PRONUNCIATION KEY

Stress. The symbol (ʹ), as in **mother** (muŧħʹər), and **redʹ wineʹ**, marks primary stress; any syllable immediately followed by (ʹ) is pronounced with greater emphasis than syllables not marked(ʹ). The symbol (ʹ), as used following the second syllables of **grandmother** (grand ondary stress; a syllable marked for secondary stress is pronounced with less emphasis than one marked (ʹ) but with more than those bearing no stress mark.

a act, bat, marry
ā age, paid, say
â(r) air, dare, Mary
ä ah, part, balm

b back, cabin, cab

ch child, teacher, beach

d do, madder, bed

e edge, set, merry
ē equal, seat, bee, mighty

ēr ear, mere

f fit, differ, puff

g give, trigger, beg

h hit, behave, hear

hw which, nowhere

i if, big, mirror, furniture
ī ice, bite, pirate, deny

j just, tragic, fudge

k keep, token, make

l low, mellow, all, bottle (botʹl)

m my, summer, him

n now, sinner, on, button (butʹn)
ng sing, Washington

o ox, bomb, wasp
ō over, boat, no

ô order, ball, raw
oi oil, joint, joy
o͝o book, tour
o͞o ooze, fool, too
ou out, loud, cow

p pot, supper, stop

r read, hurry, near

s see, passing, miss
sh shoe, fashion, push

t ten, matter, bit
th thin, ether, path

ŧħ that, either, smooth

u up, sun
û(r) urge, burn, cur

v voice, river, live

w witch, away

y yes, onion

z zoo, lazy, those
zh treasure, mirage

ə occurs in unaccented syllables to indicate the sound of the reduced vowel in
alone
system
easily
gallop
circus

ᵊ occurs between ī and **r** and between **ou** and **r** to show triphthongal quality, as in **fire** (fīᵊr), **hour** (ouᵊr)

FOREIGN SOUNDS

A as in French **ami** (A-mēʹ) [a vowel intermediate in quality between the **a** of *cat* and the **ä** of *calm*, but closer to the former]

KH as in Scottish **loch** (lôKH); German **ach** (äKH) or **ich** (iKH) [a consonant made by bringing the tongue into the position for **k** as in *coo* or **k** as in *key*, while pronouncing a strong, rasping **h**]

N as in French **bon** (bôN) [used to indicate that the preceding vowel is nasalized. Four such vowels are found in French: **un bon vin blanc** (œN bôN vaN bläN)]

Œ as in French **feu** (fœ); German **schön** (shœn) [a vowel made with the lips rounded in the position for **ō** as in *over,* while trying to say **ā** as in *able*]

R as in French **rouge** (Ro͞ozh); German **rot** (Rōt); Italian **mare** (mäʹRe); Spanish **pero** (peʹRô) [a symbol for any non-English *r,* including a trill or flap in Italian and Spanish and a sound in French and German similar to KH but pronounced with voice]

Y as in French **tu** (tY); German **über** (Yʹbər) [a vowel made with the lips rounded in position for **o͞o** as in *ooze,* while trying to say **ē** as in *east*]

ᵊ as in French **Bastogne** (bA stônʹyᵊ) [a faint prolongation of the preceding voiced consonant or glide]

ETYMOLOGY KEY

‡ probably earlier than
< descended from, borrowed from
<< descended from, borrowed from through intermediate stages not shown
> whence
? origin unknown
* unattested, reconstructed
abbr. abbreviation
abl. ablative
acc. accusative
adj. adjective, adjectival
adv. adverb, adverbial
alter. alteration
Amer. Americanism
aph. aphetic
appar. apparently
assoc. association
aug. augmentative
b. blend of, blended
c. cognate with
cf. compare
comb. form combining form
comp. comparative
contr. contraction
d. died
dat. dative
deriv. derivative
dial. dialect, dialectal
dim. diminutive
E east, eastern
equiv. equivalent
etym. etymology, etymological
fem. feminine
fig. figurative
freq. frequentative
fut. future
gen. genitive
ger. gerund, gerundive
imit. imitative
impv. imperative
indic. indicative
inf. infinitive
intransit. intransitive
irreg. irregularly
lit. literally
masc. masculine
mod. modern
N north, northern
n. noun, nominal
neut. neuter
nom. nominative
n.s. noun stem
obl. oblique
obs. obsolete
orig. origin, originally
pass. passive
perh. perhaps
pl. plural
prep. preposition
pres. present
prob. probably
pron. pronunciation, pronounced
prp. present participle
ptp. past participle
r. replacing
redupl. reduplication
repr. representing
resp. respelling, respelled
S south, southern
s. stem
sing. singular
sp. spelling, spelled
subj. subjunctive
superl. superlative
syll. syllable
trans. translation
transit. transitive
ult. ultimately
uncert. uncertain
v. verb, verbal
var. variant
voc. vocative
v.s. verb stem
W west, western

LANGUAGES

AF Anglo-French
Afr African
Afrik Afrikaans
AL Anglo-Latin
Amer American
AmerInd American Indian
AmerSp American Spanish
Ar Arabic
Aram Aramaic
Austral Australian
Bulg Bulgarian
CanF Canadian French
Celt Celtic
Chin Chinese
D Dutch
Dan Danish
E English
EGmc East Germanic
F French
Fris Frisian
G German
Gallo-Rom Gallo-Romance
Gk Greek
Gmc Germanic
Goth Gothic
Heb Hebrew
Icel Icelandic
IE Indo-European
Ir Irish
It Italian
Japn Japanese
Kor Korean
L Latin
LaF Louisiana French
LG Low German
LGk Late Greek
Lith Lithuanian
LL Late Latin
MChin Middle Chinese
MD Middle Dutch
ME Middle English
MexSp Mexican Spanish
MF Middle French
MGk Medieval Greek
MHG Middle High German
MIr Middle Irish
ML Medieval Latin
MLG Middle Low German
ModGk Modern Greek
ModHeb Modern Hebrew
MPers Middle Persian
NL Neo-Latin
Norw Norwegian
OCS Old Church Slavonic
ODan Old Danish
OE Old English
OF Old French
OFris Old Frisian
OHG Old High German
OIr Old Irish
OIt Old Italian
OL Old Latin
ON Old Norse
ONF Old North French
OPers Old Persian
OPr Old Provençal
OPruss Old Prussian
ORuss Old Russian
OS Old Saxon
OSp Old Spanish
OSw Old Swedish
PaG Pennsylvania German
Pers Persian
Pg Portuguese
Pol Polish
Pr Provençal
Rom Romance
Rum Rumanian
Russ Russian
Scand Scandinavian
Scot Scottish
ScotGael Scots Gaelic
Sem Semitic
Skt Sanskrit
Slav Slavic
Sp Spanish
SpAr Spanish Arabic
Sw Swedish
SwissF Swiss French
Turk Turkish
VL Vulgar Latin
WAfr West African
WGmc West Germanic

RANDOM HOUSE WEBSTER'S UNABRIDGED DICTIONARY

RANDOM HOUSE WEBSTER'S UNABRIDGED DICTIONARY

Second Edition

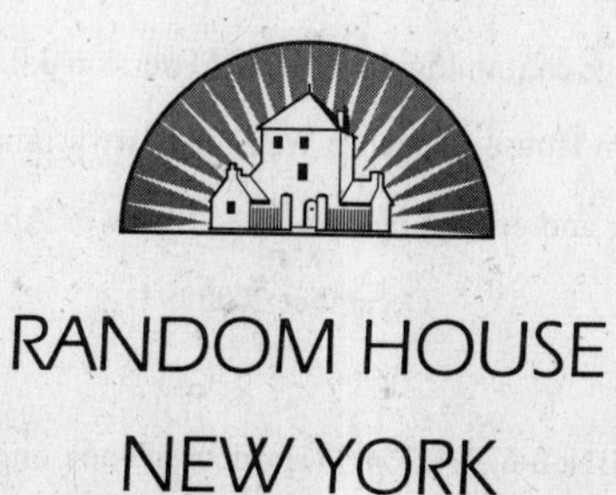

RANDOM HOUSE

NEW YORK

Random House Webster's Unabridged Dictionary, Second Edition, is a revised and updated edition of The Random House Dictionary of the English Language, Second Edition, Unabridged.

Library of Congress Cataloging-in-Publication Data as of 1997:

Random House compact unabridged dictionary
Random House Webster's Unabridged dictionary.—2nd ed.
p. cm
Rev., updated ed. of: Random House compact unabridged dictionary.
Special 2nd Ed.
ISBN 0-679-45854-9.—ISBN 0-679-45853-0
1. English language—Dictionaries.
PE1625.R293 1997 423—dc21 97-17702
CIP

Trademarks

A number of entered words which we have reason to believe constitute trademarks have been designated as such. However, no attempt has been made to designate as trademarks or service marks all terms or words in which proprietary rights might exist. The inclusion, exclusion, or definition of a word or term is not intended to affect, or to express a judgment on, the validity or legal status of the word or term as a trademark, service mark, or other proprietary term.

This book is available for special purchases in bulk by organizations and institutions, not for resale, at special discounts. Please direct your inquiries to the Random House Special Sales Department, toll free 888-591-1200 or fax 212-572-7370.

Please address inquiries about electronic licensing of this division's products, for use on a network or in software or on CD-ROM, to the Subsidiary Rights Department, Random House Reference, fax 212-940-7370.

New York Toronto London Sydney Auckland

This book is also sold in a special package containing the CD-ROM version 3.0 for Windows™ 95 and higher versions.

Visit the Random House Reference Web site at www.randomwords.com

Typeset and printed in the United States of America.

December 2000

9 8 7 6 5

ISBN: 0-679-45854-9 (Hardcover/book only)

ISBN: 0-375-40383-3 (Hardcover/book and CD-ROM package)

Contents

Random House Webster's Unabridged Dictionary

Staff: Second Edition

Sol Steinmetz, *Editorial Director*

Charles M. Levine, *Publisher*

Senior Editors
Robert B. Costello *(Text Editing)*
Enid Pearsons *(Pronunciation and Style)*
James L. Rader *(Etymology)*
Carol G. Braham
Sharon Goldstein
Keith Hollaman
Joyce O'Connor
Jesse T. Sheidlower
Eugene F. Shewmaker
P.Y. Su

Managing Editors Jennifer Dowling • Deborah M. Posner

Database Manager Constance A. Baboukis

Editors
Arthur Biderman • Dale Good • David L. Grambs • Joanne Sher Grumet • Peter Margolin • Deborah Rosenberg • Fay Webern

Pronunciation Editors
Alice Kovac Somoroff • Gloria Mihalyi Solomon • Rima Elkin McKinzey *(Contributing)*

Assistant Editors
Judith Kaplan • Lisa Riis McGowan • Edward Moran • Daniel Prior

Citation Program
Elizabeth Christensen • Bernard W. Kane • Saul Rosen

Contributing Editors
Seymour Barofsky • James B. Broderick • Olga Coren • Diane Kender Dittrick • Mark Dittrick • Stephen P. Elliott • Bonny Hart • Lyle C. Pearsons • Jerry Ralya • Stanley Schindler

Artists
PICTOGRAPH CORP.: David Behan • Ted Burwell • Dyno Lowenstein
Cartographer: Ruth Schindler

Production
Production Director: Patricia W. Ehresmann
Production Associates: Michele Purdue • Rita E. Rubin

Design
Art Director: Bernard Klein
Design Associates: LIBRA GRAPHICS, INC.:
Dorothy Gordineer • Beri Greenwald
Christine Swirnoff • Barbara Berger

Stuart Berg Flexner, *Editor in Chief Emeritus*

Leonore Crary Hauck, *Managing Editor Emerita*

PREFACE TO THE SECOND EDITION

As THE ENGLISH language has expanded and changed over the centuries, so have its dictionaries. There has been a need, and a tradition, to include more and more words and definitions from a greater variety of human endeavors and usage levels, accompanied by more detailed information about the vocabulary, its use, and its history. The Second Edition of *The Random House Dictionary of the English Language—Unabridged* carries both the history of language growth and change and the traditions of lexicography into the late 20th century.

Twenty-one years have elapsed since the first unabridged edition of *The Random House Dictionary of the English Language* was published. Its Preface pointed out the explosions of knowledge and vocabulary that, starting from the dawn of the Atomic Age, persisted into the emergent Space Age and the revolutionary social upheavals of the early 1960's. The twin explosions of knowledge and vocabulary from many sources have increased in magnitude during these past twenty-one years. Thus this Second Edition contains within its covers the transcription of a tongue that, in two decades, has again expanded enormously and, in addition, has become the most pervasive on earth: a linguistic medium of worldwide communication. With a world already anticipating the problems and wonders of the 21st century and a promise of ever more widespread use of English, this seems an ideal moment to present this completely new edition of a standard and highly regarded reference work.

In addition, during the past two decades significant and influential social and cultural movements have taken place, reverberating through our language not only as new words and meanings but in our attitudes toward language and its use. Thus recent influences that have expanded and reshaped our vocabulary and its use come not only from such obvious fields as science and technology and new forms and styles in the arts, fashion, and leisure activities, but also from history itself and from such social and cultural movements as concern with the environment, the women's movement, and a new awareness of and respect for ethnic diversity.

The growth and changes that take place in the language between succeeding editions of a dictionary, however, are reflected not only in the expanded word stock of new words and new senses of established words. Growth and change are also reflected in the language's pronunciation, syntax, morphology, and usage. It has been the aim of this Second Edition to set down such changes comprehensively and accurately, treating the First Edition as a source requiring vast expansion, sweeping revisions, and fresh analysis to meet the needs of the present day.

Several distinct features set this Second Edition apart from the First. The present edition has been expanded by some 50,000 new entries and 75,000 new definitions. Sample sentences, Usage Notes, Synonym Studies, Synonym and Antonym Lists, illustrations, and locator maps have also been increased in number, while those from the First Edition have been greatly expanded, revised, and brought up to date. This is the first unabridged American dictionary to list the dates of entry into the language of vocabulary items, and similarly to record which words are of specifically American origin. The coverage of American regional dialects has been expanded and more specific regional labeling provided (augmented by the map showing the Regions of American English on page xxvi of the front matter). In this aspect we have been fortunate in having the guidance of consultants closely associated with the various regional projects of the *Linguistic Atlas of the United States* and of the *Dictionary of American Regional English* project. To enhance this coverage, a number of Regional Variation Notes have been placed at suitable entries, pointing out regional differences in vocabulary, especially to indicate by what name certain entities (as *pail, dragonfly,* and *hero sandwich*) are known in different areas of the country. Pronunciation Notes, another new feature, take up issues of disputed usage and points of historical and social interest regarding the pronunciation of specific words. In matters of sexism, we have made every effort to make the wording of the definitions and illustrative examples gender-neutral, and to point up, in relevant Usage Notes, current usage, choices, and attitudes regarding gender-neutral and gender-specific terms. This edition also uses the new five-kingdom system of biological classification and gives the status of threatened and endangered species. Metric equivalences are now provided for weights and measurements in definitions and captions. Tables and charts are greater in number and include such useful lists as Books of the Bible, Wedding Anniversaries (and their symbols), Longest Rivers of the World, and Chief Justices of the United States Supreme Court.

Etymologies are improved well beyond historical dating and the identification of Americanisms. Many of the etymologies of the First Edition have been expanded and revised in the light of recent research and the work of our consultants, and the thorough treatment of compounds and derivatives characteristic of the original book has been augmented. A particular effort has been made to specify the contribution to English vocabulary of non-European languages, as is evident, for example, in the etymologies of words borrowed from Australian Aboriginal languages, in which more than twenty individual Australian languages are now cited, in place of the traditional but empty label "Australian Aboriginal." When the precise source of an exotic word is not known, etymologies such as "from a native word," long a staple of English-language dictionaries, have not been used to cover lack of knowledge.

There are, of course, a number of other ways in which a dictionary of this scope undergoes transformation on a wide scale. Vocabulary once confined to a specialized area becomes generalized in usage, and must be so recognized: some terms once associated only with racing cars and sports cars now apply to the design of the family car; items of clothing once worn mainly by cowboys, athletes, or explorers are in widespread, fashionable everyday use; the jargon of specific groups and activities becomes the slang of a wider social milieu and is then used by much of the general public. Important too are the substantive facts that have changed since the publication of previous unabridged dictionaries. Official population figures have been changed for geographical entries, and many entries have also undergone changes in name and political status. In addition to the many new biographical entries, all existing ones from the First Edition have been rechecked for updating, as to include death dates or changes in political positions and national affiliations. Many other facts have emerged: some planets are now known to have a different number of moons or rings than they were thought to have when the First Edition was published; some plants and animals have been reclassified as being of a different species; familiar diseases have been redefined and even renamed by medical researchers; and some medications and chemicals once considered safe now need definitions referring to their side effects or dangers.

In addition to the definitions themselves, all other facets of the original existing entries have been expanded and brought up to date. Preferences in spelling and pronunciation for many words have shifted in the last two decades, and a sizable body of words has undergone a functional shift from one part of speech to another. The changes are duly recorded in this new edition. For example, the user will find that *eon* has precedence over *aeon,* and *ameba* over *amoeba,* reflecting the current preferential usage of scientists and science writers. Further, there is a tendency to favor *naive* over *naïve;* and *firefighter, pantsuit, bypass,* and *liftoff* are more often found as solid words than as two words or hyphenated forms. It is now common to find *cubism* and *mach number* uncapitalized, *gefülte fish* respelled as *gefilte fish,* and *lasagne* and *linguini* yielding to *lasagna* and *linguine.* Abbreviations like *PTA* and *KO* now regularly appear without periods. This is not to say that earlier or alternate forms have been discarded, just that a new dictionary is responsible for recording the shifts in frequency of usage. In like manner, pinyin spellings for Chinese terms have largely superseded Wade-Giles and other transliterations; in this new edition entries for Chinese proper names are given at their most frequently encountered spellings, though alternative spellings are also entered.

Besides the many new Usage Notes, a large number of the older ones have been expanded or revised to include more background information and the latest linguistic perspective. The usage levels of all entries and definitions in the original edition, as those preceded by usage or temporal labels, have been completely reviewed and revised; thus such labels as *Slang, Informal, Archaic,* etc., reflect current usage and research.

For all the innovation and enlargement offered in the Second Edition, most of the features, having stood the test of time and the commendation of users, have been retained from its forerunner. Thus, as in the First Edition, we: (1) enter all terms, including geographical entries, biographical entries, and abbreviations, in one single alphabetical listing; (2) follow our general policy of putting the most frequently used meanings (and parts of speech) at the beginning of the entry, followed by other senses in diminishing frequency of usage, with archaic and obsolete meanings coming last; (3) show appropriate entries in italics and/or with an initial capital letter, reflecting actual usage in modern written English; and (4) include an abundance of geographical places and biographical names, people and places from the Bible, figures from mythology, titles of literary and artistic works, given names, and other items outside the generic lexicon.

The entire book has been redesigned, using new typefaces and a new page layout. Illustrations and maps are now full-column width, with a light tint to highlight most of the illustrations and charts. We hope these visual changes will help make the information easy to use and pleasing to the eye.

The overriding purpose of this Second Edition is threefold: (1) to provide the user with an accurate, accessible guide to the meanings, spellings, pronunciations, usage, and history of the words in our language—information essential to successful communication and understanding; (2) to provide a scrupulously up-to-date dictionary of record, a storehouse and mirror of the language that will serve the user not only in the present, but for years to come; (3) to bring to the user the results of the most recent, authoritative research and knowledge from scholars and experts in all fields, edited with care. The compilers of a modern dictionary, particularly one as all-embracing as the Second Edition, owe a profound debt to all the language scholars who preceded them and who, step by step through the centuries, established the traditions of modern lexicography. Our sense of gratitude additionally extends to those contemporary scholars whose research and writings help expand the boundaries of our work.

A dictionary is only as good as its staff, its citation files, and its consultants. This book has been fortunate in possessing the highest quality in all three. I would like to thank our dictionary staff and each of the contributors and consultants for their painstaking work. We owe our deepest gratitude to the late Jess Stein, who began planning and working on this book so many years ago. I would also like to thank Random House, with its tradition of excellence in publishing and its concern for the language, for literacy, and for freedom of expression, for making this book possible. In particular I am grateful to Random House executives Robert L. Bernstein, Richard E. Liebermann, and Anthony M. Schulte for their patience and their belief in the project. Finally, I thank the many teachers, librarians, writers and editors, and all the readers who, over the years, have accepted our dictionaries into their schools, libraries, homes, and offices, given us support and encouragement, and made suggestions, many of which found their way into this new book. I hope that we will continue to merit your support and invite you to continue to correspond with us. We hope you will find this dictionary useful in many ways—as a trusted and helpful guide and companion in your speaking, writing, reading, and listening, and as a complete reference book, a library of words and information. I hope it is the one book you will never finish reading—and never tire of using.

STUART BERG FLEXNER

Note on the Updated Second Edition

THE NUMEROUS updatings and revisions that have been made since publication in 1987 of the *Random House Unabridged Dictionary, Second Edition,* were greatly facilitated by the Random House Living Dictionary Project, a unique system that merges traditional lexicography with highly sophisticated computer technology. The heart of this system is a large database available to the editors for on-line editing. Dictionary entries can be corrected, updated, or altered on-screen as needed. Most significantly, new vocabulary can be added instantly. The traditional lexicographic process is laborious and time-consuming, involving the preparation, editing, and filing of thousands of slips of paper that will ultimately be assembled into the completed entries of a dictionary page. Computer technology, adapted specifically to the Random House Living Dictionary Project, now eliminates much of that prolonged labor, permitting editors to go directly from keyboarding of new material to composed pages.

This Updated Second Edition has been prepared in the sophisticated manner described above. The database of the Living Dictionary Project has been specially helpful in assembling the contents of the New-Words Section included in this edition. The updated and revised CD-ROM that is sold separately or together with the dictionary in a special package was created entirely from the Living Dictionary Project, as were the previous CD-ROMs of the *Random House Unabridged Dictionary, Second Edition.*

New-Words Section

THIS NEW-WORDS section includes about 1,000 new entries and meanings not found in the main A–Z section of the dictionary. Most of these terms have been recently borrowed or coined, such as *mad cow disease, bad hair day,* and *roofie.* Also included are a number of important biographical, geographical, and encyclopedic entries.

Entries in the new-words section that show new meanings of words already found in the main dictionary are marked with a plus sign (+) immediately after the entry word. Cross references to other entries in this section are indicated by "(in this section)" after the reference. All other cross references are to entries in the main dictionary.

These new terms represent a variety of subject categories, both general and specialized. A close look at the selection of words will reveal a great deal about our changing world. New terms have arisen largely as a result of scientific and technological advances, but social and cultural innovations have also contributed to the great expansion of the English vocabulary. A mere five years ago we did not speak about *intranets, V-chips,* or *body piercing.*

The Random House family of dictionaries has built a reputation on recording newer words faster. *Internet* and *World Wide Web* are terms that have appeared first in a Random House dictionary. The editors have taken maximum advantage of the resources available to them. One resource for new words is the large file of citations from print, broadcast, and electronic sources. A more recently developed resource is the *Random House Living Dictionary Database,* which enables editors to work on-line to add or update entries.

Most terms entered in the Random House dictionaries have passed the tests of time, frequency of occurrence, and range of use. But as editors and readers are aware, some new terms last only for the moment. Is the *macarena* a passing fad? Are *shock jock* and *soccer mom* merely nonce terms? The editors must constantly reevaluate the dictionary word list, sometimes taking out terms which are no longer common, current, or useful. For example, a previous edition of this book entered *Oi* (a type of punk rock associated with skinheads), but this edition omits it based on lack of current written or spoken evidence. However, terms may go in and out of vogue. It is interesting to note that the exclamation *duh* dates back to the 1960s and is commonly heard today, especially in the speech of young people. The term *Ebonics* was first used in the 1970s, yet most people have only recently become aware of it.

Space considerations are an issue in compiling a general dictionary, even an unabridged edition as comprehensive as this one. The size of the English vocabulary has been estimated as between half a million and one million words, but a dictionary can record only a fraction of these. Much of the new vocabulary is so technical that it belongs only in specialized dictionaries. It is generally assumed that the average person's active or speaking vocabulary ranges from 15,000 to 30,000 terms, while the passive vocabulary, the words one understands or recognizes, can exceed 100,000 items.

How do new terms originate? For centuries new words have come into English in several established ways. Most are borrowed from other languages, such as *feng shui* (from Chinese) and *karaoke* (from Japanese). Others are formed by combining or blending two or more words, such as *palmtop* and *netiquette.* The creation of abbreviations and acronyms is another common method of word formation in English. The abbreviations *SUV* and *URL* are certainly more convenient to use than the phrases they stand for; the acronyms *SLAPP* and *SQUID* are easier to pronounce or remember than their expanded forms. New words are commonly derived from existing words by the addition of a prefix or suffix. Examples of such derivatives are *antirejection, superstore,* and *incentivize.* Very often pieces of existing words are refit and rearranged in inventive ways, as illustrated by the related terms *downsize, upsize,* and *rightsize.* New terms are also created when combining forms (existing only in combination with other forms) are joined with independent words. For example, the combining form *Mc-* (extracted from "McDonald's") was joined to the existing word "job" to produce *McJob.* The outright coinage of new words not based on existing words is quite uncommon; nevertheless individuals do invent terms that are onomatopoeic, fanciful, or descriptive. Recent examples of coined words are *mondegreen* and *mosh.* A large number of coinages are names of people or places: the term *bork* is an "eponym," a word derived from a person's name. Often a word is converted to a new part of speech, as when the noun *stealth* is used as an adjective. Existing terms may be shortened to form new, often monosyllabic words: a word as recent as *Generation X* has already been clipped to *Gen X* and *euro* is a shortened form of *eurocurrency.* Back formation is a specific type of shortening in which a word is formed by dropping a suffix or other word element from an existing word. For example, *enthuse* is a back formation from "enthusiasm". As is true of any language, English is constantly evolving new idioms and expressions based on existing words, but with meanings that are not predictable from their constituent elements: to say *the jury is still out* certainly extends the meaning of "jury".

Not only does a living language add new vocabulary, but existing words change, broaden, or narrow their meanings over time. No one today uses *knave* to mean "boy", although that was the original meaning in Old English. The new senses of *holy war* and *metastasize* are examples of figurative uses of literal meanings. The new senses of *ironic, author,* and *extreme* illustrate shifted or extended meanings.

Bearing the censure associated with fads, slang, and unfamiliar usages, new terms are often fraught with controversy. Dictionary editors are objective reporters on the language, stating the observed facts of usage. At the same time they are obliged to note objections and criticism, leaving it to readers to make an informed choice. Some controversial usages have become accepted over time, but it remains to be seen how others will fare in the future. The term *challenged,* as in "physically challenged", "vertically challenged", and "ethically challenged", is considered by some to be overly euphemistic or even humorous.

As for the future of English, growth and change in language is a completely normal process. It is probably no exaggeration to assert that more new terms have come into English in the last fifty years than in any other comparable period in history, with the possible exception of the early Middle English period (1100s–1300s). Judging by its remarkable rate of growth, the English language is likely to continue to expand in the course of the 21st century. As we approach a new century and millennium, English is at its zenith in global influence and prestige. From the perspective of the 1990s, the English language is indeed alive and well.

a&b, assault and battery.

A&E, *Trademark.* Arts and Entertainment (a cable television channel).

a&r, assault and robbery.

aar, **1.** *Com.* against all risks. **2.** average annual rainfall. Also, **AAR**

AB, +Alberta, Canada (approved for postal use).

ABC, +American Broadcasting Companies (a television network).

ABD, all but dissertation: applied to a person who has completed all requirements for a doctoral degree except for the writing of a dissertation. Also, **A.B.D.**

abs (abz), *n.pl. Informal.* abdominal muscles. [1980–85, *Amer.*; by shortening]

accrd., accrued.

ACE′ inhib′itor (ās, ā′sē′ē′), any of a group of vasodilator drugs used in the treatment of hypertension and heart failure. [1980–85; *A(ngiotensin)-C(onverting) E(nzyme)*]

ac·tive-ma·trix (ak′tiv mā′triks), *adj.* of or pertaining to a high-resolution liquid-crystal display (LCD) with high contrast, used esp. for laptop computers. Cf. **passive-matrix** (in this section). [1990–95]

adapter, + *n. Computers.* See **expansion card.**

add-in (ad′in′), *n.* a component, as an expansion card or chip, added to a computer to expand its capabilities. [1985–90]

AF, +Asian female.

AFAIK, as far as I know.

agent, + *v.t.* to represent (a person or thing) as an agent; act as an agent for: *to agent a manuscript; Who agented that deal?*

Age′ of In′nocence, The, a novel (1920) by Edith Wharton.

aggressive, + *adj.* using daring or forceful methods: *aggressive treatment of infection.*

ag·i·ta (aj′i tə, ä′ji-), *n.* **1.** heartburn; indigestion. **2.** agitation; anxiety. [1980–85, *Amer.*; < It, < *agitare* < L *agitāre* AGITATE]

a-i-r, artist-in-residence.

airbrush, + *v.t.* to prettify or sanitize: *airbrushed versions of modern history.*

a·li·as·ing (ā′lē ə sing), *n.* jaggies.

a-life (ā′līf′), *n.* See **artificial life** (in this section).

all′-ter·rain′ bike′ (ôl′tə rān′). See **mountain bike** (in this section).

al′pha test′, +*Computers.* an early test of new or updated computer software conducted by the developers of the program prior to beta-testing by potential users. Cf. **beta test.**

alter′native med′icine, health care and treatment practices, including traditional Chinese medicine, chiropractic, folk medicine, and naturopathy, that minimize or eschew the use of surgery and drugs.

AM, +Asian male.

AMC, *Trademark.* American Movie Classics (a cable television channel).

Amer′ican Goth′ic, a painting (1930) by Grant Wood.

anatom′ically correct′, having representations of the sexual organs: *An anatomically correct doll was shown to the witness.* [1990–95]

AND (and), *n.* a Boolean operator that returns a positive result when both operands are positive.

Andrews, + *n.* **Julie** (*Julia Elizabeth Wells*), born 1935, U.S. actress, born in England.

an·i·me (an′ə mā′), *n.* a Japanese style of motion-picture animation, charaacterized by highly stylized, colorful art, futuristic settings, and sexuality and violence. [< Japn, borrowing of E *animation*]

An·nan (ä nän′), *n.* **Kofi,** born 1938, Ghanaian diplomat: secretary-general of the United Nations since 1997.

an·ti·a·li·as·ing (an′tē ā′lē ə sing, an′ti-), *n.* a technique for smoothing out jaggies in graphical computer output. [1990–95]

an·ti·re·jec·tion (an′tē ri jek′shən, an′ti-), *adj.* preventing the rejection of a transplanted organ: *antirejection drugs.* [1965–70]

aoi, angle of incidence.

aor, angle of reflection.

app (ap), *n. Computers* (*informal*). an application program; application software. [1985–90]

app·let (ap′lit), *n. Computers.* a small application program that can be called up for use while working in another application. [1990–95]

architecture, + *n.* a fundamental underlying design of computer hardware, software, or both.

ar′tifi′cial life′, the simulation of any aspect of life, as through computers, robotics, or biochemistry. [1990–95]

Ash·ber·y (ash′ber′ē, -bə rē), *n.* **John,** born 1927, U.S. poet.

assist′ed su′icide, suicide aided by a person, esp. a physician, who organizes the logistics of the suicide, as by providing the necessary quantities of a poison. [1985–90]

ATB, all-terrain bike.

CONCISE ETYMOLOGY KEY: <, descended or borrowed from; >, whence; b., blend of, blended; c., cognate with; cf., compare; deriv., derivative; equiv., equivalent; imit., imitative; obl., oblique; r., replacing; s., stem; sp., spelling, spelled; resp., respelling, respelled; trans., translation; ?, origin unknown; *, unattested; ‡, probably earlier than. See the full key inside the front cover.

Au, +author. Also, **au.**

au′dio book′, a recording of an oral reading of a book, often in abridged form. Also, **au′di·o·book′.** [1990–95]

Aung San Suu Kyi (oung′ sän′ sōō′ kē′), *n.* born 1945, Burmese opposition leader: Nobel peace prize 1991.

author, + *n. Computers.* the writer of a software program, esp. a hypertext or multimedia application.

au′toerot′ic asphyx′ia, asphyxia caused by intentionally strangling oneself while masturbating in order to intensify the orgasm through reduced oxygen flow to the brain. —**autoerot′ic asphyxia′tion.**

baby, + *n.* a human fetus.

ba′by bust′, a period of sharp decrease in the birthrate, as that in the United States after 1965. [1970–75, *Amer.*] —**ba′by bust′er.**

bad′ hair′ day′, a disagreeable or unpleasant day, esp. one during which one feels unattractive. [1990–95]

Ball, + *n.* **Lucille,** 1911–89, U.S. actress.

ballistic, + *adj.* **go ballistic,** *Informal.* to become overwrought or irrational: *went ballistic over the idea of a tax hike.*

balsam′ic vin′egar, a sweetish, aromatic vinegar made from the must of white grapes and aged in wood barrels. [trans. of It *aceto balsamico;* so called from its supposed medicinal effects, likened to balsam]

ban·da (bän′də), *n.* a style of Mexican dance music featuring brass instruments and having a heavy beat. [1990–95; < MexSp: lit., BAND]

Ba·nja Lu·ka (bä′nyə lōō′kə), a city in N Bosnia and Herzegovina. 183,618.

Bar·thel·me (bär′thəl mā′, -tl mē), *n.* **Donald,** 1931–89, U.S. short-story writer and novelist.

bas·ma·ti (bäs mä′tē), *n.* a variety of cultivated long-grain rice that is notably fragrant. [1845–50; < Hindi: lit., fragrant]

bay, + *n.* an open compartment in the console housing a computer's CPU in which a disk drive, tape drive, etc., may be installed. Also called **drive bay.**

BC, British Columbia, Canada (approved for postal use).

beach′ vol′leyball, volleyball played on the sand with two teams of two players each. [1990–95]

beaucoup, + *adj.* large; significant: *a beaucoup building project.*

bel·li·ni (bə lē′nē), *n.* a cocktail made with sparkling wine and peach purée. [1980–85; < It]

Bell′ Jar′, The, a novel (1963) by Sylvia Plath.

Bel′mont Stakes′ (bel′mont), a horse race for three-year-olds run annually at Elmont, N.Y., three weeks after the Preakness.

bench′ strength′, depth of talent, as on a sports team.

Ben′zi Box′ (ben′zē), *Trademark.* a brand of antitheft system for car radios that allows the radio to be removed easily from the car by the driver.

BET, *Trademark.* Black Entertainment Television (a cable television channel).

be·ta-test (bā′tə test′), *v.t. Computers.* to subject (software or hardware) to a beta test.

BF, black female.

big·foot (big′fŏŏt′), *n. Slang.* **1.** a prominent or influential person, esp. a journalist or news analyst. —*v.t.* **2.** to apply one's authority to as a bigfoot: *bigfooting his name onto an article he didn't write.* [1975–80, *Amer.*; after Big Foot]

big′ hair′, long hair worn teased and sprayed.

big′ sci′ence, scientific research requiring large capital expenditure. [1960–65]

bi·o·di·ver·si·ty (bī′ō di vûr′si tē, -dī-), *n.* diversity of plant and animal species in an environment. [1985–90, *Amer.*]

bi·op·ic (bī′ō pik′), *n.* a biographical motion picture. [1950–55; bio(graphy) + (motion) pic(ture)]

Bir·ken·stock (bûr′kən stok′), *Trademark.* a brand of sandals.

black′ bean′, any of various black-colored beans or legumes.

Blair, + *n.* **Anthony Charles Lyn·ton** (lin′tən) (*Tony*), born 1953, British political leader: prime minister since 1997.

blitz′ chess′. See **speed chess** (in this section).

blo·vi·ate (blō′vē āt′), *v.i.,* **-at·ed, -at·ing.** to speak pompously. [*Amer.;* pseudo-L alter. of BLOW to boast; pop. by W. G. HARDING]

blow′-in′, *adj.* (of a piece of advertising) inserted in but not attached to a magazine or newspaper: *blow-in cards.*

Blun·den (blun′dən), *n.* **Edmund,** 1896–1974, English poet.

blunt, + *n. Slang.* a cigar stuffed with marijuana.

blush, + *n.* rosé. Also called **blush′ wine′.**

BM, +black male.

boat′ shoe′, a moccasinlike shoe with a rubber sole that provides a firm hold on the deck of a boat. [1990–95]

bod′y dou′ble, a person whose body is shown in a movie or TV show in substitution for a leading actor, esp. in a nude scene. [1990–95]

bod′y pierc′ing, the piercing of a part of the body, as the navel, in order to insert an ornamental ring or stud. [1990–95]

Bol·ly·wood (bol′ē wŏŏd′), *n.* the motion-picture industry of India, based in Bombay. [b. *Bombay* + *Hollywood*]

boo·jie (bōō′jē), *adj. Slang.* haughty; elitist; snobbish. [1965–70, *Amer.;* shortening and alter. of BOURGEOIS]

bork (bôrk), *v.t.* to attack (a candidate or public figure) systematically, esp. in the media. [1988, *Amer.;* after Judge Robert H. *Bork,* whose appointment to the Supreme Court was blocked in 1987 after an extensive media campaign by his opponents]

bot′tom feed′er, **1.** See **bottom fisher. 2.** a person who functions or seeks to gain at the lowest level of an activity: *bottom feeders who buy undervalued stocks; social bottom feeders hanging out in seedy bars.* **3.** a person who appeals to base instincts: *Gossip columnists are the bottom feeders of journalism. Also called* ***bottom-fisher*** (for defs. 2, 3).

bot·tom-feed·ing (bot′əm fē′ding), *n.* the activities of a bottom feeder. Also called **bot·tom-fish·ing** (bot′əm fish′ing).

bot·tom-fish·er (bot′əm fish′ər), *n.* See **bottom feeder** (defs. 2, 3 in this section).

Bou·tros-Gha·li (bōō′trôs gä′lē), *n.* **Boutros,** born 1922, Egyptian diplomat: secretary-general of the United Nations 1992–1996.

bo′vine spon′gi·form encephalop′athy (spun′jə fôrm′), a fatal dementia of cattle, thought to be caused by the prion proteins implicated in Creutzfeldt-Jakob disease. Also called **mad cow disease.**

box, + *n. Slang.* a coffin.

bridge, + *adj.* (esp. of clothing) less expensive than a manufacturer's most expensive products: *showing his bridge line for the fall season.*

Brod·sky (brod′skē), *n.* **Joseph,** 1940–96, U.S. poet, born in Russia: Nobel prize 1987; U.S. poet laureate 1991.

Brook·ner (brŏŏk′nər), *n.* **Anita,** born 1928, English novelist and art historian.

Brown·son (broun′sən), *n.* **Orestes Augustus,** 1803–76, U.S. writer.

brows·er (brou′zər), *n.* **1.** a person or thing that browses. **2.** *Computers.* an application program that allows the user to examine encoded documents in a form suitable for display, esp. such a program for use on the World Wide Web.

brux (bruks), *v.i.,* **bruxed, brux·ing.** to clench and grind the teeth; gnash. [1990–95; back formation from BRUXISM]

BRV, Bravo (a cable television channel).

BST, *Biochem., Agric.* bovine somatotropin. See **bovine growth hormone.**

buf′falo wing′, a deep-fried chicken wing served in a spicy sauce and usually with celery and blue cheese. [1980–85; *Amer.;* after a restaurant in Buffalo, which popularized the dish]

bul′ly pul′pit, a position of authority or public visibility, esp. a political office, from which one may express one's views.

Burton, + *n.* **Richard** (*Richard Jenkins*), 1925–84, English actor, born in Wales.

bus′ topol′ogy, *Computers.* an arrangement of computers on a local-area network in which each computer is connected to a central cable through which data is channeled.

button, + *n. Computers.* (in a graphical user interface) any of the small, labeled, button-shaped areas upon which the user can click, as with a mouse, to choose an option.

Cain, + *n.* **James M.,** 1892–1977, U.S. novelist.

calculus, + *n.* calculation: *the calculus of political appeal.*

calling card, +a prepaid card or charge card that can be used at a public telephone instead of coins. Also called **phone card.**

Call′ of the Wild′, The, a novel (1903) by Jack London.

cam·mie (kam′ē), *n.* **1.** camouflage. **2. cammies,** a camouflage uniform; a camouflage garment or garments. [1990–95]

Campbell, + *n.* **Joseph,** 1904–87, U.S. mythologist.

Can·dom·blé (kan′dəm blā′), *n.* a religion based on the worship of Yoruba deities practiced in Brazil, esp. in the state of Bahia. [< Brazilian Pg; further orig. undetermined]

cap·el·li·ni (cap′ə lē′nē), *n.* pasta in long, very fine strands. [< It, dim. of *capello* hair]

card·mem·ber (kärd′mem′bər), *n.* a person authorized to use a credit card.

Card′ Play′ers, The, a painting (1892) by Paul Cézanne.

Carver, + *n.* **Raymond,** 1938–88, U.S. short-story writer and poet.

CBS, Columbia Broadcasting System: a television network.

CD4, *n.* a protein on the surface of T cells and other cells, functioning as a receptor for the AIDS virus antigen. [1980–85; *c(luster of) d(ifferentiation)* 4]

ce·ci·ty (sē′si tē), *n.* blindness. [1525–30; < L *caecitās,* equiv. to *caecus* blind + -ity]

cell′ phone′. See **cellular phone.**

CF, +Christian female.

chal·lenged (chal′injd), *adj.* (used as a euphemism) disabled, handicapped, or deficient (usually prec. by an adverb): *physically challenged; ethically challenged.* [1980–85, *Amer.*]

chan·nel-surf (chan′l sûrf′), *v.i.* to change from one channel on a television set to another with great or unusual frequency, esp. by using a remote control. [1985–90, *Amer.*] —**chan′nel surf′er.**

chat′ room′, *Computers.* a branch of a computer system in which participants can engage in real-time discussions with one another.

chat′tering class′, well-educated members of the upper-middle or upper class who freely express esp. liberal opinions or judgments on current issues and events. [1980–85]

child, + *n.* a human fetus.

chill′ing effect′, a discouraging or deterring effect, esp. one resulting from a restrictive law or regulation. [1965–70]

Chi·rac (shē rak′), *n.* **Jacques (René),** born 1932, prime minister of France 1974–76, 1986–88; president since 1995.

chump′ change′, *Slang.* a small or insignificant amount of money. [1965–70]

ci·gua·te·ra (sē′gwə ter′ə, sig′wə-), *n.* a tropical disease caused by ingesting a poison found in certain marine fishes. [1860-65; AmerSp < *cigua* sea snail]

city, + *n.* (*often cap.*) *Slang.* a place, person, or situation having certain features or characteristics (used in combination): *The party last night was Action City. That guy is dull city.*

CLI, cost-of-living index. Also, **cli**

clicker, + *n.* See **remote control** (def. 2).

client, + *n.* a workstation on a network that gains access to central data files, programs, and peripheral devices through a server.

Cliffs Notes (klifs), *Trademark.* a series of pamphlets with summaries and basic analyses of works of literature, intended as study aids. [after *Cliff* Hillegass, founder of Cliffs Notes, Inc.]

clin′ical tri′al, the scientific evaluation of a new treatment that has shown some benefit in animal or laboratory studies, but that has not yet been proven superior to existing therapies for people.

clip′ art′, drawings or illustrations available, as in a book or on a CD-ROM, for easy insertion into other material.

clo·chard (klō′shərd), *n.* a beggar; vagrant; tramp. [1940–45; < F, der. of *clocher* to limp << *L clopus* lame]

CM, +Christian male.

CNN, *Trademark.* Cable News Network (a cable television channel specializing in news coverage).

cob·ble[3] (kob′əl), *n. New England, New York, and New Jersey.* (esp. in placenames) a rounded hill. [1885–95; perh. < cobble[2]]

coenzyme Q 10, a naturally occurring, fat-soluble, vitaminlike enzyme found in a variety of foods and synthesized in the body: sold as a dietary supplement for its antioxidant properties.

co·hous·ing (kō hou′zing), *n.* **1.** a cooperative living arrangement in which people build a cluster of single-family houses around a common building for shared meals, child care, guest rooms, etc. **2.** the cluster of houses with the common building. [1990–95]

COM, Comedy Central (a cable television channel).

com·mand-driv·en (kə mand′driv′ən), *adj. Computers.* of or pertaining to a software program whose instructions to perform specified tasks are issued by the user as typed commands in predetermined syntax (contrasted with *menu-driven*).

compas′sion fatigue′, a lack of sympathy for suffering, as a result of continuous exposure to those in need of aid. [1980–85, *Amer.*]

compliant, + *adj.* manufactured or produced in accordance with a specified body of rules (usu. used in combination): *Energy Star–compliant computers.*

compression, + *n.* reduction of the size of computer data by efficient storage.

comp′ time′, time off from work, granted to an employee in lieu of overtime pay. [*comp(ensatory) time*]

com·put·er·phobe (kəm pyōō′tər fōb′), *n.* a person who distrusts or is intimidated by computers. [1975–80] **—com·put′er·pho′bi·a,** *n.* **—com·put′er·pho′bic,** *adj.*

content[1], + *n.* substantive information or creative material viewed in contrast to its actual or potential manner of presentation: *publishers, record companies, and other content providers; a flashy Web site, but without much content.*

control′ freak′, a person having a strong need to control his or her surroundings. [1975–80]

co·pay (kō′pā′), *n.* a fixed amount, or a percentage of the usual and customary fee for a medical service, payable by an insured to a health insurance carrier. Also called **co·pay·ment** (kō′pā′mənt). [1990–95]

cord′ blood′, blood from the placenta drawn through the newly severed umbilical cord, collected for study or for possible transfusion to treat disease in the child.

cor′porate wel′fare, financial assistance, as tax breaks or subsidies, given by the government esp. to large companies. [1990–95, *Amer.*]

Court TV, *Trademark.* a cable television channel featuring live coverage of courtroom trials.

Cree·ley (krē′lē), *n.* **Robert,** born 1926, U.S. poet.

Crichton, + *n.* **Michael,** born 1942, U.S. novelist.

crunch′ time′, a period of intense pressure. [1975–80]

cry·o·pres·er·va·tion (krī′ō prez′ər vā′shən), *n.* the storage of blood or living tissues at extremely cold temperatures, often -196 degrees Celsius. [1972; cryo- + preservation]

cryp·to·spo·ri·di·o·sis (krip′tō spôr′i dī ō′sis, -spōr′-), *n.* a disease caused by protozoan parasites of the genus *Cryptosporidia,* characterized by fever and gastrointestinal symptoms and typically spread via contaminated drinking water.

C-SPAN (sē′span′), *Trademark.* Cable Satellite Public Affairs Network (a cable television channel).

CSW, Certified Social Worker. Also, **C.S.W.**

curve, + *n.* **ahead of** (or *behind*) *the curve,* at the forefront of (or lagging behind) recent developments, trends, etc.

CW, +conventional wisdom.

cyber-, a combining form representing COMPUTER (*cybertalk; cyberart) and by extension meaning "very modern" (cyberfashion).* [extracted from cybernetics]

cy·ber·sex (sī′bər seks′), *n.* any sexual activity, display, or discussion engaged in by means of a computer. [1985–90]

cyberspace, + *n.* the realm of electronic communication.

da′ta high′way. See **information superhighway** (in this section).

day′ job′, one's regular job and main source of income, usually viewed in contrast to a speculative or irregular endeavor: *Good luck in the lottery, but don't quit your day job.*

dead′beat dad′, a father who neglects his responsibilities as a parent, esp. one who does not pay child support to his estranged wife. [1975–80]

decompression, + *n. Computers.* the restoration of data that has undergone compression to its original state.

de·hook·er (dē hŏŏk′ər), *n.* a device for removing a hook from a fish.

den′tal dam′, a flat piece of latex used to prevent the transfer of bodily fluids during cunnilingus. [after *rubber dam,* a piece of latex placed over the teeth during dental work]

derivative, + *n.* a financial contract whose value derives from the value of underlying stocks, bonds, currencies, commodities, etc.

Der·ri·da (der′ē dä′), *n.* **Jacques,** born 1930, French philosopher and literary critic, born in Algiers.

desktop, + *n. Computers.* the primary display screen of a graphical user interface, on which various icons represent files, groups of files, programs, or the like, which can be moved, accessed, added to, put away, or thrown away in ways analogous to the handling of file folders, documents, notes, etc., on a real desk.

DHEA, dehydroepiandrosterone: a steroid hormone naturally produced by the adrenal glands and sold in synthetic form as a nutritional supplement.

di′alog box′, *Computers.* (in a graphical user interface) a box, called up temporarily on the screen, that asks for user input.

did·ger·i·doo (dij′ə rē dōō′, dij′ə rē dōō′), *n., pl.* **-doos.** a musical instrument of Australian Aborigines made from a long wooden tube that is blown into to create a low drone. [1915–20; < an Aboriginal language of N Australia]

die[1], + *v.* **to die for,** stunning; remarkable: *that dress is to die for.*

dig·e·ra·ti (dij′ə rä′tē, -rā′-), *n.pl.* people skilled with or knowledgeable about computers. [1990–95; dig(ital)+(lit)erati]

digital, + *adj.* available in electronic form; readable and manipulable by computer.

diktat, + *n.* any decree or authoritative statement: *The Board of Education issued a diktat that all employees must report an hour earlier.*

DIS, the Disney Channel (a cable television channel).

Dis·ney·fy (diz′nē fī′, -ni-), *v.t.,* **-fied, -fy·ing.** to create or alter in a simplified, sentimentalized, or contrived form or manner. [1970–75, *Amer.;* Disney + -fy] **—Dis′ney·fi·ca′tion,** *n.*

dock′ing sta′tion, a small desktop cabinet, usually containing disk drives and ports for connection to peripherals, into which a laptop may be inserted so as to give it the functionality of a desktop computer.

document, + *n.* a computer data file.

dodge, + *n. Slang.* a business, profession, or occupation.

domes′tic vi′olence, acts of violence against a person living in one's household, esp. a member of one's immediate family.

do·mes·tique (dō′mes tēk′), *n. Cycling.* a member of a bicycle-racing team who assists the leader, as by setting a pace, preventing breakaways by other teams, or supplying food during a race. [1980–85; < F: lit., domestic]

don·gle (dong′gəl, dông′-), *n.* a hardware device attached to a computer without which a given software program will not run: used to prevent unauthorized use. [1980–85]

dou′ble-click′, *v.i. Computers.* to click a mouse button twice in rapid succession, as to call up a program or select a file. [1980–85] **—dou′ble click′.**

dou·la (dōō′lə), *n., pl.* **-las.** a woman who assists women during labor and after childbirth. [1975–80; < Mod Gk: female servant]

downside, + *n.* a discouraging or negative aspect.

dpi, dots per inch: a measure of resolution used esp. for printed text or images.

dream′ team′, a number of persons of the highest ability associated in some joint action: *a dream team that should easily win the Olympics; a dream team of lawyers.* [1990–95]

DRG, Diagnostic Related Grouping: a system implemented by the U.S. government for determining how much Medicare should reimburse hospitals for medical care.

drift, *v.* + **drift off,** to fall asleep gradually.

drive′ bay′, bay (in this section).

drive-by, + *adj.* **1.** occurring while driving past a person: *a drive-by shooting.* **2.** casual; superficial; offhand: *a drive-by news analysis.* **3.** involving a brief stay in a hospital, clinic, etc.: *a drive-by mastectomy.* **—***n.* **4.** a drive-by shooting.

drive′-through′ deliv′ery, childbirth after which the mother has a very brief hospital stay. Also called **drive′-by deliv′ery.** [1990–95]

drop-dead, + *adj.* being the most extreme limit or possibility: *What's the drop-dead date for handing in term papers? That is our drop-dead offer.*

dry′ beer′, beer brewed to have a higher alcohol content and a less bitter aftertaste than normal.

DSC, the Discovery Channel (a cable television channel).

duh (du; *often pronounced with a dentalized* d), *interj.* (used to express annoyance at banality, obviousness, or stupidity.) [1960–65, *Amer.*]

DUI, driving under the influence (of alcohol or drugs): often used as an official police abbreviation.

du jour, +fashionable; current: *environmentalism and other issues du jour.*

dumb, + *v.* **dumb down,** to revise to appeal or be understandable to less intelligent persons; lower the intellectual content of: *to dumb down a textbook; the dumbing down of American movies.*

Dus·sek (dōō′sek), *n.* **Jan La·di·slav** (yän lä′dyi släf), 1760–1812, Czech pianist and composer. Also, **Du·šek** (dŏŏ′shek).

DVD, digital videodisk; digital virtual disk.

eat′ing disor′der, any of various disorders, as anorexia nervosa or bulimia, characterized by severe disturbances in eating habits. [1990–95]

E·bo′la vi′rus (i bō′lə), a highly contagious virus of the family Filoviridae that causes hemorrhagic fever, gastrointestinal distress, and often death. [after *Ebola* River, Zaire, near which virus outbreak occurred in 1976]

E·bon·ics (i bon′iks), *n.* (*used with a sing. v.*) See **Black English.** Also, **e·bon·ics.** [1970–75, *Amer.;* b. of EBONY and PHONICS]

ec·o·tour·ism (ek′ō tŏŏr′iz əm, ē′kō-), *n.* tourism to places having unspoiled natural resources. [1985–90; eco- + TOURISM]

edge′ cit′y, an area on the outskirts of a city having a high density of office buildings, shopping malls, hotels, etc. [1985–90, *Amer.*]

ehr·lich·i·o·sis (ûr lik′ē ō′sis), *n.* an infection caused by bacteria of the genus *Ehrlichia,* which are thought to be transmitted to humans and animals by ticks. [after Paul *Ehrlich*]

El′mer Gan′try (gan′trē), a novel (1927) by Sinclair Lewis.

e-mail, + *n.* **1.** a message sent by e-mail: *Send me an e-mail on the idea.* **—***v.t.* **2.** to send a message to by e-mail.

EMF, electromagnetic field.

En′ergy Star′ Pro′gram, a program of the U.S. Environmental Protection Agency encouraging the manufacture of personal computers and peripherals that can reduce their energy consumption when left idle. [1990–95]

en·vi·ro (en vī′rō), *n., pl.* **-ros.** *Informal.* an environmentalist. [1985–90; by shortening]

eponym, + *n.* a word based on or derived from a person's name.

ERIC, Educational Resources Information Center.

Esch·er (esh′ər; *Du.* es′KHər), *n.* **M(au·rits) C(or·ne·lis) (mou′RITS kôr nā′lis),** 1898–1972, Dutch artist.

ESPN, *Trademark.* the Entertainment Sports Network (a cable television channel).

E′than Frome′ (frōm), a novel (1911) by Edith Wharton.

EU, European Union.

eu·ro[2] (yŏŏr′ō, yûr′-), *n., pl.* **-ros.** a proposed single monetary unit for all European countries. [1970–75; shortening of *Eurocurrency*]

Europe′an Commu′nity, **1.** an association of W European countries that includes the European Atomic Energy Community (Euratom), the European Economic Community, the European Parliament, and allied organizations. *Abbr.:* EC **2.** See **European Economic Community.**

Eu′rope′an Un′ion. See **European Community** (in this section). *Abbr.:* EU

exa-, a combining form used in the names of units of measure equal to one quintillion (10^{18}) of a given base unit. [prob. << Gk *exō-* outside, out of]

explicit, + *adj.* having sexual acts or nudity clearly depicted: *explicit movies; explicit books.*

export, + *v.t. Computers.* to save (documents, data, etc.) in a format usable by another application program.

extreme, + *adj. Chiefly Sports.* extremely dangerous or difficult: *extreme skiing.*

fac·toid + *n.* an insignificant fact. [1973, *Amer.*]

Fair′ Isle′, **1.** a banded geometrical pattern knitted into fabric with multicolored yarns. **2.** clothing featuring such a pattern.

false′-mem′o·ry syn′drome (fôls′mem′ə rē), a

CONCISE PRONUNCIATION KEY: act, cāpe, dâre, pärt; set, ēqual; if, īce; ox, ōver, ôrder, oil, bŏŏk, bōōt, out; up, ûrge; child; sing; shoe; thin, *th*at; zh as in *treasure.* ə = *a* as in *alone, e* as in *system, i* as in *easily, o* as in *gallop, u* as in *circus;* ᵊ as in *fire* (fīᵊr), *hour* (ouᵊr). l and n can serve as syllabic consonants, as in *cradle* (krād′l), and *button* (but′n). See the full key inside the front cover.

psychological condition in which a person believes that he or she remembers events that have not actually occurred. [1990–95]

false-neg•a•tive (fôls′neg′ə tiv), *n.* a test result that is incorrect because the test failed to recognize an existing condition or finding. Cf. **false-positive.**

false-pos•i•tive (fôls′poz′i tiv), *n.* a test result that is incorrect because the test indicated a condition or finding that does not exist. Cf. **false-negative.**

FAM, the Family Channel (a cable television station).

family, + *adj.* **1.** suitable or appropriate for adults and children: *a family amusement park.* **2.** not containing obscene language: *a family newspaper.*

fam′ily leave′, an unpaid leave of absence from work in order to have or take care of a baby or to care for an ailing family member. [1990–95]

fam′ily val′ues, *pl.* the moral and ethical principles traditionally upheld and transmitted within a family, as honesty, loyalty, industry, and faith.

FAQ (fak, ef′ā′kyōō′), *n., pl.* **FAQs, FAQ's.** *Chiefly Computers.* a document that introduces newcomers to a technical topic, as a newsgroup. [1985–90; *f(requently) a(sked) q(uestions)*]

far•fal•le (fär fä′lē, -lā), *n.* pasta in the shape of small bow ties with zigzag edges. [< It, pl. of *farfalla* butterfly]

fart•lek (färt′lek), *n.* a training technique, used esp. among runners, consisting of bursts of intense effort loosely alternating with less strenuous activity. [1950–55; < Sw *fart* speed + *lek* play]

fax′ mo′dem, a modem that can fax data, as documents or pictures, directly from a computer. [1985–90]

fed•ex (fed′eks′), *Informal.* —*v.t.* **1.** to send or ship by Federal Express. —*n.* **2.** a letter or parcel sent by Federal Express.

FedEx (fed′eks′), *Trademark.* Federal Express.

feng shui (fung′ shwā′), the Chinese art or practice of creating harmonious surroundings that enhance the balance of yin and yang, as in arranging furniture or determining the siting of a house. [< Chin: natural surroundings, lit., wind and water]

file•name (fīl′nām′), *n.* an identifying name given to an electronically stored computer file, conforming to limitations imposed by the operating system, as in length or restricted choice of characters.

file′ serv′er, a computer that makes files available to workstations on a network. Cf. **server** (in this section).

fil•o•vi•rus (fil′ə vī′rəs, fī′lə-), *n., pl.* **-rus•es.** any of several viruses that are members of the new virus family Filoviridae, defined by their unique appearance and reproductive strategies, as the Ebola and Marburg viruses.

Fi′nal Four′, the four remaining play-off teams that compete for the U.S. college basketball championship.

finally, + *adv.* at last; eventually; after considerable delay: *After three tries, he finally passed his driving test.*

fin•ger-point•ing (fing′gər poin′ting), *n.* the imputation of blame or responsibility.

fire′ wall′, +an integrated collection of security measures designed to prevent unauthorized electronic access to a networked computer system. Also, **fire′wall′.**

first, + *adj.* (*often cap.*) being a member of the household or an intimate acquaintance of the president of the U.S. or of the governor of a state: *the First Lady; Checkers, the first dog.*

five′-spice pow′der (fīv′spīs′), *n.* a mixture of spices used esp. in Chinese cooking, usually including cinnamon, cloves, fennel seed, pepper, and star anise. [1965–70]

flame, + *Computer Slang.* —*n.* **1.** an act or instance of angry criticism or disparagement, esp. on a computer network. —*v.t.* **2.** to insult or criticize angrily, esp. on a computer network.

flash′ mem′ory, *Computers.* a type of reprogrammable memory that retains information even with the power turned off.

flex•dol•lars (fleks′dol′ərz), *n.pl.* money given by an employer that an employee can apply to any of various employee benefits. [1990–95; FLEX[2] + DOLLAR]

flops (flops), *n.* a measure of computer speed, equal to the number of floating-point operations the computer can perform per second (used esp. in combination with *mega-, giga-, tera-*). [1985–90; *fl(oating-point) op(erations per) s(econd)*]

fo′cus group′, a representative group of people questioned together about their opinions on political issues, consumer products, etc. [1975–80]

Fo•ley (fō′lē), *adj.* of or pertaining to motion-picture sound effects or soundtracks: *a Foley artist; the Foley editor.* [after Jack Foley, sound-effect pioneer at Universal Pictures in the 1930s]

food′ court′, a space, as in a shopping mall, with a concentration of fast-food stalls and usually a common eating area. [1980–85]

Franken-, a combining form extracted from FRANKENSTEIN and used esp. before names of foods, meaning "genetically engineered": *Frankentomato.*

free-range, + *adj.* of, pertaining to, or produced by free-range animals: *free-range eggs.*

free•ware (frē′wâr′), *n.* computer software distributed without charge. Cf. **shareware.** [1980–85]

CONCISE ETYMOLOGY KEY: <, descended or borrowed from; >, whence; b., blend of, blended; c., cognate with; cf., compare; deriv., derivative; equiv., equivalent; imit., imitative; obl., oblique; r., replacing; s., stem; sp., spelling, spelled; resp., respelling, respelled; trans., translation; ?, origin unknown; *, unattested; ‡, probably earlier than. See the full key inside the front cover.

free′ weight′, a weight used for weightlifting, as a dumbbell, whose motion is not constrained by external apparatus.

fre′quent fli′er, an airline passenger registered with a program that provides bonuses, as upgrades or free flights, based esp. on distance traveled. —**fre′quent-fli′er,** *adj.*

fresh, + *adj. Slang.* exciting; appealing; great.

Friedman, + *n.* **Bruce Jay,** born 1930, U.S. novelist.

frum (frŏŏm), *adj. Yiddish.* religious; observant.

FTP, 1. File Transfer Protocol: a software protocol for exchanging information between computers over a network. **2.** any program that implements this protocol.

fudge′ fac′tor, any variable component added to an experiment, plan, or the like that can be manipulated to allow leeway for error.

fusion, + *adj.* (of food) combining usually widely differing ethnic or regional ingredients, styles, or techniques: *a restaurant serving French-Thai fusion cuisine; a fusion menu.*

FWD, 1. Also, **4WD** four-wheel drive. **2.** front-wheel drive.

gangbuster, + *adv.* **go gangbusters,** to be extremely successful: *The movie went gangbusters.*

gated, + *adj.* being a residential neighborhood protected by gates, walls, or other security measures.

gateway, + *n.* software or hardware that links two computer networks.

ga•zil•lion (gə zil′yən), *n.* an extremely large, indeterminate number. [*ga-*, var. of ka- + ZILLION]

ge•ma•tri•a (gə mā′trē ə), *n.* a cabbalistic system of interpretation of the Scriptures by substituting for a particular word another word whose letters give the same numerical sum. [1685–95; < Hebrew *gēmaṭriyā* < Gk *geōmetría* GEOMETRY]

gen•dered (jen′dərd), *adj.* characteristic of, suited to, or biased toward one gender or the other: *gendered diapers.*

ge•no•mics (jē nō′miks, -nom′iks), *n.* (*used with a sing. v.*) the study of genomes. [1985–90]

Gen X (jen′ eks′). See **Generation X.** Also, **GenX, Gen-X**

George, + *n.* **by George!** *Chiefly Brit. Informal.* (an exclamation used to express astonishment, approval, etc.)

get′-go′, *n. Slang.* the very beginning: *from the get-go.* [1965–70, *Amer.*]

Gins•burg (ginz′bûrg), *n.* **Ruth Ba•der** (bā′dər), born 1933, associate justice of the U.S. Supreme Court since 1993.

Glass, + *n.* **Philip,** born 1937, U.S. composer.

GLB, gay, lesbian, bisexual.

Godfather, The, a novel (1969) by Mario Puzo.

Go•pher (gō′fər), *n.* **1.** a protocol for a menu-based system of accessing documents on the Internet. **2.** any program that implements this protocol.

Go•rey (gôr′ē), *n.* **Edward (St. John),** born 1925, U.S. writer and illustrator.

grand′ mas′ter, 1. a chess player in the highest class of ability. **2.** a person at the highest level of ability or achievement in any field. Also, **grand′mas′ter.**

gran′ny dump′ing, the abandonment of an elderly person, esp. a relative, at a hospital, bus station, etc. [1990–95]

graphic, + *adj.* **1.** depicted in a realistic or vivid manner: *graphic sex and violence.* **2.** containing graphic descriptions: *a graphic movie.*

graph′ic design′, the art or profession of visual communication that combines images, words, and ideas to convey information to an audience, esp. to produce a specific effect.

grav•i•tas (grav′i täs′, -tas′), *n.* seriousness or sobriety, as of conduct or speech. [1920–25; < L *gravitās*; see GRAVITY]

green, + *adj.* environmentally sound or beneficial: *green computers.*

green-light (grēn′līt′), *v.t.*, **-light•ed** or *-lit, -light•ing.* to give permission to proceed; authorize: *The renovation project was green-lighted by the board of directors.*

grinch (grinch), *n.* a person or thing that spoils or dampens the pleasure of others. [1965–70; from the *Grinch,* name of a character created by Dr. Seuss (Theodor Seuss Geisel)]

Guernica, + *n.* (*italics*) a painting (1937) by Pablo Picasso.

guil•le•met (gil′ə met′; *Fr.* gēyə mā′), *n.* one of two marks (« or ») used in French, Italian, and Russian printing to enclose quotations. [< F, dim. of *Guillaume* William, prob. name of inventor]

ha•ba•ne•ro (hä′bə nâr′ō), *n., pl.* **-ros.** an extremely pungent small pepper, the fruit of a variety of *Capsicum chinense,* used in cooking. [< Sp *chile habanero* chili from Havana]

ha•lal (hə läl′), *adj.* **1.** (of an animal or its meat) slaughtered or prepared in the manner prescribed by Islamic law. **2.** of or pertaining to halal meat: *a halal butcher.* —*n.* **3.** a halal animal or halal meat. [1850–55; < Ar *ḥalāl* lawful]

half-truth, + *n.* a statement that fails to divulge the whole truth.

hang, + *v.i. Informal.* to hang out.

han•ta•vi•rus (hän′tə vī′rəs, han′-), *n., pl.* **-rus•es.** any of several viruses of the family Bunyaviridae, spread chiefly by wild rodents, that cause acute respiratory illness, kidney failure, and other syndromes. [1975–80; after the *Hantaan* River in Korea, near which the virus first afflicted Westerners in the 1950s]

happen, + *v.i. Slang.* to be very exciting or interesting: *That party was happening!*

hard′ drive′, a disk drive containing a hard disk. [1980–85]

Hard•wick (härd′wik), *n.* **Elizabeth,** born 1916, U.S. novelist and critic.

HBO, *Trademark.* Home Box Office (a cable television channel).

heads-up, + *n. Chiefly Politics.* a warning: *sending a heads-up to the Pentagon about possible attacks.*

Hea•ney (hā′nē), *n.* **Sea•mus** (shā′məs), born 1939, Irish poet: Nobel prize 1995.

heather, + *adj.* (of a yarn or fabric color) subtly flecked or mottled: *all-cotton turtlenecks in your choice of five solid colors plus heather gray and heather green.*

hedge′ fund′, *n.* an open-end investment company organized as a limited partnership and using high-risk speculative methods to obtain large profits. [1965–70]

Hel•ler (hel′ər), *n.* **Joseph,** born 1923, U.S. novelist.

hello, + *interj.* (used derisively to question the comprehension, intelligence, or common sense of the person being addressed): *You're gonna go out with him? Hello!*

Hen•ley (hen′lē), *n.* a short- or long-sleeved pullover sport shirt, usually of cotton, with a round neckband and a buttoned neckline placket that is often covered with a flap. Also called **Hen′ley shirt′.** [after a style traditionally worn by rowers at Henley-on-Thames]

Hepburn, + *n.* **Audrey,** 1929–93, U.S. actress, born in Belgium.

HF, +Hispanic female.

Hicks, + *n.* **Granville,** 1902–82, U.S. writer, educator, and editor.

High•et (hī′it), *n.* **Gilbert,** 1906–78, U.S. writer and classical scholar.

high′-oc′cu•pan•cy ve′hicle (hī′ok′yə pən sē). See **HOV** (in this section).

his•sy (his′ē), *n., pl.* **-sies.** *Slang.* a fit of anger; temper tantrum. Also called **his′sy fit′.** [1930–35, *Amer.*]

HIV positive, (of a person) diagnosed by a test as being infected with HIV.

HM, Hispanic male.

holy war, +any disagreement or argument between fanatical proponents of radically differing beliefs, opinions, etc.: *a holy war on the merits of computer operating systems; a holy war about welfare reform.*

home′ page′, *Computers.* the initial page of a site on the World Wide Web.

hor′izon′tal tast′ing, a tasting of wines from the same year but from different vineyards, producers, etc.

hor′mone replace′ment ther′apy, the administration of estrogen and progestin to alleviate symptoms of menopause and, in postmenopausal women, esp. to protect against cardiovascular disease and osteoporosis. Cf. **estrogen replacement therapy.** *Abbr.:* HRT

hot•link (hot′lingk′), *n.* a hypertext link. [1990–95]

HOV, high-occupancy vehicle: a bus, van, or car with two or more passengers. [1990–95]

HOV lane, a highway or street lane for high-occupancy vehicles, usually marked with large diamond shapes on the pavement. [1990–95]

Howe, + *n.* **Irving,** 1920–93, U.S. social historian and literary critic.

HRT, hormone replacement therapy.

HTML, HyperText Markup Language: a set of standards, a variety of SGML, used to tag the elements of a hypertext document, the standard for documents on the World Wide Web.

http, hypertext transfer protocol: a protocol for transferring hypertext documents, the standard protocol for the World Wide Web.

humanitarian, + *adj.* pertaining to the saving of human lives or to the alleviation of suffering: *a humanitarian crisis.*

human resources, +See **human resources department.**

hy•per•link (hī′pər lingk′), *n.* a hypertext link.

ice′ beer′, beer brewed at subfreezing temperatures. [1990–95]

ICS, International College of Surgeons.

ID, + *v.t.,* **ID'd** or *IDed* or *ID'ed, ID'ing* or *ID•ing.* **1.** to identify. **2.** to issue an ID to: *Go to the admissions office if you haven't been ID'd yet.*

IDE, intact dilatation and extraction.

IGY, International Geophysical Year.

il•lude (i lōōd′), *v.t.,* **-lud•ed, -lud•ing. 1.** to deceive or trick. **2.** *Obs.* **a.** to mock or ridicule. **b.** to evade. [1445–50; ME < L *illūdere* to mock, ridicule; see ILLUSION]

im•age•set•ter (im′ij set′ər), *n.* a printer, or typesetting machine, for producing professional-quality text with extremely high resolution.

impaired, + *adj. Facetious.* deficient or incompetent (prec. by a noun or adverb): *VCR-impaired; morally impaired.*

import, + *v.t. Computers.* to bring (documents, data, etc.) into one application program from another.

in•cen•ti•vize (in sen′ti vīz′), *v.t.,* **-vized, -viz•ing.** to give incentives to: *The Government should incentivize the private sector to create jobs.* [1965–70, *Amer.*]

industry, + *n.* the aggregate of work, scholarship, and ancillary activity in a particular field, often named after its principal subject: *the Mozart industry.*

in′forma′tion su′perhighway, a large-scale communications network providing a variety of often interactive services, such as text databases, electronic mail, and audio and video materials, accessed through computers, television sets, etc. Also called **data highway.** [1990–95]

informa′tion technol′ogy, the development, implementation, and maintenance of computer hardware and software systems to organize and communicate information electronically.

ink, + *n. Informal.* publicity, esp. in print media.

in′ner child′, the childlike aspect of a person's psyche, esp. when viewed as an independent entity.

intact′ dilata′tion and extrac′tion, a method of abortion used in the second or third trimester of pregnancy. *Abbr.:* IDE

In·ter·net (in′tər net′), *n.* a large computer network linking smaller computer networks worldwide (usually prec. by *the*). [1990–95]

in·tra·net (in′trə net′), a computer network with restricted access, as within a corporation, that uses software and protocols developed for the Internet. [1996]

Invis′ible Man′, The, **1.** a novel (1897) by H.G. Wells. **2.** a novel (1952) by Ralph Ellison.

ironic, + *adj.* coincidental; unexpected: *It was ironic that I was seated next to my ex-husband at the dinner.*

Jack′ Rus′sell ter′rier, any of a breed of small, compact terriers having large, erect ears and a short white coat with brown or black markings. Also called **Jack′ Rus′sell.**

Java, +*Trademark.* a programming language used to create interactive applications running over the Internet.

jerk, + *adj.* **1.** being or containing a spicy seasoning mixture flavored with allspice, used esp. in Jamaican cooking: *jerk sauce.* **2.** prepared with jerk flavorings, esp. by barbecuing or grilling; *jerk chicken.*

Jesus H. Christ, *interj. Sometimes Offensive.* (used as an expression of surprise, disappointment, astonishment, etc.) [1890–95, *Amer.;* the *H* prob. < *IHS* or *IHC,* Gk abbrev. for *Jesus,* in which the *H* (the capital Gk letter eta) is reinterpreted as the English letter H]

Jet′ Ski′, *Trademark.* a jet-propelled boat ridden like a motorcycle.

Jet·way (jet′wā′), *Trademark.* a movable passageway in an airport connecting the terminal building to an airplane.

JF, Jewish female.

JM, Jewish male.

Joe′ Six′pack (siks′pak), *Slang.* the average or typical blue-collar man. Also, **Joe′ Six′-pack.** [1975–80, *Amer.*]

John Doe, +a unidentified man: *The police were looking for a John Doe.*

ju·ku (jo͞o′ko͞o), *n., pl.* **-ku.** (in Japan) a school, attended in addition to one's regular school, where students prepare for college entrance examinations. [1980–85; < Japn]

junk DNA, segments of DNA that have no apparent genetic function. [1990–95]

jury, + *n.* **the jury is (still) out,** a decision, determination, or opinion has yet to be rendered: *The jury is still out on the President's performance.*

Ka·zin (kā′zin), *n.* **Alfred,** born 1915, U.S. literary critic.

kei·ret·su (kā ret′so͞o), *n., pl.* **-su.** (esp. in Japan) a loose coalition of business groups. [1975–80; < Japn]

ken·bei (ken′bā), *n. Japanese.* strong anti-American sentiment. [1990–95; < Japn = *ken* hate + *bei* America]

kill′er app′, a computer application that surpasses its competitors. [1990–95]

Kim Jong Il (kim′ jong′ il′), born 1942, North Korean political leader; son of Kim Il Sung.

King, + *n.* **Stephen,** born 1947, U.S. novelist and short-story writer.

klep·toc·ra·cy (klep tok′rə sē), *n., pl.* **-cies.** a government or state in which those in power exploit national resources and steal; rule by a thief or thieves. [1815–20; *klepto-* (comb. form of Gk *kléptēs* thief) + -cracy] **—klep·to·crat·ic** (klep′tə krat′ik), *adj.*

klep·to·crat (klep′tə krat′), *n.* a government official who is a thief or exploiter.

Ko·sin·ski (kə zin′skē), *n.* **Jer·zy** (jûr′zē, yezh′ē), 1933–91, U.S. novelist, born in Poland.

Ko·vàč (kô′väch), *n.* **Mi·chal** (mi′кнäl), born 1928, president of Slovakia since 1993.

ku·na (ko͞o′nə), *n., pl.* **-na.** the basic monetary unit of Croatia.

Ku·nitz (kyo͞o′nits), *n.* **Stanley,** born 1905, U.S. poet and translator.

La·can (lə käɴ′, -kän′), *n.* **Jacques,** 1901–81, French philosopher and psychoanalyst.

la-la land (lä′lä′), *n. Slang.* **1.** a state of being out-of-touch with reality. **2.** Los Angeles. [1980–85]

lao·gai (lou′gī′), *n.* the system of forced-labor camps, prisons, etc., in China. [1990–95; < Chin: lit., reform through labor]

lap′ dance′, an erotic dance by a stripteaser performed mostly in the lap of a customer. [1990–95] **—lap′-dance′,** *v.i.* —lap′ danc′ing.

Las·so (lä′sō), *n.* **Orlando di** (dē), (*Orlandus Lassus*) 1532–94, Flemish composer.

lat·te (lä′tā), *n.* hot espresso served mixed with hot milk. [1990–95; < It *(caffè) latte* (coffee with) milk]

launch, + *v.t. Computers.* to start (an application program).

legacy, + *n.* **1.** an applicant to or student at a school that was attended by a parent of the applicant. **—*adj.* 2.** of or pertaining to old or outdated computer hardware, software, or data that, while still functional, does not work well with up-to-date systems.

lep·tin (lep′tin), *n.* a hormone that is thought to suppress appetite and speed up metabolism. [1995; < Gk *leptós* small, thin + -in[2]]

LIF, Lifetime (a cable television channel).

life, + *n.* **get a life,** to improve the quality of one's social and professional life: often used in the imperative to express impatience with someone's behavior.

life′ part′ner, one member of a monogamous relationship.

light′ning chess′. See **speed chess** (in this section).

like, + *conj. Informal.* (used esp. after forms of *be* to introduce reported speech or thought): *She's like, "I don't believe it," and I'm like, "No, it's true!"*

link[1], + *n. Computers.* an object, as text or graphics, linked through hypertext to a document, another object, etc.

li·pa (lē′pə), *n., pl.* **-pa.** a monetary unit of Croatia.

lip·o·pro·tein(a) (lip′ə prō′tēn a′, -tē in ā′, lī′pə-), *n.* a plasma lipoprotein containing protein and cholesterol, high levels of which are associated with atherosclerosis.

List·serv (list′sûrv′), *n.* a specific list server: one of the most common list servers on the Internet.

list′ serv′er, *Computers.* any program that distributes messages to a mailing list. [1990–95]

lit·i·ga·tor (lit′i gā′tər), *n.* a person who litigates, esp. a courtroom lawyer.

Long′ Is′land iced′ tea′, a mixed drink of tequila, rum, vodka, gin, curaao, cola, lemon juice, and sugar.

lordosis, + *n.* a posture assumed by some female mammals during mating, in which the back arches downward.

Lowry, + *n.* **(Clarence) Malcolm (Bo·den)** (bōd′n), 1909–57, U.S. novelist, born in England.

Lp(a), lipoprotein(a).

LTR, long-term relationship.

lurk, + *v.i. Chiefly Computers.* to observe an ongoing discussion without participating in it.

ma·ca·re·na (mä′kə rā′nə, -ren′ə), *n.* (*often cap.*) a dance performed in a group line or solo and following a rhythmic pattern of arm, hand, and hip movements in time to a Spanish song. [1990–95; < Sp: fem. of *macareno* boaster, braggart]

mad′ cow′ disease′. See **bovine spongiform encephalopathy** (in this section). [1990–95]

mad-dog (mad′dôg′, -dog′), *v.t.,* **-dogged, -dog·ging.** *Slang.* to glare at threateningly. [1985–90, *Amer.*]

madeleine, + *n.* something that triggers memories or nostalgia. [in allusion to a nostalgic passage in Proust's ***Remembrance of Things Past***]

mail′ing list′, 1. a list of addresses to which mail, esp. advertisements, can be sent. **2.** *Computers.* a list of E-mail addresses to which messages, usually on a specific topic, are sent; a discussion group whose messages are distributed through E-mail: *I'm on the early American history mailing list on the Internet. Cf.* ***list server*** (in this section).

ma·jor·ly (mā′jər lē), *adv. Slang.* extremely; thoroughly: *The class was majorly hard.* [1980–85]

Malle (mal), *n.* **Lou·is** (lo͞o′ē; *Fr.* lwē), 1932–95, French film director.

man′aged care′, comprehensive health care provided by a health maintenance organization or similar system. [1985–90]

man·ga (mäng′gə, mang′-), *n.* a Japanese graphic novel, typically intended for adults, characterized by highly stylized art. [< Japn, lit., cartoon, comic strip]

marquee, + *adj.* superlative; headlining: *a marquee basketball player.*

mau-mau (mou′mou′), *v.t. Slang.* to terrorize, intimidate, or threaten. [1970; coined by Tom WOLFE in *Radical Chic and Mau-Mauing the Flak Catchers;* see Mau Mau]

MAX, Cinemax (a cable television channel).

MB, +Manitoba, Canada (approved for postal use).

MBO, management by objectives.

Mc-, +a combining form, used esp. to form nonce words, with the meaning "generic; homogenized": *McSchools that offer no individual attention; reading McNews instead of a serious newspaper.* [< *Mc(Donald's),* chain of fast-food restaurants]

Mc·Job (mək job′), *n.* an unstimulating, low-wage job with few benefits, esp. in a service industry. [1991, *Amer.;* coined by Douglas Coupland (b. 1961) in the novel *Generation X*]

MDT, 1. mean downtime. **2.** Also, **M.D.T.** mountain daylight time.

means-test (mēnz′test′), *v.t.* **1.** to subject (a person or a specific benefit) to a means test: *Government proposes to means-test Medicare.* **—*v.i.* 2.** to perform a means test: *fair and responsible means-testing.* [1960–65]

medal, + *v.i.* to receive a medal, esp. in a sporting event: *He medaled in three of four races.*

med·i·cide (med′ə sīd′), *n.* a medically assisted suicide. Cf. **assisted suicide** (in this section). [1990–95; *medi(cal)* + -CIDE]

meer·kat (mēr′kat), *n.* suricate. [1795–1805; < D: lit., monkey, appar. = *meer* sea (see mere[2]) + *kat* CAT]

Meg′an's Law′ (mā′gənz), any of various laws aimed at people convicted of sex-related crimes, requiring community notification of the release of offenders, establishment of a registry of offenders, etc. [1990–95; after *Megan* Kanka, young New Jersey girl killed by a previously convicted criminal]

-meister, a combining form meaning "a person expert in or renowned for" something specified by the initial element (often used derisively): *schlockmeister; opinionmeister; dealmeister.* [< G *Meister* master]

meme (mēm), *n.* a cultural item that is transmitted by repetition in a manner analogous to the biological transmission of genes. [1976; < Gk *mimeîsthai* to imitate, copy; coined by R. Dawkins, U.S. biologist]

Merwin, + *n.* **W(illiam) S(tanley),** born 1927, U.S. poet, translator, and writer.

mesc·lun (mes′klən), *n.* a salad consisting esp. of young, tender mixed greens. [1985–90; < F, < *mescler* to mix]

messenger, + *v.t.* to send by messenger.

met·a·fic·tion (met′ə fik′shən), *n.* fiction that discusses, describes, or analyzes a work of fiction or the conventions of fiction. [1975–80]

metastasize, + *v.i.* **1.** to spread injuriously: *Street gangs have metastasized in our city.* **2.** to transform, esp. into a dangerous form: *The KGB metastasized after the fall of the Soviet Union. Truth metastasized into lurid fantasy.*

MH, Marshall Islands (approved for postal use).

mi·cro·brew (mī′krō bro͞o′), *n.* beer brewed in a microbrewery. [1980–85]

mif·e·pris·tone (mif′ə pris′tōn), *n.* See **RU 486.** [1995; from the chemical name]

militia, + *n.* a body of citizens organized in a paramilitary group and typically regarding themselves as defenders of individual rights against the presumed interference of the federal government.

mind-bod·y (mīnd′bod′ē), *adj.* taking into account the physiological, psychic, and spiritual connections between the state of the body and that of the mind: *mind-body medicine.*

mind′ games′, psychological manipulation or strategy, used esp. to gain advantage or to intimidate. [1970–75]

min·i·stroke (min′ē strōk′), *n.* See **transient ischemic attack.**

min·i·tow·er (min′ē tou′ər), *n.* a vertical case, smaller than a tower and larger than a case for a desktop computer, designed to house a computer system standing on a floor or desk. [1990–95]

molec′ular knife′, a segment of genetic material that inhibits the reproduction of the AIDS virus by breaking up specific areas of the virus's genes. [1990–95, *Amer.*]

molest, + *v.t.* to assault sexually.

mon·de·green (mon′di grēn′), *n.* a word or phrase resulting from a misinterpretation of a word or phrase that has been heard. [1954; coined by S. Wright, British writer, fr. the line *laid him on the green,* interpreted as *Lady Mondegreen,* in a Scottish ballad]

mon·do[2] (mon′dō), *Slang.* **—*adv.* 1.** very; extremely: *mondo cool.* **—*adj.* 2.** large; big: *a mondo history paper.* [1965–70; < It *mondo* world, extracted fr. the film *Mondo Cane* (1961) and reinterpreted as an adv. in It or pseudo-It phrases such as *mondo bizarro* very bizarre, lit., bizarre world]

mo·nor·chid (mə nôr′kid), *Pathol.* **—*adj.* 1.** having or appearing to have only one testis. **—*n.* 2.** a monorchid individual. [1820-30; < NL *monorchis* (erroneous pl. *monorchides*), equiv. to mon- + *orchid-* (< Gk *orchid-;* see ORCHID)]

mo·nor·chid·ism (mə nôr′ki diz′əm), *n. Pathol.* a prenatal or postnatal condition in which one testis is absent or has not descended into the scrotum. Also, **mo·nor·chism** (mə nôr′kiz əm). [1860-65; MONORCHID + -ism]

morph, + *v.t.* to transform (an image) by computer.

mosh (mosh), *v.i. Slang.* to engage in a form of frenzied, violent dancing; slam-dance. [1980–85; perh. var. of mash[1]]

mosh′ pit′, *Slang.* an area usually in front of a stage where people mosh at rock concerts. [1985–90]

moun′tain bike′, a bicycle designed for off-road use, typically having a smaller and sturdier frame and smaller and wider tires than a standard bicycle. [1985–90] **—moun′tain bik′er. —moun′tain bik′ing.**

mouse′ pad′, *Computers.* a small typically foam rubber sheet used to provide a stable surface on which a computer mouse can be moved. [1980–85]

mouth·feel (mouth′fēl′), *n.* the tactile sensation a food gives to the mouth: *a creamy mouthfeel.* [1980–85, *Amer.*]

MPR II, a standard developed in Sweden that limits to 250 nanoteslas the electromagnetic radiation emissions from a computer monitor at a distance of a half meter.

My′ An·to·ni′a (an′tə nē′ə), a novel (1918) by Willa Cather.

n/a, +not applicable.

nail, + *n.* **1. nail in someone's** or *something's coffin,* something that hastens the demise or failure of a person or thing: *Every moment's delay is another nail in his coffin.* **—*v.t.* 2.** to accomplish perfectly: *the only gymnast to nail the dismount.*

nail-bit·er (nāl′bī′tər), *n.* **1.** a person who bites his or her nails, esp. habitually. **2.** a situation marked by anxiety or tension. [1970–75]

Nai·paul (nī′pôl′), *n.* **V(idiadhar) S(urajprasad),** born

CONCISE PRONUNCIATION KEY: act, cāpe, dâre, pärt; set, ēqual; if, īce; ox, ōver, ôrder, oil, bo͝ok, bo͞ot, out; up, ûrge; child; sing; shoe; thin, *th*at; zh as in *treasure.* ə = *a* as in *alone, e* as in *system, i* as in *easily, o* as in *gallop, u* as in *circus;* ᵊ as in *fire* (fīᵊr), *hour* (ouᵊr). l and n can serve as syllabic consonants, as in *cradle* (krād′l), and *button* (but′n). See the full key inside the front cover.

1932, English novelist and nonfiction writer, born in Trinidad.

Na′ked Lunch′, The, a novel (1959–66) by William S. Burroughs.

nan′ny tax′, the portion of Social Security and Medicare taxes paid by the employer of a nanny, gardener, or other household worker. [1990–95]

nan•o•tes•la (nan′ə tes′lə, nā′nə-), *n., pl.* **-las.** one billionth of a tesla.

native, + *adj. Computers.* **1.** designed for use with a specific type of computer: *writing native applications for 32-bit PCs.* **2.** internal to a specific application program: *to view the file in its native format.*

NAV, net asset value.

Nazi, + *n. Sometimes Offensive. (often l.c.)* a person who is fanatically dedicated to or seeks to control a specified activity, practice, etc.: *a jazz nazi who disdains other forms of music; tobacco nazis trying to ban smoking.*

NB, +New Brunswick, Canada (approved for postal use).

NBC, National Broadcasting Company: a television network.

nde, near-death experience. Also, **NDE**

N.E.A., +National Endowment for the Arts. Also, **NEA**

near′-death′ expe′rience (nēr′deth′), any experience involving a vision, as of the afterlife, reported by a resuscitated person.

necropsy, + *v.t.,* **-sied, -sy•ing.** to perform a necropsy on.

Nerf (nûrf), *Trademark.* any of various toys modeled esp. on sports equipment but made of foam rubber or other soft substances.

net[1], + *n.* **the Net,** the Internet.

Ne•tan•ya•hu (net′än yä′ho͞o), *n.* **Benjamin,** born 1949, Israeli prime minister since 1996.

net′ as′set val′ue, the price of a share in a mutual fund, equal to the total value of the fund's securities divided by the number of shares outstanding. *Abbr.:* NAV

net•i•quette (net′i kit, -ket′), *n.* the etiquette of computer networks, esp. the Internet. [1980–85; b. NETWORK + ETIQUETTE]

new•bie (no͞o′bē, nyo͞o′-), *n. Computers.* an inexperienced user of the Internet or of computers in general. [1965–70]

new′ me′dia, developing usually electronic forms of media regarded as being experimental. [1990–95]

news•group (no͞oz′gro͞op′, nyo͞oz′-), *n.* a discussion group on a specific topic, maintained on a computer network. [1985–90]

Nex•is (nek′sis), *Trademark.* a large computer database storing the text of many newspapers and magazines, accessible for a fee.

NF, +Newfoundland, Canada (approved for postal use).

NGO, 1. National Gas Outlet. **2.** Nongovernmental Organization.

niche, + *n.* **1.** a distinct segment of a market. —*adj.* **2.** of or pertaining to a distinct segment of a market.

Nin (nin), *n.* **A•na•ïs** (ə nī′əs), 1903–77, U.S. novelist and diarist.

non•start•er (non stär′tər), *n.* an issue, plan, etc., that does not get or deserve to get under way. [1905–10]

NOR (ôr), *n.* a Boolean operator that returns a positive result when both operands are negative.

NOT (not), *n.* a Boolean operator that returns a positive result if its operand is negative and a negative result if its operand is positive.

notebook, + *n.* a small, lightweight laptop computer measuring approximately 8 1/2×11 in. (22×28 cm).

noth•er (nuth′ər), *adj. Informal.* **a whole nother,** an entirely different; a whole other. [1955–60; metanalysis of *an other* or *another*]

NREM (en′rem′, non′rem′), *n.* non-REM; non-rapid eye movement.

NS, Nova Scotia, Canada (approved for postal use).

NSAID, nonsteroidal anti-inflammatory drug.

NT, Northwest Territories, Canada (approved for postal use).

object, + *n. Computers.* any item that can be individually selected or manipulated, as a picture, data file, or piece of text.

off-la•bel (ôf′lā′bəl, of′-), *adj. Informal.* of, pertaining to, or designating a drug prescribed for a particular indication even though the drug has not yet received approval from the Food and Drug Administration for that disease, condition, or symptom.

o•go•nek (ō gō′nek), *n.* a mark (˛) placed under a letter, such as Polish *a* or *e,* to mark a nasal sound; an inverted cedilla. [< Pol: lit., bobtail]

old, + *adj.* overfamiliar to the point of tedium: *Some jokes get old fast.*

o•les•tra (ō les′trə), *n.* a synthetic oil used as a substitute for dietary fat: not digested or absorbed by the human body. [1995; *ol-* (< L *oleum* oil) + *-estra,* alter. of *(poly)ester*]

Ol•son (ōl′sən), *n.* **Charles,** 1910–70, U.S. poet and essayist.

ON, +Ontario, Canada (approved for postal use).

CONCISE ETYMOLOGY KEY: <, descended or borrowed from; >, whence; b., blend of, blended; c., cognate with; cf., compare; deriv., derivative; equiv., equivalent; imit., imitative; obl., oblique; r., replacing; s., stem; sp., spelling, spelled; resp., respelling, respelled; trans., translation; ?, origin unknown; *, unattested; ‡, probably earlier than. See the full key inside the front cover.

one-note (wun′nōt′), *adj.* lacking in variety; monotonous.

on-line, + *adj.* connected by computer to one or more other computers or networks, as through a commercial electronic information service or the Internet.

On′ the Road′, a novel (1957) by Jack Kerouac.

OR (ôr), *n.* a Boolean operator that returns a positive result when either or both operands are positive.

ORV, off-road vehicle.

out, + *v.t.* to intentionally expose (a secret homosexual, a spy, etc.).

out•er•course (ou′tər kôrs′, -kōrs′), *n.* sexual activity between two or more people that does not involve penetration. [1990–95; patterned on INTERCOURSE]

out•source (out′sôrs′, -sōrs′), *v.t.,* **-sourced, -sourc•ing.** to purchase (goods) or subcontract (services) from an outside company. [1980]

o•ver•class (ō′vər klas′, -kläs′), *n.* a social stratum consisting of educated and wealthy persons considered to control the economic power of a country. [1990–95]

P.A., +Parents' Association. Also, **PA**

page, + *n. Computers.* See **Web page** (in this section).

pap•par•del•le (pap′ər del′ē, -del′ā), *n.* flat pasta cut in wide strips. [< It]

par′tial-birth′ abor′tion (pär′shəl bûrth′), (term used chiefly by opponents of abortion) See **intact dilatation and extraction** (in this section).

pas•sive-ma•trix (pas′iv mā′triks), *adj.* of or pertaining to a relatively low-resolution liquid-crystal display (LCD) with low contrast, used esp. for laptop computers. Cf. **active-matrix** (in this section). [1990–95]

patch, + *n.* an adhesive patch that applies to the skin and gradually delivers drugs or medication to the user: *using a nicotine patch to try to quit smoking.*

pa•thog•ra•phy (pə thog′rə fē), *n., pl.* **-phies.** a biography that focuses on the negative elements of its subject. [1910–20 for an earlier sense; popularized by Joyce Carol Oates, U.S. writer]

patriot, + *n.* a person who regards himself or herself as a defender, esp. of individual rights, against presumed interference by the federal government.

PC card, a small, removable, externally accessible circuit board housing a device, as a modem or disk drive, and conforming to the PCMCIA standard: used esp. for laptop computers.

PCMCIA, Personal Computer Memory Card International Association: (esp. for laptop computers) a standard for externally accessible expansion slots that accept compatible cards for enhancing the computer's functions, as by adding memory or supplying a portable modem.

PCP, +primary care physician.

PDA, personal digital assistant.

PDR, Physicians' Desk Reference.

PE, Prince Edward Island, Canada (approved for postal use).

pen•ne (pen′ā), *n., pl.* **-ne.** a type of tubular pasta having diagonally cut ends. [1970–75; < It, pl. of *penna* pen, feather, quill]

Persist′ence of Mem′ory, The, a painting (1931) by Salvador Dali.

per′sonal dig′ital assis′tant, a hand-held computer, often pen-based, that provides esp. organizational software, as an appointment calendar, and communications hardware, as a fax modem. *Abbr.:* PDA

per′sonal or′ganizer, 1. a small notebook with sections for personal information, as dates and addresses. **2.** a handheld computer that contains this information.

per′sonal train′er, a person who works one-on-one with a client to plan or implement an exercise or fitness regimen. [1990–95]

per′sonal wa′tercraft, a jet-propelled boat or boats ridden like a motorcycle. [1990–95]

peta-, a combining form used in the names of units of measure equal to one quadrillion (10^{15}) of a given base unit. [orig. uncert.]

pet′ sit′ting, the act of caring for a pet in its own home while the owner is away. —pet′ sit′ter.

phat, + *adj. Slang.* great; wonderful; terrific. [1960–65, *Amer.*; resp. of FAT]

phone′ card′. See **calling card** (in this section).

phone′ sex′, sexually explicit conversations engaged in on a telephone, usually for a fee.

Plug′ and Play′, *(sometimes l.c.)* a standard for the production of compatible computers, peripherals, and software that facilitates device installation and enables automatic configuration of the system. [1990–95]

po-faced (pō′fāst′), *adj. Chiefly Brit.* having an overly serious demeanor or attitude; humorless.

police, + *n.* people who seek to regulate a specified activity, practice, etc.: *the language police.*

po•li•cier (pô lē syā′), *n., pl.* ***-ciers*** (-syā′). *French.* a novel or film featuring detectives, crime, or the like.

Port•a•Pot•ti (pôr′tə pot′ē, pōr′-), *Trademark.* a brand of portable toilet.

post, + *n. Computers.* **1.** a message that is sent to a newsgroup. —*v.t.* **2.** to send (a message) to a newsgroup. —*v.i.* **3.** to send a message to a newsgroup.

postal, + *adj.* **go postal,** *Slang.* to lose control or go crazy.

post′er child′, 1. a child appearing on a poster for a charitable organization. **2.** a person or thing that exemplifies or represents: *She could be a poster child for good sportsmanship.* [1990–95]

postmodern, + *adj.* extremely modern; cutting-edge: *postmodern kids who grew up on MTV.*

Post•Script (pōst′skript′), *Trademark.* a page description language using scalable fonts that can be printed on a variety of appropriately equipped devices, including laser printers and professional-quality imagesetters.

Pow′er Bar′, *Trademark.* a brand of bar-shaped food intended for use esp. by athletes, having a high carbohydrate and low fat content with protein and vitamin supplements.

PQ, Quebec, Canada (approved for postal use).

Prae•to•ri•us (prē tôr′ē əs, -tōr′-), *n.* **Michael** (*Michael Schultheiss*), 1571–1621, German composer, organist, and theorist.

Preak•ness (prēk′nis), *n.* a horse race for three-year-olds run annually two weeks after the Kentucky Derby at Pimlico in Baltimore, Md.

PRF, +Puerto Rican female.

price′ point′, *n.* the price for which something is sold on the retail market, esp. in contrast to competitive prices.

PRM, Puerto Rican male.

profanity, + *n.* obscenity (defs. 2, 3).

pro•to-on•co•gene (prō′tō ong′kə jēn′), *n.* a normally present gene that appears to have a role in the regulation of normal cell growth, but that is converted to an oncogene by mutation.

PSA, prostate specific antigen: a protein, produced by the prostate, elevated levels of which may indicate the presence of cancer.

P.U.D., pickup and delivery.

PWC, See **personal watercraft** (in this section).

PYO, pick your own.

py•ra•can•tha (pī′rə kan′thə), *n., pl.* **-thas.** firethorn. [1700–10; < NL *Pyracantha* type genus < Gk *pyrákantha* kind of shrub = *pyr̂* FIRE + *ákantha* thorn]

q.m., (in prescriptions) every morning. [< L *quoque matutino*]

q.n., (in prescriptions) every night. [< L *quoque nocte*]

quant (kwänt), *n. Business Slang.* an expert in quantitative analysis. [1985–90, *Amer.*; by clipping]

quan′titative anal′ysis, + *Business.* the use of esp. computerized mathematical analysis to support decision making, make business forecasts or investment recommendations, etc.

rafter[2], + *n.* a person who travels on a raft, esp. to flee a country.

rat, + *n. Slang.* a person who frequents a specified place: *a mall rat; gym rats.*

re•al•i•ty-based (rē al′i tē bāst′), *adj.* (esp. of television) portraying or alleging to portray events as they actually happened.

real′ity check′, a corrective confronting of reality, in order to counteract one's expectations, prejudices, or the like. [1970–75]

red′ card′, *Soccer.* a red card shown by the referee to a player being sent off the field for a flagrant violation. Cf. **yellow card** (in this section).

red•shirt (red′shûrt′), *n.* **1.** a high-school or college athlete kept out of varsity competition for one year to develop skills and extend eligibility. —*v.t.* **2.** to withdraw (an athlete) from varsity competition. [1950–55, *Amer.*; from the red shirts worn in practice by such athletes]

reinvent, + *v.t.* to remake as if from the very beginning; renovate: *to reinvent government.*

repet′itive strain′ disor′der. See **repetitive strain injury** (in this section). *Abbr.:* RSD

repet′itive strain′ in′jury, any of a group of debilitating disorders, as of the hand and arm, characterized typically by pain, numbness, tingling, or loss of muscle control and caused by the stress of repeated movements. *Abbr.:* RSI

ret•ro•nym (re′trə nim), *n.* a term, such as *acoustic guitar,* coined in modification of the original referent that was used alone, such as *guitar,* to distinguish it from a later contrastive development, such as *electric guitar.* [1990–95, *Amer.*; retro- + *-nym,* as in HOMONYM]

right•size (rīt′sīz′), *v.t.,* **-sized, -siz•ing.** to adjust to an appropriate size: *Layoffs will be necessary to rightsize our workforce.* [1985–90]

road′ war′rior, *Slang.* a person who travels extensively on business. [sugg. by the film *Mad Max: The Road Warrior* (1981)]

rock′et sci′ence, 1. rocketry. **2.** something requiring great intelligence, esp. mathematical ability.

rock•u•men•ta•ry (rok′yə men′tə rē), *n.* a documentary about rock music. [1980–85; b. ROCK + DOCUMENTARY]

Rollerblade, + *v.,* **-blad•ed, -blad•ing.** *v.i. (often l.c.)* to skate on in-line skates. —**Roll′er•blad′er, roll′er•blad′er,** *n.*

roo•fie (ro͞o′fē), *n. Slang.* a powerful sedative drug that causes semiconsciousness and memory blackouts: has been implicated in date rapes. [1990–95; alter. of *Rohypnol,* brand name of this drug]

ro•shi (rō′shē), *n.* the religious leader of a group of Zen Buddhists. [< Japn *rōshi*]

Rotis′serie League′ Base′ball, *Trademark.* a game in which participants compete by running imaginary baseball teams whose results are based on the actual performances of major-league players.

RSD, repetitive strain disorder.

RSI, repetitive strain injury.

rum•bus•tious (rum bus′chəs), *adj. Chiefly Brit.* rambunctious. [prob. var. ROBUSTIOUS]

safe′ ar′ea, an area near a combat zone that is maintained as being free from military attack. Also called **safe′ ha′ven.**

same′-sex′, *adj.* of or involving a sexual relationship between two men or between two women: *same-sex marriage.* [1996]

schm-, *prefix.* (used to form jocular reduplications, as *value-schmalue, text-schmext*). *Also,* **shm-.** [< Yiddish *shm-*]

Scream, The, a painting (1937) by Edvard Munch.

screen′ sav′er, *Computers.* a program that displays a constantly shifting pattern on a display screen, used to prevent damage to the screen through continuous display of the same image.

scrunch·y (skrun′chē), *n., pl.* **scrunch·ies.** a small, round elasticized fabric band, used esp. by women to fasten the hair. Also, **scrunch′ie.** [1990–95]

self-de·liv·er·ance (self′di liv′ər əns), *n.* suicide. [1990–95]

Sem·tex (sem′teks), *n.* a plastic explosive that is easily tractable and largely odorless, used esp. by terrorists. [1980–85; name given by manufacturer; prob. from *Semtin,* town in Czech Republic where made + ex(plosive)]

se·quel·ize (sē′kwə līz′), *v.t.,* **-ized, -iz·ing.** to make a sequel to: *to sequelize a hit movie.* [1990–95]

server, + *n.* a computer that makes services, as access to data files, programs, and peripheral devices, available to workstations on a network. Cf. **client, file server** (in this section).

set-top (set′top′), *adj.* noting a device designed to sit atop a television and serve as a link to interactive communications systems: *set-top boxes that allow viewers to order movies on demand.* [1990–95]

sex′ual orienta′tion, one's natural preference in sexual partners; predilection for homosexuality, heterosexuality, or bisexuality. [1990–95]

sheesh (shēsh), *interj.* (used to express exasperation). [euphemistic shortening of *Jesus* or *shit*]

shelf′ talk′er, a cardboard, paper, or plastic advertisement of a product designed to be attached to a shelf on which the product is exhibited for sale.

Shepard, + *n.* **Sam,** born 1943, U.S. playwright, actor, and director.

SHO, Showtime (a cable television channel).

shock′ jock′, a radio disc jockey who features offensive or controversial material. [1985–90, *Amer.*]

shock′ ra′dio, broadcasting by a commercial station whose humor includes tasteless jokes, sexual innuendo, and ethnic insults. [1990–95]

sidebar, +**1.** a typographically distinct section of a page, as in a book or magazine, that amplifies or highlights the main text. **2.** a conference between the judge and lawyers out of the presence of the jury.

sil′ver bul′let, a quick solution to a difficult problem. [from the belief that vampires can be killed with a silver bullet]

sin′gle-malt′, *adj.* **1.** (of whiskey, esp. Scotch) made from unblended malt whiskey distilled at one distillery. —*n.* **2.** single-malt whiskey, esp. Scotch. [1985–90]

Sis′ter Car′rie, a novel (1900) by Theodore Dreiser.

site, + *n.* *Computers.* See **Web page** (in this section).

SK, Saskatchewan, Canada (approved for postal use).

skort (skôrt), *n.* a women's garment resembling a short skirt but having individual leg sections usually covered by a flap in front. [1985–90; b. SKIRT + short(s)]

SKU (skyo͞o), *n.* *Business.* stock-keeping unit.

slacker, + *n.* an esp. educated young person who is antimaterialistic, purposeless, apathetic, and usually works in a dead-end job. [pop. by *Slackers* (1991), film by R. Linklater]

slam[1], + *n.* a competitive, usually boisterous poetry reading.

slap[1], + *n.* **slap on the wrist,** relatively mild criticism or censure: *He got away with a slap on the wrist.*

SLAPP (slap), *n., v.,* **SLAPPed, SLAPP·ing.** —*n.* **1.** Also called **SLAPP′ suit′.** a civil lawsuit brought as an intimidation measure against an activist. —*v.t.* **2.** to bring a SLAPP against. [1988, *Amer.; S(trategic) L(awsuit) A(gainst) P(ublic) P(articipation)*]

slot, + *n.* See **expansion slot.**

s-mail (es′māl′), *n.* See **snail mail** (in this section).

smil·ey (smī′lē), *n., pl.* **-eys.** a sideways smile face, :-), or similar combination of symbols, as ;-), a winking face, or :-(, a sad face, used to communicate humor, sarcasm, sadness, etc., in an electronic message. Cf. **emoticon.** [1985–90]

snail′ mail′, *Facetious.* physical delivery of mail, as contrasted with electronic mail. Also called **s-mail.** [1980–85]

sneak·er·net (snē′kər net′), *n.* *Facetious.* the transfer of electronic information by carrying the storage medium, esp. a floppy disk, from one computer to another. [1985–90, *Amer.*]

Snyder, + *n.* **Gary,** born 1930, U.S. poet and essayist.

soc′cer mom′, a typical American suburban woman with school-age children. [1990–95, *Amer.;* so called from her practice of driving her children to soccer games]

sod[3], + *v.t.,* **sod·ded, sod·ding.** *Chiefly Brit. Slang.* **1.** to damn: *Sod the bloody bastard!* **2. sod off,** to leave (usually as an imperative): *Why don't you just sod off!*

softball, + *n.* something that can be easily dealt with: *The confirmation committee threw her a softball on that question.*

soft′ mon′ey, money contributed to a political candidate or party that is not subject to federal regulations.

Song′ of Sol′omon, a novel (1977) by Toni Morrison.

Son·tag (son′tag), *n.* **Susan,** born 1933, U.S. critic, novelist, and essayist.

south, + *adv.* *Informal.* into a state of serious decline, loss, or the like: *Sales went south during the recession.*

Spam (spam), *n., v.,* **spammed, spam·ming. 1.** *Trademark.* a canned food product consisting esp. of pork formed into a solid block. —*n.* **2.** (*l.c.*) a disruptive message posted on a computer network. —*v.t.* **3.** (*l.c.*) to send spam to. —*v.i.* **4.** (*l.c.*) to send spam. [(def. 1) < SP(ICED) + (H)AM; (other defs.) ref. to a comedy routine on *Monty Python's Flying Circus,* British TV series]

speed′ chess′, a game of chess played in a very short amount of time, usually five minutes per player for an entire game. Also called **blitz chess, lightning chess.**

spell-check (spel′chek′), *v.t.* to process (a document) with a spell checker; check the spelling of.

spi′der vein′, one of a radiating network of dilated capillaries on the skin.

Spiel·berg (spēl′bûrg), *n.* **Steven,** born 1947, U.S. film director.

spin, + *v.t.* *Slang.* to cause to have a particular bias; influence in a certain direction: *His assignment was to spin the reporters after the president's speech.*

spokes·mod·el (spōks′mod′l), *n.* a model who acts as a spokesperson. [SPOKESPERSON + MODEL (def. 6)]

sport′-u·til′i·ty ve′hicle (spôrt′yo͞o til′i tē, spōrt′-), a rugged vehicle with a trucklike chassis and four-wheel drive, designed for occasional off-road use. *Abbr.:* SUV [1990–95]

spot, + *v.t.* *Slang.* to lend: *Can you spot me twenty for tonight's game?*

spot′ reduc′ing, the usually futile effort to exercise one part of the body, as the outer thighs, in hopes of reducing the amount of fat stored in that area.

spot′ strike′, a labor strike by a local branch of a union.

SQUID (skwid), *n.* superconducting quantum interference device: a device that senses minute changes in magnetic fields, used to indicate neural activity in the brain. [1965–70]

SSN, Social Security number.

star′ an′ise, *n.* **1.** the star-shaped fruit of an East Asian evergreen tree, *Ilicium veru,* used as a spice esp. in Chinese cooking. **2.** the tree itself. [1835–40]

stealth, + *adj.* surreptitious; secret; not openly acknowledged: *a stealth hiring of the competitor's CEO; the stealth issue of the Presidential race.*

Steg·ner (steg′nər), *n.* **Wallace (Earle),** 1909–93, U.S. novelist and short-story writer.

Stella, + *n.* **Joseph,** 1887–1946, U.S. painter, born in Italy.

step′ aero′bics, (*used with a sing. or pl. v.*) aerobic exercises performed by stepping up onto and down from a stepping block. [1990–95]

Stick′y Note′, *Trademark.* a usually small piece of paper with an adhesive strip on the back that allows it to adhere to surfaces and be repositioned with ease.

stone, + *adj.* stonelike; stony; obdurate: *a stone killer; stone strength.*

stork′ park′ing, spaces reserved in a parking lot for cars driven by pregnant women or new mothers. [1996]

sto·tin (stô tēn′), *n.* a monetary unit of Slovenia.

strang′er rape′, sexual assault by an assailant upon a person he or she does not know. [1990–95]

strip′ mall′, a retail complex consisting of stores or restaurants in adjacent spaces in one long building, typically having a narrow parking area directly in front of the stores. [1990–95]

stud·ly (stud′lē), *adj.* **-li·er, -li·est.** *Slang.* virilely attractive; muscular and handsome. [1955–60]

sub·note·book (sub′nōt′bo͝ok), *n.* a laptop computer smaller and lighter than a notebook, typically weighing less than 5 pounds (2.3 kg). [1990–95, *Amer.*]

suite, + *n.* *Computers.* a group of software programs sold as a unit and usually designed to work together.

summit, + *v.t.* **1.** to reach the summit of. —*v.i.* **2.** to reach a summit: *summited after a 14-hour climb.*

su·per·church (so͞o′pər chûrch′), *n.* a church housed in an extremely large structure and containing elaborate facilities. [1990–95]

superhighway, + *n.* any very fast route or course.

su·per·mod·el (so͞o′pər mod′l), *n.* an extremely prominent and successful model who can command very high fees. [1985–90]

su·per·store (so͞o′pər stôr′, -stōr′), *n.* a very large store, esp. one stocking a wide variety of merchandise. [1940–45]

surf, + *v.i.* **1.** to search haphazardly, as for information on a computer network or an interesting program on television. —*v.t.* **2.** to search through (a computer network or TV channels) for information or entertainment.

surge′ protec′tor, a small device to protect a computer, telephone, television set, or the like from damage by high-voltage electrical surges.

SUV, *pl.* **SUVs.** sport-utility vehicle.

syntax, + *n.* *Computers.* the grammatical rules and structural patterns governing the ordered use of appropriate words and symbols for issuing commands, writing code, etc., in a particular software application or programming language.

Szym·bors·ka (sim bôrs′kä), *n.* **Wis·la·wa** (vis lä′vä), born 1923, Polish poet: Nobel prize 1996.

tag[1], + *v.t.* **1.** to write graffiti on. —*v.i.* **2.** to write graffiti.

tag·gant (tag′ənt), *n.* a nonreactive substance added to an explosive that may be traced if the explosive is used for unlawful purposes. [1990–95]

take, + *n.* **1.** an opinion or assessment: *What's your take on the candidate?* **2.** an approach; treatment: *a new take on an old idea.*

take-no-pris·on·ers (tāk′nō′priz′ə nərz, -priz′nərz), *adj.* wholeheartedly aggressive; zealous; gung-ho: *a businessman with a take-no-prisoners attitude toward dealmaking.* [1990–95]

taking, + *n.* an action by the federal government, as a regulatory ruling, that imposes a restriction on the use of private property for which the owner must be compensated.

talk, + *v.t.* *Informal.* (used only in progressive tenses) to focus on; signify or mean; talk about: *This isn't a question of a few hundred dollars—we're talking serious money.*

tar·tare (tär tär′), *adj.* (of food) served raw: *salmon tartare.* [extracted from steak tartare]

tax′-de·ferred annu′ity (taks′di fûrd′), an annuity that enables one to purchase an insurance product that will earn interest, with the tax obligation deferred until withdrawals begin, usually at retirement. *Abbr.:* TDA

T-ball (tē′bôl′), *n.* a modified form of baseball or softball in which the ball is batted off an adjustable pole or stand. [TEE[2]]

TBD, to be determined.

TBS, +*Trademark.* Turner Broadcasting System (a cable television channel).

TCP/IP, Transmission Control Protocol/Internet Protocol: a communications protocol for computer networks, the main protocol for the Internet.

TDA, tax-deferred annuity.

t.d.s., (in prescriptions) to be taken three times a day. [< L *ter die sumendum*]

technical, + *adj.* technically demanding or difficult: *a technical violin sonata; a technical ski run.*

Technicolor, + *adj.* (*often l.c.*) flamboyant or lurid, as in color, meaning, or detail.

tech·no·bab·ble (tek′nō bab′əl), *n.* incomprehensible technical language or jargon. [1980–85; patterned on PSYCHOBABBLE]

Te·ja·no (tā hä′nō, tə-), *n.* (*often l.c.*) a style of Mexican-American popular music that features the accordion and blends the polka with various forms of traditional Mexican music, now often including synthesizers and rock music. [1990–95; < AmSp: lit., Texan]

tel·e·on·o·my (tel′ē on′ə mē, tē′lē-), *n.* *Biol.* the principle that the body's structures and functions serve an overall purpose, as in assuring the survival of the organism. [1955-60; teleo- + -nomy] —**tel·e·o·nom·ic** (tel′ē ə nom′ik, tē′lē-), *adj.*

tell-all (tel′ôl′), *adj.* thoroughly revealing; candid; personal: *a tell-all biography of the movie star.*

temp, + *v.i.* *Informal.* to work as a temporary.

thigh-high (thī′hī′), *n.* a garment for the lower body, as a stocking or boot, that reaches the thigh.

thread, + *n.* *Computers.* a series of posts on a newsgroup dealing with the same subject.

three-peat (thrē′pēt, thrē pēt′), **1.** *Trademark.* a third consecutive victory, as in a major sports championship. —*v.i.* **2.** to win a third consecutive victory. [1985–90, *Amer.;* three + (re)peat]

three′-strikes′ law′ (thrē′strīks′), a law that mandates a life sentence to a felon convicted for the third time. [1990–95]

throm·bo·poi·e·tin (throm′bō poi′i tn, -poi et′n), *n.* a hormone that induces bone marrow cells to form blood platelets. [1990–95; < Gk *thrómbo(s)* clot + *poiēt(és)* maker; see -in[2]]

tick[1], + *n.* **1.** a movement in the price of a stock, bond, or option. **2.** the smallest possible tick on a given exchange.

time′ line′, **1.** a linear representation of important events in the order in which they occurred. **2.** a schedule; timetable. Also, **time′line′.** [1950–55]

tin, + *n.* *Squash.* telltale (def. 8).

tin′ cup′, **1.** a cup made out of tin, esp. one used by beggars to solicit money. **2.** a request for unearned money: *holding out a tin cup to the government.*

ti·ra·mi·su (tir′ə mē′so͞o, -mē so͞o′), *n.* an Italian dessert with coffee- and liquor-soaked layers of sponge cake alternating with mascarpone cheese and chocolate. Also, **ti′ra·mi′sù.** [< It *tiramisù,* fr. *tira* + *mi* + *sù* pick me up]

TMC, The Movie Channel (a cable television channel).

TNT, +*Trademark.* Turner Network Television (a cable television channel).

toast[1], + *n.* **be toast,** *Slang.* to be or become someone who is doomed or ruined; get into trouble: *If you're late to work again, you're toast!*

to·lar (tol′ər; *Slovenian.* tô′lär), *n.* a basic monetary unit of Slovenia.

to·pos (tō′pōs, -pos), *n., pl.* **-poi** (-poi). a convention or motif, esp. in a literary work; a rhetorical convention. [1935–40; < Gk *(koinós) tópos* (common) place]

tops, + *adv.* at a maximum; at most: *It'll take an hour, tops. I'll give you $25 for that, tops.*

CONCISE PRONUNCIATION KEY: act, cāpe, dâre, pärt; set, ēqual; if, īce; ox, ōver, ôrder, oil, bo͝ok, bo͞ot, out; up, ûrge; child; sing; shoe; thin, *th*at; zh as in *treasure.* ə = *a* as in *alone, e* as in *system, i* as in *easily, o* as in *gallop, u* as in *circus;* ᵊ as in *fire* (fīᵊr), *hour* (ouᵊr). l and n can serve as syllabic consonants, as in *cradle* (krād′l), and *button* (but′n). See the full key inside the front cover.

tower, + *n.* a vertical case designed to house a computer system standing on the floor.

track·pad (trak′pad′), *n.* a computer input device for controlling the pointer on a display screen by sliding the finger along a special surface: used chiefly in notebook computers.

trans·gen·dered (trans jen′dərd, tranz-), *adj.* **1.** appearing or attempting to be a member of the opposite sex, as a transsexual, habitual cross-dresser, or hermaphrodite. **2.** of or pertaining to a transgendered person or transgendered people: *the transgender movement.* Also, **trans·gen′der.** [1990–95]

trash, + *n. Computers.* an icon of a trash can that is used to delete files dragged onto it.

trash-talk·ing (trash′tô′king), *n.* the use of disparaging or boastful language. [1985–90, *Amer.*]

treadmill, + *n.* an exercise machine that allows the user to walk or run in place, usually on a continuous moving belt.

Tri′ple Crown′, **1.** an unofficial title held by a horse that wins the Kentucky Derby, the Preakness, and the Belmont Stakes. **2.** a usually unofficial title held by someone who wins three major awards or championships in the same year.

tuf·fet (tuf′it), *n.* **1.** a low stool; footstool. **2.** *Dial.* tuft. [1550–55]

turbocharge, + *v.t. Informal.* to speed up; accelerate.

TV-14, a television program rating advising parents that a program is unsuitable for children under the age of 14. [1997]

TV-G, a television program rating advising parents that a program is suitable for all ages. [1997]

TV-M, a television program rating advising parents that a program is for mature audiences only and unsuitable for those under the age of 17. [1997]

TV-PG, a television program rating advising parents that some material in a program may be unsuitable for children. Compare PG. [1997]

TV-Y, a television program rating advising parents that a program is appropriate for children of all ages. [1997]

TV-Y7, a television program rating advising parents that a program is appropriate for children aged 7 and above. [1997]

tweak, + *v.t.* to make a minor adjustment to: *to tweak a computer program.*

U, + *Symbol.* (on a packaged product) certified as kosher by the Union of Orthodox Hebrew Congregations.

un·dead (un′ded′), *adj.* **1.** no longer alive but animated by a supernatural force, as a vampire or zombie. —*n.* **2.** *(used with a pl. v.)* undead beings collectively (usually prec. by *the).* [1895–1900]

un·der·card (un′dər kärd′), *n.* an event or group of events preceding and supporting a featured event: *the undercard of tonight's boxing match.* [1945–50]

unfiltered, + *adj.* reality-based (in this section).

Unit′ed States′ Air′ Force′ Acad′emy, an institution at Colorado Springs, Colo., for the training of U.S. Air Force officers.

UNIX (yoo′niks), *Trademark.* a multiuser, multitasking computer operating system.

up·size (up′sīz′), *v.i., v.t.,* **-sized, -sizing.** to increase in size, as by hiring additional employees; expand: *to upsize a business.* [1985–90]

CONCISE ETYMOLOGY KEY: <, descended or borrowed from; >, whence; b., blend of, blended; c., cognate with; cf., compare; deriv., derivative; equiv., equivalent; imit., imitative; obl., oblique; r., replacing; s., stem; sp., spelling, spelled; resp., respelling, respelled; trans., translation; ?, origin unknown; *, unattested; ‡, probably earlier than. See the full key inside the front cover.

up·talk (up′tôk′), *n.* a rise in pitch at the end usually of a declarative sentence, esp. if habitual: often represented in writing by a question mark as in *Hi, I'm here to read the meter?* [1990–95]

ur′ban leg′end, a modern story of obscure origin and with little or no supporting evidence that spreads spontaneously in varying forms and often has elements of humor, moralizing, or horror: *Are there alligators living in the New York City sewer system, or is that just an urban legend?* Also called **ur′ban myth′.** [1970–75]

URL, *Computers.* Uniform Resource Locater: a protocol for specifying addresses on the Internet.

USA, +USA Network (a cable television channel).

Use·net (yo͞oz′net′, yo͞os′-), *n. Computers.* an extensive system of newsgroups: a branch of the Internet. Also, **USENET.** [1990–95; USE(RS') + NET(WORK)]

ute (yo͞ot), *n. Informal.* a utility vehicle. [1940–45]

vag′inal con′dom, a contraceptive for women, being a thin polyurethane pouch, one end of which is inserted into the vagina and the other end spread over the vulva. Also called **vag′inal pouch′.**

V-chip (vē′chip′), *n.* a computer chip or other electronic device that blocks the reception of violent or sexually explicit television shows. [1990–95; b. VIOLENT or VIOLENCE + CHIP (def. 5)]

ver′tically chal′lenged, (used as a euphemism) short in stature.

ver′tical tast′ing, a tasting of different vintages of one particular wine.

VGA, video graphics array: a high-resolution standard for displaying text, graphics, and colors on computer monitors. [1987]

vi·at·i·cal (vi at′i kəl, vē-), *adj.* **1.** of or pertaining to a viaticum. **2.** of or pertaining to a form of insurance business that pays off on the insurance policies of the terminally ill.

vin·ca (ving′kə), *n.* periwinkle². [1865–70; < NL *Vinca* type genus < LL *pervinca* periwinkle²]

visit, + *v.t.* to access, as a Web site.

V.S.O., (of brandy) very superior old.

wake-up, + *adj.* serving to arouse or excite: *a wake-up call on the problems of pollution.*

Walcott, + *n.* **Derek,** born 1930, West Indian poet and playwright: Nobel prize 1992.

Walker, + *n.* **Alice,** born 1944, U.S. novelist and short-story writer.

wean, + *v.* **wean on,** to accustom to or familiarize with something from, or as if from, childhood (usually fol. by *on*): *a brilliant student weaned on the classics; suburban kids weaned on rock music.*

web, + *n.* *(cap.) Computers.* See **World Wide Web** (in this section).

Web′ page′, *Computers.* a single, usually hypertext document on the World Wide Web that can incorporate text, graphics, sounds, etc.

Web′ site′, *Computers.* a connected group of pages on the World Wide Web regarded as a single entity, usually maintained by one person or organization and devoted to one single topic or several closely related topics. [1990–95]

Webster, + *n. Informal.* a dictionary of the English language. Also, **Web′ster's.**

wedge′ is′sue, an issue that divides or causes conflict in an otherwise unified group: *Abortion is a wedge issue for the Republican party.* [1990–95]

wedgie, + *n. Informal.* the condition of having one's underpants or other clothing uncomfortably stuck between the buttocks.

weight′ train′ing, weightlifting done as a conditioning exercise.

weight-watch·er (wāt′woch′ər), *n.* a person who is dieting to control his or her weight. [1965–70] —**weight′-watch′ing,** *adj., n.*

well·ness (wel′nis), *n.* **1.** the quality or state of being healthy, esp. as the result of deliberate effort; health. **2.** an approach to health care that emphasizes preventing illness and prolonging life, as opposed to emphasizing treating diseases. [WELL¹ (def. 13) + -NESS]

whatever, + *interj.* (used to indicate indifference to a state of affairs, situation, previous statement, etc.)

Wheelwright, + *n.* **John Brooks,** 1897–1940, U.S. poet.

white′ zin′fandel, a medium-sweet rosé wine made from zinfandel grapes.

Wilson, + *n.* **1. August,** born 1945, U.S. playwright. **2. Lan·ford** (lan′fərd), born 1937, U.S. playwright.

Win·dows (win′dōz), *Trademark.* any of several microcomputer operating systems or environments featuring a graphical user interface.

wired, + *adj.* connected electronically to one or more computer networks.

wireless, + *n.* any system or device, as a cellular phone, for transmitting messages or signals by electromagnetic waves.

wish′ing well′, a well or pool of water supposed to grant the wish of one who tosses a coin into it.

wonk, + *n.* a person who studies a subject or issue in an excessively assiduous and thorough manner: *a policy wonk.*

World′ Wide′ Web′, a system of extensively interlinked hypertext documents: a branch of the Internet. *Abbr.:* WWW [1990–95]

wrap, + *v.t.* **1.** to cover (fingernails) with a sheer silk or linen fabric, as to repair or strengthen them. —*n.* **2.** a sheer silk or linen fabric used to cover the fingernails in order to repair or strengthen them. **3.** a piece of thin, flat bread rolled around a filling and eaten as a sandwich.

WWW, World Wide Web.

XOR (eks′ôr′), *n.* a Boolean operator that returns a positive result when either but not both of its operands are positive. [(e)x(clusive) OR]

YA, young adult.

ya·da-ya·da-ya·da (yä′də yä′də yä′də), *adv.* and so on; and so forth. [1940–45]

Yam·pa (yam′pə), *n.* a river in NW Colorado, flowing W into the Green River in Dinosaur National Monument. 250 mi. (402 km) long.

yel′low card′, *Soccer.* a yellow card shown by the referee to a player being cautioned for a violation. Cf. **red card** (in this section).

yes, + *interj.* (used as a strong expression of joy, pleasure, or approval.)

Yough·io·ghe·ny (yok′ə gā′nē), *n.* a river flowing from NW Maryland through SW Pennsylvania into the Monongahela River. 135 mi. (217 km) long.

yo′-yo di′eting, a repeated cycle of weight loss followed by weight gain.

YT, Yukon Territory, Canada (approved for postal use).

Zam·bo·ni (zam bō′nē), *Trademark.* a brand of machine that smooths the surface of the ice on a rink. [1947; after Frank J. *Zamboni,* 1901–88, U.S. inventor]

Zelig, + *n.* a chameleonlike person who is unusually ubiquitous. [fr. Leonard *Zelig,* main character in *Zelig,* 1984 film by W. Allen]

ze′ro-e·mis′sion ve′hicle (zēr′ō i mish′ən), a vehicle, as an automobile, that does not directly produce atmospheric pollutants. *Abbr.:* ZEV

ZEV, zero-emission vehicle.

How to Use This Dictionary

THIS GUIDE to using the *Random House Dictionary* contains information about the Dictionary in the following order:

I. **Entries** (Range of Vocabulary Entries in the Dictionary, How to Find an Entry, Main Entries, Variants, Undefined Entries)

II. **Parts of Speech and Inflected Forms**

III. **Definitions** (Sense Division, Idioms, Cross References)

IV. **Labels** (Field Labels, Usage Labels)

V. **Etymologies** (Symbols and Abbreviations, Parentheses, Language Labels, Typefaces, Special Types of Etymologies, Treatment of Non-European Languages, Dating the Entries, Americanisms)

VI. **End-of-Entry Notes** (Synonym Lists and Studies, Antonym Lists, Usage Notes, Pronunciation Notes, Regional Variation Notes)

VII. **Pronunciation** (Approach to Pronunciations, Pronunciation System, Kinds of Symbols Used, A Guide to Pronunciation Symbols, Syllable Division and Stress in the Pronunciations)

VIII. **Supplements**

I. ENTRIES

Range of Vocabulary Entries in the Dictionary

This Dictionary contains not only words and phrases from the general vocabulary but a large number of specialized terms, as from sports, telecommunications, history, and business. It contains as well a large technical and scientific vocabulary: terms from medicine, as for current therapeutic techniques and drugs; botanical terms, from exotic flora to common houseplants; terms from astronomy, space, and physics; and terms from the expanding lexicon of computers. In addition, the book's vocabulary encompasses a variety of proper nouns—given names, names of significant people and places, names from the Bible and mythology, and select titles from the arts and literature. Also included are abbreviations, symbols, and foreign words and phrases. All these entries appear, for easy access, in a single alphabetical listing.

How To Find an Entry

Guide words. At the top of each page, on either side of the page number, are two guide words. The one at the upper left corresponds to the first **main entry** (or **headword**) on the page, while the one at the upper right corresponds to the last. The two guide words thus indicate the alphabetical range of main entry terms covered on any given page.

Spellings. For those times when someone is not sure of the spelling of a particular word, the editors have provided a list of "Sound-Spelling Correspondences in English" (p. xxxviii). Using this listing, a reader can determine how a word is likely to be spelled, based on how it is said.

Secondary entries. The user of the Dictionary should also look within an entry for variant spellings and other derived or related forms of the main entry term. In addition, some pages contain lists of undefined words beginning with the same prefix (as *un-* or *anti-*), whose meanings can be established from the sum of their parts.

Implicit entries. Many terms containing two or more words, as *rug cleaner, social change,* or *silk dress,* are self-defining. That is, their meanings can readily be understood by combining the appropriate senses of their component words. Such terms do not need to appear as entries in the Dictionary. In addition, regular plurals, like *boxes,* regular past tense forms, like *walked,* etc., are to be considered part of the lexicon even though they do not show overtly as Dictionary entries.

Main Entries

Typeface. All main entries appear flush to the left margin of the column, in large **boldface** type. Certain main entries are shown in italics, but most are entered in roman typeface. This distinction makes it easy for users of this Dictionary to ascertain the appropriate form to use for each headword, as when writing a report or academic paper. Italicized terms include book and play titles; titles of long poems and musical compositions; names of works of art, ships, and aircraft; and those foreign words and phrases that have not been naturalized or assimilated into English. Note that some main entries that appear in the Dictionary in roman type are commonly italicized for particular definitions. These definitions will be marked "(*italics*)."

count•ess (koun′tis), *n.* **1.** the wife or widow of a count

com•tesse (kôɴ tes′), *n., pl.* ***-tesses*** (-tes′). *French.* countess.

En•dym•i•on (en dim′ē ən), *n.* **1.** *Class. Myth.* a young man kept forever youthful through eternal sleep and loved by Selene. **2.** (*italics*) a narrative poem (1818) by John Keats.

Word division. To provide information about where to break words at the end of a line, the Dictionary divides entry words into syllables, using a raised centered dot. (In hyphenated compounds, the hyphen itself automatically serves to mark division between two syllables.) These divisions follow traditional American practice in the fields of editing and typesetting. Thus, although some word segments, as *-tion* and *-ble,* are never divided, entry words are primarily broken phonetically, that is, after vowels for either long or unstressed (open) syllables and after consonants for short (or closed) syllables. Capitalized acronyms, as NATO, are not divided into syllables.

Single words are normally divided into syllables at their own entries only. In multiple-word entries, the individual words are marked for stress in relation to one another but are not syllabified.

e•lec•tron•ic (i lek tron′ik, ē′lek-), *adj.* **1.** of or per-

im•ag•ing (im′ə jing), *n.* **1.** *Psychol.* a technique in

electron′ic im′aging, a system of photography

Multiple-word entries formed from components that are not entirely assimilated into English, whether or not italicized, are usually syllabified and pronounced in full, even when their component parts are pronounced elsewhere in the book.

bro•de•rie an•glaise (brō′də rē′ äng gläz′, -glez′; *Fr.* bʀôdᵊ ʀē äɴ glez′), fine white needlework done on

Readers should be cautioned that although the Dictionary shows the total number of syllables into which a word may be broken, not all syllable breaks should be used as end-of-line divisions. It is not advisable, for example, to break a word before or after a single character; one would try not to break *cit•y* or *a•lone.* And hyphenated compounds, as *country-and-western* and *habit-forming,* are best split at the hyphen. Note, too, that syllable divisions for the spelling of an entry word may not always correspond with divisions shown inside the pronunciation parentheses, as with *dou•ble* (dub′əl). These two kinds of syllable division are determined by different sets of rules.

Boldface entries are normally divided according to the first pronunciation shown, which is generally the most common one. For example, the main entry for *process* is divided after the *c: proc•ess,* although *pro•cess,* not shown and corresponding to a pronunciation less widely used in the United States, would be equally correct. However, when the pronunciation and, consequently, the division into syllables shift according to part of speech function, the Dictionary shows more than one division; syllables in the main entry are divided according to the pronunciation for the first part of speech in the entry, while appropriate division for any subsequent part of speech is shown, in boldface type, at the beginning of the definitions given for that part of speech.

prog•ress (*n.* prog′res, -rəs *or, esp. Brit.,* prō′gres; *v.* prə-gres′), *n.* **1.** a movement toward a goal or to a further or higher stage: *the progress of a student toward a degree....* —*v.i.* **pro•gress 11.** to go forward or onward in space or time: *The wagon train progressed through the valley.*

Notice that when a boldface spelling that is stressed or syllabified must break at the end of a line of Dictionary text, it usually breaks with a centered dot rather than a hyphen. The hyphen is used in these places only when it is actually part of the spelling.

broad-gauge (brôd′gāj′), *adj.* **1.** *Railroads.* of or pertaining to equipment designed for a railroad having track of a broad gauge: *broad-gauge rolling stock.* **2.** of wide scope, application, or experience: *broad-gauge efforts to improve the health of our citizens.* Also, **broad′-gauged′.** [1835–45, for earlier sense]

break-e•ven (brāk′ē′vən), *adj.* **1.** having income exactly equal to expenditure, thus showing neither profit nor loss. —*n.* **2.** See **break-even point.** Also, **break′•e′ven.** [1935–40, *Amer.*]

Identically spelled entries. Single words that are spelled identically but differ in derivation are given separate main entries. Such entries are called **homographs.** Homographs entered in lowercase roman type, with no distinguishing diacritical marks in the spelling, are marked with a small superscript number immediately following the spelled form and are given etymologies that explain their origins. Homographs that are capitalized or italicized, while entered separately, are not numbered. Near homographs, as pairs in which one of the words is spelled with *ü, ç,* or the like, and the other is spelled with those letters unmarked, are also not numbered.

rose[1] (rōz), *n., adj., v.,* **rosed, ros•ing.** —*n.* **1.** any of the wild or cultivated, usually prickly-stemmed, showy-flowered shrubs of the genus *Rosa....* [bef. 900; ME; OE *rōse* < L *rosa;* akin to Gk *rhódon* (see RHODODENDRON)] —**rose′less,** *adj.* —**rose′like′,** *adj.*

rose[2] (rōz), *v.* **1.** pt. of **rise.** **2.** *Nonstandard.* a pp. of **rise.**

Rose (rōz), *n.* **1. Billy,** 1899–1966, U.S. theatrical producer. **2.** a female given name.

ro•sé (rō zā′), *n.* a pink table wine in which the pale color is produced by removing the grape skins from the must before fermentation is completed. [1425–75; < F: lit., pink]

Word stress in multiple word entries. Although this Dictionary makes use of two kinds of stress marks, **primary stress** (′) and **secondary stress** (′), three gradations of stress can actually be shown in boldface entries: primary, secondary, and relative lack of stress. A syllable that would be pronounced with relatively heavy stress is immediately followed by a primary stress mark; a syllable pronounced with slightly less stress is immediately followed by a secondary stress mark; and a syllable that would be said with little stress remains unmarked. No stress is shown in the spellings for main entries that contain abbreviations, Roman numerals, or letters of the alphabet that are individually pronounced as such.

Knights′ of the Round′ Ta′ble, a legendary order of knights created by King Arthur.

St. Clair (sānt′ klâr′; *for 1 also* sing′klâr, sin′-) **1. Arthur,** 1736–1818, American Revolutionary War gen-

T cell, *Immunol.* any of several closely related lymphocytes, developed in the thymus, that circulate in the

The use of stress marks in any boldface entry of two or more words is intended to show the stress pattern for that entry as a unit—the usual accentual relationship among those words. It does not show the relationship of one syllable to another within an individual word. For example, the pattern ′ ′ indicates approximately equal stress: *compan′ionate mar′riage*; the pattern ′ ′ indicates that the first word receives greater stress than the second: *compan′ion cell′*; and the pattern ′ ′ shows the kind of relationship heard in utterances like *New′ York′.* Note that the usual stress for a particular word, when said in isolation, may shift when that word is used in a longer utterance: by itself, *en′do•cra′ni•al* is said with one secondary and one primary stress, but as an attributive modifier, it may change its pattern and be pronounced with two primary stresses, as in *en′docra′nial cast′.* Note, too, that because regional, individual, and circumstantial differences are characteristic of spoken discourse, readers should be aware that their own stress patterns, when different from the ones found in the book, may be equally valid.

Variants

A characteristic of the English language is the existence of alternate spellings and alternate terms. In the Dictionary, terms are usually defined at the forms a reader is most likely to find in contemporary writing, but common variant forms are shown at many entries. These forms range from simple spelling variants of the main entry (*ameba—amoeba*) through forms similar to the main entry but not identical, as those in which only the suffix differs (*exploratory—explorative*), to forms that are substantially different from the main entry (*riboflavin—vitamin B_2*). Variants, entered in boldface type, are preceded by "Also" or "Also called." Their location in an entry depends on whether they apply to the whole entry, to one part of speech only, or to particular definitions.

> **en•do•crine** (en′də krin, -krīn′, -krēn′), *Anat., Physiol.* —*adj.* Also, **en•do•cri•nal** (en′də krīn′l, -krēn′l), **en•do•crin•ic** (en′də krin′ik), **endocrinous. 1.** secreting internally into the blood or lymph.... —*n.* **3.** an internal secretion; hormone. **4.** See **endocrine gland.** Cf. **exocrine.** [1910–15; ENDO- + *-crine* < Gk *krínein* to separate]

> **pro•gram** (prō′gram, -grəm), *n., v.,* **-grammed** or **-gramed, -gram•ming** or **-gram•ing.** —*n.* **1.** a plan of action to accomplish a specified end: *a school lunch program...* —*v.i.* **15.** to plan or write a program. Also, *esp. Brit.,* **pro′gramme.** [1625–35; < LL *programma* < Gk *prógramma* public notice in writing. See PRO-[2], -GRAM[1]]

At the entry for *endocrine,* all three variants apply to the adjective part of speech only, while at the entry for *program,* the variant *programme* applies to the entire entry.

Some variant spellings are shown only at certain basic terms throughout the main vocabulary listing, but not at nearby derived forms. Thus the Dictionary gives the chiefly British variant *colour* at the entry for *color,* but does not show *colourful, colourcast,* etc., which may be inferred. Similarly, a noun ending in *-isation* is implied at *-ization* entries wherever *-ise,* another spelling variant commonly found in Great Britain, is shown for the related verb ending in *-ize.*

Main entry listings for variants. Many variant forms are entered as headwords in the main vocabulary listings, where they are not given full definitions but are cross-referred to the form that does have the definition. However, if a reader cannot find a given term, he or she should look nearby on the page for the main entry of an alternate form, since many variants whose entries would fall within 30 lines of the form that is defined do not have their own entries. (Main entries for variants may have additional full definitions for other senses.)

> **Ha•ba•na** (*Sp.* ä vä′nä), *n.* Havana.

> **nau′tical archaeol′ogy.** See **marine archaeology.**

Notice that the word "See" is used as a cross-referencing device to guide the reader to a main entry of two or more words. This is done so that such a cross reference will not be mistaken for a complete definition.

Undefined Entries

The meanings of certain terms are evident from the sum of their parts, the already defined base word plus a prefix or a suffix. There is consequently no need for the Dictionary to define all of these terms separately.

It should be understood that no group of **run-on** forms at any given entry and no **list** of prefixed terms at the bottom of a page can be considered complete. Prefixes, like *non-* and *re-,* and suffixes, like *-ly, -ity, -like,* and *-ness,* which are used to help form the undefined entries in this book, are often highly productive parts of the language. They are used to create new lexical combinations as circumstances require. The fact that a particular form of this sort cannot be found in a dictionary does not mean that it is not a "real word."

Run-on entries; root plus suffix. Run-ons are derivatives of the main entry, formed primarily by adding a suffix to the main entry form or its root, but sometimes by deleting or replacing a suffix. Run-ons can also be formed from compounds, as by adding a hyphen to a two-word entry to form an adjective. When the meaning of the run-on form can be readily understood and the term therefore does not require defining, the run-on is placed at the end of the main entry, following all definitions and any bracketed etymology, but preceding any end-of-entry notes. Each run-on or set of run-ons (the set indicating that two or more run-ons share a meaning) is preceded by a lightface dash and, when applicable, followed by one or more parts of speech.

> **bron•cho•scope** (brong′kə skōp′), *n. Med.* a lighted, flexible tubular instrument that is inserted into the trachea for diagnosis and for removing inhaled objects. [1895–1900; BRONCHO- + -SCOPE] —**bron•cho•scop•ic** (brong′kə skop′ik), *adj.* —**bron•chos•co•pist** (brong-kos′kə pist), *n.*

Since *-ic,* when attached to nouns, forms adjectives with the meaning 'of or pertaining to (the base word)', the run-on *bronchoscopic* can be assumed to mean 'of or pertaining to a bronchoscope'. The other run-ons at this entry are similarly derived by using the definitions for the individual suffixed forms.

> **as•trol•o•gy** (ə strol′ə jē), *n.* **1.** the study that assumes and attempts to interpret the influence of the heavenly bodies on human affairs. **2.** *Obs.* the science of astronomy. [1325–75; ME < L *astrologia* < Gk. See ASTRO-, -LOGY] —**as•trol′o•ger, as•trol′o•gist,** *n.* —**as•tro•log•i•cal** (as′trə loj′i kəl), **as′tro•log′ic, as•trol•o•gous** (ə strol′ə-gəs), *adj.* —**as′tro•log′i•cal•ly,** *adv.*

At the entry for *astrology,* the two noun run-ons (*astrologer, astrologist*) form one set, while the three adjective run-ons (*astrological, astrologic, astrologous*) form another.

Run-ons are usually divided into syllables and stressed. When necessary, a parenthesized pronunciation is added.

List words; prefix plus root. Just as many run-ons can be interpreted as root plus suffix, list words can be understood by adding the meaning of a root form (or a root form with suffixes) to the meaning of a prefix. These terms are so formulaic in sense that they do not warrant inclusion in the Dictionary's defined *A* to *Z* vocabulary; they have been incorporated as undefined entries for the convenience of users.

Lists can be found starting at the bottom of the page that contains the entry for each prefix. They extend, when necessary, to following pages. The vocabulary entry for each appropriate prefix includes a note explaining how the list words beginning with that prefix are to be interpreted. Lists are located at the following prefixes: *anti-, counter-, de-, half-, hyper-, inter-, mini-, mis-, multi-, non-, out-, over-, post-, pre-, pro-, pseudo-, quasi-, re-, self-, semi-, sub-, super-, trans-, ultra-, un-, under-,* and *well-.*

List words, like run-ons, are divided into syllables and stressed. Inflected forms are included in the lists wherever appropriate. However, no pronunciations are shown.

II. PARTS OF SPEECH AND INFLECTED FORMS

Parts of Speech

Single-word entries are given italicized labels, preceding a definition or group of definitions, to show grammatical function. Among the abbreviations used for the traditional parts of speech are *n., pron., adj., adv., conj., prep.,* and *interj.,* standing for noun, pronoun, adjective, adverb, conjunction, preposition, and interjection, respectively. The generalized abbreviation *v.* for verb is also used, as at the beginning of a group of verbal idiom definitions, or for verbal list words that are both transitive and intransitive, or for inflected forms, when transitivity or intransitivity is labeled at following definitions. But most verb labels are specific: *v.t.* for transitive verbs and *v.i.* for those that are intransitive. Other labels include *n.pl.* for plural nouns and *Trademark* for entries with names that are legally the property of the companies that have registered the terms.

If an entry word is used for more than one grammatical function, the appropriate part of speech label precedes each set of definitions shown for that part of speech.

> **ben•ze•noid** (ben′zə noid′), *Chem.* —*adj.* **1.** of, pertaining to, or similar to benzene, esp. with respect to structure. —*n.* **2.** any benzene compound. [1885–90; BENZENE + -OID]

Note that *benzenoid* can be an adjective (definition 1) or a noun (definition 2).

Inflected Forms

Inflected forms, as plurals for nouns or past tense and past participle forms for verbs, are available for use by speakers of English whether or not they are shown explicitly at their entries in the Dictionary. Thus *hats* is implied for *hat, looked* for *look,* etc. These are regular forms and would not be shown. The Dictionary shows inflected forms primarily for entry words that form their inflections irregularly, although some regular forms are also given.

Nouns. Plurals are shown only for **count nouns,** like *city* and *key,* that refer to things that are countable. They are not shown for **mass nouns,** like *atrophy,* since one would refer to the *atrophy,* not *atrophies,* of several persons or things. The following kinds of nouns and noun phrases show plurals: (1) nouns ending in a final *-y* that changes to *-ies* when the plural is formed, as *blasphemy: blasphemies;* (2) nouns ending in *-ey,* whether the plural is *-s* or *-ies,* as *monkey: monkeys* and *money: moneys* or *monies;* (3) nouns with plurals that are not native English formations, as *alumna: alumnae* and *alumnus: alumni;* (4) nouns with a **zero plural,** that is, with a plural identical to the singular, as *Chinese: Chinese* and *sheep: sheep;* (5) nouns changing their spellings internally to form the plural, as *louse: lice;* and (6) noun phrases or compounds, when the reader might not be sure which element is to be pluralized, as *mother-in-law: mothers-in-law, spoonful: spoonfuls,* and *solicitor general: solicitors general.*

Plurals are also shown for (7) all nouns ending in *-o, -ful,* or *-us;* (8) nouns ending in elements that usually form their plurals in a different way, like *-goose* (*mongoose: mongooses*); and (9) nouns with plurals that require information about their pronunciations, as when the voiceless (s) in *house* becomes a voiced (z) in *houses.*

All plurals, regular and irregular, are shown whenever a term can have more than one plural, and Latin names of constellations show the genitive form, as used in naming stars.

> **bass**[2] (bas), *n., pl.* (*esp. collectively*) **bass,** (*esp. referring to two or more kinds or species*) **bass•es. 1.** any of numerous edible, spiny-finned, freshwater or marine fishes of the families Serranidae and Centrarchidae. **2.** (originally) the European perch, *Perca fluviatilis.* [1375–1425; late ME *bas,* earlier *bærs,* OE *bærs* (with loss of *r* before *s* as in ASS[2], PASSEL, etc.); c. D *baars,* G *Barsch,* OSw *aghboore*]

> **O•ri•on** (ə rī′ən), *n., gen.* **Or•i•o•nis** (ôr′ē ō′nis, or′-, ə rī′ə nis) for 2. **1.** *Class. Myth.* a giant hunter who pursued the Pleiades, was eventually slain by Artemis, and was then placed in the sky as a constellation. **2.** *Astron.* the Hunter, a constellation lying on the celestial equator between Canis Major and Taurus, containing the bright stars Betelgeuse and Rigel.

Pronouns. The entire paradigm of inflections is shown at nominative pronouns.

> **I** (ī), *pron., nom.* **I,** *poss.* **my** or **mine,** *obj.* **me;** *pl. nom.* **we,** *poss.* **our** or **ours,** *obj.* **us;** *n., pl.* **I's.** —*pron.* **1.** the nominative singular pronoun, used by a speaker in referring to himself or herself.

Verbs. Past and past participle forms are shown especially for the following: (1) verbs ending in *-e,* as *examine: examined, examining,* since the final *-e* is dropped before endings are added; (2) verbs ending in *-y,* as *deny: denied, denying,* in which *y* changes to *-i* before *-ed;* (3) verbs doubling the consonant before adding inflectional endings, as *tap: tapped, tapping;* and (4) verbs forming the past or past participle other than by adding *-ed* or *-d,* as *went* for *go,* or *broke* for *break.*

Adjectives and adverbs. All adjectives and adverbs that form the comparison and superlative by adding the suffixes *-er* and *-est* will show these inflections. Examples are *green: greener, greenest* and *classy: classier, classiest.*

On the other hand, many polysyllabic adjectives and adverbs can be compared only with *more* and *most,* as the adjective *familiar,* and certain adjectives and adverbs are considered to have absolute senses that do not admit of comparison. These two groups will not show inflections.

III. DEFINITIONS

Sense Division

Order. Definitions within an entry are individually numbered in a single sequence that includes all parts of speech. In each part of speech group, the most frequently encountered meanings generally come before less common ones. Specialized senses follow those in the common vocabulary, and rare, archaic, or obsolete senses are listed last. This order may be modified slightly when it is desirable to group related meanings together.

A numbered definition can be divided into lettered subsenses, as when they share a label.

> **bronze** (bronz), *n., v.,* **bronzed, bronz•ing,** *adj.* —*n.* **1.** *Metall.* **a.** any of various alloys consisting essentially of copper and tin, the tin content not exceeding 11 percent. **b.** any of various other alloys having a large copper content. **2.** a metallic brownish color. **3.** a work of art, as a statue, statuette, bust, or medal, composed of....

Variations in form. For some meanings, the entry word is used in a form that differs slightly, as in typeface or case, from the one shown as the headword. An italicized label indicating the change—for example, (*italics*), (*cap.*), or (*l.c.*)—appears in parentheses at the beginning of the definition.

For meanings using a singular main entry in the plural form or vice versa, the changed form is spelled out at the beginning of the definition.

> **Od•ys•sey** (od′ə sē), *n., pl.* **-seys** for 2. **1.** (*italics*) an epic poem attributed to Homer, describing Odysseus's adventures in his ten-year attempt to return home to Ithaca after the Trojan War. **2.** (*often l.c.*) a long series of wanderings or adventures, esp. when filled with notable experiences, hardships, etc. —**Od′ys•se′an,** *adj.*

> **heav•en** (hev′ən), *n.* **1.** the abode of God, the angels, and the spirits of the righteous after death; the place or state of existence of the blessed after the mortal life. **2.** (*cap.*) Often, **Heavens.** the celestial powers; God. **3.** a metonym for God (used in expressions of emphasis,

surprise, etc.): *For heaven's sake!* **4. heavens, a.** (used interjectionally to express emphasis, surprise, etc.): *Heavens, what a cold room!* **b.** (*used with a singular v.*) a wooden roof or canopy over the outer stage of an Elizabethan theater. **5.** Usually, **heavens.** the sky, firmament, or expanse of space surrounding the earth.

Grammatical information. Information is included with some nouns indicating whether they are normally used with singular or plural verbs.

gym•nas•tics (jim nas′tiks), *n.* **1.** (*used with a plural v.*) gymnastic exercises. **2.** (*used with a singular v.*) the practice, art, or competitive sport of gymnastic exercises. **3.** (*used with a plural v.*) mental feats or other exercises of skill: *verbal gymnastics.* [1645–55; see GYMNASTIC, -ICS]

Additional information indicating that for a given sense the entry word is sometimes followed or preceded by a specified word, as *up* or *about*, is shown in a parenthetical phrase at the beginning of the definition.

plump¹ (plump), *adj.*, **-er, -est,** *v.* —*adj.* **1.** well filled out or rounded in form; somewhat fleshy or fat. —*v.i.* **2.** to become plump (often fol. by *up* or *out*). —*v.t.* **3.** to make plump (often fol. by *up* or *out*): *to plump up the sofa pillows.* [1475–85; earlier *plompe* dull, rude < MD *plomp* blunt, not pointed; c. MLG *plump*] **—plump′ly,** *adv.* **—plump′ness,** *n.*

If the specified word must always precede or follow the headword for a particular sense, the term is shown as an idiom.

poop² (po͞op), *v.t. Slang.* **1.** to cause to become out of breath or fatigued; exhaust: *Climbing that mountain pooped the whole group.* **2. poop out, a.** to cease from or fail in something, as from fear or exhaustion: *When the time for action came, they all pooped out and went home instead.* **b.** to break down; stop functioning: *The heater has pooped out again.* [1885–90; perh. to be identified with POOP⁴]

Idioms

Idioms, expressions whose meanings are not predictable from the usual meanings of the constituent elements, are shown in boldface type under the main entry for one of the content words in the idiom. When the idiom might feasibly be listed at either of two such words, it is fully defined at one of them and may be cross-referred to this definition at the other.

The part of speech under which an idiom is shown depends on the grammatical function of the main entry word in the idiom, and not on the grammatical function of the idiom in a sentence. Thus at *bag*, the idiom *in the bag* would be listed under the noun definitions.

Idioms are listed in alphabetical order, after all the other definitions for the part of speech under which they appear. Pronunciation and stress are not shown. Note that a single idiom may have several subsenses.

bag (bag), *n., v.,* **bagged, bag•ging,** *interj.* —*n.* **1.** a container or receptacle of leather, plastic, cloth, paper, etc., capable of being closed at the mouth; pouch.... **14. bags, a.** *Informal.* plenty; much; many (usually fol. by *of*): *bags of time; bags of money.* **b.** *Slang.* trousers. **15. bag and baggage, a.** with all one's personal property: *When they went to collect the rent, they found he had left, bag and baggage.* **b.** completely; totally: *The equipment had disappeared, bag and baggage, without even the slightest trace.* **16. bag of bones,** an emaciated person or animal. **17. bag of tricks,** a supply of expedient resources; stratagems: *Maybe they will finally be honest with us, once they've run through their bag of tricks.* **18. hold the bag,** *Informal.* to be forced to bear the entire blame, responsibility, or loss that was to have been shared: *His accomplices flew to South America on news of the theft and left him holding the bag.* **19. in the bag,** *Informal.* virtually certain; assured; definite: *Her promotion is in the bag. The sale of the house is in the bag.* **20. old bag,** *Slang.* an unattractive, often slatternly woman: *a gossipy old bag.* —*v.i.* **21.** to swell or bulge: *A stiff breeze made the sails bag out.* **22.** to hang loosely like an empty bag: *His socks bagged at the ankles.* **23.** to pack groceries or other items into a bag. —*v.t.* **24.** to cause to swell or bulge; distend: *The wind bagged the curtain.* **25.** to put into a bag. **26.** *Informal.* to kill or catch, as in hunting: *I bagged my first deer when I was a teenager.* **27.** *Theat.* clew (def. 10a). **28. bag school,** *Slang.* to be truant. Also, **bag it.** —*interj.* **29. bags!** *Brit. Slang.* (used to lay first claim to something): *Bags it! Bags, I go first!* [1200–50; 1920–25 for def. 20; ME *bagge* <ON *baggi* pack, bundle] **—bag′like′,** *adj.*

Cross References

Abbreviations, symbols, etc. Some abbreviations, symbols, acronyms, etc., are simply defined with their full, expanded forms. Some of these full forms may be sufficient to define the entries, but others are themselves shown as main entries, with more extensive definitions. Some of these definitions may in turn show the abbreviated form. Entries for chemical elements also show atomic number, atomic weight, etc.

Hidden entries. A hidden entry is enclosed in parentheses and shown in boldface within the text of a broader entry, where its definition is made clear. A main entry for an item thus defined refers the reader to the broader entry with the instruction to "See under" (the broader entry).

jun′gle fowl′, any of several East Indian, gallinaceous birds of the genus *Gallus,* as *G. gallus* **(red jungle fowl),** believed to be the ancestor of the domestic fowl. [1815–25]

red′ jun′gle fowl′. See under **jungle fowl.**

Comparisons. A "Cf." at the end of a definition, preceding one or more terms in boldface type, indicates that a user can compare the information in that definition with related information at the entries for the cross-referenced terms.

Similar cross references are used to pinpoint more specific relationships between definitions. For example, one term may be opposed to, contrasted with, or distinguished from another. These cross references are enclosed in parentheses at the end of a definition, with the entry referred to shown in italics.

elec′tromagnet′ic field′, *Elect.* the coupled electric and magnetic fields that are generated by time-varying currents and accelerated charges. Cf. **Maxwell's field equations.**

in•tra vi•res (in′trə vī′rēz), *Law.* within the legal power or authority of an individual or corporation (opposed to *ultra vires*). [1875–80; < L *intrā vīrēs* within the powers]

Illustrations. When additional helpful information can be found in an illustration, map, diagram, or table shown elsewhere in the Dictionary, the user is guided to that illustration with an instruction to "See illus. (map, diag., etc.) under (the appropriate entry term)," the latter shown in boldface.

Nean′derthal man′, a member of an extinct subspecies of powerful, physically robust humans, *Homo sapiens neanderthalensis,* that inhabited Europe and western and central Asia c100,000–40,000 B.C. See illus. under **hominid.** [1860–65]

neap¹ (nēp), *adj.* **1.** designating tides midway between spring tides that attain the least height. —*n.* **2.** neap tide. See diag. under **tide¹.** [bef. 900; ME *neep,* OE *nēp-,* in *nēpflōd* neap tide]

IV. LABELS

Field Labels

Some entries or individual definitions are restricted in use to one particular subject field, like history, or to two related fields, like chemistry and physics. These entries and definitions are appropriately labeled throughout the Dictionary. Often, however, the content of a definition will make the scope of its use sufficiently clear without overt labeling.

Usage Labels

Labels of place. Entries or definitions that are limited in use to a particular geographical location are given regional labels, like *Canadian, Chiefly Brit.,* or *South Midland U.S.* (For major U.S. labels, see map, p. xxvi.) Entries not so labeled are considered to be in general use throughout the U.S. A few terms, especially those with a somewhat rural flavor, like *agin* or *opry,* are too widespread to warrant a specific regional label. These are labeled *Dial.*

Labels of time. Not all entries and definitions are equally current. To help the user of the Dictionary discriminate between terms in contemporary use and terms of historical interest, the following labels are used:

Obs. Obsolete terms have not been in widespread use since about 1750. They may be encountered in literature written before this time.

Archaic. Entries or definitions now archaic were current roughly to 1900, but are now employed only as conscious archaisms.

Rare. This label indicates terms that, while not obsolete or archaic, are simply not often found in the contemporary idiom.

Older Use. A term with this label, though commonly used in the early part of the 20th century, is now primarily heard among older members of the population. Examples are certain slang terms from the 1920's or 1930's.

Labels of style. Entries that are not used freely as part of the standard vocabulary are given stylistic or status labels so that the reader can make useful judgments about the setting in which a term might be appropriate, the kind of speaker who might use it, the kind of communication intended, and the likely effect on the listener or reader. The following stylistic labels are used in this Dictionary:

Informal. An informal term is not likely to occur in formal, prepared speech or carefully edited writing except when used intentionally to convey a casual tone.

Nonstandard. A nonstandard term is characteristic of the speech of persons with little education and is often regarded as a marker of low social status.

Slang. Often metaphorical, slang terms may be vivid, playful, and elliptical. Much slang is ephemeral, becoming dated in a relatively short period of time, but some slang terms find their way into the standard language. Slang terms are used in formal speech and writing only for special effect.

Vulgar. Vulgar terms are considered inappropriate in many circumstances because of their association with a taboo subject. Major taboo subjects in English-speaking cultures are sex and excretion and the parts of the body associated with those functions.

Disparaging. This label indicates that a term is used with disparaging intent, as to belittle a particular racial, religious, or social group.

Offensive. This label indicates that the term so labeled is likely to be perceived as offensive by a listener or reader, whether or not any offense was intended.

Facetious. A term may be labeled "Facetious" if it is used consciously for humorous or playful effect.

Baby Talk. A term with this label is thought to be used by small children and is therefore used by adults in imitation of a child, as in speaking to babies, young children, sweethearts, or pets.

Literary. An entry term with this label is used rarely in contemporary speech or writing except to create a literary, poetic, evocative effect.

Eye Dialect. This label is used for deliberate misspellings in literature that are calculated to convey a character's lack of education or habitual use of dialectal pronunciations, but that in fact represent perfectly standard pronunciations, often the only ones in use, as the one conveyed by *wimmin,* for *women.*

Pron. Spelling. Terms with this label, which stands for "Pronunciation Spelling," differ from those labeled "Eye Dialect" in that they are not intended to convey lack of education, but merely continuous, especially rapid, speech. The label is used for such forms as *gonna* 'going to' (followed by a verb) and *lemme* 'let me', and the pronunciations they reflect, while not the only ones possible, are used by speakers at all educational and social levels, on formal as well as informal occasions.

V. ETYMOLOGIES

Etymologies in this Dictionary appear in square brackets after the definitions or, when they occur, after the variant spellings of the entry word. A full key to the symbols and abbreviations used in the etymologies appears inside the front cover of the Dictionary and on page xlii, and a concise key is given at the bottom of every left-hand page.

Symbols and Abbreviations

The following symbols and abbreviations occur with particular frequency in the etymologies.

< This symbol, meaning "from," is used to show descent from one language or group of languages to another. It is placed before a language label (e.g., < OF... < L... < Gk) in order to indicate from what source and in what form a word has entered English and to trace, in turn, the line of descent from one pre-English source to another.

diadem... [...ME *diademe* (< AF) < L *diadēma* < Gk *diádēma*...]

negative... [...< L *negātīvus* denying (see NEGATE, -IVE), r. ME *negatif* (n. and adj.) < MF < L, as above]

It is also placed between an attested word and an earlier unattested form (marked with an asterisk), signifying that the unattested form is reconstructed for an earlier unnamed stage in the development of the language in question.

cousin... [...L *consobrinus*...equiv. to *con-* CON- + *sobrīnus* second cousin (presumably orig. "pertaining to the sister") < **swesrīnos,* equiv. to **swesr-,* gradational var. of **swesor* (> *soror* SISTER) + *-*inos* -INE¹...]

This symbol is not used between words that belong to different named historical periods of the same language. It is omitted, for example, between ME and OE forms, MHG and G forms, and OF and F forms.

madder¹... [...ME *mad(d)er,* OE *mæd(e)re*...]

It is also not used before the analysis of a word—that is, before the breaking down of a word into its constituent morphemes. See **equiv. to** below.

<< This symbol is used to show descent from one language to another but with an intermediate stage omitted. It may be read as "goes back to."

tick[3]**...** [...ME *tikke, teke, tyke* (c. D *tijk*, G *Zeiche* < <L *t(h)eca*...]

> This symbol, meaning "whence," is used to indicate that the word following it is descended from the word preceding it. It generally serves the purpose of citing a modern foreign language word that is akin to the entry word.

yet... [...ME *yet(e)*, OE *gieta*, c. MHG *ieze* yet, now > G *jetzt* now]

An additional function of this symbol is to separate the stages in a sequence of sense shifts.

biretta... [...< ML *birrettum* cap, equiv. to LL *birr(us)* BIRRUS + *-ettum* -ET; appar. by shift "hooded cloak" > "hood" > "cap"...]

equiv. to This abbreviation, meaning "equivalent to," precedes the analysis of a word. It is used to show that a word is made up of the words or morphemes that follow it.

ferreous... [...< L *ferreus*, equiv. to *ferr(um)* iron + *-eus* -EOUS]

In the etymologies of Japanese and Korean loanwords that these languages have in turn borrowed from Middle Chinese, ***equiv. to*** is used to link the Middle Chinese sources and the corresponding modern Chinese words.

bonsai... [...< Japn *bon-sai* tray planting < MChin, equiv. to Chin *pén* tray + *zāi* plant, shoot]

+ This symbol is used between morphemes, the constituents of a compound or a blend, etc., in order to indicate that these are the immediate constituents of the word being analyzed.

distinctly... [DISTINCT + -LY]

boron... [BOR(AX) + (CARB)ON]

iniquity... [...ME < L *inīquitās* unevenness, unfairness, equiv. to *inīqu(us)* uneven, unfair (*in-* IN-[3] + *-īquus*, comb. form of *aequus* even, EQUAL) + *-itās* -ITY]

deriv. of This abbreviation indicates that the form preceding it—for example, a particular part of speech—is a derivative of the form that follows.

bleed... [...ME *bleden*, OE *blēdan*, deriv. of *blōd* BLOOD]

Parentheses

Parentheses are used to set off any element that is lost or replaced when constituents are joined in the derivation of an entry word or of an italicized word within an etymology.

combo... [...COMB(INATION) + -O]

compander... [...COM(PRESS) + (EX)PAND + -ER[1]]

orbicular... [...< LL *orbiculāris* circular, equiv. to L *orbicul(us)* small disk (*orbi(s)* ORB + *-culus* -CULE[1]) + *-āris* -AR[1]]

Similarly, parentheses set off entire words (and their translations) that are lost in ellipsis.

columbine[1]**...** [...< ML *columbīna (herba)* dovelike (plant)...]

A third function of parentheses is to collapse, for the sake of brevity, two or more variant spellings or forms. Hence, in the etymology below, *s(e)alm(e)* signifies that *salm, salme, sealm*, and *sealme* are all attested spellings of the Middle English word for "psalm."

psalm... [...ME *psalm(e), s(e)alm(e)*, OE *ps(e)alm*...]

A fourth function is to highlight an intermediary language that may or may not have played a role in the transmission of a form to English. In such cases, the intermediary word and the more basic etymon may both have functioned as a source, each reinforcing the other, as with words of Latin origin that also existed in French.

facility... [...late ME *facilite* (< MF) < L *facilitās*. See FACILE, -ITY]

Finally, parentheses are used to enclose the analysis of a preceding word that is itself part of a larger analysis (as with Latin *orbiculus* in the etymology of *orbicular* above), and in a variety of other situations where a subsidiary analysis or additional information is set off from other parts of the etymology.

Language Labels

Language labels, as given in the Etymology Key, precede the italicized etyma. An unlabeled form is to be understood as an English word.

harewood... [...var. of obs. *airewood*, equiv. to obs. *aire* harewood...]

A language label is shown alone without an accompanying italicized form when there is no significant difference in form or meaning between the word in the given language and the preceding word in the etymology, or the headword of the entry. In some cases an italicized word is not shown after a language label when the word is identical to one immediately following.

inland... [...ME, OE; see IN-[1], LAND]

base... [...ME < MF < L *basis*...]

Note that after an entry such as *Holy Ghost*, the etymology [ME; OE] means that the entire phrase occurs in Middle English and Old English in the form appropriate to these stages of the language; for the forms of the individual words, the reader is to consult their respective etymologies. A language label is followed by a colon and a translation when there is a difference in meaning but none in form between a word in a given language and the preceding word.

incentive... [...ME < LL *incentīvus* provocative, L: setting the tune, equiv. to *incent(us)*...]

Typefaces

Three styles of type are used in the etymologies. Roman type is used for translations, definitions, comments on grammar, and other explanatory matter.

Italic type is used for all words or parts of words (usually not entries in the Dictionary) from which the entry words are formed by derivation or composition. Foreign words, those labeled ME, OE, "obs.," "earlier," "dial.," and those, including proper names, that are not otherwise entries in the Dictionary are italicized.

Small capitals indicate a cross reference to another entry in the Dictionary where further information may be obtained about the meaning or etymology of a word. Especially frequent reference is made to numerous affixes or combining forms that correspond to common elements in pre-English words, as -ATE[1], -ION, -IVE, etc., for Latin *-ātus, -ion-, -īvus*, etc.

Special Types of Etymologies

In addition to the etymologies concerned with tracing words to their non-English sources, there are those that require only simple cross references to their parts. These are chiefly words derived within English.

developer... [...DEVELOP + -ER[1]]

singer[1]**...** [...ME; see SING, -ER[1]]

Acronyms, when not accounted for in the definition, are shown in italics with parentheses enclosing all parts but those composing the entry word.

NATO... [*N(orth) A(tlantic) T(reaty) O(rganization)*]

scuba... [*s(elf)-c(ontained) u(nderwater) b(reathing) a(pparatus)*]

Blends are shown in small capitals. Parentheses delineate the portions of words that do not enter into the blend only when the words share no phonetic material. When phonetic material is shared, the abbreviation "b." for "blend of" and the conjunction *and* are used.

brunch... [BR(EAKFAST) + (L)UNCH]

airmada... [b. AIR and ARMADA]

For entries that contain the name of an individual, the etymology generally has a cross reference to a biographical entry in the Dictionary or a brief biographical note, with the person's full name, dates, profession, and nationality, when these are known. The same information is also given on occasion for the originator of a word or phrase, especially when the originator is also the discoverer of the concept or object described in the definition.

Briggsian logarithm... [named after H. BRIGGS; see -IAN]

Alzheimer's disease... [named after Alois *Alzheimer* (1864–1915), German neurologist, who described it in 1907]

Treatment of Non-European Languages

A limited number of special symbols have been used in the etymologies of words borrowed from non-European languages, especially languages that are seldom written and have no generally accepted orthography. The symbols listed below for North American Indian languages have the same values in other etymologies. Nearly all of the symbols are those of the International Phonetic Alphabet (IPA); the full set of IPA symbols can be found in the chart under the entry **phonetic alphabet.**

Other specifics concerning the treatment of non-European languages are also given below.

1. The etyma of words borrowed from North American Indian languages are usually cited in phonemicized form in a system of transcription widely used by students of these languages. Symbols that occur in the etymologies are given below with their equivalents in the pronunciation system used in this Dictionary. When an equivalent is not available, a brief phonetic description is supplied.

ɛ = (e)
ɔ = (ô)
θ = (th)
ð = (t͟h)
č = (ch)
š = (sh)
ž = (zh)
x = (KH)
ŋ = (ng)
ɑ = tense, low, back, slightly centralized vowel (used in transcriptions of Eastern Abenaki words)
ɨ = high central vowel ("barred i")
β = voiced bilabial fricative
ɬ = voiceless lateral approximant
ƛ = voiceless lateral affricate
c = voiceless palatal stop
ɣ = voiced velar fricative
q = voiceless postvelar stop
ʔ = glottal stop
ʕ = voiced pharyngeal fricative
ḥ = voiceless pharyngeal fricative

Additionally, the following diacritic marks are used: a dot following a vowel or consonant letter (e·, k·) marks length; a hook below a vowel (ą) shows that it is nasal; a superscript *w* following a consonant (g^w) indicates that the consonant is labialized, a superscript *h* (t^h) that it is aspirate, a superscript *y* (n^y) that it is palatalized; an apostrophe directly over a consonant (k̓) shows that it is glottalized.

Examples of these symbols may be found in the etymologies for *babiche, coho, muskellunge, musquash, orenda, pogonip, potlatch, puccoon, tepee.* (Note that the acute, grave, and circumflex accents do not have a completely uniform value for transcriptions of all the languages; the interested reader is advised to consult a phonological description of the language in question.)

2. Nahuatl words are in a regularized form of the orthography of Classical Nahuatl, with the addition of macrons to mark vowel length and *h* to represent the glottal stop.

3. Quechua words are cited in a regularized form of southern Peruvian Quechua.

4. In transcriptions of Australian Aboriginal languages, the digraph *dh* represents a lamino-interdental stop.

5. In transcriptions of Khoisan words, ≠ represents an alveolar click and *!* a post-alveolar click.

6. Chinese words are given in the Beijing (Northern, Mandarin) pronunciation, spelled in pinyin, unless otherwise stated. Japanese words are cited in the Hepburn Romanization, Korean words in the McCune-Reischauer Romanization.

Dating the Entries; Americanisms

The date appearing inside the square etymology brackets refers to the time when the entry word or phrase, or an older form of it, was first recorded in English. Most dates are expressed as a spread of years, giving the time within which the earliest document containing the main entry word was written or published.

gold [bef. 900; ME; OE;...]

higgledy-piggledy [1590–1600;...]

magnetic star [1975–80]

We believe that such a spread is more useful to the Dictionary's readers than a specific date, since words do not necessarily enter the spoken language in the same year they are first written down. In many cases a term may have existed in the spoken language long before it first appeared in texts and, in any event, earlier written evidence may exist that has not yet been discovered or reported. Very old writings, especially those in Old and Middle English manuscripts, are difficult to date—often such manuscripts are copies or compilations of works composed at an unknown time. We have necessarily taken the dates of such manuscripts—as best as this can be determined by scholars—to represent the dates of their contents. For these reasons, older terms are given broader date ranges than more recent ones, and caution should be used in interpreting any entry's date.

The date refers only to a word's earliest known meaning, usually its primary or core definition, but sometimes to a long obsolete meaning or a sense of the term's immediate forerunner, as shown in the etymology.

Though most words cannot be dated precisely, many coinages can be. Thus the date for a coined word will often appear as a single year, rather than as a date spread.

snark [1876;...]

momism [coined by U.S. author Philip Wylie...(1942)]

reggae [...coined in the song "Do the Reggay" (1968)...]

Technical and scientific terms coined in another language and subsequently borrowed into English are also dated by the year of coinage, which is shown in parentheses following the language and foreign spelling (if there is one) of the word in its language of origin.

brontosaurus [< NL (1879),...]

dopa [< G *Dopa* (1917),...]

Dates are usually not given for entries that are names, as names of people and places, mythological figures, or trademarks; nor for such items as combining forms, inflected forms, most abbreviations, and spelling variants of dated words. Words derived from such names and terms will, however, often be dated:

Prussian [1555–65;...]

Wassermann test [1910–15;...]

A few terms, especially those with recent dates, are known by the editors to have existed before the date of their earliest written evidence. The dates for such words are preceded by the symbol ‡, which should read as "probably earlier than."

Americanisms, terms first recorded in the U.S. or colonial America, are indicated by the label *Amer.* after the date.

craps [1835–45, *Amer.*;...]

VI. END-OF-ENTRY NOTES

Many entries feature additional information, which cannot be covered by definitions and labels alone, concerning subtleties of sense distinction and usage, and the geographical distribution of variant forms. This information is contained in labeled notes and appears at the end of an entry, following the etymology and any derived, run-on forms.

Synonym Lists and Studies

Synonym lists and studies are preceded by **—Syn.** and may be keyed to particular definitions by number. The lists are general in nature, and the user is advised to check the entries of the individual synonyms for their precise meanings. The studies compare several terms that are closely related in meaning by describing and clarifying discriminations of a more detailed nature.

Antonym Lists

Antonym lists are preceded by **—Ant.** These lists are brief, guiding the user to the entries of antonyms where a fuller treatment may be found.

Usage Notes

Preceded by **—Usage,** these notes describe many of the disputed or problematic issues in grammar and usage, and they are intended to reflect the actual practice of speakers and writers of English at various levels of formality and in various contexts, as well as the opinions of those who, on the basis of their training and experience, have been recognized as authorities in such matters, especially teachers and editors.

Pronunciation Notes

These notes, preceded by **—Pronunciation,** discuss the regional distribution, acceptability, or history of various pronunciations of the entry word.

Regional Variation Notes

These notes constitute brief dialect studies that discuss different regional terms for the same item or different regional forms of the same word. They are preceded by **—Regional Variation.** Where relevant, cross references are given to other entries that treat regional variation.

VII. PRONUNCIATION

Approach to Pronunciations

Pronunciations, enclosed in parentheses, appear immediately following many entry forms. At any single entry, pronunciations are listed in order of frequency, insofar as that can be determined, although the difference in frequency of use between any two consecutive pronunciations may be minimal. Since print is linear and pronunciations cannot be superimposed upon one another, certain dialect patterns are shown before others as a matter of stylistic policy, as (-ôr) before (-ōr) for words like *hoarse* and *four*. Users of the Dictionary should look for pronunciations that fit most comfortably into their own dialects.

Unless otherwise labeled, all pronunciations given should be considered standard and may be used freely in all social circumstances.

Pronunciation System; Kinds of Symbols Used

The pronunciation system in this book uses diacritical marks over vowels to represent vowel quality. Thus, although it uses a type of **broad transcription,** delineating major sound divisions in English, it is not intended to represent particular sounds in an exact way. Instead, each symbol is matched with **key words,** and the system is constructed so that each user of the Dictionary, by pronouncing those key words, will automatically produce the variety of each sound appropriate to his or her own dialect. For example, while one speaker of English might say the word *cow* with a diphthong that starts with a vowel similar to the (ä) of *father*, another might use a diphthong that starts with a vowel more like the (a) of *hat.* Both speakers would respond "correctly," in the context of their own dialect patterns, to the symbol (ou), used in this book to show the pronunciation of *cow* as (kou).

The kind of diacritical system used in this Dictionary is sometimes referred to as **orthographically motivated,** because it reflects underlying fundamental sound-spelling correspondences in English. Thus, just as the stressed vowel of *divine* and the stressed vowel of *divinity* are both spelled with an *i*, the pronunciation symbols for these two sounds, (ī) and (i) respectively, are also a form of *i*, reflecting that relationship. An orthographically motivated system can therefore make efficient use of the knowledge that a native speaker of English has about the language. By contrast, using symbols from the International Phonetic Alphabet (IPA), whose symbols reflect sound-spelling correspondences in Latinate languages, the stressed vowels in *divine* and *divinity* would be rendered as [aɪ] and [ɪ].

The IPA symbols shown in the following descriptions represent approximate equivalents and are provided as an aid to users who are familiar with that system.

A Guide to Pronunciation Symbols

Vowels. In the following descriptions, **front, central,** and **back** refer to the approximate area of the mouth, on a roughly horizontal axis, in which a portion of the tongue is raised during production of a given vowel (the blade for front vowels, the central portion for central vowels, and the dorsum for back vowels). The terms **high, mid,** and **low** indicate the degree to which that raising takes place.

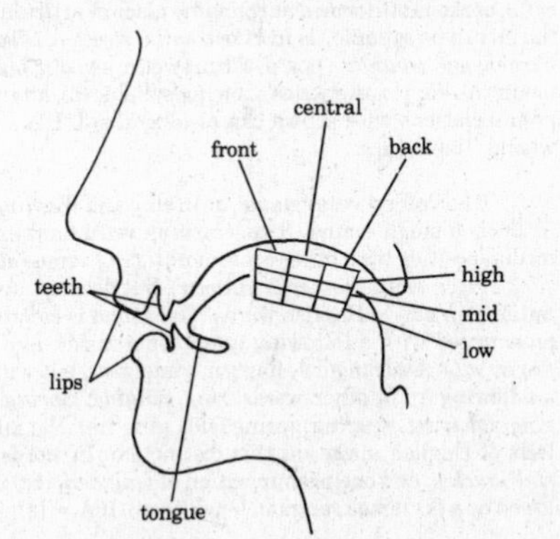

a as in *cap*, represents a "short *a*," a **low front** vowel, made with relatively lax tongue muscles. The lips are more open than for (e), but less open than for (ä). The sound is often raised toward (â) in words like *glad* and *ham.* When shown in variation with (ä), as for *ask* and *laugh*, the two symbols (a, ä) represent a range of pronunciations. IPA = [æ]

ā as in *rate*, represents the "long *a.*" It is a **mid front** vowel, made with relatively tense tongue muscles. The lips are slightly more open than for (ē) or (i), but less open than for (e). In English, the sound is typically diphthongal, especially in stressed and open syllables. IPA = [eɪ, ei, e]

â This symbol, shown with an (r) in the pronunciation key, represents the sound commonly heard before *r* in words like *air* and *dare.* It is typically a **mid front** vowel, but may actually have a range extending from the (a) of *cap* through the (e) of *bet* to the (ā) of *fade*, depending on one's dialect. The sound is commonly diphthongal and is followed by a faint schwa. In some dialects, the (r) may be dropped. IPA = [ɛə]

ä as in *calm* and *father*, represents a vowel sometimes described as **low** and **back** and sometimes as **low** and **central.** It is formed with lax tongue muscles and with the lips more open than for any other vowel. For speakers who do not distinguish between *balm* and *bomb*, this is the same sound as the one represented by (o) in this Dictionary and is also heard in *hot* and *top.* IPA = [ɑ]

e as in *get*, represents a "short *e*," typically a **mid front** vowel made with relatively lax tongue muscles. The lips are slightly more open than for (ā), but less open than for (a). In many dialects the sound is raised toward (â) before (r). IPA = [ɛ]

ē as in *fee*, represents the "long *e.*" It is a **high front** vowel formed, in stressed syllables, with relatively tense tongue muscles and with the lips more spread than for any other vowel. In unstressed syllables, as for the *y* in *pretty*, the sound may vary from one close to the (ē) of *steam* to one resembling the (i) of *Tim*, depending on the dialect. In English, the sound is often diphthongal, especially in stressed or open syllables. IPA = [i]

ēr This symbol represents the vowel plus (r) heard in *here.* In many dialects (ēr) contrasts with (ir), as heard in *mirror.* The particular vowel in words like *here* and *mirror* can range between (i) and (ē). In some dialects no contrast is made between (ēr) and (ir). Although this Dictionary shows transcriptions that reflect a distinction between the two sounds, speakers who do not make this distinction before *r* will collapse the two vowels automatically, using the key words as a guide. IPA = [ɪər, ɪɚ]

i as in *big*, represents the "short *i*," a **high front** vowel formed with relatively lax tongue muscles. The lips are slightly more open than for (ē). In this Dictionary, (i) also represents an unstressed vowel that may vary between the qualities of full (i) and (ə), the reduced vowel. This variable vowel is heard in the third syllable of *America* and the second syllable of *furniture.* IPA = [ɪ]

ī as in *bite*, represents the "long *i.*" The sound is a **fronting diphthong,** moving from **low central** or **low back** position to a **high front** position. The first vowel element is close to (ä) or between (ä) and (a), and the second element varies between (i) and (ē). IPA = [aɪ, ai]

o as in *ox* and *hot*, represents the "short *o.*" Found only in words spelled with *o*, *wa*, or *ua*, this variable symbol is included to reflect dialects that use one vowel in *bomb* and *bother* and another in *balm* and *father*, as, for example, in eastern New England. For speakers of these dialects, the sound is typically a **low back** vowel, made with relatively lax tongue muscles. The lips are slightly less open and more rounded than for (ä), but more open and less rounded than for (ô). In most of the United States, the difference between *bomb* and *balm* is collapsed, and little distinction is made, except perhaps for duration, between (o) and (ä). The (o) in this Dictionary is able to accommodate both types of dialect. IPA = [ɒ] or [ɑ]

ō as in *hope*, represents the "long *o*," a **mid back** vowel made with relatively tense tongue muscles. The lips are more rounded and less open than for (ô) and less rounded and more open than for (o͞o). In English, the sound is often diphthongal, especially in stressed or open syllables. IPA = [oʊ, ou, o]

ô as in *ought* and *fall*, represents a relatively long, typically **low back** vowel, formed with slightly tense tongue muscles. The lips are less rounded and more open than for (ō). Some dialects in North America collapse the difference between (o) and (ô). IPA = [ɔ]

oi as in *boy*, represents a fronting diphthong, moving from a low back position to a high front position, with the first vowel element roughly an (ô) and the second varying between (i) and (ē), but usually closer to (ē). IPA = [ɔɪ, ɔi]

o͝o as in *book*, represents the "short double-*o*," a **high back** vowel made with relatively lax tongue muscles. The lips are less rounded and more open than for (o͞o). Before *r*, this symbol represents the sound heard in *touring*. IPA = [ʊ]

o͞o as in *too*, represents the "long double-*o*," a **high back** vowel made with relatively tense tongue muscles. The lips are more rounded and less open than for (o͝o). IPA = [u]

ou as in *plow*, represents a **retracting diphthong,** moving from **low back** or **low central** position to a **high back** position, with the first vowel element roughly between (ä) and (a) and the second varying between an (o͝o) and an (o͞o). IPA = [aʊ, au]

u as in *cup*, represents the "short *u*," typically a **mid central** vowel formed with relatively lax tongue muscles. The lips are unrounded. In some transcription systems, it is considered a stressed variant of a schwa. IPA = [ʌ] or [ə]

û as in *turn*, represents the stressed, *r*-colored, **mid central** vowel. Since it is normally accompanied by some degree of retroflexion (that is, said with the tongue tip curled toward the palate), it is shown in the pronunciation key with the retroflex consonant (r), as (ûr). In *r*-dropping dialects, *r*-color may be minimal or absent. IPA = [ɜ]; with *r*-color, [ɝ]

ə the schwa, represents the reduced, unstressed vowel commonly heard as the sound of *a* in *alone*, *e* in *system*, *i* in *easily*, *o* in *gallop*, and *u* in *circus*. It is a **mid central** vowel formed with open lips in neutral position, neither spread nor rounded. The schwa can frequently take on some of the quality of one of the full vowels, while remaining unstressed. IPA = [ə]; with *r*-color, [ɚ]

ᵊ the superscript schwa, in transcriptions of English words, represents a faint schwa. The symbol is used following the diphthongs (ī) and (ou), when either diphthong is followed by an (r) in the same syllable, to show that the complex vowel preceding the (r) normally has triphthongal quality, as in *lyre* (līᵊr), *fire* (fīᵊr), and *tiring* (tīᵊr′ing), in contrast with *liar* (lī′ər) and *irate* (ī rāt′), and as in *flour* (flouᵊr) when pronounced so as to contrast with *flower* (flou′ər). This symbol is also used in non-English transcriptions (see below).

Consonants. The consonants of English will be described here in terms of three general articulatory features: **voice, place of articulation,** and **manner of articulation.**

A voiced consonant is one that is characteristically pronounced with audible vibration of the vocal cords. Thus voiced (b) contrasts with voiceless (p) in voice only; their place and manner of articulation are identical.

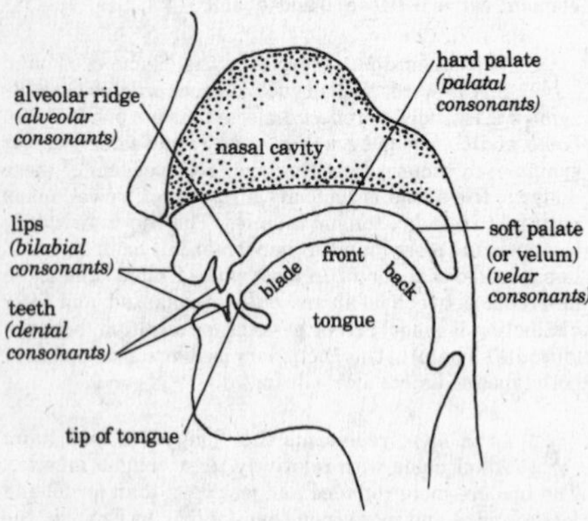

The terminology used to describe place and manner of articulation is more technical, but all the terms used here can be found, with full definitions, in the main vocabulary listing. In addition, the preceding illustration can aid in understanding the references to specific places of articulation. Labeled portions of the oral cavity correspond to the adjectives used in the descriptions; for example, "alveolar" refers to sounds made with the tip of the tongue touching or near the alveolar (or gum) ridge, "bilabial" to sounds involving the two lips, etc.

b the **voiced bilabial plosive,** as in *back, cabin,* and *cab*. Its voiceless counterpart is (p). IPA = [b]

ch the **voiceless affricate,** as in *chief, butcher,* and *beach*. It is a combination of the plosive (t) and the sibilant (or fricative) (sh), blended to form a single consonant, and is formed with the tip and blade of the tongue behind the alveolar ridge. Its voiced counterpart is (j). IPA = [tʃ]

d the **voiced alveolar plosive,** as in *do, rudder,* and *bed*. Intervocalically, especially before a relatively unstressed vowel, as in *rudder, daddy,* or *leader*, the sound is often flapped. The voiceless counterpart of (d) is (t). IPA = [d]

f the **voiceless labiodental fricative,** as in *fit, differ,* and *puff*. Its voiced counterpart is (v). IPA = [f]

g the **voiced velar plosive,** as in *give, trigger,* and *big*. This sound is commonly known as the "hard *g*." Its voiceless counterpart is (k). IPA = [g]

h the **voiceless glottal fricative,** as in *here* and *behave*. When combined with (y), as in *huge* (hyo͞oj), the (hy) represents either the two consonants (h) plus (y) in sequence or a voiceless (y), a **palatal fricative**. The combination (hl) represents the **voiceless** (l) in Welsh transcriptions. IPA = [h]

hw This symbol represents either (w) preceded by a faint (h), or a **voiceless** (w). Either sound can be heard in WH-words, as *which, when,* or *where*, when spoken by those who do not pronounce these words with the (w) of *witch, wen,* and *wear*. IPA = [hw, ʍ]

j the **voiced affricate,** as in *just, badger,* and *fudge*. It is a combination of the plosive (d) and the sibilant (or fricative) (zh), blended to form a single consonant, and is formed with the tip and blade of the tongue behind the alveolar ridge. Its voiceless counterpart is (ch). IPA = [dʒ]

k the **voiceless velar plosive,** as in *keep, coop, scoop, token,* and *make*. Its voiced counterpart is (g). IPA = [k]

l the **voiced alveolar lateral,** as in *leap, low, mellow,* and *fall*. The (l) ranges in quality from the "light" or "clear" sound usually heard when (l) is in initial position preceding a front vowel, as in *leaf*, to the "dark" sound usually heard when (l) is in final or preconsonantal position or precedes a back vowel (*call, silk,* or *loose*). When preceded by **homorganic** consonants (t), (d), or (n), consonants formed at the same place of articulation, the (l) can be syllabic, as in *little, cradle,* and *tunnel* (lit′l, krād′l, tun′l). For entries showing syllabic *l*, alternate pronunciations with schwa can also be heard. IPA = [l]; when syllabic, [l̩]

m the **voiced bilabial nasal,** as in *my, summer,* and *drum*. When preceded by **homorganic** consonants (p) or (b), consonants formed at the same place of articulation, the (m) can be syllabic, as in *cap'n* (kap′m). Syllabic *m* is not nearly as frequent as syllabic *n* or *l*. For most entries showing syllabic *m*, alternate pronunciations with schwa plus (n) can also be heard. IPA = [m]; when syllabic, [m̩]

n the **voiced alveolar nasal,** as in *now, sunny,* and *pin*. When preceded by **homorganic** consonants (t) or (d), consonants formed at the same place of articulation, the (n) can be syllabic, as in *kitten, satin, sweeten, Sweden, burden,* and *mountain* (kit′n, sat′n, swēt′n, swēd′n, bûr′dn, moun′tn). For many entries showing syllabic (n), alternate pronunciations with schwa can also be heard. IPA = [n]; when syllabic, [n̩]

ng The **voiced velar nasal,** as in *sing* and *Washington*, is a single sound. It contrasts in word final and in medial position with other consonants (*sung* versus *sun* or *sum*; *singer* versus *sinner* or *simmer*), but does not appear initially in native English words. The sound is commonly pronounced with a following (g) in some words: *wrangle, finger, youngest* (rang′gəl, fing′gər, yung′gist), but without a following (g) in other words: *ring, ringing, Springfield, gingham* (ring, ring′ing, spring′fēld′, ging′əm). Not all dialects of English maintain this distinction. In words like *sink, anchor,* and one pronunciation of *lengthen*, (ng) is followed by a (k): (singk, angk′ər, lengk′thən). IPA = [ŋ]

p the **voiceless bilabial plosive,** as in *pool, spool, supper,* and *stop*. Its voiced counterpart is (b). IPA = [p]

r While this symbol stands for a single significant consonant in the sound system of American English, it actually represents several *r*-sounds, ranging from a frictionless, retroflex consonant, as heard in most American pronunciations of *red* and *rich*, to the flapped sound heard between vowels in some British pronunciations of *very* and *worry*. In the consonant clusters (dr) and (tr), as in *dry* and *try*, the sound is often pronounced with friction, with the preceding (d) and (t) taking on affricate-like qualities. An (r) tends to affect the quality of immediately preceding sounds, as in one pronunciation of *fear*, where the target vowel is (ē) but the pronunciation is actually closer to (fiər). IPA symbols include: flapped *r*, [ɾ]; fricative and vowellike *r*, [ɹ]; trilled *r*, [r]

s the **voiceless sibilant** (or **fricative**) heard in *see, crossing,* and *kiss*. It is usually formed with the blade of the tongue close to the alveolar ridge. The breath stream is forced through a narrow groove formed by the tongue and strikes the teeth to produce a hissing sound. The voiced equivalent of (s) is (z). IPA = [s]

sh the **voiceless sibilant** (or **fricative**) heard in *she, crushing,* and *cash*. It is formed with the blade of the tongue held farther back than for (s). The breath stream is forced through a broader groove formed by the tongue and strikes the teeth to produce a hushing sound. The voiced equivalent of (sh) is (zh). IPA = [ʃ]

t the **voiceless alveolar plosive,** as in *team, steam, butter,* and *bit*. It may be released nasally, as in *button*, or laterally, as in *bottle*. Intervocalically, especially before a relatively unstressed vowel, as in *matter* and *lettuce*, or before a syllabic (l), as in *settle*, the usual sound in American English is a voiced flap virtually identical to the intervocalic (d) of *rudder*. Less often, intervocalic (t) is a voiceless flap that distinguishes *matter* from *madder*. The voiced equivalent of (t) is (d). IPA = [t]

th the **voiceless dental** (or **interdental**) **fricative,** as in *thin, ether,* and *path*. Its voiced counterpart is (*th*). IPA = [θ]

th the **voiced dental** (or **interdental**) **fricative,** as in *that, the, either,* and *smooth*. Its voiceless counterpart is (th). IPA = [ð]

v the **voiced labiodental fricative,** as in *voice, river,* and *live*. Its voiceless counterpart is (f). IPA = [v]

w the **voiced bilabial semivowel** (with secondary **velar** articulation), as in *west* and *away*. It is produced as the tongue moves from the position of an (o͞o) to the position of a following vowel. A (w) is the initial consonant in WH-words, like *which, when,* and *where*, for those who pronounce these words as homophones of *witch, wen,* and *wear*. IPA = [w]

y the **voiced palatal semivowel,** as in *yes* and *beyond*. It is produced as the tongue moves from the position of an (ē) to the position of a following vowel. IPA = [j]

z the **voiced sibilant** (or **fricative**) heard in *zoo, lazy,* and *please*. It is usually formed with the blade of the tongue close to the alveolar ridge. The breath stream is forced through a narrow groove formed by the tongue and strikes the teeth to produce a vibrating, hissing sound. The voiceless equivalent of (z) is (s). IPA = [z]

zh the **voiced sibilant** (or **fricative**) heard in *vision, pleasure,* and *mirage*. It is formed with the blade of the tongue held farther back than for (z). The breath stream is forced through a broader groove formed by the tongue and strikes the teeth to produce a vibrating hushing sound. With the exception of some loanwords (like *jabot*, from French), (zh) does not begin words in English. The voiceless equivalent of (zh) is (sh). IPA = [ʒ]

Non-English sounds. Most vowels and consonants in foreign-language pronunciations are represented by the same symbols used for English, although the actual quality of these sounds varies from language to language. Symbols in the pronunciations have been chosen to help a native speaker of English produce the sounds that are most appropriate for each language. Thus both (b) and (v) are used in Spanish pronunciations to mark a phonetic difference that a native speaker of Spanish would produce automatically and that depends on surrounding sounds, not on whether the entry is spelled with *b* or *v*. Similarly, the *d* of Spanish words may be rendered as either (d) or (*th*), depending on the phonetic environment.

Special symbols, shown below, are used only for those sounds that cannot be approximated by symbols in the English key.

A the **low vowel** heard in French *ami*. It is slightly to the front of (ä) in the French vowel system and is made with the lips open and somewhat spread. This vowel may be thought of by a speaker of English as roughly intermediate in quality between the (a) of *cat* and the (ä) of *calm*. IPA = [a]

KH This symbol represents the range of **voiceless fricatives** heard in Arabic, German, Hebrew, Scottish, Russian, etc., typically a **velar, uvular,** or **palatal** consonant. These fricatives may be articulated by bringing the tongue almost into the position of (k), but not touching the roof of the mouth, while pronouncing a strong, rasping (h). For the **velar fricative,** as in German *ach,* the tongue is brought toward the position of the (k) in *cool;* for the **palatal fricative,** as in German *ich,* the tongue is closer to the position of the (k) in *key.* Among the IPA symbols used for these various sounds are [x] for the **voiceless velar fricative** and [ç] for the **voiceless palatal fricative.**

N This symbol, as in French *bon,* is used to show that the preceding vowel is nasalized; it does not itself represent a nasal consonant. There are four nasalized vowels in French, found in the phrase *un bon vin blanc* (œN bôN vaN bläN). The usual IPA symbol is a tilde (˜), placed directly over the nasalized vowel.

Œ This symbol represents either the vowel heard in German *schön* and French *feu,* usually transcribed in IPA as [ø], or the vowel heard in the initial syllables of German *öffnen* and French *neuvième,* usually transcribed in IPA as [œ]. They are both rounded front vowels.

The former sound is made with relatively tense tongue muscles and with the lips rounded in the position for (ō) as in *over,* while trying to say (ā) as in *able.* The latter sound is made with relatively lax tongue muscles and with the lips rounded in the position for (ô) as in *ought,* while trying to say (e) as in *get.*

An English speaker may approximate an (œ) by pronouncing the vowel in *her* without any *r*-color.

R This symbol represents any non-English *r* sound and therefore does not stand for a sound with any one specific place of articulation. Since the pronunciation of *r* varies greatly from language to language, the symbol (R) is merely a token for whichever *r* is appropriate in the language being spoken. That *r* may, for example, be **flapped** (as in Spanish *pero*), **uvular** (as in the Parisian French pronunciation of *rouge*), or **trilled** (as in Italian *mare*).

Y This symbol represents either the vowel heard in the initial syllable of German *fühlen* and French *lumière,* transcribed in IPA as [y], or the one heard in the initial syllable of German *Fülle,* transcribed in IPA as [ʏ]. They are both rounded front vowels.

The former sound is made with relatively tense tongue muscles and with the lips in position for (o͞o) as in *boot,* while trying to say (ē) as in *beet.* The latter is made with relatively lax tongue muscles and with the lips in position for (o͝o) as in *cook,* while trying to say (i) as in *kick.*

ə A superscript schwa is used in foreign pronunciations to represent a sound ranging from a short, faint schwa immediately following a consonant or glide to a faint prolongation of the preceding consonant or glide, voiced or voiceless, as in French *Bastogne* or *boulevard* (ba-stôn′yᵊ, bo͞olᵊ VAR′).

Syllable Division and Stress in the Pronunciations

In the normal stream of speech, words are pronounced in a continuous flow, not as distinct syllables. Pronunciations are divided into syllables in the Dictionary, however, so that the reader may more easily sound out unfamiliar words. These divisions also aid the user to produce the appropriate phonetic variant of a given sound. For example, *mistake* is recorded as (mi stāk′) so as to avoid the pronunciation (mis-tāk′), which might sound as if the word meant 'to take badly'.

Pronunciations are also marked for stress, to reveal the relative differences in emphasis between syllables. In words of two or more syllables, a primary stress mark (′) follows the syllable having greatest stress. A secondary stress mark (′) follows a syllable having slightly less stress than primary but more stress than an unmarked syllable. A pattern in which stressed syllables alternate with unstressed ones is common in English.

de•pig•men•ta•tion (dē pig′mən tā′shən), *n. Pathol.* loss of pigment. [1885–90; DE- + PIGMENTATION]

Some unmarked syllables, when adjacent to a stressed syllable and shown with a full vowel, may have "understood" secondary stress.

de•part•men•tal•ize (di pärt men′tl īz′, dē′pärt-), *v.t.,* **-ized, -iz•ing.** to divide into departments. Also, *esp. Brit.,* **de•part•men′tal•ise′.** [1895–1900; DEPARTMENTAL + -IZE] **—de′part•men′tal•i•za′tion,** *n.*

Sound-Spelling Correspondences in English

THIS TABLE may be used when someone who wants to find a word in the Dictionary knows the pronunciation but is not sure of the spelling. Likely spellings for each sound are listed first, in boldface type, under the appropriate phonetic symbol, with other spellings following alphabetically. A vowel and an *e* separated by dots indicate a discontinuous combination that characteristically represents the "long" sound of that vowel. Thus **i...e** stands for *i* and *e* separated by any appropriate single consonant, as in *jibe, jive, pride,* or *pipe,* all of which are pronounced with (ī). Since the spellings for vowel sounds are often more difficult to determine than those for consonants, vowels and diphthongs are shown at the beginning of the table. To find a particular word, a reader should first determine the sequence of sounds and then try various spelling equivalents. The word pronounced (dis-lek′sē ə), for example, can be located once the *y* spelling has been tried for the (ĭ) sound in the first syllable, yielding *dyslexia.*

VOWELS AND DIPHTHONGS

SOUND

RHD (a) = IPA [æ]

may be spelled as:

- **a** hat
- a'a ma'am
- ach drachm
- ag diaphragm
- ai plaid
- al half
- au laugh
- ui guimpe

SOUND

RHD (ā) = IPA [eɪ, ei, e]

may be spelled as:

- **a...e** ate
- ae Gael
- ag champagne
- ai rain
- aig arraign
- ao gaol
- au gauge
- ay ray
- é exposé
- e suede
- ea steak
- ee matinee
- eh eh
- ei veil
- eig feign
- eigh sleigh
- eilles Marseilles
- es demesne
- et beret
- ey obey

SOUND

RHD (âr) = IPA [ɛər]

may be spelled as:

- **are** dare
- air chair
- aire doctrinaire
- ayer prayer
- ear wear
- eer Mynheer
- e'er ne'er
- eir their
- er mal de mer
- ere there
- ey're they're

SOUND

RHD (ä) = IPA [ɑ]

may be spelled as:

- **a** father
- à à la mode
- aa bazaar
- ah hurrah
- al calm
- half
- as faux pas
- at éclat
- au laugh
- e sergeant
- ea hearth
- oi reservoir
- ua guard

SOUND

RHD (e) = IPA [ɛ]

may be spelled as:

- **e** ebb
- a any
- ae aesthete
- ai said
- ay says
- ea leather
- eg phlegm
- ei heifer

SOUND

RHD (ē) = IPA [i]

may be spelled as:

- **ee** keep
- ae Caesar
- ay quay
- e equal
- ea team
- e'e e'en
- e...e precede
- ei receive
- eip receipt
- eo people
- ey key
- i machine
- ie field
- is debris
- oe amoeba
- uay quay
- y city

SOUND

RHD (i) = IPA [ɪ]

may be spelled as:

- **i** if
- a damage
- e England
- ee been
- ei counterfeit
- ia carriage
- ie sieve
- o women
- u business
- ui build
- y sympathetic

SOUND

RHD (ī) = IPA [aɪ, ai]

may be spelled as:

- **i...e** ice
- ai faille
- ais aisle
- ay aye
- ei stein
- eigh height
- eye eye
- ie pie
- igh high
- is island
- uy buy
- y sky
- ye lye

SOUND

RHD (o) = IPA [ɒ] or [ɑ]

may be spelled as:

- **o** box
- a wander
- quadrant
- ach yacht
- au astronaut
- eau bureaucracy
- ou cough

SOUND

RHD (ō) = IPA [oʊ, ou, o]

may be spelled as:

- **o** lo
- au mauve
- aut hautboy
- aux faux pas
- eau beau
- eaux Bordeaux
- eo yeoman
- ew sew
- o...e rote
- oa road
- oe toe
- oh oh
- ol yolk
- oo brooch
- ot depot
- ou soul
- ow flow
- owe owe

SOUND

RHD (ô) = IPA [ɔ]

may be spelled as:

- **aw** paw
- a tall
- ah Utah
- al walk
- as Arkansas
- au vault
- augh caught
- o alcohol
- oa broad
- oo floor
- ough sought

SOUND

RHD (oi) = IPA [ɔɪ, ɔi]

may be spelled as:

- **oy** boy
- awy lawyer
- eu Freud
- oi oil
- ois Iroquois
- uoy buoy

SOUND

RHD (o͝o) = IPA [ʊ]

may be spelled as:

- **oo** look
- o wolf
- oul would
- u pull

SOUND

RHD (o͞o) = IPA [u]

may be spelled as:

- **oo** ooze
- eu maneuver
- ew grew
- ieu lieu
- o move
- oe canoe
- oeu manoeuvre
- ou troupe
- u...e rule
- ue flue
- ug impugn
- ui suit

SOUND

RHD (ou) = IPA [aʊ, au]

may be spelled as:

- **ow** brow
- au landau
- ou out
- ough bough

SOUND

RHD (u) = IPA [ʌ]

may be spelled as:

- **u** pup
- o son
- oe does
- oo blood
- ou trouble

SOUND

RHD (ûr) = IPA [ɜr, ɝ]

may be spelled as:

- **ur** burn
- ear learn
- er term
- err err
- eur poseur
- ir thirsty
- or work
- our scourge
- urr purr
- yr myrtle

SOUND

RHD (yo͞o) = IPA [ju, ɪu]

may be spelled as:

- **u** utility
- eau beauty
- eu feud
- ew few
- hu huge
- ieu purlieu
- iew view
- u...e use
- ue cue
- ueue queue
- yew yew
- you you
- yu yule

SOUND

RHD (ə) = IPA [ə]

may be spelled as:

- **a** alone
- **e** system
- **i** easily
- **o** gallop
- **u** circus
- à tête-à-tête
- ai mountain
- ei mullein
- eo dungeon
- ia parliament
- io legion
- oi porpoise
- ou curious
- y Abyssinia

SOUND

RHD (ər) = IPA [ər, ɚ]

may be spelled as:

- **er** father
- ar liar
- ir elixir
- or labor
- our labour
- ur augur
- ure future
- yr martyr

CONSONANTS

SOUND

RHD (b) = IPA [b]

may be spelled as:

- **b** bed
- bb hobby
- be lobe
- bh bheesty

SOUND

RHD (ch) = IPA [tʃ]

may be spelled as:

- **ch** chief
- c cello
- che niche
- tch catch
- te righteous
- ti question
- tu natural

SOUND

RHD (d) = IPA [d]

may be spelled as:

- **d** do
- 'd we'd
- dd ladder
- de fade
- dh dhurrie
- ed pulled
- ld should

SOUND
RHD (f) = IPA [f]
may be spelled as:

f	feed
fe	life
ff	muffin
gh	tough
lf	calf
pf	pfennig
ph	physics

SOUND
RHD (g) = IPA [g]
may be spelled as:

g	give
gg	egg
gh	ghost
gu	guard
gue	plague

SOUND
RHD (h) = IPA [h]
may be spelled as:

h	hit
wh	who

SOUND
RHD (hw) = IPA [hw, ʍ]
may be spelled as:

wh	where

SOUND
RHD (hyo͞o) = IPA [hju]
may be spelled as:

hu	huge

SOUND
RHD (j) = IPA [dʒ]
may be spelled as:

j	just
ch	Greenwich
d	graduate
dg	judgment
dge	bridge
di	soldier
ge	sage
gg	exaggerate
gi	magic
jj	Hajji

SOUND
RHD (k) = IPA [k]
may be spelled as:

c	car
k	kill
cc	account
cch	bacchanal
ch	character
ck	back
cq	acquaint
cqu	lacquer
cque	sacque
cu	biscuit
gh	lough
ke	rake
kh	Sikh
lk	walk
q	Iraq
qu	liquor
que	plaque

SOUND
RHD (l) = IPA [l]
may be spelled as:

l	live
le	mile
ll	call
lle	faille
sl	lisle

SOUND
RHD (m) = IPA [m]
may be spelled as:

m	more
chm	drachm
gm	paradigm
lm	calm
mb	limb
me	home
mh	mho
mm	hammer
mn	hymn

SOUND
RHD (n) = IPA [n]
may be spelled as:

n	not
gn	gnat
kn	knife
mn	mnemonic
ne	done
nn	runner
pn	pneumatic

SOUND
RHD (ng) = IPA [ŋ]
may be spelled as:

ng	ring
n	pink
ngg	mahjongg
ngue	tongue

SOUND
RHD (p) = IPA [p]
may be spelled as:

p	pen
pe	hope
pp	stopper

SOUND
RHD (r) = IPA [r]
may be spelled as:

r	red
re	pure
rhy	rhythm
rr	carrot
rrh	catarrh
wr	wrong

SOUND
RHD (s) = IPA [s]
may be spelled as:

s	see
c	city
ce	mice
ps	psychology
sc	scene
sch	schism
se	mouse
ss	loss

SOUND
RHD (sh) = IPA [ʃ]
may be spelled as:

sh	ship
ce	ocean
ch	machine
chs	fuchsia
ci	special
psh	pshaw
s	sugar
sch	schist
sci	conscience
se	nauseous
si	mansion
ss	tissue
ssi	mission
ti	mention

SOUND
RHD (t) = IPA [t]
may be spelled as:

t	toe
bt	doubt
cht	yacht
ct	ctenophore
ed	talked
ght	bought
phth	phthisic
’t	’twas
te	bite
th	thyme
tt	bottom
tw	two

SOUND
RHD (th) = IPA [θ]
may be spelled as:

th	thin
chth	chthonian

SOUND
RHD (*th*) = IPA [ð]
may be spelled as:

th	then
the	bathe

SOUND
RHD (v) = IPA [v]
may be spelled as:

v	visit
f	of
ph	Stephen
ve	have
vv	flivver

SOUND
RHD (w) = IPA [w]
may be spelled as:

w	well
ju	marijuana
o	choir
ou	ouija
u	quiet
wh	where

SOUND
RHD (y) = IPA [j]
may be spelled as:

y	yet
i	union
j	hallelujah
ll	tortilla

SOUND
RHD (z) = IPA [z]
may be spelled as:

z	zone
s	has
sc	discern
x	xylem
zz	fuzz

SOUND
RHD (zh) = IPA [ʒ]
may be spelled as:

si	division
ge	garage
s	measure
z	azure
zi	brazier

ABBREVIATIONS USED IN THE DEFINITIONS

ab.	about
Abbr.	abbreviation
adj.	adjective
adv.	adverb
Ant.	antonym(s)
at. no.	atomic number
at. wt.	atomic weight
c	about (Latin *circa*)
cap., caps.	capital, capitals
Cap.	capital (of country or state)
Cf.	compare (Latin *confer*)
cm	centimeter, centimeters
compar.	comparative
conj.	conjunction
def., defs.	definition, definitions
E	east
esp.	especially
1st pers.	first person
fol.	followed
ft.	foot, feet
gen.	genitive
in.	inch, inches
indic.	indicative
interj.	interjection
km	kilometer, kilometers
l.c.	lower case (not capitalized)
m	meter, meters
mi.	mile, miles
mm	millimeter, millimeters
N	north
n.	noun
nom.	nominative
n.pl.	plural noun
obj.	objective
past part., pp.	past participle
pl.	plural
poss.	possessive
prec.	preceded
prep.	preposition
pres.	present tense
pres. part.	present participle
pron.	pronoun
pt.	preterit (past tense)
S	south
2nd pers.	second person
sing.	singular
sp. gr.	specific gravity
sq. cm	square centimeter, square centimeters
sq. ft.	square foot, square feet
sq. in.	square inch, square inches
sq. km	square kilometer, square kilometers
sq. mi.	square mile, square miles
sq. yd.	square yard, square yards
subj.	subjunctive
superl.	superlative
Syn.	synonym(s)
3rd pers.	third person
v.	verb
v.i.	intransitive verb
v.t.	transitive verb
W	west
yd.	yard, yards

PRONUNCIATION KEY

Stress. The symbol (′), as in **mother** (mut͟h′ər), and **red′ wine′**, marks primary stress; any syllable immediately followed by (′) is pronounced with greater emphasis than syllables not marked(′). The symbol (′), as used following the second syllables of **grandmother** (grand′mut͟h′ər), and **ice′ wa′ter**, marks secondary stress; a syllable marked for secondary stress is pronounced with less emphasis than one marked (′) but with more than those bearing no stress mark.

a act, bat, marry
ā age, paid, say
â(r) air, dare, Mary
ä ah, part, balm

b back, cabin, cab

ch child, teacher, beach

d do, madder, bed

e edge, set, merry
ē equal, seat, bee, mighty

ēr ear, mere

f fit, differ, puff

g give, trigger, beg

h hit, behave, hear

hw which, nowhere

i if, big, mirror, furniture
ī ice, bite, pirate, deny

j just, tragic, fudge

k keep, token, make

l low, mellow, all, bottle (bot′l)

m my, summer, him

n now, sinner, on, button (but′n)
ng sing, Washington

o ox, bomb, wasp
ō over, boat, no

ô order, ball, raw
oi oil, joint, joy
o͝o book, tour
o͞o ooze, fool, too
ou out, loud, cow

p pot, supper, stop

r read, hurry, near

s see, passing, miss
sh shoe, fashion, push

t ten, matter, bit
th thin, ether, path

t͟h that, either, smooth

u up, sun
û(r) urge, burn, cur

v voice, river, live

w witch, away

y yes, onion

z zoo, lazy, those
zh treasure, mirage

ə occurs in unaccented syllables to indicate the sound of the reduced vowel in alone, system, easily, gallop, circus

ᵊ occurs between **i** and **r** and between **ou** and **r** to show triphthongal quality, as in **fire** (fīᵊr), **hour** (ouᵊr)

FOREIGN SOUNDS

A as in French **ami** (A mē′) [a vowel intermediate in quality between the **a** of *cat* and the **ä** of *calm*, but closer to the former]

KH as in Scottish **loch** (lôKH); German **ach** (äKH) or **ich** (iKH) [a consonant made by bringing the tongue into the position for **k** as in *coo* or **k** as in *key*, while pronouncing a strong, rasping **h**]

N as in French **bon** (bôN) [used to indicate that the preceding vowel is nasalized. Four such vowels are found in French: **un bon vin blanc** (œN bôN vaN bläN)]

Œ as in French **feu** (fœ); German **schön** (shœn) [a vowel made with the lips rounded in the position for **ō** as in *over*, while trying to say **ā** as in *able*]

R as in French **rouge** (Ro͞ozh); German **rot** (Rōt); Italian **mare** (mä′Re); Spanish **pero** (pe′Rô) [a symbol for any non-English *r*, including a trill or flap in Italian and Spanish and a sound in French and German similar to **KH** but pronounced with voice]

Y as in French **tu** (tY); German **über** (Y′bəR) [a vowel made with the lips rounded in position for **o͞o** as in *ooze*, while trying to say **ē** as in *east*]

ᵊ as in French **Bastogne** (bA stôn′yᵊ) [a faint prolongation of the preceding voiced consonant or glide]

ETYMOLOGY KEY

‡	probably earlier than
<	descended from, borrowed from
<<	descended from, borrowed from through intermediate stages not shown
>	whence
?	origin unknown
*	unattested, reconstructed
abbr.	abbreviation
abl.	ablative
acc.	accusative
adj.	adjective, adjectival
adv.	adverb, adverbial
alter.	alteration
Amer.	Americanism
aph.	aphetic
appar.	apparently
assoc.	association
aug.	augmentative
b.	blend of, blended
c.	cognate with
cf.	compare
comb. form	combining form
comp.	comparative
contr.	contraction
d.	died
dat.	dative
deriv.	derivative
dial.	dialect, dialectal
dim.	diminutive
E	east, eastern
equiv.	equivalent
etym.	etymology, etymological
fem.	feminine
fig.	figurative
freq.	frequentative
fut.	future
gen.	genitive
ger.	gerund, gerundive
imit.	imitative
impv.	imperative
indic.	indicative
inf.	infinitive
intransit.	intransitive
irreg.	irregularly
lit.	literally
masc.	masculine
mod.	modern
N	north, northern
n.	noun, nominal
neut.	neuter
nom.	nominative
n.s.	noun stem
obl.	oblique
obs.	obsolete
orig.	origin, originally
pass.	passive
perh.	perhaps
pl.	plural
prep.	preposition
pres.	present
prob.	probably
pron.	pronunciation, pronounced
prp.	present participle
ptp.	past participle
r.	replacing
redupl.	reduplication
repr.	representing
resp.	respelling, respelled
S	south, southern
s.	stem
sing.	singular
sp.	spelling, spelled
subj.	subjunctive
superl.	superlative
syll.	syllable
trans.	translation
transit.	transitive
ult.	ultimately
uncert.	uncertain
v.	verb, verbal
var.	variant
voc.	vocative
v.s.	verb stem
W	west, western

LANGUAGES

AF	Anglo-French
Afr	African
Afrik	Afrikaans
AL	Anglo-Latin
Amer	American
AmerInd	American Indian
AmerSp	American Spanish
Ar	Arabic
Aram	Aramaic
Austral	Australian
Bulg	Bulgarian
CanF	Canadian French
Celt	Celtic
Chin	Chinese
D	Dutch
Dan	Danish
E	English
EGmc	East Germanic
F	French
Fris	Frisian
G	German
Gallo-Rom	Gallo-Romance
Gk	Greek
Gmc	Germanic
Goth	Gothic
Heb	Hebrew
Icel	Icelandic
IE	Indo-European
Ir	Irish
It	Italian
Japn	Japanese
Kor	Korean
L	Latin
LaF	Louisiana French
LG	Low German
LGk	Late Greek
Lith	Lithuanian
LL	Late Latin
MChin	Middle Chinese
MD	Middle Dutch
ME	Middle English
MexSp	Mexican Spanish
MF	Middle French
MGk	Medieval Greek
MHG	Middle High German
MIr	Middle Irish
ML	Medieval Latin
MLG	Middle Low German
ModGk	Modern Greek
ModHeb	Modern Hebrew
MPers	Middle Persian
NL	Neo-Latin
Norw	Norwegian
OCS	Old Church Slavonic
ODan	Old Danish
OE	Old English
OF	Old French
OFris	Old Frisian
OHG	Old High German
OIr	Old Irish
OIt	Old Italian
OL	Old Latin
ON	Old Norse
ONF	Old North French
OPers	Old Persian
OPr	Old Provençal
OPruss	Old Prussian
ORuss	Old Russian
OS	Old Saxon
OSp	Old Spanish
OSw	Old Swedish
PaG	Pennsylvania German
Pers	Persian
Pg	Portuguese
Pol	Polish
Pr	Provençal
Rom	Romance
Rum	Rumanian
Russ	Russian
Scand	Scandinavian
Scot	Scottish
ScotGael	Scots Gaelic
Sem	Semitic
Skt	Sanskrit
Slav	Slavic
Sp	Spanish
SpAr	Spanish Arabic
Sw	Swedish
SwissF	Swiss French
Turk	Turkish
VL	Vulgar Latin
WAfr	West African
WGmc	West Germanic

DEVELOPMENT OF MAJUSCULE								
NORTH SEMITIC	GREEK		ETR.	LATIN		MODERN		
						GOTHIC	ITALIC	ROMAN
K	∆	A	A	A	A	𝔄	*A*	A

DEVELOPMENT OF MINUSCULE					
ROMAN CURSIVE	ROMAN UNCIAL	CAROL. MIN.	MODERN		
			GOTHIC	ITALIC	ROMAN
λ	ƛ	a	𝔞	*a*	a

The first letter of the English alphabet developed from Greek *alpha* (α, A) through Etruscan and Latin. The capital (A) goes back to North Semitic *aleph,* which acquired its modern form in Greek and was retained in the Latin monumental script. The minuscule (a) derives from Latin cursive *a,* a variant form of A, through Carolingian and Florentine influence to yield both italic and roman forms.

A, a (ā), *n., pl.* **A's** or **As, a's** or **as.** **1.** the first letter of the English alphabet, a vowel. **2.** any spoken sound represented by the letter *A* or *a,* as in *bake, hat, father,* or *small.* **3.** something having the shape of an A. **4.** a written or printed representation of the letter *A* or *a.* **5.** a device, as a printer's type, for reproducing the letter *A* or *a.* **6. from A to Z,** from beginning to end; thoroughly; completely: *He knows the Bible from A to Z.* **7. not know from A to B,** to know nothing; be ignorant.

a[1] (ə; *when stressed* ā), *indefinite article.* **1.** not any particular or certain one of a class or group: *a man; a chemical; a house.* **2.** a certain; a particular: *one at a time; two of a kind; A Miss Johnson called.* **3.** another; one typically resembling: *a Cicero in eloquence; a Jonah.* **4.** one (used before plural nouns that are preceded by a quantifier singular in form): *a hundred men* (compare *hundreds of men*); *a dozen times* (compare *dozens of times*). **5.** indefinitely or nonspecifically (used with adjectives expressing number): *a great many years; a few stars.* **6.** one (used before a noun expressing quantity): *a yard of ribbon; a score of times.* **7.** any; a single: *not a one.* [ME; orig. preconsonantal phonetic var. of AN[1]]

—**Usage.** In both spoken and written English the choice of A[1] or AN[1] is determined by the initial sound of the word that follows. Before a consonant sound, A is used; before a vowel sound, AN: *a book, a rose; an apple, an opera.* Problems arise occasionally when the following word begins with a vowel letter but actually starts with a consonant sound, or vice versa. Some words beginning with the vowel letter *u* and all words beginning with the vowel letters *eu* are pronounced with a beginning consonant sound, as if the first letter were *y*: *a union; a European.* Some other spellings that begin with a vowel letter may also stand for an initial consonant sound: *a ewe; a ewer.* The words *one* and *once* and all compounds of which they are the first element begin with a *w* sound: *a one-room apartment; a once-famous actor.*

The names of the consonant letters *f, h, l, m, n, r, s,* and *x* are pronounced with a beginning vowel sound. When these letters are used as words or to form words, they are preceded by AN: *to rent an L-shaped studio; to fly an SST.* The names of the vowel letter *u* and the semivowel letters *w* and *y* are pronounced with a beginning consonant sound. When used as words, they are preceded by A: *a U-turn; The plumber installed a Y in the line.*

In some words beginning with the letter *h,* the *h* is not pronounced; the words actually begin with a vowel sound: *an hour; an honor.* When the *h* is strongly pronounced, as in a stressed syllable at the beginning of a word, it is preceded by A: *a history of the Sioux; a hero sandwich.* (In former times AN was used before strongly pronounced *h* in a stressed first syllable: *an hundred.*) Such adjectives as *historic, historical, heroic,* and *habitual,* which begin with an unstressed syllable and often with a silent or weakly pronounced *h,* are commonly preceded by AN, especially in British English. But the use of A rather than AN is widespread in both speech and writing: *a historical novel; a habitual criminal. Hotel* and *unique* are occasionally preceded by AN, but this use is increasingly old-fashioned. Although in some dialects AN has yielded to A in all cases, edited writing reflects usage as described above.

a[2] (ə; *when stressed* ā), *prep.* each; every; per: *ten cents a sheet; three times a day.* [orig. ME *a,* preconsonantal var. of ON (see A-[1]); confused with A[1]]

a[3] (ə), *prep. Pron. Spelling.* a reduced, unstressed form of **of** (often written as part of a single, unhyphenated word): *cloth a gold; time a day; kinda; sorta.* [ME; unstressed preconsonantal var. of OF[1]]

a[4] (ə), *auxiliary verb. Pron. Spelling.* a reduced, unstressed form of auxiliary **have** following some modals, as *might, should, could, would,* and *must* (usually written as part of a single, unhyphenated word): *We shoulda gone.* Cf. **of**[2]. [ME; phonetic var. of HAVE]

a[5] (ə, a, ä), *pron. Brit. Dial.* **1.** he. **2.** she. **3.** it. **4.** they. **5.** I. [ME *a, ha*]

a' (ä, ô), *adj. Scot.* all: *for a' that.* Also, **a.**

A, **1.** *Elect.* ampere; amperes. **2.** *Physics.* angstrom. **3.** answer. **4.** *Brit.* arterial (used with a road number to designate a major highway): *Take the A525 to Ruthin.*

A, *Symbol.* **1.** the first in order or in a series. **2.** (*sometimes l.c.*) (in some grading systems) a grade or mark, as in school or college, indicating the quality of a student's work as excellent or superior. **3.** (*sometimes l.c.*) (in some school systems) a symbol designating the first semester of a school year. **4.** *Music.* **a.** the sixth tone in the scale of C major or the first tone in the relative minor scale, A minor. **b.** a string, key, or pipe tuned to this tone. **c.** a written or printed note representing this tone. **d.** (in the fixed system of solmization) the sixth tone of the scale of C major, called *la.* **e.** the tonality having A as the tonic note. **5.** *Physiol.* a major blood group, usually enabling a person whose blood is of this type to donate blood to persons of group A or AB and to receive blood from persons of O or A. Cf. **ABO system.** **6.** (*sometimes l.c.*) the medieval Roman numeral for 50 or 500. Cf. **Roman numerals.** **7.** *Chem.* (formerly) argon. **8.** *Chem., Physics.* See **mass number.** **9.** *Biochem.* **a.** adenine. **b.** alanine. **10.** *Logic.* See **universal affirmative.** **11.** *Brit.* a designation for a motion picture recommended as suitable for adults. Cf. **AA** (def. 5), **U** (def. 5), **X** (def. 9). **12.** a proportional shoe width size, narrower than B and wider than AA. **13.** a proportional brassiere cup size, smaller than B and larger than AA. **14.** a quality rating for a corporate or municipal bond, lower than AA and higher than BBB.

a, *Meas.* are; ares.

a, *Symbol, Logic.* See **universal affirmative.**

Å, *Symbol, Physics.* angstrom.

A-, atomic (used in combination): *A-bomb; A-plant.*

a-[1], a reduced form of the Old English preposition *on,* meaning "on," "in," "into," "to," "toward," preserved before a noun in a prepositional phrase, forming a predicate adjective or an adverbial element (*afoot; abed; ashore; aside; away*), or before an adjective (*afar; aloud; alow*), as a moribund prefix with a verb (*acknowledge*), and in archaic and dialectal use before a present participle in *-ing* (*set the bells aringing*); and added to a verb stem with the force of a present participle (*ablaze; agape; aglow; astride;* and originally, *awry*). [ME, late OE; cf. A[2], NOWADAYS]

a-[2], a reduced form of the Old English preposition *of: akin; afresh; anew.* [ME; see A[3]]

a-[3], an old point-action prefix, not referring to an act as a whole, but only to the beginning or end: *She arose* (rose up). *They abided by their beliefs* (remained faithful to the end). [ME; OE *a-* (unstressed), *ǣ-, ā-, ō-* (stressed; see ABB, WOOF[1], OAKUM), rarely *or-* (see ORDEAL) << Gmc *uz- < unstressed IE *uss- < *ud-s, akin to OUT; in some cases confused with A-[4], as in ABRIDGE]

a-[4], var. of **ab-** before *p* and *v*: *aperient; avert.* [ME < L *ā-, a-* (var. of *ab-* AB-); in some words < F *a-* < L *ab-,* as in ABRIDGE]

a-[5], var. of **ad-,** used: (1) before *sc, sp, st* (*ascend*) and (2) in words of French derivation (often with the sense of increase, addition): *amass.* [ME, in some words < MF *a-* < L *ad-* prefix or *ad* prep. (see AD-), as in ABUT; in others < L *a-* (var. of *ad-* AD-), as in ASCEND]

a-[6], var. of **an-**[1] before a consonant, meaning "not," "without": *amoral; atonal; achromatic.*

-a[1], a plural ending of nouns borrowed from Greek and Latin: *phenomena; criteria; data; errata; genera.*

-a[2], a feminine singular ending of nouns borrowed from Latin and Greek, also used in Neo-Latin coinages to Latinize bases of any origin, and as a Latin substitute for the feminine ending *-ē* of Greek words: *anabaena; cinchona; pachysandra.*

-a[3], an ending of personal names forming feminines from masculines: *Georgia; Roberta.* [< L fem. *-a* (see -A[2]), as *Claudia,* fem. of *Claudius*]

-a[4], a suffix designating the oxide of the chemical element denoted by the stem: *alumina; ceria; thoria.* [prob. generalized from the *-a* of MAGNESIA]

A., **1.** Absolute. **2.** Academy. **3.** acre; acres. **4.** America. **5.** American. **6.** angstrom. **7.** year. [< L *annō,* abl. of *annus*] **8.** answer. **9.** before. [< L *ante*] **10.** April. **11.** Artillery.

a., **1.** about. **2.** acre; acres. **3.** active. **4.** adjective. **5.** alto. **6.** ampere; amperes. **7.** year. [< L *annō,* abl. of *annus*] **8.** anonymous. **9.** answer. **10.** before. [< L *ante*] **11.** are; ares. **12.** *Baseball.* assist; assists.

A-1 (āʹwunʹ), *adj.* See **A one.** Also, **A 1**

a·a (äʹä), *n.* basaltic lava having a rough surface. Also, **a'a.** Cf. **pahoehoe.** [1855–60; < Hawaiian *ʻaʻā*]

AA, **1.** See **administrative assistant.** **2.** See **Alcoholics Anonymous.** **3.** antiaircraft. **4.** See **author's alteration.**

AA, *Symbol.* **1.** a proportional shoe width size, narrower than A and wider than AAA. **2.** the smallest proportional brassiere cup size. **3.** a quality rating for a corporate or municipal bond, lower than AAA and higher than A. **4.** *Elect.* a battery size for 1.5 volt dry cells: diameter, 0.6 in. (1.4 cm); length, 2 in. (5 cm). **5.** *Brit.* a designation for motion pictures certified as unsuitable for children under 14 unless accompanied by an adult. Cf. **A** (def. 11), **U** (def. 5), **X** (def. 9).

āā, *Symbol.* (in prescriptions) ana[2]. Also, **āa** [< Gk *aná,* with superscript bar repr. the nasal consonant]

A.A., **1.** See **Alcoholics Anonymous.** **2.** antiaircraft. **3.** antiaircraft artillery. **4.** Associate in Accounting. **5.** See **Associate of Arts.** **6.** See **author's alteration.**

a.a., See **author's alteration.** Also, **aa**

AAA, **1.** Agricultural Adjustment Administration. **2.** Amateur Athletic Association. **3.** American Automobile Association. **4.** antiaircraft artillery. **5.** Automobile Association of America.

AAA, *Symbol.* **1.** a proportional shoe width size, narrower than AA. **2.** the highest quality rating for a corporate or municipal bond. **3.** *Elect.* a battery size for 1.5 volt dry cells: diameter, 0.4 in. (1 cm); length 1.7 in. (4.3 cm).

A.A.A., **1.** Amateur Athletic Association. **2.** American Automobile Association. **3.** Automobile Association of America.

AAAA, Amateur Athletic Association of America.

A.A.A.L., American Academy of Arts and Letters.

A.A.A.S., American Association for the Advancement of Science. Also, **AAAS**

Aa·chen (äʹkən; *Ger.* äʹKHən), *n.* a city in W Germany: coronation city of German kings 936–1531. 242,000. French, **Aix-la-Chapelle.**

A.A.E., American Association of Engineers.

A.Ae.E., Associate in Aeronautical Engineering.

A.A.E.E., American Association of Electrical Engineers.

AAES, American Association of Engineering Societies.

AAF, **1.** Allied Air Forces. **2.** (in the U.S., formerly) Army Air Forces. Also, **A.A.F.**

A.Agr., Associate in Agriculture.

aah (ä), *interj.* **1.** (used as an exclamation expressing surprise, delight, joy, etc.) —*n.* **2.** the exclamation "aah." —*v.i.* **3.** to exclaim or utter "aah": *We all oohed and aahed at the lovely birthday cake.*

CONCISE PRONUNCIATION KEY: act, cāpe, dâre, pärt; set, ēqual; if, īce; ox, ōver, ôrder, oil, bŏŏk, bōōt, out; up, ûrge; child; sing; shoe; thin, *th*at; zh as in *treasure.* ə = *a* as in *alone, e* as in *system, i* as in *easily, o* as in *gallop, u* as in *circus;* ə as in *fire* (fīər), *hour* (ouər). l and n can serve as syllabic consonants, as in *cradle* (krādʹl), and *button* (butʹn). See the full key inside the front cover.

Aal·borg (ôl′bôrg), *n.* Ålborg.

Aa·le·sund (ô′lə so͝on′), *n.* Ålesund.

aa·li·i (ä lē′ē), *n.* a bushy shrub, *Dodonaea viscosa,* of Australia, Hawaii, Africa, and tropical America, having sticky foliage. [< Hawaiian *ʻaʻaliʻi*]

Aalst (älst), *n.* Flemish name of **Alost.**

Aal·to (äl′tô), *n.* **Al·var** (äl′vär), 1898–1976, Finnish architect and furniture designer.

AAM, air-to-air missile.

a&h, *Insurance.* accident and health.

a&i, *Insurance.* accident and indemnity.

A and M, Agricultural and Mechanical (college): *Texas A and M.* Also, **A&M**

A&R, artists and repertory (used to refer to the profession of selecting recording artists, approving their repertory and performances, and arranging the distribution and promotion of the finished recording). Also, **A. & R., A-and-R**

a&s, *Insurance.* accident and sickness.

AAP, Association of American Publishers.

A.A.P.S.S., American Academy of Political and Social Science.

Aar (är), *n.* a river in central Switzerland, flowing N to the Rhine. 175 mi. (280 km) long.

Aar·au (är′ou), *n.* a town in and capital of Aargau, in N Switzerland. 15,927.

aard·vark (ärd′värk′), *n.* a large, nocturnal, burrowing mammal, *Orycteropus afer,* of central and southern Africa, feeding on ants and termites and having a long, extensile tongue, strong claws, and long ears. [1825–35; < Afrik *erdvark* < D *aardvarken,* equiv. to *aarde* EARTH + *varken* pig; see FARROW[1]]

aardvark, *Orycteropus afer,* 2 ft. (0.6 m) high at shoulder; head and body 3 ft. (0.9 m); tail to 2 ft. (0.6 m)

aard·wolf (ärd′wo͝olf′), *n., pl.* **-wolves.** a striped, hyenalike mammal, *Proteles cristatus,* of southern and eastern Africa, that feeds chiefly on insects. [1825–35; < Afrik *erdwolf* < D *aardwolf,* equiv. to *aarde* EARTH + *wolf* WOLF]

Aar·gau (är′gou), *n.* a canton in N Switzerland. 443,900; 542 sq. mi. (1400 sq. km). *Cap.:* Aarau. French, **Argovie.**

Aar·hus (ôr′ho͞os′), *n.* Århus.

Aar·on (âr′ən, ar′-), *n.* **1.** the older brother of Moses, usually regarded as the first high priest of the Hebrews. Ex. 28; 40:13–16. **2. Henry Louis** (*Hank*), born 1934, U.S. baseball player. **3.** a male given name.

Aa·ron·ic (â ron′ik, a ron′-), *adj.* **1.** of or pertaining to Aaron. **2.** pertaining or belonging to the order of Jewish priests descended from Aaron. **3.** of the second, or lesser, order of priesthood among the Mormons. **4.** priestly. Also, **Aaronical.** [1870–75; AARON + -IC]

Aa·ron·i·cal (â ron′i kəl, a ron′-), *adj.* **1.** Aaronic. **2.** of or like a high priest; pontifical. [1610–20; AARON + -ICAL]

Aa·ron·ite (âr′ə nīt′, ar′-), *n.* one of the priestly descendants of Aaron. [AARON + -ITE] **—Aar·on·it·ic** (âr′ə nit′ik, ar′-), *adj.*

Aar·on's-beard (âr′ənz bērd′, ar′-), *n.* See **rose of Sharon** (def. 2). [1540–50]

Aar′on's rod′, 1. a rod, inscribed with the name of Aaron, that miraculously blossomed and yielded almonds. Num. 17:8. Previously, the rod had changed into a serpent. Ex. 7:10. **2.** any of various plants having a tall, flowering stem, as the goldenrod or mullein. **3.** a smooth-stemmed herb, *Thermopsis caroliniana,* found from North Carolina to Georgia, having yellow flowers in stiffly erect clusters and hoary pods. **4.** *Archit.* a convex molding having regularly spaced representations of leaves or scrollwork. [1825–35 for non-Biblical use]

AARP, American Association of Retired Persons.

A.A.S., 1. Fellow of the American Academy. [< NL *Academiae Americanae Socius*] **2.** American Academy of Sciences. **3.** Associate in Applied Science.

A.A.U., Amateur Athletic Union. Also, **AAU**

A.A.U.P., 1. American Association of University Professors. **2.** American Association of University Presses. Also, **AAUP**

A.A.U.W., American Association of University Women.

A-ax·is (ā′ak′sis), *n., pl.* **A-ax·es** (ā′ak′sēz). *Crystall.* the horizontal crystallographic axis passing from front to back. Cf. **B-axis, C-axis.**

Ab (äb, äv), *n.* Av.

AB, 1. *Naut.* See **able seaman. 2.** airborne. **3.** *U.S. Air Force.* Airman Basic. **4.** antiballistic; antiballistic missile.

AB, *Symbol, Physiol.* a major blood group usually enabling a person whose blood is of this type to donate blood to persons of type AB and to receive blood from persons of type O, A, B, or AB. Cf. **ABO system.**

CONCISE ETYMOLOGY KEY: <, descended or borrowed from; >, whence; b., blend of, blended; c., cognate with; cf., compare; deriv., derivative; equiv., equivalent; imit., imitative; obl., oblique; r., replacing; s., stem; sp., spelling, spelled; resp., respelling, respelled; trans., translation; ?, origin unknown; *, unattested; ‡, probably earlier than. See the full key inside the front cover.

Ab, *Symbol.* **1.** *Chem.* alabamine. **2.** *Immunol.* antibody.

ab-, a formal element occurring in loanwords from Latin, where it meant "away from": *abdicate; abolition.* Also, **a-, abs-.** [< L *ab* (prep. and prefix) from, away, c. Gk *apó,* Skt *ápa,* G *ab,* E OF[1], OFF]

ab., 1. about. **2.** *Baseball.* (times) at bat.

A.B., 1. *Naut.* See **able seaman. 2.** See **Bachelor of Arts.** [< NL, ML *Artium Baccalaureus*] **3.** *Baseball.* (times) at bat.

a.b., *Baseball.* (times) at bat.

a·ba (ə bä′, ä′bə), *n.* **1.** a coarse, felted fabric woven of camel's or goat's hair. **2.** a loose, sleeveless outer garment made of this fabric or of silk, worn by Arabs. Also, **abba.** [1805–15; < Ar *ʻabāʼ(ah)*]

A·ba (ä bä′), *n.* a town in SE Nigeria. 177,000.

ABA, 1. Amateur Boxing Association. **2.** American Badminton Association. **3.** American Bankers Association. **4.** American Bar Association. **5.** American Basketball Association. **6.** See **American Book Award. 7.** American Booksellers Association. **8.** Associate in Business Administration. Also, **A.B.A.**

a·ba·ca (ab′ə kä′, ä′bə-), *n.* **1.** a Philippine plant, *Musa textilis.* **2.** the fiber of this plant, used in making rope, fabrics, etc. [1810–20; < Sp < Tagalog *abaká*]

ab·a·cis·cus (ab′ə sis′kəs, -kis′-), *n., pl.* **-cis·ci** (-sis′ī, -kis′kī). **1.** *Archit.* a small abacus. **2.** a tessera. Also, **abaculus.** [< NL < Gk *abakískos,* equiv. to *abak-* (s. of *ábax;* see ABACUS) + *-iskos* dim. suffix]

ab·a·cist (ab′ə sist), *n.* a person skilled in using an abacus. [1350–1400; ME *abaciste* < ML *abacista,* equiv. to L *abac(us)* ABACUS + *-ista* -IST]

a·back (ə bak′), *adv.* **1.** toward the back. **2.** *Naut.* so that the wind presses against the forward side of the sail or sails. **3. taken aback,** surprised and disconcerted: *I was taken aback by his harsh criticism.* **—adj.** *Naut.* **4.** (of a sail) positioned so that the wind presses against the forward side. **5.** (of a yard) positioned so that its sail is laid aback. [bef. 1000; ME *abak,* OE *on bæc* to the rear. See A-[1], ON, BACK[1]]

Ab·a·co (ab′ə kō′), *n.* two islands (**Great Abaco** and **Little Abaco**) in the N Bahamas. 6501; 776 sq. mi. (2010 sq. km).

a·bac·te·ri·al (ā′bak tēr′ē əl), *adj.* not caused by or free from the presence of bacteria. [1930–35; A-[6] + BACTERIAL]

a·bac·u·lus (ə bak′yə ləs), *n., pl.* **-li** (-lī′). abaciscus. [< NL; see ABACUS, -ULE]

ab·a·cus (ab′ə kəs, ə bak′əs), *n., pl.* **ab·a·cus·es, ab·a·ci** (ab′ə sī′, -kī′, ə bak′ī). **1.** a device for making arithmetic calculations, consisting of a frame set with rods on which balls or beads are moved. **2.** *Archit.* a slab forming the top of the capital of a column. See diag. under **volute.** [1350–1400; ME < L: board, counting board, reformed < Gk *ábax*]

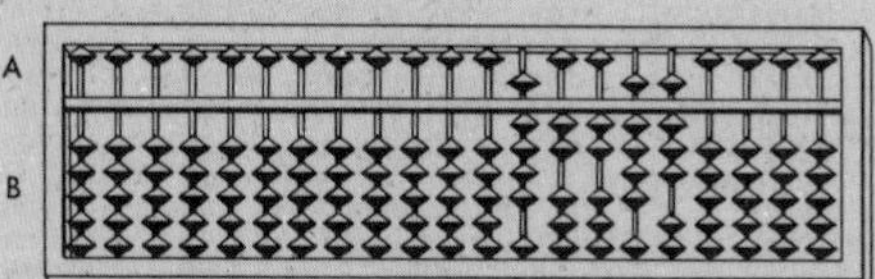

abacus (Japanese)
Each vertical column = one integer; each bead in group A = 5 when lowered; each bead in group B = 1 when raised; value of this setting is 922,980,000

A·ba·dan (ä′bə dän′, ab′ə-), *n.* a city in SW Iran, on the Shatt-al-Arab: oil refineries. 306,000.

A·bad·don (ə bad′n), *n.* **1.** Apollyon. **2.** a place of destruction; the depths of hell. [< Heb *ăbhaddōn* lit., destruction]

ab ae·ter·no (äb′ ī teʀ′nō; *Eng.* ab′ ē tûr′nō), *Latin.* from the most remote antiquity.

a·baft (ə baft′, ə bäft′), *Naut.* **—prep. 1.** to the rear of; aft of: *the fife rail abaft the mainmast.* **—adv. 2.** in the direction of the stern; astern; aft. [1225–75; ME *on baft, abaft,* equiv. to A-[1] and *on* ON + *baft,* OE *bæftan* contr. of *be* + *æftan.* See BY, AFT]

A·bag·tha (ə bag′thə), *n.* one of the seven eunuchs who served in the court of King Ahasuerus. Esther 1:10.

A·bai·lard (ᴀ bā lᴀʀ′), *n.* **Pierre** (pyeʀ), Abélard.

A·ba·kan (ä′bə kän′; *Russ.* u bu kän′), *n.* the capital of the Khakass Autonomous Region in the Russian Federation in Asia, on the Yenisei River. 128,000.

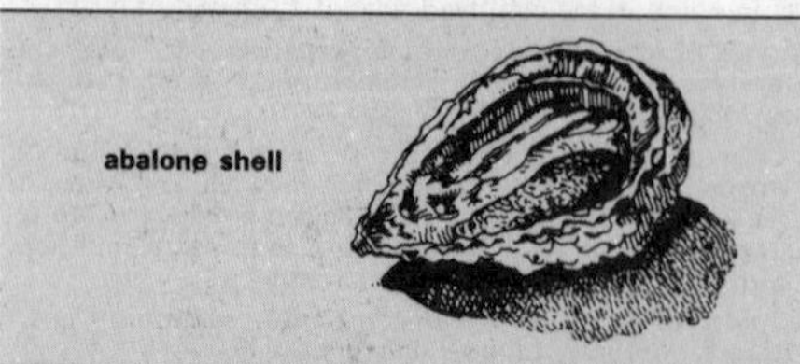

abalone shell

ab·a·lo·ne (ab′ə lō′nē), *n.* a large mollusk of the genus *Haliotis,* having a bowllike shell bearing a row of respiratory holes, the flesh of which is used for food and the shell for ornament and as a source of mother-of-pearl. [1840–50, *Amer.;* taken as sing. of California Sp *abulones,* pl. of *abulón, aulón* < a word in Rumsen, a Costanoan language formerly spoken at Monterey, California]

ab·amp (ab′amp′), *n.* *Elect.* abampere. [by shortening]

ab·am·pere (ab am′pēr, ab′am pēr′), *n.* *Elect.* the centimeter-gram-second unit of electromagnetic current, equivalent to 10 amperes. [*ab-* (prefix used for a centimeter-gram-second electromagnetic unit) + AMPERE]

a·ban·don[1] (ə ban′dən), *v.t.* **1.** to leave completely and finally; forsake utterly; desert: *to abandon one's farm; to abandon a child; to abandon a sinking ship.* **2.** to give up; discontinue; withdraw from: *to abandon a research project; to abandon hopes for a stage career.* **3.** to give up the control of: *to abandon a city to an enemy army.* **4.** to yield (oneself) without restraint or moderation; give (oneself) over to natural impulses, usually without self-control: *to abandon oneself to grief.* **5.** *Law.* to cast away, leave, or desert, as property or a child. **6.** *Insurance.* to relinquish (insured property) to the underwriter in case of partial loss, thus enabling the insured to claim a total loss. **7.** *Obs.* to banish. [1325–75; ME *abando(u)nen* < MF *abandoner* for OF (*mettre*) *a bandon* (put) under (someone's) jurisdiction, equiv. to *a* at, to (< L *ad;* see AD-) + *bandon* < Gmc **band;* see BOND[1]] **—a·ban′don·a·ble,** *adj.* **—a·ban′don·er,** *n.* **—a·ban′don·ment,** *n.*

—Syn. 1. See **desert**[2]. **2.** ABANDON, RELINQUISH, RENOUNCE mean to give up all concern in something. ABANDON means to give up or discontinue any further interest in something because of discouragement, weariness, distaste, or the like: *to abandon one's efforts.* RELINQUISH implies being or feeling compelled to give up something one would prefer to keep: *to relinquish a long-cherished desire.* RENOUNCE implies making (and perhaps formally stating) a voluntary decision to give something up: *to renounce worldly pleasures.* **3.** yield, surrender, resign, waive, abdicate. **—Ant. 1.** keep. **2.** continue; begin, start. **3.** retain.

a·ban·don[2] (ə ban′dən), *n.* a complete surrender to natural impulses without restraint or moderation; freedom from inhibition or conventionality: *to dance with reckless abandon.* [1815–25; < F, n. deriv. of *abandonner* to ABANDON[1]]

—Ant. restraint, constraint.

a·ban·doned (ə ban′dənd), *adj.* **1.** forsaken or deserted: *an abandoned building; an abandoned kitten.* **2.** unrestrained or uncontrolled; uninhibited: *She danced with abandoned enthusiasm.* **3.** utterly lacking in moral restraints; shameless; wicked: *an abandoned and dissolute ruler.* [1350–1400; ME; see ABANDON[1], -ED[2]] **—a·ban′doned·ly,** *adv.*

—Syn. 1. discarded, rejected. **3.** See **immoral.**

a·ban·don·ee (ə ban′də nē′), *n.* **1.** the party to whom a right or property is abandoned by another, esp. an insurer to whom a property has been relinquished. **2.** a person who has been abandoned. [1840–50; ABANDON[1] + -EE]

ab·ap·tis·ton (ab′ap tis′tən), *n.* *Surg.* a cone-shaped trephine designed to avoid penetration of the brain when incising the skull. [1690–1700; < Gk (*trýpanon*) *abáptiston* (trepan) not dipped, neut. of *abáptistos,* equiv. to *a-* A-[6] + *baptis-,* var. s. of *baptízein* to immerse (see BAPTIZE) + *-tos* verbal adj. suffix]

à bas (ᴀ bä′), *French.* down with. [lit., downwards, toward (the) lower (part, location); cf. ABASE]

a·base (ə bās′), *v.t.,* **a·based, a·bas·ing. 1.** to reduce or lower, as in rank, office, reputation, or estimation; humble; degrade. **2.** *Archaic.* to lower; put or bring down: *He abased his head.* [1470–80; A-[5] + BASE[2]; r. late ME *abassen,* equiv. to A-[5] + *bas* BASE[2]; r. ME *abaissen, abe(i)sen* < AF *abesser, abaisser,* OF *abaissier,* equiv. + *a-* A-[5] + *-baissier* < VL **bassiare,* v. deriv. of LL *bassus;* see BASE[2]] **—a·base′ment,** *n.* **—a·bas′er,** *n.*

—Syn. 1. humiliate, dishonor, defame, belittle.

a·based (ə bāst′), *adj.* *Heraldry.* (of a charge) lower on an escutcheon than is usual: *a bend abased.* [1645–55; ABASE + -ED[2]]

a·bash (ə bash′), *v.t.* to destroy the self-confidence, poise, or self-possession of; disconcert; make ashamed or embarrassed: *to abash someone by sneering.* [1275–1325; ME *abaishen* < dial. OF *abacher,* OF *abaissier* to put down, bring low (see ABASE), perh. conflated with AF *abaiss-,* long s. of *abair,* OF *esba(h)ir* to gape, marvel, amaze (*es-* EX-[1] + *-ba(h)ir,* alter. of *baer* to open wide, gape < VL **batāre;* cf. BAY[2], BAY[3])] **—a·bash′ment,** *n.*

—Syn. shame, discompose, embarrass.

a·bashed (ə basht′), *adj.* ashamed or embarrassed; disconcerted: *My clumsiness left me abashed.* [1300–50; ME; see ABASH, -ED[2]] **—a·bash·ed·ly** (ə bash′id lē), *adv.* **—a·bash′ed·ness,** *n.*

a·ba·sia (ə bā′zhə, -zhē ə, -zē ə), *n.* *Med.* inability to walk due to a limitation or absence of muscular coordination. Cf. **astasia.** [1885–90; < NL, equiv. to Gk *a-* A-[6] + *bat-,* verbid of *baínein* to walk + *-ia* -IA] **—a·ba·sic** (ə bā′zik, -sik), **a·bat·ic** (ə bat′ik), *adj.*

ab·a·tage (ab′ə täzh′), *n.* abattage.

a·bate (ə bāt′), *v.,* **a·bat·ed, a·bat·ing. —v.t. 1.** to reduce in amount, degree, intensity, etc.; lessen; diminish: *to abate a tax; to abate one's enthusiasm.* **2.** *Law.* **a.** to put an end to or suppress (a nuisance). **b.** to suspend or extinguish (an action). **c.** to annul (a writ). **3.** to deduct or subtract: *to abate part of the cost.* **4.** to omit: *to abate all mention of names.* **5.** to remove, as in stone carving, or hammer down, as in metalwork, (a portion of a surface) in order to produce a figure or pattern in low relief. **—v.i. 6.** to diminish in intensity, violence, amount, etc.: *The storm has abated. The pain in his shoulder finally abated.* **7.** *Law.* to end; become null and void. [1300–50; ME < MF *abatre* to beat down, equiv. to *a-* A-[5] + *batre* < LL *batere* for L *battuere* to beat; *a-* perh. also understood as A-[3]] **—a·bat′a·ble,** *adj.* **—a·bat′er;** *Law.* **a·ba′tor,** *n.*

—Syn. 1. decrease, weaken. **6.** subside. **—Ant. 1, 6.** increase, intensify.

a·bate·ment (ə bāt′mənt), *n.* **1.** the act or state of abating or the state of being abated; reduction; decrease; alleviation; mitigation. **2.** suppression or termination: *abatement of a nuisance; noise abatement.* **3.** an

amount deducted or subtracted, as from the usual price or the full tax. **4.** *Law.* **a.** a reduction of a tax assessment. **b.** the termination of a nuisance. **c.** a wrongful entry on land made by a stranger, after the owner's death and before the owner's heir or devisee has obtained possession. **d.** a decrease in the legacies of a will when the assets of an estate are insufficient to pay all general legacies in full. **5.** Also called **rebatement.** *Heraldry.* a charge or mark that, when introduced into a coat of arms, indicates the owner's disgrace. [1300–50; ME < MF; see ABATE, -MENT]
—Syn. 1. lessening, letup, diminution. **2.** end, cessation. **—Ant. 1.** intensification, increase.

ab•a•tis (ab′ə tē′, -tis, ə bat′ē, ə bat′is), *n., pl.* **ab•a•tis** (ab′ə tēz′, ə bat′ēz), **ab•a•tis•es** (ab′ə tis′iz, ə bat′ə siz). **1.** an obstacle or barricade of trees with bent or sharpened branches directed toward an enemy. **2.** a barbed wire entanglement used as an obstacle or barricade against an enemy. [1760–70; < F; OF *abateis* < VL **abatteticius,* deriv. of OF *abattre* (see ABATE)]

a•bat-jour (ä′bä zhŏŏr′; *Fr.* A bA zhōōR′), *n., pl.* **-jours** (-zhŏŏrz′; *Fr.* -zhōōR′). **1.** a device, as a skylight or reflector, for diverting light into a building. **2.** a sloping screen for cutting off the view between an interior or porch and a lower area in front of a building. [1820–30; < F: lit., it throws down (*abat*) the daylight (*jour*). See ABATE, JOURNEY]

ab•at•tage (ab′ə täzh′), *n.* the slaughter of animals, esp. the slaughter of diseased animals to prevent the infection of others. Also, **abatage.** [< F; see ABATE, -AGE]

A battery, *Electronics.* an electric battery for heating the filament or cathode heater of an electron tube. Cf. **B battery, C battery.** [1920–25]

ab•at•toir (ab′ə twär′, ab′ə twär′), *n.* a slaughterhouse. [1810–20; < F, equiv. to *abatt(re)* to slaughter (see ABATE) + *-oir* -ORY[2]]

ab•ax•i•al (ab ak′sē əl), *adj.* being or situated away from the axis: *the abaxial surface of a leaf.* [1850–55; AB- + AXIAL]

abb (ab), *n.* **1.** low-grade wool from the breech or outer edges of a fleece. **2.** yarn made from this wool. [bef. 1000; OE *ab, āweb, ōweb;* see A-[3], WOOF[1], WEB, WEAVE]

ab•ba (ə bä′, ä′bə), *n.* aba.

Ab•ba (ab′ə), *n.* (*sometimes l.c.*) **1.** a title of reverence for bishops and patriarchs in the Coptic, Ethiopian Christian, and Syriac churches. **2.** *New Testament.* an Aramaic word for *father,* used by Jesus and Paul to address God in a relation of personal intimacy. [< Aram *abbā* father]

Ab•ba (ä′bä), *n.* a female day name for Thursday. See under **day name.**

ab•ba•cy (ab′ə sē), *n., pl.* **-cies. 1.** the rank, rights, privileges, or jurisdiction of an abbot. **2.** the term of office of an abbot. [1400–50; late ME *abbacie, abbat(h)ie* < LL *abbātia* (cf. ABBEY), equiv. to *abbāt-* (see ABBOT) + *-ia* -IA]

ab•ba-dab•ba (ab′ə dab′ə), *n. Slang.* a person or thing of little importance. [perh. taken from the nonsensical refrain of a popular song "Aba Daba Honeymoon" (1904)]

Ab•bai (ä bī′), *n.* the part of the Blue Nile above Lake Tana.

Ab•bas•id (ə bas′id, ab′ə sid), *n.* a member of a dynasty of caliphs ruling at Baghdad, A.D. 750–1258, governing most of the Islamic world and claiming descent from Abbas, uncle of Muhammad. Also, **Ab•bas′sid, Ab•bas•side** (ə bas′id, ab′ə sīd′). [< Ar *(al-)′abbās* + -ID[1]]

ab•ba•tial (ə bā′shəl), *adj.* of or pertaining to an abbot, abbess, or abbey. [1635–45; < LL *abbātiālis.* See ABBACY, -AL[1]]

ab•bé (a bā′, ab′ā; *Fr.* A bā′), *n., pl.* **ab•bés** (a bāz′, ab′āz; *Fr.* A bā′). (esp. in France) **1.** a member of the secular clergy. **2.** a title of respect for any ecclesiastic or clergyman. [1520–30; < F, MF < LL *abbāte(m),* acc. of *abbās* ABBOT]

Ab′be condens′er (ä′bə, ab′ē), *Optics.* a combination of two or three lenses having a large aperture and used as a condenser for a compound microscope. [named after Ernst Abbe (1840–1905), German physicist]

Ab′be num′ber, *Optics.* the reciprocal of the dispersive power of a substance. Also called **nu-value, relative dispersion.** [see ABBE CONDENSER]

ab•bess (ab′is), *n.* a woman who is the superior of a convent of nuns. [1275–1325; ME *abbesse* < OF *abbesse, abaesse* < LL *abbātissa,* fem. of *abbās* ABBOT; r. ME *abbatisse* < LL; in turn r. OE *abadisse, abbodesse* (cf. OHG *abbatissa*) < LL **ab(b)adissa* for *abbātissa*]
—Usage. See **-ess.**

Ab•be•ville (ab′ē vil′; *for 1 also Fr.* Ab[ə] vēl′), *n.* **1.** a town in N France, on the Somme River: site of Paleolithic artifacts. 26,581. **2.** a city in S Louisiana. 12,391.

Abbe•vill•i•an (ab vil′ē ən, -vil′yən, ab′ə vil′-), *adj.* of, pertaining to, or typical of an early Lower Paleolithic industry of the middle Pleistocene Epoch in Europe, characterized by the manufacture of large flakes and hand axes; Chellean. Also, **Abbe•vill′e•an.** [< F *abbevillien* (1932); see ABBEVILLE, -IAN]

ab•bey (ab′ē), *n., pl.* **-beys. 1.** a monastery under the supervision of an abbot or a convent under the supervision of an abbess. **2.** the group of buildings comprising such a monastery or convent. **3.** the church of an abbey. [1200–50; ME *abbey(e)* < OF *abeie* < LL *abbātia* ABBACY]

Ab•bey (ab′ē), *n.* **Edwin Austin,** 1852–1911, U.S. painter and illustrator.

Ab′bey The′atre, a theater in Dublin associated with the Irish National Theatre Society (founded 1901) and the dramas of Synge, Yeats, and Lady Gregory.

Ab•bie (ab′ē), *n.* a female given name, form of **Abigail.**

ab•bot (ab′ət), *n.* a man who is the head or superior, usually elected, of a monastery. [bef. 900; ME, var. of *abbat* < L *abbāt-* (s. of *abbās*) < Gk < Aram *abbā* ABBA; r. ME, OE *abbod* (cf. OHG *abbat*) < LL *abbād-* for *abbāt-*] **—ab′bot•cy, ab′bot•ship′,** *n.*

Ab•bot (ab′ət), *n.* **1. Charles Greeley,** 1872–1973, U.S. astrophysicist. **2.** Also, **Ab′bott.** a male given name.

Ab•bots•ford (ab′əts fərd), *n.* Sir Walter Scott's residence from 1812 to 1832, near Melrose, in SE Scotland.

Ab•bott (ab′ət), *n.* **1. Berenice,** 1898–1991, U.S. photographer. **2. Edith,** 1876–1957, and her sister **Grace,** 1878–1939, U.S. social reformers. **3. Ed•ville Ger•hardt** (ed′vil gâr′härt), 1871–1938, U.S. orthopedist. **4. George,** born 1887, U.S. playwright, director, and producer. **5. Jacob,** 1803–79, and his son, **Lyman,** 1835–1922, U.S. clergymen and writers. **6. Sir John Joseph Caldwell,** 1821–93, Canadian political leader: prime minister 1891–92. **7. Robert Seng•stake** (seng′stak), 1868–1940, U.S. newspaper publisher.

Ab•boud (ä bo͞od′), *n.* **Ib•ra•him** (ib rä hēm′), born 1900, Sudanese army general and statesman: prime minister 1958–64.

abbr., abbreviation. Also, **abbrev.**

ab•bre•vi•ate (ə brē′vē āt′), *v.,* **-at•ed, -at•ing.** *—v.t.* **1.** to shorten (a word or phrase) by omitting letters, substituting shorter forms, etc., so that the shortened form can represent the whole word or phrase, as *ft.* for *foot, ab.* for *about, R.I.* for *Rhode Island, NW* for *Northwest,* or *Xn* for *Christian.* **2.** to reduce (anything) in length, duration, etc.; make briefer: *to abbreviate a speech.* *—v.i.* **3.** to use abbreviations. [1400–50; late ME *abbreviaten* < LL *abbreviātus* shortened (ptp. of *abbreviāre*), equiv. to L *ad-* AD- + *breviātus* (*brevi(s)* short + *-ātus* -ATE[1])] **—ab•bre′vi•a′tor,** *n.*
—Syn. See **shorten.**

ab•bre•vi•at•ed (ə brē′vē ā′tid), *adj.* **1.** shortened; made briefer: *The rain led to an abbreviated picnic.* **2.** (of clothing) scanty; barely covering the body: *an abbreviated bathing suit.* **3.** constituting a shorter or smaller version of: *The large car was an abbreviated limousine.* [1545–55; ABBREVIATE + -ED[2]]

ab•bre•vi•a•tion (ə brē′vē ā′shən), *n.* **1.** a shortened or contracted form of a word or phrase, used to represent the whole, as *Dr.* for *Doctor, U.S.* for *United States, lb.* for *pound.* **2.** an act of abbreviating; state or result of being abbreviated; reduction in length, duration, etc.; abridgment. [1400–50; late ME *abbreviacioun* (< MF) < LL *abbreviātiōn-* (s. of *abbreviātiō*). See ABBREVIATE, -ION]

ab•bre•vi•a•to•ry (ə brē′vē ə tôr′ē, -tōr′ē), *adj.* serving to abbreviate or shorten: *"IA" is an abbreviatory form of "Iowa."* [1840–50; ABBREVIATE + -ORY[1]]

Ab•by (ab′ē), *n.* a female given name, form of **Abigail.**

ABC (ā′bē′sē′), *n., pl.* **ABC's, ABCs.** See **ABC's** (defs. 1, 3).

ABC, atomic, biological, and chemical: *ABC warfare.*

A.B.C., **1.** Advance Booking Charter. **2.** Alcoholic Beverage Control.

ab•cou•lomb (ab ko͞o′lom, -lōm), *n. Elect.* the centimeter-gram-second unit of quantity of electricity, equivalent to 10 coulombs. [AB(AMPERE) + COULOMB]

ABC Powers, Argentina, Brazil, and Chile, usually with reference to their mediation between the U.S. and Mexico in 1914.

ABC's (ā′bē′sēz′), *n.* (*used with a plural v.*) **1.** Also, **ABC.** the alphabet. **2.** the basic skills of spelling, reading, and writing: *learning the ABC's in the early grades of school.* **3.** Also, **ABC.** the basic or elementary facts, principles, etc., of a subject: *the ABC's of electricity.* Also, **ABCs**

ABC soil, a soil with distinct A, B, and C horizons.

abd, **1.** abdomen. **2.** abdominal.

abd., **1.** abdicated. **2.** abdomen. **3.** abdominal.

Abd-el-Ka•dir (äb′del kä′dēr), *n.* 1807?–83, Algerian leader. Also, **Abd-al-Ka•dir** (äb′dal kä′dēr).

Abd-el Krim (äb′del krēm′, krim′), 1881?–1963, Moroccan chief: leader of the Riff revolts 1921, 1924.

Ab•der•hal•den (*Ger.* äp′dəR häl′dn), *n.* **E•mil** (ā′mēl), 1877–1950, Swiss chemist and physiologist.

Abd-er-Rah•man Khan (äb′dər rə män′ KHän′), 1830?–1901, amir of Afghanistan 1880–1901. Also, **Abdurrahman Khan.**

Ab•di•as (ab dī′əs), *n. Douay Bible.* Obadiah (defs. 1, 2).

ab•di•cant (ab′di kənt), *adj.* **1.** abdicating, forsaking, or deserting: *to be abdicant of one's duty.* *—n.* **2.** a person who abdicates; abdicator. [1645–55; < L *abdicant-* (s. of *abdicāns*), prp. of *abdicāre.* See ABDICATE, -ANT]

ab•di•cate (ab′di kāt′), *v.,* **-cat•ed, -cat•ing.** *—v.i.* **1.** to renounce or relinquish a throne, right, power, claim, responsibility, or the like, esp. in a formal manner: *The aging founder of the firm decided to abdicate.* *—v.t.* **2.** to give up or renounce (authority, duties, an office, etc.), esp. in a voluntary, public, or formal manner: *King Edward VIII of England abdicated the throne in 1936.* [1535–45; < L *abdicātus* renounced (ptp. of *abdicāre*), equiv. to *ab-* AB- + *dicātus* proclaimed (*dic-* (see DICTUM) + *-ātus* -ATE[1])] **—ab•di•ca•ble** (ab′di kə bəl), *adj.* **—ab•di•ca•tive** (ab′di kā′tiv, -kə-), *adj.* **—ab′di•ca′•tor,** *n.*
—Syn. 1. resign, quit. **2.** abandon, repudiate.

ab•di•ca•tion (ab′di kā′shən), *n.* the act or state of abdicating; renunciation. [1545–55; < L *abdicātiōn-* (s. of *abdicātiō*). See ABDICATE, -ION]

abdom. **1.** abdomen. **2.** abdominal.

ab•do•men (ab′də mən, ab dō′-), *n.* **1.** *Anat., Zool.* **a.** the part of the body of a mammal between the thorax and the pelvis; belly. **b.** the cavity of this part of the body containing the stomach, intestines, etc. **c.** (in nonmammalian vertebrates) a region of the body corresponding to, but not coincident with, this part or cavity. **2.** *Entomol.* the posterior section of the body of an arthropod, behind the thorax or the cephalothorax. See diag. under **insect.** [1535–45; (< MF) < L *abdōmen* belly]

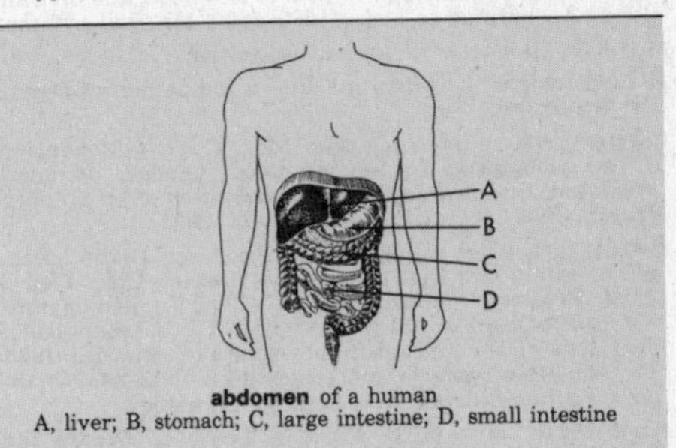

abdomen of a human
A, liver; B, stomach; C, large intestine; D, small intestine

ab•dom•i•nal (ab dom′ə nl), *adj.* **1.** of, in, on, or for the abdomen: *abdominal wall; abdominal pains.* *—n.* **2.** Usually, **abdominals.** *Informal.* the abdominal muscles. [1740–50; < L *abdōmin-,* s. of *abdōmen* ABDOMEN + -AL[1]] **—ab•dom′i•nal•ly,** *adv.*

ab•dom•i•no•plas•ty (ab dom′ə nə plas′tē), *n., pl.* **-ties.** excision of abdominal fat and skin for cosmetic purposes. [< L *abdōmin-* (see ABDOMINAL) + -O- + -PLASTY]

ab•dom•i•nous (ab dom′ə nəs), *adj.* having a large belly; potbellied. [1645–55; < L *abdōmin-* (see ABDOMINAL) + -OUS]

Ab•don (ab′don), *n.* **1.** one of the minor judges of Israel. Judges 12:13–15. **2.** a courtier of Josiah. II Chron. 34:20.

ab•duce (ab do͞os′, -dyo͞os′), *v.t.,* **-duced, -duc•ing.** *Physiol.* to draw or take away; abduct. [1530–40; < L *abdūcere,* equiv. to *ab-* AB- + *dūcere* to lead]

ab•du•cens (ab do͞o′senz, -sənz, -dyo͞o′-), *n., pl.* **ab•du•cen•tes** (ab′do͞o sen′tēz, -dyo͞o-). See **abducens nerve.** [< L, prp. of *abdūcere* to ABDUCE]

abdu′cens nerve′, *Anat.* either one of the sixth pair of cranial nerves composed of motor fibers that innervate the lateral rectus muscle of the eye. Also called **abducens, abdu′cent nerve′.** [1900–05]

ab•du•cent (ab do͞o′sənt, -dyo͞o′-), *adj. Physiol.* drawing away, as by the action of a muscle; abducting. [1705–15; < L *abdūcent-* (s. of *abdūcēns*). See ABDUCENS]

ab•duct (ab dukt′), *v.t.* **1.** to carry off or lead away (a person) illegally and in secret or by force, esp. to kidnap. **2.** *Physiol.* to move or draw away from the axis of the body or limb (opposed to *adduct*). [1825–35; < L *abductus,* ptp. of *abdūcere* to ABDUCE]

ab•duct•ee (ab duk tē′, ab′-), *n.* a person who has been abducted. [ABDUCT + -EE]

ab•duc•tion[1] (ab duk′shən), *n.* **1.** act of abducting. **2.** the state of being abducted. **3.** *Law.* the illegal carrying or enticing away of a person, esp. by interfering with a relationship, as the taking of a child from its parent. [1620–30; ABDUCT + -ION]

ab•duc•tion[2] (ab duk′shən), *n. Logic.* a syllogism whose major premise is certain but whose minor premise is probable. [1690–1700; < NL *abductiōn-* (s. of *abductiō;* trans. of Gk *apagōgḗ*). See ABDUCT, -ION]

ab•duc•tor[1] (ab duk′tər), *n.* a person who abducts. [1840–50; ABDUCT + -OR[2]]

ab•duc•tor[2] (ab duk′tər), *n.* any muscle that abducts (opposed to *adductor*). [1605–15; < NL; see ABDUCE, -TOR]

Ab•dul-A•ziz (äb′do͝ol ä zēz′), *n.* 1830–76, sultan of Turkey 1861–76 (brother of Abdul-Mejid I).

Ab•dul-Ha•mid II (äb′do͝ol hä mēd′), 1842–1918, sultan of Turkey 1876–1909.

Ab•dul-Jab•bar (äb do͞ol′jə bär′, ab-), *n.* **Ka•reem** (kə rēm′), (*Ferdinand Lewis Alcindor, Jr.*), born 1947, U.S. basketball player.

Ab•dul-Me•jid I (äb′do͝ol me jēd′), 1823–61, sultan of Turkey 1839–61 (brother of Abdul-Aziz). Also **Ab′•dul-Me•djid′ I.**

Ab•dul Rah•man (äb′do͝ol rä′män), **Tun•ku** (to͝ong′-ko͞o), 1903–90, Malaysian political leader: first prime minister of Malaya 1957–63 and prime minister of Malaysia 1963–70.

Abd•ur•rah•man Khan (äb′dər rə män′ KHän′). See **Abd-er-Rahman Khan.**

Abe (āb), *n.* a male given name, form of **Abraham.**

a•beam (ə bēm′), *adv.* **1.** *Naut., Aeron.* at right angles to the fore-and-aft line: *The vessel was sailing with the wind directly abeam.* **2.** directly abreast the middle of a ship's side. [1830–40; A-[1] + BEAM]

a•be•ce•dar•i•an (ā′bē sē dâr′ē ən), *n.* **1.** a person who is learning the letters of the alphabet. **2.** a beginner in any field of learning. *—adj.* **3.** of or pertaining to the alphabet. **4.** arranged in alphabetical order. **5.** rudimentary; elementary; primary. Also, **abecedary.** [1595–1605; < ML *abecedāriānus.* See ABECEDARY, -AN]

a•be•ce•dar•i•um (ā′bē sē dâr′ē əm), *n., pl.* **-dar•i•a** (-dâr′ē ə). a primer, esp. for teaching the alphabet. [< ML]

a•be•ce•da•ry (ā′bē sē′də rē), *n., pl.* **-ries,** *adj.* *—n.*

CONCISE PRONUNCIATION KEY: *act, cāpe, dâre, pärt; set, ēqual; if, īce; ox, ōver, ôrder, oil, bo͝ok, bo͞ot, out; up, ûrge; child; sing; shoe; thin, that;* zh as in *treasure.* ə = *a* as in *alone, e* as in *system, i* as in *easily, o* as in *gallop, u* as in *circus;* [ə] as in *fire* (fī[ə]r), *hour* (ou[ə]r). l and n can serve as syllabic consonants, as in *cradle* (krād′l), and *button* (but′n). See the full key inside the front cover.

1. abecedarian. 2. abecedarium. —*adj.* 3. abecedarian. [1570–80; < LL *abecedārius* (*a* + *be* + *ce* + *d(e)* + *-ārius* -ARY)]

a·bed (ə bed′), *adv.* 1. in bed: *to stay abed late on Sundays.* 2. confined to bed. [1200–1300; ME; see A-[1], BED]

A.B.Ed., Bachelor of Arts in Education.

A·bed·ne·go (ə bed′ni gō′), *n.* a companion of Daniel. Cf. **Shadrach.**

a·beg·ging (ə beg′ing), *adv., adj.* 1. *Archaic.* begging. 2. **go abegging,** to be unnoticed, unused, or unappreciated; find few supporters: *New ideas often go abegging.* [1350–1400; ME; see A-[1], -ING[2]]

A·bel (ā′bəl; *for 4 also Norw.* ä′bəl), *n.* 1. the second son of Adam and Eve, slain by his brother, Cain. Gen. 4. 2. **Sir Frederick Augustus,** 1827–1902, English chemist: inventor of cordite. 3. **I. W.,** 1908–87, U.S. labor leader: president of the United Steelworkers of America 1965–77. 4. **Niels Hen·rik** (nēls hen′rik), 1802–29, Norwegian mathematician. 5. a male given name.

Ab·é·lard (ab′ə lärd′; *Fr.* A bā LAR′), *n.* **Pierre** (pē-âr′; *Fr.* pyer), (*Peter Abelard*), 1079–1142, French scholastic philosopher, teacher, and theologian. His love affair with Heloïse is one of the famous romances in history. Also, **Abailard.**

a·bele (ə bēl′, ā′bəl), *n.* the white poplar tree, *Populus alba.* [1675–85; < D *abeel*, MD *abeel, aubeel* < OF *aubel, albel* < LL *albellus*, equiv. to L *alb(us)* white + *-ellus* dim. suffix]

a·be·li·a (ə bē′lē ə, ə bēl′yə), *n.* any of several shrubs belonging to the genus *Abelia*, of the honeysuckle family, having clusters of small white or pink flowers. [< NL (1818), named after Clarke *Abel* (1780–1826), British botanist; see -IA]

A·be·li·an (ə bē′lē ən, ə bēl′yən), *adj. Math.* 1. of or pertaining to Niels Henrik Abel or his theorems. 2. pertaining to an algebraic system in which an operation is commutative: *an Abelian group.* 3. pertaining to such an operation. [1905–10; ABEL + -IAN]

Abe′ Lin′coln in Illinois′, a play (1938) by Robert E. Sherwood.

A·bel-me·ho·lah (ā′bəl mi hō′lə), *n.* a city in ancient Palestine, east of the Jordan River: the home of Elisha. Judges 7:22; I Kings 4:12; 19:16.

a·bel·mosk (ā′bəl mosk′), *n.* a tropical plant, *Abelmoschus moschatus*, of the mallow family, cultivated for its musky seeds, which yield ambrette-seed oil. Also called **musk mallow.** [1765–75; < NL *abelmoschus* < Ar *ḥabb al-musk* musk seed, equiv. to *ḥabb* seed + *al* the + *musk* (< Pers; see MUSK)]

A·be·na·ki (ab′ə nak′ē, ä′bə nä′kē), *n., pl.* **-kis,** (*esp. collectively*) **-ki** for 1. 1. a member of a grouping of American Indian peoples of southern Quebec and Maine, earlier also of New Hampshire, Vermont, and northern Massachusetts. 2. any of the Eastern Algonquian languages of the Abenaki peoples. Also, **Abnaki.** Also called **Wabanaki.**

A·be·o·ku·ta (ä′bā ō′ko͞o tä), *n.* a city in SW Nigeria. 195,000.

Ab·er·crom·bie (ab′ər krom′bē, -krum′-), *n.* **Sir (Leslie) Patrick,** 1879–1957, English architect and town planner.

Ab·er·dare (ab′ər dâr′, ab′ər dâr′), *n.* a city in Mid Glamorgan, in S Wales. 37,760.

Ab·er·deen (ab′ər dēn′ *for 1, 2;* ab′ər dēn′ *for 3–6*), *n.* 1. Also called **Ab·er·deen·shire** (ab′ər dēn′shēr, -shər). a historic county in NE Scotland. 2. a seaport in NE Scotland, on the North Sea: administrative center of the Grampian region. 210,362. 3. a city in NE South Dakota. 25,956. 4. a seaport in W Washington. 18,739. 5. a town in NE Maryland. 11,533. 6. a fishhook having an extended bend. —**Ab·er·do·ni·an** (ab′ər dō′nē ən), *adj., n.*

Ab′erdeen An′gus, one of a breed of hornless beef cattle having a smooth, black coat, raised originally in Scotland. Also called **Black Angus.** [1860–65]

Ab′erdeen Prov′ing Ground′, a federal reservation and U.S. Army training center in NE Maryland, S of Aberdeen and on W Chesapeake Bay, that is the site of a military testing ground.

Ab′erdeen ter′rier. See **Scottish terrier.**

Ab·er·nath·y (ab′ər nath′ē), *n.* **Ralph (David),** 1926–90, U.S. clergyman and civil-rights leader.

ab·er·rant (ə ber′ənt, ab′ər-), *adj.* 1. departing from the right, normal, or usual course. 2. deviating from the ordinary, usual, or normal type; exceptional; abnormal. —*n.* 3. an aberrant person, thing, group, etc. [1820–30; < L *aberrant-* (s. of *aberrāns*, prp. of *aberrāre* to deviate). See AB-, ERRANT] —**ab·er′rance, ab·er′ran·cy,** *n.* —**ab·er′rant·ly,** *adv.*
—**Syn.** 1. wandering. 2. divergent, unusual.

ab·er·ra·tion (ab′ə rā′shən), *n.* 1. the act of departing from the right, normal, or usual course. 2. the act of deviating from the ordinary, usual, or normal type. 3. deviation from truth or moral rectitude. 4. mental irregularity or disorder, esp. of a minor or temporary nature; lapse from a sound mental state. 5. *Astron.* apparent displacement of a heavenly body, owing to the motion of the earth in its orbit. 6. *Optics.* any disturbance of the rays of a pencil of light such that they can no longer be brought to a sharp focus or form a clear image. 7. *Photog.* a defect in a camera lens or lens system, due to flaws in design, material, or construction, that can distort the image. [1585–95; < L *aberrātiōn-* (s. of *aberrātiō*), equiv. to *aberrāt(us)*, ptp. of *aberrāre* (see ABERRANT) + *-iōn-* -ION] —**ab′er·ra′tion·al,** *adj.*
—**Syn.** 1. wandering; deviation, divergence. 4. abnormality, eccentricity, illusion, delusion, hallucination.

ab es·se (äb es′se; *Eng.* ab es′ē), *Latin.* absent.

ab·es·sive (a bes′iv), *Gram.* —*adj.* 1. noting a case, as in Finnish, whose distinctive function is to indicate absence or lack. —*n.* 2. the abessive case. [1890–94; < L *abess(e)* to be distant + -IVE]

a·bet (ə bet′), *v.t.,* **a·bet·ted, a·bet·ting.** to encourage, support, or countenance by aid or approval, usually in wrongdoing: *to abet a swindler; to abet a crime.* [1275–1325; ME *abette* (whence OF *abeter*, unless perh. the latter, of Gmc orig., be the source for the ME), OE **ābǣtan* to hound on, equiv. to *ā-* A-[3] + *bǣtan* to BAIT, akin to BITE] —**a·bet′ment, a·bet′tal,** *n.*
—**Syn.** help, aid, assist; promote. —**Ant.** hinder, discourage.

a·be·ta·lip·o·pro·tein·e·mi·a (ā′bā tə lip′ə prō′tē-nē′mē ə, -tē ə nē′-, -li′pə-, ā′bē-), *n. Pathol.* a rare inherited disorder of fat metabolism due to an inability to synthesize betalipoproteins necessary for the transport of triglycerides, leading to diarrhea, steatorrhea, and failure to thrive. [A-[6] + BETALIPOPROTEIN + -EMIA]

a·bet·tor (ə bet′ər), *n.* a person who abets. Also, **a·bet·ter.** [1505–15; < AF *abettour.* See ABET, -OR[2]]

ab ex·tra (äb ek′strä; *Eng.* ab ek′strə), *Latin.* from the outside.

a·bey·ance (ə bā′əns), *n.* 1. temporary inactivity, cessation, or suspension: *Let's hold that problem in abeyance for a while.* 2. *Law.* a state or condition of real property in which title is not as yet vested in a known titleholder: *an estate in abeyance.* [1520–30; < AF; OF *abeance* aspiration, lit., a gaping at or toward. See A-[5], BAY[2], -ANCE]
—**Syn.** 1. remission, deferral.

a·bey·ant (ə bā′ənt), *adj.* temporarily inactive, stopped, or suspended. [1865–70; ABEY(ANCE) + -ANT]

ab·far·ad (ab far′ad, -əd), *n. Elect.* the centimeter-gram-second unit of capacitance, equivalent to 10^9 farads. [*ab-* (see ABAMPERE) + FARAD]

A.B.F.M., American Board of Foreign Missions.

Ab·ga·tha (ab′gə thə), *n. Douay Bible.* Abagtha.

ab·hen·ry (ab hen′rē), *n., pl.* **-ries.** *Elect.* the centimeter-gram-second unit of inductance, equivalent to 10^{-9} henry. [*ab-* (see ABAMPERE) + HENRY]

Ab′hi·dham′ma Pit′aka (ub′i dum′ə), *Buddhism.* See under **Pali Canon.**

ab·hom·i·na·ble (ab hom′ə nə bəl), *adj. Obs.* abominable. [1325–75; ME < ML *abhomīnābilis*, alter. of L *abōminābilis* ABOMINABLE, by assoc. with phrase *ab homine* from man, inhuman]

ab·hor (ab hôr′), *v.t.,* **-horred, -hor·ring.** to regard with extreme repugnance or aversion; detest utterly; loathe; abominate. [1400–50; late ME < L *abhorrēre* to shrink back from, shudder at, equiv. to *ab-* AB- + *horrēre* to bristle, tremble] —**ab·hor′rer,** *n.*
—**Syn.** despise. See **hate.** —**Ant.** love, admire.

ab·hor·rence (ab hôr′əns, -hor′-), *n.* 1. a feeling of extreme repugnance or aversion; utter loathing; abomination. 2. something or someone extremely repugnant or loathsome. [1650–60; ABHORR(ENT) + -ENCE]
—**Syn.** 1. execration, detestation.

ab·hor·rent (ab hôr′ənt, -hor′-), *adj.* 1. causing repugnance; detestable; loathsome: *an abhorrent deed.* 2. utterly opposed, or contrary, or in conflict (usually fol. by *to*): *abhorrent to reason.* 3. feeling extreme repugnance or aversion (usually fol. by *of*): *abhorrent of waste.* 4. remote in character (usually fol. by *from*): *abhorrent from the principles of law.* [1610–20; < L *abhorrent-* (s. of *abhorrēns*, prp. of *abhorrēre*). See ABHOR, -ENT] —**ab·hor′rent·ly,** *adv.*
—**Syn.** 1. shocking, abominable.

A·bi·a·thar (ə bī′ə thər), *n.* a priest of Israel and a companion of David. I Sam. 22:20; II Sam. 15:24–36.

A·bib (ä vēv′), *n. Chiefly Biblical.* Aviv.

a·bid·ance (ə bīd′ns), *n.* 1. the act or state of abiding. 2. conformity; compliance (usually fol. by *by*): *strict abidance by the rules.* [1640–50; ABIDE + -ANCE]

a·bide (ə bīd′), *v.,* **a·bode** or **a·bid·ed, a·bid·ing.** —*v.i.* 1. to remain; continue; stay: *Abide with me.* 2. to have one's abode; dwell; reside: *to abide in a small Scottish village.* 3. to continue in a particular condition, attitude, relationship, etc.; last. —*v.t.* 4. to put up with; tolerate; stand: *I can't abide dishonesty!* 5. to endure, sustain, or withstand without yielding or submitting: *to abide a vigorous onslaught.* 6. to wait for; await: *to abide the coming of the Lord.* 7. to accept without opposition or question: *to abide the verdict of the judges.* 8. to pay the price or penalty of; suffer for. 9. **abide by, a.** to act in accord with. **b.** to submit to; agree to: *to abide by the court's decision.* **c.** to remain steadfast or faithful to; keep: *If you make a promise, abide by it.* [bef. 1000; ME *abiden*, OE *ābidan*; c. OHG *irbītan* await, Goth *usbeisns* expectation, patience. See A-[3], BIDE] —**a·bid′er,** *n.*
—**Syn.** 1. tarry. 2. live. 3. persevere, endure. 4. bear, endure, brook; support.

a·bid·ing (ə bī′ding), *adj.* continuing without change; enduring; steadfast: *an abiding faith.* [1250–1300; ME; see ABIDE, -ING[2]] —**a·bid′ing·ly,** *adv.* —**a·bid′ing·ness,** *n.*
—**Syn.** unending, unchanging, unshakable.

Ab·i·djan (ab′i jän′; *Fr.* A bē jäN′), *n.* a seaport in and the commercial capital of the Ivory Coast. 1,850,000.

A·bie (ā′bē), *n.* a male given name, form of **Abraham.**

ab·i·ent (ab′ē ənt), *adj. Psychol.* tending to move away from a stimulus or situation. Cf. **adient.** [< L *abient-* (s. of *abiēns*, prp. of *abīre*), equiv. to *ab-* AB- + *-i-* go + *-ent-* -ENT]

à bien·tôt (A byaN tō′), *French.* see you soon; goodbye; so long.

ab·i·e·tate (ab′ē i tāt′), *n. Chem.* a salt or ester of abietic acid. [ABIET(IC ACID) + -ATE[2]]

ab′i·et′ic ac′id (ab′ē et′ik, ab′-), *Chem.* a yellow, crystalline, water-insoluble acid, $C_{20}H_{30}O_2$, obtained from the resin of a species of pine: used chiefly in driers, varnishes, and soaps. Also called **sylvic acid.** [1860–65; < L *abiet-* (s. of *abiēs*) fir + -IC]

ab·i·gail (ab′i gāl′), *n.* a lady's maid. [1645–55; after *Abigail*, name of attendant in play *The Scornful Lady* (1610), by Francis Beaumont and John Fletcher]

Ab·i·gail (ab′i gāl′), *n.* 1. the wife of Nabal and later of David. I Sam. 25. 2. a female given name: from a Hebrew word meaning "joy of the father."

A·bi·hu (ə bī′hyo͞o), *n.* a son of Aaron who, with Nadab, was destroyed by fire from heaven for disobeying the Lord. Lev. 10:1–5.

Ab·i·lene (ab′ə lēn′), *n.* a city in central Texas. 98,315.

a·bil·i·ty (ə bil′i tē), *n., pl.* **-ties.** 1. power or capacity to do or act physically, mentally, legally, morally, financially, etc. 2. competence in an activity or occupation because of one's skill, training, or other qualification: *the ability to sing well.* 3. **abilities,** talents; special skills or aptitudes: *Composing music is beyond his abilities.* [1350–1400; ME *(h)abilite* < MF < L *habilitās* aptitude, equiv. to *habili(s)* handy (see ABLE) + *-tās* -TY[2]; r. ME *ablete* < OF < L, as above]
—**Syn.** 1. capability; proficiency, expertness, dexterity. 2. ABILITY, FACULTY, TALENT denote qualifications or powers. ABILITY is a general word for power, native or acquired, enabling one to do things well: *a person of great ability; ability in mathematics.* FACULTY denotes a natural ability for a particular kind of action: *a faculty of saying what he means.* TALENT is often used to mean a native ability or aptitude in a special field: *a talent for music or art.*

-ability, a combination of **-able** and **-ity,** found on nouns corresponding to adjectives in **-able:** *capability.* [ME *-abilite* << L *-abilitās*]

abil′ity group′ing, *Educ.* tracking.

A·bim·e·lech (ə bim′ə lek′), *n.* 1. a king of Gerar, who made a peace agreement with Abraham. Gen. 20, 21. 2. a son of Gideon, who made a violent but futile attempt to become king of Shechem. Judges 8, 9.

Ab·ing·don (ab′ing dən), *n.* a town in S Oxfordshire, in S England, on the Thames: site of Benedictine abbey founded 7th century A.D. 18,596.

Ab·ing·ton (ab′ing tən), *n.* 1. a town in SE Pennsylvania. 59,084. 2. a city in SE Massachusetts. 13,517.

ab in·i·ti·o (äb i nit′ē ō′; *Eng.* ab i nish′ē ō′), *Latin.* from the beginning.

A·bin·o·am (ə bin′ō am′), *n.* the father of Barak. Judges 4:6; 12; 5:1. Also, *Douay Bible,* **A·bin·o·em** (ə bin′ō em′).

ab in·tra (äb in′trä; *Eng.* ab in′trə), *Latin.* from inside; from within.

a·bi·o·gen·e·sis (ā′bī ō jen′ə sis, ab′ē ō-), *n. Biol.* the now discredited theory that living organisms can arise spontaneously from inanimate matter; spontaneous generation. [A-[6] + BIOGENESIS; coined by T. H. Huxley in 1870] —**a·bi·o·ge·net·ic** (ā′bī ō jə net′ik, ab′ē ō-), **a′bi·o·ge·net′i·cal,** *adj.* —**a′bi·o·ge·net′i·cal·ly,** *adv.* —**a·bi·og·e·nist** (ā′bī og′ə nist, ab′ē-), *n.*

a·bi·o·gen·ic (ā′bī ō jen′ik, ab′ē ō-), *adj. Biol.* not resulting from the activity of living organisms. [1910–15; A-[6] + BIOGENIC] —**a′bi·o·gen′i·cal·ly,** *adv.*

a·bi·o·log·i·cal (ā′bī ə loj′i kəl), *adj.* not occurring or produced naturally; synthetic. [1875–80; A-[6] + BIOLOGICAL]

a·bi·o·sis (ā′bī ō′sis, ab′ē-), *n.* the absence or lack of life; a nonviable state. [A-[6] + -BIOSIS]

a·bi·ot·ic (ā′bī ot′ik, ab′ē-), *adj.* of or characterized by the absence of life or living organisms. Also, **a′bi·ot′i·cal.** [A-[6] + BIOTIC] —**a′bi·ot′i·cal·ly,** *adv.*

a·bi·ot·ro·phy (ā′bī o′trə fē, ab′ē-), *n. Pathol.* the loss of vitality in or the degeneration of certain cells or tissues, as in the aging process. [A-[6] + BIO- + -TROPHY] —**a·bi·o·troph·ic** (ā′bī ə trof′ik, -trō′fik, ab′ē-), *adj.*

ab·ir·ri·tant (ab ir′i tənt), *Med.* —*n.* 1. a soothing medication. —*adj.* 2. relieving or lessening irritation; soothing. [1875–80; AB- + IRRITANT]

ab·ir·ri·tate (ab ir′i tāt′), *v.t.,* **-tat·ed, -tat·ing.** *Med.* to make less irritable; soothe. [AB- + IRRITATE] —**ab·ir′ri·ta′tion,** *n.* —**ab·ir′ri·ta′tive,** *adj.*

Ab·i·shag (ab′ə shag′), *n.* a young maiden brought to David in his old age as a nurse and companion. I Kings 1:1–4. Also, *Douay Bible,* **Ab·i·sag** (ab′i sag′).

Ab·i·tib·i (ab′i tib′ē), *n.* 1. a lake in E Ontario and W Quebec, Canada. 369 sq. mi. (956 sq. km). 2. a river flowing N from this lake. 340 mi. (547 km) long.

A·bi·u (ə bī′yo͞o), *n. Douay Bible.* Abihu.

ab·ject (ab′jekt, ab jekt′), *adj.* 1. utterly hopeless, miserable, humiliating, or wretched: *abject poverty.* 2. contemptible; despicable; base-spirited: *an abject coward.* 3. shamelessly servile; slavish. 4. *Obs.* cast aside. [1400–50; late ME < L *abjectus* thrown down (ptp. of *abicere, abjicere*), equiv. to *ab-* AB + *-jec-* throw + *-tus* ptp. suffix] —**ab·ject′ly,** *adv.* —**ab·ject′ness, ab·ject′ed·ness,** *n.*
—**Syn.** 1. debasing, degrading; miserable. 2. base, mean, low, vile. —**Ant.** exalted.

ab·jec·tion (ab jek′shən), *n.* 1. the condition of being servile, wretched, or contemptible. 2. the act of humiliating. 3. *Mycol.* the release of spores by a fungus. [1375–1425; late ME *abjectioun* (< MF) < L *abjectiōn-*, s. of *abjectiō* casting away, equiv. to *abject(us)* (see ABJECT) + *-iōn-* -ION; or AB- + (E)JECTION]

CONCISE ETYMOLOGY KEY: <, descended or borrowed from; >, whence; b., blend of, blended; c., cognate with; cf., compare; deriv., derivative; equiv., equivalent; imit., imitative; obl., oblique; r., replacing; s., stem; sp., spelling, spelled; resp., respelling, respelled; trans., translation; ?, origin unknown; *, unattested; ‡, probably earlier than. See the full key inside the front cover.

ab·jec·tive (ab jek′tiv), *adj.* tending to degrade, humiliate, or demoralize: *the abjective influences of his early life.* [1865–70; ABJECT + -IVE]

ab·junc·tion (ab jungk′shən), *n. Mycol.* abstriction. [AB- + JUNCTION]

ab·ju·ra·tion (ab′jə rā′shən), *n.* **1.** the act of abjuring. **2.** renunciation upon oath. [1505–15; < ML *abjūrātiōn-* (s. of *abjūrātiō*); see ABJURE, -ATE[1], -ION]

ab·jure (ab jŏŏr′, -jûr′), *v.t.*, **-jured, -jur·ing. 1.** to renounce, repudiate, or retract, esp. with formal solemnity; recant: *to abjure one's errors.* **2.** to renounce or give up under oath; forswear: *to abjure allegiance.* **3.** to avoid or shun. [1400–50; late ME< L *abjūrāre* to deny on oath, equiv. to *ab-* AB- + *jūrāre* to swear; see JURY[1]] **—ab·jur′a·to′ry,** *adj.* **—ab·jur′er,** *n.*

Ab·khaz (äb käz′; *Russ.* ub KHäz′), *n.* Abkhazian.

Ab·kha·zi·a (ab kä′zhə, -zē ə; *Russ.* ub KHä′zyi yə), *n.* an autonomous republic in the Georgian Republic, on the E coast of the Black Sea. 506,000; 3360 sq. mi. (8600 sq. km). *Cap.:* Sukhumi. Also, **Ab·kha′si·a.** Formerly, **Abkhaz′ Auton′omous So′viet So′cialist Repub′lic.**

Ab·kha·zi·an (ab kä′zē ən, -zhən), *n.* a Caucasian language of Abkhazia, best known for its rich consonantism. Also, **Ab·kha′si·an.** [1865–70; ABKHAZI(A) + -AN]

abl., ablative[1].

ab·lac·tate (ab lak′tāt), *v.t.*, **-tat·ed, -tat·ing.** to wean. [< LL *ablactātus* weaned (ptp. of *ablactāre*), equiv. to *ab-* AB- + *lact-* (s. of *lac*) milk + *-ātus* -ATE[1]] **—ab′lac·ta′tion,** *n.*

à blanc (ä blängk′; *Fr.* A blän′), *French Cookery.* **1.** blanched. **2.** without browning. [< F: lit., until white]

a·blare (ə blâr′), *adv., adj.* blaring: *With trumpets ablare, the band entered the stadium.* [A[1] + BLARE]

ab·late (a blāt′), *v.*, **-lat·ed, -lat·ing.** —*v.t.* **1.** to remove or dissipate by melting, vaporization, erosion, etc.: *to ablate a metal surface with intense heat.* —*v.i.* **2.** to become ablated; undergo ablation. [1535–45; < L *ablātus* carried away (ptp. of *auferre*), equiv. to *ab-* AB- + *lātus* (ptp. of *ferre* to bear); see -ATE[1]]

ab·la·tion (a blā′shən), *n.* **1.** the removal, esp. of organs, abnormal growths, or harmful substances, from the body by mechanical means, as by surgery. **2.** the reduction in volume of glacial ice, snow, or névé by the combined processes of melting, evaporation, and calving. Cf. **alimentation** (def. 3). **3.** *Aerospace.* erosion of the protective outer surface (**ablator**) of a spacecraft or missile due to the aerodynamic heating caused by travel at hypersonic speed during reentry through the atmosphere. [1570–80; < LL *ablātiōn-* (s. of *ablātiō*). See ABLATE, -ION]

ab·la·tive[1] (ab′lə tiv), *Gram.* —*adj.* **1.** (in some inflected languages) noting a case that has among its functions the indication of place from which or, as in Latin, place in which, manner, means, instrument, or agent. —*n.* **2.** the ablative case. **3.** a word in that case, as *Troiā* in Latin *Aenēas Troiā vēnit,* "Aeneas came from Troy." [1400–50; late ME < L *ablātīvus.* See ABLATE, -IVE] **—ab·la·ti·val** (ab′lə tī′vəl), *adj.*

ab·la·tive[2] (a blā′tiv), *adj.* capable of or susceptible to ablation; tending to ablate: *the ablative nose cone of a rocket.* [1560–70; ABLATE + -IVE] **—ab·la′tive·ly,** *adv.*

ab′lative ab′solute, *Latin Gram.* a construction not dependent upon any other part of the sentence, consisting of a noun and a participle, noun and adjective, or two nouns, in which both members are in the ablative case, as Latin *viā factā,* "the road having been made." [1520–30]

ab·la·tor (a blā′tər), *n. Aerospace.* See under **ablation** (def. 3). [ABLATE + -OR[2]]

ab·laut (äb′lout, ab′-; *Ger.* äp′lout), *n. Gram.* (in Indo-European languages) regular alternation in the internal phonological structure of a word element, esp. alternation of a vowel, that is coordinated with a change in grammatical function or combination, as in English *sing, sang, sung, song;* apophony. [1840–50; < G, equiv. to *ab-* off + *Laut* sound]

a·blaze (ə blāz′), *adj.* **1.** burning; on fire: *They set the logs ablaze.* **2.** gleaming with bright lights, bold colors, etc. **3.** excited; eager; zealous; ardent. **4.** very angry. [1800–10; A-[1] + BLAZE[1]; cf. ME *on blase*]

a·ble (ā′bəl), *adj.*, **a·bler, a·blest,** *n.* —*adj.* **1.** having necessary power, skill, resources, or qualifications; qualified: *able to lift a two-hundred-pound weight; able to write music; able to travel widely; able to vote.* **2.** having unusual or superior intelligence, skill, etc.: *an able leader.* **3.** showing talent, skill, or knowledge: *an able speech.* **4.** legally empowered, qualified, or authorized. —*n.* **5.** (*usually cap.*) a code word formerly used in communications to represent the letter *A.* [1275–1325; ME < MF < L *habilis* handy, equiv. to *hab(ēre)* to have, hold + *-ilis* -ILE]
—Syn. 1. fit, fitted. ABLE, CAPABLE, COMPETENT all mean possessing adequate power for doing something. ABLE implies power equal to effort required: *able to finish in time.* CAPABLE implies power to meet or fulfill ordinary requirements: *a capable worker.* COMPETENT suggests power to meet demands in a completely satisfactory manner: *a competent nurse.* **2.** talented; skilled, clever, ingenious. **3.** apt. **—Ant. 1.** incompetent.

-able, a suffix meaning "capable of, susceptible of, fit for, tending to, given to," associated in meaning with the word **able,** occurring in loanwords from Latin (*laudable*); used in English as a highly productive suffix to form adjectives by addition to stems of any origin (*teachable; photographable*). Also, **-ble, -ible.** [ME < OF < L *-ābilis,* equiv. to *-ā-* final vowel of 1st conjugation v. stems + *-bilis*]

a·ble-bod·ied (ā′bəl bod′ēd), *adj.* having a strong, healthy body; physically fit: *Every able-bodied young man served in the armed forces.* [1615–25] **—a′ble-bod′ied·ness,** *n.*

a·ble·ism (ā′bə liz′əm), *n.* discrimination against disabled people. [1985–1990] **—a′ble·ist,** *n.*

a′ble sea′man, 1. Also called **a′ble-bodied sea′·man.** an experienced deck-department seaman qualified to perform routine sea duties. **2.** (in the British Navy and on British and U.S. merchant ships) a rating between ordinary seaman and leading seaman or boatswain's mate. *Abbr.:* A.B., AB [1695–1705]

a·bloom (ə blōōm′), *adv., adj.* in bloom; blossoming; flowering. [1850–55; A-[1] + BLOOM[1]]

A.B.L.S., Bachelor of Arts in Library Science.

ab·lu·ent (ab′lōō ənt), *adj.* **1.** serving to cleanse. —*n.* **2.** a cleansing agent. [1745–55; < L *abluent-* (s. of *abluēns,* prp. of *abluere* to wash away), equiv. to *ab-* AB- + *-lū-* comb. form of *lavere* to wash + *-ent* -ENT]

a·blush (ə blush′), *adj.* blushing; reddened. [1850–55; A-[1] + BLUSH]

ab·lut·ed (ə blōō′tid), *adj.* (of the hands, body, etc.) thoroughly washed. [1640–50; *ablute* (prob. back formation from ABLUTION) + -ED[2]]

ab·lu·tion (ə blōō′shən), *n.* **1.** a cleansing with water or other liquid, esp. as a religious ritual. **2.** the liquid thus used. **3.** a washing of the hands, body, etc. [1350–1400; ME < L *ablūtiōn-* (s. of *ablūtiō*), equiv. to *ablūt-(us),* ptp. of *abluere* (see ABLUENT) + *-iōn-* -ION] **—ab·lu′tion·ar′y,** *adj.*

a·bly (ā′blē), *adv.* in an able manner; with skill or ability; competently. [1350–1400; ME *abelli.* See ABLE, -LY]

-ably, a suffix combining **-able** and **-ly** that forms adverbs corresponding to adjectives ending in **-able:** *commendably; dependably; tolerably.* Also, **-ibly.**

ABM, antiballistic missile.

ab·mho (ab′mō), *n., pl.* **-mhos.** *Elect.* the centimeter-gram-second unit of conductance, equivalent to 10^9 mhos. [AB(AMPERE) + MHO]

ab·mo·dal·i·ty (ab′mō dal′i tē), *n., pl.* **-ties.** *Statistics.* the differing of a measurable trait in an individual case from the mean for a population. [AB- + MODALITY]

abn, airborne.

Ab·na·ki (ab nak′ē, -nä′kē), *n., pl.* **-kis,** (*esp. collectively*) **-ki.** Abenaki.

ab·ne·gate (ab′ni gāt′), *v.t.*, **-gat·ed, -gat·ing. 1.** to refuse or deny oneself (some rights, conveniences, etc.); reject; renounce. **2.** to relinquish; give up. [1650–60; < L *abnegātus* denied (ptp. of *abnegāre*). See AB-, NEGATE] **—ab′ne·ga′tion,** *n.* **—ab′ne·ga′tor,** *n.*

Ab·ner (ab′nər), *n.* **1.** the commander of the Israelite army and a cousin of Saul. I Sam. 14:50; 26:5. **2.** a male given name.

Ab′ney lev′el (ab′nē), *Survey.* a hand level for determining elevations and angles of slope.

ab·nor·mal (ab nôr′məl), *adj.* **1.** not normal, average, typical, or usual; deviating from a standard: *abnormal powers of concentration; an abnormal amount of snow; abnormal behavior.* **2.** extremely or excessively large: *abnormal profit.* [1850–55; AB- + NORMAL; r. *anormal* < ML *anōrmālus,* var. of *anōmālus* ANOMALOUS influenced by L *norma* NORM] **—ab·nor′mal·ly,** *adv.* **—ab·nor′mal·ness,** *n.*
—Syn. 1. anomalous, aberrant, irregular, deviant, unnatural, odd. See **irregular.**

ab·nor·mal·cy (ab nôr′məl sē), *n., pl.* **-cies.** abnormality. [ABNORMAL + -CY]

ab·nor·mal·i·ty (ab′nôr mal′i tē), *n., pl.* **-ties. 1.** an abnormal condition, state, or quality; irregularity; deviation. **2.** an abnormal thing or event. Also, **abnormalcy.** [1850–55; ABNORMAL + -ITY]
—Syn. anomaly, aberration, peculiarity, oddity, idiosyncrasy.

ab·nor·mal·ize (ab nôr′mə līz′), *v.t.*, **-ized, -iz·ing.** to make abnormal. Also, *esp. Brit.,* **ab·nor′mal·ise′.** [1870–75; ABNORMAL + -IZE] **—ab·nor′mal·i·za′tion,** *n.*

abnor′mal psychol′ogy, the branch of psychology that deals with modes of behavior, mental phenomena, etc., that deviate markedly from the standards believed to characterize a well-adjusted personality. [1900–05]

ab·nor·mi·ty (ab nôr′mi tē), *n., pl.* **-ties.** an abnormal condition, quality, etc.; abnormality; irregularity. [1725–35; < LL *abnormitās,* equiv. to *abnorm(is)* (*ab-* AB- + *norm(a)* rule, NORM + *-is* adj. suffix) + *-itās* -ITY]

ab·o (ab′ō), *n., pl.* **ab·os,** *adj.* (*sometimes cap.*) *Australian Disparaging and Offensive.* —*n.* **1.** an Aborigine. —*adj.* **2.** aboriginal. [1905–10; by shortening; see -O]

Å·bo (ô′bōō), *n.* Swedish name of **Turku.**

ABO, See **ABO system.**

a·board (ə bôrd′, ə bōrd′), *adv.* **1.** on board; on, in, or into a ship, train, airplane, bus, etc.: *to step aboard.* **2.** alongside; to the side. **3.** *Baseball.* on base: *a homer with two aboard.* **4. all aboard!** (as a warning to passengers entering or planning to enter a train, bus, boat, etc., just before starting) Everyone get on! **5.** into a group as a new member: *The office manager welcomed him aboard.* —*prep.* **6.** on board of; on, in, or into: *to come aboard a ship.* [1350–1400; ME *abord(e)* (see A-[1], BOARD), perh. conflated with MF *a bord*]

a·board·age (ə bôr′dij, ə bōr′-), *n. Naut.* collision between two vessels meeting side-on or at a slight angle. [ABOARD + -AGE]

a·bode[1] (ə bōd′), *n.* **1.** a place in which a person resides; residence; dwelling; habitation; home. **2.** an extended stay in a place; sojourn. [1200–50; ME *abood* a waiting, delay, stay; akin to ABIDE]

a·bode[2] (ə bōd′), *v.* a pt. and pp. of **abide.**

ab·ohm (ab ōm′, ab′ōm′), *n. Elect.* the centimeter-gram-second unit of electrical resistance, equivalent to 10^{-9} ohm. [*ab-* (see ABAMPERE) + OHM]

a·boil (ə boil′), *adv., adj.* **1.** boiling: *Make the tea as soon as the water is aboil.* **2.** in a state of excited activity: *The street was aboil with Saturday shoppers.* [1855–60; A-[1] + BOIL[1]]

a·bol·ish (ə bol′ish), *v.t.* to do away with; put an end to; annul; make void: *to abolish slavery.* [1425–75; late ME < MF *aboliss-,* long s. of *abolir* < L *abolēre* to destroy, efface, put an end to; change of conjugation perh. by assoc. with L *abolitiō* ABOLITION] **—a·bol′ish·a·ble,** *adj.* **—a·bol′ish·er,** *n.* **—a·bol′ish·ment,** *n.*
—Syn. suppress, nullify, cancel; annihilate, obliterate, extinguish; exterminate, extirpate, eliminate. ABOLISH, ERADICATE, STAMP OUT mean to do away completely with something. To ABOLISH is to cause to cease, often by a summary order: *to abolish a requirement.* STAMP OUT implies forcibly making an end to something considered undesirable or harmful: *to stamp out the opium traffic.* ERADICATE (literally, *to tear out by the roots*), a formal word, suggests extirpation, leaving no vestige or trace: *to eradicate all use of child labor.* **—Ant.** establish.

ab·o·li·tion (ab′ə lish′ən), *n.* **1.** the act of abolishing: *the abolition of war.* **2.** the state of being abolished; annulment; abrogation: *the abolition of unjust laws; the abolition of unfair taxes.* **3.** the legal prohibition and ending of slavery, esp. of slavery of blacks in the U.S. [1520–30; < L *abolitiōn-* (s. of *abolitiō*), equiv. to *abolit-(us)* effaced, destroyed, ptp. of *abolēre* (cf. ABOLISH) + *-iōn-* -ION] **—ab′o·li′tion·ar′y,** *adj.*
—Syn. 1., 2. annihilation, eradication, elimination; nullification, invalidation, revocation, repeal. **—Ant. 2.** establishment.

ab·o·li·tion·ism (ab′ə lish′ə niz′əm), *n.* the principle or policy of abolition, esp. of slavery of blacks in the U.S. [1800–10; ABOLITION + -ISM]

ab·o·li·tion·ist (ab′ə lish′ə nist), *n.* **1.** (esp. prior to the Civil War) a person who advocated or supported the abolition of slavery in the U.S. **2.** a person who favors the abolition of any law or practice deemed harmful to society: *the abolitionists who are opposed to capital punishment.* [1830–40; ABOLITION + -IST]

ab·o·li·tion·ize (ab′ə lish′ə nīz′), *v.t.*, **-ized, -iz·ing.** (esp. prior to the Civil War) to convert (persons, a region, a state, etc.) to abolitionism. Also, *esp. Brit.,* **ab′o·li′tion·ise′.** [1835–45; *Amer.;* ABOLITION + -IZE]

a·bol·la (ə bol′ə), *n., pl.* **a·bol·lae** (ə bol′ē). a woolen cloak worn by men in ancient Rome. [1865–70; < L, prob. ult. < Gk *ambolé,* syncopated var. of *anabolé* a throwing back (and about). See ANABOLISM]

ab·o·ma·sum (ab′ə mā′səm), *n., pl.* **-sa** (-sə). the fourth or true stomach of cud-chewing animals, lying next to the omasum. See diag. under **ruminant.** [1700–10; < NL; see AB-, OMASUM]

ab·o·ma·sus (ab′ə mā′səs), *n., pl.* **-si** (-sī). abomasum.

A-bomb (ā′bom′), *n.* See **atomic bomb.**

Ab·o·mey (ab′ə mā′, ə bō′mē), *n.* a city in SW Benin. 50,000.

a·bom·i·na·ble (ə bom′ə nə bəl), *adj.* **1.** repugnantly hateful; detestable; loathsome: *an abominable crime.* **2.** very unpleasant; disagreeable: *The weather was abominable last week.* **3.** very bad, poor, or inferior: *They have abominable taste in clothes.* [1325–75; ME < L *abōminābilis,* equiv. to *abōminā(rī)* to pray to avert an eventuality, despise as a bad omen, abhor (see AB-, OMEN) + *-bilis* -BLE] **—a·bom′i·na·ble·ness,** *n.* **—a·bom′i·na·bly,** *adv.*
—Syn. 1. abhorrent, horrible, revolting, foul. **2.** miserable. **—Ant. 1.** likable, admirable. **2.** delightful.

Abom′inable Snow′man, a legendary large, hairy, humanoid creature said to inhabit the Himalayas. Also called **yeti.** [1920–25; spurious trans. of a supposed Tibetan phrase *metoh kangmi,* prob. an erroneous rendering of Tibetan *mi t'om* man-bear and *k'ang mi* snowfield man]

a·bom·i·nate (ə bom′ə nāt′), *v.t.*, **-nat·ed, -nat·ing. 1.** to regard with intense aversion or loathing; abhor. **2.** to dislike strongly. [1840–50; < L *abōminātus* loathed, ptp. of *abōminārī.* See ABOMINABLE, -ATE[1]] **—a·bom′i·na′tor,** *n.*
—Syn. 1. loathe, execrate. See **hate.**

a·bom·i·na·tion (ə bom′ə nā′shən), *n.* **1.** anything abominable; anything greatly disliked or abhorred. **2.** intense aversion or loathing; detestation: *He regarded lying with abomination.* **3.** a vile, shameful, or detestable action, condition, habit, etc.: *Spitting in public is an abomination.* [1350–1400; ME *ab(h)ominacioun* < LL *abōminātiōn-* (s. of *abōminātiō*). See ABOMINATE, -ION]
—Syn. 2. hatred. **3.** corruption, depravity.

a·boon (ə bōōn′), *adv., prep. Scot. and Brit. Dial.* above. [1350–1400; ME *abone, abowne;* see ABOVE]

ab·o·ral (ab ôr′əl, -ōr′-), *adj. Anat., Zool.* opposite to or away from the mouth. [1855–60; AB- + ORAL] **—ab·o′ral·ly,** *adv.*

ab·o·rig·i·nal (ab′ə rij′ə nl), *adj.* **1.** of, pertaining to, or typical of aborigines: *aboriginal customs.* **2.** original or earliest known; native; indigenous: *the aboriginal people of Tahiti.* —*n.* **3.** aborigine (def. 1). **4.** (*cap.*) Aborigine (def. 2). [1660–70; ABORIGINE + -AL[1]] **—ab′o·rig′i·nal′i·ty,** *n.* **—ab′o·rig′i·nal·ly,** *adv.*
—Syn. 2. endemic, autochthonous, primordial.

ab o·rig·i·ne (äb ō RIG′i ne′; *Eng.* ab ô rij′ə nē′, -ō rij′-), *Latin.* from the very beginning; from the source or origin.

ab·o·rig·i·ne (ab′ə rij′ə nē), *n.* **1.** one of the original or earliest known inhabitants of a country or region. **2.** (*cap.*) Also, **Aboriginal.** Also called **Australian Aborigine.** a member of the dark-skinned people who were the earliest inhabitants of Australia. **3. aborigines,** the original, native fauna or flora of a region. [1540–50; by back formation from *aborigines* < L *Aborīginēs* a race of

CONCISE PRONUNCIATION KEY: *act, cāpe, dâre, pärt; set, ēqual; if, ice; ox, ōver, ôrder, oil, bŏŏk, bōōt, out; up, ûrge; child; sing; shoe; thin, that;* zh as in *treasure.* ə = *a* as in *alone, e* as in *system, i* as in *easily, o* as in *gallop, u* as in *circus;* ᵊ as in *fire* (fīᵊr), *hour* (ouᵊr). l and n can serve as syllabic consonants, as in *cradle* (krād′l), and *button* (but′n). See the full key inside the front cover.

pre-Roman inhabitants of Italy, prob. alter. of an earlier ethnonym by assoc. with AB ORIGINE]

a•born•ing (ə bôr′ning), *adv.* **1.** in birth; before being carried out: *The scheme died aborning.* —*adj.* **2.** being born; coming into being, fruition, realization, etc.: *A new era of architecture is aborning.* [1930–35; A-[1] + *borning* irreg. for *being born;* see BORN, -ING[2]]

a•bort (ə bôrt′), *v.i.* **1.** to bring forth a fetus from the uterus before the fetus is viable; miscarry. **2.** to develop incompletely; remain in a rudimentary or undeveloped state. **3.** to fail, cease, or stop at an early or premature stage. **4.** *Mil.* to fail to accomplish a purpose or mission for any reason other than enemy action. **5.** *Rocketry.* (of a missile) to stop before the scheduled flight is completed. —*v.t.* **6.** to cause to bring forth (a fetus) from the uterus before the fetus is viable. **7.** to cause (a pregnant female) to be delivered of a nonviable fetus. **8.** to cause to cease or end at an early or premature stage: *We aborted our vacation when the car broke down.* **9.** to terminate (a missile flight, mission, etc.) before completion. **10.** to put down or quell in the early stages: *Troops aborted the uprising.* —*n.* **11.** a missile, rocket, etc., that has aborted. [1570–80; < L *abortus* miscarried (ptp. of *aborīrī* to disappear, miscarry) equiv. to *ab-* AB- + *-or-* come into being + *-tus* ptp. suffix]

a•bor•ti•cide (ə bôr′tə sīd′), *n.* **1.** destruction of a fetus in the uterus; feticide. **2.** a drug or other agent that causes abortion. [ABORT + -I- + -CIDE]

a•bor•ti•fa•cient (ə bôr′tə fā′shənt), *adj.* **1.** causing abortion. —*n.* **2.** a drug or device used to cause abortion: *a biochemical abortifacient in pill form.* [1870–75; ABORT + -I- + -FACIENT]

a•bor•tion (ə bôr′shən), *n.* **1.** Also called **voluntary abortion.** the removal of an embryo or fetus from the uterus in order to end a pregnancy. **2.** any of various surgical methods for terminating a pregnancy, esp. during the first six months. **3.** Also called **spontaneous abortion.** miscarriage (def. 3). **4.** an immature and nonviable fetus. **5.** abortus (def. 2b). **6.** any malformed or monstrous person, thing, etc. **7.** *Biol.* the arrested development of an embryo or an organ at a more or less early stage. **8.** the stopping of an illness, infection, etc., at a very early stage. **9.** *Informal.* **a.** shambles; mess. **b.** anything that fails to develop, progress, or mature, as a design or project. [1540–50; < L *abortiōn-* (s. of *abortiō*). See ABORT, -ION]

a•bor•tion•ist (ə bôr′shə nist), *n.* **1.** a person who performs or induces abortions, esp. illegally. **2.** a person who favors or advocates abortion as a right or choice that all women should have: usually intended as an offensive term. [1870–75, *Amer.;* ABORTION + -IST]

a•bor•tion-on-de•mand (ə bôr′shən on di mand′, -mänd′, -ôn-), *n.* **1.** the right of a woman to have an abortion during the first six months of a pregnancy. **2.** an abortion performed on a woman solely at her own request. [1970–75]

abor′tion pill′, See **antigestational drug.** [1985–90]

a•bor•tive (ə bôr′tiv), *adj.* **1.** failing to succeed; unsuccessful: *an abortive rebellion; an abortive scheme.* **2.** born prematurely. **3.** imperfectly developed; rudimentary. **4.** *Med.* **a.** producing or intended to produce abortion; abortifacient. **b.** acting to halt progress of a disease. **5.** *Pathol.* (of the course of a disease) short and mild without the usual, pronounced clinical symptoms. **6.** *Bot.* (of seeds or pollen grains) imperfect; unable to germinate. [1300–50; ME < L *abortīvus.* See ABORT, -IVE] —**a•bor′tive•ly,** *adv.* —**a•bor′tive•ness,** *n.*
—**Syn. 1.** fruitless, ineffectual, bootless, unavailing, vain. —**Ant. 1.** successful.

a•bor•tus (ə bôr′təs), *n., pl.* **-tus•es. 1.** a miscarriage. **2.** *Med.* **a.** immature placental or fetal tissue prematurely passed or curetted. **b.** an aborted fetus. [< NL, L: miscarriage, equiv. to *abor(īrī)* to miscarry (see ABORT) + *-tus* suffix of v. action]

ABO system, *Physiol.* a classification of human blood based on the presence on the surface of red blood cells of one or both of two specific antigens, designated A and B, or their absence, designated O: every person has one of four possible inherited blood types, A, B, AB, or O, and has antibodies circulating in the blood that clump with any antigen that is not of that type, persons with type O thus being able to donate blood devoid of the antigens for transfusion to types A, B, and AB but able to receive only blood of type O. [1940–45]

a•bou•dik•ro (ä′bo͞o dē′krō), *n.* the wood of a sapele. [< F, said to be the name of the tree in Abe and Akye (Attié), languages of the Lagoon region of the Ivory Coast]

a•bought (ə bôt′), *v.* pt. and pp. of **aby.**

A•bou•kir (ä′bo͞o kēr′, ab′o͞o-), *n.* Abukir.

a•bou•li•a (ə bo͞o′lē ə), *n.* abulia. —**a•bou′lic,** *adj.*

a•bound (ə bound′), *v.i.* **1.** to occur or exist in great quantities or numbers: *a stream in which trout abound.* **2.** to be rich or well supplied (usually fol. by *in*): *The region abounds in coal.* **3.** to be filled; teem (usually fol. by *with*): *The ship abounds with rats.* [1325–75; ME *abounden* < L *abundāre* to overflow, equiv. to *ab-* AB- + *undāre* to move in waves; see UNDULATE] —**a•bound′ing•ly,** *adv.*

a•bout (ə bout′), *prep.* **1.** of; concerning; in regard to: *instructions about the work; a book about the Civil War.* **2.** connected or associated with: *There was an air of mystery about him.* **3.** near; close to: *a man about my height; about six o'clock.* **4.** in or somewhere near: *He is about the house.* **5.** on every side of; around: *the railing about the excavation.* **6.** on or near (one's person): *They lost all they had about them.* **7.** so as to be of use to: *Keep your wits about you.* **8.** on the verge or point of (usually fol. by an infinitive): *about to leave.* **9.** here or there; in or on: *to wander about the old castle.* **10.** concerned with; engaged in doing: *Tell me what it's about. Bring me the other book while you're about it.* —*adv.* **11.** near in time, number, degree, etc.; approximately: *It's about five miles from here.* **12.** nearly; almost: *Dinner is about ready.* **13.** nearby; not far off: *He is somewhere about.* **14.** on every side; in every direction; around: *Look about and see if you can find it.* **15.** halfway around; in the opposite direction: *to turn a car about.* **16.** from one place to another; in this place or that: *to move furniture about; important papers strewn about.* **17.** in rotation or succession; alternately: *Turn about is fair play.* **18.** in circumference: *a wheel two inches about.* **19.** *Naut.* **a.** onto a new tack. **b.** onto a new course. —*adj.* **20.** moving around; astir: *He was up and about while the rest of us still slept.* **21.** in existence; current; prevalent: *Chicken pox is about.* [bef. 900; ME *aboute(n),* OE *abūtan, onbūtan* on the outside of (*a-* A-[1] + *būtan* outside (see BUT[1], BUT[2]), equiv. to *b(e)* BY + *ūtan*), c. Goth *utana,* ON, OS *ūtan,* OFris *ūta,* OHG *ūzan(a)* outside; see OUT; cf. ABOVE, ABAFT for formation]

about′ face′, (used as a military command to perform an about-face). [1860–65, *Amer.*]

a•bout-face (*n.* ə bout′fās′, ə bout′fās′; *v.* ə bout′fās′), *n., v.,* **-faced, -fac•ing.** —*n.* **1.** *Mil.* a turn of 180° from the position of attention. **2.** a complete, sudden change in position, direction, principle, attitude, etc.: *They've done an about-face in their foreign policy.* —*v.i.* **3.** to execute an about face. **4.** to turn in the opposite direction. **5.** to switch to an opposite opinion. [1860–65, *Amer.*]

about′ ship′, (as a command) put the ship about. [1865–70]

a•bout-ship (ə bout′ship′), *v.i.,* **-shipped, -ship•ping.** *Naut.* to tack. [1680–90]

a•bove (ə buv′), *adv.* **1.** in, at, or to a higher place. **2.** overhead, upstairs, or in the sky: *My brother lives in the apartment above. A flock of birds circled above.* **3.** higher in rank, authority, or power: *She was told to speak to the person above.* **4.** higher in quantity or number: *books with 100 pages and above.* **5.** before or earlier, esp. in a book or other piece of writing; foregoing: *the remark quoted above.* Cf. **below** (def. 6). **6.** in or to heaven: *gone to her eternal rest above.* **7.** *Zool.* on the upper or dorsal side. **8.** *Theat.* upstage. Cf. **below** (def. 9). **9.** higher than zero on the temperature scale: *The temperature dropped to ten above this morning.* —*prep.* **10.** in or to a higher place than; over: *to fly above the clouds; the floor above ours.* **11.** more in quantity or number than; in excess of: *all girls above 12 years of age; The weight is above a ton.* **12.** superior in rank, authority, or standing to: *A captain is above a lieutenant.* **13.** not subject or liable to; not capable of (some undesirable action, thought, etc.): *above suspicion; to be above bad behavior.* **14.** of too fine a character for: *He is above such trickery.* **15.** rather than; in preference to: *to favor one child above the other.* **16.** beyond, esp. north of: *six miles above Baltimore.* **17.** *Theat.* upstage of. **18. above all,** most important of all; principally: *charity above all.* —*adj.* **19.** said, mentioned, or written above; foregoing: *the above explanation.* —*n.* **20.** something that was said, mentioned, or written above: *to refer to the above.* **21.** the person or persons previously indicated: *The above will all stand trial.* **22.** heaven: *truly a gift from above.* **23.** a higher authority: *an order from above.* [bef. 900; ME *above(n)* (cf. *aboon*), OE *abufan, onbufan* (A-[1], *on* + *bufan* above (c. D *boven*), equiv. to *b(e)* BY + *ufan,* c. OFris *uva,* OS *oban(a),* OHG *obana,* G *oben,* ON *ofan* above; akin to OVER); see UP; cf. ABOUT for formation]
—**Usage.** ABOVE as an adjective (*the above data*) or as a noun (*study the above*) referring to what has been mentioned earlier in a piece of writing has long been standard. A few critics object to these uses in general writing, believing that they are more appropriate in business or technical contexts; they occur, however, in all kinds of edited writing.

a•bove•board (ə buv′bôrd′, -bōrd′), *adv., adj.* in open sight; without tricks, concealment, or disguise: *Their actions are open and aboveboard.* [1610–20; ABOVE + BOARD; so called from the requirement of keeping the hands above the table or board in order to discourage possible cheating at cards]
—**Syn.** honest, straightforward. —**Ant.** devious, underhanded, sneaky.

a•bove•ground (ə buv′ground′), *adj.* **1.** situated on or above the ground. **2.** not secret or hidden; in the open: *the aboveground activities of the country's left-wing faction.* [1875–80; ABOVE + GROUND[1]]

a•bove•men•tioned (ə buv′men′shənd), *adj.* mentioned or written above: *The role was sung by the above-mentioned Mr. Phillips.* [1700–10; ABOVE + MENTION + -ED[2]]

above′ stairs′, *Chiefly Brit.* upstairs. [1750–60]

above′ the line′, *Bridge.* See under **line**[1] (def. 31).

ab o•vo (äb ō′wō; *Eng.* ab ō′vō), *Latin.* from the beginning. [lit., from the egg]

abp., archbishop.

abr., **1.** abridge. **2.** abridged. **3.** abridgment.

ab•ra•ca•dab•ra (ab′rə kə dab′rə), *n.* **1.** a mystical word or expression used in incantations, on amulets, etc., as a magical means of warding off misfortune, harm, or illness. **2.** any charm or incantation using nonsensical or supposedly magical words. **3.** meaningless talk; gibberish; nonsense. [1690–1700; < LL, prob. < LGk, perh. reflecting recitation of the initial letters of the alphabet; cf. ABECEDARY]

a•brad•ant (ə brād′nt), *adj.* **1.** having an abrasive property, effect, or quality; abrading. —*n.* **2.** an abrasive. [1875–80; ABRADE + -ANT]

a•brade (ə brād′), *v.t., v.i.,* **a•brad•ed, a•brad•ing. 1.** to wear off or down by scraping or rubbing. **2.** to scrape off. [1670–80; < L *abrādere,* equiv. to *ab-* AB- + *rādere* to scrape] —**a•brad′a•ble,** *adj.* —**a•brad′er,** *n.*

A•bra•ham (ā′brə ham′, -həm), *n.* **1.** the first of the great Biblical patriarchs, father of Isaac, and traditional founder of the ancient Hebrew nation: considered by Muslims an ancestor of the Arab peoples through his son Ishmael. **2.** a male given name: from a Hebrew word meaning "father of many."

A′braham's bos′om, heaven, considered as the reward of the righteous. Luke 16:22.

A•bram (ā′brəm), *n.* **1.** an earlier name of Abraham. Gen. 17:5. **2.** a male given name: from a Hebrew word meaning "exalted father."

a•bran•chi•ate (ā brang′kē it, -āt′), *adj. Zool.* having no gills. Also, **a•bran•chi•al** (ā brang′kē əl). [1850–55; A-[6] + Gk *bránchi(a)* (neut. pl.) gills + -ATE[1]]

a•bras•er (ə brā′zər), *n.* a machine for testing the abrasion resistance of a material. [*abrase* (< L *abrasus;* see ABRASION) + -ER[1]]

a•bra•sion (ə brā′zhən), *n.* **1.** a scraped spot or area; the result of rubbing or abrading: *abrasions on his leg caused by falling on the gravel.* **2.** the act or process of abrading. [1650–60; < ML *abrāsiōn-* (s. of *abrāsiō*), equiv. to *abrās(us)* scraped off (ptp. of *abrādere;* see ABRADE) + *-iōn-* -ION]
—**Syn. 1.** sore, scrape, lesion. **2.** rubbing, erosion.

a•bra•sive (ə brā′siv, -ziv), *n.* **1.** any material or substance used for grinding, polishing, etc., as emery, pumice, or sandpaper. —*adj.* **2.** tending to abrade; causing abrasion; abrading. **3.** tending to annoy or cause ill will; overly aggressive: *an abrasive personality.* [1870–75; < L *abrās(us)* (see ABRASION) + -IVE] —**a•bra′sive•ly,** *adv.* —**a•bra′sive•ness,** *n.*
—**Syn. 3.** harsh, rough, rasping.

a•brax•as (ə brak′səs), *n.* a word of unknown significance found on charms, esp. amulets, of the late Greco-Roman world and linked with both Gnostic beliefs and magical practices by the early church fathers. [< Gk *abráxas, abrasáx,* of obscure orig.; the combined numerical value of the Gk letters is 365, an important figure in numerology]

a•bra•zo (ä brä′thô, -sô; *Eng.* ə brä′sō), *n., pl.* ***-zos*** (-thôs, -sôs; *Eng.* -sōz). *Spanish.* an embrace, used in greeting someone.

ab•re•act (ab′rē akt′), *v.t. Psychoanal.* to remove by abreaction. [1910–15; AB- + REACT, on the model of G *abreagieren*]

ab•re•ac•tion (ab′rē ak′shən), *n. Psychoanal.* release of emotional tension achieved through recalling a repressed traumatic experience. [1910–15; AB- + REACTION, on the model of G *Abreagierung*] —**ab•re•ac•tive** (ab′rē ak′tiv), *adj.*

a•breast (ə brest′), *adv., adj.* **1.** side by side; beside each other in a line: *They walked two abreast down the street.* **2.** equal to or alongside in progress, attainment, or awareness (usually fol. by *of* or *with*): *to keep abreast of scientific developments; keeping abreast with the times.* [1590–1600; A-[1] + BREAST]

a•bri (ə brē′; *Fr.* A brē′), *n., pl.* **a•bris** (ə brēz′; *Fr.* A brē′). **1.** a shelter, esp. a dugout. **2.** *Archaeol.* a rock shelter formed by the overhang of a cliff and often containing prehistoric occupation deposits. [< F, OF, n. deriv. of *abrier* (now obs. or dial.) to shelter, shield, screen < LL *apricāre* to warm in the sun (hence, to shield from wind, cold, etc.), v. deriv. of L *apricus* sunny, warmed by the sunshine; OF *b* for *v* perh. < OPr *abriar,* or by construal of *a-* as prefix]

a•bridge (ə brij′), *v.t.,* **a•bridged, a•bridg•ing. 1.** to shorten by omissions while retaining the basic contents: *to abridge a reference book.* **2.** to reduce or lessen in duration, scope, authority, etc.; diminish; curtail: *to abridge a visit; to abridge one's freedom.* **3.** to deprive; cut off. [1350–1400; ME *abreggen, abriggen* < MF *abreg(i)er* < LL *abbreviāre* to shorten. See A-[4], ABBREVIATE] —**a•bridg′a•ble, a•bridge′a•ble,** *adj.* —**a•bridg′er,** *n.*
—**Syn. 1.** cut down; epitomize; condense, abstract, digest. See **shorten. 2.** contract, reduce. **3.** divest. —**Ant. 1.** lengthen. **2.** expand.

a•bridg•ment (ə brij′mənt), *n.* **1.** a shortened or condensed form of a book, speech, etc., that still retains the basic contents: *an abridgment of Tolstoy's* War and Peace. **2.** the act or process of abridging. **3.** the state of being abridged. **4.** reduction or curtailment: *abridgment of civil rights.* Also, **a•bridge•ment.** [1400–50; late ME *abreg(g)ement, abrygement* < MF *abregement.* See ABRIDGE, -MENT]
—**Syn. 1.** digest, epitome; compendium, synopsis, abstract, summary, précis, conspectus; syllabus, brief, outline. **2.** reduction, shortening, contraction, compression. —**Ant. 1, 2.** expansion, enlargement.

a•bris•tle (ə bris′əl), *adv., adj.* in a bristling state: *an angry dog with its hairs abristle.* [1915–20; A-[1] + BRISTLE]

a•broach (ə brōch′), *adv., adj.* **1.** opened or tapped so that the contents can flow out; broached: *The cask was set abroach.* **2.** astir; in circulation. [1350–1400; ME *abroche.* See A-[1], BROACH]

a•broad (ə brôd′), *adv.* **1.** in or to a foreign country or countries: *famous at home and abroad.* **2.** in or to another continent: *Shall we go to Mexico or abroad this summer?* **3.** out of doors; from one place to another; about: *No one was abroad in the noonday heat. The owl ventures abroad at night.* **4.** spread around; in circulation: *Rumors of disaster are abroad.* **5.** broadly; widely; far and wide. **6.** wide of the mark; in error. —*n.* **7.** a foreign land or lands: *imports from abroad.* [1225–75; ME *abrod.* See A-[1], BROAD]
—**Syn. 1.** overseas. **3.** out, outside. **4.** everywhere, rife. —**Ant. 1.** at home.

ab•ro•gate (ab′rə gāt′), *v.t.,* **-gat•ed, -gat•ing. 1.** to abolish by formal or official means; annul by an authoritative act; repeal: *to abrogate a law.* **2.** to put aside; put an end to. [1520–30; < L *abrogātus* repealed (ptp. of *abrogāre*). See AB-, ROGATION, -ATE[1]] —**ab•ro•ga•ble** (ab′rə gə bəl), *adj.* —**ab′ro•ga′tion,** *n.* —**ab′ro•ga′tive,** *adj.* —**ab′ro•ga′tor,** *n.*

CONCISE ETYMOLOGY KEY: <, descended or borrowed from; >, whence; b., blend of, blended; c., cognate with; cf., compare; deriv., derivative; equiv., equivalent; imit., imitative; obl., oblique; r., replacing; s., stem; sp., spelling, spelled; resp., respelling, respelled; trans., translation; ?, origin unknown; *, unattested; ‡, probably earlier than. See the full key inside the front cover.

—**Syn. 1.** cancel, revoke, rescind, nullify, void, invalidate. —**Ant. 1.** ratify, establish; preserve.

ab•rupt (ə brupt′), *adj.* **1.** sudden or unexpected: *an abrupt departure.* **2.** curt or brusque in speech, manner, etc.: *an abrupt reply.* **3.** terminating or changing suddenly: *an abrupt turn in a road.* **4.** having many sudden changes from one subject to another; lacking in continuity or smoothness: *an abrupt writing style.* **5.** steep; precipitous: *an abrupt descent.* **6.** *Bot.* truncate (def. 4). [1575–85; < L *abruptus* broken off (ptp. of *abrumpere*), equiv. to *ab-* AB- + *-rup-* break + *-tus* ptp. suffix] —**ab•rupt′ly,** *adv.* —**ab•rupt′ness,** *n.*
—**Syn. 1, 3.** quick, sharp. See **sudden. 2.** short, hurried, hasty, blunt. **4.** discontinuous, broken, uneven. —**Ant. 1, 3.** gradual. **2.** deliberate; patient, courteous.

ab•rup•tion (ə brup′shən), *n.* a sudden breaking off. [1600–10; < L *abruptiōn-* (s. of *abruptiō*). See ABRUPT, -ION]

abrupt′ly pin′nate, *Bot.* paripinnate.

A•bruz•zi (ə bro͞ot′sē; *It.* ä bro͞ot′tsē), *n.* **Duke of the** (*Prince Luigi Amedeo of Savoy-Aosta*), 1873–1933, Italian naval officer, mountain climber, and Arctic explorer.

A•bruz•zi e Mo•li•se (ä bro͞ot′tsē e mô lē′ze), a region in central Italy. 1,552,556; 5881 sq. mi. (15,232 sq. km). *Cap.:* Aquilla.

ABRV, Advanced Ballistic Reentry Vehicle.

ABS, antilock braking system.

ABS, *Chem.* See **ABS resin.**

abs-, var. of **ab-:** *absent; abscond.*

abs., **1.** absent. **2.** absolute. **3.** abstract.

A.B.S., **1.** American Bible Society. **2.** American Bureau of Shipping.

Ab•sa•lom (ab′sə ləm), *n.* **1.** the third and favorite son of David, who rebelled against his father and was slain by Joab. II Sam. 13–18. **2.** a male given name: from a Hebrew word meaning "father of peace."

Ab•sa′ro•ka Range′ (ab sär′ə kə), a range in S Montana and NW Wyoming: part of the Rocky Mountains. Highest peak, 13,140 ft. (4005 m).

Ab•scam (ab′skam′), *n.* the code name for an FBI investigation (1978–80) of bribery, involving members of Congress. [*Ab*(*dul Enterprises Ltd.*) + SCAM, from the name of the business used as a front by the FBI]

ab•scess (ab′ses), *n. Pathol.* a localized collection of pus in the tissues of the body, often accompanied by swelling and inflammation and frequently caused by bacteria. [1535–45; < L *abscessus* a going away, abscess, equiv. to *abscēd-*, var. s. of *abscēdere* to go away, separate off, form an abscess (*abs-* ABS- + *cēdere*; see CEDE) + *-tus* suffix of v. action, with *-dt-* > *-ss-*] —**ab′scessed,** *adj.*

ab•scind (ab sind′), *v.t.* to sever. [1650–60; < L *abscindere*, equiv. to *ab-* AB- + *scindere* to divide, tear]

ab•scise (ab sīz′), *v.i.*, **-scised, -scis•ing.** *Bot.* to separate by abscission, as a leaf from a stem. [1605–15; < L *abscīsus* cut off (ptp. of *abscīdere*), equiv. to *abs-* ABS- + *-cīdere*, comb. form of *caedere* to cut]

ab•scis′ic ac′id (ab sis′ik, -sīz′-), *Biochem.* a growth-regulating plant hormone, $C_{15}H_{20}O_4$, that promotes dormancy and the aging and abscission of leaves. [ABSCIS(SION) + -IC, on the model of the earlier name *abscisin* (see -IN[2]), coined in 1961]

ab•scis•sa (ab sis′ə), *n., pl.* **-scis•sas, -scis•sae** (-sis′ē). *Math.* (in plane Cartesian coordinates) the x-coordinate of a point: its distance from the y-axis measured parallel to the x-axis. Cf. **ordinate.** [1690–1700; fem. of L *abscissus* (ptp. of *abscindere* to ABSCIND)]

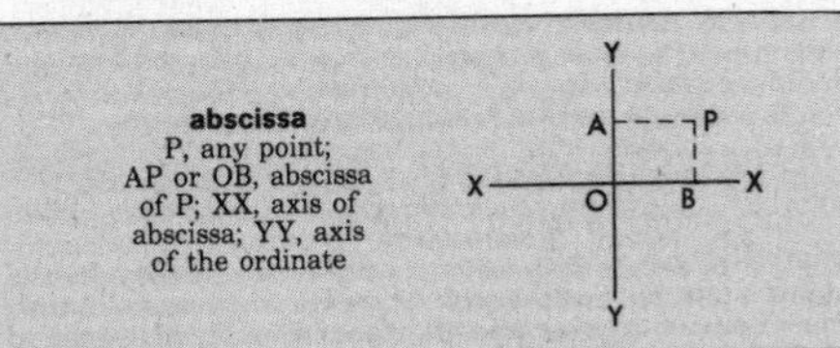

abscissa
P, any point;
AP or OB, abscissa
of P; XX, axis of
abscissa; YY, axis
of the ordinate

ab•scis•sion (ab sizh′ən, -sish′-), *n.* **1.** the act of cutting off; sudden termination. **2.** *Bot.* the normal separation of flowers, fruit, and leaves from plants. [1605–15; < L *abscissiōn-* (s. of *abscissiō*). See ABSCISSA, -ION]

abscis′sion lay′er, *Bot.* the layer of specialized, cutinized parenchyma cells that develops in the abscission zone, the disintegration of which causes abscission. Also called **separation layer.** [1915–20]

abscis′sion zone′, *Bot.* the zone at the base of a leaf petiole, fruit stalk, or branch in which the abscission layer develops.

ab•scond (ab skond′), *v.i.* to depart in a sudden and secret manner, esp. to avoid capture and legal prosecution: *The cashier absconded with the money.* [1605–15; < L *abscondere* to hide or stow away, equiv. to *abs-* ABS- + *condere* to stow (*con-* CON- + *-dere* to put; see DO[1])] —**ab•scond′er,** *n.*
—**Syn.** decamp, bolt.

ab•scond•ee (ab skon dē′, ab′-), *n.* a person who absconds; absconder. [ABSCOND + -EE]

ab•scond•ence (ab skon′dəns), *n.* hiding, esp. to avoid legal proceedings. [1875–80; ABSCOND + -ENCE]

ab•seil (äp′zil), *Mountain Climbing.* —*n.* **1.** a method of descent in which a mountain climber slides down a rope looped over or fastened to an overhead projection. —*v.i.* **2.** to descend by an abseil. [1930–35; < G *abseilen* (*ab-* down + *seilen* to rope)]

ab•sence (ab′səns), *n.* **1.** state of being away or not being present: *I acted as supervisor in his absence. Your absence was noted on the records.* **2.** period of being away: *an absence of several weeks.* **3.** failure to attend or appear when expected. **4.** lack; deficiency: *the absence of proof.* **5.** inattentiveness; preoccupation; absent-mindedness: *absence of mind.* [1350–1400; ME < MF < L *absentia.* See ABSENT, -IA]
—**Ant. 1.** presence.

ab′sence sei′zure, *Pathol.* petit mal.

ab•sent (*adj., prep.* ab′sənt; *v.* ab sent′, ab′sənt), *adj.* **1.** not in a certain place at a given time; away, missing (opposed to *present*): *absent from class.* **2.** lacking; nonexistent: *Revenge is absent from his mind.* **3.** not attentive; preoccupied; absent-minded: *an absent look on his face.* —*v.t.* **4.** to take or keep (oneself) away: *to absent oneself from a meeting.* —*prep.* **5.** in the absence of; without: *Absent some catastrophe, stock-market prices should soon improve.* [1350–1400; ME < L *absent-* (s. of *absēns*, prp. of *abesse* to be away (*ab-* AB- + *-s-* be (see IS) + *-ent-* -ENT))] —**ab•sen•ta•tion** (ab′sən tā′shən), *n.* —**ab•sent′er,** *n.* —**ab′sent•ness,** *n.*
—**Syn. 1.** out, off. —**Ant. 1.** present.

ab•sen•tee (ab′sən tē′), *n.* **1.** a person who is absent, esp. from work or school. **2.** a person who absents himself or herself, as a landowner who does not live on certain property owned or a voter who is permitted to cast a ballot by mail. [1530–40; ABSENT + -EE]

ab′sentee bal′lot, the ballot used for an absentee vote. [1930–35, *Amer.*]

ab•sen•tee•ism (ab′sən tē′iz əm), *n.* **1.** frequent or habitual absence from work, school, etc.: *rising absenteeism in the industry.* **2.** the practice of being an absentee landlord. [1820–30; ABSENTEE + -ISM]

ab′sentee land′lord, a landlord who owns but is not resident in a property.

ab′sentee vote′, a vote cast by a person who, because of absence from usual voting district, illness, or the like, has been permitted to vote by mail. [1930–35, *Amer.*] —**ab′sentee vot′er.**

ab•sen•te re•o (ab sen′te rē′ō), *Law.* in the absence of the defendant. *Abbr.:* abs. re. [< L: lit., the party to the lawsuit (or the defendant) being away]

ab•sent•ly (ab′sənt lē), *adv.* in an absent-minded manner; inattentively. [1870–75; ABSENT + -LY]

ab•sent-mind•ed (ab′sənt mīn′did), *adj.* so lost in thought that one does not realize what one is doing, what is happening, etc.; preoccupied to the extent of being unaware of one's immediate surroundings. Also, **ab′sent•mind′ed.** [1850–55] —**ab′sent-mind′ed•ly,** *adv.* —**ab′sent-mind′ed•ness,** *n.*
—**Syn.** withdrawn, musing, daydreaming, dreamy, forgetful, distracted. ABSENT-MINDED, ABSTRACTED, OBLIVIOUS all mean inattentive to immediate surroundings. ABSENT-MINDED suggests an unintentional wandering of the mind from the present: *an absent-minded committee member.* ABSTRACTED implies that the mind has been drawn away from the immediate present by reflection upon some engrossing subject: *an abstracted air.* OBLIVIOUS implies absorption in some thought that causes one to be completely forgetful of or unaware of one's surroundings: *oblivious of danger.* —**Ant.** attentive, alert, heedful, observant.

ab′sent without′ leave′, *Mil.* See **AWOL.**

ab•sinthe (ab′sinth), *n.* **1.** a green, aromatic liqueur that is 68 percent alcohol, is made with wormwood and other herbs, and has a bitter, licorice flavor: now banned in most Western countries. **2.** wormwood (def. 2). Also, **ab′sinth.** [1605–15; < F < L *absinthium* wormwood < Gk *apsínthion*] —**ab•sin′thi•al, ab•sin′thi•an,** *adj.*

ab•so•lute (ab′sə lo͞ot′, ab′sə lo͞ot′), *adj.* **1.** free from imperfection; complete; perfect: *absolute liberty.* **2.** not mixed or adulterated; pure: *absolute alcohol.* **3.** complete; outright: *an absolute lie; an absolute denial.* **4.** free from restriction or limitation; not limited in any way: *absolute command; absolute freedom.* **5.** unrestrained or unlimited by a constitution, counterbalancing group, etc., in the exercise of governmental power, esp. when arbitrary or despotic: *an absolute monarch.* **6.** viewed independently; not comparative or relative; ultimate; intrinsic: *absolute knowledge.* **7.** positive; certain: *absolute in opinion; absolute evidence.* **8.** *Gram.* **a.** relatively independent syntactically. The construction *It being Sunday* in *It being Sunday, the family went to church* is an absolute construction. **b.** (of a usually transitive verb) used without an object, as the verb *give* in *The charity asked him to give.* **c.** (of an adjective) having its noun understood, not expressed, as *poor* in *The poor are always with us.* **d.** characterizing the phonological form of a word or phrase occurring by itself, not influenced by surrounding forms, as *not* in *is not* (as opposed to *isn't*), or *will* in *they will* (as opposed to *they'll*). Cf. **sandhi. 9.** *Physics.* **a.** independent of arbitrary standards or of particular properties of substances or systems: *absolute humidity.* **b.** pertaining to a system of units, as the centimeter-gram-second system, based on some primary units, esp. units of length, mass, and time. **c.** pertaining to a measurement based on an absolute zero or unit: *absolute temperature.* **10.** *Educ.* noting or pertaining to the scale of a grading system based on an individual's performance considered as representing his or her knowledge of a given subject regardless of the performance of others in a group: *The math department marks on an absolute scale.* Cf. **curve** (def. 10). **11.** *Climatology.* noting or pertaining to the highest or lowest value of a meteorological quantity recorded during a given, usually long, period of time: *absolute maximum temperature.* **12.** *Math.* (of an inequality) indicating that the expression is true for all values of the variable, as $x^2 + 1 > 0$ for all real numbers *x*; unconditional. Cf. **conditional** (def. 6). **13.** *Computers.* machine-specific and requiring no translation (opposed to *symbolic*): *absolute coding; absolute address.* —*n.* **14.** something that is not dependent upon external conditions for existence or for its specific nature, size, etc. (opposed to *relative*). **15. the absolute, a.** something that is free from any restriction or condition. **b.** something that is independent of some or all relations. **c.** something that is perfect or complete. **d.** (in Hegelianism) the world process operating in accordance with the absolute idea. [1350–1400; ME < L *absolūtus* free, unrestricted, unconditioned (ptp. of *absolvere* to ABSOLVE), equiv. to *ab-* AB- + *solū-* loosen + *-tus* ptp. suffix] —**ab′so•lute′ness,** *n.*
—**Syn. 2.** unadulterated, sheer, unqualified, undiluted, uncontaminated. **4.** total, unconditional. ABSOLUTE, UNQUALIFIED, UTTER all mean unmodified. ABSOLUTE implies an unquestionable finality: *an absolute coward.* UNQUALIFIED means without reservations or conditions: *an unqualified success.* UTTER expresses totality or entirety: *an utter failure.* **5.** autocratic, dictatorial, totalitarian. **6.** categorical. **7.** unequivocal, definite, sure. —**Ant. 1.** imperfect, flawed. **2.** mixed, diluted, contaminated. **4.** qualified. **6.** relative.

ab′solute al′cohol, ethyl alcohol containing less than one percent by weight of water.

ab′solute al′titude, *Aeron.* the vertical distance between a flying aircraft, rocket, etc., and the point on the earth's surface directly below it, as measured by an electronic altimeter (**ab′solute altim′eter**). [1930–35]

ab′solute ceil′ing, *Aeron.* ceiling (def. 3b). [‡1915–20]

ab′solute com′plement, *Math.* complement (def. 8).

ab′solute conver′gence, *Math.* **1.** the property of an infinite series in which the series formed by replacing each term in the original series with its absolute value converges. Cf. **conditional convergence. 2.** the property of a sequence of functions in which the series whose terms are the successive differences of the elements of the sequence exhibits absolute convergence. **3.** the property of an improper integral in which the integral formed by replacing the integrand by its absolute value converges. Also called **unconditional convergence.** [1905–10]

ab′solute humid′ity, the mass of water vapor present in a unit volume of moist air. Cf. **dew point, mixing ratio, relative humidity, specific humidity.** [1865–70]

ab′solute imped′iment, *Law.* a fact or circumstance that disqualifies a person from lawful marriage.

ab′solute in′dex of refrac′tion, *Optics.* See under **index of refraction.**

ab•so•lute•ly (ab′sə lo͞ot′lē, ab′sə lo͞ot′-), *adv.* **1.** without exception; completely; wholly; entirely: *You are absolutely right.* **2.** positively; certainly. **3.** (of a transitive verb) without an object. —*interj.* **4.** (used emphatically to express complete agreement or unqualified assent): *Do you think it will work? Absolutely!* [1525–35; ABSOLUTE + -LY]
—**Syn. 1.** totally, unqualifiedly. **2.** unquestionably, unequivocally, definitely.

ab′solute mag′nitude, *Astron.* the magnitude of a star as it would appear to a hypothetical observer at a distance of 10 parsecs or 32.6 light-years. Cf. **apparent magnitude.** [1900–05]

ab′solute major′ity, **1.** a number of votes constituting more than half of the number cast. **2.** a number of voters constituting more than half of the number registered. Cf. **simple majority.**

ab′solute max′imum, *Math.* the largest value a given function assumes on a specified set. Cf. **maximum** (def. 4a).

ab′solute min′imum, *Math.* the smallest value a given function assumes on a specified set. Cf. **minimum** (def. 5a).

ab′solute mon′archy, a monarchy that is not limited or restrained by laws or a constitution.

ab′solute mu′sic, instrumental music, as a concerto or string quartet, that draws no inspiration from or makes no reference to a text, program, visual image, or title and that exists solely in terms of its musical form, structure, and elements. Also called **abstract music.** Cf. **program music.** [1885–90]

ab′solute pitch′, *Music.* **1.** the exact pitch of a tone in terms of vibrations per second. **2.** Also called **perfect pitch.** the ability to sing or recognize the pitch of a tone by ear. Cf. **relative pitch.** [1860–65]

ab′solute space′, *Physics.* space that is not affected by what occupies it or occurs within it and that provides a standard for distinguishing inertial systems from other frames of reference. [1885–90]

ab′solute tem′perature scale′, *Thermodynam.* temperature (**ab′solute tem′perature**) as measured on a scale in which the hypothetical lowest limit of physical temperatures is assigned the value zero (**ab′solute ze′ro**), as the Kelvin scale. Also called **ab′solute scale′.**

ab′solute val′ue, *Math.* **1.** the magnitude of a quantity, irrespective of sign; the distance of a quantity from zero. The absolute value of a number is symbolized by two vertical lines, as $|3|$ or $|-3|$ is 3. **2.** the square root of the sum of the squares of the real and imaginary parts of a given complex number, as $|a + bi|$ is equal to $\sqrt{a^2+b^2}$. Also called **modulus.** [1905–10]

ab′solute viscos′ity, *Physics.* See **coefficient of viscosity.**

ab′solute ze′ro, the temperature of −273.16°C (−459.69°F), the hypothetical point at which all molecular activity ceases.

ab•so•lu•tion (ab′sə lo͞o′shən), *n.* **1.** act of absolving; a freeing from blame or guilt; release from consequences, obligations, or penalties. **2.** state of being absolved. **3.** *Rom. Cath. Theol.* **a.** a remission of sin or of the punishment for sin, made by a priest in the sacrament of penance on the ground of authority received from Christ. **b.** the formula declaring such remission. **4.** *Prot. Theol.* a declaration or assurance of divine forgiveness to penitent believers, made after confession of sins. [1175–1225; ME *absolucion* < L *absolūtiōn-* (s. of *absolūtiō*) acquittal. See ABSOLUTE, -ION]

ab•so•lut•ism (ab′sə lo͞o tiz′əm), *n.* the principle, the system, or the exercise of complete and unrestricted power in government. [1745–55; ABSOLUTE + -ISM] —**ab′so•lut′ist,** *n., adj.* —**ab′so•lu•tis′tic,** *adj.* —**ab′•so•lu•tis′ti•cal•ly,** *adv.*
—**Syn. 1.** totalitarianism.

ab•so•lut•ize (ab′sə lo͞o tīz′), *v.t.,* **-ized, -iz•ing.** to render absolute; consider or declare perfect, complete, or unchangeable: *Overzealous followers absolutized his theories.* Also, *esp. Brit.,* **ab′so•lut•ise′.** [1915–20; ABSOLUTE + -IZE]

ab•sol•u•to•ry (ab sol′yə tôr′ē, -tōr′ē), *adj.* giving absolution. [1630–40; < L *absolūtōrius.* See ABSOLUTE, -TORY[1]]

ab•solve (ab zolv′, -solv′), *v.t.,* **-solved, -solv•ing. 1.** to free from guilt or blame or their consequences: *The court absolved her of guilt in his death.* **2.** to set free or release, as from some duty, obligation, or responsibility (usually fol. by *from*): *to be absolved from one's oath.* **3.** to grant pardon for. **4.** *Eccles.* **a.** to grant or pronounce remission of sins to. **b.** to remit (a sin) by absolution. **c.** to declare (censure, as excommunication) removed. [1525–35; < L *absolvere,* equiv. to *ab-* AB- + *solvere* to loosen; see SOLVE] —**ab•solv′a•ble,** *adj.* —**ab•sol′vent,** *adj., n.* —**ab•solv′er,** *n.*
—**Syn. 1.** exculpate, clear. ABSOLVE, ACQUIT, EXONERATE all mean to free from blame. ABSOLVE is a general word for this idea. To ACQUIT is to release from a specific and usually formal accusation: *The court must acquit the accused if there is not enough evidence of guilt.* To EXONERATE is to consider a person clear of blame or consequences for an act (even when the act is admitted), or to justify the person for having done it: *to be exonerated for a crime committed in self-defense.* **2.** liberate, exempt. **3.** excuse, forgive. —**Ant. 1.** blame.

ab•so•nant (ab′sə nənt), *adj.* dissonant; discordant (usually fol. by *from* or *to*): *behavior that is absonant to nature.* [1555–65; AB- + *-sonant,* as in CONSONANT, DISSONANT]

ab•sorb (ab sôrb′, -zôrb′), *v.t.* **1.** to suck up or drink in (a liquid); soak up: *A sponge absorbs water.* **2.** to swallow up the identity or individuality of; incorporate: *The empire absorbed many small nations.* **3.** to involve the full attention of; to engross or engage wholly: *so absorbed in a book that he did not hear the bell.* **4.** to occupy or fill: *This job absorbs all of my time.* **5.** to take up or receive by chemical or molecular action: *Carbonic acid is formed when water absorbs carbon dioxide.* **6.** to take in without echo, recoil, or reflection: *to absorb sound and light; to absorb shock.* **7.** to take in and utilize: *The market absorbed all the computers we could build. Can your brain absorb all this information?* **8.** to pay for (costs, taxes, etc.): *The company will absorb all the research costs.* **9.** *Archaic.* to swallow up. [1480–90; < L *absorbēre,* equiv. to *ab-*AB- + *sorbēre* to suck in, swallow] —**ab•sorb′a•ble,** *adj.* —**ab•sorb′a•bil′i•ty,** *n.*
—**Syn. 2.** assimilate, consume, devour, engulf; destroy.

ab•sorb•ance (ab sôr′bəns, -zôr′-), *n. Physics.* the capacity of a substance to absorb radiation, expressed as the common logarithm of the reciprocal of the transmittance of the substance. Also, **ab•sorb′an•cy.** [1945–50; ABSORB(ENT) + -ANCE]

ab•sorbed (ab sôrbd′, -zôrbd′), *adj.* deeply interested or involved; preoccupied: *He had an absorbed look on his face.* [1755–65; ABSORB + -ED[2]] —**ab•sorb•ed•ly** (ab sôr′bid lē, -zôr′-), *adv.* —**ab•sorb′ed•ness,** *n.*

absorbed′ dose′, *Physics.* dose (def. 4a).

ab•sor•be•fa•cient (ab sôr′bə fā′shənt, -zôr′-), *adj.* causing absorption. [1870–75; ABSORB + *-e-* (as in LIQUEFY, LIQUEFACTION) + -FACIENT]

ab•sorb•ent (ab sôr′bənt, -zôr′-), *adj.* **1.** capable of absorbing heat, light, moisture, etc.; tending to absorb. —*n.* **2.** something that absorbs: *Tons of high-powered absorbents were needed to clean up the oil spill.* [1710–20; < L *absorbent-* (s. of *absorbēns,* prp. of *absorbēre*). See ABSORB, -ENT] —**ab•sorb′en•cy,** *n.*

absorb′ent cot′ton, cotton for surgical dressings, cosmetic purposes, etc., made absorbent by removing the natural wax. [1885–90, *Amer.*]

ab•sorb•er (ab sôr′bər, -zôr′-), *n.* **1.** a person or thing that absorbs. **2.** See **shock absorber. 3.** *Physics.* a material in a nuclear reactor that absorbs neutrons without reproducing them. [1785–95; ABSORB + -ER[1]]

ab•sorb•ing (ab sôr′bing, -zôr′-), *adj.* extremely interesting; deeply engrossing: *an absorbing drama.* [1745–55; ABSORB + -ING[2]] —**ab•sorb′ing•ly,** *adv.*

absorb′ing well′, a well for draining off surface water and conducting it to absorbent earth underground. Also called **dry well, waste well.**

ab•sorp•tance (ab sôrp′təns, -zôrp′-), *n. Physics, Optics.* the ratio of the amount of radiation absorbed by a surface to the amount of radiation incident upon it. Cf. **reflectance, transmittance** (def. 2). [1930–35; trans. of G *Absorptionsvermögen.* See ABSORPTION, -ANCE]

ab•sorp•ti•om•e•ter (ab sôrp′shē om′i tər, -zôrp′-), *n.* a photoelectric instrument for measuring the concentration of a substance, as a transparent solution, by its absorption of monochromatic light. [1875–80; ABSORPTI(ON) + -O- + -METER] —**ab•sorp•ti•o•met•ric** (ab sôrp′shē ə me′trik, -zôrp′-), *adj.*

ab•sorp•tion (ab sôrp′shən, -zôrp′-), *n.* **1.** the act of absorbing. **2.** the state or process of being absorbed. **3.** assimilation; incorporation: *the absorption of small farms into one big one.* **4.** uptake of substances by a tissue, as of nutrients through the wall of the intestine. **5.** a taking in or reception by molecular or chemical action, as of gases or liquids. **6.** *Physics.* the removal of energy or particles from a beam by the medium through which the beam propagates. **7.** complete attention or preoccupation; deep engrossment: *absorption in one's work.* [1590–1600; < L *absorptiōn-* (s. of *absorptiō*), equiv. to *absorpt(us),* ptp. of *absorbēre* to ABSORB + *-iōn-* -ION]

absorp′tion band′, *Physics.* a dark band in the absorption spectrum of a substance, corresponding to a range of wavelengths for which the substance absorbs more strongly than at adjacent wavelengths. [1865–70]

absorp′tion coeffi′cient, *Physics, Optics.* a measure of the rate of decrease in the intensity of electromagnetic radiation, as light, as it passes through a given substance. [1895–1900]

absorp′tion dynamom′eter, *Elect.* a device for measuring the torque or power of an engine in a process in which the energy supplied to the device by the engine is absorbed.

absorp′tion edge′, *Physics.* a discontinuity in the graph of the absorption coefficient of a substance plotted against the wavelength of x-rays being absorbed, representing the minimum energy necessary to free electrons from particular shells of the atoms of the substance. Also called **absorp′tion discontinu′ity, absorp′tion lim′it.** [1925–29]

absorp′tion hygrom′eter, a hygrometer that uses a hygroscopic chemical to absorb atmospheric moisture.

absorp′tion neb′ula, *Astron.* See **dark nebula.**

absorp′tion spec′trum, *Physics.* the spectrum formed by electromagnetic radiation that has passed through a medium in which radiation of certain frequencies is absorbed. [1875–80]

ab•sorp•tive (ab sôrp′tiv, -zôrp′-), *adj.* able or tending to absorb; absorbent. [1655–65; < L *absorpt-* (s. of *absorptus* absorbed; see ABSORPTION) + -IVE] —**ab•sorp′tive•ly,** *adv.* —**ab•sorp′tive•ness,** *n.*

ab•sorp•tiv•i•ty (ab′sôrp tiv′i tē, -zôrp-), *n. Physics.* the property of a body that determines the fraction of incident radiation absorbed or absorbable by the body. [1860–65; ABSORPTIVE + -ITY]

ab•squat•u•late (ab skwoch′ə lāt′), *v.i.,* **-lat•ed, -lat•ing.** *Slang.* to flee; abscond: *The old prospector absquatulated with our picks and shovel.* [1820–30; pseudo-Latinism, from AB-, SQUAT, and *-ulate,* paralleling Latin-derived words with initial ABS- (e.g., ABSCOND, ABSTENTION) and final *-tulate* (e.g., CONGRATULATE)] —**ab•squat′u•lat′er,** *n.* —**ab•squat′u•la′tion,** *n.*

abs. re., *Law.* See **absente reo.**

ABS resin, *Chem.* a copolymer of acrylonitrile, butadiene, and styrene that is a tough, light, economical, heat- and stain-resistant plastic: used for telephones, boat hulls, and medical equipment. Also called **ABS**

ab•stain (ab stān′), *v.i.* **1.** to hold oneself back voluntarily, esp. from something regarded as improper or unhealthy (usually fol. by *from*): *to abstain from eating meat.* **2.** to refrain from casting one's vote: *a referendum in which two delegates abstained.* [1350–1400; ME *abste(i)nen* < MF *abstenir* << L *abstinēre,* equiv. to *abs-* ABS- + *-tinēre,* comb. form of *tenēre* to hold, keep] —**Syn. 1.** forbear; desist, cease. —**Ant. 1.** indulge.

ab•stain•er (ab stā′nər), *n.* **1.** a person who abstains from something regarded as improper or unhealthy, esp. the drinking of alcoholic beverages. **2.** a person who abstains from anything. [1525–35; ABSTAIN + -ER[1]]

ab•ste•mi•ous (ab stē′mē əs), *adj.* **1.** sparing or moderate in eating and drinking; temperate in diet. **2.** characterized by abstinence: *an abstemious life.* **3.** sparing: *an abstemious diet.* [1615–25; < L *abstēmius,* equiv. to *abs-* ABS- + *tēm-* (base of *tēmētum* intoxicating drink) + *-ius* -IOUS] —**ab•ste′mi•ous•ly,** *adv.* —**ab•ste′mi•ous•ness,** *n.*
—**Syn.** ascetic, abstinent, temperate, nonindulgent.

ab•sten•tion (ab sten′shən), *n.* **1.** an act or instance of abstaining. **2.** withholding of a vote. [1515–25; < LL *abstentiōn-* (s. of *abstentiō*), equiv. to L *abstent(us),* ptp. of *abstinēre* to ABSTAIN + *-iōn-* -ION] —**ab•sten′tious,** *adj.*

ab•sten•tion•ism (ab sten′shə niz′əm), *n.* the refusal of a government to participate in international relations or alliances that it regards as detrimental to its interests. [ABSTENTION + -ISM] —**ab•sten′tion•ist,** *n., adj.*

ab•ster•gent (ab stûr′jənt), *adj.* **1.** cleansing. **2.** purgative. —*n.* **3.** a cleansing agent, as a detergent or soap. [1605–15; < L *abstergent-,* s. of *abstergēns,* prp. of *abstergēre* to wipe off, equiv. to *abs-* ABS- + *tergēre* to wipe; see -ENT]

ab•ster•sive (ab stûr′siv), *adj.* abstergent. [1400–50; late ME (< MF) < ML *abstersivus,* equiv. to L *abstersus* (*us*), ptp. of *abstergēre* (see ABSTERGENT) + *-ivus* -IVE] —**ab•ster′sive•ness,** *n.*

ab•sti•nence (ab′stə nəns), *n.* **1.** forbearance from any indulgence of appetite, esp. from the use of alcoholic beverages: *total abstinence.* **2.** any self-restraint, self-denial, or forbearance. **3.** *Econ.* the conserving of current income in order to build up capital or savings. **4.** the state of being without a drug, as alcohol or heroin, on which one is dependent. Also, **ab′sti•nen•cy.** [1250–1300; ME < L *abstinentia.* See ABSTAIN, -ENCE] —**ab′•sti•nent,** *adj.* —**ab′sti•nent•ly,** *adv.*
—**Syn. 1.** abstemiousness, sobriety, teetotalism.

ab′stinence syn′drome, the withdrawal symptoms that occur after abstinence from a drug, esp. a narcotic, to which one is addicted.

ab′stinence the′ory, *Econ.* the theory that interest is payment for conserving current income.

abstr., 1. abstract. **2.** abstracted.

ab•stract (*adj.* ab strakt′, ab′strakt; *n.* ab′strakt; *v.* ab strakt′ *for 11–14,* ab′strakt *for 15*), *adj.* **1.** thought of apart from concrete realities, specific objects, or actual instances: *an abstract idea.* **2.** expressing a quality or characteristic apart from any specific object or instance, as *justice, poverty,* and *speed.* **3.** theoretical; not applied or practical: *abstract science.* **4.** difficult to understand; abstruse: *abstract speculations.* **5.** *Fine Arts.* **a.** of or pertaining to the formal aspect of art, emphasizing lines, colors, generalized or geometrical forms, etc., esp. with reference to their relationship to one another. **b.** (*often cap.*) pertaining to the nonrepresentational art styles of the 20th century. —*n.* **6.** a summary of a text, scientific article, document, speech, etc.; epitome. **7.** something that concentrates in itself the essential qualities of anything more extensive or more general, or of several things; essence. **8.** an idea or term considered apart from some material basis or object. **9.** an abstract work of art. **10. in the abstract,** without reference to a specific object or instance; in theory: *beauty in the abstract.* —*v.t.* **11.** to draw or take away; remove. **12.** to divert or draw away the attention of. **13.** to steal. **14.** to consider as a general quality or characteristic apart from specific objects or instances: *to abstract the notions of time, space, and matter.* **15.** to make an abstract of; summarize. **16. abstract away from,** to omit from consideration. [1400–50; late ME: withdrawn from worldly interests < L *abstractus* drawn off (ptp. of *abstrahere*). See ABS-, TRACT[1]] —**ab•stract′er,** *n.* —**ab•stract′ly,** *adv.* —**ab′stract•ness,** *n.*

ab′stract al′gebra, the branch of mathematics that deals with the extension of algebraic concepts usually associated with the real number system to other, more general systems.

ab•stract•ed (ab strak′tid), *adj.* lost in thought; deeply engrossed or preoccupied. [1605–15; ABSTRACT + -ED[2]] —**ab•stract′ed•ly,** *adv.* —**ab•stract′ed•ness,** *n.* —**Syn.** See **absent-minded.**

ab′stract expres′sionism, (*sometimes caps.*) a movement in experimental, nonrepresentational painting originating in the U.S. in the 1940's, with sources in earlier movements, and embracing many individual styles marked in common by freedom of technique, a preference for dramatically large canvases, and a desire to give spontaneous expression to the unconscious. [1950–55, *Amer.*] —**ab′stract expres′sionist.**

abstract′ing jour′nal, a periodical consisting mainly or entirely of abstracts of current works. [1955–60]

abstract′ing serv′ice, a service that provides abstracts of publications on a subject or group of related subjects, usually on a subscription basis.

ab•strac•tion (ab strak′shən), *n.* **1.** an abstract or general idea or term. **2.** the act of considering something as a general quality or characteristic, apart from concrete realities, specific objects, or actual instances. **3.** an impractical idea; something visionary and unrealistic. **4.** the act of taking away or separating; withdrawal: *The sensation of cold is due to the abstraction of heat from our bodies.* **5.** secret removal, esp. theft. **6.** absent-mindedness; inattention; mental absorption. **7.** *Fine Arts.* **a.** the abstract qualities or characteristics of a work of art. **b.** a work of art, esp. a nonrepresentational one, stressing formal relationships. [1540–50; < LL *abstractiōn-* (s. of *abstractiō*) separation. See ABSTRACT, -ION] —**ab•strac′tion•al,** *adj.*

ab•strac•tion•ism (ab strak′shə niz′əm), *n. Fine Arts.* the practice and theory of abstract art. [1905–10, for an earlier sense; ABSTRACTION + -ISM]

ab•strac•tion•ist (ab strak′shə nist), *n.* **1.** a person who produces abstract works of art. —*adj.* **2.** showing abstract characteristics in art; tending toward abstractionism. [1835–45, for earlier sense; ABSTRACTION + -IST]

ab•strac•tive (ab strak′tiv), *adj.* **1.** having the power of abstracting. **2.** pertaining to an abstract or summary. [1480–90; < ML *abstractivus.* See ABSTRACT, -IVE] —**ab•strac′tive•ly,** *adv.* —**ab•strac′tive•ness,** *n.*

ab′stract mu′sic. See **absolute music.** [1875–80]

ab′stract noun′, *Gram.* **1.** a noun denoting something immaterial and abstract, as *rest, dread,* or *transportation.* **2.** a noun formed with a suffix that imparts such a meaning, as *kindness.* Cf. **concrete noun.**

ab′stract num′ber, *Math.* a number that does not designate the quantity of any particular kind of thing. Cf. **denominate number.** [1550–60]

ab′stract of ti′tle, *Law.* an outline history of the title to a parcel of real estate, showing the original grant, subsequent conveyances, mortgages, etc. Also called **brief of title.** [1855–60]

ab′stract space′, *Math.* a space whose elements are not geometric points, esp. a function space.

ab•strict (ab strikt′), *v.i.* to undergo abstriction. [1890–95; AB- + L *strictus* bound, drawn tight; see STRICT]

ab•stric•tion (ab strik′shən), *n. Mycol.* a method of spore formation in fungi in which successive portions of the sporophore are cut off through the growth of septa; abjunction. [1640–50; AB- + STRICTION]

ab•struse (ab stro͞os′), *adj.* **1.** hard to understand; recondite; esoteric: *abstruse theories.* **2.** *Obs.* secret; hidden. [1590–1600; < L *abstrūsus* thrust away, concealed (ptp. of *abstrūdere*), equiv. to *abs-* ABS- + *trūd-* thrust + *-tus* ptp. suffix] —**ab•struse′ly,** *adv.* —**ab•struse′ness,** *n.*
—**Syn. 1.** incomprehensible, unfathomable, arcane. —**Ant. 1.** clear, uncomplicated; simple; obvious.

ab•stru•si•ty (ab stro͞o′si tē), *n., pl.* **-ties** for 2. **1.** the quality or state of being abstruse. **2.** an abstruse statement, action, etc. [1625–35; ABSTRUSE + -ITY]

ab•surd (ab sûrd′, -zûrd′), *adj.* **1.** utterly or obviously senseless, illogical, or untrue; contrary to all reason or common sense; laughably foolish or false: *an absurd explanation.* —*n.* **2.** the quality or condition of existing in a meaningless and irrational world. [1550–60; < L *absurdus* out of tune, uncouth, ridiculous. See AB-, SURD] —**ab•surd′ly,** *adv.* —**ab•surd′ness,** *n.*
—**Syn. 1.** irrational, silly, ludicrous, nonsensical. ABSURD, RIDICULOUS, PREPOSTEROUS all mean inconsistent with reason or common sense. ABSURD means utterly opposed to truth or reason: *an absurd claim.* RIDICULOUS implies that something is fit only to be laughed at, per-

haps contemptuously: *a ridiculous suggestion.* PREPOSTEROUS implies an extreme of foolishness: *a preposterous proposal.* —**Ant. 1.** logical, sensible.

ab•surd•ism (ab sûr′diz əm, -zûr′-), *n.* the philosophical and literary doctrine that human beings live in essential isolation in a meaningless and irrational world. [1945–50; ABSURD + -ISM]

ab•surd•ist (ab sûr′dist, -zûr′-), *adj.* **1.** of, pertaining to, or dealing with absurdism or the absurd. —*n.* **2.** an adherent of absurdism, esp. a writer whose work is characterized by absurdist ideas. [1950–55; ABSURD + -IST]

ab•surd•i•ty (ab sûr′di tē, -zûr′-), *n., pl.* **-ties. 1.** the state or quality of being absurd. **2.** something absurd. [1425–75; late ME *absurdite* (< MF) < LL *absurditās.* See ABSURD, -ITY]

abt., about.

A•bu-Bakr (ə bo͞o′bak′ər), *n.* A.D. 573–634, Muhammad's father-in-law and successor: first caliph of Mecca 632–634. Also, **A•bu-Bekr** (ə bo͞o′bek′ər).

a•bub•ble (ə bub′əl), *adj.* **1.** bubbling, as while cooking or boiling. **2.** characterized by intense enthusiasm or activity: *The store was abubble with last-minute shoppers.* [1865–70; A-[1] + BUBBLE]

A•bu Dha•bi (ä′bo͞o dä′bē), **1.** a sheikdom in the N United Arab Emirates, on the S coast of the Persian Gulf. 235,662. **2.** the capital of this sheikdom. 95,000. **3.** the capital of the United Arab Emirates.

A•bu Ha•ni•fa (ä bo͞o′ ha nē′fə), A.D. 699–767, Islamic scholar and founder of one of the schools of Islamic law.

a•build•ing (ə bil′ding), *adj.* in the process of building or being built. [1525–35; A-[1] + BUILD + -ING[2]]

A•bu•ja (ə bo͞o′jə), *n.* the capital of Nigeria, in the central part. 378,671.

A•bu•kir (ä′bo͞o kēr′, ab′o͞o-), *n.* a bay in N Egypt, between Alexandria and the Rosetta mouth of the Nile: French fleet defeated here by British fleet 1798. Also, **Aboukir.**

a•bu•li•a (ə byo͞o′lē ə, ə bo͞o′-), *n. Psychiatry.* a symptom of mental disorder involving impairment or loss of volition. Also, **aboulia.** [1840–50; < NL, prob. not < Gk *aboulíā* thoughtlessness, but freshly formed from A-[6], Gk *boulḗ* will, -IA] —**a•bu′lic,** *adj.*

A•bu•me•ron (ə bo͞o′mə ron′), *n.* Avenzoar.

A•bu•na (ə bo͞o′nə), *n.* (*often l.c.*) the title of the chief bishop of the Ethiopian Church. [< Ar, equiv. to *abū* father + *-nā* our]

a•bun•dance (ə bun′dəns), *n.* **1.** an extremely plentiful or oversufficient quantity or supply: *an abundance of grain.* **2.** overflowing fullness: *abundance of the heart.* **3.** affluence; wealth: *the enjoyment of abundance.* **4.** *Physics, Chem.* the number of atoms of one isotope of an element divided by the total number of atoms in a mixture of the isotopes. [1300–50; ME < MF < L *abundantia.* See ABUNDANT, -ANCE]
—**Syn. 1.** copiousness, plenteousness. See **plenty. 2.** generosity. —**Ant. 1.** scarcity.

a•bun•dant (ə bun′dənt), *adj.* **1.** present in great quantity; more than adequate; oversufficient: *an abundant supply of water.* **2.** well supplied; abounding: *a river abundant in salmon.* **3.** richly supplied: *an abundant land.* [1325–75; ME (< MF) < L *abundant-* (s. of *abundāns*) overflowing. See ABOUND, -ANT] —**a•bun′•dant•ly,** *adv.*
—**Syn. 1.** copious, profuse, overflowing. See **plentiful. 2.** teeming, rich. —**Ant. 1, 2.** sparse, scarce.

abun′dant num′ber, *Math.* a positive number that is less than the sum of all positive integers that are submultiples of it, as 12, which is less than the sum of 1, 2, 3, 4, and 6. Cf. **deficient number, perfect number.**

abun′dant year′. See under **Jewish calendar.**

ab ur•be con•di•ta (äb o͝or′be kōn′di tä′; *Eng.* ab ûr′bē kon′di tə), *Latin.* from the founding of the city (Rome, ab. 753 B.C.). *Abbr.:* A.U.C. [lit., from the city (being) founded]

A•bur•y (ā′bə rē), *n.* Avebury (def. 2).

a•bus•age (ə byo͞o′sij), *n.* improper use of words; unidiomatic or ungrammatical language. [1540–50; ABUSE + -AGE]

a•buse (*v.* ə byo͞oz′; *n.* ə byo͞os′), *v.,* **a•bused, a•bus•ing,** *n.* —*v.t.* **1.** to use wrongly or improperly; misuse: *to abuse one's authority.* **2.** to treat in a harmful, injurious, or offensive way: *to abuse a horse; to abuse one's eyesight.* **3.** to speak insultingly, harshly, and unjustly to or about; revile; malign. **4.** to commit sexual assault upon. **5.** *Obs.* to deceive or mislead. **6. abuse oneself,** to masturbate. —*n.* **7.** wrong or improper use; misuse: *the abuse of privileges.* **8.** harshly or coarsely insulting language: *The officer heaped abuse on his men.* **9.** bad or improper treatment; maltreatment: *The child was subjected to cruel abuse.* **10.** a corrupt or improper practice or custom: *the abuses of a totalitarian regime.* **11.** rape or sexual assault. **12.** *Obs.* deception. [1400–50; (v.) late ME *abusen* < MF *abuser,* v. deriv. of *abus* < L *abūsus* misuse, wasting, equiv. to *abūt(i)* to use up, misuse (*ab-* AB- + *ūti* to USE) + *-tus* suffix of v. action; (n.) late ME *abus* < MF *abus* or L *abūsus*] —**a•bus•a•ble** (ə byo͞o′zə bəl), *adj.* —**a•bus′er,** *n.*
—**Syn. 1.** misapply. **2.** ill-use, maltreat, injure, harm, hurt. **3.** vilify, vituperate, berate, scold; slander, defame, calumniate, traduce. **7.** misapplication. **8.** slander, aspersion. ABUSE, CENSURE, INVECTIVE all mean strongly expressed disapproval. ABUSE implies an outburst of harsh and scathing words against another (often one who is defenseless): *abuse directed against an opponent.* CENSURE implies blame, adverse criticism, or hostile condemnation: *severe censure of acts showing bad judgment.* INVECTIVE applies to strong but formal denunciation in speech or print, often in the public interest: *invective against graft.* —**Ant. 3, 8.** praise.

A•bu Sim•bel (ä′bo͞o sim′bel, -bəl), a former village in S Egypt, on the Nile: site of two temples of Ramses II; now inundated by Lake Nasser, created by the Aswan High Dam. Also, **Abu Sim•bil** (sim′bil). Also called **Ipsambul.**

a•bu•sive (ə byo͞o′siv), *adj.* **1.** using, containing, or characterized by harshly or coarsely insulting language: *an abusive author; abusive remarks.* **2.** treating badly or injuriously; mistreating, esp. physically: *his abusive handling of the horse.* **3.** wrongly used; corrupt: *an abusive exercise of power.* [1575–85; < LL *abūsīvus.* See ABUSE, -IVE] —**a•bu′sive•ly,** *adv.* —**a•bu′sive•ness,** *n.*

a•but (ə but′), *v.,* **a•but•ted, a•but•ting.** —*v.i.* **1.** to be adjacent; touch or join at the edge or border (often fol. by *on, upon,* or *against*): *This piece of land abuts on a street.* —*v.t.* **2.** to be adjacent to; border on; end at. **3.** to support by an abutment. [1425–75; late ME < MF, OF *abuter* touch at one end, v. deriv. of *a but* to (the) end; see A-[5], BUTT[2]]

a•bu•ti•lon (ə byo͞ot′l on′), *n.* any tropical shrub belonging to the genus *Abutilon,* of the mallow family, comprising the flowering maples. [1725–35; < NL < Ar *abūṭīlūn*]

a•but•ment (ə but′mənt), *n.* **1.** *Archit., Civ. Eng.* **a.** a masonry mass supporting and receiving the thrust of part of an arch or vault. **b.** a force that serves to abut an arch or vault. **c.** a mass, as of masonry, receiving the arch, beam, truss, etc., at each end of a bridge. **d.** a mass or structure for resisting the pressure of water on a bridge, pier, or the like. **e.** each of the parts of a canyon or the like receiving the thrusts of an arch dam. **f.** a structure for absorbing tensions from reinforcing strands for concrete being prestressed. **2.** the place where projecting parts meet; junction. **3.** *Dentistry.* a tooth or tooth root that supports or stabilizes a bridge, denture, or other prosthetic appliance. [1635–45; ABUT + -MENT]

A, abutment

a•but•tal (ə but′l), *n.* **1. abuttals, a.** those parts of one piece of land that abut on adjacent lands; boundaries. **b.** Also, **buttals.** *Law.* the boundary lines of a piece of land in relation to adjacent lands. **2.** the act or state of abutting. [1620–30; ABUT + -AL[2]]

a•but•ter (ə but′ər), *n.* a person who owns adjacent land. [1665–75, *Amer.*; ABUT + -ER[1]]

a•buzz (ə buz′), *adj.* **1.** buzzing. **2.** full of or alive with activity, talk, etc.: *The company was abuzz with rumors about the new owner.* [1855–60; A-[1] + BUZZ[1]]

abv., above.

ab•volt (ab vōlt′, ab′vōlt′), *n. Elect.* the centimeter-gram-second unit of electromotive force, equivalent to 10^{-8} volt. [*ab-* (see ABAMPERE) + VOLT[1]]

ab•watt (ab wot′, ab′wot′), *n. Elect.* the centimeter-gram-second unit of electrical power, equivalent to 10^{-7} watt. [*ab-* (see ABAMPERE) + WATT]

Ab•wehr (äp′vâr, äb′-; *Ger.* äp′vār), *n.* the German high-command service for espionage, counterintelligence, and sabotage during World War II. [< G: lit., defense (n. deriv. of *abwehren* to defend, ward off), perh. orig. in a compound such as *Spionageabwehr* counterintelligence]

a•by (ə bī′), *v., pt. and pp.* **a•bought.** —*v.t.* **1.** *Archaic.* to pay the penalty of. —*v.i. Obs.* **2.** to endure; continue. **3.** to undergo suffering as a penalty. Also, **a•bye′.** [bef. 1100; ME *abyen,* OE *ābycgan.* See A-[3], BUY]

A•by•dos (ə bī′dəs), *n.* **1.** an ancient ruined city in central Egypt, near Thebes: temples and necropolis. **2.** an ancient town in NW Asia Minor, at the narrowest part of the Hellespont.

Ab•y•la (ab′ə lə), *n.* ancient name of **Jebel Musa.**

a•bysm (ə biz′əm), *n.* an abyss. [1250–1300; ME *abi(s)me* < MF *abisme* < VL **abyssimus,* a neologistic pseudo-superl. of LL *abyssus* ABYSS]

a•bys•mal (ə biz′məl), *adj.* **1.** of or like an abyss; immeasurably deep or great. **2.** extremely or hopelessly bad or severe: *abysmal ignorance; abysmal poverty.* [1650–60; ABYSM + -AL[1]] —**a•bys′mal•ly,** *adv.*

a•byss (ə bis′), *n.* **1.** a deep, immeasurable space, gulf, or cavity; vast chasm. **2.** anything profound, unfathomable, or infinite: *the abyss of time.* **3.** (in ancient cosmogony) **a.** the primal chaos before Creation. **b.** the infernal regions; hell. **c.** a subterranean ocean. [1350–1400; earlier *abisse,* ME *abissus* < LL *abyssus* < Gk *ábyssos* bottomless, equiv. to *a-* A-[6] + *byssós* bottom of the sea]

Abyss., **1.** Abyssinia. **2.** Abyssinian.

a•byss•al (ə bis′əl), *adj.* **1.** of or like an abyss; immeasurable; unfathomable. **2.** of or pertaining to the biogeographic zone of the ocean bottom between the bathyal and hadal zones: from depths of approximately 13,000 to 21,000 ft. (4000 to 6500 m). [1685–95; < ML *abyssālis.* See ABYSS, -AL[1]]

Ab•ys•sin•i•a (ab′ə sin′ē ə), *n.* **1.** former name of **Ethiopia** (def. 1). **2.** Ethiopia (def. 2). —**Ab′ys•sin′i•an,** *adj., n.*

Abyssin′ian banan′a, a large, treelike Ethiopian plant, *Ensete ventricosum,* of the banana family, having leaves about 15 ft. (4 m) long, whitish flowers with reddish-brown bracts, and dry, inedible fruit.

Abyssin′ian cat′, a breed of domesticated cat originating in Africa, typically having grayish or brownish fur with a reddish undercoat, giving it a brindled appearance. [1875–80]

Abyssin′ian Church′. See **Ethiopian Church.**

Abyssin′ian gold′. See **Talmi gold.** [1885–90]

Abyssin′ian well′, a perforated pipe driven into the ground for pumping out collected ground water; wellpoint.

Ab•zug (ab′zo͝og), *n.* **Bella (Sa•vitz•ky)** (sə vit′skē), born 1920, U.S. politician and women's-rights activist: congresswoman 1971–76.

AC, **1.** *Real Estate.* air conditioning. **2.** *Elect.* alternating current.

Ac, *Chem.* **1.** acetate. **2.** acetyl.

Ac, *Symbol, Chem.* actinium.

ac, *Elect.* alternating current.

ac-, var. of **ad-** before *c* and *qu: accede; acquire.*

-ac, var. of **-ic** after Greek noun stems ending in *i: cardiac; maniac.* [< L *-acus* < Gk *-akos*]

A/C, **1.** *Bookkeeping.* **a.** account. **b.** account current. **2.** *Real Estate.* air conditioning. Also, **a/c**

A.C., **1.** *Real Estate.* air conditioning. **2.** *Elect.* alternating current. **3.** before Christ. [< L *ante Christum*] **4.** Army Corps. **5.** Athletic Club.

a.c., **1.** *Real Estate.* air conditioning. **2.** *Elect.* alternating current. **3.** (in prescriptions) before meals. [< L *ante cibum*]

ACA, **1.** American Camping Association. **2.** American Canoe Association. **3.** American Casting Association.

ACAA, Agricultural Conservation and Adjustment Administration.

a•ca•cia (ə kā′shə), *n.* **1.** a small tree or shrub belonging to the genus *Acacia,* of the mimosa family, having clusters of small yellow flowers. **2.** any of several other plants, as the locust tree. **3.** See **gum arabic.** [1535–45; < L < Gk *akakía* Egyptian thorn]

Aca′cia Av′enue, *Brit. Facetious.* any middle-class suburban street.

acad., **1.** academic. **2.** academy.

ac•a•deme (ak′ə dēm′, ak′ə dēm′), *n.* **1.** the campus activity, life, and interests of a college or university; the academic world. **2.** (*sometimes cap.*) any place of instruction; a school. **3.** (*cap.*) the public grove in Athens in which Plato taught. **4.** a person living in, accustomed to, or preferring the environment of a university. **5.** a scholarly or pedantic person, esp. a teacher or student. [1580–90; < L *Acadēmus* < Gk *Akádēmos* ACADEMUS]

ac•a•de•mese (ak′ə də mēz′, -mēs′, ə kad′ə-), *n.* pedantic, pretentious, and often confusing academic jargon: *a presumably scholarly article written in incomprehensible academese.* [ACADEM(IC) + -ESE]

ac•a•de•mi•a (ak′ə dē′mē ə, -dēm′yə, -dem′ē ə, -dem′yə), *n.* (*sometimes cap.*) the milieu or interests of a university, college, or academy; academe. [1945–50; < NL, L. See ACADEMY]

ac•a•dem•ic (ak′ə dem′ik), *adj.* **1.** of or pertaining to a college, academy, school, or other educational institution, esp. one for higher education: *academic requirements.* **2.** pertaining to areas of study that are not primarily vocational or applied, as the humanities or pure mathematics. **3.** theoretical or hypothetical; not practical, realistic, or directly useful: *an academic question; an academic discussion of a matter already decided.* **4.** learned or scholarly but lacking in worldliness, common sense, or practicality. **5.** conforming to set rules, standards, or traditions; conventional: *academic painting.* **6.** acquired by formal education, esp. at a college or university: *academic preparation for the ministry.* **7.** (*cap.*) of or pertaining to Academe or to the Platonic school of philosophy. —*n.* **8.** a student or teacher at a college or university. **9.** a person who is academic in background, attitudes, methods, etc.: *He was by temperament an academic, concerned with books and the arts.* **10.** (*cap.*) a person who supports or advocates the Platonic school of philosophy. **11. academics,** the scholarly activities of a school or university, as classroom studies or research projects: *more emphasis on academics and less on athletics.* [1580–90; < L *Acadēmicus* < Gk *Akadēmeikós.* See ACADEMY, ACADEME, -IC]
—**Syn. 2.** humanistic, liberal. **4.** theoretical. **5.** See **formal**[1].

ac•a•dem•i•cal (ak′ə dem′i kəl), *adj.* **1.** academic. —*n.* **2. academicals.** See **academic costume.** [1580–90; ACADEMIC + -AL[1]] —**ac′a•dem′i•cal•ly,** *adv.*

ac′adem′ic cos′tume, the ceremonial garb of the students and faculty in schools, colleges, and universities, consisting of a flat cap (mortarboard), a long, wide-sleeved gown, and sometimes a hood, worn esp. at commencement exercises. Also called **ac′adem′ic dress′.**

ac′adem′ic free′dom, **1.** freedom of a teacher to discuss or investigate any controversial social, economic, or political problems without interference or penalty from officials, organized groups, etc. **2.** freedom of a student to explore any field or hold any belief without interference from the teacher. [1900–05, *Amer.*]

ac′adem′ic gown′, a long, wide-sleeved outer garment worn as part of the academic costume.

ac•a•de•mi•cian (ak′ə də mish′ən, ə kad′ə-), *n.* **1.** a member of an association or institution for the advancement of arts, sciences, or letters. **2.** a follower or promoter of the traditional trends in philosophy, art, or literature: *Reforms were instituted over the protests of the academicians.* [1740–50; < F *académicien,* equiv. to *académic-* ACADEMIC + *-ien* -IAN]

ac•a•dem•i•cism (ak′ə dem′ə siz′əm), *n.* **1.** traditionalism or conventionalism in art, literature, etc. **2.** thoughts, opinions, and attitudes that are purely speculative. **3.** pedantic or formal quality. Also, **academism.** [1600–10; ACADEMIC + -ISM]

ac•a•dem•i•cize (ak′ə dem′ə sīz′), *v.t.*, **-cized, -ciz•ing.** academize. Also, *esp. Brit.*, **ac′a•dem′i•cise′.** [ACADEMIC + -IZE]

ac′adem′ic rank′, the rank of a faculty member in a college or university, as professor, associate professor, assistant professor, or instructor. [1875–80]

ac′adem′ic year′, the customary annual period of instruction at a college, university, etc., running approximately from September to June. Also called **school year.** [1930–35]

A•ca•dé•mie Fran•çaise (*Fr.* A KA dā mē FRÄN sez′). See **French Academy.**

A•ca•dé•mie Gon•court (*Fr.* A KA dā mē GÔN-KŌŌR′). See under **Goncourt** (def. 2).

a•cad•e•mism (ə kad′ə miz′əm), *n.* **1.** academicism. **2.** *Philos.* the philosophy of the school founded by Plato. [1720–30; ACADEME + -ISM]

a•cad•e•mize (ə kad′ə mīz′), *v.t.*, **-mized, -miz•ing.** to reduce (a subject) to a rigid set of rules, principles, precepts, etc.: *futile attempts to academize the visual arts.* Also, *esp. Brit.*, **a•cad′e•mise′.** [1865–70; ACADEM(Y) + -IZE]

Ac•a•de•mus (ak′ə dē′məs), *n.* an Arcadian whose estate became a meeting place for Athenian philosophers.

a•cad•e•my (ə kad′ə mē), *n., pl.* **-mies. 1.** a secondary or high school, esp. a private one. **2.** a school or college for special instruction or training in a subject: *a military academy.* **3.** an association or institution for the advancement of art, literature, or science: *the National Academy of Arts and Letters.* **4.** a group of authorities and leaders in a field of scholarship, art, etc., who are often permitted to dictate standards, prescribe methods, and criticize new ideas. **5. the Academy, a.** the Platonic school of philosophy or its adherents. **b.** academe (def. 3). **c.** See **French Academy. d.** See **Royal Academy.** [1470–80; < L *acadēmia* < Gk *akadḗmeia*, equiv. to *Akádēm(os)* ACADEMUS + *-eia* adj. suffix]

Acad′emy Award′, *Trademark.* an annual award given to a performer, director, technician, etc., of the motion-picture industry for superior achievement in a specific category: judged by the voting members of the Academy of Motion Picture Arts and Sciences and symbolized by the presentation of an Oscar. Cf. **Oscar.** [1940–45, *Amer.*]

A•ca•di•a (ə kā′dē ə), *n.* a former French colony in SE Canada: ceded to Great Britain 1713. French, **A•ca•die** (A KA dē′).

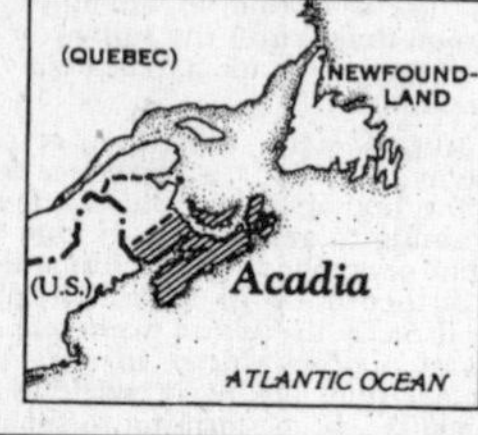

A•ca•di•an (ə kā′dē ən), *adj.* **1.** of or pertaining to Acadia or its inhabitants. —*n.* **2.** a native or inhabitant of Acadia. **3.** Cajun (def. 1). [1695–1705, *Amer.*; ACADI(A) + -AN]

Aca′dia Na′tional Park′, a national park in Maine, on Mount Desert Island. 44 sq. mi. (114 sq. km).

Aca′dian fly′catcher, a small flycatcher, *Empidonax virescens*, of eastern North America, usually having olive-green plumage above with a yellow tinge on the sides and belly. [1930–35]

Aca′dian owl′, (in former systems of nomenclature) the saw-whet owl. [1910–15]

ac•a•jou (ak′ə zhōō′, -jōō′), *n.* **1.** the wood of any of several species of mahogany. **2.** the cashew tree, its nuts, or resin. [1715–25; < F < Pg *acajú*; see CASHEW]

a•cal•cu•li•a (ā′kal kyōō′lē ə), *n. Psychiatry.* inability or loss of the ability to perform arithmetic operations. [< NL, equiv. to *a-* A-[6] + *calcul-* (see CALCULATE) + *-ia* -IA]

ac•a•leph (ak′ə lef′), *n.* (in former classifications) any coelenterate of the group Acalephae, including the sea nettles and jellyfishes. Also, **ac•a•lephe** (ak′ə lēf′). [1700–10; < NL *acalepha* < Gk *akalḗphē* stinging nettle, sea anemone]

AC and U, Association of Colleges and Universities. Also, **AC&U**

ac•an•tha•ceous (ak′ən thā′shəs), *adj.* **1.** having prickly growths. **2.** belonging to the plant family Acanthaceae. Cf. **acanthus family.** [1745–55; < NL *Acanthace(ae)* (see ACANTHUS, -ACEAE) + -OUS]

a•can•thite (ə kan′thīt), *n. Mineral.* the orthorhombic form of silver sulfide. Cf. **argentite.** [ACANTH- + -ITE[1]]

acantho-, a combining form from Greek meaning "spine," used in the formation of compound words: *acanthocephalan.* Also, *esp. before a vowel,* **acanth-.** [< Gk *akantho-*, comb. form of *ákantha* thorn]

a•can•tho•ceph•a•lan (ə kan′thə sef′ə lən), *n.* **1.** any parasitic worm of the phylum or class Acanthocephala, having a proboscis covered with recurved hooks. —*adj.* **2.** belonging or pertaining to the Acanthocephala. [1905–10; < NL *Acanthocephal(a)*, neut. pl. of *acanthocephalus* (see ACANTHO-, -CEPHALOUS) + -AN]

a•can•tho•cyte (ə kan′thə sīt′), *n. Pathol.* an abnormal red blood cell having spiny projections, found in the blood of persons with abetalipoproteinemia and certain malabsorption disorders. [1980–85; ACANTHO- + -CYTE]

a•can•tho•cy•to•sis (ə kan′thō sī tō′sis), *n.* a condition characterized by large numbers of acanthocytes in the blood. [ACANTHOCYTE + -OSIS]

ac•an•tho•di•an (ak′ən thō′dē ən), *n.* any small, spiny-finned, sharklike fish of the extinct order Acanthodii, from the Paleozoic Era. [1850–55; < NL *Acanthodi(i)* pl. of *acanthodius* (equiv. to *Acanthod(es)* a genus (< Gk *akanthṓdēs* prickly, spiny; see ACANTH-, -ODE[1]) + L *-ius*) + -AN]

a•can•thoid (ə kan′thoid), *adj.* spiny; spinous. [ACANTH- + -OID]

ac•an•thol•o•gy (ak′ən thol′ə jē), *n. Biol.* the study of spines, as in sea urchins or certain spiny-headed worms, particularly as they relate to taxonomic classification. [ACANTHO- + -LOGY] —**a•can•tho•log•i•cal** (ə kan′thə loj′i kəl), *adj.* —**ac′an•thol′o•gist,** *n.*

ac•an•thop•ter•yg•i•an (ak′ən thop′tə rij′ē ən), *adj.* **1.** belonging or pertaining to the Acanthopterygii (Acanthopteri), the group of spiny-finned fishes, including the bass and perch. —*n.* **2.** an acanthopterygian fish. [1825–35; < NL *Acanthopterygi(i)* (*acantho-* ACANTHO- + Gk *pterýgi(on)* small wing, fin + L *-ī* masc. pl. ending) + -AN]

a•can•thous (ə kan′thəs), *adj.* spinous. [ACANTH- + -OUS]

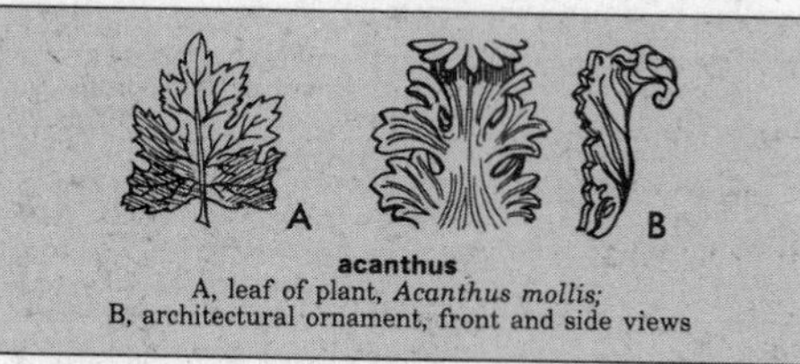

acanthus
A, leaf of plant, *Acanthus mollis;*
B, architectural ornament, front and side views

a•can•thus (ə kan′thəs), *n., pl.* **-thus•es, -thi** (-thī). **1.** any of several plants of the genus *Acanthus*, of the Mediterranean region, having spiny or toothed leaves and showy, white or purplish flowers. Cf. **acanthus family. 2.** an architectural ornament, as in the Corinthian capital, resembling the leaves of this plant. [1610–20; < NL, L < Gk *ákanthos* bear's-foot] —**a•can•thine** (ə kan′thin, -thīn), *adj.*

acan′thus fam′ily, the plant family Acanthaceae, typified by tropical herbaceous plants and shrubs having simple opposite leaves, clusters of tubular bracted flowers, and seeds sometimes dispersed by exploding fruit, including the acanthus, caricature, and shrimp plant.

a•cap•ni•a (ə kap′nē ə, ā kap′-), *n. Med.* a deficiency of carbon dioxide in the blood and tissues. [1905–10; < NL < Gk *ákapn(os)* smokeless (*a-* A-[6] + *kapnós* smoke) + *-ia* -IA; NL sense from the fact that smoke contains carbon dioxide] —**a•cap′ni•al,** *adj.*

a cap•pel•la (ä′ kə pel′ə; *It.* ä′ käp pel′lä), *Music.* **1.** without instrumental accompaniment. **2.** in the style of church or chapel music. [1875–80; < It: in the manner of a chapel (choir)]

a ca•pric•cio (ä′ kə prē′chē ō′; *It.* ä′ kä prēt′chô), *Music.* at whatever tempo or with whatever expression the performer wishes. [< It: according to caprice]

A•ca•pul•co (ak′ə pōōl′kō; *Sp.* ä′kä pōōl′kô), *n.* a seaport and resort in SW Mexico, on the Pacific. 456,700.

A′capul′co gold′, *Slang.* a strong and highly prized variety of marijuana grown in Mexico. [1965–70]

a•car•di•a (ā kär′dē ə), *n. Pathol.* congenital absence of a heart. [A-[6] + -CARDIA] —**a•car•di•ac** (ā kär′dē ak′), *adj.*

ac•a•ri (ak′ə rī′), *n.* pl. of **acarus.**

ac•a•ri•a•sis (ak′ə rī′ə sis), *n., pl.* **-ses** (-sēz′). *Pathol.* **1.** infestation with acarids, esp. mites. **2.** a skin disease caused by such infestation, as scabies. [1820–30; < NL; see ACARUS, -IASIS]

a•car•i•cide (ə kar′ə sīd′, ak′ər ə-), *n.* a substance or preparation for killing acarids. [1875–80; ACAR(US) + -I- + -CIDE] —**a•car′i•cid′al,** *adj.*

ac•a•rid (ak′ə rid), *n.* **1.** an acarine, esp. a mite of the family Acaridae. —*adj.* **2.** of or pertaining to an acarid. [1875–80; ACAR(US) + -ID[2]]

ac•a•rine (ak′ə rīn′, -rēn′, -rin), *n.* **1.** any of numerous arachnids of the order Acarina, comprising the mites and ticks. —*adj.* **2.** belonging or pertaining to the order Acarina. Also, **a•car•i•an** (ə kâr′ē ən). [1820–30; < NL *Acarina* name of the order, equiv. to *Acar(us)* name of the genus (see ACARUS) + *-ina*, neut. pl. of *-inus* -INE[1]]

Ac•ar•na•ni•a (ak′ər nā′nē ə, -nān′yə), *n.* a coastal region of the W central part of ancient Greece: now part of the province of Aetolia and Acarnania in modern Greece. Modern Greek, **Akarnanía.** —**Ac′ar•na′ni•an,** *adj., n.*

ac•a•roid (ak′ə roid′), *adj.* resembling a mite or tick. [1875–80; ACAR(US) + -OID]

ac′aroid res′in, a red or yellow resin obtained from the trunks of several grass trees, esp. *Xanthorrhoea hastilis*, used chiefly in varnishes and lacquers and as a substitute for resin. Also called **accroides gum.**

ac•a•rol•o•gy (ak′ə rol′ə jē), *n.* the branch of zoology dealing with mites and ticks. [ACAR(US) + -O- + -LOGY] —**ac′a•rol′o•gist,** *n.*

ac•a•ro•pho•bi•a (ak′ər ə fō′bē ə), *n. Psychiatry.* a pathological belief that the skin is infested with mites or insects, often leading to self-mutilation in order to eliminate the infestation. [< NL; see ACARUS, -O-, -PHOBIA]

a•car•pel•ous (ā kär′pə ləs), *adj. Bot.* having no carpels. Also, **a•car′pel•lous.** [1875–80; A-[6] + CARPEL + -OUS]

a•car•pous (ā kär′pəs), *adj. Bot.* not producing fruit; sterile; barren. [< Gk *ákarpos.* See A-[6], -CARPOUS]

ac•a•rus (ak′ər əs), *n., pl.* **-a•ri** (-ə rī′). a mite, esp. of the genus *Acarus.* [1650–60; < NL < Gk *ákari* mite]

a•cat•a•lec•tic (ā kat′l ek′tik), *Pros.* —*adj.* **1.** not catalectic; complete. —*n.* **2.** a verse having the complete number of syllables in the last foot. Cf. **catalectic, hypercatalectic.** [1580–90; < LL *acatalēcticus.* See A-[6], CATALECTIC]

a•cat•a•lep•sy (ā kat′l ep′sē), *n. Philos.* an ancient Skeptical view that no more than probable knowledge is available to human beings. [1595–1605; (< ML *acatalēpsia*) < Gk *akatalēpsía*, equiv. to *akatalēpt(eîn)* to not comprehend (v. deriv. of *akatálēptos* incomprehensible, ungraspable; see A-[6], CATALEPSY) + *-ia* -IA] —**a•cat•a•lep•tic** (ā kat′l ep′tik), *n., adj.*

a•cau•dal (ā kôd′l), *adj. Zool.* tailless. Also, **a•cau•date** (ā kô′dāt). [1855–60; A-[6] + CAUDAL]

ac•au•les•cent (ak′ô les′ənt, ā′kô-), *adj. Bot.* not caulescent; stemless; without visible stem. Also, **a•cau•line** (ā kô′lin, -līn), **a•cau•lose** (ā kô′lōs), **a•cau•lous** (ā kô′ləs). [1850–55; A-[6] + CAULESCENT] —**ac′au•les′•cence,** *n.*

a•caus•al (ā kô′zəl), *adj.* having no cause. [A-[6] + CAUSAL] —**a′caus•al′i•ty,** *n.*

acc., 1. accelerate. **2.** acceleration. **3.** accept. **4.** acceptance. **5.** accompanied. **6.** accompaniment. **7.** accordant. **8.** according. **9.** account. **10.** accountant. **11.** accusative.

Ac•cad (ak′ad, ä′käd), *n.* Akkad.

Ac•ca•di•an (ə kā′dē ən, ə kä′-), *n., adj.* Akkadian.

ACCD, American Coalition of Citizens with Disabilities.

ac•cede (ak sēd′), *v.i.*, **-ced•ed, -ced•ing. 1.** to give consent, approval, or adherence; agree; assent; *to accede to a request; to accede to the terms of a contract.* **2.** to attain or assume an office, title, or dignity; succeed (usually fol. by *to*): *to accede to the throne.* **3.** *Internat. Law.* to become a party to an agreement, treaty, or the like, by way of accession. [1400–50; late ME: to approach, adapt to < L *accēdere* to approach, assent, equiv. to *ac-* AC- + *cēdere* to go; see CEDE] —**ac•ced′ence,** *n.* —**ac•ced′er,** *n.*

—**Syn. 1.** See **agree.**

accel., accelerando.

ac•cel•er•an•do (ak sel′ə ran′dō, -rän′-; *It.* ät che′le-RÄN′dô), *adv., adj. Music.* gradually increasing in speed. [1835–45; < It < L *accelerandus*, gerundive of *accelerāre* to speed up. See ACCELERATE]

ac•cel•er•ant (ak sel′ər ənt), *n.* **1.** something that speeds up a process. **2.** *Chem.* accelerator (def. 5). **3.** a substance that accelerates the spread of fire or makes a fire more intense: *Arson was suspected when police found accelerants at the scene of the fire.* [1915–20; < L *accelerant-* (s. of *accelerāns*) hastening (prp. of *accelerāre*). See ACCELERATE]

ac•cel•er•ate (ak sel′ə rāt′), *v.*, **-at•ed, -at•ing.** —*v.t.* **1.** to cause faster or greater activity, development, progress, advancement, etc., in: *to accelerate economic growth.* **2.** to hasten the occurrence of: *to accelerate the fall of a government.* **3.** *Mech.* to change the velocity of (a body) or the rate of (motion); cause to undergo acceleration. **4.** to reduce the time required for (a course of study) by intensifying the work, eliminating detail, etc. —*v.i.* **5.** to move or go faster; increase in speed. **6.** to progress or develop faster. [1515–25; < L *accelerātus* speeded up (ptp. of *accelerāre*), equiv. to *ac-* AC- + *celer* swift + *-ātus* -ATE[1]] —**ac•cel′er•a•ble,** *adj.* —**ac•cel′er•at′ed•ly,** *adv.*

accel′erated read′er, *Educ.* a teaching device into which a page of reading material is inserted and advanced one line at a time, gradually increasing the speed to accelerate and improve one's rate of reading comprehension.

ac•cel•er•a•tion (ak sel′ə rā′shən), *n.* **1.** the act of accelerating; increase of speed or velocity. **2.** a change in velocity. **3.** *Mech.* the time rate of change of velocity with respect to magnitude or direction; the derivative of velocity with respect to time. [1525–35; < L *accelerātiōn-* (s. of *accelerātiō*). See ACCELERATE, -ION]

accelera′tion clause′, a provision of a mortgage, loan, or the like that advances the date of payment under certain circumstances. [1930–35]

accelera′tion coeffi′cient, *Econ.* the ratio of change in capital investment to the change in consumer spending. Also called **accelerator, coefficient of acceleration.** Cf. **acceleration principle.**

ac•cel•er•a•tion•ist (ak sel′ə rā′shə nist), *n. Econ.* a person, esp. an economist, who advocates or promotes the acceleration principle. [ACCELERATION + -IST]

accelera′tion of grav′ity, *Physics.* the acceleration of a falling body in the earth's gravitational field, inversely proportional to the square of the distance from the body to the center of the earth, and varying somewhat with latitude: approximately 32 ft. (9.8 m) per second per second. *Symbol:* g Also called **gravity.** [1885–90]

accelera′tion prin′ciple, *Econ.* the principle that an increase in the demand for a finished product will create a greater demand for capital goods. Also called **accel′erator prin′ciple.** [1940–45]

ac•cel•er•a•tive (ak sel′ə rā′tiv, -ər ə tiv), *adj.* tending to accelerate; increasing the velocity of. Also, **ac•cel•er•a•to•ry** (ak sel′ər ə tôr′ē, -tōr′ē). [1745–55; ACCELERATE + -IVE]

ac•cel•er•a•tor (ak sel′ə rā′tər), *n.* **1.** a person or thing that accelerates. **2.** *Auto.* a device, usually operated by the foot, for controlling the speed of an engine. **3.** *Brit.* any two- or three-wheeled motor vehicle, as a motorcycle or motor scooter. **4.** *Photog.* a chemical,

CONCISE ETYMOLOGY KEY: <, descended or borrowed from; >, whence; b., blend of, blended; c., cognate with; cf., compare; deriv., derivative; equiv., equivalent; imit., imitative; obl., oblique; r., replacing; s., stem; sp., spelling, spelled; resp., respelling, respelled; trans., translation; ?, origin unknown; *, unattested; ‡, probably earlier than. See the full key inside the front cover.

usually an alkali, added to a developer to increase the rate of development. **5.** Also called **accelerant.** *Chem.* any substance that increases the speed of a chemical change, as one that increases the rate of vulcanization of rubber or that hastens the setting of concrete, mortar, plaster, or the like. **6.** *Anat., Physiol.* any muscle, nerve, or activating substance that quickens a movement. **7.** Also called **atom smasher, particle accelerator.** *Physics.* an electrostatic or electromagnetic device, as a cyclotron, that produces high-energy particles and focuses them on a target. **8.** *Econ.* See **acceleration coefficient.** [1605–15; 1930–35 for def. 7; ACCELERATE + -OR[2]]

ac•cel•er•o•gram (ak sel′ər ə gram′), *n.* a graphic record in chart form, produced by an accelerograph in response to seismic ground motions. [1970–75; ACCELER(ATION) + -O- + -GRAM[1]]

ac•cel•er•o•graph (ak sel′ər ə graf′, -gräf′), *n.* an accelerometer containing a pendulum device for measuring and recording ground motions produced by earthquakes. [1905–10; ACCELER(ATION) + -O- + -GRAPH]

ac•cel•er•om•e•ter (ak sel′ə rom′i tər), *n.* an instrument for measuring acceleration, as of aircraft or guided missiles. [1900–05; ACCELER(ATION) + -O- + -METER]

ac•cent (*n.* ak′sent; *v.* ak′sent, ak sent′), *n.* **1.** prominence of a syllable in terms of differential loudness, or of pitch, or length, or of a combination of these. **2.** degree of prominence of a syllable within a word and sometimes of a word within a phrase: *primary accent; secondary accent.* **3.** a mark indicating stress (as (′, ′), or (ˈ, ˌ), or (′, ″), vowel quality (as French grave ˋ, acute ˊ, circumflex ˆ), form (as French *la* "the" versus *là* "there"), or pitch. **4.** any similar mark. **5.** *Pros.* **a.** regularly recurring stress. **b.** a mark indicating stress or some other distinction in pronunciation or value. **6.** a musical tone or pattern of pitch inherent in a particular language either as a feature essential to the identification of a vowel or a syllable or to the general acoustic character of the language. Cf. **tone** (def. 7). **7.** Often, **accents. a.** the unique speech patterns, inflections, choice of words, etc., that identify a particular individual: *We recognized his accents immediately. She corrected me in her usual mild accents.* **b.** the distinctive style or tone characteristic of an author, composer, etc.: *the unmistakably Brahmsian accents of the sonata; She recognized the familiar accents of Robert Frost in the poem.* **8.** a mode of pronunciation, as pitch or tone, emphasis pattern, or intonation, characteristic of or peculiar to the speech of a particular person, group, or locality: *French accent; Southern accent.* Cf. **tone** (def. 5). **9.** such a mode of pronunciation recognized as being of foreign origin: *He still speaks with an accent.* **10.** *Music.* **a.** a stress or emphasis given to certain notes. **b.** a mark noting this. **c.** stress or emphasis regularly recurring as a feature of rhythm. **11.** *Math.* **a.** a symbol used to distinguish similar quantities that differ in value, as in *b′, b″, b‴* (called *b prime, b second* or *b double prime, b third* or *b triple prime,* respectively). **b.** a symbol used to indicate a particular unit of measure, as feet (′) or inches (″), minutes (′) or seconds (″). **c.** a symbol used to indicate the order of a derivative of a function in calculus, as *f′* (called *f prime*) is the first derivative of a function *f.* **12.** words or tones expressive of some emotion. **13. accents,** words; language; speech: *He spoke in accents bold.* **14.** distinctive character or tone: *an accent of whining complaint.* **15.** special attention, stress, or emphasis: *an accent on accuracy.* **16.** a detail that is emphasized by contrasting with its surroundings: *a room decorated in navy blue with two red vases as accents.* **17.** a distinctive but subordinate pattern, motif, color, flavor, or the like: *The salad dressing had an accent of garlic.* —*v.t.* **18.** to pronounce with prominence (a syllable within a word or a word within a phrase): *to accent the first syllable of "into"; to accent the first word of "White House."* **19.** to mark with a written accent or accents. **20.** to give emphasis or prominence to; accentuate. [1520–30; < L *accentus* speaking tone, equiv. to *ac-* AC- + *-centus,* comb. form of *cantus* song (see CANTO); trans. of Gk *prosōidía* PROSODY] —**ac′cent•less,** *adj.* —**ac•cen•tu•a•ble** (ak sen′cho͞o ə bəl), *adj.*

ac′cent mark′, a mark used to indicate an accent, stress, etc., as for pronunciation or in musical notation. Cf. **diacritic** (def. 1). [1885–90]

ac•cen•tor (ak sen′tər, ak′sen-), *n.* any oscine bird of the family Prunellidae, of Europe and Asia, resembling sparrows but having more finely pointed bills, as the hedge sparrow. [1815–25; < NL: a genus of such birds, LL: one who sings with another, equiv. to L *ac-* AC- + *-centor,* comb. form of *cantor* singer; see CANTOR]

ac•cen•tu•al (ak sen′cho͞o əl), *adj.* **1.** of or pertaining to accent or stress. **2.** *Pros.* of or pertaining to poetry based on the number of stresses, as distinguished from poetry depending on the number of syllables or quantities. [1600–10; < L *accentu(s)* (see ACCENT) + -AL[1]] —**ac•cen′tu•al′i•ty,** *n.* —**ac•cen′tu•al•ly,** *adv.*

ac•cen•tu•ate (ak sen′cho͞o āt′), *v.t.,* **-at•ed, -at•ing. 1.** to give emphasis or prominence to. **2.** to mark or pronounce with an accent. [1725–35; < ML *accentuātus* intoned (ptp. of *accentuāre*). See ACCENT, -ATE[1]]

ac•cen•tu•a•tion (ak sen′cho͞o ā′shən), *n.* **1.** an act or instance of accentuating. **2.** something that is accentuated. [1820–30; < ML *accentuātiōn-* (s. of *accentuātiō*) intoning. See ACCENTUATE, -ION]

ac•cen•tu•a•tor (ak sen′cho͞o ā′tər), *n.* **1.** *Electronics.* a circuit or network inserted to provide less loss or greater gain to certain frequencies in an audio spectrum, as a preemphasis spectrum. **2.** a person or thing that accentuates. [1875–80; ACCENTUATE + -OR[2]]

ac•cept (ak sept′), *v.t.* **1.** to take or receive (something offered); receive with approval or favor: *to accept a present; to accept a proposal.* **2.** to agree or consent to; accede to: *to accept a treaty; to accept an apology.* **3.** to respond or answer affirmatively to: *to accept an invitation.* **4.** to undertake the responsibility, duties, honors, etc., of: *to accept the office of president.* **5.** to receive or admit formally, as to a college or club. **6.** to accommodate or reconcile oneself to: *to accept the situation.* **7.** to regard as true or sound; believe: *to accept a claim; to accept Catholicism.* **8.** to regard as normal, suitable, or usual. **9.** to receive as to meaning; understand. **10.** *Com.* to acknowledge, by signature, as calling for payment, and thus to agree to pay, as a draft. **11.** (in a deliberative body) to receive as an adequate performance of the duty with which an officer or a committee has been charged; receive for further action: *The report of the committee was accepted.* **12.** to receive or contain (something attached, inserted, etc.): *This socket won't accept a three-pronged plug.* **13.** to receive (a transplanted organ or tissue) without adverse reaction. Cf. **reject** (def. 7). —*v.i.* **14.** to accept an invitation, gift, position, etc. (sometimes fol. by *of*). [1350–1400; ME *accepten* < MF *accepter* < L *acceptare,* equiv. to *ac-* AC- + *-cep-* take, comb. form of *cap-* + *-t-* freq. suffix]
—**Syn. 2.** concede. **7.** acknowledge. —**Ant. 1.** reject.
—**Usage.** ACCEPT and EXCEPT are sometimes confused as verbs because of their similar pronunciations, esp. in rapid speech. ACCEPT means "to take or receive" (*I accept this trophy*), while EXCEPT means "to exclude" (*Certain types of damage are excepted from coverage in this insurance policy*).

ac•cept•a•ble (ak sep′tə bəl), *adj.* **1.** capable or worthy of being accepted. **2.** pleasing to the receiver; satisfactory; agreeable; welcome. **3.** meeting only minimum requirements; barely adequate: *an acceptable performance.* **4.** capable of being endured; tolerable; bearable: *acceptable levels of radiation.* [1350–1400; ME < LL *acceptābilis.* See ACCEPT, -ABLE] —**ac•cept′a•bil′i•ty, ac•cept′a•ble•ness,** *n.* —**ac•cept′a•bly,** *adv.*

ac•cept•ance (ak sep′təns), *n.* **1.** the act of taking or receiving something offered. **2.** favorable reception; approval; favor. **3.** the act of assenting or believing: *acceptance of a theory.* **4.** the fact or state of being accepted or acceptable. **5.** acceptation (def. 1). **6.** *Com.* **a.** an engagement to pay an order, draft, or bill of exchange when it becomes due, as by the person on whom it is drawn. **b.** an order, draft, etc., that a person or bank has accepted as calling for payment and has thus promised to pay. [1565–75; ACCEPT + -ANCE]

accept′ance race′, *Brit.* See **allowance race.**

accept′ance re′gion, *Statistics.* the set of values of a test statistic for which the null hypothesis is accepted. Cf. **rejection region.**

ac•cept•an•cy (ak sep′tən sē), *n., pl.* **-cies. 1.** the act of accepting; acceptance. **2.** a willingness to accept or receive; receptiveness. [1855–60; ACCEPT + -ANCY]

ac•cept•ant (ak sep′tənt), *adj.* willingly or readily accepting or receiving; receptive. [1590–1600; ACCEPT + -ANT]

ac•cep•ta•tion (ak′sep tā′shən), *n.* **1.** the usual or accepted meaning of a word, phrase, etc. **2.** favorable regard; approval. **3.** belief; acceptance as true or valid. [1400–50; late ME < MF. See ACCEPT, -ATION]

ac•cept•ed (ak sep′tid), *adj.* generally approved; usually regarded as normal, right, etc.: *an accepted pronunciation of a word; an accepted theory.* [1485–95; ACCEPT + -ED[2]] —**ac•cept′ed•ly,** *adv.*

accept′ed ma′sons, *Hist.* See under **Freemason** (def. 2b).

accept′ed pair′ing, a technique of advertising in which two or more competing products are compared in such a manner that certain good qualities are conceded but one product is made to appear clearly more beneficial or desirable than its competitors. [1975–80]

ac•cept•ee (ak′sep tē′), *n.* a person who is accepted, as for military service. [ACCEPT + -EE]

ac•cept•er (ak sep′tər), *n.* a person or thing that accepts. [1575–85; ACCEPT + -ER[1]]

ac•cept•ing (ak sep′ting), *adj.* amenable; open: *She was always more accepting of coaching suggestions than her teammates.* [1570–80; ACCEPT + -ING[2]] —**ac•cept′•ing•ly,** *adv.* —**ac•cept′ing•ness,** *n.*

ac•cep•tive (ak sep′tiv), *adj.* **1.** inclined to receive or accept; receptive: *She was seldom acceptive of my suggestions.* **2.** reasonably satisfactory; acceptable: *an acceptive mode of transportation.* [1590–1600; ACCEPT + -IVE, on the model of RECEPTIVE]

ac•cep•tor (ak sep′tər), *n.* **1.** accepter. **2.** *Finance.* a person who accepts a draft or bill of exchange, esp. the drawee who signs the draft or bill, confirming a willingness to pay it when due. **3.** Also called **accep′tor at′om, accep′tor impu′rity.** *Physics.* an atom of impurity in a semiconducting crystal such that the atom can capture an electron, creating a hole in a filled electron shell and thereby changing the electric conductivity of the crystal. **4.** *Chem.* an atom, ion, group of atoms, or compound that combines with, or accepts, another entity, thereby profoundly affecting physical and chemical properties: *electron acceptor; water acceptor.* [1350–1400; ME, in phrase *acceptour of persones;* ACCEPT + -OR[2], or (< AF *acceptour*) < L *acceptor,* equiv. to *accep-,* var. s. of *accipere* to receive, get (see ACCEPT) + *-tor* -TOR]

ac•cess (ak′ses), *n.* **1.** the ability, right, or permission to approach, enter, speak with, or use; admittance: *They have access to the files.* **2.** the state or quality of being approachable: *The house was difficult of access.* **3.** a way or means of approach: *The only access to the house was a rough dirt road.* **4.** *Theol.* approach to God through Jesus Christ. **5.** an attack or onset, as of a disease. **6.** a sudden and strong emotional outburst. **7.** accession. **8.** See **public-access television.** —*v.t.* **9.** to make contact with or gain access to; be able to reach, approach, enter, etc.: *Bank customers can access their checking accounts instantly through the new electronic system.* **10.** *Computers.* to locate (data) for transfer from one part of a computer system to another, generally between an external storage device and main storage. —*adj.* **11.** *Television.* (of programming, time, etc.) available to the public: *Six channels now offer access services.* [1275–1325; ME *accesse* (< OF *acces*) < L *accessus* an approach, equiv. to *acced-,* var. s. of *accēdere* to ACCEDE + *-tus* suffix of v. action]

ac•ces•sa•ry (ak ses′ə rē), *n., pl.* **-ries,** *adj. Chiefly Law.* accessory (defs. 3, 6). —**ac•ces′sa•ri•ly,** *adv.* —**ac•ces′sa•ri•ness,** *n.*

ac′cess charge′, a fee charged to long-distance telephone companies and their customers by a local telephone company for use of its lines.

ac′cess code′, a code, as of numbers or letters, that is entered into a computer, telephone, or telecommunications network so as to access a particular service.

ac•ces•si•ble (ak ses′ə bəl), *adj.* **1.** easy to approach, reach, enter, speak with, or use. **2.** that can be used, entered, reached, etc.: *an accessible road; accessible ruins.* **3.** obtainable; attainable: *accessible evidence.* **4.** open to the influence of (usually fol. by *to*): *accessible to bribery.* [1600–10; < LL *accessibilis.* See ACCESS, -IBLE] —**ac•ces′si•bil′i•ty,** *n.* —**ac•ces′si•bly,** *adv.*

ac•ces•sion (ak sesh′ən), *n.* **1.** the act of coming into the possession of a right, title, office, etc.: *accession to the throne.* **2.** an increase by something added: *an accession of territory.* **3.** something added: *a list of accessions to the college library.* **4.** *Law.* addition to property by growth or improvement. **5.** consent; agreement; approval: *accession to a demand.* **6.** *Internat. Law.* formal acceptance of a treaty, international convention, or other agreement between states. **7.** the act of coming near; approach. **8.** an attack or onset, as of a disease. —*v.t.* **9.** to make a record of (a book, painting, etc.) in the order of acquisition. **10.** to acquire (a book, painting, etc.), esp. for a permanent collection. [1580–90; < L *accessiōn-* (s. of *accessiō*) an approach, addition. See ACCESS, -ION] —**ac•ces′sion•al,** *adj.*

acces′sion num′ber, the individual number or serial designation identifying specifically any of the items, as books or records, acquired by a library, collection, or the like. Cf. **serial number.** [1875–80, *Amer.*]

ac′cess meth′od, *Computers.* a method of accessing data read from or written to an external storage medium, determined by software and the organization of data on the medium.

ac•ces•so•ri•al (ak′sə sôr′ē əl, -sōr′-), *adj.* accessory; supplementary. [1720–30; ACCESSORY + -AL[1]]

ac•ces•so•ri•us (ak′sə sôr′ē əs, -sōr′-), *n., pl.* **-so•ri•i** (-sôr′ē ī′, -sōr′-). *Anat.* any muscle, nerve, gland, etc., that reinforces the action of another. [< NL, ML: ACCESSORY]

ac•ces•so•rize (ak ses′ə rīz′), *v.,* **-rized, -riz•ing.** —*v.t.* **1.** to fit or equip with accessories: *to accessorize a car with special seat covers.* —*v.i.* **2.** to choose or wear accessories: *Well-dressed women accessorize according to the occasion.* **3.** to be suitable for accessories: *Some clothes accessorize more easily than others.* Also, *esp. Brit.,* **ac•ces′so•rise′.** [1935–39, *Amer.*; ACCESSOR(Y) + -IZE] —**ac•ces′so•ri•za′tion,** *n.*

ac•ces•so•ry (ak ses′ə rē), *n., pl.* **-ries,** *adj.* —*n.* **1.** a subordinate or supplementary part, object, or the like, used mainly for convenience, attractiveness, safety, etc., as a spotlight on an automobile or a lens cover on a camera. **2.** an article or set of articles of dress, as gloves, earrings, or a scarf, that adds completeness, convenience, attractiveness, etc., to one's basic outfit. **3.** *Law.* **a.** Also called **acces′sory before′ the fact′.** a person who, though not present during the commission of a felony, is guilty of having aided and abetted another, who committed the felony. **b.** Also called **acces′sory af′ter the fact′.** a person who knowingly conceals or assists another who has committed a felony. Cf. **principal** (def. 9b). **4.** *Anat.* See **accessory nerve.** —*adj.* **5.** contributing to a general effect; supplementary; subsidiary. **6.** *Law.* giving aid as an accessory. **7.** *Petrog.* noting any mineral whose presence in a rock has no bearing on the classification of the rock, as zircon in granite. [1400–50; late ME *accessorie* (< MF) < ML *accessōrius.* See ACCEDE, -TORY[1]] —**ac•ces′so•ri•ly,** *adv.* —**ac•ces′so•ri•ness,** *n.*
—**Syn. 1.** See **addition. 3.** accomplice.

acces′sory chro′mosome, *Genetics.* See **B chromosome.** [1900–05]

acces′sory fruit′, *Bot.* a fruit, as the apple, strawberry, or pineapple, that contains, in addition to a mature ovary and seeds, a significant amount of other tissue. Also called **false fruit, pseudocarp.** [1895–1900]

acces′sory nerve′, *Anat.* either one of the eleventh pair of cranial nerves, consisting of motor fibers from the spinal cord that innervate the pharyngeal, trapezius, and sternocleidomastoid muscles, and motor fibers from the brain that join the vagus to innervate the thoracic and abdominal viscera. Also called **spinal accessory nerve.** [1835–45]

ac′cess point′, *Library Science.* a code, term, or the like through which an entry in a bibliographic record may be found.

ac′cess road′, a road that provides access to a specific destination, as to a main highway or to a property that lies within another property. [1940–45]

ac′cess time′, *Computers.* **1.** the elapsed time from the instant that information is called from a storage unit to the instant it is received. **2.** the elapsed time from the instant that information is ready for storage to the instant it is stored. Cf. **word time.** [1945–50]

ac•cess•way (ak′ses wā′), *n.* a path, route, etc., that provides access to a specific destination or property, as to a public beach or state park. [1960–65; ACCESS + WAY]

ac•ciac•ca•tu•ra (ə chä′kə to͝or′ə; *It.* ät chäk′kä-to͞o′rä), *n., pl.* **-tu•ras, -tu•re** (-to͝or′ā, -to͝or′ē; *It.* -to͞o′-re). *Music.* a short grace note one half step below, and

CONCISE PRONUNCIATION KEY: act, cāpe, dâre, pärt; set, ēqual; *if,* ice; ox, ōver, ôrder, oil, bo͝ok, bo͞ot, out; up, ûrge; child; sing; shoe; thin, *that;* zh as in *treasure.* ə = *a* as in *alone, e* as in *system, i* as in *easily, o* as in *gallop, u* as in *circus;* ° as in *fire* (fī°r), *hour* (ou°r). l and n can serve as syllabic consonants, as in *cradle* (krād′l), and *button* (but′n). See the full key inside the front cover.

struck at the same time as, a principal note. [1875–80; < It: lit., a pounding, crushing, equiv. to *acciacc(are)* to crush, bruise (based on an echoic root *ciacc-*) + *-atura* (see -ATE[1], -URE)]

ac·ci·dence (ak′si dəns), *n.* **1.** the rudiments or essentials of a subject. **2.** *Gram.* **a.** the study of inflection as a grammatical device. **b.** the inflections so studied. [1500–1510; < L *accidentia,* neut. pl. of *accidēns* (prp. of *accidere* to fall, befall). See ACCIDENT]

ac·ci·dent (ak′si dənt), *n.* **1.** an undesirable or unfortunate happening that occurs unintentionally and usually results in harm, injury, damage, or loss; casualty; mishap: *automobile accidents.* **2.** *Law.* such a happening resulting in injury that is in no way the fault of the injured person for which compensation or indemnity is legally sought. **3.** any event that happens unexpectedly, without a deliberate plan or cause. **4.** chance; fortune; luck: *I was there by accident.* **5.** a fortuitous circumstance, quality, or characteristic: *an accident of birth.* **6.** *Philos.* any entity or event contingent upon the existence of something else. **7.** *Geol.* a surface irregularity, usually on a small scale, the reason for which is not apparent. [1350–1400; ME < L *accident-* (s. of *accidēns* happening, prp. of *accidere* to befall), equiv. to *ac-* AC- + *-cid-,* comb. form of *cad-* fall + *-ent-* -ENT]
—Syn. 1. mischance, misfortune, misadventure; contingency; disaster. **—Ant. 4.** design, intent.

ac·ci·den·tal (ak′si den′tl), *adj.* **1.** happening by chance or accident; not planned; unexpected: *an accidental meeting.* **2.** nonessential; incidental; subsidiary: *accidental benefits.* **3.** *Music.* relating to or indicating sharps, flats, or naturals. *—n.* **4.** a nonessential or subsidiary circumstance, characteristic, or feature. **5.** *Music.* a sign placed before a note indicating a chromatic alteration of its pitch. [1350–1400; ME < ML *accidentālis.* See ACCIDENT, -AL[1]] **—ac′ci·den′tal·ly,** *adv.* **—ac′ci·den′tal·ness, ac′ci·den·tal′i·ty,** *n.*
—Syn. 1. unintentional, unforeseen. ACCIDENTAL, CASUAL, FORTUITOUS all describe something outside the usual course of events. ACCIDENTAL implies occurring unexpectedly or by chance: *an accidental blow.* CASUAL describes a passing event of slight importance: *a casual reference.* FORTUITOUS is applied to events occurring without known cause, often of a fortunate or favorable nature: *a fortuitous shower of meteors.* It often also implies good luck or good fortune: *a fortuitous choice leading to rapid advancement.* **—Ant. 1.** planned, contrived.

acciden′tal death′ ben′efit, a life insurance benefit, usually in the form of a rider or policy addition, under which the proceeds are payable to the beneficiary only if the insured dies by accident. [1970–75]

ac·ci·den·tal·ism (ak′si den′tl iz′əm), *n.* **1.** a system of medicine based on the symptoms of a disease, disregarding its origin or cause. **2.** *Philos.* any theory holding that some events have no causes. [1850–55; ACCIDENTAL + -ISM] **—ac′ci·den′tal·ist,** *n., adj.*

ac′cident boat′, *Naut.* a boat kept suspended outboard so that it can be lowered immediately if someone falls overboard.

ac′cident insur′ance, insurance providing for loss resulting from accidental bodily injury. [1865–70, *Amer.*]

ac·ci·dent-prone (ak′si dənt prōn′), *adj.* tending to have more accidents or mishaps than the average person. [1925–30]

ac′cident tout′, *Brit. Slang.* See **ambulance chaser.**

ac·ci·die (ak′si dē), *n.* acedia. [1200–50; ME < ML *accidia* (alter. of LL *acēdia* ACEDIA); r. ME *accide* < OF]

ac·cip·i·ter (ak sip′i tər), *n.* a hawk of the genus *Accipiter,* having short, rounded wings and a long tail and feeding chiefly on small mammals and birds. [1870–75; < NL, L: hawk]

ac·cip·i·tral (ak sip′i trəl), *adj.* accipitrine. [1835–45; < L *accipitr-* (s. of *accipiter*) ACCIPITER + -AL[1]]

ac·cip·i·trine (ak sip′i trin, -trīn′), *adj.* **1.** of, pertaining to, or belonging to the family Accipitridae, comprising the hawks, Old World vultures, kites, harriers, and eagles. **2.** raptorial; like or related to the birds of prey. [1830–40; < L *accipitr-* (see ACCIPITRAL) + -INE[1]]

Ac·ci·us (ak′shē əs), *n.* **Lucius,** c170–c90 B.C., Roman poet and prose writer. Also, **Attius.**

ac·claim (ə klām′), *v.t.* **1.** to welcome or salute with shouts or sounds of joy and approval; applaud: *to acclaim the conquering heroes.* **2.** to announce or proclaim with enthusiastic approval: *to acclaim the new king.* *—v.i.* **3.** to make acclamation; applaud. *—n.* **4.** acclamation (defs. 1, 2). [1630–40; < L *acclāmāre.* See AC-, CLAIM] **—ac·claim′er,** *n.*

ac·cla·ma·tion (ak′lə mā′shən), *n.* **1.** a loud shout or other demonstration of welcome, goodwill, or approval. **2.** act of acclaiming. **3.** *Liturgy.* a brief responsive chant in antiphonal singing. **4.** *Eccles.* response (def. 3a). **5. by acclamation,** by an oral vote, often unanimous, expressing approval by shouts, hand-clapping, etc., rather than by formal ballot. [1535–45; < L *acclāmātiōn-* (s. of *acclāmātiō*) a shouting, equiv. to *acclāmāt(us)* (ptp. of *acclāmāre;* see ACCLAIM, -ATE[1]) + *-iōn-* -ION] **—ac·clam·a·to·ry** (ə klam′ə tôr′ē, -tōr′ē), *adj.*

ac·cli·mate (ak′lə māt′, ə klī′mit), *v.t., v.i.,* **-mat·ed, -mat·ing.** to accustom or become accustomed to a new climate or environment; adapt. [1785–95; < F *acclimater.* See AC-, CLIMATE] **—ac·cli·mat·a·ble** (ə klī′mi tə bəl), *adj.* **—ac·cli·ma·tion** (ak′lə mā′shən), *n.*

ac·cli·ma·tize (ə klī′mə tīz′), *v.t., v.i.,* **-tized, -tiz·ing.** to acclimate. Also, *esp. Brit.,* **ac·cli′ma·tise′.** [1830–40; ACCLIMATE + -IZE] **—ac·cli′ma·tiz′a·ble,** *adj.* **—ac·cli′ma·ti·za′tion,** *n.*

ac·cliv·i·ty (ə kliv′i tē), *n., pl.* **-ties.** an upward slope, as of ground; an ascent (opposed to *declivity*). [1605–15; < L *acclīvitās,* equiv. to *accliv(is)* steep (*ac-* AC- + *-clīvis,* adj. deriv. of *clīvus* slope) + *-itās* -ITY] **—ac·cliv′i·tous, ac·cli·vous** (ə klī′vəs), *adj.*

ac·co·lade (ak′ə lād′, -läd′; ak′ə lād′, -läd′), *n.* **1.** any award, honor, or laudatory notice: *The play received accolades from the press.* **2.** a light touch on the shoulder with the flat side of the sword or formerly by an embrace, done in the ceremony of conferring knighthood. **3.** the ceremony itself. **4.** *Music.* a brace joining several staves. **5.** *Archit.* **a.** an archivolt or hood molding having more or less the form of an ogee arch. **b.** a decoration having more or less the form of an ogee arch, cut into a lintel or flat arch. [1615–25; < F, deriv. of *a(c)colée* embrace (with *-ade* -ADE[1]), n. use of fem. ptp. of *a(c)coler,* OF v. deriv. of *col* neck (see COLLAR) with *a-* A-[5]] **—ac′co·lad′ed,** *adj.*

ac·co·lat·ed (ak′ə lā′tid), *adj.* (of portraits on a coin, medal, or escutcheon) overlapping and facing in the same direction; conjoined. [1875–80; < F *accol(er)* to embrace (see ACCOLADE) + -ATE[1] + -ED[2]]

ac·com·mo·date (ə kom′ə dāt′), *v.,* **-dat·ed, -dat·ing.** *—v.t.* **1.** to do a kindness or a favor to; oblige; *to accommodate a friend.* **2.** to provide suitably; supply (usually fol. by *with*): *to accommodate a friend with money.* **3.** to lend money to: *Can you accommodate him?* **4.** to provide with a room and sometimes with food. **5.** to furnish with accommodations. **6.** to have or make room for: *Will this elevator accommodate 10 people?* **7.** to make suitable or consistent; adapt: *to accommodate oneself to circumstances.* **8.** to bring into harmony; adjust; reconcile: *to accommodate differences.* *—v.i.* **9.** to become adjusted or adapted. **10.** to become reconciled; agree. [1515–25; < L *accommodātus* adjusted (ptp. of *accommodāre*), equiv. to *ac-* AC- + *commod(us)* fitting, suitable (*com-* COM- + *modus* measure, manner) + *-ātus* -ATE[1]] **—ac·com·mo·da·ble,** (ə kom′ə də bəl), *adj.*
—Syn. 1. serve, aid, assist, help, abet. See **oblige. 6.** See **contain. 7.** fit, suit. **8.** compose, harmonize. **—Ant. 1.** inconvenience.

ac·com·mo·dat·ing (ə kom′ə dā′ting), *adj.* easy to deal with; eager to help or please; obliging. [1610–20; ACCOMMODATE + -ING[2]] **—ac·com′mo·dat′ing·ly,** *adv.*

ac·com·mo·da·tion (ə kom′ə dā′shən), *n.* **1.** the act of accommodating; state or process of being accommodated; adaptation. **2.** adjustment of differences; reconciliation. **3.** *Sociol.* a process of mutual adaptation between persons or groups, usually achieved by eliminating or reducing hostility, as by compromise or arbitration. **4.** anything that supplies a need, want, favor, convenience, etc. **5.** Usually, **accommodations. a.** lodging. **b.** food and lodging. **c.** a seat, berth, or other facilities for a passenger on a train, plane, etc. **6.** readiness to aid or please others; obligingness. **7.** a loan. **8.** *Ophthalm.* the automatic adjustment by which the eye adapts itself to distinct vision at different distances. **9.** See **accommodation bill.** [1595–1605; < L *accommodātiōn-* (s. of *accommodātiō*) adjustment. See ACCOMMODATE, -ION] **—ac·com′mo·da′tion·al,** *adj.*

accommoda′tion bill′, a bill, draft, or note made, drawn, accepted, or endorsed by one person for another without consideration, to enable the second person to obtain credit or raise money. Also called **accommoda′tion pa′per.** [1815–25]

accommoda′tion col′lar, *Slang.* the arrest of a person on little or no evidence merely to fill a public or political demand for police action. [1970–75]

ac·com·mo·da·tion·ist (ə kom′ə dā′shə nist), *n.* **1.** a person who finds it expedient to adapt to the opinions or behavior of the majority of people, esp. as a means of economic or political survival. *—adj.* **2.** of, pertaining to, or characteristic of such a person: *They criticized the senator's conduct as being accommodationist.* [1960–65; ACCOMMODATION + -IST]

accommoda′tion lad′der, a portable flight of steps, usually having a small platform at each end, suspended at the side of a vessel to give access to and from boats alongside. [1760–70]

accommoda′tion line′, insurance that, by itself, would not be acceptable to an insurer but is written in connection with other policies as an accommodation to an agent or broker. [1825–35, *Amer.*]

accommoda′tion train′, *Railroads Now Rare.* a local train. [1830–40, *Amer.*]

ac·com·mo·da·tive (ə kom′ə dā′tiv), *adj.* tending to accommodate; adaptive. [1835–45; ACCOMMODATE + -IVE] **—ac·com′mo·da′tive·ness,** *n.*

ac·com·mo·da·tor (ə kom′ə dā′tər), *n.* **1.** a person or thing that accommodates. **2.** a domestic worker employed on a part-time basis or when needed. [1620–30; ACCOMMODATE + -OR[2]]

ac·com·pa·ni·ment (ə kum′pə ni mənt, ə kump′ni-), *n.* **1.** something incidental or added for ornament, symmetry, etc. **2.** *Music.* a part in a composition designed to serve as background and support for more important parts. [1725–35; ACCOMPANY + -MENT]

ac·com·pa·nist (ə kum′pə nist, ə kump′nist), *n.* *Music.* a person who plays an accompaniment. Also, **accompanyist.** [1825–35; ACCOMPAN(Y) + -IST]

ac·com·pa·ny (ə kum′pə nē), *v.,* **-nied, -ny·ing.** *—v.t.* **1.** to go along or in company with; join in action: *to accompany a friend on a walk.* **2.** to be or exist in association or company with: *Thunder accompanies lightning.* **3.** to put in company with; cause to be or go along; associate (usually fol. by *with*): *He accompanied his speech with gestures.* **4.** *Music.* to play or sing an accompaniment to or for. *—v.i.* **5.** to provide the musical accompaniment. [1425–75; late ME *accompanye* < MF *accompagnier.* See AC-, COMPANY]
—Syn. 1. ACCOMPANY, ATTEND, CONVOY, ESCORT mean to go along with someone (or something). To ACCOMPANY is to go along as an associate on equal terms: *to accompany a friend on a shopping trip.* ATTEND implies going along with, usually to render service or perform duties: *to attend one's employer on a business trip.* To CONVOY is to accompany (esp. ships) with an armed guard for protection: *to convoy a fleet of merchant vessels.* To ESCORT is to accompany in order to protect, guard, honor, or show courtesy: *to escort a visiting dignitary.*

ac·com·pa·ny·ist (ə kum′pə nē ist), *n.* accompanist.

ac·com·plice (ə kom′plis), *n.* a person who knowingly helps another in a crime or wrongdoing, often as a subordinate. [1475–85; *a(c)* of unclear orig. + late ME *complice* < MF < ML *complici-* (s. of *complex*) partner; see COMPLEX]

ac·com·plish (ə kom′plish), *v.t.* **1.** to bring to its goal or conclusion; carry out; perform; finish: *to accomplish one's mission.* **2.** to complete (a distance or period of time): *to have accomplished the age of 70; We accomplished the journey in little more than an hour.* **3.** *Archaic.* to provide polish to; perfect. [1350–1400; ME, earlier *accomplice* < MF *accompliss-,* s. of *acomplir,* equiv. to *a-* AC- + *complir* << L *complēre* to fill; see COMPLETE, -ISH[2]] **—ac·com′plish·a·ble,** *adj.* **—ac·com′plish·er,** *n.*
—Syn. 1. complete, fulfill; execute, effect. See **do**[1].

ac·com·plished (ə kom′plisht), *adj.* **1.** completed; done; effected: *an accomplished fact.* **2.** highly skilled; expert: *an accomplished pianist.* **3.** having all the social graces, manners, and other attainments of polite society. [1350–1400; ME; see ACCOMPLISH, -ED[2]]

ac·com·plish·ment (ə kom′plish mənt), *n.* **1.** an act or instance of carrying into effect; fulfillment: *the accomplishment of our desires.* **2.** something done admirably or creditably: *Space exploration is a major accomplishment of science.* **3.** anything accomplished; deed; achievement: *a career measured in a series of small accomplishments.* **4.** Often, **accomplishments. a.** a grace, skill, or knowledge expected in polite society. **b.** any acquired ability or knowledge. [1425–75; late ME; see ACCOMPLISH, -MENT. Cf. F *accomplissement*]
—Syn. 1. completion, execution. **3.** consummation. **4.** acquisition, proficiency. **—Ant. 1.** failure.

ac·cord (ə kôrd′), *v.i.* **1.** to be in agreement or harmony; agree. *—v.t.* **2.** to make agree or correspond; adapt. **3.** to grant; bestow: *to accord due praise.* **4.** *Archaic.* to settle; reconcile. *—n.* **5.** proper relationship or proportion; harmony. **6.** a harmonious union of sounds, colors, etc. **7.** consent or concurrence of opinions or wills; agreement. **8.** an international agreement; settlement of questions outstanding among nations. **9. of one's own accord,** without being asked or told; voluntarily: *We did the extra work of our own accord.* [1100–50; ME *ac(c)corden,* late OE *acordan* < OF *acorder* < VL **accordāre,* equiv. to L *ac-* AC- + *cord-* heart, mind; see CORDIAL, HEART] **—ac·cord′a·ble,** *adj.* **—ac·cord′er,** *n.*
—Syn. 1. harmonize, concur. See **correspond. 2.** reconcile. **—Ant. 1.** conflict. **3.** withhold, deny; withdraw.

ac·cord·ance (ə kôr′dns), *n.* **1.** agreement; conformity: *in accordance with the rules.* **2.** the act of according or granting: *the accordance of all rights and privileges.* [1275–1325; ME *acordance* < OF. See ACCORD, -ANCE]

ac·cord·ant (ə kôr′dnt), *adj.* agreeing; conforming; harmonious. [1275–1325; ME *acordant* < OF. See ACCORD, -ANT] **—ac·cord′ant·ly,** *adv.*

ac·cor·da·tu·ra (ə kôr′də tŏŏr′ə; *It.* äk kôr′dä tōō′rä), *n., pl.* **-tu·ras, -tu·re** (*It.* -tōō′re). *Music.* the notes to which a stringed instrument is tuned. [< It: lit., a tuning, equiv. to *accordat(o)* (ptp. of *accordare* < VL **accordāre;* see ACCORD) + *-ūra* -URE]

ac·cord·ing (ə kôr′ding), *adj.* agreeing: *according voices raised in censure.* [1350–1400; ME; see ACCORD, -ING[2]]

accord′ing as′, **1.** to the extent that; proportionately as. **2.** depending on whether; if: *I'll stay according as I have the money.* **3.** depending on how. [1475–1500]

ac·cord·ing·ly (ə kôr′ding lē), *adv.* **1.** therefore; so; in due course. **2.** in accordance; correspondingly. [1400–50; ME; see ACCORDING, -LY]
—Syn. 1, 2. consequently, hence, thus. See **therefore.**

accord′ing to′, **1.** in agreement or accord with: *according to his judgment.* **2.** consistent with; in conformity with: *to be paid according to one's experience.* **3.** on the authority of; as stated or reported by: *According to her, they have gone.* **4.** in proportion to: *He'll be charged according to his ability to pay.* **5.** contingent on: *According to the number of winners, the judges will award duplicate prizes.* [1350–1400; ME]

ac·cor·di·on (ə kôr′dē ən), *n. Music.* **1.** Also called **piano accordion.** a portable wind instrument having a large bellows for forcing air through small metal reeds, a keyboard for the right hand, and buttons for sounding single bass notes or chords for the left hand. **2.** a similar instrument having single-note buttons instead of a keyboard. *—adj.* **3.** having a fold or folds like the bellows of an accordion: *accordion roof; accordion panel.* *—v.i.* **4.** (of a door, roof, or other covering) to open by folding back or pressing together in the manner of an accordion: *The roof of the car accordions to let in sunlight and fresh air.* **5.** to fold, crush together, or collapse in the manner of an accordion. *—v.t.* **6.** to demolish by crush-

CONCISE ETYMOLOGY KEY: <, descended or borrowed from; >, whence; b., blend of, blended; c., cognate with; cf., compare; deriv., derivative; equiv., equivalent; imit., imitative; obl., oblique; r., replacing; s., stem; sp., spelling, spelled; resp., respelling, respelled; trans., translation; ?, origin unknown; *, unattested; ‡, probably earlier than. See the full key inside the front cover.

ing together lengthwise: *The impact accordioned the car beneath the truck.* [1831; < G, now sp. *Akkordion, Akkordeon* name under which the instrument was patented in Vienna in 1829; prob. < F *accord(er)* or It *accord(are)* to harmonize (see ACCORD) + F *-ion* -ION, as in G *Orchestrion* ORCHESTRION]

ac•cor•di•on-fold (ə kôr′dē ən fōld′), *v.t.* to fold into pleats resembling the bellows of an accordion: *to make a fan by accordion-folding a sheet of paper.*

ac•cor•di•on•ist (ə kôr′dē ə nist), *n.* a person who plays the accordion, esp. with skill. [ACCORDION + -IST]

accor′dion pleat′, one of a series of narrow, evenly spaced parallel pleats with alternating raised and recessed folds set into cloth or other material, usually by a commercial pleating machine. [1880–85]

ac•cost (ə kôst′, ə kost′), *v.t.* **1.** to confront boldly: *The beggar accosted me for money.* **2.** to approach, esp. with a greeting, question, or remark. **3.** (of prostitutes, procurers, etc.) to solicit for sexual purposes. —*n.* **4.** a greeting. [1570–80; < LL *accostāre* to be or put side by side. See AC-, COAST] —**ac•cost′a•ble,** *adj.*

ac•cost•ed (ə kô′stid, ə kos′tid), *adj. Heraldry.* (of animals) represented as side by side: *two dolphins accosted.* [1600–10; ACCOST + -ED[2]]

ac•couche•ment (ə ko͞osh′mənt; *Fr.* A ko͞osh mäɴ′), *n., pl.* **-ments** (-mənts; *Fr.* -mäɴ′), the confinement of childbirth; lying-in. [1800–10; < F, deriv., with *-ment* -MENT, of *accoucher* to give birth, be delivered, assist in giving birth, OF: to lie down, take to bed, equiv. to *ac-* AC- + *coucher* to put to bed; see COUCH]

ac•cou•cheur (ak′o͞o shûr′; *Fr.* A ko͞o shœʀ′), *n., pl.* **-cheurs** (-shûrz′; *Fr.* -shœʀ′). a person who assists during childbirth, esp. an obstetrician. [1750–60; < F; see ACCOUCHEMENT, -EUR]

ac•count (ə kount′), *n.* **1.** an oral or written description of particular events or situations; narrative: *an account of the meetings; an account of the trip.* **2.** an explanatory statement of conduct, as to a superior. **3.** a statement of reasons, causes, etc., explaining some event. **4.** reason; basis: *On this account I'm refusing your offer.* **5.** importance; worth; value; consequence: *things of no account.* **6.** estimation; judgment: *In his account it was an excellent piece of work.* **7.** an amount of money deposited with a bank, as in a checking or savings account: *My account is now with Third National.* **8.** Also called **charge account.** an accommodation or service extended by a business to a customer or client permitting the charging of goods or services, the returning for credit of unsatisfactory merchandise, etc.: *Do you have an account at this store? My account with the restaurant is past due.* **9.** a statement of financial transactions. **10.** *Bookkeeping.* **a.** a formal record of the debits and credits relating to the person, business, etc., named at the head of the ledger account. **b.** a balance of a specified period's receipts and expenditures. **11.** *Com.* **a.** a business relation in which credit is used. **b.** any customer or client, esp. one carried on a regular credit basis. **c.** Also called **advertising account.** the business assigned to an advertising agency by a client: *The toothpaste account was awarded to a new agency last year.* **12. call to account, a.** to hold accountable; blame; reprimand: *Call them to account for having endangered their lives.* **b.** ask for an explanation of. **13. give a good (bad,** etc.**) account of,** to do something or conduct oneself in a good (bad; etc.) manner: *She gave a good account of herself in the tennis tournament.* **14. hold to account,** to hold responsible; hold accountable or culpable: *If any of the silver is missing, I'm going to hold you to account.* **15. on account,** as an installment or a partial payment: *I can't pay the balance, but here's $10 on account.* **16. on account of, a.** by reason of; because of. **b.** for the sake of: *She saw it through on account of me.* **17. on all accounts,** in any case; under any circumstances. Also, **at all accounts. 18. on no account,** under no circumstances; absolutely not: *On no account should you buy that painting without having it appraised.* **19. take account of, a.** to make allowance for; consider: *One must take account of the difficult circumstances. Taking account of the high overhead, the price is not excessive.* **b.** to notice or observe. Also, **take into account. 20. turn to account,** to derive profit or use from; turn to advantage: *She has turned her misfortunes to account.* —*v.i.* **21.** to give an explanation (usually fol. by *for*): *to account for the accident.* **22.** to answer concerning one's conduct, duties, etc. (usually fol. by *for*): *to account for the missing typewriters.* **23.** to provide a report on money received, kept, and spent. **24.** to cause (usually fol. by *for*): *The humidity accounts for our discomfort. His reckless driving accounted for the accident.* —*v.t.* **25.** to regard; consider as: *I account myself well paid.* **26.** to assign or impute (usually fol. by *to*): *the many virtues accounted to him.* [1225–75; (n.) ME *a(c)count(e), ac(c)ompte* < AF, OF *aco(u)nte, acompte;* (v.) ME *ac(co)unten* < OF *acunter, acompter.* See AC-, COUNT[1]]
—**Syn. 1.** report, chronicle. See **narrative. 2.** justification. **5.** import, significance. **6.** consideration.

ac•count•a•bil•i•ty (ə koun′tə bil′i tē), *n.* **1.** the state of being accountable, liable, or answerable. **2.** *Educ.* a policy of holding schools and teachers accountable for students' academic progress by linking such progress with funding for salaries, maintenance, etc. [1785–95; ACCOUNT(ABLE) + -ABILITY]

ac•count•a•ble (ə koun′tə bəl), *adj.* **1.** subject to the obligation to report, explain, or justify something; responsible; answerable. **2.** capable of being explained; explicable; explainable. [1375–1425; late ME; see ACCOUNT, -ABLE] —**ac•count′a•ble•ness,** *n.* —**ac•count′a•bly,** *adv.*

ac•count•an•cy (ə koun′tn sē), *n.* the art or practice of an accountant. [1850–55; ACCOUNTAN(T) + -CY]

ac•count•ant (ə koun′tnt), *n.* a person whose profession is inspecting and auditing personal or commercial accounts. [1425–75; ACCOUNT + -ANT; r. late ME *accomptant* < MF, OF *acuntant,* prp. of *acunter* to ACCOUNT] —**ac•count′ant•ship′,** *n.*

account′ book′, a book in which personal or commercial accounts are recorded; ledger. [1690–1700]

account′ cur′rent, *pl.* **accounts current. 1.** a personal account providing for periodic settlements; current account. **2.** the periodic statement or transcript of such an account. [1675–85]

account′ exec′utive, (in an advertising agency or other service business) the manager of a client's account. [1940–45]

ac•count•ing (ə koun′ting), *n.* **1.** the theory and system of setting up, maintaining, and auditing the books of a firm; art of analyzing the financial position and operating results of a business house from a study of its sales, purchases, overhead, etc. (distinguished from *bookkeeping*). **2.** a detailed report of the financial state or transactions of a person or entity: *an accounting of the estate.* **3.** the rendering or submission of such a report. [1350–1400; ME; see ACCOUNT, -ING[1]]

account′ing machine′, a machine for performing bookkeeping functions, as arithmetic operations or vertical and horizontal tabulations. [1955–60]

account′ing pe′riod, a regular period of time, as a month or a year, for which an operative statement is drawn up.

account′ pay′able, *pl.* **accounts payable.** a liability to a creditor, carried on open account, usually for purchases of goods and services. [1935–40]

account′ receiv′able, *pl.* **accounts receivable.** a claim against a debtor, carried on open account, usually limited to debts due from the sale of goods and services. [1935–40]

ac•cou•ple•ment (ə kup′əl mənt), *n.* **1.** the act of coupling. **2.** something that couples, esp. a tie or brace in building. [1475–85; *accouple* (< MF *accopler;* see AC-, COUPLE) + *-ment* -MENT]

ac•cou•ter (ə ko͞o′tər), *v.t.* to equip or outfit, esp. with military clothes, equipment, etc. Also, *esp. Brit.,* **accoutre.** [1600–10; earlier *accou(s)tre* < F *accoutrer,* OF *acou(s)trer* to arrange, accommodate, equip, perh. < VL **accō(n)s(ū)tūrāre* to sew together, mend (see AC-, COUTURE), though loss of 2d *-ū-* is unexplained]

ac•cou•ter•ment (ə ko͞o′tər mənt, -trə-), *n.* **1.** personal clothing, accessories, etc. **2.** the equipment, excluding weapons and clothing, of a soldier. Also, *esp. Brit.,* **ac•cou′tre•ment.** [1540–50; < MF *accou(s)trement.* See ACCOUTER, -MENT]

ac•cou•tre (ə ko͞o′tər), *v.t.,* **-tred, -tring.** *Chiefly Brit.* accouter.

ac•cra (ak′rə, ə krä′), *n.* the wood of a sapele. [prob. after ACCRA]

Ac•cra (ak′rə, ə krä′), *n.* a seaport in and the capital of Ghana, on the Gulf of Guinea. 700,000. Also, **Akkra.**

ac•cred•it (ə kred′it), *v.t.* **1.** to ascribe or attribute to (usually fol. by *with*): *He was accredited with having said it.* **2.** to attribute or ascribe; consider as belonging: *an invention accredited to Edison.* **3.** to provide or send with credentials; designate officially: *to accredit an envoy.* **4.** to certify (a school, college, or the like) as meeting all formal official requirements of academic excellence, curriculum, facilities, etc. **5.** to make authoritative, creditable, or reputable; sanction. **6.** to regard as true; believe. [1610–20; earlier *acredit* < MF *acrediter.* See AC-, CREDIT] —**ac•cred′it•a•ble,** *adj.* —**ac•cred′i•ta′tion, ac•cred′it•ment,** *n.*

ac•cred•it•ed (ə kred′i tid), *adj.* **1.** officially recognized as meeting the essential requirements, as of academic excellence: *accredited schools.* **2.** provided with official credentials, as by a government: *an accredited diplomatic representative.* **3.** accepted as authoritative: *an accredited theory.* [1625–35; ACCREDIT + -ED[2]]

ac•cres•cence (ə kres′əns), *n.* continued or continuous growth. [1640–50; < ML *accrēscentia.* See ACCRESCENT, -ENCE]

ac•cres•cent (ə kres′ənt), *adj.* **1.** increasing; enlarging, expanding, or enriching. **2.** growing, as floral parts that increase in size after flowering has occurred. [1745–55; < L *accrēscent-* (s. of *accrēscēns,* prp. of *accrēscere* to grow). See AC-, CRESCENT]

ac•crete (ə krēt′), *v.,* **-cret•ed, -cret•ing,** *adj.* —*v.i.* **1.** to grow together; adhere (usually fol. by *to*). —*v.t.* **2.** to add, as by growth. —*adj.* **3.** *Bot.* grown together. [1775–85; back formation from ACCRETION]

ac•cre•tion (ə krē′shən), *n.* **1.** an increase by natural growth or by gradual external addition; growth in size or extent. **2.** the result of this process. **3.** an added part; addition: *The last part of the legend is a later accretion.* **4.** the growing together of separate parts into a single whole. **5.** *Law.* increase of property by gradual natural additions, as of land by alluvion. [1605–15; < L *accrētiōn-* (s. of *accrētiō*), equiv. to *accrēt(us),* ptp. of *accrēscere* to grow (*ac-* AC- + *crē-* grow + *-tus* ptp. suffix) + *-iōn-* -ION] —**ac•cre′tive, ac•cre′tion•ar′y,** *adj.*

accre′tion disk′, *Astron.* the rapidly spinning disk of gas that forms around the more compact component of a close binary star system as mass is transferred to the compact companion from the primary star. [1975–80]

ac•croach (ə krōch′), *v.t.* to assume to oneself without right or authority; usurp. [1275–1325; ME *acrochen* < AF *a(c)crocher* to catch hold of, seize, usurp, OF: deriv. of *croc* hook, CROOK[1] (< Gmc) with *ac-* AC-; cf. ENCROACH] —**ac•croach′ment,** *n.*

ac•croi′des gum′ (ə kroi′dēz, ak roi′-). See **acaroid resin.** [1935–40; alter. of NL *acaroides.* See ACAROID]

ac•cru•al (ə kro͞o′əl), *n.* **1.** the act or process of accruing. **2.** something accrued; accretion. [1875–80; ACCRUE + -AL[2]]

accru′al ba′sis, a method of recording income and expenses in which each item is reported as earned or incurred without regard to when actual payments are received or made. Cf. **cash basis.** [1930–35]

ac•crue (ə kro͞o′), *v.i.,* **-crued, -cru•ing. 1.** to happen or result as a natural growth, addition, etc. **2.** to be added as a matter of periodic gain or advantage, as interest on money. **3.** *Law.* to become a present and enforceable right or demand. [1425–75; late ME *acruen, acrewen,* prob. < AF *accru(e),* MF *accreu(e),* ptp. of *ac(c)reistre* to increase < L *accrēscere* grow. See AC-, CREW[1], ACCRETION] —**ac•cru′a•ble,** *adj.* —**ac•crue′ment,** *n.*
—**Syn. 1, 2.** accumulate, collect, grow, increase.
—**Ant. 1, 2.** dwindle, decrease, diminish, lessen, dissipate.

accrued′ div′idend, an accumulated unpaid dividend on preferred stock.

accrued′ expense′, an expense incurred but not yet paid, as accrued interest on notes payable. [1980–85]

accrued′ in′come, income earned but not yet received nor past due. Also called **accrued′ rev′enue.** [1980–85]

accrued′ in′terest, interest accumulated at a given time but not yet due or paid.

accrued′ liabil′ity, the amount of liability accumulated at a given time but not yet paid.

acct., 1. account. **2.** accountant.

ac•cul•tur•ate (ə kul′chə rāt′), *v.t., v.i.,* **-at•ed, -at•ing.** to alter by acculturation. [1930–35; back formation from ACCULTURATION] —**ac•cul′tur•a′tive,** *adj.*

ac•cul•tur•a•tion (ə kul′chə rā′shən), *n.* **1.** the process of adopting the cultural traits or social patterns of another group. **2.** the result of this process. [1875–80, *Amer.;* AC- + CULTURE + -ATION] —**ac•cul′tur•a′tion•al,** *adj.*

ac•cul•tur•a•tion•ist (ə kul′chə rā′shə nist), *n.* a person who studies the process of acculturation. [ACCULTURATION + -IST]

ac•cul•tur•ize (ə kul′chə rīz′), *v.t.,* **-ized, -iz•ing.** to cause (a nation, tribe, or other ethnic group) to adopt the culture of another people. Also, *esp. Brit.,* **ac•cul′tur•ise′.** [1890–95; ACCULTUR(ATION) + -IZE]

accum., accumulative.

ac•cum•bent (ə kum′bənt), *adj.* **1.** reclining; recumbent: *accumbent posture.* **2.** *Bot.* lying against something. [1650–60; < L *accumbent-* (s. of *accumbēns,* prp. of *accumbere*), equiv. to *ac-* AC- + *cumb-* (nasalized var. of *cub-* lie, recline; see COVEY) + *-ent-* -ENT] —**ac•cum′ben•cy,** *n.*

ac•cu•mu•late (ə kyo͞o′myə lāt′), *v.,* **-lat•ed, -lat•ing.** —*v.t.* **1.** to gather or collect, often in gradual degrees; heap up: *to accumulate wealth.* —*v.i.* **2.** to gather into a heap, mass, cover, etc.; form a steadily increasing quantity: *Snow accumulated in the driveway. His debts kept on accumulating.* [1520–30; < L *accumulātus* heaped up (ptp. of *accumulāre*), equiv. to *ac-* AC- + *cumul(us)* heap + *-ātus* -ATE[1]] —**ac•cu′mu•la•ble,** *adj.*

ac•cu•mu•la•tion (ə kyo͞o′myə lā′shən), *n.* **1.** act or state of accumulating; state of being accumulated. **2.** that which is accumulated; an accumulated amount, number, or mass. **3.** growth by continuous additions, as of interest to principal. [1480–90; < L *accumulātiōn-* (s. of *accumulātiō*). See ACCUMULATE, -ION]

accumula′tion point′, *Math.* a point such that every neighborhood of the point contains at least one point in a given set other than the given point. Also called **cluster point, limit point.** Cf. **strong accumulation point.**

ac•cu•mu•la•tive (ə kyo͞o′myə lā′tiv, -lə tiv), *adj.* **1.** tending to accumulate or arising from accumulation; cumulative. **2.** tending to accumulate wealth; acquisitive. [1645–55; ACCUMULATE + -IVE] —**ac•cu′mu•la′tive•ly,** *adv.* —**ac•cu′mu•la′tive•ness,** *n.*

ac•cu•mu•la•tor (ə kyo͞o′myə lā′tər), *n.* **1.** a person or thing that accumulates. **2.** a register or electric device on an arithmetic machine, as an adding machine, cash register, or digital computer, that receives a number and produces and stores the results of arithmetic operations of the given number with other numbers. **3.** *Brit.* a storage battery or storage cell. **4.** an apparatus that stores fluid at approximately the working pressure of the hydraulic or pneumatic system in which it will be employed, so that a supply of fluid is always immediately available to the system. **5.** *Mach.* (in a boiler) a vessel for storing hot fluid, ready to flash into steam. **6.** *Hydraul.* a vessel in which air is trapped and compressed by the liquid, thus storing energy to supply liquid under pressure when the demand of the system is greater than the capacity of the pump. [1685–95; < L *accumulātor,* equiv. to *accumulā(re)* to heap up (see ACCUMULATE) + *-tor* -TOR]

ac•cu•ra•cy (ak′yər ə sē), *n., pl.* **-cies. 1.** the condition or quality of being true, correct, or exact; freedom from error or defect; precision or exactness; correctness. **2.** *Chem., Physics.* the extent to which a given measurement agrees with the standard value for that measurement. Cf. **precision** (def. 6). **3.** *Math.* the degree of correctness of a quantity, expression, etc. Cf. **precision** (def. 5). [1655–65; ACCUR(ATE) + -ACY]

ac•cu•rate (ak′yər it), *adj.* **1.** free from error or defect; consistent with a standard, rule, or model; precise; exact. **2.** careful or meticulous: *an accurate typist.* [1605–15; < L *accūrātus* carefully prepared (ptp. of *accūrāre*), equiv. to *ac-* AC- + *cūr(a)* care + *-ātus* -ATE[1]] —**ac′cu•rate•ly,** *adv.* —**ac′cu•rate•ness,** *n.*
—**Syn. 1.** true, unerring. See **correct.**

ac•cu•rize (ak′yə rīz′), *v.t.,* **-rized, -riz•ing.** to improve the accuracy of (a firearm). Also, *esp. Brit.,* **ac′cu•rise′.** [ACCUR(ATE) + -IZE]

ac•curs•ed (ə kûr′sid, ə kûrst′), *adj.* **1.** under a curse; doomed; ill-fated. **2.** damnable; detestable. Also, **ac•curst** (ə kûrst′). [bef. 1000; ME *acursed,* OE *ācursod,* ptp. of *ācursian.* See A-[3], CURSE] —**ac•curs•ed•ly** (ə kûr′sid lē), *adv.* —**ac•curs′ed•ness,** *n.*

accus., accusative.

ac•cu•sal (ə kyo͞o′zəl), *n.* accusation. [1585–95; ACCUSE + -AL[2]]

ac•cu•sa•tion (ak′yo͞o zā′shən), *n.* **1.** a charge of wrongdoing; imputation of guilt or blame. **2.** the specific offense charged: *The accusation is murder.* **3.** the act of accusing or state of being accused. [1350–1400; ME *accusacion* < L *accūsātiōn-* (s. of *accūsātiō*), equiv. to *accūsāt(us),* ptp. of *accūsāre* (see ACCUSE, -ATE[1]) + *-iōn-* -ION]

ac•cu•sa•ti•val (ə kyo͞o′zə tī′vəl), *adj.* pertaining to the accusative case. [1870–75; ACCUSATIVE + -AL[1]]

ac•cu•sa•tive (ə kyo͞o′zə tiv), *adj.* **1.** *Gram.* **a.** (in certain inflected languages, as Latin, Greek, or Russian) noting a case whose distinctive function is to indicate the direct object of a verb or the object of certain prepositions. **b.** similar to such a case form in function or meaning. **2.** *Ling.* pertaining to a type of language in which there is an accusative case or in which subjects of transitive verbs behave the same way as subjects of intransitive verbs. Cf. **ergative** (def. 2). **3.** accusatory. —*n.* **4.** an accusative case. **5.** a word in an accusative case. **6.** a form or construction of similar function. [1400–50; late ME (< MF) < L *accūsātīvus,* equiv. to *ac-* AC- + *-cūsātīvus,* comb. form of *causātīvus* (see CAUSATIVE) a loan-trans. of Gk *aitiatikḗ,* in the sense of pointing to the origin or cause, accusing)] —**ac•cu′sa•tive•ly,** *adv.*

ac•cu•sa•to•ri•al (ə kyo͞o′zə tôr′ē əl, -tōr′-), *adj.* of, like, or pertaining to an accuser. [1815–25; ACCUSATORY + -AL[1]] —**ac•cu′sa•to′ri•al•ly,** *adv.*

ac•cu•sa•to•ry (ə kyo͞o′zə tôr′ē, -tōr′ē), *adj.* containing an accusation; accusing: *an accusatory look.* Also, **accusative.** [1595–1605; < L *accūsātōrius,* equiv. to *accūsā(re)* to ACCUSE + *-tōrius* -TORY[1]]

ac•cuse (ə kyo͞oz′), *v.,* **-cused, -cus•ing.** —*v.t.* **1.** to charge with the fault, offense, or crime (usually fol. by *of*): *He accused him of murder.* **2.** to find fault with; blame. —*v.i.* **3.** to make an accusation. [1250–1300; ME *ac(c)usen* < OF *acuser* < L *accūsāre* to call to account (*ac-* AC- + *-cūs-,* comb. form of *caus-;* see CAUSE)] —**ac•cus′a•ble,** *adj.* —**ac•cus′a•bly,** *adv.* —**ac•cus′ant,** *n.* —**ac•cus′ing•ly,** *adv.*
—**Syn. 1.** arraign, indict; incriminate, impeach. —**Ant. 1, 2.** exonerate.

ac•cused (ə kyo͞ozd′), *adj.* **1.** charged with a crime, wrongdoing, fault, etc.: *the accused boy.* **2.** a person charged in a court of law with a crime, offense, etc. (often prec. by *the*). [1585–95; ACCUSE + -ED[2]]

ac•cus•er (ə kyo͞o′zər), *n.* a person who accuses, esp. in a court of law: *a trial in which the accuser and accused may freely speak.* [1300–50; ME; see ACCUSE, -ER[1]]

ac•cus•tom (ə kus′təm), *v.t.* to familiarize by custom or use; habituate: *to accustom oneself to cold weather.* [1425–75; late ME < MF *acoustumer.* See AC-, CUSTOM]

ac•cus•tomed (ə kus′təmd), *adj.* **1.** customary; usual; habitual: *in their accustomed manner.* **2.** habituated; acclimated (usually fol. by *to*): *accustomed to staying up late; accustomed to the noise of the subway.* [1400–50; late ME; see ACCUSTOM, -ED[2]] —**ac•cus′tomed•ly,** *adv.* —**ac•cus′tomed•ness,** *n.*
—**Syn. 1.** characteristic, normal, regular. **2.** used (to). —**Ant. 1.** unusual. **2.** unused (to).

Ac•cu•tane (ak′yo͞o tān′), *Pharm., Trademark.* a brand of isotretinoin.

ACDA, (United States) Arms Control and Disarmament Agency.

AC/DC (ā′sē dē′sē), *adj. Slang.* sexually responsive to both men and women; bisexual. [1940–45, for an earlier sense; 1960–65 for this use]

AC/DC, *Elect.* alternating current or direct current. Also, **A.C./D.C., ac/dc, a-c/d-c, a.c.-d.c.**

ace (ās), *n., v.,* **aced, ac•ing,** *adj.* —*n.* **1.** a playing card or die marked with or having the value indicated by a single spot: *He dealt me four aces in the first hand.* **2.** a single spot or mark on a playing card or die. **3.** (in tennis, badminton, handball, etc.) **a.** Also called **service ace.** a placement made on a service. **b.** any placement. **c.** a serve that the opponent fails to touch. **d.** the point thus scored. **4.** a fighter pilot credited with destroying a prescribed number or more of enemy aircraft, usually five, in combat. **5.** a very skilled person; expert; adept: *an ace at tap dancing.* **6.** *Slang.* a one-dollar bill. **7.** *Slang.* a close friend. **8.** *Golf.* **a.** Also called **hole in one.** a shot in which the ball is driven from the tee into the hole in one stroke: *He hit a 225-yard ace on the first hole.* **b.** a score of one stroke made on such a shot: *to card an ace.* **9.** *Slang.* a barbiturate or amphetamine capsule or pill. **10.** a very small quantity, amount, or degree; a particle: *not worth an ace.* **11.** *Slang.* a grade of A; the highest grade or score. **12. ace up one's sleeve,** an important, effective, or decisive argument, resource, or advantage kept in reserve until needed. **13. be aces with,** *Slang.* to be highly regarded by: *The boss says you're aces with him.* **14. easy aces,** *Auction Bridge.* aces equally divided between opponents. **15. within an ace of,** within a narrow margin of; close to: *He came within an ace of winning.* —*v.t.* **16.** (in tennis, badminton, handball, etc.) to win a point against (one's opponent) by an ace. **17.** *Golf.* to make an ace on (a hole). **18.** *Slang.* to cheat, defraud, or take advantage of (often fol. by *out*): *to be aced out of one's inheritance; a friend who aced me out of a good job.* **19.** *Slang.* **a.** to receive a grade of A, as on a test or in a course (sometimes fol. by *out*). **b.** to complete easily and successfully: *He aced every physical fitness test they gave him.* **20. ace it,** *Slang.* to accomplish something with complete success: *a champion who could ace it every time.* —*adj.* **21.** excellent; first-rate; outstanding. [1250–1300; 1915 for def. 4; ME *as, aas* < OF *as* < L: a unit; cf. AS[2]; sense 4 after F *as* in World War I; sense 5 < 4]

ACE, American Council on Education.

-acea, *Zool.* a suffix used in the formation of names of classes and orders: *Crustacea.* [< L, neut. pl, with collective meaning, of *-āceus.* See -ACEOUS]

-aceae, *Bot.* a suffix used in the formation of names of families: *Rosaceae.* [< L, fem. pl. of *-āceus.* See -ACEOUS]

Ace′ band′age, *Trademark.* a brand of elasticized bandage, usually in a continuous strip, for securely binding an injured wrist, knee, or other joint.

ac•e•bu•to•lol (as′ə byo͞o′tl ôl′, -ol′), *n. Pharm.* a beta blocker, $C_{18}H_{28}N_2O_4$, used in the management of hypertension, angina pectoris, and cardiac arrhythmias. [1965–70; coined from components of the chemical name; see ACETYL, BUTYL]

a•ce•di•a (ə sē′dē ə), *n.* **1.** sloth (def. 1). Cf. **deadly sins. 2.** laziness or indifference in religious matters. [1600–10; < LL *acēdia* < Gk *akḗdeia,* equiv. to *akēdḗ(s)* (*a-* A-[6] + *-kēdēs,* adj. deriv. of *kêdos* care, anxiety) + *-ia* -IA]

ace-high (ās′hī′, -hī′), *adj.* **1.** (of a poker hand) having an ace as the highest card. **2.** held in high esteem: *He has an ace-high reputation.* [1875–80, *Amer.*]

ace′ in the hole′, 1. *Poker.* an ace dealt and held face down, esp. in stud poker. **2.** an advantage or a resource kept back until the proper opportunity presents itself: *His ace in the hole is his political influence.* [1920–25, *Amer.*]

A•cel•da•ma (ə sel′də mə, ə kel′-), *n.* **1.** the place near Jerusalem purchased with the bribe Judas took for betraying Jesus. Acts 1:18, 19. **2.** any place of slaughter and bloodshed. Also, **Akeldama.** [< L < Gk *Akeldamá* < Aram *ḥăqēl dəmā* field of blood]

a•cel•lu•lar (ā sel′yə lər), *adj.* **1.** being without cells. **2.** composed of tissue not divided into separate cells, as striated muscle fibers. [1935–40; A-[6] + CELLULAR]

a•ce•nes•the•sia (ā′sē nəs thē′zhə), *n. Psychiatry.* loss of the physical awareness of one's body. Also, **acoenaesthesia.** [A-[6] + CENESTHESIA]

a•cen•tric (ā sen′trik), *adj.* **1.** not centered; having no center. **2.** *Genetics.* of or pertaining to a chromosome or chromatid that lacks a centromere. Cf. **acrocentric, metacentric, telocentric.** [1850–55; A-[6] + -CENTRIC]

-aceous, a suffix with the meanings "resembling, having the nature of," "made of," occurring in loanwords from Latin (*cretaceous; herbaceous*) and forming adjectives in English on the Latin model (*ceraceous*), esp. adjectival correspondents to taxonomic names ending in **-acea** and **-aceae:** *rosaceous.* [< L *-āceus;* see -OUS]

a•ceph•a•lous (ā sef′ə ləs), *adj.* **1.** Also, **a•ce•phal•ic** (ā′sə fal′ik). *Zool.* headless; lacking a distinct head. **2.** without a leader or ruler. [1725–35; < Gk *aképhalos;* see A-[6], -CEPHALOUS]

ac•e•phate (as′ə fāt′), *n. Chem.* a white solid compound, $C_4H_{10}NO_3PS$, used as an insecticide against a wide range of plant pests, including aphids, budworms, and tent caterpillars. [ACE(TYL) + PH(OSPHOR-) + ATE[2]]

ace′ point′, the first point in backgammon. [1875–80]

a•ce•quia (ə sā′kyə; *Sp.* ä se′kyä), *n., pl.* **-quias** (-kyəz; *Sp.* -kyäs). *Southwestern U.S.* an irrigation ditch. [1835–45, *Amer.;* < Sp < Ar *al-sāqiyah* the irrigation ditch]

a•ce•ram•ic (ā′sə ram′ik), *adj.* not producing pottery: *an aceramic South American culture.* [A-[6] + CERAMIC]

ac•er•ate (as′ə rāt′, -ər it), *adj.* acerose[1]. [1840–50; < L *acer-* (by the error analyzed for ACEROSE[1]) + -ATE[1]]

a•cerb (ə sûrb′), *adj.* acerbic. [1650–60; < L *acerbus;* see ACERBIC]

ac•er•bate (*v.* as′ər bāt′; *adj.* ə sûr′bit), *v.,* **-bat•ed, -bat•ing,** *adj.* —*v.t.* **1.** to make sour or bitter. **2.** to exasperate. —*adj.* **3.** embittered. [1725–35; < L *acerbātus,* ptp. of *acerbāre* to make bitter. See ACERBIC, -ATE[1]]

a•cer•bic (ə sûr′bik), *adj.* **1.** sour or astringent in taste: *Lemon juice is acerbic.* **2.** harsh or severe, as of temper or expression: *acerbic criticism.* [1860–65; < L *acerb(us)* sour, unripe, bitterly harsh + -IC, irreg. for -OUS] —**a•cer′bi•cal•ly,** *adv.*

a•cer•bi•ty (ə sûr′bi tē), *n.* **1.** sourness, with roughness or astringency of taste. **2.** harshness or severity, as of temper or expression. [1565–75; < L *acerbitās.* See ACERBIC, -ITY]

ac•e•ro•la (as′ə rō′lə), *n.* **1.** the cherrylike fruit of a small tree, *Malpighia glabra,* of the West Indies and adjacent areas, having a high concentration of vitamin C. **2.** the tree itself. Also called **Barbados cherry, Puerto Rican cherry.** [1940–45; < AmerSp; Sp: a species of hawthorn, *Crataegus azarolus* < Ar *al-zu'rūr* the acerola]

ac•er•ose[1] (as′ə rōs′), *adj. Bot.* needle-shaped, as the leaves of the pine. Also, **acerate, acerous.** [1775–85; special sense of ACEROSE[2], by misattribution of *acer-* to L *acus* needle, whose s. is *acu-* and not *acer-* (cf. ACUTE)]

ac•er•ose[2] (as′ə rōs′), *adj.* **1.** resembling chaff. **2.** mixed with chaff. [1715–25; < L *acerōsus,* equiv. to *acer-* (s. of *acus*) chaff + *-ōsus* -OSE[1]]

ac•er•ous[1] (as′ər əs), *adj. Bot.* acerose[1]. [1840–50]

a•ce•rous[2] (ā sēr′əs), *adj. Zool.* **1.** having no antennae. **2.** having no horns. [< Gk *akerós,* equiv. to *a-* A-[6] + *-keros,* adj. deriv. of *kéras* horn; see -OUS]

a•cer•vate (ə sûr′vit, -vāt, as′ər vāt′), *adj. Bot., Mycol.* pertaining to growth, esp. of fungi, that forms a dense, heaped-up mass. [1840–50; < L *acervātus* heaped up (ptp. of *acervāre*), equiv. to *acerv(us)* heap + *-ātus* -ATE[1]] —**a•cer′vate•ly,** *adv.*

a•cer•vu•lus (ə sûr′vyə ləs), *n., pl.* **-li** (-lī′). *Mycol.* (in certain fungi) an asexual fruiting body consisting of a mat of hyphae that give rise to short-stalked conidiophores. [< NL, equiv. to L *acerv(us)* heap + *-ulus* -ULE]

a•ces•cent (ə ses′ənt), *adj.* turning sour; slightly sour; acidulous. [1725–35; < L *acēscent-* (s. of *acēscēns* souring, prp. of *acēscere*), equiv. to *ac-* sharp + *-ēscent-* -ESCENT] —**a•ces′cence, a•ces′cen•cy,** *n.*

a•ces•o•dyne (ə ses′ə dīn′), *adj.* mitigating pain; anodyne. [< Gk *akesṓdyn(os),* equiv. to *akes-* (var. s. of *akeîsthai* to heal) + *-ōdynos,* adj. comb. form of *odýnē* pain] —**ac•e•sod•y•nous** (as′ə sod′n əs), *adj.*

acet-, var. of **aceto-,** esp. before a vowel.

ac•e•tab•u•li•form (as′i tab′yə lə fôrm′), *adj. Bot., Mycol.* saucer-shaped, as the fruiting bodies of certain lichens. [1825–35; < NL; see ACETABULUM, -I-, -FORM]

ac•e•tab•u•lum (as′i tab′yə ləm), *n., pl.* **-la** (-lə). **1.** *Anat.* the socket in the hipbone that receives the head of the thighbone. See illus. under **pelvis. 2.** *Zool.* any of the suction appendages of a leech, octopus, etc. [1660–70; < L: hip socket, cup-shaped part of a plant (Pliny), lit., small cup, orig. for vinegar, equiv. to *acēt(um)* vinegar + *-ā-* by analogy with v. derivs. (cf. VOCABLE) + *-bulum* suffix denoting instrument or vessel] —**ac′e•tab′u•lar,** *adj.*

ac•e•tal (as′i tal′), *n. Chem.* **1.** Also called **diethylacetal.** a colorless, volatile, sparingly water-soluble liquid, $C_6H_{14}O_2$, having a nutlike aftertaste, obtained from acetaldehyde and ethyl alcohol: used chiefly as a solvent and in the manufacture of perfumes. **2.** any of a class of compounds of aldehydes with alcohols. [1850–55; ACET- + -AL[3]]

ac•et•al•de•hyde (as′i tal′də hīd′), *n. Chem.* a volatile, colorless, water-soluble liquid, C_2H_4O, having a pungent, fruitlike odor: used chiefly in the silvering of mirrors and in organic synthesis. Also called **ethanal.** [1875–80; ACET- + ALDEHYDE]

ac•e•tal•dol (as′i tal′dôl, -dol), *n. Chem.* aldol (def. 1). [ACETALD(EHYDE) + -OL[1]]

a•cet•am•ide (ə set′ə mīd′, as′i tam′id), *n. Chem.* a white, water-soluble, crystalline solid, C_2H_5NO, the amide of acetic acid: used chiefly in organic synthesis. Also, **a•cet•am•id** (ə set′ə mid, as′i tam′id). Also called **acetic acid amide.** [1870–75; ACET- + AMIDE]

a•ce•ta•min•o•phen (ə sē′tə min′ə fən, as′i tə-), *n. Pharm.* a crystalline substance, $C_8H_9NO_2$, used as a headache and pain reliever and to reduce fever. [1955–60; ACET- + AMINO- + PHEN(OL)]

ac•et•an•i•lide (as′i tan′l īd′), *n. Chem., Pharm.* a white, crystalline, odorless, organic powder, C_8H_9NO, produced by the action of glacial acetic acid on aniline, used chiefly in organic synthesis and formerly in the treatment of fever and headache. Also, **ac•et•an•i•lid** (as′i tan′l id). Also called **acetylaniline.** [1860–65; ACET- + ANILIDE]

a•cet•a•nis•i•dine (ə sē′tə nis′i dēn′, -din, as′i tə-), *n. Pharm.* methacetin. [ACET- + ANISE + -IDE + -INE[2]]

ac•e•tate (as′i tāt′), *n.* **1.** *Chem.* a salt or ester of acetic acid. **2.** Also called **ac′etate ray′on.** a synthetic filament, yarn, or fabric composed of a derivative of the acetic ester of cellulose, differing from viscose rayon in having greater strength when wet and greater sensitivity to high temperatures. **3.** a sheet of clear plastic film fastened over the front of artwork for protection, as an overlay, or the like. **4.** a slow-burning base material, cellulose triacetate, used for motion-picture film to minimize fire hazard during projection, and also for animation cels. [1820–30; ACET- + -ATE[2]]

a•cet•a•zo•la•mide (ə sē′tə zō′lə mīd′, -mid, -zol′ə-, as′i tə-), *n. Pharm.* a crystalline powder, $C_4H_6N_4O_3S_2$, used chiefly in the treatment of glaucoma and edema. [1950–55; ACET- + AZOLE + AMIDE]

a•ce•tic (ə sē′tik, ə set′ik), *adj.* pertaining to, derived from, or producing vinegar or acetic acid. [1800–10; ACET- + -IC]

ace′tic ac′id, *Chem.* a colorless, pungent, water-miscible liquid, $C_2H_4O_2$, the essential constituent of vinegar, produced by oxidation of acetaldehyde, bacterial action on ethyl alcohol, the reaction of methyl alcohol with carbon monoxide, and other processes: used chiefly in the manufacture of acetate fibers and in the production of numerous esters that are solvents and flavoring agents. Cf. **glacial acetic acid.** [1800–10]

ace′tic ac′id am′ide, acetamide.

ace′tic anhy′dride, *Chem.* a colorless, pungent liquid, $C_4H_6O_3$, the anhydride of acetic acid: used chiefly as a reagent and in the production of plastics, film, and fabrics derived from cellulose. [1875–80]

CONCISE ETYMOLOGY KEY: <, descended or borrowed from; >, whence; b., blend of, blended; c., cognate with; cf., compare; deriv., derivative; equiv., equivalent; imit., imitative; obl., oblique; r., replacing; s., stem; sp., spelling, spelled; resp., respelling, respelled; trans., translation; ?, origin unknown; *, unattested; ‡, probably earlier than. See the full key inside the front cover.

ace′tic e′ther, *Chem.* See **ethyl acetate.**

a•ce•ti•fy (ə sē′tə fī′, ə set′ə-), *v.t., v.i.,* **-fied, -fy•ing.** to turn into vinegar; make or become acetous. [1860–65; ACET- + -IFY] **—a•ce′ti•fi•ca′tion, ac•e•ta•tion** (as′i tā′shən), *n.* **—a•ce′ti•fi′er,** *n.*

ac•e•tim•e•ter (as′i tim′i tər), *n. Chem.* acetometer. [1870–75] **—a•ce•ti•met•ric** (ə sē′tə me′trik, as′i tə-), *adj.* **—ac′e•tim′e•try,** *n.*

ac•e•tin (as′i tin), *n. Chem.* a colorless, thick, hygroscopic liquid, $C_5H_{10}O_4$: used chiefly in the manufacture of explosives. Also called **glyceryl monoacetate, monoacetin, monoacetin.** [1870–75; ACET- + -IN²]

aceto-, a combining form with the meanings "vinegar," "acetic acid," used in the formation of compound words (*acetometer*), esp. in the names of chemical compounds in which acetic acid or the acetyl group is present (*acetophenetidin*). Also, *esp. before a vowel,* **acet-.** [< L *acēt(um)* vinegar + -O-. Cf. ACID, ACESCENT]

a•ce•to•a•ce′tic ac′id (ə sē′tō ə sē′tik, -ə set′ik, as′i tō-), *Chem.* a colorless, oily liquid, $C_4H_6O_3$, soluble in water, alcohol, and ether: used in synthetic organic chemistry. Also called **diacetic acid.** [1895–1900; ACETO- + ACETIC]

a•ce•to•bac•ter (ə sē′tə bak′tər, as′i tō-, ə sē′tə-bak′tər), *n. Bacteriol.* any of several ellipsoidal or rod-shaped aerobic bacteria of the genus *Acetobacter,* certain species of which are used in making vinegar. [< NL (1898); see ACETO-, -BACTER]

a•cet•o•in (ə set′ō in), *n. Chem.* a yellowish, pleasant-smelling liquid, $C_4H_8O_2$, obtained from various carbohydrates, as glucose, by fermentation: used chiefly in the manufacture of flavors and essences. Also called **acetylmethylcarbinol, dimethylketol.** [ACETO- + -IN²]

ac•e•tom•e•ter (as′i tom′i tər), *n. Chem.* an instrument for measuring the amount of acetic acid present in a solution. Also, **acetimeter.** [1850–55; ACETO- + -METER] **—a•ce•to•met•ri•cal** (ə sē′tə me′tri kəl, as′i-tə-), **a•ce′to•met′ric,** *adj.* **—a•ce′to•met′ri•cal•ly,** *adv.* **—ac′e•tom′e•try,** *n.*

ac•e•tone (as′i tōn′), *n. Chem.* a colorless, volatile, water-soluble, flammable liquid, C_3H_6O, usually derived by oxidation of isopropyl alcohol or by bacterial fermentation of carbohydrates: used chiefly in paints and varnishes, as a general solvent, and in organic synthesis. Also called **dimethylketone.** [1830–40; ACET- + -ONE] **—ac•e•ton•ic** (as′i ton′ik), *adj.*

ac′etone bod′y, *Biochem.* See **ketone body.** [1925–30]

a•ce•to•ne•mi•a (ə sē′tə nē′mē ə, as′i tə-), *n. Pathol.* ketonemia. [ACETONE + -EMIA]

ac•e•to•ni•trile (as′i tō nī′tril, -trēl, ə sē′tō-), *n. Chem.* a colorless, poisonous, water-soluble liquid, C_2H_3N, having an etherlike odor: used chiefly in organic synthesis and as a solvent. Also called **methyl cyanide.** [1865–70; ACETO- + NITRILE]

a•ce•to•nu•ri•a (ə sē′tō nŏŏr′ē ə, -nyŏŏr′-, as′i tō-), *n. Pathol.* ketonuria. [ACETONE + -URIA]

a•ce•to•phe•net•i•din (ə sē′tō fə net′i din, as′i tō-), *n. Pharm.* phenacetin. [1905–10; ACETO- + PHENETIDIN]

a•ce•to•phe•none (ə sē′tō fə nōn′, as′i tō-), *n. Chem.* a colorless liquid, C_8H_8O, having a sweet odor: used chiefly as a scent in the manufacture of perfume. Also called **acetylbenzene, hypnone, phenyl methyl ketone.** [1870–75; ACETO- + PHEN- + -ONE]

a•ce•to•ste•a•rin (ə sē′tō stē′ə rin, -stēr′in, as′i tō-), *n. Chem.* a waxlike, nongreasy solid, $C_{23}H_{44}O_5$: used chiefly as a food preservative and as a plasticizer. [ACETO- + STEARIN]

ac•e•tous (as′i təs, ə sē′-), *adj.* **1.** containing or producing acetic acid. **2.** sour; producing or resembling vinegar; vinegary. Also, **ac•e•tose** (as′i tōs′, ə sē′tōs). [1770–80; < LL *acētōsus.* See ACETUM, -OUS]

a•ce•tum (ə sē′təm), *n.* a preparation having vinegar or dilute acetic acid as the solvent. [< L: vinegar; cf. ACETO-]

a•ce•tyl (ə sēt′l, ə set′l, as′i tl), *adj. Chem.* containing the acetyl group. [1860–65; ACET- + -YL]

a•ce•tyl•an•i•line (ə sēt′l an′l in, -īn′, ə set′-, as′i tl-), *n. Chem.* acetanilide. [ACETYL + ANILINE]

a•cet•y•late (ə set′l āt′), *v.,* **-lat•ed, -lat•ing.** *Chem.* —*v.t.* **1.** to introduce one or more acetyl groups into (a compound). —*v.i.* **2.** to become acetylated. Also, **acetylize.** [1905–10; ACETYL + -ATE¹] **—a•cet′y•la′tion,** *n.* **—a•cet′y•la′tive,** *adj.*

a•ce•tyl•ben•zene (ə sēt′l ben′zēn, -ben zēn′, ə set′-, as′i tl-), *n. Chem.* acetophenone. [ACETYL + BENZENE]

ace′tyl chlo′ride, *Chem.* a colorless, toxic, and fuming liquid of pungent odor, C_2H_3OCl, soluble in ether, acetone, and acetic acid: used in the manufacture of dyes and pharmaceuticals.

a•ce•tyl•cho•line (ə sēt′l kō′lēn, ə set′-, as′i tl-), *n.* **1.** *Biochem.* the acetic acid ester of choline, $C_7H_{17}NO_3$, released and hydrolyzed during nerve conduction and causing muscle action by transmitting nerve impulses across synapses. **2.** *Pharm.* this substance used in its chloride form in eye surgery. *Abbr.:* ACh [1905–10; ACETYL + CHOLINE] **—a•ce•tyl•cho•lin•ic** (ə sēt′l kō lin′ik, ə set′-, as′i tl-), *adj.*

a•ce•tyl•cho•lin•es•ter•ase (ə sēt′l kō′lə nes′tə-rās′, -rāz′, ə set′-, as′i tl-), *n. Biochem.* an enzyme that hydrolyzes the neurotransmitter acetylcholine: its action is blocked by nerve gases and certain drugs. [1945–50; ACETYLCHOLINE + ESTERASE]

a•ce•tyl-co•en•zyme A (ə sēt′l kō en′zīm, ə set′-, as′i tl-), *n. Biochem.* the acetylated form of coenzyme A, formed as an intermediate in the oxidation of carbohydrates, fats, and protein in animal metabolism. Also called **a•ce•tyl-CoA** (ə sēt′l kō′ā′, ə set′-, as′i tl-). [1950–55]

a•ce•tyl•cys•te•ine (ə sēt′l sis′tē ēn′, -in, ə set′l-, as′-i tl-), *n. Pharm.* a substance, $C_5H_9NO_3S$, used in solution as an inhalant to dissolve mucus in the treatment of chronic bronchitis, asthma, and emphysema and also used as an antidote in acetaminophen poisoning. [ACETYL + CYSTEINE]

a•cet•y•lene (ə set′l ēn′, -in), *n. Chem.* a colorless gas, C_2H_2, having an etherlike odor, produced usually by the action of water on calcium carbide or by pyrolysis of natural gas: used esp. in metal cutting and welding, as an illuminant, and in organic synthesis. Also called **ethine, ethyne.** [1860–65; ACETYL + -ENE] **—a•cet•y•len•ic** (ə set′l en′ik), *adj.*

acet′ylene se′ries, *Chem.* See **alkyne series.**

a•ce′tyl•for′mic ac′id (ə sēt′l fôr′mik, ə set′-, as′-i tl-; ə sēt′l fôr′mik, ə set′-, as′i tl-), *Chem.* See **pyruvic acid.** [ACETYL + FORMIC ACID]

ace′tyl group′, *Chem.* the univalent group, CH_3CO–, derived from acetic acid. Also called **ace′tyl rad′ical.**

ac•e•tyl•ic (as′i til′ik), *adj.* of, pertaining to, or characteristic of the acetyl group. [1880–85; ACETYL + -IC]

a•cet•y•lide (ə set′l īd′), *n. Chem.* any compound derived from acetylene by the replacement of one or both of its hydrogen atoms by a metal, as silver acetylide, Ag_2Cl_2. [ACETYL + -IDE]

a•cet•y•lize (ə set′l īz′), *v.t., v.i.,* **-lized, -liz•ing.** acetylate. Also, *esp. Brit.,* **a•cet′y•lise′.** [ACETYL + -IZE] **—a•cet′y•li•za′tion,** *n.* **—a•cet′y•liz′er,** *n.*

a•ce•tyl•meth•yl•car•bi•nol (ə sēt′l meth′əl kär′bə-nôl′, -nol′, ə set′-, as′i tl-), *n. Chem.* acetoin. [ACETYL + METHYL + CARBINOL]

a•ce•tyl•sa•lic•y•late (ə sēt′l sə lis′ə lāt′, ə set′-, as′i tl-), *n. Pharm.* a salt or ester of acetylsalicylic acid. [1955–60; ACETYLSALICYL(IC ACID) + -ATE²]

a•ce′tyl•sal•i•cyl′ic ac′id (ə sēt′l sal′ə sil′ik, ə set′-, as′i tl-; ə sēt′l sal′ə sil′ik, ə set′-, as′i tl-), *Pharm.* aspirin (def. 1). [1895–1900; ACETYL + SALICYLIC ACID]

ace•y-deuc•y (ā′sē dōō′sē, -dyōō′-), *n.* **1.** a form of backgammon in which a player, upon rolling a 1–2, moves 3 and then is allowed to name and play any doublet and to roll again. —*adj.* **2.** *Slang.* A-OK; great. [1920–25; ACE + -Y² + DEUCE¹ + -Y²]

ach (äKH), *interj. German.* alas; oh.

ACH, automated clearinghouse.

ACh, *Biochem.* acetylcholine.

A•chab (ā′kab), *n. Douay Bible.* Ahab (def. 1).

A•chad (ā′kad), *n. Douay Bible.* Akkad.

A•chae•a (ə kē′ə), *n.* an ancient district in S Greece, on the Gulf of Corinth.

A•chae•an (ə kē′ən), *adj.* **1.** of or pertaining to Achaea or the Achaeans. **2.** (in the *Iliad*) Greek. —*n.* **3.** an inhabitant of Achaea. **4.** a Greek, esp. a member of the Achaean League. **5.** a member of one of the four main divisions of prehistoric Greeks, believed to have occupied the Peloponnesus and to have produced the Mycenaean culture. Cf. **Aeolian** (def. 2), **Dorian** (def. 2), **Ionian** (def. 3). [1560–70; < L *Achae(us)* (< Gk *Achaiós,* perh. reflected in Hittite *Ahhiyawa,* a country alluded to in records of the late 2nd millennium B.C.) + -AN]

Achae′an League′, a political confederation of Achaean and other Greek cities, established in the late 3rd century B.C. and dissolved by the Romans in 146 B.C.

A•chae•me•nes (ə kē′mə nēz′, ə kem′ə-), *n.* fl. 7th century B.C., Persian king: traditional founder of the Achaemenid dynasty. [< Gk *Achaiménēs* < OPers *Hachāmanish-*]

Ach•ae•me•ni•an (ak′ə mē′nē ən), *adj.* of or pertaining to the Achaemenids or their language, as recorded in cuneiform inscriptions. [1710–20; < L *Achaemeni(us)* (< Gk *Achaimén(ēs)* ACHAEMENES + L *-ius* adj. suffix) + -AN]

A•chae•me•nid (ə kē′mə nid, ə kem′ə-), *n., pl.* **A•chae•me•nids, Ach•ae•men•i•dae** (ak′ə men′i dē′), **Ach•ae•men•i•des** (ak′ə men′i dēz′). a member of the dynasty of kings in ancient Persia that ruled from c550 B.C. to 331 B.C. [ACHAEMEN(ES) + -ID¹]

ach•a•la•sia (ak′ə lā′zhə, -zhē ə, -zē ə), *n. Med.* inability of a circular muscle, esp. of the esophagus or rectum, to relax, resulting in widening of the structure above the muscular constriction. [1910–15; A-⁶ + Gk *chálas(is)* (*chala-* (s. of *chalân* to loosen) + *-sis* -SIS) + -IA]

A•chan (ā′kan), *n.* a member of the tribe of Judah who, with his family, was stoned to death for stealing forbidden spoils. Josh. 7:19–26.

A•cha•tes (ə kā′tēz), *n.* **1.** (in the *Aeneid*) the faithful companion and friend of Aeneas. **2.** a faithful friend or companion.

A•chaz (ā′kaz), *n. Douay Bible.* Ahaz.

ache (āk), *v.,* **ached, ach•ing,** *n.* —*v.i.* **1.** to have or suffer a continuous, dull pain: *His whole body ached.* **2.** to feel great sympathy, pity, or the like: *Her heart ached for the starving animals.* **3.** to feel eager; yearn; long: *She ached to be the champion. He's just aching to get even.* —*n.* **4.** a continuous, dull pain (in contrast to a sharp, sudden, or sporadic pain). [bef. 900; (v.) ME *aken,* OE *acan;* perh. metaphoric use of earlier unattested sense "drive, impel" (cf. ON *aka,* c. L *agere,* Gk *ágein*); (n.) deriv. of the v.]
—Syn. 1. hurt. **4.** See **pain.**

A•che•be (ä chā′bā), *n.* **Chin•ua** (chin′wä), born 1930, Nigerian novelist.

a•chei•la•ry (ə kī′lə rē), *adj. Bot.* achilary. [1865–70]

a•chene (ā kēn′, ə kēn′), *n. Bot.* any small, dry, hard, one-seeded, indehiscent fruit. Also, **akene.** [1835–45; < NL *achaenium,* equiv. to *a-* A-⁶ + Gk *chain-* (s. of *chaínein* to gape) + L *-ium* -IUM] **—a•che•ni•al** (ā kē′nē əl, ə kē′-), *adj.*

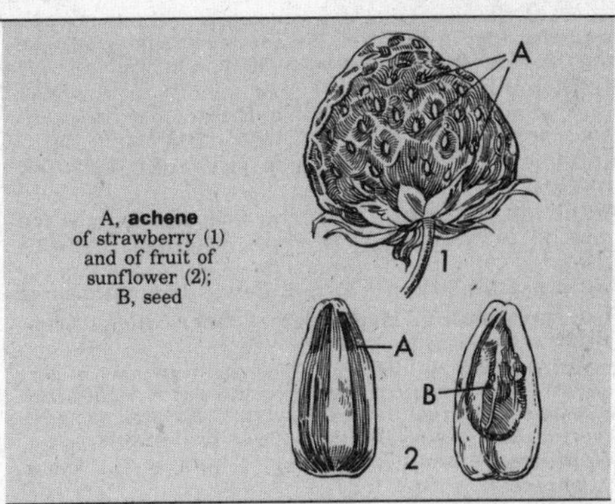

A, **achene** of strawberry (1) and of fruit of sunflower (2); B, seed

A•che•nese (ä′chə nēz′, -nēs′, ach′ə-), *pl.* **-nese.** Atjehnese.

A•cher•nar (ā′kər när′), *n. Astron.* a star of the first magnitude in the constellation Eridanus. [< Ar *ākhir al-nahr* end of the river]

Ach•er•on (ak′ə ron′), *n.* **1.** *Class. Myth.* a river in Hades over which Charon ferried the souls of the dead. **2.** the infernal regions; hell; Hades.

Ach•e•son (ach′ə sən), *n.* **1. Dean (Good•er•ham)** (gŏŏd′ər ham′, -əm), 1893–1971, U.S. statesman: Secretary of State 1949–53. **2. Edward Good•rich** (gŏŏd′-rich), 1856–1931, U.S. chemist.

A•cheu•le•an (ə shōō′lē ən), *adj.* of, pertaining to, or typical of a Lower Paleolithic culture of the middle Pleistocene Epoch, characterized by large hand axes and cleavers made by the soft hammer technique. Also, **A•cheu′li•an.** [1890–95; < F *acheuléen,* named after *St. Acheul,* N France (Somme) (where remains were found) + *-éen,* var. of *-ien* (< L *-iānus* -IAN), orig. with nouns ending in *-é*]

à che•val (A shə vAl′; *Eng.* ä′ shə val′), *French.* by horse; on horseback.

a•chieve (ə chēv′), *v.,* **a•chieved, a•chiev•ing.** —*v.t.* **1.** to bring to a successful end; carry through; accomplish: *The police crackdown on speeders achieved its purpose.* **2.** to get or attain by effort; gain; obtain: *to achieve victory.* —*v.i.* **3.** to bring about an intended result; accomplish some purpose or effect. [1275–1325; ME *acheven* < OF *achever* to finish, from phrase *a chef* to (the) head (i.e., to conclusion). See CHIEF] **—a•chiev′a•ble,** *adj.* **—a•chiev′er,** *n.*
—Syn. 1. consummate, complete; effect, execute; realize, reach. See **do¹. 2.** realize, win.

achieved′ sta′tus, *Sociol.* the social position a person gains as a result of personal effort. Cf. **ascribed status.** [1960–65]

a•chieve•ment (ə chēv′mənt), *n.* **1.** something accomplished, esp. by superior ability, special effort, great courage, etc.; a great or heroic deed: *his remarkable achievements in art.* **2.** act of achieving; attainment or accomplishment: *the achievement of one's object.* **3.** *Heraldry.* the full display of the armorial bearings of an individual or corporation. [1425–75; late ME < MF *achevement* conclusion. See ACHIEVE, -MENT]
—Syn. 1. ACHIEVEMENT, EXPLOIT, FEAT are terms for a noteworthy act. ACHIEVEMENT connotes final accomplishment of something noteworthy, after much effort and often in spite of obstacles and discouragements: *a scientific achievement.* EXPLOIT connotes boldness, bravery, and usually ingenuity: *the famous exploit of an aviator.* FEAT connotes the performance of something difficult, generally demanding skill and strength: *a feat of horsemanship.* **2.** fulfillment, realization.

achieve′ment age′, *Psychol.* the level of educational development of an individual as determined by an achievement test and based on a comparison of the examinee's score with the average score of individuals of the same chronological age. Cf. **mental age.** [1920–25]

achieve′ment quo′tient, *Psychol.* achievement age divided by chronological age, usually expressed as a multiple of 100. The achievement quotient of a ten-year-old child whose achievement age equals that of the average twelve-year-old is 1.2, or 120. *Abbr.:* AQ Cf. **intelligence quotient.** [1920–25]

achieve′ment test′, a test designed to measure the knowledge or proficiency of an individual in something that has been learned or taught, as arithmetic or typing. Cf. **intelligence test.** [1920–25]

a•chi•la•ry (ə kī′lə rē), *adj. Bot.* having no labellum or lip, or one that is undeveloped, as in the flower of certain orchids. Also, **acheilary.** [A-⁶ + CHIL- + -ARY]

Ach•ill (ak′əl), *n.* an island off the coast of NW Ireland. 14 mi. (23 km) long; 11 mi. (18 km) wide.

ach•il•le•a (ak′ə lē′ə, ə kil′ē ə), *n.* any composite plant of the genus *Achillea,* having toothed or divided leaves and flat-topped clusters of flowers, and including the yarrow and sneezewort. [< NL (Linnaeus), L *Achillēa,* fem. n. based on Gk *Achílleios* name for various plants, lit., of ACHILLES, associated with curative plants by his healing of Telephus in the Troy legends; see -A²]

A•chil•les (ə kil′ēz), *n. Class. Myth.* the greatest Greek warrior in the Trojan War and hero of Homer's *Iliad.* He killed Hector and was killed when Paris wounded him in the heel, his one vulnerable spot, with an arrow. —**Ach·il·le·an** (ak′ə lē′ən, ə kil′ē-), *adj.*

Achil′les heel′, a portion, spot, area, or the like, that is especially or solely vulnerable: *His Achilles heel is his quick temper.* Also, **Achil′les′ heel′.** [1800–10]

Achil′les re′flex. See **ankle jerk.** Also, **Achil′les′ re′flex.**

Achil′les ten′don, *Anat.* the tendon joining the calf muscles to the heel bone. Also, **Achil′les′ ten′don.** [1900–05]

A·chim·a·as (ə kim′ā as′), *n. Douay Bible.* Ahimaaz.

A·chim·e·lech (ə kim′ə lek′), *n. Douay Bible.* Ahimelech.

a·chim·e·nes (ə kim′ə nēz′), *n., pl.* **-nes.** any of several tropical American herbs of the genus *Achimenes,* cultivated for their showy, tubular flowers. [< NL (1791), alter. of L *achaemenis* < Gk *achaimenís*]

A·chi·nese (ä′chə nēz′, -nēs′, ach′ə-), *n., pl.* **-nese.** Atjehnese.

ach·ing (ā′king), *adj.* **1.** causing physical pain or distress: *treatment for an aching back.* **2.** full of or precipitating nostalgia, grief, loneliness, etc. [1200–1250; ME; see ACHE, -ING[2]] —**ach′ing·ly,** *adv.*

A·chinsk (ə chinsk′; *Russ.* ä′chyinsk), *n.* a city in the S central Russian Federation in Asia. 117,000.

a·chi·o·te (ä′chē ō′tē, -tä), *n.* annatto. Also, **a·chi·o·ta** (ä′chē ō′tä, -tə). [1790–1800; < MexSp < Nahuatl *āchiotl*]

a·chi·ral (ā kī′rəl), *adj. Chem.* not chiral.

A·chish (ā′kish), *n.* the king of the Philistine city of Gath, who twice gave refuge to David. I Sam. 21:10–15.

A·chit·o·phel (ə kit′ə fel′), *n. Douay Bible.* Ahithophel.

ach·kan (ach′kən), *n.* a close-fitting, high-necked coat, slightly flared below the waist and reaching almost to the knee, worn by men in India. [1910–15; < Hindi *ackan*]

a·chlam·y·date (ā klam′i dāt′, -dit), *adj. Zool.* not chlamydate; having neither mantle nor pallium. [1875–80; A-[6] + CHLAMYDATE]

ach·la·myd·e·ous (ak′lə mid′ē əs), *adj. Bot.* not chlamydeous; having neither calyx nor corolla. [1820–30; A-[6] + CHLAMYDEOUS]

a·chlo·ro·phyl·lous (ā klôr′ə fil′əs, ā klōr′-), *adj. Bot.* containing no chlorophyll. [A-[6] + CHLOROPHYLLOUS]

a·cho·li·a (ā kō′lē ə), *n. Pathol.* lack of a secretion of bile. [1840–50; < Gk *ácholos* lacking bile (*a-* A-[6] + *chol-* CHOL- + *-os* adj. suffix) + -IA] —**a·chol·ic** (ā kol′ik), **a·cho·lous** (ā kō′ləs, -kol′əs, ak′ə ləs), *adj.*

ach·o·lu·ri·a (ak′ə lŏŏr′ē ə), *n.* the absence of bile pigments in the urine. [1900–05; < NL < Gk *áchol(os)* (see ACHOLIA) + NL *-uria* -URIA] —**ach′o·lu′ric,** *adj.*

a·chon·drite (ā kon′drit), *n.* a meteorite containing no chondrules. [1900–05; A-[6] + CHONDRITE] —**a·chon·drit·ic** (ā′kon drit′ik), *adj.*

a·chon·dro·pla·sia (ā kon′drə plā′zhə, -zhē ə, -zē ə), *n. Pathol.* defective conversion of cartilage into bone, esp. at the epiphyses of long bones, producing a type of dwarfism. [1890–95; A-[6] + CHONDRO- + -PLASIA] —**a·chon·dro·plas·tic** (ā kon′drə plas′tik), *adj.*

a·choo (ä chōō′), *interj.* ahchoo.

ach·ro·ite (ak′rō it′), *n.* the colorless or white variety of tourmaline, often used as a gem. [< Gk *áchro(os)* colorless (*a-* A-[6] + *-chroos* colored) + -ITE[1]]

ach·ro·mat (ak′rə mat′), *n.* See **achromatic lens.** [1905–10; by shortening]

ach·ro·mate (ak′rə māt′), *n. Ophthalm.* a person unable to perceive color. [back formation from ACHROMATIC]

ach·ro·mat·ic (ak′rə mat′ik, ā′krə-), *adj.* **1.** *Optics.* **a.** free from color. **b.** able to emit, transmit, or receive light without separating it into colors. **2.** *Biol.* (of a cell structure) difficult to stain. **3.** *Music.* without accidentals or changes in key. [1760–70; A-[6] + CHROMATIC] —**ach′ro·mat′i·cal·ly,** *adv.*

ach·ro·ma·tic·i·ty (ak′rō mə tis′i tē, ā′krō-), *n. Optics.* achromatism. [1835–45; ACHROMATIC + -ITY]

ach′romat′ic lens′, *Optics.* a system of two or more lenses that is substantially free from chromatic aberration and in which the lenses are made of different substances so that the focal length of the system is the same for two or three wavelengths of light. Also called **achromat.** Cf. **crown lens, flint glass.** [‡1860–65]

ach′romat′ic prism′, *Optics.* a system of two or more prisms of different substances that deflects but does not disperse a beam of light.

a·chro·ma·tism (ā krō′mə tiz′əm), *n. Optics.* **1.** freedom from color. **2.** freedom from chromatic aberration, as in an achromatic lens. Also, **achromaticity.** [1790–1800; ACHROMAT(IC) + -ISM]

a·chro·ma·tize (ā krō′mə tīz′), *v.t.,* **-tized, -tiz·ing.** to make achromatic; deprive or free of color. Also, *esp. Brit.,* **a·chro′ma·tise′.** [1835–45; ACHROMAT(IC) + -IZE] —**a·chro′ma·ti·za′tion,** *n.*

a·chro·mat·o·phil (ā′krə mat′ə fil, ak′rə-, ā krō′mə tə-), *Biol.* —*adj.* **1.** Also, **a·chro·mat·o·phil·ic** (ā′krə mat′ə fil′ik, ak′rə-, ā krō′mə tə-). having little or no affinity for stains. —*n.* **2.** an achromatophil cell or tissue. [ACHROMAT(IC) + -O- + -PHIL]

a·chro·mat·o·phil·i·a (ā′krə mat′ə fil′ē ə, -fēl′yə, ak′rə-, ā krō′mə tə-), *n. Biol.* the property of having little or no affinity for stains. [ACHROMATOPHIL + -IA]

a·chro·ma·top·si·a (ā krō′mə top′sē ə), *n. Pathol.* color blindness (def. 2). Also, **a·chro·ma·to·pi·a** (ā krō′mə tō′pē ə), **a·chro·ma·top·sy** (ā krō′mə top′sē). [A-[6] + CHROMAT- + -OPSIA]

a·chro·ma·tous (ā krō′mə təs), *adj.* **1.** without color. **2.** having little or inadequate color; lighter in color than normal. [ACHROMAT(IC) + -OUS]

a·chro·mic (ā krō′mik), *adj.* colorless; without coloring matter. Also, **a·chro′mous.** [1755–65; A-[6] + CHROMIC]

a·chro·mo·bac·ter (ā krō′mə bak′tər), *n. Bacteriol.* any of several rod-shaped bacteria of the genus *Achromobacter,* found in soil and water. [< NL < Gk *áchrōmo(s)* colorless (*a-* A-[6] + *chrômos* color) + NL *-bacter* -BACTER]

A chromosome, *Genetics.* any chromosome belonging to the normal set characteristic of a given species. [1975–80]

Ach·ro·my·cin (ak′rō mī′sin), *Pharm., Trademark.* a brand of tetracycline.

Ach·sah (ak′sə), *n.* the daughter of Caleb who was promised in marriage to the conqueror of the city of Debir. Josh. 15:16–19; Judges 1:12–15.

Ach·tung (äkн′tŏŏng), *interj. German.* attention.

ach·y (ā′kē), *adj.,* **ach·i·er, ach·i·est.** having or causing an aching sensation: *an achy back.* [1870–75; ACHE + -Y[1]] —**ach′i·ness,** *n.*

a·cic·u·la (ə sik′yə lə), *n., pl.* **-lae** (-lē′). **1.** a needlelike part; spine, bristle, or needlelike crystal. **2.** a pl. of **aciculum.** [1875–80; < NL, LL, alter. of *acucula* ornamental pin, equiv. to L *acu-,* s. of *acus* needle (cf. ACUTE) + *-cula* -CULE[1]]

a·cic·u·lar (ə sik′yə lər), *adj.* **1.** needle-shaped. **2.** *Metall.* **a.** (of cast iron) containing ferrite in a needlelike form. **b.** (of an alloy) having a microstructure of needlelike components. [1785–95; ACICUL(A) + -AR[1]] —**a·cic·u·lar·i·ty** (ə sik′yə lar′i tē), *n.* —**a·cic′u·lar·ly,** *adv.*

a·cic·u·late (ə sik′yə lit, -lāt′), *adj.* **1.** having aciculae. **2.** marked as with needle scratches. **3.** needle-shaped; acicular. Also, **a·cic′u·lat′ed.** [1830–40; ACICUL(A) + -ATE[1]]

a·cic·u·lum (ə sik′yə ləm), *n., pl.* **-lums, -la** (-lə). **1.** an acicula. **2.** *Zool.* one of the slender, sharp stylets embedded in the parapodia of certain annelid worms, as the polychaetes. [alter. of ACICULA]

ac·id (as′id), *n.* **1.** *Chem.* a compound usually having a sour taste and capable of neutralizing alkalis and reddening blue litmus paper, containing hydrogen that can be replaced by a metal or an electropositive group to form a salt, or containing an atom that can accept a pair of electrons from a base. Acids are proton donors that yield hydronium ions in water solution, or electron-pair acceptors that combine with electron-pair donors or bases. **2.** a substance with a sour taste. **3.** something, as a remark or piece of writing, that is sharp, sour, or ill-natured: *His criticism was pure acid.* **4.** *Slang.* See **LSD** (def. 2). **5. put on the acid,** *Australian Slang.* to importune someone, as for money, sexual favors, or confidential information. —*adj.* **6.** *Chem.* **a.** belonging or pertaining to acids or the anhydrides of acids. **b.** having only a part of the hydrogen of an acid replaced by a metal or its equivalent: *an acid phosphate.* **c.** having a pH value of less than 7. Cf. **alkaline** (def. 4). **7.** sharp or biting to the taste; tasting like vinegar; sour: *acid fruits.* **8.** sharp, biting, or ill-natured in mood, manner, etc.: *an acid remark; an acid wit.* **9.** *Geol.* containing much silica. **10.** *Metall.* noting, pertaining to, or made by a process in which the lining of the furnace, or the slag that is present, functions as an acid in high-temperature reactions in taking electrons from oxide ions: usually a siliceous material, as sand or ganister. Cf. **basic** (def. 3). [1620–30; < L *acidus* sour, akin to *ācer* sharp, *acētum* vinegar, ACESCENT, ACICULA] —**ac′id·ly,** *adv.* —**ac′id·ness,** *n.*

—**Syn. 8.** acerbic, stinging, vitriolic, tart. ACID, ASTRINGENT are terms used figuratively of wit or humor. ACID suggests a sharp, biting, or ill-natured quality: *an acid joke about an opponent.* ASTRINGENT connotes severity but usually also a bracing quality, as of something applied with curative intent: *astringent criticism.*

ac′id anhy′dride, *Chem.* See under **anhydride** (def. 1).

ac·i·dan·the·ra (as′i dan′thər ə), *n.* any bulbous African plant belonging to the genus *Acidanthera,* of the iris family, having sword-shaped leaves and long tubular flowers. [< NL (1844) < Gk *akid-* (s. of *akís*) needle (c. L *acus;* see ACICULA) + NL *-anthera;* see ANTHER, -A[2]]

ac′id cell′, *1. Elect.* a cell using an acid electrolyte. **2.** See **parietal cell.**

ac′id drop′, *Brit.* a tart candy, as a sourball.

ac′id dust′, air-polluting particles of dust, usually wind-borne, having high concentrations of acid.

ac′id dye′, *Chem.* any of a class of dyes containing one or more acidic groups, as the sulfo group: used in acid solution chiefly for dyeing wool and silk. [1885–90]

ac·id-fast (as′id fast′, -fäst′), *adj.* resistant to decolorizing by acidified alcohol after staining. [1900–05] —**ac′id-fast′ness,** *n.*

ac·id-form·ing (as′id fôr′ming), *adj.* **1.** yielding acid in chemical reaction; acidic. **2.** (of food) containing a large amount of acid ash after complete oxidation. [1865–70]

ac·id-head (as′id hed′), *n. Slang.* a person who habitually takes the drug LSD. Also, **ac′id·head′.** [1965–70]

ac′id house′, *Chiefly Brit.* a style of disco music marked by heavy bass and synthesizer rhythms, often associated with the taking of LSD and MDMA. [1985–90]

a·cid·ic (ə sid′ik), *adj.* **1.** acid (def. 6). **2.** *Geol.* acid (def. 9). **3.** acid-forming (def. 1). **4.** containing acid-bearing pollutants: *Acidic runoff is poisoning the nation's rivers.* [1875–80; ACID + -IC]

a·cid·i·fy (ə sid′ə fī′), *v.t., v.i.,* **-fied, -fy·ing. 1.** to make or become acid; convert into an acid. **2.** to make or become sour. [1790–1800; ACID + -IFY] —**a·cid′i·fi′a·ble,** *adj.* —**a·cid′i·fi·ca′tion,** *n.* —**a·cid′i·fi′er,** *n.*

ac·i·dim·e·ter (as′i dim′i tər), *n. Chem.* an instrument for measuring the amount of acid in a solution. [1830–40; ACID + -I- + -METER]

ac·i·dim·e·try (as′i dim′i trē), *n. Chem.* the process of measuring the amount of acid in a solution, as with an acidimeter or by titration. [1830–40; ACID + -I- + -METRY] —**a·cid·i·met·ric** (ə sid′ə me′trik, as′i də-), **a·cid′i·met′ri·cal,** *adj.* —**a·cid′i·met′ri·cal·ly,** *adv.*

a·cid·i·ty (ə sid′i tē), *n.* **1.** the quality or state of being acid. **2.** sourness; tartness. **3.** excessive acid quality, as of the gastric juice. [1610–20; < LL *aciditās.* See ACID, -ITY]

ac·id·ize (as′i dīz′), *v.,* **-ized, -iz·ing.** —*v.t.* **1.** to impregnate with acid; acidify. —*v.i.* **2.** to become acidified. Also, *esp. Brit.,* **ac′id·ise′.** [1905–10; ACID + -IZE] —**ac′id·i·za′tion,** *n.*

ac·id-lov·ing (as′id luv′ing), *adj.* (of a plant) requiring a pH of 4.5 to 5.5 for optimal growth.

ac′id metapro′tein, *Biochem.* a metaprotein derived by means of a hydrolytic acid.

ac′id num′ber, *Chem.* a number expressing the acidity of a substance, equal to the number of milligrams of potassium hydroxide needed to neutralize the free fatty acids present in one gram of the substance. Also called **acid value.**

a·cid·o·gen·ic (ə sid′ə jen′ik, as′i də-), *adj. Biochem.* producing acid, as bacteria, or causing acidity, as of the urine. [ACID + -O- + -GENIC]

ac·i·dol·y·sis (as′i dol′ə sis), *n. Chem.* decomposition resulting from the interaction of a compound and an acid. [< NL; see ACID, -O-, -LYSIS]

a·cid·o·phil (ə sid′ə fil, as′i də-), *adj.* **1.** *Biol., Ecol.* acidophilic. —*n.* **2.** *Biol.* an acidophilic cell, tissue, organism, or substance; eosinophil. Also, **a·cid·o·phile** (ə sid′ə fīl′, as′i də-) [1895–1900; ACID + -O- + -PHIL]

a·cid·o·phil·ic (ə sid′ə fil′ik, as′i də-), *adj.* **1.** *Biol.* having an affinity for acid stains; eosinophilic. **2.** *Ecol.* thriving in or requiring an acid environment. Also, **ac·i·doph·i·lous** (as′i dof′ə ləs), **oxyphilic.** [1895–1900; ACIDOPHIL + -IC]

ac·i·doph′i·lus milk′ (as′i dof′ə ləs), a fermented milk produced by growing the bacterium *Lactobacillus acidophilus* in milk, used in medicine to alter the microbial flora of the intestinal tract under certain conditions. [1920–25; < NL; see ACID, -O-, -PHILOUS]

ac·i·do·sis (as′i dō′sis), *n. Pathol.* a blood condition in which the bicarbonate concentration is below normal. [1895–1900; < NL; see ACID, -OSIS] —**ac·i·dot·ic** (as′i-dot′ik), *adj.*

ac′id phos′phate, *Chem.* superphosphate (def. 1).

ac′id precipita′tion, meteorological precipitation that is relatively acidic. Cf. **acid rain.** [1975–80]

ac′id rad′ical, *Chem.* the remainder of an acid molecule after acidic hydrogen has been removed.

ac′id rain′, precipitation, as rain, snow, or sleet, containing relatively high concentrations of acid-forming chemicals, as the pollutants from coal smoke, chemical manufacturing, and smelting, that have been released into the atmosphere and combined with water vapor: harmful to the environment. [1855–60]

ac′id rock′, rock-'n'-roll music characterized by loud electronic distortions and strident lyrics that refer to drug-induced experiences: performances are often accompanied by animated displays of colored lights. [1965–70] —**ac′id rock′er.**

ac′id salt′, *Chem.* a salt of a polybasic acid that is only partially neutralized by a base; a salt that is also an acid. [1720–30]

ac′id soil′, a soil of acid reaction or having a predominance of hydrogen ions, tasting sour in solution.

ac′id test′, a severe and conclusive test to establish quality, genuineness, worth, etc. [1890–95]

ac′id test′ ra′tio, a ratio of cash, receivables, and marketable securities to current liabilities, used in determining credit risks.

ac·id-tongued (as′id tungd′), *adj.* bitingly critical or sarcastic; sharp-tongued: *a critic famous for his acid-tongued reviews.*

ac′id trip′, *Slang.* a psychedelic experience induced by ingesting the hallucinogen LSD. [1965–70] —**ac′id trip′per.**

a·cid·u·lant (ə sij′ə lənt), *n. Chem.* an acidulating substance. Also, **acidulent.** [1825–35; < F, n. use of prp. of *aciduler,* v. deriv. of L *acidulus.* See ACIDULOUS, -ANT]

a·cid·u·late (ə sij′ə lāt′), *v.t.,* **-lat·ed, -lat·ing. 1.** to make somewhat acid. **2.** to sour; embitter. [1725–35; ACIDUL(OUS) + -ATE[1]] —**a·cid′u·la′tion,** *n.*

a·cid·u·lent (ə sij′ə lənt), *n.* **1.** *Chem.* acidulant. —*adj.* **2.** acidulous. [1825–35]

a·cid·u·lous (ə sij′ə ləs), *adj.* **1.** slightly sour. **2.** sharp; caustic: *his acidulous criticism of the book.* **3.** moderately acid or tart; subacid. Also, **acidulent.** [1760–70; < L *acidulus.* See ACID, -ULOUS]

ac·i·du·ric (as′i dŏŏr′ik, -dyŏŏr′-), *adj.* (of bacteria) capable of growth in an acid environment. [appar. ACI(D) + L *dur(āre)* to last + -IC]

ac′id val′ue, *Chem.* See **acid number.**

ac·id-washed (as′id wosht′, -wôsht′), *adj.* (of a denim garment) processed with a bleach solution so that the color becomes faded and grayish.

ac·id·y (as′i dē), *adj.* of the nature of or resembling acid; sharp; sour: *an acidy taste.* [ACID + -Y[1]]

ac·i·er·ate (as′ē ə rāt′), *v.t.,* **-at·ed, -at·ing.** to con-

CONCISE ETYMOLOGY KEY: <, descended or borrowed from; >, whence; b., blend of, blended; c., cognate with; cf., compare; deriv., derivative; equiv., equivalent; imit., imitative; obl., oblique; r., replacing; s., stem; sp., spelling, spelled; resp., respelling, respelled; trans., translation; ?, origin unknown; *, unattested; ‡, probably earlier than. See the full key inside the front cover.

vert (iron) into steel. [1865–70; < F *aciér(er)* deriv. of *acier* steel (< VL **aciārium,* equiv. to L *aci(ēs)* sharpness + *-ārium* -ARY) + -ATE[1]] —**ac′i•er•a′tion,** *n.*

ac•i•form (as′ə fôrm′), *adj.* needle-shaped; acicular. [1840–50; < L *aci-* (comb. form of *acus* needle; cf. ACICULA) + -FORM]

ac•i•na•ceous (as′ə nā′shəs), *adj. Bot.* having many small seeds, as a grape. [1765–75; ACIN(US) + -ACEOUS]

ac•i•nac•i•form (as′ə nas′ə fôrm′), *adj. Bot.* scimitar-shaped, as a leaf. [1765–75; < L *acīnac-* (s. of *acīnacēs* < Gk *akinákēs* short sword) + -I- + -FORM]

acinaciform leaf
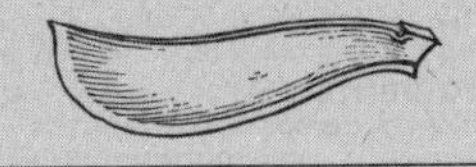

ac•i•nar•i•ous (as′ə nâr′ē əs), *adj. Bot.* covered with globose vesicles resembling grape seeds, as certain algae. [prob. < F *acinaire* (< L *acin(us)* ACINUS + F *-aire* -AIRE) + -IOUS]

a•cin•i•form (ə sin′ə fôrm′), *adj.* **1.** clustered like grapes. **2.** acinous. [1840–50; ACIN(US) + -I- + -FORM]

ac•i•nous (as′ə nəs), *adj.* consisting of acini. Also, **ac•i•nose** (as′ə nōs′). [1870–75; < L *acinōsus.* See ACINUS, -OUS]

ac•i•nus (as′ə nəs), *n., pl.* **-ni** (-nī′). **1.** *Bot.* one of the small drupelets or berries of an aggregate, baccate fruit, as the blackberry. **2.** a berry, as a grape or currant. **3.** *Anat.* **a.** a minute rounded lobule. **b.** the smallest secreting portion of a gland. [1725–35; < L: grape, berry, seed of a berry] —**ac•i•nar** (as′ə nər, -när′), **a•cin•ic** (ə sin′ik), *adj.*

-acious, a suffix forming adjectives that correspond to nouns ending in the suffixes **-acity** and **-acy:** *audacious; fallacious.* [< L *-āci-* (s. of *-āx*) adj. suffix + -OUS]

A•cis (ā′sis), *n. Class. Myth.* the lover of Galatea, killed by Polyphemus out of jealousy.

-acity, a complex noun suffix meaning "quality of" or "abounding in the characteristic of," appearing in loanwords from Latin: *tenacity.* [ME *-acite* << L *-ācitāt-* (s. of *-ācitās*). See -ACIOUS, -ITY]

ack., **1.** acknowledge. **2.** acknowledgment.

ack-ack (ak′ak′), *n. Informal.* (esp. during World War II). **1.** antiaircraft fire. **2.** antiaircraft arms. Also, **Ack′-Ack′.** [1935–40; for A.A. (abbrev. of *a(nti) a(ircraft)*) as said by British signalmen referring to sense 2]

ac•kee (ə kē′), *n.* akee.

ack•ey (ak′ē), *n., pl.* **-eys.** a silver coin minted in England in the late 18th and early 19th centuries for use in western Africa. [var. sp. of AKEE, the seeds of which served as a unit of weight]

ac•knowl•edge (ak nol′ij), *v.t.,* **-edged, -edg•ing. 1.** to admit to be real or true; recognize the existence, truth, or fact of: *to acknowledge one's mistakes.* **2.** to show or express recognition or realization of: *to acknowledge an acquaintance by nodding.* **3.** to recognize the authority, validity, or claims of: *The students acknowledged the authority of the student council.* **4.** to show or express appreciation or gratitude for: *to acknowledge a favor.* **5.** to indicate or make known the receipt of: *to acknowledge a letter.* **6.** to take notice of or reply to: *to acknowledge a greeting.* **7.** *Law.* to confirm as binding or of legal force: *to acknowledge a deed.* [1475–85; *acknowleche,* appar. either ME *aknou(en)* to recognize (OE *oncnāwan;* see A-[1], KNOW) + *-leche* n. suffix (OE **-lǣce,* by-form of *-lac;* cf. KNOWLEDGE, WEDLOCK); or b. *aknouen* and *knouleche* KNOWLEDGE; then *a-* was mistaken for AC-] —**ac•knowl′edge•a•ble,** *adj.* —**ac•knowl′edg•er,** *n.*

—**Syn. 1.** concede, confess, grant. ACKNOWLEDGE, ADMIT, CONFESS agree in the idea of declaring something to be true. ACKNOWLEDGE implies making a statement reluctantly, often about something previously denied: *to acknowledge a fault.* ADMIT especially implies acknowledging something under pressure: *to admit a charge.* CONFESS usually means stating somewhat formally an admission of wrongdoing, crime, or shortcoming: *to confess guilt; to confess an inability to understand.* —**Ant. 1.** deny, disclaim, disavow.

ac•knowl•edged (ak nol′ijd), *adj.* widely recognized; generally accepted: *an acknowledged authority on Chinese art.* [1760–70; ACKNOWLEDGE + -ED[2]] —**ac•knowl•edged•ly** (ak nol′ijd lē, -i jid-), *adv.*

ac•knowl•edg•ment (ak nol′ij mənt), *n.* **1.** an act of acknowledging. **2.** recognition of the existence or truth of something: *the acknowledgment of a sovereign power.* **3.** an expression of appreciation. **4.** a thing done or given in appreciation or gratitude. **5.** *Law.* **a.** a declaration before an official that one has executed a particular legal document. **b.** an official certificate of a formal acknowledging. **c.** public recognition by a man of an illegitimate child as his own. Also, *esp. Brit.,* **ac•knowl′•edge•ment.** [1585–95; ACKNOWLEDGE + -MENT]

ack•ton (ak′tən), *n. Armor.* acton.

ac•le (ak′lē), *n.* the hard, durable wood of a Philippine leguminous tree, *Albizzia acle,* used for making fine furniture. [< Tagalog *aklé*]

a•cleis•to•car•di•a (ə klī′stə kär′dē ə, ā klī′-), *n. Pathol.* a failure of the foramen ovale of the heart to close. [< Gk *ákleisto(s)* not closed (*a-* A-[6] + *kleis-,* var. s. of *kléiein* to close + *-tos* verbal adj. suffix) + -CARDIA]

a•clin′ic line′ (ā klin′ik), an imaginary line on the surface of the earth, close and approximately parallel to the equator, connecting all those points over which a magnetic needle shows no inclination from the horizontal. Also called **magnetic equator.** [1840–50; < Gk *aklin(ḗs)* not bending (*a-* A-[6] + *klin-,* var. s. of *klī́nein* to bend) + -IC]

A.C.L.S., American Council of Learned Societies.

ACLU, 1. See **American Civil Liberties Union. 2.** American College of Life Underwriters. Also, **A.C.L.U.**

ac•me (ak′mē), *n.* the highest point; summit; peak: *The empire was at the acme of its power.* [1610–20; < Gk *akmḗ* point, highest point, extremity] —**ac•mic** (ak′mik), **ac•mat•ic** (ak mat′ik), *adj.*

ac•me•ism (ak′mē iz′əm), *n.* a school of early 20th-century Russian poetry whose practitioners were strongly opposed to the vagueness of symbolism and strove for absolute clarity of expression through precise, concrete imagery. [< Russ *akmeízm,* equiv. to Gk *akmḗ* ACME + Russ *-izm* -ISM]

ac•mes•the•sia (ak′məs thē′zhə, -zhē ə, -zē ə), *n. Psychol.* awareness of sharp points through the sense of touch without experiencing pain. Also, **ac′maes•the′•sia.** [< Gk *akm(ḗ)* ACME + ESTHESIA]

ac•mite (ak′mīt), *n.* a rare pyroxene mineral, sodium-ferric iron silicate, $NaFe(Si_2O_6)$, found in feldspathoid rocks. [1830–40; < Gk *akm(ḗ)* sharp point + -ITE[1]]

ac•ne (ak′nē), *n. Pathol.* an inflammatory disease of the sebaceous glands, characterized by comedones and pimples, esp. on the face, back, and chest, and, in severe cases, by cysts and nodules resulting in scarring. Also called **ac′ne vul•ga′ris** (vul gâr′is, -gar′-). Cf. **rosacea.** [1820–30; < NL < LGk *aknás,* a manuscript error for *akmás,* acc. pl. of *akmḗ* facial eruption, prob. to be identified with Gk *akmḗ* ACME] —**ac′ned,** *adj.*

ac•ne•gen•ic (ak′ni jen′ik), *adj. Pathol.* causing or able to cause acne. [1975–80; ACNE + -GENIC]

ac•ne•mi•a (ak nē′mē ə), *n. Pathol.* **1.** a condition characterized by atrophy of the muscles of the calf of the leg. **2.** congenital absence of the legs. [A-[6] + *cnem-* (< Gk *knḗmē* shin) + -IA]

ac′ne rosa′cea, *Pathol.* rosacea. [1895–1900]

ac•o•asm (ak′ō az′əm), *n.* acouasm.

a•cock (ə kok′), *adv., adj.* cocked. [1840–50; A-[1] + COCK[2]]

a•coe•lo•mate (ā sē′lə māt′, ā′sē lō′mit), *Zool.* —*adj.* **1.** Also, **a•coe•lom•a•tous** (ā′sē lom′ə təs, -lō′mə-), **a•coe′lo•mous.** having no coelum. —*n.* **2.** any organism that lacks a cavity between the body wall and the digestive tract, including the flatworms, nemertines, and sea anemones. [1875–80; A-[6] + COELOMATE]

a•coe•lous (ā sē′ləs), *adj.* **1.** without a true alimentary canal. **2.** acoelomate. [A-[6] + COEL(UM) + -OUS]

a•coe•naes•the•sia (ā′sē nəs thē′zhə), *n. Psychiatry.* acenesthesia. [A-[6] + COENESTHESIA]

a•cold (ə kōld′), *adj. Archaic.* being cold or chilled. [bef. 900; ME *acolde,* OE *ācolod,* ptp. of *ācōlian* to grow cold. See A-[3], COOL, -ED[2]]

ac•o•lyte (ak′ə līt′), *n.* **1.** an altar attendant in public worship; altar boy. **2.** *Rom. Cath. Ch.* **a.** a member of the highest-ranking of the four minor orders. **b.** the order itself. Cf. **exorcist** (def. 2), **lector** (def. 2), **ostiary** (def. 1). **3.** any attendant, assistant, or follower. [1275–1325; ME *acolite* < ML *acolytus* < Gk *akólouthos* follower, attendant, equiv. to *a-* prefix denoting association + *-kolouthos,* var. of *kéleuthos* road, journey]

Ac•o•ma (ak′ə mô′, -mə, ä′kə), *n.* a Pueblo Indian village near Albuquerque, New Mexico, built on a sandstone mesa: oldest continuously inhabited location in the U.S.

A•con•ca•gua (ä′kông kä′gwä), *n.* a mountain in W Argentina, in the Andes: the highest peak in the Western Hemisphere. 22,834 ft. (6960 m).

ac•o•nite (ak′ə nīt′), *n.* any plant belonging to the genus *Aconitum,* of the buttercup family, having irregular flowers usually in loose clusters, including species with poisonous and medicinal properties. Also, **a•co•ni•tum** (ak′ə nī′təm). Cf. **monkshood, wolfsbane.** [1570–80; < L *aconītum* < Gk *akóniton* leopard's-bane, wolfsbane] —**ac•o•nit•ic** (ak′ə nit′ik), *adj.*

a•corn (ā′kôrn, ā′kərn), *n.* **1.** the typically ovoid fruit or nut of an oak, enclosed at the base by a cupule. **2.** a finial or knop, as on a piece of furniture, in the form of an acorn. [bef. 1000; ME *acorne* (influenced by CORN), r. *akern,* OE *æcern, æcren* mast, oak-mast; c. ON *akarn* fruit of wild trees, MHG *ackeran* acorn, Goth *akran* fruit, yield < Gmc **akrana-;* alleged derivation from base of ACRE is dubious if original reference was to wild trees] —**a′corned,** *adj.*

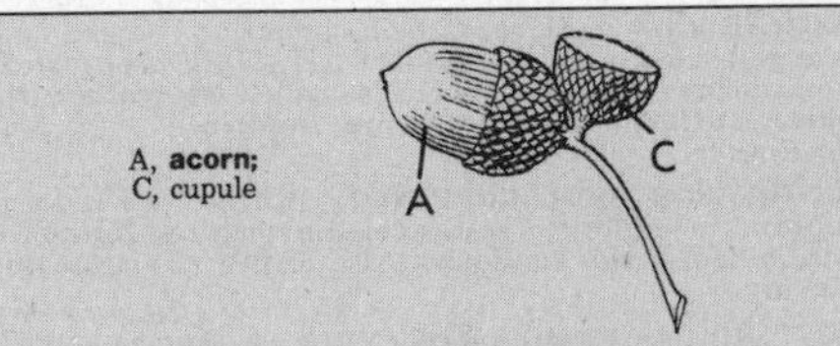

A, **acorn;**
C, cupule

a′corn bar′nacle. See under **barnacle**[1] (def. 1).

a′corn chair′, *Eng. Furniture.* a Jacobean chair having a crossrail with acorn-shaped pendants.

a′corn clock′, a mantel clock of the first half of the 19th century, having the upper part of the case shaped with a double ogee curve to resemble an acorn.

a′corn spoon′, a spoon having an acornlike ornament at the end of its stem.

a′corn squash′, an acorn-shaped variety of winter squash, growing to 18 in. (46 cm) long and 14 in. (36 cm) in diameter, having a dark-green to orange-yellow skin and yellow to orange flesh. [1935–40]

a′corn sug′ar, *Chem.* quercitol. [1895–1900]

a′corn tube′, *Electronics.* a vacuum tube, resembling an acorn in size and shape, used chiefly in ultrahigh-frequency electronic devices. [1930–35]

a′corn worm′, any of several burrowing, often brilliantly colored hemichordates of the class Enteropneusta, usually found in intertidal sand and mud, having an acorn-shaped proboscis and collar. Also, **a′corn•worm′.** [1885–90]

a•cot•y•le•don (ā′kot′l ēd′n, ā kot′-), *n.* a plant without cotyledons, therefore one belonging to a group lower than the seed plants. [1810–20; A-[6] + COTYLEDON] —**a•cot•y•le•don•ous** (ā′kot′l ēd′n əs, ā kot′-).

a•cou•asm (ə ko͞o′az əm, ak′o͞o az′-), *n. Psychiatry.* a nonverbal auditory hallucination, as a ringing or hissing. Also, **acoasm, acousma.** [< Gk *ákou(sma)* something heard (*akous-,* s. of *akoúein* to hear + *-ma* resultative n. suffix) + *-asm* as in ENTHUSIASM, ORGASM, etc.]

a•cous•ma (ə ko͞oz′mə), *n., pl.* **-mas, -ma•ta.** acouasm.

a•cous•tic (ə ko͞o′stik), *adj.* Also, **a•cous′ti•cal. 1.** pertaining to the sense or organs of hearing, to sound, or to the science of sound. **2.** (of a building material) designed for controlling sound. **3.** *Music.* **a.** of, pertaining to, or being a musical instrument whose sound is not electrically enhanced or modified. **b.** arranged for or made up of such instruments: *an acoustic solo; an acoustic group.* —*n.* **4.** *Obs.* a remedy for deafness or imperfect hearing. [1595–1605; < Gk *akoustikós.* See ACOUASM, -TIC] —**a•cous′ti•cal•ly,** *adv.*

acous′tical cloud′, one of a number of acoustic panels installed near the ceiling of a concert hall to reflect sound for improving the acoustic quality of music.

acous′tical surveil′lance, the collecting or recording of information by sound-detection methods and devices, as for intelligence purposes.

acous′tical tile′, tile made in various sizes and textures from soft, usually fibrous, sound-absorbing material, as wood, cork, or metal, and typically applied to ceilings or walls.

acous′tic cou′pler, *Computers.* a modem designed to connect a telephone handset to a computer terminal or processor. [1965–70]

acous′tic fea′ture, *Phonet.* **1.** any acoustic property of a speech sound that may be recorded and analyzed, as its fundamental frequency or formant structure. **2.** an acoustic property that defines a class of speech sounds, esp. in distinctive feature analysis, as acute, grave, or diffuse.

acous′tic feed′back, *Electronics.* (in an audio system, esp. a public-address system) the feedback of sound from a loudspeaker to a microphone, often resulting in a whistling noise caused by electrical oscillations. Also called **feedback.**

acous′tic guitar′, a traditional, unamplified guitar. Also called **Spanish guitar.** Cf. **electric guitar.**

ac•ous•ti•cian (ak′o͞o stish′ən), *n.* an acoustic engineer. [1875–80; ACOUST(ICS) + -ICIAN]

acous′tic imped′ance, *Acoustics.* the total reaction of a medium to the transmission of sound through it, expressed as the ratio of sound pressure to particle velocity at a given point in the medium.

acous′tic inert′ance, *Acoustics.* inertance. Also called **acous′tic mass′.**

acous′tic mine′, a naval mine designed to be exploded by the vibration of the propeller of a passing ship or by the sound of water along the hull. Also called **sonic mine.** Cf. **contact mine, magnetic mine.** [1940–45]

acous′tic nerve′. See **auditory nerve.**

acous′tic ohm′, *Acoustics.* the unit of acoustic impedance, equal to the impedance of a medium in which a sound pressure of one dyne per square centimeter produces a velocity of one centimeter per second.

acous′tic phonet′ics, 1. the branch of science dealing with the sounds of speech in terms of their frequency, duration, intensity, etc., esp. as analyzed by means of instruments like the sound spectrograph and the oscillograph. Cf. **articulatory phonetics. 2.** a composite branch of physics and linguistics that treats sound proper as it relates to speech. **3.** the branch of phonetics dealing with the transmission of sounds to the ear and the reception of them by the ear prior to neurological processing. Cf. **auditory phonetics.** [1930–35]

acous′tic react′ance, *Acoustics.* acoustic impedance caused by the inertia and elasticity of the transmitting medium. Also called **reactance.**

acous′tic resist′ance, *Acoustics.* acoustic impedance caused by the internal friction of the transmitting medium.

a•cous•tics (ə ko͞o′stiks), *n.* **1.** (*used with a singular v.*) *Physics.* the branch of physics that deals with sound and sound waves. **2.** (*used with a plural v.*) the qualities or characteristics of a room, auditorium, stadium, etc., that determine the audibility or fidelity of sounds in it. [1675–85; see ACOUSTIC, -ICS]

acous′tic theod′olite, *Oceanog.* an acoustic device that records a continuous vertical profile of ocean currents at a particular site. [1975–80]

acous′tic torpe′do, a torpedo guided by sound that either emanates from the target or is emitted by the torpedo and bounces off the target.

ac•ous•tim•e•ter (ak′o͞o stim′i tər), *n.* a portable electronic device for measuring noise levels, esp. those of traffic. [ACOUST(IC) + -I- + -METER]

a•cous•to•e•lec•tric (ə ko͞o′stō i lek′trik), *adj.* electroacoustic. [1965–70; ACOUSTIC + -O- + ELECTRIC]

a•cous•to•op•tics (ə ko͞o′stō op′tiks), *n.* (*used with a singular v.*) the science and technology of the interactions between sound waves and light waves passing through material media, esp. as applied to the modulation and deflection of laser beams by ultrasonic waves. [1970–75; ACOUST(IC) + -O- + OPTICS] —**a·cous′to·op′·tic, a·cous′to·op′ti·cal,** *adj.* —**a·cous′to·op′ti·cal·ly,** *adv.*

A.C.P., American College of Physicians.

acpt., acceptance.

ac·quaint (ə kwānt′), *v.t.* **1.** to make more or less familiar, aware, or conversant (usually fol. by *with*): *to acquaint the mayor with our plan.* **2.** to furnish with knowledge; inform (usually fol. by *with*): *to acquaint the manager with one's findings.* **3.** to bring into social contact; introduce (usually fol. by *with*): *She acquainted her roommate with my cousin.* [1250–1300; ME *aqueinten, acointen* < AF *acointer,* OF *acoint(i)er,* v. deriv. of *acointe* familiar, known < L *accognitus,* ptp. of *accognōscere* to recognize, equiv. to *ac-* AC- + *co-* CO- + *gni-* KNOW + *-tus* ptp. suffix]

ac·quaint·ance (ə kwān′tns), *n.* **1.** a person known to one, but usually not a close friend. **2.** the state of being acquainted. **3.** personal knowledge as a result of study, experience, etc.: *a good acquaintance with French wines.* **4.** (*used with a plural v.*) the persons with whom one is acquainted. Also, **ac·quaint′ance·ship′** (for defs. 2, 3). [1250–1300; ME *aqueinta(u)nce, acoyntaunce* < OF *acointance.* See ACQUAINT, -ANCE]
—**Syn. 1.** ACQUAINTANCE, ASSOCIATE, COMPANION, FRIEND refer to a person with whom one is in contact. An ACQUAINTANCE is someone recognized by sight or someone known, though not intimately: *a casual acquaintance.* An ASSOCIATE is a person who is often in one's company, usually because of some work, enterprise, or pursuit in common: *a business associate.* A COMPANION is a person who shares one's activities, fate, or condition: *a traveling companion; companion in despair.* A FRIEND is a person with whom one is on intimate terms and for whom one feels a warm affection: *a trusted friend.* **3.** familiarity, awareness.

acquaint′ance rape′, forced sexual intercourse with a person known to the victim. [1980–85]

ac·quaint·ed (ə kwān′tid), *adj.* **1.** having personal knowledge as a result of study, experience, etc.; informed (usually fol. by *with*): *to be acquainted with law.* **2.** brought into social contact; made familiar: *people acquainted through mutual friends.* [1250–1300; ME; see ACQUAINT, -ED[2]] —**ac·quaint′ed·ness,** *n.*

ac·quest (ə kwest′), *n. Law.* property acquired other than by inheritance, as by purchase or gift. [1605–15; < obs. F < VL **acquaesitum* that which has been acquired, n. use of **acquaesitus* (ptp. of **acquaerere* to acquire, alter. of L *acquīrere* to ACQUIRE)]

ac·qui·esce (ak′wē es′), *v.i.,* **-esced, -esc·ing.** to assent tacitly; submit or comply silently or without protest; agree; consent: *to acquiesce halfheartedly in a business plan.* [1610–20; < L *acquiēscere* to find rest in, equiv. to *ac-* AC- + *quiē-* (see QUIET[2]) + *-sc-* inchoative suffix + *-ere* inf. suffix] —**ac′qui·esc′ing·ly,** *adv.*
—**Syn.** accede, concur; capitulate.

ac·qui·es·cence (ak′wē es′əns), *n.* **1.** the act or condition of acquiescing or giving tacit assent; agreement or consent by silence or without objection; compliance (usually fol. by *to* or *in*): *acquiescence to his boss's demands.* **2.** *Law.* such neglect to take legal proceedings for such a long time as to imply the abandonment of a right. [1625–35; ACQUIESCE + -ENCE]

ac·qui·es·cent (ak′wē es′ənt), *adj.* disposed to acquiesce or consent tacitly. [1745–55; < L *acquiēscent-* (s. of *acquiēscēns,* prp. of *acquiēscere*). See ACQUIESCE, -ENT] —**ac′qui·es′cent·ly,** *adv.*

ac·quire (ə kwī^ə^r′), *v.t.,* **-quired, -quir·ing. 1.** to come into possession or ownership of; get as one's own: *to acquire property.* **2.** to gain for oneself through one's actions or efforts: *to acquire learning.* **3.** *Ling.* to achieve native or nativelike command of (a language or a linguistic rule or element). **4.** *Mil.* to locate and track (a moving target) with a detector, as radar. [1400–50; < L *acquīrere* to add to one's possessions, acquire (*ac-* AC- + *-quīrere,* comb. form of *quaerere* to search for, obtain); r. late ME *aquere* < MF *aquerre* < L] —**ac·quir′a·ble,** *adj.* —**ac·quir′a·bil′i·ty,** *n.* —**ac·quir′er,** *n.*
—**Syn. 1.** See **get. 2.** win, earn, attain; appropriate.

acquired′ char′acter, *Genetics.* a noninheritable character that results from certain environmental influences. [1875–80]

acquired′ immune′ defi′ciency syn′drome. See **AIDS.** Also, **acquired′ immunodefi′ciency syn′·drome.**

acquired′ immu′nity, *Immunol.* immunity arising from exposure to antigens. Cf. **natural immunity.**

ac·quir·ee (ə kwī^ə^r ē′), *n.* something that is acquired: *a press conference to promote the conglomerate's latest acquirees.* [ACQUIRE + -EE]

ac·quire·ment (ə kwī^ə^r′mənt), *n.* **1.** the act of acquiring, esp. the gaining of knowledge or mental attributes. **2.** Often, **acquirements.** something that is acquired, esp. an acquired ability or attainment. [1620–30; ACQUIRE + -MENT]

ac·qui·si·tion (ak′wə zish′ən), *n.* **1.** the act of acquiring or gaining possession: *the acquisition of real eatate.* **2.** something acquired; addition: *a recent acquisition to the museum.* **3.** *Ling.* the act or process of achieving mastery of a language or a linguistic rule or element: *child language acquisition; second language acquisition.* [1375–1425; ME *adquisicioun, a(c)quisicion* < L *acquīsītiōn-* (s. of *acquīsītiō*), equiv. to *acquīsīt(us),* ptp. of *acquīrere* to ACQUIRE + *-iōn-* -ION] —**ac′qui·si′tion·al,** *adj.* —**ac·quis·i·tor** (ə kwiz′i tər), *n.*

CONCISE ETYMOLOGY KEY: <, descended or borrowed from; >, whence; b., blend of, blended; c., cognate with; cf., compare; deriv., derivative; equiv., equivalent; imit., imitative; obl., oblique; r., replacing; s., stem; sp., spelling, spelled; resp., respelling, respelled; trans., translation; ?, origin unknown; *, unattested; ‡, probably earlier than. See the full key inside the front cover.

ac·quis·i·tive (ə kwiz′i tiv), *adj.* tending or seeking to acquire and own, often greedily; eager to get wealth, possessions, etc.: *our acquisitive impulses; acquisitive societies.* Also, **ac·quis·i·to·ry** (ə kwiz′i tôr′ē, -tōr′ē). [1630–40; < ML, LL *acquīsītīvus;* see ACQUISITION, -IVE] —**ac·quis′i·tive·ly,** *adv.* —**ac·quis′i·tive·ness,** *n.*
—**Syn.** covetous, grasping, avaricious.

ac·quit (ə kwit′), *v.t.,* **-quit·ted, -quit·ting. 1.** to relieve from a charge of fault or crime; declare not guilty: *They acquitted him of the crime. The jury acquitted her, but I still think she's guilty.* **2.** to release or discharge (a person) from an obligation. **3.** to settle or satisfy (a debt, obligation, claim, etc.). **4.** to bear or conduct (oneself); behave: *He acquitted himself well in battle.* **5.** to free or clear (oneself): *He acquitted himself of suspicion.* [1200–50; ME *aquiten* < AF, OF *a(c)quiter,* deriv., with *a(c)-* AC-, of *quite* free of obligations < ML *quit(t)us,* L *quiētus* QUIET[1]; cf. QUIT] —**ac·quit′ter,** *n.*
—**Syn. 1.** exculpate. See **absolve. 2.** free. —**Ant. 1.** convict.

ac·quit·tal (ə kwit′l), *n.* **1.** the act of acquitting; discharge. **2.** the state of being acquitted; release. **3.** the discharge or settlement of a debt, obligation, etc. **4.** *Law.* judicial deliverance from a criminal charge on a verdict or finding of not guilty. [1400–50; late ME *a(c)quitaille* < AF; see ACQUIT, -AL[2]]

ac·quit·tance (ə kwit′ns), *n.* **1.** the act of acquitting. **2.** the discharge of a debt or obligation. **3.** a document or receipt as evidence of the discharge of a debt or obligation. [1300–50; ME *aquitance* < OF. See ACQUIT, -ANCE]

acr-, var. of **acro-** before a vowel: *acronym.*

a·cral·de·hyde (ə kral′də hīd′), *n. Chem.* acrolein. [1865–70; < L *ācr-* (s. of *ācer*) sharp + ALDEHYDE]

a·cra·sin (ə krā′sin), *n. Mycol.* a chemotactic substance, identical with cAMP, secreted by myxamebas of cellular slime molds and attracting other myxamebas to aggregate and form a pseudoplasmodium. [1945–50; < NL *Acras(iales)* an order of cellular slime molds (*Acras(is)* a genus, so named from the lack of fusion between the cells (< Gk; see A-[6], CRASIS) + *-ales* -ALES) + -IN[2]]

a·cre (ā′kər), *n.* **1.** a common variable unit of land measure, now equal in the U.S. and Great Britain to 43,560 square feet or 1/640 square mile (4047 square meters). **2. acres, a.** lands; land: *wooded acres.* **b.** *Informal.* large quantities: *acres of Oriental rugs.* **3.** *Archaic.* a plowed or sown field. [bef. 1000; ME *aker,* OE *æcer;* c. OFris *ekker,* OS *akkar,* OHG *ackar* (G *Acker*), ON *akr,* Goth *akers,* L *ager,* Gk *agrós,* Skt *ájra-;* see also ACORN, AGRARIAN, AGRESTIC, AGRICULTURE, AGRO-]

A·cre (ä′krə *for 1;* ä′kər, ā′kər *for 2*), *n.* **1.** a state in W Brazil. 301,628; 58,900 sq. mi. (152,550 sq. km). *Cap.:* Rio Branco. **2.** a seaport in NW Israel: besieged and captured by Crusaders 1191. 38,700.

a·cre·age (ā′kər ij), *n.* **1.** extent or area in acres; acres collectively. **2.** a plot of land amounting to approximately one acre: *They bought an acreage on the outskirts of town.* [1855–60; ACRE + -AGE]

a·cred (ā′kərd), *adj.* owning many acres of land; landed. [1835–45; ACRE + -ED[3]]

a·cre-foot (ā′kər fo͝ot′), *n.* a unit of volume of water in irrigation: the amount covering one acre to a depth of one foot, equal to 43,560 cubic feet. [1900–05, *Amer.*]

a·cre-inch (ā′kər inch′), *n.* one-twelfth of an acre-foot, equal to 3630 cubic feet. [1905–10, *Amer.*]

a′cre right′, *U.S. Hist.* the right of a settler to purchase land that the settler has occupied or improved.

ac·rid (ak′rid), *adj.* **1.** sharp or biting to the taste or smell; bitterly pungent; irritating to the eyes, nose, etc.: *acrid smoke from burning rubber.* **2.** extremely or sharply stinging or bitter; exceedingly caustic: *acrid remarks.* [1705–15; < L *ācr-* (s. of *ācer*) sharp, sour + -ID[4], perh. through influence of ACID] —**a·crid·i·ty** (ə krid′i tē), **ac′rid·ness,** *n.* —**ac′rid·ly,** *adv.*

ac·ri·did (ak′ri did), *n.* locust (def. 1). [< NL *Acrididae.* equiv. to *Acrid(a)* a genus of grasshoppers (< Gk *akrid-,* s. of *akrís* grasshopper + L *-a* -A[2]) + *-idae* -ID[2]]

ac·ri·dine (ak′ri dēn′, -din), *n. Chem.* a colorless, crystalline solid, $C_{13}H_9N$, usually obtained from the anthracine fraction of coal tar: used chiefly in the synthesis of dyes and drugs. [1875–80; ACRID + -INE[2]]

ac·ri·fla·vine (ak′rə flā′vin, -vēn), *n. Chem.* an orange-brown, granular solid, $C_{14}H_{14}N_3Cl$: used chiefly in medicine as an antiseptic. Also called **neutral acriflavine, euflavine, trypaflavine neutral.** [1915–20; ACRI(DINE) + -FLAVIN]

acrifla′vine hydrochlo′ride, *Chem.* the reddish-brown, crystalline, water-soluble hydrochloride of acriflavine, used similarly. Also called **trypaflavine, flavine.**

Ac·ri·lan (ak′rə lan′), *Trademark.* a brand name for an acrylic fiber used in textiles, characterized chiefly by softness, strength, and wrinkle-resistant properties.

ac·ri·mo·ni·ous (ak′rə mō′nē əs), *adj.* caustic, stinging, or bitter in nature, speech, behavior, etc.: *an acrimonious answer; an acrimonious dispute.* [1605–15; < ML *ācrimōniōsus.* See ACRIMONY, -OUS] —**ac′ri·mo′·ni·ous·ly,** *adv.* —**ac′ri·mo′ni·ous·ness,** *n.*

ac·ri·mo·ny (ak′rə mō′nē), *n.* sharpness, harshness, or bitterness of nature, speech, disposition, etc.: *The speaker attacked him with great acrimony.* [1535–45; < L *ācrimōnia,* equiv. to *ācri-* (s. of *ācer*) sharp, sour + *-mōnia* -MONY]
—**Syn.** bitterness, animosity, spitefulness, asperity, spite. —**Ant.** goodwill, civility, kindness, politeness.

ac·ri·tarch (ak′ri tärk′), *n. Paleontol.* any of various microfossils, of unknown biological affinities, having a central cavity enclosed by a wall of chiefly organic composition. [1963; < NL *Acritarcha* (neut. pl.), irreg. < Gk *ákrit(os)* confused, doubtful (see A-[6], CRITIC) + *archḗ* beginning, origin (cf. ARCHI-)] —**ac′ri·tar′chous,** *adj.*

a·crit·i·cal (ā krit′i kəl), *adj.* **1.** not critical. **2.** *Med* (of a disease) not showing a crisis. [1860–65; A-[6] + CRIT ICAL]

acro-, a combining form with the meanings "height," "tip end," "extremities of the body," used in the formation of compound words: *acrophobia.* Also, *esp. before c vowel,* **acr-.** [< Gk, comb. form of *ákros* topmost, highest; akin to L *ācer* sharp. Cf. ACME, EAR[2]]

ac·ro·bat (ak′rə bat′), *n.* **1.** a skilled performer o gymnastic feats, as walking on a tightrope or swinging on a trapeze. **2.** a person who readily changes viewpoints or opinions. [1815–25; < F *acrobate* < Gk *akróbatos* walking on tiptoe, equiv. to *akro-* ACRO- + *-batos,* verbal adj. of *bainein* to go; F word may be recoinage, o etymological reading of the Gk word]

ac·ro·bat·ic (ak′rə bat′ik), *adj.* **1.** of, pertaining to or like an acrobat or acrobatics. **2.** having the good balance, agility, and coordination of an acrobat. Also, **ac′ro·bat′i·cal.** [1860–65; < Gk *akrobatikós.* See ACROBAT, -IC] —**ac′ro·bat′i·cal·ly,** *adv.*

ac·ro·bat·ics (ak′rə bat′iks), *n.* **1.** (*used with a plural v.*) the feats of an acrobat; gymnastics. **2.** (*used with a singular v.*) the art or practice of acrobatic feats. **3.** (*used with a plural v.*) something performed with remarkable agility and ease: *the verbal acrobatics of a habitual liar.* [1880–85; see ACROBATIC, -ICS]

ac·ro·car·pous (ak′rə kär′pəs), *adj. Bot.* having the reproductive organ at the end of the primary axis. [1860–65; < NL *acrocarpus* < Gk *akrókarpos.* See ACRO-, -CARPOUS]

ac·ro·cen·tric (ak′rə sen′trik), *adj. Genetics.* of or pertaining to any chromosome or chromatid whose centromere is closer to one end than to the other, creating two unequal chromosome arms. Cf. **acentric** (def. 2), **metacentric** (def. 2), **telocentric.** [1940–45; ACRO- + -CENTRIC]

ac·ro·ceph·a·ly (ak′rə sef′ə lē), *n. Pathol.* oxycephaly. Also, **ac·ro·ce·pha·lia** (ak′rō sə fāl′yə). [1875–80; ACRO- + -CEPHALY] —**ac·ro·ce·phal·ic** (ak′rō sə fal′ik), *adj., n.* —**ac′ro·ceph′a·lous,** *adj.*

Ac·ro·cor·inth (ak′rə kôr′inth, -kor′-), *n.* the citadel of ancient Corinth: strategic in the control of the Isthmus of Corinth; extensive ruins.

ac·ro·cy·a·no·sis (ak′rō sī′ə nō′sis), *n. Pathol.* cyanosis of the extremities, characterized by blueness and coldness of the fingers and toes. [< NL; see ACRO-, CYANOSIS]

ac·ro·dont (ak′rə dont′), *adj. Zool.* having rootless teeth fastened to the alveolar ridge of the jaws. [1840–50; ACR- + -ODONT] —**ac′ro·dont′ism,** *n.*

ac·ro·gen (ak′rə jən, -jen′), *n. Bot.* a flowerless plant growing and producing its reproductive structures at the apex only, as ferns and mosses. [1835–45; ACRO- + -GEN] —**ac·ro·gen·ic** (ak′rə jen′ik), **a·crog·e·nous** (ə kroj′ə nəs), *adj.* —**a·crog′e·nous·ly,** *adv.*

a·crog·y·nous (ə kroj′ə nəs), *adj. Bot.* having the female reproductive organ arising from the apical cell of the stem, thereby terminating its growth, as certain liverworts. Cf. **anacrogynous.** [ACRO- + -GYNOUS]

ac·ro·lect (ak′rə lekt′), *n. Ling.* the variety of language in a creole continuum that approximates most closely the standard variety of a major international language, as the English spoken in Guyana or Jamaica. Cf. **basilect, mesolect.** [1960–65; ACRO- + (DIA)LECT] —**ac′ro·lec′tal,** *adj.*

a·cro·le·in (ə krō′lē in), *n. Chem.* a yellow, flammable liquid, C_3H_4O, having a stifling odor, usually obtained by the decomposition of glycerol: used chiefly in the synthesis of commercial and pharmaceutical products. Also called **acraldehyde, acrylaldehyde, acrylic aldehyde.** [1855–60; < L *ācr-* (s. of *ācer*) sharp + *olē(re)* to smell + -IN[2]]

ac·ro·lith (ak′rə lith), *n.* a sculptured figure having the head and extremities of stone and the torso of other material. [1840–50; < L *acrolithus* < Gk *akrólithos.* See ACRO-, -LITH] —**ac′ro·lith′ic,** *adj.*

a·crol·o·gy (ə krol′ə jē), *n., pl.* **-gies.** acrophony. [< F *acrologie.* See ACRO-, -LOGY] —**ac·ro·log·ic** (ak′rə-loj′ik), *adj.* —**ac′ro·log′i·cal·ly,** *adv.*

ac·ro·meg·a·ly (ak′rə meg′ə lē), *n. Pathol.* a chronic disease characterized by enlargement of the bones of the head, the soft parts of the feet and hands, and sometimes other structures, due to excessive secretion of growth hormone by the pituitary gland. [1885–90; < F *acromégalie* < NL *acromegalia.* See ACRO-, -MEGALY] —**ac·ro·me·gal·ic** (ak′rō mə gal′ik), *adj., n.*

ac·ro·mic·ri·a (ak′rə mik′rē ə, -mī′krē ə), *n. Pathol.* abnormal smallness of the head and extremities. [< NL; see ACRO-, MICRO-, -IA]

a·cro·mi·on (ə krō′mē ən), *n., pl.* **-mi·a** (-mē ə). *Anat.* the outward end of the spine of the scapula or shoulder blade. See diag. under **shoulder.** [1605–15; < NL < Gk *akrṓmion,* equiv. to *akro-* ACRO- + *ō̃m(os)* shoulder + *-ion* n. suffix] —**a·cro′mi·al,** *adj.*

ac·ron (ak′ron, -rən), *n.* the unsegmented, preoral portion of the body of an arthropod. [< NL < Gk *ákron,* neut. sing. of *ákros;* see ACRO-] —**ac·ro·nal** (ak′rə nl), *adj.*

ac·ro·nym (ak′rə nim), *n.* **1.** a word formed from the initial letters or groups of letters of words in a set phrase or series of words, as *Wac* from *Women's Army Corps, OPEC* from *Organization of Petroleum Exporting Countries,* or *loran* from *long-range navigation.* **2.** an acrostic. —*v.t.* **3.** to make an acronym of: *The committee's name has been acronymed MIKE.* [1940–45; ACR- + -ONYM] —**ac′ro·nym′ic, a·cron·y·mous** (ə kron′ə-məs), *adj.* —**ac′ro·nym′i·cal·ly,** *adv.*

a·crop·a·thy (ə krop′ə thē), *n. Pathol.* any disease of the extremities. [ACRO- + -PATHY]

a·crop·e·tal (ə krop′i tl), *adj. Bot.* (of an inflorescence) developing upward, toward the apex. [1870–75; ACRO- + -PETAL] —**a·crop′e·tal·ly,** *adv.*

ac·ro·pho·bi·a (ak′rə fō′bē ə), *n.* a pathological fear of heights. [1890–95; < NL; see ACRO-, -PHOBIA] —**ac′ro·pho′bic,** *adj., n.*

a·croph·o·ny (ə krof′ə nē), *n., pl.* **-nies.** **1.** the use of what was originally a logogram as a phonetic symbol for the initial sound of the word the logogram represented, as, in Semitic writing, the use of a picture of a shepherd's crook to represent the sound (l), the first sound of *lamed,* the Hebrew word for a shepherd's crook. **2.** the use of a word as the name of the alphabetical symbol representing the initial sound of that word. Also, **acrology.** [1880–85; ACRO- + -PHONY] —**ac·ro·phon·ic** (ak′rə fon′ik), **ac·ro·pho·net·ic** (ak′rə fə net′ik), *adj.* —**ac′ro·phon′i·cal·ly, ac′ro·pho·net′i·cal·ly,** *adv.*

a·crop·o·lis (ə krop′ə lis), *n.* **1.** the citadel or high fortified area of an ancient Greek city. **2. the Acropolis,** the citadel of Athens and the site of the Parthenon. [1655–65; < Gk *akrópolis.* See ACRO-, -POLIS] —**ac·ro·pol·i·tan** (ak′rə pol′i tn), *adj.*

ac·ro·some (ak′rə sōm′), *n. Cell Biol.* an organelle covering the head of animal sperm and containing enzymes that digest the egg cell coating, thus permitting the sperm to enter the egg. [1895–1900; < G *Akrosoma;* see ACRO-, -SOME[3]] —**ac′ro·so′mal,** *adj.*

ac·ro·spire (ak′rə spīᵊr′), *n. Bot.* the first sprout appearing in the germination of grain; the developed plumule of the seed. [1610–20; ACRO- + SPIRE[1]; r. *akerspire,* equiv. to *aker* (OE *æchir* ear of grain) + *spire*]

ac·ro·spore (ak′rə spôr′, -spōr′), *n. Mycol.* a spore borne at the tip of a sporophore, as a basidiospore. [1865–70; < F; see ACRO-, SPORE] —**ac·ro·spo·rous** (ak′rə spôr′əs, -spōr′-, ə kros′pər əs), *adj.*

a·cross (ə krôs′, ə kros′), *prep.* **1.** from one side to the other of: *a bridge across a river.* **2.** on or to the other side of; beyond: *across the sea.* **3.** into contact with; into the presence of, usually by accident: *to come across an old friend; to run across a first edition of Byron.* **4.** crosswise of or transversely to the length of something; athwart: *coats across the bed; straddled across the boundary line.* —*adv.* **5.** from one side to another. **6.** on the other side: *We'll soon be across.* **7.** crosswise; transversely: *with arms across.* **8.** so as to be understood or learned: *He couldn't get the idea across to the class.* **9.** into a desired or successful state: *to put a business deal across.* —*adj.* **10.** being in a crossed or transverse position; crosswise: *an across pattern of supporting beams.* [1470–80; A-[1] + CROSS]

a·cross-the-board (ə krôs′thə bôrd′, -bōrd′, ə kros′-), *adj.* **1.** applying to all employees, members, groups, or categories; general: *The across-the-board pay increase means a raise for all employees.* **2.** (of a bet) covering all possibilities of winning on a given result, esp. by placing a combination bet on one horse in a race for win, place, and show. [1940–45]

a·cros·tic (ə krô′stik, ə kros′tik), *n.* **1.** a series of lines or verses in which the first, last, or other particular letters when taken in order spell out a word, phrase, etc. —*adj.* **2.** Also, **a·cros′ti·cal.** of, like, or forming an acrostic. [1580–90; < Gk *akrostichís,* equiv. to *akro-* ACRO- + *stích(os)* STICH + *-is* n. suffix] —**a·cros′ti·cal·ly,** *adv.*

ac·ro·te·ri·on (ak′rə tēr′ē on′, -ē ən), *n., pl.* **-te·ri·a** (-tēr′ē ə). acroterium. [< Gk *akrōtḗrion* topmost part, extremity, equiv. to *akrō-* ACRO- + *-tērion* suffix designating a place for]

ac·ro·te·ri·um (ak′rə tēr′ē əm), *n., pl.* **-te·ri·a** (-tēr′ē ə). *Archit.* a pedestal for a sculpture or ornament at each base or at the apex of a pediment. [Latinization of ACROTERION] —**ac′ro·te′ral, ac′ro·te′ri·al,** *adj.*

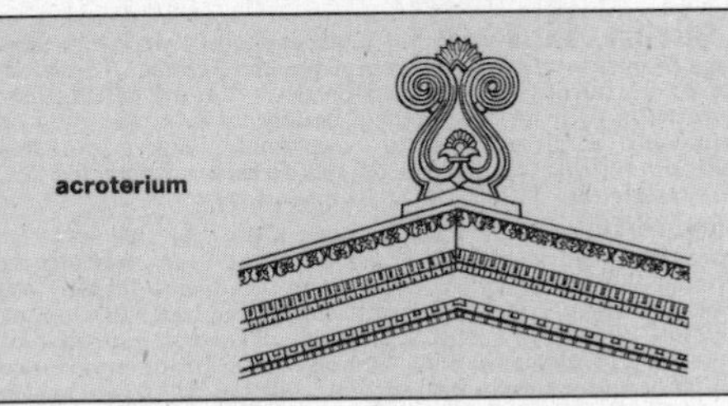
acroterium

ac·ro·tism (ak′rə tiz′əm), *n. Pathol.* absence or weakness of the pulse. [1850–55; A-[6] + Gk *krót(os)* beating or rhythmical sound + -ISM] —**a·crot·ic** (ə krot′ik), *adj.*

A·crux (ā′kruks), *n. Astron.* a star of the first magnitude in the constellation Southern Cross. [*A* (alpha) + CRUX]

ac·ryl·al·de·hyde (ak′ril al′də hīd′), *n. Chem.* acrolein. Also called **acryl′ic al′dehyde.** [ACRYL(IC) + ALDEHYDE]

a·cryl·a·mide (ə kril′ə mīd′, -mid, ak′rə lam′īd, -id), *n. Chem.* a colorless, odorless, toxic crystalline compound, C_3H_5NO, soluble in water, alcohol, and acetone: used in the synthesis of polyacrylamide and other organic materials, as textile fibers, in the processing of ore, and in the treatment of sewage. [ACRYL(IC) + AMIDE]

ac·ry·late (ak′rə lāt′, -lit), *n. Chem.* a salt or ester of an acrylic acid. [1870–75; ACRYL(IC) + -ATE[2]]

a·cryl·ic (ə kril′ik), *adj.* **1.** of or derived from acrylic acid. —*n.* **2.** See **acrylic fiber. 3.** See **acrylic resin. 4.** a paint, prepared esp. for artists, in which an acrylic resin serves as a vehicle. **5.** a painting done with this type of paint: *She sold several acrylics during the show.* [1855–60; ACR(OLEIN) + -YL + -IC]

acryl′ic ac′id, *Chem.* a colorless, corrosive liquid, $C_3H_4O_2$, having an acrid odor, usually derived from acrolein by oxidation: used esp. in the synthesis of acrylic resins. [1850–55]

acryl′ic es′ter, any of a series of esters derived from the acrylic acids.

acryl′ic fi′ber, *Chem.* any of the group of synthetic textile fibers, as Orlon, made by the polymerization of acrylonitrile as the principal component with one or more other monomers. [1950–55]

acryl′ic res′in, *Chem.* any of a group of thermoplastic resins formed by polymerizing the esters of amides of acrylic or methacrylic acid: used chiefly where transparency is desired, as in the methacrylate resins Lucite and Plexiglas. Also called **ac′rylate res′in.** [1935–40]

ac·ry·lo·ni·trile (ak′rə lō nī′tril, -trēl, -trīl), *n. Chem.* a colorless, flammable, poisonous, carcinogenic liquid, C_3H_3N, used for the production of polymers and copolymers, as rubbers, fibers, and clear plastics for beverage containers. [1890–95; ACRYL(IC) + -O- + NITRILE]

ac·ryl·yl (ak′rə lil), *adj. Chem.* containing the acrylyl group. [ACRYL(IC) + -YL]

ac′rylyl group′, *Chem.* the univalent group $C_3H_3O^-$, derived from acrylic acid. Also called **ac′rylyl rad′ical.**

A.C.S., 1. Advanced Communications System. **2.** American Cancer Society. **3.** American Chemical Society. **4.** American College of Surgeons. Also **ACS**

A.C.S.C., Association of Casualty and Surety Companies.

A/cs pay., accounts payable. Also, **a/cs pay.**

A/cs rec., accounts receivable. Also, **a/cs rec.**

act (akt), *n.* **1.** anything done, being done, or to be done; deed; performance: *a heroic act.* **2.** the process of doing: *caught in the act.* **3.** a formal decision, law, or the like, by a legislature, ruler, court, or other authority; decree or edict; statute; judgment, resolve, or award: *an act of Congress.* **4.** an instrument or document stating something done or transacted. **5.** one of the main divisions of a play or opera: *the second act of* Hamlet. **6.** a short performance by one or more entertainers, usually part of a variety show or radio or television program. **7.** the personnel of such a group: *The act broke up after 30 years.* **8.** false show; pretense; feint: *The politician's pious remarks were all an act.* **9.** *Philos.* (in scholasticism) **a.** activity in process; operation. **b.** the principle or power of operation. **c.** form as determining essence. **d.** a state of realization, as opposed to potentiality. **10. clean up one's act,** *Informal.* to begin adhering to more acceptable practices, rules of behavior, etc.: *The factory must clean up its act and treat its employees better.* **11. get** or **have one's act together,** *Informal.* to organize one's time, job, resources, etc., so as to function efficiently: *The new administration is still getting its act together.* —*v.i.* **12.** to do something; exert energy or force; be employed or operative: *He acted promptly in the emergency.* **13.** to reach, make, or issue a decision on some matter: *I am required to act before noon tomorrow.* **14.** to operate or function in a particular way; perform specific duties or functions: *to act as manager.* **15.** to produce an effect; perform a function: *The medicine failed to act.* **16.** to behave or conduct oneself in a particular fashion: *to act well under all conditions.* **17.** to pretend; feign: *Act interested even if you're bored.* **18.** to perform as an actor: *He acted in three plays by Molière.* **19.** to be capable of being performed: *His plays don't act well.* **20.** to serve or substitute (usually fol. by *for*): *In my absence the assistant manager will act for me.* —*v.t.* **21.** to represent (a fictitious or historical character) with one's person: *to act Macbeth.* **22.** to feign; counterfeit: *to act outraged virtue.* **23.** to behave as: *He acted the fool.* **24.** *Obs.* to actuate. **25. act funny,** to display eccentric or suspicious behavior. **26. act on** or **upon, a.** to act in accordance with; follow: *He acted on my advice.* **b.** to have an effect on; affect: *The stirring music acted on the emotions of the audience.* **27. act one's age,** to behave in a manner appropriate to one's maturity: *We children enjoyed our uncle because he didn't always act his age.* **28. act out, a.** to demonstrate or illustrate by pantomime or by words and gestures: *The party guests acted out stories for one another.* **b.** *Psychol.* to give overt expression to (repressed emotions or impulses) without insightful understanding: *The patients acted out early traumas by getting angry with the analyst.* **29. act up, a.** to fail to function properly; malfunction: *The vacuum cleaner is acting up again.* **b.** to behave willfully: *The children always act up in school the day before a holiday.* **c.** to become painful or troublesome, esp. after a period of improvement or remission: *My arthritis is acting up again this morning.* [1350–1400; ME *act(e)* (< MF) < L *ācta,* pl. of *āctum* something done, n. use of ptp. of *agere* to do (*āg-* ptp. s. + *-tum* neut. ptp. suffix); and directly < L *āctus* a doing (*āg-* + *-tus* suffix of v. action)]
—**Syn. 1.** feat, exploit; achievement; transaction; accomplishment. See **action. 4.** record. **6.** turn, routine. **11–15.** perform, function, work. **17, 18.** play.

ACT, 1. American College Test. **2.** Association of Classroom Teachers. **3.** Australian Capital Territory.

act. 1. acting. **2.** active. **3.** actor. **4.** actual.

ac·ta (ak′tə), *n.pl.* (*often cap.*) official records, as of acts, deeds, proceedings, transactions, or the like. [< L, neut. pl. of *āctus,* ptp. of *agere* to do; cf. ACT]

act·a·ble (ak′tə bəl), *adj.* capable of being or suitable for acting. [1840–50; ACT + -ABLE] —**act′a·bil′i·ty,** *n.*

Ac·tae·on (ak tē′ən), *n. Class. Myth.* a hunter who, for having seen Diana bathing, was changed by her into a stag and was torn to pieces by his own hounds.

Ac·ta Sanc·to·rum (äk′tä sängk tôr′o͝om), a collection of the biographies of the Christian saints and martyrs, edited by the Bollandists and arranged according to the ecclesiastical calendar.

act′ call′, *Theat.* **1.** Also called **act warning.** a call or order from the stage manager summoning performers onstage for the beginning of a performance or act. **2.** a signal summoning the audience to their seats for the beginning of a performance or act.

act′ cur′tain, *Theat.* a curtain for closing the proscenium opening between acts or scenes. Also called **act′ drop′, house curtain.**

actg., acting.

ACTH, 1. *Biochem.* a polypeptide hormone, produced by the anterior lobe of the pituitary gland, that stimulates the cortex of adrenal glands. **2.** *Pharm.* this substance, extracted from the pituitary glands of hogs and other species, in the form of its white, water-soluble powder, used for the diagnosis of diseases that impair the adrenal glands. Also called **adrenocorticotropic hormone, adrenocorticotropin.** [1940–45; *a*(*dreno*) *c*(*ortico*)*t*(*ropic*) *h*(*ormone*)]

ac·tin (ak′tən), *n. Biochem.* a globulin that is present in muscle plasma and that in connection with myosin plays an important role in muscle contraction. [1940–45; perh. ACT + -IN[2]]

actin-, var. of **actino-** before a vowel: *actinism.*

ac·ti·nal (ak′tə nl, ak tīn′l), *adj. Zool.* **1.** having tentacles or rays. **2.** pertaining to the oral area from which the arms or tentacles radiate. [1857; ACTIN- + -AL[1]; coined, with sense of def. 2, by Louis Agassiz] —**ac′ti·nal·ly,** *adv.*

act·ing (ak′ting), *adj.* **1.** serving temporarily, esp. as a substitute during another's absence; not permanent; temporary: *the acting mayor.* **2.** designed, adapted, or suitable for stage performance. **3.** provided with detailed stage directions for the performer: *an acting version of a play.* —*n.* **4.** the art, profession, or activity of those who perform in stage plays, motion pictures, etc. [1595–1605; ACT + -ING[2], -ING[1]]
—**Syn. 1.** provisional, interim.

act′ing ar′ea, *Theat.* the part of a stage used by the actors: *Confine the acting area for this scene to downstage.*

ac·tin·i·a (ak tin′ē ə), *n., pl.* **-tin·i·ae** (-tin′ē ē′), **-tin·i·as.** a sea anemone, esp. of the genus *Actinia.* [1740–50; < NL; see ACTIN-, -IA]

ac·tin·i·an (ak tin′ē ən), *adj.* **1.** belonging or pertaining to the order or suborder Actiniaria, comprising the sea anemones. —*n.* **2.** any sea anemone. [1885–90; < NL *Actini(a)* ACTINIA + -AN]

ac·tin·ic (ak tin′ik), *adj.* pertaining to actinism. [1835–45; ACTIN- + -IC] —**ac·tin′i·cal·ly,** *adv.*

actin′ic ray′, *Physics.* a ray of light of short wavelengths, as ultraviolet or violet, that produces photochemical effects. [1835–45]

ac·ti·nide (ak′tə nīd′), *n. Chem.* any element of the actinide series. [1940–45; ACTIN- + -IDE, on the model of LANTHANIDE]

ac′tinide se′ries, *Chem.* the series of radioactive elements that starts with actinium and ends with lawrencium. [1940–45]

ac·tin·i·form (ak tin′ə fôrm′), *adj. Zool.* having a radiate form. [1835–45; ACTIN- + -I- + -FORM]

ac·ti·nin (ak′tə nin), *n. Biochem.* a contractile protein of muscle. [1970–75; ACTIN + -IN[2]]

ac·tin·ism (ak′tə niz′əm), *n.* the property of radiation by which chemical effects are produced. [1835–45; ACTIN- + -ISM]

ac·tin·i·um (ak tin′ē əm), *n. Chem.* a radioactive silver-white metallic element that glows blue in the dark, resembling the rare earths in chemical behavior and valence. *Symbol:* Ac; *at. no.:* 89; *at. wt.:* 227. [1900–05; ACTIN- + -IUM]

actin′ium emana′tion, *Chem.* actinon.

actin′ium se′ries, *Chem.* the radioactive series that starts with uranium 235 and ends with a stable isotope of lead of mass number 207. [1955–60]

actino-, a combining form with the meaning "ray, beam," used in the formation of compound words, with the particular senses "radiation" in the physical sciences (*actinometer*) and "having raylike structures," "radiate in form" in biology (*actinomyces; actinopod*). Also, *esp. before a vowel,* **actin-.** [< Gk, comb. form repr. *aktís* (gen. *aktînos*) ray, beam; see -O-]

ac·ti·no·bac·il·lo·sis (ak tin′ō bas′ə lō′sis, ak′tə nō-), *n. Vet. Pathol.* an infectious disease of cattle, domestic animals, and occasionally humans, resembling actinomycosis and caused by the bacterium *Actinobacillus lignieresii.* Also called **wooden tongue.** [1900–05; < NL *actinobacill(us)* (see ACTINOBACILLUS) + -OSIS] —**ac·tin·o·bac·il·lot·ic** (ak tin′ō bas′ə lot′ik, ak′tə nō-), *adj.*

ac·tin·o·ba·cil·lus (ak tin′ō bə sil′əs, ak′tə nō-), *n., pl.* **-cil·li** (-sil′ī). *Bacteriol.* any of several spherical or rod-shaped, aerobic, parasitic bacteria of the genus *Actinobacillus,* certain species of which, as *A. mallei,* are pathogenic for animals. [< NL; see ACTINO-, BACILLUS]

ac·tin·o·chem·is·try (ak tin′ō kem′ə strē, ak′tə nō-), *n.* the branch of chemistry dealing with actinism; photochemistry. [1835–45; ACTINO- + CHEMISTRY] —**ac·tin·o·chem·i·cal** (ak tin′ō kem′i kəl, ak′tə nō-), *adj.*

ac·tin·o·der·ma·ti·tis (ak tin′ō dûr′mə tī′tis, ak′tə nō-), *n. Pathol.* inflammation of the skin caused by sunlight or other radiation. [ACTINO- + DERMATITIS]

ac·tin·o·drome (ak tin′ə drōm′), *adj.* (of a leaf) palmately veined. Also, **ac·ti·nod·ro·mous** (ak′tə nod′rə məs). [ACTINO- + -DROME]

ac·tin·o·gram (ak tin′ə gram′), *n.* the record produced by the action of an actinograph. [ACTINO- + -GRAM[1]]

ac·tin·o·graph (ak tin′ə graf′, -gräf′), *n.* a recording actinometer. [1830–40; ACTINO- + -GRAPH] —**ac·tin·o·graph·ic** (ak tin′ə graf′ik, ak′tə nō-), *adj.* —**ac·ti·nog·ra·phy** (ak′tə nog′rə fē), *n.*

ac·ti·noid (ak′tə noid′), *adj.* raylike; radiate. [1840–50; ACTIN- + -OID]

ac·tin·o·lite (ak tin′l īt′, ak′tə nl-), *n. Mineral.* a va-

CONCISE PRONUNCIATION KEY: *act, cāpe, dâre, pärt; set, ēqual; if, ice; ox, ōver, ôrder, oil, bo͝ok, bo͞ot, out; up, ûrge; child; sing; shoe; thin, that;* zh as in *treasure.* ə = *a* as in *alone, e* as in *system, i* as in *easily, o* as in *gallop, u* as in *circus;* ᵊ as in *fire* (fīᵊr), *hour* (ouᵊr). l and n can serve as syllabic consonants, as in *cradle* (krād′l), and *button* (but′n). See the full key inside the front cover.

riety of amphibole, occurring in greenish bladed crystals or in masses. [1825–35; ACTINO- + -LITE] **—ac·tin·o·lit·ic** (ak tin′l it′ik, ak′tə nl-), *adj.*

ac·ti·nol·o·gy (ak′tə nol′ə jē), *n.* the science that deals with actinism. [1855–60; ACTINO- + -LOGY]

ac·ti·nom·e·ter (ak′tə nom′i tər), *n.* a device for measuring intensity of radiation, esp. that of the sun. Cf. **actinograph.** [1825–35; ACTINO- + -METER] **—ac·tin·o·met·ric** (ak tin′ō me′trik, ak′tə nō-), **ac·tin′o·met′ri·cal,** *adj.* **—ac′ti·nom′e·try,** *n.*

ac·tin·o·mor·phic (ak tin′ō môr′fik, ak′tə nō-), *adj.* **1.** *Biol.* having radial symmetry. **2.** *Bot.* (of certain flowers, as the buttercup) divisible vertically into similar halves by each of a number of planes passing through the axis. Also, **ac·tin′o·mor′phous.** [1895–1900; ACTINO- + -MORPHIC] **—ac·tin′o·mor′phy,** *n.*

ac·tin·o·my·ces (ak tin′ō mī′sēz, ak′tə nō-), *n., pl.* **-ces.** *Bacteriol.* any of several saprophytic, filamentous, anaerobic bacteria of the genus *Actinomyces,* certain species of which are pathogenic for humans and animals. [< NL (1877), equiv. to Gk *aktino-* ACTINO- + *mýkēs* fungus (see MYCO-)] **—ac·tin′o·my·ce′tal,** *adj.*

ac·tin·o·my·cete (ak tin′ō mī′sēt, -mī sēt′, ak′tə-nō-), *n. Bacteriol.* any of several rod-shaped or filamentous, aerobic or anaerobic bacteria of the phylum Chlamydobacteriae, or in some classification schemes, the order Actinomycetales, certain species of which are pathogenic for humans and animals. [1915–20; prob. through construal of NL *Actinomycetes* (pl. of ACTINOMYCES) as an E pl. n.; see -MYCETE] **—ac·tin′o·my·cet′·ous,** *adj.*

ac·tin·o·my·cin (ak tin′ō mī′sin, ak′tə nō-), *n. Pharm.* any of a group of related antibiotics derived from several species of streptomyces bacteria, used against susceptible bacteria and fungi and in the treatment of various cancers. [ACTINOMYC(ES) + -IN[2]]

actinomycin D, *Pharm.* dactinomycin.

ac·tin·o·my·co·sis (ak tin′ō mī kō′sis, ak′tə nō-), *n. Vet. Pathol., Pathol.* an infectious, inflammatory disease caused by *Actinomyces israelii* in humans and *A. bovis* in domestic animals, and characterized by lumpy, often suppurating tumors, esp., about the jaws. Also called **lumpy jaw.** [1880–85; ACTINOMYC(ES) + -OSIS] **—ac·tin·o·my·cot·ic** (ak tin′ō mī kot′ik, ak′tə nō-), *adj.*

ac·ti·non (ak′tə non′), *n. Chem.* a chemically inert, gaseous, short-lived isotope of radon that is a member of the actinium series. *Symbol:* An; *at. no.:* 86; *at. wt.:* 219. Also called **actinium emanation.** [1925–30; < NL; see ACTINIUM, -ON[2]]

ac·tin·o·pod (ak tin′ə pod′, ak′tə nə), *n.* any protozoan of the subclass Actinopoda, including the heliozoans and radiolarians, having stiff, rodlike, radiating pseudopodia. [< NL *Actinopoda;* see ACTINO-, -POD]

ac·ti·nop·te·ryg·i·an (ak′tə nop′tə rij′ē ən), *adj.* **1.** belonging or pertaining to the Actinopterygii, a group of bony fishes. *—n.* **2.** an actinopterygian fish. [< NL *Actinopterygi(i)* (pl.) (*actino-* ACTINO- + Gk *pterýgi(on)* fin, equiv. to *pteryg-* (s. of *ptéryx* wing) + *-ion* dim. suffix) + -AN]

ac·tin·o·ther·a·py (ak tin′ō ther′ə pē, ak′tə nō-), *n. Med.* radiotherapy, esp. using ultraviolet rays. [1900–05; ACTINO- + THERAPY]

ac·tin·o·u·ra·ni·um (ak tin′ō yo͝o rā′nē əm, ak′tə-nō-), *n. Chem.* See **uranium 235.** [1925–30; ACTINO- + URANIUM]

ac·tin·o·zo·an (ak tin′ə zō′ən, ak′tə nə-), *n., adj. Zool.* anthozoan. [ACTINO- + -ZO(A) + -AN]

ac·tion (ak′shən), *n.* **1.** the process or state of acting or of being active: *The machine is not in action now.* **2.** something done or performed; act; deed. **3.** an act that one consciously wills and that may be characterized by physical or mental activity: *a crisis that demands action instead of debate; hoping for constructive action by the landlord.* **4. actions,** habitual or usual acts; conduct: *He is responsible for his actions.* **5.** energetic activity: *a man of action.* **6.** an exertion of power or force: *the action of wind upon a ship's sails.* **7.** effect or influence: *the action of morphine.* **8.** *Physiol.* a change in organs, tissues, or cells leading to performance of a function, as in muscular contraction. **9.** way or manner of moving: *the action of a machine or of a horse.* **10.** the mechanism by which something is operated, as that of a gun or a piano. **11.** a military encounter or engagement; battle, skirmish, or the like. **12.** actual engagement in fighting an enemy; military or naval combat: *He saw action in Vietnam.* **13.** *Literature.* the main subject or story, as distinguished from an incidental episode. **14.** *Theater.* **a.** an event or series of events that form part of a dramatic plot: *the action of a scene.* **b.** one of the three unities. Cf. **unity** (def. 8). **15.** the gestures or deportment of an actor or speaker. **16.** *Fine Arts.* the appearance of animation, movement, or emotion given to figures by their attitude, position, or expression. **17.** *Law.* **a.** a proceeding instituted by one party against another. **b.** the right of bringing it. **18.** *Slang.* **a.** interesting or exciting activity, often of an illicit nature: *He gave us some tips on where the action was.* **b.** gambling or the excitement of gambling: *The casino usually offers plenty of action.* **c.** money bet in gambling, esp. illegally. **19.** *Eccles.* **a.** a religious ceremony, esp. a Eucharistic service. **b.** the canon of the Mass. **c.** those parts of a service of worship in which the congregation participates. **20. in action, a.** performing or taking part in a characteristic act: *The school baseball team is in action tonight.* **b.** working; functioning: *His rescuing the child was bravery in action.* **21. out of action,** removed from action, as by sudden disability: *The star halfback is out of action with a bad knee.* **22. piece of the action,** *Informal.* a share of the proceeds or profits: *Cut me in for a piece of the action.* **23. take action, a.** to start doing something: *As soon as we get his decision, we'll take action.* **b.** to start a legal procedure. *—adj.* **24.** characterized by brisk or dynamic action: *an action car; an action melodrama.* [1300–50; < L *āctiōn-* (s. of *āctiō*), equiv. to *āct-(us)* (ptp.; see ACT) + *-iōn-* -ION; r. ME *accioun* < AF < L] **—ac′tion·less,** *adj.*

—Syn. 1. movement, operation. **2.** ACTION, ACT, DEED mean something done. ACTION applies esp. to the doing, ACT to the result of the doing. An ACTION usually lasts through some time and consists of more than one act: *to take action on a petition.* An ACT is single: *an act of kindness.* DEED emphasizes the finished or completed quality of an act; it may imply an act of some note, good or bad: *an irrevocable deed; a deed of daring.* **4.** behavior. **12.** brush, encounter, fight, skirmish. See **battle. 15.** plot. **—Ant. 1.** rest, inactivity.

ACTION (ak′shən), *n. U.S. Govt.* an independent agency created in 1971 to administer domestic volunteer programs. [named by analogy with the acronymic names of other agencies, but itself not an acronym]

ac·tion·a·ble (ak′shə nə bəl), *adj.* **1.** furnishing ground for a lawsuit. **2.** liable to a lawsuit. **3.** ready to go or be put into action; ready for use: *to retrieve actionable copy from a computer.* [1585–95; ACTION + -ABLE] **—ac′tion·a·bil′i·ty,** *n.* **—ac′tion·a·bly,** *adv.*

ac′tion grant′, funds awarded by the federal government on a competitive basis to cities that submit plans for urban development and are able to show that such plans have the cooperation and endorsement of private investors.

ac′tion line′, a telephone line maintained by a newspaper, television station, or other medium to provide the public a ready means of expressing complaints or obtaining information about matters of vital interest. [1970–75]

ac′tion paint′ing, 1. (*sometimes caps.*) Also called **tachism.** a style of American abstract expressionist painting typified esp. in the works of Jackson Pollack and Willem de Kooning in the 1940's, in which the furiously energetic and free application of the paint is seen as being expressive of the psychological and emotional state of the artist at the moment of creation. **2.** See **abstract expressionism.** [1950–55, *Amer.*] **—ac′tion paint′er.**

ac′tion poten′tial, *Physiol.* the change in electrical potential that occurs between the inside and outside of a nerve or muscle fiber when it is stimulated, serving to transmit nerve signals. Cf. **nerve impulse.** [1925–30]

ac′tion re′play, *Brit.* See **instant replay.** [1970–75]

ac′tion report′er, a news reporter who reports to the public on matters of special interest to the consumer.

Ac·tis (ak′tis), *n. Class. Myth.* a son of Rhoda and Helius who, when banished from his home for fratricide, fled to Egypt, where he taught astrology. The Colossus of Rhodes was built in his honor.

Ac·ti·um (ak′tē əm, -shē əm), *n.* a promontory in NW ancient Greece: Antony and Cleopatra were defeated by Octavian and Agrippa in a naval battle near here in 31 B.C. **—Ac·ti·an** (ak′tē ən, -shē ən), *adj.*

ac·ti·vate (ak′tə vāt′), *v.t.,* **-vat·ed, -vat·ing. 1.** to make active; cause to function or act. **2.** *Physics.* **a.** to render more reactive; excite: *to activate a molecule.* **b.** to induce radioactivity. **3.** to aerate (sewage) in order to accelerate decomposition of impure organic matter by microorganisms. **4.** *Chem.* **a.** to make (carbon, a catalyst, molecules, etc.) more active. **b.** to hasten (reactions) by various means, as heating. **5.** to place (a military unit or station) on an active status in an assigned capacity. [1620–30; ACTIVE + -ATE[1]] **—ac′ti·va′tion,** *n.*

—Syn. 1. actuate, start, turn on, set going. **—Ant. 1.** stop, halt, check.

ac′tivated alu′mina, *Chem.* alumina in the form of granules having many fine pores, used to adsorb water and various gases.

ac′tivated car′bon, *Chem.* a form of carbon having very fine pores: used chiefly for adsorbing gases or solutes, as in various filter systems for purification, deodorization, and decolorization. Also called **ac′tivated char′coal.** [1920–25]

ac′tivated mine′, a mine with a secondary fuze designed to explode if the mine is tampered with.

ac′tivated sludge′, sludge (def. 8).

activa′tion anal′ysis, *Chem.* a method for the qualitative and quantitative determination of trace amounts of various elements by measuring the characteristic radioactive decay induced by neutron bombardment. Also called **neutron activation analysis.** [1945–50]

ac·ti·va·tor (ak′tə vā′tər), *n.* **1.** a person or thing that activates. **2.** *Chem., Biochem.* a catalyst. **3.** any impurity in a mineral that causes luminescence. Cf. **inhibitor** (def. 3). **4.** *Orthodontics.* a removable appliance, usually of hard plastic, that is worn in the mouth instead of a fixed appliance to help align the teeth and improve the relationship of the lower jaw to the upper. [ACTIVATE + -OR[2]]

ac·tive (ak′tiv), *adj.* **1.** engaged in action; characterized by energetic work, participation, etc.; busy: *an active life.* **2.** being in a state of existence, progress, or motion: *active hostilities.* **3.** involving physical effort and action: *active sports.* **4.** having the power of quick motion; nimble: *active as a gazelle.* **5.** characterized by action, motion, volume, use, participation, etc.: *an active market in wheat; an active list of subscribers.* **6.** causing activity or change; capable of exerting influence (opposed to *passive*): *active treason.* **7.** effective (opposed to *inert*): *active ingredients.* **8.** *Gram.* noting or pertaining to a voice of verbal inflection in which typically the subject of the sentence is represented as performing the action expressed by the verb (opposed to *passive*): *Writes* in *He writes a letter every day* is an active verb form. **9.** requiring or giving rise to action; practical: *an active course.* **10.** (of a volcano) in eruption. **11.** *Accounting.* profitable; busy: *active accounts.* **12.** requiring personal effort or attention; not automatic: *an active alarm system.* **13.** interest-bearing: *active paper.* **14.** *Med.* acting quickly; producing immediate effects: *active remedies.* **15.** *Sociol.* (of a crowd) engaging in purposeful activity, often of a militant nature. Cf. **expressive** (def. 4). **16.** *Aerospace.* able to transmit signals: *an active communications satellite.* **17.** *Electronics.* (of a device or system) acting as a source of electrical energy, as a generator, or capable of amplifying or converting voltages or currents, as a transistor or diode. **18.** (of a solar heating system) accumulating and distributing solar heat by mechanical means. **19.** *Mil.* serving on active duty. *—n.* **20.** *Gram.* **a.** the active voice. **b.** a form or construction in the active voice. **21.** an active person, member, subscriber, etc.: *The circular was mailed only to the actives on our list.* **22.** *Informal.* something showing considerable action or activity: *On the stock market there was heavy trading in the actives.* [1300–50; < L *āctīvus* (see ACT, -IVE); r. ME *actif* < MF < L] **—ac′tive·ly,** *adv.* **—ac′tive·ness,** *n.*

—Syn. 1. acting; working; operative. **3.** ACTIVE, ENERGETIC, STRENUOUS, VIGOROUS imply a liveliness and briskness in accomplishing something. ACTIVE suggests quickness and diligence as opposed to laziness or dilatory methods: *an active and useful person.* ENERGETIC suggests forceful and intense, sometimes nervous, activity: *conducting an energetic campaign.* STRENUOUS implies arduous and zealous activity with a sense of urgency: *a strenuous effort.* VIGOROUS suggests strong, effective activity: *using vigorous measures to accomplish an end.* **4.** agile, sprightly. **—Ant. 1.** lazy. **5.** sluggish.

ac′tive du′ty, *Mil.* the status of full-time service: *on active duty.* Also called **ac′tive serv′ice.**

ac′tive hy′drogen, *Chem.* See **atomic hydrogen.**

ac′tive immu′nity, *Immunol.* immunity in an organism resulting from its own production of antibody or lymphocytes. Cf. **passive immunity.** [1910–15]

ac′tive lay′er, (in arctic or subarctic regions) the layer of soil, above the permafrost, that thaws during the summer.

ac′tive mass′, *Chem.* the effective concentration of a substance. [1905–10]

ac′tive rea′son, *Aristotelianism.* an activity of intellect, embodying universal truth, potentially present in the mind of every individual, and when present, forming the only immortal part of the individual. Cf. **passive reason.**

ac′tive site′, *Biochem.* the part of an enzyme that interacts with the substrate during catalysis. [1960–65]

ac′tive sun′, *Astron.* **1.** the sun at a maximum of solar activity, occurring every 11 years. **2.** solar activity, superimposed on an unchanging background. Cf. **quiet sun, solar cycle.** [1975–80]

ac′tive trans′port, the movement of ions or molecules across a cellular membrane from a lower to a higher concentration, requiring the consumption of energy. [1960–65]

ac·tive·wear (ak′tiv wâr′), *n.* sportswear (def. 1). Also, **ac′tive wear′.** [ACTIVE + WEAR]

ac·tiv·ism (ak′tə viz′əm), *n.* **1.** the doctrine or practice of vigorous action or involvement as a means of achieving political or other goals, sometimes by demonstrations, protests, etc. **2.** *Philos.* **a.** a theory that the essence of reality is pure activity, esp. spiritual activity, or process. **b.** a theory that the relationship between the mind and the objects of perception depends upon the action of the mind. [1905–10; < G *Aktivismus.* See ACTIVE, -ISM]

ac·tiv·ist (ak′tə vist), *n.* **1.** an especially active, vigorous advocate of a cause, esp. a political cause. *—adj.* **2.** of or pertaining to activism or activists: *an activist organization for environmental concern.* **3.** advocating or opposing a cause or issue vigorously, esp. a political cause: *Activist opponents of the President picketed the White House.* [1905–10; ACTIVE + -IST]

ac·tiv·i·ty (ak tiv′i tē), *n., pl.* **-ties. 1.** the state or quality of being active: *There was not much activity in the stock market today. He doesn't have enough physical activity in his life.* **2.** a specific deed, action, function, or sphere of action: *social activities.* **3.** work, esp. in elementary grades at school, that involves direct experience by the student rather than textbook study. **4.** energetic activity; animation; liveliness. **5.** a use of energy or force; an active movement or operation. **6.** normal mental or bodily power, function, or process. **7.** *Physical Chem.* the capacity of a substance to react, corrected for the loss of reactivity due to the interaction of its constituents. **8.** *Physics.* **a.** the number of atoms of a radioactive substance that disintegrate per unit of time, usually expressed in curies. **b.** radioactivity. **9.** an organizational unit or the function it performs. [1520–30; (< MF) < ML *āctīvitās.* See ACTIVE, -ITY]

ac·tiv·ize (ak′tə vīz′), *v.t.,* **-ized, -iz·ing.** to make active; activate. Also, *esp. Brit.,* **ac′tiv·ise′.** [ACTIVE + -IZE] **—ac′tiv·i·za′tion,** *n.*

ac·to (ak′tō; *Sp.* äk′tô), *n., pl.* **-tos** (-tōz; *Sp.* -tôs). *Southwest U.S.* a short, realistic play, usually in Spanish, that dramatizes the social and economic problems of Chicanos. [< Sp: ACT]

act′ of faith′, an act that demonstrates or tests the strength of a person's convictions, as an important personal sacrifice. Cf. **auto-da-fé.**

act′ of God′, *Law.* a direct, sudden, and irresistible action of natural forces such as could not reasonably have been foreseen or prevented, as a flood, hurricane, earthquake, or other natural catastrophe. [1855–60]

Act′ of Par′liament clock′. See **Parliament clock.**

Act′ of Tolera′tion, *Eng. Hist.* the statute (1689) granting religious freedom to dissenting Protestants upon meeting certain conditions. Also called **Toleration Act.**

Act′ of Uniform′ity, *Eng. Hist.* any of the three

CONCISE ETYMOLOGY KEY: <, descended or borrowed from; >, whence; b., blend of, blended; c., cognate with; cf., compare; deriv., derivative; equiv., equivalent; imit., imitative; obl., oblique; r., replacing; s., stem; sp., spelling, spelled; resp., respelling, respelled; trans., translation; ?, origin unknown; *, unattested; ‡, probably earlier than. See the full key inside the front cover.

statutes (1549, 1559, 1662) regulating public worship services in the Anglican Church, esp. the act of 1662 requiring the use of the Book of Common Prayer. Also called **Uniformity Act.**

act′ of war′, an act of aggression by a country against another with which it is nominally at peace.

ac·to·my·o·sin (ak′tə mī′ə sin), *n. Biochem.* a complex protein, consisting of myosin and actin, that is the major constituent of skeletal muscle and is thought to interact with ATP to cause muscle contraction. [1940–45; ACT(IN) + -O- + MYOSIN]

ac·ton (ak′tən), *n. Armor.* a quilted garment worn under mail in the 13th and 14th centuries; gambeson. Also, **ackton, aketon.** [1250–1300; ME < AF *aketoun,* OF *a(u)queton* < OSp *algodon* < SpAr < Ar *al-quṭun* the cotton]

Ac·ton (ak′tən), *n.* **1. Lord** (*John Emerich Edward Dalberg-Acton,* 1st Baron), 1834–1902, English historian. **2.** a former municipal borough in SE England, now part of the London borough of Ealing: center of Puritanism at the time of Cromwell. **3.** a city in NE Massachusetts. 17,544.

ac·tor (ak′tər), *n.* **1.** a person who acts in stage plays, motion pictures, television broadcasts, etc. **2.** a person who does something; participant. [1350–1400; ME < L *āctor,* equiv. to *āg-* (see ACT) + *-tor* -TOR]

Ac·tor (ak′tər), *n. Class. Myth.* a brother of King Augeas, sometimes believed to be the father, by Molione, of Eurytus and Cteatus. Cf. **Moliones.**

Ac·tor·i·dae (ak tôr′i dē′), *n.pl. Class. Myth.* Moliones.

ac·tor·ish (ak′tər ish), *adj.* exaggeratedly theatrical; affected: *a stagy, actorish voice.* [ACTOR + -ISH[1]]

ac·tor-man·ag·er (ak′tər man′ə jər), *n.* a leading actor who produces and usually stars in his or her own productions: *Sir Henry Irving was one of the first actor-managers.* [1860–65]

ac·tor-proof (ak′tər pro͞of′), *adj. Theat.* (of a role or script) effective even if poorly acted. [1890–95; ACTOR + -PROOF]

Ac′tors′ Eq′uity Associa′tion, a labor union for stage actors, founded in 1912 and affiliated with the AFL-CIO.

ACTP, American College Testing Program.

ac·tress (ak′tris), *n.* a woman who acts in stage plays, motion pictures, television broadcasts, etc., esp. professionally. [1580–90; ACT(O)R + -ESS]
—Usage. See **-ess.**

ac·tress·y (ak′trə sē), *adj.* self-consciously stagy in style or manner; exaggeratedly theatrical: *an actressy reading that distorted the character of Ophelia.* [1895–1900; ACTRESS + -Y[1]]

Acts′ of the Apos′tles, a book of the New Testament. Also called **Acts.**

ac·tu·al (ak′cho͞o əl), *adj.* **1.** existing in act or fact; real: *an actual case of heroism; actual expenses.* **2.** existing now; present; current: *The ship's actual position is 22 miles due east of Miami.* **3.** *Obs.* pertaining to or involving acts or action. [1275–1325; < LL *āctuālis,* equiv. to L *āctu-* (s. of action n. *āctus;* see ACT) + *-ālis* -AL[1]; r. ME *actuel* < MF < L] **—ac′tu·al·ness,** *n.*
—Syn. 1. genuine, authentic, veritable. See **real**[1]. **—Ant. 1.** unreal, fictional.

ac′tual cost′, the cost of a product based on incurred costs of material and labor required in its production. Cf. **standard cost.**

ac·tu·al·ism (ak′cho͞o ə liz′əm), *n. Philos.* the doctrine that all reality is animate or in motion. [1855–60; ACTUAL + -ISM] **—ac′tu·al·ist,** *n., adj.* **—ac′tu·al·is′tic,** *adj.*

ac·tu·al·i·ty (ak′cho͞o al′i tē), *n., pl.* **-ties. 1.** actual existence; reality. **2.** an actual condition or circumstance; fact: *Space travel is now an actuality.* [1350–1400; ME *actualite* < ML *āctuālitās.* See ACTUAL, -ITY]

ac·tu·al·i·za·tion (ak′cho͞o ə lə zā′shən), *n.* **1.** the act or process of actualizing. **2.** *Psychol.* self-actualization. [1815–25; ACTUALIZE + -ATION]

ac·tu·al·ize (ak′cho͞o ə līz′), *v.t.,* **-ized, -iz·ing.** to make actual or real; turn into action or fact. Also, *esp. Brit.,* **ac′tu·al·ise′.** [1800–10; ACTUAL + -IZE]

ac·tu·al·ly (ak′cho͞o ə lē), *adv.* as an actual or existing fact; really. [1400–50; late ME; see ACTUAL, -LY]

ac′tual sin′, *Theol.* any sin committed by an individual of his or her free will, as contrasted with original sin.

ac·tu·ar·y (ak′cho͞o er′ē), *n., pl.* **-ar·ies. 1.** *Insurance.* a person who computes premium rates, dividends, risks, etc., according to probabilities based on statistical records. **2.** (formerly) a registrar or clerk. [1545–55; < L *āctuārius* shorthand writer, clerk, var. (with *u* of the action n. *āctus* ACT) of *āctārius* (*āct(a)* deeds, documents + *-ārius* -ARY)] **—ac·tu·ar·i·al** (ak′cho͞o âr′ē əl), **ac′tu·ar′i·an,** *adj.* **—ac′tu·ar′i·al·ly,** *adv.*

ac·tu·ate (ak′cho͞o āt′), *v.t.,* **-at·ed, -at·ing. 1.** to incite or move to action; impel; motivate: *actuated by selfish motives.* **2.** to put into action; start a process; turn on: *to actuate a machine.* [1590–1600; < ML *āctuātus*) reduced to action (ptp. of *āctuāre*), equiv. to L *āctu(s)* (see ACT) + *-ātus* -ATE[1]] **—ac′tu·a′tion,** *n.*

ac·tu·a·tor (ak′cho͞o ā′tər), *n.* **1.** a person or thing that actuates. **2.** a servomechanism that supplies and transmits a measured amount of energy for the operation of another mechanism or system. [1860–65; ACTUATE + -OR[2]]

act′ warn′ing, *Theat.* **1.** notification from the manager advising the performers of the amount of time left before they must appear onstage. **2.** See **act call** (def. 1).

ac·u·ate (ak′yo͞o it, -āt′), *adj.* sharpened; pointed. [1425–75; late ME < L *acu(s)* needle (cf. ACICULA, ACUTE) + -ATE[1]]

A·cuff (ā′kuf), *n.* **Roy (Claxton),** 1903–92, U.S. country-and-western singer and composer.

a·cu·i·ty (ə kyo͞o′i tē), *n.* sharpness; acuteness; keenness: *acuity of vision; acuity of mind.* [1375–1425; late ME *acuite* < OF < ML, LL *acuitās,* equiv. to L *acu(ere)* to sharpen or *acū(tus)* sharpened (see ACUTE) + *-itās* -ITY]

a·cu·le·ate (ə kyo͞o′lē it, -āt′), *adj.* **1.** *Biol.* having or being any sharp-pointed structure. **2.** having a slender ovipositor or sting, as the hymenopterous insects. **3.** pointed; stinging. Also, **a·cu′le·at′ed.** [1595–1605; < L *acūleātus.* See ACULEUS, -ATE[1]]

a·cu·le·us (ə kyo͞o′lē əs) *n., pl.* **-le·i** (-lē ī′). **1.** Also, **acus.** the modified ovipositor or sting of certain hymenopterous insects. **2.** prickle (def. 2). [1820–30; < L: sting, barb, equiv. to *acu(s)* needle + *-leus* n. suffix]

a·cu·men (ə kyo͞o′mən, ak′yə-), *n.* keen insight; shrewdness: *remarkable acumen in business matters.* [1525–35; < L *acūmen* sharpness, equiv. to *acū-* (s. of *acuere* to sharpen; see ACUTE) + *-men* n. suffix] **—a·cu·mi·nous** (ə kyo͞o′mə nəs), *adj.*

a·cu·mi·nate (*adj.* ə kyo͞o′mə nit, -nāt′; *v.* ə kyo͞o′mə-nāt′), *adj., v.,* **-nat·ed, -nat·ing.** —*adj.* **1.** *Bot., Zool.* pointed; tapering to a point. —*v.t.* **2.** to make sharp or keen. [1595–1605; < L *acūminātus* (ptp. of *acūmināre*), equiv. to *acūmin-* (s. of *acūmen*) ACUMEN + *-ātus* -ATE[1]] **—a·cu′mi·na′tion,** *n.*

ac·u·pres·sure (ak′yo͝o presh′ər), *n.* **1.** a type of massage in which finger pressure on the specific bodily sites described in acupuncture therapy is used to promote healing, alleviate fatigue, etc. **2.** *Med.* a procedure for stopping blood flow from an injured blood vessel. [1855–60; ACU(PUNCTURE) + PRESSURE]

ac·u·punc·ture (*n.* ak′yo͝o pungk′chər; *v.* ak′yo͝o-pungk′chər, ak′yo͝o pungk′-), *n., v.,* **-tured, -tur·ing.** —*n.* **1.** a Chinese medical practice or procedure that treats illness or provides local anesthesia by the insertion of needles at specified sites of the body. —*v.t.* **2.** to perform acupuncture on. [1675–85; < L *acū* with a needle (abl. of *acus* needle) or *acu-* (as comb. form of *acus*) + PUNCTURE]

ac·u·punc·tur·ist (ak′yo͝o pungk′chər ist), *n.* a person, as a physician, chiropractor, or layperson, who practices acupuncture. [1950–55; ACUPUNCTURE + -IST]

a·cus (ā′kəs), *n., pl.* **a·cus. 1.** *Surg.* a needle, esp. one used in a surgical operation. **2.** aculeus (def. 1). [< L]

ac·u·sec·tor (ak′yo͝o sek′tər), *n. Surg.* a needle for cutting tissue by means of a high-frequency electric current. [< NL; see ACUS, SECTOR] **—ac′u·sec′tion,** *n.*

a·cut·ance (ə kyo͞ot′ns), *n.* a measure of the sharpness with which a film can reproduce the edge of an object. [ACUTE + -ANCE]

a·cute (ə kyo͞ot′), *adj.* **1.** sharp or severe in effect; intense: *acute sorrow; an acute pain.* **2.** extremely great or serious; crucial; critical: *an acute shortage of oil.* **3.** (of disease) brief and severe (opposed to *chronic*). **4.** sharp or penetrating in intellect, insight, or perception: *an acute observer.* **5.** extremely sensitive even to slight details or impressions: *acute eyesight.* **6.** sharp at the end; ending in a point. **7.** *Geom.* **a.** (of an angle) less than 90°. See diag. under **angle. b.** (of a triangle) containing only acute angles. See diag. under **triangle. 8.** consisting of, indicated by, or bearing the mark ´, placed over vowel symbols in some languages to show that the vowels or the syllables they are in are pronounced in a certain way, as in French that the quality of an *e* so marked is close; in Hungarian that the vowel is long; in Spanish that the marked syllable bears the word accent; in Ibo that it is pronounced with high tones; or in classical Greek, where the mark originated, that the syllable bears the word accent and is pronounced, according to the ancient grammarians, with raised pitch (opposed to *grave*): *the acute accent; an acute e.* —*n.* **9.** the acute accent. [1560–70; < L *acūtus* sharpened, ptp. of *acuere* (*acū-,* v. stem, akin to *acus* needle, *ācer* sharp + *-tus* ptp. suffix)] **—a·cute′ly,** *adv.* **—a·cute′ness,** *n.*
—Syn. 3. sudden, distressing, violent. **4.** keen, astute, discerning, perceptive, intelligent, perspicacious; sharp-witted, clever, smart, bright, ingenious, brilliant; knowing, wise, sage, sagacious, sapient. ACUTE, PENETRATING, SHREWD imply a keenness of understanding, perception, or insight. ACUTE suggests particularly a clearness of perception and a realization of related meanings: *an acute intellect.* PENETRATING adds the idea of depth of perception and a realization of implications: *a wise and penetrating judgment.* SHREWD adds the idea of knowing how to apply practically (or to one's own advantage) what one perceives and understands: *wary and shrewd.*

acute′ ante′rior poliomyeli′tis, *Pathol.* poliomyelitis.

acute′ bisec′trix, *Crystall.* See under **bisectrix** (def. 1).

a·cute-care (ə kyo͞ot′kâr′), *adj.* (of a hospital) providing emergency services and general medical and surgical treatment for acute disorders rather than long-term residential care for chronic illness. [1975–80]

acute′ glauco′ma. See under **glaucoma.**

acute′ nec′rotizing gingivi′tis, trench mouth. *Abbr.:* ANG

a·cu·ti·lin·gual (ə kyo͞ot′ə ling′gwəl), *adj. Zool.* having a sharply pointed tongue or mouth, as certain bees. [< L *acūt(us)* ACUTE + -I- + LINGUAL]

ACV, 1. Also, **A.C.V.** actual cash value. **2.** air cushion vehicle: any of various vehicles that ride over water or terrain on a cushion of air generated by downward-thrusting fans and are pushed forward by one or more air propellers.

ACW, *Radio.* alternating continuous waves.

-acy, a suffix of nouns of quality, state, office, etc., many of which accompany adjectives in *-acious* or nouns or adjectives in *-ate*: *fallacy; papacy; legacy; delicacy; piracy.* [< L *-ācia, -ātia* (sp. interchangeably in ML, reflecting the Rom merger of the forms); these are in turn complexes of *-āc-* and *-āt-* -ATE[1] + *-ia* -Y[3]. Cf. -CRACY]

a·cy·clic (ā sī′klik, ā sik′lik), *adj.* **1.** not cyclic: *an acyclic flower; acyclic compounds.* **2.** *Chem.* of or pertaining to a compound that does not contain a closed chain or ring of atoms (contrasted with *cyclic*). [1875–80; A-[6] + CYCLIC]

acy′clic ter′pene, *Chem.* See under **terpene** (def. 2).

a·cy·clo·vir (ā sī′klō vēr′, -klə-), *n. Pharm.* a crystalline compound, $C_8H_{11}N_5O_3$, used as an antiviral drug in the treatment of herpes infections. [1980–85; perh. *acyclo(guanosine)* an earlier name for the compound (A-[6] + CYCLO- + *guanosine* a nucleotide) + VIR(US) or VIR(AL)]

ac·yl (as′il, -ēl), *adj. Chem.* containing the acyl group. [1895–1900; < G: an organic radical derived from an acid; see ACID, -YL]

ac·yl·ate (as′ə lāt′), *v.t.,* **-at·ed, -at·ing.** *Chem.* to introduce the acyl group into (a compound). [ACYL + -ATE[1]] **—ac′yl·a′tion,** *n.*

ac′yl group′, *Chem.* the univalent group RCO–, where R is any organic group attached to one bond of the carbonyl group. Also called **ac′yl rad′ical.**

a·cyl·o·in (ə sil′ō in, as′ə loin′, as′ə lō′in), *n. Chem.* a hydroxy ketone of the general formula RCOCHOHR, where R is an element or group. [ACYL + (BENZ)OIN]

ad[1] (ad), *n.* **1.** advertisement. **2.** advertising: *an ad agency.* [1835–45; by shortening]

ad[2] (ad), *n. Tennis.* **1.** advantage (def. 5). **2. ad in,** the advantage being scored by the server. **3. ad out,** the advantage being scored by the receiver. [1945–50; by shortening]

ad[3] (ad), *prep.* (in prescriptions) to; up to. [< L]

ad-, a prefix occurring in loanwords from Latin, where it meant "toward" and indicated direction, tendency, or addition: *adjoin.* Usually assimilated to the following consonant; see **a-**[5], **ac-, af-, ag-, al-, an-**[2], **ap-**[1], **ar-, as-, at-.** [< L *ad, ad-* (prep. and prefix) to, toward, at, about; c. AT[1]]

-ad[1], **1.** a suffix occurring in loanwords from Greek denoting a group or unit comprising a certain number, sometimes of years: *dyad; triad.* **2.** a suffix meaning "derived from," "related to," "concerned with," "associated with" (*oread*), introduced in loanwords from Greek (*Olympiad; oread*), used sporadically in imitation of Greek models, as *Dunciad,* after *Iliad.* [Gk *-ad-* (s. of *-as*), specialization of fem. adjective-forming suffix, often used substantively]

-ad[2], var. of **-ade**[1]: *ballad.*

-ad[3], *Anat., Zool.* a suffix forming adverbs from nouns signifying parts of the body, denoting a direction toward that part: *dextrad; dorsad; mediad.* [< L *ad* toward, anomalously suffixed to the noun; introduced as a suffix by Scottish anatomist John Barclay (1758–1826) in 1803]

ad., 1. adverb. **2.** advertisement.

A.D., 1. active duty. **2.** in the year of the Lord; since Christ was born: *Charlemagne was born in* A.D. *742.* [< L *annō Dominī*] **3.** art director. **4.** assembly district. **5.** assistant director. **6.** athletic director. **7.** average deviation.
—Usage. Because ANNO DOMINI means "in the year of the Lord," its abbreviation A.D. was originally placed before rather than after a date: *The Roman conquest of Britain began in* A.D. *43* (or *began* A.D. *43*). In edited writing, it is still usually placed before the date. But, by analogy with the position of B.C. "before Christ," which always appears after a date (*Caesar was assassinated in 44* B.C.), A.D. is also frequently found after the date in all types of writing, including historical works: *The Roman emperor Claudius I lived from 10* B.C. *to 54* A.D. Despite its literal meaning, A.D. is also used to designate centuries, being placed after the specified century: *the second century* A.D.

a.d., 1. after date. **2.** before the day. [< L *ante diem*] **3.** autograph document.

A·da (ā′də), *n.* **1.** a city in central Oklahoma. 14,509. **2.** *Douay Bible.* Adah. **3.** a female given name: from a Germanic word meaning "noble."

A·da (ā′də), *n. Computers.* a programming language particularly suited to real-time applications: developed for use by the U.S. Department of Defense. [named after Augusta *Ada* (Byron), Countess of Lovelace (1815–37), English mathematician, who assisted Charles Babbage in developing a precursor of the modern computer]

ADA, 1. adenosine deaminase. **2.** American Dental Association. **3.** American Diabetes Association **4.** Americans for Democratic Action.

A.D.A., 1. American Dental Association. **2.** American

Diabetes Association. **3.** Americans for Democratic Action.

A·da·ba·zar (ä′də bə zär′), *n.* former name of **Adapazari.**

ad ab·sur·dum (ad ab sûr′dəm), to the point of absurdity. [< L: to (the) absurd]

a·dac·ty·lous (ā dak′tl əs), *adj. Zool.* having no fingers or toes. [1855–60; A-[6] + -DACTYLOUS]

A·dad (ä′däd), *n.* Babylonian god of storms and wind.

ADAD (ā′dad), *n.* a coded card or other device that when inserted into a telephone allows the user to reach a number without dialing. [*a(utomatic telephone) d(ialing-)a(nnouncing) d(evice)*]

ADA deficiency. See **adenosine deaminase deficiency.**

ad·age (ad′ij), *n.* a traditional saying expressing a common experience or observation; proverb. [1540–50; < F < L *adagium,* equiv. to *ad-* AD- + *ag-* (s. of *āio* I say) + *-ium* -IUM] —**a·da·gi·al** (ə dā′jē əl), *adj.*

a·da·gio (ə dä′jō, -zhē ō′; *It.* ä dä′jô), *adv., adj., n., pl.* **-gios.** —*adv.* **1.** *Music.* in a leisurely manner; slowly. —*adj.* **2.** *Music.* slow. —*n.* **3.** *Music.* an adagio movement or piece. **4.** *Dance.* **a.** a sequence of well-controlled, graceful movements performed as a display of skill. **b.** a duet by a man and a woman or mixed trio emphasizing difficult technical feats. **c.** (esp. in ballet) a love-duet sequence in a pas de deux. [1740–50; < It, for *ad agio* at ease; *agio* < OPr *ais* or OF *aise* (see EASE)]

A·dah (ā′də), *n.* **1.** one of the two wives of Lamech. Gen. 4:19. **2.** the wife of Esau, and the mother of Eliphaz, Gen. 36:2, 4, 10, 12, 16.

Ad·am (ad′əm *for 1, 3, 5–8;* A dän′ *for 2, 4*), *n.* **1.** the name of the first man: husband of Eve and progenitor of the human race. Gen. 2:7; 5:1–5. **2. A·dolphe Charles** (A dôlf′ shARl), 1803–56, French composer of comic opera and ballet music. **3. James,** 1730–94, and his brother **Robert,** 1728–92, English architects and furniture designers. **4. Lam·bert Si·gis·bert** (län beR′ sē zhez beR′), 1700–59, and his brother **Ni·cho·las Sé·bas·tien** (nē kô lä′ sā bäs tyaN′), 1705–78, French sculptors. **5.** a male given name. **6. not know from Adam,** to be unacquainted with: *He says hello to us every morning, but we don't know him from Adam.* **7. the old Adam,** the natural tendency toward sin: *He attributed his wild outburst to the old Adam in him.* —*adj.* **8.** of or pertaining to the style of architecture, decoration, or furnishings associated with Robert and James Adam, characterized by free adaptation of ancient Roman forms and interiors treated with delicate ornament generally painted in light, vivid colors. [< Heb *ādhām* lit., man]

Ad·a·ma (ad′ə mə), *n. Douay Bible.* Admah.

Ad·am-and-Eve (ad′əm ən ēv′, -ənd-), *n.* the puttyroot. [1780–90]

ad·a·mant (ad′ə mənt, -mant′), *adj.* **1.** utterly unyielding in attitude or opinion in spite of all appeals, urgings, etc. **2.** too hard to cut, break, or pierce. —*n.* **3.** any impenetrably or unyieldingly hard substance. **4.** a legendary stone of impenetrable hardness, formerly sometimes identified with the diamond. [bef. 900; ME < OF *adamaunt* < L *adamant-* (s. of *adamas*) hard metal (perh. steel), diamond < Gk, equiv. to *a-* A-[6] + *-damant-* verbal adj. of *damân* to tame, conquer; r. OE *athamans* (< ML) and ME *aymont* < MF *aimant* < VL **adimant-* < L] —**ad·a·man·cy** (ad′ə mən sē), **ad′a·mance,** *n.* —**ad′a·mant·ly,** *adv.*
—**Syn. 1.** inflexible, rigid, uncompromising. —**Ant. 1.** flexible, easygoing, yielding.

ad·a·man·tane (ad′ə man′tān), *n. Chem.* a white crystalline alicyclic hydrocarbon, $C_{10}H_{16}$, consisting of four fused cyclohexane rings, with the carbon atoms arranged as in the diamond lattice. Cf. **amantadine.** [< F; see ADAMANT, -ANE; so called from the diamondlike arrangement of the carbon atoms]

ad·a·man·tine (ad′ə man′tēn, -tin, -tīn), *adj.* **1.** utterly unyielding or firm in attitude or opinion. **2.** too hard to cut, break, or pierce. **3.** like a diamond in luster. [1200–1250; ME < L *adamantinus* < Gk *adamántinos.* See ADAMANT, -INE[1]]

Ad·a·ma·wa-East·ern (ad′ə mä′wə ē′stərn), *n.* a branch of the Niger-Congo family of languages, centered in Nigeria, Cameroon, Chad, and the Central African Republic, including Sango and Zande.

Ad′am Bede′ (bēd), a novel (1859) by George Eliot.

A·dam de la Halle (A dän də lA Al′), c1240–87, French troubadour: composer.

ADAMHA, Alcohol, Drug Abuse, and Mental Health Administration.

A·dam·ic (ə dam′ik, ad′ə mik), *adj.* pertaining to or suggestive of Adam. Also, **A·dam′i·cal.** [1650–60; ADAM + -IC] —**A·dam′i·cal·ly,** *adv.*

Ad·am·ite (ad′ə mīt′), *n.* **1.** a descendant of Adam; human being. **2.** a nudist. [1620–30; ADAM + -ITE[1]] —**Ad·am·it·ic** (ad′ə mit′ik), **Ad′am·it′i·cal,** *adj.*

Ad·ams (ad′əmz), *n.* **1. Abigail (Smith),** 1744–1818, U.S. social and political figure (wife of John Adams). **2. Ansel,** 1902–84, U.S. photographer. **3. Brooks,** 1848–1927, U.S. historian and political scientist (son of Charles Francis Adams and brother of Henry Brooks Adams). **4. Charles Francis,** 1807–86, U.S. statesman: minister to Great Britain 1861–68 (son of John Quincy Adams). **5. Franklin P(ierce)** (*"F.P.A."*), 1881–1960, U.S. author and columnist. **6. Henry (Brooks),** 1838–1918, U.S. historian, writer, and teacher (son of Charles Francis Adams). **7. James Trus·low** (trus′lō), 1878–1949, U.S. historian. **8. John,** 1735–1826, 2nd president of the U.S. 1797–1801: a leader in the American Revolution. **9. John Michael Geoffrey Man·ning·ham** (man′ing əm), (*"Tom"*), 1931–85, Barbadian political leader: prime minister 1976–85. **10. John Quin·cy** (kwin′zē, -sē), 1767–1848, 6th president of the U.S. 1825–29; Secretary of State 1817–25 (son of John Adams). **11. Lé·o·nie Fuller** (lā ō′nē), born 1899, U.S. poet. **12. Maude** (*Maude Kiskadden*), 1872–1953, U.S. actress. **13. Roger,** 1889–1971, U.S. chemist. **14. Samuel,** 1722–1803, American statesman: a leader in the American Revolution. **15. Samuel Hopkins,** 1874–1958, U.S. journalist and novelist. **16. Walter Sydney,** 1876–1956, U.S. astronomer. **17. Mount.** a mountain in SW Washington, in the Cascade Range. 12,307 ft. (3751 m). **18.** a mountain in N New Hampshire, in the White Mountains. 5798 ft. (1767 m). **19.** a city in W Massachusetts. 10,381.

Ad′am's ale′, *Facetious.* water. [1635–45]

Ad′am's ap′ple, 1. a projection of the thyroid cartilage at the front of the neck that is more prominent in men than in women. **2.** See **crape jasmine.** [1745–55]

Ad′am's Bridge′, an island chain in the Gulf of Mannar between NW Sri Lanka and SE India; ownership divided between Sri Lanka and India. 30 mi. (48 km) long.

Ad′am's cup′, *Chiefly New Eng.* See **pitcher plant.**

ad·ams·ite (ad′əm zīt′), *n. Chem., Mil.* a yellow irritant smoke, containing a poisonous form of arsenic and used as a harassing agent. Also called **phenarsazine chloride, diphenylaminechlorarsine.** [1920–25; named after R. ADAMS; see -ITE[1]]

Ad·am's-nee·dle (ad′əmz nēd′l), *n.* a yucca, *Yucca filamentosa,* grown as an ornamental, having sword-shaped leaves and a tall spike of creamy-white, bell-shaped flowers. [1750–60, *Amer.*]

Ad′ams-Stokes′ syn′drome (ad′əmz stōks′), *Pathol.* See **Stokes-Adams syndrome.** Also called **Ad′·ams-Stokes′ disease′.**

A·da·na (ä′dä nä′), *n.* a city in S Turkey, on the Seyhan River. 347,000. Also called **Seyhan.**

A·da·pa·za·ri (ä′də pä′zə rē′), *n.* a city in NW Turkey, SE of Istanbul. 101,590. Formerly, **Adabazar.**

a·dapt (ə dapt′), *v.t.* **1.** to make suitable to requirements or conditions; adjust or modify fittingly: *They adapted themselves to the change quickly. He adapted the novel for movies.* —*v.i.* **2.** to adjust oneself to different conditions, environment, etc.: *to adapt easily to all circumstances.* [1605–15; < L *adaptāre* to fit, adjust, perh. via F *adapter.* See AD-, APT] —**a·dapt′ed·ness,** *n.*
—**Syn. 1.** fit, accommodate, suit, reconcile, conform; modify, rework, convert. See **adjust.**

a·dapt·a·ble (ə dap′tə bəl), *adj.* **1.** capable of being adapted. **2.** able to adjust oneself readily to different conditions: *an adaptable person.* [1790–1800; ADAPT + -ABLE] —**a·dapt′a·bil′i·ty, a·dapt′a·ble·ness,** *n.*

ad·ap·ta·tion (ad′əp tā′shən), *n.* **1.** the act of adapting. **2.** the state of being adapted; adjustment. **3.** something produced by adapting: *an adaptation of a play for television.* **4.** *Biol.* **a.** any alteration in the structure or function of an organism or any of its parts that results from natural selection and by which the organism becomes better fitted to survive and multiply in its environment. **b.** a form or structure modified to fit a changed environment. **c.** the ability of a species to survive in a particular ecological niche, esp. because of alterations of form or behavior brought about through natural selection. **5.** *Physiol.* the decrease in response of sensory receptor organs, as those of vision, touch, temperature, olfaction, audition, and pain, to changed, constantly applied, environmental conditions. **6.** *Ophthalm.* the regulating by the pupil of the quantity of light entering the eye. **7.** Also, **a·dap·tion** (ə dap′shən). *Sociol.* a slow, usually unconscious modification of individual and social activity in adjustment to cultural surroundings. [1600–10; < ML *adaptātiōn-* (s. of *adaptātiō*), equiv. to L *adaptāt(us)* (ptp. of *adaptāre* to ADAPT; see -ATE[1]) + *-iōn-* -ION] —**ad′ap·ta′tion·al,** *adj.* —**ad′ap·ta′tion·al·ly,** *adv.*

a·dapt·er (ə dap′tər), *n.* **1.** a person or thing that adapts. **2.** a connector for joining parts or devices having different sizes, designs, etc., enabling them to be fitted or to work together. **3.** an accessory to convert a machine, tool, or part to a new or modified use. Also, **a·dap′tor.** [1795–1805; ADAPT + -ER[1]]

a·dap·tive (ə dap′tiv), *adj.* serving or able to adapt; showing or contributing to adaptation: *the adaptive coloring of a chameleon.* [1815–25; ADAPT + -IVE] —**a·dap′tive·ly,** *adv.* —**a·dap′tive·ness,** *n.* —**ad·ap·tiv·i·ty** (ad′ap tiv′i tē), *n.*

adap′tive op′tics, the branch of optics that compensates for image distortions, esp. by means of flexible mirrors or membranes.

adap′tive radia′tion, *Biol.* the diversification of an ancestral group of organisms into a variety of related forms specialized to fit different environments or ways of life, each often further diversifying into more specialized types. [1900–05]

A·dar (ə där′; *Seph. Heb.* ä däR′; *Ashk. Heb.* ä′däR), *n.* the sixth month of the Jewish calendar. [< Heb *ădhār*]

ad ar·bi·tri·um (äd är bi′tRē ŏŏm′; *Eng.* ad är bi′trē əm), *Latin.* at pleasure; at will. [lit., at (one's) control or decision]

Adar′ She′ni (*Eng., Ashk. Heb.* shā′nē; *Seph. Heb.* shä nē′), an intercalary month of the Jewish calendar, added between Adar and Nisan; Veadar. [< Heb *ădhār shēnī* Adar the Second]

ad a·stra per a·spe·ra (äd ä′stRä per ä′spe Rä′; *Eng.,* ad as′trə pər as′pər ə), *Latin.* to the stars through difficulties: motto of Kansas.

a·dat (ä′dät), *n.* the native law traditional in Indonesia. [< Javanese < Ar *ʿadālah* (court of) equity]

ad·ax·i·al (ad ak′sē əl), *adj. Bot., Mycol.* situated on the side toward the axis or stem. [1895–1900; AD- + AXIAL]

a·daz·zle (ə daz′əl), *adj.* dazzling; glitteringly bright: *a street adazzle with Christmas displays.* [1825–35; A-[1] + DAZZLE]

A.D.B., accidental death benefit.

ADC, 1. advanced developing countries. **2.** Aid to Dependent Children. **3.** Air Defense Command.

A.D.C., aide-de-camp.

ad cap·tan·dum vul·gus (äd käp tän′dŏŏm wŏŏl′gŏŏs; *Eng.* ad kap tan′dəm vul′gəs), *Latin.* in order to please the mob. [lit., for courting the crowd]

Ad′cock anten′na (ad′kok), *Electronics.* an antenna used for direction-finding, consisting of a pair of vertical dipoles. [‡1955–60; named after its inventor]

ADD, attention deficit disorder.

add (ad), *v.t.* **1.** to unite or join so as to increase the number, quantity, size, or importance: *to add two cups of sugar; to add a postscript to her letter; to add insult to injury.* **2.** to find the sum of (often fol. by *up*): *Add this column of figures. Add up the grocery bills.* **3.** to say or write further. **4.** to include (usually fol. by *in*): *Don't forget to add in the tip.* —*v.i.* **5.** to perform the arithmetic operation of addition: *children learning to add and subtract.* **6.** to be or serve as an addition (usually fol. by *to*): *His illness added to the family's troubles.* **7. add up, a.** to make the desired, expected, or correct total: *These figures don't add up right.* **b.** to seem reasonable or consistent; be in harmony or accord: *Some aspects of the story didn't add up.* **8. add up to,** to signify; indicate: *The evidence adds up to a case of murder.* —*n.* **9.** *Journalism.* copy added to a completed story. [1325–75; ME *adden* < L *addere,* equiv. to *ad-* AD- + *-dere* to put (comb. form; see DO[1])] —**add′a·ble, add′i·ble,** *adj.* —**add′ed·ly,** *adv.*
—**Syn. 1.** affix, append, attach, adjoin. **2.** total, sum.

add., 1. (in prescriptions) **a.** add. [< L *adde*] **b.** let there be added. [< L *addantur*] **2.** addenda. **3.** addition. **4.** additional. **5.** address.

ad dam·num (ad dam′nəm), *Law.* a formal and specific claim by a plaintiff for damages. [< L: lit., for financial loss]

Ad·dams (ad′əmz), *n.* **1. Charles (Samuel),** 1912–88, U.S. cartoonist. **2. Jane,** 1860–1935, U.S. social worker and writer: Nobel peace prize 1931.

ad·dax (ad′aks), *n.* a large, pale-colored antelope, *Addax nasomaculatus,* of North Africa, with loosely spiraled horns. [1685–95; < L, presumably < some language of ancient North Africa]

addax,
Addax nasomaculatus, 3½ ft. (1.1 m) high at shoulder; horns 3½ ft. (1.1 m); head and body 5½ ft. (1.7 m); tail 1 ft. (0.3 m)

add′ed en′try, *Library Science.* an access point in a catalog or bibliography that is other than the main entry and may be less complete than the main entry. Cf. **main entry.** [1955–60]

add′ed line′. See **ledger line.**

add′ed ti′tle page′, a title page preceding or following the main title page of a book, often giving a series title or the book title in another language. [1975–80]

add′ed-val′ue tax′ (ad′id val′yōō). See **value-added tax.** [1965–70]

ad·dend (ad′end, ə dend′), *n. Math.* **1.** any of a group of numbers or terms added together to form a sum. **2.** (formerly) a number that is added to another in forming a sum. Cf. **augend.** [1905–10; shortening of ADDENDUM]

ad·den·da (ə den′də), *n.* **1.** a pl. of **addendum. 2.** (*used with a singular v.*) a list of things to be added: *The addenda in the back of the book runs to thirty pages.*

ad·den·dum (ə den′dəm), *n., pl.* **-da** (-də) for 1, 2; **-dums** for 3. **1.** a thing to be added; an addition. **2.** an appendix to a book. **3.** *Mach.* **a.** the radial distance between the tip of a gear tooth and the pitch circle of a gear or the pitch line of a rack. Cf. **dedendum. b.** Also called **adden′dum cir′cle.** an imaginary circle touching the tips of the teeth on a gear. [1785–95; neut. sing. of L *addendus* to be added, gerundive of *addere* to ADD]

ad·der[1] (ad′ər), *n.* **1.** the common European viper, *Vipera berus.* **2.** any of various other venomous or harmless snakes resembling the viper. [bef. 950; late ME; r. ME *nadder* (*a nadder* becoming *an adder* by misdivision; cf. APRON), OE *nǣddre;* c. OS *nādra,* OHG *nātara* (G *Natter*), ON *nathra* snake, Goth *nadrs* adder, OIr *nathir* snake, L *natrix* water snake]

add·er[2] (ad′ər), *n.* a person or thing that adds. [1570–80; ADD + -ER[1]]

ad·der's-mouth (ad′ərz mouth′), *n., pl.* **-mouths** (-mouthz′, -mouths′). **1.** any of several North American, terrestrial orchids of the genus *Malaxis,* having tiny white or greenish flowers. **2.** See **rose pogonia.** [1830–40, *Amer.*]

ad·der's-tongue (ad′ərz tung′), *n.* **1.** a fern of the

CONCISE ETYMOLOGY KEY: <, descended or borrowed from; >, whence; b., blend of, blended; c., cognate with; cf., compare; deriv., derivative; equiv., equivalent; imit., imitative; obl., oblique; r., replacing; s., stem; sp., spelling, spelled; resp., respelling, respelled; trans., translation; ?, origin unknown; *, unattested; ‡, probably earlier than. See the full key inside the front cover.

genus *Ophioglossum*, having one or sometimes two sterile leaves and a fruiting spike. **2.** any of several American dogtooth violets.

ad•dict (*n.* ad′ikt; *v.* ə dikt′), *n.* **1.** a person who is addicted to an activity, habit, or substance: *a drug addict.* —*v.t.* **2.** to cause to become physiologically or psychologically dependent on an addictive substance, as alcohol or a narcotic. **3.** to habituate or abandon (oneself) to something compulsively or obsessively: *a writer addicted to the use of high-flown language; children addicted to video games.* [1520–30; < L *addictus* assigned, surrendered (ptp. of *addicere*, equiv. to *ad-* AD- + *dic-* (var. s. of *dīcere* to fix, determine) + *-tus* ptp. suffix)]
—Syn. 1. adherent, devotee; fanatic; junkie.

ad•dict•ed (ə dik′tid), *adj.* devoted or given up to a practice or habit or to something psychologically or physically habit-forming (usually fol. by *to*): *to be addicted to drugs.* [1550–60; ADDICT + -ED²] **—ad•dict′•ed•ness,** *n.*

ad•dic•tion (ə dik′shən), *n.* the state of being enslaved to a habit or practice or to something that is psychologically or physically habit-forming, as narcotics, to such an extent that its cessation causes severe trauma. [1595–1605; < L *addictiōn-* (s. of *addictiō*) a giving over, surrender. See ADDICT, -ION]

ad•dic•tive (ə dik′tiv), *adj.* **1.** producing or tending to cause addiction: *an addictive drug.* **2.** more than normally susceptible to addiction: *an addictive personality.* [1935–40; ADDICT + -IVE] **—ad•dic′tive•ness,** *n.*

Ad•die (ad′ē), *n.* a female given name, form of **Adeline.**

add′ing machine′, a machine capable of adding numbers and sometimes capable of performing the other arithmetic functions of subtraction, multiplication, and division: such machines are now obsolescent, having been replaced in most applications by electronic calculators. [1870–75, *Amer.*]

Ad•ding•ton (ad′ing tən), *n.* **Henry, Viscount Sidmouth** (sid′məth), 1757–1844, British statesman: prime minister 1801–04.

ad•di•o (äd dē′ô), *interj. Italian.* good-bye.

Ad•dis A•ba•ba (äd′dis ä′bə bä′; *Eng.* ad′is ab′ə bə), a city in and the capital of Ethiopia, in the central part. 1,161,267.

Ad•di•son (ad′ə sən), *n.* **1. Joseph,** 1672–1719, English essayist and poet. **2. Thomas,** 1793–1860, English physician. **3.** a town in NE Illinois. 28,836.

Ad•di•so•ni•an (ad′ə sō′nē ən), *adj.* **1.** of, pertaining to, or characteristic of Joseph Addison or his works. **2.** fluent and clear in literary style. **3.** of or pertaining to Addison's disease. —*n.* **4.** one who studies the works of Joseph Addison. [ADDISON + -IAN]

Ad′dison's disease′, *Pathol.* a disease characterized by asthenia, low blood pressure, and a brownish coloration of the skin, due to decreased secretion of cortisol from the adrenal cortex, resulting in hypoadrenalism. [1855–60; named after T. ADDISON, who described it]

ad•dit•a•ment (ə dit′ə mənt), *n.* something added; an addition. [1400–50; late ME < L *additāmentum*, equiv. to *addit(us)* (ptp.) added (see ADDITION) + *-ā-* (by analogy with verbal derivatives such as *ornāmentum* ORNAMENT) + *-mentum* -MENT] **—ad•dit•a•men•ta•ry** (ə dit′ə men′tə rē), *adj.*

ad•di•tion (ə dish′ən), *n.* **1.** the act or process of adding or uniting. **2.** the process of uniting two or more numbers into one sum, represented by the symbol +. **3.** the result of adding. **4.** something added. **5.** a wing, room, etc., added to a building, or abutting land added to real estate already owned. **6.** *Chem.* a reaction in which two or more substances combine to form another compound. **7. in addition to,** as well as; besides: *In addition to directing the play, she designed most of the scenery.* [1350–1400; ME *addicio(u)n* < L *additiōn-* (s. of *additiō*), equiv. to *addit(us)*, ptp. of *addere* to ADD (*ad-* AD- + *di-* put + *-tus* ptp. suffix) + *-iōn-* -ION]
—Syn. 1. joining. **3, 4.** increase, enlargement; increment; accession. **4.** supplement; appendix. ADDITION, ACCESSORY, ADJUNCT, ATTACHMENT mean something joined onto or used with something else. ADDITION is the general word, carrying no implication of size, importance, or kind, but merely that of being joined to something previously existing: *an addition to an income, to a building, to one's cares.* An ACCESSORY is a subordinate addition to a more important thing, for the purpose of aiding, completing, ornamenting, etc.: *accessories to a costume.* An ADJUNCT is a subordinate addition that aids or assists a main thing or person but is often separate: *a second machine as an adjunct to the first.* An ATTACHMENT is an accessory part that may be easily connected and removed: *a sewing machine attachment for pleating.*

ad•di•tion•al (ə dish′ə nl), *adj.* added; more; supplementary: *additional information.* [1630–40; ADDITION + -AL¹] **—ad•di′tion•al•ly,** *adv.*

addi′tion com′pound, *Chem.* adduct (def. 2). [1920–25]

addi′tion pol′ymer, *Chem.* a polymer formed by the direct reaction of two or more monomers, and with no resulting water or other by-product.

addi′tion polymeriza′tion, *Chem.* See under **polymerization** (def. 2).

addi′tion reac′tion, *Chem.* a reaction in which part of a compound is added to one end of a double or triple bond, while the rest adds to the other end, converting it, respectively, to a single or double bond.

ad•di•tive (ad′i tiv), *n.* **1.** something that is added, as one substance to another, to alter or improve the general quality or to counteract undesirable properties: *an additive that thins paint.* **2.** *Nutrition.* **a.** Also called **food additive.** a substance added directly to food during processing, as for preservation, coloring, or stabilization. **b.** something that becomes part of food or affects it as a result of packaging or processing, as debris or radiation. —*adj.* **3.** characterized or produced by addition; cumulative: *an additive process.* **4.** *Math.* (of a function) having the property that the function of the union or sum of two quantities is equal to the sum of the functional values of each quantity; linear. [1690–1700; < LL *additīvus.* See ADDITAMENT, -IVE] **—ad′di•tive•ly,** *adv.*

ad′ditive col′or, *Photog.* red, green, or blue-violet, as used in the additive process of color photography. Also called **ad′ditive pri′mary.** [1905–10]

ad′ditive group′, *Math.* a group in which the operation of the group is addition.

ad′ditive iden′tity, *Math.* an element that when added to a given element in a specified set leaves that element unchanged, as zero in the real-number system. [1955–60]

ad′ditive in′verse, *Math.* the number in the set of real numbers that when added to a given number will yield zero: *The additive inverse of 2 is −2.* [1955–60]

ad′ditive proc′ess, a process of color photography in which the colors are formed by the combination of red, green, and blue-violet. Cf. **subtractive process.** [1930–35]

ad•di•to•ry (ad′i tôr′ē, -tōr′ē), *adj.* capable of or tending to make an addition; additional; supplementary. [1650–60; ADDIT(ION) + -ORY¹]

ad•dle (ad′l), *v.*, **-dled, -dling,** *adj.* —*v.t., v.i.* **1.** to make or become confused. **2.** to make or become rotten, as eggs. —*adj.* **3.** mentally confused; muddled. **4.** rotten: *addle eggs.* [bef. 1000; ME *adel* rotten, OE *adela* liquid, filth; c. MLG *adele* liquid manure]

ad•dle•brained (ad′l brānd′), *adj.* having a muddled or confused mind; foolish, silly, or illogical. [1865–70; ADDLE + BRAIN + -ED³]

ad•dle•pat•ed (ad′l pā′tid), *adj.* addlebrained. [1620–30; ADDLE + PATE + -ED³]

addn., addition.

addnl., additional.

add-on (ad′on′, -ôn′), *n.* **1.** a device or unit added to equipment or a construction: *an add-on to a computer; a nice add-on to an old house.* **2.** an extra charge: *Add-ons for taxes and tour guide fees boosted the price of the vacation to $2,500.* **3.** an additional item, as a rider or provision: *This is just another legislative add-on.* **4.** anything added on: *a hi-fi system that can be augmented with add-ons like extra speakers.* —*adj.* **5.** being installed or provided as an add-on: *an add-on speaker system.* [1945–50; n. and adj. use of v. phrase *add on*]

ad•dress (*n.* ə dres′, ad′res; *v.* ə dres′), *n., v.,* **-dressed** or **-drest, -dress•ing.** —*n.* **1.** a speech or written statement, usually formal, directed to a particular group of persons: *the President's address on the state of the economy.* **2.** a direction as to the intended recipient, written on or attached to a piece of mail. **3.** the place or the name of the place where a person, organization, or the like is located or may be reached: *What is your address when you're in Des Moines?* **4.** manner of speaking to persons; personal bearing in conversation. **5.** skillful and expeditious management; ready skill; dispatch: *to handle a matter with address.* **6.** *Computers.* a label, as an integer, symbol, or other set of characters, designating a location, register, etc., where information is stored in computer memory. **7.** *Govt.* a request to the executive by the legislature to remove a judge for unfitness. **8.** Usually, **addresses.** attentions paid by a suitor or lover; courtship. **9.** (*usually cap.*) the reply to the King's speech in the English Parliament. **10.** *Obs.* preparation. —*v.t.* **11.** to direct a speech or written statement to: *to address an assembly.* **12.** to use a specified form or title in speaking or writing to: *Address the President as "Mr. President."* **13.** to direct to the attention: *He addressed his remarks to the lawyers in the audience.* **14.** to apply in speech (used reflexively, usually fol. by *to*): *He addressed himself to the leader.* **15.** to deal with or discuss: *to address the issues.* **16.** to put the directions for delivery on: *to address a letter.* **17.** *Com.* to consign or entrust to the care of another, as agent or factor. **18.** to direct the energy or efforts of (usually fol. by *to*): *He addressed himself to the task.* **19.** to direct (data) to a specified location in an electronic computer. **20.** *Golf.* to take a stance and place the head of the club behind (the ball) preparatory to hitting it. **21.** *Obs.* to woo; court. **22.** *Archaic.* to give direction to; aim. **23.** *Obs.* to prepare. —*v.i. Obs.* **24.** to make an appeal. **25.** to make preparations. [1300–50; ME *adressen* to adorn < MF *adresser.* See A-⁵, DRESS] **—ad•dress′er, ad•dres′sor,** *n.*
—Syn. 1. discourse, lecture. See **speech. 5.** adroitness, cleverness, ingenuity, tact.

ad•dress•a•ble (ə dres′ə bəl), *adj.* **1.** capable of being addressed. **2.** *Television.* (of a cable-TV system) capable of addressing or calling up any available channel. **3.** *Computers.* (of stored information) capable of being accessed. [1950–55; ADDRESS + -ABLE]

ad•dress•ee (ad′re sē′, ə dre sē′), *n.* the person, company, or the like to whom a piece of mail is addressed. [1670–80, *Amer.*; ADDRESS + -EE]

address′ing machine′, a machine for printing addresses on envelopes, labels, etc. [1860–65]

Ad•dres•so•graph (ə dres′ə graf′, -gräf′), *Trademark.* a machine designed for the rapid, automatic addressing of mail in large quantities.

ad•duce (ə dōōs′, ə dyōōs′), *v.t.,* **-duced, -duc•ing.** to bring forward in argument or as evidence; cite as pertinent or conclusive: *to adduce reasons in support of a constitutional amendment.* [1610–20; < L *addūcere* to bring into, equiv. to *ad-* AD- + *dūcere* to lead] **—ad•duce′a•ble, ad•duc′i•ble,** *adj.* **—ad•duc′er,** *n.*

ad•du•cent (ə dōō′sənt, ə dyōō′-), *adj. Physiol.* drawing toward, as by the action of a muscle; adducting. [1685–95; < L *addūcent-* (s. of *addūcēns*), prp. of *addūcere.* See ADDUCE, -ENT]

ad•duct (*v.* ə dukt′; *n.* ad′ukt), *v.t.* **1.** *Physiol.* to move or draw toward the axis of the body or one of its parts (opposed to *abduct*). —*n.* **2.** Also called **addition compound.** *Chem.* a combination of two or more independently stable compounds by means of van der Waals' forces, coordinate bonds, or covalent bonds. Cf. **clathrate** (def. 2), **inclusion complex.** [1830–40; < L *adductus* drawn to, ptp. of *addūcere*; see ADDUCE] **—ad•duc′tive,** *adj.*

ad•duc•tion (ə duk′shən), *n.* **1.** *Physiol.* the action of an adducent muscle. **2.** the act of adducing. [1630–40; < ML *adductiōn-* (s. of *adductiō*). See ADDUCT, -ION]

ad•duc•tor (ə duk′tər), *n.* any muscle that adducts (opposed to *abductor*). [1740–50; < NL, LL: conductor. See ADDUCE, -TOR]

Ade (ād), *n.* **George,** 1866–1944, U.S. humorist.

-ade¹, **1.** a suffix found in nouns denoting action or process or a person or persons acting, appearing in loanwords from French and sometimes from Spanish (*cannonade; fusillade; renegade*), but also attached to native stems: *blockade; escapade; masquerade.* **2.** a noun suffix indicating a drink made of a particular fruit, normally a citrus: *lemonade.* [< F < Pr, Sp, or Upper It *-ada* < L *-āta*, fem. of *-ātus* -ATE¹; or < Sp *-ado* < L *-ātus* -ATE¹]

-ade², a collective suffix like **-ad¹**: *decade.* [< F < Gk; see AD¹]

a•deem (ə dēm′), *v.t. Law.* to revoke (a legacy) by ademption. [1835–45; < L *adimere* to take away, deprive of, confiscate, equiv. to *ad-* AD- + *-imere*, comb. form of *emere* to take, buy; sp. conformed to REDEEM]

Ad•e•laide (ad′l ād′), *n.* **1.** a city in and the capital of South Australia, in Australia. 882,520. **2.** a female given name: from a Germanic word meaning "nobility."

a•de•lan•ta•do (ad′l än tä′dō; *Sp.* ä′the län tä′thô), *n., pl.* **-dos** (-dōz; *Sp.* -thôs). *Hist.* **1.** a governor of a province in Spain or of a Spanish colonial province. **2.** any of the early explorers, conquerors, or colonizers in Spanish America. [1835–45, *Amer.*; < Sp, n. use of ptp. of *adelantar* to go forward, deriv. of *adelante* in front (*a-* (< L *ad-* AD-) + *delante* before, for *denante* < LL *dē in ante*)]

A•dele (ə del′), *n.* a female given name: from a Germanic word meaning "noble." Also, **A•del•a.** (ə del′ə, ad′l ə).

a•del•gid (ə del′jid), *n.* any of various homopterous insects of the family Adelgidae, as *Adelges abietis* **(spruce gall aphid)** and *Pineus pinifoliae* **(pine leaf aphid),** that feed and form galls on conifers. [< NL *Adelgidae*, equiv. to *Adelg(es)* a genus name (appar. < Gk *ádel(os)* unseen, invisible (*a-* A-⁶ + *dêlos* visible, clear) + NL *-ges* < ?: unexplained by the name's originator) + *-idae* -ID²]

A•dé′lie Coast′ (ə dā′lē; *Fr.* A dā lē′), a coastal region of Antarctica, south of Australia: claimed by France.

Adé′lie pen′guin, a penguin, *Pygoscelis adeliae*, occurring in large colonies in Antarctica. Also, **Ade′lie pen′guin.** Also called **Adélie.** [1905–10]

Ad•e•line (ad′l īn′; *Dan.* ä′də lē′nə; *Fr.* ADᵊ lēn′; *Ger.* ä də lē′nə), *n.* a female given name, form of **Adele.** Also, **Ad•e•li•na** (ad′l ē′nə, -ī′nə).

-adelphous, *Bot.* a combining form meaning "having stamens growing together in bundles," of the number specified by the initial element: *monadelphous.* [< NL < Gk *-adelphos*, adj. deriv. of *adelphós* brother or *adelphḗ* sister; see -OUS]

a•demp•tion (ə demp′shən), *n. Law.* the failure of a legacy because the subject matter no longer belongs to the testator's estate at death. [1580–90; < L *ademptiōn-* (s. of *ademptiō*) a taking away, equiv. to *adempt(us)* (*ad-* AD- + *em(p)-*, s. of *emere* to take + *-tus* ptp. suffix) + *-iōn-* -ION]

A•den (äd′n, ād′n), *n.* **1.** a seaport in and the economic capital of the Republic of Yemen, in the S part: formerly the center of a British colony. 318,000. **2. Colony of.** Also called **State of Aden.** a former British colony on the Gulf of Aden and a member of the former Federation of South Arabia. 75 sq. mi. (194 sq. km). **3. Protectorate of,** former name, until 1962, of the former Protectorate of South Arabia. **4. Gulf of,** an arm of the Arabian Sea between the E tip of Africa and the Arabian Peninsula.

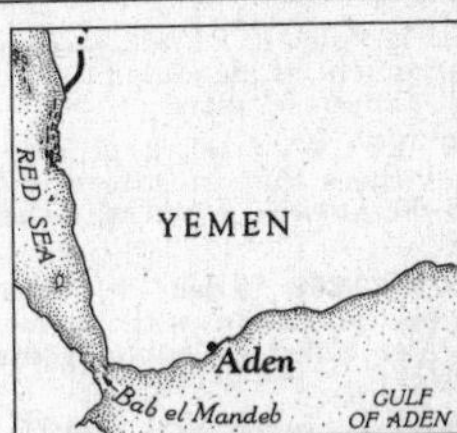

aden-, var. of **adeno-** before a vowel: *adenitis.*

A•de•nau•er (ad′nouᵊr, -nou ər, ad′n ouᵊr, -ou′ər; *Ger.* äd′n ou′ər), *n.* **Kon•rad** (kon′rad; *Ger.* kôn′rät), 1876–1967, chancellor of the West German Federal Republic 1949–63.

ad•e•nec•to•my (ad′n ek′tə mē), *n., pl.* **-mies.** surgical excision of a gland. [ADEN- + -ECTOMY]

A•den•ese (äd′n ēz′, -ēs′), *n., pl.* **-ese.** Adeni.

A•den•i (äd′n ē), *n.* a native or inhabitant of Aden.

ad•e•nine (ad′n in, -ēn′, -īn′), *n. Biochem.* a purine base, $C_5H_5N_5$, one of the fundamental components of nucleic acids, as DNA, in which it forms a base pair with

CONCISE PRONUNCIATION KEY: act, cāpe, dâre, pärt; set, ēqual; if, īce; ox, ōver, ôrder, oil, bŏŏk, bōōt, out; up, ûrge; child; sing; shoe; thin, *th*at; zh as in *treasure.* ə = *a* as in *alone*, *e* as in *system*, *i* as in *easily*, *o* as in *gallop*, *u* as in *circus*; ᵊ as in *fire* (fīᵊr), *hour* (ouᵊr). l and n can serve as syllabic consonants, as in *cradle* (krād′l), and *button* (but′n). See the full key inside the front cover.

thymine, and RNA, in which it pairs with uracil. *Symbol:* A [1880–85; < G *Adenin;* see ADEN-, -INE[2]]

ad•e•ni•tis (ad′n ī′tis), *n. Pathol.* lymphadenitis. [1840–50; ADEN- + -ITIS]

adeno-, a combining form meaning "gland," used in the formation of compound words: *adenovirus.* Also, *esp. before a vowel,* **aden-.** [< Gk, comb. form of *adḗn* gland; akin to L *inguen* groin]

ad•e•no•car•ci•no•ma (ad′n ō kär′sə nō′mə), *n., pl.* **-mas, -ma•ta** (-mə tə). *Pathol.* **1.** a malignant tumor arising from secretory epithelium. **2.** a malignant tumor of glandlike structure. [1885–90; ADENO- + CARCINOMA] —**ad•e•no•car•ci•nom•a•tous** (ad′n ō kär′sə nom′ə təs, -nō′mə-), *adj.*

ad•e•no•hy•poph•y•sis (ad′n ō hī pof′ə sis), *n., pl.* **-ses** (-sēz′). *Anat.* See under **pituitary gland.** [1930–35; ADENO- + HYPOPHYSIS] —**ad•e•no•hy•poph•y•se•al** (ad′n ō hī pof′ə sē′əl, -zē′-), **ad•e•no•hy•po•phys•i•al** (ad′n ō hī′pə fiz′ē əl), *adj.*

ad•e•noid (ad′n oid′), *n.* **1.** Usually, **adenoids.** an enlarged mass of lymphoid tissue in the upper pharynx, often obstructing breathing through the nasal passages. See diag. under **tonsil.** —*adj.* **2.** of or pertaining to the lymph glands. **3.** of or pertaining to the adenoids. [1830–40; < Gk *adenoeidḗs.* See ADEN-, -OID]

ad•e•noi•dal (ad′n oid′l), *adj.* **1.** of or pertaining to the adenoids; adenoid. **2.** having the adenoids enlarged, esp. to a degree that interferes with normal breathing. **3.** being characteristically pinched and nasal in tone quality: *a high-pitched, adenoidal voice.* [1915–20; ADENOID + -AL[1]]

ad•e•noid•ec•to•my (ad′n oi dek′tə mē), *n., pl.* **-mies.** *Surg.* surgical removal of the adenoids. [1905–10; ADENOID + -ECTOMY]

ad•e•noid•i•tis (ad′n oi dī′tis), *n. Pathol.* inflammation of the adenoid tissue. [ADENOID + -ITIS]

ad•e•nol•o•gy (ad′n ol′ə jē), *n. Med.* the branch of medicine dealing with the development, structure, function, and diseases of glands. [1745–55; ADENO- + -LOGY] —**ad•en•o•log•i•cal** (ad′n ə loj′i kəl), *adj.*

ad•e•no•ma (ad′n ō′mə), *n., pl.* **-mas, -ma•ta** (-mə tə). *Pathol.* **1.** a benign tumor originating in a secretory gland. **2.** a benign tumor of glandlike structure. [1865–70; < NL; see ADEN-, -OMA] —**ad•e•nom•a•tous** (ad′n om′ə təs, -ō′mə-), *adj.*

ad•e•nop•a•thy (ad′n op′ə thē), *n. Pathol.* enlargement or disease of the glands, esp. the lymphatic glands. [1875–80; ADENO- + -PATHY]

ad•e•no•sar•co•ma (ad′n ō sär kō′mə), *n., pl.* **-mas, -ma•ta** (-mə tə). *Pathol.* a complex tumor containing both glandular and connective tissues. Also called **sarcoadenoma.** [ADENO- + SARCOMA]

a•den•o•sine (ə den′ə sēn′, -sin), *n. Biochem.* a white, crystalline, water-soluble nucleoside, $C_{10}H_{13}N_5O_4$, of adenine and ribose. [1905–10; < G *Adenosin,* b. *Adenin* ADENINE and *Ribose* RIBOSE]

aden′osine ar•a•bin′o•side (ar′ə bin′ə sīd′, ə rab′ə nə-), *Pharm.* vidarabine.

aden′osine cy′clic mon•o•phos′phate (mon′ə fos′fāt). See **cyclic AMP.** [MONO- + PHOSPHATE]

aden′osine deam′inase, an enzyme that catalyzes the conversion of adenosine to inosine and ammonia. *Abbr.:* ADA

aden′osine deam′inase defi′ciency, a severe immune system disorder caused by a genetic inability to produce adenosine deaminase. Also called **ADA deficiency.**

aden′osine diphos′phate, *Biochem.* See **ADP** (def. 1). [1945–50]

aden′osine mon•o•phos′phate (mon′ə fos′fāt), *Biochem.* See **AMP.** [1945–50; MONO- + PHOSPHATE]

aden′osine tri•phos′pha•tase (trī fos′fə tās′, -āz′), *Biochem.* ATPase. [1940–45; TRIPHOSPHATE + -ASE]

aden′osine triphos′phate, *Biochem.* See **ATP.** [1935–40]

ad•e•no•sis (ad′n ō′sis), *n. Pathol.* **1.** abnormal development or enlargement of glandular tissue. **2.** any disease of a gland. [ADEN- + -OSIS]

ad•e•no•vi•rus (ad′n ō vī′rəs), *n., pl.* **-rus•es.** any of a group of DNA viruses that cause eye and respiratory diseases. [1955–60; ADENO- + VIRUS] —**ad′e•no•vi′ral,** *adj.*

a•den′yl•ate cy′clase (ə den′l it, -āt′, ad′n l-), *Biochem.* an enzyme that catalyzes the conversion of ATP to cyclic AMP. Also called **ad′e•nyl cy′clase** (ad′n il). [1965–70; ADEN(INE) + -YL + ATE[2]]

ad′e•nyl′ic ac′id (ad′n il′ik, ad′-). See **AMP.** [1890–95; ADEN(INE) + -YL + -IC]

A•de•od•a•tus I (ā′dē od′ə təs), Deusdedit.

Adeodatus II, **Saint,** died A.D. 676, pope 672–676.

ad•e•pha•gia (ad′ə fā′jə, -jē ə), *n. Pathol.* bulimia (def. 1). [< Gk *adēphagía,* equiv. to *hádē(n), ádē(n)* to satiety + *-phagia* -PHAGIA]

a•dept (*adj.* ə dept′; *n.* ad′ept, ə dept′), *adj.* **1.** very skilled; proficient; expert: *an adept juggler.* —*n.* **ad•ept 2.** a skilled or proficient person; expert. [1655–65; < ML *adeptus* one who has attained (the secret of transmuting metals), n. use of L ptp. of *adipīscī* to attain to (*ad-* AD- + *-ep-,* comb. form of *ap-* in *aptus* APT + *-tus* ptp. suffix)] —**a•dept′ly,** *adv.* —**a•dept′ness,** *n.*

ad•e•qua•cy (ad′i kwə sē), *n., pl.* **-cies.** the state or quality of being adequate; sufficiency for a particular purpose. [1800–10; ADEQU(ATE) + -ACY]

ad•e•quate (ad′i kwit), *adj.* **1.** as much or as good as necessary for some requirement or purpose; fully sufficient, suitable, or fit (often fol. by *to* or *for*): *This car is adequate to our needs. adequate food for fifty people.* **2.** barely sufficient or suitable: *Being adequate is not good enough.* **3.** *Law.* reasonably sufficient for starting legal action: *adequate grounds.* [1610–20; < L *adaequātus* matched (ptp. of *adaequāre*). See AD-, EQUAL, -ATE[1]] —**ad′e•quate•ly,** *adv.* —**ad′e•quate•ness,** *n.*
—**Syn. 1.** satisfactory, competent, sufficient, enough; capable.

-ades, a suffix occurring in loanwords from Greek, the plural of **-ad**[1]: *Hyades; Pleiades.* [< Gk *-ades.* See -AD[1]]

ad•es•sive (ad es′iv), *Gram.* —*adj.* **1.** locative. —*n.* **2.** the locative case. [1855–60; < L *adess(e)* to be present (*ad-* AD- + *esse* to be) + -IVE]

ad e•un•dem gra•dum (ad ē un′dəm grā′dəm, grä′-), to, of, or in the same rank or standing: pertaining to a university recognizing the academic credentials of a student transferring from another university by granting the student comparable status. [< NL, L]

à deux (ä dœ′; *Fr.* A dœ′), **1.** being between two persons in intimate relationship: *dinner à deux.* **2.** intimately with just two persons present: *dined by candlelight à deux.* [< F: of or for two; two at a time]

ad ex•tre•mum (äd ek strā′mo͝om; *Eng.* ad ek strē′məm), *Latin.* to the extreme; at last; finally.

ADF, automatic direction finder.

ad fin., *Latin.* to, toward, or at the end. [*ad finem*]

ad•freeze (ad frēz′), *v.t.,* **-froze, -fro•zen, -freez•ing.** to adhere through the binding power of ice. [AD- + FREEZE]

ad glo•ri•am (äd glō′rē äm′; *Eng.* ad glôr′ē am′, -glōr′-), *Latin.* for glory.

ADH, *Biochem.* antidiuretic hormone. Cf. **vasopressin.**

ad•here (ad hēr′), *v.,* **-hered, -her•ing.** —*v.i.* **1.** to stay attached; stick fast; cleave; cling (usually fol. by *to*): *The mud adhered to his shoes.* **2.** *Physics.* (of two or more dissimilar substances) to be united by a molecular force acting in the area of contact. **3.** to be devoted in support or allegiance; be attached as a follower or upholder (usually fol. by *to*): *to adhere to a party.* **4.** to hold closely or firmly (usually fol. by *to*): *to adhere to a plan.* **5.** *Obs.* to be consistent. —*v.t.* **6.** to cause to adhere; make stick: *Glue will adhere the tiles to the wallboard.* [1590–1600; < ML *adhērēre* for L *adhaerēre* (*ad-* AD- + *haerēre* to stick, cling), perh. via MF *adhérer*] —**ad•her′a•ble,** *adj.* —**ad•her′er,** *n.*
—**Syn. 1.** See **stick.** —**Ant. 1.** part, loosen.

ad•her•ence (ad hēr′əns, -her′-), *n.* **1.** the quality of adhering; steady devotion, support, allegiance, or attachment: *adherence to a party; rigid adherence to rules.* **2.** the act or state of adhering; adhesion. [< ML *adhērentia.* See ADHERE, -ENCE]

ad•her•end (ad hēr′ənd, -her′-, ad′hi rend′), *n. Chem.* any substance bonded to another by an adhesive. [1945–50; ADHERE + *-end* (< L *-endum* ger. suffix)]

ad•her•ent (ad hēr′ənt, -her′-), *n.* **1.** a person who follows or upholds a leader, cause, etc.; supporter; follower. —*adj.* **2.** sticking; clinging; adhering: *an adherent substance.* **3.** bound by contract or other formal agreement: *the nations adherent to the Geneva Convention.* **4.** *Biol.* adnate. **5.** *Gram.* standing before and modifying a noun; attributive. [1350–1400; ME < ML *adhērent-* for L *adhaerent-* (s. of *adhaerēns,* prp. of *adhaerēre*). See ADHERE, -ENT] —**ad•her′ent•ly,** *adv.*
—**Syn. 1.** disciple, devotee, fan. See **follower.**

ad•he•sion (ad hē′zhən), *n.* **1.** the act or state of adhering; state of being adhered or united: *the adhesion of parts united by growth.* **2.** steady or devoted attachment, support, etc.; adherence. **3.** assent; concurrence. **4.** *Physics.* the molecular force of attraction in the area of contact between unlike bodies that acts to hold them together. Cf. **cohesion** (def. 2). **5.** *Pathol.* **a.** the abnormal union of adjacent tissues. **b.** the tissue involved. **6.** *Bot.* the union of normally separate parts. **7.** *Railroads.* **a.** the frictional resistance of rails to the tendency of driving wheels to slip. **b.** See **factor of adhesion.** [1615–25; < ML *adhēsiōn-* for L *adhaesiōn-* (s. of *adhaesiō*) a clinging, equiv. to *adhaes(us),* ptp. of *adhaerēre* to ADHERE + *-iōn-* -ION] —**ad•he′sion•al,** *adj.*

ad•he•sive (ad hē′siv, -ziv), *adj.* **1.** coated with glue, paste, mastic, or other sticky substance: *adhesive bandages.* **2.** sticking fast; sticky; clinging. **3.** *Physics.* of or pertaining to the molecular force that exists in the area of contact between unlike bodies and that acts to unite them. —*n.* **4.** a substance that causes something to adhere, as glue or rubber cement. **5.** See **adhesive tape. 6.** *Philately.* a postage stamp with a gummed back, as distinguished from one embossed or printed on an envelope or card. [1660–70; ADHES(ION) + -IVE] —**ad•he′sive•ly,** *adv.* —**ad•he′sive•ness,** *n.*

adhe′sive band′age, a bandage consisting of a small pad of gauze affixed to a strip of adhesive tape.

adhe′sive bind′ing. See **perfect binding.** [1950–55]

adhe′sive fac′tor, *Railroads.* See **factor of adhesion.**

adhe′sive plas′ter, adhesive tape, esp. in wide sheets.

adhe′sive tape′, cotton or other fabric coated with an adhesive substance, used for covering minor injuries on the skin, holding a bandage in place, etc. [1930–34]

ad•hib•it (ad hib′it), *v.t.* **1.** to take or let in; admit. **2.** to use or apply. **3.** to attach. [1520–30; < L *adhibitus* brought (ptp. of *adhibēre* to bring to), equiv. to *ad-* AD- + *-hibi-* (comb. form of *habēre* to hold, have) + *-tus* ptp. suffix] —**ad•hi•bi•tion** (ad′hə bish′ən), *n.*

ad hoc (ad hok′; *Lat.* äd hōk′), **1.** for the special purpose or end presently under consideration: *a committee formed ad hoc to deal with the issue.* **2.** concerned or dealing with a specific subject, purpose, or end: *The ad hoc committee disbanded after making its final report.* [1550–60; < L *ad hōc* for this]

ad hock•er•y (ad hok′ə rē), reliance on temporary solutions rather than on consistent, long-term plans. Also, **ad hoc•er•y** (ad hok′ə rē), **ad hoc•ism** (ad hok′iz əm). [1960–65; AD HOC + -ERY]

ad ho•mi•nem (äd hō′mi nem′; *Eng.* ad hom′ə nəm), *Latin.* **1.** appealing to one's prejudices, emotions, or special interests rather than to one's intellect or reason. **2.** attacking an opponent's character rather than answering his argument. [lit., to the man]

ad•i•a•bat (ad′ē ə bat′), *n.* a line on a thermodynamic chart relating the pressure and temperature of a substance undergoing an adiabatic change. [back formation from ADIABATIC]

ad•i•a•bat•ic (ad′ē ə bat′ik, ā′dī ə-), *adj.* occurring without gain or loss of heat (opposed to *diabatic*): *an adiabatic process.* [1875–80; < Gk *adiábat(os)* incapable of being crossed (*a-* A-[6] + *dia-* DIA- + *ba-* (s. of *bainein* to cross) + *-tos* verbal adj. suffix) + -IC; cf. DIABATIC] —**ad′i•a•bat′i•cal•ly,** *adv.*

ad′iabat′ic chart′, a graph for the analysis of adiabatic processes. Also called **ad′iabat′ic di′agram.**

a•di•ac•tin•ic (ā′dī ak tin′ik), *adj.* (of a medium) not capable of transmitting actinic rays. [1875–80; A-[6] + DIACTINIC]

ad•i•ad•o•cho•ki•ne•sia (ad′ē ad′ə kō ki nē′zhə, -zhē ə, -zē ə, -kī nē′-), *n. Med.* the inability to perform rapidly alternating muscular movements, as flexion and extension. Also, **ad•i•ad′o•cho•ki•ne•sis,** (ad′ē ad′ə kō ki nē′sis, -kī nē′-), **ad′i•ad′o•ko•ki•ne′sia, ad′i•ad′o•ko•ki•ne′sis.** Cf. **diadochokinesia.** [A-[6] + Gk *diádocho(s)* successor (*dia-* DIA- + *doch-,* var. s. of *déchesthai* to receive + *-os* adj. suffix) + -KINESIA]

ad•i•aph•o•re•sis (ad′ē af′ə rē′sis, ə dī′ə fə-), *n. Med.* absence or reduction of perspiration. [A-[6] + DIAPHORESIS]

ad•i•aph•o•ret•ic (ad′ē af′ə ret′ik, ə dī′ə fə-), *Med.* —*adj.* **1.** preventing or reducing perspiration. —*n.* **2.** an adiaphoretic agent. [A-[6] + DIAPHORETIC]

ad•i•aph•or•ism (ad′ē af′ə riz′əm), *n.* tolerance of actions or beliefs not specifically prohibited in the Scriptures; indifferentism. [1865–70; ADIAPHOR(OUS) + -ISM] —**ad′i•aph′o•rist,** *n.* —**ad′i•aph′o•ris′tic,** *adj.*

ad•i•aph•o•rous (ad′ē af′ər əs), *adj.* doing neither good nor harm, as a medicine. [1625–35, for earlier sense; < Gk *adiáphoros,* equiv. to *a-* A-[6] + *diáphoros* different (*dia-* DIA- + *-phoros* -PHOROUS)]

A•die (ā′dē), *n.* a female given name.

ad•i•ent (ad′ē ənt), *adj. Psychol.* tending to move toward a stimulus. Cf. **abient.** [< L *adient-* (s. of *adiēns* approaching, prp. of *adīre*), equiv. to *ad-* AD- + *-i-* go + *-ent-* -ENT]

a•dieu (ə do͞o′, ə dyo͞o′; *Fr.* A dyœ′), *interj., n., pl.* **a•dieus, a•dieux** (ə do͞oz′, ə dyo͞oz′; *Fr.* A dyœ′). —*interj.* **1.** good-bye; farewell. —*n.* **2.** the act of leaving or departing; farewell. [1325–75; ME < MF, equiv. to *a* (< L *ad* to) + *dieu* (< L *deus* god)]

A•di•ge (ä′dē je), *n.* a river in N Italy, flowing SE to the Adriatic Sea. 220 mi. (354 km) long.

A•di•ghe (ä′di gā′, ä′di gā′; *Russ.* u di gyā′), *n.* Adygei.

A•di•granth (ä′di grunt′), *n.* Granth.

ad inf., ad infinitum. Also, **ad infin.**

ad in•fi•ni•tum (ad in′fə nī′təm, ad′ in-), to infinity; endlessly; without limit. [< L]

ad init., ad initium.

ad i•ni•ti•um (ad′ i nish′ē əm), at the beginning. [< L]

ad int., ad interim.

ad in•te•rim (ad in′tə rim), in the meantime. [< L: lit., for the time between]

ad•i•os (ad′ē ōs′, ä′dē-; *Sp.* ä thyôs′), *interj.* good-bye; farewell. [1830–40, *Amer.;* < Sp: lit., to God; cf. ADIEU]

adip-, var. of **adipo-** before a vowel: *adipic.*

ad•i•pate (ad′ə pāt′), *n. Chem.* **1.** a salt or ester of adipic acid. **2.** an alkyd resin derived from adipic acid. [ADIP(IC) + -ATE[2]]

a•dip′ic ac′id (ə dip′ik), *Chem.* a white, crystalline, slightly water-soluble solid, $C_6H_{10}O_4$, used chiefly in the synthesis of nylon. Also called **hexanedioic acid.** [ADIP- + -IC]

adipo-, a combining form with the meaning "fat, fatty tissue," used in the formation of compound words: *adipocere.* Also, *esp. before a vowel,* **adip-.** [< L *adip-* (see ADIPOSE) + -O-]

ad•i•po•cere (ad′ə pō sēr′), *n.* a waxy substance produced by the decomposition of dead animal bodies in moist burial places or under water. [1795–1805; < F *adipocire,* equiv. to *adipo-* ADIPO- + *cire* wax < L *cēra;* E e by assoc. with *cēra;* cf. CERE[2]] —**ad•i•poc•er•ous** (ad′ə pos′ər əs), *adj.*

ad•i•poc•er•ite (ad′ə pos′ə rīt′), *n.* hatchettite. [ADIPOCERE + -ITE[1]]

ad•i•po•cyte (ad′ə pō sīt′), *n.* See **fat cell.** [ADIPO- + -CYTE]

ad•i•po•ni•trile (ad′ə pō nī′tril, -trēl, -tril), *n. Chem.* a colorless liquid, $C_6H_8N_2$, used chiefly as an intermediate in the manufacture of nylon. [ADIPO- + NITRILE]

ad•i•po•pex•i•a (ad′ə pō pek′sē ə), *n. Biochem.* lipopexia. Also, **ad•i•po•pex•is** (ad′ə pō pek′sis). [ADIPO- + Gk *-pexia* -PEXY] —**ad′i•po•pec′tic, ad′i•po•pex′ic,** *adj.*

ad•i•pose (ad′ə pōs′), *adj.* **1.** fatty; consisting of,

CONCISE ETYMOLOGY KEY: <, descended or borrowed from; >, whence; b., blend of, blended; c., cognate with; cf., compare; deriv., derivative; equiv., equivalent; imit., imitative; obl., oblique; r., replacing; s., stem; sp., spelling, spelled; resp., respelling, respelled; trans., translation; ?, origin unknown; *, unattested; ‡, probably earlier than. See the full key inside the front cover.

resembling, or relating to fat. —*n.* **2.** animal fat stored in the fatty tissue of the body. [1735–45; < L *adip-*, s of *adeps* fat, lard + -OSE[1]] —**ad′i·pose′ness, ad·i·pos·i·ty** (ad′ə pos′i tē), **ad′i·po′sis,** *n.*

ad′ipose fin′, a small, fleshy fin, usually lacking rays, behind the main dorsal fin in trouts, catfishes, and other bony fishes.

ad′ipose tis′sue, loose connective tissue in which fat cells accumulate. [1850–55]

Ad·i·ron·dack (ad′ə ron′dak), *n., pl.* **-dacks,** (*esp. collectively*) **-dack. 1.** a member of an Algonquian people living mainly north of the St. Lawrence River. **2. Adirondacks.** See **Adirondack Mountains.** [‡1865–70, *Amer.*]

Adiron′dack chair′, a sturdy armchair for outdoor use, made of wide wooden slats, with a sloping back and a seat often slanting down toward it.

Ad′iron′dack Moun′tains, a mountain range in NE New York: a part of the Appalachian Mountains. Highest peak, Mt. Marcy, 5344 ft. (1629 m). Also called **Adirondacks.**

ad·it (ad′it), *n.* **1.** an entrance or a passage. **2.** Also called **entry.** *Mining.* a nearly horizontal passage leading into a mine. **3.** an approach or access. [1595–1605; < L *aditus* an approach, equiv. to *ad-* AD- + *-i-* (s. of *ire* to go) + *-tus* suffix of v. action]

A·dit·ya (ä′dit yə), *n. Hinduism.* one of the Vedic gods, the sons of Aditi. Cf. **Asura.** [< Skt *āditya* (or *ādityāḥ* pl.), deriv. of *aditi* a goddess (orig. a deified abstraction, lit., the absence of binding)]

adj., 1. adjacent. **2.** adjective. **3.** adjoining. **4.** adjourned. **5.** adjudged. **6.** adjunct. **7.** *Banking.* adjustment. **8.** adjutant.

Adj.A., Adjunct in Arts.

ad·ja·cen·cy (ə jā′sən sē), *n., pl.* **-cies. 1.** Also, **adja′cence.** the state of being adjacent; nearness. **2.** Usually, **adjacencies.** things, places, etc., that are adjacent. **3.** *Radio and Television.* a broadcast or announcement immediately preceding or following another. [1640–50; < LL *adjacentia.* See ADJACENT, -ENCY]

ad·ja·cent (ə jā′sənt), *adj.* **1.** lying near, close, or contiguous; adjoining; neighboring: *a motel adjacent to the highway.* **2.** just before, after, or facing: *a map on an adjacent page.* [1400–50; late ME < L *adjacent-* (s. of *adjacēns,* prp. of *adjacēre* to adjoin), equiv. to *ad-* AD- + *jac-* lie + *-ent-* -ENT] —**ad·ja′cent·ly,** *adv.*
—**Syn. 1.** abutting, juxtaposed, touching. See **adjoining.** —**Ant.** distant.

adja′cent an′gles, *Geom.* two angles having the same vertex and having a common side between them.

ad·jec·ti·val (aj′ik tī′vəl), *adj.* **1.** of, pertaining to, or used as an adjective. **2.** describing by means of many adjectives; depending for effect on intensive qualification of subject matter, as a writer, style, or essay. [1790–1800; ADJECTIVE + -AL[1]] —**ad′jec·ti′val·ly,** *adv.*

ad·jec·tive (aj′ik tiv), *n.* **1.** *Gram.* any member of a class of words that in many languages are distinguished in form, as partly in English by having comparative and superlative endings, or by functioning as modifiers of nouns, as *good, wise, perfect.* —*adj.* **2.** pertaining to or functioning as an adjective; adjectival: *the adjective use of a noun.* **3.** not able to stand alone; dependent. **4.** *Law.* concerning methods of enforcement of legal rights, as pleading and practice (opposed to *substantive*). **5.** (of dye colors) requiring a mordant or the like to render them permanent (opposed to *substantive*). [1350–1400; ME < LL *adjectīvum,* neut. of *adjectīvus,* equiv. to *adject(us)* attached, added, ptp. of *ad(j)icere* (*ad-* AD- + *-jec-,* comb. form of *jac-* throw + *-tus* ptp. suffix) + *-īvus* -IVE] —**ad′jec·tive·ly,** *adv.*

ad′jective clause′, *Gram.* a relative clause that modifies a noun or pronoun, as *who saw us* in *It was she who saw us.*

ad′jective phrase′, *Gram.* a group of words including an adjective and its complements or modifiers that functions as an adjective, as *too openly critical of the administration.*

ad·join (ə join′), *v.t.* **1.** to be close to or in contact with; abut on: *His property adjoins the lake.* **2.** to attach or append; affix. —*v.i.* **3.** to be in connection or contact: *the point where the estates adjoin.* [1275–1325; ME *a(d)joinen* < MF *ajoindre.* See AD-, JOIN]

ad·join·ing (ə joi′ning), *adj.* being in contact at some point or line; located next to another; bordering; contiguous: *the adjoining room; a row of adjoining town houses.* [1485–95; ADJOIN + -ING[2]]
—**Syn.** ADJOINING, ADJACENT, BORDERING all mean near or close to something. ADJOINING implies touching, having a common point or line: *an adjoining yard.* ADJACENT implies being nearby or next to something else: *all the adjacent houses; adjacent angles.* BORDERING means having a common boundary with something: *the farm bordering on the river.* —**Ant.** separated.

ad·joint (aj′oint), *n. Math.* **1.** a square matrix obtained from a given square matrix and having the property that its product with the given matrix is equal to the determinant of the given matrix times the identity matrix. **2.** Also called **Hermitian conjugate, transposed conjugate.** the matrix obtained from a given matrix by interchanging rows and columns and by replacing each element by its complex conjugate. [AD- + JOINT]

ad′joint differen′tial equa′tion, *Math.* a differential equation obtained from a given differential equation and having the property that any solution of one equation is an integrating factor of the other.

ad·journ (ə jûrn′), *v.t.* **1.** to suspend the meeting of (a club, legislature, committee, etc.) to a future time, another place, or indefinitely: *to adjourn the court.* **2.** to defer or postpone to a later time: *They adjourned the meeting until the following Monday.* **3.** to defer or postpone (a matter) to a future meeting of the same body. **4.** to defer or postpone (a matter) to some future time, either specified or not specified. —*v.i.* **5.** to postpone, suspend, or transfer proceedings. **6.** to go to another place: *to adjourn to the parlor.* [1300–50; ME *ajo(u)rnen* < MF *ajo(u)rner,* equiv. to *a-* AD- + *jorn-* < L *diurnus* daily; see JOURNAL, JOURNEY]

ad·journ·ment (ə jûrn′mənt), *n.* the act of adjourning or the state or period of being adjourned. [1635–45; < AF *adjournement,* MF. See ADJOURN, -MENT]

adjt., adjutant.

ad·judge (ə juj′), *v.t.,* **-judged, -judg·ing. 1.** to declare or pronounce formally; decree: *The will was adjudged void.* **2.** to award or assign judicially: *The prize was adjudged to him.* **3.** to decide by a judicial opinion or sentence: *to adjudge a case.* **4.** to sentence or condemn: *He was adjudged to die.* **5.** to deem; consider; think: *It was adjudged wise to avoid war.* [1325–75; ME *ajugen* < MF *ajug(i)er* < L *adjūdicāre.* See ADJUDICATE]

ad·ju·di·cate (ə jo͞o′di kāt′), *v.,* **-cat·ed, -cat·ing.** —*v.t.* **1.** to pronounce or decree by judicial sentence. **2.** to settle or determine (an issue or dispute) judicially. —*v.i.* **3.** to sit in judgment (usually fol. by *upon*). [1690–1700; < L *adjūdicātus* (ptp. of *adjūdicāre*). See AD-, JUDGE, -ATE[1]] —**ad·ju·di·ca·tive** (ə jo͞o′di kā′tiv, -kə tiv), **ad·ju·di·ca·to·ry** (ə jo͞o′di kə tôr′ē, -tōr′ē), *adj.* —**ad·ju′di·ca′tor,** *n.*

ad·ju·di·ca·tion (ə jo͞o′di kā′shən), *n.* **1.** an act of adjudicating. **2.** *Law.* **a.** the act of a court in making an order, judgment, or decree. **b.** a judicial decision or sentence. **c.** a court decree in bankruptcy. [1685–95; < LL *adjūdicātiōn-* (s. of *adjūdicātiō*). See ADJUDICATE, -ION]

ad·ju·gate (aj′o͝o git, -gāt′), *n. Math. Now Rare.* adjoint (def. 1). [AD- + (CON)JUGATE]

ad·junct (aj′ungkt), *n.* **1.** something added to another thing but not essential to it. **2.** a person associated with lesser status, rank, authority, etc., in some duty or service; assistant. **3.** a person working at an institution, as a college or university, without having full or permanent status: *My lawyer works two nights a week as an adjunct, teaching business law at the college.* **4.** *Gram.* a modifying form, word, or phrase depending on some other form, word, or phrase, esp. an element of clause structure with adverbial function. —*adj.* **5.** joined or associated, esp. in an auxiliary or subordinate relationship. **6.** attached or belonging without full or permanent status: *an adjunct surgeon on the hospital staff.* [1580–90; < L *adjunctus* joined to (ptp. of *adjungere*), equiv. to *ad-* AD- + *jung-* (nasal var. of *jug-* YOKE[1]) + *-tus* ptp. suffix] —**ad·junct′ly,** *adv.*
—**Syn. 1.** appendix, supplement. See **addition. 2.** aide, attaché.

ad·junc·tion (ə jungk′shən), *n.* addition of an adjunct. [1595–1605; < L *adjunctiōn-* (s. of *adjunctiō*). See ADJUNCT, -ION]

ad·junc·tive (ə jungk′tiv), *adj.* forming an adjunct. [1745–55; ADJUNCT + -IVE] —**ad·junc′tive·ly,** *adv.*

ad′junct profes′sor, a professor employed by a college or university for a specific purpose or length of time and often part-time. [1820–30]

ad·ju·ra·tion (aj′ə rā′shən), *n.* **1.** an earnest request; entreaty. **2.** a solemn or desperate urging or counseling: *an adjuration for all citizens of the beleaguered city to take shelter.* [1605–15; < L *adjūrātiōn-* (s. of *adjūrātiō*), equiv. to *adjūrāt(us),* ptp. of *adjūrāre* to ADJURE + *-iōn-* -ION]

ad·jure (ə jo͝or′), *v.t.,* **-jured, -jur·ing. 1.** to charge, bind, or command earnestly and solemnly, often under oath or the threat of a penalty. **2.** to entreat or request earnestly or solemnly. [1350–1400; ME < L *adjūrāre.* See AD-, JURY] —**ad·jur·a·to·ry** (ə jo͝or′ə tôr′ē, -tōr′ē), *adj.* —**ad·jur′er, ad·ju′ror,** *n.*

ad·just (ə just′), *v.t.* **1.** to change (something) so that it fits, corresponds, or conforms; adapt; accommodate: *to adjust expenses to income.* **2.** to put in good working order; regulate; bring to a proper state or position: *to adjust an instrument.* **3.** to settle or bring to a satisfactory state, so that parties are agreed in the result: *to adjust our differences.* **4.** *Insurance.* to determine the amount to be paid in settlement of (a claim). **5.** to systematize. **6.** *Mil.* to correct the elevation or deflection of (a gun). —*v.i.* **7.** to adapt oneself; become adapted: *They had no problems in adjusting at the new school.* [1350–1400; ME *ajusten* < AF *ajuster,* OF *aj(o)uster* to make conform to, v. deriv., with *a-* A-[5], of *juste* right, JUST[1], influenced in sense by *ajouter, ajoster* to add < LL *adjuxtāre;* see AD-, JUXTA-]
—**Syn. 2.** set; repair, fix. ADJUST, ADAPT, ALTER in their literal meanings imply making necessary or desirable changes (as in position, shape, or the like). To ADJUST is to move into proper position for use: *to adjust the eyepiece of a telescope.* To ADAPT is to make a change in character, to make something useful in a new way: *to adapt a paper clip for a hairpin.* To ALTER is to change the appearance but not the use: *to alter the height of a table.* **3.** arrange; rectify; reconcile.

ad·just·a·bil·i·ty (ə jus′tə bil′i tē), *n.* **1.** the quality of being adjustable: *a reclining chair with infinite adjustability.* **2.** the ability, esp. of a child, to adjust to new surroundings; adaptability: *to observe the child's adjustability to her foster home.* [ADJUST + -ABILITY]

ad·just·a·ble (ə jus′tə bəl), *adj.* **1.** capable of being adjusted: *adjustable seat belts.* **2.** (of loans, mortgages, etc.) having a flexible rate, as one based on money market interest rates or on the rate of inflation or cost of living. **3.** (esp. of life insurance) having flexible premiums and coverage, based on the insuree's current needs and ability to pay. —*n.* **4.** any rate, expense, income, etc., that varies unpredictably: *Luckily, his chief income is not made up of adjustables. Allow some money in your budget for the adjustables.* [1765–75; ADJUST + -ABLE] —**ad·just′a·bly,** *adv.*

ad·just·a·ble-pitch (ə jus′tə bəl pich′), *adj.* (of a marine or aircraft propeller) having blades whose pitch can be changed while the propeller is stationary, chiefly to suit various conditions of navigation or flight. Cf. **controllable-pitch.** [1905–10]

ad·just′a·ble-rate mort′gage (ə jus′tə bəl rāt′), a mortgage that provides for periodic changes in the interest rate, based on changing market condtions. *Abbr.:* ARM

adjust′able span′ner, *Brit.* See **monkey wrench** (def. 1).

ad·just·ed (ə jus′tid), *adj.* **1.** arranged or fitted properly: *Properly adjusted shelving will accommodate books of various heights.* **2.** adapted to surroundings or circumstances (often used in combination): *a well-adjusted child.* [1665–75; ADJUST + -ED[2]]

adjust′ed gross′ in′come, (in U.S. income-tax returns) the total of an individual's wages, salaries, interest, dividends, etc., minus allowable deductions. *Abbr.:* AGI

ad·just·er (ə jus′tər), *n.* **1.** a person or thing that adjusts. **2.** an insurance company representative who investigates claims and makes settlement recommendations based on the estimate of the damages and the company's liability. Also, **adjustor.** [1665–75; ADJUST + -ER[1]]

ad·jus·tive (ə jus′tiv), *adj.* concerned with making, or controlling adjustments: *to settle in a chair with adjustive motions; a thermostat with an adjustive dial.* [1880–85; ADJUST + -IVE]

ad·just·ment (ə just′mənt), *n.* **1.** the act of adjusting; adaptation to a particular condition, position, or purpose. **2.** the state of being adjusted; orderly relation of parts or elements. **3.** a device, as a knob or lever, for adjusting: *the adjustments on a television set.* **4.** the act of bringing something into conformity with external requirements: *the adjustment of one's view of reality.* **5.** harmony achieved by modification or change of a position: *They worked out an adjustment of their conflicting ideas.* **6.** *Sociol.* a process of modifying, adapting, or altering individual or collective patterns of behavior so as to bring them into conformity with other such patterns, as with those provided by a cultural environment. **7.** *Insurance.* the act of ascertaining the amount of indemnity that the party insured is entitled to receive under the policy, and of settling the claim. **8.** a settlement of a disputed account or claim. **9.** a change or concession, as in price or other terms, in view of minor defect or the like. [1635–45; ADJUST + -MENT] —**ad·just·ment·al** (ə just men′tl), *adj.*

adjust′ment disor′der, *Psychiatry.* a mental disorder that occurs as a maladaptive reaction to an episode of psychological, social, or physical stress, as divorce or a natural disaster.

ad·jus·tor (ə jus′tər), *n.* adjuster. [ADJUST + -OR[2]]

ad·ju·tan·cy (aj′ə tən sē), *n., pl.* **-cies.** The office or rank of an adjutant: *His adjutancy allows him certain privileges.* [1765–75; ADJUT(ANT) + -ANCY]

ad·ju·tant (aj′ə tənt), *n.* **1.** *Mil.* a staff officer who assists the commanding officer in issuing orders. **2.** *Mil. Brit.* an executive officer. **3.** an assistant. **4.** See **adjutant stork.** [1590–1600; < L *adjūtant-* (s. of *adjūtāns,* prp. of *adjūtāre* to help, assist), equiv. to *ad-* AD- + *jū-* (var. s. of *juvāre* to help) + *-t-* freq. suffix + *-ant-* -ANT]

ad′jutant gen′eral, *pl.* **adjutants general. 1.** *U.S. Army.* **a. the Adjutant General,** the chief administrative officer of the Army. **b.** an adjutant of a unit having a general staff, usually an officer of the Adjutant General's Corps. **2.** a high, often the highest, officer of the National Guard of a state or territory.

ad′jutant stork′, a large Indian stork, *Leptoptilus dubius,* having a pinkish-brown neck and bill, a large naked pouch under the throat, and a military gait. Also called **adjutant, ad′jutant bird′.**

ad·ju·vant (aj′ə vənt), *adj.* **1.** serving to help or assist; auxiliary. **2.** *Med.* utilizing drugs, radiation therapy, or other means of supplemental treatment following cancer surgery. —*n.* **3.** a person or thing that aids or helps. **4.** anything that aids in removing or preventing a disease, esp. a substance added to a prescription to aid the effect of the main ingredient. **5.** *Immunol.* a substance admixed with an immunogen in order to elicit a more marked immune response. [1600–10; < L *adjuvant-* (s. of *adjuvāns,* prp. of *adjuvāre*), equiv. to *ad-* AD- + *juv-* (s. of *juvāre* to help) + *-ant-* -ANT]

ad ka·len·das Grae·cas (äd kä len′däs GRĪ′käs; *Eng.* ad kə len′dəs grē′kəs), *Latin.* at no time; never: from the fact that the Greeks did not reckon dates by calends. [lit., at the Greek calends]

ADL, Anti-Defamation League (of B'nai B'rith). Also, **A.D.L.**

Ad·lai (ad′lē, -lā, -lī), *n.* a male given name.

Ad·ler (ad′lər; *for 1–3 also* äd′lər), *n.* **1. Alfred,** 1870–1937, Austrian psychiatrist and psychologist. **2. Cyrus,** 1863–1940, U.S. religious leader and Jewish scholar. **3. Felix,** 1851–1933, U.S. educator, reformer, and writer. **4. Kurt (Herbert),** 1905–77, U.S. orchestra conductor, born in Austria. **5. Lawrence Cecil** (*"Larry"*), born 1914, U.S. harmonica player. **6. Mortimer (Jerome),** 1902–91, U.S. philosopher, educator, and author. **7. Peter Hermann,** 1899–1990, U.S. orchestra conductor, born in Czechoslovakia.

Ad·le·ri·an (ad lēr′ē ən), *adj.* of or pertaining to Alfred Adler or his doctrines, esp. in respect to the belief that behavior is determined by compensation for feelings of inferiority. [1930–35; ADLER + -IAN]

ad lib (ad lib′, ad′), **1.** something improvised in speech, music, etc.: *Was that joke part of your speech or an ad lib?* **2.** at one's pleasure; without restriction. **3.** freely; as needed; without stint: *Water can be given to the patients ad lib.* [1810–20; see AD LIBITUM]

ad-lib (ad lib′, ad′-), *v.*, **-libbed, -lib•bing,** *adj.* —*v.t.* **1.** to improvise all or part of (a speech, a piece of music, etc.): *to ad-lib one's lines.* —*v.i.* **2.** to act, speak, etc., without preparation: *Throughout the play he had to ad-lib constantly.* —*adj.* **3.** impromptu; extemporaneous: *ad-lib remarks to hecklers.* [1915–20, *Amer.*; v. use of AD LIB] —**ad-lib′ber,** *n.*

ad lib., See **ad libitum.**

ad lib•i•tum (ad lib′i təm; *Lat.* äd lib′i to͝om′), **1.** at one's pleasure. **2.** *Music.* not obligatory or indispensable. *Abbr.:* ad lib. [1695–1705; < L]

ad li•tem (ad′ lī′tem), *Law.* for the particular action or proceeding: *a guardian ad litem.* [1760–70; < L; cf. LITIGATE]

ad lit•te•ram (äd lit′te räm′; *Eng.* ad lit′ə ram′), *Latin.* to the letter; exactly.

ad loc., at or to the place. [< L *ad locum*]

Adm., **1.** admiral. **2.** admiralty. Also, **ADM**

adm., **1.** administration. **2.** administrative. **3.** administrator. **4.** admission.

Ad•mah (ad′mə), *n.* one of the cities that was destroyed along with Sodom and Gomorrah. Deut. 29:23.

ad ma•jo•rem De•i glo•ri•am (äd mä yô′rem de′ē glô′rē äm′), *Latin.* for the greater glory of God: motto of the Jesuits.

ad•man (ad′man′, -mən), *n., pl.* **-men** (-men′, -mən). **1.** Also called **advertising man.** one whose profession is writing, designing, or selling advertisements. **2.** a printer or compositor who specializes in setting advertisements. [1905–10; AD[1] + MAN[1] or -MAN]

ad•mass (ad′mas′), *Chiefly Brit.* —*n.* **1.** high-pressure marketing in which mass-media advertising is used to reach large numbers of people. —*adj.* **2.** characteristic of or relating to admass. [1950–55; AD[1] + MASS]

ad•meas•ure (ad mezh′ər), *v.t.*, **-ured, -ur•ing.** **1.** to measure off or out; apportion. **2.** *Naut.* to measure the dimensions and capacity of a vessel, as for official registration. [1300–50; ME *amesuren* < MF *amesurer,* with AD- r. A-[5]; see MEASURE] —**ad•meas′ur•er,** *n.*

ad•meas•ure•ment (ad mezh′ər mənt), *n.* **1.** the process of measuring. **2.** the number, dimensions, or measure of anything. **3.** apportionment. [1590–1600; ADMEASURE + -MENT]

Ad•me•te (ad mē′tē), *n. Class. Myth.* a daughter of Eurystheus for whom Hercules took the golden girdle of Ares from Hippolyte.

Ad•me•tus (ad mē′təs), *n. Class. Myth.* a Thessalian king, one of the Argonauts and husband of Alcestis.

admin., administration.

ad•min•i•cle (ad min′i kəl), *n.* an aid; auxiliary. [1550–60; < L *adminiculum* prop, support (*ad-* AD- + *-min-* prob. to be identified with the base of *ēminēre* to stick out, protrude (see EMINENT) + *-i-* -I- + *-culum* -CLE[2])] —**ad•mi•nic•u•lar** (ad′mə nik′yə lər), **ad•mi•nic•u•lar•y** (ad′mə nik′yə ler′ē), *adj.*

ad•min•is•ter (ad min′ə stər), *v.t.* **1.** to manage (affairs, a government, etc.); have executive charge of: *to administer the law.* **2.** to bring into use or operation: *to administer justice; to administer last rites.* **3.** to make application of; give: *to administer medicine.* **4.** to supervise the formal taking of (an oath or the like). **5.** *Law.* to manage or dispose of, as a decedent's estate by an executor or administrator or a trust estate by a trustee. —*v.i.* **6.** to contribute assistance; bring aid or supplies (usually fol. by *to*): *to administer to the poor.* **7.** to perform the duties of an administrator: *She administers quite effectively.* [1325–75; < L *administrāre* to assist, carry out, manage the affairs of (see AD-, MINISTER); r. ME *amynistre* (with A-[5]) < MF *aministrer*] —**ad•min•is•trant** (ad min′ə strənt), *n.*
—**Syn. 1.** conduct, control, execute; direct, superintend, supervise, oversee. See **rule. 2.** distribute, supply, furnish.

admin′istered price′, a price that is determined administratively rather than by changes in supply and demand.

ad•min•is•te•ri•al (ad min′ə stēr′ē əl), *adj.* of or concerned with administration; administrative: *administerial matters.* [1840–50; ADMINISTER + -IAL, on the model of MINISTERIAL]

ad•min•is•tra•ble (ad min′ə strə bəl), *adj.* capable of being administered: *a bureaucracy so vast that it's no longer administrable.* [1810–20; ADMINISTR(ATE) + -ABLE]

ad•min•is•trate (ad min′ə strāt′), *v.t.*, **-trat•ed, -trat•ing.** to administer. [1630–40; < L *administrātus,* ptp. of *administrāre* to ADMINISTER; see -ATE[1]]

ad•min•is•tra•tion (ad min′ə strā′shən), *n.* **1.** the management of any office, business, or organization; direction. **2.** the function of a political state in exercising its governmental duties. **3.** the duty or duties of an administrator in exercising the executive functions of the position. **4.** the management by an administrator of such duties. **5.** a body of administrators, esp. in government. **6.** (*often cap.*) the executive branch of the U.S. government as headed by the President and in power during his or her term of office: *The Administration has threatened to veto the new bill. The Reagan administration followed President Carter's.* **7.** the period of service of a governmental administrator or body of governmental administrators. **8.** any group entrusted with executive or administrative powers: *the administration of a college.* **9.** *Law.* management of a decedent's estate by an executor or administrator, or of a trust estate by a trustee. **10.** an act of dispensing, esp. formally: *administration of the sacraments.* **11.** supervision of the taking of an oath or the like. **12.** application, as of a salve or medicine. [1275–1325; ME *administracio(u)n* < L *administrātiōn-* (s. of *administrātiō*) service. See ADMINISTRATE, -ION] —**ad•min′is•tra′tion•al,** *adj.*

ad•min•is•tra•tive (ad min′ə strā′tiv, -strə-), *adj.* pertaining to administration; executive: *administrative ability.* [1725–35; < L *administrātīvus.* See ADMINISTRATE, -IVE] —**ad•min′is•tra′tive•ly,** *adv.*

admin′istrative assis′tant, a person employed to aid an executive, as in a corporate department, by coordinating such office services and procedures as the supervision, maintenance, and control of the flow of work and programs, personnel, budgeting, records, etc., for the entire department.

admin′istrative coun′ty, *Brit.* a principal administrative division in Great Britain, usually not coextensive with traditional county boundaries. [1945–50]

admin′istrative law′, the body of rules and principles that governs the duties and operations of federal or state administrative agencies, as commissions and boards. [1890–95]

ad•min′is•tra•tive-law′ judge′ (ad min′ə strā′tiv-lô′), an official of a federal or state agency who hears, weighs, and decides on evidence in administrative proceedings, and makes recommendations for any necessary legal action.

admin′istrative leave′, leave, as from a government agency or department, arranged by special permission or directive: *During the investigation she was placed on administrative leave with pay.*

ad•min•is•tra•tor (ad min′ə strā′tər), *n.* **1.** a person who manages or has a talent for managing. **2.** *Law.* a person appointed by a court to take charge of the estate of a decedent, but not appointed in the decedent's will. [1400–50; late ME < L *administrātor,* equiv. to *administrā(re)* (see ADMINISTER) + *-tor* -TOR] —**ad•min′is•tra′tor•ship′,** *n.*

ad•min•is•tra•trix (ad min′ə strā′triks, ad′min ə-, ad min′ə strā′-), *n., pl.* **-is•tra•tri•ces** (-ə strā′trə sēz′, -ə strə trī′sēz). *Law.* a woman who is an administrator. [1620–30; < ML *administrātrix,* fem. of ADMINISTRATOR; see -TRIX]
—**Usage.** See **-trix.**

ad•mi•ra•ble (ad′mər ə bəl), *adj.* **1.** worthy of admiration; inspiring approval, reverence, or affection. **2.** excellent; first-rate. [1590–1600; < L *admīrābilis.* See ADMIRE, -ABLE] —**ad′mi•ra•ble•ness, ad′mi•ra•bil′i•ty,** *n.* —**ad′mi•ra•bly,** *adv.*
—**Syn. 1.** estimable, praiseworthy. —**Ant. 1.** unworthy; disreputable; reprehensible.

ad′mirable bolete′, an edible mushroom, *Boletus mirabilis,* of Rocky Mountain and Pacific northwestern evergreen forests, having a dark-red, scaly or woolly cap with yellow pores and a stout stem.

Ad′mirable Crich′ton, The (krīt′n), a comedy (1902) by Sir James M. Barrie.

ad•mi•ral (ad′mər əl), *n.* **1.** the commander in chief of a fleet. **2.** a naval officer of the highest rank. **3.** a naval officer of a high rank: the grades in the U.S. Navy are fleet admiral, admiral, vice-admiral, and rear admiral. **4.** *Obs.* the flagship of an admiral. **5.** *Brit.* a master who directs a fishing fleet. **6.** any of several often brightly colored butterflies of the family Nymphalidae, as *Vanessa atalanta* (**red admiral**). [1175–1225; ME, var. of *amiral* < OF < Ar *amīr al* commander of the; *-d-* < ML *admīrābilis mundī* for Ar *amīr al-mu'minīn* commander of the faithful; or with replacement of A-[5] by AD-, as in ADMINISTER] —**ad′mi•ral•ship′,** *n.*

Ad′miral of the Fleet′, an officer of the highest rank in the British navy.

ad•mi•ral•ty (ad′mər əl tē), *n., pl.* **-ties,** *adj.* —*n.* **1.** the office or jurisdiction of an admiral. **2.** the officials or the department of state having charge of naval affairs, as in Great Britain. **3.** a court dealing with maritime questions, offenses, etc. **4.** maritime law. **5. the Admiralty,** the official building, in London, of the British commissioners for naval affairs. —*adj.* **6.** of or pertaining to admiralty law. [1300–50; ME *amiralty* < MF. See ADMIRAL, -TY[2]]

ad′miralty cloth′, *Brit.* melton cloth, used for coats and jackets, esp. for the naval service.

Ad′miralty Is′lands, a group of islands in the SW Pacific, N of New Guinea: part of Papua New Guinea. 27,600; ab. 800 sq. mi. (2070 sq. km).

ad′miralty law′. See **maritime law.** [1930–35]

ad′miralty met′al, an alloy of not less than 70 percent copper, about 1 percent tin, small amounts of other elements, and the balance zinc; tin brass. Also called **ad′miralty brass′, ad′miralty bronze′.**

Ad′miralty mile′, *Brit.* See **nautical mile.** [1900–05]

Ad′miralty Range′, a mountain range in Antarctica, NW of the Ross Sea.

ad•mi•ra•tion (ad′mə rā′shən), *n.* **1.** a feeling of wonder, pleasure, or approval. **2.** the act of looking on or contemplating with pleasure: *admiration of fine paintings.* **3.** an object of wonder, pleasure, or approval: *The dancer was the admiration of everyone.* **4.** *Archaic.* wonder; astonishment. [1400–50; late ME *admiracion* < L *admīrātiōn-* (s. of *admīrātiō*). See ADMIRE, -ATION] —**ad•mi•ra•tive** (ad mī′rə tiv, ad′mə rā′-), *adj.* —**ad•mi′ra•tive•ly,** *adv.*
—**Syn. 1.** approval; esteem, regard; affection. —**Ant. 1.** condemnation.

ad•mire (ad mīᵊr′), *v.*, **-mired, -mir•ing.** —*v.t.* **1.** to regard with wonder, pleasure, or approval. **2.** to regard with wonder or surprise (usually used ironically or sarcastically): *I admire your audacity.* —*v.i.* **3.** to feel or express admiration. **4.** *Dial.* to take pleasure; like or desire: *I would admire to go.* **5. be admiring of,** *Chiefly South Midland and Southern U.S.* to admire: *He's admiring of his brother's farm.* [1580–90; < L *admīrārī,* equiv. to *ad-* AD- + *mīrārī* (in ML *mīrāre*) to wonder at, admire] —**ad•mir′er,** *n.*
—**Syn. 1.** esteem, revere, venerate. —**Ant. 1.** despise.

ad•mir•ing (ad mīᵊr′ing), *adj.* displaying or feeling admiration: *admiring looks.* [1620–30; ADMIRE + -ING[2]] —**ad•mir′ing•ly,** *adv.*

ad•mis•si•ble (ad mis′ə bəl), *adj.* **1.** that may be allowed or conceded; allowable: *an admissible plan.* **2.** capable or worthy of being admitted: *admissible evidence.* [1605–15; < L *admiss-* (see ADMISSION) + -IBLE; or < F, formed from same elements] —**ad•mis′si•bil′i•ty, ad•mis′si•ble•ness,** *n.* —**ad•mis′si•bly,** *adv.*

ad•mis•sion (ad mish′ən), *n.* **1.** the act of allowing to enter; entrance granted by permission, by provision or existence of pecuniary means, or by the removal of obstacles: *the admission of aliens into a country.* **2.** right or permission to enter: *granting admission to the rare books room.* **3.** the price paid for entrance, as to a theater or ball park. **4.** an act or condition of being received or accepted in a position, profession, occupation, or office; appointment: *admission to the bar.* **5.** confession of a charge, an error, or a crime; acknowledgment: *His admission of the theft solved the mystery.* **6.** an acknowledgment of the truth of something. **7.** a point or statement admitted; concession. [1400–50; late ME < L *admissiōn-* (s. of *admissiō*), equiv. to *admiss-,* var. s. of *admittere* to ADMIT + *-iōn-* -ION]
—**Syn. 1.** See **entrance**[1]. **2.** access.

ad•mis•sive (ad mis′iv), *adj.* tending to admit. [1770–80; < L *admiss(us)* (see ADMISSION) + -IVE]

ad•mit (ad mit′), *v.*, **-mit•ted, -mit•ting.** —*v.t.* **1.** to allow to enter; grant or afford entrance to: *to admit a student to college.* **2.** to give right or means of entrance to: *This ticket admits two people.* **3.** to permit to exercise a certain function or privilege: *admitted to the bar.* **4.** to permit; allow. **5.** to allow or concede as valid: *to admit the force of an argument.* **6.** to acknowledge; confess: *He admitted his guilt.* **7.** to grant in argument; concede: *The fact is admitted.* **8.** to have capacity for: *This passage admits two abreast.* —*v.i.* **9.** to permit entrance; give access: *This door admits to the garden.* **10.** to grant opportunity or permission (usually fol. by *of*): *The contract admits of no other interpretation.* [1375–1425; < L *admittere,* equiv. to *ad-* AD- + *mittere* to send, let go; r. late ME *amitte,* with A-[5] (instead of *ad-*) < MF *amettre* < L, as above] —**ad•mit′ta•ble, ad•mit′ti•ble,** *adj.* —**ad•mit′ter,** *n.*
—**Syn. 1.** receive. **6.** own, avow. See **acknowledge.**

ad•mit•tance (ad mit′ns), *n.* **1.** permission or right to enter: *admittance into the exhibit room.* **2.** an act of admitting. **3.** actual entrance. **4.** *Elect.* the measure of the ability of a circuit to conduct an alternating current, consisting of two components, conductance and susceptance; the reciprocal of impedance, expressed in mhos. *Symbol:* Y [1585–95; ADMIT + -ANCE]
—**Syn. 1.** access. See **entrance**[1].

ad•mit•ted•ly (ad mit′id lē), *adv.* by acknowledgment; by one's own admission; confessedly: *He was admittedly the one who had lost the documents.* [1795–1805; ADMITTED + -LY]

ad•mit•tee (ad mit ē′, ad mit′ē), *n.* a person who has been or is going to be admitted: *Every admittee must present a ticket at the door.* [ADMIT + -EE]

ad•mix (ad miks′), *v.t., v.i.*, **-mixed** or **-mixt, -mix•ing.** to mingle with or add to something else. [1525–35; AD- + MIX, modeled on L *admiscēre* (*admixtus* ptp.)]

ad•mix•ture (ad miks′chər), *n.* **1.** the act of mixing; state of being mixed. **2.** anything added; any alien element or ingredient: *This is a pure product; there are no admixtures.* **3.** a compound containing an admixture. [1595–1605; < L *admixt(us)* + -URE, on the model of MIXTURE]

ad•mon•ish (ad mon′ish), *v.t.* **1.** to caution, advise, or counsel against something. **2.** to reprove or scold, esp. in a mild and good-willed manner: *The teacher admonished him about excessive noise.* **3.** to urge to a duty; remind: *to admonish them about their obligations.* [1275–1325; late ME *admonish, amonesche, admonesse, amoness,* ME *a(d)monest* (with *-t* later taken as ptp. suffix) < AF, OF *amonester* < VL **admonestāre,* appar. deriv. of L *admonēre* to remind, give advice to (source of *-est-* uncert.), equiv. to *ad-* AD- + *monēre* to remind, warn] —**ad•mon′ish•er,** *n.* —**ad•mon′ish•ing•ly,** *adv.* —**ad•mon′ish•ment,** *n.*
—**Syn. 1.** See **warn. 2.** rebuke, censure, upbraid. See **reprimand.**

ad•mo•ni•tion (ad′mə nish′ən), *n.* **1.** an act of admonishing. **2.** counsel, advice, or caution. **3.** a gentle reproof. **4.** a warning or reproof given by an ecclesiastical authority. [1350–1400; < L *admonitiōn-* (s. of *admonitiō*); see AD-, MONITION; r. late ME *amonicioun* < AF < L; see ADMONISH]

ad•mon•i•tor (ad mon′i tər), *n.* an admonisher. [1540–50; < L; see AD-, MONITOR] —**ad•mon•i•to•ri•al** (ad mon′i tôr′ē əl, -tōr′-), *adj.*

ad•mon•i•to•ry (ad mon′i tôr′ē, -tōr′ē), *adj.* tending or serving to admonish; warning: *an admonitory gesture.* [1585–95; < ML *admonitōrius.* See AD-, MONITORY] —**ad•mon′i•to′ri•ly,** *adv.*

admov., (in prescriptions) **1.** apply. [< L *admovē*] **2.** let it be applied. [< L *admoveātur*]

Ad•nah (ad′nə), *n.* **1.** a Manassite deserter from Saul's to David's army. I Chron. 12:20. **2.** a commander in King Jehosaphat's army. II Chron. 17:14.

CONCISE ETYMOLOGY KEY: <, descended or borrowed from; >, whence; b., blend of, blended; c., cognate with; cf., compare; deriv., derivative; equiv., equivalent; imit., imitative; obl., oblique; r., replacing; s., stem; sp., spelling, spelled; resp., respelling, respelled; trans., translation; ?, origin unknown; *, unattested; ‡, probably earlier than. See the full key inside the front cover.

d·nate (ad′nāt), *adj. Biol.* grown fast to something; ongenitally attached. [1655–65; < L *adnātus,* i.e., *d(g)nātus,* r. *agnātus* AGNATE]

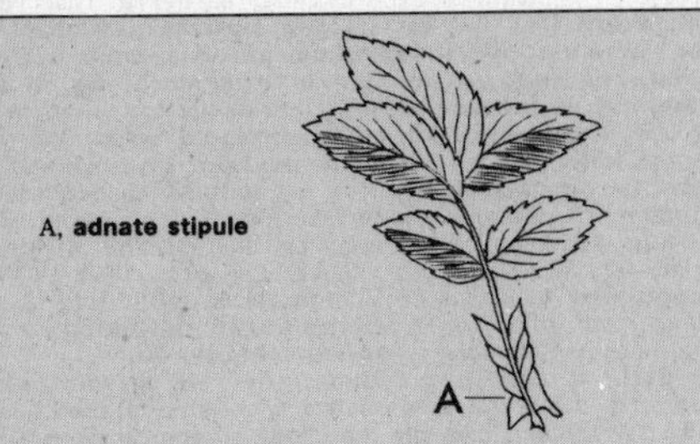

A, **adnate stipule**

d·na·tion (ad nā′shən), *n.* adnate condition. [1835–45; < L *adnātiōn-,* for *agnātiōn-* AGNATION; see ADNATE]

d nau·se·am (ad nô′zē əm, -am′), to a sickening or disgusting degree. [< L: lit., to seasickness]

d·nex·a (ad nek′sə), *n.pl. Anat.* parts added, attached, or adjunct to another or others, as the eyelids and tear glands in relation to the eyeball. [1895–1900; < L, neut. pl. of *adnexus* physically attached, joined, ptp. of *adnectere* to attach; see AD-, NEXUS] —**ad·nex′al,** *adj.*

d·nom·i·nal (ad nom′ə nl), *Gram.* —*adj.* **1.** of, pertaining to, or used as the modifier of a noun, as *new* in *the new theater, on the corner* in *the house on the corner,* or *the mayor's* in *the mayor's reputation.* **2.** of or pertaining to an adnoun. —*n.* **3.** a word or phrase that modifies a noun. [1835–45; AD- + NOMINAL, on the model of ADVERBIAL]

d·noun (ad′noun′), *n. Gram.* an adjective used as a noun, as *meek* in *Blessed are the meek;* absolute adjective. [1745–55; AD(JECTIVE) + NOUN]

·do (ə do͞o′), *n.* busy activity; bustle; fuss. [1250–1300; ME (north) *at do,* a phrase equiv. to *at* to (< ON, which used *at* with the inf.) + *do* DO[1]]
—**Syn.** flurry; confusion, upset, excitement; hubbub, noise, turmoil. ADO, TO-DO, COMMOTION, STIR, TUMULT suggest a great deal of fuss and noise. ADO implies a confused bustle of activity, a considerable emotional upset, and a great deal of talking: *Much Ado About Nothing.* TO-DO, now more commonly used, may mean merely excitement and noise and may be pleasant or unpleasant: *a great to-do over a movie star.* COMMOTION suggests a noisy confusion and babble: *commotion at the scene of an accident.* STIR suggests excitement and noise, with a hint of emotional cause: *The report was followed by a tremendous stir in the city.* TUMULT suggests disorder with noise and violence: *a tumult as the mob stormed the Bastille.* —**Ant.** calm, peace, tranquillity.

·do·be (ə dō′bē), *n.* **1.** sun-dried brick made of clay and straw, in common use in countries having little rainfall. **2.** a yellow silt or clay, deposited by rivers, used to make bricks. **3.** a building constructed of adobe. **4.** a dark, heavy soil, containing clay. [1750–60; *Amer.;* < Sp < Ar *al-ṭub* the brick < Coptic *to:o:be* brick < Egyptian Demotic *tb* < Egyptian Hieroglyphic *ḏbt*]

do′be flat′, a plain consisting of adobe deposited by short-lived rainfall or thaw streams, usually having a smooth or unmarked surface. [1920–25; *Amer.*]

·do-E·ki·ti (ä′dō ek′i tē′, -ä′ki-), *n.* a town in SE Nigeria. 213,000.

d·o·les·cence (ad′l es′əns), *n.* **1.** the transitional period between puberty and adulthood in human development, extending mainly over the teen years and terminating legally when the age of majority is reached; youth. **2.** the process or state of growing to maturity. **3.** a period or stage of development, as of a society, preceding maturity. [1400–50; late ME < MF < L *adolēscentia.* See ADOLESCENT, -ENCE]

d·o·les·cent (ad′l es′ənt), *adj.* **1.** growing to manhood or womanhood; youthful. **2.** having the characteristics of adolescence or of an adolescent. —*n.* **3.** an adolescent person. [1475–85; < L *adolēscent-* (s. of *adolēscēns* growing up, prp. of *adolēscere*), equiv. to *adol(ē)-* (see ADULT) + *-ēsc-* -ESCE + *-ent-* -ENT] —**ad′·o·les′cent·ly,** *adv.*
—**Syn. 1.** immature, young. **3.** youth, teenager, minor.

Ad·olf (ad′olf, ā′dolf; *Ger.* ä′dôlf), *n.* a male given name: from Germanic words meaning "noble" and "wolf." Also, **Ad′olph, Ad′olphe, A·dol·phus** (ə dol′fəs).

·do·nai (*Seph.* ä′dô nī′; *Ashk.* ä′dō noi′), *n. Hebrew.* a title of reverence for God, serving also as a substitute pronunciation of the Tetragrammaton. Also, ***A·do·noy*** (ä′dō noi′). [lit., my Lord; spoken in place of the ineffable name YAHWEH]

·don·ic (ə don′ik), *adj.* **1.** *Pros.* noting a verse consisting of a dactyl (—⏑⏑) followed by a spondee (——) or trochee (—⏑). **2.** of or like Adonis. —*n.* **3.** *Pros.* an Adonic verse or line. [1670–80; < ML *Adōnicus.* See ADONIS, -IC]

Ad·o·ni·jah (ad′n ī′jə), *n.* a son of David, put to death at the order of Solomon. II Sam. 3:4; I Kings 2:19–25. Also, *Douay Bible,* **Ad·o·ni·as.** (ad′n ī′əs).

·don·is (ə don′is, ə dō′nis), *n.* **1.** *Class. Myth.* a youth slain by a wild boar but permitted by Zeus to pass four months every year in the lower world with Persephone, four with Aphrodite, and four wherever he chose. **2.** a very handsome young man. [1615–25 for def. 2]

·don O·lam (ä dōn′ ō läm′), *Judaism.* a liturgical prayer or hymn expressing the faith of Israel in God, often sung in unison usually at the close of a service. [< Heb *ădhōn ʿōlām* lit., Lord of the world]

·dopt (ə dopt′), *v.t.* **1.** to choose or take as one's own; make one's own by selection or assent: *to adopt a nickname.* **2.** to take and rear (the child of other parents) as one's own child, specifically by a formal legal act. **3.** to take or receive into any kind of new relationship: *to adopt a person as a protégé.* **4.** to select as a basic or required textbook or series of textbooks in a course. **5.** to vote to accept: *The House adopted the report.* **6.** to accept or act in accordance with (a plan, principle, etc.). **7. adopt out,** to place (a child) for adoption: *The institution may keep a child or adopt it out.* [1490–1500; (< MF *adopter*) < L *adoptāre,* equiv. to *ad-* AD- + *optāre* to OPT] —**a·dopt′er,** *n.*

a·dopt·a·ble (ə dop′tə bəl), *adj.* **1.** capable of being adopted; suitable or eligible for adoption: *an adoptable child; a resolution found to be adoptable.* —*n.* **2.** a child who is considered suitable for adoption: *fewer adoptables than in previous years.* [1835–45; ADOPT + -ABLE] —**a·dopt′a·bil′i·ty,** *n.*

a·dopt·ee (ə dop tē′, ad′op-), *n.* a person who is adopted. [1890–95; ADOPT + -EE]

a·dop·tion (ə dop′shən), *n.* **1.** the act of adopting: *the adoption of a new amendment.* **2.** the state of being adopted. [1300–50; ME *adopcioun* < L *adoptiōn-,* s. of *adoptiō.* See AD-, OPTION] —**a·dop′tion·al,** *adj.*

a·dop·tive (ə dop′tiv), *adj.* **1.** of or involving adoption. **2.** acquired or related by adoption: *an adoptive father or son.* **3.** tending to adopt. [1400–50; < L *adoptīvus;* see ADOPT, -IVE; r. late ME *adoptife* < MF *adoptif*] —**a·dop′tive·ly,** *adv.*
—**Usage.** Although ADOPTIVE in the sense "acquired or related by adoption" can refer to either parent or child in such a relationship, ADOPTIVE is customarily applied to the parent (*her adoptive mother*) and *adopted* to the child (*their adopted son*).

adop′tive immu′nity, passive immunity resulting from the administration of sensitized lymphocytes from an immune donor.

a·dor·a·ble (ə dôr′ə bəl, ə dōr′-), *adj.* **1.** very attractive or delightful; charming: *What an adorable hat!* **2.** worthy of being adored. [1605–15; < L *adōrābilis.* See ADORE, -ABLE] —**a·dor′a·ble·ness, a·dor′a·bil′i·ty,** *n.* —**a·dor′a·bly,** *adv.*

ad·o·ra·tion (ad′ə rā′shən), *n.* **1.** the act of paying honor, as to a divine being; worship. **2.** reverent homage. **3.** fervent and devoted love. [1535–45; < L *adōrātiōn-* (s. of *adōrātiō*) worship. See ADORE, -ATION]

a·dore (ə dôr′, ə dōr′), *v.,* **a·dored, a·dor·ing.** —*v.t.* **1.** to regard with the utmost esteem, love, and respect; honor. **2.** to pay divine honor to; worship: *to adore God.* **3.** to like or admire very much: *I simply adore the way your hair is done!* —*v.i.* **4.** to worship. [1275–1325; < L *adōrāre* to speak to, pray, worship, equiv. to *ad-* AD- + *ōrāre* to speak, beg (see ORAL); r. ME *aour(i)e* < OF *aourer* < L] —**a·dor′er,** *n.* —**a·dor′ing·ly,** *adv.*
—**Syn. 1.** idolize; reverence, revere, venerate. —**Ant. 1.** abhor.

a·dorn (ə dôrn′), *v.t.* **1.** to decorate or add beauty to, as by ornaments: *garlands of flowers adorning their hair.* **2.** to make more pleasing, attractive, impressive, etc.; enhance: *Piety adorned Abigail's character.* [1325–75; ME *adornen* < L *adōrnāre,* equiv. to *ad-* AD- + *ōrnāre* to dress (see ORNATE); r. late ME *aourne* < MF < L] —**a·dorn′er,** *n.* —**a·dorn′ing·ly,** *adv.*
—**Syn. 1.** beautify; deck, bedeck; bedizen, array.

a·dorn·ment (ə dôrn′mənt), *n.* **1.** something that adds attractiveness; ornament; accessory: *the adornments and furnishings of a room.* **2.** ornamentation; embellishment: *personal adornment.* [1470–80; ADORN + -MENT; r. late ME *aournement* < MF]

a·dor·no (ə dôr′nō), *n., pl.* **-nos.** *Ceram.* relief ornament applied to a piece. [< Sp, n. deriv. of *adornar* < L *adōrnāre* to ADORN]

A·dou·la (ä do͞o′lə), *n.* **Cy·rille** (sē ril′), 1922–78, African statesman: premier of the Democratic Republic of the Congo (now Zaire) 1961–64.

A·do·wa (ä′do͝o wä′), *n.* Aduwa.

a·down (ə doun′), *adv., prep. Archaic.* down. [bef. 1000; ME *adoun,* OE *of dūne* off the hill. See A-[2], DOWN[2]]

a·doze (ə dōz′), *adv., adj.* dozing; napping: *a cat adoze by the fireside.* [1845–50; A-[1] + DOZE[1]]

ADP, 1. Also called **adenosine diphosphate, adenosinediphosphoric acid.** *Biochem.* an ester of adenosine and pyrophosphoric acid, $C_{10}H_{12}N_5O_3H_3P_2O_7$, derived from ATP, and serving to transfer energy during glycolysis. **2.** automatic data processing: the processing of data by computers or related devices, using techniques that reduce human intervention to a minimum. Cf. **EDP, IDP.** [1940–45]

ad part. dolent., (in prescriptions) to the painful parts. [< L *ad partēs dolentēs*]

ad pa·tres (äd pä′tres; *Eng.* ad pā′trēz), *Latin.* dead. [lit., to the fathers]

ad·per·son (ad′pûr′sən), *n.* a copywriter, account executive, or other person employed in advertising. [1975–80; AD(MAN) + -PERSON]
—**Usage.** See **-person.**

ad quem (äd kwem′; *Eng.* ad kwem′), *Latin.* at or to which; the end toward which something tends.

A·dram·me·lech (ə dram′ə lek′), *n.* **1.** one of the gods worshiped by the Sepharvites. II Kings 17:31. Cf. **Anammelech. 2.** a son of Sennacherib. II Kings 19:37. Also, *Douay Bible,* **A·dram′e·lech′.**

A·dras·tus (ə dras′təs), *n. Class. Myth.* a king of Argos and leader of the Seven against Thebes. Also, **A·dras′tos.**

ad rem (ad rem′; *Lat.* äd rem′), **1.** relevant; pertinent: *an ad rem remark.* **2.** without digressing; in a straightforward manner: *to reply ad rem.* [< L: lit., to the matter]

adren-, var. of **adreno-** before a vowel: *adrenergic.*

ad·re·nal (ə drēn′l), —*adj.* **1.** of or produced by the adrenal glands. **2.** situated near or on the kidneys; suprarenal. —*n.* **3.** See **adrenal gland.** [1870–75; AD- + L *rēn-* (s. of *rēnēs* kidneys) + -AL[1]] —**ad·re′nal·ly,** *adv.*

adre′nal gland′, *Anat.* one of a pair of ductless glands, located above the kidneys, consisting of a cortex, which produces steroidal hormones, and a medulla, which produces epinephrine and norepinephrine. Also called **suprarenal gland.** See diag. under **kidney.** [1870–75]

A·dren·al·in (ə dren′l in), *Pharm., Trademark.* epinephrine (def. 2).

a·dren·a·line (ə dren′l in, -ēn′), *n. Biochem, Pharm.* epinephrine (def. 1). [1900–05; ADRENAL + -INE[1]]

ad·re·nal·ize (ə drēn′l īz′), *v.t.,* **-ized, -iz·ing.** to stir to action; excite: *The promise of victory adrenalized the team.* Also, *esp. Brit.,* **ad·re′nal·ise′.** [ADRENAL(INE) + -IZE]

ad·ren·er·gic (ad′rə nûr′jik), *adj.* **1.** of or like epinephrine in effect. **2.** releasing epinephrine. **3.** activated by epinephrine or any of various substances having epinephrinelike activity. —*n.* **4.** a drug or other agent having an epinephrinelike effect. Cf. **cholinergic.** [1930–35; ADREN- + -ERGIC]

adreno-, a combining form representing **adrenal** or **adrenaline** in compound words: *adrenocortical.* Also, *esp. before a vowel,* **adren-.**

a·dre·no·cor·ti·cal (ə drē′nō kôr′ti kəl), *adj.* of, pertaining to, or produced by the cortex of the adrenal gland. [1935–40; ADRENO- + CORTICAL]

a·dre·no·cor·ti·co·ster·oid (ə drē′nō kôr′ti kō-ster′oid, -stēr′-), *n. Biochem.* any of a group of steroid hormones produced by the cortex of the adrenal gland. [1960–65; ADRENO- + CORTICOSTEROID]

a·dre·no·cor·ti·co·trop·ic (ə drē′nō kôr′ti kō trop′-ik, -trō′pik), *adj.* stimulating the adrenal cortex. Also, **a·dre·no·cor·ti·co·troph·ic** (ə drē′nō kôr′ti kō trof′ik, -trō′fik). [1935–40; ADRENO- + CORTICO- + -TROPIC]

adre′nocor′ticotrop′ic hor′mone. See **ACTH.** Also called **a·dre·no·cor·ti·co·tro·pin** (ə drē′nō kôr′ti-kō trō′pin). [1935–40]

a·dre·no·re·cep·tor (ə drē′nō ri sep′tər), *n. Biochem., Physiol.* a receptor that binds with epinephrine, norepinephrine, or related compounds. [ADRENO- + RECEPTOR]

a·dret (a drā′), *n.* a side of a mountain receiving direct sunlight. [1930–35; < F < Pr (Dauphiné, Provence) *adre(i)t,* OPr *adreg, adret* lit., good, suitable (i.e., the good side of the mountain for vineyards, etc.); see ADROIT]

A·dri·a·my·cin (ā′drē ə mī′sin), *Pharm., Trademark.* a brand of doxorubicin.

A·dri·an (ā′drē ən), *n.* **1. Edgar Douglas,** 1889–1977, English physiologist: Nobel prize for medicine 1932. **2. (Gilbert),** 1903–59, U.S. fashion and costume designer. **3.** Hadrian. **4.** a city in SE Michigan. 21,186. **5.** a male given name: from a Latin word meaning "from Hadria," an ancient city in northern Italy.

Adrian I, died A.D. 795, pope 772–795. Also, **Hadrian I.**

Adrian II, Italian ecclesiastic: pope A.D. 867–872. Also, **Hadrian II.**

Adrian III, Saint, Italian ecclesiastic: pope A.D. 884–885. Also, **Hadrian III.**

Adrian IV, (*Nicholas Breakspear*), c1100–59, only Englishman to become pope, 1154–59. Also, **Hadrian IV.**

Adrian V, died 1276, Italian ecclesiastic: pope 1276. Also, **Hadrian V.**

Adrian VI, 1459–1523, Dutch ecclesiastic: pope 1522–23. Also, **Hadrian VI.**

A·dri·an·o·ple (ā′drē ə nō′pəl), *n.* Edirne.

A′driano′ple red′, a medium red color. Also called **Levant red, Turkey red.**

A·dri·an·op·o·lis (ā′drē ə nop′ə lis), *n.* former name of **Edirne.**

A·dri·at·ic (ā′drē at′ik, ad′rē-), *adj.* **1.** of or pertaining to the Adriatic Sea. —*n.* **2.** See **Adriatic Sea.**

A′driat′ic Sea′, an arm of the Mediterranean between Italy and the Balkan Peninsula. Also called **Adriatic.**

A·dri·enne (ā′drē en′, -ən; *Fr.* A drē en′), *n.* a female given name: derived from *Adrian.*

a·drift (ə drift′), *adj., adv.* **1.** floating without control; drifting; not anchored or moored: *The survivors were adrift in the rowboat for three days.* **2.** lacking aim, direction, or stability. [1615–25; A-[1] + DRIFT]

a·droit (ə droit′), *adj.* **1.** expert or nimble in the use of

CONCISE PRONUNCIATION KEY: act, cāpe, dâre, pärt; set, ēqual; *if,* ice; ox, ōver, ôrder, oil, bo͝ok, bo͞ot, out; up, ûrge; child; sing; shoe; thin, *that;* zh as in *treasure.* ə = *a* as in *alone, e* as in *system, i* as in *easily, o* as in *gallop, u* as in *circus;* ᵊ as in *fire* (fīᵊr), *hour* (ouᵊr). l and n can serve as syllabic consonants, as in *cradle* (krād′l), and *button* (but′n). See the full key inside the front cover.

the hands or body. **2.** cleverly skillful, resourceful, or ingenious: *an adroit debater.* [1645–55; < F, OF: elegant, skillful, equiv. to *a-* A-[5] + *droit, dreit* straight, just, correct < L *dīrēctus;* see DIRECT] **—a·droit′ly,** *adv.* **—a·droit′ness,** *n.*

—Syn. 1. skillful, clever; deft, apt, adept. **1, 2.** See **dexterous. —Ant. 1.** clumsy.

à droite (A DRWAT′), *French.* to the right.

ADS, American Dialect Society.

a.d.s., autograph document, signed.

ad·sci·ti·tious (ad′si tish′əs), *adj.* added or derived from an external source; additional. [1610–20; < L *a(d)scīt(us)* derived, assumed, foreign (ptp. of *a(d)scīscī*), equiv. to *ad-* AD- + *scī-* (s. of *scīre* to know) + *-tus* ptp. suffix + -ITIOUS] **—ad′sci·ti′tious·ly,** *adv.*

ad·script (ad′skript), *adj.* **1.** written after (distinguished from *subscript*). **—n. 2.** an adscript character. Cf. **inferior** (def. 11), **superior** (def. 12). [1715–25; < L *a(d)scrīptus* (ptp. of *ascrībere* to ASCRIBE), equiv. to *ad-* AD- + *scrīptus* written; see SCRIPT]

ad·scrip·tion (ad skrip′shən), *n.* ascription.

ad·sorb (ad sôrb′, -zôrb′), *v.t. Physical Chem.* to gather (a gas, liquid, or dissolved substance) on a surface in a condensed layer: *Charcoal will adsorb gases.* [1880–85; AD- + (AB)SORB] **—ad·sorb′a·ble,** *adj.* **—ad·sorb′a·bil′i·ty,** *n.* **—ad·sorb′ent,** *adj., n.* **—ad·sorp·tion** (ad sôrp′shən, -zôrp′-), *n.* **—ad·sorp′tive,** *adj.* **—ad·sorp′tive·ly,** *adv.*

ad·sorb·ate (ad sôr′bāt, -bit, -zôr′-), *n.* a substance that is adsorbed. [1925–30; ADSORB + -ATE[1]]

adst. feb., (in prescriptions) when fever is present. [< L *adstante febre*]

ad·stra·tum (ad′strā′təm, -strat′əm), *n., pl.* **-stra·ta** (-strā′tə, -strat′ə). *Historical Ling.* a substratum or superstratum. [AD- + STRATUM]

ad·su′ki bean′ (ad so͞o′kē, -zo͞o′-). See **adzuki bean.**

ad·sum (äd′so͝om; *Eng.* ad′sum), *interj. Latin.* I am present.

ADTS, Automated Data and Telecommunications Service.

a du·e (ä do͞o′ā; *It.* ä do͞o′e), *Music.* **1.** together; in unison. **2.** divisi. [< It: lit., by two]

ad·u·la·res·cent (aj′ə lə res′ənt), *adj.* (of certain gemstones, esp. adularia) having a milky, bluish luster. [ADULAR(IA) + -ESCENT] **—ad′u·la·res′cence,** *n.*

ad·u·lar·i·a (aj′ə lâr′ē ə), *n. Mineral.* a sometimes opalescent variety of orthoclase formed at a low temperature. [1790–1800; < It < F *adulaire,* named after *Adula* a mountain group in Switzerland; see -ARY]

ad·u·late (aj′ə lāt′), *v.t.,* **-lat·ed, -lat·ing.** to show excessive admiration or devotion to; flatter or admire servilely. [1770–80; back formation from *adulation,* ME < MF < L *adūlātiōn-* (s. of *adūlātiō*) servile flattery, fawning, equiv. to *adūlāt(us),* ptp. of *adūlārī, -āre* to fawn upon (of dogs), appar. a nominal deriv., with *ad-* AD-, of an otherwise unattested base + *-iōn-* -ION] **—ad′u·la′tion,** *n.* **—ad′u·la′tor,** *n.* **—ad·u·la·to·ry** (aj′ə lə tôr′ē, -tōr′ē), *adj.*

a·dult (ə dult′, ad′ult), *adj.* **1.** having attained full size and strength; grown up; mature: *an adult person, animal, or plant.* **2.** of, pertaining to, or befitting adults. **3.** intended for adults; not suitable for children: *adult entertainment.* **—n. 4.** a person who is fully grown or developed or of age. **5.** a full-grown animal or plant. **6.** a person who has attained the age of maturity as specified by law. [1525–35; 1925–30 for def. 3; < L *adultus* grown (ptp. of *adolēre* to make grow), equiv. to *ad-* AD- + *ul-* (identical with base *al-* in ALIMENT, *ol-* in PROLIFIC) + *-tus* ptp. suffix] **—a·dult′hood,** *n.* **—a·dult′like′,** *adj.* **—a·dult′ly,** *adv.* **—a·dult′ness,** *n.*

adult′ educa′tion, a program of noncredit courses for adults regardless of previous education, offered typically by a university extension or institute. Also called **continued education, continuing education.** [1850–55]

a·dul·ter·ant (ə dul′tər ənt), *n.* **1.** a substance that adulterates. **—adj. 2.** adulterating. [1745–55; < L *adulterant-* (s. of *adulterāns,* prp. of *adulterāre*), equiv. to *ad-* AD- + *-ulter* (see ADULTERATE) + *-ant-* -ANT]

a·dul·ter·ate (*v.* ə dul′tə rāt′; *adj.* ə dul′tər it, -tə rāt′), *v.,* **-at·ed, -at·ing,** *adj.* **—v.t. 1.** to debase or make impure by adding inferior materials or elements; use cheaper, inferior, or less desirable goods in the production of (any professedly genuine article): *to adulterate food.* **—adj. 2.** adulterated. **3.** adulterous (def. 1). [1580–90; < L *adulterātus* mixed, adulterated (ptp. of *adulterāre*), equiv. to *ad-* AD- + *-ulter* (perh. comb. form of *alter* other; see ALTER) + *-ātus* -ATE[1]] **—a·dul′ter·a′tor,** *n.*

a·dul·ter·a·tion (ə dul′tə rā′shən), *n.* **1.** the act or process of adulterating. **2.** the state of being adulterated. **3.** something adulterated. [1500–10; < L *adulterātiōn-* (s. of *adulterātiō*); see ADULTERATE, -ION]

a·dul·ter·er (ə dul′tər ər), *n.* a person who commits adultery. [1350–1400; earlier *adulter* adulterer (< L, back formation from *adulterāre* to defile; see ADULTERATE) + -ER[1]; r. ME *avouter, avoutrer* < OF < L]

a·dul·ter·ess (ə dul′tər is, -tris), *n.* a woman who commits adultery. [1350–1400; ADULTER(ER) + -ESS; r. ME *avoutresse*]

—Usage. See **-ess.**

a·dul·ter·ine (ə dul′tə rēn′, -tə rīn′), *adj.* **1.** characterized by adulteration; spurious. **2.** born of adultery. **3.** of or involving adultery. [1535–45; < L *adulterīnus,* equiv. to *adulter* adulterer, counterfeiter (see ADULTERER) + *-īnus* -INE[1]]

a·dul·ter·ous (ə dul′tər əs), *adj.* characterized by or involved in adultery; illicit: *an adulterous relationship.* [1400–50; ADULTER(Y) + -OUS; r. late ME *avoutrious*] **—a·dul′ter·ous·ly,** *adv.*

a·dul·ter·y (ə dul′tə rē), *n., pl.* **-ter·ies.** voluntary sexual intercourse between a married person and someone other than his or her lawful spouse. [1325–75; ME *adulterie* < L *adulterium,* equiv. to *adulter* (see ADULTERER) + *-ium* -IUM; r. ME *a(d)vouterie* < OF *avoutrie* < L, with *ad-* AD- r. *a* A-[5]]

adult′ home′, any of various private residences for former state psychiatric patients, supervised by a department of a state or city government. [1975–1980]

adult′ on′set diabe′tes, diabetes (def. 4).

adult′ res′piratory distress′ syn′drome, *Pathol.* See **respiratory distress syndrome** (def. 2). *Abbr.:* ARDS

ad·um·bral (a dum′brəl), *adj.* shadowy; shady. [1835–45; AD- + L *umbr(a)* shade, shadow + -AL[1]]

ad·um·brate (a dum′brāt, ad′əm brāt′), *v.t.,* **-brat·ed, -brat·ing. 1.** to produce a faint image or resemblance of; to outline or sketch. **2.** to foreshadow; prefigure. **3.** to darken or conceal partially; overshadow. [1575–85; < L *adumbrātus* shaded (ptp. of *adumbrāre*), equiv. to *ad-* AD- + *umbr(a)* shade, shadow + *-ātus* -ATE[1]] **—ad′um·bra′tion,** *n.*

ad·um·bra·tive (a dum′brə tiv, ad′əm brā′tiv), *adj.* foreshadowing; sketchy; faintly indicative. [1830–40; ADUMBRATE + -IVE] **—ad·um′bra·tive·ly,** *adv.*

a·dunc (ə dungk′), *adj.* curved inward; hooked. [1620–30; < L *aduncus,* equiv. to *ad-* AD- + *uncus* hook, barb] **—a·dun·ci·ty** (ə dun′si tē), *n.*

a·dust (ə dust′), *adj.* **1.** dried or darkened as by heat. **2.** burned; scorched. **3.** *Archaic.* gloomy in appearance or mood. [1400–50; late ME < L *adustus* (ptp. of *adūrere*), equiv. to *ad-* AD- + *us-* (base of *ūrere* to burn) + *-tus* ptp. suffix]

ad u·trum·que pa·ra·tus (äd o͞o tro͝om′kwe pä rä′to͝os; *Eng.* ad yo͞o trum′kwē pə rā′təs), *Latin.* ready for either alternative.

A·du·wa (ä′do͞o wä′), *n.* a town in N Ethiopia: Italians defeated 1896. 15,712. Also, **Adowa.**

Adv., **1.** Advent. **2.** Advocate

adv., **1.** ad valorem. **2.** advance. **3.** adverb. **4.** adverbial. **5.** adverbially. **6.** adversus. **7.** advertisement. **8.** advertising. **9.** adviser. **10.** advisory.

Ad·vai·ta (əd vī′tə), *n. Hinduism.* one of the two principal Vedantic schools, asserting the existence of Brahman alone, whose appearance as the world is an illusion resulting from ignorance. Cf. **dvaita** (def. 2). [< Skt]

ad val., ad valorem.

ad va·lo·rem (ad və lôr′əm, -lōr′-), in proportion to the value (used esp. of duties on imports that are fixed at a percentage of the value as stated on the invoice). [< L: lit., according to the worth]

ad valo′rem tax′, a tax levied according to the value of the property, merchandise, etc., being taxed. [1690–1700]

ad·vance (ad vans′, -väns′), *v.,* **-vanced, -vanc·ing,** *n., adj.* **—v.t. 1.** to move or bring forward: *The general advanced his troops to the new position.* **2.** to bring into consideration or notice; suggest; propose: *to advance reasons for a tax cut.* **3.** to improve; further: *to advance one's interests.* **4.** to raise in rank; promote: *The board of directors advanced him to president.* **5.** to raise in rate or amount; increase: *to advance the price.* **6.** to bring forward in time; accelerate: *to advance growth; to advance clocks one hour.* **7.** to supply beforehand; furnish on credit or before goods are delivered or work is done. **8.** to furnish as part of a stock or fund. **9.** to supply or pay in expectation of reimbursement: *They advanced her $5000 against future royalties.* **10.** to schedule at a later time or date: *to advance a meeting from early to late fall.* **11.** *Informal.* to do advance publicity for: *to advance a rock singer's personal appearances; the most heavily advanced sports event in history.* **12.** *Archaic.* to raise, as a banner. **—v.i. 13.** to move or go forward; proceed: *The troops advanced.* **14.** to increase in quantity, value, price, etc.: *His stock advanced three points.* **15.** (of a color, form, etc., on a flat surface) to move toward or be perceived as moving toward an observer, esp. as giving the illusion of space. Cf. **recede**[1] (def. 3). **16.** to improve or make progress. **17.** to grow or rise in importance, status, etc.: *to advance in rank.* **18.** *Informal.* to provide publicity; do promotion: *He was hired to advance for a best-selling author.* **—n. 19.** a forward movement; progress in space: *the advance of the troops to the border.* **20.** promotion; improvement in importance, rank, etc.: *his advance to the position of treasurer.* **21.** Usually, **advances. a.** attempts at forming an acquaintanceship, reaching an agreement, or the like, made by one party. **b.** actions or words intended to be sexually inviting. **22.** addition to price; rise in price: *an advance on cottons.* **23.** *Com.* **a.** a giving beforehand; a furnishing of something before an equivalent is received: *An advance on his next month's salary permitted him to pay his debt on time.* **b.** the money or goods thus furnished: *He received $100 as an advance against future delivery.* **24.** *Journalism.* **a.** copy prepared before the event it describes has occurred: *The morning papers carried advances on the ceremony, which will take place tonight.* **b.** a press release, wire-service dispatch, or the like, as one containing the text or partial text of a speech, sent to arrive in advance of the event to which it is related. Cf. **release copy. 25.** the leading body of an army. **26.** *Mil.* (formerly) the order or a signal to advance. **27.** *Informal.* **a.** publicity done before the appearance of a noted person, a public event, etc.: *She was hired to do advance for the candidate.* **b.** a person hired to do advance publicity for an event: *He is regarded as the best advance in the business.* **28.** *Auto. Mach.* an adjustment made in the setting of the distribu tor of an internal-combustion engine to generate th spark for ignition in each cylinder earlier in the cycle Cf. **retard** (def. 5). **29.** *Geol.* a seaward movement o the shoreline. **30. in advance,** ahead of time; before hand: *You must get your tickets in advance.* **31. in ad vance of,** in front of; before: *Heralds walked in advanc of the king.* **—adj. 32.** going or placed before: *an ad vance section of a train.* **33.** made or given ahead o time: *an advance payment on a loan.* **34.** issued ahea of time: *an advance copy of the President's speech.* **35** having gone beyond others or beyond the averag [1200–50; ME *avauncen* < AF, OF *avanc(i)er* < V **abantiāre,* v. deriv. of LL *abante* in front (of) (L *a* away from, off + *ante* before); AD- by mistaking *a-* fo A-[5] in the 16th cent.] **—ad·vanc′ing·ly,** *adv.*

—Syn. 2. adduce, propound; offer. **3.** forward, pro mote. **6.** force; quicken, hasten, speed up. **9.** lend, loan **13.** ADVANCE, MOVE ON, PROCEED all imply movemen forward. ADVANCE applies to forward movement, esp. to ward an objective: *to advance to a platform.* PROCEE emphasizes movement, as from one place to another, an often implies continuing after a halt: *to proceed on one' journey.* MOVE ON is similar in meaning to PROCEED; i does not, however, imply a definite goal: *The crowd wa told to move on.* **16.** thrive, flourish; prosper. **20** growth, advancement. **21.** overture, proposal; offer tender. **24.** prepublication. **25.** spearhead. **—Ant. 1 2.** withdraw. **13.** retreat. **17.** decrease.

ad·vanced (ad vanst′, -vänst′), *adj.* **1.** placed ahea or forward: *with one foot advanced.* **2.** ahead or far o further along in progress, complexity, knowledge, skill etc.: *an advanced class in Spanish; to take a course i advanced mathematics; Our plans are too advanced t make the change now.* **3.** pertaining to or embodyin ideas, practices, attitudes, etc., taken as being more en lightened or liberal than the standardized, established or traditional: *advanced theories of child care; the mor advanced members of the artistic community.* **4.** fa along in time: *the advanced age of most senators.* [1425–75; late ME; see ADVANCE, -ED[2]]

advanced′ cred′it, academic credit allowed by an educational institution to an entering student for previously completed studies taken at another recognized institution.

advanced′ degree′, an academic degree conferred for completion of requirements beyond the undergraduate college level, as M.S. or Ph.D. [1950–55]

advanced′ stand′ing, **1.** credit for studies completed elsewhere, granted to a student by a college or university. **2.** the higher academic status of a student granted such credit. [1780–90]

advance′ fee′. See **front money** (def. 3).

advance′ guard′, a body of troops going before the main force to clear the way, guard against surprise, etc. [1750–60]

advance′ man′, advance (def. 27b). Also, **ad·vance′·man′.** [1925–30]

ad·vance·ment (ad vans′mənt, -väns′-), *n.* **1.** an act of moving forward. **2.** promotion in rank or standing; preferment: *She had high hopes for advancement in the company.* **3.** *Law.* money or property given by one person during his or her lifetime to another that is considered an anticipation of an inheritance and is therefore to be deducted from any share that the recipient may have in a donor's estate. [1250–1300; ME *avauncement* < AF, OF *avancement.* See ADVANCE, -MENT]

ad·vanc·er (ad van′sər, -vän′-), *n.* **1.** a person or thing that advances. **2.** the second branch of the antlers of a buck. [1490–1500; see ADVANCE, -ER[1]]

ad·van·tage (ad van′tij, -vän′-), *n., v.,* **-taged, -tag·ing. —n. 1.** any state, circumstance, opportunity, or means specially favorable to success, interest, or any desired end: *the advantage of a good education.* **2.** benefit; gain; profit: *It will be to his advantage to learn Chinese before going to China.* **3.** superiority or ascendancy (often fol. by *over* or *of*): *His height gave him an advantage over his opponent.* **4.** a position of superiority (often fol. by *over* or *of*): *their advantage in experienced players.* **5.** *Tennis.* the first point scored after deuce. **6. have the advantage of,** to be in a superior or advantageous position; possess an advantage over: *By virtue of independent wealth, he has the advantage of his opponents.* **7. take advantage of, a.** to make use of for gain: *to take advantage of an opportunity.* **b.** to impose upon, esp. unfairly, as by exploiting a weakness: *to take advantage of someone.* **8. to advantage,** to good effect; advantageously: *The paintings were arranged to advantage on one wall.* **—v.t. 9.** to be of service to; yield profit or gain to; benefit. **10.** to cause to advance; further; promote: *Such action will advantage our cause.* **11.** to prove beneficial to; profit: *It would advantage him to work harder.* [1300–50; ME *ava(u)ntage* < AF, OF *avantage,* equiv. to *avant* before (see ADVANCE) + *-age* -AGE; for *ad-* see ADVANCE]

—Syn. 2. ADVANTAGE, BENEFIT, PROFIT all mean something that is of use or value. ADVANTAGE is anything that places one in an improved position, esp. in coping with competition or difficulties: *It is to one's advantage to have traveled widely.* BENEFIT is anything that promotes the welfare or improves the state of a person or group: *a benefit to society.* PROFIT is any valuable, useful, or helpful gain: *profit from trade or experience.* **9.** serve, avail, help, aid.

advan′tage court′, *Tennis.* the receiver's left-hand service court, into which the ball is served when one side has the advantage.

ad·van·taged (ad van′tijd, -vän′-), *adj.* **1.** having greater resources or better skills, education, facilities, etc.: *She is more advantaged than her cousin.* **2.** having sufficient or abundant income, natural resources, etc.; affluent: *the advantaged nations.* **—n. 3.** (*used with a plural v.*) advantaged people collectively (usually prec.

CONCISE ETYMOLOGY KEY: <, descended or borrowed from; >, whence; b., blend of, blended; c., cognate with; cf., compare; deriv., derivative; equiv., equivalent; imit., imitative; obl., oblique; r., replacing; s., stem; sp., spelling, spelled; resp., respelling, respelled; trans., translation; ?, origin unknown; *, unattested; ‡, probably earlier than. See the full key inside the front cover.

y the): *a luxury cruise that only the advantaged could* ford. [1595–1605; ADVANTAGE + -ED[3]]

l•van•ta•geous (ad′vən tā′jəs), *adj.* providing an dvantage; furnishing convenience or opportunity; faorable; profitable; useful; beneficial: *an advantageous* osition; *an advantageous treaty.* [1590–1600; ADVAN-AGE + -OUS; cf. F *avantageux,* It *avantaggioso*] **—ad′•an•ta′geous•ly,** *adv.* **—ad′van•ta′geous•ness,** *n.*

l•vect (ad vekt′), *v.t.* to move by the process of ad-ection. [back formation from ADVECTION]

l•vec•tion (ad vek′shən), *n.* **1.** *Meteorol.* the hori-ontal transport of atmospheric properties (distinguished om *convection*). **2.** the horizontal flow of air, water, tc. [1905–10; < L *advectiōn-* (s. of *advectiō*), equiv. to *dvect(us),* ptp. of *advehere* (*ad-* AD- + *vec-,* var. s. of *ehere* to carry, bring + *-tus* ptp. suffix) + *-iōn-* -ION] **-ad•vec′tive,** *adj.*

dvec′tion fog′, *Meteorol.* fog caused by the move-ent of warm, moist air over a cold surface. [1940–45]

l•vent (ad′vent), *n.* **1.** a coming into place, view, or eing; arrival: *the advent of the holiday season.* **2.** (*usu-lly cap.*) the coming of Christ into the world. **3.** (*cap.*) e period beginning four Sundays before Christmas, ob-erved in commemoration of the coming of Christ into e world. **4.** (*usually cap.*) See **Second Coming.** 125–75; ME < L *adventus* arrival, approach, equiv. to *d-* AD- + *ven-* (s. of *venīre* to come) + *-tus* suffix of erbal action]
—Syn. 1. onset, beginning, commencement, start.

d•vent•ist (ad′ven tist, ad ven′-), *n.* **1.** Also called **econd Adventist.** a member of any of certain Chris-an denominations that maintain that the Second dvent of Christ is imminent. *—adj.* **2.** of or pertaining Adventists. [1835–45; ADVENT + -IST] **—Ad′vent•sm,** *n.*

d•ven•ti•ti•a (ad′ven tish′ē ə, -tish′ə), *n. Anat.* the xternal covering of an organ or other structure, derived om connective tissue, esp. the external covering of a lood vessel. [1875–80; < L *adventicia,* neut. pl. of *ad-entīcius* ADVENTITIOUS] **—ad′ven•ti′tial,** *adj.*

d•ven•ti•tious (ad′vən tish′əs), *adj.* **1.** associated with something by chance rather than as an integral art; extrinsic. **2.** *Bot., Zool.* appearing in an abnormal r unusual position or place, as a root. [1595–1605; < L *dventīcius* lit., coming from without, external, equiv. to *d-* AD- + *ven-* (s. of *venīre* to come) + *-t(us)* ptp. suffix *-īcius* -ITIOUS] **—ad′ven•ti′tious•ly,** *adv.* **—ad′ven-i′tious•ness,** *n.*

d•ven•tive (ad ven′tiv), *Bot., Zool.* *—adj.* **1.** not na-ive and usually not yet well established, as exotic plants r animals. *—n.* **2.** an adventive plant or animal. 1595–1605, for an earlier sense; < L *advent(us)* advance, ncursion (see ADVENT) + -IVE] **—ad•ven′tive•ly,** *adv.*

d′vent Sun′day, the first Sunday in Advent.

d•ven•ture (ad ven′chər), *n., v.,* **-tured, -tur•ing.** *—n.* **1.** an exciting or very unusual experience. **2.** par-icipation in exciting undertakings or enterprises: *the pirit of adventure.* **3.** a bold, usually risky undertaking; azardous action of uncertain outcome. **4.** a commercial r financial speculation of any kind; venture. **5.** *Obs.* **a.** eril; danger; risk. **b.** chance; fortune; luck. *—v.t.* **6.** to isk or hazard. **7.** to take the chance of; dare. **8.** to enture to say or utter: *to adventure an opinion.* *—v.i.* **.** to take the risk involved. **10.** to venture; hazard. 1200–50; ME *aventure* < AF, OF < VL **adventūra* what must happen, fem. (orig. neut. pl.) of L *adventūrus* ut. participle of *advenīre* to arrive; *ad-* AD- r. *a-* A-[5]. See DVENT, -URE] **—ad•ven′ture•ful,** *adj.*

dven′ture play′ground, *Brit.* a children's play-round, often in a somewhat desolate urban area, that tilizes derelict industrial or commercial items or prod-cts for equipment, as used tires for swings and wooden rates for tunnels. [1965–70]

d•ven•tur•er (ad ven′chər ər), *n.* **1.** a person who as, enjoys, or seeks adventures. **2.** a seeker of fortune n daring enterprises; soldier of fortune. **3.** a person who undertakes great commercial risk; speculator. **4.** a erson who seeks power, wealth, or social rank by un-crupulous or questionable means: *They thought John was an adventurer and after their daughter's money.* **5.** *usually cap.*) a member of Camp Fire, Inc., who is be-ween the ages of 9 and 11. [1475–85; ADVENTURE + ER[1]]

d•ven•ture•some (ad ven′chər səm), *adj.* bold; dar-ng; adventurous. [1725–35; ADVENTURE + -SOME[1]] **—ad•ven′ture•some•ly,** *adv.* **—ad•ven′ture•some-ess,** *n.*

d•ven•tur•ess (ad ven′chər is), *n.* **1.** a woman who chemes to win social position, wealth, etc., by unscrupu-ous or questionable means. **2.** a woman who is an ad-enturer. [1745–55; ADVENTUR(ER) + -ESS]
—Usage. See **-ess.**

d•ven•tur•ism (ad ven′chə riz′əm), *n.* **1.** defiance or isregard of accepted standards of behavior. **2.** rash or rresponsible policies, methods, or actions, esp. in politi-al or international affairs. [1835–45; ADVENTURE + ISM, as trans. of Russ *avantyurizm*] **—ad•ven′tur•ist,** . **—ad•ven′tur•is′tic,** *adj.*

d•ven•tur•ous (ad ven′chər əs), *adj.* **1.** inclined or willing to engage in adventures; enjoying adventures. **2.** ull of risk; requiring courage; hazardous: *an adventur-us undertaking.* [1300–50; ME *aventurous* < MF *aven-ur(e)os.* See ADVENTURE, -OUS] **—ad•ven′tur•ous•ly,** *dv.* **—ad•ven′tur•ous•ness,** *n.*
—Syn. 1. bold, daring, venturous, venturesome.

d•verb (ad′vûrb), *n. Gram.* any member of a class of words that in many languages are distinguished in form, s *partly* in English by the ending *-ly,* or by functioning s modifiers of verbs or clauses, and in some languages, s Latin and English, also as modifiers of adjectives or ther adverbs or adverbial phrases, as *very, well, quickly.* dverbs typically express some relation of place, time, nanner, attendant circumstance, degree, cause, infer-nce, result, condition, exception, concession, purpose, or neans. [1520–30; < L *adverbium,* equiv. to *ad-* AD- + *verb(um)* word, VERB + *-ium* -IUM; calque of Gk *epír-rhēma*] **—ad′verb•less,** *adj.*

ad′verb clause′, *Gram.* a subordinate clause that functions as an adverb within a main clause.

ad•ver•bi•al (ad vûr′bē əl), *adj.* **1.** of, pertaining to, or used as an adverb. *—n.* **2.** a word or group of words functioning as an adverb. **—ad•ver′bi•al•ly,** *adv.* [1605–15; < L *adverbi(um)* ADVERB + -AL[1]; cf. LL *adver-biālis*]

ad ver•bum (äd wer′bo͝om; *Eng.* ad vûr′bəm), *Latin.* to the word; exact in wording according to an original.

ad•ver•sar•y (ad′vər ser′ē), *n., pl.* **-sar•ies,** *adj.* *—n.* **1.** a person, group, or force that opposes or attacks; op-ponent; enemy; foe. **2.** a person, group, etc., that is an opponent in a contest; contestant. **3. the Adversary,** the devil; Satan. *—adj.* Also, *esp. Brit.,* **ad•ver•sar•i•al** (ad′vər sâr′ē əl). **4.** of or pertaining to an adversary. **5.** involving adversaries, as plaintiff and defendant in a legal proceeding: *an adversary trial.* [1300–50; ME *ad-versarie* < L *adversārius,* equiv. to *advers(us)* (see AD-VERSE) + *-ārius* -ARY; r. ME *adversere* < AF] **—ad′ver-sar′i•ness,** *n.*
—Syn. 1. ADVERSARY, ANTAGONIST mean a person or a group contending against another. ADVERSARY suggests an enemy who fights determinedly, continuously, and re-lentlessly: *a formidable adversary.* ANTAGONIST suggests one who, in hostile spirit, opposes another, often in a particular contest or struggle: *a duel with an antagonist.* **—Ant. 1.** ally.

ad•ver•sar•y•ism (ad′vər ser′ē iz′əm), *n.* an atti-tude, as in labor-management negotiations, that any op-position to demands indicates an unwillingness of one side to cooperate and bargain in good faith. [ADVERSARY + -ISM]

ad•ver•sa•tive (ad vûr′sə tiv), *adj.* **1.** expressing con-trariety, opposition, or antithesis: *"But" is an adversa-tive conjunction.* *—n.* **2.** an adversative word or propo-sition. [1525–35; < LL *adversātīvus,* equiv. to *adversāt(us)* (ptp. of *adversārī* to resist; see ADVERSE, -ATE[1]) + *-īvus* -IVE] **—ad•ver′sa•tive•ly,** *adv.*

adver′sative asyn′deton, *Rhet.* a staccato effect produced by omitting adversative connectives from be-tween two or more items forming a group, as in "I liked all there was to buy in the store . . . I didn't get any-thing." Cf. **copulative asyndeton.**

ad•verse (ad vûrs′, ad′vûrs), *adj.* **1.** unfavorable or antagonistic in purpose or effect: *adverse criticism.* **2.** opposing one's interests or desire: *adverse circumstances.* **3.** being or acting in a contrary direction; opposed or op-posing: *adverse winds.* **4.** opposite; confronting: *the ad-verse page.* [1350–1400; ME < AF, OF *advers* < L *ad-versus* hostile (ptp. of *advertere*), equiv. to *ad-* AD- + *vert-* turn + *-tus* ptp. suffix, with *-tt-* > *-s-*] **—ad•verse′ly,** *adv.* **—ad•verse′ness,** *n.*
—Syn. 1. hostile, inimical, unfriendly. **2.** unfavorable; unlucky, unfortunate; disastrous, calamitous, cata-strophic. See **contrary.** **—Ant. 1–3.** favorable.
—Usage. The adjectives ADVERSE and AVERSE are re-lated both etymologically and semantically, each having "opposition" as a central sense. ADVERSE is seldom used of people but rather of effects or events, and it usually conveys a sense of hostility or harmfulness: *adverse re-views; adverse winds; adverse trends in the economy.* Re-lated nouns are *adversity* and *adversary: Adversities breed bitterness. His adversaries countered his every move.* AVERSE is used of persons and means "feeling op-posed or disinclined"; it often occurs idiomatically with a preceding negative to convey the opposite meaning "willing or agreeable," and is not interchangeable with ADVERSE in these contexts: *We are not averse to holding another meeting.* The related noun is *aversion: She has a strong aversion to violence.* AVERSE is usually followed by *to,* in older use occasionally by *from.*

adverse′ posses′sion, *Law.* the open and exclusive occupation and use of someone else's real property with-out permission of the owner continuously for a period of years prescribed by law, thereafter giving title to the oc-cupier-user.

adverse′ selec′tion, *Insurance.* the process of sin-gling out potential customers who are considered higher risks than the average. Also called **antiselection.**

ad•ver•si•ty (ad vûr′si tē), *n., pl.* **-ties** for 2. **1.** ad-verse fortune or fate; a condition marked by misfortune, calamity, or distress: *A friend will show his or her true colors in times of adversity.* **2.** an adverse or unfortu-nate event or circumstance: *You will meet many adversi-ties in life.* [1200–50; ME *adversite* (< AF) < L *adver-sitās.* See ADVERSE, -ITY]
—Syn. 1. catastrophe, disaster; trouble, misery. **2.** See **affliction.** **—Ant. 1.** prosperity.

ad•vert[1] (ad vûrt′), *v.i.* **1.** to remark or comment; refer (usually fol. by *to*): *He adverted briefly to the news of the day.* **2.** to turn the attention (usually fol. by *to*): *The committee adverted to the business at hand.* [1375–1425; late ME *a(d)verten* < OF *a(d)vertir* << L *adver-tere* to pay attention, equiv. to *ad-* AD- + *vertere* to turn; AD- r. *a-* A-[5]]
—Syn. 1. allude.

ad•vert[2] (ad′vərt), *n. Chiefly Brit. Informal.* adver-tisement. [by shortening]

ad•vert•ence (ad vûr′tns), *n.* **1.** the act of being or becoming advertent; heedfulness. **2.** advertency. [1350–1400; ME; see ADVERT[1], -ENCE]

ad•vert•en•cy (ad vûr′tn sē), *n., pl.* **-cies.** **1.** the state or quality of being advertent. **2.** advertence. [1640–50; ADVERT(ENT) + -ENCY]

ad•vert•ent (ad vûr′tnt), *adj.* attentive; heedful. [1665–75; < L *advertent-* (s. of *advertēns,* prp. of *adver-tere*), equiv. to *ad-* AD- + *vert-* turn + *-ent-* -ENT] **—ad•vert′ent•ly,** *adv.*

ad•ver•tise (ad′vər tīz′, ad′vər tīz′), *v.,* **-tised, -tis•ing.** *—v.t.* **1.** to announce or praise (a product, service, etc.) in some public medium of communication in order to induce people to buy or use it: *to advertise a new brand of toothpaste.* **2.** to give information to the public about; announce publicly in a newspaper, on radio or tel-evision, etc.: *to advertise a reward.* **3.** to call attention to, in a boastful or ostentatious manner: *Stop advertising yourself!* **4.** *Obs.* to give notice, advice, or information to; inform: *I advertised him of my intention.* **5.** *Obs.* to admonish; warn. *—v.i.* **6.** to ask for something by plac-ing a notice in a newspaper, over radio or television, etc.: *to advertise for a house to rent.* **7.** to offer goods for sale or rent, solicit funds, etc., by means of advertisements: *It pays to advertise.* **8.** *Cards.* **a.** *Poker.* to bluff so as to make the bluff obvious. **b.** *Rummy.* to discard a card in order to induce an opponent to discard one of the same suit or denomination. Also, **advertize.** [1400–50; late ME *advertisen* < MF *advertiss-,* long s. of *avertir* < VL **advertīre,* L *advertere* to ADVERT[1]; the expected ME **advertishen* prob. conformed to ADVERTISEMENT or the suffix -IZE] **—ad•ver•tis•a•ble** (ad′vər tī′zə bəl, ad′vər-tī′-), *adj.* **—ad′ver•tis′er,** *n.*

ad•ver•tise•ment (ad′vər tīz′mənt, ad vûr′tis mənt, -tiz-), *n.* **1.** a paid announcement, as of goods for sale, in newspapers or magazines, on radio or television, etc. **2.** a public notice, esp. in print. **3.** the action of making generally known; a calling to the attention of the public: *The news of this event will receive wide advertisement.* Also, **ad′ver•tize′ment.** [1425–75; late ME < MF *aver-tissement.* See ADVERTISE, -MENT]

ad•ver•tis•ing (ad′vər tī′zing), *n.* **1.** the act or prac-tice of calling public attention to one's product, service, need, etc., esp. by paid announcements in newspapers and magazines, over radio or television, on billboards, etc.: *to get more customers by advertising.* **2.** paid an-nouncements; advertisements. **3.** the profession of plan-ning, designing, and writing advertisements. Also, **ad′•ver•tiz′ing.** [1520–30; ADVERTISE + -ING[1]]

ad′vertising account′, account (def. 11c).

ad′vertising a′gency, an agency employed by ad-vertisers to plan, design, place, and supervise their ad-vertisements or advertising campaigns. [1840–50, *Amer.*]

ad′vertising man′, adman (def. 1).

ad•ver•tize (ad′vər tīz′, ad′vər tīz′), *v.t., v.i.,* **-tized, -tiz•ing.** advertise. **—ad•ver•tiz•a•ble** (ad′vər tī′zə bəl, ad′vər tī′-), *adj.* **—ad′ver•tiz′er,** *n.*

ad•ver•to•ri•al (ad′vər tôr′ē əl, -tōr′-), *n.* an ex-tended newspaper or magazine text advertisement that promotes the advertiser's product or services or special point of view but resembles an editorial in style and lay-out. [b. ADVERTISEMENT and EDITORIAL]

ad•vice (ad vīs′), *n.* **1.** an opinion or recommendation offered as a guide to action, conduct, etc.: *I shall act on your advice.* **2.** a communication, esp. from a distance, containing information: *Advice from abroad informs us that the government has fallen. Recent diplomatic ad-vices have been ominous.* **3.** an official notification, esp. one pertaining to a business agreement: *an overdue ad-vice.* [1250–1300; late ME *advise;* r. ME *avis* (with *ad-* AD- for *a-* A-[5]) < OF *a vis* (taken from the phrase *ce m'est a vis* that is my impression, it seems to me) < L *ad* (see AD-) + *vīsus* (see VISAGE)]
—Syn. 1. admonition, warning, caution; guidance; urging. ADVICE, COUNSEL, RECOMMENDATION, SUGGES-TION, PERSUASION, EXHORTATION refer to opinions urged with more or less force as worthy bases for thought, opinion, conduct, or action. ADVICE is a practical recom-mendation as to action or conduct: *advice about purchas-ing land.* COUNSEL is weighty and serious advice, given after careful deliberation: *counsel about one's career.* RECOMMENDATION is weaker than advice and suggests an opinion that may or may not be acted upon: *Do you think he'll follow my recommendation?* SUGGESTION im-plies something more tentative than a recommendation: *He did not expect his suggestion to be taken seriously.* PERSUASION suggests a stronger form of advice, urged at some length with appeals to reason, emotion, self-inter-est, or ideals: *His persuasion changed their minds.* EX-HORTATION suggests an intensified persuasion or admo-nition, often in the form of a discourse or address: *an impassioned exhortation.* **2.** intelligence, word. **3.** no-tice, advisory.

advice′ and consent′, *U.S. Govt.* a phrase in the Constitution (Article II, Section 2) allowing the Senate to restrain presidential powers of appointment and treaty-making. [1780–90]

advice′ boat′, a fast boat for conveying messages; dispatch boat. [1660–70]

Ad•vil (ad′vil), *Pharm., Trademark.* a brand of ibu-profen.

ad•vis•a•ble (ad vī′zə bəl), *adj.* **1.** proper to be ad-vised or recommended; desirable or wise, as a course of action: *Is it advisable for me to write to him?* **2.** open to or desirous of advice. [1640–50; ADVISE + -ABLE] **—ad•vis′a•bil′i•ty, ad•vis′a•ble•ness,** *n.* **—ad•vis′a•bly,** *adv.*
—Syn. 1. expedient, politic, proper, fit, suitable, pru-dent, sensible, judicious.

ad•vise (ad vīz′), *v.,* **-vised, -vis•ing.** *—v.t.* **1.** to give counsel to; offer an opinion or suggestion as worth fol-lowing: *I advise you to be cautious.* **2.** to recommend as desirable, wise, prudent, etc.: *He advised secrecy.* **3.** to give (a person, group, etc.) information or notice (often fol. by *of*): *The investors were advised of the risk. They advised him that this was their final notice.* *—v.i.* **4.** to take counsel; consult (usually fol. by *with*): *I shall advise with my friends.* **5.** to offer counsel; give advice: *I shall act as you advise.* [1275–1325; late ME; r. ME *avisen*

< AF, OF *aviser,* v. deriv. of *avis* opinion (< *a vis;* see ADVICE)]
—Syn. 1. counsel, admonish, caution. **2.** suggest. **3.** inform, notify, apprise, acquaint. **4.** confer, deliberate, discuss, consult.

ad•vised (ad vīzd′), *adj.* **1.** considered (usually used in combination): *ill-advised; well-advised.* **2.** informed; apprised: *The President was kept thoroughly advised.* [1275–1325; ME; see ADVISE, -ED[2]] **—ad•vis•ed•ness** (ad-vī′zid nis), *n.*

ad•vis•ed•ly (ad vī′zid lē), *adv.* after careful or thorough consideration; deliberately. [1425–75; late ME *avisedli;* see ADVISED, -LY]

ad•vis•ee (ad vī zē′, ad′-), *n. Educ.* one of a group of students assigned to a faculty adviser for help in selection of a course of studies. [1815–25; ADVISE + -EE]

ad•vise•ment (ad vīz′mənt), *n.* careful deliberation or consideration; consultation: *The petition was taken under advisement.* [1300–50; ADVISE + -MENT; r. ME *avisement* < OF]

ad•vis•er (ad vī′zər), *n.* **1.** one who gives advice. **2.** *Educ.* a teacher responsible for advising students on academic matters. **3.** a fortuneteller. Also, **ad•vi′sor.** [1605–15; ADVISE + -ER[1]] **—ad•vis′er•ship′,** *n.*

ad•vi•so•ry (ad vī′zə rē), *adj., n., pl.* **-ries.** *—adj.* **1.** of, giving, or containing advice: *an advisory letter from a stockbroker.* **2.** having the power or duty to advise: *an advisory council.* *—n.* **3.** a report on existing or predicted conditions, often with advice for dealing with them: *an investment advisory.* **4.** an announcement or bulletin that serves to advise and usually warn the public, as of some potential hazard: *a health advisory; a travelers' advisory.* **5.** an announcement from the U.S. National Weather Service to keep the public informed about the progress of a potentially dangerous weather condition: *hurricane advisory; tornado advisory.* Cf. **warning** (def. 3), **watch** (def. 23). [1770–80; ADVISE + -ORY[1]] **—ad•vi′so•ri•ly,** *adv.*

advi′sory opin′ion, *Law.* a formal opinion that is given on a point of law by a court, judge, or judges on request from a legislature or government official, contrasted with an opinion in a case at law where the point is being adjudicated.

ad vi•tam (äd wē′täm; *Eng.* ad vī′tam), *Latin.* for life.

ad vi•vum (äd wē′wo͝om; *Eng.* ad vī′vəm), *Latin.* to that which is alive.

ad•vo•caat (ad′vō kät′), *n.* a Dutch liqueur made with brandy, sugar, and eggs. [1930–35; < D, short for *advocatenborrel* drink that lubricates the throat of a lawyer, equiv. to *advocaat* lawyer (see ADVOCATE) + *-en-* connective + *borrel* drink, nip < ?]

ad•vo•ca•cy (ad′və kə sē), *n., pl.* **-cies.** the act of pleading for, supporting, or recommending; active espousal: *He was known for his advocacy of states' rights.* [1375–1425; late ME *advocacye* < ML *advocātia.* See ADVOCATE, -ACY]

ad•vo•cate (*v.* ad′və kāt′; *n.* ad′və kit, -kāt′), *v.,* **-cat•ed, -cat•ing,** *n.* *—v.t.* **1.** to speak or write in favor of; support or urge by argument; recommend publicly: *He advocated higher salaries for teachers.* *—n.* **2.** a person who speaks or writes in support or defense of a person, cause, etc. (usually fol. by *of*): *an advocate of peace.* **3.** a person who pleads for or in behalf of another; intercessor. **4.** a person who pleads the cause of another in a court of law. [1300–50; < L *advocātus* legal counselor (orig. ptp. of *advocāre* to call to one's aid), equiv. to *ad-* AD- + *voc-* call (akin to *vōx* VOICE) + *-ātus* -ATE[1]; r. ME *avocat* < MF] **—ad′vo•ca′tive,** *adj.* **—ad′vo•ca′tor,** *n.*
—Syn. 2. champion, proponent, backer. **4.** lawyer, attorney, counselor, counsel; barrister; solicitor.

ad•vo•ca•tion (ad′və kā′shən), *n.* **1.** *Scot. Law.* the action of a superior court in calling before itself or reviewing an action originally brought before an inferior court. **2.** *Obs.* **a.** advocacy. **b.** the act of summoning. [1400–50; late ME < L *advocātiōn-,* s. of *advocātiō;* see ADVOCATE, -ION]

ad•voc•a•to•ry (ad vok′ə tôr′ē, -tōr′ē, ad′və kə-, ad′və kā′tə rē), *adj.* of or pertaining to an advocate or his or her functions. [1860–65; ADVOCATE + -ORY[1]]

ad•vo•ca•tus di•a•bo•li (äd′vô kä′to͞os dē ä′bô lē′), *Medieval Latin.* See **devil's advocate** (def. 2).

ad•vow•son (ad vou′zən), *n. Eng. Eccles. Law.* the right of presentation of a candidate to a benefice or church office. [1250–1300; < AF; r. ME *avoweisoun* < AF, OF *avoeson* << L *advocātiōn-.* See ADVOCATION]

advt., advertisement.

A•dy•gei (ä′də gā′, ä′də gā′; *Russ.* u di gyā′), *n.* **1.** Official name, **A′dygei Auton′omous Re′gion.** an autonomous region in the Russian Federation, part of the Krasnodar territory, in the NW Caucasus Mountains. 410,000; 1505 sq. mi. (3903 sq. km). *Cap.:* Maikop. **2.** a Circassian language spoken in the Adygei Autonomous Region. Also, **Adighe, A′dy•ghe.**

ad•y•tum (ad′i təm), *n., pl.* **-ta** (-tə). **1.** (in ancient worship) a sacred place that the public was forbidden to enter; an inner shrine. **2.** the most sacred or reserved part of any place of worship. [1665–75; < L < Gk *ádyton* (place) not to be entered, equiv. to *a-* A-[6] + *-dyton,* neut. of *-dytos,* verbid of *dýein* to enter]

adz (adz), *n.* **1.** an axlike tool, for dressing timbers roughly, with a curved, chisellike steel head mounted at a right angle to the wooden handle. *—v.t.* **2.** to dress or shape (wood) with an adz. Also, **adze.** [bef. 900; ME *ad(e)se,* OE *adesa;* **ad-es-,* of obscure orig., appears to be formed like AX, and might by assoc. with the latter have lost **w-;* if so, < Gmc **wad-,* c. Lith *vedegà* adz]

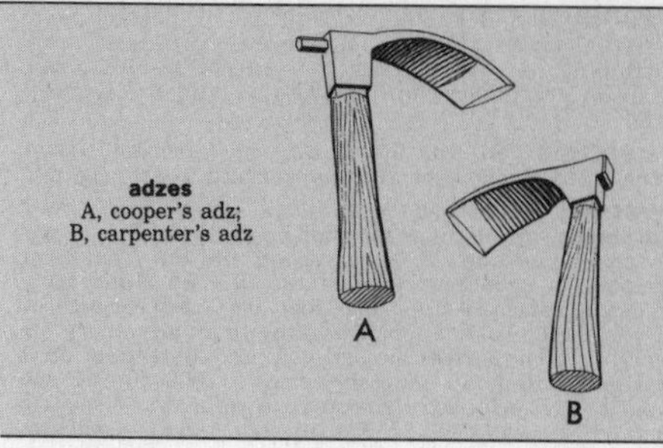

adzes
A, cooper's adz;
B, carpenter's adz

adze (adz), *n., v.t.,* **adzed, adz•ing.** adz.

A•dzhar•i•stan (ə jär′ə stan′; *Russ.* u jə ryi stän′), *n.* an autonomous republic in the Georgian Republic, in Transcaucasia. 355,000; 1080 sq. mi. (3000 sq. km). *Cap.:* Batumi. Formerly, **A•dzhar′ Auton′omous So′viet So′cialist Repub′lic** (ə jär′; *Russ.* u jär′).

ad•zu′ki bean′ (ad zo͞o′kē), **1.** a bushy plant, *Vigna (Phaseolus) angularis,* widely cultivated in Asia. **2.** the edible bean of this plant, from which a flour is made. Also, **adsuki bean.** [< Japn *azuki,* earlier *aduki*]

ae (ā), *adj. Scot.* one. [ME (Scots) ā-, OE *ān* ONE; cf. A[1]]

AE, 1. account executive. **2.** AE **3.** American English.

Æ, pen name of George William Russell. Also, **AE, A.E.**

æ, the ash, an early English ligature representing a vowel sound like that of *a* in modern *bad.* The long *ǣ* continued in use until about 1250, but was finally replaced by *e.* The short *æ* was given up by 1150, being replaced usually by *a* but sometimes by *e.*

ae, a digraph or ligature appearing in Latin and Latinized Greek words. In English words of Latin or Greek origin, *ae* is now usually represented by *e,* except generally in proper names (*Caesar*), in words belonging to Roman or Greek antiquities (*aegis*), and in modern words of scientific or technical use (*aecium*). Also, **æ.**

ae-. for words with initial **ae-,** see also **e-.**

ae., at the age of; aged. [< L *aetātis*]

A.E., 1. Agricultural Engineer. **2.** Associate in Education. **3.** Associate in Engineering. **4.** AE

a.e., *Math.* See **almost everywhere.**

-aea, var. of **-ea:** *Athenaea.*

A.E.A., 1. Actors' Equity Association. **2.** Also, **AEA** *Brit.* Atomic Energy Authority.

Ae•ac•i•des (ē as′i dēz′), *n., pl.* **-dae** (-dē′). *Class. Myth.* a patronymic for any of the descendants of Aeacus, as Achilles, Peleus, and Telamon.

Ae•a•cus (ē′ə kəs), *n. Class. Myth.* a judge in Hades, a son of Zeus and grandfather of Achilles.

Ae•ae•a (ē ē′ə), *n. Class. Myth.* **1.** the island inhabited by Circe. **2.** Circe (def. 1).

-aean, a combination of **-aea** and **-an:** *Athenaean.*

A.E. and P., Ambassador Extraordinary and Plenipotentiary.

AEC, See **Atomic Energy Commission.**

A.E.C., *Insurance.* additional extended coverage.

aech•me•a (ēk mē′ə, ēk′mē ə), *n.* any of various epiphytic bromeliads of the genus *Aechmea,* native to tropical America, having stiff, spiny leaves and clusters of red, yellow, or blue flowers: popular as a houseplant. [< NL (1794), prob. based on Gk *aichmḗeis* armed with a spear, deriv. of *aichmḗ* spear point, spear; see -A[2]]

ae•cid•i•um (ē sid′ē əm), *n., pl.* **ae•cid•i•a** (ē sid′ē ə). *Mycol.* an aecium in which the spores are always formed in chains and enclosed in a cup-shaped peridium. [1865–70; < NL; see AECIUM, -IDIUM]

ae•ci•o•spore (ē′sē ə spôr′, -spōr′, ē′shē-), *n. Mycol.* a spore borne by an aecium. [1875–80; AECI(UM) + -O- + SPORE]

ae•ci•um (ē′sē əm, ē′shē-), *n., pl.* **ae•ci•a** (ē′sē ə, ē′shē ə). *Mycol.* the fruiting body of rust fungi, which bears chainlike or stalked spores. [< NL < Gk *aikía* assault, injury; see -IUM] **—ae′ci•al,** *adj.*

A.Ed., Associate in Education.

ae•de•a•gus (ē dē′ə gəs), *n., pl.* **-gi** (-gī′, -jī′). the phallus of a male insect. Also, **aedoeagus.** [< NL < Gk *aidoî(a)* genitals + *agós* leader (deriv. of *ágein* to lead)] **—ae•de′a•gal,** *adj.*

a•e•des (ā ē′dēz), *n.* **1.** See **yellow-fever mosquito.** **2.** any mosquito of the genus *Aedes.* Also, **a•ë′des.** [< NL (1818) < Gk *aēdḗs* distasteful, unpleasant, equiv. to *a-* A-[6] + *-ēdēs,* comb. form of *hēdýs* sweet, akin to *hēdonḗ* pleasure. See SWEET]

ae•dic•u•la (ē dik′yə lə), *n., pl.* **-lae** (-lē′). aediculé.

ae•di•cule (ē′di kyo͞ol′, ed′i-), *n.* **1.** a small building. **2.** a small construction, as a shrine, designed in the form of a building. Also, **aedicula, edicule.** [1825–35; < L *aedicula,* equiv. to *aedi-* (s. of *aedēs*) temple, shrine (akin to Gk *aíthein* to blaze, *aithḗr* bright upper sky, ETHER) + *-cula* -CULE[1]]

ae•dile (ē′dīl), *n. Rom. Hist.* one of a board of magistrates in charge of public buildings, streets, markets, games, etc. Also, **edile.** [1570–80; < L *aedīlis,* equiv. to *aedi-* (s. of *aedēs;* see AEDICULE) + *-īlis* -ILE] **—ae′dile•ship′,** *n.* **—ae•dil•i•tian** (ēd′l ish′ən), *adj.*

ae•doe•a•gus (ē dē′ə gəs), *n., pl.* **-gi** (-gī′, -jī′). aedeagus.

A•ë•don (ā ēd′n), *n. Class. Myth.* a daughter of Pa[r]dareus who mistakenly killed her son. Zeus took pity o[n] her and turned her into a nightingale.

Ae.E., Aeronautical Engineer.

Ae•ë•tes (ē ē′tēz), *n. Class. Myth.* a king of Colchi[s], father of Medea and custodian of the Golden Fleece.

A.E.F., American Expeditionary Forces; American E[x]peditionary Force. Also, **AEF**

Ae•ga′di•an Is′lands (i gā′dē ən), Egadi. Also, **Ae[•]ga′de•an Is′lands.**

Ae•ga•tes (i gā′tēz), *n.* ancient name of **Egadi.**

Ae•ge•an (i jē′ən), *adj.* **1.** pertaining to the Aegea[n] Sea or Islands. **2.** pertaining to or denoting the prehis[-]toric civilization that preceded the historic Hellenic pe[-]riod and flourished on the various islands and nearb[y] regions of the Aegean Sea, as at Crete and Argolis. *—*[*n.*] **3. the.** See **Aegean Sea.** [< L *Aegae(us)* (< G[k] *Aigaîos*) + -AN]

Aege′an Is′lands, the islands of the Aegean Sea, i[n]cluding the Dodecanese, Cyclades, and Sporades.

Aege′an Sea′, an arm of the Mediterranean Sea be[-]tween Greece and Turkey. Also called **the Aegean.**

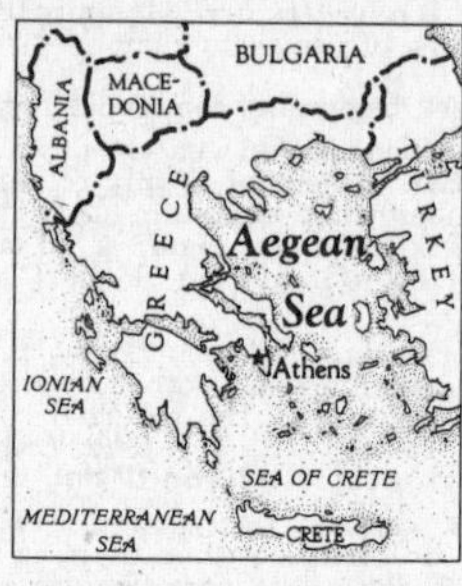

Ae•gi•na (ē jī′nə, i jē′-), *n.* **1.** *Class. Myth.* a daughte[r] of Asopus and Metope who was abducted by Zeus an[d] bore him a son, Aeacus. **2. Gulf of.** See **Saronic Gul[f].** **3.** an island in the Saronic Gulf. 32 sq. mi. (83 sq. km[).] **4.** a seaport on this island. 5704. Modern Greek, **Aíyin[a]** (for defs. 2–4). **—Ae•gi•ne•tan** (ē′jə nēt′n), *adj.*

Ae•gir (e′jir), *n. Scand. Myth.* a sea god, husband o[f] Ran, and host at feast of the gods spoiled by Lok[i]. [< ON *Ægir,* akin to ON *ā* river, water, Goth *ahw[a]* water, L *aqua*]

ae•gir•ite (ā′gə rīt′, ē′jə-), *n.* a mineral, mainly sodi[-]um-ferric iron silicate, $NaFe(Si_2O_6)$, occurring in feld[-]spathoid rocks in slender prismatic crystals. Also, **ae•gir•ine** (ā′gə rēn′, ē′jə-). [1830–40; AEGIR + -ITE[2]]

ae•gis (ē′jis), *n.* **1.** *Class. Myth.* the shield or breast[-]plate of Zeus or Athena, bearing at its center the head o[f] the Gorgon. **2.** protection; support: *under the imperi[al] aegis.* **3.** sponsorship; auspices: *a debate under the aegi[s] of the League of Women Voters.* Also, **egis.** [1695–170[5]; < L < Gk *aigís* shield of Zeus or Athena, prob. fro[m] *aig-* (s. of *aíx* goat) + *-is* n. suffix, from a type of shiel[d] made of goatskin]
—Syn. 3. patronage.

Ae•gis•thus (ē jis′thəs), *n. Class. Myth.* a cousin o[f] Agamemnon who seduced Clytemnestra, Agamemnon'[s] wife, and was later killed by Orestes.

Ae•gi•um (ē′jē əm), *n.* a town in ancient Achaea, or the Gulf of Corinth: the Achaean League met here.

Ae•gos•pot•a•mi (ē′gəs pot′ə mī′), *n.* a river in an[-]cient Thrace, flowing into the Hellespont: near its mouth the Athenian fleet was defeated by Lysander, 405 B.C., i[n] the last battle of the Peloponnesian War.

ae•gro•tat (ē′grō tat′, ē grō′tat), *n. Brit.* an unclas[-]sified degree granted a university student who has fulfilled all requirements for graduation but was pre[-]vented by illness from attending the final examinations [1860–65; < L *aegrōtat* lit., he is sick (pres. 3rd sing. o[f] *aegrōtāre*), equiv. to *aegrōt(us)* sick (*aeg(e)r* sick + *-ōtu[s]* adj. suffix) + *-at* 3rd sing. ending]

Ae•gyp•to•pith•e•cus (i jip′tō pith′i kəs, -pə thē′-kəs), *n.* a genus of extinct anthropoid ape of the Oligo[-]cene Period known from remains found in Egypt. [< N[L] (1965), equiv. to L *Aegypt(us)* EGYPT + NL *-o-* *-o-* + *pi[-]thecus* ape < Gk *píthēkos*]

Æl•fric (al′frik), *n.* (*"Ælfric Grammaticus"; "Ælfri[c] the Grammarian"*) A.D. c955–c1020, English abbot and writer.

ae•lu•ro•phile (ē lo͝or′ə fīl′, i lo͝or′-), *n.* ailurophile. **—ae•lu•ro•phil•ic** (ē lo͝or′ə fil′ik, i lo͝or′-), *adj.*

ae•lu•ro•phil•i•a (ē lo͝or′ə fil′ē ə, i lo͝or′-), *n.* ailurophilia.

ae•lu•ro•phobe (ē lo͝or′ə fōb′, i lo͝or′-), *n.* ailurophobe. **—ae•lu′ro•pho′bic,** *adj.*

ae•lu•ro•pho•bi•a (ē lo͝or′ə fō′bē ə, i lo͝or′-), *n.* ailurophobia.

-aemia, var. of **-emia:** *anaemia.*

-aena, var. of **-ena:** *hyaena.*

Ae•ne•as (i nē′əs), *n. Class. Myth.* a Trojan hero, the reputed ancestor of the Romans: protagonist of the *Aeneid.*

Aene′as Sil′vi•us (sil′vē əs), **1.** Also, **Aene′as Syl′vius.** literary name of **Pius II.** **2.** *Rom. Legend.* a king of Alba Longa.

Ae•ne•id (i nē′id), *n.* a Latin epic poem by Vergil, recounting the adventures of Aeneas after the fall of Troy.

A•e•ne•o•lith•ic (ā ē′nē ō lith′ik), *adj.* Chalcolithic. Also, **Eneolithic.** [1900–05; AENE(OUS) + -O- + -LITHIC]

•e•ne•ous (ā ē′nē əs), *adj.* bronze-colored: *an aeneus beetle.* Also, **a•ë′ne•ous.** [1805–15; < L *aēneus,* quiv. to *aēn(us)* of bronze (*ae(s)* bronze + *-n-* adj. uffix) + *-eus* -EOUS]

.Eng., Associate in Engineering.

e•o•li•a (ē ō′lē ə), *n.* Aeolis.

e•o•li•an (ē ō′lē ən), *adj.* **1.** Also, **Aeolic.** belonging o a branch of the Greek race named after Aeolus, its egendary founder. —*n.* **2.** a member of one of the four nain divisions of the prehistoric Greeks. Cf. **Achaean** def. 5), **Dorian** (def. 2), **Ionian** (def. 3). **3.** Aeolic. Also, **olian.** [1580–90; < L *Aeoli(i)* (< Gk *Aioleîs* the Aeolins, with change of suffix) + -AN]

e•o•li•an (ē ō′lē ən), *adj.* **1.** pertaining to Aeolus, or o the winds in general. **2.** (*usually l.c.*) of or caused by he wind; wind-blown. [1595–1605; *Aeoli(us)* pertaining o AEOLUS + *-an* -AN]

eo′lian harp′, a box with an opening across which re stretched a number of strings of equal length that re tuned in unison and sounded by the wind. Also called **eo′lian lyre′, wind harp.** [1785–95]

eo′lian mode′, *Music.* an authentic church mode epresented on the white keys of a keyboard instrument y an ascending scale from A to A.

e•ol•ic (ē ol′ik), *n.* **1.** the Greek dialect of ancient Aeolis and Thessaly; Aeolian. —*adj.* **2.** *Archit.* noting r pertaining to a capital used in the Greek territories of he eastern Aegean in the 7th and 6th centuries B.C., aving two volutes rising from a shaft in opposite direcions, and often having below them two convex rings of eaf ornament in the form of water-lily buds. **3.** Aeolian def. 1). Also, **Eolic.** [1730–40; < L *Aeolicus* < Gk *Aiolikós,* equiv. to *Aioleús* (pl. *Aioleîs*) + *-ikos* -IC]

e•ol•i•pile (ē ol′ə pīl′), *n.* **1.** a round vessel caused to otate by the force of tangentially escaping steam: an arly example of jet propulsion. **2.** a device for injecting he vapors of heated alcohol into a laboratory furnace. Also, **ae•ol′i•pyle′, eolipile.** [1650–60; < L *aeolipilae* alls of AEOLUS, alter. of *aeolipylae* gates of AEOLUS, quiv. to *Aeolī* (gen. sing. of AEOLUS) + *pylae,* pl. of *pyla* < Gk *pýlē* gate]

e•o•lis (ē′ə lis), *n.* an ancient coastal region and Greek colony in NW Asia Minor: settled by Aeolians. Also, **Aeolia.**

e•o•lo•trop•ic (ē′ə lō trop′ik, -trō′pik), *adj. Physics.* ot isotropic; anisotropic. [1865–70; < Gk *aiólo(s)* fickle, hangeful + -TROPIC] —**ae•o•lot•ro•py** (ē′ə lo′trə pē), **ae′o•lot′ro•pism,** *n.*

e•o•lus (ē′ə ləs), *n. Class. Myth.* **1.** the ruler of the vinds. **2.** the eponymous founder of the Aeolian nation.

e•on (ē′ən, ē′on), *n.* **1.** (in Gnosticism) one of a class f powers or beings conceived as emanating from the Supreme Being and performing various functions in the operations of the universe. **2.** eon. [1640–50; < LL < Gk *aiṓn* space of time, age]

e•o•ni•an (ē ō′nē ən), *adj.* eternal; everlasting. Also, **eonian.** [1755–65; < Gk *aiṓni(os)* (*aiṓn* AEON + *-ios* adj. uffix) + -AN]

e•py•or•nis (ē′pē ôr′nis), *n.* an extinct genus of ratte birds, best known from the Pleistocene Epoch of Madagascar, having massive legs and rudimentary vings, and growing to a height of 8 ft. (2.4 m). [< NL 1850) < Gk *aipý(s)* steep, lofty, + *órnīs* bird]

eq., equal. [< L *aequālis*]

e•quo a•ni•mo (ī′kwō ä′ni mō′; *Eng.* ē′kwō an′əmō′), *Latin.* with an even mind; with composure.

e•quor•in (ē kwôr′in, ē kwor′-), *n. Biochem., Histol.* protein, secreted by certain jellyfish, that produces a lue light upon binding with calcium. [1965–70; < NL *Aequor(ea)* a genus of jellyfish that produces such a protein (L: fem. of *aequoreus* of the sea, equiv. to *aequor* evel surface, the sea + *-eus* -EOUS) + -IN[2]]

er-, var. of **aero-** before a vowel: *aerate.*

e•rar•i•an (ē râr′ē ən), *Rom. Hist.* —*adj.* **1.** of or ertaining to the aerarium. —*n.* **2.** a member of the owest class of Roman citizens, who paid a poll tax but id not vote. [1840–50; < L *aerāri(us)* (see AERARIUM) + AN]

e•rar•i•um (ē râr′ē əm), *n., pl.* **ae•rar•i•a** (ē râr′ē ə). he state treasury in ancient Rome. [< L, equiv. to *aer-* s. of *aes* bronze, money) + *-ārium* -ARY]

er•ate (âr′āt, ā′ə rāt′), *v.t.,* **-at•ed, -at•ing.** **1.** to exose to the action or effect of air or to cause air to circuate through: *to aerate milk in order to remove odors.* **2.** o change or treat with air or a gas, esp. with carbon dixide. **3.** *Physiol.* to expose (a medium or tissue) to air, s in the oxygenation of the blood in respiration. [1785–5; < L *āer-* AER- + -ATE[1]] —**aer•a′tion,** *n.*

er•a•tor (âr′ā tər, ā′ə rā′-), *n.* **1.** an apparatus for erating water or other fluids. **2.** a device for introducng air into a bin of wheat or other grain in order to prevent the accumulation of moisture, keeping it free of ungi and insects. [1860–65; AERATE + -OR[2]]

er•en•chy•ma (â reng′kə mə, â ren′-), *n. Bot.* a tissue in certain aquatic plants, consisting of thin-walled ells and large intercellular spaces adapted for internal irculation of air. [1895–1900; < NL; see AER-, PARENCHYMA]

e•re per•en•ni•us (ī′RE pe REN′ni ōōs′; *Eng.* ēr′ē ə ren′ē əs), *Latin.* more lasting than bronze.

eri-, var. of **aero-** before an element of Latin origin: *eriferous.*

er•i•a (ēr′ē ə), *n.* an area in the northern hemisphere f Mars.

er•i•al (*adj.* âr′ē əl, ā ēr′ē əl; *n.* âr′ē əl), *adj.* **1.** of, n, or produced by the air: *aerial currents.* **2.** inhabiting r frequenting the air: *aerial creatures.* **3.** operating on track or cable elevated above the ground: *an aerial ski lift up the mountainside.* **4.** reaching far into the air; high; lofty: *aerial spires.* **5.** partaking of the nature of air; airy. **6.** unsubstantial; visionary: *aerial fancies.* **7.** having a light and graceful beauty; ethereal: *aerial music.* **8.** *Biol.* growing in the air, as the adventitious roots of some trees. **9.** pertaining to or used for, against, or in aircraft. **10.** supplied or performed by means of aircraft: *aerial support; aerial reconnaissance.* —*n.* **11.** a radio or television antenna. **12.** *Football.* See **forward pass.** [1595–1605; 1900–05 for def. 11; < L *āeri(us)* of the air (< Gk *āérios,* equiv. to *āer-* (s. of *āḗr* AIR[1]) + *-ios* adj. suffix) + -AL[1]] —**aer′i•al•ly,** *adv.* —**aer′i•al•ness,** *n.*

aer•i•al•ist (âr′ē ə list, ā ēr′ē ə-), *n.* **1.** a trapeze artist. **2.** *Slang.* a burglar who gains entrance to a building or apartment by leaping from rooftop to rooftop, sliding down ropes, or the like. [1900–05; AERIAL + -IST]

aer•i•al•i•ty (âr′ē al′i tē, ā ēr′-), *n.* unsubstantial quality. [1850–55; AERIAL + -ITY]

aer′ial lad′der, an extensible ladder used for reaching heights, esp. from a hook-and-ladder truck.

aer′ial mine′, **1.** *Mil.* a mine designed to be dropped from the air into water. **2.** a bomb or land mine designed to be dropped by parachute. [1905–10]

aer′ial mosa′ic, *Survey.* mosaic (def. 4).

aer′ial perspec′tive, a technique of rendering depth or distance in painting by modifying the tone or hue and distinctness of objects perceived as receding from the picture plane, esp. by reducing distinctive local colors and contrasts of light and dark to a uniform light bluish-gray color. Also called **atmospheric perspective.** [1725–35]

aer′ial pho′tograph, a photograph taken from an aircraft or satellite in flight. Also called **aerophoto, air photograph.** [1895–1900] —**aer′ial photog′raphy.**

aer′ial rail′way, tramway (def. 4). [1885–90]

aer′ial sur′vey, **1.** a survey made from above, as from an aircraft, a high point, etc. **2.** a survey that maps an area by means of aerial photography, photogrammetry, and the like. [1915–20]

aer′ial tank′er, a multiengined aircraft designed to refuel other aircraft in flight.

aer′ial tram′way, tramway (def. 4). [1900–05]

aer•ie (âr′ē, ēr′ē), *n.* **1.** the nest of a bird of prey, as an eagle or a hawk. **2.** a lofty nest of any large bird. **3.** a house, fortress, or the like, located high on a hill or mountain. **4.** *Obs.* the brood in a nest, esp. of a bird of prey. Also, **aery, eyrie, eyry.** [1575–85; < AF, OF *airie,* equiv. to *aire* (< L *ager* field, presumably "nest" in VL; see ACRE) + *ie* -Y[3]; cf. ML *aerea, aeria* aerie, brood < OF *aire*]

aer•if•er•ous (â rif′ər əs), *adj.* conveying air, as the bronchial tubes. [1680–90; AERI- + -FEROUS]

aer•i•fi•ca•tion (âr′ə fi kā′shən, ā ēr′-), *n.* **1.** an act of combining with air. **2.** the state of being filled with air. [1840–50; AERI- + -FICATION]

aer•i•form (âr′ə fôrm′, ā ēr′-), *adj.* **1.** having the form or nature of air; gaseous. **2.** unsubstantial; unreal. [1780–90; AERI- + -FORM]

aer•i•fy (âr′ə fī′, ā ēr′-), *v.t.,* **-fied, -fy•ing.** **1.** to aerate. **2.** to make aeriform; convert into vapor. [1840–50; AERI- + -FY]

aer•o (âr′ō), *adj.* **1.** of or for aircraft. **2.** of or pertaining to aeronautics. [1895–1900; AERO- used as free form]

aero-, a combining form meaning "air," used in formation of compound words: *aerodrome.* Also, **aer-, aeri-.** [< Gk, equiv. to *āer-* (s. of *āḗr* AIR[1]) + *-o-* -O-]

aero., **1.** aeronautic; aeronautical. **2.** aeronautics. **3.** aerospace.

aer•o•bac•ter (âr′ō bak′tər), *n.* any of several short, rod-shaped, Gram-negative bacteria of the genus *Aerobacter,* free living in nature and also normally inhabiting the intestinal tracts of humans and other animals. [< NL (1900); see AERO-, -BACTER]

aer•o•bal•lis•tics (âr′ō bə lis′tiks), *n.* (*used with a singular v.*) the science of ballistics combined with that of aerodynamics and dealing primarily with the motion through the atmosphere of rockets, guided missiles, and other projectiles. [1945–50; AERO- + BALLISTICS] —**aer′o•bal•lis′tic,** *adj.*

aer•o•bat (âr′ə bat′), *n.* a person who performs aerobatics. [1855–60; AERO- + (ACRO)BAT]

aer•o•bat•ics (âr′ə bat′iks), *n.* **1.** (*used with a plural v.*) stunts performed in flight by an airplane, glider, or the like. **2.** (*used with a singular v.*) the art or technique of performing such stunts. [1915–20; AERO- + (ACRO)BATICS] —**aer′o•bat′ic,** *adj.*

aer•obe (âr′ōb), *n.* an organism, esp. a bacterium, that requires air or free oxygen for life (opposed to *anaerobe*). [1875–80; AER- + (MICR)OBE]

Aer•o•bee (âr′ə bē′), *n.* a U.S. two-stage, liquid-propellant sounding rocket developed in the 1940's that carried scientific instruments and occasionally biological specimens into the upper stratosphere. [*Aero(jet Engineering Corporation)* developer of the rocket + (*Bumble)bee* cover name for the Navy project to produce such rockets]

aer•o•bic (â rō′bik), *adj.* **1.** (of an organism or tissue) requiring the presence of air or free oxygen for life. **2.** pertaining to or caused by the presence of oxygen. **3.** of or utilizing the principles of aerobics: *aerobic exercises; aerobic dances.* [1880–85; AEROBE + -IC] —**aer•o′bi•cal•ly,** *adv.*

aero′bic danc′ing, a system of exercises combining aerobics with dance steps and usually done to music. [1975–80]

aer•o•bics (â rō′biks), *n.* **1.** Also called **aero′bic ex′ercises.** (*used with a plural v.*) any of various sustained exercises, as jogging, rowing, swimming, or cycling, that stimulate and strengthen the heart and lungs, thereby improving the body's utilization of oxygen. **2.** (*used with a singular v.*) a physical fitness program based on such exercises: *Aerobics is a good way to get your body in shape.* [1965–70; see AEROBIC, -ICS; prob. shortened from *aerobic exercises* on the model of CALISTHENICS]

aer•o•bi•ol•o•gy (âr′ō bī ol′ə jē), *n.* the study of the dispersion of airborne biological materials, as pollen, spores, microorganisms, or viruses. [1935–40; AERO- + BIOLOGY]

aer•o•bi•o•sis (âr′ō bī ō′sis), *n. Biol.* life in an environment containing oxygen or air. [1895–1900; < NL; see AERO-, -BIOSIS] —**aer•o•bi•ot•ic** (âr′ō bī ot′ik), *adj.* —**aer′o•bi•ot′i•cal•ly,** *adv.*

aer•o•cul•ture (âr′ə kul′chər), *n. Agric.* a method of growing plants without soil by suspending them above sprays that constantly moisten the roots with water and nutrients. Cf. **geoponics, hydroponics.** [AERO- + (AGRI)CULTURE]

aer•o•don•tal•gia (âr′ō don tal′jə, -jē ə), *n. Dentistry.* a toothache caused by lowered barometric pressure, as in high-altitude flight. [AER- + ODONTALGIA]

aer•o•drome (âr′ə drōm′), *n. Chiefly Brit.* airdrome. [1905–10; AERO- + -DROME]

aer•o•dy•nam•i•cist (âr′ō dī nam′ə sist), *n.* an expert in aerodynamics. [1925–30; AERODYNAMIC + -IST]

aer•o•dy•nam•ics (âr′ō dī nam′iks), *n.* (*used with a singular v.*) the branch of mechanics that deals with the motion of air and other gases and with the effects of such motion on bodies in the medium. Cf. **aerostatics** (def. 1). [1830–40; AERO- + DYNAMICS] —**aer′o•dy•nam′ic, aer′o•dy•nam′i•cal,** *adj.* —**aer′o•dy•nam′i•cal•ly,** *adv.*

aer′odynam′ic trajec′tory, *Rocketry.* the path of an object, as a rocket, when the air is dense enough to modify the course of flight significantly.

aer′odynam′ic wave′ drag′, *Aeron.* the restraining force on a supersonic aircraft caused by shock waves. Also called **wave drag.**

aer•o•dyne (âr′ə dīn′), *n.* any heavier-than-air aircraft deriving its lift mainly from aerodynamic forces. [1905–10; back formation from AERODYNAMIC; see DYNE]

aer•o•e•las•tic (âr′ō i las′tik), *adj. Aeron.* (of an airframe) **1.** of, pertaining to, or resulting from aerodynamic forces: *tests to determine the aeroelastic stress on a building.* **2.** deformable by aerodynamic forces. [1930–35; AERO- + ELASTIC] —**aer•o•e•las•tic•i•ty** (âr′ō i la-stis′i tē, -ē′la-), *n.*

aer•o•e•las•tics (âr′ō i las′tiks), *n.* (*used with a singular v.*) *Aeron.* the study of aeroelastic phenomena. [see AEROELASTIC, -ICS]

aer•o•em•bo•lism (âr′ō em′bə liz′əm), *n. Pathol.* **1.** an obstruction of the circulatory system caused by air, as may arise during surgery. **2.** Also called **the bends, caisson disease, decompression sickness.** an acute condition caused by a rapid substantial decrease in atmospheric pressure, as in high-altitude flying and coming up from deep-sea diving, characterized by the formation of nitrogen bubbles in the blood, severe pain in the lungs and joints, and neurological impairment. [1935–40; AERO- + EMBOLISM]

aer•o•foil (âr′ə foil′), *n. Brit.* airfoil. [AERO- + FOIL[2]]

aer•o•gel (âr′ə jel′), *n. Chem.* a gel formed by the dispersion of air in a solidified matrix; a solid foam, as Styrofoam. [1920–25; AERO- + GEL]

aer•o•gen•ic (âr′ə jen′ik), *adj.* producing gas, as certain bacteria. Also, **aer•og•e•nous** (â roj′ə nəs). [AERO- + -GENIC] —**aer′o•gen′i•cal•ly,** *adv.*

aer•o•gram (âr′ə gram′), *n.* **1.** a radiogram. **2.** *Older Use.* a message carried by aircraft; an airmail letter. **3.** *Meteorol.* **a.** a diagram for analyzing thermodynamic processes in the atmosphere. **b.** the record of an aerograph. **4.** aérogramme. [1895–1900; AERO- + -GRAM[1]]

aé•ro•gramme (âr′ə gram′), *n.* a sheet of lightweight paper, bearing an official postal stamp imprint, that is folded to form its own envelope and can be sent via airmail at a special, low rate because of its standard size, light weight, and lack of enclosures. Also, **aerogram, aer′o•gramme′.** Cf. **air letter.** [1895–1900; < F; see AERO-, -GRAM[1]]

aer•o•graph (âr′ə graf′, -gräf′), *n. Meteorol.* any automatic recording instrument for atmospheric measurement that is carried aloft by aircraft. [AERO- + -GRAPH]

aer•og•ra•phy (â rog′rə fē), *n.* the study of the air or atmosphere. [1745–55; AERO- + -GRAPHY] —**aer•og′ra•pher,** *n.* —**aer•o•graph•ic** (âr′ə graf′ik), **aer′o•graph′i•cal,** *adj.*

aer•o•lite (âr′ə līt′), *n.* a meteorite consisting mainly of stony matter. Also, **aer•o•lith** (âr′ə lith). [1805–15; AERO- + -LITE] —**aer•o•lit•ic** (âr′ə lit′ik), *adj.*

aer•ol•o•gy (â rol′ə jē), *n.* **1.** the branch of meteorology involving the observation of the atmosphere by means of balloons, airplanes, etc. **2.** (in former use by the U.S. Navy) meteorology. [1745–55; AERO- + -LOGY] —**aer•o•log•ic** (âr′ə loj′ik), **aer′o•log′i•cal,** *adj.* —**aer•ol′o•gist,** *n.*

aer•o•mag•net•ic (âr′ō mag net′ik), *adj.* of, pertaining to, or based on an aerial survey of the earth's magnetic field: *an aeromagnetic map.* [1945–50; AERO- + MAGNETIC]

CONCISE PRONUNCIATION KEY: *act, cāpe, dâre, pärt; set, ēqual; if, īce; ox, ōver, ôrder, oil, bŏŏk, bōōt, out; up, ûrge; child; sing; shoe; thin, that;* zh as in *treasure.* ə = *a* as in *alone, e* as in *system, i* as in *easily, o* as in *gallop, u* as in *circus;* ə as in *fire* (fīər), *hour* (ouər). l and n can serve as syllabic consonants, as in *cradle* (krād′l), and *button* (but′n). See the full key inside the front cover.

aer·o·man·cy (âr′ə man′sē), *n.* the prediction of future events from observation of weather conditions. [1350–1400; ME. See AERO-, -MANCY] **—aer′o·man′cer,** *n.* **—aer′o·man′tic,** *adj.*

aer·o·ma·rine (âr′ō mə rēn′), *adj. Aeron.* relating to navigation of aircraft above the ocean. [1915–20; AERO- + MARINE]

aer·o·me·chan·ic (âr′ō mə kan′ik), *n.* **1.** an aviation mechanic. —*adj.* **2.** of or pertaining to aeromechanics. [1895–1900; AERO- + MECHANIC]

aer·o·me·chan·ics (âr′ō mə kan′iks), *n.* (*used with a singular v.*) the mechanics of air or gases. [1895–1900; AERO- + MECHANICS] **—aer′o·me·chan′i·cal,** *adj.*

aer·o·med·i·cal (âr′ə med′i kəl), *adj.* of or pertaining to the science or practice of aviation medicine. [1935–40; AERO- + MEDICAL]

aer·o·med·i·cine (âr′ə med′ə sən), *n.* See **aviation medicine.** [AERO- + MEDICINE]

aer·o·me·te·or·o·graph (âr′ə mē′tē ər ə graf′, -gräf′, -mē′tē ôr′ə-, -or′ə-), *n.* a meteorograph for use in aircraft. [1940–45; AERO- + METEOROGRAPH]

aer·om·e·ter (â rom′i tər), *n.* an instrument for determining the weight, density, etc., of air or other gases. [1785–95; AERO- + -METER] **—aer·o·met·ric** (âr′ə me′trik), *adj.* **—aer·om·e·try** (â rom′i trē), *n.*

aeron., aeronautics.

aer·o·naut (âr′ə nôt′, -not′), *n.* **1.** the pilot of a balloon or other lighter-than-air aircraft. **2.** a traveler in an airship. [1775–85; < F *aéronaute* < Gk *āero-* AERO- + *naútēs* sailor; cf. NAUTICAL, ARGONAUT]

aer·o·nau·ti·cal (âr′ə nô′ti kəl, -not′i-), *adj.* of aeronautics or aeronauts. Also, **aer′o·nau′tic.** [AERONAUT + -ICAL] **—aer′o·nau′ti·cal·ly,** *adv.*

aeronau′tical engineer′ing. See under **aerospace engineering.** **—aeronau′tical engineer′.**

aer·o·nau·tics (âr′ə nô′tiks, -not′iks), *n.* (*used with a singular v.*) the science or art of flight. [1820–25; < NL *aeronautica* or F *aéronautique;* see AERO-, NAUTICAL, -ICS]

ae·ron·o·my (â ron′ə mē), *n.* the study of chemical and physical phenomena in the upper atmosphere. [1955–60; AERO- + -NOMY]

aer·o·pause (âr′ə pôz′), *n. Aeron.* the indefinite boundary in the upper atmosphere beyond which the air is too thin for conventional aircraft to operate. [1950–55; AERO- + PAUSE]

A·ër·o·pe (ā er′ə pē′), *n. Class. Myth.* the wife of Atreus, seduced by her brother-in-law Thyestes.

aer·o·pha·gia (âr′ə fā′jə, -jē ə), *n. Psychiatry.* swallowing of air, sometimes due to nervousness or anxiety. [1900–05; AERO- + -PHAGIA] **—aer·oph·a·gist** (â rof′ə-jist), *n.*

aer·o·phi·lat·e·ly (âr′ō fi lat′l ē), *n.* the study or collection of airmail stamps, cancellations, etc. [AERO- + PHILATELY] **—aer·o·phil·a·tel·ic** (âr′ō fil′ə tel′ik), *adj.* **—aer′o·phi·lat′e·list,** *n.*

aer·o·pho·bi·a (âr′ə fō′bē ə), *n. Psychiatry.* an abnormal fear of drafts of air, gases, or airborne matter. [1765–75; AERO- + -PHOBIA] **—aer·o·pho·bic** (âr′ə fō′bik, -fob′ik), *adj.*

aer·o·phone (âr′ə fōn′), *n.* any musical wind instrument. [1875–80; AERO- + -PHONE]

aer·o·phore (âr′ə fôr′, -fōr′), *n.* a portable device filled with compressed air and used in cases of asphyxia or the like. [1875–80; AERO- + -PHORE]

aer·o·pho·to (âr′ō fō′tō), *n., pl.* **-tos.** See **aerial photograph.** [AERO- + PHOTO] **—aer·o·pho·tog·ra·phy** (âr′ō fə tog′rə fē), *n.*

aer·o·phyte (âr′ə fīt′), *n. Bot.* epiphyte. [1830–40; AERO- + -PHYTE]

aer·o·plane (âr′ə plān′), *n. Chiefly Brit.* airplane. [1870–75; < F *aéroplane,* equiv. to *aéro-* AERO- + *-plane,* appar. fem. of *plan* flat, level (< L *plānus;* cf. PLAIN[1]), perh. by assoc. with *forme plane;* appar. coined and first used by French sculptor and inventor Joseph Pline in 1855]

aer·o·pon·ics (âr′ə pon′iks), *n.* (*used with a singular v.*) aeroculture. [AERO- + (GEO)PONICS, on the model of HYDROPONICS]

aer·o·pulse (âr′ə puls′), *n.* See **pulsejet engine.** [AERO- + PULSE]

aer·o·scep·sy (âr′ə skep′sē), *n. Zool.* perception of atmospheric conditions, as the perception of odors by the antennae of insects. Also, **aer·o·scep·sis** (âr′ō skep′sis). [1825–35; AERO- + *-scepsy* < Gk *sképsis* observation, perception, equiv. to *skep-* (s. of *sképtesthai* to observe, examine; cf. SKEPTIC) + *-sis* -SIS]

aer·o·si·nus·i·tis (âr′ō sī′nə sī′tis), *n. Med.* inflammation of the nasal sinuses caused by the effect on the sinuses of changes in atmospheric pressure. Also called **barosinusitus.** [AERO- + SINUSITIS]

aer·o·sol (âr′ə sôl′, -sol′), *n.* **1.** *Physical Chem.* a system of colloidal particles dispersed in a gas; smoke or fog. **2.** a liquid substance, as a disinfectant or deodorant, sealed in a metal container under pressure with an inert gas or other activating agent and released as a spray or foam through a push-button valve or nozzle: *an aerosol for cleaning ovens.* **3.** See **aerosol bomb.** —*adj.* **4.** of or containing a liquid or gas under pressure for dispensing as a spray or foam: *a deodorant available in aerosol cans.* [1920–25; AERO- + SOL[4]]

CONCISE ETYMOLOGY KEY: <, descended or borrowed from; >, whence; b., blend of, blended; c., cognate with; cf., compare; deriv., derivative; equiv., equivalent; imit., imitative; obl., oblique; r., replacing; s., stem; sp., spelling, spelled; resp., respelling, respelled; trans., translation; ?, origin unknown; *, unattested; ‡, probably earlier than. See the full key inside the front cover.

aer′osol bomb′, a metal receptacle, containing an inert gas under pressure, that sprays an insecticide, disinfectant, or the like when the gas is released by opening a valve. [1940–45]

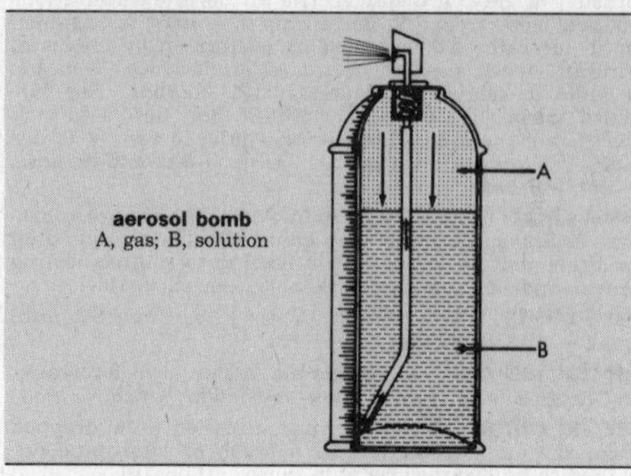

aerosol bomb
A, gas; B, solution

aer·o·sol·ize (âr′ə sô līz′, -so-), *v.t.,* **-ized, -iz·ing.** **1.** to disperse or discharge as an aerosol. **2.** to contain or pack in aerosol form. Also, *esp. Brit.,* **aer′o·sol·ise′.** [1940–45; AEROSOL + -IZE] **—aer′o·sol·i·za′tion,** *n.*

aer·o·space (âr′ō spās′), *n.* **1.** the atmosphere and the space beyond considered as a whole. **2.** the industry concerned with the design and manufacture of aircraft, rockets, missiles, spacecraft, etc., that operate in aerospace. —*adj.* **3.** of or pertaining to aerospace or the aerospace industry. [1955–60; AERO- + SPACE]

aer′ospace engineer′ing, the branch of engineering that deals with the design, development, testing, and production of aircraft and related systems (**aeronautical engineering**) and of spacecraft, missiles, rocket-propulsion systems, and other equipment operating beyond the earth's atmosphere (**astronautical engineering**). **—aer′ospace engineer′.**

aer·o·sphere (âr′ə sfēr′), *n. Aeron.* (not in technical use) atmosphere. [1910–15; AERO- + -SPHERE]

aer·o·stat (âr′ə stat′), *n.* any lighter-than-air aircraft, as a balloon or dirigible. [1775–85; AERO- + -STAT]

aer·o·stat·ic (âr′ə stat′ik), *adj.* **1.** of or pertaining to aerostatics. **2.** of, or capable of supporting, aerostats. Also, **aer′o·stat′i·cal.** [1775–85; AERO- + STATIC]

aer·o·stat·ics (âr′ə stat′iks), *n.* (*used with a singular v.*) **1.** the branch of statics that deals with gases in equilibrium and with gases and bodies in the gases in equilibrium with one another. Cf. **aerodynamics.** **2.** the science of lighter-than-air aircraft. [1745–55; see AEROSTATIC, -ICS]

aer·o·sta·tion (âr′ə stā′shən), *n. Aeron.* the science or art of operating aerostats. [1775–85; AEROSTAT + -ION]

aer·o·ther·a·peu·tics (âr′ō ther′ə pyōō′tiks), *n.* (*used with a singular v.*) the branch of therapeutics that deals with the curative use of air or of artificially prepared atmospheres. Also, **aer·o·ther·a·py** (âr′ō ther′ə-pē). [AERO- + THERAPEUTICS]

aer·o·ther·mo·dy·nam·ics (âr′ō thûr′mō dī nam′iks), *n.* (*used with a singular v.*) aerodynamics dealing with conditions where there are significant heat exchanges in gases or significant thermal effects between gas and solid surfaces, as in very high-speed, generally supersonic flight. [1940–45; AERO- + THERMODYNAMICS] **—aer′o·ther′mo·dy·nam′ic,** *adj.*

aer′o·ti′tis me′dia (âr′ə tī′tis, âr′-), temporary deafness and pain arising from traumatic inflammation of the middle ear, caused by a rapid change in barometric pressure, as a rise in ambient cabin pressure in an aircraft descending from high altitude for landing. Also called **aer′o·ti′tis.** [AER- + OTITIS MEDIA]

aer·o·tow (âr′ə tō′), *v.t.* **1.** to tow (an aircraft) through the air. —*n.* **2.** the act of aerotowing. [AERO- + TOW[1]]

aer·o·train (âr′ə trān′), *n.* an experimental high-speed train that rides on a cushion of air over a concrete guide track in the shape of an inverted T and is propelled by one or more propellers or jet engines. Also called **hovertrain.** [1965–70; AERO- + TRAIN]

aer·ot·ro·pism (â ro′trə piz′əm), *n. Biol.* growth or movement in the direction of a supply of air or oxygen. [AERO- + -TROPISM] **—aer·o·trop·ic** (âr′ə trop′ik), *adj.*

ae·ru·gi·nous (i rōō′jə nəs, ī rōō′-), *adj.* bluish-green; like verdigris. [1595–1605; < L *aerūginōsus,* equiv. to *aerūgin-* (s. of *aerūgō*) AERUGO + *-ōsus* -OUS]

ae·ru·go (i rōō′gō, ī rōō′-), *n.* verdigris. [1745–55; < L, equiv. to *aer-* (s. of *aes* AES) + *-ūgō* suffix used in forming names of rusts and surface growths; cf. FERRUGINOUS, LANUGO]

aer·y[1] (âr′ē, ā′ə rē), *adj.,* **aer·i·er, aer·i·est.** ethereal; aerial. Also, **aër′y.** [1580–90; < L *āerius* < Gk *āérios,* equiv. to *āer-* AER- + *-ios* adj. suffix] **—aer′i·ly,** *adv.*

aer·y[2] (âr′ē, ēr′ē), *n., pl.* **aer·ies.** aerie.

aes (ēz), *n.* any of various early forms of bronze or copper money used in ancient Rome. Cf. **as**[2] (def. 1). [< L: copper, bronze, money made from them, money in general; see ORE]

æsc (ash), *n.* ash[2] (def. 3).

Aes·chi·nes (es′kə nēz′ *or, esp. Brit.,* ē′skə-), *n.* 389–314 B.C., Athenian orator: rival of Demosthenes.

Aes·chy·lus (es′kə ləs *or, esp. Brit.,* ē′skə-), *n.* 525–456 B.C., Greek poet and dramatist. **—Aes·chy·le·an** (es′kə lē′ən *or, esp. Brit.,* ē′skə-), *adj.*

Aes·cu·la·pi·an (es′kyə lā′pē ən *or, esp. Brit.,* ē′skə-), *adj.* **1.** pertaining to Aesculapius. **2.** medical; medicinal. —*n.* **3.** a physician; doctor. Also, **Esculapia**[n] [1615–25; AESCULAPI(US) + -AN]

Aes·cu·la·pi·us (es′kyə lā′pē əs *or, esp. Brit.,* ē′skə-), *n.* the ancient Roman god of medicine and healing. C[f.] **Asclepius.**

aes·cu·lin (es′kyə lin), *n. Chem.* esculin.

Ae·sir (ā′sir, ā′zir), *n.* (*often l.c.*) (*used with a plural v*[*.*]) *Scand. Myth.* the principal race of gods, led by Odin an[d] living at Asgard. Cf. **Vanir.** [< ON, pl. of *āss* god; c. O[E] *ōs* god, *Os-* in proper names (as *Ōswald*), OHG *Ans-* i[n] proper names (as *Anselm*); akin to Skt *asura* lord]

Ae·sop (ē′səp, ē′sop), *n.* c620–c560 B.C., Greek write[r] of fables.

Ae·so·pi·an (ē sō′pē ən, ē sop′ē-), *adj.* **1.** of, pertair[ning] to, or characteristic of Aesop or his fables: *a sto*[*ry*] *that points an Aesopian moral.* **2.** conveying meanir[ng] by hint, euphemism, innuendo, or the like: *In the cand*[*i*]*date's Aesopian language, "soft on Communism" was* [*to*] *be interpreted as "Communist sympathizer."* Also, **A**[**e**]**sop·ic** (ē sop′ik). [1870–75; < LL *Aesōpi(us)* + -AN]

aes·the·sia (es thē′zhə, -zhē ə, -zē ə), *n.* esthesi[a]. Also, **aes·the·sis** (es thē′sis).

aes·thete (es′thēt *or, esp. Brit.,* ēs′-), *n.* **1.** a perso[n] who has or professes to have refined sensitivity towar[d] the beauties of art or nature. **2.** a person who affect[s] great love of art, music, poetry, etc., and indifference t[o] practical matters. Also, **esthete.** [1880–85; < Gk *ais*[-]*thētēs* one who perceives, equiv. to *aisthē-* (var. s. of *ais*[-]*thánesthai* to perceive) + *-tēs* n. suffix denoting agen[t]] **—Syn.** **1.** connoisseur. **2.** dilettante.

aes·thet·ic (es thet′ik *or, esp. Brit.,* ēs-), *adj.* **1.** per[-]taining to a sense of the beautiful or to the science o[f] aesthetics. **2.** having a sense of the beautiful; character[-]ized by a love of beauty. **3.** pertaining to, involving, o[r] concerned with pure emotion and sensation as oppose[d] to pure intellectuality. —*n.* **4.** a philosophical theory o[r] idea of what is aesthetically valid at a given time an[d] place: *the clean lines, bare surfaces, and sense of spa*[*ce*] *that bespeak the machine-age aesthetic.* **5.** aesthetic[s.] **6.** *Archaic.* the study of the nature of sensation. Als[o,] **esthetic.** [1815–25; < NL *aestheticus* < Gk *aisthētikó*[*s*] equiv. to *aisthēt(és)* (see AESTHETE) + *-ikos* -IC] **—Syn.** **2.** discriminating, cultivated, refined.

aes·thet·i·cal (es thet′i kəl *or, esp. Brit.,* ēs-), *adj.* o[f] or relating to aesthetics. Also, **esthetical.** [1790–180[0;] see AESTHETIC, -AL[1]]

aes·thet·i·cal·ly (es thet′ik lē *or, esp. Brit.,* ēs-), *adv.* **1.** according to aesthetics or its principles. **2.** in an aes[-]thetic manner. Also, **esthetically.** [1820–30; AESTHETI[-]CAL + -LY]

aesthet′ic dis′tance, a degree of detachment fro[m] or nonidentification with the characters or circumstance[s] of a work of art, permitting the formation of judgmen[t] based on aesthetic rather than extra-aesthetic criteri[a.] [1935–40]

aes·the·ti·cian (es′thi tish′ən *or, esp. Brit.,* ēs′-), *n.* [a] person who is versed in aesthetics. Also, **esthetician**[.] [1820–30; AESTHETIC + -IAN; see -ICIAN]

aes·thet·i·cism (es thet′ə siz′əm *or, esp. Brit.,* ēs-), *n.* **1.** the acceptance of artistic beauty and taste as a funda[-]mental standard, ethical and other standards being sec[-]ondary. **2.** an exaggerated devotion to art, music, or po[-]etry, with indifference to practical matters. **3.** a lat[e] Victorian movement in British and American art charac[-]terized by a dedicatedly eclectic search for beauty and b[y] an interest in old English, Japanese, and classical ar[t.] Also, **estheticism.** [1855–60; AESTHETIC + -ISM]

aes·thet·ics (es thet′iks *or, esp. Brit.,* ēs-), *n.* (*use*[*d*] *with a singular v.*) **1.** the branch of philosophy dealin[g] with such notions as the beautiful, the ugly, the sublim[e,] the comic, etc., as applicable to the fine arts, with a vie[w] to establishing the meaning and validity of critical judg[-]ments concerning works of art, and the principles under[-]lying or justifying such judgments. **2.** the study of th[e] mind and emotions in relation to the sense of beauty[.] Also, **esthetics.** [1815–25; see AESTHETIC, -ICS]

aes·ti·val (es′tə vəl, e stī′- *or, esp. Brit.,* ē′stə-, ē stī′-), *adj.* estival.

aes·ti·vate (es′tə vāt′ *or, esp. Brit.,* ē′stə-), *v.i.,* **-va**[**t**]**ed, -vat·ing.** estivate. **—aes′ti·va′tion,** *n.* **—aes′ti**[**·**]**va′tor,** *n.*

aet., at the age of. Also, **aetat.** [< L *aetātis*]

ae·ta·tis su·ae (ī tä′tis sōō′ī; *Eng.* ē tā′tis sōō′ē) *Latin.* in a certain year of one's age.

ae·tha·li·um (ē thā′lē əm), *n., pl.* **-li·a** (-lē ə). *Mycol.* [a] large, plump, pillow-shaped fruiting body of certai[n] myxomycetes, formed by the aggregation of plasmodi[a] into a single functional mass. [< NL, orig. a genus o[f] Myxomycetes containing such a body < Gk *aithal(os)* o[r] *aithál(ē)* thick smoke, soot (akin to *aithein* to kindle[,] burn) + NL *-ium* -IUM; so named from the smokelik[e] spores]

aeth·el·ing (ath′ə ling, ath′-), *n.* atheling.

Aeth·el·stan (ath′əl stan′), *n.* Athelstan. Also, **Ethel**[**-**]**stan.**

ae·ther (ē′thər), *n.* **1.** ether (defs. 3–5). **2.** (*cap.*) th[e] ancient Greek personification of the clear upper air o[f] the sky. **—ae·the·re·al** (i thēr′ē əl), **ae·ther·ic** (i ther′ik), *adj.*

ae·thon (ē′thon), *n. Chem.* See **triethyl orthofor**[**-**]**mate.** [< L < Gk *aíthōn* burning]

ae·ti·ol·o·gy (ē′tē ol′ə jē), *n., pl.* **-gies.** etiology **—ae·ti·o·log·ic** (ē′tē ə loj′ik), **ae′ti·o·log′i·cal** *adj* **—ae′ti·o·log′i·cal·ly,** *adv.* **—ae′ti·ol′o·gist,** *n.*

Aet·na (et′nə), *n.* **Mount.** See **Etna, Mount.**

Ae·to·li·a (ē tō′lē ə), *n.* an ancient district in W[.] Greece, now part of the province of Aetolia and Acar[-]nania. See map under **Delphi.** Modern Greek, **Aitolía**[.] **—Ae·to′li·an,** *adj., n.*

e·to·lus (ēt′l əs), *n. Class. Myth.* son of Endymion and founder of Aetolia.

F, **1.** Air Force. **2.** Anglo-French.

f-, var. of **ad-** before *f: affect.*

f., **1.** Africa. **2.** African.

.F., **1.** Air Force. **2.** Anglo-French. **3.** audio frequency.

.f., audio frequency.

.F.A., Associate in Fine Arts.

.F.A.M., Ancient Free and Accepted Masons.

·far (ə fär′), *adv.* **1.** from, at, or to a distance; far away (usually fol. by *off*): *He saw the castle afar off.* —*n.* **2. from afar,** from a long way off: *The princess saw him riding toward her from afar.* [1125–75; ME *a fer,* on *ferr;* r. OE *feorran.* See A-[1] (perh. also A-[2] for the meaning "from"), FAR]

·far (ä′fär), *n., pl.* **A·fars, A·fa·ra** (ə fär′ə), (*esp. collectively*) **A·far** for 1. **1.** a member of a nomadic Muslim people living in Eritrea, Djibouti, and northern Ethiopia. **2.** the Northern Cushitic language spoken by the Afars. Also called **Danakil.**

·fars′ and Is′sas (ə färz′ ənd ē′säz), **French Territory of the,** a former name of **Djibouti** (def. 1).

FB, Air Force Base.

.F.B., American Federation for the Blind.

FBF, See **American Farm Bureau Federation.**

FC, **1.** American Football Conference. **2.** American Foxhound Club. **3.** Association Football Club. **4.** automatic flight control. **5.** automatic frequency control.

FDC, Aid to Families with Dependent Children. Also, **.F.D.C.**

·feard (ə fērd′), *adj. Brit. and Midland and Southern U.S.* afraid. Also, **a·feared′.** [bef. 1000; ME *afered,* OE *āfǣred* frightened (ptp. of *āfǣran*). See A-[3], FEAR, -ED[2]]

·fe·brile (ā fē′brəl, ā feb′rəl), *adj.* without fever; feverless. [1870–75; A-[6] + FEBRILE]

ff (af), *prep., adv. Scot.* off.

ff., **1.** affirmative. **2.** affix.

f·fa·ble (af′ə bəl), *adj.* **1.** pleasantly easy to approach and to talk to; friendly; cordial; warmly polite: *an affable and courteous gentleman.* **2.** showing warmth and friendliness; benign; pleasant: *an affable smile.* 1530–40; < L *affābilis* that can be spoken to, courteous, equiv. to *af-* AF- + *fā-* speak (see FATE) + *-bilis* -BLE, perh. via MF] —**af′fa·bil′i·ty, af′fa·ble·ness,** *n.* —**af′fa·bly,** *adv.*

—**Syn. 1.** See **civil.**

f·fair (ə fâr′), *n.* **1.** anything done or to be done; anything requiring action or effort; business; concern: *an affair of great importance.* **2. affairs,** matters of commercial or public interest or concern; the transactions of public or private business or finance: *affairs of state; Before taking such a long trip you should put all your affairs in order.* **3.** an event or a performance; a particular action, operation, or proceeding: *When did this affair happen?* **4.** thing; matter (applied to anything made or existing, usually with a descriptive or qualifying term): *Our new computer is an amazing affair.* **5.** a private or personal concern; a special function, business, or duty: *That's none of your affair.* **6.** an intense amorous relationship, usually of short duration. **7.** an event or happening that occasions or arouses notoriety, dispute, and often public scandal; incident: *the Congressional bribery affair.* **8.** a party, social gathering, or other organized festive occasion: *The awards ceremony is the biggest affair on the school calendar.* [1250–1300; earlier *affaire* < F, OF *afaire* for *a faire* to do, equiv. to *a* < L *ad* to) + *faire* << L *facere;* r. ME *afere* < OF]

f·faire d'a·mour (A feʀ dA mōōʀ′), *pl.* ***af·faires d'a·mour*** (A feʀ dA mōōʀ′). *French.* a love affair. Also called ***af·faire′.***

f·faire de coeur (A feʀ də kœʀ′), *pl.* ***af·faires de coeur*** (A feʀ də kœʀ′). *French.* a love affair. Also called **affaire.** [lit., affair of the heart]

f·faire d'hon·neur (A feʀ dô nœʀ′), *pl.* ***af·faires d'hon·neur*** (A feʀ dô nœʀ′). *French.* a duel. [lit., affair of honor]

f·fect[1] (*v.* ə fekt′; *n.* af′ekt), *v.t.* **1.** to act on; produce an effect or change in: *Cold weather affected the crops.* **2.** to impress the mind or move the feelings of: *The music affected him deeply.* **3.** (of pain, disease, etc.) to attack or lay hold of. —*n.* **4.** *Psychol.* feeling or emotion. **5.** *Psychiatry.* an expressed or observed emotional response: *Restricted, flat, or blunted affect may be a symptom of mental illness, especially schizophrenia.* **6.** *Obs.* affection; passion; sensation; inclination; inward disposition or feeling. [1350–1400; ME < L *affectus* acted upon, subjected to; mental or emotional state (ptp. and action n. of *afficere*), equiv. to *af-* AF- + *fec-* (comb. form of *facere* to make, do) + *-tus* action n. suffix or *-tus* ptp. suffix] —**af·fect′a·ble,** *adj.* —**af·fect′a·bil′i·ty,** *n.*

—**Syn. 1.** influence, sway; modify, alter. **2.** touch, stir.

—**Usage.** AFFECT[1] and EFFECT, each both noun and verb, share the sense of "influence," and because of their similarity in pronunciation are sometimes confused in writing. As a verb AFFECT[1] means "to act on" or "to move" (*His words affected the crowd so deeply that many wept*); AFFECT[2] means "to pretend" or "to assume" (*new students affecting a nonchalance they didn't feel*). The verb EFFECT means "to bring about, accomplish": *Her administration effected radical changes.* The noun EFFECT means "result, consequence": *the serious effects of the oil spill.* The noun AFFECT[1] pronounced with the stress on the first syllable, is a technical term in psychology and psychiatry. AFFECT[2] is not used as a noun.

f·fect[2] (ə fekt′), *v.t.* **1.** to give the appearance of; pretend or feign: *to affect knowledge of the situation.* **2.** to assume artificially, pretentiously, or for effect: *to affect a Southern accent.* **3.** to use, wear, or adopt by preference; choose; prefer: *the peculiar costume he affected.* **4.** to assume the character or attitude of: *to affect the freethinker.* **5.** (of things) to tend toward habitually or naturally: *a substance that affects colloidal form.* **6.** (of animals and plants) to occupy or inhabit; live in or on: *Lions affect Africa. Moss affects the northern slopes.* **7.** *Archaic.* **a.** to have affection for; fancy. **b.** to aim at; aspire to. —*v.i.* **8.** *Obs.* to incline, tend, or favor (usually fol. by *to*): *He affects to the old ways.* [1400–50; late ME < MF *affecter* < L *affectāre* to strive after, feign (freq. of *afficere* to do to), equiv. to *af-* AF- + *fec-* (see AFFECT[1]) + *-tāre* freq. suffix] —**af·fect′·er,** *n.*

—**Syn. 1.** See **pretend.**

—**Usage.** See **affect**[1].

af·fec·ta·tion (af′ek tā′shən), *n.* **1.** an effort to appear to have a quality not really or fully possessed; the pretense of actual possession: *an affectation of interest in art; affectation of great wealth.* **2.** conspicuous artificiality of manner or appearance; effort to attract notice by pretense, assumption, or any assumed peculiarity. **3.** a trait, action, or expression characterized by such artificiality: *a man of a thousand affectations.* **4.** *Obs.* **a.** strenuous pursuit, desire, or aspiration. **b.** affection; fondness: *his affectation of literature.* [1540–50; < L *affectātiōn-* (s. of *affectātiō*) a striving after, equiv. to *affectāt(us),* ptp. of *affectāre* to AFFECT[2] (see -ATE[1]) + *-iōn-* -ION]

—**Syn. 2.** pretension, airs, mannerisms, pose. —**Ant. 2.** artlessness, simplicity, sincerity.

af·fect·ed[1] (ə fek′tid), *adj.* **1.** acted upon; influenced. **2.** influenced in a harmful way; impaired, harmed, or attacked, as by climate or disease. **3.** (of the mind or feelings) impressed; moved; touched: *She was deeply affected by their generosity.* [1570–80; AFFECT[1] + -ED[2]]

af·fect·ed[2] (ə fek′tid), *adj.* **1.** assumed artificially; unnatural; feigned: *affected sophistication; an affected British accent.* **2.** assuming or pretending to possess that which is not natural: *Her affected wealth and social pedigree are so obviously false that it's embarrassing.* **3.** inclined or disposed: *well affected toward the speaker's cause.* **4.** held in affection; fancied: *a novel much affected by our grandparents.* [1525–35; AFFECT[2] + -ED[2]] —**af·fect′ed·ly,** *adv.* —**af·fect′ed·ness,** *n.*

af·fect·ing (ə fek′ting), *adj.* moving or exciting the feelings or emotions. [1555–65; AFFECT[1] + -ING[2]] —**af·fect′ing·ly,** *adv.*

—**Syn.** touching, pathetic, piteous, stirring.

af·fec·tion[1] (ə fek′shən), *n.* **1.** fond attachment, devotion, or love: *the affection of a parent for an only child.* **2.** Often, **affections. a.** emotion; feeling; sentiment: *over and above our reason and affections.* **b.** the emotional realm of love: *a place in his affections.* **3.** *Pathol.* a disease, or the condition of being diseased; abnormal state of body or mind: *a gouty affection.* **4.** the act of affecting; act of influencing or acting upon. **5.** the state of being affected. **6.** *Philos.* a contingent, alterable, and accidental state or quality of being. **7.** the affective aspect of a mental process. **8.** bent or disposition of mind. **9.** *Obs.* bias; prejudice. [1200–50; ME < OF < L *affectiōn-* (s. of *affectiō*) disposition or state of mind or body; see AFFECT[1], -ION] —**af·fec′tion·less,** *adj.*

—**Syn. 1.** liking, friendliness, amity, fondness, friendship. See **love.** —**Ant. 1.** dislike.

af·fec·tion[2] (ə fek′shən), *n. Obs.* affectation (defs. 1–3). [1525–35; AFFECT[2] + -ION]

af·fec·tion·al (ə fek′shə nl), *adj.* relating to or implying affection. [1855–60; AFFECTION[1] + -AL[1]] —**af·fec′tion·al·ly,** *adv.*

af·fec·tion·ate (ə fek′shə nit), *adj.* **1.** showing, indicating, or characterized by affection or love; fondly tender: *an affectionate embrace.* **2.** having great affection or love; warmly attached; loving: *your affectionate brother.* **3.** *Obs.* **a.** strongly disposed or inclined. **b.** passionate; headstrong. **c.** biased; partisan. [1485–95; AFFECTION[1] + -ATE[1], on the model of PASSIONATE] —**af·fec′tion·ate·ly,** *adv.* —**af·fec′tion·ate·ness,** *n.*

—**Syn. 1.** loving, fond.

af·fec·tive (af′ek tiv), *adj.* **1.** of, caused by, or expressing emotion or feeling; emotional. **2.** causing emotion or feeling. [1540–50; < ML *affectīvus,* equiv. to L *affect(us)* (action n.; see AFFECT[1]) + *-īvus* -IVE] —**af′fec·tive·ly,** *adv.* —**af·fec·tiv·i·ty** (af′ek tiv′i tē), *n.*

af′fective disor′der, *Psychiatry.* any mental disorder, as depressive disorder, bipolar disorder, or cyclothymia, in which a major disturbance of feelings or emotions is predominant.

af′fective fal′lacy, a proposition in literary criticism that a poem should be analyzed and described in terms of its own internal structure and not in terms of the emotional response it arouses in the reader. [1945–50]

af·fect·less (af′ekt lis), *adj.* lacking feeling or emotion; indifferent to the suffering of others: *an affectless, futuristic drama in which the human characters are virtually robots.* [1965–70; AFFECT[1] + -LESS] —**af′fect·less·ly,** *adv.* —**af′fect·less·ness,** *n.*

af·fen·pin·scher (af′ən pin′shər), *n.* one of a breed of toy dogs having a dense, wiry, red or gray coat with tufts of hair around the eyes, nose, and chin, cropped ears, and a docked tail. Also called **monkey pinscher, monkey dog.** [1900–05; < G, equiv. to *Affen* (comb. form of *Affe* APE) + *Pinscher* terrier]

af·fer·ent (af′ər ənt), *Physiol.* —*adj.* **1.** bringing to or leading toward an organ or part, as a nerve or arteriole (opposed to *efferent*). —*n.* **2.** a nerve carrying a message toward the central nervous system. [1830–40; < L *afferent-* (s. of *afferēns,* prp. of *afferre*), equiv. to *af-* AF- + *fer-* (s. of *ferre* to carry) + *-ent-* -ENT] —**af′fer·ent·ly,** *adv.*

af·fet·tuo·so (ə fech′ōō ō′sō; *It.* äf′fet twô′zô), *adj., adv., n., pl.* **-sos.** *Music.* —*adj., adv.* **1.** with affection and tenderness (a musical direction). —*n.* **2.** a composition or movement of gentle, tender character. [1715–25; < It: affecting, moving < L *affectuōsus,* equiv. to *affectu(s)* AFFECT[1] + *-ōsus* -OUS]

af·fi·ance (ə fī′əns), *v.,* **-anced, -anc·ing,** *n.* —*v.t.* **1.** to pledge by promise of marriage; betroth. —*n. Archaic.* **2.** a pledging of faith, as a marriage contract. **3.** trust; confidence; reliance. [1300–50; ME < MF *afiance,* equiv. to *afi(er)* to pledge faith, declare on oath, betroth (< ML *affīdāre,* equiv. to *ad-* AD- + **fīdāre,* for L *fīdere* to trust; see CONFIDE) + *-ance* -ANCE]

af·fi·anced (ə fī′ənst), *adj.* betrothed; engaged. [1570–80; AFFIANCE + -ED[2]]

af·fi·ant (ə fī′ənt), *n. Law.* a person who makes an affidavit. [1800–10, *Amer.;* obs. v. *affy* to confide (< MF *afier;* see AFFIANCE) + -ANT]

af·fiche (A fēsh′), *n., pl.* ***af·fiches*** (A fēsh′). *French.* a notice posted in a public place; poster.

af·fi·cio·na·do (ə fish′yə nä′dō), *n., pl.* **-dos.** aficionado.

af·fi·da·vit (af′i dā′vit), *n. Law.* a written declaration upon oath made before an authorized official. [1615–25; < ML *affīdāvit* (he) has declared on oath, perf. 3rd sing. of *affīdāre;* see AFFIANCE]

af·fil·i·ate (*v.* ə fil′ē āt′; *n.* ə fil′ē it, -āt′), *v.,* **-at·ed, -at·ing,** *n.* —*v.t.* **1.** to bring into close association or connection: *The research center is affiliated with the university.* **2.** to attach or unite on terms of fellowship; associate (usually fol. by *with* in U.S. usage, by *to* in Brit. usage): *to affiliate with the church.* **3.** to trace the descent, derivation, or origin of: *to affiliate a language.* **4.** to adopt. **5.** *Law.* to fix the paternity of, as an illegitimate child: *The mother affiliated her child upon John Doe.* —*v.i.* **6.** to associate oneself; be intimately united in action or interest. —*n.* **7.** a branch organization. **8.** *Com.* **a.** a business concern owned or controlled in whole or in part by another concern. **b.** a subsidiary. **9.** a person who is affiliated; associate; auxiliary. [1755–65; < L *affīliātus* adopted as son (ptp. of *affīliāre*), equiv. to *af-* AF- + *fīli(us)* son + *-ātus* -ATE[1]] —**af·fil·i·a·ble** (ə fil′ē ə bəl), *adj.* —**af·fil·i·a·tive** (ə fil′ē ā′tiv, -fil′ē ə-), *adj.*

af·fil·i·at·ed (ə fil′ē ā′tid), *adj.* being in close formal or informal association; related: *a letter sent to all affiliated clubs; a radio network and its affiliated local stations.* [1785–95; AFFILIATE + -ED[2]]

af·fil·i·a·tion (ə fil′ē ā′shən), *n.* the act of affiliating; state of being affiliated or associated. [1745–55; < ML *affīliātiōn-* (s. of *affīliātiō*); see AFFILIATE, -ION]

affilia′tion or′der, *Brit. Law.* a court order requiring the father of an illegitimate child to make child-support payments. [1830–40]

af·fil′i·a·tive drive′ (ə fil′ē ə tiv, -ā′tiv), the urge to form friendships and attachments, typically prompting a person to attend social gatherings and join organizations as a way of preventing loneliness and gaining emotional security. [AFFILIATE + -IVE]

af·fi·nal (a fīn′l, ə fīn′l, af′in l), *adj.* related by or concerning marriage. [1600–10; < L *affīn(is)* a relative + AL[1]. See AFFINITY]

af·fine (a fīn′, ə fīn′, af′in), *n.* **1.** a person related to one by marriage. —*adj. Math.* **2.** assigning finite values to finite quantities. **3.** of or pertaining to a transformation that maps parallel lines to parallel lines and finite points to finite points. [1500–10; < F *affin* related < L *affīnis* akin, neighboring] —**af·fine′ly,** *adv.*

af·fined (ə fīnd′), *adj.* **1.** closely related or connected. **2.** bound; obligated. [1590–1600; AFFINE + -ED[3]]

af′fine geom′etry, the branch of geometry dealing with affine transformations. [1915–20]

af′fine group′, *Math.* the group of all affine transformations of a finite-dimensional vector space.

af·fin·i·tive (ə fin′i tiv), *adj.* characterized by affinity; closely related or associated. [1645–55; AFFINIT(Y) + -IVE]

af·fin·i·ty (ə fin′i tē), *n., pl.* **-ties,** *adj.* —*n.* **1.** a natural liking for or attraction to a person, thing, idea, etc. **2.** a person, thing, idea, etc., for which such a natural liking or attraction is felt. **3.** relationship by marriage or by ties other than those of blood (distinguished from *consanguinity*). **4.** inherent likeness or agreement; close resemblance or connection. **5.** *Biol.* the phylogenetic relationship between two organisms or groups of organisms resulting in a resemblance in general plan or structure, or in the essential structural parts. **6.** *Chem.* the force by which atoms are held together in chemical compounds. —*adj.* **7.** of or pertaining to persons who share the same interests: *to arrange charter flights for opera lovers and other affinity groups.* [1275–1325; ME *affinite* < MF < L *affīnitās* connection by marriage. See AFFINE, -ITY]

—**Syn. 1.** partiality, fondness; sympathy, leaning, bent. **4.** similarity, compatibility. —**Ant. 1.** dislike, aversion. **4.** dissimilarity, disparity.

affin′ity card′, a credit card issued in conjunction with an organization, as a university or sports club. [1985–90]

af·firm (ə fûrm′), *v.t.* **1.** to state or assert positively; maintain as true: *to affirm one's loyalty to one's country; He affirmed that all was well.* **2.** to confirm or ratify: *The appellate court affirmed the judgment of the lower court.* **3.** to assert solemnly: *He affirmed his innocence.* **4.** to express agreement with or commitment to; uphold; support: *to affirm human rights.* —*v.i.* **5.** *Law.* **a.** to state something solemnly before a court or magistrate, but without oath. **b.** to ratify and accept a voidable transaction. **c.** (of an appellate court) to determine that the action of the lower court shall stand. [1300–50; < L *affirmāre,* equiv. to *af-* AF- + *firmāre* to make firm (see FIRM[1]); r. ME *a(f)fermen* < MF *afermer* < L] —**af·firm′a·ble,** *adj.* —**af·firm′a·bly,** *adv.* —**af·firm′er,** *n.* —**af·firm′ing·ly,** *adv.*

—**Syn. 1.** aver, asseverate, depose, testify. See **declare. 2.** approve, endorse. —**Ant. 1.** deny.

CONCISE PRONUNCIATION KEY: *act, cāpe, dâre, pärt; set, ēqual; if, ice; ox, ōver, ôrder, oil, bŏŏk, bōōt, out; up, ûrge; child; sing; shoe; thin, that;* zh as in *treasure.* ə = *a* as in *alone, e* as in *system, i* as in *easily, o* as in *gallop, u* as in *circus;* ° as in *fire* (fī°r), *hour* (ou°r). l and n can serve as syllabic consonants, as in *cradle* (krād′l), and *button* (but′n). See the full key inside the front cover.

af·firm·ance (ə fûr′məns), *n.* affirmation. [1350–1400; ME *affermance* < MF; see AFFIRM, -ANCE]

af·firm·ant (ə fûr′mənt), *n.* a person who affirms. [1740–50; AFFIRM + -ANT]

af·fir·ma·tion (af′ər mā′shən), *n.* **1.** the act or an instance of affirming; state of being affirmed. **2.** the assertion that something exists or is true. **3.** something that is affirmed; a statement or proposition that is declared to be true. **4.** confirmation or ratification of the truth or validity of a prior judgment, decision, etc. **5.** *Law.* a solemn declaration accepted instead of a statement under oath. [1535–45; < L *affirmātiōn-* (s. of *affirmātiō*), equiv. to *affirmāt(us)* (ptp. of *affirmāre* to AFFIRM) + *-iōn-* -ION]

af·firm·a·tive (ə fûr′mə tiv), *adj.* **1.** affirming or assenting; asserting the truth, validity, or fact of something. **2.** expressing agreement or consent; assenting: *an affirmative reply.* **3.** positive; not negative. **4.** *Logic.* noting a proposition in which a property of a subject is affirmed, as "All men are happy." —*n.* **5.** something that affirms or asserts; a positive statement or proposition; affirmation. **6.** a reply indicating assent, as *Yes* or *I do.* **7.** a manner or mode that indicates assent: *a reply in the affirmative.* **8.** the side, as in a debate, that affirms or defends a statement that the opposite side denies or attacks: *to speak for the affirmative.* —*interj.* **9.** (used to indicate agreement, assent, etc.): *"Is this the right way to Lake George?" "Affirmative."* [1400–50; < L *affirmātīvus*, equiv. to *affirmāt-* (see AFFIRMATION) + *-īvus* -IVE; r. late ME *affirmatyff* < MF < L] —**af·firm′a·tive·ly,** *adv.*

affirm′ative ac′tion, the encouragement of increased representation of women and minority-group members, esp. in employment. [1960–65] —**af·firm′a·tive-ac′tion,** *adj.*

affirm′ative flag′, *Naut.* a flag having five horizontal stripes, blue, white, red, white, and blue, from top to bottom, signifying "yes": letter C in the International Code of Signals.

af·firm·a·to·ry (ə fûr′mə tôr′ē, -tōr′ē), *adj.* affirmative. [1645–55; AFFIRMAT(ION) + -ORY[1]]

affirm′ing gun′. See **informing gun.**

af·fix (*v.* ə fiks′; *n.* af′iks), *v.t.* **1.** to fasten, join, or attach (usually fol. by *to*): *to affix stamps to a letter.* **2.** to put or add on; append: *to affix a signature to a contract.* **3.** to impress (a seal or stamp). **4.** to attach (blame, reproach, ridicule, etc.). —*n.* **5.** something that is joined or attached. **6.** *Gram.* a bound inflectional or derivational element, as a prefix, infix, or suffix, added to a base or stem to form a fresh stem or a word, as *-ed* added to *want* to form *wanted,* or *im-* added to *possible* to form *impossible.* Cf. **combining form.** [1525–35; < L *affixus* fastened to (ptp. of *affigere*), equiv. to *af-* AF- + *fīg-* fasten + *-sus,* var. of *-tus* ptp. suffix] —**af·fix′a·ble,** *adj.* —**af·fix·al** (a fik′səl), **af·fix·i·al** (a fik′sē əl), *adj.* —**af·fix′er,** *n.* —**af·fix′ment,** *n.*

af·fix·a·tion (af′ik sā′shən), *n.* **1.** affixture. **2.** *Gram.* the process of inflection or derivation that consists of adding an affix. [1850–55; AFFIX + -ATION]

af·fix·ture (ə fiks′chər), *n.* the act of affixing; attachment. Also, **affixation.** [1785–95; b. obs. *affixion* (see AFFIX, -ION) and FIXTURE]

af·flat·ed (ə flā′tid), *adj.* having inspiration; inspired. [1840–50; obs. *afflate* to inspire (< L *afflātus,* ptp. of *afflāre;* see AFFLATUS) + -ED[2]]

af·fla·tus (ə flā′təs), *n.* **1.** inspiration; an impelling mental force acting from within. **2.** divine communication of knowledge. [1655–65; < L *afflātus* a breathing on, equiv. to *af-* AF- + *flā-* (s. of *flāre* to BLOW[2]) + *-tus* suffix of v. action]

af·flict (ə flikt′), *v.t.* **1.** to distress with mental or bodily pain; trouble greatly or grievously: *to be afflicted with arthritis.* **2.** *Obs.* **a.** to overthrow; defeat. **b.** to humble. [1350–1400; ME *afflicten* < L *afflīctus* distressed, ptp. of *affligere* to cast down (*af-* AF- + *flig-* knock + *-tus* ptp. suffix); r. ME *aflight* < MF *aflit* < L. See INFLICT] —**af·flict′ed·ness,** *n.* —**af·flict′er,** *n.*
—**Syn. 1.** vex, harass, torment, plague.

af·flic·tion (ə flik′shən), *n.* **1.** a state of pain, distress, or grief; misery: *They sympathized with us in our affliction.* **2.** a cause of mental or bodily pain, as sickness, loss, calamity, or persecution. [1300–50; ME *affliccioun* < L *afflīctiōn-* (s. of *afflīctiō*). See AFFLICT, -ION] —**af·flic′tion·less,** *adj.*
—**Syn. 2.** mishap, trouble, tribulation, calamity, catastrophe, disaster. AFFLICTION, ADVERSITY, MISFORTUNE, TRIAL refer to an event or circumstance that is hard to bear. A MISFORTUNE is any adverse or unfavorable occurrence: *He had the misfortune to break his leg.* AFFLICTION suggests not only a serious misfortune but the emotional effect of this: *Blindness is an affliction.* ADVERSITY suggests a calamity or distress: *Job remained patient despite all his adversities.* TRIAL emphasizes the testing of one's character in undergoing misfortunes, trouble, etc.: *His son's conduct was a great trial to him.*
—**Ant. 1.** relief, comfort, solace.

af·flic·tive (ə flik′tiv), *adj.* characterized by or causing pain, distress, or grief; distressing. [1605–15; AFFLICT + -IVE] —**af·flic′tive·ly,** *adv.*

af·flu·ence (af′lo͞o əns *or, often,* ə flo͞o′-), *n.* **1.** abundance of money, property, and other material goods; riches; wealth. **2.** an abundant supply, as of thoughts or words; profusion. **3.** a flowing to or toward; afflux. [1350–1400; ME < MF < L *affluentia,* equiv. to *af-* AF- + *flu-* flow + *-entia* -ENCE]

af·flu·en·cy (af′lo͞o ən sē *or, often,* ə flo͞o′-), *n., pl.* **-cies.** affluence (def. 2). [1655–65; see AFFLUENCE, -ENCY]

CONCISE ETYMOLOGY KEY: <, descended or borrowed from; >, whence; b., blend of, blended; c., cognate with; cf., compare; deriv., derivative; equiv., equivalent; imit., imitative; obl., oblique; r., replacing; s., stem; sp., spelling, spelled; resp., respelling, respelled; trans., translation; ?, origin unknown; *, unattested; ‡, probably earlier than. See the full key inside the front cover.

af·flu·ent (af′lo͞o ənt *or, often,* ə flo͞o′-), *adj.* **1.** having an abundance of wealth, property, or other material goods; prosperous; rich: *an affluent person.* **2.** abounding in anything; abundant. **3.** flowing freely: *an affluent fountain.* —*n.* **4.** a tributary stream. **5.** an affluent person: *a luxurious resort appealing to young affluents.* [1400–50; late ME < MF < L *affluent-* (s. of *affluēns* rich; orig. prp. of *affluere*), equiv. to *af-* AF- + *flu-* flow + *-ent* -ENT] —**af′flu·ent·ly,** *adv.*
—**Syn. 1.** See **rich. 2.** teeming.

af·flux (af′luks), *n.* **1.** something that flows to or toward a point: *an afflux of blood to the head.* **2.** the act of flowing to or toward; flow. [1605–15; < ML *affluxus,* deriv. of L *affluere;* see AFFLUENT, FLUX]

af·ford (ə fôrd′, ə fōrd′), *v.t.* **1.** to be able to do, manage, or bear without serious consequence or adverse effect: *The country can't afford another drought.* **2.** to be able to meet the expense of; have or be able to spare the price of: *Can we afford a trip to Europe this year? The city can easily afford to repair the street.* **3.** to be able to give or spare: *He can't afford the loss of a day.* **4.** to furnish; supply: *The transaction afforded him a good profit.* **5.** to be capable of yielding or providing: *The records afford no explanation.* **6.** to give or confer upon: *to afford great pleasure to someone.* [bef. 1050; ME *aforthen, iforthen,* OE *geforthian* to further, accomplish, equiv. to *ge-* Y- + *forth* FORTH + *-ian* inf. suffix]

af·ford·a·ble (ə fôr′də bəl), *adj.* **1.** that can be afforded; believed to be within one's financial means: *attractive new cars at affordable prices.* —*n.* **2.** Usually, **affordables.** items, expenses, etc., that one can afford: *a variety of affordables for your gift list.* [1865–70; AFFORD + -ABLE] —**af·ford′a·bil′i·ty,** *n.* —**af·ford′a·bly,** *adv.*

af·for·est (ə fôr′ist, ə for′-), *v.t.* to convert (bare or cultivated land) into forest, originally for the purpose of providing hunting grounds. [1495–1505; < ML *afforēstāre,* equiv. to *af-* AF- + *forēst(is)* FOREST + *-āre* inf. suffix] —**af·for′est·a′tion, af·for′est·ment,** *n.*

af·fran·chise (ə fran′chīz), *v.t.,* **-chised, -chis·ing.** to free from a state of dependence, servitude, or obligation. [1450–1500; late ME < MF *afranchiss-,* long s. of *afranchir,* v. deriv., with *a-* A-[5], of *franc* free; see FRANK[1]] —**af·fran′chise·ment,** *n.*

af·fray (ə frā′), *n.* **1.** a public fight; a noisy quarrel; brawl. **2.** *Law.* the fighting of two or more persons in a public place. —*v.t.* **3.** *Archaic.* to frighten. [1275–1325; ME < AF *afray* (n.), *afrayer* (v.), OF *esfrei* (n.), *esfreer* (v.) < VL **exfridāre* to break the peace, equiv. to *ex-* EX-[1] + *-frid-* peace (< Gmc; cf. G *Friede*) + *-āre* inf. suffix]
—**Syn. 1.** row, fracas, altercation, melee.

af·fray·er (ə frā′ər), *n.* a person who engages in an affray; brawler. [1545–55; AFFRAY + -ER[1]]

af·freight (ə frāt′), *v.t.* to charter (a ship) as a freight carrier. [1840–50; < F *affréter* (resp. by influence of *freight*), equiv. to *a-* A-[5] (< L *ad-* AD-) + *fréter* to hire a ship, deriv. of *fret* FREIGHT, OF < MD] —**af·freight′er,** *n.* —**af·freight′ment,** *n.*

af·fri·cate (*n.* af′ri kit; *v.* af′ri kāt′), *n., v.,* **-cat·ed, -cat·ing.** *Phonet.* —*n.* **1.** Also called **affricative.** a speech sound comprising occlusion, plosion, and frication, as either of the *ch*-sounds in *church* and the *j*-sound in *joy.* —*v.t.* **2.** to change the pronunciation of (a stop) to an affricate, esp. by releasing (the stop) slowly. [1875–85; < L *affricātus* rubbed against (ptp. of *affricāre*), equiv. to *af-* AF- + *fric-* (see FRICTION) + *-ātus* -ATE[1]]

af·fri·ca·tion (af′ri kā′shən), *n.* *Phonet.* the act or process of changing a stop sound to an affricate. [1930–40; AFFRICATE + -ION]

af·fric·a·tive (ə frik′ə tiv, af′rə kā′-), *Phonet.* —*n.* **1.** affricate (def. 1). —*adj.* **2.** of or pertaining to an affricate. **3.** articulated as an affricate. [AFFRICATE + -IVE]

af·fright (ə frīt′), *Archaic.* —*v.t.* **1.** to frighten. —*n.* **2.** sudden fear or terror; fright. **3.** a source of terror. **4.** the act of terrifying. [bef. 1000; ME *afrighten,* OE *āfyrhtan,* equiv. to *ā-* A-[3] + *fyrhtan* to FRIGHT]

af·front (ə frunt′), *n.* **1.** a personally offensive act or word; deliberate act or display of disrespect; intentional slight; insult: *an affront to the king.* **2.** an offense to one's dignity or self-respect. —*v.t.* **3.** to offend by an open manifestation of disrespect or insolence: *His speech affronted all of us.* **4.** to make ashamed or confused; embarrass. **5.** *Archaic.* to front; face; look on. **6.** *Obs.* to meet or encounter face to face; confront. [1300–50; ME *afrounten* < MF *af(f)ronter* to strike in the face < VL **affrontāre,* deriv. of L phrase *ad frontem* at or toward the forehead (as the seat of one's feelings or dignity). See AD-, FRONT] —**af·front′ed·ly,** *adv.* —**af·front′ed·ness,** *n.* —**af·front′er,** *n.* —**af·front′ing·ly,** *adv.*
—**Syn. 1.** impertinence; contumely, scorn; indignity, abuse, outrage. See **insult. 3.** insult, slight, abuse.

af·fron·tive (ə frun′tiv), *adj.* *Archaic.* insulting; offensive. [1650–60; AFFRONT + -IVE] —**af·fron′tive·ness,** *n.*

afft., affidavit.

af·fu·sion (ə fyo͞o′zhən), *n.* the pouring on of water or other liquid, as in the rite of baptism. [1605–15; < LL *affūsiōn-* (s. of *affūsiō* a pouring upon), equiv. to *affūs(us)* (ptp. of *affundere;* see AF-, FUSE[2]) + *-iōn-* -ION]

AFGE, American Federation of Government Employees.

Afgh., Afghanistan. Also, **Afg.**

Af·ghan (af′gan, -gən), *n.* **1.** Also, **Afghani.** a native or inhabitant of Afghanistan. **2.** Pashto. **3.** (*l.c.*) a soft woolen blanket, crocheted or knitted, usually in a geometric pattern. **4.** Also called **Af′ghan hound′.** one of a breed of swift hunting hounds having a long, narrow head and a long, silky coat. —*adj.* **5.** of Afghanistan or its people or language.

Af·ghan·i (af gan′ē, -gä′nē), *n.* **1.** Afghan (def. 1). **2.** Pashto. **3.** (*l.c.*) a coin and monetary unit of Afghanistan, equal to 100 puls. *Abbr.:* Agh. [1925–30; < Pe *Afghān* AFGHAN + *-ī* suffix of appurtenance]

Af·ghan·i·stan (af gan′ə stan′), *n.* a republic in ce tral Asia, NW of India and E of Iran. 12,700,000; 250,0 sq. mi. (647,500 sq. km). *Cap.:* Kabul.

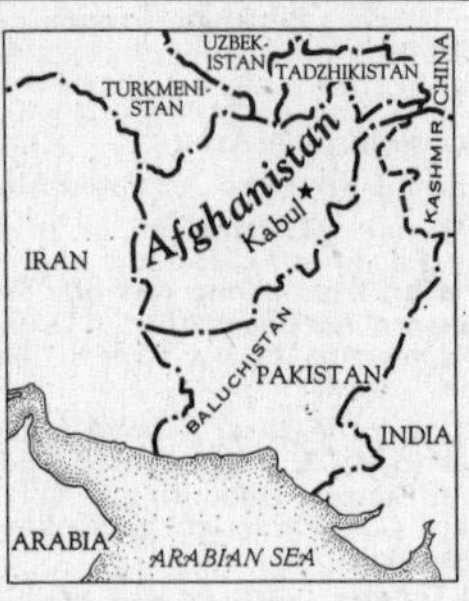

a·fi·cio·na·da (ə fish′yə nä′də; *Sp.* ä fē′thyô nä′th ä fē′syô-), *n., pl.* **-das** (-dəz; *Sp.* -thäs). a woman who an ardent devotee; fan; enthusiast. [1950–55; < Sp: fe of *aficionado* AFICIONADO]

a·fi·cio·na·do (ə fish′yə nä′dō; *Sp.* ä fē′thyô nä′th ä fē′syô-), *n., pl.* **-dos** (-dōz; *Sp.* -thōs). an ardent dev tee; fan, enthusiast. Also, **afficionado.** [1835–45; < lit., amateur, ptp. in *-ado* -ATE[1] of *aficionar* to engend affection, equiv. to *afición* AFFECTION[1] + *-ar* inf. suff

a·field (ə fēld′), *adv.* **1.** abroad; away from home. off the beaten path; far and wide: *to go afield in on reading.* **3.** off the mark: *His criticism was tota afield.* **4.** in or to the field or countryside. **5.** beyo the range or field of one's experience, knowledge, a quaintanceship, etc.: *a philosophy far afield of previo philosophical thought.* [bef. 1000; ME *afelde,* OE *felda.* See A-[1], FIELD]

a·fi·ko·men (ä′fē kō′mən), *n.* *Judaism.* a piece matzo broken off from the center one of the three ma zoth set before the leader of a Seder: it is hidden by t leader and later searched for by the children, with t finder, usually the youngest, receiving a reward. [189 95; < Yiddish *afikoymen* < Heb *aphīgōmān* < Gk *ep kōmion* revel, n. use of neut. of *epikōmios* of a rev equiv. to *epi-* EPI- + *kôm(os)* revel + *-ios* adj. suffix

a·fire (ə fīər′), *adj.* **1.** on fire: *to set a house afire.* aflame (def. 2). [1175–1225; ME; see A-[1], FIRE]

A1c, airman, first class.

AFL, 1. See **American Federation of Labor. 2.** Ame ican Football League.

A.F.L., See **American Federation of Labor.** Also, **A of L.**

a·flame (ə flām′), *adj.* **1.** on fire; ablaze: *The hou was all aflame.* **2.** eager and excited: *I was aflame wi curiosity.* [1545–55; A-[1] + FLAME]

af·la·tox·in (af′lə tok′sin), *n.* any of various relat mycotoxins produced by a species of *Aspergillus,* co monly *A. flavus,* found as a contaminant in moldy grai and meals, as in rice and peanut meal, and suspected causing liver cancer in humans and other anima [1960–65; *A(spergillus) fla(vus)* (species name; see ASPE GILLUS, FLAVO-) + TOXIN]

AFL-CIO, See **American Federation of Labor a Congress of Industrial Organizations.**

a·float (ə flōt′), *adv., adj.* **1.** floating or borne on t water; in a floating condition: *The ship was set aflo* **2.** on board a ship, boat, raft, etc.; at sea: *cargo aflo and ashore.* **3.** covered with water; flooded; awash: *T main deck was afloat.* **4.** moving without being guid or controlled; drifting. **5.** passing from place to place; circulation: *A rumor is afloat.* **6.** free of major troub esp. financially solvent: *to keep a venture afloat.* [b 1000; ME, OE *on flote.* See A-[1], FLOAT]

a·flut·ter (ə flut′ər), *adj.* in a flutter. [1820–30; A-[1] FLUTTER]

AFM, 1. American Federation of Musicians. **2.** aud frequency modulation: a method for recording hig fidelity stereo sound on home videotape recorders a on video discs.

a·fo·cal (ā fō′kəl), *adj.* *Optics.* pertaining to or havi no finite focal point, as a telescope. [A-[6] + FOCAL]

A·fog·nak (ə fôg′nak, ə fog′-), *n.* an island off sout ern Alaska, in the Gulf of Alaska, N of Kodiak Islan 721 sq. mi. (1867 sq. km).

à fond (A FÔN′), *French.* to or toward the botto thoroughly; fully.

a·foot (ə fo͝ot′), *adv., adj.* **1.** on foot; walking: *I car afoot.* **2.** astir; in progress: *There is mischief afo* [1175–1225; ME *a fote, on fote.* See A-[1], FOOT]

a·fore (ə fôr′, ə fōr′), *adv., prep., conj.* *Older Use.* b fore. [bef. 900; late ME; ME *aforne, aforen,* OE *foran.* See A-[1], FORE[1]]

a·fore·hand (ə fôr′hand′, ə fōr′-), *adv.* *Older U* beforehand. [1400–50; late ME. See AFORE, HAND]

a·fore·men·tioned (ə fôr′men′shənd, ə fōr′-; ə fôr men′shənd, ə fōr′-), *adj.* cited or mentioned earlier previously. [1580–90; AFORE + MENTION + -ED[2]]

a·fore·said (ə fôr′sed′, ə fōr′-), *adj.* said or me tioned earlier or previously. [1375–1425; late ME; s AFORE, SAID[1]]

a·fore·thought (ə fôr′thôt′, ə fōr′-), *adj.* **1.** thoug of previously; premeditated (usually used predicatively *with malice aforethought.* —*n.* **2.** premeditation; fo thought. [1575–85; AFORE + THOUGHT[2]]

a·fore·time (ə fôr′tīm′, ə fōr′-), *adv.* **1.** in time pa in a former time; previously. —*adj.* **2.** former; previous. [1525–35; AFORE + TIME]

a for·ti·o·ri (ä fôr′tē ō′rē; *Eng.* ā fôr′shē ôr′ī, ā fôr′shē ōr′ī), *Latin.* for a still stronger reason; even more certain; all the more.

a·foul (ə foul′), *adv., adj.* **1.** in a state of collision or entanglement: *a ship with its shrouds afoul.* **2. run** or **come** or **fall afoul of, a.** to become entangled with: *The boat ran afoul of the seaweed.* **b.** to come into conflict with: *The business had fallen afoul of the new government regulations.* [1800–10, *Amer.*; A-[1] + FOUL]

AFP, alphafetoprotein.

Afr, African.

Afr-, var. of **Afro-** before a vowel: *Afrasian.*

Afr., **1.** Africa. **2.** African.

A.-Fr., Anglo-French.

a·fraid (ə frād′), *adj.* **1.** feeling fear; filled with apprehension: *afraid to go.* **2.** feeling regret, unhappiness, or the like: *I'm afraid we can't go on Monday.* **3.** feeling reluctance, unwillingness, distaste, or the like: *He seemed afraid to show his own children a little kindness.* [var. sp. of *affrayed,* ptp. of AFFRAY to disturb, frighten]
—**Syn. 1.** scared, fearful, disquieted, apprehensive, timid, timorous. AFRAID, ALARMED, FRIGHTENED, TERRIFIED all indicate a state of fear. AFRAID implies inner apprehensive disquiet: *afraid of the dark.* ALARMED implies that the feelings are aroused through realization of some imminent or unexpected danger to oneself or others: *alarmed by* (or *about*) *someone's illness.* FRIGHTENED means shocked with sudden, but usually short-lived, fear, esp. that arising from apprehension of physical harm: *frightened by an accident.* TERRIFIED suggests the emotional reaction when one is struck with a violent, overwhelming fear: *terrified by an earthquake.* —**Ant. 1.** bold, confident, fearless.

A-frame (ā′frām′), *n.* **1.** any upright, rigid supporting frame in the form of a triangle or an inverted V, as V. **2.** a building constructed principally of such a frame, with a steep gabled roof resting directly on a foundation. [1960–65]

Af·ra·mer·i·can (af′rə mer′i kən), *adj., n.* Afro-American. [AFR- + AMERICAN]

Af·ra·sia (af rā′zhə, -shə), *n.* N Africa and SW Asia considered together. [AFR- + ASIA]

Af·ra·sian (af rā′zhən, -shən), *adj.* **1.** of Afrasia. **2.** of mixed African and Asian descent. —*n.* **3.** the offspring of an African and an Asian. [AFRASI(A) + -AN]

af·reet (af′rēt, ə frēt′), *n. Arabian Myth.* a powerful evil demon or monster. Also, **afrit.** [1795–1805; < dial. Ar *ʿafrīt* < Pahlavi *āfrītan* creature]

a·fresh (ə fresh′), *adv.* anew; once more; again: *to start afresh.* [1500–10; A-[2] + FRESH]

Af·ric (af′rik), *adj.* African. [1580–90; < L *Āfricus,* equiv. to *Āfr-,* s. of *Āfer* African + *-icus* -IC]

Af·ri·ca (af′ri kə), *n.* **1.** a continent S of Europe and between the Atlantic and Indian oceans. 551,000,000; ab. 11,700,000 sq. mi. (30,303,000 sq. km). —*adj.* **2.** African.

Af·ri·can (af′ri kən), *adj.* **1.** Also, **Africa.** of or from Africa; belonging to the black peoples of Africa —*n.* **2.** a native or inhabitant of Africa. **3.** (loosely) a black or other person of African ancestry. [< L *Āfricānus,* equiv. to *Āfric(us)* AFRIC + *-ānus* -AN; cf. ME *Aufrican,* OE *Africanas* (nom. pl.)] —**Af′ri·can·ness,** *n.*

Af·ri·ca·na (af′ri kan′ə, -kä′nə, -kā′nə), *n.* (*used with a plural v.*) **1.** artifacts or artistic or literary works of any of the nations of Africa reflecting geographical, historical, or cultural development. **2.** a collection of materials, as books and documents, on African history or culture. [1905–10; AFRIC(A) or AFRIC(AN) + -ANA]

Af·ri·can-A·mer·i·can (af′ri kən ə mer′i kən), *n.* **1.** a black American of African descent. —*adj.* **2.** of or pertaining to African-Americans. Also, **Afro-American.** [1860–65, *Amer.*]
—**Usage.** See **black.**

Af′rican cher′ry-or·ange (cher′ē ôr′inj, -or′-), a citrus shrub or small tree, *Citropsis schweinfurthi,* of Africa, having a limelike but sweet fruit.

Af′rican dai′sy, any of several composite plants native to Africa, esp. of the genera *Arctotis, Gerbera,* and *Lonas,* having showy, daisylike flowers.

Af·ri·can·der (af′ri kan′dər), *n.* Afrikander.

Af′rican dom′inoes, *Slang* (*disparaging and offensive*). dice, esp. as used in the game of craps. [1920–25, *Amer.*]

Af′rican el′ephant. See under **elephant** (def. 1).

Af′rican grape′, *Slang* (*offensive*). a watermelon.

Af′rican gray′. See **gray parrot.**

Af′rican green′ mon′key. See **green monkey.**

Af′rican hon′eybee. See **killer bee** (def. 1).

Af·ri·can·ism (af′ri kə niz′əm), *n.* **1.** something that is characteristic of African culture or tradition. **2.** a word, term, or the like, that has been adopted from an African language. **3.** African culture, ideals, or advancement. [1635–45; AFRICAN + -ISM]

Af·ri·can·ist (af′ri kə nist), *n.* a person who specializes in and studies the cultures or languages of Africa. [1890–95; AFRICAN + -IST]

Af·ri·can·ize (af′ri kə nīz′), *v.t.,* **-ized, -iz·ing. 1.** to replace the European or white staff of (an organization in Africa) with black Africans. **2.** to bring under African, esp. black African, influence or to adapt to African needs. Also, *esp. Brit.,* **Af′ri·can·ise′.** [1850–55; *Amer.*; AFRICAN + -IZE] —**Af′ri·can·i·za′tion,** *n.*

Af′ri·can·ized hon′eybee (af′ri kə nīzd′). See **killer bee** (def. 2).

Af′rican lil′y, lily-of-the-Nile.

Af′rican li′on hound′. See **Rhodesian ridgeback.**

Af′rican mahog′any, 1. a large tree, *Khaya ivorensis,* of western Africa, having hard wood resembling true mahogany, widely used in cabinetmaking and boatbuilding. **2.** any of several related or similar African hardwood trees. **3.** the wood of any of these trees. [1835–45]

Af′rican mar′igold, a bushy composite plant, *Tagetes erecta,* of Mexico, having pinnate leaves and large yellow or orange flower heads. Also called **Aztec marigold.** [1830–40]

Af′rican mil′let, 1. a grass, *Eleusine coracana,* of Asia and Africa, having round fruit with a loose husk, grown as a cereal and as an ornamental. **2.** See **pearl millet.** [1835–45]

Af′rican mon′goose, ichneumon.

Af′rican Plate′, *Geol.* a major tectonic division of the earth's crust, comprising the African continent as well as adjacent ocean basins.

Af′rican sleep′ing sick′ness, *Pathol.* See **sleeping sickness** (def. 1).

Af·ri·can·thro·pus (af′ri kan′thrə pəs, -kan thrō′pəs), *n.* a genus of hominids of eastern Africa, assumed from a number of now lost skull fragments to have been a form of archaic *Homo*: no longer in technical use. [< NL (1939), equiv. to *Afric(a)* AFRICA + Gk *ánthrōpos* man, human being]

Af′rican trypanosomi′asis, *Pathol.* See **sleeping sickness** (def. 1).

Af′rican vi′olet, a popular house plant, *Saintpaulia ionantha,* of the gesneriad family, having hairy leaves and showy violet, pink, or white flowers. [1940–45]

Af′rican yel′lowwood, a tree, *Podocarpus elongatus,* of tropical Africa and the mountains of southern Africa, having globe-shaped fruit, grown as an ornamental.

Af·ri·kaans (af′ri käns′, -känz′), *n.* **1.** Also called **the Taal.** an official language of South Africa, developed out of the speech of 17th-century settlers from Holland and still very like Dutch. —*adj.* **2.** of or pertaining to Afrikaans or Afrikaners. [1895–1900; < D, equiv. to *Afrikaan* native of Africa + *-s* -ISH[1]]

Af·ri·kan·der (af′ri kan′dər), *n.* **1.** one of a breed of red beef cattle, raised originally in southern Africa, well adapted to high temperatures. **2.** *Archaic.* Afrikaner. Also, **Africander.** [see AFRIKANER]

Af·ri·ka·ner (af′ri kä′nər, -kan′ər), *n.* an Afrikaans-speaking native of South Africa of European, esp. Dutch, descent. Also, **Af′ri·kaa′ner.** [1815–1825; < Afrik, earlier *Afrikaander,* equiv. to *Afrikaan* AFRICAN + *-er* -ER[1], with *-d-* from *Hollander*]

Af·ri·ka·ner·ism (af′ri kä′nə riz′əm, -kan′ə-), *n.* a word, term, or usage peculiar to or originating among Afrikaners. [1930–35; AFRIKANER + -ISM]

af·rit (af′rēt, ə frēt′), *n.* afreet.

Af·ro (af′rō), *adj., n., pl.* **-ros.** —*adj.* **1.** of or pertaining to Afro-Americans or to black traditions, culture, etc.: *Afro societies; Afro hair styles.* —*n.* **2.** a hair style originating with black persons, in which the hair is allowed to grow naturally and to acquire a bushy appearance. [1965–70; independent use of AFRO-]

Afro-, a combining form of **Africa**: *Afro-American; Afro-Asiatic.* Also, *esp. before a vowel,* **Afr-.** [< L *Āfr-* (s. of *Āfer* an African) + -o-]

Af·ro-A·mer·i·can (af′rō ə mer′i kən), *n., adj.* See **African-American.** [1850–55, *Amer.*]
—**Usage.** See **black.**

Af′ro-Amer′ican Eng′lish. See **Black English** (def. 1).

Af′ro-Amer′ican stud′ies. See **black studies.** [1965–70]

Af·ro-A·sian (af′rō ā′zhən, -shən), *adj.* of or pertaining to the nations of Africa and Asia or their peoples. [1950–55]

Af·ro·a·si·at·ic (af′rō ā′zhē at′ik, -ā′shē-, -ā′zē-), *adj.* **1.** of, belonging to, or pertaining to Afroasiatic; Hamito-Semitic. —*n.* **2.** Also called **Hamito-Semitic.** a family of languages including as subfamilies Semitic, Egyptian, Berber, Cushitic, and Chadic. Cf. **family** (def. 14). Also, **Af′ro-A′si·at′ic.** [1955–60; AFRO- + ASIATIC]

Af·ro·cen·tric (af′rō sen′trik), *adj.* centered on Africa or on African-derived cultures, as those of Brazil, Cuba, and Haiti: *Afrocentric art.* [1985–90] —**Af′ro·cen′trism,** *n.* —**Af′ro·cen′trist,** *n.*

Af·ro-Cu·ban (af′rō kyōō′bən), *adj.* **1.** combining elements of black African culture with those of Cuban culture. —*n.* **2.** percussive Latin music originating in Cuba and showing strong African rhythmic influence. [1945–50]

Af·ro-pop (af′rō pop′), *n.* African pop music played on electric instruments and inspired by Western pop or soul music. [1985–90]

af·ror·mo·si·a (af′rôr mō′zē ə, -zhə, -rôr-), *n.* **1.** a tree, *Pericopsis elata* (or *Afrormosia elata*), of western Africa, having wood that resembles teak and is used in cabinetwork. **2.** the wood of this tree. [< NL (1906), orig. the genus name, equiv. to L *Āfr-,* s. of *Āfer* (adj.) African + NL *Ormosia* a genus to which the plant was first attributed (irreg. from Gk *hórmos* necklace + NL *-ia* -IA; so called because the seeds of the plant were strung as necklaces)]

A.F.S., American Field Service.

AFSC, See **American Friends Service Committee.** Also, **A.F.S.C.**

AFSCME, American Federation of State, County, and Municipal Employees.

aft[1] (aft, äft), *Naut., Aeron.* —*adv.* **1.** at, close to, or toward the stern or tail: *Stow the luggage aft.* —*adj.* **2.** situated toward or at the stern or tail: *The aft sail was luffing.* [bef. 950; ME *afte,* OE *æftan* from behind, equiv. to *æf-* opposite + *-t-* suffix of uncertain value + *-an* suffix marking motion from; c. OFris *efta,* OS, OHG *aftan,* Goth *aftana,* ON *aptan,* Gk *opís(s)ō* behind; not akin to Gk *apó* OFF]

aft[2] (aft, äft), *adv. Scot.* oft.

aft., afternoon.

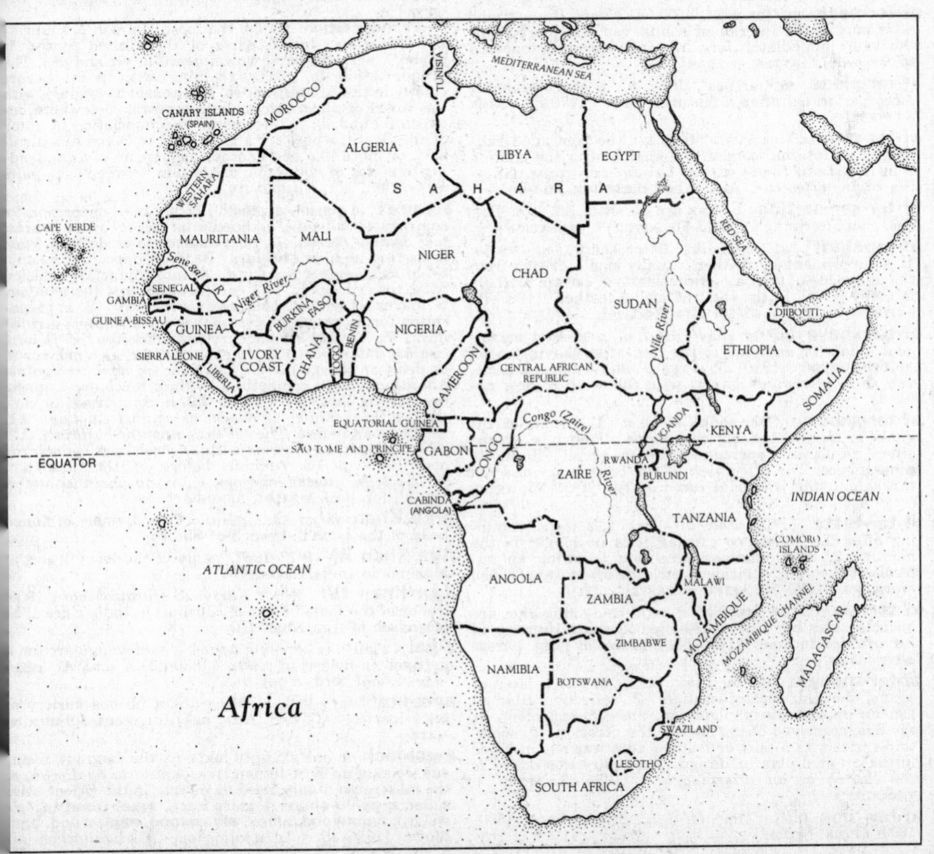

CONCISE PRONUNCIATION KEY: act, cāpe, dâre, pärt; set, ēqual; if, īce; ox, ōver, ôrder, oil, bŏŏk, bōōt, out; up, ûrge; child; sing; shoe; thin, *th*at; zh as in *treasure.* ə = *a* as in *alone,* *e* as in *system,* *i* as in *easily,* *o* as in *gallop,* *u* as in *circus;* ᵊ as in *fire* (fīᵊr), *hour* (ouᵊr). l and n can serve as syllabic consonants, as in *cradle* (krād′l), and *button* (but′n). See the full key inside the front cover.

A.F.T., American Federation of Teachers.

af·ter (af′tər, äf′-), *prep.* **1.** behind in place or position; following behind: *men lining up one after the other.* **2.** later in time than; in succession to; at the close of: *Tell me after supper. Day after day he came to work late.* **3.** subsequent to and in consequence of: *After what has happened, I can never return.* **4.** below in rank or excellence; nearest to: *Milton is usually placed after Shakespeare among English poets.* **5.** in imitation of or in imitation of the style of: *to make something after a model; fashioned after Raphael.* **6.** in pursuit or search of; with or in desire for: *I'm after a better job. Run after him!* **7.** concerning; about: *to inquire after a person.* **8.** with the name of; for: *He was named after his uncle.* **9.** in proportion to; in accordance with: *He was a man after the hopes and expectations of his father.* **10.** according to the nature of; in conformity with; in agreement or unison with: *He was a man after my own heart. He swore after the manner of his faith.* **11.** subsequent to and notwithstanding; in spite of: *After all their troubles, they still manage to be optimistic.* **12. after all,** despite what has occurred or been assumed previously; nevertheless: *I've discovered I can attend the meeting after all.* —*adv.* **13.** behind; in the rear: *Jill came tumbling after.* **14.** later in time; afterward: *three hours after; happily ever after.* —*adj.* **15.** later in time; next; subsequent; succeeding: *In after years we never heard from him.* **16.** *Naut., Aeron.* **a.** farther aft. **b.** located closest to the stern or tail; aftermost: *after hold; after mast.* **c.** including the stern or tail: *the after part of a hull.* —*conj.* **17.** subsequent to the time that: *after the boys left.* —*n.* **18. afters,** *Brit. Informal.* the final course of a meal, as pudding, ice cream, or the like; dessert. [bef. 900; ME; OE *æfter;* c. OFris *efter,* OS, OHG *after,* Goth *aftaro,* ON *eptir;* equiv. to *æf-* (see AFT) + *-ter* suffix of comparison and polarity (c. Gk *-teros*)]
—**Syn. 1.** See **behind.**

af·ter·beat (af′tər bēt′, äf′-), *n.* a secondary, weaker half of a musical beat. [1905–10; AFTER + BEAT]

af·ter·birth (af′tər bûrth′, äf′-), *n.* the placenta and fetal membranes expelled from the uterus after childbirth. [1580–90; AFTER + BIRTH]

af·ter·bod·y (af′tər bod′ē, äf′-), *n., pl.* **-bod·ies. 1.** *Naut.* the portion of a ship's hull aft of the middle body. **2.** *Aeron.* the rear part of an aircraft's fuselage. **3.** *Rocketry.* the part of a guided missile behind the nose cone, usually unprotected against reentry heat. [AFTER + BODY]

af·ter·brain (af′tər brān′, äf′-), *n.* the metencephalon. [1605–15; AFTER + BRAIN]

af·ter·burn·er (af′tər bûr′nər, äf′-), *n.* **1.** *Aeron.* a device placed within, or attached to the exit of, a jet-engine exhaust pipe to produce afterburning. **2.** a device for burning exhaust fumes from an internal-combustion engine, as of an automobile. [1945–50; AFTER + BURNER]

af·ter·burn·ing (af′tər bûr′ning, äf′-), *n.* **1.** *Aeron.* combustion in an afterburner that results from the injection of fuel into the exhaust gases of a jet engine to produce additional thrust with more efficient fuel consumption. **2.** *Rocketry.* an irregular burning of residual fuel in some rocket motors after the cessation of the main burning. [1885–90; AFTER + BURNING, trans. of G *Nachbrennen*]

af·ter·care (af′tər kâr′, äf′-), *n. Med.* the care and treatment of a convalescent patient. [1755–65; AFTER + CARE]

af·ter·cast (af′tər kast′, äf′tər käst′), *n. Foundry.* **1.** a casting made from a mold that was itself made from an original casting. **2.** an exact impression, usually in plaster, made of a permanent mold or die after the production of castings is finished. [AFTER + CAST[1]]

af·ter·clap (af′tər klap′, äf′-), *n.* an unexpected repercussion. [1300–50; ME; cf. LG *achterklap;* see AFTER, CLAP[1]]

af·ter·cool·er (af′tər kōō′lər, äf′-), *n.* a device for cooling compressed air or gases to reduce their volume or temperature. [1900–05; AFTER + COOLER]

af·ter·damp (af′tər damp′, äf′-), *n.* an irrespirable mixture of gases, consisting chiefly of carbon dioxide and nitrogen, left in a mine after an explosion or fire. [1855–60; AFTER + DAMP]

af·ter·deck (af′tər dek′, äf′-), *n. Naut.* the weather deck of a vessel behind the bridge house or midship section. [1895–1900; AFTER + DECK]

af·ter-din·ner (af′tər din′ər, äf′-), *adj.* immediately following dinner: *an after-dinner speech.* [1570–80]

af·ter·ef·fect (af′tər i fekt′, äf′-), *n.* **1.** a delayed effect; an effect that follows at some interval after the stimulus that produces it. **2.** *Med.* a result appearing after the first effect due to an agent, usually a drug, has gone. [1810–20; AFTER + EFFECT]

af·ter·glow (af′tər glō′, äf′-), *n.* **1.** the glow frequently seen in the sky after sunset; afterlight. **2.** a second or secondary glow, as in heated metal before it ceases to become incandescent. **3.** the pleasant remembrance of a past experience, glory, etc.: *She basked in the afterglow of her stage triumph.* **4.** phosphorescence (def. 3). [1870–75; AFTER + GLOW]

af·ter·growth (af′tər grōth′, äf′-), *n.* a second growth, as of crops or timber, after one harvesting, cutting, etc.; second crop. [1810–20; AFTER + GROWTH]

af·ter·guard (af′tər gärd′, äf′-), *n. Naut. Slang.* **1.** the owner of a yacht or his guests. **2.** the officers quartered in the stern of a vessel. [1820–30; AFTER + GUARD]

af·ter·heat (af′tər hēt′, äf′-), *n. Physics.* the heat generated by radioactivity remaining in a nuclear reactor after it has been shut down. [1970–75; AFTER + HEAT]

af·ter-hours (af′tər ou°rz′, -ou′ərz, äf′-), *adj.* occurring, engaged in, or operating after the normal or legal closing time for business: *an after-hours drinking club.* [1925–30]

af·ter·im·age (af′tər im′ij, äf′-), *n. Psychol.* a visual image or other sense impression that persists after the stimulus that caused it is no longer operative. [1875–80; trans. of G *Nachbild;* see AFTER, IMAGE]

af·ter·life (af′tər līf′, äf′-), *n.* **1.** Also called **future life.** life after death. **2.** the later part of a person's life: *the remarkably productive afterlife of Thomas Jefferson.* [1585–95; AFTER + LIFE]

af·ter·light (af′tər līt′, äf′-), *n.* **1.** the light visible in the sky after sunset; afterglow. **2.** a view of past events; retrospect. [1890–95; AFTER + LIGHT[1]]

af·ter·mar·ket (af′tər mär′kit, äf′-), *n.* **1.** the market for replacement parts, accessories, and equipment for the care or enhancement of the original product, esp. an automobile, after its sale to the consumer: *The company holds a large share in the automotive radio aftermarket.* **2.** any additional market created by a product after the primary market: *Television is the perfect aftermarket for old movies.* **3.** *Stock Exchange.* See **secondary market.** [1935–40; AFTER + MARKET]

af′ter mast′, the aftermost mast of a sailing vessel.

af·ter·math (af′tər math′, äf′-), *n.* **1.** something that results or follows from an event, esp. one of a disastrous or unfortunate nature; consequence: *the aftermath of war; the aftermath of the flood.* **2.** a new growth of grass following one or more mowings, which may be grazed, mowed, or plowed under. [1515–25; AFTER + *math* a mowing, OE *mǣth;* c. OHG *mād* (G *Mahd*); akin to MOW[1]]
—**Syn. 1.** outcome, result, upshot.

af·ter·most (af′tər mōst′, äf′- *or, esp. Brit.,* äf′tər məst), *adj.* **1.** *Naut.* farthest aft; aftmost: *The aftermost sail is called a spanker.* **2.** hindmost; last. [bef. 900; AFTER + -MOST; r. ME *aftermest,* itself r. OE *æftemest,* equiv. to *æfteme-* (c. Goth *aftuma* last; *æfte* (see AFT) + *-m-* superl. suffix) + *(-e)st* -EST[1]]

af·ter·noon (*n.* af′tər nōōn′, äf′-; *adj.* af′tər nōōn′, äf′-, af′-, äf′-), *n.* **1.** the time from noon until evening. **2.** the latter part: *the afternoon of life.* —*adj.* **3.** pertaining to the latter part of the day. [1250–1300; ME; see AFTER, NOON]

af·ter·noon·er (af′tər nōō′nər, äf′-), *n. Informal.* **1.** a person or thing that appears, flourishes, etc., in the afternoon: *One of radio's favorite afternooners is a soap opera.* **2.** a baseball game or other event that takes place in the afternoon. [1905–10; AFTERNOON + -ER[1]]

Afternoon′ of a Faun′, The. See ***L'Après-midi d'un Faune.***

af·ter·noons (af′tər nōōnz′, äf′-), *adv.* in or during any or every afternoon: *He slept late and worked afternoons.* [1895–1900, *Amer.;* AFTERNOON + -S[1]]

afternoon′ watch′, *Naut.* the watch from noon until 4 P.M.

af·ter·pain (af′tər pān′, äf′-), *n. Med.* pain due to continuing contractions of the uterus following childbirth. [1550–60; AFTER + PAIN]

af·ter·peak (af′tər pēk′, äf′-), *n. Naut.* the extreme after part of the interior of a hull, esp. that part below the water immediately forward of the sternpost (opposed to *forepeak*). [AFTER + PEAK[1]]

af·ter·piece (af′tər pēs′, äf′-), *n.* a short dramatic piece performed after a featured play. [1770–80; AFTER + PIECE]

af·ter-run (af′tər run′, äf′-), *n.* the continued running of an internal-combustion engine after the ignition is switched off: *Heavy carbon buildup can cause annoying engine after-run.* Also called **dieseling, run-on.**

af·ter·sen·sa·tion (af′tər sen sā′shən, äf′-), *n. Psychol.* an afterimage. [1865–70; AFTER + SENSATION]

af·ter·shaft (af′tər shaft′, äf′tər shäft′), *n. Ornith.* **1.** a supplementary feather, usually small, arising from the underside of the base of the shafts of certain feathers in many birds. **2.** the shaft of such a feather. [1865–70; AFTER + SHAFT] —**af′ter·shaft′ed,** *adj.*

af·ter·shave (af′tər shāv′, äf′-), *n.* a scented, astringent lotion for applying to the face after shaving. Also, **af′ter-shave′.** [1920–25; AFTER + SHAVE, orig. adjectival, as in *aftershave lotion,* with following n. now deleted]

af·ter·shock (af′tər shok′, äf′-), *n.* **1.** a small earthquake or tremor that follows a major earthquake. **2.** the effect, result, or repercussion of an event; aftermath; consequence: *The aftershock of the bankruptcy was felt throughout the financial community.* [1890–95; AFTER + SHOCK[1]]

af·ter·taste (af′tər tāst′, äf′-), *n.* **1.** a taste remaining after the substance causing it is no longer in the mouth. **2.** the remaining sensation following an unpleasant experience, incident, etc.: *the aftertaste of a bad marriage.* [1820–30; AFTER + TASTE]

af·ter·tax (af′tər taks′, äf′-), *adj.* remaining after applicable taxes have been deducted: *a sharp decrease in her aftertax income.* [1950–55; adj. use of prep. phrase *after tax(es)*]

af·ter·thought (af′tər thôt′, äf′-), *n.* **1.** a later or second thought; reconsideration. **2.** reflection after an act; an appropriate explanation, answer, expedient, or the like, conceived of too late for the occasion. **3.** something added, as a part or feature, that was not included in the original plan or design: *The vestry was added to the church as an afterthought.* [1655–65; AFTER + THOUGHT[1]]

af·ter·time (af′tər tīm′, äf′-), *n.* future time. [1590–1600; AFTER + TIME]

af·ter·treat·ment (af′tər trēt′mənt, äf′-), *n.* a chemical treatment to which a fabric is subjected immediately after being dyed, for increasing the fastness of the color. [1825–35; AFTER + TREATMENT]

af·ter·ward (af′tər wərd, äf′-), *adv.* at a later or subsequent time; subsequently. Also, **af′ter·wards.** [bef. 1000; ME; OE *æfterweard,* alter. (with *-r-* of *æfter* AFTER) of *æfteweard,* equiv. to *æfte-, æftan* AFT + *-weard* -WARD]

af·ter·word (af′tər wûrd′, äf′-), *n.* a concluding section, commentary, etc., as of a book, treatise, or the like; closing statement. Cf. **foreword.** [1885–90; AFTER + WORD]

af·ter·world (af′tər wûrld′, äf′-), *n.* the future world, esp. the world after death. [1590–1600; AFTER + WORLD]

af·ter·years (af′tər yērz′, äf′-), *n.pl.* the years following a specified event: *Often, in afteryears, I have regretted my hasty decision.* [1805–15; AFTER + YEAR + -S[3]]

aft·most (aft′mōst′, -məst, äft′-), *adj. Naut.* aftermost (def. 1).

af·to·sa (af tō′sə, -zə), *n.* See **foot-and-mouth disease.** [< Sp *(fiebre) aftosa* APHTHOUS (FEVER)]

AFTRA, American Federation of Television and Radio Artists. Also, **A.F.T.R.A.**

A·fyon (ä fyôn′), *n.* a city in W Turkey. 51,660. Also called **Afyon′ Ka·ra·hi·sar′** (kär′ə hi sär′).

ag (ag), *adj., n. Informal.* agriculture: *ag courses; to major in ag.* [by shortening]

Ag, *Symbol, Chem.* silver. [< L *argentum*]

ag-, var. of **ad-** before *g: agglutinate.*

Ag., August.

ag., agriculture.

A.G., 1. Adjutant General. **2.** Attorney General. Also **AG**

a·ga (ä′gə), *n.* (in Turkey and other Muslim countries) **1.** a title of honor, usually implying respect for age. **2.** a general. Also, **agha.** [1590–1600; < Turk *ağa* lord]

Ag·a·bus (ag′ə bəs), *n.* a Christian prophet who predicted a great famine. Acts 11:28.

A·ga·da (*Seph. Heb.* ä gä dä′, *Ashk. Heb.* ə gä′də), *n.* Aggadah.

A·ga·de (ə gä′də), *n.* Akkad (def. 2).

A·ga·dir (ä′gä dēr′), *n.* a seaport in SW Morocco: destroyed by earthquake in 1960; new town rebuilt S of original site. 1,220,600.

A·gag (ā′gag), *n.* an Amalekite king who was captured and spared by Saul but later killed by Samuel. I Sam. 15.

a·gain (ə gen′, ə gān′), *adv.* **1.** once more; another time; anew; in addition: *Will you spell your name again please?* **2.** in an additional case or instance; moreover besides; furthermore. **3.** on the other hand: *It might happen, and again it might not.* **4.** back; in return; in reply: *to answer again.* **5.** to the same place or person: *to return again.* **6. again and again,** with frequent repetition; often: *They went over the same arguments again and again.* **7. as much again,** twice as much: *She earns as much again as I do.* [bef. 900; ME *agayn, ageyn,* OE *ongegn* opposite (to), equiv. to *on* ON, in (see A-[1]) + *gegn* straight; c. OHG *ingagan, ingegin* (G *entgegen*), ON *igegn*]
—**Pronunciation.** By far the most common pronunciation of AGAIN, in all parts of the United States, is (ə gen′), with the same vowel heard in *yet* and *pep.* The pronunciation (ə gān′), rhyming with *pain,* occurs chiefly in the Atlantic states. AGAIN said as (ə gin′), with the vowel of *pit* or *sip,* or with a vowel somewhere between (e) and (i), is the common pronunciation in much of the South, where (e) and (i) tend to become neutralized, or more like one another, before (m) and (n), leading to a lack of noticeable distinction between such pairs as *pen* and *pin, ten* and *tin.*

a·gainst (ə genst′, ə gānst′), *prep.* **1.** in opposition to; contrary to; adverse or hostile to: *twenty votes against ten; against reason.* **2.** in resistance to or defense from: *protection against burglars.* **3.** in an opposite direction to: *to ride against the wind.* **4.** into contact or collision with; toward; upon: *The rain beat against the window.* **5.** in contact with: *to lean against the wall.* **6.** in preparation for; in provision for: *money saved against a rainy day.* **7.** having as background: *a design of flowers against a dark wall.* **8.** in exchange for; as a balance to or debit or charge on: *He asked for an advance against his salary.* **9.** in competition with: *a racehorse running against his own record time.* **10.** in comparison or contrast with: *a matter of reason as against emotion.* **11.** beside; near; before: *The car is against the building.* **12. over against,** in contrast with: *the rich over against the poor.* —*conj.* **13.** *Archaic.* before; by the time that. [1125–75; ME *agens, ageynes,* equiv. to *ageyn* AGAIN + *-es* -S[1]; for *-t* cf. WHILST, AMONGST]

A·ga Khan (ä′gə kän′), *Islam.* the divinely ordained head of the Isma'ili branch of Shi'ism.

Aga Khan III, 1877–1957, leader of the Isma'ili sect of Muslims in India 1885–1957.

Aga Khan IV, *(Shah Karim al-Husainy)* born 1936, leader of the Isma'ili sect of Muslims in India since 1957 (grandson of Aga Khan III).

a·gal (ə gäl′), *n.* (among Arabs) a cord wound around a kaffiyeh to hold it in place. [1850–55; < dial. Ar *'agal* var. of *'iqāl* cord, rope]

ag·a·lite (ag′ə līt′), *n. Mineral.* a fibrous variety of talc. [perh. < Gk *agá* (Attic *agé*) fragment, splinter + -LITE]

a·gal·loch (ə gal′ək, ag′ə lok′), *n.* the fragrant, resinous wood of an East Indian tree, *Aquilaria agallocha,* of the mezereum family, used as incense in the Orient. Also called **a·gal·lo·chum** (ə gal′ə kəm), **ag·al·wood** (ag′əl wŏŏd′), **agilawood, aloes, aloeswood, eaglewood, lign aloes.** [1625–35; < LL *agallochon* < Gk *agállochon* (al-

CONCISE ETYMOLOGY KEY: <, descended or borrowed from; >, whence; b., blend of, blended; c., cognate with; cf., compare; deriv., derivative; equiv., equivalent; imit., imitative; obl., oblique; r., replacing; s., stem; sp., spelling, spelled; resp., respelling, respelled; trans., translation; ?, origin unknown; *, unattested; ‡, probably earlier than. See the full key inside the front cover.

tered by influence of *agállein* to decorate); ult. of Dravidian orig.; see EAGLEWOOD]

ag·a·ma (ag′ə mə), *n.* any of numerous agamid lizards of the genus *Agama*, many of which are brilliantly colored and have the ability to change the color of the skin. [1810–20; < NL < Carib]

A·ga·ma (ä′gə mə), *n. Hinduism, Buddhism.* any of the Tantric writings. [< Skt *āgama* tradition, traditional work]

Ag·a·me·de (ag′ə mē′dē), *n. Class. Myth.* a daughter of Augeas noted for her skill at using herbs for healing.

Ag·a·mem·non (ag′ə mem′non, -nən), *n.* **1.** *Class. Myth.* a king of Mycenae, a son of Atreus and brother of Menelaus. He led the Greeks in the Trojan War and was murdered by Clytemnestra, his wife, upon his return from Troy. **2.** (*italics*) a tragedy (458 B.C.) by Aeschylus. Cf. ***Oresteia.*** [< Gk *Agamémnon-* (s. of *Agamémnōn*), < **Agaménmon-*, equiv. to *aga-* great + *men-* (truncation of MENELAUS, meaning king) + *-mon-* suffix used in shortened names]

a·gam·ete (ā gam′ēt, ā′gə mēt′), *n. Cell Biol.* an asexual reproductive cell, as a spore, that forms a new organism without fusion with another cell. [1915–20; < Gk *agámet(os)* unmarried, equiv. to *a-* A-[6] + *-gametos* married, deriv. of *gamétēs*; see GAMETE]

a·gam·ic (ə gam′ik), *adj.* **1.** *Biol.* **a.** asexual. **b.** occurring without sexual union; germinating without impregnation; not gamic. **2.** *Bot., Mycol.* cryptogamic. Also, **ag·a·mous** (ag′ə məs). [1840–50; < Gk *ágam(os)* unwed (*a-* A-[6] + *gámos* marriage) + -IC] **—a·gam′i·cal·ly,** *adv.*

ag·a·mid (ag′ə mid), *n.* **1.** any of numerous Old World lizards of the family Agamidae, related to the iguanids. *—adj.* **2.** belonging or pertaining to the Agamidae. [1885–90; < NL *Agamidae*; see AGAMA, -ID[2]]

a·gam·ma·glob·u·li·ne·mi·a (ā′gam ə glob′yə lə nē′mē ə), *n. Pathol.* a condition of the blood, either congenital or acquired, in which there is near or complete absence of gamma globulin and a failure of the body to form antibodies, resulting in a frequent occurrence of infectious disease. [1950–55; A-[6] + GAMMA GLOBULIN + -EMIA] **—a′gam·ma·glob′u·li·ne′mic,** *adj.*

ag·a·mo·gen·e·sis (ag′ə mō jen′ə sis, ā′gam ə-), *n. Biol.* asexual reproduction by buds, offshoots, cell division, etc. [1860–65; < Gk *ágamo(s)* (see AGAMIC) + -GENESIS] **—ag·a·mo·ge·net·ic** (ag′ə mō jə net′ik, ā′gam ə-), *adj.* **—ag′a·mo·ge·net′i·cal·ly,** *adv.*

ag·a·mo·sper·my (ag′ə mō spûr′mē, ā gam′ə-), *n. Biol.* any form of reproduction, as parthenogenesis, apogamy, and apospory, that involves the sex cell but takes place without fertilization or meiosis. [1940–45; < Gk *ágam(os)* (see AGAMIC) + -O- + -SPERM + -Y[3]]

ag·a·my (ag′ə mē), *n.* the absence of a rule dictating marriage choices within a social group. [1790–1800; < Gk *agamía*, equiv. to *ágam(os)* (see AGAMIC) + *-ia* -Y[3]]

A·gá·ña (ä gä′nyä), *n.* a seaport in and the capital of Guam. 2119.

ag·a·pan·thus (ag′ə pan′thəs), *n., pl.* **-thus·es.** any of several plants of the genus *Agapanthus*, of the amaryllis family, native to Africa, having sword-shaped leaves and umbels of blue or white flowers. Cf. **lily-of-the-Nile.** [< NL (1789) < Gk *agáp(ē)* love + *ánthos* flower]

a·gape[1] (ə gāp′, ə gap′), *adv., adj.* **1.** with the mouth wide open, as in wonder, surprise, or eagerness: *We stood there agape at the splendor.* **2.** wide open: *his mouth agape.* [1660–70; A-[1] + GAPE]

a·ga·pe[2] (ä gä′pā, ä′gə pā′, ag′ə-), *n., pl.* **-pae** (-pī, -pī′, -pē′), **-pai** (-pī, -pī′) for 3. **1.** the love of God or Christ for humankind. **2.** the love of Christians for other persons, corresponding to the love of God for humankind. **3.** unselfish love of one person for another without sexual implications; brotherly love. **4.** See **love feast** (defs. 1, 2). [1600–10; < Gk *agápē* love]

Ag·a·pe·tus I (ag′ə pē′təs), **Saint,** died A.D. 536, Italian ecclesiastic: pope 535–536.

Agapetus II, died A.D. 955, Italian ecclesiastic: pope 946–955.

a·gar (ä′gär, ag′ər), *n.* **1.** Also, **a′gar-a′gar.** Also called **Chinese gelatin, Chinese isinglass, Japanese gelatin, Japanese isinglass.** a gelatinlike product of certain seaweeds, used for solidifying certain culture media, as a thickening agent for ice cream and other foods, as a substitute for gelatin, in adhesives, as an emulsifier, etc. **2.** *Biol.* a culture medium having an agar base. [1885–90; < Malay *agaragar* seaweed from which a gelatin is rendered, or the gelatin itself]

A·gar (ā′gär), *n. Douay Bible.* Hagar.

ag·a·ric (ag′ə rik, ə gar′ik), *n.* any fungus of the family Agaricaceae, including several common edible mushrooms. [1525–35; < NL *Agaricus* genus name < Gk *agarikós* (adj.) pertaining to *Agaría*, a town in Sarmatis; neut. *agarikón* used as n., name of some fungi]

a·gar·i·ca·ceous (ə gar′ə kā′shəs), *adj.* belonging to the Agaricaceae, a family of fungi including mushrooms having blade-shaped gills on the underside of the cap. [< NL *Agaricace(ae)* (see AGARIC, -ACEAE) + -OUS]

ag′aric ac′id, *Chem.* a white, microcrystalline, water-soluble powder, $C_{22}H_{40}O_7$: formerly used in medicine to stop excessive perspiration. Also, **ag′a·ric′ic ac′id** (ag′ə ris′ik, ag′-). [1875–80]

a·gar·i·cin (ə gar′ə sin, -sən), *n. Chem.* an impure form of agaric acid: formerly used in medicine as an agent for stopping excessive perspiration. [AGARIC + -IN[2]]

ag′aric min′eral. See **rock milk.** [1830–40]

a·gar·i·cus (ə gar′i kəs), *n., pl.* **-cus·es.** any mushroom of the genus *Agaricus*, comprising the meadow mushrooms and a commercially grown species, *A. brunnescens.* [< NL. See AGARIC]

ag·a·ri·ta (ag′ə rē′tə, ä′gə-), *n.* a tall shrub, *Mahonia trifoliolata*, of the barberry family, of southwestern North America, having stiff, oblong leaflets with spiny teeth and a red fruit used in jelly. Also, **algerita.** [1885–90, *Amer.*; < MexSp *agrito*, prob. deriv. of Sp *agrio* bitter, OSp *agro* < L *ācer-* (s. of *ācer* sharp)]

a·gar·ose (ä′gə rōs′, -rōz′), *n. Chem.* a substance obtained from agar and used for chromatographic separations. [1965–70; AGAR + -OSE[2]]

Ag·as·siz (ag′ə sē; *for 2 also Fr.* A GA SĒ′), *n.* **1. Alexander,** 1835–1910, U.S. oceanographer and marine zoologist, born in Switzerland. **2.** his father, **(Jean) Louis (Ro·dolphe)** (zhäɴ lwē RÔ dôlf′), 1807–73, U.S. zoologist and geologist, born in Switzerland. **3. Lake,** a lake existing in the prehistoric Pleistocene Epoch in central N America. 700 mi. (1127 km) long.

A·gas·tro·phus (ə gas′trə fəs), *n.* (in the *Iliad*) a son of Paeon who was slain by Diomedes.

A·gas·tya (ä′gəs tyə), *n.* the legendary Aryan sage who introduced the Vedas to southern India.

ag·a·ta (ag′ə tə), *n.* an American art glass having a mottled, glossy, white and rose surface. [< It: AGATE < L *achātēs*]

ag·ate (ag′it), *n.* **1.** a variegated chalcedony showing curved, colored bands or other markings. **2.** a playing marble made of this substance, or of glass in imitation of it. **3.** *Print.* a 5½-point type of a size between pearl and nonpareil. Cf. **ruby** (def. 5). [1150–1200; ME *ac(c)ate, achate, agaten* (cf. D *agaat*, OS *agāt*, OHG *agat*), appar. < OF *agathe* or It *agata* (initial stress) << ML *achātēs* < Gk *achā́tēs*] **—ag′ate·like′, ag′a·toid′,** *adj.*

ag′ate line′, a measure of advertising space, 1/14 of an inch deep and one column wide. [1880–85]

ag·ate·ware (ag′it wâr′), *n.* **1.** steel or iron household ware enameled in an agatelike pattern. **2.** pottery variegated to resemble agate. [1855–60; AGATE + WARE[1]]

Ag·a·tha (ag′ə thə), *n.* a female given name: from a Greek word meaning "good."

Ag·a·tho (ag′ə thō′), *n.* **Saint,** died A.D. 681, Sicilian ecclesiastic: pope 678–681.

A·gath·o·cles (ə gath′ə klēz′), *n.* 361–289 B.C., tyrant of Syracuse 317–289.

Ag·a·thon (ag′ə thon′), *n.* c450–c400 B.C., Greek poet and dramatist.

ag·at·ize (ag′ə tīz′), *v.t.,* **-ized, -iz·ing.** to change into or make like agate. Also, *esp. Brit.,* **ag′at·ise′.** [AGATE + -IZE]

à gauche (A gōsh′), *French.* on or to the left-hand side.

a·ga·ve (ə gä′vē, ə gä′-), *n.* any of numerous American plants belonging to the genus *Agave*, of the agave family, species of which are cultivated for economic or ornamental purposes: *A. arizonica*, of central Arizona, is an endangered species. [< NL (Linnaeus) < Gk *agauḗ*, fem. of *agauós* noble, brilliant]

aga′ve fam′ily, the plant family Agavaceae, characterized by herbaceous or woody plants having rhizomes, a basal cluster of toothed, sword-shaped leaves, and a tall, dense spike of flowers, including the agave, century plant, dracaena, sansevieria, sisal, and yucca.

Ag·a·wam (ag′ə wom′), *n.* a city in W central Massachusetts. 26,271.

a·gaze (ə gāz′), *adj.* staring intently; gazing: *The children were agaze at the Christmas tree.* [1400–50; late ME. See A-[1], GAZE]

ag·ba (ag′bə), *n.* **1.** a tropical tree, *Gossweilerodendron balsamiferum*, of the legume family. **2.** the hard, strong, mahoganylike wood of this tree, used for veneers. [1915–20; < Edo *ágbá*]

AGC, 1. advanced graduate certificate. **2.** automatic gain control. Also, **A.G.C.**

agcy., agency.

age (āj), *n., v.,* **aged, ag·ing** or **age·ing.** *—n.* **1.** the length of time during which a being or thing has existed; length of life or existence to the time spoken of or referred to: *trees of unknown age; His age is 20 years.* **2.** a period of human life, measured by years from birth, usually marked by a certain stage or degree of mental or physical development and involving legal responsibility and capacity: *the age of discretion; the age of consent; The state raised the drinking age from 18 to 21 years.* **3.** the particular period of life at which a person becomes naturally or conventionally qualified or disqualified for anything: *He was over age for military duty.* **4.** one of the periods or stages of human life: *a person of middle age.* **5.** advanced years; old age: *His eyes were dim with age.* **6.** a particular period of history, as distinguished from others; a historical epoch: *the age of Pericles; the Stone Age; the age of electronic communications.* **7.** the period of history contemporary with the span of an individual's life: *He was the most famous architect of the age.* **8.** a generation or a series of generations: *ages yet unborn.* **9.** a great length of time: *I haven't seen you for an age. He's been gone for ages.* **10.** the average life expectancy of an individual or of the individuals of a class or species: *The age of a horse is from 25 to 30 years.* **11.** *Psychol.* the level of mental, emotional, or educational development of a person, esp. a child, as determined by various tests and based on a comparison of the individual's score with the average score for persons of the same chronological age. **12.** *Geol.* **a.** a period of the history of the earth distinguished by some special feature: *the Ice Age.* **b.** a unit of geological time, shorter than an epoch, during which the rocks comprising a stage were formed. **13.** any of the successive periods in human history divided, according to Hesiod, into the golden, silver, bronze, heroic, and iron ages. **14.** *Cards.* **a.** *Poker.* the first player at the dealer's left. Cf. **edge** (def. 10a). **b.** See **eldest hand. 15. of age,** *Law.* **a.** being any of several ages, usually 21 or 18, at which certain legal rights, as voting or marriage, are acquired. **b.** being old enough for full legal rights and responsibilities. *—v.i.* **16.** to grow old: *He is aging rapidly.* **17.** to mature, as wine, cheese, or wood: *a heavy port that ages slowly.* *—v.t.* **18.** to make old; cause to grow or seem old: *Fear aged him overnight.* **19.** to bring to maturity or a state fit for use: *to age wine.* **20.** to store (a permanent magnet, a capacitor, or other similar device) so that its electrical or magnetic characteristics become constant. [1225–75; (n.) ME < AF, OF *aage, eage*, equiv. to *aé* (< L *aetātem* acc. of *ae(vi)tās* age; *aev(um)* time, lifetime + *-itās* -ITY) + *-age* -AGE; (v.) ME *agen*, deriv. of the n.]
—Syn. 6. AGE, EPOCH, ERA, PERIOD all refer to an extent of time. AGE usually implies a considerable extent of time, esp. one associated with a dominant personality, influence, characteristic, or institution: *the age of chivalry.* EPOCH and ERA are often used interchangeably to refer to an extent of time characterized by changed conditions and new undertakings: *an era (or epoch) of invention.* EPOCH sometimes refers especially to the beginning of an era: *the steam engine—an epoch in technology.* A PERIOD may be long or short, but usually has a marked condition or feature: *the glacial period; a period of expansion.* **17.** ripen, mellow, develop.

-age, a suffix typically forming mass or abstract nouns from various parts of speech, occurring originally in loanwords from French (*voyage; courage*) and productive in English with the meanings "aggregate" (*coinage; peerage; trackage*), "process" (*coverage; breakage*), "the outcome of" as either "the fact of" or "the physical effect or remains of" (*seepage; wreckage; spoilage*), "place of living or business" (*parsonage; brokerage*), "social standing or relationship" (*bondage; marriage; patronage*), and "quantity, measure, or charge" (*footage; shortage; tonnage; towage*). [ME < OF < L *-āticum*, neut. of *-āticus* adj. suffix; an extension of L *-āta* -ATE[1], whose range of senses it reflects closely]

Ag.E., Agricultural Engineer.

A.G.E., Associate in General Education.

a·ged (ā′jid *for 1, 2, 5, 6;* ājd *for 1, 3, 4*), *adj.* **1.** having lived or existed long; of advanced age; old: *an aged man; an aged tree.* **2.** pertaining to or characteristic of old age: *aged wrinkles.* **3.** of the age of: *a man aged 40 years.* **4.** brought to maturity or mellowness, as wine, cheese, or wood: *aged whiskey.* **5.** *Phys. Geog.* old; approaching the state of peneplain. *—n.* **6.** (*used with a plural v.*) old people collectively (usually prec. by *the*): *We must have improved medical care for the aged.* [1375–1425; late ME. See AGE, -ED[2]] **—a′ged·ly,** *adv.* **—a′ged·ness,** *n.*
—Syn. 1. ancient. See **old.** **—Ant. 1.** young.

agee (ə jē′) *adv. Brit. Dial.* to one side; awry. Also, **ajee.** [1790–1800; A-[1] + GEE]

A·gee (ā′jē), *n.* **James,** 1909–55, U.S. author, scenarist, and film critic.

age′ group′, persons of approximately the same age and often of the same sex, nationality, educational or social background, etc. [1900–05]

age·ing (ā′jing), *n.* aging.

age·ism (ā′jiz əm), *n.* **1.** discrimination against persons of a certain age group. **2.** a tendency to regard older persons as debilitated, unworthy of attention, or unsuitable for employment. [1965–70; AGE + -ISM, on the model of SEXISM, RACISM, etc.] **—age′ist,** *adj., n.*

Ag·e·la·us (aj′ə lā′əs), *n. Class. Myth.* **1.** the herdsman of Priam who raised Paris. **2.** a son of Hercules and Omphale. **3.** (in the *Iliad*) a son of Phradmon who was killed by Diomedes. **4.** (in the *Odyssey*) one of the suitors of Penelope.

age·less (āj′lis), *adj.* **1.** not aging or appearing to age. **2.** lasting forever; eternal; undying: *the ageless beauty of Greek sculpture.* [1645–55; AGE + -LESS] **—age′less·ly,** *adv.* **—age′less·ness,** *n.*

age·long (āj′lông′, -long′), *adj.* lasting for an age. [1800–10; AGE + LONG]

age·mate (āj′māt′), *n.* a person of about the same age as another: *The student is far behind her agemates in reading comprehension.* [1575–85; AGE + MATE[1]]

A·ge·na (ə jē′nə), *n. Rocketry.* a U.S. upper stage, with a restartable liquid-propellant engine, used with various booster stages to launch satellites into orbit around the earth and send probes to the moon and planets: also used as a docking target in the Gemini program.

A·ge·nais (AZHᵊ NE′), *n.* an ancient region of SW France. Also, **A·ge·nois** (AZHᵊ NWA′).

a·gen·cy (ā′jən sē), *n., pl.* **-cies. 1.** an organization, company, or bureau that provides some service for another: *a welfare agency.* **2.** a company having a franchise to represent another. **3.** a governmental bureau, or an office that represents it. **4.** the place of business of an agent. **5.** See **Indian agency. 6.** an administrative division of a government. **7.** the duty or function of an agent. **8.** the relationship between a principal and his or her agent. **9.** the state of being in action or of exerting power; operation: *the agency of Providence.* **10.** a means of exerting power or influence; instrumentality: *nominated by the agency of friends.* [1650–60; < ML *agentia*, equiv. to L *ag-* (root of *agere* to do, act, manage) + *-entia* -ENCY]
—Syn. 10. intercession, good offices.

A′gency for Interna′tional Devel′opment. See **AID**

a′gency shop′, a shop in which the union represents all workers in the bargaining unit and collects dues and fees from nonunion members. [1945–50]

a•gen•da (ə jen′də), *n., formally a pl. of* **agendum,** *but usually used as a sing. with pl.* **-das** *or* **-da.** a list, plan, outline, or the like, of things to be done, matters to be acted or voted upon, etc.: *The chairman says we have a lengthy agenda this afternoon.* [1745–55; < L, pl. of *agendum* that which is to be done, ger. of *agere* to do; the pl. orig. carried a collective sense denoting the various items to be transacted] **—a•gen′da•less,** *adj.*
—Usage. AGENDA, "things to be done," is the plural of the Latin gerund *agendum* and is used today in the sense "a plan or list of matters to be acted upon." In that sense it is treated as a singular noun; its plural is usually *agendas: The agenda is ready for distribution. The agendas of last year's meetings are printed in the official minutes.* The singular AGENDUM, meaning "an item on an agenda," is rare.

a•gen•dum (ə jen′dəm), *n., pl.* **-da** (-də), **-dums. 1.** an agenda. **2.** something that is to be done. **3.** an item on an agenda. [1895–1900; < L, ger. of *agere* to do]
—Usage. See **agenda.**

a•gen•e•sis (ā jen′ə sis), *n. Pathol.* **1.** absence of or failed development of a body part. **2.** sterility; impotence; barrenness. Also, **a•ge•ne•sia** (ā′jə nē′zhə, -zhē ə -sē ə). [1850–55; < NL; see A-⁶, GENESIS] **—a•ge•net•ic** (ā′jə net′ik), *adj.*

a•ge•nize (ā′jə nīz′), *v.t.,* **-nized, -niz•ing.** to bleach (flour) with nitrogen trichloride. Also, *esp. Brit.,* **a′ge•nise′.** [1945–50; *agene* U.S. trade name for nitrogen trichloride + -IZE]

a•gent (ā′jənt), *n.* **1.** a person or business authorized to act on another's behalf: *Our agent in Hong Kong will ship the merchandise. A best-selling author needs a good agent.* **2.** a person or thing that acts or has the power to act. **3.** a natural force or object producing or used for obtaining specific results: *Many insects are agents of fertilization.* **4.** an active cause; an efficient cause. **5.** a person who works for or manages an agency. **6.** a person who acts in an official capacity for a government or private agency, as a guard, detective, or spy: *an FBI agent; the secret agents of a foreign power.* **7.** a person responsible for a particular action: *Who was the agent of this deed?* **8.** *Gram.* a form or construction, usually a noun or noun phrase, denoting an animate being that performs or causes the action expressed by the verb, as *the police* in *The car was found by the police.* **9.** See **Indian agent. 10.** a representative of a business firm, esp. a traveling salesperson; canvasser; solicitor. **11.** *Chem.* a substance that causes a reaction. **12.** *Pharm.* a drug or chemical capable of eliciting a biological response. **13.** *Pathol.* any microorganism capable of causing disease. **14.** *Brit.* a campaign manager; an election agent. **—*adj.* 15.** acting; exerting power (opposed to *patient*). [1570–80; < L *agent-* (s. of *agēns* (prp.) doing), equiv. to *ag-* (root of *agere* to do) + *-ent-* -ENT]
—Syn. 1. representative, deputy. **3.** means.

a•gent-gen•er•al (ā′jənt jen′ər əl), *n., pl.* **a•gents-gen•er•al. 1.** a chief representative. **2.** a person sent to England from a British dominion to represent the interests of the dominion. [1910–15]

a•gen•tial (ā jen′shəl), *adj.* **1.** pertaining to an agent or agency. **2.** *Gram.* agentive. [1870–75; AGENT + -IAL]

a•gen•ti•val (ā′jən tī′vəl), *adj.* agentive. [AGENTIVE + -AL¹]

a•gen•tive (ā′jən tiv), *adj. Gram.* **1.** pertaining to, or productive of, a form that indicates an agent or agency. **2.** (in case grammar) pertaining to the semantic role or case of a noun phrase that indicates the volitional or primary causer of the action expressed by a verb. **—*n.* 3.** an agentive word or suffix. **4.** the agentive case. [AGENT + -IVE]

a′gent noun′, *Gram.* a noun denoting the doer of an action, as *editor* or *jogger.* [1875–80]

A′gent Or′ange, a powerful herbicide and defoliant containing trace amounts of dioxin, a toxic impurity suspected of causing serious health problems, including cancer and genetic damage, in some persons exposed to it and birth defects in their offspring: used by U.S. armed forces during the Vietnam War to defoliate jungles. [1965–70; so called from the color of the identifying stripe on the drums in which it was stored]

a•gent pro•vo•ca•teur (ā′jənt prə vok′ə tûr′; *Fr.* A ZHÄN PRÔ VÔ KA TŒR′), *pl.* **a•gents pro•vo•ca•teurs** (ā′jənts prə vok′ə tûr′; *Fr.* A ZHÄN PRÔ VÔ KA TŒR′). a secret agent hired to incite suspected persons to some illegal action, outbreak, etc., that will make them liable to punishment. [1875–80; < F: inciting agent; see PROVOCATION, -EUR]

a•gent•ry (ā′jən trē), *n., pl.* **-ries.** the profession, business, or activities of an agent: *one of the cleverest spies in the history of foreign agentry.* [1920–25; AGENT + -RY]

Age′ of Aquar′ius, an astrological era believed to bring increased spirituality and harmony on earth. Also called **Aquarian Age.** [1965–70]

age′ of consent′, the age at which a person becomes legally competent to consent to marriage or sexual intercourse. [1800–10]

age′ of discre′tion, *Law.* the age at which a person becomes legally responsible for certain acts and competent to exercise certain powers.

Age′ of Rea′son, 1. any period in history, esp. the 18th century in France, England, etc., characterized by a critical approach to religious, social, and philosophical matters that seeks to repudiate beliefs or systems not based on or justifiable by reason. **2.** (*l.c.*) the age at which a person is considered capable of distinguishing between right and wrong.

CONCISE ETYMOLOGY KEY: <, descended or borrowed from; >, whence; b., blend of, blended; c., cognate with; cf., compare; deriv., derivative; equiv., equivalent; imit., imitative; obl., oblique; r., replacing; s., stem; sp., spelling, spelled; resp., respelling, respelled; trans., translation; ?, origin unknown; *, unattested; ‡, probably earlier than. See the full key inside the front cover.

age-old (āj′ōld′), *adj.* ancient; from time immemorial: *an age-old tradition.* [1900–05]

ag•er•a•tum (aj′ə rā′təm, ə jer′ə-), *n.* **1.** any of several composite plants of the genus *Ageratum,* esp. *A. houstonianum,* having heart-shaped leaves and small, dense, blue, lavender, or white flower heads, often grown in gardens. **2.** any of various other composite plants, as the mistflower, having blue or white flowers. [1560–70; < NL; L *agēraton* < Gk *agḗraton,* neut. of *agḗratos* unaging, equiv. to *a-* A-⁶ + *gērat-* (s. of *gêras*) old age + -os adj. suffix]

A•ges•i•la•us II (ə jes′ə lā′əs), 444?–c360 B.C., king of Sparta c400–c360.

a•geu•si•a (ə gyo͞o′zē ə, -zhē ə, -zhə), *n. Pathol.* loss or impairment of the sense of taste. Also, **a•geu•sti•a** (ə gyo͞o′stē ə). [1840–50; < NL, equiv. to A-⁶ + *geus-* (var. s. of Gk *geúesthai* to taste) + *-ia* -Y³] **—a•geu•sic** (ə gyo͞o′zik, -sik), *adj.*

Ag•ga•dah (*Seph. Heb.* ä gä dä′; *Ashk. Heb.* ə gä′də), *n.* the nonlegal or narrative material, as parables, maxims, or anecdotes, in the Talmud and other rabbinical literature, serving either to illustrate the meaning or purpose of the law, custom, or Biblical passage being discussed or to introduce a different, unrelated topic. Also, **Ag•ga•da′, Agada, Haggadah.** [< Heb *haggādhāh,* deriv. of *higgīdh* to narrate; see HAGGADAH] **—Ag•gad•ic, ag•gad•ic** (ə gad′ik, ə gä′dik), *adj.*

ag•ger (aj′ər), *n.* **1.** Also called **double tide.** *Oceanog.* **a.** a high tide in which the water rises to a certain level, recedes, then rises again. **b.** a low tide in which the water recedes to a certain level, rises slightly, then recedes again. **2.** (in ancient Roman building) an earthen mound or rampart, esp. one having no revetment. [1350–1400; ME: heap, pile < L: rubble, mound, rampart, equiv. to *ag-* AG- + *-ger,* base of *gerere* to carry, bring]

Ag•ge•us (ə gē′əs), *n. Douay Bible.* Haggai.

ag•gie¹ (ag′ē), *n.* agate (def. 2). [1875–80]

ag•gie² (ag′ē), *n.* (*sometimes cap.*) *Informal* **1.** an agriculture college. **2.** a student at an agricultural college. [1900–05, *Amer.;* AG(RICULTURAL) + -IE]

Ag•gie (ag′ē), *n.* a female given name, form of **Agatha** or **Agnes.**

ag•gior•na•men•to (ə jôr′nə men′tō; *It.* äd jôr′nä men′tô), *n., pl.* **-ti** (-tē). the act of bringing something up to date to meet current needs. [1960–65; < It, equiv. to *aggiorna(re)* to revise, update (*ag-* AG- + *-giornare,* v. deriv. of *giorno* day < L *diurnus;* see ADJOURN) + *-mento* -MENT]

ag•glom•er•ate (*v.* ə glom′ə rāt′; *adj., n.* ə glom′ər it, -ə rāt′), *v.,* **-at•ed, -at•ing,** *adj., n.* **—*v.t., v.i.* 1.** to collect or gather into a cluster or mass. **—*adj.* 2.** gathered together into a cluster or mass. **3.** *Bot.* crowded into a dense cluster, but not cohering. **—*n.* 4.** a mass of things clustered together. **5.** rock composed of rounded or angular volcanic fragments. [1675–85; < L *agglomerātus* (ptp. of *agglomerāre*), equiv. to *ag-* AG- + *glomer-* (s. of *glomus* ball of yarn) + *-ātus* -ATE¹] **—ag•glom•er•a•tive** (ə glom′ə rā′tiv, -ər ə tiv), *adj.* **—ag•glom′er•a′tor,** *n.*
—Syn. 1. assemble, amass, accumulate. **—Ant. 1.** disperse, scatter.

ag•glom•er•a•tion (ə glom′ə rā′shən), *n.* **1.** a jumbled cluster or mass of varied parts. **2.** the act or process of agglomerating. [1765–75; AGGLOMERATE + -ION]
—Syn. 1. jumble, conglomeration, aggregation, conglomerate, agglomerate, aggregate.

ag•glu•ti•nant (ə glo͞ot′n ənt), *adj.* **1.** uniting, as glue; causing adhesion. **—*n.* 2.** an agglutinating agent. [1675–85; < L *agglūtinant-* (s. of *agglūtināns,* prp. of *agglūtināre*), equiv. to *agglūtin-* (see AGGLUTINATE) + *-ant* -ANT]

ag•glu•ti•nate (*v.* ə glo͞ot′n āt′; *adj.* ə glo͞ot′n it, -āt′), *v.,* **-nat•ed, -nat•ing,** *adj.* **—*v.t., v.i.* 1.** to unite or cause to adhere, as with glue. **2.** *Immunol.* to clump or cause to clump, as bacteria or blood platelets. **3.** *Ling.* to form by agglutination. **—*adj.* 4.** united by or as by glue. **5.** agglutinative. [1535–45; < L *agglūtinātus* (ptp. of *agglūtināre*), equiv. to *ag-* AG- + *glūtin-* (s. of *glūten* glue) + *-ātus* -ATE¹] **—ag•glu•ti•na•bil•i•ty** (ə glo͞ot′n ə bil′i tē), *n.* **—ag•glu′tin•a•ble,** *adj.*

ag•glu•ti•na•tion (ə glo͞ot′n ā′shən), *n.* **1.** the act or process of uniting by glue or other tenacious substance. **2.** the state of being thus united; adhesion of parts. **3.** that which is united; a mass or group cemented together. **4.** *Immunol.* the clumping of bacteria, red blood cells, or other cells, due to the introduction of an antibody. **5.** *Ling.* a process of word formation in which morphemes, each having one relatively constant shape, are combined without fusion or morphophonemic change, and in which each grammatical category is typically represented by a single morpheme in the resulting word, esp. such a process involving the addition of one or more affixes to a base, as in Turkish, in which *ev* means "house," *ev-den* means "from a house," and *ev-ler-den* means "from houses." [1535–45; AGGLUTINATE + -ION]

ag•glu•ti•na•tive (ə glo͞ot′n ā′tiv, ə glo͞ot′n ə-), *adj.* **1.** tending or having power to agglutinate or unite: *an agglutinative substance.* **2.** *Ling.* pertaining to or notting a language, as Turkish, characterized by agglutination. Cf. **inflectional** (def. 2), **isolating.** [1625–35; AGGLUTINATE + -IVE]

ag•glu•ti•nin (ə glo͞ot′n in), *n. Immunol.* an antibody that causes agglutination. [1895–1900; AGGLUTIN(ATE) + -IN²]

ag•glu•tin•o•gen (ag′lo͞o tin′ə jən, -jen′, ə glo͞ot′n ə-), *n. Immunol.* an antigen that causes the production of agglutinins. [1900–05; AGGLUTIN(ATE) + -O- + -GEN] **—ag•glu•tin•o•gen•ic** (ag′lo͞o tin′ə jen′ik, ə glo͞ot′n ə-), *adj.*

ag•grade (ə grād′), *v.t.,* **-grad•ed, -grad•ing.** *Phys. Geog.* to raise the grade or level of (a river valley, a stream bed, etc.) by depositing detritus, sediment, or th[e] like. Cf. **degrade.** [1895–1900; AG- + GRADE] **—ag•gra•da•tion** (ag′rə dā′shən), *n.* **—ag′gra•da′tion•al,** *adj.*

ag•gran•dize (ə gran′dīz, ag′rən dīz′), *v.t.,* **-dized, -diz•ing. 1.** to widen in scope; increase in size or inten[sity]; enlarge; extend. **2.** to make great or greater i[n] power, wealth, rank, or honor. **3.** to make (something) appear greater. Also, *esp. Brit.,* **ag•gran′dise.** [1625–3[5]; < F *aggrandiss-* (long s. of *aggrandir* to magnify), equiv. to *ag-* AG- + *grand* (see GRAND) + *-iss* -ISH², irreg[.] equated with -IZE¹] **—ag•gran•dize•ment** (ə gran′diz mənt), *n.* **—ag•gran•diz•er** (ə gran′dī zər, ag′rən dī′-), *n.*
—Syn. 2. inflate, strengthen, exalt. **3.** magnify. **—Ant. 1.** reduce. **2.** diminish. **3.** minimize.

ag•gra•vate (ag′rə vāt′), *v.t.,* **-vat•ed, -vat•ing. 1.** t[o] make worse or more severe; intensify, as anything evil, disorderly, or troublesome: *to aggravate a grievance; t[o] aggravate an illness.* **2.** to annoy; irritate; exasperate: *His questions aggravate her.* **3.** to cause to become irri[tated] or inflamed: *The child's constant scratching ag[gravated the rash.* [1425–75; late ME < L *aggravātu[s]* (ptp. of *aggravāre*), equiv. to *ag-* AG- + *grav-* (se[e] GRAVE²) + *-ātus* -ATE¹; cf. AGGRIEVE] **—ag′gra•va′tive** *adj.* **—ag′gra•va′tor,** *n.*
—Syn. 1. heighten, increase. AGGRAVATE, INTENSIF[Y] both mean to increase in degree. To AGGRAVATE is t[o] make more serious or more grave: *to aggravate a dan[ger,] an offense, a wound.* To INTENSIFY is perceptibly t[o] increase intensity, force, energy, vividness, etc.: *to inten[sify] heat, color, rage.* **2.** anger, vex, rile. **—Ant. 1** alleviate.
—Usage. The two most common senses of AGGRAVAT[E] are "to make worse" and "to annoy or exasperate." Bot[h] senses first appeared in the early 17th century at almos[t] the same time; the corresponding two senses of the nou[n] AGGRAVATION also appeared then. Both senses of AGGRAVATE and AGGRAVATION have been standard since the[n.] The use of AGGRAVATE to mean "annoy" is sometimes ob[jected to because it departs from the etymological mean[ing] "to make heavier," and in formal speech and writin[g] the sense "annoy" is somewhat less frequent than "t[o] make worse." The noun AGGRAVATION meaning "annoy[ance"] occurs in all types of speech and writing.

ag•gra•vat•ed (ag′rə vā′tid), *adj. Law.* characterize[d] by some feature defined by law that enhances the crime, as the intention of the criminal or the special vulnerabil[ity] of the victim: *aggravated assault; aggravated rape.* [1540–50; AGGRAVATE + -ED²]

ag•gra•vat•ing (ag′rə vā′ting), *adj.* causing or full o[f] aggravation: *I've had an aggravating day.* [1630–40; AG[GRAVATE] + -ING²] **—ag′gra•vat′ing•ly,** *adv.*

ag•gra•va•tion (ag′rə vā′shən), *n.* **1.** an increase i[n] intensity, seriousness, or severity; act of making worse: *an aggravation of pain.* **2.** the state of being ag[gravated.] **3.** something that causes an increase in inten[sity,] degree, or severity. **4.** annoyance; exasperation: *Johnny causes me so much aggravation!* **5.** a source o[r] cause of annoyance or exasperation: *Johnny's such a[n] aggravation to her!* [1475–85; < ML *aggravātiōn-* (s. of *aggravātiō*); see AGGRAVATE, -ION]
—Usage. See **aggravate.**

ag•gre•gate (*adj., n.* ag′ri git, -gāt′; *v.* ag′ri gāt′), *adj., n., v.,* **-gat•ed, -gat•ing. —*adj.* 1.** formed by th[e] conjunction or collection of particulars into a whole mas[s] or sum; total; combined: *the aggregate amount of indebt[edness.]* **2.** *Bot.* **a.** (of a flower) formed of florets col[lected] in a dense cluster but not cohering, as the daisy. **b.** (of a fruit) composed of a cluster of carpels belonging to the same flower, as the raspberry. **3.** *Geol.* (of a rock) consisting of a mixture of minerals separable by me[chanical] means. **—*n.* 4.** a sum, mass, or assemblage o[f] particulars; a total or gross amount: *the aggregate of al[l] past experience.* **5.** a cluster of soil granules not large[r] than a small crumb. **6.** any of various loose, particulat[e] materials, as sand, gravel, or pebbles, added to a cement[-]ing agent to make concrete, plaster, etc. **7.** *Math.* se[e] (def. 110). **8. in the aggregate,** taken or considered a[s] a whole: *In the aggregate, our losses have been relativel[y] small.* **—*v.t.* 9.** to bring together; collect into one sum, mass, or body. **10.** to amount to (the number of): *Th[e] guns captured will aggregate five or six hundred.* **—*v.i.* 11.** to combine and form a collection or mass. [1375–1425; late ME < L *aggregātus* (ptp. of *aggregāre*), equiv. to *ag-* AG- + *greg-* (s. of *grex* flock) + *-ātus* -ATE¹] **—ag•gre•ga•ble** (ag′ri gə bəl), *adj.* **—ag′gre•gate•ly** *adv.* **—ag′gre•gate•ness,** *n.* **—ag•gre•ga•to•ry** (ag′ri gə tôr′ē, -tōr′ē), *adj.*
—Syn. 1. added, complete, whole. **9.** assemble, amass, accumulate, gather.

ag•gre•ga•tion (ag′ri gā′shən), *n.* **1.** a group or mas[s] of distinct or varied things, persons, etc.: *an aggregatio[n] of complainants.* **2.** collection into an unorganize[d] whole. **3.** the state of being so collected. **4.** *Biol., Ecol.* a group of organisms of the same or different species liv[-]ing closely together but less integrated than a society. [1540–50; < ML *aggregātiōn-* (s. of *aggregātiō*); see AGGREGATE, -ION] **—ag′gre•ga′tion•al,** *adj.*

ag•gre•ga•tive (ag′ri gā′tiv), *adj.* **1.** of or pertainin[g] to an aggregate. **2.** forming or tending to form an ag[gregate.] [1635–45; AGGREGATE + -IVE] **—ag′gre•ga′tive•ly,** *adv.*

ag•gress (ə gres′), *v.i.* **1.** to commit the first act o[f] hostility or offense; attack first. **2.** to begin to quarrel. **—*v.t.* 3.** to behave aggressively toward; attack (often fol. by *upon*): *wild animals aggressing their prey.* [1565–75; < L *aggressus* (ptp. of *aggredī* to attack), equiv. to *ag-* AG- + *gred-* (see GRADE) + *-tus* ptp. suffix]

ag•gres•sion (ə gresh′ən), *n.* **1.** the action of a state in violating by force the rights of another state, particu[-]larly its territorial rights; an unprovoked offensive, attack, invasion, or the like: *The army is prepared to sto[p] any foreign aggression.* **2.** any offensive action, attack, or procedure; an inroad or encroachment: *an aggressio[n] upon one's rights.* **3.** the practice of making assaults o[r] attacks; offensive action in general. **4.** *Psychiatry.* over[t] or suppressed hostility, either innate or resulting from continued frustration and directed outward or against oneself. [1605–15; < L *aggressiōn-* (s. of *aggressiō*), equiv. to *aggress(us)* (see AGGRESS) + *-iōn-* -ION] —**Ant. 1.** peacefulness.

ag•gres•sive (ə gres′iv), *adj.* **1.** characterized by or tending toward unprovoked offensives, attacks, invasions, or the like; militantly forward or menacing: *aggressive acts against a neighboring country.* **2.** making an all-out effort to win or succeed; competitive: *an aggressive basketball player.* **3.** vigorously energetic, esp. in the use of initiative and forcefulness: *an aggressive salesperson.* **4.** boldly assertive and forward; pushy: *an aggressive driver.* **5.** emphasizing maximum growth and capital gains over quality, security, and income: *an aggressive mutual fund.* [1815–25; AGGRESS(ION) + -IVE] —**ag•gres′sive•ly,** *adv.* —**ag•gres′sive•ness, ag•gres•siv•i•ty** (ag′re siv′i tē), *n.*
—**Syn. 1.** pugnacious, militant. **2.** forceful, enterprising, assertive. —**Ant. 1.** friendly. **2.** retiring, shy, timid, hesitant.

ag•gres•sor (ə gres′ər), *n.* a person, group, or nation that attacks first or initiates hostilities; an assailant or invader. [1670–80; < LL, L *aggred-* (s. of *aggredī* to attack; see AGGRESS) + *-tor* -TOR]

ag•grieve (ə grēv′), *v.t.,* **-grieved, -griev•ing. 1.** to oppress or wrong grievously; injure by injustice. **2.** to afflict with pain, anxiety, etc. [1250–1300; ME *agreven* < MF *agrever* < L *aggravāre* to make heavy, worsen, equiv. to *ag-* AG- + *grav-* (see GRAVE[2]) + *-āre* inf. suffix; cf. AGGRAVATE] —**ag•grieve′ment,** *n.*

ag•grieved (ə grēvd′), *adj.* **1.** wronged, offended, or injured: *He felt himself aggrieved.* **2.** *Law.* deprived of legal rights or claims. **3.** troubled; worried; disturbed; unhappy. [1250–1300; ME; see AGGRIEVE, -ED[2]] —**ag•griev•ed•ly** (ə grē′vid lē), *adv.* —**ag•griev′ed•ness,** *n.*
—**Syn. 1.** abused, harmed, wounded.

ag•gro (ag′rō), *n. Brit. and Australian Informal.* **1.** aggressiveness, esp. that of an urban youth gang or gang member. **2.** trouble; irritation. [1965–70; construed as a shortening of either AGGRAVATION or AGGRESSION (or AGGRESSIVE); see -O]

Agh., Afghani (def. 3).

a•gha (ä′gə), *n.* aga.

a•ghast (ə gast′, ə gäst′), *adj.* struck with overwhelming shock or amazement; filled with sudden fright or horror: *They stood aghast at the sight of the plane crashing.* [1225–75; ME *agast* frightened, ptp. of *agasten,* equiv. to *a-* A-[3] + *gasten,* OE *gǣstan* to frighten, earlier **gāstjan* < Gmc causative **gaistjan;* see GHOST]

AGI, See **adjusted gross income.**

ag•i•la•wood (ag′ə lə wo͝od′), *n.* agalloch. [1690–1700; *agila* (< Pg *aguila;* see EAGLEWOOD) + WOOD[1]]

ag•ile (aj′əl, -īl), *adj.* **1.** quick and well-coordinated in movement; lithe: *an agile leap.* **2.** active; lively: *an agile person.* **3.** marked by an ability to think quickly; mentally acute or aware: *She's 95 and still very agile.* [1570–80; earlier *agil* < L *agilis,* equiv. to *ag-* (base of *agere* to do) + *-ilis* -ILE] —**ag′ile•ly,** *adv.* —**ag′ile•ness,** *n.*
—**Syn. 1.** nimble, sprightly. **2.** brisk, spry. —**Ant. 1.** awkward. **2.** sluggish, lethargic.

a•gil•i•ty (ə jil′i tē), *n.* **1.** the power of moving quickly and easily; nimbleness: *exercises demanding agility.* **2.** the ability to think and draw conclusions quickly; intellectual acuity. [1375–1425; late ME *agilite* < MF < L *agilitās.* See AGILE, -ITY]

a•gin (ə gin′), *prep. Dial.* against; opposed to. [1815–25; see AGAIN]

Ag•in•court (aj′in kôrt′, -kōrt′; *Fr.* A zhan ko͞or′), *n.* a village in N France, near Calais: victory of the English over the French 1415. 276.

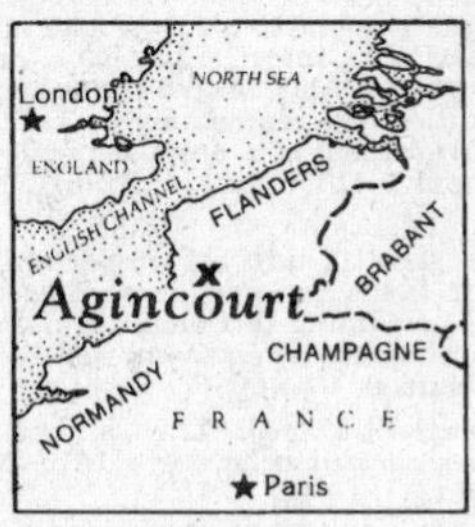

a•gin•ner (ə gin′ər), *n. Informal.* a person who opposes a plan, proposed legislation, or any drastic change: *He won the election by appealing to the aginners.* [AGIN + -ER[1]]

ag•i•o (aj′ē ō′), *n., pl.* **-os. 1.** a premium on money in exchange. **2.** an allowance for the difference in value of two currencies. **3.** an allowance given or taken on bills of exchange from other countries, as to balance exchange expenses. **4.** agiotage. [1675–85; < It *a(g)gio* exchange, premium, ult. < MGk *allágion,* deriv. of Gk *allagḗ* lit., change, barter; cf. Venetian *azo,* ML *lazius*]

ag•i•o•tage (aj′ē ə tij), *n.* the business of dealing in foreign exchange. [1820–30; < F, equiv. to *agiot(er)* to speculate (*agiot* exchange < It *aggio* AGIO) + *-age* -AGE]

a•gist (ə jist′), *v.t.* to feed or pasture (livestock) for a fee. [1590–1600; < AF, MF *agister* to give lodgings to, equiv. to *a-* A-[5] + *gister* to lodge, lie < Gmc; cf. OE *giestian* to lodge, deriv. of *giest* GUEST] —**a•gist′er, a•gis′tor,** *n.*

a•gist•ment (ə jist′ment), *n. Obs.* **1.** the act of agisting. **2.** a contract or an agreement to agist. **3.** the fee paid or the profit made in agisting. [1605–15; AGIST + -MENT]

agit., (in prescriptions) shake, stir. [< L *agitā*]

ag•i•tate (aj′i tāt′), *v.,* **-tat•ed, -tat•ing.** —*v.t.* **1.** to move or force into violent, irregular action: *The hurricane winds agitated the sea.* **2.** to shake or move briskly: *The machine agitated the mixture.* **3.** to move to and fro; impart regular motion to. **4.** to disturb or excite emotionally; arouse; perturb: *a crowd agitated to a frenzy by impassioned oratory; a man agitated by disquieting news.* **5.** to call attention to by speech or writing; discuss; debate: *to agitate the question.* **6.** to consider on all sides; revolve in the mind; plan. —*v.i.* **7.** to arouse or attempt to arouse public interest and support, as in some political or social cause or theory: *to agitate for the repeal of a tax.* [1580–90; < L *agitātus* (ptp. of *agitāre* to set in motion), equiv. to *ag-* (root of *agere* to drive) + *-it-* freq. suffix + *-ātus* -ATE[1]] —**ag•i•ta•ble** (aj′i tə bəl), *adj.* —**ag′i•ta′tive,** *adj.*
—**Syn. 1.** disturb, toss. **3.** wave. **4.** ruffle, fluster, roil. **5.** dispute. —**Ant. 1.** calm, soothe.

ag•i•tat•ed (aj′i tā′tid), *adj.* excited; disturbed. —**ag′i•tat′ed•ly,** *adv.*

ag′itated depres′sion, *Psychiatry.* a severe depression accompanied by constant restlessness.

ag•i•ta•tion (aj′i tā′shən), *n.* **1.** the act or process of agitating; state of being agitated: *She left in great agitation.* **2.** persistent urging of a political or social cause or theory before the public. **3.** Also called **psychomotor agitation.** psychological and physical restlessness, manifested by pacing, hand-wringing, or other activity, sometimes occurring as a symptom of severe depression, schizophrenia, or other mental disorder. [1560–70; < L *agitātiōn-* (s. of *agitātiō*); see AGITATE, -ION] —**ag′i•ta′•tion•al,** *adj.*
—**Syn. 1.** tumult, storm; unrest, disquiet; struggle, conflict; perturbation, ado. AGITATION, DISTURBANCE, EXCITEMENT, TURMOIL imply inner unrest, uneasiness, or apprehension. AGITATION implies a shaken state of emotions, usually perceptible in the face or movements: *With evident agitation she opened the telegram.* DISTURBANCE implies an inner disquiet caused by worry, indecision, apprehension, or the like: *Long-continued mental disturbance is a cause of illness.* EXCITEMENT implies a highly emotional state caused by either agreeable or distressing circumstances: *excitement over a proposed trip, unexpected good news, a fire.* TURMOIL suggests such a struggle or conflict of emotions that one is unable to think consecutively: *Her thoughts were in a hopeless turmoil.* **2.** debate, discussion, argument.

a•gi•ta•to (aj′i tä′tō; *It.* ä′jē tä′tô), *adj. Music.* agitated; restless or hurried in movement or style. [1885–90; < It < L *agitātus.* See AGITATE]

ag•i•ta•tor (aj′i tā′tər), *n.* **1.** a person who stirs up others in order to upset the status quo and further a political, social, or other cause: *The boss said he would fire any union agitators.* **2.** a machine or device for agitating and mixing. [1730–40; AGITATE + -OR[2]] —**ag•i•ta•to•ri•al** (aj′i tə tôr′ē əl, -tōr′-), *adj.*

ag•it•prop (aj′it prop′), *n.* **1.** agitation and propaganda, esp. for the cause of communism. **2.** (*often cap.*) an agency or department, as of a government, that directs and coordinates agitation and propaganda. **3.** Also, **ag′it•prop′ist.** a person who is trained or takes part in such activities. —*adj.* **4.** of or pertaining to agitprop. [1930–35; < Russ *Agitpróp,* orig. for *Agitatsiónno-propagandístskiĭ otdél* Agitation Propaganda Section (of the Central Committee, or a local committee, of the Communist Party); subsequently the head of such a section, or in compound names of political education organs, as *agitpropbrigáda,* etc.]

A•gla•ia (ə glā′ə, ə glī′ə), *n. Class. Myth.* one of the Graces. [< Gk: splendor, beauty]

A•gla′o•phon of Tha′sos (ə glou′ə fon′), fl. 6th to 5th centuries B.C., Greek painter: father and teacher of Polygnotus.

a•glare (ə glâr′), *adj., adv.* glaring; blazing: *The sky was aglare with spotlights.* [1870–75; A-[1] + GLARE[1]]

a•gleam (ə glēm′), *adj.* gleaming; bright; radiant: *a city agleam with lights.* [1865–70; A-[1] + GLEAM]

ag•let (ag′lit), *n.* **1.** a metal tag or sheath at the end of a lace used for tying, as of a shoelace. **2.** (in the 16th and 17th centuries) an ornament at the end of a point or other ribbon used to secure a garment. **3.** aiguillette (def. 1). Also, **aiglet.** [1400–50; late ME < MF *aiguillette,* equiv. to *aiguille* needle (see AIGUILLE) + *-ette* -ET]

a•gley (ə glē′, ə glā′, ə glī′), *adv. Chiefly Scot.* off the right line; awry; wrong. Also, **a•gly′.** [1775–85; A-[1] + *gley* GLEE[2]]

a•glim•mer (ə glim′ər), *adj.* glimmering; shining faintly or unsteadily. [1855–60; A-[1] + GLIMMER]

a•glint (ə glint′), *adj.* displaying bright points of light, as by reflection; glittering: *a diamond tiara aglint under the ballroom lights.* [1875–80; A-[1] + GLINT]

a•glis•ten (ə glis′ən), *adj.* refulgent; glistening. [1890–95; A-[1] + GLISTEN]

a•glit•ter (ə glit′ər), *adj.* glittering; sparkling. [1860–65; A-[1] + GLITTER]

a•glos•si•a (ə glô′sē ə, ā glô′-, ə glos′ē ə, ā glos′-), *n.* **1.** *Pathol.* absence of the tongue, esp. when congenital. **2.** inability to speak. [< Gk: want of eloquence, equiv. to *a-* A-[6] + *glôss(a)* tongue + *-ia* -Y[3]]

a•glow (ə glō), *adj.* glowing: *a house aglow with lights; a face aglow with happiness.* [1810–20; A-[1] + GLOW]

a•glu•con (ə glo͞o′kon), *n. Biochem.* an aglycon, esp. one combined with glucose to form a glycoside. Also, **a•glu•cone** (ə glo͞o′kōn). [1920–25; < Gk *a-* together + *gluk-* (var. transliteration of *glyk-,* s. of *glykýs*) sweet + *-on;* see -ONE]

a•gly•con (ə glī′kon), *n. Biochem.* a noncarbohydrate group, usually an alcohol or phenol, combined with a sugar to form a glycoside. Also, **a•gly•cone** (ə glī′kōn). Cf. **aglucon.** [1920–25; see AGLUCON]

AGM, air-to-ground missile.

ag•ma (ag′mə), *n.* **1.** (in Latin and Greek) the velar nasal consonant sound, esp. in those forms where it was represented by the letter *g* or by *gamma.* **2.** eng. [< LGk; Gk: fracture]

AGMA, American Guild of Musical Artists. Also, **A.G.M.A.**

ag•mi•nate (ag′mə nit, -nāt′), *adj.* aggregated together. Also, **ag′mi•nat′ed.** [1855–60; < L *agmin-* (s. of *agmen*) army on march, throng, crowd + -ATE[1]]

ag•nail (ag′nāl′) *n.* **1.** hangnail. **2.** whitlow. [bef. 950; ME; OE *angnægl,* equiv. to *ang-* tight, hard, painful + *nægl* corn (on foot), NAIL]

ag•nate (ag′nāt), *n.* **1.** a relative whose connection is traceable exclusively through males. **2.** any male relation on the father's side. —*adj.* **3.** related or akin through males or on the father's side. **4.** allied or akin. [1525–35; < L *agnātus* paternal kinsman, var. of *ad-(g)nātus* born to (ptp. of *adgnāscī*), equiv. to *ad-* AD- + *-gnā* be born + *-tus* ptp. suffix] —**ag•nat•ic** (ag nat′ik), **ag•nat′i•cal,** *adj.* —**ag•nat′i•cal•ly,** *adv.* —**ag•na•tion** (ag nā′shən), *n.*

Ag•na•tha (ag′nə thə), *n.* the class of vertebrates comprising the lampreys, hagfishes, and several extinct forms, having no jaws or paired appendages. [1875–80; < NL, equiv. to Gk *a-* A-[6] + *-gnatha,* neut. pl. of *-gnathos* -GNATHOUS]

ag•na•than (ag′nə thən), *n.* **1.** any member of the vertebrate class Agnatha. —*adj.* **2.** agnathous. [AGNATH(A) + -AN]

ag•na•thous (ag′nə thəs), *adj. Zool.* **1.** having no jaws. **2.** belonging or pertaining to the class Agnatha. Also, **agnathan, ag′na•thic.** [1875–80; see AGNATHA, -OUS]

ag•nel (A nyel′), *n., pl.* **ag•neaux** (A nyō′). a gold coin of France of the 13th–16th centuries, bearing the figure of a lamb. [< MF: lit., lamb < L *agnellus,* dim. of *agnus* lamb]

Ag•nes (ag′nis), *n.* **1. Saint,** A.D. 292?–304?, Roman Catholic child martyr. **2.** a female given name: from a Greek word meaning "chaste."

Ag•new (ag′no͞o, -nyo͞o), *n.* **1. David Hayes,** 1818–92, U.S. surgeon. **2. Spi•ro T(heodore)** (spēr′ō), 1918–96, U.S. politician: vice president 1969–73; resigned 1973.

Ag•ni (ug′nē; *Eng.* ag′nē), *n. Hindu Myth.* the god of fire, one of the three chief divinities of the Vedas. [< Skt: fire, the fire-god; akin to L *ignis,* Russ *ogónʹ* fire]

ag•nize (ag nīz′, ag′nīz), *v.t.,* **-nized, -niz•ing.** *Archaic.* to recognize; acknowledge; own. Also, *esp. Brit.,* **ag•nise′.** [1525–35; < L *agn(ōscere)* to recognize (*a(d)-* AD- + *(g)nōscere* to come to know, equiv. to *gnō-* know + *-scere* -ESCE) + -IZE, modeled on COGNIZE, RECOGNIZE]

a•gno•lot•ti (an′yə lot′ē; *It.* ä′nyô lôt′tē), *n.* (*used with a singular or plural v.*) *Italian Cookery.* a dish of small pasta shaped like half moons and usually filled with tortellini stuffing: boiled and served in broth or with a sauce. [< It: filled disc-shaped or rectangular pasta, pl. of *agnolotto, agnellotto,* prob. alter of **anegliotto,* var. of *anellotto,* equiv. to *anell(o)* ring (< L *ānellus,* dim. of *ānus* ring) + *-otto* n. suffix, here perh. with dim. force; *-o-* internally may reflect Upper It form such as Pavia dial. *agnulòt*]

ag•no•men (ag nō′mən), *n., pl.* **-nom•i•na** (-nom′ə nə). **1.** an additional, fourth name given to a person by the ancient Romans in allusion to some achievement or other circumstance, as "Africanus" in "Publius Cornelius Scipio Africanus." Cf. **cognomen** (def. 3). **2.** a nickname. [1745–55; < LL, equiv. to *ad-* AD- + *nōmen* name, with alter. to *ag-* through influence of *agnōscere;* see AGNIZE] —**ag•nom•i•nal** (ag nom′ə nl), *adj.*

Ag•non (ag′non), *n.* **Shmu•el Yo•sef** (shmo͞o′el yō′səf, -zəf), (*Samuel Josef Czaczkes*), 1888–1970, Israeli novelist and short-story writer, born in Poland: Nobel prize 1966.

ag•no•sia (ag nō′zhə, -zhē ə, -zē ə), *n. Psychiatry.* partial or total inability to recognize objects by use of the senses. [1895–1900; < Gk *agnōsía* ignorance, equiv. to *ágnōt(os)* unknown (see AGNOSTIC) + *-ia* -Y[3]]

ag•nos•tic (ag nos′tik), *n.* **1.** a person who holds that the existence of the ultimate cause, as God, and the essential nature of things are unknown and unknowable, or that human knowledge is limited to experience. **2.** a person who denies or doubts the possibility of ultimate knowledge in some area of study. —*adj.* **3.** of or pertaining to agnostics or agnosticism. **4.** asserting the uncertainty of all claims to knowledge. [< Gk *ágnōst(os),* var. of *ágnōtos* not known, incapable of being known (*a-* A-[6] + *gnōtós* known, adj. deriv. from base of *gignṓskein* to know) + -IC, after GNOSTIC; said to have been coined by T.H. Huxley in 1869] —**ag•nos′ti•cal•ly,** *adv.*
—**Syn. 1.** See **atheist.**

ag•nos•ti•cism (ag nos′tə siz′əm), *n.* **1.** the doctrine or belief of an agnostic. **2.** an intellectual doctrine or attitude affirming the uncertainty of all claims to ultimate knowledge. [1870–75; AGNOSTIC + -ISM]

Ag•nus De•i (ag′nəs dē′ī, de′ē; ä′nyo͝os de′ē), **1.** *Eccles.* **a.** a figure of a lamb as emblematic of Christ. **b.** such a representation with the nimbus inscribed with the cross about its head, and supporting the banner of the cross. **2.** a prayer addressed to Christ as Savior preceding the communion in the Mass. **3.** a musical setting of this prayer. [< L: lamb of God]

a•go (ə gō′), *adj.* **1.** gone; gone by; past (usually prec. by a noun): *five days ago.* —*adv.* **2.** in past time; in the past: *All this happened long ago.* [bef. 1000; ME *ago(n),* OE *āgān,* ptp. of *āgān* to go by, pass, equiv. to *ā-* A-[3] + *gān* to GO[1]]

CONCISE PRONUNCIATION KEY: *act, cāpe, dâre, pärt; set, ēqual; if, īce; ox, ōver, ôrder, oil, bo͝ok, bo͞ot, out; up, ûrge; child; sing; shoe; thin, that;* zh as in *treasure.* ə = *a* as in *alone, e* as in *system, i* as in *easily, o* as in *gallop, u* as in *circus;* ° as in *fire* (fī°r), *hour* (ou°r). l and n can serve as syllabic consonants, as in *cradle* (krād′l), and *button* (but′n). See the full key inside the front cover.

a•gog (ə gog′), *adj.* **1.** highly excited by eagerness, curiosity, anticipation, etc. —*adv.* **2.** in a state of eager desire; excitedly. [1535–45; var. of *on gog* (in phrase *set on gog* rouse, stir up) < MF *en gogues;* see À GOGO] —**Syn. 1.** awestruck, enthralled.

-agog, var. of **-agogue.**

a•gog•ic (ə goj′ik, ə gō′jik), *n. Music.* stress given to a note through prolonged duration. Also called **agog′ic ac′cent.** [1890–95; < Gk *agōg(ḗ)* course + -IC (modeled on G *agogisch*)]

a•gog•ics (ə goj′iks, ə gō′jiks), *n.* (*usually used with a singular v.*) *Music.* the theory that accent within a musical phrase can be produced by modifying the duration of certain notes rather than by increasing dynamic stress. [1920–25; see AGOGIC ACCENT, -ICS] —**a•gog′ic,** *adj.*

à go•go (ə gō′gō′), as much as you like; to your heart's content; galore (used esp. in the names of cabarets, discotheques, and the like): *They danced all night at the Mistral à gogo.* Also, **à Go′go, à go′-go.** [1960–65; < F, MF; *gogo* perh. by redupl. and alter. of *gogue* witticism, jest (F *goguette*), expressive word of obscure orig.]

-agogue, a combining form with the meaning "leader, bringer," of that named by the initial element, occurring in loanwords from Greek (*demagogue; pedagogue*); used also in medical terms that denote substances inducing the expulsion or secretion of that named by the initial element (*cholagogue; hemagogue*). Also, **-agog.** [< Gk *-agōgos, -ē, -on,* akin to *ágein* to lead, c. L *agere* to lead, drive, ON *aka* to carry, convey]

ag•on (ag′ōn, -on, ä gōn′), *n., pl.* **a•go•nes** (ə gō′nēz). **1.** (in ancient Greece) a contest in which prizes were awarded in any of a number of events, as athletics, drama, music, poetry, and painting. **2.** (*italics*) *Greek.* (in ancient Greek drama) a formalized debate or argumentation, esp. in comedy: usually following the *proagon* and preceding the *parabasis.* **3.** *Literature.* conflict, esp. between the protagonist and the antagonist. [1650–60; < Gk *agṓn* struggle, contest]

ag•o•nal (ag′ə nl), *adj.* of, pertaining to, or symptomatic of agony, esp. paroxysmal distress, as the death throes. [1600–10; AGON(Y) + -AL[1]]

a•gone (ə gôn′, ə gon′), *adv., adj. Archaic.* ago.

a•gon•ic (ā gon′ik), *adj. Math. Now Rare.* not forming an angle. [1800–65; < Gk *ágōn(os)* (*a-* A-[6] + *gōn-* deriv. s. akin to *góny* KNEE) + -IC]

agon′ic line′, an imaginary line on the surface of the earth connecting all points at which the declination of the magnetic field of the earth is zero. [1860–65]

ag•o•nist (ag′ə nist), *n.* **1.** a person engaged in a contest, conflict, struggle, etc., esp. the protagonist in a literary work. **2.** a person who is torn by inner conflict. **3.** *Physiol.* a contracting muscle whose action is opposed by another muscle. Cf. **antagonist** (def. 3). **4.** *Pharm.* a chemical substance capable of activating a receptor to induce a full or partial pharmacological response. Cf. **antagonist** (def. 5). [1620–30; < LL *agōnista* < Gk *agōnistḗs* contestant, equiv. to *agṓn* AGON + *-istēs* -IST]

ag•o•nis•tic (ag′ə nis′tik), *adj.* **1.** combative; striving to overcome in argument. **2.** straining for effect: *agonistic humor.* **3.** of or pertaining to ancient Greek athletic contests. **4.** *Ethology.* pertaining to the range of activities associated with aggressive encounters between members of the same species, including threat, attack, appeasement, or retreat. Also, **ag′o•nis′ti•cal.** [1640–50; < Gk *agōnistikós,* equiv. to *agōnist(ḗs)* AGONIST + *-ikos* -IC] —**ag′o•nis′ti•cal•ly,** *adv.*

ag•o•nize (ag′ə nīz′), *v.,* **-nized, -niz•ing.** —*v.i.* **1.** to suffer extreme pain or anguish; be in agony. **2.** to put forth great effort of any kind. —*v.t.* **3.** to distress with extreme pain; torture. Also, *esp. Brit.,* **ag′o•nise′.** [1575–85; < ML *agōnizāre* < Gk *agōnízesthai* to struggle (for a prize), equiv. to *agōn-* AGON + *-izesthai* -IZE]

ag•o•nized (ag′ə nīzd′), *adj.* involving or accompanied by agony or severe struggle: *an agonized effort.* [1575–85; AGONIZE + -ED[2]] —**ag•o•niz•ed•ly** (ag′ə nī′zid lē), *adv.*

ag•o•niz•ing (ag′ə nī′zing), *adj.* accompanied by, filled with, or resulting in agony or distress: *We spent an agonizing hour waiting to hear if the accident had been serious or not.* [1660–70; AGONIZE + -ING[2]] —**ag′o•niz′ing•ly,** *adv.*

ag•o•ny (ag′ə nē), *n., pl.* **-nies. 1.** extreme and generally prolonged pain; intense physical or mental suffering. **2.** a display or outburst of intense mental or emotional excitement: *an agony of joy.* **3.** the struggle preceding natural death: *mortal agony.* **4.** a violent struggle. **5.** (*often cap.*) *Theol.* the sufferings of Christ in the garden of Gethsemane. [1350–1400; ME *agonye* (< AF) < LL *agōnia* < Gk, equiv. to *agṓn* AGON + *-ia* -Y[3]] —**Syn. 1.** anguish, torment, torture. See **pain. 2.** paroxysm. —**Ant. 1.** comfort, ease, pleasure.

ag′ony col′umn, a section or column in a newspaper containing advertisements by individuals seeking missing relatives or lost pets or possessions, announcing the end of a marriage, etc. [1860–65]

ag•o•ra[1] (ag′ər ə), *n., pl.* **-o•rae** (-ə rē′). (in ancient Greece) **1.** a popular political assembly. **2.** the place where such an assembly met, originally a marketplace or public square. **3. the Agora,** the chief marketplace of Athens, center of the city's civic life. [1590–1600; < Gk *agorá* marketplace, equiv. to *agor-* (var. s. of *ageírein* to gather together < a pre-Hellenic IE substratum language, equiv. to *a(d)-* AD- + **gher-* grasp, c. Skt *harṣate,* fetch) + *-ā* n. ending]

a•go•ra[2] (ä gôr′ə, -gōr′ə; *Seph. Heb.* ä gô RÄ′), *n., pl.* **a•go•rot** (ä gôr′ōt, -gōr′-; *Seph. Heb.* ä gô RÔT′). an aluminum coin and monetary unit of Israel, the 100th part of a shekel: replaced the prutah as the fractional unit in 1960. Also, **agura.** [< Heb]

ag•o•ra•pho•bi•a (ag′ər ə fō′bē ə), *n. Psychiatry.* an abnormal fear of being in crowds, public places, or open areas, sometimes accompanied by anxiety attacks. [1870–75; AGORA + -PHOBIA]

ag•o•ra•pho•bic (ag′ər ə fō′bik), *adj.* **1.** of, pertaining to, or characteristic of agoraphobia: *She couldn't leave the house for years because of agoraphobic panic.* —*n.* **2.** Also, **ag•o•ra•pho•bi•ac** (ag′ər ə fō′bē ak′). a person who suffers from agoraphobia. [1880–85; AGORA + -PHOBIC]

a•gou•ta (ə gō͞o′tə), *n. Zool.* the Haitian solenodon, *Solenodon paradoxus.* [< F < Sp *aguta* < Taino]

a•gou•ti (ə gō͞o′tē), *n., pl.* **-tis, -ties. 1.** any of several short-haired, short-eared, rabbitlike rodents of the genus *Dasyprocta,* of South and Central America and the West Indies, destructive to sugar cane. **2.** an irregularly barred pattern of the fur of certain rodents. **3.** an animal having fur of this pattern. [1725–35; < F < Sp *agutí* < Tupian *agutí, agoutí, acutí*]

agouti, *Dasyprocta aguti,* length 20 in. (51 cm)

a•gou•ty (ə gō͞o′tē), *n., pl.* **-ties.** agouti.

agr., 1. agricultural. **2.** agriculture.

A•gra (ä′grə), *n.* a city in SW Uttar Pradesh, in N India: site of the Taj Mahal. 637,785.

a•graffe (ə graf′), *n.* **1.** a small cramp iron. **2.** a clasp, often richly ornamented, for clothing or armor. **3.** a device, as a hook, for preventing vibration in the section of a piano string between the pin and the bridge. **4.** (in classical architecture) a sculptural relief on the face of a keystone. Also, **a•grafe** (ə graf′). [1660–70; < F, var. of *agrafe,* n. deriv. of *agrafer* to hook, equiv. to *a-* A-[5] + *grafe* hook, cramp iron, prob. < Gmc; see GRAPE]

A•gram (ä′grAm), *n.* German name of **Zagreb.**

a•gram•ma•tism (ā gram′ə tiz′əm, ə gram′-), *n. Pathol.* a type of aphasia, usually caused by cerebral disease, characterized by an inability to construct a grammatical or intelligible sentence while retaining the ability to speak single words. Also called **a•gram•ma•pha•sia** (ā gram′ə fā′zhə, -zē ə, ə gram′-), **ag•ram•mat•i•ca** (ag′rə mat′i kə), **a•gram•ma•to•lo•gi•a** (ā gram′ə tl ō′jē ə, ə gram′-). [1880–85; < Gk *agrámmat(os)* illiterate (*a-* A-[6] + *grammat-* (s. of *grámma* letter) + *-os* adj. suffix) + -ISM]

à grands frais (A GRÄN FRE′), *French.* at great cost or expense.

a•gran•u•lo•cy•to•sis (ə gran′yə lō sī tō′sis), *n. Pathol.* a serious, acute blood disease, sometimes related to drug or radiation therapy, characterized by extreme leukopenia, fever, and ulcerations of the mucous membranes. [1925–30; A-[6] + GRANULOCYTE + -OSIS]

ag•ra•pha (ag′rə fə), *n.* (*used with a singular or plural v.*) the sayings of Jesus as recorded in the writings of the early Christians and in those parts of the New Testament other than the Gospels. [1885–90; < Gk, neut. pl. of *ágraphos,* equiv. to *a-* A-[6] + *graph-* (s. of *gráphein* to write) + *-os* adj. suffix; i.e., not written down (directly)]

a•graph•i•a (ā graf′ē ə, ə graf′-), *n. Pathol.* a cerebral disorder characterized by total or partial inability to write. [1870–75; < NL; see A-[6], -GRAPHY] —**a•graph′ic,** *adj.*

a•grar•i•an (ə grâr′ē ən), *adj.* **1.** relating to land, land tenure, or the division of landed property: *agrarian laws.* **2.** pertaining to the advancement of agricultural groups: *an agrarian movement.* **3.** composed of or pertaining to farmers: *an agrarian co-op.* **4.** rural; agricultural. **5.** growing in fields; wild: *an agrarian plant.* —*n.* **6.** a person who favors the equal division of landed property and the advancement of agricultural groups. [1610–20; < L *agrāri(us)* (*agr-* s. of *ager* field, ACRE + *-ārius* -ARY) + -AN; cf. AGRESTAL] —**a•grar′i•an•ly,** *adv.*

a•grar•i•an•ism (ə grâr′ē ə niz′əm), *n.* a movement for the equal division of landed property and for the promotion of agricultural interests. [1800–10; AGRARIAN + -ISM]

a•grav•ic (ə grav′ik, ā grav′-), *adj.* pertaining to a state or region in which the effect of gravity is zero. [A-[6] + GRAV(ITY) + -IC]

a•gré•a•tion (A GRĀ A SYÔN′), *n., pl.* **-tions** (-SYÔN′). *French.* the procedure followed by a government for determining the acceptability to a foreign government of a proposed envoy.

a•gree (ə grē′), *v.,* **a•greed, a•gree•ing.** —*v.i.* **1.** to have the same views, emotions, etc.; harmonize in opinion or feeling (often fol. by *with*): *I don't agree with you.* **2.** to give consent; assent (often fol. by *to*): *He agreed to accompany the ambassador. Do you agree to the conditions?* **3.** to live in concord or without contention; get along together. **4.** to come to one opinion or mind; come to an arrangement or understanding; arrive at a settlement: *They have agreed on the terms of surrender.* **5.** to be consistent; harmonize (usually fol. by *with*): *This story agrees with hers.* **6.** to correspond; conform; resemble (usually fol. by *with*): *The play does not agree with the book.* **7.** to be suitable; comply with a preference or an ability to digest (usually fol. by *with*): *The food did not agree with me.* **8.** *Gram.* to correspond in inflectional form, as in number, case, gender, or person; to show agreement. In *The boy runs, boy* is a singular noun and *runs* agrees with it in number. —*v.t.* **9.** to concede; grant (usually fol. by a noun clause): *I agree that he is the ablest of us.* **10.** *Chiefly Brit.* to consent to or concur with: *We agree the stipulations. I must agree your plans.* [1350–1400; ME *agre, agreen* < AF, OF *agre(e)r* from phrase *a gre* at pleasure, at will; *a* < L *ad* to, at; *gre* < L *grātum* (see GREE[2])] —**a•gree′ing•ly,** *adv.*

—**Syn. 1.** AGREE, CONSENT, ACCEDE, ASSENT, CONCUR all suggest complying with the idea, sentiment, or action of someone. AGREE, the general term, suggests compliance in response to any degree of persuasion or opposition: *to agree to go; to agree to a meeting, to a wish, request, demand, ultimatum.* CONSENT, applying to rather important matters, conveys an active and positive idea; it implies making a definite decision to comply with someone's expressed wish: *to consent to become engaged.* ACCEDE, a more formal word, also applies to important matters and implies a degree of yielding to conditions: *to accede to terms.* ASSENT conveys a more passive idea; it suggests agreeing intellectually or verbally with someone's assertion, request, etc.: *to assent to a speaker's theory, to a proposed arrangement.* To CONCUR is to show accord in matters of opinion, as of minds independently running along the same channels: *to concur in a judgment about a painting.* **5.** See **correspond.** —**Ant. 2.** refuse, decline. **5.** disagree.

a•gree•a•ble (ə grē′ə bəl), *adj.* **1.** to one's liking; pleasing: *agreeable manners; an agreeable sensation.* **2.** willing or ready to agree or consent: *Are you agreeable to my plans for Saturday?* **3.** suitable; conformable (usually fol. by *to*): *practice agreeable to theory.* [1350–1400; ME *agreable* < AF. See AGREE, -ABLE] —**a•gree′a•bil′i•ty, a•gree′a•ble•ness,** *n.* —**a•gree′a•bly,** *adv.*

—**Syn. 1.** pleasant, likable, accommodating, gracious, amiable. **3.** compatible, harmonious.

a•greed (ə grēd′), *adj.* arranged or set by common consent: *They met at the agreed time.* [1375–1425; late ME. See AGREE, -ED[2]]

a•gree•ment (ə grē′mənt), *n.* **1.** the act of agreeing or of coming to a mutual arrangement. **2.** the state of being in accord. **3.** an arrangement that is accepted by all parties to a transaction. **4.** a contract or other document delineating such an arrangement. **5.** unanimity of opinion; harmony in feeling: *agreement among the members of the faculty.* **6.** *Gram.* correspondence in number, case, gender, person, or some other formal category between syntactically connected words, esp. between one or more subordinate words and the word or words upon which they depend; selection by one word of the matching formal subclass, or category, in another word syntactically construed with the first. **7.** See **collective agreement. 8.** *Law.* **a.** an expression of assent by two or more parties to the same object. **b.** the phraseology, written or oral, of an exchange of promises. [1375–1425; late ME *agrement* < MF. See AGREE, -MENT]

—**Syn. 3.** understanding, accord, concurrence. AGREEMENT, BARGAIN, COMPACT, CONTRACT all suggest a binding arrangement between two or more parties. AGREEMENT ranges in meaning from mutual understanding to binding obligation. BARGAIN applies particularly to agreements about buying and selling but also to haggling over terms in an agreement. COMPACT applies to treaties or alliances between nations or to solemn personal pledges. CONTRACT is used especially in law and business for such agreements as are legally enforceable. **8.** settlement, treaty, pact.

a•gré•gé (ä′gre zhā′; *Fr.* A GRĀ ZHĀ′), *n., pl.* **-gés** (-zhāz′; *Fr.* -ZHĀ′). a degree awarded by a French university, based on a competitive examination given by the state and qualifying the recipient for the highest teaching positions in a lycée or for the rank of professor in a school of law or medicine. [< F: lit., aggregated, i.e., admitted to membership]

a•gré•ment (ä′grā mänt′; *Fr.* A GRĀ MÄN′), *n., pl.* **-ments** (-mänts′; *Fr.* -MÄN′). **1.** *Music.* ornament (def. 9). **2. agréments.** Also, **a•gré•mens** (A GRĀ MÄN′). agreeable qualities or circumstances. **3.** the official approval by a government of a proposed envoy from a foreign government. [1705–15; < F: lit., pleasure; see AGREEMENT]

a•gres•tal (ə gres′tl), *adj.* of or pertaining to plants growing wild in fields and uncultivated areas. [1600–10; < L *agrest(is)* pertaining to fields, rural, rustic (by dissimilation from **agrestris,* equiv. to *agr-,* s. of *ager* field + *-estris* adj. suffix) + -AL[1]]

a•gres•tic (ə gres′tik), *adj.* **1.** rural; rustic. **2.** unpolished; awkward: *agrestic behavior.* [1610–20; < L *agrest(is)* (see AGRESTAL) + -IC]

agri-, a combining form with the meaning "agriculture, farming," used in the formation of compound words: *agribusiness.* [extracted from AGRICULTURE, with *agri* taken as a comb. form with the linking vowel -I-]

ag•ri•biz (ag′rə biz′), *n. Informal.* agribusiness. [AGRI- + BIZ]

ag•ri•busi•ness (ag′rə biz′nis), *n.* the businesses collectively associated with the production, processing, and distribution of agricultural products. Also, **agrobusiness.** [1950–55; *Amer.;* AGRI- + BUSINESS]

agric., 1. agricultural. **2.** agriculture.

ag•ri•chem•i•cal (ag′ri kem′i kəl), *n.* **1.** any chemical used in agricultural production, as commercial fertilizers, pesticides, and feed supplements. —*adj.* **2.** of or pertaining to such a chemical. Also, **agrochemical.** [1935–40; AGRI- + CHEMICAL]

A•gric•o•la (ə grik′ə lə), *n.* **1. Geor•gi•us** (jôr′jē əs, jē ôr′-), (*Georg Bauer*), 1494–1555, German historian, physician, and pioneer in mineralogy. **2. Gnae•us Jul•ius** (nē′əs), A.D. 37–93, Roman general: governor of Britain.

agricul′tural a′gent. See **county agent.** [1945–50; *Amer.*]

agricul′tural ant′. See **harvester ant.** [1865–70, *Amer.*]

CONCISE ETYMOLOGY KEY: <, descended or borrowed from; >, whence; b., blend of, blended; c., cognate with; cf., compare; deriv., derivative; equiv., equivalent; imit., imitative; obl., oblique; r., replacing; s., stem; sp., spelling, spelled; resp., respelling, respelled; trans., translation; ?, origin unknown; *, unattested; ‡, probably earlier than. See the full key inside the front cover.

agricul′tural engineer′ing, the branch of engineering involved with the design of farm machinery, with soil management, land development, and mechanization and automation of livestock farming, and with the efficient planting, harvesting, storage, and processing of farm commodities. [1910–15]

ag•ri•cul•ture (ag′ri kul′chər), *n.* **1.** the science, art, or occupation concerned with cultivating land, raising crops, and feeding, breeding, and raising livestock; farming. **2.** the production of crops, livestock, or poultry. **3.** agronomy. [1425–75; late ME < MF < L *agricultūra*, equiv. to *agrī* (gen. sing. of *ager*) field + *cultūra* CULTURE] —**ag′ri•cul′tur•al,** *adj.* —**ag′ri•cul′tur•al•ly,** *adv.*

ag•ri•cul•tur•ist (ag′ri kul′chər ist), *n.* **1.** a farmer. **2.** an expert in agriculture. Also, **ag•ri•cul•tur•al•ist** (ag′ri kul′chər ə list). [1750–60; AGRICULTURE + -IST]

A•gri•gen•to (ä′grē jen′tô), *n.* a city in S Italy. 480,068. Formerly, **Girgenti.**

ag•ri•mo•ny (ag′rə mō′nē), *n., pl.* **-nies. 1.** any plant belonging to the genus *Agrimonia*, of the rose family, esp. the perennial *A. eupatoria*, having pinnate leaves and small, yellow flowers. **2.** any of certain other plants, as hemp agrimony or bur marigold. [1350–1400; late ME < L *agrimōnia*, metathetic var. (perh. by assoc. with *ager* field) of *argemōnia* < Gk *argemṓnē* poppy; r. ME *egremoyne* < MF *aigremoine* < L, as above]

A•gri•nion (ä grē′nyôn), *n.* a city in W Greece. 32,415.

ag•ri•ol•o•gy (ag′rē ol′ə jē), *n.* the comparative study of nonliterate cultures. [1875–80; < Gk *ágrio(s)* uncultivated, wild (*agr(ós)* field + *-ios* adj. suffix) + -LOGY] —**ag•ri•o•log•i•cal** (ag′rē ə loj′i kəl), *adj.* —**ag′ri•ol′o•gist,** *n.*

A•gri•o•pe (ə grī′ə pē′), *n. Class. Myth.* Eurydice.

A•grip•pa (ə grip′ə), *n.* **Marcus Vip•sa•ni•us** (vip sā′nē əs), 63–12 B.C., Roman statesman, general, and engineer: defeated Antony and Cleopatra at Actium.

Ag•rip•pi•na II (ag′rə pī′nə, -pē′-), A.D. 16?–59?, mother of the Roman emperor Nero and sister of Caligula.

A•gri•us (ā′grē əs), *n. Class. Myth.* **1.** one of the Gigantes. **2.** a centaur who attacked Hercules. **3.** a son of Circe and Odysseus. **4.** the father of Thersites.

agro-, a combining form meaning "field," "soil," "crop production," used in the formation of compound words: *agronomy.* [< Gk, comb. form of *agrós* tilled land. See ACRE]

ag•ro•bac•te•ri•a (ag′rō bak tēr′ē ə), *n.pl., sing.* **-te•ri•um** (-tēr′ē əm). *Bacteriol.* short rod-shaped aerobic bacteria of the genus *Agrobacterium*, that cause plant diseases, as crown gall. [< NL; see AGRO-, BACTERIA]

ag•ro•bi•ol•o•gy (ag′rō bī ol′ə jē), *n.* the quantitative science of plant life and plant nutrition. [AGRO- + BIOLOGY] —**ag•ro•bi•o•log•ic** (ag′rō bī′ə loj′ik), **ag′ro•bi′o•log′i•cal,** *adj.* —**ag′ro•bi′o•log′i•cal•ly,** *adv.* —**ag′ro•bi•ol′o•gist,** *n.*

ag•ro•busi•ness (ag′rə biz′nis), *n.* agribusiness. [AGRO- + BUSINESS]

ag•ro•chem•i•cal (ag′rə kem′i kəl), *n., adj.* agrichemical. [1935–40; AGRO- + CHEMICAL]

ag•ro•ec•o•nom•ic (ag′rō ek′ə nom′ik, -ē′kə-), *adj.* of or pertaining to a nation's agricultural economy, the financial problems of farmers as a group, etc.: *mounting pressures on the agro-economic system.*

ag•ro•in•dus•tri•al•ize (ag′rō in dus′trē ə līz′), *v.,* **-ized, -iz•ing.** —*v.t.* **1.** to industrialize the agriculture of: *to agro-industrialize a developing nation.* **2.** to convert or organize into an agro-industry: *to agro-industrialize livestock production.* —*v.i.* **3.** to become an agroindustry. Also, *esp. Brit.,* **ag′ro•in•dus′tri•al•ise′.** —**ag′ro•in•dus′tri•al•i•za′tion,** *n.*

ag•ro•in•dus•try (ag′rō in′də strē), *n., pl.* **-tries.** the large-scale production, processing, and packaging of food using modern equipment and methods. Also, **ag′ro•in′dus•try.** [1965–70] —**ag•ro•in•dus•tri•al, ag•ro•in•dus•tri•al** (ag′rō in dus′trē əl), *adj.* —**ag•ro•in•dus′tri•al•ist, ag′ro•in•dus′tri•al•ist,** *n.*

a•grol•o•gy (ə grol′ə jē), *n.* the branch of soil science dealing esp. with the production of crops. [1915–20; AGRO- + -LOGY] —**ag•ro•log•ic** (ag′rə loj′ik), **ag′ro•log′i•cal,** *adj.*

ag•ro•ma•ni•a (ag′rə mā′nē ə, -mān′yə), *n. Psychiatry.* an abnormal desire to live alone, esp. in an isolated area. [AGRO- + -MANIA]

agron., agronomy.

a•gron•o•my (ə gron′ə mē), *n.* the science of soil management and the production of field crops. Also, **ag•ro•nom•ics** (ag′rə nom′iks). [1805–15; AGRO- + -NOMY] —**ag′ro•nom′ic, ag′ro•nom′i•cal,** *adj.* —**ag′ro•nom′i•cal•ly,** *adv.* —**a•gron′o•mist,** *n.*

ag•ros•tog•ra•phy (ag′rə stog′rə fē), *n., pl.* **-phies.** a treatise on grasses. [< Gk *ágrōst(is)* (see AGROSTOLOGY), + -O- + -GRAPHY] —**ag′ros•tog′ra•pher,** *n.* —**a•gros•to•graph•ic** (ə gros′tə graf′ik), **a•gros′to•graph′i•cal,** *adj.*

ag•ros•tol•o•gy (ag′rə stol′ə jē), *n.* the branch of botany dealing with grasses. [1840–50; < Gk *ágrōst(is)* name of certain grasses + -O- + -LOGY] —**a•gros•to•log•ic** (ə gros′tl oj′ik), **a•gros′to•log′i•cal,** *adj.* —**ag′ros•tol′o•gist,** *n.*

ag•ro•tech•ni•cian (ag′rō tek nish′ən), *n.* a specialist in the science and technology of agriculture, farm production, or the like. [1975–80; AGRO- + TECHNICIAN]

ag•ro•tech•nol•o•gy (ag′rō tek nol′ə jē), *n.* the technology of agriculture, as the methods or machinery needed for efficient production. [1970–75; AGRO- + TECHNOLOGY] —**ag′ro•tech•nol′o•gist,** *n.*

a•ground (ə ground′), *adv., adj.* on or into the ground; in a stranded condition or state: *The ship ran aground.* [1250–1300; ME. See A-[1], GROUND]

A.G.S., Associate in General Studies.

agst., against.

Agt., agent. Also, **agt.**

A•gua•dil•la (ä′gwə dē′ə; *Sp.* ä′gwä thē′yä), *n.* a seaport in NW Puerto Rico. 56,600.

a•guar•dien•te (ä gwär′dē en′tē; *Sp.* ä′gwär thyen′te), *n.* **1.** a type of brandy made in Spain and Portugal. **2.** a liquor, popular in South and Central America, made from sugar cane. **3.** (in Spanish-speaking countries) any distilled spirit. [1815–25, *Amer.*; < Sp, contr. of *agua ardiente* lit., fiery water; see AQUA, ARDENT]

A•guas•ca•lien•tes (ä′gwäs kä lyen′tes), *n.* **1.** a state in central Mexico. 430,000; 2499 sq. mi. (6470 sq. km). **2.** a city in and the capital of this state. 238,700.

a•gue (ā′gyōō), *n.* **1.** *Pathol.* a malarial fever characterized by regularly returning paroxysms, marked by successive cold, hot, and sweating fits. **2.** a fit of fever or shivering or shaking chills, accompanied by malaise, pains in the bones and joints, etc.; chill. [1250–1300; ME < MF, short for *fievre ague* acute fever < L *febris acūta*] —**a′gue•like′,** *adj.*

a•gue•weed (ā′gyōō wēd′), *n.* **1.** a boneset, *Eupatorium perfoliatum.* See illus. under **boneset. 2.** a gentian, *Gentianella quinquefolia,* having bristly blue flowers. [1885–90, *Amer.*; AGUE + WEED[1]]

A•gui•nal•do (ä′gē näl′dô), *n.* **E•mi•lio** (e mē′lyô), 1869–1964, Filipino leader during the Spanish-American war: opposed to U.S. occupation.

a•gu•ish (ā′gyōō ish), *adj.* **1.** producing, resembling, or resulting from ague. **2.** easily affected by or subject to fits of ague. **3.** shaking; quivering. [1610–20; AGUE + ISH[1]] —**a′gu•ish•ly,** *adv.*

A•gul•has (ə gul′əs; *Port.* ä gōō′lyəsh), *n.* **Cape,** the southernmost point of Africa.

Agul′has Cur′rent, a warm ocean current flowing S along the SE coast of Africa. Also called **Mozambique Current.**

A•gung (ä′gŏŏng), *n.* a volcano on NE Bali, in Indonesia: erupted 1963. 10,300 ft. (3139 m).

a•gu•ra (ä gŏŏr′ə), *n., pl.* **a•gu•rot** (ä gŏŏr′ōt). agora[2].

A•gus•tín I (*Sp.* ä′gōō stēn′). See **Itúrbide, Agustín de.**

ah (ä), *interj.* (used as an exclamation of pain, surprise, pity, complaint, dislike, joy, etc., according to the manner of utterance.)

Ah, ampere-hour. Also, **a.h.**

A.H., in the year of the Hegira; since the Hegira (A.D. 622). [< NL *annō Hejirae*]

a•ha (ä hä′, ə hä′), *interj.* (used as an exclamation of triumph, mockery, contempt, irony, surprise, etc., according to the manner of utterance.)

AHA, American Heart Association.

A.H.A., 1. American Historical Association. **2.** American Hospital Association.

A•hab (ā′hab), *n.* **1.** a king of Israel and husband of Jezebel, reigned 874?–853? B.C. I Kings 16–22. **2.** captain of the ship *Pequod* and tragic hero of Melville's *Moby Dick,* obsessed with the pursuit of the white whale.

A•had Ha•am (*Seph. Heb.* ä KHäd′ hä äm′), pen name of Asher Ginzberg.

a•han•ka•ra (ə hung kär′ə), *n. Hinduism, Buddhism.* the false identification of the purusha, or true inner self, with the body, the mind, or the outside world. [< Skt *ahaṅkāra* ego consciousness, equiv. to *aham* I + *-kāra* making or producing (a sound), saying, as in *sītkāra* making the sound *sīt*]

A•has•u•e•rus (ə haz′yōō ēr′əs, ə has′-, ə hazh′ōō-; *Seph. Heb.* ä KHäsh′ve RÔSH′; *Ashk. Heb.* ä′KHəsh vā′RƏSH), *n.* a king of ancient Persia, known to the Greeks as Xerxes: husband of the Biblical Esther.

AHAUS, Amateur Hockey Association of the United States.

à haute voix (A ōt VWA′), *French.* aloud; loudly.

A•haz (ā′haz), *n.* a king of Judah, 735?–715? B.C. II Kings 16; II Chron. 28:9.

A•ha•zi•ah (ā′ə zī′ə, ā′ha-), *n.* **1.** a son of Ahab and his successor as king of Israel, reigned 853?–852? B.C. I Kings 22:40. **2.** a king of Judah, 846? B.C. II Kings 8:24.

ah•choo (ä chōō′), *interj.* (used to represent the sound of a person sneezing.) Also, **achoo, hachoo, kerchoo.**

A.H.E., Associate in Home Economics.

a•head (ə hed′), *adv.* **1.** in or to the front; in advance of; before: *Walk ahead of us.* **2.** in a forward direction; onward; forward: *The line of cars moved ahead slowly.* **3.** into or for the future: *Plan ahead.* **4.** so as to register a later time: *to set the clock ahead.* **5.** at or to a different time, either earlier or later: *to push a deadline ahead one day from Tuesday to Monday; to push a deadline ahead one day from Tuesday to Wednesday.* **6.** onward toward success; to a more advantageous position; upward in station: *There's a young man who is sure to get ahead.* **7. ahead of, a.** in front of; before: *He ran ahead of me.* **b.** superior to; beyond: *materially ahead of other countries.* **c.** in advance of; at an earlier time than: *We got there ahead of the other guests.* **8. be ahead, a.** to be winning: *Our team is ahead by two runs.* **b.** to be in a position of advantage; be benefiting: *His score in mathematics is poor, but he's ahead in foreign languages.* [1590–1600; A-[1] + HEAD]

a•hem (*pronounced with a small scraping sound accompanied or followed by a nasal; spelling pron.* ə hem′, hem), *interj.* (an utterance similar to the sound of clearing one's throat, used to attract attention, express doubt or a mild warning, etc.)

AHF, *Biochem.* See **antihemophilic factor.**

A•hid•jo (ä ē jō′), *n.* **Ah•ma•dou** (ä mä dōō′), born 1924, statesman: president of Cameroon since 1960.

A•hi•e•zer (ā′hī ē′zər), *n.* **1.** a Danite who assisted Moses with the census and was head of the tribe of Dan in the wilderness. Num. 1:12; 2:35; 10:25. **2.** a Benjaminite chief of a body of archers who came to David's aid while he was hiding from Saul. I Chron. 12:3.

A•him•a•az (ə him′ā az′), *n.* a priest who supported David during the revolt of Absalom. II Sam. 18:19–32.

A•him•e•lech (ə him′ə lek′), *n.* a priest who was killed by Saul for helping David. I Sam. 21:1–9; 22:9–23.

a•him•sa (ə him′sä, ə hing′-), *n. Hinduism.* the principle of noninjury to living beings. [1870–75; < Skt, equiv. to *a-* not, without (c. A-[6]) + *hiṁsā* injury, akin to *hánti* (he) slays, Gk *phónos* murder]

A•hir (ə hēr′), *n.* a member of the caste of cowherds and milkmen in India. [< Hindi < Skt *abhīra*]

A•hi•ra (ə hī′rə), *n.* a Naphtalite who assisted Moses with the census in the wilderness. Num. 1:15; 2:29.

A•hi•shar (ə hī′shär), *n.* a chamberlain in Solomon's household. I Kings 4:6.

a•his•tor•ic (ā′hi stôr′ik, -stor′-), *adj.* without concern for history or historical development; indifferent to tradition. Also, **a′his•tor′i•cal.** [1935–40; A-[6] + HISTORIC]

A•hith•o•phel (ə hith′ə fel′), *n.* an adviser to David who later turned against him by joining the rebellion of Absalom. II Sam. 15–17.

ah•ki•o (ä′kē ō′), *n.* pulka. [< Finnish]

AHL, American Hockey League.

Ah•ma•di (ä′mə dē′), *n. Islam.* a member of the Ahmadiya.

Ah•ma•di•ya (ä′mə dē′yə), *n. Islam.* a modern sect, divided into an older group **(Qadianis)** and a newer group **(Lahore party).** [< Ar *aḥmadiyah* lit., followers of *Aḥmad,* i.e., Muhammad]

Ah•med•a•bad (ä′məd ə bäd′), *n.* a city in E Gujarat, in W India, N of Bombay: a former state capital. 1,741,522. Also, **Ah′mad•a•bad′.**

Ah•med•na•gar (ä′məd nug′ər), *n.* a city in W Maharashtra, in W India, E of Bombay. 117,275. Also, **Ah′mad•na′gar.**

Ah•mose I (ä′mōs), 1580–1557 B.C., founder of the New Kingdom of ancient Egypt.

Ahn′felt's sea′weed (än′felts), a red alga, *Ahnfeltia plicata,* common along the coasts of North America and Europe, having brownish, bushlike branches. [after N. Ahnfelt (1801–[illegible]), Swedish botanist]

a•hold (ə hōld′), *n.* **1.** *Informal.* a hold or grasp (often fol. by *of*): *He took ahold of my arm. Grab ahold!* **2. get ahold of,** *Informal.* See **hold** (def. 51). —*adv.* **3.** *Naut. Archaic.* close to the wind and on a single tack: *to keep a vessel ahold.* [1600–10; A-[1] + HOLD[1] (n.)]

-aholic, a combining form extracted from **alcoholic,** occurring as the final element in compounds, often facetious nonce words, with the sense "a person who has an addiction to or obsession with some object or activity": *workaholic; chargeaholic.* Also, **-holic.** [by extraction, with *a* replacing *o* as the sp. of the unstressed vowel]

a•holt (ə hōlt′), *n. Older Use.* ahold.

A•hom (ä′hōm), *n.* an extinct Thai language of Assam.

A horizon, *Geol.* the topsoil in a soil profile. Cf. **B horizon, C horizon.** [1935–40]

a•horse (ə hôrs′), *adj., adv.* on horseback: *to escape ahorse.* [1855–60; A-[1] + HORSE]

a•hoy (ə hoi′), *interj. Naut.* (used as a call to hail another ship, attract attention, etc.) [1745–55; var. of HOY. Cf. AHA, AHEM]

AHQ, 1. Air Headquarters. **2.** Army Headquarters.

AHRA, American Hot Rod Association.

Ah•ri•man (ä′ri mən), *n. Zoroastrianism.* See **Angra Mainyu.**

AHSA, American Horse Shows Association.

Aht•na (ät′nə), *n., pl.* **-nas,** (*esp. collectively*) **-na** for 1. **1.** a member of a group of Indians inhabiting the Copper River Valley in southeastern Alaska. **2.** the Athabaskan language of the Ahtna. Also, **Ah•te•na** (ät′n ə, ät′nə), **Atna.** [< Russ *Atna* a name for the Copper River < Ahtna *ʔatnaʔ* the lower Copper River (place-name of obscure orig.)]

a•hu (ä′hōō), *n.* a stone heap or platform used by the Polynesians as a marker or memorial. [< Hawaiian]

a•hull (ə hul′), *adj. Naut.* **1.** (of a sailing vessel) with all sails furled and the helm lashed to head into the wind, as in heavy weather. **2.** abandoned, with decks awash. [1575–85; A-[1] + HULL[2]]

A•hu•na Var•ya (ä′hŏŏ nä vär′yä), *Zoroastrianism.* the best-known and most frequently recited prayer: equivalent to the Lord's Prayer for Christians. Also called **A•hun•var** (ä′hŏŏn vär′).

a•hun•gered (ə hung′gərd), *adj. Archaic.* very hungry. [1375–1425; late ME *ahungred,* equiv. to *a-* A-[2] + *hungred* (ptp. of *hungren* to HUNGER), modeled on ATHIRST]

A•hu•ra (ä′hŏŏ rə), *n. Zoroastrianism, Hinduism.* generic title for benevolent deities in Zoroastrianism or evil deities in Hinduism. Also, **Asura.**

A′hura Maz′da, *Zoroastrianism.* the supreme creative deity, the creator of Gayomart whose omnipotence is challenged by Angra Mainyu. Also called **Mazda, Ohrmazd, Ormazd, Ormuzd.**

A•huz•zath (ə huz′ath), *n.* a friend of Abimelech with whom he journeyed from Gerar to make a covenant with Isaac in Beersheba. Gen. 26:26–31.

Ah•ve•nan•maa (äKH′ve nän mä′), *n.* (*used with a plural v.*) Finnish name of the **Åland Islands.**

Ah•waz (ä wäz′), *n.* a city in and the capital of Khuzistan, in W Iran. 329,006. Also, **Ah•vaz′.**

Ah′, Wil′derness!, a comedy (1933) by Eugene O'Neill.

a•i[1] (ä′ē), *n., pl.* **a•is** (ä′ēz). a three-toed sloth, *Bradypus tridactylus,* inhabiting forests of southern Venezuela, the Guianas, and northern Brazil, having a diet apparently restricted to the leaves of the trumpet-tree, and sounding a high-pitched cry when disturbed. [1685–95; < Pg < Tupi]

ai[2] (ī), *interj.* (used as an utterance of pity, pain, anguish, etc.)

AI, **1.** See **Amnesty International. 2.** See **artificial insemination. 3.** See **artificial intelligence.** Also, **A.I.**

A.I.A., **1.** American Institute of Architects. **2.** American Insurance Association.

A•ias (ä′yas, ī′as), *n.* Ajax (defs. 1–3).

AIAW, Association of Intercollegiate Athletics for Women.

A.I.C., American Institute of Chemists.

AIChE, American Institute of Chemical Engineers. Also, **A.I.Ch.E.**

aid (ād), *v.t.* **1.** to provide support for or relief to; help: *to aid the homeless victims of the fire.* **2.** to promote the progress or accomplishment of; facilitate. —*v.i.* **3.** to give help or assistance. —*n.* **4.** help or support; assistance. **5.** a person or thing that aids or furnishes assistance; helper; auxiliary. **6. aids,** *Manège.* **a.** Also called **natural aids.** the means by which a rider communicates with and controls a horse, as the hands, legs, voice, and shifts in weight. **b.** Also called **artificial aids.** the devices by means of which a rider increases control of a horse, as spurs, whip, and martingale. **7.** aide-de-camp. **8.** See **foreign aid. 9.** a payment made by feudal vassals to their lord on special occasions. **10.** *Eng. Hist.* (after 1066) any of several revenues received by a king in the Middle Ages from his vassals and other subjects, limited by the Magna Charta to specified occasions. [1375–1425; (n.) late ME *ayde* < AF, OF *aide,* n. deriv. of *aid(i)er* < L *adjūtāre* to help (freq. of *adjuvāre*), equiv. to *ad-* AD- + *-jū-* help + *-t-* freq. suffix + *-āre* inf. suffix; (v.) < AF, OF *aid(i)er* < L, as above] —**aid′er,** *n.* —**aid′ful,** *adj.* —**aid′less,** *adj.*
—**Syn. 1.** See **help. 2.** abet, back, foster, advance. **4.** succor; relief; subsidy, grant. —**Ant. 2.** hinder, frustrate.
—**Usage.** Although the nouns AID and AIDE both have among their meanings "an assisting person," the spelling AIDE is increasingly used for the sense "helper, assistant": *One of the senator's aides is calling.* AIDE in military use is short for *aide-de-camp.* It is also the spelling in *nurse's aide.*

AID (ād), *n. U.S. Govt.* the division of the United States International Development Cooperation Agency that coordinates the various foreign aid programs with U.S. foreign policy: established in 1961. [*A(gency for) I(nternational) D(evelopment)*]

AID, **1.** American Institute of Decorators. **2.** American Institute of Interior Designers. **3.** Also, **A.I.D.** *Brit.* artificial insemination donor.

A•i•da (ä ē′də), *n.* **1.** (*italics*) an opera (1871) by Giuseppe Verdi. **2.** a female given name. Also, **A•ï′da.**

aid-de-camp (ād′də kamp′), *n., pl.* **aids-de-camp.** aide-de-camp.

aide (ād), *n.* **1.** See **nurse's aide. 2.** an aide-de-camp. **3.** an assistant or helper, esp. a confidential one. [1770–80, *Amer.*; < F: helper; see AID]
—**Usage.** See **aid.**

aide-de-camp (ād′də kamp′), *n., pl.* **aides-de-camp.** a subordinate military or naval officer acting as a confidential assistant to a superior, usually to a general officer or admiral. Also, **aid-de-camp.** [1660–70; < F: lit., camp helper; see AID, DE, CAMP]

aide-mé•moire (ād′mem wär′; *Fr.* ed mā mwAR′), *n., pl.* **aides-mé•moire** (ādz′mem wär′; *Fr.* ed mā mwAR′). a memorandum summarizing a discussion, agreement, or action. [1840–50; < F: lit., (that which) aids (the) memory]

aid•man (ād′man′, -mən), *n., pl.* **-men** (-men′, -mən). a military medical corpsman trained to provide initial emergency treatment. [1940–45; AID + MAN[1]]

A•i•do•ne•us (ā′i dō′nē əs, -nyōōs), *n. Class. Myth.* a king of Thesprotia.

Ai•dos (ī′dos), *n.* the ancient Greek personification of modesty, respect, and shame. [< Gk *aidṓs*]

AIDS (ādz), *n. Pathol.* a disease of the immune system characterized by increased susceptibility to opportunistic infections, as pneumocystis carinii pneumonia and candidiasis, to certain cancers, as Kaposi's sarcoma, and to neurological disorders: caused by a retrovirus and transmitted chiefly through blood or blood products that enter the body's bloodstream, esp. by sexual contact or contaminated hypodermic needles. Cf. **AIDS virus.** [1982; *a(cquired) i(mmune) d(eficiency) s(yndrome)*]

AIDS′-re•lat•ed com′plex (ādz′ri lā′tid), *Pathol.* a syndrome caused by the AIDS virus and characterized primarily by chronically swollen lymph nodes and persistent fever: sometimes a precursor of AIDS. *Abbr.:* ARC

AIDS′-related vi′rus, a variant of the AIDS virus. *Abbr.:* ARV

aid′ sta′tion, *Mil.* a medical installation located in a forward or isolated position in the field for providing routine or emergency medical treatment to the troops.

AIDS′ vi′rus, a variable retrovirus that invades and inactivates helper T cells of the immune system and is a cause of AIDS and AIDS-related complex: variants were identified in several laboratories and independently named lymphadenopathy-associated virus **(LAV),** human T-cell lymphotropic virus type 3 **(HTLV-3),** and AIDS-related virus **(ARV),** the name human immunodeficiency virus **(HIV)** being subsequently proposed by an international taxonomy committee.

A•ie•a (ä′ē ä′ä), *n.* a town on S Oahu, in Hawaii. 32,879.

ai•glet (ā′glit), *n.* aglet.

ai•grette (ā′gret, ā gret′), *n.* **1.** a plume or tuft of feathers, esp. the back plume of any of various herons, arranged as a head ornament. **2.** a jeweled ornament depicting or suggesting this, usually worn in the hair or on a hat. [1635–45; < F, equiv. to *aigr-* (< Gmc; cf. OHG *heiger* heron) + *-ette* -ETTE. See EGRET, HERON]

ai•guille (ā gwēl′, ā′gwēl), *n.* a needlelike rock mass or mountain peak. [1810–20; < F: lit., needle < VL **acūcula,* alter. of LL *acucula,* equiv. to *acu(s)* needle + *-cula* -CULE[1]; cf. ACICULA]

ai•guil•lette (ā′gwi let′), *n.* **1.** an ornamental tagged cord or braid on the shoulder of a uniform; aglet. **2.** a long thin slice of cooked meat, esp. a narrow strip cut lengthwise from the breast of a fowl. [1810–20; < F; see AIGUILLE, -ETTE] —**ai′guil•let′ted,** *adj.*

Ai•ken (ā′kən), *n.* **1. Conrad (Potter),** 1889–1973, U.S. poet. **2.** a city in SW South Carolina. 14,978. **3.** a male given name.

ai•ki•do (ī kē′dō; *Japn.* ī′kē dô′), *n.* a Japanese form of self-defense utilizing wrist, joint, and elbow grips to immobilize or throw one's opponent. [1960–65; < Japn *aikidō,* equiv. to *ai* to coordinate + *ki* breath control + *dō* way (< MChin; see JUDO)]

ail (āl), *v.t.* **1.** to cause pain, uneasiness, or trouble to. —*v.i.* **2.** to be unwell; feel pain; be ill: *He's been ailing for some time.* [bef. 950; ME *ail, eilen,* OE *eglan* to afflict (c. MLG *egelen* annoy, Goth *-agljan*), deriv. of *egle* painful; akin to Goth *agls* shameful, Skt *aghám* evil, pain]
—**Syn. 1.** bother, annoy, distress.

ai•lan•thus (ā lan′thəs), *n., pl.* **-thus•es.** any tree belonging to the genus *Ailanthus,* of the quassia family, esp. *A. altissima,* widely grown in cities. Cf. **tree of heaven.** [1788; < NL *Ailantus, Ailanthus* (*th* by assoc. with Gk *ánthos* flower) < Central Moluccan *ai lanit(o), ai lanit(e),* equiv. to *ai* tree, wood + *lanit* sky + *-o, -e* a definite article] —**ai•lan′thic,** *adj.*

ailan′thus silk′worm, a green silkworm, *Samia walkeri,* introduced into the U.S. from China, that feeds on the leaves of the ailanthus. [1865–70]

Ai•leen (ā lēn′; *Irish* ī lēn′), *n.* a female given name, form of **Helen.**

ai•ler•on (ā′lə ron′), *n.* **1.** *Aeron.* a movable surface, usually near the trailing edge of a wing, that controls the roll of the airframe or effects maneuvers, as banks and the like. **2.** a wall at the end of a roof with a single slope, as that of a church aisle. [1905–10; < F, equiv. to *ail(e)* (see AISLE) + *-eron* dim. suffix]

ai′leron roll′, *Aeron.* a roll consisting of one or more rotations, usually controlled by the use of ailerons.

ai•lette (ā let′), *n. Armor.* either of two standing pieces of metal or cuir-bouilli, attached to the shoulders as an ornament or as a means of displaying the wearer's arms: used c1275–c1350. [< MF, dim. of *aile* wing. See AISLE, -ETTE]

Ai•ley (ā′lē), *n.* **Alvin,** born 1931, U.S. dancer and choreographer.

ail•ing (ā′ling), *adj.* **1.** sickly; unwell. **2.** unsound or troubled: *a financially ailing corporation.* [1590–1600; AIL + -ING[2]]

ail•ment (āl′mənt), *n.* a physical disorder or illness, esp. of a minor or chronic nature. [1700–10; AIL + -MENT]

ai•lu•ro•phile (ī lŏŏr′ə fīl′, ā lŏŏr′-), *n.* a person who likes cats; cat fancier. Also, **aelurophile.** [1925–30; < Gk *aílouro(s)* cat + -PHILE] —**ai•lu•ro•phil•ic** (ī lŏŏr′ə fil′ik, ā lŏŏr′-), *adj.*

ai•lu•ro•phil•i•a (ī lŏŏr′ə fil′ē ə, ā lŏŏr′-), *n.* a liking for cats, as by cat fanciers. Also, **aelurophilia.** [< Gk *aílouro(s)* cat + -PHILIA]

ai•lu•ro•phobe (ī lŏŏr′ə fōb′, ā lŏŏr′-); *n.* **1.** a person who has an abnormal fear of cats. **2.** a person who detests cats. Also, **aelurophobe.** [1905–10; < Gk *aílouro(s)* cat + -PHOBE] —**ai•lu′ro•pho′bic,** *adj.*

ai•lu•ro•pho•bi•a (ī lŏŏr′ə fō′bē ə, ā lŏŏr′-), *n. Psychiatry.* an abnormal fear of cats. Also, **aelurophobia.** [1905–10; < Gk *aílouro(s)* cat + -PHOBIA]

aim (ām), *v.t.* **1.** to position or direct (a firearm, ball, arrow, rocket, etc.) so that, on firing or release, the discharged projectile will hit a target or travel along a certain path. **2.** to intend or direct for a particular effect or purpose: *to aim a satire at snobbery.* —*v.i.* **3.** to point or direct a gun, punch, etc., toward: *He aimed at the target but missed it.* **4.** to strive; try (usually fol. by *to* or *at*): *We aim to please. They aim at saving something every month.* **5.** to intend: *She aims to go tomorrow.* **6.** to direct efforts, as toward an object: *The satire aimed at modern greed.* **7.** *Obs.* to estimate; guess. —*n.* **8.** the act of aiming or directing anything at or toward a particular point or target. **9.** the direction in which a weapon or missile is pointed; the line of sighting: *within the cannon's aim.* **10.** the point intended to be hit; thing or person aimed at: *to miss one's aim.* **11.** something intended or desired to be attained by one's efforts; purpose: *whatever his aim in life may be.* **12.** *Obs.* conjecture; guess. **13. take aim,** to sight a target: *to take aim and fire.* [1275–1325; late ME *aimen* < AF *a(e)smer, eimer,* OF *aesmer* < VL **adaestimāre,* equiv. to L *ad-* AD- + *aestimāre* (see ESTIMATE); r. ME *amen* < OF (dial.) *amer* < L *aestimāre*] —**aim′er,** *n.* —**aim′ful,** *adj.* —**aim′ful•ly,** *adv.*
—**Syn. 1.** point. **8.** sighting. **10.** target, objective. **11.** goal; intent, design. AIM, END, OBJECT all imply something that is the goal of one's efforts. AIM implies that toward which one makes a direct line, refusing to be diverted from it: *a nobleness of aim; one's aim in life.* END emphasizes the goal as a cause of efforts: *the end for which one strives.* OBJECT emphasizes the goal as that toward which all efforts are directed: *the object of years of study.*

AIM (ām), *n.* American Indian Movement.

ai•mak (ī′mak, ā′mak), *n.* **1.** one of the 18 largest regions into which the Mongolian People's Republic is divided for administrative purposes. **2.** a clanlike group among Mongolian peoples. [< Mongolian *aimag*]

A.I.M.E., **1.** American Institute of Mining Engineers. **2.** Association of the Institute of Mechanical Engineers.

Ai•mee (ā′mē), *n.* a female given name.

aim′ing point′, the point at which a gun or bombsight is aimed in order to strike a desired target, often a point in advance of or behind the actual target. [1905–10]

aim•less (ām′lis), *adj.* without aim; purposeless. [1620–30; AIM + -LESS] —**aim′less•ly,** *adv.* —**aim′•less•ness,** *n.*

A.I.M.U., American Institute of Marine Underwriters.

ain (ān), *adj. Scot.* own. [1700–25; repr. OE *ǣgen* or ON *eiginn;* r. ME (Scots) *awyn, awne,* OE *āgen;* see OWN]

Ain (aN), *n.* a department in E France. 376,477; 2249 sq. mi. (5825 sq. km). *Cap.:* Bourg.

‘ain (īn, ān), *n.* **1.** the 18th letter of the Arabic alphabet. **2.** the voiced pharyngeal constrictive consonant represented by this letter. [< Ar *‘ayn*]

AInd, Anglo-Indian (def. 4).

Ai•nei•as (i nē′əs), *n. Class. Myth.* Greek form of **Aeneas.**

ain't (ānt), **1.** *Nonstandard except in some dialects.* am not; are not; is not. **2.** *Nonstandard.* have not; has not; do not; does not; did not. [1770–80; var. of *amn't* (contr. of AM NOT) by loss of *m* and raising with compensatory lengthening of *a;* cf. AREN'T]
—**Usage.** As a substitute for *am not, is not,* and *are not* in declarative sentences, AIN'T is more common in uneducated speech than in educated, but it occurs with some frequency in the informal speech of the educated, especially in the southern and south-central states. This is especially true of the interrogative use of *ain't I?* as a substitute for the formal and—to some—stilted *am I not?* or for *aren't I?,* considered by some to be ungrammatical, or for the awkward—and rare in American speech—*amn't I?* Some speakers avoid any of the preceding forms by substituting *Isn't that so (true, the case)?* AIN'T occurs in humorous or set phrases: *Ain't it the truth! She ain't what she used to be. It ain't funny.* The word is also used for emphasis: *That just ain't so!* It does not appear in formal writing except for deliberate effect in such phrases or to represent speech. As a substitute for *have not* or *has not* and—occasionally in Southern speech—*do not, does not,* and *did not,* it is nonstandard except in similar humorous uses: *You ain't heard nothin' yet!* See also **aren't.**

Ain•tab (īn täb′), *n.* former name of **Gaziantep.**

Ai•nu (ī′nōō), *n., pl.* **-nus,** (*esp. collectively*) **-nu. 1.** a member of an aboriginal population of northernmost Japan, having lighter skin and hairier bodies than other Japanese. **2.** the language of the Ainus.

ai•o•li (ī ō′lē, ā ō′-; *Fr.* A yô lē′), *n. Cookery.* a garlic-flavored mayonnaise of Provence, served with fish and seafood and often with vegetables. [1895–1900; < F *aïoli* < Pr, equiv. to *ai* garlic (< L *allium*) + *oli* oil (< L *oleum;* see OIL)]

A•io•ra (ə yôr′ə, ə yōr′ə), *n.* (*sometimes used with a plural v.*) a festival of ancient Attica at which dolls were swung from trees to commemorate Erigone's suicide by hanging. [< Gk *Aiṓra* lit., swing (n.), akin to *aeírein* to lift, *aeíresthai* to hang, be suspended]

AIP, American Institute of Physics.

air[1] (âr), *n.* **1.** a mixture of nitrogen, oxygen, and minute amounts of other gases that surrounds the earth and forms its atmosphere. **2.** a stir in the atmosphere; a light breeze. **3.** overhead space; sky: *The planes filled the air.* **4.** circulation; publication; publicity: *to give air to one's theories.* **5.** the general character or complexion of anything; appearance: *His early work had an air of freshness and originality.* **6.** the peculiar look, appearance, and bearing of a person: *There is an air of mystery about him.* **7. airs,** affected or unnatural manner; manifestation of pride or vanity; assumed haughtiness: *He acquired airs that were insufferable to his friends.* **8.** *Music.* **a.** a tune; melody. **b.** the soprano or treble part. **c.** an aria. **d.** Also, **ayre.** an Elizabethan art song. **9.** aircraft as a means of transportation: *to arrive by air; to ship goods by air.* **10.** *Informal.* air conditioning or an air-conditioning system: *The price includes tires, radio, and air.* **11.** *Radio.* the medium through which radio waves are transmitted. **12.** *Archaic.* breath. **13. clear**

CONCISE ETYMOLOGY KEY: <, descended or borrowed from; >, whence; b., blend of, blended; c., cognate with; cf., compare; deriv., derivative; equiv., equivalent; imit., imitative; obl., oblique; r., replacing; s., stem; sp., spelling, spelled; resp., respelling, respelled; trans., translation; ?, origin unknown; *, unattested; ‡, probably earlier than. See the full key inside the front cover.

the air, to eliminate dissension, ambiguity, or tension from a discussion, situation, etc.: *The staff meeting was intended to help clear the air.* **14. get the air,** *Informal.* **a.** to be rejected, as by a lover. **b.** to be dismissed, as by an employer: *He had worked only a few days when he got the air.* **15. give (someone) the air,** *Informal.* **a.** to reject, as a lover: *He was bitter because she gave him the air.* **b.** to dismiss, as an employee. **16. in the air,** in circulation; current: *There's a rumor in the air that we're moving to a new location.* **17. into thin air,** completely out of sight or reach: *He vanished into thin air.* **18. off the air, a.** not broadcasting: *The station goes off the air at midnight.* **b.** not broadcast; out of operation as a broadcast: *The program went off the air years ago.* **c.** (of a computer) not in operation. **19. on the air, a.** in the act of broadcasting; being broadcast: *The program will be going on the air in a few seconds.* **b.** (of a computer) in operation. **20. put on airs,** to assume an affected or haughty manner: *As their fortune increased, they began to put on airs.* **21. take the air, a.** to go out-of-doors; take a short walk or ride. **b.** *Slang.* to leave, esp. hurriedly. **c.** to begin broadcasting. **22. up in the air, a.** Also, **in the air.** undecided or unsettled: *The contract is still up in the air.* **b.** *Informal.* angry; perturbed: *There is no need to get up in the air over a simple mistake.* **23. walk** or **tread on air,** to feel very happy; be elated. —*v.t.* **24.** to expose to the air; give access to the open air; ventilate (often fol. by *out*): *We air the bedrooms every day.* **25.** to expose ostentatiously; bring to public notice; display: *to air one's opinions; to air one's theories.* **26.** to broadcast or televise. —*v.i.* **27.** to be exposed to the open air (often fol. by *out*): *Open the window and let the room air out.* **28.** to be broadcast or televised. —*adj.* **29.** operating by means of air pressure or by acting upon air: *an air drill; an air pump.* **30.** of or pertaining to aircraft or to aviation: *air industry.* **31.** taking place in the air; aerial: *air war.* [1150–1200; ME *eir* < OF *air* < L *āēr-* (acc. *āerem*) < Gk *āer-* (s. of *āḗr*) the lower atmosphere; conflated with (esp. for defs. 4 and 5) F *air,* OF *aire* nature, character < L *ager* field (cf. ACRE) and *ārea* threshing floor, clearing, AREA; and with (for def. 7) F *air* < It *aria* ARIA] —**air′like′,** *adj.*
—**Syn. 2.** See **wind**[1]. **5, 6.** impression, aspect. **6.** aura, demeanor, attitude. See **manner**[1].

air[2] (âr), *Scot.* —*adj.* **1.** early. —*adv.* **2.** *Obs.* before; previously. [see ERE]

A·ïr (ä′ēr), *n.* a region in N Niger, in the Sahara: low massif and oases. ab. 30,000 sq. mi. (77,700 sq. km). Also called **Asben.**

air′ alert′, 1. the act of flying while waiting for combat orders or for enemy airplanes to appear. **2.** the signal to take stations for such action. [1940–45]

air′ arm′, the aviation section of a national military force, including aircraft, base and support facilities, and personnel. [1915–20]

air′ attaché′, a commissioned officer or warrant officer of an air force serving on the staff of an ambassador or minister.

air′ bag′, an inflatable plastic bag mounted under the dashboard or on the back of the front seat of a car: it cushions the driver and passengers by inflating automatically in the event of collision. [1830–40, for an earlier sense]

air′ ball′, *Basketball.* a missed shot that fails to touch the rim, net, or backboard.

air′ base′, 1. an operations center for units of an air force. **2.** *Aerial Photogrammetry.* **a.** a line joining two camera stations. **b.** the length of this line. **3.** the distance between the points on the ground over which an aerial photograph is taken. [1915–20]

air′ bat′tery, a set of two or more air cells connected together to supply electricity.

air′ bed′, a bed made by inflating a mattresslike bag.

air′ bell′, *Glassmaking.* an air bubble formed in glass during blowing and often retained as a decorative element. [1960–65]

air·bill (âr′bil′), *n.* See **air waybill.**

air′ blad′der, 1. a vesicle or sac containing air. **2.** Also called **gas bladder, swim bladder.** *Ichthyol.* a gas-filled sac located against the roof of the body cavity of most bony fishes, originally functioning only as a lung, now serving in many higher fishes to regulate hydrostatic pressure. [1725–35]

air′ blast′, a jet of air produced mechanically. [1885–90]

air·boat (âr′bōt′), *n.* **1.** a small open boat having a very shallow draft and driven by a caged airplane propeller mounted above the rear transom, capable of traveling at relatively high speeds through shallow water, swamps, etc. —*v.i.* **2.** to go or travel in an airboat. [1865–70, for an earlier sense; AIR(CRAFT) + BOAT]

air·borne (âr′bôrn′, -bōrn′), *adj.* **1.** carried by the air, as pollen or dust. **2.** in flight; aloft: *The plane was airborne by six o'clock.* **3.** *Mil.* (of ground forces) carried in airplanes or gliders: *airborne infantry.* **4.** *Aeron.* (of an aircraft) supported entirely by the atmosphere; flying. [1635–45; AIR[1] + BORNE]

air′borne alert′, a state of military alert wherein combat-equipped aircraft are flying and prepared for action.

air′borne command′ post′, *Mil.* any of several converted commercial aircraft equipped with special communications and code gear, intended as flying bunkers for the President, Secretary of Defense, military commanders, or their designated replacements.

air·bound (âr′bound′), *adj.* stopped up by air. [1910–15; AIR[1] + -BOUND[1]]

air′ brake′, 1. a brake or system of brakes operated by compressed air. **2.** *Aeron.* a device for reducing the air speed of an aircraft by increasing its drag. **3.** a device for stopping the sails of a windmill by disrupting the flow of air around them. [1870–75, *Amer.*]

air·bra·sive (âr′brā′siv, -ziv), *Dentistry.* —*n.* **1.** an instrument for cutting tooth structure by means of a stream of abrasive particles under gas or air pressure. —*adj.* **2.** noting or pertaining to the technique of using this instrument. [1940–45; AIR[1] + (A)BRASIVE]

air-breathe (âr′brēth′), *v.i.,* **-breathed** (-brētht′), **-breath·ing.** (of an engine, aircraft, missile, etc.) to take in air from the atmosphere to oxidize the fuel for combustion. [AIR[1] + BREATHE]

air-breath·er (âr′brē′thər), *n.* an aircraft, missile, or submarine engine that requires air from the atmosphere for the combustion of its fuel. Also, **air′breath′er.**

air′ brick′, a ceramic or metal unit the size of a brick, open at the sides for admitting air to a building interior.

air·brush (âr′brush′), *n.* **1.** an atomizer for spraying paint. —*v.t.* **2.** to paint or decorate, using an airbrush: *to airbrush murals; to airbrush silk kimonos.* **3.** to remove or alter by or as by means of an airbrush: *to airbrush facial lines from a photograph.* [1885–90; AIR[1] + BRUSH[1]]

air·burst (âr′bûrst′), *n.* the explosion of a bomb or shell in midair. [1915–20; AIR[1] + BURST]

air·bus (âr′bus′), *n.* a short-range or medium-range commercial passenger airplane, esp. one that is part of a frequent shuttlelike service between two popular destinations. Also, **air′ bus′.** [1905–10; AIR[1] + BUS[1]]

air′ car′go, cargo transported or to be transported by an air carrier.

air′ car′rier, 1. a commercial carrier utilizing aircraft as its means of transport; an airline, as for passengers or freight. **2.** an aircraft meeting specified requirements, for use by an airline. [1915–20]

air′ cas′ing, a casing for the funnel of a powered vessel, large enough to provide an air space all around the funnel.

air′ cas′tle. See **castle in the air.**

air·cav (âr′kav′), *n. Mil. Slang.* See **air cavalry.** [‡1965–70; by shortening]

air′ cav′alry, an infantry or reconnaissance unit transported by air to combat areas. Also called **sky cavalry.** [1915–20, *Amer.*]

air′ cav′alryman, a soldier assigned to the air cavalry. [1915–20]

air′ cell′, 1. *Anat., Zool., Bot.* a cavity or receptacle containing air. **2.** *Elect.* a cell in which the positive electrode is depolarized by the oxygen in the air. [1780–90]

air′ cham′ber, 1. a chamber containing air, as in a pump, lifeboat, or organic body. **2.** Also called **air cushion.** a compartment of a hydraulic system containing air that by its elasticity equalizes the pressure and flow of liquid within the system. [1840–50]

air′ chief′ mar′shal, *Brit.* an air force commander of a rank comparable to an army general. [1915–20]

air′ clean′er, a filtering device for removing impurities from air: *Many cars have air cleaners with replaceable filters.* [1925–30]

air′ coach′, coach (def. 4). [1945–50]

air′ cock′, *Mach.* a special type of valve for controlling the flow of air. [1790–1800]

air′ command′, *U.S. Air Force.* a unit of command that is higher than an air force.

air′ com′modore, *Brit.* an air force officer of a rank comparable to an army brigadier general. [1915–20]

air-con·di·tion (âr′kən dish′ən), *v.t.* **1.** to furnish with an air-conditioning system. **2.** to treat (air) with such a system. [1930–35]

air′ condi′tioner, an air-conditioning device. [1905–10]

air′ condi′tioning, 1. a system or process for controlling the temperature, humidity, and sometimes the purity of the air in an interior, as of an office, theater, laboratory, or house, esp. one capable of cooling. **2.** an air-conditioning system or unit. [1905–10] —**air′-con·di′tion·ing,** *adj.*

air′ conduc′tion, *Med.* transmission of sound vibrations to the eardrum through the external auditory meatus (opposed to *bone conduction*).

air′ consign′ment note′, *Chiefly Brit.* See **air waybill.**

air-cool (âr′ko͞ol′), *v.t.* **1.** *Mach.* to remove the heat of combustion, friction, etc., from (a machine, engine, or device), as by air streams flowing over an engine jacket. **2.** to cool by means of air conditioning. [1895–1900] —**air′-cooled′,** *adj.*

air-core (âr′kôr′, -kōr′), *adj. Elect.* having a nonmagnetic core, as one of fiber or plastic, encircled by a coil (**air′-core coil′**), or containing one or more such coils: *air-core transformer.* [1890–95]

Air′ Corps′, *U.S. Army.* **1.** (before July 26, 1947) a branch of the U.S. Army concerned with military aviation. **2.** (before May 1, 1942) the name for the Army Air Forces.

air′ cor′ridor, corridor (def. 6). [1920–25]

air′ cov′er, 1. the use of aircraft to protect ground or naval military operations. **2.** the protection given by such aircraft.

air·craft (âr′kraft′, -kräft′), *n., pl.* **-craft.** any machine supported for flight in the air by buoyancy or by the dynamic action of air on its surfaces, esp. powered airplanes, gliders, and helicopters. [1840–50; AIR[1] + CRAFT]

air′craft car′rier, a warship equipped with a large open deck for the taking off and landing of warplanes and with facilities to carry, service, and arm them. [1915–20]

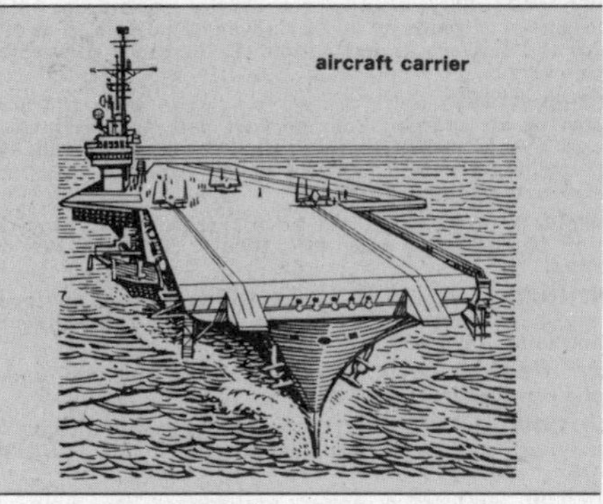
aircraft carrier

air′craft observ′er, *U.S. Army.* observer (def. 4).

air·crafts·man (âr′krafts′mən, -kräfts′-), *n., pl.* **-men.** *Brit.* a person holding the rank of noncommissioned officer in the RAF. Also, **air′craft′man.** [1915–20; AIRCRAFT + 's[1] + -MAN]
—**Usage.** See **-man.**

air·crafts·wom·an (âr′krafts′wo͝om′ən, -kräfts′-), *n., pl.* **-wom·en.** *Brit.* a woman holding a noncommissioned rank in the RAF. [1935–40; AIRCRAFT + 's[1] + -WOMAN]
—**Usage.** See **-woman.**

air·crew (âr′kro͞o′), *n. U.S. Air Force.* the crew of an aircraft. Also, **air′ crew′.** [1920–25; AIR[1] + CREW]

air·crew·man (âr′kro͞o′mən), *n., pl.* **-men.** a member of an aircrew. [AIRCREW + -MAN]

air′ cur′tain, compressed air directed, usually downward, across a doorway so as to form a shield to exclude drafts, insects, etc.

air′ cush′ion, 1. an inflatable, airtight cushion. **2.** See **air chamber** (def. 2). **3.** an air bag. [1830–40] —**air′-cush′ioned,** *adj.*

air′ cush′ion ve′hicle. See **ACV** (def. 2). Also, **air′-cushion ve′hicle.** [1960–65]

air′ cyl′inder, a cylinder containing air, esp. one equipped with a piston and used as a device for checking the recoil of a gun.

air′ dam′, *Auto.* a spoiler mounted at the front of an automobile to reduce air flow on the underside of the chassis to increase stability. [1970–75]

air·date (âr′dāt′), *n. Radio and Television.* the date of a broadcast or scheduled broadcast. [1970–75; AIR[1] + DATE[1]]

air′ divi′sion, *U.S. Air Force.* a unit of command within an air force, usually composed of two or more wings.

Air·drie (âr′drē), *n.* a city in central Scotland, near Glasgow. 37,908.

air′ drill′, a drill powered by compressed air.

air·drome (âr′drōm′), *n.* a landing field for airplanes that has extensive buildings, equipment, shelters, etc.; airport. Also, *esp. Brit.,* **aerodrome.** [1915–20; AIR[1] + -DROME]

air·drop (âr′drop′), *v.,* **-dropped, -drop·ping,** *n.* —*v.t.* **1.** to drop (persons, equipment, etc.) by parachute from an aircraft in flight. —*n.* **2.** the act or process of airdropping. [1945–50; AIR[1] + DROP] —**air′-drop′pa·ble,** *adj.*

air-dry (âr′drī′), *v.,* **-dried, -dry·ing,** *adj.* —*v.t., v.i.* **1.** to dry by exposure to the air. —*adj.* **2.** dry beyond further evaporation. [1855–60]

air′ duct′, an enclosure, usually of sheet metal, that conducts heated or conditioned air. [1865–70]

-aire, a suffix that forms nouns denoting a person characterized by or occupied with that named by the stem, occurring in loanwords from French: *concessionaire; doctrinaire; legionnaire; millionaire.* [< F < L *-ārius* -ARY, a learned doublet of the F suffix *-ier* -EER, -IER[2]]

Aire·dale (âr′dāl′), *n.* one of a breed of large terriers having a wiry, black-and-tan coat and a docked tail. Also called **Aire′dale ter′rier.** [1875–80; short for *Airedale terrier;* so called from the name of a district in Yorkshire where the dogs were bred]

Airedale
23 in. (58 cm) high
at shoulder

CONCISE PRONUNCIATION KEY: *act, cāpe, dâre, pärt; set, ēqual; if, īce; ox, ōver, ôrder, oil, bo͝ok, bo͞ot, out; up, ûrge; child; sing; shoe; thin, ŧħat;* zh as in *treasure.* ə = *a* as in *alone, e* as in *system, i* as in *easily, o* as in *gallop, u* as in *circus;* ᵊ as in *fire* (fīᵊr), *hour* (ouᵊr). l and n can serve as syllabic consonants, as in *cradle* (krād′l), and *button* (but′n). See the full key inside the front cover.

air′ equiv′alent, *Physics.* a measure of the effectiveness of a material in absorbing nuclear radiation, expressed as the thickness of an air layer (at 0° C and 1 atmosphere) causing the same absorption.

air′ express′, **1.** an express service for shipping small packages of goods by air: includes ground pickup at origin and delivery at destination. **2.** the goods shipped by this service.

air-ex•press (âr′ik spres′), *v.t.* **1.** to send or transport by air express: *Your package will be air-expressed and should reach its destination tomorrow.* —*adj.* **2.** pertaining to, using, or sent by air express: *Your air-express package just arrived.*

air•fare (âr′fâr′), *n.* the price charged for transportation by airplane. Also, **air′ fare′.** [1915–20; AIR[1] + FARE]

air•field (âr′fēld′), *n.* a level area, usually equipped with hard-surfaced runways, on which airplanes take off and land. [1930–35; AIR[1] + FIELD]

air′ fleet′, a group of military aircraft, usually under one commander. [1905–10]

air•flow (âr′flō′), *n.* the air flowing past or through a moving body, as an airplane or automobile. [1910–15; AIR[1] + FLOW]

air•foil (âr′foil′), *n. Aeron.* any surface, as a wing, aileron, or stabilizer, designed to aid in lifting or controlling an aircraft by making use of the air currents through which it moves. [1920–25; AIR[1] + FOIL[2]]

Air′ Force′, **1.** the U.S. department consisting of practically all military aviation forces, established July 26, 1947. **2.** (*l.c.*) a similar department in any military organization. **3.** (*l.c.*) (formerly) the largest unit in the U.S. Army Air Forces. **4.** (*l.c.*) a unit of U.S. Air Force command between an air division and an air command. **5.** (*sometimes l.c.*) the military unit of a nation charged with carrying out military operations in the air. **6.** *Brit.* Royal Air Force. [1915–1920]

Air′ Force′ Cross′, a decoration for heroism in combat, reserved for U.S. Air Force personnel.

Air′ Force′ One′, one of several specially equipped and fitted jet airliners maintained by the Air Force for use by the president of the U.S. and designated Air Force One when carrying the president.

air•frame (âr′frām′), *n.* the framework and external covering of an airplane, rocket, etc. [1930–35; AIR(PLANE) + FRAME]

air′ freight′, **1.** a system of transporting freight by aircraft: *Ship it by air freight.* **2.** freight transported by aircraft. **3.** the charge for such transportation. Also, **air′freight′.** [1925–30] —**air′ freight′er.**

air•freight (âr′frāt′), *n.* **1.** See **air freight.** —*v.t.* **2.** to send or ship by air freight: *to airfreight French bread to the U.S.* —*v.i.* **3.** to ship cargo by air freight: *During the truckers' strike we had to airfreight.* —*adj.* **4.** of, pertaining to, or involved in air freight: *the airfreight business.* [1925–30; AIR[1] + FREIGHT]

air′ fresh′ener, an aerosol spray, liquid deodorizer, or other preparation used to remove odors and freshen the air in a room. [1945–50]

air′ gap′, *Elect.* the space between two objects magnetically related, as between the rotor and the stator in a dynamo, or between two objects electrically related, as between the electrode and the tip of a spark plug. [1895–1900]

air′ gas′, *Chem.* See **producer gas.**

air′ gauge′, a gauge for measuring air pressure. [1835–45]

air•glow (âr′glō′), *n.* a dim light from the upper atmosphere caused by emissions from atoms and molecules ionized by solar radiation: observed at night (**nightglow**), during the day (**dayglow**), and at twilight (**twilight glow**), with each having slightly different characteristics. [1950–55; AIR[1] + GLOW]

air′ gun′, a gun operated by compressed air.

air′ ham′mer, a pneumatic hammer, usually portable.

air′ har′bor, a harbor for hydroplanes, esp. seaplanes.

air-hard•en•ing (âr′här′dn ing), *adj. Metall.* noting any metal, esp. alloy steel, that can be hardened from above its transformation point by cooling in air. [1905–10]

air•head[1] (âr′hed′), *n.* an area in enemy territory or in threatened friendly territory, seized by airborne troops for bringing in supplies and additional troops by airdrop or landing. [AIR[1] + (BEACH)HEAD]

air•head[2] (âr′hed′), *n. Slang.* a scatterbrained, stupid, or simple-minded person; dolt. [‡1975–80; AIR[1] + HEAD] —**air′head′ed,** *adj.*

air′ hoist′, a pneumatic hoist. [1910–15]

air′ hole′, **1.** an opening to admit or discharge air. **2.** a natural opening in the frozen surface of a river or pond. **3.** See **air pocket.** [1760–70]

air′ horn′, a horn activated by compressed air. Also, **air′horn′.**

air•hose (âr′hōz′), *n.* a hose for conducting air under pressure, as one connected to an air pump, an air brake, or a scuba tank. [1905–10; AIR[1] + HOSE]

air′ hun′ger, deep, rapid, and labored breathing caused by an increased respiratory drive due to abnormally low blood oxygen levels, as in severe heart failure or asthma.

air•i•ly (âr′ə lē), *adv.* **1.** in a gay or breezy manner; jauntily. **2.** lightly; delicately. [1760–70; AIR(Y) + -ILY]

CONCISE ETYMOLOGY KEY: <, descended or borrowed from; >, whence; b., blend of, blended; c., cognate with; cf., compare; deriv., derivative; equiv., equivalent; imit., imitative; obl., oblique; r., replacing; s., stem; sp., spelling, spelled; resp., respelling, respelled; trans., translation; ?, origin unknown; *, unattested; ‡, probably earlier than. See the full key inside the front cover.

air•i•ness (âr′ē nis), *n.* **1.** openness to the air: *the airiness of a balcony facing the sea.* **2.** sprightliness of manner: *a ballet marked by airiness and deft movement.* **3.** snobbishness; affectation. [1735–45; AIRY + -NESS]

air•ing (âr′ing), *n.* **1.** an exposure to the air, as for drying. **2.** a public discussion or disclosure, as of ideas, proposals, or facts. **3.** a walk, drive, exercise period, etc., in the open air, esp. to promote health. **4.** the act of broadcasting on radio or television: *The new comedy program will have its first airing this Friday night.* [1600–10; AIR[1] + -ING[1]]

air′ injec′tion, injection of liquid fuel into the cylinder of an internal-combustion engine, esp. a diesel, by means of a jet of compressed air. Cf. **solid injection.**

air•ish (âr′ish), *adj. South Midland and Southern U.S.* given to putting on airs. [1940–45; *air(s)* (see AIR[1]) + -ISH[1]]

air′ jack′et, **1.** an envelope of enclosed air around part of a machine, as for checking the transmission of heat. **2.** *Brit.* See **life jacket.** [1905–10]

air′ kiss′, a pursing of the lips in a pretended kiss, as when parting on the telephone or touching cheeks in greeting. [1985–90]

air′ lance′, *Mach.* a lance using an air blast.

air-lance (âr′lans′, -läns′), *v.t.,* **-lanced, -lanc•ing.** to clean with an air lance.

air′ lane′, a route regularly used by airplanes; airway. Also called **skyway.** [1910–15]

air′-launched cruise′ mis′sile (âr′lôncht′, -läncht′), *Mil.* a winged, jet-powered missile designed to be launched from an aircraft and to fly toward the target at low altitude on automatic guidance, with a range of almost 2500 mi. (4023 km). *Abbr.:* ALCM, A.L.C.M.

air′ lay′er, **1.** to treat a plant by means of air layering. **2.** to use air layering to propagate a plant. **3.** a plant, commonly a young one, that has been propagated by air layering.

air′ lay′ering, *Hort.* a method of propagating a plant by girdling or cutting part way into a stem or branch and packing the area with a moist medium, as sphagnum moss, stimulating root formation so that the stem or branch can be removed and grown as an independent plant. [1895–1900; AIR LAYER + ING[1]]

air•less (âr′lis), *adj.* **1.** lacking air. **2.** that is without fresh air; stuffy: *a dark, airless hallway.* **3.** that is without a breeze; still: *an airless July day.* [1595–1605; AIR[1] + -LESS] —**air′less•ness,** *n.*

air′ let′ter, **1.** an airmail letter. **2.** a sheet of very lightweight stationery for use in airmail. Cf. **aérogramme.** [1915–20]

air•lift (âr′lift′), *n.* Also, **air′ lift′.** **1.** a system for transporting persons or cargo by aircraft, esp. in an emergency. **2.** the persons or cargo so transported. **3.** the act or process of transporting such a load. **4.** a pump for raising liquids by the pressure of air forced into the pump chamber. —*v.t.* **5.** to transport (persons or cargo) by airlift. —*adj.* **6.** of or pertaining to an airlift or airlifts: *to increase the army's airlift capacity.* [1940–45; AIR[1] + LIFT]

air•lift•er (âr′lif′tər), *n.* a large aircraft specially designed to transport heavy cargo and to land on and take off from a relatively short runway. [AIRLIFT + -ER[1]]

air•light (âr′līt′), *n.* light scattered or diffused in the air by dust, haze, etc., esp. as it limits the visibility of distant, dark objects by causing them to blend with the background sky. [AIR[1] + LIGHT[1]]

air-line (âr′lin′), *adj.* straight; direct; traveling a direct route: *Some railroads advertise air-line routes between stations.* [1805–15, *Amer.*]

air•line (âr′lin′), *n.* **1.** *Aeron.* **a.** a system furnishing air transport, usually scheduled, between specified points. **b.** the airplanes, airports, etc., of such a system. **c.** Often, **airlines.** a company that owns or operates such a system. **2.** a direct line; beeline. **3.** an airhose used to pipe air to a deep-sea diver, pneumatic drill, etc. —*adj.* **4.** of or on an airline. [1910–15; AIR[1] + LINE[1]]

air•lin•er (âr′li′nər), *n.* a passenger aircraft operated by an airline. [1905–10; AIR[1] + LINER[1]]

air′ lock′, **1.** *Civ. Eng.* an airtight chamber permitting passage to or from a space, as in a caisson, in which the air is kept under pressure. **2.** the impedance in the functioning of a pump or a system of piping caused by the presence of an air bubble; vapor lock. [1855–60]

air-lock (âr′lok′), *v.t.* to place in or confine to an air lock: *to air-lock divers before they descend.* [1855–60]

air′ log′, **1.** *Aeron.* a device for recording the distance traveled by an aircraft, relative to the air through which it moves. **2.** *Rocketry.* a device for regulating the range of a guided missile. [1925–30]

air-logged (âr′lôgd′, -logd′), *adj.* (of a pump or system of piping) hindered in its functioning by an air lock; air-bound.

air•ma•da (âr mä′də, -mā′-), *n.* a large fleet or flight of airplanes assigned to a specific mission: *shipping lanes guarded by a giant airmada overhead.* [1950–55; b. AIRPLANE and ARMADA]

air•mail (âr′māl′), *n.* **1.** the system, esp. a government postal system, of sending mail by airplane. **2.** a letter, package, etc., sent by this system. **3.** a stamp authorizing delivery of mail by this system. —*adj.* **4.** of or pertaining to airmail. —*adv.* **5.** by airmail: *Send all overseas letters airmail.* —*v.t.* **6.** to send via airmail: *I airmailed the package yesterday.* Also, **air′-mail′.** [1910–15; AIR[1] + -MAIL[1]]

air•man (âr′mən), *n., pl.* **-men.** **1.** an aviator. **2.** *U.S. Air Force.* an enlisted person of one of the three lowest ranks (**air′man ba′sic, airman, air′man first′ class′**). **3.** a member of a military aircrew. **4.** (in other countries) an enlisted person in the air force. [1870–75, for an earlier sense; AIR[1] + -MAN, on the model of SEAMAN]

air•man•ship (âr′mən ship′), *n.* the knowledge and ability needed to control and navigate an aircraft. [1860–65; AIR[1] + -MANSHIP]

Air′man's Med′al, a U.S. Air Force award for heroism, not involving combat, available to any member of the U.S. or friendly armed forces serving with the USAF.

air′ map′, a map constructed from aerial photographs.

air′ mar′shal, *Brit.* an air force officer of a rank comparable to an army lieutenant general. [1915–20]

air′ mass′, a body of air covering a relatively wide area, exhibiting approximately uniform properties through any horizontal section. [1890–95]

air′ mat′tress, a mattress, usually of plastic or rubber, that can be inflated for use, as in camping, and deflated for storage. [1925–30]

Air′ Med′al, an award for heroism or meritorious action involving an aerial military operation: personnel from any branch of the U.S. armed forces are eligible. [authorized by Congress in 1942]

air′ me′ter, a small, sensitive anemometer of the windmill type.

air′ mile′, See **international nautical mile.** [1915–20]

air-mind•ed (âr′min′did), *adj.* **1.** interested in aviation or aeronautics. **2.** favoring increased use of aircraft. [1925–30] —**air′-mind′ed•ness,** *n.*

Air′ Min′istry, (in England) the department of government administering all civil and military matters concerning aviation.

air•mo•bile (âr′mō′bəl, -bēl *or, esp. Brit.,* -bil), *adj.* transportable or transported to combat areas by helicopters: *airmobile troops; airmobile corps.* [1960–65, *Amer.*; AIR[1] + MOBILE]

Air′ Na′tional Guard′, a national guard organization similar to and coordinate with the U.S. Air Force.

air′ observ′er, *U.S. Army.* observer (def. 3).

air•pack (âr′pak′), *n.* an apparatus consisting of a face mask connected to a portable air supply, as an air tank that can be strapped to one's back, used esp. by firefighters and search teams in areas of smoke, poisonous fumes, intense heat, etc. [AIR[1] + PACK[1]]

air•park (âr′pärk′), *n.* a small airport for private planes, esp. one located near an industrial park or other commercial center. [1925–30; AIR[1] + PARK]

air′ pas′sage, **1.** a space occupied or traversed by air. **2.** travel by air. **3.** accommodations for an air trip: *to book air passage for Hong Kong.* [1830–40]

air′ pho′tograph. See **aerial photograph.** —**air′ photog′raphy.**

air•pipe (âr′pip′), *n.* an airhose connecting the mouthpiece of scuba diving equipment to its air supply. [1665–75, for an earlier sense; AIR[1] + PIPE[1]]

air′ pi′racy, the hijacking of an airplane; skyjacking. [1945–50] —**air′ pi′rate.**

air′ pis′tol, a pistol that utilizes compressed air rather than ignited gunpowder to propel a single shot, often a pellet. [1955–60]

air•plane (âr′plān′), *n.* **1.** a heavier-than-air aircraft kept aloft by the upward thrust exerted by the passing air on its fixed wings and driven by propellers, jet propulsion, etc. **2.** any similar heavier-than-air aircraft, as a glider or helicopter. Also, *esp. Brit.,* **aeroplane.** [1870–75, for an earlier sense; alter. of AEROPLANE, with AIR[1] r. AERO-]

air′plane car′rier, an aircraft carrier.

air′plane cloth′, **1.** a strong cotton cloth of plain weave treated with dope and formerly used as a covering for the wings and fuselages of airplanes. **2.** a similar, lighter-weight fabric for shirts and pajamas.

air′plane spin′, *Wrestling.* a maneuver in which a wrestler, grasping an opponent by the head and crotch, lifts the opponent's body crosswise overhead, lowers it to the shoulders for support, then spins around and throws the opponent back over the head to the mat.

air′plane turn′, *Skiing.* a midair turn made in the middle of a jump. [‡1975–80]

air′ plant′, **1.** an epiphyte. **2.** Also called **life plant.** a tropical plant, *Kalanchoe pinnata,* of the stonecrop family, having pale green flowers tinged with red and new plants sprouting at the leaf notches. [1835–45, *Amer.*]

air•play (âr′plā′), *n.* the act or an instance of broadcasting recorded material over radio or television. [1965–70; AIR[1] + PLAY]

air′ plot′, **1.** *Aeron.* the calculation of the ground position of an aircraft by first determining its air position from its speed in the air and heading information, and then correcting for wind effects. **2.** the room or rooms from which aircraft are directed aboard an aircraft carrier. Also, **air′plot′.** [1940–45]

air′ plug′, a plug making an airtight seal to a vent.

air′ pock′et, (not in technical use) a nearly vertical air current that can cause an aircraft to experience a sudden change in altitude, usually a decrease. Also called **air hole.** [1910–15]

Air′ Police′, an organization of personnel in the U.S. Air Force or Air National Guard serving as police. *Abbr.:* AP, A.P. [1940–45]

air•port[1] (âr′pôrt′, -pōrt′), *n.* a tract of land or water with facilities for the landing, takeoff, shelter, supply, and repair of aircraft, esp. one used for receiving or discharging passengers and cargo at regularly scheduled times. [1915–20; AIR[1] + PORT[1], on the model of SEAPORT]

air•port[2] (âr′pôrt′, -pōrt′), *n. Naut.* a porthole designed to be opened to the outside air. [1780–90; AIR[1] + PORT[4]]

air′port code′, a three-letter abbreviation of the names of the world's major airports, used esp. as an identifier for routing baggage.

AIRPORT CODES OF SELECTED WORLD CITIES

	Code
Amsterdam, the Netherlands	AMS
Athens, Greece	ATH
Atlanta	ATL
Baltimore	BWI
Beijing (Peking), China	PEK
Berlin, Germany: Tegel	TXL
Bombay, India	BOM
Boston	BOS
Brussels, Belgium	BRU
Buenos Aires, Argentina: Ezeiza	EZE
Cairo, Egypt	CAI
Chicago: O'Hare	ORD
Chicago: Midway	MDW
Copenhagen, Denmark	CPH
Dallas/Ft. Worth	DFW
Delhi, India	DEL
Denver	DEN
Detroit	DTW
Frankfurt, Germany	FRA
Geneva, Switzerland	GVA
Hong Kong	HKG
Honolulu	HNL
Jerusalem, Israel	JRS
Las Vegas	LAS
Lisbon, Portugal	LIS
London, United Kingdom: Heathrow	LHR
London, United Kingdom: Gatwick	LGW
Los Angeles	LAX
Madrid, Spain	MAD
Melbourne, Australia	MEL
Mexico City, Mexico	MEX
Miami	MIA
Montreal, Canada: Dorval	YUL
Moscow, Russian Federation: Sheremetyevo	SVO
Nairobi, Kenya	NBO
Naples, Italy	NAP
New York: JFK (Kennedy) International	JFK
New York: La Guardia	LGA
New York: Newark	EWR
Orlando	MCO
Paris, France: Charles de Gaulle	CDG
Paris, France: Orly	ORY
Philadelphia	PHL
Phoenix	PHX
Pittsburgh	PIT
Rio de Janeiro, Brazil	GIG
Rome, Italy: Leonardo da Vinci (Fiumicino)	FCO
San Francisco	SFO
Shannon, Ireland	SNN
St. Louis	STL
Seattle	SEA
Singapore	SIN
Stockholm, Sweden: Arlanda	ARN
Sydney, Australia	SYD
Tel Aviv, Israel	TLV
Tokyo, Japan: Narita	NRT
Toronto, Canada: Lester B. Pearson International	YYZ
Washington, D.C.: Dulles International	IAD
Washington, D.C.: National	DCA
Zurich, Switzerland	ZRH

air′ pota′to, a vine, *Dioscorea bulbifera,* of southeastern Asia, having tubers weighing several pounds and growing in the leaf axils.

air′ pow′er, the total military capability of a nation for operations involving the use of aircraft and missiles. [1905–10]

air′ pres′sure, the force exerted by air, whether compressed or unconfined, on any surface in contact with it. Cf. **atmospheric pressure.** [1870–75]

air•proof (âr′pro͞of′), *adj.* **1.** impervious to air. —*v.t.* **2.** to make impervious to air. [AIR[1] + -PROOF]

air′ pump′, 1. an apparatus for drawing in, compressing, or exhausting air. **2.** (*caps.*) *Astron.* the constellation Antlia. [1650–60]

air′ raid′, a raid by aircraft, esp. for bombing a particular area. [1910–15] —**air′-raid′,** *adj.* —**air′ raid′er.**

air′-raid shel′ter, an indoor or other protected area specifically designated as a shelter during an air raid. Cf. **bomb shelter.** [1915–20]

air′-raid war′den, a civilian having special duties during an air-raid alert, as directing people to air-raid shelters. [1935–40]

air′ ri′fle, an air gun with rifled bore. [1900–05, *Amer.*]

air′ right′, 1. a right of way in the air space above a property owner's land and the immovable property on it, subject to the public right of air navigation above the property at a legally prescribed altitude. **2.** such a right sold or leased for use or occupation, esp. on a support elevated above an immovable property, as for the erection of an office building over a railroad track. [1920–25]

air′ route′, a designated route for aircraft flying between particular ground locations at specified minimum altitudes. [1910–15]

air′ sac′, 1. a sac containing air. **2.** alveolus (def. 2). **3.** any of certain cavities in a bird's body connected with the lungs. **4.** a saclike dilation of the wall of a trachea in many insects. [1820–30]

air′ scoop′, an air intake that projects into the airflow around a motor vehicle or aircraft in such a way as to provide a steady flow of air for combustion or ventilation. [1915–20]

air•screw (âr′skro͞o′), *n. Brit.* an airplane propeller. [1890–95; AIR[1] + SCREW]

air′ serv′ice, 1. the services performed by an airline, as flights between various destinations to transport passengers, freight, and mail. **2.** (*caps.*) (formerly) the air arm of the U.S. military forces. [1920–25]

air′ shaft′, 1. See **air well. 2.** *Mining.* a ventilating shaft. [1685–95]

air•shed (âr′shed′), *n. Meteorol.* a geographical area within which the air frequently is confined or channeled, with all parts of the area thus being subject to similar conditions of air pollution. [1910–15; AIR[1] + (WATER)SHED]

air•ship (âr′ship′), *n.* a self-propelled, lighter-than-air aircraft with means of controlling the direction of flight; dirigible. Cf. **blimp.** [1810–20, for an earlier sense; AIR[1] + SHIP]

air-ship (âr′ship′), *v.t.,* **-shipped, -ship•ping.** to send or ship via aircraft: *to air-ship machine parts overseas.* [1950–1955] —**air′-ship′pa•ble,** *adj.*

air•show (âr′shō′), *n.* a fair that features aircraft performing aerial stunts. [1910–15; AIR[1] + SHOW]

air′ show′er, a shower of secondary cosmic radiation, caused by the interaction of cosmic radiation or gamma radiation with the atmosphere. Also called **shower.** [1955–60]

air•sick (âr′sik′), *adj.* afflicted with airsickness. [1775–85; AIR[1] + SICK]

air•sick•ness (âr′sik′nis), *n.* a feeling of nausea and dizziness, sometimes accompanied by vomiting, as a result of the motion of the aircraft in which one is traveling. Cf. **motion sickness.** [1775–85; AIR[1] + SICKNESS]

air′ sign′, *Astrol.* any of the three astrological signs, Gemini, Libra, or Aquarius, that are grouped together because of the shared attributes of intellect and gregariousness. Cf. **triplicity.**

air-slake (âr′slāk′), *v.t.,* **-slaked, -slak•ing.** to slake (lime or the like) with moist air.

air′ sleeve′, windsock.

air′ sock′, windsock.

air′ space′, 1. a space occupied by air. **2.** the amount of breathing air in a room or other enclosed space. **3.** the region of the atmosphere above a municipality, state, or nation, over which it has jurisdiction. **4.** the region of the atmosphere above a plot of ground, to which the owner has rights or access. Also, **air′space′** (for defs. 3, 4). [1900–05]

air•speed (âr′spēd′), *n.* the forward speed of an aircraft relative to the air through which it moves. Also, **air′ speed′.** Cf. **groundspeed.** [1905–10; AIR[1] + SPEED]

air′speed in′dicator, *Aeron.* a flight instrument showing the airspeed of an aircraft. *Abbr.:* ASI

air-spray (âr′sprā′), *adj.* pertaining to compressed-air spraying devices or to liquids used in them. —**air′-sprayed′,** *adj.*

air′ spray′er, a pneumatic sprayer.

air′ spring′, *Mach.* a springlike support utilizing the compressibility of air confined behind a piston in a cylinder.

air′ stack′, stack (def. 13).

air′ sta′tion, an airfield having facilities for sheltering and servicing aircraft. [1910–15]

air•stream (âr′strēm′), *n.* any localized airflow. Also, **air′ stream′, air′-stream′.** [1865–70; AIR[1] + STREAM]

air′ strike′, the bombing or strafing of a city, enemy force, etc., by military aircraft: *The air strike devastated the enemy's submarine base.* Also, **air′strike′.** [1940–45]

air•strip (âr′strip′), *n.* **1.** a small landing field having only one runway. **2.** a temporary or auxiliary aircraft runway. [1940–45; AIR[1] + STRIP[2]]

air-su•pe•ri•or•i•ty (âr′sə pēr ē ôr′i tē, -or′-, -so͝o-), *adj.* designating a fighter aircraft built for long patrol capability at high altitudes and supersonic speeds, with air-to-air combat as its principal mission. [1930–35]

air′ switch′, *Elect.* a switch in which the interruption of the circuit occurs in air.

air′ sys′tem, 1. a system of refrigeration utilizing air as a coolant. **2.** any group of devices operated or controlled by air under pressure or vacuum.

airt (ârt; *Scot.* ärt), *Chiefly Scot.* —*n.* **1.** a direction. —*v.t.* **2.** to point out the way; direct; guide. Also, **airth** (ârth; *Scot.* ärth). [1400–50; late ME (Scots) *a(i)rt* < ScotGael *àird* point, quarter of the compass; c. Gk *árdis* arrowhead. The borrowing of Scots *airt* from ScotGael *àird* is exact since ScotGael *d* is totally voiceless and *àird* sounds like E *arch*]

air′ tax′i, a small aircraft for passengers, cargo, and mail operated, either on a scheduled or nonscheduled basis, along short routes not serviced by large airlines. [1915–20, *Amer.*]

air′ tee′. See **wind tee.**

air•tight (âr′tīt′), *adj.* **1.** preventing the entrance or escape of air or gas. **2.** having no weak points or openings of which an opponent may take advantage: *an airtight contract.* [1750–60; AIR[1] + TIGHT] —**air′tight′ly,** *adv.* —**air′tight′ness,** *n.*

air•time (âr′tīm′), *n.* **1.** the particular time that a program is broadcast or scheduled for broadcast: *The airtime for the newscast is 10 P.M.* **2.** the time during which a broadcast takes place: *The airtime for the new show is from 10 to 10:30 P.M.* **3.** a block of such time sold by a radio or television station to an advertiser, allotted to a political candidate, etc.: *The company bought three minutes of airtime.* Also, **air′ time′.** [1940–45; AIR[1] + TIME]

air-to-air (âr′to͞o âr′, -tə-), *adj.* **1.** operating between airborne objects, esp. aircraft: *air-to-air missiles; air-to-air communication.* —*adv.* **2.** from one aircraft, missile, or the like, to another while in flight: *They refueled air-to-air.* [1940–45]

air-to-sur•face (âr′tə sûr′fəs), *adj.* **1.** operating or directed from a flying aircraft to the surface: *air-to-surface missiles.* —*adv.* **2.** from a flying aircraft to the surface of the earth: *They released the rockets air-to-surface.* Also called **air-to-ground** (âr′tə ground′). [1955–60]

air′ traf′fic, aircraft moving in flight or on airport runways. [1910–15]

air′-traf′fic control′ (âr′traf′ik), a government service that facilitates the safe and orderly movement of aircraft within and between airports by receiving and processing data from radar and devices that monitor local weather conditions and by maintaining radio contact with pilots. [1930–35] —**air′-traf′fic control′ler.**

air′ train′. See **sky train.**

air-trans•port•a•ble (âr′trans pôr′tə bəl, -pōr′-), *adj.* that can be transported by aircraft: *air-transportable equipment.* —**air′ transportabil′ity.**

air′ trap′, trap[1] (def. 4).

air′ tur′bine, a turbine operated by air under pressure.

air′ twist′, a serpentine motif within the stem of a goblet, produced by extending and twisting an air bubble during glass blowing. [1895–1900] —**air′-twist′ed,** *adj.*

air′ valve′, a device for controlling the flow of air, as from a pipe or tank.

air va•rié (âr′ vâr′ē ā′; *Fr.* ER VA RYĀ′), *Music.* a melody with variations. [< F]

air′ ves′icle, *Bot.* a large, air-filled pocket, chiefly in plants that float on water, as kelps.

air′ vice-mar′shal (vīs′mär′shəl, vīs′-), *Brit.* an air force officer of a rank comparable to an army major general. [1915–20]

air′ war′, 1. military operations by combatants involving the use of aircraft. **2.** those phases or aspects of a war in which aircraft play a part. [1910–15]

air•wash (âr′wosh′, -wôsh′), *v.t.* **1.** to cool (a roof or the like) with a current of air. —*n.* **2.** a current of air for cooling a roof or the like. [1945–50; AIR[1] + WASH]

air•waves (âr′wāvz′), *n.pl.* the media of radio and television broadcasting: *The airwaves were filled with news flashes about the crisis.* [1895–1900, for earlier sense; AIR[1] + *waves* (pl. of WAVE)]

air•way (âr′wā′), *n.* **1.** an air route equipped with emergency landing fields, beacon lights, radio beams, etc. **2.** a passageway by which air passes from the nose or mouth to the air sacs of the lungs. **3.** *Med.* a tubelike device used to maintain adequate, unobstructed respiration, as during general anesthesia. **4.** any passage in a mine used for purposes of ventilation; an air course. **5. airways, a.** the band of frequencies, taken collectively, used by radio broadcasting stations: *The news was sent out over the airways immediately.* **b.** airwaves. **c.** airline (def. 1c). [1905–10; AIR[1] + WAY]

air′ way′bill, a nonnegotiable shipping document evidencing the contract between shipper and air carrier for transportation and delivery of cargo. *Abbr.:* AWB Also, **air′way′bill′.** Also called **airbill, waybill;** *esp. Brit.,* **air consignment note, consignment note.**

air′ well′, a ventilating shaft in a building. Also called **air shaft.**

air•wom•an (âr′wo͝om′ən), *n., pl.* **-wom•en.** a woman who pilots an aircraft. [1910–15; AIR[1] + -WOMAN] —**Usage.** See **-woman.**

air′ wood′, timber dried naturally by contact with the open air. [1670–80]

air•wor•thy (âr′wûr′thē), *adj.,* **-thi•er, -thi•est.** (of an aircraft) meeting established standards for safe flight; equipped and maintained in condition to fly. [1820–30; AIR[1] + -WORTHY] —**air′wor′thi•ness,** *n.*

air•y (âr′ē), *adj.,* **air•i•er, air•i•est. 1.** open to a free current of fresh air; breezy: *airy rooms.* **2.** consisting of or having the character of air; immaterial: *airy phantoms.* **3.** light in appearance; thin: *airy garments.* **4.** light in manner; sprightly; lively: *airy songs.* **5.** light in movement; graceful; delicate: *an airy step.* **6.** light as air; unsubstantial; unreal; imaginary: *airy dreams.* **7.** visionary; speculative. **8.** performed in the air; aerial. **9.** lofty; high in the air. **10.** putting on airs; affected; snobbish: *an airy debutante posing for society photographers.* [1350–1400; ME *ayery;* see AIR[1], -Y[1]] —**Syn. 4.** jaunty, merry. **6.** fanciful, illusory.

Air′y disc′ (âr′ē), *Optics.* the bright central part of the diffraction pattern of light from a point source that is diffracted by a circular aperture. [named after Sir George Biddel Airy (1801–92)]

air•y-fair•y (âr′ē fâr′ē), *adj.* **1.** *Informal.* **a.** delicate or lovely: *an airy-fairy actress; an airy-fairy nightgown.* **b.** not based on reality or concerned with mundane affairs; unrealistic: *airy-fairy ideas about spending a fortune that isn't even his.* **2.** *Slang.* effeminate; swishy.

[perh. orig. in the phrase "airy, fairy Lilian" in Tennyson's poem "Lilian" (1830)]

A•i•sha (ä′ē shä′ *for 1;* ä ē′shə *for 2*), *n.* **1.** A.D. 613?–678, favorite wife of Muhammad (daughter of Abu-Bekr). **2.** a female given name: from a Swahili word meaning "life."

AISI, American Iron and Steel Institute.

AISI steel, any steel made to conform to the standard chemical compositions generally accepted by the U.S. steel industry and its principal customers.

aisle (īl), *n.* **1.** a walkway between or along sections of seats in a theater, classroom, or the like. **2.** *Archit.* **a.** a longitudinal division of an interior area, as in a church, separated from the main area by an arcade or the like. **b.** any of the longitudinal divisions of a church or the like. **3. in the aisles,** (of an audience) convulsed with laughter. [1350–1400; alter. (with *ai* < F *aile* wing) of earlier *isle* (with *s* from ISLE), *ile;* r. ME *ele* < MF < L *āla* wing, c. AXLE. See ALA] —**aisled,** *adj.*

Aisne (ān; *Fr.* en), *n.* **1.** a river in N France, flowing NW and W to the Oise. 175 mi. (280 km) long. **2.** a department in N France. 533,862. 2868 sq. mi. (7430 sq. km). *Cap.:* Laon.

ait (āt), *n. Brit. Dial.* a small island, esp. in a river. Also, **eyot.** [bef. 900; ME *eyt,* OE *ȳgett,* dim. of *ieg, ig* island, c. MLG *ō, ōge, ou(we),* OHG *ouwa,* ON *ey.* See ISLAND]

aitch (āch), *n.* the letter *H, h.* [ME *ache* < OF *ache* < LL **hacca* or **accha;* r. *ha*]

aitch•bone (āch′bōn′), *n.* **1.** the rump bone, as of beef. **2.** the cut of beef that includes this bone. Also, **edgebone.** [1480–90; earlier *hach-boon* (with spurious *h-*); *(h)ach* var. by misdivision as *an (h)ach(e)* of *a nache* rump < MF < VL **natica,* fem. of **naticus* of the rump, equiv. to L *nati(s)* rump, NATES + *-cus* adj. suffix]

Ait•ken (āt′kən), *n.* **1. Robert Grant,** 1864–1951, U.S. astronomer. **2. William Maxwell.** See **Beaverbrook, William Maxwell Aitken.**

Ai•to•lí•a (e′tô lē′ä), *n.* Modern Greek name of **Aetolia.**

A•i•us Lo•cu•tius (ā′ē əs lō kyo͞o′shəs), *Rom. Legend.* a disembodied voice that warned the Romans of a coming invasion by the Gauls.

Aix-en-Pro•vence (ek sän prô väns′; *Eng.* āks′änprə väns′), *n.* a city in SE France, N of Marseilles. 114,014. Also called **Aix** (eks; *Eng.* āks).

Aix-la-Cha•pelle (eks lȧ shȧ pel′; *Eng.* āks′lä shäpel′), *n.* French name of **Aachen.**

Aix-les-Bains (eks lā baN′; *Eng.* āks′lä bānz′), *n.* a town in SE France, N of Chambéry. 22,293.

Aí•yi•na (e′yē nä), *n.* Modern Greek name of **Aegina** (defs. 2–4).

A•jac•cio (ä yät′chô), *n.* a seaport in and the capital of Corsica: the birthplace of Napoleon I. 51,770.

A•jan•ta (ə jun′tə), *n.* a village in N Maharashtra, in W central India: caves and shrines containing Buddhist frescoes and sculptures.

a•jar[1] (ə jär′), *adj., adv.* neither entirely open nor entirely shut; partly open: *The door was ajar.* [1350–1400; ME *on char* on the turn; see A-[1], CHAR[3]]

a•jar[2] (ə jär′), *adv., adj.* in contradiction to; at variance with: *a story ajar with the facts.* [1545–55; for *at jar* at discord; cf. JAR[3] (n.)]

A•jax (ā′jaks), *n.* **1.** Also called **Great Ajax, Telamonian Ajax.** *Class. Myth.* a Greek hero in the Trojan War who rescued the body of Achilles and killed himself out of jealousy when Odysseus was awarded the armor of Achilles. **2.** Also called **A′jax the Less′er.** *Class. Myth.* a Locrian king, noted for his fighting during the Trojan War, who was said to have been killed in a shipwreck as punishment for violating a shrine of Athena. **3.** (*italics*) a tragedy (c440 B.C.) by Sophocles. **4.** a town in S Ontario, in S Canada. 20,774. Also, **Aias** (for defs. 1–3).

a•jee (ə jē′), *adv. Brit. Dial.* agee.

a•jin•gle (ə jing′gəl), *adv., adj.* jingling.

a•ji•va (ə jē′və), *n. Jainism.* all in the universe that is not jiva, as space, time, matter, and those things by which rest and motion are possible to objects. [< Skt *ajīva* without life, equiv. to *a-* A-[6] + *jīva* living]

A•ji•vi•ka (ä jē′vi kə), *n.* a member of a former Indian sect originating in the 5th century B.C. as a heretical offshoot of Jainism: a disciple of Gosala. [< Skt *ājīvika*]

Aj•mer (uj mēr′), *n.* a city in central Rajasthan, in NW India. 262,480.

Aj•mer-Mer•wa•ra (uj mēr′mer wär′ə), *n.* a former province in NW India. 2400 sq. mi. (6216 sq. km).

A•jodh•ya (ə yōd′yə), *n.* a city in E Uttar Pradesh, in N India; a suburb of Faizabad: one of the seven most sacred Hindu centers.

à jour (ä′ zho͝or′; *Fr.* A zho͞oR′), of or pertaining to objects that are pierced, perforated, or decorated with an openwork pattern. Also, **a•jou•ré** (ä′zho͞o rā′; *Fr.* A zho͞o Rā′). [< F: lit., (open) to daylight]

a•ju•ga (aj′ə gə), *n.* any of various plants of the genus *Ajuga,* having usually blue flowers and often cultivated as a ground cover. Also called **bugle, bugleweed.** [< NL (Linnaeus), equiv. to *a-* A-[6] + L *jug(um)* YOKE + *-a* -A[2]]

AK, Alaska (approved esp. for use with zip code).

CONCISE ETYMOLOGY KEY: <, descended or borrowed from; >, whence; b., blend of, blended; c., cognate with; cf., compare; deriv., derivative; equiv., equivalent; imit., imitative; obl., oblique; r., replacing; s., stem; sp., spelling, spelled; resp., respelling, respelled; trans., translation; ?, origin unknown; *, unattested; ‡, probably earlier than. See the full key inside the front cover.

a.k., *Slang (vulgar).* ass-kisser.

a.k.a., also known as: *According to police records he is Joe Smith a.k.a. "Baby Face Smith" and Joseph Smathers.* Also, **AKA, aka** [1945–50]

A•ka•ba (ä′kə bə, ak′ə-), *n.* Aqaba. [1945–50]

a•ka•la (ə kä′lə), *n.* a Hawaiian shrub or climber, *Rubus macraei,* bearing a large, red, edible raspberry. [< Hawaiian *ʻākala*]

A•kan (ä′kän), *n., pl.* **A•kans,** (*esp. collectively*) **A•kan** for 2. **1.** a language of the Kwa branch of Niger-Congo spoken in much of Ghana and parts of the Ivory Coast. **2.** a member of any of various Akan-speaking peoples, including the Ashanti and Fanti.

A•kar•na•ní•a (ä kär nä nē′ä), *n.* Modern Greek name of **Acarnania.**

a•ka•sha (ä kä′shə), *n.* (in the philosophies of India) the ether, regarded as including material and nonmaterial entities in a common medium. [< Skt *ākāśa*]

A•ka•shi (ä kä′shē), *n.* a city on W Honshu, in Japan. 254,873.

ak•a•this•ia (ak′ə thizh′ə, -thiz′ē ə), *n.* a state of motor restlessness, sometimes produced by neuroleptic medication, that ranges from a feeling of inner distress to an inability to sit still. [1900–05; < Czech *akathisie* < Gk *a-* A-[6] + *káthis(is)* sitting (n. deriv. of *kathízein* to seat, make sit, take one's seat; *kat-* CAT- + *hízein* to seat, akin to SIT[1]) + NL *-ia* -IA]

Ak•bar (ak′bär), *n.* (*"the Great"*) (*Jalal-ud-Din Mohammed*) 1542–1605, Mogul emperor of India 1556–1605.

A.K.C., American Kennel Club.

ake (āk), *v.i.,* **aked, ak•ing,** *n. Obs.* ache.

a•ke•a•ke (ä′kē ä′kē), *n.* aalii. [< Maori]

ak•e•bi (ak′ə bē), *n.* a climbing vine, *Akebia quinata,* of eastern Asia, bearing inconspicuous flowers and purple, edible berries, grown as an ornamental in the U.S. [< Japn]

a•kee (ə kē′), *n.* a tropical tree, *Blighia sapida,* of the soapberry family, cultivated for the edible aril of its seeds. Also, **ackee.** [1785–95; allegedly < Kru]

a•ke•la (ə kē′lə), *n.* (in the Cub Scouts) a pack leader. [after *Akela,* leader of the wolf pack in *The Jungle Books* by Kipling]

A•kel•da•ma (ə kel′də mə), *n.* Aceldama.

Ake•ley (āk′lē), *n.* **Carl Ethan,** 1864–1926, U.S. naturalist, explorer, and sculptor.

a•kene (ā kēn′, ə kēn′), *n.* achene.

ake•ton (ak′tən), *n. Armor.* acton.

Akh (äk), *n. Egyptian Myth.* the transfigured and beatified spirit of a dead person. [vocalization of Egyptian *ʾḫ* spirit of the dead]

A•khe•ta•ton (ä′kə tät′n), *n.* the capital of ancient Egypt under the reign of Amenhotep IV: its excavated site is at the modern village of Tell el Amarna.

Ak•hi•sar (äk′hi sär′), *n.* a town in W Turkey, NE of Izmir. 47,856. Ancient, **Thyatira.**

Akh•ma•to•va (äk mä′tə və; *Russ.* ukh mä′tə və), *n.* **An•na** (an′ə; *Russ.* ä′nə), (*Anna Andreyevna Gorenko*), 1889–1966, Russian poet.

Akh•na•ton (äk nät′n), *n.* See **Amenhotep IV.**

a•ki•a•po•la•au (ä kē′ä pō′lä ou′), *n.* a rare yellow Hawaiian honeycreeper, *Hemignathus munroi,* having a long slender down-curved upper bill and a short straight lower bill. [< Hawaiian *ʻakiapolaʻau*]

A•ki•ba ben Jo•seph (ä kē′bä ben jō′zəf, -səf, ə kē′və), A.D. c50–c135, rabbi and scholar: systematizer of Jewish oral law on which the Mishnah is based. Also called **A•ki′ba.**

A•ki•hi•to (ä′ki hē′tō; *Japn.* ä kē′hē tô′), *n.* born 1933, emperor of Japan since 1989 (son of Hirohito).

A•kil (ä kēl′), *n.* a male given name: from an Arabic word meaning "one who uses reason."

a•kim•bo (ə kim′bō), *adj., adv.* with hand on hip and elbow bent outward: *to stand with arms akimbo.* [1375–1425; late ME *in kenebowe* < ON **i keng boginn* bent into a crook (*i* in, *keng* acc. of *kengr* hook, *boginn* ptp. of *bjūga* to bend)]

Ak′i•mis′ki Is′land (ak′ə mis′kē, ak′-), an island in SW James Bay, in the SE Northwest Territories, in S central Canada. ab. 898 sq. mi. (2326 sq. km).

a•kin (ə kin′), *adj.* **1.** of kin; related by blood (usually used predicatively): *cousins who were too closely akin for marriage.* **2.** allied by nature; having the same properties: *Something akin to vertigo was troubling her.* **3.** having or showing an affinity; kindred: *They are emotionally but not intellectually akin.* [1580–90; see A-[2], KIN]
—**Syn. 2.** cognate; similar, analogous, comparable, parallel.

a•ki•ne•sia (ā′ki nē′zhə, -kī-), *n. Pathol.* absence, loss, or impairment of the power of voluntary movement. Also, **a•ki•ne•sis** (ā′ki nē′sis, -kī-, ā kin′ə sis). [< NL < Gk *akīnēsíā;* see A-[6], -KINESIA] —**a•ki•net•ic** (ā′kinet′ik, -kī-), *adj.*

ak•i•nete (ak′ə nēt′, ā ki′nēt), *n.* (in certain algae) a nonmotile, asexual spore formed within a cell, the wall of which is fused to that of the parent cell. Cf. **aplanospore.** [< Gk *akínētos* without movement, equiv. to *a-* A-[6] + *kīnētos* moving, deriv. of *kīnein* to move]

a′kinet′ic mut′ism, *Pathol., Psychiatry.* a state of apparent alertness with normal eye movements but no speech or other voluntary motion, usually due to a stroke.

A•kins (ā′kinz), *n.* **Zo•ë** (zō′ē), 1886–1958, U.S. playwright.

A•ki•ta (ə kē′tə), *n.* **1.** a seaport on N Honshu, in N Japan, on the Sea of Japan. 284,830. **2.** (*sometimes l.c.*) one of a Japanese breed of large, muscular dogs having a broad head with erect ears, a stiff coat of brown, red, black, or brindle color, and a long tail curled over its back, originally bred for hunting, now often used as a guard dog.

Akita (def. 2) 26 in. (66 cm) high at shoulder

Ak•kad (ak′ad, ä′käd), *n.* Also, **Accad. 1.** one of the ancient kingdoms of Mesopotamia, the northern division of Babylonia. **2.** Also called **Agade.** a city in and the capital of this kingdom, one of the three cities of Nimrod's kingdom. Gen. 10:10. —*adj.* **3.** Akkadian.

Ak•ka•di•an (ə kā′dē ən, ə kä′-), *n.* **1.** the eastern Semitic language, now extinct, of Assyria and Babylonia, written with a cuneiform script. **2.** one of the Akkadian people. **3.** *Obs.* Sumerian. —*adj.* **4.** of or belonging to Akkad. **5.** of or pertaining to the eastern Semitic language called Akkadian. **6.** *Obs.* Sumerian. Also, **Accadian.** [1850–55; AKKAD + -IAN]

Ak•ker•man (ä′kər män′, ä′kər män′; *Russ.* u kyirmän′), *n.* former name of **Belgorod-Dnestrovsky.**

Ak•kra (ak′rə, ə krä′), *n.* Accra.

Ak•mo•linsk (äk′mə linsk′; *Russ.* uk mô′lyinsk), *n.* former name of **Tselinograd.**

Ak•ron (ak′rən), *n.* a city in NE Ohio. 237,177.

Ak•ro•tí•ri (ak′rō tēr′ē), *n.* the remains of an ancient Minoan city on the island of Thera in the Aegean Sea, where abundant pottery and frescoes of the second millennium B.C. have been excavated.

Ak•sum (äk′so͞om), *n.* the capital of an ancient Ethiopian kingdom, ruled by Himyaritic emigrants from Arabia. Also, **Axum.**

Ak•tyu•binsk (äk tyo͞o′binsk; *Russ.* uk tyo͞o′byinsk), *n.* a city in NW Kazakhstan. 191,000.

A•kur•ey•ri (ä′kə râr′ē; *Icel.* ä′kYR ā′Ri), *n.* a city in N Iceland. 12,643.

A•ku•ta•ga•wa (ä ko͞o′tä gä′wä), *n.* **Ryu•no•su•ke** (Ryo͞o nô′so͞o ke′), 1892–1927, Japanese short-story writer and essayist.

ak•va•vit (äk′vä vēt′), *n.* aquavit.

Ak•yab (ak yab′, ak′yab), *n.* former name of **Sittwe.**

al (äl), *n.* See **Indian mulberry.** [< Hindi *āl*]

Al (al), *n.* a male given name: form of **Albert, Alfred, Aloysius.**

à l′, form of **à la** used for either gender before a vowel or *h.*

al-, var. of **ad-** before *l: allure.*

Al-, a word in Arabic names meaning "family" or "the house of": *Al-Saud, or the members of the house of Saud.* [< Ar *āl* family]

-al[1], a suffix with the general sense "of the kind of, pertaining to, having the form or character of" that named by the stem, occurring in loanwords from Latin (*autumnal; natural; pastoral*), and productive in English on the Latin model, usually with bases of Latin origin (*accidental; seasonal; tribal*). Originally, **-al**[1] was restricted to stems not containing an *-l-* (cf. **-ar**[1]); recent lapses in this rule have produced semantically distinct pairs, as *familiar* and *familial.* Cf. **-ical, -ial.** [< L *-ālis, -āle;* often r. ME *-el* < OF]

-al[2], a suffix forming nouns from verbs, usually verbs of French or Latin origin: *denial; refusal.* [< L *-āle* (sing.), *-ālia* (pl.), nominalized neut. of *-ālis* -AL[1]; often r. ME *-aille* < OF < L *-ālia*]

-al[3], *Chem.* a suffix indicating that a compound contains an aldehyde group: *chloral.* [presumed to be short for ALDEHYDE]

AL, 1. Alabama (approved esp. for use with zip code). **2.** Anglo-Latin.

Al, *Symbol, Chem.* aluminum.

AL., Anglo-Latin.

al., 1. other things. [< L *alia*] **2.** other persons. [< L *aliī*]

A.L., 1. *Baseball.* American League. **2.** American Legion. **3.** Anglo-Latin.

a.l., autograph letter.

à la (ä′ lä, ä′ lə; *Fr.* A lA), **1.** according to; in the manner of: *a short poem à la Ogden Nash.* **2.** *Cookery.* **a.** prepared in the manner of, to the taste of, or by: *chicken à la provençale.* **b.** prepared with the ingredient of. Also, **a la.** [1580–90; < F: short for *à la mode de* in the style of]

a•la (ā′lə), *n., pl.* **a•lae** (ā′lē). **1.** a wing. **2.** a winglike part, process, or expansion, as of a bone, shell, seed, or stem. **3.** either of the two side petals of a flower in the legume family, as the pea. **4.** (in an ancient Roman house) a small room, as an alcove, opening into a larger room or courtyard. [1730–40; < L *āla* wing, armpit, shoulder, repr. **aks-lā,* deriv. of same base as *axis* axle (see AXIS[1]); see AXLE]

A•la (ä′lä), *n.* **Hus•sein** (ho͞o sān′), 1888–1964, Iranian statesman and diplomat: premier in 1951 and from 1955 to 1957.

Ala, *Biochem.* alanine.

Ala., Alabama.

A.L.A., **1.** American Library Association. **2.** Associate in Liberal Arts. **3.** Authors League of America. **4.** Automobile Legal Association.

Al•a•bam•a (al′ə bam′ə), *n.* **1.** a state in the SE United States. 3,890,061; 51,609 sq. mi. (133,670 sq. km). *Cap.:* Montgomery. *Abbr.:* AL (for use with zip code), Ala. **2.** a river flowing SW from central Alabama to the Mobile River. 315 mi. (505 km) long. **—Al•a•bam•i•an** (al′ə bam′ē ən), **Al′a•bam′an,** *adj., n.*

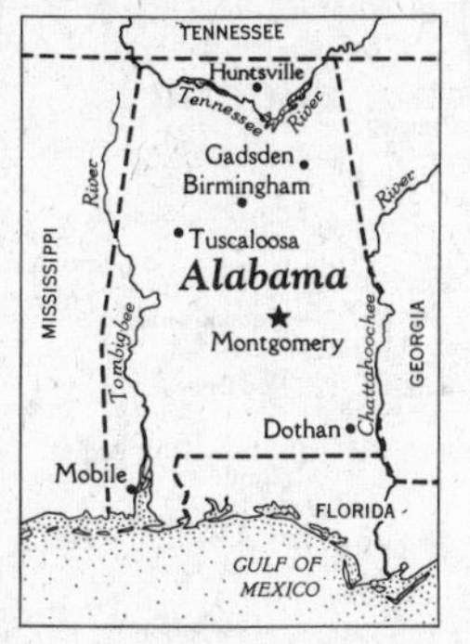

al•a•bam•ine (al′ə bam′ēn, -in), *n. Chem.* (formerly) astatine. *Symbol:* Ab [1930–35; ALABAM(A) + -INE²]

al•a•ban•dite (al′ə ban′dīt), *n.* a rare mineral, manganese sulfide, MnS, occurring in a massive form and having a cubical lattice structure. [see ALMANDINE, -ITE¹]

à l'a•ban•don (A lA bäN dôN′), *French.* carelessly; recklessly. [lit., with abandon]

al•a•bas•ter (al′ə bas′tər, -bä′stər), *n.* **1.** a finely granular variety of gypsum, often white and translucent, used for ornamental objects or work, such as lamp bases, figurines, etc. **2.** Also called **Oriental alabaster.** a variety of calcite, often banded, used or sold as alabaster. *—adj.* Also, **al•a•bas•trine** (al′ə bas′trin). **3.** made of alabaster: *an alabaster column.* **4.** resembling alabaster; smooth and white: *her alabaster throat.* [1350–1400; < L < Gk *alábastros;* r. ME *alabastre* < MF < L]

al•a•bas•tos (al′ə bas′tos, -təs, -bä′stos, -stəs), *n., pl.* **-bas•toi** (-bas′toi, -bä′stoi). alabastron.

al•a•bas•tron (al′ə bas′tron, -trən, -bä′stron, -strən), *n., pl.* **-bas•tra** (-bas′trə, -bä′strə), **-bas•trons.** *Gk. and Rom. Antiq.* a jar characteristically having an elongated shape, narrow neck, flat-rimmed mouth, and rounded base requiring a stand or support, chiefly used for fragrant ointments. Also, **alabastos, alabastrum.** Cf. **aryballos, askos, lekythos.** [1840–50; < Gk *alábastron* alabaster vase]

al•a•bas•trum (al′ə bas′trəm, -bä′strəm), *n., pl.* **-bas•tra** (-bas′trə, -bä′strə), **-bas•trums.** alabastron.

à la bonne heure (A lA bô nœʀ′), *French.* **1.** at the right moment. **2.** well and good; just right; excellent. [lit., at the good hour]

à la broche (A lA bʀôsh), *French.* cooked on a skewer.

à la carte (ä′ lə kärt′, al′ə; *Fr.* A lA kaʀt′), with a separate price for each dish offered on the menu: *dinner à la carte.* Cf. **prix fixe, table d'hôte.** [1820–30; < F: according to the menu; see CARTE²]

a•lack (ə lak′), *interj. Archaic.* (used as an exclamation of sorrow, regret, or dismay.) Also, **a•lack•a•day** (ə lak′ə dā′). [presumably AH + LACK. Cf. AHA, AHEM, ALAS]

a•lac•ri•ty (ə lak′ri tē), *n.* **1.** cheerful readiness, promptness, or willingness: *We accepted the invitation with alacrity.* **2.** liveliness; briskness. [1500–10; < L *alacritās,* equiv. to *alacri(s)* lively + *-tās-* -TY²] **—a•lac′ri•tous,** *adj.*
—Syn. 1. eagerness, keenness; fervor, zeal. **2.** sprightliness, agility.

A•la Dagh (ä′lä däкн′), **1.** a mountain range in S Turkey: highest peak, ab. 11,000 ft. (3350 m). **2.** a mountain range in E Turkey: highest peak, ab. 11,500 ft. (3500 m).

A•lad•din (ə lad′n), *n.* (in *The Arabian Nights' Entertainments*) the son of a poor widow in China. He becomes the possessor of a magic lamp and ring with which he can command a jinn to do his bidding.

a•lae (ā′lē), *n.* pl. of **ala.**

à la fran•çaise (A lA fʀäN sez′), *French.* in or according to the French manner or style.

A•la•gez (*Armenian.* u′lə gyôs′), *n.* **Mount.** See **Aragats, Mount.**

A•la•go•as (ä′lə gō′əs), *n.* a state in NE Brazil. 1,987,673; 10,674 sq. mi. (27,650 sq. km). *Cap.:* Maceió.

A•la•göz (ä′lä gœz′), *n.* Turkish name of Mount Aragats.

A•lai′ Moun′tains (ə lī′; *Russ.* u lī′), a mountain range in SW Kirghizia (Kyrgyzstan): part of the Tien Shan Mountains; highest peak, ab. 19,000 ft. (5790 m).

A•la•jue•la (ä′lä hwe′lä), *n.* a city in central Costa Rica. 36,736.

à la king (ä′ lə king′, al′ə), (of cooked fowl, fish, etc.) diced and served in a cream sauce containing mushrooms, pimiento, or green pepper: *chicken à la king.* [1915–20]

a•la•la (ä′lä lä′), *n.* a dull, brownish-tinged crow that occurs only in Hawaii. [< Hawaiian *ʻalalā;* as homonymous v., to caw, scream]

Al•al•co•me•neus (al′al kə mēn′yəs), *n. Class. Myth.* the first man: he reared Athena and reconciled Zeus and Hera. Also, **Al′al•ko•me′neus.** **—Al′al•co•me′ne•an, Al′al•ko•me′ne•an,** *adj.*

a•la•li•a (ə lā′lē ə, ə lāl′yə), *n. Pathol.* an inability to speak. [1875–80; A-⁶ + Gk *lalia* talk, chatter, equiv. to *lal(leîn)* to talk, chatter + *-ia* -Y³]

A•la•mán (ä′lä män′), *n.* **Lu•cas** (lo͞o′käs), 1792–1853, Mexican historian and politician.

Al•a•man•ni (al′ə man′ī), *n.pl.* Alemanni.

Al•a•man•nic (al′ə man′ik), *n., adj.* Alemannic.

al•a•me•da (al′ə mā′də), *n.* **1.** *Chiefly Southwestern U.S.* a public walk shaded with trees. **2.** (in Latin America) a boulevard, park, or public garden having such a walk. [1790–1800; < Sp, equiv. to *álam(o)* poplar (see ALAMO) + *-eda* < L *-ētum* suffix denoting a grove or stand of trees]

Al•a•me•da (al′ə mē′də, -mā′-), *n.* a city in W California. 63,852.

A•la•mein (al′ə mān′), *n.* See **El Alamein.**

à l'a•mé•ri•caine (ä lə mer′i kān′, -ken′; *Fr.* A lA-mā ʀē ken′), *French Cookery.* prepared with tomatoes, garlic, wine, shallots, and herbs: *lobster à l'américaine.* [< F: in the American style]

al•a•mi•qui (al′ə mə kē′), *n.* almique (def. 3).

al•a•mo (al′ə mō′, ä′lə-), *n., pl.* **-mos.** *Southwestern U.S.* a poplar. [1830–40; < Sp *álamo* poplar, ult. < a pre-Roman language of Iberia]

Al•a•mo (al′ə mō′), *n.* a Franciscan mission in San Antonio, Texas, besieged by Mexicans on February 23, 1836, during the Texan war for independence and taken on March 6, 1836, with its entire garrison killed.

à la mode (ä′ lə mōd′, al′ə-; *Fr.* A lA môd′), **1.** in or according to the fashion. **2.** *Cookery.* **a.** (of pie or other dessert) served with a portion of ice cream, often as a topping: *apple pie à la mode.* **b.** (of beef) larded and braised or stewed with vegetables, herbs, etc., and served with a rich brown gravy. Also, **a′ la mode′, alamode.** [1640–50; < F]

al•a•mode (al′ə mōd′), *n.* **1.** a lightweight, glossy silk fabric used in the manufacture of scarfs, hoods, etc. **2.** See **à la mode.**

Al•a•mo•gor•do (al′ə mə gôr′dō), *n.* a city in S New Mexico: first atomic bomb exploded in the desert ab. 50 mi. (80 km) NW of here, July 16, 1945. 24,024.

à la mort (A lA môʀ′), *French.* **1.** mortally ill. **2.** melancholy; dispirited. **3.** grievously; fatally. [lit., to the death]

Al•an (al′ən), *n.* a male given name: from a Celtic word meaning "harmony."

Al•an-a-dale (al′ən ə dāl′), *n.* Allan-a-dale.

à l'an•cienne (A läN syen′), *French.* in or according to the old-fashioned manner or style.

Å′land Is′lands (ä′lənd, ô′lənd; *Swed.* ō′länd′), a group of Finnish islands in the Baltic Sea, between Sweden and Finland. 22,608; 572 sq. mi. (1480 sq. km). Finnish, **Ahvenanmaa.**

à l'an•glaise (ä′ läng glāz′, -glez′; *Fr.* A läN glez′) **1.** (*italics*) *French.* in the English manner or style. **2.** *French Cookery.* boiled in water or white stock: *chicken à l'anglaise; vegetables à l'anglaise.* [< F]

A•la•ni (ə lā′nī, ə lä′nē), *n.pl.* a nomadic Iranian people who flourished in the 2nd–4th centuries A.D. and are ancestors of the present-day Ossets. Also called **A•lans** (ə lānz′, ə länz′).

al•a•nine (al′ə nēn′, -nin), *n. Biochem.* any of several isomers of a colorless, crystalline, water-soluble amino acid, $CH_3CH(NH_2)COOH$, found in many proteins and produced synthetically: used chiefly in biochemical research. *Abbr.:* Ala; *Symbol:* A [1860–65; AL(DEHYDE) + *-an-* (arbitrarily inserted) + -INE²]

Al-A•non (al′ə non′), *n.* a support and discussion group for the relatives of people suffering from alcoholism, usually operated in conjunction with Alcoholics Anonymous.

al′ant starch′ (al′ənt, ə lant′), *Chem.* inulin. [< G, OHG, perh. < VL **iluna,* alter. of L *inula* (see INULIN)]

al•a•nyl (al′ə nil), *Chem.* *—n.* **1.** the acyl group of alanine. *—adj.* **2.** of or pertaining to such a group. [ALA-N(INE) + (AC)YL]

a•lap•a (ə lap′ə), *n. Rom. Cath. Ch., Anglican Ch.* the light blow on the cheek delivered by the bishop in a confirmation service. [< L: a slap]

a•lar (ā′lər), *adj.* **1.** pertaining to or having wings; alary. **2.** winglike; wing-shaped. **3.** *Anat., Bot.* axillary. [1830–40; < L *ālāris,* equiv. to *āl(a)* ALA + *-āris* -AR¹]

A•lar (ā′lär), *Trademark.* a brand of daminozide.

A•lar•cón (ä′lär kôn′), *n.* **Pe•dro An•to•nio** (pe′thʀô än tô′nyô), (*Pedro Antonio Alarcón y Ariza*), 1833–91, Spanish novelist, short-story writer, and diplomat.

Al•a•ric (al′ər ik), *n.* A.D. c370–410, king of the Visigoths: captured Rome 410.

à la ri•gueur (A lA ʀē gœʀ′), *French.* to the fullest extent; literally. [lit., in strictness]

a•larm (ə lärm′), *n.* **1.** a sudden fear or distressing suspense caused by an awareness of danger; apprehension; fright. **2.** any sound, outcry, or information intended to warn of approaching danger: *Paul Revere raced through the countryside raising the alarm that the British were coming.* **3.** an automatic device that serves to call attention, to rouse from sleep, or to warn of fire, smoke, an intruder, etc. **4.** a warning sound; signal for attention. **5.** *Animal Behav.* any sound, outcry, chemical discharge, action, or other signal that functions to draw attention to a potential predator. **6.** *Fencing.* an appeal or a challenge made by a step or stamp on the ground with the advancing foot. **7.** *Archaic.* a call to arms. *—v.t.* **8.** to make fearful or apprehensive; distress. **9.** to warn of danger; rouse to vigilance and swift measures for safety. **10.** to fit or equip with an alarm or alarms, as for fire, smoke, or robbery: *to alarm one's house and garage.* [1350–1400; ME *alarme, alarom* < MF < OIt *allarme,* n. from phrase *all'arme* to (the) arms. See ARM²] **—a•larm′a•ble,** *adj.* **—a•larm•ed•ly** (ə lär′mid lē), *adv.*
—Syn. 1. consternation; terror, panic. See **fear. 8.** See **frighten.**

alarm′ clock′, a clock with a bell or buzzer that can be set to sound at a particular time, as to awaken someone. [1690–1700]

a•larm•ing (ə lär′ming), *adj.* causing alarm or fear: *an alarming case of pneumonia; an alarming lack of respect.* [1670–80; ALARM + -ING²] **—a•larm′ing•ly,** *adv.*

a•larm•ist (ə lär′mist), *n.* **1.** a person who tends to raise alarms, esp. without sufficient reason, as by exaggerating dangers or prophesying calamities. *—adj.* **2.** of or like an alarmist. [1795–1805; ALARM + -IST] **—a•larm′ism,** *n.*

alarm′ reac′tion, *Physiol.* the first stage of the general adaptation syndrome, in which the body responds to stress by exhibiting shock. [1935–40]

a•lar•um (ə lar′əm, ə lär′-), *n. Archaic.* alarm.

alar′ums and excur′sions, 1. (esp. in Elizabethan drama) military action, as representative fragments of a battle, sound effects of trumpets, or clash of arms: used as a stage direction. **2.** any noisy, frantic, or disorganized activity. [1585–95]

a•la•ry (ā′lə rē, al′ə-), *adj.* **1.** of or pertaining to wings. **2.** *Biol.* wing-shaped. [1650–60; < L *ālārius,* equiv. to *āl(a)* ALA + *-ārius* -ARY]

a•las (ə las′, ə läs′), *interj.* (used as an exclamation to express sorrow, grief, pity, concern, or apprehension of evil.) [1225–75; ME < OF *(h)a las!,* equiv. to *(h)a* AH + *las* wretched < L *lassus* weary; cf. ALACK]

Alas., Alaska.

al-Ash•ʻa•ri (al′ash ə rē′), **A•bu 'l-Ha•san** (ä′bo͞o al ha san′), A.D. c873–936, the formulator of the classical synthesis in Islamic philosophical theology known as Ashʻarism.

A•las•ka (ə las′kə), *n.* **1.** a state of the United States in NW North America. 400,481; 586,400 sq. mi. (1,519,000 sq. km). *Cap.:* Juneau. *Abbr.:* AK (for use with zip code), Alas. **2. Gulf of,** a gulf of the Pacific, on the coast of S Alaska. **—A•las′kan,** *adj., n.*

Alas′ka cod′. See **Pacific cod.**

Alas′ka crab′. See **king crab** (def. 2).

Alas′ka Cur′rent, an ocean current flowing counterclockwise in the Gulf of Alaska.

A•las′ka-Ha•wai′i time′ (ə las′kə hə wī′ē, -wä′ē, -wä′yə), the civil time officially adopted for the region of the 150th meridian, which includes the states of Alaska and Hawaii; two hours behind Pacific time. Also called **Alas′ka-Hawai′i Stand′ard Time′, Alaska time, Alaska Standard Time, Hawaii time, Hawaii Standard Time.**

Alas′ka High′way, a highway in NW Canada and Alaska, extending from E British Columbia to Fairbanks: built as a U.S. military supply route 1942. 1523 mi. (2452 km) long. Also called **Alcan Highway.**

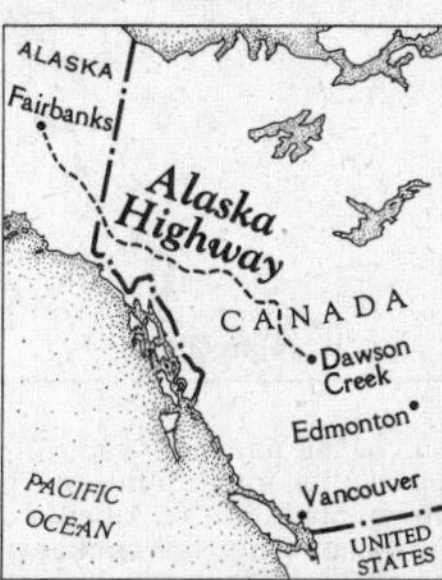

CONCISE PRONUNCIATION KEY: act, cāpe, dâre, pärt; set, ēqual; if, īce; ox, ōver, ôrder, oil, bo͝ok, bo͞ot, out; up, ûrge; child; sing; shoe; thin, *th*at; zh as in *treasure.* ə = *a* as in *alone,* *e* as in *system,* *i* as in *easily,* *o* as in *gallop,* *u* as in *circus;* ᵊ as in *fire* (fīᵊr), *hour* (ouᵊr). l and n can serve as syllabic consonants, as in *cradle* (krād′l), and *button* (but′n). See the full key inside the front cover.

Alas′kan king′ crab′. See **king crab** (def. 2). Also, **Alas′ka king′ crab′.** [1980–85]

Alas′kan mal′amute, one of an Alaskan breed of large dogs having a dense, coarse coat, raised originally by Alaskan Eskimos for drawing sleds. [1935–40]

Alas′ka Penin′sula, a peninsula in SW Alaska. 500 mi. (800 km) long.

Alas′ka pol′lock. See **walleye pollock.**

Alas′ka Pur′chase, **1.** purchase of the territory of Alaska by the U.S. from Russia in 1867 for $7,200,000. Cf. **Seward's Folly. 2.** the territory itself.

Alas′ka Range′, a mountain range in S Alaska. Highest peak, Mt. McKinley, 20,300 ft. (6190 m).

Alas′ka time′. See **Alaska-Hawaii time.** Also called **Alas′ka Stand′ard Time′.** [1945–50]

Al•as•tair (al′ə stər, -stâr′), *n.* a male given name.

a•late (ā′lāt), *adj.* Also, **a′lat•ed. 1.** having wings; winged. **2.** having membranous expansions like wings. **—*n.* 3.** the winged form of an insect when both winged and wingless forms occur in the species. [1660–70; < L *ālātus*, equiv. to *āl(a)* ALA + *-ātus* -ATE[1]]

Al•a•teen (al′ə tēn′), *n.* a support organization of teenage children of alcoholic parents, usually operated in conjunction with Alcoholics Anonymous.

Al•a•va (al′ə və), *n.* **Cape,** a cape in NW Washington: westernmost point in the contiguous U.S.

à la vapeur (A LA VA pœR′), *French.* steamed.

′Al•a•wite (al′ə wēt′, al′ə wēt′), *n. Islam.* a member of a Shi'ite sect inhabiting the coastal district of Latakia in northwest Syria. Also, **′Al•a•wi** (al′ə wē). Also called **Nusairi.** [< Ar *'Alawī* + -ITE[1]]

alb (alb), *n. Eccles.* a linen vestment with narrow sleeves, worn chiefly by priests, now invariably white in the Western Church but any color in the Eastern Church. [bef. 1100; ME *albe, (h)aube* (< MF), OE *albe* < L *alba (vestis)* white (garment); cf. D *albe*, OHG *alba* (G *Albe*)]

Alb., **1.** Albania. **2.** Albanian. **3.** Albany. **4.** Alberta.

alb., (in prescriptions) white. [< L *albus*]

al•ba (äl′bə, al′-), *n.* a Provençal troubadour poem or love song, typically about the parting of lovers at dawn. [1815–25; < OPr: dawn < L, fem. of *albus* white]

Al•ba (al′bə; *Sp.* äl′vä), *n.* **Duke of.** See **Alva, Fernando Alvarez de Toledo.**

Alba., Alberta.

Al•ba•ce•te (äl′vä the′te), *n.* a city in SE Spain. 92,233.

al•ba•core (al′bə kôr′, -kōr′), *n., pl.* (*esp. collectively*) **-core,** (*esp. referring to kinds or species*) **-cores. 1.** a long-finned tuna, *Thunnus alalunga*, of warm or temperate seas, the flesh of which is valued for canning. **2.** any of various tunalike fishes. [1570–80; < Pg *albacora* << North African Ar *al-bakūrah* the tuna]

Al•ba Lon•ga (al′bə lông′gə, long′-), a city of ancient Latium, SE of Rome: legendary birthplace of Romulus and Remus.

Al•ba•my•cin (al′bə mī′sin), *Pharm., Trademark.* a brand of novobiocin.

Al•ban (ôl′bən, al′-), *n.* **Saint,** 3rd century A.D., first English martyr.

Al•ba•ne•se (al′bə nā′zə, -sə, -zē, äl′-; *It.* äl′bä ne′ze), *n.* **Li•cia** (lē′chē ə; *It.* lē′chä), born 1913, Italian operatic soprano.

Al•ba•ni•a (al bā′nē ə, -bān′yə), *n.* **1.** a republic in S Europe, in the Balkan Peninsula, W of Macedonia and NW of Greece. 2,400,000; 10,632 sq. mi. (27,535 sq. km). *Cap.:* Tirana. **2.** *Obs.* Scotland.

Al•ba•ni•an (al bā′nē ən, -bān′yən, ôl-), *adj.* **1.** pertaining to Albania, its inhabitants, or their language. **—*n.* 2.** a native or inhabitant of Albania or Albany, N.Y. **3.** the Indo-European language spoken in Albania and adjacent areas. [1590–1600; ALBANI(A) + -AN]

CONCISE ETYMOLOGY KEY: <, descended or borrowed from; >, whence; b., blend of, blended; c., cognate with; cf., compare; deriv., derivative; equiv., equivalent; imit., imitative; obl., oblique; r., replacing; s., stem; sp., spelling, spelled; resp., respelling, respelled; trans., translation; ?, origin unknown; *, unattested; ‡, probably earlier than. See the full key inside the front cover.

Al•ba•ny (ôl′bə nē), *n.* **1.** a city in and the capital of New York, in the E part, on the Hudson. 101,727. **2.** a city in SW Georgia. 73,934. **3.** a city in W Oregon. 26,546. **4.** a seaport in SW Australia: resort. 15,222. **5.** a city in W California, on San Francisco Bay. 15,130. **6.** a river in central Canada, flowing E from W Ontario to James Bay. 610 mi. (980 km) long.

Al′bany Con′gress, *Amer. Hist.* a meeting of delegates from seven American colonies, held in 1754 at Albany, New York, at which Benjamin Franklin proposed a plan **(Al′bany Plan′ of Un′ion)** for unifying the colonies.

al•ba•rel•lo (al′bə rel′ō), *n., pl.* **-rel•los, -rel•li** (-rel′ē). a majolica jar of the 15th and 16th centuries, cylindrical with a waist slightly narrower than the ends, used in Spain and Italy for keeping dry drugs. [1870–75; < It, prob. dim. of *albero* poplar << L *albus* white]

al•bar•i•um (al bâr′ē əm), *n.* a stucco used in ancient times, made from powdered marble and lime mortar and often polished. [< L: stucco, neut. sing. of *albārius* pertaining to stucco, equiv. to *alb(us)* white + *-ārius* -ARY]

Al•ba•teg•ni•us (al′bə teg′nē əs), *n.* Latin name of **Battani.**

al•ba•tross (al′bə trôs′, -tros′), *n.* **1.** any of several large, web-footed sea birds of the family Diomedeidae that have the ability to remain aloft for long periods. Cf. **wandering albatross. 2.** a seemingly inescapable moral or emotional burden, as of guilt or responsibility. **3.** something burdensome that impedes action or progress. **4.** *Textiles.* **a.** a lightweight worsted fabric with a crepe or pebble finish. **b.** a plain-weave cotton fabric with a soft nap surface. [1675–85; var. of *algatross* frigate bird < Pg *alcatraz* pelican, prob. < Ar *al-ghaṭṭāṣ* a kind of sea eagle, lit., the diver; *-b-* for *-g-* perh. by assoc. with L *albus* white (the bird's color)]

albatross, *Diomedea exulans,* length 4 ft. (1.2 m); wingspread to 12 ft. (3.7 m)

Al-Bat•ta•ni (al bə tä′nē), *n.* Battani.

Al•bay (äl bī′), *n.* former name of **Legaspi.**

al•be•do (al bē′dō), *n., pl.* **-dos. 1.** *Astron.* the ratio of the light reflected by a planet or satellite to that received by it. **2.** *Meteorol.* such a ratio for any part of the earth's surface or atmosphere. **3.** the white, inner rind of a citrus fruit. [1855–60; < LL *albēdō* whiteness, equiv. to *alb(us)* white + *-ēdō* n. suffix; cf. TORPEDO]

al•be•dom•e•ter (al′bi dom′i tər), *n.* an instrument that measures the albedo of a surface. [ALBEDO + -METER]

Al•bee (ôl′bē), *n.* **Edward,** born 1928, U.S. playwright.

al•be•it (ôl bē′it), *conj.* although; even if: *a peaceful, albeit brief retirement.* [1350–1400; ME *al be it* al(though) it be]

Al•be•marle (al′bə märl′), *n.* a city in central North Carolina. 15,130.

Al′bemarle Sound′, an inlet of the Atlantic Ocean, in NE North Carolina. 60 mi. (97 km) long.

Al•bé•niz (äl ve′nēth; *Eng.* äl bā′nēs, al-), *n.* **I•sa•ac** (ē′sä äk′; *Eng.* ī′zək), 1860–1909, Spanish composer and pianist.

al•ber•go (äl beR′gô), *n., pl.* ***-ghi*** (-gē). *Italian.* an inn or hotel.

Al•ber•ich (äl′bər iKH), *n. Teutonic Legend.* a king of the dwarfs, the possessor of the tarnkappe and of the treasure of the Nibelungs.

Al•be•ro•ni (äl′be Rô′nē), *n.* **Giu•lio** (jo͞o′lyô), 1664–1752, Italian cardinal and statesman: prime minister of Spain 1715–19.

Al•bert (al′bərt), *n.* **1. Carl (Bert),** born 1908, U.S. politician: Speaker of the House 1971–77. **2. Prince** (*Albert Francis Charles Augustus Emanuel, Prince of Saxe-Coburg-Gotha*), 1819–61, consort of Queen Victoria. **3. Lake.** Also called **Albert Nyanza.** a lake in central Africa, between Uganda and Zaire: a source of the Nile. 100 mi. (160 km) long; 2061 sq. mi. (5338 sq. km); 2030 ft. (619 m) above sea level. **4.** a male given name: from Old High German words meaning "noble" and "bright."

Albert I, 1875–1934, king of the Belgians 1909–34.

Albert II, 1397–1439, king of Germany and emperor of the Holy Roman Empire 1438–39.

Al•ber•ta (al bûr′tə), *n.* **1.** a province in W Canada. 1,799,771; 255,285 sq. mi. (661,190 sq. km). *Cap.:* Edmonton. *Abbr.:* Alba., Alta. **2.** a female given name, form of **Albertine. —Al•ber′tan,** *adj., n.*

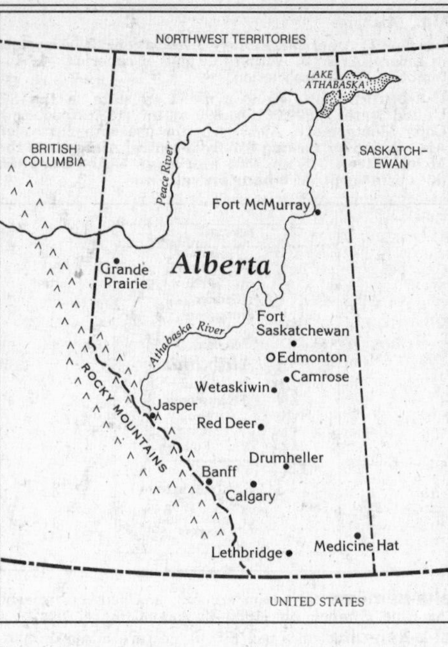

Al•bert, d′ (dal′bərt; *Ger.* däl′beRt; *Fr.* dAl beR′), **Eu•gen** (*Ger.* oi gän′) **Eu•gène** (*Fr.* œ zhen′) **Francis Charles,** 1864–1932, German-French pianist and composer, born in Scotland.

Al′bert Ed′ward, a mountain in SE New Guinea, in the Owen Stanley Range. 13,030 ft. (3972 m).

Al•ber•ti (äl beR′tē), *n.* **1. Le•on Bat•ti•sta** (le ôn′ bät tē′stä), 1404–72, Italian architect, artist, musician, and poet. **2. Ra•fa•el** (Rä fä el′), born 1902, Spanish poet.

Al•ber•ti bass (al bûr′tē bās′, äl ber′-), *Music.* a reiterated broken-chord figure used as an accompaniment, esp. in 18th-century rococo keyboard music. [1875–80; named after Domenico *Alberti* (ca. 1710–40), Italian musician]

Al•ber•tine (al′bər tēn′; *Fr.* Al beR tēn′; *Ger.* äl′ber-tē′nə), *n.* a female given name: derived from *Albert.* Also, **Al•ber•ti•na** (al′bər tē′nə).

Al′bert Lea′, a city in S Minnesota. 19,190.

Al′bert Ny•an′za (nī an′zə, nyän′zä). See **Albert, Lake.**

Al•ber•tus Mag•nus (al bûr′təs mag′nəs), **Saint** (*Albert von Böllstadt*) (*"Albert the Great," "the Universal Doctor"*), 1193?–1280, German scholastic philosopher: teacher of Saint Thomas Aquinas. **—Al•ber•tist** (al-bûr′tist, al′bər-), *n.*

Al•bert•ville (*Fr.* Al beR vēl′ *for 1;* al′bərt vil′ *for 2*), *n.* **1.** former name of **Kalemie. 2.** a town in NE Alabama. 12,039.

al•ber•type (al′bər tīp′), *n. Print. Now Rare.* collotype. [1870–75; after Joseph *Albert* (1825–86), Austrian photographer; see -TYPE]

al•bes•cent (al bes′ənt), *adj.* becoming white; whitish. [1825–35; < L *albēscent-* (s. of *albēscēns*, prp. of *albēscere*), equiv. to *alb(us)* white + *-ēscent-* -ESCENT] **—al•bes′cence,** *n.*

Al•bi (Al bē′), *n.* a city in and the capital of Tarn, in S France: center of the Albigenses. 49,456.

Al•bi•gen•ses (al′bi jen′sēz), *n.pl.* members of a Catharistic sect in the south of France that arose in the 11th century and was exterminated in the 13th century by a crusade **(Albigen′sian Crusade′)** and the Inquisition. [< ML *Albigēnsēs*, pl. of *Albigēnsis*, equiv. to *Albig(a)* ALBI + *-ēnsis* -ENSIS] **—Al•bi•gen•si•an** (al′bi jen′sē ən, -shən), *adj., n.* **—Al′bi•gen′si•an•ism,** *n.*

al•bi•nism (al′bə niz′əm), *n.* the state or condition of being an albino. [1830–40; ALBIN(O) + -ISM] **—al′bi•nis′tic,** *adj.*

al•bi•no (al bī′nō *or, esp. Brit.,* -bē′-), *n., pl.* **-nos. 1.** a person with pale skin, light hair, pinkish eyes, and visual abnormalities resulting from a hereditary inability to produce the pigment melanin. **2.** an animal or plant with a marked deficiency in pigmentation. **3.** *Philately.* an embossed stamp accidentally left without ink. [1770–80; < Pg, equiv. to *alb(o)* white (< L *albus*) + *-ino* -INE[1]] **—al•bin•ic** (al bin′ik), **al•bi•nal** (al′bə nl), *adj.*

al•bi•not•ic (al′bə not′ik), *adj. Pathol.* **1.** of or pertaining to albinism. **2.** afflicted with albinism or partial albinism. [1870–75; ALBIN(O) + -OTIC, prob. on the model of MELANOTIC]

Al•bi•nus (al bī′nəs), *n.* Alcuin.

Al•bi•on (al′bē ən), *n.* **1.** Alebion. **2.** a city in S Michigan. 11,059. **3.** *Literary.* Britain.

al•bite (al′bīt), *n. Mineral.* the sodium end member of the plagioclase feldspar group, light-colored and found in alkalic igneous rocks. [1835–45; < L *alb(us)* white + -ITE[1]] **—al•bit•ic** (al bit′ik), *adj.*

Al•bi•zu Cam•pos (äl bē′so͞o käm′pôs), **Pe•dro** (pe′-thrô), 1891–1964, Puerto Rican political leader.

al•biz•zi•a (al biz′ē ə, -bit′sē ə), *n.* any of several trees and shrubs belonging to the genus *Albizia*, of the legume family, native to warm regions of the Old World, having feathery pinnate leaves, densely clustered flowers, and flat pods. [1772; < NL, after Filippo delgi *Albizzi,* a Tuscan nobleman who introduced the silk tree into Italy in the mid-18th century; see -IA]

ALBM, air-launched ballistic missile.

Al•boin (al′boin, -bō in), *n.* died A.D. 573?, king of the Langobards 561?–573?

Al•bo•rak (äl′bô räk′, -bŏŏ-), *n. Islam.* the white horse that Muhammad rode to heaven. [< Ar *al-Buraq* < Aram *bārag, barqā* mount of the Messiah < Pahlavi *bārak* a fabulous steed]

Ål•borg (ôl′bôrg), *n.* a seaport in NE Jutland, in Denmark. 154,582. Also, **Aalborg.**

Al•bright (ôl′brīt), *n.* **1. Ivan (Le Lor•raine)** (lə lō-rān′, lō-), 1897–1983, U.S. painter. **2. Ten•ley (Emma)** (ten′lē), born 1935, U.S. figure skater. **3. William Fox•well** (foks′wel, -wəl), 1891–1971, U.S. archaeologist and biblical historian.

al•bronze (al′bronz′), *n.* See **aluminum bronze.**

al-Bu•kha•ri (al′bŏŏ KHär′ē), *n.* **Muhammad ibn Is•ma•'il** (ib′ən is mä′ēl), A.D. 810–870, a collector of the Hadith.

al•bum (al′bəm), *n.* **1.** a bound or loose-leaf book consisting of blank pages, pockets, envelopes, etc., for storing or displaying photographs, stamps, or the like, or for collecting autographs. **2.** a phonograph record or set of records containing several musical selections, a complete play, opera, etc.: *Her album of folk songs will be out next month.* **3.** the package or container for such a record or records: *The album has a pocket for each record.* **4.** a printed book containing an anthology of writings, reproductions of artwork, musical compositions, etc. [1645–55; 1955–60 for def. 2; < L: neut. sing. of *albus* white, i.e., a blank (tablet) painted white for writing on]

al•bu•men (al byŏŏ′mən), *n.* **1.** the white of an egg. **2.** *Bot.* the nutritive matter around the embryo in a seed. **3.** *Biochem.* albumin. [1590–1600; < LL, equiv. to *alb(us)* white, with s. in *-ū-* + *-men* n. suffix]

al•bu•me•nize (al byŏŏ′mə nīz′), *v.t.,* **-nized, -niz•ing.** to treat with an albuminous solution. Also, *esp. Brit.,* **al•bu′me•nise′.** [ALBUMEN + -IZE] **—al•bu′me•ni•za′tion,** *n.* **—al•bu′me•niz′er,** *n.*

albu′men pa′per, *Photog.* a printing paper coated with albumen, salt, and citric acid and sensitized with silver nitrate, used c1850–80.

albu′men plate′, a flexible zinc or aluminum printing plate coated with a photosensitive compound, used in offset printing of usually fewer than 50,000 copies. Cf. **deep-etch plate.**

al•bu•min (al byŏŏ′mən), *n. Biochem.* any of a class of simple, sulfur-containing, water-soluble proteins that coagulate when heated, occurring in egg white, milk, blood, and other animal and vegetable tissues and secretions. Also, **albumen.** [ALBUM(EN) + -IN[2]]

al•bu•mi•nate (al byŏŏ′mə nāt′), *n. Biochem.* a compound resulting from the action of an alkali or an acid upon albumin. [1855–60; ALBUMIN + -ATE[2]]

albu′min col′or, (in textile printing) a color fixed to a fabric by an albuminous mordant.

al•bu•mi•nize (al byŏŏ′mə nīz′), *v.t.,* **-nized, -niz•ing.** albumenize. Also, *esp. Brit.,* **al•bu′mi•nise′.**

al•bu•mi•noid (al byŏŏ′mə noid′), *Biochem.* —*n.* **1.** any of a class of simple proteins, as keratin, gelatin, or collagen, that are insoluble in all neutral solvents; scleroprotein. —*adj.* **2.** resembling albumen or albumin. [1855–60; ALBUMIN + -OID] **—al•bu′mi•noi′dal,** *adj.*

al•bu•mi•nous (al byŏŏ′mə nəs), *adj.* of, containing, or resembling albumen. Also, **al•bu•mi•nose** (al byŏŏ′mə nōs′). [1785–95; < LL *albūmin-,* s. of *albūmen* ALBUMEN + -OUS]

al•bu•mi•nu•ri•a (al byŏŏ′mə nŏŏr′ē ə, -nyŏŏr′-), *n. Pathol.* the presence of albumin in the urine. [1835–45; ALBUMIN + -URIA] **—al•bu′mi•nu′ric,** *adj.*

al•bum-o•ri•ent•ed (al′bəm ôr′ē ən tid, -ōr′-), *adj.* of or designating a format featuring rock songs from LPs and CDs rather than singles, esp. mainstream rock music.

Al•bu•quer•que (al′bə kûr′kē; *for 1 also Port.* ôl′bŏŏ-keR′kə), *n.* **1. Af•fon•so de** (ə fôN′sŏŏ də), 1453–1515, founder of the Portuguese empire in the East. **2.** a city in central New Mexico. 331,767.

al•bur•num (al bûr′nəm), *n. Bot.* sapwood. [1655–65; < L, equiv. to *alb(us)* white + *-urnum* neut. n. suffix] **—al•bur′nous,** *adj.*

al•bu•te•rol (al byŏŏ′tə rôl′, -rol′), *n. Pharm.* a selective sympathomimetic bronchodilator, $C_{13}H_{21}NO_3$, inhaled to relax bronchial muscles and ease breathing during an asthma attack. [appar. coined from components of the chemical name]

alc., alcohol.

Al•cae•us (al sē′əs), *n.* **1.** fl. c600 B.C., Greek poet of Mytilene. **2.** *Class. Myth.* a son of Androgeus and a grandson of Minos.

al•ca•hest (al′kə hest′), *n.* alkahest.

Al•ca•ic (al kā′ik), *adj.* **1.** pertaining to Alcaeus or to certain meters or a form of strophe or stanza used by, or named after, him. —*n.* **2. Alcaics,** Alcaic verses or strophes. [1620–30; < LL *Alcaicus* < Gk *Alkaïkós,* equiv. to *Alka(îos)* ALCAEUS + *-ikos* -IC]

al•cai•de (al kī′dē; *Sp.* äl kī′the), *n., pl.* **-cai•des** (-kī′dēz; *Sp.* -kī′thes). (in Spain, Portugal, Southwestern U.S., etc.) **1.** a commander of a fortress. **2.** a jailer; the warden of a prison. Also, **alcayde.** [1495–1505; < Sp < Ar *al-qā'id* the leader]

Al•ca•ids (al kā′idz), *n.pl. Class. Myth.* the descendants of Alcaeus.

al•cal•de (al kal′dē; *Sp.* äl käl′the), *n., pl.* **-des** (-dēz; *Sp.* -thes). (in Spain and Southwestern U.S.) a mayor having judicial powers. Also, **al•cade** (al kād′). [1605–15; < Sp < Ar *al-qāḍī* the judge]

al•ca•lig•e•nes (al′kə lij′ə nēz′), *n., pl.* **-nes.** *Bacteriol.* any of several rod-shaped aerobic or facultatively anaerobic bacteria of the genus *Alcaligenes,* found in the intestinal tract of humans and other vertebrates and in dairy products. [1919; < NL < F *alcali-* ALKALI + Gk *-genēs;* see -GEN]

Al•can•dre (al kan′drē), *n.* (in the *Odyssey*) the wife of Polybus who received Helen and Menelaus on their way home from Troy.

Al′can High′way (al′kan). See **Alaska Highway.**

Al•cath•o•us (al kath′ō əs), *n. Class. Myth.* **1.** a son of Pelops and Hippodamia who married Euachme and became king of Megara. **2.** (in the *Iliad*) a Trojan chieftain slain by Idomeneus.

Al•ca•traz (al′kə traz′), *n.* a small island in W California, in San Francisco Bay: site of a U.S. penitentiary 1933–63.

al•cay•de (al kī′dē; *Sp.* äl kī′the), *n., pl.* **-cay•des** (-kī′dēz; *Sp.* -kī′thes). alcaide.

Al•cá•zar (al′kə zär′, al kaz′ər; *Sp.* äl kä′thäR), *n.* **1.** the palace of the Moorish kings in Seville, Spain: later used by Spanish kings. **2.** (*l.c.*) a castle or fortress of the Spanish Moors. [< Sp < Ar *al* the + *qaṣr* < L *castrum* CASTLE, stronghold]

Al•ceste (al sest′), *n.* an opera (1767) by Christoph Willibald Gluck.

Al•ces•tis (al ses′tis), *n.* **1.** Also, **Alkestis.** *Class. Myth.* the wife of Admetus who gave up her life in order that the Fates might save the life of Admetus and later was brought back from Hades by Hercules. **2.** (*italics*) a tragedy (438 B.C.) by Euripides.

alchem., alchemy.

al•che•mist (al′kə mist), *n.* a person who is versed in or practices alchemy. [1350–1400; ME *alkamist;* prob. < ML *alchymista,* equiv. to *alchym(ia)* ALCHEMY + *-ista* -IST]

Alchemist, The, a comedy (1610) by Ben Jonson.

al•che•mize (al′kə mīz′), *v.t.,* **-mized, -miz•ing.** to change by or as by alchemy; transmute: *to alchemize lead into gold.* Also, *esp. Brit.,* **al′che•mise′.** [1595–1605; ALCHEM(Y) + -IZE]

al•che•my (al′kə mē), *n., pl.* **-mies** for 2. **1.** a form of chemistry and speculative philosophy practiced in the Middle Ages and the Renaissance and concerned principally with discovering methods for transmuting baser metals into gold and with finding a universal solvent and an elixir of life. **2.** any magical power or process of transmuting a common substance, usually of little value, into a substance of great value. [1325–1375; earlier *alchimie* < OF *alquemie* < ML *alchymia* < Ar *al* the + *kīmiyā'* < Gk *kēmeía* transmutation; r. ME *alconomye,* equiv. to *alk(imie)* + *(astr)onomye* ASTRONOMY] **—al•chem•ic** (al kem′ik), **al•chem′i•cal, al•che•mis•tic** (al′kə mis′tik), **al′che•mis′ti•cal,** *adj.* **—al•chem′i•cal•ly,** *adv.*

al•che•rin•ga (al′chə ring′gə), *n.* dreamtime. [1895–1900; < Aranda *aljerreŋe*]

Al•chuine (al′kwin), *n.* Alcuin.

Al•ci•bi•a•des (al′sə bī′ə dēz′), *n.* 450?–404 B.C., Athenian politician and general. **—Al′ci•bi′a•de′an,** *adj.*

al•cid (al′sid), *adj.* **1.** Also, **al•ci•dine** (al′si dīn′). of, pertaining, or belonging to the family Alcidae, comprising the auks, murres, puffins, etc. —*n.* **2.** a bird of the family Alcidae. [< NL *Alcidae* name of the family, equiv. to *Alc(a)* an auk genus (< Scand; see AUK) + *-idae* -ID[2]]

Al•ci•des (al sī′dēz), *n.* Hercules (def. 1).

Al•cim•e•de (al sim′i dē′), *n. Class. Myth.* the mother of Jason.

Al•ci•me•des (al′sə mē′dēz), *n. Class. Myth.* a son of Jason and Medea.

Al•cim•e•don (al sim′i don′), *n. Class. Myth.* **1.** an Arcadian hero whose daughter, Philao, was seduced by Hercules. **2.** (in the *Iliad*) a son of Laerces who was a captain of the Myrmidons under Patroclus.

Al•cin•dor (al sin′dər), *n.* **(Ferdinand) Lew(is, Jr.),** original name of Kareem Abdul-Jabbar.

Al•cin•o•üs (al sin′ō əs), *n.* (in the *Odyssey*) king of the Phaeacians and father of Nausicaä and Laodamas.

Al•cith•o•ë (al sith′ō ē′), *n. Class. Myth.* a daughter of Minyas who was driven mad for mocking Dionysus.

ALCM, See **air-launched cruise missile.** Also, **A.L.C.M.**

Alc•mae•on (alk mē′ən), *n. Class. Myth.* a son of Amphiaraus and Eriphyle who commanded the second expedition against Thebes. He killed his mother for sending his father to certain death and was driven mad by the Furies.

Alc•man′ic verse′ (alk man′ik), *Pros.* a form of verse used in Greek drama and Latin dramatic poetry, composed in dactylic tetrameter. [< Gk *Alkmanikós* equiv. to *Alkmán* Alcman, a Greek lyric poet (late 7th cent. B.C.) + *-ikos* -IC]

Alc•me•ne (alk mē′nē), *n. Class. Myth.* the mother of Hercules by Zeus, who had assumed the form of Amphitryon, her husband. Also, **Alkmene, Alc•me•na** (alk mē′nə).

alco-, a combining form representing **alcohol** in compound words (*alcogas*), sometimes with the sense "using alcohol as fuel" (*alcoboat; alcotruck*). [by false analysis of ALCOHOL as *alco-* (an assumed comb. form with -o-) + *-hol*]

al•co•hol (al′kə hôl′, -hol′), *n.* **1.** Also called **ethyl alcohol, grain alcohol, ethanol, fermentation alcohol.** a colorless, limpid, volatile, flammable, water-miscible liquid, C_2H_5OH, having an etherlike odor and pungent, burning taste, the intoxicating principle of fermented liquors, produced by yeast fermentation of certain carbohydrates, as grains, molasses, starch, or sugar, or obtained synthetically by hydration of ethylene or as a by-product of certain hydrocarbon syntheses: used chiefly as a solvent in the extraction of specific substances, in beverages, medicines, organic synthesis, lotions, tonics, colognes, rubbing compounds, as an automobile radiator antifreeze, and as a rocket fuel. Cf. **denatured alcohol, methyl alcohol. 2.** whiskey, gin, vodka, or any other intoxicating liquor containing this liquid. **3.** *Chem.* any of a class of chemical compounds having the general formula ROH, where R represents an alkyl group and –OH a hydroxyl group, as in methyl alcohol, CH_3OH, or ethyl alcohol, C_2H_5OH. [1535–45; < NL < ML < Ar *al-kuḥl* the powdered antimony, the distillate]

al•co•hol•ate (al′kə hô lāt′, -ho-; al′kə hô′lit, -hol′it), *n. Chem.* **1.** any of a class of compounds, analogous to hydrates, containing chemically combined alcohol, as chloral alcoholate, $C_4Cl_3H_7O_2$. **2.** alkoxide. [1860–65; ALCOHOL + -ATE[2]]

al•co•hol•ic (al′kə hô′lik, -hol′ik), *adj.* **1.** of, pertaining to, or of the nature of alcohol. **2.** containing or using alcohol. **3.** caused by alcohol. **4.** suffering from alcoholism. **5.** preserved in alcohol. —*n.* **6.** *Pathol.* a person suffering from alcoholism. **7.** a person addicted to intoxicating drinks. [1780–90; ALCOHOL + -IC] **—al′co•hol′i•cal•ly,** *adv.*
—Syn. 6. See **drunkard.**

al•co•hol•ic•i•ty (al′kə hô lis′i tē, -ho-), *n.* alcoholic quality or strength. [1870–75; ALCOHOLIC + -ITY]

alcohol′ic psycho′sis, any of a group of major mental disorders, as delirium tremens, Wernicke-Korsakoff syndrome, and hallucinosis, associated with organic brain injury due to alcohol.

Alcohol′ics Anon′ymous, an organization of alcoholics whose purpose is to stay sober and help others recover from the disease of alcoholism. *Abbr.:* AA, A.A.

al•co•hol•ism (al′kə hô liz′əm, -ho-), *n. Pathol.* a chronic disorder characterized by dependence on alcohol, repeated excessive use of alcoholic beverages, the development of withdrawal symptoms on reducing or ceasing intake, morbidity that may include cirrhosis of the liver, and decreased ability to function socially and vocationally. [1855–60; ALCOHOL + -ISM]

al•co•hol•ize (al′kə hô līz′, -ho-), *v.t.,* **-ized, -iz•ing. 1.** to convert into an alcohol. **2.** to treat or saturate with an alcohol. **3.** to place under the influence of alcoholic beverages; make drunk; besot. Also, *esp. Brit.,* **al′co•hol•ise′.** [1680–90; ALCOHOL + -IZE] **—al′co•hol′i•za′tion,** *n.*

al•co•hol•om•e•ter (al′kə hô lom′i tər, -ho-), *n.* an instrument for finding the percentage of alcohol in a liquid. [1855–60; ALCOHOL + -O- + -METER] **—al•co•hol•o•met•ric** (al′kə hô′lə me′trik, -hol′ə-), **al′co•hol′o•met′ri•cal,** *adj.* **—al′co•hol•om′e•try,** *n.*

al•co•hol•y•sis (al′kə hô′lə sis, -hol′ə-), *n. Chem.* chemical decomposition resulting from the interaction of a compound and an alcohol. [ALCOHOL + -LYSIS] **—al•co•hol•yt•ic** (al′kə hô lit′ik, -ho-), *adj.*

Al•con (al′kon), *n. Class. Myth.* **1.** a noted archer who helped Hercules abduct the cattle of Geryon. **2.** a Trojan warrior who wounded Odysseus while trying to seize the body of Achilles and who was later killed by Odysseus.

Al•cor (al kôr′), *Astron.* a star, the fifth-magnitude companion of Mizar in the handle of the Big Dipper. [perh. < Ar *al-khawr* the low ground]

Al•co•ran (al′kô rän′, -ran′, -kō-), *n.* Alkoran. **—Al′co•ran′ic,** *adj.*

Al•co•ran•ist (al′kô rä′nist, -ran′ist, -kō-), *n. Islam.* a person who believes in an absolutely literal interpretation of the Koran. [ALCORAN + -IST]

Al•cott (ôl′kət, -kot), *n.* **1. (Amos) Bron•son** (bron′sən), 1799–1888, U.S. educator and philosopher. **2.** his daughter **Louisa May,** 1832–88, U.S. author. **3.** a male given name.

al•cove (al′kōv), *n.* **1.** a recess or small room adjacent to or opening out of a room: *a dining alcove.* **2.** a recess in a room for a bed, bookcases, or the like. **3.** any recessed space, as a bower in a garden. [1670–80; < F *alcôve* < Sp *alcoba* < Ar *al-qubbah* the dome]
—Syn. nook, bay.

Al•cuin (al′kwin), *n.* (*Ealhwine Flaccus*) A.D. 735–804, English theologian and scholar: teacher and adviser of Charlemagne. Also, **Alchuine.** Also called **Albinus.**

al•cy•o•nar•i•an (al′sē ə nâr′ē ən), *n.* **1.** any anthozoan coelenterate of the subclass Alcyonaria, as corals and sea anemones, having the tentacles and other body parts in branches or segments of eight. —*adj.* **2.** belonging or pertaining to the Alcyonaria. [1875–80; < NL *Alcyonari(a)* (< Gk *alkyón(ion)* a type of coral named from its resemblance to the nest of the kingfisher (*alkyṓn*) + L *-āria* -ARY) + -AN]

Al•cy•o•ne (al sī′ə nē′), *n.* **1.** a third-magnitude star in the constellation Taurus: brightest star in the Pleiades. **2.** Also, **Halcyon, Halcyone.** *Class. Myth.* a daughter of Aeolus who, with her husband, Ceyx, was transformed into a kingfisher.

Al•cy•o•neus (al sī′ə nyŏŏs′, -nəs), *n. Class. Myth.* **1.** a giant who threw a stone at Hercules and was killed when Hercules hit the stone back with his club. **2.** a giant who, invulnerable in his own country, was dragged by Hercules to another country and there killed.

Ald., Alderman. Also, **ald.**

Al•da (äl′də, ôl′-, al′-), *n.* **1. Frances,** 1885–1952, U.S. operatic singer. **2.** a male or female given name.

Al•dan (ul dän′), *n.* a river in the Russian Federation in Asia, flowing NE from the Yabloni Mountains to the Lena. ab. 1500 mi. (2415 km) long.

Al•deb•a•ran (al deb′ər ən), *n.* a first-magnitude star,

CONCISE PRONUNCIATION KEY: act, cāpe, dâre, pärt; set, ēqual; *if,* īce; ox, ōver, ôrder, oil, bŏŏk, bōōt, out; up, ûrge; child; sing; shoe; thin, *that;* zh as in *treasure.* ə = *a* as in *alone, e* as in *system, i* as in *easily, o* as in *gallop, u* as in *circus;* ᵊ as in *fire* (fīᵊr), *hour* (ouᵊr). l and n can serve as syllabic consonants, as in *cradle* (krād′l), and *button* (but′n). See the full key inside the front cover.

orange in color, in the constellation Taurus. [< Ar *al* the + *dabarān* follower (of the Pleiades)]

al•de•hyde (al′də hīd′), *n. Chem.* any of a class of organic compounds containing the group −CHO, which yields acids when oxidized and alcohols when reduced. [1840–50; < NL *al(cohol) dehyd(rogenātum)* dehydrogenated alcohol] —**al′de•hy′dic,** *adj.*

Al•den (ôl′dən), *n.* **1. John,** 1599?–1687, Pilgrim settler in Plymouth, Massachusetts, 1620. **2.** a male or female given name: from an Old English word meaning "old friend."

al den•te (al den′tā, -tē; *It.* äl den′te), (esp. of pasta) cooked so as not to be too soft; firm to the bite: *spaghetti al dente.* [1945–50; It: lit., to the tooth]

al•der (ôl′dər), *n.* **1.** any shrub or tree belonging to the genus *Alnus,* of the birch family, growing in moist places in northern temperate or colder regions and having toothed, simple leaves and flowers in catkins. **2.** any of various trees or shrubs resembling an alder. [bef. 900; ME *alder, aller,* OE *alor, al(e)r;* c. ON *ǫlr,* MLG *al(l)er* < Gmc **áluső;* akin to MHG *alze* < Gmc **alúső,* OHG *elira, erila* (G *Erle*) < Gmc **áliső,* MLG *els(e)* < Gmc **alísō,* hence Gmc **álus, alísō;* cf. Pol *olcha,* Russ *ol′khá* < IE dial. **alisā;* Lith *alksnis,* L *alnus* < IE dial. **alsnos*]

Al•der (äl′dər; *Ger.* äl′dəʀ), *n.* **Kurt** (kûrt; *Ger.* ko͝oʀt), 1902–58, German chemist: Nobel prize 1950.

al′der buck′thorn, a shrub or small tree, *Frangula alnus,* of Eurasia and northern Africa, having nonedible red fruit that turns black when ripe. [1860–65]

al•der•fly (ôl′dər flī′), *n., pl.* **-flies.** any of several dark-colored neuropterous insects of the family Sialidae, the larvae of which are aquatic and predacious on other aquatic insects. [1820–30; ALDER + FLY[2]]

al′der fly′catcher, a North American flycatcher, *Empidonax alnorum,* of alder thickets and other moist areas, that has greenish-brown upper parts and whitish underparts and is almost indistinguishable except by voice from *E. traillii* (**willow flycatcher**).

al•der•man (ôl′dər mən), *n., pl.* **-men. 1.** a member of a municipal legislative body, esp. of a municipal council. **2.** (in England) one of the members, chosen by the elected councilors, in a borough or county council. **3.** *Early Eng. Hist.* **a.** a chief. **b.** (later) the chief magistrate of a county or group of counties. **4.** *Northern U.S. Slang.* a pot belly. [bef. 900; ME; OE *(e)aldormann,* equiv. to *ealdor* chief, patriarch (*eald* OLD + *-or* n. suffix) + *mann* MAN[1]] —**al′der•man•cy, al′der•man•ship′,** *n.* —**al•der•man•ic** (ôl′dər man′ik), *adj.*
—Usage. See **-man.**

al•der•man•ry (ôl′dər mən rē), *n., pl.* **-ries.** the district, office, or rank of an alderman. [1200–50; ME *aldermanrie.* See ALDERMAN, -RY]

Al•der•ney (ôl′dər nē), *n.* **1.** one of the Channel Islands in the English Channel. 1785; 3 sq. mi. (8 sq. km). **2.** any of several breeds of cattle raised originally in the Channel Islands, as the Jersey or Guernsey.

al•der•per•son (ôl′dər pûr′sən), *n.* a member of a municipal legislative body, esp. of a municipal council. [ALDER(MAN) + -PERSON]
—Usage. See **-person.**

Al•der•shot (ôl′dər shot′), *n.* **1.** a city in NE Hampshire, in S England, SW of London. 33,111. **2.** a large military training center there.

al•der•wom•an (ôl′dər wo͝om′ən), *n., pl.* **-wom•en.** a woman who is a member of a municipal legislative body, esp. of a municipal council. [1550–60, for earlier sense; ALDER(MAN) + -WOMAN]
—Usage. See **-woman.**

al•di•carb (al′di kärb′), *n. Chem.* a crystalline compound, $C_7H_{14}N_2O_2S$, used on plants as a systemic insecticide, miticide, and nematocide. [(PROPION)ALD(EHYDE) + -I- + CARB(ON)]

Al•dine (ôl′dīn, -dēn), *adj.* **1.** of or from the press of Aldus Manutius and his family in Venice, c1490–1597, noted for compactly printed editions of the classics. —*n.* **2.** an Aldine or other early edition. **3.** any of several styles of printing types modeled on those designed by Aldus, esp. italic. [1795–1805; < It *aldino,* equiv. to *Ald(o* Manuzio; see MANUTIUS, ALDUS) + *-ino* -INE[1]]

Al•ding•ton (ôl′ding tən), *n.* **Richard,** 1892–1962, English poet, novelist, and composer.

Aldm., Alderman. Also, **aldm.**

al•do•hex•ose (al′dō hek′sōs), *n. Chem.* any of several hexoses in which one carbon atom is part of an aldehyde structure. [1905–10; ALD(EHYDE) + -O- + HEXOSE]

al•dol (al′dôl, -dol), *n. Chem.* **1.** Also called **acetaldol.** a colorless, syrupy, water-soluble liquid, $C_4H_8O_2$, formed by the condensation of acetaldehyde: used chiefly in the manufacture of rubber vulcanizers and accelerators, and in perfumery. **2.** any of a class of compounds containing both an alcohol and an aldehyde functional group, formed by a condensation reaction between aldehyde or ketone molecules. [1870–75; ALD(EHYDE) + -OL]

al•dol•ase (al′də lās′, -lāz′), *n. Biochem.* any of a group of enzymes catalyzing reversible aldol condensations. [1935–40; < G *Aldolase;* see ALDOL, -ASE]

Al•do•met (al′də met′), *Pharm., Trademark.* a brand of methyldopa.

al•dose (al′dōs), *n. Chem.* a sugar containing the aldehyde group or its hemiacetal equivalent. [1890–95; ALD(EHYDE) + -OSE[2]]

al•do•ste•rone (al′dō sti rōn′, al′dō sti rōn′, al dos′tə rōn′), *n. Biochem.* a hormone produced by the cortex of the adrenal gland, instrumental in the regulation of sodium and potassium reabsorption by the cells of the tubular portion of the kidney. [1950–55; ALD(EHYDE) + -O- + STER(OL) + -ONE]

CONCISE ETYMOLOGY KEY: <, descended or borrowed from; >, whence; b., blend of, blended; c., cognate with; cf., compare; deriv., derivative; equiv., equivalent; imit., imitative; obl., oblique; r., replacing; s., stem; sp., spelling, spelled; resp., respelling, respelled; trans., translation; ?, origin unknown; *, unattested; ‡, probably earlier than. See the full key inside the front cover.

al•do•ster•on•ism (al′dō ster′ə niz′əm, al dos′tə rō-), *n. Pathol.* an abnormality of the body's electrolyte balance, caused by excessive secretion of aldosterone by the adrenal cortex and characterized by hypertension, low serum potassium, excessive urination, and alkalosis. Also called **hyperaldosteronism.** [1950–55; ALDOSTERONE + -ISM]

Al•drich (ôl′drich), *n.* **Thomas Bailey,** 1836–1907, U.S. short-story writer, poet, and novelist.

Al•dridge (ôl′drij), *n.* **Ira Frederick** (*"the African Roscius"*), 1804?–67, U.S. actor, primarily in Europe.

al•drin (ôl′drin), *n. Chem.* a brown, water-insoluble, toxic solid consisting of more than 95 percent of the chlorinated hydrocarbon $C_{12}H_8Cl_6$: used as an insecticide. [1949; named after Kurt ALDER; see -IN[2]]

Al•drin (ôl′drin), *n.* **Edwin Eugene, Jr.** (*"Buzz"*), born 1930, U.S. astronaut.

Al•dus Ma•nu•ti•us (ôl′dəs mə no͞o′shē əs, -nyo͞o′-, al′dəs). See **Manutius, Aldus.**

ale (āl), *n.* **1.** a malt beverage, darker, heavier, and more bitter than beer, containing about 6 percent alcohol by volume. **2.** *Brit.* beer. [bef. 950; ME; OE *(e)alu* (gen. *ealoth*); c. OS *alo-,* MD *ale, ael,* ON *ǫl;* Lith *alùs,* OCS *olŭ;* Finnish, Estonian *olut;* areal word of North Europe]

A.L.E., *Insurance.* additional living expense.

A•le•a (ā′lē ə), *n.* **1.** *Class. Myth.* an epithet of Athena referring to a sanctuary built in her honor by Aleus. **2.** an ancient city on the E border of Arcadia, near Argolis.

A•le•ar•di (ä′le är′dē), *n.* **Count A•le•ar•do** (ä′le är′dô), 1812–78, Italian poet and patriot.

a•le•a•to•ry (ā′lē ə tôr′ē, -tōr′ē, al′ē-), *adj.* **1.** *Law.* depending on a contingent event: *an aleatory contract.* **2.** of or pertaining to accidental causes; of luck or chance; unpredictable: *an aleatory element.* **3.** *Music.* employing the element of chance in the choice of tones, rests, durations, rhythms, dynamics, etc. Also, **a•le•a•tor•ic** (ā′lē ə tôr′ik, -tor′-, al′ē-). [1685–95; < L *āleātōrius,* equiv. to *āleātōr-* (s. of *āleātor* gambler (*āle(a)* game of chance + *-ātor* -ATOR) + *-ius* adj. suffix; see -TORY[1]]

a′leatory po′em. See **cut-up poem.**

A•le•bi•on (ə lē′bē on′), *n. Class. Myth.* a son of Poseidon who, with his brother Dercynus, was killed by Hercules while attempting to steal the cattle that Hercules had taken from Geryon. Also, **Albion.**

al•ec[1] (al′ik), *n. Obs.* **1.** a herring. **2.** a sauce or relish made from small herring or anchovies. [1510–20; < L *(h)al(l)ec* fish sauce]

al•ec[2] (al′ik), *n. Australian.* a simpleton or fool. [1920–25; cf. SMART-ALECK; sense shift perh. orig. from ironic usage]

Al•ec (al′ik), *n.* a male given name, form of **Alexander.** Also, **Al′eck.**

a•lec•i•thal (ā les′ə thəl), *adj. Embryol.* having little or no yolk in the cytoplasm of the egg or ovum. Also, **a•le•cith•ic** (ā′lə sith′ik). [1875–80; A-[6] + Gk *lékith(os)* yolk + -AL[1]]

A•lec•to (ə lek′tō), *n. Class. Myth.* one of the Furies.

a•lec•try•o•man•cy (ə lek′trē ə man′sē), *n.* an ancient form of divination, using a rooster to select grains of food placed on letters of the alphabet. Also, **a•lec•to•ro•man•cy** (ə lek′tə rō man′sē). [1675–85; < Gk *alektryṓ(n)* rooster + -MANCY]

a•lee (ə lē′), *adv., adj. Naut.* upon or toward the lee side of a vessel; away from the wind (opposed to *aweather*). [1350–1400; ME. See A-[1], LEE[1]]

al•e•gar (al′ə gər, ā′lə-), *n. Brit. Informal.* ale vinegar; sour ale. [1535–45; ALE + (VIN)EGAR]

A•le•gre•te (ô li gʀe′ti), *n.* a city in SW Brazil. 63,945.

ale•house (āl′hous′), *n., pl.* **-hous•es** (-hou′ziz). a tavern where ale or beer is sold; bar; pub. [bef. 1000; ME, OE. See ALE, HOUSE]

A•lei•chem (ä lā′кнem), *n.* **Sho•lom** (shô′ləm) or **Sho•lem** (shō′lem, -ləm) or **Sha•lom** (shä lōm′), (pen name of *Solomon Rabinowitz*), 1859–1916, Russian author of Yiddish novels, plays, and short stories; in the U.S. from 1906.

a•lei•chem sha•lom (*Seph.* ä le кнem′ shä lôm′; *Ashk.* ə lā′кнəm shô′ləm), *Hebrew.* a conventional greeting, meaning "peace to you": used in reply to the greeting *shalom aleichem.*

A•lei•xan•dre (ä′lā ksän′dʀe), *n.* **Vi•cen•te** (bē then′te), 1898–1984, Spanish poet: Nobel prize 1977.

A•le•ksan•dra Fyo•do•rov•na (al′ik zan′drə fyô′də-rôv′nə, -rov′-, -zän′-; *Russ.* u lyi ksän′dʀə fyô′də ʀəv-nə). See **Alexandra Feodorovna.**

A•le•ksan•dro•pol (*Russ.* u lyi ksun dʀô′pəl), *n.* a former name of **Gumri.**

A•le•ksan•drovsk (*Russ.* u lyi ksän′drəfsk), *n.* former name of **Zaporozhye.**

A•le•mán (ä′le män′), *n.* **1. Ma•te•o** (mä te′ô), 1547?–1610, Spanish novelist. **2. Mi•guel** (mē gel′), born 1902, president of Mexico 1946–52.

Al•e•man•ni (al′ə man′ī), *n.* (*used with a plural v.*) a confederation of Germanic tribes, first recorded in the 3rd century A.D., that settled in the area between the Rhine, Main, and Danube rivers, and made harassing attacks against the Roman Empire. Also, **Alamanni.** [< L, of Gmc orig.; c. Goth *alamans* totality of humankind, equiv. to *ala-* ALL (see ALMIGHTY) + *mann-* MAN[1]]

Al•e•man•nic (al′ə man′ik), *n.* **1.** the high German speech of Switzerland, Alsace, and southwestern Germany. Cf. **Bavarian** (def. 3). —*adj.* **2.** of or pertaining to Alemannic or the Alemanni. Also, **Alamannic.** [1770–80; < L *Alamannicus:* see ALEMANNI, -IC]

A•lem•bert, d′ (dal′əm bâr′; *Fr.* da län beʀ′), **Jean Le Rond** (zhäɴ lə ʀôɴ′), 1717?–83, French mathematician, philosopher, and writer: associate of Diderot.

a•lem•bic (ə lem′bik), *n.* **1.** a vessel with a beaked cap or head, formerly used in distilling. **2.** anything that transforms, purifies, or refines. [1350–1400; ME, var. of *alambic* < ML *alambicus* < dial. Ar *al* the *anbīq* still < Gk *ámbix* cup]

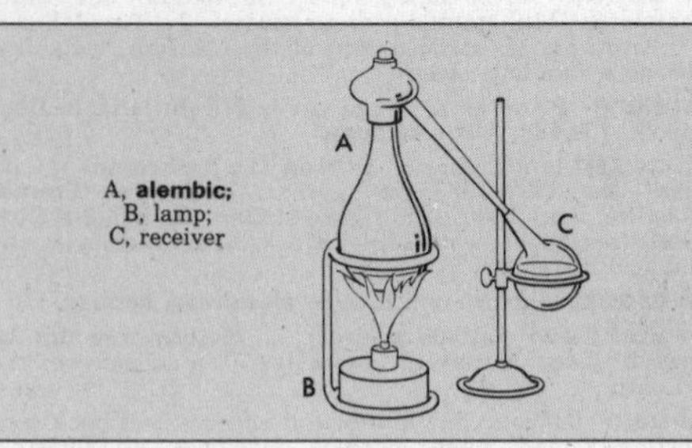

A, **alembic;** B, lamp; C, receiver

A•len•çon (a län sôɴ′; *Eng.* ə len′sən, -son), *n.* a city in and the capital of Orne, in NW France: lace manufacture. 34,666.

Alen′çon lace′, 1. Also called **point d'Alençon.** a delicate needlepoint lace having a solid design outlined with twisted yarn on a background of hexagonal mesh. **2.** a machine reproduction of this lace, with a cordlike outline. [1855–60]

A•lene (ā lēn′), *n.* a female given name, form of **Helen.**

a•leph (ä′lif; *Heb.* ä′lef), *n.* **1.** the first letter of the Hebrew alphabet. **2.** the glottal stop consonant or, alternatively, long vowel represented by this letter. [1250–1300; ME < Heb *ālep̄h,* akin to *eleph* ox]

a•leph-null (ä′lif nul′), *n. Math.* the cardinal number of the set of all positive integers; the smallest transfinite cardinal number. Also called **a•leph-ze•ro** (ä′lif zēr′ō). [1905–10]

A•lep•po (ə lep′ō), *n.* a city in NW Syria. 710,636. French, **A•lep** (a lep′).

Alep′po gall′, a nutlike gall produced by gall wasps on certain oaks in western Asia and eastern Europe, used as a source of astringent and tannic and gallic acids.

Alep′po grass′. See **Johnson grass.**

Alep′po pine′, a pine tree, *Pinus halepensis,* native to the Mediterranean area, that is planted as an ornamental and is a source of turpentine. [1930–35]

a•ler•ce (ə lėr′sə), *n.* **1.** the wood of the sandarac tree. **2.** a Chilean evergreen tree, *Fitzroya cupressoides,* having furrowed, reddish bark and overlapping leaves. **3.** an incense cedar, *Austrocedrus chilensis,* of Chile. [1835–45; < Sp < Ar *al-arz* the cypress]

a•le•ri•on (ə lēr′ē ən, -on′), *n. Heraldry.* an eagle displayed, usually represented without a beak or legs. [1595–1605; < F *alérion* << Frankish **adalaron-;* c. OHG *adelare* noble eagle (G *Adler* eagle), from distinction made in falconry between noble and ignoble birds of prey, equiv. to *adal* noble + **aron-* eagle; see ERNE]

a•lert (ə lûrt′), *adj.* **1.** fully aware and attentive; wide-awake; keen: *an alert mind.* **2.** swift; agile; nimble. —*n.* **3.** an attitude of vigilance, readiness, or caution, as before an expected attack. **4.** a warning or alarm of an impending military attack, a storm, etc.: *We'd just boarded the bus when the alert sounded.* **5.** the period during which such a warning or alarm is in effect. **6. on the alert,** on guard against danger; in readiness; vigilant: *The state police are on the alert for an escaped convict believed to be in the area.* —*v.t.* **7.** to warn (troops, ships, etc.) to prepare for action. **8.** to warn of an impending raid, attack, storm, etc.: *The radio alerted coastal residents to prepare for the hurricane.* **9.** to advise or warn; cause to be on guard: *to alert gardeners to the dangers of some pesticides.* [1590–1600; 1940–45 for def. 4; < It *all'erta,* equiv. to *all(a)* to, on the + *erta* lookout, watchtower, orig. fem. of *erto,* ptp. of *ergere* < L *ērigere* to ERECT] —**a•lert′ly,** *adv.* —**a•lert′ness,** *n.*
—Syn. 1. awake, wary, observant. ALERT, VIGILANT, WATCHFUL imply a wide-awake attitude, as of someone keenly aware of his or her surroundings. ALERT describes a ready and prompt attentiveness together with a quick intelligence: *The tourist was alert and eager to see the sights.* VIGILANT suggests some immediate necessity for keen, active observation, and for continuing alertness: *Knowing the danger, the scout was unceasingly vigilant.* WATCHFUL suggests carefulness and preparedness: *watchful waiting.* **2.** brisk, lively, quick, active, sprightly, spirited. **—Ant. 1.** unaware.

-ales, *Bot.* a suffix of names of orders: *Cycadales.* [< L pl. of *-ālis* -AL[1]]

A•le•si•a (ə lē′zhē ə, -zhə), *n.* an ancient city and fortress in Gaul: Caesar captured Vercingetorix here 52 B.C.

Al•es•san•dra (al′ə san′drə, -sän′-; *It.* ä′les sän′dʀä), *n.* a female given name, Italian form of **Alexandra.**

A•les•san•dri (ä′le sän′drē), *n.* **1. Jor•ge** (hôʀ′he), 1896–1986, Chilean engineer and statesman: president 1958–64. **2. Ar•tu•ro** (äʀ to͞o′ʀô), 1868–1950, Chilean lawyer and statesman: president 1920–24, 1925, 1932–38.

A•les•san•dri•a (ä′les sän′dʀē ä), *n.* a city in NW Italy, in Piedmont. 102,774.

Al•es•san•dro (al′i san′drō), *n.* **Victor Nicholas,** 1915–76, U.S. orchestra conductor.

Å•le•sund (ô′lə so͝on′), *n.* a seaport in W Norway. 40,816. Also, **Aalesund.**

A•le•tes (ə lē′tēz), *n. Class. Myth.* **1.** a son of Clytemnestra and her lover Aegisthus. He became ruler of Mycenae after the death of his parents. **2.** a descendant of Hercules who conquered Corinth.

Al•e•the•a (al′ə thē′ə), *n.* a female given name: from a Greek word meaning "truth."

Al•e•thi•a (al′ə thē′ə), *n.* the ancient Greek personification of truth.

a•le•thi•ol•o•gy (ə lē′thē ol′ə jē), *n.* the branch of logic dealing with truth and error. [1830–40; < Gk *alḗthei(a)* truth (*alēthḗ(s)* true + *-ia* -IA) + -o- + -LOGY] —**a•le•thi•o•log•ic** (ə lē′thē ə loj′ik), **a•le′thi•o•log′i•cal,** *adj.* —**a•le′thi•ol′o•gist,** *n.*

a•lette (ə let′), *n.* **1.** (in classical architecture) a part of a pier, flanking a pilaster or engaged column and supporting either impost of an arch. **2.** a small wing of a building. **3.** either jamb of a doorway. [1810–20; < F, var. of AILETTE]

à l'étuvée (A lā ty vā′), *French.* stewed.

a•leu•ro•man•cy (ə lŏŏr′ə man′sē), *n.* (in ancient times) the use of flour as a means of divination. [1650–60; < F *aleuromancie* (see ALEURONE, -MANCY), alter. of Gk *aleuromanteîon* divination by meal]

al•eu•rone (al′yə rōn′, ə lŏŏr′ōn), *n.* (in the seeds of cereal plants) protein granules **(al′eurone grains′)** found in a single layer of cells **(al′eurone lay′er)** in the outermost portion of the endosperm. Also, **al•eu•ron** (al′yə ron′, ə lŏŏr′on). [1865–70; < Gk *áleuron* flour, meal] —**al•eu•ron•ic** (al′yŏŏ ron′ik), *adj.*

A•le•us (ā′lē əs), *n. Class. Myth.* a king of Tegea and the father of Amphidamas, Auge, Cepheus, and Lycurgus.

Al•eut (ə lōōt′, al′ē ōōt′), *n.* **1.** Also, **Aleutian.** a member of a people native to the Aleutian Islands and the western Alaska Peninsula who are related physically and culturally to the Eskimos. **2.** the language of the Aleuts, distantly related to Eskimo: a member of the Eskimo-Aleut family.

A•leu•tian (ə lōō′shən), *adj.* **1.** of or pertaining to the Aleutian Islands. —*n.* **2.** Aleut (def. 1). **3. Aleutians.** See **Aleutian Islands.**

Aleu′tian Cur′rent, a current in the Pacific Ocean that flows eastward between latitudes 40° and 50° N. Also called **Subarctic Current.**

Aleu′tian Is′lands, an archipelago extending SW from the Alaska Peninsula: part of Alaska. Also called **Aleutians.**

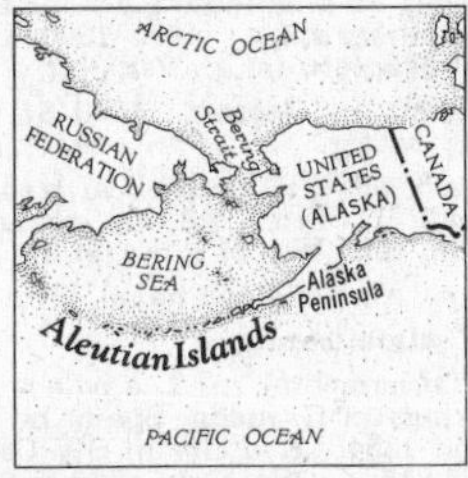

Aleu′tian Range′, a mountain range extending along the eastern coast of the Alaska Peninsula. Highest peak, Mt. Katmai, 6715 ft. (2047 m).

A lev•el (ā′ lev′əl), *Brit.* **1.** a public examination requiring advanced knowledge in a subject and taken at the end of secondary school, usually two years after O level. **2.** a pass in this examination. [1950–55; *A(dvanced) level*]

al•e•vin (al′ə vən), *n. Ichthyol.* a fry, esp. a salmon, whose yolk is depleted. [1865–70; < F, OF << VL **allevamen,* equiv. to L *allevā(re)* to lift up, raise (prob. in VL: to bring up, rear; *al-* AL- + *levāre* to raise; see LEVER) + *-men* resultative n. suffix; cf. It dial. *alvam* calf]

ale•wife[1] (āl′wīf′), *n., pl.* **-wives.** a North American fish, *Alosa pseudoharengus,* resembling a small shad. [1625–35, *Amer.*; earlier *allowes,* perh. influenced by ALEWIFE[2], prob. < F *alose* shad < Gallo-Latin *alausa*]

ale•wife[2] (āl′wīf′), *n., pl.* **-wives.** a woman who owns or operates an alehouse. [1350–1400; ME; see ALE, WIFE]

Al•ex (al′iks), *n.* a male given name, form of **Alexander.**

A•lex•a (ə lek′sə), *n.* a female given name, form of **Alexandra.**

al•ex•an•der (al′ig zan′dər, -zän′-), *n.* (*often cap.*) a cocktail made with crème de cacao with gin or brandy **(brandy alexander)** and sweet cream. [1925–30; prob. after the proper name]

Al•ex•an•der (al′ig zan′dər, -zän′-), *n.* **1.** See **Alexander the Great. 2.** Also, **Alexandros.** *Class. Myth.* Homeric name for Paris. **3. Franz** (frants, franz, fränts), 1891–1964, U.S. psychoanalyst, born in Hungary. **4. Grover Cleveland,** 1887–1950, U.S. baseball player. **5. Sir Harold R. L. G.** (*Alexander of Tunis*), 1891–1969, English field marshal. **6. Samuel,** 1859–1938, British philosopher. **7. William,** 1726–83, general in the American Revolution. **8.** a male given name: from a Greek word meaning "defender of men."

Alexander I, 1. Saint, pope A.D. 106?–115. **2.** (*Aleksandr Pavlovich*) 1777–1825, czar of Russia 1801–25. **3.** (*Alexander Obrenovich* or *Aleksandar Obrenović*) 1876–1903, king of Serbia 1889–1903. **4.** 1888–1934, king of Yugoslavia 1921–34 (son of Peter I of Serbia).

Alexander I Island, an island off the coast of Antarctica, in the Bellingshausen Sea.

Alexander II, 1. died 1073, Italian ecclesiastic: pope 1061–1073. **2.** (*Aleksandr Nikolaevich*) 1818–81, czar of Russia 1855–81.

Alexander III, 1. died 1181, Italian ecclesiastic: pope 1159–81. **2.** (*Aleksandr Aleksandrovich*) 1845–94, czar of Russia 1881–94.

Alexander IV, (*Rinaldo Conti*) died 1261, Italian ecclesiastic: pope 1254–61.

Alexander V, 1340?–1410, Cretan ecclesiastic: pope 1409–10.

Alexander VI, (*Rodrigo Borgia*) 1431?–1503, Italian ecclesiastic: pope 1492–1503 (father of Cesare and Lucrezia Borgia).

Alexander VII, (*Fabio Chigi*) 1599–1667, Italian ecclesiastic: pope 1655–67.

Alexander VIII, (*Pietro Ottoboni*) 1610–91, Italian ecclesiastic: pope 1689–91.

Alexan′der Archipel′ago, an archipelago off the coast of SE Alaska.

Al′exan′der Cit′y, a city in E Alabama. 13,807.

Alexan′der Nev′ski (al′ig zan′dər nev′skē, nef′-, -zän′-; *Russ.* u lyi ksän′dʀ nyef′skyē), (*Aleksandr Nevski*) 1220?–63, Russian prince, national hero, and saint.

al•ex•an•ders (al′ig zan′dərz, -zän′-), *n., pl.* **-ders.** (*used with a singular or plural v.*) **1.** a tall plant, *Angelica atropurpurea,* of the parsley family, having broad clusters of small white flowers. **2.** a related plant, *Smyrnium olusatrum,* having yellowish flowers. [prob. < F *alexandre(s)*; cf. ME *alisaundre* (< OF), OE *alexandre* < ML (*petroselīnum*) *Alexandrīnum* a name for *Smyrnium olusatrum,* and synonymous with ML *petroselinum Macedonicum,* appar. through assoc. of Macedonia with Alexander the Great; cf. PARSLEY]

Alexan′der Se•ve′rus (sə vēr′əs), A.D. 208?–235, Roman emperor 222–235.

Al•ex•an•der•son (al′ig zan′dər sən), *n.* **Ernst F. W.** (ûrnst), 1878–1975, U.S. engineer and inventor.

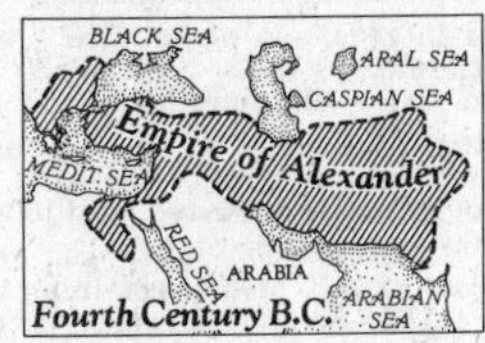

Fourth Century B.C.

Alexan′der the Great′, 356–323 B.C., king of Macedonia 336–323: conqueror of Greek city-states and of the Persian empire from Asia Minor and Egypt to India.

Al•ex•an•dra (al′ig zan′drə, -zän′-), *n.* **1.** 1844–1925, queen consort of Edward VII of England. **2.** *Class. Myth.* Cassandra (def. 1). **3.** a female given name: derived from *Alexander.*

A•le•xan•dra Feo•do•rov•na (al′ig zan′drə fyô′də rôv′nə, -rov′-, -zän′-; *Russ.* u lyi ksän′drə fyô′də rəvnə), 1872–1918, empress of Russia (wife of Nicholas II). Also, **Aleksandra Fyodorovna.**

Al•ex•an•dret•ta (al′ig zan dret′ə, -zän-), *n.* former name of **Iskenderun.**

Al•ex•an•dri•a (al′ig zan′drē ə, -zän′-), *n.* **1.** Arabic, **Al-Iskandarīyah.** a seaport in N Egypt, in the Nile delta: founded in 332 B.C. by Alexander the Great; ancient center of learning. 2,201,000. **2.** a city in NE Virginia, S of the District of Columbia. 103,217. **3.** a city in central Louisiana, on the Red River. 51,565.

Al•ex•an•dri•an (al′ig zan′drē ən, -zän′-), *adj.* **1.** of Alexandria, esp. Alexandria, Egypt. **2.** of or pertaining to the schools of philosophy, literature, and science in ancient Alexandria. **3.** Alexandrine. —*n.* **4.** a native or inhabitant of Alexandria, esp. Alexandria, Egypt. [1575–85; ALEXANDRI(A) + -AN]

Alexan′dria sen′na. See under **senna** (def. 2).

Al•ex•an•dri•na (al′ig zan drē′nə, -zän-), *n.* a female given name, form of **Alexandra.**

Al•ex•an•drine (al′ig zan′drin, -drēn, -zän′-), *Pros.* —*n.* **1.** (*often l.c.*) a verse or line of poetry of twelve syllables. —*adj.* **2.** (*often l.c.*) of or pertaining to such a verse or line. [1580–90; < MF *alexandrin,* after *Alexandre,* from the use of this meter in an Old French poem on Alexander the Great; see -INE[1]]

Al•ex•an•drine (al′ig zan′drin, -drēn, -zän′-), *adj.* of or pertaining to Alexandria, Egypt. [1490–1500; ALEXANDR(IA) + -INE[1]]

Al′exan′drine rat′. See **roof rat.**

Al•ex•an•dri•nus (al′ig zan drē′nəs, -drī′-, -zän-), *n.* the Greek uncial codex, dating from the early 5th century A.D., originally containing the complete text of the Greek Old and New Testaments. Cf. **codex.** [< L: lit., of ALEXANDRIA (Egypt); so called from its origin; see -INE[1]]

al•ex•an•drite (al′ig zan′drīt, -zän′-), *n. Mineral.* a variety of chrysoberyl, green by daylight and red-violet by artificial light, used as a gem. [1830–40; named after ALEXANDER I of Russia; see -ITE[1]]

Al•ex•an•dros (al′ig zan′dros, -drōs), *n. Class. Myth.* Alexander (def. 2).

A•le•xan•drou•po•lis (ä′le ksän drōō′pô lēs), *n.* a seaport in W Thrace, in NE Greece. 22,995. Formerly, **Dede Agach.**

a•lex•i•a (ə lek′sē ə), *n. Pathol.* a neurologic disorder marked by loss of the ability to understand written or printed language, usually resulting from a brain lesion or a congenital defect. Also called **word blindness.** [1875–80; A-[6] + Gk *léx(is)* speech (*leg-* s. of *légein* to speak + *-sis* -SIS) + -IA; altered meaning by assoc. of *-lex-* with LEXICON, etc.]

A•lex•ian (ə lek′shən, -sē ən), *n. Rom. Cath. Ch.* a member of a congregation of brothers founded for the care of the sick at Mechlin, Brabant, in the 15th century. [named after Saint *Alexius* of Edessa, 5th-century Christian; see -AN]

A•lex•i•ar•es (ə lek′sē âr′ēz), *n. Class. Myth.* a son of Hercules and Hebe.

A•lex•i•ca•cus (ə lek′si kā′kəs), *n. Class. Myth.* an epithet of Apollo, meaning "averter of evil," in reference to his dispelling a plague that afflicted the Athenian forces in the Peloponnesian War.

a•lex•in (ə lek′sin) *n, Immunol.* complement (def. 10). [1890–95; < Gk *aléx(ein)* to ward off + -IN[2]] —**al•ex•in•ic** (al′ek sin′ik), *adj.*

a•lex•i•phar•mic (ə lek′sə fär′mik), *Med.* —*adj.* **1.** warding off poisoning or infection; antidotal; prophylactic. —*n.* **2.** an alexipharmic agent, esp. an internal antidote. [1665–75; obs. *alexipharm(ac)* antidote (< Gk *alexiphármakon,* equiv. to *alexi-* averter (see ALEXIN) + *phármakon* poison, drug) + -IC; see PHARMACY]

A•lex•is (ə lek′sis), *n.* a male or female given name: from a Greek word meaning "helper."

A•lex•is Mi•khai•lo•vich (ə lek′sis mi kī′lə vich; *Russ.* myi KHī′lə vyich), (*Aleksei Mikhailovich*) 1629–76, czar of Russia 1645–76 (father of Peter I).

A•lex•is Ni•ko•la•ye•vich (ə lek′sis nik′ə lī′ə vich; *Russ.* nyi ku lä′yi vyich), (*Aleksei Nikolayevich*), 1904–18, son of Nicholas II of Russia, heir apparent to the Russian throne: executed in the Russian Bolshevik Revolution.

a•lex•i•thy•mi•a (ā′lek sə thī′mē ə), *n. Psychiatry.* difficulty in experiencing, expressing, and describing emotional responses. [A-[6] + Gk *léxi(s)* speech (see ALEXIA) + -THYMIA]

A•lex•i•us I (ə lek′sē əs), (*Alexius Comnenus*) 1048–1118, emperor of the Byzantine Empire 1081–1118.

ale•yard (āl′yärd′), *n.* yard-of-ale. [ALE + YARD[1]]

Alf (alf; *Nor.* älf), *n.* a male given name, form of **Alfred.**

al•fa (al′fə), *n.* a word used in communications to represent the letter *A.* Also, **ALFA.** [1950–55; var. sp. of ALPHA]

Al•fa (al′fə), *n. Mil.* the NATO name for a class of nuclear-powered Soviet attack submarine having a titanium hull and a submerged speed of more than 40 knots.

al•fal•fa (al fal′fə), *n.* a plant, *Medicago sativa,* of the legume family, usually having bluish-purple flowers, originating in the Near East and widely cultivated as a forage crop. Also called **lucerne, purple medic.** [1835–45; < Sp, var. of *alfalfez* < SpAr *al* the + *faṣfaṣah* < Pers *ispist* lucerne]

alfal′fa but′terfly, a sulfur butterfly, *Colias eurytheme,* having orange wings edged with black, the larvae of which feed on alfalfa and other legumes. Also called **orange sulfur.**

alfal′fa wee′vil, a European weevil, *Hypera postica,* now also widely distributed in North America, that is an important pest, primarily of alfalfa, in both the larval and adult stages. [1910–15]

Al Fa•ra•bi (al′ fä rä′bē), died A.D. 950, Arab philosopher. Also called **Al•fa•ra•bi•us** (al′fə rā′bē əs).

Al•fa•ro (äl fä′rô), *n.* **(Fla•vio) E•loy** (flä′vyô e loi′), 1864–1912, Ecuadorian political leader: president 1897–1901, 1907–11.

Al Fa•tah (äl′ fä tä′), a guerrilla group within the Palestine Liberation Organization. [1965–70; < Ar *al* the + acronym from the name of the organization *Ḥ(arakat) T(aḥrīr) F(ilastīn)* Movement for the Liberation of Palestine, with play on *fataḥ* conquer]

Alf•heim (alv′hām′), *n. Scand. Myth.* the domain of elves. [< ON *Alfheimr,* equiv. to *alf-* (s. of *alfr*) ELF + *heimr* world, HOME]

Al•fie (al′fē), *n.* a male given name, form of **Alfred.**

Al•fie•ri (äl fye′ʀē), *n.* **Count Vit•to•rio** (vēt tô′ʀyô), 1749–1803, Italian dramatist and poet.

al•fil•a•ri•a (al fil′ə rē′ə), *n.* a European plant, *Erodium cicutarium,* of the geranium family, grown for forage in the U.S. Also called **pin clover.** [1865–70, *Amer.*; < Sp *alfilerillo,* equiv. to *alfiler* pin (< Ar *al-khilāl* the pin) + *-illo* dim. suffix]

al fi•ne (al fē′nā; *It.* äl fē′ne), *Music.* to the end (a direction, as after a *da capo* or *dal segno,* to continue to *fine,* the indicated end). [< It]

al•fi•sol (al′fə sôl′, -sol′), *n.* a fertile soil of humid regions that occurs worldwide, esp. where native broadleaf forests were established, and is highly productive for agriculture. [1970–75; *alf-* (according to the U.S. Soil Conservation Service, initiator of the term, a "meaningless syllable") + -I- + -SOL]

Alfonso I, (*Alfonso Henriques*), 1109?–85, first king of Portugal 1139–85.

Al•fon•so X (al fon′sō, -zō; *Sp.* äl fôn′sô), (*"Alfonso the Wise"*) 1221–84, king of Castile 1252–84.

Alfonso XII, 1857–85, king of Spain 1874–85.

Alfonso XIII, 1886–1941, king of Spain 1886–1930.

al•for•ja (al fôr′jə; *Sp.* äl fôʀ′hä), *n., pl.* **-jas** (-jəz; *Sp.* -häs). *Southwestern U.S.* **1.** a saddlebag, esp. one made of leather. **2.** a cheek pouch. [1605–15; < Sp < Ar *al-khurj* the pair of saddlebags]

Al•fred (al′fred, -frid), *n.* a male given name: from the Old English words meaning "elf" and "counsel."

CONCISE PRONUNCIATION KEY: act, cāpe, dâre, pärt; set, ēqual; if, ice; ox, ōver, ôrder, oil, bŏŏk, bōōt, out; up, ûrge; child; sing; shoe; thin, *th*at; zh as in *treasure.* ə = *a* as in *alone, e* as in *system, i* as in *easily, o* as in *gallop, u* as in *circus;* ᵊ as in *fire* (fīᵊr), *hour* (ouᵊr). l and n can serve as syllabic consonants, as in *cradle* (krād′l), and *button* (but′n). See the full key inside the front cover.

Al′fred the Great′, A.D. 849–899, king of the West Saxons 871–899.

al•fres•co (al fres′kō), *adv.* **1.** out-of-doors; in the open air: *to dine alfresco.* —*adj.* **2.** outdoor: *an alfresco café.* Also, **al fres′co.** [1745–55; < It: in the cool, in a cool place. See FRESCO]

Al•fur (al′fo͝or, -fyo͝or), *n.* a member of an aboriginal people of eastern Indonesia, esp. of the Moluccas, whose features show both Malayan and Papuan characteristics. [1875–80]

al-Fus•tat (al fo͞o stat′), *n.* a city in N Egypt, near the modern city of Cairo, founded in the 7th century A.D. Also, **El Fostat, el-Fustat.** Also called **Old Cairo.**

Alf•vén (äl vān′, al-), *n.* **Han•nes (O•lof Gö•sta)** (hän′nes o͞o′lôf yœ′stä), born 1908, Swedish physicist: Nobel prize 1970.

Alfvén′ wave′, a type of oscillation of plasma particles, consisting of transverse waves propagating along the magnetic field lines in a plasma. Also called **magnetohydrodynamic wave.** [named after Hannes O. G. ALFVÉN]

Alg., **1.** Algerian. **2.** Algiers.

alg., algebra.

al•gae (al′jē), *n.pl., sing.* **-ga** (-gə). any of numerous groups of chlorophyll-containing, mainly aquatic eukaryotic organisms ranging from microscopic single-celled forms to multicellular forms 100 ft. (30 m) or more long, distinguished from plants by the absence of true roots, stems, and leaves and by a lack of nonreproductive cells in the reproductive structures: classified into the six phyla Euglenophyta, Chrysophyta, Pyrrophyta, Chlorophyta, Phaeophyta, and Rhodophyta. Cf. **blue-green algae.** [< NL, pl. of L *alga* seaweed] —**al′gal,** *adj.*

Al•gar (al′gər), *n.* a male given name.

Al′ga•roth pow′der (al′gə rôth′, -roth′). See **antimony oxychloride.** [1795–1805; part trans. of F *poudre d'algaroth* powder of algaroth < It *algarotto,* named after Vittorio *Algarotto* (d. 1604), Italian physician]

al•gar•ro•ba (al′gə rō′bə), *n.* **1.** any of certain mesquites, esp. *Prosopis juliflora,* having pinnate leaves and yellowish flowers. **2.** the beanlike pod of this plant. **3.** the carob tree or fruit. Also, **al′ga•ro′ba.** [1835–45; < Sp < Ar *al* the + *kharrūbah* CAROB]

Al-Ga•zel (al′gə zel′), *n.* Ghazzali.

al•ge•bra (al′jə brə), *n.* **1.** the branch of mathematics that deals with general statements of relations, utilizing letters and other symbols to represent specific sets of numbers, values, vectors, etc., in the description of such relations. **2.** any of several algebraic systems, esp. a ring in which elements can be multiplied by real or complex numbers **(linear algebra)** as well as by other elements of the ring. **3.** any special system of notation adapted to the study of a special system of relationship: *algebra of classes.* [1535–45; < ML < Ar *al-jabr* lit., restoration]

al•ge•bra•ic (al′jə brā′ik), *adj.* **1.** of, occurring in, or utilizing algebra. **2.** *Math.* of or pertaining to an element that is the root of a polynomial equation with coefficients from some given field: *$\sqrt{2}$ is algebraic over the field of real numbers.* **3.** using arbitrary letters or symbols in place of the letters, symbols, or numbers of an actual application. Also, **al′ge•bra′i•cal.** [1655–65; ALGEBRA + -IC] —**al′ge•bra′i•cal•ly,** *adv.*

algebra′ically closed′ field′, *Math.* a field in which every polynomial equation with coefficients that are elements of the field has at least one root in the field, as the field of complex numbers.

algebra′ic equa′tion, *Math.* an equation in the form of a polynomial having a finite number of terms and equated to zero, as $2x^3 + 4x^2 - x + 7 = 0$.

algebra′ic exten′sion, *Math.* a field containing a given field such that every element in the first field is algebraic over the given field. Cf. **extension field.**

al′gebra′ic func′tion, *Math.* a function that can be expressed as a root of an equation in which a polynomial, in the independent and dependent variables, is set equal to zero.

algebra′ic geom′etry, *Math.* the study of sets that are defined by algebraic equations. [1895–1900]

al′gebra′ic num′ber, *Math.* **1.** a root of an algebraic equation with integral coefficients. **2.** root[1] (def. 10b). [1930–35]

algebra′ic opera′tion, any of the mathematical operations of addition, subtraction, multiplication, division, raising to a power, or extraction of a root. [1930–35]

algebra′ic topol′ogy, *Math.* the branch of mathematics that deals with the application of algebraic methods to topology, esp. the study of homology and homotopy.

al•ge•bra•ist (al′jə brā′ist), *n.* an expert in algebra. [1665–75; ALGEBRA + -IST]

al′gebra of sets′, *Math.* a nonempty collection of sets having the property that the union of two sets of the collection is a set of the collection and the complement of each set of the collection is a set in the collection. Cf. **Boolean ring.**

Al•ge•ci•ras (al′ji sir′əs; *Sp.* äl′he thē′räs), *n.* a seaport in S Spain, in Andalusia, on the Strait of Gibraltar. 81,662.

Al•ger (al′jər), *n.* **1. Horatio, Jr.,** 1834–99, U.S. novelist: author of a series of books for boys. **2.** a male given name.

CONCISE ETYMOLOGY KEY: <, descended or borrowed from; >, whence; b., blend of, blended; c., cognate with; cf., compare; deriv., derivative; equiv., equivalent; imit., imitative; obl., oblique; r., replacing; s., stem; sp., spelling, spelled; resp., respelling, respelled; trans., translation; ?, origin unknown; *, unattested; ‡, probably earlier than. See the full key inside the front cover.

Al•ge•ri•a (al jēr′ē ə), *n.* a republic in NW Africa: formerly comprised 13 departments of France; gained independence 1962. 16,200,000; 919,352 sq. mi. (2,381,122 sq. km). *Cap.:* Algiers.

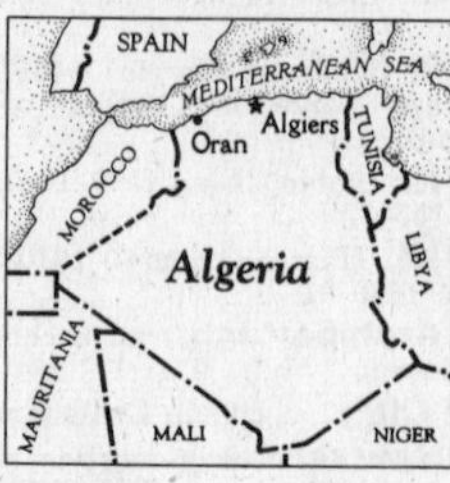

Al•ge•ri•an (al jēr′ē ən), *adj.* **1.** of or pertaining to Algeria or its inhabitants. —*n.* **2.** a native or inhabitant of Algeria. Also, **Algerine.** [1870–75; ALGERI(A) + -AN]

Alge′rian stripe′, a fabric woven with alternate stripes of coarse cotton and silk, usually cream-colored.

al•ge•ri•enne (al jēr′ē en′), *n.* a brightly striped woolen fabric used for tents, awnings, curtains, etc. Also, **algerine.** [< F *algérienne,* fem. of *algérien* ALGERIAN, from the fact that the fabric is made in Algeria]

Al•ge•rine (al′jə rēn′), *adj.* **1.** Algerian. —*n.* **2.** Algerian. **3.** (*l.c.*) a pirate. **4.** (*l.c.*) algerienne. [1650–60; ALGER(IA) + -INE[1]]

al•ge•ri•ta (al′gə rē′tə), *n.* agarita.

Al•ger•non (al′jər nən, -non′), *n.* a male given name: from an Old North French word meaning "whiskered."

al•ge•si•a (al jē′zē ə, -sē ə), *n. Med.* sensitivity to pain; hyperesthesia. [< NL < Gk *álgēs(is)* feeling of pain + NL *-ia* -IA] —**al•ge•sic** (al jē′zik, -sik), *adj.*

al•ge•sim•e•ter (al′ji sim′i tər), *n.* an instrument for determining the sensitiveness of the skin to a painful stimulus. Also, **al•ge•si•om•e•ter** (al jē′sē om′i tər, -zē-). [ALGESI(A) + -METER]

al•get•ic (al jet′ik), *adj. Med.* pertaining to or causing pain; painful. [1875–80; < Gk *algē-* (s. of *algeîn* to suffer pain) + -TIC]

Al-Ghaz•za•li (al′ga zä′lē), *n.* Ghazzali.

Al•ghe•ro (äl gâr′ō), *n.* a seaport in W Sardinia. 30,697.

-algia, var. of **algo-** as final element of a compound word: *neuralgia.* Also, **-algy.** [< NL < Gk; see ALGO-, -IA]

al•gi•cide (al′jə sīd′), *n.* a substance or preparation for killing algae. [1900–05; ALG(AE) + -I- + -CIDE] —**al′gi•cid′al,** *adj.*

al•gid (al′jid), *adj.* cold; chilly. [1620–30; < L *algidus* cold] —**al•gid′i•ty, al′gid•ness,** *n.*

Al•gie (al′jē), *n.* a male given name, form of **Algernon.**

Al•giers (al jērz′), *n.* **1.** a seaport in and the capital of Algeria, in the N part. 1,839,000. **2.** one of the former Barbary States in N Africa: now modern Algeria.

al•gin (al′jin), *n. Chem.* any hydrophilic, colloidal substance found in or obtained from various kelps, as alginic acid or one of its soluble salts. [1880–85; ALG(AE) + -IN[2]]

al•gi•nate (al′jə nāt′), *n.* a salt of alginic acid. [1935–40; ALGIN + -ATE[2]]

al′gin fi′ber, *Chem.* an alkali-soluble fiber produced by injecting a fine stream of alkaline algin into an aqueous solution of a metallic salt, used chiefly in the manufacture of fine threads.

al•gin′ic ac′id (al jin′ik), *Chem.* an insoluble, colloidal acid, $(C_6H_8O_6)_n$, found in the cell walls of various kelps, esp. brown kelps, known chiefly in the form of its salts, and used as a thickening or stabilizing agent in foodstuffs, esp. ice cream, and for sizing paper. [1885–90; ALGIN + -IC]

algo-, a combining form meaning "pain," used in the formation of compound words: *algophobia.* [comb. form repr. Gk *álgos*]

al•goid (al′goid), *adj.* like algae. [1870–75; ALG(AE) + -OID]

Al′gol (al′gol, -gôl), *n.* a star of the second magnitude in the constellation Perseus: the first known and most famous eclipsing binary star. Also called **Demon Star.** [1350–1400; ME < Ar, equiv. to *al* the + *ghūl* GHOUL; as trans. of Gk (Ptolemy) *gorgónion* the head of the Gorgon Medusa, held by Perseus]

ALGOL (al′gol, -gôl), *n. Computers.* a computer language in which information is expressed in algebraic notation and according to the rules of Boolean algebra. [1955–60; *algo(rithmic) l(anguage)*]

al•go•lag•ni•a (al′gə lag′nē ə), *n. Psychiatry.* sexual pleasure derived from enduring or inflicting pain, as in masochism or sadism. [1900–05; < G *Algolagnie,* equiv. to *algo-* ALGO- + *-lagnie* < Gk *lagneía* lust] —**al′go•lag′nic,** *adj.* —**al′go•lag′nist,** *n.*

al•gol•o•gy (al gol′ə jē), *n.* the branch of botany dealing with algae. [1840–50; ALG(AE) + -O- + -LOGY] —**al•go•log•i•cal** (al′gə loj′i kəl), *adj.* —**al′go•log′i•cal•ly,** *adv.* —**al•gol′o•gist,** *n.*

al•gom•e•ter (al gom′i tər), *n.* a device for determining sensitiveness to pain caused by pressure. [1890–95; ALGO- + -METER] —**al•go•met•ric** (al′gə me′trik), **al′go•met′ri•cal,** *adj.* —**al′go•met′ri•cal•ly,** *adv.* —**al•gom′e•try,** *n.*

Al•gon•ki•an (al gong′kē ən), *adj., n., pl.* **-ans,** (*esp. collectively*) **-an.** —*adj.* **1.** *Geol.* Proterozoic (def. 1). **2.** Algonquian. —*n.* **3.** *Geol.* Proterozoic (def. 2). **4.** Algonquian.

Al•gon•kin (al gong′kin), *n., pl.* **-kins,** (*esp. collectively*) **-kin,** *adj.* —*n.* **1.** Algonquin. **2.** Algonquian. —*adj.* **3.** Algonquian. **4.** Algonquin.

Al•gon•qui•an (al gong′kē ən, -kwē ən), *n., pl.* **-ans,** (*esp. collectively*) **-an** for 2, *adj.* —*n.* **1.** a family of languages spoken now or formerly by American Indians in an area extending from Labrador westward to the Rocky Mountains, west-southwestward through Michigan and Illinois, and southwestward along the Atlantic coast to Cape Hatteras, including esp. Arapaho, Blackfoot, Cheyenne, Cree, Fox, Massachusett, Micmac, Ojibwa, and Powhatan. Cf. **family** (def. 14). **2.** a member of an Algonquian-speaking tribe. —*adj.* **3.** of or pertaining to Algonquian or its speakers. Also, **Algonkian, Algonkin, Algonquin.** [1885–90, *Amer.;* ALGONQUI(N) + -AN]

Al•gon•quin (al gong′kin, -kwin), *n., pl.* **-quins,** (*esp. collectively*) **-quin** for 1, 3, *adj.* —*n.* **1.** a member of a group of North American Indian tribes formerly along the Ottawa River and the northern tributaries of the St. Lawrence. **2.** their speech, a dialect of Ojibwa, of the Algonquian family of languages. **3.** Algonquian. —*adj.* **4.** Algonquian. Also, **Algonkin.** [1615–25; < F; earlier *Algoumequin,* presumably < an Algonquian language]

Algon′quin Park′, a provincial park in S Canada, in SE Ontario. 2741 sq. mi. (7100 sq. km).

al•goph•a•gous (al gof′ə gəs), *adj.* feeding on algae, as certain insects. [ALG(AE) + -O- + -PHAGOUS]

al•go•pho•bi•a (al′gə fō′bē ə), *n. Psychiatry.* an abnormal dread of pain. [1895–1900; ALGO- + -PHOBIA]

al•go•rism (al′gə riz′əm), *n. Math. Now Rare.* **1.** the Arabic system of arithmetical notation (with the figures 1, 2, 3, etc.). **2.** the art of computation with the Arabic figures, one to nine, plus the zero; arithmetic. **3.** algorithm. [1200–1250; < ML *algorismus* < Ar *al* the + *kh(u)wārizmī* (surname of a 9th-century Muslim mathematician), equiv. to *khwārizm* KHIVA + *-ī* suffix of appurtenance; r. ME *augrim, algrim* < MF < ML] —**al′go•ris′mic,** *adj.*

al•go•rithm (al′gə rith′əm), *n.* a set of rules for solving a problem in a finite number of steps, as for finding the greatest common divisor. [1890–95; var. of ALGORISM, by assoc. with Gk *arithmós* number. See ARITHMETIC] —**al′go•rith′mic,** *adj.*

al′gorith′mic lan′guage, *Computers.* See **ALGOL.** [1955–60; ALGORITHM + -IC]

al•gra•phy (al′grə fē), *n. Print.* (formerly) an offset process employing an aluminum plate instead of a stone. Also called **aluminography.** [1895–1900; AL(UMINUM) + -GRAPHY] —**al•graph•ic** (al graf′ik), *adj.*

Al•gren (ôl′grin), *n.* **Nelson,** 1909–81, U.S. novelist and short-story writer.

al•gum (al′gəm, ôl′-), *n.* a Biblical tree, possibly the red sandalwood. II Chron. 2:8. Cf. **almug.** [1570–80; < Heb *algūmīm* (pl.), var. of *almuggīm*]

Al•gy (al′jē), *n.* a male given name, form of **Algernon.**

-algy, var. of **-algia:** *coxalgy.*

Al•ham•bra (al ham′brə), *n.* **1.** a palace and citadel of the Moorish kings in Granada, Spain: built chiefly between 1248 and 1354. **2.** a city in SW California, near Los Angeles. 64,615. [< Sp < Ar *al-ḥamrā′* lit., the red]

Al•ham•bresque (al′ham bresk′), *adj.* resembling the elaborately fanciful style of ornamentation of the Alhambra in Spain. [1860–65; ALHAMBR(A) + -ESQUE]

Al-Hil•lah (el hil′ə) *n.* Hilla.

Al Hu•fuf (al ho͞o fo͞of′), Hofuf.

A•li (ä′lē, ä lē′ *for 1–4;* ä lē′ *for* 5), *n.* **1.** (*′Alī ibn-abu-Talib*) (*"the Lion of God"*) A.D. c600–661, Arab caliph (cousin and son-in-law of Muhammad). **2.** See **Mehemet Ali. 3. Mohammed,** 1909–63, Pakistani statesman and diplomat. **4.** See **Mohammed Ali, Maulana. 5. Muhammad** (*Cassius Marcellus Clay, Jr.*), born 1942, U.S. boxer: world heavyweight champion 1964–67, 1974–78, 1978–79.

a•li•as (ā′lē əs), *n., pl.* **-as•es,** *adv.* —*n.* **1.** a false name used to conceal one's identity; an assumed name: *The police files indicate that "Smith" is an alias for Simpson.* —*adv.* **2.** at another time; in another place; in other circumstances; otherwise. "Simpson *alias* Smith" means that Simpson in other circumstances has called himself Smith. [1525–35; < L *aliās* (adv.): at another time, otherwise; cf. ELSE]
—**Syn. 1.** nom de guerre; nom de plume, pseudonym.

a•li•as dic•tus (ä′lē äs dik′to͞os; *Eng.* ā′lē əs dik′təs), *Latin.* otherwise called; alias.

A•li Ba•ba (ä′lē bä′bä, al′ē bab′ə), the poor woodcutter, hero of a tale in *The Arabian Nights' Entertainments,* who uses the magic words "Open sesame" to open the door to the cave in which the Forty Thieves had hidden their treasure.

al•i•bi (al′ə bī′), *n., pl.* **-bis,** *v.* —*n.* **1.** *Law.* the defense by an accused person of having been elsewhere at the time an alleged offense was committed. **2.** an excuse, esp. to avoid blame. **3.** a person used as one's excuse: *My sick grandmother was my alibi for missing school.* —*v.i.* **4.** *Informal.* to give an excuse; offer a defense: *to alibi for being late.* —*v.t.* **5.** *Informal.* **a.** to provide an alibi for (someone): *He alibied his friend out of a fix.* **b.** to make or find (one's way) by using alibis: *to alibi one's way out of work.* [1720–30; < L *alibī* (adv.): in or at another place]
—**Syn. 2.** explanation, reason, justification.
—**Usage.** ALIBI in Latin is an adverb meaning "in or at another place." Its earliest English uses, in the 18th century, are in legal contexts, both as an adverb and as a noun meaning "a plea of having been elsewhere." The extended noun senses "excuse" and "person used as one's excuse" developed in the 20th century in the United States and occur in all but the most formal writing. As a verb ALIBI occurs mainly in informal use.

al•i•ble (al′ə bəl), *adj. Archaic.* nutritive; nourishing. [1650–60; < L *alibilis,* equiv. to *al(ere)* to feed + *-ibilis* -IBLE] —**al′i•bil′i•ty,** *n.*

Al•i•can•te (al′ə kan′tē; *Sp.* ä′lē kän′te), *n.* a seaport in SE Spain, on the Mediterranean. 184,716.

Al•ice (al′is), *n.* **1.** a city in S Texas. 20,961. **2. the.** See **Alice Springs. 3.** a female given name: from a Germanic word meaning "of noble rank."

Al′ice blue′, a pale grayish-blue color. [1920–25, *Amer.*; named after *Alice* Longworth (daughter of Theodore Roosevelt)]

Al•ice-in-Won•der•land (al′is in wun′dər land′), *adj.* resembling a dream or fantasy; unreal: *an Alice-in-Wonderland world of incompleted projects and wishful thinking.* [1920–25]

Al′ice's Adven′tures in Won′derland, a story for children (1865) by Lewis Carroll. Also called ***Al′ice in Won′derland.***

Al′ice's fern′. See **Hartford fern.**

Al′ice Springs′, a town in Northern Territory, in central Australia. 13,400. Also called **the Alice.** Formerly, **Stuart.**

A•li•cia (ə lish′ə, ə lish′ē ə, ə lē′shə, -shē ə), *n.* a female given name, form of **Alice.**

Al•ick (al′ik), *n.* a male given name, form of **Alexander.**

al•i•cy•clic (al′ə sī′klik, -sik′lik), *adj. Chem.* of or noting organic compounds essentially aliphatic in chemical behavior but differing structurally in that the essential carbon atoms are connected in a ring instead of a chain. Also, **cycloaliphatic.** [1890–95; ALI(PHATIC) + CYCLIC]

al•i•dade (al′i dād′), *n. Survey.* **1.** (in plane-tabling) a straightedge having a telescopic sight or other means of sighting parallel to the straightedge. **2.** the entire upper part of a theodolite or transit, including the telescope, its supports, the level vials, the circle-reading device, and the spindle. Also, **al•i•dad** (al′i dad′). [1400–50; var. of *alhidade* < ML *alhidada* < Ar *al-'iḍādah* the turning radius (like a clock hand) of a circle; r. late ME *allydatha* (< OSp *alhidada*)]

al•ien (āl′yən, ā′lē ən), *n.* **1.** a resident born in or belonging to another country who has not acquired citizenship by naturalization (distinguished from *citizen*). **2.** a foreigner. **3.** a person who has been estranged or excluded. **4.** a creature from outer space; extraterrestrial. *—adj.* **5.** residing under a government or in a country other than that of one's birth without having or obtaining the status of citizenship there. **6.** belonging or relating to aliens: *alien property.* **7.** unlike one's own; strange; not belonging to one: *alien speech.* **8.** adverse; hostile; opposed (usually fol. by *to* or *from*): *ideas alien to modern thinking.* **9.** extraterrestrial. [1300–50; ME < MF < L *aliēnus,* equiv. to **alies-* (*ali-,* base of *alius* other + *-es-* n. suffix) + *-nus* adj. suffix]
—Syn. 1. immigrant. **2.** See **stranger. 3.** outcast. **7.** exotic, foreign.

al•ien•a•ble (āl′yə nə bəl, ā′lē ə-), *adj. Law.* capable of being sold or transferred. [1605–15; ALIEN + -ABLE] **—al′ien•a•bil′i•ty,** *n.*

al•ien•age (āl′yə nij, ā′lē ə-), *n.* **1.** the state of being an alien. **2.** the legal status of an alien. Also called **alienism.** [1800–10; ALIEN + -AGE]

al•ien•ate (āl′yə nāt′, ā′lē ə-), *v.t.,* **-at•ed, -at•ing. 1.** to make indifferent or hostile: *He has alienated his entire family.* **2.** to turn away; transfer or divert: *to alienate funds from their intended purpose.* **3.** *Law.* to transfer or convey, as title, property, or other right, to another: *to alienate lands.* [1400–50; late ME < L *aliēnātus* (ptp. of *aliēnāre*), equiv. to *aliēn(us)* ALIEN + *-ātus* -ATE[1]] **—al′ien•a′tor,** *n.*
—Syn. 1. See **estrange.**

al•ien•a•tion (āl′yə nā′shən, ā′lē ə-), *n.* **1.** the act of alienating. **2.** the state of being alienated. **3.** *Law.* a transfer of the title to property by one person to another; conveyance. **4.** the state of being withdrawn or isolated from the objective world, as through indifference or disaffection. **5.** *Statistics.* the lack of correlation in the variation of two measurable variates over a population. [1350–1400; ME < L *aliēnātiōn-* (s. of *aliēnātiō*), equiv. to *aliēnāt(us)* (see ALIENATE) + *-iōn-* -ION] **—al′ien•a′tive,** *adj.*

aliena′tion of affec′tions, *Law.* the estrangement by a third person of one spouse from the other.

al•ien•ee (āl′yə nē′, ā′lē ə-), *n. Law.* a person to whom property is alienated. [1525–35; obs. *alien* (v.), ME *alienen* + -EE]

al′ien hand′ syn′drome, a neurological disorder in which the movements of the left and right hands are not coordinated. [1991]

a•li•e•ni ge•ne•ris (ä′li ā′nē ge′ne ris; *Eng.* ā′lī ē′nī jen′ər is, ā′lē-), *Latin.* of another kind.

a•li•e•ni ju•ris (ā′lī ē′nī jŏŏr′is, ā′lē-), *Law.* under the control of another, as a lunatic or infant. Cf. **sui juris.** [< L: lit., of another's law]

al•ien•ism (āl′yə niz′əm, ā′lē ə-), *n.* alienage. [1800–10, *Amer.*; ALIEN + -ISM]

al•ien•ist (āl′yə nist, ā′lē ə-), *n.* **1.** (formerly) a doctor specializing in the treatment of mental illness. **2.** an expert witness in a sanity trial. [1860–65; ALIEN(ATION) + -IST; cf. F *aliéniste* in same sense]

al•ien•or (āl′yə nər, ā′lē ə-, āl′yə nôr′, ā′lē ə-), *n. Law.* a person who transfers property. Also, **al•ien•er** (āl′yə nər, ā′lē ə-). [1545–55; obs. *alien* (v.), ME *alienen* + -OR[2]; r. *alienour* < AF (cf. F *aliéneur*) < LL *aliēnātor.* See ALIENATE, -TOR]

a•lif (ä′lif), *n.* **1.** the first letter of the Arabic alphabet. **2.** the glottal stop consonant represented by this letter. [< Ar; see ALEPH]

al•i•form (al′ə fôrm′, ā′lə-), *adj.* wing-shaped; winglike; alar. [1830–40; AL(A) + -I- + -FORM]

A•li•garh (ä′lē gur′, al′ə gär′), *n.* a city in W Uttar Pradesh, in N India. 254,008.

a•light[1] (ə līt′), *v.i.,* **a•light•ed** or **a•lit, a•light•ing. 1.** to dismount from a horse, descend from a vehicle, etc. **2.** to settle or stay after descending: *The bird alighted on the tree.* **3.** to encounter or notice something accidentally. [bef. 1000; ME *alighten,* OE *ālihtan,* equiv. to *ā-* A-[3] + *lihtan* to relieve (orig. an animal mount) of weight, LIGHT[2])]

a•light[2] (ə līt′), *adv., adj.* **1.** provided with light; lighted up. **2.** on fire; burning. [bef. 1000; now taken as A-[1] + LIGHT[1]; orig. ptp. of *alight* to light up (ME *alihten,* OE *onlihtan,* equiv. to *on* A-[1] + *lihtan* to LIGHT[1])]

a•lign (ə līn′), *v.t.* **1.** to arrange in a straight line; adjust according to a line. **2.** to bring into a line or alignment. **3.** to bring into cooperation or agreement with a particular group, party, cause, etc.: *He aligned himself with the liberals.* **4.** to adjust (two or more components of an electronic circuit) to improve the response over a frequency band, as to align the tuned circuits of a radio receiver for proper tracking throughout its frequency range, or a television receiver for appropriate wide-band responses. *—v.i.* **5.** to fall or come into line; be in line. **6.** to join with others in a cause. Also, **aline.** [1685–95; < F *aligner,* equiv. to *a-* A-[5] + *ligner* < L *lineāre,* deriv. of *līnea* LINE[1]] **—a•lign′er,** *n.*
—Syn. 1, 2. straighten.

align′ing punch′, a drift for aligning rivet holes.

a•lign•ment (ə līn′mənt), *n.* **1.** an adjustment to a line; arrangement in a straight line. **2.** the line or lines so formed. **3.** the proper adjustment of the components of an electronic circuit, machine, etc., for coordinated functioning: *The front wheels of the car are out of alignment.* **4.** a state of agreement or cooperation among persons, groups, nations, etc., with a common cause or viewpoint. **5.** a ground plan of a railroad or highway. **6.** *Archaeol.* a line or an arrangement of parallel or converging lines of upright stones or menhirs. Also, **alinement.** [1780–90; ALIGN + -MENT; r. earlier *alignement* < F]

align′ment chart′, *Math.* nomogram. [1910–15]

a•li•go•té (*Fr.* A lē gô tā′; *Eng.* al′i gō tā′), *n.* **1.** a white grape of Burgundy. **2.** the dry white wine made from this grape. [1910–15; < F, appar. n. use of ptp. of OF *(h)aligoter, harigoter* to tear up, shred (see HARICOT[2], HARRY); sense development unclear]

a•like (ə līk′), *adv.* **1.** in the same manner or form; similarly: *They treated all customers alike.* **2.** to the same degree; equally: *All three were guilty alike.* *—adj.* **3.** having resemblance or similarity; having or showing no marked or important difference: *He thinks all politicians are alike.* [bef. 950; ME *alyke* < Scand; cf. ON *álíkr,* c. OE *onlic,* OHG *analīh;* r. ME *ilich,* OE *gelīc,* c. OS *gilīk,* OHG *gilīh* (G *gleich*), Goth *galeiks,* ON *(g)líkr;* see LIKE[1]] **—a•like′ness,** *n.*

al•i•ment (*n.* al′ə mənt; *v.* al′ə ment′), *n.* **1.** that which nourishes; nutriment; food. **2.** that which sustains; means of support. *—v.t.* **3.** to sustain; support. [1470–80; < L *alimentum,* equiv. to *al(ere)* to feed + *-i-* -I- + *-mentum* -MENT] **—al′i•men′tal,** *adj.* **—al′i•men′tal•ly,** *adv.*
—Syn. 1. nourishment. **1, 2.** sustenance.

al•i•men•ta•ry (al′ə men′tə rē), *adj.* **1.** concerned with the function of nutrition; nutritive. **2.** pertaining to food. **3.** providing sustenance or maintenance. [1605–15; < L *alimentārius.* See ALIMENT, -ARY]

alimen′tary canal′, *Anat., Zool.* a tubular passage functioning in the digestion and absorption of food and the elimination of food residue, beginning at the mouth and terminating at the anus. [1755–65]

al•i•men•ta•tion (al′ə men tā′shən), *n.* **1.** nourishment; nutrition. **2.** maintenance; support. **3.** addition to the volume of a glacial mass, chiefly by the accumulation of ice, snow, or névé. Cf. **ablation** (def. 2). [1580–90; < ML *alimentātiōn-* (s. of *alimentātiō*). See ALIMENT, -ATION]

al•i•men•ta•tive (al′ə men′tə tiv), *adj.* nourishing; nutritive. [1880–85; ALIMENT + -ATIVE] **—al′i•men′ta•tive•ly,** *adv.* **—al′i•men′ta•tive•ness,** *n.*

al•i•mo•ny (al′ə mō′nē), *n.* **1.** *Law.* an allowance paid to a person by that person's spouse or former spouse for maintenance, granted by a court upon a legal separation or a divorce or while action is pending. **2.** supply of the means of living; maintenance. [1645–55; < L *alimōnia* nourishment, sustenance, deriv. of *alimōn-* (s. of *alimō*), equiv. to *ali-* (see ALIMENT) + *-mōn-* action n. suffix parallel to *-mentum* -MENT] **—al′i•mo′nied,** *adj.*

à l'im•pro•viste (A lan prô vēst′), *French.* all of a sudden; unexpectedly; suddenly.

A′li Muham′mad of Shiraz′. See **Bab ed-Din.**

a•line (ə līn′), *v.t., v.i.,* **a•lined, a•lin•ing.** align. **—a•line′ment,** *n.* **—a•lin′er,** *n.*

A•line (ə lēn′, al′ēn), *n.* a female given name, form of **Adeline.**

A-line (ā′līn′), *n.* **1.** (esp. in women's clothing) a cut of garment consisting basically of two A-shaped panels for the front and back, designed to give increasing fullness toward the hemline. **2.** a garment having such a cut. *—adj.* **3.** being of such design or cut: *an A-line coat; an A-line dress.* [1960–65]

a•li•no•tum (ā′lə nō′təm, al′ə-), *n., pl.* **-ta** (-tə). the plate to which the wings are attached on the notum of an insect. [< NL, equiv. to L *āl(a)* ALA + *-i-* -I- + Gk *nôton* back]

Al•i•oth (al′ē oth′), *n. Astron.* a star of the second magnitude in the constellation Ursa Major. [< Ar < ?]

A•li Pa•sha (ä′lē pä shä′), (*Arslan*) 1741–1822, Turkish pasha and ruler of Albania 1787?–1820.

al•i•ped (al′ə ped′), *Zool.* *—adj.* **1.** having the toes connected by a winglike membrane, as a bat. *—n.* **2.** an aliped animal. [1725–35; < L *ālipēd-* (s. of *ālipēs* wing-footed). See ALA, -PED]

al•i•phat•ic (al′ə fat′ik), *adj. Chem.* pertaining to nonaromatic hydrocarbon compounds in which the constituent carbon atoms can be straight-chain, branched chain, or cyclic, as in alicyclic compounds; saturated, as in the paraffins; or unsaturated, as in the olefins and alkynes. [1885–90; < Gk *aleiphat-* (s. of *áleiphar* oil, fat) + -IC]

al•ip•te•ri•on (al′ip tēr′ē ən), *n., pl.* **-te•ri•a** (-tēr′ē ə). (in an ancient Roman bath) a room for anointment. Also called **elaeothesium, unctuarium.** [< Gk *aleiptḗrion,* equiv. to *aleipt(hein)* to anoint + *-tērion* place for]

al•i•quant (al′i kwənt), *adj. Math. Now Rare.* contained in a number or quantity, but not dividing it evenly: *An aliquant part of 16 is 5.* [1685–95; < L *aliquantus* more or less great, equiv. to *ali-* differently + *quantus* great]

Al•i•quip•pa (al′i kwip′ə), *n.* a borough in W Pennsylvania. 17,094.

al•i•quot (al′i kwət), *adj.* **1.** *Math.* forming an exact proper divisor: *An aliquot part of 15 is 5.* **2.** *Chem., Pharm.* comprising a known fraction of a whole and constituting a sample: *an aliquot quantity of acid for analysis.* *—n.* **3.** an aliquot part. [1560–70; < L, equiv. to *ali-* some other + *quot* as many as]

-alis, a suffix occurring in scientific names from Latin: *borealis.* [< L *-ālis;* see -AL[1]]

Al-Is•kan•da•rî•yah (äl is kän drē′yä), *n.* Arabic name of **Alexandria.**

Al•i•son (al′ə sən), *n.* a female given name, form of **Alice.**

A•lis•sa (ə lis′ə), *n.* a female given name: from a Hebrew word meaning "joy." Also, **A•li•sa** (ə lē′sə).

a•list (ə list′), *adj. Naut.* (of a vessel) inclined to one side; heeling or listing. [A-[1] + LIST[1]]

a•lis vo•lat pro•pri•is (ä′lis wō′lät prō′prē is; *Eng.* ā′lis vō′lat prō′prē is), *Latin.* She flies with her own wings (motto of Oregon).

a•lit (ə lit′), *v.* a pt. and pp. of **alight**[1].

a•lit•er•ate (ā lit′ər it), *n.* **1.** a person who is able to read but rarely chooses to do so: *Schools are worried about producing aliterates who prefer television to books.* *—adj.* **2.** of, pertaining to, or characteristic of aliterates. [see A-[6], LITERATE] **—a•lit′er•a•cy,** *n.*

a•li•tur•gi•cal (ā′li tûr′ji kəl), *adj.* designating those days on which the celebration of certain liturgies, esp. the Eucharist, is forbidden. Also, **a′li•tur′gic.** [1870–75; A-[6] + LITURGICAL]

a•li•un•de (ā′lē un′dē), *adv., adj. Chiefly Law.* not part of or derivable from the document or instrument itself: *evidence aliunde.* [< L: from another person or place, equiv. to *ali(us)* other + *unde* whence]

a•live (ə līv′), *adj.* **1.** having life; living; existing; not dead or lifeless. **2.** living (used for emphasis): *the proudest man alive.* **3.** in a state of action; in force or operation; active: *to keep hope alive.* **4.** full of energy and spirit; lively: *Grandmother's more alive than most of her contemporaries.* **5.** having the quality of life; vivid; vibrant: *The room was alive with color.* **6.** *Elect.* live[2] (def. 17). **7. alive to,** alert or sensitive to; aware of: *City planners are alive to the necessity of revitalizing deteriorating neighborhoods.* **8. alive with,** filled with living things; swarming; teeming: *The room was alive with mosquitoes.* **9. look alive!** pay attention! move quickly!: *Look alive! We haven't got all day.* [bef. 1000; ME; OE *on life* in LIFE; see A-[1]] **—a•live′ness,** *n.*
—Syn. 4. active. **—Ant. 1.** dead. **3.** defunct. **4.** lifeless.

a•li•yah (*Seph. Heb., Eng.* ä′lē ä′; *for 1 also Ashk. Heb.* ä lē′ô *or, Eng.,* ə lē′ə), *n., pl.* **a•li•yahs, a•li•yos** (ä′lē yäz′; *for 1 also Ashk. Heb.* ä lē′ôz *or, Eng.,* ə lē′əz), **a•li•yot** (*Seph. Heb.* ä′lē ôt′). **1.** the act of proceeding to the reading table in a synagogue for the reading of a portion from the Torah. **2.** the immigration of Jews to Israel, either as individuals or in groups. **3.** any of the major waves of Jewish immigration to Palestine or Israel. [< Heb: *'ălīyyāh* lit., ascent, rise]

a•liz•a•rin (ə liz′ər in), *n. Chem.* a solid appearing reddish-orange as crystals and brownish-yellow as powder, $C_{14}H_8O_4$, one of the earliest known dyes, formerly obtained in its natural state from madder and now derived from anthraquinone: used chiefly in the synthesis of other dyes. Also, **a•liz•a•rine** (ə liz′ər in, -ə rēn′). [1825–35; < F *alizarine,* equiv. to *alizar(i)* (< Sp < Ar *al* the + *'aṣārah* juice) + *-ine* -INE[1]]

aliz′arin crim′son, a pigment used in painting, derived from anthraquinone and characterized by its red color and transparency.

alk., 1. alkali. **2.** alkaline.

al•ka•hest (al′kə hest′), *n.* the universal solvent sought by the alchemists. Also, **alcahest.** [1635–45; < late ML *alchahest;* prob. coinage of Paracelsus] **—al′ka•hes′tic, al′ka•hes′ti•cal,** *adj.*

al•ka•le•mi•a (al′kə lē′mē ə), *n. Pathol.* abnormal alkalinity of the blood. [1920–25; ALKAL(I) + -EMIA]

al•ka•les•cent (al′kə les′ənt), *adj.* tending to become alkaline; slightly alkaline. [1725–35; ALKAL(I) + -ESCENT] **—al′ka•les′cence, al′ka•les′cen•cy,** *n.*

al•ka•li (al′kə lī′), *n., pl.* **-lis, -lies,** *adj.* *—n.* **1.** *Chem.* **a.** any of various bases, the hydroxides of the alkali metals and of ammonium, that neutralize acids to form salts and turn red litmus paper blue. **b.** any of various other more or less active bases, as calcium hydroxide. **c.** (not in technical use) an alkali metal. **d.** *Obs.* any of various other compounds, as the carbonates of sodium and potassium. **2.** *Agric.* a soluble mineral salt or a mixture of soluble salts, present in some soils, esp. in arid regions, and detrimental to the growing of most crops. *—adj.* **3.** *Chem.* alkaline. [1300–50; ME *alkaly* < MF *alcali* < dial. Ar *al-qalī,* var. of Ar *qily* saltwort ashes]

al′kali blue′, *Chem.* any of the class of blue pigments

CONCISE PRONUNCIATION KEY: *act, cāpe, dâre, pärt; set, ēqual; if, īce; ox, ōver, ôrder, oil, bŏŏk, bōōt, out; up, ûrge; child; sing; shoe; thin, that;* zh *as in treasure.* ə = *a* as in *alone, e* as in *system, i* as in *easily, o* as in *gallop, u* as in *circus;* ᵊ as in *fire* (fīᵊr), *hour* (ouᵊr). l and n can serve as syllabic consonants, as in *cradle* (krād′l), and *button* (but′n). See the full key inside the front cover.

having the highest tinting strength, by weight, of all known blue pigments: used chiefly in the manufacture of printing inks.

al·kal·ic (al kal′ik), *adj. Geol.* (of igneous rock) containing a relatively high percentage of sodium and potassium alkali. [1725–35, in sense "alkaline;" ALKAL(I) + -IC]

al′kali flat′, a level area, as a dry lake bed, in which evaporation has concentrated alkali minerals, as sodium sulfates and carbonates. Cf. **salt flat.** [1870–75, *Amer.*]

al·ka·li·fy (al′kə lə fī′, al kal′ə-), *v.*, **-fied, -fy·ing.** *Chem.* —*v.t.* **1.** to alkalize. —*v.i.* **2.** to become alkaline. [1825–35; ALKALI + -FY] —**al′ka·li·fi′a·ble,** *adj.*

al′kali grass′, a plant, *Zigadenus elegans*, of central and western North America, having tough, wiry, bluish-green leaves and greenish flowers. [1865–70, *Amer.*]

al·ka·li-lov·ing (al′kə lī luv′ing), *adj.* (of a plant) requiring a pH of 7.1 to 9 for optimal growth.

al′kali met′al, *Chem.* any of the group of univalent metals including potassium, sodium, lithium, rubidium, cesium, and francium, whose hydroxides are alkalis. [1880–85]

al′kali metapro′tein, *Biochem.* a metaprotein derived by means of a hydrolytic alkali.

al·ka·lim·e·ter (al′kə lim′i tər), *n. Physical Chem.* an instrument for determining the quantity of carbon dioxide. [1820–30; ALKALI + -METER] —**al·ka·li·met·ric** (al′kə lə me′trik), **al′ka·li·met′ri·cal,** *adj.* —**al′ka·li·met′ri·cal·ly,** *adv.* —**al′ka·lim′e·try,** *n.*

al·ka·line (al′kə līn′, -lin), *adj. Chem.* **1.** of or like an alkali. **2.** containing an alkali. **3.** having the properties of an alkali. **4.** having a pH value greater than 7. Cf. **acid** (def. 5c). [1670–80; ALKAL(I) + -INE[1]]

al′kaline earth′, *Chem.* any of the oxides of barium, radium, strontium, calcium, and, sometimes, magnesium. [1810–20]

al′ka·line-earth′ met′al (al′kə līn′ûrth′, -lin-), *Chem.* any of the group of bivalent metals including barium, radium, strontium, calcium, and, usually, magnesium, the hydroxides of which are alkalis but less soluble than those of the alkali metals. [1900–05]

al′kaline phos′phatase, *n. Biochem.* a phosphatase active in an alkaline medium. [1945–50]

al·ka·lin·i·ty (al′kə lin′i tē), *n. Chem.* alkaline condition; the quality that constitutes an alkali. [1780–90; ALKALINE + -ITY]

al′kali rock′, *Mineral.* any igneous rock with a marked preponderance of alkali and a low percentage of silica.

al′kali soil′, soil that has either a high degree of alkalinity or a high percentage of sodium, or both, so that most crops cannot be grown in it profitably. [1910–15]

al·ka·lize (al′kə līz′), *v.t., v.i.*, **-lized, -liz·ing.** *Chem.* to make or become alkaline. Also, **al′ka·lin·ize′;** *esp. Brit.*, **al′ka·lise′, al′ka·lin·ise′.** [1740–50; ALKAL(I) + -IZE] —**al′ka·liz′a·ble,** *adj.* —**al′ka·li·za′tion,** *n.* —**al′ka·liz′er,** *n.*

al·ka·loid (al′kə loid′), *Biochem., Chem., Pharm.* —*n.* **1.** any of a large class of organic, nitrogen-containing ring compounds of vegetable origin and sometimes synthesized, some of which are liquid but most of which are solid, that have a bitter taste, that are usually water-insoluble and alcohol-soluble, that combine with acids without the loss of a water molecule to form water-soluble hydrochlorides, hydrobromides, or the like, and that usually exhibit pharmacological action, as nicotine, morphine, or quinine. —*adj.* **2.** resembling an alkali; alkaline. [1825–35; ALKAL(I) + -OID]

al·ka·loi·dal (al′kə loid′l), *adj.* of, pertaining to, or derived from alkaloids. [1875–80; ALKALOID + -AL[1]]

al·ka·lo·sis (al′kə lō′sis), *n. Pathol.* a condition of the blood and other body fluids in which the bicarbonate concentration is above normal, tending toward alkalemia. [1910–15; ALKAL(I) + -OSIS] —**al·ka·lot·ic** (al′kə-lot′ik), *adj.*

al·kane (al′kān), *n. Chem.* any member of the alkane series. [1895–1900; ALK(YL) + -ANE]

al′kane se′ries, *Chem.* the homologous series of saturated, aliphatic hydrocarbons having the general formula C_nH_{2n+2}, as methane, CH_4, or ethane, C_2H_6. Also called **methane series, paraffin series.** [1945–50]

al·ka·net (al′kə net′), *n.* **1.** a European plant, *Alkanna tinctoria*, of the borage family. **2.** the root of this plant, yielding a red dye. **3.** the dye itself. **4.** any of several similar hairy plants, as the bugloss, *Anchusa officinalis*, or a puccoon of the genus *Lithospermum*. [1300–50; ME < OSp *alcaneta*, equiv. to *alcan(a)* henna (plant) (< ML *alchanna* < Ar *al* the + *hinnā′* henna) + *-eta* dim. suffix]

al·kane·thi·ol (al′kān thī′ôl, -ol), *n. Chem.* any compound containing an alkyl group joined to a mercapto group, as methyl mercaptan or methanethiol, CH_3SH. [ALKANE + THIOL]

al·kan·nin (al kan′in), *n. Chem.* a dark red, amorphous, water-insoluble powder, $C_{16}H_{16}O_5$, obtained from the root of the alkanet: used chiefly for coloring fats, oils, and pharmaceuticals. [< NL *alkann(a)* < ML *alchanna* (see ALKANET) + -IN[2]]

al·kap·ton (al kap′ton, -tən), *n. Biochem.* See **homogentisic acid.** [1885–90; AL(KALI) + Gk *kápt(ein)* to gulp + -ON]

al·kap·to·nu·ri·a (al kap′tə no͝or′ē ə, -nyo͝or′-), *n. Pathol.* excessive excretion of homogentisic acid in the urine, caused by a hereditary abnormality of the metabolism of tyrosine and phenylalanine. [1885–90; ALKAPTON + -URIA]

al·ke·ken·gi (al′kə ken′jē), *n.* the winter cherry plant or fruit. [1400–50; late ME < ML < Ar *al* the + *kākanj* ground cherry < Pers]

al·kene (al′kēn), *n. Chem.* any member of the alkene series. [1895–1900; ALK(YL) + -ENE]

al′kene se′ries, *Chem.* the homologous series of unsaturated, aliphatic hydrocarbons containing one double bond and having the general formula C_nH_{2n}, as ethylene, $H_2C{=}CH_2$. Also called **ethylene series, olefin series.**

al·ker·mes (al kûr′mēz), *n.* a Mediterranean liqueur made from brandy flavored with nutmeg, cinnamon, cloves, and other spices, and colored red with kermes or cochineal. [1595–1605; < Sp < Ar *al* the + *qirmiz* KERMES]

Al·kes·tis (al kes′tis), *n. Class. Myth.* Alcestis (def. 1).

al·kine (al′kīn), *n. Chem.* alkyne.

Alk·maar (älk′mär), *n.* a city in the W Netherlands: cheese market. 73,766.

Alk·me·ne (alk mē′nē), *n. Class. Myth.* Alcmene.

Al·ko·ran (al′kô rän′, -ran′, -kō-), *n.* the Koran. Also, **Alcoran.** [1325–75; < Ar *al-qur′ān* lit., reading (aloud); r. ME *alkaro(u)n* < MF or ML]

alk·ox·ide (al kok′sīd, -sid), *n. Chem.* a compound formed from an alcohol by the replacement of the hydrogen of the hydroxyl group with a metal, as sodium methoxide, CH_3ONa, from methyl alcohol, CH_3OH. Also called **alcoholate.** [ALK(YL) + OX(Y)-[2] + -IDE]

alk·ox·y (al kok′sē), *adj. Chem.* of or containing a univalent organic radical consisting of an alkyl group attached to oxygen. [1920–25; ALK(YL) + OXY-[2]]

Al Ku·fa (al ko͞o′fə, -fa), Kufa.

al·ky (al′kē), *n., pl.* **-kies.** *Slang.* **1.** an alcoholic. **2.** alcohol. [1840–50; resp. of ALC(OHOL) + -Y[2]]

al·kyd (al′kid), *Chem. n.* **1.** Also called **al′kyd res′in.** any of a group of sticky resins derived from dicarboxylic acids, as phthalic or maleic acid, in reaction with polyvalent alcohols, as glycol or glycerol: used chiefly in adhesives and paints. —*adj.* **2.** made of or containing an alkyd. [1925–30; ALKY(L) + (ACI)D]

al·kyl (al′kəl), *Chem.* —*adj.* **1.** containing an alkyl group. —*n.* **2.** an alkyl group. [1880–85; < G, equiv. to *Alk(ohol)* ALCOHOL + *-yl* -YL]

al·kyl·ate (al′kə lāt′), *n., v.*, **-at·ed, -at·ing.** *Chem.* —*n.* **1.** a substance produced by adding one or more alkyl groups to a compound. —*v.t.* **2.** to add one or more alkyl groups to (a compound). [1885–90; ALKYL + -ATE[1]]

al′kylating drug′, *Pharm.* any of various potentially cytotoxic, carcinogenic, and mutagenic substances: used therapeutically to destroy cells, esp. proliferating cancer cells.

al·kyl·a·tion (al′kə lā′shən), *n. Chem.* **1.** the replacement of a hydrogen atom in an organic compound by an alkyl group. **2.** the addition of a paraffin to an olefin, done in the manufacture of gasoline. [1895–1900; ALKYL + -ATION]

al′kyl group′, *Chem.* any of a series of univalent groups of the general formula C_nH_{2n+1}, derived from aliphatic hydrocarbons, as the methyl group, CH_3-, or ethyl group, C_2H_5-. Also called **al′kyl rad′ical.**

al′kyl hal′ide, *Chem.* a compound with the type formula RX, where R is an alkyl group and X is a halogen. [1895–1900]

al·kyl·ic (al kil′ik), *adj.* of, pertaining to, or characteristic of an alkyl group. [ALKYL + -IC]

al·kyne (al′kīn), *n. Chem.* any member of the alkyne series. Also, **alkine.** [1880–85; ALK(YL) + -INE[2], altered to *-yne*]

al′kyne se′ries, *Chem.* the homologous series of unsaturated, aliphatic hydrocarbons containing one triple bond and having the general formula, C_nH_{2n-2}, as acetylene, $HC{\equiv}CH$. Also called **acetylene series.**

all (ôl), *adj.* **1.** the whole of (used in referring to quantity, extent, or duration): *all the cake; all the way; all year.* **2.** the whole number of (used in referring to individuals or particulars, taken collectively): *all students.* **3.** the greatest possible (used in referring to quality or degree): *with all due respect; with all speed.* **4.** every: *all kinds; all sorts.* **5.** any; any whatever: *beyond all doubt.* **6.** nothing but; only: *The coat is all wool.* **7.** dominated by or as if by the conspicuous possession or use of a particular feature: *The colt was all legs. They were all ears, listening attentively to everything she said.* **8.** *Chiefly Pennsylvania German.* all gone; consumed; finished: *The pie is all.*
—*pron.* **9.** the whole quantity or amount: *He ate all of the peanuts. All are gone.* **10.** the whole number; every one: *all of us.* **11.** everything: *Is that all you want to say? All is lost.*
—*n.* **12.** one's whole interest, energy, or property: *to give one's all; to lose one's all.* **13.** (*often cap.*) the entire universe. **14. above all,** before everything else; chiefly: *Above all, the little girl wanted a piano.* **15. after all,** in spite of the circumstances; notwithstanding: *He came in time after all.* **16. all in all, a.** everything considered; in general: *All in all, her health is greatly improved.* **b.** altogether: *There were twelve absentees all in all.* **c.** everything; everything regarded as important: *Painting became his all in all.* **17. all in hand,** *Print., Journ.* (of the copy for typesetting a particular article, book, issue, etc.) in the possession of the compositor. **18. and all,** together with every other associated or connected attribute, object, or circumstance: *What with the snow and all, we may be a little late.* **19. at all, a.** in the slightest degree: *I wasn't surprised at all.* **b.** for any reason: *Why bother at all?* **c.** in any way: *no offense at all.* **20. for all (that),** in spite of; notwithstanding: *For all that, it was a good year.* **21. in all,** all included; all together: *a hundred guests in all.* **22. once and for all,** for the last time; finally: *The case was settled once and for all when the appeal was denied.*
—*adv.* **23.** wholly; entirely; completely: *all alone.* **24.** only; exclusively: *He spent his income all on pleasure.* **25.** each; apiece: *The score was one all.* **26.** *Archaic.* even; just. **27. all at once.** See **once** (def. 14). **28. all but,** almost; very nearly: *These batteries are all but dead.* **29. all in,** *Northern and Western U.S.* very tired; exhausted: *We were all in at the end of the day.* **30. all in the wind,** *Naut.* too close to the wind. **31. all out,** with all available means or effort: *We went all out to win the war.* **32. all over, a.** finished; done; ended. **b.** everywhere; in every part. **c.** in every respect; typically. **33. all standing,** *Naut.* **a.** in such a way and so suddenly that sails or engines are still set to propel a vessel forward: *The ship ran aground all standing.* **b.** fully clothed: *The crew turned in all standing.* **c.** fully equipped, as a vessel. **34. all that,** remarkably; entirely; decidedly (used in negative constructions): *It's not all that different from your other house.* **35. all the better,** more advantageous; so much the better: *If the sun shines it will be all the better for our trip.* **36. all there,** *Informal.* mentally competent; not insane or feeble-minded: *Some of his farfetched ideas made us suspect that he wasn't all there.* **37. all the same.** See **same** (def. 8). **38. all told.** See **told** (def. 2). **39. all up, a.** *Print., Journ.* (of copy) completely set in type. **b.** *Informal.* with no vestige of hope remaining: *It's all up with George—they've caught him.* [bef. 900; ME *al*, pl. *alle*; OE *eal(l)*; c. Goth *alls*, ON *allr*, OFris, D, MLG *al*, OS, OHG *al(l)* (G *all*); if < **ol-no-*, equiv. to Welsh *oll* and akin to OIr *uile* < **ol-io-*; cf. ALMIGHTY]
—**Syn. 2.** every one of, each of. **23.** totally, utterly, fully.
—**Usage.** Expressions like *all the farther* and *all the higher* occur chiefly in informal speech: *This is all the farther the bus goes. That's all the higher she can jump.* Elsewhere *as far as* and *as high as* are generally used: *This is as far as the bus goes. That's as high as she can jump.*
Although some object to the inclusion of *of* in such phrases as *all of the students* and *all of the contracts* and prefer to omit it, the construction is entirely standard.
See also **already, alright, altogether.**

all-, var. of **allo-** before a vowel: *allonym.*

al·la bre·ve (ä′lə brev′ā; *It.* äl′lä bre′ve), *Music.* using the half note as the basic time unit; 2/2 time. *Symbol:* ₵ Also called **cut time.** Cf. **common time.** [1800–10; < It: in short time, accelerated. See BRIEF]

Al·lah (al′ə, ä′lə), *n. Islam.* the Supreme Being; God. [< Ar *Allāh*, akin to *ilāh* god]

Al·lah·a·bad (al′ə hə bad′, ä′lə hä bäd′), *n.* a city in SE Uttar Pradesh, in N India, on the Ganges. 513,997.

al·la·man·da (al′ə man′də), *n.* any of several tropical American shrubs or woody vines belonging to the genus *Allamanda*, of the dogbane family, having showy yellow or purple flowers, and often used for ornamental plantings. [1790–1800; < NL, named after Jean-Nicolas-Sébastien *Allamand* (1713–87), Swiss naturalist; see -A[2]]

al·la mar·cia (ä′lə mär′chə; *It.* äl′lä mär′chä), *Music.* like a march; in the manner of a march. [< It. See MARCH]

all-A·mer·i·can (ôl′ə mer′i kən), *adj.* **1.** representing the entire United States. **2.** composed exclusively of American members or elements. **3.** selected as the best in the United States, as in a sport: *the all-American college football team of 1983.* —*n.* **4.** an all-American player or performer. [1885–90, *Amer.*]

Al·lan (al′ən), *n.* a male given name.

Al·lan-a-Dale (al′ən ə dāl′), *n.* (in English balladry) a member of Robin Hood's band who carried off his sweetheart just before she was to be forced into marriage with an aged knight. Also, **Alan-a-dale.**

al·lan·ite (al′ə nīt′), *n. Mineral.* a member of the epidote group, a silicate of calcium, cerium, aluminum, and iron, occurring chiefly in brown-to-black masses or prismatic crystals. [1835–45; named after Thomas *Allan* (1777–1833), English mineralogist; see -ITE[1]] —**al·la·nit·ic** (al′ə nit′ik), *adj.*

al·l'an·ti·ca (äl′län tē′kä), *adv. Italian.* in the manner of the ancients.

al·lan·to·ic (al′ən tō′ik), *adj.* of or pertaining to the allantois. [1830–40; ALLANTO(IS) + -IC]

al·lan·toid (ə lan′toid), *adj.* **1.** Also, **al·lan·toi·dal** (al′ən toid′l). allantoic. —*n.* **2.** the allantois. [1625–35; < Gk *allantoeidḗs*, equiv. to *allant-* (s. of *allâs* sausage) + *-oeidēs* -OID]

al·lan·to·in (ə lan′tō in), *n. Biochem., Pharm.* a white powder, $C_4H_6N_4O_3$, produced by oxidation of uric acid and the major excretory product of purine degradation in many vertebrates: used medicinally to heal skin ulcers and in lotions, lipsticks, etc., for its soothing effect. [1835–45; ALLANTO(IS) + -IN[2]; so named because it is found in the fluid of the allantois]

al·lan·to·is (ə lan′tō is, -tois), *n. Embryol., Zool.* a vascular, extraembryonic membrane of birds, reptiles, and certain mammals that develops as a sac or diverticulum from the ventral wall of the hindgut. [1640–50; < NL < Gk *allantoeidḗs*, wrongly taken for pl. and given a sing., on the model of words like *hērōis* (sing.), *hērōides* (pl.)]

al·la pri·ma (ä′lə prē′mə), *Fine Arts.* a painting technique in which a canvas is completed in one session, often having a thickly applied impasto. [< It: lit., at the first]

al·lar·gan·do (ä′lär gän′dō, -gan′-; *It.* äl′lär gän′dô), *adj. Music.* becoming slower and broader. [1890–95; < It: *al* to the + *largando* broadening. See LARGE]

all-a·round (ôl′ə round′), *adj.* **1.** able to do many things; versatile: *an all-around player.* **2.** broadly applicable; not specialized: *an all-around education.* **3.** inclusive; comprehensive; complete: *an all-around failure.* Also, **all-round.** [1720–30]

CONCISE ETYMOLOGY KEY: <, descended or borrowed from; >, whence; b., blend of, blended; c., cognate with; cf., compare; deriv., derivative; equiv., equivalent; imit., imitative; obl., oblique; r., replacing; s., stem; sp., spelling, spelled; resp., respelling, respelled; trans., translation; ?, origin unknown; *, unattested; ‡, probably earlier than. See the full key inside the front cover.

al-Lat (äl lät′), *n.* a pre-Islamic Arabian goddess personifying the sun and considered to be a daughter of Allah.

al•la•tive (al′ə tiv), *Gram.* —*adj.* **1.** noting a case, as in Finnish, whose distinctive function is to indicate place to or toward which. —*n.* **2.** the allative case. [1860–65; < L *allāt(us)* (*al-* AL- + *lātus* suppletive ptp. of *ferre* to bring; cf. ALLEY[1]) + -IVE]

al•la vos•tra sa•lu•te (äl′lä vôs′trä sä lo͞o′te), *Italian.* to your health (used as a toast).

al•lay (ə lā′), *v.t.,* **-layed, -lay•ing. 1.** to put (fear, doubt, suspicion, anger, etc.) to rest; calm; quiet. **2.** to lessen or relieve; mitigate; alleviate: *to allay pain.* [bef. 1000; ME *aleyen,* OE *ālecgan* to put down, allay (*ā-* A-[3] + *lecgan* to LAY[1]); sp. *-ll-* shows influence of the now obs. *allege* (< AF, OF *aleg(i)er;* see ALLEGE) to alleviate, allay] —**al•lay′er,** *n.*
—**Syn. 1.** soften, assuage. ALLAY, MODERATE, SOOTHE mean to reduce excitement or emotion. TO ALLAY is to lay to rest or lull to a sense of security, possibly by making the emotion seem unjustified: *to allay suspicion, anxiety, fears.* To MODERATE is to tone down any excess and thus to restore calm: *to moderate the expression of one's grief.* To SOOTHE is to exert a pacifying or tranquilizing influence: *to soothe a terrified child.* **2.** lighten, mollify, temper, ease. —**Ant. 1.** excite.

all′ clear′, the signal that an air raid or other danger is over. [1915–20]

all-day (ôl′dā′), *adj.* taking up, extending through, lasting for, or occurring continually during a day, esp. the hours of daylight; daylong: *an all-day tour of the city; an all-day lollipop.* Cf. **all-night.** [1865–70]

al•le•cret (al′i kret′), *n.* a half suit of light plate armor. [1530–40; < MF *halecret,* perh. < G *Hals* neck]

al•le•ga•tion (al′i gā′shən), *n.* **1.** the act of alleging; affirmation. **2.** an assertion made with little or no proof. **3.** an assertion made by a party in a legal proceeding, which the party then undertakes to prove. **4.** a statement offered as a plea, excuse, or justification. [1375–1425; late ME < L *allēgātiōn-* (s. of *allēgātiō*), equiv. to *allēgāt(us),* ptp. of *allēgāre* to adduce in support of a plea (*al-* AL- + *-lēgāre,* deriv. of *lēx* law; see LEGAL) + *-iōn-* -ION]
—**Syn. 1, 2.** charge, accusation; claim, contention.

al•lege (ə lej′), *v.t.,* **-leged, -leg•ing. 1.** to assert without proof. **2.** to declare with positiveness; affirm; assert: *to allege a fact.* **3.** to declare before a court or elsewhere, as if under oath. **4.** to plead in support of; offer as a reason or excuse. **5.** *Archaic.* to cite or quote in confirmation. [1275–1325; ME *alleg(g)en,* prob. < OF *aleguer* (< ML, L *allēgāre* to adduce in support of a plea; see ALLEGATION), conflated with AF, OF *aleg(i)er* to justify, free, lit., to lighten (< LL *alleviāre;* see ALLEVIATE); homonymous ME v. *alleg(g)en,* with literal sense of OF *aleg(i)er,* replaced by ALLAY in 16th cent.] —**al•lege′a•ble,** *adj.* —**al•leg′er,** *n.*
—**Syn. 1.** See **maintain. 2.** state, asseverate, aver. **3.** attest. —**Ant. 2.** deny.

al•leged (ə lejd′, ə lej′id), *adj.* **1.** declared or stated to be as described; asserted: *The alleged murderer could not be located for questioning.* **2.** doubtful; suspect; supposed: *The alleged cure-all produced no results when it was tested by reputable doctors.* [1400–50; late ME; see ALLEGE, -ED[2]]

al•leg•ed•ly (ə lej′id lē), *adv.* according to what is or has been alleged. [1870–75; ALLEGED + -LY]

Al•le•ghe•ny (al′i gā′nē), *n.* a river flowing NW from Pennsylvania into SW New York and then S through W Pennsylvania, joining the Monongahela at Pittsburgh to form the Ohio River. 325 mi. (525 km) long. —**Al′le•ghe′ni•an, Al′le•gha′ni•an,** *adj.*

Al′leghe′ny bar′berry, a shrub, *Berberis canadensis,* of North America, resembling the common barberry of Europe, but having leaves with grayish undersides.

Al′leghe′ny Moun′tains, a mountain range in Pennsylvania, Maryland, West Virginia, and Virginia: a part of the Appalachian Mountains. Also called **Al′le•ghe′nies.**

Al′leghe′ny spurge′, a low, shrubby evergreen plant, *Pachysandra procumbens,* having spikes of white or purplish flowers, native to the southeastern U.S. and widely cultivated as a ground cover. [1935–40]

al•le•giance (ə lē′jəns), *n.* **1.** the loyalty of a citizen to his or her government or of a subject to his or her sovereign. **2.** loyalty or devotion to some person, group, cause, or the like. [1350–1400; ME *aliegiaunce,* equiv. to *a-* prob. A-[5] + *liege* LIEGE + *-aunce* -ANCE; cf. MF *ligeance*]
—**Syn.** See **loyalty.** —**Ant. 1.** treason. **2.** treachery.

al•le•giant (ə lē′jənt), *adj.* **1.** loyal; faithful. —*n.* **2.** a faithful follower; adherent: *allegiants of religious cults.* [1605–15; ALLEGI(ANCE) + -ANT]

al•le•gor•i•cal (al′i gôr′i kəl, -gor′-), *adj.* consisting of or pertaining to allegory; of the nature of or containing allegory; figurative: *an allegorical poem; an allegorical meaning.* Also, **al′le•gor′ic.** [1520–30; < LL *allēgoricus* (< Gk *allēgorikós;* see ALLEGORY, -IC) + -AL[1]] —**al′le•gor′i•cal•ly,** *adv.* —**al′le•gor′i•cal•ness,** *n.*

al•le•go•rist (al′i gôr′ist, -gōr′-, al′i gər ist), *n.* a person who uses or writes allegory. [1675–85; ALLEGOR(IZE) + -IST]

al•le•go•ris•tic (al′i gə ris′tik), *adj.* writing or using allegory; interpreting in an allegorical sense. [ALLEGORIST + -IC]

al•le•go•rize (al′i gə rīz′), *v.,* **-rized, -riz•ing.** —*v.t.* **1.** to make into an allegory; narrate allegorically. **2.** to understand in an allegorical sense; interpret allegorically. —*v.i.* **3.** to use allegory. Also, *esp. Brit.,* **al′le•go•rise′.** [1425–75; late ME < LL *allēgorizāre;* see ALLEGORY, -IZE] —**al′le•go•ri•za′tion,** *n.* —**al′le•go•riz′er,** *n.*

al•le•go•ry (al′ə gôr′ē, -gōr′ē), *n., pl.* **-ries. 1.** a representation of an abstract or spiritual meaning through concrete or material forms; figurative treatment of one subject under the guise of another. **2.** a symbolical narrative: *the allegory of* Piers Plowman. **3.** emblem (def. 3). [1350–1400; ME *allegorie* < L *allēgoria* < Gk *allēgoría,* deriv. of *allēgoreîn* to speak so as to imply something other. See ALLO-, AGORA; Gk *agoreúein* to speak, proclaim, orig. meant to act (e.g., speak) in the assembly]

Al•le•gra (ə leg′rə; *It.* äl le′grä), *n.* a female given name.

al•le•gret•to (al′i gret′ō; *It.* äl′le gret′tô), *adj., adv., n., pl.* **-tos.** *Music.* —*adj., adv.* **1.** light, graceful, and moderately fast in tempo. —*n.* **2.** an allegretto movement. [1730–40; < It, equiv. to *allegr(o)* ALLEGRO + *-etto* -ET]

al•le•gro (ə lā′grō, ə leg′rō; *It.* äl le′grô), *adj., adv., n., pl.* **-gros.** *Music.* —*adj., adv.* **1.** brisk or rapid in tempo. —*n.* **2.** an allegro movement. [1625–35; < It < L *alacer* brisk. Cf. ALACRITY]

Al•le•gro, L′ (lä lā′grō, la-). See ***L'Allegro.***

al•lele (ə lēl′), *n. Genetics.* any of several forms of a gene, usually arising through mutation, that are responsible for hereditary variation. [1930–35; < G *Allel,* appar. as shortening of G equivalents of ALLELOMORPH or *allelomorphic gene; allelo-* < Gk *allēlo-,* comb. form of *allḗlōn* of/to one another, reciprocally] —**al•lel•ic** (ə lē′lik, ə lel′ik), *adj.* —**al•lel′ism,** *n.*

allele′ fre′quency, *Genetics.* See **gene frequency.**

al•le•lo•morph (ə lē′lə môrf′, ə lel′ə-), *n.* allele. [1900–05; < Gk *allēlo-* (see ALLELE) + -MORPH] —**al•le′lo•mor′phic,** *adj.* —**al•le′lo•mor′phism,** *n.*

al•le•lop•a•thy (ə lē lop′ə thē, al′ə lop′-), *n. Bot.* suppression of growth of a plant by a toxin released from a nearby plant of the same or another species. [1940–45; < F *allélopathie;* see ALLELE, -PATHY] —**al•le•lo•path•ic** (ə lē′lə path′ik, ə lel′ə-), *adj.*

al•le•lu•ia (al′ə lo͞o′yə), *interj.* **1.** praise ye the Lord; hallelujah. —*n.* **2.** a song of praise to God. [1175–1225; ME < LL < Gk *allēlouïá* < Heb *halălūyāh* praise ye Yahweh] —**al•le•lu•iat•ic** (al′ə lo͞o yat′ik), *adj.*

al•le•mande (al′ə mand′, -mänd′, al′ə mand′, -mänd′; *Fr.* al[ə] mäɴd′), *n., pl.* **-mandes** (-mandz′, -mändz′, -mandz′, -mändz′; *Fr.* -mäɴd′). **1.** a 17th- and 18th-century dance in slow duple time. **2.** a piece of music based on its rhythm, often following the prelude in the classical suite. **3.** a figure performed in a quadrille. **4.** a German folk dance in triple meter, similar to the ländler. [1675–85; < F, short for *danse allemande* German dance]

al′lemande sauce′, a velouté thickened and enriched with egg yolk. Also, **Al′lemande sauce′.** [1820–30; fem. of F *allemand* German]

all-em•brac•ing (ôl′em brā′sing), *adj.* covering or applying to all; all-inclusive; blanket: *an all-embracing definition.* Also, **all-encompassing.** [1820–30]

al•le•mont•ite (al′ə mon′tīt), *n.* a white to gray, brittle mineral, antimony arsenide, AsSb, occurring in reniform masses: formerly used as an ore of arsenic. [1830–40; named after *Allemont* (place in France where found); see -ITE[1]]

Al•len (al′ən), *n.* **1. (Charles) Grant (Blair•fin•die)** (blâr fin′dē), (*"Cecil Power," "J. Arbuthnot Wilson"*), 1848–99, British philosophical writer and novelist. **2. Ethan,** 1738–89, American soldier in the Revolutionary War: leader of the "Green Mountain Boys" of Vermont. **3. Fred** (*John Florence Sullivan*), 1894–1956, U.S. comedian. **4. Frederick Lewis,** 1890–1954, U.S. historian and editor. **5. Gracie** (*Grace Ethel Cecile Rosalie Allen*), 1905–64, U.S. comedian (partner and wife of George Burns). **6. Richard,** 1760–1831, U.S. clergyman: a founder of the African Methodist Episcopal Church. **7. (William) Her•vey** (hûr′vē), 1889–1949, U.S. novelist, poet, and biographer. **8. Woody** (*Allen Stewart Konigsberg*), born 1935, U.S. comedian, author, actor, and filmmaker. **9.** a male given name.

Al•len•by (al′ən bē), *n.* **Edmund Henry Hyn•man** (hin′mən), **1st Viscount,** 1861–1936, British field marshal: commander of British forces in Egypt in World War I and conqueror of Jerusalem (1917).

all-en•com•pass•ing (ôl′en kum′pə sing), *adj.* all-embracing.

Al•len•de Gos•sens (ä yen′de gô′sens), **Salvador,** 1908–73, Chilean political leader: president 1970–73.

Al•len′de me′teorite (ä yen′dā), *Astron.* a carbonaceous chondrite meteorite that fell over northern Mexico in 1969: one of the largest recorded falls of a stony meteorite. [after Pueblito de *Allende,* village in Chihuahua, Mexico, near where pieces of it were recovered]

Al′len Park′, a city in SE Michigan. 34,196.

Al′len screw′, a screw turned by means of an axial hexagonal hole in its head. [formerly a trademark]

Al•len•stein (ä′lən shtīn′), *n.* German name of **Olsztyn.**

Al•len•town (al′ən toun′), *n.* a city in E Pennsylvania. 103,758.

Al′len wrench′, a wrench for Allen screws, formed from a piece of hexagonal bar stock bent to a right angle. See illus. under **wrench.** [formerly a trademark]

Al•lep•pey (ə lep′ē), *n.* a port in SW Kerala, in S India, on the Arabian Sea. 160,166.

al•ler•gen (al′ər jən, -jen′), *n. Immunol.* any substance, often a protein, that induces an allergy: common allergens include pollen, grasses, dust, and some medications. [1910–15; ALLER(GY) + -GEN]

al•ler•gen•ic (al′ər jen′ik), *adj.* causing allergic sensitization. [1910–15; ALLERGEN + -IC] —**al•ler•ge•nic•i•ty** (al′ər jə nis′i tē), *n.*

al•ler•gic (ə lûr′jik), *adj.* **1.** of or pertaining to allergy: *an allergic reaction to wool.* **2.** having an allergy. **3.** *Informal.* having a strong dislike or aversion: *He's allergic to most modern music.* [1910–15; ALLERG(Y) + -IC]

aller′gic rhini′tis, *Pathol.* a condition characterized by head congestion, sneezing, tearing, and swelling of the nasal mucous membranes, caused by an allergic reaction. Cf. **hay fever.**

al•ler•gist (al′ər jist), *n.* a physician specializing in the diagnosis and treatment of allergies. [1930–35; ALLERG(Y) + -IST]

al•ler•gy (al′ər jē), *n., pl.* **-gies. 1.** an abnormal reaction of the body to a previously encountered allergen introduced by inhalation, ingestion, injection, or skin contact, often manifested by itchy eyes, runny nose, wheezing, skin rash, or diarrhea. **2.** hypersensitivity to the reintroduction of an allergen. Cf. **anaphylaxis. 3.** *Informal.* a strong dislike or aversion, as toward a person or activity: *He has an allergy to hard work.* [1910–15; < Gk *áll(os)* other + *-ergy* < Gk *-ergia,* equiv. to *érg(on)* activity + *-ia* -Y[3]]

al•le•thrin (al′ə thrin), *n. Chem.* a clear, amber, viscous liquid, $C_{19}H_{26}O_3$, used as an insecticide. [1945–50; ALL(YL) + (*pyr*)*ethrin,* equiv. to *Pyrethr(um)* name of a genus of composite plants + -IN[2]]

al•le•vi•ant (ə lē′vē ənt), *n.* something that alleviates a condition. [ALLEVI(ATE) + -ANT]

al•le•vi•ate (ə lē′vē āt′), *v.t.,* **-at•ed, -at•ing.** to make easier to endure; lessen; mitigate: *to alleviate sorrow; to alleviate pain.* [1425–75; late ME *alleviaten* < LL *alleviātus* (ptp. of *alleviāre*), equiv. to *al-* AL- + *levi(s)* light, not heavy + *-ātus* -ATE[1]]
—**Syn.** lighten, diminish, abate, relieve, assuage. —**Ant.** increase, strengthen; aggravate, intensify.

al•le•vi•a•tion (ə lē′vē ā′shən), *n.* **1.** the act of alleviating. **2.** something that alleviates or palliates. [1615–25; < ML *alleviātiōn-* (s. of *alleviātiō*), equiv. to *alleviāt(us)* (see ALLEVIATE) + *-iōn-* -ION]

al•le•vi•a•tive (ə lē′vē ā′tiv, -ə tiv), *adj.* **1.** Also, **al•le•vi•a•to•ry** (ə lē′vē ə tôr′ē, -tōr′ē). serving to alleviate; palliative. —*n.* **2.** *Obs.* alleviation (def. 2). [1665–75; ALLEVIATE + -IVE]

al•le•vi•a•tor (ə lē′vē ā′tər), *n.* **1.** a person or thing that alleviates. **2.** (in a pipeline) an airtight box, having a free liquid surface, for cushioning the shock of water hammer. [1805–15; ALLEVIATE + -OR[2]]

all-ex•pense (ôl′ik spens′), *adj.* including all necessary or usual expenses, as the full cost of a trip, tour, or the like: *a two-week all-expense tour of Mexico.* Also, **all-ex•pens•es-paid** (ôl′ik spen′siz pād′).

al•ley[1] (al′ē), *n., pl.* **-leys. 1.** a passage, as through a continuous row of houses, permitting access from the street to backyards, garages, etc. **2.** a narrow back street. **3.** a walk, as in a garden, enclosed with hedges or shrubbery. **4.** *Bowling.* **a.** a long, narrow, wooden lane or floor along which the ball is rolled. **b.** (*often pl.*) a building for bowling. **c.** See **bowling green. 5.** *Tennis.* the space on each side of a tennis court between the doubles sideline and the service or singles sideline. **6.** *Rare.* an aisle. **7. up** or **down one's alley,** *Informal.* in keeping with or satisfying one's abilities, interests, or tastes: *If you like science fiction, this book will be right up your alley.* [1350–1400; ME *al(e)y* < MF *alee* walk, passage, deriv. of fem. of *ale,* ptp. of *aler* to walk (F *aller*), prob. < VL **allāri,* regularized from *allātus,* the suppletive ptp. of *afferre* to bring (pass. *afferri* to be moved, conveyed, to betake oneself); F *aller* often allegedly < L *ambulāre* to walk (see AMBLE), but this offers grave phonetic problems, since the *m* and *b* would not normally be lost]
—**Syn. 2.** See **street.**

al•ley[2] (al′ē), *n., pl.* **-leys.** *Chiefly Northeastern U.S.* a choice, large playing marble. [1710–20; prob. AL(ABASTER) + -Y[2], sp. to conform with ALLEY[1]]

al′ley cat′, a homeless, usually mongrel, cat that scavenges for food in alleys, streets, etc. [1900–05]

al•ley-oop (al′ē o͞op′), *interj.* **1.** (used as a shout of encouragement, exhortation, or the like, esp. when coordinating efforts to lift a heavy object. —*n.* **2.** *Basketball.* a quick-score play in which a high, arching pass is made to a teammate close to the basket, who leaps to catch the ball and in midair drops or stuffs it through the basket.

al•ley•way (al′ē wā′), *n.* **1.** an alley or lane. **2.** a narrow passageway. [1780–90, *Amer.;* ALLEY[1] + WAY]

all-fired (ôl′fī[ə]rd′), *adj., superl.* **-fired•est,** *adv. Informal.* —*adj.* **1.** tremendous; extreme; excessive: *He had the all-fired gall to quit in the middle of the job.* —*adv.* **2.** Also, **all-fired•ly** (ôl′fī[ə]rd′lē, -fī′rid-). extremely; excessively: *Don't be so all-fired sure of yourself.* [1825–35; prob. euphemism for *hell-fired*]

All′ Fools′ Day′. See **April Fools' Day.** [1705–15]

All′ for Love′, a drama in blank verse (1678) by Dryden.

all′ fours′, 1. all four limbs or extremities; the four legs or feet of an animal or both arms and both legs or both hands and both feet of a person: *The cat rolled off the ledge but landed on all fours.* **2.** (*used with a singular v.*) Also called **high-low-jack, old sledge, pitch, seven-up.** *Cards.* a game for two or three players or two partnerships in which a 52-card pack is used, the object being to win special scoring values for the highest trump, the lowest trump, the jack, the ace, the ten, and the face cards. **3. on all fours, a.** in conformity with; corresponding exactly with. **b.** (of a person) on the hands and feet, or the hands and knees: *I had to go on all fours to squeeze through the low opening.* [1555–65]

CONCISE PRONUNCIATION KEY: act, cāpe, dâre, pärt; set, ēqual; if, ice; ox, ōver, ôrder, oil, bo͝ok, bo͞ot, out; up, ûrge; child; sing; shoe; thin, *th*at; zh as in *treasure.* ə = *a* as in *alone, e* as in *system, i* as in *easily, o* as in *gallop, u* as in *circus;* [ə] as in *fire* (fī[ə]r), *hour* (ou[ə]r). l and n can serve as syllabic consonants, as in *cradle* (krād′l), and *button* (but′n). See the full key inside the front cover.

all′ hail′, *Archaic.* a salutation of greeting or welcome. [1350–1400; ME]

All·hal·low·mas (ôl′hal′ō məs), *n. Archaic.* See **All Saints' Day.** [bef. 1100; ME *alhalwemesse,* OE *ealra hālgena mæsse* mass of all saints]

All·hal·lows (ôl′hal′ōz), *n.* See **All Saints' Day.** [bef. 1000]

Allhal′lows Eve′, Halloween. Also called **All′ Hal′low E′ven.** [1550–60]

All·hal·low·tide (ôl′hal′ō tīd′), *n. Archaic.* the time or season of All Saints' Day. [1540–50; ALLHALLOW(s) + TIDE[1]]

all·heal (ôl′hēl′), *n.* **1.** valerian (def. 1). **2.** any of several plants once believed to have extensive curative powers, as the selfheal, *Prunella vulgaris.* [1590–1600; ALL + HEAL]

al·li·a·ceous (al′ē ā′shəs), *adj.* **1.** *Bot.* belonging to the genus *Allium* (formerly the family Alliaceae). Cf. **allium.** **2.** having the odor or taste of garlic, onion, etc. [1785–95; < L *alli(um)* garlic + -ACEOUS]

al·li·ance (ə lī′əns), *n.* **1.** the act of allying or state of being allied. **2.** a formal agreement or treaty between two or more nations to cooperate for specific purposes. **3.** a merging of efforts or interests by persons, families, states, or organizations: *an alliance between church and state.* **4.** the persons or entities so allied. **5.** marriage or the relationship created by marriage between the families of the bride and bridegroom. **6.** correspondence in basic characteristics; affinity: *the alliance between logic and metaphysics.* [1250–1300; ME *aliance* < OF, equiv. to *ali(er)* to ALLY + *-ance* -ANCE]
—**Syn. 1.** association; coalition, combination, bloc; partnership; affiliation. ALLIANCE, CONFEDERATION, LEAGUE, UNION all mean the joining of states for mutual benefit or to permit the joint exercise of functions. An ALLIANCE may apply to any connection entered into for mutual benefit. LEAGUE usually suggests closer combination or a more definite object or purpose. CONFEDERATION applies to a permanent combination for the exercise in common of certain governmental functions. UNION implies an alliance so close and permanent that the separate states or parties become essentially one. **2.** pact, compact.

Al·li·ance (ə lī′əns), *n.* a city in NE Ohio. 24,315.

Alli′ance for Prog′ress, a program of foreign aid presented by President Kennedy to help solve the economic and social problems of Latin America.

al·lied (ə līd′, al′īd), *adj.* **1.** joined by treaty, agreement, or common cause: *allied nations.* **2.** related; kindred: *allied species.* **3.** (*cap.*) of or pertaining to the Allies. [1250–1300; ME; see ALLY, -ED[2]]
—**Syn. 2.** akin.

Al·lier (A lyā′), *n.* **1.** a river flowing N from S France to the Loire. ab. 250 mi. (400 km) long. **2.** a department in central France. 378,406; 2850 sq. mi. (7380 sq. km). *Cap.:* Moulins.

al·lies (al′īz, ə līz′), *n.* **1.** pl. of **ally. 2.** (*cap.*) (in World War I) the powers of the Triple Entente (Great Britain, France, Russia), with the nations allied with them (Belgium, Serbia, Japan, Italy, etc., not including the United States), or, loosely, with all the nations (including the United States) allied or associated with them as opposed to the Central Powers. **3.** (*cap.*) the 26 nations that fought against the Axis in World War II and, with subsequent additions, signed the charter of the United Nations in San Francisco in 1945. **4.** (*cap.*) the member nations of NATO.

al·li·gate (al′i gāt′), *v.t.,* **-gat·ed, -gat·ing.** *Obs.* to attach; bind. [1535–45; < L *alligātus* (ptp. of *alligāre*), equiv. to *al-* AL- + *lig-* bind (see LIGATURE) + *-ātus* -ATE[1]]

al·li·ga·tor (al′i gā′tər), *n.* **1.** either of two broad-snouted crocodilians of the genus *Alligator,* of the southeastern U.S. and eastern China. **2.** (loosely) any broad-snouted crocodilian, as a caiman. **3.** *Metall.* a machine for bringing the balls of iron from a puddling furnace into compact form so that they can be handled. **4.** *Jazz.* an enthusiastic fan of swing. —*v.i.* **5.** (of paint, varnish, or the like) to crack and acquire the appearance of alligator hide, as from weathering or improper application to a surface. **6.** *Metalworking.* (of a rolled metal slab) to split and curl up and down at one end; fishmouth. [1560–70; < Sp *el lagarto* the lizard < VL **ille* that + **lacartus,* for L *lacertus* LIZARD]

alligator, *Alligator mississippiensis,* length 17 ft. (5.2 m)

al′ligator clip′, *Elect.* a type of terminal for making temporary electrical connections, consisting of a cliplike device with long, narrow jaws that resemble those of an alligator. Also called **al′ligator clamp′.** [1940–45]

al·li·ga·tor·fish (al′i gā′tər fish′), *n., pl.* (*esp. collectively*) **-fish,** (*esp. referring to two or more kinds or species*) **-fish·es. 1.** a slender marine fish, *Aspidophoroides monopterygius,* of Atlantic seas, having overlapping plates covering the body. **2.** any of several related fishes of the family Agonidae. [1765–75, *Amer.*; ALLIGATOR + FISH]

al′ligator gar′, a large, heavily scaled fish, *Lepisosteus spatula,* with an elongated body and long snout, found mainly in shallow weedy fresh water in the southeastern U.S. [1815–25, *Amer.*]

al′ligator liz′ard, any of several lizards of the genera *Algaria* and *Gerrhonotus,* of western North America, having shinglelike scales and a fold along each side that permits expansion.

al′ligator pear′, avocado (def. 1). [1755–65; *alligator,* alter. by folk etym. of Sp *avocado* or AmerSp *aguacate* (see AVOCADO)]

al′ligator shear′, heavy shears for cutting metal slabs.

al′ligator snap′ping tur′tle, a large American snapping turtle, *Macroclemys temmincki,* having three prominent ridges on its shell and a wormlike process on the floor of the mouth used to attract prey. Also called **al′ligator snap′per.** [1790–1800, *Amer.*]

al′ligator wrench′, *Mach.* a wrench having a V-shaped pair of serrated jaws set at right angles to the shank for turning cylindrical or irregularly shaped parts. [1935–40]

all-im·por·tant (ôl′im pôr′tnt), *adj.* extremely or vitally important; essential. [1830–40]

all-in (ôl′in′), *adj.* **1.** *Wrestling.* without restrictions; with virtually every type of hold permitted. **2.** *Jazz.* performed by all members of the group; played ensemble: *An all-in refrain followed the solos.* **3.** *Brit.* with extras included; inclusive: *at the all-in rate.* [1885–90]

all-in·clu·sive (ôl′in klo͞o′siv), *adj.* including everything; comprehensive. [1880–85]

Al·ling·ham (al′ing əm), *n.* **Margery,** 1904–66, English mystery writer.

all-in-one (ôl′in wun′), *n.* an undergarment that combines a girdle and brassiere in one piece.

al·li·sion (ə lizh′ən), *n. Law.* the striking of one ship by another. [1625–35; < LL *allīsiōn-* (s. of *allīsiō*), equiv. to *allis(us)* struck at, ptp. of *allīdere* (*al-* AL- + *-līd-* strike (comb. form of *laed-*; see LESION) + *-tus* ptp. suffix) + *-iōn-* -ION]

Al·li·son (al′ə sən), *n.* **1. Donald** (*Donnie*), born 1939, and his brother, **Robert** (*Bobby*), born 1937, U.S. racing-car drivers. **2.** a female given name, form of **Alice.**

al·lit·er·ate (ə lit′ə rāt′), *v.,* **-at·ed, -at·ing.** —*v.i.* **1.** to show alliteration: *In "Round and round the rugged rock the ragged rascal ran," the "r" alliterates.* **2.** to use alliteration: *Swinburne often alliterates.* —*v.t.* **3.** to compose or arrange with alliteration: *He alliterates the "w's" in that line.* [1810–20; back formation from ALLITERATION] —**al·lit′er·a′tor,** *n.*

al·lit·er·a·tion (ə lit′ə rā′shən), *n.* **1.** the commencement of two or more stressed syllables of a word group either with the same consonant sound or sound group **(consonantal alliteration),** as in *from stem to stern,* or with a vowel sound that may differ from syllable to syllable **(vocalic alliteration),** as in *each to all.* Cf. **consonance** (def. 4a). **2.** the commencement of two or more words of a word group with the same letter, as in *apt alliteration's artful aid.* [1650–60; < ML *alliterātiōn-,* s. of *alliterātiō,* equiv. to *al-* AL- + *literātiō,* modeled after *obliterātiō* OBLITERATION but intended to convey a deriv. of *littera* letter]

al·lit·er·a·tive (ə lit′ə rā′tiv, -ər ə tiv), *adj.* pertaining to or characterized by alliteration: *alliterative verse.* [1755–65; ALLITERAT(ION) + -IVE] —**al·lit′er·a′tive·ly,** *adv.* —**al·lit′er·a′tive·ness,** *n.*

al·li·um (al′ē əm), *n.* **1.** any bulbous plant belonging to the genus *Allium,* of the amaryllis family, having an onion odor and flowers in a round cluster, including the onion, leek, shallot, garlic, and chive. **2.** a substance occurring in garlic bulbs that has antibiotic properties. [1800–10; < NL, L: garlic]

all·mouth (ôl′mouth′), *n., pl.* **-mouths** (-mouthz′, mouths′). angler (def. 3). [ALL + MOUTH; i.e., big mouth]

all·ness (ôl′nis), *n.* the quality or state of universality or totality. [1645–55; ALL + -NESS]

all-night (ôl′nīt′), *adj.* **1.** taking up, extending through, or occurring continually during an entire night; nightlong: *an all-night vigil.* **2.** open all night, as for business; providing services, accommodations, etc., at all hours of the night: *an all-night restaurant.* [1520–30]

all-night·er (ôl′nī′tər), *n. Informal.* **1.** something that lasts, is available, or is open for business throughout the night: *The poker game turned into an all-nighter. Are any of the grocery stores all-nighters?* **2.** an act of staying up all night, as to study or finish a task: *I had to pull an all-nighter to get the paper done on time.* [1890–95; *all night* + -ER[1]]

allo-, a combining form meaning "other," used in the formation of compound words (*allotrope*) and in chemistry to denote the more stable of two geometric isomers. Also (except in chemistry), *esp. before a vowel,* **all-.** [< Gk, comb. form of *állos* other; c. L *alius,* ELSE]

allo., allegro.

al·lo·an·ti·bod·y (al′ō an′ti bod′ē, -an′tē-), *n., pl.* **-bod·ies.** *Immunol.* an antibody that reacts with an antigen from a genetically different individual of the same species. [1965–70; ALLO- + ANTIBODY]

al·lo·an·ti·gen (al′ō an′ti jən, -jen′), *n. Immunol.* an antigen present in some but not all individuals of the same species, as those in different human blood groups. [1965–70; ALLO- + ANTIGEN]

al·lo·bar·ic (al′ə bar′ik), *adj. Meteorol.* of or pertaining to change in atmospheric pressure: *allobaric wind.* [ALLO- + BARIC[2]]

al·lo·ca·ble (al′ə kə bəl), *adj.* that can be allocated. Also, **al′lo·cat′a·ble.** [1915–19; ALLOC(ATE) + -ABLE]

al·lo·cate (al′ə kāt′), *v.t.,* **-cat·ed, -cat·ing. 1.** to set apart for a particular purpose; assign or allot: *to allocate funds for new projects.* **2.** to fix the place of; locate. [1630–40; < ML *allocātus* (ptp. of *allocāre*), equiv. to *al-* AL- + *loc(us)* place + *-ātus* -ATE[1]] —**al′lo·ca′tor,** *n.*
—**Syn. 1.** See **assign.**

al·lo·ca·tion (al′ə kā′shən), *n.* **1.** the act of allocating; apportionment. **2.** the state of being allocated. **3.** the share or portion allocated. **4.** *Accounting.* a system of dividing expenses and incomes among the various branches, departments, etc., of a business. [1525–35; < ML *allocātiōn-* (s. of *allocātiō*), equiv. to *allocāt(us)* (see ALLOCATE) + *-iōn-* -ION] —**al′lo·ca′tive,** *adj.*

al·lo·cher (al′ə ker′), *n. Ling.* any of the variant forms of a chereme. Cf. **chereme.** [ALLO- + CHER(EME), on the model of ALLOPHONE, ALLOMORPH]

al·lo·chro·mat·ic (al′ə krə mat′ik, -krō-), *adj.* **1.** *Physical Chem.* pertaining to or having photochemical properties resulting from an impurity or from exposure to radiation. **2.** *Mineral.* (of a mineral) having no color in itself but bearing colored impurities. Cf. **idiochromatic.** [1875–80; ALLO- + CHROMATIC]

al·loch·thon (ə lok′thən, -thon), *n. Geol.* a geological formation not formed in the region where found and moved to its present location by tectonic forces. Cf. **autochthon** (def. 3). [1940–45; back formation from ALLOCHTHONOUS]

al·loch·tho·nous (ə lok′thə nəs), *adj. Geol.* (of rocks, minerals, etc.) not formed in the region where found. Cf. **autochthonous** (def. 4). [1910–15; ALLO- + *-chthonous,* modeled after AUTOCHTHONOUS]

al·lo·cu·tion (al′ə kyo͞o′shən), *n.* **1.** a formal speech, esp. one of an incontrovertible or hortatory nature. **2.** a pronouncement delivered by the pope to a secret consistory, esp. on a matter of policy or of general importance. [1605–15; < L *allocūtiōn-* (s. of *allocūtiō*), equiv. to *allocūt(us),* ptp. of *alloquī* to speak to, address (*al-* AL- + *locū-* speak + *-tus* ptp. suffix) + *-iōn-* -ION]

al·lo·di·al (ə lō′dē əl), *adj.* free from the tenurial rights of a feudal overlord. Also, **alodial.** [1650–60; < ML *allodiālis,* equiv. to *allōdi(um)* ALLODIUM + *-ālis* -AL[1]] —**al·lo′di·al′i·ty,** *n.* —**al·lo′di·al·ly,** *adv.*

al·lo·di·um (ə lō′dē əm), *n., pl.* **-di·a** (-dē ə). land owned absolutely; land owned and not subject to any rent, service, or other tenurial right of an overlord. Also, **alodium.** Also called **al·lod** (al′od, -əd), **alod.** [1620–30; < ML < Frankish **allōd-* (*all* ALL + *-ōd* patrimony, c. ON *ōth-* in *ōthal,* Goth *-ōth-* in *haim-ōthli,* OS *ōth-* in *ōthil,* OE, OFris *ēth-* in *ēthel,* akin (by gradation) to *ath-* of ATHELING) + ML *-ium* -IUM]

al·log·a·my (ə log′ə mē), *n.* cross-fertilization in plants (opposed to *autogamy*). [1875–80; ALLO- + -GAMY] —**al·log′a·mous,** *adj.*

al·lo·ge·ne·ic (al′ō jə nē′ik), *adj. Immunol.* (of cells, tissues, etc.) related but sufficiently dissimilar in genotype to interact antigenically: *allogeneic graft.* Also, **allogenic.** [1885–90; ALLO- + GENE + -IC] —**al′lo·ge·ne′i·cal·ly,** *adv.*

al·lo·gen·ic (al′ə jen′ik), *adj.* **1.** *Geol.* (of a constituent of a rock) formed elsewhere than in the rock where it is found. Cf. **authigenic. 2.** *Immunol.* allogeneic. [1885–90; ALLO- + -GENIC] —**al′lo·gen′i·cal·ly,** *adv.*

al·lo·graft (al′ə graft′, -gräft′), *n. Surg.* a tissue or organ obtained from one member of a species and grafted to a genetically dissimilar member of the same species. Also called **allotransplant, homograft, homotransplant.** Cf. **autograft, syngraft, xenograft.** [1960–65; ALLO- + GRAFT]

al·lo·graph (al′ə graf′, -gräf′), *n.* **1.** *Ling.* a variant form of a grapheme that is in complementary distribution or free variation with another form of the same grapheme, as *t* and *T* or *n* in *run* and *nn* in *runner;* an orthographic contextual variant. Cf. **grapheme. 2.** writing or a signature inscribed by one person for another, as distinguished from autograph. **3.** a deed or other legal document not in the writing of any of the persons who are party to it. [1950–55; ALLO- + -GRAPH, on the model of ALLOPHONE] —**al·lo·graph·ic** (al′ə graf′ik), *adj.*

al·lom·er·ism (ə lom′ə riz′əm), *n. Chem.* variability in chemical constitution without change in crystalline form. [1880–85; ALLO- + -MER + -ISM] —**al·lom′er·ous,** *adj.*

al·lom·er·ize (ə lom′ə rīz′), *v.i.,* **-ized, -iz·ing.** *Chem.* to undergo allomerism. Also, *esp. Brit.,* **al·lom′er·ise′.** [ALLO- + -MER + -IZE] —**al·lom′er·i·za′tion,** *n.*

al·lom·e·try (ə lom′i trē), *n. Biol.* **1.** growth of a part of an organism in relation to the growth of the whole organism or some part of it. **2.** the measurement or study of this growth. Also, **al·loi·om·e·try** (al′oi om′i-trē). [1935–40; ALLO- + -METRY] —**al·lo·met·ric** (al′ə-me′trik), **al·loi·o·met·ric** (ə loi′ə me′trik), *adj.*

al·lo·morph (al′ə môrf′), *n.* **1.** any of two or more different forms of the same chemical compound. **2.** *Ling.* one of the alternate contextually determined phonological shapes of a morpheme, as *en* in *oxen,* which is an allomorph of the English plural morpheme. Cf. **morph. 3.** *Mineral.* paramorph. [1865–70; ALLO- + -MORPH] —**al′lo·mor′phic,** *adj.*

al·lo·mor·phism (al′ə môr′fiz əm), *n. Chem.* variability in crystalline form without change in chemical constitution. Cf. **paramorphism.** [1865–70; ALLOMORPH + -ISM]

all′ on′, *Fox Hunting.* the cry uttered by a whipper-in to signify that all the hounds are accounted for.

al·longe (ə lunj′; *Fr.* A lônzh′), *n., pl.* **al·long·es** (ə lun′jiz; *Fr.* A lônzh′). *Law.* a paper annexed to a negotiable instrument, for endorsements too numerous or lengthy to be contained in the original. [1860–65; < F: lengthening; see LUNGE[1]]

CONCISE ETYMOLOGY KEY: <, descended or borrowed from; >, whence; b., blend of, blended; c., cognate with; cf., compare; deriv., derivative; equiv., equivalent; imit., imitative; obl., oblique; r., replacing; s., stem; sp., spelling, spelled; resp., respelling, respelled; trans., translation; ?, origin unknown; *, unattested; ‡, probably earlier than. See the full key inside the front cover.

al·lon·gé (*Fr.* A lôN zhā′), *adj. Ballet.* performed with the body and one arm stretched forward: *an arabesque allongé.* [1660–70; < F: lit., extended, lengthened, ptp. of *allonger*]

al·lo·nym (al′ə nim), *n.* **1.** the name of another person taken by an author as a pen name. Cf. **pseudonym. 2.** a work published under a name that is not that of the author. [1865–70; ALL- + -ONYM; cf. PSEUDONYM] **—al·lon·y·mous** (ə lon′ə məs), *adj.* **—al·lon′y·mous·ly,** *adv.*

al·lo·path (al′ə path′), *n.* a person who practices or favors allopathy. Also, **al·lop·a·thist** (ə lop′ə thist). [1820–30; < G, back formation from *Allopathie* ALLOPATHY]

al·lop·a·thy (ə lop′ə thē), *n.* the method of treating disease by the use of agents that produce effects different from those of the disease treated (opposed to *homeopathy*). [1835–45; < G *Allopathie.* See ALLO-, -PATHY] **—al·lo·path·ic** (al′ə path′ik), *adj.* **—al′lo·path′i·cal·ly,** *adv.*

al·lo·pat·ric (al′ə pa′trik), *adj. Biol., Ecol.* originating in or occupying different geographical areas. [1940–45; ALLO- + Gk *patr(ía)* fatherland (*patḗr* father + *-ia* n. suffix) + -IC] **—al′lo·pat′ri·cal·ly,** *adv.* **—al·lop·a·try** (ə lop′ə trē), *n.*

al·lo·pe·lag·ic (al′ō pə laj′ik), *adj.* (of a marine organism) living or growing at different depths. [< G *allopelagisch.* See ALLO-, PELAGIC]

al·lo·phan·a·mide (al′ə fan′ə mīd′, -mid), *n. Chem.* biuret. [< Gk *allophan(ḗs),* appearing otherwise (see ALLOPHANE) + AMIDE]

al·lo·phane (al′ə fān′), *n.* a clay mineral, an amorphous hydrous silicate of aluminum, occurring in blue, green, or yellow, resinous to earthy masses. [1835–45; < Gk *allophanḗs,* equiv. to *allo-* ALLO- + *phan-* (s. of *phainesthai* to appear) + *-ēs* adj. suffix]

al·lo·phone (al′ə fōn′), *n. Phonet.* any of the members of a class of speech sounds that, taken together, are commonly felt to be a phoneme, as the *t*-sounds of *toe, stow, tree, hatpin, catcall, cats, catnip, button, metal, city;* a speech sound constituting one of the phonetic manifestations or variants of a particular phoneme. [1930–35; ALLO- + PHONE²] **—al·lo·phon·ic** (al′ə fon′ik), *adj.* **—al′lo·phon′i·cal·ly,** *adv.*

al·lo·phyl·i·an (al′ə fil′ē ən, -fil′yən), *adj. Archaic.* **1.** (of languages, esp. those of Europe and Asia) neither Indo-European nor Semitic. —*n.* **2.** Turanian (defs. 3, 4). [1835–45; < LL *allophyl(us)* (< Gk *allóphylos,* equiv. to *allo-* ALLO- + *phŷl(ē)* tribe + *-os* adj. suffix) + -IAN; *phylḗ,* akin to *phŷlon* race (see PHYLUM)]

al·lo·plas·ty (al′ə plas′tē), *n., pl.* **-ties.** *Surg.* implantation of a synthetic material to replace a diseased or damaged body tissue or organ. [ALLO- + -PLASTY]

al·lo·pol·y·ploid (al′ə pol′ə ploid′), *Biol.* —*adj.* **1.** having more than two haploid sets of chromosomes that are dissimilar and derived from different species. —*n.* **2.** an allopolyploid cell or organism. Cf. **autopolyploid.** [1925–30; ALLO- + POLYPLOID] **—al·lo·pol·y·ploi·dy** (al′ə pol′ə ploi′dē), *n.*

al·lo·pu·ri·nol (al′ə pyŏŏr′ə nôl′, -nol′), *n. Pharm.* a substance, $C_5H_4N_4O$, used primarily in the treatment of chronic gout to decrease the synthesis of uric acid. [1960–65; appar. ALLO- + PURINE + -OL¹]

all′-or-none′ law′ (ôl′ər nun′), *Physiol.* the principle that under given conditions the response of a nerve or muscle fiber to a stimulus at any strength above the threshold is the same: the muscle or nerve responds completely or not at all. [1895–1900]

all-or-noth·ing (ôl′ər nuth′ing), *adj.* not allowing for qualification or compromise; either fully or not at all operative: *an all-or-nothing approach.* [1755–65]

al·lo·saur (al′ə sôr′), *n.* a carnivorous dinosaur of the genus *Antrodemus* (formerly *Allosaurus*), from the late Jurassic Period of North America, that was about 30 ft. (9 m) long. [< NL *Allosaurus* (1877). See ALLO-, -SAUR]

al·lo·ster·ic (al′ə ster′ik, -stēr′-), *adj. Biochem.* pertaining to regulation of the rate of an enzymatic process. [1960–65; ALLO- + STERIC] **—al′lo·ster′i·cal·ly,** *adv.*

al·lot (ə lot′), *v.t.,* **-lot·ted, -lot·ting. 1.** to divide or distribute by share or portion; distribute or parcel out; apportion: *to allot the available farmland among the settlers.* **2.** to appropriate for a special purpose: *to allot money for a park.* **3.** to assign as a portion; set apart; dedicate. [1425–75; earlier *alot,* late ME *alotten* < MF *aloter,* equiv. to *a-* A-⁵ + *lot* LOT (< Gmc) + *-er* inf. suffix] **—al·lot′ta·ble,** *adj.* **—al·lot′ter,** *n.*
—Syn. 1. See **assign.**

al·lot·ment (ə lot′mənt), *n.* **1.** the act of allotting. **2.** a portion or thing allotted; a share granted. **3.** (in U.S. military use) the portion of pay that an officer or enlisted person authorizes to be paid directly to another person, as a dependent, or an institution, as an insurance company. **4.** *Brit.* a plot of land rented to a gardener. [1565–75; ALLOT + -MENT; cf. F *allotement*]
—Syn. 2. measure, lot, ration.

al·lo·trans·plant (al′ō trans′plant′, -plänt′), *n.* allograft. [1965–70; ALLO- + TRANSPLANT]

al·lot·ri·o·mor·phic (ə lo′trē ə môr′fik), *adj. Petrog.* xenomorphic (def. 1). [1885–90; < Gk *allótrio(s)* belonging to another + -MORPHIC]

al·lo·trope (al′ə trōp′), *n. Chem.* one of two or more existing forms of an element: *Graphite and diamond are allotropes of carbon.* [1885–90; ALLO- + -TROPE]

al·lo·trop·ic (al′ə trop′ik, -trō′pik), *adj.* pertaining to or characterized by allotropy. Also, **al′lo·trop′i·cal.** [1875–80; ALLOTROP(Y) + -IC] **—al′lo·trop′i·cal·ly,** *adv.* **—al·lo·tro·pic·i·ty** (al′ə trə pis′i tē), *n.*

al·lot·ro·py (ə lo′trə pē), *n. Chem.* a property of certain elements, as carbon, sulfur, and phosphorus, of existing in two or more distinct forms; allomorphism. Also, **al·lot′ro·pism.** [1840–50; ALLO- + -TROPY]

all′ ot·ta·va (äl′ ə tä′və; *It.* äl′lôt tä′vä), *Music.* a direction (8va), placed above or below the staff to indicate that the passage covered is to be played one octave higher or lower respectively. [1815–25; < It: lit., at the octave]

al·lot·tee (ə lot ē′), *n.* a person to whom something is allotted. [1840–50; ALLOT + -EE]

al·lo·type (al′ə tīp′), *n.* **1.** *Biol.* a type specimen of the sex opposite to that of the holotype. **2.** *Immunol.* an antibody of a given class having certain molecular sites shared by only some members of a species and therefore acting as an antigen to other members of the same species. [1915–20; ALLO- + TYPE; in immunological sense, prob. back formation from *allotypy* < F *allotypie,* coined in 1956] **—al·lo·typ·ic** (al′ə tip′ik), *adj.* **—al′lo·typ′i·cal·ly,** *adv.* **—al·lo·typ·y** (al′ə tī′pē), *n.*

all-out (ôl′out′), *adj.* using all one's resources; complete; total: *an all-out effort.* [1905–10; adj. use of *all out* utterly, completely, ME *al out*]
—Syn. unstinting, exhaustive, unremitting.

all·ov·er (ôl′ō′vər), *adj.* **1.** extending or repeated over the entire surface, as a decorative pattern. —*n.* **2.** a fabric with an allover pattern. [1570–80; ALL + OVER]

al·low (ə lou′), *v.t.* **1.** to give permission to or for; permit: *to allow a student to be absent; No swimming allowed.* **2.** to let have; give as one's share; grant as one's right: *to allow a person $100 for expenses.* **3.** to permit by neglect, oversight, or the like: *to allow a door to remain open.* **4.** to admit; acknowledge; concede: *to allow a claim.* **5.** to take into consideration, as by adding or subtracting; set apart: *to allow an hour for changing trains.* **6.** *Older Use.* to say; think. **7.** *Archaic.* to approve; sanction. —*v.i.* **8.** to permit something to happen or to exist; admit (often fol. by *of*): *to spend more than one's budget allows; a premise that allows of only one conclusion.* **9. allow for,** to make concession or provision for: *to allow for breakage.* [1250–1300; ME *alowen* < AF *al(l)o(u)er* to place, allot, allow, OF *aloer* to place < LL *allocāre;* see AL-, LOCUS; the older sense "approve, sanction" and ME sense "praise" prob. by taking the AF v. as repr. ML, L *adlaudāre* to praise; see AD-, LAUD]
—Syn. 1. ALLOW, LET, PERMIT imply granting or conceding the right of someone to do something. ALLOW and PERMIT are often interchangeable, but PERMIT is the more positive. ALLOW implies complete absence of an attempt, or even an intent, to hinder. PERMIT suggests formal or implied assent or authorization. LET is the familiar, conversational term for both ALLOW and PERMIT.
—Ant. 1. forbid, prohibit.

al·low·a·ble (ə lou′ə bəl), *adj.* **1.** that may be allowed; legitimate; permissible: *an allowable tax deduction.* —*n.* **2.** something, as an action or amount, that is allowed. **3.** *Ecol.* See **allowable cut.** [1350–1400; ME < MF *alouable.* See ALLOW, -ABLE] **—al·low′a·ble·ness,** *n.* **—al·low′a·bly,** *adv.*

allow′able cut′, *Ecol.* the amount of a natural resource, as grain or oil, that may be harvested or taken from the earth within a specified period, as limited by law for conservation. Also called **allowable, permissible yield, prescribed cut.**

al·low·ance (ə lou′əns), *n., v.,* **-anced, -anc·ing.** —*n.* **1.** the act of allowing. **2.** an amount or share allotted or granted. **3.** a sum of money allotted or granted for a particular purpose, as for expenses: *Her allowance for the business trip was $200.* **4.** a sum of money allotted or granted to a person on a regular basis, as for personal or general living expenses: *The art student lived on an allowance of $300 a month. When I was in first grade, my parents gave me an allowance of 50 cents a week.* **5.** an addition or deduction based on an extenuating or qualifying circumstance: *an allowance for profit; an allowance for depreciation.* **6.** acknowledgment; concession: *the allowance of a claim.* **7.** sanction; tolerance: *the allowance of slavery.* **8.** *Mach.* a prescribed difference in dimensions of two closely fitting mating parts with regard to minimum clearance or maximum interference. Cf. **tolerance** (def. 6a). **9.** *Coining.* tolerance (def. 7). **10. make allowance** or **allowances (for), a.** to take mitigating factors or circumstances into consideration. **b.** to pardon; excuse. **c.** to reserve time, money, etc.; allow for: *Make allowance for souvenirs on the return trip.* —*v.t.* **11.** to place on a fixed allowance, as of food or drink. **12.** to allocate (supplies, rations, etc.) in fixed or regular amounts. [1350–1400; ME *alouance* < MF. See ALLOW, -ANCE]
—Syn. 2. allotment. **4.** stipend. **7.** permission, authorization, approval, sufferance.

allow′ance race′, *Horse Racing.* a race in which each horse is assigned a specified weight according to age, record of past performance, sex, etc.

Al·lo·way (al′ə wā′), *n.* a hamlet in SW Scotland, near Ayr: birthplace of Robert Burns.

al·lowed (ə loud′), *adj. Physics.* involving a change in quantum numbers, permitted by the selection rules: *allowed transition.* [ALLOW + -ED²]

al·low·ed·ly (ə lou′id lē), *adv.* by general allowance or admission; admittedly. [1595–1605; ALLOWED + -LY]

al·lox·an (ə lok′sən), *n. Biochem.* a white crystalline pyrimidine derivative, $C_4H_2O_4N_2$, used in biomedical research to induce diabetes in laboratory animals. [< G, equiv. to *All(antoïn)* ALLANTOIN + *Ox(alsäure)* OXALIC ACID + *-an* -AN; coined by J. von LIEBIG in 1838]

al·loy (*n.* al′oi, ə loi′; *v.* ə loi′), *n.* **1.** a substance composed of two or more metals, or of a metal or metals with a nonmetal, intimately mixed, as by fusion or electrodeposition. **2.** a less costly metal mixed with a more valuable one. **3.** standard; quality; fineness. **4.** admixture, as of good with evil. **5.** anything added that serves to reduce quality or purity. —*v.t.* **6.** to mix (metals or metal with nonmetal) so as to form an alloy. **7.** to reduce in value by an admixture of a less costly metal. **8.** to debase, impair, or reduce by admixture; adulterate. [1590–1600; < MF *aloi,* OF *alei,* n. deriv. of *aleier* to combine < L *alligāre* to bind up, equiv. to *al-* AL- + *ligāre* to bind (see ALLY, LIGAMENT); r. earlier *allay,* ME < AF *allai*]
—Syn. 4. fusion, blend, composite.

al′loy steel′, carbon steel to which various elements, as chromium, cobalt, copper, manganese, molybdenum, nickel, tungsten, or vanadium, have been added in sufficient amounts to obtain desirable physical and chemical properties. [1900–05]

all-pass (ôl′pas′, -päs′), *adj. Radio.* (of a network, transducer, etc.) transmitting signals without significant attenuation of any frequencies.

all′-points bul′letin (ôl′points′), a broadcast alert from one police station to all others in an area, state, etc., as with instructions to arrest a particular suspect or suspects. *Abbr.:* APB

All·port (ôl′pôrt, -pōrt), *n.* **Gordon W(illard),** 1897–1967, U.S. psychologist and educator.

all-pow·er·ful (ôl′pou′ər fəl), *adj.* having or exercising exclusive and unlimited authority; omnipotent. [1685–95]

all-pur·pose (ôl′pûr′pəs), *adj.* for every purpose: *an all-purpose detergent.* [1925–30]

All′ Qui′et on the West′ern Front′, (German, *Im Westen nichts Neues*), a novel (1929) by Erich Maria Remarque.

all′ right′, 1. safe; sound: *Are you all right?* **2.** yes; very well; OK: *All right, I'll go with you.* **3.** (used as an interrogative or interrogative tag) OK?; do you agree?: *We'll deal with this problem tomorrow, all right?* **4.** satisfactory; acceptable: *His performance was all right, but I've seen better.* **5.** satisfactorily; acceptably: *His work is coming along all right.* **6.** without fail; certainly: *You'll hear about this, all right!* **7.** *Informal.* reliable; good: *That fellow is all right.* **8. (a) bit of all right,** *Brit.* quite satisfactory (used as an understatement): *The way he saved that child's life was a bit of all right.* [1100–50; orig. adv. phrase; cf. ME *al ri(g)ht* indeed, straightway, at once, late OE *eall riht* just (as)]
—Usage. See **alright.**

all-right (ôl′rīt′), *adj. Informal.* agreeable, acceptable, or commendable: *an all-right plan.* [1815–25]

all-round (ôl′round′), *adj.* all-around.

all-round·er (ôl′roun′dər), *n.* a person of great versatility or wide-ranging skills: *The job needs an all-rounder who knows sales, accounting, and something about computers.* [1855–60; *all (a)round* + -ER¹]

All′ Saints′ Day′, a church festival celebrated November 1 in honor of all the saints; Allhallows. [1570–80]

all·seed (ôl′sēd′), *n.* any of various many-seeded plants, as the goosefoot, *Chenopodium polyspermum,* and the knotgrass, *Polygonum aviculare.* [1815–25; ALL + SEED]

All′ Souls′ Day′, a day of solemn prayer for all dead persons, observed by Roman Catholics and certain Anglicans, usually on November 2. [1550–60]

all·spice (ôl′spīs′), *n.* **1.** the dried, unripe berries of an aromatic tropical American tree, *Pimenta dioica,* used whole or ground as a spice. **2.** the tree itself. Also called **pimento.** [1615–25; ALL + SPICE]

all-star (ôl′stär′), *adj.* **1.** consisting of athletes chosen as the best at their positions from all teams in a league or region: *Our quarterback was chosen for the all-star team.* **2.** consisting entirely of star performers: *an all-star cast.* —*n.* **3.** *Sports.* a player selected for an all-star team. [1885–90, *Amer.*]

all-state (ôl′stāt′), *adj.* selected on the basis of merit to represent one's state, often in a competition: *an all-state debater; a pitcher on the all-state team.* Also, **all′-State′.**

All·ston (ôl′stən), *n.* **Washington,** 1799–1843, U.S. painter, novelist, and poet.

All's′ Well′ That Ends′ Well′, a comedy (1602?) by Shakespeare.

all′-ter·rain′ ve′hicle (ôl′tə rān′), a vehicle with treads, wheels, or both, designed to traverse varied, uneven terrain as well as roads. *Abbr.:* ATV [1965–70]

All′ the King's′ Men′, a novel (1946) by Robert Penn Warren.

all-time (ôl′tīm′), *adj.* **1.** never surpassed or greater: *Production will reach an all-time high.* **2.** regarded as such in its entire history: *an all-time favorite song.* [1910–15]

al·lude (ə lo͞od′), *v.i.,* **-lud·ed, -lud·ing. 1.** to refer casually or indirectly; make an allusion (usually fol. by to): *He often alluded to his poverty.* **2.** to contain a casual or indirect reference (usually fol. by *to*): *The letter alludes to something now forgotten.* [1525–35; < L *allūdere* to play beside, make a playful allusion to, equiv. to *al-* AL- + *lūdere* to play]
—Syn. hint, intimate, suggest.

al·lure¹ (ə lo͝or′), *v.,* **-lured, -lur·ing,** *n.* —*v.t.* **1.** to attract or tempt by something flattering or desirable. **2.** to fascinate; charm. —*v.i.* **3.** to be attractive or tempting. —*n.* **4.** fascination; charm; appeal. [1375–1425; late ME *aluren* < MF *alurer,* equiv. to *a-* A-⁵ + *lurer* to LURE] **—al·lur′er,** *n.*
—Syn. 1. entice, lure. **2.** enchant, entrance, captivate. **4.** glamor, attraction.

al·lure² (al′yo͝or, -yər), *n.* alure.

CONCISE PRONUNCIATION KEY: act, cāpe, dâre, pärt; set, ēqual; *if,* ice; ox, ōver, ôrder, oil, bo͝ok, bo͞ot, out; up, ûrge; child; sing; shoe; thin, *th*at; zh as in *treasure.* ə = *a* as in *alone, e* as in *system, i* as in *easily, o* as in *gallop, u* as in *circus;* ᵊ as in *fire* (fīᵊr), *hour* (ouᵊr). l and n can serve as syllabic consonants, as in *cradle* (krād′l), and *button* (but′n). See the full key inside the front cover.

al•lure•ment (ə lo͝or′mənt), *n.* **1.** fascination; charm. **2.** the means of alluring. **3.** the act or process of alluring. [1540–50; ALLURE[1] + -MENT]

al•lur•ing (ə lo͝or′ing), *adj.* **1.** very attractive or tempting; enticing; seductive. **2.** fascinating; charming. [1525–35; ALLURE[1] + -ING[2]] —**al•lur′ing•ly,** *adv.* —**al•lur′ing•ness,** *n.*

al•lu•sion (ə lo͞o′zhən), *n.* **1.** a passing or casual reference; an incidental mention of something, either directly or by implication: *an allusion to Shakespeare.* **2.** the act of alluding. **3.** *Obs.* a metaphor; parable. [1540–50; < LL *allūsiōn-* (s. of *allūsiō*), equiv. to *allūs(us)*, ptp. of *allūdere* (see ALLUDE; *al-* AL- + *lūd-* play + *-tus* ptp. suffix) + *-iōn-* -ION]

al•lu•sive (ə lo͞o′siv), *adj.* **1.** having reference to something implied or inferred; containing, abounding in, or characterized by allusions. **2.** *Obs.* metaphorical; symbolic; figurative. [1595–1605; ALLUS(ION) + -IVE] —**al•lu′sive•ly,** *adv.* —**al•lu′sive•ness,** *n.*

al•lu•vi•al (ə lo͞o′vē əl), *adj.* **1.** of or pertaining to alluvium. —*n.* **2.** alluvial soil. **3.** *Australia.* gold-bearing alluvial soil. [1795–1805; ALLUVI(UM) + -AL[1]]

allu′vial fan′, *Physical Geog.* a fan-shaped alluvial deposit formed by a stream where its velocity is abruptly decreased, as at the mouth of a ravine or at the foot of a mountain. Also called **allu′vial cone′.** [1870–75]

allu′vial plain′, a level or gently sloping surface formed of sediments laid down by streams, generally during flooding. [1955–60]

al•lu•vi•on (ə lo͞o′vē ən), *n.* **1.** *Law.* a gradual increase of land on a shore or a river bank by the action of water, whether from natural or artificial causes. **2.** overflow; flood. **3.** *Now Rare.* alluvium. [1530–40; < L *alluviōn-* (s. of *alluviō* an overflowing), equiv. to *al-* AL- + *-luv-*, base of *-luere*, comb. form of *lavere* to wash) + *-iōn-* -ION]

al•lu•vi•um (ə lo͞o′vē əm), *n., pl.* **-vi•ums, -vi•a** (-vē ə). **1.** a deposit of sand, mud, etc., formed by flowing water. **2.** the sedimentary matter deposited thus within recent times, esp. in the valleys of large rivers. [1655–65; < L, n. use of neut. of *alluvius* washed against, equiv. to *alluv-* (see ALLUVION) + *-ius, -ium* adj. suffix; see -IUM]

all-weath•er (ôl′weth′ər), *adj.* **1.** designed to operate or be usable in any type of weather: *an all-weather coat; an all-weather shelter.* **2.** capable of resisting damage from exposure to any climatic conditions; weatherproof: *an all-weather paint.* **3.** in or including all types of weather: *years of all-weather experience in the Arctic.* [1955–60]

al•ly (*v.* ə lī′; *n.* al′ī, ə lī′), *v.*, **-lied, -ly•ing,** *n., pl.* **-lies.** —*v.t.* **1.** to unite formally, as by treaty, league, marriage, or the like (usually fol. by *with* or *to*): *Russia allied itself to France.* **2.** to associate or connect by some mutual relationship, as resemblance or friendship. —*v.i.* **3.** to enter into an alliance; join; unite. —*n.* **4.** a person, group, or nation that is associated with another or others for some common cause or purpose: *Canada and the United States were allies in World War II.* **5.** *Biol.* a plant, animal, or other organism bearing an evolutionary relationship to another, often as a member of the same family: *The squash is an ally of the watermelon.* **6.** a person who associates or cooperates with another; supporter. [1250–1300; ME *alien* < AF *al(l)ier, aillier,* OF *alier* < L *alligāre* to bind to. See ALLOY] —**al•li′a•ble,** *adj.*
—**Syn. 1.** unify, join, combine, wed. **4.** partner, confederate. **6.** friend, aide, accomplice, accessory, assistant, abettor; colleague, coadjutor, auxiliary, helper.
—**Ant. 4, 6.** enemy, foe, adversary.

-ally, an adverbial suffix attached to certain adjectives with stems in *-ic* that have no forms ending in *-ical*: *terrifically.* [-AL[1] + -LY]

all-year (ôl′yēr′), *adj.* **1.** taking up, extending through, or occurring continually during a year: *an all-year activity.* **2.** open all year, as for business or occupancy: *an all-year resort.* **3.** usable or productive during all parts of a year: *all-year pasture; all-year fishing grounds.*

al•lyl (al′il), *Chem.* —*adj.* **1.** containing the allyl group. —*n.* **2.** the allyl group. [1850–55; < L *all(ium)* garlic + -YL]

al′lyl al′cohol, *Chem.* a colorless liquid, C_3H_6O, having a pungent, mustardlike odor irritating to the skin and mucous membranes, usually obtained from allyl chloride by hydrolysis: used chiefly in organic synthesis in the manufacture of resins, plasticizers, and pharmaceuticals. Also called **propenyl alcohol.**

al′lyl cap′roate, *Chem.* a colorless to pale yellow liquid, $C_9H_{16}O_2$, having a pineapple odor: used chiefly as a scent in the manufacture of flavorings and perfume.

al′lyl chlo′ride, *Chem.* a colorless, volatile, flammable liquid, C_3H_5Cl, having a pungent odor, derived from propylene by chlorination: used chiefly in the synthesis of allyl alcohol, resins, and pharmaceuticals.

al′lyl group′, *Chem.* the univalent group C_3H_5, derived from propylene. Also called **al′lyl rad′ical.**

al•lyl•ic (ə lil′ik), *adj.* of, pertaining to, or characteristic of the allyl group. [1855–60; ALLYL + -IC]

al′lyl mercap′tan, *Chem.* a colorless liquid, C_3H_6S, having a strong, garlicky odor, used in the manufacture of pharmaceuticals.

al′lyl res′in, *Chem.* any of a class of thermosetting resins made from allyl alcohol and a dibasic acid, used chiefly as adhesives for laminated materials.

CONCISE ETYMOLOGY KEY: <, descended or borrowed from; >, whence; b., blend of, blended; c., cognate with; cf., compare; deriv., derivative; equiv., equivalent; imit., imitative; obl., oblique; r., replacing; s., stem; sp., spelling, spelled; resp., respelling, respelled; trans., translation; ?, origin unknown; *, unattested; ‡, probably earlier than. See the full key inside the front cover.

al′lyl sul′fide, *Chem.* a colorless or pale yellow, water-insoluble liquid, $C_6H_{10}S$, having a garlicky odor, used chiefly in flavoring. Also called **diallyl sulfide, thioallyl ether.**

al•lyl•thi•o•u•re•a (al′il thī′ō yo͞o rē′ə, -yo͝or′ē ə), *n. Chem.* thiosinamine. [< NL; see ALLYL, THIOUREA]

ALM, audio-lingual method.

Al•ma (al′mə; *for 1 also Fr.* al mä′), *n.* **1.** a town in SE Quebec, in SE Canada. 25,638. **2.** a female given name: from a Latin word meaning "kind."

Al•ma-A•ta (al′mə ə tä′; *Russ.* ul mä′u tä′), *n.* a city in and the capital of Kazakhstan, in the SE part. 910,000. Formerly, **Verny.**

Al•ma•dén (äl′mä then′), *n.* a town in Spain: mercury mines. 10,774.

Al•ma•gest (al′mə jest′), *n.* **1.** (*italics*) a Greek work on astronomy by Ptolemy. **2.** (*l.c.*) any of various medieval works of a like kind, as on astrology or alchemy. [1350–1400; ME *almageste* < MF < Ar *al* the + *majisṭī* < Gk *megístē (sýntaxis)* greatest (composition)]

al•mah (al′mə), *n.* (in Egypt) a woman or girl who dances or sings professionally. Also, **al′ma, alme, almeh.** [< Egyptian Ar *ʿalmah*, var. of Ar *ʿālimah* lit., knowledgeable]

al•ma ma•ter (äl′mə mä′tər, al′-; al′mə mā′tər), **1.** a school, college, or university at which one has studied and, usually, from which one has graduated. **2.** the official anthem of a school, college, or university. [< L: nourishing (i.e., dear) mother]

al•ma•nac (ôl′mə nak′), *n.* **1.** an annual publication containing a calendar for the coming year, the times of such events and phenomena as anniversaries, sunrises and sunsets, phases of the moon, tides, etc., and other statistical information and related topics. **2.** a publication containing astronomical or meteorological information, usually including future positions of celestial objects, star magnitudes, and culmination dates of constellations. **3.** an annual reference book of useful and interesting facts relating to countries of the world, sports, entertainment, etc. [1350–1400; ME *almenak* < ML *almanach* < SpAr *al* the + *manākh* calendar < ?]

Al•ma•nach de Go•tha (ôl′mə nak′ də goth′ə; *Ger.* äl′mä näkн′ də gō′tä; *Fr.* al mа nа′ də gō tä′), a publication giving statistical information on European royalty.

Al Ma•nam•ah (al mə nam′ə), Manama.

al•man•dine (al′mən dēn′, -dīn′, -din), *n.* a mineral, red iron aluminum garnet. [1670–80; < F, MF < ML *alamandina, alabandina* a precious stone, prob. a kind of garnet, equiv. to *Alaband(a)* a town in Asia Minor + *-ina*, fem. of *-īnus* -INE[1]; cf. ME *alabaundaryne, alemaundine*; cf. ALABANDITE]

al•man•dite (al′mən dīt′), *n.* almandine. [1830–40; ALMAND(INE) + -ITE[1]]

Al•ma-Tad•e•ma (al′mə tad′ə mə), *n.* **Sir Lawrence,** 1836–1912, English painter, born in the Netherlands.

al•me (al′me), *n.* almah. Also, **al′meh.**

Al•mei•da (äl mā′də), *n.* **Fran•cis•co de** (fʀäɴ sēsh′-ko͞o də), 1450?–1510, Portuguese military leader: first Portuguese viceroy in India.

al•me•mar (äl mē′mär), *n.* bimah. [< Ar *al* the + *minbar* stand, platform]

Al•me•rí•a (äl′me ʀē′ä), *n.* a seaport in S Spain, on the Mediterranean. 114,510. —**Al•me•ri•an** (al′mə rē′-ən), *adj., n.*

al•mer•y (ä′mə rē), *n., pl.* **-er•ies.** *Rare.* ambry.

Al•me•tyevsk (äl′mə tyefsk′; *Russ.* ul mye′tyifsk), *n.* a city in the W central RSFSR, in the W Soviet Union in Asia, SE of Kazan. 110,000.

al•might•y (ôl mī′tē), *adj.* **1.** having unlimited power; omnipotent, as God. **2.** having very great power, influence, etc.: *The almighty press condemned him without trial.* **3.** *Informal.* extreme; terrible: *He's in an almighty fix.* —*adv.* **4.** *Informal.* extremely: *It's almighty hot.* —*n.* **5. the Almighty,** God. [bef. 900; ME; OE *ælmihtig, ealmihtig*, equiv. to *æl-, eal-* ALL (c. ON *al-* < **ol-o-*) + *mihtig* (*miht, meaht* MIGHT[2] + *-ig* -Y[1]); cf. ALEMANNI] —**al•might′i•ly,** *adv.* —**al•might′i•ness,** *n.*
—**Syn. 1.** supreme, sovereign, all-powerful.

almight′y dol′lar, money regarded as a major goal in life or as the basis of power: *Love of the almighty dollar has ruined many people.* [1830–40, *Amer.*]

al•mi•que (al′mə kē′), *n.* **1.** a West African tree, *Manilkara albescens*, of the sapodilla family. **2.** the hard, reddish-brown wood of this tree, used for making furniture. **3.** Also, **alamiqui.** a Cuban solenodon, *Solenodon cubanus.* [< AmerSp *almiquí*, prob. two distinct words, both of obscure orig.; supposed connection between the animal's name and Sp *almizcle* musk or (*ratón*) *almizclero* muskrat is prob. specious]

al•mi•rah (al mī′rə), *n. Anglo-Indian.* a wardrobe, cabinet, or cupboard. [1875–80; << Pg *almario* < L *armārium* ARMARIUM]

Al•mo•had (al′mə had′), *n.* a member of a Muslim dynasty ruling in Spain and northern Africa during the 12th and 13th centuries. Also, **Al•mo•hade** (al′mə hād′, -hād′). [< Ar *al-muwaḥḥid* lit., the one who professes the unity of God]

al•mon (al′mōn, am′ən), *n.* **1.** a Philippine, dipterocarpaceous tree, *Shorea eximia.* **2.** the hard, yellowish-white wood of this tree, used for making furniture. [< Bisayan]

al•mond (ä′mənd, am′ənd; *spelling pron.* al′mənd), *n.* **1.** the nutlike kernel of the fruit of either of two trees, *Prunus dulcis* **(sweet almond)** or *P. dulcis amara* **(bitter almond),** which grow in warm temperate regions. **2.** the tree itself. **3.** a delicate, pale tan. **4.** anything shaped like an almond, esp. an ornament. —*adj.* **5.** of the color, taste, or shape of an almond. **6.** made or flavored with almonds: *almond cookies.* [1250–1300; ME *almande* < OF (dial.) *alemande*, prob. by transposition of *-la* < LL *amandula*, with assimilative replacement of the unfamiliar cluster and adaptation to a known suffix, repr. L *amygdala* < Gk *amygdálē*; r. OE *amigdal* < L] —**al′mond•like′, al′mond•y,** *adj.*

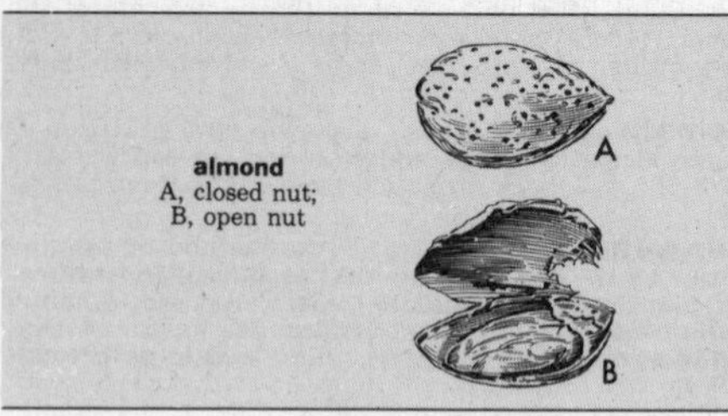

almond
A, closed nut;
B, open nut

al′mond bark′, a type of candy consisting of sheets or fairly thick pieces of semisweet or milk chocolate to which almonds or almond pieces have been added.

al′mond cake′, *Chem.* the residue of almonds from which oil has been expressed.

al•mond-eyed (ä′mənd īd′, am′ənd-; *spelling pron.* al′mənd īd′), *adj.* having long or narrow, oval-shaped eyes. [1865–70]

al′mond meal′, *Chem.* the meal obtained by pulverizing blanched almonds, used chiefly in the manufacture of perfume and cosmetics.

al′mond milk′, a creamy mixture of blanched almonds, sugar, and water, blended to a smooth paste and sieved.

al′mond oil′, *Chem.* **1.** Also called **sweet almond oil, expressed almond oil.** a colorless to pale yellow fatty oil expressed from the seeds of the sweet almond, used in preparing perfumes and confections. **2.** Also called **bitter almond oil.** a colorless to yellow, poisonous oil obtained by steam distillation from the almond meal of bitter almond seeds: used chiefly in the manufacture of cosmetics, medicines, and perfumes. [1835–45]

al•mond-shaped (ä′mənd shāpt′, am′ənd-; *spelling pron.* al′mənd shāpt′), *adj.* having an oval shape usually pointed at one or both ends.

al•mon•er (al′mə nər, ä′mə-), *n.* **1.** a person whose function or duty is the distribution of alms on behalf of an institution, a royal personage, a monastery, etc. **2.** *Brit.* **a.** a hospital official who determines the amount due for a patient's treatment. **b.** a social worker in a hospital. [1250–1300; ME *almoiner, aumoner* (with insertion of *l* under influence of ALMS) < OF *aumon(i)er* << LL *eleēmosynārius* ELEEMOSYNARY]

al′moner's cup′board. See **livery cupboard.**

al•mon•ry (al′mən rē, ä′mən-), *n., pl.* **-ries.** the place where an almoner resides or where alms are distributed. [1175–1225; ME *aumonerie* < OF (see ALMONER, -RY); r. ME *aumery*]

Al•mo•ra•vid (al′mə rä′vid, al môr′ə-, -mōr′-), *n.* a member of a Muslim dynasty ruling in Spain and northern Africa from 1056 to 1147. Also, **Al•mo•ra•vide** (al-môr′ə vīd′, -mōr′-, al′mə rä′vīd). [< Sp < Ar *al-murābit* lit., the occupant of a fortified convent]

al•most (ôl′mōst, ôl mōst′), *adv.* very nearly; all but: *almost every house; almost the entire symphony; to pay almost nothing for a car; almost twice as many books.* [bef. 1000; ME; OE (*e*)*al māst*, var. of *æl mǣst* nearly]
—**Syn.** ALMOST (MOST), NEARLY, WELL-NIGH all mean within a small degree of or short space of. ALMOST implies very little short of: *almost exhausted; almost home.* MOST is colloquial for ALMOST. NEARLY implies a slightly greater distance or degree than ALMOST: *nearly well; nearly to the city.* WELL-NIGH, a more literary word, implies a barely appreciable distance or extent: *well-nigh forgotten; well-nigh home.*
—**Usage.** See **most.**

al′most ev′erywhere, *Math.* everywhere in a given set except on a subset with measure zero. *Abbr.:* a.e.

al′most period′ic func′tion, *Math.* a function that repeats its values approximately at almost equally spaced intervals of its domain.

al•mous (ä′məs, ô′məs), *n.* (*used with a plural v.*) *Brit. Dial.* alms. [1250–1300; ME *almus* < Scand; cf. ON *ǫlmusa* ALMS]

alms (ämz), *n.* (*used with a singular or plural v.*) money, food, or other donations given to the poor or needy; anything given as charity: *The hands of the beggars were outstretched for alms.* [bef. 1000; ME *almes, almesse*, OE *ælmesse* (cf. OS *alamōsna*, OHG *alamuosa*, D *aalmoes*; OSp *almosna*) << LL *eleēmosyna* < Gk *eleēmosýnē* compassion, alms, deriv. of *éleos* pity. See ELEEMOSYNARY]

alms•giv•er (ämz′giv′ər), *n.* a person who gives alms. [1625–35; ALMS + GIVER] —**alms′giv′ing,** *n.*

alms•house (ämz′hous′), *n., pl.* **-hous•es** (-hou′ziz). *Chiefly Brit.* **1.** a house endowed by private charity for the reception and support of the aged or infirm poor. **2.** (formerly) a poorhouse. [1350–1400; ME *almes hous.* See ALMS, HOUSE]

alms•man (ämz′mən), *n., pl.* **-men.** **1.** a person supported by or receiving alms. **2.** *Archaic.* a person who gives alms. [bef. 1000; ME *almes man*, OE *ælmesman*; see ALMS, -MAN]
—**Usage.** See **-man.**

alms•wom•an (ämz′wo͝om′ən), *n., pl.* **-wom•en.** **1.** a woman supported by alms. **2.** *Archaic.* a woman who gives alms. [ALMS + WOMAN]
—**Usage.** See **-woman.**

al•mu•can•tar (al′myo͞o kan′tər), *n. Astron.* a circle

on the celestial sphere parallel to the horizon; the locus of all points of a given altitude. Also called **parallel of altitude.** [1350–1400; prob. < ML *almucantarath* < Ar *al-muqanṭarāt* the almucantars, equiv. to *al* the + *muqanṭarāt* sundial, deriv. of *qanṭarah* arch; r. *almicanter,* ME *almicanteras* (pl.) < MF *almicantarath* < ML]

al•muce (al′myo͞os), *n.* a furred hood or hooded cape with long ends hanging down in front, formerly worn by the clergy. Also, **amice.** [< MF *almuce, aumuce.* See AMICE[2]]

al•mug (al′məg, ôl′-), *n. Bible.* a tree, possibly the red sandalwood. I Kings 10:12. Cf. **algum.** [1605–15; cf. ALGUM]

al•ni•co (al′ni kō′), *n.* a permanent-magnet alloy having aluminum, nickel, and cobalt as its principal ingredients. [AL(UMINUM) + NI(CKEL) + CO(BALT)]

Al•o•a•dae (al′ō ā′dē), *n.pl. Class. Myth.* Ephialtes and Otus, the sons of Poseidon and Iphimedia, raised by Aloeus. Also, **Aloidae.**

Al-O•beid (al′ō bād′), *n.* See **El Obeid.**

a•lo•di•um (ə lō′dē əm), *n., pl.* **-di•a** (-dē ə). allodium. Also called **al•od** (al′od, -əd). **—a•lo′di•al,** *adj.* **—a•lo′•di•al′i•ty,** *n.* **—a•lo′di•al•ly,** *adv.*

al•oe (al′ō), *n., pl.* **-oes. 1.** any chiefly African shrub belonging to the genus *Aloe,* of the lily family, certain species of which yield a fiber. **2.** See **aloe vera. 3.** See **century plant. 4. aloes,** (*used with a singular v.*) agalloch. [bef. 950; ME *alōe, alow, alewen;* OE *al(u)we, alewe* (cf. OS, OHG *ālōe*) < L *aloē* < Gk *alóē,* perh. < South Asia via Heb] **—al•o•et•ic** (al′ō et′ik), *adj.*

al•oes•wood (al′ōz wo͝od′), *n.* agalloch. [1865–70]

A•lo•e•us (ə lō′ē əs, ə lō′yo͞os), *n. Class. Myth.* a son of Poseidon, husband of Iphimedia, and foster father of Otus and Ephialtes. Cf. **Aloadae.**

al′oe ver′a (ver′ə, vēr′ə), any aloe of the species *Aloe vera,* the fleshy leaves of which yield a juice used as an emollient ingredient of skin lotions and for treating burns. [< NL: lit., true aloe]

a•loft (ə lôft′, ə loft′), *adv.* **1.** high up; far above the ground. **2.** *Naut.* **a.** on the masts; in the rigging; overhead. **b.** (on a square-rigged sailing ship) in the upper rigging, specifically, on or above the lower yards (opposed to *alow*). **3.** in or into the air. —*prep.* **4.** on or at the top of: *flags flying aloft the castle.* [1150–1200; ME *o loft;* < ON *ā lopt* in the air; see A-[1], LOFT]

A•lo•gi (ā lō′gī), *n.* (*used with a singular or plural v.*) a group of Christians in the 2nd century A.D. who rejected the doctrine of the Logos. [1150–1200; < ML < Gk *álogoi,* pl. of *álogos,* equiv. to *a-* A-[6] + *-logos,* adj. deriv. of *lógos* speech, word, the Word]

a•lo•gia (ə lō′jə, -jē ə), *n. Pathol.* aphasia. [< NL < Gk *álog(os)* (< *a-* A-[6] + *-logos,* adj. deriv. of *lógos* speech, akin to *légein* to speak) + NL *-ia* -IA]

a•log•i•cal (ā loj′i kəl), *adj.* beyond the scope of logic or logical reasoning: *alogical philosophical speculations.* [1685–95; A-[6] + LOGICAL] **—a•log′i•cal•ly,** *adv.*

a•lo•ha (ə lō′ə, ä lō′hä), *n., interj.* **1.** hello; greetings. **2.** farewell. —*adj.* **3.** friendly; hospitable; welcoming: *The aloha spirit prevails throughout the islands.* [1890–95; < Hawaiian]

alo′ha shirt′. See **Hawaiian shirt.** Also, **Alo′ha shirt′.** [1935–40, *Amer.*]

Alo′ha State′, Hawaii (used as a nickname).

Al•o•i•dae (al′ō ī′dē), *n.pl. Class. Myth.* Aloadae.

al•o•in (al′ō in), *n. Pharm.* an intensely bitter, crystalline, water-soluble powder composed of the active principles of and obtained from aloe, used chiefly as a purgative. [1835–45; ALOE + -INE[2]]

a•lone (ə lōn′), *adj.* (used predicatively) **1.** separate, apart, or isolated from others: *I want to be alone.* **2.** to the exclusion of all others or all else: *One cannot live by bread alone.* **3.** unique; unequaled; unexcelled: *He is alone among his peers in devotion to duty.* **4. leave alone, a.** to allow (someone) to be by himself or herself: *Leave him alone—he wants to rest.* **b.** to refrain from annoying or interfering with: *The youngsters wouldn't leave the dog alone, and he finally turned on them.* **5. let alone, a.** to refrain from annoying or interfering with. **b.** not to mention: *He was too tired to walk, let alone run.* **6. let well enough alone,** to be satisfied with the existing situation; refrain from attempting to change conditions: *Marriages are often destroyed by relatives who will not let well enough alone.* —*adv.* **7.** solitarily; solely: *She prefers to live alone.* **8.** only; exclusively. **9.** without aid or help: *The baby let go of the side of the crib and stood alone.* [1250–1300; ME *al one* ALL (wholly) ONE] **—a•lone′ness,** *n.*
—Syn. 1. single, solitary; unaccompanied, unattended. ALONE, LONE, LONELY, LONESOME all imply being without companionship or association. ALONE is colorless unless reinforced by ALL; it then suggests solitariness or desolation: *alone in the house; all alone on an island.* LONE is somewhat poetic or is intended humorously: *a lone sentinel.* LONELY implies a sad or disquieting feeling of isolation. LONESOME connotes emotion, a longing for companionship. **—Ant. 1.** accompanied.
—Usage. 4, 5. See **leave**[1].

a•long (ə lông′, ə long′), *prep.* **1.** through, on, beside, over, or parallel to the length or direction of; from one end to the other of: *to walk along a highway; to run a border along a shelf.* **2.** during; in the course of: *Somewhere along the way I lost my hat.* **3.** in conformity or accordance with: *I plan to revise the article along the lines suggested.* —*adv.* **4.** by the length; lengthwise; parallel to or in a line with the length or direction: *He ran along beside me.* **5.** with a progressive motion; onward: *The police ordered the line to move along.* **6.** (of time) some way on: *along toward evening.* **7.** in company; in agreement (usually fol. by *with*): *I'll go along with you. He planned the project along with his associates.* **8.** as a companion; with one: *She took her brother along.* **9.** from one person or place to another: *The order was passed along from the general to the captain and from the captain to a private.* **10.** at or to an advanced place or state: *Work on the new ship is quite far along.* **11.** as an accompanying item; on hand: *Bring along your umbrella.* **12. all along,** all the time; throughout: *I knew all along that it was a lie.* **13. along of,** *Chiefly Southern U.S. and Brit. Dial.* **a.** owing to; because of: *We weren't invited, along of your rudeness.* **b.** in company with: *You come along of me to the store.* **14. be along,** *Informal.* to arrive at a place; come: *They should be along soon.* **15. get along.** See **get** (def. 33). [bef. 900; ME; OE *andlang,* equiv. to *and-* (c. OS, ON *and-,* Goth *and(a)-,* OHG *ant-,* prefix with orig. sense "facing"; cf. ANSWER) + *lang* LONG[1]]

a•long•ships (ə lông′ships′, ə long′-), *adj., adv. Naut.* in the fore-and-aft line of a vessel. [1680–90; ALONG + SHIP + -S[1]]

a•long•shore (ə lông′shôr′, -shōr′, ə long′-), *adv., adj.* by or along the shore or coast. [1770–80; ALONG + SHORE[1]]

a•long•side (ə lông′sīd′, ə long′-), *adv.* **1.** along, by, at, or to the side of something: *We brought the boat alongside.* —*prep.* **2.** beside; by the side of: *The dog ran alongside me all the way.* **3.** *Informal.* **alongside of,** compared with: *Alongside of his brother, he is no student at all.* [1700–10; ALONG + SIDE[1]]

A•lon•so (ə lon′zō; *Sp.* ä lôn′sô), *n.* **1. Alicia** (*Alicia Ernestina de la Caridad del Cobre Martínez Hoyo*), born 1921, Cuban ballerina. **2. Dá•ma•so** (dä′mä sô′), 1898–1990, Spanish poet, critic, and philologist. **3.** Also, **A•lon′zo.** a male given name, Spanish form of **Alphonso.**

a•loof (ə lo͞of′), *adv.* **1.** at a distance, esp. in feeling or interest; apart: *They always stood aloof from their classmates.* —*adj.* **2.** reserved or reticent; indifferent; disinterested: *Because of his shyness, he had the reputation of being aloof.* [1525–35; A-[1] + *loof* LUFF windward] **—a•loof′ly,** *adv.* **—a•loof′ness,** *n.*
—Syn. 2. cool, detached; distant, standoffish; snobbish, haughty, disdainful. **—Ant. 1.** near. **2.** warm, open, gregarious, outgoing.

Al•o•pe (al′ō pē′), *n. Class. Myth.* a daughter of Cercyon who was raped by Poseidon and bore a son, Hippothous.

al•o•pe•ci•a (al′ə pē′shē ə, -sē ə), *n. Pathol.* loss of hair; baldness. [1350–1400; ME < L < Gk *alōpekía* mange in foxes, equiv. to *alōpek-* (s. of *alṓpēx*) fox + *-ia* -IA] **—al•o•pe•cic** (al′ə pē′sik), *adj.*

alope′cia ar•e•a′ta (ar′ē ā′tə, -ä′tə), *Pathol.* loss of hair in circumscribed patches. [< NL: circumscribed alopecia]

à l'o•range (ä′ lô ränzh′; *Fr.* A lô RÄNZH′), *French Cookery.* prepared or served with slices of orange, orange peel, or an orange-flavored sauce: *duck à l'orange.* [< F: with orange]

A•lost (*Fr.* A lôst′), *n.* a city in central Belgium, NW of Brussels. 45,241. Flemish, **Aalst.**

a•loud (ə loud′), *adv.* **1.** with the normal tone and volume of the speaking voice, as distinguished from whisperingly: *They could not speak aloud in the library.* **2.** vocally, as distinguished from mentally: *He read the book aloud.* **3.** with a loud voice; loudly: *to cry aloud in grief.* [1325–75; ME; see A-[1], LOUD]

Al-Oued (al wed′), *n.* See **El Oued.**

a•lou•et•te (A lwet′ *or, for 2,* A lo͞o e′tə; *Eng.* al′o͞o-et′ə, ä′lo͞o-), *n., pl.* **a•lou•et•tes** (A lwet′; *Eng.* al′o͞o et′-əz, ä′lo͞o-) for 1. **1.** *French.* a lark. **2.** (*cap.*) a French children's song for group singing.

a•low[1] (ə lō′), *adv. Naut.* **1.** below decks. **2.** (on a square-rigged sailing ship) in the lower rigging, specifically, below the lower yards (opposed to *aloft*). [1350–1400; earlier, downward, lower down, ME *aloue;* see A-[1], LOW[1]]

a•low[2] (ə lō′), *adj., adv. Northern Brit. Dial.* ablaze; aflame. Also, **a•lowe′.** [1150–1200; ME *o loghe, a lowe;* see A-[1], LOW[3]]

Al•o•y•sius (al′ō ish′əs), *n.* a male given name: from a Germanic word meaning "famous warrior."

alp (alp), *n.* a high mountain. [1635–1645; back formation from ALPS]

A.L.P., American Labor Party. Also, **ALP**

alpaca, *Lama pacos,* 3½ ft. (1.1 m) high at shoulder; total height 5 ft. (1.5 m); length 3½ ft. (1.1 m)

al•pac•a (al pak′ə), *n.* **1.** a domesticated South American hoofed mammal, *Lama pacos,* having long, soft, silky fleece, related to the llama and believed to be a variety of the guanaco. **2.** the fleece of this animal. **3.** a fabric or yarn made of it. **4.** a glossy, commonly black woolen fabric with cotton warp. **5.** a crepe fabric made of rayon and acetate yarn in imitation of alpaca wool cloth. [1805–15; < Sp < Aymara *allpaqa*]

Al•pe•na (al pē′nə), *n.* a city in NE Michigan, on Lake Huron. 12,214.

al•pen•glow (al′pən glō′), *n.* a reddish glow often seen on the summits of mountains just before sunrise or just after sunset. [1870–75; < G *Alpenglühen,* with GLOW r. G *glühen*]

al•pen•horn (al′pən hôrn′), *n.* a long, powerful horn of wood or bark, with a cupped mouthpiece and a curved bell at opposite ends, used by Swiss herders and mountaineers. Also called **alphorn.** [1860–65; < G, equiv. to *Alpen* ALPS + *Horn* HORN]

al•pen•stock (al′pən stok′), *n.* a strong staff with an iron point, used by mountain climbers. [1820–30; < G, equiv. to *Alpen* ALPS + *Stock* staff]

Alpes-de-Haute Pro•vence (Alp də ōt PRÔ VÄNS′), a department in SE France. 112,178; 2698 sq. mi. (6990 sq. km). *Cap.:* Digne. Formerly, **Basses-Alpes.**

Alpes-Ma•ri•times (Alp MA RĒ tēm′), *n.* a department in SE France. 816,681; 1527 sq. mi. (3955 sq. km). *Cap.:* Nice.

al•pes•trine (al pes′trin), *adj. Bot.* subalpine (def. 2). [1875–80; < ML *alpestr(is)* (L *Alp(ēs)* the Alps + *-estris* adj. suffix; see TERRESTRIAL) + -INE[1]]

al•pha (al′fə), *n.* **1.** the first letter of the Greek alphabet (A, α). **2.** the vowel sound represented by this letter. **3.** the first; beginning. **4.** (*cap.*) *Astron.* used to designate the brightest star in a constellation. **5.** *Chem.* one of two or more isomeric compounds. **6.** the first in a series of related items: frequently used in chemistry and physics. **7.** *Chiefly Brit.* a mark or grade corresponding to an A. Cf. **beta** (def. 8), **gamma** (def. 9). —*adj.* **8.** (esp. of animals) having the highest rank of its sex in a dominance hierarchy: *the alpha female.* **9.** *Chem.* pertaining or linked to the carbon atom closest to a particular group in an organic molecule. [< L < Gk *álpha* < Sem; cf. ALEPH]

al•pha-ad•ren•er•gic (al′fə ad′rə nûr′jik), *adj.* of or pertaining to an alpha receptor. [1965–70]

al′pha-adrener′gic recep′tor, *Physiol.* See **alpha receptor.**

al′pha and ome′ga, 1. the beginning and the end. Rev. 1:8. **2.** the basic or essential element or elements: *the alpha and omega of political reform.*

al•pha•bet (al′fə bet′, -bit), *n.* **1.** the letters of a language in their customary order. **2.** any system of characters or signs with which a language is written: *the Greek alphabet.* **3.** any such system for representing the sounds of a language: *the phonetic alphabet.* **4.** first elements; basic facts; simplest rudiments: *the alphabet of genetics.* **5. the alphabet,** a system of writing, developed in the ancient Near East and transmitted from the northwest Semites to the Greeks, in which each symbol ideally represents one sound unit in the spoken language, and from which most alphabetical scripts are derived. [1375–1425; late ME *alphabete* < LL *alphabētum,* alter. of Gk *alphábētos.* See ALPHA, BETA]

al′pha-be′ta brass′ (al′fə bā′tə, -bē′-), an alloy of from 55 to 61 percent copper with from 39 to 45 percent zinc. Also called **Muntz metal.** [1915–20]

al′phabet code′, a list of easily distinguishable words, each representing a letter of the alphabet, used in radio and telephonic communications.

al•pha•bet•i•cal (al′fə bet′i kəl), *adj.* **1.** in the order of the letters of the alphabet: *alphabetical arrangement.* **2.** pertaining to, expressed by, or using an alphabet: *alphabetical writing.* Also, **al′pha•bet′ic.** [1560–70; ALPHABET + -ICAL] **—al′pha•bet′i•cal•ly,** *adv.*

al•pha•bet•ize (al′fə bi tīz′), *v.t.,* **-ized, -iz•ing. 1.** to put or arrange in alphabetical order. **2.** to express by or furnish with an alphabet. Also, *esp. Brit.,* **al′pha•bet•ise′.** [1865–70; ALPHABET + -IZE] **—al•pha•bet•i•za•tion** (al′fə bet′ə zā′shən, -bi tə-), *n.* **—al′pha•bet•iz′er,** *n.*

al′phabet soup′, a soup containing small noodles in the shapes of letters of the alphabet. [1905–10]

al′pha block′er, *Pharm.* any of various substances that interfere with the action of the alpha receptors. Also, **al′pha-block′er.** Cf. **beta blocker. —al′•pha-block′ing,** *adj.*

al′pha brass′, any alloy of copper and zinc, a homogeneous solid solution containing more than 64 percent copper. [1915–20]

Al′pha Centau′ri, *Astron.* a triple-star system that is the brightest celestial object in the constellation Centaurus. Also called **Rigel Kentaurus.** [< NL: Alpha of Centaurus]

al′pha decay′, *Physics.* a radioactive process in which an alpha particle is emitted from the nucleus of an atom, decreasing its atomic number by two. [1935–40]

al•pha-fe•to•pro•tein (al′fə fē′tō prō′tēn, -tē in), *n. Biochem.* a serum protein produced during pregnancy, useful in the prenatal diagnosis of multiple births or birth defects. *Abbr.:* AFP [1970–75; ALPHA + FET(US) + -O- + PROTEIN]

al′pha glob′ulin, a blood plasma protein that is separable from other globulins by electrophoresis. [1920–25]

al′pha he′lix, *Biochem.* the rodlike spatial configuration of many protein molecules in which the polypeptide backbone is stabilized by hydrogen bonds between amino acids in successive helical turns. [1950–55]

al•pha-in•ter•fer•on (al′fə in′tər fēr′on), *n. Pharm.* interferon (def. 2).

al′pha i′ron, *Metall.* the magnetic allotrope of iron, stable below 910°C and having a body-centered cubic space lattice. [1880–90]

al′pha-ke′to·glu·tar′ic ac′id (al′fə kē′tō glo͞o tar′ik, al′fə kē′-), *Biochem.* a dibasic keto acid, $C_5H_6O_5$, that occurs as an intermediate in the Krebs' cycle and in protein metabolism. [1905–10; KETO- + *glutaric* (*acid*), prob. b. GLUTEN (as in GLUTAMIC ACID) and *pyrotartaric acid;* see PYRO-, TARTARIC]

al·pha-naph·thol (al′fə naf′thôl, -thol, -nap′-), *n. Chem.* See under **naphthol.**

al′pha-naph′thyl group′ (al′fə naf′thil, -nap′-, al′-), *Chem.* See **naphthyl group** (def. 1). Also called **al′pha-naph′thyl rad′ical.**

al·pha-naph·thyl·thi·o·u·re·a (al′fə naf′thil thī′ō yo͞o rē′ə, -yo͝or′ē ə, -nap′-), *n. Chem.* See **ANTU.** [ALPHA + NAPHTHYL + THIOUREA]

al·pha·nu·mer·ic (al′fə no͞o mer′ik, -nyo͞o-), *adj. Computers.* (of a set of characters) including letters, numbers, and, often, special characters, as punctuation marks: *alphanumeric code.* Also, **al·pha·mer·ic** (al′fə mer′ik), **al′pha·nu·mer′i·cal, al′pha·mer′i·cal.** [1950–55; ALPHA(BET) + NUMERIC(AL)] —**al′pha·nu·mer′i·cal·ly, al′pha·mer′i·cal·ly,** *adv.*

al′pha par′ticle, *Physics.* a positively charged particle consisting of two protons and two neutrons, emitted in radioactive decay or nuclear fission; the nucleus of a helium atom. [1900–05]

al′pha-par′ti·cle scat′tering (al′fə pär′ti kəl), *Physics.* See **Rutherford scattering.** [1900–05]

al′pha priv′ative, the prefix *a-* or, before a vowel, *an-*, used in Greek and English to express negation or absence. [1580–90]

al′pha ray′, *Physics.* a stream of alpha particles. Also called **al′pha radia′tion.** [1900–05]

al′pha recep′tor, a site on a cell that, upon interaction with epinephrine or norepinephrine, controls vasoconstriction, intestinal relaxation, pupil dilation, and other physiological processes. Also, **al′pha-re·cep′tor.** Also called **alpha-adrenergic receptor.** Cf. **beta receptor.** [1960–65]

al′pha rhythm′, a pattern of slow brain waves (**al′pha waves′**) in normal persons at rest with closed eyes, thought by some to be associated with an alert but daydreaming mind. [1935–40; earlier *alpha waves,* trans. of G *Alphawellen,* term used by their discoverer, German physician Hans Berger (1873–1941)]

al′pha-stan′nic ac′id (al′fə stan′ik, al′-). *Chem.* See under **stannic acid.**

al′pha test′, *Psychol.* a set of mental tests designed to measure the general intelligence of individuals able to read and write, used by the U.S. Army in World War I. Cf. **beta test.**

al·pha·to·coph·e·rol (al′fə tō kof′ə rôl′, -rol′), *n. Biochem.* vitamin E.

al·phit·o·man·cy (al fit′ə man′sē), *n.* the use of barley meal as a means of divination. [1645–55; < Gk *álphito*(*n*) barley + -MANCY, prob. influenced by Gk *alphitómantis* one who divines from barley meal]

Al′phonse and Gas′ton, marked by a ritualistic courtliness in which two often competing participants graciously but stubbornly defer to each other: *a kind of Alphonse and Gaston act in which each man insisted the other go through the doorway first.* Also, **Al′phonse-and-Gas′ton.** [after the title characters of a cartoon strip by American cartoonist Frederick Burr Opper (1857–1937), which first appeared in 1905]

Al·phon·so (al fon′sō, -zō), *n.* a male given name: from Germanic words meaning "noble" and "ready." Also, **Al·phonse** (al′fons, -fonz′; *Fr.* al fôɴs′).

alp·horn (alp′hôrn′), *n.* alpenhorn.

al·pine (al′pīn, -pin), *adj.* **1.** of, pertaining to, on, or part of any lofty mountain. **2.** very high; elevated. **3.** (*cap.*) of, pertaining to, on, or part of the Alps. **4.** *Bot.* growing on mountains above the limit of tree growth: *alpine plants.* **5.** (*often cap.*) of or pertaining to downhill skiing or a competitive downhill skiing event. Cf. **Nordic** (def. 3). **6.** (*cap.*) *Anthropol.* having the features characteristic of an Alpine. —*n.* **7.** (*cap.*) *Anthropol.* a member of a Caucasoid people found in central Europe and characterized by heavy body build, medium complexion, and straight to wavy hair. [1600–10; < L *Alpīnus,* equiv. to *Alp*(*ēs*) (pl.) the ALPS + *-īnus* -INE[1]] —**al′pine·ly,** *adv.*

Al′pine azal′ea, a low, branching shrub, *Loiseleuria procumbens,* of northern regions, having evergreen leaves and clusters of white or pink flowers. [1930–35]

al′pine bis′tort. See under **bistort** (def. 2).

Al′pine combined′, a competition for Alpine skiers in a combination of downhill and slalom races, the winner having the highest total score.

Al′pine cur′rant. See **mountain currant.**

al′pine fir′, a fir, *Abies lasiocarpa,* of the Rocky Mountains, yielding a soft, brittle wood used for making boxes, crates, etc. [1895–1900]

al′pine gar′den, a rock garden. [1940–45]

Al′pine i′bex, an ibex, *Capra ibex,* of the Alps and Apennines, having long, heavy horns with transverse ridges.

al′pine tun′dra, a tundra that is treeless because of high elevation rather than high latitude.

al·pin·ism (al′pə niz′əm), *n.* (*often cap.*) mountain climbing, esp. in the Alps. [1880–85; < F *alpinisme.* See ALPINE, -ISM]

al·pin·ist (al′pə nist), *n.* (*often cap.*) **1.** a mountain climber, esp. in the Alps. **2.** a downhill skier, esp. one engaging in competitive slalom and downhill events. [1880–85; < F *alpiniste.* See ALPINE, -IST]

al·pra·zo·lam (al prā′zə lam′), *n. Pharm.* a potent benzodiazepine, $C_{17}H_{13}ClN_4$, used in the treatment of certain anxiety states. [laboratory coinage of unexplained orig.]

Alps (alps), *n.* (*used with a plural v.*) a mountain range in S Europe, extending from France through Switzerland and Italy into Austria, Slovenia, and Croatia. Highest peak, Mont Blanc, 15,781 ft. (4810 m).

al·read·y (ôl red′ē), *adv.* **1.** by this or that time; previously; prior to or at some specified or implied time: *When we came in, we found they had already arrived.* **2.** now; so soon; so early: *Is it noon already?* **3.** *Informal.* (used as an intensifier to express exasperation or impatience): *Let's go already!* [1350–1400; ME *al redy* ALL READY; what orig. meant "completely (ALL) ready" and modified the subject (*The porter all ready was there*) was taken adverbially as modifying the predicate (*The porter already was there,* meaning "from an earlier time")]

—**Usage.** Although ALREADY and ALL READY are often indistinguishable in speech, the written forms have distinct meanings and uses. The phrase ALL READY means "entirely ready" or "prepared" (*I was all ready to leave on vacation*). ALREADY means "previously" (*The plane had already left the airport*) or "so soon" (*Is it lunchtime already?*).

al·right (ôl rīt′), *adv.* all right.

—**Usage.** The form ALRIGHT as a one-word spelling of the phrase ALL RIGHT in all of its senses probably arose by analogy with such words as *already* and *altogether.* Although ALRIGHT is a common spelling in written dialogue and in other types of informal writing, ALL RIGHT is used in more formal, edited writing.

ALS, See **amyotrophic lateral sclerosis.**

a.l.s., autograph letter, signed.

Al·sace (al sas′, -sās′, al′sas, -sās; *Fr.* al zas′), *n.* a region and former province of France between the Vosges and the Rhine. Ancient, **Alsatia.** Cf. **Alsace-Lorraine.**

Al·sace-Lor·raine (al′sas lô rān′, -lō-, -sās-; *Fr.* al zas lô ren′), *n.* a region in NE France, including the former provinces of Alsace and Lorraine: part of Germany 1871–1919, 1940–45. 3,976,276; 5607 sq. mi. (14,522 sq. km). —**Al′sace-Lor·rain′er,** *n.*

Al·sa·tia (al sā′shə), *n.* **1.** name formerly given to the Whitefriars district in London, England, which was a sanctuary for debtors and lawbreakers. **2.** ancient name of **Alsace.**

Al·sa·tian (al sā′shən), *adj.* **1.** of or pertaining to Alsace or its inhabitants. **2.** of or pertaining to Alsatia. —*n.* **3.** a native or inhabitant of Alsace. **4.** a resident or native of Alsatia. **5.** Also called **Alsa′tian dog′.** *Chiefly Brit.* German shepherd. [1685–95; < ML *Alsati*(*a*) Alsace + -AN]

al′sike clo′ver (al′sīk, -sik, ôl′-), a European clover, *Trifolium hybridum,* having pink flowers, grown in the U.S. for forage. Also called **al′sike.** [1850–55; after *Alsike,* near Uppsala, Sweden]

Al·sip (ôl′sip), *n.* a town in NE Illinois. 17,134.

Al Si·rat (al si rät′), *Islam.* **1.** the correct path of religion. **2.** the bridge, fine as a razor's edge, over which all who enter paradise must pass. [< Ar, equiv. to *al* the + *ṣirāṭ* road < L (*via*) *strāta* paved (way). See STREET]

al·so (ôl′sō), *adv.* **1.** in addition; too; besides; as well: *He was thin, and he was also tall.* **2.** likewise; in the same manner: *Since you're having another cup of coffee, I'll have one also.* —*conj.* **3.** and: *He was mean, also ugly.* [1125–75; ME; OE (*e*)*alswā* ALL (wholly or quite) SO[1]; the meaning ALL SO "wholly" thus implies replication, and therefore "additionally, besides"]

—**Syn. 1.** moreover.

Al·sop (ôl′səp), *n.* **Joseph W(right),** born 1910, U.S. political journalist and writer.

al·so-ran (ôl′sō ran′), *n.* **1.** *Sports.* **a.** (in a race) a contestant who fails to win or to place among the first three finishers. **b.** an athlete or team whose performance in competition is rarely, if ever, a winning or near-winning one. **2.** *Informal.* a person who loses a contest, election, or other competition. **3.** *Informal.* a person who attains little or no success: *For every great artist there are a thousand also-rans.* [1895–1900]

Al·ston (ôl′stən), *n.* a male given name.

alt (alt) *Music.* —*adj.* **1.** high. —*n.* **2.** **in alt,** in the first octave above the treble staff. [1525–35; < Pr < L *altum,* n. use of neut. of *altus* high]

alt-, var. of **alti-** before a vowel: *altazimuth.*

alt., **1.** alteration. **2.** alternate. **3.** altitude. **4.** alto.

Alta., Alberta.

Al·ta·de·na (al′tə dē′nə), *n.* a town in SW California, near Los Angeles. 40,510.

Al·tai (al′tī; *Russ.* ul tī′), *n.* a territory of the Russian Federation in central Asia. 2,675,000; 101,000 sq. mi. (261,700 sq. km). *Cap.:* Barnaul. Also, **Altay.**

Al·tai (al′tī), *n., pl.* **-tais,** (*esp. collectively*) **-tai** for 1. **1.** a member of a grouping of peoples living mainly in the Gorno-Altai Autonomous Region of the Russian Federation. **2.** the Turkic language of the Altai.

Al·ta·ic (al tā′ik), *n.* **1.** the Turkic, Mongolian, and Tungusic language families collectively, spoken over a broad expanse of Eurasia, from southeastern Europe to the Pacific: variously considered to be a single, genetically related family, with Japanese and Korean sometimes also included, or a group of languages with shared typologies and histories, but not genetically akin. —*adj.* **2.** of or belonging to Altaic. **3.** of or pertaining to the Altai Mountains. Also, **Al·ta·ian** (al tā′ən, -tī-). [1825–35; ALTA(I) + -IC]

Al′tai Moun′tains, a mountain range in central Asia, mostly in Mongolia, China, Kazakhstan, and the S Russian Federation. Highest peak, Belukha, 15,157 ft. (4506 m). Also, **Altay Mountains.**

Al·tair (al′târ, -tīᵊr, al târ′, -tīᵊr′), *n.* a first-magnitude star in the constellation Aquila. [< Ar (*al-nasr*) *al-ṭā'ir* (the) flying (eagle)]

Al·ta·mi·ra (al′tə mēr′ə; *Sp.* äl′tä mē′rä), *n.* a cave in northern Spain, near Santander, noted for its Upper Paleolithic polychrome paintings of bison, deer, and pigs.

Al′ta·monte Springs′ (al′tə mont′), a city in central Florida. 22,028.

al·tar (ôl′tər), *n.* **1.** an elevated place or structure, as a mound or platform, at which religious rites are performed or on which sacrifices are offered to gods, ancestors, etc. **2.** *Eccles.* See **communion table.** **3.** (*cap.*) *Astron.* the constellation Ara. **4.** (in a dry dock) a ledge for supporting the feet of shorings. **5.** **lead to the altar,** to marry: *After a five-year courtship, he led her to the altar.* [bef. 1000; ME *alter, altar* (influenced by L), *auter* (< OF *aut*(*i*)*er*), OE *alter* (OE also *altar;* cf. MD *outaer,* OS, ON *altari,* OHG *altāri*) < L *altāria* (pl.), of disputed origin and formation, but prob. akin to L *adolēre* to ritually burn, Umbrian *uřetu* let it burn]

al·tar·age (ôl′tər ij), *n.* **1.** *Eccles.* **a.** offerings made upon an altar of a church. **b.** offerings made to a church. **2.** an honorarium paid to a priest for services at the altar from offerings and gifts. **3.** endowments for the saying of Masses for deceased persons, often at a particular altar. [1350–1400; ME *awterage* < AF, OF *auterage.* See ALTAR, -AGE]

al′tar board′, *Coptic Church.* an elaborately carved wooden panel, placed in a recess on top of an altar during the Mass, on which the chalice and paten rest.

al′tar boy′, acolyte (def. 1). [1765–75]

al′tar bread′, bread for use in a Eucharistic service. [1840–50]

al′tar call′, an evangelist preacher's invitation at the end of the sermon, asking people to come forward to acknowledge a conversion. [1945–50]

al′tar card′, *Rom. Cath. Ch.* one of three cards having certain portions of the Mass printed on them, placed upright on the altar to assist the memory of the celebrant. [1840–50]

al′tar cloth′, a cloth covering for an altar. [1150–1200; ME]

al′tar of repose′, *Rom. Cath. Ch.* a pedestal or niche upon which the sacraments are preserved from Maundy Thursday to Good Friday. [1870–75]

al·tar·piece (ôl′tər pēs′), *n.* a painted or carved screen behind or above the altar or communion table in Christian churches; reredos. [1635–45; ALTAR + PIECE]

al′tar rail′, the rail in front of an altar, separating the sanctuary from those parts of the church that are in front of it. [1855–60]

al′tar stand′. See **missal stand.**

al′tar stone′, mensa. Also called **al′tar slab′.** [1275–1325; ME *awterston*]

al′tar wine′. See **sacramental wine.**

Al·tay (al′tī; *Russ.* ul tī′), *n.* Altai.

Al′tay Moun′tains. See **Altai Mountains.**

alt·az·i·muth (al taz′ə məth), *n. Astron.* an instrument for determining both the altitude and the azimuth of a heavenly body. [1855–60; ALT(ITUDE) + AZIMUTH]

altaz′imuth mount′ing, a mounting with two axes, to allow movement in both horizontal and vertical planes, used with telescopes, antennas, and precise surveying instruments. [1875–80]

Alt·dorf (ält′dôrf′), *n.* a town in and the capital of Uri, in central Switzerland, near Lucerne: legendary home of William Tell. 8600.

Alt·dor·fer (ält′dôr′fər), *n.* **Al·brecht** (äl′brekht), c1480–1538, German painter.

al·ter (ôl′tər), *v.t.* **1.** to make different in some particular, as size, style, course, or the like; modify: *to alter a coat; to alter a will; to alter course.* **2.** to castrate or spay. —*v.i.* **3.** to change; become different or modified. [1350–1400; ME < OF *alterer* < LL *alterāre* to change, worsen, deriv. of L *alter* other] —**al′ter·er,** *n.*

—**Syn. 1.** See **adjust, change.**

Al·ter (ôl′tər), *n.* **David,** 1807–81, U.S. physicist.

alter., alteration.

al·ter·a·ble (ôl′tər ə bəl), *adj.* capable of being altered. [1520–30; ALTER + -ABLE] —**al′ter·a·bil′i·ty, al′ter·a·ble·ness,** *n.* —**al′ter·a·bly,** *adv.*

al·ter·ant (ôl′tər ənt), *adj.* **1.** causing or producing alteration. —*n.* **2.** something that produces alteration. [1620–30; < LL *alterant-* (s. of *alterāns* changing, prp. of *alterāre*), equiv. to *alter* other + *-ant-* -ANT]

al·ter·a·tion (ôl′tə rā′shən), *n.* **1.** the act or process of altering; the state of being altered: *Alteration will improve the dress.* **2.** a change; modification or adjustment: *There has been an alteration in our plans.* [1350–

CONCISE ETYMOLOGY KEY: <, descended or borrowed from; >, whence; b., blend of, blended; c., cognate with; cf., compare; deriv., derivative; equiv., equivalent; imit., imitative; obl., oblique; r., replacing; s., stem; sp., spelling, spelled; resp., respelling, respelled; trans., translation; ?, origin unknown; *, unattested; ‡, probably earlier than. See the full key inside the front cover.

1400; ME *alteracioun* < ML *alterātiōn-* (s. of *alterātiō*). See ALTER, -ATION]

al•ter•a•tive (ôl′tə rā′tiv, -tər ə tiv), *adj.* **1.** tending to alter. **2.** *Med. Obs.* gradually restoring healthy bodily functions. —*n.* **3.** *Med. Obs.* an alterative remedy. [1350–1400; ME < ML *alterātīvus.* See ALTER, -ATIVE]

al•ter•cate (ôl′tər kāt′), *v.i.,* **-cat•ed, -cat•ing.** to argue or quarrel with zeal, heat, or anger; wrangle. [1530–40; < L *altercātus* (ptp. of *altercārī* to quarrel), equiv. to **alterc(us)* a disputing (*alter* other + *-cus* formative suffix) + *-ātus* -ATE[1]]

al•ter•ca•tion (ôl′tər kā′shən), *n.* a heated or angry dispute; noisy argument or controversy. [1350–1400; ME *altercacioun* < L *altercātiōn-* (s. of *altercātiō*). See ALTERCATE, -ION]
—**Syn.** quarrel, disagreement, clash; squabble, tiff.

al′tered chord′, *Music.* a chord in which at least one tone has been changed from its normal pitch in the key.

al′tered state′ of con′sciousness, any modification of the normal state of consciousness or awareness, including drowsiness or sleep and also states created by the use of alcohol, drugs, hypnosis, or techniques of meditation. [1970–75]

al•ter e•go (ôl′tər ē′gō, eg′ō, al′-), **1.** a second self; a perfect substitute or deputy: *His adviser acts as his alter ego during his absence.* **2.** an inseparable friend. **3.** another aspect of one's self. [1530–40; < L (Cicero), prob. trans. of Gk *állos egṓ, héteros egṓ* another I]

al•ter i•dem (äl′ter ē′dem; *Eng.* ôl′tər ī′dem, al′-), *Latin.* another exactly the same.

al•tern (ôl′tərn, al′-), *adj. Archaic.* alternate; following one another. [1635–45; < L *altern(us)* interchangeable, alternating, equiv. to *alter* the other (see ALTER) + *-nus* adj. suffix]

al•ter•nant (ôl′tûr nənt, al′- *or, esp. Brit.,* ôl tûr′nənt, al-), *adj.* **1.** alternating; alternate. —*n.* **2.** *Ling.* a variant form that exists in alternation with another or others. [1630–40; < L *alternant-* (s. of *alternāns,* prp. of *alternāre*). See ALTERN, -ANT]

al•ter•nate (*v.* ôl′tər nāt′, al′-; *adj., n.* ôl′tər nit, al′-), *v.,* **-nat•ed, -nat•ing,** *adj., n.* —*v.i.* **1.** to interchange repeatedly and regularly with one another in time or place; rotate (usually fol. by *with*): *Day alternates with night.* **2.** to change back and forth between conditions, states, actions, etc.: *He alternates between hope and despair.* **3.** to take turns: *My sister and I alternated in doing the dishes.* **4.** *Elect.* to reverse direction or sign periodically. **5.** *Ling.* to occur as a variant in alternation with another form. —*v.t.* **6.** to perform or do in succession or one after another: *to alternate comedy acts; to alternate jogging and walking.* **7.** to interchange successively or regularly: *to alternate hot and cold compresses.* —*adj.* **8.** being in a constant state of succession or rotation; interchanged repeatedly one for another: *Winter and summer are alternate seasons.* **9.** reciprocal; mutual: *alternate acts of kindness.* **10.** every second one of a series: *Read only the alternate lines.* **11.** constituting an alternative: *The alternate route is more scenic.* **12.** alternative (defs. 4, 6). **13.** *Bot.* **a.** placed singly at different heights on the axis, on each side in succession, or at definite angular distances from one another, as leaves. **b.** opposite to the intervals between other organs: *petals alternate with sepals.* —*n.* **14.** a person authorized to fill the position, exercise the duties, etc., of another who is temporarily absent; substitute. **15.** *Theat.* **a.** either of two actors who take turns playing the same role. **b.** an understudy. **16.** alternative. [1505–15; < L *alternātus* (ptp. of *alternāre*). See ALTERN, -ATE[1]] —**al′ter•nate•ly,** *adv.* —**al′ter•nate•ness,** *n.* —**al′ter•nat′ing•ly,** *adv.*

al′ternate an′gles, *Geom.* two nonadjacent angles made by the crossing of two lines by a third line, both angles being either interior or exterior, and being on opposite sides of the third line. [1650–60]

al′ternate host′, *Ecol.* a host, other than the usual or primary host, on which a parasitic organism can sustain itself.

al′ternate plum′age, *Ornith.* (of birds having more than one plumage in their cycle of molts) the plumage of the second molt, usually brighter than the basic plumage.

al′ternate straight′, *Poker.* See **skip straight.**

al′ternating cur′rent, an electric current that reverses direction at regular intervals, having a magnitude that varies continuously in sinusoidal manner. *Abbr.:* ac Cf. **direct current.** [1830–40]

al′ternating group′, *Math.* the subgroup consisting of all even permutations, of the group of all permutations of a finite set. Cf. **symmetric group.** [1905–10]

al′ternating light′, *Navig.* a beacon showing different colors in succession.

al′ternating se′ries, *Math.* a series, usually infinite, in which successive terms have opposite signs, as $1 - \frac{1}{2} + \frac{1}{4} - \frac{1}{8} + \cdots$.

al′ternating volt′age, *Elect.* a voltage that reverses direction in regular cycles.

al•ter•na•tion (ôl′tər nā′shən, al′-), *n.* **1.** the act or process of alternating or the state of being alternated. **2.** alternate succession; repeated rotation: *the alternation of the seasons.* **3.** *Elect.* a single fluctuation in the absolute value of an alternating current or voltage from zero to a maximum and back to zero, being equal to one half cycle. **4.** *Ling.* variation in the form of a linguistic unit as it occurs in different environments or under different conditions, as between the *-ed* and *-en* forms of the past participle in *danced* and *spoken* or between the (t) and (d) pronunciations of the past tense suffix *-ed* in *hopped* and *rubbed.* [1605–15; < LL *alternātiōn-* (s. of *alternātiō*). See ALTERNATE, -ION]

alterna′tion of genera′tions, *Biol.* the alternation in an organism's life cycle of dissimilar reproductive forms, esp. the alternation of sexual with asexual reproduction. [1855–60]

al•ter•na•tive (ôl tûr′nə tiv, al-), *n.* **1.** a choice limited to one of two or more possibilities, as of things, propositions, or courses of action, the selection of which precludes any other possibility: *You have the alternative of riding or walking.* **2.** one of the things, propositions, or courses of action that can be chosen: *The alternative to riding is walking.* **3.** a possible or remaining course or choice: *There was no alternative but to walk.* —*adj.* **4.** affording a choice of two or more things, propositions, or courses of action. **5.** (of two things, propositions, or courses) mutually exclusive so that if one is chosen the other must be rejected: *The alternative possibilities are neutrality and war.* **6.** employing or following nontraditional or unconventional ideas, methods, etc.; existing outside the establishment: *an alternative newspaper; alternative lifestyles.* **7.** *Logic.* (of a proposition) asserting two or more choices, at least one of which is true. Also, **alternate** (for defs. 1–4, 6). [1580–90; ALTERNATE + -IVE] —**al•ter′na•tive•ly,** *adv.* —**al•ter′na•tive•ness, al•ter′na•tiv′i•ty,** *n.*
—**Syn. 1.** option, selection. See **choice.**

alter′native conjunc′tion, *Gram.* a conjunction, as *or,* that expresses an alternative relationship between the words, phrases, or clauses it connects. [1930–35]

alter′native en′ergy, energy, as solar, wind, or nuclear energy, that can replace or supplement traditional fossil-fuel sources, as coal, oil, and natural gas. [1970–75]

alter′native hypoth′esis, (in the statistical testing of a hypothesis) the hypothesis to be accepted if the null hypothesis is rejected.

alter′native ques′tion, *Gram.* a question that offers the listener a choice of two or more alternatives and is characterized by rising intonation on each alternative except for the final one, which has falling intonation, as *Would you like coffee, tea, or soda?*

alter′native school′, any public or private school having a special curriculum, esp. an elementary or secondary school offering a more flexible program of study than a traditional school. [1970–75]

alter′native soci′ety, a society or social group that espouses values different from those of the established social order. [1970–75]

al•ter•na•tor (ôl′tər nā′tər, al′-), *n. Elect.* a generator of alternating current. [1890–95; ALTERNATE + -OR[2]]

Alt•geld (ôlt′geld), *n.* **John Peter,** 1847–1902, U.S. politician, born in Germany: governor of Illinois 1892–96: made controversial decision to pardon those convicted in Haymarket Riot.

Al•thae•a (al thē′ə), *n. Class. Myth.* wife of Oeneus and mother of Toxeus, Tydeus, Meleager, and Deianira.

al•the•a (al thē′ə), *n.* **1.** the rose of Sharon, *Hibiscus syriacus.* **2.** any plant belonging to the genus *Althaea,* of the mallow family, having lobed leaves and showy flowers in a spikelike cluster, including the hollyhocks and marsh mallows. Also, **al•thae′a.** [1660–70; < NL, L *althaea* < Gk *althaía* marsh mallow]

Al•the•a (al thē′ə), *n.* a female given name: from a Greek word meaning "wholesome."

Al•thing (äl′thing, ôl′-), *n.* the parliament of Iceland, consisting of an upper and a lower house. [< ON; see ALL, THING[2]]

al•tho (ôl ŧħō′), *conj. Pron. Spelling.* although.

alt•horn (alt′hôrn′), *n.* a valved brass musical instrument, varying in shape, that is the alto member of the cornet family. Also called **alto horn, mellophone.** [1855–60; ALT + HORN]

al•though (ôl ŧħō′), *conj.* in spite of the fact that; even though; though. [1275–1325; ME *al thogh* ALL (adv.) even + THOUGH]
—**Syn.** notwithstanding (that), even if, albeit (that).

alti-, a combining form with the meaning "high," used in the formation of compound words: *altigram, altitude.* Also, ALTO-; *esp. before a vowel,* **alt-.** [ME < L *alti-* comb. form of *altus* high]

al•ti•graph (al′ti graf′, -gräf′), *n.* an altimeter equipped with a device for recording its measurements on a graph. [ALTI- + -GRAPH]

al•tim•e•ter (al tim′i tər, al′tə mē′tər), *n.* **1.** a sensitive aneroid barometer that is graduated and calibrated, used chiefly in aircraft for finding distance above sea level, terrain, or some other reference point by a comparison of air pressures. **2.** any device used for the same purpose that operates by some other means, as by radio waves. [1820–30; ALTI- + -METER]

al•tim•e•try (al tim′i trē), *n.* the science of measuring altitudes, as by altimeters. [1690–1700; ALTI- + -METRY] —**al•ti•met•ri•cal** (al′tə me′tri kəl), *adj.* —**al′ti•met′ri•cal•ly,** *adv.*

al•ti•plane (al′tə plān′), *n. Geol.* an elevated terrace or plateau sculptured by periglacial geomorphic processes. Also, **altiplano.** [1915–20; alter. of ALTIPLANO under influence of PLANE[1]]

Al•ti•pla•no (al′tə plä′nō; *for 1 also Sp.* äl′tē plä′nô), *n., pl.* **-nos** for 2. **1.** a plateau region in South America, situated in the Andes of Argentina, Bolivia, and Peru. **2.** (*l.c.*) *Geol.* altiplane. [< AmerSp, equiv. to *alti-* ALTI- + Sp *plano* PLAIN[1]]

al•tis•si•mo (al tis′ə mō′; *It.* äl tēs′sē mô′), *Music.* —*adj.* **1.** very high. —*n.* **2. in altissimo,** in the second octave above the treble staff. [1810–20; < It: lit., highest, equiv. to *alt(o)* high + *-issimo* superl. suffix]

al•ti•tude (al′ti to͞od′, -tyo͞od′), *n.* **1.** the height of anything above a given planetary reference plane, esp. above sea level on earth. **2.** extent or distance upward; height. **3.** *Astron.* the angular distance of a heavenly body above the horizon. **4.** *Geom.* **a.** the perpendicular distance from the vertex of a figure to the side opposite the vertex. **b.** the line through the vertex of a figure perpendicular to the base. **5.** Usually, **altitudes.** a high place or region: *mountain altitudes.* **6.** high or important position, rank, etc. [1350–1400; ME < L *altitūdō;* see ALTI-, -TUDE] —**al•ti•tu•di•nous** (al′ti to͞od′n əs, -tyo͞od′-), *adj.*
—**Syn. 1.** elevation. **1, 2.** See **height.** —**Ant. 2.** depth.

al′titude cham′ber, *Aeron.* a chamber for simulating the conditions of air pressure and temperature for a given altitude in order to test the behavior of people and equipment in such an environment. [1930–35]

al′titude di′al, an adjustable sundial utilizing the altitude of the sun, at a given latitude and time of year, as a means of telling the time.

al′titude sick′ness, *Pathol.* a condition affecting some persons at high altitudes, caused by insufficient oxygen in the blood and characterized by dizziness, nausea, and shortness of breath. [1915–20]

al•ti•tu•di•nal (al′ti to͞od′n l, -tyo͞od′-), *adj.* relating to altitude or height. [1770–80; < L *altitūdin-* (s. of *altitūdō*) ALTITUDE + -AL[1]]

al•to (al′tō), *n., pl.* **-tos,** *adj. Music.* —*n.* **1.** the lowest female voice; contralto. **2.** the highest male voice; countertenor. **3.** a singer with such a voice. **4.** a musical part for such a voice. **5.** the second highest of the four parts of a mixed vocal chorus, or the voices or persons singing this part. **6.** the second highest instrument in a family of musical instruments, as the viola in the violin family or the althorn in the cornet family. —*adj.* **7.** of, pertaining to, or having the tonal range of the alto. **8.** (of a musical instrument) second highest in a family of musical instruments: *alto saxophone.* [1775–85; < It < L *altus* high]

alto-, var. of **alti-:** *altostratus.*

al′to clef′, *Music.* a sign locating middle C on the third line of the staff. Also called **viola clef.** See illus. under **clef, C clef.** [1875–80]

al•to•cu•mu•lus (al′tō kyo͞o′myə ləs), *n., pl.* **-lus.** *Meteorol.* a cloud of a class characterized by globular masses or rolls in layers or patches, the individual elements being larger and darker than those of cirrocumulus and smaller than those of stratocumulus: of medium altitude, about 8000–20,000 ft. (2450–6100 m). [1890–95; ALTO- + CUMULUS]

al′to flute′, a large flute pitched a perfect fourth lower than an ordinary flute. [1930–35]

al•to•geth•er (ôl′tə geŧħ′ər, ôl′tə geŧħ′ər), *adv.* **1.** wholly; entirely; completely; quite: *altogether fitting.* **2.** with all or everything included: *The debt amounted altogether to twenty dollars.* **3.** with everything considered; on the whole: *Altogether, I'm glad it's over.* —*n.* **4. in the altogether,** *Informal.* nude: *When the phone rang she had just stepped out of the bathtub and was in the altogether.* [1125–75; var. of ME *altogeder.* See ALL, TOGETHER]
—**Syn. 1.** utterly, totally, absolutely.
—**Usage.** The forms ALTOGETHER and ALL TOGETHER, though often indistinguishable in speech, are distinct in meaning. The adverb ALTOGETHER means "wholly, entirely, completely": *an altogether confused scene.* The phrase ALL TOGETHER means "in a group": *The children were all together in the kitchen.* This ALL can be omitted without seriously affecting the meaning: *The children were together in the kitchen.*

al′to horn′, althorn.

al•to•ist (al′tō ist), *n.* a performer on the alto saxophone. [ALTO + -IST]

Al•ton (ôl′tn), *n.* **1.** a city in SW Illinois. 34,171. **2.** a male given name.

Al•to•na (äl′tō nä), *n.* a metropolitan district of Hamburg, West Germany: formerly an independent city.

Al•too•na (al to͞o′nə), *n.* a city in central Pennsylvania. 57,078.

al•to-re•lie•vo (al′tō ri lē′vō), *n., pl.* **-vos.** See **high relief.** [1710–20; < It *alto rilievo* high relief]

al•to•stra•tus (al′tō strā′təs, -strat′əs), *n., pl.* **-tus.**

CONCISE PRONUNCIATION KEY: act, cāpe, dâre, pärt; set, ēqual; *if,* īce; ox, ōver, ôrder, oil, bo͝ok, bo͞ot, out; up, ûrge; child; sing; shoe; thin, ŧħat; zh as in *treasure.* ə = *a* as in *alone, e* as in *system, i* as in *easily, o* as in *gallop, u* as in *circus;* ᵊ as in *fire* (fīᵊr), *hour* (ouᵊr). l and n can serve as syllabic consonants, as in *cradle* (krād′l), and *button* (but′n). See the full key inside the front cover.

Meteorol. a cloud of a class characterized by a generally uniform gray sheet or layer, lighter in color than nimbostratus and darker than cirrostratus: of medium altitude, about 8000–20,000 ft. (2450–6100 m). [1890–95; ALTO- + STRATUS]

al·tri·cial (al trish′əl), *adj. Zool.* (of an animal species) helpless at birth or hatching and requiring parental care for a period of time (opposed to *precocial.*) [1870–75; < L *altrīc-*, s. of *altrīx* wet nurse, nourisher (*al(ere)* to nourish (cf. ALIMENT) + *-trix* -TRIX) + -AL[1]]

al·tru·ism (al′tro͞o iz′əm), *n.* **1.** the principle or practice of unselfish concern for or devotion to the welfare of others (opposed to *egoism*). **2.** *Animal Behav.* behavior by an animal that may be to its disadvantage but that benefits others of its kind, as a warning cry that reveals the location of the caller to a predator. [1850–55; < F *altruisme,* equiv. to *autru(i)* others (< VL **alterui,* obl. form of L *alter* other (>F *autre*), with *-ui* from *cui* to whom; *-l-* restored from L *alter*) + *-isme* -ISM; popularized through trans. of A. Comte, who perh. coined it, on the model of *égoïsme* EGOISM]

al·tru·ist (al′tro͞o ist), *n.* a person unselfishly concerned for or devoted to the welfare of others (opposed to *egoist*). [1865–70; < F *altruiste;* see ALTRUISM, -IST]

al·tru·is·tic (al′tro͞o is′tik), *adj.* **1.** unselfishly concerned for or devoted to the welfare of others (opposed to *egoistic*). **2.** *Animal Behav.* of or pertaining to behavior by an animal that may be to its disadvantage but that benefits others of its kind, often its close relatives. [1850–55; ALTRU(ISM) + -ISTIC] —**al′tru·is′ti·cal·ly,** *adv.*
—**Syn. 1.** charitable, generous, philanthropic; benevolent, unselfish. —**Ant. 1.** self-centered, selfish, mean.

Al·tus (al′təs), *n.* a city in SW Oklahoma. 23,101.

ALU, *Computers.* arithmetic/logic unit: the part of a central processing unit that performs arithmetic and logical operations.

Al-U·bay·yid (al′o͝o bā′id), *n.* Arabic name of **El Obeid.**

al·u·del (al′yo͝o del′), *n. Chem.* one of a series of pear-shaped vessels of earthenware or glass, open at both ends and fitted one above the other, for recovering the sublimates produced during sublimation. [1550–60; < MF < Sp < Ar *al* the + *uthāl,* var. of *ithāl,* pl. of *athlah* piece of apparatus]

al·u·la (al′yə lə), *n., pl.* **-lae** (-lē′). **1.** Also called **bastard wing, spurious wing.** the group of three to six small, rather stiff feathers growing on the first digit, pollex, or thumb of a bird's wing. **2.** a membranous lobe at the base of each wing of a dipterous insect. [1765–75; < NL, equiv. to L *āl(a)* wing + *-ula* -ULE] —**al′u·lar,** *adj.*

al·um[1] (al′əm), *n. Chem.* **1.** Also called **potash alum, potassium alum.** a crystalline solid, aluminum potassium sulfate, $K_2SO_4 \cdot Al_2(SO_4)_3 \cdot 24H_2O$, used in medicine as an astringent and styptic, in dyeing and tanning, and in many technical processes. **2.** one of a class of double sulfates analogous to the potassium alum, as aluminum ammonium sulfate, having the general formula $R_2SO_4 \cdot X_2(SO_4)_3 \cdot 24H_2O$, where R is a univalent alkali metal or ammonium, and X one of a number of trivalent metals. **3.** (not in technical use) aluminum sulfate. [1275–1325; ME < AF < L *alūmen;* r. OE *alefne, ælifnæ* < OWelsh (cf. MWelsh *elyf*) < L *alūmini-* (s. of *alūmen*)]

a·lum[2] (ə lum′), *n. Informal.* an alumna or alumnus. [by shortening]

alum., *Chem.* aluminum.

alumin-, var. of **alumino-,** esp. before a vowel.

a·lu·mi·na (ə lo͞o′mə nə), *n.* the natural or synthetic oxide of aluminum, Al_2O_3, occurring in nature in a pure crystal form as corundum. Also called **aluminum oxide.** [1780–90; < L *alūmin-*, s. of *alūmen* ALUM[1] + -A[4]]

alu′mina cement′, a quick-setting cement with a large bauxite content.

a·lu·mi·nate (ə lo͞o′mə nit′, -nāt′), *n. Chem.* a salt of the acid form of aluminum hydroxide, containing the group AlO_2^- or AlO_3^{-3}. [1725–35; ALUMIN- + -ATE[2]]

alu′mina trihy′drate, *Chem.* See **aluminum hydroxide.**

a·lu·mi·nif·er·ous (ə lo͞o′mə nif′ər əs), *adj.* containing or yielding aluminum. [ALUMIN- + -I- + -FEROUS]

a·lu·mi·nite (ə lo͞o′mə nīt′), *n.* a mineral, hydrous aluminum sulfate, $Al_2(SO_4)(OH)_4 \cdot 7H_2O$, occurring in white, chalky masses. Also called **websterite.** [1865–70; ALUMIN- + -ITE[1]]

al·u·min·i·um (al′yə min′ē əm), *n., adj. Chiefly Brit.* aluminum.

a·lu·mi·nize (ə lo͞o′mə nīz′), *v.t.,* **-nized, -niz·ing.** to treat with aluminum. Also, *esp. Brit.,* **a·lu′mi·nise′.** [1855–60; ALUMIN- + -IZE] —**a·lu′mi·ni·za′tion,** *n.*

alumino-, a combining form of **aluminum,** used esp. before a consonant: *aluminosilicate.* Also, *esp. before a vowel,* **alumin-.**

a·lu·mi·nog·ra·phy (ə lo͞o′mə nog′rə fē), *n. Print.* algraphy. [1930–35; ALUMINO- + -GRAPHY] —**a·lu·mi·no·graph·ic** (ə lo͞o′mə nə graf′ik), *adj.*

a·lu·mi·no·sil·i·cate (ə lo͞o′mə nō sil′ə kit, -kāt′), *n.* any naturally occurring or synthetically produced aluminum silicate containing alkali-metal or alkaline-earth-metal ions, as a feldspar, zeolite, or beryl. [ALUMINO- + SILICATE]

a·lu·mi·no·ther·my (ə lo͞o′mə nə thûr′mē), *n. Metall.* a process of producing high temperatures by causing finely divided aluminum to react with the oxygen from another metallic oxide. Also, **a·lu′mi·no·ther′mics.** [1910–15; ALUMINO- + -THERMY]

a·lu·mi·nous (ə lo͞o′mə nəs), *adj.* of the nature of or containing alum or alumina. [1535–45; < F *alumineux* or L *alūminōsus;* see ALUM[1], -OUS] —**a·lu·mi·nos·i·ty** (ə lo͞o′mə nos′i tē), *n.*

a·lu·mi·num (ə lo͞o′mə nəm), *n.* **1.** *Chem.* a silver-white metallic element, light in weight, ductile, malleable, and not readily corroded or tarnished, occurring combined in nature in igneous rock, shale, clay, and most soil: used in alloys and for lightweight utensils, castings, airplane parts, etc. *Abbr.:* alum.; *Symbol:* Al; *at. wt.:* 26.98; *at. no.:* 13; *sp. gr.:* 2.70 at 20°C. —*adj.* **2.** of, pertaining to, or containing aluminum: *an aluminum frying pan.* Also, *esp. Brit.,* **aluminium.** [1812; < NL, alter., by Humphry Davy, of *alumium,* which was first proposed; *aluminium* formed after other metals in *-ium.* See ALUMINA, -IUM] —**al·u·min·ic** (al′yə min′ik), *adj.*

alu′minum ac′etate, *Chem.* a compound that in the form of its normal salt, $Al(C_2H_3O_2)_3$, obtained as a white, water-soluble, amorphous powder, is used chiefly in medicine as an astringent and as an antiseptic, and in the form of its basic salt, $Al(C_2H_3O_2)_2OH$, obtained as a white, crystalline, water-insoluble powder, is used chiefly in the textile industry as a waterproofing agent, as a fireproofing agent, and as a mordant.

alu′minum ammo′nium sul′fate, *Chem.* a crystalline solid, $AlNH_4(SO_4)_2 \cdot 12H_2O$, used chiefly as a size in the manufacture of paper; alum. Also called **ammonium alum, ammonia alum.**

alu′minum bo′rate, *Chem.* a white, granular, water-insoluble powder, $2Al_2O_3 \cdot B_2O_3 \cdot 3H_2O$, used chiefly in the manufacture of crown glass.

alu′minum borohy′dride, *Chem.* a volatile liquid, $Al(BH_4)_3$, that ignites spontaneously in air and reacts vigorously with water to form hydrogen, used chiefly in organic synthesis.

alu′minum brass′, an alloy of about 75 percent copper, 2 percent aluminum, small amounts of other elements, and the balance zinc. [1905–10]

alu′minum bronze′, any of several alloys containing a high percentage of copper with from 5 to 11 percent aluminum and varying amounts of iron, nickel, manganese, and other elements. Also called **albronze.** [1870–80]

alu′minum car′bide, *Chem.* a yellow, crystalline solid, Al_4C_3, that reacts with water to form methane.

alu′minum chlo′ride, *Chem.* a yellow-white, crystalline, water-soluble solid that in its white hydrated form, $AlCl_3 \cdot 6H_2O$, is used chiefly as a wood preservative and in its yellow-white anhydrous form, $AlCl_3$, chiefly as a catalyst. [1865–70]

alu′minum fluosil′icate, *Chem.* a white, water-soluble powder, $Al_2(SiF_6)_3$, used in the manufacture of optical glass and of synthetic sapphires and rubies.

alu′minum gly′cin·ate (glī′sə nāt′), *Pharm.* a white, bland-tasting powder, $C_2H_6AlNO_4$, that is used as an antacid. [GLYCINE + -ATE[2]]

alu′minum hydrox′ide, *Chem.* a crystalline, water-insoluble powder, $Al(OH)_3$ or $Al_2O_3 \cdot 3H_2O$, obtained chiefly from bauxite: used in the manufacture of glass, ceramics, and printing inks, in dyeing, and in medicine as an antacid and in the treatment of ulcers. Also called **alumina trihydrate, alu′minum hy′drate, hydrated alumina.** [1870–75]

alu′minum monoste′arate, *Chem.* a white, water-insoluble powder, $Al(OH)_2C_{18}H_{35}O_2$, used as a drier in paints and as a thickener in lubricating oils.

alu′minum ni′trate, *Chem.* a white, crystalline, water-soluble solid, $Al(NO_3)_3 \cdot 9H_2O$, used chiefly as a mordant in dyeing cotton.

alu′minum ox′ide, alumina.

alu′minum sil′icate, any of a group of naturally occurring, water-insoluble substances, obtained from clay or synthesized, containing varying amounts of oxides of aluminum and silicon, Al_2O_3 and Si_2O_3, and used in the manufacture of glass, ceramics, paints, printing inks, rubber, and plastics. Cf. **mullite.**

alu′minum soap′, *Chem.* any of the salts formed by higher carboxylic acids and aluminum, as aluminum oleate, aluminum palmitate, and aluminum stearate.

alu′minum sul′fate, *Chem.* a white, crystalline, water-soluble solid, $Al_2(SO_4)_3$, used chiefly as a water-purifying agent, as a mordant, and as a size in the manufacture of paper. [1865–70]

a·lum·na (ə lum′nə), *n., pl.* **-nae** (-nē, -nī). a woman who is a graduate or former student of a specific school, college, or university. [1880–85, *Amer.;* < L: foster daughter, pupil; fem. of ALUMNUS]
—**Usage.** See **alumnus.**

a·lum·nus (ə lum′nəs), *n., pl.* **-ni** (-nī, -nē). **1.** a graduate or former student of a specific school, college, or university. **2.** a former associate, employee, member, or the like: *He invited all the alumni of the library staff to the party.* [1635–45; < L: foster son, pupil, equiv. to *al-* (s. of *alere* to feed, support) + *-u-* (< stem-vowel **-o-* in interior syllable) + *-m(i)nus,* orig. passive participial suffix (cf. ADULT, OLD), akin to Gk *-menos;* see PHENOMENON]
—**Usage.** ALUMNUS (in Latin a masculine noun) refers to a male graduate or former student; the plural is ALUMNI. An ALUMNA (in Latin a feminine noun) refers to a female graduate or former student; the plural is ALUMNAE. Traditionally, the masculine plural ALUMNI has been used for groups composed of both sexes and is still widely so used: *the alumni of Indiana University.* Sometimes, to avoid any suggestion of sexism, both terms are used for mixed groups: *the alumni/alumnae of Indiana University* or *the alumni and alumnae of Indiana University.* While not quite equivalent in meaning, the terms *graduate* and *graduates* avoid the complexities of the Latin forms and eliminate any need for using a masculine plural form to refer to both sexes.

Al′um Rock′ (al′əm), a town in W central California, near San Jose. 16,890.

al·um·root (al′əm ro͞ot′, -ro͝ot′), *n.* **1.** any of several North American plants belonging to the genus *Heuchera,* of the saxifrage family, esp. *H. americana,* having mottled foliage and greenish-white flowers. **2.** the root of any of these plants, used as an astringent. [1805–15, *Amer.;* ALUM[1] + ROOT[1]]

A·lun·dum (ə lun′dəm), *Trademark.* a brand name for a substance consisting of fused alumina, used chiefly as an abrasive and as a refractory.

al·u·nite (al′yə nīt′), *n.* a mineral, a hydrous sulfate of potassium and aluminum, $KAl_3(SO_4)_2(OH)_6$, commonly occurring in fine-grained masses. Also called **alumstone** (al′əm stōn′). [1865–70; < F *alun* (< L *alūmen* ALUM[1]) + -ITE[1]]

a·lu·no·gen (ə lo͞o′nə jən), *n.* a mineral, hydrous sulfate of aluminum, $Al_2(SO_4)_3 \cdot 18H_2O$, occurring as a white, fibrous crust on quarry or mine walls. [1865–70; < F *alun* (see ALUNITE) + -O- + -GEN]

al·ure (al′yo͝or, -yər), *n.* a passageway, as the walk along one side of a cloister. Also, **allure.** [1250–1300; ME, also *al(o)ur* < OF *aleure* passage, equiv. to *ale* walk (see ALLEY[1]) + *-ure* -URE]

al·u·ta·ceous (al′yə tā′shəs), *adj.* **1.** *Zool.* covered with minute cracks or wrinkles and having a pale, leathery-brown color. **2.** having the color of soft brown leather. [1870–75; < LL *alūtācius,* equiv. to L *alūt(a)* leather softened with alum + *-ācius* -ACIOUS (altered to -ACEOUS); L *alūta* appears to be a ptp. (*alū-* + *-ta,* fem. of *-tus*) akin to *alū-* in *alūmen* ALUM[1]]

al-'Uz·za (äl o͞oz′zä), *n.* a pre-Islamic Arabian goddess personifying the planet Venus and considered to be a daughter of Allah.

Al·va (al′və; *Sp.* äl′vä), *n.* **1.** Also, **Alba. Fer·nan·do Al·va·rez de To·le·do** (fer nän′dô äl′vä reth′ the tô le′thô), **Duke of,** 1508–82, Spanish general who suppressed a Protestant rebellion in the Netherlands in 1567. **2.** a male or female given name.

Al·var (äl′vär), *n.* (*sometimes l.c.*) *Hinduism.* (in southern India) a holy person of the Vaishnava sect. [< Tamil *āḻvār,* deriv. of *āṛ-* sink, be absorbed (as in contemplation)]

Al·va·ra·do (äl′vä rä′thô), *n.* **1. A·lon·so de** (ä lôn′sô the), c1490–1554, Spanish soldier in the conquests of Mexico and Peru: governor of Cuzco 1552?–54. **2. Pe·dro de** (pe′thrô the), 1495–1541, Spanish soldier: chief aide of Cortés in conquest of Mexico; governor of Guatemala 1530–34.

Al·va·rez (al′və rez′), *n.* **Luis Walter,** born 1911, U.S. physicist: Nobel prize 1968.

Ál·va·rez Quin·te·ro (äl′vä reth′ kēn te′rô), **Joaquín** (hwä kēn′), 1873–1944, and his brother **Se·ra·fín** (se′rä fēn′), 1871–1938, Spanish dramatists and coauthors.

Al·va·ro (äl vä′rô), *n.* **Cor·ra·do** (kôr rä′dô), c1890–1956, Italian journalist and novelist.

al·ve·at·ed (al′vē ā′tid), *adj.* having the vaulted shape of a beehive. [1615–25; < L *alveāt(us)* (equiv. to *alve(us)* concave vessel, trough (*alv(us)* belly + *-eus* n. suffix) + *-ātus* -ATE[1]) + -ED[2]]

alveol-, var. of **alveolo-** before a vowel: *alveolectomy.*

al·ve·o·la (al vē′ə lə), *n., pl.* **-lae** (-lē′). *Bot., Zool.* **1.** a small cavity, cell, or pit on the surface of an organ. **2.** an alveolus. [< NL; L *alveolus;* see ALVEOLUS]

al·ve·o·lar (al vē′ə lər), *adj.* **1.** *Anat., Zool.* of or pertaining to an alveolus or to alveoli. **2.** *Phonet.* articulated with the tongue touching or close to the alveolar ridge, as English *t, d, n;* gingival. —*n.* **3.** *Phonet.* an alveolar sound. [1790–1800; ALVEOL- + -AR[1]] —**al·ve′o·lar·ly,** *adv.*

alve′olar arch′, the part of the upper or lower jawbone in which the teeth are set. [1895–1900]

alve′olar ridge′, the ridgelike border of the upper and lower jaws containing the sockets of the teeth. Also called **alve′olar proc′ess.** See diag. under **mouth.**

al·ve·o·late (al vē′ə lit, -lāt′), *adj.* having alveoli; deeply pitted, as a honeycomb. Also, **al·ve′o·lat′ed.** [1830–40; < L *alveolātus.* See ALVEOLUS, -ATE[1]] —**al·ve′o·la′tion,** *n.*

alveolo-, a combining form of **alveolus:** *alveolopalatal.* Also, *esp. before a vowel,* **alveol-.**

al·ve·o·lus (al vē′ə ləs), *n., pl.* **-li** (-lī′). **1.** a little cavity, pit, or cell, as a cell of a honeycomb. **2.** an air cell of the lungs, formed by the terminal dilation of tiny air passageways. **3.** one of the terminal secretory units of a racemose gland. **4.** the socket within the jawbone in which the root or roots of a tooth are set. [1700–10; < L, equiv. to *alve(us)* concave vessel + *-olus* -OLE[1]]

al·ve·o·pal·a·tal (al′vē ō pal′ə tl), *Phonet.* —*adj.* **1.** articulated with the blade or front of the tongue approaching or touching the front of the hard palate near its junction with the alveolar ridge; having a primary palatal articulation and a secondary alveolar articulation. —*n.* **2.** an alveopalatal sound. Also, **al·ve·o·lo·pal·a·tal** (al vē′ə lō pal′ə tl). [1940–45; shortening of *alveolopalatal,* equiv. to ALVEOLO- + PALATAL]

Al·vin (al′vin), *n.* **1.** a town in S Texas. 16,515. **2.** a male given name: from Old English words meaning "elf" and "friend."

al·vine (al′vin, -vīn), *adj. Med. Obs.* of or pertaining to the belly; intestinal. [1745–55; < L *alvīnus,* equiv. to *alv(us)* belly + *-īnus* -INE[1]]

Al·vi·ra (al vī′rə, -vēr′ə), *n.* a female given name, form of **Elvira.** Also, **Al·ve·ra** (al vēr′ə).

al·way (ôl′wā), *adv. Archaic.* always. [bef. 900; ME *allwaye, alle wey;* OE *ealneweg,* equiv. to *ealne* (acc. sing. masc. of *eal* ALL) + *weg* WAY; the acc. denoted duration]

al·ways (ôl′wāz, -wēz), *adv.* **1.** every time; on every occasion; without exception: *He always works on Saturday.* **2.** all the time; continuously; uninterruptedly:

CONCISE ETYMOLOGY KEY: <, descended or borrowed from; >, whence; b., blend of, blended; c., cognate with; cf., compare; deriv., derivative; equiv., equivalent; imit., imitative; obl., oblique; r., replacing; s., stem; sp., spelling, spelled; resp., respelling, respelled; trans., translation; ?, origin unknown; *, unattested; ‡, probably earlier than. See the full key inside the front cover.

There is always some pollution in the air. **3.** forever: *Will you always love me?* **4.** in any event; at any time; if necessary: *She can always move back with her parents.* [1200–50; ME *alwayes, alleweyes, alles weis,* gen. (denoting distribution; cf. ONCE) of *all wei; alle-* lost its gen. ending and was treated as a compounding element under influence of *alle wey* ALWAY. See ALL, WAY, ALWAY, -S[1]]
—Syn. 1. regularly, invariably, consistently. **2, 3.** perpetually, everlastingly, continuously. Both ALWAYS and EVER refer to uniform or perpetual continuance. ALWAYS often expresses or implies repetition as producing the uniformity or continuance: *The sun always rises in the east.* EVER implies an unchanging sameness throughout: *Natural law is ever to be reckoned with.*

Al•win (al′win), *n.* a male given name. Also, **Al′wyn.**

al•wite (ôl′wīt), *adj. Armor.* white (def. 14).

Al•y•at•tes (al′ē at′ēz), *n.* king of Lydia c617–560 B.C.

Al•yce (al′is), *n.* a female given name.

Al′yce clo′ver, a plant, *Alysicarpus vaginalis,* of the legume family, native to central Asia and grown in warm regions as forage. [1940–45; prob. by folk etym. from NL *Alysicarpus* the genus name, equiv. to Gk *(h)alysi-* (comb. form of *hálysis* chain) + Gk *-karpos* -CARPOUS]

Al•y•son (al′ə sən), *n.* a female given name, form of **Alice.**

a•lys•sum (ə lis′əm), *n.* **1.** any of various plants belonging to the genus *Alyssum,* of the mustard family, having clusters of small yellow or white flowers. **2.** any of several related plants of the genus *Aurinia,* as *A. saxatilis,* a widely cultivated species with yellow flowers. **3.** See **sweet alyssum.** [1545–55; < NL; L *alysson* < Gk, neut. of *ályssos* curing (canine) madness, equiv. to *a-* A-[6] + *lýss(a)* madness + *-os* adj. suffix]

Alz′hei•mer's disease′ (älts′hī mərz, alts′-, ôlts′-), *Pathol.* a common form of dementia of unknown cause, usually beginning in late middle age, characterized by memory lapses, confusion, emotional instability, and progressive loss of mental ability. [named after Alois *Alzheimer* (1864–1915), German neurologist, who described it in 1907]

am (am; *unstressed* əm, m), *v.* 1st pers. sing. pres. indic. of **be.** [before 900; ME; OE *am, eam, eom;* c. Goth *im,* ON, Armenian *em,* OIr *am,* Gk *eimí,* Hittite, early Lith *esmi,* OCS *yesmĭ,* Albanian *jam,* Skt *asmi* < IE *Hes- be + *-m 1st pers. sing. + *-i now; cf. IS]

AM, 1. *Electronics.* amplitude modulation: a method of impressing a signal on a radio carrier wave by varying its amplitude. **2.** *Radio.* a system of broadcasting by means of amplitude modulation. **3.** of, pertaining to, or utilizing such a system. Cf. **FM** [1935–40]

Am, *Symbol, Chem.* americium.

Am., 1. America. **2.** American.

A/m, ampere per meter.

A.M., 1. See **a.m. 2.** See **Master of Arts.** [< L *Artium Magister*]

a.m., 1. before noon. **2.** the period from midnight to noon, esp. the period of daylight prior to noon: *Shall we meet Saturday a.m.?* **3.** a morning newspaper, sometimes issued shortly before midnight. Cf. **p.m.** [1755–65; < L *ante merīdiem*]
—Usage. The abbreviation A.M. for Latin *ante meridiem,* meaning "before noon," refers to the period from midnight until noon. One minute before noon is 11:59 a.m. One minute after noon is 12:01 p.m. Many people distinguish between noon and midnight by saying *12 noon* and *12 midnight.* Expressions combining A.M. with morning (*6 a.m. in the morning*) and P.M. with *afternoon, evening,* or *night* (*9 p.m. at night*) are redundant and occur most often in casual speech and writing. Both *a.m.* and *p.m.* sometimes appear in capital letters, especially in printed matter.

a•ma (ä′mä), *n., pl.* **a•mas, a•ma.** a Japanese diver, usually a woman, who tends underwater oyster beds used in the cultivation of pearls. [1945–50; < Japn, of uncert. orig.]

-ama, var. of **-orama,** occurring as the final element in compounds when the first element is a disyllable ending in *-r,* used so that the entire word maintains the same number of syllables as **panorama**: *rollerama; Futurama.*

A.M.A., 1. American Management Association. **2.** American Medical Association. **3.** American Motorcycle Association.

Am•a•belle (am′ə bel′), *n.* a female given name. Also, **Am•a•bel•la** (am′ə bel′ə).

a•ma•dan (ä′mə dôn′), *n. Irish.* fool. [< Ir *amadán,* dim. (with suffix *-án*) of *amaid* a foolish woman < **anmed′* witless (< **an-man-t-i;* cf. MENTAL[1]), crossed with **ameth* (< **ambi-bito-;* cf. OIr *baéth* foolish) very foolish]

am•a•da•vat (am′ə də vat′), *n.* avadavat.

Am•a•dis (am′ə dis), *n. Medieval Romance.* a knight-errant, model of the chivalric hero.

Am′a•dis of Gaul′, (Spanish, *Amadís de Gaula*), a Spanish romance of the second half of the 15th century by García de Montalvo, possibly based on Portuguese and French material of the late medieval period.

A•ma•do (ə mä′dō; *Port.* ä mä′do͞o), *n.* **Jor•ge** (*Port.* zhôʀ′zhə), born 1912, Brazilian novelist.

A•ma•dor Guer•re•ro (ä′mä thôʀ′ geʀ ʀe′ʀô), **Ma•nuel** (mä nwel′), 1833–1909, Panamanian political leader: first president of Panama 1904–08.

am•a•dou (am′ə do͞o′), *n.* a spongy substance prepared from fungi, *Polyporus* (*Fomes*) *fomentarius* and allied species, growing on trees, used as tinder and in surgery. [1805–15; < F, MF, appar. n. deriv. of *amadouer* to coax, influence by flattery. v. deriv. of Pr, OPr *amadou(r)* lover < L *amātōr-,* s. of *amātor* (see AMATEUR); name is usually explained by the conventional assoc. between love and highly combustible substances]

A•ma•ga•sa•ki (ä′mä gä sä′kē), *n.* a city on SW Honshu, in S Japan. 523,657.

a•mah (ä′mə, am′ə), *n.* (in India and the Far East) **1.** a baby's nurse, esp. a wet nurse. **2.** a female servant; maid. [1830–40; < Pg *ama* nurse, governess < ML *amma* wet nurse, perh. alter. of L *mamma* breast]

a•main (ə mān′), *adv. Archaic.* **1.** with full force. **2.** at full speed. **3.** suddenly; hastily. **4.** exceedingly; greatly. [1530–40; A-[1] + MAIN[1]]

a•ma•ki•hi (ä′mä kē′hē), *n., pl.* **-his.** a small Hawaiian honeycreeper, *Hemignathus virens,* having mainly olive-green plumage above with a dark mark extending from the eye to the beak. [< Hawaiian *'amakihi*]

amal., 1. amalgamate. **2.** amalgamated. Also, **amalg.**

a•ma•la•ka (ä mul′ə kə), *n.* (in Hindu architecture) the bulbous finial of a sikhara. [< Skt *āmalaka* the myrobalan tree]

Am•a•lek (am′ə lek′), *n.* **1.** the son of Eliphaz and grandson of Esau. Gen. 36:12; I Chron. 1:36. **2.** a nomadic tribe or nation descended from Amalek and hostile to Israel. Num. 24:20.

Am•a•lek•ite (am′ə lek′it, ə mal′i kīt′), *n., pl.* **-ites,** (*esp. collectively*) **-ite,** *adj.* —*n.* **1.** a member of the tribe of Amalek. Gen. 36:12. —*adj.* **2.** of or pertaining to the Amalekites. [< Heb *'ămālēq* AMALEK + -ITE[1]]

a•mal•gam (ə mal′gəm), *n.* **1.** an alloy of mercury with another metal or metals. **2.** an alloy that consists chiefly of silver mixed with mercury and variable amounts of other metals and is used as a dental filling. **3.** a rare mineral, an alloy of silver and mercury, occurring as silver-white crystals or grains. **4.** a mixture or combination: *His character is a strange amalgam of contradictory traits.* [1425–75; late ME *amalgam(e)* < MF < ML < dial. Ar *al* the + *malgham* < Gk *málagma* softening agent, equiv. to *malak-* (s. of *malássein* to soften) + *-ma* n. suffix]

a•mal•ga•mate (ə mal′gə māt′), *v.,* **-mat•ed, -mat•ing.** —*v.t.* **1.** to mix or merge so as to make a combination; blend; unite; combine: *to amalgamate two companies.* **2.** *Metall.* to mix or alloy (a metal) with mercury. —*v.i.* **3.** to combine, unite, merge, or coalesce. **4.** to blend with another metal, as mercury. [1635–45; AMALGAM + -ATE[1]] **—a•mal′ga•ma•ble,** *adj.* **—a•mal′ga•ma′tive,** *adj.* **—a•mal′ga•ma′tor,** *n.*
—Syn. 1. mingle, commingle, unify. **—Ant. 1.** separate, part, divide.

a•mal•ga•ma•tion (ə mal′gə mā′shən), *n.* **1.** the act or process of amalgamating. **2.** the state or result of being amalgamated. **3.** *Com.* a consolidation of two or more corporations. **4.** *Metall.* the extraction of precious metals from their ores by treatment with mercury. [1605–15; AMALGAM + -ATION]

amal′gam gild′ing. See **fire gilding.**

A•mal•ia (ə māl′yə, am′ə lē′ə), *n.* a female given name.

Am•al•thae•a (am′əl thē′ə), *n. Class. Myth.* a nymph who brought up the infant Zeus on the milk of a goat: in some versions she is the goat rather than a nymph. Also, **Amalthea.**

Am•al•the•a (am′əl thē′ə), **1.** *Class. Myth.* Amalthaea. **2.** *Astron.* a small natural satellite of the planet Jupiter.

A•man (ā′mən), *n. Douay Bible.* Haman.

A•man′a Church′ Soci′ety (ə man′ə), a religious group founded in Germany in 1714, moved to New York State in 1843, and then to Iowa in 1855, where its villages have flourished as cooperative corporations since 1932.

A•man•da (ə man′də), *n.* a female given name: from a Latin word meaning "beloved."

a•man•dine (ä′mən dēn′, am′ən-), *adj.* (of food) served or prepared with almonds: *trout amandine.* [1835–45; < F; see ALMOND, -INE[2]]

am•a•ni•ta (am′ə nī′tə, -nē′-), *n.* any agaricaceous fungus of the genus *Amanita,* comprised chiefly of poisonous species. [1821; < NL < Gk *amānîtai* (pl.) kind of fungi]

A•man•ite (ə man′īt), *n.* a member of the Amana Church Society. [AMAN(A CHURCH SOCIETY) + -ITE[1]]

a•man•ta•dine (ə man′tə dēn′), *n. Pharm.* a water-soluble crystalline substance, $C_{10}H_{17}NHCl$, used as an antiviral and antiparkinsonian drug. [1960–65; coinage appar. based on the chemical name *1-aminoadamantane;* see AMINO-, ADAMANTANE]

a•man•u•en•sis (ə man′yo͞o en′sis), *n., pl.* **-ses** (-sēz). a person employed to write what another dictates or to copy what has been written by another; secretary. [1610–20; < L (*servus*) *āmanuēnsis,* equiv. to *ā-* A-[4] + *manu-,* s. of *manus* hand + *-ēnsis* -ENSIS]

A•ma•pá (ä′mä pä′), *n.* a federal territory in N Brazil. 175,634; 51,177 sq. mi. (132,550 sq. km). *Cap.:* Macapá.

am•a•ranth (am′ə ranth′), *n.* **1.** an imaginary, undying flower. **2.** any plant of the genus *Amaranthus,* some species of which are cultivated as food and some for their showy flower clusters or foliage. Cf. **amaranth family. 3.** *Chem.* a purplish-red, water-soluble powder, $C_{20}H_{11}N_2O_{10}Na_3$, an azo dye used chiefly to color pharmaceuticals, food, and garments. **4.** purpleheart. [1545–55; < L *amarantus,* alter. of Gk *amáranton* unfading flower, n. use of neut. sing. of *amárantos,* equiv. to *a-* A-[6] + *maran-* (s. of *maraínein* to fade) + *-tos* verbal adj. suffix; *-th-* < Gk *ánthos* flower]

am•a•ran•tha•ceous (am′ə ran thā′shəs), *adj.* belonging to the plant family Amaranthaceae. Cf. **amaranth family.** [1830–40; < NL *Amaranthace(ae)* (*Amaranth(us)* AMARANTH + *-aceae* -ACEAE) + -OUS]

am′aranth fam′ily, the plant family Amaranthaceae, typified by herbaceous, often weedy plants having alternate or opposite leaves and small, chaffy flowers without petals in brightly colored dense clusters, including the cockscomb, pigweed, and amaranth.

am•a•ran•thine (am′ə ran′thin, -thīn), *adj.* **1.** of or like the amaranth. **2.** unfading; everlasting: *a woman of amaranthine loveliness.* **3.** of purplish-red color. [1660–70; AMARANTH + -INE[1]]

am•a•relle (am′ə rel′), *n.* any variety of the sour cherry, *Prunus cerasus,* having colorless juice. [< G < ML *amārellum,* equiv. to L *amār(us)* bitter + *-ellum* -ELLE]

am•a•ret•to (am′ə ret′ō, ä′mə-), *n.* an Italian liqueur with a slightly bitter almond flavor. [1975–80; < It, dim. of *amaro* bitter < L *amārus*]

Am•a•ril•lo (am′ə ril′ō), *n.* a city in NW Texas. 149,230.

A•mar•na (ə mär′nə), *adj.* (*sometimes l.c.*) of or pertaining to the period in ancient Egyptian history described on cuneiform tablets (**Amar′na tab′lets**) that were found in 1887 at Tell el Amarna and contain the correspondence (**Amar′na let′ters**) from neighboring kings and governors to Amenhotep IV and his father Amenhotep III.

am•a•ryl•li•da•ceous (am′ə ril′i dā′shəs), *adj.* belonging to the plant family Amaryllidaceae. Cf. **amaryllis family.** [1830–40; < NL *Amaryllidace(ae)* (*amaryllid-,* s. of *amaryllis* AMARYLLIS + *-aceae* -ACEAE) + -OUS]

am•a•ryl•lis (am′ə ril′is), *n.* **1.** any of several bulbous plants of the genus *Hippeastrum,* esp. *H. puniceum,* which has large red or pink flowers and is popular as a houseplant. Cf. **amaryllis family. 2.** Also called **belladonna lily, naked lady.** a related plant, *Amaryllis belladonna,* having clusters of usually rose-colored flowers. **3.** any of several other similar or related plants. **4.** (*cap.*) a shepherdess or country girl, esp. in classical and later pastoral poetry. [1785–95; < L: name of a shepherdess in Vergil's *Eclogues*]

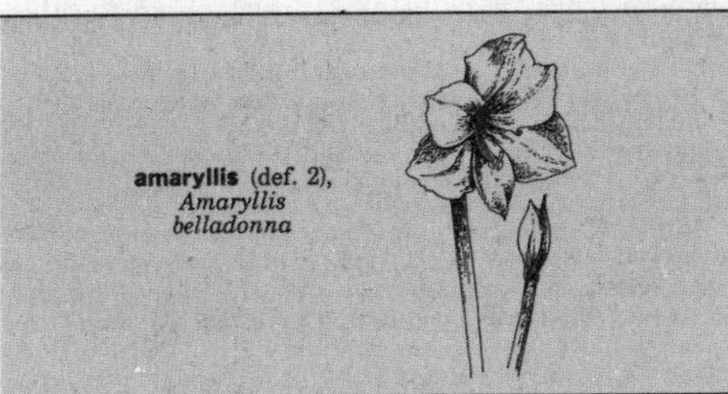
amaryllis (def. 2), *Amaryllis belladonna*

Am•a•ryl•lis (am′ə ril′is), *n.* a female given name.

amaryl′lis fam′ily, the plant family Amaryllidaceae, typified by herbaceous plants having alternate or basal lance-shaped leaves, bulbs or corms, and showy, lilylike flowers and including the amaryllis, daffodil, onion and its relatives, and snowdrop.

A•mar•yn•ceus (ə mar′in syo͞os′), *n.* (in the *Iliad*) a king of Messene who ruled Elis with Augeas and who was slain by Nestor in a war against the Pylians.

A•ma•sa (ə mā′sə, am′ə sə), *n.* the commander of Absalom's army and later of David's army. II Sam. 17:25; 19:13.

Am•a•si•as (am′ə sī′əs), *n. Douay Bible.* Amaziah.

a•mass (ə mas′), *v.t.* **1.** to gather for oneself; collect as one's own: *to amass a huge amount of money.* **2.** to collect into a mass or pile; gather: *He amassed his papers for his memoirs.* —*v.i.* **3.** to come together; assemble: *crowds amassing for the parade.* [1475–85; < F *amasser,* equiv. to *a-* A-[5] + *masse* MASS + *-er* inf. suffix] **—a•mass′a•ble,** *adj.* **—a•mass′er,** *n.* **—a•mass′ment,** *n.*
—Syn. 1. accumulate. **2.** assemble, aggregate.

A•ma•ta (ə mā′tə), *n. Rom. Legend.* the mother, by Latinus, of Lavinia.

a•mate[1] (ə māt′), *v.t.,* **a•mat•ed, a•mat•ing.** *Archaic.* to dismay; daunt. [1275–1325; ME < MF *amatir,* equiv. to *a-* A-[5] + *matir* to subdue, deriv. of *mat* subdued, dull. See MAT[3]]

a•mate[2] (ə māt′), *v.t.,* **a•mat•ed, a•mat•ing.** *Obs.* to be a mate to. [1590–1600; A-[1] + MATE[1]]

A•ma•te•ra•su (ä′mä te rä′so͞o), *n.* the Japanese Shinto goddess personifying the sun.

am•a•teur (am′ə cho͝or′, -chər, -tər, am′ə tûr′), *n.* **1.** a person who engages in a study, sport, or other activity for pleasure rather than for financial benefit or professional reasons. Cf. **professional. 2.** an athlete who has never competed for payment or for a monetary prize. **3.** a person inexperienced or unskilled in a particular activity: *Hunting lions is not for amateurs.* **4.** a person who admires something; devotee; fan: *an amateur of the cinema.* —*adj.* **5.** characteristic of or engaged in by an amateur; nonprofessional: *an amateur painter; amateur tennis.* [1775–85; < F, MF < L *amātor* lover, equiv. to *amā-* (s. of *amāre* to love) + *-tor* -TOR, replaced by F *-teur* (< L *-tōr-,* obl. s. of *-tor*); see -EUR]
—Syn. 2. nonprofessional. **3.** dilettante, tyro, novice.

am•a•teur•ish (am′ə cho͝or′ish, -chûr′-, -tyo͝or′-, -tûr′-), *adj.* characteristic of an amateur, esp. in having the faults or deficiencies of an amateur; inept: *Though an enthusiastic violinist, he gave an amateurish performance.* [1860–65; AMATEUR + -ISH[1]] **—am′a•teur′ish•ly,** *adv.* **—am′a•teur′ish•ness,** *n.*

am•a•teur•ism (am′ə cho͞o riz′əm, -tyo͞o-, -chə-, -tə-, am′ə tûr′iz əm), *n.* the practice, quality, or character of an amateur or amateurish performance. [1865–70; AMATEUR + -ISM]

am′ateur night′, 1. an entertainment featuring amateur performers, often in competition for prizes. **2.** *In-*

CONCISE PRONUNCIATION KEY: *act, cāpe, dâre, pärt; set, ēqual; if, ice; ox, ōver, ôrder, oil, bo͝ok, bo͞ot, out; up, ûrge; child; sing; shoe; thin, that;* zh as in *treasure.* ə = *a* as in *alone, e* as in *system, i* as in *easily, o* as in *gallop, u* as in *circus;* ᵊ as in *fire* (fīᵊr), *hour* (ouᵊr). l and n can serve as syllabic consonants, as in *cradle* (krād′l), and *button* (but′n). See the full key inside the front cover.

formal. an example of or situation marked by flagrant ineptitude: *Critics say it's been amateur night at the embassy since the new ambassador took over.* Also called **am′ateur hour′.** [1930–35]

Am·a·thi (am′ə thī′), *n. Douay Bible.* Amittai.

A·ma·ti (ä mä′tē), *n.* **1. Ni·co·lò** (nē′kô lô′), 1596–1684, Italian violinmaker, one of a famous family of 16th- and 17th-century violinmakers: teacher of Antonio Stradivari. **2.** a violin made by a member of this family.

am·a·tive (am′ə tiv), *adj.* disposed to love; amorous. [1630–40; < ML *amātīvus,* equiv. to *amāt(us)* (ptp. of *amāre* to love) + *-īvus* -IVE] **—am′a·tive·ly,** *adv.* **—am′a·tive·ness,** *n.*

A·ma·to (ə mä′tō; *It.* ä mä′tô), *n.* **Pa·squa·le** (pə skwä′lē, -lā; *It.* päs kwä′le), 1879–1942, Italian operatic baritone.

am·a·tol (am′ə tôl′, -tol′), *n. Chem.* an explosive mixture of ammonium nitrate and TNT. [1915–20; AM(MONIUM) + connective *-a-* + (TRINITRO)TOL(UENE)]

am·a·to·ry (am′ə tôr′ē, -tōr′ē), *adj.* of or pertaining to lovers or lovemaking; expressive of love: *amatory poems; an amatory look.* Also, **am′a·to′ri·al.** [1590–1600; < L *amātōrius,* equiv. to *amā-* (s. of *amāre* to love) + *-tōrius* -TORY[1]] **—am′a·to′ri·al·ly,** *adv.*

am·a·tun·gu·la (am′ə tung′gyə lə), *n.* See **Natal plum.** [< Zulu *amathungulu,* pl. of *i(li)thungulu* fruit of the Natal plum (or < a cognate Nguni word)]

am·au·ro·sis (am′ô rō′sis), *n.* partial or total loss of sight, esp. in the absence of a gross lesion or injury. [1650–60; < Gk: darkening, hindrance to sight, equiv. to *amaur(ós)* dim, dark + *-ōsis* -OSIS] **—am·au·rot·ic** (am′ô rot′ik), *adj.*

a·maze (ə māz′), *v.,* **a·mazed, a·maz·ing,** *n.* **—*v.t.*** **1.** to overwhelm with surprise or sudden wonder; astonish greatly. **2.** *Obs.* to bewilder; perplex. **—*v.i.*** **3.** to cause amazement: *a new art show that delights and amazes.* **—*n.*** **4.** *Archaic.* amazement. [bef. 1000; ME *amasen,* OE *āmasian* to confuse, stun, astonish. See A-[3], MAZE] **—Syn. 1.** astound, dumfound, stun, flabbergast. See **surprise.**

a·mazed (ə māzd′), *adj.* greatly surprised; astounded; suddenly filled with wonder: *The magician made the dove disappear before our amazed eyes.* [1200–50; ME; see AMAZE, -ED[2]] **—a·maz·ed·ly** (ə mā′zid lē), *adv.* **—a·maz′ed·ness,** *n.*

a·maze·ment (ə māz′mənt), *n.* **1.** overwhelming surprise or astonishment. **2.** *Obs.* **a.** stupefaction; frenzy. **b.** perplexity. **c.** consternation. [1590–1600; AMAZE + -MENT]

Am·a·zi·ah (am′ə zī′ə), *n.* a son and successor of Joash as king of Judah. II Kings 14.

a·maz·ing (ə mā′zing), *adj.* causing great surprise or sudden wonder. [1520–30; AMAZE + -ING[2]] **—a·maz′·ing·ly,** *adv.*

Am·a·zon (am′ə zon′, -zən), *n.* **1.** a river in N South America, flowing E from the Peruvian Andes through N Brazil to the Atlantic Ocean: the largest river in the world in volume of water carried. 3900 mi. (6280 km) long. **2.** *Class. Myth.* one of a race of female warriors said to dwell near the Black Sea. **3.** one of a fabled tribe of female warriors in South America. **4.** (*often l.c.*) a tall, powerful, aggressive woman. **5.** See **Amazon ant. 6.** any of several green parrots of the genus *Amazona,* of tropical America, often kept as pets. [< L *Amazōn* < Gk *Amazṓn,* of obscure orig.]

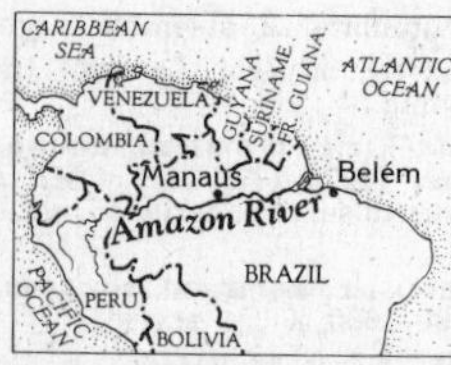

Am′azon ant′, any of several ants of the genus *Polyergus* that raid the nests of other species, carrying off and enslaving the young.

A·ma·zo·nas (am′ə zō′nəs), *n.* a state in NW Brazil. 1,406,354; 601,769 sq. mi. (1,558,582 sq. km). *Cap.:* Manáos.

Am·a·zo·ni·a (am′ə zō′nē ə), *n.* the region around the Amazon, in N South America.

Am·a·zo·ni·an (am′ə zō′nē ən), *adj.* **1.** (of a woman) characteristic of or like an Amazon; powerful and aggressive; warlike. **2.** pertaining to the Amazon River or the country adjacent to it. **—*n.*** **3.** a native or inhabitant of the area adjoining the Amazon River. [1585–95; AMAZON + -IAN]

Am·a·zo·nis (am′ə zō′nis), *n.* an area on the equator of Mars.

am·a·zon·ite (am′ə zə nīt′), *n. Mineral.* a green feldspar, a variety of microcline, used as an ornamental material. Also called **Am′azon stone′.** [1595–1605; AMAZON (river) + -ITE[1]]

Am′azon par′rot, any of several tropical American green parrots of the genus *Amazona,* popular as pets.

Amb., Ambassador. Also, **amb.**

am·ba (am′bə), *n.* anba.

CONCISE ETYMOLOGY KEY: <, descended or borrowed from; >, whence; b., blend of, blended; c., cognate with; cf., compare; deriv., derivative; equiv., equivalent; imit., imitative; obl., oblique; r., replacing; s., stem; sp., spelling, spelled; resp., respelling, respelled; trans., translation; ?, origin unknown; *, unattested; ‡, probably earlier than. See the full key inside the front cover.

am·ba·ges (am bā′jēz), *n. Archaic.* (*used with a plural v.*) winding, roundabout paths or ways. [1350–1400; ME < L *ambāgēs* (pl.) circuits, equiv. to *amb(i)-* AMBI- + *-āg-* (comb. form of *agere* to move) + *-ēs* pl. ending; cf. INDAGATE]

am·ba·gious (am bā′jəs), *adj.* roundabout; circuitous: *ambagious reasoning.* [1650–60; < L *ambāgiōsus,* equiv. to *ambāgi-* (s. of *ambāgēs* AMBAGES) + *-ōsus* -OUS] **—am·ba′gious·ly,** *adv.* **—am·ba′gious·ness,** *n.*

Am·ba·la (əm bä′lə), *n.* a city in N Haryana, in N India. 102,519.

am·ba·rel·la (am′bə rel′ə), *n.* See **Otaheite apple.** [< Sinhalese *æmbarælla* < Skt *āmravāṭaka* a kind of tree]

am·ba·ry (am bär′ē), *n.* kenaf. Also, **am·ba′ri.** [< Deccan Hindi or Marathi *ambāṛī*]

am·bas·sa·dor (am bas′ə dər, -dôr′), *n.* **1.** a diplomatic official of the highest rank, sent by one sovereign or state to another as its resident representative (**ambas′sador extraor′dinary and plenipoten′·tiary**). **2.** a diplomatic official of the highest rank sent by a government to represent it on a temporary mission, as for negotiating a treaty. **3.** a diplomatic official serving as permanent head of a country's mission to the United Nations or some other international organization. **4.** an authorized messenger or representative. *Abbr.:* Amb., amb. [1325–75; ME *am-, embass(i)adour, imbassadore* < AF *ambassateur, ambassaduer* < It *ambassatore,* dial. It *ambassadore,* equiv. to *ambass-* (see EMBASSY) *-atore, -adore* < L *-ātōrem* acc. of *-ātor* -ATOR] **—am·bas·sa·do·ri·al** (am bas′ə dôr′ē əl, -dōr′-), *adj.* **—am·bas′sa·do′ri·al·ly,** *adv.* **—am·bas′·sa·dor·ship′,** *n.*

am·bas·sa·dor-at-large (am bas′ə dər ət lärj′, -dôr′), *n., pl.* **am·bas·sa·dors-at-large.** an ambassador who is not assigned to a particular diplomatic post but is appointed on a special mission. [1905–10]

Ambassadors, The, a novel (1903) by Henry James.

am·bas·sa·dress (am bas′ə dris), *n.* **1.** a woman who is an ambassador. **2.** the wife of an ambassador. [1585–95; AMBASSAD(O)R + -ESS]
—Usage. See **-ess.**

am·batch (am′bach), *n.* an Egyptian tree, *Aeschynomene elaphroxylon,* of the legume family, having a light-colored, spongy wood. [1860–65; perh. < a source akin to Amharic *əmb(w)ac'o,* name for *Rumex alismafolius*]

Am·ba·to (äm bä′tô), *n.* a city in central Ecuador, ab. 8500 ft. (2590 m) above sea level. 77,955.

Am·bed·kar (äm bed′kär), *n.* **Bhim·rao Ram·ji** (bēm′rou räm′jē), 1893–1956, Indian politician and jurist.

am·beer (am′bēr), *n. Chiefly South Midland and Southern U.S.* tobacco juice. [1755–65; *Amer.*; earlier, water soaked in cut tobacco refuse; perh. b. AMBER and BEER, alluding to its color and foaminess]

am·ber (am′bər), *n.* **1.** a pale yellow, sometimes reddish or brownish, fossil resin of vegetable origin, translucent, brittle, and capable of gaining a negative electrical charge by friction and of being an excellent insulator: used for making jewelry and other ornamental articles. **2.** the yellowish-brown color of resin. **—*adj.*** **3.** of the color of amber; yellowish-brown: *amber fields of grain.* **4.** made of amber: *amber earrings.* [1350–1400; ME *ambre* < OF < ML *ambra* < Ar *'anbar* ambergris; confusion of the dissimilar substances perh. because both were rare, valuable, and found on seacoasts] **—am′ber·like′, am′ber·y, am′ber·ous,** *adj.*

Am·ber (am′bər), *n.* a female given name.

am·ber·fish (am′bər fish′), *n., pl.* (*esp. collectively*) **-fish,** (*esp. referring to two or more kinds or species*) **-fish·es.** amberjack. [1665–75; AMBER + FISH]

am·ber·gris (am′bər grēs′, -gris), *n.* an opaque, ash-colored secretion of the sperm whale intestine, usually found floating on the ocean or cast ashore: used in perfumery. [1375–1425; < MF *ambre gris* gray amber (see AMBER); r. late ME *imbergres*]

am·ber·i·na (am′bə rē′nə), *n.* an American art glass having transparent colors ranging from pale amber to ruby. [formerly a trademark]

Am′ber Is′lands, (in ancient geography) a name given by the Greeks in later times to the islands in the North Sea. Cf. **Electrides.**

am·ber·jack (am′bər jak′), *n., pl.* (*esp. collectively*) **-jack,** (*esp. referring to two or more kinds or species*) **-jacks.** any of several yellow to coppery fork-tailed fishes of the genus *Seriola,* as *S. dumerili* of warm Atlantic waters. Also called **amberfish.** [1890–95; AMBER (color) + JACK[1] (kind of fish)]

am·ber·oid (am′bə roid′), *n.* synthetic amber made by compressing pieces of various resins at a high temperature. Also, **ambroid.** [1895–1900; AMBER + -OID]

ambi-, a prefix occurring in loanwords from Latin, meaning "both" (*ambiguous*) and "around" (*ambient*); used in the formation of compound words: *ambitendency.* [< L; akin to Gk *amphí,* Albanian *mbë,* OIr *imb, imb-,* Welsh, OBreton *am, am-* (var. *em-*), Gaulish *amb(i)-* (see EMBASSY), OHG *umbi* (> G *um*), OE *ymb(e)-,* Skt *abhítas* around. Cf. AMPHI-]

am·bi·ance (am′bē əns; *Fr.* äɴ byäɴs′), *n., pl.* **-bi·anc·es** (-bē ən siz; *Fr.* -byäɴs′). **1.** the mood, character, quality, tone, atmosphere, etc., particularly of an environment or milieu: *The restaurant had a delightful ambiance.* **2.** that which surrounds or encompasses; environment. Also, **ambience.** [< F, equiv. to *ambi(ant)* surrounding (MF, also *ambient* < L; see AMBIENT) + *-ance* -ANCE]
—Syn. 1. See **environment.**

am·bi·dex·ter (am′bi dek′stər), *adj.* **1.** *Archaic.* ambidextrous. **—*n.*** **2.** *Obs.* an ambidextrous person. [1525–35; < LL; see AMBI-, DEXTER] **—am′bi·dex′tral,** *adj.*

am·bi·dex·ter·i·ty (am′bi dek ster′i tē), *n.* **1.** ambidextrous ease, skill, or facility. **2.** unusual cleverness. **3.** duplicity; deceitfulness. [1645–55; AMBIDEXTER + -ITY]

am·bi·dex·trous (am′bi dek′strəs), *adj.* **1.** able to use both hands equally well: *an ambidextrous surgeon.* **2.** unusually skillful; facile: *an ambidextrous painter, familiar with all media.* **3.** double-dealing; deceitful. **4.** *Slang.* bisexual. [1640–50; AMBIDEXT(E)R + -OUS] **—am′bi·dex′trous·ly,** *adv.* **—am′bi·dex′trous·ness,** *n.*

am·bi·ence (am′bē əns; *Fr.* äɴ byäɴs′), *n., pl.* **-bi·enc·es** (-bē ən siz; *Fr.* -byäɴs′). ambiance. [1885–90]

am·bi·ent (am′bē ənt), *adj.* **1.** of the surrounding area or environment: *The tape recorder picked up too many ambient noises. The temperature in the display case was 20° lower than the ambient temperature.* **2.** completely surrounding; encompassing: *the ambient air.* [1590–1600; (< MF) < L *ambient-* (s. of *ambiēns,* prp. of *ambīre* to go around), equiv. to *amb-* AMBI- + *-i-* go + *-ent-* -ENT]

am′bient air′ stand′ard, the highest concentration of a specific air pollutant at a particular outdoor location, in a specified unit of time, that is not considered hazardous to humans: *The ambient air standard for gas X is 3 parts per million per hour.* [1970–75]

am·bien·te (äm byen′te), *n. Spanish.* atmosphere; ambiance.

am·bi·gu·i·ty (am′bi gyōō′i tē), *n., pl.* **-ties. 1.** doubtfulness or uncertainty of meaning or intention: *to speak with ambiguity; an ambiguity of manner.* **2.** an unclear, indefinite, or equivocal word, expression, meaning, etc.: *a contract free of ambiguities; the ambiguities of modern poetry.* [1375–1425; late ME *ambiguite* < L *ambiguitās,* equiv. to *ambigu(us)* AMBIGUOUS + *-itās* -ITY]

am·big·u·ous (am big′yōō əs), *adj.* **1.** open to or having several possible meanings or interpretations; equivocal: *an ambiguous answer.* **2.** *Ling.* (of an expression) exhibiting constructional homonymity; having two or more structural descriptions, as the sequence *Flying planes can be dangerous.* **3.** of doubtful or uncertain nature; difficult to comprehend, distinguish, or classify: *a rock of ambiguous character.* **4.** lacking clearness or definiteness; obscure; indistinct: *an ambiguous shape; an ambiguous future.* [1520–30; < L *ambiguus,* equiv. to *ambig(ere)* be uncertain (*amb-* AMBI- + *-igere* comb. form of *agere* to drive, lead, act) + *-uus* deverbal adj. suffix; see -OUS] **—am·big′u·ous·ly,** *adv.* **—am·big′u·ous·ness,** *n.*
—Syn. 1. AMBIGUOUS, EQUIVOCAL, CRYPTIC, ENIGMATIC describe conditions or statements not clear in meaning. AMBIGUOUS can refer to a statement, act, or attitude that is capable of two or more often contradictory interpretations, usually accidentally or unintentionally so: *an ambiguous passage in the preamble.* EQUIVOCAL, usually applied to spoken as well as written language, also means susceptible of two or more interpretations, and it usually suggests a deliberate intent to mislead by avoiding clarity: *saving face with an equivocal response to an embarrassing question.* CRYPTIC usually refers to intentional obscurity, especially in language, and often implies a private or hidden meaning but stresses resultant mystification or puzzlement: *a cryptic remark that left us struggling to interpret his intention.* ENIGMATIC focuses on perplexity resulting from a mysterious or imponderable event or utterance, often one of great importance or deep significance: *prophetic texts so enigmatic that their meaning has been disputed for centuries.*

am·bi·lat·er·al (am′bi lat′ər əl), *adj.* of, pertaining to, or affecting both sides. [AMBI- + LATERAL] **—am′bi·lat′er·al′i·ty,** *n.* **—am′bi·lat′er·al·ly,** *adv.*

am·bi·sex·trous (am′bi sek′strəs), *adj.* **1.** *Informal.* **a.** sexually attracted to both sexes; bisexual. **b.** used by or suitable for either sex; unisex: *ambisextrous hair styles.* **2.** held in common by both sexes, esp. sexual characteristics. [1965–70; b. SEX and AMBIDEXTROUS]

am·bi·sex·u·al (am′bi sek′shōō əl), *adj., n.* bisexual (defs. 2, 4). [1935–40; AMBI- + SEXUAL] **—am′bi·sex′u·al′i·ty,** *n.*

am·bi·sin·is·ter (am′bi sin′ə stər), *adj.* clumsy or unskillful with both hands. Also, **am·bi·sin·is·trous** (am′bi·sin′is trəs, -bē si nis′trəs). [AMBI- + SINISTER]

am·bi·son·ics (am′bi son′iks), *n.* (*used with a sing. v.*) a system of sound reproduction that uses a combination of channels and speakers to produce an effect of surrounding the listener with the sound. [1970–75; AMBI- + SON(IC) + -ICS] **—am′bi·son′ic,** *adj.*

am·bi·syl·lab·ic (am′bē si lab′ik), *adj. Phonet.* (of a single speech sound or cluster) shared phonetically by two contiguous syllables, as the single *n*-sound of *any* or the *pl*-cluster of *grappling.* [AMBI- + SYLLABIC]

am·bit (am′bit), *n.* **1.** circumference; circuit. **2.** boundary; limit. **3.** a sphere of operation or influence; range; scope: *the ambit of such an action.* [1350–1400; ME < L *ambitus* a going around, equiv. to *amb-* AMBI- + *itus* a going (*i-* (s. of *ire* to go) + *-tus* suffix of v. action)]

am·bi·tend·en·cy (am′bi ten′dən sē), *n., pl.* **-cies.** *Psychol.* ambivalence, esp. when acted out; a tendency to contradictory behavior arising from conflicting impulses. [AMBI- + TENDENCY]

am·bi·tion (am bish′ən), *n.* **1.** an earnest desire for some type of achievement or distinction, as power, honor, fame, or wealth, and the willingness to strive for its attainment: *Too much ambition caused him to be disliked by his colleagues.* **2.** the object, state, or result desired or sought after: *The crown was his ambition.* **3.** desire for work or activity; energy: *I awoke feeling tired and utterly lacking in ambition.* **—*v.t.*** **4.** to seek after earnestly; aspire to. [1300–50; ME *ambicio(u)n* (< MF) < L *ambitiōn-* (s. of *ambitiō*), equiv. to *amb-* AMBI- + *-i-* go + *-t-* ptp. suffix + *-iōn-* -ION] **—am·bi′tion·less,** *adj.* **—am·bi′tion·less·ly,** *adv.*
—Syn. 1. aspiration, yearning, longing. **2.** goal, aim. **3.** drive, force.

am•bi•tious (am bish′əs), *adj.* **1.** having ambition; eagerly desirous of achieving or obtaining success, power, wealth, a specific goal, etc.: *ambitious students.* **2.** showing or caused by ambition: *an ambitious attempt to break the record.* **3.** strongly desirous; eager: *ambitious of love and approval.* **4.** requiring exceptional effort, ability, etc.: *an ambitious program for eliminating all slums.* [1350–1400; ME < L *ambitiōsus,* equiv. to *ambiti(ō)* AMBITION + *-ōsus* -OUS] **—am•bi′tious•ly,** *adv.* **—am•bi′tious•ness,** *n.*
—Syn. 1. AMBITIOUS, ASPIRING, ENTERPRISING describe a person who wishes to rise above his or her present position or condition. The AMBITIOUS person wishes to attain worldly success, and puts forth effort toward this end: *ambitious for social position.* The ENTERPRISING person, interested especially in wealth, is characterized by energy and daring in undertaking projects. The ASPIRING person wishes to rise (mentally or spiritually) to a higher level or plane, or to attain some end above ordinary expectations. **—Ant. 1.** apathetic, lackadaisical.

am•biv•a•lence (am biv′ə ləns), *n.* **1.** uncertainty or fluctuation, esp. when caused by inability to make a choice or by a simultaneous desire to say or do two opposite or conflicting things. **2.** *Psychol.* the coexistence within an individual of positive and negative feelings toward the same person, object, or action, simultaneously drawing him or her in opposite directions. Also, **am•biv′a•len•cy.** [1910–15; AMBI- + VALENCE] **—am•biv′•a•lent,** *adj.* **—am•biv′a•lent•ly,** *adv.*

am•bi•ver•sion (am′bi vûr′zhən, -shən, am′bi vûr′-), *n. Psychol.* a state intermediate between extroversion and introversion. [1925–30; AMBI- + *-version,* as in EXTROVERSION, INTROVERSION] **—am•bi•ver•sive** (am′bi vûr′siv), *adj.*

am•bi•vert (am′bi vûrt′), *n. Psychol.* one whose personality type is intermediate between extrovert and introvert. [1925–30; AMBI- + *-vert,* as in EXTROVERT, INTROVERT]

am•ble (am′bəl), *v.,* **-bled, -bling,** *n.* **—***v.i.* **1.** to go at a slow, easy pace; stroll; saunter: *He ambled around the town.* **2.** (of a horse) to go at a slow pace with the legs moving in lateral pairs and usually having a four-beat rhythm. **—***n.* **3.** an ambling gait. **4.** a slow, easy walk or gentle pace. **5.** a stroll. [1350–1400; ME < MF *ambler* < L *ambulāre* to walk, equiv. to *amb-* AMBI- + *-ulāre* to step (**-el-* + s. vowel *-ā-*; c. Welsh *el-* may go, Gk *elaúnein* to set in motion)] **—am′bler,** *n.* **—am′•bling•ly,** *adv.*

Am•bler (am′blər), *n.* **Eric,** born 1909, English suspense novelist.

am•blyg•o•nite (am blig′ə nit′), *n.* a mineral, a lithium aluminum fluorophosphate, $Li(AlF)PO_4$: an ore of lithium. [1840–50; < Gk *amblygṓn(ios)* (*amblý(s)* blunt, obtuse + *gōní(a)* angle + *-os* adj. suffix) + -ITE[1]]

am•bly•o•pi•a (am′blē ō′pē ə), *n. Ophthalm.* dimness of sight, without apparent organic defect. [1700–10; < NL < Gk *amblyōpía,* equiv. to *amblý(s)* dull + *-ōpia* -OPIA] **—am•bly•op•ic** (am′blē op′ik), *adj.*

am•bly•o•scope (am′blē ə skōp′), *n.* an instrument used to train an amblyopic eye to function properly. [< Gk *amblý(s)* dull, dim-sighted + -O- + -SCOPE]

am•bly•pod (am′blə pod′), *n.* one of the primitive ungulate mammals of the extinct order Pantodonta, from the Paleocene and Eocene epochs, having a massive body and short legs. [< NL *Amblypoda* < Gk *amblý(s)* blunt + *-poda* -PODA]

am•bo (am′bō), *n., pl.* **-bos.** (in an early Christian church) a raised desk, or either of two such desks, from which the Gospels or Epistles were read or chanted. Also, **ambon.** [1635–45; < ML *ambō(n)* < Gk *ámbōn* edge, rim, pulpit]

am•bo•cep•tor (am′bə sep′tər), *n. Immunol. Now Rare.* hemolysin. [1900–05; < L *ambō* both (akin to AMBI-) + (RE)CEPTOR]

Am•boi•na (am boi′nə), *n.* Ambon.

Amboi′na wood′, 1. the hard, heavy wood of a tree, *Pterocarpus indicus,* of southern Asia, having a curly or mottled grain. **2.** the tree itself. Also, **Amboy′na wood′.** [1860–65]

Am•boise (äN bwäz′), *n.* a town in central France, E of Tours: castle. 11,116.

am•bon (am′bon), *n., pl.* **am•bo•nes** (am bō′nēz). ambo.

Am•bon (äm′bôn), *n.* **1.** an island in the central Moluccas, in E Indonesia. 72,679; 314 sq. mi. (813 sq. km). **2.** a seaport on this island. 56,037. Also, **Amboina.**

Am•bo•nese (am′bə nēz′, -nēs′), *n., pl.* **-nese** for 1, *adj.* **—***n.* **1.** a native or inhabitant of Ambon. **2.** the Austronesian language, having several dialects, spoken by the people of Ambon. **3.** a Malay dialect spoken as a lingua franca in the central Moluccas. **—***adj.* **4.** of or pertaining to Ambon, its people, or their language. Also, **Am•boi•nese** (am′boi nēz′, -nēs′). [1860–65; AMBON + -ESE]

ambrette′ seed′ (am bret′), the seed of the abelmosk. [< F *ambrette.* See AMBER, -ETTE]

am•brette′-seed oil′ (am bret′sēd′), a yellow oil expressed from ambrette seeds, used as a fixative in the manufacture of perfume.

am•bret•to•lide (am bret′l īd′), *n. Chem.* a colorless liquid, $C_{16}H_{28}O_2$, having a strong musky odor, used as a fixative in the manufacture of perfume. [AMBRETTE + -OLE + -IDE]

am•broid (am′broid), *n.* amberoid.

Am•brose (am′brōz), *n.* **1. Saint,** A.D. 340?–397, bishop of Milan 374–397. **2.** a male given name: from a Greek word meaning "immortal."

Am′brose Chan′nel, a ship channel at the entrance to New York harbor, near Sandy Hook. 7½ mi. (12 km) long.

am•bro•sia (am brō′zhə), *n.* **1.** *Class. Myth.* the food of the gods. Cf. **nectar** (def. 3). **2.** something especially delicious to taste or smell. **3.** a fruit dessert made of oranges and shredded coconut and sometimes pineapple. [1545–55; < L < Gk: immortality, food of the gods, n. use of fem. of *ambrósios,* equiv. to *a-* A-[6] + *-mbros-* (comb. form of *brotós* MORTAL; akin to L *mortuus* dead, MURDER) + *-ios* adj. suffix; r. ME *ambrose, ambrosie* < OF *ambroise* < L]

ambro′sia bee′tle. See **bark beetle.** [1895–1900; *ambrosia* in reference to the beetles' food, a coating formed by a fungus which they cultivate]

am•bro•sial (am brō′zhəl), *adj.* **1.** exceptionally pleasing to taste or smell; especially delicious or fragrant. **2.** worthy of the gods; divine. Also, **ambrosian.** [1590–1600; AMBROSI(A) + -AL[1]] **—am•bro′sial•ly,** *adv.*

Am•bro•sian (am brō′zhən), *adj.* **1.** *Rom. Cath. Ch.* **a.** pertaining to the religious congregations under the protection of Saint Ambrose. **b.** pertaining to the ancient liturgy of the church of Milan. **2.** (*l.c.*) ambrosial.

Ambro′sian chant′, the liturgical chant, established by Saint Ambrose, characterized by ornamented, often antiphonal, singing. Also called **Milanese chant.**

am•bro•type (am′brə tīp′), *n. Photog.* an early type of photograph, made by placing a glass negative against a dark background. [1850–55, *Amer.*; < Gk *ámbro(tos)* immortal (see AMBROSIA) + -TYPE]

am•bry (am′brē), *n., pl.* **-bries. 1.** Also called **armarium.** *Eccles.* a recess in the wall of a church or a cupboard in the sacristy where sacred vessels, books, vestments, etc., are kept. **2.** *Chiefly Brit. Dial.* a storeroom, closet, or pantry. **3.** *Obs.* any of various types of closet or cupboard with doors and shelves. Also, **aumbry.** [1200–1250; ME *aumry, almerie, almarie* < OF *aumaire, almarie* < ML *almārium,* dissimilated var. of *armārium* < L. See ARMARIUM]

ambs•ace (āmz′ās′, amz′-), *n. Archaic.* **1.** the lowest throw at dice, the double ace. **2.** bad luck; misfortune. **3.** the smallest amount or distance. Also, **amesace.** [1250–1300; ME *ambes as* < OF < L *ambas* both + *as* unit; see ACE]

am•bu•lac•rum (am′byə lak′rəm, -lā′krəm), *n., pl.* **-lac•ra** (-lak′rə, -lā′krə). one of the radial areas in an echinoderm, as the sea urchin, bearing the tube feet by which the creature moves. [1830–40; < NL, L: alley, walking place, equiv. to *ambulā-* (s. of *ambulāre* to walk) + *-crum* n. suffix denoting means] **—am′bu•lac′ral,** *adj.*

am•bu•lance (am′byə ləns), *n.* **1.** a specially equipped motor vehicle, airplane, ship, etc., for carrying sick or injured people, usually to a hospital. **2.** (formerly) a field hospital. [1800–10; < F, equiv. to (*hôpital*) *ambul(ant)* walking (hospital) + *-ance* -ANCE. See AMBULANT]

am′bulance chas′er, *Disparaging.* a lawyer who seeks accident victims as clients and encourages them to sue for damages. [1895–1900, *Amer.*] **—am′bulance chas′ing.**

am•bu•lant (am′byə lənt), *adj.* **1.** moving from place to place; itinerant; shifting. **2.** *Med.* ambulatory (def. 4). [1645–55; (< F) < L *ambulant-* (s. of *ambulāns,* prp. of *ambulāre* to walk). See AMBLE]

am•bu•lante (am′byə länt′; *Fr.* äN BY läNt′), *n., pl.* **-lantes** (-länts′; *Fr.* -läNt′). a portable tea table, used in 18th-century France. [< F: lit., walking, fem. of *ambulant,* prp. of *ambuler* < L *ambulāre.* See AMBLE]

am•bu•late (am′byə lāt′), *v.i.,* **-lat•ed, -lat•ing.** to walk about or move from place to place. [1615–25; < L *ambulātus* (ptp. of *ambulāre* to walk), equiv. to *ambul-* (see AMBLE) + *-ātus* -ATE[1]] **—am′bu•la′tion,** *n.* **—am′bu•la′tor,** *n.*

am•bu•la•to•ry (am′byə lə tôr′ē, -tōr′ē), *adj., n., pl.* **-ries. —***adj.* **1.** of, pertaining to, or capable of walking: *an ambulatory exploration of the countryside.* **2.** adapted for walking, as the limbs of many animals. **3.** moving about or from place to place; not stationary: *an ambulatory tribe.* **4.** Also, **ambulant.** *Med.* **a.** not confined to bed; able or strong enough to walk: *an ambulatory patient.* **b.** serving patients who are able to walk: *an ambulatory care center.* **5.** *Law.* not fixed; alterable or revocable: *ambulatory will.* **—***n.* **6.** Also called **deambulatory.** *Archit.* **a.** an aisle surrounding the end of the choir or chancel of a church. **b.** the covered walk of a cloister. [1615–25; < L *ambulātōrius,* equiv. to *ambulā-,* s. of *ambulāre* (see AMBLE) + *-tōrius* -TORY[1]] **—am′bu•la•to′ri•ly,** *adv.*

am•bu•lette (am′byə let′), *n.* a specially equipped motor vehicle for transporting convalescing or handicapped people. [1980–85; AMBUL(ANCE) + -ETTE]

am•bus•cade (am′bə skād′, am′bə skād′), *n., v.,* **-cad•ed, -cad•ing. —***n.* **1.** an ambush. **—***v.i.* **2.** to lie in ambush. **—***v.t.* **3.** to attack from a concealed position; ambush. [1575–85; < MF *embuscade,* alter. (under influence of OF *embuschier;* see AMBUSH) of MF *emboscade* < OIt *imboscata,* fem. ptp. of *imboscare,* v. deriv. with *in-* IN-[2] of *bosco* wood, forest < Gmc **bosk-* BUSH[1]] **—am′bus•cad′er,** *n.*

am•bus•ca•do (am′bə skā′dō), *n., pl.* **-dos.** *Obs.* ambuscade. [1585–95; pseudo-Sp alter. of AMBUSCADE]

am•bush (am′bo͝osh), *n.* Also, **am′bush•ment. 1.** an act or instance of lying concealed so as to attack by surprise: *The highwaymen waited in ambush near the road.* **2.** an act or instance of attacking unexpectedly from a concealed position. **3.** the concealed position itself: *They fired from ambush.* **4.** those who attack suddenly and unexpectedly from a concealed position. **—***v.t.* **5.** to attack from ambush. [1250–1300; (v.) ME *enbuss(h)en* < MF *embuschier* to place men in ambush, lit., to set in the woods, equiv. to *em-* IM-[1] + *busch-* (< VL **busca* wood, forest < Gmc **busk-* heavy stick) + *-ier* inf. suffix; (n.) earlier *enbusshe* < MF *embusche,* deriv. of the v.] **—am′bush•er,** *n.* **—am′bush•like′,** *adj.*

am′bush bug′, any of several carnivorous bugs of the family Phymatidae, inhabiting tropical areas in the Americas and Asia, that lie concealed in flowers to prey on insects.

am•bys•to•mid (am bis′tə mid), *n.* **1.** Also called **mole salamander.** any of various small- to moderate-sized salamanders of the genus *Ambystoma,* terrestrial or semiaquatic, inhabiting North America from New England to Florida and westward to Texas. **—***adj.* **2.** of or pertaining to the ambystomids. Cf. **axolotl.** [1940–45; < NL *Ambystom(a)* genus name (*amby-,* prob. erroneous for Gk *amblý(s)* blunt, dull + *-stoma* -STOME) + -ID[2]]

Am•chit•ka (am chit′kə), *n.* an island off the coast of SW Alaska, in the W part of the Aleutian Islands; site of U.S. air base during World War II. 40 mi. (64 km) long.

A.M.D.G., for the greater glory of God: motto of the Jesuits. Also **AMDG** [< L *ad mājōrem Deī glōriam*]

amdt., amendment.

A.M.E., 1. Advanced Master of Education. **2.** African Methodist Episcopal.

a•me•ba (ə mē′bə), *n., pl.* **-bas, -bae** (-bē). **1.** any of numerous freshwater, marine, or parasitic one-celled protozoa of the order Amoebida, characterized by a granular nucleus surrounded by a jellylike mass of cytoplasm that forms temporary extensions, or pseudopodia, by which the organism moves, engulfs food particles, and forms food vacuoles. **2.** a protozoan of the genus *Amoeba,* inhabiting bottom vegetation of freshwater ponds and streams: used widely in laboratory studies. Also, **amoeba.** [< NL *amoeba* < Gk *amoibḗ* change, alternation, akin to *ameíbein* to exchange] **—a•me′ba•like′,** *adj.*

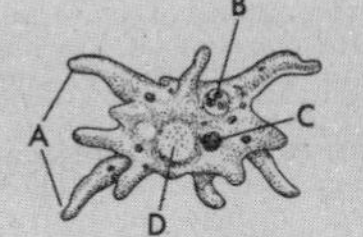

ameba
A, pseudopods;
B, food vacuole;
C, nucleus; D, contractile vacuole

am•e•bi•a•sis (am′ə bī′ə sis), *n. Pathol.* **1.** infection with *Entamoeba histolytica* or other pathogenic ameba. **2.** See **amebic dysentery.** Also, **amoebiasis.** [1900–05; AMEB(A) + -IASIS]

a•me•bic (ə mē′bik), *adj.* **1.** of, pertaining to, or resembling an ameba. **2.** characterized by or due to the presence of amebas, as certain diseases. Also, **amoebic.** [AMEB(A) + -IC]

ame′bic dys′entery, *Pathol.* a type of dysentery caused by the protozoan *Entamoeba histolytica,* characterized esp. by ulceration of the large intestine. Also called **amebiasis, intestinal amebiasis, ame′bic coli′•tis.** [1890–95]

a•me•bo•cyte (ə mē′bə sīt′), *n. Zool.* a migratory, ameboid cell found in many invertebrates that functions in excretion, assimilation, etc. Also, **amoebocyte.** [AMEB(A) + -O- + -CYTE]

a•me•boid (ə mē′boid), *adj. Biol.* resembling or related to amebas. Also, **amoeboid.** [AMEB(A) + -OID] **—a•me′boid•ism,** *n.*

âme dam•née (äm′ dä nā′), *pl.* **âmes dam•nées** (äm′ dä nā′). *French.* a person who is willingly or blindly the tool of another person. [lit., damned soul]

AMEDS, Army Medical Service. Also, **AMedS**

a•meer (ə mēr′), *n.* emir.

a•meer•ate (ə mēr′it, -āt), *n.* emirate.

a•mei•o•sis (ā′mī ō′sis), *n. Cell Biol.* aberrant meiosis in which only an equational division occurs, as in parthenogenesis. [< NL; see A-[6], MEIOSIS] **—a•mei•ot•ic** (ā′mī ot′ik), *adj.*

a•mel•i•a (ə mel′ē ə, ā mē′lē ə), *n. Pathol.* the congenital absence of one or more limbs. [1970–75; A-[6] + -MELIA]

A•mel•ia (ə mēl′yə), *n.* a female given name: from a Germanic word meaning "industrious."

a•mel•io•rate (ə mēl′yə rāt′, ə mē′lē ə-), *v.t., v.i.,* **-rat•ed, -rat•ing.** to make or become better, more bearable, or more satisfactory; improve; meliorate. [1760–70; A-[5] + MELIORATE] **—a•mel′io•ra•ble,** *adj.* **—a•mel′io•ra•ble•ness,** *n.* **—a•mel′io•rant,** *n.* **—a•mel′io•ra′•tive, a•mel•io•ra•to•ry** (ə mēl′yər ə tôr′ē, -tōr′ē, ə mē′lē ə-), *adj.* **—a•mel′io•ra′tor,** *n.*
—Syn. amend, better. See **improve. —Ant.** worsen.

a•mel•io•ra•tion (ə mēl′yə rā′shən, ə mē′lē ə-), *n.* **1.** an act or instance of ameliorating; the state of being ameliorated. **2.** something that ameliorates; an improvement. **3.** melioration (def. 1). [1790–1800; AMELIORATE + -ION]
—Ant. depreciation, pejoration.

am•e•lo•blast (am′ə lō blast′), *n. Anat.* one of a layer of enamel-secreting cells covering the dentin of a developing tooth. [1875–80; (EN)AMEL + -O- + -BLAST] **—am′e•lo•blas′tic,** *adj.*

a•men (ā′men′, ä′men′), *interj.* **1.** it is so; so be it (used after a prayer, creed, or other formal statement to express solemn ratification or agreement). **—***adv.* **2.** verily; truly. **—***n.* **3.** an utterance of the interjection "amen." **4.** a musical setting for such an utterance. **5.** an expression of concurrence or assent: *The committee gave its amen to the proposal.* [bef. 1000; ME, OE < LL < Gk < Heb *āmēn* certainty, certainly]

A•men (ä′mən), *n. Egyptian Myth.* a primeval deity worshiped esp. at Thebes, the personification of air or breath represented as either a ram or a goose (later identified with Amen-Ra). Also, **Amon.**

a•me•na•ble (ə mē′nə bəl, ə men′ə-), *adj.* **1.** ready or willing to answer, act, agree, or yield; open to influence, persuasion, or advice; agreeable; submissive; tractable: *an amenable servant.* **2.** liable to be called to account;

answerable; legally responsible: *You are amenable for this debt.* **3.** capable of or agreeable to being tested, tried, analyzed, etc. [1590–1600; < AF, equiv. to MF *amen(er)* to lead to (*a-* A-[5] + *mener* < LL *mināre* for L *minārī* to drive) + *-able* -ABLE] **—a·me′na·bil′i·ty, a·me′na·ble·ness,** *n.* **—a·me′na·bly,** *adv.*
—Syn. 1. manageable, docile, easy. **3.** open, subject.
—Ant. 1. stubborn, recalcitrant.

amen′ cor′ner, *Chiefly Midland and Southern U.S.* a place in some Protestant churches, usually at one side of the pulpit, occupied by worshipers leading the responsive amens of the congregation. [1855–60, *Amer.*]

a·mend (ə mend′), *v.t.* **1.** to alter, modify, rephrase, or add to or subtract from (a motion, bill, constitution, etc.) by formal procedure: *Congress may amend the proposed tax bill.* **2.** to change for the better; improve: *to amend one's ways.* **3.** to remove or correct faults in; rectify. *—v.i.* **4.** to grow or become better by reforming oneself: *He amends day by day.* [1175–1225; ME *amenden* < OF *amender* < L *ēmendāre* to correct, equiv. to *ē-* E- + *mend(a)* blemish + *-āre* inf. suffix] **—a·mend′a·ble,** *adj.* **—a·mend′er,** *n.*
—Syn. 2. ameliorate, better. **3.** AMEND, EMEND both mean to improve by correcting or by freeing from error. AMEND is the general term, used of any such correction in detail: *to amend spelling, punctuation, grammar.* EMEND usually applies to the correction of a text in the process of editing or preparing for publication; it implies improvement in the sense of greater accuracy: *He emended the text of the play by restoring the original reading.* **4.** improve, ameliorate. **—Ant. 2, 4.** worsen.

a·mend·a·tory (ə men′də tôr′ē, -tōr′ē), *adj.* serving to amend; corrective. [1780–90, *Amer.*; < LL *ēmendātōrius* (with *a-* for *e-* from AMEND). See EMENDATOR, -TORY[1]]

a·mende ho·no·ra·ble (ə mend′ on′ər ə bəl; *Fr.* A mäɴ dô nô RA′blᵊ), *pl.* **a·mendes ho·no·ra·bles** (ə mendz′ on′ər ə bəl; *Fr.* A mäɴ dô nô RA′blᵊ). a formal apology to a person whose honor has been offended. [1660–70; < F; see AMENDS, HONORABLE]

a·mend·ment (ə mend′mənt), *n.* **1.** the act of amending or the state of being amended. **2.** an alteration of or addition to a motion, bill, constitution, etc. **3.** a change made by correction, addition, or deletion: *The editors made few amendments to the manuscript.* **4.** *Hort.* a soil-conditioning substance that promotes plant growth indirectly by improving such soil qualities as porosity, moisture retention, and pH balance. [1250–1300; ME < OF *amendement.* See AMEND, -MENT]

a·mends (ə mendz′), *n.* (*used with a singular or plural v.*) **1.** reparation or compensation for a loss, damage, or injury of any kind; recompense. **2.** *Obs.* improvement; recovery, as of health. **3. make amends,** to compensate, as for an injury, loss, or insult: *I tried to make amends for the misunderstanding by sending her flowers.* [1275–1325; ME *amendes* < MF, pl. of *amende* reparation, n. deriv. of *amender* to AMEND]
—Syn. 1. redress, restitution.

Amen′ glass′ (ā′men′, ä′men′), a British glass of the mid-18th century, having engraved on it a sentiment favoring the cause of the Old Pretender, concluded with the word "Amen." [1920–25]

A·men·ho·tep III (ä′mən hō′tep, am′ən-), king of Egypt 1411?–1375 B.C. Also called **Am·e·no·phis III** (am′ə nō′fis).

Amenhotep IV, died 1357? B.C., king of Egypt 1375?–1357?: reformer of ancient Egyptian religion (son of Amenhotep III). Also called **Amenophis IV, Akhnaton, Ikhnaton.**

a·men·i·ty (ə men′i tē, ə mē′ni-), *n., pl.* **-ties. 1.** an agreeable way or manner; courtesy; civility: *the graceful amenities of society.* **2.** any feature that provides comfort, convenience, or pleasure: *The house has a swimming pool, two fireplaces, and other amenities.* **3.** the quality of being pleasing or agreeable in situation, prospect, disposition, etc.; pleasantness: *the amenity of the Caribbean climate.* **4. amenities,** lavatory; bathroom: used as a euphemism. [1400–50; late ME *amenite* < AF < L *amoenitās,* equiv. to *amoen(us)* pleasing + *-itās* -ITY]

a·men·or·rhe·a (ā men′ə rē′ə, ə men′-), *n. Pathol.* absence of the menses. Also, **a·men′or·rhoe′a.** [1795–1805; A-[6] + MENO- + -RRHEA] **—a·men′or·rhe′al, a·men′or·rhoe′al, a·men′or·rhe′ic, a·men′or·rhoe′ic,** *adj.*

A·men-Ra (ä′mən rä′), *n. Egyptian Myth.* a god in whom Amen and Ra were combined: the god of the universe and the supreme Egyptian god during the period of Theban political supremacy. Also, **Amon-Ra.**

a men·sa et tho·ro (ā men′sə et thôr′ō, thōr′ō), *Law.* pertaining to or noting a divorce that forbids husband and wife to live together but does not dissolve the marriage bond. [1590–1600; < L: lit., from board and bed. See MENSAL[2], TORUS]

a·men·sa·lism (ā men′sə liz′əm), *n. Ecol.* a relationship between two species of organisms in which the individuals of one species adversely affect those of the other and are unaffected themselves. [prob. A-[6] + (COM)MENSAL + -ISM]

am·ent[1] (am′ənt, ā′mənt), *n. Bot.* catkin. [1785–95; < NL, L *āmentum* strap, thong]

a·ment[2] (ā′ment, ā′mənt), *n.* a person who has amentia. [1890–95; < L *āment-* (s. of *āmēns* out of one's mind, mad), equiv. to *ā-* A-[4] + *ment-;* see MENTAL] **—a·men·tal** (ā men′tl), *adj.*

am·en·ta·ceous (am′ən tā′shəs), *adj. Bot.* **1.** consisting of an ament. **2.** bearing aments. [1730–40; AMENT[1] + -ACEOUS]

a·men·tia (ā men′shə, ə men′-), *n. Psychiatry.* lack of intellectual development; imbecility; severe mental retardation. [1350–1400; ME < L, equiv. to *āment-* (see AMENT[2]) + *-ia* -IA]

am·en·tif·er·ous (am′ən tif′ər əs), *adj. Bot.* bearing aments or catkins. [1850–55; AMENT[1] + -I- + -FEROUS]

Amer., 1. America. **2.** Also, **Amer** American.

Am·er·a·sian (am′ə rā′zhən, -shən), *n.* **1.** the offspring of an American and an Asian, esp. one whose father is American. *—adj.* **2.** of mixed American and Asian descent. Also, **Am′er-A′sian.** [1950–55; AMER(ICAN) + ASIAN]

a·merce (ə mûrs′), *v.t.,* **a·merced, a·merc·ing. 1.** to punish by imposing a fine not fixed by statute. **2.** to punish by inflicting any discretionary or arbitrary penalty. [1250–1300; ME *amercy* < AF *amerci(er)* to fine, repr. (*estre*) *a merci* (to be) at (someone's) mercy. See A-[5], MERCY] **—a·merce′a·ble,** *adj.* **—a·merce′ment,** *n.* **—a·merc′er,** *n.*

A·mer·i·ca (ə mer′i kə), *n.* **1.** See **United States. 2.** See **North America. 3.** See **South America. 4.** Also called **the Americas.** North and South America, considered together.

Amer′ica First′ Commit′tee, a political pressure group that during 1940–41 urged the U.S. not to oppose fascism in Europe or enter World War II.

Amer′ica First′er (fûr′stər), *Informal.* a member or supporter of the America First Committee. [1935–40; *America First* + -ER[1]]

A·mer·i·can (ə mer′i kən), *adj.* **1.** of or pertaining to the United States of America or its inhabitants: *an American citizen.* **2.** of or pertaining to North or South America; of the Western Hemisphere: *the American continents.* **3.** of or pertaining to the aboriginal Indians of North and South America, usually excluding the Eskimos, regarded as being of Asian ancestry and marked generally by reddish to brownish skin, black hair, dark eyes, and prominent cheekbones. *—n.* **4.** a citizen of the United States of America. **5.** a native or inhabitant of the Western Hemisphere. **6.** an Indian of North or South America. **7.** See **American English. 8.** a steam locomotive having a four-wheeled front truck, four driving wheels, and no rear truck. See table under **Whyte classification.** [1570–80; AMERIC(A) + -AN] **—A·mer′i·can·ly,** *adv.* **—A·mer′i·can·ness,** *n.*

American, The, a novel (1877) by Henry James.

A·mer·i·ca·na (ə mer′i kan′ə, -kä′nə, -kā′nə), *n.* **1.** (*often used with a plural v.*) books, papers, maps, etc., relating to America, esp. to its history, culture, and geography. **2.** (*used with a singular v.*) a collection of such materials. [1835–45, *Amer.*; AMERIC(A) + -ANA]

Amer′ican al′oe. See **century plant.** [1725–35]

Amer′ican Antislav′ery Soci′ety, *U.S. Hist.* a society, founded in 1833 and led by William Lloyd Garrison, to abolish slavery.

Amer′ican Associa′tion of Retired′ Per′sons, an organization of retirement-age persons (aged 50 or over) devoted to informing its members of all rights and benefits to which they are entitled. *Abbr.:* AARP

Amer′ican Beau′ty, an American variety of rose, periodically bearing large crimson blossoms. [1855–60, *Amer.*]

Amer′ican Bi′ble Soci′ety, a society founded in New York City in 1816 to bring about worldwide dissemination of the Bible.

Amer′ican bi′son, bison (def. 1). [1885–90, *Amer.*]

Amer′ican bit′tern. See under **bittern** (def. 1). [1805–15, *Amer.*]

Amer′ican blight′. See under **woolly aphid** (def. 1). [1805–15]

Amer′ican bond′, a brickwork bond having a course of headers between five or six courses of stretchers. Also called **common bond.** See illus. under **bond.**

Amer′ican Book′ Award′, any of several awards given annually since 1980 to an author whose book is judged the best in its category: administered by the Association of American Publishers. *Abbr.:* ABA, A.B.A. Cf. **National Book Award.**

Amer′ican brook′lime. See under **brooklime.**

Amer′ican buf′falo, bison (def. 1). [1885–90, *Amer.*]

Amer′ican chair′, *Brit.* See **Hitchcock chair.**

Amer′ican chame′leon. See under **chameleon** (def. 2). [1880–85, *Amer.*]

Amer′ican cheese′, a type of processed cheddar-style cheese made in the U.S. [1795–1805, *Amer.*]

Amer′ican chest′nut. See under **chestnut** (def. 1). [1775–85, *Amer.*]

Amer′ican Civ′il Lib′erties Un′ion, an organization founded in 1920 to defend the civil rights of all U.S. citizens. *Abbr.:* ACLU, A.C.L.U.

Amer′ican Civ′il War′, the war in the U.S. between the North and the South, 1861–65.

Amer′ican cloth′, *Brit.* oilcloth. [1855–60]

Amer′ican cock′roach, a large, reddish-brown cockroach, *Periplaneta americana,* found originally in the southern U.S. but now widely distributed.

Amer′ican Col′lege Test′, a standardized aptitude examination for college admission, developed by the American College Testing Program, consisting of multiple-choice tests in English, mathematics, natural-science reading, and social-studies reading as well as a personal student-profile section, graded on a scale of 0 to 36 and according to percentile rank. *Abbr.:* ACT. Cf. **Scholastic Aptitude Test.**

Amer′ican cop′per. See under **copper**[1] (def. 4).

Amer′ican cot′ton. See **upland cotton.** Also called **Amer′ican up′land cot′ton.**

Amer′ican cow′slip. See **shooting star** (def. 2). [1780–90, *Amer.*]

Amer′ican crab′ ap′ple, a twiggy, stiff-branched tree, *Malus coronaria,* of southern central North America, having small fruit and rose-colored flowers that change to white. Also called **garland crab apple, sweet crab apple.**

Amer′ican cran′berry. See under **cranberry** (def. 1).

Amer′ican depos′itory receipt′, *Stock Exchange.* a negotiable receipt similar to a stock certificate, registered in the owner's name and showing ownership of shares in a foreign company, held by a foreign branch of a U.S. bank or its overseas correspondent bank.

Amer′ican Directoire′, a style of American furniture making and related crafts from c1805 to c1815, corresponding to the French Directoire and English Regency styles.

Amer′ican dog′ tick′, a common tick, *Dermacentor variabilis,* that is the vector of Rocky Mountain spotted fever in the eastern U.S. and also carries tularemia. Also called **wood tick.**

Amer′ican Dream′, 1. the ideals of freedom, equality, and opportunity traditionally held to be available to every American. **2.** a life of personal happiness and material comfort as traditionally sought by individuals in the U.S. [1930–35]

Amer′ican ea′gle, the bald eagle, esp. as depicted on the great seal of the U.S. [1775–85, *Amer.*]

Amer′ican elk′, elk (def. 2). [1765–75, *Amer.*]

Amer′ican elm′, an elm, *Ulmus americana,* of North America, cultivated for shade and ornament: state tree of Massachusetts, Nebraska, and North Dakota. [1775–85]

Amer′ican Em′pire, a style of American furniture making and related crafts from c1815 to c1840, corresponding to the French Empire and late English Regency styles.

Amer′ican Eng′lish, the English language as spoken and written in the U.S. [1800–10, *Amer.*]

Amer′ican Expedi′tionary Forc′es, troops sent to Europe by the U.S. Army during World War I. *Abbr.:* A.E.F., AEF

Amer′ican Farm′ Bu′reau Federa′tion, an organization founded in 1920 to promote the interests of farmers, esp. through state and national legislation. *Abbr.:* AFBF

Amer′ican Federa′tion of La′bor, a federation of trade unions organized in 1886: united with the Congress of Industrial Organizations 1955. *Abbr.:* A.F.L., AFL, A.F. of L.

Amer′ican Federa′tion of La′bor and Con′gress of Indus′trial Organiza′tions, a federation of trade unions formed in 1955 by merger. *Abbr.:* AFL-CIO

Amer′ican flag′fish, flagfish (def. 1).

Amer′ican Fork′, a town in central Utah. 12,417.

Amer′ican fox′hound, one of an American breed of medium-sized dogs having a smooth, glossy coat usually black, tan, and white in color, a square-cut muzzle, hanging ears, and a moderately high-set tail, used for hunting both in packs or individually, tailing the game by scent. Cf. **English foxhound.** [1890–95]

Amer′ican fried′ pota′toes. See **home fries.** Also called **Amer′ican fries′.**

Amer′ican Friends′ Serv′ice Commit′tee, a social-service organization founded 1917 by the Religious Society of Friends: Nobel peace prize 1947. *Abbr.:* AFSC, A.F.S.C.

Amer′ican globe′flower, a plant, *Trollius laxus,* of the buttercup family, of the northeastern and Great Lakes coastal areas of the U.S., having solitary, yellowish-green flowers.

Amer′ican High′land, a region in Antarctica, W of Enderby Land and E of Wilkes Land: discovered 1939.

Amer′ican hol′ly. See under **holly** (def. 1). [1775–85; *Amer.*]

Amer′ican horn′beam. See under **hornbeam.** [1775–85, *Amer.*]

Amer′ican In′dian, 1. Indian (def. 1). **2.** Amerind (def. 2). *Abbr.:* AmerInd [1725–35]
—Usage. See **Indian.**

Amer′ican ip′ecac, a plant, *Gillenia stipulata,* of the rose family, of the eastern coast of the U.S., having white flowers on long stalks.

A·mer·i·can·ism (ə mer′i kə niz′əm), *n.* **1.** a custom, trait, or thing peculiar to the United States of America or its citizens. **2.** a word, phrase, or other language feature that is especially characteristic of the English language as spoken or written in the U.S. **3.** devotion to or preference for the U.S. and its institutions. **4.** anything, as a custom or word, peculiar to America. [1775–85, *Amer.*; AMERICAN + -ISM]

A·mer·i·can·ist (ə mer′i kə nist), *n.* **1.** a student of America, esp. of its history, culture, and geography. **2.** a specialist in the cultures or languages of American Indians. **3.** a specialist in American literature. **4.** a person who favors the U.S., its policies, etc. [1880–85; AMERICAN + -IST] **—A·mer′i·can·is′tic,** *adj.*

Amer′ican i′vy. See **Virginia creeper.** [1775–85, *Amer.*]

A·mer·i·can·ize (ə mer′i kə nīz′), *v.t., v.i.,* **-ized, -iz·ing.** to make or become American in character; assimilate to the customs and institutions of the U.S. Also, *esp. Brit.,* **A·mer′i·can·ise′.** [1790–1800, *Amer.*; AMERICAN + -IZE] **—A·mer′i·can·i·za′tion,** *n.* **—A·mer′i·can·iz′er,** *n.*

Amer′ican kes′trel, a small American falcon, *Falco*

CONCISE ETYMOLOGY KEY: <, descended or borrowed from; >, whence; b., blend of, blended; c., cognate with; cf., compare; deriv., derivative; equiv., equivalent; imit., imitative; obl., oblique; r., replacing; s., stem; sp., spelling, spelled; resp., respelling, respelled; trans., translation; ?, origin unknown; *, unattested; ‡, probably earlier than. See the full key inside the front cover.

sparverius, that preys esp. on grasshoppers and small mammals. Also called **sparrow hawk.**

Amer′ican La′bor par′ty, a U.S. political party (1936–56) organized in New York City to gain independent political status for the labor and liberal factions of the Democratic party.

Amer′ican League′, one of the two major professional U.S. baseball leagues, established in 1900. *Abbr.:* A.L.

Amer′ican Le′gion, a society, organized in 1919, composed of veterans of the armed forces of the U.S.

Amer′ican lin′den. See under **linden** (def. 1).

Amer′ican lo′tus. See **water chinquapin** (def. 1).

Amer′ican mar′ten. See **pine marten** (def. 2).

Amer′ican mul′berry. See under **mulberry** (def. 2).

Amer′ican Na′tional Stand′ards In′stitute, a U.S. organization that recommends standards for many products in various industries. *Abbr.:* ANSI

A·mer·i·ca·no (ə mer′i kan′ō, -kä′nō), *n., pl.* **-nos.** a cocktail made with bitters, sweet vermouth, and soda water. Also called **Amer′ica′no cock′tail.** [1940–45; < Sp: American]

A·mer·i·can·ol·o·gist (ə mer′i kə nol′ə jist), *n.* a foreign expert or specialist in American cultural or political matters: *a leading Americanologist in the Kremlin.* [1965–70; AMERICAN + -OLOG(Y) + -IST]

Amer′ican or′gan, a reed organ having a suction bellows that draws the air in through the reeds. [1875–80]

Amer′ican par′ty. See under **know-nothing** (def. 3). Also called **Know-Nothing party.**

Amer′ican pit′ bull′ ter′rier. See **American Staffordshire terrier.**

Amer′ican plan′, (in hotels) a system of paying a single fixed rate that covers room and all meals. *Abbr.:* AP Cf. **European plan.** [1795–1805, *Amer.*]

Amer′ican red′start. See under **redstart** (def. 2). [1800–10, *Amer.*]

Amer′ican Revised′ Ver′sion, a revision of the Bible, based chiefly on the Revised Version of the Bible, published in the U.S. in 1901. Also called **American Standard Version.**

Amer′ican Revolu′tion, the war between Great Britain and its American colonies, 1775–83, by which the colonies won their independence.

Amer′ican rig′, a rig for drilling oil and gas wells by using a chisel bit dropped from a considerable height.

Amer′ican sa′ble, 1. the pine marten, *Martes americana,* of the U.S. and Canada. **2.** the fur of this animal.

Amer′ican sad′dle horse′, one of a breed of horses, raised originally in the U.S., that have high-stepping gaits and are bred to the three-gaited or five-gaited type. Also called **saddle horse.** [1920–25]

Amer′ican Samo′a, the part of Samoa belonging to the U.S., comprising mainly Tutuila and the Manua Islands. 29,000; 76 sq. mi. (197 sq. km). *Cap.:* Pago Pago. *Abbr.:* AS (for use with zip code). Cf. **Samoa, Western Samoa.**

Amer′ican sen′na. See **wild senna.** [1775–85, *Amer.*]

Amer′ican short′hair cat′, one of a breed of medium-sized, muscular shorthaired domestic cats with a broad head and a short, thick coat.

Amer′ican Sign′ Lan′guage, a visual-gesture language, having its own semantic and syntactic structure, used by deaf people in the U.S. and English-speaking parts of Canada. *Abbr.:* ASL Also called **Ameslan.** [1960–65]

Amer′ican smoke′ tree′, a small tree, *Cotinus obovatus,* of the cashew family, of the central southern U.S., having yellowish flowers and clusters of fleshy fruit with silky plumes. Also called **chittamwood.**

Amer′ican Span′ish, Spanish as used in Latin America. *Abbr.:* AmerSp

Amer′ican Staf′fordshire ter′rier, one of an American breed of strong, muscular terriers, originally developed in England, with a short, close-lying, stiff coat of any color or combination of colors except solid white. Also called **American pit bull terrier, pit bull terrier.** Formerly, **Staffordshire terrier.** [1965–70]

Amer′ican Stand′ard Code′ for Informa′tion In′terchange. See **ASCII.**

Amer′ican Stand′ard Ver′sion. See **American Revised Version.**

Amer′ican star′, *Heraldry.* mullet[2].

Amer′ican Stock′ Exchange′, the second largest stock exchange in the U.S., located in New York City. *Abbr.:* ASE, A.S.E. Also called **AMEX, Amex.** Formerly, **New York Curb Exchange.** Cf. **New York Stock Exchange.**

Amer′ican Trag′edy, An, a novel (1925) by Theodore Dreiser.

Amer′ican trypanosomi′asis, *Pathol.* See **Chagas' disease.**

Amer′ican twist′, *Tennis.* a service in which the ball is spun so as to bounce high and to the left of the receiver. Also called **kick serve.**

Amer′ican wa′ter span′iel, one of an American breed of medium-sized water spaniels having a thick, curly chocolate-colored or liver-colored coat. [1945–50]

Amer′ican way′faring tree′, hobblebush.

Amer′ican wood′bine. See under **woodbine** (def. 2).

Amer′ican worm′seed. See **Mexican tea.**

Amer′ica's Cup′, 1. an international yachting trophy, originally offered as the Hundred Guinea Cup in 1851, but renamed for the yacht *America,* winner of it that year. **2.** the yacht race itself, the oldest and most prestigious event in international sailing, now restricted to 12-meter yachts.

am·er·i·ci·um (am′ə rish′ē əm), *n. Chem.* a transuranic element, one of the products of high-energy helium bombardment of uranium and plutonium. *Symbol:* Am; *at. no.:* 95. [1945–50, *Amer.*; AMERIC(A) + -IUM]

A·mer·i·cus (ə mer′i kəs), *n.* a city in SW central Georgia. 16,120.

A·me·ri·go Ves·puc·ci (ə mer′i gō′ ve spo͞o′chē, -spyo͞o′-; *It.* ä′me rē′gô ves po͞ot′chē). See **Vespucci, Amerigo.**

Am·er·ind (am′ə rind), *n.* **1.** Indian (def. 1). **2.** any of the indigenous languages of the American Indians. [1895–1900, *Amer.*; AMER(ICAN) + IND(IAN)] —**Am′er·in′dic,** *adj.*
—**Usage.** See **Indian.**

AmerInd, American Indian. Also, **Amer. Ind.**

Am·er·in·di·an (am′ə rin′dē ən), *n.* **1.** Indian (def. 1). —*adj.* **2.** of or pertaining to Amerindians. [AMER(ICAN) + INDIAN]
—**Usage.** See **Indian.**

am·er·is·tic (am′ə ris′tik, ā′me ris′-), *adj. Bot.* not divided into parts; having no meristem. [< Gk *amérist-(os)* undivided (*a-* A-[6] + *meristós* divided) + -IC] —**am′er·ism,** *n.*

A·mers·foort (ä′mərz fôrt′, -fōrt′, -mərs-), *n.* a city in the central Netherlands. 88,365.

AmerSp, American Spanish.

A′mer·y Ice′ Shelf′ (ā′mə rē), an ice barrier in Antarctica, in the SW Indian Ocean, bordered by Enderby Land on the N and American Highland on the W.

Ames (āmz), *n.* a city in central Iowa. 45,775.

ames·ace (āmz′ās′, amz′-), *n.* ambsace.

Ames·bur·y (āmz′ber′ē, -bə rē), *n.* a town in NE Massachusetts. 13,971.

A·me·sha Spen·ta (ä′me shə spen′tə), *Zoroastrianism.* any of the personified attributes of Ahura Mazda. Also called **Spenta Amesha.** [< Avestan, equiv. to *amesha* angel + *spenta* good]

Am·e·slan (am′ə slan′, am′slan), *n.* See **American Sign Language.** [1970–75, *Amer.*]

Ames′ test′, a test that exposes a strain of bacteria to a chemical compound in order to determine the mutagenic potential of the compound. [1975–80; after U.S. biochemist Bruce N. Ames (born 1928), who developed the test]

a·met·a·bol·ic (ā′met ə bol′ik), *adj. Zool.* undergoing slight or no metamorphosis. Also, **a·me·tab·o·lous** (ā′mə tab′ə ləs). [1865–70; A-[6] + METABOLIC]

am·e·thyst (am′ə thist), *n.* **1.** a purple or violet quartz, used as a gem. **2.** a purplish tint. —*adj.* **3.** having the color of amethyst. **4.** containing or set with an amethyst or amethysts: *an amethyst brooch.* [1250–1300; < L *amethystus* < Gk *améthystos* not intoxicating, not intoxicated (so called from a belief that it prevented drunkenness), equiv. to *a-* A-[6] + *methys-* (var. s. of *methýein* to intoxicate; see METHYLENE) + *-tos* verbal adj. suffix; r. ME *ametist* < AF *ametiste* < L] —**am·e·thys·tine** (am′ə this′tin, -tīn), *adj.* —**am′e·thyst·like′,** *adj.*

am·e·tro·pi·a (am′i trō′pē ə), *n. Ophthalm.* faulty refraction of light rays by the eye, as in astigmatism or myopia. [1875–80; < Gk *ámetr(os)* unmeasured (*a-* A-[6] + *métr(on)* measure + *-os* adj. suffix) + -OPIA] —**am·e·trop·ic** (am′i trop′ik, -trō′pik), *adj.*

AMEX (am′eks), *n.* See **American Stock Exchange.** Also, **Amex**

am/fm (ā′em′ef′em′), *adj.* (of a radio) able to receive both AM and FM stations. Also, **AM/FM**

AMG, Allied Military Government.

Am·ha·ra (äm här′ə), *n.* **1.** a former kingdom in E Africa: now a province in NW Ethiopia. *Cap.:* Gondar. **2.** a member of an agricultural, Amharic-speaking Christian people of central Ethiopia descended from Semites who began conquering the land in the sixth century B.C.

Am·har·ic (am har′ik, äm här′-), *n.* **1.** the Semitic language that is the official language of Ethiopia. —*adj.* **2.** of or pertaining to this language or its speakers. [1590–1600; AMHAR(A) + -IC]

Am·herst (am′ərst), *n.* **1. Jeffrey, Baron,** 1717–97, British field marshal: governor general of British North America 1760–63. **2.** a city in W Massachusetts. 33,229. **3.** a town in N Ohio. 10,638. **4.** a town in central Nova Scotia, in SE Canada. 10,263.

a·mi (A mē′; *Eng.* a mē′, ä mē′), *n., pl.* ***a·mis*** (A mē′; *Eng.* a mēz′, ä mēz′). *French.* **1.** a friend, esp. a male friend. **2.** a boyfriend or male lover.

a·mi·a·ble (ā′mē ə bəl), *adj.* **1.** having or showing pleasant, good-natured personal qualities; affable: *an amiable disposition.* **2.** friendly; sociable: *an amiable greeting; an amiable gathering.* **3.** agreeable; willing to accept the wishes, decisions, or suggestions of another or others. **4.** *Obs.* lovable or lovely. [1300–50; ME < MF < LL *amīcābilis* AMICABLE] —**a′mi·a·bil′i·ty, a′mi·a·ble·ness,** *n.* —**a′mi·a·bly,** *adv.*

am·i·an·thus (am′ē an′thəs), *n. Mineral.* a fine variety of asbestos, with delicate, flexible filaments. [1660–70; < L *amiantus* < Gk *amíantos,* equiv. to *a-* A-[6] + *mian-* (s. of *miaínein* to defile, make impure) + *-tos* verbal adj. suffix] —**am·i·an·thine** (am′ē an′thən, -thīn), *adj.* —**am′i·an′thoid, am′i·an·thoi′dal,** *adj.*

am·ic (am′ik), *adj. Chem.* of or pertaining to an amide or amine. [1860–65; AM(IDE) or AM(INE) + -IC]

am·i·ca·ble (am′i kə bəl), *adj.* characterized by or showing goodwill; friendly; peaceable: *an amicable settlement.* [1425–75; late ME < LL *amīcābilis,* equiv. to *amīc(us)* friend, friendly + *-ābilis* -ABLE; cf. AMIABLE] —**am′i·ca·bil′i·ty, am′i·ca·ble·ness,** *n.* —**am′i·ca·bly,** *adv.*
—**Syn.** agreeable.

am′icable num′ber, *Math.* either of a pair of positive integers in which each member is equal to the sum of the submultiples of the other, as 220 and 284.

am·ice[1] (am′is), *n. Eccles.* an oblong vestment, usually of white linen, worn about the neck and shoulders and partly under the alb. [1200–50; ME *amice(s)* < OF *amis, amys,* pl. of *amit* < L *amictus* mantle, cloak, equiv. to *amic-,* base of *amicīre* to wrap around (*am-* AMBI- + *-ic-,* comb. s. of *iacere* to throw) + *-tus* n. suffix of verbal action (hence, orig. the act of wrapping around)]

am·ice[2] (am′is), *n.* almuce. [late ME *amisse* < MF *aumusse, aumuce* < Sp *almucio* < L *almucia, almucium*]

A·mi′ci prism′ (ə mē′chē), *Optics.* a compound prism that spreads out incident white light into a spectrum but produces no deviation of the central color of the dispersed beam. Also called **direct-vision prism, roof prism.** [named after G. B. *Amici* (1784–1863), Italian astronomer]

a·mi·cus (ə mī′kəs, ə mē′-), *adj. Law.* of, pertaining to, or representing an amicus curiae: *The church stated its official position in an amicus brief.* [by shortening]

a·mi·cus cu·ri·ae (ə mī′kəs kyo͝or′ē ē′, ə mē′kəs kyo͝or′ē ī′), *pl.* **a·mi·ci cu·ri·ae** (ə mī′kī kyo͝or′ē ē′, ə mē′kē kyo͝or′ē ī′). *Law.* a person, not a party to the litigation, who volunteers or is invited by the court to give advice upon some matter pending before it. Also called **friend of the court.** [1605–15; < NL]

a·mi·cus hu·ma·ni ge·ne·ris (ä mē′ko͞os ho͞o mä′nē ge′ne ris; *Eng.* ə mī′kəs hyo͞o mā′nī jen′ə ris, ə mē′kəs hyo͞o mä′nē), *Latin.* a philanthropist. [lit., friend of the human race]

a·mi·cus us·que ad a·ras (ä mē′ko͞os o͞os′kwe äd ä′räs; *Eng.* ə mī′kəs us′kwē ad ā′ras, ə mē′-), *Latin.* a friend to the last degree.

a·mid (ə mid′), *prep.* **1.** in the middle of; surrounded by; among: *to stand weeping amid the ruins.* **2.** during; in or throughout the course of. Also, **amidst.** [bef. 1000; ME *amidde,* OE *amiddan,* for *on middan* in (the) middle. See A-[1], MID[1]]
—**Syn. 1.** See **among.**

amid-, var. of **amido-** before a vowel: *amidase.* [1870–75]

A·mi·da (ä′mi də), *n. Buddhism.* a Buddha who rules over paradise, enjoying endless and infinite bliss. Cf. **Pure Land.**

A·mi·dah (ä mē′dä), *n. Judaism.* a liturgical prayer that is recited in standing position at each of the three daily services and consists of three opening blessings, three closing blessings, and one intermediate blessing on the Sabbath and holy days and 13 intermediate blessings on other days. [< Heb *ʿămīdhāh* a standing]

am·i·dase (am′i dās′, -dāz′), *n. Biochem.* an enzyme that catalyzes the hydrolysis of an acid amide. [1920–25; AMID- + -ASE]

am·i·date (am′i dāt′), *v.t.,* **-dat·ed, -dat·ing.** *Chem.* to convert into an amide. [AMID- + -ATE[1]] —**am′i·da′tion,** *n.*

am·ide (am′īd, -id), *n. Chem.* **1.** a metallic derivative of ammonia in which the $-NH_2$ group is retained, as potassium amide, KNH_2. **2.** an organic compound obtained by replacing the $-OH$ group in acids by the $-NH_2$ group. **3.** an organic compound formed from ammonia by replacing a hydrogen atom by an acyl group. [1840–50; AM(MONIA) + -IDE] —**a·mid·ic** (ə mid′ik), *adj.*

am·i·din (am′i din), *n.* the soluble matter of starch. [1825–35; < ML *amid(um)* starch (alter. of L *amylum;* see AMYL) + -IN[2]]

am·i·dine (am′i dēn′, -din), *n. Chem.* any of a group of compounds containing the CN_2H_3 group, some of which have marked pharmacological action. [AMID- + -INE[2]]

am·i·di·no·hy·dra·zone (am′i dē′nō hī′drə zōn′), *n.* any of a group of pesticides, originally developed as antimalarial and antitubercular drugs, that impair cell respiration in cockroaches, red ants, and other insects. [shortening and alter. of the chemical name]

amido-, 1. a combining form used in the names of chemical compounds in which the $-NH_2$ group united with an acid radical is present: *amidocyanogen.* **2.** (erroneously) amino-. Also, *esp. before a vowel,* **amid-.** [AMIDE + -O-]

a·mi·do·gen (ə mē′də jən, -jen′, ə mid′ə-), *n. Chem.* (formerly) the $-NH_2$ group. [1840–50; AMIDO- + -GEN]

am·i·dol (am′i dôl′, -dol′), *n. Chem.* a colorless, crystalline powder, $C_6H_8N_2O\cdot 2HCl$, derived from phenol, used chiefly as a photographic developer. [1890–95; AMID- + -OL[1]]

a·mid·ships (ə mid′ships′), *adv.* **1.** in or toward the middle part of a ship or aircraft; midway between the ends. **2.** along the central fore-and-aft line of a ship or aircraft. **3.** in or toward the center of anything: *a long, narrow office with a desk placed amidships.* —*adj.* **4.** of, pertaining to, or located in the middle part of a ship or aircraft. Also, **a·mid′ship′.** [1685–95; AMID + SHIP + -S[1]]

a·midst (ə midst′), *prep.* amid. [1250–1300; ME *amiddes;* see AMID, -S[1]; for *-t* see AGAINST, AMONGST, etc.]

a·mie (A mē′; *Eng.* a mē′, ä mē′), *n., pl.* ***a·mies*** (A mē′; *Eng.* a mēz′, ä mēz′). *French.* **1.** a female friend. **2.** a girlfriend or female lover.

Am·i·ens (am′ē ənz; *Fr.* A myaN′), *n.* a city in and the

CONCISE PRONUNCIATION KEY: act, cāpe, dâre, pärt; set, ēqual; if, īce; ox, ōver, ôrder, oil, bo͝ok, bo͞ot, out; up, ûrge; child; sing; shoe; thin, *th*at; zh as in *treasure.* ə = *a* as in *alone, e* as in *system, i* as in *easily, o* as in *gallop, u* as in *circus;* ′ as in *fire* (fī′r), *hour* (ou′r). l and n can serve as syllabic consonants, as in *cradle* (krād′l), and *button* (but′n). See the full key inside the front cover.

capital of Somme, in N France: cathedral; battles 1914, 1918, 1944. 135,992.

a•mi•ga (ə mē′gə, ä mē′-; *Sp.* ä mē′gä), *n., pl.* **-gas** (-gəz; *Sp.* -gäs). a female friend. [< Sp; fem. of AMIGO]

a•mi•go (ə mē′gō, ä mē′-; *Sp.* ä mē′gô), *n., pl.* **-gos** (-gōz; *Sp.* -gôs). a friend, esp. a male friend. [1830–40, *Amer.*; < Sp < L *amīcus*]

am•i•ka•cin (am′i kā′sin), *n. Pharm.* a wide-spectrum semisynthetic antibiotic, $C_{22}H_{43}N_5O_{13}$, used in the treatment of infections, esp. those caused by susceptible Gram-negative bacilli. [perh. AMI(NOGLUCOSIDE) + *ka(namy)cin (D)*, the antibiotic from which amikacin is derived; (*Streptomyces*) *kanamyc(eticus)* a bacterium that produces kanamycin + -IN[2]]

a•mil•o•ride (ə mil′ə rīd′), *n. Pharm.* a potassium-sparing diuretic, $C_6H_8ClN_7O$, used in the treatment of hypertension. [perh. *(di)ami(no-6-ch)lor(opyrazinam)-ide*, part of its chemical name]

a•mim•i•a (ā mim′ē ə), *n. Med.* the inability to express ideas by means of gestures or signs. [< NL, equiv. to *a-* A-[6] + Gk *mîm(os)* actor, mimic + *-ia* -IA]

A•min (ä mēn′), *n.* **I•di** (ē′dē), (*Idi Amin Dada*), born 1925?, Ugandan dictator: president 1971–79; in exile from 1979.

amin-, var. of **amino-** before a vowel.

A•mi•nah (ä mē′nə), *n.* a female given name: from an Arabic word meaning "honest and faithful." Also, **A•mi′•na.**

am•i•nase (am′ə nās′, -nāz′), *n. Biochem.* any of a group of enzymes that catalyze the hydrolysis of amino compounds, releasing the amino group and liberating nitrogen. [AMIN- + -ASE]

am•i•nate (am′ə nāt′), *v.t.*, **-nat•ed, -nat•ing.** *Chem.* to introduce an amino group into (a compound). [AMINE + -ATE[1]] —**am′i•na′tion,** *n.*

A′min•di′vi Is′lands (ä′min dē′vē, ä′min-), a group of islands in the NE Laccadive Islands, off the SW coast of India. 3.75 sq. mi. (9.71 sq. km).

a•mine (ə mēn′, am′in), *n. Chem.* any of a class of compounds derived from ammonia by replacement of one or more hydrogen atoms with organic groups. [1860–65; AM(MONIUM) + -INE[2]] —**a•min•ic** (ə mē′nik, ə min′ik), *adj.* —**a•min•i•ty** (ə min′i tē), *n.*

-amine, var. of **amino-** as final element of a compound word: *Dramamine.*

a•mi•no (ə mē′nō, am′ə nō′), *adj. Chem.* containing the amino group. [1900–05; independent use of AMINO-]

amino-, a combining form used in the names of chemical compounds in which the amino group is present: *aminobenzene.* Also, **-amine**; *esp. before a vowel,* **amin-.** [AMINE + -O-]

a•mi′no•a•ce′tic ac′id (ə mē′nō ə sē′tik, -set′ik, am′ə nō′-, ə mē′nō-, am′ə nō-), *Chem.* glycine. [1885–90; AMINO- + ACETIC ACID]

ami′no ac′id, *Biochem.* any of a class of organic compounds that contains at least one amino group, $-NH_2$, and one carboxyl group, $-COOH$: the alpha-amino acids, $RCH(NH_2)COOH$, are the building blocks from which proteins are constructed. Cf. **essential amino acid.** [1895–1900]

a•mi′no-ac′id dat′ing (ə mē′nō as′id, am′ə nō′-), a method used to date an organic geological or archaeological specimen, as a fossil or mummified body, by determining how much change has occurred in the amino-acid structure of that specimen. [1970–75]

a•mi•no•ac•id•u•ri•a (ə mē′nō as′i dŏŏr′ē ə, -dyŏŏr′-, am′ə nō-), *n. Physiol.* excess amino acids in the urine, as in certain kidney diseases. [AMINO ACID + -URIA]

a•mi•no•ben•zene (ə mē′nō ben′zēn, -ben zēn′, am′-ə nō-), *n. Chem.* aniline (def. 1). [1900–05; AMINO- + BENZENE]

a•mi′no•ben•zo′ic ac′id (ə mē′nō ben zō′ik, am′ə-nō′-, ə mē′nō-, am′ə nō-), *Chem.* any of three isomers having the formula $C_7H_7NO_2$, derived from benzoic acid, esp. the para isomer, para-aminobenzoic acid. [1900–05; AMINO- + BENZOIC ACID]

a•mi•no•carb (ə mē′nō kärb′, am′ə nō-), *n. Chem.* a crystalline compound, $C_{11}H_{16}N_2O_2$, used as a nonsystemic insecticide on various food crops and forest growth. [AMINO- + CARB(AMATE), components of the full chemical name]

a•mi′no•cit′ric ac′id (ə mē′nō si′trik, am′ə nō′-, ə mē′nō-, am′ə nō-), *Biochem.* an amino acid, $C_6H_9O_7N$, that is a component of calf thymus ribonucleoprotein. [AMINO- + CITRIC]

a•mi•no•cy•clo•hex•ane (ə mē′nō sī′klə hek′sān, -sik′lə-, am′ə nō-), *n. Chem.* cyclohexylamine. [AMINO- + CYCLOHEXANE]

a•mi•no•glu•teth•i•mide (ə mē′nō glōō teth′ə mīd′, am′ə nō-), *n. Pharm.* a hormone antagonist, $C_{13}H_{16}N_2O_2$, used in the treatment of Cushing's syndrome and breast cancer. [appar. from selected and rearranged syllables of *aminophenyl* and *ethylglutarimide*, components of its full chemical name]

a•mi•no•gly•co•side (ə mē′nō glī′kə sīd′, am′ə nō-), *Pharm.* —*adj.* **1.** of or pertaining to amino sugars in glycosidic linkage. —*n.* **2.** any of a group of bacterial antibiotics having aminoglycoside structure. [AMINO- + GLYCOSIDE]

ami′no group′, *Chem.* the univalent group, $-NH_2$. Also called **ami′no rad′ical.**

a•mi•no•pep•ti•dase (ə mē′nō pep′ti dās′, -dāz′, am′ə nō-), *n. Biochem.* any of several intestinal hydrolytic enzymes that remove an amino acid from the end of a peptide chain having a free amino group. Cf. **carboxypeptidase.** [AMINO- + PEPTIDASE]

a•mi•no•phe•nol (ə mē′nō fē′nôl, -nol, am′ə nō-), *n. Chem.* a white crystalline substance, C_6H_7NO, occurring in three isomers, meta-, ortho-, and para-aminophenol: used as an intermediate for dyes and as a photographic developer. [AMINO- + PHENOL]

a•mi•no•phyl•line (ə mē′nō fil′in, -ēn, am′ə nō-), *n. Pharm.* a theophylline derivative, $C_{16}H_{24}N_{10}O_4$, used chiefly to relieve bronchial spasm in asthma, in the treatment of certain heart conditions, and as a diuretic. [1955–60; AMINO- + (THEO)PHYLLINE]

a•mi•no•plast (ə mē′nə plast′, am′ə nō-), *n. Chem.* See **amino resin.** [1935–40; AMINO- + PLAST(IC)]

ami′no res′in, *Chem.* any of the class of thermosetting resins formed by the interaction of an amine, as urea, and an aldehyde, as formaldehyde: used chiefly as adhesives for laminated materials and as coatings for paper and textiles. Also called **aminoplast.**

a•mi′no•suc•cin′ic ac′id (ə mē′nō sək sin′ik, am′-ə nō′-, ə mē′nō-, am′ə nō-), *Biochem.* See **aspartic acid.** [AMINO- + SUCCINIC ACID]

a•mi•no•su•gar (ə mē′nō shŏŏg′ər, am′ə nō-), *n. Biochem.* a monosaccharide with an amino or substituted amino group in place of a nonglycosidic hydroxyl group. [AMINO- + SUGAR]

a•mi•no•trans•fer•ase (ə mē′nō trans′fə rās′, -rāz′, am′ə nō-), *n. Biochem.* transaminase. [1960–65; AMINO- + TRANSFERASE]

am•i•o•dar•one (am′ē ō dar′ōn), *n. Pharm.* a substance, $C_{25}H_{29}I_2NO_3$, used in the treatment of heart arrhythmias. [laboratory coinage of unexplained orig.]

a•mir (ə mēr′), *n.* emir. [1605–15; < Ar *amīr* commander; see EMIR]

a•mir•ate (ə mēr′it, -āt), *n.* emirate. [AMIR + -ATE[3]]

A•mis (ā′mis), *n.* **Kingsley,** 1922–95, English novelist.

A•mish (ä′mish, am′ish), *adj.* **1.** of or pertaining to any of the strict Mennonite groups, chiefly in Pennsylvania, Ohio, Indiana, and Canada, descended from the followers of Jakob Ammann, a Swiss Mennonite bishop of the 17th century. —*n.* **2.** the Amish people. [1835–45, *Amer.*; < G *amisch*, after Jakob *Ammann*; see -ISH[1]]

a•miss (ə mis′), *adv.* **1.** out of the right or proper course, order, or condition; improperly; wrongly; astray: *Did I speak amiss?* **2. take amiss,** to be offended at or resentful of (something not meant to cause offense or resentment); misunderstand: *I couldn't think of a way to present my view so that no one would take it amiss.* —*adj.* (usually used predicatively) **3.** improper; wrong; faulty: *I think something is amiss in your calculations.* [1200–50; ME *amis*, equiv. to *a-* A-[1] + *mis* wrong. See MISS[1]]
—**Syn. 1.** inappropriately, unsuitably. **3.** mistaken, erroneous; awry, askew. —**Ant. 1.** rightly, properly. **3.** correct, true.

A•mi•tā•bha (u′mi tä′bə), *n. Sanskrit.* Amida.

am•i•tate (am′i tāt′, -tit), *n. Anthropol.* a close social relationship between a paternal aunt and her niece. [< L *amit(a)* paternal aunt + -ATE[3]]

am•i•to•sis (am′i tō′sis, ā′mī-), *n. Biol.* the direct method of cell division, characterized by simple cleavage of the nucleus without the formation of chromosomes. [1890–95; A-[6] + MITOSIS] —**am•i•tot•ic** (am′i tot′ik, ā′mī-), *adj.* —**am′i•tot′i•cal•ly,** *adv.*

am•i•trip•ty•line (am′i trip′tə lēn′, -lin′, -lin), *n. Pharm.* a white crystalline powder, $C_{20}H_{23}N$, used to treat depression and enuresis. [perh. AMI(NO)- + TRYPT(OPHAN) + (METH)YL + -INE[2]]

A•mit•tai (ə mit′ī), *n.* the father of Jonah. II Kings 14:25.

am•i•ty (am′i tē), *n.* **1.** friendship; peaceful harmony. **2.** mutual understanding and a peaceful relationship, esp. between nations; peace; accord. [1400–50; late ME *amit(i)e* < MF *amitie*, OF *amiste(t)* < VL **amīcitāt-*, s. of *amīcitās*, deriv. of L *amīcus.* See AMI, AMIABLE, -ITY]

Am•i•ty (am′i tē), *n.* a female given name.

A.M.L.S., Master of Arts in Library Science.

Am•man (ä män′, ä′män), *n.* a city in and the capital of Jordan, in the W part. 615,000. Also called **Rabbath Ammon.**

Am•ma•na•ti (ä′mə nä′tē; *It.* äm′mä nä′tē), *n.* **Bar•to•lom•me•o** (bär′tô lôm me′ô), 1511–92, Italian architect and sculptor.

am•me•ter (am′mē′tər), *n. Elect.* an instrument for measuring current in amperes. [1880–85; AM(PERE) + -METER]

Am•mi•a•nus (am′ē ā′nəs), *n.* **Mar•cel•li•nus** (mär′-sə lī′nəs), A.D. c325–c398, Roman historian.

am•mine (am′ēn, ə mēn′), *n. Chem.* **1.** a compound containing one or more ammonia molecules in coordinate linkage. **2.** any coordination compound containing one or more ammonia molecules bonded to a metal ion. [1895–1900; AMM(ONIA) + -INE[2]]

am•mi•no (am′ə nō′, ə mē′nō), *adj. Chem.* containing or pertaining to an ammine. [independent use of AMMINE + -O-]

Am•mi•shad•dai (am′ə shad′ī), *n.* the father of Ahiezer, the Danite. Num. 1:12; 2:25. Also, *Douay Bible,* **Ammi•sad•dai** (am′ə sad′ī, -sad′ā ī′).

am•mo (am′ō), *n. Informal.* ammunition. [AMM(UNITION) + -O]

am•mo•cete (am′ə sēt′), *n.* the larval stage of a lamprey. Also, **am′mo•coete′.** [1855–60; < NL *ammocoetes* lit., something bedded in sand < Gk *ámmo(s)* sand + *koítē* bed]

Am•mon (am′ən), *n.* **1.** the classical name of the Egyptian divinity Amen, whom the Greeks identified with Zeus, the Romans with Jupiter. **2.** the ancient country of the Ammonites, east of the Jordan River.

am•mo•nal (am′ə nal′), *n.* a high explosive consisting chiefly of powdered aluminum, ammonium nitrate, and TNT. [1900–05; AMMON(IUM) + AL(UMINUM)]

am•mo•nate (am′ə nāt′), *n. Chem.* ammoniate (def. 2). —**am′mo•na′tion,** *n.*

ammoni-, var. of **ammonio-**, esp. before a vowel.

am•mo•nia (ə mōn′yə, ə mō′nē ə), *n. Chem.* **1.** a colorless, pungent, suffocating, highly water-soluble, gaseous compound, NH_3, usually produced by the direct combination of nitrogen and hydrogen gases: used chiefly for refrigeration and in the manufacture of commercial chemicals and laboratory reagents. **2.** Also called **ammonia solution, ammonia water, aqua ammoniae, aqua ammonia, aqueous ammonia.** this gas dissolved in water; ammonium hydroxide. [1790–1800; < NL, so called as being obtained from sal *ammoniac.* See AMMONIAC]

ammo′nia al′um, *Chem.* See **aluminum ammonium sulfate.**

am•mo•ni•ac (ə mō′nē ak′), *n.* **1.** Also, **am•mo•ni•a•cum** (am′ə nī′ə kəm). See **gum ammoniac.** —*adj.* **2.** ammoniacal. [1375–1425; late ME *armoniac, ammoniak* < L *ammōniacum* < Gk *ammōniakón* (neut. of *ammōniakós* of AMMON; see -I-, -AC), applied to a salt and a gum resin prepared near the Shrine of Ammon in Libya]

am•mo•ni•a•cal (am′ə nī′ə kəl), *adj.* **1.** consisting of, containing, or using ammonia. **2.** like ammonia. Also, **ammoniac.** [1725–35; AMMONIAC + -AL[1]]

ammo′nia liq′uor, *Chem.* a concentrated solution of ammonia, ammonium compounds, and sulfur compounds, obtained as a by-product in the destructive distillation of bituminous coal. Also, **ammoni′acal liq′uor.** Also called **gas liquor.**

ammo′nia solu′tion, *Chem.* ammonia (def. 2).

am•mo•ni•ate (ə mō′nē āt′), *v.*, **-at•ed, -at•ing,** *n. Chem.* —*v.t.* **1.** to treat or cause to unite with ammonia. —*n.* **2.** Also, **ammonate.** a compound formed by adding ammonia in stoichiometric proportions to another compound, as $CaCl_2{\cdot}8NH_3$ or $CuSO_4{\cdot}4NH_3$. [1835–45; AMMONI(A) + -ATE[1] (def. 1), -ATE[2] (def. 2)] —**am•mo′ni•a′•tion,** *n.*

ammo′nia wa′ter, *Chem.* ammonia (def. 2). [1900–05]

am•mon•ic (ə mon′ik, ə mō′nik), *adj.* of or pertaining to ammonia or ammonium. Also, **am•mon′i•cal.** [1865–70; AMMON(IA) + -IC]

am•mon•i•fi•ca•tion (ə mon′ə fi kā′shən, ə mō′nə-), *n.* **1.** the act of impregnating with ammonia, as in the manufacture of fertilizer. **2.** the state of being so impregnated. **3.** the formation of ammonia or its compounds by decomposition of organic matter. [1885–90; AMMONI(A) + -FICATION]

am•mon•i•fy (ə mon′ə fī′, ə mō′nə-), *v.*, **-fied, -fy•ing.** —*v.t.* **1.** to combine or impregnate with ammonia. **2.** to form into ammonia or ammonium compounds. —*v.i.* **3.** to become ammonified; produce ammonification. [1910–15; AMMONI(A) + -FY] —**am•mon′i•fi′er,** *n.*

ammonio-, a combining form representing **ammonia** or **ammonium** in compound words: *ammonioferric.* Also, *esp. before a vowel,* **ammoni-.**

am•mo′ni•o•fer′ric ox′alate (ə mō′nē ō fer′ik, ə mō′-), *Chem.* See **ferric ammonium oxalate.** [AMMONIO- + FERRIC]

am•mo•nite[1] (am′ə nīt′), *n.* the coiled, chambered fossil shell of an ammonoid. [1700–10; < NL *Ammonites* < ML *(cornū) Ammōn(is)* (lit., horn of AMMON) + *-ītes* -ITE[1]; fossil so called from its resemblance to the horn of Jupiter Ammon] —**am•mo•nit•ic** (am′ə nit′ik), *adj.* —**am•mon•i•toid** (ə mon′i toid′), *adj.*

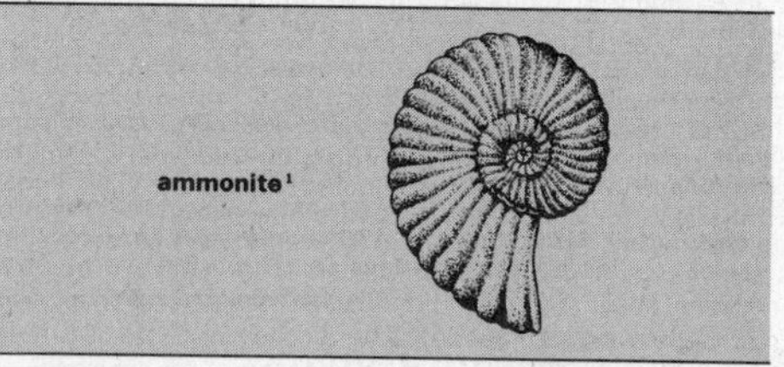
ammonite[1]

am•mo•nite[2] (am′ə nīt′), *n.* a nitrogenous mixture consisting chiefly of dried animal fats, usually obtained from livestock carcasses, and used as a fertilizer. [1600–10; AMMO(NIUM) + NIT(RAT)E]

Am•mon•ite (am′ə nīt′), *n.* **1.** an inhabitant of Ammon. —*adj.* **2.** of or pertaining to the Ammonites. [1605–15; AMMON + -ITE[1]] —**Am′mon•it′ish,** *adj.*

am•mo•ni•um (ə mō′nē əm), *n. Chem.* the univalent ion, NH_4^+, or group, NH_4, which plays the part of a metal in the salt formed when ammonia reacts with an acid. [< NL; see AMMONIA, -IUM; coined by J. J. Berzelius in 1808]

ammo′nium ac′etate, *Chem.* a white, crystalline, deliquescent, water-soluble solid, $NH_4(C_2H_3O_2)$, used chiefly in the manufacture of dyes and meat preservatives.

ammo′nium al′um, *Chem.* See **aluminum ammonium sulfate.**

ammo′nium bicar′bonate, *Chem.* a white, crystalline, water-soluble powder, NH_4HCO_3, used chiefly in the manufacture of baking powder.

ammo′nium bifluor′ide, *Chem.* a white, crystalline, water-soluble, poisonous solid, NH_4HF_2, used chiefly for cleaning and sterilizing brewing and dairy equipment.

CONCISE ETYMOLOGY KEY: <, descended or borrowed from; >, whence; b., blend of, blended; c., cognate with; cf., compare; deriv., derivative; equiv., equivalent; imit., imitative; obl., oblique; r., replacing; s., stem; sp., spelling, spelled; resp., respelling, respelled; trans., translation; ?, origin unknown; *, unattested; ‡, probably earlier than. See the full key inside the front cover.

ammo′nium binox′alate, *Chem.* a colorless, crystalline, water-soluble, poisonous solid, $C_2H_5NO_4 \cdot H_2O$, used chiefly for removing ink stains from fabrics.

ammo′nium car′bamate, *Chem.* a white, crystalline, water-soluble, extremely volatile powder, $CH_6N_2O_2$, used as a fertilizer.

ammo′nium car′bonate, *Chem.* a water-soluble mixture of ammonium bicarbonate and ammonium carbamate, occurring either as a white powder or in colorless, hard, crystalline masses: used chiefly in the manufacture of smelling salts and baking powder. [1880–85]

ammo′nium chlo′ride, *Chem., Pharm.* a white, crystalline, water-soluble powder, NH_4Cl, which produces a cooling sensation on the tongue, used chiefly in the manufacture of dry cells, in electroplating, and in medicine as an expectorant. Also called **sal ammoniac.** [1865–70]

ammo′nium chrome′ al′um, *Chem.* See **chrome alum** (def. 1).

ammo′nium chro′mic sul′fate, *Chem.* See **chrome alum** (def. 1).

ammo′nium cy′anate, *Chem.* a white, crystalline solid, CH_4N_2O, soluble in alcohol, that is converted into urea when heated.

ammo′nium hydrox′ide, *Chem.* a basic compound, NH_4OH, existing only in solution, formed by dissolving ammonia gas in water. Cf. **ammonia.** [1900–05]

ammo′nium lac′tate, *Chem.* a colorless to yellow, water-soluble, syrupy liquid, $C_3H_9NO_3$, used chiefly in electroplating.

ammo′nium ni′trate, *Chem.* a white, crystalline, water-soluble powder, NH_4NO_3, usually produced by reacting nitric acid with vaporous ammonia: used chiefly in explosives, fertilizers, freezing mixtures, and in the manufacture of nitrous oxide. [1880–85]

ammo′nium phos′phate, *Chem.* **1.** See **monoammonium phosphate. 2.** (loosely) diammonium phosphate.

ammo′nium pur′pu·rate (pûr′pyər it, -pyə rāt′), *Chem.* murexide. [PURPUR(IC) + -ATE[2]]

ammo′nium salt′, *Chem.* any salt containing the NH_4^+ ion, formed by the neutralization of ammonium hydroxide by an acid.

ammo′nium sel′enate, *Chem.* a colorless, crystalline, water-soluble solid, $(NH_4)_2SeO_4$, used as a mothproofing agent.

ammo′nium ste′arate, *Chem.* a tan, waxlike, water-insoluble solid, $C_{18}H_{39}NO_2$, used chiefly in the manufacture of cosmetics.

ammo′nium sul′fate, *Chem.* a white, crystalline, water-soluble solid, $(NH_4)_2SO_4$, used chiefly as a fertilizer. [1800–85]

ammo′nium thiocy′anate, *Chem.* a colorless, crystalline, deliquescent, water-soluble solid, CH_4N_2S, used chiefly as a herbicide and as a fixative in textile printing.

ammo′nium thiosul′fate, *Chem.* a white, crystalline, water-soluble solid, $(NH_4)_2S_2O_3$, used chiefly in the manufacture of cleaning compounds for alloys having a tin or lead base.

am·mo·no (am′ə nō′), *adj. Chem.* of, containing, or derived from ammonia. [independent use of AMMONO-]

ammono-, a combining form representing **ammonia** in compound words: *ammonolysis.*

am·mo·noid (am′ə noid′), *n.* any cephalopod mollusk of the extinct order Ammonoidea, from the Devonian to the Cretaceous periods, having a coiled, chambered shell. [1880–85; < NL *Ammonoidea,* equiv. to *Ammon(ites)* name of the order + *-oidea* -OIDEA; see AMMONITE[2]]

am·mo·nol·y·sis (am′ə nol′ə sis), *n., pl.* **-ses** (-sēz′). *Chem.* decomposition in which ammonia is resolved into other compounds by being a source of H^+ and NH_2. [1910–15; AMMONO- + -LYSIS] **—am·mo·no·lit·ic** (ə mōn′l it′ik, am′ə nl-), *adj.*

am·mo·no·lyze (ə mōn′l īz′), *v.,* **-lyzed, -lyz·ing.** *Chem.* —*v.t.* **1.** to subject to ammonolysis. —*v.i.* **2.** to undergo ammonolysis. [1930–35; AMMONOL(YSIS) + -IZE]

am·moph·i·lous (ə mof′ə ləs), *adj. Biol.* living or growing in sand. [1875–80; < Gk *ámmo(s)* sand + -PHILOUS]

am·mu·ni·tion (am′yə nish′ən), *n.* **1.** the material fired, scattered, dropped, or detonated from any weapon, as bombs or rockets, and esp. shot, shrapnel, bullets, or shells fired by guns. **2.** the means of igniting or exploding such material, as primers, fuzes, and gunpowder. **3.** any material, means, weapons, etc., used in any conflict: *a crude ammunition of stones.* **4.** information, advice, or supplies to help defend or attack a viewpoint, argument, or claim: *Give me some ammunition for the debate.* **5.** *Obs.* any military supplies. [1620–30; < MF *amonitions, amunitions* (pl.) military supplies (*a-* A-[5] + *munition* < L; see MUNITION), or < F *la munition,* wrongly analyzed as *l'amunition*]

Amn, *Air Force.* airman.

am·ne·sia (am nē′zhə), *n.* loss of a large block of interrelated memories; complete or partial loss of memory caused by brain injury, shock, etc. [1780–90; < NL < Gk *amnēsía,* var. of *amnēstía* oblivion; perhaps learnedly formed from *mnē-,* s. of *mimnḗskesthai* to remember (cf. MNEMONIC) + *-s-* + *-ia* -IA. See AMNESTY] **—am·nes·tic** (am nes′tik), *adj.*

am·ne·si·ac (am nē′zhē ak′, -zē-), *n.* **1.** a person affected by amnesia. —*adj.* **2.** Also, **am·ne·sic** (am-nē′sik, -zik). displaying the symptoms of amnesia. [1910–15; AMNESI(A) + -AC, after such pairs as MANIA, MANIAC]

am·nes·ty (am′nə stē), *n., pl.* **-ties,** *v.,* **-tied, -ty·ing.** —*n.* **1.** a general pardon for offenses, esp. political offenses, against a government, often granted before any trial or conviction. **2.** *Law.* an act of forgiveness for past offenses, esp. to a class of persons as a whole. **3.** a forgetting or overlooking of any past offense. —*v.t.* **4.** to grant amnesty to; pardon. [1570–80; (< MF *amnestie*) < Gk *amnēstía* oblivion, equiv. to *ámnēst(os)* forgetting (*a-* A-[6] + *mnēs-* remember + *-tos* verbal adj. suffix) + *-ia* -Y[3]]
—Syn. 1. See **pardon.**

Am′nesty Interna′tional, an independent worldwide organization working against human-rights violations and for the release of persons imprisoned for political or religious dissent; Nobel peace prize 1977. *Abbr.:* AI, A.I.

am·ni·o (am′nē ō′), *n., pl.* **-ni·os.** *Informal.* amniocentesis. [1985–90; by shortening]

am·ni·o·cen·te·sis (am′nē ō sen tē′sis), *n., pl.* **-ses** (-sēz). a surgical procedure for obtaining a sample of amniotic fluid from the amniotic sac in the uterus of a pregnant woman by inserting a hollow needle through the abdominal wall, used in diagnosing certain genetic defects or possible obstetric complications. [1955–60; *amnio-* (as comb. form of AMNION) + CENTESIS]

am·ni·og·ra·phy (am′nē og′rə fē), *n., pl.* **-phies.** an x-ray examination of the amniotic sac after the injection of an opaque solution, performed to permit visualization of the umbilical cord and the placenta. [1965–70; *amnio-* (as comb. form of AMNION) + -GRAPHY]

am·ni·on (am′nē ən), *n., pl.* **-ni·ons, -ni·a** (-nē ə). **1.** *Anat., Zool.* the innermost of the embryonic or fetal membranes of reptiles, birds, and mammals; the sac in which the embryo is suspended. **2.** *Zool.* a similar membrane of insects and other invertebrates. [1660–70; < Gk, equiv. to *amn(ós)* lamb (see YEAN) + *-ion* dim. suffix]

am·ni·ote (am′nē ōt′), *n.* any vertebrate of the group Amniota, comprising the reptiles, birds, and mammals, characterized by having an amnion during the embryonic stage. Cf. **anamniote.** [< NL *amniota;* see AMNION, -OTE]

am·ni·ot·ic (am′nē ot′ik), *adj. Anat., Zool.* of, pertaining to, or having an amnion. Also, **am·ni·on·ic** (am′-nē on′ik), **am·nic** (am′nik). [1815–25; AMNI(ON) + -OTIC]

am′niot′ic flu′id, *Anat., Zool.* the watery fluid in the amnion, in which the embryo is suspended.

amn't (ant, am′ənt), am not.
—Usage. See **ain't.**

am·o·bar·bi·tal (am′ō bär′bi tal′, -tôl′), *n. Pharm.* a colorless, crystalline barbiturate, $C_{11}H_{18}N_2O_3$, used chiefly as a sedative. [1945–50; AM(YL) + -O- + BARBITAL]

a·moe·ba (ə mē′bə), *n., pl.* **-bas, -bae** (-bē). ameba.

am·oe·bae·an (am′ə bē′ən), *adj. Pros.* alternately responsive, as verses in dialogue. Also, **am′oe·be′an.** [1650–60; < L *amoebae(us)* antiphonal (< Gk *amoibaîos* interchanging, equiv. to *amoib(ḗ)* alternation (cf. AMEBA) + *-aios* adj. suffix) + -AN]

am·oe·bi·a·sis (am′ə bī′ə sis), *n. Pathol.* amebiasis.

a·moe·bic (ə mē′bik), *adj.* amebic.

a·moe·bo·cyte (ə mē′bə sīt′), *n.* amebocyte.

a·moe·boid (ə mē′boid), *adj.* ameboid. **—a·moe′·boid·ism,** *n.*

a·mok (ə muk′, ə mok′), *n.* **1.** (among members of certain Southeast Asian cultures) a psychic disturbance characterized by depression followed by a manic urge to murder. —*adv.* **2. run** or **go amok.** See **amuck** (def. 1). —*adj.* **3.** amuck. Also, **amuck.** [1865–70; < Malay *amuk*]

a·mo·le (ə mō′lā; *Sp.* ä mô′le), *n., pl.* **-les** (-lāz; *Sp.* -les). *Southwestern U.S.* **1.** the root of any of several plants, as Mexican species of agaves, used as a substitute for soap. **2.** any such plant itself. [< MexSp < Nahuatl *ahmōlli* soap]

A·mon (ä′mən), *n. Egyptian Myth.* Amen.

a·mong (ə mung′), *prep.* **1.** in, into, or through the midst of; in association or connection with; surrounded by: *He was among friends.* **2.** in the midst of, so as to influence: *missionary work among the local people.* **3.** with a share for each of: *Divide the cigars among you.* **4.** in the number, class, or group of; of or out of: *That is among the things we must do.* **5.** by all or with the whole of; by most or with many of: *popular among the people.* **6.** by the joint or reciprocal action of: *Settle it among yourselves.* **7.** each with the other; mutually: *They quarreled among themselves.* **8.** familiar to or characteristic of: *a proverb among the Spanish.* [bef. 1000; ME; OE *amang, onmang* for *on gemang, on gemonge* (dat. of *gemong* crowd, akin to *mengan* to mix) in (the) group (of); akin to MINGLE]
—Syn. AMONG and BETWEEN suggest a relationship that is not necessarily physical: *among the crowd; between two pillars; They don't have much sense among them. Between you and me, I don't like any of them.* AMID, a more literary word, implies being in the middle of a place or surrounded by something: *to stand amid ruins.*
—Usage. See **between.**

a·mongst (ə mungst′, ə mungkst′), *prep. Chiefly Brit.* among. [1200–50; earlier *amonges,* ME *amonges,* equiv. to *among* AMONG + *-es* adv. gen. suffix; excrescent *-t* as in AGAINST]

A-mon-Ra (ä′mən rä′), *n. Egyptian Myth.* Amen-Ra.

a·mon·til·la·do (ə mon′tl ä′dō, -tē ä′-; *Sp.* ä môn′tē-lyä′thô, -yä′thô), *n.* a pale, dry Spanish sherry. [1815–25; < Sp, equiv. to *a* to, near (< L *ad*) + *Montill(a)* (see MONTILLA) + *-ado* -ATE[1]]

A·mor (ä′môr), *n.* Cupid. [< L: love; see AMOROUS]

a·mo·ra (ə môr′ə, ə mōr′ə), *n., pl.* **a·mo·ra·im** (ä′mô-rä′im, ä′mō-). (*often cap.*) *Judaism.* one of a group of Jewish scholars, active in the rabbinical academies of Palestine and Babylonia from the 3rd to the 6th centuries A.D., whose commentaries on and interpretations of the Mishnah comprise the Palestinian and Babylonian Gemaras. Cf. **sabora, tanna.** [< Heb *āmōrā'* interpreter]

a·mor·al (ā môr′əl, a môr′-, ā mor′-, a mor′-), *adj.* **1.** not involving questions of right or wrong; without moral quality; neither moral nor immoral. **2.** having no moral standards, restraints, or principles; unaware of or indifferent to questions of right or wrong: *a completely amoral person.* [1880–85; A-[6] + MORAL] **—a·mor′al·ism,** *n.* **—a·mo·ral·i·ty** (ā′mə ral′i tē, am′ə-), *n.* **—a·mor′al·ly,** *adv.*
—Syn. See **immoral.**

A′mor as′teroid, *Astron.* one of a small group of asteroids whose orbits approach but do not cross that of the earth: named after the first such asteroid discovered (1932). Cf. **Apollo asteroid.**

AMORC, Ancient Mystic Order Rosae Crucis. See under **Rosicrucian** (def. 2).

am·o·ret·to (am′ə ret′ō; *It.* ä′mô ret′tô), *n., pl.* **-ret·ti** (-ret′ē; *It.* -ret′tē). a little cupid. [1590–1600; < It, equiv. to *amor(e)* love (< L *amōrem,* acc. of *amor*) + *-etto* -ET; cf. AMOUR]

a·mo·ri·no (am′ə rē′nō; *It.* ä′mô rē′nô), *n., pl.* **-ni** (-nē). *Fine Arts.* a putto represented as an infant cupid. [1855–60; < It, equiv. to *amor(e)* love (see AMORETTO) + *-ino* dim. suffix (< L *-inus* adj. suffix)]

am·o·rist (am′ər ist), *n.* **1.** a person who is devoted to love and lovemaking. **2.** a person who writes about love. [1575–85; < L *amor* love + -IST] **—am′o·ris′tic,** *adj.*

Am·o·rite (am′ə rīt′), *n.* **1.** a member of one of the principal tribes, or nations, of Canaan before its conquest by the Israelites. II Sam. 12:26–31. **2.** the Semitic language of the Amorites. [1600–10; < Heb *ĕmōr(i)* Amorites + -ITE[1]]

a·mo·ro·so (ä′mə rō′sō; *Sp.* ä′mô rô′sô), *n.* a medium dry sherry of Spain. [1610–20; < Sp: AMOROUS]

am·o·rous (am′ər əs), *adj.* **1.** inclined or disposed to love, esp. sexual love: *an amorous disposition.* **2.** showing or expressing love: *an amorous letter.* **3.** of or pertaining to love: *amorous poetry.* **4.** being in love; enamored: *She smiled and at once he became amorous of her.* [1275–1325; ME < MF < L *amōrōsus,* equiv. to *amor* love + *-ōsus* -OSE[1], -OUS] **—am′o·rous·ly,** *adv.* **—am′·o·rous·ness, am·o·ros·i·ty** (am′ə ros′i tē), *n.*
—Syn. 1. loving; amatory.

a·mor pa·tri·ae (ä′mōr pä′trē ī′; *Eng.* ā′môr pā′-trē ē′), *Latin.* love of one's country; patriotism.

a·mor·phism (ə môr′fiz əm), *n.* **1.** the state or quality of being amorphous. **2.** *Obs.* nihilism (def. 3). [1850–55; < G *Amorphismus* < Gk *ámorph(os)* AMORPHOUS + *-ismos* -ISM]

a·mor·phous (ə môr′fəs), *adj.* **1.** lacking definite form; having no specific shape; formless: *the amorphous clouds.* **2.** of no particular kind or character; indeterminate; having no pattern or structure; unorganized: *an amorphous style; an amorphous personality.* **3.** *Petrog., Mineral.* occurring in a mass, as without stratification or crystalline structure. **4.** *Chem.* not crystalline. **5.** *Biol.* having structural components that are not clearly differentiated, as the nuclear material in certain bacteria. [1725–35; < Gk *ámorphos* shapeless. See A-[6], -MORPH, -OUS] **—a·mor′phous·ly,** *adv.* **—a·mor′·phous·ness,** *n.*

a·mort (ə môrt′), *adj. Archaic.* spiritless; lifeless. [1580–90; < F *à mort* at (the point of) death. See A-[5], MORT]

amort., amortization.

am·or·ti·za·tion (am′ər tə zā′shən, ə môr′-), *n.* **1.** an act or instance of amortizing a debt or other obligation. **2.** the sums devoted to this purpose. Also, **amortizement.** [1665–75; < ML *a(d)mortizātiōn-* (s. of *admortizātiō*). See AMORTIZE, -ATION]

am·or·tize (am′ər tīz′, ə môr′tīz), *v.t.,* **-tized, -tiz·ing.** **1.** *Finance.* **a.** to liquidate or extinguish (a mortgage, debt, or other obligation), esp. by periodic payments to the creditor or to a sinking fund. **b.** to write off a cost of (an asset) gradually. **2.** *Old Eng. Law.* to convey to a corporation or church group; alienate in mortmain. Also, *esp. Brit.,* **am′or·tise′.** [1375–1425; ME *amortisen* < AF, OF *amortiss-,* long s. of *amortir* lit., to kill, die < VL **a(d)mortire* (deriv. of L *mors,* s. *mort-* death, with *ad-* AD-); -IZE later r. *-is(s)-,* prob. by assoc. with AL *a(d)mortizāre*] **—am′or·tiz′a·ble,** *adj.*

am·or·tize·ment (am′ər tīz′mənt, ə môr′tiz-), *n.* **1.** a sloping top on a buttress, pillar, etc. **2.** an architectural feature, as a gable, at the top of a façade. **3.** amortization. Also, **a·mor·tisse·ment** (ə môr′tiz mənt). [1610–20; AMORTIZE + -MENT, after MF or AF *amortissement*]

A·mo·ry (ā′mə rē), *n.* a male or female given name.

A·mos (ā′məs), *n.* **1.** a Minor Prophet of the 8th century B.C. **2.** a book of the Bible bearing his name. **3.** a male given name: from a Hebrew word meaning "burden."

am·o·site (am′ə sīt′), *n. Mineral.* an asbestine variety of anthophyllite, rich in iron, formerly used as a heat-resistant material. [1915–20; *A(sbestos) M(ine) o(f) S(outh Africa)* + -ITE[1]]

a·mount (ə mount′), *n.* **1.** the sum total of two or more quantities or sums; aggregate. **2.** the sum of the principal and interest of a loan. **3.** quantity; measure: *a great amount of resistance.* **4.** the full effect, value, or significance. —*v.i.* **5.** to total; add (usually fol. by *to*): *The repair bill amounts to $300.* **6.** to reach, extend, or be equal in number, quantity, effect, etc.; be equivalent (usually fol. by *to*): *It is stated differently but amounts to the same thing.* **7.** to develop into; become (usually fol.

by *to*): *With his intelligence, he should amount to something when he grows up.* [1250–1300; ME *amounten, amunten* < AF *amo(u)nter, amunter,* OF *amonter* lit., to go up, ascend, prob. *a-* A-[5] + *monter* (see MOUNT[1]); E n. use of v. from early 18th cent.]

—**Usage.** The traditional distinction between AMOUNT and NUMBER is that AMOUNT is used with mass or uncountable nouns (*the amount of paperwork; the amount of energy*) and NUMBER with countable nouns (*a number of songs; a number of days*). Although objected to, the use of AMOUNT instead of NUMBER with countable nouns occurs in both speech and writing, especially when the noun can be considered as a unit or group (*the amount of people present; the amount of weapons*) or when it refers to money (*the amount of dollars paid; the amount of pennies in the till*).

amount′ at risk′, *Insurance.* the difference between the reserve of a life-insurance policy and its face amount.

a·mour (ə mŏŏr′), *n.* **1.** a love affair. **2.** an illicit or secret love affair. [1250–1300; ME < MF, OF *amo(u)r,* repr. a dial. form or < OPr < L *amōrem* acc. of *amor* love, equiv. to *am(āre)* to love + *-or* -OR[1]; cf. AMORETTO]

a·mour-pro·pre (A MOOR PRÔ′PRᵊ), *n. French.* self-esteem; self-respect. [lit., self-love]

am·ox·i·cil·lin (am ok′sə sil′in, ə mok′-), *n. Pharm.* a semisynthetic penicillin, $C_{16}H_{19}N_3O_5S$, taken orally as a broad-spectrum antibiotic. [1970–75; perh. *am(inohydr)ox(yphenyl)* part of its chemical name + (PEN)ICILLIN]

A·moy (ä moi′, am′oi), *n.* **1.** Xiamen. **2.** a Fukienese dialect spoken in and around Xiamen, as well as on Taiwan and Hainan.

amp[1] (amp), *n. Elect.* ampere. [1885–90; by shortening]

amp[2] (amp), *n. Informal.* amplifier. [1960–65; by shortening]

amp[3] (amp), *n. Slang.* **1.** amputation. **2.** amputee. [by shortening]

AMP, *Biochem.* a white, crystalline, water-soluble nucleotide, $C_{10}H_{12}N_5O_3H_2PO_4$, obtained by the partial hydrolysis of ATP or of ribonucleic acid, yielding on hydrolysis adenine, ribose, and orthophosphoric acid. Also called **adenosine monophosphate, adenylic acid.** [1950–55; *a(denosine) m(ono) p(hosphate)*]

amp., *Elect.* **1.** amperage. **2.** ampere; amperes.

AMPAS, Academy of Motion Picture Arts and Sciences.

am·pe·lop·sis (am′pə lop′sis), *n.* any climbing, woody vine or shrub belonging to the genus *Ampelopsis,* of the grape family, having small greenish flowers and inedible berries. [1803; < NL < Gk *ámpel(os)* grapevine + *ópsis* -OPSIS]

Am·pe·los (am′pə los′), *n. Class. Myth.* a satyr who was placed among the stars by Dionysus.

am·per·age (am′pər ij, am pēr′-), *n. Elect.* the strength of an electric current measured in amperes. *Abbr.:* amp. [1890–95; AMPERE + -AGE]

am·pere (am′pēr, am pēr′), *n. Elect.* the base SI unit of electrical current, equivalent to one coulomb per second, formally defined to be the constant current which if maintained in two straight parallel conductors of infinite length, of negligible circular cross section, and placed one meter apart in vacuum, would produce between these conductors a force equal to 2×10^{-7} newton per meter of length. *Abbr.:* A, amp. Also, **am′père.** [1881; named after A. M. AMPÈRE]

Am·père (am′pēr; *Fr.* äN peR′), *n.* **An·dré Ma·rie** (än′drā mə rē′; *Fr.* äN dRā′ MA Rē′), 1775–1836, French physicist. —**Am·per·i·an** (am pēr′ē ən, -per′-), *adj.*

am·pere-hour (am′pēr ouᵊr′, -ou′ər, am pēr′-), *n. Elect.* a unit of electric charge noting the amount of electricity transferred by a current of one ampere in one hour, equal to 3600 coulombs. *Abbr.:* Ah, amp-hr, amp. hr. [1880–85]

Am′père's law′, *Physics.* the law that a magnetic field induced by an electric current is, at any point, directly proportional to the product of the current intensity and the length of the current conductor, inversely proportional to the square of the distance between the point and the conductor, and perpendicular to the plane joining the point and the conductor. [named after A. M. AMPÈRE]

am·pere-turn (am′pēr tûrn′, am pēr′-), *n. Elect.* **1.** one complete convolution of a conducting coil, through which one ampere of current passes. **2.** the magnetomotive force produced by one ampere passing through one complete turn or convolution of a coil. *Abbr.:* At [1880–85]

am·per·o·met·ric (am′pēr ə me′trik, am pēr′ə-), *adj. Elect.* pertaining to or involving the measurement of an electric current. [1940–45; AMPERE + -O- + METRIC[1]]

amperomet′ric titra′tion, *Chem.* titration in which the end point is determined by measuring the amperage of an electric current of given voltage that is passed through the solution. [1940–45]

am·per·sand (am′pər sand′, am′pər sand′), *n.* a character or symbol (& or &) for *and: Smith & Jones, Inc.* [1820–30; contr. of *and per se and* lit., (the symbol) & by itself (stands for) and; see PER SE]

am·phet·a·mine (am fet′ə mēn′, -min), *n. Pharm.* a racemic drug, $C_9H_{13}N$, that stimulates the central nervous system: used chiefly to lift the mood in depressive states and to control the appetite in cases of obesity. [1935–40; A(LPHA) + M(ETHYL) + PH(ENYL) + ET(HYL) + AMINE]

CONCISE ETYMOLOGY KEY: <, descended or borrowed from; >, whence; b., blend of, blended; c., cognate with; cf., compare; deriv., derivative; equiv., equivalent; imit., imitative; obl., oblique; r., replacing; s., stem; sp., spelling, spelled; resp., respelling, respelled; trans., translation; ?, origin unknown; *, unattested; ‡, probably earlier than. See the full key inside the front cover.

amphi-, a prefix occurring in loanwords from Greek (*amphibious*); on this model, used with the meaning "two," "both," "on both sides," in the formation of compound words: *amphiaster.* [< Gk, comb. form of *amphí* on both sides; c. L *amb(i)-* AMBI-, Albanian *mbë;* akin to OE *ymb(e)-* around]

Am·phi·a·ra·us (am′fē ə rā′əs), *n. Class. Myth.* a hero who joined the Seven against Thebes, although he knew that his death was fated: deified after death.

am·phi·ar·thro·sis (am′fē är thrō′sis), *n., pl.* **-ses** (-sēz). *Anat.* a joint permitting only slight motion, as that between the vertebrae. [1830–40; AMPHI- + Gk *árthrōsis* articulation. See ARTHRO-, -OSIS] —**am′phi·ar·thro′di·al,** *adj.*

am·phi·as·ter (am′fē as′tər), *n. Cell Biol.* the achromatic spindle with two asters that forms during mitosis. [1880–85; AMPHI- + -ASTER[2]]

Am·phib·i·a (am fib′ē ə), *n.* the class comprising the amphibians. [1600–10; < NL < Gk *amphíbia (zôia)* (animals) living a double life, neut. pl. of *amphíbios.* See AMPHIBIOUS]

am·phib·i·an (am fib′ē ən), *n.* **1.** any cold-blooded vertebrate of the class Amphibia, comprising frogs and toads, newts and salamanders, and caecilians, the larvae being typically aquatic, breathing by gills, and the adults being typically semiterrestrial, breathing by lungs and through the moist, glandular skin. **2.** an amphibious plant. **3.** an airplane designed for taking off from and landing on both land and water. **4.** Also called **amtrac.** a flat-bottomed, armed, military vehicle, equipped with both tracks and a rudder, that can travel either on land or in water, used chiefly for landing assault troops. —*adj.* **5.** belonging or pertaining to the Amphibia. **6.** amphibious (def. 2). [1630–40; < L *amphibi(a),* neut. pl. of *amphibius* (adj.) (see AMPHIBIOUS) + -AN]

am·phi·bi·ot·ic (am′fi bī ot′ik), *adj. Zool.* living on land during the adult stage and in water during a larval stage. [AMPHI- + BIOTIC]

am·phib·i·ous (am fib′ē əs), *adj.* **1.** living or able to live both on land and in water; belonging to both land and water. **2.** Also, **amphibian.** capable of operating on both land and water: *amphibious vehicles.* **3.** of or pertaining to military operations by both land and naval forces against the same object, esp. to a military attack by troops landed by naval ships. **4.** trained or organized to fight, or fighting, on both land and sea: *amphibious troops.* **5.** combining two qualities, kinds, traits, etc.; of or having a mixed or twofold nature. [1635–45; < L *amphibius* < Gk *amphíbios* living a double life. See AMPHI-, BIO-, -OUS] —**am·phib′i·ous·ly,** *adv.* —**am·phib′i·ous·ness,** *n.*

am·phi·bole (am′fə bōl′), *n. Mineral.* any of a complex group of hydrous silicate minerals, containing chiefly calcium, magnesium, sodium, iron, and aluminum, and including hornblende, tremolite, asbestos, etc., occurring as important constituents of many rocks. [1600–10; < F < LL *amphibolus* AMPHIBOLOUS]

am·phi·bol·ic (am′fə bol′ik), *adj.* equivocal; uncertain; changing; ambiguous. [1850–55; AMPHIBOL(Y) + -IC]

am·phib·o·lite (am fib′ə līt′), *n. Petrog.* a metamorphic rock composed mainly of amphibole and plagioclase. [1825–35; AMPHIBOLE + -ITE[1]] —**am·phib·o·lit·ic** (am fib′ə lit′ik), *adj.*

am·phi·bol·o·gy (am′fə bol′ə jē), *n., pl.* **-gies.** amphiboly. [1325–75; ME *amphibologie* < LL *amphibologia.* See AMPHIBOLY, -LOGY] —**am·phib·o·log·i·cal** (am fib′ə loj′i kəl), *adj.* —**am·phib′o·log′i·cal·ly,** *adv.*

am·phib·o·lous (am fib′ə ləs), *adj.* ambiguous or equivocal, esp. when due to the uncertain grammatical construction of a word or phrase. [1635–45; < L *amphibolus* < Gk *amphíbolos* thrown on both sides, ambiguous, equiv. to *amphi-* AMPHI- + *-bol-* (verbid of *bállein* to throw) + *-os* -OUS]

am·phib·o·ly (am fib′ə lē), *n., pl.* **-lies.** ambiguity of speech, esp. from uncertainty of the grammatical construction rather than of the meaning of the words, as in *The Duke yet lives that Henry shall depose.* Also called **amphibology.** [1580–90; < L *amphibolia* < Gk. See AMPHIBOLOUS, -Y[3]]

am·phi·brach (am′fə brak′), *n. Pros.* a trisyllabic foot, the arrangement of the syllables of which is short, long, short in quantitative meter, or unstressed, stressed, unstressed in accentual meter. Thus, *together* is an accentual amphibrach. [1580–90; < L *amphibrachus* < Gk *amphíbrachys* short before and after (*amphi-* AMPHI- + *brachýs* short); cf. AMPHIMACER] —**am′phi·brach′ic,** *adj.*

am·phi·car·pous (am′fi kär′pəs), *adj. Bot.* producing two kinds of fruit that differ either in form or in time of ripening. Also, **am′phi·car′pic.** [1865–70; AMPHI- + -CARPOUS]

am·phi·ce·lous (am′fə sē′ləs), *adj. Anat., Zool.* concave on both sides, as the bodies of the vertebrae of fishes. Also, **am′phi·coe′lous.** [1865–70; < Gk *amphíkoilos* hollow at both ends. See AMPHI-, -CELE[2], -OUS]

am·phi·chro·ic (am′fi krō′ik), *adj. Chem.* giving either of two colors, one with acids and one with alkalis. Also, **am·phi·chro·mat·ic** (am′fi krō mat′ik, -krə-). [1875–80; AMPHI- + -CHROIC]

am·phic·ty·on (am fik′tē ən), *n.* a deputy to the council of an amphictyony. [1580–90; back formation from *amphictyons* < Gk *amphiktýones,* orig. *amphiktíones* neighbors, equiv. to *amphi-* AMPHI- + *-kti-* inhabit + *-ones* n. suffix (pl.)]

Am·phic·ty·on (am fik′tē ən), *n. Class. Myth.* a son of Deucalion and Pyrrha who seized the throne of Attica and who, in devising a plan for avoiding disputes at his council meetings, became the first man to mix water with wine.

am·phic·ty·on·ic (am fik′tē on′ik), *adj.* of or pertaining to an amphictyon or an amphictyony. [1745–55; < Gk *amphiktyonikós.* See AMPHICTYON, -IC]

am·phic·ty·o·ny (am fik′tē ə nē), *n., pl.* **-nies.** (in ancient Greece) any of the leagues of states, esp. the league at Delphi, united for mutual protection and the worship of a common deity. [1825–35; < Gk *Amphiktyonía.* See AMPHICTYON, -Y[3]]

Am·phid·a·mas (am fid′ə məs), *n. Class. Myth.* **1.** a son of Aleus who, with his brother Cepheus, joined the Argonauts. **2.** (in the *Iliad*) a king of Cythera.

am·phi·dip·loid (am′fi dip′loid), *n. Biol.* a plant having the sum of the chromosome numbers of two parental species, owing to the doubling of the chromosomes in a hybrid of two species. [1925–30; AMPHI- + DIPLOID]

am·phi·dro·mi·a (am′fi drō′mē ə), *n.* a family festival in ancient Athens in honor of the birth of a child, during which the child received its name. [< Gk, equiv. to *amphídrom(os)* running about (see AMPHI-, -DROME) + *-ia* -IA]

am′phi·drom′ic point′ (am′fi drom′ik, am′-), *Oceanog.* a point of almost zero tidal fluctuation on the ocean surface, represented on a chart of cotidal lines by a point from which these lines radiate. [1935–40; < Gk *amphídrom(os)* running both ways + -IC; see AMPHI-, -DROME]

am·phig·e·nous (am fij′ə nəs), *adj.* (of certain parasitic fungi) growing on both sides of leaves. [1825–35; AMPHI- + -GENOUS] —**am·phig′e·nous·ly,** *adv.*

am·phi·go·ry (am′fi gôr′ē, -gōr′ē), *n., pl.* **-ries.** a meaningless or nonsensical piece of writing, esp. one intended as a parody. Also, **amphigouri.** [1800–10; < F *amphigouri,* equiv. to *amphi-* AMPHI- + *gouri;* perh. modeled on F equiv. of PHANTASMAGORIA] —**am·phi·gor·ic** (am′fə gôr′ik, -gor′-), *adj.*

am·phi·gou·ri (am′fi gŏŏr′ē), *n., pl.* **-ris.** amphigory.

am·phi·kar·y·on (am′fi kar′ē on′, -ē ən), *n. Biol.* a diploid nucleus. Cf. **hemikaryon.** [AMPHI- + Gk *káryon* nut] —**am′phi·kar′y·ot′ic,** *adj.*

Am·phil·o·chus (am fil′ə kəs), *n. Class. Myth.* a seer, the son of Amphiaraus and Eriphyle, and the brother of Alcmaeon.

am·phim·a·cer (am fim′ə sər), *n. Pros.* a trisyllabic foot, the arrangement of the syllables of which is long, short, long in quantitative meter, or stressed, unstressed, stressed in accentual meter, as *anodyne,* an accentual amphimacer. [1580–90; < L *amphimacrus* < Gk *amphímakros* long at both ends. See AMPHI-, MACRO-; cf. AMPHIBRACH]

Am·phim·a·rus (am fim′ər əs), *n. Class. Myth.* a son of Poseidon, sometimes believed to be the father, by Urania, of the poet Linus.

am·phi·mix·is (am′fə mik′sis), *n., pl.* **-mix·es** (-mik′sēz). **1.** *Biol.* the merging of the nuclei of the sperm and egg cells; sexual reproduction. **2.** *Psychoanal.* the combining of anal and genital eroticism in the development of sexuality. [1890–95; AMPHI- + Gk *míxis* a mingling, equiv. to *mig-* (s. of *mígnynai* to mix) + *-sis* -SIS] —**am·phi·mic·tic** (am′fə mik′tik), *adj.* —**am′phi·mic′ti·cal·ly,** *adv.*

Am·phin·o·me (am fin′ə mē′), *n. Class. Myth.* a maiden who, along with her sister Evadne, was deceived by Medea into murdering their father, Pelias.

Am·phin·o·mus (am fin′ə məs), *n.* (in the *Odyssey*) Penelope's favorite suitor.

Am·phi·on (am fī′ən, am′fē-), *n. Class. Myth.* a son of Antiope by Zeus, and the husband of Niobe. With his twin brother, Zethus, he built the walls of Thebes, charming the stones into place with his lyre. —**Am·phi·on·ic** (am′fī on′ik, -fē-), *adj.*

am·phi·ox·us (am′fē ok′səs), *n., pl.* **-ox·i** (-ok′sī), **-ox·us·es.** *Zool.* lancelet. [1830–40; < NL: lit., sharp at both ends < Gk *amphi-* AMPHI- + *oxýs* pointed]

am·phi·path·ic (am′fə path′ik), *adj. Chem.* (of a molecule) having two different affinities, as a polar end that is attracted to water and a nonpolar end that is repelled by it. [1970–75; AMPHI- + -PATHIC]

am·phi·phile (am′fə fīl′), *n. Biochem.* any of many organic compounds, as a surfactant, detergent, bile salt, or phospholipid, composed of hydrophilic and hydrophobic portions. [1970–75; AMPHI- + -PHILE] —**am·phi·phil·ic** (am′fə fil′ik), *adj.*

am·phi·ploid (am′fə ploid′), *n.* a hybrid organism having a diploid set of chromosomes from each parental species. [1940–45; AMPHI- + -PLOID]

am·phi·pod (am′fə pod′), *n.* **1.** any of numerous small, flat-bodied crustaceans of the group Amphipoda, including the beach fleas, sand hoppers, etc. —*adj.* **2.** of or pertaining to the amphipods. [1825–35; < NL *Amphipoda;* see AMPHI-, -POD]

am·phip·ro·style (am fip′rə stīl′, am′fə prō′stīl), *adj.* (of a classical temple) prostyle on both fronts. [1700–10; < L *amphiprostylus* < Gk *amphipróstylos.* See AMPHI-, PROSTYLE] —**am·phip′ro·sty′lar,** *adj.*

am·phis·bae·na (am′fəs bē′nə), *n., pl.* **-nae** (-nē), **-nas.** **1.** any of numerous worm lizards of the genus *Amphisbaena.* **2.** *Class. Myth.* a serpent having a head at each end of its body and the ability to move forward or backward. [1350–1400; ME *amphibena* < NL, L < Gk *amphísbaina* a serpent that moves forward or backward, equiv. to *amphis* both ways + *baín(ein)* to go + *-a* n. suffix] —**am′phis·bae′ni·an, am′phis·bae′nic, am′phis·bae′noid, am′phis·bae′nous,** *adj.*

am·phis·ci·ans (am fish′ē ənz, -fish′ənz), *n.pl. Archaic.* inhabitants of the tropics. Also, **am·phis·ci·i** (am fish′ē ī′). [1615–25; < ML *Amphisci(i)* (< Gk *amphískioi,* pl. of *amphískios* (adj.) casting a shadow both ways, equiv. to *amphi-* AMPHI- + *skí(a)* shadow + *-os* adj. suffix) + *-ans,* pl. of -AN]

am·phi·sty·lar (am′fə stī′lər), *adj. Archit.* **1.** (of a classical temple) having columns on both fronts. **2.** having columns at both sides. [1900–05; AMPHI- + Gk *stŷl(os)* pillar + -AR[1]]

am•phi•thal•a•mus (am′fə thal′ə məs), *n., pl.* **-mi** (-mī′). (in an ancient Greek house) a room adjoining the thalamus. [< L < Gk *amphithálamos*. See AMPHI-, THALAMUS]

am•phi•the•a•ter (am′fə thē′ə tər, -thēᵊ′tər), *n.* **1.** an oval or round building with tiers of seats around a central open area, as those used in ancient Rome for gladiatorial contests. **2.** any similar place for public contests, games, performances, exhibitions, etc.; an arena, stadium, or auditorium. **3.** a room having tiers of seats arranged around a central area, in which students and other observers can view surgery, hear lectures, etc. **4.** *Brit.* **a.** the first section of seats in the gallery of a theater. **b.** a designated section of seats in any part of a theater. **5.** a level area of oval or circular shape surrounded by rising ground. Also, **am′phi•the′a•tre.** [1540–50; < L *amphitheātrum* < Gk *amphithéātron*. See AMPHI-, THEATER] —**am•phi•the•at•ric** (am′fə thē a′trik), **am′phi•the•at′ri•cal,** *adj.* —**am′phi•the•at′ri•cal•ly,** *adv.*

am•phi•the•ci•um (am′fə thē′shē əm), *n., pl.* **-ci•a** (-shē ə). **1.** *Bot.* the layer or one of the layers of cells in the capsule of a moss surrounding the spores. **2.** *Mycol.* (in certain lichens) a layer of cells that surrounds the fungal apothecium. [< NL < Gk *amphi-* AMPHI- + *thēkíon* (*thḗk*(*ē*) case, cover + *-ion* dim. suffix)] —**am•phi•the•cial** (am′fə thē′shəl, -shē əl, -sē əl), *adj.*

Am•phith•e•mis (am fith′ə mis), *n. Class. Myth.* a son of Apollo and Acacallis.

am•phi•thu•ron (am′fə thŏŏr′on), *n., pl.* **-thu•ra** (-thŏŏr′ə), **-thu•rons.** amphithyra (def. 1).

am•phi•thy•ra (äm fē′thē rä; *Eng.* am fith′ər ə), *n., pl.* **-ra. 1.** Also, **amphithyron, am•phi•thu•ra** (am′fə-thŏŏr′ə), **amphithuron.** *Gk. Orth. Ch.* a divided curtain in front of the door of the iconostasis. **2.** pl. of **amphithyron.** [< LGk, equiv. to *amphi-* AMPHI- + *thýra* door]

am•phi•thy•ron (äm fē′thē rôn; *Eng.* am fith′ə ron′), *n., pl.* **-phi•thy•ra** (-fē′thē rä; *Eng.* -fith′ər ə), **-phi•thy•rons.** amphithyra (def. 1). Also, **amphithuron.**

am•phit•ri•chate (am fi′tri kit), *adj.* (of bacteria) having a single flagellum at each end. Also, **am•phit′ri•chous.** [< Gk *amphi-* AMPHI- + *trich-* (s. of *thríx* hair) + -ATE[1]]

Am•phi•tri•te (am′fi trī′tē), *n.* an ancient Greek sea goddess, a daughter of Nereus and the wife of Poseidon.

am•phit•ro•pous (am fi′trə pəs), *adj. Bot.* (of an ovule) inverted so that the funicle is in the middle of one side. [1835–45; AMPHI- + -TROPOUS]

Am•phit•ru•o (am fi′trōō ō′), *n.* a comedy (c200 B.C.) by Plautus.

Am•phit•ry•on (am fi′trē ən), *n. Class. Myth.* the husband of the virtuous Alcmene, whom Zeus seduced by assuming the form of Amphitryon, resulting in the birth of Hercules.

Amphitryon 38, a play (1938) by Jean Giraudoux.

am•phi•u•ma (am′fē yōō′mə), *n.* an aquatic, eellike salamander of the genus *Amphiuma,* of the southeastern U.S., having two pairs of very small feet. [< NL *Amphiuma* name of the genus, prob. irreg. formation. See AMPHI-, PNEUMA]

am•pho•gen•ic (am′fə jen′ik), *adj. Biol.* producing both male and female offspring. Also, **am•phog•e•nous** (am foj′ə nəs). [*ampho-* (< Gk *amphō-*; see AMPHI-) + -GENIC] —**am•phog•e•ny** (am foj′ə nē), *n.*

am•pho•lyte (am′fə līt′), *n. Chem.* an ampholytic substance. [AMPHO(TERIC) + (ELECTRO)LYTE]

am•pho•lyt•ic (am′fə lit′ik), *adj. Chem.* capable of ionizing into both anions and cations; amphoteric. [AMPHOLYTE + -IC]

am•pho•ra (am′fər ə), *n., pl.* **-pho•rae** (-fə rē′), **-pho•ras.** *Gk. and Rom. Antiq.* a large two-handled storage jar having an oval body, usually tapering to a point at the base, with a pair of handles extending from immediately below the lip to the shoulder: used chiefly for oil, wine, etc., and, set on a foot, as a commemorative vase awarded the victors in contests such as the Panathenaic games. Cf. **pelike, stamnos.** [1300–50; ME < L < Gk *amphoreús,* equiv. to *am*(*phi*)- AMPHI- + *phoreús* bearer (i.e., handle), akin to *phérein* to bear] —**am′pho•ral,** *adj.*

am•phor•ic (am fôr′ik, -for′-), *adj.* resembling the deep, hollow sound made by blowing across the mouth of a large, narrow-necked, empty bottle: *amphoric breathing.* [1830–40; AMPHOR(A) + -IC] —**am•pho•ric•i•ty** (am′fə ris′i tē), *n.*

am•pho•ris•kos (am′fə ris′kəs), *n., pl.* **-koi** (-koi). *Gk. and Rom. Antiq.* a miniature amphora. [< Gk, equiv. to *amphor*(*eús*) AMPHORA + *-iskos* dim. suffix]

am•pho•ter•ic (am′fə ter′ik), *adj. Chem.* capable of functioning either as an acid or as a base. [1840–50; < Gk *amphóter*(*os*) (comp. of *ámphō* both; c. L *ambō*) + -IC]

am•pho•ter•i•cin (am′fə ter′ə sin), *n. Pharm.* an amphoteric antibiotic produced by the bacterium *Streptomyces nodosus* and used in the treatment of fungal infections. [1950–55; AMPHOTERIC + -IN[2]]

amp-hr, *Elect.* ampere-hour. Also, **amp. hr.**

am•pi•cil•lin (am′pə sil′in), *n. Pharm.* a broad-spectrum semisynthetic penicillin, $C_{16}H_{19}N_3O_4S$, effective against certain susceptible Gram-positive and Gram-negative bacteria. [1965–70; prob. *am*(*inobenzyl*)-*p*(*en*)*icillin,* an alternate chemical name]

am•ple (am′pəl), *adj.,* **-pler, -plest. 1.** fully sufficient or more than adequate for the purpose or needs; plentiful; enough: *an ample supply of water; ample time to finish.* **2.** of sufficient or abundant measure; liberal; copious: *an ample reward.* **3.** of adequate or more than adequate extent, size, or amount; large; spacious; roomy: *ample storage space.* [1400–50; late ME < AF < L *amplus* wide, large] —**am′ple•ness,** *n.*

—**Syn. 1.** See **plentiful. 2.** generous, free, abounding, lavish, plenteous, overflowing. AMPLE, LIBERAL, COPIOUS, PROFUSE describe degrees of abundant provision. AMPLE implies a plentiful provision: *to give ample praise.* LIBERAL implies provision from a generous supply (more than AMPLE but less than COPIOUS): *Liberal amounts of food were distributed to the needy.* COPIOUS implies an apparently inexhaustible and lavish abundance: *a copious flow of tears.* PROFUSE implies a still more unrestrained abundance of provision or flow: *profuse in his apologies.* **3.** extensive, vast, great, capacious. —**Ant. 2.** scanty, meager.

am•plex•i•caul (am plek′si kôl′), *adj. Bot.* clasping the stem, as some leaves do at their base. [1750–60; < NL *amplexicaulis,* equiv. to L *amplex*(*us*) embrace (see AMPLEXUS) + *-i-* -I- + *caulis* stem (see COLE)]

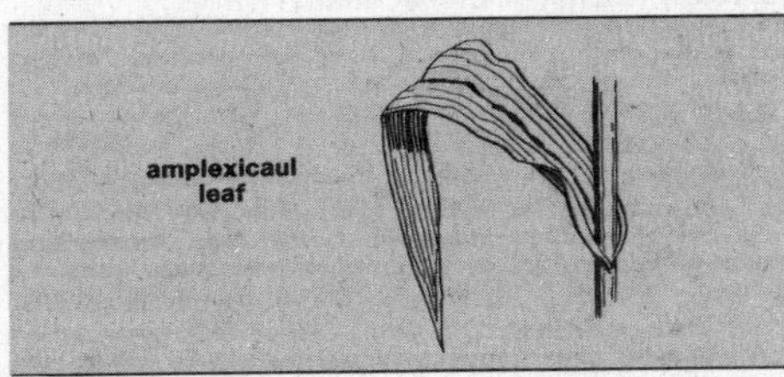

am•plex•i•fo•li•ate (am′plek sə fō′lē it, -āt′, am-plek′-), *adj. Bot.* having amplexicaul leaves. [1875–80; *amplexi-* (see AMPLEXICAUL) + FOLIATE]

am•plex•us (am plek′səs), *n., pl.* **-us•es, -us.** the clasping posture of fertilization in frogs and toads. [1925–30; < NL, L: embrace, equiv. to *amplect*(*i*) to embrace (*am-,* var. of *ambi-* AMBI- + *plecti,* deponent of *plectere* to plait, twine; cf. COMPLEX, PLEXUS) + *-tus* suffix of v. action]

am•pli•ate (am′plē it, -āt′), *adj.* enlarged; dilated. [1505–15; < L *ampliātus* extended (ptp. of *ampliāre*). See AMPLE, -I-, -ATE[1]]

am•pli•a•tion (am′plē ā′shən), *n. Archaic.* an enlarging or extending; amplification. [1500–10; < L *ampliātiōn-* (s. of *ampliātiō*) an extending. See AMPLIATE, -ION]

am•pli•dyne (am′pli dīn′), *n. Elect.* a direct-current generator with a rotating armature, capable of magnifying a small amount of power supplied to the field winding of the device and using the amplified power to operate an attached, direct-current motor. [1935–40; AMPLI(FIER) + DYNE]

am•pli•fi•ca•tion (am′plə fi kā′shən), *n.* **1.** the act of amplifying or the state of being amplified. **2.** expansion of a statement, narrative, etc., as for rhetorical purposes: *In the revision, the story underwent considerable amplification.* **3.** a statement, narrative, etc., so expanded: *The text of the second edition was an amplification.* **4.** the matter or substance used to expand an idea, statement, or the like: *He added an extra paragraph to his speech as an amplification.* **5.** *Elect.* increase in the strength of current, voltage, or power. **6.** *Genetics.* See **gene amplification.** [1540–50; < L *amplificātiōn-* (s. of *amplificātiō*). See AMPLE, -I-, -FICATION]

am•plif•i•ca•to•ry (am plif′i kə tôr′ē, -tōr′ē), *adj.* of the nature of enlargement or extension, as of a statement, narrative, etc. [1840–50; < L *amplificā*(*re*) to increase (see AMPLIFY) + -TORY[1]]

am•pli•fi•er (am′plə fī′ər), *n.* **1.** a person or thing that amplifies or enlarges. **2.** an electronic component or circuit for amplifying power, current, or voltage. [1540–50; AMPLIFY + -ER[1]]

am•pli•fy (am′plə fī′), *v.,* **-fied, -fy•ing.** —*v.t.* **1.** to make larger, greater, or stronger; enlarge; extend. **2.** to expand in stating or describing, as by details or illustrations; clarify by expanding. **3.** *Elect.* to increase the amplitude of; cause amplification in. **4.** *Archaic.* to exaggerate. —*v.i.* **5.** to discourse at length; expatiate or expand one's remarks, speech, etc. (usually fol. by *on*): *The preacher amplified on the theme of brotherly love.* [1375–1425; late ME *amplifyen* < MF *amplifier* < L *amplificāre* to increase, augment. See AMPLE, -IFY] —**am′pli•fi′a•ble,** *adj.*

—**Syn. 1.** increase, intensify, heighten. **2.** widen, broaden, develop. —**Ant. 1.** contract, reduce. **2.** condense, abridge.

am•pli•tude (am′pli tōōd′, -tyōōd′), *n.* **1.** the state or quality of being ample, esp. as to breadth or width; largeness; greatness of extent. **2.** large or full measure; abundance; copiousness. **3.** mental range, scope, or capacity. **4.** *Physics.* the absolute value of the maximum displacement from a zero value during one period of an oscillation. **5.** *Elect.* the maximum deviation of an alternating current from its average value. **6.** *Astron.* the arc of the horizon measured from the east or west point to the point where a vertical circle through a heavenly body would intersect the horizon. **7.** *Math.* argument (def. 8b). [1540–50; < L *amplitūdō.* See AMPLE, -I-, -TUDE]

am′plitude modula′tion, *Electronics, Radio.* See **AM.** [1920–25]

am•ply (am′plē), *adv.* in an ample manner; sufficiently or abundantly: *He apologized amply for his error. They were amply supplied with food.* [1550–60; AMP(LE) + -LY]

am•pule (am′pyōōl, -pōōl), *n. Med.* a sealed glass or plastic bulb containing solutions for hypodermic injection. Also, **am′pul, am′poule.** [1175–1225; < F < L *ampulla* AMPULLA; r. ME *ampulle* < OF < L; r. OE *ampella, ampulla* < L]

am•pul•la (am pul′ə, -pŏŏl′ə), *n., pl.* **-pul•lae** (-pul′ē, -pŏŏl′ē). **1.** *Anat.* a dilated portion of a canal or duct, esp. of the semicircular canals of the ear. **2.** *Zool., Bot.* any flask-shaped structure. **3.** *Eccles.* **a.** a vessel for the wine and water used at the altar. **b.** a vessel for holding consecrated oil. **4.** a two-handled bottle having a somewhat globular shape, made of glass or earthenware, used by the ancient Romans for holding oil, wine, or perfumes. **5.** *Ichthyol.* See **ampulla of Lorenzini.** [< NL, L, equiv. to *amphor*(*a*) AMPHORA + *-la* dim. suffix, with normal vowel reduction and Gk *ph* rendered as *p*]

am•pul•la•ceous (am′pə lā′shəs), *adj.* like an ampulla; bottle-shaped. Also, **am•pul•lar** (am pul′ər, -pŏŏl′-), **am•pul•la•ry** (am pul′ə rē, -pŏŏl′-, am′pə ler′-ē). [1770–80; < L *ampullāceus.* See AMPULLA, -ACEOUS]

ampul′la of Lo•ren•zi′ni (lôr′ən zē′nē), *Ichthyol.* any of an array of electroreceptors in the head of sharks, skates, and rays capable of detecting weak electrical signals produced by muscular activity in other creatures. [after Italian physician Stefano *Lorenzini* (fl. 1678), who first described them]

am•pul•lu•la (am pul′yə lə, -pŏŏl′-), *n., pl.* **-lae** (-lē′). *Anat.* a small ampulla. [< NL; see AMPULLA, -ULE]

am•pu•tate (am′pyŏŏ tāt′), *v.t.,* **-tat•ed, -tat•ing. 1.** to cut off (all or part of a limb or digit of the body), as by surgery. **2.** to prune, lop off, or remove: *Because of space limitations the editor amputated the last two paragraphs of the news report.* **3.** *Obs.* to prune, as branches of trees. [1630–40; < L *amputātus* pruned, trimmed (ptp. of *amputāre*), equiv. to *am*(*bi*) around (cf. AMBI-) + *put-* trim + *-ātus* -ATE[1]] —**am′pu•ta′tion,** *n.* —**am′•pu•ta′tive,** *adj.* —**am′pu•ta′tor,** *n.*

am•pu•tee (am′pyŏŏ tē′), *n.* a person who has lost all or part of an arm, hand, leg, etc., by amputation. [1905–10; AMPUT(ATED) + -EE, modeled on F *amputé,* ptp. of *amputer* to amputate]

Am•py•cus (am′pi kəs), *n. Class. Myth.* a son of Pelias, husband of Chloris, and father of Mopsus. Also, **Am•pyx** (am′piks).

Am•ram (am′ram), *n.* the father of Aaron and Moses. Ex. 6:20.

Am•ra•tian (am rā′shən), *adj.* of, pertaining to, or belonging to the predynastic Chalcolithic culture that flourished in Upper Egypt about 3800 B.C., characterized by the working of raw gold, the use of copper, and the burial of the dead in shallow graves. [named after (El) *Amra,* site of archaeological discoveries in Upper Egypt; see -IAN (*-t-* is hiatus-filling)]

Am•ri (am′rī), *n. Douay Bible.* Omri.

am•ri•none (am′rə nōn′), *n. Pharm.* a potent substance, $C_{10}H_9N_3O$, used in the treatment of congestive heart failure. [perh. AM(INO-) + (*py*)*ri*(*di*)*none* components of its chemical name; see PYRIDINE, -ONE]

am•ri•ta (əm rē′tə), *n. Hindu Myth.* **1.** the beverage of immortality. **2.** the immortality conferred by this beverage. Also, **am•ree′ta.** [1800–10; < Skt, equiv. to *a-* not (see A-[6]) + *mṛta* dead (*mṛ* die + *-ta* verbid suffix); akin to Gk *ámbrotos* IMMORTAL]

Am•rit•sar (əm rit′sər), *n.* a city in NW Punjab, in NW India: site of the holiest shrine of the Sikh religion. 432,663.

AMS, Agricultural Marketing Service.

A.M.S., Army Medical Staff.

Am•ster•dam (am′stər dam′; *for 1 also Du.* äm′stər-däm′), *n.* **1.** a city in and the official capital of the Netherlands. 712,294. Cf. **Hague, The. 2.** a city in E New York. 21,872.

A.M.S.W., Master of Arts in Social Work.

amt (amt, ämt), *n.* an administrative division in Denmark. [< Dan < G; OHG *ambaht, ampacht* (neut.) service, akin to *ampacht* (masc.) < Gallo-L *ambactus* servant; see EMBASSY]

AMT, alternative minimum tax.

amt., amount.

A.M.T., 1. Associate in Mechanical Technology. **2.** Associate in Medical Technology. **3.** Master of Arts in Teaching.

am•trac (am′trak′), *n.* amphibian (def. 4). Also, **am′•track′.** [1940–45; AM(PHIBIOUS) + TRAC(TOR)]

Am•trak (am′trak′), *n.* a government-subsidized public corporation created by Congress in 1970 to operate a national intercity passenger railroad system through contracts with existing railroads. [*Am*(*erican*) *tra*(*vel on trac*)*k*]

amu, See **atomic mass unit.** Also, **AMU**

a•muck (ə muk′), *adv.* **1. run** or **go amuck, a.** to rush about in a murderous frenzy: *The maniac ran amuck in the crowd, shooting at random.* **b.** to rush about wildly; lose self-control: *When the nightclub* *caught fire the patrons ran amuck, blocking the exits.* —*adj.* **2.** mad with murderous frenzy. —*n.* **3.** amok. [1510–20; var. of AMOK]

A·mu Dar·ya (ä′mo͞o där′yə; *Russ.* u mo͞o′ du RYä′), a river in central Asia, flowing NW from the Pamirs to the Aral Sea. ab. 1400 mi. (2250 km) long. Also called **Oxus.**

a·mu·gis (ä mo͞o′gēs), *n.* **1.** a Philippine tree, *Koordersiodendron pinnatum,* of the cashew family. **2.** the hard, reddish wood of this tree, used in the construction of houses, ships, etc. [< Tagalog]

am·u·let (am′yə lit), *n.* a small object worn to ward off evil, harm, or illness or to bring good fortune; protecting charm. [1595–1605; (< MF *amulete*) < L *amulētum*]
—**Syn.** talisman.

A·mu·li·us (ə myo͞o′lē əs), *n. Rom. Legend.* a son of Proca who revolted against his brother Numitor and seized the throne of Alba Longa.

A·mund·sen (ä′mənd sən; *Norw.* ä′mo͝on sən), *n.* **Ro·ald** (rō′äl), 1872–1928, Norwegian explorer: discovered the South Pole in 1911.

A·mur (ä mo͝or′; *Russ.* u MOOR′), *n.* a river in E Asia, forming most of the boundary between N Manchuria and the SE Russian Federation, flowing into the Sea of Okhotsk. ab. 2700 mi. (4350 km) long. Chinese, **Heilong Jiang.**

a·mur·ca (ə mûr′kə), *n.* the lees or sediment of olive oil. [< L < Gk *amórgē*]

Amur′ cork′ tree′, an Asiatic cork tree, *Phellodendron amurense,* of the rue family, having a deeply ridged, corky bark.

Amur′ priv′et, a northern Chinese shrub, *Ligustrum amurense,* of the olive family, having hairy leaves and white flowers.

A.Mus., Associate in Music.

A.Mus.D., Doctor of Musical Arts.

a·muse (ə myo͞oz′), *v.t.,* **a·mused, a·mus·ing. 1.** to hold the attention of (someone) pleasantly; entertain or divert in an enjoyable or cheerful manner: *She amused the guests with witty conversation.* **2.** to cause mirth, laughter, or the like, in: *The comedian amused the audience with a steady stream of jokes.* **3.** to cause (time, leisure, etc.) to pass agreeably. **4.** *Archaic.* to keep in expectation by flattery, pretenses, etc. **5.** *Obs.* **a.** to engross; absorb. **b.** to puzzle; distract. [1470–80; < MF *amuser* to divert, amuse; see A-[5], MUSE] —**a·mus′a·ble,** *adj.* —**a·mus′er,** *n.*
—**Syn. 1.** please, charm, cheer. AMUSE, DIVERT, ENTERTAIN mean to occupy the attention with something pleasant. That which AMUSES is usually playful or humorous and pleases the fancy. DIVERT implies turning the attention from serious thoughts or pursuits to something light, amusing, or lively. That which ENTERTAINS usually does so because of a plan or program that engages and holds the attention by being pleasing and sometimes instructive.

a·mused (ə myo͞ozd′), *adj.* **1.** pleasurably entertained, occupied, or diverted. **2.** displaying amusement: *an amused expression on her face.* **3.** aroused to mirth. [1590–1600; AMUSE + ED[2]] —**a·mus·ed·ly** (ə myo͞o′zid lē), *adv.*

a·muse·ment (ə myo͞oz′mənt), *n.* **1.** anything that amuses; pastime; entertainment. **2.** the act of amusing. **3.** the state of being amused; enjoyment. [1595–1605; < MF; see AMUSE, -MENT]
—**Syn. 1.** diversion, game. **3.** recreation, delight.

amuse′ment park′, a large park equipped with such recreational devices as a merry-go-round, Ferris wheel, roller coaster, etc., and usually having booths for games and refreshments. [1905–10]

amuse′ment tax′, a tax levied on such forms of entertainment as motion pictures, theater, etc., and included in the total admission price. Cf. **cabaret tax.**

a·mu·si·a (ā myo͞o′zē ə), *n. Med.* the inability to produce or comprehend music or musical sounds. [< NL < Gk *amousía* state of being without the Muses, especially song. See A-[6], MUSE, -IA]

a·mus·ing (ə myo͞o′zing), *adj.* **1.** pleasantly entertaining or diverting: *an amusing speaker.* **2.** causing laughter or mirth; humorously entertaining: *an amusing joke.* [1590–1600; AMUSE + -ING[2]] —**a·mus′ing·ly,** *adv.* —**a·mus′ing·ness,** *n.*
—**Syn. 1.** charming, cheering, lively. **2.** laughable, delightful, funny. AMUSING, COMICAL, DROLL describe that which causes mirth. That which is AMUSING is quietly humorous or funny in a gentle, good-humored way: *The baby's attempts to talk were amusing.* That which is COMICAL causes laughter by being incongruous, witty, or ludicrous: *His huge shoes made the clown look comical.* DROLL adds to COMICAL the idea of strange or peculiar, and sometimes that of sly or waggish humor: *the droll antics of a kitten; a droll imitation.*

a·mu·sive (ə myo͞o′ziv), *adj.* amusing; entertaining. [1720–30; AMUSE + -IVE] —**a·mu′sive·ly,** *adv.* —**a·mu′sive·ness,** *n.*

AMVETS (am′vets′), *n.* an organization of U.S. veterans of World War II and more recent wars, founded in 1944. [*Am*(*erican*) *Vet*(*eran*)*s*]

a·my (ā′mē), *n., pl.* **a·mies.** *Slang.* a vial of amyl nitrate. [by shortening]

A·my (ā′mē), *n.* a female given name: from a French word meaning "beloved."

A·my·clas (ə mī′klas, -kləs), *n. Class. Myth.* **1.** a son of Lacedaemon and Sparta. **2.** a son of Niobe and Amphion.

CONCISE ETYMOLOGY KEY: <, descended or borrowed from; >, whence; b., blend of, blended; c., cognate with; cf., compare; deriv., derivative; equiv., equivalent; imit., imitative; obl., oblique; r., replacing; s., stem; sp., spelling, spelled; resp., respelling, respelled; trans., translation; ?, origin unknown; *, unattested; ‡, probably earlier than. See the full key inside the front cover.

Am·y·cus (am′i kəs), *n. Class. Myth.* a son of Poseidon and one of the Meliae, known for his ruthlessness and his skill at boxing.

am·y·e·li·a (am′ī ē′lē ə, -el′ē ə, am′ē-), *n. Med.* congenital absence of the spinal cord. [< NL < Gk *amyél*(*os*) marrowless (see A-[6], MYEL-) + *-ia* -IA] —**am·y·el·ic** (am′ī el′ik, am′ē-), **a·my·e·lous** (ə mī′ə ləs), *adj.*

a·myg·da·la (ə mig′də lə), *n., pl.* **-lae** (-lē′). *Anat.* **1.** an almond-shaped part, as a tonsil. **2.** a ganglion of the limbic system adjoining the temporal lobe of the brain and involved in emotions of fear and aggression. [bef. 950; < ML: almond, tonsil, L: almond < Gk *amygdálē*; r. ME *amygdal,* OE *amigdal* almond < L *amygdalon* < Gk *amygdalon*; cf. ALMOND]

a·myg·da·la·ceous (ə mig′də lā′shəs), *adj.* belonging or pertaining to the Amygdalaceae, a family of plants bearing fruit containing a single hard seed. [1850–55; < NL *Amygdalace*(*ae*) plant family name (see AMYGDALA, -ACEAE) + -OUS]

a·myg·da·late (ə mig′də lit, -lāt′), *adj.* pertaining to, resembling, or made of almonds. [1650–60; < L *amygdal*(*a*) ALMOND + -ATE[1]]

am·yg·dal·ic (am′ig dal′ik), *adj.* **1.** of almonds. **2.** *Chem.* of or derived from amygdalin or amygdalic acid. [1855–60; < L *amygdal*(*a*) ALMOND + -IC]

am′ygdal′ic ac′id, *Chem.* See **mandelic acid.**

a·myg·da·li·form (ə mig′də lə fôrm′), *adj.* almond-shaped. [< L *amygdal*(*a*) ALMOND + -I- + -FORM]

a·myg·da·lin (ə mig′də lin), *n. Chem., Pharm.* a white, bitter-tasting, water-soluble, glycosidic powder, $C_{20}H_{27}NO_{11}$, usually obtained from bitter almond seeds and the leaves of plants of the genus *Prunus* and related genera: used chiefly in medicine as an expectorant. [1645–55; < L *amygdal*(*a*) ALMOND + -IN[2]]

a·myg·da·line (ə mig′də lin, -līn′), *adj.* of, pertaining to, or resembling an almond. [1725–35; < L *amygdalinus* < Gk *amygdálinos* of almonds. See AMYGDALA, -INE[1]]

a·myg·da·loid (ə mig′də loid′), *n. Petrol.* **1.** a volcanic rock in which rounded cavities formed by the expansion of gas or steam have later become filled with deposits of various minerals. —*adj.* Also, **a·myg′da·loi′dal. 2.** (of rocks) containing amygdules. **3.** almond-shaped. **4.** *Anat.* of or pertaining to an amygdala. [1785–95; < L *amygdal*(*a*) ALMOND + -OID]

a·myg·dule (ə mig′do͞ol, -dyo͞ol), *n. Petrol.* one of the mineral nodules in an amygdaloid. [1875–80; AMYGD(ALA) + -ULE]

am·yl (am′il, ā′mil), *Chem.* —*adj.* **1.** containing an amyl group; pentyl. —*n.* **2.** an amyl group. [1840–50; < Gk *ám*(*ylon*) starch (see AMYLO-) + -YL, with haplology of *am*(*yl*)*-yl*]

amyl-, var. of **amylo-,** esp. before a vowel.

am·y·la·ceous (am′ə lā′shəs), *adj.* of the nature of starch; starchy. [1820–30; AMYL- + -ACEOUS]

am′yl ac′etate, *Chem.* See **banana oil** (def. 1). Also called **am′yl·a·ce′tic e′ther** (am′il ə sē′tik, -set′ik, am′-). [1865–70]

am′yl al′cohol, *Chem.* a colorless liquid, $C_5H_{12}O$, consisting of a mixture of two or more isomeric alcohols, derived from the pentanes, and used as a solvent and intermediate for organic synthesis: the main component of fusel oil. [1860–65]

am·yl·ase (am′ə lās′, -lāz′), *n. Biochem.* **1.** any of a widely distributed class of enzymes that catalyze the hydrolysis of starch, glycogen, and related polysaccharides to oligosaccharides, maltose, or glucose. **2.** any of several digestive enzymes that break down starches. [1890–95; AMYL- + -ASE]

am·yl·ene (am′ə lēn′), *n. Chem.* any of five unsaturated isomeric hydrocarbons having the formula C_5H_{10}. [1855–60; AMYL + -ENE]

am′yl group′, *Chem.* any of several univalent, isomeric groups having the formula C_5H_{11}–, whose derivatives are found in fusel oil, fruit extracts, etc. Also called **amyl radical.**

a·myl·ic (ə mil′ik), *adj.* of, pertaining to, or characterized by the amyl group. [1855–60; AMYL + -IC]

am′yl ni′trite, *Pharm.* a yellowish, fragrant, flammable liquid, $C_5H_{11}NO_2$, used in medicine chiefly as a vasodilator, esp. in the treatment of angina pectoris: misused by inhalation as a stimulant, esp. of sexual sensation. Also called **isoamyl nitrite.**

amylo-, a combining form representing **amylum** in compound words: *amylolysis.* Also, *esp. before a vowel,* **amyl-.** [comb. form of Gk *ámylon* starch, n. use of neut. of *ámylos* not milled (*a-* A-[6] + *mýl*(*ē*) mill + *-os* adj. suffix)]

a·myl·o·gen (ə mil′ə jən, -jen′), *n. Chem.* the water-soluble part of a starch granule. [1875–80; AMYLO- + -GEN]

am·y·loid (am′ə loid′), *n.* **1.** *Biochem.* a waxy, translucent substance, composed primarily of protein fibers, that is deposited in various organs of animals in certain diseases. **2.** a nonnitrogenous food consisting esp. of starch. —*adj.* **3.** Also, **am′y·loi′dal.** of, resembling, or containing amylum. [1855–60; AMYL- + -OID]

am·y·loi·do·sis (am′ə loi dō′sis), *n., pl.* **-ses** (-sēz). *Pathol.* **1.** a deposit of amyloid in tissues or organs. **2.** the diseased state resulting from this deposit. [1895–1900; AMYLOID + -OSIS]

am·y·lol·y·sis (am′ə lol′ə sis), *n. Biochem.* the conversion of starch into sugar. [1885–90; AMYLO- + -LYSIS] —**am·y·lo·lyt·ic** (am′ə lō lit′ik), *adj.*

am·y·lo·pec·tin (am′ə lō pek′tin), *n.* the insoluble or gel component of starch that forms a paste with water, but does not solidify, and that turns red in iodine. Cf. **amylose.** [1900–05; AMYLO- + PECTIN]

am·y·lo·plast (am′ə lō plast′), *n. Bot.* a starch-forming granule in plants; leucoplast. [1885–90; AMYLO- + -PLAST]

am·yl·ose (am′ə lōs′), *n.* the soluble or sol component of starch that forms a stiff gel at ordinary temperatures and turns blue in iodine. Cf. **amylopectin.** [1875–80; AMYL- + -OSE[2]]

am′yl pro′pionate, *Chem.* a colorless liquid, $C_8H_{16}O_2$, having an applelike odor, used chiefly as a scent in the manufacture of flavorings and perfume.

am′yl rad′ical, *Chem.* See **amyl group.**

am′yl sul′fide, *Chem.* See **diamyl sulfide.**

am·y·lum (am′ə ləm), *n.* starch (def. 1). [1550–60; < L < Gk *ámylon* starch. See AMYLO-]

Am·yn·tor (am′in tôr′), *n. Class. Myth.* a king of Ormenium who refused to give his daughter Astydamia to Hercules and who was slain by Hercules.

a·my·o·to·ni·a (ā′mī ə tō′nē ə, ā mī′-), *n. Pathol.* myatonia. [1915–20; < NL; see A-[6], MYOTONIA] —**a·my·a·ton·ic** (ā′mī ə ton′ik, ā mī′-), *adj.*

a·my·o·troph′ic lat′eral sclero′sis (ā′mī ə trof′ik, -trō′fik, ā mī′ə-), *Pathol.* an incurable disease of unknown cause in which progressive degeneration of motor neurons in the brain stem and spinal cord leads to atrophy and eventually complete paralysis of the voluntary muscles. *Abbr.:* ALS Also called **Lou Gehrig's disease.** [1885–90; A-[6] + MYO- + -TROPHIC]

Am·y·tal (am′i tôl′, -tal′), *Pharm., Trademark.* a brand of amobarbital.

Am·y·tha·on (am′ə thā′on), *n. Class. Myth.* the son of Cretheus and Tyro who supported Jason's claim to the throne of Iolcus.

a·myx·or·rhe·a (ā mik′sə rē′ə), *n. Med.* the absence of the normal secretion of mucus. Also, **a·myx′or·rhoe′a.** [< NL; see A-[6], MYXO-, -RRHEA]

an[1] (ən; *when stressed* an), *indefinite article.* the form of **a** before an initial vowel sound (*an arch; an honor*) and sometimes, esp. in British English, before an initial unstressed syllable beginning with a silent or weakly pronounced *h*: *an historian.* [bef. 950; ME; OE *ān* ONE in a weakened sense]
—**Usage.** See **a**[1].

an[2] (ən; *when stressed* an), *conj.* **1.** *Pron. Spelling.* and. **2.** *Archaic.* if. Also, **an', 'n, 'n'.** [1125–75; ME, unstressed phonetic var. of AND]

An (än), *n.* the Sumerian god of heaven: the counterpart of the Akkadian Anu.

an-[1], a prefix occurring before stems beginning with a vowel or *h* in loanwords from Greek, where it means "not," "without," "lacking" (*anarchy; anecdote*); used in the formation of compound words: *anelectric.* Also, *before a consonant,* **a-.** [< Gk. See A-[6], IN-[3], UN-[1]]

an-[2], var. of **ad-** before *n: announce.*

an-[3], var. of **ana-** before a vowel: *anion.*

-an, a suffix occurring originally in adjectives borrowed from Latin, formed from nouns denoting places (*Roman; urban*) or persons (*Augustan*), and now productively forming English adjectives by extension of the Latin pattern. Attached to geographic names, it denotes provenance or membership (*American; Chicagoan; Tibetan*), the latter sense now extended to membership in social classes, religious denominations, etc., in adjectives formed from various kinds of noun bases (*Episcopalian; pedestrian; Puritan; Republican*) and membership in zoological taxa (*acanthocephalan; crustacean*). Attached to personal names, it has the additional senses "contemporary with" (*Elizabethan; Jacobean*) or "proponent of" (*Hegelian; Freudian*) the person specified by the noun base. The suffix **-an,** and its variant **-ian,** also occurs in a set of personal nouns, mainly loanwords from French, denoting one who engages in, practices, or works with the referent of the base noun (*comedian; grammarian; historian; theologian*); this usage is esp. productive with nouns ending in **-ic** (*electrician; logician; technician*). See **-ian** for relative distribution with that suffix. Cf. **-enne, -ean, -arian, -ician.** [ME < L *-ānus, -āna, -ānum*; in some words r. *-ain, -en* < OF < L]

AN, Anglo-Norman. Also, **A.-N.**

An, *Symbol, Chem.* actinon.

an., in the year. [< L *annō*]

A.N., 1. Anglo-Norman. **2.** Associate in Nursing.

an·a[1] (an′ə, ä′nə), *n.* **1.** a collection of miscellaneous information about a particular subject, person, place, or thing. **2.** an item in such a collection, as an anecdote, a memorable saying, etc. [1720–30; independent use of -ANA]

an·a[2] (an′ə), *adv.* (of ingredients in pharmaceutical prescriptions) in equal quantities; of each. *Symbol:* āā, āa [1490–1500; < ML < Gk *aná* of each]

ana-, a prefix in loanwords from Greek, where it means "up," "against," "back," "re-": *anabasis;* used in the formation of compound words: *anacardiaceous.* Also, *esp. before a vowel,* **an-.** [< Gk, comb. form of *aná*; no necessary relation to ON]

-ana, a suffix that forms collective nouns denoting an assembly of items, as household objects, art, books, or maps, or a description of such items, as a bibliography, all of which are representative of or associated with the place, person, or period named by the stem: *Americana; Shakespeareana; Victoriana.* Also, **-iana.** [< L, neut. pl. of *-ānus* -AN]

A.N.A., 1. American Newspaper Association. **2.** American Nurses Association. **3.** Association of National Advertisers. Also, **ANA**

an·a·bae·na (an′ə bē′nə), *n.* any of the freshwater algae of the genus *Anabaena,* commonly occurring in masses and often contaminating drinking water, giving it a fishy odor and taste. [< NL < Gk *anabain*(*ein*) to go up (*ana-* ANA- + *bainein* to go) + L *-a* -A[2]]

an·a·ban·tid (an′ə ban′tid), *n.* **1.** any of several fishes of the family Anabantidae, comprising the labyrinth fishes. —*adj.* **2.** belonging or pertaining to the family Anabantidae. [< NL *Anabantidae* < *anabant-* (s. of *Anabas* ANABAS) + *-idae* -ID[2]]

An·a·bap·tist (an′ə bap′tist), *n.* **1.** a member of any of various Protestant sects, formed in Europe after 1520, that denied the validity of infant baptism, baptized believers only, and advocated social and economic reforms as well as the complete separation of church and state. **2.** *Archaic.* Baptist (def. 1). —*adj.* **3.** of or pertaining to Anabaptists or Anabaptism. [1525–35; < NL *anabaptista* < ML *anabapt(izāre)* to rebaptize (< LGk *anabaptízein;* see ANA-, BAPTIZE) + *-ista* -IST] —**An′a·bap′·tism,** *n.* —**An′a·bap·tis′ti·cal·ly,** *adv.*

an·a·bas (an′ə bas′), *n.* any small fish of the genus *Anabas,* of ponds and swamps in Africa and southeastern Asia. Cf. **climbing perch.** [1835–45; < NL < Gk, aorist participle of *anabaínein* to go up. See ANABAENA]

a·nab·a·sine (ə nab′ə sēn′, -sin), *n. Chem.* a colorless, poisonous liquid, $C_{10}H_{14}N_2$, used as an insecticide. [< NL *Anabas(is)* genus name (see ANA-, BASIS) + -INE[2]]

a·nab·a·sis (ə nab′ə sis), *n., pl.* **-ses** (-sēz′). **1.** a march from the coast into the interior, as that of Cyrus the Younger against Artaxerxes II, described by Xenophon in his historical work *Anabasis* (379–371 B.C.). **2.** *Literary.* any military expedition or advance. Cf. **katabasis.** [1700–10; < Gk: a stepping up. See ANA-, BASIS]

an·a·bat·ic (an′ə bat′ik), *adj. Meteorol.* **1.** pertaining to an uphill wind produced by the effects of local heating. Cf. **katabatic. 2.** (formerly) pertaining to any upward-moving air current. [1805–15; < Gk *anabatikós* pertaining to climbing or to a climber, equiv. to *anaba-* (s. of *anabaínein;* see ANABAENA) + *-tikos* -TIC]

an·a·bi·o·sis (an′ə bī ō′sis), *n.* a bringing back to consciousness; reanimation after apparent death. [1885–90; < NL < Gk *anabíōsis* a coming back to life, equiv. to *anabiō-,* var. s. of *anabioûn* to return to life (see ANA-, BIO-) + *-sis* -SIS] —**an·a·bi·ot·ic** (an′ə bī ot′ik), *adj.*

an·a·bleps (an′ə bleps′), *n.* See **four-eyed fish.** [1777; < NL, the genus name, coinage based on Gk *anablépein* to look up, equiv. to *ana-* ANA- + *blépein* to see]

an′abol′ic ster′oid, a synthetic derivative of testosterone, sometimes used by athletes to help increase weight and strength. [1960–65]

a·nab·o·lism (ə nab′ə liz′əm), *n. Biol., Physiol.* constructive metabolism; the synthesis in living organisms of more complex substances from simpler ones (opposed to *catabolism*). [1885–90; ANA- + (META)BOLISM] —**an·a·bol·ic** (an′ə bol′ik), *adj.*

a·nab·o·lite (ə nab′ə līt′), *n. Biol., Physiol.* a product of anabolic action. [ANABOL(ISM) + -ITE[1]]

an·a·branch (an′ə branch′, -bränch′), *n.* a stream branching off from a river and rejoining it further downstream. [1825–35; short for *anastomotic branch.* See ANASTOMOSIS]

an·a·can·thous (an′ə kan′thəs), *adj. Bot.* having no spines or thorns. [< Gk *anákanthos* thornless. See AN-[1], ACANTHOUS]

an·a·car·di·a·ceous (an′ə kär′dē ā′shəs), *adj.* belonging to the Anacardiaceae, the cashew family of plants. Cf. **cashew family.** [1850–55; < NL *Anacardiace(ae)* plant family name (see ANA-, CARDI-, -ACEAE) + -OUS]

a·nach·a·ris (ə nak′ər is), *n.* elodea.

a·nach·ro·nism (ə nak′rə niz′əm), *n.* **1.** something or someone that is not in its correct historical or chronological time, esp. a thing or person that belongs to an earlier time: *The sword is an anachronism in modern warfare.* **2.** an error in chronology in which a person, object, event, etc., is assigned a date or period other than the correct one: *To assign Michelangelo to the 14th century is an anachronism.* Cf. **parachronism, prochronism.** [1640–50; < L *anachronismus* < Gk *anachronismós* a wrong time reference, equiv. to *anachron(ízein)* to make a wrong time reference (see ANA-, CHRON-, -IZE) + *-ismos* -ISM] —**an·a·chron·i·cal·ly** (an′ə kron′ik lē), *adv.*

a·nach·ro·nis·tic (ə nak′rə nis′tik), *adj.* pertaining to or containing an anachronism. Also, **a·nach′ro·nis′ti·cal.** [1765–75; ANACHRON(ISM) + -ISTIC] —**a·nach′ro·nis′ti·cal·ly,** *adv.*

a·nach·ro·nous (ə nak′rə nəs), *adj.* misplaced in time; anachronistic. [1850–55; ANACHRON(ISM) + -OUS] —**a·nach′ro·nous·ly,** *adv.*

an·a·cid·i·ty (an′ə sid′i tē), *n. Med.* the abnormal absence of hydrochloric acid in the stomach. [AN-[1] + ACIDITY]

an·a·clas·tic (an′ə klas′tik), *adj. Optics.* (formerly) of or pertaining to refraction. [1690–1700; < Gk *anáklast(os)* bent back (verbal adj. of *anaklâ* to refract, equiv. to *ana-* ANA- + *klân* to break) + -IC]

An·a·cle·tus (an′ə klē′təs), *n.* fl. 1st century A.D., pope 76–88. Also called **Cletus.**

an·a·cli·sis (an′ə klī′sis), *n. Psychoanal.* the choice of an object of libidinal attachment on the basis of a resemblance to early childhood protective and parental figures. [< Gk *anáklisis* a reclining, equiv. to *anakli-,* var. s. of *anaklínein* to lean (something) upon (*ana-* ANA- + *klínein* to lean) + *-sis* -SIS]

an·a·clit·ic (an′ə klit′ik), *adj. Psychoanal.* exhibiting or pertaining to anaclisis. [1920–25; < Gk *anáklit(os)* for reclining (*anakli-* (see ANACLISIS) + *-tos* verbal adj. suffix) + -IC]

an·a·coe·no·sis (an′ə si nō′sis), *n., pl.* **-ses** (-sēz). *Rhet.* a figure of speech in which an appeal is made to one's listeners or opponents for their opinion or judgment as to the subject under discussion. [1580–90; < ML < Gk *anakoínōsis,* equiv. to *anakoinō-,* var. s. of *anakoinoûn* to impart (*ana-* ANA- + *koinoûn* to make common, deriv. of *koinós* CENO-[2]) + *-sis* -SIS]

an·a·co·lu·thi·a (an′ə kə lo͞o′thē ə), *n. Rhet.* lack of grammatical sequence or coherence, esp. in a sentence. [1855–60; < L < Gk *anakolouthía.* See ANACOLUTHON, -IA] —**an′a·co·lu′thic,** *adj.* —**an′a·co·lu′thi·cal·ly,** *adv.*

an·a·co·lu·thon (an′ə kə lo͞o′thon), *n., pl.* **-tha** (-thə). *Rhet.* **1.** a construction involving a break in grammatical sequence, as *It makes me so—I just get angry.* **2.** an instance of anacoluthia. [1700–10; < Gk *anakólouthon,* neut. of *anakólouthos* not following, equiv. to *an-* AN-[1] + *akólouthos* marching together (*a-* together + *kolouth-,* gradational var. of *keleuth-* road, march + *-os* adj. suffix)]

an·a·con·da (an′ə kon′də), *n.* **1.** a South American boa, *Eunectes murinus,* that often grows to a length of more than 25 ft. (7.6 m). **2.** any large boa. **3.** *Cards.* a variety of poker in which each player is dealt seven cards, discards two, and turns up one of the remaining five before each betting round. [1760–70; misapplication of a name orig. used for a snake of Sri Lanka; earlier *anacandaia* < Sinhalese *henakandayā* kind of snake]

An·a·con·da (an′ə kon′də), *n.* a city in SW Montana. 12,518.

An·a·cos·ti·a (an′ə kôs′tē ə, -kos′-), *n.* a section of the District of Columbia, in the SE part.

Anacos′tia Riv′er, a river in the District of Columbia flowing into the Potomac River. ab. 24 mi. (39 km) long.

an·a·cous·tic (an′ə ko͞o′stik), *adj.* of or pertaining to the upper portion of the earth's atmosphere and to interplanetary space, where sound cannot be transmitted because molecules are too far apart to serve as a transmitting medium. [AN-[1] + ACOUSTIC]

A·nac·re·on (ə nak′rē ən), *n.* c570–c480 B.C., Greek writer, esp. of love poems and drinking songs.

A·nac·re·on·tic (ə nak′rē on′tik), *adj.* **1.** (*sometimes l.c.*) of or in the manner of Anacreon. **2.** (*sometimes l.c.*) convivial and amatory. —*n.* **3.** (*l.c.*) an Anacreontic poem. [1650–60; < L *Anacreonticus,* equiv. to *Anacreont-* (< Gk *Anakreont-,* s. of *Anakréōn*) ANACREON + *-icus* -IC] —**A·nac′re·on′ti·cal·ly,** *adv.*

an·a·crog·y·nous (an′ə kroj′ə nəs), *adj. Bot.* having the female sex organs arising from any cell below the apex of the stem, thereby not terminating its growth, as certain liverworts. Cf. **acrogynous.** [AN-[1] + ACROGYNOUS]

an·a·cru·sis (an′ə kro͞o′sis), *n., pl.* **-cru·ses** (-kro͞o′sēz). **1.** *Pros.* an unstressed syllable or syllable group that begins a line of verse but is not counted as part of the first foot. **2.** *Music.* the note or notes preceding a downbeat; upbeat. [1825–35; < L < Gk *anákrousis,* equiv. to *anakroú(ein)* to strike up, push back (*ana-* ANA- + *kroúein* to strike, push) + *-sis* -SIS] —**an·a·crus·tic** (an′ə krus′tik), *adj.* —**an′a·crus′ti·cal·ly,** *adv.*

an·a·cu·sis (an′ə kyo͞o′sis), *n. Med.* total deafness. [< NL; see AN-[3], ACOUSTIC, -SIS] —**an′a·cu′sic,** *adj.*

an·a·dam′a bread′ (an′ə dam′ə), a yeast-raised bread having corn meal and molasses among its ingredients: a traditional food of colonial America. [1910–15; orig. obscure; the various anecdotes ascribing it to a permutation of "Anna damn her" or "Anna's damn bread" are purely folk etymologies]

an·a·dem (an′ə dem′), *n. Archaic.* a garland or wreath for the head. [1595–1605; < L *anadēm(a)* headband < Gk, deriv. of *anadeîn* to bind up (*ana-* ANA- + *dē-* verbid s. of *deîn* to bind) + *-ma* n. suffix]

an·a·de·ni·a (an′ə dē′nē ə, -dēn′yə), *n. Pathol.* **1.** deficient glandular activity. **2.** absence of glands. [< NL; see AN-[1], ADEN-, -IA]

an·a·di·plo·sis (an′ə di plō′sis), *n. Rhet.* repetition in the first part of a clause or sentence of a prominent word from the latter part of the preceding clause or sentence, usually with a change or extension of meaning. [1580–90; < L < Gk, equiv. to *anadiplō-,* var. s. of *anadiploûsthai* to be doubled back + *-sis* -SIS. See ANA-, DIPLOSIS]

a·nad·ro·mous (ə nad′rə məs), *adj.* (of fish) migrating from salt water to spawn in fresh water, as salmon of the genera *Salmo* and *Oncorhynchus* (distinguished from *catadromous*). [1745–55; < Gk *anádromos* running upward. See ANA-, -DROME, -OUS]

A·na·dyr′ Range′ (ä′nə dēr′, an′ə-; *Russ.* u nu-DIR′), a mountain range in NE Siberia in the Russian Federation: a part of the Kolyma Range.

a·nae·mi·a (ə nē′mē ə), *n.* anemia.

a·nae·mic (ə nē′mik), *adj.* anemic.

an·aer·obe (an′ə rōb′, an âr′ōb), *n.* an organism, esp. a bacterium, that does not require air or free oxygen to live (opposed to *aerobe*). [1875–80; AN-[1] + AEROBE]

an·aer·o·bic (an′ə rō′bik, an′â-), *adj.* **1.** (of an organism or tissue) living in the absence of air or free oxygen. **2.** pertaining to or caused by the absence of oxygen. [1880–85; ANAEROBE + -IC] —**an′aer·o′bi·cal·ly,** *adv.*

an·aes·the·sia (an′əs thē′zhə), *n. Med., Pathol.* anesthesia. —**an·aes·thet·ic** (an′əs thet′ik), *adj., n.* —**an·aes·the·tist** (ə nes′thi tist *or, esp. Brit.,* ə nēs′-), *n.*

an·aes·the·si·ol·o·gy (an′əs thē′zē ol′ə jē), *n.* anesthesiology. —**an·aes′the·si·ol′o·gist,** *n.*

an·aes·the·tize (ə nes′thi tīz′ *or, esp. Brit.,* ə nēs′-), *v.t.,* **-tized, -tiz·ing.** anesthetize. Also, *esp. Brit.,* **an·aes′the·tise′.** —**an·aes′the·ti·za′tion,** *n.*

an·a·gen·e·sis (an′ə jen′ə sis), *n.* **1.** *Biol.* the progressive evolution of a species. Cf. **catagenesis. 2.** *Physiol.* the regeneration of tissue. [1875–80; < NL; see ANA-, GENESIS] —**an·a·ge·net·ic** (an′ə jə net′ik), **an′a·ge·net′i·cal,** *adj.*

an·a·glyph (an′ə glif), *n.* **1.** an ornament sculptured or embossed in low relief, as a cameo. **2.** *Optics.* a composite picture printed in two colors that produces a three-dimensional image when viewed through spectacles having lenses of corresponding colors. [1645–55; < Gk *anáglyphos* wrought in low relief. See ANA-, GLYPH] —**an′a·glyph′ic, an′a·glyph′i·cal, an·a·glyp·tic** (an′ə glip′tik), **an′a·glyp′ti·cal,** *adj.* —**a·nag·ly·phy** (ə nag′lə fē, an′ə glif′ē), *n.*

an·a·glyph·o·scope (an′ə glif′ə skōp′), *n. Optics.* a pair of spectacles for viewing an anaglyph. [ANAGLYPH + -O- + SCOPE]

an·ag·no·ri·sis (an′ag nôr′ə sis, -nōr′-), *n., pl.* **-ses** (-sēz′). (in ancient Greek tragedy) the critical moment of recognition or discovery, esp. preceding peripeteia. [1790–1800; < L < Gk, equiv. to *anagnōrí(zein)* to know again (*ana-* ANA- + *gnōr-,* c. L *-gnōr-* in *ignōrāre* to IGNORE + *-izein* -IZE) + *-sis* -SIS; perh. *gnōr-* from adj. deriv. **gnō-ró-* knowing]

an·a·go·ge (an′ə gō′jē, an′ə gō′jē), *n.* **1.** a spiritual interpretation or application of words, as of Scriptures. **2.** a form of allegorical interpretation of Scripture that seeks hidden meanings regarding the future life. Also, **anagogy.** [< LL < Gk *anagōgḗ* an uplifting, equiv. to *an-* AN-[3] + *agōgḗ,* fem. of *agōgós* leading; see -AGOGUE]

an·a·gog·ic (an′ə goj′ik), *adj.* **1.** of or pertaining to an anagoge. **2.** *Psychol.* deriving from, pertaining to, or reflecting the moral or idealistic striving of the unconscious: *anagogic image; anagogic interpretation.* Also, **an′a·gog′i·cal.** [1350–1400; ME < ML *anagogicus.* See ANAGOGE, -IC] —**an′a·gog′i·cal·ly,** *adv.*

an·a·go·gy (an′ə gō′jē, an′ə gō′jē), *n., pl.* **-gies.** anagoge. [1400–50; late ME *anagogie* < ML *anagōgia,* for LL *anagōgē* ANAGOGE]

an·a·gram (an′ə gram′), *n., v.,* **-grammed, -gram·ming.** —*n.* **1.** a word, phrase, or sentence formed from another by rearranging its letters: *"Angel" is an anagram of "glean."* **2. anagrams,** (*used with a singular v.*) a game in which the players build words by transposing and, often, adding letters. —*v.t.* **3.** to form (the letters of a text) into a secret message by rearranging them. **4.** to rearrange (the letters of a text) so as to discover a secret message. [1580–90; prob. < MF *anagramme* < NL *anagramma.* See ANA-, -GRAM[1]] —**an·a·gram·mat·ic** (an′ə grə mat′ik), **an′a·gram·mat′i·cal,** *adj.* —**an′a·gram·mat′i·cal·ly,** *adv.*

an·a·gram·ma·tize (an′ə gram′ə tīz′), *v.t., v.i.,* **-tized, -tiz·ing.** to transpose into an anagram. Also, *esp. Brit.,* **an′a·gram′ma·tise′.** [1585–95; < Gk *anagrammatízein* to transpose letters, equiv. to *ana-* ANA- + *grammat-* (s. of *grámma*) letter + *-izein* -IZE] —**an·a·gram·ma·tism** (an′ə gram′ə tiz′əm), *n.* —**an′a·gram′·ma·tist,** *n.*

An·a·heim (an′ə hīm′), *n.* a city in SW California, SE of Los Angeles. 221,847.

A·ná·huac (ə nä′wäk; *Sp.* ä nä′wäk), *n.* the central plateau of Mexico, between the Sierra Madre Occidental and the Sierra Madre Oriental ranges (3700 to 9000 ft.; 1128 to 2743 m): center of former Aztec civilization.

An·a·kim (an′ə kim), *n.pl.* tall people or giants who lived in S Palestine and were destroyed or scattered after the arrival of the Hebrews. Num. 13:28, 31; Deut. 2:21; 9:2.

a·nal (ān′l), *adj.* **1.** of, pertaining to, involving, or near the anus. **2.** *Psychoanal.* **a.** of or pertaining to the second stage of psychosexual development, during which gratification is derived from the retention or expulsion of feces. **b.** of or pertaining to an anal character. **c.** of or pertaining to gratification derived from stimulation of the anus. [1760–70; AN(US) + -AL[1]] —**a′nal·ly,** *adv.*

anal., 1. analogous. **2.** analogy. **3.** analysis. **4.** analytic.

a′nal char′acter, *Psychoanal.* a group of personality traits including meticulousness, compulsiveness, and rigidity, believed to be associated with excessive preoccupation with the anal phase as a child, with effects lingering into adulthood.

a·nal·cite (ə nal′sīt, an′l sīt′), *n.* a white or slightly colored zeolite mineral, $Na(AlSi_2O_6){\cdot}H_2O$, generally found in crystalline form. Also, **a·nal·cime** (ə nal′sēm, -sīm, -sim). [1795–1805; < Gk *análk(imos)* weak (*an-* AN-[1] + *álkimos* strong) + -ITE[1]]

an·a·lects (an′l ekts′), *n.pl.* selected passages from the writings of an author or of different authors. Also, **an·a·lec·ta** (an′l ek′tə). [1615–25; < L *analecta* < Gk *análekta,* neut. pl. of *análektos* (verbal adj. of *analégein* to pick up, gather up), equiv. to *ana-* ANA- + *-lek-* gather (var. of *-leg-*) + *-tos* verbal adj. suffix] —**an′a·lec′tic,** *adj.*

An′alects of Confu′cius, The, (Chinese, *Lun Yü*) a compilation of the discourses, maxims, and aphorisms of Confucius, dating from the 4th century B.C.

an·a·lem·ma (an′l em′ə), *n., pl.* **an·a·lem·mas, an·a·lem·ma·ta** (an′l em′ə tə). a scale shaped like the figure 8, showing the declination of the sun and the equation of time for each day of the year. [1645–55; < L: pedestal of a sundial, sundial < Gk *análēmma* support] —**an·a·lem·mat·ic** (an′l e mat′ik), *adj.*

an·a·lep·tic (an′l ep′tik), *Med.* —*adj.* **1.** restoring; invigorating; giving strength after disease. **2.** awakening, esp. from drug stupor. —*n.* **3.** a pharmacological substance that stimulates the central nervous system and also acts as an anticonvulsant. [1655–65; < Gk *analēptikós* restorative, equiv. to *analēp-,* var. s. of *analambánein* to restore (*ana-* ANA- + *lambánein* to take) + *-tikos* -TIC]

a′nal fin′, the median, unpaired fin on the ventral margin between the anus and the caudal fin in fishes. See diag. under **fish.**

an·al·ge·si·a (an′l jē′zē ə, -sē ə), *n. Med.* absence of sense of pain. [1700–10; < NL < Gk *analgēsía* painlessness, equiv. to *analgēt(os)* without pain (*an-* AN-[1] + *álg(os)* pain + *-ētos* adj. suffix) + *-ia* -IA]

an·al·ge·sic (an′l jē′zik, -sik), *Med.* —*n.* **1.** a remedy

CONCISE PRONUNCIATION KEY: act, cāpe, dâre, pärt; set, ēqual; *if,* īce; ox, ōver, ôrder, oil, bo͝ok, bo͞ot, out; up, ûrge; child; sing; shoe; thin, *that;* zh as in *treasure.* ə = *a* as in *alone, e* as in *system, i* as in *easily, o* as in *gallop, u* as in *circus;* ᵊ as in *fire* (fīᵊr), *hour* (ouᵊr). l and n can serve as syllabic consonants, as in *cradle* (krād′l), and *button* (but′n). See the full key inside the front cover.

that relieves or allays pain. —*adj.* **2.** of, pertaining to, or causing analgesia. [1870–75; ANALGES(IA) + -IC]

a•nal•i•ty (ā nal′i tē), *n., pl.* **-ties.** *Psychoanal.* the condition or quality of having an anal character; collectively, the personality traits characteristic of the anal stage of psychosexual development. [1935–40; ANAL + -ITY]

an•a•log (an′l ôg′, -og′), *n.* **1.** analogue. —*adj.* **2.** of or pertaining to a mechanism that represents data by measurement of a continuous physical variable, as voltage or pressure.

an′alog clock′, a clock that represents time by the position of hands on a dial. Cf. **digital clock.**

an′alog comput′er, a computer that represents data by measurable quantities, as voltages or, formerly, the rotation of gears, in order to solve a problem, rather than by expressing the data as numbers. Cf. **digital computer.** [1945–50, *Amer.*]

an•a•log•i•cal (an′l oj′i kəl), *adj.* based on, involving, or expressing an analogy. Also, **an′a•log′ic.** [1560–70; < L *analogic(us)* (< Gk *analogikós*; see ANALOGY, -IC) + -AL[1]] —**an′a•log′i•cal•ly,** *adv.* —**an′a•log′i•cal•ness,** *n.*

a•na•lo•gi•on (ä′nä lô′yē ôn; *Eng.* an′l ō′jē on′), *n., pl.* **-gi•a** (-yē ä; *Eng.* -jē ə), **-gi•ons.** *Gk. Orth. Ch.* a lectern. [< Gk *analogeîon,* deriv. of *analégesthai* to read through (*ana-* ANA- + *légein* to gather, collect, speak)]

a•nal•o•gism (ə nal′ə jiz′əm), *n.* reasoning or argument by analogy. [1650–60; ANALOG(Y) + -ISM]

a•nal•o•gist (ə nal′ə jist), *n.* **1.** a person who employs or argues from analogy. **2.** a person who seeks analogies. [1830–40; ANALOG(IZE) + -IST] —**a•nal′o•gis′tic,** *adj.*

a•nal•o•gize (ə nal′ə jīz′), *v.,* **-gized, -giz•ing.** —*v.i.* **1.** to make use of analogy in reasoning, argument, etc. **2.** to be analogous; show analogy. —*v.t.* **3.** to make analogous; show an analogy between: *to analogize a dog to a cat.* Also, *esp. Brit.,* **a•nal′o•gise′.** [1645–55; ANALOG(Y) + -IZE]

a•nal•o•gous (ə nal′ə gəs), *adj.* **1.** having analogy; corresponding in some particular: *A brain and a computer are analogous.* **2.** *Biol.* corresponding in function, but not evolved from corresponding organs, as the wings of a bee and those of a hummingbird. [1640–50; < L *analogus* < Gk *análogos* proportionate, equiv. to *ana-* ANA- + *lóg(os)* ratio + *-os* adj. suffix; see -OUS] —**a•nal′o•gous•ly,** *adv.* —**a•nal′o•gous•ness,** *n.*
—**Syn. 1.** similar, alike, like, comparable, akin.
—**Ant. 1.** dissimilar.

an′alog record′ing, 1. a method of sound recording in which an input audio waveform is converted to an analogous waveform. **2.** a record or audiotape made by this method. Cf. **digital recording.**

an•a•logue (an′l ôg′, -og′), *n.* **1.** something having analogy to something else. **2.** *Biol.* an organ or part analogous to another. **3.** *Chem.* one of a group of chemical compounds similar in structure but different in respect to elemental composition. **4.** a food made from vegetable matter, esp. soybeans, that has been processed to taste and look like another food, as meat or dairy, and is used as a substitute for it. Also, **analog.** [1820–30; < F < Gk *análogon,* neut. of *análogos* ANALOGOUS; r. earlier *analogon* < Gk]

an′alog watch′, a watch that represents time by the position of hands on a dial. Cf. **digital watch.**

a•nal•o•gy (ə nal′ə jē), *n., pl.* **-gies. 1.** a similarity between like features of two things, on which a comparison may be based: *the analogy between the heart and a pump.* **2.** similarity or comparability: *I see no analogy between your problem and mine.* **3.** *Biol.* an analogous relationship. **4.** *Ling.* **a.** the process by which words or phrases are created or re-formed according to existing patterns in the language, as when *shoon* was re-formed as *shoes,* when *-ize* is added to nouns like *winter* to form verbs, or when a child says *foots* for *feet.* **b.** a form resulting from such a process. **5.** *Logic.* a form of reasoning in which one thing is inferred to be similar to another thing in a certain respect, on the basis of the known similarity between the things in other respects. [1530–40; < L *analogia* < Gk. See ANALOGOUS, -Y[3]]
—**Syn. 1.** comparison, likeness, resemblance, similitude, affinity. **2.** correspondence.

anal′ogy test′, a reasoning test in which the subject is required to supply the missing term in a relationship of the form "A is to B as Y is to ______."

an•al•pha•bet (an al′fə bet′, -bit), *n.* a person who cannot read or write; illiterate. [1660–70; back formation from ANALPHABETIC]

an•al•pha•bet•ic (an′al fə bet′ik, an al′-), *adj.* **1.** not alphabetic: *an analphabetic arrangement of letters.* **2.** unable to read or write; illiterate: *analphabetic peoples.* **3.** *Phonet.* of or constituting a system of phonetic transcription, as the one devised by Otto Jespersen, that for each sound indicates by separate sets of symbols the articulator, the point of articulation, and the size and shape of the mouth opening. —*n.* **4.** an illiterate person; analphabet. [1660–70; < Gk *analphábēt(os)* not knowing the alphabet (*an-* AN-[1] + *alphábēt(os)* ALPHABET + *-os* adj. suffix) + -IC]

a′nal phase′, *Psychoanal.* the second stage of psychosexual development during which the child, usually at two years of age, becomes preoccupied with defecation.

a′nal reten′tive. 1. having an anal character. **2.** a person who is anal retentive.

a′nal vein′, one of several veins in the rear portion of the wing of an insect.

CONCISE ETYMOLOGY KEY: <, descended or borrowed from; >, whence; b., blend of, blended; c., cognate with; cf., compare; deriv., derivative; equiv., equivalent; imit., imitative; obl., oblique; r., replacing; s., stem; sp., spelling, spelled; resp., respelling, respelled; trans., translation; ?, origin unknown; *, unattested; ‡, probably earlier than. See the full key inside the front cover.

a•nal•y•sand (ə nal′ə sand′, -zand′), *n. Psychiatry.* a person undergoing psychoanalysis. [1930–35; ANALYSE + *-and* as in MULTIPLICAND]

an•a•lyse (an′l īz′), *v.t.,* **-lysed, -lys•ing.** *Chiefly Brit.* analyze.

a•nal•y•sis (ə nal′ə sis), *n., pl.* **-ses** (-sēz′). **1.** the separating of any material or abstract entity into its constituent elements (opposed to *synthesis*). **2.** this process as a method of studying the nature of something or of determining its essential features and their relations: *the grammatical analysis of a sentence.* **3.** a presentation, usually in writing, of the results of this process: *The paper published an analysis of the political situation.* **4.** a philosophical method of exhibiting complex concepts or propositions as compounds or functions of more basic ones. **5.** *Math.* **a.** an investigation based on the properties of numbers. **b.** the discussion of a problem by algebra, as opposed to geometry. **c.** the branch of mathematics consisting of calculus and its higher developments. **d.** a system of calculation, as combinatorial analysis or vector analysis. **e.** a method of proving a proposition by assuming the result and working backward to something that is known to be true. Cf. **synthesis** (def. 4). **6.** *Chem.* **a.** intentionally produced decomposition or separation of materials into their ingredients or elements, as to find their kind or quantity. **b.** the ascertainment of the kind or amount of one or more of the constituents of materials, whether obtained in separate form or not. Cf. **qualitative analysis, quantitative analysis. 7.** psychoanalysis. **8.** *Computers.* See **systems analysis.** [1575–85; < NL < Gk, equiv. to *analý(ein)* to loosen up (*ana-* ANA- + *lýein* to loosen) + *-sis* -SIS]

anal′ysis of var′iance, *Statistics.* a procedure for resolving the total variance of a set of variates into component variances that are associated with defined factors affecting the variates. Also called **variance analysis.** [1935–40]

anal′ysis si′tus, *Math. Now Rare.* topology (defs. 1, 2). [1905–10]

an•a•lyst (an′l ist), *n.* **1.** a person who analyzes or who is skilled in analysis. **2.** a psychoanalyst. **3.** *Computers.* See **systems analyst.** [1650–60; < F *analyste,* equiv. to *analyse* ANALYSIS + *-iste* -IST, by haplology from **analysiste*]

analyt., analytical.

an•a•lyt•ic (an′l it′ik), *adj.* **1.** pertaining to or proceeding by analysis (opposed to *synthetic*). **2.** skilled in or habitually using analysis. **3.** (of a language) characterized by a relatively frequent use of function words, auxiliary verbs, and changes in word order to express syntactic relations, rather than of inflected forms. Cf. **synthetic** (def. 3), **polysynthetic** (def. 1). **4.** *Logic.* (of a proposition) necessarily true because its denial involves a contradiction, as "All husbands are married." **5.** *Math.* **a.** (of a function of a complex variable) having a first derivative at all points of a given domain; holomorphic; regular. **b.** (of a curve) having parametric equations that represent analytic functions. **c.** (of a proof) using analysis. Also, **an′a•lyt′i•cal.** [1580–90; < ML *analyticus* < Gk *analytikós,* equiv. to *analy-* (see ANALYSIS) + *-tikos* -TIC] —**an′a•lyt′i•cal•ly,** *adv.*

analyt′ical bal′ance, a precision balance having a sensitivity of 0.1 milligram.

analyt′ical chem′istry, the subdivision of chemistry dealing with the qualitative and quantitative determination of chemical components of substances. [1875–80]

analyt′ical cub′ism, (*sometimes caps.*) *Fine Arts.* the early phase of cubism, chiefly characterized by a pronounced use of geometric shapes and by a tendency toward a monochromatic use of color. Cf. **synthetic cubism.**

analyt′ical en′try, *Library Science.* a bibliographic record of part of an item for which a comprehensive bibliographic record has been made, as a single play or essay in an anthology, a subject in a comprehensive work, or a part of a multivolume set of books. [1955–60]

analyt′ic continua′tion, *Math.* **1.** a method of finding a function that coincides with a given analytic function in a domain and that remains analytic in a larger domain. **2.** any function found by this method. [1955–60]

analyt′ic geom′etry, a branch of mathematics in which algebraic procedures are applied to geometry and position is represented analytically by coordinates. Also called **coordinate geometry.** [1820–30]

an•a•lyt•ics (an′l it′iks), *n.* (*used with a singular v.*) *Logic.* the science of logical analysis. [1580–90; see ANALYTIC, -ICS]

an•a•ly•tique (an′l i tēk′), *n. Archit.* an elevation drawing of a façade, surrounded by a decorative arrangement composed of drawings of the important details and sometimes a plan or section of the façade. [< F: ANALYTIC]

an•a•lyze (an′l īz′), *v.t.,* **-lyzed, -lyz•ing. 1.** to separate (a material or abstract entity) into constituent parts or elements; determine the elements or essential features of (opposed to *synthesize*): *to analyze an argument.* **2.** to examine critically, so as to bring out the essential elements or give the essence of: *to analyze a poem.* **3.** to examine carefully and in detail so as to identify causes, key factors, possible results, etc. **4.** to subject to mathematical, chemical, grammatical, etc., analysis. **5.** to psychoanalyze: *a patient who has been analyzed by two therapists.* Also, *esp. Brit.,* **analyse.** [1595–1605; back formation from ANALYSIS (or from its L or Gk sources), with *-ys-* taken as -IZE] —**an′a•lyz′a•ble,** *adj.* —**an′a•lyz′a•bil′i•ty,** *n.* —**an′a•ly•za′tion,** *n.*
—**Syn. 1.** break down. **2.** explicate. —**Ant. 1.** synthesize.

an′alyzed rhyme′, *Pros.* the use of assonance and consonance in a complex pattern at the ends of alternate lines of a quatrain, as in *head, mat, met, had.*

an•a•lyz•er (an′l ī′zər), *n.* **1.** a person, machine, or device that analyzes. **2.** *Optics.* a polarizing device, often a Nicol prism, that indicates the direction of vibration of light by selecting and transmitting only the component of linearly polarized light in that direction. [1620–30; ANALYZE + -ER[1]]

A•nam (ə nam′), *n.* Annam.

A•nam•mel•ech (ə nam′ə lek′), *n.* one of the gods worshiped by the Sepharvites. II Kings 17:31. Also, *Douay Bible,* **A•nam′el•ech′.** Cf. **Adrammelech** (def. 1).

an•am•ne•sis (an′am nē′sis), *n., pl.* **-ses** (-sēz). **1.** the recollection or remembrance of the past; reminiscence. **2.** *Platonism.* recollection of the Ideas, which the soul had known in a previous existence, esp. by means of reasoning. **3.** the medical history of a patient. **4.** *Immunol.* a prompt immune response to a previously encountered antigen, characterized by more rapid onset and greater effectiveness of antibody and T cell reaction than during the first encounter, as after a booster shot in a previously immunized person. **5.** (*often cap.*) a prayer in a Eucharistic service, recalling the Passion, Resurrection, and Ascension of Christ. [1650–60; < NL < Gk *anámnēsis* remembrance, equiv. to *ana(mi)mnē(skein)* to remember (*ana* ANA- + *mimnēskein* to call to mind) + *-sis* -SIS] —**an•am•nes•tic** (an′am nes′tik), *adj.* —**an′am•nes′ti•cal•ly,** *adv.*

an•am•ni•ote (an am′nē ōt′), *n.* any of the vertebrates of the group Anamnia (Anamniota), comprising the cyclostomes, fishes, and amphibians, characterized by the absence of an amnion during the embryonic stage. Cf. **amniote.** [< NL *Anamniota.* See AN-[1], AMNIOTE]

an•a•mor•phic (an′ə môr′fik), *adj.* **1.** *Optics.* having or producing unequal magnifications along two axes perpendicular to each other. **2.** of, pertaining to, or created by anamorphosis or anamorphism. [1900–05; ANAMORPH(ISM) + -IC]

an′amor′phic lens′, *Motion Pictures, Optics.* **1.** a compound lens or system of lenses that compresses the camera image in the horizontal direction during filming, so that a wide-screen image can fit on the width of conventional 35-mm film. **2.** a similar system used in projection that horizontally expands the compressed image back to its original wide-screen aspect ratio. [1950–55]

an•a•mor•phism (an′ə môr′fiz əm), *n. Geol.* metamorphism, usually occurring deep under the earth's surface, that changes simple minerals to complex minerals. Cf. **katamorphism.** [1830–40; ANA- + -MORPHISM]

an•a•mor•pho•scope (an′ə môr′fə skōp′), *n.* a curved mirror or other optical device for giving a correct image of a picture or the like distorted by anamorphosis. [1880–85; ANAMORPHO(SIS) + -SCOPE]

an•a•mor•pho•sis (an′ə môr′fə sis, -môr fō′sis), *n., pl.* **-ses** (-sēz′, -sēz). **1.** a drawing presenting a distorted image that appears in natural form under certain conditions, as when viewed at a raking angle or reflected from a curved mirror. **2.** the method of producing such a drawing. **3.** *Zool., Entomol.* the gradual change in form from one type to another during the evolution of a group of organisms. **4.** (in certain arthropods) metamorphosis in which body parts or segments are added to those already present. [1720–30; < Gk, equiv. to *anamorphō-* (var. s. of *anamorphoûn* to transform; see ANA-, MORPHO-) + *-sis* -SIS]

a•nan•da (ä′nən də), *n. Hinduism.* perfect bliss. Cf. **Sat-cit-ananda.** [< Skt *ānanda-* joy, happiness]

A•nan•da (ä′nən də), *n.* fl. early 5th century B.C., favorite disciple of Gautama Buddha.

an•an•drous (ə nan′drəs, an an′-), *adj. Bot.* having no stamens. [1840–50; < Gk *ánandros* manless, equiv. to *an-* AN-[1] + *andr-* (s. of *anḗr*) man + *-os*; see -OUS]

An•a•ni•as (an′ə nī′əs), *n.* **1.** a man who was struck dead for lying. Acts. 5:1–5. **2.** a chronic liar.

an•an•kas′tic personal′ity (an′ən kas′tik, an′-ang-), a personality syndrome characterized by obsessional or compulsive traits. [< Gk *anankastikós* compulsory, coercive, equiv. to *anankast(ós)* forced (adj. deriv. of *anankázein* to force, compel, v. deriv. of *anánkē* force, necessity) + *ikos* -IC]

An•an•ke (ə nang′kē, ə nan′kē), *n. Astron.* a small natural satellite of the planet Jupiter. [< Gk *anánkē* necessity, force]

an•an•thous (ə nan′thəs, an an′-), *adj. Bot.* having no flowers. [1865–70; < Gk *ananth(ḗs)* without flowers (*an-* AN-[1] + *anth(ós)* flower + *-ēs* adj. suffix) + -OUS]

an•a•pest (an′ə pest′), *n. Pros.* a foot of three syllables, two short followed by one long in quantitative meter, and two unstressed followed by one stressed in accentual meter, as in *for the nonce.* Also, **an′a•paest′.** [1580–90; < L *anapaestus* < Gk *anápaistos* struck back, reversed (as compared with a dactyl), equiv. to *ana-* ANA- + *pais-* (var. s. of *paíein* to strike) + *-tos* ptp. suffix] —**an′a•pes′tic, an′a•paes′tic,** *adj.* —**an′a•pes′ti•cal•ly, an′a•paes′ti•cal•ly,** *adv.*

an•a•phase (an′ə fāz′), *n. Biol.* the stage in mitosis or meiosis following metaphase in which the daughter chromosomes move away from each other to opposite ends of the cell. [1885–90; ANA- + PHASE] —**an′a•pha′sic,** *adj.*

a•naph•o•ra (ə naf′ər ə), *n.* **1.** Also called **epanaphora.** *Rhet.* repetition of a word or words at the beginning of two or more successive verses, clauses, or sentences. Cf. **epistrophe** (def. 1), **symploce. 2.** *Gram.* the use of a word as a regular grammatical substitute for a preceding word or group of words, as the use of *it* and *do* in *I know it and he does too.* Cf. **cataphora. 3.** (*sometimes cap.*) *Eastern Ch.* **a.** the prayer of oblation and consecration in the Divine Liturgy during which the Eucharistic elements are offered. **b.** the part of the ceremony during which the Eucharistic elements are offered as an oblation. [1580–90; < LL < Gk: a bringing back, repeating, equiv. to *ana-* ANA- + *-phora,* akin to *phérein* to carry, bring; cf. -PHORE, -PHOROUS] —**a•naph′o•ral,** *adj.*

an•a•phor•ic (an′ə fôr′ik, -for′-), *adj. Gram.* referring back to or substituting for a preceding word or group of words: *anaphoric reference.* [1910–15; ANAPHOR(A) + -IC] —**an′a•phor′i•cal•ly,** *adv.*

an•aph•ro•di•sia (an af′rə dē′zhə, -dizh′ə, -diz′ē ə), *n. Psychiatry.* diminished sexual desire. [< Gk *anaphrodisía* inability to inspire love; see AN-[1], APHRODISIA]

an•aph•ro•dis•i•ac (an af′rə dē′zē ak′, -diz′ē-), *Med.* —*adj.* **1.** capable of diminishing sexual desire. —*n.* **2.** an anaphrodisiac agent. [1815–25; AN-[1] + APHRODISIAC]

an′aphylac′tic shock′, *Pathol.* a severe and sometimes fatal allergic reaction to a foreign substance, esp. a protein, as serum or bee venom, to which an individual has become sensitized, often involving rapid swelling, acute respiratory distress, and collapse of circulation. [1905–10]

an•a•phy•lax•is (an′ə fə lak′sis), *n. Pathol.* exaggerated allergic reaction to a foreign protein resulting from previous exposure to it. [1905–10; ANA- + (PRO)PHYLAXIS] —**an•a•phy•lac•tic** (an′ə fə lak′tik), *adj.* —**an′a•phy•lac′ti•cal•ly,** *adv.*

an•a•pla•sia (an′ə plā′zhə, -zhē ə, -zē ə), *n. Pathol.* the loss of structural differentiation within a cell or group of cells. [1905–10; ANA- + -PLASIA]

an•a•plas•mo•sis (an′ə plaz mō′sis), *n. Vet. Pathol.* a disease of cattle caused by a blood-infecting protozoan parasite, *Anaplasma marginale,* transmitted by bloodsucking flies and ticks. [< NL *Anaplasm(a)* genus name (see ANA-, PLASMA) + -OSIS]

an•a•plas•tic (an′ə plas′tik), *adj. Pathol.* **1.** (of cells) having reverted to a more primitive form. **2.** of or pertaining to anaplasty. [1875–80; < Gk *anáplast(os)* moldable, plastic (see ANA-, -PLAST) + -IC]

an•a•plas•ty (an′ə plas′tē), *n., pl.* **-ties.** *Surg.* reconstruction or restoration, esp. by plastic surgery, of a lost or injured part. [1875–80; < Gk *anáplast(os)* (see ANAPLASTIC) + -Y[3]; cf. -PLASTY]

A•ná•po•lis (ä nä′po͝o lis), *n.* a city in central Brazil. 83,848.

an•ap•o•phys•i•al (an′ə pə fiz′ē əl, ə nap′ə-), *adj.* of or pertaining to an anapophysis. [1865–70; ANAPOPHYSI(S) + -AL[1]]

an•a•poph•y•sis (an′ə pof′ə sis), *n., pl.* **-ses** (-sēz′). *Anat.* a small process of a vertebra, esp. of a lumbar or thoracic vertebra. [1850–55; AN-[3] + APOPHYSIS]

a•nap•sid (ə nap′sid), *adj.* **1.** belonging or pertaining to the Anapsida, a subclass of reptiles, extinct except for the turtles, characterized by having no opening in the temporal region of the skull. —*n.* **2.** a reptile of the subclass Anapsida. Cf. **diapsid.** [1930–35; < NL *Anapsida,* equiv. to *an-* AN-[1] + *-apsida,* pl. of *-apsidum,* neut. adj. deriv. of Gk *apsís, hapsis* loop, arch (referring to the opening in the skull); see APSIS]

an•ap•tot•ic (an′ap tot′ik), *adj. Archaic.* (of languages) tending to become uninflected, in accordance with a theory that languages evolve from uninflected to inflected and back. [1840–50; AN-[3] + *aptote* (< Gk *áptōton,* n. use of neut. of *áptōtos* uninflected, not falling, equiv. to *a-* A-[6] + *ptōtós* falling, verbal of *píptein* to fall) + -IC]

an•ap•tyx•is (an′ap tik′sis, an′ap-), *n., pl.* **-tyx•es** (-tik′sēz). epenthesis of a vowel. [1880–85; < NL < Gk, equiv. to *anaptyk-* (s. of *anaptýssein* to unfold, equiv. to *ana-* ANA- + *ptýssein* to fold) + *-sis* -SIS] —**an•ap•tyc•tic** (an′ap tik′tik, an′ap-), **an′ap•tyc′ti•cal,** *adj.*

A•na•pur•na (an′ə po͝or′nə, -pûr′-), *n.* Annapurna.

an•arch (an′ärk), *n. Archaic.* anarchist. [1880–85; back formation from ANARCHY]

an•ar•chic (an är′kik), *adj.* **1.** of, like, or tending to anarchy. **2.** advocating anarchy. **3.** not regulated by law; lawless: *Anarchic bands pillaged the countryside.* Also, **an•ar′chi•cal.** [1780–90; < F *anarchique,* or ANARCH(Y) + -IC] —**an•ar′chi•cal•ly,** *adv.*

an•ar•chism (an′ər kiz′əm), *n.* **1.** a doctrine urging the abolition of government or governmental restraint as the indispensable condition for full social and political liberty. **2.** the methods or practices of anarchists, as the use of violence to undermine government. **3.** anarchy. [1635–45; ANARCH(Y) + -ISM]

an•ar•chist (an′ər kist), *n.* **1.** a person who advocates or believes in anarchy or anarchism. **2.** a person who seeks to overturn by violence all constituted forms and institutions of society and government, with no purpose of establishing any other system of order in the place of that destroyed. **3.** a person who promotes disorder or excites revolt against any established rule, law, or custom. [1670–80; ANARCH(Y) + -IST] —**an′ar•chis′tic,** *adj.*

an•ar•cho•syn•di•cal•ism (an′ər kō sin′di kə liz′əm, an är′kō-), *n.* syndicalism. [1925–30] —**an′ar•cho•syn′di•cal•ist,** *n., adj.*

an•ar•chy (an′ər kē), *n.* **1.** a state of society without government or law. **2.** political and social disorder due to the absence of governmental control: *The death of the king was followed by a year of anarchy.* **3.** a theory that regards the absence of all direct or coercive government as a political ideal and that proposes the cooperative and voluntary association of individuals and groups as the principal mode of organized society. **4.** confusion; chaos; disorder: *Intellectual and moral anarchy followed his loss of faith.* [1530–40; (< MF *anarchie* or ML *anarchia*) < Gk, *anarchía* lawlessness, lit., lack of a leader, equiv. to *ánarch(os)* leaderless (*an-* AN-[1] + *arch(ós)* leader + -os adj. suffix) + *-ia* -Y[3]]

an•ar•thri•a (an är′thrē ə), *n. Pathol.* loss of articulate speech. [1880–85; < NL, perh. via G; see AN-[1], ARTHR-, -IA] —**an•ar•thric** (an är′thrik), *adj.*

an•ar•throus (an är′thrəs), *adj.* **1.** *Zool.* having no joints or articulated limbs. **2.** (esp. in Greek grammar) used without the article. [1800–10; < Gk *ánarthros* jointless. See AN-[1], ARTHR-, -OUS] —**an•ar′throus•ly,** *adv.* —**an•ar′throus•ness,** *n.*

an•a•sar•ca (an′ə sär′kə), *n. Pathol.* a pronounced, generalized edema. [1350–1400; ME (< MF) < ML, repr. Gk phrase *anà sárka* lit., throughout the body] —**an′a•sar′cous,** *adj.*

A•na•sa•zi (ä′nə sä′zē), *n., pl.* **-zis,** (*esp. collectively*) **-zi** for 2. **1.** a Basket Maker-Pueblo culture of the plateau region of northern Arizona and New Mexico and of southern Utah and Colorado, dating probably from A.D. 100 to 1300. **2.** a member of the people producing this culture. —*adj.* **3.** of, pertaining to, or characteristic of this culture or its people: *the Anasazi communities.* [term introduced in 1936 by U.S. archaeologist Alfred V. Kidder (1885–1963) < Navajo *ʼanaasází* ancient inhabitants of the Pueblo ruins, lit., aliens' ancestors (*ʼanaa-* enemy, alien + *-sází* ancestor(s), ancestral)]

an•as•pid (ə nas′pid), *n. Paleontol.* any member of an extinct order, Anaspida, of small, freshwater jawless fishes of the Silurian and Devonian periods, characterized by a single nostril, narrow rows of scales, and, usually, an armor-plated head. [< NL *Anaspida* name of the order, equiv. to *an-* AN-[3] + Gk *aspid-* (s. of *aspís* shield) + *-a* neut. pl. n. ending]

An•a•sta•sia (an′ə stā′zhə, ä′nə stä′shə; *Russ.* u nustä′syi yə), *n.* **1. Ni•ko•la•iev•na Ro•ma•nov** (*Russ.* nyi ku lä′yiv nə RU mä′nəf), **Grand Duchess,** 1901–?, daughter of Nicholas II: believed executed by the Bolsheviks in 1918 with other members of the Romanov family. **2.** a female given name.

a•nas•ta•sis (ə nas′tə sis), *n., pl.* **-ses** (-sēz′). a representation, in Byzantine art, of Christ harrowing hell. [< Gk *anástasis* a raising up, removal. See ANA-, STASIS]

An•as•ta•sius I (an′ə stā′shəs, -shē əs), A.D. c430–518, emperor of the Eastern Roman Empire 491–518.

an•as•tig•mat (ə nas′tig mat′, an′ə stig′mat), *n. Optics.* a compound lens corrected for the aberrations of astigmatism and curvature of field. [1885–90; < G, back formation from *anastigmatisch* ANASTIGMATIC]

an•as•tig•mat•ic (an′ə stig mat′ik, a nas′tig-), *adj. Optics.* (of a lens) not having astigmatism; forming point images of a point object located off the axis of the lens; stigmatic. [1885–90; AN-[1] + ASTIGMATIC]

a•nas•to•mose (ə nas′tə mōz′), *v.t., v.i.,* **-mosed, -mos•ing.** *Physiol., Anat., Geol.* to communicate or connect by anastomosis. [1690–1700; back formation from ANASTOMOSIS]

a•nas•to•mo•sis (ə nas′tə mō′sis), *n., pl.* **-ses** (-sēz). **1.** *Anat.* communication between blood vessels by means of collateral channels, esp. when usual routes are obstructed. **2.** *Biol., Geol.* connection between parts of any branching system, as veinlets in a leaf or branches of a stream. **3.** *Surg., Pathol.* a joining of or opening between two organs or spaces that normally are not connected. [1605–15; < NL < Gk: opening. See ANA-, STOMA, -OSIS] —**a•nas•to•mot•ic** (ə nas′tə mot′ik), *adj.*

a•nas•tro•phe (ə nas′trə fē), *n. Rhet.* inversion of the usual order of words. [1570–80; < Gk: turning back. See ANA-, STROPHE]

an•a•sty•lo•sis (an′ə stī lō′sis), *n., pl.* **-ses** (-sēz). the restoration of a ruined monument or building by reassembling fallen parts and, when necessary, incorporating new materials. [1955–60; ANA- + Gk *stȳ́lōsis,* deriv. of *styloûn* to prop with pillars; see STYLO-, -OSIS]

anat., 1. anatomical. **2.** anatomist. **3.** anatomy.

a•nat•a•bine (ə nat′ə bēn′, -bin), *n. Chem.* a liquid alkaloid, $C_{10}H_{12}N_2$, obtained from tobacco. [ANA- + Sp *tab(aco)* TOBACCO + -INE[2]]

an•a•tase (an′ə tās′, -tāz′), *n. Mineral.* a naturally occurring crystalline form of titanium dioxide, TiO_2. Also called **octahedrite.** [1835–45; < F < Gk *anátasis,* equiv. to *ana-* ANA- + *ta-* (var. s. of *teínein* to stretch) + *-sis* -SIS]

an•a•tex•is (an′ə tek′sis), *n., pl.* **-tex•es** (-tek′sēz). *Geol.* the process by which igneous rock remelts into magma. [< NL < Gk *anátēxis* a melting, equiv. to *anatḗk(ein)* to melt down (*ana-* ANA- + *tḗkein* to thaw) + *-sis* -SIS]

a•nath•e•ma (ə nath′ə mə), *n., pl.* **-mas. 1.** a person or thing detested or loathed: *That subject is anathema to him.* **2.** a person or thing accursed or consigned to damnation or destruction. **3.** a formal ecclesiastical curse involving excommunication. **4.** any imprecation of divine punishment. **5.** a curse; execration. [1520–30; < L < Gk: a thing accursed, devoted to evil, orig. devoted, equiv. to *ana(ti)thé(nai)* to set up + *-ma* n. suffix]

a•nath•e•mat•ic (ə nath′ə mat′ik), *adj.* loathsome; disgusting; hateful. Also, **a•nath′e•mat′i•cal.** [1840–50; < Gk *anathemat-* (s. of *anáthema;* see ANATHEMA) + -IC] —**a•nath′e•mat′i•cal•ly,** *adv.*

a•nath•e•ma•tize (ə nath′ə mə tīz′), *v.,* **-tized, -tiz•ing.** —*v.t.* **1.** to pronounce an anathema against; denounce; curse. —*v.i.* **2.** to pronounce anathemas; curse. Also, *esp. Brit.,* **a•nath′e•ma•tise′.** [1560–70; (< MF) < LL *anathematizāre* to put under the ban, curse, detest < Gk *anathematízein* to bind by a curse, make accursed, equiv. to *anathemat-* (s. of *anáthema*) + *-izein* -IZE] —**a•nath′e•ma•ti•za′tion,** *n.* —**a•nath′e•ma•tiz′er,** *n.*

an•a•tine (an′ə tīn′, -tin), *adj.* **1.** of or pertaining to the family Anatidae, comprising the swans, geese, and ducks. **2.** resembling a duck. [1860–65; < L *anatīnus* of, pertaining to a duck, equiv. to *anat-* (s. of *anas*) duck + *-īnus* -INE[1]]

a•nat•man (ə nät′mən), *n. Sanskrit.* anatta.

An•a•tol (an′ə tōl′), *n.* a male given name: from a Greek word meaning "sunrise." Also, **An′a•tole′.**

An•a•to•li•a (an′ə tō′lē ə), *n.* a vast plateau between the Black and the Mediterranean seas: in ancient usage, synonymous with the peninsula of Asia Minor; in modern usage, applied to Turkey in Asia. Cf. **Asia Minor.**

An•a•to•li•an (an′ə tō′lē ən), *adj.* **1.** of or pertaining to Anatolia, its inhabitants, or their language. **2.** of, pertaining to, or belonging to the Anatolian group or family of languages. —*n.* **3.** a native or inhabitant of Anatolia. **4.** any of various Turkish dialects spoken in Anatolia. **5.** a group or family of extinct languages that includes cuneiform Hittite and its nearest congeners, as Lycian, Lydian, and Luwian. **6.** a variety of Turkish rug woven in Anatolia. [1580–90; ANATOLI(A) + -AN]

An•a•tol•ic (an′ə tol′ik), *adj., n.* Anatolian. [1850–55; ANATOL(IA) + -IC]

an•a•tom•i•cal (an′ə tom′i kəl), *adj.* of or pertaining to anatomy. Also, **an′a•tom′ic.** [1580–90; < LL *anatomic(us)* (< Gk *anatomikós;* see ANATOMY, -IC) + -AL[1]] —**an′a•tom′i•cal•ly,** *adv.*

anatom′ical pathol′ogy, the branch of pathology dealing with the morphologic changes in the tissues, both gross and microscopic; pathological anatomy. —**an•a•tom•i•co•path•o•log•i•cal** (an′ə tom′i kō path′ə loj′i kəl), *adj.*

a•nat•o•mist (ə nat′ə mist), *n.* **1.** a specialist in anatomy. **2.** a person who analyzes all the parts or elements of something with particular care: *an anatomist of public-school systems and their problems.* [1560–70; ANATOM(Y) + -IST or < MF *anatomiste*]

a•nat•o•mize (ə nat′ə mīz′), *v.t.,* **-mized, -miz•ing. 1.** to cut apart (an animal or plant) to show or examine the position, structure, and relation of the parts; display the anatomy of; dissect. **2.** to examine in great detail; analyze minutely: *The couple anatomized their new neighbor.* Also, *esp. Brit.,* **a•nat′o•mise′.** [1400–50; late ME < MF *anatomiser* or < ML *anatomizāre.* See ANATOMY, -IZE] —**a•nat′o•miz′a•ble,** *adj.* —**a•nat′o•mi•za′tion,** *n.* —**a•nat′o•miz′er,** *n.*

a•nat•o•my (ə nat′ə mē), *n., pl.* **-mies. 1.** the science dealing with the structure of animals and plants. **2.** the structure of an animal or plant, or of any of its parts. **3.** dissection of all or part of an animal or plant in order to study its structure. **4.** a plant or animal that has been or will be dissected, or a model of such a dissected organism. **5.** a skeleton. **6.** *Informal.* the human body. **7.** an analysis or minute examination. [1350–1400; ME < L *anatomia* < Gk *anatom(ḗ)* a cutting up (*ana-* ANA- + *tom-* cut (var. of *tem-*) + *-ē* n. suffix) + *-ia* -Y[3]]

Anat′omy of Mel′ancholy, The, a philosophical treatise (1621) by Robert Burton.

an•a•tox•in (an′ə tok′sin), *n.* toxoid. [1920–25; ANA- + TOXIN]

a•nat•ro•pous (ə na′trə pəs), *adj. Bot.* (of an ovule) inverted at an early stage of growth, so that the micropyle is turned toward the funicle and the embryonic root is at the opposite end. [1840–50; ANA- + -TROPOUS]

an•at•ta (un′ət tä′), *n. Buddhism.* the doctrine asserting the nonexistence of a personal and immortal soul. Sanskrit, ***anatman.*** Cf. **Three Signs of Being.** [< Pali: lit., breathless]

a•nat•to (ə nat′ō, ä nä′tō), *n., pl.* **-tos.** annatto.

An•ax (an′aks), *n. Class. Myth.* one of the Gigantes and father of Asterius.

An•ax•ag•o•ras (an′ak sag′ər əs), *n.* 500?–428 B.C., Greek philosopher. —**An•ax•ag•o•re•an** (an′ak sag′ə rē′ən), *adj.*

An•ax•ar•e•te (an′ak sar′i tē′), *n. Class. Myth.* a princess turned to stone for scorning the love of a commoner.

An•ax•ib•i•a (an′ak sib′ē ə), *n. Class. Myth.* **1.** a daughter of Atreus and Aërope, and the sister of Agamemnon and Menelaus. **2.** the wife of Nestor.

A•nax•i•man•der (ə nak′sə man′dər), *n.* 611?–547? B.C., Greek astronomer and philosopher. —**A•nax•i•man•dri•an** (ə nak′sə man′drē ən), *adj.*

An•ax•im•e•nes (an′ak sim′ə nēz′), *n.* fl. 6th century B.C., Greek philosopher at Miletus.

an•ba (an′bə), *n.* father: a title of a clergyman or saint in the Coptic Church. Also, **amba.** [< Ar < Coptic *apa, abba* < Syriac *abbā* father]

ANC, 1. African National Congress. **2.** Army Nurse Corps.

anc., ancient.

An•cae•us (an sē′əs), *n. Class. Myth.* **1.** a son of Poseidon who joined the Argonauts and became helmsman of the *Argo.* **2.** a descendant of Lycurgus who, among the Argonauts, was second in strength only to Hercules.

An•cas•ter (an′kas tər, ang′-), *n.* a town in S Ontario, in S Canada. 14,255.

-ance, a suffix used to form nouns either from adjectives in *-ant* or from verbs: *brilliance; appearance.* [ME < OF < L *-antia* -ANCY, equiv. to *-ant-* -ANT + *-ia* -Y[3]]

an•ces•tor (an′ses tər *or, esp. Brit.,* -sə stər), *n.* **1.** a person from whom one is descended; forebear; progenitor. **2.** *Biol.* the actual or hypothetical form or stock from which an organism has developed or descended. **3.** an object, idea, style, or occurrence serving as a prototype, forerunner, or inspiration to a later one: *The balloon is an ancestor of the modern dirigible.* **4.** a person who serves as an influence or model for another; one from whom mental, artistic, spiritual, etc., descent is claimed: *a philosophical ancestor.* **5.** *Law.* a person from whom an heir derives an inheritance. [1250–1300; ME *ancestre* < OF (with *t* developed between *s* and *r*) < L *antecessor* ANTECESSOR]

an′cestor wor′ship, *Anthropol.* (in certain societies) the veneration of ancestors whose spirits are frequently held to possess the power to influence the affairs of the living. [1850–55]

an•ces•tral (an ses′trəl), *adj.* **1.** pertaining to ancestors; descending or claimed from ancestors: *an ancestral home.* **2.** serving as a forerunner, prototype, or inspiration. [1425–75; late ME *aunce(s)trel* < MF, equiv. to *ancestre* ANCESTOR + *-el* -AL[1]] —**an•ces′tral•ly,** *adv.*

CONCISE PRONUNCIATION KEY: *act, cāpe, dâre, pärt; set, ēqual; if, īce; ox, ōver, ôrder, oil, bo͝ok, bo͞ot, out; up, ûrge; child; sing; shoe; thin,* t͟h*at;* zh *as in treasure.* ə = *a as in alone, e as in system, i as in easily, o as in gallop, u as in circus;* ᵊ *as in fire* (fīᵊr), *hour* (ouᵊr). l *and* n *can serve as syllabic consonants, as in cradle* (krād′l), *and button* (but′n). *See the full key inside the front cover.*

an•ces•tress (an′ses tris *or, esp. Brit.,* -sə stris), *n.* a woman from whom a person is descended. [1570–80; ANCEST(O)R + -ESS]
—Usage. See **-ess.**

an•ces•try (an′ses trē *or, esp. Brit.,* -sə strē), *n., pl.* **-tries. 1.** family or ancestral descent; lineage. **2.** honorable or distinguished descent: *famous by title and ancestry.* **3.** a series of ancestors: *His ancestry settled Utah.* **4.** the inception or origin of a phenomenon, object, idea, or style. **5.** the history or developmental process of a phenomenon, object, idea, or style. [1300–50; ME, equiv. to *ancestre* ANCESTOR + -Y[3]; r. ME *aunce(s)trie* < AF]
—Syn. 1. pedigree, genealogy, stock. **3.** family, line.

An•ch'ing (än′ching′), *n. Wade-Giles.* Anqing.

an•chor (ang′kər), *n.* **1.** any of various devices dropped by a chain, cable, or rope to the bottom of a body of water for preventing or restricting the motion of a vessel or other floating object, typically having broad, hooklike arms that bury themselves in the bottom to provide a firm hold. **2.** any similar device for holding fast or checking motion: *an anchor of stones.* **3.** any device for securing a suspension or cantilever bridge at either end. **4.** any of various devices, as a metal tie, for binding one part of a structure to another. **5.** a person or thing that can be relied on for support, stability, or security; mainstay: *Hope was his only anchor.* **6.** *Radio and Television.* a person who is the main broadcaster on a program of news, sports, etc., and who usually also serves as coordinator of all participating broadcasters during the program; anchorman or anchorwoman; anchorperson. **7.** *Television.* a program that attracts many viewers who are likely to stay tuned to the network for the programs that follow. **8.** *Slang.* automotive brakes. **9.** *Mil.* a key position in defense lines. **10.** Also, **anchorman.** *Sports.* **a.** the person on a team, esp. a relay team, who competes last. **b.** the person farthest to the rear on a tug-of-war team. **11. at anchor,** held in place by an anchor: *The luxury liner is at anchor in the harbor.* **12. drag anchor,** (of a vessel) to move with a current or wind because an anchor has failed to hold. **13. drop anchor,** to anchor a vessel: *They dropped anchor in a bay to escape the storm.* **14. weigh anchor,** to raise the anchor: *We will weigh anchor at dawn.* —*v.t.* **15.** to hold fast by an anchor. **16.** to fix or fasten; affix firmly: *The button was anchored to the cloth with heavy thread.* **17.** to act or serve as an anchor for: *He anchored the evening news.* —*v.i.* **18.** to drop anchor; lie or ride at anchor: *The ship anchored at dawn.* **19.** to keep hold or be firmly fixed: *The insect anchored fast to its prey.* **20.** *Sports, Radio and Television.* to act or serve as an anchor. [bef. 900; ME *anker, ancre,* OE *ancor, ancer, ancra* (cf. OFris, MD, MLG *anker*) < L *anc(h)ora* < Gk *ánkyra*] **—an′chor•a•ble,** *adj.* **—an′chor•less,** *adj.* **—an′chor•like′,** *adj.*

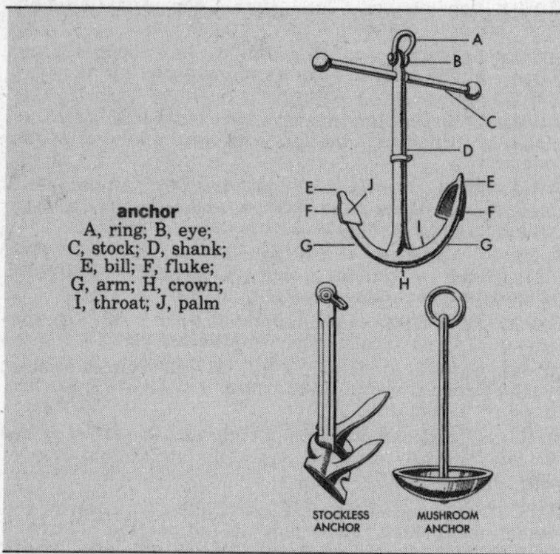

anchor
A, ring; B, eye; C, stock; D, shank; E, bill; F, fluke; G, arm; H, crown; I, throat; J, palm

an•chor•age (ang′kər ij), *n.* **1.** that portion of a harbor or area outside a harbor suitable for anchoring or in which ships are permitted to anchor. **2.** a charge for occupying such an area. **3.** the act of anchoring or the state of being anchored. **4.** that to which anything is fastened. **5.** a means of anchoring or making fast. **6.** something that can be relied on: *The Bible is her anchorage.* **7.** (in a suspension bridge) a massive masonry or concrete construction securing a cable at each end. **8.** *Dentistry.* **a.** an abutment. **b.** the locking in of a tooth filling by means of an undercut. [1400–50; late ME *ankerage.* See ANCHOR, -AGE]

An•chor•age (ang′kər ij), *n.* a seaport in S Alaska: earthquake 1964. 173,017.

an′chor ball′, *Naut.* a day shape consisting of a black ball not less than 2 ft. (0.6 m) in diameter, displayed in the fore rigging of a vessel at anchor.

an′chor bed′, *Naut.* a sloping, slightly projecting platform on the forecastle of a ship, for supporting an anchor when not in use. Also called **billboard.**

an′chor bell′, a bell rung in foggy weather by a vessel at anchor.

an′chor bend′. See **fisherman's bend.**

an′chor bolt′, any of several kinds of bolts inserted and fixed in masonry as a hold for timbers, shelves, etc. [1870–75]

CONCISE ETYMOLOGY KEY: <, descended or borrowed from; >, whence; b., blend of, blended; c., cognate with; cf., compare; deriv., derivative; equiv., equivalent; imit., imitative; obl., oblique; r., replacing; s., stem; sp., spelling, spelled; resp., respelling, respelled; trans., translation; ?, origin unknown; *, unattested; ‡, probably earlier than. See the full key inside the front cover.

an′chor buoy′, a buoy used to indicate the location of an underwater anchor.

an′chor deck′, *Naut.* a small forecastle housing the machinery for operating the anchors of a ship.

an′chor escape′ment, *Horol.* an escapement in which wedge-shaped pallets engage with an escape wheel having pointed teeth, usually facing in the direction of revolution, so that the escape wheel recoils slightly at every release. Also called **recoil escapement.** See diag. under **escapement.** [1850–55]

an•cho•ress (ang′kər is), *n.* a woman who is an anchorite. [1350–1400; late ME *anchoryse,* ME *ankres,* equiv. to *ancre* ANCHORITE + *-es* -ESS]
—Usage. See **-ess.**

an•cho•ret (ang′kər it, -kə ret′), *n.* anchorite. [1735–45; var. of ANCHORITE, with final vowel directly reflecting LL or LGk sp.] **—an•cho•ret•ic** (ang′kə ret′ik), *adj.* **—an′cho•ret′ism,** *n.*

an′chor ice′, ice formed below the surface of a body of water that attaches either to a submerged object or to the bottom. Also called **bottom ice, ground ice.** [1805–15, *Amer.*]

an•cho•rite (ang′kə rīt′), *n.* a person who has retired to a solitary place for a life of religious seclusion; hermit. Also, **anchoret.** [1400–50; late ME *anc(h)orite,* conflation of ME *ancre* (OE *ancra, ancer*) and OF *anacorite* or ML *anachōrīta* < LGk *anachōrētés,* equiv. to Gk *anachōrē-,* s. of *anachōreîn* to withdraw (*ana-* ANA- + *chōreîn* to give way, v. deriv. of *chôros* space) + *-tēs* agent suffix; OE forms < OIr **ancharae* < LL *anachōrēta* < LGk] **—an•cho•rit•ic** (ang′kə rit′ik), *adj.* **—an′cho•rit′i•cal•ly,** *adv.* **—an•cho•rit•ism** (ang′kə rī tiz′əm), *n.*

an′chor knot′. See **fisherman's bend.**

an′chor light′, *Naut.* a 32-point light, visible from at least two miles away, shown at night near the bow and not more than 20 ft. (6 m) above the deck of a vessel lying at anchor. Also called **riding light.**

an•chor•man (ang′kər man′, -mən), *n., pl.* **-men** (-men′, -mən). **1.** *Sports.* anchor (def. 10). **2.** *Radio and Television.* a man who anchors a program of news, sports, etc.; anchor. [1910–15 for def. 1; 1955–60 for def. 2; ANCHOR + MAN[1]]
—Usage. See **-man.**

an•chor•per•son (ang′kər pûr′sən), *n. Radio and Television.* a man or woman who anchors a program of news, sports, etc.; anchor. [1970–75; ANCHOR(MAN) + -PERSON]
—Usage. See **-person.**

an′chor plant′, a South American shrub, *Colletia cruciata,* of the buckthorn family, having flattened green branches and yellowish-white flowers.

an′chor pock′et, *Naut.* a recess in the bow of a vessel, for housing a stockless anchor.

an′chor ring′, *Geom. Now Rare.* torus (def. 2a). [1860–65]

an′chor shot′, *Naut.* See **grapple shot.** [1905–10]

an′chor span′, (on a suspension or cantilever bridge) a span from an anchorage to the nearest pier or tower.

an′chor watch′, *Naut.* a deck watch maintained by the crew of a ship at anchor. [1875–80]

an•chor•wom•an (ang′kər wo͝om′ən), *n., pl.* **-wom•en.** *Radio and Television.* a woman who anchors a program of news, sports, etc.; anchor. [1970–75; ANCHOR(MAN) + -WOMAN]
—Usage. See **-woman.**

an•chor•y (ang′kə rē, ang′krē), *adj. Heraldry.* ancré. [alter. of F *ancré* by influence of ANCHOR]

an•cho•vet•a (an′chō vet′ə, -chə-), *n.* an anchovy, *Cetengraulis mysticetus,* found along the Pacific coast from British Columbia to Lower California, used for bait. [1935–40; < Sp, equiv. to *anchov(a)* ANCHOVY + *-eta* < L *-itta* dim. suffix]

an•cho•vy (an′chō vē, -chə-, an chō′vē), *n., pl.* **-vies.** any small, marine, herringlike fish of the family Engraulidae, esp. *Engraulis encrasicholus,* found in the Mediterranean Sea, often preserved in oil and used in salads, spreads, etc., or packaged in paste form. [1590–1600; < F or Ibero-Romance < Genoese *anchua, anchova* < VL **apiu(v)a,* var. of L *apua* (Pliny) < Gk *aphýē* fry of various fishes]

an′chovy pear′, **1.** the fruit of a West Indian tree, *Grias cauliflora,* somewhat resembling the mango. **2.** the tree itself. [1690–1700]

an•chu•sa (ang kyo͞o′sə, -zə, an cho͞o′-), *n.* any plant of the genus *Anchusa,* of the borage family, several species of which are cultivated for their blue or purplish flowers that resemble forget-me-nots. Also called **alkanet.** [< NL, L *anchūsa* dyer's bugloss < Gk *ánchousa*]

an•chu•sin (ang kyo͞o′sin), *n.* a red coloring matter obtained from the root of the alkanet, *Alkanna tinctoria.* [1860–65; < NL *Anchus(a)* ANCHUSA + -IN[2]]

anchylo-, var. of **ancylo-.**

An•cienne-Lo•rette (*Fr.* äɴ syen lô ret′), *n.* a town in S Quebec, in E Canada. 11,694.

an•cienne no•blesse (äɴ syen nô bles′), *French.* the ancient nobility, esp. of the *ancien régime.*

an•cien ré•gime (äɴ syaɴ rā zhēm′), *pl.* ***an•ciens ré•gimes*** (äɴ syaɴ rā zhēm′). *French.* **1.** the political and social system of France before the revolution of 1789. **2.** the system of government during this period.

an•cient[1] (ān′shənt), *adj.* **1.** of or in time long past, esp. before the end of the Western Roman Empire A.D. 476: *ancient history.* **2.** dating from a remote period; of great age: *ancient rocks; ancient trees.* **3.** very old; aged: *an ancient folk tale.* **4.** being old in wisdom and experience; venerable. **5.** old-fashioned or antique. —*n.* **6.** a person who lived in ancient times. **7.** one of the classical writers of antiquity. **8.** a very old or aged person, esp. if venerable or patriarchal. **9. ancients, a.** the civilized peoples, nations, or cultures of antiquity, as the Greeks, Romans, Hebrews, and Egyptians (usually prec. by *the*). **b.** the writers, artists, and philosophers of ancient times, esp. those of Greece and Rome. [1300–50; ME *auncien* < AF; OF *ancien* < VL **antiānus,* equiv. to L *ante(ā)* before (see ANTE-) + *-ānus* -AN; late ME forms with *-t* developed by confusion with the prp. ending *-nt* (see -ENT)] **—an′cient•ness,** *n.*
—Syn. 2, 3. ANCIENT, ANTIQUATED, ANTIQUE, OLD-FASHIONED refer to something dating from the past. ANCIENT implies existence or first occurrence in a distant past: *an ancient custom.* ANTIQUATED connotes something too old or no longer useful: *an antiquated building.* ANTIQUE suggests a curious or pleasing quality in something old: *antique furniture.* OLD-FASHIONED may disparage something as being out of date or may approve something old as being superior: *an old-fashioned hat; old-fashioned courtesy.* **—Ant. 2, 3.** new, modern.

an•cient[2] (ān′shənt), *n. Obs.* **1.** the bearer of a flag. **2.** a flag, banner, or standard; ensign. [1545–55; var. of ENSIGN by confusion with ANCIENT[1]]

An′cient Ar′abic Or′der of No′bles of the Mys′tic Shrine′. See under **Shriner.**

an′cient his′tory, **1.** the study or a course of study of history before the end of the Western Roman Empire A.D. 476. **2.** information or an event of the recent past that is common knowledge or is no longer pertinent: *Last week's news is ancient history.* **3.** an event, as in a person's life, that occurred in the remote past and has no practical relationship with the present: *She was my best friend in high school, but that's ancient history now.* [1585–95]

an•cient•ly (ān′shənt lē), *adv.* in ancient times; of old. [1495–1505; ANCIENT[1] + -LY]

An′cient Mys′tic Or′der Ro′sae Cru′cis (rō′zē kro͞o′sis). See under **Rosicrucian** (def. 2). *Abbr.:* AMORC

An′cient of Days′, the Supreme Being; God.

an′cient regime′. See ***ancien régime.***

an•cient•ry (ān′shən trē), *n.* **1.** *Archaic.* **a.** ancient character or style. **b.** ancient times. **2.** *Obs.* **a.** ancient lineage. **b.** old people. [1540–50; ANCIENT[1] + -RY]

an•ci•le (an sī′lē, äng kē′lā), *n., pl.* **an•cil•i•a** (an sil′ē ə, äng kil′-). *Rom. Religion.* **1.** a shield given by Mars to Numa Pompilius as the palladium of Rome. **2.** any of 11 counterfeits of this shield, carried with it on ceremonial occasions. [1590–1600; < L *ancīle,* traditionally said to be equiv. to *an-* (var. of *ambi-* AMBI- before *c-*) + *-cīle* (*-cīd-* comb. form of *caed(ere)* to cut (cf. -CIDE) + **-sl-* n. suffix + *-e,* earlier **-i,* s. vowel for compounds), referring to the deep indentations in the waist of the shield]

an•cil•la (an sil′ə), *n., pl.* **-las. 1.** an accessory; auxiliary or adjunct. **2.** *Archaic.* a maidservant. [1870–75; < L: female slave, maid, prob. *anc-* + *-illa* dim. suffix, by reanalysis of *ancula* maid < **anquola,* equiv. to *an-* (see ANCILE) + **-quola,* n. deriv. of a v. base **quel-* turn about, hence "one who circles around"; c. Gk *amphípolos* attendant]

an•cil•lar•y (an′sə ler′ē *or, esp. Brit.,* an sil′ə rē), *adj., n., pl.* **-lar•ies.** —*adj.* **1.** subordinate; subsidiary. **2.** auxiliary; assisting. —*n.* **3.** something that serves in an ancillary capacity: *Slides, records, and other ancillaries can be used with the basic textbook.* [1660–70; < L *ancill(a)* (see ANCILLA) + -ARY; cf. L *ancillāris* having the status of a female slave, with *-āris* -AR[1]]

an•cip•i•tal (an sip′i tl), *adj. Bot., Zool.* two-edged: *ancipital stems.* [1785–95; < L *ancipit-* (s. of *anceps;* an- (see ANCILE) + *-cipit-* comb. form of *caput* head) + -AL[1]]

An•co•hu•ma (äng′kō o͞o′mä), *n.* a peak of Mount Sorata. Cf. **Sorata, Mount.**

an•con (ang′kon), *n.; pl.* **an•co•nes** (ang kō′nēz). **1.** the elbow. **2.** *Archit.* a bracket or console, as one supporting part of a cornice. [1700–10; < L < Gk *ankṓn* elbow] **—an•co•nal** (ang kōn′l), **an•co•ne•al** (ang kō′nē əl), *adj.* **—an′con•oid′,** *adj.*

A, ancon

an•co•na (än kô′nä; *Eng.* ang kō′nə), *n., pl.* ***-ne*** (-ne), *Eng.* **-nas.** *Italian.* an altarpiece, usually consisting of a painted panel or panels, reliefs, or statues set in an elaborate frame. [1870–75]

An•co•na (än kô′nä), *n.* **1.** a seaport in E Italy, on the Adriatic Sea. 107,922. **2.** one of a Mediterranean breed of chickens having mottled black-and-white plumage.

an•cré (ang′krā), *adj. Heraldry.* (of a cross) having the end of each limb divided and carved outward like the flukes of an anchor; moline: *a cross ancré.* Also, **anchory.** [< F, equiv. to *anchre* ANCHOR + *-é* (< L *-ātus* -ATE[1])]

An•cus Mar•ci•us (ang′kəs mär′shē əs, -shəs), *Rom. Legend.* a king of Rome, during whose reign the first bridge across the Tiber was constructed.

-ancy, a combination of **-ance** and **-y,** used to form nouns denoting state or quality: *brilliancy.* [< L *-antia,* equiv. to *-ant-* -ANT (*-ā-* thematic vowel + *-nt-* prp. suffix) + *-ia* -Y[3]]

ancylo-, a combining form meaning "hook," "joint," used in the formation of technical terms: *ancylostomiasis.* Also, **anchylo-, ankylo-.** [comb. form repr. Gk *ankýlos* crooked, curved, equiv. to *ánk(os)* bend (c. L *uncus* bent, ANGLE[2]) + *-ylos* adjective-forming suffix]

and (and; *unstressed* ənd, ən, *or, esp. after a homorganic consonant,* n), *conj.* **1.** (used to connect grammatically coordinate words, phrases, or clauses) along or together with; as well as; in addition to; besides; also; moreover: *pens and pencils.* **2.** added to; plus: *2 and 2 are 4.* **3.** then: *He read for an hour and went to bed.* **4.** also, at the same time: *to sleep and dream.* **5.** then again; repeatedly: *He coughed and coughed.* **6.** (used to imply different qualities in things having the same name): *There are bargains and bargains, so watch out.* **7.** (used to introduce a sentence, implying continuation) also; then: *And then it happened.* **8.** *Informal.* to (used between two finite verbs): *Try and do it. Call and see if she's home yet.* **9.** (used to introduce a consequence or conditional result): *He felt sick and decided to lie down for a while. Say one more word about it and I'll scream.* **10.** but; on the contrary: *He tried to run five miles and couldn't. They said they were about to leave and then stayed for two more hours.* **11.** (used to connect alternatives): *He felt that he was being forced to choose between his career and his family.* **12.** (used to introduce a comment on the preceding clause): *They don't like each other—and with good reason.* **13.** *Archaic.* if: *and you please.* Cf. **an**². **14. and so forth,** and the like; and others; et cetera: *We discussed traveling, sightseeing, and so forth.* **15. and so on,** and more things or others of a similar kind; and the like: *It was a summer filled with parties, picnics, and so on.* —*n.* **16.** an added condition, stipulation, detail, or particular: *He accepted the job, no ands or buts about it.* **17.** conjunction (def. 5b). [bef. 900; ME; OE *and, ond;* c. OS, OHG *ant,* OFris, Goth *and,* Icel *and-;* akin to G *und,* D *en,* Skt *anti*]

—Usage. Both AND and BUT, and to a lesser extent OR and so, are common as transitional words at the beginnings of sentences in all types of speech and writing: *General Jackson thought the attack would come after darkness. And he was right.* Any objection to this practice probably stems from the overuse of such sentences by inexperienced writers. When one of these words begins a sentence or an independent clause within a sentence, it is not followed by a comma unless the comma is one of a pair setting off a parenthetical element that follows: *John is popular, and he seems to be well adjusted. But, appearances to the contrary, he is often depressed.* See also **and/or, et cetera, try.**

An·da·lu·sia (an′dl o͞o′zhə, -shē ə), *n.* **1.** Spanish, **Andalucía** (än′dä lo͞o thē′ä, -sē′ä). a region in S Spain, bordering on the Atlantic Ocean and the Mediterranean Sea. 33,712 sq. mi. (87,314 sq. km). **2.** a city in S Alabama. 10,415. **—An′da·lu′sian,** *adj., n.*

an·da·lu·site (an′dl o͞o′sīt), *n. Mineral.* an orthorhombic form of aluminum silicate, Al_2SiO_5, found in schistose rocks. [1830–40; named after ANDALUSIA, where it was first found; see -ITE¹]

An·da·man (an′də mən), *adj.* **1.** Also, **Andamanese.** of or pertaining to the Andaman Islands, the Andamanese people, or their language. —*n.* **2.** Andamanese (def. 1).

An′daman and Nic′o·bar Is′lands (nik′ə bär′, nik′ə bär′), a union territory of India, comprising the Andaman and Nicobar island groups in the E part of the Bay of Bengal, SW of Burma. 188,254; 3143 sq. mi. (8140 sq. km). *Cap.:* Port Blair.

An·da·man·ese (an′də mə nēz′, -nēs′), *n., pl.* **-ese,** *adj.* —*n.* **1.** Also, **Andaman.** Also called **An′daman Is′lander.** a member of a physically distinctive people that comprise the indigenous population of the Andaman Islands. **2.** the language of the Andamanese, of uncertain genetic affiliation. —*adj.* **3.** Andaman (def. 1). [1860–65; ANDAMAN + -ESE]

An′daman Is′lands, a group of islands of India in the E part of the Bay of Bengal, W of the Malay Peninsula, part of Andaman and Nicobar Islands. 157,821; 2508 sq. mi. (6496 sq. km).

An′daman Sea′, a part of the Bay of Bengal, E of the Andaman and Nicobar Islands. 300,000 sq. mi. (777,000 sq. km).

an·da·men·to (an′də men′tō; *It.* än′dä men′tô), *n., pl.* **-tos,** *It.* **-ta** (-tä). *Music.* **1.** an extended fugue subject. **2.** an episode in a fugue. [< It, equiv. to *anda(re)* to walk (see ANDANTE) + *-mento* -MENT]

an·dan·te (än dän′tā, an dan′tē; *It.* än dän′te), *adj., adv., n., pl.* **-tes.** *Music.* —*adj., adv.* **1.** moderately slow and even. —*n.* **2.** an andante movement or piece. [1735–45; < It: lit., walking, prp. of *andare* to walk, go (see -ANT); etym. disputed, but often alleged: < VL **ambitare,* deriv. of L *ambitus* circular motion, roundabout journey (see AMBIT); perh., alternatively, early L borrowing < Gaulish **andā-,* akin to L *pandere* to spread (hence, stride); cf. *passus* step, pace (action n. **pand-tu-*), equiv. to OIr *ēs* footprint, track]

an·dan·ti·no (än′dän tē′nō, an′dan-; *It.* än′dän tē′nô), *adj., adv., n., pl.* **-nos,** *It.* **-ni** (-nē). *Music.* —*adj., adv.* **1.** slightly faster than andante. —*n.* **2.** an andantino movement or piece. [1810–20; < It, equiv. to *andan(te)* ANDANTE + *-ino* dim. suffix]

AND′ cir′cuit (and), *Computers.* a circuit that is energized only when all of its inputs are energized.

An·de·an (an dē′ən, an′dē-), *adj.* of or like the Andes. [1830–40; ANDE(S) + -AN]

Ande′an con′dor. See under **condor** (def. 1).

Ande′an deer′, huemul.

An·der·lecht (än′dər lekht′), *n.* a city in central Belgium, near Brussels. 103,796.

An·der·sen (an′dər sən), *n.* **Hans Christian** (hanz), 1805–75, Danish author, esp. of fairy tales.

An·der·sen Nex·ö (ä′nər sən nik′sœ). See **Nexö, Martin Andersen.**

An·der·son (an′dər sən), *n.* **1. Carl David,** 1905–91, U.S. physicist: discoverer of the positron; Nobel prize 1936. **2. Dame Judith,** born 1898, Australian actress in the U.S. **3. Marian,** 1902–93, U.S. contralto. **4. Maxwell,** 1888–1959, U.S. dramatist. **5. Philip Warren,** born 1923, U.S. physicist: developer of solid-state circuitry; Nobel prize 1977. **6. Sherwood,** 1876–1941, U.S. novelist and short-story writer. **7.** a city in central Indiana. 64,695. **8.** a city in NW South Carolina. 27,313.

An·der·son·ville (an′dər sən vil′), *n.* a village in SW Georgia: site of a Confederate military prison. 267.

An·des (an′dēz), *n.* (*used with a plural v.*) a mountain range in W South America, extending ab. 4500 mi. (7250 km) from N Colombia and Venezuela S to Cape Horn. Highest peak, Aconcagua, 22,834 ft. (6960 m).

an·de·sine (an′də zēn′), *n.* a mineral, intermediate in the plagioclase feldspar group, having a play of colors and usually found as crystals in igneous rocks. [1860–65; named after ANDES; see -INE²]

an·des·ite (an′də zīt′), *n.* a dark-colored volcanic rock composed essentially of plagioclase feldspar and one or more mafic minerals, as hornblende or biotite. [1840–50; named after ANDES; see -ITE¹] **—an·de·sit·ic** (an′də-zit′ik), *adj.*

An′des light′ning, an electrical discharge of the corona type, occurring over mountains when the atmosphere is electrically disturbed. Also called **An′des glow′, An′des lights′.**

An·dhra Pra·desh (än′drə prə dāsh′), a state in SE India, formed from portions of Madras and Hyderabad states 1956. 48,630,000; 105,963 sq. mi. (274,444 sq. km). *Cap.:* Hyderabad.

an·dia·mo (än dyä′mô), *interj. Italian.* let's go; hurry up.

An·die (an′dē), *n.* a male or female given name.

An·di·ki·thi·ra (an′di ki thēr′ə; *Gk.* än′dē kē′thē rä), *n.* Antikythera.

and·i·ron (and′ī′ərn), *n.* one of a pair of metal stands, usually of iron or brass, for holding logs in a fireplace. [1250–1300; ME *aundyr(n)e,* AF *aundyre,* with the 2d syll. taken as ME *ire, iren* IRON < OF *andier,* allegedly < Gaulish **anderos* young animal (through known use of animals' heads as decorations on andirons), though supposed relation between this word and Middle Welsh *anneir,* Breton *annoer* heifer, OIr *ainder* young woman, poses serious phonetic problems]
—Regional Variation. See **dog iron, firedog.**

andirons

An·di·zhan (än′di zhän′; *Russ.* un dyi zhän′), *n.* a city in E Uzbekistan, SE of Tashkent. 230,000.

and/or (and′ôr′), *conj.* (used to imply that either or both of the things mentioned may be affected or involved): *insurance covering fire and/or wind damage.*
—Usage. The combination AND/OR is used primarily in business and legal writing: *All dwellings and/or other structures on the property are included in the contract.* Because of these business and legal associations, some object to the use of this combination in general writing, where it occasionally occurs: *She spends much of her leisure time entertaining and/or traveling.* In such writing, either AND or OR is usually adequate. If a greater distinction is needed, another phrasing is available: *Would you like cream or sugar, or both?*

an·do·ro·ba (an′də rō′bə), *n.* carapa. [< Pg *andiroba* < Tupi *nhandiroba*]

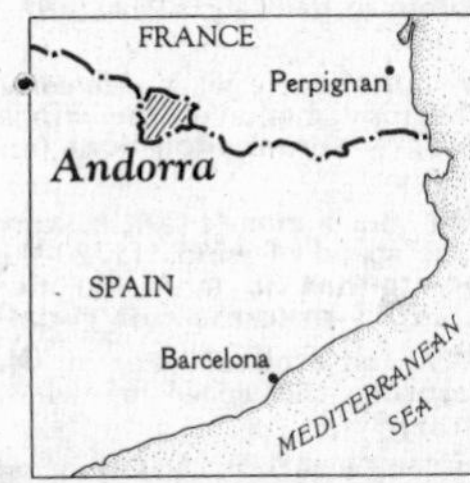

An·dor·ra (an dôr′ə, -dor′ə; *Sp.* än dôr′rä), *n.* **1.** a republic in the E Pyrenees between France and Spain, under the joint suzerainty of France and the Spanish Bishop of Urgel. 26,558; 191 sq. mi. (495 sq. km). **2.** Also called **An·dor·ra la Ve·lla** (*Catalan.* än dôr′rä lä ve′-lyä). a city in and the capital of this republic. 7926. French, **An·dorre** (äɴ dôr′). **—An·dor′ran,** *adj., n.*

An·do·ver (an′dō vər, -də-), *n.* a city in NE Massachusetts. 26,370.

andr-, var. of **andro-** before a vowel: *android.*

An·dra·da e Sil·va (äɴ drä′də e sēl′və), **Jo·sé Bo·ni·fa·cio de** (zhô ze′ bô′nē fä′syo͞o di), 1763–1838, Brazilian statesman and scientist: architect of Brazilian independence.

an·dra·dite (an′drə dīt′), *n.* a mineral, calcium-iron garnet, $Ca_3Fe_2Si_3O_2$, occurring in brown, green, or black crystals. [1830–40; named after J. B. de ANDRADA E SILVA; see -ITE¹]

an·dra·go·gy (an′drə gō′jē, -goj′ē), *n.* the methods or techniques used to teach adults. [ANDR- + (PED)AGOGY; see -AGOGUE, -Y³]

An·drás·sy (an dras′ē; *Hung.* on′drä shē), *n.* **1. Count Julius,** 1823–90, Hungarian statesman. **2.** his son, **Count Julius** (*Gyula*), 1860–1929, Hungarian statesman.

An·dré (än′drā *or, for 1,* an′drē; *for 2 also Fr.* äɴ-drā′), *n.* **1. John,** 1751–80, British major hanged as a spy by the Americans in the Revolutionary War: plotted the betrayal of West Point with Benedict Arnold. **2.** a male given name, French form of **Andrew.**

An·dre·a (an′drē ə, än′-, än drā′ə), *n.* a male or female given name, Latinized form of **Andrew.**

An·dre·a del Sar·to (än drā′ə del sär′tō; *It.* än-dre′ä del sär′tô), **1.** (*Andrea Domenico d'Annolo di Francesco*) 1486–1531, Italian painter. **2.** (*italics*) a dramatic monologue (1855) by Robert Browning.

An·dre·a′nof Is′lands (an′drē an′ôf, -of, än′drē ä′-nôf, -nof; *Russ.* un dryi yä′nəf), a group of islands in the W part of the Aleutian Islands. 1432 sq. mi. (3710 sq. km).

An·dret·ti (an dret′ē), *n.* **Mario (Gabriel),** born 1940, U.S. racing-car driver.

An·drew (an′dro͞o), *n.* **1.** one of the 12 apostles of Jesus. Mark 3:18; John 1:40–42. **2.** a male given name: from a Greek word meaning "manly."

An·drewes (an′dro͞oz), *n.* **Lancelot,** 1555–1626, English theologian: one of the translators of the Authorized Version of the Bible.

An′drew of Crete′, A.D. c650–730, Greek poet and Orthodox archbishop of Crete.

An·drews (an′dro͞oz), *n.* **1. Charles Mc·Lean** (mə klān′), 1863–1943, U.S. historian and author. **2. Frank Maxwell,** 1884–1943, U.S. Air Force general. **3. Roy Chapman,** 1884–1960, U.S. naturalist, explorer, and author. **4.** a city in NW Texas. 11,061.

An·dre·yev (än drā′əf; *Russ.* un drye′yif), *n.* **Le·o·nid Ni·ko·la·e·vich** (lē′ə nid nik′ə lī′ə vich; *Russ.* lyi u-nyēt′ nyi ku lä′yi vyich), 1871–1919, Russian novelist, short-story writer, and playwright.

An·drić (än′drich), *n.* **I·vo** (ē′vô), 1892–1975, Yugoslavian poet, novelist, and short-story writer: Nobel prize 1961.

andro-, a combining form meaning "male," used in the formation of compound words: *androsterone.* Also, **andr-.** [< Gk *andró(s),* gen. of *anḗr* man; akin to Skt *nar-,* Albanian *njerí* person, L *Nero* NERO]

an·dro·cen·tric (an′drə sen′trik), *adj.* centered on, emphasizing, or dominated by males or masculine interests: *an androcentric society; an androcentric religion.* [1900–05; ANDRO- + -CENTRIC, on the model of ETHNOCENTRIC] **—an′dro·cen′trism,** *n.* **—an′dro·cen′trist,** *n.*

An·dro·cles (an′drə klēz′), *n. Rom. Legend.* a slave who was spared in the arena by a lion from whose foot he had long before extracted a thorn. Also, **An·dro·clus** (an′drə kləs).

An′drocles and the Li′on, a comedy (1913) by G. B. Shaw.

an·dro·clin·i·um (an′drə klin′ē əm), *n., pl.* **-clin·i·a** (-klin′ē ə). *Bot.* clinandrium. [< NL, equiv. to *andro-* ANDRO- + *-clinium* < Gk *klínion,* dim. of *klínē* bed; see -IUM]

an·dro·co·ni·um (an′drə kō′nē əm), *n., pl.* **-ni·a** (-nē ə). a scale on the forewing of certain male butterflies from which an odor attractive to females is emitted. [1875–80; < NL, equiv. to *andro-* ANDRO- + *-conium* < Gk *kónion,* neut. of *kónios* dusty (*kóni(s)* dust + *-os* adj. suffix)]

an·droc·ra·cy (an drok′rə sē), *n.* social and political rule by men. [ANDRO- + -CRACY] **—an·dro·crat·ic** (an′drə krat′ik), *adj.*

an·dro·di·oe·cious (an′drō dī ē′shəs), *adj. Bot.* having staminate and monoclinous flowers on separate plants of the same species. [1875–80; ANDRO- + DIOECIOUS] **—an·dro·di·oe·cism** (an′drō dī ē′siz əm), *n.*

an·droe·ci·um (an drē′shē əm), *n., pl.* **-ci·a** (-shē ə). *Bot.* the stamens of a flower collectively. [1830–40; < NL < Gk *andr-* ANDR- + *oikíon,* dim. of *oîkos* house] **—an·droe·cial** (an drē′shəl), *adj.*

an·dro·gen (an′drə jən, -jen′), *n. Biochem.* any substance, as testosterone or androsterone, that promotes male characteristics. [1935–40; ANDRO- + -GEN] **—an·dro·gen·ic** (an′drə jen′ik), *adj.*

an·drog·e·nous (an droj′ə nəs), *adj. Biol.* pertaining to the production of or tending to produce male offspring. [1750–60; ANDRO- + -GENOUS]

An·drog·e·us (an droj′ē əs, -yo͞os), *n. Class. Myth.* a son of Minos and Pasiphaë who fell victim to Athenian King Aegeus: in revenge, Minos waged war on the Athenians and forced them to send a tribute of seven maidens and seven youths to the Minotaur every nine years.

an·dro·gyne (an′drə jīn′), *n.* **1.** an androgynous plant. **2.** an androgynous person, as one who chooses unisex clothing. **3.** a female pseudohermaphrodite. **4.** a being of ambiguous sexual identity; one that combines major aspects of both the male and the female. [1545–55; < MF < L *androgynus* < Gk *andrógynos* hermaphrodite, equiv. to *andro-* ANDRO- + *gyn-* GYN- + *-os* masc. n. suffix]

an·drog·y·nous (an droj′ə nəs), *adj.* **1.** being both male and female; hermaphroditic. **2.** having both masculine and feminine characteristics. **3.** having an ambiguous sexual identity. **4.** neither clearly masculine nor clearly feminine in appearance: *the androgynous look of many rock stars.* **5.** *Bot.* having staminate and pistillate flowers in the same inflorescence. [1620–30; ANDROGYNE + -OUS] **—an·drog′y·ny,** *n.*

an·droid (an′droid), *n.* an automaton in the form of a human being. [1720–30; < NL *androidēs.* See ANDR-, -OID]

an·drol·o·gy (an drol′ə jē), *n.* the study of the functions and diseases peculiar to males, esp. of the reproductive organs. [1970–75; ANDRO- + -LOGY]

An·drom·a·che (an drom′ə kē′), *n.* **1.** *Class. Myth.* the wife of Hector and mother of Astyanax. **2.** (*italics*) a tragedy (c419 B.C.) by Euripides.

An·dro·maque (äN drô mAk′), *n.* a tragedy (1667) by Racine.

an·drom·e·da (an drom′i də), *n.* See **Japanese andromeda.** [special use of ANDROMEDA]

An·drom·e·da (an drom′i də), *n., gen.* **-dae** (-dē′) for 2. **1.** *Class. Myth.* an Ethiopian princess, the daughter of Cassiopeia and wife of Perseus, by whom she had been rescued from a sea monster. **2.** *Astron.* a northern constellation between Pisces and Cassiopeia.

Androm′eda gal′axy, *Astron.* a spiral galaxy, appearing to the naked eye as a fuzzy oval patch in the constellation Andromeda; it is a close neighbor to our own galaxy.

Androm′eda strain′, an infectious pathogen that mutates unpredictably into new forms and shows extreme resistance to destruction by conventional means. [1970–75; after such a pathogen in a novel of the same name (1969) by U.S. author Michael Crichton (born 1942)]

an·dro·mo·noe·cious (an′drō mə nē′shəs), *adj. Bot.* having staminate and monoclinous flowers on the same plant. [1875–80; ANDRO- + MONOECIOUS] **—an·dro·mo·noe·cism** (an′drō mə nē′siz əm), *n.*

an·dron (an′dron), *n.* **1.** (in an ancient Greek house) an apartment for men, esp. one for banqueting. **2.** (in an ancient Roman house) a passage between two peristyles. [< Gk, equiv. to *andr-* ANDR- + *-ōn* n. suffix]

An·dron (an′dron), *n. Class. Myth.* a son of Anius who was given the power of prophecy by Apollo. Also, **Andrus.**

an·dro·phore (an′drə fôr′, -fōr′), *n. Bot.* a stalk or column supporting the stamens, formed by the fusion of their filaments. [1815–25; ANDRO- + -PHORE]

An·dro·pov (an drō′ pôf, -pof; *Russ.* un dʀô′ pəf), *n.* a former name (1984–90) of **Rybinsk.**

An·dros (an′drəs), *n.* **1. Sir Edmund,** 1637–1714, British governor in the American colonies, 1686–89, 1692–98. **2.** the largest island in the Bahamas, in the W part of the group. 8845; 1600 sq. mi. (4144 sq. km).

an·dros·a·ce (an dros′ə kē′, -ə sē′), *n.* any plant of the genus *Androsace,* of the primrose family, having basal leaves and white or reddish flowers. [< NL < Gk *andrósakes* a marine plant (perh. equiv. to *andrós* (gen. of *anḗr* man) + *-akes,* deriv. of *ákos* cure); prob. misconstrued by Linnaeus as a compound with Gk *sákos* shield]

An·dros·cog·gin (an′drə skog′in), *n.* a river flowing from NE New Hampshire through SW Maine into the Kennebec River. 171 mi. (275 km) long.

an·dro·sphinx (an′drə sfingks′), *n., pl.* **-sphinx·es, -sphin·ges** (-sfin′jēz). a sphinx with the head of a man. [1600–10; < Gk; see ANDRO-, SPHINX]

an·dro·spore (an′drə spôr′, -spōr′), *n. Bot.* the zoospore of certain algae that develops into a small male plant producing antherozoids. [1860–65; ANDRO- + SPORE]

an·dros·ter·one (an dros′tə rōn′), *n. Biochem.* a sex hormone, $C_{19}H_{30}O_2$, usually present in male urine. [1930–35; ANDRO- + STER(OL) + -ONE]

An·drou·et du Cer·ceau (äN dʀōō e dy seʀ sō′), **1. Jacques** (zhäk), (*Jacques Androuet*), c1510–84, architect, author, and illustrator of architectural books. **2.** his sons, **Bap·tiste** (bA tēst′), c1544–1602, and **Jacques,** died 1614, French architects. **3. Jean** (zhäN), died c1650, architectural designer (son of Baptiste Androuet du Cerceau).

-androus, a combining form meaning "male," occurring as final element of a compound word: *polyandrous.* [< NL *-andrus.* See ANDR-, -OUS]

An·drus (an′drəs), *n. Class. Myth.* Andron.

-andry, a combining form occurring in nouns corresponding to adjectives ending in **-androus:** *polyandry.* [< Gk *-andria.* See ANDR-, -Y[3]]

An·dva·ri (än′dwä rē), *n. Scand. Legend.* a dwarf from whom Loki extorted a treasure, including a magic ring, to give to Hreidmar as wergild for the killing of Otter: Andvari then cursed all those who would possess the treasure.

An·dy (an′dē), *n.* **1.** a male given name, form of **Andrew. 2.** a female given name, form of **Andrea.**

ane (ān), *adj., n., pron. Chiefly Scot.* one. [1350–1400; ME (North) *an,* var. of *on* ONE]

-ane, *Chem.* a suffix used in names of hydrocarbons of the methane or paraffin series: *propane.* [< L *-ānus* -AN]

a·near (ə nēr′), *adv., prep. Archaic.* near. [1725–35; *a-* (semantically empty, perh. by analogy with AFAR; cf. APAST) + NEAR]

an·ec·dot·age[1] (an′ik dō′tij), *n.* anecdotes collectively. [1815–25; ANECDOTE + -AGE]

an·ec·dot·age[2] (an′ik dō′tij), *n. Facetious.* the state of being advanced in age and strongly inclined to tell reminiscent anecdotes: *Grandfather is in his anecdotage.* [1815–25; b. ANECDOTE and DOTAGE]

an·ec·do·tal (an′ik dōt′l, an′ik dōt′l), *adj.* **1.** pertaining to, resembling, or containing anecdotes: *an anecdotal history of jazz.* **2.** (of the treatment of subject matter in representational art) pertaining to the relationship of figures or to the arrangement of elements in a scene so as to emphasize the story content of a subject. Cf. **narrative** (def. 6). **3.** based on personal observation, case study reports, or random investigations rather than systematic scientific evaluation: *anecdotal evidence.* [1830–40; ANECDOTE + -AL[1]] **—an′ec·do′tal·ism,** *n.* **—an′ec·do′tal·ly,** *adv.*

an·ec·dote (an′ik dōt′), *n.* a short account of a particular incident or event of an interesting or amusing nature, often biographical. [1670–80; < NL *anecdota* or F *anecdotes* < LGk, Gk *anékdota* things unpublished (referring esp. to Procopius' unpublished memoirs of Justinian and Theodora), neut. pl. of *anékdotos,* equiv. to *an-* AN-[1] + *ékdotos* given out, verbal adj. of *ekdidónai* to give out, publish (*ek-* EC- + *didónai* to give)]

an·ec·dot·ic (an′ik dot′ik), *adj.* **1.** anecdotal. **2.** fond of telling anecdotes. Also, **an′ec·dot′i·cal.** [1780–90; ANECDOTE + -IC] **—an′ec·dot′i·cal·ly,** *adv.*

an·ec·dot·ist (an′ik dō′tist), *n.* a collector or teller of anecdotes. Also, **an·ec·do·tal·ist** (an′ik dōt′l ist). [1830–40; ANECDOTE + -IST]

an·e·cho·ic (an′e kō′ik), *adj.* (of a recording chamber, television studio, or the like) characterized by an unusually low degree of reverberation; echo-free. [1945–50; AN-[1] + ECHOIC]

an·e·lace (an′l ās′), *n.* a short sword having a double-edged blade tapering sharply to a point: worn by civilians from the 13th to the 16th centuries. Also, **anlace.** [1250–1300; ME *an(e)las* < OF *ale(s)naz* (by metathesis), deriv. of *alesne* awl < OHG *alasna.* See AWL]

an·e·las·tic·i·ty (an′i la stis′i tē, an ē′la stis′-), *n. Physics.* the property of a solid in which deformation depends on the time rate of change of stress as well as on the stress itself. [AN-[1] + ELASTICITY] **—an·e·las·tic** (an′i las′tik), *adj.*

a·nele (ə nēl′), *v.t.,* **a·neled, a·nel·ing.** *Archaic.* to administer extreme unction to. [1275–1325; ME *anelien,* equiv. to *an-* ON + *elien* to oil, equiv. to *el-* (OE *ele* oil < L *oleum*) + *-i-* thematic vowel + *-en* (OE *-an*) inf. ending]

an·e·lec·tric (an′i lek′trik), *adj. Elect.* not capable of acquiring a static electric charge when subjected to friction. [1820–30; AN-[1] + ELECTRIC]

a·ne·mi·a (ə nē′mē ə), *n.* **1.** *Pathol.* a quantitative deficiency of the hemoglobin, often accompanied by a reduced number of red blood cells and causing pallor, weakness, and breathlessness. **2.** a lack of power, vigor, vitality, or colorfulness: *His writing suffers from anemia.* Also, **anaemia.** [1800–10; < NL < Gk *anaimía* want of blood. See AN-[1], -EMIA]

a·ne·mic (ə nē′mik), *adj.* **1.** *Pathol.* suffering from anemia. **2.** lacking power, vigor, vitality, or colorfulness; listless; weak: *an anemic effort.* Also, **anaemic.** [1830–40; ANEM(IA) + -IC] **—a·ne′mi·cal·ly,** *adv.*

anemo-, a combining form meaning "wind": *anemograph.* [< Gk, comb. form of *ánemos;* c. L *animus* breath; akin to Skt *anilas*]

a·nem·o·chore (ə nem′ə kôr′, -kōr′), *n.* an anemochorous plant, seed, or spore. [ANEMO- + *-chore* < Gk *chōreîn* to spread]

an·e·moch·o·rous (an′ə mok′ər əs), *adj.* **1.** (of a fruit, seed, or spore) adapted for dispersion by wind. **2.** (of a plant) having anemochorous fruits, seeds, or spores, as the dandelion. Also, **a·ne·mo·cho·ric** (ə nē′mə kôr′ik, -kōr′-). [ANEMOCHORE + -OUS]

a·nem·o·gram (ə nem′ə gram′), *n.* an anemographic record. [1870–75; ANEMO- + -GRAM[1]]

a·nem·o·graph (ə nem′ə graf′, -gräf′), *n.* a recording anemometer. [1860–65; ANEMO- + -GRAPH] **—a·nem·o·graph·ic** (ə nem′ə graf′ik), *adj.* **—a·nem′o·graph′i·cal·ly,** *adv.*

an·e·mol·o·gy (an′ə mol′ə jē), *n. Meteorol. Now Rare.* the study of the movements of the winds. [1785–95; ANEMO- + -LOGY] **—an·e·mo·log·i·cal** (an′ə mə loj′i kəl), *adj.*

an·e·mom·e·ter (an′ə mom′i tər), *n.* any instrument for measuring the speed of wind. [1720–30; ANEMO- + -METER] **—an·e·mo·met·ric** (an′ə mō me′trik), **an′e·mo·met′ri·cal,** *adj.* **—an′e·mo·met′ri·cal·ly,** *adv.*

an·e·mom·e·try (an′ə mom′i trē), *n. Meteorol.* the science of measuring the speed of wind. [1840–50; ANEMO- + -METRY]

a·nem·o·ne (ə nem′ə nē′), *n.* **1.** any of various plants belonging to the genus *Anemone,* of the buttercup family, having petallike sepals and including several wild species with white flowers as well as others cultivated for their showy flowers in a variety of colors. **2.** See **sea anemone.** [1545–55; < L < Gk: lit., daughter of the wind, equiv. to *ánem(os)* wind + *-ōnē* fem. patronymic suffix; see -ONE]

anem′one fish′, any of several small colorful damselfishes of the genus *Amphiprion,* as the clown anemone fish, that occur in association with certain tropical marine anemones.

an·e·moph·i·lous (an′ə mof′ə ləs), *adj. Bot., Mycol.* fertilized by wind-borne pollen or spores. [1870–75; ANEMO- + -PHILOUS] **—an′e·moph′i·ly,** *n.*

a·nem·o·scope (ə nem′ə skōp′), *n. Meteorol.* any instrument showing the existence and direction of the wind. [1700–10; ANEMO- + -SCOPE]

an·e·mo·sis (an′ə mō′sis), *n., pl.* **-ses** (-sēz). See **wind shake** (def. 1). [ANEMO- + -SIS]

an·e·mo·tax·is (an′ə mə tak′sis), *n.* oriented movement in response to a current of air. [ANEMO- + -TAXIS]

an·e·mot·ro·pism (an′ə mo′trə piz′əm), *n. Biol.* orientation in response to a current of air. [1895–1900; ANEMO- + TROPISM] **—an·e·mo·trop·ic** (an′ə mə trop′ik, -trō′pik), *adj.*

an·en·ceph·a·ly (an′en sef′ə lē), *n. Med.* congenital absence of part or all of the brain. Also, **an·en·ce·pha·lia** (an′en sə fāl′yə, an′-). [1825–35; < NL; see AN-[1], ENCEPHAL-, -Y[3]] **—an·en·ce·phal·ic** (an′en sə fal′ik, an en′-), **an′en·ceph′a·lous,** *adj.*

a·nenst (ə nenst′), *prep. Brit. Dial.* anent (def. 2). [ME *anenist,* equiv. to *anen* (see ANENT) + *-is* adv. gen. suffix + excrescent *-t*]

a·nent (ə nent′), *prep.* **1.** in regard to; about; concerning. **2.** *Brit.* beside; in line with. [bef. 900; ME var. (with excrescent *-t;* see ANCIENT) of *anen,* OE *on emn, on efen* on EVEN[1] (ground), with, beside]

an·ep·i·graph·ic (an ep′ə graf′ik), *adj.* (of a coin, artifact, etc.) without a legend or inscription. Also, **an·e·pig·ra·phous** (an′ə pig′rə fəs). [AN-[1] + EPIGRAPHIC]

an·er·gy (an′ər jē), *n.* **1.** *Pathol.* deficiency of energy. **2.** *Immunol.* lack of immunity to an antigen. [< NL *anergia.* See AN-[1], ERGO-[1], -Y[3]] **—a·ner·gic** (a nûr′jik, an′ər-), *adj.*

an·er·oid (an′ə roid′), *adj.* **1.** using no fluid. **—*n.* 2.** See **aneroid barometer.** [1840–50; A-[6] + Gk *nēr(ós)* wet, fluid (akin to *nân* to flow) + -OID]

an′eroid bar′ograph, *Meteorol.* an aneroid barometer equipped with an automatic recording mechanism. Also called **an·er·oid·o·graph** (an′ə roi′də graf′, -gräf′).

an′eroid barom′eter, a device for measuring atmospheric pressure, often specially calibrated for use as an altimeter, consisting of a box or chamber partially exhausted of air, having an elastic top and a pointer to indicate the degree of compression of the top caused by the external air. Cf. **mercury barometer.** [1840–50]

an′eroid cap′sule, *Meteorol.* a box or chamber of thin metal, partially exhausted of air, used in the aneroid barometer and pressure altimeter.

anes (āns), *adv. Chiefly Scot.* once. [ME, OE, equiv. to *ān* ONE + *-es* adv. gen. suffix]

an·es·the·sia (an′əs thē′zhə), *n.* **1.** *Med.* general or local insensibility, as to pain and other sensation, induced by certain interventions or drugs to permit the performance of surgery or other painful procedures. **2.** *Pathol.* general loss of the senses of feeling, as pain, heat, cold, touch, and other less common varieties of sensation. **3.** *Psychiatry.* absence of sensation due to psychological processes, as in conversion disorders. Also, **anaesthesia.** [1715–25; < NL < Gk *anaisthēsía* want of feeling. See AN-[1], ESTHESIA]

an·es·the·sim·e·ter (ə nes′thə sim′i tər), *n. Med.* **1.** a device for measuring the amount of anesthetic given by inhalation. **2.** an esthesiometer. Also, **an·es·the·si·om·e·ter** (an′is thē′zē om′i tər). [1855–60; ANESTHESI(A) + -METER]

an·es·the·si·ol·o·gist (an′əs thē′zē ol′ə jist), *n.* a physician who specializes in anesthesiology. Also, **anaesthesiologist.** [1940–45; ANESTHESIOLOG(Y) + -IST]

an·es·the·si·ol·o·gy (an′əs thē′zē ol′ə jē), *n.* the science of administering anesthetics. Also, **anaesthesiology.** [1910–15; ANESTHESI(A) + -O- + -LOGY]

an·es·thet·ic (an′əs thet′ik), *n.* **1.** a substance that produces anesthesia, as halothane, procaine, or ether. **—*adj.* 2.** pertaining to or causing physical insensibility. **3.** physically insensitive: *an anesthetic state.* Also, **anaesthetic.** [1840–50, *Amer.;* < Gk *anaísthēt(os)* without feeling, senseless + -IC; see AN-[1], ESTHETIC] **—an′es·thet′i·cal·ly,** *adv.*

an·es·the·tist (ə nes′thi tist), *n.* a person who administers anesthetics, usually a specially trained doctor or nurse. Also, **anaesthetist.** [1880–85; ANESTHET(IZE) + -IST]

an·es·the·tize (ə nes′thi tīz′), *v.t.,* **-tized, -tiz·ing.** to render physically insensible, as by an anesthetic. Also, **anaesthetize;** *esp. Brit.,* **an·es′the·tise′.** [1840–50; < Gk *anaísthēt(os)* (see ANESTHETIC) + -IZE] **—an·es′the·ti·za′tion,** *n.*

an·es·trous (an es′trəs), *adj.* **1.** not showing estrus. **2.** of or pertaining to anestrus. Also, **anoestrous.** [1905–10; AN-[1] + ESTROUS]

an·es·trus (an es′trəs), *n. Zool.* (of a female mammal) the interval of sexual inactivity between two periods of heat or rut. Also, **anoestrus.** [1925–30; AN-[1] + ESTRUS]

an·e·thole (an′ə thōl′), *n. Chem., Pharm.* a white, crystalline powder, $C_{10}H_{12}O$, having a sweet taste, obtained from anise or fennel oils or synthesized: used chiefly in perfumes, dentifrices, flavoring, synthesis of anisaldehyde, and in medicine as an antiseptic and carminative. Also called **anise camphor.** [1860–65; < Gk *ánēth(on)* dill, anise + -OLE[2]]

A·ne·to (ä ne′tô), *n.* **Pi·co de** (pē′kô the), Spanish name of **Pic de Nethou.**

a·neuch (ə nōōKH′), *adj., n., adv., interj. Scot.* enough.

a·neu·ri·a (ə nŏŏr′ē ə, ə nyŏŏr′-), *n.* neurasthenia. [< NL; see AN-[1], NEUR-, -IA] **—a·neu′ric,** *adj.*

an·eu·rin (an′yə rin), *n. Biochem.* thiamine. Also, **an·eu·rine** (an′yə rēn′). [1930–35; AN-[1] + NEUR- + -IN[2]]

A·neu·rin (ə nī′rin), *n.* a male given name.

an·eu·rysm (an′yə riz′əm), *n. Pathol.* a permanent cardiac or arterial dilatation usually caused by weakening of the vessel wall. Also, **an′eu·rism.** [1650–60; < Gk *aneúrysma* dilation, equiv. to *aneurys-* (var. s. of *aneurýnein* to dilate; see AN-³, EURY-) + *-ma* n. suffix] —**an′·eu·rys′mal, an′eu·ris′mal,** *adj.* —**an′eu·rys′mal·ly, an′eu·ris′mal·ly,** *adv.*

a·new (ə nōō′, ə nyōō′), *adv.* **1.** over again; again; once more: *to play the tune anew.* **2.** in a new form or manner: *to write the story anew.* [bef. 1000; ME *onew, of newe;* see A-², OE of *niowe,* prob. modeled on OF *de neuf;* r. OE *edniwe* once more]

ANF, *Biochem.* atrial natriuretic factor.

An·fin·sen (an′fin sən), *n.* **Christian Boeh·mer** (bā′mər, bō′-), born 1916, U.S. biochemist: Nobel prize for chemistry 1972.

an·frac·tu·os·i·ty (an frak′chōō os′i tē), *n.* **1.** the state or quality of being anfractuous. **2.** a channel, crevice, or passage full of windings and turnings. [1590–1600; < L *anfrāctuōs(us)* winding (*anfrāctu(s)* a bend (see AMBI-, FRACTO-) + *-ōsus* -OSE¹) + -ITY]

an·frac·tu·ous (an frak′chōō əs), *adj.* characterized by windings and turnings; sinuous; circuitous: *an anfractuous path.* [1615–25; back formation from ANFRACTUOSITY]

ANG, 1. acute necrotizing gingivitis; trench mouth. **2.** Air National Guard.

an·ga (ung′gə), *n.* any of the eight practices of Yoga, including the abstentions, mandatory actions, posture, breath control, control of the senses, concentration, meditation, and contemplation. Cf. **antaranga.** [< Skt *aṅga* (pl.)]

an·ga·kok (ang′gə kok′), *n.* a shaman in Eskimo society. Also, **an′ge·kok′.** [1760–70; < G < Inuit (Greenlandic) *angeqok*]

An·ga·ra (äng′gə rä; *Russ.* un gu rä′), *n.* a river in the S Russian Federation in Asia, flowing NW from Lake Baikal to the Yenisei River: called Upper Tunguska in its lower course. 1151 mi. (1855 km) long.

An·garsk (äng gärsk′; *Russ.* un gärsk′), *n.* a city in the S Russian Federation in Asia, near Lake Baikal. 239,000.

an·ga·ry (ang′gə rē), *n. Internat. Law.* the right of a belligerent state to seize and use the property of neutrals for purposes of warfare, subject to payment of full compensation. [1875–80; < LL *angaria* service to a lord < Gk *angareía* couriership, equiv. to *ángaros* official courier (< OPers) + *-eia* -Y³]

an·gel (ān′jəl), *n.* **1.** one of a class of spiritual beings; a celestial attendant of God. In medieval angelology, angels constituted the lowest of the nine celestial orders (seraphim, cherubim, thrones, dominations or dominions, virtues, powers, principalities or princedoms, archangels, and angels). **2.** a conventional representation of such a being, in human form, with wings, usually in white robes. **3.** a messenger, esp. of God. **4.** a person who performs a mission of God or acts as if sent by God: *an angel of mercy.* **5.** a person having qualities generally attributed to an angel, as beauty, purity, or kindliness. **6.** a person whose actions and thoughts are consistently virtuous. **7.** an attendant or guardian spirit. **8.** a deceased person whose soul is regarded as having been accepted into heaven. **9.** *Informal.* a person who provides financial backing for some undertaking, as a play or political campaign. **10.** an English gold coin issued from 1470 to 1634, varying in value from 6s. 8d. to 10s. and bearing on its obverse a figure of the archangel Michael killing a dragon. **11.** *Slang.* an image on a radar screen caused by a low-flying object, as a bird. —*v.t.* **12.** *Informal.* to provide financial backing for. [bef. 950; 1890–95 for def. 9; ME *a(u)ngel* (< AF, OF) < LL *angelus* < NT Gk *ángelos* messenger of God, special use of Gk *ángelos* messenger; r. OE *engel* < L, as above]

An·gel (ān′jəl; *Sp.* än hel′), *n.* a male or female given name.

An·ge·la (an′jə lə), *n.* a female given name: from a Greek word meaning "messenger."

An·ge·la Me·ri·ci (än′je lä me rē′chē), **Saint,** 1474–1540, Italian ecclesiastic, founder of the Ursuline order.

an′gel bed′, 1. *Fr. Furniture.* a bed having a suspended or bracketed canopy of less than full length. Cf. **duchesse bed. 2.** *U.S. Furniture.* a bed without posts, as a truckle bed. [1700–10]

an′gel dust′, *Slang.* phencyclidine. [1965–70]

An·ge·le·no (an′jə lē′nō), *n., pl.* **-nos,** *adj.* —*n.* **1.** Also called **Los Angeleno.** a native or inhabitant of Los Angeles: *a cheering crowd of Angelenos.* —*adj.* **2.** of or pertaining to Los Angeles.

An·ge·les (an′jə ləs; *Sp.* äng′he les′), *n.* a city in the Philippines, on S central Luzon. 188,834.

An′gel Falls′, a waterfall in SE Venezuela: world's highest. 3212 ft. (979 m) high.

an·gel·fish (ān′jəl fish′), *n., pl.* (*esp. collectively*) **-fish,** (*esp. referring to two or more kinds or species*) **-fish·es. 1.** a South American freshwater fish, genus *Pterophyllum,* often kept in aquariums. Cf. **scalare. 2.** See **angel shark.** [1660–70; ANGEL + FISH]

an′gel food′ cake′, a white sponge cake with a light, delicate texture obtained by using stiffly beaten egg whites and cream of tartar. Also called **an′gel cake′.** [1880–85, *Amer.*; after the white color of the cake]

an′gel hair′, 1. Also called **capelli d'angelo.** *Italian Cookery.* a type of very thin pasta. **2.** a Christmas-tree decoration consisting of long, fine threads of white spun glass. **3.** a type of building insulation made of spun glass. Also, **angel's hair.**

an·gel·hood (ān′jəl hŏŏd′), *n.* **1.** the state or condition of being an angel; angelic nature. **2.** angels collectively: *the angelhood of heaven.* **3.** an angelic being. [1830–40; ANGEL + -HOOD]

an·gel·ic (an jel′ik), *adj.* **1.** of or belonging to angels: *the angelic host.* **2.** like or befitting an angel, esp. in virtue, beauty, etc.: *angelic sweetness.* Also, **an·gel′i·cal.** [1350–1400; ME *angelyk* < LL *angelicus* < Gk *angelikós.* See ANGEL, -IC] —**an·gel′i·cal·ly,** *adv.* —**an·gel′i·cal·ness,** *n.*
—**Syn. 1.** ethereal, celestial, saintly, beatific, seraphic, cherubic. —**Ant. 2.** fiendish, diabolic.

an·gel·i·ca (an jel′i kə), *n.* **1.** Also called **archangel.** any plant belonging to the genus *Angelica,* of the parsley family, esp. *A. archangelica,* cultivated in Europe for its aromatic odor and medicinal root and for its stalks, which are candied and eaten. **2.** the candied stalks of this plant. [1570–80; < ML (*herba*) *angelica* ANGELIC (herb)]

An·gel·i·ca (an jel′i kə), *n.* a female given name.

angel′ica tree′, 1. Hercules-club (def. 2). **2.** See **prickly ash** (def. 1). [1775–85, *Amer.*]

An·ge·li·co (an jel′i kō′; *It.* än je′lē kô), *n.* **Fra** (frä; *It.* frä), (*Giovanni da Fiesole*), 1387–1455, Italian painter. —**An·gel·i·can** (an jel′i kən), *adj.*

An·ge·li·na (an′jə lē′nə, -lī′-), *n.* a female given name, form of **Angela.** Also, **An·ge·line** (an′jə lēn′).

an·ge·lique (an′jə lēk′), *n.* **1.** a South American tree, *Dicorynia paraensis,* of the legume family. **2.** the hard, reddish-brown wood of this tree, used in shipbuilding. [< F: plant of *Angelica* genus. See ANGELIC]

An·gé·lique (an′jə lēk′; *Fr.* än zhā lēk′), *n.* a female given name.

An·gell (ān′jəl), *n.* **1. James Row·land** (rō′lənd), 1869–1949, U.S. educator. **2. Norman** (*Sir Ralph Norman Angell Lane*), 1874–1967, English pacifist, economist, and writer: Nobel peace prize 1933. **3.** a male or female given name.

an′gel light′, *Archit.* (in an English Perpendicular window) a compartment, approximately triangular, formed by the arch of the window, an arch of a lower tier of tracery, and a mullion of an upper tier of tracery.

An·ge·lo (an′jə lō′), *n.* a male given name.

An′gel of Death′, Azrael (def. 1).

an·gel·ol·o·gy (ān′jə lol′ə jē), *n.* a doctrine or theory concerning angels. [1745–55; ANGEL + -O- + -LOGY]

an′gel's hair′. See **angel hair.**

an′gel shark′, any shark of the genus *Squatina,* found in warm and temperate shore waters, having a depressed, flat body and large, winglike pectoral fins.

an·gel's-trum·pet (ān′jəlz trum′pit), *n.* any of several plants belonging to the genera *Brugmansia* and *Datura,* of the nightshade family, having large, trumpet-shaped flowers in a variety of colors.

An·ge·lus (an′jə ləs), *n. Rom. Cath. Ch.* **1.** a devotion in memory of the Annunciation. **2.** Also called **An′·gelus bell′.** the bell tolled in the morning, at noon, and in the evening to indicate the time when the Angelus is to be recited. Also, **an′ge·lus.** [1720–30; < LL, from the first word of the service: *Angelus* (*dominī nūntiāvit Mariae*). See ANGEL]

An′gelus Si·le′si·us (si lē′shē əs, -zhē əs, sī-), (*Johannes Scheffler*) 1627–77, German poet.

an·ger (ang′gər), *n.* **1.** a strong feeling of displeasure and belligerence aroused by a wrong; wrath; ire. **2.** *Chiefly Brit. Dial.* pain or smart, as of a sore. **3.** *Obs.* grief; trouble. —*v.t.* **4.** to arouse anger or wrath in. **5.** *Chiefly Brit. Dial.* to cause to smart; inflame. —*v.i.* **6.** to become angry: *He angers with little provocation.* [1150–1200; ME < Scand; cf. ON *angr* sorrow, grief, akin to OHG *angust* (G *Angst* fear), L *angor* anguish] —**an′·ger·less,** *adj.*
—**Syn. 1.** resentment, exasperation; choler, bile, spleen. ANGER, FURY, INDIGNATION, RAGE imply deep and strong feelings aroused by injury, injustice, wrong, etc. ANGER is the general term for a sudden violent displeasure: *a burst of anger.* INDIGNATION implies deep and justified anger: *indignation at cruelty or against corruption.* RAGE is vehement anger: *rage at being frustrated.* FURY is rage so great that it resembles insanity: *the fury of an outraged lover.* **4.** displease, vex, irritate, exasperate, infuriate, enrage, incense, madden.

an·ger·ly (ang′gər lē), *adv.* **1.** *Archaic.* angrily. **2.** *Obs.* hurtfully; painfully. [1325–75; ME; see ANGER, -LY]

An·ge·ro·na (an′jə rō′nə), *n.* the ancient Roman goddess of anguish. Also, **An·ge·ro·ni·a** (an′jə rō′nē ə).

An·gers (an′jərz, ang′gərz; *Fr.* än zhā′), *n.* a city in and capital of Maine-et-Loire, in W France. 163,191.

An·ge·vin (an′jə vin), *adj.* **1.** of or pertaining to Anjou or its inhabitants. **2.** relating to the counts of Anjou or their descendants, esp. those who ruled in England, or to the period during which they ruled. —*n.* **3.** an inhabitant of Anjou. **4.** a member of an Angevin royal house, esp. that of the Plantagenets in England. Also, **An·ge·vine** (an′jə vin, -vīn′).

angi-, var. of **angio-** before a vowel.

An·gie (an′jē), *n.* a male or female given name, form of **Angel.**

an·gi·na (an jī′nə; *in Med. often* an′jə nə), *n. Pathol.* **1.** any attack of painful spasms characterized by sensations of choking or suffocating. **2.** See **angina pectoris. 3.** any disease of the throat or fauces. [1580–90; < L *angina* quinsey, for **ancina* < Gk *anchónē,* strangulation, hanging, influenced by L *ang(ere)* to throttle (see ANGER)]

an·gi·nal (an jīn′l, an′jə nl), *adj.* of, noting, or pertaining to angina, esp. angina pectoris. Also, **an·gi·nous** (an jī′nəs), **an·gi·nose** (an′jə nōs′, an jī′nōs). [1805–15; ANGIN(A) + -AL¹]

angi′na pec′to·ris (pek′tə ris), *Pathol.* a syndrome characterized by paroxysmal, constricting pain below the sternum, most easily precipitated by exertion or excitement and caused by ischemia of the heart muscle, usually due to a coronary artery disease, as arteriosclerosis. [1760–70; < NL: angina of the chest]

angio-, a learned borrowing from Greek meaning "vessel," "container," used in the formation of compound words: *angiosperm.* Also, esp. *before a vowel,* **angi-.** [< Gk, comb. form repr. *angeîon,* equiv. to *áng(os)* vessel, vat, shell + *-eion* dim. suffix]

an·gi·o·blast (an′jē ə blast′), *n. Embryol.* one of several mesenchymal cells capable of developing into the endothelium of the blood vessels. [ANGIO- + -BLAST] —**an′gi·o·blas′tic,** *adj.*

an·gi·o·car·di·og·ra·phy (an′jē ō kär′dē og′rə fē), *n., pl.* **-phies.** x-ray examination of the heart and its blood vessels following intravenous injection of radiopaque fluid; coronary angiography. [1935–40; ANGIO- + CARDIOGRAPHY] —**an·gi·o·car·di·o·graph·ic** (an′jē ō kär′dē ə graf′ik), *adj.*

an·gi·o·carp (an′jē ə kärp′), *n.* a plant bearing an angiocarpous fruit. [ANGIO- + -CARP]

an·gi·o·car·pous (an′jē ō kär′pəs), *adj.* **1.** (of a fruit) partially or wholly enclosed in a shell, involucre, or husk. **2.** (of a fungus or lichen) having the fruiting body immersed or enclosed in the thallus. Also, **an′gi·o·car′pic.** Cf. **gymnocarpous.** [1830–40; ANGIO- + -CARPOUS]

an·gi·o·gen·e·sis (an′jē ō jen′ə sis), *n. Biol.* the formation and development of blood vessels. [ANGIO- + -GENESIS] —**an′gi·o·gen′ic,** *adj.*

an·gi·o·gen·in (an′jē ō jen′in, -oj′ə nin), *n.* a small, single-chain protein, resembling ribonuclease in structure, that stimulates the formation of new blood vessels. [presumably ANGIOGEN(IC) + -IN²]

an·gi·o·gram (an′jē ə gram′), *n.* an x-ray produced by angiography. [1930–35; ANGIO- + -GRAM¹]

an·gi·og·ra·phy (an′jē og′rə fē), *n.* x-ray examination of blood vessels or lymphatics following injection of a radiopaque substance. [1720–30; ANGIO- + -GRAPHY] —**an·gi·o·graph·ic** (an′jē ə graf′ik), *adj.*

an·gi·o·ker·a·to·ma (an′jē ō ker′ə tō′mə), *n., pl.* **-mas, -ma·ta** (-mə tə). *Pathol.* a skin disease characterized by clusters of dilated blood vessels and by thickened skin, forming warty growths, esp. on the scrotum, fingers, and toes. [1965–70; ANGIO- + KERATOMA]

an·gi·ol·o·gy (an′jē ol′ə jē), *n.* the branch of anatomy dealing with blood vessels and lymphatics. [1700–10; ANGIO- + -LOGY]

an·gi·o·ma (an′jē ō′mə), *n., pl.* **-mas, -ma·ta** (-mə tə). *Pathol.* a benign tumor consisting chiefly of dilated or newly formed blood vessels (**hemangioma**) or lymph vessels (**lymphangioma**). [1870–75; ANGI- + -OMA] —**an·gi·om·a·tous** (an′jē om′ə təs, -ō′mə-), *adj.*

an·gi·o·plas·ty (an′jē ə plas′tē), *n., pl.* **-ties.** *Surg.* the repair of a blood vessel, as by inserting a balloon-tipped catheter to unclog it or by replacing part of the vessel with either a piece of the patient's own tissue or a prosthetic device: *coronary angioplasty to widen an artery blocked by plaque.* [ANGIO- + -PLASTY]

an·gi·o·sar·co·ma (an′jē ō sär kō′mə), *n., pl.* **-mas, -ma·ta** (-mə tə). *Pathol.* malignant overgrowth of vascular tissue. [ANGIO- + SARCOMA]

an·gi·o·sperm (an′jē ə spûrm′), *n. Bot.* a plant having its seeds enclosed in an ovary; a flowering plant. Cf. **gymnosperm.** [ANGIO- + -SPERM]

an·gi·o·sper·mous (an′jē ō spûr′məs), *adj.* of or pertaining to an angiosperm; having enclosed seeds. [1725–35; ANGIOSPERM + -OUS]

an·gi·o·ten·sin (an′jē ō ten′sin), *n. Biochem.* any of three oligopeptides occurring in plasma, an inactive form (**angiotensin I**) and two varieties (**angiotensin II** and **angiotensin III**) that elevate blood pressure and stimulate the adrenal cortex to secrete aldosterone. [1960–65; prob. ANGIO(TONIN) + (HYPER)TENSIN, earlier names for the substances]

an·gi·ya (än jē′ə), *n.* a short-sleeved bodice that ends just below the breasts, worn by Muslim women in India. [< Gujarati *āgiyo* or a cognate word in another Indo-Aryan language]

Ang·kor (ang′kôr, -kōr), *n.* a vast assemblage of ruins of the Khmer empire, near the modern city of Siem Reap in NW Cambodia: many elaborately carved and decorated temples, stone statues, gateways, and towers.

Ang′kor Thom′ (tôm), the site of the ruined capital city of the Khmer empire, at Angkor.

Ang′kor Wat′ (wät, vät), the largest and best preserved Khmer temple in the Angkor complex of ruins. Also, **Ang′kor Vat′** (vät).

Angl., 1. Anglican. **2.** Anglicized.

an·glaise (äng gläz′, -glez′), *n.* **1.** an old English country-dance. **2.** a dance form in quick duple time, occasionally constituting part of an 18th-century instrumental suite. [< F, fem. of *anglais* English]

an·gle[1] (ang′gəl), *n., v.,* **-gled, -gling.** —*n.* **1.** *Geom.* **a.** the space within two lines or three or more planes diverging from a common point, or within two planes diverging from a common line. **b.** the figure so formed. **c.** the amount of rotation needed to bring one line or plane into coincidence with another, generally measured in radians or in degrees, minutes, and seconds, as in 12° 10′ 30″, which is read as 12 degrees, 10 minutes, and 30 seconds. **2.** an angular projection; a projecting corner: *the angles of a building.* **3.** a viewpoint; standpoint: *He looked at the problem only from his own angle.* **4.** *Journalism.* **a.** slant (def. 11). **b.** the point of view from which copy is written, esp. when the copy is intended to interest a particular audience: *The financial editor added a supplementary article from the investor's angle.* **5.** one aspect of an event, problem, subject, etc.: *The accountant emphasized the tax angle of the leasing arrangement.* **6.** *Motion Pictures, Photog.* See **angle shot. 7.** *Informal.* a secret motive: *She's been too friendly lately—what's her angle?* **8.** *Astrol.* any of the four interceptions of the equatorial circle by the two basic axes, the horizon and the meridian: commonly identified by the compass directions. **9.** See **angle iron** (def. 2). **10.** *Slang.* **play the angles,** to use every available means to reach one's goal: *A second-rate talent can survive only by playing all the angles.* —*v.t.* **11.** to move or bend in an angle. **12.** to set, fix, direct, or adjust at an angle: *to angle a spotlight.* **13.** *Journalism.* to write or edit in such a way as to appeal to a particular audience; slant: *She angled her column toward teenagers.* —*v.i.* **14.** to turn sharply in a different direction: *The road angles to the right.* **15.** to move or go in angles or at an angle: *The trout angled downstream.* [1350–1400; ME < MF < L *angulus,* of unclear orig.]

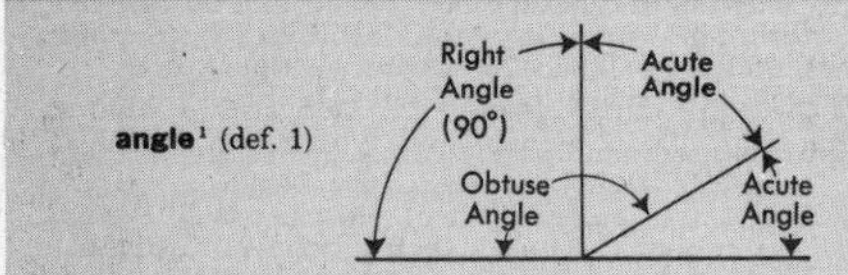
angle[1] (def. 1)

an·gle[2] (ang′gəl), *v.,* **-gled, -gling,** *n.* —*v.i.* **1.** to fish with hook and line. **2.** to attempt to get something by sly or artful means; fish: *to angle for a compliment.* —*n.* **3.** *Archaic.* a fishhook or fishing tackle. [bef. 900; ME v. *angelen,* n. *angel, angul,* OE *angel, angul;* c. Fris, D *angel,* OS, OHG *angul* (> G *Angel*), ON *ǫngull;* Gk *ankýlos* bent, Skt *ankuśá-* hook; akin to OE *anga,* OHG *ango,* L *uncus,* Gk *ónkos* hook; relation, if any, to L *angulus* ANGLE[1] not clear]

An·gle (ang′gəl), *n.* a member of a West Germanic people that migrated from Sleswick to Britain in the 5th century A.D. and founded the kingdoms of East Anglia, Mercia, and Northumbria. As early as the 6th century their name was extended to all the Germanic inhabitants of Britain. [< OE *Angle* pl. (var. of *Engle*) tribal name of disputed orig.; perh. akin to ANGLE[2] if meaning was fisher folk, coastal dwellers]

an′gle bar′. See **angle iron** (def. 2).

an′gle board′, a board serving as a gauge for an angle planed across the end of other boards.

an′gle brack′et, one of two marks < or > used in printing to enclose parenthetical matter, interpolations, etc. [1955–60]

an′gle cleat′, a short length of angle iron used as a bracket. Also called **seat angle.**

an′gle-clo·sure glauco′ma (ang′gəl klō′zhər), *Ophthalm.* See under **glaucoma.**

an′gle col′lar, *Shipbuilding.* stapling.

an·gled (ang′gəld), *adj.* **1.** having an angle or angles. **2.** *Heraldry.* **a.** noting an interrupted partition line having the two parts offset and a line at right angles connecting them. **b.** (of an ordinary) having an edge or edges so formed. [1565–75; ANGLE[1] + -ED[3]]

an·gle·doz·er (ang′gəl dō′zər), *n.* a bulldozer having an angled moldboard for pushing earth to one side. [formerly a trademark]

an′gle i′ron, 1. an iron or steel bar, brace, or cleat in the form of an angle. **2.** Also called **angle, angle bar, L bar, L beam.** a piece of structural iron or steel having a cross section in the form of an L. See illus. under **shape.** [1850–55]

an′gle of attack′, 1. Also called, *esp. Brit.,* **angle of incidence.** *Aeron.* the acute angle between the chord of an aircraft wing or other airfoil and the direction of the relative wind. **2.** *Railroads.* the angular attitude of a wheel flange to the rail, esp. on curves. [1905–10]

an′gle of climb′, *Aeron.* the angle between the axis of motion of a climbing aircraft and the horizontal plane.

an′gle of depres′sion, *Survey.* depression (def. 11). [1780–90]

an′gle of devia′tion, *Optics.* the angle equal to the difference between the angle of incidence and the angle of refraction of a ray of light passing through the surface between one medium and another of different refractive index. Also called **deviation.** [1825–35]

an′gle of dip′, dip[1] (def. 32).

an′gle of eleva′tion, *Survey.* elevation (def. 8a). [1780–90]

CONCISE ETYMOLOGY KEY: <, descended or borrowed from; >, whence; b., blend of, blended; c., cognate with; cf., compare; deriv., derivative; equiv., equivalent; imit., imitative; obl., oblique; r., replacing; s., stem; sp., spelling, spelled; resp., respelling, respelled; trans., translation; ?, origin unknown; *, unattested; ‡, probably earlier than. See the full key inside the front cover.

an·gle-off (ang′gəl ôf′, -of′), *n.* **1.** the angle formed by the line of flight of an aerial target and the line of sight on a gun of an attacking aircraft. **2.** the angle formed by the line of flight of an attacking aircraft and that of an aerial target. [ANGLE[1] + OFF]

an′gle of in′cidence, 1. Also called **incidence.** *Optics, Physics.* the angle that a straight line, ray of light, etc., meeting a surface, makes with a normal to the surface at the point of meeting. **2.** (on an airplane) the angle, usually fixed, between a wing or tail root chord and the axis of the fuselage. **3.** *Chiefly Brit.* See **angle of attack** (def. 1). [1620–30]

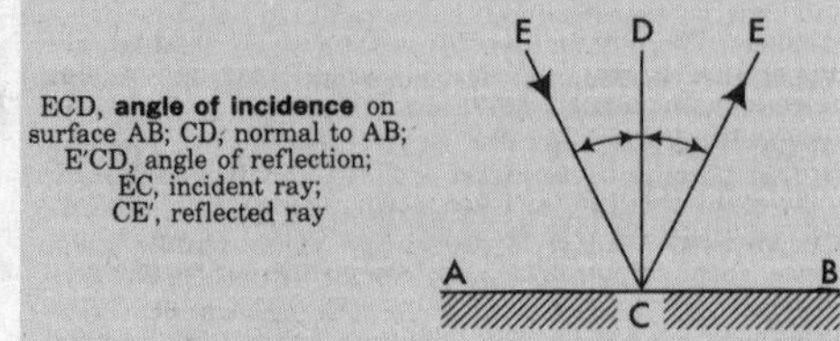
ECD, **angle of incidence** on surface AB; CD, normal to AB; E′CD, angle of reflection; EC, incident ray; CE′, reflected ray

an′gle of lag′, *Physics, Elect.* the phase difference, expressed in degrees, by which one sinusoidal function moves behind a second having the same period, as alternating current moving behind the alternating voltage.

an′gle of lead′ (lēd), *Physics, Elect.* the phase difference, expressed in degrees, by which one sinusoidal function is moving ahead of a second having the same period, as alternating voltage moving ahead of the alternating current.

an′gle of pitch′, *Aeron.* the acute angle between the longitudinal axis of an aircraft or spacecraft and the direction of the wind relative to the vehicle.

an′gle of polariza′tion, *Optics.* See under **Brewster's law.**

an′gle of reflec′tion, *Physics.* the angle that a ray of light or the like, reflected from a surface, makes with a normal to the surface at the point of reflection. See diag. under **angle of incidence.** [1630–40]

an′gle of refrac′tion, *Physics, Optics.* the angle between a refracted ray and a line drawn normal to the interface between two media at the point of refraction. See diag. under **refraction.** [1765–75]

an′gle of repose′, *Geol.* the maximum slope, measured in degrees from the horizontal, at which loose solid material will remain in place without sliding. Cf. **angle of slide.** [1875–80]

an′gle of roll′, *Aeron.* the acute angle between the lateral axis of an aircraft or spacecraft and a horizontal plane.

an′gle of slide′, *Geol.* the minimum slope, measured in degrees from the horizontal, at which loose solid material will start to slide or flow. Cf. **angle of repose.** [1930–35]

an′gle of stall′, *Aeron.* See **critical angle** (def. 2).

an′gle of view′, *Optics.* the angle formed at a nodal point of a lens by the intersection of two lines drawn from the opposite ends of an image produced by the lens.

an′gle of yaw′, *Aeron.* the acute angle between the longitudinal axis of an aircraft or spacecraft and a given reference direction, as viewed from above.

an′gle plate′, an angular metal plate or casting for clamping and supporting work in metalworking machines.

an·gle·pod (ang′gəl pod′), *n.* a southern U.S. twining plant, *Gonolobus gonocarpos,* of the milkweed family, having angled or winged pods. [ANGLE[1] + POD[1]; so called from its shape]

an·gler (ang′glər), *n.* **1.** a person who fishes with a hook and line. **2.** a person who gets or tries to get something through scheming. **3.** Also called **allmouth, anglerfish, goosefish, lotte, monkfish.** any large pediculate fish of the family Lophiidae, esp. *Lophius americanus,* found along the Atlantic coast of America, having an immense mouth and a large, depressed head to which is attached a wormlike filament for luring prey. **4.** Also called **anglerfish.** any of various related fishes of the order Lophiiformes. [1545–55; ANGLE[2] + -ER[1]]

an·gler·fish (ang′glər fish′), *n., pl.* (*esp. collectively*) **-fish,** (*esp. referring to two or more kinds or species*) **-fish·es.** angler (defs. 3, 4). [1645–55; ANGLER + FISH]

An·gle·sey (ang′gəl sē), *n.* an island and historic county in Gwynedd, in NW Wales.

an′gle shot′, *Motion Pictures, Photog.* a picture taken with the camera pointed obliquely at the subject, sometimes causing distortion of perspective and proportion. Also called **angle.** [1935–40]

an·gle·site (ang′gəl sīt′), *n.* a mineral, lead sulfate, $PbSO_4$, found in massive deposits and in colorless or variously tinted crystals: a minor ore of lead. [1830–40; named after ANGLESEY where it was first found; see -ITE[1]]

an·gle·smith (ang′gəl smith′), *n.* a blacksmith skilled in forging angle irons, beams, etc., into various forms used in shipbuilding. [ANGLE[1] + SMITH]

An·gle·ton (ang′gəl tən), *n.* a town in S Texas. 13,929.

an·gle·wing (ang′gəl wing′), *n.* any of several nymphalid butterflies, esp. of the genus *Polygonia,* having angular notches on the outer edges of the forewings. [1900–05, *Amer.;* ANGLE[1] + WING]

an·gle·worm (ang′gəl wûrm′), *n. Chiefly Northern, North Midland, and Western U.S.* an earthworm, as used for bait in angling. [1825–35, *Amer.;* ANGLE[2] + WORM]
—Regional Variation. See **earthworm.**

An·gli·a (ang′glē ə), *n.* Latin name of **England.**

An·gli·an (ang′glē ən), *adj.* **1.** Also, **Anglic.** of or relating to the Angles or to East Anglia. —*n.* **2.** an Angle. **3.** the northern and central group of Old English dialects, spoken in Northumbria and Mercia. [1720–30; ANGLI(A) + -AN]

An·glic (ang′glik), *n.* **1.** the English language in a simplified spelling devised by R. E. Zachrisson (1880–1937), a Swedish philologist, to make English easier to use as an auxiliary language. About 40 of the most frequent words are kept in their usual spellings; the rest of the vocabulary is spelled phonetically with letters of the traditional 26-letter alphabet. —*adj.* **2.** Anglian (def. 1). [1865–70; < ML *Anglicus* English, equiv. to LL *Angl(us)* Angle, Germanic-speaking inhabitant of Britain (L *Anglii* a continental tribe mentioned by Tacitus; cf. ANGLE) + *-icus* -IC]

An·gli·can (ang′gli kən), *adj.* **1.** of or pertaining to the Church of England. **2.** related in origin to and in communion with the Church of England, as various Episcopal churches in other parts of the world. **3.** English (def. 1). —*n.* **4.** a member of the Church of England or of a church in communion with it. **5.** a person who upholds the system or teachings of the Church of England. [1625–35; < ML *Anglicānus* English. See ANGLIC, -AN] —**An′gli·can·ly,** *adv.*

An′glican chant′, a harmonized, strictly metrical chant to which canticles, psalms, and other liturgical texts are sung in the Anglican Church.

An′glican Church′, the Church of England and those churches that are in communion with it and each other and that share essentially its doctrines and order, as the Church of Ireland, the Episcopal Church of Scotland, the Church of Wales, and the Protestant Episcopal Church in the U.S.

An·gli·can·ism (ang′gli kə niz′əm), *n.* the doctrines, principles, or system of the Anglican Church. [1840–50; ANGLICAN + -ISM]

An·gli·ce (ang′glə sē), *adv.* in English; as the English would say it; according to the English way: *Córdoba, Anglice "Cordova."* [1595–1605; < ML, equiv. to *Anglic(us)* English (see ANGLIC) + *-e* adv. suffix]

An·gli·cism (ang′glə siz′əm), *n.* (*sometimes l.c.*) **1.** a Briticism. **2.** the state of being English; characteristic English quality. **3.** a word, idiom, or characteristic feature of the English language occurring in or borrowed by another language. **4.** any custom, manner, idea, etc., characteristic of the English people. [1635–45; < ML *Anglic(us)* English + -ISM]

An·gli·cist (ang′glə sist), *n.* an authority on the English language or English literature. [1865–70; < ML *Anglic(us)* English + -IST]

An·gli·cize (ang′glə sīz′), *v.t., v.i.,* **-cized, -ciz·ing.** (*sometimes l.c.*) to make or become English in form or character: *to Anglicize the pronunciation of a Russian name.* Also, *esp. Brit.,* **An′gli·cise′.** [1700–10; < ML *Anglic(us)* English + -IZE] —**An′gli·ci·za′tion,** *n.*

An·gli·fy (ang′glə fī′), *v.t.,* **-fied, -fy·ing.** (*sometimes l.c.*) to Anglicize. [1745–55, *Amer.;* ANGLE + -IFY] —**An′gli·fi·ca′tion,** *n.*

an·gling (ang′gling), *n.* the act or art of fishing with a hook and line, usually attached to a rod. [1490–1500; ANGLE[2] + -ING[1]]

An·glist (ang′glist), *n.* Anglicist. [1885–90; < G < ML *Angl(ia)* England + G *-ist* -IST]

Ang·lis·tics (ang glis′tiks), *n.* (*used with a singular v.*) the study of the English language and of literature written in English. [1925–30; < G *Anglistik,* equiv. to *Anglist* ANGLIST + *-ik* -ICS]

An·glo (ang′glō), *n., pl.* **-glos,** *adj.* —*n.* **1.** a white American of non-Hispanic descent, as distinguished esp. from an American of Mexican or Spanish descent. **2.** (*sometimes l.c.*) an English-speaking person in a place where English is not the language of the majority. —*adj.* **3.** of, pertaining to, or characteristic of Anglos. [1835–45; independent use of ANGLO-]

Anglo-, a combining form of **English:** *Anglo-Norman; Anglo-Catholic.* [< LL *Angl(us)* (see ANGLIC) + -O-]

An·glo-A·mer·i·can (ang′glō ə mer′i kən), *adj.* **1.** belonging to, relating to, or involving England and America, esp. the United States, or the people of the two countries: *the Anglo-American policy toward Russia.* **2.** of or pertaining to Anglo-Americans. —*n.* **3.** a native or descendant of a native of England who has settled in or become a citizen of America, esp. of the United States. [1730–40, *Amer.*] —**An′glo-A·mer′i·can·ism,** *n.*

An·glo-Aus·tral·ian (ang′glō ô strāl′yən), *adj.* **1.** belonging, relating to, or involving England and Australia, or the people of the two countries. —*n.* **2.** a native or descendant of a native of England who has settled in Australia.

An·glo-Cath·o·lic (ang′glō kath′ə lik, -kath′lik), *n.* **1.** an adherent of Anglo-Catholicism. **2.** a member of the Church of England, as distinguished from a Roman Catholic or member of the Greek or Russian Orthodox churches. —*adj.* **3.** of or pertaining to Anglo-Catholicism or Anglo-Catholics. [1830–40]

An·glo-Ca·thol·i·cism (ang′glō kə thol′ə siz′əm), *n.* **1.** the tradition or form of worship in the Anglican Church that emphasizes Catholicity, the apostolic succession, and the continuity of all churches within the communion with pre-Reformation Christianity as well as the importance of liturgy and ritual. **2.** the religion of the Church of England, as distinguished from that of the Roman Catholic, Greek Orthodox, or Russian Orthodox churches.

An′glo-E·gyp′tian Sudan′ (ang′glō i jip′shən), former name of **Sudan.**

An·glo-French (ang′glō french′), *adj.* **1.** belonging to, relating to, or involving England and France, or the people of the two countries. **2.** of or pertaining to the Anglo-French dialect. —*n.* **3.** Also called **Anglo-Norman.** the dialect of French current in England from the

Norman Conquest to the end of the Middle Ages. *Abbr.:* AF, A.F. [1850–55]

An•glo-Gal•lic (ang′glō gal′ik), *adj. Numis.* noting or pertaining to the coins or series of coins issued by the English kings from Henry II to Henry VIII for their French domains. [1750–60]

An•glo-In•di•an (ang′glō in′dē ən), *adj.* **1.** belonging to, relating to, or involving England and India, esp. as politically associated: *Anglo-Indian treaties.* **2.** of or pertaining to Anglo-Indians or their speech. —*n.* **3.** a person of English and Indian ancestry. **4.** the speech of such persons, characterized by the Anglicizations of Indian words. *Abbr.:* AInd **5.** a person of English birth or citizenship living in India. [1805–15, *Amer.*]

An•glo-I•rish (ang′glō ī′rish), *n.* **1.** persons of English descent living in Ireland. **2.** Hiberno-English. —*adj.* **3.** of or pertaining to the Anglo-Irish or their speech. **4.** Hiberno-Saxon. [1785–95]

An•glo-Lat•in (ang′glō lat′n), *n.* Medieval Latin as used in England. *Abbr.:* AL, AL., A.L. [1785–95]

An•glo•ma•ni•a (ang′glə mā′nē ə, -mān′yə), *n.* an intense admiration of, interest in, or tendency to imitate English institutions, manners, customs, etc. [1780–90, *Amer.*; ANGLO- + MANIA] —**An•glo•ma•ni•ac** (ang′glō-mā′nē ak′), *n.* —**An•glo•ma•ni•ac•al** (ang′glō mə nī′ə-kəl), *adj.*

An•glo-Nor•man (ang′glō nôr′mən), *adj.* **1.** pertaining to the period, 1066–1154, when England was ruled by Normans. **2.** of or pertaining to Anglo-Normans or the Anglo-Norman dialect. —*n.* **3.** a Norman who settled in England after 1066, or a descendant of one. **4.** Anglo-French (def. 3). [1725–35]

An•glo•phile (ang′glə fīl′, -fil), *n.* a person who is friendly to or admires England or English customs, institutions, etc. Also, **An•glo•phil** (ang′glə fil). [1865–70; ANGLO- + -PHILE] —**An′glo•phil•ism,** *n.*

An•glo•phil•ia (ang′glə fil′ē ə), *n.* a strong admiration or enthusiasm for England, its people, and things English. [1895–90; ANGLO- + -PHILIA] —**An•glo•phil•i•ac** (ang′glə fil′ē ak′), **An′glo•phil′ic,** *adj.*

An•glo•phobe (ang′glə fōb′), *n.* a person who hates or fears England or anything English. [1865–70; ANGLO- + -PHOBE]

An•glo•pho•bi•a (ang′glə fō′bē ə), *n.* a hatred or fear of England or anything English. [1785–95, *Amer.*; ANGLO- + -PHOBIA] —**An•glo•pho•bi•ac** (ang′glə fō′bē-ak′), **An′glo•pho′bic,** *adj.*

An•glo•phone (ang′glə fōn′), (*sometimes l.c.*) *n.* **1.** an English-speaking person, esp. a native speaker of English. —*adj.* **2.** of or pertaining to speakers of English. [1965–70; ANGLO- + -PHONE]

An•glo-Sax•on (ang′glō sak′sən), *n.* **1.** an English person of the period before the Norman Conquest. **2.** See **Old English** (def. 1). **3.** the original Germanic element in the English language. **4.** plain and simple English, esp. language that is blunt, monosyllabic, and often rude or vulgar. **5.** a person whose native language is English. **6.** a person of English descent. **7.** (in the U.S.) a person of colonial descent or British origin. —*adj.* **8.** of, pertaining to, or characteristic of the Anglo-Saxons. **9.** of or pertaining to Anglo-Saxon. **10.** English-speaking; British or American. **11.** (of words, speech, or writing) blunt, monosyllabic, and often vulgar. [1605–15; based on NL, ML *Anglo-Saxōnēs, Anglī Saxōnēs* (pl.); from 10th cent., collective name for WGmc-speaking people of Britain (cf. OE *Angulseaxan*); see ANGLE, SAXON]

An•glo-Sax•on•ism (ang′glō sak′sə niz′əm), *n.* Saxonism. [1855–60; ANGLO-SAXON + -ISM]

An′glo-Ve•ne′tian glass′ (ang′glō və nē′shən), glassware made in England from the late 16th to the late 17th centuries in imitation of Venetian models.

ang•ma (ang′mə), *n.* agma.

An•go•la (ang gō′lə), *n.* Formerly, **Portuguese West Africa.** a republic in SW Africa: formerly an overseas province of Portugal; gained independence Nov. 11, 1975. 5,500,000; 481,226 sq. mi. (1,246,375 sq. km). *Cap.:* Luanda. —**An•go′lan,** *adj., n.*

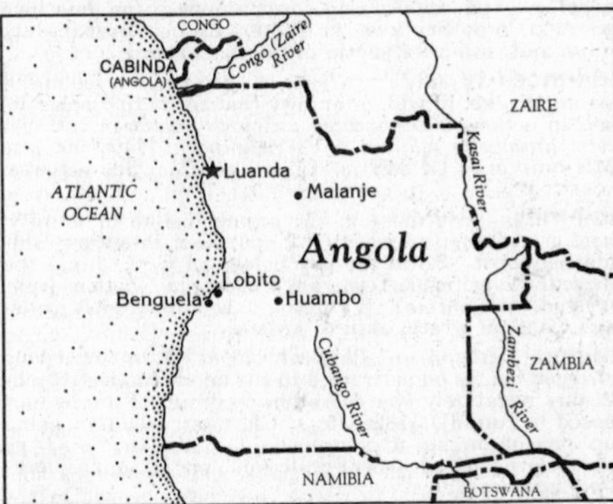

An•go•lese (ang′gə lēz′, -lēs′), *n., pl.* **-lese.** a member of any of the tribes residing in Angola. [ANGOL(A) + -ESE]

an•gon (ang′gon), *n.* a spear having a long, narrow iron shaft and a small, usually barbed tip, associated mainly with Frankish and Saxon grave finds of the 5th through 8th centuries A.D. [1870–75; < LGk *ángōn* < Gmc; cf. OHG *ango* prong, tip, hook, OE *anga,* ON *angi;* akin to ANGLE²]

an•gor (ang′gər), *n. Med.* **1.** extreme distress or mental anguish, usually of physical origin. **2.** angina. [1400–50; late ME < L: suffocation. See ANGER]

An•go•ra (ang gôr′ə, -gōr′ə, an- *for 1–3, 5–7;* ang-gôr′ə, -gōr′ə, ang′gər ə *for 4*), *n.* **1.** See **Angora cat. 2.** (*often l.c.*) Also, **Angora wool.** the hair of the Angora goat or of the Angora rabbit. **3.** (*often l.c.*) yarn, fabric, or a garment made from this hair. **4.** Ankara. **5.** See **Angora goat. 6.** See **Angora rabbit.** —*adj.* **7.** (*usually l.c.*) made from a yarn or fabric of the hairs of the Angora goat or Angora rabbit: *an angora sweater.* [1825–35; var. of ANKARA]

Ango′ra cat′, a long-haired variety of the domestic cat, raised originally in Angora, having a long body, pointed head, and bushy tail. Also called **Angora.** [1810–20]

Ango′ra goat′, a variety of domestic goat, raised originally in Angora, having long, silky hair called mohair. Also called **Angora.** [1825–35]

Ango′ra rab′bit, one of a breed of rabbits raised chiefly in Europe for its long, silky hair. Also called **Angora.** [1840–50]

Ango′ra wool′, Angora (def. 2). [1870–75]

an′gos•tu′ra bark′ (ang′gə stŏŏr′ə, -styŏŏr′ə, ang′-), the bitter, aromatic bark of either of two South American citrus trees, *Galipea officinalis* or *G. cusparia,* used in medicine and in the preparation of liqueurs and bitters. Also called **an′gos•tu′ra.** [1785–95; after *Angostura* (now Ciudad Bolívar), town in central Venezuela]

An•gou•mois (äng′gōōm wä′; *Fr.* än gōō mwa′), *n.* a region and former province of W France: famous as source of cognac.

Angoumois′ grain′ moth′, a gelechiid moth, *Sitotroga cerealella,* the larvae of which feed on stored corn and other grains.

An•gra do He•ro•ís•mo (*Port.* äng′grə dŏŏ e′rŏŏ-ēzh′mŏŏ), a seaport on and the capital of the island of Terceira in the Azores: former capital of the Azores. 85,650.

An•gra Main•yu (ang′rə mīn′yōō), *Zoroastrianism.* the evil spirit who contends against Spenta Mainyu. Also called **Ahriman.**

Angr•bo•da (äng′gər bō′də, -bô′-), *n. Scand. Myth.* a giantess who was the mother of Loki's children, Fenrir and Hel, and also of the Midgard serpent. [< ON *Angrbotha* lit., one who announces misfortune, equiv. to *angr* misfortune + *botha* to announce]

an•gry (ang′grē), *adj.,* **-gri•er, -gri•est. 1.** feeling or showing anger or strong resentment (usually fol. by *at, with,* or *about*): *to be angry at the dean; to be angry about the snub.* **2.** expressing, caused by, or characterized by anger; wrathful: *angry words.* **3.** *Chiefly New Eng. and Midland U.S.* inflamed, as a sore; exhibiting inflammation. **4.** (of an object or phenomenon) exhibiting a characteristic or creating a mood associated with anger or danger, as by color, sound, force, etc.: *an angry sea; the boom of angry guns.* [1275–1325; ME. See ANGER, -Y¹] —**an′gri•ly,** *adv.* —**an′gri•ness,** *n.*
—**Syn. 1.** irate, incensed, enraged, infuriated, furious, mad; provoked, irritated. —**Ant. 1.** calm.

an′gry young′ man′, 1. (*often cap.*) one of a group of British writers of the late 1950's and the 1960's whose works reflect strong dissatisfaction with, frustration by, and rebellion against tradition and society. **2.** any author writing in this manner.

angst (ängkst), *n., pl.* **äng•ste** (engk′stə). a feeling of dread, anxiety, or anguish. [1840–50; < G *Angst* fear, anxiety, OHG *angust* (c. MLG *angest,* MD *anxt*), equiv. to *ang-* (akin to *eng* narrow, constricted) + *-st* abstract nominal suffix, perh. a conglomerate of a suffix **-os-* + **-ti-* suffix forming abstracts]

ang•strom (ang′strəm), *n.* (*often cap.*) a unit of length, equal to one tenth of a millimicron, or one ten millionth of a millimeter, primarily used to express electromagnetic wavelengths. *Symbol:* Å; *Abbr.:* A Also called **ang′strom u′nit, Ang′strom u′nit.** [1895–1900; named after A. J. ÅNGSTRÖM]

Ång•ström (ang′strəm; *Swed.* ông′strœm), *n.* **An•ders Jo•nas** (an′dərz jō′nəs; *Swed.* än′dərs yōō′näs), 1814–74, Swedish astronomer and physicist.

An•guier (än gyā′), *n.* **Fran•çois** (frän swa′), 1604–69, and his brother **Mi•chel** (mē shel′), 1614–86, French sculptors.

An•guil•la (ang gwil′ə), *n.* an island in the N Leeward Islands, in the E West Indies; a British dependency. 6500; 34 sq. mi. (88 sq. km). Cf. **St. Kitts-Nevis-Anguilla.**

an•guil•li•form (ang gwil′ə fôrm′), *adj.* having the shape or form of an eel. [1685–95; < L *anguill(a)* eel (*angu(is)* snake + *-illa* dim. suffix) + -I- + -FORM]

an•guine (ang′gwin), *adj.* pertaining to or resembling a snake. [1650–60; < L *anguinus* pertaining to a snake, equiv. to *angu(is)* snake, serpent + *-inus* -INE¹]

an•guish (ang′gwish), *n.* **1.** excruciating or acute distress, suffering, or pain: *the anguish of grief.* —*v.t.* **2.** to inflict with distress, suffering, or pain. —*v.i.* **3.** to suffer, feel, or exhibit anguish: *to anguish over the loss of a loved one.* [1175–1225; ME *anguisse* < OF < L *angustia* tight place, equiv. to *angust(us)* narrow + *-ia* -IA; cf. ANXIOUS; akin to ANGER]
—**Syn. 1.** agony, torment, torture. See **pain.** —**Ant. 1.** delight, comfort, relief.

an•guished (ang′gwisht), *adj.* **1.** feeling, showing, or accompanied by anguish. **2.** resulting from or produced by anguish. [1350–1400; ME; see ANGUISH, -ED³]

an•gu•lar (ang′gyə lər), *adj.* **1.** having an angle or angles. **2.** consisting of, situated at, or forming an angle. **3.** of, pertaining to, or measured by an angle. **4.** *Physics.* pertaining to quantities related to a revolving body that are measured in reference to its axis of revolution. **5.** bony, lean, or gaunt: *a tall, angular man.* **6.** acting or moving awkwardly. **7.** stiff in manner; unbending. Also, **angulose, angulous.** [1590–1600; < L *angulāris* having corners or angles, equiv. to *angul(us)* ANGLE¹ + *-āris* -AR¹] —**an′gu•lar•ly,** *adv.* —**an′gu•lar•ness,** *n.*
—**Ant. 1.** curved. **5.** rotund. **6.** graceful.

an′gular accelera′tion, *Physics.* the time rate of change of angular velocity of a rotating body. [1880–85]

an′gular diam′eter, *Astron.* the angle that the apparent diameter of a celestial object subtends at the eye of the observer. [1870–75]

an′gular disper′sion, *Optics.* a measure of the angular separation of light rays of different wavelength or color traversing a prism or diffraction grating, equal to the rate of change of the angle of deviation with respect to the change in wavelength.

an′gular displace′ment, *Physics.* the amount of rotation of a point, line, or body in a specified direction about an axis.

an′gular fre′quency, *Physics.* a measure of the frequency of an object varying sinusoidally equal to 2π times the frequency in cycles per second and expressed in radians per second. *Symbol:* π [1925–30]

an′gular house′, any of the four astrological houses that begin at the angles: the first, fourth, seventh, and tenth houses, that correspond, respectively, to self, home, others, and career. Cf. **cadent house, succedent house.** [1975–80]

an•gu•lar•i•ty (ang′gyə lar′i tē), *n., pl.* **-ties. 1.** the quality of being angular. **2. angularities,** sharp corners; angular outlines: *the angularities of the coastline.* [1635–45; ANGULAR + -ITY]

an′gular leaf′ spot′, *Plant Pathol.* a disease of plants, characterized by angular, watery spots on the leaves and fruit, caused by any of several bacteria, as *Pseudomonas lachrymans.*

an′gular magnifica′tion, *Optics.* the ratio of the angle subtended at the eye by the image formed by an optical instrument to the angle subtended at the eye by the object being viewed.

an′gular meas′ure, *Math.* **1.** the units used to measure angles. Cf. **angle¹** (def. 1c). **2.** the number of such units in a given angle.

an′gular momen′tum, *Physics.* the product of the moment of inertia of a body about an axis and its angular velocity with respect to the same axis. Also called **moment of momentum.** [1865–70]

an′gular veloc′ity, *Physics.* the time rate of change of angular position of a rotating body, usually expressed in radians per second or radians per minute. [1810–20]

an•gu•late (ang′gyə lit, -lāt′), *adj.* of angular form; angled: *angulate stems.* Also, **an′gu•lat′ed.** [1785–95; < L *angulātus* having angles. See ANGLE¹, -ATE¹] —**an′gu•late•ly,** *adv.* —**an′gu•late•ness,** *n.*

an•gu•la•tion (ang′gyə lā′shən), *n.* **1.** an angular part, position, or formation. **2.** the exact measurement of angles. **3.** Also called **comma position.** *Skiing.* a position for traversing a slope in which the skis are edged into the hill by bending the knees toward the hill and leaning the upper body away from the hill, with all weight on the downhill ski. [1865–70; ANGULATE + -ION]

an•gu•lous (ang′gyə ləs), *adj.* angular. Also, **an•gu•lose** (ang′gyə lōs′). [1650–60; < L *angulōsus.* See ANGLE¹, -OUS] —**an•gu•los•i•ty** (ang′gyə los′i tē), *n.*

An•gus (ang′gəs), *n.* **1.** Formerly, **Forfar.** a historic county in E Scotland. **2.** See **Aberdeen Angus. 3.** a male given name.

An′gus Og′ (ōg), *Irish Myth.* the god of love and beauty, the patron deity of young men and women.

An•halt (än′hält), *n.* a former state in central Germany, now part of Saxony-Anhalt.

an•har•mon•ic (an′här mon′ik), *adj. Physics.* of or pertaining to an oscillating system that is not undergoing simple harmonic motion. [AN-¹ + HARMONIC; modeled on F *anharmonique*]

an′harmon′ic ra′tio, *Math.* See **cross ratio.** [1860–65]

an•he•do•ni•a (an′hē dō′nē ə), *n. Psychol.* lack of pleasure or of the capacity to experience it. [1895–1900; < Gk *an-* AN-¹ + *hēdon(ḗ)* pleasure + *-ia* -IA] —**an•he•don•ic** (an′hē don′ik), *adj.*

an•he•dral (an hē′drəl), *adj. Petrog.* xenomorphic (def. 1). [1895–1900; AN-¹ + -HEDRAL]

an•hi•dro•sis (an′hi drō′sis, -hī-), *n. Med.* the deficiency or absence of perspiration; adiaphoresis. Also, **an′hy•dro′sis.** [< NL; see AN-¹, HIDROSIS] —**an•hi•drot•ic, an•hy•drot•ic** (an′hi drot′ik, -hī-), *adj.*

an•hin•ga (an hing′gə), *n.* any of various totipalmate swimming birds of the family Anhingidae, having a very long and flexible neck. Also called **snakebird, water turkey.** [1760–70; < Pg < Tupi *ayingá*]

An•hui (än′hwē′), *n. Pinyin, Wade-Giles.* a province in E China. 35,000,000; 54,015 sq. mi. (139,899 sq. km). *Cap.:* Hefei. Also, *Older Spelling,* **An•hwei** (än′hwā′).

anhyd., *Chem.* anhydrous.

anhydr-, var. of **anhydro-** before a vowel.

an•hy•dre•mi•a (an′hī drē′mē ə), *n. Med.* an abnormal decrease in the volume of the blood, due to loss of water. [ANHYDR- + -EMIA] —**an′hy•dre′mic,** *adj.*

an•hy•dride (an hī′drīd, -drid), *n. Chem.* **1.** a compound formed by removing water from a more complex compound: an oxide of a nonmetal **(acid anhydride)** or a metal **(basic anhydride)** that forms an acid or a base, respectively, when united with water. **2.** a compound from which water has been abstracted. [1860–65; ANHYDR- + -IDE]

an•hy•drite (an hī′drīt), *n.* a mineral, anhydrous calcium sulfate, $CaSO_4$, usually occurring in whitish or slightly colored masses. [1825–35; ANHYDR- + -ITE[1]]

anhydro-, *Chem.* a combining form representing **anhydride** in compound words: *anhydroglucose.* Also, *esp. before a vowel,* **anhydr-.**

an•hy•drous (an hī′drəs), *adj. Chem.* with all water removed, esp. water of crystallization. [1810–20; < Gk *ánydros* waterless (with etymological *h* restored). See AN-[1], HYDRO-[1], -OUS]

a•ni (ä′nē, ä nē′), *n., pl.* **a•nis.** any of several black, tropical American cuckoos of the genus *Crotophaga,* having a compressed, bladelike bill. [1820–30; < Sp or Pg < Tupi or Guarani]

An′i•ak′chak Cra′ter (an′ē ak′chak, an′-), an active volcanic crater on the Alaskan Peninsula, with a diameter of 6 mi. (10 km).

a•ni•a•ni•au (ä′nē ä′nē ou′), *n.* a small Hawaiian honeycreeper, *Loxops parva,* occurring in the high forests of Kauai. Also called **lesser amakihi.** [< Hawaiian *'ania-niau*]

a•nic•ca (ə nik′ə), *n. Buddhism.* the cycle of birth, growth, decay, and death through which every living thing must pass. Cf. **Three Signs of Being.** [< Pali < Skt *anitya* not everlasting, equiv. to *a-* A-[6] + *nitya* eternal]

An•i•ce•tus (an′ə sē′təs), *n.* **Saint,** pope A.D. 155?–166?.

an•i•con•ic (an′ī kon′ik), *adj.* **1.** not employing or permitting images, idols, etc.: *an aniconic religion.* **2.** not forming an image. **3.** of or pertaining to aniconism. [1890–95; AN-[1] + ICONIC]

an•i•con•ism (an ī′kə niz′əm), *n.* **1.** opposition to the use of idols or images. **2.** the worship of objects symbolic of but not depicting a deity. [1905–10; AN[1]- + ICON + -ISM]

a•nigh (ə nī′), *Chiefly New Eng. and Midland U.S. Older Use.* —*prep.* **1.** near; close to. —*adv.* **2.** nearby; close by. [1765–75; *a-* (as in ANEAR) + NIGH]

An•ik (an′ik), *n.* one of a series of Canadian geosynchronous communications satellites that provide telephone and television transmissions. [1970–75; < Inuit (Quebec, Labrador dial.) *anik* older brother]

an•il (an′l), *n.* **1.** a West Indian shrub, *Indigofera suffruticosa,* of the legume family, having elongated clusters of small, reddish-yellow flowers and yielding indigo. **2.** indigo; deep blue. [1575–85; < Pg < Ar *an-nīl,* equiv. to *al* the + *nīl* indigo < Skt *nīlī* indigo (*nīl(a)* dark blue + *-ī* fem. n. suffix)]

an•ile (an′īl, ā′nīl), *adj.* of or like a foolish, doddering old woman. [1645–55; < L *anīlis* pertaining to an old woman, equiv. to *an(us)* old woman + *-īlis* -ILE] —**a•nil•i•ty** (ə nil′i tē), *n.*

an•i•lide (an′l id, -īd′), *n. Chem.* any compound containing the univalent group C_6H_5NH–, derived from aniline, as acetanilide, C_8H_9NO. [1860–65; < G *Anilid.* See ANIL, -IDE] —**an•i•lid•ic** (an′ə lid′ik), *adj.*

an•i•line (an′l in, -īn′), *n.* **1.** Also called **an′iline oil′, aminobenzine, phenylamine.** *Chem.* a colorless, oily, slightly water-soluble liquid, $C_6H_5NH_2$, usually derived from nitrobenzene by reduction: used chiefly in the synthesis of dyes and drugs. —*adj.* **2.** pertaining to or derived from aniline: *aniline colors.* Also, **an•i•lin** (an′l-in). [1840–50; ANIL + -INE[2]]

an′iline black′, *Chem.* the black dye obtained by the oxidation of aniline hydrochloride, used for dyeing textiles, esp. cotton.

an′iline dye′, *Chem.* any of a large number of synthetic dyes derived from aniline, usually obtained from coal tar. [1860–65]

an′iline hydrochlo′ride, *Chem.* a white, crystalline, water-soluble solid, $C_6H_5NH_2 \cdot HCl$, used chiefly as an intermediate in the manufacture of dyes, esp. aniline black.

a•ni•lin•gus (ā′nl ing′gəs), *n.* oral stimulation of the anus. [1945–50; AN(US) + -I- + (CUNNI)LINGUS]

anim., *Music.* animato.

an•i•ma (an′ə mə), *n.* **1.** soul; life. **2.** (in the psychology of C. G. Jung) **a.** the inner personality that is turned toward the unconscious of the individual (contrasted with *persona*). **b.** the feminine principle, esp. as present in men (contrasted with *animus*). [1920–25; < L: breath, vital force, soul, spirit]

an•i•mad•ver•sion (an′ə mad vûr′zhən, -shən), *n.* **1.** an unfavorable or censorious comment: *to make animadversions on someone's conduct.* **2.** the act of criticizing. [1590–1600; < L *animadversiōn-* (s. of *animadversiō*) a heeding, censure, equiv. to *animadvers(us)* (ptp. of *animadvertere* to heed, censure; see ANIMADVERT) + *-iōn-* -ION] —**an′i•mad•ver′sion•al,** *adj.*

an•i•mad•vert (an′ə mad vûrt′), *v.i.* **1.** to comment unfavorably or critically (usually fol. by *on* or *upon*): *to animadvert at length upon his faulty use of English.* —*v.t.* **2.** *Obs.* to take cognizance or notice of. [1630–40; < L *animadvertere* to heed, censure, equiv. to *anim(um),* acc. of *animus* (see ANIMUS) + *advertere* to ADVERT] —**an′i•mad•vert′er,** *n.*

an•i•mal (an′ə məl), *n.* **1.** any member of the kingdom Animalia, comprising multicellular organisms that have a well-defined shape and usually limited growth, can move voluntarily, actively acquire food and digest it internally, and have sensory and nervous systems that allow them to respond rapidly to stimuli: some classification schemes also include protozoa and certain other single-celled eukaryotes that have motility and animallike nutritional modes. **2.** any such living thing other than a human being. **3.** a mammal, as opposed to a fish, bird, etc. **4.** the physical, sensual, or carnal nature of human beings; animality: *the animal in every person.* **5.** an inhuman person; brutish or beastlike person: *She married an animal.* **6.** thing: *A perfect job? Is there any such animal?* —*adj.* **7.** of, pertaining to, or derived from animals: *animal fats.* **8.** pertaining to the physical, sensual, or carnal nature of humans, rather than their spiritual or intellectual nature: *animal needs.* [1300–50; ME (< OF) < L, n. deriv. (with loss of final vowel and shortening of *ā*) of *animāle,* neut. of *animālis* living, animate, equiv. to *anim(a)* air, breath + *-ālis* -AL[1]; E adj. also directly < L *animālis*] —**an•i•mal•ic** (an′ə mal′ik), **an•i•ma•li•an** (an′ə mā′lē ən, -māl′yən), *adj.*

—**Syn. 1, 2.** ANIMAL, BEAST, BRUTE refer to sentient creatures as distinct from minerals and plants; figuratively, they usually connote qualities and characteristics below the human level. ANIMAL is the general word; figuratively, it applies merely to the body or to animallike characteristics: *An athlete is a magnificent animal.* BEAST refers to four-footed animals; figuratively, it suggests a base, sensual nature: *A glutton is a beast.* BRUTE implies absence of ability to reason; figuratively, it connotes savagery as well: *a drunken brute.* **5.** monster. **8.** fleshly, physical; beastly, brutal. See **carnal.**

an′imal behav′ior, 1. behavior (def. 2). **2.** a branch of biology that deals with the behavior of animals, encompassing such fields as ethology, comparative psychology, behavioral ecology, and sociobiology. —**an′imal behav′iorist.**

an′imal black′, any of various black pigments, as boneblack or ivory black, obtained from calcined animal matter. [1870–75]

an′imal char′coal, carbon obtained from the carbonization of organic tissue of animals.

an′imal crack′er, a small cookie in the shape of an animal. [1895–1900]

an•i•mal•cule (an′ə mal′kyōōl), *n.* **1.** a minute or microscopic animal, nearly or quite invisible to the naked eye, as an infusorian or rotifer. **2.** *Archaic.* a tiny animal, as a mouse or fly. [1590–1600; < NL *animalculum* a small animal. See ANIMAL, -CULE[1]] —**an•i•mal•cu•lar** (an′ə mal′kyə lər), **an•i•mal•cu•line** (an′ə mal′kyə lin), **an′i•mal′cu•lous,** *adj.*

an•i•mal•cu•lum (an′ə mal′kyə ləm), *n., pl.* **-la** (-lə). animalcule. [1670–80]

an′imal faith′, nonrational belief in the existence of a fully knowable world outside the mind. [1920–25]

An′imal Farm′, a political satire (1945) by George Orwell.

an′imal heat′, *Physiol.* heat produced in a living animal by any of various metabolic activities. [1770–80]

an′imal hus′bandry, the science of breeding, feeding, and tending domestic animals, esp. farm animals. —**an′imal hus′bandman.** [1915–20]

An•i•ma•li•a (an′ə mā′lē ə, -māl′yə), *n.* (*used with a plural v.*) *Biol.* the taxonomic kingdom comprising all animals. [< NL, L: pl. of *animal* ANIMAL]

an•i•mal•ism (an′ə mə liz′əm), *n.* **1.** preoccupation with or motivation by sensual, physical, or carnal appetites rather than moral, spiritual, or intellectual forces. **2.** the theory that human beings lack a spiritual nature. [1825–35; ANIMAL(IZE) + -ISM]

an•i•mal•ist (an′ə mə list), *n.* **1.** a person driven by animal appetites; sensualist. **2.** an advocate of the theory of animalism. [1830–40; ANIMAL + -IST] —**an′i•mal•is′tic,** *adj.*

an•i•mal•i•ty (an′ə mal′i tē), *n.* **1.** the state of being an animal. **2.** the animal nature or instincts of human beings. **3.** See **animal kingdom.** [1605–15; ANIMAL + -ITY, modeled on CARNALITY]

an•i•mal•ize (an′ə mə līz′), *v.t.,* **-ized, -iz•ing. 1.** to excite the animal passions of; brutalize; sensualize. **2.** *Fine Arts.* to represent in animal form or endow with animal features. Also, *esp. Brit.,* **an′i•mal•ise′.** [1735–45; ANIMAL + -IZE] —**an′i•mal•i•za′tion,** *n.*

an′imal king′dom, the animals of the world collectively. Cf. **mineral kingdom, plant kingdom.** [1840–50]

an•i•mal•ly (an′ə mə lē), *adv.* physically. [1590–1600; ANIMAL + -LY]

an′imal mag′netism, 1. the power to attract others through one's physical presence, bearing, energy, etc. **2.** the indefinite power, presumably innate in some persons, that enables one to induce hypnosis. Also called **biomagnetism.** [1775–85]

an′imal park′, a zoo in which wild animals are housed and displayed in large open spaces designed to resemble their native habitats. [1970–75]

an′imal pole′, *Biol.* the formative part of an ovum, having the greatest amount of cytoplasm and containing the nucleus. Cf. **vegetal pole.** [1885–90]

an′imal rights′, the rights of animals, claimed on ethical grounds, to the same humane treatment and protection from exploitation and abuse that are accorded to humans. [1975–80]

an′imal shel′ter, an establishment, esp. one supported by charitable contributions, that provides a temporary home for dogs, cats, and other animals that are offered for adoption.

an′imal spir′its, exuberance arising from an excess of energy; vivacity and good humor: *The children romped on the lawn, full of animal spirits.* [1535–45]

an′imal starch′, *Biochem.* glycogen. [1855–60]

an′imal war′den, dogcatcher.

an•i•mate (*v.* an′ə māt′; *adj.* an′ə mit), *v.,* **-mat•ed, -mat•ing,** *adj.* —*v.t.* **1.** to give life to; make alive: *God animated the dust.* **2.** to make lively, vivacious, or vigorous; give zest or spirit to: *Her presence animated the party.* **3.** to fill with courage or boldness; encourage: *to animate weary troops.* **4.** to move or stir to action; motivate: *He was animated by religious zeal.* **5.** to give motion to: *leaves animated by a breeze.* **6.** to prepare or produce as an animated cartoon: *to animate a children's story.* —*adj.* **7.** alive; possessing life: *animate creatures.* **8.** lively: *an animate expression of joy.* **9.** of or relating to animal life. **10.** able to move voluntarily. **11.** *Ling.* belonging to a syntactic category or having a semantic feature that is characteristic of words denoting beings regarded as having perception and volition (opposed to *inanimate*). [1375–1425; late ME *animat* < L *animātus* filled with breath or air, quickened, animated (ptp. of *animāre*). See ANIMA, -ATE[1]] —**an′i•mate•ly,** *adv.* —**an′i•mate•ness,** *n.* —**an′i•mat′ing•ly,** *adv.*

—**Syn. 1.** vivify, quicken, vitalize. **2.** energize, fortify. ANIMATE, INVIGORATE, STIMULATE mean to enliven. To ANIMATE is to create a liveliness: *Health and energy animated his movements.* To INVIGORATE means to give physical vigor, to refresh, to exhilarate: *Mountain air invigorates.* To STIMULATE is to arouse a latent liveliness on a particular occasion: *Alcohol stimulates.* **3.** inspire, inspirit, hearten, arouse, exhilarate.

an•i•mat•ed (an′ə mā′tid), *adj.* **1.** full of life, action, or spirit; lively; vigorous: *an animated debate on the death penalty.* **2.** made or equipped to move or give the appearance of moving in an animallike fashion: *animated puppets.* **3.** containing representations of animals or mechanical objects that appear to move as real ones do: *an animated window display.* [1525–35; ANIMATE + -ED[2]] —**an′i•mat′ed•ly,** *adv.*

an′imated cartoon′, a motion picture consisting of a sequence of drawings, each so slightly different that when filmed and run through a projector the figures seem to move. [1910–15]

an′imated oat′, an oat, *Avena sterilis,* of the Mediterranean region, having spikelets that twist or move when exposed to sudden moisture, due to the hygroscopic action of the awns.

an•i•mat•ic (an′ə mat′ik), *Advertising.* —*n.* **1.** a preliminary form of a television commercial consisting of a series of drawings with a voice-over, prepared chiefly for test-marketing. —*adj.* **2.** of or pertaining to animatics. [perh. b. ANIMATE or ANIMATION and AUTOMATIC, prob. on the model of *photomatic* a similar commercial made by filming still photographs, based on *Photomaton* the trademark name of a kind of automatic camera]

an•i•ma•tion (an′ə mā′shən), *n.* **1.** animated quality; liveliness; vivacity; spirit: *to talk with animation.* **2.** an act or instance of animating or enlivening. **3.** the state or condition of being animated. **4.** the process of preparing animated cartoons. [1590–1600; 1910–15 for def. 4; (< MF) < L *animātiōn-* (s. of *animātiō* a bestowing of life). See ANIMATE, -ION]

an•i•ma•tism (an′ə mə tiz′əm), *n.* the attribution of consciousness to inanimate objects and natural phenomena. [1895–1900; ANIMATE + -ISM]

a•ni•ma•to (ä′nə mä′tō, an′ə-; *It.* ä′nē mä′tô), *adj. Music.* animated; lively. *Abbr.:* anim. [1715–25; < It < L. See ANIMATE]

an•i•ma•tor (an′ə mā′tər), *n.* **1.** a person or thing that animates. **2.** an artist who draws animated cartoons. Also, **an′i•mat′er.** [1625–35; < LL; see ANIMATE, -TOR]

an•i•ma•tron•ics (an′ə mə tron′iks), *n.* (*used with a sing. v.*) the technology connected with the use of electronics to animate puppets or other figures, as for motion pictures. [1975–80; b. ANIMATE and ELECTRONICS] —**an′i•ma•tron′ic,** *adj.*

a•nime (ə nēm′), *n. Armor.* an articulated cuirass of the 16th century. [< MF, alter. of *lamine* cuirass, thin plate of metal (with *l* taken as the definite article and metathesis of nasals) < L *lāmina* LAMINA]

an•i•mé (an′ə mā′, -mē), *n.* any of various resins or copals, esp. that from *Hymenaea courbaril,* a tree of tropical America, used in making varnish, scenting pastilles, etc. Also, **a•ni•mi** (ə nē′mē). [1570–80; < F < Sp or Pg *anime,* of uncert. orig.]

an•i•mism (an′ə miz′əm), *n.* **1.** the belief that natural objects, natural phenomena, and the universe itself possess souls. **2.** the belief that natural objects have souls that may exist apart from their material bodies. **3.** the doctrine that the soul is the principle of life and health. **4.** belief in spiritual beings or agencies. [1825–35; < L *anim(a)* (see ANIMA) + -ISM] —**an′i•mist,** *adj.* —**an′i•mis′tic,** *adj.*

a•ni•mis o•pi•bus•que pa•ra•ti (ä′ni mis ō′pi-bōōs′kwe pä rä′tē; *Eng.* an′ə məs ō′pə bus′kwē pə rā′tī, ō′pə bus′kwā pə rä′tē), *Latin.* prepared in mind and resources: motto of South Carolina.

an•i•mos•i•ty (an′ə mos′i tē), *n., pl.* **-ties.** a feeling of strong dislike, ill will, or enmity that tends to display itself in action: *a deep-seated animosity between two sisters; animosity against one's neighbor.* [1400–50; late ME *animosite* (< MF) < LL *animōsitās.* See ANIMUS, -OSE[1], -ITY]

an•i•mus (an′ə məs), *n.* **1.** strong dislike or enmity; hostile attitude; animosity. **2.** purpose; intention; animating spirit. **3.** (in the psychology of C. G. Jung) the masculine principle, esp. as present in women (contrasted with *anima*). [1810–20; < L: mind, spirit, courage, passion, wrath; akin to ANIMA]

an•i•on (an′ī′ən), *n. Physical Chem.* **1.** a negatively charged ion, as one attracted to the anode in electrolysis. **2.** any negatively charged atom or group of atoms (opposed to *cation*). [1825–35; < Gk, neut. of *aniṓn* going up (prp. of *aniénai* to go up), equiv. to *an-* AN-[3] + *-i-* go + *-ōn* prp. suffix] —**an•i•on•ic** (an′ī on′ik), *adj.* —**an′i•on′i•cal•ly,** *adv.*

anion′ic deter′gent, *Chem.* any of a class of synthetic compounds whose anions are alkali salts, as soap, or whose ions are ammonium salts.

an•is (ä′nēs), *n.* a variety of anisette made esp. in Spain and Latin America. [< Sp (*aceite de*) *anís* lit., oil of ANISE]

an•is•al•de•hyde (an′ə sal′də hīd′), *n. Chem.* a colorless, oily, aromatic liquid, the para form of $C_8H_8O_2$, having a vanillalike odor: used chiefly in the manufacture of cosmetics and perfume, and as an intermediate in organic synthesis. Also called **anisic aldehyde.** [ANISE + ALDEHYDE]

CONCISE ETYMOLOGY KEY: <, descended or borrowed from; >, whence; b., blend of, blended; c., cognate with; cf., compare; deriv., derivative; equiv., equivalent; imit., imitative; obl., oblique; r., replacing; s., stem; sp., spelling, spelled; resp., respelling, respelled; trans., translation; ?, origin unknown; *, unattested; ‡, probably earlier than. See the full key inside the front cover.

an•ise (an′is), *n.* **1.** a Mediterranean plant, *Pimpinella anisum,* of the parsley family, having loose umbrels of small yellowish-white flowers that yield aniseed. **2.** aniseed. [1350–1400; ME *anis* < OF < L *anisum* < Gk *ánison*] —**a•nis•ic** (ə nis′ik), *adj.*

an′ise cam′phor, anethole. [1860–65]

an•i•seed (an′ə sēd′, an′is sēd′), *n.* the aromatic seed of anise, the oil of which (**an′ise oil′, an′iseed oil′, oil of anise**) is used in the manufacture of anethole, in medicine as a carminative and expectorant, and in cookery and liqueurs for its licoricelike flavor. [1350–1400; ME *anece seed.* See ANISE, SEED]

an•is•ei•ko•ni•a (an′ə sī kō′nē ə), *n. Ophthalm.* a defect of vision in which the images at the retinas are unequal in size. [1930–35; < NL; see ANISO-, EIKON, -IA] —**an•is•ei•kon•ic** (an′ə sī kon′ik), *adj.*

an•i•sette (an′ə set′, -zet′, an′ə set′, -zet′), *n.* a cordial or liqueur flavored with aniseed. [1830–40; < F, short for *anisette de Bordeaux.* See ANISE, -ETTE]

anis′ic al′cohol, *Chem.* See **anisyl alcohol.**

anis′ic al′dehyde, *Chem.* anisaldehyde.

aniso-, a combining form meaning "unequal," "uneven," used in the formation of compound words: *anisogamous.* [< Gk, comb. form of *ánisos;* see AN-[1], ISO-]

an•i•so•car•pic (an ī′sə kär′pik, an′ī-), *adj. Bot.* (of a flower) having a lower number of carpels than of other floral parts. [AN-[1] + ISOCARPIC]

an•i•so•co•ri•a (an ī′sə kôr′ē ə, -kōr′-, an′ī-), *n. Ophthalm.* inequality in the size of the pupils. [1900–05; ANISO- + Gk *kór(ē)* pupil + -IA]

an•i•so•dac•ty•lous (an ī′sə dak′tl əs, an′ī-), *adj.* **1.** *Zool.* having the toes unlike, or unequal in number. **2.** *Ornith.* having three toes directed forward and one backward. Also, **an•i′so•dac′tyl.** [ANISO- + -DACTYLOUS]

an•i•so•ga•mete (an ī′sō gə mēt′, -gam′ēt, an′ī sō-gam′ēt), *n. Biol.* either of a pair of unlike gametes, usually differing in size. [ANISO- + GAMETE] —**an•i•so•ga•met•ic** (an ī′sō gə met′ik, an′ī-), *adj.*

an•i•sog•a•mous (an′ī sog′ə məs), *adj. Biol.* reproducing by the fusion of dissimilar gametes or individuals, usually differing in size. Also, **an•i•so•gam•ic** (an ī′sə-gam′ik, an′ī-). [1900–05; ANISO- + -GAMOUS]

an•i•sog•a•my (an′ī sog′ə mē), *n. Biol.* the union of anisogametes. [1890–95; ANISO- + -GAMY]

an•i•sole (an′ə sōl′), *n. Chem.* a colorless, water-insoluble liquid, C_7H_8O, having a pleasant, aromatic odor, used chiefly in perfumery and organic synthesis, and as a vermicide. Also called **methyl phenyl ether, methoxybenzene.** [1860–65; ANISE + -OLE[2]]

an•i•so•met•ric (an ī′sə me′trik, an′ī-), *adj.* **1.** not isometric; of unequal measurement. **2.** *Mineral.* (of a crystal) having axes of different lengths (opposed to *equant*). [1865–70; AN-[1] + ISOMETRIC]

an•i•so•phyl•lous (an ī′sə fil′əs, an′ī-), *adj. Bot.* having leaves of different shapes or sizes. [1875–80; ANISO- + -PHYLLOUS] —**an•i′so•phyl′ly,** *n.*

an•i•sop•ter•an (an′ī sop′tər ən), *adj.* belonging or pertaining to the suborder Anisoptera, comprising the dragonflies. [< NL *Anisopter(a)* (see ANISO-, -PTEROUS) + -AN]

an•i•so•trop•ic (an ī′sə trop′ik, -trō′pik, an′ī-), *adj.* **1.** *Physics.* of unequal physical properties along different axes. Cf. **isotropic** (def. 1). **2.** *Bot.* of different dimensions along different axes. [1875–80; AN-[1] + ISOTROPIC] —**an′i•so•trop′i•cal•ly,** *adv.* —**an•i•sot•ro•py** (an′ī so′trə pē), **an′i•sot′ro•pism,** *n.*

an′i•syl ac′etate (an′ə sil), *Chem.* a colorless liquid, the para form of $C_{10}H_{12}O_3$, having a lilaclike odor, used chiefly as a scent in the manufacture of perfume. [ANISE + -YL]

an′isyl al′cohol, *Chem.* a colorless liquid, the para form of $C_8H_{10}O_2$, having a hawthornlike odor, used chiefly as a scent in the manufacture of perfume. Also, **anisic alcohol.** [1860–65]

A•ni•ta (ə nē′tə), *n.* a female given name: Spanish form of **Anna.**

An•jou (an′jo͞o; *Fr.* äɴ zho͞o′), *n.* **1.** a region and former province in W France, in the Loire Valley. **2.** a firm-fleshed green-skinned variety of pear. **3.** a town in S Quebec, in E Canada. 36,596.

An•ka•ra (ang′kər ə; *Turk.* äng′kä rä), *n.* a city in and the capital of Turkey, in the central part. 1,522,350. Also, **Angora.**

An′ka•ra′tra Moun′tains (äng′kə rä′trə, -trə, äng′-), a mountain range in central Madagascar: highest peak, 8675 ft. (2644 m).

An•ke•ny (ang′kə nē), *n.* a town in central Iowa. 15,429.

an•ker•ite (ang′kə rīt′), *n.* a carbonate mineral related to dolomite but with iron replacing part of the magnesium. [1835–45; named after M. J. *Anker* (d. 1843), Austrian mineralogist; see -ITE[1]]

ankh (angk), *n. Egyptian Art.* a tau cross with a loop at the top, used as a symbol of generation or enduring life. [1885–90; < Egyptian *ʿnḫ* live; appar. at least partially homophonous with word for "sandal strap," hence stylized picture of sandal strap became symbol for life]

An•king (än′king′), *n. Older Spelling.* Anqing.

an•kle (ang′kəl), *n.* **1.** (in humans) the joint between the foot and the leg, in which movement occurs in two planes. **2.** the corresponding joint in a quadruped or bird; hock. **3.** the slender part of the leg above the foot. [bef. 1000; ME *ankel, enkel* (c. MLG, D *enkel,* OHG *anchal, enchil,* ON *ǫkkul*); ME *anclowe,* OE *ancléow(e)* (c. MLG *anclef,* D *anklāw,* OHG *anchlāo*)]

an•kle•bone (ang′kəl bōn′), *n.* the talus. [1350–1400; ME; see ANKLE, BONE[1]]

an•kle-deep (ang′kəl dēp′), *adj.* **1.** high enough to reach or cover the ankles: *ankle-deep mud.* **2.** deeply involved or entangled: *He is ankle-deep in financial troubles.* —*adv.* **3.** as high as the ankles: *Rain water ran ankle-deep.* [1755–65]

an′kle jerk′, a reflex extension of the foot, caused by contraction of the muscles of the calf, resulting from a sharp tap on the Achilles tendon; Achilles reflex. [1885–90]

an•klet (ang′klit), *n.* **1.** a sock that reaches just above the ankle. **2.** an ornamental circlet worn around the ankle. [1810–20; ANKLE + -LET]

an•klung (ang′klung), *n.* a southeast Asian rhythm instrument consisting of a set of bamboo tubes that are tuned in octaves and slide in the grooves of a frame shaken by the performer. [< Javanese *angklung*]

an•kus (ang′kəs, ung′kəsh), *n., pl.* **-kus, -kus•es.** an elephant goad of India with a spike and a hook at one end. [1885–90; < Hindi; akin to ANGLE[2]]

ankylo-, var. of **ancylo-:** *ankylosis.*

an•ky•lo•glos•si•a (ang′kə lō glô′sē ə, -glos′ē ə), *n. Pathol.* tongue-tie. [ANKYLO- + Gk *glôss(a)* tongue + -IA]

an•ky•lo•saur (ang′kə lō sôr′), *n.* any of several herbivorous dinosaurs of the suborder Ankylosauria, from the Cretaceous Period, having the body covered with thick, bony plates. Also called **armored dinosaur.** [1905–10; < NL *Ankylosauria* name of the suborder. See ANKYLO-, -SAUR, -IA]

an•ky•lose (ang′kə lōs′), *v.t., v.i.,* **-losed, -los•ing.** to unite or grow together, as the bones of a joint or the root of a tooth and its surrounding bone. [1780–90; back formation from ANKYLOSIS]

an′kylosing spondyli′tis, *Pathol.* a degenerative inflammatory disease, most common in young men, characterized by back pain and impaired mobility of the spinal column.

an•ky•lo•sis (ang′kə lō′sis), *n.* **1.** *Pathol.* abnormal adhesion of the bones of a joint. **2.** *Anat.* the union or consolidation of two or more bones or other hard tissues into one. [1705–15; < Gk: a stiffening of the joints. See ANKYLO-, -OSIS] —**an•ky•lot•ic** (ang′kə lot′ik), *adj.*

an•ky•lo•sto•mi•a•sis (ang′kə lō stə mī′ə sis, -los-tə-), *n. Pathol.* hookworm (def. 2). [1885–90; < NL, equiv. to *Ancylostom(a)* a genus of hookworm (see ANCYLO-, STOMA) + *-iasis* -IASIS]

an•lace (an′lis), *n.* anelace.

an•la•ge (än′lä gə), *n., pl.* **-gen** (-gən), **-ges.** (*sometimes cap.*) **1.** *Embryol.* an embryonic area capable of forming a structure: the primordium, germ, or bud. **2.** *Psychol.* an inherited predisposition to certain traits or to a particular character development. [1890–95; < G *Anlage* foundation, basis, as n. deriv. of *anlegen* to lay on or out, apply, equiv. to *an-* ON + *legen* to LAY[1]]

an•laut (än′lout′), *n., pl.* **-lau•te** (-lou′tə), **-lauts.** *Ling.* **1.** initial position in a word, esp. as a conditioning environment in sound change. **2.** a sound in this position. Cf. **auslaut, inlaut.** [1880–85; < G, equiv. to *an-* ON + *Laut* sound, as n. deriv. of *anlauten* to begin (with a given sound)]

Ann (an), *n.* a female given name, form of **Anna.**

ann., **1.** annals. **2.** annuity. **3.** years. [< L *annī*]

an•na (ä′nə), *n.* **1.** a former cupronickel coin of Pakistan, the 16th part of a rupee: last issued in 1960. **2.** a former cupronickel coin of India, the 16th part of a rupee. [1720–30; < Hindi *ānā*]

An•na (an′ə), *n.* **1.** *Douay Bible.* Hannah. **2.** a female given name: from a Hebrew word meaning "grace."

An•na•ba (an nä′bə), *n.* a seaport in NE Algeria: site of Hippo Regius. 152,006. Formerly, **Bône.**

An•na•bel (an′ə bel′), *n.* a female given name. Also, **An′na•belle′.**

an•na•berg•ite (an′ə bûr′gīt), *n.* a mineral, hydrous nickel arsenate, $Ni_3As_2O_8·8H_2O$, occurring in apple-green masses and isomorphous with erythrite. [named after *Annaberg,* a town in E Germany where first found; see -ITE[1]]

An′na Chris′tie (kris′tē), a play (1921) by Eugene O'Neill.

An Na•fud (an′ na fo͞od′). See **Nefud Desert.**

An•na I•va•nov•na (ä′nə ē vä′nəv nə), 1693–1740, empress of Russia 1730–40.

An-Na•jaf (an naj′af), *n.* Najaf.

An•na Ka•ren•i•na (an′ə kə ren′ə nə; *Russ.* ä′nə ku ʀʏe′nyi nə), a novel (1875–76) by Leo Tolstoy.

an•nal•ist (an′l ist), *n.* a chronicler of events, esp. yearly ones; historian. [1605–15; ANNAL(S) + -IST, or < F *annaliste*] —**an′nal•is′tic,** *adj.* —**an′nal•is′ti•cal•ly,** *adv.*

an•nals (an′lz), *n.* (*used with a plural v.*) **1.** a record of events, esp. a yearly record, usually in chronological order. **2.** historical records generally: *the annals of war.* **3.** a periodical publication containing the formal reports of an organization or learned field. [1555–65; (< MF) < L *annālēs (librī)* lit., yearly (books), pl. of *annālis* continuing for a year, annual, equiv. to *ann(us)* a year + *ālis* -AL[1]]
—**Syn. 1, 2.** chronicles, history.

An•nam (ə nam′), *n.* a former kingdom and French protectorate along the E coast of French Indochina: now part of Vietnam. Also, **Anam.**

An•na•mese (an′ə mēz′, -mēs′), *adj., n., pl.* **-mese.** —*adj.* **1.** of or pertaining to Annam, its people, or their language. —*n.* Also, **An•nam•ite** (an′ə mīt′). **2.** a native of Annam. **3.** former name of the language **Vietnamese.** [1820–30; ANNAM + -ESE]

An•nap•o•lis (ə nap′ə lis), *n.* a seaport in and the capital of Maryland, in the central part, on Chesapeake Bay: U.S. Naval Academy. 31,740.

Annap′olis Roy′al, a town in W Nova Scotia, in SE Canada, on an arm of the Bay of Fundy: the first settlement in Canada 1605. 738. Formerly, **Port Royal.**

An•na•pur•na (an′ə po͝or′nə, -pûr′-), *n.* **1.** *Hinduism.* Devi (def. 2). **2.** a mountain in N Nepal, in the Himalayas. 26,503 ft. (8078 m). Also, **Anapurna.**

Ann Ar•bor (an är′bər), a city in SE Michigan. 107,316.

An•na•tol (an′ə tōl′), *n.* a male given name.

an•nat•to (ə nat′ō, ə nä′tō), *n., pl.* **-tos. 1.** a small tree, *Bixa orellana,* of tropical America. **2.** Also, **arnatto.** a yellowish-red dye obtained from the pulp enclosing the seeds of this tree, used for coloring fabrics, butter, varnish, etc. Also, **anatto.** Also called **achiote.** [1675–85; < Carib]

Anne (an), *n.* **1.** 1665–1714, queen of England 1702–14 (daughter of James II of England). **2.** a female given name, form of **Anna.**

an•neal (ə nēl′), *v.t.* **1.** to heat (glass, earthenware, metals, etc.) to remove or prevent internal stress. **2.** to free from internal stress by heating and gradually cooling. **3.** to toughen or temper. **4.** *Biochem.* to recombine (nucleic acid strands) at low temperature after separating by heat. **5.** to fuse colors onto (a vitreous or metallic surface) by heating. —*n.* **6.** an act, instance, or product of annealing. [bef. 1000; ME *anelen,* OE *anǣlan* to kindle, equiv. to *an-* ON + *ǣlan* to burn, akin to *āl* fire] —**an•neal′er,** *n.*

Anne′ Bol•eyn′ (bo͝o lin′, bo͝ol′in). See **Boleyn, Anne.**

an•nec•tent (ə nek′tənt), *adj. Zool.* connecting or linking, as a group of animals transitional between two other species, families, classes, etc. Also, **an•nec′tant.** [1820–30; < L *annectent-* (s. of *annectēns* tying to, prp. of *annectere*), equiv. to *an-* AN-[2] + *nect-* bind + *-ent-* -ENT]

An•ne•cy (anə sē′), *n.* a city in and the capital of Haute-Savoie, in SE France. 54,954.

Anne de Beau•jeu (*Fr.* an′ də bō zhœ′). See **Anne of France.**

an•ne•lid (an′l id), *n.* **1.** any segmented worm of the phylum Annelida, including the earthworms, leeches, and various marine forms. —*adj.* **2.** belonging or pertaining to the Annelida. Also, **an•nel•i•dan** (ə nel′i dn). [1825–35; see ANNELIDA]

An•nel•i•da (ə nel′i də), *n.* the phylum comprising the annelids. [1825–35; < NL, equiv. to *annel-* (< F *annelés* lit., ringed ones, pl. ptp. of *anneler* to ring, deriv. of OF *an(n)el* ring < L *ānellus,* dim. of *ānus* ring, ANUS) + *-ida* -ID[2]]

An•nen•sky (ə nen′skē; *Russ.* ä′nyin skyə), *n.* **In•no•ken•ty Fyo•do•ro•vich** (ē nu kyen′ti fyô′də ʀə vyich), 1856–1909, Russian poet. Also, **An•nen′ski.**

Anne′ of Aus′tria, 1601–66, queen consort of Louis XIII of France: regent during minority of her son Louis XIV.

Anne′ of Bohe′mia, 1366–94, queen consort of Richard II of England.

Anne′ of Brit′tany, 1477–1514, wife of Maximilian I of Austria 1490–91; queen consort of Charles VIII of France 1491–98; queen consort of Louis XII of France 1499–1514. French, **Anne de Bre•tagne** (an də bʀə tan′yᵊ).

Anne′ of Cleves′, 1515–57, fourth wife of Henry VIII of England.

Anne′ of Den′mark, 1574–1619, queen consort of James I of England.

Anne′ of France′, (*Anne de Beaujeu*) 1460–1522, daughter of Louis XI of France: regent during the minority of her brother Charles VIII 1483–91.

An•nette (ə net′, a net′; *Fr.* a net′), *n.* a female given name, form of **Anne.**

an•nex (*v.* ə neks′, an′eks; *n.* an′eks, -iks), *v.t.* **1.** to attach, append, or add, esp. to something larger or more important. **2.** to incorporate (territory) into the domain of a city, country, or state: *Germany annexed part of Czechoslovakia.* **3.** to take or appropriate, esp. without permission. **4.** to attach as an attribute, condition, or consequence. —*n.* Also, *esp. Brit.,* **an′nexe. 5.** something annexed. **6.** a subsidiary building or an addition to a building: *The emergency room is in the annex of the main building.* **7.** something added to a document; appendix; supplement: *an annex to a treaty.* [1350–1400; (v.) ME < AF, OF *annexer* < ML *annexāre,* deriv. of L *annexus* tied to, ptp. of *annectere* (see ANNECTENT); (n.) < F *annexe* or n. use of v.] —**an•nex′a•ble,** *adj.*

an•nex•a•tion (an′ik sā′shən, -ek-), *n.* **1.** the act or an instance of annexing, esp. new territory. **2.** the fact of being annexed. **3.** something annexed. [1605–15; < ML *annexātiōn-* (s. of *annexātiō*), equiv. to *annexāt(us)* joined to (ptp. of *annexāre;* see ANNEX, -ATE[1]) + *-iōn-* -ION] —**an′nex•a′tion•al,** *adj.*

an•nex•a•tion•ism (an′ik sā′shə niz′əm, an′ek-), *n.* the theory or practice of taking over another country's

CONCISE PRONUNCIATION KEY: act, cāpe, dâre, pärt; set, ēqual; if, īce; ox, ōver, ôrder, oil, bo͝ok, bo͞ot, out; up, ûrge; child; sing; shoe; thin, *that;* zh as in *treasure.* ə = *a* as in *alone, e* as in *system, i* as in *easily, o* as in *gallop, u* as in *circus;* ᵊ as in *fire* (fīᵊr), *hour* (ouᵊr). l and n can serve as syllabic consonants, as in *cradle* (krād′l), and *button* (but′n). See the full key inside the front cover.

territory, esp. by force. [1840–50; ANNEXATION + -ISM] —**an′nex·a′tion·ist,** *n., adj.*

An Nhon (än′ nôn′), a city in S central Vietnam. 117,000. Formerly, **Binh Dinh.**

An·nie (an′ē), *n.* a female given name, form of **Ann, Anna,** or **Anne.**

An′nie Oak′ley (ōk′lē), a free ticket, as to a theater; pass. [allegedly so called because such tickets, punched to prevent resale, resembled the playing cards used as targets by Annie OAKLEY]

an·ni·hi·la·ble (ə nī′ə lə bəl), *adj.* that can be annihilated. [1670–80; ANNIHIL(ATE) + -ABLE] —**an·ni′hi·la·bil′i·ty,** *n.*

an·ni·hi·late (ə nī′ə lāt′), *v.t.,* **-lat·ed, -lat·ing. 1.** to reduce to utter ruin or nonexistence; destroy utterly: *The heavy bombing almost annihilated the city.* **2.** to destroy the collective existence or main body of; wipe out: *to annihilate an army.* **3.** to annul; make void: *to annihilate a law.* **4.** to cancel the effect of; nullify. **5.** to defeat completely; vanquish: *Our basketball team annihilated the visiting team.* [1350–1400; ME *adnichilat(e)* destroyed < LL *annihilātus* brought to nothing, annihilated (ptp. of *annihilāre*) (L *an-* AN-² + *nihil* nothing + *-ātus* -ATE¹)] —**an·ni·hi·la·tive** (ə nī′ə lā′tiv, -ə lə-), **an·ni·hi·la·to·ry** (ə nī′ə lə tôr′ē, -tōr′ē), *adj.*
—**Syn. 1.** ravage, devastate, desolate. **1, 2.** smash, obliterate, demolish.

an·ni·hi·la·tion (ə nī′ə lā′shən), *n.* **1.** the act or an instance of annihilating. **2.** the state of being annihilated; extinction; destruction. **3.** *Physics.* **a.** Also called **pair annihilation.** the process in which a particle and antiparticle unite, annihilate each other, and produce one or more photons. Cf. **positronium. b.** the conversion of rest mass into energy in the form of electromagnetic radiation. [1630–40; (< F) < LL *annihilātiōn-* (s. of *annihilātiō*). See ANNIHILATE, -ION]

annihila′tion radia′tion, *Physics.* electromagnetic radiation produced by the coalescence and mutual annihilation of a positron and an electron, each pair forming two photons having a minimum energy of 0.5 million electron volts each. [1960–65]

an·ni·hi·la·tor (ə nī′ə lā′tər), *n.* **1.** a person or thing that annihilates. **2.** *Math.* the set of all linear functionals that map to zero all elements of a given subset of a vector space. [1690–1700; ANNIHILATE + -OR²]

An·nis·ton (an′ə stən), *n.* a city in E Alabama. 29,523.

anniv., anniversary.

an·ni·ver·sa·ry (an′ə vûr′sə rē), *n., pl.* **-ries,** *adj.* —*n.* **1.** the yearly recurrence of the date of a past event: *the tenth anniversary of their marriage.* **2.** the celebration or commemoration of such a date. **3.** See **wedding anniversary.** —*adj.* **4.** returning or recurring each year; annual. **5.** pertaining to an anniversary: *an anniversary gift. Abbr.:* anniv. [1200–50; ME *anniversarie* (< AF) < ML (*diēs*) *anniversāria* anniversary (day), L *anniversārius* recurring yearly, equiv. to *anni-* (comb. form of *annus* year) + *vers(us)* turned, ptp. of *vertere* (*vert-* turn + *-tus* ptp. suffix) + *-ārius* -ARY]

anniver′sary reac′tion, a psychological reaction, as depression, occurring at a regularly fixed time and associated with the recollection of an emotionally upsetting past experience, as loss of a loved one.

an·no ae·ta·tis su·ae (än′nō ī tä′tis sōō′ī; *Eng.* an′ō i tā′tis sōō′ē), *Latin.* in the year of his age; in the year of her age.

an·no Dom·i·ni (an′ō dom′ə nī′, -nē′, ä′nō). See **A.D.**

an·no He·ji·rae (an′ō hi jī′rē, hej′ə rē′, ä′nō). See **A.H.** [1885–90]

an·no mun·di (än′nō mōōn′dē; *Eng.* an′ō mun′dī, -dē), *Latin.* in the year of the world.

an·no·na (ə nō′nə), *n.* any of various trees and shrubs of the genus *Annona,* native to tropical America, and grown for their edible fruits. Cf. **annona family.** [< NL < AmerSp *anona, anon,* allegedly < Arawak (Hispaniola)]

an·no·na·ceous (an′ə nā′shəs), *adj.* belonging to the plant family Annonaceae. Cf. **annona family.** [< NL *Annonace(ae)* (see ANNONA, -ACEAE) + -OUS]

anno′na fam′ily, the plant family Annonaceae, characterized by tropical trees and shrubs bearing simple alternate leaves, solitary or clustered dull-colored flowers, and edible fruit, and including the cherimoya, custard apple, and sweetsop.

an·no reg·ni (än′nō reg′nē; *Eng.* an′ō reg′nī, -nē), *Latin.* in the year of the reign.

annot., 1. annotated. **2.** annotation. **3.** annotator.

an·no·tate (an′ə tāt′), *v.,* **-tat·ed, -tat·ing.** —*v.t.* **1.** to supply with critical or explanatory notes; comment upon in notes: *to annotate the works of Shakespeare.* —*v.i.* **2.** to make annotations or notes. [1725–35; < L *annotātus* noted down (ptp. of *annotāre*), equiv. to *an-* AN-² + *notātus* noted, marked; see NOTE, -ATE¹] —**an′·no·ta′tive, an·no·ta·to·ry** (an′ə tā′tə rē, -tə tôr′ē, -tōr′ē; ə nō′tə tôr′ē, -tōr′ē), *adj.* —**an′no·ta′tor,** *n.*

an·no·tat·ed (an′ə tā′tid), *adj.* supplied with or containing explanatory notes, textual comments, etc.: *an annotated edition of Milton's poetry.* [1800–10; ANNOTATE + -ED²]

an·no·ta·tion (an′ə tā′shən), *n.* **1.** a critical or explanatory note or body of notes added to a text. **2.** the act of annotating. **3.** note (def. 1). *Abbr.:* annot. [1425–75; < L *annotātiōn-* (s. of *annotātiō*). See ANNOTATE, -ION]

an·not·i·nous (ə not′n əs, a not′-), *adj. Bot.* one year old. [1830–40; < L *annōtinus,* equiv. to *annō* (in the) year, abl. of *annus* year + *-tinus* suffix forming adjs. from advs. of time (cf. PRISTINE); see -OUS]

an·nounce (ə nouns′), *v.,* **-nounced, -nounc·ing.** —*v.t.* **1.** to make known publicly or officially; proclaim; give notice of: *to announce a special sale.* **2.** to state the approach or presence of: *to announce guests; to announce dinner.* **3.** to make known to the mind or senses. **4.** to serve as an announcer of: *The mayor announced the program.* **5.** to state; declare. **6.** to state in advance; declare beforehand. **7.** to write, or have printed, and send a formal declaration of an event, esp. a social event, as a wedding. —*v.i.* **8.** to be employed or serve as an announcer, esp. of a radio or television broadcast: *She announces for the local radio station.* **9.** to declare one's candidacy, as for a political office (usually fol. by *for*): *We are hoping that he will announce for governor.* [1490–1500; < MF *anoncer* < L *annūntiāre,* equiv. to *an-* AN-² + *nūntiāre* to announce, deriv. of *nūntius* messenger] —**an·nounce′a·ble,** *adj.*
—**Syn. 1.** declare, report, promulgate. ANNOUNCE, PROCLAIM, PUBLISH mean to communicate something in a formal or public way. To ANNOUNCE is to give out news, often of something expected in the future: *to announce a lecture series.* To PROCLAIM is to make a widespread and general announcement of something of public interest: *to proclaim a holiday.* To PUBLISH is to make public in an official way, now esp. by printing: *to publish a book.*

an·nounce·ment (ə nouns′mənt), *n.* **1.** public or formal notice announcing something: *The announcement appeared in the newspapers.* **2.** the act of announcing. **3.** a short message or commercial, esp. a commercial spoken on radio or television. **4.** a card or piece of formal stationery containing a formal declaration of an event, as a wedding. [1790–1800; < F *anoncement.* See ANNOUNCE, -MENT]

an·nounc·er (ə noun′sər), *n.* a person who announces, esp. one who introduces programs, presents news items, reads advertisements, and does other similar assignments over radio or television. [1605–15; 1920–25 in radio use; ANNOUNCE + -ER¹]

an·no ur·bis con·di·tae (än′nō ŏŏr′bis kōn′di tī′; *Eng.* an′ō ûr′bis kon′di tē′), *Latin.* See **A.U.C.** (def. 2).

an·noy (ə noi′), *v.t.* **1.** to disturb or bother (a person) in a way that displeases, troubles, or slightly irritates. **2.** to molest; harm. —*v.i.* **3.** to be bothersome or troublesome. —*n.* **4.** *Archaic.* an annoyance. [1250–1300; (v.) ME *an(n)oien, enoien* < AF, OF *anoier, anuier* to molest, harm, tire < LL *inodiāre* to cause aversion, from L phrase *mihi in odiō est . . .* I dislike . . .; cf. IN-², ODIUM, ENNUI, NOISOME; (n.) ME *a(n)noi, ennoi* < AF, OF *a(n)nui,* etc., deriv. of the v.] —**an·noy′er,** *n.*
—**Syn. 1.** harass, pester. See **bother, worry.** —**Ant. 1.** comfort, calm, soothe.

an·noy·ance (ə noi′əns), *n.* **1.** a person or thing that annoys; nuisance: *Unwanted visitors are an annoyance.* **2.** an act or instance of annoying. **3.** the feeling of being annoyed. [1350–1400; ME < MF; see ANNOY, -ANCE]

an·noy·ing (ə noi′ing), *adj.* causing annoyance; irritatingly bothersome: *annoying delays.* [1325–75; ME; see ANNOY, -ING²] —**an·noy′ing·ly,** *adv.* —**an·noy′·ing·ness,** *n.*

an·nu·al (an′yōō əl), *adj.* **1.** of, for, or pertaining to a year; yearly: *annual salary.* **2.** occurring or returning once a year: *an annual celebration.* **3.** *Bot.* living only one growing season, as beans or corn. **4.** performed or executed during a year: *the annual course of the sun.* **5.** *Entomol.* living or lasting but one season or year, as certain insects or colonies of insects. —*n.* **6.** *Bot.* a plant living only one year or season. **7.** a book, report, etc., published annually. [1350–1400; < LL *annuālis,* equiv. to L *annu(us)* yearly (deriv. of *annus* circuit of the sun, year) + *-ālis* -AL¹; r. ME *annuel* < AF < L] —**an′nu·al·ly,** *adv.*

an·nu·al·ize (an′yōō ə līz′), *v.,* **-ized, -iz·ing.** —*v.t.* **1.** to calculate for or as for an entire year: *Investors earned an annualized rate of seven percent paid quarterly.* —*v.i.* **2.** to be annualized. Also, *esp. Brit.,* **an′nu·al·ise′.** [ANNUAL + -IZE]

an′nual par′allax. See under **parallax** (def. 2).

an′nual report′, a document reporting to stockholders on management and operations and containing fiscal information, published yearly by a publicly held corporation as required by federal law.

an′nual ring′, an annual formation of wood in plants, consisting of two concentric layers, one of springwood and one of summerwood. See diag. under **stem**¹. Also called **growth ring, tree ring.** [1875–80]

an′nual wage′. See **guaranteed annual wage.**

an·nu·i·tant (ə nōō′i tnt, ə nyōō′-), *n.* a person who receives an annuity. [1710–20; ANNUIT(Y) + -ANT]

an·nu·it coep·tis (än′nōō it koip′tis; *Eng.* an′yōō it sep′tis), *Latin.* He (God) has favored our undertakings: a motto on the reverse of the great seal of the U.S. (adapted from Vergil's *Aeneid* IX:625).

an·nu·i·ty (ə nōō′i tē, ə nyōō′-), *n., pl.* **-ties. 1.** a specified income payable at stated intervals for a fixed or a contingent period, often for the recipient's life, in consideration of a stipulated premium paid either in prior installment payments or in a single payment. **2.** the right to receive such an income, or the duty to make such a payment or payments. [1400–50; late ME < AF *annuité, annualté* < ML *annuitās,* equiv. to L *annu(us)* yearly (deriv. of *annus* year) + *-itās* -ITY]

annu′ity cer′tain, *pl.* **annuities certain.** an annuity payable for a certain number of years regardless of any contingency.

an·nul (ə nul′), *v.t.,* **-nulled, -nul·ling. 1.** (esp. of laws or other established rules, usages, etc.) to make void or null; abolish; cancel; invalidate: *to annul a marriage.* **2.** to reduce to nothing; obliterate. **3.** to cancel (a regularly scheduled train, plane, social event, etc.) for one day or one time only. [1375–1425; late ME < AF *annuler* < LL *adnūllāre* render null (calque of Gk *exoudeneîn*), equiv. to *ad-* AD- + *-nullāre,* v. deriv. of L *nūllus* no, not any] —**an·nul′la·ble,** *adj.*
—**Syn. 1.** nullify; rescind, repeal.

an·nu·lar (an′yə lər), *adj.* **1.** having the form of a ring. **2.** (of a carpenter's nail) having a series of concentric grooves to improve holding power. [1565–75; < L *annulāris,* equiv. to *annul(us)* ring (var. of *ānulus*) + *-āris* -AR¹] —**an′nu·lar′i·ty,** *n.* —**an′nu·lar·ly,** *adv.*

an′nular clock′, a clock in the form of a vase, ball, etc., having the hours painted on a ring rotating beneath a pointer.

an′nular eclipse′, an eclipse of the sun in which a portion of its surface is visible as a ring surrounding the dark moon. Cf. **total eclipse.** [1720–30]

an′nular gear′, *Mach.* See **internal gear.**

an′nular lig′ament, *Anat.* the ligamentous envelope surrounding a part, as the joints of the wrist or ankle or the head of the radius. [1835–45]

an·nu·late (an′yə lit, -lāt′), *adj.* **1.** formed of ringlike segments, as an annelid worm. **2.** having rings or ringlike bands. Also, **an′nu·lat′ed.** [1820–30; < L *annulātus,* var. of *ānulātus* ringed, equiv. to *ānul(us)* ring + *-ātus* -ATE¹] —**an′nu·la′tion,** *n.*

an·nu·let (an′yə lit), *n.* **1.** Also called **bandelet, bandlet, square and rabbet.** *Archit.* an encircling band, molding, or fillet, as on the shaft of a column. **2.** *Entomol.* a ring, usually colored, around or on the surface of an organ. **3.** *Heraldry.* a ring, represented as a voided roundel, used esp. as the cadence mark of a fifth son. [1565–75; < L *annul(us)* ring (see ANNULUS) + -ET; r. earlier *anlet* < AF *anelet,* dim. of OF *anel* ring < L *ānellus* ring]

an·nul·ment (ə nul′mənt), *n.* **1.** the act of annulling, esp. the formal declaration that annuls a marriage. **2.** *Psychoanal.* a mental process by which unpleasant or painful ideas are abolished from the mind. [1485–95; ANNUL + -MENT or < MF *annulement*]

an·nu·lose (an′yə lōs′), *adj.* furnished with or composed of rings: *annulose animals.* [1820–30; < NL *annulōsus.* See ANNULUS, -OSE¹]

an·nu·lus (an′yə ləs), *n., pl.* **-li** (-lī′), **-lus·es. 1.** a ring; a ringlike part, band, or space. **2.** *Geom.* the space between two concentric circles on a plane. **3.** the veil remnant on a mushroom stalk. See illus. under **mushroom. 4.** a growth ring, as on the cross section of a tree trunk, that can be used to estimate age. [1555–65; < L, var. of *ānulus,* equiv. to *ān(us)* ring + *-ulus* -ULE]

an·nun·ci·ate (ə nun′sē āt′), *v.t.,* **-at·ed, -at·ing.** to announce. [1350–1400; < ML *annūnciātus,* for L *annūntiātus,* ptp. of *annūntiāre* to make known. See ANNOUNCE, -ATE¹] —**an·nun′ci·a·ble,** *adj.* —**an·nun′ci·a′tive, an·nun·ci·a·to·ry** (ə nun′sē ə tôr′ē, -tōr′ē), *adj.*

an·nun·ci·a·tion (ə nun′sē ā′shən), *n.* **1.** (*often cap.*) the announcement by the angel Gabriel to the Virgin Mary of her conception of Christ. **2.** (*cap.*) a representation of this in art. **3.** (*cap.*) Also called **Lady Day.** the church festival on March 25 in memory of this. **4.** an act or instance of announcing; proclamation: *the annunciation of a new foreign policy.* [1350–1400; ME *an(n)unciacio(u)n* (< AF) < ML *annūnciātiōn-,* s. of *annūnciātiō,* for LL *adnūntiātiō;* see ANNUNCIATE, -ION]

Annuncia′tion lil′y. See **Madonna lily.** [1875–80]

an·nun·ci·a·tor (ə nun′sē ā′tər), *n.* **1.** an announcer. **2.** a signaling apparatus, generally used in conjunction with a buzzer, that displays a visual indication when energized by electric current. [1745–55; *annūntiātor;* see ANNUNCIATE, -TOR] —**an·nun·ci·a·to·ry** (ə nun′sē ə tôr′ē, -tōr′ē), *adj.*

An·nun·zio, d′ (dän nōōn′tsyô), **Ga·bri·e·le** (gä′brē e′le). See **D'Annunzio, Gabriele.**

an·nus mi·ra·bi·lis (än′nŏŏs mi rä′bi lis; *Eng.* an′əs mə rab′ə lis), *pl.* ***an·ni mi·ra·bi·les*** (än′nē mi rä′bi les′; *Eng.* an′ī mə rab′ə lēz′, an′ē), *Latin.* year of wonders; wonderful year.

Ann·wfn (än′ŏŏvn), *n. Welsh Myth.* the other world; the land of fairies. Also, **Ann·wn** (än′ŏŏn).

ano-¹, a combining form of **anus** or **anal:** *anorectal.*

ano-², a combining form meaning "up," "upper," "upward": *anoopsia.* [< Gk, comb. form of *ánō*]

a·no·a (ə nō′ə), *n.* a small forest buffalo, *Bubalus* (*Anoa*) *depressicornis,* of the island of Celebes, having a brown coat and straight, sharp-tipped horns: an endangered species. Also called **dwarf buffalo.** [1840–50; < Indonesian Malay < Makassarese *anuang*]

an·ode (an′ōd), *n.* **1.** the electrode or terminal by which current enters an electrolytic cell, voltaic cell, battery, etc. **2.** the negative terminal of a voltaic cell or battery. **3.** the positive terminal, electrode, or element of an electron tube or electrolytic cell. [1825–35; < Gk *ánodos* way up, equiv. to *an-* AN-³ + *hodós* way, road]

an′ode dark′ space′, *Physics.* the dark region between the anode glow and the anode in a vacuum tube, occurring when the pressure is low.

an′ode glow′, *Physics.* the luminous region between the positive column and the anode dark space in a vacuum tube, occurring when the pressure is low.

an′ode ray′, *Physics.* See **positive ray.**

an′ode resist′ance, *Electronics.* (of a vacuum tube at a given level of output) the ratio of a small change in voltage of the anode to the corresponding small change in anode current. Also called **plate resistance.**

an·od·ic (an od′ik), *adj.* pertaining to an anode or the phenomena in its vicinity. [1830–40; ANODE + -IC] —**an·od′i·cal·ly, an·od·al·ly** (a nōd′l ē), *adv.*

an·o·dize (an′ə dīz′), *v.t.,* **-dized, -diz·ing.** *Chem.* to coat a metal, esp. magnesium or aluminum, with a protective film by chemical or electrolytic means. Also, *esp. Brit.,* **an′o·dise′.** [1930–35; ANODE + -IZE] —**an′o·di·za′tion,** *n.*

an·o·don·tia (an′ə don′shə, -shē ə), *n. Dentistry.* congenital absence of teeth. [AN-¹ + -ODONT + -IA]

CONCISE ETYMOLOGY KEY: <, descended or borrowed from; >, whence; b., blend of, blended; c., cognate with; cf., compare; deriv., derivative; equiv., equivalent; imit., imitative; obl., oblique; r., replacing; s., stem; sp., spelling, spelled; resp., respelling, respelled; trans., translation; ?, origin unknown; *, unattested; ‡, probably earlier than. See the full key inside the front cover.

an•o•dyne (an′ə dīn′), *n.* **1.** a medicine that relieves or allays pain. **2.** anything that relieves distress or pain: *The music was an anodyne to his grief.* —*adj.* **3.** relieving pain. **4.** soothing to the mind or feelings. [1535–45; < L *anōdynus* < Gk *anṓdynos* painless, equiv. to *an-* AN-[1] + *ōdyn-* (s. of *odýnē* pain, with lengthening of *o*) + -*os* adj. suffix] —**an•o•dyn•ic** (an′ə din′ik), *adj.*

an•o•e•sis (an′ō ē′sis), *n.* a state of mind consisting of pure sensation or emotion without cognitive content. [1900–05; A-[6] + NOESIS] —**an•o•et•ic** (an′ō et′ik), *adj.*

an•oes•trous (an es′trəs, -ē′strəs), *adj.* anestrous.

an•oes•trus (an es′trəs, -ē′strəs), *n.* anestrus.

a•noi•a (ə noi′ə), *n.* extreme mental deficiency. Also called **an•o•e•sia** (an′ō ē′shə, -shē ə, -zē ə). [< Gk, equiv. to *áno(os)* not understanding (*a-* A-[6] + *nó(os)* mind + -*os* adj. suffix) + -*ia* -IA]

a•noint (ə noint′), *v.t.* **1.** to rub or sprinkle on; apply an unguent, ointment, or oily liquid to. **2.** to smear with any liquid. **3.** to consecrate or make sacred in a ceremony that includes the token applying of oil: *He anointed the new high priest.* **4.** to dedicate to the service of God. [1300–50; ME *anoynten,* deriv. of *anoynt, enoynt* (ptp.) < OF *enoint* < L *inūnctus* anointed (ptp. of *inungere*), equiv. to *in-* IN-[2] + *ung-* smear with oil + -*tus* ptp. suffix] —**a•noint′er,** *n.* —**a•noint′ment,** *n.*

anoint′ing of the sick′, *Rom. Cath. Ch.* a sacrament consisting of anointment with oil and the recitation of prayer, administered by a priest to a person who is very ill or dying. Formerly, **extreme unction.** Also called **last rites.** [1880–85]

A•no•ka (ə nō′kə), *n.* a city in E Minnesota. 15,634.

a•no•le (ə nō′lē), *n.* any of numerous chiefly insectivorous New World lizards of the genus *Anolis,* related to the iguana, that have the ability to change the color of their skin among a wide range of green and brown shades. See illus. under **lizard.** [1895–1900; var. of *anoli* < Carib]

an•o•lyte (an′l īt′), *n.* (in electrolysis) the portion of the electrolyte in the immediate vicinity of the anode. [1885–90; ANO(DE) + (ELECTRO)LYTE]

a•nom•a•lism (ə nom′ə liz′əm), *n. Rare.* **1.** the state or quality of being anomalous. **2.** an anomaly. [1660–70; < Gk *anṓmal(os)* ANOMALOUS + -ISM]

a•nom•a•lis•tic (ə nom′ə lis′tik), *adj.* of or pertaining to an anomaly. [1760–70; ANOMAL(Y) + -ISTIC] —**a•nom′a•lis′ti•cal•ly,** *adv.*

anom′alis′tic month′, *Astron.* See under **month** (def. 5). [1760–70]

anom′alis′tic year′, *Astron.* the average interval between consecutive passages of the earth through the perihelion, equivalent to 365.26 days. [1870–75]

a•nom•a•lous (ə nom′ə ləs), *adj.* **1.** deviating from or inconsistent with the common order, form, or rule; irregular; abnormal: *Advanced forms of life may be anomalous in the universe.* **2.** not fitting into a common or familiar type, classification, or pattern; unusual: *He held an anomalous position in the art world.* **3.** incongruous or inconsistent. **4.** *Gram.* irregular. [1640–50; (< ML, LL *anōmalus*) < Gk *anṓmalos* irregular, equiv. to *an-* AN-[1] + *homalós* even, with *ō* by analogy with other Gk privatives (cf. ANOPHELES); see HOMO-, -OUS] —**a•nom′a•lous•ly,** *adv.* —**a•nom′a•lous•ness,** *n.*

anom′alous disper′sion, *Physics.* a sudden change in the refractive index of a material for wavelengths in the vicinity of absorption bands in the spectrum of the material. [1880–85]

anom′alous Zee′man effect′, *Physics, Optics.* See under **Zeeman effect.**

a•nom•a•ly (ə nom′ə lē), *n., pl.* **-lies.** **1.** a deviation from the common rule, type, arrangement, or form. **2.** someone or something anomalous: *With his quiet nature, he was an anomaly in his exuberant family.* **3.** an odd, peculiar, or strange condition, situation, quality, etc. **4.** an incongruity or inconsistency. **5.** *Astron.* a quantity measured in degrees, defining the position of an orbiting body with respect to the point at which it is nearest to or farthest from its primary. **6.** *Meteorol.* the amount of deviation of a meteorological quantity from the accepted normal value of that quantity. **7.** *Gram.* irregularity. [1565–75; < L *anōmalia* < Gk *anōmalía,* equiv. to *anṓmal(os)* ANOMALOUS + -*ia* -IA]
—**Syn. 1, 2.** abnormality, exception, peculiarity.

a•no•mi•a (ə nō′mē ə), *n. Med.* the inability to name objects or to recognize the written or spoken names of objects. [< NL, irreg. < Gk *a-* A-[6] + L *nōm(en)* NAME + -*ia* -IA]

an•o•mie (an′ə mē′), *n. Sociol.* a state or condition of individuals or society characterized by a breakdown or absence of social norms and values, as in the case of uprooted people. Also, **an′o•my.** [1930–35; < F < Gk *anomía* lawlessness. See A-[6], -NOMY] —**a•nom•ic** (ə nom′ik), *adj.*

an•o•mite (an′ə mīt′), *n. Mineral.* a variety of mica, similar to biotite but differing in optical orientation. [< Gk *ánom(os)* lawless (*a-* A-[6] + *nóm(os)* law + -*os* adj. suffix) + -ITE[1]]

a•non (ə non′), *adv.* **1.** in a short time; soon. **2.** at another time. **3.** *Archaic.* at once; immediately. **4. ever and anon,** now and then; occasionally. [bef. 1000; ME *anon, anoon,* OE *on āne* in ONE (course), i.e., straightaway]

anon., **1.** anonymous. **2.** anonymously. [1730–40]

an•o•nych•i•a (an′ə nik′ē ə), *n. Med.* congenital absence of the nails. [< NL < Gk *an-* AN-[1] + *onych-* (s. of *ónyx* nail; see ONYX) + -*ia* -IA]

an•o•nym (an′ə nim), *n.* **1.** an assumed or false name. **2.** an anonymous person or publication. [1805–15; < F *anonyme* < Gk *anṓnymos* ANONYMOUS]

an•o•nym•i•ty (an′ə nim′i tē), *n., pl.* **-ties.** **1.** the state or quality of being anonymous. **2.** an anonymous person: *some fine poetry attributed to anonymities.* [1810–20; ANONYM(OUS) + -ITY, or < F *anonymité*]

a•non•y•mous (ə non′ə məs), *adj.* **1.** without any name acknowledged, as that of author, contributor, or the like: *an anonymous letter to the editor; an anonymous donation.* **2.** of unknown name; whose name is withheld: *an anonymous author.* **3.** lacking individuality, unique character, or distinction: *an endless row of drab, anonymous houses.* [1595–1605; < L *anōnymus* < Gk *anṓnymos,* equiv. to *an-* AN-[1] + -*ōnym(a)* (var. of *ónyma*) -ONYM (earlier (*a*)*n-* with vowel lengthening; cf. ANOPHELES) + -*os* adj. suffix; see -OUS] —**a•non′y•mous•ness,** *n.* —**a•non′y•mous•ly,** *adv.*

a•noph•e•les (ə nof′ə lēz′), *n., pl.* **-les.** any mosquito of the genus *Anopheles,* certain species of which are vectors of the parasite causing malaria in humans, distinguished from other mosquitoes by the absence of breathing tubes in the larvae and by the head-downward stance of the adult while resting or feeding. Cf. **culex.** [1895–1900; < NL < Gk *anōphelḗs* useless, hurtful, harmful, equiv. to *an-* AN-[1] + -*ōpheles-* var. s. of *óphelos* profit; earlier (*a*)*n-* (with vowel lengthening) + *opheles-,* written in Mycenaean Gk as *nopere*] —**a•noph•e•line** (ə nof′ə lin′, -lin), *adj., n.*

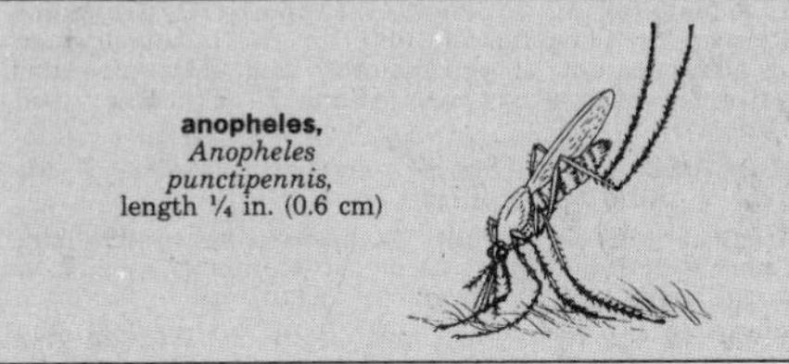
anopheles, *Anopheles punctipennis,* length ¼ in. (0.6 cm)

an•o•pi•a (an ō′pē ə), *n. Ophthalm.* absence of sight, esp. when due to a structural defect in or absence of an eye. [AN-[1] + -OPIA]

an•o•pis•tho•graph (an′ə pis′thə graf′, -gräf′), *n.* a manuscript, parchment, or book having writing on only one side of the leaves. Cf. **opisthograph.** [1870–75; AN-[1] + OPISTHOGRAPH] —**an′o•pis′tho•graph′ic,** *adj.* —**an′o•pis′tho•graph′i•cal•ly,** *adv.*

an•o•rak (an′ə rak′, ä′nə räk′), *n.* **1.** a hooded pullover jacket originally made of fur and worn in the arctic, now made of any weather-resistant fabric. **2.** a jacket patterned after this, made of any weather-resistant material and worn widely. [1920–25; < Inuit (Greenlandic) *annoraaq*]

an•o•rec•tal (an′ə rek′tl), *adj.* of, pertaining to, or associated with the anus and rectum. [ANO-[1] + RECTAL]

an•o•rec•tic (an′ə rek′tik), *adj.* **1.** Also, **an′o•rec′tous.** having no appetite. **2.** causing a loss of appetite. —*n.* **3.** an anorectic substance, as a drug; anorexiant. Also, **an•o•ret•ic** (an′ə ret′ik), **anorexic.** [1895–1900; AN-[1] + ORECTIC]

an•o•rex•i•a (an′ə rek′sē ə), *n.* **1.** loss of appetite and inability to eat. **2.** *Psychiatry.* See **anorexia nervosa.** [1590–1600; < NL < Gk, equiv. to *an-* AN-[1] + *órex(is)* longing (*oreg-* reach after + -*sis* -SIS) + -*ia* -IA]

anorex′ia ner•vo′sa (nûr vō′sə), *Psychiatry.* an eating disorder primarily affecting adolescent girls and young women, characterized by pathological fear of becoming fat, distorted body image, excessive dieting, and emaciation. Cf. **bulimia, bulimarexia.** [1870–75; < NL: nervous anorexia]

an•o•rex•i•ant (an′ə rek′sē ənt, an′ə-), *n. Med.* a substance, as a drug, for causing loss of appetite. [ANOREXI(A) + -ANT]

an•o•rex•ic (an′ə rek′sik), *n.* **1.** a person suffering from anorexia or esp. anorexia nervosa. —*adj.* **2.** anorectic. [1960–65; ANOREX(IA) + -IC]

an•or•gas•mi•a (an′ôr gaz′mē ə), *n.* inability to experience sexual orgasm. Also, **an′or•gas′my.** [AN-[1] + ORGASM + -IA] —**an′or•gas′mic,** *adj.*

an•or•thite (an ôr′thīt), *n. Mineral.* a white or gray feldspar mineral, $CaAl_2Si_2O_8$, calcic plagioclase. [1825–35; AN-[1] + ORTH- + -ITE[1]] —**an•or•thit•ic** (an′ôr thit′ik), *adj.*

an•or•tho•clase (an ôr′thə klās′, -klāz′), *n. Mineral.* a variety of microcline, rich in sodium and sometimes having a play of color: sometimes considered a variety of orthoclase. [AN-[1] + ORTHOCLASE]

an•or•tho•site (an ôr′thə sīt′), *n. Petrol.* a granular plutonic rock composed largely of labradorite or a more calcic feldspar. [1860–65; < F *anorthose* anorthoclase (*an-* AN-[1] + Gk *orthós* straight) + -ITE[1]] —**an•or•tho•sit•ic** (an ô′thə sit′ik), *adj.*

a•no•scope (ā′nə skōp′), *n. Med.* proctoscope. [ANO-[1] + -SCOPE]

an•os•mi•a (an oz′mē ə, -os′-), *n. Pathol.* absence or loss of the sense of smell. [1805–15; < NL < Gk *an-* AN-[1] + *osm(ḗ)* smell (akin to *ózein* to smell) + -*ia* -IA] —**an•os•mat•ic** (an′əz mat′ik), **an•os′mic,** *adj.*

an•oth•er (ə nuth′ər), *adj.* **1.** being one more or more of the same; further; additional: *another piece of cake.* **2.** different; distinct; of a different period, place, or kind: *at another time; another man.* **3.** very similar to; of the same kind or category as: *What we need today is another Thomas Jefferson.* —*pron.* **4.** one more; an additional one: *That first hot dog tasted so good I'd like another.* **5.** a different one; something different: *going from one house to another.* **6.** one like the first: *one copy for her and another for him.* **7.** a person other than oneself or the one specified: *He told her he loved another.* [1175–1225; ME; see AN[1], OTHER]

an•oth•er-guess (ə nuth′ər ges′), *adj. Archaic.* of another kind. [1615–25; earlier *anothergets, anothergates,* orig. as gen. of phrase *another gate* another kind (see GATE[2]); resp. by assoc. with GUESS]

A•nouilh (A nōō′yə), *n.* **Jean** (zhäN), born 1910, French dramatist.

an•our•ous (ə nōōr′əs), *adj.* anurous.

an•ov•u•lant (an ov′yə lənt, -ō′vyə-), *adj.* **1.** of, characterized by, or pertaining to a lack of or suppression of ovulation. —*n.* **2.** a substance that suppresses ovulation. [1965–70; AN-[1] + OVUL(ATE) + -ANT]

an•ov•u•la•tion (an′ov yə lā′shən, -ō vyə-, an ov′yə, -ō′vyə-), *n.* the absence of ovulation. [1965–70; AN-[1] + OVULATION]

an•ov•u•la•to•ry (an ov′yə lə tôr′ē, -tōr′ē, -ō′vyə-), *adj.* **1.** not associated with, not caused by, or not exhibiting ovulation. **2.** inhibiting ovulation. Also, **an•ov•u•lar** (an ov′yə lər, -ō′vyə-). [1930–35; AN-[1] + OVULATE + -ORY[1]]

an•ox•e•mi•a (an′ok sē′mē ə), *n.* a deficiency of oxygen in the arterial blood. Also, **an′ox•ae′mi•a.** [1885–90; AN-[1] + OX(YGEN) + -EMIA] —**an′ox•e′mic, an′ox•ae′mic,** *adj.*

an•ox•i•a (an ok′sē ə, ə nok′-), *n.* **1.** an abnormally low amount of oxygen in the body tissues; hypoxia. **2.** the mental and physical disturbances that occur as a result of hypoxia. [1930–35; AN-[1] + OX(YGEN) + -IA] —**an•ox′ic,** *adj.*

ANPA, American Newspaper Publishers Association.

An•qing (än′ching′), *n. Pinyin.* a city in S Anhui province, in E China, on the Chang Jiang: former capital of Anhui. 160,000. Also, **Anch′ing, Anking.**

ANS, American Name Society.

ans., answer.

an•sa (an′sə), *n., pl.* **-sae** (-sē). **1.** *Archaeol.* a looped handle, esp. of a vase. **2.** *Astron.* either of the apparent extremities of the rings of Saturn or of other planets, esp. when viewed from the earth or from spacecraft under certain conditions, when they look like two handles. [1655–65; < L]

An•sar (an′sär), *n.* (*sometimes l.c.*) (*used with a plural v.*) **1.** the first inhabitants of Medina to accept Islam. **2.** any of those who helped Muhammad after he began his preaching. [< Ar *anṣār,* pl. of *nāṣir* helper] —**An•sar′i•an,** *adj.*

an•sate (an′sāt), *adj.* having a handle or handlelike part. [1890–95; < L *ansātus* having a handle. See ANSA, -ATE[1]]

an′sate cross′, ankh. [1775–85]

An•schau•ung (än′shou ŏŏng′, -əng), *n. Philos.* direct or immediate intuition or perception of sense data with little or no rational interpretation. [1855–60; < G: view, equiv. to *anschau(en)* to view (*an-* on, at + *schauen* to look) + -*ung* -ING[1]]

An•schluss (än′shlŏŏs), *n.* union, esp. the political union of Austria with Germany in 1938. [1920–25; < G: consolidation, joining together, equiv. to *an-* on, to + *Schluss* a closing]

An•selm (an′selm), *n.* **1. Saint,** 1033–1109, archbishop of Canterbury: scholastic theologian and philosopher. **2.** Also, **An•sel** (an′səl, -sel). a male given name: from Germanic words meaning "divine" and "helmet."

an•ser•ine (an′sə rīn′, -rin), *adj.* **1.** of or pertaining to the subfamily Anserinae, of the family Anatidae, comprising the true geese. **2.** resembling a goose; gooselike. **3.** stupid; foolish; silly. Also, **an′ser•ous.** [1830–40; < L *anserīnus* of, pertaining to geese, equiv. to *anser* GOOSE + -*inus* -INE[1]]

An•ser•met (*Fr.* äN seR me′), *n.* **Er•nest** (eR nest′), 1883–1969, Swiss symphony orchestra conductor.

Ans•gar (ans′gär), *n.* **Saint** ("*Apostle of the North*"), 801–865, French Benedictine priest and missionary: patron saint of Scandinavia. Also, **Ans•kar** (an′skär).

Ans•gar•i•us (ans gâr′ē əs), *n.* Latin name of **Ansgar.**

An•shan (än′shän′), *n. Pinyin, Wade-Giles.* a city in E Liaoning province, in NE China. 1,500,000.

ANSI, See **American National Standards Institute.**

An•son (an′sən), *n.* a male given name.

An•so•ni•a (an sō′nē ə, -sōn′yə), *n.* a city in SW Connecticut. 19,039.

an•stoss (*Ger.* än′shtôs), *n., pl.* **-stös•se** (*Ger.* -shtœ sə). (in the philosophy of Fichte) any of the six successive steps by which the absolute ego attains self-knowledge. [< G *Anstoss* impetus, collision]

an•swer (an′sər, än′-), *n.* **1.** a spoken or written reply or response to a question, request, letter, etc.: *He sent an answer to my letter promptly.* **2.** a correct response to a question asked to test one's knowledge. **3.** an equivalent or approximation: *a singing group that tried to be the French answer to the Beatles.* **4.** an action serving as a reply or response: *The answer was a volley of fire.* **5.** a solution to a problem, esp. in mathematics. **6.** a reply to a charge or accusation. **7.** *Law.* a pleading in which a party responds to his or her opponent's statement of position, esp. the defendant's reply to the plaintiff's complaint. **8.** *Music.* the entrance of a fugue subject, usually on the dominant, either slightly altered or transposed exactly after each presentation in the tonic. —*v.i.* **9.** to speak or write in response; make answer; reply. **10.** to respond by an act or motion: *He answered with a nod. The champion answered with a right to the jaw.* **11.** to act or suffer in consequence of (usually fol. by *for*). **12.** to be or declare oneself responsible or accountable (usually fol. by *for*): *I will answer for his safety.* **13.** to be satisfactory or serve (usually fol. by *for*): *His cane answered for a baseball bat.* **14.** to conform; correspond (usually fol. by *to*): *The prisoner answered to the description issued by the police.* —*v.t.* **15.** to speak or write in

CONCISE PRONUNCIATION KEY: *act, cāpe, dâre, pärt; set, ēqual; if, īce; ox, ōver, ôrder, oil, bŏŏk, bōōt, out; up, ûrge; child; sing; shoe; thin, that;* zh as in *treasure.* ə = *a* as in *alone, e* as in *system, i* as in *easily, o* as in *gallop, u* as in *circus;* ə as in *fire* (fīər), *hour* (ouər). l and n can serve as syllabic consonants, as in *cradle* (krād′l), and *button* (but′n). See the full key inside the front cover.

response to; reply to: *to answer a person; to answer a question.* **16.** to act or move in response to: *Answer the doorbell. We answered their goal with two quick goals of our own.* **17.** to solve or present a solution of. **18.** to serve or fulfill: *This will answer the purpose.* **19.** to discharge (a responsibility, claim, debt, etc.). **20.** to conform or correspond to; be similar or equivalent to: *This dog answers your description.* **21.** to atone for; make amends for. **22.** to reply or respond favorably to: *I would like to answer your request but am unable to do so.* **23. answer back,** to reply impertinently or rudely: *Well-behaved children do not answer back when scolded.* **24. answer the helm,** *Naut.* (of a vessel) to maneuver or remain steady according to the position of the rudder. [bef. 900; ME *andswerien,* OE *andswerian, andswarian* deriv. of *andswaru* an answer, equiv. to *and-* opposite, facing (cf. AND, ALONG) + Gmc **swarō,* deriv. of SWEAR] **—an′swer·er,** *n.* **—an′swer·less,** *adj.*
—Syn. 1. riposte. ANSWER, REJOINDER, REPLY, RESPONSE, RETORT all mean words used to meet a question, remark, charge, etc. An ANSWER is a return remark: *an answer giving the desired information.* A REJOINDER is a quick, usually clever answer or remark made in reply to another's comment, not to a question. REPLY usually refers to a direct or point-by-point response to a suggestion, proposal, question, or the like: *a reply to a letter.* A RESPONSE often suggests an answer to an appeal, exhortation, etc., or an expected or fixed reply: *a response to inquiry; a response in a church service.* A RETORT implies a keen, prompt answer, esp. one that turns a remark upon the person who made it: *a sharp retort.* **6.** defense, plea.

an·swer·a·ble (an′sər ə bəl, än′-), *adj.* **1.** liable to be asked to give account; responsible: *He is answerable to a committee for all his decisions.* **2.** capable of being answered: *a question answerable by mail.* **3.** proportionate; correlative (usually fol. by *to*). **4.** corresponding; suitable (usually fol. by *to*): *The amount is not answerable to my needs.* [1540–50; ANSWER + -ABLE] **—an′swer·a·bil′i·ty, an′swer·a·ble·ness,** *n.* **—an′swer·a·bly,** *adv.*

an·swer·back (an′sər bak′, än′-), *n.* **1.** a reply or answering message from a computer or other electronic device, as by means of teletypewriter or simulated voice. *—adj.* **2.** of, constituting, or providing an answerback: *a computer with answerback capability.* [n. use of v. phrase *answer back*]

an′swering machine′, an electronic device that is attached to a telephone and that automatically answers callers with a prerecorded message and records their messages for later playback. Also called **telephone answering machine.** [1975–80]

an′swering pen′nant, *Naut.* one of the flags of the International Code of Signals, a pennant of three red and two white vertical stripes, flown at the dip while a message is being interpreted and close up when it is understood. Also called **code flag.**

an′swering serv′ice, a service providing operators who answer a subscriber's telephone and take messages when the subscriber does not answer. [1960–65]

an′swer print′, a motion-picture film print composed of picture and sound, used for evaluation. [1935–40]

ant (ant), *n.* **1.** any of numerous black, red, brown, or yellow social insects of the family Formicidae, of worldwide distribution esp. in warm climates, having a large head with inner jaws for chewing and outer jaws for carrying and digging, and living in highly organized colonies containing wingless female workers, a winged queen, and, during breeding seasons, winged males, some species being noted for engaging in warfare, slavemaking, or the cultivation of food sources. **2. have ants in one's pants,** *Slang.* to be impatient or eager to act or speak. [bef. 1000; ME *am(e)te, em(e)te,* OE *ǣmette;* c. MLG *āmete, ēm(e)te,* MD *amete,* OHG *āmeiza* (ā- A-[3] + *meizan* to beat, cut, c. Albanian *mih* (he) digs), G *Ameise.* See EMMET, MITE[1]] **—ant′like′,** *adj.*

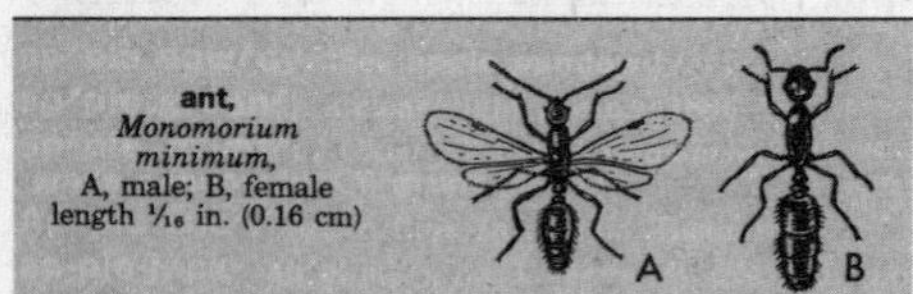

ant, *Monomorium minimum,* A, male; B, female length 1/16 in. (0.16 cm)

an't (ant, änt, ānt), **1.** *Chiefly Brit. Dial.* contraction of *am not.* **2.** *Dial.* ain't. [1700–10; see AIN'T; AREN'T]

ant-, var. of **anti-** before a vowel or *h: antacid; anthelmintic.*

-ant, a suffix forming adjectives and nouns from verbs, occurring originally in French and Latin loanwords (*pleasant; servant*) and productive in English on this model; **-ant** has the general sense "characterized by or serving in the capacity of" that named by the stem (*ascendant; pretendant*), esp. in the formation of nouns denoting human agents in legal actions or other formal procedures (*tenant; defendant; applicant; contestant*). In technical and commercial coinages, **-ant** is a suffix of nouns denoting impersonal physical agents (*propellant; lubricant; deodorant*). In general, **-ant** can be added only to bases of Latin origin, with a very few exceptions, as *coolant.* See also **-ent.** [< L *-ant-,* prp. s. of verbs in *-āre;* in many words < F *-ant* < L *-ant-* or *-ent-* (see -ENT); akin to ME, OE *-and-, -end-,* prp. suffix]

ant., **1.** antenna **2.** antonym.

Ant., Antarctica.

CONCISE ETYMOLOGY KEY: <, descended or borrowed from; >, whence; b., blend of, blended; c., cognate with; cf., compare; deriv., derivative; equiv., equivalent; imit., imitative; obl., oblique; r., replacing; s., stem; sp., spelling, spelled; resp., respelling, respelled; trans., translation; ?, origin unknown; *, unattested; ‡, probably earlier than. See the full key inside the front cover.

an·ta (an′tə), *n., pl.* **-tae** (-tē). *Archit.* a rectangular pier or pilaster, esp. one formed by thickening the end of a masonry wall. [1745–55; deduced < L *antae* pilasters (in pl. only)]

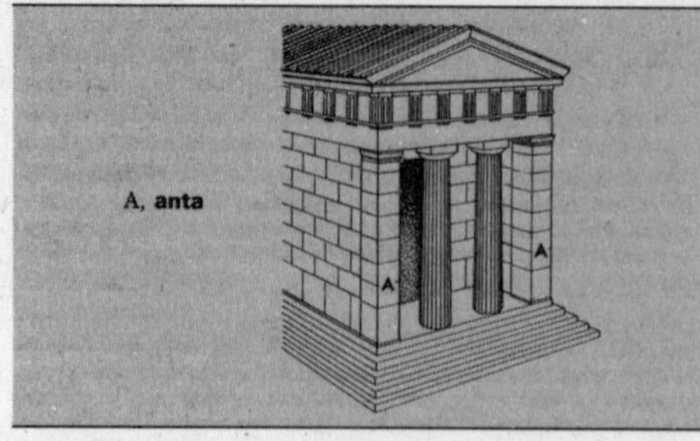

A, anta

ANTA (an′tə), *n.* a privately supported organization, chartered by Congress in 1935, for the encouragement and advancement of professional and nonprofessional theater. [*A(merican) N(ational) T(heatre and) A(cademy)*]

Ant·a·buse (an′tə byo͞os′, -byo͞oz′), *Pharm., Trademark.* a brand of disulfiram.

ant·ac·id (ant as′id), *adj.* **1.** preventing, neutralizing, or counteracting acidity, as of the stomach. *—n.* **2.** an antacid agent. [1725–35; ANT- + ACID]

An·tae·us (an tē′əs), *n. Class. Myth.* an African giant who was invincible when in contact with the earth but was lifted into the air by Hercules and crushed. **—An·tae′an,** *adj.*

an·tag·o·nism (an tag′ə niz′əm), *n.* **1.** an active hostility or opposition, as between unfriendly or conflicting groups: *the antagonism between the liberal and the conservative parties.* **2.** an opposing force, principle, or tendency: *Her plan to become an actress met with the antagonism of her family.* **3.** *Physiol.* an opposing action, as by one muscle in relation to another. **4.** the opposing action of substances, as drugs, that when taken together decrease the effectiveness of at least one of them (contrasted with *synergism*). **5.** *Ecol.* **a.** a relationship between two species of organisms in which the individuals of each species adversely affect the other, as in competition. **b.** the inhibition of the growth of one type of organism by a different type that is competing for the same ecological niche. [1835–40; (< F *antagonisme*) < Gk *antagṓnisma.* See ANTAGONIZE, -ISM]
—Syn. 1. conflict, friction, strife. **2.** animosity.

an·tag·o·nist (an tag′ə nist), *n.* **1.** a person who is opposed to, struggles against, or competes with another; opponent; adversary. **2.** the adversary of the hero or protagonist of a drama or other literary work: *Iago is the antagonist of Othello.* **3.** *Physiol.* a muscle that acts in opposition to another. Cf. **agonist** (def. 3). **4.** *Dentistry.* a tooth in one jaw that articulates during mastication or occlusion with a tooth in the opposing jaw. **5.** *Pharm.* a drug that counteracts the effects of another drug. [1590–1600; < LL *antagōnista* < Gk *antagōnistḗs.* See ANTAGONIZE, -IST]
—Syn. 1. contestant, enemy, foe. See **adversary.**
—Ant. 1. ally, friend.

an·tag·o·nis·tic (an tag′ə nis′tik), *adj.* **1.** acting in opposition; opposing, esp. mutually. **2.** hostile; unfriendly. [1625–35; ANTAGONIST + -IC] **—an·tag′o·nis′ti·cal·ly,** *adv.*

an·tag·o·nize (an tag′ə nīz′), *v.,* **-nized, -niz·ing.** *—v.t.* **1.** to make hostile or unfriendly; make an enemy or antagonist of: *His speech antagonized many voters.* **2.** to act in opposition to; oppose. *—v.i.* **3.** *Rare.* to act antagonistically. Also, *esp. Brit.,* **an·tag′o·nise′.** [1625–35; < Gk *antagōnízesthai* to contend against, dispute with. See ANT-, AGONIZE] **—an·tag′o·niz′a·ble,** *adj.* **—an·tag′o·ni·za′tion,** *n.*

An·ta·ki·ya (än′tä kē′yä), *n.* Arabic name of **Antioch.**

An·ta·kya (än tä′kyä), *n.* Turkish name of **Antioch.**

ant·al·ka·li (ant al′kə lī′), *n., pl.* **-lis, -lies.** something that neutralizes alkalis or counteracts alkalinity. Also, **antalkaline.** [1825–35; ANT- + ALKALI]

ant·al·ka·line (ant al′kə līn′, -lin), *adj.* **1.** preventing, neutralizing, or counteracting alkalinity. *—n.* **2.** antalkali. [1805–15; ANT- + ALKALINE]

An·tal·ya (än täl′yä), *n.* a seaport in SW Turkey. 130,759.

ant·an·a·clas·is (ant′an ə klas′is), *n. Rhet.* a form of speech in which a key word is repeated and used in a different, and sometimes contrary, way for a play on words, as in *The craft of a politician is to appear before the public without craft.* [1640–50; < Gk *antanáklasis* lit., echo, reflection, equiv. to *ant-* ANT- + *ana-* ANA- + *klásis* a breaking, bending (see -CLASE, -CLASIS)]

An·ta·na·na·ri·vo (än′tə nä′nə rē′vō, an′tə nan′ə-), *n.* a city in and the capital of Madagascar, in the central part. 650,000. Formerly, **Tananarive.**

ant·a·pex (ant ā′peks), *n., pl.* **-a·pex·es, -ap·i·ces** (-ap′ə sēz′, -ā′pə-). *Astron.* the point exactly opposite in direction to the solar apex; the point away from which the solar system is moving and toward which the stars appear to be converging, located in the constellation Columba. [1885–90; ANT- + APEX]

an·tar·an·ga (un′tər ung′gə), *n.* (*used with a plural v.*) *Yoga.* the three angas pertaining to the mind: dharana or concentration, dhyana or meditation, and samadhi or contemplation. [< Skt *antaraṅga*]

ant·arc·tic (ant ärk′tik, -är′tik), *adj.* **1.** of, at, or near the South Pole. *—n.* **2. the Antarctic,** the Antarctic Ocean and Antarctica. [1325–75; < L *antarcticus* < Gk *antarktikós* (see ANT-, ARCTIC); r. ME *antartik* (< MF) < ML *antarticus*]

Ant·arc·ti·ca (ant ärk′ti kə, -är′ti-), *n.* the continent surrounding the South Pole: almost entirely covered by an ice sheet. ab. 5,000,000 sq. mi. (12,950,000 sq. km). Also called **Antarctic Continent.** See map below.

Antarc′tic Cir′cle, an imaginary line drawn parallel to the equator, at 23° 28′ N of the South Pole: between the South Frigid Zone and the South Temperate Zone. See diag. under **zone.**

Antarc′tic Circumpo′lar Cur′rent, an ocean current flowing from west to east around Antarctica. Also called **West Wind Drift.**

Antarc′tic Con′tinent, Antarctica.

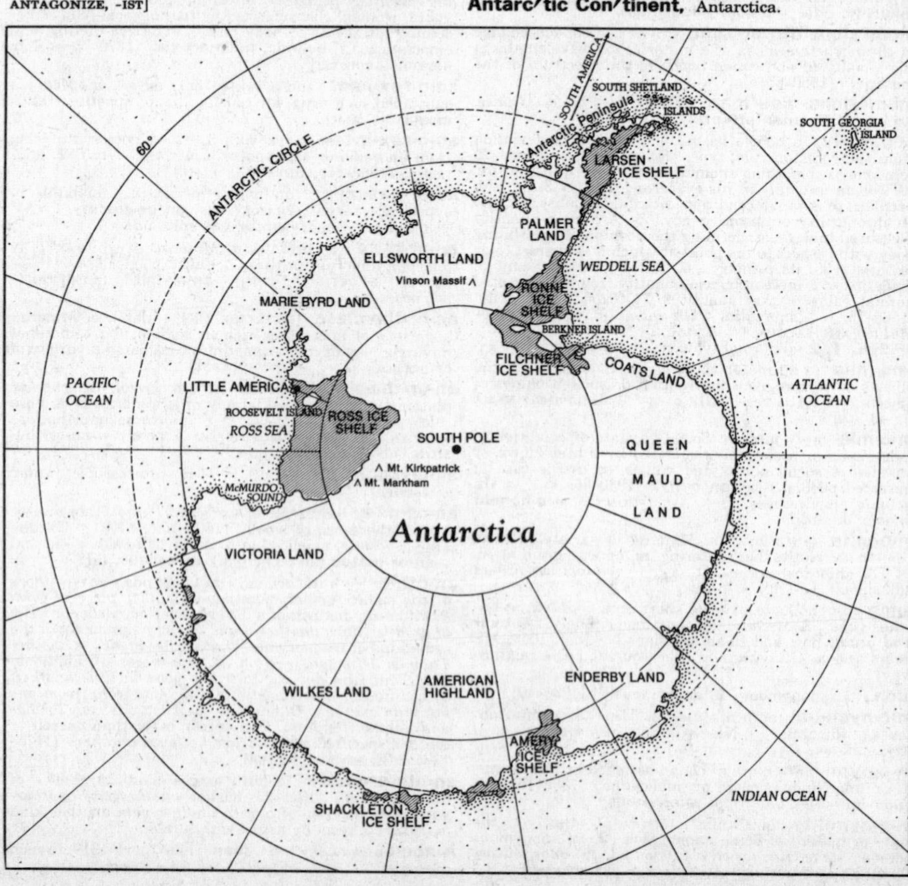

Antarc′tic Conver′gence, the fairly well-defined boundary that exists between the cold antarctic waters and the warmer waters to the north and can be traced around the world.

Antarc′tic O′cean, the waters surrounding Antarctica, comprising the southernmost parts of the Pacific, Atlantic, and Indian oceans.

Antarc′tic Penin′sula, a peninsula in Antarctica, S of South America. Cf. **Graham Land, Palmer Peninsula.**

Antarc′tic Plate′, a major tectonic division of the earth's crust, comprising Antarctica and adjacent ocean basins (the South Indian, Southeast Pacific, and Atlantic-Indian basins) and bounded on the north by the Nazca, South American, African, Indo-Australian, and Pacific plates.

Antarc′tic Zone′, the section of the earth's surface lying between the Antarctic Circle and the South Pole. See diag. under **zone.**

An•tar•es (an târ′ēz, -tar′-), *n. Astron.* a red supergiant star of the first magnitude in the constellation Scorpius.

ant•ar•thrit•ic (ant′är thrit′ik), *adj., n. Pharm., Med.* antiarthritic. [1700–10; ANT- + ARTHRITIC]

ant•asth•mat•ic (ant′az mat′ik, -as-), *Med.* —*adj.* **1.** relieving or preventing asthma or an asthmatic paroxysm. —*n.* **2.** an antasthmatic agent. [1675–85; ANT- + ASTHMATIC]

ant•a•troph•ic (ant′ə trof′ik, -trō′fik), *Med.* —*adj.* **1.** preventing or curing atrophy. —*n.* **2.** an antatrophic agent. [1805–15; ANT- + ATROPHIC]

ant′ bear′, aardvark. [1545–55]

ant•bird (ant′bûrd′), *n.* any of numerous passerine birds of the family Formicariidae, of the New World tropics, many species of which follow army ant swarms to feed on insects disturbed by the ants. [ANT + BIRD]

ant′ cow′, an aphid that excretes honeydew and is tended by honeydew-gathering ants. [1870–75]

an•te (an′tē), *n., v.,* **-ted** or **-teed, -te•ing.** —*n.* **1.** *Poker.* a fixed but arbitrary stake put into the pot by each player before the deal. **2.** an amount of money paid in advance to insure an individual's share in a joint business venture. **3.** *Informal.* an individual's share of the total expenses incurred by a group. **4.** *Informal.* the price or cost of something. —*v.t.* **5.** *Poker.* to put (one's initial stake) into the pot. **6.** to produce or pay (one's share) (usually fol. by *up*): *He anted up his half of the bill.* —*v.i.* **7.** *Poker.* to put one's initial stake into the pot. **8.** *Informal.* to pay (usually fol. by *up*). [1830–40, *Amer.*; independent use of ANTE-]

ante-, a prefix meaning "before," used in the formation of compound words: *anteroom; antebellum; antedate.* [< L, prefixal form of prep. and adv. *ante* (see ANCIENT); akin to Gk *antí,* OE *and-* against, toward, opposite. See ANSWER, AND, ANTI-]

ant•eat•er (ant′ē′tər), *n.* **1.** any of several mammals of the family Myrmecophagidae, having a long, tapered snout, extensile tongue, and powerful front claws and feeding chiefly on ants and termites. Cf. **giant anteater, silky anteater, tamandua. 2.** the aardvark. **3.** a pangolin. **4.** an echidna. **5.** See **banded anteater.** [1755–65; ANT + EATER]

an•te•bel•lum (an′tē bel′əm), *adj.* before or existing before the war, esp. the American Civil War. [1860–65; < L *ante bellum* before the war]

an•te•cede (an′tə sēd′), *v.t.,* **-ced•ed, -ced•ing.** to go before, in time, order, rank, etc.; precede: *Shakespeare antecedes Milton.* [1615–25; < L *antecēdere* to go before, precede, excel, surpass. See ANTE-, CEDE]

an•te•ced•ence (an′tə sēd′ns), *n.* **1.** the act of going before; precedence. **2.** priority. **3.** *Astron.* (of a planet) apparent retrograde motion. [1525–35; ANTECEDE + -ENCE]

an•te•ced•en•cy (an′tə sēd′n sē), *n.* the quality or condition of being antecedent. [1590–1600; ANTECED(ENT) + -ENCY]

an•te•ced•ent (an′tə sēd′nt), *adj.* **1.** preceding; prior: *an antecedent event.* —*n.* **2.** a preceding circumstance, event, object, style, phenomenon, etc. **3. antecedents, a.** ancestors. **b.** the history, events, characteristics, etc., of one's earlier life: *Little is known about his birth and antecedents.* **4.** *Gram.* a word, phrase, or clause, usually a substantive, that is replaced by a pronoun or other substitute later, or occasionally earlier, in the same or in another, usually subsequent, sentence. In *Jane lost a glove and she can't find it, Jane* is the antecedent of *she* and *glove* is the antecedent of *it.* **5.** *Math.* **a.** the first term of a ratio; the first or third term of a proportion. **b.** the first of two vectors in a dyad. **6.** *Logic.* the conditional element in a proposition, as "Caesar conquered Gaul," in "If Caesar conquered Gaul, he was a great general." [1350–1400; ME (< MF) < L *antecēdent-* (s. of *antecēdēns*) going before, prp. of *antecēdere* to ANTECEDE; see -ENT] —**an•te•ce•den•tal** (an′tə sē den′tl), *adj.* —**an′te•ced′ent•ly,** *adv.*
—**Syn. 1.** precursory, preexistent. **2.** precursor, forerunner, ancestor. —**Ant. 1.** subsequent. **2.** successor.

an•te•ces•sor (an′tə ses′ər), *n.* a person who goes before; predecessor. [1375–1425; late ME *antecessour* (< MF) < L *antecessor* he who goes before, a predecessor, equiv. to *anteced-,* var. s. of *antecēdere* (see ANTECEDE) + *-tor* -TOR; cf. ANCESTOR]

an•te•cham•ber (an′tē chām′bər), *n.* a chamber or room that serves as a waiting room and entrance to a larger room or an apartment; anteroom. [1650–60; earlier *antichamber* < F *antichambre,* as trans. of It *anticamera,* equiv. to *anti-* (< L *ante-* ANTE-) + *camera* CHAMBER]

an•te•chap•el (an′tē chap′əl), *n.* a room or hall before the entrance to a chapel. [1695–1705; ANTE- + CHAPEL]

an•te•choir (an′tē kwīᵊr′), *n.* an enclosed space in front of the choir of a church. Also called **forechoir.** [1885–90; ANTE- + CHOIR]

an•te-Chris•tum (än′te krē′stŏŏm; *Eng.* an′tē kris′təm), *adj. Latin.* before Christ. *Abbr.:* A.C.

an•te•court (an′tē kôrt′, -kōrt′), *n. Rare.* a forecourt. [1685–95; ANTE- + COURT]

an•te•date (*v.* an′ti dāt′, an′ti dāt′; *n.* an′ti dāt′), *v.,* **-dat•ed, -dat•ing,** *n.* —*v.t.* **1.** to be of older date than; precede in time: *The Peruvian empire antedates the Mexican empire.* **2.** predate (def. 1). **3.** to assign to an earlier date: *to antedate a historical event.* **4.** to cause to return to an earlier time: *to antedate one's thoughts by remembering past events.* **5.** to cause to happen sooner; accelerate: *The cold weather antedated their departure from the country.* **6.** *Archaic.* to take or have in advance; anticipate. —*n.* **7.** a prior date. [1570–80; earlier *antidate* < MF *antidater,* deriv. of *antidate* a date earlier than the true date (by assoc. with *anté-* ANTE-), orig. a date put in place of another date; see ANTE-, DATE[1]]

an•te•di•lu•vi•an (an′tē di lo͞o′vē ən), *adj.* **1.** of or belonging to the period before the Flood. Gen. 7, 8. **2.** very old, old-fashioned, or out of date; antiquated; primitive: *antediluvian ideas.* —*n.* **3.** a person who lived before the Flood. **4.** a very old or old-fashioned person or thing. [1640–50; ANTE- + L *diluvi(um)* a flood, DELUGE + -AN]

an′tedilu′vian pa′triarch. See under **patriarch** (def. 1).

an•te•fix (an′tə fiks′), *n., pl.* **-fix•es, -fix•a** (-fik′sə). *Archit.* **1.** an upright ornament at the eaves of a tiled roof, to conceal the foot of a row of convex tiles that cover the joints of the flat tiles. **2.** an ornament above the top molding of a cornice. [1825–35; < L *antefixa,* neut. pl. of *antefixus* fastened in front, equiv. to *ante-* ANTE- + *fixus* ptp. of *figere* to FIX] —**an′te•fix′al,** *adj.*

an•te•flex•ion (an′tə flek′shən), *n. Pathol.* a bending forward of an organ, esp. of the body of the uterus. [1855–60; ANTE- + L *flexiōn-* (s. of *flexiō*) a bending; see FLEXION]

ant′ egg′, the white pupa or larva of an ant, sold dried as food for pet fish, birds, turtles, etc.

an•te•hall (an′tē hôl′), *n.* a room or hall serving as a waiting room and entrance to a larger hall. [1840–50; ANTE- + HALL]

an•te•lope (an′tl ōp′), *n., pl.* **-lopes,** (*esp. collectively*) **-lope. 1.** any of several ruminants of the family Bovidae, chiefly of Africa and Asia, having permanent, hollow, unbranched horns. **2.** leather made from the hide of such an animal. **3.** pronghorn. [1400–50; late ME *antelop* < MF < ML *antalopus* < MGk *anthólops* a fabulous beast described by Eustathius of Antioch (d. 337); orig. of word unknown] —**an′te•lo′pi•an, an•te•lo•pine** (an′tl ō′pin, -pīn), *adj.*

an•te•me•rid•i•an (an′tē mə rid′ē ən), *adj.* **1.** occurring before noon. **2.** of or pertaining to the forenoon. [1650–60; ANTE- + MERIDIAN]

an•te me•rid•i•em (an′tē mə rid′ē əm, -em′). See **a.m.** [1555–65]

an•te•mor•tem (an′tē môr′təm), *adj.* before death: *an antemortem confession.* Also, **an′te-mor′tem, an′te mor′tem.** [1880–85; < L]

an•te•mun•dane (an′tē mun dān′, -mun′dān), *adj.* before the creation of the world. [1725–35; ANTE- + MUNDANE]

an•te•na•tal (an′tē nāt′l), *adj.* prenatal: *an antenatal clinic.* [1810–20; ANTE- + NATAL] —**an′te•na′tal•ly,** *adv.*

an•te•nave (an′tē nāv′), *n.* a porch or narthex before the nave of a church. [1820–30; ANTE- + NAVE[1]]

an•te-Ni•cene (an′tē nī sēn′, -nī′sēn), *adj.* of or pertaining to the Christian church or period before the Nicene Council of A.D. 325. Also, **an•te-Ni•cae•an** (an′tē nī sē′ən).

an•ten•na (an ten′ə), *n., pl.* **-ten•nas** for 1, **-ten•nae** (-ten′ē) for 2. **1.** a conductor by which electromagnetic waves are sent out or received, consisting commonly of a wire or set of wires; aerial. **2.** *Zool.* one of the jointed, movable, sensory appendages occurring in pairs on the heads of insects and most other arthropods. See diag. under **insect.** [1640–50; < L: a sailyard] —**an•ten′nal,** *adj.*

anten′na array′, a directional antenna or system of antennas for radio transmission or reception. Also called **array.** [1935–40]

anten′nal gland′. See **green gland.**

an•ten•na•ry (an ten′ə rē), *adj. Zool.* **1.** of, pertaining to, or resembling an antenna. **2.** bearing antennae; antennate. [1830–40; ANTENN(A) + -ARY[1]]

an•ten•nate (an′tə nit, -nāt′), *adj. Zool.* having antennae. [ANTENN(AE) + -ATE[1]]

an•ten•ni•fer (an ten′ə fər), *n. Zool.* a pivotal projection at the rim of an antennal socket. [ANTENN(A) + -I- + -FER]

an•ten•nule (an ten′yo͞ol), *n. Zool.* a small antenna, esp. one of the foremost pair of a crustacean. [1835–45; ANTENN(A) + -ULE] —**an•ten•nu•lar** (an ten′yə lər), **an•ten•nu•lar•y** (an ten′yə ler′ē), *adj.*

an•te•num•ber (an′tē num′bər), *n.* a number that immediately precedes another: *Three is the antenumber of four.* [1620–30; ANTE- + NUMBER]

an•te•nup•tial (an′tē nup′shəl), *adj.* before marriage: *an antenuptial agreement.* [1810–20; ANTE- + NUPTIAL]

an•te•or•bit•al (an′tē ôr′bi tl), *adj. Anat.* situated in front of the eye. [1830–40; ANTE- + ORBITAL]

an•te•par•tum (an′tē pär′təm), *adj. Obstet.* of or noting the period prior to childbirth; before delivery. Cf. **postpartum.** [1905–10; < L]

an•te•past (an′ti past′), *n. Archaic.* a foretaste; appetizer. [1580–90; ANTE- + L *pāstus* food (orig. ptp. of *pāscere* to feed), equiv. to *pās-* feed + *-tus* ptp. suffix]

an•te•pen•di•um (an′tē pen′dē əm), *n., pl.* **-di•a** (-dē ə). the decoration of the front of an altar, as a covering of silk or a painted panel. [1690–1700; < ML; see ANTE-, PEND, -IUM]

an•te•pe•nult (an′tē pē′nult, -pi nult′), *n.* the third syllable from the end in a word, as *te* in *antepenult.* [1575–85; < L (*syllaba*) *antepaenultima* the second (syllable) from the last, fem. of *antepaenultimus* standing before the penult. See ANTE-, PENULT]

an•te•pe•nul•ti•mate (an′tē pi nul′tə mit), *adj.* **1.** third from the end. **2.** of or pertaining to an antepenult. —*n.* **3.** an antepenult. [1720–30; ANTEPENULT + (ULT)IMATE]

an•te•porch (an′tē pôrch′, -pōrch′), *n.* an outer porch. [1615–25; ANTE- + PORCH]

an•te•por•ti•co (an′tē pôr′ti kō′, -pōr′-), *n., pl.* **-coes, -cos.** a lesser portico preceding a main portico. [1830–40; ANTE- + PORTICO]

an•te•pran•di•al (an′tē pran′dē əl), *adj.* preprandial. [1840–50; ANTE- + PRANDIAL]

an•te•pro•hi•bi•tion (an′tē prō′ə bish′ən), *adj.* before prohibition. [ANTE- + PROHIBITION]

an•te•ri•or (an tēr′ē ər), *adj.* **1.** situated before or at the front of; fore (opposed to *posterior*). **2.** going before in time or sequence; preceding; earlier: *events anterior to the outbreak of war.* **3.** *Ling.* (in distinctive feature analysis) articulated in the region extending from the alveolar ridge to the lips; alveolar, dental, or labial. **4.** (in animals and embryos) pertaining to or toward the head or forward end of the body. **5.** (in humans) pertaining to or toward the front plane of the body, equivalent to the ventral surface of quadrupeds. **6.** *Bot.* on the front side and away from the main axis, as the lower lip of a flower. [1535–45; < L, comp. of *ante* before, formed on model of POSTERIOR] —**an•te•ri•or•i•ty** (an tēr′ē ôr′i tē, -or′-), *n.* —**an•te′ri•or•ly,** *adv.*

ante′rior pitu′itary, *Anat.* See under **pituitary gland.**

ante′rior pitu′itary luteotro′pin, *Biochem.* prolactin.

ante′rior tooth′, *Dentistry.* a tooth in the front of the mouth; an incisor or cuspid.

antero-, a combining form with the meaning "situated in front, fore," used in the formation of compound words: *anteroparietal.* [ANTER(IOR) + -O-]

an•te•room (an′tē ro͞om′, -rŏŏm′), *n.* **1.** a room that admits to a larger room. **2.** a waiting room. [1755–65; ANTE- + ROOM]

an•ter•o•pa•ri•et•al (an′tə rō pə rī′i tl), *adj. Anat.* situated in a forward part or on the wall of an organ or cavity. [ANTERO- + PARIETAL]

An•te•ros (an′tə ros′), *n.* **1.** *Class. Myth.* a brother of Eros, most often regarded as the avenger of unrequited love. **2.** Anterus.

An•ter•us (an′tər əs), *n.* **Saint,** pope A.D. 235–236. Also, **Anteros.**

an•te•type (an′tē tīp′), *n.* an earlier form; prototype. [1605–15; ANTE- + TYPE]

an•te•ver•sion (an′tē vûr′zhən, -shən), *n. Pathol.* a tipping forward of an organ, as the uterus. [1850–55; ANTE- + VERSION]

an•te•vert (an′tē vûrt′), *v.t. Pathol.* to displace (the uterus or other body organ) by tipping forward. [1640–50; < L *antevertere* to go before, precede, equiv. to *ante* ANTE- + *vertere* to turn]

anth-, var. of **antho-** esp. before a vowel.

An•the•a (an thē′ə), *n.* a female given name: from a Greek word meaning "flowery."

An•theil (an′tīl), *n.* **George,** 1900–59, U.S. composer.

ant•he′lic arc′, (ant hē′lik, an thē′-), a rare halo occurring at the sun's elevation but in the opposite part of the sky. [ANTHEL(ION) + -IC]

ant•he•li•on (ant hē′lē ən, an thē′-), *n., pl.* **-li•a** (-lē ə). a luminous, white spot occasionally appearing at the sun's elevation but in the opposite part of the sky. [1660–70; < LGk *anthḗlion,* neut. of *anthḗlios* opposite the sun, equiv. to *ant-* ANT- + *hḗli(os)* the sun + *-os* adj. suffix]

ant•hel•min•tic (ant′hel min′tik, an′thel-), *Pharm.* —*adj.* **1.** of or pertaining to a substance capable of destroying or eliminating parasitic worms, esp. human intestinal helminths. —*n.* **2.** any such substance. [1675–85; ANT- + HELMINT(H)IC]

an•them (an′thəm), *n.* **1.** a song, as of praise, devotion, or patriotism: *the national anthem of Spain; our college anthem.* **2.** a piece of sacred vocal music, usually with words taken from the Scriptures. **3.** a hymn sung alternately by different sections of a choir or congregation. —*v.t.* **4.** to celebrate with or in an anthem. [bef. 1000; ME *antem,* OE *antemn(e), antefne* < LL *antefana, antiphōna* (fem. sing.) < Gk *antíphōna* (see ANTIPHON); sp. with *h* prob. by assoc. with HYMN, with pron. then changed to reflect sp.]

an•the•ma (an thē′mə, an′thə-), *n., pl.* **an•the•ma•ta** (an thē′mə tə, -them′ə tə), **an•the•mas.** *Pathol.* **1.** exanthema. **2.** an eruption of the skin. [< Gk *ánthēma* efflorescence, equiv. to *ánthē,* verbid s. of *anthein* to bloom (see ANTHO-) + *-ma* n. suffix of result]

an•the•mi•on (an thē′mē ən), *n., pl.* **-mi•a** (-mē ə). an ornament of floral forms in a flat radiating cluster, as in architectural decoration, vase painting, etc. Also called **honeysuckle ornament.** [1860–65; < Gk *anthémion,* equiv. to *ánthem(on)* flower + *-ion* dim. suffix; see ANTHO-]

CONCISE PRONUNCIATION KEY: act, cāpe, dâre, pärt; set, ēqual; if, ice; ox, ōver, ôrder, oil, bŏŏk, bo͞ot, out; up, ûrge; child; sing; shoe; thin, *th*at; zh as in *treasure.* ə = *a* in *alone,* e as in *system,* i as in *easily,* o as in *gallop,* u as in *circus;* ᵊ as in *fire* (fīᵊr), *hour* (ouᵊr). l and n can serve as syllabic consonants, as in *cradle* (krād′l), and *button* (but′n). See the full key inside the front cover.

an•ther (an′thər), *n. Bot.* the pollen-bearing part of a stamen. See diag. under **flower.** [1545–55; < NL *anthēra* < L < Gk, fem. of *antherós* flowery; see ANTHESIS] —**an′ther•al,** *adj.* —**an′ther•less,** *adj.*

an•ther•id•i•um (an′thə rid′ē əm), *n., pl.* **-ther•id•i•a** (-thə rid′ē ə). *Bot., Mycol.* a male reproductive structure producing gametes, occurring in ferns, mosses, fungi, and algae. [1850–55; < NL; see ANTHER, -IDIUM] —**an′ther•id′i•al,** *adj.*

an•ther•o•zo•id (an′thər ə zō′id, an′thər ə zoid′), *n. Bot., Mycol.* the motile male gamete produced in an antheridium. [1850–55; ANTHER + -O- + Z(O)OID]

an•the•sis (an thē′sis), *n., pl.* **-ses** (-sēz). *Bot.* the period or act of expansion in flowers, esp. the maturing of the stamens. [1825–35; < NL < Gk *ánthēsis* bloom, equiv. to *anthē-* (verbid s. of *antheîn* to bloom) + *-sis* -SIS]

An•thes•te•ri•a (an′thə stēr′ē ə), *n.* (*sometimes used with a plural v.*) one of the ancient Athenian festivals composing the Dionysia; a spring festival celebrating flowers and new wine. —**An•thes•te•ri•ac** (an′thə-stēr′ē ak′), *adj.*

ant•hill (ant′hil′), *n.* a mound of earth, leaves, etc., formed by a colony of ants in digging or constructing their underground nest. [1250–1300; ME *amete hulle, ampte hille;* see ANT, HILL]

antho-, a combining form meaning "flower," used in the formation of compound words: *anthophore.* [< Gk, comb. form of *ánthos* flower]

an•tho•car•pous (an′thə kär′pəs), *adj.* (of a fruit) having accessory or enlarged tissue, as the apple or strawberry. [1825–35; ANTHO- + -CARPOUS]

an•tho•cy•a•nin (an′thə sī′ə nin), *n. Biochem.* any of a class of water-soluble pigments that give flowers the colors ranging from red to blue. Also, **an•tho•cy•an** (an′-thə sī′ən). [1830–40; ANTHO- + CYANIN(E)]

an•tho•di•um (an thō′dē əm), *n., pl.* **-di•a** (-dē ə). *Bot.* a flower head or capitulum, esp. the head of a composite plant. See illus. under **inflorescence.** [1855–60; < NL < Gk *anthṓd(ēs)* flowerlike (*ánth(os)* a flower + *-ōdēs* -ODE[1]) + L *-ium* -IUM]

anthol., anthology.

an•thol•o•gize (an thol′ə jīz′), *v.,* **-gized, -giz•ing.** —*v.i.* **1.** to compile an anthology. —*v.t.* **2.** to make an anthology of; include in an anthology. Also, *esp. Brit.,* **an•thol′o•gise′.** [1890–95; ANTHOLOG(Y) + -IZE] —**an•thol′o•giz′er,** *n.*

an•thol•o•gy (an thol′ə jē), *n., pl.* **-gies. 1.** a book or other collection of selected writings by various authors, usually in the same literary form, of the same period, or on the same subject: *an anthology of Elizabethan drama; an anthology of modern philosophy.* **2.** a collection of selected writings by one author. [1630–40; < L *anthologia* < Gk: collection of poems, lit., gathering of flowers, equiv. to *anthológ(os)* flower-gathering (*antho-* ANTHO- + *-logos,* adj. deriv. of *légein* to pick up, collect) + *-ia* -IA] —**an•tho•log•i•cal** (an′thə loj′i kəl), *adj.* —**an′tho•log′i•cal•ly,** *adv.* —**an•thol′o•gist,** *n.*

An•tho•ny (an′tə nē *for 1, 2;* an′thə nē *for 3;* an′thə-nē *or, esp. Brit.,* -tə- *for 4*), *n.* **1.** See **Antony, Mark. 2. Saint,** A.D. 251?–356?, Egyptian hermit: founder of Christian monasticism. **3. Susan Brow•nell** (brou′nel), 1820–1906, U.S. reformer and suffragist. **4.** a male given name: from Latin *Antonius,* a family name.

An′thony dol′lar, a cupronickel coin of the U.S., equal to one dollar, bearing a portrait of Susan B. Anthony on its obverse: first issued in 1979.

An′tho•ny of Pad′ua (an′tə nē, -thə-), **Saint,** 1195–1231, Franciscan monk and preacher in Italy and France.

an•thoph•i•lous (an thof′ə ləs), *adj.* **1.** Also, **an•thoph•a•gous** (an thof′ə gəs). feeding on flowers, as certain insects. **2.** attracted by or living among flowers. [1880–85; ANTHO- + -PHILOUS]

an•tho•phore (an′thə fôr′, -fōr′), *n. Bot.* a form of floral stalk, produced by the elongation of the internode between the calyx and the corolla, and bearing the corolla, stamens, and pistil. [1830–40; < Gk *anthophóros* flower-bearing, blooming. See ANTHO-, -PHORE]

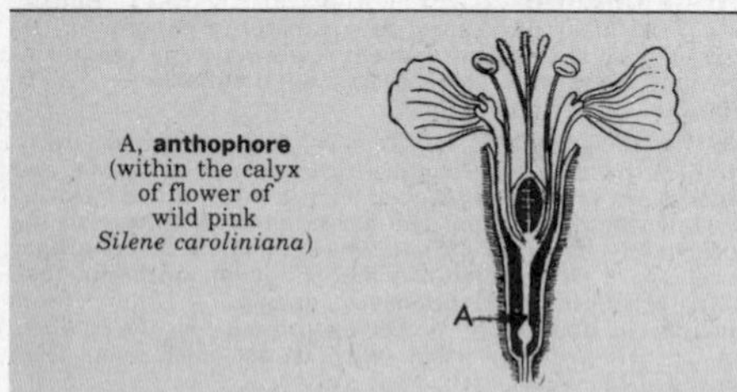

A, **anthophore** (within the calyx of flower of wild pink *Silene caroliniana*)

an•tho•phyl•lite (an′thə fil′īt), *n.* a mineral, magnesium-iron silicate, $(Mg,Fe)_7(Si_8O_{22})(OH)_2$, occurring in schists in lamellar or fibrous clove-brown crystals. [1835–45; < NL *anthophyll(um)* clove (see ANTHO-, -PHYL) + -ITE[1]] —**an•tho•phyl•lit•ic** (an′thə fə lit′ik), *adj.*

-anthous, a combining form meaning "having flowers," of the type or number specified by the initial element, used in the formation of compound words: *monanthous.* [< Gk *ánth(os)* flower + -OUS]

CONCISE ETYMOLOGY KEY: <, descended or borrowed from; >, whence; b., blend of, blended; c., cognate with; cf., compare; deriv., derivative; equiv., equivalent; imit., imitative; obl., oblique; r., replacing; s., stem; sp., spelling, spelled; resp., respelling, respelled; trans., translation; ?, origin unknown; *, unattested; ‡, probably earlier than. See the full key inside the front cover.

an•tho•zo•an (an′thə zō′ən), *n.* **1.** any marine coelenterate of the class Anthozoa, comprising colonial and solitary polyps and including corals, sea anemones, sea pens, etc. —*adj.* **2.** Also, **an′tho•zo′ic.** belonging or pertaining to the anthozoans. [1885–90; < NL *Anthozo(a)* (see ANTHO-, -ZOA) + -AN]

anthrac-, a combining form meaning "coal," "carbon," "carbuncle," used in the formation of compound words: *anthracosis; anthracnose; anthracoid.* Also, *esp. before a consonant,* **anthraco-.** [< L *anthrac-* < Gk *anthrak-* (s. of *ánthrax*). See ANTHRAX]

an•thra•cene (an′thrə sēn′), *n. Chem.* a colorless, crystalline powder, $C_{14}H_{12}$, obtained from coal tar and having a violet fluorescence: used chiefly as a source of anthraquinone and alizarin, and in the process of measuring radioactive materials. [1860–65; ANTHRAC- + -ENE]

an•thra•cite (an′thrə sīt′), *n.* a mineral coal containing little of the volatile hydrocarbons and burning almost without flame; hard coal. Also called **an′thracite coal′.** [1810–15; prob. < F < L (Pliny) *anthracītis* kind of coal. See ANTHRAC-, -ITE[1]] —**an•thra•cit•ic** (an′thrə sit′ik), **an•thra•cit•ous** (an′thrə sī′təs), *adj.*

an•thrac•nose (an thrak′nōs), *n. Plant. Pathol.* a disease of plants characterized by restricted, discolored lesions, caused by a fungus. [1885–90; < F; see ANTHRAC-, NOSO-]

anthraco-, var. of **anthrac-** before a consonant.

an•thra•coid (an′thrə koid′), *adj.* **1.** resembling anthrax. **2.** resembling coal or charcoal; carbonlike. [1880–85; ANTHRAC- + -OID]

an•thra•co•sil•i•co•sis (an′thrə kō sil′i kō′sis), *n. Pathol.* a form of pneumoconiosis occurring in miners, caused by the inhalation of coal and siliceous particles. Also, **an•thra•sil•i•co•sis** (an′thrə sil′i kō′sis). [< NL; see ANTHRACO-, SILICOSIS]

an•thra•co•sis (an′thrə kō′sis), *n. Pathol.* **1.** the deposition of coal dust in the lungs; asymptomatic pneumoconiosis. **2.** See **black lung.** [1830–40; < NL; see ANTHRAC-, -OSIS] —**an•thra•cot•ic** (an′thrə kot′ik), *adj.*

an•thran•i•late (an thran′l āt′, -it, an′thrə nil′āt, -it), *n. Chem.* a salt or ester of anthranilic acid. [ANTHRANIL(IC ACID) + -ATE[2]]

an′thra•nil′ic ac′id (an′thrə nil′ik, an′-), *Chem.* a yellowish crystalline compound, $C_7H_7NO_2$, soluble in hot water, alcohol, and ether: used in the manufacture of dyes, pharmaceuticals, and perfumes. [ANTHR(ACENE) + ANIL(INE) + -IC]

an•thra•qui•none (an′thrə kwə nōn′, -kwē′nōn, -kwin′ōn), *n. Chem.* a yellow, water-insoluble, crystalline powder, $C_{14}H_8O_2$, usually derived from anthracene or phthalic anhydride: used chiefly in the manufacture of anthraquinone dyes. [1880–85; ANTHRA(CENE) + QUINONE]

an′thraquinone′ dye′, *Chem.* any of the class of dyes derived from anthraquinone, used for dyeing textiles, esp. cotton, rayon, and silk.

an•thrax (an′thraks), *n., pl.* **-thra•ces** (-thrə sēz′). *Pathol.* **1.** an infectious, often fatal disease of cattle, sheep, and other mammals, caused by *Bacillus anthracis,* transmitted to humans by contaminated wool, raw meat, or other animal products. **2.** a malignant carbuncle that is the diagnostic lesion of anthrax disease in humans. [1350–1400; ME *antrax* malignant boil or growth < L *anthrax* carbuncle < Gk *ánthrax* a coal, carbuncle]

anthrop., **1.** anthropological. **2.** anthropology.

an•throp•ic (an throp′ik), *adj.* of or pertaining to human beings or their span of existence on earth. Also, **an•throp′i•cal.** [1795–1805; < Gk *anthrōpikós* human. See ANTHROPO-, -IC]

anthropo-, a learned borrowing from Greek meaning "human," used in the formation of compound words: *anthropometry.* [< Gk, comb. form of *ánthrōpos* human being, man]

an•thro•po•cen•tric (an′thrə pō sen′trik), *adj.* **1.** regarding the human being as the central fact of the universe. **2.** assuming human beings to be the final aim and end of the universe. **3.** viewing and interpreting everything in terms of human experience and values. [1860–65; ANTHROPO- + -CENTRIC] —**an′thro•po•cen′•tri•cal•ly,** *adv.*

an•thro•po•cen•tric•i•ty (an′thrə pō sen tris′i tē), *n., pl.* **-ties. 1.** the state or quality of being anthropocentric. **2.** an anthropocentric interpretation of the universe. [1955–60; ANTHROPOCENTRIC + -ITY]

an•thro•po•cen•trism (an′thrə pō sen′triz əm), *n.* an anthropocentric theory or view. [1905–10; ANTHROPOCENTR(IC) + -ISM]

an•thro•po•gen•e•sis (an′thrə pō jen′ə sis), *n.* the genesis or development of the human race, esp. as a subject of scientific study. Also, **an•thro•pog•e•ny** (an′thrə-poj′ə nē). [ANTHROPO- + GENESIS] —**an•thro•po•ge•net•ic** (an′thrə pō jə net′ik), *adj.*

an•thro•po•gen•ic (an′thrə pə jen′ik), *adj.* caused or produced by humans: *anthropogenic air pollution.* [1885–90; ANTHROPO- + -GENIC]

an•thro•po•ge•og•ra•phy (an′thrə pō jē og′rə fē), *n.* a branch of anthropology dealing with the geographical distribution of humankind and the relationship between human beings and their environment. [1645–55; ANTHROPO- + GEOGRAPHY] —**an′thro•po•ge•og′ra•pher,** *n.* —**an•thro•po•ge•o•graph•ic** (an′thrə pō jē′ə graf′-ik), **an′thro•po•ge′o•graph′i•cal,** *adj.*

an•thro•pog•ra•phy (an′thrə pog′rə fē), *n.* the branch of anthropology that describes the varieties of humankind and their geographical distribution. [1560–70; ANTHROPO- + -GRAPHY] —**an•thro•po•graph•ic** (an′thrə pə graf′ik), *adj.*

an•thro•poid (an′thrə poid′), *adj.* **1.** resembling humans. **2.** belonging or pertaining to the primate suborder Anthropoidea, characterized by a relatively flat face, dry nose, small immobile ears, and forward-facing eyes, comprising humans, apes, Old World monkeys, and New World monkeys. Cf. **prosimian.** —*n.* **3.** See **anthropoid ape.** [1825–35; < Gk *anthrōpoeidḗs* in the shape of a man. See ANTHROPO-, -OID] —**an′thro•poi′dal,** *adj.*

an′thropoid ape′, any tailless ape of the families Pongidae and Hylobatidae, anatomically resembling humans, and comprising the gorillas, chimpanzees, orangutans, gibbons and siamangs. [1830–40]

anthropol., anthropology.

an•thro•pol•a•try (an′thrə pol′ə trē), *n.* the worship of a human being as a god. [1650–60; ANTHROPO- + -LATRY] —**an′thro•pol′a•ter,** *n.* —**an•thro•pol•a•tric** (an′thrə pol′ə trik, -pə la′trik), *adj.*

anthropolog′ical linguis′tics, the study of language in relation to culture, including the recording and analysis of the languages of nonliterate societies.

an•thro•pol•o•gist (an′thrə pol′ə jist), *n.* a person who specializes in anthropology. [1790–1800; ANTHROPOLOG(Y) + -IST]

an•thro•pol•o•gy (an′thrə pol′ə jē), *n.* **1.** the science that deals with the origins, physical and cultural development, biological characteristics, and social customs and beliefs of humankind. **2.** the study of human beings' similarity to and divergence from other animals. **3.** the science of humans and their works. **4.** Also called **philosophical anthropology.** the study of the nature and essence of humankind. [1585–95; ANTHROPO- + -LOGY] —**an•thro•po•log•i•cal** (an′thrə pə loj′i kəl), **an′thro•po•log′ic,** *adj.* —**an′thro•po•log′i•cal•ly,** *adv.*

an•thro•pom•e•ter (an′thrə pom′i tər), *n. Anthropol.* an instrument that consists of a calibrated, vertical rod to which are attached two horizontal arms, one fixed and one movable, for measuring the human trunk and limbs. [1880–85; ANTHROPO- + -METER]

an•thro•pom•e•try (an′thrə pom′i trē), *n.* the measurement of the size and proportions of the human body. [1830–40; ANTHROPO- + -METRY] —**an•thro•po•met•ric** (an′thrə pə me′trik, -pō-), **an′thro•po•met′ri•cal,** *adj.* —**an′thro•po•met′ri•cal•ly,** *adv.* —**an′thro•pom′e•trist,** *n.*

an•thro•po•mor•phic (an′thrə pə môr′fik), *adj.* **1.** ascribing human form or attributes to a being or thing not human, esp. to a deity. **2.** resembling or made to resemble a human form: *an anthropomorphic carving.* Also, **an′thro•po•mor′phous.** [1820–30; ANTHROPO- + -MORPHIC] —**an′thro•po•mor′phi•cal•ly, an′thro•po•mor′phous•ly,** *adv.*

an•thro•po•mor•phism (an′thrə pə môr′fiz əm), *n.* an anthropomorphic conception or representation, as of a deity. [1745–55; ANTHROPO- + -MORPHISM] —**an′•thro•po•mor′phist,** *n.*

an•thro•po•mor•phize (an′thrə pə môr′fīz), *v.t., v.i.,* **-phized, -phiz•ing.** to ascribe human form or attributes to (an animal, plant, material object, etc.). Also, *esp. Brit.,* **an′thro•po•mor′phise.** [1835–45; ANTHROPOMORPH(OUS) + -IZE] —**an′thro•po•mor′phi•za′•tion,** *n.*

an•thro•po•mor•pho•sis (an′thrə pə môr′fə sis), *n.* transformation into human form. [1860–65; ANTHROPO- + (META)MORPHOSIS]

an•thro•pon•o•my (an′thrə pon′ə mē), *n.* the science dealing with the laws regulating the development of the human organism in relation to other organisms and to environment. Also, **an•thro•po•nom•ics** (an′thrə pə-nom′iks). [ANTHROPO- + -NOMY] —**an′thro•po•nom′i•cal,** *adj.* —**an′thro•pon′o•mist,** *n.*

an•throp•o•nym (an throp′ə nim), *n.* a personal name. [1955–60; ANTHROP(O)- + -ONYM]

an•thro•pon•y•my (an′thrə pon′ə mē), *n.* the study of personal names. [1935–40; ANTHROPONYM + -Y[3], on the model of TOPONYMY]

an•thro•pop•a•thy (an′thrə pop′ə thē), *n.* ascription of human passions or feelings to a being or beings not human, esp. to a deity. Also, **an′thro•pop′a•thism.** [1640–50; < ML *anthrōpopatheia* < Gk *anthrōpopátheia* humanness. See ANTHROPO-, -PATHY] —**an•thro•po•path•ic** (an′thrə pə path′ik), *adj.*

an•thro•poph•a•gi (an′thrə pof′ə jī′, -gī′), *n.pl., sing.* **-a•gus** (-ə gəs). eaters of human flesh; cannibals. [1545–55; < L, pl. of *anthrōpophagus* cannibal < Gk *anthrōpophágos* man-eating. See ANTHROPO-, -PHAGE, -PHAGOUS]

an•thro•poph•a•gite (an′thrə pof′ə jīt′), *n.* an eater of human flesh; cannibal. [1595–1605; < L *anthrōpophag(us)* (see ANTHROPOPHAGI) + -ITE[1]]

an•thro•poph•a•gy (an′thrə pof′ə jē), *n.* the eating of human flesh; cannibalism. [1630–40; < Gk *anthrōpophagía.* See ANTHROPO-, -PHAGY] —**an•thro•po•phag•ic** (an′thrə pə faj′ik, -fā′jik), **an′thro•po•phag′i•cal, an•thro•poph•a•gous** (an′thrə pof′ə gəs), *adj.* —**an′thro•poph′a•gous•ly,** *adv.*

an•thro•pos•co•py (an′thrə pos′kə pē), *n.* physiognomy (def. 2). [1840–50; ANTHROPO- + -SCOPY]

an•thro•pos•o•phy (an′thrə pos′ə fē), *n.* a philosophy based on the teachings of Rudolf Steiner (1861–1925) which maintains that, by virtue of a prescribed method of self-discipline, cognitional experience of the spiritual world can be achieved. [1910–15; < G *Anthroposophie.* See ANTHROPO-, -SOPHY] —**an•thro•po•soph•i•cal** (an′-thrə pə sof′i kəl), **an′thro•po•soph′ic,** *adj.*

an•throp•o•sphere (an throp′ə sfēr′, an′thrə pə-), *n. Ecol.* noosphere.

an•thu•ri•um (an thŏŏr′ē əm), *n.* any tropical American plant belonging to the genus *Anthurium,* of the arum family, certain species of which are cultivated for their glossy red heart-shaped bract surrounding a rodlike spike of tiny yellow flowers. [1829; < NL *Anthurium,* equiv. to *anth-* ANTH- + *-urium* < Gk *our(á)* tail + NL *-ium* -IUM]

an•ti (an′tī, an′tē), *n., pl.* **-tis.** a person who is opposed to a particular practice, party, policy, action, etc. [1780–90; by shortening of words prefixed with ANTI-]

anti-, a prefix meaning "against," "opposite of," "antiparticle of," used in the formation of compound words (*anticline*); used freely in combination with elements of any origin (*antibody; antifreeze; antiknock; antilepton*). Also, *before a vowel,* **ant-.** [ME < L < Gk, prefixal use of *antí;* akin to Skt *ánti* opposite, L *ante,* MD *ende* (> D *en* and), E *an-* in ANSWER. Cf. ANTE-, AND]
—Note. The lists at the bottom of this and following pages provide the spelling, syllabification, and stress for words whose meanings may easily by inferred by combining the meanings of ANTI- and an attached base word, or base word plus a suffix. Appropriate parts of speech are also shown. Words prefixed by ANTI- that have special meanings or uses are entered in their proper alphabetical places in the main vocabulary or as derived forms run on at the end of a main vocabulary entry.

an•ti•a•bor•tion (an′tē ə bôr′shən, an′tī-), *adj.* **1.** opposed to abortion or the legalization of abortion. *—n.* **2.** opposition to abortion, esp. legalized abortion. [1965–70; ANTI- + ABORTION] **—an′ti•a•bor′tion•ist,** *n.*

an•ti•ag•ing (an′tē ā′jing, an′tī-), *adj.* effective in retarding the effects of aging: *Chemists hope to produce an antiaging drug.* Also, **an′ti•age′ing.** [ANTI- + AGE (v.) + -ING[1]]

an•ti•air•craft (an′tē âr′kraft′, -kräft′, an′tī-), *adj.* **1.** designed for or used in defense against enemy aircraft. *—n.* **2.** artillery used against enemy aircraft. **3.** a military organization operating and servicing antiaircraft artillery. **4.** shellfire from antiaircraft artillery: *The planes flew through heavy antiaircraft.* [1910–15; ANTI- + AIRCRAFT]

an•ti•al•co•hol•ism (an′tē al′kə hô liz′əm, -ho-, an′tī-), *n.* opposition to excessive drinking of alcoholic beverages. [ANTI- + ALCOHOLISM] **—an′ti•al′co•hol′ic,** *adj.* **—an′ti•al′co•hol•ist,** *n.*

an•ti•al•ler•gen•ic (an′tē al′ər jen′ik, an′tī-), *adj.* **1.** not aggravating an allergy; intended or prepared for those suffering from an allergy: *antiallergenic cosmetics.* *—n.* **2.** an antiallergenic substance. Also, **an•ti•al•ler•gic** (an′tē ə lûr′jik, an′tī-). [ANTI- + ALLERGENIC]

an•ti-A•mer•i•can (an′tē ə mer′i kən, an′tī-), *adj.* **1.** opposed or hostile to the United States of America, its people, its principles, or its policies. *—n.* **2.** an anti-American person. [1765–75, *Amer.,* in sense "anticolonial"; ANTI- + AMERICAN] **—an′ti-A•mer′i•can•ism,** *n.*

an•ti•an•ti•bod•y (an′tē an′ti bod′ē, an′tī-), *n. Immunol.* antibody that combines with another antibody. [ANTI- + ANTIBODY]

an•ti•anx•i•e•ty (an′tē ang zī′i tē, an′tī-), *adj.* tending to prevent or relieve anxiety. [1960–65; ANTI- + ANXIETY]

antianxi′ety drug′, *Pharm.* any of various substances, as benzodiazepines, that are primarily used to treat various forms of anxiety and psychosomatic conditions. Also called **anxiolytic, minor tranquilizer.**

an•ti•ar (an′tē är′), *n.* **1.** the upas tree. **2.** Also, **an•ti•a•rin** (an′tē ər in). an arrow poison prepared from the sap of the upas tree. [1860–65; said to be < Java Malay *ancar*]

an•ti•ar•rhyth•mic (an′tē ə rith′mik, -ə rith′-, an′tī-), *Pharm.* *—adj.* **1.** of or pertaining to any substance that prevents, inhibits, or alleviates heartbeat irregularities. *—n.* **2.** any such substance, as lidocaine. [1950–55; ANTI- + ARRHYTHMIC]

an•ti•art (an′tē ärt′, an′tī-), *n.* art, as dada, based on total rejection of established artistic practices and aesthetic values in favor of those that are arbitrary, shocking, and meaningless. [1940–45; ANTI- + ART[1]] **—an′ti•art′ist,** *n., adj.*

an•ti•at•om (an′tē at′əm, an′tī-), *n. Physics.* an atom of antimatter. [1965–70; ANTI- + ATOM]

an•ti•aux•in (an′tē ôk′sin, an′tī-), *n. Biochem.* a substance that inhibits the growth-regulating function of an auxin. [1950–55; ANTI- + AUXIN]

an•ti•bac•chi•us (an′ti bə kī′əs), *n., pl.* **-chi•i** (-kī′ī, -kī′ē). *Pros.* a foot of three syllables that in quantitative meter consists of two long syllables followed by a short one, and that in accentual meter consists of two stressed syllables followed by an unstressed one. Cf. **bacchius.** [1580–90; < LL < Gk *antibákcheios.* See ANTI-, BACCHIUS] **—an•ti•bac•chic** (an′ti bak′ik), *adj.*

an•ti•bac•te•ri•al (an′tē bak tēr′ē əl, an′tī-), *adj.* destructive to or inhibiting the growth of bacteria. [1895–1900; ANTI- + BACTERIAL]

an•ti•bal•lis•tic (an′tē bə lis′tik, an′tī-), *adj. Mil.* designed to detect, intercept, or destroy ballistic missiles: *an antiballistic missile.* [1955–60; ANTI- + BALLISTIC]

An′tiballis′tic Mis′sile Trea′ty, an agreement between the U.S. and U.S.S.R., signed May 26, 1972, limiting the number of ABM deployment areas, launchers, and interceptors.

an•ti•bar•y•on (an′tē bar′ē on′, an′tī-), *n. Physics.* the antiparticle of a baryon, having baryon number −1 and charge, strangeness, and other quantum numbers opposite in sign to those of the baryon. [ANTI- + BARYON]

An•tibes (äɴ tēb′), *n.* a seaport in SE France, SW of Nice: preserved ruins of 4th-century B.C. Roman town. 56,309.

an•ti•bil•ious (an′tē bil′yəs, an′tī-), *adj.* serving to prevent or cure biliousness. [1810–20; ANTI- + BILIOUS]

an•ti•bi•o•sis (an′tē bī ō′sis, an′tī-), *n. Biol.* an association between organisms that is injurious to one of them. [1895–1900; ANTI- + -BIOSIS]

an•ti•bi•ot•ic (an′ti bī ot′ik, -bē-, an′tē-, -tī-), *Biochem., Pharm.* *—n.* **1.** any of a large group of chemical substances, as penicillin or streptomycin, produced by various microorganisms and fungi, having the capacity in dilute solutions to inhibit the growth of or to destroy bacteria and other microorganisms, used chiefly in the treatment of infectious diseases. *—adj.* **2.** of or involving antibiotics. [1855–60, for an earlier sense; ANTI- + BIOTIC] **—an′ti•bi•ot′i•cal•ly,** *adv.*

an•ti•black (an′tē blak′, an′tī-), *adj.* resistant or antagonistic to black people or their values or objectives: *antiblack sentiment among some reactionary groups.* [1950–55; ANTI- + BLACK] **—an′ti•black′ism,** *n.*

an•ti•blas•tic (an′tē blas′tik, an′tī-), *adj. Biol.* antagonistic to growth. [ANTI- + -BLAST + -IC]

an•ti•bod•y (an′ti bod′ē), *n., pl.* **-bod•ies.** **1.** any of numerous Y-shaped protein molecules produced by B cells as a primary immune defense, each molecule and its clones having a unique binding site that can combine with the complementary site of a foreign antigen, as on a virus or bacterium, thereby disabling the antigen and signaling other immune defenses. *Abbr.:* Ab **2.** antibodies of a particular type collectively. Also called **immunoglobulin.** [1895–1900; ANTI- + BODY]

an′ti•bod•y-me′di•at•ed immu′nity (an′ti bod′ē mē′dē ā′tid, an′tē-), *Immunol.* immunity conferred to an individual through the activity of B cells and their progeny, which produce circulating antibodies in response to the presence of a foreign substance and recognize the substance upon renewed exposure. Also called **humoral immunity.** Cf. **cell-mediated immunity.**

an•ti•bug•ging (an′tē bug′ing, an′tī-), *adj.* **1.** designed to detect and alert a person to the use of a secret listening device: *to install antibugging equipment.* **2.** designed to prevent or counteract the use of a secret listening device. [ANTI- + BUG[1] + -ING[1]]

an•ti•bus•er (an′tē bus′ər, an′tī-), *n.* a person who opposes the busing of students to achieve racial balance in public schools. Also, **an′ti•bus′ser.** [1970–75, *Amer.;* ANTIBUS(ING) + -ER[1]]

an•ti•bus•ing (an′tē bus′ing, an′tī-), *adj.* opposing legislation that requires the busing of students from one school or school district to another to achieve racial balance in public schools. Also, **an′ti•bus′sing.** [1965–70, *Amer.;* ANTI- + BUSING]

an•tic (an′tik), *n., adj., v.,* **-ticked, -tick•ing.** *—n.* **1.** Usually, **antics. a.** a playful trick or prank; caper. **b.** a grotesque, fantastic, or ludicrous gesture, act, or posture. **2.** *Archaic.* **a.** an actor in a grotesque or ridiculous presentation. **b.** a buffoon; clown. **3.** *Obs.* **a.** a grotesque theatrical presentation; ridiculous interlude. **b.** a grotesque or fantastic sculptured figure, as a gargoyle. *—adj.* **4.** ludicrous; funny. **5.** fantastic; odd; grotesque: *an antic disposition.* *—v.i.* **6.** *Obs.* to perform antics; caper. [1520–30; earlier *antike, antique* < It *antico* ancient (< L *anticus, antiquus;* see ANTIQUE), appar. taken to mean "grotesque," as used in descriptions of fantastic figures found in Roman ruins] **—an′ti•cal•ly,** *adv.*

an•ti•can•cer (an′tē kan′sər, an′tī-), *adj.* for or used in the prevention or treatment of cancer: *an anticancer drug.* [1925–30; ANTI- + CANCER]

an•ti•car•i•ous (an′tē kâr′ē əs, -kar′-, an′tī-), *adj. Dentistry.* preventing or retarding caries. [ANTI- + CARIOUS]

an•ti•cat•a•lase (an′tē kat′l ās′, -āz′, an′tī-), *n. Biochem.* a substance that inhibits the enzymatic action of a catalase. [ANTI- + CATALASE]

an•ti•cat•a•lyst (an′tē kat′l ist, an′tī-), *n. Chem.* an inhibitor. [1920–25; ANTI- + CATALYST]

an•ti•ca•thex•is (an′tē kə thek′sis, an′tī-), *n. Psychoanal.* a change from one emotion to its opposite, as from hate to love. [ANTI- + CATHEXIS]

an•ti•cath•ode (an′tē kath′ōd, an′tī-), *n.* the positive plate of an x-ray or other electron tube serving as the target for electrons coming from the cathode, which cause it to emit high-frequency radiations. [1905–10; ANTI- + CATHODE]

an•ti•cav•i•ty (an′tē kav′i tē, an′tī-), *adj.* designed to prevent the occurrence of cavities in teeth: *an anticavity toothpaste.* [ANTI- + CAVITY]

an•ti•cen•ter (an′tē sen′tər, an′tī-), *n.* **1.** *Geol.* the point on the surface of the earth diametrically opposite the epicenter of an earthquake. **2.** *Astron.* the point on the celestial sphere diametrically opposite the galactic center. [ANTI- + CENTER]

an•ti•chlor (an′ti klôr′, -klōr′), *n. Chem.* any of various substances, esp. sodium thiosulfate, used for removing excess chlorine from paper pulp, textile, fiber, etc., after bleaching. [1865–70; ANTI- + CHLOR(INE)] **—an•ti•chlo•ris•tic** (an′ti klō ris′tik, -klō-), *adj.*

an•ti•choice (an′tē chois′, an′tī-), *adj.* opposed to the concept that a pregnant woman has the right to choose abortion. [ANTI- + CHOICE]

an•ti•cho•lin•er•gic (an′ti kō′lə nûr′jik, -kol′ə-), *Biochem., Pharm.* *—adj.* **1.** of or pertaining to a substance that opposes the effects of acetylcholine; interfering with the passage of parasympathetic nerve impulses. Cf. **cholinolytic.** *—n.* **2.** an anticholinergic substance, as a drug. [1940–45; ANTI- + *cholinergic,* equiv. to CHOLINE + -ERGIC]

an•ti•cho•lin•es•ter•ase (an′tē kō′lə nes′tə rās′, -rāz′, -kol′ə-, an′tī-), *n. Biochem., Pharm.* an enzyme or drug that blocks the action of acetylcholinesterase, thereby increasing the stimulating effect of acetylcholine on the muscles. [1950–55; ANTI- + CHOLINESTERASE]

An•ti•christ (an′ti krīst′), *n. Theol.* **1.** a particular personage or power, variously identified or explained, who is conceived of as appearing in the world as the principal antagonist of Christ. **2.** (*sometimes l.c.*) an opponent of Christ; a person or power antagonistic to Christ. **3.** (*often l.c.*) a disbeliever in Christ. **4.** (*often l.c.*) a false Christ. [bef. 1150; ME, OE < LL *Antichristus* < LGk *Antíchristos* the Antichrist. See ANTI-, CHRIST]

an•tich•thon (an tik′thon, -thən), *n., pl.* **-tho•nes** (-thə nēz′). counterearth. [1645–55; < L *antichthonēs* (pl.) < Gk *antíchthones* the antipodes, equiv. to *anti* ANTI- + *chthon-* (s. of *chthṓn*) earth + *-es* pl. n. suffix]

an•tic•i•pant (an tis′ə pənt), *adj.* **1.** anticipative (usually fol. by *of*): *We were eagerly anticipant of her arrival.* *—n.* **2.** a person who anticipates. [1620–30; < L *anticipant-* (s. of *anticipāns,* prp. of *anticipāre*) taking before, equiv. to *anti-* (var. of *ante-* ANTE-) + *-cip-* (comb. form of *capere* to take) + *-ant-* -ANT]

an•tic•i•pate (an tis′ə pāt′), *v.t.,* **-pat•ed, -pat•ing.** **1.** to realize beforehand; foretaste or foresee: *to anticipate pleasure.* **2.** to expect; look forward to; be sure of: *to anticipate a favorable decision.* **3.** to perform (an action) before another has had time to act. **4.** to answer (a question), obey (a command), or satisfy (a request) before it is made: *He anticipated each of my orders.* **5.** to nullify, prevent, or forestall by taking countermeasures in advance: *to anticipate a military attack.* **6.** to consider or mention before the proper time: *to anticipate more difficult questions.* **7.** to be before (another) in doing, thinking, achieving, etc.: *Many modern inventions were anticipated by Leonardo da Vinci.* **8.** *Finance.* **a.** to expend (funds) before they are legitimately available for use. **b.** to discharge (an obligation) before it is due. *—v.i.* **9.** to think, speak, act, or feel an emotional response in advance. [1525–35; < L *anticipātus* taken before, fore, anticipated (ptp. of *anticipāre*), equiv. to *anti-* (var. of *ante-* ANTE-) + *-cip-* (comb. form of *capere* to take) + *-ātus* -ATE[1]] **—an•tic′i•pat′a•ble,** *adj.* **—an•tic′i•pa′•tor,** *n.*

CONCISE PRONUNCIATION KEY: *act, cāpe, dâre, pärt; set, ēqual; if, īce; ox, ōver, ôrder, oil, bo͝ok, bo͞ot, out; up, ûrge; child; sing; shoe; thin, that;* zh as in *treasure.* ə = *a* as in *alone, e* as in *system, i* as in *easily, o* as in *gallop, u* as in *circus;* ᵊ as in *fire* (fīᵊr), *hour* (ouᵊr). l and n can serve as syllabic consonants, as in *cradle* (krād′l), and *button* (but′n). See the full key inside the front cover.

an′ti•a•buse′, *adj.*
an′ti•ac′a•dem′ic, *adj., n.*
an′ti•ad•min′is•tra′tion, *n., adj.*
an′ti•ag•glu′ti•nant, *adj., n.*
an′ti•ag•glu′ti•na′tion, *adj.*
an′ti•ag•glu′ti•na′tive, *adj.*
an′ti•ag•gres′sion, *adj.*
an′ti•ag•gres′sive, *adj.;* **-ly,** *adv.;* **-ness,** *n.*
an′ti•an′a•phy•lac′tic, *adj., n.*
an′ti•an′nex•a′tion, *adj.*
an′ti•an′nex•a′tion•ist, *n., adj.*
an′ti•a•part′heid, *n., adj.*
an′ti•aph′ro•dis′i•ac′, *adj., n.*
an′ti-Ar′ab, *adj., n.*
an′ti•ar′is•toc′ra•cy, *adj., n., pl.* **-cies.**
an′ti•a•ris′to•crat′ic, *adj.*
an′ti•a•ris′to•crat′i•cal, *adj.;* **-ly,** *adv.*
an′ti-Ar′is•to•te′lian, *adj., n.*
an′ti-Ar′is•to•te′lian•ism, *n.*
an′ti•ar′mor, *adj.*
an′ti•ar•thrit′ic, *adj., n.*
an′ti•as•sim′i•la′tion, *n., adj.*
an′ti•asth•mat′ic, *adj., n.*
an′ti•a′the•ism, *adj., n.*
an′ti•a′the•ist, *n., adj.*
an′ti•a′the•is′tic, *adj.*
an′ti•a′the•is′ti•cal, *adj.;* **-ly,** *adv.*
an′ti-Aus•tral′ian, *adj., n.*
an′ti-Aus′tri•a, *adj.*
an′ti-Aus′tri•an, *adj., n.*
an′ti•au•thor′i•tar′i•an, *adj.*
an′ti•au•thor′i•tar′i•an•ism, *n.*
an′ti•au•thor′i•ty, *adj.*
an′ti-Bi′ble, *adj.*
an′ti-Bib′li•cal, *adj.;* **-ly,** *adv.*
an′ti-Bol′she•vik, *n., adj.*
an′ti-Bol′she•vism, *n.*
an′ti-Bol′she•vist, *n., adj.*
an′ti-Bol′she•vis′tic, *adj.*
an′ti•bour•geois′, *n., pl.* **-geois′,** *adj.*
an′ti•boy′cott, *n., adj.*
an′ti-Brit′ish, *adj., n.*
an′ti•bu′rea•crat′ic, *adj.*
an′ti•bur′gla•ry, *adj.*
an′ti•busi′ness, *adj.*
an′ti-Cal′vin•ism, *n.*
an′ti-Cal′vin•ist, *n., adj.*
an′ti-Cal′vin•is′tic, *adj.*
an′ti-Cal′vin•is′ti•cal, *adj.*
an′ti•cap′i•tal•ism, *n.*
an′ti•cap′i•tal•ist, *n., adj.*
an′ti•cap′i•tal•is′tic, *adj.*
an′ti•cap′i•tal•is′ti•cal•ly, *adv.*
an′ti•car•cin′o•gen, *n.*
an′ti•car′cin•o•gen′ic, *adj.*
an′ti•caste′, *adj.*
an′ti•cat′a•lyt′ic, *adj., n.*
an′ti•cat′a•lyt′i•cal•ly, *adv.*
an′ti-Cath′o•lic, *adj., n.*
an′ti-Ca•thol′i•cism, *n.*
an′ti•cen•so′ri•al, *adj.*
an′ti•cen•so′ri•ous, *adj.;* **-ly,** *adv.;* **-ness,** *n.*
an′ti•cen′sor•ship′, *adj.*
an′ti•cen′tral•ism, *n.*
an′ti•cen′tral•ist, *n., adj.*
an′ti•cen′tral•i•za′tion, *adj., n.*
an′ti•cer′e•mo′ni•al, *adj.;* **-ly,** *adv.*
an′ti•cer′e•mo′ni•al•ism, *n.*
an′ti•cer′e•mo′ni•al•ist, *n., adj.*
an′ti•cer′e•mo′ni•ous, *adj.;* **-ly,** *adv.;* **-ness,** *n.*
an′ti-Chris′tian, *adj.*
an′ti•church′, *adj.*
an′ti•cig′a•rette′, *adj.*
an′ti•civ′ic, *adj.*
an′ti•civ′il, *adj.*
an′ti•ci•vil′ian, *adj.*
an′ti•clas′si•cal, *adj.;* **-ly,** *adv.;* **-ness,** *n.*
an′ti•clas′si•cal•ism, *n.*
an′ti•clas′si•cal•ist, *n., adj.*
an′ti•clas′si•cism, *n.*
an′ti•clas′si•cist, *n., adj.*
an′ti•cler′gy, *adj.*
an′ti•cling′, *adj.*
an′ti•clog′ging, *adj.*
an′ti•co•ag′u•lat′ing, *adj.*
an′ti•co•ag′u•la′tion, *n., adj.*
an′ti•co•ag′u•la′tor, *n.*
an′ti•col•li′sion, *adj.*
an′ti•com•mer′cial, *adj.;* **-ly,** *adv.;* **-ness,** *n.*
an′ti•com•mer′cial•ism, *n.*
an′ti•com•mer′cial•ist, *n., adj.*
an′ti•com•mer′cial•is′tic, *adj.*
an′ti•com•mer′ci•al′i•ty, *n.*
an′ti•com′mu•nism, *n.*
an′ti•com′mu•nist, *n., adj.*
an′ti•com′mu•nis′tic, *adj.*
an′ti•com′mu•nis′ti•cal, *adj.;* **-ly,** *adv.*
an′ti•com•pet′i•tive, *adj.;* **-ly,** *adv.;* **-ness,** *n.*
an′ti•con•fed′er•a′tion•ism, *n.*
an′ti•con•fed′er•a′tion•ist, *n., adj.*
an′ti•con•fed′er•a′tive, *adj.*
an′ti•con•form′ist, *n.*
an′ti•con•form′i•ty, *n., pl.* **-ties.**
an′ti-Con•fu′cian, *n., adj.*
an′ti-Con•fu′cian•ism, *n.*
an′ti•con•scrip′tion, *n.*
an′ti•con′ser•va′tion, *n., adj.*
an′ti•con′ser•va′tion•ism, *n.*
an′ti•con′ser•va′tion•ist, *n.*
an′ti•con•serv′a•tism, *n.*
an′ti•con•serv′a•tive, *adj., n.;* **-ly,** *adv.;* **-ness,** *n.*

—**Syn. 1.** See **expect. 5.** preclude, obviate.
—**Usage.** Despite claims that ANTICIPATE should only be used to mean "to perform (an action) or respond to (a question, etc.) in advance" or "to forestall," it has been used widely since the 18th century as a synonym for *expect,* often with an implication of pleasure: *We anticipate a large turnout at the next meeting.* This use is standard in all types of speech and writing.

an•tic•i•pa•tion (an tis′ə pā′shən), *n.* **1.** the act of anticipating or the state of being anticipated. **2.** realization in advance; foretaste. **3.** expectation or hope. **4.** previous notion; slight previous impression. **5.** intuition, foreknowledge, or prescience. **6.** *Law.* a premature withdrawal or assignment of money from a trust estate. **7.** *Music.* a tone introduced in advance of its harmony so that it sounds against the preceding chord. [1540–50; (< MF) < L *anticipātiōn-* (s. of *anticipātiō*), equiv. to *anticipāt(us)* (ptp.; see ANTICIPATE) + *-iōn-* -ION]

A, **anticipation** (def. 7)

an•tic•i•pa•tive (an tis′ə pā′tiv, -pə tiv), *adj.* anticipating or tending to anticipate; expressing, revealing, or containing anticipation: *an anticipative action; an anticipative look.* [1655–65; ANTICIPATE + -IVE] —**an•tic′•i•pa′tive•ly,** *adv.*

an•tic•i•pa•to•ry (an tis′ə pə tôr′ē, -tōr′ē), *adj.* of, showing, or expressing anticipation. [1660–70; ANTICIPATE + -ORY[1]] —**an•tic′i•pa•to′ri•ly,** *adv.*

antic′ipatory assimila′tion. See **regressive assimilation.**

an•ti•clas•tic (an′tē klas′tik, an′tī-), *adj. Math.* (of a surface) having principal curvatures of opposite sign at a given point. Cf. **synclastic.** [1865–70; ANTI- + CLASTIC]

an•ti•cler•i•cal (an′tē kler′i kəl, an′tī-), *adj.* opposed to the influence and activities of the clergy or the church in secular or public affairs. [1835–45; ANTI- + CLERICAL] —**an′ti•cler′i•cal•ism,** *n.* —**an′ti•cler′i•cal•ist,** *n.*

an•ti•cli•mac•tic (an′tē klī mak′tik, -klə-, an′tī-), *adj.* of, like, pertaining to, or expressing anticlimax. [1895–1900; ANTI + CLIMACTIC] —**an′ti•cli•mac′ti•cal•ly,** *adv.*

an•ti•cli•max (an′ti klī′maks), *n.* **1.** an event, conclusion, statement, etc., that is far less important, powerful, or striking than expected. **2.** a descent in power, quality, dignity, etc.; a disappointing, weak, or inglorious conclusion: *After serving as President, he may find life in retirement an anticlimax.* **3.** a noticeable or ludicrous descent from lofty ideas or expressions to banalities or commonplace remarks: *We were amused by the anticlimax of the company's motto: "For God, for country, and for Acme Gasworks."* [1720–30; ANTI- + CLIMAX]

an•ti•cli•nal (an′ti klīn′l), *adj.* **1.** inclining in opposite directions from a central axis. **2.** *Geol.* **a.** inclining downward on both sides from a median line or axis, as a fold of rock strata. **b.** pertaining to such a fold. [1825–35; < Gk *antiklín(ein)* to lean against each other (*anti-* ANTI- + *klínein* to LEAN[1]) + -AL[1]]

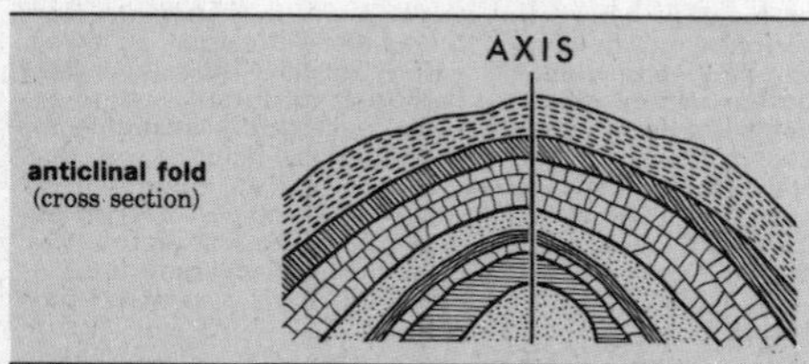

anticlinal fold (cross section)

CONCISE ETYMOLOGY KEY: <, descended or borrowed from; >, whence; b., blend of, blended; c., cognate with; cf., compare; deriv., derivative; equiv., equivalent; imit., imitative; obl., oblique; r., replacing; s., stem; sp., spelling, spelled; resp., respelling, respelled; trans., translation; ?, origin unknown; *, unattested; ‡, probably earlier than. See the full key inside the front cover.

an•ti•cline (an′ti klīn′), *n. Geol.* an anticlinal rock structure. [1860–65; back formation from ANTICLINAL]

an•ti•cli•no•ri•um (an′ti klī nôr′ē əm, -nōr′-), *n., pl.* **-no•ri•a** (-nôr′ē ə, -nōr′-). *Geol.* a compound anticline, consisting of a series of subordinate anticlines and synclines, the whole having the general contour of an arch. [1870–75 < NL; see ANTICLINE, -ORIUM]

an•ti•clock•wise (an′ti klok′wīz′), *adj., adv. Chiefly Brit.* counterclockwise. [1895–1900; ANTI- + CLOCKWISE]

an•ti•clot•ting (an′tē klot′ing, an′tī-), *adj. Biochem., Pharm.* anticoagulant (def. 1). [ANTI- + CLOTTING]

an•tic•ly (an′tik lē), *adv.* in an antic manner. [1550–60; ANTIC + -LY]

an•ti•co•ag•u•lant (an′tē kō ag′yə lənt, an′tī-), *Biochem., Pharm.* —*adj.* **1.** Also, **an•ti•co•ag•u•la•tive** (an′tē kō ag′yə lā′tiv, -lə tiv, an′tī-). preventing coagulation, esp. of blood. —*n.* **2.** an anticoagulant agent, as heparin. [1900–05; ANTI- + COAGULANT]

an•ti•co•don (an′tē kō′don, an′tī-), *n. Genetics.* a sequence of three nucleotides in a region of transfer RNA that recognizes a complementary coding triplet of nucleotides in messenger RNA during translation by the ribosomes in protein biosynthesis. Cf. **codon.** [1960–65; ANTI- + CODON]

an•ti•co•lo•ni•al (an′tē kə lō′nē əl, an′tī-), *adj.* **1.** opposing colonialism. —*n.* **2.** a person or country that actively opposes colonialism. [ANTI- + COLONIAL]

an•ti•co•lo•ni•al•ism (an′tē kə lō′nē ə liz′əm, an′tī-), *n.* opposition to colonialism. [ANTICOLONIAL + -ISM] —**an′ti•co•lo′ni•al•ist,** *n., adj.*

An′ti-Com′in•tern Pact′ (an′tē kom′in tûrn′, -kom′in tûrn′, an′tī-), a pact formed in 1936, based on agreements between Germany and Japan to oppose communism and the Third International: Italy and Spain subsequently became signatories.

an•ti•com•mu•ta•tive (an′tē kə myōō′tə tiv, -kom′-yə tā′-, an′tī-), *adj. Math.* **1.** (of a binary operation) having the property that one term operating on a second is equal to the negative of the second operating on the first, as $ab = -ba$. **2.** (of two matrices) defined by an anticommutative operation. [ANTI- + COMMUTATIVE]

an•ti•co•ro•na (an′tē kə rō′nə), *n.* a luminous edging around the shadow of an observer or the point where his or her shadow would fall, as thrown by the sun upon a cloud or fog bank. Also called **Brocken bow, glory.** [ANTI- + CORONA]

an•ti•cor•ro•sive (an′tē kə rō′siv, an′tī-), *n.* **1.** something that prevents or counteracts corrosion. —*adj.* **2.** Also, **an′ti•cor•ro′sion.** preventing or counteracting corrosion. [1815–25; ANTI- + CORROSIVE] —**an′ti•cor•ro′sive•ly,** *adv.* —**an′ti•cor•ro′sive•ness,** *n.*

An•ti•cos•ti (an′tə kô′stē, -kos′tē), *n.* an island at the head of the Gulf of St. Lawrence in E Canada, in E Quebec province. 494; 135 mi. (217 km) long; 3043 sq. mi. (7880 sq. km).

an′ti•cre•pus′cu•lar arch′ (an′tē kri pus′kyə lər, an′tī-, an′tē-, an′tī-). See **antitwilight arch.** [ANTI- + CREPUSCULAR]

an•ti•cryp•tic (an′tē krip′tik, an′tī-), *adj. Zool.* serving to conceal an animal from its prey. Cf. **procryptic.** [1885–90; ANTI- + CRYPTIC] —**an′ti•cryp′ti•cal•ly,** *adv.*

an•ti•cum (an tī′kəm), *n., pl.* **-ca** (-kə). pronaos. [< NL, appar. neut. of L *antīcus, antīquus* pertaining to the front, existing previously, ancient (see ANTIQUE); NL sense by analogy with L *postīcum* POSTICUM]

an•ti•cy•cli•cal (an′tē sī′kli kəl, -sik′li-, an′tī-), *adj.* not conforming to or following a cycle: *anticyclical sales that rise when the economy fades.* Also, **an′ti•cy′clic.** [ANTI- + CYCLICAL] —**an′ti•cy′cli•cal•ly,** *adv.*

an•ti•cy•clo•gen•e•sis (an′tē sī′klō jen′ə sis, an′tī-), *n. Meteorol.* the intensification or development of an anticyclone. Cf. **anticyclolysis.** [ANTICYCLO(NE) + GENESIS]

an•ti•cy•clol•y•sis (an′tē sī klol′ə sis, an′tī-), *n. Meteorol.* the weakening or extinction of an anticyclone. Cf. **anticyclogenesis.** [ANTICYCLO(NE) + -LYSIS]

an•ti•cy•clone (an′tē sī′klōn, an′tī-), *n. Meteorol.* a circulation of winds around a central region of high atmospheric pressure, clockwise in the Northern Hemisphere, counterclockwise in the Southern Hemisphere. Cf. **cyclone** (def. 1), **high** (def. 41). [1875–80; ANTI- + CYCLONE] —**an•ti•cy•clon•ic** (an′tē sī klon′ik, an′tī-), *adj.*

an•ti•de•pres•sant (an′tē di pres′ənt, an′tī-), *Pharm.* —*adj.* **1.** of or pertaining to a substance that is used in the treatment of mood disorders, as characterized by various manic or depressive affects. —*n.* **2.** Also called **energizer, psychic energizer.** any such substance, as a tricyclic antidepressant, MAO inhibitor, or lithium. Also, **an′ti•de•pres′sant, an•ti•de•pres•sive** (an′tē di pres′-iv, an′tī-). [1960–65; ANTI- + DEPRESSANT]

an•ti•de•riv•a•tive (an′tē də riv′ə tiv, an′tī-), *n.* See **indefinite integral.** [1940–45; ANTI- + DERIVATIVE]

an•ti•des•ic•cant (an′tē des′i kənt, an′tī-), *n. Hort.* a substance or material applied to a plant, as by spraying, to inhibit moisture loss during transplanting. [ANTI- + DESICCANT]

an•ti•dis•es•tab•lish•men•tar•i•an (an′tē dis′ə-stab′lish mən târ′ē ən, an′tī-), *n.* **1.** a person who advocates antidisestablishmentarianism. —*adj.* **2.** of or pertaining to antidisestablishmentarianism. [ANTI- + DISESTABLISHMENT + -ARIAN]

an•ti•dis•es•tab•lish•men•tar•i•an•ism (an′tē dis′-ə stab′lish mən târ′ē ə niz′əm, an′tī-), *n.* opposition to the withdrawal of state support or recognition from an established church, esp. the Anglican Church in 19th-century England. [ANTI- + DISESTABLISHMENT + -ARIAN + -ISM]

an•ti•di•u•ret•ic (an′tē dī′ə ret′ik), *Biochem., Pharm.* —*adj.* **1.** of or pertaining to a substance that suppresses the formation of urine. —*n.* **2.** any such substance. [1940–45; ANTI- + DIURETIC]

an′tidiuret′ic hor′mone, *Biochem.* vasopressin. *Abbr.:* ADH

an•ti•do•ron (än dē′thô rôn; *Eng.* an′tē dôr′on, -dōr′-), *n.* **1.** Also called **holy bread.** *Gk. Orth. Ch.* bread blessed and distributed to the congregation at the end of the liturgy. **2.** *Eastern Ch.* eulogia (def. 1). [1840–50; < LGk *antidôron* return gift, equiv. to *anti-* ANTI- + *dôron* gift, deriv. of *didónai* to give]

an•ti•dote (an′ti dōt′), *n., v.,* **-dot•ed, -dot•ing.** —*n.* **1.** a medicine or other remedy for counteracting the effects of poison, disease, etc. **2.** something that prevents or counteracts injurious or unwanted effects: *Good jobs are the best antidote to teenage crime.* —*v.t.* **3.** to counteract with an antidote: *Medication was given to antidote the poison the child had swallowed.* [1400–50; late ME (< MF) < L *antidotum* < Gk *antídoton* something given against (i.e., for counteracting), equiv. to *anti-* ANTI- + *dotón* neut. of *dotós* given, verbid of *didónai* to give; akin to DATUM] —**an′ti•dot′al, an•ti•dot•i•cal** (an′ti dot′i kəl), *adj.* —**an′ti•dot′al•ly, an′ti•dot′i•cal•ly,** *adv.*

an•ti•drom•ic (an′ti drom′ik), *adj. Physiol.* conducting nerve impulses in a direction opposite to the usual one. [1905–10; ANTI- + -DROME + -IC] —**an′ti•drom′i•cal•ly,** *adv.*

an•ti•drug (an′tē drug′, an′tī-), *adj.* opposing or restricting the use of narcotics or other drugs of abuse: *to enact stricter antidrug laws.* [1965–70; ANTI- + DRUG]

an•ti•dump•ing (an′tē dum′ping, an′tī-), *adj.* intended to discourage the dumping of imported commodities, esp. by imposing extra customs duties: *antidumping measures against foreign steel.* [1910–15; ANTI- + DUMPING]

an•ti•e•lec•tron (an′tē i lek′tron, an′tī-), *n. Physics.* a positron. [ANTI- + ELECTRON]

an•ti•e•met•ic (an′tē ə met′ik, an′tī-), *Pharm.* —*adj.* **1.** of or pertaining to a substance that is useful in the suppression of nausea or vomiting. —*n.* **2.** any such substance. [ANTI- + EMETIC]

an•ti•en•er•gis•tic (an′tē en′ər jis′tik, an′tī-), *adj.* opposing or resisting applied energy. [ANTI- + ENERG(IZE) + -ISTIC]

an•ti•en•zyme (an′tē en′zīm, an′tī-), *n. Biochem.* a substance that inhibits or counteracts the action of an enzyme. [1900–05; ANTI- + ENZYME] —**an•ti•en•zy•mat•ic** (an′tē en′zī mat′ik, -zi-, an′tī-), **an•ti•en•zy•mic** (an′tē en zī′mik, -zim′ik, an′tī-), *adj.*

an•ti•es•tab•lish•ment (an′tē i stab′lish mənt, an′-tī-), *adj.* opposed to or working against the existing power structure or mores, as of society or government: *Antiestablishment candidates promised to disband the army, Congress, and the cabinet if elected.* [1955–60; ANTI- + ESTABLISHMENT]

an•ti•es•tab•lish•men•tar•i•an (an′tē i stab′lish-mən târ′ē ən, an′tī-), *n.* **1.** a person who supports or advocates antiestablishmentarianism. —*adj.* **2.** of, pertaining to, or characteristic of antiestablishmentarianism. [ANTI- + ESTABLISHMENTARIAN]

an•ti•es•tab•lish•men•tar•i•an•ism (an′tē i stab′-

an′ti•con′sti•tu′tion, *adj.*
an′ti•con′sti•tu′tion•al, *adj.;* **-ly,** *adv.*
an′ti•con′sti•tu′tion•al•ism, *n.*
an′ti•con′sti•tu′tion•al•ist, *adj., n.*
an′ti•con•sum′er, *n., adj.*
an•ti•con•sum′er•ism, *n.*
an′ti•con•ta′gious, *adj.;* **-ly,** *adv.;* **-ness,** *n.*
an•ti•con•ven′tion, *adj.*
an′ti•con•ven′tion•al, *adj.;* **-ly,** *adv.*
an•ti•con•ven′tion•al•ism, *n.*
an′ti•con•ven′tion•al•ist, *n., adj.*
an•ti•con•vul′sant, *adj., n.*
an′ti•cor′por•ate, *adj.;* **-ly,** *adv.;* **-ness,** *n.*
an′ti•cor•rup′tion, *n., adj.*
an′ti•cos•met′ics, *adj.*
an′ti•cre•a′tion, *adj.*
an′ti•cre•a′tion•al, *adj.*
an′ti•cre•a′tion•ism, *n.*
an′ti•cre•a′tion•ist, *n., adj.*
an′ti•cre•a′tive, *adj.;* **-ly,** *adv.;* **-ness,** *n.*
an′ti•cre′a•tiv′i•ty, *n.*
an′ti•crime′, *adj.*
an′ti•crit′i•cal, *adj.;* **-ly,** *adv.;* **-ness,** *n.*
an′ti•cru′el•ty, *adj.*
an′ti•cult′, *n., adj.*
an′ti•cul′tur•al, *adj.;* **-ly,** *adv.*
an′ti•cul′ture, *n.*
an′ti•cyn′ic, *n., adj.*
an′ti•cyn′i•cal, *adj.;* **-ly,** *adv.*
an′′ti•cyn′i•cism, *n.*
an′ti•danc′ing, *adj.*
an′ti-Dar′win, *adj.*
an′ti-Dar•win′i•an, *n., adj.*
an′ti-Dar′win•ism, *n.*
an′ti-Dar′win•ist, *n., adj.*
an′ti•deg′ra•da′tion, *adj.*
an′ti•de•moc′ra•cy, *n., pl.* **-cies,** *adj.*
an′ti•dem′o•crat′, *n.*
an′ti•dem′o•crat′ic, *adj.*
an′ti•dem′o•crat′i•cal, *adj.;* **-ly,** *adv.*
an′ti•de•pres′sion, *adj., n.*
an′ti•de•seg′re•ga′tion, *adj.*
an′ti•de•vel′op•ment, *adj.*
an′ti•di′a•bet′ic, *adj.*
an′ti•di′ar•rhe′al, *adj.*
an′ti•di•lu′tion, *adj.*
an′ti•di•lu′tive, *adj.*
an′ti•diph′the•rit′ic, *adj., n.*
an′ti•dis•crim′i•na′tion, *adj.*
an′ti•dis′si•dent, *n., adj.*
an′ti•di•vorce′, *adj.*
an′ti•dog•mat′ic, *adj.*
an′ti•dog•mat′i•cal, *adj.;* **-ly,** *adv.*
an′ti•dog′ma•tism, *n.*
an′ti•dog′ma•tist, *n., adj.*
an′ti•do•mes′tic, *adj.*
an′ti•do•mes′ti•cal•ly, *adv.*
an′ti•draft′, *adj.*
an′ti•dy•nas′tic, *adj.*
an′ti•dy•nas′ti•cal, *adj.;* **-ly,** *adv.*
an′ti•dy′nas•ty, *adj.*
an′ti•eaves′drop′ping, *adj.*
an′ti•ec•cle′si•as′tic, *n., adj.*
an′ti•ec•cle′si•as′ti•cal, *adj.;* **-ly,** *adv.*
an′ti•ec•cle′si•as′ti•cism, *n.*
an′ti•ec′o•nom′ic, *adj.*
an′ti•ed′u•ca′tion, *adj.*
an′ti•ed′u•ca′tion•al, *adj.;* **-ly,** *adv.*
an′ti•ed′u•ca′tion•al•ist, *n.*
an′ti•ed′u•ca′tion•ist, *n., adj.*
an′ti•e•gal′i•tar′i•an, *adj.*
an′ti•e′go•ism, *n.*
an′ti•e′go•ist, *n.*
an′ti•e′go•is′tic, *adj.*
an′ti•e′go•is′ti•cal, *adj.;* **-ly,** *adv.*
an′ti•e′go•tism, *n.*
an′ti•e′go•tist, *n., adj.*
an′ti•e′go•tis′tic, *adj.*
an′ti•e′go•tis′ti•cal, *adj.;* **-ly,** *adv.*
an′ti•e•lite′, *n., adj*
an′ti•e•lit′ism, *n.*
an′ti•e•lit′ist, *n., adj.*
an′ti•em•pir′ic, *n., adj.*
an′ti•em•pir′i•cal, *adj.;* **-ly,** *adv.*
an′ti•em•pir′i•cism, *n.*
an′ti•em•pir′i•cist, *n., adj.*
an′ti-Eng′lish, *adj.*
an′ti•en•thu′si•asm, *n.*
an′ti•en•thu′si•ast′, *n.*
an′ti•en•thu′si•as′tic, *adj.*
an′ti•en•thu′si•as′ti•cal•ly, *adv.*
an′ti•en•vi′ron•men′tal•ist, *n., adj.*
an′ti•ep′i•lep′tic, *adj., n.*
an′ti•e•ro′sion, *adj.*
an′ti•e•ro′sive, *adj.*
an′ti•e•rot′ic, *adj.*
an′ti•es′tro•gen, *n.*
an′ti•es′tro•gen′ic, *adj.*
an′ti-Eu′rope, *adj.*
an′ti-Eu′ro•pe′an, *adj., n.*
an′ti-Eu′ro•pe′an•ism, *n.*
an′ti•ev′o•lu′tion, *adj.*
an′ti•ev′o•lu′tion•al, *adj.;* **-ly,** *adv.*
an′ti•ev′o•lu′tion•ar′y, *adj.*
an′ti•ev′o•lu′tion•ist, *n., adj.*
an′ti•ev′o•lu′tion•is′tic, *adj.*
an′ti•ex•pan′sion, *adj.*

lish mən târ′ē ə niz′əm, an′tī-), *n.* a policy or attitude that views a nation's power structure as corrupt, repressive, exploitive, etc. [ANTIESTABLISHMENTARIAN + -ISM]

An•tie•tam (an tē′təm), *n.* a creek flowing from S Pennsylvania through NW Maryland into the Potomac: Civil War battle fought near here at Sharpsburg, Maryland, in 1862.

an•ti•fe•brile (an′tē fē′brəl, -feb′rəl, an′tī-), *Biochem., Pharm.* —*adj.* **1.** efficacious against fever; febrifuge; antipyretic. —*n.* **2.** an antifebrile agent. [1655–65; ANTI- + FEBRILE]

an•ti•fe•brin (an′tē fē′brin, -feb′rin, an′tī-), *n. Pharm.* acetanilide. [ANTI- + FEBR(ILE) + -IN[2]]

An•ti•fed•er•al•ist (an′tē fed′ər ə list, -fed′rə-, an′tī-), *n.* **1.** *U.S. Hist.* a member or supporter of the Antifederal party. **2.** (*l.c.*) an opponent of federalism. [1780–90; *Amer.*; ANTI- + FEDERALIST] —**An′ti•fed′er•al•ism,** *n.*

An•ti•fed′er•al par′ty (an′tē fed′ər əl, -fed′rəl, an′tī-), *U.S. Hist.* the party that, before 1789, opposed the adoption of the proposed Constitution and after that favored its strict construction. Cf. **States' rights.**

an•ti•feed•ant (an′tē fēd′nt, an′tī-), *n.* a chemical agent that causes a pest, as an insect, to stop eating. [1970–75; ANTI- + FEED + -ANT]

an•ti•fer•ro•mag•net (an′tē fer′ō mag′nit, an′tī-), *n. Physics.* an antiferromagnetic substance. [1935–40; ANTI- + FERROMAGNET]

an•ti•fer•ro•mag•net•ic (an′tē fer′ō mag net′ik, an′tī-), *adj.* noting or pertaining to a substance in which, at sufficiently low temperatures, the magnetic moments of adjacent atoms point in opposite directions. Cf. **diamagnetic, ferrimagnetic, ferromagnetic, paramagnetic.** [1935–40; ANTI- + FERROMAGNETIC] —**an•ti•fer•ro•mag•ne•tism** (an′tē fer′ō mag′ni tiz′əm, an′tī-), *n.*

an•ti•fer•til•i•ty (an′tē fər til′i tē, an′tī-), *adj. Pharm.* of or pertaining to a substance that inhibits the ability to produce offspring; contraceptive. [ANTI- + FERTILITY]

an•ti•foam•ing (an′tē fō′ming, an′tī-), *adj.* preventing the development of or reducing foam. [1930–35; ANTI- + FOAM + -ING[2]]

an•ti•fog (an′tē fog′, -fôg′, an′tī-), *adj.* preventing or resisting the buildup of moisture on a surface: *an antifog fluid for camera lenses.* [ANTI- + FOG]

an•ti•fog•gant (an′tē fog′ənt, -fô′gənt, an′tī-), *n. Photog.* a chemical that prevents or minimizes fogging. [ANTIFOG + -ANT]

an•ti•fog•ger (an′tē fog′ər, -fô′gər, an′tī-), *n. Informal.* an antifoggant. [ANTIFOG + -ER[1]]

an•ti•for•eign•ism (an′tē fôr′ə niz′əm, -for′-, an′tī-), *n.* the policy or practice of showing hostility toward foreigners, foreign customs, etc. [ANTI- + FOREIGNISM] —**an′ti•for′eign,** *adj.*

an•ti•foul•ing (an′tē fou′ling, an′tī-), *adj. Naut.* (of a coating, process, or the like) preventing the accumulation of barnacles, algae, etc., on underwater surfaces: *The marines now use an antifouling chemical on all marine hulls.* [1865–70; ANTI- + FOUL + -ING[1]]

antifoul′ing paint′, *Naut.* paint applied to the portion of a hull below the waterline to poison or discourage marine animals and plants that would otherwise cling to it. [1865–70]

an•ti•freeze (an′ti frēz′, an′tē-), *n.* a liquid used in the radiator of an internal-combustion engine to lower the freezing point of the cooling medium. [1910–15; ANTI- + FREEZE]

an•ti•fric•tion (an′tē frik′shən, an′tī-), *n.* **1.** something that prevents or reduces friction; lubricant. —*adj.* **2.** tending to prevent or reduce friction. [1830–40; ANTI- + FRICTION] —**an′ti•fric′tion•al,** *adj.*

antifric′tion al′loy, a metallic alloy, as Babbitt metal or bearing bronze, having antifriction qualities.

antifric′tion bear′ing, *Mach.* See **rolling-element bearing.**

an•ti•gay (an′tē gā′, an′tī-), *adj.* opposed or hostile to homosexuals or to homosexual social reforms and institutions, etc. [ANTI- + GAY]

an•ti•gen (an′ti jən, -jen′), *n.* **1.** *Immunol.* any substance that can stimulate the production of antibodies and combine specifically with them. **2.** *Pharm.* any commercial substance that, when injected or absorbed into animal tissues, stimulates the production of antibodies. **3.** antigens of a particular type collectively. [1905–10; ANTI(BODY) + -GEN] —**an•ti•gen•ic** (an′ti-jen′ik), *adj.* —**an′ti•gen′i•cal•ly,** *adv.* —**an•ti•ge•nic•i•ty** (an′ti jə nis′i tē), *n.*

antigen′ic deter′minant, *Immunol.* determinant (def. 3). [1905–10]

an•ti•ges•ta′tion•al drug′ (an′tē jes tā′ shə nəl, an′tī-), a drug that averts a pregnancy by preventing the fertilized egg from becoming implanted in the uterine wall.

an•ti•glob•u•lin (an′tē glob′yə lin, an′tī-), *n. Immunol.* an antibody produced by an animal in reaction to the introduction of globulin from another animal. [1905–10; ANTI- + GLOBULIN]

an•ti•god•lin (an′ti god′lin), *adj. Southern and Western U.S.* **1.** lopsided or at an angle; out of alignment. **2.** diagonal or cater-cornered. Also, **an•ti•gog•lin** (an′ti-gog′lin). [1895–1900; perh. ANTI- + *gogglin,* repr. prp. of Brit. dial. *goggle* to shake, tremble; var. with *d* perh. by dissimilation, reinforced by folk etym. as "against God"]

An•tig•o•ne (an tig′ə nē′), *n.* **1.** *Class. Myth.* a daughter of Oedipus and Jocasta who defied her uncle, King Creon, by performing funeral rites over her brother, Polynices, and was condemned to be immured alive in a cave. **2.** (*italics*) a tragedy (c440 B.C.) by Sophocles.

An•tig•o•nus I (an tig′ə nəs), (*Cyclops*) 382?–301 B.C., Macedonian general under Alexander the Great.

Antigonus II, (*Gonatus*) c319–239 B.C., king of Macedonia 283–239 (son of Demetrius I).

an•tig•o•rite (an tig′ə rīt′), *n. Mineral.* a variety of serpentine occurring in a brownish-green lamellar form. [1860–65; named after *Antigorio* valley in N Italy where first found + -ITE[1]]

an•ti•gov•ern•ment (an′tē guv′ərn mənt, -ər mənt, an′tī-), *adj.* **1.** opposed to or in rebellion against an existing government. **2.** of or pertaining to a political group, military force, etc., seeking to replace or overthrow an existing government. [ANTI- + GOVERNMENT] —**an′ti•gov′ern•men′tal,** *adj.*

an•ti•grav•i•ty (an′tē grav′i tē, an′tī-), *n.* **1.** *Physics.* the antithesis of gravity; a hypothetical force by which a body of positive mass would repel a body of negative mass. **2.** (not in technical use) a controllable force that can be made to act against the force of gravity. —*adj.* **3.** (not in technical use) counteracting the force of gravity: *The antigravity drive in this spaceship will enable us to reach Polaris.* [1940–45; ANTI- + GRAVITY]

an•ti-G′ suit′ (an′tē jē′, an′tī-), *Aeron., Aerospace.* a garment for fliers and astronauts designed to exert pressure on the abdomen and thighs to prevent or retard the pooling of blood below the heart under the influence of excessive head-to-toe acceleration forces. Also called **G-suit.** [1940–45; *G* repr. *gravity*]

An•ti•gua (an tē′gə), *n.* **1.** one of the Leeward Islands, in the E West Indies. 108 sq. mi. (280 sq. km). —**An•ti′•guan,** *adj., n.*

Anti′gua and Barbu′da, an island state comprising Antigua and two smaller islands: a member of the former West Indies Associated States; formerly a British crown colony; gained independence 1981. 79,000; 171 sq. mi. (442 sq. km). *Cap.:* St. John's.

an•ti•ha•la•tion (an′tē hā lā′shən, -ha-, an′tī-), *Photog.* —*n.* **1.** the process of treating a film base with a light-absorbing substance to prevent refraction of light from the rear of the film. —*adj.* **2.** resistant to halation. [1900–05; ANTI- + HALATION]

an•ti•he•lix (an′tē hē′liks, an′tī-), *n., pl.* **-hel•i•ces** (-hel′ə sēz′), **-he•lix•es.** *Anat.* the inward curving ridge of the auricle of the ear. See diag. under **ear.** [1715–25; ANTI- + HELIX; r. *anthelix* < Gk, equiv. to *ant-* ANT- + *hélix* HELIX]

an•ti•he•mo•phil′ic fac′tor (an′tē hē′mə fil′ik, -hem′ə-), *Biochem.* a protein that is essential to normal blood clotting and is lacking or deficient in persons having hemophilia A. *Abbr.:* AHF Also called **factor VIII.** [1945–50; ANTI- + HEMOPHILIC]

an•ti•he•ro (an′tē hēr′ō, an′tī-), *n., pl.* **-roes.** a protagonist who lacks the attributes that make a heroic figure, as nobility of mind and spirit, a life or attitude marked by action or purpose, and the like. [1705–15; ANTI- + HERO] —**an•ti•her•o•ism,** (an′tē her′ō iz′əm, an′tī-), *n.*

an•ti•he•ro•ic (an′tē hi rō′ik, an′tī-), *adj.* **1.** (of a protagonist) possessing the characteristics of an antihero. **2.** (of a literary work) having an antihero as its protagonist. [1875–80; ANTI- + HEROIC]

an•ti•her•o•ine (an′tē her′ō in, an′tī-), *n.* a female protagonist, as in a novel or play, whose attitudes and behavior are not typical of a conventional heroine. [1905–10; ANTI- + HEROINE]

an•ti•his•ta•mine (an′ti his′tə mēn′, -min), *n. Biochem., Pharm.* any of certain compounds or medicines that neutralize or inhibit the effect of histamine in the body, used chiefly in the treatment of allergic disorders and colds. [1930–35; ANTI- + HISTAMINE]

an•ti•his•ta•min•ic (an′tē his′tə min′ik, an′tī-), *Biochem., Pharm.* —*adj.* **1.** of or pertaining to an antihistamine or its effect. —*n.* **2.** an antihistaminic agent, as a drug. [1945–50; ANTIHISTAMINE + -IC]

an•ti•hu•man (an′tē hyōō′mən *or, often,* -yōō′-, an′-tī-), *adj.* against or opposed to human beings or human values. [1850–55; ANTI- + HUMAN]

an•ti•hy•per•ten•sive (an′tē hī′pər ten′siv, an′tī-), *Med., Pharm.* —*adj.* **1.** acting to reduce hypertension: *an antihypertensive drug, diet, or regimen.* —*n.* **2.** a drug, as a diuretic, used to treat hypertension.

an•ti•ic•er (an′tē ī′sər), *n.* **1.** a device used to prevent the forming of ice, as on an airplane propeller. **2.** a fluid used in such a device. [1930–35]

an•ti-id (an′tē id′, an′tī-), *n. Immunol. Informal.* an anti-idiotypic antibody. [by shortening]

an•ti-id•i•o•type (an′tē id′ē ə tīp′, an′tī-), *n. Immunol.* a molecular arrangement on an antibody that is the counterpart of that on a different antibody, thus making one an antigen to the other. —**an•ti-id•i•o•typ•ic** (an′tē id′ē ə tip′ik, an′tī-), *adj.*

an•ti-im•pe•ri•al•ist (an′tē im pēr′ē ə list, an′tī-), *n.* **1.** an opponent of imperialism. —*adj.* **2.** opposed to imperialism. [1895–1900] —**an′ti-im•pe′ri•al•ism,** *n.* —**an′ti-im•pe′ri•al•is′tic,** *adj.*

an•ti-in•fec•tive (an′tē in fek′tiv, an′tī-), *Pharm.* —*adj.* **1.** of or pertaining to a substance used in the treatment of an infection. —*n.* **2.** any such substance, as bacitracin. —**an′ti-in•fec′tive•ness,** *n.*

an•ti-in•flam•ma•to•ry (an′tē in flam′ə tôr′ē, -tōr′ē, an′tī-), *adj., n., pl.* **-ries.** —*adj.* **1.** acting to reduce certain signs of inflammation, as swelling, tenderness, fever, and pain. —*n.* **2.** *Pharm.* a medication, as aspirin, used to reduce inflammation. [1955–60]

an•ti-in•tel•lec•tu•al (an′tē in′tl ek′chōō əl, an′tī-), *n.* **1.** a person opposed to or hostile toward intellectuals and the modern academic, artistic, social, religious, and other theories associated with them. **2.** a person who believes that intellect and reason are less important than actions and emotions in solving practical problems and understanding reality. —*adj.* **3.** of, pertaining to, or characteristic of anti-intellectuals or their beliefs. Also, **an′ti-in′tel•lec′tu•al•ist.** [1935–40] —**an′ti-in′tel•lec′tu•al•ism,** *n.* —**an′ti-in′tel•lec′tu•al•is′tic,** *adj.* —**an′ti-in′tel•lec′tu•al′i•ty,** *n.*

an•ti•knock (an′tē nok′, an′tī-), *adj.* noting or pertaining to any material added to fuel for an internal-combustion engine to eliminate or minimize knock. [1920–25; ANTI- + KNOCK]

An•ti•ky•ther•a (an′ti ki thēr′ə; *Gk.* än′dē kē′thē rä), *n.* an island in the E Mediterranean, NW of Crete: archaeological site. 8½ sq. mi. (22 sq. km). Also, **Andikithira.**

an•ti-Lea•guer (an′tē lē′gər, an′tī-), *n. Hist.* a person who opposed the League of Nations or U.S. participation in it.

An•ti-Leb•a•non (an′tē leb′ə nən), *n.* a mountain range in SW Asia, between Syria and Lebanon, E of the Lebanon Mountains.

CONCISE PRONUNCIATION KEY: *act, cāpe, dâre, pärt; set, ēqual; if, īce; ox, ōver, ôrder, oil, bŏŏk, bōōt, out; up, ûrge; child; sing; shoe; thin, that;* zh as in *treasure.* ə = *a* as in *alone, e* as in *system, i* as in *easily, o* as in *gallop, u* as in *circus;* ° as in *fire* (fī°r), *hour* (ou°r). l and n can serve as syllabic consonants, as in *cradle* (krād′l), and *button* (but′n). See the full key inside the front cover.

an′ti•ex•pan′sion•ism, *n.*
an′ti•ex•pan′sion•ist, *n., adj.*
an′ti•ex•pres′sion•ism, *n.*
an′ti•ex•pres′sion•ist, *n., adj.*
an′ti•ex•pres′sion•is′tic, *adj.*
an′ti•ex•pres′sive, *adj.;* **-ly,** *adv.;* **-ness,** *n.*
an′ti•fam′i•ly, *adj.*
an′ti•fas′cism, *n.*
an′ti•fas′cist, *n., adj.*
an′ti•fash′ion, *n., adj.*
an′ti•fash′ion•a•ble, *adj.*
an′ti•fa•tigue′, *adj.*
an′ti•fe′male, *adj.*
an′ti•fem′i•nine, *adj.;* **-ly,** *adv.;* **-ness,** *n.*
an′ti•fem′i•nism, *n.*
an′ti•fem′i•nist, *n., adj.*
an′ti•fem′i•nis′tic, *adj.*
an′ti•feu′dal, *adj.*
an′ti•feu′dal•ism, *n.*
an′ti•feu′dal•ist, *n.*
an′ti•feu′dal•is′tic, *adj.*
an′ti•feu′dal•i•za′tion, *adj., n.*
an′ti•fil′i•bus′ter, *n., adj.*
an′ti•fluor′i•da′tion, *n., adj.*
an′ti•fluor′i•da′tion•ist, *n.*
an′ti•fore•clo′sure, *n., adj.*
an′ti•for′mal•ist, *n., adj.*
an′ti-France′, *adj.*
an′ti•fraud′, *adj.*
an′ti-French′, *adj.*
an′ti-Freud′, *adj.*
an′ti-Freud′i•an, *adj., n.*
an′ti-Freud′i•an•ism, *n.*
an′ti•fun′da•men′tal•ism, *n.*
an′ti•fun′da•men′tal•ist, *n., adj.*
an′ti•fun′gal, *adj.*
an′ti•gam′bling, *adj.*
an′ti-Ger′man, *n., adj.*
an′ti-Ger•man′ic, *adj.*
an′ti-Ger′man•ism, *n.*
an′ti-Ger′man•i•za′tion, *adj., n.*
an′ti•glare′, *adj.*
an′ti•gnos′tic, *adj., n.*
an′ti•gnos′ti•cal, *adj.*
an′ti•graft′, *adj.*
an′ti•gram•mat′i•cal, *adj.;* **-ly,** *adv.;* **-ness,** *n.*
an′ti•grav′i•ta′tion, *adj.*
an′ti•grav′i•ta′tion•al, *adj.;* **-ly,** *adv.*
an′ti-Greece′, *adj.*
an′ti-Greek′, *adj., n.*
an′ti•growth′, *adj.*
an′ti•guer•ril′la, *n., adj.*
an′ti•gun′, *adj.*
an′ti•he•gem′o•nism, *n.*
an′ti•he•gem′o•ny, *n., pl.* **-nies,** *adj.*
an′ti•hi′er•ar′chal, *adj.*
an′ti•hi′er•ar′chic, *adj.*
an′ti•hi′er•ar′chi•cal, *adj.;* **-ly,** *adv.*
an′ti•hi′er•ar′chism, *n.*
an′ti•hi′er•ar′chy, *n., pl.* **-chies,** *adj.*
an′ti•hi′jack, *adj.*
an′ti•his•tor′i•cal, *adj.;* **-ly,** *adv.;* **-ness,** *n.*
an′ti•ho′mo•sex′u•al, *adj.*
an′ti•ho′mo•sex′u•al′i•ty, *n., adj.*
an′ti•hu′man•ism, *n.*
an′ti•hu′man•ist, *n., adj.*
an′ti•hu′man•is′tic, *adj.*
an′ti•hu•man′i•tar′i•an, *adj., n.*
an′ti•hu•man′i•ty, *n., pl.* **-ties.**
an′ti•hunt′ing, *n., adj.*
an′ti•hy′gi•en′ic, *adj.*
an′ti•hy′gi•en′i•cal•ly, *adv.*
an′ti•hy′per•ten′sion, *adj.*
an′ti•hyp•not′ic, *adj., n.*
an′ti•hyp•not′i•cal•ly, *adv.*
an′ti•hys•ter′ic, *n., adj.*
an′ti-i•de′al•ism, *n.*
an′ti-i•de′al•ist, *n., adj.*
an′ti-i•de′al•is′tic, *adj.*
an′ti-i•de′al•is′ti•cal•ly, *adv.*
an′ti-i′de•o•log′i•cal, *adj.;* **-ly,** *adv.*
an′ti•im′mi•gra′tion, *adj.*
an′ti-in•cum′bent, *adj., n.*
an′ti-in•dem′ni•ty, *adj.*
an′ti-in•duc′tion, *adj.*
an′ti-in•duc′tive, *adj.;* **-ly,** *adv.;* **-ness,** *n.*
an′ti-in•fla′tion, *n., adj.*
an′ti-in•fla′tion•ar′y, *adj.*
an′ti-in•som′ni•ac′, *adj., n.*
an′ti-in′sti•tu′tion•al, *adj.;* **-ly,** *adv.*
an′ti-in′te•gra′tion, *adj.*
an′ti-I′rish, *adj., n., pl.* **-I′rish.**
an′ti-i′so•la′tion, *adj.*
an′ti-i′so•la′tion•ism, *n.*
an′ti-i′so•la′tion•ist, *n., adj.*
an′ti-Is•rae′li, *n., adj.*
an′ti-I•tal′ian, *adj., n.*
an′ti-I•tal′ian•ism, *n.*
an′ti•itch′, *adj.*
an′ti-Jap′a•nese′, *adj., n., pl.* **-nese′.**
an′ti-Jes′u•it, *n., adj.*
an′ti-Jes′u•it′ic, *adj.*
an′ti-Jes′u•it′i•cal, *adj.;* **-ly,** *adv.*
an′ti-Jes′u•it•ism, *n.*
an′ti-Jes′u•it•ry, *n.*
an′ti-Jew′ish, *adj.*
an′ti-Ju•da′ic, *adj.*
an′ti-Ju′da•ism, *n.*
an′ti-Ju′da•ist, *n., adj.*
an′ti-Ju′da•is′tic, *adj.*
an′ti•kick′back′, *adj.*

an•ti•le•gom•e•na (an′ti lə gom′ə nə), *n.* (*used with a singular v.*) a group of books in the New Testament, generally held to be uncanonical by the early church. Cf. **homologumena.** [1840–50; < Gk: things spoken against, neut. pl. of *antilegómenos* (pass. prp. of *antilégein* to speak against), equiv. to *anti-* ANTI- + *lego-* speak + *-menos* pass. prp. suffix]

an•ti•lep•ton (an′tē lep′ton, an′tī-), *n. Physics.* the antiparticle of a lepton. Cf. **antineutrino, muon, positron, tau lepton.** [ANTI- + LEPTON]

an•ti•life (an′tē līf′, an′tī-), *adj.* **1.** antagonistic or indifferent to a normal life. **2.** regarded as opposing the life force because of advocating abortion, birth control, etc. [1925–30; ANTI- + LIFE] **—an′ti•lif′er,** *n.*

An•til•les (an til′ēz), *n.* (*used with a plural v.*) a chain of islands in the West Indies, divided into two parts, the one including Cuba, Hispaniola, Jamaica, and Puerto Rico **(Greater Antilles),** the other including a large arch of smaller islands to the SE and S **(Lesser Antilles** or **Caribees). —An•til•le•an** (an til′ē ən, an′tl ē′-), *adj.*

Antil′les Cur′rent, a warm ocean current flowing NW along the N coast of the Greater Antilles and joining the Florida Current off the SW coast of Florida.

An•til•o•chus (an til′ə kəs), *n. Class. Myth.* a son of Nestor and a trusted friend of Achilles.

an′ti•lock brake′ (an′tē lok′, an′ti-), a brake equipped with a computer-controlled device that prevents the wheel from locking. [1985–1990]

an•ti•log (an′ti lôg′, -log), *n. Math.* antilogarithm. [by shortening]

an•ti•log•a•rithm (an′ti lô′gə rith′əm, -rith′-, -log′ə-), *n. Math.* the number of which a given number is the logarithm; antilog [1790–1800; ANTI- + LOGARITHM] **—an′ti•log′a•rith′mic,** *adj.*

an•til•o•gism (an til′ə jiz′əm), *n. Logic.* a group of three inconsistent propositions, two of which are premises of a syllogism that contradict the third. [1900–05; < LGk *antilogismós*, equiv. to *anti-* ANTI- + *logismós* calculation, deriv. of *logízesthai* to calculate, deriv. of *lógos* reckoning] **—an•til′o•gis′tic,** *adj.* **—an•til′o•gis′ti•cal•ly,** *adv.*

an•til•o•gy (an til′ə jē), *n., pl.* **-gies.** a contradiction in terms or ideas. [1605–15; < Gk *antilogía* controversy, discussion. See ANTI-, -LOGY]

an•ti•ma•cas•sar (an′ti mə kas′ər), *n.* a small covering, usually ornamental, placed on the backs and arms of upholstered furniture to prevent wear or soiling; a tidy. [1850–55; ANTI- + MACASSAR (OIL)]

An•tim•a•chus (an tim′ə kəs), *n.* **1.** Also called **the Colophonian.** fl. c410 B.C. Greek poet. **2.** (in the *Iliad*) a chieftain who believed that the Trojans should not return Helen to Menelaus.

an•ti•mag•net•ic (an′tē mag net′ik, an′tī-), *adj.* **1.** resistant to magnetization. **2.** (of a precision instrument, watch, etc.) having the critical parts composed of antimagnetic materials, and hence not seriously affected in accuracy by exposure to magnetic fields. [1945–50; ANTI- + MAGNETIC]

an•ti•man•ic (an′tē man′ik, -mā′nik, an′tī-), *adj.* **1.** preventing, curing, or palliating the symptoms of mania. —*n.* **2.** *Pharm.* a pharmacological substance used to treat mania, as lithium. [ANTI- + MANIC]

An•ti-Ma•son (an′tē mā′sən, an′tī-), *n. U.S. Hist.* a member of the Anti-Masonic party or a supporter of its principles. **—An•ti-Ma•son•ic** (an′tē mə son′ik, an′tī-), *adj.* **—An′ti-Ma′son•ry,** *n.*

An′ti-Mason′ic par′ty, *U.S. Hist.* a former political party (1826–35) that opposed Freemasonry in civil affairs.

an•ti•masque (an′ti mask′, -mäsk′), *n.* a comic or grotesque performance, as a dance, presented before or between the acts of a masque. Also, **an′ti•mask′.** [1605–15; ANTI- + MASQUE; r. *antemask*; see ANTE-, MASK] **—an′ti•mas′quer, an′ti•mask′er,** *n.*

an•ti•mat•ter (an′tē mat′ər, an′tī-), *n. Physics.* matter composed only of antiparticles, esp. antiprotons, antineutrons, and positrons. [1950–55; ANTI- + MATTER]

CONCISE ETYMOLOGY KEY: <, descended or borrowed from; >, whence; b., blend of, blended; c., cognate with; cf., compare; deriv., derivative; equiv., equivalent; imit., imitative; obl., oblique; r., replacing; s., stem; sp., spelling, spelled; resp., respelling, respelled; trans., translation; ?, origin unknown; *, unattested; ‡, probably earlier than. See the full key inside the front cover.

an•ti•men•si•on (än′dē mēn′sē ôn; *Eng.* an′ti men′sē-on′), *n., pl.* **-si•a** (-sē ä; *Eng.* -sē ə). *Gk. Orth. Ch.* a consecrated linen or silk cloth, kept on an altar, to which is sewn a linen or silk bag containing relics of saints. Also, **antimensium.** [< ML *antimēnsium* < MGk *antimínsion, antimḗsion*, equiv. to Gk *anti-* ANTI- + L *mēns(a)* table + Gk *-ion* n. suffix]

an•ti•men•si•um (an′ti men′sē əm), *n., pl.* **-si•a** (-sē ə). antimension.

an•ti•mere (an′tə mēr′), *n. Zool.* **1.** a segment or division of the body having a corresponding segment or division that is opposite to it relative to the longitudinal axis of the body. **2.** a similar part in a radially symmetrical animal. [1875–80; ANTI- + -MERE] **—an•ti•mer•ic** (an′tə mer′ik), *adj.* **—an•tim•er•ism** (an tim′ə riz′əm), *n.*

an•ti•me•tab•o•lite (an′tē mə tab′ə līt′, an′tī-), *n.* **1.** *Biochem.* any substance that interferes with growth of an organism by competing with or substituting for an essential nutrient in an enzymatic process. —*adj.* **2.** *Pharm.* of or pertaining to certain substances used to prevent or reduce the proliferation of cells, esp. cancer cells, by interfering with normal metabolic activity. Also, **an•ti•met•a•bol•ic** (an′tē met′ə bol′ik, an′tī-). [1940–45; ANTI- + METABOLITE]

an•ti•mil•i•tant (an′tē mil′i tənt, an′tī-) *adj.* **1.** opposing military power, esp. its increase or development or the influence of military leaders. —*n.* **2.** a person who opposes military power, esp. its increase or development: *Antimilitants demonstrated against nuclear weaponry.* [ANTI- + MILITANT]

an•ti•mis•sile (an′tē mis′əl, an′tī- *or, esp. Brit.*, -mis′-īl), *adj.* **1.** designed or used in defense against guided enemy missiles. —*n.* **2.** a ballistic device for seeking and destroying enemy missiles. Also, **an′ti-mis′sile.**

antimis′sile mis′sile, a ballistic missile for seeking and destroying missiles in flight. [1955–60]

an•ti•mi•tot•ic (an′tē mī tot′ik, -mi-, an′tī-), *Biochem., Pharm.* —*adj.* **1.** of or pertaining to certain substances capable of arresting the process of cell division. —*n.* **2.** any such substance, as certain drugs used to destroy cancer cells. [1965–70; ANTI- + MITOTIC]

an•ti•mo•nate (an′tə mə nāt′), *n. Chem.* a salt containing pentavalent antimony and oxygen, as potassium antimonate, $KSb(OH)_6$. Also, **an•ti•mo•ni•ate** (an′tə-mō′nē āt′, -it). [1850–55; ANTIMON(Y) + -ATE[2]]

an•ti•mo•nic (an′tə mō′nik, -mon′ik), *adj. Chem.* of or containing antimony, esp. in the pentavalent state. [1825–35; ANTIMON(Y) + -IC]

an′timo′nic ac′id, *Chem.* See **antimony pentoxide.** [1825–35]

an•ti•mo•nide (an′tə mə nīd′, -nid), *n. Chem.* a binary compound containing antimony and a second element, usually a metal. [1860–65; ANTIMON(Y) + -IDE]

an•ti•mo•nous (an′tə mə nəs, -mō′nəs), *adj. Chem.* of or containing antimony, esp. in the trivalent state. Also, **an•ti•mo•ni•ous** (an′tə mō′nē əs). [1825–35; ANTIMON(Y) + -OUS]

an•ti•mon•soon (an′tē mon so͞on′), *n. Meteorol.* a current of air lying above a monsoon and moving in an opposite direction. [ANTI- + MONSOON]

an•ti•mo•ny (an′tə mō′nē), *n. Chem.* a brittle, lustrous, white metallic element occurring in nature free or combined, used chiefly in alloys and in compounds in medicine. *Symbol:* Sb; *at. no.:* 51; *at. wt.:* 121.75. [1375–1425; late ME *antimonie* < ML *antimōnium*, perh. < dial. Ar *uthmud*] **—an′ti•mo′ni•al,** *adj., n.*

antimony 124, *Chem.* the radioactive isotope of antimony having a mass number of 124 and a half-life of 60 days, used chiefly as a tracer.

an′timony hy′dride, *Chem.* stibine.

an•ti•mo•nyl (an′tə mə nil, an tim′ə-), *n. Chem.* the univalent group –SbO, believed to exist in certain compounds, as antimony potassium tartrate, $K(SbO)C_4H_4O_6$. [ANTIMON(Y) + -YL]

an′timony oxychlo′ride, *Chem.* a white, water-insoluble powder, SbOCl, used chiefly in the manufacture of antimony salts. Also called **Algaroth powder.**

an′timony pen•ta•sul′fide (pen′tə sul′fīd), *Chem.* a deep-yellow, water-insoluble powder, Sb_2S_5, used chiefly as a pigment in oil and water colors.

an′timony pent•ox′ide (pen tok′sīd), *Chem.* a white or yellowish, water-insoluble powder, Sb_2O_5, used chiefly in the synthesis of antimonates. Also called **antimonic acid.**

an′timony potas′sium tar′trate, *Chem.* See **ta[rtar] emetic.** Also, **an′timonyl potas′sium tar′trate.**

an′timony sul′fate, *Chem.* a white, crystallin[e] deliquescent, water-insoluble solid, $Sb_2(SO_4)_3$, use[d] chiefly in the manufacture of explosives.

an′timony sul′fide, *Chem.* **1.** See **antimony pe[n]tasulfide. 2.** See **antimony trisulfide.**

an′timony triflu′oride, *Chem.* a white to grayish white, crystalline, hygroscopic, water-soluble, poisonou[s] solid, SbF_3, used chiefly in dyeing textiles.

an′timony trisul′fide, *Chem.* a black or orang[e] red, crystalline, water-insoluble solid, Sb_2S_3, used chief[ly] as a pigment in paints and in the manufacture of fire works and matches.

an′timony yel′low. See **Naples yellow. —an′t[i]mo′ny-yel′low,** *adj.*

an•ti•mu•ta•gen•ic (an′tē myo͞o′tə jen′ik, an′tī-), *ad[j.]* *Genetics.* capable of reducing the frequency of mutatio[n] [ANTI- + MUTAGENIC]

an•ti•ne•o•plas•tic (an′tē nē′ō plas′tik, an′tī-), *Med Pharm.* —*adj.* **1.** destroying, inhibiting, or preventin[g] the growth or spread of neoplasms. —*n.* **2.** an antineo[-] plastic substance. [1965–70; ANTI- + NEOPLASTIC]

an•ti•neu•tri•no (an′tē no͞o trē′nō, -nyo͞o-, an′tī-), *n.* *pl.* **-nos.** *Physics.* the antiparticle of a neutrino, distin[-] guished from the neutrino by having clockwise rathe[r] than counterclockwise spin when observing in the direc[-] tion of motion. [1930–35; ANTI- + NEUTRINO]

an•ti•neu•tron (an′tē no͞o′tron, -nyo͞o′-, an′tī-), *n* *Physics.* **1.** an elementary particle having no charge an[d] having a mass and spin equal to that of the neutron bu[t] with magnetic moment opposite to that of the neutro[n] the antiparticle of the neutron. —*adj.* **2.** Also, **an[′] ti-neu′tron.** opposing the building, stockpiling, or use o[f] neutron bombs: *The antineutron lobby was outnum[-] bered.* [1940–45; ANTI- + NEUTRON]

ant•ing (an′ting), *n.* the placing of ants among th[e] feathers, done by certain birds apparently to kill para[-] sites. [1935–40; ANT + -ING[1], as trans. of G *Einemsen*]

an•ti•node (an′ti nōd′), *n. Physics.* the region of maxi[-] mum amplitude between two adjacent nodes in a stand[-] ing wave. [1880–85; ANTI- + NODE] **—an′ti•nod′al,** *ad[j.]*

an•ti•noise (an′tē noiz′, an′tī-), *adj.* designed to re[-] duce or ban excessively loud sound, as of jet engines o[r] traffic: *antinoise legislation.* [1905–10; ANTI- + NOISE]

an•ti•no•mi•an (an′ti nō′mē ən), *n.* a person wh[o] maintains that Christians are freed from the moral la[w] by virtue of grace as set forth in the gospel. [1635–45 < ML *Antinom(i)* name of sect (pl. of *Antinomus* oppo[-] nent of (the moral) law < Gk *antí* ANTI- + *nómos* law + -IAN] **—an′ti•no′mi•an•ism,** *n.*

an•tin•o•my (an tin′ə mē), *n., pl.* **-mies. 1.** oppositio[n] between one law, principle, rule, etc., and another. **2** *Philos.* a contradiction between two statements, both ap[-] parently obtained by correct reasoning. [1585–95; < L *antinomia* < Gk *antinomía* a contradiction betwee[n] laws. See ANTI-, -NOMY] **—an•ti•nom•ic** (an′ti nom′ik) **an′ti•nom′i•cal,** *adj.*

An•tin•o•us (an tin′ō əs), *n. Class. Myth.* the chie[f] suitor of Penelope, killed by Odysseus upon his retur[n] from Troy.

an•ti•nov•el (an′tē nov′əl, an′tī-), *n.* a literary wor[k] in which the author rejects the use of traditional ele[-] ments of novel structure, esp. in regard to developmen[t] of plot and character. [1955–60; ANTI- + NOVEL[1]]

an•ti•nu•cle•ar (an′tē no͞o′klē ər, -nyo͞o′- *or by metathesis*, -kyə lər), *adj.* **1.** opposed to the building stockpiling, or use of nuclear weapons. **2.** opposed to the building or use of nuclear power plants: *Antinuclea[r] demonstrators picketed the power plant.* [1955–60; ANTI + NUCLEAR]
—Pronunciation. See **nuclear.**

an•ti•nu•cle•on (an′tē no͞o′klē on′, -nyo͞o′-, an′tī-), *n* *Physics.* an antiproton or an antineutron. [1945–50 ANTI- + NUCLEON]

an•ti•nuke (an′tē no͞ok′, -nyo͞ok′, an′tī-), *Informal* —*adj.* **1.** antinuclear. —*n.* **2.** Also, **an′ti•nuk′er.** a person who supports antinuclear programs.

an•ti•nu•tri•ent (an′tē no͞o′trē ənt, -nyo͞o′-, an′tī-), *n* *Biochem.* a substance that interferes with the utilization of one or more nutrients by the body, as oxalate and phytate, which prevent calcium absorption. [ANTI- + NUTRIENT] **—an•ti•nu•tri•tive** (an′tē no͞o′trə tiv, -nyo͞o′-, an′tī-), *adj.*

an′ti•la′bor, *adj.*
an′ti•la′bour, *adj.*
an′ti-Lat′in, *adj.*
an′ti-Lat′in•ism, *n.*
an′ti•league′, *adj.*
an′ti•left′, *adj.*
an′ti•left′ist, *adj.*
an′ti•lep′ro•sy, *adj.*
an′ti•leu•ke′mic, *adj., n.*
an′ti•lev′el•ing, *adj.*
an′ti•lev′el•ling, *adj.*
an′ti•lib′er•al, *adj., n.*; **-ly,** *adv.*; **-ness,** *n.*
an′ti•lib′er•al•ism, *n.*
an′ti•lib′er•al•ist, *n., adj.*
an′ti•lib′er•al•is′tic, *adj.*
an′ti•lib′er•tar′i•an, *adj., n.*
an′ti•liq′uor, *adj.*
an′ti•lit′er•a•cy, *adj.*
an′ti•lit′er•ate, *adj., n.*; **-ly,** *adv.*
an′ti•lit′ter, *adj.*
an′ti•lit′ter•ing, *adj.*
an′ti•li•tur′gic, *adj.*
an′ti•li•tur′gi•cal, *adj.*; **-ly,** *adv.*
an′ti•lit′ur•gist, *n.*
an′ti•lit′ur•gy, *adj.*
an′ti•lot′ter•y, *adj.*
an′ti•lynch′ing, *adj.*
an′ti•mach′i•na′tion, *adj.*
an′ti•ma•chine′, *adj.*
an′ti•ma•chin′er•y, *adj.*
an′ti•ma′cho, *adj.*
an′ti•male′, *n., adj.*
an′ti-Mal•thu′si•an, *adj., n.*
an′ti-Mal•thu′si•an•ism, *n.*
an′ti•man′, *adj.*
an′ti•man′age•ment, *adj., n.*
an′ti•ma•te′ri•al•ism, *n.*
an′ti•ma•te′ri•al•ist, *n., adj.*
an′ti•ma•te′ri•al•is′tic, *adj.*
an′ti•ma•te′ri•al•is′ti•cal•ly, *adv.*
an′ti•mech′an•ism, *n.*
an′ti•mech′an•ist, *n., adj.*
an′ti•mech′a•nis′tic, *adj.*
an′ti•mech′a•nis′ti•cal•ly, *adv.*
an′ti•mech′a•ni•za′tion, *adj.*
an′ti•med′i•cal, *adj.*; **-ly,** *adv.*
an′ti•med′i•ca′tion, *adj.*
an′ti•med′i•ca′tive, *adj.*
an′ti•med′i•cine, *adj.*
an′ti•me′di•ae′val, *adj.*; **-ly,** *adv.*
an′ti•me′di•ae′val•ism, *n.*
an′ti•me′di•ae′val•ist, *n., adj.*
an′ti•me′di•e′val, *adj.*; **-ly,** *adv.*
an′ti•me′di•e′val•ism, *n.*
an′ti•me′di•e′val•ist, *n., adj.*
an′ti•merg′er, *adj.*
an′ti•merg′ing, *adj.*
an′ti•met′a•phys′i•cal, *adj.*; **-ly,** *adv.*
an′ti•meth′od, *adj.*
an′ti•me•thod′ic, *adj.*
an′ti•me•thod′i•cal, *adj.*; **-ly,** *adv.*; **-ness,** *n.*
an′ti-Mex′i•can, *n., adj.*
an′ti•mil′i•ta•rism, *n.*
an′ti•mil′i•ta•rist, *n., adj.*
an′ti•mil′i•ta•ris′tic, *adj.*
an′ti•mil′i•ta•ris′ti•cal•ly, *adv.*
an′ti•mil′i•tar′y, *adj.*
an′ti•min′is•te′ri•al, *adj.*; **-ly,** *adv.*
an′ti•min′is•te′ri•al•ist, *n., adj.*
an′ti•mis′ce•ge•na′tion, *n., adj.*
an′ti•mod′ern, *adj., n.*; **-ly,** *adv.*; **-ness,** *n.*
an′ti•mod′ern•ism, *n.*
an′ti•mod′ern•ist, *n., adj.*
an′ti•mod′ern•is′tic, *adj.*
an′ti•mod′ern•i•za′tion, *adj.*
an′ti•mon′arch, *adj., n.*
an′ti•mo•nar′chal, *adj.*; **-ly,** *adv.*
an′ti•mo•nar′chi•al, *adj.*
an′ti•mo•nar′chic, *adj.*
an′ti•mo•nar′chi•cal, *adj.*; **-ly,** *adv.*
an′ti•mon′ar•chism, *n.*
an′ti•mon′ar•chist, *n., adj.*
an′ti•mon′ar•chis′tic, *adj.*
an′ti•mon′ar•chy, *adj.*
an′ti•mo•nop′o•lism, *n.*
an′ti•mo•nop′o•list, *n., adj.*
an′ti•mo•nop′o•lis′tic, *adj.*
an′ti•mo•nop′o•li•za′tion, *adj.*
an′ti•mo•nop′o•ly, *adj.*
an′ti•mor′al, *adj.*
an′ti•mor′al•ism, *n.*
an′ti•mor′al•ist, *n., adj.*
an′ti•mor′al•is′tic, *adj.*
an′ti•mo•ral′i•ty, *adj.*
an′ti•mo′ti•va′tion•al, *adj.*
an′ti•mu′sic, *n., adj.*
an′ti•mu′si•cal, *adj.*; **-ly,** *adv.*; **-ness,** *n.*
an′ti•mys′tic, *adj., n.*
an′ti•mys′ti•cal, *adj.*; **-ly,** *adv.*; **-ness,** *n.*
an′ti•mys′ti•cism, *n.*
an′ti•nar•cot′ic, *adj., n.*
an′ti•nar•cot′ics, *adj.*
an′ti•na′tion•al, *adj.*; **-ly,** *adv.*
an′ti•na′tion•al•ism, *n.*
an′ti•na′tion•al•ist, *n., adj.*
an′ti•na•tion•al•is′tic, *adj.*
an′ti•na•tion•al•is′ti•cal•ly, *adv.*
an′ti•na′tion•al•i•za′tion, *adj.*
an′ti•nat′u•ral, *adj.*; **-ly,** *adv.*; **-ness,** *n.*
an′ti•nat′u•ral•ism, *n.*
an′ti•nat′u•ral•ist, *n., adj.*
an′ti•nat′u•ral•is′tic, *adj.*
an′ti•na′ture, *adj., n.*
an′ti•nau′se•ant, *adj., n.*

n·ti·och (an′tē ok′), *n.* **1.** Arabic, **Antakiya.** Turkish, **Antakya.** a city in S Turkey: capital of the ancient kingdom of Syria 300–64 B.C. 66,520. **2.** a city in W California. 43,559. —**An·ti·o·chi·an** (an′tē ō′kē ən), *n., adj.*

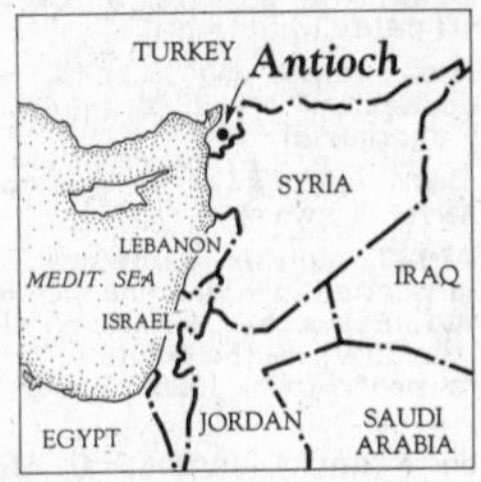

n·ti·o·chus III (an tī′ə kəs), *("the Great")* 241?–187 B.C., king of Syria 223–187.

ntiochus IV, *(Antiochus Epiphanes)* died 164? B.C., king of Syria 175–164?.

n·ti·o·don·tal·gic (an′tē ō′don tal′jik, an′tī-), *Dentistry.* —*adj.* **1.** relieving the pain of a toothache. —*n.* **2.** a toothache remedy. Also, **antodontalgic.** [1810–20; ANTI- + ODONTALGIC]

n·ti·ox·i·dant (an′tē ok′si dənt, an′tī-), *n.* **1.** *Chem.* any substance that inhibits oxidation, as a substance that inhibits oxidative deterioration of gasoline, rubbers, plastics, soaps, etc. **2.** *Biochem.* an enzyme or other organic substance, as vitamin E or beta carotene, that is capable of counteracting the damaging effects of oxidation in animal tissues. —*adj.* **3.** *Chem.* of or pertaining to an antioxidant. [1925–30; ANTI- + *oxidant* (OXID(IZE) + -ANT)]

n·ti·o·zon·ant (an′tē ō′zō nənt, an′tī-), *n. Chem.* an admixture to natural or synthetic rubber for preventing ozonolysis. [1950–55; ANTI- + *ozonant* (OZON(IZE) + -ANT)]

n·ti·par·a·be·ma (an′ti par′ə bē′mə), *n., pl.* **-ma·ta** (-mə tə). either of two chapels at the west end of an Armenian or Byzantine church. [ANTI- + NGk *parabêma* < Gk *para-* PARA-[1] + LGk *bêma* BEMA]

n·ti·par·al·lel (an′tē par′ə lel′, an′tī-), *adj. Math, Physics.* (of two vectors) pointing in opposite directions. [1650–60; ANTI- + PARALLEL]

n·ti·par·ti·cle (an′tē pär′ti kəl, an′tī-), *n. Physics.* a particle all of whose properties, as mass, spin, or charge, have the same magnitude as but, where appropriate, the opposite sign of a specific elementary particle; neutral pions, photons, and gravitons are considered to be their own antiparticles: *The positron is the antiparticle of the electron.* Cf. **antimatter, annihilation** (def. 3). [1930–35; ANTI- + PARTICLE]

n·ti·pas·to (an′ti pä′stō, -pas′tō; *It.* än′tē päs′tô), *n., pl.* **-pas·tos, -pas·ti** (-pä′stē, -pas′tē; *It.* -päs′tē). *Italian Cookery.* a course of appetizers consisting of an assortment of foods, as olives, anchovies, sliced sausage, peppers, and artichoke hearts. [1580–90; < It, equiv. to *anti-* (< L *ante-* ANTE-) + *pasto* food < L *pāstus* pasturage, feeding ground, orig. the act of feeding, equiv. to *pās-* s. of *pāscere* to feed + *-tus* suffix of v. action]

n·tip·a·ter (an tip′ə tər), *n.* 398?–319 B.C., Macedonian statesman and general: regent of Macedonia 334–323.

n·ti·pa·thet·ic (an′ti pə thet′ik, an tip′ə-), *adj.* **1.** opposed, averse, or contrary; having or showing antipathy: *They were antipathetic to many of the proposed changes* **2.** causing or likely to cause antipathy: *The new management was antipathetic to all of us.* Also, **an′·ti·pa·thet′i·cal.** [1630–40; < Gk *antipathēs* opposed in feeling (*anti-* + *-pathēs,* adj. deriv. of *páthos* PATHOS), with *-etic* by analogy with PATHETIC] —**an′ti·pa·thet′i·cal·ly,** *adv.* —**an′ti·pa·thet′i·cal·ness,** *n.*

n·tip·a·thy (an tip′ə thē), *n., pl.* **-thies. 1.** a natural, basic, or habitual repugnance; aversion. **2.** an instinctive contrariety or opposition in feeling. **3.** an object of natural aversion or habitual dislike. [1595–1605; < L *antipathīa* < Gk *antipátheia.* See ANTI-, -PATHY] —**an·tip′a·thist,** *n.*
—**Syn. 1.** disgust, abhorrence, detestation, hatred. See **aversion.** —**Ant. 1.** attraction.

n·ti·pe·dal (an′ti pēd′l), *adj.* (in a mollusk) located opposite the foot. [ANTI- + PEDAL]

an·ti·per·i·stal·sis (an′tē per′i stôl′sis, -stal′-, an′tī-), *n. Physiol.* reversed peristaltic action of the intestines, by which their contents are carried upward. [ANTI- + PERISTALSIS] —**an·ti·per·i·stal·tic** (an′tē per′i stal′tik, an′tī-), *adj.*

an·ti·per·son·nel (an′tē pûr′sə nel′, an′tī-), *adj. Mil.* used against enemy personnel rather than against mechanized vehicles, matériel, etc.: *antipersonnel bombs.* [1935–40; ANTI- + PERSONNEL]

an·ti·per·spi·rant (an′ti pûr′spər ənt), *n.* an astringent preparation for reducing perspiration, usually containing aluminum or zirconium and used to prevent body odor and clothing stains. [1940–45; ANTI- + PERSPIRE + -ANT]

an·ti·phlo·gis·tic (an′tē flō jis′tik, an′tī-), *Med., Pharm.* —*adj.* **1.** acting against inflammation or fever. —*n.* **2.** an antiphlogistic agent. [1735–45; ANTI- + PHLOGISTIC]

an·ti·phon (an′tə fon′), *n.* **1.** a verse or song to be chanted or sung in response. **2.** *Eccles.* **a.** a psalm, hymn, or prayer sung in alternate parts. **b.** a verse or a series of verses sung as a prelude or conclusion to some part of the service. [1490–1500; < ML *antiphōna* responsive singing < Gk *(tà) antíphōna,* neut. pl. of *antíphōnos* sounding in answer, equiv. to *anti-* ANTI- + *phōn(ē)* sound + *-os* adj. suffix. Cf. ANTHEM]

an·tiph·o·nal (an tif′ə nl), *adj.* **1.** pertaining to antiphons or antiphony; responsive. —*n.* **2.** an antiphonary. [1685–95; ANTIPHON + -AL[1]] —**an·tiph′o·nal·ly,** *adv.*

an·tiph·o·nar·y (an tif′ə ner′ē), *n., pl.* **-nar·ies.** a book of antiphons. [1425–75; late ME < ML *antiphōnārium;* learned borrowing r. earlier versions, which had undergone changes: ME *anfenere, antefenar, antiphoner(e),* OE *antefnere* (cf. MD *antiffenaer,* MLG *antifenēr,* OHG *antiphenere*) < ML. See ANTIPHON, -ARY]

an·tiph·o·ny (an tif′ə nē), *n., pl.* **-nies. 1.** alternate or responsive singing by a choir in two divisions. **2.** a psalm, verse, etc., so sung; antiphon. **3.** a responsive musical utterance. [1585–95; ANTIPHON + -Y[3]] —**an·ti·phon·ic** (an′tə fon′ik), *adj.* —**an′ti·phon′i·cal·ly,** *adv.*

an·tiph·ra·sis (an tif′rə sis), *n. Rhet.* the use of a word in a sense opposite to its proper meaning. [1525–35; < L < Gk, deriv. of *antiphrázein* to speak the opposite (*anti-* ANTI- + *phrázein* to speak); see PHRASE, SIS] —**an·ti·phras·tic** (an′ti fras′tik), **an′ti·phras′ti·cal,** *adj.* —**an′ti·phras′ti·cal·ly,** *adv.*

An·ti·phus (an′tə fəs), *n. Class. Myth.* **1.** (in the *Iliad*) a Trojan ally, the son of Talaemenes and a nymph. **2.** a Greek commander who sailed from Troy with Odysseus and was devoured by Polyphemus.

an·ti·plas·tic (an′tē plas′tik, an′tī-), *adj.* allaying or preventing the growth of new tissue. [ANTI- + PLASTIC]

an·tip·o·dal (an tip′ə dl), *adj.* **1.** *Geog.* on the opposite side of the globe; pertaining to the antipodes. **2.** diametrically opposite: *twin brothers with antipodal personalities.* **3.** *Bot.* (in a developing ovule) of or at the end opposite to the micropyle: *antipodal nuclei.* [1640–50; ANTIPODE + -AL[1]]

an·ti·pode (an′ti pōd′), *n.* a direct or exact opposite. [1540–50; back formation from ANTIPODES]

an·tip·o·des (an tip′ə dēz′), *n.pl.* **1.** places diametrically opposite each other on the globe. **2.** those who dwell there. [1350–1400; ME < L < Gk *(hoi) antípodes* lit., (those) with the feet opposite (pl. of *antípous*), equiv. to *anti-* ANTI- + *-podes,* nom. pl. of *poûs* FOOT] —**an·tip·o·de·an** (an tip′ə dē′ən), *adj., n.*

An·tip·o·des (an tip′ə dēz′), *n.* (*used with a plural v.*) a group of islands SE of and belonging to New Zealand. 24 sq. mi. (62 sq. km).

an·ti·po·et·ic (an′tē pō et′ik, an′tī-), *adj.* of or pertaining to elements or techniques used in a poem not conventionally thought to be suitable or traditional. [1840–50; ANTI- + POETIC]

an·ti·pole (an′ti pōl′), *n.* the opposite pole. [1815–25; ANTI- + POLE]

an·ti·pol·lu·tion (an′tē pə lo͞o′shən, an′tī-), *adj.* designed to prevent or reduce environmental pollution: *antipollution laws; an antipollution campaign.* [1920–25; ANTI- + POLLUTION] —**an′ti·pol·lu′tion·ist,** *n.*

an·ti·pope (an′ti pōp′), *n.* a person who is elected or claims to be pope in opposition to another held to be canonically chosen. [1570–80; ANTI- + POPE; r. *antipape* < ML *antipāpa,* modeled on *Antichrīstus* ANTICHRIST]

an·ti·pov·er·ty (an′tē pov′ər tē, an′tī-), *adj.* designed or directed to reduce or abolish poverty (used esp. in describing certain governmental programs). [ANTI- + POVERTY]

an·ti·pro·lif·er·a·tion (an′tē prə lif′ə rā′shən), *adj.* **1.** opposing an increase in nuclear weapons, esp. in allowing additional countries to obtain them. **2.** taking or containing measures to curb nuclear proliferation: *to sign the antiproliferation treaty.* [1975–80; ANTI- + PROLIFERATION]

an·ti·pro·lif·er·a·tive (an′tē prō lif′ə rā′tiv, an′tī-), *Pharm.* —*adj.* **1.** of or pertaining to a substance used to prevent or retard the spread of cells, esp. malignant cells, into surrounding tissues. —*n.* **2.** any such substance. [ANTI- + PROLIFERATIVE]

an·ti·pro·ton (an′tē prō′ton, an′tī-), *n. Physics.* an elementary particle having negative charge equal in magnitude to that of the electron and having the same mass and spin as a proton; the antiparticle of the proton. [1935–40; ANTI- + PROTON]

an·ti·pru·rit·ic (an′tē pro͞o rit′ik, an′tī-), *Med., Pharm.* —*adj.* **1.** relieving or preventing itching. —*n.* **2.** an antipruritic agent. [1875–80; ANTI- + PRURITIC]

an·ti·psy·chot·ic (an′tē sī kot′ik, an′tī-), *Pharm.* —*adj.* **1.** of or pertaining to any of various substances used in the treatment of psychosis, esp. schizophrenia, and acute or severe states of mania, depression, or paranoia. —*n.* **2.** Also called **major tranquilizer, neuroleptic.** any such substance, as the phenothiazines. [1950–55; ANTI- + PSYCHOTIC]

an·ti·py·ret·ic (an′tē pī ret′ik, an′tī-), *Med., Pharm.* —*adj.* **1.** checking or preventing fever. —*n.* **2.** an antipyretic agent. [1675–85; ANTI- + PYRETIC] —**an·ti·py·re·sis** (an′tē pī rē′sis, an′tī-), *n.*

an·ti·py·rot·ic (an′tē pī rot′ik, an′tī-), *Med., Pharm.* —*adj.* **1.** relieving the pain and stimulating the healing of burns. —*n.* **2.** an antipyrotic agent. [1830–40; ANTI- + Gk *pyrōtikós* burning, equiv. to *pyrō-,* verbid s. of *pyroûn* to burn + *-tikos* -TIC]

antiq., **1.** antiquarian. **2.** antiquary. **3.** antiquity.

an·ti·quar·i·an (an′ti kwâr′ē ən), *adj.* **1.** pertaining to antiquaries or to the study of antiquities. **2.** of, dealing in, or interested in old or rare books. —*n.* **3.** an antiquary. **4.** a size of drawing and writing paper, 31 × 53 or 29 × 52 inches. [1600–10; < L *antiquāri(us)* (see ANTIQUARY) + -AN] —**an′ti·quar′i·an·ism,** *n.*

an·ti·quark (an′tē kwôrk′, -kwärk′, an′tī-), *n. Physics.* the antiparticle of a quark. [ANTI- + QUARK]

an·ti·quar·y (an′ti kwer′ē), *n., pl.* **-quar·ies. 1.** an expert on or student of antiquities. **2.** a collector of antiquities. [1555–65; < L *antiquārius* a student of the past, equiv. to *antiqu(us)* ancient, old (see ANTIQUE) + *-ārius* -ARY]

an·ti·quate (an′ti kwāt′), *v.t.,* **-quat·ed, -quat·ing. 1.** to make obsolete, old-fashioned, or out of date by replacing with something newer or better: *This latest device will antiquate the ice-cube tray.* **2.** to design or create in an antique style; cause to appear antique. [1400–50; late ME *antiquat* old < ML *antiquātus* old, ancient, ptp. of *antiquāre* to put in an earlier state, v. deriv. of L *antiquus;* see ANTIQUE] —**an′ti·qua′tion,** *n.*

an·ti·quat·ed (an′ti kwā′tid), *adj.* **1.** continued from, resembling, or adhering to the past; old-fashioned: *antiquated attitudes.* **2.** no longer used; obsolete or obsolescent: *The spinning wheel is an antiquated machine.* **3.** aged; old: [1615–25; ANTIQUATE + -ED[2]] —**an′ti·qua′·ted·ness,** *n.*
—**Syn.** See **ancient**[1].

an·tique (an tēk′), *adj., n., v.,* **-tiqued, -ti·quing.** —*adj.* **1.** of or belonging to the past; not modern. **2.** dating from a period long ago: *antique furniture.* **3.** noting or pertaining to automobiles approximately 25 years old or more. **4.** in the tradition, fashion, or style of an earlier period; old-fashioned; antiquated. **5.** of or belonging to the ancient Greeks and Romans. **6.** (of paper) neither calendered nor coated and having a rough surface. **7.** ancient. —*n.* **8.** any work of art, piece of furniture, decorative object, or the like, created or produced in a former period, or, according to U.S. customs laws, 100 years before date of purchase. **9.** the antique style, usually Greek or Roman, esp. in art. **10.** *Print.* a style of type. —*v.t.* **11.** to make or finish (something, esp. furniture) in imitation of antiques. **12.** to emboss

CONCISE PRONUNCIATION KEY: act, cāpe, dâre, pärt; set, ēqual; *if,* īce; ox, ōver, ôrder, oil, bo͝ok, bo͞ot, out; up, ûrge; child; sing; shoe; thin, *that;* zh as in *treasure.* ə = *a* as in *alone, e* as in *system, i* as in *easily, o* as in *gallop, u* as in *circus;* ᵊ as in *fire* (fīᵊr), *hour* (ouᵊr). l and n can serve as syllabic consonants, as in *cradle* (krād′l), and *button* (but′n). See the full key inside the front cover.

an′ti-Na′zi, *n., adj.*
an′ti-Ne′gro, *adj., n., pl.* **-groes.**
an′ti-Ne′gro·ism, *n.*
an′ti·nep′o·tism, *n.*
an′ti·neu·ral′gic, *adj., n.*
an′ti·neu·rit′ic, *adj., n.*
an′ti·neu′tral, *adj., n.;* **-ly,** *adv.*
an′ti·neu′tral·ism, *n.*
an′ti·neu·tral′i·ty, *n.*
an′ti·ni′hil·ism, *n.*
an′ti·ni′hil·ist, *n., adj.*
an′ti·ni′hil·is′tic, *adj.*
an′ti-Nor′dic, *adj.*
an′ti·nor′mal, *adj.;* **-ness,** *n.*
an′ti·nor·mal′i·ty, *n.*
an′ti·o·be′si·ty, *adj., n., pl.* **-ties.**
an′ti·ob·scen′i·ty, *n., pl.* **-ties,** *adj.*
an′ti-o′pen-shop′, *n.*
an′ti·op′ti·mism, *n.*
an′ti·op′ti·mist, *n., adj.*
an′ti·op′ti·mis′tic, *adj.*
an′ti·op′ti·mis′ti·cal, *adj.;* **-ly,** *adv.*
an′ti·or′gan·i·za′tion, *n.*
an′ti-O′ri·en′tal, *adj., n.*
an′ti-O′ri·en′tal·ism, *n.*
an′ti-O′ri·en′tal·ist, *n., adj.*
an′ti·or′tho·dox′, *adj.;* **-ly,** *adv.*
an′ti·or′tho·dox′y, *n.*
an′ti·ox′i·diz′er, *n.*
an′ti·ox′i·diz′ing, *adj.*
an′ti·ox′y·gen·at′ing, *adj.*
an′ti·ox′y·gen·a′tion, *n.*
an′ti·ox′y·gen·a′tor, *n.*
an′ti·pac′i·fism, *n.*
an′ti·pac′i·fist, *n., adj.*
an′ti·pac′i·fis′tic, *adj.*
an′ti·pa′pa·cy, *adj.*
an′ti·pa′pal, *adj.*
an′ti·pa′pal·ist, *n., adj.*
an′ti·pa′pism, *n.*
an′ti·pa′pist, *n., adj.*
an′ti·pa·pis′tic, *adj.*
an′ti·pa·pis′ti·cal, *adj.*
an′ti·par′a·sit′ic, *n., adj.*
an′ti·par′a·sit′i·cal, *adj.;* **-ly,** *adv.*
an′ti·par′lia·ment, *adj.*
an′ti·par′lia·men′ta·ry, *adj.*
an′ti·path′o·gen, *n.*
an′ti·path′o·gene′, *n.*
an′ti·path′o·gen′ic, *adj.*
an′ti·pa′tri·arch′, *n.*
an′ti·pa′tri·ar′chal, *adj.;* **-ly,** *adv.*
an′ti·pa′tri·ar′chy, *n., pl.* **-chies.**
an′ti·pa′tri·ot, *n.*
an′ti·pa′tri·ot′ic, *adj.*
an′ti·pa′tri·ot′i·cal·ly, *adv.*
an′ti·pa′tri·ot·ism, *n.*
an′ti·pes′ti·lence, *adj.*
an′ti·pes′ti·lent, *adj.;* **-ly,** *adv.*
an′ti·pes′ti·len′tial, *adj.*
an′ti·phil′o·soph′ic, *adj.*
an′ti·phil′o·soph′i·cal, *adj.;* **-ly,** *adv.*
an′ti·phi·los′o·phism, *n.*
an′ti·phi·los′o·phy, *adj., n., pl.* **-phies.**
an′ti·phys′i·cal, *adj.;* **-ly,** *adv.;* **-ness,** *n.*
an′ti·pill′, *n.*
an′ti·pi′ra·cy, *n., pl.* **-cies,** *adj.*
an′ti·plague′, *n., adj.*
an′ti-Pla′to, *adj.*
an′ti-Pla·ton′ic, *adj.*
an′ti-Pla·ton′i·cal·ly, *adv.*
an′ti-Pla′to·nism, *n.*
an′ti-Pla′to·nist, *n., adj.*
an′ti·pleas′ure, *n., adj.*
an′ti·poach′ing, *adj.*
an′ti·po·et′i·cal, *adj.;* **-ly,** *adv.*
an′ti·po′lar, *adj.*
an′ti-Pol′ish, *n., adj.*
an′ti·po·lit′i·cal, *adj.;* **-ly,** *adv.*
an′ti·pol′i·tics, *adj.*
an′ti·pop′er·y, *n.*
an′ti·pop′u·lar, *adj.*
an′ti·pop′u·lar·i·za′tion, *adj., n.*
an′ti-Pop′u·lism, *n.*
an′ti-Pop′u·list, *n., adj.*
an′ti·porn′, *adj.*
an′ti·por′no·graph′ic, *adj.*
an′ti·por·nog′ra·phy, *n., adj.*
an′ti·prag·mat′ic, *adj.*
an′ti·prag·mat′i·cal, *adj.;* **-ly,** *adv.*
an′ti·prag·mat′i·cism, *n.*
an′ti·prag′ma·tism, *n.*
an′ti·prag′ma·tist, *n., adj.*
an′ti·pred′a·tor, *n.*
an′ti·prel′a·tism, *n.*
an′ti·prel′a·tist, *n., adj.*
an′ti·priest′, *adj.*
an′ti·priest′hood, *adj.*
an′ti·pro·duc′tive, *adj.;* **-ly,** *adv.;* **-ness,** *n.*
an′ti·pro′duc·tiv′i·ty, *adj., n.*
an′ti·prof′i·teer′ing, *adj.*
an′ti·pro·gres′sion·ist, *n., adj.*
an′ti·pro·gres′sive, *adj.*
an′ti·pro′hi·bi′tion, *adj., n.*
an′ti·pro′hi·bi′tion·ist, *n., adj.*
an′ti·pros′ti·tu′tion, *adj., n.*
an′ti·pro·tec′tion·ist, *n., adj.*
an′ti-Prot′es·tant, *n., adj.*
an′ti-Prot′es·tant·ism, *n.*
an′ti·pro′to·zo′al, *adj., n.*
an′ti·psalm′ist, *n., adj.*

(an image, design, letters, or the like) on paper or fabric. —*v.i.* **13.** to shop for or collect antiques: *She spent her vacation antiquing in Boston.* [1520–30; earlier also *anticke* (< MF *antique*) < L *antīquus, antīcus* in front, existing earler, ancient; cf. ANTIC, POSTICUM] —**an·tique′ly,** *adv.* —**an·tique′ness,** *n.*
—**Syn. 1.** bygone, archaic. **2.** old, obsolete, obsolescent. See **ancient**[1].

an′tique glass′. See **pot metal** (def. 4).

an·ti·quer (an tē′kər), *n.* **1.** a person who takes a special interest in antiques; a collector of antiquities; antiquary. **2.** a person who simulates antique furniture by using processes that give an appearance of age, wear, etc., to recently manufactured pieces. [ANTIQUE + -ER[1]]

an·tiq·ui·ty (an tik′wi tē), *n., pl.* **-ties. 1.** the quality of being ancient; ancientness: *a bowl of great antiquity.* **2.** ancient times; former ages: *the splendor of antiquity.* **3.** the period of history before the Middle Ages. **4.** the peoples, nations, tribes, or cultures of ancient times. **5.** Usually, **antiquities.** something belonging to or remaining from ancient times, as monuments, relics, or customs. [1350–1400; ME *antiquite* < AF < L *antīquitās,* equiv. to *antīqu(us)* old (see ANTIQUE) + *-itās* -ITY]

an·ti·rad·i·cal (an′tē rad′i kəl, an′tī-), *adj.* opposed to radicalism or radicals. [1865–70; ANTI- + RADICAL]

an·ti·re·ces·sion·ar·y (an′tē ri sesh′ə ner′ē, an′tī-), *adj.* used to counteract or offset the economic effects of a recession: *the President's antirecessionary program.* [‡1970–75, *Amer.*; ANTI- + RECESSIONARY]

an·ti·re·flec′tion coat′ing (an′tē ri flek′shən, an′tī-), *Optics.* a thin film consisting of one or more layers of transparent material applied to lenses to reduce reflection. [ANTI- + REFLECTION]

an·ti·re·flex·ive (an′tē ri flek′siv, an′tī-), *adj. Math.* noting a relation in which no element is in relation to itself, as "less than." [ANTI- + REFLEXIVE]

An·ti·re·mon·strant (an′tē ri mon′strənt, an′tī-), *n.* a member or supporter of that party in the Dutch Calvinistic Church which opposed the Remonstrants or Arminians. [ANTI- + REMONSTRANT]

an·ti·rent (an′tē rent′, an′tī-), *adj.* noting or pertaining to a political party (1839–47) in New York that opposed the payment of rents to patroons. [1835–45; *Amer.*; ANTI- + RENT[1]] —**an′ti·rent′er,** *n.* —**an′ti·rent′ism,** *n.*

an·ti·res·o·nance (an′tē rez′ə nəns, an′tī-), *n. Physics.* a phenomenon in an electric, acoustic, or other such system in which the impedance is tending to infinity. [1920–25; ANTI- + RESONANCE]

an′ti·roll′ bar′ (an′tē rōl′, an′tī-), *Auto.* **1.** See **roll bar. 2.** See **stabilizer bar.** [1965–70; ANTI- + ROLL]

an·ti·rust (an′tē rust′, an′tī-, an′ti rust′), *adj.* **1.** preventing or resisting rust. **2.** rustproof. —*n.* **3.** something that prevents or resists rust. [ANTI- + RUST]

An·ti-Sa·loon′ League′ of Amer′ica (an′tē sə-lo͞on′, an′tī-), a national organization, founded in 1893 in Ohio, advocating the prohibition of the manufacture and sale of alcoholic beverages.

An·ti·sa·na (än′tē sä′nä), *n.* **Mount,** an active volcano in N central Ecuador, near Quito. 18,885 ft. (5756 m).

an·ti·sat·el·lite (an′tē sat′l īt′, an′tī-), *adj.* (of a weapon or weapon system) designed to destroy an enemy's orbiting satellite. *Abbr.:* ASAT [1960–65; ANTI- + SATELLITE]

an·ti·scor·bu·tic (an′tē skôr byo͞o′tik, an′tī-), *Med., Pharm.* —*adj.* **1.** efficacious against scurvy. —*n.* **2.** an antiscorbutic agent, as ascorbic acid. [1715–25; ANTI- + SCORBUTIC]

an·ti·se·lec·tion (an′tē si lek′shən, an′tī-), *n. Insurance.* See **adverse selection.** [ANTI- + SELECTION]

an·ti-Sem·ite (an′tē sem′īt, an′tī- *or, esp. Brit.,* -sē′-mīt), *n.* a person who discriminates against or is prejudiced or hostile toward Jews. [1880–85] —**an·ti-Se·mit·ic** (an′tē sə mit′ik, an′tī-), *adj.* —**an′ti-Se·mit′i·cal·ly,** *adv.*

an·ti-Sem·i·tism (an′tē sem′i tiz′əm, an′tī-), *n.* discrimination against or prejudice or hostility toward Jews. [1880–85]

CONCISE ETYMOLOGY KEY: <, descended or borrowed from; >, whence; b., blend of, blended; c., cognate with; cf., compare; deriv., derivative; equiv., equivalent; imit., imitative; obl., oblique; r., replacing; s., stem; sp., spelling, spelled; resp., respelling, respelled; trans., translation; ?, origin unknown; *, unattested; ‡, probably earlier than. See the full key inside the front cover.

an·ti·sense (an′tē sens′, an′tī-), *adj.* of or pertaining to a gene that is derived from RNA or complementary DNA, is inserted in reverse orientation into a strand of DNA, and is used in genetic engineering to regulate genetic expression of a trait. [1985–90]

an·ti·sep·sis (an′tə sep′sis), *n.* destruction of the microorganisms that produce sepsis or septic disease. [1870–75; ANTI- + SEPSIS]

an·ti·sep·tic (an′tə sep′tik), *adj.* **1.** pertaining to or affecting antisepsis. **2.** free from or cleaned of germs and other microorganisms. **3.** exceptionally clean or neat. **4.** free of contamination or pollution. —*n.* **5.** an antiseptic agent. [1745–55; ANTI- + SEPTIC]

an·ti·sep·ti·cal·ly (an′tə sep′tik lē), *adv.* with the aid of antiseptics. [1880–85; ANTISEPTIC + -AL[1] + -LY]

an·ti·sep·ti·cize (an′ti sep′tə sīz′), *v.t.,* **-cized, -cizing.** to treat with antiseptics. Also, *esp. Brit.,* **an′ti·sep′ti·cise′.** [1905–10; ANTISEPTIC + -IZE]

an·ti·se·rum (an′tə sēr′əm), *n., pl.* **-se·rums, -se·ra** (-sēr′ə). a serum containing antibodies, as antitoxins or agglutinins, obtained by inoculation of animals and used for injection into other animals to provide immunity to a specific disease. [1900–05; ANTI- + SERUM]

an·ti·sex·ist (an′tē sek′sist, an′tī-), *adj.* **1.** opposing sexism. —*n.* **2.** a person who opposes sexism. [1980–85; ANTI- + SEXIST]

an·ti·skat·ing (an′tē skā′ting, an′tī-), *adj.* of or pertaining to a control or adjustment on a record player that counteracts the tendency of the tone arm to be pulled inward by centripetal force. [ANTI- + SKATE[1] + -ING[1]]

an·ti·skid (an′tē skid′, an′tī-), *adj. Auto.* designed or constructed to prevent the skidding of a vehicle, esp. by reducing hydraulic pressure in the brake system to prevent the brakes from locking. [1900–05; ANTI- + SKID]

an·ti·slav·er·y (an′tē slā′və rē, -slāv′rē, an′tī-), *n.* **1.** opposition to slavery, esp. black slavery. —*adj.* **2.** of or pertaining to antislavery. [1810–20, *Amer.*; ANTI- + SLAVERY]

an·ti·smog (an′tē smog′, -smôg′, an′tī-), *adj.* designed to reduce smog by reducing the pollutants released into the earth's atmosphere: *an antismog device for a car's exhaust.* [1965–70; ANTI- + SMOG]

an·ti·smok·ing (an′tē smō′king, an′tī-), *adj.* opposed to or promoting the discontinuance of the smoking of tobacco: *an antismoking campaign launched by a health agency.* [1960–65; ANTI- + *smoking* (see SMOKE (v.), -ING[1])]

an·ti·so·cial (an′tē sō′shəl, an′tī-), *adj.* **1.** unwilling or unable to associate in a normal or friendly way with other people: *He's not antisocial, just shy.* **2.** antagonistic, hostile, or unfriendly toward others; menacing; threatening: *an antisocial act.* **3.** opposed or detrimental to social order or the principles on which society is constituted: *antisocial behavior.* **4.** *Psychiatry.* of or pertaining to a pattern of behavior in which social norms and the rights of others are persistently violated. —*n.* **5.** a person exhibiting antisocial traits. [1790–1800; ANTI- + SOCIAL] —**an′ti·so′ci·al′i·ty,** *n.* —**an′ti·so′cial·ly,** *adv.*

an·ti·so·cial·ist (an′tē sō′shə list, an′tī-), *n.* **1.** a person who opposes socialism. —*adj.* **2.** Also, **an′ti·so′cial·is′tic.** opposing socialism, made up of antisocialists, etc.: *Antisocialist forces marched on the capital.* [1860–65; ANTI- + SOCIALIST]

antiso′cial personal′ity, a personality disorder, beginning early in life, characterized by chronic and continuous antisocial behavior in which the rights of others are violated, as by lying, stealing, or aggressive sexual behavior.

an·ti·so·lar (an′tē sō′lər, an′tī-), *adj. Astron.* (on the celestial sphere) opposite the sun. [ANTI- + SOLAR]

an·ti·stat (an′ti stat′), *n. Chem.* an antistatic agent. [by shortening]

an·ti·stat·ic (an′tē stat′ik, an′tī-), *adj.* pertaining to a material or procedure that disperses, or inhibits the accumulation of, static charges on textiles, phonograph records, paper products, etc. [1935–40; ANTI- + STATIC]

An·tis·the·nes (an tis′thə nēz′), *n.* 444?–365? B.C., Greek philosopher: founder of the Cynic school.

an·ti·sto·ry (an′tē stôr′ē, -stōr′ē, an′tī-), *n., pl.* **-ries.** a narrative of short-story length that makes no effort to follow a plot and ignores structural conventions, character motivations, and the like. [ANTI- + STORY[1]]

an·tis·tro·phe (an tis′trə fē), *n.* **1.** the part of an ancient Greek choral ode answering a previous strophe, sung by the chorus when returning from left to right. **2.** the movement performed by the chorus while singing a antistrophe. **3.** *Pros.* the second of two metrically corr sponding systems in a poem. Cf. **strophe** (def. 3). [154 50; < Gk: a turning about. See ANTI-, STROPHE] —**an·ti·stroph·ic** (an′tə strof′ik, -strō′fik), **an·tis′tro·phal,** *ac* —**an′ti·stroph′i·cal·ly,** *adv.*

an·ti·su·dor·if·ic (an′tē so͞o′də rif′ik, an′tī-), *Me* —*n.* **1.** an antiperspirant. —*adj.* **2.** inhibiting perspira tion. [ANTI- + SUDORIFIC]

an′ti·sway′ bar′ (an′tē swā′, an′tī-). *Auto.* See **sta bilizer bar.** [ANTI- + SWAY]

an·ti·sym·met·ric (an′tē si me′trik, an′tī-), *ac Math.* noting a relation in which one element's depen ence on a second implies that the second element is n dependent on the first, as the relation "greater than Also, **an′ti·sym·met′ri·cal.** [1920–25; ANTI- + SYMME RIC]

an·ti·tank (an′tē tangk′, an′tī-), *adj. Mil.* designe for use against tanks or other armored vehicles: *antitan gun.* [1915–20; ANTI- + TANK]

an·ti·ter·ror·ist (an′tē ter′ər ist, an′tī-), *adj.* used designed to combat terrorism: *antiterrorist tactic* [1960–65; ANTI- + TERRORIST] —**an′ti·ter′ror·ism,** *n.*

an·tith·e·sis (an tith′ə sis), *n., pl.* **-ses** (-sēz′). **1.** op position; contrast: *the antithesis of right and wrong.* the direct opposite (usually fol. by *of* or *to*): *Her behavio was the very antithesis of cowardly.* **3.** *Rhet.* **a.** th placing of a sentence or one of its parts against anothe to which it is opposed to form a balanced contrast ideas, as in "Give me liberty or give me death." **b.** th second sentence or part thus set in opposition, as "c give me death." **4.** *Philos.* See under **Hegelian diale tic.** [1520–30; < L < Gk: opposition, equiv. to *anti(ti thé(nai)* to oppose + *-sis* -SIS. See ANTI-, THESIS]

an·ti·thet·ic (an′tə thet′ik), *adj.* **1.** of the nature or involving antithesis. **2.** directly opposed or co trasted; opposite. Also, **an′ti·thet′i·cal.** [1575–85; < G *antithetikós,* equiv. to *anti(ti)thé(nai)* to set in oppos tion + *-tikos* -TIC] —**an′ti·thet′i·cal·ly,** *adv.*

an·ti·torque′ ro′tor (an′tē tôrk′, an′tī-), *Aeron.* (o certain helicopters) a small rotor on the tail, turning i the vertical plane and providing a thrust whose torqu opposes and compensates for the torque of the mai rotor. [ANTI- + TORQUE]

an·ti·tox·ic (an′ti tok′sik, an′tē-), *adj.* **1.** counteract ing toxic influences. **2.** of or serving as an antitoxi [1885–90; ANTI- + TOXIC]

an·ti·tox·in (an′ti tok′sin, an′tē-), *n.* **1.** a substanc formed in the body, that counteracts a specific toxin. the antibody formed in immunization with a given toxi used in treating certain infectious diseases or in immu nizing against them. [1890–95; ANTI- + TOXIN]

an·ti·trade (an′ti trād′), *n.* **1.** **antitrades,** wester winds lying above the trade winds in the tropics. —*ad* **2.** noting or pertaining to such a wind. [1850–55; ANTI + TRADE]

an·tit·ra·gus (an ti′trə gəs), *n., pl.* **-gi** (-jī′). *Anat.* process of the external ear. See diag. under **ear.** [1835 45; < NL < Gk *antítragos.* See ANTI-, TRAGUS]

an·ti·trust (an′tē trust′, an′tī-), *adj.* opposing or in tended to restrain trusts, monopolies, or other larg combinations of business and capital, esp. with a view t maintaining and promoting competition: *antitrust legis lation.* [1885–90, *Amer.*; ANTI- + TRUST]

an·ti·trust·er (an′tē trus′tər, an′tī-), *n. Informal.* person who opposes business trusts and favors unre strained competition among businesses. [1945–50; ANTI TRUST + -ER[1]]

an·ti·tus·sive (an′tē tus′iv, an′tī-), *Pharm.* —*adj.* **1** of or pertaining to a substance that is used to suppres coughing. —*n.* **2.** any such substance, as codeine [1905–10; ANTI- + TUSSIVE]

an·ti·twi′light arch′ (an′tē twī′līt, an′tī-), a narrov band, pink or with a purple cast, that sometimes appear at twilight just above the horizon opposite the sun. Als called **anticrepuscular arch.** [ANTI- + TWILIGHT]

an·ti·type (an′ti tīp′), *n.* something that is foreshad owed by a type or symbol, as a New Testament even prefigured in the Old Testament. [1605–15; < ML *an titypus* < LGk *antítypos* (impression) answering to a die See ANTI-, TYPE] —**an·ti·typ·ic** (an′ti tip′ik), **an′ti typ′i·cal,** *adj.* —**an′ti·typ′i·cal·ly,** *adv.*

an·ti·un·ion (an′tē yo͞on′yən, an′tī-), *adj.* opposed t trade unions or unionism. [1805–15, *Amer.*; ANTI- + UNION] —**an′ti·un′ion·ism,** *n.* —**an′ti·un′ion·ist,** *n.*

an′ti·pu′ri·tan, *n., adj.*
an′ti-Pu′ri·tan, *n., adj.*
an′ti-Pu′ri·tan·ism, *n.*
an′ti·ra′bies, *adj., n.*
an′ti·ra′cial, *adj.;* **-ly,** *adv.*
an′ti·rac′ing, *adj.*
an′ti·ra′cism, *n.*
an′ti·ra′cist, *n., adj.*
an′ti·rack′e·teer′ing, *adj.*
an′ti·ra′dar, *n., adj.*
an′ti·ra′di·ant, *adj.*
an′ti·ra′di·at′ing, *adj.*
an′ti·ra′di·a′tion, *adj.*
an′ti·rad′i·cal·ism, *n.*
an′ti·rape′, *adj., n.*
an′ti·ra′tion·al, *adj.;* **-ly,** *adv.*
an′ti·ra′tion·al·ism, *n.*
an′ti·ra′tion·al·ist, *n., adj.*
an′ti·ra′tion·al·is′tic, *adj.*
an′ti·ra′tion·al′i·ty, *n., adj.*
an′ti·re·act′ing, *adj.*
an′ti·re·ac′tion, *adj., n.*
an′ti·re·ac′tion·ar′y, *n., pl.* **-ar′ies,** *adj.*
an′ti·re·ac′tive, *adj.*
an′ti·re′al·ism, *n.*
an′ti·re′al·ist, *n., adj.*
an′ti·re′al·is′tic, *adj.*
an′ti·re′al·is′ti·cal·ly, *adv.*
an′ti·re·al′i·ty, *n.*
an′ti·re·ces′sion, *n., adj.*
an′ti·red′, *adj.*
an′ti·re·duc′er, *n.*
an′ti·re·duc′ing, *adj., n.*
an′ti·re·duc′tion, *adj.*
an′ti·re·duc′tive, *adj.*
an′ti·re·flec′tive, *adj.;* **-ly,** *adv.;* **-ness,** *n.*
an′ti·re·form′, *adj.*
an′ti·re·form′er, *n.*
an′ti·re·form′ing, *adj., n.*
an′ti·re·form′ist, *n., adj.*
an′ti·reg′u·la·to′ry, *adj.*
an′ti·re·li′gion, *adj.*
an′ti·re·li′gion·ist, *n., adj.*
an′ti·re·lig′i·os′i·ty, *n.*
an′ti·re·li′gious, *adj.;* **-ly,** *adv.*
an′ti·re·pub′li·can, *adj., n.*
an′ti·re·pub′li·can·ism, *n.*
an′ti·re·sis′tant, *adj., n.;* **-ly,** *adv.*
an′ti·res′to·ra′tion, *adj.*
an′ti·re·vi′sion·ist, *n., adj.*
an′ti·rev′o·lu′tion, *adj.*
an′ti·rev′o·lu′tion·ar′y, *n., pl.* **-ar·ies,** *adj.*
an′ti·rev′o·lu′tion·ist, *n.*
an′ti·rheu·mat′ic, *adj., n.*
an′ti·rights′, *n., adj.*
an′ti·ri′ot, *adj., n.*
an′ti·rit′u·al, *adj.*
an′ti·rit′u·al·ism, *n.*
an′ti·rit′u·al·ist, *n., adj.*
an′ti·rit′u·al·is′tic, *adj.*
an′ti·rob′ber·y, *adj.*
an′ti-Ro′man, *adj., n.*
an′ti·ro·mance′, *adj.*
an′ti·ro·man′tic, *adj., n.*
an′ti·ro·man′ti·cism, *n.*
an′ti·ro·man′ti·cist, *n., adj.*
an′ti-Ro′man·ist, *n.*
an′ti·roy′al, *adj.*
an′ti·roy′al·ism, *n.*
an′ti·roy′al·ist, *n., adj.*
an′ti-Rus′sia, *adj.*
an′ti-Rus′sian, *adj., n.*
an′ti·sag′, *adj.*
an′ti-Scan′di·na′vi·a, *adj.*
an′ti·scep′tic, *n.*
an′ti·scep′ti·cal, *adj.*
an′ti·scep′ti·cism, *n.*
an′ti·scho·las′tic, *adj., n.*
an′ti·scho·las′ti·cal·ly, *adv.*
an′ti·scho·las′ti·cism, *n.*
an′ti·school′, *adj.*
an′ti·sci′ence, *adj., n.*
an′ti·sci′en·tif′ic, *adj.*
an′ti·sci′en·tif′i·cal·ly, *adv.*
an′ti·scrip′tur·al, *adj.*
an′ti-Scrip′ture, *adj.*
an′ti·se′cre·cy, *adj.*
an′ti·se·di′tion, *adj.*
an′ti·seg′re·ga′tion, *n., adj.*
an′ti·sen′si·tiv′i·ty, *n., pl.* **-ties,** *adj.*
an′ti·sen′si·tiz′er, *n.*
an′ti·sen′si·tiz′ing, *adj.*
an′ti·sen′su·al′i·ty, *n., pl.* **-ties,** *adj.*
an′ti·sen′su·ous, *adj.;* **-ly,** *adv.;* **-ness,** *n.*
an′ti·sen′ti·men′tal, *adj.;* **-ly,** *adv.*
an′ti·sep′a·ra·tist, *n.*
an′ti-Serb′, *adj., n.*
an′ti·sex′, *adj.*
an′ti·sex′ism, *n.*
an′ti·sex′u·al, *adj.;* **-ly,** *adv.*
an′ti·sex′u·al′i·ty, *n., adj.*
an′ti·shock′, *adj., n.*
an′ti·shop′lift′ing, *adj.*
an′ti·sic′ca·tive, *adj.*
an′ti·skep′tic, *n.*
an′ti·skep′ti·cal, *adj.*
an′ti·skep′ti·cism, *n.*
an′ti·skid′ding, *adj.*
an′ti·sky′jack′ing, *adj.*
an′ti-Slav′, *n.*
an′ti-Slav′ic, *adj., n.*
an′ti·sleep′, *adj.*
an′ti·slip′, *adj.*
an′ti·smoke′, *adj., n.*
an′ti·smok′er, *n.*
an′ti·smug′gling, *adj.*

ın·ti·u·to·pi·a (an′tē yo͞o tō′pē ə, an′tī-), *n.* **1.** dys-topia. **2.** a literary work that describes an antiutopia. [1965–70; ANTI- + UTOPIA] —**an′ti·u·to′pi·an,** *adj., n.*

ın·ti·ven·in (an′tē ven′in, an′tī-), *n.* **1.** an antitoxin present in the blood of an animal following repeated in-jections of venom. **2.** the antitoxic serum obtained from such blood. [1890–95; earlier *antiven(ene)* (ANTI- + *ve-nene* < L *venēnum* potion, poison; see VENOM) + -IN[2]]

ın·ti·vi·ta·min (an′tē vī′tə min, an′tī- *or, Brit.,* -vit′-ə min), *n. Biochem.* any substance that interferes with the action of a vitamin. [1925–30; ANTI- + VITAMIN]

ın·ti·viv·i·sec·tion·ist (an′tē viv′ə sek′shə nist, an′-tī-), *n.* **1.** a person who opposes vivisection. —*adj.* **2.** Also, **an′ti·viv′i·sec′tion.** of, pertaining to, or charac-teristic of antivivisectionists or their policies. [1880–85; ANTI- + VIVISECTION + -IST] —**an′ti·viv′i·sec′tion·ism,** *n.*

ın·ti·white (an′tē hwīt′, -wīt′, an′tī-), *adj.* **1.** preju-diced or discriminating against or hostile toward white people. **2.** reflecting or promoting such feelings: *anti-white demonstrations.* [1905–10; ANTI- + WHITE]

ın·ti·world (an′tē wûrld′, an′tī-), *n.* Often, **anti-worlds.** *Physics.* a hypothetical world composed of anti-matter. [ANTI- + WORLD]

ın·ti·xe·roph·thal′mic vi′tamin (an′tē zēr′of-thal′mik, an′tī-), *Biochem.* See **vitamin A.** [ANTI- + XEROPHTHALM(IA) + -IC]

ınt·ler (ant′lər), *n.* one of the solid deciduous horns, usually branched, of an animal of the deer family. 1350–1400; ME *aunteler* < MF *antoillier* < VL **an-teoculārem (rāmum),* acc. sing of **anteoculāris (rāmus)* anteocular (branch of a stag's horn). See ANTE-, OCULAR] —**ant′ler·less,** *adj.*

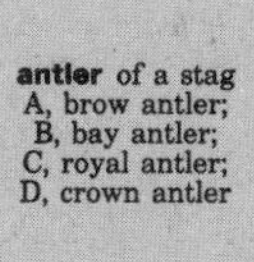

antler of a stag
A, brow antler;
B, bay antler;
C, royal antler;
D, crown antler

ınt·lered (ant′lərd), *adj.* **1.** having antlers. **2.** deco-rated with antlers. [1810–20; ANTLER + -ED[3]]

ınt·ler·ite (ant′lə rīt′), *n.* an emerald to blackish-green mineral, hydrous copper sulfate, $Cu_3(OH)_4SO_4$, a major copper ore in Chile. [after the *Antler* Mine, Mo-have Co., Arizona, from where samples were first de-scribed in 1889; see -ITE[1]]

ınt·li·a (ant′lē ə), *n., gen.* **-li·ae** (-lē ē′) for 1, *pl.* **-li·ae** -lē ē′) for 2. **1.** *Astron.* the Air Pump, a small southern constellation between Vela and Hydra. **2.** (*l.c.*) *Entomol.* the proboscis of a lepidopterous insect. [< L *antlia* pump, machine for drawing water < Gk *antlía* bilgewa-ter, a ship's hold, equiv. to *ántl(os)* the hold (of a ship), bilge water + *-ia* -IA] —**ant·li·ate** (ant′lē āt′), *adj.*

ınt′ li′on, any of several insects belonging to the fam-ily Myrmeleontidae, of the order Neuroptera, the larvae of which dig a pit in sand where they lie in wait to prey upon ants or other insects that lose their footing. Also, **ınt′li′on.** [1805–15]

ın·to·don·tal·gic (an′tō don tal′jik), *adj., n. Den-tistry.* antiodontalgic.

ın·to·fa·gas·ta (än′tō fə gä′stə; *Sp.* än′tô fä gäs′tä), *n.* a seaport in N Chile. 149,720.

ın·toine (an′twän; *Fr.* äN twAN′), *n.* **1. An·dré** (äN-dRā′), 1858–1943, French theatrical director, manager, and critic. **2. Père** (peR) (*Francisco Ildefonso Mareno*), 1748–1829, Roman Catholic priest in Louisiana: tried to establish an Inquisition. **3.** a male given name: French form of **Anthony.**

ın·toi·nette (an′twə net′, -tə-; *Fr.* äN twA net′), *n.* **1. Ma·rie** (mə rē′; *Fr.* mA Rē′), 1755–93, queen of France 1774–93: wife of Louis XVI. **2.** a female given name: derived from *Antoine*

ın·ton (an′ton, -tən), *n.* a male given name, form of **Anthony.**

ın·to·nel·lo da Mes·si·na (än′tô nel′lô dä mes sē′-nä), (*Antonello di Giovanni degli Antonj*) 1430?–79, Sicilian painter.

An·to·ni·a (an tō′nē ə, -tōn′yə), *n.* a female given name: derived from *Antonius.*

an·to·nin·i·a·nus (an′tə nin′ē ā′nəs), *n., pl.* **-ni** (-nī). a Roman coin of the 3rd century A.D., originally of silver but later debased. [< L *Antōniniānus* pertaining to ANTONINUS, equiv. to *Antōnīn(us)* + *-iānus* -IAN]

An·to·ni·nus (an′tə nī′nəs), *n.* **Marcus Aurelius.** See **Marcus Aurelius.**

Antoni′nus Pi′us (pī′əs), A.D. 86–161, emperor of Rome 138–161.

An·to·nio·ni (än′tô nyô′nē; *Eng.* an tō′nē ō′nē), *n.* **Mi·chel·an·ge·lo** (*It.* mē′kel än′je lô; *Eng.* mī′kəl an′jə lō′, mik′əl-), born 1912, Italian film director.

An·to·ni·us (an tō′nē əs), *n.* **Marcus.** See **Antony, Mark.**

an·to·no·ma·sia (an′tə nə mā′zhə), *n.* **1.** *Rhet.* the identification of a person by an epithet or appellative that is not the person's name, as *his lordship.* **2.** the use of the name of a person who was distinguished by a par-ticular characteristic, as Don Juan or Annie Oakley, to designate a person or group of persons having the same characteristic. [1580–90; < L < Gk, verbid of *anto-nomázein* to call by a new name, equiv. to *ant-* ANT- + *onomat-* s. of *ónoma* NAME + *-ia* -IA] —**an·to·no·mas·tic** (an′tə nō mas′tik), **an′to·no·mas′ti·cal,** *adj.* —**an′-to·no·mas′ti·cal·ly,** *adv.*

An·to·ny (an′tə nē), *n.* **1. Mark** (*Marcus Antonius*), 83?–30 B.C., Roman general: friend of Caesar; member of the second triumvirate and rival of Octavian. **2.** a male given name.

An′tony and Cleopa′tra, a tragedy (1606–07?) by Shakespeare.

an·to·nym (an′tə nim), *n.* a word opposite in meaning to another. *Fast* is an antonym of *slow.* Cf. **synonym** (def. 1). [1865–70; ANT- + (SYN)ONYM] —**an·ton·y·mous** (an ton′ə məs), **an′to·nym′ic,** *adj.* —**an·ton′y·my,** *n.*

ant-pip·it (ant′pip′it), *n.* gnateater.

an·tre (an′tər), *n.* a cavern; cave. [1595–1605; < MF < L *antrum.* See ANTRUM]

An·trim (an′trim), *n.* **1.** a county in NE Northern Ire-land. 355,716; 1098 sq. mi. (2844 sq. km). *Co. seat:* Belfast. **2.** an administrative district in this county. 35,000; 217 sq. mi. (563 sq. km).

An·tron (an′tron), *Trademark.* a brand of nylon textile fiber that is lightweight and strong, used in making du-rable materials for upholstery, draperies, carpets, etc.

an·trorse (an trôrs′), *adj. Bot., Zool.* bent or directed forward or upward. [1855–60; < NL *antrorsus,* equiv. to *antr-* (as presumed base of L *anterior* ANTERIOR) + *-orsus,* extracted from L *intrōrsus* INTRORSE] —**an·trorse′ly,** *adv.*

an·trum (an′trəm), *n., pl.* **-tra** (-trə). *Anat.* a cavity in a body organ, esp. a bone. [1720–30; < L < Gk *ántron* cave] —**an′tral,** *adj.*

ant·shrike (ant′shrīk′), *n.* any of several antbirds, esp. of the genus *Thamnophilus,* superficially resem-bling the shrike. [ANT(BIRD) + SHRIKE]

Ant·si·ra·ne (änt′sə rä′nā), *n.* Diego-Suarez.

ants·y (ant′sē), *adj.,* **ants·i·er, ants·i·est.** *Informal.* **1.** unable to sit or stand still; fidgety: *The children were bored and antsy.* **2.** apprehensive, uneasy, or nervous: *I'm a little antsy since hearing those storm warnings.* [1950–55; ANT + -S[3] + -Y[1]; cf. -SY] —**ants′i·ness,** *n.*

ant-thrush (ant′thrush′), *n.* any of several antbirds, esp. of the genus *Formicarius.* [1860–65; ANT(BIRD) + THRUSH[1]]

ANTU (an′to͞o), *Trademark.* a brand of gray, water-insoluble, poisonous powder, $C_{11}H_{10}N_2S$, used for killing rodents; alpha-naphthylthiourea.

An·tung (än′do͝ong′; *Eng.* an to͝ong′), *n. Wade-Giles.* **1.** former name of **Dandong. 2.** a former province of China, in Manchuria.

Ant·werp (ant′wərp), *n.* **1.** a seaport in N Belgium, on the Scheldt. 209,200. **2.** a province in N Belgium. 1,559,269; 1104 sq. mi. (2860 sq. km). French, **Anvers.** Flemish, **Ant·wer·pen** (änt′veR pən).

Ant′werp blue′, any of several iron-blue pigments, usually containing a considerable amount of extender. [1825–35]

ant·wren (ant′ren′), *n.* any of several small antbirds, esp. of the genus *Myrmotherula.* [1815–25; ANT + WREN]

A·nu (ä′no͞o), *n.* the Akkadian god of heaven.

A·nu·bis (ə no͞o′bis, ə nyo͞o′-), *n. Egyptian Religion.* the god of tombs and weigher of the hearts of the dead: represented as having the head of a jackal.

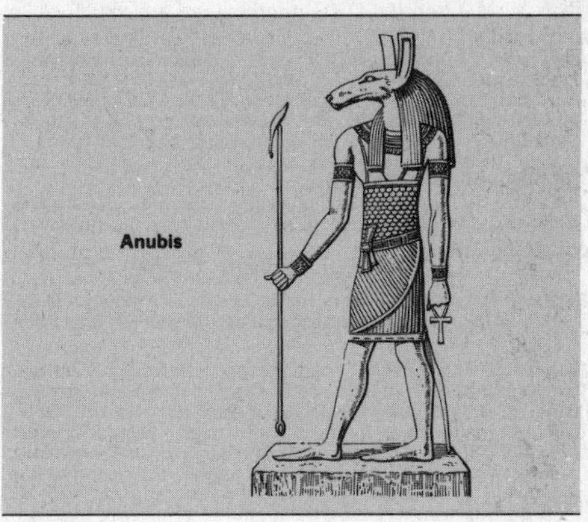

Anubis

a·nu·cle·ate (ā no͞o′klē it, ā nyo͞o′-), *adj. Cell Biol.* having no nucleus. Also, **a·nu·cle·at·ed** (ā no͞o′klē ā′tid, ā nyo͞o′-). [A-[6] + NUCLEATE]

a·nu·cle·o·late (ā no͞o′klē ə lāt′, -lit, ā nyo͞o′-; ā′no͞o klē′ə lāt′, -lit, ā′nyo͞o-), *adj.* lacking a nucleolus or nucleoli. [A-[6] + NUCLEOLATE]

-anum, a suffix occurring in scientific words of Latin origin: *laudanum.* [< L, neut. of *-ānus* -AN]

A number 1. See **A one** (def. 2). [1835–45]

A·nun·na·ki (ä no͝on′nä kē), *n.* (*used with a plural v.*) various unnamed Sumerian deities who constituted the divine assembly presided over by An and Enlil and of whom seven were judges in the afterworld.

A·nu·ra·dha·pu·ra (ə no͝or′ə də po͝or′ə, un′o͝o rä′-də-), *n.* a city in N central Sri Lanka: ruins of ancient Buddhist temples. 30,000.

an·u·ran (ə no͝or′ən, ə nyo͝or′-), *n.* **1.** any amphibian of the order Anura, comprising the frogs and toads. —*adj.* **2.** belonging or pertaining to the Anura. [< NL *Anur(a)* (*an-* AN-[1] + Gk *-oura,* neut. pl. of *-ouros* -tailed, deriv. of *ourá* tail) + -AN]

an·u·re·sis (an′yə rē′sis), *n.* retention of urine in the bladder. [1895–1900; AN-[1] + Gk *oúrēsis* urination (see URETER, -SIS)] —**an·u·ret·ic** (an′yə ret′ik), *adj.*

an·u·ri·a (ə no͝or′ē ə, ə nyo͝or′-, an yo͝or′-), *n. Med.* the absence or suppression of urine. [1830–40; < NL; see AN-[1], -URIA] —**an·u′ric,** *adj.*

an·u·rous (an′yər əs, ə no͝or′əs, ə nyo͝or′-), *adj. Zool.* having no tail. Also, **anourous.** [1830–40; see ANURAN, -OUS]

a·nus (ā′nəs), *n., pl.* **a·nus·es.** *Anat.* the opening at the lower end of the alimentary canal, through which the solid refuse of digestion is excreted. See diag. under **intestine.** [1650–60; < L *ānus* ring, anus]

-anus, a suffix occurring in scientific words of Latin or-igin: *Platanus.* [< L *-ānus;* see -AN]

An·vers (äN veR′), *n.* French name of **Antwerp.**

anvil (def. 1)

an·vil (an′vil), *n.* **1.** a heavy iron block with a smooth face, frequently of steel, on which metals, usually heated until soft, are hammered into desired shapes. **2.** any-thing having a similar form or use. **3.** the fixed jaw in certain measuring instruments. **4.** Also called **an′vil cloud′, an′vil top′.** *Meteorol.* incus (def. 2). **5.** a musi-

CONCISE PRONUNCIATION KEY: *act, cāpe, dâre, pärt; set, ēqual; if, īce; ox, ōver, ôrder, oil, bo͝ok, bo͞ot, out; up, ûrge; child; sing; shoe; thin, that;* zh as in *treasure.* ə = *a* as in *alone, e* as in *system, i* as in *easily, o* as in *gallop, u* as in *circus;* ᵊ as in *fire* (fīᵊr), *hour* (ouᵊr). l and n can serve as syllabic consonants, as in *cradle* (krād′l), and *button* (but′n). See the full key inside the front cover.

·′ti·smut′, *adj.*
·′ti·snob′, *n.*
·′ti·so·ci′e·tal, *adj.;* **-ly,** *adv.*
·′ti-Soc′ra·tes, *adj.*
·′ti-So·crat′ic, *adj.*
·′ti·soph′ism, *n.*
·′ti·soph′ist, *n., adj.*
·′ti·so·phis′tic, *adj.*
·′ti·so·phis′ti·ca′tion, *n.*
·′ti·soph′ist·ry, *n.*
·′ti·sop′o·rif′ic, *adj., n.*
·′ti-So′vi·et, *n., adj.*
·′ti-Spain′, *adj.*
·′ti-Span′ish, *adj.*
·′ti·spas·mod′ic, *adj., n.*
·′ti·spec′u·la′tion, *n., adj.*
·′ti·spec′u·la′tive, *adj.;* **-ly,** *adv.;* **-ness,** *n.*
·′ti·spend′ing, *adj.*
·′ti·spir′it·u·al, *adj.;* **-ly,** *adv.*
·′ti·spir′it·u·al·ism, *n.*
·′ti·spir′it·u·al·ist, *n., adj.*
·′ti·spir′it·u·al·is′tic, *adj.*
an′ti·split′ting, *adj.*
an′ti·spread′er, *n.*
an′ti·spread′ing, *adj.*
an′ti·stall′ing, *adj.*
an′ti·state′, *adj.*
an′ti·stat′ic, *adj.*
an′ti·stat′ism, *n.*
an′ti·stat′ist, *n., adj.*
an′ti·ste·ril′i·ty, *adj.*
an′ti·stim′u·lant, *adj., n.*
an′ti·stim′u·la′tion, *n.*
an′ti·sto′ry, *n., pl.* **-ries.**
an′ti·stress′, *adj.*
an′ti·strike′, *adj.*
an′ti·strik′er, *n.*
an′ti·struc′tur·al·ist, *n., adj.*
an′ti·stu′dent, *n., adj.*
an′ti·style′, *n.*
an′ti·sub′ma·rine′, *adj.*
an′ti·sub′si·dy, *n., pl.* **-dies.**
an′ti·sub·ver′sion, *n.*
an′ti·suf′frage, *adj.*
an′ti·suf′fra·gist, *n., adj.*
an′ti·su′i·cide, *adj.*
an′ti·su′per·nat′ur·al, *adj., n.*
an′ti·su′per·nat′ur·al·ism, *n.*
an′ti·su′per·nat′ur·al·ist, *n., adj.*
an′ti·su′per·nat′ur·al·is′tic, *adj.*
an′ti-Swe′den, *adj.*
an′ti-Swe′dish, *adj.*
an′ti·sym′me·try, *adj., n.*
an′ti·syn′di·cal·ism, *n.*
an′ti·syn′di·cal·ist, *n., adj.*
an′ti·syn′di·ca′tion, *adj.*
an′ti·syn′od, *adj.*
an′ti·syph′i·lit′ic, *adj., n.*
an′ti·take′o′ver, *adj., n.*
an′ti·tank′, *adj.*
an′ti·tar′nish, *adj.*
an′ti·tar′nish·ing, *adj.*
an′ti·tar·tar′ic, *adj.*
an′ti·tax′, *adj.*
an′ti·tax·a′tion, *adj.*
an′ti·tech′no·log′i·cal, *adj.*
an′ti·tech·nol′o·gist, *n.*
an′ti·tech·nol′o·gy, *n.*
an′ti·tem′per·ance, *adj.*
an′ti·ter′ror·ism, *adj.*
an′ti-Teu′ton, *adj., n.*
an′ti-Teu·ton′ic, *adj.*
an′ti·theft′, *adj.*
an′ti·the′o·lo′gian, *n., adj.*
an′ti·the′o·log′i·cal, *adj.*
an′ti·the·ol′o·giz′ing, *adj.*
an′ti·the·ol′o·gy, *adj.*
an′ti·the′o·ret′i·cal, *adj.;* **-ly,** *adv.*
an′ti·thy′roid, *adj., n.*
an′ti·to·bac′co, *adj.*
an′ti·ton′ic, *adj., n.*
an′ti·to·tal′i·tar′i·an, *adj.*
an′ti·tra·di′tion, *adj.*
an′ti·tra·di′tion·al, *adj.;* **-ly,** *adv.*
an′ti·tra·di′tion·al·ist, *n., adj.*
an′ti-Trin′i·tar′i·an, *adj., n.*
an′ti-Trin′i·tar′i·an·ism, *n.*
an′ti·tu·ber′cu·lar, *adj.*
an′ti·tu·ber′cu·lo′sis, *adj.*
an′ti·tu·ber′cu·lous, *adj.*
an′ti·tu′mor, *adj., n.*
an′ti·tu′mor·al, *adj.*
an′ti-Turk′ish, *adj.*
an′ti·ty′phoid, *adj.*
an′ti·ul′cer, *adj.*
an′ti·un′em·ploy′ment, *adj.*
an′ti·u′ni·ver′si·ty, *adj., n.*
an′ti·ur′ban, *adj.*
an′ti·u·til′i·tar′i·an, *adj., n.*
an′ti·u·til′i·tar′i·an·ism, *n.*
an′ti·vac′ci·na′tion, *adj.*
an′ti·vac′ci·na′tion·ist, *n.*
an′ti·vac′cin·ist, *n.*
an′ti·ver′ti·cal·ist, *n.*
an′ti·vi′o·lence, *adj.*
an′ti·vi′ral, *adj.*
an′ti·vi′rus, *adj., n.*
an′ti·war′, *adj.*
an′ti·wel′fare, *adj.*
an′ti-West′, *adj.*
an′ti-West′ern, *adj.*
an′ti·whal′ing, *adj.*
an′ti·wom′an, *adj., n., pl.* **-wom′en.**
an′ti·wrin′kle, *adj.*
an′ti-Zi′on·ism, *n.*
an′ti-Zi′on·ist, *n., adj.*

cal percussion instrument having steel bars that are struck with a wooden or metal beater. **6.** *Anat.* incus (def. 1). [bef. 900; ME *anvelt, anfelt,* OE *anfilt(e), anfealt;* c. MD *anvilte,* OHG *anafalz.* See ON, FELT[2]]

anx•i•e•ty (ang zī′i tē), *n., pl.* **-ties. 1.** distress or uneasiness of mind caused by fear of danger or misfortune: *He felt anxiety about the possible loss of his job.* **2.** earnest but tense desire; eagerness: *He had a keen anxiety to succeed in his work.* **3.** *Psychiatry.* a state of apprehension and psychic tension occurring in some forms of mental disorder. [1515–25; < L *anxietās,* equiv. to *anxi(us)* ANXIOUS + *-etās,* var. of *-itās* before a vowel]
—Syn. 1. fear, foreboding; worry, disquiet. See **apprehension. —Ant. 1.** certainty, serenity, tranquillity.

anxi′ety neuro′sis, *Psychiatry.* a neurotic disorder characterized by pervasive anxiety. [1900–05]

anx•i•o•lyt•ic (ang′zē ə lit′ik), *adj.* **1.** anxiety relieving. *—n.* **2.** See **antianxiety drug.** [1960–65; ANXI(ETY) + -O- + -LYTIC]

anx•ious (angk′shəs, ang′-), *adj.* **1.** full of mental distress or uneasiness because of fear of danger or misfortune; greatly worried; solicitous: *Her parents were anxious about her poor health.* **2.** earnestly desirous; eager (usually fol. by an infinitive or *for*): *anxious to please; anxious for our happiness.* **3.** attended with or showing solicitude or uneasiness: *anxious forebodings.* [1615–25; < L *anxius* worried, distressed, deriv. of *angere* to strangle, pain, distress; cf. ANGUISH, -OUS] **—anx′ious•ly,** *adv.* **—anx′ious•ness,** *n.*
—Usage. The earliest sense of ANXIOUS (in the 17th century) was "troubled" or "worried": *We are still anxious for the safety of our dear sons in battle.* Its meaning "earnestly desirous, eager" arose in the mid-18th century: *We are anxious to see our new grandson.* Some insist that ANXIOUS must always convey a sense of distress or worry and object to its use in the sense of "eager," but such use is fully standard.

anx′ious seat′, 1. Also called **anx′ious bench′.** *Chiefly North Atlantic States and Southern and South Midland U.S.* a seat reserved at a revival meeting for those troubled by conscience and eager for spiritual assistance. **2.** a state of anxiety, esp. about the outcome of a vote, negotiation, etc.: *Strikers have been in the anxious seat for the last three days.* [1810–20, *Amer.*]

an•y (en′ē), *adj.* **1.** one, a, an, or some; one or more without specification or identification: *If you have any witnesses, produce them. Pick out any six you like.* **2.** whatever or whichever it may be: *cheap at any price.* **3.** in whatever quantity or number, great or small; some: *Do you have any butter?* **4.** every; all: *Any schoolboy would know that. Read any books you find on the subject.* **5.** (following a negative) at all: *She can't endure any criticism.* *—pron.* **6.** an unspecified person or persons; anybody; anyone: *He does better than any before him.* **7.** a single one or ones; an unspecified thing or things; a quantity or number: *We don't have any left.* *—adv.* **8.** in whatever degree; to some extent; at all: *Do you feel any better?* **9. any which way,** in any manner whatever; indifferently or carelessly: *Doing your work any which way is just not good enough.* [bef. 950; ME *eni, ani,* OE *ǣnig* (OE *ān* ONE + *-ig* -Y[1])]
—Syn. 3. See **some.**
—Usage. See **anybody, anyone, anyplace, anyway, either, they.**

An•yang (än′yäng′), *n. Pinyin, Wade-Giles.* a city in N Henan province, in E China: site of the ancient city of Yin, the center of the Shang dynasty, dated c1350–1027 B.C. 225,000. Also, **An′-yang′.**

an•y•bod•y (en′ē bod′ē, -bud′ē), *pron., n., pl.* **-bod•ies.** *—pron.* **1.** any person. **2. anybody's guess,** a matter of conjecture: *It's anybody's guess why she quit.* *—n.* **3.** a person of some importance: *If you're anybody, you'll receive an invitation.* [1250–1300; ME *ani bodi.* See ANY, BODY]
—Usage. The pronoun ANYBODY is always written as one word: *Is anybody home? There isn't anybody in the office.* The two-word noun phrase ANY BODY means "any group" (*Any body of students will include a few dissidents*) or "any physical body": *The search continued for a week despite the failure to find any body.* If the word *a* can be substituted for *any* without seriously affecting the meaning, the two-word noun phrase is called for: *a body of students; failure to find a body.* If the substitution cannot be made, the spelling is ANYBODY. ANYBODY is less formal than ANYONE. See also **anyone, each, they.**

an•y•how (en′ē hou′), *adv.* **1.** in any way whatever. **2.** in any case; at all events. **3.** in a careless manner; haphazardly. [1730–40; ANY + HOW]

an•y•more (en′ē môr′, -mōr′), *adv.* **1.** any longer. **2.** nowadays; presently. [1350–1400; ME *ani more* any longer]
—Usage. The adverb ANYMORE meaning "any longer" or "nowadays" is most commonly spelled as one word. It is used in negative constructions and in some types of questions: *Sally doesn't work here anymore. Do you play tennis anymore?* In some dialects, chiefly South Midland in origin, it is found in positive statements meaning "nowadays": *Baker's bread is all we eat anymore. Anymore we always take the bus.* Its use at the beginning of a sentence is almost exclusive to speech or to representations of speech.

an•yon (an′yon), *n.* an elementary particle or particlelike excitation having properties intermediate between those of bosons and fermions. [1983; ANY + -ON[1]]

an•y•one (en′ē wun′, -wən), *pron.* any person at all; anybody: *Did anyone see the accident?* [1350–1400; ME *ani on.* See ANY, ONE]
—Usage. ANYONE as a pronoun meaning "anybody" or "any person at all" is written as one word: *Does anyone have the correct time?* The two-word phrase ANY ONE means "any single member of a group of persons or things" and is often followed by *of: Can any one of the members type? Any one of these books is exciting reading.* ANYONE is somewhat more formal than ANYBODY. See also **each, they.**

an•y•place (en′ē plās′), *adv.* anywhere. [1915–20; ANY + PLACE]
—Usage. The adverb ANYPLACE is most often written as one word: *Anyplace you look there are ruins.* It occurs mainly in informal speech and only occasionally in writing. ANYWHERE is by far the more common form in formal speech and edited writing. The same holds true, respectively, of the adverbial pairs EVERYPLACE and EVERYWHERE; NOPLACE and NOWHERE; and SOMEPLACE and SOMEWHERE. The two-word noun phrases ANY PLACE, EVERY PLACE, NO PLACE, and SOME PLACE occur, however, in all contexts: *We can build the house in any place we choose. There's no place like home.*

an•y•road (en′ē rōd′), *adv. Brit. Slang.* anyway; anyhow. [1885–90]

an•y•thing (en′ē thing′), *pron.* **1.** any thing whatever; something, no matter what: *Do you have anything for a toothache?* *—n.* **2.** a thing of any kind. **3. anything goes,** any type of conduct, dress, speech, etc., is considered acceptable or valid or is likely to be encountered and tolerated: *That resort is a place where anything goes!* *—adv.* **4.** in any degree; to any extent; in any way; at all: *Does it taste anything like chocolate?* **5. anything but,** in no degree or respect; not in the least: *The plans were anything but definite.* [bef. 900; ME *ani thing, eni thing,* OE *ǣnig thing.* See ANY, THING[1]]

an•y•time (en′ē tīm′), *adv.* **1.** at any time; regardless of hour, date, etc.; whenever. **2.** invariably; without doubt or exception; always: *I can do better than that anytime.* [1780–90; ANY + TIME]

an•y•way (en′ē wā′), *adv.* **1.** in any case; anyhow; nonetheless; regardless: *Whether you like it or not, I'm going anyway.* **2.** (used to continue or resume the thread of a story or account): *Anyway, we finally found a plumber who could come right over.* [1150–1200; ME *ani wei.* See ANY, WAY]
—Usage. The adverb ANYWAY is spelled as one word: *It was snowing hard, but we drove to the play anyway.* The two-word phrase ANY WAY means "in any manner": *Finish the job any way you choose.* If the words "in the" can be substituted for "any," the two-word phrase is called for: *Finish the job in the way you choose.* If the substitution cannot be made, the spelling is ANYWAY.

an•y•ways (en′ē wāz′), *adv. Nonstandard.* anyway.

an•y•where (en′ē hwâr′, -wâr′), *adv.* **1.** in, at, or to any place. **2.** to any extent; to some degree: *Does my answer come anywhere near the right one?* **3. get anywhere,** to achieve success: *You'll never get anywhere with that attitude!* *—n.* **4.** any place or direction: *They knew the attack could come from anywhere.* [1350–1400; ME *anywher(e), aniquar.* See ANY, WHERE]
—Usage. See **anyplace.**

an•y•wheres (en′ē hwârz′, -wârz′), *adv. Nonstandard.* anywhere. [1765–75; ANYWHERE + -S[1]]

an•y•wise (en′ē wīz′), *adv.* in any way or respect. [bef. 1000; ME *ani wise,* OE *on ǣnige wīsan* in any wise. See ANY, WISE[2]]

An•za (än′sä), *n.* **Juan Bau•tis•ta de** (hwän bou tēs′tä the), 1735–88, Spanish frontiersman and army officer, born in Mexico: explored western coast of U.S.

An•zac (an′zak), *n.* **1.** a member of the Australian and New Zealand Army Corps during World War I. **2.** a soldier from Australia or New Zealand. **3.** any Australian or New Zealander. [1910–15]

An′zac Day′, April 25, a national day of remembrance in Australia and New Zealand commemorating the Anzac landing on Gallipoli, Turkey, in 1915, the first major engagement of Australian and New Zealand forces in World War I.

An•zen•gru•ber (än′tsən grōō′bər), *n.* **Lud•wig** (lōōt′viḵ, lōōd′-), 1839–89, Austrian playwright and novelist.

An•zhe•ro-Su•dzhensk (un zhe′rə sōō′jinsk), *n.* a city in the S Russian Federation in central Asia. 105,000.

An•zi•o (an′zē ō′; *It.* än′tsyô), *n.* a town in Italy, S of Rome on the Tyrrhenian coast: site of Allied beachhead in World War II. 23,421.

ANZUS (an′zəs), *n.* Australia, New Zealand, and the United States, esp. as associated in the mutual defense treaty **(ANZUS Pact** or **ANZUS Treaty)** of 1952.

A/O, 1. account of. **2.** and others. Also, **a/o**

AOA, Administration on Aging.

ao dai (ou′ dī′, ô′ dī′), *n., pl.* **ao dais.** a costume composed of a long tunic with side slits over wide trousers, worn by Vietnamese women as traditional dress. [< Vietnamese *áo dài* lit., long garment]

A•oe•de (ā ē′dē), *n. Class. Myth.* one of the original three Muses; the Muse of song. Also, **A•oi•de** (ā oi′dē). Cf. **Melete, mneme** (def. 2).

AOH, Ancient Order of Hibernians.

A-OK (ā′ō kā′), *adj., adv. Informal.* OK; perfect: *an A-OK rocket launching.* Also, **A-O.K., A′-O•kay′.** [1955–60]

A•o•ki (ä ô′kē), *n.* **Shu•zo** (shōō′zô), 1844–1914, first Japanese ambassador to U.S., 1905–09.

a•o•le (ä ō′lā), *adv. Hawaiian.* no; not at all. [< Hawaiian *ʻaʻole*]

A•o•mo•ri (ä′ô môʀē), *n.* a seaport on N Honshu, in N Japan. 287,609.

A one (ā′ wun′), **1.** noting a vessel regarded by a shipping-classification society as being equipped to the highest standard and with equipment maintained in first-class condition. **2.** Also, **A number one.** *Informal.* first-class; excellent; superior: *The meals there are A one.* Also, **A-one, A 1, A-1** [1830–40]

AOR, 1. *Law.* advice of rights. **2.** Album-Oriented Radio. **3.** Album-Oriented Rock.

A•o•ran•gi (ä′ō räng′gē), *n.* See **Cook, Mount.**

a•o•rist (ā′ə rist), *Gram.* *—n.* **1.** a verb tense, as in Classical Greek, expressing action or, in the indicative mood, past action, without further limitation or implication. *—adj.* **2.** of or in this tense. [1575–85; < Gk *aóristos* unlimited, equiv. to *a-* A-[6] + (*h*)*oristós* limited (*horizein* (base of *horízein* to bound, limit; see HORIZON) + *-tos* adj. suffix)]

a•o•ris•tic (ā′ə ris′tik), *adj.* **1.** *Gram.* pertaining to the aorist. **2.** indefinite; indeterminate. [1840–50; AORIST + -IC] **—a′o•ris′ti•cal•ly,** *adv.*

a•or•ta (ā ôr′tə), *n., pl.* **-tas, -tae** (-tē). *Anat.* the main trunk of the arterial system, conveying blood from the left ventricle of the heart to all of the body except the lungs. See illus. under **heart.** [1570–80; < ML < Gk *aortḗ* the great artery, lit., something hung, carried; akin to *aeírein* to lift, carry] **—a•or′tic, a•or′tal,** *adj.*

aor′tic arch′, *Embryol.* one member of a series of paired curved blood vessels that arise in the embryo from the ventral aorta, pass around the pharynx through the branchial arches, and join with the dorsal aorta to form the great vessels of the head and neck. [1900–05]

aor′tic insuffi′ciency, *Pathol.* abnormal closure of the aortic valve resulting in regurgitation of blood to the left ventricle. Also called **aor′tic incom′petence.**

aor′tic steno′sis, *Pathol.* abnormal narrowing of the aorta, esp. of its orifice, usually as a result of rheumatic fever or embryologic anomalies.

aor′tic valve′, *Anat.* a semilunar valve between the aorta and the left ventricle of the heart that prevents the blood from flowing back into the left ventricle.

a•or•ti•tis (ā′ôr tī′tis), *n. Pathol.* inflammation of the aorta. [1835–45; < NL; see AORTA, -ITIS]

a•or•to•cla•sia (ā ôr′tə klā′zhə, -zhē ə), *n. Pathol.* rupture of the aorta. [AORT(A) + -O- + *-clasia* < Gk *klás(is)* a breaking (see -CLASIS) + -IA]

a•or•tog•ra•phy (ā′ôr tog′rə fē), *n., pl.* **-phies.** x-ray examination of the aorta following injection of radiopaque dye. [1930–35; AORT(A) + -O- + -GRAPHY] **—a•or•to•graph•ic** (ā ôr′tə graf′ik), *adj.*

A.O.U., American Ornithologists' Union.

a•ou•dad (ä′ōō dad′), *n.* a wild sheep, *Ammotragus lervia,* of northern Africa, having a long fringe of hair on the throat, chest, and forelegs. Also called **Barbary sheep.** [1860–65; < F < Berber, equiv. to *a-* masc. sing. prefix + *udad* ram]

AP, 1. See **adjective phrase. 2.** *Education.* Advanced Placement. **3.** See **Air Police. 4.** See **American plan. 5.** antipersonnel. Also, **A.P.**

ap-[1], var. of **ad-** before *p: appear.*

ap-[2], var. of **apo-** before a vowel or *h: aphelion.*

Ap., 1. Apostle. **2.** Apothecaries'. **3.** April.

A/P, 1. account paid. **2.** accounts payable. **3.** authority to pay or purchase. Also, **a/p**

a.p., 1. additional premium. **2.** author's proof.

a•pa (ə pä′), *n.* a tree, *Eperua falcata,* of tropical America, having reddish-brown wood used in the construction of houses. [< Tupi]

A•pa (ä′pä), *n.* a river in central South America that flows W along the E Paraguay-SW Brazil border to the Paraguay River. ab. 125 mi. (200 km) long.

APA, 1. American Psychiatric Association. **2.** American Psychological Association.

A.P.A., 1. American Philological Association. **2.** American Protective Association. **3.** American Protestant Association. **4.** American Psychiatric Association. **5.** American Psychological Association. **6.** Associate in Public Administration.

a•pace (ə pās′), *adv.* with speed; quickly; swiftly. [1275–1325; ME *a pas(e)* at a (good) pace. See A-[1], PACE]

a•pache (ə päsh′, ə pash′; *Fr.* A pASh′), *n., pl.* **a•paches** (ə pä′shiz, ə pash′iz; *Fr.* A pASh′). a Parisian gangster, rowdy, or ruffian. [1735–45, *Amer.*; < APACHE]

A•pach•e (ə pach′ē), *n., pl.* **A•pach•es,** (*esp. collectively*) **A•pach•e. 1.** a member of an Athabaskan people of the southwestern U.S. **2.** any of the several Athabaskan languages of Arizona and the Rio Grande basin. **3.** *Mil.* a two-man U.S. Army helicopter designed to attack enemy armor with rockets or a 30mm gun and equipped for use in bad weather and in darkness. [1915–20; < MexSp, perh. < Zuni *ʔa·paču* Navajos, presumably applied formerly to the Apacheans (Navajos and Apaches) generally]

A•pach•e•an (ə pach′ē ən), *n.* **1.** a subgroup of the Athabaskan language family comprising the languages of the Apache tribes and the Navajo. **2.** a speaker of an Apachean language. [APACHE + -AN]

a•pache′ dance′ (ə päsh′, ə pash′ *or, often* ə pach′ē), a vigorous dance representing a Parisian apache dancing in a rough, domineering way with his woman.

Apach′e plume′, a low shrub, *Fallugia paradoxa,* of the rose family, of southwestern North America, having white flowers and fruit heads of feathery tufts. [1885–90, *Amer.*]

Ap′a•lach′ee Bay′ (ap′ə lach′ē, ap′-), a bay of the Gulf of Mexico, on the coast of NW Florida. ab. 30 mi. (48 km) wide.

Ap•a•lach•i•co•la (ap′ə lach′ə kō′lə), *n.* a river flowing S from NW Florida into the Gulf of Mexico. 90 mi. (145 km) long.

ap•a•nage (ap′ə nij), *n.* appanage.

CONCISE ETYMOLOGY KEY: <, descended or borrowed from; >, whence; b., blend of, blended; c., cognate with; cf., compare; deriv., derivative; equiv., equivalent; imit., imitative; obl., oblique; r., replacing; s., stem; sp., spelling, spelled; resp., respelling, respelled; trans., translation; ?, origin unknown; *, unattested; ‡, probably earlier than. See the full key inside the front cover.

·pa·pa·ne (ä′pä pä′nā), *n.* a small, deep crimson Ha- aiian honeycreeper, *Himatione sanguinea,* having lack wings, tail, and bill. [< Hawaiian *ʻapapane*]

pa·ra·vid·ya (ə pär′ə vid′yä), *n. Hinduism.* intel- ectual knowledge. Cf. **paravidya.** [< Skt]

pa·re·jo (ap′ə rā′ō, -rā′hō, ä′pə-; *Sp.* ä′pä RE′hô), ., *pl.* ***-jos*** (-ōz, -hōz; *Sp.* -hôs). *Spanish.* a Mexican acksaddle formed of stuffed leather cushions. [lit., reparation (i.e., equipment)]

·par·ri (ä pär′RĒ), *n.* a seaport on N Luzon, in the N hilippines. 45,070.

·part (ə pärt′), *adv.* **1.** into pieces or parts; to pieces: *take a watch apart; an old barn falling apart from ecay.* **2.** separately in place, time, motion, etc.: *New 'ork and Tokyo are thousands of miles apart. Our birth- ays are three days apart.* **3.** to or at one side, with re- pect to place, purpose, or function: *to put money apart r education; to keep apart from the group out of pride.* . separately or individually in consideration: *each fac- r viewed apart from the others.* **5.** aside (used with a erund or noun): *Joking apart, what do you think?* **6.** **part from,** aside from; in addition to; besides: *Apart rom other considerations, time is a factor.* **7. take part, a.** to disassemble: *to take a clock apart.* **b.** *Infor- ıal.* to criticize; attack: *She was taken apart for her con- roversial stand.* **c.** to subject to intense examination: *He ill take your feeble excuses apart.* —*adj.* **8.** having in- ependent or unique qualities, features, or characteris- cs (usually used following the noun it modifies): *a class part.* [1350–1400; ME < OF *a part* to one side. See A-⁵, ART] —**a·part′ness,** *n.*

·part·heid (ə pärt′hāt, -hīt), *n.* **1.** (in the Republic of outh Africa) a rigid policy of segregation of the non- hite population. **2.** any system or practice that sepa- ates people according to race, caste, etc. [1945–50; Afrik, equiv. to *apart* APART + *-heid* -HOOD]

·part·ment (ə pärt′mənt), *n.* **1.** a room or a group of elated rooms, among similar sets in one building, de- igned for use as a dwelling. **2.** a building containing or ıade up of such rooms. **3.** any separated room or group f rooms in a house or other dwelling: *We heard cries rom an apartment at the back of the house.* **4. apart- nents,** *Brit.* a set of rooms used as a dwelling by one erson or one family. [1635–45; < F *appartement* < It *ppartamento,* equiv. to *apparta(re)* to separate, divide . deriv. of *a parte* APART, to one side) + *-mento* -MENT] **-a·part·men·tal** (ə pärt men′tl), *adj.*
—**Syn. 1.** APARTMENT, COMPARTMENT agree in denot- ng a space enclosed by partitions or walls. APARTMENT, owever, emphasizes the idea of separateness or privacy: *ne's own apartment.* COMPARTMENT suggests a section f a larger space: *compartments in a ship's hold, in an range crate.*

part′ment hotel′, a hotel that rents furnished partments or suites suitable for housekeeping, on a eekly or more permanent basis, and usually supplies all otel services. [1900–05, *Amer.*]

part′ment house′, a building containing a number f residential apartments. Also called **apart′ment uild′ing.** [1870–75, *Amer.*]

·part·ment·ize (ə pärt′mən tīz′), *v.t.,* **-ized, -iz·ing.** . to build apartments on or in: *to apartmentize the owntown area.* **2.** to convert into apartments: *The old ıansion has recently been apartmentized.* Also, *esp. rit.,* **a·part′ment·ise′.** [APARTMENT + -IZE]

·past (ə past′, ə päst′), *prep. Chiefly South Midland .S. and Newfoundland.* past; beyond. [1890–95; *a-* semantically empty, perh. a generalization of adverbial -¹) + PAST; cf. ANEAR, ANIGH]

p·as·tron (ə pas′trən, -tron), *n., pl.* **-tra** (-trə). *Astron.* he point at which the stars of a binary system are far- hest apart (opposed to *periastron*). [< NL < Gk *ap-* P-² + *ástron* star, constellation; on the model of APO- EE]

p·a·tet·ic (ap′ə tet′ik), *adj. Zool.* assuming colors nd forms that effect deceptive camouflage. [1885–90; Gk *apatētikós* fallacious, equiv. to *apatē-* (var. s. of *pateúein* to deceive) + *-tikos* -TIC]

p·a·thet·ic (ap′ə thet′ik), *adj.* **1.** having or showing ttle or no emotion: *apathetic behavior.* **2.** not inter- sted or concerned; indifferent or unresponsive: *an apa- hetic audience.* Also, **ap′a·thet′i·cal.** [1735–45; PATH(Y) + (PATH)ETIC] —**ap′a·thet′i·cal·ly,** *adv.*
—**Syn. 1.** unfeeling, impassive, cool. **2.** uninterested, nconcerned. —**Ant. 1.** emotional. **2.** concerned.

p·a·thy (ap′ə thē), *n., pl.* **-thies. 1.** absence or sup- ression of passion, emotion, or excitement. **2.** lack of nterest in or concern for things that others find moving r exciting. **3.** Also, **ap·a·thei·a, ap·a·thi·a** (ap′ə thē′ə). *toicism.* freedom from emotion of any kind. [1595– 605; (< F) < L *apathia* < Gk *apátheia* insensibility to uffering, equiv. to *apathe-* (s. of *apathḗs*) unfeeling (*a-* -⁶ + *pathe-,* var. s. of *páthos* PATHOS) + *-ia* -IA]
—**Syn. 1.** coolness. **2.** See **indifference.** —**Ant. 1.** rdor; fervor.

p·a·tite (ap′ə tīt′), *n.* a common mineral, calcium uorophosphate, $Ca_5FP_3O_{12}$, occurring in individual rystals and in masses and varying in color, formerly sed in the manufacture of phosphate fertilizers. [1795– 805; < Gk *apát(ē)* trickery, fraud, deceit + -ITE¹]

PB, See **all-points bulletin.**

PC, 1. *Pharm.* aspirin, phenacetin, and caffeine: a ompound formerly used in headache and cold remedies. *Facetious.* any all-purpose cure. **3.** See **armored ersonnel carrier.** Also, **A.P.C.** (for defs. 1, 2).

pe (āp), *n., v.,* **aped, ap·ing.** —*n.* **1.** any of a group of nthropoid primates characterized by long arms, a broad hest, and the absence of a tail, comprising the family ongidae **(great ape),** which includes the chimpanzee, orilla, and orangutan, and the family Hylobatidae **esser ape),** which includes the gibbon and siamang. (loosely) any primate except humans. **3.** an imitator; imic. **4.** *Informal.* a big, ugly, clumsy person. —*v.t.* to imitate; mimic: *to ape another's style of writing.* **6. go ape,** *Slang.* to become violently emotional: *When she threatened to leave him, he went ape.* **7. go ape over,** *Slang.* to be extremely enthusiastic about: *They go ape over old rock music.* [bef. 900; ME; OE *apa;* c. OS *apo,* ON *api,* OHG *affo* (G *Affe*)] —**ape′like′,** *adj.*

a·peak (ə pēk′), *Naut.* —*adj.* **1.** more or less vertical. **2.** (of a dropped anchor) as nearly vertical as possible without being free of the bottom. **3.** (of an anchored vessel) having the anchor cable as nearly vertical as possible without freeing the anchor. —*adv.* **4.** vertically. Also, **a·peek′.** [1590–1600; A-¹ + PEAK¹]

ape′ hang′ers, *Slang.* a pair of very high, angled handlebars on some customized motorcycles. [1960–65]

A·pel·doorn (ä′pəl dōrn′, -dôrn′), *n.* a city in central Netherlands. 140,769.

A·pel·les (ə pel′ēz), *n.* 360?–315? B.C., Greek painter.

ape-man (āp′man′), *n., pl.* **-men. 1.** a hypothetical primate representing a transitional form between true humans and the anthropoid apes, considered by some as constituting the genus *Australopithecus.* **2.** a human assumed to have been reared by apes. [1875–80]

Ap′en·nine Moun′tains (ap′ə nīn′), Apennines.

Ap·en·nines (ap′ə nīnz′), *n.* (*used with a plural v.*) a mountain range in Italy, extending across the length of the entire peninsula from NW to SW. Highest peak, Monte Corno, 9585 ft. (2922 m).

A·pe·pi (ä′pe pē), *n. Egyptian Myth.* Apophis. [vocalization of Egyptian *ʼpp;* cf. Coptic *apho:ph*]

a·per·çu (A PER SY′), *n., pl.* ***-çus*** (-SY′). *French.* **1.** a hasty glance; a glimpse. **2.** an immediate estimate or judgment; understanding; insight. **3.** an outline or summary. [lit., perceived]

a·per·i·ent (ə pēr′ē ənt), *Med.* —*adj.* **1.** having a mild purgative or laxative effect. —*n.* **2.** a medicine or food that acts as a mild laxative. Also called **aperitive.** [1620–30; < L *aperient-* (s. of *aperiēns* opening, prp. of *aperīre* to open), equiv. to *aperi-* (appar. *ap-,* var. of *ab-* AB- + *-eri-*) + *-ent-* -ENT; the base *-eri-,* perh. with an earlier shape **twery-* or **twery-,* occurs only in this verb and *operīre* to close (see COVER, OPERCULUM)]

a·pe·ri·od·ic (ā′pēr ē od′ik), *adj.* **1.** not periodic; irregular. **2.** *Physics.* of or pertaining to vibrations or oscillations with no apparent period. [1875–80; A-⁶ + PERIODIC] —**a′pe·ri·od′i·cal·ly,** *adv.* —**a·pe·ri·o·dic·i·ty** (ā pēr′ē ə dis′i tē), *n.*

a·pé·ri·tif (ä per′i tēf′, ə per′-; *Fr.* A pā RE tēf′), *n., pl.* **-tifs** (-tēfs′; *Fr.* -tēf′). **1.** a small drink of alcoholic liquor taken to stimulate the appetite before a meal. **2.** Also called **apé′ritif wine′.** a wine served as an appetizer or cocktail. [1890–95; < F (*vin*) *apéritif;* see APERITIVE]

a·per·i·tive (ə per′i tiv), *Med.* —*adj.* **1.** aperient. **2.** having a stimulating effect on the appetite. —*n.* **3.** an aperient. **4.** an appetite stimulant. [1575–85; < ML *aperitīvus,* var. of LL *apertīvus,* equiv. to L *apert-* (see APERTURE) + *-īvus* -IVE]

ap·er·tom·e·ter (ap′ər tom′i tər), *n. Optics.* an instrument for measuring the angular and numerical aperture of the objective lens of a microscope. [1875–80; APERT(URE) + -O- + -METER]

ap·er·ture (ap′ər chər), *n.* **1.** an opening, as a hole, slit, crack, gap, etc. **2.** Also called **ap′erture stop′.** *Optics.* an opening, usually circular, that limits the quantity of light that can enter an optical instrument. [1400–50; late ME < L *apertūra* an opening, equiv. to *apert(us)* opened (ptp. of *aperīre; aper(i)-* (see APERIENT) + *-tus* ptp. suffix) + *-ūra* -URE] —**ap·er·tur·al** (ap′ər chŏŏr′- əl), *adj.* —**ap′er·tured,** *adj.*

ap′erture mask′, *Television.* See **shadow mask.**

ap·er·ture-pri·or·i·ty (ap′ər chər prī ôr′i tē, -or′-), *adj. Photog.* of or pertaining to a semiautomatic exposure system in which the photographer presets the aperture and the camera selects the shutter speed. Also, **ap·er·ture-pre·ferred** (ap′ər chər pri fûrd′). Cf. **shutter-priority.**

ap′erture ra′tio, *Optics.* See **relative aperture.** [1885–90]

ap′erture syn′thesis, (in radio astronomy) a technique that combines the inputs of a set of radio telescopes to obtain a greater resolution of images than is possible with a single member of the set. [1960–65]

ap·er·y (ā′pə rē), *n., pl.* **-er·ies. 1.** apish behavior; mimicry. **2.** a silly trick. [1610–20; APE + -ERY]

a·pet·al·ous (ā pet′l əs), *adj. Bot.* having no petals. [1700–10; < NL *apetalus.* See A-⁶, PETALOUS] —**a·pet′a·lous·ness, a·pet′a·ly,** *n.*

a·pex (ā′peks), *n., pl.* **a·pex·es, a·pi·ces** (ā′pə sēz′, ap′ə-). **1.** the tip, point, or vertex; summit. **2.** climax; peak; acme: *His election to the presidency was the apex of his career.* **3.** *Astron.* See **solar apex.** [1595–1605; < L]

APEX (ā′peks), *n.* a type of international air fare offering reduced rates for extended stays that are booked in advance. [1970–75; *A(dvance) P(urchase) Ex(cursion)*]

Ap·gar (ap′gär), *n.* **Virginia,** 1909–74, U.S. physician: developed test to evaluate health of newborns.

Ap′gar score′, a numerical measure of the physical health of a newborn infant derived by evaluating heart rate, muscle tone, respiratory effort, response to stimulation, skin color, and other physiological indicators. [named after V. APGAR]

aph., aphetic.

a·phaer·e·sis (ə fer′ə sis), *n.* apheresis. —**aph·ae·ret·ic** (af′ə ret′ik), *adj.*

a·pha·gi·a (ə fā′jē ə), *n. Pathol.* difficulty or pain in swallowing. [1865–70; A-⁶ + -PHAGIA]

a·pha·ki·a (ə fā′kē ə), *n. Ophthalm.* lack or loss of the lens of the eye. Also, **a·pha·cia** (ə fā′shə, -shē ə, -sē ə). [1860–65; < NL, equiv. to *a-* A-⁶ + Gk *phak(ós)* lentil (for sense see LENS) + -IA] —**a·pha′kic, a·pha·cic** (ə fā′sik), **a·pha·cial** (ə fā′shəl), *adj.*

aph·a·nite (af′ə nīt′), *n. Petrog.* a fine-grained igneous rock having such compact texture that the constituent minerals cannot be detected with the naked eye. [1860–65; < Gk *aphan(ḗs)* unseen, hidden, invisible (*a-* A-⁶ + *phanēs,* adj. deriv. of *phainein* to bring to light, disclose) + -ITE¹] —**aph·a·nit·ic** (af′ə nit′ik), *adj.*

a·pha·sia (ə fā′zhə), *n. Pathol.* the loss of a previously held ability to speak or understand spoken or written language, due to disease or injury of the brain. [1865–70; < Gk: speechlessness, equiv. to *a-* A-⁶ + *phat(ós)* spoken (deriv. of *phánai* to speak) + *-ia* -IA]

a·pha·sic (ə fā′zik, -sik), *Pathol.* —*adj.* **1.** pertaining to or affected with aphasia. —*n.* **2.** Also, **a·pha·si·ac** (ə fā′zē ak′). a person affected with aphasia. [1865–70; APHAS(IA) + -IC]

a·phe·li·on (ə fē′lē ən, ə fēl′yən, ap hē′lē ən), *n., pl.* **a·phe·li·a** (ə fē′lē ə, ə fēl′yə, ap hē′lē ə). *Astron.* the point in the orbit of a planet or a comet at which it is farthest from the sun. Cf. **perihelion.** [1650–60; Hellenized form of NL *aphēlium* < Gk **aphḗlion* (*diástēma*) off-sun (distance), neut. of **aphḗlios* (adj.), equiv. to *ap-* AP-² + *hḗli(os)* sun + *-os* adj. suffix. See APOGEE] —**a·phe′li·an,** *adj.*

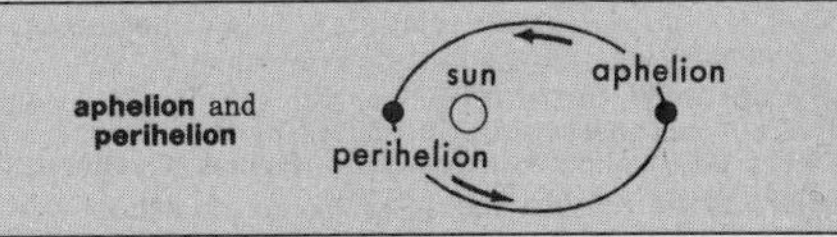

aphelion and **perihelion**

a·phe·li·o·trop·ic (a fē′lē ə trop′ik, -trō′pik, ap- hē′-), *adj. Bot.* turning or growing away from the sun. [1875–80; AP-² + HELIOTROPIC] —**a·phe′li·o·trop′i·cal·ly,** *adv.*

a·phe·li·ot·ro·pism (ə fē′lē o′trə piz′əm, ap hē′lē-), *n.* apheliotropic tendency or type of growth. [1875–80; APHELIOTROP(IC) + -ISM]

a·phe·mi·a (ə fē′mē ə), *n. Med.* a type of aphasia characterized by the inability to express ideas in spoken words. [1860–65; < Gk *a-* A-⁶ + *phḗm(ē)* speech + *-ia* -IA]

a·pher·e·sis (ə fer′ə sis *for 1;* af′ə rē′sis *for 2*), *n.* **1.** Also, **aphaeresis.** the loss or omission of one or more letters or sounds at the beginning of a word, as in *squire* for *esquire,* or *count* for *account.* **2.** *Med.* the withdrawal of whole blood from the body, separation of one or more components, and return by transfusion of remaining blood to the donor. [1605–15; < LL *aphaeresis* < Gk *aphaíresis* a taking away, equiv to *aphairé(ìn)* to take away (*ap-* AP-² + *haireîn* to snatch) + *-sis* -SIS] —**aph·e·ret·ic** (af′ə ret′ik), *adj.*

aph·e·sis (af′ə sis), *n. Historical Ling.* the disappearance or loss of an unstressed initial vowel or syllable. [1880; < Gk *áphesis* a letting go, equiv. to *aphe-* (var. s. of *aphiénai* to let go, set free; *ap-* AP-² + *hiénai* to send) + *-sis* -SIS]

a·phet·ic (ə fet′ik), *adj.* pertaining to or due to aphesis. [1875–80; < Gk *áphet(os)* freed, discharged (*aphe-* (see APHESIS) + *-tos* ptp. suffix) + -IC] —**a·phet′i·cal·ly,** *adv.*

a·phid (ā′fid, af′id), *n.* any of numerous tiny soft-bodied insects of the family Aphididae of worldwide distribution, that suck the sap from the stems and leaves of various plants, some developing wings when overcrowding occurs: an important pest of many fruit trees and vegetable crops. Also called **plant louse.** [1880–85; back formation from APHIDES, pl. of APHIS] —**a·phid·i·an** (ə fid′ē ən), *adj., n.* —**a·phid′i·ous,** *adj.*

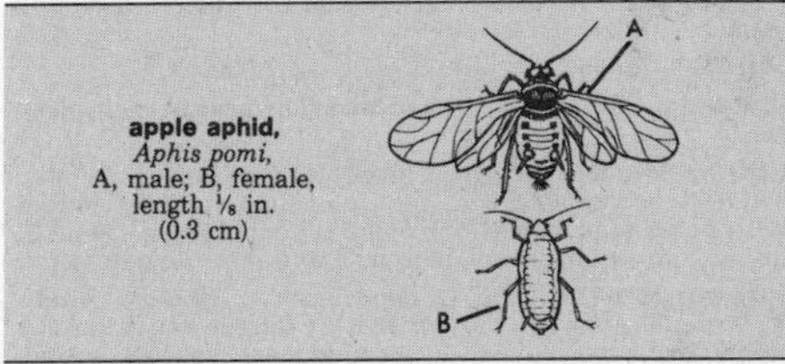

apple aphid, *Aphis pomi,* A, male; B, female, length ⅛ in. (0.3 cm)

a′phid li′on, the larva of a lacewing, usually predaceous on aphids. Also, **a′phis li′on.**

a·phis (ā′fis, af′is), *n., pl.* **a·phi·des** (ā′fi dēz′, af′i-). an aphid, esp. of the genus *Aphis.* [1765–75; < NL, first recorded in a Gk lexicon of 1523 as *áphis,* with the L gloss *cimex* bedbug; perh. orig. a misreading of Gk *kóris* bug]

APHIS, Animal and Plant Health Inspection Service.

a·pho·ni·a (ā fō′nē ə), *n. Pathol.* loss of voice, esp. due to an organic or functional disturbance of the vocal organs. [1770–80; < NL < Gk: speechlessness. See A-⁶, PHON-, -IA]

a·phon·ic (ā fon′ik, ā fō′nik), *adj.* **1.** mouthed but not spoken; noiseless; silent. **2.** *Phonet.* **a.** lacking phonation; unvoiced. **b.** without voice; voiceless. **3.** *Pathol.* affected with aphonia. —*n.* **4.** *Pathol.* a person who is affected with aphonia. [1820–30; < Gk *áphōn(os)* voiceless (see APHONIA) + -IC]

aph·o·rism (af′ə riz′əm), *n.* a terse saying embodying a general truth, or astute observation, as "Power tends to corrupt, and absolute power corrupts absolutely" (Lord Acton). [1520–30; F *aphorisme* < LL *aphorismus* < Gk *aphorismós* definition, equiv. to *aphor(ízein)* to

CONCISE PRONUNCIATION KEY: *act, cāpe, dâre, pärt; set, ēqual; if, īce; ox, ōver, ôrder, oil, bŏŏk, bōōt, out; up, ûrge; child; sing; shoe; thin, that;* zh as in *treasure.* ə = *a* as in *alone, e* as in *system, i* as in *easily, o* as in *gallop, u* as in *circus;* ə as in *fire* (fīər), *hour* (ouər). l and n can serve as syllabic consonants, as in *cradle* (krād′l), and *button* (but′n). See the full key inside the front cover.

define (see APHORIZE) + *-ismos* -ISM] —**aph′o·ris′mic, aph·o·ris·mat·ic** (af′ə riz mat′ik), *adj.*

aph·o·rist (af′ər ist), *n.* a person who makes or uses aphorisms. [1705–15; APHOR(IZE) + -IST]

aph·o·ris·tic (af′ə ris′tik), *adj.* **1.** of, like, or containing aphorisms: *His sermons were richly aphoristic.* **2.** given to making or quoting aphorisms. [1745–55; < Gk *aphoristikós.* See APHORIST, -IC] —**aph′o·ris′ti·cal·ly,** *adv.*

aph·o·rize (af′ə rīz′), *v.i.,* **-rized, -riz·ing.** to utter aphorisms; write or speak in aphorisms. Also, *esp. Brit.,* **aph′o·rise′.** [1660–70; < Gk *aphorízein* to mark off, define, determine, equiv. to *ap-* AP-[2] + *horízein* to limit, define; see HORIZON] —**aph′o·riz′er,** *n.*

a·pho·tic (ā fō′tik), *adj.* lightless; dark. [1900–05; A-[6] + PHOTIC]

aph·ro·di·sia (af′rə dē′zhə, -dizh′ə, -diz′ē ə), *n.* sexual desire. [1820–30; < NL < Gk, neut. pl. of *aphrodísios* of Aphrodite. See APHRODISIAC]

aph·ro·dis·i·ac (af′rə dē′zē ak′, -diz′ē ak′), *adj.* **1.** Also, **aph·ro·di·si·a·cal** (af′rə də zī′ə kəl, -sī′-). arousing sexual desire. —*n.* **2.** an aphrodisiac food, drug, potion, or other agent that arouses sexual desire. [1710–20; < Gk *aphrodisiakós* relating to love or desire, equiv. to *aphrodísi(os)* of Aphrodite + *-akos* -AC]

Aph·ro·di·te (af′rə dī′tē), *n.* the ancient Greek goddess of love and beauty, identified by the Romans with Venus. Also called **Anadyomene, Cypris, Cytherea.**

Aphrodi′te of Me′los. See **Venus de Milo.**

Aph′rodi′te Ter′ra, *Astron.* a large plateau region that stretches approximately halfway around the middle latitude of Venus.

aph′thous fe′ver (af′thəs, ap′thəs). See **foot-and-mouth disease.** [< L *ap(h)th(ae)* thrush (< Gk *áphthai,* pl. of *áphtha* spot, speck) + -OUS]

a·phyl·lous (ā fil′əs), *adj. Bot.* naturally leafless. [1820–30; < NL *aphyllus* < Gk *áphyllos* leafless. See A-[6], -PHYLLOUS] —**a′phyl·ly,** *n.*

API, American Petroleum Institute. Also, **A.P.I.**

A·pi·a (ä pē′ä, ä′pē ä′), *n.* a seaport in and the capital of Western Samoa, on N Upolu. 30,593.

a·pi·a·ceous (ā′pē ā′shəs), *adj.* belonging to the Apiaceae, an alternative name for the plant family Umbelliferae. Cf. **parsley** (def. 4). [1830–40; < NL *Apiace(ae)* (*Api(um)* a genus (L: celery, parsley) + *-aceae* -ACEAE) + -OUS]

a·pi·an (ā′pē ən), *adj.* of or pertaining to bees. [1860–65; < L *api(s)* bee + -AN; cf. L *apiānus* muscat]

a·pi·ar·i·an (ā′pē âr′ē ən), *adj.* relating to bees or to the breeding and care of bees. [1795–1805; APIARY + -AN]

a·pi·a·rist (ā′pē ə rist), *n.* a person who keeps an apiary. [1810–20; APIAR(Y) + -IST]

a·pi·ar·y (ā′pē er′ē), *n., pl.* **-ar·ies.** a place in which a colony or colonies of bees are kept, as a stand or shed for beehives or a bee house containing a number of beehives. [1645–55; < L *apiārium* beehive, equiv. to *api(s)* bee + *-ārium* -ARY]

a·pi·cal (ā′pi kəl, ap′i-), *adj.* **1.** of, at, or forming the apex. **2.** *Phonet.* (of a speech sound) articulated principally with the aid of the tip of the tongue, as *t* or *d.* —*n.* **3.** *Phonet.* an apical sound. [1820–30; < L *apic-* (s. of *apex*) APEX + -AL[1]] —**a′pi·cal·ly,** *adv.*

a′pical dom′inance, *Bot.* suppression of the development of lateral buds in a growing plant shoot, caused by hormones produced in the tip of the plant shoot. [1945–50]

a′pical mer′istem, meristem at the apex of a root or shoot.

a·pi·ces (ā′pə sēz′, ap′ə-), *n.* a pl. of **apex.**

apico-, a combining form of **apex** or **apical:** *apicodental.*

a·pi·co·al·ve·o·lar (ā′pi kō al vē′ə lər, ap′i-), *Phonet.* —*adj.* **1.** articulated with the tip of the tongue in contact with or in approximation to the alveolar ridge. —*n.* **2.** an apicoalveolar speech sound. [APICO- + ALVEOLAR]

a·pi·co·den·tal (ā′pi kō den′tl, ap′i-), *Phonet.* —*adj.* **1.** articulated with the tip of the tongue touching the upper front teeth. —*n.* **2.** an apicodental speech sound. [APICO- + DENTAL]

a·pi·co·ec·to·my (ā′pi kō ek′tə mē, ap′i-), *n., pl.* **-mies.** *Dentistry.* a surgical procedure to remove the end of a tooth root in endodontic therapy. [APICO- + -ECTOMY]

a·pic·u·late (ə pik′yə lit, -lāt′), *adj. Bot.* tipped with a short, abrupt point, as a leaf. [1820–30; < NL *apiculātus.* See APICULUS, -ATE[1]]

a·pi·cul·ture (ā′pi kul′chər), *n.* beekeeping, esp. on a commercial scale for the sale of honey. [1860–65; < L *api(s)* bee + CULTURE] —**a′pi·cul′tur·al,** *adj.* —**a′pi·cul′tur·ist,** *n.*

a·pic·u·lus (ə pik′yə ləs, ā pik′-), *n., pl.* **-li** (-lī′). *Bot.* a small point or tip. [1860–65; < NL, equiv. to *apic-* (s. of *apex*) APEX + *-ulus* -ULE]

a·piece (ə pēs′), *adv.* for each piece, thing, or person; for each one; each: *We ate an orange apiece. The cakes cost a dollar apiece.* [1425–75; late ME *a pease.* See A[2], PIECE]

à pied (A pyā′), *French.* afoot; walking; on foot.

a·pi·ol·o·gy (ā′pē ol′ə jē), *n.* the scientific study of bees, esp. honeybees. [< L *api(s)* bee + -O- + -LOGY] —**a′pi·ol′o·gist,** *n.*

CONCISE ETYMOLOGY KEY: <, descended or borrowed from; >, whence; b., blend of, blended; c., cognate with; cf., compare; deriv., derivative; equiv., equivalent; imit., imitative; obl., oblique; r., replacing; s., stem; sp., spelling, spelled; resp., respelling, respelled; trans., translation; ?, origin unknown; *, unattested; ‡, probably earlier than. See the full key inside the front cover.

A·pis (ä′pis), *n. Egyptian Religion.* a sacred bull worshiped at Memphis: identified originally with Ptah and later assimilated with Osiris to form the Ptolemaic Serapis. Also called **Hapi, Hap.**

ap·ish (ā′pish), *adj.* **1.** having the qualities, appearance, or ways of an ape. **2.** slavishly imitative. **3.** foolishly affected; silly. [1525–35; APE + -ISH[1]] —**ap′ish·ly,** *adv.* —**ap′ish·ness,** *n.*

a·piv·or·ous (ā piv′ər əs), *adj. Zool.* feeding on bees, as certain birds. [< L *api(s)* bee + -VOROUS]

APL, *Computers.* an interactive programming language having concise notations for operations on entire arrays of numbers and characters. [1965–70; *A P(rogramming) L(anguage)*]

a·pla·cen·tal (ā′plə sen′tl, ap′lə-), *adj. Zool.* having or forming no placenta, as the marsupials and monotremes. [1855–60; A-[6] + PLACENTAL]

ap·la·coph·o·ran (ap′lə kof′ər ən), *n. Zool.* solenogaster. [< NL *Aplacophor(a)* the class name (*a-* A-[6] + Gk *plak-,* s. of *pláx* flat object, tablet + *-o-* -O- + *-phora,* neut. pl. of *-phoros* bearing, -PHOROUS) + -AN]

ap·la·nat·ic (ap′lə nat′ik), *adj. Optics.* free from spherical aberration and coma. [1785–95; A-[6] + Gk *planá(ein)* to wander + -TIC. See PLANET] —**ap′la·nat′i·cal·ly,** *adv.*

a·pla·net·ic (ā′plə net′ik), *adj. Biol.* having no motility. [A-[6] + Gk *planēt(ós)* wandering (see PLANET) + -IC; cf. APLANATIC]

a·plan·o·ga·mete (ā plan′ə gə mēt′, ā plan′ə gə mēt′, ā′plan ə gam′ēt), *n. Cell Biol.* a nonmotile gamete. [1885–90; < Gk *aplan(ḗs)* unmoving (see A-[6], PLANET) + -O- + GAMETE]

a·plan·o·spore (ā plan′ə spôr′, -spōr′), *n.* (in certain algae and fungi) a nonmotile, asexual spore formed within a cell, the wall of which is distinct from that of the parent cell. Cf. **akinete.** [*aplano-* (see APLANOGAMETE) + SPORE]

a·pla·sia (ə plā′zhə), *n. Pathol.* defective development or congenital absence of a limb, organ, or other body part. [1880–85; A-[6] + -PLASIA] —**a·plas·tic** (ā plas′tik), *adj.*

aplas′tic ane′mia, *Pathol.* severe anemia due to destruction or depressed functioning of the bone marrow, usually resulting from bone cancer, radiation, or the toxic effects of certain drugs or chemicals. [1930–35; A-[6] + -PLASTIC]

a·plen·ty (ə plen′tē), *Informal.* —*adj.* **1.** in sufficient quantity; in generous amounts (usually used following the noun it modifies): *He had troubles aplenty.* —*adv.* **2.** sufficiently; enough; more than sparingly: *He howled aplenty when hurt.* Also, **a-plen′ty.** [1820–30; A-[1] + PLENTY]

ap·lite (ap′lit), *n. Petrol.* a fine-grained granite composed essentially of feldspar and quartz. [1875–80; *apl-* (var. of HAPLO-) + ITE[1]] —**ap·lit·ic** (ap lit′ik), *adj.*

a·plomb (ə plom′, ə plum′), *n.* **1.** imperturbable self-possession, poise, or assurance. **2.** the perpendicular, or vertical, position. [1820–30; < F *à plomb* according to the plummet, i.e., straight up and down, vertical position]
—**Syn. 1.** composure, equanimity, imperturbability.
—**Ant. 1.** confusion, discomposure; doubt, uncertainty.

apmt., appointment.

ap·ne·a (ap′nē ə, ap nē′ə), *n. Pathol.* **1.** a temporary suspension of breathing, occurring in some newborns (**infant apnea**) and in some adults during sleep (**sleep apnea**). **2.** asphyxia. Also, **ap′noe·a.** [1710–20; < NL *apnoea* < Gk *ápnoia,* equiv. to *ápno(os)* breathless (*a-* A-[6] + *pno-,* var. s. of *pneîn* to breathe + *-os* adj. suffix) + *-ia* -IA] —**ap′ne·al, ap·ne′ic, ap′noe·al, ap·noe′ic,** *adj.*

ap·neus·tic (ap nōō′stik, -nyōō′-), *adj. Entomol.* having no open spiracles, as the tracheal systems of certain aquatic insect larvae. [A-[6] + Gk *pneustikós* pertaining to breathing, equiv. to *pneust(os) (verbal of *pneîn* to breathe) + *-ikos* -IC]

A·po (ä′pô), *n.* an active volcano in the S Philippines, on S Mindanao: highest peak in the Philippines. 9690 ft. (2954 m).

apo-, a prefix occurring originally in loanwords from Greek, where it was joined to verbs, deverbal forms, and other parts of speech. Among its functions in Greek, **apo-** has the spatial sense "away, off, apart" (*apogee; apocope; apostasy; apostrophe*); it occurs with deverbals that denote a response or defense (*apodosis; apology*) and is found on verbs having perfective force relative to a corresponding simple verb (*apoplexy; aposiopesis*). In modern scientific coinages in English and other languages, **apo-** marks things that are detached, separate, or derivative (*apocarpous; apoenzyme*). Also, *esp. before a vowel,* **ap-.** [< Gk, prefixal use of *apó;* akin to OFF, Skt *apa,* L *ab*]

A.P.O., Army & Air Force Post Office. Also, **APO**

Apoc., **1.** Apocalypse. **2.** Apocrypha. **3.** Apocryphal.

a·poc·a·lypse (ə pok′ə lips), *n.* **1.** (*cap.*) revelation (def. 4). **2.** any of a class of Jewish or Christian writings that appeared from about 200 B.C. to A.D. 350 and were assumed to make revelations of the ultimate divine purpose. **3.** a prophetic revelation, esp. concerning a cataclysm in which the forces of good permanently triumph over the forces of evil. **4.** any revelation or prophecy. **5.** any universal or widespread destruction or disaster: *the apocalypse of nuclear war.* [1125–75; ME < LL *apocalypsis* < Gk *apokálypsis* revelation, equiv. to *apokalýp(tein)* to uncover, reveal (*apo-* APO- + *kalýptein* to cover, conceal) + *-sis* -SIS]

a·poc·a·lyp·tic (ə pok′ə lip′tik), *adj.* **1.** of or like an apocalypse; affording a revelation or prophecy. **2.** pertaining to the Apocalypse or biblical book of Revelation. **3.** predicting or presaging imminent disaster and total or universal destruction: *the apocalyptic vision of some contemporary writers.* Also, **a·poc′a·lyp′ti·cal.** [1620–30; < LGk *apokalyptikós,* equiv. to *apokalýpt(ein)* to uncover, disclose (see APOCALYPSE) + *-ikos* -IC] —**a·poc′a·lyp′ti·cal·ly,** *adv.*

a·poc·a·lyp·ti·cism (ə pok′ə lip′tə siz′əm), *n. Theol.* **1.** any doctrine concerning the end of the temporal world, esp. one based on the supposed prophetic passages in the Revelation of St. John the Divine. **2.** the millennial doctrine of the Second Advent and personal reign of Jesus Christ on earth. [1880–85; APOCALYPTIC + -ISM]

a·poc·a·lyp·tist (ə pok′ə lip′tist), *n.* **1.** a writer of apocalyptic literature. **2.** a person who adheres to the teachings of apocalyptic literature concerning the signs and events preceding the end of the world. **3.** a person who holds to any teachings that predict a catastrophic end to the world. [1825–35; APOCALYPT(IC) + -IST]

ap·o·carp (ap′ə kärp′), *n. Bot.* a female element of a flower having separate carpels. [APO- + -CARP]

ap·o·car·pous (ap′ə kär′pəs), *adj. Bot.* having the carpels separate. [1820–30; APO- + -CARPOUS] —**ap′o·car′py,** *n.*

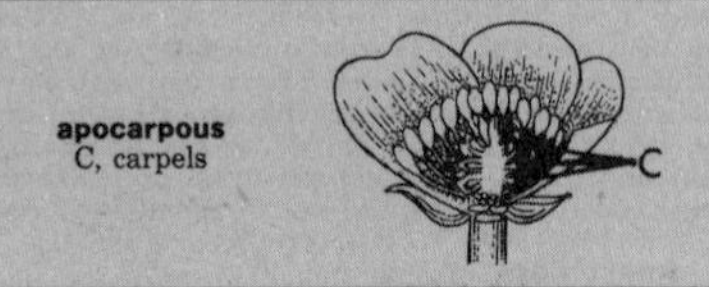

apocarpous
C, carpels

ap·o·ca·tas·ta·sis (ap′ō kə tas′tə sis), *n.* **1.** the state of being restored or reestablished; restitution. **2.** the doctrine that Satan and all sinners will ultimately be restored to God. Also, **apokatastasis.** Cf. **universalism** (def. 3). [1670–80; < L < Gk: a setting up again. See APO-, CATASTASIS] —**ap·o·cat·a·stat·ic** (ap′ə kat′ə stat′ik), *adj.*

ap·o·cen·ter (ap′ə sen′tər), *n. Astron.* the point in the orbit of a heavenly body farthest from a primary other than the earth or the sun. Cf. **pericenter.** [1900–05; APO- + CENTER] —**ap′o·cen′tric,** *adj.* —**ap·o·cen·tric·i·ty** (ap′ə sen tris′i tē), *n.*

ap·o·chro·mat·ic (ap′ə krō mat′ik, -ō krə-), *adj. Optics.* corrected for spherical aberration at two wavelengths or colors and for chromatic aberration at three wavelengths. [1885–90; APO- + CHROMATIC] —**ap·o·chro·ma·tism** (ap′ə krō′mə tiz′əm), *n.*

a·poc·o·pate (ə pok′ə pāt′), *v.t.,* **-pat·ed, -pat·ing.** to shorten by apocope. [1850–55; v. use of *apocopate* (adj.) curtailed, docked. See APOCOPE, -ATE[1]] —**a·poc′o·pa′tion,** *n.*

a·poc·o·pe (ə pok′ə pē′), *n.* loss or omission of the last letter, syllable, or part of a word. [1585–95; < LL < Gk *apokopḗ* a cutting off, equiv. to *apokóp(tein)* to cut off (*apo-* APO- + *kóptein* to cut) + *-ē* n. suffix] —**ap·o·cop·ic** (ap′ə kop′ik), *adj.*

ap·o·crine (ap′ə krin, -krīn′, -krēn′), *adj. Physiol.* **1.** of or pertaining to certain glands whose secretions are acted upon by bacteria to produce the characteristic odor of perspiration (distinguished from *eccrine*). **2.** of or pertaining to such secretions: *apocrine sweat.* [1925–30; < Gk *apokrínein* to set apart, equiv. to *apo-* APO- + *krínein* to separate, choose; formed as if with -INE[1] prob. on the model of ENDOCRINE]

a·poc·ry·pha (ə pok′rə fə), *n.* (*often used with a singular v.*) **1.** (*cap.*) a group of 14 books, not considered canonical, included in the Septuagint and the Vulgate as part of the Old Testament, but usually omitted from Protestant editions of the Bible. See table under **Bible.** **2.** various religious writings of uncertain origin regarded by some as inspired, but rejected by most authorities. **3.** writings, statements, etc., of doubtful authorship or authenticity. Cf. **canon**[1] (defs. 6, 7, 9). [1350–1400; ME < LL < Gk, neut. pl. of *apókryphos* hidden, unknown, spurious, equiv. to *apokryph-* (base of *apokrýptein* to hide away; see APO-, CRYPT) + *-os* adj. suffix]

a·poc·ry·phal (ə pok′rə fəl), *adj.* **1.** of doubtful authorship or authenticity. **2.** *Eccles.* **a.** (*cap.*) of or pertaining to the Apocrypha. **b.** of doubtful sanction; uncanonical. **3.** false; spurious: *He told an apocryphal story about the sword, but the truth was later revealed.* [1580–90; APOCRYPH(A) + -AL[1]] —**a·poc′ry·phal·ly,** *adv.* —**a·poc′ry·phal·ness,** *n.*

a·poc·y·na·ceous (ə pos′ə nā′shəs), *adj.* belonging to the Apocynaceae, the dogbane family of plants. Cf. **dogbane family.** [1880–85; < NL *Apocyn(um)* genus name (< Gk *apókynon* dogbane: *apo-* APO- + *kyn-* (s. of *kýōn* dog) + *-on* n. suffix) + -ACEOUS]

ap·o·dal (ap′ə dl), *adj. Zool.* **1.** having no distinct feet or footlike members. **2.** belonging or pertaining to the orders Apoda and Apodes, comprising various groups of animals without limbs. Also, **apodous.** [1760–70; < Gk *apod-,* s. of *ápous* footless (see A-[6], -POD) + -AL[1]]

a·po·deip·non (ä pô thēp′nôn; *Eng.* ap′ə dīp′non), *n., pl.* **-deip·na** (-thēp′nä; *Eng.* -dīp′nə). *Gk. Orth. Ch.* compline. [< MGk; Gk *apo-* APO- + *deîpnon* meal]

a·pod·e·ma (ə pod′ə mə), *n., pl.* **a·pod·e·mas, ap·o·dem·a·ta** (ap′ə dem′ə tə) apodeme.

ap·o·deme (ap′ə dēm′), *n.* a ridgelike ingrowth of the exoskeleton of an arthropod that supports the internal organs and provides the attachment points for the muscles. [1850–55; < NL *apodema,* equiv. to *apo-* APO- + *-dema* < Gk *démas* body] —**a·pod·e·mal** (ə pod′ə məl), **ap·o·dem·a·tal** (ap′ə dem′ə tl), *adj.*

ap·o·dic·tic (ap′ə dik′tik), *adj.* **1.** incontestable because of having been demonstrated or proved to be demonstrable. **2.** *Logic.* (of a proposition) necessarily true or logically certain. Also, **ap·o·deic·tic** (ap′ə dīk′tik), **ap′o·dic′ti·cal.** [1645–55; < L *apodicticus* < Gk *apodeiktikós* proving fully. See APO-, DEICTIC] —**ap′o·dic′ti·cal·ly, ap′o·deic′ti·cal·ly,** *adv.*

·pod·o·sis (ə pod′ə sis), *n., pl.* **-ses** (-sēz′). the clause ›xpressing the consequence in a conditional sentence, often beginning with *then,* as "then I will" in "If you go, hen I will." Cf. **protasis** (def. 1). [1630–40; < LL < Gk: a returning, answering clause, equiv. to *apo(di)dó(nai)* to give back (*apo-* APO- + *didónai* to give) + *-sis* -SIS]

p·o·dous (ap′ə dəs), *adj.* apodal. [APOD(AL) + -OUS]

p·o·en·zyme (ap′ō en′zīm), *n. Biochem.* the protein component that with a coenzyme forms a complete enzyme. [1935–40; < F; see APO-, ENZYME]

p·o·fer·ri·tin (ap′ō fer′i tin), *n. Biochem.* a homogeneous protein, found esp. in the intestinal mucosa and the liver, that interacts with a ferric hydroxide-ferric phosphate complex to form ferritin. [APO- + FERRITIN]

·pog·a·my (ə pog′ə mē), *n. Bot., Mycol.* the asexual development of a sporophyte from a cell or cells of the gametophyte other than the egg. [1875–80; APO- + -GAMY] —**ap·o·gam·ic** (ap′ə gam′ik), **a·pog′a·mous,** *adj.* —**ap′o·gam′i·cal·ly, a·pog′a·mous·ly,** *adv.*

p·o·gee (ap′ə jē′), *n.* **1.** *Astron.* the point in the orbit of a heavenly body, esp. the moon, or of a man-made satellite at which it is farthest from the earth. Cf. **perigee. 2.** the highest or most distant point; climax. 1585–95; alter. (after F *apogée*) of earlier *apogaeum* < L < Gk *apógaion* (*diástema*) off-earth (distance), neut. of *apógaios* (adj.), equiv. to *apo-* APO- + *gáïos* of the earth, deriv. of *gaîa,* var. of *gê* the earth] —**ap′o·ge′al, ap′o·ge′an, ap′o·ge′ic,** *adj.*

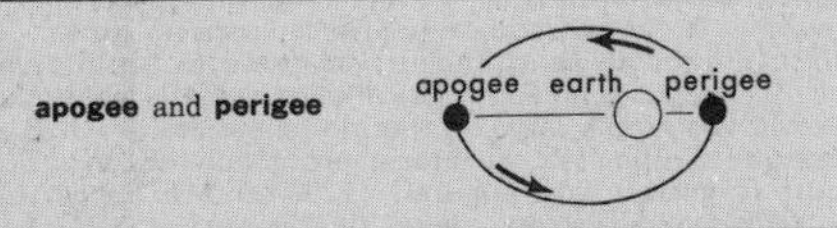

apogee and perigee

p·o·ge·ot·ro·pism (ap′ə jē o′trə piz′əm), *n. Biol.* growth or orientation away from the earth; negative geotropism. [1875–80; APO- + GEOTROPISM] —**ap·o·ge·o·trop·ic** (ap′ə jē′ə trop′ik, -trō′pik), *adj.* —**ap′o·ge′o·trop′i·cal·ly,** *adv.*

p·o·graph (ap′ə graf′, -gräf′), *n.* transcript (defs. 1, 2). [1595–1605; < L *apographon* < Gk *apógraphon,* n. use of neut. of *apógraphos* (adj.) copied. See APO-, -GRAPH] —**ap·o·graph·ic** (ap′ə graf′ik), **ap′o·graph′i·cal,** *adj.*

point (A pwaN′), *French.* **1.** just in time. **2.** (of cooking) to a turn; perfectly. **3.** (of meat) cooked medium.

p·o·ka·tas·ta·sis (ap′ō kə tas′tə sis), *n.* apocatastasis. —**ap·o·kat·a·stat·ic** (ap′ə kat′ə stat′ik), *adj.*

p·o·lip·o·pro·tein (ap′ə lip′ə prō′tēn, -tē in, -lī′pə-), *n. Biochem.* the lipid-free protein portion of a lipoprotein. [APO- + LIPOPROTEIN]

·po·lit·i·cal (ā′pə lit′i kəl), *adj.* **1.** not political; of no political significance: *an apolitical organization.* **2.** not involved or interested in politics. [1950–55; A-[6] + POLITICAL] —**a′po·lit′i·cal·ly,** *adv.*

·pol·li·naire (ə pol′ə nâr′; *Fr.* A pô lē neR′), *n.* **Guillaume** (gē yōm′), (*Wilhelm Apollinaris de Kostrowitzky*), 1880–1918, French poet and art critic, born in Italy.

·pol·lo (ə pol′ō), *n., pl.* **-los** for 2, 3. **1.** the ancient Greek and Roman god of light, healing, music, poetry, prophecy, and manly beauty; the son of Leto and brother of Artemis. **2.** a very handsome young man. **3.** *Aerospace.* one of a series of U.S. spacecraft designed to carry astronauts to the moon and back.

Apollo

pol′lo as′teroid, *Astron.* one of a number of asteroids whose orbits cross that of the earth. Cf. **Amor asteroid, Aten asteroid.**

pol′lo Belvedere′, a Roman marble statue, possibly a copy of a Greek original of the 4th–1st centuries B.C.

p·ol·lo·ni·an (ap′ə lō′nē ən), *adj.* **1.** pertaining to the cult of Apollo. **2.** (*l.c.*) serene, calm, or well-balanced; poised and disciplined. **3.** (*l.c.*) having the properties of or preferring classic beauty. Cf. **Dionysian** (def. 2). [1655–65; < Gk *apollṓni(os)* of APOLLO + -AN]

p·ol·lo·ni·us Dys·co·lus (ap′ə lō′nē əs dis′kə ləs), died A.D. c140. Greek grammarian.

·pol·lyon (ə pol′yən), *n.* the destroyer; the angel of the bottomless pit; Abaddon. Rev. 9:11. [< Gk *apollýōn* prp. of *apollýnai* to utterly destroy), equiv. to *ap-* AP-[2] + *olly-* destroy + *-ōn* prp. suffix]

·pol·o·get·ic (ə pol′ə jet′ik), *adj.* **1.** containing an apology or excuse for a fault, failure, insult, injury, etc.: *An apologetic letter to his creditors explained the delay.* **2.** defending by speech or writing. **3.** willing or eager to apologize. **4.** sorry; regretful. Also, **a·pol′o·get′i·cal.** [1400–50; late ME *apologetik* a formal defense (< MF) < LL *apologēticus* written defense, defensive < Gk *apologētikós* fit for defense, equiv. to *apologē-* (var. s. of *apologeîsthai* to speak in defense; see APOLOGIA) + *-tikos* -TIC] —**a·pol′o·get′i·cal·ly,** *adv.*

a·pol·o·get·ics (ə pol′ə jet′iks), *n.* (*used with a singular v.*) the branch of theology concerned with the defense or proof of Christianity. [1725–35; see APOLOGETIC, -ICS]

ap·o·lo·gi·a (ap′ə lō′jē ə), *n.* **1.** an apology, as in defense or justification of a belief, idea, etc. **2.** *Literature.* a work written as an explanation or justification of one's motives, convictions, or acts. [1775–85; < LL < Gk: a speaking in defense. See APO-, LOG-, -IA]

Ap·o·lo·gi·a pro Vi·ta Su·a (ap′ə lō′jē ə prō vī′tə so͞o′ə, vē′tə), a religious autobiography (1864) of Cardinal John Henry Newman.

a·pol·o·gist (ə pol′ə jist), *n.* **1.** a person who makes a defense in speech or writing of a belief, idea, etc. **2.** *Eccles.* **a.** Also, **a·pol·o·gete** (ə pol′ə jēt′). a person skilled in apologetics. **b.** one of the authors of the early Christian apologies in defense of the faith. [1630–40; APOLOG(Y) + -IST or < F *apologiste*]

a·pol·o·gize (ə pol′ə jīz′), *v.i.,* **-gized, -giz·ing. 1.** to offer an apology or excuse for some fault, insult, failure, or injury: *He apologized for accusing her falsely.* **2.** to make a formal defense in speech or writing. Also, *esp. Brit.,* **a·pol′o·gise′.** [1590–1600; APOLOG(Y) + -IZE] —**a·pol′o·giz′er,** *n.*

ap·o·logue (ap′ə lôg′, -log′), *n.* **1.** a didactic narrative; a moral fable. **2.** an allegory. [1545–55; (< MF) < L *apologus* < Gk *apólogos* fable. See APO-, -LOGUE] —**ap′o·log′al,** *adj.*

a·pol·o·gy (ə pol′ə jē), *n., pl.* **-gies. 1.** a written or spoken expression of one's regret, remorse, or sorrow for having insulted, failed, injured, or wronged another: *He demanded an apology from me for calling him a crook.* **2.** a defense, excuse, or justification in speech or writing, as for a cause or doctrine. **3.** (*cap., italics*) a dialogue by Plato, centering on Socrates' defense before the tribunal that condemned him to death. **4.** an inferior specimen or substitute; makeshift: *The tramp wore a sad apology for a hat.* [1400–50; earlier *apologie,* late ME *apologe* (< MF) < LL *apologia* < Gk; see APOLOGIA]
—**Syn. 2.** vindication. See **excuse.**

ap·o·lune (ap′ə lo͞on′), *n. Aerospace.* the point in a lunar orbit that is farthest from the moon. Cf. **perilune.** [1965–70; APO- + *-lune* < L *lūna* moon, on the model of APOGEE, etc.]

ap·o·mict (ap′ə mikt), *n. Biol.* an organism produced by apomixis. [1935–40; back formation from *apomictic,* equiv. to APO- + Gk *mikt(os)* mixed + -IC]

ap·o·mix·is (ap′ə mik′sis), *n., pl.* **-mix·es** (-mik′sēz). *Biol.* any of several types of asexual reproduction, as apogamy or parthenogenesis. [1910–15; < NL < Gk *apo-* APO- + *mixis* a mixing, equiv. to *mig(nýnai)* to mix + *-sis* -SIS] —**ap·o·mic·tic** (ap′ə mik′tik), **ap′o·mic′ti·cal,** *adj.* —**ap′o·mic′ti·cal·ly,** *adv.*

ap·o·mor·phine (ap′ə môr′fēn, -fin), *n. Pharm.* an alkaloid, $C_{17}H_{17}NO_2$, derived from morphine and used as a fast-acting emetic. Also, **ap·o·mor·phin** (ap′ə môr′fin). [1885–90; APO- + MORPHINE]

ap·o·neu·ro·sis (ap′ə no͝o rō′sis, -nyo͝o-), *n., pl.* **-ses** (-sēz). *Anat.* a whitish, fibrous membrane that connects a muscle to a bone or fascia. [1670–80; < Gk *aponeúrōsis* the part of a muscle becoming a tendon, equiv. to *aponeurō-,* var. s. of *aponeuroûn* to change to tendon (see APO-, NEURON) + *-sis* -SIS] —**ap·o·neu·rot·ic** (ap′ə-no͝o rot′ik, -nyo͝o-), *adj.*

ap·o·pemp·tic (ap′ə pemp′tik), *adj.* **1.** pertaining to leave-taking or departing; valedictory. —*n.* **2.** *Obs.* a farewell address; valedictory. [1745–55; < Gk *apopemptikós* of, pertaining to sending away, equiv. to *apopémp(ein)* to send away, dismiss (*apo-* APO- + *pémpein* to send, dispatch) + *-tikos* -TIC]

a·poph·a·sis (ə pof′ə sis), *n. Rhet.* denial of one's intention to speak of a subject that is at the same time named or insinuated, as "I shall not mention Caesar's avarice, nor his cunning, nor his morality." [1650–60; < LL < Gk: a denial, equiv. to *apópha(nai)* to say no, deny (*apo-* APO- + *phánai* to say) + *-sis* -SIS]

A·po·phis (ə pō′fis), *n. Egyptian Myth.* a demon serpent of darkness whom Ra, as sun god, destroys every morning at dawn. Also, **Apepi.** [< Gk *Apophis* < Egyptian; see APEPI]

a·poph·o·ny (ə pof′ə nē), *n., pl.* **-nies.** ablaut. [1880–85; APO- + -PHONY] —**ap·o·phon·ic** (ap′ə fon′ik), *adj.*

ap·o·phthegm (ap′ə them′), *n.* apothegm. —**ap·o·phtheg·mat·ic** (ap′ə theg mat′ik), **ap′o·phtheg·mat′i·cal,** *adj.*

a·poph·y·ge (ə pof′i jē′), *n. Archit.* **1.** a small, concave, outward curve joining the shaft of a column, esp. a classical column, to its base. **2.** Also called **hypophyge.** a similar curve joining the shaft of a column to its capital. Also, **apophysis.** [1555–65; < Gk *apophygḗ* escape, equiv. to *apophyg-* (var. s. of *apopheúgein* to flee; *apo-* APO- + *pheúgein* to flee; akin to -FUGE) + *-ē* n. suffix]

a·poph·yl·lite (ə pof′ə līt′, ap′ə fil′īt), *n.* a hydrous potassium and calcium silicate mineral occurring in white crystals. [1800–10; APO- + -PHYLL + -ITE[1]]

a·poph·y·sis (ə pof′ə sis), *n., pl.* **-ses** (-sēz′). **1.** *Anat., Bot.* an outgrowth; process; projection or protuberance. **2.** *Archit.* apophyge. [1605–15; < NL < Gk: offshoot, equiv. to *apo-* APO- + *phýsis* growth, equiv. to *phý(ein)* to bring forth + *-sis* -SIS] —**a·poph·y·sate** (ə pof′ə sit, -sāt′), *adj.* —**ap·o·phys·e·al, ap·o·phys·i·al** (ap′ə fiz′ē-əl, ə pof′ə sē′əl), **a·poph·y·sar·y** (ə pof′ə ser′ē), *adj.*

ap·o·plec·tic (ap′ə plek′tik), *adj.* Also, **ap′o·plec′ti·cal. 1.** of or pertaining to apoplexy. **2.** having or inclined to apoplexy. **3.** intense enough to threaten or cause apoplexy: *an apoplectic rage.* —*n.* **4.** a person having or predisposed to apoplexy. [1605–15; < LL *apoplēcticus* < Gk *apoplēktikós* pertaining to a (paralytic) stroke, equiv. to *apóplēkt(os)* struck down (verbal of *apoplḗssein*) + *-ikos* -IC] —**ap′o·plec′ti·cal·ly,** *adv.*

ap·o·plex·y (ap′ə plek′sē), *n. Pathol.* **1.** stroke (def. 6). **2.** a sudden, usually marked loss of bodily function due to rupture or occlusion of a blood vessel. **3.** a hemorrhage into an organ cavity or tissue. [1350–1400; ME *apoplexie* < LL < Gk, equiv. to *apóplēkt(os)* (see APOPLECTIC) + *-ia* -Y[3]] —**ap·o·plec·ti·form** (ap′ə plek′tə-fôrm′), **ap′o·plec′toid,** *adj.*

ap·o·pyle (ap′ə pīl′), *n. Zool.* (in sponges) a pore in each of the saclike chambers formed by the evagination of the body wall, through which water passes into the excurrent canals. Cf. **prosopyle.** [1885–90; APO- + Gk *pýlē* gate, entrance; see PYLON]

a·po·ri·a (ə pôr′ē ə, ə pōr′-), *n., pl.* **a·po·ri·as, a·po·ri·ae** (ə pôr′ē ē′, ə pōr′-). **1.** *Rhet.* the expression of a simulated or real doubt, as about where to begin or what to do or say. **2.** *Logic, Philos.* a difficulty encountered in establishing the theoretical truth of a proposition, created by the presence of evidence both for and against it. [1580–90; < LL < Gk: state of being at a loss, equiv. to *ápor(os)* impassable (see A-[6], PORE[2]) + *-ia* -IA]

a·port (ə pôrt′, ə pōrt′), *adv. Naut.* on or toward the port side. [1620–30; A-[1] + PORT[2]]

ap·o·se·mat·ic (ap′ə sə mat′ik), *adj. Zool.* colored or constructed in a way that indicates special capabilities for defense. [1885–90; APO- + SEMATIC] —**ap′o·se·mat′i·cal·ly,** *adv.*

ap·o·si·o·pe·sis (ap′ə sī′ə pē′sis), *n., pl.* **-ses** (-sēz). *Rhet.* a sudden breaking off in the midst of a sentence, as if from inability or unwillingness to proceed. [1570–80; < LL < Gk: lit., a full silence, equiv. to *aposiōpē-* (verbal s. of *aposiōpáein* to be fully silent; *apo-* APO- + *siōpáein* to be silent) + *-sis* -SIS] —**ap·o·si·o·pet·ic** (ap′ə sī′ə pet′ik), *adj.*

ap·o·spor·y (ap′ə spôr′ē, -spōr′ē, ə pos′pə rē), *n. Bot.* the development of a gametophyte from a sporophyte without meiosis. [1880–85; APO- + SPOR- + -Y[3]] —**ap·o·spor·ic** (ap′ə spôr′ik, -spor′-), **a·pos·por·ous** (ə pos′-pər əs, ap′ə spôr′əs, -spor′-), *adj.*

a·pos·ta·sy (ə pos′tə sē), *n., pl.* **-sies.** a total desertion of or departure from one's religion, principles, party, cause, etc. [1350–1400; ME *apostasye* (< AF) < LL *apostasia* < Gk: a standing away, withdrawing, equiv. to *apóstas(is)* (*apo-* APO- + *sta-* STAND + *-sis* -SIS) + *-ia* -IA]

a·pos·tate (ə pos′tāt, -tit), *n.* **1.** a person who forsakes his religion, cause, party, etc. —*adj.* **2.** of or characterized by apostasy. [1300–50; ME < LL *apostata* < Gk *apostátēs,* equiv. to *aposta-* (see APOSTASY) + *-tēs* n. suffix] —**ap·o·stat·i·cal·ly** (ap′ə stat′ik lē), *adv.*

a·pos·ta·tize (ə pos′tə tīz′), *v.i.,* **-tized, -tiz·ing.** to commit apostasy. Also, *esp. Brit.,* **a·pos′ta·tise′.** [1545–55; < LL *apostatizāre.* See APOSTATE, -IZE] —**a·pos·ta·tism** (ə pos′tə tiz′əm), *n.*

a pos·te·ri·o·ri (ā′ po stēr′ē ôr′ī, -ōr′ī, -ôr′ē, -ōr′ē), **1.** from particular instances to a general principle or law; based upon actual observation or upon experimental data: *an a posteriori argument that derives the theory from the evidence.* Cf. **a priori** (def. 1). **2.** not existing in the mind prior to or independent of experience. Cf. **a priori** (def. 2). [1615–25; < L: lit., from the one behind. See A-[4], POSTERIOR]

a·pos·til (ə pos′til), *n.* a marginal annotation or note. Also, **a·pos′tille.** [1520–30; < MF *apostille,* n. deriv. of *apostiller* to add marginal notes, deriv., with *a-* A-[5], of ML *postilla* marginal note, perh. from the phrase *post illa* (*verba*) after these (words), with *illa* construed as the L dim. suffix]

ap·o·stilb (ap′ə stilb′), *n. Optics.* a unit of luminance equal to one ten thousandth of a lambert. [APO- + STILB]

a·pos·tle (ə pos′əl), *n.* **1.** any of the early followers of Jesus who carried the Christian message into the world. **2.** (*sometimes cap.*) any of the original 12 disciples called by Jesus to preach the gospel: Simon Peter, the brothers James and John, Andrew, Philip, Bartholomew, Matthew, Thomas, James the son of Alpheus, Thaddaeus, Simon the Zealot, Judas Iscariot. **3.** the first or the best-known Christian missionary in any region or country. **4.** *Eastern Ch.* one of the 70 disciples of Jesus. **5.** the title of the highest ecclesiastical official in certain Protestant sects. **6.** (among the Jews of the Christian epoch) a title borne by persons sent on foreign missions. **7.** one of the 12 administrative officials of the Mormon Church. **8.** a pioneer of any reform movement. **9.** *Naut.* a knighthead, esp. one having its top projecting and used as a bitt or bollard. [bef. 950; ME, var. of *apostel, apostol,* OE *apostol* (cf. OFris *apostol,* OHG *apostol(o),* G *Apostel*) < LL *apostolus* < Gk *apóstolos* lit., one who is sent out; akin to *apostéllein* to send off; see APO-. Cf., with loss of initial unstressed *a-,* ME *postle, postel,* OE *postol* (> ON *postuli*) OHG *postul*] —**a·pos′tle·hood′, a·pos′tle·ship′,** *n.*

a·pos·tle·bird (ə pos′əl bûrd′), *n.* an omnivorous bird, *Struthidea cinerea,* of eastern Australia, that has chiefly dark gray-brown plumage with white tail markings and is noted for its habit of traveling in groups of about 12 related individuals. Also, **apos′tle bird′.** [1930–35; APOSTLE + BIRD]

Apos′tle pitch′er, a stoneware pitcher decorated in relief with figures of the apostles.

apos′tle plant′, a plant, *Neomarica northiana,* of the

iris family, native to Brazil, having large, fragrant white and violet flowers, and often cultivated as a houseplant.

Apos′tles′ Creed′, a creed, dating back to about A.D. 400, traditionally ascribed to Christ's apostles and having widespread acceptance in the Christian church. It begins "I believe in God the Father Almighty."

Apos′tle spoon′, a spoon having at the end of the handle the figure of one of the 12 apostles, formerly given as a christening present. [1605–15]

a•pos•to•late (ə pos′tl it, -āt′), *n.* **1.** the dignity or office of an apostle. **2.** *Rom. Cath. Ch.* **a.** the dignity and office of the pope as head of the Apostolic See. **b.** the mission of bishops in their dioceses. **c.** an organization of the laity devoted to the mission of the Church. [1635–45; < LL *apostolātus* the office of an apostle, equiv. to LL *apostol(us)* APOSTLE + *-ātus* -ATE[3]]

ap•os•tol•ic (ap′ə stol′ik), *adj.* **1.** of or characteristic of an apostle. **2.** pertaining to or characteristic of the 12 apostles. **3.** derived from the apostles in regular succession. **4.** of or pertaining to the pope; papal. Also, **ap′os•tol′i•cal.** [1540–50; < LL *apostolicus* < Gk *apostolikós*, equiv. to *apóstol(os)* APOSTLE + *-ikos* -IC] —**ap′os•tol′i•cal•ly,** *adv.* —**a•pos•tol•i•cism** (ap′ə stol′ə siz′əm), *n.* —**a•pos•to•lic•i•ty** (ə pos′tl is′i tē), **ap′os•tol′i•cal•ness,** *n.*

ap′ostol′ic age′, the earliest period of Christianity, lasting through the death of the last apostle. [1840–50]

Ap′ostol′ic Church′, **1.** the Christian church as founded by the apostles. **2.** See **Apostolic See** (def. 2). [1540–50]

ap′ostol′ic del′egate, a representative of the pope in a country that has no regular diplomatic relations with the Vatican. Cf. **nuncio.** [1905–10]

Ap′ostol′ic Fa′thers, **1.** the fathers of the early Christian church whose lives overlapped those of any of the apostles. **2.** the collection of works attributed to them. [1820–30]

Ap′ostol′ic See′, **1.** the Church of Rome, traditionally founded by St. Peter. **2.** Also called **Apostolic Church.** a church founded by an apostle. [1585–95]

apostol′ic succes′sion, *Rom. Cath. Ch., Orth. Ch., Anglican Ch.* the unbroken line of succession beginning with the apostles and perpetuated through bishops, considered essential for orders and sacraments to be valid. [1830–40]

ap′ostol′ic vic′ar. See **vicar apostolic.**

A•pos•to•los (ä pôs′tô lôs; *Eng.* ə pos′tl os′), *n. Gk. Orth. Ch.* **1.** a book containing parts of the Epistles and parts of the Acts of the Apostles. **2.** a reading from this book. [< LGk, Gk: APOSTLE]

a•pos•tro•phe[1] (ə pos′trə fē), *n.* the sign ('), as used: to indicate the omission of one or more letters in a word, whether unpronounced, as in *o'er* for *over*, or pronounced, as in *gov't* for *government;* to indicate the possessive case, as in *man's;* or to indicate plurals of abbreviations and symbols, as in *several M.D.'s, 3's.* [1580–90; < MF (with pron. later altered by confusion with APOSTROPHE[2]), r. earlier *apostrophus* < LL (> MF) < Gk *apóstrophos* (*prosōidía*) eliding (mark), lit., (mark) of turning away, verbid of *apostréphein* to turn away, equiv. to *apo-* APO- + *stréphein* to turn; see STROPHE] —**ap•os•troph•ic** (ap′ə strof′ik, -strō′fik), *adj.*

a•pos•tro•phe[2] (ə pos′trə fē), *n. Rhet.* a digression in the form of an address to someone not present, or to a personified object or idea, as "O Death, where is thy sting?" [1525–35; < LL < Gk *apostrophḗ* a turning away, equiv. to *apostroph-* (verbid of *apostréphein;* see APOSTROPHE[1]) + *-ē* n. suffix] —**ap•os•troph•ic** (ap′ə strof′ik, -strō′fik), *adj.*

a•pos•tro•phize (ə pos′trə fīz′), *v.,* **-phized, -phiz•ing.** *Rhet.* —*v.t.* **1.** to address by apostrophe. —*v.i.* **2.** to utter an apostrophe. Also, *esp. Brit.,* **a•pos′tro•phise′.** [1605–15; APOSTROPHE[2] + -IZE]

apoth′ecaries' meas′ure, a system of units used chiefly in compounding and dispensing liquid drugs. In the U.S. 60 minims (♏) = 1 fluid dram (f ʒ); 8 fluid drams = 1 fluid ounce (f ℥); 16 fluid ounces = 1 pint (O.); 8 pints = 1 gallon (C.) (231 cubic inches). In Great Britain 20 minims = 1 fluid scruple; 3 fluid scruples = 1 fluid dram; 8 fluid drams = 1 fluid ounce; 20 fluid ounces = 1 pint; 8 pints = 1 imperial gallon (277.42 cubic inches). [1895–1900]

apoth′ecaries' weight′, a system of weights used chiefly in compounding and dispensing drugs: 20 grains = 1 scruple (℈); 3 scruples = 1 dram (ʒ); 8 drams = 1 ounce (℥); 12 ounces = 1 pound. The grain, ounce, and pound are the same as in troy weight, the grain alone being the same as in avoirdupois weight. [1755–65]

a•poth•e•car•y (ə poth′ə ker′ē), *n., pl.* **-car•ies.** **1.** a druggist; a pharmacist. **2.** a pharmacy or drugstore. **3.** (esp. in England and Ireland) a druggist licensed to prescribe medicine. [1325–75; ME (< OF) < ML *apothēcārius* seller of spices and drugs, LL: shopkeeper, equiv. to L *apothēc(a)* shop, storehouse (< Gk *apothḗkē;* see APO-, THECA) + *-ārius* -ARY]

apoth′ecary jar′, a small, covered jar, formerly used by druggists to hold pharmaceuticals, now chiefly in household use to hold spices, candies, cosmetics, etc., and sometimes decorated, as a lamp base or flower vase.

ap•o•the•ci•um (ap′ə thē′shē əm, -sē-), *n., pl.* **-ci•a** (-shē ə, -sē ə). *Bot., Mycol.* the fruit of certain lichens and fungi: usually an open, saucer-shaped or cup-shaped body, the inner surface of which is covered with a layer that bears asci. [1820–30; < NL < Gk *apo-* APO- + *thēkíon,* equiv. to *thḗk(ē)* case (see THECA) + *-ion* dim. suffix] —**ap•o•the•cial** (ap′ə thē′shəl), *adj.*

ap•o•thegm (ap′ə them′), *n.* a short, pithy, instructive saying; a terse remark or aphorism. Also, **apophthegm.** [1545–55; earlier *apothegma* < Gk *apóphthegma,* equiv. to *apophtheg-* (var. s. of *apophthéngesthai* to speak out; *apo-* APO- + *phthéngesthai* to speak) + *-ma* n. suffix] —**ap•o•theg•mat•ic** (ap′ə theg mat′ik), **ap′o•theg•mat′i•cal,** *adj.* —**ap′o•theg•mat′i•cal•ly,** *adv.*

ap•o•them (ap′ə them′), *n. Geom.* a perpendicular from the center of a regular polygon to one of its sides. [1855–60; < F *apothème,* prob. on the model of Gk *hypóthema* base; see APO-, THEME]

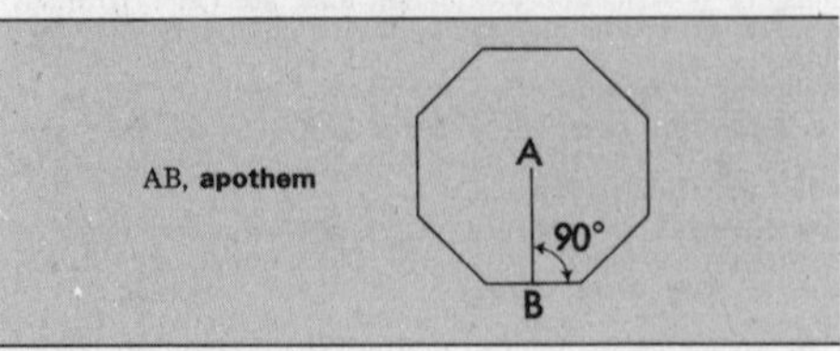

a•poth•e•o•sis (ə poth′ē ō′sis, ap′ə thē′ə sis), *n., pl.* **-ses** (-sēz, -sēz′). **1.** the elevation or exaltation of a person to the rank of a god. **2.** the ideal example; epitome; quintessence: *This poem is the apotheosis of lyric expression.* [1570–80; < LL < Gk. See APO-, THEO-, -OSIS]

a•poth•e•o•size (ə poth′ē ə sīz′, ap′ə thē′ə sīz′), *v.t.,* **-sized, -siz•ing.** to deify; glorify. [1750–60; APOTHEOS(IS) + -IZE]

ap•o•tro•pa•ic (ap′ə trə pā′ik), *adj.* intended to ward off evil. [1880–85; < Gk *apotrópai(os)* averting evil (see APO-, TROPE) + -IC] —**ap′o•tro•pa′i•cal•ly,** *adv.*

ap•o•tro•pa•ism (ap′ə trə pā′iz əm), *n.* the use of magic and ritualistic ceremony to anticipate and prevent evil. [< Gk *apotrópai(on)* object that averts evil (see APOTROPAIC) + -ISM]

app., **1.** apparatus. **2.** apparent. **3.** appendix. **4.** applied. **5.** appointed. **6.** approved. **7.** approximate.

ap•pal (ə pôl′), *v.t.,* **-palled, -pal•ling.** appall.

Ap•pa•la•chi•a (ap′ə lā′chē ə, -chə, -lach′ē ə, -lach′ə), *n.* **1.** *Geol.* a Paleozoic landmass, the erosion of which provided the sediments to form the rocks of the Appalachian Mountains. **2.** a region in the E United States, in the area of the S Appalachian Mountains, usually including NE Alabama, NW Georgia, NW South Carolina, E Tennessee, W Virginia, E Kentucky, West Virginia, and SW Pennsylvania.

Ap•pa•la•chi•an (ap′ə lā′chē ən, -chən, -lach′ē ən, lach′ən), *adj.* **1.** of or pertaining to the Appalachian Mountains. **2.** of or pertaining to the region of Appalachia, its inhabitants, or their culture. **3.** *Geol.* of or pertaining to the orogeny and accompanying intrusion that occurred in eastern North America during the Pennsylvanian and Permian periods. —*n.* **4.** a native or inhabitant of Appalachia, esp. one of predominantly Scotch-Irish, English, or German ancestry who exemplifies the characteristic cultural traditions of this region.

Ap′pala′chian Moun′tains, a mountain range in E North America, extending from S Quebec province to N Alabama. Highest peak, Mt. Mitchell, 6684 ft. (2037 m). Also called **Ap′pa•la′chi•ans.**

Ap′pala′chian Spring′, a dance (1944) choreographed by Martha Graham, with musical score by Aaron Copland.

Ap′pala′chian tea′, **1.** the leaves of any of certain plants of the genus *Ilex* of the eastern U.S., as the shrub *I. glabra,* sometimes used as a tea. **2.** a plant yielding such leaves. [1905–10, *Amer.*]

Ap′pala′chian trail′, a hiking trail extending through the Appalachian Mountains from central Maine to N Georgia. 2050 mi. (3300 km) long.

ap•pall (ə pôl′), *v.t.* to fill or overcome with horror, consternation, or fear; dismay: *He was appalled by the damage from the fire. I am appalled at your mistakes.* Also, **appal.** [1275–1325; ME < MF *ap(p)allir* to grow or make pale, equiv. to *a-* A-[5] + *pal(l)ir* in same sense; see PALE[1]]
—**Syn.** horrify, daunt. See **frighten.**

ap•pall•ing (ə pô′ling), *adj.* causing dismay or horror: *an appalling accident; an appalling lack of manners.* [1810–20; APPALL + -ING[2]] —**ap•pall′ing•ly,** *adv.*

Ap•pa•loo•sa (ap′ə lo͞o′sə), *n.* one of a hardy breed of riding horses, developed in the North American West, having a mottled hide, vertically striped hoofs, and eyes that show a relatively large proportion of white. [1920–25, *Amer.;* orig. uncert.; perh. to be identified with *Opelousa* a Louisiana Indian tribal name (cf. *Opelousas poney,* recorded in a G text of 1849), though the breed is traditionally associated with the Nez Percé Indians and the Palouse River (W Idaho)]

ap•pa•nage (ap′ə nij), *n.* **1.** land or some other source of revenue assigned for the maintenance of a member of the family of a ruling house. **2.** whatever belongs rightfully or appropriately to one's rank or station in life. **3.** a natural or necessary accompaniment; adjunct. Also, **apanage.** [1595–1605; < MF, OF *apanage, apeinaige,* equiv. to *apan(er)* to endow (a younger son or daughter) with a maintenance (< ML *appānāre; ap-* AP-[1] + *-pānāre,* v. deriv. of L *pānis* bread; cf. OPr *apanar* to nourish) + *-age* -AGE]

appar., **1.** apparent. **2.** apparently.

ap•pa•rat (ap′ə rat′, ä′pə rät′), *n.* an organization or existing power structure, esp. a political one: *a position of leadership within the party apparat; The chess apparat is not eager to change tournament rules.* [1940–45; < Russ *apparát* orig., scientific apparatus < G < L *apparātus.* See APPARATUS]

ap•pa•rat•chik (ä′pə rä′chik; *Russ.* u pu rät′chyik), *n., pl.* **-chiks;** *Russ.* **-chi•ki** (-chyi kyē). a member of an apparat, esp. in a Communist country. [1940–45; < Russ *apparátchik,* equiv. to *apparát* APPARAT + *-chik* agent suffix]

ap•pa•rat•us (ap′ə rat′əs, -rā′təs), *n., pl.* **-tus, -tus•es.** **1.** a group or combination of instruments, machinery, tools, materials, etc., having a particular function or intended for a specific use: *Our town has excellent fire-fighting apparatus.* **2.** any complex instrument or mechanism for a particular purpose. **3.** any system or systematic organization of activities, functions, processes, etc., directed toward a specific goal: *the apparatus of government; espionage apparatus.* **4.** *Physiol.* a group of structurally different organs working together in the performance of a particular function: *the digestive apparatus.* [1620–30; < L *apparātus* equipment, orig. the act of equipping, preparation, equiv. to *apparā(re)* to prepare (*ap-* AP-[1] + *parāre;* see PREPARE) + *-tus* suffix of v. action]
—**Syn.** **2.** machine, appliance, device, contraption, contrivance.

ap•pa•ra•tus crit•i•cus (ap′ə rat′əs krit′i kəs, -rā′-təs; *Lat.* äp′pä rä′to͞os krit′i ko͞os′), supplementary information, as variant readings, added to a text to provide material for study or criticism. [1860–65; < NL: critical apparatus]

ap•par•el (ə par′əl), *n., v.,* **-eled, -el•ing** or (*esp. Brit.*) **-elled, -el•ling.** —*n.* **1.** clothing, esp. outerwear; garments; attire; raiment. **2.** anything that decorates or covers. **3.** superficial appearance; aspect; guise. **4.** *Naut.* the masts, sails, anchor, etc., used to equip a vessel. **5.** *Eccles.* a piece of embroidery, usually oblong, on certain vestments, esp. on the alb or amice. —*v.t.* **6.** to dress or clothe. **7.** to adorn; ornament. **8.** *Naut.* to equip (a vessel) with apparel. [1200–50; ME *appareillen* < OF *apareillier* to make fit, fit out < VL **appariculāre,* equiv. to *ap-* AP-[1] + **paricul(us)* a fit (see PAR, -CULE[1]) + *-ā-* thematic vowel + *-re* inf. suffix]
—**Syn.** **1.** clothes, dress, garb, costume, habiliments, vesture. **6.** outfit, array, deck out.

ap•par•ent (ə par′ənt, ə pâr′-), *adj.* **1.** readily seen; exposed to sight; open to view; visible: *The crack in the wall was readily apparent.* **2.** capable of being easily perceived or understood; plain or clear; obvious: *The solution to the problem was apparent to all.* **3.** according to appearances, initial evidence, incomplete results, etc.; ostensible rather than actual: *He was the apparent winner of the election.* **4.** entitled to a right of inheritance by birth, indefeasible except by one's death before that of the ancestor, to an inherited throne, title, or other estate. Cf. **heir apparent, heir presumptive.** [1350–1400; < L *appārent-* (s. of *appārēns* appearing; see APPEAR, -ENT); r. ME *aparant* < MF] —**ap•par′ent•ly,** *adv.* —**ap•par′ent•ness,** *n.*
—**Syn.** **1.** discernible. **2.** open, conspicuous, manifest, unmistakable. APPARENT, EVIDENT, OBVIOUS, PATENT all refer to something easily perceived. APPARENT applies to that which can readily be seen or perceived: *an apparent effort.* EVIDENT applies to that which facts or circumstances make plain: *His innocence was evident.* OBVIOUS applies to that which is unquestionable, because of being completely manifest or noticeable: *an obvious change of method.* PATENT, a more formal word, applies to that which is open to view or understanding by all: *a patent error.* —**Ant.** **2.** concealed, obscure.

appar′ent can′dlepower, *Optics.* a measure of the luminous intensity of an extended source of light in terms of the candlepower of a point source of light that has an equivalent luminous intensity when placed at the same distance as the extended source.

ap•pa•ren•te•ment (A PA RÄNT[a] MÄN′), *n., pl.* **-ments** (-MÄN′). *Fr. Govt.* a coalition formed between political parties during an election. [< F: alliance, coalition, equiv. to *apparent(er)* to make part of the family, ally, connect (*ap-* AP-[1] + *-parenter,* v. deriv. of *parent* PARENT, relative) + *-ment* -MENT]

appar′ent mag′nitude, *Astron.* the magnitude of a star as it appears to an observer on the earth. Cf. **absolute magnitude.** [1870–75]

appar′ent so′lar day′, *Astron.* the period of time between two successive passages of the sun's center across the same meridian. [1910–15]

appar′ent time′, *Astron.* local time measured by the hour angle of the sun. Cf. **mean solar time.** [1685–95]

appar′ent wind′ (wind), the velocity of air as measured from a moving object, as a ship.

ap•pa•ri•tion (ap′ə rish′ən), *n.* **1.** a supernatural appearance of a person or thing, esp. a ghost; a specter or phantom; wraith: *a ghostly apparition at midnight.* **2.** anything that appears, esp. something remarkable or startling: *the surprising apparition of cowboys in New York City.* **3.** an act of appearing; manifestation. **4.** *Astron.* the appearance or time when a comet, esp. a periodic one, is visible: *the 1986 apparition of Halley's comet.* [1400–50; late ME *apparicio(u)n* < AF, OF < LL *appāritiōn-* (s. of *appāritiō,* as calque of Gk *epipháneia* EPIPHANY), equiv. to L *appārit(us)* (ptp. of *appārēre;* see APPEAR) + *-iōn-* -ION] —**ap′pa•ri′tion•al,** *adj.*
—**Syn.** **1.** spirit, shade. APPARITION, PHANTASM, PHANTOM are terms for a supernatural appearance. An APPARITION of a person or thing is an immaterial appearance that seems real, and is generally sudden or startling in its manifestation: *an apparition of a headless horseman.* Both PHANTOM and PHANTASM denote an illusory appearance, as in a dream; the former may be pleasant, while the latter is usually frightening: *a phantom of loveliness, a monstrous phantasm.*

ap•par•i•tor (ə par′i tər), *n.* (in ancient Rome) a subordinate official of a magistrate or of the court. [1250–1300; ME *apparitour* < L *appāritor,* equiv. to *appāri-* (var. s. of *appārēre* to serve, attend, lit., to be seen; see APPEAR) + *-tor* -TOR]

ap•pas•sio•na•to (ə pä′sē ə nä′tō, ə pash′ə-; *It.* äpɔäs′syô nä′tô), *adj. Music.* impassioned; with passion or strong feeling. [< It; see AP-[1], PASSION, -ATE[1]]

ppd., approved.

p·peal (ə pēl′), *n.* **1.** an earnest request for aid, support, sympathy, mercy, etc.; entreaty; petition; plea. **2.** a request or reference to some person or authority for a decision, corroboration, judgment, etc. **3.** *Law.* **a.** an application or proceeding for review by a higher tribunal. **b.** (in a legislative body or assembly) a formal question as to the correctness of a ruling by a presiding officer. **c.** *Obs.* a formal charge or accusation. **4.** the power or ability to attract, interest, amuse, or stimulate the mind or emotions: *The game has lost its appeal.* **5.** *Obs.* a summons or challenge. —*v.i.* **6.** to ask for aid, support, mercy, sympathy, or the like; make an earnest entreaty: *The college appealed to its alumni for funds.* **7.** *Law.* to apply for review of a case or particular issue to a higher tribunal. **8.** to have need of or ask for proof, a decision, corroboration, etc. **9.** to be especially attractive, pleasing, interesting, or enjoyable: *The red hat appeals to me.* —*v.t.* **10.** *Law.* **a.** to apply for review of (a case) to a higher tribunal. **b.** *Obs.* to charge with a crime before a tribunal. **11. appeal to the country,** *Brit.* See **country** (def. 11). [1250–1300; (v.) ME *a(p)pelen* < AF, OF *a(p)peler* < L *appellāre* to speak to, address, equiv. to *ap-* AP-[1] + *-pellāre,* iterative s. of *pellere* to push, beat against; (n.) ME *ap(p)el* < AF, OF *apel,* n. deriv. of *ap(p)eler*] —**ap·peal′a·bil′i·ty,** *n.* —**ap·peal′a·ble,** *adj.* —**ap·peal′er,** *n.*

—**Syn. 1.** prayer, supplication, invocation. **2.** suit, solicitation. **4.** attraction. **6.** request, ask. APPEAL, ENTREAT, PETITION, SUPPLICATE mean to ask for something wished for or needed. APPEAL and PETITION may concern groups and formal or public requests. ENTREAT and SUPPLICATE are usually more personal and urgent. To APPEAL is to ask earnestly for help or support, on grounds of reason, justice, common humanity, etc.: *to appeal for contributions to a cause.* To PETITION is to ask by written request, by prayer, or the like, that something be granted: *to petition for more playgrounds.* ENTREAT suggests pleading: *The captured knight entreated the king not to punish him.* To SUPPLICATE is to beg humbly, usually from a superior, powerful, or stern (official) person: *to supplicate that the lives of prisoners be spared.*

p·peal·ing (ə pē′ling), *adj.* evoking or attracting interest, desire, curiosity, sympathy, or the like; attractive. 1400–50; late ME; see APPEAL, -ING[2]] —**ap·peal′ing·ly,** *adv.* —**ap·peal′ing·ness,** *n.*

ppeal′ play′, *Baseball.* an appeal by the team in the field to the umpire regarding a possible base-running infraction, such as failure to touch a base or leaving it to score before a fly is caught, that is considered only when the defending team tags the runner or base in question before making the appeal.

p·pear (ə pēr′), *v.i.* **1.** to come into sight; become visible: *A man suddenly appeared in the doorway.* **2.** to have the appearance of being; seem; look: *to appear wise.* **3.** to be obvious or easily perceived; be clear or made clear by evidence: *It appears to me that you are right.* **4.** to come or be placed before the public; be published: *Her biography appeared last year.* **5.** to perform publicly, as in a play, dance, etc.: *He appeared as the king in the play.* **6.** to attend or be present, esp. to arrive late or stay but a short time: *He appeared at the party but left quickly.* **7.** to come into being; be created, invented, or developed: *Speech appears in the child's first or second year.* **8.** *Law.* to come formally, esp. as a party or counsel, to a proceeding before a tribunal, authority, etc. 1250–1300; ME *ap(p)eren* < AF, OF *aper-,* tonic s. of *apare(i)r, apparoir* < L *appārēre* be seen, appear, equiv. to *ap-* AP-[1] + *pārēre* be visible]

—**Syn. 1.** emerge, arise. **2.** See **seem.**

p·pear·ance (ə pēr′əns), *n.* **1.** the act or fact of appearing, as to the eye or mind or before the public: *the unannounced appearance of dinner guests; the last appearance of Caruso in Aïda; her first appearance at a stockholders' meeting.* **2.** the state, condition, manner, or style in which a person or object appears; outward look or aspect: *a table of antique appearance; a man of noble appearance.* **3.** outward show or seeming; semblance: *to avoid the appearance of coveting an honor.* **4.** *Law.* the coming into court of either party to a suit or action. **5. appearances,** outward impressions, indications, or circumstances: *By all appearances, he enjoyed himself.* **6.** *Philos.* the sensory, or phenomenal, aspect of existence to an observer. **7.** *Archaic.* an apparition. **8. keep up appearances,** to maintain a public impression of decorum, prosperity, etc., despite reverses, unfavorable conditions, etc.: *They tried to keep up appearances after losing all their money.* **9. make an appearance,** to come; arrive: *He didn't make an appearance until after midnight.* **10. put in an appearance,** to attend a gathering or meeting, esp. for a very short time: *The author put in an appearance at the cocktail party on her way to dinner.* [1350–1400; APPEAR + -ANCE; r. ME *aparance* < AF, OF < LL *appārentia,* neut. pl. of L *appārēns* APPARENT]

—**Syn. 1.** arrival, coming, advent. **2.** demeanor, presence. APPEARANCE, ASPECT, GUISE refer to the way in which something outwardly presents itself to view. APPEARANCE refers to the outward look: *the shabby appearance of his car.* ASPECT refers to the appearance at some particular time or in special circumstances; it often has emotional implications, either ascribed to the object itself or felt by the beholder: *In the dusk the forest had a terrifying aspect.* GUISE suggests a misleading appearance, assumed for an occasion or a purpose: *under the guise of friendship.* **3.** face, pretense.

p·pease (ə pēz′), *v.t.,* **-peased, -peas·ing. 1.** to bring to a state of peace, quiet, ease, calm, or contentment; pacify; soothe: *to appease an angry king.* **2.** to satisfy, allay, or relieve; assuage: *The fruit appeased his hunger.* **3.** to yield or concede to the belligerent demands of (a nation, group, person, etc.) in a conciliatory effort, sometimes at the expense of justice or other principles. 1300–50; ME *apesen* < AF *apeser,* OF *apais(i)er,* equiv. to *a-* A-[5] + *paisi-* PEACE + *-er* inf. suffix] —**ap·peas′a·ble,** *adj.* —**ap·peas′a·ble·ness,** *n.* —**ap·peas′a·bly,** *adv.* —**ap·pease′ment,** *n.* —**ap·peas′er,** *n.* —**ap·peas′ing·ly,** *adv.*

—**Syn. 1.** calm, placate. **3.** APPEASE, CONCILIATE, PROPITIATE imply trying to preserve or obtain peace. To APPEASE is to make anxious overtures and often undue concessions to satisfy the demands of someone with a greed for power, territory, etc.: *Chamberlain tried to appease Hitler at Munich.* To CONCILIATE is to win an enemy or opponent over by displaying a willingness to be just and fair: *When mutual grievances are recognized, conciliation is possible.* To PROPITIATE is to admit a fault, and, by trying to make amends, to allay hostile feeling: *to propitiate an offended neighbor.* —**Ant. 1.** enrage. **2.** increase, arouse, sharpen. **3.** defy.

ap·pel (ə pel′, a pel′; *Fr.* A pel′), *n., pl.* **ap·pels** (ə pelz′, a pelz′; *Fr.* A pel′). *Fencing.* **1.** a tap or stamp of the foot, formerly serving as a warning of one's intent to attack, but now also used as a feint. **2.** a sharp stroke with the blade used for the purpose of procuring an opening. [< F; see APPEAL]

ap·pel·lant (ə pel′ənt), *n.* **1.** a person who appeals. **2.** *Law.* a party that appeals to a higher tribunal. —*adj.* **3.** of or pertaining to an appeal; appellate. [1400–50; late ME *appellaunt* < AF; OF *apelant,* prp. of *apeler* to APPEAL; see -ANT]

ap·pel·late (ə pel′it), *adj. Law.* **1.** of or pertaining to appeals. **2.** having the power or authority to review and decide appeals, as a court. [1720–30; < L *appellātus* called upon, named, appealed to (ptp. of *appellāre*), equiv. to *ap-* AP-[1] + *pell-* move, go + *-ātus* -ATE[1]]

appel′late divi′sion, *Law.* the section of a court that hears appeals, sometimes existing as an intermediate court between a trial court and a court of last resort.

ap·pel·la·tion (ap′ə lā′shən), *n.* **1.** a name, title, or designation. **2.** appellative (def. 1). **3.** the act of naming. [1400–50; late ME *appelacion* < OF < L *appellātiōn-* (s. of *appellātiō*) a naming, equiv. to *appellāt(us)* (see APPELLATE) + *-iōn-* -ION]

ap·pel·la·tion con·trô·lée (A pe lA syôN′ kôN trō-lā′), (of a French wine) having use of its name or designation controlled by the government with respect to the region of production, the variety of grapes used, and the level of quality maintained. [< F: controlled appellation]

ap·pel·la·tive (ə pel′ə tiv), *n.* **1.** a descriptive name or designation, as *Bald* in *Charles the Bald.* **2.** a common noun. —*adj.* **3.** designative; descriptive. **4.** tending toward or serving for the assigning of names: *the appellative function of some primitive rites.* **5.** pertaining to a common noun. [1375–1425; late ME (< MF) < LL *appellātīvus.* See APPELLATE, -IVE] —**ap·pel′la·tive·ly,** *adv.* —**ap·pel′la·tive·ness,** *n.*

ap·pel·lee (ap′ə lē′), *n. Law.* the defendant or respondent in an appellate proceeding. [1525–35; < AF, OF *apelé,* ptp. of *apeler* to APPEAL; see -EE]

ap·pel·lor (ə pel′ôr, ap′ə lôr′), *n. Brit. Law.* **1.** a person who prosecutes in an appellate proceeding. **2.** *Obs.* a person who accuses another in a criminal appeal. [1400–50; late ME *apelour* < AF, OF *apeleor* < L *appellātor* appellant. See APPELLATE, -TOR]

ap·pend (ə pend′), *v.t.* **1.** to add as a supplement, accessory, or appendix; subjoin: *to append a note to a letter.* **2.** to attach or suspend as a pendant. **3.** to sign a document with; affix: *to append one's signature to a will.* [1640–50; < L *appendere,* equiv. to *ap-* AP[1] + *-pendere* to hang (transit.)]

ap·pend·age (ə pen′dij), *n.* **1.** a subordinate part attached to something; an auxiliary part; addition. **2.** *Anat., Zool.* any member of the body diverging from the axial trunk. **3.** *Bot., Mycol.* any subsidiary part superadded to another part. **4.** a person in a subordinate or dependent position, esp. a servile or parasitic follower. [1640–50; APPEND + -AGE] —**ap·pend′aged,** *adj.*

ap·pend·ant (ə pen′dənt), *adj.* **1.** attached or suspended; annexed. **2.** associated as an accompaniment or consequence: *the salary appendant to a position.* **3.** *Law.* pertaining to a legal appendant. —*n.* **4.** a person or thing attached or added. **5.** *Law.* any subordinate possession or right historically annexed to or dependent on a greater one and automatically passing with it, as by sale or inheritance. Also, **ap·pend′ent.** [1350–1400; ME *ap(p)endaunt* (in legal sense) < AF, prp. of *apendre* to belong (to), befit < ML *appendēre,* equiv. to L *ap-* AP-[1] + *pendēre* to hang (intransit.); later senses by assoc. with APPEND] —**ap·pend′ance, ap·pend′an·cy, ap·pend′ence, ap·pend′en·cy,** *n.*

ap·pen·dec·to·my (ap′ən dek′tə mē), *n., pl.* **-mies.** *Surg.* excision of the vermiform appendix. [1890–95; APPEND(IX) + -ECTOMY]

ap·pen·di·ceal (ap′ən dish′əl, ə pen′di sē′əl), *adj.* of or pertaining to the vermiform appendix. Also, **ap·pen·di·cal** (ə pen′di kəl), **ap·pen·di·cial** (ap′ən dish′əl). [1905–10; < L *appendic-* (see APPENDIX) + *-eal,* var. of -IAL]

ap·pen·di·cec·to·my (ə pen′də sek′tə mē), *n., pl.* **-mies.** *Chiefly Brit.* appendectomy.

ap·pen·di·ci·tis (ə pen′də sī′tis), *n. Pathol.* inflammation of the vermiform appendix. [1885–90, *Amer.*; < NL, equiv. to L *appendic-* (s. of *appendix*) APPENDIX + NL *-ītis* -ITIS]

ap·pen·di·cle (ə pen′di kəl), *n.* a small appendage. [1605–15; < L *appendicula* small appendage, equiv. to *appendic-* (see APPENDIX) + *-ula* -ULE]

ap·pen·dic·u·lar (ap′ən dik′yə lər), *adj.* **1.** of or pertaining to an appendage or limb. **2.** *Anat.* appendiceal. [1645–55; < L *appendicul(a)* APPENDICLE + -AR[1]]

ap·pen·dic·u·late (ap′ən dik′yə lit, -lāt′), *adj. Bot., Zool.* **1.** having appendages. **2.** forming an appendage or appendicle. [1825–35; < L *appendicul(a)* APPENDICLE + -ATE[1]]

ap·pen·dix (ə pen′diks), *n., pl.* **-dix·es, -di·ces** (-də sēz′). **1.** supplementary material at the end of a book, article, document, or other text, usually of an explanatory, statistical, or bibliographic nature. **2.** an appendage. **3.** *Anat.* **a.** a process or projection. **b.** See **vermiform appendix. 4.** *Aeron.* the short tube at the bottom of a balloon bag, by which the intake and release of buoyant gas is controlled. [1535–45; < L: appendage, equiv. to *append(ere)* to APPEND + *-ix* (equiv. to *-ic-* n. suffix + *-s* nom. sing. ending)]

—**Syn. 1.** addendum, adjunct. APPENDIX, SUPPLEMENT both mean material added at the end of a book. An APPENDIX gives useful additional information, but even without it the rest of the book is complete: *In the appendix are forty detailed charts.* A SUPPLEMENT, bound in the book or published separately, is given for comparison, as an enhancement, to provide corrections, to present later information, and the like: *A yearly supplement is issued.*

—**Usage.** APPENDICES, a plural borrowed directly from Latin, is sometimes used, especially in scholarly writing, to refer to supplementary material at the end of a book.

ap·pen·tice (ə pen′tis, a pen′-), *n.* penthouse (def. 4). [1610–20; < F *appentis,* OF *apentiz;* see PENTHOUSE]

Ap·pen·zell (ap′ən zel′; *Ger.* ä′pən tsel′), *n.* **1.** a canton in NE Switzerland, divided into two independent areas. Cf. **Appenzell Ausser Rhoden, Appenzell Inner Rhoden. 2.** a town in and the capital of Appenzell Inner Rhoden. 5200. **3.** (*often l.c.*) a type of embroidery, used chiefly on fine hankerchiefs.

Ap·pen·zell Aus·ser Rho·den (*Ger.* ä′pən tsel′ ou′sər rōd′n), a demicanton in NE Switzerland: Protestant. 47,400; 94 sq. mi. (245 sq. km). *Cap.:* Herisau.

ap·pen·zel·ler (ap′ən zel′ər; *Ger.* ä′pən tsel′ər), *n.* a cow's milk cheese, originally made in the canton of Appenzell in Switzerland. [< G, short for *Appenzeller Käse* Appenzell cheese]

Ap·pen·zell In·ner Rho·den (*Ger.* ä′pən tsel′ in′ər rōd′n), a demicanton in NE Switzerland: Catholic. 13,400. 66 sq. mi. (170 sq. km). *Cap.:* Appenzell.

ap·per·ceive (ap′ər sēv′), *v.t.,* **-ceived, -ceiv·ing.** *Psychol.* **1.** to have conscious perception of; comprehend. **2.** to comprehend (a new idea) by assimilation with the sum of one's previous knowledge and experience. [1250–1300; ME < OF *aperceivre.* See AP-[1], PERCEIVE]

ap·per·cep·tion (ap′ər sep′shən), *n. Psychol.* **1.** conscious perception. **2.** the act or process of apperceiving. [1745–55; (< F) < NL (Leibnitz) *apperceptiōn-,* s. of *apperceptiō.* See AP-[1], PERCEPTION] —**ap′per·cep′tive,** *adj.* —**ap′per·cep′tive·ly,** *adv.*

ap·per·son·a·tion (a pûr′sə nā′shən, ə pûr′-), *n. Psychiatry.* the unconscious assumption of the personality characteristics of another, usually well known, person. Also, **ap·per·son·i·fi·ca·tion** (ap′ər son′ə fi kā′shən). [1930–35; AP-[1] + PERSONATION, modeled on G *Appersonierung*]

ap·per·tain (ap′ər tān′), *v.i.* to belong as a part, right, possession, attribute, etc.; pertain or relate (usually fol. by *to*): *privileges that appertain to members of the royal family.* [1350–1400; ME *a(p)perte(y)nen* < OF *apertenir.* See AP-[1], PERTAIN]

ap·pe·stat (ap′ə stat′), *n.* a presumed region in the human brain, possibly the hypothalamus, that functions to adjust appetite. [APPE(TITE) + -STAT]

ap·pe·tence (ap′i təns), *n.* **1.** intense desire; strong natural craving; appetite. **2.** instinctive inclination or natural tendency. **3.** material or chemical attraction or affinity. Also, **appetency.** [1600–10; *appete* (obs.) to seek for, long for (< L *appetere,* equiv. to *ap-* AP-[1] + *petere* to seek) + -ENCE; or < F *appétence*] —**ap′pe·tent,** *adj.*

ap·pe·ten·cy (ap′i tən sē), *n., pl.* **-cies.** appetence. [1620–30; < L *appetentia* a craving for, equiv. to *appetent-* (s. of *appetēns,* prp. of *appetere;* see APPETENCE) + *-ia* -IA; see -ENCY]

ap·pe·tite (ap′i tīt′), *n.* **1.** a desire for food or drink: *I have no appetite for lunch today.* **2.** a desire to satisfy any bodily need or craving. **3.** a desire or liking for something; fondness; taste: *an appetite for power; an appetite for pleasure.* [1275–1325; ME *appetit* (< AF) < L *appetītus* natural desire, equiv. to *appetī-* (var. s. of *appetere;* see APPETENCE) + *-tus* suffix of v. action]

—**Syn. 1–3.** longing, hunger. **1, 3.** thirst. **2.** inclination, wish. **3.** relish, gusto, zest. —**Ant. 1–3.** satiety.

ap·pe·ti·tive (ap′i tī′tiv), *adj.* pertaining to appetite. [1570–80; APPETITE + -IVE]

ap′petitive behav′ior, *Ethology.* activity that increases the likelihood of satisfying a specific need, as restless searching for food by a hungry predator (distinguished from *consummatory behavior*). [1950–55]

ap·pe·tiz·er (ap′i tī′zər), *n.* **1.** a small portion of a food or drink served before or at the beginning of a meal to stimulate the desire to eat. **2.** any small portion that stimulates a desire for more or that indicates more is to follow: *The first game was an appetizer to a great football season.* [1860–65; APPETIZ(ING) + -ER[1]]

ap·pe·tiz·ing (ap′i tī′zing), *adj.* **1.** appealing to or stimulating the appetite; savory. **2.** appealing; tempting. [1645–55; APPET(ITE) + -IZE + -ING[2], as trans. of F *appétissant*] —**ap′pe·tiz′ing·ly,** *adv.*

—**Syn. 1.** See **palatable.**

CONCISE PRONUNCIATION KEY: *act, cāpe, dâre, pärt; set, ēqual; if, īce; ox, ōver, ôrder, oil, bŏŏk, bōōt, out; up, ûrge; child; sing; shoe; thin, that;* zh as in *treasure.* ə = *a* as in *alone, e* as in *system, i* as in *easily, o* as in *gallop, u* as in *circus;* ə as in *fire* (fīər), *hour* (ouər). l and n can serve as syllabic consonants, as in *cradle* (krād′l), and *button* (but′n). See the full key inside the front cover.

Ap·pia (*Fr.* A pyA′), *n.* **A·dolphe** (*Fr.* A dôlf′), 1862–1928, Swiss stage designer and theatrical producer.

Ap′pi·an Way′ (ap′ē ən), an ancient Roman highway extending from Rome to Brundisium (now Brindisi): begun 312 B.C. by Appius Claudius Caecus. ab. 350 mi. (565 km) long.

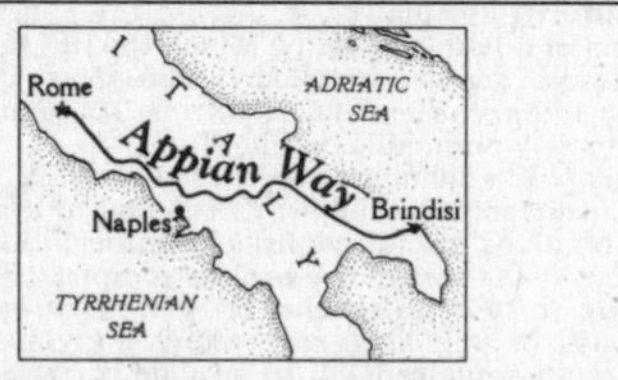

appl., **1.** appeal. **2.** applicable. **3.** applied.

ap·pla·nate (ap′lə nāt′, a plā′nāt), *adj. Biol.* having a horizontally flattened form. [< NL *applānātus* flattened; see AP-[1], PLANATE]

ap·plaud (ə plôd′), *v.i.* **1.** to clap the hands as an expression of approval, appreciation, acclamation, etc.: *They applauded wildly at the end of the opera.* **2.** to express approval; give praise; acclaim. —*v.t.* **3.** to clap the hands so as to show approval, appreciation, etc., of: *to applaud an actor; to applaud a speech.* **4.** to praise or express approval of: *to applaud a person's ambition.* [1530–40; < L *applaudere,* equiv. to *ap-* AP-[1] + *plaudere* to clap the hands] —**ap·plaud′er,** *n.* —**ap·plaud′ing·ly,** *adv.*

ap·plaud·a·ble (ə plô′də bəl), *adj.* worthy of praise or applause; estimable; admirable: *applaudable efforts to save the environment.* [APPLAUD + -ABLE] —**ap·plaud′a·bly,** *adv.*

ap·plause (ə plôz′), *n.* **1.** hand clapping as a demonstration of approval, appreciation, acclamation, or the like. **2.** any positive expression of appreciation or approval; acclamation. [1590–1600; < L *applausus* struck upon, applauded (ptp. of *applaudere*), equiv. to *ap-* AP-[1] + *plaud-* clap + *-tus* ptp. suffix] —**ap·plau·sive** (ə plô′siv, -ziv), *adj.*

ap·ple (ap′əl), *n.* **1.** the usually round, red or yellow, edible fruit of a small tree, *Malus sylvestris,* of the rose family. **2.** the tree, cultivated in most temperate regions. **3.** the fruit of any of certain other species of tree of the same genus. **4.** any of these trees. **5.** any of various other similar fruits, or fruitlike products or plants, as the custard apple, love apple, May apple, or oak apple. **6.** anything resembling an apple in size and shape, as a ball, esp. a baseball. **7.** *Bowling.* an ineffectively bowled ball. **8.** *Slang.* a red capsule containing a barbiturate, esp. secobarbital. [bef. 900; ME *appel,* OE *æppel;* c. OFris, D *appel,* OS *apl, appul,* OHG *apful* (G *Apfel*), Crimean Goth *apel* < Gmc **aplu* (akin to ON *epli* < **aplja*ⁿ); OIr *ubull* (neut.), Welsh *afal,* Breton *aval* < pre-Celtic **ǫblu;* Lith *óbuolas, -ỹs,* Latvian *âbuol(i)s* (with reshaped suffix), OPruss *woble,* perh. Thracian (*din*)*upla,* (*sin*)*upyla* wild pumpkin, OCS (*j*)*ablŭko* (repr. **ablŭ-ko,* neut.) < Balto-Slavic **āblu-.* Cf. AVALON]

ap′ple bee′, *Chiefly New Eng.* a social gathering at which apples are prepared for drying. [1820–30, *Amer.*]

ap′ple blos′som, the flower of the apple tree: the state flower of Arkansas and Michigan. [1815–25]

ap′ple bran′dy, applejack (def. 1). [1770–80, *Amer.*]

ap′ple but′ter, apples stewed to a paste, spiced, sometimes sweetened, and served as a spread or condiment. [1765–75, *Amer.*]

ap·ple·cart (ap′əl kärt′), *n.* **1.** a pushcart used by a vendor of apples. **2.** **upset the** or **someone's applecart,** to ruin plans or arrangements; spoil something: *He was making a fantastic profit until a competitor upset the applecart by cutting prices.* [1780–90; APPLE + CART]

ap′ple dow′dy. See **apple pandowdy.**

ap′ple green′, a clear, light green. [1805–15]

ap′ple grunt′, *Chiefly Eastern Massachusetts.* See **apple pandowdy.** Cf. **grunt** (def. 6).

Ap′ple Isle′, *Australian. Informal.* Tasmania.

ap·ple·jack (ap′əl jak′), *n.* **1.** a brandy distilled from fermented cider; apple brandy. **2.** fermented cider. **3.** an alcoholic beverage consisting of the unfrozen liquid that remains after freezing fermented cider. **4.** *Chiefly North Carolina and Brit. Dial.* an apple turnover. [1810–20, *Amer.;* APPLE + JACK[1]]

ap·ple·knock·er (ap′əl nok′ər), *n. Slang.* **1.** *Northern U.S.* a rustic. **2.** a farm laborer, esp. a fruit picker. [1910–15; APPLE + KNOCKER; from the practice of picking apples by knocking them from trees]

ap′ple mag′got. See **railroad worm.** [1865–70, *Amer.*]

ap′ple of dis′cord, *Class. Myth.* a golden apple inscribed "For the fairest," thrown by Eris, goddess of discord, among the gods. Its award by Paris to Aphrodite caused events that led to the Trojan War. Cf. **Helen, Paris.** [1640–50]

ap′ple of one's eye′, something or someone very precious or dear: *His new baby girl was the apple of his eye.* [orig. in reference to the pupil of one's eye (in OE simply *æppel;* cf. OHG *apful* with similar sense); later misunderstood]

ap′ple of Peru′, a plant, *Nicandra physalodes,* of the nightshade family, having large blue flowers.

CONCISE ETYMOLOGY KEY: <, descended or borrowed from; >, whence; b., blend of, blended; c., cognate with; cf., compare; deriv., derivative; equiv., equivalent; imit., imitative; obl., oblique; r., replacing; s., stem; sp., spelling, spelled; resp., respelling, respelled; trans., translation; ?, origin unknown; *, unattested; ‡, probably earlier than. See the full key inside the front cover.

ap′ple pandow′dy, *Chiefly New Eng.* a deep-dish apple pie or cobbler, usually sweetened with molasses. Also called **pandowdy, apple dowdy.** [1820–30, *Amer.*]

ap·ple-pie (ap′əl pī′), *adj.* pertaining to or embodying traditional American values: *apple-pie virtues; an apple-pie issue that no politician could vote against.*

ap′ple-pie′ bed′, a bed that has been short-sheeted as a joke. Also called **pie bed.** [1770–80]

ap′ple-pie or′der, excellent or perfect order: *Her desk is always in apple-pie order.* [1770–80]

ap·ple-pol·ish (ap′əl pol′ish), *Informal.* —*v.i.* **1.** to curry favor with someone, esp. in an obsequious or flattering manner. —*v.t.* **2.** to curry favor with (someone). [1930–35] —**ap′ple pol′isher.** —**ap′ple-pol′ish·er,** *n.*

ap·ples (ap′əlz), *adj. Australian Slang.* well or fine; under control.

ap·ple·sauce (ap′əl sôs′), *n.* **1.** apples stewed to a soft pulp and sometimes sweetened or spiced with cinnamon. **2.** *Slang.* nonsense; bunk. [1730–40; APPLE + SAUCE]

Ap·ple·seed (ap′əl sēd′), *n.* **Johnny** (*John Chapman*), 1774–1845, American pioneer and orchardist: prototype for character in American folklore.

Ap′ples of the Hesper′ides, *Class. Myth.* the golden apples given to Hera as a wedding gift. They were in the safekeeping of the Hesperides and of the dragon Ladon.

ap′ple suck′er, a small homopterous insect, *Psyllia mali,* originally of Europe, that is a serious pest of apple crops.

Ap·ple·ton (ap′əl tən), *n.* **1.** **Sir Edward Victor,** 1892–1965, British physicist: Nobel prize 1947. **2.** a city in E Wisconsin. 59,032.

Ap′pleton lay′er, *Geophysics.* See under **F layer.** [1930–35; named after Sir E. V. APPLETON]

ap′ple tree′ bor′er, **1.** Also called **flatheaded apple tree borer.** the larva of a metallic wood-boring beetle, *Chrysobothris femorata,* that bores into the wood of apple and other fruit trees. **2.** Also called **roundheaded apple tree borer.** the larva of a long-horned beetle, *Saperda candida,* that bores into the wood of apple and other fruit trees. [1830–40, *Amer.*]

Ap′ple Val′ley, a town in SE Minnesota. 21,818.

ap·pli·ance (ə plī′əns), *n., v.,* **-anced, -anc·ing.** —*n.* **1.** an instrument, apparatus, or device for a particular purpose or use. **2.** a piece of equipment, usually operated electrically, esp. for use in the home or for performance of domestic chores, as a refrigerator, washing machine, or toaster. **3.** the act of applying; application. **4.** *Archaic.* a measure; stratagem. **5.** *Obs.* compliance. —*v.t.* **6.** to equip with appliances: *a fully applianced kitchen.* [1555–65; APPLY + -ANCE]

appli′ance garage′, a kitchen compartment or cabinet designed for housing frequently used small electric appliances. [1985–90]

ap·pli·ca·ble (ap′li kə bəl, ə plik′ə-), *adj.* applying or capable of being applied; relevant; suitable; appropriate: *an applicable rule; a solution that is applicable to the problem.* [1400–50; < L *applic(āre)* to APPLY + -ABLE, or < MF *applicable,* ML *applicābilis;* r. late ME *appliable*] —**ap′pli·ca·bil′i·ty, ap′pli·ca·ble·ness,** *n.* —**ap′pli·ca·bly,** *adv.*
—**Syn.** fitting, proper, germane, pertinent.

ap·pli·cant (ap′li kənt), *n.* a person who applies for or requests something; a candidate: *an applicant for a position.* [1475–85; < L *applicant-* (s. of *applicāns* applying, prp. of *applicāre*). See APPLY, -ANT]

ap·pli·ca·tion (ap′li kā′shən), *n.* **1.** the act of putting to a special use or purpose: *the application of common sense to a problem.* **2.** the special use or purpose to which something is put: *a technology having numerous applications never thought of by its inventors.* **3.** the quality of being usable for a particular purpose or in a special way; relevance: *This has no application to the case.* **4.** the act of requesting. **5.** a written or spoken request or appeal for employment, admission, help, funds, etc.: *to file an application for admission to a university.* **6.** a form to be filled out by an applicant, as for a job or a driver's license. **7.** close attention; persistent effort: *Application to one's studies is necessary.* **8.** an act or instance of spreading on, rubbing in, or bringing into contact: *the application of a compress to a wound; a second application of varnish.* **9.** a salve, ointment, or the like, applied as a soothing or healing agent. **10.** *Computers.* a type of job or problem that lends itself to processing or solution by computer: *Inventory control is a common business application.* [1375–1425; late ME *applicacio(u)n* (< MF) < L *applicātiōn-* (s. of *applicātiō*), equiv. to *applicāt(us)* applied (ptp. of *applicāre* to APPLY) + *-iōn-* -ION]
—**Syn.** **1.** utilization. **3.** aptitude, suitability, pertinence. **4.** solicitation, petition. **7.** assiduity, industry, persistence, perseverance. See **effort.**

applica′tion pro′gram, *Computers.* a program used for a particular application (opposed to *system program*). Also, **applica′tions pro′gram.** Also called **applica′tion soft′ware, applica′tions soft′ware.** —**applica′tion pro′grammer.** —**applica′tion pro′gramming.**

ap·pli·ca·tive (ap′li kā′tiv, ə plik′ə-), *adj.* usable or capable of being used; practical; applicatory. [1630–40; *applicate* (now obs.) to apply (see APPLICATION) + -IVE] —**ap′pli·ca′tive·ly,** *adv.*

ap·pli·ca·tor (ap′li kā′tər), *n.* a simple device, as a rod, spatula, or the like, for applying medication, cosmetics, glue, or any other substance not usually touched with the fingers. [1650–60; *applicate* (see APPLICATIVE) + -OR[2]]

ap·pli·ca·to·ry (ap′li kə tôr′ē, -tōr′ē, ə plik′ə-), *adj.* fitted for application or use; practical. [1530–40; *applicate* (see APPLICATIVE) + -ORY[1]] —**ap′pli·ca·to′ri·ly,** *adv.*

ap·plied (ə plīd′), *adj.* **1.** having a practical purpose c use; derived from or involved with actual phenomen (distinguished from *theoretical,* opposed to *pure*): *applie mathematics; applied science.* **2.** of or pertaining t those arts or crafts that have a primarily utilitaria function, or to the designs and decorations used in thes arts. [1490–1500; APPLY + -ED[2]]

applied′ kinemat′ics, *Mech.* kinematics (def. 2 [‡1960–65]

applied′ linguis′tics, **1.** linguistic theory as applie to such fields as lexicography, psychology, the teachir of reading, the creation of orthographies, and esp. lar guage teaching. **2.** the study of practical applications linguistics, as to telephone engineering, data processin and data retrieval. [1955–60]

ap·pli·qué (ap′li kā′), *n., v.,* **-quéd, -qué·ing.** —*n.* ornamentation, as a cutout design, that is sewn on to c otherwise applied to a piece of material. **2.** work s formed. **3.** a decorative feature, as a sconce, applied to surface. —*v.t.* **4.** to apply as appliqué to. [1835–4 < F: applied, fastened to, ptp. of *appliquer* to APPLY]

ap·ply (ə plī′), *v.,* **-plied, -ply·ing.** —*v.t.* **1.** to mak use of as relevant, suitable, or pertinent: *to apply a th ory to a problem.* **2.** to put to use, esp. for a particula purpose: *to apply pressure to open a door.* **3.** to brin into action; use; employ: *He applied the brakes and skic ded to a stop.* **4.** to use a label or other designatio *Don't apply any such term to me.* **5.** to use for or assig to a specific purpose: *He applied a portion of his sala each week to savings.* **6.** to put into effect: *They applie the rules to new members only.* **7.** to devote or emplc diligently or with close attention: *to apply one's mind a problem; to apply oneself to a task.* **8.** to place in co tact with; lay or spread on: *to apply paint to a wall; apply a bandage to a wound.* **9.** to bring into physic contact with or close proximity to: *to apply a match gunpowder.* **10.** to credit to, as an account: *to apply $ to his account at the store.* —*v.i.* **11.** to be pertinen suitable, or relevant: *The argument applies to the cas The theory doesn't apply.* **12.** to make an application c request; ask: *to apply for a job; to apply for a raise.* **1** to lay or spread on: *The plastic coating is easy to app on any surface.* **14.** to be placed or remain in contac *This paint doesn't apply very easily.* [1350–1400; M *ap(p)lien* < AF, OF *ap(p)lier* < L *applicāre,* equiv. t *ap-* AP-[1] + *plicāre* to fold; see PLY[2]] —**ap·pli′a·ble,** *ad* —**ap·pli′a·ble·ness,** *n.* —**ap·pli′a·bly,** *adv.* —**ap·pli· er,** *n.*
—**Syn.** **3.** utilize. **5.** appropriate, allot, assign, ded cate. **12.** petition, sue, entreat.

appmt., appointment.

ap·pog·gia·tu·ra (ə poj′ə to͝or′ə, -tyo͝or′ə; *It.* äj pôd′jä to͞o′rä), *n. Music.* a note of embellishment pre ceding another note and taking a portion of its tim [1745–55; < It: a propping, equiv. to *appoggiat(o),* ptp. c *appoggiare* to support (see AP-[1], PODI(UM), -ATE[1]) + *-ur* -URE]

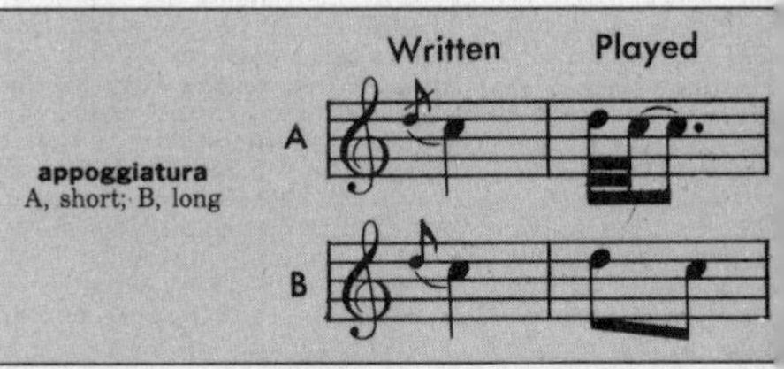

appoggiatura
A, short; B, long

ap·point (ə point′), *v.t.* **1.** to name or assign to a pos tion, an office, or the like; designate: *to appoint a ne treasurer; to appoint a judge to the bench.* **2.** to dete mine by authority or agreement; fix; set: *to appoint time for the meeting.* **3.** *Law.* to designate (a person) take the benefit of an estate created by a deed or wil **4.** to provide with what is necessary; equip; furnis *They appointed the house with all the latest devices.* *Archaic.* to order or establish by decree or command; o dain; constitute: *laws appointed by God.* **6.** *Obs.* to poi at by way of censure. —*v.i.* **7.** *Obs.* to ordain; resolv determine. [1325–75; ME *apointen* < MF *apointe* equiv. to *a-* A-[5] + *pointer* to POINT] —**ap·point′a·bl** *adj.* —**ap·point′er,** *n.*
—**Syn.** **1.** choose, select. **2.** prescribe, establis
—**Ant.** **1.** dismiss, discharge.

ap·point·ed (ə poin′tid), *adj.* **1.** by, through, or as result of an appointment (often in contrast with *electe*) *an appointed official.* **2.** predetermined; arranged; se *They met at the appointed time in the appointed plac* **3.** provided with what is necessary; equipped; furnishe *a beautifully appointed office.* [1525–35; APPOINT -ED[2]]

ap·point·ee (ə poin tē′, ap′oin tē′), *n.* **1.** a perso who is appointed. **2.** a beneficiary under a legal a pointment. [1720–30; APPOINT + -EE, as trans. of F *a pointé*]

ap·poin·tive (ə poin′tiv), *adj.* **1.** pertaining to c filled by appointment: *an appointive office.* **2.** havir the ability or authority to appoint: *appointive powe* [1880–85, *Amer.;* APPOINT + -IVE]

ap·point·ment (ə point′mənt), *n.* **1.** a fixed mutu agreement for a meeting; engagement: *We made an a pointment to meet again.* **2.** a meeting set for a specif time or place: *I'm late for my appointment.* **3.** the act appointing, designating, or placing in office: *to fill a v cancy by appointment.* **4.** an office, position, or the lik to which a person is appointed: *He received his appoin ment as ambassador to Italy.* **5.** Usually, **appoin ments.** equipment, furnishings, or accouterments. **appointments,** accouterments for a soldier or a hors **7.** *Manège.* a horse-show class in which the contesta need not be a member of a hunt but must wear regul

tion hunt livery. Cf. **Corinthian** (def. 9). **8.** *Archaic.* decree; ordinance. [1375–1425; late ME *apoynt(e)ment* < MF *ap(p)ointement.* See APPOINT, -MENT]
—Syn. 1, 2. assignation, rendezvous, tryst, date. **4.** APPOINTMENT, OFFICE, POST, STATION all refer to kinds of duty or employment. APPOINTMENT refers to a position to which one is assigned, as by a high government official. OFFICE often suggests a position of trust or authority. POST is usually restricted to a military or other public position, as of a diplomat, although it may also refer to a teaching position. Both POST and STATION may refer to the place where a person is assigned to work.

Appoint′ment in Samar′ra, a novel (1934) by John O'Hara.

ap•poin•tor (ə poin′tər; ə poin tôr′, ap′oin-), *n. Law.* a person who exercises a power of appointment of property. [1880–85; APPOINT + -OR²]

Ap•po•mat•tox (ap′ə mat′əks), *n.* **1.** a town in central Virginia where Lee surrendered to Grant on April 9, 1865, ending the Civil War. **2.** a river flowing E from E central Virginia to the James River. 137 mi. (220 km) long.

ap•por•tion (ə pôr′shən, ə pōr′-), *v.t.* to distribute or allocate proportionally; divide and assign according to some rule of proportional distribution: *to apportion expenses among the three men.* [1565–75; < MF *apportionner,* equiv. to *ap-* AP-¹ + *portionner* to PORTION] **—ap•por′tion•a•ble,** *adj.* **—ap•por′tion•er,** *n.*

ap•por•tion•ment (ə pôr′shən mənt, ə pōr′-), *n.* **1.** the act of apportioning. **2.** the determination of the number of members of the U.S. House of Representatives according to the proportion of the population of each state to the total population of the U.S. **3.** the apportioning of members of any other legislative body. [1620–30; APPORTION + -MENT]

ap•pose (ə pōz′), *v.t.,* **-posed, -pos•ing. 1.** to place side by side, as two things; place next to; juxtapose. **2.** to put or apply (one thing) to or near to another. [1585–95; by analogy with COMPOSE, PROPOSE, etc. < L *appōnere* to place near, set alongside, equiv. to *ap-* AP-¹ + *pōnere* to place] **—ap•pos′a•bil′i•ty,** *n.* **—ap•pos′a•ble,** *adj.* **—ap•pos′er,** *n.*

ap•po•site (ap′ə zit, ə poz′it), *adj.* suitable; well-adapted; pertinent; relevant; apt: *an apposite answer.* [1615–25; < L *appositus* added to, put near (ptp. of *appōnere*), equiv. to *ap-* AP-¹ + *positus* placed (*posi-* place + *-tus* ptp. suffix)] **—ap′po•site•ly,** *adj.* **—ap′po•site•ness,** *n.*

ap•po•si•tion (ap′ə zish′ən), *n.* **1.** the act of placing together or bringing into proximity; juxtaposition. **2.** the addition or application of one thing to another thing. **3.** *Gram.* a syntactic relation between expressions, usually consecutive, that have the same function and the same relation to other elements in the sentence, the second expression identifying or supplementing the first. In *Washington, our first president,* the phrase *our first president* is in apposition with *Washington.* **4.** *Biol.* growth of a cell wall by the deposition of new particles in layers on the wall. Cf. **intussusception** (def. 2). [1400–50; late ME *apposicioun* < LL *appositiōn-* (s. of *appositiō*) < L *apposit(us)* (see APPOSITE) + *-iōn-* -ION] **—ap′po•si′tion•al,** *adj.* **—ap′po•si′tion•al•ly,** *adv.*

ap•pos•i•tive (ə poz′i tiv), *Gram.* —*n.* **1.** a word or phrase in apposition. —*adj.* **2.** placed in apposition. **3.** (of an adjective or adjectival phrase) directly following the noun it modifies. [1685–95; APPOSIT(ION) + -IVE] **—ap•pos′i•tive•ly,** *adj.*

ap•prais•al (ə prā′zəl), *n.* **1.** the act of estimating or judging the nature or value of something or someone. **2.** an estimate of value, as for sale, assessment, or taxation; valuation. **3.** an estimate or considered opinion of the nature, quality, importance, etc: *the critics' appraisal of pop art; an incorrect appraisal of public opinion.* Also, **ap•praise′ment.** [1810–20; APPRAISE + -AL²]

ap•praise (ə prāz′), *v.t.,* **-praised, -prais•ing. 1.** to estimate the monetary value of; determine the worth of; assess: *We had an expert appraise the house before we bought it.* **2.** to estimate the nature, quality, importance, etc.: *He tried to appraise the poetry of John Updike.* [1400–50; late ME *apraysen* to set a value on, prob. a conflation of *aprisen* to APPRIZE¹ and *preisen* to PRAISE (with sense of PRIZE²)] **—ap•prais′a•ble,** *adj.* **—ap•prais′er,** *n.* **—ap•prais′ing•ly,** *adv.* **—ap•prais′ive,** *adj.*

ap•pre•ci•a•ble (ə prē′shē ə bəl, -shə bəl), *adj.* sufficient to be readily perceived or estimated; considerable: *There is an appreciable difference between socialism and communism.* [1810–20; APPRECI(ATE) + -ABLE] **—ap•pre′ci•a•bly,** *adv.*

ap•pre•ci•ate (ə prē′shē āt′), *v.,* **-at•ed, -at•ing. 1.** to be grateful or thankful for: *They appreciated his thoughtfulness.* —*v.t.* **2.** to value or regard highly; place a high estimate on: *to appreciate good wine.* **3.** to be fully conscious of; be aware of; detect: *to appreciate the dangers of a situation.* **4.** to raise in value. —*v.i.* **5.** to increase in value: *Property values appreciated yearly.* [1645–55; < ML *appreciātus* valued, appraised, LL *appretiātus* (ptp. of *appretiāre*) appraised, equiv. to L *ap-* AP-¹ + *preti(um)* PRICE + *-ātus* -ATE¹] **—ap•pre′ci•at′•ing•ly,** *adv.* **—ap•pre′ci•a′tor,** *n.*
—Syn. 2. APPRECIATE, ESTEEM, PRIZE, VALUE imply holding something in high regard. To APPRECIATE is to exercise wise judgment, delicate perception, and keen insight in realizing the worth of something. To ESTEEM is to feel respect combined with a warm, kindly feeling. To VALUE is to attach importance to a thing because of its worth (material or otherwise). To PRIZE is to value highly and cherish.

ap•pre•ci•a•tion (ə prē′shē ā′shən), *n.* **1.** gratitude; thankful recognition: *They showed their appreciation by giving him a gold watch.* **2.** the act of estimating the qualities of things and giving them their proper value. **3.** clear perception or recognition, esp. of aesthetic quality: *a course in art appreciation.* **4.** an increase or rise in the value of property, goods, etc. **5.** critical notice; evaluation; opinion, as of a situation, person, etc. **6.** a critique or written evaluation, esp. when favorable. [1600–10; earlier *appretiation* < LL *appretiāt(us)* (see APPRECIATE) + -ION, or < F *appréciation*] **—ap•pre′ci•a′tion•al,** *adj.*

ap•pre•cia•tive (ə prē′shə tiv, -shē ə-, -shē ā′-), *adj.* feeling or showing appreciation: *an appreciative audience at the concert.* [1690–1700; APPRECIATE + -IVE] **—ap•pre′cia•tive•ly,** *adv.* **—ap•pre′cia•tive•ness,** *n.*

ap•pre•ci•a•to•ry (ə prē′shē ə tôr′ē, -tōr′ē, -shə-), *adj.* appreciative. [1810–20; APPRECIATE + -ORY¹] **—ap•pre′ci•a•to′ri•ly,** *adv.*

ap•pre•hend (ap′ri hend′), *v.t.* **1.** to take into custody; arrest by legal warrant or authority: *The police apprehended the burglars.* **2.** to grasp the meaning of; understand, esp. intuitively; perceive. **3.** to expect with anxiety, suspicion, or fear; anticipate: *apprehending violence.* —*v.i.* **4.** to understand. **5.** to be apprehensive, suspicious, or fearful; fear. [1350–1400; ME *apprehenden* < L *apprehendere* to grasp, equiv. to *ap-* AP-¹ + *prehendere* to seize (*pre-* PRE- + *-hendere* to grasp)] **—ap′pre•hend′er,** *n.*

ap•pre•hen•si•ble (ap′ri hen′sə bəl), *adj.* capable of being understood. [1625–35; < LL *apprehēnsibilis* < L *apprehēns(us)* grasped (ptp. of *apprehendere*), equiv. to *apprehend-* (see APPREHEND) + *-t(us)* ptp. suffix + *-ibilis* -IBLE] **—ap′pre•hen′si•bil′i•ty,** *n.* **—ap′pre•hen′•si•bly,** *adv.*

ap•pre•hen•sion (ap′ri hen′shən), *n.* **1.** anticipation of adversity or misfortune; suspicion or fear of future trouble or evil. **2.** the faculty or act of apprehending, esp. intuitive understanding; perception on a direct and immediate level. **3.** acceptance of or receptivity to information without passing judgment on its validity, often without complete comprehension. **4.** a view, opinion, or idea on any subject. **5.** the act of arresting; seizure. [1350–1400; ME (< OF) < LL *apprehēnsiōn-* (s. of *apprehēnsiō*), equiv. to *apprehens-* (see APPREHENSIBLE) + *-iōn-* -ION]
—Syn. 1. alarm, worry, uneasiness; suspicion. APPREHENSION, ANXIETY, MISGIVING imply an unsettled and uneasy state of mind. APPREHENSION is an active state of fear, usually of some danger or misfortune: *apprehension before opening a telegram.* ANXIETY is a somewhat prolonged state of apprehensive worry: *anxiety because of a reduced income.* MISGIVING implies a dubious uncertainty or suspicion, as well as uneasiness: *to have misgivings about the investment.* **5.** capture. **—Ant. 1.** composure, tranquillity. **5.** release.

ap•pre•hen•sive (ap′ri hen′siv), *adj.* **1.** uneasy or fearful about something that might happen: *apprehensive for the safety of the mountain climbers.* **2.** quick to learn or understand. **3.** perceptive; discerning (usually fol. by *of*). [1350–1400; ME < ML *apprehēnsīvus.* See APPREHENSIBLE, -IVE] **—ap′pre•hen′sive•ly,** *adv.* **—ap′pre•hen′sive•ness,** *n.*

ap•pren•tice (ə pren′tis), *n., v.,* **-ticed, -tic•ing.** —*n.* **1.** a person who works for another in order to learn a trade: *an apprentice to a plumber.* **2.** *Hist.* a person legally bound through indenture to a master craftsman in order to learn a trade. **3.** a learner; novice; tyro. **4.** *U.S. Navy.* an enlisted person receiving specialized training. **5.** a jockey with less than one year's experience who has won fewer than 40 races. —*v.t.* **6.** to bind to or place with an employer, master craftsman, or the like, for instruction in a trade. —*v.i.* **7.** to serve as an apprentice: *He apprenticed for 14 years under a master silversmith.* [1300–50; ME *ap(p)rentis* < AF, OF *ap(p)rentiz* < VL **apprenditīcius,* equiv. to **apprendit(us)* (for L *apprehēnsus;* see APPREHENSIBLE) + L *-īcius* suffix forming adjs. from ptps., here nominalized] **—ap•pren′tice•ship′,** *n.*

ap•pressed (ə prest′), *adj.* pressed closely against or fitting closely to something. [1785–95; < L *appress(us)* pressed to (ptp. of *apprimere*), equiv. to *ap-* AP-¹ + *pressus* (see PRESS¹) + -ED²]

ap•pres•so•ri•um (ap′re sôr′ē əm, -sōr′-), *n., pl.* **-so•ri•a** (-sôr′ē ə, -sōr′-). *Mycol.* a flattened and thickened tip of a hyphal branch, formed by some parasitic fungi, that facilitates penetration of the host plant. [1895–1900; < NL, equiv. to L *appress(us)* (see APPRESSED) + *-ōrium* -ORIUM]

ap•prise¹ (ə prīz′), *v.t.,* **-prised, -pris•ing.** to give notice to; inform; advise (often fol. by *of*): *to be apprised of the death of an old friend.* Also, **apprize.** [1685–95; < F *appris* taught, informed, ptp. of *apprendre;* see APPREHEND]

ap•prise² (ə prīz′), *v.t.,* **-prised, -pris•ing.** *Obs.* appraise.

ap•prize¹ (ə prīz′), *v.t.,* **-prized, -priz•ing.** *Obs.* appraise. [1400–50; late ME *aprisen* < MF *apris(i)er,* equiv. to *a-* A-⁵ + *prisier* to PRIZE²] **—ap•priz′er,** *n.*

ap•prize² (ə prīz′), *v.t.,* **-prized, -priz•ing.** apprise¹.

ap•pro (ap′rō), *n. Brit. Informal.* (of a purchase) approval: *on appro.* [1870–75; APPR(OVAL) + -O]

ap•proach (ə prōch′), *v.t.* **1.** to come near or nearer to: *The cars slowed down as they approached the intersection.* **2.** to come near to in quality, character, time, or condition; to come within range for comparison: *As a poet he hardly approaches Keats.* **3.** to present, offer, or make a proposal or request to: *to approach the president with a suggestion.* **4.** to begin work on; set about: *to approach a problem.* **5.** to make advances to; address. **6.** to bring near to something. —*v.i.* **7.** to come nearer; draw near: *A storm is approaching.* **8.** to come near in character, time, amount, etc.; approximate. —*n.* **9.** the act of drawing near: *the approach of a train.* **10.** nearness or close approximation: *a fair approach to accuracy.* **11.** any means of access, as a road or ramp: *the approaches to a city.* **12.** the method used or steps taken in setting about a task, problem, etc.: *His approach to any problem was to prepare an outline.* **13.** the course to be followed by an aircraft in approaching for a landing or in joining a traffic pattern: *The plane's approach to the airport was hazardous.* **14.** Sometimes, **approaches.** a presentation, offer, or proposal. **15. approaches,** *Mil.* works for protecting forces in an advance against a fortified position. **16.** Also called **approach shot.** *Golf.* a stroke made after teeing off, by which a player attempts to get the ball onto the putting green. **17.** *Bowling.* **a.** the steps taken and the manner employed in delivering the ball: *He favors a four-step approach.* **b.** the area behind the foul line, from which the ball is delivered. [1275–1325; (v.) ME *a(p)prochen* < AF, OF *a(p)rocher* < LL *adpropiāre,* v. deriv., with *ad-* AD-, of L *propius* nearer (comp. of *prope* near), r. L *appropinquāre;* (n.) late ME *approche,* deriv. of the v.] **—ap•proach′er,** *n.* **—ap•proach′less,** *adj.*
—Syn. 1. near, close with. **3.** sound out. **—Ant. 6.** withdraw.

ap•proach•a•ble (ə prō′chə bəl), *adj.* **1.** capable of being approached; accessible. **2.** (of a person) easy to meet, know, talk with, etc. [1565–75; APPROACH + -ABLE] **—ap•proach′a•bil′i•ty, ap•proach′a•ble•ness,** *n.*

approach′ light′, *Aeron.* one of a series of lights installed along the projected centerline of an airport runway to assist a pilot in aligning the aircraft during the approach to landing at night. [1925–30]

approach′ shot′, 1. *Tennis.* a hard, forcing shot usually made deep into the opponent's court, allowing the player to move in toward the net for an offensive volley. **2.** *Golf.* approach (def. 16). [1875–80]

ap•pro•bate (ap′rə bāt′), *v.t.,* **-bat•ed, -bat•ing.** to approve officially. [1400–50; late ME < L *approbātus* approved (ptp. of *approbāre*), equiv. to *ap-* AP-¹ + *probātus* proved; see PROBATE] **—ap′pro•ba′tor,** *n.*

ap•pro•ba•tion (ap′rə bā′shən), *n.* **1.** approval; commendation. **2.** official approval or sanction. **3.** *Obs.* conclusive proof. [1350–1400; ME (< MF) < L *approbātiōn-* (s. of *approbātiō*). See APPROBATE, -ION]

ap•pro•ba•tive (ap′rə bā′tiv, ə prō′bə-), *adj.* approving; expressing approbation. Also, **ap•pro•ba•to•ry** (ə prō′bə tôr′ē, -tōr′ē). [1605–15; < ML *approbātīvus.* See APPROBATE, -IVE] **—ap′pro•ba′tive•ness,** *n.*

ap•pro•pri•a•ble (ə prō′prē ə bəl), *adj.* capable of being appropriated; liable to be appropriated. [1640–50; APPROPRI(ATE) + -ABLE]

ap•pro•pri•ate (*adj.* ə prō′prē it; *v.* ə prō′prē āt′), *adj., v.,* **-at•ed, -at•ing.** —*adj.* **1.** suitable or fitting for a particular purpose, person, occasion, etc.: *an appropriate example; an appropriate dress.* **2.** belonging to or peculiar to a person; proper: *Each played his appropriate part.* —*v.t.* **3.** to set apart, authorize, or legislate for some specific purpose or use: *The legislature appropriated funds for the university.* **4.** to take to or for oneself; take possession of. **5.** to take without permission or consent; seize; expropriate: *He appropriated the trust funds for himself.* **6.** to steal, esp. to commit petty theft. [1515–25; < LL *appropriātus* made one's own (ptp. of *appropriāre*), equiv. to L *ap-* AP-¹ + *propri(us)* one's own + *-ātus* -ATE¹] **—ap•pro′pri•ate•ly,** *adv.* **—ap•pro′•pri•ate•ness,** *n.* **—ap•pro′pri•a•tive** (ə prō′prē ā′tiv, -ə tiv), *adj.* **—ap•pro′pri•a′tive•ness,** *n.* **—ap•pro′pri•a′tor,** *n.*
—Syn. 1. befitting, apt, meet, felicitous, suited, proper, due, becoming, pertinent. **3.** apportion, allocate, assign. **—Ant. 1.** unsuitable, inept.

ap•pro•pri•a•tion (ə prō′prē ā′shən), *n.* **1.** the act of appropriating. **2.** anything appropriated for a special purpose, esp. money. **3.** an act of a legislature authorizing money to be paid from the treasury for a specified use. **4.** the money thus authorized: *a large appropriation for aid to libraries.* [1325–75; ME (< MF) < LL *appropriātiōn-* (s. of *appropriātiō*). See APPROPRIATE, -ION]

ap•prov•a•ble (ə pro͞o′və bəl), *adj.* **1.** capable of being approved. **2.** worthy of being approved; commendable. [1400–50; late ME. See APPROVE, -ABLE] **—ap•prov′a•bil′i•ty,** *n.* **—ap•prov′a•bly,** *adv.*

ap•prov•al (ə pro͞o′vəl), *n.* **1.** the act of approving; approbation. **2.** formal permission or sanction. **3.** *Philately.* one of a group of selected stamps sent by a dealer to a prospective customer for examination and either purchase or return. **4. on approval,** without obligation to buy unless satisfactory to the customer upon trial or examination and, otherwise, returnable: *We ship merchandise on approval.* [1680–90; APPROVE + -AL²]

ap•prove (ə pro͞ov′), *v.,* **-proved, -prov•ing.** —*v.t.* **1.** to speak or think favorably of; pronounce or consider agreeable or good; judge favorably: *to approve the policies of the administration.* **2.** to consent or agree to: *Father approved our plan to visit Chicago.* **3.** to confirm or sanction formally; ratify: *The Senate promptly approved the bill.* **4.** *Obs.* **a.** to demonstrate; show. **b.** to make good; attest. **c.** to prove by trial. **d.** to convict. —*v.i.* **5.** to speak or consider favorably (sometimes fol. by *of*): *Mother didn't approve of him. The boss wouldn't approve of the plan. He said that he approved.* [1300–50; ME *a(p)proven* < AF, OF *aprover* < L *approbāre,* equiv. to *ap-* AP-¹ + *probāre* to PROVE] **—ap•prov′ed•ly,** *adv.* **—ap•prov′ed•ness,** *n.* **—ap•prov′ing•ly,** *adv.*
—Syn. 1. appreciate, esteem. APPROVE, COMMEND, PRAISE mean to have, and usually to express, a favorable opinion. To APPROVE is to have a very good opinion, expressed or not, of someone or something: *He approved the new plan.* To COMMEND is to speak or write approv-

CONCISE PRONUNCIATION KEY: *act, cāpe, dâre, pärt; set, ēqual; if, īce; ox, ōver, ôrder, oil, bo͝ok, bo͞ot, out; up, ûrge; child; sing; shoe; thin, that;* zh as in *treasure.* ə = *a* as in *alone, e* as in *system, i* as in *easily, o* as in *gallop, u* as in *circus;* ᵊ as in *fire* (fīᵊr), *hour* (ouᵊr). l and n can serve as syllabic consonants, as in *cradle* (krād′l), and *button* (but′n). See the full key inside the front cover.

ingly, often formally and publicly, to congratulate or honor for something done: *to commend a worker for a job well done.* To PRAISE is to speak or write, often in glowing and emotional terms, about one or more persons, actions, plans, etc.: *to praise someone's courage.* **2, 3.** authorize, endorse, validate. **—Ant. 2, 3.** reject.

approved′ school′, (in Britain) a government school for delinquent boys or girls. [1930–35]

ap•prov•er (ə pro͞o′vər), *n.* **1.** a person who approves. **2.** *Old Eng. Law.* an accomplice to a felony who confesses his or her guilt and gives evidence against his or her confederates. [1350–1400; ME; see APPROVE, -ER[1]]

approx., 1. approximate. **2.** approximately.

ap•prox•i•mal (ə prok′sə məl), *adj. Anat.* near or adjacent. [AP-[1] + PROXIMAL]

ap•prox•i•mant (ə prok′sə mənt), *n. Phonet.* **1.** an articulation in which one articulator is close to another, but not sufficiently so to form a stop or a fricative. **2.** a sound characterized by such an articulation, as (w), (y), (r), (l), or a vowel. [APPROXIM(ATE) + -ANT]

ap•prox•i•mate (*adj.* ə prok′sə mit; *v.* ə prok′sə māt′), *adj., v.,* **-mat•ed, -mat•ing.** **—adj. 1.** near or approaching a certain state, condition, goal, or standard. **2.** nearly exact; not perfectly accurate or correct: *The approximate time was 10 o'clock.* **3.** near; close together. **4.** very similar; nearly identical. **—v.t. 5.** to come near to; approach closely to: *to approximate an ideal.* **6.** to estimate: *We approximated the distance at three miles.* **7.** to simulate; imitate closely: *The motions of the stars can be approximated in a planetarium.* **8.** to bring near. **—v.i. 9.** to come near in position, character, amount, etc. [1400–50; late ME < LL *approximātus* drawn near to, approached (ptp. of *approximāre*). See AP-[1], PROXIMATE] **—ap•prox′i•mate•ly,** *adv.*

ap•prox•i•ma•tion (ə prok′sə mā′shən), *n.* **1.** a guess or estimate: *Ninety-three million miles is an approximation of the distance of the earth from the sun.* **2.** nearness in space, position, degree, or relation; proximity; closeness. **3.** *Math., Physics.* a result that is not necessarily exact, but is within the limits of accuracy required for a given purpose. [1400–50; late ME *approximacioun* (< MF) < ML *approximātiōn-,* s. of *approximātiō.* See APPROXIMATE, -ION] **—ap•prox′i•ma′tive,** *adj.*

appt., 1. appoint. **2.** appointed. **3.** appointment.

apptd., appointed.

ap•pulse (ə puls′), *n.* **1.** energetic motion toward a point. **2.** the act of striking against something. **3.** *Astron.* the approach or occurrence of conjunction between two celestial bodies. [1620–30; < L *appulsus* driven to, landed (ptp. of *appellere*), equiv. to *ap-* AP-[1] + *pul-* (var. s. of *pellere* to drive, push) + *-sus,* var. of *-tus* ptp. suffix] **—ap•pul′sive,** *adj.* **—ap•pul′sive•ly,** *adv.*

ap•pur•te•nance (ə pûr′tn əns), *n.* **1.** something subordinate to another, more important thing; adjunct; accessory. **2.** *Law.* a right, privilege, or improvement belonging to and passing with a principal property. **3. appurtenances,** apparatus; instruments. [1350–1400; ME < AF, equiv. to *ap-* AP-[1] + *-purtenance* a belonging; see PURTENANCE]

ap•pur•te•nant (ə pûr′tn ənt), *adj.* **1.** appertaining or belonging; pertaining. **—n. 2.** an appurtenance. [1350–1400; ME (see APPURTENANCE, -ANT); r. ME *apertinent* < LL *appertinent-* (s. of *appertinēns,* prp. of *appertinēre*). See AP-[1], PERTINENT]

APR, annual percentage rate. Also, **A.P.R.**

Apr., April.

a•prax•i•a (ə prak′sē ə, ā prak′-), *n. Pathol.* a disorder of the nervous system, characterized by an inability to perform purposeful movements, but not accompanied by a loss of sensory function or paralysis. [1885–90; < NL; see A-[6], PRAXIS, -IA] **a•prac•tic** (ə prak′tik, ā prak′-), **a•prax′ic,** *adj.*

a•près (ä′prā, ap′rā), *prep.* after; following (used in combination): *après-tennis clothes.* [1955–60; extracted from *après-ski* < F: after-ski(ing)]

A•près-mi•di d'un Faune, L' (*Fr.* lᴀ pʀe mē dē′ dœɴ fōn′). See ***L'Après-midi d'un Faune.***

a•près moi le dé•luge (ᴀ pʀe mwᴀ′ lə dā lʏzh′), *French.* after me, the deluge (attributed to Louis XV, adapted from *après nous le déluge* "after us the deluge," credited to Madame de Pompadour: said in reference to signs of the approaching Revolution).

A•pres•o•line (ə pres′ə lēn′), *Pharm., Trademark.* a brand of hydralazine.

a•près-ski (ä′prā skē′, ap′rā-), *n.* **1.** the period of relaxation that follows skiing: *menus suitable for après-ski.* **—adj. 2.** pertaining to or suitable for such a time: *après-ski clothes; an après-ski party.* [1950–55; < F, equiv. to *après* after + *ski* SKI, skiing]

ap•ri•cot (ap′ri kot′, ā′pri-), *n.* **1.** the downy, yellow, sometimes rosy fruit, somewhat resembling a small peach, of the tree *Prunus armeniaca.* **2.** the tree itself. **3.** a pinkish yellow or yellowish pink. **4.** Also called **wild apricot.** *Chiefly South Midland U.S.* the maypop vine and its fruit; passionfruit. [1545–55; < MF *abricot* < Pg *albricoque* or Sp *albar(i)coque* < Ar *al* the + *barqūq* < MGk < LL *praecoquum,* for L *(persicum) praecox* lit., early-ripening peach, perh. referring to the apricot (see PEACH[1], PRECOCIOUS); r. earlier *abrecock* < Pg or Sp; later *p* for MF *b* perh. < L *praecox*]

A•pril (ā′prəl), *n.* **1.** the fourth month of the year, containing 30 days. *Abbr.:* Apr. **2.** a female given name. [bef. 1150; ME < L *Aprīlis* (adj., as modifying *mēnsis* month), prob. based on Etruscan *apru* APHRODITE < Gk *Aphrodítē;* r. ME *Averil* (< OF *avril* < L), in its turn replacing late OE *aprilis* (< L)]

CONCISE ETYMOLOGY KEY: <, descended or borrowed from; >, whence; b., blend of, blended; c., cognate with; cf., compare; deriv., derivative; equiv., equivalent; imit., imitative; obl., oblique; r., replacing; s., stem; sp., spelling, spelled; resp., respelling, respelled; trans., translation; ?, origin unknown; *, unattested; ‡, probably earlier than. See the full key inside the front cover.

A′pril fool′, 1. the victim of a practical joke or trick on April Fools' Day. **2.** a practical joke or trick played on that day. [1680–90]

A′pril Fools′ Day′, April 1, a day when practical jokes or tricks are played on unsuspecting people. Also called **All Fools' Day.** [1825–35]

a pri•o•ri (ā′ prī ôr′ī, -ōr′ī, ā′ prē ôr′ē, -ōr′ē, ä′ prē-ôr′ē, -ōr′ē), **1.** from a general law to a particular instance; valid independently of observation. Cf. **a posteriori** (def. 1). **2.** existing in the mind prior to and independent of experience, as a faculty or character trait. Cf. **a posteriori** (def. 2). **3.** not based on prior study or examination; nonanalytic: *an a priori judgment.* [1645–55; < L: lit., from the one before. See A-[4], PRIOR] **—a•pri•or•i•ty** (ā′prī ôr′i tē, -or′-), *n.*

a•pri•o•rism (ā′prī ôr′iz əm, -ōr′-, ā′prē-, ä′prē-), *n. Philos.* belief in, or reliance upon, a priori reasoning, arguments, or principles. [1870–75; prob. trans. of D *apriorisme.* See A PRIORI, -ISM] **—a′pri•or′ist,** *n.* **—a•pri•o•ris•tic** (ā prī′ə ris′tik), *adj.* **—a•pri′o•ris′ti•cal•ly,** *adv.*

a•pron (ā′prən), *n.* **1.** a garment covering part of the front of the body and tied at the waist, for protecting the wearer's clothing: *a kitchen apron.* **2.** *Anglican Ch.* a similar garment extending to the knees, worn by bishops, deans, and archdeans. **3.** a metal plate or cover, usually vertical, for a machine, mechanism, artillery piece, etc., for protecting those who operate it. **4.** a continuous conveyor belt for bulk materials, consisting of a chain of steel plates. **5.** (in a lathe) a part of the carriage holding the clutches and gears moving the toolholder. **6.** a paved or hard-packed area abutting an airfield's buildings and hangars, where planes are parked, loaded, or the like. **7.** a broad paved area used for parking cars, as at the end of a driveway. **8.** *Civ. Eng.* **a.** any device for protecting a surface of earth, as a riverbank, from the action of moving water. **b.** a platform to receive the water falling over a dam. **9.** the part of a stage floor in front of the curtain line. **10.** *Furniture.* skirt (def. 6). **11.** the outer border of a green of a golf course. **12.** the part of the floor of a boxing ring that extends outside the ropes. **13.** Also called **skirt.** a flat, broad piece of interior window trim immediately beneath the sill. See diag. under **double-hung. 14.** a strip of metal set into masonry and bent down to cover the upper edge of flashing; counterflashing. **15.** the open part of a pier for loading and unloading vessels. **16.** *Naut.* (in a wooden vessel) a piece reinforcing the stem on the after side and leading down to the deadwood. **17.** *Geol.* a deposit of gravel and sand at the base of a mountain or extending from the edges of a glacier. **18.** the frill of long hairs on the throat and chest of certain long-haired dogs, as the collie. **19.** a structure erected around another structure, as for reinforcement or decoration: *a high fence surrounded by a wire apron buried in the ground.* **—v.t. 20.** to put an apron on; furnish with an apron. **21.** to surround in the manner of an apron: *The inner city is aproned by low-cost housing.* [1275–1325; 1925–30 for def. 6; 1900–05 for def. 8; ME *napron* (by later misconstruing *a napron* as *an apron*) < MF *naperon,* equiv. to *nape* tablecloth (< L *mappa* napkin; cf. MAP) + *-ron* dim. suffix]

a′pron piece′, (in a staircase) a header receiving the ends of rough strings, carriage pieces, and the joists of landings. Also called **pitching piece.** [1855–60]

a′pron strings′, 1. the strings on an apron, used for securing it around one's person. **2. tie to someone's apron strings,** to make or be dependent on or dominated by someone: *He has never married because he's tied to his mother's apron strings.* [1535–45]

ap•ro•pos (ap′rə pō′), *adv.* **1.** fitting; at the right time; to the purpose; opportunely. **2.** *Obs.* by the way. **3. apropos of,** with reference to; in respect or regard to: *apropos of the preceding statement.* **—adj. 4.** opportune; pertinent: *apropos remarks.* [1660–70; < F *à propos* lit., to purpose < L *ad prōpositum.* See AD-, PROPOSITION]

à pro•pos de rien (ᴀ pʀô pō də ʀyaɴ′), *French.* apropos of nothing; with reference to nothing in particular.

a•pro•tic (ā prō′tik), *adj. Chem.* not containing dissociable hydrogen. [A-[6] + PROT(ON) + -IC]

a•prowl (ə proul′), *adj.* moving about in stealthy search; covertly stalking or hunting; prowling (usually used predicatively): *The sudden silence in the jungle gave warning that some huge carnivore was aprowl.* [A-[1] + PROWL]

A.P.S., 1. American Peace Society. **2.** American Philatelic Society. **3.** American Philosophical Society. **4.** American Physical Society. **5.** American Protestant Society.

A.P.S.A., American Political Science Association.

Ap•sa•ras (up′sər əs), *n., pl.* **-sa•ras•es** (-sər ə siz). **1.** *Hindu Myth.* a supernatural female being, either the mistress of a soul in paradise or a succubus. **2.** a representation of such a being. [< Skt]

apse (aps), *n.* **1.** *Archit.* a semicircular or polygonal termination or recess in a building, usually vaulted and used esp. at the end of a choir in a church. See diag. under **basilica. 2.** *Astron.* an apsis. [1815–25; var. of APSIS] **—ap•si•dal** (ap′si dl), *adj.* **—ap′si•dal•ly,** *adv.*

apse′ line′, *Astron.* See **line of apsides.**

ap′sidal mo′tion, *Astron.* the rotation of the major axis of an eccentric orbit in the plane of the orbit. [1955–60]

ap•sid•i•ole (ap sid′ē ōl′), *n.* a small apse, esp. one attached to a larger apse or a transept. [1885–90; < F *absidiole,* equiv. to *abside* APSIS (< ML *absid-,* s. of *absis*) + *-i-* -I- + *-ole* -OLE[1]]

ap•sis (ap′sis), *n., pl.* **-si•des** (-si dēz′). **1.** *Astron.* either of two points in an eccentric orbit, one **(higher apsis)** farthest from the center of attraction, the other **(lower apsis)** nearest to the center of attraction. **2.** *Archit.* an apse. [1595–1605; < L < Gk *hapsís* (felloe of) a wheel, arch, vault, orig., fastening, equiv. to *háp(tein)* to fasten + *-sis* -SIS]

Ap star (ā′pē′), *Astron.* a peculiar A star whose emission spectrum is characterized by abnormally strong lines of certain ionized metals. [1970–75; *A* (star) + *p* (abbr. for PECULIAR STAR)]

Ap•su (äp′so͞o), *n.* an Akkadian god: the consort of Tiamat and the father of the gods.

Ap•syr•tus (ap sûr′təs), *n. Class. Myth.* a son of Aeëtes, killed by his sister Medea, who, while fleeing with Jason, threw pieces of her brother's body into the sea so that her father, in pursuing her, might be delayed while picking them up.

apt (apt), *adj.* **1.** inclined; disposed; given; prone: *too apt to slander others.* **2.** likely: *Am I apt to find him at home?* **3.** unusually intelligent; able to learn quickly and easily: *an apt pupil.* **4.** suited to the purpose or occasion; appropriate: *an apt metaphor; a few apt remarks on world peace.* **5.** *Archaic.* prepared; ready; willing. [1350–1400; ME (< AF) < L *aptus* fastened, fitted, fitting, appropriate, equiv. to *ap-* fasten, attach + *-tus* ptp. suffix] **—apt′ly,** *adv.* **—apt′ness,** *n.*
—Syn. 1. liable. **2.** See **likely. 3.** clever, bright, adaptable; handy, adroit, dexterous, skillful. **4.** fitting, meet, germane, felicitous. APT, PERTINENT, RELEVANT all refer to something suitable or fitting. APT means to the point and particularly appropriate: *an apt comment.* PERTINENT means pertaining to the matter in hand: *a pertinent remark.* RELEVANT means directly related to and important to the subject: *a relevant opinion.*
—Usage. Some usage guides insist that APT followed by an infinitive can or should be used to mean only "inclined, disposed": *He is apt to ignore matters he regards as unimportant.* In fact, APT is standard in all varieties of speech and writing as a synonym for *likely* in contexts that suggest probability without any implication of a natural disposition toward: *Hostilities are apt to break out if the confrontation is not soon resolved. She is apt to arrive almost any time now.* See also **liable.**

apt., *pl.* **apts.** apartment.

ap•ter•al (ap′tər əl), *adj. Archit.* **1.** (of a classical temple) not having a surrounding colonnade; not peripteral. **2.** (of a church) having no aisles. **3.** (of a church façade) revealing no aisles. [1825–35; < Gk *ápter(os)* wingless (*a-* A-[6] + *-pteros* -PTEROUS) + -AL[1]]

ap•te•ri•um (ap tēr′ē əm), *n., pl.* **-te•ri•a** (-tēr′ē ə). *Ornith.* one of the featherless portions of the skin of a bird. Cf. **pteryla.** [1865–70; < NL; see A-[6], PTER-, -IUM] **—ap•te′ri•al,** *adj.*

ap•ter•ous (ap′tər əs), *adj.* **1.** *Zool.* wingless, as some insects. **2.** *Bot.* without membranous expansions, as a stem. [1765–75; < Gk *ápteros* wingless. See A-[6], -PTEROUS]

ap•te•ryg•i•al (ap′tə rij′ē əl), *adj. Zool.* having no wings, fins, or limbs, as snakes and eels. [1900–05; A-[6] + Gk *pteryg-* (s. of *ptéryx* wing) + -IAL]

ap•ter•y•gote (ap ter′i gōt′, ap′tər-), *adj.* belonging or pertaining to the Apterygota, a subclass of primitive wingless insects that undergo little or no metamorphosis. Also, **ap•ter•y•go•tous** (ap ter′i gō′təs). [< NL *Apterygota* name of the subclass, equiv. to *a-* A-[6] + *Pterygota* < Gk, neut. pl. of *pterygōtós* winged, deriv. of *pteryg-* (s. of *ptéryx*) wing]

ap•ter•yx (ap′tə riks), *n.* kiwi (def. 1). [1805–15; < NL: the genus name, equiv. to Gk *a-* A-[6] + *-pteryx,* adj. use of *ptéryx* wing]

ap•ti•tude (ap′ti to͞od′, -tyo͞od′), *n.* **1.** capability; ability; innate or acquired capacity for something; talent: *She has a special aptitude for mathematics.* **2.** readiness or quickness in learning; intelligence: *He was placed in honors classes because of his general aptitude.* **3.** the state or quality of being apt; special fitness. [1400–50; late ME (< MF) < LL *aptitūdō.* See APT, -I-, -TUDE] **—ap′ti•tu′di•nal,** *adj.* **—ap′ti•tu′di•nal•ly,** *adv.*

ap′titude test′, any of various tests given to measure abilities, as manual dexterity, visual acuity, reasoning, or verbal comprehension, and used to assist in the selection of a career. [1920–25]

Ap•u•le•ius (ap′yə lē′əs), *n.* **Lucius,** born A.D. 125?, Roman philosopher and satirist.

A•pu•lia (ə pyo͞ol′yə), *n.* a department in SE Italy. 3,828,322; 7442 sq. mi. (19,275 sq. km). *Cap.:* Bari. Italian, **Puglia. —A•pu′lian,** *adj.*

a pun•ta d'ar•co (ä po͝on′tə där′kō; *It.* ä po͞on′tä dän′kô), *Music.* (of performance of a musical passage for a stringed instrument) with the point of the bow. [< It; see AD-, POINT, ARC]

A•pu•re (ä po͞o′ʀe), *n.* a river flowing E from W Venezuela to the Orinoco. ab. 500 mi. (805 km) long.

A•pu•rí•mac (ä′po͞o ʀē′mäk), *n.* a river flowing NW from S Peru to the Ucayali River. ab. 550 mi. (885 km) long.

A•pus (ā′pəs), *n., gen.* **Ap•o•dis** (ap′ə dis). *Astron.* the Bird of Paradise, a southern constellation between Octans and Triangulum Australe. [< NL < Gk *ápous* name applied to various swallowlike birds, lit., footless, equiv. to *a-* A-[6] + *-pous* -footed, adj. deriv. of *poús* foot; cf. -POD]

apx., appendix.

ap•y•rase (ap′ə rās′, -rāz′), *n. Biochem.* a relatively nonspecific ATPase occurring in plants and molds. [1940–45; *a(denyl)pyr(ophosphat)ase;* see ADENYLPYROPHOSPHATE, -ASE]

a•py•ret•ic (ā′pī ret′ik), *adj. Pathol.* free from fever. [1835–45; A-[6] + PYRETIC]

AQ, *Psychol.* See **achievement quotient.**

aq., water. [< L *aqua*]

A·qa·ba (ä′kə bə, ak′ə-), *n.* **1.** a seaport in SW Jordan, at the N end of the Gulf of Aqaba. 10,000. **2. Gulf of,** an arm of the Red Sea, between Saudi Arabia and Egypt. 100 mi. (160 km) long. Also, **Akaba.**

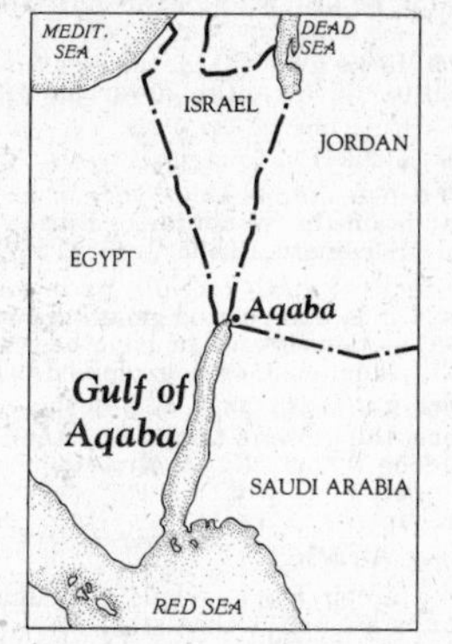

aq. bull., (in prescriptions) boiling water. [< L *aqua bulliēns*]

aq. comm., (in prescriptions) common water. [< L *aqua commūnis*]

aq. dest., (in prescriptions) distilled water. [< L *aqua dēstillāta*]

aq. ferv., (in prescriptions) hot water. [< L *aqua fervēns*]

aq·ua (ak′wə, ä′kwə), *n., pl.* **aq·uae** (ak′wē, ä′kwē), **aq·uas,** *adj.* —*n.* **1.** *Chiefly Pharm.* **a.** water. **b.** a liquid. **c.** a solution, esp. in water. **2.** a light greenish-blue color. —*adj.* **3.** having the color aqua. [1350–1400; ME < L: water]

aqua-, var. of **aqui-.** [prob. orig. attributive use of AQUA, or generalized from words in which it is etymologically the head noun of a phrase, as AQUAMARINE, AQUATINT]

aq′ua am·mo′ni·ae (ə mō′nē ē′), ammonia (def. 2). Also, **aq′ua ammo′nia.** [< NL: lit., water of ammonia]

aq·ua·cade (ak′wə kād′, ä′kwə-), *n.* an elaborate aquatic performance or exhibition consisting of swimming, diving, etc., usually accompanied by music [1935–40; AQUA- + -CADE]

aq·ua·cul·ture (ak′wə kul′chər, ä′kwə-), *n.* the cultivation of aquatic animals and plants, esp. fish, shellfish, and seaweed, in natural or controlled marine or freshwater environments; underwater agriculture. Also, **aquiculture.** [1865–70; AQUA- + (AGRI)CULTURE] —**aq′ua·cul′tur·al,** *adj.* —**aq′ua·cul′tur·ist,** *n.*

Aq·ua·dag (ak′wə dag′, ä′kwə-), *Chem., Trademark.* a colloidal suspension of graphite in water, used as a conductor and lubricant.

aq·uae·ma·na·le (ak′wē mə nā′lē, ä′kwē-), *n., pl.* **-na·li·a** (-nā′lē ə). aquamanile.

aq·ua·farm (ak′wə färm′, ä′kwə-), *n.* a body of water, usually a tract of shallow water along the shore of a bay or inlet, used for aquaculture. [1965–70; AQUA- + FARM] —**aq′ua·farm′ing,** *n.*

aq′ua for′tis, *Chem.* See **nitric acid.** [1595–1605; < L: lit., strong water]

Aq·ua-Lung (ak′wə lung′, ä′kwə-), *Trademark.* a brand of underwater breathing apparatus for a swimmer or skin-diver, consisting of a cylinder of compressed air that is strapped to the back, a flexible tube connecting the cylinder with the swimmer's mouth, and an automatic pressure regulator that controls the flow of air into the lungs.

aq·ua·ma·na·le (ak′wə mə nā′lē, ä′kwə-), *n., pl.* **-na·li·a** (-nā′lē ə). aquamanile.

aq·ua·ma·ni·le (ak′wə mə nī′lē, ä′kwə mə nē′lā), *n., pl.* **-ni·les** (-nī′lēz, -nē′lās), **-nil·i·a** (-nil′ē ə). **1.** a medieval ewer, often made in grotesque animal forms. **2.** *Eccles.* a basin used by a celebrant for washing the hands during the saying of the Mass. Also, **aquaemanale, aquamanale.** [1870–75; < ML, LL: alter. (perh. by assoc. with *manus* hand) of L *aquimināle, aquae mānāle* ewer, equiv. to *aquae,* gen. of *aqua* water + *mānāle* (or *manāle*), perh. deriv. of *mānāre* to flow, pour]

aq·ua·ma·rine (ak′wə mə rēn′, ä′kwə-), *n.* **1.** a transparent, light-blue or greenish-blue variety of beryl, used as a gem. **2.** light blue-green or greenish blue. [1590–1600; < L *aqua marina* sea water (named from its color). See AQUA, MARINE]

aq·ua·naut (ak′wə nôt′, -not′, ä′kwə-), *n.* **1.** an undersea explorer, esp. one who skin-dives from or lives for an extended period of time in a submerged dwelling. **2.** a skin-diver. [1880–85; AQUA- + *-naut,* on the model of AERONAUT, ASTRONAUT, etc.]

aq·ua·plane (ak′wə plān′, ä′kwə-), *n., v.,* **-planed, -plan·ing.** —*n.* **1.** a board that skims over water when towed at high speed by a motorboat, used to carry a rider in aquatic sports. —*v.i.* **2.** to ride an aquaplane. **3.** hydroplane (def. 7). [1910–15; AQUA- + (AIR)PLANE] —**aq′ua·plan′er,** *n.*

aq′ua pu′ra (pyo͝or′ə), pure water. [1930–35; < L]

aq′ua re′gi·a (rē′jē ə), *Chem.* a yellow, fuming liquid composed of one part nitric acid and three to four parts hydrochloric acid: used chiefly to dissolve metals as gold, platinum, or the like. Also called **nitrohydrochloric acid.** [1600–10; < NL: lit., royal water]

aq·ua·relle (ak′wə rel′, ä′kwə-; *Fr.* A KWA REL′), *n., pl.* **-relles** (-relz′; *Fr.* -REL′). **1.** a watercolor. **2.** *Print.* a printed picture that has been colored manually by applying watercolor through stencils, each color requiring a different stencil. [1865–70; < F < It *acquarella* (now obs.) watercolor, equiv. to L *aquār(ius)* of water (see AQUARIUM) + It *-ella* -ELLE] —**aq′ua·rel′list,** *n.*

A·quar·i·an (ə kwâr′ē ən), *adj.* **1.** Also, **Aquarius.** of or pertaining to Aquarius, or to the Age of Aquarius. —*n.* **2.** *Astrol.* a person born under Aquarius, the eleventh sign of the zodiac; an Aquarius. [1965–70; AQUARI(US) + -AN]

Aquar′ian Age′. See **Age of Aquarius.**

Aq·ua·rids (ak′wə rids, ä′kwə-), *n.* (*used with a plural v.*) either of two collections of meteors comprising meteor showers having their apparent origin in the constellation Aquarius and visible either in early May (**Eta Aquarids**) or late July (**Delta Aquarids**). [AQUAR(IUS) + -ID¹]

a·quar·ist (ə kwâr′ist), *n.* a curator, collector, or ichthyologist associated with an aquarium. [1890–95; AQUAR(IUM) + -IST]

a·quar·i·um (ə kwâr′ē əm), *n., pl.* **a·quar·i·ums, a·quar·i·a** (ə kwâr′ē ə). **1.** a glass-sided tank, bowl, or the like, in which fish or other living aquatic animals or plants are kept. **2.** a building or institution in which fish or other aquatic animals or plants are kept for exhibit, study, etc. [1840–50; b. L *aquārius* of or for water (*aqu(a)* water + *-ārius* -ARY) and VIVARIUM; cf. -ARIUM] —**a·quar′i·al,** *adj.*

A·quar·i·us (ə kwâr′ē əs), *n., gen.* **A·quar·i·i** (ə kwâr′ē ī′) for 1, *adj.* —*n.* **1.** *Astron.* the Water Bearer, a zodiacal constellation between Pisces and Capricornus. **2.** *Astrol.* **a.** the eleventh sign of the zodiac: the fixed air sign. See illus. under **zodiac. b.** a person born under this sign, usually between January 20th and February 18th; an Aquarian. —*adj.* **3.** Aquarian.

a·quat·ic (ə kwat′ik, ə kwot′-), *adj.* **1.** of, in, or pertaining to water. **2.** living or growing in water: *aquatic plant life.* **3.** taking place or practiced on or in water: *aquatic sports.* —*n.* **4.** an aquatic plant or animal. **5. aquatics,** sports practiced on or in water. [1480–90; < L *aquāticus,* equiv. to *aqu(a)* water + *-āticus* (see -ATE¹, -IC); r. late ME *aquatyque* < MF < L, as above] —**a·quat′i·cal·ly,** *adv.*

aq·ua·tint (ak′wə tint′, ä′kwə-), *n.* **1.** a process imitating the broad flat tints of ink or wash drawings by etching a microscopic crackle on the copperplate intended for printing. **2.** an etching made by this process. —*v.t., v.i.* **3.** to etch in aquatint. [1775–85; var. of *aqua-tinta* < It *acqua tinta* lit., tinted water. See AQUA, TINT] —**aq′ua·tint′er, aq′ua·tint′ist,** *n.*

aq·ua·tone (ak′wə tōn′, ä′kwə-), *n.* **1.** a lithographic process for printing by offset from a metal plate coated with photosensitized gelatin. **2.** a print so produced. [AQUA- + TONE]

aq·ua·vit (ä′kwə vēt′, ak′wə-), *n.* a dry spirit, esp. of Scandinavia, made from redistilled grain or potato alcohol and usually flavored with caraway seeds. Also, **akvavit.** [1885–90; < Dan, Sw, Norw *akvavit, aquavit* < L *aqua vit(ae)* water of life]

aq′ua vi′tae (vī′tē, vē′tē), **1.** alcohol. **2.** spirituous liquor, as brandy or whiskey. [1375–1425; late ME *aqua vite* < L: water of life; cf. AQUAVIT, WHISKEY]

aq·ue·duct (ak′wi dukt′), *n.* **1.** *Civ. Eng.* **a.** a conduit or artificial channel for conducting water from a distance, usually by means of gravity. **b.** a bridgelike structure that carries a water conduit or canal across a valley or over a river. **2.** *Anat.* a canal or passage through which liquids pass. [< ML *aquēductus* < L *aquae ductus* a drawing off of water. See AQUA, DUCT]

aq′ueduct of Syl′vi·us (sil′vē əs), *Anat.* a canal in the midbrain, connecting the third and fourth ventricles of the brain. [named after *Sylvius,* Latinized name of Jacques Dubois (d. 1555), French anatomist]

a·que·ous (ā′kwē əs, ak′wē-), *adj.* **1.** of, like, or containing water; watery: *an aqueous solution.* **2.** (of rocks or sediments) formed of matter deposited in or by water. [1635–45; AQU(A) + -EOUS] —**a′que·ous·ly,** *adv.* —**a′que·ous·ness,** *n.*

a′queous ammo′nia, ammonia (def. 2).

a′queous hu′mor, *Anat.* the limpid watery fluid that fills the space between the cornea and the crystalline lens in the eye. [1635–45]

aqui-, a combining form meaning "water," used in the formation of compound words: *aquiclude; aquiculture; aquifer.* Also, **aqua-.** [< L, comb. form of *aqua* water]

aq·ui·clude (ak′wi klo͞od′), *n.* any geological formation that absorbs and holds water but does not transmit it at a sufficient rate to supply springs, wells, etc. [AQUI- + *-clude* < L *clūdere,* var. of *claudere* to CLOSE]

aq·ui·cul·ture (ak′wi kul′chər), *n.* **1.** hydroponics. **2.** aquaculture. [1865–70; AQUI- + (AGRI)CULTURE] —**aq′ui·cul′tur·al,** *adj.* —**aq′ui·cul′tur·ist,** *n.*

aq·ui·fer (ak′wə fər), *n.* any geological formation containing or conducting ground water, esp. one that supplies the water for wells, springs, etc. [1900–05; prob. < F *aquifère* (adj.); see AQUI-, -FER]

A·quil·a (ak′wə lə, ə kwil′ə), *n., gen.* **A·quil·ae** (ə kwil′ē, ak′wə lē). the Eagle, a northern constellation south of Cygnus, containing the bright star Altair.

Aq·ui·la (ä′kwə lə; *It.* ä′kwē lä), *n.* a city in central Italy. 300,950. Also called **L'Aquila, A·qui·la de·gli A·bruz·zi** (ä′kwē lä de′lyē ä bro͞ot′tsē).

aq·ui·le·gi·a (ak′wə lē′jē ə, ä′kwə-), *n.* any plant belonging to the genus *Aquilegia,* of the buttercup family, comprising the columbines. [1570–80; < NL, ML, var. of *aquilēia* columbine]

A·qui·le·ia (ä′kwē le′yä), *n.* an ancient Roman city at the northern end of the Adriatic: founded in 181 B.C.; destroyed by Attila in A.D. 452.

aq·ui·line (ak′wə lin′, -lin), *adj.* **1.** (of the nose) shaped like an eagle's beak; hooked. **2.** of or like the eagle. [1640–50; (< F) < L *aquilīnus.* See AQUILA, -INE¹] —**aq·ui·lin·i·ty** (ak′wə lin′i tē), *n.*

Aq·ui·lo (ak′wə lō′), *n.* the ancient Roman personification of the north wind. Cf. **Boreas.**

A·qui·nas (ə kwī′nəs), *n.* **Saint Thomas** (*"the Angelic Doctor"*), 1225?–74, Italian scholastic philosopher: a major theologian of the Roman Catholic Church. —**A·qui′nist,** *n.*

A·qui·no (ä kē′nō), *n.* **Co·ra·zon C.** (kôr′ə zon′, kor′-), born 1933, Philippine political leader: president 1986–92.

a·quí se ha·bla es·pa·ñol (ä kē′ se ä′blä es′pä-nyôl′), *Spanish.* Spanish is spoken here.

Aq·ui·taine (ak′wi tān′; *Fr.* A kē ten′), *n.* a lowland region in SW France, formerly an ancient Roman province and medieval duchy. Latin, **Aq·ui·ta·ni·a** (ak′wi-tā′nē ə).

a·quiv·er (ə kwiv′ər), *adj.* in a state of trepidation or vibrant agitation; trembling; quivering (usually used predicatively): *The bamboo thicket was aquiver with small birds and insects. The exciting news set me aquiver.* [1880–85; A-¹ + QUIVER¹]

a quo (ä kwō′; *Eng.* ā kwō′), *Latin.* from which; following from: used as a point of departure, as for an idea or plan.

ar-, var. of **ad-** before *r: arrear.*

-ar¹, var. of the adjective-forming suffix **-al¹,** joined to words in which an *l* precedes the suffix: *circular; lunar; singular.* [< L *-āris;* r. ME *-er* < AF, OF < L *-āris*]

-ar², var. of **-er²,** often under the influence of a spelling with *-ar-* in a cognate Latin noun: *burglar; cellar; collar; mortar; poplar; scholar; vicar; vinegar.*

-ar³, var. of **-er¹** on the model of **-ar²,** used in the formation of nouns of agency: *liar; beggar.*

AR, **1.** annual return. **2.** Arkansas (approved esp. for use with zip code). **3.** Army Regulation; Army Regulations.

Ar, Arabic.

Ar, *Symbol, Chem.* argon.

Ar., **1.** Arabic. **2.** Aramaic.

ar., **1.** arrival. **2.** arrive; arrives.

A/R, **1.** account receivable. **2.** accounts receivable. Also, **a/r**

A.R., **1.** annual return. **2.** Army Regulation; Army Regulations.

a.r., *Insurance.* all risks.

A·ra (â′rə, âr′ə), *n., gen.* **A·rae** (â′rē, âr′ē). *Astron.* the Altar, a southern constellation between Triangulum Australe and Scorpius. [< L *āra* altar]

ARA, Agricultural Research Administration.

A.R.A., **1.** American Railway Association. **2.** Associate of the Royal Academy.

Ar·ab (ar′əb), *n.* **1.** a member of a Semitic people inhabiting Arabia and other countries of the Middle East. **2.** a member of any Arabic-speaking people. **3.** See **Arabian horse. 4.** *Sometimes Offensive.* a street peddler (esp. in Baltimore). **5.** See **street Arab.** —*adj.* **6.** of or pertaining to Arabs. **7.** Arabian. **8.** Arabic. [1625–35; back formation from L *Arabs* (taken as pl.) < Gk *Áraps* Arabian, an Arabian or Arab]

Arab., **1.** Arabia. **2.** Arabian. **3.** Arabic.

Ar·ab-A·mer·i·can (ar′əb ə mer′i kən), *n.* **1.** a citizen or resident of the U.S. of Arab birth or descent. —*adj.* **2.** of or pertaining to an Arab-American.

ar·a·ban (ar′ə ban′), *n. Biochem.* a pentosan, found chiefly in vegetable gums, that yields arabinose upon hydrolysis. [1890–95; ARAB(INOSE) + *-an;* see -ANE]

Ar·a·bel (ar′ə bel′), *n.* a female given name.

ar·a·besque (ar′ə besk′), *n.* **1.** *Fine Arts.* a sinuous, spiraling, undulating, or serpentine line or linear motif. **2.** a pose in ballet in which the dancer stands on one leg with one arm extended in front and the other leg and arm extended behind. **3.** a short, fanciful musical piece, typically for piano. **4.** any ornament or ornamental object, as a rug or mosaic, in which flowers, foliage, fruits, vases, animals, and figures are represented in a fancifully combined pattern. —*adj.* **5.** decorated with or characterized by arabesques: *arabesque design.* [1605–15; < F < It *arabesco* ornament in Islamic style, lit., Arabian, equiv. to *arab(o)* ARAB + *-esco* -ESQUE] —**ar′a·besque′ly,** *adv.*

A·ra·bi·a (ə rā′bē ə), *n.* a peninsula in SW Asia, including Saudi Arabia, Yemen, Oman, the United Arab Emirates, Qatar, and Kuwait: divided in ancient times into Arabia Deserta, Arabia Petraea, and Arabia Felix.

CONCISE PRONUNCIATION KEY: act, cāpe, dâre, pärt; set, ēqual; if, īce; ox, ōver, ôrder, oil, bo͝ok, bo͞ot, out; up, ûrge; child; sing; shoe; thin, *that;* zh as in *treasure.* ə = *a* as in *alone, e* as in *system, i* as in *easily, o* as in *gallop, u* as in *circus;* ᵊ as in *fire* (fīᵊr), *hour* (ouᵊr). l and n can serve as syllabic consonants, as in *cradle* (krād′l), and *button* (but′n). See the full key inside the front cover.

17,800,000; ab. 1,000,000 sq. mi. (2,600,000 sq. km). Also called **Ara′bian Penin′sula.**

Ara′bia De·ser′ta (di zûr′tə), an ancient division of Arabia, in the N part between Syria and Mesopotamia.

Ara′bia Fe′lix (fē′liks), an ancient division of Arabia, in the S part: sometimes restricted to Yemen.

A·ra·bi·an (ə rā′bē ən), *adj.* **1.** of or pertaining to Arabia or its inhabitants. **2.** Arab. **3.** Arabic. —*n.* **4.** an inhabitant of Arabia. **5.** an Arab. **6.** See **Arabian horse.** [1350–1400; ARABI(A) + -AN]

Ara′bian cam′el, the dromedary.

Ara′bian cof′fee. See **arabica coffee.**

Ara′bian Des′ert, 1. a desert in Egypt between the Nile valley and the Red Sea. ab. 80,000 sq. mi. (207,000 sq. km). **2.** the desert region in the N part of the Arabian peninsula.

Ara′bian Gulf′. See **Persian Gulf.**

Ara′bian horse′, one of a breed of horses, raised originally in Arabia and adjacent countries, noted for intelligence, grace, and speed. Also called **Arab, Arabian.** [1730–40]

Ara′bian jas′mine, a climbing shrub, *Jasminum sambac,* of India, having hairy branches and very fragrant white flowers that turn purple with age, used in making jasmine tea; sampaguita.

Ara′bian Nights′ Entertain′ments, The, a collection of Eastern folk tales derived in part from Indian and Persian sources and dating from the 10th century A.D. Also called ***The Thousand and One Nights.***

Ara′bian Sea′, the NW arm of the Indian Ocean between India and Arabia.

Ara′bia Pe·trae′a (pi trē′ə), an ancient division of Arabia, in the NW part.

Ar·a·bic (ar′ə bik), *adj.* **1.** of, belonging to, or derived from the language or literature of the Arabs. **2.** noting, pertaining to, or in the alphabetical script used for the writing of Arabic probably since about the fourth century A.D., and adopted with modifications by Persian, Urdu, and many other languages. A distinguishing feature of this script is the fact that etymologically short vowels are not normally represented. **3.** Arab. **4.** Arabian. —*n.* **5.** a Semitic language that developed out of the language of the Arabians of the time of Muhammad, now spoken in countries of the Middle East and North Africa. *Abbr.:* Ar **6.** the standard literary and classical language as established by the Koran. [1350–1400; ME *arabik* < L *Arabicus* Arabian, equiv. to *Arab(ia)* + *-icus* -IC]

a·rab′i·ca cof′fee (ə rab′i kə), **1.** a tree, *Coffea arabica,* of the madder family, the principal species of coffee cultivated in Latin America and the chief coffee tree of commerce. **2.** the seeds of this tree. **3.** the beverage made from the ground seeds. Cf. **robusta coffee.** Also, **Arab′ica cof′fee.** Also called **Arabian coffee.** [< NL *arabica* the species name, L: fem of *Arabicus* ARABIC]

A·rab·i·cize (ə rab′ə sīz′), *v.t., v.i.,* **-cized, -ciz·ing. 1.** (of a language or a linguistic feature) to make or become Arabic in form. **2.** Arabize. Also, *esp. Brit.,* **A·rab′·i·cise′.** [1870–75; ARABIC + -IZE] —**A·rab′i·ci·za′·tion,** *n.*

Ar′abic nu′merals, the characters 0, 1, 2, 3, 4, 5, 6, 7, 8, 9, in general European use since the 12th century. See table under **Roman numerals.** Also, **Ar′abic fig′ures.** [1840–50]

a·rab·i·nose (ə rab′ə nōs′, ar′ə bə-), *n. Chem.* a white, crystalline, water-soluble solid, $C_5H_{10}O_5$, obtained from plant gums or made synthetically from glucose, used chiefly as a culture medium in bacteriology. Also called **pectin sugar, pectinose.** [1880–85; *arabin* the soluble essence of certain gums ((GUM) ARAB(IC) + -IN[2]) + -OSE[2]] —**a·rab·i·nos·ic** (ə rab′ə nos′ik, ar′ə bə-), *adj.*

ar·a·bin·o·side (ar′ə bin′ə sīd′, ə rab′ə nə-), *n. Biochem.* a glycoside of arabinose, esp. any of those used in antiviral therapy as structural analogs of ribonucleosides. [1925–30; ARABINOSE + -IDE]

ar·a·bis (ar′ə bis), *n.* any plant of the genus *Arabis,* including the rock cresses. [1570–80; < NL < Gk *árabis* (s. *arabid-*) Arabian mustard (deriv. with *arab-,* as in *Arabía* Arabia, *Áraps* Arab, etc.); prob. applied to the plant because it grows in rocky or sandy soil]

Ar·ab·ist (ar′ə bist), *n.* **1.** a person who specializes in or studies the Arabic language or Arab culture. **2.** a supporter of Arab interests, esp. in international affairs. [1745–55; ARAB + -IST]

Ar·ab·ize (ar′ə bīz′), *v.t., v.i.,* **-ized, -iz·ing.** to place or come under Arab influence or domination: *Middle Eastern countries began to Arabize their oil industries.* Also, *esp. Brit.,* **Ar′ab·ise′.** [1880–85; ARAB + -IZE] —**Ar′ab·i·za′tion,** *n.*

ar·a·ble (ar′ə bəl), *adj.* **1.** capable of producing crops; suitable for farming; suited to the plow and for tillage: *arable land; arable soil.* —*n.* **2.** land that can be or is cultivated. [1375–1425; < L *arābilis,* equiv. to *arā(re)* to plow + *-bilis* -BLE; r. late ME *erable,* equiv. to *er(en)* to plow (OE *erian*) + *-able* -ABLE] —**ar′a·bil′i·ty,** *n.*

Ar′ab League′, a confederation formed in 1945 by Egypt, Iraq, Lebanon, Saudi Arabia, Syria, Jordan, and Yemen and later joined by Libya, Sudan, Morocco, Tunisia, Kuwait, Algeria, Bahrain, Mauritania, Oman, Qatar, Somalia, and the United Arab Emirates.

Ar′ab Le′gion, a police force (1920–56) under British supervision, responsible for keeping order among desert tribesmen in Trans-Jordan.

CONCISE ETYMOLOGY KEY: <, descended or borrowed from; >, whence; b., blend of, blended; c., cognate with; cf., compare; deriv., derivative; equiv., equivalent; imit., imitative; obl., oblique; r., replacing; s., stem; sp., spelling, spelled; resp., respelling, respelled; trans., translation; ?, origin unknown; *, unattested; ‡, probably earlier than. See the full key inside the front cover.

Ar′ab Repub′lic of E′gypt, Egypt (def. 1).

Ar·a·by (ar′ə bē), *n. Literary.* Arabia. [1125–75; ME *Arabye* < OF *Arabie* < L *Arabia*]

ar·a-C (ar′ə sē′), *n. Pharm.* cytarabine. [perh. as abbrev. of the alternate name *aracytidine,* appar. a coinage based on the chemical name *beta-cytosine arabinoside;* see CYTOSINE, ARABINOSIDE]

A·ra·ca·ju (ä′Rə kä′zhōō), *n.* a seaport in E Brazil. 299,622.

a·ra·ca·ri (är′ə sär′ē), *n.* any of several small toucans of the genus *Pteroglossus,* having strongly serrate bills and yellow underparts marked with black and red. [< Pg *araçari* < Tupi *arasári*]

A·ra·ca·tu·ba (ä′Rə sə tōō′bə), *n.* a city in SE Brazil. 95,946.

a·ra·ceous (ə rā′shəs), *adj. Bot.* belonging to the plant family Araceae. Cf. **arum family.** [< NL *Arace(ae)* (see ARUM, -ACEAE) + -OUS]

ar·a·chid·ic (ar′ə kid′ik), *adj. Chem.* of or derived from arachidic acid. Also, **a·rach·ic** (ə rak′ik). [1850–55; *arachid-* (< NL, s. of *Arachis* the groundnut genus, irreg. < Gk *arakís,* dim. of *árakos* a leguminous plant, prob. *Lathyrus arnuus*) + -IC]

ar′achid′ic ac′id, *Chem.* a white, crystalline, water-insoluble solid, $C_{20}H_{40}O_2$, obtained from peanut oil: used chiefly in the manufacture of lubricants, plastics, and waxes. [1870–75]

ar′a·chi·don′ic ac′id (ar′ə ki don′ik, ar′-), *Biochem.* an essential fatty acid, $C_{20}H_{32}O_2$, found in the lipids of most tissues, that is a precursor in the synthesis of prostaglandins, prostacyclins, and related effectors. [1910–15; ARACHID(IC) + -ONIC]

ar′a·chis oil′ (ar′ə kis). See **peanut oil.** [1885–90]

A·rach·ne (ə rak′nē), *n. Class. Myth.* a Lydian woman who challenged Athena to a weaving contest and was changed into a spider for her presumption.

a·rach·nid (ə rak′nid), *n.* **1.** any wingless, carnivorous arthropod of the class Arachnida, including spiders, scorpions, mites, ticks, and daddy-longlegs, having a body divided into two parts, the cephalothorax and the abdomen, and having eight appendages and no antennae. Cf. **insect.** —*adj.* **2.** belonging or pertaining to the arachnids. [1865–70; < NL *Arachnida* < Gk *aráchn(ē)* spider, spider's web + NL *-ida* -IDA] —**a·rach·ni·dan** (ə rak′ni dən), *adj., n.*

a·rach·noid (ə rak′noid), *adj.* **1.** resembling a spider's web. **2.** of or belonging to the arachnids. **3.** *Anat.* of or pertaining to the arachnoid membrane. **4.** *Bot.* formed of or covered with long, delicate hairs or fibers. —*n.* **5.** an arachnid. **6.** *Anat.* the serous membrane forming the middle of the three coverings of the brain and spinal cord. Cf. **dura mater, meninges, pia mater.** [1745–55; < NL *arachnoides* < Gk *arachnoeidḗs* cobweblike. See ARACHNID, -OID]

A·rad (ä räd′), *n.* **1.** a city in W Rumania, on the Mures River. 171,110. **2.** a town in southern Israel: site of ancient Canaanite town. 11,600.

a·rae·o·style (ə rē′ə stīl′), *adj. Archit.* having an intercolumniation of four diameters. See illus. under **intercolumniation.** Also, **areostyle.** [1555–65; < L *araeostylus* < Gk *araióstylos* with few columns, equiv. to *araió(s)* thin, few + *-stylos* -STYLE[2]]

a·rae·o·sys·tyle (ə rē′ə sis′tīl), *adj. Archit.* having an intercolumniation alternately of two and four diameters. Also, **areosystyle.** [1825–35; AERO(STYLE) + SYSTYLE]

Ar·a·fat (ar′ə fat′, är′ə fät′), *n.* **Ya·sir** (yä′sər, -sir, yas′ər), born 1929, Palestinian leader: head of the Palestine Liberation Organization.

ʿAr·a·fat (är′ə fat′, ar′ə fat′), *n.* a hill 15 mi. (24 km) southeast of Mecca, in Saudi Arabia: site of Muslim pilgrimages.

A′ra·fu′ra Sea′ (är′ə fŏŏr′ə, är′ə-), a part of the Pacific between N Australia and SW New Guinea.

Ar·a·gats (ar′ə gats′; *Russ.* u Rʊ gäts′), *n.* **Mount,** an extinct volcano in NW Armenia. 13,435 ft. (4095 m). Also called **Mount Alagez.** Turkish, **Alagöz.**

A·ra′go man′ (ə rä′gō, ə rag′ō, ar′ə gō′), the skeletal remains of *Homo erectus* of the middle Pleistocene Epoch found in a cave in the French Pyrenees. Also called **Tautauvel man.** [after the name of the cave (F *La Caune de l'Arago*), near the village of Tautavel (Pyrénées-Orientales)]

A·ra·gon (A RA gôN′ *for 1;* ar′ə gon′ *for 2*), *n.* **1. Louis** (lwē), 1897–1982, French novelist, poet, and journalist. **2.** Spanish, **A·ra·gón** (ä′rä gôn′), a region in NE Spain: formerly a kingdom; later a province. 18,181 sq. mi. (47,089 sq. km).

Ar·a·go·nese (ar′ə gə nēz′, -nēs′), *adj., n., pl.* **-nese.** —*adj.* **1.** of Aragon, its people, or their language. —*n.* **2.** a native or inhabitant of Aragon. **3.** the dialect of Spanish spoken in Aragon. [1505–15; ARAGON (the province) + -ESE]

a·rag·o·nite (ə rag′ə nīt′, ar′ə gə-), *n.* a mineral, orthorhombic calcium carbonate, $CaCO_3$, chemically identical with calcite but differing in crystallization and in having a higher specific gravity and less marked cleavage. [1795–1805; named after ARAGON (the province, where first found) + -ITE[1]]

A·ra·gua·rí (ä′Rə gwə Rē′), *n.* a city in central Brazil. 59,798.

A·ra·gua·ya (ä′Rə gwä′yä), *n.* a river flowing N from central Brazil to the Tocantins River. ab. 1100 mi. (1770 km) long.

ar·ak (ar′ək, ə rak′), *n.* arrack.

A·ra·kan Yo·ma (är′ə kän′ yō′mə, ar′ə kan′), a mountain range on the W border of Burma (Myanmar). Highest peak, Saramati, 12,633 ft. (3851 m).

a·ra·li·a (ə rā′lē ə, ə räl′yə), *n.* any of various plants of the genus *Aralia* and related genera, several of which are cultivated as houseplants or have been used medicinally. [< NL (Linnaeus), of unexplained orig.]

a·ra·li·a·ceous (ə rā′lē ā′shəs), *adj. Bot.* belonging to the Araliaceae, the ginseng family of plants. Cf. **ginseng family.** [1865–70; < NL *Araliace(ae)* (see ARALIA, -ACEAE) + -OUS]

A·ral·lu (ä rä′lōō), *n.* the ancient Babylonian world of the dead. Also, **A·ra′lu.**

Ar′al Sea′ (ar′əl; *Russ.* u Räl′), an inland sea between Kazakhstan and Uzbekistan, E of the Caspian Sea. 26,166 sq. mi. (67,770 sq. km). Also called **Lake Aral.** Russian, **A·ral·sko·ye Mo·re** (u Räl′skə yə mô′Ryə).

A·ram (ā′ram, âr′əm), *n.* Biblical name of ancient Syria. See map under **Philistia.**

Aram, Aramaic (def. 1).

Aram., Aramaic.

-arama, var. of **-orama,** occurring as the final element in compounds when the first element is a monosyllable, used so that the entire word maintains the same number of syllables as **panorama:** *foodarama; dancearama,*

Ar·a·ma·ic (ar′ə mā′ik), *n.* **1.** Also, **Aramean, Aramaean.** a northwest Semitic language that from c300 B.C.–A.D. 650 was a lingua franca for nearly all of SW Asia and was the everyday speech of Syria, Mesopotamia, and Palestine. *Abbr.:* Aram Cf. **Biblical Aramaic.** —*adj.* **2.** pertaining to Aram, or to the languages spoken there. **3.** noting or pertaining to the alphabetical, or perhaps syllabic, script used for the writing of Aramaic from about the ninth century B.C. and from which were derived the Hebrew, Arabic, Armenian, Pahlavi, Uighur, and many other scripts, probably including Brahmi. [1825–35; < Gk *aramaî(os)* of ARAM + -IC, modeled on *Hebraic*]

A·ram·bu·ru (ä′Räm bōō′Rōō), *n.* **Pe·dro E·u·ge·nio** (pe′thRô e′ōō he′nyô), 1903–70, president of Argentina 1955–58.

Ar·a·me·an (ar′ə mē′ən), *n.* **1.** a Semite of the division associated with Aram. **2.** Aramaic (def. 1). Also, **Ar′a·mae′an.** [1825–35; < L *Aramae(us)* (< Gk *aramaîos* of ARAM) + -AN]

ar·a·mid (ar′ə mid), *n. Chem.* any of a class of synthetic aromatic long-chain polyamides capable of extrusion into fibers having resistance to high temperatures and great strength. [prob. AR(OMATIC) + *-amid,* resp. of AMIDE]

A·ran·da (ə ran′də, ə rän′-), *n., pl.* **-das,** (*esp. collectively*) **-da** for 1. **1.** a member of an Australian aboriginal people living in the vicinity of Alice Springs, Northern Territory. **2.** the language of the Aranda. Also, **Arunta.**

a·ra·ne·id (ə rā′nē id), *n.* a member of the order Araneae (Araneida), comprising the spiders. [1895–1900; < NL *Araneida,* equiv. to *Arane(a)* a genus (L *arānea;* see ARANEOSE) + *-ida* -IDA]

a·ra·ne·ose (ə rā′nē ōs′), *adj.* arachnoid, esp. as a plant. Also, **a·ra·ne·ous** (ə rā′nē əs). [1875–80; < L *araneōsus* pertaining to a spider, equiv. to *arāne(a)* spider, spiderweb, cobweb (akin to Gk *aráchnē* spider) + *-ōsus* -OSE[1]]

A·ra·nha (ä Rä′nyä), *n.* **Os·wal·do** (ôs wäl′dô), 1894–1960, Brazilian politician.

Ar′an Is′lands (ar′ən), a group of three islands off the W central coast of Ireland. ab. 18 sq. mi. (47 sq. km).

A·ran·rhod (ä Rän′Rôd), *n. Welsh Legend.* the daughter of the goddess Dôn and the mother of Lleu Llaw Gyffes.

A·ran·ya·ka (ä run′yə kə), *n. Hinduism.* one of a class of the Vedic texts that, together with the Upanishads, make up the closing portions of the Brahmanas. [< Skt: a forest book]

A·rap·a·ho (ə rap′ə hō′), *n., pl.* **-hos,** (*esp. collectively*) **-ho. 1.** a member of a tribe of North American Indians of Algonquian speech stock, once dwelling in the Colorado plains and now in Oklahoma and Wyoming. **2.** an Algonquian language, the language of the Arapaho.

A·rap·a·hoe (ə rap′ə hō′), *n., pl.* **-hoes,** (*esp. collectively*) **-hoe.** Arapaho.

ar·a·pai·ma (ar′ə pī′mə), *n.* a large freshwater fish, *Arapaima gigas,* of Brazil and Guiana, reputed to reach a length of 15 ft. (4.5 m) and a weight of 500 lb. (225 kg). [1830–40; < Pg < Tupi]

Ar·a·pesh (är′ə pesh′), *n., pl.* **-pesh·es,** (*esp. collectively*) **-pesh.** a member of a Papuan people of Papua New Guinea.

Ar·a·rat (ar′ə rat′), *n.* a mountain in E Turkey, near the borders of Iran and Armenia: traditionally considered the landing place of Noah's Ark. 16,945 ft. (5165 m). Also called **Mount Ararat.**

a·ra·ro·ba (ar′ə rō′bə), *n.* the wood of a Brazilian, leguminous tree, *Andira araroba,* from which Goa powder is derived. **1.** *Pharm.* See **Goa powder.** [< Pg < Tupi, perh. var. of *araribá*]

A·ras (ä räs′ *for 1;* ar′əs *for 2*), *n.* **1.** Ancient, **Araxes.** a river in SW Asia, flowing from E Turkey along part of the boundary between NW Iran and Armenia and Azerbaijan into the Kura River. ab. 660 mi. (1065 km) long. **2.** *Class. Myth.* the first king of Phliasia.

A·ra·tus of Sic·y·on (ə rā′təs əv sish′ē on′, sis′-, ə rä′-), 271–213 B.C., Greek general: leader of the Achaean League.

A·rau·can (ə rô′kən), *n., pl.* **-cans,** (*esp. collectively*) **-can,** *adj.* Araucanian. [< Sp *araucano,* equiv. to *Arauc(o)* province in central Chile + *-ano* -AN]

Ar·au·ca·na (ar′ə kä′nə), *n.* **1.** any of numerous varieties of domestic chickens derived from South American wild fowl, noted for producing pale blue, green, or pinkish eggs. **2.** a breed of Araucana, developed in the U.S., having ear tufts and no tail. Also called **Easter egg chicken.** [< AmerSp, fem. of *araucano;* see ARAUCAN]

Ar·au·ca·ni·a (ar′ô kā′nē ə; *Sp.* ä′rou kä′nyä), *n.* a region in central Chile.

Ar·au·ca·ni·an (ar′ô kā′nē ən), *n.* **1.** a member of an Indian people of central Chile. **2.** the language of the Araucanians, spoken in central Chile and northern Argentina. —*adj.* **3.** pertaining to the Araucanians or to their language. [1900–05; ARAUCANI(A) + -AN]

ar·au·car·i·a (ar′ô kâr′ē ə), *n.* any of several coniferous trees of the genus *Araucaria,* of warm regions. Cf. **monkey puzzle, Norfolk Island pine.** [1825–35; < NL, named after *Arauc(o)* province in central Chile; see -ARIA] —**ar′au·car′i·an,** *adj.*

Ar·a·wak (ar′ə wäk′, -wak′), *n., pl.* **-waks,** (*esp. collectively*) **-wak. 1.** a member of an Indian people once widespread in the Antilles but now confined to northeastern South America. **2.** the language of the Arawaks.

Ar·a·wak·an (ar′ə wä′kən, -wak′ən), *n.* **1.** a family of numerous and widely scattered languages spoken formerly from Florida to Chile but now only in South America. **2.** a member of a group of Indian peoples who spoke these languages. —*adj.* **3.** of or belonging to this language family or its speakers or to the Arawak.

Ar·awn (är′oun), *n. Welsh Myth.* the lord of Annwfn.

A·ra·xá (ä′rä shä′), *n.* a city in E Brazil. 32,798.

A·rax·es (ə rak′sēz), *n.* ancient name of **Aras.**

arb (ärb), *n.* an arbitrager. [1980–85; by shortening]

ar·ba kan·foth (*Seph.* är bä′ kän fôt′; *Ashk.* är′bə-kän′fəs), *Hebrew.* a rectangular piece of cloth with fringes at the four corners and a hole in the center for the head, worn under the clothes by Orthodox Jewish males. Also, ***ar·ba′ kan·fot′,*** *Ashk.* ***ar′ba kan′fos.*** Also called ***tallith katan.*** [*arbaʿ kənāphōth* lit., four corners]

ar·ba·lest (är′bə list), *n.* a powerful medieval crossbow with a steel bow, used to shoot stones, metal balls, arrows, etc. Also, **ar′ba·list.** [bef. 1100; < OF *arbaleste* < OPr < LL *arcuballista* (see ARC, BALLISTA); r. ME, late OE *arblast* < OF] —**ar·ba·lest·er, ar·ba·list·er** (är′bə-lis′tər), *n.*

Ar·be·la (är bē′lə), *n.* an ancient city of Assyria, E of the Tigris, on the site of modern Erbil: headquarters of Darius III before his defeat by Alexander the Great at Gaugamela 331 B.C.

Ar·bil (ir′bil), *n.* Erbil.

ar·bi·ter (är′bi tər), *n.* **1.** a person empowered to decide matters at issue; judge; umpire. **2.** a person who has the sole or absolute power of judging or determining. [1350–1400; ME *arbitour, arbitre* < AF, OF < L *arbiter*]

ar·bi·ter e·le·gan·ti·ae (är′bi ter′ ā′le gän′tē ī′; *Eng.* är′bi tər el′ə gan′shē ē′), *Latin.* a judge of elegance or matters of taste. Also, ***ar·bi·ter e·le·gan·ti·a·rum*** (är′bi ter′ ā′le gän′tē ä′ro͝om; *Eng.* är′bi tər el′-ə gan′shē âr′əm).

ar·bi·tra·ble (är′bi trə bəl), *adj.* capable of arbitration; subject to the decision of an arbiter or arbitrator: *an arbitrable dispute.* [1525–35; (< MF) < L *arbitr(āri)* to decide (see ARBITRATE) + -ABLE]

ar·bi·trage (är′bi träzh′ *for 1, 3;* är′bi trij *for 2*), *n., v.,* **-traged, -trag·ing.** —*n.* **1.** *Finance.* the simultaneous purchase and sale of the same securities, commodities, or foreign exchange in different markets to profit from unequal prices. **2.** *Archaic.* arbitration. —*v.i.* **3.** *Finance.* to engage in arbitrage. [1470–80; < MF, equiv. to *arbitr(er)* to arbitrate, regulate (< L *arbitrārī;* see ARBITRATE) + *-age* -AGE]

ar·bi·trag·er (är′bi trä′zhər), *n.* a person who engages in arbitrage. Also, **ar·bi·tra·geur** (är′bi trä zhûr′). [1865–70; < F *arbitrageur,* equiv. to *arbitrage* ARBITRAGE + *-eur* -EUR]

ar·bi·tral (är′bi trəl), *adj.* pertaining to an arbiter or to arbitration. [1600–10; (< OF) < LL *arbitrālis.* See ARBITER, -AL[1]]

ar·bit·ra·ment (är bi′trə mənt), *n.* **1.** the act of arbitrating; arbitration. **2.** the decision or sentence pronounced by an arbiter. **3.** the power of absolute and final decision. Also, **arbitrement.** [1375–1425; late ME < ML *arbitrāmentum,* equiv. to L *arbitrā(rī)* to ARBITRATE + *-mentum* -MENT; r. ME *arbitrement* < AF < ML]

ar·bi·trar·y (är′bi trer′ē), *adj., n., pl.* **-trar·ies.** —*adj.* **1.** subject to individual will or judgment without restriction; contingent solely upon one's discretion: *an arbitrary decision.* **2.** decided by a judge or arbiter rather than by a law or statute. **3.** having unlimited power; uncontrolled or unrestricted by law; despotic; tyrannical: *an arbitrary government.* **4.** capricious; unreasonable; unsupported: *an arbitrary demand for payment.* **5.** *Math.* undetermined; not assigned a specific value: *an arbitrary constant.* —*n.* **6. arbitraries,** *Print.* (in Britain) peculiar (def. 9). [1400–50; late ME < L *arbitrārius* uncertain (i.e., depending on an arbiter's decision). See ARBITER, -ARY] —**ar·bi·trar·i·ly** (är′bi trer′ə lē, är′bi trâr′-), *adv.* —**ar′bi·trar′i·ness,** *n.*

ar·bi·trate (är′bi trāt′), *v.,* **-trat·ed, -trat·ing.** —*v.t.* **1.** to decide as arbitrator or arbiter; determine. **2.** to submit to arbitration; settle by arbitration: *to arbitrate a dispute.* —*v.i.* **3.** to act as arbitrator or arbiter; decide between opposing or contending parties or sides. **4.** to submit a matter to arbitration. [1580–90; < L *arbitrātus* decided, judged (ptp. of *arbitrārī*), equiv. to *arbit(e)r* ARBITER + *-ātus* -ATE[1]] —**ar′bi·tra′tive,** *adj.*

ar·bi·tra·tion (är′bi trā′shən), *n.* **1.** the hearing and determining of a dispute or the settling of differences between parties by a person or persons chosen or agreed to by them: *Rather than risk a long strike, the union and management agreed to arbitration.* **2.** *Internat. Law.* the application of judicial methods to the settlement of international disputes. [1350–1400; ME < L *arbitrātiōn-* (s. of *arbitrātiō*), equiv. to *arbitrāt(us)* (see ARBITRATE) + *-iōn-* -ION] —**ar′bi·tra′tion·al,** *adj.* —**ar′bi·tra′tion·ist,** *n.*
—**Syn. 1.** See **mediation.**

Arbitration, The, a comedy (c300 B.C.) by Menander, extant only as a fragment.

arbitra′tion bar′, *Metall.* a bar of cast iron used as a sample for the batch to which it belongs.

ar·bi·tra·tor (är′bi trā′tər), *n.* a person chosen to decide a dispute or settle differences, esp. one formally empowered to examine the facts and decide the issue. [1400–50; late ME *arbitratour* < LL; see ARBITRATE, -TOR]

ar·bit·re·ment (är bi′trə mənt), *n.* arbitrament.

ar·bi·trer (är′bi trər), *n. Obs.* arbitrator. [1350–1400; ME *arbitrour* < AF < LL *arbitrātōr-;* see ARBITRATOR]

ar·bi·tress (är′bi tris), *n.* a woman who is an arbiter. [1300–50; ME < MF *arbitresse,* equiv. to *arbitre* ARBIT(E)R + *-esse* -ESS]
—**Usage.** See **-ess.**

Ar·blay, d′ (där′blā; *Fr.* dar blā′), **Madame Frances.** See **Burney, Frances.**

ar·bor[1] (är′bər), *n.* **1.** a leafy, shady recess formed by tree branches, shrubs, etc. **2.** a latticework bower intertwined with climbing vines and flowers. **3.** *Obs.* a grass plot; lawn; garden; orchard. Also, *esp. Brit.,* **arbour.** [1350–1400; ME *(h)erber* < AF, OF *(h)erbier* HERBARIUM; resp. with *-or* under the influence of ARBOR[3]]

ar·bor[2] (är′bər), *n.* **1.** *Mach.* **a.** a bar, shaft, or axis that holds, turns, or supports a rotating cutting tool or grinding wheel, often having a tapered shank fitting tightly into the spindle of a machine tool. Cf. **mandrel. b.** a beam, shaft, axle, or spindle. **2.** *Metall.* a reinforcing member of a core or mold. [1650–60; resp., by assoc. with ARBOR[3], of earlier *arber, arbre* < F, OF < L *arbor* wooden beam or part in an olive press, tree]

ar·bor[3] (är′bər), *n., pl.* **ar·bo·res** (är′bə rēz′). *Bot.* a tree. [1660–70; < NL, L: tree.] —**ar′bo·resque′,** *adj.*

Ar′bor Day′, a day, varying in date but always in the spring, observed in certain states of the U.S. by the planting of trees. [1870–75, *Amer.*]

ar·bo·re·al (är bôr′ē əl, -bōr′-), *adj.* **1.** of or pertaining to trees; treelike. **2.** Also, **arboreous.** living in or among trees. **3.** *Zool.* adapted for living and moving about in trees, as the limbs and skeleton of opossums, squirrels, monkeys, and apes. [1660–70; < L *arbore(us)* of trees (*arbor* tree + *-eus* -EOUS) + -AL[1]] —**ar·bo′re·al·ly,** *adv.*

ar·bored (är′bərd), *adj.* **1.** furnished with an arbor. **2.** lined with trees; shaded. Also, *esp. Brit.,* **arboured.** [ARBOR[1] + -ED[3]]

ar·bo·re·ous (är bôr′ē əs, -bōr′-), *adj.* **1.** abounding in trees; wooded. **2.** arboreal (def. 2). **3.** arborescent. [1640–50; < L *arboreus* of trees, equiv. to *arbor* tree + *-eus* -EOUS]

ar·bo·res·cent (är′bə res′ənt), *adj.* treelike in size and form. [1665–75; < L *arborēscent-* (s. of *arborēscēns*), prp. of *arborēscere* to grow into a tree. See ARBOR[3], -ESCENT] —**ar′bo·res′cence,** *n.* —**ar′bo·res′cent·ly,** *adv.*

ar·bo·re·tum (är′bə rē′təm), *n., pl.* **-tums, -ta** (-tə). a plot of land on which many different trees or shrubs are grown for study or display. [1830–40; < L *arborētum* a plantation of trees, equiv. to *arbor* tree + *-ētum* suffix denoting place where a given plant grows (cf. ALAMEDA)]

ar·bor·i·cul·ture (är′bər i kul′chər är bôr′-, -bōr′-), *n.* the cultivation of trees and shrubs. [1820–30; ARBOR[3] + (AGRI)CULTURE] —**ar′bor·i·cul′tur·al,** *adj.*

ar·bor·ist (är′bər ist), *n.* a specialist in the cultivation and care of trees and shrubs, including tree surgery, the diagnosis, treatment, and prevention of tree diseases, and the control of pests. [1570–80; ARBOR[3] + -IST]

ar·bor·i·za·tion (är′bər ə zā′shən), *n.* **1.** a treelike appearance, as in certain minerals or fossils. **2.** *Anat.* the branchlike appearance characteristic of certain nerve-cell outgrowths. [1785–95; ARBOR[3] + -IZATION]

ar·bor·ous (är′bər əs), *adj.* of or pertaining to trees. [1660–70; ARBOR[3] + -OUS]

ar·bor vi·tae (är′bər vī′tē), *Anat.* a treelike appearance in a vertical section of the cerebellum, due to the arrangement of the white and gray nerve tissues.

ar·bor·vi·tae (är′bər vī′tē), *n.* **1.** any of several ornamental or timber-producing evergreen trees belonging to the genus *Thuja,* of the cypress family, native to North America and eastern Asia, having a scaly bark and scalelike leaves on branchlets. **2.** *Anat.* See **arbor vitae.** [1655–65 for def. 1; 1790–1800 for def. 2; < L: tree of life]

ar·bour (är′bər), *n. Chiefly Brit.* arbor[1].

ar·bo·vi·rus (är′bə vī′rəs), *n., pl.* **-rus·es.** any of several groups of RNA-containing viruses that are transmitted by bloodsucking arthropods, as ticks, fleas, or mosquitoes, and may cause encephalitis, yellow fever, or dengue fever. [1955–60; *ar(thropod-) bo(rne) virus*]

arbtrn., arbitration.

Ar·buth·not (är buth′nət, är′bəth not′), *n.* **John,** 1667–1735, Scottish satirist and physician: friend of Alexander Pope and Jonathan Swift.

ar·bu·tus (är byo͞o′təs), *n., pl.* **-tus·es. 1.** any of the evergreen shrubs or trees belonging to the genus *Arbutus,* of the heath family, esp. *A. unedo,* of southern Europe, with scarlet berries, cultivated for ornament and food. **2.** See **trailing arbutus.** [1545–55; < NL, L: the wild strawberry tree]

arc (ärk), *n., v.,* **arced** (ärkt) or **arcked, arc·ing** (är′-king) or **arck·ing.** —*n.* **1.** *Geom.* any unbroken part of the circumference of a circle or other curved line. **2.** Also called **electric arc.** *Elect.* a luminous bridge formed in a gap between two electrodes. Cf. **spark**[1] (def. 2). **3.** *Astron.* the part of a circle representing the apparent course of a heavenly body. **4.** anything bow-shaped. —*v.i.* **5.** to form an electric arc. **6.** to move in a curve suggestive of an arc. [1350–1400; ME *ark* < L *arcus* bow, arch, curve]

ARC (ärk), *n. Pathol.* See **AIDS-related complex.**

ARC, American Red Cross. Also, **A.R.C.**

ar·ca (är′kə), *n., pl.* **-cae** (-sē). a chest for valuables, used in medieval Spain and Italy. [< L: chest, box. See ARK]

ar·cade (är kād′), *n., v.,* **-cad·ed, -cad·ing.** —*n.* **1.** *Archit.* **a.** a series of arches supported on piers or columns. **b.** an arched, roofed-in gallery. Cf. **colonnade. 2.** an arched or covered passageway, usually with shops on each side. **3.** an establishment, public area, etc., containing games of a mechanical and electronic type, as pinball and video games, that can be played by a customer for a fee. **4.** an ornamental carving, as on a piece of furniture, in the form of a row of arches. —*v.t.* **5.** to provide with an arcade. [1725–35; < F < It *arcata* arch, equiv. to *arc(o)* arch (see ARC) + *-ata* -ATE[1]]

ar·cad·ed (är kā′did), *adj.* **1.** decorated with an arcade: *an arcaded entryway.* **2.** housed in an arcade: *arcaded shops.* [1795–1805; ARCADE + -ED[3]]

arcade′ game′, a game or type of game available in arcades.

Ar·ca·di·a (är kā′dē ə), *n.* **1.** a mountainous region of ancient Greece, traditionally known for the contented pastoral innocence of its people. **2.** any real or imaginary place offering peace and simplicity. **3.** a city in SW California, E of Los Angeles. 45,994.

Ar·ca·di·an (är kā′dē ən), *adj.* **1.** of Arcadia. **2.** rural, rustic, or pastoral, esp. suggesting simple, innocent contentment. —*n.* **3.** a native of Arcadia. **4.** the dialect of ancient Greek spoken in Arcadia. [1580–90; ARCADI(A) + -AN] —**Ar·ca′di·an·ism,** *n.* —**Ar·ca′di·an·ly,** *adv.*

Ar·ca·do-Cyp·ri·an (är kā′dō sip′rē ən), *n.* an ancient language group of eastern Greece.

Ar·ca·dy (är′kə dē), *n. Literary.* Arcadia. [earlier *Arcadie* < L *Arcadia* < Gk *Arkadía*]

ar·cane (är kān′), *adj.* known or understood by very few; mysterious; secret; obscure; esoteric: *She knew a lot about Sanskrit grammar and other arcane matters.* [1540–50; (< MF) < L *arcānus,* equiv. to *arc(ēre)* to shut up, keep (deriv. of *arca* a chest, box) + *-ānus* -AN]

ar·can·ist (är kā′nist), *n.* a person professing special secret knowledge concerning ceramics, esp. concerning the making of porcelain. [1900–05; ARCAN(UM) + -IST]

ar·ca·num (är kā′nəm), *n., pl.* **-na** (-nə). **1.** Often, **arcana.** a secret; mystery. **2.** a supposed great secret of nature that the alchemists sought to discover. **3.** a secret and powerful remedy. [1590–1600; < L, neut. (used as n.) of *arcānus* ARCANE]

ar·ca·num ar·ca·no·rum (är kä′no͞om är′kä nō′-ro͞om; *Eng.* är kā′nəm är′kə nôr′əm, -nōr′-), *Latin.* secret of secrets.

Ar·ca·ro (är kâr′ō), *n.* **Edward** (*Eddie*), born 1916, U.S. jockey.

Ar·cas (är′kəs), *n. Class. Myth.* a son of Zeus and Callisto, the ancestor of the Arcadians who was set among the stars with his mother as the Little Bear and the Great Bear respectively.

Ar·ca·ta (är kā′tə), *n.* a town in NW California. 12,338.

ar·ca·ture (är′kə chər), *n. Archit.* **1.** an arcade of small dimensions. **2.** a blind arcade, as a series of arches superimposed on the walls of a building for decoration. [< ML *arcāt(a)* an arch (see ARCADE) + -URE]

arc-back (ärk′bak′), *n. Electronics.* an undesirable phenomenon, occurring in rectifier tubes, in which current flows in the reverse direction, from anode to cathode, as a result of arcing, limiting the usable voltage of the tube.

arc-bou·tant (ARK boo tän′), *n., pl.* ***arcs-bou·tants*** (ARK boo tän′). *French.* See **flying buttress.** [lit., thrusting arch]

arc cos, See **arc cosine.**

arc′ cose′cant, *Trig.* the angle, measured in radians, that has a cosecant equal to a given number. *Abbr.:* arc csc; *Symbol:* csc^{-1} Also called **inverse cosecant.** [1905–10]

arc′ co′sine, *Trig.* the angle, measured in radians, that has a cosine equal to a given number. *Abbr.:* arc cos; *Symbol:* cos^{-1} Also called **inverse cosine.** [1905–10]

arc cot, See **arc cotangent.**

arc′ cotan′gent, *Trig.* the angle, measured in radians, that has a cotangent equal to a given number. *Abbr.:* arc cot *Symbol:* cot^{-1} Also called **inverse cotangent.** [1905–10]

arc csc, See **arc cosecant.**

Arc, d′ (dARK), **Jeanne** (zhän). See **Joan of Arc.**

Arc de Tri·omphe (ARK də trē ôNf′), an arch, located in Paris, begun in 1806 by Napoleon in honor of his victorious armies and completed in 1836. The unknown soldier of France and the eternal flame were placed beneath the arch after World War I. Also, **Arc de Tri·omphe de l′É·toile′** (ARK də trē ôNf′ də lā twAl′). [< F: arch of triumph]

Ar·ce (är′sē), *n. Class. Myth.* a daughter of Thaumas and the sister of Iris and the Harpies. Zeus took away her wings when she aided the Titans in their war against him.

Ar·cel·la (är sel′ə), *n.* a genus of freshwater, ameboid protozoa that secrete a hard, umbrellalike shell having a single opening through which the pseudopodia extend. [1838; < NL, equiv. to L *arc(a)* a chest, box + *-ella* dim. suffix]

Ar·ces·i·la·us (är ses′ə lā′əs), *n.* 316–241 B.C., Greek philosopher.

Ar·ces·i·us (är ses′ē əs), *n. Class. Myth.* a son of Zeus and Euryodia, father of Laertes, and grandfather of Odysseus.

arc·form (ärk′fôrm′), *adj. Naut.* noting a type of cargo-ship construction in which the sides have the form of arcs so drawn that the greatest breadth is at load waterline, the purpose being to promote the flow of water to the propeller with an easy bilge and without loss of capacity. [ARC + -FORM]

arc′ fur′nace, a furnace in which heat is generated by an electric arc.

one type of primitive arch; flat; segmental; stilted; blunt; equilateral; lancet; Gothic; 3-centered or basket-handle; 4-centered or Tudor; ogee; rampant; bell; horseshoe; cusped; Florentine

arches

arch[1] A, abutment; S, springer; V, voussoir; K, keystone; Ex., extrados; P, pier; I, impost; In., intrados

RISE SPAN

arch[1] (ärch), *n.* **1.** *Archit.* **a.** a curved masonry construction for spanning an opening, consisting of a number of wedgelike stones, bricks, or the like, set with the narrower side toward the opening in such a way that forces on the arch are transmitted as vertical or oblique stresses on either side of the opening. **b.** an upwardly curved construction, as of steel or timber functioning in the manner of a masonry arch. **c.** a doorway, gateway, etc., having a curved head; an archway. **d.** the curved head of an opening, as a doorway. **2.** any overhead curvature resembling an arch. **3.** something bowed or curved; any bowlike part: *the arch of the foot.* **4.** a device inserted in or built into shoes for supporting the arch of the foot. **5.** a dam construction having the form of a barrel vault running vertically with its convex face toward the impounded water. **6.** *Glassmaking.* **a.** a chamber or opening in a glassmaking furnace. **b.** See **pot arch.** —*v.t.* **7.** to cover with a vault, or span with an arch: *the rude bridge that arched the flood.* **8.** to throw or make into the shape of an arch or vault; curve: *The horse arched its neck.* —*v.i.* **9.** to form an arch: *elms arching over the road.* **10.** *Naut.* hog (def. 16). [1250–1300; ME *arch(e)* < OF *arche* < VL **arca,* fem. var. of L *arcus* ARC]

arch[2] (ärch), *adj.* **1.** playfully roguish or mischievous: *an arch smile.* **2.** cunning; crafty; sly. —*n.* **3.** *Obs.* a person who is preeminent; a chief. [independent use of ARCH-[1]]

arch-[1], a combining form that represents the outcome of **archi-** in words borrowed through Latin from Greek in the Old English period; it subsequently became a productive form added to nouns of any origin, which thus denote individuals or institutions directing or having authority over others of their class (*archbishop; archdiocese; archpriest*). More recently, **arch-[1]** has developed the senses "principal" (*archenemy; archrival*) or "prototypical" and thus exemplary or extreme (*archconservative*); nouns so formed are almost always pejorative. [ME; OE *arce-, ærce-, erce-* (> ON *erki-*) < L *archi-* < Gk (see ARCHI-); but D *aarts-,* MLG *erse-,* MHG, G *Erz-* < ML *arci-,* and Goth *ark-* directly < Gk. Cf. ARCHANGEL]

arch-[2], var. of **archi-** before a vowel: *archangel; archenteron.*

-arch, a combining form meaning "chief, leader, ruler," used in the formation of compound words: *monarch; matriarch; heresiarch.* [< Gk *-archos* or *-archēs,* as comb. forms of *árchos* leader; cf. ARCHI-]

Arch., Archbishop.

arch., **1.** archaic. **2.** archaism. **3.** archery. **4.** archipelago. **5.** architect. **6.** architectural. **7.** architecture. **8.** archive; archives.

Ar·chae·an (är kē′ən), *adj. Geol.* Archean.

ar·chae·bac·te·ri·a (är′kē bak tēr′ē ə), *n. pl., sing.* **-te·ri·um** (-tēr′ē əm). a group of microorganisms, including the methanogens and certain halophiles and thermoacidophiles, that have RNA sequences, coenzymes, and a cell wall composition that are different from all other organisms: considered to be an ancient form of life that evolved separately from the bacteria and blue-green algae and sometimes classified as a kingdom. Also, **ar·chae·o·bac·te·ri·a** (är′kē ō bak tēr′ē ə). [1977; < NL, equiv. to *archae-,* irreg. for *archaeo-* ARCHAEO- (perh. an erroneous Latinizing of Gk *arche-* ARCHE-) + *bacteria* BACTERIA]

archaeo-, a combining form meaning "ancient," used in the formation of compound words: *archaeopteryx; archaeology.* Also, **archeo-.** [< Gk, comb. form of *archaîos,* equiv. to *arch-* (see ARCHI-) + *-aios* adj. suffix]

ar·chae·o·as·tron·o·my (är′kē ō ə stron′ə mē), *n.* the branch of archaeology that deals with the apparent use by prehistoric civilizations of astronomical techniques to establish the seasons or the cycle of the year, esp. as evidenced in the construction of megaliths and other ritual structures. Also, **archeoastronomy.** Also called **astroarchaeology, megalithic astronomy.** [1970–75; ARCHAEO- + ASTRONOMY] —**ar′chae·o·as·tron′o·mer,** *n.* —**ar·chae·o·as·tro·nom·i·cal** (är′kē ō as′trə nom′i kəl), *adj.*

Ar·chae·o·cy·a·thid (är′kē ō sī′ə thid, är kē′ə-), *n.* one of the marine invertebrates of the extinct phylum Archaeocyatha, widely distributed during the Cambrian Period, having a limy, typically conical or cylindrical skeleton composed of sievelike inner and outer walls. [< NL *Archaeocyath(us)* genus name (*archaeo-* ARCHAEO- + L *cyathus* ladle < Gk *kýathos*) + -ID[2]]

ar·chae·o·cyte (är′kē ə sīt′), *n.* archeocyte.

archaeol., **1.** archaeological. **2.** archaeology.

ar·chae·o·log·i·cal (är′kē ə loj′i kəl), *adj.* of or pertaining to archaeology. Also, **ar′chae·o·log′ic, archeological, archeologic.** [1775–85; < Gk *archaiologik(ós)* (see ARCHAEOLOGY, -IC) + -AL[1]] —**ar′chae·o·log′i·cal·ly,** *adv.*

ar·chae·ol·o·gy (är′kē ol′ə jē), *n.* **1.** the scientific study of historic or prehistoric peoples and their cultures by analysis of their artifacts, inscriptions, monuments, and other such remains, esp. those that have been excavated. **2.** *Rare.* ancient history; the study of antiquity. Also, **archeology.** [1600–10; < Gk *archaiología* the discussion of antiquities. See ARCHAEO-, -LOGY] —**ar′chae·ol′o·gist,** *n.*

ar·chae·o·mag′ne·tism dat′ing (är′kē ō mag′ni tiz′əm), the dating of archaeological specimens by determination of the magnetic alignment of objects containing ferromagnetic materials, as baked clay pots, within undisturbed archaeological sites. Also, **archeomagnetism dating.** [ARCHAEO- + MAGNETISM]

ar·chae·om·e·try (är′kē om′i trē), *n.* the branch of archaeology that deals with the dating of archaeological specimens through specific techniques, as radiocarbon dating and amino-acid dating. Also, **archeometry.** [1960–65; ARCHAEO- + -METRY] —**ar′chae·om′e·trist,** *n.*

ar·chae·op·ter·yx (är′kē op′tə riks), *n.* a reptilelike fossil bird of the genus *Archaeopteryx,* from the late Jurassic Period, having teeth and a long, feathered, vertebrate tail. Cf. **protoavis.** [1855–60; < NL < Gk *archaio-* ARCHAEO- + *ptéryx* wing]

archaeopteryx, *Archaeopteryx lithographica,* approx. 19 in. (48 cm)

Ar·chae·o·zo·ic (är′kē ə zō′ik), *adj., n. Geol.* Archeozoic.

ar·cha·ic (är kā′ik), *adj.* **1.** marked by the characteristics of an earlier period; antiquated: *an archaic manner; an archaic notion.* **2.** (of a linguistic form) commonly used in an earlier time but rare in present-day usage except to suggest the older time, as in religious rituals or historical novels. Examples: *thou; wast; methinks; forsooth.* **3.** forming the earliest stage; prior to full development: *the archaic period of psychoanalytic research.* **4.** (*often cap.*) pertaining to or designating the style of the fine arts, esp. painting and sculpture, developed in Greece from the middle 7th to the early 5th century B.C., chiefly characterized by an increased emphasis on the human figure in action, naturalistic proportions and anatomical structure, simplicity of volumes, forms, or design, and the evolution of a definitive style for the narrative treatment of subject matter. Cf. **classical** (def. 6), **Hellenistic** (def. 5). **5.** primitive; ancient; old: *an archaic form of animal life.* [1825–35; (< F) < Gk *archaïkós* antiquated, old-fashioned, equiv. to *archaî(os)* old + *-ikos* -IC] —**ar·cha′i·cal·ly,** *adv.*

archa′ic *Ho′mo,* **1.** collectively, the very robust, regionally differentiated human populations that lived in Europe, Asia, the Middle East, and Africa from 35,000 to 200,000 years ago. **2.** any physically robust, premodern form of the genus *Homo,* including *Homo sapiens neanderthalensis* (Neanderthal man), *Homo erectus,* and their intermediate forms and regional variants. See illus. under **hominid.**

archa′ic smile′, *Fine Arts.* a conventional representation of the mouth characterized by slightly upturned corners of the lips, found esp. on Greek sculpture produced prior to the 5th century B.C. [1900–05]

ar·cha·ism (är′kē iz′əm, -kā-), *n.* **1.** something archaic, as a word or expression. **2.** the use of what is archaic, as in literature or art: *The archaism of the novelist's style provided a sense of the period.* **3.** the survival or presence of something from the past: *The art of letter writing is becoming an archaism.* Also, **ar·cha·i·cism** (är kā′ə siz′əm). [1635–45; earlier *archaismus* < L < Gk *archaïsmós.* See ARCHAIZE, -ISM] —**ar′cha·ist,** *n.* —**ar′cha·is′tic,** *adj.*

ar·cha·ize (är′kē īz′, -kā-), *v.,* **-ized, -iz·ing.** —*v.t.* **1.** to give an archaic appearance or quality to: *The poet archaized her work with many Elizabethan words.* —*v.i.* **2.** to use archaisms. Also, *esp. Brit.,* **ar′cha·ise′.** [1840–50; < Gk *archaḯzein* to imitate the language of ancient authors. See ARCHAEO-, -IZE] —**ar′cha·iz′er,** *n.*

arch·an·gel (ärk′ān′jəl), *n.* **1.** *Theol.* a chief or principal angel; in medieval angelology one of the nine orders of celestial attendants on God. Cf. **angel** (def. 1). **2.** angelica (def. 1). [bef. 1000; early ME *arc(h)angel* < AF, OF *arc(h)ang(e)le* < LL *archangelus* < Gk *archángelos;* r. OE *hēahengel;* see HIGH, ARCH-[1], ANGEL] —**arch·an·gel·ic** (ärk′an jel′ik), **arch′an·gel′i·cal,** *adj.*

Arch·an·gel (ärk′ān′jəl), *n.* **1.** Russian, **Arkhangelsk.** a seaport in the NW Russian Federation in Europe, on Dvina Bay. 385,000. **2. Gulf of.** former name of **Dvina Bay.**

arch·banc (*Fr.* ARsh bäN′), *n., pl.* **-bancs** (-bäN′). archebanc.

arch′ beam′, a crowned metal beam, as of the deck of a ship.

arch·bish·op (ärch′bish′əp), *n.* a bishop of the highest rank who presides over an archbishopric or archdiocese. [bef. 900; ME; OE *arcebiscop* (*arce-* ARCH-[1] + *biscop* BISHOP), modeled on LL *archiepiscopus* < Gk *archiepískopos;* r. OE *hēahbisceop* (see HIGH)]

arch·bish·op·ric (ärch′bish′əp rik), *n.* the see, diocese, or office of an archbishop. [bef. 1000; ME *archebischopric,* OE *arcebisceopriċe,* equiv. to *arcebisceop* ARCHBISHOP + *rīce* region, realm; c. ON *rīki,* Goth *reiki,* OHG *rihki* (G *Reich*)]

arch′ board′, *Naut.* a distinctive area at the upper part of a stern, curving upward toward the center and giving the name and port of the vessel within a carved and painted frame; escutcheon.

Archbp., Archbishop.

arch′ brace′, *Carpentry.* a curved brace, esp. one of a pair used to give the effect of an arch in a roof frame.

arch·con·fra·ter·ni·ty (ärch′kon frə tûr′ni tē), *n., pl.* **-ties.** *Rom. Cath. Ch.* a confraternity having the right to associate itself with confraternities that are similar to it, and to impart to them its privileges and indulgences. [1630–40; < It *arciconfraternità.* See ARCH-[1], CONFRATERNITY]

arch·con·serv·a·tive (ärch′kən sûr′və tiv), *adj.* **1.** consistently holding extremely conservative views:

CONCISE ETYMOLOGY KEY: <, descended or borrowed from; >, whence; b., blend of, blended; c., cognate with; cf., compare; deriv., derivative; equiv., equivalent; imit., imitative; obl., oblique; r., replacing; s., stem; sp., spelling, spelled; resp., respelling, respelled; trans., translation; ?, origin unknown; *, unattested; ‡, probably earlier than. See the full key inside the front cover.

publisher of the city's archconservative newspaper. —*n.* **2.** a person who holds extremely conservative views. [‡1960–65; ARCH-[1] + CONSERVATIVE]

archd., **1.** archdeacon. **2.** archduke. Also, **Archd.**

arch′ dam′, a dam resisting the pressure of impounded water by an arch principle, esp. a dam having in plan the form of a single arch abutted by natural rock formations.

arch•dea•con (ärch′dē′kən), *n.* **1.** an ecclesiastic, ranking next below a bishop and having charge of the temporal and external administration of a diocese, with jurisdiction delegated from the bishop. **2.** *Rom. Cath. Ch.* a title of honor conferred only on a member of a cathedral chapter. [bef. 1000; ME *archideken,* OE *arcediacon* < LL *archidiāconus* < Gk *archidiákonos.* See ARCH-[1], DEACON] —**arch′dea′con•ate, arch′dea′con•ship′,** *n.*

arch•dea•con•ry (ärch′dē′kən rē), *n., pl.* **-ries.** the jurisdiction, residence, or office of an archdeacon. [1545–55; ARCHDEACON + -RY]

arch•di•o•cese (ärch′dī′ə sēs′, -sis), *n.* the diocese of an archbishop. [1835–45; ARCH-[1] + DIOCESE] —**arch•di•oc•e•san** (ärch′dī os′ə sən), *adj.*

arch•du•cal (ärch′do͞o′kəl, -dyo͞o′-), *adj.* of or pertaining to an archduke or an archduchy. [1655–65; earlier *archiducal* < F. See ARCHI-, DUCAL]

arch•duch•ess (ärch′duch′is), *n.* **1.** the wife of an archduke. **2.** a princess of the Austrian imperial family. [1610–20; ARCH-[1] + DUCHESS, modeled on F *archiduchesse*]
—**Usage.** See **-ess.**

arch•duch•y (ärch′duch′ē), *n., pl.* **-duch•ies.** the domain of an archduke or an archduchess. [1670–80; ARCH-[1] + DUCHY, modeled on F *archeduché* (now *archiduché*)]

arch•duke (ärch′do͞ok′, -dyo͞ok′), *n.* a title of the sovereign princes of the former ruling house of Austria. [1520–30; earlier *archeduke* < F *archeduc* (now *archiduc*). See ARCH-[1], DUKE]

arch•duke•dom (ärch′do͞ok′dəm, -dyo͞ok′-), *n.* **1.** an archduchy. **2.** the office or rank of an archduke. [1520–30; ARCHDUKE + -DOM]

arche-, a combining form meaning "prior, original, first" (*archegonium; archetype*); in scientific coinages, a synonym of **archi-** (*archesporium*). [< Gk, by-form of *archi-* ARCHI-]

Arch. E., Architectural Engineer.

Ar•che•an (är kē′ən), *adj. Geol.* noting or pertaining to rocks of the Archeozoic portion of the Precambrian Era. Also, **Archaean.** [1870–75; < Gk *archaî(os)* ancient (see ARCHAEO-) + -AN]

arche•banc (ARSH bäN′), *n., pl.* **-bancs** (-bäN′), *Fr. Furniture.* a bench or settle of the medieval and Renaissance periods, wide enough for several persons and having a seat with a chest beneath, arms at the ends, and a high back. Also, **archbanc.** [< F; see ARCH[1], ARCA, BANK[3]]

arched (ärcht), *adj.* **1.** made, covered, or spanned with an arch or arches. **2.** having the form of an arch. **3.** *Heraldry.* noting an ordinary or partition line formed as a slight curve. [1575–85; ARCH[1] + -ED[3]]

arched′ truss′, a truss having an archlike form but unlike a true arch in that it is free to move horizontally at its base, as in expanding or contracting because of temperature changes. Cf. **braced arch.**

ar•che•go•ni•um (är′ki gō′nē əm), *n., pl.* **-ni•a** (-nē ə). *Bot.* the female reproductive organ in ferns, mosses, etc. [1850–55; < NL, equiv. to *archegon-* (< Gk *archégonos* first of a race; see ARCHE-, GONO-) + *-ium* < Gk *-ion* dim. suffix] —**ar′che•go′ni•al, ar•che•go•ni•ate** (är′ki-gō′nē it, -āt′), *adj.*

Ar•chem•o•rus (är kem′ər əs), *n. Class. Myth.* Opheltes.

arch•en•ceph•a•lon (är′ken sef′ə lon′), *n. Embryol.* the primitive forebrain region of the embryo, anterior to the notochord, that gives rise to the midbrain and forebrain. [ARCH-[2] + ENCEPHALON]

arch•en•e•my (ärch′en′ə mē), *n., pl.* **-mies. 1.** a chief enemy. **2.** Satan; the Devil. [1540–50; ARCH-[1] + ENEMY]

arch•en•ter•on (är ken′tə ron′), *n., pl.* **-ter•a** (-tər ə). *Embryol.* the primitive enteron or digestive cavity of a gastrula. Also called **primitive gut.** [1875–80; ARCH-[2] + ENTERON] —**arch•en•ter•ic** (är′kən ter′ik), *adj.*

archeo-, var. of **archaeo-:** *Archeozoic.*

ar•che•o•as•tron•o•my (är′kē ō ə stron′ə mē), *n.* archaeoastronomy. —**ar′che•o•as•tron′o•mer,** *n.* —**ar•che•o•as•tro•nom•i•cal** (är′kē ō as′trənom′i kəl), *adj.*

ar•che•o•cyte (är′kē ə sīt′), *n. Zool.* (in sponges) a type of amoebocyte capable of developing into other types of cells, esp. reproductive cells. Also, **archaeocyte.** [1885–90; ARCHEO- + -CYTE]

ar•che•ol•o•gy (är′kē ol′ə jē), *n.* archaeology. —**ar•che•o•log•i•cal** (är′kē ə loj′i kəl), **ar′che•o•log′ic,** *adj.* —**ar′che•o•log′i•cal•ly,** *adv.* —**ar′che•ol′o•gist,** *n.*

ar•che•o•mag′ne•tism dat′ing (är′kē ō mag′nitiz′əm). See **archaeomagnetism dating.**

ar•che•om•e•try (är′kē om′i trē), *n.* archaeometry. —**ar′che•om′e•trist,** *n.*

Ar•che•o•zo•ic (är′kē ə zō′ik), *Geol.* —*adj.* **1.** noting or pertaining to the earlier half of the Precambrian Era, from about 5 billion to 2.5 billion years ago, during which the earliest datable rocks were formed and from which the oldest known fossil forms, blue-green algae and bacteria, have been recovered. See table under **geologic time.** —*n.* **2.** the Archeozoic division of geologic time or the rock systems formed then. Also, **Archaeozoic.** [1870–75; ARCHEO- + Gk *zō(ḗ)* life + -IC]

Ar•chep•tol•e•mus (är′kep tol′ə məs), *n.* (in the *Iliad*) the son of Iphitus who served as a charioteer for Hector.

arch•er (är′chər), *n.* **1.** a person who shoots with a bow and arrow; bowman. **2.** (*cap.*) *Astron., Astrol.* the constellation or sign of Sagittarius. **3.** an archerfish. [1250–1300; ME < AF; OF *archier* < LL *arcuārius,* equiv. to *arcu-,* s. of *arcus* bow (see ARC) + *-ārius* -ARY]

Ar•cher (är′chər), *n.* **1. William,** 1856–1924, Scottish playwright, drama critic, and translator. **2.** a male given name.

ar•cher•fish (är′chər fish′), *n., pl.* (*esp. collectively*) **-fish,** (*esp. referring to two or more kinds or species*) **-fish•es. 1.** a small fish, *Toxotes jaculatrix,* of brackish and fresh waters in southeastern Asia, that preys upon shoreside spiders and insects by spitting drops of water at them and knocking them into the water. **2.** any of several closely related fishes of the family Toxotidae. [1885–90; ARCHER + FISH]

ar•cher•y (är′chə rē), *n.* **1.** the art, practice, or skill of an archer. **2.** archers collectively, as in an army. **3.** the equipment of an archer, as bows and arrows. [1350–1400; ME *archerye* < MF *archerie,* equiv. to *arch(i)er* ARCHER + *-ie* -Y[3]]

Arch′es Na′tional Park′, a national park in E Utah: natural arch formations. 114 sq. mi. (295 sq. km).

ar•che•spore (är′kə spôr′, -spōr′), *n. Bot.* the primitive cell, or group of cells, that give rise to the cells from which spores are derived. [1900–05; ARCHE- + SPORE] —**ar′che•spo′ri•al,** *adj.*

ar•che•spo•ri•um (ar′kə spôr′ē əm, -spōr′-), *n., pl.* **-spo•ri•a** (-spôr′ē ə, -spōr′-). *Bot.* archespore. [< NL]

ar•chet•to (är ket′ō), *n., pl.* **-tos.** *Ceram.* a tool, consisting of a bow strung with wire, for trimming excess material from a piece being modeled. [< It, equiv. to *arc(o)* bow (see ARC) + *-etto* -ET]

ar•che•type (är′ki tīp′), *n.* **1.** the original pattern or model from which all things of the same kind are copied or on which they are based; a model or first form; prototype. **2.** (in Jungian psychology) a collectively inherited unconscious idea, pattern of thought, image, etc., universally present in individual psyches. [1595–1605; < L *archetypum* an original < Gk *archétypon* a model, pattern (neut. of *archétypos* of the first mold, equiv. to *arche-* ARCHE- + *týp(os)* mold, TYPE + *-os* adj. suffix)] —**ar•che•typ•al** (är′ki tī′pəl), **ar•che•typ•i•cal** (är′ki tip′i-kəl), **ar′che•typ′ic,** *adj.* —**ar′che•typ′al•ly, ar′che•typ′i•cal•ly,** *adv.*

arch•fiend (ärch′fēnd′), *n.* **1.** a chief fiend. **2.** Satan. [1660–70; ARCH-[1] + FIEND]

arch′ head′, *Mach.* a vertical, arc-shaped member fixed to the end of a walking beam, for supporting a chain from which a pump rod or the like is suspended in such a way as to let it rise and fall vertically.

archi-, **1.** a combining form with the general sense "first, principal," that is prefixed to nouns denoting things that are earliest, most basic, or bottommost (*archiblast; archiphoneme; architrave*); or denoting individuals who direct or have authority over others of their class, usually named by the base noun (*archimandrite; architect*). Also, esp. *before a vowel,* **arch-.** Cf. **arch-[1], arche-.** [< Gk, comb. form akin to *archḗ* beginning, *árchos* leader, *árchein* to be the first, command]

Ar•chi•bald (är′chə bôld′, -bəld), *n.* a male given name: from a Germanic word meaning "distinguished and bold."

ar•chi•ben•thos (är′kə ben′thos), *n.* the ocean bottom between the littoral and abyssal zones: from depths of approximately 200 ft. (60 m) to 3300 ft. (1000 m). [ARCHI- + BENTHOS]

ar•chi•blast (är′kə blast′), *n. Biol.* the formative part of the egg, as distinguished from the part that nourishes the embryo. [1875–80; ARCHI- + -BLAST]

ar•chi•blas•tic (är′kə blas′tik), *adj.* of, pertaining to, or derived from an archiblast. [1880–85; ARCHIBLAST + -IC]

ar•chi•carp (är′ki kärp′), *n. Bot.* the female sex organ in various ascomycete fungi. [1885–90; ARCHI- + -CARP]

ar•chi•di•ac•o•nal (är′ki dī ak′ə nl), *adj.* of or pertaining to an archdeacon or to the office of an archdeacon. [1645–55; < LL *archidiācon(us)* ARCHDEACON + -AL[1]]

Ar•chie (är′chē), *n.* a male given name, form of **Archibald.**

Ar′chie Bun′ker, a poorly educated blue-collar worker, holding ultraconservative, racist, and male-chauvinist opinions. [from a character in the American television series "All in the Family" which premiered in 1971] —**Ar′chie Bun′ker•ism** (bung′kə riz′əm).

ar•chi•e•pis•co•pa•cy (är′kē i pis′kə pə sē), *n.* a form of church government in which power is vested in archbishops. [1635–45; < LL *archiepiscop(us)* ARCHBISHOP + -ACY]

ar•chi•e•pis•co•pal (är′kē i pis′kə pəl), *adj.* of or pertaining to an archbishop or to the office of an archbishop. [1605–15; < ML *archiepiscopālis,* equiv. to LL *archiepiscop(us)* ARCHBISHOP + L *-ālis* -AL[1]] —**ar′chi•e•pis′co•pal′i•ty,** *n.* —**ar′chi•e•pis′co•pal•ly,** *adv.*

ar′chiepis′copal cross′. See **patriarchal cross.**

ar•chi•e•pis•co•pate (är′kē ə pis′kə pit, -pāt′), *n.* **1.** the tenure of office of an archbishop. **2.** the jurisdiction of an archbishop.

ar•chil (är′kil), *n.* orchil.

Ar•chi•lo•chi•an (är′kə lō′kē ən), *adj. Pros.* of or pertaining to a form of poetic meter devised by the Greek Archilochus in which various types of meter are combined in the same line or couplet, as a dactylic tetrameter plus a trochaic tripody. [1745–55; < Gk *archilócheі(os)* (equiv. to *Archíloch(os)* ARCHILOCHUS + *-eios* adj. suffix) + -AN]

Ar•chil•o•chus (är kil′ə kəs), *n.* fl. c650 B.C., Greek poet.

ar•chi•mage (är′kə māj′), *n.* a great magician. [1545–55; ARCHI- + MAGE]

ar•chi•man•drite (är′kə man′drīt), *n. Eastern Ch.* **1.** the head of a monastery; an abbot. **2.** a superior abbot, having charge of several monasteries. **3.** a title given to distinguished celibate priests. [1585–95; < LL *archimandrīta* < LGk *archimandrítēs* abbot, equiv. to Gk *archi-* ARCHI- + LGk *mándr(a)* monastery (Gk: fold, enclosure) + *-ītēs* -ITE[1]]

Ar•chi•me•de•an (är′kə mē′dē ən, -mi dē′ən), *adj.* **1.** of, pertaining to, or discovered by Archimedes. **2.** *Math.* of or pertaining to any ordered field, as the field of real numbers, having the property that for any two unequal positive elements there is an integral multiple of the smaller which is greater than the larger. [1805–15; ARCHIMEDE(S) + -AN]

Ar•chi•me•des (är′kə mē′dēz), *n.* 287?–212 B.C., Greek mathematician, physicist, and inventor: discovered the principles of specific gravity and of the lever.

Ar′chime′des′ prin′ciple, *Physics.* the law that a body immersed in a fluid is buoyed up by a force (**buoyant force**) equal to the weight of the fluid displaced by the body.

Ar′chime′des′ screw′, a device consisting essentially of a spiral passage within an inclined cylinder for raising water to a height when rotated. Also, **Ar′•chime′dean screw′.** Also called **water snail.** [1860–65]

ar•chine (är shēn′), *n.* arshin.

arch•ing (är′ching), *n.* arched work or formation. [1670–80; ARCH[1] + -ING[1]]

ar•chi•pel•a•go (är′kə pel′ə gō′), *n., pl.* **-gos, -goes. 1.** a large group or chain of islands: *the Malay Archipelago.* **2.** any large body of water with many islands. **3. the Archipelago,** the Aegean Sea. [1495–1505; alter. (ARCHI- for *arci-*) of It *arcipelago,* alter. of *Egeopelago* the Aegean Sea < Gk *Aigaîon pélagos*] —**ar•chi•pe•lag•ic** (är′kə pə laj′ik), **ar•chi•pe•la•gi•an** (är′kə pə lā′jē-ən, -jən), *adj.*

Ar•chi•pen•ko (är′kə peng′kō; *Russ.* UR KHYē′pyin-kə), *n.* **A•le•ksan•der Por•fir•ie•vich** (al′ig zan′dər pər-fēr′ə vich, -zän′-; *Russ.* u lyi ksändR′ puR fyē′ryi-vyich), 1887–1964, U.S. sculptor, born in Russia.

ar•chi•pho•neme (är′kə fō′nēm, är′kə fō′nēm), *n. Ling.* **1.** an abstract phonological unit consisting of the distinctive features common to two phonemes that differ only in that one has a distinctive feature lacking in the other. The archiphoneme is said to be realized when in a certain position an otherwise phonemic opposition is neutralized; thus, in German, while *p* and *b* are separate phonemes differing only in the distinctive feature of voicing, in final position the voicing or unvoicing of the labial stop is nondistinctive, and the *p*-sound of *leib* "body" may be called the realization of the archiphoneme. **2.** such a unit occurring in a position where the contrast between two or more phonemes is neutralized. [1935–40; < G *Archiphonem* or < F *archiphonème,* term first used by R. Jakobson in 1929; see ARCHI-, PHONEME]

Ar•chi•pié•la•go de Co•lón (är′chē pye′lä gô′ the kô lôn′), Spanish name of **Galápagos Islands.**

archit., architecture.

ar•chi•tect (är′ki tekt′), *n.* **1.** a person who engages in the profession of architecture. **2.** a person professionally engaged in the design of certain large constructions other than buildings and the like: *landscape architect; naval architect.* **3.** the deviser, maker, or creator of anything: *the architects of the Constitution of the United States.* —*v.t.* **4.** to plan, organize, or structure as an architect: *The house is well architected.* [1555–65; < L *architectus* < Gk *architéktōn,* equiv. to Gk *archi-* ARCHI- + *tektōn* builder, craftsman]

ar•chi•tec•ton•ic (är′ki tek ton′ik), *adj.* **1.** of or pertaining to the principles of architecture. **2.** resembling architecture, esp. in its highly organized manner or technique of structure: *the architectonic perfection of his new novel.* [1635–45; < L *architectonicus* < Gk *architektonikós,* of belonging to architecture. See ARCHI-, TECTONIC] —**ar•chi•tec•ton′i•cal•ly,** *adv.*

ar•chi•tec•ton•ics (ar′ki tek ton′iks), *n.* (*used with a singular v.*) the science of planning and constructing buildings. [1650–60; see ARCHITECTONIC, -ICS]

ar′chitect's ta′ble. See **drawing table.**

ar•chi•tec•tur•al (är′ki tek′chər əl), *adj.* **1.** of or pertaining to architecture: *architectural metals.* **2.** conforming to the basic principles of architecture. **3.** having the qualities of architecture; characteristic of architecture; structural; architectonic. [1755–65; ARCHITECTURE + -AL[1]] —**ar′chi•tec′tur•al•ly,** *adv.*

architec′tural bronze′, a brass alloy of about 57 percent copper, 41 percent zinc, and 2 percent lead.

ar•chi•tec•ture (är′ki tek′chər), *n.* **1.** the profession of designing buildings, open areas, communities, and other artificial constructions and environments, usually with some regard to aesthetic effect. Architecture often includes design or selection of furnishings and decorations, supervision of construction work, and the examination, restoration, or remodeling of existing buildings. **2.** the character or style of building: *the architecture of Paris; Romanesque architecture.* **3.** the action or process of building; construction. **4.** the result or product of architectural work, as a building. **5.** buildings collectively. **6.** the structure of anything: *the architecture of a novel.* [1555–65; (< MF) < L *architectūra.* See ARCHITECT, -URE]

ar′chitecture par·lan′te (pär län′tē), the architecture of buildings that, in their plans or elevations, create an image that suggests their functions. [< F: lit., talking architecture]

ar·chi·trave (är′ki trāv′), *n. Archit.* **1.** the lowermost member of a classical entablature, resting originally upon columns. See diag. under **column. 2.** a molded or decorated band framing a panel or an opening, esp. a rectangular one, as of a door or window. [1555–65; MF < It; see ARCHI-, TRAVE[1]] **—ar′chi·tra′val,** *adj.* **—ar′·chi·traved′,** *adj.*

ar·chi·val (är kī′vəl), *adj.* of or pertaining to archives or valuable records; contained in or comprising such archives or records. [1840–50; ARCHIVE + -AL[1]]

ar·chive (är′kīv), *n., v.,* **-chived, -chiv·ing.** *—n.* **1.** Usually, **archives.** documents or records relating to the activities, business dealings, etc., of a person, family, corporation, association, community, or nation. **2. archives,** a place where public records or other historical documents are kept. **3.** any extensive record or collection of data: *The encyclopedia is an archive of world history. The experience was sealed in the archive of her memory.* *—v.t.* **4.** to place or store in an archive: *to vote on archiving the city's historic documents.* [1595–1605; orig., as pl. < F *archives* < L *archī(v)a* < Gk *archeîa,* orig. pl. of *archeîon* public office, equiv. to *arch(ḗ)* magistracy, office + *-eion* suffix of place]

ar·chi·vist (är′kə vist, -kī-), *n.* a person responsible for preserving, organizing, or servicing archival material. [1745–55; < F *archiviste.* See ARCHIVE, -IST]

ar·chi·volt (är′kə vōlt′), *n. Archit.* a molded or decorated band following the extrados of an arch or forming an archlike frame for an opening. [1725–35; < F *archivolte* < It *archivolto* < ML **archivoltum,* Latinization of OF *arvol* < LL *arcus volūtus* vaulted arch; see ARCH[1], VAULT[1]]

arch·lute (ärch′lo͞ot′), *n.* a lute with two pegboxes, one for the stopped strings and the other for the bass strings, which run outside the fingerboard. [1720–30; ARCH-[1] + LUTE, modeled on It *archiliuto*]

arch·ly (ärch′lē), *adv.* in an arch or roguish manner. [1655–65; ARCH[2] + -LY]

arch·ness (ärch′nis), *n.* roguishness; sauciness. [1700–10; ARCH[2] + -NESS]

Arch′ of Tri′umph. See **Arc de Triomphe.**

ar·chon (är′kon), *n.* **1.** a higher magistrate in ancient Athens. **2.** any ruler. [1650–60; < Gk *árchōn* magistrate, ruler, n. use of prp. of *árchein* to be first, rule; see ARCHI-] **—ar′chon·ship′,** *n.*

ar·cho·saur (är′kə sôr′), *n.* any reptile of the subclass Archosauria, including the dinosaurs, pterosaurs, and crocodilians and characterized by two pairs of openings in the temporal region of the skull. [1965–70; < NL *Archosaurus,* taken as sing. of *Archosauria,* equiv. to Gk *archo-,* comb. form of *archós* ruler, chief + *saûr(os)* -SAUR + NL *-ia* -IA] **—ar′cho·sau′ri·an,** *adj.*

arch·priest (ärch′prēst′), *n.* **1.** a priest holding first rank, as among the members of a cathedral chapter or among the clergy of a district outside the episcopal city. **2.** *Rom. Cath. Ch.* a priest acting as superior of the Roman Catholic secular clergy in England, first appointed in 1598 and superseded by a vicar apostolic in 1623. [1350–1400; ME *archeprest* (modeled on LL *archipresbyter* < Gk *archipresbýteros*). See ARCH-[1], PRIEST] **—arch′priest′hood,** *n.* **—arch′priest′ship,** *n.*

arch·ri·val (ärch′rī′vəl), *n.* a chief rival. [ARCH-[1] + RIVAL]

arch·see (ärch′sē′), *n.* archbishopric. [1605–15; ARCH-[1] + SEE[2]]

arch′ support′, a rigid support placed inside a shoe so that its molded form fits the arch of the foot and relieves strain on the muscles of the foot while walking, standing, etc. [1935–40]

archt., architect.

arch·way (ärch′wā′), *n. Archit.* **1.** an entrance or passage under an arch. **2.** a covering or enclosing arch. [1795–1805; ARCH[1] + WAY]

Ar·chy (är′chē), *n.* a male given name, form of **Archibald.**

-archy, a combining form meaning "rule," "government," forming abstract nouns usually corresponding to personal nouns ending in **-arch:** *monarchy; oligarchy.* [ME *-archie* < L *-archia* < Gk, equiv. to *arch(os)* or *-arch(ēs)* -ARCH + *-ia* -Y[3]]

ar·ci·form (är′sə fôrm′), *adj.* resembling an arch in appearance. [1830–40; < L *arci-* (comb. form of *arcus* bow; see ARC) + -FORM]

Ar·cim·bol·di (är′chim bōl′dē; *It.* är′chēm bôl′dē), *n.* **Giu·sep·pe** (jə sep′ē; *It.* jo͞o zep′pe), 1527–93, Italian painter.

Ar·ci·nie·gas (är sē nye′gäs), *n.* **Ger·mán** (her-män′), born 1900, Colombian author, editor, and diplomat.

arcked (ärkt), *v.* a pt. and pp. of **arc.**

arck·ing (är′king), *v.* a ppr. of **arc.**

arc′ light′, 1. Also, **arc′ lamp′.** a lamp in which the light source is a high-intensity electric arc either between carbon rods in air or between metal electrodes in a xenon gas atmosphere enclosed in a quartz bulb. **2.** the light produced by such a lamp. Cf. **carbon arc, xenon arc.** [1875–80, *Amer.*]

ar·co (är′kō), *adv. Music.* (of the performance of a passage for stringed instruments) with the bow. [1730–40; < It: bow < L *arcus.* See ARC]

CONCISE ETYMOLOGY KEY: <, descended or borrowed from; >, whence; b., blend of, blended; c., cognate with; cf., compare; deriv., derivative; equiv., equivalent; imit., imitative; obl., oblique; r., replacing; s., stem; sp., spelling, spelled; resp., respelling, respelled; trans., translation; ?, origin unknown; *, unattested; ‡, probably earlier than. See the full key inside the front cover.

Arc′ of Lo′witz (lō′vits), *Meteorol.* a halo or arc of light, occurring infrequently, which extends diagonally downward from a 22° parhelion. Also, **Lowitz arc.** [named after Tobias *Lowitz* (1757–1804), German-born chemist, who published a description of a halo display observed in St. Petersburg in 1790]

arc·o·graph (är′kə graf′, -gräf′), *n. Geom.* an instrument for drawing arcs, having a flexible arc-shaped part adjusted by an extensible straight bar connecting its sides. [1815–25; ARC + -O- + -GRAPH]

ar·co·so·li·um (är′kə sō′lē əm), *n., pl.* **-li·a** (-lē ə). (in Roman catacombs) an arched recess for a sarcophagus. [1875–80; < NL, equiv. to L *arc(us)* ARC + *-o-* -O- + *solium* sarcophagus]

A.R.C.S., 1. Associate of the Royal College of Science. **2.** Associate of the Royal College of Surgeons.

arc sec, See **arc secant.**

arc′ se′cant, *Trig.* the angle, measured in radians, that has a secant equal to a given number. *Abbr.:* arc sec; *Symbol:* sec^{-1} Also called **inverse secant.** [1905–10]

arc′ sec′ond, *Astron.* second[2] (def. 4). Also, **arc′-sec′ond.**

arc sin, See **arc sine.**

arc′ sine′, *Trig.* the angle, measured in radians, that has a sine equal to a given number. *Abbr.:* arc sin; *Symbol:* sin^{-1} Also called **inverse sine.** [1905–10]

arc′ spec′trum, *Physics.* a spectrum formed from the light produced by an electric arc, characteristic of the gas or vapor through which the arc passes.

arc tan, See **arc tangent.**

arc′ tan′gent, *Trig.* the angle, measured in radians, that has a tangent equal to a given number. *Abbr.:* arc tan; *Symbol:* tan^{-1} Also called **inverse tangent.** [1905–10]

arc·tic (ärk′tik *or, esp. for* 7, är′tik), *adj.* **1.** (*often cap.*) of, pertaining to, or located at or near the North Pole: *the arctic region.* **2.** coming from the North Pole or the arctic region: *an arctic wind.* **3.** characteristic of the extremely cold, snowy, windy weather north of the Arctic Circle; frigid; bleak: *an arctic winter.* **4.** suitable for use in the arctic: *arctic boots.* **5.** extremely cold in manner, atmosphere, etc.: *a look of arctic disdain.* *—n.* **6.** (*often cap.*) the region lying north of the Arctic Circle or of the northernmost limit of tree growth; the polar area north of the timber line. **7. arctics,** warm, waterproof overshoes. [1350–1400; < L *arcticus* < Gk *arktikós* northern, lit., of the Bear, equiv. to *árkt(os)* bear (see URSA MAJOR) + *-ikos* -IC; r. ME *artik* < MF *artique* < L] **—arc′ti·cal·ly,** *adv.*

Arc′tic char′, a salmonid, *Salvelinus alpinus,* that inhabits arctic lakes and streams throughout the Northern Hemisphere: considered a food delicacy. Also, **arc′·tic char′.** [1900–05]

Arc′tic Cir′cle, an imaginary line drawn parallel to the equator, at 23°28′ S of the North Pole: between the North Frigid Zone and the North Temperate Zone. See diag. under **zone.**

Arc′tic Cur′rent. See **Labrador Current.**

Arc′tic dai′sy, a daisy, *Chrysanthemum arcticum,* of arctic regions, having asterlike heads of white or lilac flowers. Also, **arc′tic dai′sy.** Also called **aster daisy.**

Arc′tic fox′, a thickly furred, short-eared fox, *Alopex lagopus,* of the arctic regions, brownish gray in summer and white in winter. Also, **arc′tic fox′.** Also called **white fox.** [1765–75]

Arc′tic O′cean, an ocean N of North America, Asia, and the Arctic Circle. ab. 5,540,000 sq. mi. (14,350,000 sq. km).

arc·ti·col·o·gist (ärk′ti kol′ə jist, är′-), *n.* a person who specializes in arcticology. [ARCTICOLOG(Y) + -IST]

arc·ti·col·o·gy (ärk′ti kol′ə jē, är′-), *n.* the scientific study of the Polar Regions. [ARCTIC + -O- + -LOGY]

Arc′tic seal′, rabbit fur that has been sheared and dyed to simulate sealskin. Also, **arc′tic seal′.**

Arc′tic tern′, a tern, *Sterna paradisaea,* resembling the common tern, that breeds in arctic and north temperate regions and winters in antarctic regions. Also, **arc′tic tern′.** [1880–85]

Arc′tic Zone′, the section of the earth's surface lying between the Arctic Circle and the North Pole. See diag. under **zone.**

Arc·to·gae·a (ärk′tə jē′ə), *n.* a biogeographical division comprising the Holarctic and Paleotropical regions. Also, **Arc′to·ge′a.** [1865–70; < NL, equiv. to *arcto-* (< Gk *arkto-* comb. form of *árktos;* see ARCTIC) + *gaea* (< Gk *gaîa* land, earth)] **—Arc′to·gae′an, Arc′to·ge′·an, Arc′to·gae′al, Arc′to·ge′al, Arc′to·gae′ic, Arc′·to·ge′ic,** *adj.*

arc·to·phile (ärk′tə fīl′), *n.* a person who is very fond of and is usually a collector of teddy bears. [< Gk *arkto-,* comb. form of *arktós* bear + -PHILE]

Arc·tu·rus (ärk to͝or′əs, -tyo͝or′-), *n. Astron.* a first-magnitude star in the constellation Boötes. [1352–75; < L < Gk *Arktoûros,* equiv. to *árkt(os)* bear + *-oûros* keeper; r. ME *arture* < MF] **—Arc·tu′ri·an,** *adj.*

ar·cu·ate (är′kyo͞o it, -āt′), *adj.* bent or curved like a bow. Also, **ar′cu·at′ed.** [1620–30; < L *arcuātus* bent like a bow, curved (ptp. of *arcuāre*), equiv. to *arcu-,* s. of *arcus* bow + *-ātus* -ATE[1]] **—ar′cu·ate·ly,** *adv.*

ar·cu·a·tion (är′kyo͞o ā′shən), *n.* **1.** the state of being bent or curved. **2.** the use of arches in building. **3.** a system or grouping of arches. [1690–1700; < L *arcuātiōn-* (s. of *arcuātiō*) a curving, equiv. to *arcuāt(us)* curved (see ARCUATE) + *-iōn-* -ION]

ar·cus (är′kəs), *n., pl.* **-cus.** *Meteorol.* a dense, horizontal, roll-shaped cloud sometimes occurring at the lower front portion of a cumulonimbus. Also called **roll cloud.** [< L: bow, arch]

ar·cus se·ni·lis (är′kəs sə nī′lis), *Ophthalm.* the appearance of a yellowish-gray lipid ring around the margin of the cornea, occurring in aging persons. [1785–95; < L *arcus senīlis* lit., old man's bow]

arc′ weld′ing, welding by means of the heat of an electric arc. Also called **electric arc welding.** [1930–35]

-ard, a suffix forming nouns that denote persons who regularly engage in an activity, or who are characterized in a certain way, as indicated by the stem; now usually pejorative: *coward; dullard; drunkard; wizard.* Also, **-art.** [ME < OF, prob. extracted from Frankish compound personal names; cf. OHG *Adalhart* (F *Alard*), *Bernhart* (F *Bernard*), with 2d element *-hart* lit., strong, hardy, HARD (c. OE *-heard* in names), often merely as intensifier of quality denoted in 1st element.]

ar·deb (är′deb), *n.* a unit of capacity used for dry measure in Egypt and neighboring countries, officially equivalent in Egypt to 5.62 U.S. bushels, but varying greatly in different localities. [1860–65; < dial. Ar *ardabb* << Aram *'rdb,* perh. < OPers; cf. Egyptian Demotic *'rtb,* late Akkadian *ardabu,* Elamite *irtiba,* Syriac *'arṭba,* Gk *artábē,* Ar *'irdabb* << Aram]

Ar·dèche (AR desh′), *n.* a department in SE France. 257,065; 2145 sq. mi. (5555 sq. km). *Cap.:* Privas.

ar·de·id (är′dē id), *adj.* belonging or pertaining to the family Ardeidae, comprising the herons and bitterns. [< NL *Ardeidae* name of the family, equiv. to *Arde(a)* name of the genus (L: heron) + *-idae* -ID[2]]

Ar·del·la (är del′ə), *n.* a female given name. Also, **Ar·delle** (är del′).

Ar·den (är′dn), *n.* **1. Forest of,** a forest district in central England, in N Warwickshire: scene of Shakespeare's *As You Like It.* **2. Elizabeth,** 1891–1966, U.S. cosmetician, born in Canada.

Ar·dennes (är den′; *Fr.* AR den′), *n.* **1. Forest of,** a wooded plateau region in W Europe, in NE France, SE Belgium, and Luxembourg: World War I battle 1914; World War II battle 1944–45. **2.** a department in NE France. 309,306; 2028 sq. mi. (5255 sq. km). *Cap.:* Mézières.

ar·dent (är′dnt), *adj.* **1.** having, expressive of, or characterized by intense feeling; passionate; fervent: *an ardent vow; ardent love.* **2.** intensely devoted, eager, or enthusiastic; zealous: *an ardent theatergoer. an ardent student of French history.* **3.** vehement; fierce: *They were frightened by his ardent, burning eyes.* **4.** burning, fiery, or hot: *the ardent core of a star.* [1325–75; < L *ārdent-* (s. of *ārdēns,* prp. of *ārdēre* to burn), equiv. to *ārd-* burn + *-ent-* -ENT; r. ME *ardant* < MF] **—ar′·dent·ly,** *adv.* **—ar·den·cy** (är′dn sē), **ar′dent·ness,** *n.*
—Syn. 1. fervid, eager, impassioned. **2.** avid.

ar′dent spir′its, strong alcoholic liquors made by distillation, as brandy, whiskey, or gin. [1790–1800]

Ard·more (ärd′môr, -mōr), *n.* a city in S Oklahoma. 23,689.

ar·dor (är′dər), *n.* **1.** great warmth of feeling; fervor; passion: *She spoke persuasively and with ardor.* **2.** intense devotion, eagerness, or enthusiasm; zeal: *his well-known ardor for Chinese art.* **3.** burning heat. Also, *esp. Brit.,* **ar′dour.** [1350–1400; ME < L, equiv. to *ārd(ēre)* to burn + *-or* -OR[1]; r. ME *ardure* < OF *ardur* < L, as above; 17th century *ardour* < AF < L, as above]
—Syn. 1. fervency, spirit, earnestness, intensity.

ARDS, *Pathol.* adult respiratory distress syndrome. See **respiratory distress syndrome** (def. 2).

ar·du·ous (är′jo͞o əs *or, esp. Brit.,* är′dyo͞o-), *adj.* **1.** requiring great exertion; laborious; difficult: *an arduous undertaking.* **2.** requiring or using much energy and vigor; strenuous: *making an arduous effort.* **3.** hard to climb; steep: *an arduous path up the hill.* **4.** hard to endure; full of hardships; severe: *an arduous winter.* [1530–40; < L *arduus* erect, steep, laborious; see -OUS] **—ar′du·ous·ly,** *adv.* **—ar′du·ous·ness,** *n.*
—Syn. 1. hard, toilsome, onerous, wearisome, burdensome, exhausting. **—Ant. 1.** easy.

are[1] (är; *unstressed* ər), *v.* pres. indic. pl. and 2nd pers. sing. of **be.** [bef. 900; ME *aren, are, arn,* OE (Northumbrian) *aron;* c. ON *eru,* 3rd pers. pl. See ART[2]]

are[2] (âr, är), *n.* a surface measure equal to 100 square meters, or 119.6 square yards; $\frac{1}{100}$ of a hectare. *Abbr.:* a [1810–20; < F < L *ārea.* See AREA]

ar·e·a (âr′ē ə), *n.* **1.** any particular extent of space or surface; part: *the dark areas in the painting; the dusty area of the room.* **2.** a geographical region; tract: *the Chicago area; the unsettled areas along the frontier.* **3.** any section reserved for a specific function: *the business area of a town; the dining area of a house.* **4.** extent, range, or scope: *inquiries that embrace the whole area of science.* **5.** field of study, or a branch of a field of study: *Related areas of inquiry often reflect borrowed notions.* **6.** a piece of unoccupied ground; an open space. **7.** the space or site on which a building stands; the yard attached to or surrounding a house. **8.** *Brit.* areaway (def. 1). **9.** the quantitative measure of a plane or curved surface; two-dimensional extent. **10.** *Anat.* a zone of the cerebral cortex having a specific function: *The damage to Broca's area affected his speech.* [1530–40; < L *ārea* vacant piece of level ground, open space in a town, threshing floor; perh. akin to *ārēre* to be dry. See ARID] **—ar′·e·al,** *adj.* **—ar′e·al·ly,** *adv.*

ar′ea bomb′ing, aerial bombing in which bombs are dropped over the general area of a target. Cf. **pattern bombing, precision bombing.** [1940–45]

ar′ea code′, a three-digit code that identifies one of the telephone areas into which the U.S. and certain other countries are divided and that precedes the local telephone number when dialing a call between areas. [1960–65]

ar′eal veloc′ity, *Astron.* a measure of the velocity of one celestial body in orbit about another, equal to the area swept out per unit time by the vector joining the two bodies. [1960–65]

ar′ea o·pa′ca (ō pā′kə), *Embryol.* the opaque area of the blastoderm surrounding the area pellucida. [< NL]

ar′ea pel·lu′ci·da (pə lo͞o′si də), *Embryol.* the translucent central area of the blastoderm of birds and reptiles within which the embryo develops. [< NL]

ar′ea rug′, a rug designed to cover only part of a floor.

ar′ea stud′y, anthropological or sociological research intended to gather and relate data on various aspects of a geographical region and its inhabitants, as natural resources, history, language, institutions, or cultural and economic characteristics.

ar′ea vas·cu·lo′sa (vas′kyə lō′sə), *Embryol.* that part of the area opaca in which the blood cells and vessels are formed. [< NL; see AREA, VASCULUM, -OSE[1]]

ar′ea vit·el·li′na (vit′l ī′nə), *Embryol.* the nonvascular part of the area opaca surrounding the area vasculosa. [< NL: vitelline area]

ar·e·a·way (âr′ē ə wā′), *n.* **1.** a sunken area leading to a basement entrance, or in front of basement windows. **2.** a passageway, esp. one between buildings.

a·re·ca (ə rē′kə, ar′i-), *n.* any tropical Asian palm of the genus *Areca,* as the betel palm. [1500–10; < NL (earlier E sps. reflect Pg or F); all ult. < Malayalam *aṭaykka*]

are′ca nut′. See **betel nut.**

A·re·ci·bo (är′ə sē′bō; *Sp.* ä′re sē′bô), *n.* a seaport in N Puerto Rico. 83,300.

Areci′bo Observ′atory, a radio-astronomy and ionospheric observatory near Arecibo, Puerto Rico: site of one of the world's largest single-dish radio telescopes, 1000 ft. (305 m) in diameter.

a·re·co·line (ə rē′kə lēn′, -lin, ə rek′ə-, ar′i kə-), *n.* a toxic alkaloid obtained from the seeds of the areca, used in veterinary medicine as an agent for killing and expelling intestinal worms. [AREC(A) + -OL[1] + -INE[2]]

a·re·li·gious (ā′ri lij′əs), *adj.* unconcerned with or indifferent to religious matters. [A-[6] + RELIGIOUS]

a·re·na (ə rē′nə), *n.* **1.** the oval space in the center of a Roman amphitheater for gladiatorial combats or other performances. **2.** a central stage, ring, area, or the like, used for sports or other forms of entertainment, surrounded by seats for spectators: *a circus arena.* **3.** a building housing an arena. **4.** a field of conflict, activity, or endeavor: *the arena of politics.* [1620–30; < L (*h*)*arēna* sand, sandy place, area sanded for combat]

ar·e·na·ceous (ar′ə nā′shəs), *adj.* **1.** *Geol., Petrol.* (of rocks) sandlike; sandy. **2.** *Bot.* growing in sand. [1640–50; < L (*h*)*arēnāceus.* See ARENA, -ACEOUS]

Are′na Chap′el, a private chapel in Padua containing a fresco cycle painted (1305–06) by Giotto. Also called **Scrovegni Chapel.**

are′na the′ater, a theater with seats arranged on at least three sides around a central stage. Also called **theater-in-the-round.** [1940–45]

ar·en·a·vi·rus (är′en ä′vī′rəs), *n., pl.* **-rus·es.** any of various RNA-containing viruses of the family Arenaviridae, usu. transmitted to humans by contact with excreta of infected rodents. [1971; earlier *arenovirus* (1970) < L (*h*)*arēn*(*a*) sand + -o- + VIRUS; so called from the RNA granules seen in cross sections of the virion]

Ar·endt (âr′ənt, är′-), *n.* **Hannah,** 1906–75, U.S. author, political scientist, and teacher, born in Germany.

ar·e·nic·o·lous (ar′ə nik′ə ləs), *adj.* inhabiting sand. [1850–55; < L (*h*)*arēn*(*a*) (see ARENA) + -I- + -COLOUS]

ar·e·nite (ar′ə nīt′, ə rē′-), *n. Geol.* psammite. [< L (*h*)*arēn*(*a*) sand + -ITE[1]]

ar·e·nose (ar′ə nōs′), *adj.* sandy; gritty. Also, **ar·e·nous** (ar′ə nəs), **a·ren·u·lous** (ə ren′yə ləs). [1400–50; late ME *arenous* < L (*h*)*arēnōsus* sandy. See ARENA, -OSE[1]] **—ar·e·nos·i·ty** (ar′ə nos′i tē), *n.*

A·ren·sky (ə ren′skē; *Russ.* u ryen′skyĕ), *n.* **An·ton Ste·pa·no·vich** (un tôn′ styi pä′nə vyich), 1861–1906, Russian composer.

aren't (ärnt, är′ənt), **1.** contraction of *are not.* **2.** contraction of *am not* (used interrogatively). [as contr. of *am not,* a doublet of AIN'T (without raising of the vowel), sp. *aren't* by r-less speakers; *ar* was later substituted for the long *a* by speakers who regularly pronounce preconsonantal *r*]
—Usage. The social unacceptability of *ain't,* the historical contraction of *am not,* has created a gap in the pattern of verbal contractions. *I'm not,* the alternative to *I ain't,* has no corresponding interrogative form except *ain't I.* In questions, *ain't I* is often avoided by the use of AREN'T I: *I'm right, aren't I? Aren't I on the list?* This AREN'T is simply a different outcome of the same historical development that yielded *ain't,* but the fact that it is spelled and pronounced like the contraction of *are not* (as in *You are staying, aren't you?*) apparently gives it, for some, an acceptability that *ain't* lacks. The use of AREN'T I is objected to by others because a declarative counterpart, I AREN'T, does not exist. Many speakers, however, prefer AREN'T I to the uncontracted, rather formal *am I not.* See also **ain't, contraction.**

areo-, a combining form meaning "the planet Mars," used in the formation of compound words: *areocentric.* [< Gk *Áreo*(*s*), gen. of *Árēs* ARES]

ar·e·o·cen·tric (âr′ē ō sen′trik), *adj. Astron.* centered on the planet Mars. [1875–80; AREO- + CENTRIC]

a·re·o·la (ə rē′ə lə), *n., pl.* **-lae** (-lē′), **-las.** *Biol.* **1.** a ring of color, as around the human nipple. **2.** a small interstice, as between the fibers of connective tissue. [1655–65; < L, equiv. to *āre*(*a*) AREA + *-ola* OLE[1]] **—a·re′o·lar,** *adj.* **—a·re·o·late** (ə rē′ə lit, -lāt′), **a·re·o·lat·ed** (ə rē′ə lā′tid), *adj.* **—ar·e·o·la·tion** (âr′ē ə lā′shən), *n.*

ar·e·ole (âr′ē ōl′), *n. Biol.* an areola. [1855–60; < F *aréole* < L *āreola* a small open space. See AREOLA]

ar·e·ol·o·gy (âr′ē ol′ə jē), *n. Astron.* the observation and study of the planet Mars. [AREO- + -LOGY] **—ar·e·o·log·ic** (âr′ē ə loj′ik), **ar·e·o·log′i·cal,** *adj.* **—ar′e·o·log′i·cal·ly,** *adv.* **—ar′e·ol′o·gist,** *n.*

Ar·e·op·a·gite (ar′ē op′ə jit′, -gīt′), *n. Gk. Hist.* a member of the council of the Areopagus. [< L *Areopagītēs* < Gk *Areiopagítēs* a member of the AREOPAGUS; see -ITE[1]] **—Ar·e·op·a·git·ic** (ar′ē op′ə jit′ik), *adj.*

Ar·e·op·a·gus (ar′ē op′ə gəs), *n.* **1.** a hill in Athens, Greece, W of the Acropolis. **2.** *Gk. Hist.* the council that met on this hill, originally having wide public functions but later becoming a purely judicial body. **3.** any high tribunal. [< L < Gk *Áreios págos* hill of Ares]

a·re·o·style (ə rē′ə stīl′, ar′ē ō-), *adj.* araeostyle.

a·re·o·sys·tyle (ə rē′ə sis′tīl, ar′ē ō-), *adj.* araeosystyle.

A·re·qui·pa (ar′ə kē′pä; *Sp.* ä′re kē′pä), *n.* a city in S Peru. 302,316.

Ar·es (âr′ēz), *n.* the ancient Greek god of war, a son of Zeus and Hera, identified by the Romans with Mars.

a·re·te (är′i tā′), *n.* the aggregate of qualities, as valor and virtue, making up good character. [< Gk *aretḗ*]

a·rête (ə rāt′), *n. Phys. Geog., Geol.* a sharp rugged mountain ridge, produced by glaciation. [1860–65; < F; OF *areste* sharp ridge < L *arista* awn, ear of wheat]

ar·e·thu·sa (ar′ə thōō′zə), *n.* **1.** Also called **dragon's mouth, swamp pink.** an orchid, *Arethusa bulbosa,* of eastern North America, having a solitary pink flower with a blotched, fringed lip: now rare. **2.** (*cap.*) *Class. Myth.* a nymph who was changed into a spring to save her when she was being pursued by the river god Alpheus. [1810–20; (< NL) < Gk *Aréthousa*]

A·re·ti·no (är′i tē′nō; *It.* ä′re tē′nô), *n.* **Pie·tro** (pye′trô), 1492–1556, Italian satirist and dramatist.

A·rez·zo (ə ret′sō; *It.* ä ret′tsô), *n.* a city in central Italy. 312,514.

arf (ärf), *interj.* (used to imitate the bark of a dog).

arf·ved·son·ite (är′vid sə nīt′), *n. Mineral.* a sodium-rich amphibole, occurring in green to black crystals in alkalic rocks. [1830–40; named after J. A. *Arfvedson* (d. 1841), Swedish chemist; see -ITE[1]]

Arg, *Biochem.* arginine.

Arg., Argentina.

ar·gal[1] (är′gəl), *n. Chem.* argol.

ar·gal[2] (är′gəl), *n.* argali.

ar·gal[3] (är′gəl), *conj., adv. Literary.* therefore: used facetiously to indicate that the reasoning that had gone before or the conclusion that follows is specious or absurd. [1595–1605; prob. repr. a popular early mod. E pron. of L *ergō* ERGO, with *ĕr* > *ar,* laxing of *ō,* and excrescent *l*]

ar·ga·li (är′gə lē), *n., pl.* **-li.** a wild sheep, *Ovis ammon,* of Asia, having long, curved horns that typically form an open, outwardly extended spiral: rare or endangered. Also, **argal.** [1770–80; < Mongolian: female mountain sheep]

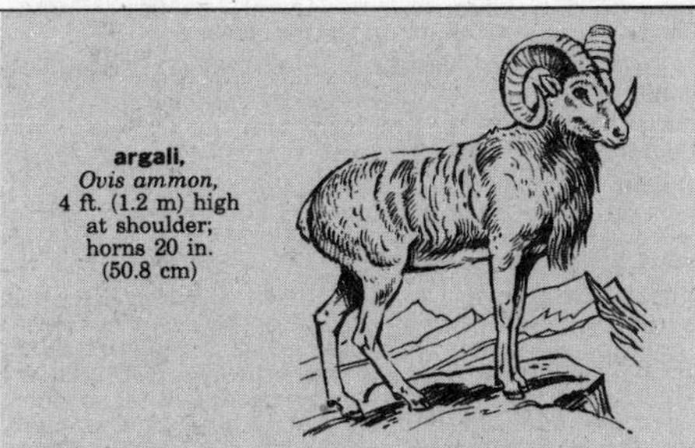

argali, *Ovis ammon,* 4 ft. (1.2 m) high at shoulder; horns 20 in. (50.8 cm)

Ar·gall (är′gôl, -gəl), *n.* **Sir Samuel,** 1572–1639, British explorer: colonial governor of Virginia 1617–19.

Ar′gand burn′er (är′gand, -gänd, -gənd), a type of oil or gas burner in which air is fed directly into the flame through a metal tube inside a cylindrical wick. [1780–90; named after Aimé *Argand* (1750–1803), Swiss scientist]

Ar′gand di′agram, *Math.* a Cartesian coordinate system consisting of two perpendicular axes for graphing complex numbers, the real part of a number being plotted along the horizontal axis and the imaginary part along the vertical axis. Cf. **imaginary axis, real axis.** [1905–10; named after Jean-Robert *Argand* (1768–1822), Swiss mathematician]

Ar′gand lamp′, an oil lamp with a chimney, having a tubular wick that permits air to reach the center of the flame. [1795–1805; named after A. *Argand.* See ARGAND BURNER]

ar·ga·sid (är′gə sid), *n.* **1.** any of the numerous ticks of the family Argasidae, comprising the soft ticks. **—*adj.*** **2.** belonging or pertaining to the family Argasidae. [< NL *Argasidae* name of the family, equiv. to *Argas* a genus, perh. irreg. < Gk *argós* not working, idle (see ARGON) + *-idae* -ID[2]]

Ar·ge·lan·der (är′gə län′dər), *n.* **Frie·drich Wil·helm Au·gust** (frē′drikh vil′helm ou′gŏŏst), 1799–1875, German astronomer.

ar·gent (är′jənt), *n.* **1.** *Heraldry.* the tincture or metal silver. **2.** *Archaic.* **a.** silver. **b.** something silvery or white. **3.** *Obs.* money. **—*adj.*** **4.** like silver; silvery white. **5.** *Heraldry.* of the tincture or metal silver: *a lion argent.* [1400–50; late ME *argentum* < L: silver, money]

argent-, var. of **argento-,** esp. before a vowel. Also, **argenti-.**

ar·gen·tal (är jen′tl), *adj.* of, pertaining to, containing, or resembling silver. [1810–20; ARGENT- + -AL[1]]

ar·gen·te·ous (är jen′tē əs), *adj.* silvery. Also, **ar·gen·tate** (är′jən tāt′). [1880–85; < L *argenteus.* See ARGENT-, -EOUS]

Ar·gen·teuil (ar zhän tœ′yᵊ), *n.* a city in N France, on the Seine near Paris. 103,141.

ar·gen·tic (är jen′tik), *adj. Chem.* of or containing silver and having a valence greater than the corresponding argentous compound. [1865–70; ARGENT- + -IC]

ar·gen·tif·er·ous (är′jən tif′ər əs), *adj.* silver-bearing. [1795–1805; < L *argent*(*um*) silver + -I- + -FEROUS]

Ar·gen·ti·na (är′jən tē′nə; *Sp.* är′hen tē′nä), *n.* a republic in S South America. 27,862,771; 1,084,120 sq. mi. (2,807,870 sq. km). *Cap.:* Buenos Aires. Also called **the Argentine.** Official name, **Ar′gentine Repub′lic.**

ar·gen·tine[1] (är′jən tin, -tīn′), *adj.* **1.** pertaining to or resembling silver. **—*n.*** **2.** a silvery substance, esp. one obtained from fish scales, used in making imitation pearls. [1400–50; late ME (< AF) < L *argentīnus* silvery. See ARGENT, -INE[1]]

ar·gen·tine[2] (är′jən tin, -tīn′), *n.* any of various silvery marine fishes, esp. those of the genus *Argentina.* [1530–40; < NL *Argentina* genus name, L, fem. of *argentīnus* silvery. See ARGENTINE[1]]

Ar·gen·tine (är′jən tēn′, -tīn′), *n.* **1.** a native or inhabitant of Argentina. **2.** Argentina (usually prec. by *the*): *They vacationed in the Argentine.* **—*adj.*** **3.** of or pertaining to Argentina. Also, **Ar·gen·tin·e·an** (är′jən tin′ē ən) (for defs. 1, 3).

Ar′gentine ant′, a small brown ant, *Iridomyrmex humilis,* introduced into the southern U.S. from South America: a household and fruit pest. [1905–10]

ar·gen·tite (är′jən tīt′), *n.* a dark lead-gray sectile mineral, silver sulfide, Ag_2S, occurring in crystals and as formless aggregates: an important ore of silver. [1830–40; ARGENT- + -ITE[1]]

argento-, a combining form meaning "silver," used in the formation of compound words: *argento-cuprous sulfide.* Also, **argenti-;** *esp. before a vowel,* **argent-.** [< L *argent*(*um*) + -o-]

ar·gen·tous (är jen′təs), *adj. Chem.* containing univalent silver, as argentous chloride, AgCl.

ar·gen·tum (är jen′təm), *n. Chem.* silver. *Symbol:* Ag [< L]

ar·ghool (är gōōl′), *n.* an Arabian wind instrument of the oboe family, consisting of two pipes, one of which is a drone. [< dial. Ar *arghūl*]

Ar·gie (är′jē), *n. Chiefly Brit. Slang* (*often disparaging*). an Argentine. Also, **Argy.** [ARG(ENTINEAN) + -IE]

ar·gil (är′jil), *n.* clay, esp. potter's clay. [1350–1400; ME *argilla* < L < Gk *árgillos,* equiv. to *arg*(*ós*) white + *-il*(*l*)*os* n. suffix]

ar·gil·la·ceous (är′jə lā′shəs), *adj.* **1.** *Geol., Petrol.* of the nature of or resembling clay; clayey. **2.** containing a considerable amount of clayey matter. [1725–35; < L *argillāceus* clayish. See ARGIL, -ACEOUS]

ar·gil·lite (är′jə līt′), *n.* any compact sedimentary rock composed mainly of clay materials; clay stone. [1785–95; < L *argill*(*a*) ARGIL + -ITE[1]] **—ar·gil·lit·ic** (är′jə lit′ik), *adj.*

ar·gi·nase (är′jə nās′, -nāz′), *n. Biochem.* a liver enzyme that converts arginine to urea. [1900–05; < G *Arginase;* see ARGININE, -ASE]

CONCISE PRONUNCIATION KEY: *act, cāpe, dâre, pärt; set, ēqual; if, ice; ox, ōver, ôrder, oil, bŏŏk, bōōt, out; up, ûrge; child; sing; shoe; thin, that;* zh as in *treasure.* ə = *a* as in *alone, e* as in *system, i* as in *easily, o* as in *gallop, u* as in *circus;* ᵊ as in *fire* (fīᵊr), *hour* (ouᵊr). l and n can serve as syllabic consonants, as in *cradle* (krād′l), and *button* (but′n). See the full key inside the front cover.

ar·gi·nine (är′jə nēn′, -nīn′, -nin), *n. Biochem.* an essential amino acid, $C_6H_{14}N_4O_2$: the free amino acid increases insulin secretion and is converted to urea in the liver by arginase. *Abbr.:* Arg; *Symbol:* R [1885–90; < G *Arginin,* a name unexplained by its originators]

Ar·give (är′jīv, -gīv), *adj.* **1.** of or pertaining to Argos. **2.** Greek. —*n.* **3.** a native of Argos. **4.** a Greek. [1590–1600; < L *Argīvus* < Gk *Argeîos* of Argos]

ar·gle-bar·gle (är′gəl bär′gəl), *n. Chiefly Brit.* argybargy. [1870–75; redupl. of *argle,* var. of ARGUE]

Ar·go (är′gō), *n., gen.* **Ar·gus** (är′gəs) for 1. **1.** *Astron.* a very large southern constellation, now divided into Vela, Carina, Puppis, and Pyxis, four separate constellations lying largely south of Canis Major. **2.** (*italics*) *Class. Myth.* the ship in which Jason sailed in quest of the Golden Fleece. —**Ar·go′an,** *adj.*

ar·gol (är′gəl), *n.* a crude tartar, produced as a by-product in casks by the fermentation of wine grapes, used as a mordant in dyeing, in the manufacture of tartaric acid, and in fertilizers. Also, **argal.** [1350–1400; ME *argul, argoile* < AF *argoil* << L *argilla* ARGIL]

Ar·go·lis (är′gə lis), *n.* **1.** an ancient district in SE Greece. **2. Gulf of,** a gulf of the Aegean, in SE Greece. ab. 30 mi. (48 km) long. —**Ar·gol·ic** (är gol′ik), **Ar·go·li·an** (är gō′lē ən), **Ar′go·lid,** *adj.*

ar·gon (är′gon), *n. Chem.* a colorless, odorless, chemically inactive, monatomic, gaseous element that, because of its inertness, is used for filling fluorescent and incandescent lamps and vacuum tubes. *Symbol:* Ar; *at. no.:* 18; *at. wt.:* 39.948. [1890–95; < Gk, neut. of *argós* inactive, not working, idle, contr. of *aergós* equiv. to *a-* A-[6] + *érg(on)* work + *-os* adj. suffix]

Ar·go·naut (är′gə nôt′, -not′), *n.* **1.** *Class. Myth.* a member of the band of men who sailed to Colchis with Jason in the ship *Argo* in search of the Golden Fleece. **2.** (*sometimes l.c.*) a person in quest of something dangerous but rewarding; adventurer. **3.** a person who moved to California during the gold rush of 1849. **4.** (*l.c.*) See **paper nautilus.** [< L *Argonauta* < Gk *Argonaútēs* crewman of the ship ARGO; see NAUTICAL] —**Ar′go·nau′tic,** *adj.*

Ar′gonne For′est (är′gon, är gon′; *Fr.* AR gôn′), a wooded region in NE France: battles, World War I, 1918; World War II, 1944. Also called **Ar·gonne** (AR gôn′).

Ar·gos (är′gos, -gəs), *n.* **1.** an ancient city in SE Greece, on the Gulf of Argolis: a powerful rival of Sparta, Athens, and Corinth.

ar·go·sy (är′gə sē), *n., pl.* **-sies.** **1.** a large merchant ship, esp. one with a rich cargo. **2.** a fleet of such ships. **3.** an opulent supply. [1570–80; earlier *ragusy* < It (*nave*) *ragusea* (ship) of RAGUSA]

ar·got (är′gō, -gət), *n.* **1.** a specialized idiomatic vocabulary peculiar to a particular class or group of people, esp. that of an underworld group, devised for private communication and identification: *a Restoration play rich in thieves' argot.* **2.** the special vocabulary and idiom of a particular profession or social group: *sociologists' argot.* [1855–60; < F, n. deriv. of *argoter* to quarrel, deriv. L *ergō* ERGO with v. suffix *-oter*] —**ar·got·ic** (är got′ik), *adj.*

Ar·go·vie (AR gô vē′), *n.* French name of **Aargau.**

ar·gu·a·ble (är′gyo͞o ə bəl), *adj.* **1.** susceptible to debate, challenge, or doubt; questionable: *Whether this is the best plan of action or not is arguable.* **2.** susceptible to being supported by convincing or persuasive argument: *Admirers agree that it is arguable he is the finest pianist of his generation.* [1605–15; ARGUE + -ABLE] —**ar′gu·a·bly,** *adv.*

ar·gue (är′gyo͞o), *v.,* **-gued, -gu·ing.** —*v.i.* **1.** to present reasons for or against a thing: *He argued in favor of capital punishment.* **2.** to contend in oral disagreement; dispute: *The Senator argued with the President about the new tax bill.* —*v.t.* **3.** to state the reasons for or against: *The lawyers argued the case.* **4.** to maintain in reasoning: *to argue that the news report must be wrong.* **5.** to persuade, drive, etc., by reasoning: *to argue someone out of a plan.* **6.** to show; prove; imply; indicate: *His clothes argue poverty.* [1275–1325; ME < AF, OF *arguer* < L *argūtāre, -ārī,* freq. of *arguere* to prove, assert, accuse (ML: argue, reason), though L freq. form attested only in sense "babble, chatter"] —**ar′gu·er,** *n.*
—**Syn. 1., 2.** ARGUE, DEBATE, DISCUSS imply using reasons or proofs to support or refute an assertion, proposition, or principle. ARGUE implies presenting one's reasons: *The scientists argued for a safer testing procedure;* it may also imply disputing in an angry or excited way: *His parents argue all the time.* To DISCUSS is to present varied opinions and views: *to discuss ways and means.* To DEBATE is to interchange formal (usually opposing) arguments, esp. on public questions: *to debate a proposed amendment.*

CONCISE ETYMOLOGY KEY: <, descended or borrowed from; >, whence; b., blend of, blended; c., cognate with; cf., compare; deriv., derivative; equiv., equivalent; imit., imitative; obl., oblique; r., replacing; s., stem; sp., spelling, spelled; resp., respelling, respelled; trans., translation; ?, origin unknown; *, unattested; ‡, probably earlier than. See the full key inside the front cover.

Ar·güe·das (AR gwe′thäs), *n.* **Al·ci·des** (äl sē′thes), 1879–1946, Bolivian author, sociologist, and statesman.

ar·gu·fy (är′gyə fī′), *v.t., v.i.,* **-fied, -fy·ing.** *Chiefly South Midland and Southern U.S.* to argue, dispute, or wrangle. [1745–55; ARGUE + -FY] —**ar′gu·fi′er,** *n.*

ar·gu·ment (är′gyə mənt), *n.* **1.** an oral disagreement; verbal opposition; contention; altercation: *a violent argument.* **2.** a discussion involving differing points of view; debate: *They were deeply involved in an argument about inflation.* **3.** a process of reasoning; series of reasons: *I couldn't follow his argument.* **4.** a statement, reason, or fact for or against a point: *This is a strong argument in favor of her theory.* **5.** an address or composition intended to convince or persuade; persuasive discourse. **6.** subject matter; theme: *The central argument of his paper was presented clearly.* **7.** an abstract or summary of the major points in a work of prose or poetry, or of sections of such a work. **8.** *Math.* **a.** an independent variable of a function. **b.** Also called **amplitude.** the angle made by a given vector with the reference axis. **c.** the angle corresponding to a point representing a given complex number in polar coordinates. Cf. **principal argument. 9.** *Computers.* a variable in a program, to which a value will be assigned when the program is run: often given in parentheses following a function name and used to calculate the function. **10.** *Obs.* **a.** evidence or proof. **b.** a matter of contention. [1325–75; ME (< OF) < L *argūmentum.* See ARGUE, -MENT]
—**Syn. 1.** ARGUMENT, CONTROVERSY, DISPUTE imply the expression of opinions for and against some idea. An ARGUMENT usually arises from a disagreement between two persons, each of whom advances facts supporting his or her own point of view. A CONTROVERSY or a DISPUTE may involve two or more persons. A DISPUTE is an oral contention, usually brief, and often of a heated, angry, or undignified character: *a violent dispute over a purchase.* A CONTROVERSY is an oral or written expression of contrary opinions, and may be dignified and of some duration: *a political controversy.*

ar·gu·men·ta·tion (är′gyə men tā′shən), *n.* **1.** the process of developing or presenting an argument; reasoning. **2.** discussion; debate; disputation: *The lengthy argumentation tired many listeners.* **3.** a discussion dealing with a controversial point. **4.** the setting forth of reasons together with the conclusion drawn from them. **5.** the premises and conclusion so set forth. **6.** argument (def. 5). [1400–50; late ME *argumentacioun* (< MF) < L *argūmentātiōn-* (s. of *argūmentātiō*). See ARGUMENT, -ATION] —**ar′gu·men·ta′tious,** *adj.*

ar·gu·men·ta·tive (är′gyə men′tə tiv), *adj.* **1.** fond of or given to argument and dispute; disputatious; contentious: *The law students were an unusually argumentative group.* **2.** of or characterized by argument; controversial: *an argumentative attitude toward political issues.* **3.** *Law.* arguing or containing arguments suggesting that a certain fact tends toward a certain conclusion. [1635–45; ARGUMENT + -ATIVE] —**ar′gu·men′ta·tive·ly,** *adv.* —**ar′gu·men′ta·tive·ness,** *n.*

ar′gument from design′, *Philos.* See **teleological argument.**

ar·gu·men·tum (är′gyə men′təm), *n., pl.* **-ta** (-tə). argument (def. 3). [< L]

Ar·gun (är go͞on′), *n. Older Spelling.* a river in NE Asia, forming part of the boundary between the Russian Federation and China. ab. 450 mi. (725 km) long. Also called **Ergun He.**

Ar·gus (är′gəs), *n.* **1.** *Class. Myth.* a giant with 100 eyes, set to guard the heifer Io: his eyes were transferred after his death to the peacock's tail. **2.** a son of Phrixus and builder of the *Argo.* **3.** (in the *Odyssey*) Odysseus' faithful dog, who recognized his master after twenty years and immediately died. **4.** any observant or vigilant person; a watchful guardian. **5.** (*l.c.*) Also, **ar′gus pheas′ant.** any of several brilliantly marked Malayan pheasants of the *Argusianus* or *Rheinardia* genera. [< L < Gk *Árgos,* deriv. of *argós* bright, shining]

Ar·gus-eyed (är′gəs īd′), *adj.* having keen eyes; vigilant; watchful.

ar′gus tor′toise bee′tle. See under **tortoise beetle.**

ar·gu·ta (är gyo͞o′tə), *n.* the green, smooth-skinned, edible fruit of an Asian vine, *Actinidia arguta.* [< NL, the species name, fem of L *argūtus* pungent, sharp, producing a clear, constant sound, ptp. of *arguere;* see ARGUE]

Ar·gy (är′jē), *n., pl.* **-gies.** Argie.

ar·gy-bar·gy (är′gē bär′gē), *n., pl.* **-gies.** *Chiefly Brit.* a vigorous discussion or dispute. [1595–1605; see ARGLE-BARGLE]

ar·gyle (är′gīl), (*often cap.*) *adj.* **1.** (of knitted articles) having a diamond-shaped pattern in two or more colors. —*n.* **2.** a diamond-shaped pattern of two or more colors, used in knitting socks, sweaters, etc. **3.** a sock having this pattern. [1790–1800; var. of ARGYLL; so called because orig. patterned after the tartan of this clan]

Ar·gyll (är gīl′), *n.* a historic county in W Scotland. Also called **Ar·gyll·shire** (är gīl′shēr, -shər).

Ar·gy·rol (är′jə rôl′, -rol′), *Pharm., Trademark.* See **mild silver protein.**

Ar·hat (AR′hət), *n.* a Buddhist who has attained Nirvana through rigorous discipline and ascetic practices. Cf. **Bodhisattva.** Also, **Ar·hant** (är′hənt). [1865–70; < Skt: meriting respect, deriv. of *arhati* (he) merits] —**Ar′hat·ship′,** *n.*

År·hus (ôr′ho͞os), *n.* a seaport in E Jutland, in Denmark. 245,941. Also, **Aarhus.**

a·rhyth·mi·a (ə rith′mē ə, ə rith′-), *n. Pathol.* arrhythmia. —**a·rhyth·mic** (ə rith′mik, ə rith′-), **a·rhyth′mi·cal,** *adj.* —**a·rhyth′mi·cal·ly,** *adv.*

a·ri·a (är′ē ə, âr′ē ə), *n.* **1.** an air or melody. **2.** an elaborate melody sung solo with accompaniment, as in an opera or oratorio. [1735–45; < It; see AIR[1]]

A·ri·a (âr′ē ə, ə rī′ə), *n. Class. Myth.* a nymph, the mother of Miletus, by Apollo.

-aria, a suffix occurring in scientific terms of Latin origin, esp. in names of biological genera and groups: *filaria.* [< L: fem. sing. or neut. pl. of *-ārius* -ARY]

a·ri·a da ca·po (är′ē ə də kä′pō), *pl.* **arias da capo.** an operatic aria in three sections with the first and third sections alike and the middle section contrasting. [< It: lit., air from the head, i.e., beginning]

Ar·i·ad·ne (ar′ē ad′nē), *n.* **1.** *Class. Myth.* a daughter of Minos and Pasiphaë who gave Theseus the thread by which he escaped from the labyrinth: deserted by Theseus on Naxos, she became the bride of Dionysus. **2.** a female given name.

Ar·i·an (âr′ē ən, ar′-), *adj.* **1.** of or pertaining to Arius or Arianism. —*n.* **2.** an adherent of Arianism. [1525–35; < LL *Ariānus* of, pertaining to ARIUS; see -AN]

Ar·i·an (âr′ē ən, ar′-), *adj., n.* Aryan.

-arian, a suffix forming personal nouns corresponding to Latin adjectives ending in *-ārius* or English adjectives or nouns ending in **-ary** (*librarian; proletarian; Rotarian; seminarian; sexagenarian; veterinarian*); subsequently productive in English with other Latinate stems, forming nouns denoting a person who supports, advocates, or practices a doctrine, theory, or set of principles associated with the base word: *authoritarian; establishmentarian; totalitarian; vegetarian.* [< L *-āri(us)* or -ARY + -AN]

Ar·i·ane (ar′ē an′; *Fr.* A RYAN′), *n.* **1.** *Rocketry.* a French-built, three-stage, liquid-propellant rocket for launching satellites into orbit around the earth. **2.** a female given name, French form of **Ariadne.**

Ar·i·an·ism (âr′ē ə niz′əm, ar′-), *n. Theol.* the doctrine, taught by Arius, that Christ the Son was not consubstantial with God the Father. [1590–1600; ARIAN + -ISM] —**Ar′i·an·is′tic, Ar′i·an·is′ti·cal,** *adj.*

A·ri·ca (ə rē′kə; *Sp.* ä RĒ′kä), *n.* **1.** a seaport in N Chile. 112,300. **2.** See under **Tacna-Arica.**

ar·id (ar′id), *adj.* **1.** being without moisture; extremely dry; parched: *arid land; an arid climate.* **2.** barren or unproductive because of lack of moisture: *arid farmland.* **3.** lacking interest or imaginativeness; sterile; jejune: *an arid treatment of an exciting topic.* [1645–55; (< F) < L *āridus,* equiv. to *ār(ēre)* to be dry + *-idus* -ID[4]; cf. ASH[1]] —**a·rid·i·ty** (ə rid′i tē), **ar′id·ness,** *n.* —**ar′id·ly,** *adv.*
—**Syn. 1.** See **dry. 3.** tedious, dreary, vapid, uninspired, uninspiring.

a·rid·i·fi·ca·tion (ə rid′ə fi kā′shən), *n.* the process by which a humid region becomes increasingly dry, as by climatic change or human interference with the ecology. Cf. **desertification.** [ARID + -I- + -FICATION]

a·rid·i·sol (ə rid′ə sôl′, -sol′), *n.* a soil type common to the world's deserts, poor in organic matter and rich in salts. [1970–75; ARID + -I- + -SOL]

arid′ity in′dex, a number indicating how much more precipitation could be lost by evapotranspiration if it were available than is actually lost at a given location.

A·riège (A RYEZH′), *n.* a department in S France. 137,857; 1893 sq. mi. (4905 sq. km). *Cap.:* Foix.

ar·i·el (âr′ē əl), *n.* a mountain gazelle of Arabia, *Gazella gazella arabica:* almost extinct. Also, **ar′iel gazelle′.** [1825–35; < dial. Ar *aryal*]

Ar·i·el (âr′ē əl), *n.* **1.** (in Shakespeare's *Tempest*) a spirit of the air who is required to use his magic to help Prospero. **2.** *Astron.* one of the moons of the planet Uranus. **3.** *Aerospace.* one of a series of British satellites that studied the ionosphere, cosmic rays, and x-rays. **4.** Also, **Ar·i·elle** (ar′ē el′, âr′-). a female given name. **5.** a male given name.

Ar·ies (âr′ēz, -ē ēz′), *n., gen.* **A·ri·e·tis** (ə rī′i tis). **1.** *Astron.* the Ram, a zodiacal constellation between Pisces and Taurus. **2.** *Astrol.* **a.** the first sign of the zodiac: the cardinal fire sign. See illus. under **zodiac. b.** a person born under this sign, usually between March 21st and April 19th. [1350–1400; ME < L: ram]

ar·i·et·ta (ar′ē et′ə; *It.* ä′RE et′tä), *n., pl.* **-et·tas, -et·te** (-et′ə; *It.* -et′te). *Music.* a short aria. Also, **ar·i·ette** (ar′ē et′). [1735–45; < It, equiv. to *ari(a)* ARIA + *-etta* -ETTE]

a·ri·ga·to (ä′RE gä′tô; *Eng.* är′ē gä′tō), *interj. Japanese.* thank you. [1965–70]

a·right (ə rīt′), *adv.* rightly; correctly; properly: *I want to set things aright.* [bef. 1000; ME; OE *ariht, on riht.* See A-[1], RIGHT]

A·rik·a·ra (ə rik′ər ə), *n., pl.* **-ras,** (*esp. collectively*) **-ra** for 1. **1.** a member of a group of North American Indians of Pawnee origin who now inhabit the Dakota region. **2.** the Caddoan language spoken by the Arikara.

a·ri·ki (ä rē′kē), *n., pl.* **-ki.** (in Polynesia) a chief or king. [< Maori]

ar·il (ar′il), *n. Bot.* a usually fleshy appendage or covering of certain seeds, as of the bittersweet, *Celastrus scandens,* or the nutmeg. [1785–95; < NL *arillus;* ML: grape seed, prob. erroneously for *armillus,* with same sense; cf. Upper It dial. *armella, arma* kernel, pit of a fruit, It *animella* edible insides of an animal < L *anima* lit., spirit (hence, the insides of a thing), with *-illa* dim. suffix; see ANIMA] —**ar′il·loid′,** *adj.*

ar·il·late (ar′ə lāt′, -lit), *adj. Bot.* having an aril. [1825–35; < NL *arill(us)* ARIL + -ATE[1]]

Ar·i·ma·thae·a (ar′ə mə thē′ə), *n.* a town in ancient Palestine. Matt. 27:57. Also, **Ar′i·ma·the′a.** —**Ar′i·ma·thae′an, Ar′i·ma·the′an,** *adj.*

A·rim·i·num (ə rim′ə nəm), *n.* ancient name of **Rimini.**

A·ri·on (ə rī′ən), *n.* **1.** fl. 7th century B.C., Greek poet: inventor of the dithyramb. **2.** *Class. Myth.* a winged horse often believed to be the offspring of Poseidon and Demeter.

ar•i•ose (ar′ē ōs′, ar′ē ōs′), *adj.* characterized by melody; songlike. [1735–45; Anglicized var. of ARIOSO]

a•rio•so (är′ē ō′sō, ar′-; *It.* ä ryô′sô), *adj., adv., n., pl.* **-sos.** *Music.* —*adj., adv.* **1.** in the manner of an air or melody. —*n.* **2.** an arioso composition or section. [1735–45; < It: lit., songlike. See ARIA, -OSE[1]]

A•ri•os•to (är′ē os′tō, -ō′stō, ar′-; *It.* ä′rē ôs′tô), *n.* **Lu•do•vi•co** (lo͞o′dô vē′kô), 1474–1533, Italian poet: author of *Orlando Furioso.*

Ar•i•o•vis•tus (ar′ē ō vis′təs), *n.* fl. c71–58 B.C., Germanic leader of the Suevi.

-aris, a suffix occurring in scientific terms: *Polaris.* [< L *-āris;* see -AR[1]]

a•rise (ə rīz′), *v.i.,* **a•rose, a•ris•en** (ə riz′ən), **a•ris•ing. 1.** to get up from sitting, lying, or kneeling; rise: *He arose from his chair when she entered the room.* **2.** to awaken; wake up: *He arose at sunrise to get an early start to the beach.* **3.** to move upward; mount; ascend: *A thin curl of smoke arose lazily from the cabin.* **4.** to come into being, action, or notice; originate; appear; spring up: *New problems arise daily.* **5.** to result or proceed; spring or issue (sometimes fol. by *from*): *It is difficult to foresee the consequences that may arise from this action. After such destruction many problems in resettlement often arise.* [bef. 900; ME *arisen,* OE *ārisan;* c. Goth *ur-reisan.* See A-[3], RISE]
—Syn. 3. climb. **4.** emerge, flow, emanate.

a•ris•ta (ə ris′tə), *n., pl.* **-tae** (-tē). **1.** *Bot.* a bristlelike appendage of the spikelets of grains or grasses; an awn. **2.** *Entomol.* a prominent bristle on the antenna of some dipterous insects. [1685–95; < L: awn, beard or ear of grain; cf. ARÊTE]

A•ris•ta (ä rēs′tä), *n.* **Ma•ria•no** (mä ryä′nô), 1802–55, Mexican general: president of Mexico 1851–53.

ar•is•tarch (ar′ə stärk′), *n.* a severe critic. [1615–25; after ARISTARCHUS of Samothrace, who, in editing Homer, rejected many lines as spurious interpolations] —**Ar′i•star′chi•an,** *adj.*

Ar•is•tar•chus (ar′ə stär′kəs), *n.* **1. of Samos.** late 3rd century B.C., Greek astronomer. **2. of Samothrace.** c216–144 B.C., Greek philologist and critic. **3.** an extremely bright crater in the second quadrant of the face of the moon: about 29 miles (47 km) in diameter from crest to crest.

a•ris•tate (ə ris′tāt), *adj.* **1.** *Bot.* having aristae; awned. **2.** *Zool.* tipped with a bristle. [1830–40; < LL *aristātus* awned. See ARISTA, -ATE[1]]

Ar•is•ti•des (ar′ə stī′dēz), *n.* ("*the Just*") 530?–468? B.C., Athenian statesman and general.

Ar•is•tip•pus (ar′ə stip′əs), *n.* 435?–356? B.C., Greek philosopher: founder of the Cyrenaic school of philosophy.

a•ris•to (ə ris′tō), *n., pl.* **-tos.** *Chiefly Brit. Informal.* aristocrat. [1860–65; by shortening; cf. -O]

aristo-, a learned borrowing from Greek meaning "best," occurring either in direct loans (*aristocratic*), or in the formation of compound words: *aristotype.* [< Gk, comb. form of *áristos* best, superl. of *ari-* prob. a term specifying at first the upper class of society, the warrior caste; cf. ARES, perh. ARYAN]

ar•is•toc•ra•cy (ar′ə stok′rə sē), *n., pl.* **-cies. 1.** a class of persons holding exceptional rank and privileges, esp. the hereditary nobility. **2.** a government or state ruled by an aristocracy, elite, or privileged upper class. **3.** government by those considered to be the best or most able people in the state. **4.** a governing body composed of those considered to be the best or most able people in the state. **5.** any class or group considered to be superior, as through education, ability, wealth, or social prestige. [1555–65; (< MF *aristocratie*) < ML *aristocracia* (var. of *-tia*) < Gk *aristokratía* rule of the best. See ARISTO-, -CRACY]

a•ris•to•crat (ə ris′tə krat′, ar′ə stə-), *n.* **1.** a member of an aristocracy, esp. a noble. **2.** a person who has the tastes, manners, etc., characteristic of members of an aristocracy. **3.** an advocate of an aristocratic form of government. **4.** anything regarded as the best, most elegant, or most stylish of its kind: *the aristocrat of California wines.* [1770–80; < F *aristocrate,* back formation from *aristocratie* ARISTOCRACY]
—Syn. 1. patrician, peer, lord.

a•ris•to•crat•ic (ə ris′tə krat′ik, ar′ə stə-), *adj.* **1.** of or pertaining to government by an aristocracy. **2.** belonging to or favoring the aristocracy. **3.** characteristic of an aristocrat; having the manners, values, or qualities associated with the aristocracy: *aristocratic bearing; aristocratic snobbishness.* Also, **a•ris′to•crat′i•cal.** [1595–1605; < Gk *aristokratikós* pertaining to ARISTOCRACY; see -IC] —**a•ris′to•crat′i•cal•ly,** *adv.* —**a•ris′to•crat′i•cal•ness, a•ris′to•crat′ic•ness,** *n.*

a•ris•to•lo•chi•a•ceous (ə ris′tl ō′kē ā′shəs), *adj.* belonging to the Aristolochiaceae, the birthwort family of plants. Cf. **birthwort family.** [< NL *Aristolochi(a)* genus name (< Gk *aristolócheia* birthwort, lit., best childbirth, from the herb's supposed effects; see ARISTO-, LOCHIA) + -ACEOUS]

Ar•is•toph•a•nes (ar′ə stof′ə nēz′), *n.* 448?–385? B.C., Athenian comic dramatist. —**A•ris•to•phan•ic** (ə ris′tə-fan′ik), *adj.*

Ar•is•tot•e•les (ar′ə stot′l ēz′), *n.* a walled plain in the first quadrant of the face of the moon: about 60 miles (97 km) in diameter.

Ar•is•to•te•lian (ar′ə stə tēl′yən, -tē′lē ən, ə ris′tə-) *adj.* **1.** of, pertaining to, based on, or derived from Aristotle or his theories. —*n.* **2.** a follower of Aristotle. Also, **Ar′is•to•te′lean.** [1600–10; < L *Aristoteli(us)* < Gk *Aristotéleios* of ARISTOTLE + -AN]

Ar•is•to•te•lian•ism (ar′ə stə tēl′yə niz′əm, -tē′lē ə-, ə ris′tə-), *n.* **1.** the philosophy of Aristotle. **2.** emphasis upon deduction and upon investigation of concrete and particular things and situations. [1835–45; ARISTOTELIAN + -ISM]

Ar′istote′lian log′ic, 1. the logic of Aristotle, esp. in the modified form taught in the Middle Ages. **2.** See **traditional logic.** [1830–40]

Ar•is•tot•le (ar′ə stot′l), *n.* 384–322 B.C., Greek philosopher: pupil of Plato; tutor of Alexander the Great.

Ar′istotle Con′templating the Bust′ of Ho′mer, a painting (1653) by Rembrandt.

Ar′istot′le's lan′tern, *Zool.* a complex arrangement of muscles and calcareous teeth and plates forming an eversible organ in most echinoids, functioning in mastication. [so called from a reference by Aristotle to a sea urchin resembling in shape certain lanterns]

a•ris•to•type (ə ris′tə tīp′), *n.* **1.** a process of photographic printing in which paper coated with silver chloride in gelatin is used. **2.** a print made by this process. [ARISTO- + -TYPE]

arith., 1. arithmetic. **2.** arithmetical.

ar•ith•man•cy (ar′ith man′sē), *n.* divination by the use of numbers, esp. by the number of letters in names. Also, **a•rith•mo•man•cy** (ə rith′mə man′sē, ar′ith-). [1570–80; < NL *arithmomantia* < Gk *arithmó(s)* number + *manteía* -MANCY]

a•rith•me•tic (*n.* ə rith′mə tik; *adj.* ar′ith met′ik), *n.* **1.** the method or process of computation with figures: the most elementary branch of mathematics. **2.** Also called **higher arithmetic, theoretical arithmetic.** the theory of numbers; the study of the divisibility of whole numbers, the remainders after division, etc. **3.** a book on this subject. —*adj.* **4.** Also, **ar′ith•met′i•cal.** of or pertaining to arithmetic. [1200–50; < L *arithmētica,* fem. sing. of *arithmēticus* < Gk *arithmētikḗ* (*téchnē*) (art, skill) of numbers, equiv. to *arithmé(ein)* to reckon + *-t(o)-* verbal adj. + *-ikē* -IC; r. ME *arsmet(r)ike* < OF *arismetique* < ML *arismētica,* with *s* for LGk *th*] —**ar′ith•met′i•cal•ly,** *adv.*

a•rith•me•ti•cian (ə rith′mi tish′ən, ar′ith-), *n.* an expert in arithmetic. [1550–60; < MF *arithmeticien;* see ARITHMETIC, -IAN]

ar′ith•met′ic/log′ic u′nit (ar′ith met′ik loj′ik), *Computers.* See **ALU.**

ar′ithmet′ic mean′, *Statistics.* the mean obtained by adding several quantities together and dividing the sum by the number of quantities: *the arithmetic mean of 1, 5, 2, and 8 is 4.* Also called **average.** [1790–1800]

arithmet′ic progres′sion, a sequence in which each term is obtained by the addition of a constant number to the preceding term, as 1, 4, 7, 10, 13, and 6, 1, −4, −9, −14. Also called **ar′ithmet′ic se′ries.** [1585–95]

-arium, a suffix occurring in loanwords from Latin, which often denote a location or receptacle (*armarium; caldarium; solarium; vivarium*). It has limited productivity in English, esp. in words denoting an artificial environment for plants or animals, on the model of *vivarium* or *herbarium: aquarium; insectarium; terrarium.* Cf. -ary. [< L *-ārium;* see -ARY]

A•ri•us (ə rī′əs, âr′ē-), *n.* died A.D. 336, Christian priest at Alexandria: founder of Arianism.

a ri•ve•der•ci (ä′ rē ve deR′chē), *Italian.* arrivederci.

Ariz., Arizona.

Ar•i•zo•na (ar′ə zō′nə), *n.* a state in SW United States. 2,717,866; 113,909 sq. mi. (295,025 sq. km). *Cap.:* Phoenix. *Abbr.:* AZ (for use with zip code), Ariz. —**Ar′i•zo′nan, Ar•i•zo•ni•an** (ar′ə zō′nē ən), *adj., n.*

Ar•ju•na (är′jə nə; *Skt.* uR′jo͝o nə), *n. Hinduism.* the chief hero of the *Bhagavad-Gita,* befriended by Krishna, who appears as his charioteer and advises him on duty and the immortality of the soul.

ark (ärk), *n.* **1.** (*sometimes cap.*) Also called **Noah's Ark.** the large boat built by Noah in which he saved himself, his family, and a pair of every kind of creature during the Flood. Gen. 6–9. **2.** Also called **ark of the covenant.** a chest or box containing the two stone tablets inscribed with the Ten Commandments, carried by the Israelites in their wanderings in the desert after the Exodus: the most sacred object of the tabernacle and the Temple in Jerusalem, where it was kept in the holy of holies. **3.** a place of protection or security; refuge; asylum. **4.** (*cap.*) *Judaism.* See **Holy Ark. 5.** a flatboat formerly used on the Mississippi River and its tributaries. **6.** *Naut.* See **life car. 7.** *Archaic.* a chest or box. [bef. 850; ME *ark(e),* erke, OE *arc, earc(e)* (cf. OFris *erke, arke,* Dark, OHG, Goth *arka,* ON *ǫrk*) < L *arca* chest, coffer, deriv. of *arcēre* to safeguard, c. Hittite *ḫark-* hold, possess]

Ark., Arkansas.

Ar•ka•del•phia (är′kə del′fē ə), *n.* a city in central Arkansas. 10,005.

Ar•kan•sas (är′kən sô′; *also for 2* ar kan′zəs), *n.* **1.** state in S central United States; 2,285,513. 53,103 sq. mi. (137,537 sq. km). *Cap.:* Little Rock. *Abbr.:* AR (for use with zip code), Ark. **2.** a river flowing E and SE from central Colorado into the Mississippi in SE Arkansas. 1450 mi. (2335 km) long. —**Ar•kan•san** (är kan′zən), **Ar•kan•si•an** (är kan′zē ən), *n., adj.*

Ar•kan′sas Cit′y (är kan′zəs), a city in S Kansas. 13,201.

Ar′kansas tooth′pick, *Slang.* a bowie knife or similar sharp knifelike implement.

Ar•kan•saw•yer (är′kən sô′yər, -soi′ər), *n. Informal.* an Arkansan. [1905–10, *Amer.;* ARKANSAS + -YER, with *s* respelled as *y* on model of SAWYER]

Ar•khan•gelsk (uR кнän′gyilsk), *n.* Russian name of **Archangel.**

Ar•kie (är′kē), *n. Often Disparaging.* a migrant worker originally from Arkansas. [1925–30; ARK(ANSAS) + -IE]

ark′ of the cov′enant, ark (def. 2).

ar•kose (är′kōs), *n.* a granular sedimentary rock composed of quartz and feldspar or mica; a feldspathic sandstone. [1830–40; < F] —**ar•ko′sic,** *adj.*

ark′ shell′, any marine bivalve of the family Arcidae, esp. of the genus *Arca,* characterized by a heavy shell with a toothed hinge and a deep, boatlike inner surface. [1850–55]

ark•wright (ärk′rīt′), *n.* a maker of chests, boxes, or coffers. [ARK + WRIGHT]

Ark•wright (ärk′rīt′), *n.* **Sir Richard,** 1732–92, English inventor of the spinning jenny.

ark′wright fur′niture, late medieval English furniture of simple construction.

ARL, Association of Research Libraries.

Arl•berg (äRl′berk′), *n.* **1.** a mountain pass in W Austria. 5946 ft. (1812 m) high. **2.** a tunnel beneath this pass.

Ar•leen (är lēn′), *n.* a female given name.

Ar•len (är′lən), *n.* **1. Harold** (*Hymen Arluck*), born 1905, U.S. songwriter. **2. Michael** (*Dikran Kouyoumdjian*), 1895–1956, English novelist, born in Bulgaria. **3.** a male given name.

Ar•lene (är lēn′), *n.* a female given name.

Arles (ärlz; *Fr.* aRl), *n.* a city in SE France, on the Rhone River: Roman ruins. 50,345.

Ar•ling•ton (är′ling tən), *n.* **1.** a county in NE Virginia, opposite Washington, D.C.: national cemetery. 152,599. **2.** a city in N Texas. 160,123. **3.** a city in E Massachusetts. 48,219. **4.** a town in SE New York. 11,305.

Ar′lington Heights′, a city in NE Illinois, near Chicago. 66,116.

Ar′lington Na′tional Cem′etery, a national cemetery located in Arlington, Virginia, across the Potomac from Washington, D.C.: site of the Tomb of the Unknown Soldier.

Ar•liss (är′lis), *n.* **George,** 1868–1946, English actor.

arm[1] (ärm), *n.* **1.** the upper limb of the human body, esp. the part extending from the shoulder to the wrist. **2.** the upper limb from the shoulder to the elbow. **3.** the forelimb of any vertebrate. **4.** some part of an organism like or likened to an arm. **5.** any armlike part or attachment, as the tone arm of a phonograph. **6.** a covering for the arm, esp. a sleeve of a garment: *the arm of a coat.* **7.** an administrative or operational branch of an organization: *A special arm of the government will investigate.* **8.** *Naut.* any of the curved or bent pieces of an anchor, terminating in the flukes. See diag. under **anchor. 9.** an armrest. **10.** an inlet or cove: *an arm of the sea.* **11.** a combat branch of the military service, as the infantry, cavalry, or field artillery. **12.** power; might; strength; authority: *the long arm of the law.* **13.** *Typography.* either of the extensions to the right of the vertical line of a K or upward from the vertical stem of a Y. **14. an arm and a leg,** a great deal of money: *Our night on the town cost us an arm and a leg.* **15. arm in arm,** with arms linked together or intertwined: *They walked along arm in arm.* **16. at arm's length,** not on familiar or friendly terms; at a distance: *He's the kind of person you pity but want to keep at arm's length.* **17. in the arms of Morpheus,** asleep: *After a strenuous day, he was soon in the arms of Morpheus.* **18. on the arm,** *Slang.* free of charge; gratis: *an investigation of policemen who ate lunch on the arm.* **19. put the arm on,** *Slang.* **a.** to solicit or borrow money from: *She put the arm on me for a generous contribution.* **b.** to use force or violence on; use strong-arm tactics on: *If they don't cooperate, put the arm on them.* **20. twist someone's arm,** to use force or coercion on someone. **21. with open arms,** cordially; with warm hospitality: *a country that receives immi-*

CONCISE PRONUNCIATION KEY: act, cāpe, dâre, pärt; set, ēqual; *if,* īce; ox, ōver, ôrder, oil, bo͝ok, bo͞ot, out; up, ûrge; child; sing; shoe; thin, *th*at; zh as in *treasure.* ə = a as in *alone,* e as in *system,* i as in *easily,* o as in *gallop,* u as in *circus;* ᵊ as in *fire* (fīᵊr), *hour* (ouᵊr). l and n can serve as syllabic consonants, as in *cradle* (krād′l), and *button* (but′n). See the full key inside the front cover.

grants with open arms. [bef. 900; ME; OE *earm;* c. Goth *arms,* ON *armr,* OFris *erm,* D, OS, OHG *arm* (G *Arm*) arm; L *armus,* Serbo-Croatian *rȁme, rȁmo* shoulder; akin to Skt *īrmá,* Avestan *arəma-,* OPruss *irmo* arm; not akin to L *arma* ARM²] —**armed,** *adj.* —**arm′like′,** *adj.*

arm² (ärm), *n.* **1.** Usually, **arms.** weapons, esp. firearms. **2. arms,** *Heraldry.* the escutcheon, with its divisions, charges, and tinctures, and the other components forming an achievement that symbolizes and is reserved for a person, family, or corporate body; armorial bearings; coat of arms. **3. bear arms, a.** to carry weapons. **b.** to serve as a member of the military or of contending forces: *His religious convictions kept him from bearing arms, but he served as an ambulance driver with the Red Cross.* **4. take up arms,** to prepare for war; go to war: *to take up arms against the enemy.* **5. under arms,** ready for battle; trained and equipped: *The number of men under arms is no longer the decisive factor in warfare.* **6. up in arms,** ready to take action; indignant; outraged: *There is no need to get up in arms over such a trifle.* —*v.i.* **7.** to enter into a state of hostility or of readiness for war. —*v.t.* **8.** to equip with weapons: *to arm the troops.* **9.** to activate (a fuze) so that it will explode the charge at the time desired. **10.** to cover protectively. **11.** to provide with whatever will add strength, force, or security; support; fortify: *He was armed with statistics and facts.* **12.** to equip or prepare for any specific purpose or effective use: *to arm a security system; to arm oneself with persuasive arguments.* **13.** to prepare for action; make fit; ready. [1200–50 for v.; 1300–50 for n.; (v.) ME *armen* < AF, OF *armer* < L *armāre* to arm, v. deriv. of *arma* (pl.) tools, weapons (not akin to ARM¹); (n.) ME *armes* (pl.) << L *arma,* as above] —**arm′less,** *adj.*
—**Syn. 12.** outfit. —**Ant. 9.** deactivate, disarm.

ARM, See **adjustable-rate mortgage.**

Arm, Armenian.

Arm., **1.** Armenian. **2.** Armorican.

Ar.M., Master of Architecture. [< NL *Architecturae Magister*]

Ar·ma·da (är mä′də, -mā′-), *n.* **1.** Also called **Invincible Armada, Spanish Armada.** the fleet sent against England by Philip II of Spain in 1588. It was defeated by the English navy and later dispersed and wrecked by storms. **2.** (*l.c.*) any fleet of warships. **3.** (*l.c.*) a large group or force of vehicles, airplanes, etc.: *an armada of transport trucks.* [1525–35; < Sp < L *armāta* armed forces, neut. pl. of *armātus* (ptp. of *armāre* to equip with arms). See ARM², -ATE¹]

Arma′da chest′, an iron or iron-bound strongbox of the 17th or 18th century.

nine-banded armadillo, *Dasypus novemcinctus,* 8 in. (20 cm) high at shoulder; head and body 1½ ft. (0.5 m); tail 1 ft. (0.3 m)

ar·ma·dil·lo (är′mə dil′ō), *n., pl.* **-los.** any of several burrowing, chiefly nocturnal mammals constituting the family Dasypodidae, ranging from the southern U.S. through South America, having strong claws and a jointed protective covering of bony plates: used in certain areas for food. [1570–80; < Sp, equiv. to *armad(o)* armed (< L *armātus;* see ARM², -ATE¹) + *-illo* < L *-illus* dim. suffix]

Ar·ma·ged·don (är′mə ged′n), *n.* **1.** the place where the final battle will be fought between the forces of good and evil (probably so called in reference to the battlefield of Megiddo. Rev. 16:16). **2.** the last and completely destructive battle: *The arms race can lead to Armageddon.* **3.** any great and crucial conflict.

Ar·magh (är mä′), *n.* **1.** a county in S Northern Ireland. 133,969; 489 sq. mi. (1267 sq. km). *Co. seat:* Armagh. **2.** an administrative district in this county. 46,850; 261 sq. mi. (676 sq. km).

Ar·mag·nac (är′mən yak′; *Fr.* AR mä nyak′), *n.* a dry brandy distilled in the district of Armagnac in SW France. [1840–50]

ar·ma·ment (är′mə mənt), *n.* **1.** the arms and equipment with which a military unit or military apparatus is supplied. **2.** a land, sea, or air force equipped for war. **3.** armor (def. 5). **4.** Usually, **armaments.** military strength collectively: *the armaments race; a country without armaments.* **5.** the process of equipping or arming for war. [1690–1700; < L *armāmenta* fittings, equiv. to *armā(re)* to fit out (see ARM²) + *-menta* (pl.) -MENT]

ar·ma·men·tar·i·um (är′mə mən târ′ē əm, -men-), *n., pl.* **-tar·i·a** (-târ′ē ə). **1.** the aggregate of equipment, methods, and techniques available to one for carrying out one's duties: *The stethescope is still an essential part of the physician's armamentarium.* **2.** a fruitful source of devices or materials available or used for an undertaking: *The new arts center is an armamentarium for creative activity.* [1855–60; < L *armāmentārium* armory, equiv. to *armāment(a)* (see ARMAMENT) + *-ārium* -ARIUM]

Ar·mand (är′mənd; *Fr.* AR män′), *n.* a male given name, French form of **Herman.**

ar·mar·i·an (är mâr′ē ən), *n. Hist.* a monk in charge of the library and scriptorium in a monastery. [1840–50; < ML *armāri(us),* equiv. to *armāri(a)* library, orig. neut. pl., deriv. of L *armārium* (see ARMARIUM) + -AN]

ar·mar·i·um (är mâr′ē əm), *n., pl.* **-mar·i·a** (-mâr′ē ə). ambry (def. 1). [< L: cupboard, safe, equiv. to *arm(a)* weapons, tools + *-ārium* -ARIUM]

ar·ma·ture (är′mə chər), *n.* **1.** armor. **2.** *Biol.* the protective covering of an animal or plant, or any part serving for defense or offense. **3.** *Elect.* **a.** the part of an electric machine that includes the main current-carrying winding and in which the electromotive force is induced. **b.** the pivoted part of an electric device, as a buzzer or relay, that is activated by a magnetic field. **c.** the iron or steel applied across the poles of a permanent magnet to close it, or across the poles of an electromagnet to transmit a mechanical force. See illus. under **electromagnet.** **4.** *Sculpture.* a skeletal framework built as a support on which a clay, wax, or plaster figure is constructed. [1535–45; (< MF) < L *armātūra* an outfit, armor, equiv. to *armāt(us)* equipped (see ARM², -ATE¹) + *-ūra* -URE]

ar′mature reac′tion, *Elect.* a change in the magnetic field of a dynamo caused by the magnetic field induced by the current flowing through the armature.

Ar·ma·vir (är′mə vēr′; *Russ.* UR mu vyēR′), *n.* a city in the SW Russian Federation, E of Krasnodar. 162,000.

arm·band (ärm′band′), *n.* a fabric band worn around the upper arm as a badge or symbol; brassard. [1790–1800; ARM¹ + BAND²]

arm·chair (ärm′châr′), *n.* **1.** a chair with sidepieces or arms to support a person's forearms or elbows. —*adj.* **2.** theorizing without the benefit of practical experience: *an armchair football coach.* **3.** participating or experiencing indirectly or vicariously: *an armchair traveler.* [1625–35; ARM¹ + CHAIR]

armed (ärmd), *adj.* **1.** bearing firearms; having weapons: *a heavily armed patrol.* **2.** maintained by arms: *armed peace.* **3.** involving the use of weapons: *armed conflict.* **4.** equipped: *The students came armed with their pocket calculators.* **5.** (esp. of an animal) covered protectively, as by a shell. **6.** fortified; made secure: *Armed by an inveterate optimism, he withstood despair.* **7.** (of an artillery shell, bomb, missile, etc.) having the fuze made operative. [1250–1300; ME; see ARM², -ED²]

armed′ bull′head, pogge.

armed′ forc′es, military, naval, and air forces, esp. of a nation or of a number of nations. Also called **armed′ serv′ices.** [1685–95]

Armed′ Forc′es Day′, the third Saturday in May, observed in some areas of the U.S. as a holiday in honor of all branches of the armed forces. [1965–70]

armed′ neutral′ity, military preparedness without commitment, esp. as the expressed policy of a neutral nation in wartime; readiness to counter with force an invasion of rights by any belligerent power. [1770–80]

armed′ rob′bery, a robbery in which the robber is armed with a dangerous weapon. [1975–80]

Armen., Armenian.

Ar·me·ni·a (är mē′nē ə, -mēn′yə; *for 3 also Sp.* är me′nyä), *n.* **1.** an ancient country in W Asia: now divided between Armenia, Turkey, and Iran. **2.** Also called **Arme′nian Repub′lic.** a republic in Transcaucasia, S of Georgia and W of Azerbaijan. 3,031,000; ab. 11,500 sq. mi. (29,800 sq. km). *Cap.:* Yerevan. **3.** a city in W central Colombia. 135,615.

Ar·me·ni·an (är mē′nē ən, -mēn′yən), *adj.* **1.** of or pertaining to Armenia, its inhabitants, or their language. —*n.* **2.** a native of Armenia. **3.** the language of the Armenians, an Indo-European language written in a distinctive script dating from the 5th century. *Abbr.:* Arm [1710–20; ARMENI(A) + -AN]

Arme′nian Church′, a Monophysite church organized in 1899 in the U.S. Also called **Arme′nian Apostol′ic Church′.**

Ar·men·tières (AR män tyeR′; *Eng.* är′mən tērz′, -tyâr′), *n.* a city in extreme N France: World War I battles 1914, 1918. 27,473.

ar·met (är′met), *n. Armor.* a completely enclosed helmet having a visor and hinged cheek pieces fastened under the chin. Cf. **close helmet.** [1500–10; < MF, equiv. to *arme* ARM² + *-et* -ET]

arm·ful (ärm′fo͝ol′), *n., pl.* **-fuls.** **1.** as much as a person can hold or carry in an arm or both arms. **2.** *Informal.* a girl or woman with a well-rounded figure. **3.** *Informal.* an obstreperous child; handful. [1570–80; ARM¹ + -FUL]
—**Usage. 1.** See **-ful.**

arm·guard (ärm′gärd′), *n.* **1.** a band of leather or other material worn about the wrist or lower part of the arm for protection and support. **2.** *Archery.* bracer². [ARM¹ + GUARD]

arm·hole (ärm′hōl′), *n.* an opening in a garment, for the arm. [1275–1325; ME *arm-hol* armpit. See ARM¹, HOLE]

ar·mi·ger (är′mi jər), *n.* **1.** a person entitled to armorial bearings. **2.** an armorbearer to a knight; a squire. [1755–65; < ML: squire, L: armorbearer (n.), armorbearing (adj.), equiv. to *armi-* (comb. form of *arma* ARM²) + *-ger* bearing, base of *gerere* to carry, wear] —**ar·mig·er·al** (är mij′ər əl), *adj.*

ar·mig·er·ous (är mij′ər əs), *adj.* bearing or entitled to use a coat of arms. [1725–35; ARMIGER + -OUS]

ar·mill (är′mil), *n.* a garment resembling a stole, worn by a British king at his coronation. Also, **ar′mil, armilla.** [1425–75; late ME *armille* bracelet < MF < L *armilla.* See ARMILLARY]

ar·mil·la (är mil′ə), *n., pl.* **-mil·lae** (-mil′ē, -mil′ī), **-mil·las.** armill.

ar·mil·lar′i·a root′ rot′ (är′mə lâr′ē ə), a widespread rot caused by the honey mushroom, *Armillariella mellea,* seriously damaging to the roots of various hardwoods, conifers, and other trees. [< NL *Armillaria* an earlier name for the genus, equiv. to L *armill(a)* bracelet (referring to the braceletlike frill on such mushrooms; see ARMILLARY) + *-aria,* fem. of *-arius* -ARY]

ar·mil·lar·y (är′mə ler′ē, är mil′ə rē), *adj.* consisting of hoops or rings. [1655–65; < L *armill(a)* bracelet, hoop (*arm(us)* shoulder (see ARM¹) + *-illa* dim. suffix) + -ARY]

ar′millary sphere′, *Astron.* an ancient instrument consisting of an arrangement of rings, all of which are circles of the same sphere, used to show the relative positions of the celestial equator, ecliptic, and other circles on the celestial sphere. [1550–60]

arm′ing chest′, a chest for holding armor and weapons.

Ar·min·i·an·ism (är min′ē ə niz′əm), *n. Theol.* the doctrinal teachings of Jacobus Arminius or his followers, esp. the doctrine that Christ died for all people and not only for the elect. Cf. **Calvinism** (def. 1). [1610–20; J. ARMINI(US) + -AN + -ISM] —**Ar·min′i·an,** *adj., n.*

Ar·min·i·us (är min′ē əs), *n.* **1.** (*Hermann*) 17? B.C.–A.D. 21, Germanic hero who defeated Roman army A.D. 9. **2. Ja·co·bus** (jə kō′bəs), (*Jacob Harmensen*), 1560–1609, Dutch Protestant theologian.

ar·mip·o·tent (är mip′ə tnt), *adj. Archaic.* strong in battle. [1350–1400; < L *armipotent-* (s. of *armipotēns* potent in arms). See ARM², -I-, POTENT]

ar·mi·stice (är′mə stis), *n.* a temporary suspension of hostilities by agreement of the warring parties; truce: *World War I ended with the armistice of 1918.* [1655–65; < F < ML *armistitium,* equiv. to L *armi-* (comb. form of *arma* ARM²) + *-stitium* a stopping (*stit-* (var. s. of *sistere* to stop; see STAND) + *-ium* -IUM)]

Ar′mistice Day′, former name of **Veterans Day.** [1915–20]

Ar·mi·tage (är′mi tij), *n.* **Kenneth,** born 1916, English sculptor.

arm·less (ärm′lis), *adj.* lacking an arm or arms: *The* Venus de Milo *is an armless statue.* [1350–1400; ME; see ARM¹, -LESS] —**arm′less·ness,** *n.*

arm·let (ärm′lit), *n.* **1.** an ornamental band worn on the arm, esp. a bracelet worn high on the arm, rather than on the wrist. **2.** a little inlet or arm: *an armlet of the sea.* [1525–35; ARM¹ + -LET]

arm·load (ärm′lōd′), *n. Chiefly Midland U.S.* armful (def. 1). [ARM¹ + LOAD]

arm·lock (ärm′lok′), *n.* any hold in which a wrestler's arm is rendered immobile, often by the opponent twisting the arm. [1900–05; ARM¹ + LOCK¹]

ar·moire (ärm wär′, ärm′wär), *n.* a large wardrobe or movable cupboard, with doors and shelves. [1565–75; < MF; OF b. *armaire* and *aumoire* AMBRY]

ar·mor (är′mər), *n.* **1.** any covering worn as a defense against weapons. **2.** a suit of armor. **3.** a metallic sheathing or protective covering, esp. metal plates, used on warships, armored vehicles, airplanes, and fortifications. **4.** mechanized units of military forces, as armored divisions. **5.** Also called **armament.** any protective covering, as on certain animals, insects, or plants. **6.** any quality, characteristic, situation, or thing that serves as protection: *A chilling courtesy was his only armor.* **7.** the outer, protective wrapping of metal, usually fine, braided steel wires, on a cable. —*v.t.* **8.** to cover or equip with armor or armor plate. Also, *esp. Brit.,* **armour.** [1250–1300; ME *armo(u)r, armure* < AF *armour(e), armure* OF *armëure* < L *armātūra* ARMATURE; assimilated, in ME and AF, to nouns ending in *-our* -OR²] —**ar′mor·less,** *adj.*

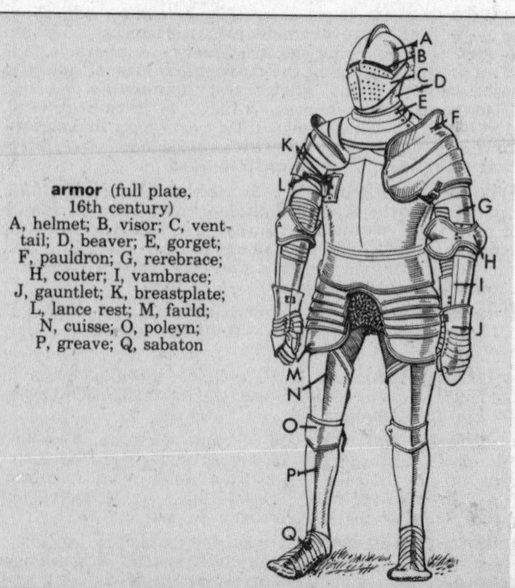

armor (full plate, 16th century) A, helmet; B, visor; C, ventail; D, beaver; E, gorget; F, pauldron; G, rerebrace; H, couter; I, vambrace; J, gauntlet; K, breastplate; L, lance rest; M, fauld; N, cuisse; O, poleyn; P, greave; Q, sabaton

ar•mor•bear•er (är′mər bâr′ər), *n.* a male attendant bearing the armor or arms of a warrior or knight. [1605–15; ARMOR + BEARER]

ar•mor-clad (är′mər klad′), *adj.* covered with armor. [1860–65; ARMOR + CLAD]

ar•mored (är′mərd), *adj.* **1.** protected by armor or armor plate. **2.** provided with or using armored equipment, as tanks or armored cars: *an armored unit; an armored patrol.* [1595–1605; ARMOR + -ED[3]]

ar′mored ca′ble, electric cable covered by a protective metallic wrapping. [1895–1900]

ar′mored car′, **1.** an armorplated truck with strong locks and doors, and usually portholes for guards to shoot through, for transporting money and valuables, as to and from banks. **2.** a military combat and reconnaissance vehicle with wheels, light armor, and usually machine guns. [1910–15]

ar′mored di′nosaur, ankylosaur.

ar′mored personnel′ car′rier, a tracked military vehicle with a steel or aluminum hull used to transport troops in combat and usually fitted with light armament. *Abbr.:* APC

ar′mored rope′, rope made of wire-wrapped hempen strands that is used in salvage work.

ar′mored scale′, any of numerous insects constituting the family Diaspididae, the largest group of scale insects, which includes many important pests of various trees and shrubs, as the San Jose scale. [1900–05]

ar•mor•er (är′mər ər), *n.* **1.** a maker or repairer of arms or armor. **2.** a person who manufactures, repairs, or services firearms. **3.** an enlisted person in charge of the upkeep of small arms, machine guns, ammunition, and the like. [1350–1400; ME; r. ME *armurer* < AF, OF *armurier.* See ARMOR, -ER[2]]

ar•mo•ri•al (är môr′ē əl, -mōr′-), *adj.* **1.** of or pertaining to heraldry or heraldic bearings. **2.** bearing a coat or coats of arms: *a set of armorial china.* —*n.* **3.** a book containing heraldic bearings and devices. [1570–80; ARMORY + -AL[1]]

Ar•mor•i•ca (är môr′i kə, -mor′-), *n.* an ancient region in NW France, corresponding generally to Brittany.

Ar•mor•i•can (är môr′i kən, -mor′-), *adj.* **1.** of or pertaining to Armorica. —*n.* **2.** a native of Armorica. **3.** Breton (def. 2). Also **Ar•mor′ic.** [ARMORIC(A) + -AN]

ar•mor•ist (är′mər ist), *n.* a person who is an expert at heraldry. [1580–90; ARMOR + -IST]

ar•mor•ize (är′mə rīz′), *v.t.,* **-ized, -iz•ing.** to equip with armor or other protective devices: *to armorize a car with bulletproof glass.* [‡1975–80; ARMOR + -IZE]

ar•mor-pierc•ing (är′mər pēr′sing), *adj.* (of bullets, artillery shells, etc.) designed especially for piercing armor. [1895–1900]

ar′mor plate′, a plate or plating of specially hardened steel used to cover warships, tanks, aircraft, fortifications, etc., to protect them from enemy fire. Also, **ar′•mor plat′ing.** —**ar′mor-plat′ed,** *adj.* [1860–65]

ar•mor•y (är′mə rē), *n., pl.* **-mor•ies.** **1.** a storage place for weapons and other war equipment. **2.** a building that is the headquarters and drill center of a military unit. **3.** a place where arms and armor are made; an armorer's shop. **4.** *Heraldry.* the art of blazoning arms. **5.** heraldry. **6.** arms or armor collectively. **7.** *Archaic.* heraldic bearings or arms. [1300–50; ME *armerie, armur(i)e* < MF *armoierie,* equiv. to OF *armoi(er)* to bear arms (deriv. of *armes* ARM[2]) + *-erie* -ERY]

Ar′mory Show′, an international art show held in a New York City armory in 1913: considered a landmark in the public and critical acceptance of modern art.

ar•mour (är′mər), *n. Chiefly Brit.* armor.
—**Usage.** See **-our.**

Ar•mour (är′mər), *n.* **Philip Dan•forth** (dan′fôrth, -fōrth), 1832–1901, U.S. meat-packing industrialist.

arm•pad (ärm′pad′), *n.* a small cushion forming part of the arm of a chair, sofa, or the like. Also called **manchette.** [ARM[1] + PAD[1]]

arm•patch (ärm′pach′), *n.* an insignia, badge, slogan, or the like sewn on the sleeve of a uniform shirt or jacket or affixed to an armband to indicate one's affiliation, sponsorship, rank, etc. [ARM[1] + PATCH[1]]

arm•pit (ärm′pit′), *n.* the hollow under the arm at the shoulder; axilla. [1300–50; ME; see ARM[1], PIT[1]]

arm•rest (ärm′rest′), *n.* a projecting, often padded support for the forearm, as at the side of a chair or sofa or between seats in a theater, car, or airplane. Also called **arm.** [1885–90; ARM[1] + REST[1]]

Arms′ and the Man′, a comedy (1898) by G. B. Shaw.

arms′ control′, **1.** any plan, treaty, or agreement to limit the number, size, or type of weapons or armed forces of the participating nations. **2.** the measures taken to limit the weapons systems or armed forces.

arm•scye (ärm′sī, -zī), *n.* the armhole opening in a garment. Also, **arms•eye** (ärmz′ī′). [ARM[1] + *scye* armhole (orig. Scot, Ulster dial. s(e)y, *sie,* of uncert. orig.); reanalyzed by folk etym. as "arm's eye"]

arm's-length (ärmz′lengkth′, -length′), *adj.* not closely or intimately connected or associated; distant; remote: *an arm's-length relationship.* [1645–55]

arms′ race′, competition between countries to achieve superiority in quantity and quality of military arms. [1935–40]

arm′stand dive′ (ärm′stand′), a dive starting from a handstand at the end of a springboard or a platform with the diver's back to the water. [‡1975–80; ARM[1] + STAND]

Arm•strong (ärm′strông′), *n.* **1.** (**Daniel**) **Louis** ("*Satchmo*"), 1900–71, U.S. jazz trumpeter and bandleader. **2. Edwin Howard,** 1890–1954, U.S. electrical engineer and inventor: developed frequency modulation. **3. Henry** (*Henry Jackson*), 1912–88, U.S. boxer: world featherweight champion 1937–38; world lightweight champion 1938–39; world welterweight champion 1938–40. **4. Neil A.,** born 1930, U.S. astronaut: first person to walk on the moon, July 20, 1969.

arm-twist (ärm′twist′), *v.t.* to subject to arm-twisting: *The unions arm-twisted the government into negotiating by threatening widespread strikes.* [back formation from ARM-TWISTING] —**arm′-twist′er,** *n.*

arm-twist•ing (ärm′twis′ting), *n.* the use of threat, coercion, or other forms of pressure and persuasion to achieve one's purpose: *It took a lot of arm-twisting but he finally agreed to work this weekend.* Also, **arm′•twist′ing.** [1945–50]

ar•mure (är′myər), *n.* a woolen or silk fabric woven with a small, raised pattern. [1875–80; < F. See ARMOR]

arm-wres•tle (ärm′res′əl), *v.t., v.i.,* **-tled, -tling.** to engage in arm wrestling. —**arm′ wres′tler.**

arm′ wres′tling, a form of wrestling in which two opponents, usually facing each other across a table, rest their right or left elbows on the table and, placing their corresponding forearms upward and parallel, grip each other's hand, the object being to force the opponent's hand down so that it touches the table. Also, **arm′-wres′tling.** Also called **Indian wrestling.**

ar•my (är′mē), *n., pl.* **-mies.** **1.** the military forces of a nation, exclusive of the navy and in some countries the air force. **2.** (in large military land forces) a unit consisting typically of two or more corps and a headquarters. **3.** a large body of persons trained and armed for war. **4.** any body of persons organized for any purpose: *an army of census takers.* **5.** a very large number or group of something; a great multitude; a host: *the army of the unemployed.* [1350–1400; ME *armee* < MF < L *armāta.* Cf. ARMADA]

Ar′my Air′ Forc′es, *U.S. Army.* a unit comprising almost all aviation, with its personnel, equipment, etc.: it became part of the Air Force on July 26, 1947.

ar′my ant′, any of the chiefly tropical ants of the suborder Dorylinae that travel in vast swarms, preying mainly on other insects. Also called **driver ant, legionary ant.** [1870–75]

ar′my brat′, *Informal.* the child of an army officer or enlisted person, esp. one who has grown up on army bases or in military communities.

ar′my corps′, corps (def. 1b). [1840–50]

ar′my cut′worm, the larva of a noctuid moth, *Chorizagrotis auxiliaris,* that is a pest of wheat and alfalfa in the Plains states.

ar′my-na′vy store′ (är′mē nā′vē), a retail store selling a stock of surplus army, naval, and other military apparel and goods, often at bargain rates. [1945–50]

ar′my of occupa′tion, an army occupying conquered territory to maintain order and to ensure the carrying out of peace or armistice terms.

Ar′my of the Poto′mac, *U.S. Hist.* **1.** Union forces, trained and organized by Gen. George B. McClellan, that guarded Washington, D.C., against a Confederate invasion across the Potomac and fought battles in the eastern sector during the Civil War. **2.** Confederate forces from the Alexandria, Potomac, and Shenandoah districts from mid-1861 to mid-1862: later known as Army of Northern Virginia.

Ar′my of the Unit′ed States′, the army or armies referred to in the U.S. Constitution, esp. consisting of the Regular Army, National Guard, and Army Reserve. Cf. **United States Army.**

ar•my•worm (är′mē wûrm′), *n.* **1.** the caterpillar of a noctuid moth, *Pseudaletia unipuncta,* that often travels in large numbers over a region, destroying crops of wheat, corn, etc. **2.** any of the larvae of several related moths having similar habits. [1735–45, *Amer.;* ARMY + WORM]

ar•nat•to (är nat′ō, -nä′tō), *n., pl.* **-tos.** annatto (def. 2).

Arndt (ärnt), *n.* **Ernst Mo•ritz** (ernst mō′rits), 1769–1860, German poet and historian.

Arne (ärn), *n.* **Thomas Augustine,** 1710–78, English composer of operas and songs.

Ar•nel (är nel′), *Trademark.* a brand of fiber manufactured from cellulose triacetate.

Arn•hem (ärn′hem, är′nəm), *n.* a city in the central Netherlands, on the Rhine River: World War II battle 1944. 128,717.

Arn′hem Land′ (är′nəm), a region in N Northern Territory, Australia: site of Aborigine reservation. Also, **Arn′hem-land′.**

ar•ni•ca (är′ni kə), *n.* **1.** any composite plant of the genus *Arnica,* having opposite leaves and yellow flower heads. **2.** a tincture of the flowers of *A. montana,* of Europe, and other species of *Arnica,* formerly used as an external application in sprains and bruises. [1745–55; < NL < ?]

Ar•no (är′nō; *for 2 also It.* äʀ′nô), *n.* **1. Peter** (*Curtis Arnoux Peters*), 1904–68, U.S. cartoonist and author. **2.** a river flowing W from central Italy to the Ligurian Sea. 140 mi. (225 km) long.

Ar•nold (är′nld), *n.* **1. Benedict,** 1741–1801, American general in the Revolutionary War who became a traitor. **2. Sir Edwin,** 1832–1904, English poet and journalist. **3. Henry H.** ("*Hap*"), 1886–1950, U.S. general. **4. Matthew,** 1822–88, English essayist, poet, and literary critic. **5.** his father, **Thomas,** 1795–1842, English clergyman, educator, historian, and writer. **6. Thur•man Wesley** (thûr′mən), 1891–1969, U.S. lawyer and writer. **7.** a town in E Missouri. 19,141. **8.** a male given name: from Germanic words meaning "eagle" and "power."

Ar•nold•son (är′nld sən; *Sw.* äʀ′no͝old sôn′), *n.* **Klas Pon•tus** (kläs pôn′təs), 1844–1916, Swedish author and politician: Nobel peace prize 1908.

Ar•nulf (är′no͝olf), *n.* A.D. 850?–899, emperor of the Holy Roman Empire 887–899: crowned 896.

ar•oid (ar′oid, âr′-), *Bot.* —*adj.* **1.** araceous. —*n.* **2.** any plant of the arum family. [1875–80; AR(UM) + -OID]

a•roint (ə roint′), *imperative verb. Obs.* begone: *Aroint thee, varlet!* [1595–1605; of uncert. orig.]

a•ro•ma (ə rō′mə), *n.* **1.** an odor arising from spices, plants, cooking, etc., esp. an agreeable odor; fragrance. **2.** (of wines and spirits) the odor or bouquet. **3.** a pervasive characteristic or quality. [1175–1225; < L < Gk: spice; r. ME *aromat* < OF < L *arōmat-* (s. of *arōma*)]
—**Syn. 1.** See **perfume.**

a•ro•ma•ther•a•py (ə rō′mə ther′ə pē), *n.* **1.** the use of fragrances to affect or alter a person's mood or behavior. **2.** treatment of facial skin by the application of fragrant floral and herbal substances. [1980–85]

ar•o•mat•ic (ar′ə mat′ik), *adj.* **1.** having an aroma; fragrant or sweet-scented; odoriferous. **2.** *Chem.* of or pertaining to an aromatic compound or compounds. —*n.* **3.** a plant, drug, or medicine yielding a fragrant aroma, as sage or certain spices and oils. **4.** See **aromatic compound.** [1325–75; ME *aromatyk* (< MF) < LL *arōmaticus* < Gk *arōmatikós.* See AROMA, -IC] —**ar′o•mat′i•cal•ly,** *adv.* —**ar′o•mat′ic•ness,** *n.*

ar′omat′ic com′pound, *Chem.* an organic compound that contains one or more benzene or equivalent heterocyclic rings: many such compounds have an agreeable odor. [1865–70]

ar•o•ma•tic•i•ty (ar′ə mə tis′i tē, ə rō′mə-), *n.* **1.** the quality or state of being aromatic. **2.** *Chem.* the property of being or resembling any of the aromatic compounds. [AROMATIC + -ITY]

ar′omat′ic spir′its of ammo′nia, *Pharm.* a nearly colorless liquid containing ammonia, ammonium carbonate, alcohol, and aromatic oils, used orally as an antacid and carminative and, by inhalation, as a stimulant in the treatment of faintness. Also, **ar′omat′ic spir′it of ammo′nia.**

a•ro•ma•ti•za•tion (ə rō′mə tə zā′shən), *n. Chem.* the conversion of aliphatic or alicyclic compounds to aromatic hydrocarbons. [1595–1605; (< F) < ML *arōmatizātiōn-* (s. of *arōmatizātiō*); see AROMATIZE, -ATION]

a•ro•ma•tize (ə rō′mə tīz′), *v.t.,* **-tized, -tiz•ing.** to make aromatic or fragrant. Also, *esp. Brit.,* **a•ro′ma•tise′.** [1400–50; late ME (< MF) < LL *arōmatizāre* < Gk *arōmatízein* to spice. See AROMA, -IZE] —**a•ro′•ma•tiz′er,** *n.*

Ar•on (âr′ən, ar′-), *n.* a male given name.

A•ron Ko•desh (*Seph.* ä ʀôn′ kô′desh; *Ashk.* ôʀ′ōn kō′desh), *Hebrew.* See **Holy Ark.**

A•roos•took (ə ro͞os′to͝ok, -tik), *n.* a river flowing NE from N Maine to the St. John River. 140 mi. (225 km) long.

a•rose (ə rōz′), *v.* pt. of **arise.**

a•round (ə round′), *adv.* **1.** in a circle, ring, or the like; so as to surround a person, group, thing, etc.: *The crowd gathered around.* **2.** on all sides; about: *His land is fenced all around.* **3.** in all directions from a center or point of reference: *He owns the land for miles around.* **4.** in a region or area neighboring a place: *all the country around.* **5.** in circumference: *The tree was 40 inches around.* **6.** in a circular or rounded course: *to fly around and around.* **7.** through a sequence or series, as of places or persons: *to show someone around.* **8.** through a recurring period, as of time, esp. to the present or a particular time: *when spring rolls around again.* **9.** by a circuitous or roundabout course: *The driveway to the house goes around past the stables.* **10.** to a place or point, as by a circuit or circuitous course: *to get around into the navigable channel.* **11.** with a rotating course or movement: *The wheels turned around.* **12.** in or to another or opposite direction, course, opinion, etc.: *Sit still and don't turn around. After our arguments, she finally came around.* **13.** back into consciousness: *The smelling salts brought her around.* **14.** in circulation, action, etc.; about: *He hasn't been around lately.* **15.** somewhere near or about; nearby: *I'll be around if you need me.* **16.** to a specific place: *He came around to see me.* **17. been around,** having had much worldly experience: *He's been around and isn't likely to be taken in.* —*prep.* **18.** about; on all sides; encircling; encompassing: *a halo around his head.* **19.** so as to encircle, surround, or envelop: *to tie paper around a package.* **20.** on the edge, border, or outer part of: *a skirt with fringe around the bottom.* **21.** from place to place in; about: *to get around town.* **22.** in all or various directions from: *to look around one.* **23.** in the vicinity of: *the country around Boston.* **24.** approximately; about: *It's around five o'clock.* **25.** here and there in: *There are many cafés around the city.* **26.** somewhere in or near: *to stay around the house.* **27.** to all or various parts of: *to wander around the country.* **28.** so as to make a circuit about or partial circuit to the other side of: *to go around the lake; to sail around a cape.* **29.** reached by making a turn or partial circuit about: *the church around the corner.* **30.** so as to revolve or rotate about a center or axis: *the earth's motion around its axis.* **31.** personally close to: *Only the few advisers around the party leader understood his real motives.* **32.** so as to get by a difficulty: *They got around the lack of chairs by sitting on the floor.* **33.** so as to have a foundation in: *The novel is built around a little-known historical event.* [1250–1300; ME *around(e).* See A-[1], ROUND]

a•round-the-clock (ə round′thə klok′), *adj.* continuing without pause or interruption: *an around-the-clock guard on the prisoner.* Also, **round-the-clock.**

a•rouse (ə rouz′), *v.,* **a•roused, a•rous•ing.** —*v.t.* **1.** to stir to action or strong response; excite: *to arouse a crowd; to arouse suspicion.* **2.** to stimulate sexually. **3.**

to awaken; wake up: *The footsteps aroused the dog.* —*v.i.* **4.** to awake or become aroused: *At dawn the farmers began to arouse.* [1585–95; A-[3] + ROUSE[1], modeled on ARISE] —**a·rous′a·bil′i·ty,** *n.* —**a·rous′a·ble,** *adj.* —**a·rous·al** (ə rou′zəl), *n.* —**a·rous′er,** *n.*
—**Syn. 1.** animate; inspirit, inspire; incite, provoke, instigate; stimulate, kindle, fire. —**Ant. 1.** calm.

Arp (ärp), *n.* **1. Bill,** pen name of Charles Henry Smith. **2. Hans** (häns) or **Jean** (zhäN), 1888?–1966, French painter and sculptor.

ARP, *Stock Exchange.* adjustable-rate preferred.

Ár·pád (är′päd), *n.* died A.D. 907, Hungarian national hero.

ar·peg·gi·ate (är pej′ē āt′), *v.t.,* **-at·ed, -at·ing.** *Music.* to sound the notes of (a chord) in succession. [ARPEGGI(O) + -ATE]

ar·peg·gi·a·tion (är pej′ē ā′shən), *n.* the writing or playing of arpeggios. [1885–90; ARPEGGI(O) + -ATION]

ar·peg·gi·o (är pej′ē ō′, -pej′ō), *n., pl.* **-gi·os.** *Music.* **1.** the sounding of the notes of a chord in rapid succession instead of simultaneously. **2.** a chord thus sounded. Also called **broken chord.** [1735–45; < It: lit., a harping, n. deriv. of *arpeggi(are)* to play on the harp (< Gmc; cf. OE *hearpi(g)an* to harp)] —**ar·peg′gi·at′ed, ar·peg′gi·oed′,** *adj.*

ar·pent (är′pənt; *Fr.* AR päN′), *n., pl.* **-pents** (-pənts; *Fr.* -päN′). an old French unit of area equal to about one acre (0.4 hectare). It is still used in the province of Quebec and in parts of Louisiana. [1570–80; < MF < L *arepennis* half-acre < Gaulish; akin to MIr *airchenn* unit of area]

Ar·pi·no (är pē′nō), *n.* **Gerald (Peter),** born 1928, U.S. choreographer.

ar·que·bus (är′kwə bəs), *n., pl.* **-bus·es.** harquebus.

ar·que·bus·ier (är′kwə bə sēr′, -kə-), *n.* harquebusier.

arr., 1. arranged. **2.** arrangement. **3.** arrival. **4.** arrive; arrived.

ar·rack (ar′ək, ə rak′), *n.* any of various spirituous liquors distilled in the East Indies and other parts of the East and Middle East from the fermented sap of toddy palms, or from fermented molasses, rice, or other materials. Also, **arak.** [1595–1605; < Ar *'araq* lit., sweat, juice; see RAKI]

ar·rah (ar′ə), *interj. Irish.* (used as an expression of surprise or excitement.) [< Ir *ara*]

ar·raign (ə rān′), *v.t.* **1.** to call or bring before a court to answer to an indictment. **2.** to accuse or charge in general; criticize adversely; censure. [1275–1325; ME *arainen* < AF *arainer,* OF *araisnier,* equiv. to *a-* A-[5] + *raisnier* < VL **ratiōnāre* to talk, reason; see RATIO] —**ar·raign′er,** *n.*

ar·raign·ment (ə rān′mənt), *n.* **1.** an act of arraigning or the state of being arraigned. **2.** a calling into question or a finding fault, esp. with respect to the value or virtue of something; critical examination. [1400–50; late ME *arainement* < MF *araisnement.* See ARRAIGN, -MENT]

Ar·ran (ar′ən), *n.* an island in SW Scotland, in the Firth of Clyde. 3705; 166 sq. mi. (430 sq. km).

ar·range (ə rānj′), *v.,* **-ranged, -rang·ing.** —*v.t.* **1.** to place in proper, desired, or convenient order; adjust properly: *to arrange books on a shelf.* **2.** to come to an agreement or understanding regarding: *The two sides arranged the sale of the property.* **3.** to prepare or plan: *to arrange the details of a meeting.* **4.** *Music.* to adapt (a composition) for a particular style of performance by voices or instruments. —*v.i.* **5.** to make plans or preparations: *They arranged for a conference on Wednesday.* **6.** to make a settlement; come to an agreement: *to arrange with the coal company for regular deliveries.* [1325–75; ME *arayngen* < MF *arangier,* equiv. to *a-* A-[5] + *rangier* to RANGE] —**ar·range′a·ble,** *adj.* —**ar·rang′er,** *n.*
—**Syn. 1.** array; group, sort, dispose; classify.

ar·range·ment (ə rānj′mənt), *n.* **1.** an act of arranging; state of being arranged. **2.** the manner or way in which things are arranged: *a tactful arrangement of the seating at dinner.* **3.** a final settlement; adjustment by agreement: *The arrangement with the rebels lasted only two weeks.* **4.** Usually, **arrangements.** preparatory measures; plans; preparations: *They made arrangements for an early departure.* **5.** something arranged in a particular way: *a floral arrangement; the arrangement of chairs for the seminar.* **6.** *Music.* **a.** the adaptation of a composition to voices or instruments, or to a new purpose. **b.** a piece so adapted. **7. final arrangements,** the planning or scheduling of funeral services and burial: *Final arrangements are still pending.* [1720–30; < F; see ARRANGE, -MENT]

ar·rant (ar′ənt), *adj.* **1.** downright; thorough; unmitigated; notorious: *an arrant fool.* **2.** wandering; errant. [1350–1400; ME, var. of ERRANT] —**ar′rant·ly,** *adv.*
—**Syn. 1.** thoroughgoing, utter, confirmed, flagrant.

ar·ras[1] (ar′əs), *n.* **1.** a rich tapestry. **2.** a tapestry weave. **3.** a wall hanging, as a tapestry or similar object. **4.** *Theat.* a curtain suspended loosely across a stage and used as a backdrop or part of a stage setting. [1375–1425; late ME, named after ARRAS] —**ar′rased,** *adj.*

ar·ras[2] (är′äs; *Sp.* är′räs), *n.* (*used with a singular v.*) a gift presented at marriage by a husband to his wife in consideration of her dowry. [< Sp: lit., earnest money. See EARNEST[2]]

Ar·ras (ar′əs; *Fr.* A räs′), *n.* a city in and capital of Pas-de-Calais, in N France: battles in World War I. 50,386.

Ar·rau (ə rou′; *Sp.* är rou′), *n.* **Clau·di·o** (klô′dē ō′; *Sp.* klou′thyô), 1903–91, Chilean pianist.

ar·ray (ə rā′), *v.t.* **1.** to place in proper or desired order; marshal: *Napoleon arrayed his troops for battle.* **2.** to clothe with garments, esp. of an ornamental kind; dress up; deck out: *She arrayed herself in furs and diamonds.* —*n.* **3.** order or arrangement, as of troops drawn up for battle. **4.** military force, esp. a body of troops. **5.** a large and impressive grouping or organization of things: *He couldn't dismiss the array of facts.* **6.** regular order or arrangement; series: *an array of figures.* **7.** a large group, number, or quantity of people or things: *an impressive array of scholars; an imposing array of books.* **8.** attire; dress: *in fine array.* **9.** an arrangement of interrelated objects or items of equipment for accomplishing a particular task: *thousands of solar cells in one vast array.* **10.** *Math., Statistics.* **a.** an arrangement of a series of terms according to value, as from largest to smallest. **b.** an arrangement of a series of terms in some geometric pattern, as in a matrix. **11.** *Computers.* a block of related data elements, each of which is usually identified by one or more subscripts. **12.** *Radio.* See **antenna array.** [1250–1300; ME *arrayen* < AF *arayer,* OF *are(y)er* < Gmc; cf. OE *ārǣdan* to prepare, equiv. to *ā-* A-[3] + *rǣde* ready] —**ar·ray′er,** *n.*
—**Syn. 1.** arrange, range, order, dispose. **2.** apparel, dress, attire; ornament, adorn, decorate. **3.** disposition. **5.** show, exhibit, exhibition. **8.** raiment.

ar·ray·al (ə rā′əl), *n.* **1.** an act of arraying. **2.** something that is arrayed. [1810–20; ARRAY + -AL[2]]

ar·rear (ə rēr′), *n.* **1.** Usually, **arrears.** the state of being behind or late, esp. in the fulfillment of a duty, promise, obligation, or the like. **2.** Often, **arrears.** something overdue in payment; a debt that remains unpaid. [1300–50; n. use of *arrear* (adv., now obs.), ME *arere* behind < MF << L *ad retrō.* See AD-, RETRO-]

ar·rear·age (ə rēr′ij), *n.* **1.** the state or condition of being in arrears. **2.** Often, **arrearages.** arrears; amount or amounts overdue. **3.** *Archaic.* a thing or part kept in reserve. [1275–1325; ME *arerage* < OF. See ARREAR, -AGE]

ar·re·not·o·ky (ar′ə not′ə kē), *n.* arrhenotoky. —**ar′re·not′o·kous,** *adj.*

ar·rest (ə rest′), *v.t.* **1.** to seize (a person) by legal authority or warrant; take into custody: *The police arrested the burglar.* **2.** to catch and hold; attract and fix; engage: *The loud noise arrested our attention.* **3.** to check the course of; stop; slow down: *to arrest progress.* **4.** *Med.* to control or stop the active progress of (a disease): *The new drug did not arrest the cancer.* —*n.* **5.** the taking of a person into legal custody, as by officers of the law. **6.** any seizure or taking by force. **7.** an act of stopping or the state of being stopped: *the arrest of tooth decay.* **8.** *Mach.* any device for stopping machinery; stop. **9. under arrest,** in custody of the police or other legal authorities: *They placed the suspect under arrest at the scene of the crime.* [1275–1325; (v.) ME *aresten* < AF, MF *arester,* < VL **arrestāre* to stop (see AR-, REST[2]); (n.) ME *arest(e)* < AF, OF, n. deriv. of v.] —**ar·rest′a·ble,** *adj.* —**ar·rest′ment,** *n.*
—**Syn. 1.** apprehend. **2.** secure, rivet, occupy. **3.** stay. See **stop. 5.** detention, apprehension, imprisonment. **7.** stoppage, halt, stay, check.

ar·rest·ant (ə res′tənt), *n. Entomol.* a substance that interrupts the normal development of an insect. [1960–65; ARREST + -ANT]

ar·rest·ee (ə res tē′), *n.* a person who is under arrest. [1840–50, for earlier sense; ARREST + -EE]

ar·rest·er (ə res′tər), *n.* **1.** Also, **ar·res′tor.** a person or thing that arrests. **2.** *Elect.* See **lightning arrester.** [1400–50; late ME *arester.* See ARREST, -ER[1]]

ar·rest·ing (ə res′ting), *adj.* **1.** attracting or capable of attracting attention or interest; striking: *an arresting smile.* **2.** making or having made an arrest: *the arresting officer.* [ARREST + -ING[2]] —**ar·rest′ing·ly,** *adv.*

arrest′ing gear′, any mechanism or device for bringing something to a stop, as an airplane landing on an aircraft carrier. [1950–55]

ar·res·tive (ə res′tiv), *adj.* tending to arrest or take hold of the attention, interest, etc. [1825–35; ARREST + -IVE]

Ar′re·tine ware′ (ar′ə tin′, -tēn′), a red-glazed terracotta pottery produced in Tuscany from 100 B.C. to A.D. 100 and widely traded. Also called **terra sigillata.** [1775–85; < L *Arrētinus,* deriv. of *Arrētium* (modern Arezzo), a town in Tuscany where such pottery was made; see -INE[1]]

arrgt., arrangement.

Ar·rhe·ni·us (är rā′nē o͝os′), *n.* **Svan·te Au·gust** (svän′te ou′go͞ost), 1859–1927, Swedish physicist and chemist: Nobel prize for chemistry 1903.

ar·rhe·not·o·ky (ar′ə not′ə kē), *n.* parthenogenesis in which only males are produced. Also, **arrenotoky.** [< Gk *arrhenotokía,* equiv. to *arrhenotók(os)* bearing male offspring (*arrhēno-* male + *tók(os)* offspring + *-os* adj. suffix) + *-ia* -Y[3]] —**ar′rhe·not′o·kous,** *adj.*

ar·rhyth·mi·a (ə rith′mē ə, ā rith′-), *n. Pathol.* any disturbance in the rhythm of the heartbeat. Also, **arhythmia.** [1885–90; < NL < Gk *arrhythmía.* See A-[6], RHYTHM, -IA] —**arrhyth·mic** (ə rith′mik, ā rith′-), **ar·rhyth′mi·cal,** *adj.* —**ar·rhyth′mi·cal·ly,** *adv.*

ar·ric·cia·to (är′ē chä′tō; *It.* är′Rēt chä′tô), *n., pl.* **-tos, -ti** (-tē). arriccio. [< It; see ARRICIO, -ATE[1]]

ar·ric·cio (ə rē′chō; *It.* är Rēt′chô), *n., pl.* **-cios, -ci** (-chē). (formerly in fresco painting) a second coat of plaster, somewhat finer than the first coat, applied over the entire surface and on which the drawing for the fresco is done. Also, **arricciato.** Also called **brown coat.** Cf. **intonaco.** [< It, deriv. of *arricciare* to curl up, make grooves in (*a-* A-[5] + *-ricciare,* v. deriv. of *riccio* hedgehog < L *ēricius*]

ar·ride (ə rīd′), *v.t.,* **-rid·ed, -rid·ing.** *Obs.* to be agreeable or pleasing to. [1590–1600; < L *arridēre* to smile upon, please, equiv. to *ar-* AR- + *rīdēre* to smile, laugh; see RIDICULE]

ar·ri·ère-ban (ar′ē er′ban′; *Fr.* A RyeR bäN′), *n., pl.* **-bans** (-banz′; *Fr.* -bäN′). **1.** a group of vassals who owed military service, esp. to French kings. **2.** the summoning by a medieval ruler of all vassals and free men for military service. [1515–25; < F, alter. (by assoc. with *arrière* behind, rear; see ARREAR) of OF *arban, herban* < Gmc; cf. OHG *hari* army, *ban* BAN[2]]

ar·rière-garde (A RyeR GARD′), *n. French.* **1.** rear guard. **2.** a group that is behind or out-of-date in any field, esp. in one of the arts. Cf. **avant-garde.**

ar·rière-pen·sée (A RyeR päN sā′) *n., pl.* ***-pen·sées*** (-päN sā′). *French.* a mental reservation; hidden motive.

Ar Ri·mal (är′ ri mäl′). See **Rub' al Khali.**

ar·ris (ar′is), *n. Archit.* **1.** a sharp ridge, as between adjoining channels of a Doric column. **2.** the line, ridge, or hip formed by the meeting of two surfaces at an exterior angle. Also called **piend.** [1670–80; < MF *areste;* see ARÊTE]

ar·ri·val (ə rī′vəl), *n.* **1.** an act of arriving; a coming: *His arrival was delayed by traffic.* **2.** the reaching or attainment of any object or condition: *arrival at a peace treaty.* **3.** the person or thing that arrives or has arrived: *First arrivals will be the first seated.* [1350–1400; ARRIVE + -AL[2]; r. ME *arivaille* < MF]
—**Syn. 1.** advent.

ar·rive (ə rīv′), *v.,* **-rived, -riv·ing.** —*v.i.* **1.** to come to a certain point in the course of travel; reach one's destination: *He finally arrived in Rome.* **2.** to come to be near or present in time: *The moment to act has arrived.* **3.** to attain a position of success, power, achievement, fame, or the like: *After years of hard work, she has finally arrived in her field.* **4.** *Archaic.* to happen: *It arrived that the master had already departed.* —*v.t.* **5.** *Obs.* to reach; come to. **6. arrive at, a.** to come to a place after traveling; reach. **b.** to attain the objective in a course or process: *to arrive at a conclusion.* [1175–1225; ME *a(r)riven* < OF *a(r)river* < VL **arrīpāre* to come to land, v. deriv. of L *ad rīpam* to the riverbank; cf. RIVER[1]] —**ar·riv′er,** *n.*

ar·ri·vé (ar′ē vā′; *Fr.* A Rē vā′), *n., pl.* **-vés** (-vāz′; *Fr.* -vā′). a person who has swiftly gained wealth, status, success, or fame. [1920–25; < F: lit., arrived, n. use of ptp. of *arriver* to ARRIVE]

ar·ri·ve·der·ci (äR′Rē ve deR′chē), *interj. Italian.* until we see each other again; good-bye for the present. Also, ***a rivederci.***

ar·ri·vism (ar′ə viz′əm), *n.* the conduct or condition of an arriviste. [1935–40; < F *arrivisme;* see ARRIVE, -ISM]

ar·ri·viste (ar′ē vēst′; *Fr.* A Rē vēst′), *n., pl.* **-vistes** (-vēsts′; *Fr.* -vēst′). a person who has recently acquired unaccustomed status, wealth, or success, esp. by dubious means and without earning concomitant esteem. [1900–05; < F; see ARRIVE, -IST]

ar·ro·ba (ə rō′bə; *Sp. and Port.* är Rô′bä), *n., pl.* **-bas** (-bəz; *Sp. and Port.* -bäs). **1.** a Spanish and Portuguese unit of weight of varying value, equal to 25.37 pounds avoirdupois (9.5 kilograms) in Mexico and to 32.38 pounds avoirdupois (12 kilograms) in Brazil. **2.** a unit of liquid measure of varying value, used esp. in Spain and commonly equal (when used for wine) to 4.26 U.S. gallons (16.1 liters). [1590–1600; < Sp < Ar *al rub'* the fourth part, i.e., a quarter of the *qinṭār;* see QUINTAL]

ar·ro·gance (ar′ə gəns), *n.* offensive display of superiority or self-importance; overbearing pride. Also, **ar′·ro·gan·cy.** [1275–1325; ME < MF < L *arrogantia* presumption. See ARROGANT, -ANCE]
—**Syn.** haughtiness, insolence, disdain. —**Ant.** humility, modesty, diffidence.

ar′rogance of pow′er, presumption on the part of a nation that its power gives it the right to intervene in the affairs of less powerful nations. [1965–70]

ar·ro·gant (ar′ə gənt), *adj.* **1.** making claims or pretensions to superior importance or rights; overbearingly assuming; insolently proud: *an arrogant public official.* **2.** characterized by or proceeding from arrogance: *arrogant claims.* [1350–1400; ME < L *arrogant-* (s. of *arrogāns*) presuming, prp. of *arrogāre.* See ARROGATE, -ANT] —**ar′ro·gant·ly,** *adv.*
—**Syn. 1.** presumptuous, haughty, imperious, brazen. See **proud.** —**Ant. 1.** meek. **2.** modest, humble.

ar·ro·gate (ar′ə gāt′), *v.t.,* **-gat·ed, -gat·ing. 1.** to claim unwarrantably or presumptuously; assume or appropriate to oneself without right: *to arrogate the right to make decisions.* **2.** to attribute or assign to another; ascribe. [1530–40; < L *arrogātus* appropriated, assumed, questioned (ptp. of *arrogāre*), equiv. to *arrog-* (*ar-* AR- + *rog(āre)* to ask, propose) + *-ātus* -ATE[1]] —**ar′ro·gat′ing·ly,** *adv.* —**ar′ro·ga′tion,** *n.* —**ar′ro·ga′tor,** *n.*

ar·ron·disse·ment (ə ron′dis mənt, ar′ən dēs′-; *Fr.* A RôN dēs mäN′), *n., pl.* **-ments** (-mənts; *Fr.* -mäN′). **1.** the largest administrative division of a French department, comprising a number of cantons. **2.** an administrative district of certain large cities in France. [1800–10; < F, equiv. to *arrondiss-* (var. s. of *arrondir* to round out; see A-[5], ROUND) + *-ment* -MENT]

ar·row (ar′ō), *n.* **1.** a slender, straight, generally pointed missile or weapon made to be shot from a bow and equipped with feathers at the end of the shaft near the nock, for controlling flight. **2.** anything resembling

CONCISE ETYMOLOGY KEY: <, descended or borrowed from; >, whence; b., blend of, blended; c., cognate with; cf., compare; deriv., derivative; equiv., equivalent; imit., imitative; obl., oblique; r., replacing; s., stem; sp., spelling, spelled; resp., respelling, respelled; trans., translation; ?, origin unknown; *, unattested; ‡, probably earlier than. See the full key inside the front cover.

an arrow in form, function, or character. **3.** a linear figure having a wedge-shaped end, as one used on a map or architectural drawing, to indicate direction or placement. **4.** (*cap.*) *Astron.* the constellation Sagitta. **5.** See **broad arrow.** —*v.t.* **6.** to indicate the proper position of (an insertion) by means of an arrow (often fol. by *in*): *to arrow in a comment between the paragraphs.* [bef. 900; ME *arewe, arwe,* OE *earh;* c. ON *ǫr* (pl. *ǫrvar*), Goth *arhwazna;* Gmc **arhwō* (fem.), akin to L *arcus* (gen. *arcūs*) bow, ARC; thus L **arku-* bow, pre-Gmc **arku-ā* belonging to the bow] —**ar′row·less,** *adj.* —**ar′row·like′,** *adj.*

Ar·row (ar′ō), *n.* **Kenneth Joseph,** born 1921, U.S. economist: Nobel prize 1972.

ar′row ar′um, a North American plant, *Peltandra virginica,* of wet areas, having large, arrow-shaped leaves and inconspicuous flowers enclosed in a narrow, pointed spathe. Also called **tuckahoe.** [1855–60, *Amer.*]

ar·row·head (ar′ō hed′), *n.* **1.** the head or tip of an arrow, usually separable from the shaft and conventionally wedge-shaped. **2.** anything resembling or having the conventional shape of an arrowhead. **3.** any aquatic or bog plant of the genus *Sagittaria,* having usually arrowhead-shaped leaves and clusters of white flowers. **4.** any of several other plants having arrowhead-shaped leaves. **5.** the dartlike form in an egg-and-dart ornament. [1350–1400; ME *arwe he(ve)d;* see ARROW, HEAD]

ar·row·root (ar′ō ro͞ot′, -ro͝ot′), *n.* **1.** a tropical American plant, *Maranta arundinacea,* the rhizomes of which yield a nutritious starch. **2.** the starch itself. **3.** any of several other plants yielding a similar starch. **4.** the starch of these plants, used in cooking as a binder or thickener. [1690–1700; so called from use of its root in treatment of wounds made by poisoned arrows]

Ar·row·smith (ar′ō smith′), *n.* a novel (1925) by Sinclair Lewis.

ar·row·wood (ar′ō wo͝od′), *n.* any of several shrubs or small trees, esp. of the genus *Viburnum,* having tough, straight shoots formerly used for arrows. [1700–10, *Amer.;* so called from its use in making arrows]

ar·row·worm (ar′ō wûrm′), *n.* any small, translucent marine worm of the phylum (or class) Chaetognatha, having lateral and caudal fins. Also called **glassworm.** [1885–90; so called from a fancied resemblance to an arrow]

ar·row·y (ar′ō ē), *adj.* **1.** resembling or suggesting an arrow, as in slimness or swiftness. **2.** consisting of arrows. [1630–40; ARROW + -Y[1]]

ar·roy·o (ə roi′ō), *n., pl.* **-os.** (chiefly in southwest U.S.) a small steep-sided watercourse or gulch with a nearly flat floor: usually dry except after heavy rains. [1800–10, *Amer.;* < Sp; akin to L *arrūgia* mine shaft]

Arroy′o Gran′de, a town in SW California. 11,290.

ar·roz con pol·lo (ä rôth′ kôn pô′lyō, ä rôs′ kôn pô′yō), a Spanish dish of chicken cooked with rice, onions, and saffron, and sometimes tomatoes, often garnished with pimientos and peas. [1935–40; < Sp: rice with chicken]

Ar′ru Is′lands (ä′ro͞o). See **Aru Islands.**

ARS, 1. advanced record system. **2.** Agricultural Research Service.

Ar·sa·ces I (är′sə sēz′, är sā′sēz), founder of the Parthian empire c250 B.C.

Ars An·ti·qua (ärz′ an tē′kwə, ärs′-), *Music.* the style of composition characteristic of the 13th century, esp. in France. Cf. **Ars Nova.** [< ML: ancient art]

arse (ärs), *n. Slang (vulgar).* ass[2] (defs. 1, 2). [see ASS[2]]

arsen-, var. of **arseno-,** esp. before a vowel.

ar·se·nal (är′sə nl, ärs′nəl), *n.* **1.** a place of storage or a magazine containing arms and military equipment for land or naval service. **2.** a government establishment where military equipment or munitions are manufactured. **3.** a collection or supply of weapons or munitions. **4.** a collection or supply of anything; store: *He came to the meeting with an impressive arsenal of new research data.* [1500–10; (< MF) < It *arzanale* < Upper Italian (Venetian) *arzanà* dockyard < Ar *dār ṣinā'ah* workshop (lit., house of handwork); initial *d* prob. taken as a form of the prep. *di* from]

ar·se·nate (är′sə nāt′, -nit), *n.* a salt or ester of arsenic acid. [1790–1800; ARSEN- + -ATE[2]]

ar·se·nic (*n.* är′sə nik, ärs′nik; *adj.* är sen′ik), *n.* **1.** a grayish-white element having a metallic luster, vaporizing when heated, and forming poisonous compounds. *Symbol:* As; *at. wt.:* 74.92; *at. no.:* 33. **2.** See **arsenic trioxide. 3.** a mineral, the native element, occurring in white or gray masses. —*adj.* **4.** of or containing arsenic, esp. in the pentavalent state. [1350–1400; ME *arsenicum* < L < Gk *arsenikón* orpiment, n. use of neut. of *arsenikós* virile (*ársēn* male, strong + *-ikos* -IC), prob. alter. of Oriental word (perh. < **arznig,* metathetic var. of Syriac *zarnig*) by folk etym.]

arsen′ic ac′id, *Chem.* a white, crystalline, water-soluble powder, $H_3AsO_4\cdot\frac{1}{2}H_2O$, used chiefly in the manufacture of arsenates. [1795–1805]

ar·sen·i·cal (är sen′i kəl), *adj.* **1.** containing or relating to arsenic. —*n.* **2.** any of a group of pesticides, drugs, or other compounds containing arsenic. [1595–1605; ARSENIC + -AL[1]]

ar′senic disul′fide, *Chem.* an orange-red, water-insoluble, poisonous powder, As_4S_4, As_2S_2, or AsS, used chiefly in the manufacture of fireworks. Also called **ar′senic mon·o·sul′fide** (mon′ə sul′fīd).

ar′senic trichlo′ride, *Chem.* a colorless or yellow, oily, poisonous liquid, $AsCl_3$, used chiefly as an intermediate in the manufacture of organic arsenicals. Also called **butter of arsenic.**

ar′senic triox′ide, *Chem.* a white, tasteless, amorphous, slightly water-soluble, poisonous powder, As_2O_3, used chiefly in the manufacture of pigments and glass and as an insecticide or weed-killer; arsenous acid. Also called **arsenic.**

ar′senic trisul′fide, *Chem.* a yellow or red crystalline substance, As_2S_3, occurring in nature as the mineral orpiment, and used as a pigment **(king's yellow)** and in pyrotechnics. [1905–10]

ar·se·nide (är′sə nīd′, -nid), *n. Chem.* a compound containing two elements of which arsenic is the negative one, as silver arsenide, Ag_3As. [1860–65; ARSEN- + -IDE]

ar·se·ni·ous (är sē′nē əs), *adj. Chem.* arsenous. [ARSEN- + -IOUS]

ar·se·nite (är′sə nīt′), *n. Chem.* a salt or ester of arsenous acid. [1790–1800; ARSEN- + -ITE[1]]

ar·se·niu·ret·ted (är sē′nyə ret′id, -sen′yə-), *adj. Chem.* combined with arsenic so as to form an arsenide. Also, **ar·se′niu·ret′ed.** [1805–15; ARSENI(C) + -URET + -ED[3]]

arse′niuretted hy′drogen, *Chem.* arsine (def. 1). [1805–15]

ar·se·no (är′sə nō′), *adj. Chem.* containing the arseno group. [adj. use of ARSENO-]

arseno-, a combining form representing **arsenic** or **arseno group** in the formation of compound words: *arsenopyrite.* Also, *esp. before a vowel,* **arsen-.** [ARSEN(IC) + -O-]

ar′seno group′, *Chem.* the bivalent group $-As{=}As-$. Also called **ar′seno rad′ical.**

ar·sen·o·lite (är sen′l īt′), *n.* a mineral, arsenic trioxide, As_2O_3, occurring usually as a white incrustation on arsenical ores. [1850–55; ARSENO- + -LITE]

ar·se·no·py·rite (är′sə nō pī′rīt, är sen′ə-), *n.* a common mineral, iron arsenic sulfide, FeAsS, occurring in silver-white to steel-gray crystals or masses: an ore of arsenic. Also called **mispickel.** [1880–85; ARSENO- + PYRITE]

ar·se·nous (är′sə nəs), *adj. Chem.* **1.** containing arsenic in the trivalent state, as arsenous chloride, $AsCl_3$. **2.** of or derived from arsenous acid. Also, **arsenious.** [1790–1800; ARSEN- + -OUS]

ar′senous ac′id, *Chem.* **1.** a hypothetical acid, H_3AsO_3 or $HAsO_2$, found only in solution or in the form of its salts. **2.** See **arsenic trioxide.** [1790–1800]

ars est ce·la·re ar·tem (ärs est ke lä′re är′tem; *Eng.* ärz est sə lā′rē är′təm, -lâr′ē, ärs), *Latin.* it is art to conceal art; true art conceals the means by which it is achieved.

ars gra·ti·a ar·tis (ärs′ grä′tē ä′ är′tis; *Eng.* ärz′ grā′shē ə är′tis, ärs), *Latin.* art for art's sake.

ar·shin (är shēn′), *n.* a Russian unit of length equal to 28 in. (71 cm). Also, **ar·shine′.** [1725–35; < Russ *arshin* < Tatar *aršin* or a cognate Turkic word << Pers]

ar·sine (är sēn′, är′sēn, -sin), *n. Chem.* **1.** Also called **arseniuretted hydrogen.** a colorless, flammable, slightly water-soluble gas, AsH_3, having a fetid, garlic-like odor, used in chemical warfare. **2.** any derivative of this compound in which one or more hydrogen atoms are replaced by organic groups. [1875–80; ARS(ENIC) + -INE[2]]

ar·si·no (är sē′nō), *adj. Chem.* containing the arsino group. [ARSINE + -O-, construed as adj.]

arsi′no group′, *Chem.* the univalent group H_2As-. Also called **arsi′no rad′ical.**

ar·sis (är′sis), *n., pl.* **-ses** (-sēz). **1.** *Music.* the upward stroke in conducting; upbeat. Cf. **thesis** (def. 4). **2.** *Pros.* **a.** the part of a metrical foot that bears the ictus or stress. **b.** (less commonly) a part of a metrical foot that does not bear the ictus. Cf. **thesis** (def. 5). [1350–1400; ME: raising the voice < L < Gk, equiv. to *ar-* (s. of *aírein* to raise, lift) + *-sis* -SIS]

ars lon·ga, vi·ta bre·vis (ärs lông′gä wē′tä bre′wis; *Eng.* ärz lông′gə vī′tə brē′vis, brev′is, vē′tə, ärs), *Latin.* art is long, life is short.

Ars No·va (ärz′ nō′və, ärs′), *Music.* the style of composition characteristic of the 14th century in France and Italy. Cf. **Ars Antiqua.** [< ML: new art]

ar·son (är′sən), *n. Law.* the malicious burning of another's house or property, or in some statutes, the burning of one's own house or property, as to collect insurance. [1670–80; < AF, OF < LL *ārsiōn-* (s. of *ārsiō*) a burning, equiv. to *ārs-* (L *ārd(ere)* to burn (cf. ARDENT) + *-t(us)* ptp. suffix) + *-iōn-* -ION] —**ar′son·ous,** *adj.*

ar·son·ist (är′sə nist), *n.* a person who commits arson. [1860–65; ARSON + -IST]

ars·phen·a·mine (ärs fen′ə mēn′, -min), *n. Pharm.* a yellow, crystalline powder, $C_{12}H_{12}N_2O_2As_2\cdot 2HCl\cdot 2H_2O$, formerly used to treat diseases caused by spirochete organisms, esp. syphilis and trench mouth: first known as "606." [1915–20; ARS(ENIC) + PHEN(YL) + AMINE]

ars po·e·ti·ca (ärz′ pō et′i kə, ärs′), **1.** a treatise on the art of poetry or poetics. **2.** (*cap., italics*) a poem (c20 B.C.) by Horace, setting forth his precepts for the art of poetry.

ar·sy-var·sy (är′sē vär′sē), *Informal.* —*adj.* **1.** wrong end foremost; completely backward: *an arsy-varsy way of doing things.* —*adv.* **2.** in a backward or thoroughly mixed-up fashion: *The papers are all filed arsy-varsy.* Also, **ar·sy-ver·sy** (är′sē vûr′sē). [1530–40; prob. alter. of L *vice versa* (see VICE VERSA), with ARSE substituted to make a facetious rhyming compound; for L *versa* > *varsy,* cf. ARGAL[3]]

art[1] (ärt), *n.* **1.** the quality, production, expression, or realm, according to aesthetic principles, of what is beautiful, appealing, or of more than ordinary significance. **2.** the class of objects subject to aesthetic criteria; works of art collectively, as paintings, sculptures, or drawings: *a museum of art; an art collection.* **3.** a field, genre, or category of art: *Dance is an art.* **4.** the fine arts collectively, often excluding architecture: *art and architecture.* **5.** any field using the skills or techniques of art: *advertising art; industrial art.* **6.** (in printed matter) illustrative or decorative material: *Is there any art with the copy for this story?* **7.** the principles or methods governing any craft or branch of learning: *the art of baking; the art of selling.* **8.** the craft or trade using these principles or methods. **9.** skill in conducting any human activity: *a master at the art of conversation.* **10.** a branch of learning or university study, esp. one of the fine arts or the humanities, as music, philosophy, or literature. **11. arts, a.** (*used with a singular v.*) the humanities: *a college of arts and sciences.* **b.** (*used with a plural v.*) See **liberal arts. 12.** skilled workmanship, execution, or agency, as distinguished from nature. **13.** trickery; cunning: *glib and devious art.* **14.** studied action; artificiality in behavior. **15.** an artifice or artful device: *the innumerable arts and wiles of politics.* **16.** *Archaic.* science, learning, or scholarship. [1175–1225; ME < OF, acc. of *ars* < L *ars* (nom.), *artem* (acc.)]

art[2] (ärt), *v. Archaic.* 2nd pers. sing. pres. indic. of **be.** [bef. 950; ME; OE *eart,* equiv. to *ear-* (see ARE[1]) + *-t* ending of 2nd pers. sing.]

Art (ärt), *n.* a male given name, form of **Arthur.**

ART, *Ling.* article: often used to represent the class of determiners, including words such as *this, that,* and *some* as well as the articles *a, an,* and *the.*

-art, var. of **-ard:** *braggart.*

art., *pl.* **arts.** for 1. **1.** article; articles. **2.** artificial. **3.** artillery. **4.** artist.

ar·tal (är′täl), *n.* pl. of **rotl.**

Ar·taud (ar tō′), *n.* **An·to·nin** (äɴ tô naɴ′), 1896–1948, French actor, poet, and drama critic.

Ar·ta·xerx·es I (är′tə zûrk′sēz), *("Longimanus"),* died 424 B.C., king of Persia 464–24.

Artaxerxes II *("Mnemon"),* died 359? B.C., king of Persia 404?–359?.

art′ dec′o, a style of decorative art developed originally in the 1920's with a revival in the 1960's, marked chiefly by geometric motifs, curvilinear forms, sharply defined outlines, often bold colors, and the use of synthetic materials, as plastics. Also, **Art′ Dec′o.** Also called **deco, Deco.** [1965–70; < F *Art Déco,* shortened from *Exposition Internationale des Arts Décoratifs et Industriels Modernes,* an exposition of modern decorative and industrial arts held in Paris, France, in 1925]

art′ direc′tor, 1. *Motion Pictures, Television.* the person who determines the staging requirements for a production and often designs the sets or supervises their building and dressing. **2.** Also called **art′ ed′itor.** a person who is responsible for the selection, execution, production, etc., of graphic art for a publication, advertising agency, or the like. **3.** See **artistic director.** [1930–35]

ar·te·fact (är′tə fakt′), *n.* artifact.

ar·tel (är tel′), *n.* (in Russia or the Soviet Union) a peasants' or workers' cooperative; an association of workers or peasants for collective effort. [1880–85; < Russ *artél',* perh. ult. < a deriv. of Turkic *ort-* middle (cf. Turk *ortak* partner, *ortaklık* association), though identity of suffixed element(s) unclear]

Ar·te·mis (är′tə mis), *n.* **1.** Also called **Cynthia.** an ancient Greek goddess, the daughter of Leto and the sister of Apollo, characterized as a virgin huntress and associated with the moon. Cf. **Diana. 2.** a female given name.

ar·te·mis·i·a (är′tə miz′ē ə, -mizh′-, -mish′-), *n.* any of several composite plants of the genus *Artemisia,* having aromatic foliage and small disk flowers, including the sagebrush, wormwood, and mugwort. [1350–1400; ME: mugwort < L < Gk, equiv. to *Artemis* Artemis + *-ia* -IA]

Ar·te·movsk (ur tyô′məfsk), *n.* a city in E Ukraine. 89,000. Formerly, **Bakhmut.**

arteri-, var. of **arterio-,** esp. before a vowel.

ar·te·ri·al (är tēr′ē əl), *adj.* **1.** *Physiol.* pertaining to the blood in the pulmonary vein, in the left side of the heart, and in most arteries, having been oxygenated during its passage through the lungs and being normally bright red. **2.** *Anat.* of, pertaining to, or resembling the arteries. **3.** being or constituting a main route, channel, or other course of flow or access, often with many branches: *an arterial highway; an arterial drainage system.* —*n.* **4.** a main route, channel, or other course of flow or access: *funds to resurface the main arterials of the city.* [1375–1425; late ME (< MF) < ML *artēriālis.* See ARTERY, -AL[1]] —**ar·te′ri·al·ly,** *adv.*

ar·te·ri·al·ize (är tēr′ē ə līz′), *v.t.,* **-ized, -iz·ing.** *Physiol.* to convert (venous blood) into arterial blood by the action of oxygen in the lungs. Also, *esp. Brit.,* **ar·te′ri·al·ise′.** [1825–35; ARTERIAL + -IZE] —**ar·te′ri·al·i·za′tion,** *n.*

arterio-, a combining form meaning "artery," used in the formation of compound words: *arteriosclerosis.* Also, *esp. before a vowel,* **arteri-.** [< Gk *artērio-,* comb. form of *artēría* windpipe, ARTERY]

ar·te·ri·o·gram (är tēr′ē ə gram′), *n.* an x-ray produced by arteriography. [1880–85; ARTERIO- + -GRAM[1]]

ar·te·ri·og·ra·phy (är tēr′ē og′rə fē), *n., pl.* **-phies.** *Med.* x-ray examination of an artery or arteries following injection of a radiopaque substance. Cf. **angiography.** [1835–45; ARTERIO- + -GRAPHY] —**ar·te·ri·o·graph·ic** (är tēr′ē ə graf′ik), *adj.*

ar·te·ri·ole (är tēr′ē ōl′), *n. Anat.* any of the smallest branches of an artery, terminating in capillaries. [1830–40; < NL *artēriola,* equiv. to L *artēri(a)* ARTERY + *-ola* -OLE[1]] —**ar·te·ri·o′lar,** *adj.*

ar·te·ri·o·scle·ro·sis (är tēr′ē ō sklə rō′sis), *n.* degenerative changes in the arteries, characterized by thickening of the vessel walls and accumulation of calcium with consequent loss of elasticity and lessened blood flow. Cf. **atherosclerosis.** [1885–90; < NL. See ARTERIO-, SCLEROSIS] —**ar·te·ri·o·scle·rot·ic** (är tēr′ē ō sklə rot′ik), *adj.*

ar·te·ri·ot·o·my (är tēr′ē ot′ə mē), *n., pl.* **-mies.** *Surg.* the incision or opening into the lumen of an artery for the removal of a clot, embolus, or the like, or, formerly, for bloodletting. [1625–35; ARTERIO- + -TOMY]

ar·te·ri·o·ve·nous (är tēr′ē ō vē′nəs), *adj. Anat.* of or pertaining to an artery and a vein; having characteristics of both arteries and veins. [1875–80; ARTERIO- + VENOUS]

ar·te·ri·tis (är′tə rī′tis), *n.* inflammation of an artery. [1830–40; ARTER(IO)- + -ITIS]

ar·ter·y (är′tə rē), *n., pl.* **-ter·ies. 1.** *Anat.* a blood vessel that conveys blood from the heart to any part of the body. **2.** a main channel or highway, esp. of a connected system with many branches. [1350–1400; ME < L *artēria* < Gk: windpipe, artery. See AORTA]

Ar·te·sia (är tē′zhə), *n.* **1.** a city in S California. 14,301. **2.** a city in SE New Mexico. 10,385.

ar·te·sian (är tē′zhən), *adj.* noting, pertaining to, or characteristic of an artesian well. [1820–30; < F *artésien* pertaining to ARTOIS (OF *Arteis* Artois + *-ien* -IAN), after the wells of this kind in the region]

arte′sian well′, a well in which water rises under pressure from a permeable stratum overlaid by impermeable rock. [1855–60]

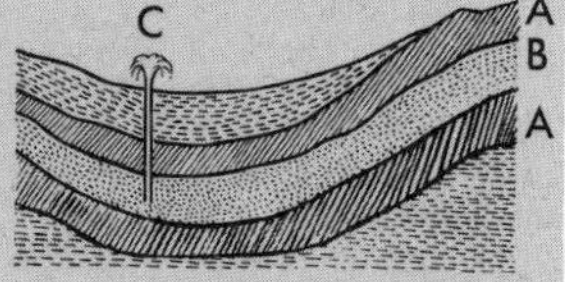

artesian well (cross section) A, impermeable strata; B, permeable stratum; C, artesian boring and well

Ar·te·veld (är′tə velt′), *n.* **1. Ja·cob van** (yä′kôp vän), 1290?–1345, Flemish statesman. **2.** his son, **Phi·lip van** (fē′lip vän), 1340?–82, Flemish revolutionist and political leader. Also, **Ar·te·vel·de** (är′tə vel′də).

art′ film′, a motion picture made primarily for aesthetic reasons rather than commercial profit, often of an experimental nature or having an unconventional or highly symbolic content, aimed typically at a limited audience. [1925–30]

art′ form′, 1. the more or less established structure, pattern, or scheme followed in shaping an artistic work: *The sonata, the sonnet, and the novel are all art forms.* **2.** a medium for artistic expression: *ballet, sculpture, opera, and other art forms.* **3.** a medium other than the artistic regarded as having highly developed or systematized rules, procedures, or formulations: *international diplomacy regarded as an art form.* [1865–70]

art·ful (ärt′fəl), *adj.* **1.** slyly crafty or cunning; deceitful; tricky: *artful schemes.* **2.** skillful or clever in adapting means to ends; ingenious: *an artful choice of metaphors and similes.* **3.** done with or characterized by art or skill: *artful acting; artful repairs.* **4.** *Archaic.* artificial. [1605–15; ART[1] + -FUL] —**art′ful·ly,** *adv.* —**art′ful·ness,** *n.*

art′ glass′, 1. (in the late 19th and early 20th centuries) any of the several varieties of glass using combinations of colors, special effects of opaqueness and transparency, etc., to create an aesthetic effect. **2.** any of the objects made of such glass, as lamps, vases, and the like. [1925–30]

art′ histor′ical, of or pertaining to the history of art or to its study: *art historical documents on 16th-century painting.* Also, **art′-his·tor′i·cal.** [1930–35]

art′ house′, a motion-picture theater specializing in the exhibition of art films. Also called **art theater.** [1950–55]

arthr-, var. of **arthro-** before a vowel.

ar·thral·gia (är thral′jə), *n. Pathol.* pain in a joint. [1840–50; ARTHR- + -ALGIA] —**ar·thral′gic,** *adj.*

ar·threc·to·my (är threk′tə mē), *n., pl.* **-mies.** *Surg.* erasion (def. 2b). [ARTHR- + -ECTOMY]

ar·thrit·ic (är thrit′ik), *adj.* **1.** Also, **ar·thrit′i·cal.** of, pertaining to, or afflicted with arthritis. —*n.* **2.** a person afflicted with arthritis. [1325–75; < L *arthrīticus* < Gk *arthrītikós* (see ARTHR-, -ITIC); r. ME *artetik* < OF *artetique* < L, as above] —**ar·thrit′i·cal·ly,** *adv.*

ar·thri·tis (är thrī′tis), *n.* acute or chronic inflammation of a joint, often accompanied by pain and structural changes and having diverse causes, as infection, crystal deposition, or injury. Cf. **bursitis, gout, osteoarthritis, rheumatoid arthritis.** [1535–45; < NL < Gk: gout. See ARTHRO-, -ITIS]

arthro-, a combining form meaning "joint," "jointed," used in the formation of compound words: *arthropod.* Also, *esp. before a vowel,* **arthr-.** [< Gk, comb. form of *árthron* a joint; akin to L *artus* (see ARTICLE)]

Ar·thro·bac·ter (är′thrō bak′tər), *n. Bacteriol.* a genus of rod-shaped or spherical bacteria found in the soil. [1947; < NL; see ARTHRO-, -BACTER]

ar·throd·e·sis (är throd′ə sis), *n., pl.* **-ses** (-sēz′). permanent surgical immobilization of a joint. Also called **artificial ankylosis.** [1900–05; ARTHRO- + Gk *désis* binding together, equiv. to *dé(ein)* to bind + *-sis* -SIS]

CONCISE ETYMOLOGY KEY: <, descended or borrowed from; >, whence; b., blend of, blended; c., cognate with; cf., compare; deriv., derivative; equiv., equivalent; imit., imitative; obl., oblique; r., replacing; s., stem; sp., spelling, spelled; resp., respelling, respelled; trans., translation; ?, origin unknown; *, unattested; ‡, probably earlier than. See the full key inside the front cover.

ar·thro·di·a (är thrō′dē ə), *n., pl.* **-di·ae** (-dē ē′). *Anat.* a joint, as in the carpal articulations, in which the surfaces glide over each other in movement. Also called **gliding joint.** [1625–35; < Gk *arthrōdía,* equiv. to *arthrṓd(ēs)* jointed (*árthr(on)* joint + *-ōdēs* -ODE[1]) + *-ia* -IA] —**ar·thro′di·al, ar·throd·ic** (är throd′ik), *adj.*

ar·thro·dire (är′thrə dīᵊr′), *n.* any of numerous fishes of the extinct order Arthrodira, widely distributed during the Devonian Period, having the anterior part of the body covered by a shield of bony plates. [< NL *Arthrodira,* equiv. to *arthro-* ARTHRO- + *-dira* < Gk *deirḗ* neck, throat] —**ar·thro·di·ran** (är′thrə dī′rən), **ar′thro·di′rous,** *adj.*

ar·thro·gram (är′thrə gram′), *n.* an x-ray photograph produced by arthrography. [ARTHRO- + -GRAM[1]]

ar·throg·ra·phy (är throg′rə fē), *n.* x-ray examination of a joint following injection of a radiopaque substance. [1855–60; ARTHRO- + -GRAPHY]

ar·thro·mere (är′thrə mēr′), *n. Zool.* any of the segments or parts of a jointed animal. [ARTHRO- + -MERE] —**ar·thro·mer·ic** (är′thrə mer′ik), *adj.*

ar·throp·a·thy (är throp′ə thē), *n.* disease of the joints. [1875–80; ARTHRO- + -PATHY] —**ar·thro·path·ic** (är′thrə path′ik), *adj.*

ar·thro·plas·ty (är′thrə plas′tē), *n.* the surgical repair of a joint or the fashioning of a movable joint, using the patient's own tissue or an artificial replacement. [1885–90; ARTHRO- + -PLASTY]

ar·thro·pod (är′thrə pod′), *n.* **1.** any invertebrate of the phylum Arthropoda, having a segmented body, jointed limbs, and usually a chitinous shell that undergoes moltings, including the insects, spiders and other arachnids, crustaceans, and myriapods. —*adj.* **2.** Also, **ar·throp·o·dal** (är throp′ə dl), **ar·throp·o·dan** (är throp′ə dn), **ar·throp·o·dous** (är throp′ə dəs). belonging or pertaining to the Arthropoda. [1875–80; < NL *Arthropoda;* see ARTHRO-, -POD]

Ar·throp·o·da (är throp′ə də), *n.* the phylum comprising the arthropods. [1865–70; < NL; see ARTHRO-, PODA]

ar·thro·scope (är′thrə skōp′), *n.* a tubelike instrument utilizing fiber optics to examine and treat the inside of a joint. [ARTHRO- + -SCOPE]

ar·thros·co·py (är thros′kə pē), *n.* the use of an arthroscope to diagnose an injury to or disease of a joint or to perform minor surgery on a joint. [1930–35; ARTHRO- + -SCOPY] —**ar·thro·scop·ic** (är′thrə skop′ik), *adj.*

ar·thro·sis[1] (är thrō′sis), *n. Anat.* junction of two or more bones of the skeleton; joint. [1625–35; < Gk *árthrōsis* joining, articulation, equiv. to *arthrō-* (var. s. of *arthroûn* to fasten by a joint; see ARTHRO-) + *-sis* -SIS]

ar·thro·sis[2] (är thrō′sis), *n. Pathol.* degenerative joint disease. [ARTHR- + -OSIS]

ar·thro·spore (är′thrə spôr′, -spōr′), *n. Biol.* **1.** an isolated vegetative cell that has passed into a resting state, occurring in bacteria and not regarded as a true spore. **2.** one of a number of spores of various fungi and certain blue-green algae, united in the form of a string of beads, formed by fission. [1890–95; ARTHRO- + SPORE] —**ar·thro·spor·ic** (är′thrə spôr′ik, -spor′-), **ar·thros·po·rous** (är thros′pər əs, är′thrə spôr′əs, -spōr′-), *adj.*

Ar·thur (är′thər), *n.* **1. Chester Alan,** 1830–86, 21st president of the U.S. 1881–85. **2.** legendary king in ancient Britain: leader of the Knights of the Round Table. **3.** a male given name.

Ar·thu·ri·an (är thŏŏr′ē ən), *adj.* of or pertaining to King Arthur, who, with his knights, formed the subject of a large part of medieval romance: *Arthurian legends.* [1850–55; ARTHUR + -IAN]

Ar·thus′ reac′tion (är tōō′siz), *Immunol.* a severe, local immune reaction to the injection of an antigen in a sensitized host. Also called **Arthus′ phenom′enon.** [after Nicolas-Maurice *Arthus* (1862–1945), French physiologist, who discovered it in 1903]

ar·ti·choke (är′ti chōk′), *n.* **1.** a tall, thistlelike composite plant, *Cynara scolymus,* native to the Mediterranean region, of which the numerous scalelike bracts and receptacle of the immature flower head are eaten as a vegetable. **2.** the large, rounded, closed flower head itself. **3.** See **Jerusalem artichoke.** Also called **globe artichoke** (for defs. 1, 2). [1525–35; < Upper It *articiocco,* var. (by dissimilation) of *arcicioco, arcicioffo* < **arcarcioffo* < OSp *alcarchofa* < dial. Ar *al-kharshūf* the artichoke]

artichoke, *Cynara scolymus*

ar·ti·cle (är′ti kəl), *n., v.,* **-cled, -cling.** —*n.* **1.** a written composition in prose, usually nonfiction, on a specific topic, forming an independent part of a book or other publication, as a newspaper or magazine. **2.** an individual object, member, or portion of a class; an item or particular: *an article of food; articles of clothing.* **3.** something of indefinite character or description: *What is that article?* **4.** an item for sale; commodity. **5.** *Gram.* any member of a small class of words, or, as in Swedish or Rumanian, affixes, found in certain languages, as English, French, and Arabic, that are linked to nouns and that typically have a grammatical function identifying the noun as a noun rather than describing it. In English the definite article is *the,* the indefinite article is *a* or *an,* and their force is generally to impart specificity to the noun or to single out the referent from the class named by the noun. **6.** a clause, item, point, or particular in a contract, treaty, or other formal agreement; a condition or stipulation in a contract or bargain: *The lawyers disagreed on the article covering plagiarism suits.* **7.** a separate clause or provision of a statute. **8.** *Slang.* a person. **9.** *Archaic.* a subject or matter of interest, thought, business, etc. **10.** *Obs.* a specific or critical point of time; juncture or moment: *the article of death.* —*v.t.* **11.** to set forth in articles; charge or accuse specifically: *They articled his alleged crimes.* **12.** to bind by articles of covenant or stipulation: *to article an apprentice.* [1200–50; ME < AF, ML *articulus* article of faith, L: joint, limb, member, clause, grammatical article, equiv. to *arti-* (comb. form of *artus* joint; akin to ARTHRO-, ARM[2]) + *-culus* -CULE[1]]

ar·ti·cled (är′ti kəld), *adj.* bound by the terms of apprenticeship: *an articled clerk.* [1570–80; ARTICLE + -ED[2]]

ar′ticle of faith′, a fundamental belief; tenet. Also called **ar′ticle of belief′.** [1400–50; late ME]

ar′ticles of agree′ment, *Naut.* a contract between the captain of a ship and a crew member regarding stipulations of a voyage, signed prior to and upon termination of a voyage. Also called **shipping articles.**

Ar′ticles of Confedera′tion, the first constitution of the 13 American states, adopted in 1781 and replaced in 1789 by the Constitution of the United States.

Ar′ticles of War′, the body of laws and legal procedures of the U.S. Army and Air Force, replaced in 1951 by the Uniform Code of Military Justice.

ar·tic·u·lar (är tik′yə lər), *adj.* of or pertaining to the joints. [1400–50; late ME < L *articulāris* pertaining to the joints. See ARTICLE, -AR[1]] —**ar·tic′u·lar·ly,** *adv.*

ar·tic·u·late (*adj., n.* är tik′yə lit; *v.* är tik′yə lāt′), *adj., v.,* **-lat·ed, -lat·ing,** *n.* —*adj.* **1.** uttered clearly in distinct syllables. **2.** capable of speech; not speechless. **3.** using language easily and fluently; having facility with words: *an articulate speaker.* **4.** expressed, formulated, or presented with clarity and effectiveness: *an articulate thought.* **5.** made clear, distinct, and precise in relation to other parts: *an articulate form; an articulate shape; an articulate area.* **6.** (of ideas, form, etc.) having a meaningful relation to other parts: *an articulate image.* **7.** having parts or distinct areas organized into a coherent or meaningful whole; unified: *an articulate system of philosophy.* **8.** *Zool.* having joints or articulations; composed of segments. —*v.t.* **9.** to utter clearly and distinctly; pronounce with clarity. **10.** *Phonet.* to make the movements and adjustments of the speech organs necessary to utter (a speech sound). **11.** to give clarity or distinction to: *to articulate a shape; to articulate an idea.* **12.** *Dentistry.* to subject to articulation. **13.** to unite by a joint or joints. **14.** to reveal or make distinct: *an injection to articulate arteries so that obstructions can be observed by x-ray.* —*v.i.* **15.** to pronounce clearly each of a succession of speech sounds, syllables, or words; enunciate: *to articulate with excessive precision.* **16.** *Phonet.* to articulate a speech sound. **17.** *Anat., Zool.* to form a joint. **18.** *Obs.* to make terms of agreement. —*n.* **19.** a segmented invertebrate. [1545–55; < L *articulātus,* ptp. of articulāre to divide into distinct parts. See ARTICLE, -ATE[1]] —**ar·tic·u·la·ble** (är tik′yə lə bəl), *adj.* —**ar·tic′u·late·ly,** *adv.* —**ar·tic′u·late·ness, ar·tic·u·la·cy** (är tik′yə lə sē), *n.* —**ar·tic·u·la·tive** (är tik′yə lā′tiv, -lə tiv), *adj.*
—**Syn. 4.** expressive. See **eloquent. 9.** enunciate.
—**Ant. 4.** inarticulate, unintelligible. **9.** mumble.

ar·tic·u·lat·ed (är tik′yə lā′tid), *adj.* **1.** made clear or distinct: *articulated sounds.* **2.** having a joint or joints; jointed: *an articulated appendage.* **3.** (of a vehicle) built in sections that are hinged or otherwise connected so as to allow flexibility of movement: *an articulated bus; an articulated locomotive.* [1545–55; ARTICULATE + -ED[2]]

artic′ulated joint′, 1. *Anat.* a flexible joint. **2.** an artificial appendage, limb, or the like, esp. one activated and controlled by a computer, as the mechanical arm of a robot. **3.** a device by which two or more sections of a vehicle are linked together so as to allow greater capacity, flexibility of movement, etc. [1955–60]

artic′ulated lor′ry, *Brit.* a tractor-trailer truck.

ar·tic·u·la·tion (är tik′yə lā′shən), *n.* **1.** an act or the process of articulating: *the articulation of a form; the articulation of a new thought.* **2.** *Phonet.* **a.** the act or process of articulating speech. **b.** the adjustments and movements of speech organs involved in pronouncing a particular sound, taken as a whole. **c.** any one of these adjustments and movements. **d.** any speech sound, esp. a consonant. **3.** the act of jointing. **4.** a jointed state or formation; a joint. **5.** *Bot.* **a.** a joint or place between two parts where separation may take place spontaneously, as at the point of attachment of a leaf. **b.** a node in a stem, or the space between two nodes. **6.** *Anat., Zool.* a joint, as the joining or juncture of bones or of the movable segments of an arthropod. **7.** *Dentistry.* **a.** the positioning of teeth in a denture, usually on an articulator, for correct occlusion. **b.** the bringing of opposing tooth surfaces into contact with each other. **c.** the relations of the upper and lower natural or artificial teeth in occlusion. **8.** a measure of the effectiveness of a telephonic transmission system in reproducing speech comprehensibly, expressed as the percentage of speech units uttered that is correctly understood. [1400–50; late ME *articulacio(u)n* < MF < L *articulātiōn-,* s. of *articulātiō.* See ARTICULATE, -ION] —**ar·tic·u·la·to·ry** (är tik′yə lə tôr′ē, -tōr′ē), *adj.* —**ar·tic′u·la·to′ri·ly,** *adv.*

ar·tic·u·la·tor (är tik′yə lā′tər), *n.* **1.** a person or thing that articulates. **2.** *Phonet.* a movable organ, as the tongue, lips, or uvula, the action of which is involved in the production of speech sounds. Cf. **place of articulation. 3.** *Dentistry.* a mechanical device, representing the jaws, to which casts may be attached: used in the making of dentures. [1770–80; ARTICULATE + -OR[2]]

artic′ulatory fea′ture, *Phonet.* a property of a speech sound based on its voicing or on its place or manner of articulation in the vocal tract, as voiceless, bilabial, or stop used in describing the sound (p).

artic′ulatory phonet′ics, the branch of phonetics dealing with the motive processes and anatomy involved in the production of the sounds of speech. Cf. **acoustic phonetics** (def. 1), **auditory phonetics, physiological phonetics.** [1950–55]

Ar·tie (är′tē) *n.* a male given name, form of **Arthur.**

ar·ti·fact (är′tə fakt′), *n.* **1.** any object made by human beings, esp. with a view to subsequent use. **2.** a handmade object, as a tool, or the remains of one, as a shard of pottery, characteristic of an earlier time or cultural stage, esp. such an object found at an archaeological excavation. **3.** any mass-produced, usually inexpensive object reflecting contemporary society or popular culture: *artifacts of the pop rock generation.* **4.** a substance or structure not naturally present in the matter being observed but formed by artificial means, as during preparation of a microscope slide. **5.** a spurious observation or result arising from preparatory or investigative procedures. **6.** any feature that is not naturally present but is a product of an extrinsic agent, method, or the like: *statistical artifacts that make the inflation rate seem greater than it is.* Also, **artefact.** [1815–25; var. of *artefact* < L phrase *arte factum* (something) made with skill. See ART, FACT] **—ar·ti·fac·tu·al** (är′tə fak′cho͞o əl), *adj.*

ar·ti·fac·ti·tious (är′tə fak tish′əs), *adj.* of, pertaining to, or of the nature of an artifact. [ARTIFACT + -ITIOUS]

ar·ti·fice (är′tə fis), *n.* **1.** a clever trick or stratagem; a cunning, crafty device or expedient; wile. **2.** trickery; guile; craftiness. **3.** cunning; ingenuity; inventiveness: *a drawing-room comedy crafted with artifice and elegance.* **4.** a skillful or artful contrivance or expedient. [1525–35; < AF < L *artificium* craftsmanship, art, craftiness, equiv. to *arti-*, comb. form of *ars* ART[1] + *-fic-*, comb. form of *facere* to DO[1], make + *-ium* + -IUM]
—Syn. 1. subterfuge. See **trick. 2.** deception, deceit, art, duplicity. See **cunning.**

ar·tif·i·cer (är tif′ə sər), *n.* **1.** a person who is skillful or clever in devising ways of making things; inventor. **2.** a skillful or artistic worker; craftsperson. [1350–1400; ME < AF *artificer*, perh. < ML *artificiārius*; see ARTIFICE, -ER[2]]

ar·ti·fi·cial (är′tə fish′əl), *adj.* **1.** made by human skill; produced by humans (opposed to *natural*): *artificial flowers.* **2.** imitation; simulated; sham: *artificial vanilla flavoring.* **3.** lacking naturalness or spontaneity; forced; contrived; feigned: *an artificial smile.* **4.** full of affectation; affected; stilted: *artificial manners; artificial speech.* **5.** made without regard to the particular needs of a situation, person, etc.; imposed arbitrarily; unnatural: *artificial rules for dormitory residents.* **6.** *Biol.* based on arbitrary, superficial characteristics rather than natural, organic relationships: *an artificial system of classification.* **7.** *Jewelry.* manufactured to resemble a natural gem, in chemical composition or appearance. Cf. **assembled, imitation** (def. 11), **synthetic** (def. 6). [1350–1400; ME < L *artificiālis* contrived by art; see ARTIFICE, -AL[1]] **—ar′ti·fi′cial·ly,** *adv.* **—ar′ti·fi′cial·ness,** *n.*
—Syn. 1. synthetic. **2, 3.** counterfeit, factitious. **4.** pretentious. **—Ant. 2.** genuine, real.

ar′tifi′cial aids′, *Manège.* aid (def. 6b). [1930–35]

artifi′cial ankylo′sis, arthrodesis.

ar′tifi′cial blood′, a chemical emulsion, capable of carrying oxygen and carbon dioxide, for temporary use as a blood substitute in medical emergencies or when a patient objects to blood transfusions on religious grounds. [1970–75]

ar′tifi′cial ear′. See **cochlear implant.**

ar′tifi′cial eye′, a manufactured eye of glass, plastic, or other material, usually hemispherical or cup-shaped, worn cosmetically over a blind eye or in the socket of a lost eye and sometimes attached to muscles to provide movement.

ar′tifi′cial gene′, *Genetics.* a duplicate gene synthesized in the laboratory by combining nucleotides in a sequence characteristic of the copied gene. [1970–75]

ar′tifi′cial grav′ity, a simulated gravity or sensation of weight established within a spacecraft by means of the craft's rotation, acceleration, or deceleration. [1955–60]

artifi′cial harmon′ics, *Music.* (*used with a plural v.*) harmonics of a note produced on a stringed instrument by lightly touching a stopped sounded string. Cf. **natural harmonics.**

ar′tifi′cial heart′, any of various four-chambered devices, modeled on the human heart, that pump blood by attachment to a power source and that are constructed for temporary external use or for implantation as a temporary or permanent heart replacement.

artifi′cial hori′zon, 1. a level, as a surface of mercury, used in determining the altitudes of stars. Cf. **level** (def. 7). **2.** the bubble in a sextant or octant for aerial use. **3.** Also called **flight indicator, gyro horizon.** *Aeron.* an instrument that indicates the banking and pitch of an aircraft with respect to the horizon. [1795–1805]

artifi′cial insemina′tion, the injection of semen into the vagina or uterus by means of a syringe or the like rather than by coitus. *Abbr.:* AI [1895–1900]

artifi′cial intel′ligence, the capacity of a computer to perform operations analogous to learning and decision making in humans, as by an expert system, a program for CAD or CAM, or a program for the perception and recognition of shapes in computer vision systems. *Abbr.:* AI, A.I. [1965–70]

ar·ti·fi·ci·al·i·ty (är′tə fish′ē al′i tē), *n., pl.* **-ties. 1.** artificial quality. **2.** an artificial thing or trait: *artificialities of speech.* [1755–65; ARTIFICIAL + -ITY]

ar′tifi′cial kid′ney, a mechanical device that operates outside the body and substitutes for the kidney by removing waste products from the blood. Also called **hemodialyzer.** Cf. **dialysis** (def. 3). [1910–15]

ar′tifi′cial lan′guage, 1. an invented language, as opposed to a hereditary one, intended for a special use, as in international communication, a secret society, or computer programming. **2.** code (def. 11). [1860–65]

ar′tifi′cial per′son, *Law.* See under **person** (def. 11).

artifi′cial radioactiv′ity, *Physics.* radioactivity introduced into a nonradioactive substance by bombarding the substance with charged particles. Also called **induced radioactivity.**

artifi′cial real′ity, See **virtual reality.** [1985–90]

artifi′cial respira′tion, the stimulation of natural respiratory functions in persons whose breathing has failed or in newborn infants by artificially forcing air into and out of the lungs. Cf. **cardiopulmonary resuscitation.** [1850–55]

artifi′cial selec′tion, a process in the breeding of animals and in the cultivation of plants by which the breeder chooses to perpetuate only those forms having certain desirable inheritable characteristics.

ar′tifi′cial turf′, any of various synthetic, carpetlike materials made to resemble turf and used as a playing surface for football and baseball fields, to cover patios, etc. [1960–65]

Ar·ti·gas (äʀ tē′gäs), *n.* **Jo·sé Ger·va·sio** (hô se′ heʀ vä′syô), 1764–1850, Uruguayan soldier and patriot.

ar·til·ler·y (är til′ə rē), *n.* **1.** mounted projectile-firing guns or missile launchers, mobile or stationary, light or heavy, as distinguished from small arms. **2.** the troops or the branch of an army concerned with the use and service of such weapons. **3.** the science that treats of the use of such weapons. [1350–1400; ME *artil(le)rie, artelry, art(u)ry* armaments, ballistic engines < AF, MF *artillerie*, equiv. to OF *artill(ier)* to equip, arm, alter., by assoc. with *art* ART[1], of *atill(i)er* to set in order, put on armor (< VL **apticulāre*, deriv. of L *aptāre* to put on (armor, ornaments, etc.; see ADAPT); *-i-* for expected *-ei-* perh. by assoc. with *atirier*; see ATTIRE) + *-erie* -ERY]

ar·til·ler·y·man (är til′ə rē mən), *n., pl.* **-men.** a soldier serving in an artillery unit of the army. Also, **ar·til·ler·ist** (är til′ər ist). [1625–35; ARTILLERY + -MAN]

artil′lery plant′, a spreading, tropical American plant, *Pilea microphylla*, of the nettle family, having small, fleshy leaves and green flowers, grown as a curiosity because the pollen is discharged explosively when dry.

artio-, a combining form meaning "even number," used in the formation of compound words: *artiodactyl.* [< Gk *ártio(s)* even (in number), perfect; akin to L *ars* art, Skt *arthya* suitable, rich]

ar·ti·o·dac·tyl (är′tē ō dak′til), *adj.* **1.** *Zool.* having an even number of toes or digits on each foot. **—*n.* 2.** a hoofed, even-toed mammal of the order Artiodactyla, comprising the pigs, hippopotamuses, camels, deer, giraffes, pronghorns, sheep, goats, antelope, and cattle. Cf. **perissodactyl.** [1840–50; < NL; see ARTIO-, DACTYL] **—ar′ti·o·dac′ty·lous,** *adj.*

ar·ti·san (är′tə zən), *n.* a person skilled in an applied art; a craftsperson. [1530–40; < F < It *artigiano*, equiv. to L *artīt(us)* trained in arts and crafts (ptp. of *artīre*; see ART[1], -ITE[2]) + It *-iano* (< L *-iānus*) -IAN] **—ar′ti·san·al,** *adj.* **—ar′ti·san·ship′,** *n.*
—Syn. See **artist.**

art·ist (är′tist), *n.* **1.** a person who produces works in any of the arts that are primarily subject to aesthetic criteria. **2.** a person who practices one of the fine arts, esp. a painter or sculptor. **3.** a person whose trade or profession requires a knowledge of design, drawing, painting, etc.: *a commercial artist.* **4.** a person who works in one of the performing arts, as an actor, musician, or singer; a public performer: *a mime artist; an artist of the dance.* **5.** a person whose work exhibits exceptional skill. **6.** a person who is expert at trickery or deceit: *He's an artist with cards.* **7.** *Obs.* an artisan. [1575–85; < MF *artiste* < ML *artista* master of arts. See ART[1], -IST]
—Syn. 1. ARTIST, ARTISAN are persons having superior skill or ability, or who are capable of producing superior work. An ARTIST is a person engaged in some type of fine art. An ARTISAN is engaged in a craft or applied art.

ar·tiste (är tēst′; *Fr.* aʀ tēst′), *n., pl.* **-tistes** (-tēsts′; *Fr.* -tēst′). an artist, esp. an actor, singer, dancer, or other public performer. [1815–25; < F; see ARTIST]

ar·tis·tic (är tis′tik), *adj.* **1.** conforming to the standards of art; satisfying aesthetic requirements: *artistic productions.* **2.** showing skill or excellence in execution: *artistic workmanship.* **3.** exhibiting taste, discriminating judgment, or sensitivity: *an artistic arrangement of flowers; artistic handling of a delicate diplomatic situation.* **4.** exhibiting an involvement in or appreciation of art, esp. the fine arts: *He had wide-ranging artistic interests.* **5.** involving only aesthetic considerations, usually taken as excluding moral, practical, religious, political, or similar concerns: *artistic principles.* **6.** of art or artists: *artistic works.* **7.** of, like, or thought of as characteristic of an artist: *an artistic temperament.* Also, **ar·tis′ti·cal.** [1745–55; ARTIST + -IC] **—ar·tis′ti·cal·ly,** *adv.*

artis′tic direc′tor, a person who is responsible for the administration of a theater or ballet company, opera house, etc. [1925–30]

art·ist·ry (är′ti strē), *n.* **1.** artistic workmanship, effect, or quality. **2.** artistic ability. [1865–70; ARTIST + -RY]

art·less (ärt′lis), *adj.* **1.** free from deceit, cunning, or craftiness; ingenuous: *an artless child.* **2.** not artificial; natural; simple; uncontrived: *artless beauty; artless charm.* **3.** lacking art, knowledge, or skill. **4.** poorly made; inartistic; clumsy; crude: *an artless translation.* [1580–90; ART[1] + -LESS] **—art′less·ly,** *adv.* **—art′less·ness,** *n.*
—Syn. 1. naive, unsophisticated, guileless, open, frank, plain, unaffected, candid, sincere. **—Ant. 1.** cunning.

art′ lin′ing, *Print.* a system for aligning type in which the baseline is established some distance above the bottom of the body to accommodate letters with unusually long descenders. Cf. **standard lining, title lining.**

art·mo·bile (ärt′mə bēl′), *n.* a truck trailer outfitted to transport and exhibit works of art in areas without access to museums. [1965–70; ART[1] + -MOBILE]

art nou·veau (ärt′ no͞o vō′, är′; *Fr.* aʀ no͞o vō′), (*often caps.*) *Fine Arts.* a style of fine and applied art current in the late 19th and early 20th centuries, characterized chiefly by curvilinear motifs often derived from natural forms. [1900–05; < F: lit., new art]

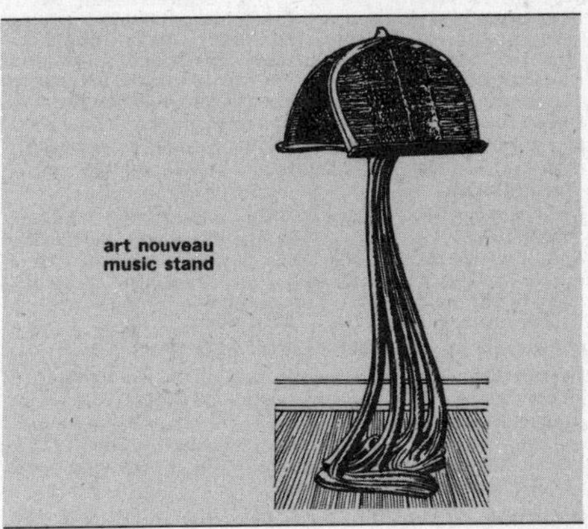

art nouveau music stand

Art′ of Love′, The, (Latin, *Ars Amatoria*), a series of poems in three books (1? B.C) by Ovid.

Ar·tois (aʀ twä′), *n.* a former province in N France: artesian wells.

ar·to·pho·ri·on (är′tô fô′ʀē ôn; *Eng.* är′tə fôr′ē on′, -fōr′-), *n., pl.* **-pho·ri·a** (-fô′ʀē ä; *Eng.* -fôr′ē ə, -fōr′-). *Gk. Orth. Ch.* pyx (def. 1a). [< MGk, Gk: basket for bread, equiv. to *arto-* (comb. form of *ártos* cake, bread) + *-phorion* (akin to *phérein* to bear)]

ar·to·type (är′tə tīp′), *n. Print.* collotype. [1875–80; ART[1] + -O- + TYPE]

art′ rock′, a type of rock music, often with poetic lyrics, characterized by sophisticated harmonic, dynamic, and technical complexity based on forms derived from classical music and requiring performers of considerable training and skill.

arts′ and crafts′, the handcrafting and decoration of esp. utilitarian objects. [1885–90]

Arts′ and Crafts′ Move′ment, a movement, originating in England c1860 as a reaction against poor-quality mass-produced goods, that sought to revive earlier standards of workmanship and design, conceiving of decoration and craftsmanship as a single entity to be applied to the handcrafted production of both utilitarian and decorative objects, and that produced furniture, textiles, wallpaper, jewelry, and other items, often decorated with floral motifs. [1935–40]

art′ song′, a song intended primarily to be sung in recital, typically set to a poem, and having subtly interdependent vocal and piano parts. Cf. **lied.** [1885–90]

art·sy (ärt′sē), *adj.,* **-si·er, -si·est.** *Informal.* **1.** arty. **2.** artsy-craftsy. [1900–05; ART[1] + -SY or ART[1] + -S[3] + -Y[1]] **—art′si·ness,** *n.*

Ar·tsy·ba·shev (*Russ.* uʀ tsi bä′shyif), *n.* **Mi·kha·il** (*Russ.* myi KHU yēl′). See **Artzybashev, Mikhail.**

art·sy-craft·sy (ärt′sē kraft′sē, -kräft′-), *adj. Informal.* **1.** pretending to artistry and craftsmanship or to an interest in arts and crafts: *an artsy-craftsy chair; an artsy-craftsy person.* **2.** cloyingly charming: *The shop has an artsy-craftsy décor.* Also, **arty-crafty.** [1925–30; from ARTS AND CRAFTS; see ARTSY]

art·sy-fart·sy (ärt′sē färt′sē), *adj. Slang* (*vulgar*). arty. Also, **art·y-fart·y** (är′tē fär′tē). [1975–1980; rhyming compound from ART[1], FART, -SY]

art′ the′ater. See **art house.** [1920–25]

art′ un′ion, *Australian.* a lottery, originally a non-government lottery with works of art as prizes.

Ar·tur (är′tər, -to͝or), *n.* a male given name.

art·ware (ärt′wâr′), *n.* **1.** an article of china, porcelain, glass, or the like, prized for its artistry and collected as an art object: *a rare collection of artwares.* **2.** such articles collectively. [ART[1] + WARE[1]]

art·work (ärt′wûrk′), *n.* **1.** *Print.* **a.** the elements that constitute a mechanical, as type, proofs, and illustrations. **b.** a mechanical; paste-up. **2.** the production of artistic or craft objects. **3.** the object so produced. [1875–80; ART[1] + WORK]

art·y (är′tē), *adj.,* **art·i·er, art·i·est.** *Informal.* characterized by a showy, pretentious, and often spurious display of artistic interest, manner, or mannerism. Also, **artsy.** [1900–05; ART[1] + -Y[1]] **—art′i·ly,** *adv.* **—art′i·ness,** *n.*

Ar·ty (är′tē), *n.* a male given name, form of **Arthur.**

Arty., Artillery.

art·y-craft·y (är′tē kraf′tē, -kräf′-), *adj. Informal.* artsy-craftsy.

Ar·tzy·ba·sheff (ärt′si bä′shif; *Russ.* ᴜʀ tsi bä′shyif), *n.* **Bor·is Mi·khai·lo·vich** (bôr′is mi kī′lə vich, bor′-; *Russ.* bu ʀyēs′ myi ᴋʜī′lə vyich), 1899–1965, U.S. illustrator and writer, born in Russia.

Ar·tzy·ba·shev (ᴜʀ tsi bä′shyif), *n.* **Mi·kha·il** (myi-ᴋʜu yēl′), 1878–1927, Russian writer. Also, **Artsybashev.**

ARU, *Computers.* See **audio response unit.**

A·ru·ba (ä ro͞o′bä), *n.* an island in the Netherlands Antilles, in the West Indies, off the NW coast of Venezuela. 62,788; 69 sq. mi. (179 sq. km).

a·ru·gu·la (ə ro͞o′gə lə), *n.* a Mediterranean plant, *Eruca vesicaria sativa,* of the mustard family, having pungent leaves used in salads. Also called **rocket, roquette.** [1965–70; appar. < an Upper It dial. form, akin to Lombard *arigola,* Venetian *rucola* < L *ērūca* name for *Eruca sativa* (cf. It *ruca*), with dim. suffix *-ola* < L *-ula* -ᴜʟᴇ; cf. ʀᴏᴄᴋᴇᴛ[2]]

A′ru Is′lands (är′o͞o), an island group in Indonesia, SW of New Guinea. 3306 sq. mi. (8565 sq. km). Also, **Arru Islands.**

ar′um fam′ily (âr′əm), *n.* the plant family Araceae, characterized by herbaceous plants having numerous tiny flowers on a fleshy spike above or sheathed by a large spathe, and including the anthurium, calla lily, jack-in-the-pulpit, and philodendron. [1545–55; < L < Gk *áron* wake-robin] —**ar′um·like′,** *adj.*

ar′um lil′y, calla (def. 1). [1855–60]

Ar·un·del (ar′ən dl; *locally* ärn′dl), *n.* a town in S West Sussex, in S England: castle. 2382.

a·run·di·na·ceous (ə run′də nā′shəs), *adj. Bot.* pertaining to or like a reed or cane; reedlike; reedy. [1650–60; < NL, equiv. to L *(h)arundin-* (s. of *harundō* reed) + *-āceus* -ᴀᴄᴇᴏᴜs]

A·run·ta (ə run′tə), *n., pl.* **tas,** (*esp. collectively*) **-ta.** Aranda.

A·ru·ru (ä ro͞o′ro͞o), *n.* the Akkadian goddess personifying earth, who assisted Marduk in the creation of human beings: the counterpart of the Sumerian Ki.

A·ru·sha (ə ro͞o′shə), *n.* a city in N Tanganyika, in Tanzania. 33,000.

a·rus·pex (ə rus′peks), *n., pl.* **-pi·ces** (-pə sēz′). haruspex.

a·rus·pi·cy (ə rus′pə sē), *n.* haruspicy.

A·ru·wi·mi (är′o͞o wē′mē), *n.* a river in Zaïre, flowing SW and W into the Zaire River. ab. 800 mi. (1300 km) long.

A.R.V., **1.** AIDS-related virus. See under **AIDS virus. 2.** See **American Revised Version.**

Ar·vad·a (är vad′ə), *n.* a city in central Colorado, near Denver. 84,576.

ARVN (är′vin), *n.* (in the Vietnam War) a soldier in the army of South Vietnam. [1965–70; *A(rmy of the) R(epublic of) V(iet) N(am)*]

ar·vo (är′vō), *n. Australian Slang.* afternoon. [1930–35; ᴀғ(ᴛᴇʀɴᴏᴏɴ) + -ᴏ, with voicing of *-f-*; *ar* is r-less speaker's representation of low back vowel]

ar·y (âr′ē), *adj. Chiefly Midland and Southern U.S.* **1.** any; anyone. **2.** none, not any; nary. [1810–20; alter. of *e'er a* ever a, in sense "any"]

-ary, a suffix occurring originally in loanwords from Classical and Medieval Latin, on adjectives (*elementary; honorary; stationary; tributary*), personal nouns (*actuary; notary; secretary*), or nouns denoting objects, esp. receptacles or places (*library; rosary; glossary*). The suffix has the general sense "pertaining to, connected with" the referent named by the base; it is productive in English, sometimes with the additional senses "contributing to," "for the purpose of," and usually forming adjectives: *complimentary; visionary; revolutionary; inflationary.* [ME *-arie* < L *-ārius, -a, -um;* E personal nouns reflect *-ārius,* objects and places *-ārium* or *-āria;* inherited and adopted F forms of this suffix are -ᴇʀ[2], -ᴇᴇʀ, -ɪᴇʀ[2], -ᴀɪʀᴇ; cf. -ᴇʀ[1]]

Ar·y·an (âr′ē ən, âr′yən, ar′-), *n.* **1.** *Ethnol.* a member or descendant of the prehistoric people who spoke Indo-European. **2.** (in Nazi doctrine) a non-Jewish Caucasian, esp. of Nordic stock. **3.** (formerly) Indo-European. **4.** (formerly) Indo-Iranian. —*adj.* **5.** of or pertaining to an Aryan or the Aryans. **6.** (formerly) Indo-European. **7.** (formerly) Indo-Iranian. Also, **Arian.** [1785–95; < Skt *ārya* of high rank (adj.), aristocrat (n.) + -ᴀɴ]

Ar·y·an·ize (âr′ē ə nīz′, âr′yə-, ar′-), *v.t.,* **-ized, -iz·ing.** (in Nazi doctrine) to remove all non-Aryan persons from (office, business, etc.). Also, *esp. Brit.,* **Ar′y·an·ise′.** [1855–60; ᴀʀʏᴀɴ + -ɪᴢᴇ]

ar·y·bal·los (ar′ə bal′əs), *n., pl.* **-bal·loi** (-bal′oi). *Gk. and Rom. Antiq.* an oil jar, characterized by a spherical body, flat-rimmed mouth, and often a single handle extending from the lip to the shoulder of the jar, used chiefly for fragrant ointments. Cf. **alabastron, askos, lekythos.** [1840–50; < Gk *arýballos* a draw-purse, equiv. to *arý(ein)* to draw + *-ballos,* akin to *ballántion* purse] —**ar′y·bal′loid,** *adj.*

aryballos

ᴄᴏɴᴄɪsᴇ ᴇᴛʏᴍᴏʟᴏɢʏ ᴋᴇʏ: <, descended or borrowed from; >, whence; b., blend of, blended; c., cognate with; cf., compare; deriv., derivative; equiv., equivalent; imit., imitative; obl., oblique; r., replacing; s., stem; sp., spelling, spelled; resp., respelling, respelled; trans., translation; ?, origin unknown; *, unattested; ‡, probably earlier than. See the full key inside the front cover.

ar·y·bal·lus (ar′ə bal′əs), *n., pl.* **-bal·li** (-bal′ī). aryballos.

ar·y·ep·i·glot·tic (ar′ē ep′ə glot′ik), *adj. Anat.* pertaining to or connecting the arytenoid cartilage and the epiglottis. [1895–1900; < Gk *arý(ein)* to draw, pull + ᴇᴘɪɢʟᴏᴛᴛ(ɪs) + -ɪᴄ]

ar·yl (ar′il), *adj. Chem.* containing an aryl group. [1905–10; ᴀʀ(ᴏᴍᴀᴛɪᴄ) + -ʏʟ]

ar·yl·a·mine (ar′il ə mēn′, -am′in), *n. Chem.* any of a group of amines in which one or more of the hydrogen atoms of ammonia are replaced by aromatic groups. [ᴀʀʏʟ + -ᴀᴍɪɴᴇ]

ar·yl·ate (ar′ə lāt′), *v.t.,* **-at·ed, -at·ing.** *Chem.* to introduce one or more aryl groups into (a compound). [ᴀʀʏʟ + -ᴀᴛᴇ[1]] —**ar′yl·a′tion,** *n.*

ar′yl group′, *Chem.* any organic group derived from an aromatic hydrocarbon by the removal of a hydrogen atom, as phenyl, C_6H_5-, from benzene, C_6H_6. Also called **ar′yl rad′ical.** [1905–10]

ar·y·te·noid (ar′i tē′noid, ə rit′n oid′), *Anat.* —*adj.* **1.** pertaining to either of two small cartilages on top of the cricoid cartilage at the upper, back part of the larynx. **2.** pertaining to the muscles connected with these cartilages. **3.** pertaining to the glands in the aryepiglottic fold of the larynx. —*n.* **4.** an arytenoid cartilage, muscle, or gland. [1685–95; < Gk *arytainoeidḗs* lit., ladle-shaped, equiv. to *arýtain(a)* ladle, pitcher, funnel + *-oeidēs* -ᴏɪᴅ] —**ar·y·te·noi·dal** (ar′i tn oid′l), *adj.*

as[1] (az; *unstressed* əz), *adv.* **1.** to the same degree, amount, or extent; similarly; equally: *I don't think it's as hot and humid today as it was yesterday.* **2.** for example; for instance: *Some flowers, as the rose, require special care.* **3.** thought to be or considered to be: *the square as distinct from the rectangle; the church as separate from the state.* **4.** in the manner (directed, agreed, promised, etc.): *She sang as promised. He left as agreed.* **5. as well.** See **well**[1] (def. 11). **6. as well as.** See **well**[1] (def. 12). —*conj.* **7.** (used correlatively after an adjective or adverb prec. by an adverbial phrase, the adverbial *as,* or another adverb) to such a degree or extent that: *It came out the same way as it did before. You are as good as you think you are.* **8.** (without antecedent) in the degree, manner, etc., of or that: *She's good as gold. Do as we do.* **9.** at the same time that; while; when: *as you look away.* **10.** since; because: *As you are leaving last, please turn out the lights.* **11.** though: *Questionable as it may be, we will proceed.* **12.** with the result or purpose: *He said it in a voice so loud as to make everyone stare.* **13.** *Informal.* (in dependent clauses) that: *I don't know as I do.* **14.** *Midland and Southern U.S. and Brit. Dial.* than. **15. as . . . as,** (used to express similarity or equality in a specified characteristic, condition, etc., as between one person or thing and another): *as rich as Croesus.* **16. as far as,** to the degree or extent that: *It is an excellent piece of work, as far as I can tell.* **17. as for** or **to,** with respect to; in reference to: *As for staying away, I wouldn't think of it.* **18. as good as, a.** equivalent to; in effect; practically: *as good as new.* **b.** true to; trustworthy as: *as good as his word.* **19. as how,** *Chiefly Midland and Southern U.S.* that; if; whether: *He allowed as how it was none of my business. I don't know as how I ought to interfere.* **20. as if** or **though,** as it would be if: *It was as if the world had come to an end.* **21. as is,** in whatever condition something happens to be, esp. referring to something offered for sale in a flawed, damaged, or used condition: *We bought the table as is.* **22. as it were,** in a way; so to speak: *He became, as it were, a man without a country.* **23. as long as.** See **long**[1] (def. 39). **24. as of,** beginning on; on and after; from: *This price is effective as of June 23.* **25. as regards,** with regard or reference to; concerning: *As regards the expense involved, it is of no concern to him.* **26. as such, a.** as being what is indicated; in that capacity: *An officer of the law, as such, is entitled to respect.* **b.** in itself or in themselves: *The position, as such, does not appeal to him, but the salary is a lure.* **27. as yet,** up to the present time; until now: *As yet, no one has thought of a solution.* —*pron.* **28.** (used relatively) that; who; which (usually prec. by *such* or *the same*): *I have the same trouble as you had.* **29.** a fact that: *She did her job well, as can be proved by the records.* **30.** *New England, Midland, and Southern U.S.* who; whom; which; that: *Them as has gets.* —*prep.* **31.** in the role, function, or status of: *to act as leader.* [bef. 1000; ME *as, als, alse, also,* OE *alswā, ealswā* all so (see ᴀʟsᴏ), quite so, quite as, as; c. MD *alse* (D *als*), OHG *alsō* (MHG *ālsō, ālse, als,* G *also* so, *als* as, if, because)]

—**Syn. 10.** See **because.**

—**Usage.** As a conjunction, one sense of ᴀs is "because": *As she was bored, Sue left the room.* As also has an equally common use in the sense "while, when": *As the parade passed by, the crowd cheered and applauded.* These two senses sometimes result in ambiguity: *As the gates were closed, he walked away.* (When? Because?)

As . . . ᴀs is standard in both positive and negative constructions: *The fleet was as widely scattered then as it had been at the start of the conflict. Foreign service is not as attractive as it once was.* So . . . ᴀs is sometimes used in negative constructions (. . . *not so attractive as it once was*) and in questions (*"What is so rare as a day in June?"*).

The phrase ᴀs ғᴀʀ ᴀs generally introduces a clause: *As far as money is concerned, the council has exhausted all its resources.* In some informal speech and writing, ᴀs ғᴀʀ ᴀs is treated as a preposition and followed only by an object: *As far as money, the council has exhausted all its resources.*

As ᴛᴏ as a compound preposition has long been standard though occasionally criticized as a vague substitute for *about, of, on,* or *concerning: We were undecided as to our destination.* As ᴛᴏ sometimes occurs at the beginning of a sentence, where it introduces an element that would otherwise have less emphasis: *As to his salary, that too will be reviewed.* As ᴛᴏ ᴡʜᴀᴛ and ᴀs ᴛᴏ ᴡʜᴇᴛʜᴇʀ are sometimes considered redundant but have long been standard: *an argument as to what department was responsible.* See also **all, because, farther, like, so**[1].

as[2] (as), *n., pl.* **as·ses** (as′iz). **1.** a copper coin and early monetary unit of ancient Rome, originally having a nominal weight of a pound of 12 ounces: discontinued c80 ʙ.ᴄ. **2.** a unit of weight equal to 12 ounces. [1595–1605; < L]

AS, 1. American Samoa (approved esp. for use with zip code). **2.** Anglo-Saxon. **3.** antisubmarine.

As, *Symbol, Chem.* arsenic (def. 1).

as-, var. of **ad-** before *s: assert.*

AS., Anglo-Saxon.

A.S., 1. Associate in Science. **2.** Anglo-Saxon.

A.-S., Anglo-Saxon.

A·sa (ā′sə), *n.* a king of Judah, 913?–873? ʙ.ᴄ. I Kings 15:8–24.

ASA, 1. Acoustical Society of America. **2.** American Standards Association: former name of the American National Standards Institute. **3.** the numerical exposure index of a photographic film under the system adopted by the American Standards Association, used to indicate the light sensitivity of the film's emulsion.

as·a·fet·i·da (as′ə fet′i də), *n. Chem.* a soft, brown, lumpy gum resin having a bitter, acrid taste and an obnoxious odor, obtained from the roots of several Near Eastern plants belonging to the genus *Ferula,* of the parsley family: formerly used in medicine as a carminative and antispasmodic. Also, **a′sa·foet′i·da, asfetida.** Also called **devil's dung, food of the gods.** [1350–1400; ME < ML *asafoetida,* equiv. to *asa* (< Pers *azā* mastic, gum) + L *foetida,* fem. of *foetidus* ғᴇᴛɪᴅ]

A·sa·hi·ga·wa (ä′sä hē′gä wä), *n.* a city on W central Hokkaido, in N Japan. 352,620. Also, **A·sa·hi·ka·wa** (ä′sä hē′kä wä).

a·sa·na (ä′sə nə), *n.* any of the postures in a yoga exercise. [< Skt]

A·san·sol (ä′sən sōl′), *n.* a city in NW West Bengal, in E India. 155,968.

A·san·te (ə san′tē, ə sän′-), *n., pl.* **-tes,** (*esp. collectively*) **-te.** Ashanti.

ASAP, as soon as possible. Also, **A.S.A.P., a.s.a.p.**

A·sa·rah Be·te·vet (*Seph. Heb.* ä sä ʀä′ bə te′vet; *Ashk. Heb.* ä sô′ʀə bə tā′vās), a Jewish fast day observed on the 10th day of the month of Tevet in memory of the beginning of the siege of Jerusalem in 586 ʙ.ᴄ. by the Babylonians under King Nebuchadnezzar. Also, **Asarah′ Bete′bet.**

as·a·ro·tum (as′ə rō′təm), *n., pl.* **-ta** (-tə). (in ancient Roman architecture) a painted pavement. [Latinization of neut. sing. of Gk *asárōtos* lit., unswept (once in Pliny, designating a floor paved in mosaic resembling table scraps), equiv. to *a-* ᴀ-[6] + *sarō-,* verbid s. of *saroûn* to sweep clean + *-tos* verbal adj. suffix]

as·a·rum (as′ər əm), *n. Chem.* the dried rhizome and roots of wild ginger that yield an acrid resin and a volatile, aromatic oil, used chiefly as a flavoring. [< L < Gk *ásaron* hazelwort, wild spikenard]

A·sat (u′sut), *n. Hinduism.* (in Vedic mythology) the realm of nonexistence, populated by demons. Cf. **sat**[2] (def. 1).

ASAT (ā′sat′), *n.* antisatellite.

asb., asbestos.

As·ben (äs ben′), *n.* Aïr.

as·bes·tos (as bes′təs, az-), *n.* **1.** *Mineral.* a fibrous mineral, either amphibole or chrysotile, formerly used for making incombustible or fireproof articles. **2.** a fabric woven from asbestos fibers, formerly used for theater curtains, firefighters' gloves, etc. **3.** *Theat.* a fireproof curtain. Also, **as·bes′tus.** [1350–1400; < L < Gk: lit., unquenched, equiv. to *a-* ᴀ-[6] + *sbestós* (*sbes-* var. s. of *sbennýnai* to quench + *-tos* ptp. suffix); r. ME *asbeston, albeston* < MF < L] —**as·bes·tine** (as bes′tin, az-), **as·bes′tous,** *adj.* —**as·bes′toid, as′bes·toi′dal,** *adj.*

asbes′tos cement′, a compound of asbestos fiber and Portland cement formerly used for various nonstructural building purposes. [1885–90]

as·bes·to·sis (as′be stō′sis, az′-), *n. Pathol.* a lung disease caused by the inhalation of asbestos dust. [1925–30; < NL; see ᴀsʙᴇsᴛᴏs, -ᴏsɪs]

As·björn·sen (äs′byŭʀn sən), *n.* **Pe·ter Chris·ten** (pā′təʀ ᴋʀɪs′tən), 1812–85, Norwegian naturalist and folklorist.

ASBM, See **air-to-surface ballistic missile.** Also, **A.S.B.M.**

As·bur·y (az′bə rē), *n.* **Francis,** 1745–1816, English missionary: first bishop of the Methodist Church in America.

As′bur·y Park′ (az′ber′ē, -bə rē), a city in E New Jersey: seashore resort. 17,015.

ASC, American Society of Cinematographers. Also, **A.S.C.**

asc-, var. of **asco-** before a vowel or *h: Aschelminthes.*

ASCAP (as′kap), *n.* American Society of Composers, Authors, and Publishers.

a·scared (ə skârd′), *adj. Chiefly Midland and Southern U.S.* afraid; scared. [1905–10; *a-* prefix attached to ptps. (cf. Brit. dial. *a-* with same function; see ʏ-) + sᴄᴀʀᴇᴅ]

as·ca·ri·a·sis (as′kə rī′ə sis), *n. Pathol.* infestation with ascarids, esp. *Ascaris lumbricoides.* [1885–90; < NL; see ᴀsᴄᴀʀɪᴅ, -ɪᴀsɪs]

as·ca·rid (as′kə rid), *n.* **1.** any nematode of the family Ascaridae; roundworm. **2.** ascaris. [< NL *Ascaridae.* See ᴀsᴄᴀʀɪs, -ɪᴅᴀᴇ]

as·car·i·dole (ə skar′i dōl′), *n. Chem.* a liquid, $C_{10}H_{16}O_2$, constituting the active principle of chenopodium oil, used chiefly as a catalyst in polymerization reactions. [1905–10; ᴀsᴄᴀʀɪᴅ + -ᴏʟᴇ]

as•ca•ris (as′kə ris), *n., pl.* **as•car•i•des** (a skar′i dēz′). any parasitic roundworm of the genus *Ascaris,* found in the human small intestine and causing colic and diarrhea. Also, **ascarid.** [< NL (Linnaeus), the genus < Gk *ascarís* intestinal worm; cf. earlier, late ME *ascarides* (pl.) < ML < Gk]

as•cend (ə send′), *v.i.* **1.** to move, climb, or go upward; mount; rise: *The airplane ascended into the clouds.* **2.** to slant upward. **3.** to rise to a higher point, rank, or degree; proceed from an inferior to a superior degree or level: *to ascend to the presidency.* **4.** to go toward the source or beginning; go back in time. **5.** *Music.* to rise in pitch; pass from any tone to a higher one. —*v.t.* **6.** to go or move upward upon or along; climb; mount: *to ascend a lookout tower; to ascend stairs.* **7.** to gain or succeed to; acquire: *to ascend the throne.* [1350–1400; ME *ascenden* < AF *ascendre* < L *ascendere* to climb up, equiv. to *a-* A-[5] + *-scendere,* comb. form of *scandere* to climb. See SCAN] —**as•cend′a•ble, as•cend′i•ble,** *adj.*
—**Syn. 1.** soar. **6.** See **climb.** —**Ant. 1, 6.** descend.

as•cend•an•cy (ə sen′dən sē), *n.* the state of being in the ascendant; governing or controlling influence; domination. Also, **as•cend′en•cy, as•cend′ance, as•cend′ence.** [1705–15; ASCEND(ANT) + -ANCY]
—**Syn.** primacy, predominance, command, sovereignty, mastery, supremacy.

as•cend•ant (ə sen′dənt), *n.* **1.** a position of dominance or controlling influence: possession of power, superiority, or preeminence: *With his rivals in the ascendant, he soon lost his position.* **2.** an ancestor; forebear. **3.** *Astrol.* the point of the ecliptic or the sign and degree of the zodiac rising above the eastern horizon at the time of a birth or event: the cusp of the first house. —*adj.* **4.** ascending; rising. **5.** superior; predominant. **6.** *Bot.* directed or curved upward. Also, **as•cend′ent.** [1350–1400; ME *ascendent* < L *ascendent-* (s. of *ascendēns*) climbing up. See ASCEND, -ENT, -ANT]

as•cend•er (ə sen′dər), *n.* **1.** a person or thing that ascends or causes ascension. **2.** *Print.* **a.** the part of a lowercase letter, as b, d, f, h, that rises above x-height. **b.** a letter rising above x-height, as b, d, f, h, etc. [1615–25; ASCEND + -ER[1]]

as•cend•ing (ə sen′ding), *adj.* **1.** moving upward; rising. **2.** *Bot.* growing or directed upward, esp. obliquely or in a curve from the base. [1350–1400; ME; see ASCEND, -ING[2]] —**as•cend′ing•ly,** *adv.*

ascend′ing co′lon (kō′lən), *Anat.* the first portion of the colon, beginning at the cecum in the lower right abdominal cavity and continuing upward along the right posterior abdominal wall to approximately the lower ribs. See diag. under **intestine.** [1855–60]

ascend′ing node′, *Astron.* the node through which an orbiting body passes as it moves to the north (opposed to *descending node*).

ascend′ing rhythm′. See **rising rhythm.** [1900–05]

As•ce•nez (as′kə nēz′), *n. Douay Bible.* Ashkenaz.

as•cen•sion (ə sen′shən), *n.* **1.** the act of ascending; ascent. **2. the Ascension,** the bodily ascending of Christ from earth to heaven. **3.** *(cap.)* See **Ascension Day.** [1300–50; ME *ascencioun* (< AF) < L *ascēnsiōn-* (s. of *ascēnsiō*), equiv. to *ascēns(us)* risen up (ptp. of *ascendere,* equiv. to *ascend-* climb up (see ASCEND) + *-tus* ptp. suffix) + *-iōn-* -ION] —**as•cen′sion•al,** *adj.*

As•cen•sion (ə sen′shən), *n.* a British island in the S Atlantic Ocean: constituent part of St. Helena. 1130; 34 sq. mi. (88 sq. km).

Ascen′sion Day′, the 40th day after Easter, commemorating the Ascension of Christ; Holy Thursday. [1325–75; ME]

as•cen•sive (ə sen′siv), *adj.* ascending; rising. [1640–50; ASCENS(ION) + -IVE]

as•cent (ə sent′), *n.* **1.** an act of ascending; upward movement; a rising movement: *the ascent of a balloon.* **2.** movement upward from a lower to a higher state, degree, grade, or status; advancement: *His ascent to the governorship came after a long political career.* **3.** the act of climbing or traveling up: *Three climbers attempted the ascent of Mount Rainier.* **4.** the way or means of ascending; upward slope; acclivity. **5.** a movement or return toward a source or beginning. **6.** the degree of inclination; gradient: *a steep ascent.* [1590–1600; deriv. of ASCEND, on the model of DESCENT]

as•cer•tain (as′ər tān′), *v.t.* **1.** to find out definitely; learn with certainty or assurance; determine: *to ascertain the facts.* **2.** *Archaic.* to make certain, clear, or definitely known. [1400–50; late ME, var. of *assertain, acertain* < MF *acertain-* (tonic s. of *acertener* to make certain), equiv. to *a-* A-[5] + *certain* CERTAIN] —**as′cer•tain′a•ble,** *adj.* —**as′cer•tain′a•bly,** *adv.* —**as′cer•tain′er,** *n.* —**as′cer•tain′ment,** *n.*
—**Syn. 1.** See **learn.**

as•ce•sis (ə sē′sis), *n., pl.* **-ses** (-sēz). askesis.

as•cet•ic (ə set′ik), *n.* **1.** a person who dedicates his or her life to a pursuit of contemplative ideals and practices extreme self-denial or self-mortification for religious reasons. **2.** a person who leads an austerely simple life, esp. one who abstains from the normal pleasures of life or denies himself or herself material satisfaction. **3.** (in the early Christian church) a monk; hermit. —*adj.* Also, **as•cet′i•cal. 4.** pertaining to asceticism. **5.** rigorously abstinent; austere: *an ascetic existence.* **6.** exceedingly strict or severe in religious exercises or self-mortification. [1640–50; < Gk *askētikós* subject to rigorous exercise, hardworking, equiv. to *askē-* (see ASKESIS) + *-tikos* -TIC] —**as•cet′i•cal•ly,** *adv.*
—**Syn. 3.** anchorite, recluse; cenobite. **5.** strict, frugal, plain. **6.** fanatic. —**Ant. 5.** self-indulgent.

as•cet•i•cism (ə set′ə siz′əm), *n.* **1.** the manner of life, practices, or principles of an ascetic. **2.** the doctrine that a person can attain a high spiritual and moral state by practicing self-denial, self-mortification, and the like. **3.** rigorous self-denial; extreme abstinence; austerity. [1640–50; ASCETIC + -ISM]

Asch (ash), *n.* **Sho•lom** (shô′ləm) or **Sho•lem** (shô′ləm, -lem), 1880–1957, U.S. author, born in Poland.

As•cham (as′kəm), *n.* **Roger,** 1515–68, English scholar and writer: tutor of Queen Elizabeth I.

Asc•hel•min•thes (ask′hel min′thēz), *n. Zool.* a major grouping (formerly a phylum) of small-to-microscopic pseudocoelomate organisms, as the rotifers, nematodes, and gastrotriches, all of which are now classified as separate phyla. [< NL; see ASC-, HELMINTH, -ES[1]]

Asch′heim-Zon′dek test′ (äsh′hīm tson′dek, -zon′-), *Med.* a test used to detect whether a woman is pregnant by noting the effect on the ovaries of an immature mouse or rabbit injected with her urine. Also called **A-Z test.** [named after S. *Aschheim* (1878–1965), German gynecologist, and B. *Zondek* (1891–1966), Israeli gynecologist born in Germany]

A′schoff bod′y (ä′shôf), *Pathol.* any of the spindle-shaped nodules found in heart tissue and associated with the myocarditis of rheumatic fever. Also, **A′schoff nod′ule.** [named after Ludwig *Aschoff* (d. 1942), German pathologist]

as•ci (as′ī), *n.* pl. of **ascus.**

as•cid•i•an (ə sid′ē ən), *Zool.* —*n.* **1.** any solitary or colonial tunicate of the class Ascidiacea, exhibiting in the larval stage the vertebrate characteristics of a notocord and hollow nerve cord. —*adj.* **2.** belonging or pertaining to the class Ascidiacea. [1855–60; < NL *Ascidi(um)* a tunicate genus (see ASCIDIUM) + -AN]

as•cid•i•um (ə sid′ē əm), *n., pl.* **-cid•i•a** (-sid′ē ə). *Bot., Mycol.* a baglike or pitcherlike part. [1760–70; < NL < Gk *askídion* a small bag, equiv. to *ask(ós)* bag + *-idion* -IDIUM]

as•cig•er•ous (ə sij′ər əs), *adj. Mycol.* of or pertaining to asci. [1820–30; ASC(US) + -I- + -GEROUS]

ASCII (as′kē), *n.* a standard code, consisting of 128 7-bit combinations, for characters stored in a computer or to be transmitted between computers. [*A(merican) S(tandard) C(ode for) I(nformation) I(nterchange)*]

as•ci•tes (ə sī′tēz), *n. Pathol.* accumulation of serous fluid in the peritoneal cavity; dropsy of the peritoneum. [1350–1400; ME *aschites* < ML < Gk *askítēs (hýdrōps)* abdominal (dropsy), equiv. to *ask(ós)* belly + *-itēs* -ITE[1]] —**as•cit•ic** (ə sit′ik), **as•cit′i•cal,** *adj.*

as•cle•pi•a•da•ceous (ə sklē′pē ə dā′shəs), *adj.* belonging to the Asclepiadaceae, the milkweed family of plants. Cf. **milkweed family.** [1875–80; < NL *Asclepiadace(ae)* (*Asclepiad-,* s. of *Asclepias* the type genus (L < Gk *asklēpiás* a plant, perh. the swallowwort, deriv. of *Asklēpiós* ASCLEPIUS) + *-aceae* -ACEAE) + -OUS]

As•cle•pi•a•de•an (ə sklē′pē ə dē′ən), *Class. Pros.* —*adj.* **1.** noting or pertaining to a verse consisting of a spondee, two or three choriambi, and an iamb. —*n.* **2.** an Asclepiadean verse. [1700–10; < Gk *Asklēpiádei(os)* pertaining to *Asclepiades,* 3rd-century Greek poet to whom the verse was attributed + -AN]

As•cle•pi•us (ə sklē′pē əs), *n. Class. Myth.* a son of Apollo and the ancient Greek god of medicine and healing, worshiped by the Romans as Aesculapius.

asco-, a combining form meaning "sac," used in the formation of compound words: *ascomycete.* Also, *esp. before a vowel,* **asc-.** [< Gk *asko-,* comb. form of *askós* wineskin, bladder, belly]

as•co•carp (as′kə kärp′), *n. Mycol.* (in ascomycetous fungi) the fruiting body bearing the asci, as an apothecium or perithecium. [1885–90; ASCO- + -CARP] —**as′co•carp′ous,** *adj.*

as•cog•e•nous (ə skoj′ə nəs), *adj. Mycol.* of, pertaining to, or producing asci. [ASCO- + -GENOUS]

as•co•go•ni•um (as′kə gō′nē əm), *n., pl.* **-ni•a** (-nē ə). *Mycol.* **1.** the female sexual organ in certain ascomycetous fungi. **2.** the portion of the archicarp in certain ascomycetous fungi that receives the antheridial nuclei and puts out the hyphae bearing the asci. [1870–75; ASCO- + -GONIUM] —**as′co•go′ni•al,** *adj.*

as•co•ma (a skō′mə), *n., pl.* **-ma•ta** (-mə tə), *Mycol.* a fruiting body that bears asci. [< NL; see ASCUS, -OMA]

as•co•my•cete (as′kə mī′sēt, -mī sēt′), *n. Mycol.* any fungus of the phylum Ascomycota (or class Ascomycetes), including the molds and truffles, characterized by bearing the sexual spores in a sac (as distinguished from *basidiomycete*). Also called **sac fungus.** [1855–60; < NL; see ASCO-, -MYCETE]

as•co•my•ce•tous (as′kə mī sē′təs), *adj. Mycol.* belonging or pertaining to the Ascomycota. [1865–70; ASCOMYCETE + -OUS]

as•con (as′kon), *n.* a type of sponge having an oval shape and a thin body wall with pores leading directly into the spongocoel. Cf. **leucon, sycon.** [alter. of Gk *askós;* see ASCO-]

as•co•noid (as′kə noid′), *adj.* pertaining to or resembling an ascon. [ASCON + -OID]

a•scor•bate (ə skôr′bāt, -bit), *n. Chem.* a salt or other derivative of ascorbic acid. [1940–45; ASCORB(IC) + -ATE[2]]

a•scor′bic ac′id (ə skôr′bik), *Biochem.* a white, crystalline, water-soluble vitamin, $C_6H_8O_6$, occurring naturally in citrus fruits, green vegetables, etc., and often produced synthetically, essential for normal metabolism: used in the prevention and treatment of scurvy, and in wound-healing and tissue repair. Also called **antiscorbutic acid, vitamin C.** [1930–35; A-[6] + SCORB(UT)IC]

as•co•spore (as′kə spôr′, -spōr′), *n. Mycol.* a spore formed within an ascus. [1870–75; ASCO- + SPORE] —**as•co•spor•ic** (as′kə spôr′ik, -spor′-), **as•cos•po•rous** (as kos′pər əs, as′kə spôr′-, -spōr′-), *adj.*

as•cot (as′kət, -kot), *n.* a necktie or scarf with broad ends, tied and arranged so that the ends are laid flat, one across the other, sometimes with a pin to secure them. [1905–10; so called from the fashionable dress worn at the ASCOT races]

ascot

As•cot (as′kət), *n.* a village in SE Berkshire, in S England: annual horse races.

as•cribe (ə skrīb′), *v.t.,* **-cribed, -crib•ing. 1.** to credit or assign, as to a cause or source; attribute; impute: *The alphabet is usually ascribed to the Phoenicians.* **2.** to attribute or think of as belonging, as a quality or characteristic: *They ascribed courage to me for something I did out of sheer panic.* [1400–50; late ME < L *ascrībere,* equiv. to *a-* A-[5] + *scrībere* to SCRIBE[2]; r. ME *ascrive* < MF. See SHRIVE] —**a•scrib′a•ble,** *adj.*
—**Syn. 1.** See **attribute.**

ascribed′ sta′tus, *Sociol.* the social position assigned to a person on the basis of age, sex, race, etc. Cf. **achieved status.** [1965–70]

as•crip•tion (ə skrip′shən), *n.* **1.** the act of ascribing. **2.** a statement ascribing something, esp. praise to the Deity. Also, **adscription.** [1590–1600; < L *ascrīptiōn-* (s. of *ascrīptiō*) a written addition. See A-[5], SCRIPT, -ION]

as•crip•tive (ə skrip′tiv), *adj.* pertaining to, involving, or indicating ascription, esp. the attribution of qualities or characteristics. [1640–50; ASCRIPT(ION) + -IVE; cf. L *a(d)scrīptīvus* supernumerary, DESCRIPTIVE, PROSCRIPTIVE] —**as•crip′tive•ly,** *adv.*

ASCS, Agricultural Stabilization and Conservation Service.

ASCU, Association of State Colleges and Universities.

as•cus (as′kəs), *n., pl.* **as•ci** (as′ī, -kī, -kē). *Mycol.* the sac in ascomycetes in which the sexual spores are formed. [1820–30; < NL < Gk *askós* bag, sac]

asdic (az′dik), *n. Brit.* sonar. [1935–40; *A(nti-)S(ubmarine) D(etection) I(nvestigation) C(ommittee)*]

ASE, See **American Stock Exchange.** Also, **A.S.E.**

-ase, a suffix used in the names of enzymes: *oxidase.* [extracted from DIASTASE]

a•sea (ə sē′), *adj., adv.* **1.** to or toward the sea; seaward. **2.** at sea. See **sea** (def. 10). [1855–60; A-[1] + SEA]

ASEAN, Association of Southeast Asian Nations. Also, **A.S.E.A.N.**

a•seis•mic (ā sīz′mik, -sīs′-), *adj. Geol.* free from earthquakes. [1880–85; A-[6] + SEISMIC]

a•se•i•ty (ə sē′i tē, ā sē′-), *n. Metaphys.* existence originating from and having no source other than itself. [1685–95; < ML *aseitās,* equiv. to L *ā sē* from oneself + *-itās* -ITY]

a•se•mi•a (ə sē′mē ə), *n. Psychiatry.* inability to comprehend or use communicative symbols, as words or gestures. [< Gk *ásēm(os)* signless (*a-* A-[6] + *sêm(a)* sign + *-os* adj. suffix) + *-ia* -IA] —**a•sem•ic** (ə sem′ik), *adj.*

As•e•nath (as′ə nath′), *n.* the wife of Joseph and the mother of Manasseh and Ephraim. Gen. 41:45; 46:20. Also, *Douay Bible,* **As•e•neth** (as′ə neth′).

a•sep•sis (ə sep′sis, ā sep′-), *n.* **1.** absence of the microorganisms that produce sepsis or septic disease. **2.** *Med.* methods, as sterile surgical techniques, used to assure asepsis. [1890–95; A-[6] + SEPSIS]

a•sep•tate (ā sep′tāt), *adj. Bot., Mycol.* without a separating wall or membrane. [A-[6] + SEPTATE]

a•sep•tic (ə sep′tik, ā sep′-), *adj.* **1.** free from the living germs of disease, fermentation, or putrefaction. —*n.* **2.** a product, as milk or fruit juice, that is marketed in an aseptic package or container. **3. aseptics,** *(used with a singular v.)* a system of packaging sterilized products in airtight containers so that freshness is preserved for several months. [1855–60; A-[6] + SEPTIC] —**a•sep′ti•cal•ly,** *adv.* —**a•sep•ti•cism** (ə sep′tə siz′əm, ā sep′-), *n.*

asep′tic meningi′tis, *Pathol.* a mild form of meningitis usually caused by one of several viruses, characterized by headache, fever, and neck stiffness.

A•ser (ā′sər), *n. Douay Bible.* Asher (def. 1).

a•sex•u•al (ā sek′sho͞o əl), *adj.* **1.** *Biol.* **a.** having no sex or sexual organs. **b.** independent of sexual processes, esp. not involving the union of male and female germ cells. **2.** free from or unaffected by sexuality: *an asexual friendship.* [1820–30; A-[6] + SEXUAL] —**a•sex•u•al•i•ty** (ā sek′sho͞o al′i tē), *n.* —**a•sex′u•al•ly,** *adv.*

a•sex•u•al•ize (ā sek′sho͞o ə līz′), *v.t.,* **-ized, -iz•ing.** to make incapable of reproduction, as by castrating. Also, *esp. Brit.,* **a•sex′u•al•ise′.** [ASEXUAL + -IZE] —**a•sex′u•al•i•za′tion,** *n.*

asex′ual reproduc′tion, *Biol.* reproduction, as budding, fission, or spore formation, not involving the union of gametes.

A•se•yev (ä sā′ev, -ef; *Russ.* u sye′yif), *n.* **Ni•ko•lay Ni•ko•la•e•vich** (nik′ə lī′ nik′ə lī′ə vich; *Russ.* nyi ku-lī′ nyi ku lä′yi vyich), 1889–1963, Russian poet.

CONCISE PRONUNCIATION KEY: act, cāpe, dâre, pärt; set, ēqual; *if,* ice; ox, ōver, ôrder, oil, bo͝ok, bo͞ot, out; up, ûrge; child; sing; shoe; thin, *that;* zh as in *treasure.* ə = *a* as in *alone, e* as in *system, i* as in *easily, o* as in *gallop, u* as in *circus;* ə as in *fire* (fīər), *hour* (ouər). l and n can serve as syllabic consonants, as in *cradle* (krād′l), and *button* (but′n). See the full key inside the front cover.

as·fet·i·da (as fet′i də), *n.* asafetida.

As·gard (äs′gärd, as′-), *n. Scand. Myth.* the home of the Aesir and location of Valhalla and the palaces of the individual gods: connected with the earth by the rainbow bridge, Bifrost. [< ON *Ásgarthr*, equiv. to *ās* god (c. OE *ōs*) + *garthr* yard; see GARTH]

asgd., assigned.

Ás·geirs·son (äs′gâr sən), *n.* **As·geir** (äs′gâr), 1894–1972, Icelandic statesman: president 1952–68.

asgmt., assignment.

ash[1] (ash), *n.* **1.** the powdery residue of matter that remains after burning. **2.** Also called **volcanic ash.** *Geol.* finely pulverized lava thrown out by a volcano in eruption. **3.** a light, silvery-gray color. **4. ashes, a.** deathlike grayness; extreme pallor suggestive of death. **b.** ruins, esp. the residue of something destroyed; remains; vestiges: *the ashes of their love; the ashes of the past.* **c.** mortal remains, esp. the physical or corporeal body as liable to decay. **d.** anything, as an act, gesture, speech, or feeling, that is symbolic of penance, regret, remorse, or the like. [bef. 950; ME *a(i)sshe*, OE *asce, æsce;* c. Fris *esk*, D *asch*, ON, OHG *aska* (G *Asche*), Goth *azgo* < Gmc **askōn-* (with Goth unexplained); akin to L *ārēre* be dry (see ARID), Tocharian *ās-* get dry, Skt *āsa-* ashes, Hittite *hassi* on the hearth; < IE **HaHs-*] **—ash′i·ness,** *n.* **—ash′less,** *adj.*

ash[2] (ash), *n.* **1.** any of various trees of the genus *Fraxinus*, of the olive family, esp. *F. excelsior*, of Europe and Asia, or *F. americana* **(white ash)**, of North America, having opposite, pinnate leaves and purplish flowers in small clusters. **2.** the tough, straight-grained wood of any of these trees, valued as timber. **3.** Also, **aesc.** the symbol "æ." [bef. 900; ME *asshe*, OE *æsc;* c. Fris *esk*, MLG, MD *asch*, OS, OHG *asc* (G *Esche*, with altered vowel from the adj. deriv. *eschen*, MHG *eschîn*), ON *askr;* akin to L *ornus*, Welsh *onnen*, Russ *yásen′*, Czech *jasan*, Lith *úosis*, Armenian *hatsʰi;* Albanian *ah* beech; < IE **Hₒes-*]

A·sha (ush′ə), *n. Zoroastrianism.* the cosmic principle of order, justice, righteousness, and truth. Cf. **Drug.**

As·hab (äs′häb), *n.pl., sing.* **Sa·hib** (sä′ib, -ēb). *Islam.* those associating with Muhammad at any time in his life. Cf. **Ansar, Muhajirun.**

a·shake (ə shāk′), *adj.* shaking (usually used predicatively): *The very hills were ashake with the violence of the storm.* [1855–60; A-[1] + SHAKE]

a·shamed (ə shāmd′), *adj.* **1.** feeling shame; distressed or embarrassed by feelings of guilt, foolishness, or disgrace: *He felt ashamed for having spoken so cruelly.* **2.** unwilling or restrained because of fear of shame, ridicule, or disapproval: *They were ashamed to show their work.* **3.** *Chiefly Midland U.S.* (esp. of children) bashful; timid. [bef. 1000; orig. ptp. of earlier *ashame* (v.) to be ashamed, ME, OE *āscamian*, equiv. to *ā-* A-[3] + *scamian* to SHAME] **—a·sham·ed·ly** (ə shā′mid lē), *adv.* **—a·sham′ed·ness,** *n.*
—Syn. 1. ASHAMED, HUMILIATED, MORTIFIED refer to a condition or feeling of discomfort or embarrassment. ASHAMED focuses on the sense of one's own responsibility for an act, whether it is foolish, improper, or immoral: *He was ashamed of his dishonesty. She was ashamed of her mistake.* HUMILIATED stresses a feeling of being humbled or disgraced, without any necessary implication of guilt: *He was humiliated by the king.* Both words are used equally in situations in which one is felt to be responsible for the actions of another: *Robert felt humiliated by his daughter's behavior. Mom was ashamed of the way I looked.* MORTIFIED represents an intensification of the feelings implied by the other two words: *She was mortified by her clumsiness.* **—Ant. 1, 2.** proud.

A·shan·ti (ə shan′tē, ə shän′-), *n., pl.* **-tis,** (esp. collectively) **-ti** for 2. **1.** a former native kingdom and British colony in W Africa: now a region of Ghana. 1,505,049; 9700 sq. mi. (25,123 sq. km). *Cap.:* Kumasi. **2.** a native or inhabitant of Ashanti. **3.** the dialect of Akan spoken by the people of Ashanti. Also, **Asante.**

Ash·ʿa·rism (ash′ə riz′əm), *n. Islam.* the classical synthesis of Islamic philosophical theology, formulated by al-Ashʿari. [< Ar *al-Ashʿar(ī)* AL-ASHʿARI + -ISM] **—Ash′ʿa·rite′,** *n.*

ash-blond (ash′blond′), *adj.* pale, grayish blond: *ash-blond hair.* Also, **ash′-blonde′.** [1900–05] **—ash′ blond′, ash′ blonde′.**

Ash·bur·ton (ash′bûr tn), *n.* **1st Baron.** See **Baring, Alexander.**

ash·cake (ash′kāk′), *n. Chiefly South Midland and Southern U.S.* cornbread baked in hot ashes. [1800–10; ASH[1] + CAKE]

ash·can (ash′kan′), *n.* **1.** a large metal barrel, can, or similar receptacle for ashes, garbage, or refuse. **2.** *Slang.* a depth charge. **3.** *Motion Pictures.* an arc light of 1000 watts, enclosed in a reflector. [1895–1900; ASH[1] + CAN[2]]

ash′can school′, *(often caps.) Fine Arts.* a group of American painters of the early 20th century whose genre paintings were derived from city life.

ash′ col′or. See **ash gray.** [1570–80]

Ash·croft (ash′krôft, -kroft), *n.* **Dame Peggy** *(Edith Margaret Emily Ashcroft)*, 1907–91, English actress.

Ash·dod (ash′dod; *Seph. Heb.* äsh dôd′), *n.* a town in W Israel: an important ancient Philistine city; early center of Christianity. 64,400. Also, **Esdud.** Greek, **Azotos.**

Ashe (ash), *n.* **Arthur (Robert, Jr.),** 1943–93, U.S. tennis player.

CONCISE ETYMOLOGY KEY: <, descended or borrowed from; >, whence; b., blend of, blended; c., cognate with; cf., compare; deriv., derivative; equiv., equivalent; imit., imitative; obl., oblique; r., replacing; s., stem; sp., spelling, spelled; resp., respelling, respelled; trans., translation; ?, origin unknown; *, unattested; ‡, probably earlier than. See the full key inside the front cover.

Ashe·bor·o (ash′bûr ō, -bur ō), *n.* a town in central North Carolina. 15,252.

ash·en[1] (ash′ən), *adj.* **1.** ash-colored; gray. **2.** extremely pale; drained of color; pallid: *His face was ashen.* **3.** consisting of ashes. [1350–1400; ME; see ASH[1], -EN[2]] **—Syn. 1.** ashy. **2.** pasty, colorless.

ash·en[2] (ash′ən), *adj.* **1.** pertaining to the ash tree or its timber. **2.** made of wood from the ash tree. [bef. 1000; ME, OE; see ASH[2], -EN[2]]

ash′en light′, *Astron.* a faint glow visible on the unlighted side of the planet Venus in its crescent phase.

Ash·er (ash′ər), *n.* **1.** a son of Jacob and Zilpah. Gen. 30:12–13. **2.** one of the 12 tribes of Israel traditionally descended from him. **3.** a male given name.

A·she·rah (ə shēr′ə), *n., pl.* **A·she·rim** (ə shēr′im), **A·she·rahs** for 2. **1.** an ancient Semitic goddess, sometimes identified with Ashtoreth and Astarte, worshiped by the Phoenicians and Canaanites. **2.** any of various upright wooden objects serving as a sacred symbol of Asherah.

Ash·er·ite (ash′ə rīt′), *n.* a member of the tribe of Asher. [ASHER + -ITE[1]]

Ashe·ville (ash′vil), *n.* a city in W North Carolina. 53,281.

ash′ fall′, *Geol.* **1.** a rain of airborne ash resulting from a volcanic eruption. **2.** the deposit produced by such an event. Also, **ash′fall′.**

ash′ flow′, *Geol.* an avalanche of volcanic ash.

ash′ gray′, pale gray resembling the color of ashes. Also called **ash color.** [1790–1800]

A·shi·ka·ga (ä′shē kä′gä), *n.* a member of a powerful family in Japan that ruled as shoguns 1338–1573.

Ash·ke·naz (ash′kə naz′), *n.* **1.** a son of Gomer and grandson of Japheth. Gen 10:1–3; I Chron. 1:6. **2.** an ancient kingdom in eastern Armenia.

Ashk., Ashkenazic.

Ash·ke·naz·im (äsh′kə nä′zim), *n.pl., sing.* **-naz·i** (-nä′zē). Jews of central and eastern Europe, or their descendants, distinguished from the Sephardim chiefly by their liturgy, religious customs, and pronunciation of Hebrew. [1830–40; < post-Biblical Heb *ashkənazzim*, pl. of *ashkənazzī*, equiv. to *ashkənaz* ASHKENAZ + *-ī* suffix of appurtenance] **—Ash′ke·naz′ic,** *adj.*

Ash·ke·na·zy (äsh′kə nä′zē), *n.* **Vladimir (Da·vi·do·vich)** (də vē′də vich), born 1937, Russian pianist in western Europe since 1963.

Ash·kha·bad (äsh′kə bäd′; *Russ.* ush KHU bät′), *n.* a city in and the capital of Turkmenistan, in the S part. 312,000. Formerly, **Poltoratsk.**

Ash·land (ash′lənd), *n.* **1.** a city in NE Kentucky, on the Ohio River. 27,064. **2.** a city in N central Ohio. 20,326. **3.** a town in SW Oregon. 14,943.

ash·lar (ash′lər), *n.* **1.** *Masonry.* **a.** a squared building stone cut more or less true on all faces adjacent to those of other stones so as to permit very thin mortar joints. **b.** such stones collectively. **c.** masonry made of them. **2.** *Carpentry.* a short stud between joists and sloping rafters, esp. near the eaves. **—***v.t.* **3.** to face with ashlars. Also, **ash′ler.** [1325–75; ME *ascheler* < MF *aissel(i)er* < L *axillāris*, equiv. to *axill(a)* (*axis* board, plank, AXIS + *-illa* dim. suffix) + *-āris* -AR[1]; cf. -AR[2]]

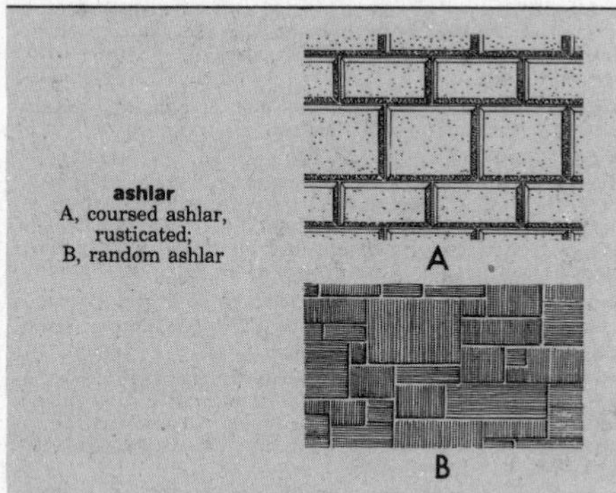

ashlar
A, coursed ashlar, rusticated;
B, random ashlar

ash·lar·ing (ash′lər ing), *n.* ashlar (def. 1b). [1725–35; ASHLAR + -ING[1]]

ash′lar line′, a horizontal line, indicated at a building site with a taut string, that corresponds to the exterior surface plane of a masonry wall.

Ash·ley (ash′lē), *n.* a male or female given name.

ash·man (ash′man′), *n., pl.* **-men.** a person who collects and disposes of ashes, garbage, and refuse. [1615–25; ASH[1] + MAN[1]]

a·shore (ə shôr′, ə shōr′), *adv.* **1.** to the shore; onto the shore: *The schooner was driven ashore.* **2.** on the shore; on land rather than at sea or on the water: *The captain has been ashore for two hours.* [1580–90; A-[1] + SHORE[1]]

ash·pit (ash′pit′), *n.* a receptacle in the bottom of a fireplace, under a barbecue, or the like, for the accumulation of ashes. [1790–1800; ASH[1] + PIT[1]]

ash·ram (äsh′rəm), *n.* **1.** a secluded building, often the residence of a guru, used for religious retreat or instruction in Hinduism. **2.** the persons instructed there. Also, **asrama.** [1915–20; < Skt *āśrama*]

Ash-Shay·tān (ash′shī tän′), *n.* (in Muslim usage) Satan; the devil. Also, **Shaytan, Shaitan, Sheitan.** [< Ar *al-Shayṭān;* see SATAN]

Ash·ta·bu·la (ash′tə byōō′lə), *n.* a port in NE Ohio, on Lake Erie. 23,449.

Ash·ton (ash′tən), *n.* **Sir Frederick** *(William)*, born 1906, English dancer and choreographer, born in Ecuador.

Ash·ton-un·der-Lyne (ash′tən un′dər līn′), *n.* a borough in Greater Manchester metropolitan county, in W England. 48,865.

Ash·to·reth (ash′tə reth′), *n.* an ancient Semitic goddess, identified with the Phoenician Astarte. [< Heb *ʿashtōreth* < Phoenician *ʿashtart.* See ASTARTE]

ash·tray (ash′trā′), *n.* a receptacle for tobacco ashes of smokers. [1885–90; ASH[1] + TRAY]

A·shur (ä′shŏŏr *for 1;* ash′ər *for 2*), *n.* **1.** Assur. **2.** a male given name.

ʿAsh·u·ra′ (ash′ŏŏ rä), *n.* **1.** the tenth of the month of Muharram, an important fast day for Sunni Muslims. **2.** (among Shiʿite Muslims) the anniversary of the martyrdom of Hussein. [< Ar *ʿĀshūrāʾ*]

A·shur·ba·ni·pal (ä′shŏŏr bä′nē päl′), *n.* died 626? B.C., king of Assyria 668?–626? B.C. Also, **Assurbanipal.**

A·shur·na·sir·pal II (ä′shŏŏr nä′zir päl′), *("the Merciless")* died 859? B.C., warrior king of Assyria 884?–859 B.C. Also, **Assurnasirpal II, A·shur-na·sir-a·pal II** (ä′shŏŏr nä′zir ä päl′).

Ash·wau·be·non (ash wô′bə non′), *n.* a town in E Wisconsin. 14,486.

Ash′ Wednes′day, the first day of Lent. [1250–1300]

ash·y (ash′ē), *adj.,* **ash·i·er, ash·i·est. 1.** ash-colored; pale; wan: *an ashy complexion.* **2.** of or resembling ashes: *an ashy residue.* **3.** sprinkled or covered with ashes. [1350–1400; ME *asshy.* See ASH[1], -Y[1]]

ASI, *Aeron.* airspeed indicator.

A·sia (ā′zhə, ā′shə), *n.* a continent bounded by Europe and the Arctic, Pacific, and Indian oceans. 2,896,700,000; ab. 16,000,000 sq. mi. (41,440,000 sq. km). See map on next page.

A·sia·dol·lar (ā′zhə dol′ər, ā′shə-), *n.* a U.S. dollar deposited in or credited to Asian banks and used in the money markets of the region. Cf. **Eurodollar.** [1970–75; ASIA + DOLLAR]

A′sia Mi′nor, a peninsula in W Asia between the Black and Mediterranean seas, including most of Asiatic Turkey. Cf. **Anatolia.**

A·sian (ā′zhən, ā′shən), *adj.* **1.** of, belonging to, or characteristic of Asia or its inhabitants. **—***n.* **2.** a native of Asia. [1555–65; < L *Asiānus* < Gk *Asiānós.* See ASIA, -AN]

A·sian-A·mer·i·can (ā′zhən ə mer′i kən, ā′shən-), *n.* **1.** a citizen or resident of the U.S. of Asian birth or descent. **—***adj.* **2.** of or pertaining to Asian-Americans or their culture.

A·si·at·ic (ā′zhē at′ik, ā′shē-, ā′zē-), *n., adj. Sometimes Offensive.* Asian. [1625–35; < L *Asiāticus* < Gk *Asiātikós.* See ASIA, -ATIC] **—A′si·at′i·cal·ly,** *adv.*

A′siat′ic bee′tle. See **oriental beetle.**

A′siat′ic chol′era, *Pathol.* cholera (def. 1). [1825–35]

A′siat′ic el′ephant, Indian elephant. See under **elephant.** [1925–30]

a·side (ə sīd′), *adv.* **1.** on or to one side; to or at a short distance apart; away from some position or direction: *to turn aside; to move the chair aside.* **2.** away from one's thoughts or consideration: *to put one's cares aside.* **3.** in reserve; in a separate place, as for safekeeping; apart; away: *to put some money aside for a rainy day.* **4.** away from a present group, esp. for reasons of privacy; off to another part, as of a room; into or to a separate place: *He took him aside and talked business.* **5.** in spite of; put apart; notwithstanding: *all kidding aside; unusual circumstances aside.* **6. aside from, a.** apart from; besides; excluding: *Aside from her salary, she receives money from investments.* **b.** except for: *They had no more food, aside from a few stale rolls.* **—***n.* **7.** a part of an actor's lines supposedly not heard by others on the stage and intended only for the audience. **8.** words spoken so as not to be heard by others present. **9.** a temporary departure from a main theme or topic, esp. a parenthetical comment or remark; short digression. [1350–1400; ME; see A-[1], SIDE[1]]

a·sid·er·ite (ə sid′ə rīt′), *n.* an iron-free meteorite consisting of friable material. [A-[6] + SIDERITE]

As·i·mov (az′ə môf′, -mof′), *n.* **Isaac,** 1920–92, U.S. science and science-fiction writer, born in Russia.

A·si·ne (a sē′nā), *n.* an ancient town in S Greece, on the Gulf of Argolis.

as·i·nine (as′ə nīn′), *adj.* **1.** foolish, unintelligent, or silly; stupid: *It is surprising that supposedly intelligent people can make such asinine statements.* **2.** of or like an ass: *asinine obstinacy; asinine features.* [1600–10; < L *asinīnus*, equiv. to *asin(us)* ASS[1] + *-īnus* -INE[1]] **—as′i·nine′ly,** *adv.* **—as·i·nin·i·ty** (as′ə nin′i tē), *n.* **—Syn. 1.** See **foolish.**

A·sir (ä sēr′), *n.* a district in SW Saudi Arabia.

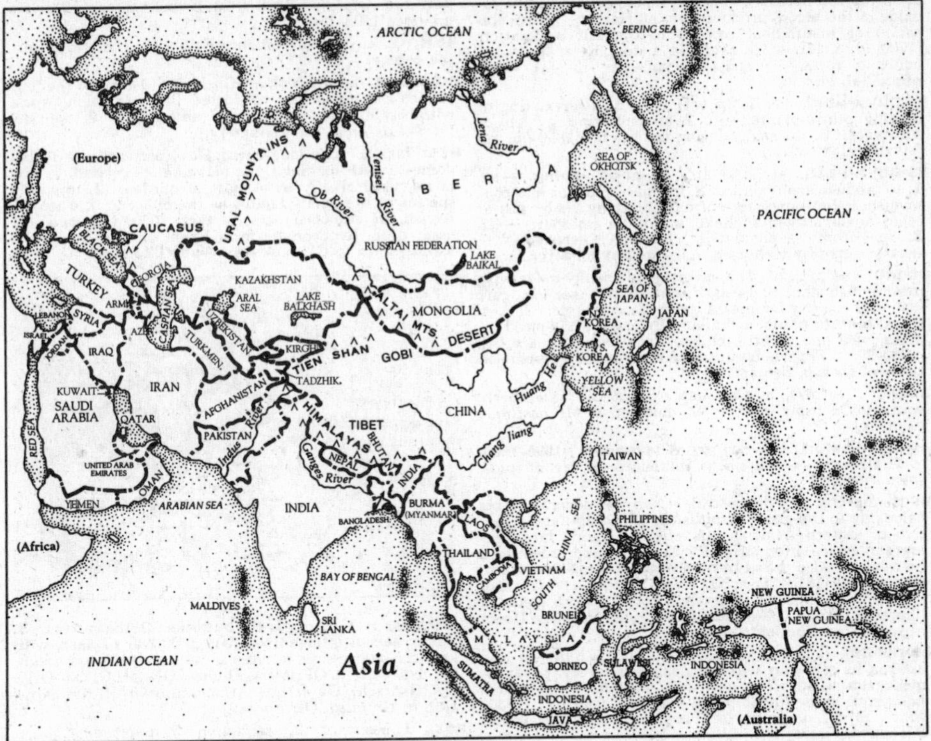

Asia

-asis, a suffix occurring in scientific, esp. medical, words from Greek: *psoriasis.* [< L < Gk *-iā-* v.s. + *-sis* -SIS]

ask (ask, äsk), *v.t.* **1.** to put a question to; inquire of: *I asked him but he didn't answer.* **2.** to request information about: *to ask the way.* **3.** to try to get by using words; request: *to ask advice; to ask a favor.* **4.** to solicit from; request of: *Could I ask you a favor? Ask her for advice.* **5.** to demand; expect: *What price are they asking? A little silence is all I ask.* **6.** to set a price of: *to ask $20 for the hat.* **7.** to call for; need; require: *This experiment asks patience.* **8.** to invite: *to ask guests to dinner.* **9.** *Archaic.* to publish (banns). —*v.i.* **10.** to make inquiry; inquire: *to ask about a person.* **11.** to request or petition (usually fol. by *for*): *to ask for leniency; to ask for food.* **12. ask for it,** to risk or invite trouble, danger, punishment, etc., by persisting in some action or manner: *He was asking for it by his abusive remarks.* [bef. 900; ME *asken, axen,* OE *āscian, āxian;* c. OFris *āskia,* OS *ēscon,* OHG *eiscōn* (G *heischen*), Skt *icchati* (he) seeks] —**ask′er,** *n.*
—**Syn. 1.** question, interrogate. **3, 11.** sue, appeal. **4.** beseech, beg, entreat. **10.** See **inquire.** —**Ant. 1, 10.** answer.

Ask (äsk), *n. Scand. Myth.* the first man, made by the gods from an ash tree. Cf. **Embla.** [< ON *Askr;* see ASH²]

a•skance (ə skans′), *adv.* **1.** with suspicion, mistrust, or disapproval: *He looked askance at my offer.* **2.** with a side glance; sidewise; obliquely. Also, **a•skant** (ə skant′). [1520–30; earlier *a scanche, a sca(u)nce;* of obscure orig.]
—**Syn. 1.** skeptically, suspiciously.

as•ka•rel (as′kə rel′), *n. Chem.* any of the class of synthetic, nonflammable, liquid dielectrics used chiefly for insulation in transformers. [of obscure orig.]

as•ka•ri (as′kə rē), *n., pl.* **-ris, -ri.** a native African police officer or soldier, esp. one serving a colonial administration. [1885–90; < Swahili < Ar *ʿaskarī* soldier, equiv. to *ʿaskar* army (< Pers *lashkar;* cf. LASCAR) + *-ī* suffix of appurtenance]

as•ke•sis (ə skē′sis), *n., pl.* **-ses** (-sēz). strict self-discipline or self-control, as for religious or meditative purposes. Also, **ascesis.** [1870–75; Gk *askēsis* exercise, training, equiv. to *askē-* (var. s. of *askeîn* to practice, train) + *-sis* -SIS]

a•skew (ə skyōō′), *adv.* **1.** to one side; out of line; in a crooked position; awry: *to wear one's hat askew; to hang a picture askew.* **2.** with disapproval, scorn, contempt, etc.; disdainfully: *They looked askew at the painting.* —*adj.* **3.** crooked; awry: *Your clothes are all askew.* [1565–75; A-¹ + SKEW] —**a•skew′ness,** *n.*

ask′ing bid′, *Bridge.* a conventional bid by which a bidder asks for specific information about the strength of his or her partner's hand in a given suit. [1935–40]

ask′ing price′, the price originally demanded by the seller, as before any reduction resulting from bargaining, discount, etc. [1745–55]

Ask•ja (äsk′yä), *n.* a volcano in E central Iceland. 4754 ft. (1449 m).

as•kos (as′kos), *n., pl.* **-koi** (-koi). *Gk. and Rom. Antiq.* an oil or wine jar, characterized by an ellipsoidal body and a short, flanged spout from which a thin handle extends in an arc to join the back of the jar. Cf. **alabastron, aryballos, lekythos.** [< Gk *áskos*]

ASL, 1. American Shuffleboard League. **2.** See **American Sign Language. 3.** American Soccer League.

ASLA, American Society of Landscape Architects.

a•slant (ə slant′, ə slänt′), *adv.* **1.** at a slant; slantingly; obliquely. —*adj.* **2.** slanting or on a slant; oblique. —*prep.* **3.** slantingly across; athwart. [1250–1300; ME *on slont, on slent* on slope, at a SLANT]

As•laug (äs′loug), *n. Scand. Legend.* (in the *Volsunga Saga*) daughter of Brynhild and Sigurd, wife of Ragnar Lodbrok. [< ON *Āslaug*]

a•sleep (ə slēp′), *adv.* **1.** in or into a state of sleep: *He fell asleep quickly.* **2.** into a dormant or inactive state; to rest: *Their anxieties were put asleep.* **3.** into the state of death. —*adj.* **4.** sleeping: *He is asleep.* **5.** dormant; inactive. **6.** (of the foot, hand, leg, etc.) numb. **7.** dead. [bef. 1000; ME *o slæpe, aslepe,* OE *on slǣpe;* see A-¹, SLEEP]

a•slope (ə slōp′), *adv.* **1.** at a slope; aslant; slantingly; diagonally. —*adj.* **2.** sloping. [1350–1400; ME; see A-¹, SLOPE]

ASM, air-to-surface missile.

As•ma•ra (äs mär′ə), *n.* a city in and the capital of Eritrea, in N Ethiopia. 276,355.

ASME, American Society of Mechanical Engineers.

As•mo•de•us (az′mə dē′əs, as′-), *n. Jewish Demonology.* an evil spirit. [< L *Asmodaeus* < Gk *Asmodaîos* < Heb *ashmədhai*]

As•mo•ne•an (az′mə nē′ən), *n.* Hasmonean. Also, **As′mo•nae′an.**

ASN, Army service number.

Asn, *Biochem.* asparagine.

As•nières (ä nyer′), *n.* a city in N central France, near Paris. 75,679.

a•so•cial (ā sō′shəl), *adj.* **1.** not sociable or gregarious; withdrawn from society. **2.** indifferent to or averse to conforming to conventional standards of behavior. **3.** inconsiderate of others; selfish; egocentric. [1880–85; A-⁶ + SOCIAL]

A•so•ka (ə sō′kə), *n.* died 232 B.C., Buddhist king in India 269?–232? B.C.

a•so•ma•tous (ā sō′mə təs, ə sō′-), *adj.* having no material body; incorporeal. [1725–35; < LL *asōmatus* < Gk *asṓmatos* bodiless, equiv. to *a-* A-⁶ + *sōmatos,* adj. deriv. of *sôma* body; see SOMA, -OUS]

a•so•ni•a (ə sō′nē ə), *n. Pathol.* tone deafness. [< NL; see A-⁶, -SONOUS, -IA]

A•so•san (ä′sô sän′), *n.* a volcano in SW Japan, in central Kyushu. 5225 ft. (1593 m); crater 12 mi. (19 km) across.

asp¹ (asp), *n.* **1.** any of several venomous snakes, esp. the Egyptian cobra or the horned viper. **2.** *Archaeol.* uraeus. [1300–50; back formation from ME *aspis* (taken as pl.) < L < Gk *aspís* orig., shield] —**asp′ish,** *adj.*

asp² (asp), *n., adj.* aspen. [bef. 900; ME *aspe, apse,* OE *æsp(e), æps(e);* c. MLG *aspe,* OHG *aspa* (G *Espe,* with altered vowel < OHG adj. *espîn*), ON *ǫsp;* akin to Latvian *apse,* Russ *osína,* Czech *osika* < North European IE **aps-.* See ASPEN]

ASP, American selling price.

Asp, *Biochem.* aspartic acid.

as•par•a•gi•nase (ə spar′ə jə nās′, -nāz′), *n. Biochem., Pharm.* an enzyme that catalyzes the conversion of asparagine to aspartic acid and ammonia, used in the treatment of acute lymphocytic leukemia. [1960–65; ASPARAGINE + -ASE]

as•par•a•gine (ə spar′ə jēn′, -jin), *n.* a white, crystalline, amino acid, $NH_2COCH_2CH(NH_2)COOH$, soluble in water, obtained from certain plants, esp. legumes, and used chiefly as a nutrient in culture media for certain bacteria. *Abbr.:* Asn; *Symbol:* N [1805–15; < F; see ASPARAGUS, -INE²]

as•par′a•gin′ic ac′id (ə spar′ə jin′ik, ə spar′-), *Biochem.* See **aspartic acid.** Also, **as′par•ag′ic ac′id** (as′pə raj′ik, as′-). [ASPARAGINE + -IC]

as•par•a•gus (ə spar′ə gəs), *n.* **1.** any plant of the genus *Asparagus,* of the lily family, esp. *A. officianalis,* cultivated for its edible shoots. **2.** the shoots, eaten as a vegetable. [bef. 1000; < L < Gk *asp(h)áragos;* r. OE *sparagi* (< ML) and later *sperage, sparrowgrass*] —**as•pa•rag•i•nous** (as′pə raj′ə nəs), *adj.*

aspar′agus bean′, a trailing, long-stemmed Asian vine, *Vigna unguiculata sesquipedalis,* of the legume family, having yellow or violet flowers and very long pods. Also called **yard-long bean.** [1855–60, *Amer.*]

aspar′agus bee′tle, either of two leaf beetles of the genus *Crioceris* that feed on the asparagus plant in both the larval and adult stages. [1805–15]

aspar′agus fern′, a fernlike climbing vine, *Asparagus setaceus,* of southern Africa, having very small, whitish flowers and pea-sized, purplish-black berries. Also called **fern asparagus.**

aspar′agus fern′ cat′erpillar. See **beet armyworm.**

as•par•tame (ə spär′tām, a spär′-, as′pər tām′), *n.* a white, crystalline, odorless, slightly water-soluble noncarbohydrate powder, $C_{14}H_{18}N_2O_5$, synthesized from amino acids, that is 150–200 times as sweet as sugar: used as a low-calorie sugar substitute in soft drinks, table sweeteners, and other food products. [1970–75; *aspart(yl phenyl)a(linine) m(ethyl) e(ster),* the powder's chemical name]

as•par•tate (ə spär′tāt), *n. Biochem.* a salt or ester formed from aspartic acid. [1860–65; ASPART(IC ACID) + -ATE²]

as•par′tic ac′id (ə spär′tik), *Biochem.* a nonessential amino acid, $C_4H_7NO_4$, produced by the hydrolysis of asparagine and proteins, found chiefly in young sugar cane and sugar-beet molasses, and used in the preparation of culture media and as a dietary supplement. *Abbr.:* Asp; *Symbol:* D Also called **aminosuccinic acid.** [1830–40; ASPAR(AGUS) + -TIC]

As•pa•sia (a spā′shə, -zhə), *n.* c470–410 B.C., Athenian courtesan, mistress of Pericles.

A.S.P.C.A., American Society for the Prevention of Cruelty to Animals.

as•pect (as′pekt), *n.* **1.** appearance to the eye or mind; look: *the physical aspect of the country.* **2.** nature; quality; character: *the superficial aspect of the situation.* **3.** a way in which a thing may be viewed or regarded; interpretation; view: *both aspects of a decision.* **4.** part; feature; phase: *That is the aspect of the problem that interests me most.* **5.** facial expression; countenance: *He wore an aspect of gloom. Hers was an aspect of happy optimism.* **6.** bearing; air; mien: *warlike in aspect.* **7.** view commanded; exposure: *The house has a southern aspect.* **8.** the side or surface facing a given direction: *the dorsal aspect of a fish; the northern aspect of the house.* **9.** *Gram.* **a.** a category or interrelated set of categories for which the verb is inflected in some languages, typically to indicate the duration, repetition, completion, or quality of the action or state denoted by the verb. **b.** a set of syntactic devices, as in the English perfect with *have* in *I have gone,* with functions similar to such inflections. **c.** any of the members or instances of these categories or sets: *the Latin perfect aspect; the Russian imperfect aspect.* **d.** the meaning of, or meaning typical of, such a category or construction. **e.** such categories or constructions, or their meanings collectively. **10.** *Astrol.* **a.** the angular distance between two points as seen from the earth, primarily derived by dividing the 360 degrees of the zodiac by the integers 1 through 12. **b.** the influence of any two planets or groups of planets located at such points. **11.** *Archaic.* a look; glance. [1350–1400; ME < L *aspectus* appearance, visible form, the action of looking at, equiv. to *aspec-* (var. s. of *aspicere* to observe, look at; *a-* A-⁵ + *-spicere,* comb. form of *specere* to see) + *-tus* suffix of v. action]
—**Syn. 1.** See **appearance. 7.** prospect, outlook.

as•pec•tant (ə spek′tənt), *adj. Heraldry.* (of birds, fish, and animals other than beasts of prey) face to face; respectant. [< L *aspectant-* (s. of *aspectāns,* prp. of *aspectāre* to gaze at, freq. of *aspicere*). See ASPECT, -ANT]

as′pect ra′tio, 1. *Aeron.* the ratio of the span of an airfoil to its mean chord. **2.** *Television.* the ratio of the width of an image to its height, usually the ratio 4 to 3. **3.** *Naval Archit.* the ratio of the height of a rudder to its fore-and-aft length. **4.** *Rocketry.* **a.** Also called **fineness ratio, slenderness ratio.** the ratio of the mean diameter of the body of a rocket or missile to its length. **b.** the ratio of the length of the combustion chamber of a rocket motor to its diameter. [1905–10]

as•pec•tu•al (a spek′chōō əl), *adj. Gram.* **1.** of, pertaining to, or producing a particular aspect or aspects. **2.** used as or like a form inflected for a particular aspect. [1645–55; < L *aspectu-,* s. of *aspectus* ASPECT + -AL¹]

as•pen (as′pən), *n.* **1.** any of various poplars, as *Populus tremula,* of Europe, and *P. tremuloides* **(quaking aspen)** or *P. alba* **(white aspen),** of America, having soft wood and alternate ovate leaves that tremble in the slightest breeze. —*adj.* **2.** of or pertaining to the aspen. **3.** trembling or quivering, like the leaves of the aspen. [1350–1400; ME *aspen* (adj.), OE *æspen;* c. OFris *espen* (adj.), *espenbeam,* MD *espenboom,* OHG *espîn* (adj.). See ASP², -EN²]

As•pen (as′pən), *n.* a town in central Colorado: ski resort. 3678.

CONCISE PRONUNCIATION KEY: *act, cāpe, dâre, pärt; set, ēqual; if, īce; ox, ōver, ôrder, oil, bŏŏk, bōōt, out; up, ûrge; child; sing; shoe; thin, that;* zh as in *treasure.* ə = *a* as in *alone, e* as in *system, i* as in *easily, o* as in *gallop, u* as in *circus;* ° as in *fire* (fī°r), *hour* (ou°r). l and n can serve as syllabic consonants, as in *cradle* (krād′l), and *button* (but′n). See the full key inside the front cover.

As/pen Hill/, a city in central Maryland. 47,455.

as·per[1] (as/pər), *n.* a former silver coin of Turkey and Egypt: later a money of account equal to 1/120 of a piaster. [1580–90; < It *aspero* < MGk *áspron* lit., white coin, n. use of neut. of *áspros* white]

as·per[2] (as/pər), *adj. Obs.* harsh; rough. [1325–75; < L: rough; r. ME *aspre* < MF]

as·per·ate (as/pə rāt/), *v.t.*, **-at·ed, -at·ing.** to make rough, harsh, or uneven: *a voice asperated by violent emotion.* [1650–60; < L *asperātus* (ptp. of *asperāre*). See ASPER[2], -ATE[1]]

As·per·ges (ə spûr/jēz), *n. Rom. Cath. Ch.* the rite of sprinkling the altar, clergy, and people with holy water before High Mass. [< L: thou shalt sprinkle (2nd pers. sing. fut. of *aspergere*). See A-[5], SPARGE]

as·per·gil·lo·sis (as/pər jə lō/sis), *n., pl.* **-ses** (-sēz). an infection or disease caused by a mold of the genus *Aspergillus,* characterized by granulomatous lesions of the lungs, skin, etc. [1895–1900; < F *aspergillose;* see ASPERGILLUS, -OSIS]

as·per·gil·lum (as/pər jil/əm), *n., pl.* **-gil·la** (-jil/ə), **-gil·lums.** *Rom. Cath. Ch.* a brush or instrument for sprinkling holy water; aspersorium. [1640–50; < NL, equiv. to L *asperg(ere)* to besprinkle (see A-[5], SPARGE) + *-illum* dim. suffix]

as·per·gil·lus (as/pər jil/əs), *n., pl.* **-gil·li** (-jil/ī). *Mycol.* any fungus of the genus *Aspergillus,* having sporophores with a bristly, knoblike top. [1840–50; < NL: alter. of ASPERGILLUM]

as·per·i·ty (ə sper/i tē), *n., pl.* **-ties.** **1.** harshness or sharpness of tone, temper, or manner; severity; acrimony: *The cause of her anger did not warrant such asperity.* **2.** hardship; difficulty; rigor: *the asperities of polar weather.* **3.** roughness of surface; unevenness. **4.** something rough or harsh. [1200–50; late ME *asperite* (< AF) < L *asperitās,* equiv. to *asper* rough + *-itās* -ITY; r. ME *asprete* < AF, OF < L]
—Syn. 1. acerbity, bitterness, astringency. **—Ant. 1.** affability, cheerfulness.

as·perse (ə spûrs/), *v.t.*, **-persed, -pers·ing. 1.** to attack with false, malicious, and damaging charges or insinuations; slander. **2.** to sprinkle; bespatter. [1480–90; < L *aspersus* besprinkled (ptp. of *aspergere*), equiv. to *a-* A-[5] + *-sper-* (comb. form of *spar-,* var. of *sparg-* SPARGE) + *-sus,* var. of *-tus* ptp. suffix] **—as·pers/er,** *n.* **—as·per/sive,** *adj.* **—as·per/sive·ly,** *adv.*
—Syn. 1. malign, abuse, traduce.

as·per·sion (ə spûr/zhən, -shən), *n.* **1.** a damaging or derogatory remark or criticism; slander: *casting aspersions on a campaign rival.* **2.** the act of slandering; vilification; defamation; calumniation; derogation: *Such vehement aspersions cannot be ignored.* **3.** the act of sprinkling, as in baptism. **4.** *Archaic.* a shower or spray. [1545–55; (< MF) < L *aspersiōn-* (s. of *aspersiō*) a sprinkling. See ASPERSE, -ION]
—Syn. 1. censure, reproach.

as·per·so·ri·um (as/pər sôr/ē əm, -sōr/-), *n., pl.* **-so·ri·a** (-sôr/ē ə, -sōr/-), **-so·ri·ums.** *Rom. Cath. Ch.* **1.** a vessel for holding holy water. See illus. under **stoup. 2.** aspergillum. [1860–65; < ML; see ASPERSE, -TORY[2]]

as·phalt (as/fôlt *or, esp. Brit.,* -falt), *n.* **1.** any of various dark-colored, solid, bituminous substances, native in various areas of the earth and composed mainly of hydrocarbon mixtures. **2.** a similar substance that is the by-product of petroleum-cracking operations. **3.** a mixture of such substances with gravel, crushed rock, or the like, used for paving. *—v.t.* **4.** to cover or pave with asphalt. *—adj.* **5.** of, pertaining to, or containing asphalt: *asphalt tile.* [1275–1325; earlier *asphaltos, -um* < L < Gk *ásphaltos, -on,* akin to *asphalízein* to make firm, to secure; r. ME *aspaltoun* << Gk *ásphalton*] **—as·phal/tic,** *adj.* **—as/phalt·like/,** *adj.*

as·phal·tene (as fôl/tēn *or, esp. Brit.,* -fal/-), *n. Chem.* any of the constituents of a bitumen, as asphalt, that are insoluble in pentane, hexane, or naphthalene. Cf. **petrolene.** [1830–40; ASPHALT + -ENE]

as·phal·tite (as fôl/tit, as/fôl tīt/ *or, esp. Brit.,* as-fal/-, as/fal-), *n.* a natural, solid hydrocarbon having a melting point higher than that of asphalt. [1815–25; < Gk *asphaltītēs.* See ASPHALT, -ITE[1]]

as/phalt jun/gle, any large, crowded city or urban area regarded as a dangerous place where people are engaged in a struggle for survival. [appar. coined by George Ade in a fable published in 1917; popularized by a novel of the same title (1949) by W.R. Burnett (born 1899), U.S. novelist and screenwriter]

as/phalt pa/per, paper treated with asphalt, as to increase toughness or water resistance.

as/phalt rock/, *Geol.* a rock formation, usually of limestone or sandstone, containing large amounts of bitumens.

as·phal·tum (as fôl/təm *or, esp. Brit.,* -fal/-), *n.* asphalt. [< NL < Gk *ásphalton* ASPHALT]

a·spher·i·cal (ā sfer/i kəl), *adj. Optics.* (of a reflecting surface or lens) deviating slightly from a perfectly spherical shape and relatively free from aberrations. Also, **a·spher/ic.** [1920–25; A-[6] + SPHERICAL]

as·pho·del (as/fə del/), *n.* **1.** any of various southern European plants of the genera *Asphodelus* and *Asphodeline,* of the lily family, having white, pink, or yellow flowers in elongated clusters. **2.** any of various other plants, as the daffodil. [1590–1600; < L *asphodelus* < Gk *asphódelos* the asphodel. See DAFFODIL]

as·phyx·i·a (as fik/sē ə), *n. Pathol.* the extreme condition caused by lack of oxygen and excess of carbon dioxide in the blood, produced by interference with respiration or insufficient oxygen in the air; suffocation. [1700–10; < NL < Gk *asphyxía* a stopping of the pulse, equiv. to *a-* A-[6] + *sphýx(is)* pulse + *-ia* -IA] **—as·phyx/i·al,** *adj.*

as·phyx·i·ant (as fik/sē ənt), *adj.* **1.** asphyxiating or tending to asphyxiate. *—n.* **2.** an asphyxiating agent or substance. **3.** an asphyxiating condition. [1850–55; ASPHYXI(ATE) + -ANT]

as·phyx·i·ate (as fik/sē āt/), *v.*, **-at·ed, -at·ing.** *—v.t.* **1.** to produce asphyxia in. **2.** to cause to die or lose consciousness by impairing normal breathing, as by gas or other noxious agents; choke; suffocate; smother. *—v.i.* **3.** to become asphyxiated. [1830–40; ASPHYXI(A) + -ATE[1]] **—as·phyx/i·a/tion,** *n.* **—as·phyx/i·a/tor,** *n.*

as·pic[1] (as/pik), *n.* **1.** a savory jelly usually made with meat or fish stock and gelatin, chilled and used as a garnish and coating for meats, seafoods, eggs, etc. **2.** Also called **tomato aspic.** a similar jelly made with spiced tomato juice and gelatin, chilled and served as a salad. [1780–90; < F; perh. because the form or color resembled those of an asp. See ASPIC[2]]

as·pic[2] (as/pik), *n. Obs.* asp[1]. [1520–30; < F, perh. equiv. to OF *asp(e)* ASP[1] + *-ic,* modeled on MF *basilique* BASILISK]

as·pic[3] (as/pik), *n.* See **great lavender.** [1595–1605; < F; OF *espic* < ML *spicus* spikenard, L: var. of *spīca, spīcum* SPIKE[2]]

as·pi·dis·tra (as/pi dis/trə), *n.* any of several plants belonging to the genus *Aspidistra,* of the lily family, native to eastern Asia, esp. *A. eliator,* having large evergreen leaves often striped with white, and grown as a houseplant. Also called **barroom plant, cast-iron plant, iron plant.** [1815–25; < NL, equiv. to *aspid-* (< Gk: s. of *aspís* shield) + *-istra,* extracted from *Tupistra* genus of liliaceous plants < Gk *typís* mallet + L *-tra* pl. of *-trum* n. suffix denoting instrument]

as·pir·ant (ə spīər/ənt, as/pər ənt), *n.* **1.** a person who aspires, as one who seeks or desires a career, advancement, status, etc.: *The aspirants for foundation grants had yet to prove themselves.* *—adj.* **2.** aspiring. [1730–40; (< F) < L *aspīrant-* (s. of *aspīrāns,* prp. of *aspīrāre*). See ASPIRE, -ANT]

as·pi·ra·ta (as/pə rā/tə), *n., pl.* **-tae** (-tē). *Gk. Grammar.* a voiceless stop accompanied by strong aspiration, as *φ, θ, χ.* [< LL (*littera*) *aspīrāta* aspirated (letter); see ASPIRATE]

as·pi·rate (*v.* as/pə rāt/; *n., adj.,* as/pər it), *v.*, **-rat·ed, -rat·ing,** *n., adj.* *—v.t.* **1.** *Phonet.* **a.** to articulate (a speech sound, esp. a stop) so as to produce an audible puff of breath, as with the first *t* of *total,* the second *t* being unaspirated. **b.** to articulate (the beginning of a word or syllable) with an *h*-sound, as in *which,* pronounced (hwich), or *hitch* as opposed to *witch* or *itch.* **2.** *Med.* **a.** to remove (a fluid) from a body cavity by use of an aspirator or suction syringe. **b.** to inhale (fluid or a foreign body) into the bronchi and lungs, often after vomiting. **3.** to draw or remove by suction. *—n.* **4.** *Phonet.* a speech sound having as an obvious concomitant an audible puff of breath, as initial stop consonants or initial *h*-sounds. **5.** *Med.* the substance or contents that have been aspirated. *—adj.* **6.** *Phonet.* (of a speech sound) pronounced with or accompanied by aspiration; aspirated. [1660–70; < L *aspīrātus* breathed upon (ptp. of *aspīrāre*). See ASPIRE, -ATE[1]]

as·pi·ra·tion (as/pə rā/shən), *n.* **1.** strong desire, longing, or aim; ambition: *intellectual aspirations.* **2.** a goal or objective desired: *The presidency is the traditional aspiration of young American boys.* **3.** act of aspirating; breath. **4.** *Phonet.* **a.** articulation accompanied by an audible puff of breath, as in the *h*-sound of *how,* or of *when* (hwen), or in the release of initial stops, as in the *k*-sound of *key.* **b.** the use of an aspirate in pronunciation. **5.** *Med.* **a.** the act of removing a fluid, as pus or serum, from a cavity of the body, by a hollow needle or trocar connected with a suction syringe. **b.** the act of inhaling fluid or a foreign body into the bronchi and lungs, often after vomiting. [1375–1425; late ME (< MF) < L *aspīrātiōn-* (s. of *aspīrātiō*). See ASPIRATE, -ION] **—as/pi·ra/tion·al,** *adj.*
—Syn. 1. yearning, craving.

as·pi·ra·tor (as/pə rā/tər), *n.* **1.** an apparatus or device employing suction. **2.** *Hydraul.* a suction pump that operates by the pressure differential created by the high-speed flow of a fluid past an intake orifice. **3.** *Med.* an instrument for removing body fluids by suction. [1860–65; ASPIRATE + -OR[2]]

as·pir·a·to·ry (ə spīər/ə tôr/ē, -tōr/ē), *adj.* pertaining to or suited for aspiration. [1860–65; ASPIRATE + -ORY[1]]

as·pire (ə spīər/), *v.i.*, **-pired, -pir·ing. 1.** to long, aim, or seek ambitiously; be eagerly desirous, esp. for something great or of high value (usually fol. by *to, after,* or an infinitive): *to aspire after literary immortality; to aspire to be a doctor.* **2.** *Archaic.* to rise up; soar; mount; tower. [1425–75; late ME (< MF *aspirer*) < L *aspīrāre* to breathe upon, pant after, equiv. to *a-* A-[5] + *spīrāre* to breathe, blow] **—as·pir/er,** *n.* **—as·pir/ing·ly,** *adv.*
—Syn. 1. yearn.

as·pi·rin (as/pər in, -prin), *n., pl.* **-rin, -rins. 1.** *Pharm.* a white, crystalline substance, $C_9H_8O_4$, derivative of salicylic acid, used as an anti-inflammatory agent and to relieve the pain of headache, rheumatism, gout, neuralgia, etc.; acetylsalicylic acid. **2.** an aspirin tablet: *I took two aspirin and went right to bed.* [1899; orig. G trademark, equiv. to *A(cetyl)* ACETYL + *Spir(säure)* salicylic acid (see SPIRAEA) + *-in* -IN[2]]

a·sprawl (ə sprôl/), *adv., adj.* being in a sprawling state or posture: *The body lay asprawl among the wreckage.* [1875–80; A-[1] + SPRAWL]

a·squint (ə skwint/), *adv., adj.* with an oblique glance or squint; askance; slyly; dubiously. [1200–50; ME, equiv. to *a-* A-[1] + *squint,* of uncert. orig.]

As·quith (as/kwith), *n.* **Herbert Henry** (*1st Earl of Oxford and Asquith*), 1852–1928, British statesman: prime minister 1908–16.

ASR, 1. airport surveillance radar. **2.** *U.S. Navy.* air-sea rescue.

a·sra·ma (ä/shrə mə), *n. Hinduism.* **1.** any of the four phases of the ideally conducted life: education, work, withdrawal from society, and asceticism. **2.** ashram. [< Skt *āśrama.* See ASHRAM]

ass[1] (as), *n.* **1.** a long-eared, slow, patient, sure-footed domesticated mammal, *Equus asinus,* related to the horse, used chiefly as a beast of burden. **2.** any wild species of the genus *Equus,* as the onager. **3.** a stupid, foolish, or stubborn person. [bef. 1000; ME *asse,* OE *assa,* prob. hypocoristic form based on OIr *asan* < L *asinus;* akin to Gk *ónos* ass] **—ass/like/,** *adj.*

ass[1], *Equus asinus,* 3½ ft. (1.1 m) high at shoulder head and body 7 ft. (2 m); tail 1½ ft. (0.5 m)

ass[2] (as), *n. Vulgar.* **1.** the buttocks. **2.** the rectum. **3.** *Slang.* sexual intercourse. [bef. 1000; var of ARSE, with loss of *r* before *s,* as in PASSEL, CUSS, etc.; ME *ars, er(e)s,* OE *ærs, ears;* c. OFris *ers,* D *aars,* ON, MLG, OS, OHG *ars* (G *Arsch*), Gk *órrhos,* Armenian *oṙkh,* Hittite *arras;* akin to Gk *ourá,* OIr *err* tail]

ass., 1. assistant. **2.** association. **3.** assorted.

As·sad (ä säd/), *n.* **Ha·fez al** (hä fez/ el), born 1928?, Syrian military and political leader: president since 1971.

as·sa·gai (as/ə gī/), *n., pl.* **-gais,** *v.t.*, **-gaied, -gai·ing.** assegai.

as·sa·i[1] (ə sī/; *It.* äs sä/ē), *adv. Music.* very: *allegro assai* (very quick). [1715–25; < It: lit., enough << L *ad* (up) to + *satis* enough. See ASSET]

as·sa·i[2] (ə sä/ē), *n.* any of several slender Brazilian palms of the genus *Euterpe,* esp. *E. edulis,* a species bearing a purple fruit from which a beverage is made by infusion. [1895–1900; < Pg < Tupi *assaí*]

as·sail (ə sāl/), *v.t.* **1.** to attack vigorously or violently; assault. **2.** to attack with arguments, criticism, ridicule, abuse, etc.: *to assail one's opponent with slander.* **3.** to undertake with the purpose of mastering: *He assailed his studies with new determination.* **4.** to impinge upon; make an impact on; beset: *His mind was assailed by conflicting arguments. The light assailed their eyes.* [1175–1225; ME *asaylen* < OF *asalir* < LL *assalīre,* equiv. to L *as-* AS- + *salīre* to leap, spring] **—as·sail/a·ble,** *adj.* **—as·sail/a·ble·ness,** *n.* **—as·sail/er,** *n.* **—as·sail/ment,** *n.*
—Syn. 1. See **attack. 2.** asperse, malign.

as·sail·ant (ə sā/lənt), *n.* **1.** a person who attacks. *—adj.* **2.** *Archaic.* assailing; attacking; hostile. [1525–35; < MF *assaillant.* See ASSAIL, -ANT]

As·sam (as sam/), *n.* a state in NE India. 17,810,000; 85,012 sq. mi. (220,181 sq. km). *Cap.:* Shillong.

As·sa·mese (as/ə mēz/, -mēs/), *adj., n., pl.* **-mese.** *—adj.* **1.** of or pertaining to Assam, its inhabitants, or their language. *—n.* **2.** a native or inhabitant of Assam. **3.** an Indic language of Assam. [1820–30; ASSAM + -ESE]

Assam/ States/, a group of former states in NE India, most of which are now part of the state of Assam.

as·sas·sin (ə sas/in), *n.* **1.** a murderer, esp. one who kills a politically prominent person for fanatical or monetary reasons. **2.** (*cap.*) one of an order of Muslim fanatics, active in Persia and Syria from about 1090 to 1272, whose chief object was to assassinate Crusaders. [1525–35; < ML *assassīnī* (pl.) < Ar *ḥashshāshīn* eaters of HASHISH]

as·sas·si·nate (ə sas/ə nāt/), *v.t.*, **-nat·ed, -nat·ing. 1.** to kill suddenly or secretively, esp. a politically prominent person; murder premeditatedly and treacherously. **2.** to destroy or harm treacherously and viciously: *to assassinate a person's character.* [1590–1600; ASSASSIN + -ATE[1]] **—as·sas/si·na/tion,** *n.* **—as·sas/si·na/tive,** *adj.* **—as·sas/si·na/tor,** *n.*
—Syn. 1. slay.

assas/sin bug/, any of numerous bugs of the family Reduviidae, feeding chiefly on other insects but including some forms that are bloodsucking parasites of mammals. Also called **reduviid.** [1890–95]

As/sa·teague Is/land (as/ə tēg/), a narrow island in SE Maryland and E Virginia on Chincoteague Bay: annual wild pony roundup. 33 mi. (53 km) long.

as·sault (ə sôlt/), *n.* **1.** a sudden, violent attack; onslaught: *an assault on tradition.* **2.** *Law.* an unlawful physical attack upon another; an attempt or offer to do violence to another, with or without battery, as by holding a stone or club in a threatening manner. **3.** *Mil.* the stage of close combat in an attack. **4.** rape[1]. *—v.t.* **5.** to make an assault upon; attack; assail. [1200–50; ME *asaut* < OF < ML *assaltus* (r. L *assultus*), equiv. to L *as-* AS- + *saltus* a leap (*sal(īre)* to leap + *-tus* suffix of v. action)] **—as·sault/a·ble,** *adj.* **—as·sault/er,** *n.*
—Syn. 1. onset, charge; invasion, aggression. **5.** See **attack.**

CONCISE ETYMOLOGY KEY: <, descended or borrowed from; >, whence; b., blend of, blended; c., cognate with; cf., compare; deriv., derivative; equiv., equivalent; imit., imitative; obl., oblique; r., replacing; s., stem; sp., spelling, spelled; resp., respelling, respelled; trans., translation; ?, origin unknown; *, unattested; ‡, probably earlier than. See the full key inside the front cover.

assault′ and bat′tery, *Law.* an assault with an actual touching or other violence upon another. [1580–90]

assault′ boat′, a portable boat used for landing troops on beaches and for crossing rivers. Also called **storm boat.** [1940–45]

as·saul·tive (ə sôl′tiv), *adj.* tending or seeming to assault; physically aggressive: *the assaultive behavior of the inmates; the assaultive manner of some rock bands.* [1950–55; ASSAULT + -IVE] **—as·saul′tive·ly,** *adv.* **—as·saul′tive·ness,** *n.*

assault′ jack′et, a protective jacketlike garment, armored so as to resist bullets, knives, etc., worn esp. by police officers for defense against attack.

assault′ ri′fle, 1. a military rifle capable of both automatic and semiautomatic fire, utilizing an intermediate-power cartridge. **2.** a nonmilitary weapon modeled on the military assault rifle, usu. modified to allow only semiautomatic fire. [1970–75]

as·say (*v.* a sā′; *n.* as′ā, a sā′), *v.t.* **1.** to examine or analyze: *to assay a situation; to assay an event.* **2.** *Metall.* to analyze (an ore, alloy, etc.) in order to determine the quantity of gold, silver, or other metal in it. **3.** *Pharm.* to subject (a drug) to an analysis for the determination of its potency or composition. **4.** to judge the quality of; assess; evaluate: *to assay someone's efforts.* **5.** to try or test; put to trial: *to assay one's strength; to assay one's debating abilities.* **6.** to attempt; try; essay: *to assay a dance step.* —*v.i.* **7.** to contain, as shown by analysis, a certain proportion of usually precious metal. —*n.* **8.** *Metall.* determination of the amount of metal, esp. gold or silver, in an ore, alloy, etc. **9.** a substance undergoing analysis or trial. **10.** a detailed report of the findings in assaying a substance. **11.** *Archaic.* examination; trial; attempt; essay. [1250–1300; ME < MF; var. of ESSAY] **—as·say′a·ble,** *adj.* **—as·say′er,** *n.*

as′say cup′, a small wine cup for tasting wine to be offered to another person. [1520–30]

as′say groove′, (in silverwork) a furrow left in a piece by the digging out of metal for assay.

as′say of′fice, a local testing station for assaying ore, as gold or silver, esp. a government station maintained in connection with the registration of mineral claims, purchases of gold, or the like. [1765–75]

as′say ton′, a unit of weight used in assaying ore, equivalent to 29.167 grams. [1880–85]

ass·back·wards (as′bak′wərdz), *adv. Slang (sometimes vulgar).* **1.** in an order or way reverse from the usual: *You've sewn the sleeve on assbackwards.* **2.** in a manner incongruously or preposterously counter to what is customary, probable, or feasible: *The plan fell apart because everything leading up to it was handled assbackwards.* Also, **ass′back′ward.** [1935–40; ASS[2] + BACKWARDS]

asse (as), *n.* See **Cape fox.**

as·se·gai (as′ə gī′), *n., pl.* **-gais,** *v.,* **-gaied, -gai·ing.** —*n.* **1.** the slender javelin or spear of the Bantu-speaking people of southern Africa. **2.** a southern African tree, *Curtisia dentata,* of the dogwood family, from whose wood such spears are made. —*v.t.* **3.** to pierce with an assegai. Also, **assagai.** [1615–25; earlier *azagaia* < Pg < Ar *az zaghāyah,* equiv. to *al* the + Berber *zaghāyah* assegai]

as·sem·blage (ə sem′blij; *for 3, 4 also Fr.* A säɴ blAzh′), *n.* **1.** a group of persons or things gathered or collected; an assembly; collection; aggregate. **2.** the act of assembling; state of being assembled. **3.** *Fine Arts.* **a.** a sculptural technique of organizing or composing into a unified whole a group of unrelated and often fragmentary or discarded objects. **b.** a work of art produced by this technique. Cf. **collage, found object, ready-made** (def. 4). **4.** *Archaeol.* the aggregate of artifacts and other remains found on a site, considered as material evidence in support of a theory concerning the culture or cultures inhabiting it. [1695–1705; < F; see ASSEMBLE, -AGE]

as·sem·blag·ist (ə sem′blə jist, as′äm blä′zhist), *n.* an artist who produces works of art using the techniques of assemblage. [1960–65; ASSEMBLAGE + -IST]

as·sem·ble (ə sem′bəl), *v.,* **-bled, -bling.** —*v.t.* **1.** to bring together or gather into one place, company, body, or whole. **2.** to put or fit together; put together the parts of: *to assemble information for a report; to assemble a toy from a kit.* **3.** *Computers.* compile (def. 4). —*v.i.* **4.** to come together; gather; meet: *We assembled in the auditorium.* [1200–50; ME < OF *assembler* < VL **assimulāre* to bring together, equiv. to L *as-* AS- + *simul* together + *-ā-* thematic vowel + *-re* inf. suffix]
—Syn. 1. convene, convoke. See **gather. 2.** connect. See **manufacture. 4.** congregate, convene.

as·sem·blé (*Fr.* A säɴ blā′), *n., pl.* **-blés** (*Fr.* -blā′). *Ballet.* a jump in which the dancer throws one leg up, springs off the other, and lands with both feet together. [< F, ptp. of *assembler* to ASSEMBLE]

as·sem·bled (ə sem′bəld), *adj.* noting an artificial gem formed of two or more parts, as a doublet or triplet, at least one of which is a true gemstone. [1585–95; ASSEMBLE + -ED[2]]

as·sem·bler (ə sem′blər), *n.* **1.** a person or thing that assembles. **2.** *Computers.* **a.** Also called **assembly routine.** a language processor that translates symbolic assembly language into equivalent machine language. **b.** See **assembly language.** [1625–35; ASSEMBLE + -ER[1]]

Assem′blies of God′, the largest American Pentecostal denomination, formed in 1914 by the merger of various Pentecostal churches and marked by faith healing and speaking in tongues. Also, **Assembly of God.**

as·sem·bly (ə sem′blē), *n., pl.* **-blies. 1.** an assembling or coming together of a number of persons, usually for a particular purpose: *The principal will speak to all the students at Friday's assembly.* **2.** a group of persons gathered together, usually for a particular purpose, whether religious, political, educational, or social. **3.** (*often cap.*) *Govt.* a legislative body, esp. the lower house of the legislature in certain states of the U.S.: *a bill before the assembly; the New York State Assembly.* **4.** *Mil.* **a.** a signal, as by drum or bugle, for troops to fall into ranks or otherwise assemble. **b.** the movement of forces, tanks, soldiers, etc., scattered by battle or battle drill, toward and into a small area. **5.** the putting together of complex machinery, as airplanes, from interchangeable parts of standard dimensions. **6.** *Mach.* a group of machine parts, esp. one forming a self-contained, independently mounted unit. Cf. **subassembly.** [1275–1325; ME *assemblee* < MF, lit., (that which is) assembled, fem. ptp. of *assembler* to ASSEMBLE]
—Syn. 1, 2. assemblage, gathering, congress, meeting. See **convention. 2.** throng. **3.** congress, representatives.

assem′bly dis′trict, *U.S.* one of a fixed number of districts into which a state is divided, each district electing one member to the lower house of the state legislature. Cf. **Congressional district, senatorial district.** [1870–75, *Amer.*]

assem′bly lan′guage, a computer language most of whose expressions are symbolic equivalents of the machine-language instructions of a particular computer. [1960–65]

assem′bly line′, an arrangement of machines, tools, and workers in which a product is assembled by having each perform a specific, successive operation on an incomplete unit as it passes by in a series of stages organized in a direct line. Also called **production line.** [1910–15, *Amer.*]

as·sem·bly·man (ə sem′blē mən), *n., pl.* **-men.** (*sometimes cap.*) a member of a legislative assembly, esp. a member of the lower house of the legislature in certain states of the U.S. [1640–50; ASSEMBLY + -MAN]
—Usage. See **-man.**

Assem′bly of God′. See **Assemblies of God.**

Assem′bly of the No′tables, notable (def. 5).

as·sem·bly·per·son (ə sem′blē pûr′sən), *n.* (*sometimes cap.*) a member of a legislative assembly, esp. a member of the lower house of the legislature in certain states of the U.S. [ASSEMBLY(MAN) + -PERSON]
—Usage. See **-person.**

assem′bly plant′, a factory where parts for a complete unit are put together, as in automobile manufacturing.

assem′bly routine′, *Computers.* assembler (def. 2a).

as·sem·bly·wom·an (ə sem′blē wo͝om′ən), *n., pl.* **-wom·en.** (*sometimes cap.*) a woman who is a member of a legislative assembly, esp. a member of the lower house of the legislature in certain states of the U.S. [1965–70, *Amer.*; ASSEMBLY(MAN) + WOMAN]
—Usage. See **-woman.**

as·sent (ə sent′), *v.i.* **1.** to agree or concur; subscribe to (often fol. by *to*): *to assent to a statement.* **2.** to give in; yield; concede: *Assenting to his demands, I did as I was told.* —*n.* **3.** agreement, as to a proposal; concurrence. **4.** acquiescence; compliance. [1250–1300; ME *asenten* < OF *asenter* < L *assentārī,* equiv. to *as-* AS- + *sen(t)-* (see SCENT) + *-t-* freq. suffix + *-ā-* thematic vowel + *-rī* inf. suffix] **—as·sent′ing·ly,** *adv.* **—as·sen′tive,** *adj.* **—as·sen′tive·ness,** *n.* **—as·sen′tor, as·sent′er,** *n.*
—Syn. 1, 2. acquiesce. See **agree.**

as·sen·ta·tion (as′en tā′shən), *n.* the practice of assenting readily, esp. obsequiously. [1475–85; < L *assentātiōn-* (s. of *assentātiō*). See ASSENT, -ATION]

As·ser (ä′sər), *n.* **To·bi·as** (tō bī′əs; *Du.* tô bē′äs), 1838–1913, Dutch jurist and statesman: Nobel peace prize 1911.

as·sert (ə sûrt′), *v.t.* **1.** to state with assurance, confidence, or force; state strongly or positively; affirm; aver: *He asserted his innocence of the crime.* **2.** to maintain or defend (claims, rights, etc.). **3.** to state as having existence; affirm; postulate: *to assert a first cause as necessary.* **4. assert oneself,** to insist on one's rights, declare one's views forcefully, etc.: *The candidate finally asserted himself about property taxes.* [1595–1605; < L *assertus* joined to, defended, claimed (ptp. of *asserere*), equiv. to *as-* AS- + *ser-* (see SERIES) + *-tus* ptp. suffix] **—as·sert′er, as·ser′tor,** *n.* **—as·sert′i·ble,** *adj.*
—Syn. 1. asseverate, avow, maintain. See **declare. 2.** uphold, support. See **maintain. —Ant. 1.** deny.

as·sert·ed (ə sûr′tid), *adj.* resting on a statement or claim unsupported by evidence or proof; alleged: *The asserted value of the property was twice the amount anyone offered.* [1675–85; ASSERT + -ED[2]] **—as·sert′ed·ly,** *adv.*

as·ser·tion (ə sûr′shən), *n.* **1.** a positive statement or declaration, often without support or reason: *a mere assertion; an unwarranted assertion.* **2.** an act of asserting. [1375–1425; late ME *assercion* < L *assertiōn-* (s. of *assertiō*). See ASSERT, -ION] **—as·ser′tion·al,** *adj.*

as·ser·tive (ə sûr′tiv), *adj.* **1.** confidently aggressive or self-assured; positive: aggressive; dogmatic: *He is too assertive as a salesman.* **2.** having a distinctive or pronounced taste or aroma. [1555–65; ASSERT + -IVE] **—as·ser′tive·ly,** *adv.* **—as·ser′tive·ness,** *n.*
—Syn. 1. forceful, decisive, forward.

asser′tiveness train′ing, a type of behavior therapy in which people are taught appropriate methods of asserting themselves in various situations through honest and direct expression of both positive and negative feelings. [1970–75]

as·ser·to·ry (ə sûr′tə rē), *adj.* stated positively; affirmative: *an assertory proposition.* [1610–20; ASSERT + -ORY[1]] **—as·ser′to·ri·ly,** *adv.*

as·ses[1] (as′iz), *n.* pl. of **ass**[1].

as·ses[2] (as′iz), *n.* pl. of **as**[2].

as′ses′ bridge′, *Geom.* See **pons asinorum.**

as·sess (ə ses′), *v.t.* **1.** to estimate officially the value of (property, income, etc.) as a basis for taxation. **2.** to fix or determine the amount of (damages, a tax, a fine, etc.): *The hurricane damage was assessed at six million dollars.* **3.** to impose a tax or other charge on. **4.** to estimate or judge the value, character, etc., of; evaluate: *to assess one's efforts.* [1400–50; late ME *assessen* < ML *assessāre* to assess a tax, deriv. of L *assessus* seated beside (a judge) (ptp. of *assidēre*), equiv. to *as-* AS- + *sed-* (s. of *sedēre* to SIT) + *-tus* ptp. suffix] **—as·sess′a·ble,** *adj.*

assessed′ val′ue, the value of something as determined by an assessor, esp. the value of real property.

as·sess·ment (ə ses′mənt), *n.* **1.** the act of assessing; appraisal; evaluation. **2.** an official valuation of property for the purpose of levying a tax; an assigned value. **3.** an amount assessed as payable. [1530–40; ASSESS + -MENT]

as·ses·sor (ə ses′ər), *n.* **1.** a person who makes assessments, esp. for purposes of taxation. **2.** an adviser or assistant to a judge, esp. one serving as a specialist in some field. **3.** *Archaic.* **a.** a person who shares another's position, rank, or dignity. **b.** a person sitting beside another in an advisory capacity; an advisory associate. [1350–1400; ME *assessour* < ML *assessor* one who assesses taxes, L: a judge's helper. See ASSESS, -TOR] **—as·ses·so·ri·al** (as′ə sôr′ē əl, -sōr′-), *adj.* **—as·ses′sor·ship′,** *n.*

as·set (as′et), *n.* **1.** a useful and desirable thing or quality: *Organizational ability is an asset.* **2.** a single item of ownership having exchange value. **3. assets, a.** items of ownership convertible into cash; total resources of a person or business, as cash, notes and accounts receivable, securities, inventories, goodwill, fixtures, machinery, or real estate (opposed to *liabilities*). **b.** *Accounting.* the items detailed on a balance sheet, esp. in relation to liabilities and capital. **c.** all property available for the payment of debts, esp. of a bankrupt or insolvent firm or person. **d.** *Law.* property in the hands of an heir, executor, or administrator, that is sufficient to pay the debts or legacies of a deceased person. [1525–35; back formation from *assets,* in phrase *have assets,* lit., have enough (to pay obligations) < AF, OF *asez* enough. See ASSAI[1]] **—as′set·less,** *adj.*

as·sev·er·ate (ə sev′ə rāt′), *v.t.,* **-at·ed, -at·ing.** to declare earnestly or solemnly; affirm positively; aver. [1785–95; < L *assevērātus* spoken in earnest (ptp. of *assevērāre*), equiv. to *as-* AS- + *sevēr-* (see SEVERE) + *-ātus* -ATE[1]]

as·sev·er·a·tion (ə sev′ə rā′shən), *n.* **1.** the act of asseverating. **2.** an emphatic assertion. [1550–60; < L *assevērātiōn-* (s. of *assevērātiō*). See ASSEVERATE, -ION] **—as·sev·er·a·tive** (ə sev′ə rā′tiv, -ər ə tiv), **as·sev·er·a·to·ry** (ə sev′ər ə tôr′ē, -tōr′ē), *adj.* **—as·sev′er·a′tive·ly,** *adv.*

ass·hole (as′hōl′), *n. Vulgar.* **1.** anus. **2.** *Slang.* **a.** a stupid, mean, or contemptible person. **b.** the worst part of a place or thing. —*adj.* **3.** *Slang.* stupid, mean, or contemptible. [1350–1400; ME *arshole* anus; see ASS[2], HOLE]

As·shur (ä′sho͝or), *n.* Assur.

as·sib·i·late (ə sib′ə lāt′), *v.,* **-lat·ed, -lat·ing.** *Phonet.* —*v.t.* **1.** to change into or pronounce with the accompaniment of a sibilant sound or sounds. —*v.i.* **2.** to change by assibilation. **3.** to become a sibilant or a sound containing a sibilant. [1835–45; < L *assibilātus* murmured, whispered at, hissed (ptp. of *assibilāre*). See AS-, SIBILATE] **—as·sib′i·la′tion,** *n.*

As·si·de·an (as′i dē′ən), *n. Judaism.* a member of a sect, characterized by its religious zeal and piety, that flourished in the 2nd century B.C. during the time of the Maccabees and vigorously resisted the Hellenization of Jewish culture and religion. Also, **As′si·dae′an, Hasidean, Hasidaean.** [1605–15; < Gk *Assidaî(oi)* (pl.) (< Heb *hasīdhīm* pious ones; cf. HASID) + -AN]

as·si·du·i·ty (as′i do͞o′i tē, -dyo͞o′-), *n., pl.* **-ties. 1.** constant or close application or effort; diligence; industry. **2. assiduities,** devoted or solicitous attentions. [1595–1605; < L *assiduitās.* See ASSIDUOUS, -ITY]

as·sid·u·ous (ə sij′o͞o əs), *adj.* **1.** constant; unremitting: *assiduous reading.* **2.** constant in application or effort; working diligently at a task; persevering; industrious; attentive: *an assiduous student.* [1530–40; < L *assiduus,* equiv. to *assid(ēre)* to sit near, beside, dwell close to (see ASSESS) + *-uus* deverbal adj. suffix; see -OUS] **—as·sid′u·ous·ly,** *adv.* **—as·sid′u·ous·ness,** *n.*
—Syn. 1. continuous, tireless, persistent. **2.** studious, diligent, sedulous. **—Ant. 1, 2.** inconstant, lazy.

as·sign (ə sīn′), *v.t.* **1.** to give or allocate; allot: *to assign rooms at a hotel.* **2.** to give out or announce as a task: *to assign homework.* **3.** to appoint, as to a post or duty: *to assign one to guard duty.* **4.** to designate; name; specify: *to assign a day for a meeting.* **5.** to ascribe; attribute; bring forward: *to assign a cause.* **6.** *Law.* to transfer: *to assign a contract.* **7.** *Mil.* to place permanently on duty with a unit or under a commander. —*v.i.* **8.** *Law.* to transfer property, esp. in trust or for the benefit of creditors. —*n.* **9.** Usually, **assigns.** *Law.* a person to whom the property or interest of another is or may be transferred; assignee: *my heirs and assigns.* [1250–1300; ME *assignen* < OF *assigner* < L *assignāre.* See AS-, SIGN] **—as·sign′er;** *Chiefly Law.* **as·sign·or** (ə sī nôr′, as′ə nôr′), *n.*
—Syn. 1. ASSIGN, ALLOCATE, ALLOT mean to apportion or measure out. To ASSIGN is to distribute available things, designating them to be given to or reserved for

CONCISE PRONUNCIATION KEY: act, cāpe, dâre, pärt; set, ēqual; *if,* ice; ox, ōver, ôrder, oil, bo͝ok, bo͞ot, out; up, ûrge; child; sing; shoe; thin, that; zh as in *treasure.* ə = *a* as in *alone, e* as in *system, i* as in *easily, o* as in *gallop, u* as in *circus;* ᵊ as in *fire* (fīᵊr), *hour* (ouᵊr). l and n can serve as syllabic consonants, as in *cradle* (krād′l), and *button* (but′n). See the full key inside the front cover.

specific persons or purposes: *to assign duties.* To ALLOCATE is to earmark or set aside parts of things available or expected in the future, each for a specific purpose: *to allocate income to various types of expenses.* To ALLOT implies making restrictions as to amount, size, purpose, etc., and then apportioning or assigning: *to allot spaces for parking.* **4.** fix, determine. **5.** adduce, allege, advance, show, offer.

as•sign•a•ble (ə sī′nə bəl), *adj.* **1.** capable of being specified: *The word has no assignable meaning in our language.* **2.** capable of being attributed: *This work is assignable to a 12th-century poet.* **3.** *Law.* capable of being assigned. [1250–1300; ME; see ASSIGN, -ABLE] **—as•sign′a•bil′i•ty,** *n.* **—as•sign′a•bly,** *adv.*

as•sig•nat (as′ig nat′; *Fr.* A sē nyA′), *n., pl.* **as•sig•nats** (as′ig nats′; *Fr.* A sē nyA′). *Fr. Hist.* one of the notes issued as paper currency from 1789 to 1796 by the revolutionary government on the security of confiscated lands. [1780–90; < F < L *assignātus* assigned (ptp. of *assignāre*). See ASSIGN, -ATE[1]]

as•sig•na•tion (as′ig nā′shən), *n.* **1.** an appointment for a meeting, esp. a lover's secret rendezvous. **2.** the act of assigning; assignment. [1400–50; late ME *assignacioun* < L *assignātiōn-* (s. of *assignātiō*). See ASSIGN, -ATION]

assigned′ coun′sel, any private lawyer designated by a city or county court to represent indigent defendants in criminal cases at public expense. Cf. **public defender.**

assigned′ risk′, *Insurance.* a risk that, under state law, is assigned to an insurer from a pool of insurers who would not otherwise accept it. [1945–50]

as•sign•ee (ə sī nē′, as′ə nē′), *n. Law.* a person to whom some right or interest is transferred, either for his or her own enjoyment or in trust. [1275–1325; ME *assigne* < MF, n. use of ptp. of *assigner* to ASSIGN; see -EE]

as•sign•ment (ə sīn′mənt), *n.* **1.** something assigned, as a particular task or duty: *She completed the assignment and went on to other jobs.* **2.** a position of responsibility, post of duty, or the like, to which one is appointed: *He left for his assignment in the Middle East.* **3.** an act of assigning; appointment. **4.** *Law.* **a.** the transference of a right, interest, or title, or the instrument of transfer. **b.** a transference of property to assignees for the benefit of creditors. [1350–1400; ME *assignement* < ML *assignāmentum.* See ASSIGN, -MENT] **—Syn. 1, 2.** obligation, job. **1.** See **task.**

as•sim•i•la•ble (ə sim′ə lə bəl), *adj.* capable of being assimilated. [1640–50; < ML *assimilābilis,* equiv. to L *assimilā(re)* (see ASSIMILATE) + *-bilis* -BLE] **—as•sim′i•la•bil′i•ty,** *n.*

as•sim•i•late (*v.* ə sim′ə lāt′; *n.* ə sim′ə lit, -lāt′), *v.,* **-lat•ed, -lat•ing,** *n.* **—***v.t.* **1.** to take in and incorporate as one's own; absorb: *He assimilated many new experiences on his European trip.* **2.** to bring into conformity with the customs, attitudes, etc., of a group, nation, or the like; adapt or adjust: *to assimilate the new immigrants.* **3.** *Physiol.* to convert (food) to substances suitable for incorporation into the body and its tissues. **4.** to cause to resemble (usually fol. by *to* or *with*). **5.** to compare; liken (usually fol. by *to* or *with*). **6.** *Phonet.* to modify by assimilation. **—***v.i.* **7.** to be or become absorbed. **8.** to conform or adjust to the customs, attitudes, etc., of a group, nation, or the like: *The new arrivals assimilated easily and quickly.* **9.** *Physiol.* (of food) to be converted into the substance of the body; be absorbed into the system. **10.** to bear a resemblance (usually fol. by *to* or *with*). **11.** *Phonet.* to become modified by assimilation. **—***n.* **12.** something that is assimilated. [1570–80; < L *assimilātus* likened to, made like (ptp. of *assimilāre*), equiv. to *as-* AS- + *simil-* (see SIMILAR) + *-ātus* -ATE[1]] **—as•sim′i•la′tor,** *n.*

as•sim•i•la•tion (ə sim′ə lā′shən), *n.* **1.** the act or process of assimilating; state or condition of being assimilated. **2.** *Physiol.* the conversion of absorbed food into the substance of the body. **3.** *Bot.* the total process of plant nutrition, including photosynthesis and the absorption of raw materials. **4.** *Sociol.* the merging of cultural traits from previously distinct cultural groups, not involving biological amalgamation. **5.** *Phonet.* the act or process by which a sound becomes identical with or similar to a neighboring sound in one or more defining characteristics, as place of articulation, voice or voicelessness, or manner of articulation, as in (gram′pä) for *grandpa.* Cf. **dissimilation** (def. 2). [1595–1605; < L *assimilātiōn-* (s. of *assimilātiō*). See ASSIMILATE, -ION]

as•sim•i•la•tion•ism (ə sim′ə lā′shə niz′əm), *n.* the practice or policy of assimilating or encouraging the assimilation of people from all races and cultures: *The family at first resisted the assimilationism of the New World.* [1950–55; ASSIMILATION + -ISM] **—as•sim′i•la′•tion•ist,** *n., adj.*

as•sim•i•la•tive (ə sim′ə lā′tiv, -lə tiv), *adj.* characterized by assimilation; assimilating. Also, **as•sim•i•la•to•ry** (ə sim′ə lə tôr′ē, -tōr′ē). [1520–30; < ML *assimilātīvus.* See ASSIMILATE, -IVE] **—as•sim′i•la′tive•ness,** *n.*

As•sin•i•boin (ə sin′ə boin′), *n., pl.* **-boins,** (*esp. collectively*) **-boin. 1.** a member of a Siouan people of northeastern Montana and adjacent parts of Canada. **2.** the dialect of Dakota spoken by the Assiniboin Indians. [1675–85; < CanF *Assiniboine* < Ojibwa (Saulteaux dial.) *assini·-pwa·n* lit., stone Sioux (equiv. to Proto-Algonquian **a?senyi* stone + **pwa·θa* enemy tribesman)]

As•sin•i•boine (ə sin′ə boin′), *n.* a river in S Canada, flowing S and E from SE Saskatchewan into the Red River in S Manitoba. 450 mi. (725 km) long.

CONCISE ETYMOLOGY KEY: <, descended or borrowed from; >, whence; b., blend of, blended; c., cognate with; cf., compare; deriv., derivative; equiv., equivalent; imit., imitative; obl., oblique; r., replacing; s., stem; sp., spelling, spelled; resp., respelling, respelled; trans., translation; ?, origin unknown; *, unattested; ‡, probably earlier than. See the full key inside the front cover.

As•si•si (ə sē′zē; *It.* äs sē′zē), *n.* a town in E Umbria, in central Italy: birthplace of St. Francis of Assisi. 24,002.

as•sist (ə sist′), *v.t.* **1.** to give support or aid to; help: *Please assist him in moving the furniture.* **2.** to be associated with as an assistant or helper. **—***v.i.* **3.** to give aid or help. **4.** to be present, as at a meeting or ceremony. **—***n.* **5.** *Sports.* **a.** *Baseball.* a play that helps to put out a batter or base runner. **b.** *Basketball, Ice Hockey.* a play that helps a teammate in gaining a goal. **c.** the official credit scored for such plays. **6.** a helpful act: *She finished her homework without an assist from her father.* **7.** *Mach.* an electrical, hydraulic, or mechanical means of increasing power, efficiency, or ease of use: *a luxury automobile equipped with assists for brakes, steering, windows, and seat adjustment.* [1505–15; < L *assistere* to stand by, help, equiv. to *as-* AS- + *sistere* to (cause to) stand (*si-* reduplicative prefix + *-ste-* (var. of *sta-* STAND) + *-re* inf. suffix)] **—as•sist′er;** *Chiefly Law,* **as•sis′tor,** *n.* **—as•sist′ive,** *adj.* **—Syn. 1.** sustain, abet, befriend; back, promote. See **help. —Ant. 1.** hinder, frustrate.

as•sis•tance (ə sis′təns), *n.* the act of assisting; help; aid; support. [1375–1425; late ME *assistence* < ML *assistentia.* See ASSIST, -ENCE, -ANCE]

as•sis•tant (ə sis′tənt), *n.* **1.** a person who assists or gives aid and support; helper. **2.** a person who is subordinate to another in rank, function, etc.; one holding a secondary rank in an office or post: *He was assistant to the office manager.* **3.** something that aids and supplements another. **4.** a faculty member of a college or university who ranks below an instructor and whose responsibilities usually include grading papers, supervising laboratories, and assisting in teaching. **—***adj.* **5.** assisting; helpful. **6.** serving in an immediately subordinate position; of secondary rank: *an assistant coach.* [1400–50; late ME *assistent* < L *assistent-* (s. of *assistēns,* prp. of *assistere* to ASSIST); see -ENT, -ANT] **—Syn. 2.** aide, adjutant.

assis′tant profes′sor, a teacher in a college or university who ranks above an instructor and below an associate professor. [1850–55, *Amer.*] **—assis′tant profes′sorship.**

as•sis•tant•ship (ə sis′tənt ship′), *n.* a form of financial aid awarded to a student studying for a graduate degree at a college or university in which the student assists a professor, usually in academic or laboratory work. [1690–1700; ASSISTANT + -SHIP]

As•siut (ä syōōt′), *n.* Asyut.

as•size (ə sīz′), *n.* **1.** Usually, **assizes.** a trial session, civil or criminal, held periodically in specific locations in England, usually by a judge of a superior court. **2.** an edict, ordinance, or enactment made at a session of a legislative assembly. **3.** an inquest before members of a jury or assessors; a judicial inquiry. **4.** an action, writ, or verdict of an assize. **5.** judgment: *the last assize; the great assize.* **6.** a statute for the regulation and control of weights and measures or prices of general commodities in the market. [1250–1300; ME *asise* < OF: a sitting, n. use of fem. of *asis* seated at (ptp. of *aseeir*), equiv. to *a-* A-[5] + *-sis* < L *sēssum* (*sed-* s. of *sedēre* to SIT + *-tus* ptp. suffix)]

ass-kick (as′kik′), *v.i. Slang (vulgar).* to kick ass. See **kick** (def. 16). **—ass′-kick′er,** *n.*

ass-kiss•ing (as′kis′ing), *n. Slang (vulgar).* the practice or an instance of attempting to curry favor by the excessive use of compliments, praise, or the like. **—ass′-kiss′er,** *n.*

assn., association. Also, **Assn.**

assoc., 1. associate. **2.** associated. **3.** association.

as•so•ci•a•ble (ə sō′shē ə bəl, -sē-, -shə bəl), *adj.* **1.** capable of being associated. **2.** (of a nation or state) belonging to an economic association. **—***n.* **3.** an associable nation or state. [1605–15; ASSOCI(ATE) + -ABLE] **—as•so′ci•a•bil′i•ty, as•so′ci•a•ble•ness,** *n.*

as•so•ci•ate (*v.* ə sō′shē āt′, -sē-; *n., adj.,* ə sō′shē it, -āt′, -sē-), *v.,* **-at•ed, -at•ing,** *n., adj.* **—***v.t.* **1.** to connect or bring into relation, as thought, feeling, memory, etc.: *Many people associate dark clouds with depression and gloom.* **2.** to join as a companion, partner, or ally: *to associate oneself with a cause.* **3.** to unite; combine: *coal associated with shale.* **—***v.i.* **4.** to enter into union; unite. **5.** to keep company, as a friend, companion, or ally: *He was accused of associating with known criminals.* **6.** to join together as partners or colleagues. **—***n.* **7.** a person who shares actively in anything as a business, enterprise, or undertaking; partner; colleague; fellow worker: *He consulted with his associates before proceeding further.* **8.** a companion or comrade: *my most intimate associates.* **9.** a confederate; an accomplice or ally: *criminal associates.* **10.** anything usually accompanying or associated with another; an accompaniment or concomitant. **11.** a person who is admitted to a subordinate degree of membership in an association or institution: *an associate of the Royal Academy.* **—***adj.* **12.** connected, joined, or related, esp. as a companion or colleague; having equal or nearly equal responsibility: *an associate partner.* **13.** having subordinate status; without full rights and privileges: *an associate member.* **14.** allied; concomitant. [1400–50; late ME < L *associātus* joined to, united with (ptp. of *associāre*), equiv. to *as-* AS- + *soci-* (see SOCIAL) + *-ātus* -ATE[1]; cf. AF *associer* (v.), *associé* (n.)] **—as•so′ci•ate•ship′,** *n.* **—Syn. 1.** link. **7, 8.** See **acquaintance. —Ant. 1.** dissociate. **7–9.** adversary.

asso′ciated state′, a nation with limited sovereignty, esp. a former colony that now assumes responsibility for domestic affairs but continues to depend on the colonial ruler for defense and foreign policy. Also, **asso′ciate state′.** [1955–60]

Asso′ciate of Arts′, a degree granted esp. by junior colleges after completion of two years of study. *Abbr.:* A.A. Also called **asso′ciate's degree′.**

asso′ciate profes′sor, a teacher in a college or university who ranks above an assistant professor and below a professor. [1815–25] **—asso′ciate profes′•sorship.**

as•so•ci•a•tion (ə sō′sē ā′shən, -shē-), *n.* **1.** an organization of people with a common purpose and having a formal structure. **2.** the act of associating or state of being associated. **3.** friendship; companionship: *Their close association did not last long.* **4.** connection or combination. **5.** the connection or relation of ideas, feelings, sensations, etc.; correlation of elements of perception, reasoning, or the like. **6.** an idea, image, feeling, etc., suggested by or connected with something other than itself; an accompanying thought, emotion, or the like; an overtone or connotation: *My associations with that painting are of springlike days.* **7.** *Ecol.* a group of plants of one or more species living together under uniform environmental conditions and having a uniform and distinctive aspect. **8.** *Chem.* a weak form of chemical bonding involving aggregation of molecules of the same compound. **9.** See **touch football. 10.** *Astron.* See **stellar association.** [1525–35; (< MF) < ML *associātiōn-* (s. of *associātiō*). See ASSOCIATE, -ION] **—as•so′ci•a′tion•al,** *adj.* **—Syn. 1.** alliance, union; society, company; band. **3.** fellowship.

associa′tion ar′ea, any of the regions of the cerebral cortex of the brain connected by numerous nerve fibers to all parts of both cerebral hemispheres and coordinating such higher activities as learning and reasoning. Also called **associa′tion cor′tex.** [1905–10]

associa′tion fi′ber, *Anat.* any of several nerve fibers connecting different areas of the cerebral cortex in the same hemisphere. [1875–80]

asso′cia′tion foot′ball, *Brit.* soccer. [1860–65]

as•so•ci•a•tion•ism (ə sō′sē ā′shə niz′əm, -shē ā′-), *n. Psychol.* any of several theories that explain complex psychological phenomena as being built up from the association of simple sensations, stimuli and responses, or other behavioral or mental elements considered as primary. Cf. **sensationism.** [1830–40, *Amer.*; ASSOCIATION + -ISM] **—as•so′ci•a′tion•ist,** *adj., n.* **—as•so′ci•a′•tion•is′tic,** *adj.*

associa′tion of stars′. *Astron.* See **stellar association.**

as•so•ci•a•tive (ə sō′shē ā′tiv, -sē-, -shə tiv), *adj.* **1.** pertaining to or resulting from association. **2.** tending to associate or unite. **3.** *Math., Logic.* **a.** (of an operation on a set of elements) giving an equivalent expression when elements are grouped without change of order, as $(a + b) + c = a + (b + c)$. **b.** having reference to this property: *associative law of multiplication.* [1805–15; ASSOCIATE + -IVE] **—as•so•ci•a•tive•ly** (ə sō′shē ā′tiv-lē, -ə tiv-, -sē-), *adv.* **—as•so•ci•a•tiv•i•ty** (ə sō′shē ə tiv′i tē, -sē-, -shə tiv′-), **as•so′ci•a′tive•ness,** *n.*

as•soil (ə soil′), *v.t. Archaic.* **1.** to absolve; acquit; pardon. **2.** to atone for. [1250–1300; ME *asoilen* < AF *asoiler,* OF *asoilier,* var. of *asoldre* < L *absolvere* to ABSOLVE] **—as•soil′ment,** *n.*

as•so•lu•ta (as′ə lōō′tə; *It.* äs′sô lōō′tä), *adj.* absolute; supreme: *a prima ballerina assoluta.* [< It, fem. of *assoluto* < L *absolūtus* ABSOLUTE]

as•so•nance (as′ə nəns), *n.* **1.** resemblance of sounds. **2.** Also called **vowel rhyme.** *Pros.* rhyme in which the same vowel sounds are used with different consonants in the stressed syllables of the rhyming words, as in *penitent* and *reticence.* **3.** partial agreement or correspondence. [1720–30; < F, equiv. to *asson(ant)* sounding in answer (see AS-, SONANT) + *-ance* -ANCE] **—as′so•nant,** *adj., n.* **—as•so•nan•tal** (as′ə nan′tl), **as′so•nan′tic,** *adj.*

as•sort (ə sôrt′), *v.t.* **1.** to distribute, place, or arrange according to kind or class; classify; sort. **2.** to furnish with a suitable assortment or variety of goods; make up of articles likely to suit a demand. **3.** *Archaic.* to group with others of the same or similar kind; connect or identify as of a similar class; associate (usually fol. by *with*). **—***v.i.* **4.** to agree in sort or kind; be matched or suited. **5.** to associate; consort. [1480–90; < MF *assorter.* See AS-, SORT] **—as•sort′a•tive, as•sort′ive,** *adj.* **—as•sort′a•tive•ly,** *adv.* **—as•sort′er,** *n.*

assort′ative mat′ing, *Animal Behav., Psychol.* the reproductive pairing of individuals that have more traits in common than would likely be the case if mating were random (contrasted with *disassortative mating*). Cf. **panmixia.** [1895–1900]

as•sort•ed (ə sôr′tid), *adj.* **1.** consisting of different or various kinds; miscellaneous: *assorted flavors; assorted sizes.* **2.** consisting of selected kinds; arranged in sorts or varieties: *rows of assorted vegetables.* **3.** matched; suited. [1790–1800; ASSORT + -ED[2]]

as•sort•ment (ə sôrt′mənt), *n.* **1.** the act of assorting; distribution; classification. **2.** a collection of various kinds of things; a mixed collection. [1605–15; ASSORT + -MENT]

ASSR, Autonomous Soviet Socialist Republic. Also, **A.S.S.R.**

asst., assistant.

as•suage (ə swāj′, ə swāzh′), *v.t.,* **-suaged, -suag•ing. 1.** to make milder or less severe; relieve; ease; mitigate: *to assuage one's grief; to assuage one's pain.* **2.** to appease; satisfy; allay; relieve: *to assuage one's hunger.* **3.** to soothe, calm, or mollify: *to assuage his fears; to assuage her anger.* [1250–1300; ME *aswagen* < OF *asouagier* < VL **assuāviāre,* equiv. to L *as-* AS- + *suāviāre,* v. deriv. of L *suāvis* agreeable to the taste, pleasant (cf. SUAVE; akin to SWEET)] **—as•suage′ment,** *n.* **—as•suag′er,** *n.* **—Syn. 1.** alleviate, lessen. **—Ant.** intensify.

As•suan (as′wän; *Arab.* äs wän′), *n.* Aswan. Also, **As•souan′.**

as•sua•sive (ə swā′siv), *adj.* soothing; alleviative. [1700–10; AS- + (PER)SUASIVE]

As•su•e•rus (as′o͞o er′əs, -ēr′-), *n. Douay Bible.* Ahasuerus.

as•sum•a•ble (ə so͞o′mə bəl), *adj.* capable of being assumed, as an office or an obligation: *Assumable mortgages are hard to find these days.* [1775–85; ASSUME + -ABLE] **—as•sum′a•bil′i•ty,** *n.* **—as•sum′a•bly,** *adv.*

as•sume (ə so͞om′), *v.t.,* **-sumed, -sum•ing. 1.** to take for granted or without proof; suppose; postulate; posit: *to assume that everyone wants peace.* **2.** to take upon oneself; undertake: *to assume an obligation.* **3.** to take over the duties or responsibilities of: *to assume the office of treasurer.* **4.** to take on (a particular character, quality, mode of life, etc.); adopt: *He assumed the style of an aggressive go-getter.* **5.** to take on; be invested or endowed with: *The situation assumed a threatening character.* **6.** to pretend to have or be; feign: *to assume a humble manner.* **7.** to appropriate or arrogate; seize; usurp: *to assume a right to oneself; to assume control.* **8.** to take upon oneself (the debts or obligations of another). **9.** *Archaic.* to take into relation or association; adopt. —*v.i.* **10.** to take something for granted; presume. [1400–50; late ME (< AF *assumer*) < L *assūmere* to take to, adopt, equiv. to *as-* AS- + *sūmere* to take up; see CONSUME] **—as•sum′er,** *n.*
—Syn. 1. presuppose. **6.** See **pretend.**

as•sumed (ə so͞omd′), *adj.* **1.** adopted in order to deceive; fictitious; pretended; feigned: *an assumed name; an assumed air of humility.* **2.** taken for granted; supposed: *His assumed innocence proved untrue.* **3.** usurped. [1615–25; ASSUME + -ED^{2}] **—as•sum•ed•ly** (ə so͞o′mid lē), *adv.*

assumed′ bond′, a bond issued by one corporation and assumed as an obligation by another.

as•sum•ing (ə so͞o′ming), *adj.* taking too much for granted; presumptuous. [1595–1605; ASSUME + -ING^{2}] **—as•sum′ing•ly,** *adv.*

as•sump•sit (ə sump′sit), *n. Law.* **1.** a legal action for a breach of contract or promise not under seal. **2.** an actionable promise. [1605–15; < L: he has taken upon himself, he has undertaken]

as•sump•tion (ə sump′shən), *n.* **1.** something taken for granted; a supposition: *a correct assumption.* **2.** the act of taking for granted or supposing. **3.** the act of taking to or upon oneself. **4.** the act of taking possession of something: *the assumption of power.* **5.** arrogance; presumption. **6.** the taking over of another's debts or obligations. **7.** *Eccles.* **a.** (*often cap.*) the bodily taking up into heaven of the Virgin Mary. **b.** (*cap.*) a feast commemorating this, celebrated on August 15. [1250–1300; ME *assumpcioun, assompcioun, assumsion* < L *assūmptiōn-* (s. of *assūmptiō*), equiv. to *assūmpt(us)* taken up (ptp. of *assūmere;* see ASSUME) + *-iōn-* -ION]
—Syn. 1, 2. presupposition. **1.** hypothesis, conjecture, guess, postulate, theory. **3.** presumption. **5.** effrontery, forwardness.

As•sump•tion•ist (ə sump′shə nist), *n.* See **Augustinian of the Assumption.** [ASSUMPTION + -IST]

as•sump•tive (ə sump′tiv), *adj.* **1.** taken for granted. **2.** characterized by assumption: *an assumptive statement.* **3.** presumptuous. [1605–15; < L *assūmptīvus,* equiv. to *assūmpt(us)* (ptp.) (see ASSUMPTION) + *-īvus* -IVE] **—as•sump′tive•ly,** *adv.*

As•sur (as′ər), *n.* the god of war and supreme national god of Assyria. Also, **Ashur, Asshur, Asur.**

as•sur•ance (ə sho͝or′əns, -shûr′-), *n.* **1.** a positive declaration intended to give confidence: *He received assurances of support for the project.* **2.** promise or pledge; guaranty; surety: *He gave his assurance that the job would be done.* **3.** full confidence; freedom from doubt; certainty: *to act in the assurance of success.* **4.** freedom from timidity; self-confidence; belief in one's abilities: *She acted with speed and assurance.* **5.** presumptuous boldness; impudence. **6.** *Chiefly Brit.* insurance. [1325–75; ME *ass(e)ura(u)nce* < MF *ass(e)urance.* See ASSURE, -ANCE]
—Syn. 2. warranty, oath. **3.** See **trust. 4.** See **confidence. 5.** effrontery, impertinence, nerve, cheek.
—Ant. 3–5. uncertainty.

As•sur•ba•ni•pal (ä′so͝or bä′nē päl′), *n.* Ashurbanipal.

as•sure (ə sho͝or′, ə shûr′), *v.t.,* **-sured, -sur•ing. 1.** to declare earnestly to; inform or tell positively; state with confidence to: *She assured us that everything would turn out all right.* **2.** to cause to know surely; reassure: *He assured himself that no one was left on the bus.* **3.** to pledge or promise; give surety of; guarantee: *He was assured a job in the spring.* **4.** to make (a future event) sure; ensure: *This contract assures the company's profit this month.* **5.** to secure or confirm; render safe or stable: *to assure a person's position.* **6.** to give confidence to; encourage. **7.** *Chiefly Brit.* to insure, as against loss. [1325–75; ME *as(e)uren, assuren* < OF *aseurer* < LL *assēcūrāre,* equiv. to L *as-* AS- + *sēcūr-* (see SECURE) + *-ā-* thematic vowel + *-re* inf. suffix] **—as•sur′er, as•su′ror,** *n.*

as•sured (ə sho͝ord′, ə shûrd′), *adj.* **1.** guaranteed; sure; certain; secure: *an assured income.* **2.** bold; confident; authoritative: *His art was both assured and facile.* **3.** boldly presumptuous. **4.** *Chiefly Brit.* insured, as against loss. —*n.* **5.** *Insurance.* **a.** the beneficiary under a policy. **b.** the person whose life or property is covered by a policy. [1325–75; ME; see ASSURE, -ED^{2}] **—as•sur•ed•ly** (ə sho͝or′id lē, ə shûr′-), *adv.* **—as•sur′ed•ness,** *n.*

as•sur•gent (ə sûr′jənt), *adj. Bot.* curving upward, as leaves; ascendant. [1570–80; < L *assurgent-* (s. of *assurgēns* rising up, prp. of *assurgere*). See AS-, SURGENT] **—as•sur′gen•cy,** *n.*

As•sur•na•sir•pal II (ä′so͝or nä′zir päl′). See **Ashurnasirpal II.**

Assyr., Assyrian.

As•syr•i•a (ə sir′ē ə), *n.* an ancient empire in SW Asia: greatest extent from ab. 750 to 612 B.C. *Cap.:* Nineveh.

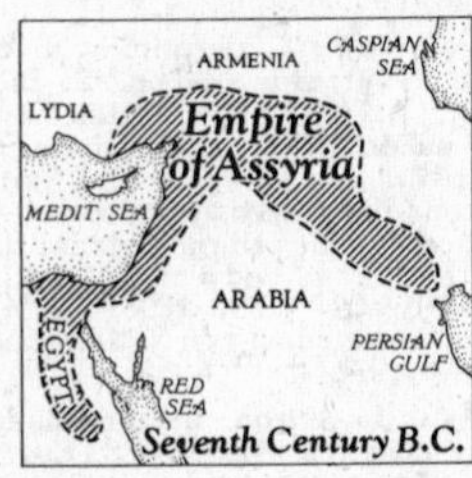

As•syr•i•an (ə sir′ē ən), *adj.* **1.** of or pertaining to Assyria, its inhabitants, or their language. —*n.* **2.** a native or an inhabitant of Assyria. **3.** the dialect of Akkadian spoken in Assyria. Cf. **Akkadian** (def. 1). [1585–95; ASSYRI(A) + -AN]

As•syr•i•ol•o•gy (ə sir′ē ol′ə jē), *n.* the study of the history, language, etc., of the ancient Assyrians. [1820–30; ASSYRI(A) + -O- + -LOGY] **—As•syr•i•o•log•i•cal** (ə sir′ē ə loj′i kəl), *adj.* **—As•syr′i•ol′o•gist,** *n.*

As•syr•o-Bab•y•lo•ni•an (ə sir′ō bab′ə lō′nē ən), *adj.* **1.** of or pertaining to Assyria and Babylonia. —*n.* **2.** the language of Assyria and Babylonia; Akkadian. [1825–35; ASSYR(IA) + -O- + BABYLONIAN]

AST, Atlantic Standard Time. See under **standard time.** Also, **A.S.T., a.s.t.**

A•staire (ə stâr′), *n.* **Fred,** 1899–1987, U.S. dancer and actor.

A star, *Astron.* a blue to white star, as Altair, Sirius, or Vega, having a surface temperature between 7500 and 10,000 K and an absorption spectrum dominated by Balmer-series lines of hydrogen. Cf. **spectral type.**

a•star•board (ə stär′bərd), *adv. Naut.* toward or on the starboard side. [1620–30; A-^{1} + STARBOARD]

As•tar•te (a stär′tē), *n.* **1.** an ancient Semitic deity, goddess of fertility and reproduction worshiped by the Phoenicians and Canaanites. **2.** (*l.c.*) Also called **chestnut clam.** any of several marine bivalve mollusks of the genus *Astarte,* having a somewhat triangular, chestnut-brown shell.

a•sta•sia (ə stā′zhə, -zhē ə, -zē ə), *n. Med.* inability to stand due to a limitation or absence of muscular coordination. Cf. **abasia.** [1885–90; < Gk *astasía* instability, equiv. to *ástat(os)* (see ASTATIC) + *-ia* -IA]

a•stat•ic (ā stat′ik), *adj.* **1.** unstable; unsteady. **2.** *Physics.* having no tendency to take a definite position or direction. [1820–30; < Gk *ástat(os)* not steadfast, unstable (*a-* A-^{6} + *statós* standing) + -IC; see STATIC] **—a•stat′i•cal•ly,** *adv.* **—a•stat•i•cism** (ā stat′ə siz′əm), *n.*

astat′ic galvanom′eter, *Elect.* a galvanometer that is unaffected by the earth's magnetic field and is used for measuring small currents. [1865–70]

as•ta•tine (as′tə tēn′ -tin), *n. Chem.* a rare element of the halogen family. *Symbol:* At; *at. no.:* 85. [1945–50; < Gk *ástat(os)* not steadfast, unstable (see ASTATIC) + -INE^{2}]

as•ter (as′tər), *n.* **1.** any composite plant of the genus *Aster,* having rays varying from white or pink to blue around a yellow disk. **2.** a plant of some allied genus, as the China aster. **3.** *Cell Biol.* a structure formed in a cell during mitosis, composed of astral rays radiating about the centrosome. **4.** *Furniture.* sunflower (def. 2). [1595–1605; < L < Gk *astḗr* STAR]

aster,
Aster novae-angliae

-aster^{1}, a diminutive or pejorative suffix denoting something that imperfectly resembles or mimics the true thing: *criticaster; poetaster; oleaster.* [< L]

-aster^{2}, *Chiefly Biol.* a combining form with the meaning "star," used in the formation of compound words: *diaster.* [< Gk *astḗr* STAR; cf. ASTRO-]

as•ter•a•ceous (as′tə rā′shəs), *adj. Bot.* belonging to the Asteraceae, an alternative name for the plant family Compositae. Cf. **composite family.** [1875–80; ASTER + -ACEOUS]

as′ter dai′sy. See **Arctic daisy.**

a•ster•e•og•no•sis (ə ster′ē og nō′sis, ā ster′-, ə stēr′-, ā stēr′-), *n. Pathol.* the inability to determine the shape of an object by touching or feeling it. [1895–1900; A-^{6} + STEREO- + -GNOSIS]

as•te•ri•at•ed (a stēr′ē ā′tid), *adj. Mineral.* exhibiting asterism. [1810–20; < Gk *astéri(os)* starry (deriv. of *astḗr* ASTER) + -ATE^{1} + -ED^{2}]

as•ter•isk (as′tə risk), *n.* **1.** a small starlike symbol (*), used in writing and printing as a reference mark or to indicate omission, doubtful matter, etc. **2.** *Ling.* the figure of a star (*) used to mark an utterance that would be considered ungrammatical or otherwise unacceptable by native speakers of a language, as in **I enjoy to ski.* **3.** *Historical Ling.* the figure of a star (*) used to mark a hypothetical or reconstructed form that is not attested in a text or inscription. **4.** something in the shape of a star or asterisk. —*v.t.* **5.** to mark with an asterisk: *to asterisk a word that requires a footnote.* [1350–1400; ME < L *asteriscus* < Gk *asterískos* small star, equiv. to *aster-,* s. of *astḗr* STAR + *-iskos* dim. suffix] **—as′ter•isk•less,** *adj.*
—Pronunciation. While ASTERISK is usually said as (as′tə risk), with the (s) sound in the final syllable preceding the (k), a metathesized pronunciation is also heard, in which the (s) and (k) change places, producing (as′tə riks). This pronunciation, resulting in part from analogy with plural forms like *kicks* and *sticks,* can sometimes lead to a false analysis of (as′tə riks) as a plural pronunciation, with a corresponding singular (as′tə rik). The metathesized pronunciation, although occasionally heard among educated speakers, is usually considered nonstandard, as is the pronunciation with no (s) in the final syllable.

as•ter•ism (as′tə riz′əm), *n.* **1.** *Astron.* **a.** a group of stars. **b.** a constellation. **2.** *Mineral.* a property of some crystallized minerals of showing a starlike luminous figure in transmitted light or, in a cabochon-cut stone, by reflected light. **3.** three asterisks (⁂ or ⁎⁎⁎) printed to draw attention to a passage it precedes. [1590–1600; < Gk *asterism(ós)* a marking with stars. See ASTERISK, -ISM] **—as′ter•is′mal,** *adj.*

a•stern (ə stûrn′), *adv.* **1.** in a position behind a specified vessel or aircraft: *The cutter was following close astern.* **2.** in a backward direction: *The steamer went astern at half speed.* [1620–30; A-^{1} + STERN^{2}]

a•ster•nal (ā stûr′nl), *adj. Anat., Zool.* not reaching to or connected with the sternum. [1840–50; A-^{6} + STERNAL]

as•ter•oid (as′tə roid′), *n.* **1.** Also called **minor planet.** *Astron.* any of the thousands of small bodies of from 480 miles (775 km) to less than one mile (1.6 km) in diameter that revolve about the sun in orbits lying mostly between those of Mars and Jupiter. **2.** *Zool.* an asteroidean; a starfish. —*adj.* **3.** starlike. [1795–1805; < Gk *asteroeidḗs* starry, starlike. See ASTERISK, -OID] **—as′ter•oi′dal,** *adj.*

as′teroid belt′, *Astron.* the region of space between the orbits of Mars and Jupiter in which most asteroids are located.

As•ter•oi•de•a (as′tə roi′dē ə), *n.* the class comprising the starfishes. [< NL, equiv. to *Aster(ias)* a starfish genus (< Gk *asterías* starry, deriv. of *astḗr* STAR) + *-oidea* -OIDEA]

as•ter•oi•de•an (as′tə roi′dē ən), *n.* **1.** an echinoderm of the class Asteroidea, comprising the starfishes. —*adj.* **2.** belonging or pertaining to the Asteroidea. [ASTEROIDE(A) + -AN]

As•te•ro•pae•us (as′tə rō pē′əs), *n.* (in the *Iliad*) a Trojan ally slain by Achilles.

as′ter yel′lows, *Plant Pathol.* a dwarfing and yellowing of asters and various other plants, caused by a mycoplasma transmitted by a leafhopper. [1920–25]

as•the•ni•a (as thē′nē ə), *n.* lack or loss of strength; weakness. [1795–1805; < NL < Gk *asthéneia* weakness, equiv. to *asthene-,* s. of *asthenḗs* (*a-* A-^{6} + *sthene-,* var. s. of *sthénos* strength) + *-ia* -IA]

as•then•ic (as then′ik), *adj.* **1.** of, pertaining to, or characterized by asthenia; weak. **2.** (of a physical type) having a slight build or slender body structure. Cf. **athletic** (def. 5), **pyknic** (def. 1). —*n.* **3.** a person of the asthenic type. [1780–90; < Gk *asthenikós,* equiv. to *asthen-* (see ASTHENIA) + *-ikos* -IC]

as•the•no•pi•a (as′thə nō′pē ə), *n. Ophthalm.* a fatigue or tiring of the eyes, usually characterized by discomfort, dimness of vision, and headache, caused by overuse of the visual organs, dysfunction of the ocular muscles, and incorrect refraction. [< Gk *asthen(ḗs)* frail (see ASTHENIA) + -OPIA] **—as•the•nop•ic** (as′thə nop′ik), *adj.*

as•then•o•sphere (as then′ə sfēr′), *n. Geol.* the region below the lithosphere, variously estimated as being from fifty to several hundred miles (eighty-five to several hundred kilometers) thick, in which the rock is less rigid than that above and below but rigid enough to transmit transverse seismic waves. [1910–15; < Gk *asthen(ḗs)* frail (see ASTHENIA) + -O- + -SPHERE]

asth•ma (az′mə, as′-), *n. Pathol.* a paroxysmal, often allergic disorder of respiration, characterized by bronchospasm, wheezing, and difficulty in expiration, often accompanied by coughing and a feeling of constriction in the chest. Also called **bronchial asthma.** [1350–1400; ME < Gk: a panting (akin to *aázein* to breathe hard); r. ME *asma* < ML < Gk *ásthma*]

asth•mat•ic (az mat′ik, as-), *adj.* Also, **asth•mat′i•cal. 1.** suffering from asthma. **2.** pertaining to asthma: *an asthmatic wheeze.* —*n.* **3.** a person suffering from asthma. [1535–45; < L *asthmaticus* < Gk *asthmatikós,* equiv. to *asthmat-* (s. of *ásthma*) ASTHMA + *-ikos* -IC] **—asth•mat′i•cal•ly,** *adv.*

As•ti (ä′stē; *Eng.* as′tē), *n.* a city in the Piedmont region of Italy, S of Turin: center of wine-producing region. 76,950.

as•tig•mat•ic (as′tig mat′ik), *Ophthalm.* —*adj.* **1.** pertaining to, exhibiting, or correcting astigmatism. —*n.*

2. a person who has astigmatism. [1840–50; A-[6] + STIGMATIC] —**as′tig·mat′i·cal·ly,** *adv.*

a·stig·ma·tism (ə stig′mə tiz′əm), *n.* **1.** Also called **a·stig·mi·a** (ə stig′mē ə). *Ophthalm.* a refractive error of the eye in which parallel rays of light from an external source do not converge on a single focal point on the retina. **2.** *Optics.* an aberration of a lens or other optical system in which the image of a point is spread out along the axis of the system. [1840–50; ASTIGMAT(IC) + -ISM]

a·stig·ma·tiz·er (ə stig′mə tī′zər), *n.* *Optics.* a cylindrical lens used in a rangefinder to draw out the point image of a point source into a line. [A-[6] + STIGMATIZER]

as·tig·mat·o·scope (as′tig mat′ə skōp′), *n.* *Ophthalm.* an instrument for determining the presence and severity of astigmatism. [ASTIGMAT(ISM) + -O- + -SCOPE]

a·stig·ma·tos·co·py (ə stig′mə tos′kə pē), *n., pl.* **-pies.** *Ophthalm.* examination by means of an astigmatoscope. [ASTIGMAT(ISM) + -O- + -SCOPY]

as·tig·mom·e·ter (as′tig mom′i tər), *n.* *Ophthalm.* an apparatus for measuring the degree of astigmatism. Also, **a·stig·ma·tom·e·ter** (ə stig′mə tom′i tər). [ASTIGM(ATISM) + -O- + -METER] —**as′tig·mom′e·try, a·stig′ma·tom′e·try,** *n.*

a·stig·mo·scope (ə stig′mə skōp′), *n.* *Ophthalm.* astigmatoscope.

a·stil·be (ə stil′bē), *n.* any plant of the genus *Astilbe,* of the saxifrage family, having spirelike clusters of small white, pink, or reddish flowers. [1825; < NL, equiv. to *a-* A-[6] + Gk *stilbḗ,* fem. of *stilbós* glittering]

a·stir (ə stûr′), *adj.* **1.** moving or stirring, esp. with much activity or excitement: *The field was astir with small animals, birds, and insects.* **2.** up and about; out of bed. [bef. 1000; ME, OE; see A-[1], STIR[1]]

As′ti spu·man′te, a sweet, sparkling Italian white wine with a muscat flavor. Also, **As′ti Spu·man′te.** [< It: lit., effervescent Asti; see ASTI, SPUME, -ANT]

ASTM, American Society for Testing Materials. Also, **A.S.T.M.**

As·to·lat (as′tl at′, -ät′), *n.* a place in the Arthurian romances, possibly in Surrey, England.

a·stom·a·tous (ā stom′ə təs, ā stō′mə-), *adj.* *Zool., Bot.* having no mouth, stoma, or stomata. [1850–55; A-[6] + STOMATOUS]

As·ton (as′tən), *n.* **Francis William,** 1877–1945, English physicist and chemist: Nobel prize for chemistry 1922.

As′ton dark′ space′, *Physics.* the dark region between the cathode and the cathode glow in a vacuum tube, occurring when the pressure is low. [named after F. W. ASTON]

as·ton·ied (ə ston′ēd), *adj.* *Archaic.* dazed; bewildered; filled with consternation. [1300–50; ME, ptp. of *astonyen* to ASTONISH; see -ED[2]]

as·ton·ish (ə ston′ish), *v.t.* to fill with sudden and overpowering surprise or wonder; amaze: *Her easy humor and keen intellect astonished me.* [1525–35; ME *astonyen, astonen,* prob. < dial. OF *astoner, OF *estoner < VL *extonāre, for L *attonāre* to strike with lightning, equiv. to *ex-* EX-[1], *at-* AT- + *tonāre* to THUNDER; extended by -ISH[2], perh. reflecting AF *astonir < dial. OF] —**as·ton′ished·ly,** *adv.* —**as·ton′ish·er,** *n.*
—**Syn.** astound, startle, shock. See **surprise.**

as·ton·ish·ing (ə ston′i shing), *adj.* causing astonishment or surprise; amazing: *an astonishing victory; an astonishing remark.* [1520–30; ASTONISH + -ING[2]] —**as·ton′ish·ing·ly,** *adv.* —**as·ton′ish·ing·ness,** *n.*

as·ton·ish·ment (ə ston′ish mənt), *n.* **1.** overpowering wonder or surprise; amazement: *He looked with astonishment at his friends.* **2.** an object or cause of amazement. [1570–80; ASTONISH + -MENT]

As·tor (as′tər), *n.* **1. John Jacob,** 1763–1848, U.S. capitalist and fur merchant. **2. Nancy (Lang·horne)** (lang′hôrn′, -ərn), **Viscountess,** 1879–1964, first woman member of Parliament in England.

as·tound (ə stound′), *v.t.* **1.** to overwhelm with amazement; astonish greatly; shock with wonder or surprise. —*adj.* **2.** *Archaic.* astonished; astounded. [1275–1325; ME *astoun(e)d,* ptp. of *astonen,* var. of *astonyen* to ASTONISH] —**as·tound′ment,** *n.*
—**Syn. 1.** See **surprise.**

as·tound·ing (ə stoun′ding), *adj.* capable of overwhelming with amazement; stunningly surprising. [1580–90; ASTOUND + -ING[2]] —**as·tound′ing·ly,** *adv.*

astr., **1.** astronomer. **2.** astronomical. **3.** astronomy.

as·tra·chan (as′trə kən, -kan′), *n.* **1.** astrakhan. **2.** (*cap.*) *Hort.* a tart, usually red or yellow variety of apple.

a·strad·dle (ə strad′l), *adv., adj., prep.* astride with one leg on each side of; astride: *sitting astraddle a fence.* [1695–1705; A-[1] + STRADDLE]

as·tra·gal (as′trə gəl), *n.* *Archit., Furniture.* **1.** a small convex molding cut into the form of a string of beads. Cf. **bead and reel.** **2.** a plain convex molding; bead. **3.** a molding attached to one or both meeting stiles of a pair of double doors in order to prevent drafts. [1555–65; < L *astragalus* < Gk *astrágalos* a vertebra, the huckle-bone, a molding, a kind of vetch; in pl., dice (i.e., huckle-bones)]

as·trag·a·lus (a strag′ə ləs), *n., pl.* **-li** (-lī′). *Zool.* (in higher vertebrates) one of the proximal bones of the tarsus; talus. [1535–45; < NL; see ASTRAGAL] —**as·trag′a·lar,** *adj.*

as·tra·khan (as′trə kən, -kan′), *n.* **1.** a fur of young lambs, with lustrous, closely curled wool, from Astrakhan. **2.** Also called **as′trakhan cloth′.** a fabric with curled pile resembling astrakhan fur. Also, **astrachan.** [1760–70]

As·tra·khan (as′trə kan′; *Russ.* u STRU KHÄN′), *n.* a city in the S Russian Federation in Europe, at the mouth of the Volga. 461,000.

as·tral (as′trəl), *adj.* **1.** pertaining to or proceeding from the stars; stellar; star-shaped. **2.** *Biol.* pertaining to, consisting of, or resembling an aster; having a discoid, radiate flower head. **3.** *Theosophy.* noting a supersensible substance pervading all space and forming the substance of a second body **(astral body)** belonging to each individual. It accompanies the individual through life, is able to leave the human body at will, and survives the individual after death. [1595–1605; (< MF) < LL *astrālis,* equiv. to L *ast(rum)* star (< Gk *ástron*) + *-ālis* -AL[1]] —**as′tral·ly,** *adv.*

as′tral bod′y, **1.** *Astron.* a star, planet, comet, or other heavenly body. **2.** *Theosophy.* See under **astral** (def. 3). [1685–95]

As·tran·gi·a (ə strān′jē ə), *n.* a genus of corals forming small, encrusting colonies, found in shallow waters off both coasts of the U.S. [1848; < NL < Gk *ástr(on)* STAR + *angeî(on)* vessel + *-a* -A[2]]

as·tra·pho·bi·a (as′trə fō′bē ə), *n.* *Psychiatry.* an abnormal fear of thunder and lightning. Also, **as·tra·po·pho·bi·a** (as′trə pə fō′bē ə). [< Gk *astra(pḗ)* lightning + -PHOBIA]

a·stray (ə strā′), *adv., adj.* **1.** out of the right way; off the correct or known road, path, or route: *Despite specific instructions, they went astray and got lost.* **2.** away from that which is right; into error, confusion, or undesirable action or thought: *They were led astray by their lust for money.* [1250–1300; ME *astraye* < AF *astraié, OF *estraié,* ptp. of *estraier;* see STRAY]

as·trict (ə strikt′), *v.t.* **1.** to bind fast; constrain. **2.** to bind morally or legally. [1505–15; < L *astrictus* drawn together, bound, tightened (ptp. of *astringere*), equiv. to *a-* A-[5] + *strig-* (var. s. of *stringere* to draw) + *-tus* ptp. suffix. See ASTRINGE] —**as·tric′tion,** *n.*

As·trid (as′trid; *Norw.* äs′trē), *n.* a female given name: from Scandinavian, meaning "divine strength."

a·stride (ə strīd′), *prep.* **1.** with a leg on each side of; straddling: *She sat astride the horse.* **2.** on both sides of: *Budapest lies astride the river.* **3.** in a dominant position within: *Napoleon stands astride the early 19th century like a giant.* —*adv., adj.* **4.** in a posture of striding or straddling; with legs apart or on either side of something. [1655–65; A-[1] + STRIDE]

as·tringe (ə strinj′), *v.t.,* **-tringed, -tring·ing.** to compress; bind together; constrict. [1515–25; < L *astringere* to draw together, equiv. to *a-* A-[5] + *stringere* to draw; see STRINGENT]

as·trin·gent (ə strin′jənt), *adj.* **1.** *Med.* contracting; constrictive; styptic. **2.** harshly biting; caustic: *his astringent criticism.* **3.** stern or severe; austere. **4.** sharply incisive; pungent: *astringent wit.* —*n.* **5.** *Med.* a substance that contracts the tissues or canals of the body, thereby diminishing discharges, as of mucus or blood. **6.** a cosmetic that cleans the skin and constricts the pores. [1535–45; < L *astringent-* (s. of *astringēns*) prp. of *astringere* to ASTRINGE; see -ENT] —**as·trin′gen·cy,** *n.* —**as·trin′gent·ly,** *adv.*
—**Syn. 2, 3.** sharp, harsh, rigorous. See **acid.**

as·trin·ger (as′trin jər), *n.* *Falconry.* a person who trains and flies short-winged hawks, as the goshawk. Also, **austringer, ostringer.** [1425–75; late ME *ostringer,* alter., with intrusive *n,* as in PASSENGER, of MF *ostricier,* deriv. of *ostour* hawk < ML *auceptor,* L *acceptor,* alter. of *accipiter* ACCIPITER]

as·tri·on·ics (as′trē on′iks), *n.* (*used with a singular v.*) *Rocketry.* the science dealing with the application of electronics to astronautics. [ASTR(O)- + -I- + (ELECTR)ONICS]

astro-, a combining form with the meaning "pertaining to stars or celestial bodies, or to activities, as spaceflight, taking place outside the earth's atmosphere," used in the formation of compound words: *astronautics; astrophotography.* Cf. **cosmo-.** [< Gk, comb. form of *ástron* a star, constellation, akin to *astḗr* STAR; cf. ASTER, -ASTER[2]]

as·tro·ar·chae·ol·o·gy (as′trō är′kē ol′ə jē), *n.* archaeoastronomy. Also, **as′tro·ar′che·ol′o·gy.** [1970–75; ASTRO- + ARCHAEOLOGY]

as·tro·bi·ol·o·gy (as′trō bī ol′ə jē), *n.* (not in technical use) exobiology. [1950–55; ASTRO- + BIOLOGY] —**as·tro·bi·o·log·i·cal** (as′trō bī′ə loj′i kəl), *adj.*

as·tro·bleme (as′trə blēm′), *n.* *Geol.* an erosional scar on the earth's surface, produced by the impact of a cosmic body, as a meteorite or asteroid. Cf. **crater** (def. 2). [1965–70; < ASTRO- + *-bleme* (< Gk *blêma* shot, wound)]

as·tro·chem·is·try (as′trō kem′ə strē), *n.* a branch of astronomy and chemistry dealing with the chemical composition and evolution of the universe and its parts. [1970–75; ASTRO- + CHEMISTRY] —**as·tro·chem·i·cal** (as′trō kem′i kəl), *adj.* —**as′tro·chem′i·cal·ly,** *adv.*

as·tro·cyte (as′trə sīt′), *n.* *Cell Biol.* a star-shaped neuroglial cell of ectodermal origin. [1895–1900; ASTRO- + -CYTE] —**as·tro·cyt·ic** (as′trə sit′ik), *adj.*

as·tro·dome (as′trə dōm′), *n.* a transparent dome on top of the fuselage of an aircraft, through which observations are made for celestial navigation. Also called **as′tro hatch′** (as′trō). [1940–45; ASTRO- + DOME]

as·tro·dy·nam·ics (as′trō dī nam′iks), *n.* (*used with a singular v.*) the science dealing with the paths of space vehicles. [1950–55; ASTRO- + DYNAMICS]

as·tro·gate (as′trə gāt′), *v.i., v.t.,* **-gat·ed, -gat·ing.** to navigate in outer space. [ASTRO- + (NAVI)GATE] —**as′tro·ga′tion,** *n.* —**as′tro·ga′tor,** *n.*

as·tro·ge·ol·o·gy (as′trō jē ol′ə jē), *n.* the science dealing with the structure and composition of planets and other bodies in the solar system. [ASTRO- + GEOLOGY] —**as·tro·ge·o·log·ic** (as′trō jē′ə loj′ik), *adj.*

as·tro·graph (as′trə graf′, -gräf′), *n.* a navigational device for projecting altitude curves of the stars and planets onto charts or plotting sheets. [ASTRO- + -GRAPH] —**as·tro·graph·ic** (as′trə graf′ik), *adj.* —**as·trog·ra·phy** (ə strog′rə fē), *n.*

as·troid (as′troid), *n.* *Geom.* a hypocycloid with four cusps. [ASTR(O)- + -OID]

as′tro·in·er′tial guid′ance (as′trō i nûr′shəl). See **celestial guidance.**

astrol., **1.** astrologer. **2.** astrological. **3.** astrology.

as·tro·labe (as′trə lāb′), *n.* an astronomical instrument for taking the altitude of the sun or stars and for the solution of other problems in astronomy and navigation: used by Greek astronomers from about 200 B.C. and by Arab astronomers from the Middle Ages until superseded by the sextant. [1325–75; ME, var. of *astrolabie* < ML *astrolabium* < LGk *astrolábion,* Gk *astrolábon* (neut. of *astrolábos,* adj. used as n.), equiv. to *ástro(n)* STAR + *lab-* (var. s. of *lambánein* to take, seize) + *-on* neut. suffix] —**as·tro·lab·i·cal** (as′trə lab′i kəl, -lā′bi-), *adj.*

as·trol·o·gy (ə strol′ə jē), *n.* **1.** the study that assumes and attempts to interpret the influence of the heavenly bodies on human affairs. **2.** *Obs.* the science of astronomy. [1325–75; ME < L *astrologia* < Gk. See ASTRO-, -LOGY] —**as·trol′o·ger, as·trol′o·gist,** *n.* —**as·tro·log·i·cal** (a′strə loj′i kəl), **as′tro·log′ic, as·trol·o·gous** (ə strol′ə gəs), *adj.* —**as′tro·log′i·cal·ly,** *adv.*

as·tro·man·cy (as′trə man′sē), *n.* divination by means of the stars. [1645–55; < ML *astromantia* < Gk *astromanteia.* See ASTRO-, -MANCY] —**as′tro·man′cer,** *n.* —**as′tro·man′tic,** *adj.*

as·tro·me·te·or·ol·o·gy (as′trō mē′tē ə rol′ə jē), *n.* the study of the theoretical effects of astronomical bodies and forces on the earth's atmosphere. [1860–65; ASTRO- + METEOROLOGY] —**as·tro·me·te·or·o·log·i·cal** (as′trō mē′tē ər ə loj′i kəl), *adj.* —**as′tro·me′te·or·ol′o·gist,** *n.*

as′tromet′ric bi′nary, *Astron.* a binary star that can be recognized as such because of its undulating proper motion. [1975–80]

as·trom·e·try (ə strom′i trē), *n.* the branch of astronomy that deals with the measurement of the positions and motions of the celestial bodies. Also called **positional astronomy.** [1865–70; ASTRO- + -METRY] —**as·tro·met·ric** (as′trō me′trik), **as′tro·met′ri·cal,** *adj.*

astron., **1.** astronomer. **2.** astronomical. **3.** astronomy.

as·tro·naut (as′trə nôt′, -not′), *n.* a person engaged in or trained for spaceflight. [1925–30; ASTRO- + (AERO)NAUT, prob. via F *astronaute;* see ASTRONAUTICAL]

as·tro·nau·ti·cal (as′trə nô′ti kəl, -not′i-), *adj.* of or pertaining to astronautics or astronauts. Also, **as′tro·nau′tic.** [*astronautic* (< F *astronautique,* equiv. to *astronaute* (*astro-* ASTRO- + *-naute* < Gk *naútēs* sailor, on the model of *aéronaute* AERONAUT) + *-ique* -IC) + -AL[1]] —**as′tro·nau′ti·cal·ly,** *adv.*

astronau′tical engineer′ing. See under **aerospace engineering.** —**astronau′tical engineer′.**

as·tro·nau·tics (as′trə nô′tiks, -not′iks), *n.* (*used with a singular v.*) the science of or technology involved in travel beyond the earth's atmosphere, including interplanetary and interstellar flight. [1925–30; see ASTRONAUTICAL, -ICS]

as·tro·nav·i·ga·tion (as′trō nav′i gā′shən), *n.* See **celestial navigation.** [1940–45; ASTRO- + NAVIGATION] —**as′tro·nav′i·ga′tor,** *n.*

as·tron·o·mer (ə stron′ə mər), *n.* an expert in astronomy; a scientific observer of the celestial bodies. [1325–75; ME; see ASTRONOMY, -ER[1]]

Astron′omer Roy′al, **1.** the chief astronomer of England, appointed by the British Crown. **2.** the chief astronomer of Scotland, director of the Royal Edinburgh Observatory. [1895–1900]

as·tro·nom·i·cal (as′trə nom′i kəl), *adj.* **1.** of, pertaining to, or connected with astronomy. **2.** extremely large; exceedingly great; enormous: *It takes an astronomical amount of money to build a car factory.* Also, **as′tro·nom′ic.** [1550–60; < L *astronomic(us)* (< Gk *astronomikós;* see ASTRONOMY, -IC) + -AL[1]] —**as′tro·nom′i·cal·ly,** *adv.*

as′tronom′ical clock′, **1.** a clock indicating or representing the movements of the sun or planets, the phases of the moon, or the sky visible at a given time, used as a means of establishing time or for additional information, as locating celestial bodies or timing their movement. **2.** a clock used for observing the apparent time of the meridian passages of heavenly bodies. [1855–60]

astronom′ical frame′ of ref′erence, *Physics.* a frame of reference in which the sun or center of mass of the universe is fixed and which does not rotate with respect to the fixed stars.

astronom′ical refrac′tion, *Astron.* refraction (def. 3).

as′tronom′ical tel′escope, a telescope having an objective with a long focal length and an eyepiece with a short focal length, usually used for observing celestial bodies. Also called **Kepler telescope.** [1880–85]

as′tronom′ical tri′angle, the spherical triangle formed by the great circles connecting a celestial object, the zenith, and the celestial pole. [1915–20]

as′tronom′ical twi′light, either of two periods of partial darkness, after sunset or before sunrise, when the center of the sun is more than 6° but less than 18° below the horizon.

as′tronom′ical u′nit, *Astron.* a unit of length, equal to the mean distance of the earth from the sun:

approximately 93 million miles (150 million km). *Abbr.:* AU [1900–05]

as′tronom′ical year′, year (def. 4b). [1855–60]

as•tron•o•my (ə stron′ə mē), *n.* the science that deals with the material universe beyond the earth's atmosphere. [1175–1225; ME *astronomie* (< AF) < L *astronomia* < Gk. See ASTRO-, -NOMY]

as•tro•pho•tog•ra•phy (as′trō fə tog′rə fē), *n.* the photography of stars and other celestial objects. [1855–60; ASTRO- + PHOTOGRAPHY] **—as′tro•pho•tog′ra•pher,** *n.* **—as•tro•pho•to•graph•ic** (as′trō fō′tə graf′ik), *adj.*

as•tro•pho•tom•e•try (as′trō fō tom′i trē), *n.* the measurement of the intensity of light of celestial objects. [ASTRO- + PHOTOMETRY] **—as•tro•pho•to•met•ric** (as′trō fō′tə me′trik), **as′tro•pho′to•met′ri•cal,** *adj.* **—as′tro•pho′to•met′ri•cal•ly,** *adv.*

as•tro•phys•ics (as′trō fiz′iks), *n.* (*used with a singular v.*) the branch of astronomy that deals with the physical properties of celestial bodies and with the interaction between matter and radiation in the interior of celestial bodies and in interstellar space. [1885–90; ASTRO- + PHYSICS] **—as′tro•phys′i•cal,** *adj.* **—as•tro•phys•i•cist** (as′trō fiz′ə sist), *n.*

as•tro•sphere (as′trə sfēr′), *n. Biol.* **1.** the central portion of an aster, in which the centrosome lies. **2.** the whole aster exclusive of the centrosome. [1895–1900; ASTRO- + SPHERE]

As•tro•turf (as′trə tûrf′), *Trademark.* a brand of carpetlike covering made of vinyl and nylon to resemble turf, used for athletic fields, patios, etc.

As•tu•ri•an (a stŏŏr′ē ən, a styŏŏr′-), *adj.* **1.** of or pertaining to Asturias, its people, or their language. —*n.* **2.** a native or inhabitant of Asturias. **3.** the dialect of Spanish spoken in Asturias. [1605–15; < Sp *asturiano.* See ASTURIAS, -AN]

As•tu•ri•as (a stŏŏr′ē əs, a styŏŏr′-; *Sp.* äs tōō′ryäs), *n.* **1. Mi•guel Án•gel** (mē gel′ äng′hel), 1899–1974, Guatemalan novelist, poet, and short-story writer: Nobel prize 1967. **2.** a former kingdom and province in NW Spain.

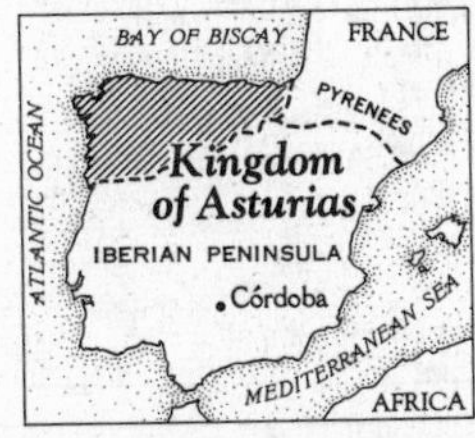

as•tute (ə stōōt′, ə styōōt′), *adj.* **1.** of keen penetration or discernment; sagacious: *an astute analysis.* **2.** clever; cunning; ingenious; shrewd: *an astute merchandising program; an astute manipulation of facts.* [1605–15; < L *astūtus* shrewd, sly, cunning, equiv. to *astū-* (s. of *astus*) cleverness + *-tus* adj. suffix] **—as•tute′ly,** *adv.* **—as•tute′ness,** *n.*
—Syn. 1. smart, quick, perceptive. **2.** artful, crafty, wily, sly.

a•sty•lar (ā stī′lər), *adj. Archit.* without columns. [1835–45; < Gk *ástyl(os)* without columns (*a-* A-[6] + *stŷl(os)* pillar + *-os* adj. suffix) + -AR[1]]

ASU, American Students Union.

A•sun•ción (ä′sōōn syôn′, -thyôn′), *n.* a city in and the capital of Paraguay, in the S part. 400,000.

a•sun•der (ə sun′dər), *adv., adj.* **1.** into separate parts; in or into pieces: *Lightning split the old oak tree asunder.* **2.** apart or widely separated: *as wide asunder as the polar regions.* [bef. 1000; ME; OE *on sundrum* apart. See A-[1], SUNDRY]

A supply, *Electronics.* a battery or other source of power for heating the filament or cathode heater of an electron tube. Cf. **B supply, C supply.**

A•sur (as′ər, ä′sŏŏr), *n.* Assur.

A•su•ra (us′ŏŏ rə), *n.* **1.** (in Indian mythology) a god or demon. **2.** *Zoroastrianism.* Ahura. [< Skt: mighty Lord; later (by reanalysis as *a-* + *-sura*) taken to mean "demon," as opposed to *sura* (by back formation) "god"]

A.S.V., American Standard Version. Also, **ASV**

A.S.W., Association of Scientific Workers.

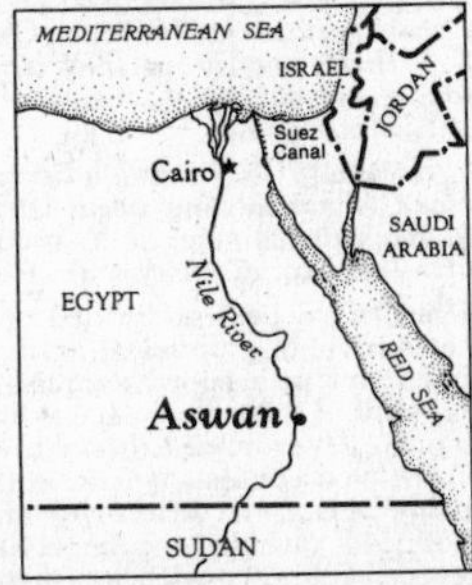

As•wan (as′wän; *Arab.* äs wän′), *n.* **1.** Ancient, **Syene.** a city in SE Egypt, on the Nile. 246,000. **2.** a dam near this city, extending across the Nile. 6400 ft. (1950 m) long. Also, **As•wân′, Assuan, Assouan.**

a•swarm (ə swôrm′), *adj.* filled, as by objects, organisms, etc., esp. in motion; teeming (usually used predicatively): *The garden was aswarm with bees; a night sky aswarm with stars.* [1880–85; A-[1] + SWARM[1]]

a•swirl (ə swûrl′), *adj., adv.* moving in a swirling pattern or motion: *dancers aswirl to the waltz music.* [1875–80; A-[1] + SWIRL]

a•swoon (ə swōōn′), *adj., adv.* being in a swoon: *the duchess aswoon on the couch in despair.* [1300–50; ME *aswowe(n), aswowne,* alter. (with initial vowel taken as A-[1]) of *i swone(n), in swoue(n),* reanalysis, as a prep. phrase, of *iswouen,* OE *geswōgen* fainted; see Y-, SWOON]

a•syl•lab•ic (ā′si lab′ik), *adj.* not syllabic. [1745–55; A-[6] + SYLLABIC]

a•sy•lum (ə sī′ləm), *n.* **1.** (esp. formerly) an institution for the maintenance and care of the mentally ill, orphans, or other persons requiring specialized assistance. **2.** an inviolable refuge, as formerly for criminals and debtors; sanctuary: *He sought asylum in the church.* **3.** *Internat. Law.* **a.** a refuge granted an alien by a sovereign state on its own territory. **b.** a temporary refuge granted political offenders, esp. in a foreign embassy. **4.** any secure retreat. [1400–50; late ME; < L < Gk *ásylon* sanctuary, equiv. to *a-* A-[6] + *sŷlon* right of seizure]
—Syn. 2. haven, shelter, retreat.

a•sym•met•ric (ā′sə me′trik, as′ə-), *adj.* **1.** not identical on both sides of a central line; unsymmetrical; lacking symmetry: *Most faces are asymmetric.* **2.** (of a logical or mathematical relation) holding true of members of a class in one order but not in the opposite order, as in the relation "being an ancestor of." **3.** *Chem.* **a.** having an unsymmetrical arrangement of atoms in a molecule. **b.** noting a carbon atom bonded to four different atoms or groups. **c.** (of a polymer) noting an atom or group that is within a polymer chain and is bonded to two different atoms or groups that are external to the chain. Also, **a′sym•met′ri•cal.** [1870–75; A-[6] + SYMMETRIC] **—a′sym•met′ri•cal•ly,** *adv.*

a•sym•me•try (ā sim′i trē), *n.* the quality or state of being asymmetric. [1645–55; < Gk *asymmetría* lack of proportion. See A-[6], SYMMETRY]

a•symp•to•mat•ic (ā simp′tə mat′ik, ā′simp-), *adj.* showing no evidence of disease. [1930–35; A-[6] + SYMPTOMATIC] **—a•symp′to•mat′i•cal•ly,** *adv.*

as•ymp•tote (as′im tōt′), *n. Math.* a straight line approached by a given curve as one of the variables in the equation of the curve approaches infinity. [1650–60; < Gk *asýmptōtos,* equiv. to *a-* A-[6] + *sýmptōtos* falling together (*sym-* SYM- + *ptōtós* falling, deriv. of *ptō-,* var. s. of *píptein* to fall + *-tos* verbal suffix)]

as•ymp•tot•ic (as′im tot′ik), *adj. Math.* **1.** of or pertaining to an asymptote. **2.** (of a function) approaching a given value as an expression containing a variable tends to infinity. **3.** (of two functions) so defined that their ratio approaches unity as the independent variable approaches a limit or infinity. **4.** (of a formula) becoming increasingly exact as a variable approaches a limit, usually infinity. **5.** coming into consideration as a variable approaches a limit, usually infinity: *asymptotic property; asymptotic behavior.* Also, **as′ymp•tot′i•cal.** [1665–75; ASYMPTOTE + -IC] **—as′ymp•tot′i•cal•ly,** *adv.*

as′ymptot′ic free′dom, *Physics.* a property of the force between quarks, according to quantum chromodynamics, such that they behave almost like free particles when they are close together within a hadron.

a•syn•ap•sis (ā′si nap′sis), *n., pl.* **-ses** (-sēz). *Genetics.* failure of the pairing of homologous chromosomes during meiosis. [1925–30; A-[6] + SYNAPSIS]

a•syn•chro•nism (ā sing′krə niz′əm), *n.* a lack of synchronism or coincidence in time. Also, **a•syn′chro•ny.** [1870–75; A-[6] + SYNCHRONISM]

a•syn•chro•nous (ā sing′krə nəs), *adj.* **1.** not occurring at the same time. **2.** (of a computer or other electrical machine) having each operation started only after the preceding operation is completed. **3.** *Computers, Telecommunications.* of or pertaining to operation without the use of fixed time intervals (opposed to *synchronous*). [1740–50; A-[6] + SYNCHRONOUS] **—a•syn′chro•nous•ly,** *adv.*

asyn′chronous transmis′sion, electronic communication between digital devices, as two separate computers that run at different speeds, that requires start and stop bits for each character transmitted.

a•syn•de•ton (ə sin′di ton′, -tən), *n.* **1.** *Rhet.* the omission of conjunctions, as in "He has provided the poor with jobs, with opportunity, with self-respect." **2.** *Library Science.* the omission of cross references, esp. from a catalog. [1580–90; < L < Gk, n. use of neut. of *asýndetos* not linked (*a-* A-[6] + *syndé(ein)* to link + *-tos* verbid suffix)] **—as•yn•det•ic** (as′in det′ik), *adj.* **—as′yn•det′i•cal•ly,** *adv.*

a•syn•er•gy (ā sin′ər jē), *n. Med.* defective coordination between parts, as muscles or limbs, that normally act in unison. Also, **a•sy•ner•gia** (ā′si nûr′jə, -jē ə). [1855–60; A-[6] + SYNERGY]

A•syn•jur (ä′sin yŏŏr′), *n.pl., sing.* **-ja** (-yä′), **-je** (-yə′). (*often l.c.*) *Scand. Myth.* the goddesses of the Aesir, led by Frigg.

a•syn•tac•tic (ā′sin tak′tik), *adj. Gram.* (of compounds) consisting of morphemes that are combined differently from their mode of combination as separate words in a phrase, as *bookstore,* which is an asyntactic compound, while the same elements are combined syntactically in *store for books.* [1875–80; A-[6] + SYNTACTIC]

As′ You′ Like′ It′, a comedy (1599?) by Shakespeare.

A•syut (ä syōōt′), *n.* a city in central Egypt, on the Nile. 284,000. Also, **A•syût′, Assiut.**

at[1] (at; *unstressed* ət, it), *prep.* **1.** (used to indicate a point or place occupied in space); in, on, or near: *to stand at the door; at the bottom of the barrel.* **2.** (used to indicate a location or position, as in time, on a scale, or in order): *at zero; at noon; at age 65; at the end; at the lowest point.* **3.** (used to indicate presence or location): *at home; at hand.* **4.** (used to indicate amount, degree, or rate): *at great speed; at high altitudes.* **5.** (used to indicate a direction, goal, or objective); toward: *Aim at the mark. Look at that.* **6.** (used to indicate occupation or involvement): *at work; at play.* **7.** (used to indicate a state or condition): *at ease; at peace.* **8.** (used to indicate a cause or source): *She was annoyed at his stupidity.* **9.** (used to indicate a method or manner): *He spoke at length.* **10.** (used to indicate relative quality or value): *at one's best; at cost.* **11. be at (someone),** to be sexually aggressive toward (a person): *She's pregnant again because he's at her morning, noon, and night.* **12. where it's at,** *Informal.* the place where the most interesting or exciting things happen: *Emma says that Rome is definitely where it's at now.* [bef. 900; ME; OE *æt;* c. OFris *et,* ON, OS, Goth *at,* OHG *az,* L, Old Welsh, Old Breton *ad,* Gk *a-* (< a pre-Hellenic IE substratum language), Oscan, OIr, Gaulish, Phrygian *ad-*]

at[2] (ät, at), *n.* a money of account of Laos, the 100th part of a kip. [1950–55; < Lao; cf. Thai *ʔàt* formerly, a copper coin worth one eighth of a fúang, ult. < Pali *aṭṭha* EIGHT]

at-, var. of **ad-** before *t: attend.*

AT, **1.** achievement test. **2.** antitank.

At, ampere-turn.

At, *Symbol, Chem.* astatine.

at., **1.** atmosphere. **2.** atomic. **3.** attorney.

A.T., Atlantic time.

-ata[1], a plural suffix occurring in loanwords from Latin, forming nouns used esp. in names of zoological groups: *Vertebrata.* [< L, neut. pl. of *-ātus* -ATE[1], originally adj. in L, then substantivized in NL.]

-ata[2], a plural suffix occurring in loanwords from Greek: *stomata.* [< Gk *t*-stems, *-mata* result of, state of, act of; cf. -MENT]

A.T.A., Associate Technical Aide.

A•ta•ba•li•pa (ä′tä bä′lē pä′), *n.* Atahualpa.

At•a•brine (at′ə brin, -brēn′), *Pharm., Trademark.* a brand of quinacrine.

A′ta•ca′ma Des′ert (at′ə kam′ə, at′-, ä′tə kä′mə, ä′tə-; *Sp.* ä′tä kä′mä), an arid region in N Chile: rich nitrate deposits. ab. 600 mi. (960 km) long; ab. 70,000 sq. mi. (181,300 sq. km).

at•a•cam•ite (at′ə kam′īt, ə tak′ə mīt′), *n.* a mineral, hydrated chloride of copper, $Cu_2Cl(OH)_3$, occurring in a green, granular form: a minor ore of copper. [1830–40; named after ATACAMA DESERT; see -ITE[1]]

a•tac•tic (ā tak′tik), *adj. Chem.* (of a polymer) not stereospecific; lacking tacticity. [1955–60; A-[6] + *-tactic,* back formation from TACTICITY]

at•a•ghan (at′ə gan′, -gən), *n.* yataghan.

A•ta•hual•pa (ä′tä wäl′pä), *n.* c1500–33, last Incan king of Peru (son of Huayna Capac). Also, **Atabalipa.**

A•tak•a•pa (ə tak′ə pə, -pä′, -pô′), *n., pl.* **-pas,** (*esp. collectively*) **-pa.** **1.** a member of an American Indian people living along the coast of Louisiana. **2.** the language of the Atakapa Indians.

At•a•lan•ta (at′l an′tə), *n. Class Myth.* a virgin huntress who promised to marry the man who could win a foot race against her but lost to Hippomenes when she stopped to retrieve three golden apples of Aphrodite that he dropped in her path. Also, **At•a•lan•te** (at′l an′tē). Cf. **Melanion.**

at•a•man (at′ə mən), *n., pl.* **-mans.** the elected chief of a Cossack village or military force. [1825–35; < Russ *atamán,* ORuss *vatamanŭ,* prob. alter. of a Turkic word with the personal suffix *-man;* identity of initial element disputed]

at′a•mas′co lil′y (at′ə mas′kō, at′-), a plant, *Zephyranthes atamasco,* of the amaryllis family, of the southeastern U.S., bearing a single white lilylike flower sometimes tinged with purple. Also called **fairy lily.** [1620–30, *Amer.*; earlier *attamusco* < Virginia Algonquian]

at•ar (at′ər, -är), *n.* attar (def. 1).

At•a•rax (at′ə raks′), *Pharm., Trademark.* a brand of hydroxyzine.

at•a•rax•i•a (at′ə rak′sē ə), *n.* a state of freedom from emotional disturbance and anxiety; tranquillity. Also, **at•a•rax•y** (at′ə rak′sē). [1595–1605; < L < Gk: calmness, equiv. to *atarák(tos)* unmoved (*a-* A-[6] + *tarak-,* var. s. of *tarássein* to disturb + *-tos* verbid suffix) + *-s(is)* -SIS + *-ia* -IA] **—at•a•rac•tic** (at′ə rak′tik), **at′a•rax′ic,** *adj., n.*

A•tas•ca•de•ro (ə tas′kə dâr′ō), *n.* a town in SW California. 15,930.

A•ta•türk (at′ə tûrk′, ä tä tûrk′), *n.* See **Kemal Atatürk.**

a•tav•ic (ə tav′ik), *adj.* atavistic. [1865–70; ATAV(ISM) + -IC, modeled on F *atavique*]

at•a•vism (at′ə viz′əm), *n.* **1.** *Biol.* **a.** the reappearance in an individual of characteristics of some remote ancestor that have been absent in intervening generations. **b.** an individual embodying such a reversion. **2.** reversion to an earlier type; throwback. [1825–35; < L *atav(us)* remote ancestor (*at-,* akin to *atta* familiar name for a grandfather + *avus* grandfather, forefather) + -ISM] **—at′a•vist,** *n.*

at•a•vis•tic (at′ə vis′tik), *adj.* of, pertaining to, or characterized by atavism; reverting to or suggesting the characteristics of a remote ancestor or primitive type. [1870–75; ATAV(ISM) + -ISTIC] **—at′a•vis′ti•cal•ly,** *adv.*

CONCISE PRONUNCIATION KEY: act, cāpe, dâre, pärt; set, ēqual; *if,* īce; ox, ōver, ôrder, oil, bŏŏk, bōōt, out; up, ûrge; child; sing; shoe; thin, *th*at; zh as in *treasure.* ə = a as in *alone,* e as in *system,* i as in *easily,* o as in *gallop,* u as in *circus;* ᵊ as in *fire* (fīᵊr), *hour* (ouᵊr), l and n can serve as syllabic consonants, as in *cradle* (krād′l), and *button* (but′n). See the full key inside the front cover.

a•tax•i•a (ə tak′sē ə), *n. Pathol.* loss of coordination of the muscles, esp. of the extremities. Also, **a•tax•y** (ə tak′sē, a tak′-). Cf. **tabes dorsalis.** [1605–15; < NL < Gk: indiscipline, equiv. to *a-* A-[6] + *táx(is)* -TAXIS + *-ia* -IA] —**a•tax′ic,** *adj.*

At•ba•ra (ät′bə rə, at′-), *n.* **1.** a river in NE Africa, flowing NW from NW Ethiopia to the Nile in E Sudan. ab. 500 mi. (800 km) long. **2.** a city in NE Sudan. 62,407.

ATC, 1. Air Traffic Control. **2.** Air Transport Command.

Atch•i•son (ach′ə sən), *n.* a city in NE Kansas, on the Missouri River. 11,407.

ate (āt; *Brit.* et), *v.* pt. of **eat.**

A•te (ā′tē, ä′tā), *n.* an ancient Greek goddess personifying the fatal blindness or recklessness that produces crime and the divine punishment that follows it. [< Gk, special use of *átē* reckless impulse, ruin, akin to *aáein* to mislead, harm]

ATE, equipment that makes a series of tests automatically. [*a(utomatic) t(est) e(quipment)*]

-ate[1], a suffix occurring in loanwords from Latin, its English distribution paralleling that of Latin. The form originated as a suffix added to *a*-stem verbs to form adjectives (*separate*). The resulting form could also be used independently as a noun (*advocate*) and came to be used as a stem on which a verb could be formed (*separate; advocate*). In English the use as a verbal suffix has been extended to stems of non-Latin origin: *calibrate; acierate.* [< L *-ātus* (masc.), *-āta* (fem.), *-ātum* (neut.), equiv. to *-ā-* thematic vowel + *-tus, -ta, -tum* ptp. suffix]

-ate[2], *Chem.* a specialization of **-ate[1],** used to indicate a salt of an acid ending in **-ic,** added to a form of the stem of the element or group: *nitrate; sulfate.* Cf. **-ite[1].** [< L *-ātum,* neut. of *-ātus* -ATE[1]]

-ate[3], a suffix occurring in nouns borrowed from Latin, and in English coinages from Latin bases, that denotes offices or functions (*consulate; triumvirate*), as well as institutions or collective bodies (*senate; electorate*); sometimes extended to denote a person who exercises such a function (*magistrate; potentate*), an associated place (*consulate*), or a period of office or rule (*protectorate*). Joined to stems of any origin, **-ate[3]** signifies the office, term of office, or territory of a ruler or official (*khanate; caliphate; shogunate*). [< L *-ātus* (gen. *-ātūs*), generalized from v. derivs. such as *augurātus* office of an augur (*augurā(re)* to foretell by augury + *-tus* suffix of v. action), construed as deriv. of *augur* AUGUR]

A Team, *Mil.* a unit composed of 12 U.S. Special Forces soldiers.

a•tef-crown (ä′tef kroun′), *n.* a symbolic headdress of certain Egyptian gods, as Osiris, and of Egyptian kings, consisting of a tall conical cap flanked by two plumes and bearing representations of the uraeus and the sun. [*atef,* vocalization of Egyptian *yt* father + the *f*-symbol (a horned viper), orig. taken as part of the word, but now thought to be a nonphonetic determinative]

at•e•lec•ta•sis (at′l ek′tə sis), *n. Pathol.* **1.** incomplete expansion of the lungs at birth, as from lack of breathing force. **2.** collapse of the lungs, as from bronchial obstruction. [1855–60; < NL; see ATELIOSIS, ECTASIS] —**at•e•lec•tat•ic** (at′l ek tat′ik), *adj.*

a•te•lei•o•sis (ə tē′lē ō′sis), *n. Pathol.* ateliosis.

at•el•ier (at′l yā′, at′l yā′; *Fr.* AT[ə] lyā′), *n., pl.* **at•el•iers** (at′l yāz′, at′l yāz′; *Fr.* AT[ə] lyā′). a workshop or studio, esp. of an artist, artisan, or designer. [1830–40; < F: lit., pile of chips (hence, workshop); OF *astele* chip (< LL *astella,* dim. of L *astula,* var. of *assula* splinter, equiv. to *ass(is)* plank + *-ula* -ULE) + *-ier* -IER[2]]

a•te•li•o•sis (ə tē′lē ō′sis, ə tel′ē-), *n. Pathol.* a form of infantilism caused by pituitary malfunction, characterized by a childish face and voice and associated physical underdevelopment, but not affecting intelligence. Also, **ateleiosis.** [1900–05; < Gk *ateleí(a)* imperfection, incompletion (see A-[6], TELE-[2], -IA) + -OSIS] —**a•tel•i•ot•ic** (ə tel′ē ot′ik), *adj.*

a tem•po (ä tem′pō; *It.* ä tem′pô), *Music.* resuming the speed obtained preceding ritardando or accelerando. [1730–40; < It: in (the regular) time]

a•tem•po•ral (ā tem′pər əl, ā tem′prəl), *adj.* free from limitations of time. [1865–70; A-[6] + TEMPORAL[1]]

A•ten (ät′n), *n.* Aton.

A′ten as′teroid, *Astron.* one of a small group of asteroids whose orbits cross that of the earth and whose semimajor axes are smaller than that of the earth. Cf. **Apollo asteroid.**

a•ten•o•lol (ə ten′ə lôl′, -lol′), *n. Pharm.* a synthetic beta blocker, $C_{14}H_{22}N_2O_3$, used in the management of hypertension, angina pectoris, and cardiac arrhythmias and, topically, in the treatment of glaucoma. [laboratory coinage of unexplained orig.]

a ter•go (ä teR′gō), *Latin.* at or toward the back; from behind; in the rear.

A•te•ri•an (ə tēr′ē ən), *adj. Archaeol.* of or indicating a Middle Paleolithic industry of northwestern Africa and the Sahara, characterized by the production of tanged points and bifacially worked leaf-shaped points of varying sizes. [1925–30; < F *atérien,* after the type-site, Bir el Ater, Algeria; see -IAN]

à terre (*Fr.* A teR′), *Ballet.* on the ground. [1920–25; < F]

A•tes•te (ə tes′tē), *n.* ancient name of **Este.**

Ath•a•bas•ka (ath′ə bas′kə), *n.* **1. Lake,** a lake in W Canada, in NW Saskatchewan and NE Alberta. ab. 200 mi. (320 km) long; ab. 3000 sq. mi. (7800 sq. km). **2.** a river in W Canada flowing NE from W Alberta to Lake Athabaska. 765 mi. (1230 km) long.

Ath•a•bas•kan (ath′ə bas′kən), *n.* **1.** a family of languages spoken by American Indians in most of inland northwest Canada and Alaska, in coastal Oregon and California, and in Arizona and the Rio Grande basin, and including esp. Navajo, Apache, and Chipewyan. Cf. **family** (def. 14). **2.** a member of any of various American Indian peoples speaking Athabaskan. —*adj.* **3.** belonging to or characteristic of the Athabaskans. Also, **Ath′a•bas′can, Athapaskan, Athapascan.** [1770–80; earlier *Athapasca(s),* introduced as a term for the Canadian Athabaskans (< Woods Cree *ahδapaska·w* Lake Athabaska, lit., there are reeds here and there < Proto-Algonquian **a·θlap(y)-* net, reticulated + **-ašk-* plant + derivational elements) + -AN]

Ath•a•li•ah (ath′ə lī′ə), *n.* a daughter of Ahab and Jezebel and usurper of the throne of Judah, reigned 842–837 B.C. II Kings 11:1–3. Also, *Douay Bible,* **Ath′a•li′a.**

ath•a•na•sia (ath′ə nā′zhə), *n.* deathlessness; immortality. Also, **a•than•a•sy** (ə than′ə sē). [1820–30; < Gk *athanasía,* equiv. to *athánat(os)* deathless (*a-* A-[6] + *thánatos* death) + *-ia* -IA, with *ti* > *si*]

Ath•a•na•sian (ath′ə nā′zhən), *adj.* **1.** of or pertaining to Athanasius or to the doctrines ascribed to him. —*n.* **2.** *Theol.* a follower of Athanasius or a believer in the Athanasian Creed. [1580–90; ATHANASI(US) + -AN]

Ath′ana′sian Creed′, a creed or formulary of Christian faith, of unknown authorship, formerly ascribed to Athanasius. [1580–90]

Ath•a•na•sius (ath′ə nā′shəs), *n.* **Saint,** A.D. 296?–373, bishop of Alexandria: opponent of Arianism.

ath•a•nor (ath′ə nôr′), *n. Alchemy.* a digester furnace with a self-feeding fuel supply contained in a towerlike contrivance, ensuring a constant, durable temperature. [1425–75; late ME << Ar *at tannūr* the furnace]

Ath•a•pas•kan (ath′ə pas′kən), *n., adj.* Athabaskan. Also, **Ath′a•pas′can.**

ath•ar (ath′ər, -är), *n.* attar (def. 1).

A•thar•va-Ve•da (ə tär′və vā′də, -vē′də), *n. Hinduism.* one of the Samhitas, a collection of mantras and formulas, some showing pre-Vedic influence. Cf. **Veda.**

a•the•ism (ā′thē iz′əm), *n.* **1.** the doctrine or belief that there is no God. **2.** disbelief in the existence of a supreme being or beings. [1580–90; < Gk *áthe(os)* godless + -ISM]

a•the•ist (ā′thē ist), *n.* a person who denies or disbelieves the existence of a supreme being or beings. [1565–75; < Gk *áthe(os)* godless + -IST]
—**Syn.** ATHEIST, AGNOSTIC, INFIDEL, SKEPTIC refer to persons not inclined toward religious belief or a particular form of religious belief. An ATHEIST is one who denies the existence of a deity or of divine beings. An AGNOSTIC is one who believes it impossible to know anything about God or about the creation of the universe and refrains from commitment to any religious doctrine. INFIDEL means an unbeliever, especially a nonbeliever in Islam or Christianity. A SKEPTIC doubts and is critical of all accepted doctrines and creeds.

a•the•is•tic (ā′thē is′tik), *adj.* pertaining to or characteristic of atheists or atheism; containing, suggesting, or disseminating atheism: *atheistic literature; atheistic people.* Also, **a′the•is′ti•cal.** [1625–35; ATHEIST + -IC] —**a′the•is′ti•cal•ly,** *adv.* —**a′the•is′tic•ness,** *n.*

Ath•el (ath′əl), *n.* a male given name.

ath•el•ing (ath′ə ling, *a*th′-), *n. Early Eng. Hist.* a man of royal blood; a prince. [bef. 1000; ME; OE *ætheling* (c. OHG *ediling, adalung,* OS *ethiling*), equiv. to *æthel(u)* noble family (c. OHG *adoul,* G *Adel,* OS *athal(i),* ON *athal* nature; akin to Tocharian *atäl* man) + *-ing* -ING[3]]

Ath•el•stan (ath′əl stan′), *n.* A.D. 895?–940, king of England 925–940.

ath′el tree′, an evergreen tree or large shrub, *Tamarix aphylla,* native to desert regions of western Asia and northern Africa, having small, pink flowers in terminal clusters, widely planted as a windbreak and ornamental. Also called **salt tree.** [< Ar *athlah*]

a•the•mat•ic (ā′thē mat′ik), *adj.* inflected without a thematic vowel. [1890–95; A-[6] + THEMATIC]

Athena

A•the•na (ə thē′nə), *n.* **1.** Also, **A•the•ne** (ə thē′nē). Also called **Pallas, Pallas Athena.** the virgin deity of the ancient Greeks worshiped as the goddess of wisdom, fertility, the useful arts, and prudent warfare. At her birth she sprang forth fully armed from the head of her father, Zeus. Cf. **Minerva. 2.** a female given name.

ath•e•nae•um (ath′ə nē′əm, -nā′-), *n.* **1.** an institution for the promotion of literary or scientific learning. **2.** a library or reading room. **3.** (*cap.*) a sanctuary of Athena at Athens, built by the Roman emperor Hadrian, and frequented by poets and scholars. Also, **ath′e•ne′•um.** [1720–30; < L < Gk *Athḗnaion* temple of Athena, where poets read their works]

Ath•e•nae•us (ath′ə nē′əs, -nā′-), *n.* late 2nd century A.D., Greek philosopher and rhetorician at Naucratis in Egypt.

Athenae′us of At•ta•lei′a (at′l ī′ə), Greek physician in Rome, fl. A.D. c40–65.

Ath•e•nag•o•ras I (ath′ə nag′ər əs; *Gk.* ä thē′nä gô′räs), (*Aristocles Spyrou*) 1886–1972, Archbishop Ecumenical of Constantinople and Ecumenical Patriarch of the Greek Orthodox Church 1948–72.

A•the•nai (ä thē′ne), *n.* Greek name of **Athens.**

A•the•ni•an (ə thē′nē ən), *adj.* **1.** pertaining to Athens, Greece. —*n.* **2.** a native or citizen of Athens, Greece. [1580–90; < L *Athēni(ēnsis)* of Athens + -AN; see -ENSIS]

A•thé•nienne (ä′tān yen′; *Fr.* A tā nyen′), *n., pl.* **A•thé•niennes** (ä′tān yenz′; *Fr.* A tā nyen′). a small, decorative stand in the form of an antique tripod, used esp. in France in the Louis XVI and Empire periods. [< F, fem. of *athénien* ATHENIAN]

Ath•ens (ath′inz), *n.* **1.** Greek, **Athenai.** a city in and the capital of Greece, in the SE part. 885,136. **2. Greater,** a metropolitan area comprising the city of Athens, Piraeus, and several residential suburbs. 2,530,000. **3.** a city in N Georgia. 42,549. **4.** a city in S Ohio. 19,743. **5.** a town in N Alabama. 14,558. **6.** a town in S Tennessee. 12,080. **7.** a town in E Texas. 10,197. **8.** any city that is compared to Athens, esp. as a cultural center: *the Athens of the Midwest.*

ath•er•ec•to•my (ath′ə rek′tə mē), *n., pl.* **-mies.** the removal of plaque from an artery by means of a tiny rotating cutting blade inserted through a catheter. [ATHER(OMA) + -ECTOMY]

ath•er•ine (ath′ə rīn′, -ər in), *adj.* **1.** belonging or pertaining to the family Atherinidae, comprising the silversides. —*n.* **2.** an atherine fish. [1760–70; < NL *Atherina* a genus of the family < Gk *atherínē* smelt]

athero-, a combining form representing **atheroma** or **atheromatous** in compound words: *atherosclerosis.* [< Gk *athḗr(ē)* gruel (see ATHEROMA) + -O-]

ath•er•o•gen•ic (ath′ə rō jen′ik), *adj. Pathol.* capable of producing atheromatous plaques in arteries. [1950–55; ATHERO- + -GENIC]

ath•er•o•ma (ath′ə rō′mə), *n., pl.* **-mas, -ma•ta** (-mə tə). *Pathol.* **1.** a sebaceous cyst. **2.** a mass of yellowish fatty and cellular material that forms in and beneath the inner lining of the arterial walls. [1700–10; < NL, L: a tumor filled with gruellike matter < Gk *athérōma,* equiv. to *athḗr(ē)* gruel + *-ōma* -OMA] —**ath•er•om•a•tous** (ath′ə rom′ə təs, -rō′mə-), *adj.*

ath•er•o•scle•ro•sis (ath′ə rō sklə rō′sis, *a*th′-), *n. Pathol.* a common form of arteriosclerosis in which fatty substances form a deposit of plaque on the inner lining of arterial walls. [1905–10; < G *Atherosklerose;* see ATHERO-, SCLEROSIS] —**ath•er•o•scle•rot•ic** (ath′ə rō sklə rot′ik, *a*th′-), *adj.* —**ath′er•o•scle•rot′i•cal•ly,** *adv.*

Ath•er•ton (ath′ər tən), *n.* **Gertrude (Franklin)** (*Gertrude Franklin Horn*), 1857–1948, U.S. novelist.

ath•e•to•sis (ath′i tō′sis), *n. Pathol.* a condition, chiefly in children, of slow, involuntary, wormlike movements of the fingers, toes, hands, and feet, usually resulting from a brain lesion. [1870–75; < Gk *áthet(os)* not placed (*a-* A-[6] + *thetós,* equiv. to *the-* (s. of *tithénai* to set, put) + *-tos* verbid suffix) + -OSIS] —**ath′e•to′sic, ath•e•tot•ic** (ath′i tot′ik), *adj.*

a•thirst (ə thûrst′), *adj.* **1.** having a keen desire; eager (often fol. by *for*): *She has long been athirst for European travel.* **2.** *Archaic.* thirsty. [bef. 1000; ME *athurst, ofthurst,* OE *ofthyrst,* ptp. of *ofthyrstan.* See A-[2], THIRST]

ath•lete (ath′lēt), *n.* a person trained or gifted in exercises or contests involving physical agility, stamina, or strength; a participant in a sport, exercise, or game requiring physical skill. [1520–30; < L *āthlēta* < Gk *āthlētḗs,* equiv. to *āthlē-* (var. s. of *āthleîn* to contend for a prize, deriv. of *âthlos* a contest) + *-tēs* suffix of agency]
—**Pronunciation.** ATHLETE, ATHLETIC, and ATHLETICS, normally pronounced (ath′lēt), (ath let′ik), and (ath let′iks), are heard frequently with an epenthetic schwa, an intrusive unstressed vowel inserted between the first and second syllables: (ath′ə lēt′), (ath′ə let′ik), and (ath′ə let′iks). The pronunciations containing the extra syllable are usually considered nonstandard, in spite of their widespread use on radio and television. Pronunciations with similarly intrusive vowels are also heard, though with less currency, for other words, as (fil′əm)

CONCISE ETYMOLOGY KEY: <, descended or borrowed from; >, whence; b., blend of, blended; c., cognate with; cf., compare; deriv., derivative; equiv., equivalent; imit., imitative; obl., oblique; r., replacing; s., stem; sp., spelling, spelled; resp., respelling, respelled; trans., translation; ?, origin unknown; *, unattested; ‡, probably earlier than. See the full key inside the front cover.

for *film*, (el′əm) for *elm*, and (är′thə rī′tis) for *arthritis*, rather than the standard (film), (elm), and (är thrī′tis).

ath′lete's foot′, *Pathol.* a contagious disease, caused by a fungus that thrives on moist surfaces; ringworm of the feet. [1925–30, *Amer.*]

ath′lete's heart′, nonpathological enlargement of the heart resulting from intensive aerobic exercise. Also, **athlet′ic heart′.**

ath•let•ic (ath let′ik), *adj.* **1.** physically active and strong; good at athletics or sports: *an athletic child.* **2.** of, like, or befitting an athlete. **3.** of or pertaining to athletes; involving the use of physical skills or capabilities, as strength, agility, or stamina: *athletic sports; athletic training.* **4.** for athletics: *an athletic field.* **5.** *Psychol.* (of a physical type) having a sturdy build or well-proportioned body structure. Cf. **asthenic** (def. 2), **pyknic** (def. 1). [1595–1605; < L *āthlēticus* < Gk *āthlētikós.* See ATHLETE, -IC] —**ath•let′i•cal•ly,** *adv.* —**ath•let•i•cism** (ath let′ə siz′əm), *n.*
—**Pronunciation.** See **athlete.**

ath•let•ics (ath let′iks), *n.* **1.** (*usually used with a plural v.*) athletic sports, as running, rowing, or boxing. **2.** *Brit.* track-and-field events. **3.** (*usually used with a singular v.*) the practice of athletic exercises; the principles of athletic training. [1595–1605; see ATHLETIC, -ICS]
—**Pronunciation.** See **athlete.**

athlet′ic shoe′, **1.** a shoe designed to be worn for sports, exercising, or recreational activity, as racquetball, jogging, or aerobic dancing. **2.** sneaker (def. 1).

athlet′ic support′er, jockstrap. [1925–30]

ath•o•dyd (ath′ə did), *n.* a ramjet. [1925–30; *a(ero)-th(erm)ody(namic) d(uct)*]

Ath•ol (ath′ôl, -əl), *n.* **1.** a city in central Massachusetts. 10,634. **2.** a male given name.

at-home (at hōm′), *n.* **1.** Also, **at home′.** a reception of visitors at certain hours at one's home. —*adj.* **2.** done or used in the home; intended for one's home: *a new line of at-home computers; at-home assignments for free-lance workers.* [1740–45]

-athon, a suffix extracted from **marathon,** occurring as the final element in compounds which have the general sense "an event, as a sale or contest, drawn out to unusual length, often until a prearranged goal, as the contribution of a certain amount of money, is reached": *walkathon; readathon.* Also, **-a-thon, -thon.**

ath•o•nite (ath′ə nīt′), *adj.* of or relating to Mount Athos. [1885–90; < L *Athōn-,* s. of *Athōs* (< Gk *Athṓs* ATHOS) + -ITE[1]]

Ath•os (ath′ōs, ā′thos; *Gk.* ä′thôs), *n.* **Mount, 1.** the easternmost of three prongs of the peninsula of Chalcidice, in NE Greece: site of an autonomous theocracy constituted of 20 monasteries. 1713; 131 sq. mi. (340 sq. km); ab. 35 mi. (56 km) long. **2.** a headland on this peninsula. 6350 ft. (1935 m) long.

a•thrill (ə thril′), *adj.* affected with a sudden wave of keen emotion or excitement; tingling (usually used predicatively): *After the first surprise, he found himself athrill with a sense of discovery.* [1875–80; A-[1] + THRILL]

ath•ro•cyte (ath′rə sīt′), *n. Cell Biol.* a cell that ingests foreign particles and retains them in suspension in the cytoplasm. [1935–40; < Gk *(h)athró(os)* gathered together + -CYTE] —**ath′ro•cy•to′sis,** *n.*

a•thwart (ə thwôrt′), *adv.* **1.** from side to side; crosswise. **2.** *Naut.* **a.** at right angles to the fore-and-aft line; across. **b.** broadside to the wind because of equal and opposite pressures of wind and tide: *a ship riding athwart.* **3.** perversely; awry; wrongly. —*prep.* **4.** from side to side of; across. **5.** *Naut.* across the direction or course of. **6.** in opposition to; contrary to. [1425–75; late ME; see A-[1], THWART]

a•thwart•ships (ə thwôrt′ships′), *adv. Naut.* from one side of a ship to the other. [1710–20; ATHWART + SHIP + -S[1]]

a•tilt (ə tilt′), *adj., adv.* **1.** with a tilt or inclination; tilted: *Hold the bottle slightly atilt.* **2.** with the lance in hand in tilting. [1555–65; A-[1] + TILT[1]]

a•tin•gle (ə ting′gəl), *adj.* tingling; stimulated. [1850–55; A-[1] + TINGLE]

-ation, a combination of **-ate**[1] and **-ion,** used to form nouns from stems in **-ate**[1] (*separation*); on this model, used independently to form nouns from stems of other origin: *starvation.* [< L *-ātiōn-* (s. of *-ātiō*), equiv. to *-ā-* s. vowel + *-tiōn-* -TION]

a•tip•toe (ə tip′tō′), *adv., adj.* **1.** standing or walking on tiptoe (usually used predicatively). **2.** eagerly expectant, as anticipating a desired event or arrival: *waiting atiptoe for the mail.* **3.** moving with caution or stealth, as avoiding calling attention to one's presence: *She walked atiptoe through the sleeping house.* [1570–80; A-[1] + TIPTOE]

A•ti•tlán (ä′tē tlän′), *n.* **Lake,** a crater lake in SW Guatemala, 4700 ft. (1433 m) above sea level. ab. 53 sq. mi. (137 sq. km).

-ative, a combination of **-ate**[1] and **-ive,** used to form adjectives from stems in **-ate**[1] (*regulative*); on this model, because of the frequency and productivity of **-ate**[1], used independently to form adjectives from stems of other origin: *normative.* [< L *-ātivus,* equiv. to *-āt(us)* -ATE[1] + *-īvus* -IVE]

Atj•eh•nese (ach′ə nēz′, -nēs′), *n., pl.* **-nese** for 1. **1.** a member of an indigenous Muslim people of northernmost Sumatra. **2.** the Austronesian language spoken by the Atjehnese. Also, **Achenese, Achinese.**

At′ka mack′erel (at′kə), a black-banded mackerel, *Pleurogrammus monopterygius,* of northern Pacific seas. [1890–95; named after *Atka,* an island in SW Alaska near the fishing grounds]

At•kins (at′kinz), *n., pl.* **-kins** for 2. **1. Chester** (*"Chet"*), born 1924, U.S. country-and-western singer and musician. **2.** See **Tommy Atkins.**

At•kin•son (at′kin sən), *n.* **1. Sir Harry Albert,** 1831–92, New Zealand statesman, born in England: prime minister 1876–77, 1883–84, 1887–91. **2. (Justin) Brooks,** 1894–1984, U.S. drama critic, journalist, and author. **3. Theodore Francis** (*Ted*), born 1916, U.S. jockey.

Atl., Atlantic.

At•lan•ta (at lan′tə), *n.* a city in and the capital of Georgia, in the N part. 425,022.

at•lan•tal (at lan′tl), *adj. Anat.* of or pertaining to the atlas. [1795–1805; < NL *atlant-* (see ATLANTIC) + -AL[1]]

At•lan•te•an (at′lan tē′ən, -lən-), *adj.* **1.** pertaining to the demigod Atlas. **2.** having the strength of Atlas: *He was of monumental girth and Atlantean power.* **3.** pertaining to Atlantis. [1660–70; < L *Atlantē(us)* (< Gk *Atlánteios* of ATLAS, equiv. to *Atlant-,* s. of *Átlās* + *-eios* adj. suffix) + -AN]

at•lan•tes (at lan′tēz), *n.* pl. of **atlas** (def. 5).

At•lan•tic (at lan′tik), *adj.* **1.** of or pertaining to the Atlantic Ocean. **2.** of, pertaining to, or situated on the eastern seaboard of the U.S.: *the Atlantic states.* **3.** of or pertaining to the countries bordering the Atlantic Ocean, esp. those of North America and Europe. **4.** of or pertaining to the North Atlantic Treaty Organization or its members: *the Atlantic Alliance.* —*n.* **5.** See **Atlantic Ocean. 6.** *Railroads.* a steam locomotive having a four-wheeled front truck, four driving wheels, and a two-wheeled rear truck. See table under **Whyte classification.** [1350–1400; ME < L *Atlanticum* (*mare*) the Atlantic (ocean), neut. of *Atlanticus* < Gk *Atlantikós* of (Mount) ATLAS, equiv. to *Atlant-* (s. of *Átlās*) + *-ikos* -IC]

Atlan′tic Char′ter, the joint declaration of President Roosevelt and Prime Minister Churchill (August 14, 1941) resulting from a conference at sea, setting forth the peace aims of their governments for the period following World War II. The declaration was later endorsed by a number of countries and incorporated in the purposes of the United Nations.

Atlan′tic Cit′y, a city in SE New Jersey: seashore resort. 40,199.

Atlan′tic croak′er. See under **croaker** (def. 2). [1945–50]

Atlan′tic Intracoast′al Wa′terway. See under **Intracoastal Waterway.**

At•lan•ti•cist (at lan′tə sist), *n.* a supporter of close military, political, and economic cooperation between Western Europe and the U.S. [1965–70; ATLANTIC + -IST] —**At•lan′ti•cism,** *n.*

Atlan′tic O′cean, an ocean bounded by North America and South America in the Western Hemisphere and by Europe and Africa in the Eastern Hemisphere. ab. 31,530,000 sq. mi. (81,663,000 sq. km); with connecting seas ab. 41,000,000 sq. mi. (106,100,000 sq. km); greatest known depth, 30,246 ft. (9219 m).

Atlan′tic Pact′. See **North Atlantic Treaty.**

Atlan′tic Prov′inces, the Canadian provinces bordering the Atlantic Ocean, comprising New Brunswick, Newfoundland, Nova Scotia, and Prince Edward Island.

Atlan′tic puf′fin. See under **puffin.**

Atlan′tic rid′ley, ridley (def. 1).

Atlan′tic salm′on, a valuable food and game fish, *Salmo salar,* mainly of northern coastal Atlantic waters or, when spawning, in freshwater streams tributary to the ocean. [1900–05]

Atlan′tic time′. See under **standard time.** Also called **Atlan′tic Stand′ard Time′.** [1905–10]

At•lan•tis (at lan′tis), *n.* a legendary island, first mentioned by Plato, said to have existed in the Atlantic Ocean west of Gibraltar and to have sunk beneath the sea, but linked by some modern archaeologists with the island of Thera, the surviving remnant of a much larger island destroyed by a volcanic eruption c1500 B.C. Cf. **Akrotiri.**

at•las (at′ləs), *n., pl.* **at•las•es** for 1–3, **at•lan•tes** (at lan′tēz) for 5. **1.** a bound collection of maps. **2.** a bound volume of charts, plates, or tables illustrating any subject. **3.** *Anat.* the first cervical vertebra, which supports the head. **4.** a size of drawing or writing paper, 26 × 34 or 33 inches. **5.** Also called **telamon.** *Archit.* a sculptural figure of a man used as a column. Cf. **caryatid.** [1580–90 in sense "prop, support"; as name for a collection of maps, said to be from illustrations of Atlas supporting the globe in early books of this kind]

At•las (at′ləs), *n., pl.* **At•las•es** for 2, 4. **1.** *Class. Myth.* a Titan, son of Iapetus and brother of Prometheus and Epimetheus, condemned to support the sky on his shoulders: identified by the ancients with the Atlas Mountains. **2.** a person who supports a heavy burden; a mainstay. **3. Charles** (*Angelo Siciliano*), 1894–1972, U.S. body-building advocate, born in Italy. **4.** a liquid-propellant booster rocket, originally developed as the first U.S. ICBM, used with Agena or Centaur upper stages to launch satellites into orbit around the earth and send probes to the moon and planets; also used to launch the Mercury spacecraft into orbit around the earth.

At′las ce′dar, an evergreen tree, *Cedrus atlantica,* native to northern Africa, having in its widely cultivated forms bluish-green leaves and light-brown cones.

At′las Moun′tains, a mountain range in NW Africa, extending through Morocco, Algeria, and Tunisia. Highest peak, Mt. Tizi, 14,764 ft. (4500 m).

at•latl (ät′lät′l), *n. Archaeol.* spear-thrower (def. 2). [1870–75; < Nahuatl *ahtlatl*]

At•li (ät′lē), *n. Scand. Legend.* Attila, king of the Huns: represented in the *Volsunga Saga* as the brother of Brynhild and the second husband of Gudrun, whose brothers he killed in order to get the Nibelung treasure. Cf. **Etzel.**

ATM, See **automated-teller machine.**

atm., 1. atmosphere; atmospheres. **2.** atmospheric.

At/m, ampere-turns per meter.

at. m. See **atomic mass.**

at•man (ät′mən), *n. Hinduism.* **1.** the principle of life. **2.** the individual self, known after enlightenment to be identical with Brahman. **3.** (*cap.*) the World Soul, from which all individual souls derive, and to which they return as the supreme goal of existence. Also, **at•ma** (ät′mə). [1775–85; < Skt *ātman* breath, self]

atmo-, a combining form meaning "air," used in the formation of compound words: *atmosphere.* [< Gk, comb. form of *atmós* vapor, smoke]

at•mol•y•sis (at mol′ə sis), *n., pl.* **-ses** (-sēz′). a process for separating gases or vapors of different molecular weights by transmission through a porous substance. [1865–70; ATMO- + -LYSIS]

at•mom•e•ter (at mom′i tər), *n.* an instrument for measuring the rate at which water evaporates. Also called **evaporimeter.** [1805–15; ATMO- + -METER]

at•mom•e•try (at mom′i trē), *n.* the science of measuring the rate at which water evaporates. [ATMO- + -METRY]

at•mo•phile (at′mə fīl′), *Geol.* —*adj.* **1.** (of a chemical element in the earth) having an affinity for the atmosphere, as neon or helium. —*n.* **2.** an atmophile element. [ATMO- + -PHILE]

At′mos clock′ (at′məs), *Trademark.* a brand of self-winding clock utilizing variations of temperature acting on a mercury thermometer to create an imbalance within the winding drum.

at•mos•phere (at′məs fēr′), *n., v.,* **-phered, -pher•ing.** —*n.* **1.** the gaseous envelope surrounding the earth; the air. **2.** this medium at a given place. **3.** *Astron.* the gaseous envelope surrounding a heavenly body. **4.** *Chem.* any gaseous envelope or medium. **5.** a conventional unit of pressure, the normal pressure of the air at sea level, about 14.7 pounds per square inch (101.3 kilopascals), equal to the pressure exerted by a column of mercury 29.92 in. (760 mm) high. *Abbr.:* atm. **6.** a surrounding or pervading mood, environment, or influence: *an atmosphere of impending war; a very tense atmosphere.* **7.** the dominant mood or emotional tone of a work of art, as of a play or novel: *the chilly atmosphere of a ghost story.* **8.** a distinctive quality, as of a place; character: *The old part of town has lots of atmosphere.* —*v.t.* **9.** to give an atmosphere to: *The author had cleverly atmosphered the novel for added chills.* [1630–40; < NL *atmosphaera.* See ATMO-, -SPHERE] —**at′mos•phere′less,** *adj.*

at•mos•pher•ic (at′məs fer′ik, -fēr′-), *adj.* **1.** pertaining to, existing in, or consisting of the atmosphere: *atmospheric vapors.* **2.** caused by, produced by, or operated on by the atmosphere: *atmospheric storms.* **3.** resembling or suggestive of the atmosphere; having muted tones and softened or indistinct outlines; hazy: *atmospheric effects.* **4.** having or producing an emotional atmosphere: *atmospheric quality; atmospheric lighting.* Also, **at′mos•pher′i•cal.** [1775–85; ATMOSPHERE + -IC] —**at′mos•pher′i•cal•ly,** *adv.*

at′mospher′ic bound′ary lay′er. See **surface boundary layer.**

at′mospher′ic brak′ing, *Rocketry.* a technique of reentry in which the vehicle is maneuvered in the upper atmosphere so as to lose velocity by utilizing drag without overheating.

atmospher′ic electric′ity, static electricity produced by charged particles in the atmosphere.

at′mospher′ic en′gine, an early form of single-acting engine in which the power stroke is provided by atmospheric pressure acting upon a piston in an exhausted cylinder. [1815–25]

atmospher′ic inver′sion, *Meteorol.* inversion (def. 12).

atmospher′ic perspec′tive. See **aerial perspective.**

at′mospher′ic pres′sure, *Meteorol.* **1.** the pressure exerted by the earth's atmosphere at any given point, being the product of the mass of the atmospheric column of the unit area above the given point and of the gravitational acceleration at the given point. **2.** a value of standard or normal atmospheric pressure, equivalent to the pressure exerted by a column of mercury 29.92 in. (760 mm) high, or 1013 millibars (101.3 kilopascals). Also called **barometric pressure.** Cf. **sea-level pressure.** [1655–65]

at•mos•pher•ics (at′məs fer′iks, -fēr′-), *n.* **1.** (*used with a plural v.*) *Radio and Television.* noise in a radio receiver or randomly distributed white spots or bands on the screen of a television receiver, caused by interference from natural electromagnetic disturbances in the atmosphere. **2.** (*used with a singular v.*) the study of such phenomena; sferics. **3.** (*used with a plural v.*) mood or atmosphere; ambience: *The atmospherics of the conference were cordial.* [1900–05; see ATMOSPHERIC, -ICS]

at′mospher′ic tide′, *Meteorol.* a movement of atmospheric masses caused by the gravitational attraction of the sun and moon and by daily solar heating. [1825–35]

at′mospher′ic win′dow, *Astron.* any of the wavelengths at which electromagnetic radiation from space can penetrate the earth's atmosphere. [1965–70]

At•na (ät′nə), *n.* Ahtna.

at. no. See **atomic number.**

CONCISE PRONUNCIATION KEY: act, cāpe, dâre, pärt; set, ēqual; if, īce; ox, ōver, ôrder, oil, bo͝ok, bo͞ot, out; up, ûrge; child; sing; shoe; thin, that; zh as in *treasure.* ə = *a* as in *alone, e* as in *system, i* as in *easily, o* as in *gallop, u* as in *circus;* ə as in *fire* (fīər), *hour* (ouər). l and n can serve as syllabic consonants, as in *cradle* (krād′l), and *button* (but′n). See the full key inside the front cover.

at•oll (at′ôl, -ol, -ōl, ə tôl′, ə tol′, ə tōl′), *n.* a ring-shaped coral reef or a string of closely spaced small coral islands, enclosing or nearly enclosing a shallow lagoon. [1615–25; earlier *atollon* < F: a word used in early descriptions of the Maldive Island atolls; said to be Divehi (Indo-Aryan language of the Maldives) *atoḷu*]

at•om (at′əm), *n.* **1.** *Physics.* **a.** the smallest component of an element having the chemical properties of the element, consisting of a nucleus containing combinations of neutrons and protons and one or more electrons bound to the nucleus by electrical attraction; the number of protons determines the identity of the element. **b.** an atom with one of the electrons replaced by some other particle: *muonic atom; kaonic atom.* **2.** *Energy.* this component as the source of nuclear energy. **3.** a hypothetical particle of matter so minute as to admit of no division. **4.** anything extremely small; a minute quantity. [1350–1400; ME *attomos, athomus* < L *atomus* < Gk *átomos,* n. use of *átomos* undivided, equiv. to *a-* A-[6] + *tomós* divided, verbal of *témnein* to cut]
—**Syn. 4.** shred, speck, scintilla, iota, jot, whit.

at′om bomb′. See **atomic bomb.** [1940–45]

at•om-bomb (at′əm bom′), *v.t.* **1.** to bomb (a target) with an atomic bomb. —*v.i.* **2.** to atom-bomb a target. [1940–45]

a•tom•ic (ə tom′ik), *adj.* **1.** of, pertaining to, resulting from, or using atoms, atomic energy, or atomic bombs: *an atomic explosion.* **2.** propelled or driven by atomic energy: *an atomic submarine.* **3.** *Chem.* existing as free, uncombined atoms. **4.** extremely minute. Also, **a•tom′i•cal.** [1670–80; ATOM + -IC] —**a•tom′i•cal•ly,** *adv.*

atom′ic age′, the period in history initiated by the first use of the atomic bomb and characterized by atomic energy as a military, political, and industrial factor. [1940–45]

atom′ic bomb′, **1.** a bomb whose potency is derived from nuclear fission of atoms of fissionable material with the consequent conversion of part of their mass into energy. **2.** a bomb whose explosive force comes from a chain reaction based on nuclear fission in U-235 or plutonium. Also, **atom bomb.** Also called **A-bomb, fission bomb.** [1910–15]

atom′ic clock′, an extremely accurate electronic clock regulated by the resonance frequency of atoms or molecules of certain substances, as cesium. [1935–40]

atom′ic cock′tail, *Informal.* an oral dose of a radioactive substance used in the treatment or diagnosis of cancer.

atom′ic en′ergy. See **nuclear energy.** [1905–10]

Atom′ic En′ergy Commis′sion, a former federal agency (1946–75) created to regulate the development of the U.S. atomic energy program: functions transferred to the Nuclear Regulatory Commission. *Abbr.:* AEC

atom′ic hy′drogen, *Chem.* hydrogen in the form of single atoms, rather than molecules, which makes it extremely reactive. Also called **active hydrogen.**

at•o•mic•i•ty (at′ə mis′i tē), *n. Chem.* **1.** the number of atoms in a molecule of a gas. **2.** valence. [1860–65; ATOMIC + -ITY]

atom′ic mass′, *Chem.* the mass of an isotope of an element measured in units formerly based on the mass of one hydrogen atom taken as a unit or on 1/16 the mass of one oxygen atom, but after 1961 based on 1/12 the mass of the carbon-12 atom. *Abbr.:* at. m. [1895–1900]

atom′ic mass′ u′nit, *Physics.* **1.** Also called **dalton.** a unit of mass, equal to 1/12 the mass of the carbon-12 atom and used to express the mass of atomic and subatomic particles. **2.** (formerly) a unit of mass, equal to 1/16 the mass of an oxygen atom having atomic mass 16. *Abbr.:* amu, AMU [1950–55]

atom′ic num′ber, the number of positive charges or protons in the nucleus of an atom of a given element, and therefore also the number of electrons normally surrounding the nucleus. *Abbr.:* at. no.; *Symbol:* Z Also called **proton number.** [1815–25]

atom′ic or′bital, *Physics, Chem.* See under **orbital** (def. 2).

atom′ic pile′, *Physics.* reactor (def. 4). [1940–45]

atom′ic pow′er. See **nuclear power.** [1940–45]

atom′ic reac′tor, *Physics.* reactor (def. 4).

a•tom•ics (ə tom′iks), *n.* (*used with a singular v.*) *Informal.* the branch of physics that deals with atoms, esp. atomic energy. [see ATOMIC, -ICS]

atom′ic struc′ture, *Physics.* the structure of an atom, theoretically consisting of a positively charged nucleus surrounded and neutralized by negatively charged electrons revolving in orbits at varying distances from the nucleus, the constitution of the nucleus and the arrangement of the electrons differing with various chemical elements. [1895–1900]

atom′ic the′ory, **1.** *Physics, Chem.* any of several theories describing the structure, behavior, and other properties of the atom and its component parts. **2.** *Philos.* atomism (def. 1). [1840–50]

atom′ic u′nit of length′, *Physics.* See **Bohr radius.**

atom′ic vol′ume, *Chem.* the atomic weight of an element divided by its density. *Abbr.:* at. vol.

atom′ic weight′, *Chem.* the average weight of an atom of an element, formerly based on the weight of one hydrogen atom taken as a unit or on 1/16 the weight of an oxygen atom, but after 1961 based on 1/12 the weight of the carbon-12 atom. *Abbr.:* at. wt. [1820–30]

CONCISE ETYMOLOGY KEY: <, descended or borrowed from; >, whence; b., blend of, blended; c., cognate with; cf., compare; deriv., derivative; equiv., equivalent; imit., imitative; obl., oblique; r., replacing; s., stem; sp., spelling, spelled; resp., respelling, respelled; trans., translation; ?, origin unknown; *, unattested; ‡, probably earlier than. See the full key inside the front cover.

at•om•ism (at′ə miz′əm), *n.* **1.** Also called **atomic theory.** *Philos.* the theory that minute, discrete, finite, and indivisible elements are the ultimate constituents of all matter. **2.** *Psychol.* a method or theory that reduces all psychological phenomena to simple elements. [1670–80; ATOM + -ISM] —**at′om•ist,** *n.* —**at′om•is′tic, at′•om•is′ti•cal,** *adj.* —**at′om•is′ti•cal•ly,** *adv.*

at•om•ize (at′ə mīz′), *v.,* **-ized, -iz•ing.** —*v.t.* **1.** to reduce to atoms. **2.** to reduce to fine particles or spray. **3.** to destroy (a target) by bombing, esp. with an atomic bomb. —*v.i.* **4.** to split into many sections, groups, factions, etc.; fragmentize: *Critics say the group has atomized around several leaders. Also, esp. Brit.,* **at′om•ise′.** [1670–80; ATOM + -IZE] —**at′om•i•za′tion,** *n.*

at•om•iz•er (at′ə mī′zər), *n.* an apparatus for reducing liquids to a fine spray, as for medicinal or cosmetic application. [1860–65; ATOMIZE + -ER[1]]

at′om smash′er, *Physics.* accelerator (def. 7). [1935–40]

at•o•my[1] (at′ə mē), *n., pl.* **-mies. 1.** an atom; mote. **2.** a small creature; pygmy. [1585–95; sing. use of L *atomī,* pl. of *atomus* ATOM]

at•o•my[2] (at′ə mē), *n., pl.* **-mies.** a skeleton. [1590–1600; var. of ANATOMY (taken as *an atomy*)]

A•ton (ät′n), *n. Egyptian Religion.* a solar deity declared by Amenhotep IV to be the only god, represented as a solar disk with rays ending in human hands. Also, **Aten.**

a•ton•al (ā tōn′l), *adj. Music.* of, pertaining to, or marked by atonality. [1920–25; A-[6] + TONAL] —**a•ton′•al•is′tic,** *adj.* —**a•ton′•al•ly,** *adv.*

a•ton•al•ism (ā tōn′l iz′əm), *n. Music.* **1.** atonality. **2.** a note, phrase, etc., that seems harsh or discordant. [1925–30; ATONAL + -ISM] —**a•ton′al•ist,** *n.*

a•to•nal•i•ty (ā′tō nal′i tē), *n. Music.* **1.** the absence of key or tonal center. **2.** an atonal principle or style of composition. [1920–25; ATONAL + -ITY]

a•tone (ə tōn′), *v.,* **a•toned, a•ton•ing.** —*v.i.* **1.** to make amends or reparation, as for an offense or a crime, or for an offender (usually fol. by *for*): *to atone for one's sins.* **2.** to make up, as for errors or deficiencies (usually fol. by *for*): *to atone for one's failings.* **3.** *Obs.* to become reconciled; agree. —*v.t.* **4.** to make amends for; expiate: *He atoned his sins.* **5.** *Obs.* to bring into unity, harmony, concord, etc. [1545–55; back formation from ATONEMENT] —**a•ton′a•ble, a•tone′a•ble,** *adj.* —**a•ton′•er,** *n.* —**a•ton′ing•ly,** *adv.*

a•tone•ment (ə tōn′mənt), *n.* **1.** satisfaction or reparation for a wrong or injury; amends. **2.** (*sometimes cap.*) *Theol.* the doctrine concerning the reconciliation of God and humankind, esp. as accomplished through the life, suffering, and death of Christ. **3.** *Christian Science.* the experience of humankind's unity with God exemplified by Jesus Christ. **4.** *Archaic.* reconciliation; agreement. [1505–15; from phrase *at one* in harmony + -MENT, as trans. of ML *adūnāmentum;* cf. ME *onement* unity]

a•ton•ic (ə ton′ik, ā ton′-), *adj.* **1.** *Phonet.* **a.** unaccented. **b.** *Obs.* voiceless. **2.** *Pathol.* characterized by atony. —*n.* **3.** *Gram.* an unaccented word, syllable, or sound. [1720–30; A-[6] + TONIC; in pathology sense, ATON(Y) + -IC]

at•o•nic•i•ty (at′n is′i tē, ā′tō nis′-), *n. Pathol.* lack of tone; atony. [1895–1900; ATONIC + -ITY]

at•o•ny (at′n ē), *n.* **1.** *Pathol.* lack of tone or energy; muscular weakness, esp. in a contractile organ. **2.** *Phonet.* lack of stress accent. Also, **a•to•ni•a** (ə tō′nē ə, ā tō′-). [1685–95; < LL *atonia* < Gk, deriv. of *átonos* unaccented, languid, lit., toneless. See A-[6], TONE]

a•top (ə top′), *adj., adv.* **1.** on or at the top. —*prep.* **2.** on the top of: *atop the flagpole.* [1650–60; A-[1] + TOP[1]]

a•top•ic (ā top′ik, ə top′-), *adj.* **1.** of or pertaining to atopy. **2.** ectopic. [1920–25; ATOP(Y) + -IC]

at•o•py (at′ə pē), *n.* an allergy, involving an inherited immunoglobulin of the IgE type, that predisposes a person to certain allergic responses, as atopic dermatitis. [1920–25; < Gk *atopía* extraordinariness, equiv. to *átop(os)* out of place, unusual (see A-[6], TOPO-) + *-ia* -Y[3]]

-ator, a combination of **-ate**[1] and **-or**[2] that forms nouns corresponding to verbs ending in **-ate**[1], denoting a human agent (*agitator; mediator; adjudicator*) or nonhuman entity, esp. a machine (*incubator; regulator; vibrator*) performing the function named by the verb. Cf. **-tor, -or**[2]. [< L *-ātor,* orig. not a suffix, but the termination of nouns formed with *-tor* -TOR from verbs whose stems ended in *-ā-;* in English, Latin loanwords ending in *-ātor* have been reanalyzed as derivatives of the past participles in *-tus* (see -ATE[1]) and a suffix *-or* (see -OR[2]), and many new English nouns derived from English verbs based on Latin past participles (e.g., VIBRATOR from VIBRATE)]

-atory, a combination of **-ate**[1] and **-ory**[1] or **-ory**[2], used infrequently as an independent suffix with the same senses as **-ory**[1] and **-ory**[2]: *affirmatory; observatory.* [< L *-ātōrius, -a, -um,* orig. the termination of adjectives formed with *-tōrius* (see -TORY[1], TORY[2]) and verbs whose stems ended in *-ā-;* reanalyzed in English in the same way as -ATOR]

a•tox•ic (ā tok′sik), *adj.* not toxic. [A-[6] + TOXIC]

ATP, *Biochem.* adenosine triphosphate: an ester of adenosine and triphosphoric acid, $C_{10}H_{12}N_5O_4H_4P_3O_9$, formed esp. aerobically by the reaction of ADP and an orthophosphate during oxidation, or by the interaction of ADP and phosphocreatine or certain other substrates, and serving as a source of energy for physiological reactions, esp. muscle contraction. [1940–45]

ATPase (ā′tē′pē′ās, -āz), *n. Biochem.* adenosine triphosphatase: any of several enzymes that catalyze the hydrolysis of ATP to ADP and phosphate. [1945–50; ATP + -ASE]

at•ra•bil•ious (a′trə bil′yəs), *adj.* **1.** gloomy; morose; melancholy; morbid. **2.** irritable; bad-tempered; splenetic. Also, **at′ra•bil′iar.** [1645–55; < L *ātra bīli(s)* black bile + -OUS] —**at′ra•bil′ious•ness,** *n.*

A•tra•ha•sis (ä′trä hä′sis), *n.* a legendary Akkadian sage who built a boat in which he and his family, servants, and chattels escaped the Deluge. Cf. **Ziusudra.**

at•ra•zine (a′trə zēn′), *n. Chem.* a white crystalline compound, $C_8H_{14}N_5Cl$, used as an herbicide to control weeds, esp. in corn crops. [1960–65; A(MINO-) +TR(I)A-ZINE]

A•trek (ə trek′, ä trek′), *n.* a river arising in NE Iran, flowing W, then along the Iran-Turkmenistan border, and through Turkmenistan into the Caspian Sea. ab. 300 mi. (485 km) long. Also, **A•trak** (ə trak′, ä trak′).

a•trem•ble (ə trem′bəl), *adv.* in a trembling state. [1855–60; A-[1] + TREMBLE]

a•tre•sia (ə trē′zhə, -zhē ə), *n. Med.* the congenital absence, or the pathological closure, of an opening, passage, or cavity. [1800–10; < NL < Gk *a-* A-[6] + *trēs(is)* perforation + *-ia* -IA] —**a•tre•sic** (ə trē′zik, -sik), **a•tret•ic** (ə tret′ik), *adj.*

A•tre•us (ā′trē əs, ā′tryōōs), *n. Class. Myth.* the father of Plisthenes, Agamemnon, Menelaus, and Anaxibia upon whose house Thyestes pronounced a curse.

a′trial na′triuret′ic fac′tor, any of several peptide hormones that are released by the atria of the heart in response to an abnormal increase in blood volume and that modulate blood pressure and the excretion of sodium, potassium, and water. *Abbr.:* ANF Also called **atriopeptin, auriculin.**

a•trich•i•a (ā trik′ē ə, ə trik′-), *n. Med.* congenital absence or loss of hair. Also, **at•ri•cho•sis** (a′trə kō′sis). [< NL; see A-[6], TRICH-, -IA]

a•tri•o•ven•tric•u•lar (ā′trē ō ven trik′yə lər), *adj. Anat.* of or pertaining to the atria and ventricles of the heart. *Abbr.:* AV, A-V [1855–60; < NL *atrio-* (comb. form of *atrium* heart chamber; see ATRIUM, -O-) + VENTRICULAR]

a′trioventric′ular bun′dle, *Anat.* a bundle of specialized muscle fibers regulating the heartbeat by conducting impulses from the right atrium to the ventricles. Also called **bundle of His.**

a′trioventric′ular node′, *Anat.* a small mass of muscular fibers at the base of the wall between the atria, conducting impulses received from the sinoatrial node by way of the atrioventricular bundles and, under certain conditions, functioning for the sinoatrial node as pacemaker of the heart. *Abbr.:* A-V node. [1930–35]

a•trip (ə trip′), *adj. Naut.* **1.** aweigh. **2.** (of a sail) in position and ready for trimming. **3.** (of a yard) hoisted and ready to be fastened in position. **4.** (of an upper mast) unfastened and ready for lowering. [1620–30; A-[1] + TRIP]

a•tri•um (ā′trē əm), *n., pl.* **a•tri•a** (ā′trē ə), **a•tri•ums. 1.** *Archit.* **a.** Also called **cavaedium.** the main or central room of an ancient Roman house, open to the sky at the center and usually having a pool for the collection of rain water. **b.** a courtyard, flanked or surrounded by porticoes, in front of an early or medieval Christian church. See diag. under **basilica. c.** a skylit central court in a contemporary building or house. **2.** *Anat.* either of the two upper chambers on each side of the heart that receive blood from the veins and in turn force it into the ventricles. See illus. under **heart.** [1570–80; < L (in anatomical sense < NL)] —**a′tri•al,** *adj.*

at•ro•ce•ru•le•ous (a′trō sə rōō′lē əs, -rōōl′yəs), *n.* a deep blue-black color. Also, **at′ro•ce•ru′le•us, at′ro•coe•ru′le•us.** [< L *ātr-,* s. of *āter* black + -O- + *caeruleus* azure; see CERULEAN, -OUS]

a•tro•cious (ə trō′shəs), *adj.* **1.** extremely or shockingly wicked, cruel, or brutal: *an atrocious crime.* **2.** shockingly bad or tasteless; dreadful; abominable: *an atrocious painting; atrocious manners.* [1660–70; ATROCI(TY) + -OUS] —**a•tro′cious•ly,** *adv.* —**a•tro′•cious•ness,** *n.*
—**Syn. 1.** felonious, heinous, monstrous, diabolical, devilish. **2.** execrable; detestable.

atro′cious assault′ and bat′tery, *Law.* **1.** an assault involving the actual wounding and maiming of another person. **2.** See **aggravated assault.** [1930–35]

a•troc•i•ty (ə tros′i tē), *n., pl.* **-ties. 1.** the quality or state of being atrocious. **2.** an atrocious act, thing, or circumstance. [1525–35; < L *atrōcitās,* equiv. to *atrōci-* (s. of *atrōx*) fierce + *-tās* -TY[2]]

à trois (A TRWÄ′), *French.* for, among, or composed of three persons collectively (usually used following the word it modifies): *a secret shared* à trois.

At•ro•pa•te•ne (a′trə pə tē′nə), *n.* See **Media Atropatene.**

at•ro•phied (a′trə fēd), *adj.* exhibiting or affected with atrophy; wasted; withered; shriveled: *an atrophied arm; an atrophied talent.* [1590–1600; ATROPHY + -ED[2]]

at•ro•phy (a′trə fē), *n., v.,* **-phied, -phy•ing.** —*n.* **1.** Also, **a•tro•phi•a** (ə trō′fē ə). *Pathol.* a wasting away of the body or of an organ or part, as from defective nutrition or nerve damage. **2.** degeneration, decline, or decrease, as from disuse: *He argued that there was a progressive atrophy of freedom and independence of thought.* —*v.t., v.i.* **3.** to affect with or undergo atrophy. [1590–1600; earlier *atrophie* (< MF) < LL *atrophia* < Gk, equiv. to *átroph(os)* not fed (see A-[6], TROPHO-) + *-ia* -IA] —**a•troph•ic** (ə trof′ik, ə trō′fik), *adj.*

at•ro•pine (a′trə pēn′, -pin), *n. Pharm.* a poisonous crystalline alkaloid, $C_{17}H_{23}NO_3$, obtained from belladonna and other plants of the nightshade family, that prevents the response of various body structures to certain types of nerve stimulation: used chiefly to relieve spasms, to lessen secretions, and, topically, to dilate the pupil of the eye. [1830–40; < NL *Atrop(a)* belladonna genus (< Gk *átropos;* see ATROPOS) + -INE[2]]

at•ro•pism (a′trə piz′əm), *n. Pathol.* poisoning resulting from atropine or belladonna. Also, **at•ro•pin•ism** (a′trə pə niz′əm). [1875–80; ATROP(INE) + -ISM]

At·ro·pos (a′trə pos′), *n. Class. Myth.* the Fate who cuts the thread of life. [< Gk: lit., not turning, hence, inflexible. See A-[6], -TROPE]

a·try (ə trī′), *adj. Naut.* lying to under a trysail in heavy weather; trying. [1605–15; A-[1] + TRY]

ATS, Auxiliary Territorial Service (organized in 1941 for women serving in the British army; became part of army in 1949 as WRAC).

A.T.S., **1.** American Temperance Society. **2.** American Tract Society. **3.** American Transport Service.

att., **1.** attached. **2.** attention. **3.** attorney.

at·ta·boy (at′ə boi′), *interj. Informal.* (used as an enthusiastic expression of encouragement or approval to a boy, man, or male animal.) [1905–10, *Amer.*; alleged to be a reduced form of *that's a boy* or *that's the boy*]

at·tac·ca (ə tä′kə, ə tak′ə; *It.* ät täk′kä), *v.* (used as an imperative) *Music.* begin immediately (directing a performer to go without pause to the next section). [< It: impv. of *attaccare* to ATTACK]

at·tach (ə tach′), *v.t.* **1.** to fasten or affix; join; connect: *to attach a photograph to an application with a staple.* **2.** to join in action or function; make part of: *to attach oneself to a group.* **3.** *Mil.* to place on temporary duty with or in assistance to a military unit. **4.** to include as a quality or condition of something: *One proviso is attached to this legacy.* **5.** to assign or attribute: *to attach significance to a gesture.* **6.** to bind by ties of affection or regard: *You always attach yourself to people who end up hurting you.* **7.** *Law.* to take (persons or property) by legal authority. **8.** *Obs.* to lay hold of; seize. —*v.i.* **9.** to adhere; pertain; belong (usually fol. by *to* or *upon*): *No blame attaches to him.* [1300–50; ME *atachen* < AF *atacher* to seize, OF *atachier* to fasten, alter. of *estachier* to fasten with or to a stake, equiv. to *estach(e)* (< Gmc **stakka* STAKE) + *-ier* inf. suffix] —**at·tach′a·ble,** *adj.* —**at·tach′er,** *n.*
—**Syn. 1.** subjoin, append, add, annex. —**Ant. 1.** detach.

at·ta·ché (a ta shā′, at′ə- *or, esp. Brit.,* ə tash′ā), —*n.* **1.** a diplomatic official attached to an embassy or legation, esp. in a technical capacity: *a commercial attaché; a cultural attaché.* **2.** a military officer who is assigned to a diplomatic post in a foreign country in order to gather military information: *an air attaché; an army attaché; a naval attaché.* **3.** Also, **at′ta·che′.** See **attaché case.** [1825–35; < F: lit., attached, ptp. of *attacher* to ATTACH]

attaché′ case′, a flat, usually rigid, rectangular briefcase for carrying business papers, documents, or the like. Also called **dispatch case.** [1900–05]

at·tached (ə tacht′), *adj.* **1.** joined; connected; bound. **2.** having a wall in common with another building (opposed to *detached*): *an attached house.* **3.** *Zool.* permanently fixed to the substratum; sessile. [1545–55; ATTACH + -ED[2]]

at·tach·ment (ə tach′mənt), *n.* **1.** an act of attaching or the state of being attached. **2.** a feeling that binds one to a person, thing, cause, ideal, or the like; devotion; regard: *a fond attachment to his cousin; a profound attachment to the cause of peace.* **3.** something that attaches; a fastening or tie: *the attachments of a harness; the attachments of a pair of skis.* **4.** an additional or supplementary device: *attachments for an electric drill.* **5.** *Law.* seizure of property or person by legal authority, esp. seizure of a defendant's property to prevent its dissipation before trial or to acquire jurisdiction over it. **6.** something attached, as a document added to a letter. [1400–50; late ME *attachement* seizure < AF. See ATTACH, -MENT]
—**Syn. 2.** love, devotedness. **3.** junction, connection. **4.** See **addition.**

at·tack (ə tak′), *v.t.* **1.** to set upon in a forceful, violent, hostile, or aggressive way, with or without a weapon; begin fighting with: *He attacked him with his bare hands.* **2.** to begin hostilities against; start an offensive against: *to attack the enemy.* **3.** to blame or abuse violently or bitterly. **4.** to direct unfavorable criticism against; criticize severely; argue with strongly: *He attacked his opponent's statement.* **5.** to try to destroy, esp. with verbal abuse: *to attack the mayor's reputation.* **6.** to set about (a task) or go to work on (a thing) vigorously: *to attack housecleaning; to attack the hamburger hungrily.* **7.** (of disease, destructive agencies, etc.) to begin to affect. —*v.i.* **8.** to make an attack; begin hostilities. —*n.* **9.** the act of attacking; onslaught; assault. **10.** a military offensive against an enemy or enemy position. **11.** *Pathol.* seizure by disease or illness: *an attack of indigestion.* **12.** the beginning or initiating of any action; onset. **13.** an aggressive move in a performance or contest. **14.** the approach or manner of approach in beginning a musical phrase. [1590–1600; earlier *atta(c)que* < MF *atta(c)quer* < It *attaccare* to attack, ATTACH] —**at·tack′a·ble,** *adj.* —**at·tack′er,** *n.*
—**Syn. 1.** storm, charge. ATTACK, ASSAIL, ASSAULT, MOLEST all mean to set upon someone forcibly, with hostile or violent intent. ATTACK is the most general word and applies to a beginning of hostilities, esp. those definitely planned: *to attack from ambush.* ASSAIL implies vehement, sudden, and sometimes repeated attack: *to assail with weapons or with gossip.* ASSAULT almost always implies bodily violence: *to assault with intent to kill.* To MOLEST is to harass, to threaten, or to assault: *He was safe, and where no one could molest him.* **4.** censure; impugn, oppugn, abuse. **9.** onset, encounter. —**Ant. 1, 4.** defend. **9.** defense.

attack′ dog′, a dog trained to attack on command, as for protection or to aid in the apprehension of criminals. [1965–70]

at·ta·girl (at′ə gûrl′), *interj. Informal.* (used as an enthusiastic expression of encouragement or approval to a girl, woman, or female animal.) [1905–10; see ATTABOY, GIRL]

at·tain (ə tān′), *v.t.* **1.** to reach, achieve, or accomplish; gain; obtain: *to attain one's goals.* **2.** to come to or arrive at, esp. after some labor or tedium; reach: *to attain the age of 96; to attain the mountain peak.* —*v.i.* **3.** to arrive at or succeed in reaching or obtaining something (usually fol. by *to* or *unto*): *to attain to knowledge.* **4.** to reach in the course of development or growth: *These trees attain to remarkable height.* [1300–50; ME *atei(g)nen* < AF, OF *ateign-* (s. of *ateindre*) < VL **attangere* (for L *attingere*), equiv. to L *at-* AT- + *tangere* to touch] —**at·tain′er,** *n.*
—**Syn. 1.** secure. See **gain**[1]. —**Ant. 1, 2.** miss.

at·tain·a·ble (ə tā′nə bəl), *adj.* capable of being attained. [1640–50; ATTAIN + -ABLE] —**at·tain′a·bil′i·ty, at·tain′a·ble·ness,** *n.*

at·tain·der (ə tān′dər), *n.* **1.** the legal consequence of judgment of death or outlawry for treason or felony, involving the loss of all civil rights. **2.** *Obs.* dishonor. [1425–75; late ME, n. use of AF *attaindre* to convict, OF *ataindre* to convict, ATTAIN]

at·tain·ment (ə tān′mənt), *n.* **1.** an act of attaining. **2.** something attained; a personal acquirement; achievement. [1350–1400; ME *attenement.* See ATTAIN, -MENT]
—**Syn. 2.** accomplishment.

at·taint (ə tānt′), *v.t.* **1.** *Law.* to condemn by a sentence or a bill or act of attainder. **2.** to disgrace. **3.** *Archaic.* to accuse. **4.** *Obs.* to prove the guilt of. —*n.* **5.** *Obs.* a stain; disgrace; taint. [1250–1300; ME *ataynte,* deriv. of *ataynt* convicted < AF, OF, ptp. of *ataindre* to convict, ATTAIN]

at·tain·ture (ə tān′chər), *n. Obs.* **1.** attainder. **2.** imputation. [1530–40; ATTAINT + -URE, modeled on ML *attinctūra*]

At·ta·lid (at′l id), *n., pl.* **At·ta·lids, At·tal·i·dae** (ə tal′i dē′). any of a line of kings, usually named Attalus or Eumenes, that ruled Pergamum, in Asia Minor, 282–133 B.C. [presumably after *Attalus* (< Gk *Áttalos*), father of Philetaerus (d. 263 B.C.), founder of the kingdom; see -ID[1]]

At·ta·lus I (at′l əs), (*Soter*) king of Pergamum 241–197 B.C.

Attalus II, (*Philadelphus*) king of Pergamum c159–138 B.C.

Attalus III, (*Philometor*) king of Pergamum 138–133 B.C.

at·ta·pul·gite (at′ə pul′jit), *n.* a clay mineral, basic hydrous silicate of magnesium and aluminum, the active ingredient of fuller's earth. [named after *Attapulgus,* town in SW Georgia, U.S., near source of supply; see -ITE[1]]

at·tar (at′ər), *n.* **1.** Also, **atar, athar, ottar, otto.** a perfume or essential oil obtained from flowers or petals. **2.** Also called **at′tar of ros′es.** See **rose oil.** [1790–1800; short for Pers *'atar-gūl* attar of roses, akin to *'atara* to smell sweet, *'iṭr* fragrance (< Ar)]

at·tem·per (ə tem′pər), *v.t. Archaic.* **1.** to modify or moderate by mixing or blending with something different or opposite. **2.** to regulate or modify the temperature of. **3.** to soothe; mollify; mitigate. **4.** to accommodate; adapt (usually fol. by *to*). [1325–75; ME *attemperen* < L *attemperāre* to adjust (see AT-, TEMPER); r. ME *atempren* < MF *attemprer* < L, as above]

at·tempt (ə tempt′), *v.t.* **1.** to make an effort at; try; undertake; seek: *to attempt an impossible task; to attempt to walk six miles.* **2.** *Archaic.* to attack; move against in a hostile manner: *to attempt a person's life.* **3.** *Archaic.* to tempt. —*n.* **4.** an effort made to accomplish something: *He made an attempt to swim across the lake.* **5.** an attack or assault: *an attempt upon the leader's life.* [1350–1400; ME < AF *atempter* < L *attemptāre* to test, tamper with. See AT-, TEMPT] —**at·tempt′a·bil′i·ty,** *n.* —**at·tempt′a·ble,** *adj.* —**at·tempt′er,** *n.*
—**Syn. 1.** See **try.** **4.** try, endeavor.

at·tend (ə tend′), *v.t.* **1.** to be present at: *to attend a lecture; to attend church.* **2.** to go with as a concomitant or result; accompany: *Fever may attend a cold. Success attended her hard work.* **3.** to take care of; minister to; devote one's services to: *The nurse attended the patient daily.* **4.** to wait upon; accompany as a companion or servant: *The retainers attended their lord.* **5.** to take charge of; watch over; look after; tend; guard: *to attend one's health.* **6.** to listen to; give heed to. **7.** *Archaic.* to wait for; expect. —*v.i.* **8.** to take care or charge: *to attend to a sick person.* **9.** to apply oneself: *to attend to one's work.* **10.** to pay attention; listen or watch attentively; direct one's thought; pay heed: *to attend to a speaker.* **11.** to be present: *She is a member but does not attend regularly.* **12.** to be present and ready to give service; wait (usually fol. by *on* or *upon*): *to attend upon the Queen.* **13.** to follow; be consequent (usually fol. by *on* or *upon*). **14.** *Obs.* to wait. [1250–1300; ME *atenden* < AF, OF *atendre* < L *attendere* to bend to, notice. See AT-, TEND[1]] —**at·tend′er,** *n.* —**at·tend′ing·ly,** *adv.*
—**Syn. 4.** See **accompany.**

at·tend·ance (ə ten′dəns), *n.* **1.** the act of attending. **2.** the persons or number of persons present: *an attendance of more than 300 veterans.* **3. dance attendance,** to be obsequious in one's attentions or service; attend constantly: *He was given a larger office and several assistants to dance attendance on him.* [1325–75; ME < AF, MF. See ATTEND, -ANCE]

attend′ance of′ficer. See **truant officer.**

at·tend·ant (ə ten′dənt), *n.* **1.** a person who attends another, as to perform a service. **2.** *Chiefly Brit.* an usher or clerk. **3.** a corollary or concomitant thing or quality. **4.** a person who is present, as at a meeting. —*adj.* **5.** being present or in attendance; accompanying. **6.** consequent; concomitant; associated; related: *winter holidays and attendant parties; war and its attendant evils; poverty and its attendant hardships.* [1350–1400; ME < MF, prp. of *attendre* to notice, await. See ATTEND, -ANT] —**at·tend′ant·ly,** *adv.*
—**Syn. 1.** escort, companion, comrade; follower, retainer, servant. **3.** accompaniment, consequence.

at·tend·ee (ə ten dē′, at′en-, ə ten′dē), *n.* a person who is present at a specific time or place: *a conference with thousands of attendees.* [1935–40; ATTEND + -EE]

at·tend·ing (ə ten′ding), *adj.* (of a physician) **1.** having primary responsibility for a patient. **2.** holding a staff position in an accredited hospital. [1580–90; ATTEND + -ING[2]]

at·tent (ə tent′), *adj. Archaic.* attentive; intent. [1275–1325; ME < L *attentus* attentive (ptp. of *attendere*), equiv. to *atten(d)-* (see ATTEND) + *-tus* ptp. suffix] —**at·tent′ly,** *adv.*

at·ten·tion (*n.* ə ten′shən; *interj.* ə ten′shun′), *n.* **1.** the act or faculty of attending, esp. by directing the mind to an object. **2.** *Psychol.* **a.** a concentration of the mind on a single object or thought, esp. one preferentially selected from a complex, with a view to limiting or clarifying receptivity by narrowing the range of stimuli. **b.** a state of consciousness characterized by such concentration. **c.** a capacity to maintain selective or sustained concentration. **3.** observant care; consideration: *Individual attention is given to each child.* **4.** civility or courtesy: *attention to a guest.* **5.** notice or awareness: *His deliberate cough caught the waiter's attention.* **6. attentions,** acts of courtesy or devotion indicating affection, as in courtship. **7.** *Mil.* **a.** an erect position with eyes to the front, arms to the sides, and heels together (often used as a command). [1325–75; ME *attencioun* < L *attentiōn-* (s. of *attentiō*). See ATTENT, -ION] —**at·ten′tion·al,** *adj.*

atten′tion def′icit disor′der, a developmental disorder of children characterized by inattention, impulsiveness, distractibility, and often hyperactivity. [1980–85]

at·ten·tion-get·ting (ə ten′shən get′ing), *adj.* conspicuously drawing attention to something or someone: *an attention-getting device; attention-getting behavior.*

atten′tion line′, a line of text after the address on a piece of correspondence, directing it to a particular person or department. [1920–25]

atten′tion span′, the interval during which an individual can concentrate, as on a single object, idea, or activity. [1930–35]

at·ten·tive (ə ten′tiv), *adj.* **1.** characterized by or giving attention; observant: *an attentive audience.* **2.** thoughtful of others; considerate; polite; courteous: *an attentive host.* [1375–1425; late ME (Scots) < MF; see ATTENT, -IVE] —**at·ten′tive·ly,** *adv.* —**at·ten′tive·ness,** *n.*
—**Syn. 1.** heedful, mindful, aware, alert, awake, watchful. —**Ant. 1.** indifferent, apathetic, unconcerned.

at·ten·u·ant (ə ten′yo͞o ənt), *n.* a medicine or agent that thins the blood. [1595–1605; < L *attenuant-* (s. of *attenuāns* thinning, prp. of *attenuāre*). See AT-, TENUIS, -ANT]

at·ten·u·ate (*v.* ə ten′yo͞o āt′; *adj.* ə ten′yo͞o it, -āt′), *v.,* **-at·ed, -at·ing,** *adj.* —*v.t.* **1.** to weaken or reduce in force, intensity, effect, quantity, or value: *to attenuate desire.* **2.** to make thin; make slender or fine. **3.** *Bacteriol., Immunol.* to render less virulent, as a strain of pathogenic virus or bacterium. **4.** *Electronics.* to decrease the amplitude of (an electronic signal). —*v.i.* **5.** to become thin or fine; lessen. —*adj.* **6.** weakened; diminishing. **7.** *Bot.* tapering gradually to a narrow extremity. [1520–30; < L *attenuātus* (ptp. of *attenuāre* to thin, reduce). See AT-, TENUIS, -ATE[1]]

at·ten·u·a·tion (ə ten′yo͞o ā′shən), *n.* **1.** the act of attenuating or the state of being attenuated. **2.** the process by which a virus, bacterium, etc., changes under laboratory conditions to become harmless or less virulent. **3.** *Physics.* a decrease in a property, as energy, per unit area of a wave or a beam of particles, occurring as the distance from the source increases as a result of absorption, scattering, spreading in three dimensions, etc. [1585–95; (< MF) < L *attenuātiōn-* (s. of *attenuātiō*). See ATTENUATE, -ION]

at·ten·u·a·tor (ə ten′yo͞o ā′tər), *n. Electronics.* a device for decreasing the amplitude of an electronic signal. [1920–25; ATTENUATE + -OR[2]]

at·test (ə test′), *v.t.* **1.** to bear witness to; certify; declare to be correct, true, or genuine; declare the truth of, in words or writing, esp. affirm in an official capacity: *to attest the truth of a statement.* **2.** to give proof or evidence of; manifest: *His works attest his industry.* **3.** to put on oath. —*v.i.* **4.** to testify or bear witness (often fol. by *to*): *to attest to the reliability of an employee.* —*n.* **5.** *Archaic.* witness; testimony; attestation. [1590–1600; (< MF *attester*) < L *attestārī* to bear witness to, equiv. to *at-* AT- + *testārī* (*test(is)* a witness + *-ā-* thematic vowel + *-rī* inf. suffix)] —**at·test′a·ble,** *adj.* —**at·test′ant,** *n.* —**at·test′er, at·tes′tor, at·tes·ta·tor** (ə tes′tā tər, at′e stā′-), *n.* —**at·tes′tive,** *adj.*

at·tes·ta·tion (at′e stā′shən), *n.* **1.** an act of attesting. **2.** an attesting declaration; testimony; evidence. [1540–50; (< MF) < L *attestātiōn-* (s. of *attestātiō*). See ATTEST, -ATION] —**at·tes·ta·tive** (ə tes′tə tiv), *adj.*

attest′ed form′, a linguistic form actually in use or found in written records, in contrast to one that is hypothesized or reconstructed.

att. gen., attorney general.

at·tic (at′ik), *n.* **1.** the part of a building, esp. of a house, directly under a roof; garret. **2.** a room or rooms in an attic. **3.** a low story or decorative wall above an entablature or the main cornice of a building. **4.** *Anat.* the upper part of the tympanic cavity of the ear. [1690–1700; special use of ATTIC]

At·tic (at′ik), *adj.* **1.** of, pertaining to, or characteristic of Greece or of Athens. **2.** (*often l.c.*) displaying simple elegance, incisive intelligence, and delicate wit. —*n.* **3.** the dialect of ancient Attica that became the standard language of Classical Greek literature in the 5th and 4th centuries B.C. [1555–65; < L *Atticus* < Gk *Attikós*]

At·ti·ca (at′i kə), *n.* **1.** a region in SE Greece, surrounding Athens: under Athenian rule in ancient times. **2.** a town in W New York: state prison. 2659.

At′tic base′, (in classical architecture) a base for a column, consisting of an upper and a lower torus separated by a scotia between two fillets. [1720–30]

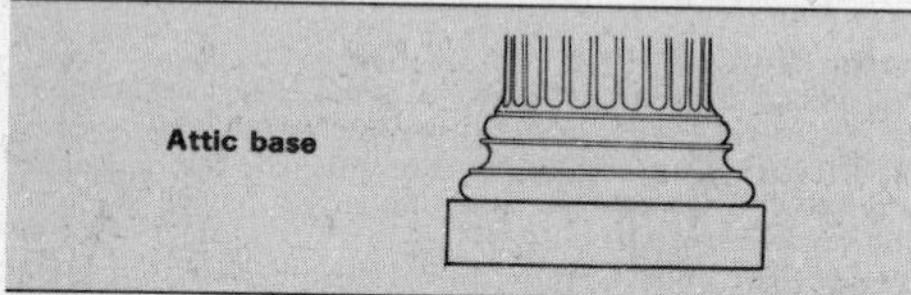

at·ti·cism (at′ə siz′əm), *n.* (*often cap.*) **1.** the style or idiom of Attic Greek occurring in another dialect or language. **2.** attachment to Athens or to the style, customs, etc., of the Athenians. **3.** concise and elegant expression, diction, or the like. [1605–15; < Gk *Attikismós* a siding with Athens, an Attic expression. See ATTIC, -ISM] **—at′ti·cist,** *n.*

at·ti·cize (at′ə sīz′), *v.,* **-cized, -ciz·ing.** (*often cap.*) —*v.i.* **1.** to affect Attic style, usages, etc.; intermingle with Attic elements. **2.** to favor or side with the Athenians. —*v.t.* **3.** to make conformable to Attic usage. Also, *esp. Brit.,* **at′ti·cise′.** [1600–10; < Gk *attikízein* to speak Attic, side with Athens. See ATTIC, -IZE]

at′tic salt′, dry, delicate wit. Also called **at′tic wit′.**

At·ti·la (at′l ə, ə til′ə), *n.* (*"Scourge of God"*) A.D. 406?–453, king of the Huns who invaded Europe: defeated by the Romans and Visigoths in 451 at Châlons-sur-Marne in France.

at·tin·gent (ə tin′jənt), *adj. Archaic.* touching; in contact. [1570–80; < L *attingent-* (s. of *attingēns* touching, prp. of *attingere*), equiv. to *at-* AT- + *-ting-* (comb. form of *tang-* touch) + *-ent-* -ENT] **—at·tin′gence, at·tin′·gen·cy,** *n.*

at·tire (ə tīər′), *v.,* **-tired, -tir·ing,** *n.* —*v.t.* **1.** to dress, array, or adorn, esp. for special occasions, ceremonials, etc. —*n.* **2.** clothes or apparel, esp. rich or splendid garments. **3.** the horns of a deer. [1250–1300; (v.) ME *atiren* < AF *atirer,* OF *atirier,* v. deriv. of *a tire* into a row or rank (see A-[3], TIER[1]); (n.) ME *atir* < AF, n. deriv. of the v.]

at·tire·ment (ə tīər′mənt), *n. Obs.* dress; attire. [1560–70; ATTIRE + -MENT]

at·ti·tude (at′i to͞od′, -tyo͞od′), *n.* **1.** manner, disposition, feeling, position, etc., with regard to a person or thing; tendency or orientation, esp. of the mind: *a negative attitude; group attitudes.* **2.** position or posture of the body appropriate to or expressive of an action, emotion, etc.: *a threatening attitude; a relaxed attitude.* **3.** *Aeron.* the inclination of the three principal axes of an aircraft relative to the wind, to the ground, etc. **4.** *Ballet.* a pose in which the dancer stands on one leg, the other bent behind. [1660–70; < F < It *attitudine* < LL *aptitūdini-* (s. of *aptitūdō*) APTITUDE] **—at′ti·tu′di·nal,** *adj.*
—Syn. 2. See **position.**

at·ti·tu·di·nar·i·an (at′i to͞od′n âr′ē ən, -tyo͞od′-), *n.* a person who assumes attitudes or poses for effect. [1745–55; *attitudin-* (see ATTITUDE; by analogy with nouns ending in the L suffix *-tūdō,* s. *-tūdin-* -TUDE) + -ARIAN] **—at′ti·tu′di·nar′i·an·ism,** *n.*

at·ti·tu·di·nize (at′i to͞od′n īz′, -tyo͞od′-), *v.i.,* **-nized, -niz·ing.** to assume attitudes; pose for effect. Also, *esp. Brit.,* **at′ti·tu′di·nise′.** [1775–85; *attitudin-* (see ATTITUDINARIAN) + -IZE] **—at′ti·tu′di·niz′er,** *n.*

At·ti·us (at′ē əs), *n.* **Lucius.** See **Accius, Lucius.**

At·tle·bor·o (at′l bûr′ō, -bur′ō), *n.* a city in SE Massachusetts. 34,196.

Att·lee (at′lē), *n.* **Clement (Richard),** 1883–1967, British statesman: prime minister 1945–51.

attn., attention.

atto-, a combining form that enters into compounds denoting a unit one-quintillionth (10^{-18}) the size of the unit named by the stem. [< Dan or Norw *att(en)* eighteen + -O-]

at·torn (ə tûrn′), *Law.* —*v.i.* **1.** to acknowledge the relation of a tenant to a new landlord. —*v.t.* **2.** to turn over to another; transfer. [1425–75; late ME *attournen* < AF *attourner,* OF *atourner* to turn over to. See AT-, TURN] **—at·torn′ment,** *n.*

CONCISE ETYMOLOGY KEY: <, descended or borrowed from; >, whence; b., blend of, blended; c., cognate with; cf., compare; deriv., derivative; equiv., equivalent; imit., imitative; obl., oblique; r., replacing; s., stem; sp., spelling, spelled; resp., respelling, respelled; trans., translation; ?, origin unknown; *, unattested; ‡, probably earlier than. See the full key inside the front cover.

at·tor·ney (ə tûr′nē), *n., pl.* **-neys. 1.** a lawyer; attorney-at-law. **2.** an attorney-in-fact; agent. [1250–1300; ME < AF *attourne* lit., (one who is) turned to, i.e., appointed, ptp. of *attourner* to ATTORN] **—at·tor′ney·ship′,** *n.*

at·tor·ney-at-law (ə tûr′nē ət lô′), *n., pl.* **at·tor·neys-at-law.** *Law.* an officer of the court authorized to appear before it as a representative of a party to a legal controversy. [1530–40]

attor′ney gen′eral, *pl.* **attorneys general, attorney generals. 1.** the chief law officer of a country or state and head of its legal department. **2.** (*caps.*) the head of the U.S. Department of Justice: a member of the president's cabinet. [1575–85]

at·tor·ney-in-fact (ə tûr′nē in fakt′), *n., pl.* **at·tor·neys-in-fact.** *Law.* a person authorized by power of attorney to act on the authorizer's behalf outside a court of law.

at·tract (ə trakt′), *v.t.* **1.** to draw by a physical force causing or tending to cause to approach, adhere, or unite; pull (opposed to *repel*): *The gravitational force of the earth attracts smaller bodies to it.* **2.** to draw by appealing to the emotions or senses, by stimulating interest, or by exciting admiration; allure; invite: *to attract attention; to attract admirers by one's charm.* —*v.i.* **3.** to possess or exert the power of attraction. [1400–50; late ME < L *attractus* drawn to (ptp. of *attrahere*), equiv. to *at-* AT- + *trac-* (var. s. of *trahere* to draw) + *-tus* ptp. suffix] **—at·tract′a·ble,** *adj.* **—at·tract′a·ble·ness,** *n.* **—at·tract′ing·ly,** *adv.*

at·tract·ant (ə trak′tənt), *n.* an attracting agent or substance; lure: *the sex attractant of the cockroach; a synthetic attractant used to bait insect traps.* [1915–20; ATTRACT + -ANT]

at·trac·tion (ə trak′shən), *n.* **1.** the act, power, or property of attracting. **2.** attractive quality; magnetic charm; fascination; allurement; enticement: *the subtle attraction of her strange personality.* **3.** a person or thing that draws, attracts, allures, or entices: *The main attraction was the after-dinner speaker.* **4.** a characteristic or quality that provides pleasure; attractive feature: *The chief attractions of the evening were the good drinks and witty conversation.* **5.** *Physics.* the electric or magnetic force that acts between oppositely charged bodies, tending to draw them together. **6.** an entertainment offered to the public. [1375–1425; late ME *attraccioun* (< AF) < ML *attractiōn-* (s. of *attractiō*). See ATTRACT, -ION] **—at·trac′tion·al·ly,** *adv.*
—Syn. 2. appeal, lure. **6.** show, spectacle.

at·trac·tive (ə trak′tiv), *adj.* **1.** providing pleasure or delight, esp. in appearance or manner; pleasing; charming; alluring: *an attractive personality.* **2.** arousing interest or engaging one's thought, consideration, etc.: *an attractive idea; an attractive price.* **3.** having the quality of attracting. [1375–1425; late ME *attractif* (< MF) < LL *attractīvus* of a medicine with drawing power. See ATTRACT, -IVE] **—at·trac′tive·ly,** *adv.* **—at·trac′tive·ness,** *n.*

attrac′tive nui′sance, 1. *Law.* a doctrine of tort law under which a person who creates or permits to exist on his or her land a dangerous condition attractive to children, as an unfenced swimming pool, is liable for their resulting injuries, even though the injured are trespassers. **2.** a hazardous condition or object to which this doctrine is applicable.

at·trac·tor (ə trak′tər), *n.* **1.** a person or thing that attracts. **2.** *Physics.* a state or behavior toward which a dynamic system tends to evolve, represented as a point or orbit in the system's phase space. [1645–55]

attrib., 1. attribute. **2.** attributive. **3.** attributively.

at·trib·ute (*v.* ə trib′yo͞ot; *n.* a′trə byo͞ot′), *v.,* **-ut·ed, -ut·ing,** *n.* —*v.t.* **1.** to regard as resulting from a specified cause; consider as caused by something indicated (usually fol. by *to*): *She attributed his bad temper to ill health.* **2.** to consider as a quality or characteristic of the person, thing, group, etc., indicated: *He attributed intelligence to his colleagues.* **3.** to consider as made by the one indicated, esp. with strong evidence but in the absence of conclusive proof: *to attribute a painting to an artist.* **4.** to regard as produced by or originating in the time, period, place, etc., indicated; credit; assign: *to attribute a work to a particular period; to attribute a discovery to a particular country.* —*n.* **5.** something attributed as belonging to a person, thing, group, etc.; a quality, character, characteristic, or property: *Sensitivity is one of his attributes.* **6.** something used as a symbol of a particular person, office, or status: *A scepter is one of the attributes of a king.* **7.** *Gram.* a word or phrase that is syntactically subordinate to another and serves to limit, identify, particularize, describe, or supplement the meaning of the form with which it is in construction. In *the red house, red* is an attribute of *house.* **8.** *Fine Arts.* an object associated with or symbolic of a character, office, or quality, as the keys of St. Peter or the lion skin of Hercules. **9.** *Philos.* (in the philosophy of Spinoza) any of the essential qualifications of God, thought and extension being the only ones known. Cf. **mode**[1] (def. 4b). **10.** *Logic.* (in a proposition) that which is affirmed or denied concerning the subject. **11.** *Obs.* distinguished character; reputation. [1350–1400; ME < L *attribūtus* allotted, assigned, imputed to (ptp. of *attribuere*), equiv. to *at-* AT- + *tribū-* (s. of *tribuere* to assign (to tribes), classify, ascribe; see TRIBE) + *-tus* ptp. suffix] **—at·trib′ut·a·ble,** *adj.* **—at·trib′ut·er, at·trib′u·tor,** *n.*
—Syn. 1. ATTRIBUTE, ASCRIBE, IMPUTE imply definite origin. ATTRIBUTE and ASCRIBE are often used interchangeably, to imply that something originates with a definite person or from a definite cause. ASCRIBE, however, has neutral implications; whereas, possibly because of an association with tribute, ATTRIBUTE is coming to have a complimentary connotation: *to ascribe an accident to carelessness; to attribute one's success to a friend's encouragement.* IMPUTE has gained uncomplimentary connotations, and usually means to accuse or blame someone or something as a cause or origin: *to impute an error to him.* **5.** See **quality.**

at·tri·bu·tion (a′trə byo͞o′shən), *n.* **1.** the act of attributing; ascription. **2.** something ascribed; an attribute. **3.** *Numis.* a classification for a coin, based on its distinguishing features, as date, design, or metal. **4.** *Archaic.* authority or function assigned, as to a ruler, legislative assembly, delegate, or the like. [1425–75; late ME (< MF) < L *attribūtiōn-* (s. of *attribūtiō* assignment). See ATTRIBUTE, -ION]

at·trib·u·tive (ə trib′yə tiv), *adj.* **1.** pertaining to or having the character of attribution or an attribute. **2.** *Gram.* of or pertaining to an adjective or noun that is directly adjacent to, in English usually preceding, the noun it modifies, without any intervening linking verb, as the adjective *sunny* in *a sunny day* or the noun *television* in *a television screen.* —*n.* **3.** *Gram.* an attributive word, esp. an adjective. [1600–10; ATTRIBUTE or ATTRIBUT(ION) + -IVE; cf. MF *attributif*] **—at·trib′u·tive·ly,** *adv.* **—at·trib′u·tive·ness,** *n.*

at·trit (ə trit′), *v.t.,* **-trit·ted, -trit·ting.** to wear down (an opposing military force) by numerical superiority in troops or firepower. [1750–60; back formation from ATTRITION]

at·trite (ə trīt′), *adj., v.,* **-trit·ed, -trit·ing.** —*adj.* **1.** Also, **at·trit′ed.** worn by rubbing or attrition. —*v.t.* **2.** to make smaller by attrition. [1615–25; < L *attrītus* rubbed against, rubbed away, worn away (ptp. of *atterere*), equiv. to *at-* AT- + *tri-* (var. s. of *terere* to rub) + *-tus* ptp. suffix] **—at·trite′ness,** *n.*

at·tri·tion (ə trish′ən), *n.* **1.** a reduction or decrease in numbers, size, or strength: *Our club has had a high rate of attrition because so many members have moved away.* **2.** a wearing down or weakening of resistance, esp. as a result of continuous pressure or harassment: *The enemy surrounded the town and conducted a war of attrition.* **3.** a gradual reduction in work force without firing of personnel, as when workers resign or retire and are not replaced. **4.** the act of rubbing against something; friction. **5.** a wearing down or away by friction; abrasion. **6.** *Theol.* imperfect contrition. See under **contrition** (def. 2). [1325–75; ME < L *attrītiōn-* (s. of *attrītiō*) friction. See ATTRITE, -ION] **—at·tri′tion·al,** *adj.* **—at·tri′·tive** (ə trī′tiv), *adj.*

At·tu (at′o͞o′), *n.* the westernmost of the Aleutian Islands: Japanese occupation 1942–43.

At·tucks (at′əks), *n.* **Cris·pus** (kris′pəs), 1723?–70, American patriot, probably a fugitive slave, killed in the Boston Massacre.

at·tune (ə to͞on′, ə tyo͞on′), *v.t.,* **-tuned, -tun·ing. 1.** to bring into accord, harmony, or sympathetic relationship; adjust: *He has attuned himself to living in the quiet country.* **2.** *Archaic.* to tune or bring into harmony, as a musical instrument. [1590–1600; AT- + TUNE]

atty., attorney.

Atty. Gen., Attorney General.

A·tum (ä′təm), *n. Egyptian Religion.* a primeval god who by himself begot Shu and Tefnut: the original god of the Ennead.

ATV, See **all-terrain vehicle.**

at. vol., See **atomic volume.**

a·twain (ə twān′), *adv. Archaic.* in twain; in two; apart. [1350–1400; ME; see A-[1], TWAIN]

At·wa·ter (at′wô′tər, -wot′ər), *n.* **1.** a town in central California. 17,530. **2.** a male given name.

at·weel (ə twēl′, at wēl′), *adv. Scot.* surely. [1760–70; aph. var. of phrase (*I*) *wat weel* (I) know well. See WOT, WELL[1]]

a·tween (ə twēn′), *prep., adv. Dial.* between. [1350–1400; ME *atwen,* prob. on the model of other synonymous pairs, as *afore, before,* etc.; see A-[1], BETWEEN]

a·twit·ter (ə twit′ər), *adj.* excited; nervous; aflutter; twittering: *They were atwitter at the prospect of meeting a Hollywood star.* [1825–35; A-[1] + TWITTER]

At·wood (at′wo͝od′), *n.* **Margaret (Eleanor),** born 1939, Canadian poet and novelist.

At′wood's machine′, *Physics.* a device consisting of two unequal masses connected by a string passed over a pulley, used to illustrate the laws of motion. [named after George Atwood (1746–1807), English mathematician who invented it]

at. wt., See **atomic weight.**

a·typ·i·cal (ā tip′i kəl), *adj.* not typical; not conforming to the type; irregular: *atypical behavior; a flower atypical of the species.* Also, **a·typ′ic.** [1880–85; A-[6] + TYPICAL] **—a′typ·i·cal′i·ty,** *n.* **—a·typ′i·cal·ly,** *adv.*

au (ō), *pl.* ***aux*** (ō). *French.* to the; at the; with the. Cf. **à la.**

AU, See **astronomical unit.**

Au, *Symbol, Chem.* gold. [< L *aurum*]

A.U., angstrom unit. Also, **a.u.**

A.U.A., American Unitarian Association.

au·bade (ō bad′, ō bäd′; *Fr.* ō BAD′), *n., pl.* **au·bades** (ō badz′, ō bädz′; *Fr.* ō BAD′). *Music.* a piece sung or played outdoors at dawn, usually as a compliment to someone. [1670–80; < F, MF, equiv. to *aube* (< Pr *alba* song about the parting of two lovers at dawn < VL, n. use of fem. of L *albus* white, clear) + *-ade* -ADE[1]]

Au·ba·nel (ō BA nel′), *n.* **Thé·o·dore** (tā ô dôr′), 1829–86, French poet.

Aube (ōb), *n.* **1.** a river in N France, flowing NW to the Seine. 125 mi. (200 km) long. **2.** a department in NE France. 284,823; 2327 sq. mi. (6025 sq. km). *Cap.:* Troyes.

Au·ber (ō BER′), *n.* **Da·niel Fran·çois Es·prit** (dA nyel′ fRäN SWA′ es pRē′), 1782–1871, French composer.

au·berge (ō bârzh′; *Fr.* ō beRzh′), *n., pl.* **au·berges** (ō bâr′zhiz; *Fr.* ō beRzh′). an inn; hostel. [1770–80; < F, MF < Pr, Franco-Provencal *aubergo* hostelry, OPr *alberga, alberja* encampment, hut, n. deriv. of *albergar,* dissimilated form of *arbergar* to lodge, shelter < VL < EGmc **haribergōn* to shelter an armed force (*hari-* army + *bergōn* to shelter); cf. HARBINGER, HARBOR < a WGmc cognate of the same verb]

au·ber·gine (ō′bər zhēn′, -jēn′, ō′ber-; ō′bər zhēn′, -jēn′, ō′ber-), *n.* **1.** *Chiefly Brit.* eggplant. **2.** a dark purplish color. [1785–95; < F < Catalan *albergínia* < Ar *al* the + *bādhinjān* eggplant < Pers *bādingān* perh. < Indo-Aryan; cf. Skt *vātiṅgaṇaḥ*]

Au·ber·vil·liers (ō beʀ vē lyā′), *n.* a town in N France, a suburb of Paris. 72,997.

Au·brey (ô′brē), *n.* **1.** **John,** 1626–97, English antiquary. **2.** a male given name: from Germanic words meaning "elf" and "ruler."

au·bre·tia (ô brē′tə, -shə, -shē ə, ō brē′-), *n.* any of several plants belonging to the genus *Aubrietia,* of the mustard family, forming dense mats and having numerous small, purplish flowers. [1763; < NL, named after Claude *Aubriet* (1651–1743), French painter of plants and animals; see -A[2]]

au·burn (ô′bərn), *n.* **1.** a reddish-brown or golden-brown color. —*adj.* **2.** having auburn color: *auburn hair.* [1400–50; late ME *abo(u)rne* blond < MF, OF *auborne, alborne* < L *alburnus* whitish. See ALBURNUM]

Au·burn (ô′bərn), *n.* **1.** a city in central New York: state prison. 32,548. **2.** a city in E Alabama. 28,471. **3.** a city in W central Washington. 26,417. **4.** a city in SW Maine, on the Androscoggin River. 23,128. **5.** a city in central Massachusetts. 14,845.

Au·bus·son (ō′bə sən, -sôN′; *Fr.* ō bʏ sôN′), *n.* an ornate rug constructed in a flat tapestry weave, often in pastel colors. [1960–65; after *Aubusson,* town in central France where made]

A.U.C., **1.** from the founding of the city (of Rome in 753? B.C.). The year 360 A.U.C. would be the 360th year after the founding of Rome. [< L *ab urbe conditā*] **2.** in the year from the founding of the city (of Rome in 753? B.C.). [< L *annō urbis conditae*]

Auck·land (ôk′lənd), *n.* a seaport on N North Island, in New Zealand. 797,406.

au con·traire (ō kôN tʀeʀ′), *French.* **1.** on the contrary. **2.** on the opposite or adverse side.

au cou·rant (ō′ ko͞o räN′; *Fr.* ō ko͞o ʀäN′), **1.** up-to-date. **2.** fully aware or familiar; cognizant. [< F: lit., in the current]

auc·tion (ôk′shən), *n.* **1.** Also called **public sale.** a publicly held sale at which property or goods are sold to the highest bidder. **2.** *Cards.* **a.** See **auction bridge. b.** (in bridge or certain other games) the competitive bidding to fix a contract that a player or players undertake to fulfill. —*v.t.* **3.** to sell by auction (often fol. by *off*): *He auctioned off his furniture.* [1585–95; < L *auctiōn-* (s. of *auctiō*) an increase, esp. in the bidding at a sale, equiv. to *auct(us)* increased, ptp. of *augēre* (*aug-* increase + *-tus* ptp. suffix) + *-iōn-* -ION] —**auc′tion·a·ble,** *adj.* —**auc′tion·ar′y,** *adj.*

auc′tion block′, **1.** Also called **block.** a platform from which an auctioneer sells: *the old courthouse where slaves were sold from the auction block.* **2. put on the auction block,** to offer for sale at auction; offer to sell to the highest bidder. Also, **put on the block.** [1840–50, *Amer.*]

auc′tion bridge′, a variety of bridge in which odd tricks won in excess of the number named in the contract are scored toward game. Cf. **contract** (def. 5). [1905–10]

auc·tion·eer (ôk′shə nēr′), *n.* **1.** a person who conducts sales by auction. —*v.t.* **2.** to auction (something). [1700–10; AUCTION + -EER]

auc′tion pi′nochle, **1.** a variety of pinochle for three to five players in which, for every hand, there are three active players, each dealt 15 cards, with the highest bidder winning the contract and playing against the other two active opponents. **2.** pinochle in which players bid to name trump.

auc′tion pitch′, *Cards.* a variety of all fours in which players bid to determine the trump or pitch.

auc·to·ri·al (ôk tôr′ē əl, -tōr′-, ouk′-), *adj.* of, by, or pertaining to an author: *auctorial changes made in the manuscript margin; auctorial rights.* [1815–25; < L *auctor* AUTHOR + -IAL]

au·cu·ba (ô′kyə bə), *n.* any shrub of the genus *Aucuba,* native to Asia, having evergreen leaves, clusters of purple flowers, and brightly colored berries. [1783; < NL, appar. < Japn *a(w)o-ku* being green + *-ba* comb. form of *ha* leaf (earlier *fa,* *pa); cf. the Japn name for the shrub *ao-ki* < *a(w)o* green + *ki(y)* tree (earlier *koi)]

aud., **1.** audit. **2.** auditor.

au·da·cious (ô dā′shəs), *adj.* **1.** extremely bold or daring; recklessly brave; fearless: *an audacious explorer.* **2.** extremely original; without restriction to prior ideas; highly inventive: *an audacious vision of the city's bright future.* **3.** recklessly bold in defiance of convention, propriety, law, or the like; insolent; brazen. **4.** lively; unrestrained; uninhibited: *an audacious interpretation of her role.* [1540–50; AUDACI(TY) + -OUS] —**au·da′cious·ly,** *adv.* —**au·da′cious·ness,** *n.*
—**Syn. 1.** courageous, intrepid, dauntless, venturesome. **3.** unabashed, shameless; impertinent, forward. —**Ant. 1.** cowardly.

au·dac·i·ty (ô das′i tē), *n., pl.* **-ties. 1.** boldness or daring, esp. with confident or arrogant disregard for personal safety, conventional thought, or other restrictions. **2.** effrontery or insolence; shameless boldness: *His questioner's audacity shocked the lecturer.* **3.** Usually, **audacities.** audacious acts or statements. [1400–50; late ME *audacite* < L *audāc-,* s. of *audāx* daring (adj.) + *-ite* -ITY]
—**Syn. 1.** nerve, spunk, grit, temerity, foolhardiness. **2.** impudence, impertinence, brashness. —**Ant. 1, 2.** discretion, prudence.

Aude (ōd), *n.* a department in S France. 272,366; 2449 sq. mi. (6345 sq. km). *Cap.:* Carcassonne.

Au·den (ôd′n), *n.* **W(ys·tan) H(ugh)** (wis′tən), 1907–73, English poet in the U.S.

Aud·hum·la (oud′ho͝om lä, -hum-), *n. Scand. Myth.* a cow, owned by Ymir and born like him from drops of the melting primeval ice: its licking of a mass of salty ice exposed the first god, Buri. Also, **Aud·hum·bla** (oud′ho͝om blä, -lä, -hum-). [< ON *Authum(b)la,* equiv. to *auth(r)* wealth + *humla* a polled cow]

au·di·al (ô′dē əl), *adj.* of or pertaining to the sense of hearing; aural. [AUDI(O)- + -AL[1]]

au·di·ble (ô′də bəl), *adj.* **1.** capable of being heard; loud enough to be heard; actually heard. —*n.* **2.** Also called **automatic, checkoff.** *Football.* a play called at the line of scrimmage to supersede the play originally agreed upon as the result of a change in strategy. [1520–30; < LL *audibilis,* equiv. to L *audī(re)* to hear + *-bilis* -BLE] —**au′di·bil′i·ty, au′di·ble·ness,** *n.* —**au′di·bly,** *adv.*

Au·die (ô′dē), *n.* a female or male given name.

au·di·ence (ô′dē əns), *n.* **1.** the group of spectators at a public event; listeners or viewers collectively, as in attendance at a theater or concert: *The audience was respectful of the speaker's opinion.* **2.** the persons reached by a book, radio or television broadcast, etc.; public: *Some works of music have a wide and varied audience.* **3.** a regular public that manifests interest, support, enthusiasm, or the like; a following: *Every art form has its audience.* **4.** opportunity to be heard; chance to speak to or before a person or group; a hearing. **5.** a formal interview with a sovereign, high officer of government, or other high-ranking person: *an audience with the pope.* **6.** the act of hearing, or attending to, words or sounds. [1325–75; ME < MF < L *audientia.* See AUDIENT, -ENCE]
—**Usage.** See **collective noun.**

au′dience room′, a room for holding formal interviews or hearings. [1780–90]

au′dience share′, the percentage of households with television sets in use or tuned to a particular station during a specific period of time. [1970–75]

au·dile (ô′dil, -dīl), *n. Psychol.* a person in whose mind auditory images, rather than visual or motor images, are predominant or unusually distinct. [1885–90; AUD(ITORY) + -ILE]

aud·ing (ô′ding), *n.* the process of listening to and comprehending spoken language. [1945–50; < L *aud(ire)* to hear + -ING[1]]

au·di·o (ô′dē ō′), *adj.* **1.** *Electronics.* designating an electronic apparatus using audio frequencies: *audio amplifier.* **2.** of, pertaining to, or employed in the transmission, reception, or reproduction of sound. **3.** of or pertaining to frequencies or signals in the audible range. —*n.* **4.** *Television.* **a.** the audio elements of television (distinguished from *video*). **b.** the circuits in a receiver for reproducing sound. **c.** the audio part of a television broadcast. **5.** the field of sound recording, transmission, reception, and reproduction. [1920–25; independent use of AUDIO-]

audio-, a combining form used in the formation of compound words, with the meanings: "sound within the range of human hearing" (*audiometer*); "hearing" (*audiology*); "sound reproduction" (*audiophile*). [< L *audi-* (s. of *audīre* to hear) + -O-]

au′dio cassette′, a cassette containing audiotape. [1970–75]

au·di·o·disk (ô′dē ō disk′), *n.* See under **record** (def. 17). Also, **au′dio disk′, au′di·o·disc′.** [1980–85; AUDIO- + DISK]

au′dio fre′quency, *Acoustics, Electronics.* a frequency between 15 Hz and 20,000 Hz, within the range of normally audible sound. [1910–15]

au·di·o·gen·ic (ô′dē ə jen′ik), *adj.* caused by sound. [1940–45; AUDIO- + -GENIC]

au·di·o·gram (ô′dē ə gram′), *n. Med.* the graphic record produced by an audiometer. [1925–30; AUDIO- + -GRAM[1]]

au·di·o·lin·gual (ô′dē ō ling′gwəl), *adj.* pertaining to listening comprehension and speaking, esp. in learning a foreign language. [1955–60]

audio-lin′gual meth′od, a technique of foreign-language instruction that emphasizes audio-lingual skills over reading and writing and is characterized by extensive use of pattern practice.

au·di·ol·o·gy (ô′dē ol′ə jē), *n.* the study of hearing disorders, including evaluation of hearing function and rehabilitation of patients with hearing impairments. [1945–50; AUDIO- + -LOGY] —**au·di·o·log·i·cal** (ô′dē ə loj′i kəl), **au′di·o·log′ic,** *adj.* —**au′di·ol′o·gist,** *n.*

au·di·om·e·ter (ô′dē om′i tər), *n. Med.* an instrument for gauging and recording acuity of hearing. Also called **sonometer.** [1875–80; AUDIO- + -METER]

au·di·om·e·try (ô′dē om′i trē), *n. Med.* the testing of hearing by means of an audiometer. [1885–90; AUDIO- + -METRY] —**au·di·o·met·ric** (ô′dē ə me′trik), *adj.* —**au′di·o·met′ri·cal·ly,** *adv.*

au·di·on (ô′dē ən, -on′), *n. Electronics.* an early type of triode. [formerly a trademark]

au·di·o·phile (ô′dē ə fīl′), *n.* a person who is especially interested in high-fidelity sound reproduction. [1950–55; AUDIO- + -PHILE]

au′dio response′ u′nit, *Computers.* **1.** a device that enables a computer to give a spoken response by generating sounds similar to human speech. **2.** a similar device that selects from a vocabulary of prerecorded words. *Abbr.:* ARU

au·di·o·tape (ô′dē ō tāp′), *n.* magnetic tape for recording sound (distinguished from *videotape*). [1960–65; AUDIO- + TAPE]

au·di·o·vis·u·al (ô′dē ō vizh′o͞o əl), *adj.* **1.** of, pertaining to, involving, or directed at both hearing and sight: *audiovisual facilities; audiovisual techniques.* —*n.* **2.** Usually, **audiovisuals.** See **audiovisual aids.** Also, **au′di·o·vis′u·al.** [1935–40; AUDIO- + VISUAL] —**au′di·o·vis′u·al·ly,** *adv.*

au′diovis′ual aids′, training or educational materials directed at both the sense of hearing and the sense of sight; films, recordings, photographs, etc., used in classroom instruction, library collections, or the like. [1935–40]

au·di·phone (ô′də fōn′), *n. Med.* a kind of diaphragm held against the upper teeth to assist hearing by transmitting sound vibrations to the auditory nerve. [1875–80, *Amer.*; AUDI(O)- + -PHONE, modeled on TELEPHONE]

au·dit (ô′dit), *n.* **1.** an official examination and verification of accounts and records, esp. of financial accounts. **2.** a report or statement reflecting an audit; a final statement of account. **3.** the inspection or examination of a building or other facility to evaluate or improve its appropriateness, safety, efficiency, or the like: *An energy audit can suggest ways to reduce home fuel bills.* **4.** *Archaic.* a judicial hearing. **5.** *Obs.* an audience. —*v.t.* **6.** to make an audit of; examine (accounts, records, etc.) for purposes of verification: *The accountants audited the company's books at the end of the fiscal year.* **7.** to attend (classes, lectures, etc.) as an auditor. **8.** to make an audit of (a building or other facility) to evaluate or improve its safety, efficiency, or the like. —*v.i.* **9.** to examine and verify an account or accounts by reference to vouchers. [1400–50; late ME *audite* < L *auditus* the sense or act of hearing, equiv. to *audi(re)* to hear + *-tus* suffix of v. action] —**au′dit·a·ble,** *adj.*

au·di·tion (ô dish′ən), *n.* **1.** a trial hearing given to a singer, actor, or other performer to test suitability for employment, professional training or competition, etc. **2.** a reading or other simplified rendering of a theatrical work, performed before a potential backer, producer, etc. **3.** the act, sense, or power of hearing. **4.** something that is heard. —*v.t., v.i.* **5.** to try or compete in an audition: *to audition aspiring actors; to audition for the leading role.* [1590–1600; (< MF) < L *auditiōn-* (s. of *auditiō* hearing). See AUDITIVE, -ION] —**au·di′tion·er,** *n.*

au·di·tion·ee (ô dish′ə nē′), *n.* a person who competes or takes part in an audition. [AUDITION (v.) + -EE]

au·di·tive (ô′di tiv), *adj.* auditory. [1400–50; late ME *auditif* (< MF) < ML *auditīvus,* equiv. to L *audit(us)* ptp. of *audire* to hear + *-īvus* -IVE]

au·di·tor (ô′di tər), *n.* **1.** a person appointed and authorized to examine accounts and accounting records, compare the charges with the vouchers, verify balance sheet and income items, and state the result. **2.** a university student registered for a course without credit and without obligation to do work assigned to the class. **3.** a hearer; listener. [1300–50; ME *auditour* < AF < L *auditor* hearer, equiv. to *audi(re)* to hear + *-tor* -TOR] —**au′di·tor·ship′,** *n.*

au·di·to·ri·um (ô′di tôr′ē əm, -tōr′-), *n., pl.* **-to·ri·ums, -to·ri·a** (-tôr′ē ə, -tōr′-). **1.** the space set apart for the audience in a theater, school, or other public building. **2.** a building for public gatherings; hall. [1720–30; < L: lecture hall; see AUDITOR, -TORY[2]]

au·di·to·ry (ô′di tôr′ē, -tōr′ē-), *adj., n., pl.* **-ries.** —*adj.* **1.** *Anat., Physiol.* pertaining to hearing, to the sense of hearing, or to the organs of hearing. **2.** perceived through or resulting from the sense of hearing: *auditory hallucinations.* —*n. Archaic.* **3.** an assembly of hearers; audience. **4.** an auditorium, esp. the nave of a church. [1350–1400; ME < LL *auditōrius* relating to hearing. See AUDITOR, -TORY[1]] —**au′di·to′ri·ly, au′di·to′ri·al·ly,** *adv.*

au′ditory apha′sia, *Pathol.* aphasia in which there is no comprehension of spoken words; word deafness.

au′ditory canal′, *Anat.* the narrow passageway from the outer ear to the eardrum. [1895–1900]

au′ditory nerve′, *Anat.* either one of the eighth pair of cranial nerves, consisting of sensory fibers that conduct impulses from the organs of hearing and from the semicircular canals to the brain. Also called **acoustic nerve.** [1715–25]

au′ditory phonet′ics, the branch of phonetics dealing with the physiological processes involved in the reception of speech. Cf. **acoustic phonetics, articulatory phonetics, physiological phonetics.**

au′ditory ves′icle, *Embryol.* the pouch that is formed by the invagination of an ectodermal placode and that develops into the internal ear. Also called **otic vesicle, otocyst.**

au′dit trail′, **1.** *Accounting.* the process or an instance of cross-referring each bookkeeping entry to its source in order to facilitate checking its accuracy. **2.** *Computers.* a track of a particular item of output data back through the processing steps that produced it to the corresponding input data. [1965–70]

Au·drey (ô′drē), *n.* a female given name: from Old English words meaning "noble" and "strength."

Au·du·bon (ô′də bon′, -bən), *n.* **John James,** 1785–1851, U.S. naturalist who painted and wrote about the birds of North America.

Au′dubon Soci′ety, a society founded in 1905 for the preservation of wildlife, esp. of birds. [named after J. J. AUDUBON]

Au′dubon's war′bler. See under **yellow-rumped warbler.** [1830–40, *Amer.*; named after J. J. AUDUBON]

Au·er (ou′ər), *n.* **Le·o·pold** (lē′ə pōld′; *Hung.* lä′ô pôlt′), 1845–1930, Hungarian violinist and teacher.

Au·er·bach (ou′ər bäk′, our′-; *for 2 also Ger.* ou′əʀ bäKH′), *n.* **1. Arnold** ("*Red*"), born 1917, U.S. basketball coach and manager. **2. Ber·thold** (beʀ′tōlt), 1812–82, German novelist.

au fait (ō fe′), *French.* having experience or practical knowledge of a thing; expert; versed. [lit., to the fact]

CONCISE PRONUNCIATION KEY: act, cāpe, dâre, pärt; set, ēqual; if, īce; ox, ōver, ôrder, oil, bo͝ok, bo͞ot, out; up, ûrge; child; sing; shoe; thin, *th*at; zh as in *treasure.* ə = *a* as in *alone, e* as in *system, i* as in *easily, o* as in *gallop, u* as in *circus;* ᵊ as in *fire* (fīᵊr), *hour* (ouᵊr). l and n can serve as syllabic consonants, as in *cradle* (krād′l), and *button* (but′n). See the full key inside the front cover.

Auf•klä•rung (ouf′kle′ro͝ong), *n. German.* **1.** enlightenment. **2.** *Europ. Hist.* the Enlightenment.

au fond (ō fôɴ′), *French.* at bottom or to the bottom; thoroughly; in reality; fundamentally.

auf Wie•der•seh•en (ouf vē′dər zā′ən), *German.* until we meet again; good-bye for the present.

Aug., August.

aug., **1.** augmentative. **2.** augmented.

Au•ge (ô′jē), *n. Class. Myth.* a daughter of King Aleus who became a priestess of Athena. After being raped by Hercules she bore a son, Telephus.

Au•ge•an (ô jē′ən), *adj.* **1.** resembling the Augean stables in filthiness or degradation. **2.** difficult and unpleasant: *an Augean chore.* [1590–1600; < L *Augē(us)* of AUGEAS (Gk *Augei(ās)* + *-us* adj. suffix) + -AN]

Auge′an sta′bles, *Class. Myth.* the stables in which King Augeas kept 3000 oxen, and which had not been cleaned for 30 years. The cleaning of these stables was accomplished by Hercules, who diverted the river Alpheus through them.

Au•ge•as (ô′jē əs, ô jē′əs), *n.* king of the Epeans in Elis and one of the Argonauts. Cf. **Augean stables.**

au•gend (ô′jend, ô jend′), *n. Math.* a number to which another is added in forming a sum. Cf. **addend** (def. 2). [1905–10; < L *augendum* a thing to be increased, n. use of neut. of *augendus* to be increased, ger. of *augēre* to increase]

au•ger (ô′gər), *n.* **1.** *Carpentry.* **a.** a bit, as for a brace. **b.** a boring tool, similar to but larger than a gimlet, consisting of a bit rotated by a transverse handle. **2.** See **earth auger. 3.** a device consisting of a shaft with a broad helical flange rotating within a cylindrical casing to force bulk materials from one end to the other. **4.** snake (def. 3a). [bef. 900; ME *nauger* (*a nauger* misdivided as *an auger;* cf. ADDER, APRON), OE *nafogār* navepiercer (c. ON *nafarr,* OS *nabugēr,* MD *navegeer,* OHG *nabagēr*), equiv. to *nafa* NAVE[2] + *gār* spear; cf. GORE[3], GARLIC]

au′ger bit′, an auger having a square tang at its upper end and rotated by a brace, used for boring through wood. See illus. under **bit.**

Au•ger′ effect′ (ō zhā′), *Physics.* a nonradiative process in which an atom in an excited state undergoes a transition to a lower state by the emission of a bound electron **(Auger′ elec′tron)** rather than by the emission of an x-ray. Also called **autoionization.** [1930–35; named after Pierre V. *Auger* (b. 1899), French physicist]

au•ger-eyed (ô′gər īd′), *Chiefly South Midland U.S.* having sharp or piercing vision.

Auger′ show′er, *Astron.* a very large cosmic ray shower caused by a primary cosmic ray entering the earth's atmosphere. [see AUGER EFFECT]

aught[1] (ôt), *n.* **1.** anything whatever; any part: *for aught I know.* —*adv.* **2.** *Archaic.* in any degree; at all; in any respect. Also, **ought.** [bef. 1000; ME *aught, ought,* OE *āht, āwiht, ōwiht,* equiv. to *ā, ō* ever + *wiht* thing, WIGHT[1]]

aught[2] (ôt), *n.* a cipher (0); zero. Also, **ought.** [*a naught,* taken as *an aught* (cf. AUGER). See NAUGHT]

aught[3] (ôᴋʜt), *v.t. Scot.* **1.** to own; possess. **2.** to owe (someone or something); be obligated to. —*adj.* **3.** possessed of. —*n.* **4.** *Archaic.* **a.** ownership; possession. **b.** property; a possession. [bef. 1000; ME; OE *æht;* c. OHG *ēht,* Goth *aihts;* akin to OWE, OWN]

aught[4] (ôᴋʜt), *adj. Scot.* **1.** eight. **2.** eighth. [ME *aghte, aughte,* var. of *eighte;* see EIGHT]

aught•lins (ôᴋʜt′linz), *adv. Scot.* oughtlins. [AUGHT[2] + *-lin* (var. of -LING[2]) + -S[1]]

Au•gier (ō zhyā′), *n.* **Guil•laume Vic•tor É•mile** (gē-yōm′ vēk tôr′ ā mēl′), 1820–89, French dramatist.

au•gite (ô′jīt), *n.* a silicate mineral, chiefly of calcium, magnesium, iron, and aluminum: a dark-green to black variety of monoclinic pyroxene, characteristic of basic rocks. [1780–90; < L *augitis* a kind of precious stone < Gk, equiv. to *aug(ḗ)* sunlight + *-itis,* fem. of *-ítēs* -ITE[1]] —**au•git•ic** (ô jit′ik), *adj.*

aug•ment (*v.* ôg ment′; *n.* ôg′ment), *v.t.* **1.** to make larger; enlarge in size, number, strength, or extent; increase: *His salary is augmented by a small inheritance.* **2.** *Music.* **a.** to raise (the upper note of an interval or chord) by a half step. **b.** to double the note values of (a theme): *In the fugue's development the subject is augmented.* **3.** *Gram.* to add an augment to. **4.** *Heraldry.* to grant an augmentation to (a coat of arms). —*v.i.* **5.** to become larger. —*n.* **6.** *Gram.* a prefixed vowel or a lengthening of the initial vowel that characterizes certain forms in the nonpresent inflection of verbs in Greek, Sanskrit, Armenian, and Phrygian. [1375–1425; late ME *au(g)menten* < AF, MF *au(g)menter* < LL *augmentāre* to increase, deriv. of *augmentum* an increase (*aug(ēre)* to increase (akin to EKE) + *-mentum* -MENT) + *-ā-* thematic vowel + *-re* inf. ending] —**aug•ment′a•ble,** *adj.* —**Syn. 1.** swell. See **increase. 5.** increase.

aug•men•ta•tion (ôg′men tā′shən), *n.* **1.** the act of augmenting; state of being augmented. **2.** that by which anything is augmented. **3.** *Music.* modification of a theme by increasing the time value of all its notes. **4.** *Heraldry.* an addition to a coat of arms granted to a person by a sovereign power in recognition of a notable action. [1425–75; late ME (< AF) < LL *augmentātiōn-* (s. of *augmentātiō*). See AUGMENT, -ATION; r. late ME *aumentacion* < MF]

aug•ment•a•tive (ôg men′tə tiv), *adj.* **1.** serving to augment. **2.** *Gram.* pertaining to or productive of a form denoting increased size or intensity. In Spanish the augmentative suffix *-ón* is added to a word (as *silla* "chair") to indicate increased size, as in *sillón* "armchair." —*n.* **3.** *Gram.* an augmentative element or formation. [1495–1505; AUGMENT + -ATIVE; r. *augmentatif* < MF] —**aug•men′ta•tive•ly,** *adv.*

augment′ed ro′man. See **Initial Teaching Alphabet.**

augment′ed sixth′, *Music.* **1.** an interval greater than a major sixth by a chromatic half step. **2.** any of various chords having this as the characteristic interval.

aug•ment•er (ôg men′tər), *n.* **1.** a person or thing that augments. **2.** *Aviation, Rocketry.* any auxiliary device, as an afterburner, for additional thrust from the exhaust of a jet or rocket engine. Also, **aug•men′tor.** [1525–35; AUGMENT + -ER[1], -OR[2]]

au grat•in (ō grät′n, ō grat′n, ô grät′n, ô grat′n; *Fr.* ō gʀa taɴ′), *Cookery.* cooked or baked with a topping of either browned bread crumbs and butter or grated cheese, or with both. [1800–10; < F: lit., with the scraping, i.e., the burnt part]

Augs•burg (ôgz′bûrg; *Ger.* ouks′bo͝ork), *n.* a city in Bavaria, in S Germany. 247,700.

Augs′burg Confes′sion, the statement of beliefs and doctrines of the Lutherans, formulated by Melanchthon and endorsed by the Lutheran princes, which was presented at the Diet of Augsburg in 1530 and which became the chief creed of the Lutheran Church. Also called **Augustan Confession.**

au•gur[1] (ô′gər), *n.* **1.** one of a group of ancient Roman officials charged with observing and interpreting omens for guidance in public affairs. **2.** soothsayer; prophet. —*v.t.* **3.** to divine or predict, as from omens; prognosticate. **4.** to serve as an omen or promise of; foreshadow; betoken: *Mounting sales augur a profitable year.* —*v.i.* **5.** to conjecture from signs or omens; predict. **6.** to be a sign; bode: *The movement of troops augurs ill for the peace of the area.* [1540–50; < L *augur* (var. of *auger*) a diviner, soothsayer, deriv. of *augēre* to AUGMENT with orig. implication of "prosper"; cf. AUGUST]

au•gur[2] (ô gər), *Western U.S.* —*v.i.* **1.** to argue, talk, or converse. —*n.* **2.** an excessively talkative person. [1920–25; metathetic var. of ARGUE; n. perh. by assoc. with AUGER]

au•gu•ry (ô′gyə rē), *n., pl.* **-ries. 1.** the art or practice of an augur; divination. **2.** the rite or ceremony of an augur. **3.** an omen, token, or indication. [1325–75; ME < L *augurium* soothsaying, equiv. to *augur* AUGUR + *-ium* -IUM] —**au′gu•ral,** *adj.*

au•gust (ô gust′), *adj.* **1.** inspiring reverence or admiration; of supreme dignity or grandeur; majestic: *an august performance of a religious drama.* **2.** venerable; eminent: *an august personage.* [1655–65; < L *augustus* sacred, grand, akin to *augēre* to increase. See EKE] —**au•gust′ly,** *adv.* —**au•gust′ness,** *n.*

Au•gust (ô′gəst), *n.* **1.** the eighth month of the year, containing 31 days. *Abbr.:* Aug. **2.** a male given name, form of **Augustus.** [bef. 1100; ME < L *Augustus* (named after AUGUSTUS); r. OE *Agustus* < L, as above]

Au•gus•ta (ô gus′tə, ə gus′-), *n.* **1.** a city in E Georgia, on the Savannah River. 47,532. **2.** a city in and the capital of Maine, in the SW part, on the Kennebec River. 21,819. **3.** a female given name.

Au•gus•ta•les (ô′gə stā′lēz), *n.pl.* (in ancient Rome) local officials, usually freedmen, appointed in various towns for the worship of deified emperors. [< L, pl. of *Augustālis.* See AUGUSTUS, -AL[1]]

Au•gus•tan (ô gus′tən, ə gus′-), *adj.* **1.** of or pertaining to Augustus Caesar, the first Roman emperor, or to the age **(Augus′tan Age′)** in which he flourished, which marked the golden age of Latin literature. **2.** of or pertaining to the neoclassic period, esp. of 18th-century English literature. —*n.* **3.** an author in an Augustan age. [1695–1705; < L *Augustānus.* See AUGUSTUS, -AN]

Augus′tan Confes′sion. See **Augsburg Confession.**

Au•gus•tine (ô′gə stēn′, ô gus′tin, ə gus′-), *n.* **1. Saint,** A.D. 354–430, one of the Latin fathers in the early Christian Church; author; bishop of Hippo in N Africa. **2. Saint,** (*Austin*) died A.D. 604, Roman monk: headed group of missionaries who landed in England A.D. 597 and began the conversion of the English to Christianity; first archbishop of Canterbury 601–604. **3.** a male given name, form of **Augustus.**

Au•gus•tin•i•an (ô′gə stin′ē ən), *adj.* **1.** pertaining to St. Augustine of Hippo, to his doctrines, or to any religious order following his rule. —*n.* **2.** *Rom. Cath. Ch.* a member of any of several religious orders deriving their name and rule from St. Augustine. **3.** a person who adopts the views or doctrines of St. Augustine. [1595–1605; AUGUSTINE + -IAN] —**Au′gus•tin′i•an•ism, Au•gus•tin•ism** (ô gus′tə niz′əm), *n.*

Augustin′ian of the Assump′tion, a member of a Roman Catholic congregation founded in 1847 in France, engaged in missionary and educational work. Also called **Assumptionist.**

Au•gus•tus (ô gus′təs, ə gus′-), *n.* **1.** Also called **Octavian** (before 27 B.C.) (*Gaius Julius Caesar Octavianus, Augustus Caesar*), 63 B.C.–A.D. 14, first Roman emperor 27 B.C.–A.D. 14: reformer, patron of arts and literature; heir and successor to Julius Caesar. **2.** a title of office given to rulers of the Roman Republic after Octavianus. **3.** a male given name. [< L: AUGUST, a title given to Octavian when he became emperor]

au jus (ō zho͞os′, ō jo͞os′; *Fr.* ō zhʏ′), (of meat) served in the natural juices that flow from the meat as it cooks. [1915–20; < F: lit., with the gravy. See JUICE]

auk (ôk), *n.* any of several usually black-and-white diving birds of the family Alcidae, of northern seas, having webbed feet and small wings. Cf. **great auk, razor-billed auk.** [1665–75; < Scand; cf. ON *alka*]

razor-billed auk,
Alca torda,
length 1½ ft. (0.46 m)

auk•let (ôk′lit), *n.* any of several small auks of the coasts of the North Pacific, as *Aethia cristatella* **(crested auklet),** having a crest of recurved plumes. [1885–90; AUK + -LET]

au lait (ō lā′; *Fr.* ō le′), *French Cookery.* prepared or served with milk. [< F: lit., with the milk. See LACT-]

Au•lard (ō lᴀʀ′), *n.* **Fran•çois Vic•tor Al•phonse** (fʀäɴ swa′ vēk tôʀ′ al fôɴs′), 1849–1928, French historian.

auld (ôld), *adj. Scot. and North Eng.* old.

auld lang syne (ôld′ lang zīn′, sīn′), *Scot. and North Eng.* **1.** old times, esp. times fondly remembered. **2.** old or long friendship. [lit., old long since, i.e., old long-ago (days)]

au•lic (ô′lik), *adj.* of or pertaining to a royal court. [1695–1705; < L *aulicus* < Gk *aulikós* courtly, equiv. to *aul(ḗ)* hall, court + *-ikos* -IC]

au′lic coun′cil, a personal council of the Holy Roman Emperor, exercising chiefly judicial powers.

Au•li•e A•ta (ou′lē ä′ ə tä′; *Russ.* ʊ lyi ye′ u tä′), former name of **Dzhambul.**

au•lo•phyte (ô′lə fīt′), *n.* a free-living plant growing on or in another plant. [< Gk *aulo-,* comb. form of *aulós* (see AULOS) + -PHYTE]

au•los (ô′los), *n., pl.* **-loi** (-loi). an ancient Greek wind instrument, a double pipe played with a double reed. [< Gk *aulós* tube, pipe, flute]

AUM, air-to-underwater missile.

Aum (ōm), *n. Hinduism.* Om.

aum•bry (am′brē), *n., pl.* **-bries.** ambry.

au•mil•dar (ô′mil där′, ô′mil där′), *n.* (in India) **1.** a manager or agent. **2.** a collector of revenue. [1770–80; < Hindi *amaldār* < Pers, equiv. to Ar *'amal* work + Pers *-dar* agent suffix, lit., holder, holding]

au na•tu•rel (ō′ nach′ə rel′; *Fr.* ō na tʏ ʀel′), **1.** in the natural state. **2.** naked; nude. **3.** cooked plainly. **4.** uncooked. [< F]

aune (ōn), *n.* an old French unit of measure for fabrics, equivalent to about 47 in. (119 cm). [1700–10; < F; OF *aulne* < Frankish **alina* (c. OHG *elina,* OE *eln*). See ELL[2]]

aunt (ant, änt), *n.* **1.** the sister of one's father or mother. **2.** the wife of one's uncle. **3.** *Chiefly New England and South Midland U.S.* (used as a term of respectful address to an older woman who is not related to the speaker). **4.** *Slang.* an aging male homosexual. [1250–1300; ME *aunte* < AF, for OF *ante* < L *amita* father's sister, old fem. ptp. of *amāre* to love, i.e., beloved] —**aunt′like′,** *adj.*

—**Pronunciation.** The usual vowel of AUNT in the United States is the (a) of *rant* except in New England and eastern Virginia, where it is commonly the "New England broad *a,*" a vowel similar to French (ᴀ) and having a quality between the (a) of *hat* and the (ä) of *car.* The vowel (ä) itself is also used. In New England and eastern Virginia (ä) or the (ᴀ)-like sound occur in AUNT in the speech of all social groups, even where a "broad *a*" is not used in words like *dance* and *laugh.* Elsewhere, the "broader" *a* is chiefly an educated pronunciation, fostered by the schools with only partial success ("Your relative isn't an insect, is she?"), and is sometimes regarded as an affectation. AUNT with the vowel of *paint* is chiefly South Midland United States and is limited to folk speech.

The (a) pronunciation of AUNT was brought to America before British English developed the (ä) in such words as *aunt, dance,* and *laugh.* In American English, (ä) is most common in the areas that maintained the closest cultural ties with England after the (ä) pronunciation developed there in these words.

aunt•ie (an′tē, än′-), *n. Informal.* aunt. Also, **aunty.** [1785–95; AUNT + -IE]

Aunt′ Jemi′ma, *Slang (disparaging and offensive).* a black woman considered by other blacks to be subservient to or to curry favor with whites. Cf. **Uncle Tom.** [1885–90; after the trademarked name of a brand of pancake mixes and associated products, featuring a picture of a black female cook on the packaging]

Aunt′ Sal′ly, *Chiefly Brit.* a person who is a ready target for criticism or focus for disputation. [1860–65; so called from the figure used as a target at fairs]

aunt•y (an′tē, än′-), *n., pl.* **aunt•ies.** auntie.

au pair (ō pâr′), **1.** a person, usually a young foreign visitor, employed to take care of children, do housework, etc., in exchange for room and board: *We sent the children to the beach with the au pair.* **2.** of, pertaining to, or employed under such an arrangement: *an au pair girl.* [1965–70; < F, lit., equal, even (*au* contr. of *à le* at the + *pair* equal (n.); cf. PAIR), referring to the equal exchange of work for room and board]

au poi•vre (ō pwa′vʀᵊ), *French Cookery.* spiced with peppercorns or ground black pepper: *steak au poivre.* [< F: with pepper]

aur-[1], var. of **auri-**[1], esp. before a vowel.

aur-[2], var. of **auri-**[2], esp. before a vowel.

CONCISE ETYMOLOGY KEY: <, descended or borrowed from; >, whence; b., blend of, blended; c., cognate with; cf., compare; deriv., derivative; equiv., equivalent; imit., imitative; obl., oblique; r., replacing; s., stem; sp., spelling, spelled; resp., respelling, respelled; trans., translation; ?, origin unknown; *, unattested; ‡, probably earlier than. See the full key inside the front cover.

au·ra (ôr′ə), *n., pl.* **au·ras** or, for 3, **au·rae** (ôr′ē). **1.** a distinctive and pervasive quality or character; air; atmosphere: *an aura of respectability; an aura of friendliness.* **2.** a subtly pervasive quality or atmosphere seen as emanating from a person, place, or thing. **3.** *Pathol.* a sensation, as of lights or a current of warm or cold air, preceding an attack of migraine or epilepsy. [1350–1400; ME < L < Gk: breath (of air)]

Au·ra (ôr′ə), *n. Class. Myth.* a companion of Artemis who bore twins to Dionysus. Zeus changed her into a spring because, in a fit of madness, she had killed one of her children.

au·ral[1] (ôr′əl), *adj.* of or pertaining to an aura. [1865–70; AUR(A) + -AL[1]]

au·ral[2] (ôr′əl), *adj.* of or pertaining to the ear or to the sense of hearing. [1840–50; < L *aur(is)* the ear + -AL[1]] —**au′ral·ly,** *adv.*

au·ral-o·ral (ôr′əl ôr′əl, ôr′əl ōr′-), *adj.* audio-lingual.

au·ra·mine (ôr′ə mēn′, -min), *n. Chem.* a yellow, crystalline solid, $C_{17}H_{22}ClN_3$, soluble in water, alcohol, and ether, used chiefly as a dye for paper and leather. [1880–85; < L *aur(um)* gold + AMINE]

Au·rang·zeb (ôr′əng zeb′), *n.* 1618–1707, Mogul emperor of Hindustan 1658–1707. Also, **Aurungzeb.**

au·ran·o·fin (ô ran′ə fin′), *n. Pharm.* a gold-containing compound, $C_{20}H_{34}AuO_9PS$, used orally in the treatment of rheumatoid arthritis. [coinage appar. based on AURUM; following syllables unexplained]

au·rar (oi′rär), *n.* pl. of **eyrir.**

au·re·a me·di·o·cri·tas (ou′rä ä′ me′dē ōk′ri täs′; *Eng.* ôr′ē ə mē′dē ok′ri tas′, -təs, -med′ē-), *Latin.* the golden mean.

au·re·ate (ôr′ē it, -āt′), *adj.* **1.** golden or gilded. **2.** brilliant; splendid. **3.** characterized by an ornate style of writing or speaking. [1400–50; late ME *aureat* < LL *aureātus* decorated with gold, equiv. to L *aure(us)* golden, of gold (*aur(um)* gold + *-eus* adj. suffix) + *-ātus* -ATE[1]] —**au′re·ate·ly,** *adv.* —**au′re·ate·ness,** *n.*

au′reate lan′guage, a style of poetic diction, used originally in 15th-century English poetry, characterized by the use of ornate phrases and Latinized coinages.

au·re·li·a (ô rē′lē ə, ô rēl′yə), *n.* See **moon jellyfish.** [1590–1600; < NL]

Au·rel·ia (ô rēl′yə), *n.* a female given name: from Latin *Aurelianus,* a family name.

Au·re·li·an (ô rē′lē ən, ô rēl′yən), *n.* (*Lucius Domitius Aurelianus*) A.D. 212?–275, Roman emperor 270–275.

Au·re·li·us (ô rē′lē əs, ô rēl′yəs), *n.* **Marcus.** See **Marcus Aurelius.**

au′rene glass′ (ôr′ēn), an iridescent American art glass colored gold and blue. [formerly a trademark]

au·re·ole (ôr′ē ōl′), *n.* **1.** a radiance surrounding the head or the whole figure in the representation of a sacred personage. **2.** any encircling ring of light or color; halo. **3.** *Astron.* corona (def. 3). **4.** *Geol.* a zone of altered country rock around an igneous intrusion. Also, **au·re·o·la** (ô rē′ə lə, ə rē′-). [1175–1225; ME < L *aureola* (*corona*) golden (crown), equiv. to *aure(us)* golden (see AUREATE) + *-ola,* fem. of *-olus* -OLE[1]]

au·re·o·lin (ô rē′ə lin, ə rē′-), *n.* a pigment used in painting, consisting of potassium cobaltinitrite and characterized by its brilliant yellow hue, transparency, and permanence. Also called **cobalt yellow.** [1875–80; < L *aureol(us)* golden, of gold (see AUREOLE) + -IN[2]] —**au·re·o·line** (ô rē′ə lin, -lin′, ə rē′-), *adj.*

Au·re·o·my·cin (ôr′ē ō mī′sin), *Pharm., Trademark.* a brand of chlortetracycline.

au·re·us (ôr′ē əs), *n., pl.* **au·re·i** (ôr′ē ī′). a gold coin and monetary unit of ancient Rome, from Caesar to Constantine I. [1600–10; < L: lit., golden]

au re·voir (ō rə vwar′; *Eng.* ō′ rə vwär′), *French.* until we see each other again; good-bye for the present.

auri-[1], a combining form meaning "gold": *auriferous.* Also, *esp. before a vowel,* **aur-.** [< L *aur(um)* + *-i-* -I-]

auri-[2], a combining form meaning "ear": *auriform.* Also, *esp. before a vowel,* **aur-.** [< L *auris* EAR[1]]

au·ric (ôr′ik), *adj. Chem.* of or containing gold in the trivalent state. [1830–40; < L *aur(um)* gold + -IC]

au·ri·cle (ôr′i kəl), *n.* **1.** *Anat.* **a.** the projecting outer portion of the ear; pinna. **b.** Also called **auricular appendage.** an ear-shaped appendage projecting from each atrium of the heart. **c.** (loosely) the atrium. **2.** *Bot., Zool.* a part like or likened to an ear. [1645–55; < L *auricula* the (external) ear, ear lobe. See AURI-[2], -CLE[1]] —**au′ri·cled,** *adj.*

au·ric·u·lar (ô rik′yə lər), *adj.* **1.** of or pertaining to the ear or to the sense of hearing; aural. **2.** perceived by or addressed to the ear; made in private: *an auricular confession.* **3.** dependent on hearing; understood or known by hearing: *auricular evidence.* **4.** shaped like an ear; auriculate. **5.** *Anat.* pertaining to an auricle of the heart. **6.** *Ornith.* pertaining to certain often modified feathers that cover and protect the opening of a bird's ear. —*n.* **7.** Usually, **auriculars.** *Ornith.* feathers that cover and protect the opening of a bird's ear. [1535–45; < LL *auriculāris* of, pertaining to the ear. See AURICLE, -AR[1]] —**au·ric′u·lar·ly,** *adv.*

auric′ular append′age, auricle (def. 1b).

au·ric·u·lar·i·a (ô rik′yə lâr′ē ə), *n., pl.* **-lar·i·ae** (-lâr′ē ē′), **-lar·i·as.** the bilaterally symmetrical, ciliated larva of a holothurian. [< NL; see AURICLE, -ARIA]

au·ric·u·late (ô rik′yə lit, -lāt′), *adj.* **1.** having auricles or earlike parts. **2.** shaped like an ear. [1705–15; < L *auricul(a)* AURICLE + -ATE[1]] —**au·ric′u·late·ly,** *adv.*

au·ric·u·lin (ô rik′yə lin), *n. Biochem.* See **atrial natriuretic factor.** [1980–85; perh. AURICUL(AR APPENDAGE) + -IN[2]]

au·ric·u·lo·ven·tric·u·lar (ô rik′yə lō ven trik′yə lər), *adj. Anat.* atrioventricular. [*auriculo-* (comb. form of AURICLE) + VENTRICULAR]

au·rif·er·ous (ô rif′ər əs), *adj.* yielding or containing gold. [1720–30; < L *aurifer* gold-bearing (see AURI-[1], -FER) + -OUS]

au·ri·form (ôr′ə fôrm′), *adj.* shaped like an ear, as the shell of certain mollusks. [1810–20; AURI-[2] + -FORM]

au·ri·fy (ôr′ə fī′), *v.t.,* **-fied, -fy·ing. 1.** to cause to appear golden; gild: *Dawn came, and sunlight aurified the lead-gray ocean.* **2.** to transmute into gold. [1645–55; AURI-[1] + -FY] —**au·rif·ic** (ô rif′ik), *adj.* —**au′ri·fi·ca′tion,** *n.*

Au·ri·ga (ô rī′gə), *n., gen.* **-gae** (-jē). *Astron.* the Charioteer, a northern constellation between Perseus and Gemini, containing the bright star Capella. [1400–50; late ME < L: charioteer]

Au·ri·gnac (ô rē nyak′), *n.* a village in S France: many prehistoric artifacts found in area. 1149.

Au·ri·gna·cian (ôr′in yā′shən), *adj.* of, belonging to, or typical of an Upper Paleolithic industry with characteristic stone and bone artifacts that is distributed from western France to eastern Europe and the Middle East. [1910–15; AURIGNAC + -IAN]

Au·ri·ol (ôr′ē ōl′, -ôl′; *Fr.* ō ryôl′), *n.* **Vin·cent** (vin′sənt; *Fr.* van sän′), 1884–1966, French statesman: president 1947–54.

au·ri·scope (ôr′ə skōp′), *n. Med.* otoscope. [1850–55; AURI-[2] + -SCOPE] —**au·ri·scop·ic** (ôr′ə skop′ik), *adj.* —**au′ri·scop′i·cal·ly,** *adv.*

au·rist (ôr′ist), *n.* a physician specializing in the treatment of ear diseases; otologist. [1670–80; AUR-[2] + -IST]

Au·ro·bin·do (ôr′ə bin′dō), *n.* **Sri** (*Sri Aurobindo Ghose*), 1872–1950, Indian scholar and spiritual leader.

au·rochs (ôr′oks), *n., pl.* **-rochs. 1.** a large, black European wild ox, *Bos primigenius:* extinct since 1627. **2.** (not used scientifically) the European bison. [1760–70; < G, var. (now obs.) of *Auerochs,* MHG *ūrochse,* OHG *ūrohso,* equiv. to *ūr* (c. OE *ūr* bison) + *ohso* ox]

aurochs (def. 2)

Au·ro·ra (ô rôr′ə, ô rōr′ə, ə rôr′ə, ə rōr′ə), *n.* **1.** the ancient Roman goddess of the dawn. Cf. **Eos. 2.** (*l.c.*) dawn. **3.** (*l.c.*) *Meteorol.* a radiant emission from the upper atmosphere that occurs sporadically over the middle and high latitudes of both hemispheres in the form of luminous bands, streamers, or the like, caused by the bombardment of the atmosphere with charged solar particles that are being guided along the earth's magnetic lines of force. **4.** a city in central Colorado, near Denver. 158,588. **5.** a city in NE Illinois. 81,293. **6.** a female given name. [1350–1400; ME < L *aurōra* dawn, dawn goddess, EAST]

auro′ra aus·tra′lis (ô strā′lis), *Meteorol.* the aurora of the Southern Hemisphere. Also called **southern lights.** [1735–45; < NL: southern aurora; see AUSTRAL]

auro′ra bo·re·al′is (bôr′ē al′is, -ā′lis, bōr′-), *Meteorol.* the aurora of the Northern Hemisphere. Also called **northern lights, auro′ra polar′is.** [1621; < NL: northern aurora; see BOREAL]

au·ro·ral (ô rôr′əl, ô rōr′-, ə rôr′-, ə rōr′-), *adj.* **1.** of or like the dawn. **2.** pertaining to the aurora borealis or aurora australis. [1545–55; AUROR(A) + -AL[1]] —**au·ro′ral·ly,** *adv.*

auro′ral zone′, the region surrounding the north or south geomagnetic pole in which the auroral phenomena take place.

au·ro·re·an (ô rôr′ē ən, ô rōr′-, ə rôr′-, ə rōr′-), *adj.* belonging to the dawn; auroral. [1810–20; AUROR(A) + -EAN]

aur·ous (ôr′əs), *adj.* **1.** *Chem.* of or containing gold in the univalent state. **2.** of or containing gold. [1860–65; AUR-[1] + -OUS]

au·rum (ôr′əm), *n. Chem.* gold. *Symbol:* Au [1490–1500; < L: gold]

Au·rung·zeb (ôr′əng zeb′), *n.* Aurangzeb.

AUS, Army of the United States. Also, **A.U.S.**

Aus., 1. Austria. **2.** Austrian.

Au·sa·ble (ô sā′bəl), *n.* a river in NE New York, flowing NE through a gorge (**Ausa′ble Chasm′**) into Lake Champlain. 20 mi. (32 km) long.

Ausch·witz (oush′vits), *n.* a town in SW Poland: site of Nazi concentration camp during World War II. 39,600. Polish, **Oświęcim.**

aus·cul·tate (ô′skəl tāt′), *v.t., v.i.,* **-tat·ed, -tat·ing.** *Med.* to examine by auscultation. [1860–65; back formation from AUSCULTATION] —**aus·cul·ta·tive** (ô′skəl tā′tiv, ô skul′tə-), **aus·cul·ta·to·ry** (ô skul′tə tôr′ē, -tōr′ē), *adj.* —**aus′cul·ta′tor,** *n.*

aus·cul·ta·tion (ô′skəl tā′shən), *n. Med.* the act of listening, either directly or through a stethoscope or other instrument, to sounds within the body as a method of diagnosis. [1625–35; < L *auscultātiōn-* (s. of *auscultātiō*) a listening, attending to, equiv. to *auscultāt(us)* listened to (ptp. of *auscultāre; aus-* (var. s. of *auris* ear) + *-cultā-* of uncert. sense and orig. + *-tus* ptp. suffix) + *-iōn-* -ION]

Aus·land·er (ous′lan′dər, ô′slan′-), *n.* foreigner; alien; outlander. [< G *Ausländer;* see OUT-, LAND, -ER[1]]

aus·laut (ous′lout′), *n., pl.* **-lau·te** (-lou′tə), **-lauts.** *Ling.* **1.** final position in a word, esp. as a conditioning environment in sound change. **2.** a sound in this position. Cf. **anlaut, inlaut.** [1880–85; < G, equiv. to *aus-* OUT- + *Laut* sound, as n. deriv. of *auslauten* to end (with a given sound)]

Aus·le·se (ous′lā zə), *n.* (*often l.c.*) a wine made in Germany from carefully selected ripe grapes. [< G: lit., selection]

aus·pex (ô′speks), *n., pl.* **aus·pi·ces** (ô′spə sēz′). an augur of ancient Rome. [1590–1600; < L: one who observes birds, soothsayer, diviner, equiv. to *au-,* base of *avis* bird + *-spex* watcher (*spec-,* s. of *specere* to look at) + *-s* nom. sing. suffix]

aus·pi·cate (ô′spi kāt′), *v.t.,* **-cat·ed, -cat·ing.** to initiate with ceremonies calculated to ensure good luck; inaugurate. [1595–1605; < L *auspicātus* consecrated by auguries (ptp. of *auspicārī*), equiv. to *auspic-* (s. of AUSPEX) + *-ātus* -ATE[1]]

aus·pice (ô′spis), *n., pl.* **aus·pic·es** (ô′spə siz). **1.** Usually, **auspices.** patronage; support; sponsorship: *under the auspices of the Department of Education.* **2.** Often, **auspices.** a favorable sign or propitious circumstance. **3.** a divination or prognostication, originally from observing birds. [1525–35; < F < L *auspicium* a bird-watching, divination from flight of birds, equiv. to *auspic-* (s. of AUSPEX) + *-ium* -IUM]

aus·pi·cial (ô spish′əl), *adj.* **1.** of or pertaining to auspices: *auspicial rites.* **2.** auspicious. [1605–15; < L *auspici(um)* AUSPICE + -AL[1]]

aus·pi·cious (ô spish′əs), *adj.* **1.** promising success; propitious; opportune; favorable: *an auspicious occasion.* **2.** favored by fortune; prosperous; fortunate. [1600–10; < L *auspici(um)* AUSPICE + -OUS] —**aus·pi′cious·ly,** *adv.* —**aus·pi′cious·ness,** *n.*

Aus·sie (ô′sē, *or, esp. Brit.,* oz′ē, ô′zē), *n. Informal.* an Australian. [1890–95; AUS(TRALIAN) + -IE]

Aust., 1. Austria. **2.** Austria-Hungary. **3.** Austrian.

aus·tem·per (ôs′tem′pər), *v.t.* to harden (steel) by heating and quenching to render it austenitic. [AUS(TENITE) + TEMPER]

Aus·ten (ô′stən), *n.* **Jane,** 1775–1817, English novelist.

aus·ten·ite (ô′stə nīt′), *n. Metall.* **1.** a solid solution of carbon or of carbon and other elements in gamma iron, having a face-centered cubic lattice at all temperatures. **2.** an allotrope of iron, stable between 910°C and 1400°C and having a face-centered cubic lattice; gamma iron. [1900–05; named after Sir W. C. Roberts-*Austen* (1843–1902), English metallurgist; see -ITE[1]]

aus·ten·it·ic (ô′stə nit′ik), *adj.* (of an iron alloy) consisting mainly of austenite. [1900–05; AUSTENITE + -IC]

aus·ten·it·ize (ô′stə ni tīz′), *v.t.,* **-ized, -iz·ing.** *Metall.* to form austenite in (a ferrous alloy) by heating. Also, *esp. Brit.,* **aus′ten·it·ise′.** [AUSTENITE + -IZE]

Aus·ter (ô′stər), *n. Literary.* the south wind personified. [1325–75; ME < L]

aus·tere (ô stēr′), *adj.* **1.** severe in manner or appearance; uncompromising; strict; forbidding: *an austere teacher.* **2.** rigorously self-disciplined and severely moral; ascetic; abstinent: *the austere quality of life in the convent.* **3.** grave; sober; solemn; serious: *an austere manner.* **4.** without excess, luxury, or ease; simple; limited; severe: *an austere life.* **5.** severely simple; without ornament: *austere writing.* **6.** lacking softness; hard: *an austere bed of straw.* **7.** rough to the taste; sour or harsh in flavor. [1300–50; ME (< AF) < L *austērus* < Gk *austērós* harsh, rough, bitter] —**aus·tere′ly,** *adv.* —**aus·tere′ness,** *n.*
—**Syn. 4.** AUSTERE, BLEAK, SPARTAN, STARK all suggest lack of ornament or adornment and of a feeling of comfort or warmth. AUSTERE usually implies a purposeful avoidance of luxury or ease: *simple, stripped-down, austere surroundings.* BLEAK adds a sense of forbidding coldness, hopelessness, depression: *a bleak, dreary, windswept plain.* SPARTAN, somewhat more forceful than *austere,* implies stern discipline and rigorous, even harsh, avoidance of all that is not strictly functional: *a life of Spartan simplicity.* STARK shares with BLEAK a sense of grimness and desolation: *the stark cliff face.* —**Ant. 4.** luxurious, comfortable, lush; sybaritic.

aus·ter·i·ty (ô ster′i tē), *n., pl.* **-ties. 1.** austere quality; severity of manner, life, etc.; sternness. **2.** Usually, **austerities.** ascetic practices: *austerities of monastery life.* **3.** strict economy. [1300–50; ME *austerite* < AF, OF *austerite* < L *austēritās.* See AUSTERE, -ITY]
—**Syn. 1.** harshness, strictness, asceticism, rigor. **2.** See **hardship.** —**Ant. 1.** leniency.

Aus·ter·litz (ô′stər lits; *Ger.* ous′tər lits), *n.* a town in S Moravia, in the SE Czech Republic: Russian and Austrian armies defeated by Napoleon I 1805. Czech, **Slavkov.**

Aus·tin (ô′stən), *n.* **1. Alfred,** 1835–1913, English poet: poet laureate 1896–1913. **2. John,** 1790–1859, English writer on law. **3. John Lang·shaw** (lang′shô), 1911–60, British philosopher. **4. Mary (Hunter),** 1868–1934, U.S. novelist, playwright, and short-story writer. **5. Stephen Fuller,** 1793–1836, American colonizer in Texas. **6. Warren Robinson,** 1877–1962, U.S. diplomat. **7.** See **Augustine, Saint** (def. 2). **8.** a city in and the capital of Texas, in the central part, on the Colorado River. 345,496. **9.** a city in SE Minnesota. 23,020. **10.** a male given name, form of **Augustus.**

Aus′tin fri′ar, one of the Hermits of St. Augustine. [1860–65]

austr-, var. of **austro-** before a vowel.

CONCISE PRONUNCIATION KEY: *act, cāpe, dâre, pärt; set, ēqual; if, īce; ox, ōver, ôrder, oil, bo͝ok, bo͞ot, out; up, ûrge; child; sing; shoe; thin, that;* zh as in *treasure.* ə = *a* as in *alone, e* as in *system, i* as in *easily, o* as in *gallop, u* as in *circus;* ə as in *fire* (fīər), *hour* (ouər). l and n can serve as syllabic consonants, as in *cradle* (krād′l), and *button* (but′n). See the full key inside the front cover.

aus·tral[1] (ô′strəl), *adj.* **1.** southern. **2.** (*cap.*) Australian. [1350–1400; ME < L *austrālis* southern, equiv. to *Aust(e)r* AUSTER + *-ālis* -AL[1]]

aus·tral[2] (ous trȧl′), *n., pl.* **-tra·les** (-trȧ′les). a monetary unit of Argentina, equal to 100 centavos: replaced the peso in 1985. [< Sp; see AUSTRAL[1]]

Austral, Australian (def. 6).

Austral., **1.** Australasia. **2.** Australia. **3.** Australian.

Aus·tral·a·sia (ô′strə lā′zhə, -shə), *n.* Australia, New Zealand, and neighboring islands in the S Pacific Ocean. [AUSTRAL(IA) + ASIA] —**Aus′tral·a′sian,** *adj., n.*

Aus·tral·ia (ô strāl′yə), *n.* **1.** a continent SE of Asia, between the Indian and the Pacific oceans. 14,576,330; 2,948,366 sq. mi. (7,636,270 sq. km). **2. Commonwealth of,** a member of the Commonwealth of Nations, consisting of the federated states and territories of Australia and Tasmania. 14,995,287; 2,974,581 sq. mi. (7,704,165 sq. km). *Cap.:* Canberra. See map below.

Austral′ia Cur′rent, a branch of the South Equatorial Current flowing SW from around Fiji to the E coast of Australia and then S along the coast.

Austral′ia Day′, a legal holiday in Australia, the first Monday after January 25, commemorating the landing of the British in 1788. Formerly, **Foundation Day.**

Aus·tral·ian (ô strāl′yən), *adj.* **1.** of or pertaining to Australia, its inhabitants, or their languages. **2.** *Zoogeog.* belonging to a geographical division comprising Australia, New Zealand, Tasmania, Celebes, the Moluccas, Papua New Guinea, and adjacent smaller islands. **3.** *Phytogeog.* belonging or pertaining to a geographical division comprising Australia and Tasmania. —*n.* **4.** a native or inhabitant of Australia. **5.** an Aborigine of Australia. **6.** the phylum of languages spoken by the Aborigines of Australia, consisting of more than a hundred languages. *Abbr.:* Austral, Austral. [AUSTRALI(A) + -AN]

Austral′ian Aborig′ine, aborigine (def. 2).

Austral′ian Alps′, a mountain range in SE Australia. Highest peak, Mt. Kosciusko, 7328 ft. (2234 m).

Austral′ian Antarc′tic Ter′ritory, an outlying territory of Australia located S of latitude 60°S. 2,360,000 sq. mi. (6,112,000 sq. km).

Austral′ian bal′lot, a ballot containing the names of all the candidates for public office, handed to the voter at the polling station to be marked in secret: so called because it originated in Australia. Cf. **Indiana ballot, Massachusetts ballot, office-block ballot.** [1885–90, *Amer.*]

Austral′ian blue′bell creep′er, an evergreen twining shrub, *Sollya heterophylla,* of western Australia, having nodding blue flowers in terminal clusters. [1895–1900]

Austral′ian Cap′ital Ter′ritory, a federal territory on the continent of Australia in the SE part: includes Canberra, capital of the Commonwealth of Australia. 221,609; 939 sq. mi. (2430 sq. km). Formerly, **Federal Capital Territory.**

Austral′ian cat′tle dog′, one of an Australian breed of medium-sized herding dogs with a blue, blue-mottled, or red-speckled coat, developed by cross breeding the Australian kelpie, dingo, and collie. [1925–30]

Austral′ian crawl′, *Swimming.* a crawl in which the swimmer kicks twice with one leg for each stroke of the opposite arm. [1905–10]

Austral′ian dou′bles, *Tennis.* an unusual formation in doubles in which the server's partner is positioned on the same side of the court as the server. [1970–75]

Austral′ian fan′ palm′, a fan palm, *Livistona australis,* of Australia, having a slender, reddish-brown trunk, spiny leafstalks, and round fruit.

Austral′ian Il′la·war·ra Short′horn (il′ə wôr′ə, -wor′ə), a breed of dual-purpose cattle originally bred to withstand dry conditions in Australia. [*Illawarra,* district of E New South Wales]

Aus·tral·ian·ize (ô strāl′yə nīz′), *v.t., v.i.,* **-ized, -iz·ing.** to make or become Australian in speech, manners, practices, etc. Also, *esp. Brit.,* **Aus·tral′ian·ise′.** [1880–85; AUSTRALIAN + -IZE]

Austral′ian kel′pie, one of an Australian breed of medium-sized sheepherding dogs having a short, harsh, straight coat in a combination of colors that can include black, red, tan, fawn, chocolate, or smoke blue, probably developed by crossbreeding between the border collie and dingo. [alleged to be the name of an early example of the breed]

Austral′ian pine′. See **Norfolk Island pine.** [1915–20]

Austral′ian Rules′ foot′ball, a variation of rugby played almost exclusively in Australia, engaging two teams of eighteen players each on an oval-shaped field about 180 yards (165 m) long with four upright posts at each end, the object being to kick a rugby ball between these posts. [1930–35]

Austral′ian rye′ grass′. See **Italian rye grass.**

Austral′ian tea′ tree′, a shrubby Australian tree, *Leptospermum laevigatum,* of the myrtle family, having lance-shaped leaves and white, bell-shaped flowers.

Austral′ian ter′rier, one of an Australian breed of small working terriers having a rough coat, either silver black or blue black with tan markings on the head and tail, a topknot, erect ears, and a docked tail, originally bred for herding sheep and guarding mines. [1905–10]

Aus·tra·loid (ô′strə loid′), *n.* **1.** *Anthropol.* a descriptive category including principally the Australian Aborigines and sometimes including Papuans, Melanesians, various small-statured peoples, as Negritos, of the Philippines, Malay Peninsula, and Andaman Islands, and some of the tribes of central and southern India. —*adj.* **2.** pertaining to or having the characteristics of the Australoids. Also, **Aus·tra·li·oid** (ô strā′lē oid′). [1860–65; var. of *Australioid.* See AUSTRALIA, -OID]

aus·tra·lo·pith·e·cine (ô strā′lō pith′ə sēn′, -sīn′, -pə thē′sin, -sīn′, ô′strə-), *n.* **1.** (*sometimes cap.*) a member of the extinct genus *Australopithecus.* —*adj.* **2.** of, pertaining to, or resembling the genus *Australopithecus* or its members. [1935–40; AUSTRALOPITHEC(US) + -INE[1]]

Aus·tra·lo·pith·e·cus (ô strā′lō pith′i kəs, -pə thē′-kəs, ô′strə-), *n.* an extinct genus of small-brained, large-toothed bipedal hominids that lived in Africa between one and four million years ago. Cf. **australopithecine.** [< NL (1905), equiv. to *austral(is)* AUSTRAL + -o- -o- + *pithēcus* < Gk *píthēkos* ape]

Australopith′ecus a·far·en′sis (ə fä ren′sis), **1.** an extinct species of early hominid whose fossil remains were discovered in Ethiopia and have been dated at between 3.5 and 4 million years of age. **2.** a fossil belonging to this species. Cf. **Lucy.** See illus. under **hominid.** [1978; < NL; after the *Afar* region of Ethiopia, where Lucy was found; see AFAR, -ENSIS]

Australopith′ecus af·ri·ca′nus (af′ri kä′nəs, -kan′əs), **1.** an extinct species of gracile hominid, formerly known as *Plesianthropus transvaalensis,* that lived in southern Africa about three million years ago. **2.** a fossil belonging to this species. See illus. under **hominid.** [1925; < NL; see AFRICAN]

Australopith′ecus boi·sei′ (boi sā′), **1.** an extinct species of very rugged, large-toothed bipedal hominid, formerly known as *Zinjanthropus boisei,* that lived in eastern Africa one to two million years ago. **2.** a fossil belonging to this species. See illus. under **hominid.** [< NL; *boisei* after Charles Boise, a benefactor of L.S.B. Leakey, who described and named the original finds in 1959]

Australopith′ecus ro·bus′tus (rō bus′təs), **1.** an extinct species of large-toothed bipedal hominid that lived in southern Africa c1.5–2 million years ago: formerly classified as the genus *Paranthropus.* **2.** a fossil belonging to this species. See illus. under **hominid.** [< NL; see ROBUST]

Aus·tral·orp (ô′strə lôrp′), *n.* one of an Australian breed of chickens valued for egg production. [1920–25; AUSTRAL(IAN) + ORP(INGTON)]

Aus·tra·sia (ô strā′zhə, -shə), *n.* the E part of the former kingdom of the Franks, comprising parts of what is now NE France, W Germany, and Belgium. *Cap.:* Metz.

Aus·tri·a (ô′strē ə), *n.* a republic in central Europe. 7,555,333; 32,381 sq. mi. (83,865 sq. km). *Cap.:* Vienna. German, **Österreich.** —**Aus′tri·an,** *adj., n.*

Aus·tri·a-Hun·ga·ry (ô′strē ə hung′gə rē), *n.* a monarchy (1867–1918) in central Europe that included the empire of Austria, the kingdom of Hungary, and various crown lands. —**Aus·tro-Hun·gar·i·an** (ô′strō-hung gâr′ē ən), *adj., n.*

Aus′trian pine′, a widely cultivated pine, *Pinus nigra,* native to Europe and Asia Minor, growing to a height of more than 100 ft. (30 m), often planted as a windbreak. [1930–35]

Aus′trian shade′, a window shade in which the fabric falls in a series of puffy festoons created by vertical rows of shirring.

aus·trin·ger (ô′strin jər), *n.* astringer.

Austro-, a combining form of **Austria:** *Austro-Hungarian.*

austro-, a combining form meaning "south," used in the formation of compound words: *Austronesia.* Also, *esp. before a vowel,* **austr-.** [< L *aust(e)r* the south, the south wind + -o-]

Aus·tro·a·si·at·ic (ô′strō ā′zhē at′ik, -shē-), *n.* **1.** a family of languages spoken in SE Asia and the lands

around the Bay of Bengal and consisting principally of Vietnamese, Khmer, Mon, Khasi, Nicobarese, and the Munda languages. *—adj.* **2.** of or pertaining to Austroasiatic. [1920–25; AUSTRO- + ASIATIC]

Aus·tro·ne·sia (ô′strō nē′zhə, -shə), *n.* the islands of the central and S Pacific. [AUSTRO- + Gk *nês*(os) island + *-ia* -IA]

Aus·tro·ne·sian (ô′strō nē′zhən, -shən), *n.* **1.** Also called **Malayo-Polynesian.** a family of languages spoken in the Malay Peninsula, Indonesia, the Philippines, Vietnam, Taiwan, Madagascar, and Oceania. *—adj.* **2.** of or pertaining to Austronesia or the Austronesian family of languages; Malayo-Polynesian. [1900–05; AUSTRONESI(A) + -AN]

Aus′tro-Prus′sian War′ (ô′strō prush′ən), the war (1866) in which Prussia, Italy, and some minor German states opposed Austria, Saxony, Hanover, and the states of southern Germany. Also called **Seven Weeks' War.**

aut-, var. of **auto-**[1] before a vowel: *autacoid.*

au·ta·coid (ô′tə koid′), *n. Physiol.* any physiologically active internal secretion, esp. one of uncertain classification, as histamine or prostaglandin. [1910–15; AUT- + Gk *ák*(os) remedy + -OID] **—au′ta·coi′dal,** *adj.*

au·tarch (ô′tärk), *n.* an absolute ruler; autocrat; tyrant. [1860–65; < Gk *aútarchos,* n. use of *aútarchos* autocratic, equiv. to *aut-* AUT- + *-archos* -ARCH]

au·tar·chy (ô′tär kē), *n., pl.* **-chies. 1.** absolute sovereignty. **2.** an autocratic government. **3.** autarky. [1655–65; < Gk *autarchía* self-rule. See AUT-, -ARCHY] **—au·tar′chic, au·tar′chi·cal,** *adj.* **—au·tar′chi·cal·ly,** *adv.* **—au′tar·chist,** *n.*

au·tar·ky (ô′tär kē), *n., pl.* **-kies. 1.** the condition of self-sufficiency, esp. economic, as applied to a nation. **2.** a national policy of economic independence. Also, **autarchy.** [1610–20; < Gk *autárkeia,* equiv. to *aut-* AUT- + *arke-* suffice + *-ia* -IA] **—au·tar′kic, au·tar′ki·cal,** *adj.* **—au·tar′ki·cal·ly,** *adv.* **—au′tar·kist,** *n.*

aut Cae·sar, aut ni·hil (out kī′särʀ out ni′hil; *Eng.* ôt sē′zər ôt nī′hil), *Latin.* either a Caesar or nothing; all or nothing.

au·te·cism (ô tē′siz əm), *n.* autoecism. **—au·te·cious** (ô tē′shəs), *adj.* **—au·te′cious·ly,** *adv.* **—au·te′cious·ness,** *n.*

aut·e·col·o·gy (ô′tə kol′ə je), *n.* a branch of ecology dealing with the individual organism or species in relation to its environment. Cf. **synecology.** [1905–10; AUT- + ECOLOGY] **—aut·ec·o·log·ic** (ôt′ek ə loj′ik, -ē kə-), **aut′ec·o·log′i·cal,** *adj.* **—aut′ec·o·log′i·cal·ly,** *adv.*

Au·teuil (ō tœ′yᵊ), *n.* a former town, now part of Paris, France: noted for residences of Boileau, Talleyrand, Molière, La Fontaine, and other eminent people.

au·teur (ō tûr′; *Fr.* ō tœʀ′), *n., pl.* **au·teurs** (ō tûrz′; *Fr.* ō tœʀ′). a filmmaker whose individual style and complete control over all elements of production give a film its personal and unique stamp. [1960–65; < F: lit., author, originator < L *auctor.* See AUTHOR] **—au·teur′·ism,** *n.* **—au·teur′ist,** *adj., n.*

auteur′ the′ory, (in film criticism) a theory that the director is the chief creator of a film and gives it an individual style that is evident in all aspects of the finished product. [1960–65]

auth., **1.** authentic. **2.** author. **3.** authority. **4.** authorized.

au·then·tic (ô then′tik), *adj.* **1.** not false or copied; genuine; real: *an authentic antique.* **2.** having the origin supported by unquestionable evidence; authenticated; verified: *an authentic document of the Middle Ages; an authentic work of the old master.* **3.** entitled to acceptance or belief because of agreement with known facts or experience; reliable; trustworthy: *an authentic report on poverty in Africa.* **4.** *Law.* executed with all due formalities: *an authentic deed.* **5.** *Music.* **a.** (of a church mode) having a range extending from the final to the octave above. Cf. **plagal. b.** (of a cadence) consisting of a dominant harmony followed by a tonic. **6.** *Obs.* authoritative. [1300–50; < LL *authenticus* < Gk *authentikós* original, primary, at first hand, equiv. to *authént(ēs)* one who does things himself (*aut-* AUT- + *-hentēs* doer) + *-ikos* -IC; r. ME *autentik* (< AF) < ML *autenticus*] **—au·then′ti·cal·ly,** *adv.*
—Syn. 1–3. AUTHENTIC, GENUINE, REAL, VERITABLE share the sense of actuality and lack of falsehood or misrepresentation. AUTHENTIC carries a connotation of authoritative certification that an object is what it is claimed to be: *an authentic Rembrandt sketch.* GENUINE refers to objects or persons having the characteristics or source claimed or implied: *a genuine ivory carving.* REAL, the most general of these terms, refers to innate or actual—as opposed to ostensible—nature or character: *In real life, plans often miscarry. A real diamond will cut glass.* VERITABLE, derived from the Latin word for truth, suggests the general truthfulness but not necessarily the literal or strict correspondence with reality of that which it describes; it is often used metaphorically: *a veritable wizard of finance.*

au·then·ti·cal (ô then′ti kəl), *adj. Archaic.* authentic. [1525–35; AUTHENTIC + -AL[1]]

au·then·ti·cate (ô then′ti kāt′), *v.t.,* **-cat·ed, -cat·ing. 1.** to establish as genuine. **2.** to establish the authorship or origin of conclusively or unquestionably, chiefly by the techniques of scholarship: *to authenticate a painting.* **3.** to make authoritative or valid. [1565–75; < ML *authenticātus* made authentic (ptp. of *authenticāre*). See AUTHENTIC, -ATE[1]] **—au·then′ti·cat′a·ble,** *adj.* **—au·then′ti·ca′tion,** *n.*
—Syn. 1. confirm, validate, substantiate.

au·then·ti·ca·tor (ô then′ti kā′tər), *n.* **1.** a person or thing that authenticates. **2.** *Cryptography.* a code used to authenticate a previously transmitted code. [1860–65; AUTHENTICATE + -OR[2]]

au·then·tic·i·ty (ô′then tis′i tē, ô′thən-), *n.* the quality of being authentic; genuineness. [1650–60; AUTHENTIC + -ITY]

au·thi·gen·ic (ô′thi jen′ik), *adj. Geol.* (of a constituent of a rock) formed in the rock where it is found. Cf. **allogenic** (def. 1). [1885–90; < G *Authigen* < Gk *authigenēs* native to a specific place (*aûthi* there + *-genēs* born) + -IC; see GENIC]

au·thor (ô′thər), *n.* **1.** a person who writes a novel, poem, essay, etc.; the composer of a literary work, as distinguished from a compiler, translator, editor, or copyist. **2.** the literary production or productions of a writer: *to find a passage in an author.* **3.** the maker of anything; creator; originator: *the author of a new tax plan.* *—v.t.* **4.** to write; be the author of: *He authored a history of the Civil War.* **5.** to originate; create a design for: *She authored a new system for teaching chemistry.* [1250–1300; earlier *auct(h)or* < L *auctor* writer, progenitor, equiv. to *aug(ēre)* to increase, AUGMENT + *-tor* -TOR; r. ME *auto(u)r* < AF, for OF *autor* < L, as above] **—au·tho·ri·al** (ô thôr′ē əl, ô thōr′-), *adj.* **—au′thor·less,** *adj.*

au′thor cat′alog, *Library Science.* a catalog whose entries are listed by author, editor, compiler, translator, or other party considered to have responsibility for the creation or assembly of the work specified. [1910–15]

au·thor·ess (ô′thər is), *n.* a woman who is an author. [1485–95; AUTHOR + -ESS]
—Usage. See **-ess.**

au·thor·i·tar·i·an (ə thôr′i târ′ē ən, ə thor′-), *adj.* **1.** favoring complete obedience or subjection to authority as opposed to individual freedom: *authoritarian principles; authoritarian attitudes.* **2.** of or pertaining to a governmental or political system, principle, or practice in which individual freedom is held as completely subordinate to the power or authority of the state, centered either in one person or a small group that is not constitutionally accountable to the people. **3.** exercising complete or almost complete control over the will of another or of others: *an authoritarian parent.* *—n.* **4.** a person who favors or acts according to authoritarian principles. [1875–80; AUTHORIT(Y) + -ARIAN] **—au·thor′i·tar′i·an·ism,** *n.*

au·thor·i·ta·tive (ə thôr′i tā′tiv, ə thor′-), *adj.* **1.** having due authority; having the sanction or weight of authority: *an authoritative opinion.* **2.** substantiated or supported by documentary evidence and accepted by most authorities in a field: *an authoritative edition of Shakespeare; an authoritative treatment of a subject.* **3.** having an air of authority; accustomed to exercising authority; positive; peremptory; dictatorial: *said with an authoritative air.* [1595–1605; AUTHORIT(Y) + -ATIVE] **—au·thor′i·ta′tive·ly,** *adv.* **—au·thor′i·ta′tive·ness,** *n.*
—Syn. 1. official. **3.** dogmatic, authoritarian.

au·thor·i·ty (ə thôr′i tē, ə thor′-), *n., pl.* **-ties. 1.** the power to determine, adjudicate, or otherwise settle issues or disputes; jurisdiction; the right to control, command, or determine. **2.** a power or right delegated or given; authorization: *Who has the authority to grant permission?* **3.** a person or body of persons in whom authority is vested, as a governmental agency. **4.** Usually, **authorities.** persons having the legal power to make and enforce the law; government: *They finally persuaded the authorities that they were not involved in espionage.* **5.** an accepted source of information, advice, etc. **6.** a quotation or citation from such a source. **7.** an expert on a subject: *He is an authority on baseball.* **8.** persuasive force; conviction: *She spoke with authority.* **9.** a statute, court rule, or judicial decision that establishes a rule or principle of law; a ruling. **10.** right to respect or acceptance of one's word, command, thought, etc.; commanding influence: *the authority of a parent; the authority of a great writer.* **11.** mastery in execution or performance, as of a work of art or literature or a piece of music. **12.** a warrant for action; justification. **13.** testimony; witness. [1200–50; earlier *auct(h)oritie* < L *auctōritās;* r. ME *autorite* < OF < L. See AUTHOR, -ITY]
—Syn. 1. rule, power, sway. AUTHORITY, CONTROL, INFLUENCE denote a power or right to direct the actions or thoughts of others. AUTHORITY is a power or right, usually because of rank or office, to issue commands and to punish for violations: *to have authority over subordinates.* CONTROL is either power or influence applied to the complete and successful direction or manipulation of persons or things: *to be in control of a project.* INFLUENCE is a personal and unofficial power derived from deference of others to one's character, ability, or station; it may be exerted unconsciously or may operate through persuasion: *to have influence over one's friends.* **3.** sovereign, arbiter.

author′ity control′, *Library Science.* the establishment and maintainance of consistent forms of terms, as of names, subjects, and titles, to be used as headings in bibliographic records.

author′ity fig′ure, a person whose real or apparent authority over others inspires or demands obedience and emulation: *Parents, teachers, and police officers are traditional authority figures for children.*

author′ity file′, *Library Science.* a file, either on cards or in machine-readable format, in which decisions involving bibliographic records, particularly for form of entry, are recorded to establish a precedent or rule for subsequent decisions and to provide for consistency of entries. [1975–80]

au·thor·i·za·tion (ô′thər ə zā′shən), *n.* **1.** the act of authorizing. **2.** permission or power granted by an authority; sanction. **3.** a legislative act authorizing money to be spent for government programs that specifies a maximum spending level without provision for actual funds. [1600–10; AUTHORIZE + -ATION]

au·thor·ize (ô′thə rīz′), *v.t.,* **-ized, -iz·ing. 1.** to give authority or official power to; empower: *to authorize an employee to sign purchase orders.* **2.** to give authority for; formally sanction (an act or proceeding): *Congress authorized the new tax on tobacco.* **3.** to establish by authority or usage: *an arrangement long authorized by etiquette books.* **4.** to afford a ground for; warrant; justify. Also, *esp. Brit.,* **au′thor·ise′.** [1350–1400; earlier *auctorize* < ML *auctōrizāre;* r. ME *autorisen* < MF *autoriser* < ML. See AUTHOR, -IZE] **—au′thor·iz′a·ble,** *adj.* **—au′thor·iz′er,** *n.*

au·thor·ized (ô′thə rīzd′), *adj.* **1.** given or endowed with authority: *an authorized agent.* **2.** duly sanctioned. [AUTHORIZE + -ED[2]]

au′thorized cap′ital, the aggregate par value or the total subscription price of all equity shares of a corporation authorized to be issued under its charter. [1910–15]

Au′thorized Ver′sion, an English version of the Bible prepared in England under James I and published in 1611. Also called **King James Version.**

au·thors (ô′thərz), *n.* (*used with a singular v.*) a card game for two or more persons that is played with a 52-card pack, the object being to take the largest number of tricks consisting of four cards of the same denomination. [1865–70, *Amer.;* pl. of AUTHOR]

au′thor's altera′tion, a correction or change made in typeset copy that is not a correction of an error introduced by the compositor. *Abbr.:* AA, A.A., a.a., aa Cf. **printer's error.**

au·thor·ship (ô′thər ship′), *n.* **1.** origin, esp. with reference to an author, creator, producer, etc., of a work: *establishing the authorship of early medieval manuscripts.* **2.** the occupation or career of writing books, articles, etc. [1700–10; AUTHOR + -SHIP]

Auth. Ver., Authorized Version (of the Bible).

au·tism (ô′tiz əm), *n.* **1.** *Psychiatry.* a pervasive developmental disorder of children, characterized by impaired communication, excessive rigidity, and emotional detachment. **2.** a tendency to view life in terms of one's own needs and desires. [1910–15; AUT- + -ISM] **—au′·tist,** *n.* **—au·tis·tic** (ô tis′tik), *adj.* **—au·tis′ti·cal·ly,** *adv.*

au·to (ô′tō), *n., pl.* **-tos.** automobile. [1895–1900, *Amer.;* by shortening]

auto-[1], a combining form meaning "self," "same," "spontaneous," used in the formation of compound words: *autograph.* Also, *esp. before a vowel,* **aut-.** [< Gk, comb. form of *autós* self]

auto-[2], a combining form representing **automobile** in compound words: *autocade.* [see AUTO]

auto-[3], a combining form representing **automatic** in compound words: *autoalarm; autofeed; autofocus.* Sometimes also taken as an adjective: *auto enlarger; auto stop control.*

auto., **1.** automatic. **2.** automobile. **3.** automotive.

au·to·a·nal·y·sis (ô′tō ə nal′ə sis), *n.* **1.** *Psychoanal.* self-analysis. **2.** *Chem.* analysis by an autoanalyzer. [1890–95; AUTO-[1] + ANALYSIS]

au·to·an·a·lyz·er (ô′tō an′l ī′zər), *n.* a device that performs chemical analysis automatically. [AUTO-[3] + ANALYZER]

au·to·an·ti·bod·y (ô′tō an′ti bod′ē, -an′tē-), *n., pl.* **-bod·ies.** *Immunol.* an antibody that an organism produces against any of its own tissues, cells, or cell components. [1905–10; AUTO-[1] + ANTIBODY]

au·to·an·ti·gen (ô′tō an′ti jən, -jen′), *n. Immunol.* an antigen of one's own cells or cell products. Also called **self-antigen.** [AUTO-[1] + ANTIGEN]

au·to·bahn (ô′tə bän′; *Ger.* ou′tō bän′), *n., pl.* **-bahns, -bahn·en** (-bä′nən). (in Germany and Austria) a superhighway; expressway. [1935–40; < G, equiv. to *Auto* AUTO + *Bahn* road, way]

au·to·bi·o (ô′tō bī′ō), *n, pl.* **-bi·os.** *Informal.* autobiography. [by shortening]

au·to·bi·og (ô′tō bī og′), *n. Informal.* autobiography. [by shortening]

au·to·bi·o·graph·i·cal (ô′tə bī′ə graf′i kəl, ô′tō-), *adj.* marked by or dealing with one's own experiences or life history; of or in the manner of an autobiography: *autobiographical material; an autobiographical novel.* Also, **au′to·bi′o·graph′ic.** [1820–30; AUTO-[1] + BIOGRAPHICAL] **—au′to·bi′o·graph′i·cal·ly,** *adv.*

au·to·bi·og·ra·phy (ô′tə bī og′rə fē, -bē-, ô′tō-), *n., pl.* **-phies.** a history of a person's life written or told by that person. [1790–1800; AUTO-[1] + BIOGRAPHY] **—au′·to·bi·og′ra·pher,** *n.*

Autobiography of Alice B. Toklas, The (tok′ləs, tōk′ləs), a memoir (1933) by Gertrude Stein.

au·to·bus (ô′tō bus′), *n., pl.* **-bus·es, -bus·ses.** bus[1] (def. 1). [1895–1900, *Amer.;* AUTO-[2] + BUS]

au·to·cade (ô′tə kād′), *n.* a procession or parade of automobiles; motorcade. [AUTO-[2] + -CADE]

au·to·ca·tal·y·sis (ô′tō kə tal′ə sis), *n., pl.* **-ses** (-sēz′). *Chem., Biochem.* catalysis caused by a catalytic agent formed during a reaction. [1890–95; AUTO-[1] + CATALYSIS] **—au·to·cat·a·lyt·ic** (ô′tō kat′l it′ik), *adj.* **—au′to·cat′a·lyt′i·cal·ly,** *adv.*

au·to·ca·thar·sis (ô′tō kə thär′sis), *n. Psychiatry.* a therapeutic process designed to free unconscious disturbances by having the patient write about his or her experiences, impressions, etc. [AUTO-[1] + CATHARSIS]

au·to·ceph·a·lous (ô′tə sef′ə ləs), *adj. Eastern Ch.* **1.** (of a church) having its own head or chief bishop, though in communion with other Orthodox churches. **2.** (of a bishop) subordinate to no superior authority; self-governing. [1860–65; < LGk *autoképhalos* having its own head. See AUTO-[1], -CEPHALOUS]

au·to·ceph·a·ly (ô′tə sef′ə lē), *n.* the state of being autocephalous. [AUTOCEPHAL(OUS) + -Y[3]]

au·to·chrome (ô′tə krōm′), *n. Photog.* a material once used for color photography, consisting of a photographic emulsion applied over a multicolored screen of minute starch grains dyed red, green, and blue-violet. [1905–10; AUTO-[1] + -CHROME]

au•toch•thon (ô tok′thən), *n., pl.* **-thons, -tho•nes** (-thə nēz′). **1.** an aboriginal inhabitant. **2.** *Ecol.* one of the indigenous animals or plants of a region. **3.** *Geol.* a geological formation formed in the region where found. Cf. **allochthon.** [1640–50; < Gk *autóchthōn* of the land itself, equiv. to *auto-* AUTO-[1] + *chthṓn* the earth, land, ground]

au•toch•tho•nous (ô tok′thə nəs), *adj.* **1.** pertaining to autochthons; aboriginal; indigenous (opposed to *heterochthonous*). **2.** *Pathol.* **a.** found in the part of the body in which it originates, as a cancerous lesion. **b.** found in a locality in which it originates, as an infectious disease. **3.** *Psychol.* of or pertaining to ideas that arise independently of the individual's own train of thought and seem instead to have some alien or external agency as their source. **4.** *Geol.* (of rocks, minerals, etc.) formed in the region where found. Cf. **allochthonous.** Also, **au•toch′tho•nal, au•toch•thon•ic** (ô′tok thon′ik). [1795–1805; AUTOCHTHON + -OUS] —**au•toch′tho•nism, au•toch′tho•ny,** *n.* —**au•toch′tho•nous•ly,** *adv.* —**au•toch′tho•nous•ness,** *n.*

au•to•cide (ô′tō sīd′), *n.* suicide by crashing the vehicle one is driving. [1965–70; AUTO-[2] + -CIDE]

au•to•clave (ô′tə klāv′), *n., v.,* **-claved, -clav•ing.** —*n.* **1.** a heavy vessel for conducting chemical reactions under high pressure. **2.** See **pressure cooker. 3.** *Med., Bacteriol.* an apparatus in which steam under pressure effects sterilization. —*v.t.* **4.** to place in an autoclave. [1875–80; < F, equiv. to *auto-* AUTO-[1] + *clave* < L *clāv-,* s. of *clāvis* key and *clāvus* nail]

au•to•col•li•ma•tion (ô′tō kol′ə mā′shən), *n. Optics.* the process used in an autocollimator. [AUTO-[1] + COLLIMATION]

au•to•col•li•ma•tor (ô′tō kol′ə mā′tər), *n. Optics.* an instrument combining the functions of a telescope and collimator, for detecting and measuring very small deviations in a beam of light. [AUTO-[3] + COLLIMATOR]

au•to•cor•re•la•tion (ô′tō kôr′ə lā′shən, -kor′-), *n. Statistics.* the correlation of an ordered series of observations with the same series displaced by the same number of terms. [1945–50; AUTO-[1] + CORRELATION]

au′to court′, motel. [1930–35]

au•toc•ra•cy (ô tok′rə sē), *n., pl.* **-cies. 1.** government in which one person has uncontrolled or unlimited authority over others; the government or power of an absolute monarch. **2.** a nation, state, or community ruled by an autocrat. **3.** unlimited authority, power, or influence of one person in any group. [1645–55; < Gk *autokráteia* power over oneself, sole power, equiv. to *autokrat(ḗs)* AUTOCRAT + *-eia* -IA; see -CRACY]

au•to•crat (ô′tə krat′), *n.* **1.** an absolute ruler, esp. a monarch who holds and exercises the powers of government as by inherent right, not subject to restrictions. **2.** a person invested with or claiming to exercise absolute authority. **3.** a person who behaves in an authoritarian manner; a domineering person. [1795–1805; < Gk *autokratḗs* self-ruling, ruling alone, equiv. to *auto-* AUTO-[1] + *krat-* (s. of *krátos* power) + *-ēs* adj. suffix]

au•to•crat•ic (ô′tə krat′ik), *adj.* **1.** pertaining to or of the nature of autocracy or of an autocrat; absolute: *autocratic government.* **2.** like an autocrat; tyrannical; despotic; domineering. Also, **au′to•crat′i•cal.** [1815–25; AUTOCRAT + -IC] —**au′to•crat′i•cal•ly,** *adv.*

au•to•cross (ô′tō krôs′, -kros′), *n. Auto.* gymkhana (def. 2). [1960–65; AUTO-[2] + (MOTO)CROSS]

au•to-da-fé (ô′tō də fā′), *n., pl.* **au•tos-da-fé.** the public declaration of the judgment passed on persons tried in the courts of the Spanish Inquisition, followed by the execution by the civil authorities of the sentences imposed, esp. the burning of condemned heretics at the stake. [1715–25; < Pg: ACT of the FAITH, as trans. of ML *actus fideī*]

au•to-de•struct (ô′tō di strukt′), *v.i.* self-destruct. [1970–75] —**au′to-de•struc′tion,** *n.* —**au′to-de•struc′tive,** *adj.*

au•to-di•al (ô′tō dī′əl, -dīl′), *n.* See under **auto-dialer.**

au•to-di•al•er (ô′tō dī′ə lər, -dī′lər), *n.* a telephone device that makes possible a service feature (**au′to-dial′**) whereby a call is automatically made in response to a brief input signal from the user, as the pressing of a button. Also called **automatic dialer.**

au•to•di•dact (ô′tō dī′dakt, -dī dakt′), *n.* a person who has learned a subject without the benefit of a teacher or formal education; a self-taught person. [1525–35; < Gk *autodídaktos* self-taught; see AUTO-, DIDACTIC] —**au′to•di•dac′tic,** *adj.* —**au′to•di•dac′ti•cal•ly,** *adv.*

au•to•dyne (ô′tə dīn′), *n. Electronics.* a type of heterodyne circuit containing a vacuum tube or transistor that acts simultaneously as a detector and oscillator. [1915–20; AUTO-[1] + DYNE]

au•toe•cism (ô tē′siz əm), *n. Mycol.* the development of the entire life cycle of a parasitic fungus on a single host or group of hosts. Also, **autecism.** Also called **ametoecism.** [AUT- + *oec-* (< Gk *oik-,* s. of *oîkos* house) + -ISM] —**au•toe•cious** (ô tē′shəs), *adj.* —**au•toe′cious•ly,** *adv.* —**au•toe′cious•ness,** *n.*

au•to•e•rot•ic (ô′tō i rot′ik), *adj.* producing sexual excitement or pleasure without association with another person or external stimulation. [1895–1900; AUTO-[1] + EROTIC] —**au′to•e•rot′i•cal•ly,** *adv.*

au•to•e•rot•i•cism (ô′tō i rot′ə siz′əm), *n.* the arousal and satisfaction of sexual excitement within or by oneself, as by masturbation. Also, **au•to•er•o•tism** (ô′tō er′ə tiz′əm). [1895–1900; AUTO-[1] + EROTICISM]

au•to•fo•cus (ô′tō fō′kəs), *adj.* **1.** having the ability to focus automatically: *an autofocus lens; an autofocus camera.* —*n.* **2.** such an ability. Also, **au′to-fo′cus.** [1955–60; AUTO-[3] + FOCUS]

au•tog•a•my (ô tog′ə mē), *n.* **1.** pollination of the ovules of a flower by its own pollen; self-fertilization (opposed to *allogamy*). **2.** conjugation in an individual organism by division of its nucleus into two parts that in turn reunite to form a zygote. [1875–80; AUTO-[1] + -GAMY] —**au•tog′a•mous, au•to•gam•ic** (ô′tō gam′ik), *adj.*

au•to•ge•net•ic (ô′tō jə net′ik), *adj.* **1.** self-generated. [1885–90; AUTO-[1] + GENETIC] —**au′to•ge•net′i•cal•ly,** *adv.*

au′to•gen′ic train′ing (ô′tō jen′ik, ô′tō-), a relaxation technique utilizing self-suggestion, breathing exercises, and meditation. [1960–65; AUTO-[1] + -GENIC]

au•tog•e•nous (ô toj′ə nəs), *adj.* **1.** self-produced; self-generated. **2.** *Physiol.* pertaining to substances generated in the body. **3.** *Metall.* self-fused, without the addition of solder or the application of an adhesive: *an autogenous weld between two pieces of the same metal.* [1840–50; < Gk *autogen(ḗs)* self-produced (see AUTO-[1], -GEN) + -OUS] —**au•tog′e•nous•ly,** *adv.*

au•to•gi•ro (ô′tə jī′rō), *n., pl.* **-ros.** an aircraft with an unpowered, horizontally rotating propeller on a shaft above the fuselage that provides lift for the machine, with forward propulsion being provided by a conventional propeller: superseded in most applications by the helicopter. Also, **au′to•gy′ro.** Also called **gyrocopter, gyroplane.** [1920–25; formerly a trademark]

au•to•graft (ô′tə graft′, -gräft′), *n. Surg.* a tissue or organ that is grafted into a new position on the body of the individual from which it was removed. Also called **autoplast, autotransplant.** Cf. **allograft, syngraft, xenograft.** [1915–20; AUTO-[1] + GRAFT[1]]

au•to•graph (ô′tə graf′, -gräf′), *n.* **1.** a person's own signature: *He collects autographs of artists.* **2.** something written in a person's own hand, as a manuscript or letter. —*adj.* **3.** written by a person's own hand: *an autograph letter.* **4.** containing autographs: *an autograph album.* —*v.t.* **5.** to write one's name on or in; sign: *to autograph a book.* **6.** to write with one's own hand. [1630–40; < L *autographum,* n. use of neut. of L *autographus* written with one's own hand < Gk *autógraphos.* See AUTO-[1], -GRAPH] —**au•to•graph•ic** (ô′tə graf′ik), **au′to•graph′i•cal,** *adj.* —**au′to•graph′i•cal•ly,** *adv.*

au•tog•ra•phy (ô tog′rə fē), *n.* **1.** the act of writing by one's own hand. **2.** autographs collectively. [1635–45; AUTO-[1] + -GRAPHY]

Au•to•harp (ô′tō härp′), *Trademark.* a zither having buttons that when depressed damp all strings except those to be sounded, the undamped strings being strummed to produce simple chords.

au•to•hyp•no•sis (ô′tō hip nō′sis), *n.* self-induced hypnosis or hypnotic state. [1900–05; AUTO-[1] + HYPNOSIS] —**au•to•hyp•not•ic** (ô′tō hip not′ik), *adj.* —**au′to•hyp•not′i•cal•ly,** *adv.*

au•toi•cous (ô toi′kəs), *adj. Bot.* having the male and female organs on the same plant. [AUT- + *oic-* (< Gk *oik-,* s. of *oîkos* house) + -OUS]

au•to•ig•ni•tion (ô′tō ig nish′ən), *n.* **1.** *Auto.* the spontaneous ignition of fuel when introduced into the combustion chamber of an internal-combustion engine, as a result either of glowing carbon in the chamber or of the heat of compression. **2.** See **spontaneous combustion.** [AUTO-[1] + IGNITION]

autoigni′tion point′, *Chem.* the minimum temperature at which a substance will undergo spontaneous combustion. Also called **ignition point, ignition temperature.**

au•to•im•mune (ô′tō i myo͞on′), *adj. Immunol.* of or pertaining to the immune response of an organism against any of its own tissues, cells, or cell components. [1950–55; AUTO-[1] + IMMUNE] —**au′to•im•mu′ni•ty,** *n.*

autoimmune′ disease′, *Pathol.* a disease resulting from a disordered immune reaction in which antibodies are produced against one's own tissues, as systemic lupus erythematosus or rheumatoid arthritis. [1960–65]

au•to•im•mu•ni•za•tion (ô′tō im′yə nə zā′shən, -i myo͞o′-), *n. Immunol.* antibody production by an organism in response to and against any of its own tissues, cells, or cell components. Also called **autosensitization.** [1905–10; AUTO-[1] + IMMUNIZATION]

au•to•in•fec•tion (ô′tō in fek′shən), *n. Pathol.* **1.** reinfection by a pathogen that is already in the body. **2.** infection caused by transfer of a pathogen from one part of the body to another. [1900–05; AUTO-[1] + INFECTION]

au•to•in•oc•u•la•tion (ô′tō i nok′yə lā′shən), *n.* inoculation of a healthy part with an infective agent from a diseased part of the same body. [AUTO-[1] + INOCULATION] —**au•to•in•oc•u•la•ble** (ô′tō i nok′yə lə bəl), *adj.* —**au′to•in•oc′u•la•bil′i•ty,** *n.*

au•to•in•tox•i•ca•tion (ô′tō in tok′sə kā′shən), *n. Pathol.* poisoning with toxic substances formed within the body, as during intestinal digestion. Also called **autotoxemia, autotoxaemia, autotoxicosis.** [1885–90; AUTO-[1] + INTOXICATION]

au•to•i•on•i•za•tion (ô′tō ī′ə nə zā′shən), *n. Physics.* See **Auger effect.** [AUTO-[1] + IONIZATION]

au•to•ist (ô′tō ist), *n.* motorist (def. 1). [1900–05, *Amer.;* AUTO-[2] + -IST]

au•to•ki•ne•sis (ô′tō ki nē′sis, -kī-), *n. Physiol.* voluntary movement. [1895–1900; AUTO-[1] + KINESIS] —**au•to•ki•net•ic** (ô′tō ki net′ik, -kī-), *adj.*

au′tokinet′ic effect′, *Psychol.* apparent motion of a single point of light or a small object when presented on a dark field and observed continuously. Also called **au′tokinet′ic illu′sion.** [1930–35]

au′to lift′, a device, often powered hydraulically, for raising a vehicle so that the underside is accessible for inspection and repair.

au•to•li•thog•ra•phy (ô′tō li thog′rə fē), *n.* a lithographic technique by which the artist draws or traces with a brush and pen directly on a stone or plate. [1870–75; AUTO-[1] + LITHOGRAPHY]

au•to•load•er (ô′tō lō′dər), *n.* a firearm with an automatic loading mechanism. [AUTO-[3] + LOADER]

au•to•load•ing (ô′tō lō′ding), *adj.* semiautomatic (def. 2). [1920–25; AUTO-[3] + LOAD + -ING[2]]

au•tol•o•gous (ô tol′ə gəs), *adj.* from the same organism: *an autologous graft.* [1920–25; AUTO-[1] + *-logous* (see -LOGY, -OUS), on the model of HOMOLOGOUS]

Au•tol•y•cus (ô tol′i kəs), *n. Class. Myth.* a thief, the son of Hermes and Chione, and the grandfather of Odysseus. He possessed the power of changing the shape of whatever he stole and of making it and himself invisible.

au•tol•y•sate (ô tol′ə sāt′), *n. Biochem.* a substance produced by autolysis. [1925–30; AUTOLYS(IS) + -ATE[2]]

au•to•ly•sin (ôt′l ī′sin, ô tol′ə-), *n.* any agent producing autolysis. [1960–65; AUTOLYS(IS) + -IN[2]]

au•tol•y•sis (ô tol′ə sis), *n. Biochem.* the breakdown of plant or animal tissue by the action of enzymes contained in the tissue affected; self-digestion. [1900–05; AUTO-[1] + -LYSIS] —**au•to•lyt•ic** (ôt′l it′ik), *adj.*

au•to•lyze (ôt′l īz′), *v.,* **-lyzed, -lyz•ing.** *Biochem.* —*v.t.* **1.** to cause to undergo autolysis. —*v.i.* **2.** to undergo autolysis. Also, *esp. Brit.,* **au′to•lyse′.** [1900–05; back formation from AUTOLYSIS, on the model of ANALYZE]

au•to•mak•er (ô′tō mā′kər), *n.* an automobile manufacturer. [1900–05; AUTO-[2] + MAKER] —**au′to•mak′ing,** *n.*

au•to•ma•nip•u•la•tion (ô′tō mə nip′yə lā′shən), *n.* physical stimulation of one's own genitals. [1960–65; AUTO-[1] + MANIPULATION]

Au•to•mat (ô′tə mat′), *Trademark.* a type of self-service restaurant in which customers obtain food from small compartments by depositing the required number of coins in slots so that the doors can be opened.

au•tom•a•ta (ô tom′ə tə), *n.* a pl. of **automaton.**

au•to•mate (ô′tə māt′), *v.,* **-mat•ed, -mat•ing.** —*v.t.* **1.** to apply the principles of automation to (a mechanical process, industry, office, etc.). **2.** to operate or control by automation. **3.** to displace or make obsolete by automation (often fol. by *out*): *The unskilled jobs are going to be automated out.* —*v.i.* **4.** to install automatic procedures, as for manufacturing or servicing; follow or utilize the principles of automation: *Many banks have begun to automate.* [1950–55; back formation from AUTOMATION] —**au′to•mat′a•ble,** *adj.*

au′to•mat•ed-tell′er machine′ (ô′tə mā′tid tel′ər), an electronic banking machine that dispenses cash, accepts deposits, and performs other services when a customer inserts a plastic card and pushes the proper coded buttons. *Abbr.:* ATM Also called **au′tomated tell′er, automatic-teller machine, cash machine, money machine.** [1980–85]

au•to•mat•ic (ô′tə mat′ik), *adj.* **1.** having the capability of starting, operating, moving, etc., independently: *an automatic sprinkler system.* **2.** *Physiol.* occurring independently of volition, as certain muscular actions; involuntary. **3.** done unconsciously or from force of habit; mechanical: *an automatic application of the brakes.* **4.** occurring spontaneously: *automatic enthusiasm.* **5.** (of a firearm, pistol, etc.) utilizing the recoil or part of the force of the explosive to eject the spent cartridge shell, introduce a new cartridge, cock the arm, and fire it repeatedly. —*n.* **6.** a machine that operates automatically. **7.** See **automatic rifle. 8.** See **automatic pistol. 9.** *Football.* audible (def. 2). **10.** See **automatic pilot. 11.** See **automatic transmission. 12.** an automobile equipped with automatic transmission. **13. on automatic,** being operated or controlled by or as if by an automatic device. [1740–50; < Gk *autómat(os)* self-moving (see AUTOMATON) + -IC] —**au′to•mat′i•cal•ly,** *adv.* —**au•to•ma•tic•i•ty** (ô′tə mə tis′i tē), *n.*
—**Syn. 2.** AUTOMATIC, INVOLUNTARY, SPONTANEOUS all mean not under the control of the will. That which is AUTOMATIC, however, is an invariable reaction to a fixed type of stimulus: *The patella reflex is automatic.* That which is INVOLUNTARY is an unexpected response that varies according to the occasion, circumstances, mood, etc.: *an involuntary cry of pain.* That which is SPONTANEOUS arises from immediate stimuli and usually involves an expression of strong feeling: *a spontaneous roar of laughter.*

au′tomat′ic da′ta proc′essing. See **ADP.**

au′tomat′ic di′aler, auto-dialer.

au′tomat′ic drive′. See **automatic transmission.**

au′tomat′ic pi′lot, *Aeron.* an airborne electronic control system that automatically maintains a preset heading and attitude. Also called **automatic, autopilot, gyropilot, robot.** [1915–20]

au′tomat′ic pis′tol, a type of pistol having a mechanism that throws out the empty shell, puts in a new one, and prepares the pistol to be fired again. Also called **automatic.** [1875–80]

au′tomat′ic re′dial, a telephone service feature whereby the last number dialed is automatically called again, either after a specified time or when activated by the user. Also called **redial.**

au′tomat′ic ri′fle, a type of light machine gun capable of firing automatically or in single shots. Also called **automatic, machine rifle.** [1875–80]

au′tomatic-tell′er machine′. See **automated-teller machine.** Also called **au′tomat′ic tell′er.**

au′tomat′ic track′ing, *Electronics.* a radar tracking system in which an automatic device uses the echo signal from the tracked object to keep the radar con-

CONCISE ETYMOLOGY KEY: <, descended or borrowed from; >, whence; b., blend of, blended; c., cognate with; cf., compare; deriv., derivative; equiv., equivalent; imit., imitative; obl., oblique; r., replacing; s., stem; sp., spelling, spelled; resp., respelling, respelled; trans., translation; ?, origin unknown; *, unattested; ‡, probably earlier than. See the full key inside the front cover.

stantly beamed on target and to compute the range of the object.

automat′ic transmis′sion, an automotive transmission requiring either very little or no manual shifting of gears. Also called **automatic, automatic drive.** [1945–50]

au′tomat′ic writ′ing, writing performed without apparent intent or conscious control, esp. to achieve spontaneity or uncensored expression. [1880–85]

au•to•ma•tion (ô′tə mā′shən), *n.* **1.** the technique, method, or system of operating or controlling a process by highly automatic means, as by electronic devices, reducing human intervention to a minimum. **2.** a mechanical device, operated electronically, that functions automatically, without continuous input from an operator. **3.** act or process of automating. **4.** the state of being automated. [1945–50; AUTOM(ATIC OPER)ATION]

au•tom•a•tism (ô tom′ə tiz′əm), *n.* **1.** the action or condition of being automatic; mechanical or involuntary action. **2.** *Philos.* the doctrine that all activities of animals, or of humans and animals, are entirely controlled by physical or physiological causes in which consciousness takes no part. **3.** *Physiol.* the involuntary functioning of an organic process, esp. muscular, without apparent neural stimulation. **4.** *Psychol.* **a.** the performance of an act or actions without the performer's awareness or conscious volition. **b.** such an act, as sleepwalking. **5.** a method of producing pictorial art, as paintings and collages, associated chiefly with the dadaists and surrealists, in which the artist strives to allow the impulses of the unconscious to guide the hand in matters of line, color, and structure without the interference of conscious choice. [1880–85; < Gk *automatismós* a happening of itself. See AUTOMATON, -ISM] **—au•tom′a•tist,** *n., adj.*

au•tom•a•tize (ô tom′ə tīz′), *v.t.,* **-tized, -tiz•ing. 1.** to make automatic. **2.** automate. Also *esp. Brit.,* **au•tom′a•tise′.** [1830–40; AUTOMAT(IC) + -IZE] **—au•tom′a•tist,** *n.* **—au•tom′a•ti•za′tion,** *n.*

au•to•mat•o•graph (ô′tə mat′ə graf′, -gräf′), *n.* a device for recording involuntary bodily movements. [1890–95; < Gk *autómato(s)* self-moving (see AUTOMATON) + -GRAPH]

au•tom•a•ton (ô tom′ə ton′, -tn), *n., pl.* **-tons, -ta** (-tə). **1.** a mechanical figure or contrivance constructed to act as if by its own motive power; robot. **2.** a person or animal that acts in a monotonous, routine manner, without active intelligence. **3.** something capable of acting automatically or without an external motive force. [1605–15; < L: automatic device < Gk, n. use of neut. of *autómatos* spontaneous, acting without human agency, equiv. to *auto-* AUTO-[1] + *-matos,* adj. deriv. from base of *memonénai* to intend, *ménos* might, force] **—au•tom′a•tous,** *adj.*

au•to•mech•an•ism (ô′tō mek′ə niz′əm), *n.* an automatic mechanical system or component, esp. a device that operates automatically under predetermined conditions. [AUTO-[3] + MECHANISM]

au•to•mo•bile (ô′tə mə bēl′, ô′tə mə bēl′, ô′tə mō′bēl, -bəl), *n.* **1.** a passenger vehicle designed for operation on ordinary roads and typically having four wheels and a gasoline or diesel internal-combustion engine. *—adj.* **2.** automotive. [1865–70; < F: lit., self-movable (vehicle). See AUTO-[1], MOBILE] **—au•to•mo•bil•ist** (ô′tə mə-bē′list, -mō′bi list), *n.*

automobile′ insur′ance, insurance covering loss or damages arising from the operation or ownership of an automobile.

au•to•mor•phic (ô′tə môr′fik), *adj. Petrog.* idiomorphic (def. 1). [1870–75; AUTO-[1] + -MORPHIC] **—au′to•mor′phi•cal•ly,** *adv.*

au•to•mor•phism (ô′tə môr′fiz əm), *n. Math.* an isomorphism from a given set to itself. Cf. **inner automorphism, outer automorphism.** [1870–75; AUTO-[1] + MORPH- + -ISM]

au•to•mo•tive (ô′tə mō′tiv, ô′tə mō′tiv), *adj.* **1.** pertaining to the design, operation, manufacture, or sale of automobiles: *automotive parts.* **2.** propelled by a self-contained motor, engine, or the like. *—n.* **3.** *Informal.* an industry, store department, etc., specializing in appliances and parts for cars, trucks, and other motorized vehicles: *You may find what you're looking for in automotive.* [1860–65; AUTO-[1] + MOTIVE]

au•to•nom•ic (ô′tə nom′ik), *adj.* **1.** autonomous. **2.** of or pertaining to the autonomic nervous system. **3.** *Physiol.* under the control of the autonomic nervous system. **4.** *Cell Biol.* produced by internal forces or causes; spontaneous. Also, **au′to•nom′i•cal.** [1825–35; AUTONOM(Y) + -IC] **—au′to•nom′i•cal•ly,** *adv.*

au′tonom′ic nerv′ous sys′tem, the system of nerves and ganglia that innervates the blood vessels, heart, smooth muscles, viscera, and glands and controls their involuntary functions, consisting of sympathetic and parasympathetic portions. [1895–1900]

au•ton•o•mism (ô ton′ə miz′əm), *n.* the belief in or a movement toward autonomy. [1870–75; AUTONOM(Y) + -ISM] **—au•ton′o•mist,** *adj., n.*

au•ton•o•mous (ô ton′ə məs), *adj.* **1.** *Govt.* **a.** self-governing; independent; subject to its own laws only. **b.** pertaining to an autonomy. **2.** having autonomy; not subject to control from outside; independent: *a subsidiary that functioned as an autonomous unit.* **3.** *Biol.* **a.** existing and functioning as an independent organism. **b.** spontaneous. [1790–1800; < Gk *autónomos* with laws of one's own, independent, equiv. to *auto-* AUTO-[1] + *nóm(os)* law, custom + *-os* adj. suffix] **—au•ton′o•mous•ly,** *adv.*

auton′omous pho′neme, *Ling.* a phoneme that is defined or determined by its contrast in sound with other phonemes, without reference to its role in morphology or any other level of linguistic analysis beyond the phonetic level. Also called **taxonomic phoneme.** Cf. **systematic phoneme.**

auton′omous syn′tax, *Ling.* an approach of generative grammar in which the syntactic component of a grammar is viewed as existing or operating independently of the semantic component and abstract syntactic representation is not equivalent to semantic representation.

au•ton•o•my (ô ton′ə mē), *n., pl.* **-mies. 1.** independence or freedom, as of the will or one's actions: *the autonomy of the individual.* **2.** the condition of being autonomous; self-government, or the right of self-government; independence: *The rebels demanded autonomy from Spain.* **3.** a self-governing community. [1615–25; < Gk *autonomía* independence, equiv. to *autónom(os)* AUTONOMOUS + *-ia* -Y[3]] **—au•ton′o•mist,** *n.*

au•to•nym (ô′tə nim), *n.* **1.** a person's own name. Cf. **pseudonym. 2.** a book published under the real name of the author. [1865–70; AUT- + -ONYM]

au•to•ox•i•da•tion (ô′tō ok′si dā′shən), *n. Chem.* autoxidation.

au•to•pha•gia (ô′tə fā′jə, -jē ə), *n. Physiol.* **1.** controlled digestion of damaged organelles within a cell. **2.** the maintenance of bodily nutrition by the metabolic breakdown of some bodily tissues. Also, **au•toph•a•gy** (ô tof′ə jē). [AUTO-[1] + -PHAGIA] **—au•to•phag•ic** (ô′tə-faj′ik), *adj.*

au•to•phyte (ô′tə fīt′), *n. Ecol.* any organism that synthesizes its own food, as a photosynthetic plant. Cf. **heterophyte.** [AUTO-[1] + -PHYTE] **—au•to•phyt•ic** (ô′tə fit′ik), *adj.* **—au′to•phyt′i•cal•ly,** *adv.*

au•to•pi•lot (ô′tō pī′lət), *n.* See **automatic pilot.** [AUTO-[3] + PILOT]

au•to•plast (ô′tə plast′), *n. Surg.* autograft. [1880–85; AUTO-[1] + -PLAST]

au•to•plas•ty (ô′tə plas′tē), *n., pl.* **-ties.** *Surg.* the repair of defects with tissue from another part of the patient's body. [1850–55; AUTO-[1] + -PLASTY] **—au′to•plas′tic,** *adj.*

au•to•pol•y•ploid (ô′tə pol′ə ploid′), *Biol.* *—adj.* **1.** having more than two haploid sets of chromosomes that are derived from the same ancestral species. *—n.* **2.** an autopolyploid cell or organism. Cf. **allopolyploid.** [1925–30; AUTO-[1] + POLYPLOID] **—au′to•pol′y•ploi′dy,** *n.*

au•to•po•tam•ic (ô′tō pə tam′ik), *adj.* (of an organism) living or growing only in flowing freshwater streams. [AUTO-[1] + POTAMIC]

au•top•sy (ô′top sē, ô′təp-), *n., pl.* **-sies,** *v.,* **-sied, -sy•ing.** *—n.* **1.** inspection and dissection of a body after death, as for determination of the cause of death; post-mortem examination. **2.** an analysis of something after it has been done or made. *—v.t.* **3.** to perform an autopsy on. [1645–55; (< MF *autopsie*) < Gk *autopsía* a seeing with one's own eyes, equiv. to *aut-* AUT- + *óps(is)* -OPSIS + *-ia* -Y[3]] **—au′top•sist,** *n.*

au′to rac′ing, the sport of racing automobiles in which drivers compete against each other on a course designed for racing or on closed public roads. [‡1965–70]

au•to•ra•di•o•graph (ô′tə rā′dē ə graf′, -gräf′), *n.* a picture revealing the presence of radioactive material, the film being laid directly on the object to be tested. Also, **au•to•ra•di•o•gram** (ô′tə rā′dē ə gram′). Also called **radioautograph.** [1900–05; AUTO-[1] + RADIOGRAPH] **—au•to•ra•di•o•graph•ic** (ô′tə rā′dē ə graf′ik), *adj.* **—au′to•ra′di•o•graph′i•cal•ly,** *adv.*

au•to•ra•di•og•ra•phy (ô′tō rā′dē og′rə fē), *n.* the technique or process of making autoradiographs. Also called **radioautography.** [1940–45; AUTO-[1] + RADIOGRAPHY]

au•to•reg•u•la•tion (ô′tō reg′yə lā′shən), *n.* the continual automatic adjustment or self-regulation of a biochemical, physiological, or ecological system to maintain a stable state. [1965–70; AUTO-[1] + REGULATION] **—au•to•reg•u•la•tive** (ô′tō reg′yə lā′tiv, -lə tiv), **au•to•reg•u•la•to•ry** (ô′tō reg′yə lə tôr′ē, -tōr′ē), *adj.* **—au′to•reg′u•la′tive•ly,** *adv.*

au•to•ro•ta•tion (ô′tō rō tā′shən), *n. Aeron.* the condition of flight occurring when lift is derived solely from the action of air upon the unpowered rotor of a moving helicopter or autogiro. [1915–20; AUTO-[1] + ROTATION] **—au′to•ro•ta′tion•al,** *adj.*

au•to•route (ô′tō ro͞ot′; *Fr.* ō tō ro͞ot′), *n., pl.* **-routes** (-ro͞ots′; *Fr.* -ro͞ot′). a principal highway, esp. in France and French-speaking Canada. [1960–65; < F; see AUTO, ROUTE]

au•to•sche•di•asm (ô′tō skē′dē az′əm), *n.* something that is improvised or extemporized. [1835–45; < Gk *autoschediasma,* deriv., with *-(s)ma* resultative n. suffix, of *autoschediázein* to extemporize, v. deriv. of *autoschédios* hand-to-hand, offhand, improvised, equiv. to *auto-* AUTO-[1] + *schédios* near, casual, offhand, deriv. of *schedón* (adv.) near, close by, akin to *échein* to hold, possess] **—au′to•sche′di•ast′,** *n.* **—au′to•sche′di•as′tic, au′to•sche′di•as′ti•cal,** *adj.*

au•to•sen•si•ti•za•tion (ô′tō sen′si tə zā′shən), *n. Immunol.* autoimmunization. [AUTO-[1] + SENSITIZATION]

au•to•sex•ing (ô′tō sek′sing), *n.* breeding, esp. of domestic fowl, to reveal sexual characteristics at birth or hatching in order to separate males from females. [1935–40; AUTO-[1] + SEX + -ING[2]]

au•to•some (ô′tə sōm′), *n. Genetics.* any chromosome other than a sex chromosome. Also called **euchromosome.** [1905–10; AUTO-[1] + -SOME[3]] **—au′to•so′mal,** *adj.* **—au′to•so′mal•ly,** *adv.*

au•to•sta•bil•i•ty (ô′tō stə bil′i tē), *n. Mach.* the ability of a mechanism to maintain a stable performance, due either to the mechanics of its structure or to built-in automatic control devices. [AUTO-[1] + STABILITY]

au•to•stra•da (ô′tō strä′də; *It.* ou′tô strä′dä), *n., pl.* **-stra•das,** *It.* **-stra•de** (-strä′de). (in Italy) a divided highway connecting major cities. [1925–30; < It, equiv. to *auto* AUTO + *strada* road, highway << L (*via*) *strāta;* see STREET]

au•to•sug•ges•tion (ô′tō səg jes′chən, -sə-), *n. Psychol.* suggestion arising from oneself, as the repetition of verbal messages as a means of changing behavior. [1885–90; AUTO-[1] + SUGGESTION] **—au′to•sug•gest′i•ble,** *adj.* **—au′to•sug•gest′i•bil′i•ty,** *n.* **—au′to•sug•ges′tion•ist,** *n.* **—au′to•sug•ges′tive,** *adj.*

au•to•tel•ic (ô′tə tel′ik), *adj. Philos.* (of an entity or event) having within itself the purpose of its existence or happening. Cf. **heterotelic.** [1900–05; AUTO-[1] + TELIC] **—au′to•tel′ism,** *n.*

au•tot•o•mize (ô tot′ə mīz′), *v.,* **-mized, -miz•ing.** *—v.i.* **1.** to undergo autotomy. *—v.t.* **2.** to effect autotomy of (a part). Also *esp. Brit.,* **au•tot′o•mise′.** [1900–05; AUTOTOM(Y) + -IZE]

au•tot•o•my (ô tot′ə mē), *n., pl.* **-mies. 1.** *Zool.* **a.** separation of a body part. **b.** self-amputation of a damaged or trapped appendage. **2.** the performance of surgery upon oneself. [1895–1900; AUTO-[1] + -TOMY] **—au•to•tom•ic** (ô′tə tom′ik), **au•tot′o•mous,** *adj.*

au•to•tox•e•mi•a (ô′tō tok sē′mē ə), *n. Pathol.* autointoxication. Also, **au′to•tox•ae′mi•a.** [1885–90; AUTO-[1] + TOXEMIA]

au•to•tox•i•co•sis (ô′tə tok′si kō′sis), *n. Pathol.* autointoxication. [AUTO-[1] + TOXICOSIS]

au•to•tox•in (ô′tə tok′sin), *n. Pathol.* a toxin or poisonous chemical formed within the body and acting against it. [1890–95; AUTO-[1] + TOXIN] **—au′to•tox′ic,** *adj.*

au•to•trans•form•er (ô′tō trans fôr′mər), *n. Elect.* a transformer having a single coil that serves as both a primary coil and a secondary coil. [1890–95; AUTO-[1] + TRANSFORMER]

au•to•trans•fu•sion (ô′tō trans fyo͞o′zhən), *n.* infusion of a patient's own blood, either collected and returned to the body during surgery or transfused from a stored supply. [1960–65; AUTO-[1] + TRANSFUSION]

au•to•trans•plant (ô′tə trans′plant′, -plänt′), *n. Surg.* autograft. [1905–10; AUTO-[1] + TRANSPLANT] **—au′to•trans′plan•ta′tion,** *n.*

au•to•troph (ô′tə trof′, -trōf′), *n. Biol.* any organism capable of self-nourishment by using inorganic materials as a source of nutrients and using photosynthesis or chemosynthesis as a source of energy, as most plants and certain bacteria and protists. Cf. **heterotroph.** [1935–40; back formation from *autotrophic;* see AUTO-[1], TROPHIC] **—au′to•troph′ic,** *adj.*

au•to•truck (ô′tō truk′), *n.* a motor truck. [1895–1900, *Amer.;* AUTO-[2] + TRUCK]

au•to•type (ô′tə tīp′), *n.* **1.** facsimile (defs. 1, 2). **2.** *Photog.* **a.** a process for producing permanent prints in a carbon pigment. **b.** a print made by this process. [1850–55; AUTO-[1] + TYPE] **—au•to•typ•ic** (ô′tə tip′ik), *adj.* **—au•to•typ•y** (ô′tə tī′pē), *n.*

au•to•work•er (ô′tō wûr′kər), *n.* a worker employed in the manufacture of automobiles, esp. on the assembly line of an automobile plant. [1940–45; AUTO-[2] + WORKER]

au•tox•i•da•tion (ô tok′si dā′shən), *n. Chem.* **1.** the oxidation of a compound by exposure to air. **2.** an oxidation reaction in which another substance, in addition to air and the compound being oxidized, must be present. Also, **autooxidation.** [AUT- + OXIDATION]

au•tox•i•da•tion-re•duc•tion (ô tok′si dā′shən ri-duk′shən), *n. Chem.* disproportionation.

au•tres temps, au•tres mœurs (ō trᵊ tän′ ō trᵊ mœr′, mœrs′), *French.* other times, other customs.

au•tumn (ô′təm), *n.* **1.** the season between summer and winter; fall. In the Northern Hemisphere it is from the September equinox to the December solstice; in the Southern Hemisphere it is from the March equinox to the June solstice. **2.** a time of full maturity, esp. the late stages of full maturity or, sometimes, the early stages of decline: *to be in the autumn of one's life.* [1325–75; < L *autumnus;* r. ME *autumpne* < MF *autompne* < L]

au•tum•nal (ô tum′nl), *adj.* **1.** belonging to or suggestive of autumn; produced or gathered in autumn: *autumnal colors.* **2.** past maturity or middle life. [1630–40; < L *autumnālis.* See AUTUMN, -AL[1]] **—au•tum′nal•ly,** *adv.*

autum′nal e′quinox, 1. See under **equinox** (def. 1). **2.** Also called **autum′nal point′.** the position of the sun at the time of the autumnal equinox. [1670–80]

au′tumn cro′cus, any of several bulbous plants of the genus *Colchicum,* of the lily family, esp. *C. autumnale,* bearing showy, crocuslike white, pink, or purple flowers in autumn. Also called **meadow saffron;** *Brit.,* **naked ladies.** [1905–10]

au•tun•ite (ôt′n īt′, ō tun′īt), *n.* a yellow mineral, a hydrous calcium uranium phosphate, $CaU_2P_2O_{12}{\cdot}8H_2O$, occurring in crystals as nearly square tablets: a minor ore of uranium. [1850–55; named after *Autun,* city in E France near source of supply; see -ITE[1]]

Au•vergne (ō vârn′, ō vûrn′; *Fr.* ō vernʸᵊ), *n.* a former province in central France. See map under **Gascony.**

au vol (ō vol′), *Falconry.* a cry used to encourage a hawk to fly. [< F: to the flight. See VOLLEY]

aux (ō), *French.* pl. of **au.**

AUX, *Ling.* auxiliary verb: used to represent a phrase structure constituent that may include such verbal elements as tense and mood markers as well as auxiliaries. Also, **Aux**

aux-, var. of **auxo-,** esp. before a vowel: *auxin.*

aux., auxiliary; auxiliaries. Also, **aux, auxil.**

CONCISE PRONUNCIATION KEY: act, cāpe, dâre, pärt; set, ēqual; *if,* ice; ox, ōver, ôrder, oil, bo͝ok, bo͞ot, out; up, ûrge; child; sing; shoe; thin, that; zh as in *treasure.* ə = a as in *alone,* e as in *system,* i as in *easily,* o as in *gallop,* u as in *circus;* ᵊ as in *fire* (fīᵊr), *hour* (ouᵊr). l and n can serve as syllabic consonants, as in *cradle* (krād′l), and *button* (but′n). See the full key inside the front cover.

Aux Cayes (ō kā′), former name of **Les Cayes.**

aux·e·sis (ôg zē′sis, ôk sē′-), *n. Biol.* growth, esp. that resulting from an increase in cell size. Cf. **merisis.** [1570–80; < Gk: increase, equiv. to *auxē-* verbid s. of *aúxein* to increase + *-sis* -SIS]

aux·et·ic (ôg zet′ik, ôk set′-), *Biol.* —*adj.* **1.** pertaining to or promoting auxesis. —*n.* **2.** an auxetic agent. [1730–40; < Gk *auxētikos* increasing, equiv. to *auxēt(ós)* increased (deriv. of *aúxein;* see AUXESIS) + *-ikos* -IC]

aux·il·ia·ry (ôg zil′yə rē, -zil′ə-), *adj., n., pl.* **-ries.** —*adj.* **1.** additional; supplementary; reserve: *an auxiliary police force.* **2.** used as a substitute or reserve in case of need: *The hospital has an auxiliary power system in case of a blackout.* **3.** (of a boat) having an engine that can be used to supplement the sails: *an auxiliary yawl.* **4.** giving support; serving as an aid; helpful: *The mind and emotions are auxiliary to each other. Passion is auxiliary to art.* —*n.* **5.** a person or thing that gives aid of any kind; helper. **6.** an organization allied with, but subsidiary to, a main body of restricted membership, esp. one composed of members' relatives: *The men's club and the ladies' auxiliary were merged into one organization.* **7.** See **auxiliary verb. 8. auxiliaries,** foreign troops in the service of a nation at war. **9.** *Navy.* a naval vessel designed for other than combat purposes, as a tug, supply ship, or transport. **10.** *Naut.* a sailing vessel carrying an auxiliary propulsion engine or engines. [1595–1605; < L *auxiliārius* assisting, aiding, helping, equiv. to *auxili(um)* aid, help *(aux(us)* increased, augmented (ptp. of *augēre: aug-* increase + *-sus,* var. of *-tus* ptp. suffix) + *-ilium* n. suffix) + *-ārius* -ARY]
—**Syn. 2.** backup, ancillary, secondary. **5.** aide, ally, assistant; help.

auxil′iary equa′tion, *Math.* See **characteristic equation** (def. 1b.).

auxil′iary lan′guage, a language, as Esperanto, Swahili, or English, used for intercommunication by speakers of various other languages. [1900–05]

auxil′iary raft′er, 1. a rafter reinforcing a principal rafter. **2.** a rafter reinforcing a diagonal member of a queen post truss. Also called **cushion rafter.**

auxil′iary stor′age, *Computers.* See **secondary storage.** Also called **auxil′iary mem′ory.**

auxil′iary tone′, *Music.* a melodic ornamental tone following a principal tone by a step above or below and returning to the principal tone; embellishment. Also called **auxil′iary note′.**

auxil′iary verb′, a word used in construction with and preceding certain forms of other verbs, as infinitives or participles, to express distinctions of tense, aspect, mood, etc., as *did* in *Did you go?, am* in *I am listening, have* in *We have spoken,* or *can* in *They can see.* Also called **helping verb.** [1755–65]

aux·i·lyt·ic (ôk′sə lit′ik), *adj. Biochem.* promoting lysis or increasing lytic action. [AUX- + -I- + -LYTIC]

aux·in (ôk′sin), *n. Biochem.* a class of substances that in minute amounts regulate or modify the growth of plants, esp. root formation, bud growth, and fruit and leaf drop. [1930–35; AUX- + -IN[2]] —**aux·in′ic,** *adj.*

Aux·o (ôk′sō), *n. Class. Myth.* one of the Graces worshiped at Athens.

auxo-, a combining form meaning "growth," "increase," used in the formation of compound words: *auxochrome.* Also, *esp. before a vowel,* **aux-.** [< Gk *aúx(ein)* to grow, increase (var. of *auxánein*) + -O-]

aux·o·car·di·a (ôk′sə kär′dē ə), *n. Pathol.* enlargement of the heart, as by hypertrophy or dilatation. [AUXO- + -CARDIA]

aux·o·chrome (ôk′sə krōm′), *n. Chem.* any radical or group of atoms that intensifies the color of a substance. [1890–95; AUXO- + CHROME] —**aux′o·chrom′·ic,** *adj.*

aux·o·troph (ôk′sə trof′, -trōf′), *n. Biol.* a mutant organism, esp. a microorganism, that has a nutritional requirement not shared by the parent organism. Cf. **prototroph** (def. 1). [1950–55; back formation from *auxotrophic;* see AUXO-, TROPHIC] —**aux′o·troph′ic,** *adj.*

Av (äv, ôv), *n.* the eleventh month of the Jewish calendar. Also, **Ab.** Cf. **Jewish calendar.** [< Heb *ābh*]

AV, 1. arteriovenous. **2.** atrioventricular. **3.** audiovisual.

av., 1. avenue. **2.** average. **3.** See **avoirdupois weight.**

A-V, 1. atrioventricular. **2.** audiovisual.

A/V, 1. Also, **a.v.** ad valorem. **2.** audiovisual.

A.V., 1. Artillery Volunteers. **2.** audiovisual. **3.** Authorized Version (of the Bible).

a·va (ə vä′, ə vô′), *adv. Scot.* of all; at all. Also, **a·va′.**

A·va (ā′və), *n.* a female given name.

av·a·da·vat (av′ə də vat′), *n.* a waxbill, *Estrilda amandava,* native to Asia, having in the male scarlet plumage with white dots on the sides and breast: raised as a cage bird. Also, **amadavat.** [1770–80; earlier *amaduvad,* after *Amidavad,* a 17th century name (perh. < Pg) for AHMEDABAD, in Gujarat, from where the birds were first exported]

a·vail (ə vāl′), *v.t.* **1.** to be of use or value to; profit; advantage: *All our efforts availed us little in trying to effect a change.* —*v.i.* **2.** to be of use; have force or efficacy; serve; help: *His strength did not avail against the hostile onslaught.* **3.** to be of value or profit. **4. avail oneself of,** to use to one's advantage: *They availed themselves of the opportunity to hear a free concert.* —*n.* **5.** advantage; use; efficacy; effective use in the achievement of a goal or objective: *His belated help will be of little or no avail.* **6. avails,** *Archaic.* profits or proceeds. [1250–1300; ME *availe,* equiv. to *a-* A-[2] + *vaile* < OF *vail-* (s. of *valoir*) < L *valēre* to be of worth] —**a·vail′·ing·ly,** *adv.*

a·vail·a·ble (ə vā′lə bəl), *adj.* **1.** suitable or ready for use; of use or service; at hand: *I used whatever tools were available.* **2.** readily obtainable; accessible: *available resources.* **3.** having sufficient power or efficacy; valid. **4.** *Archaic.* efficacious; profitable; advantageous. [1425–75; late ME; see AVAIL, -ABLE] —**a·vail′a·bil′i·ty, a·vail′a·ble·ness,** *n.* —**a·vail′a·bly,** *adv.*
—**Syn. 1.** accessible, usable, handy. —**Ant. 1.** unavailable.

avail′able light′, *Photog., Fine Arts.* the natural or usual light on a subject.

av·a·lanche (av′ə lanch′, -länch′), *n., v.,* **-lanched, -lanch·ing.** —*n.* **1.** a large mass of snow, ice, etc., detached from a mountain slope and sliding or falling suddenly downward. **2.** anything like an avalanche in suddenness and overwhelming quantity: *an avalanche of misfortunes; an avalanche of fan mail.* **3.** Also called **Townsend avalanche.** *Physics, Chem.* a cumulative ionization process in which the ions and electrons of one generation undergo collisions that produce a greater number of ions and electrons in succeeding generations. —*v.i.* **4.** to come down in, or like, an avalanche. —*v.t.* **5.** to overwhelm with an extremely large amount of anything; swamp. [1755–65; < F < dial. (Savoy) *avalantse,* alter. (by assoc. with *avaler* to descend rapidly) of *laventse* < pre-L (perh. Ligurian) **lavanca,* or reshaping of LL *labina* landslide (deriv. of L *labī* to slide) with a pre-L suffix *-anca*]

av′alanche lil′y, either of two plants, *Erythronium grandiflorum* or *E. montanum,* of the lily family, of the mountains of northwestern North America, having nodding yellow or white flowers. [1910–15, *Amer.;* appar. so called because it is found near the snow line or the edge of glaciers]

av′alanche wind′ (wind), the wind that is created in front of an avalanche.

A·va·lo·ki·te·sva·ra (uv′ə lō′ki tāsh′vər ə), *n. Buddhism.* a male Bodhisattva, widely revered and identified with various persons and gods. Cf. **Kwan-Yin.**

Av·a·lon (av′ə lon′), *n. Celtic Legend.* an island, represented as an earthly paradise in the western seas, to which King Arthur and other heroes were carried at death. Also, **Av′al·lon′.** [< ML *(insula) avallonis* (Geoffrey of Monmouth) (island) of Avallon, lit., apple tree (island) < a British Celt s. for apple tree, c. Welsh *afall* (pl. collective), Middle Breton *avallenn* (sing.), OIr *aball* (fem.) < **ab̥ol-n-,* c. Slavic **(j)ablanĭ;* see APPLE]

Av′alon Penin′sula, a peninsula in SE Newfoundland, in E Canada: surrounded on three sides by the Atlantic Ocean. ab. 3579 sq. mi. (9270 sq. km).

a·vant-garde (ə vänt′gärd′, ə vant′-, av′änt-, ä′vänt-; *Fr.* A VÄN GARD′), *n.* **1.** the advance group in any field, esp. in the visual, literary, or musical arts, whose works are characterized chiefly by unorthodox and experimental methods. —*adj.* **2.** of or pertaining to the experimental treatment of artistic, musical, or literary material. **3.** belonging to the avant-garde: *an avant-garde composer.* **4.** unorthodox or daring; radical. [1475–85; in sense "vanguard"; < F: lit., fore-guard. See VANGUARD] —**a·vant′-gard′ist,** *n.*

a·vant-gard·ism (ə vänt′gär′diz əm, ə vant′-, av′änt-, ä′vänt-), *n.* the attitudes, techniques, etc., of the cultural avant-garde. [1945–50; AVANT-GARDE + -ISM]

A·van·ti (ə vun′tē), *n.* **Kingdom of,** an ancient Aryan kingdom of W central India, with its capital near modern Ujjain; flourished in the 6th–4th centuries B.C.

A·var (ä′vär), *n.* a member of a people, probably originating in Asia, who settled in Dacia A.D. c555, later occupied Pannonia, and invaded other parts of central and eastern Europe before their decline in the 9th century.

av·a·rice (av′ər is), *n.* insatiable greed for riches; inordinate, miserly desire to gain and hoard wealth. [1250–1300; ME < OF < L *avāritia,* equiv. to *avār(us)* greedy + *-itia* -ICE]
—**Syn.** cupidity.

av·a·ri·cious (av′ə rish′əs), *adj.* characterized by avarice; greedy; covetous. [1425–75; late ME; see AVARICE, -IOUS] —**av′a·ri′cious·ly,** *adv.* —**av′a·ri′cious·ness,** *n.*
—**Syn.** AVARICIOUS, COVETOUS, GREEDY, RAPACIOUS share the sense of desiring to possess more of something than one already has or might in normal circumstances be entitled to. AVARICIOUS often implies a pathological, driven greediness for money or other valuables and usually suggests a concomitant miserliness: *the cheerless dwelling of an avaricious usurer.* COVETOUS implies a powerful and usually illicit desire for the property or possessions of another: *The book collector was openly covetous of my rare first edition.* GREEDY, the most general of these terms, suggests a naked and uncontrolled desire for almost anything—food and drink, money, emotional gratification: *embarrassingly greedy for praise.* RAPACIOUS, stronger and more assertive than the other terms, implies an aggressive, predatory, insatiable, and unprincipled desire for possessions and power: *a rapacious frequenter of tax sales and forced auctions.*

a·vast (ə vast′, ə väst′), *imperative verb. Naut.* (used as a command to stop or cease): *Avast heaving!* [1675–85; perh. < D *houd vast* hold fast (see HOLD[1], FAST[1])]

av·a·tar (av′ə tär′, av′ə tär′), *n.* **1.** *Hindu Myth.* the descent of a deity to the earth in an incarnate form or some manifest shape; the incarnation of a god. **2.** an embodiment or personification, as of a principle, attitude, or view of life. [1775–85; < Skt *avatāra* a passing down, equiv. to *ava* down + *-tāra* a passing over]

a·vaunt (ə vônt′, ə vänt′), *adv. Archaic.* away; hence. [1275–1325; ME < MF *avant* to the front < LL *ab ante* before (L: from before). See AB-, ANTE-]

A.V.C., 1. American Veterans' Committee. **2.** automatic volume control. Also, **AVC**

avdp., See **avoirdupois weight.**

a·ve (ä′vā, ā′vē), *interj.* **1.** hail; welcome. **2.** farewell; good-bye. —*n.* **3.** the salutation "ave." **4.** *(cap.)* See **Ave Maria.** [1200–50; ME < L: impv. 2d sing. of *avēre* to be well, fare well]

Ave., avenue. Also, **ave.**

a·ve at·que va·le (ä′we ät′kwe wä′le; *Eng.* ā′vē at′kwē vā′lē, ä′vā ät′kwä vä′lā), *Latin.* hail and farewell.

Ave·bur·y (āv′bə rē), *n.* **1. Baron.** See **Lubbock, Sir John. 2.** Also, **Abury.** a village in Wiltshire, England: site of one of the largest ceremonial megalithic structures in Europe.

a·vec plai·sir (A vek ple zēr′), *French.* with pleasure.

Av·e·don (av′i don′), *n.* **Richard,** born 1923, U.S. photographer.

A·ve·lla·ne·da (ä ve′yä ne′thä), *n.* a city in E Argentina, near Buenos Aires. 330,654.

A·ve Ma·ri·a (ä′vā mə rē′ə), **1.** *(italics.)* the first two words of the Latin version of a prayer in the Roman Catholic Church, based on the salutation of the angel Gabriel to the Virgin Mary and the words of Elizabeth to her. **2.** a recitation of this prayer. **3.** the bead or beads on a rosary used to count off each prayer as spoken. Also called **Hail Mary.** [1200–50; ME; see AVE]

av·e·na·ceous (av′ə nā′shəs), *adj. Bot.* of or like oats. [1765–75; < L *avēnāceus,* equiv. to *avēn(a)* oats + *-āceus* -ACEOUS]

a·venge (ə venj′), *v.t.,* **a·venged, a·veng·ing. 1.** to take vengeance or exact satisfaction for: *to avenge a grave insult.* **2.** to take vengeance on behalf of: *He avenged his brother.* [1325–75; ME *avengen* < OF *avengier,* equiv. to *a-* A-[5] + *vengier* < L *vindicāre;* see VINDICATE] —**a·venge′ful,** *adj.* —**a·veng′er,** *n.* —**a·veng′ing·ly,** *adv.*
—**Syn.** vindicate. AVENGE, REVENGE both imply to inflict pain or harm in return for pain or harm inflicted on oneself or those persons or causes to which one feels loyalty. The two words were formerly interchangeable, but have been differentiated until they now convey widely diverse ideas. AVENGE is now restricted to inflicting punishment as an act of retributive justice or as a vindication of propriety: *to avenge a murder by bringing the criminal to trial.* REVENGE implies inflicting pain or harm to retaliate for real or fancied wrongs; a reflexive pronoun is often used with this verb: *Iago wished to revenge himself upon Othello.* —**Ant. 1.** forgive.

av·ens (av′inz), *n., pl.* **-ens.** any of various plants of the genus *Geum,* of the rose family, having yellow, white, or red flowers. [1200–50; ME *avence* < OF < ML *avencia* kind of clover]

av·en·tail (av′ən tāl′), *n. Armor.* **1.** Also called **camail.** a mail tippet suspended from the lower edges of a 14th-century basinet as a protection for the neck, throat, and shoulders. **2.** ventail. [1300–50; ME < AF *aventaille,* equiv. to *a-* (< ?) + *ventaille* VENTAIL]

Av·en·tine (av′ən tīn′, -tin), *n.* **1.** one of the seven hills on which ancient Rome was built. —*adj.* **2.** of or pertaining to the Aventine. [1615–25; < L *Aventīnus (mōns)* the Aventine (hill)]

a·ven·tu·rine (ə ven′chə rēn′, -rin), *n.* **1.** an opaque, brown glass containing fine, gold-colored particles. **2.** any of several varieties of minerals, esp. quartz or feldspar, spangled with bright particles of mica, hematite, or other minerals. Also, **a·ven′tu·rin.** Also called **goldstone.** [1805–15; < F, equiv. to *aventure* chance (see ADVENTURE) + *-ine* -INE[2]; so called because metal particles are introduced into the molten glass pell-mell *(à l'aventure)*]

av·e·nue (av′ə nyōō′, -nōō′), *n.* **1.** a wide street or main thoroughfare. **2.** a means of access or attainment: *avenues of escape; avenues to greater power.* **3.** a way or means of entering into or approaching a place: *the various avenues to India.* **4.** *Chiefly Brit.* **a.** a wide, usually tree-lined road, path, driveway, etc., through grounds to a country house or monumental building. **b.** a suburban, usually tree-lined residential street. [1590–1600; < F, lit., approach, n. use of fem. ptp. of *avenir* < L *advenīre* to come to. See A-[5], VENUE]
—**Syn. 1.** See **street.**

Av·en·zo·ar (av′ən zō′ər, -zō är′), *n.* 1091?–1162, Arab physician and writer in Spain: founder of Almohad dynasty. Also called **Abumeron.**

a·ver (ə vûr′), *v.t.,* **a·verred, a·ver·ring. 1.** to assert or affirm with confidence; declare in a positive or peremptory manner. **2.** *Law.* to allege as a fact. [1350–1400; ME < MF *averer* < ML *adverāre,* equiv. to *ad-* AD- + *-vēr-* (< L *vērus* true) + *-ā-* thematic vowel + *-re* inf. suffix]
—**Syn.** See **maintain.**

av·er·age (av′ər ij, av′rij), *n., adj., v.,* **-aged, -ag·ing.** —*n.* **1.** a quantity, rating, or the like that represents or approximates an arithmetic mean: *Her golf average is in the 90's. My average in science has gone from B to C this semester.* **2.** a typical amount, rate, degree, etc.; norm. **3.** *Statistics.* See **arithmetic mean. 4.** *Math.* a quantity intermediate to a set of quantities. **5.** *Com.* **a.** a charge paid by the master of a ship for such services as pilotage or towage. **b.** an expense, partial loss, or damage to a ship or cargo. **c.** the incidence of such an expense or loss to the owners or their insurers. **d.** an equitable apportionment among all the interested parties of such an expense or loss. Cf. **general average, particular average. 6. on the** or **an average,** usually; typically: *She can read 50 pages an hour, on the average.* —*adj.* **7.** of or pertaining to an average; estimated by

CONCISE ETYMOLOGY KEY: <, descended or borrowed from; >, whence; b., blend of, blended; c., cognate with; cf., compare; deriv., derivative; equiv., equivalent; imit., imitative; obl., oblique; r., replacing; s., stem; sp., spelling, spelled; resp., respelling, respelled; trans., translation; ?, origin unknown; *, unattested; ‡, probably earlier than. See the full key inside the front cover.

average; forming an average: *The average rainfall there is 180 inches.* **8.** typical; common; ordinary: *The average secretary couldn't handle such a workload. His grades were nothing special, only average.* —*v.t.* **9.** to find an average value for (a variable quantity); reduce to a mean: *We averaged the price of milk in five neighborhood stores.* **10.** (of a variable quantity) to have as its arithmetic mean: *Wheat averages 56 pounds to a bushel.* **11.** to do or have on the average: *He averages seven hours of sleep a night.* —*v.i.* **12.** to have or show an average: *to average as expected.* **13. average down,** to purchase more of a security or commodity at a lower price to reduce the average cost of one's holdings. **14. average out, a.** to come out of a security or commodity transaction with a profit or without a loss. **b.** to reach an average or other figure: *His taxes should average out to about a fifth of his income.* **15. average up,** to purchase more of a security or commodity at a higher price to take advantage of a contemplated further rise in prices. [1485–95; earlier *averay* charge on goods shipped, orig. duty (< MF *avarie* < OIt *avaria* < Ar *'awārīyah* damaged merchandise), with -AGE r. *-ay*] —**av′er·age·a·ble,** *adj.* —**av′er·age·ly,** *adv.* —**av′er·age·ness,** *n.*

av′erage devia′tion. See **mean deviation.**

av′erage life′, *Physics.* See **mean life.**

av′erage rev′enue, the total receipts from sales divided by the number of units sold, frequently employed in price theory in conjunction with marginal revenue.

av′eraging light′ me′ter, *Photog.* an exposure meter that evaluates light measured from all parts of the picture area to generate an average reading. Cf. **center-weighted light meter.**

A·ve Re·gi·na Coe·lo·rum (ä′vā ri jē′nə che lôr′əm, -lōr′-), a Latin hymn in honor of the Virgin Mary as Queen of Heaven. [lit., Hail, Queen of Heaven]

A·ver·il (ā′vər il), *n.* a male given name. Also, **A′ver·ell.**

a·ver·ment (ə vûr′mənt), *n.* **1.** the act of averring. **2.** a positive statement. [1400–50; late ME *averrement* < MF. See AVER, -MENT]

A·ver·nus (ə vûr′nəs), *n.* **1.** a lake near Naples, Italy, looked upon in ancient times as an entrance to hell, from whose waters vile-smelling vapors arose, supposedly killing birds flying over it. **2.** hell. [< L < Gk *áornos* birdless, equiv. to *a-* A-[6] + *órn(is)* bird + *-os* adj. suffix] —**A·ver′nal,** *adj.*

A·ver·ro·ës (ə ver′ō ēz′), *n.* 1126?–98, Arab philosopher in Spain. Also, **A·ver′rho·ës′.**

Av·er·ro·ism (av′ə rō′iz əm, ə ver′ō-), *n.* the philosophy of Averroës, largely based on Aristotelianism and asserting the unity of an active intellect common to all human beings while denying personal immortality. Also, **Av′er·rho′ism.** [1745–55; AVERRO(ËS) + -ISM] —**Av′·er·ro′ist, Av′er·rho′ist,** *n.* —**Av′er·ro·is′tic, Av′er·rho·is′tic,** *adj.*

a·verse (ə vûrs′), *adj.* having a strong feeling of opposition, antipathy, repugnance, etc.; opposed: *He is not averse to having a drink now and then.* [1590–1600; (< MF) < L *āversus* turned away, averted (ptp. of *āvertere*), equiv. to *ā-* A-[4] + *vert-* turn + *-tus* ptp. suffix] —**a·verse′ly,** *adv.* —**a·verse′ness,** *n.*
—**Syn.** unwilling, loath. See **reluctant.** —**Ant.** inclined, eager.
—**Usage.** See **adverse.**

a·ver·sion (ə vûr′zhən, -shən), *n.* **1.** a strong feeling of dislike, opposition, repugnance, or antipathy (usually fol. by *to*): *a strong aversion to snakes and spiders.* **2.** a cause or object of dislike; person or thing that causes antipathy: *His pet aversion is guests who are always late.* **3.** *Obs.* the act of averting; a turning away or preventing. [1590–1600; < L *āversiōn-* (s. of *āversiō*), equiv. to *āvers(us)* turned away (see AVERSE) + *-iōn-* -ION]
—**Syn. 1.** distaste, abhorrence, disgust. AVERSION, ANTIPATHY, LOATHING connote strong dislike or detestation. AVERSION is an unreasoning desire to avoid that which displeases, annoys, or offends: *an aversion to* (or *toward*) *cats.* ANTIPATHY is a distaste, dislike, or disgust toward something: *an antipathy toward* (or *for*) *braggarts.* LOATHING connotes a combination of hatred and disgust, or detestation: *a loathing for* (or *toward*) *hypocrisy, a criminal.* —**Ant. 1.** predilection.

a·ver·sive (ə vûr′siv, -ziv), *adj.* **1.** of or pertaining to aversion. **2.** of or pertaining to aversive conditioning. —*n.* **3.** a reprimand, punishment, or agent, used in aversive conditioning: *Antabuse is a commonly used aversive in the treatment of alcoholism.* [1590–1600; AVERS(ION) + -IVE] —**a·ver′sive·ly,** *adv.* —**a·ver′sive·ness,** *n.*

aver′sive condi′tioning, *Psychol., Psychiatry.* a type of behavior conditioning in which noxious stimuli are associated with undesirable or unwanted behavior that is to be modified or abolished, as the use of nausea-inducing drugs in the treatment of alcoholism. Also called **aver′sive ther′apy, aver′sion ther′apy.**

a·vert (ə vûrt′), *v.t.* **1.** to turn away or aside: *to avert one's eyes.* **2.** to ward off; prevent: *to avert evil; to avert an accident.* [1400–50; late ME < MF *avertir* << L *āvertere*, equiv. to *ā-* A-[4] + *vertere* to turn] —**a·vert′·ed·ly,** *adv.* —**a·vert′er,** *n.* —**a·vert′i·ble, a·vert′a·ble,** *adj.*

A·ver·tin (ə vûr′tin), *Pharm., Trademark.* a brand of tribromoethanol.

A·ver·y (ā′və rē), *n.* **1. Milton,** 1893–1965, U.S. painter. **2.** a male given name: from Old English words meaning "elf" and "favor."

A·ves (ā′vēz), *n.* (*used with a plural v.*) a class of vertebrates comprising the birds. [1895–1900; < NL; L, pl. of *avis* bird]

A·ves·ta (ə ves′tə), *n.* a collection of sacred Zoroastrian writings, including the Gathas.

A·ves·tan (ə ves′tən), *n.* **1.** an ancient East Iranian language of the Indo-European family, the language of all the Avesta but the Gathas. Cf. **Gathic** (def. 1). —*adj.* **2.** of or pertaining to the Avesta or its language. [1855–60; AVEST(A) + -AN]

A·vey·ron (A vā RÔN′), *n.* a department in S France. 278,306; 3387 sq. mi. (8770 sq. km). *Cap.:* Rodez.

AVF, all-volunteer force: referring to an armed force made up solely of volunteers during a period when there is no military draft, as the U.S. armed forces since the Vietnam War.

avg., average.

av·gas (av′gas′), *n. Aviation.* gasoline for use in piston-engined aircraft. [1940–45; AV(IATION) + GAS(OLINE)]

av·go·lem·o·no (äv′gō lem′ə nō′; *Gk.* äv′gô le′mô-nô), *n. Greek Cookery.* a soup or sauce made with beaten eggs, lemon juice, and usually chicken broth. [1960–65; ModGk *augolémono*, equiv. to *augó, abgó* egg (pron. *avγó*), classical Gk *tò ōión* the egg, pl. *tà ōiá* (cf. OO-), altered by fusion of article and noun, *v* and *γ* filling vocalic hiatus, merger of sing. and pl. forms, and separation of the article as *t'* + *-lemono* var. (in compounds) of *lemóni* lemon < It *limone* << Pers; see LEMON]

avi-, a combining form meaning "bird," used in the formation of compound words: *aviculture.* [< L, comb. form of *avis*]

a·vi·an (ā′vē ən), *adj.* of or pertaining to birds. [1865–70; AVI- + -AN]

a′vian diphthe′ria, *Vet. Pathol.* See **fowl pox.**

a′vian influen′za, an acute, usually fatal viral disease of chickens and other domestic and wild birds except pigeons, characterized by sudden onset of symptoms including fever, swollen head and neck, bluish-black comb and wattle, and difficult respiration. Also called **bird plague, fowl plague.**

a·vi·an·ize (ā′vē ə nīz′), *v.t.*, **-ized, -iz·ing.** *Microbiol.* to diminish the infectivity of (a virus) by repeated culturing in chick embryos. Also *esp. Brit.*, **a′vi·an·ise′.** [AVIAN + -IZE]

a′vian leuko′sis, *Vet. Pathol.* leukosis.

a′vian pneu·mo·en·ceph·a·li′tis (no͞o′mō en sef′ə lī′tis, nyo͞o′-), *Vet. Pathol.* See **Newcastle disease.**

a′vian pox′, *Vet. Pathol.* See **fowl pox.**

a·vi·ar·y (ā′vē er′ē), *n., pl.* **-ar·ies.** a large cage or a house or enclosure in which birds are kept. [1570–80; < L *aviārium* a place where birds are kept, n. use of neut. of *aviārius* pertaining to birds. See AVI-, -ARY] —**a·vi·a·rist** (ā′vē ə rist), *n.*

a·vi·ate (ā′vē āt′, av′ē-), *v.t., v.i.*, **-at·ed, -at·ing.** to fly or fly in an aircraft. [1885–90; back formation from AVIATION]

a·vi·a·tion (ā′vē ā′shən, av′ē-), *n.* **1.** the design, development, production, operation, and use of aircraft, esp. heavier-than-air aircraft. **2.** military aircraft. [1865–70; < F; see AVI-, -ATION] —**a·vi·at·ic** (ā′vē at′ik, av′ē-), *adj.*

avia′tion badge′, wings.

avia′tion cadet′, one who trains to become an officer in an air force. [1940–45]

avia′tion med′icine, the branch of medicine dealing with the psychological, physiological, and pathological effects of flying in airplanes. Also called **aeromedicine.**

a·vi·a·tor (ā′vē ā′tər, av′ē-), *n.* a pilot of an airplane or other heavier-than-air aircraft. [1885–90; AVI- + -ATOR, modeled on F *aviateur*]

a′viator glass′es, eyeglasses with metal frames, and often tinted lenses, contoured to suggest the goggles once worn by aviators. [1965–70]

a·vi·a·trix (ā′vē ā′triks, av′ē-), *n., pl.* **-a·tri·ces** (-ā′trə sēz′, -ə trī′sēz). a woman who is a pilot; aviator. Also, **a·vi·a·tress, a·vi·a·trice** (ā′vē ā′tris). [1925–30; AVIAT(OR) + -TRIX]
—**Usage.** See **-trix.**

A·vi·ce·brón (ä′vē the brôn′, -se-), *n.* (*Solomon ben Judah ibn-Gabirol*) 1021?–58, Jewish poet and philosopher in Spain.

Av·i·cen·na (av′ə sen′ə), *n.* A.D. 980–1037, Islamic physician and philosopher, born in Persia.

a·vic·u·lar·i·um (ə vik′yə lâr′ē əm), *n., pl.* **-lar·i·a** (-lâr′ē ə). *Zool.* a protective zooid of a bryozoan colony, having movable jaws that can be snapped shut. [< NL; see AVI-, -CULE[1], -ARIUM] —**a·vic′u·lar′i·an,** *adj.*

a·vi·cul·ture (ā′vi kul′chər), *n.* the rearing or keeping of birds. [1875–80; AVI- + CULTURE] —**a′vi·cul′tur·ist,** *n.*

av·id (av′id), *adj.* **1.** enthusiastic; ardent; dedicated; keen: *an avid moviegoer.* **2.** keenly desirous; eager; greedy (often fol. by *for* or *of*): *avid for pleasure; avid of power.* [1760–70; < L *avidus*, equiv. to *av(ēre)* to crave + *-idus* -ID[4]] —**av′id·ly,** *adv.* —**av′id·ness,** *n.*
—**Syn.** AVID, EAGER, KEEN all share the sense of strongly desirous. AVID suggests a desire akin to greed, so strong as to be insatiable: *driven by an avid need for fame and recognition.* EAGER implies a desire that is strong and impatient but less than overpowering: *eager to try his hand at new tasks.* KEEN carries a sense of zest and active, alert desire: *an amateur painter, ever keen to try new techniques.*

av·i·din (av′i din, ə vid′in), *n. Biochem.* a protein, found in the white of egg, that combines with and prevents the action of biotin, thus injuring the animal that consumes it in excess by producing biotin deficiency. [1940–45; AVID + (BIOT)IN; so named from its affinity for biotin]

a·vid·i·ty (ə vid′i tē), *n.* **1.** eagerness; greediness. **2.** enthusiasm or dedication. [1400–50; late ME *avidite* < MF < L *aviditās*. See AVID, -ITY]

a·vid·ya (ə vid′yä), *n. Hinduism, Buddhism.* ignorance of the identity of oneself with Brahman, resulting in imprisonment within the cycle of birth and death. Cf. **vidya.** [< Skt *avidyā* ignorance, equiv. to *a-* A-[6] + *vidyā*; see VIDYA]

a·vi·fau·na (ā′və fô′nə, av′ə), *n.* the birds of a given region, considered as a whole. [1870–75; AVI- + FAUNA] —**a′vi·fau′nal,** *adj.* —**a′vi·fau′nal·ly,** *adv.*

av·i·ga·tion (av′i gā′shən), *n.* aerial navigation. [AVI- + (NAVI)GATION] —**av′i·ga′tor,** *n.*

A·vi·gnon (A vē nyôN′), *n.* a city in and the capital of Vaucluse, in SE France, on the Rhone River: papal residence 1309–77. 93,024.

A·vi·la Ca·ma·cho (ä′vē lä′ kä mä′chô), **Ma·nuel** (mä nwel′), 1897–1955, president of Mexico 1940–46.

a vin·cu·lo mat·ri·mo·ni·i (ā ving′kyə lō′ ma′tri-mō′nē ī′, -nē ē′), *Law.* pertaining to or noting a divorce that absolutely dissolves the marriage bond and releases husband and wife from all matrimonial obligations: *a divorce a vinculo matrimonii.* [< L: from the bond of marriage]

a·vi·on·ics (ā′vē on′iks, av′ē-), *n.* **1.** (*used with a singular v.*) the science and technology of the development and use of electrical and electronic devices in aviation. **2.** (*used with a plural v.*) the devices themselves. [1945–50; AVI(ATION) + (ELECTR)ONICS] —**a′vi·on′ic,** *adj.*

a·vi·o·pho·bi·a (ā′vē ə fō′bē ə, av′ē-), *n. Psychiatry.* fear of flying in an airplane or other aircraft. [perh. AVI(ATION) + -O- + -PHOBIA]

a·vir·u·lent (ā vir′yə lənt, ā vir′ə-), *adj.* (of organisms) having no virulence, as a result of age, heat, etc.; nonpathogenic. [1895–1900; A-[6] + VIRULENT] —**a·vir′u·lence,** *n.*

A·vis (ā′vis), *n.* a female given name: from a Latin word meaning "bird."

a·vi·so (ə vī′zō), *n., pl.* **-sos.** a boat used esp. for carrying dispatches; dispatch boat. [1625–35; < Sp, n. deriv. of *avisar* to ADVISE]

a·vi·ta·min·o·sis (ā vī′tə mə nō′sis), *n. Pathol.* any disease caused by a lack of vitamins. [1910–15; A-[6] + VITAMIN + -OSIS] —**a·vi·ta·min·ot·ic** (ā vī′tə mə not′ik), *adj.*

A·viv (ä vēv′), *n. Chiefly Biblical.* the seventh month of the Jewish year, equivalent to Nisan of the modern Jewish calendar. Ex. 34:18. Also, **Abib.** [< Heb *ābhībh* lit., ear of grain]

Av·lo·na (av lō′nə), *n.* former name of **Vlorë.**

avn., aviation.

A-V node. See **atrioventricular node.** Also, **AV node.**

a·vo (ä′vo͞o), *n., pl.* **a·vos.** a money of account of Macao, the 100th part of a pataca. [1905–10; < Pg: lit., trifle, shortening of *oitavo* eighth; see OCTAVE]

av·o·ca·do (av′ə kä′dō, ä′və-), *n., pl.* **-dos. 1.** Also called **alligator pear.** a large, usually pear-shaped fruit having green to blackish skin, a single large seed, and soft, light-green pulp, borne by the tropical American tree *Persea americana* and its variety *P. adrymifolia,* often eaten raw, esp. in salads. **2.** the tree itself. [1690–1700; alter. of Sp *abogado* lit., lawyer (see ADVOCATE), by confusion with MexSp *aguacate* < Nahuatl *āhuacatl* avocado, testicle; cf. ALLIGATOR PEAR]

avocado, *Persea americana*

av·o·ca·tion (av′ə kā′shən), *n.* **1.** something a person does in addition to a principal occupation, esp. for pleasure; hobby: *Our doctor's avocation is painting.* **2.** a person's regular occupation, calling, or vocation. **3.** *Archaic.* diversion or distraction. [1520–30; < L *āvocātiōn-* (s. of *āvocātiō*) a calling away. See A-[4], VOCATION] —**av′·o·ca′tion·al,** *adj.* —**av′o·ca′tion·al·ly,** *adv.*

av·o·cet (av′ə set′), *n.* any of several long-legged, web-footed shorebirds constituting the genus *Recurvirostra,* having a long, slender, upward-curving bill. [1760–70; < F *avocette*, prob. erroneous sp. for NL *avosetta* < It < Upper It (< Venetian)]

av·o·di·re (av′ə də rā′), *n.* the hard, light-colored wood of a West African tree, *Turraeanthus africana,* of the mahogany family, used for making furniture. [1930–35; < F *avodiré*, said to be < Agni, a Kwa language of the Ivory Coast]

A·vo·ga·dro (ä′və gä′drō; *It.* ä′vô gä′dRô), *n.* **Count A·ma·de·o** (ä′mä de′ô), 1776–1856, Italian physicist and chemist.

A′voga′dro's law′, *Chem.* the principle that equal volumes of all gases at the same temperature and pressure contain the same number of molecules. Thus, the molar volume of all ideal gases at 0° C and a pressure of 1 atm. is 22.4 liters. [1870–75; named after A. AVOGADRO]

A′voga′dro's num′ber, *Chem.* the constant, 6.02 $\times 10^{23}$, representing the number of atoms in a gram atom or the number of molecules in a gram molecule. *Symbol:* N Also called **A′voga′dro con′stant.** Cf. **Loschmidt's number.** [1925–30; see AVOGADRO'S LAW]

a·void (ə void′), *v.t.* **1.** to keep away from; keep clear

of; shun: *to avoid a person; to avoid taxes; to avoid danger.* **2.** to prevent from happening: *to avoid falling.* **3.** *Law.* to make void or of no effect; invalidate. **4.** *Obs.* to empty; eject or expel. [1250–30; ME *avoiden* < AF *a-voider,* equiv. to *a-* A-^{4} + *voider* to VOID] —**a•void′a•ble,** *adj.* —**a•void′a•bly,** *adv.* —**a•void′er,** *n.*
—**Syn. 1.** elude. AVOID, ESCAPE mean to come through a potentially harmful or unpleasant experience, without suffering serious consequences. To AVOID is to succeed in keeping away from something dangerous or undesirable: *to avoid meeting an enemy.* ESCAPE suggests encountering peril but coming through it safely: *to escape drowning.* —**Ant. 1.** confront, face, encounter.

a•void•ance (ə void′ns), *n.* **1.** the act of avoiding or keeping away from: *the avoidance of scandal; the avoidance of one's neighbors.* **2.** *Law.* a making void; annulment. [1350–1400; ME < AF; see AVOID, -ANCE]

avoid′ance play′, *Bridge.* a play by the declarer designed to prevent a particular opponent from taking the lead.

avoir., See **avoirdupois weight.**

av•oir•du•pois (av′ər də poiz′), *n.* **1.** See **avoirdupois weight. 2.** *Informal.* bodily weight: *He carries around a lot of excess avoirdupois.* [1250–1300; ME *avoir de pois* lit., property of weight < OF, equiv. to *avoir* (earlier *aveir* < L *habēre* to have) + *de* (< L *dē*) + *pois* (earlier *peis* < L *pēnsum*)]

avoirdupois′ weight′, the system of weights in British and U.S. use for goods other than gems, precious metals, and drugs: 27$\frac{11}{32}$ grains = 1 dram; 16 drams = 1 ounce; 16 ounces = 1 pound; 112 pounds (Brit.) or 100 pounds (U.S.) = 1 hundredweight; 20 hundredweight = 1 ton. The pound contains 7000 grains. *Abbr.:* av.; avdp.; avoir. [1610–20]

A•von (ā′vən, av′ən *for 1–4;* ā′von *for 5*), *n.* **1.** a river in central England, flowing SE past Stratford-on-Avon to the Severn. 96 mi. (155 km) long. **2.** a river in S England, flowing W to the mouth of the Severn. ab. 75 mi. (120 km) long. **3.** a river in S England, flowing S to the English Channel. ab. 60 mi. (100 km) long. **4.** a county in SW England, 919,600; 520 sq. mi. (1346 sq. km.) **5.** a town in N Connecticut. 11,201.

A′von Lake′ (ā′von), a town in N Ohio. 13,222.

à vo•tre san•té (A vô′TR^{ə} säN tā′), *French.* to your health.

a•vouch (ə vouch′), *v.t.* **1.** to make frank acknowledgment or affirmation of; declare or assert with positiveness. **2.** to assume responsibility for; vouch for; guarantee. **3.** to admit; confess. [1350–1400; ME *avouchen* < MF *avouchier* < L *advocāre.* See A-^{5}, VOUCH, ADVOCATE] —**a•vouch′er,** *n.* —**a•vouch′ment,** *n.*

a•vow (ə vou′), *v.t.* to declare frankly or openly; own; acknowledge; confess; admit: *He avowed himself an opponent of all alliances.* [1150–1200; ME *avowen* < OF *avoue(r)* < L *advocāre.* See ADVOCATE] —**a•vow′a•ble,** *adj.* —**a•vow′er,** *n.*

a•vow•al (ə vou′əl), *n.* an open statement of affirmation; frank acknowledgment or admission. [1720–30; AVOW + -AL^{2}]

a•vowed (ə voud′), *adj.* acknowledged; declared: *an avowed enemy.* [1300–50; ME; see AVOW, -ED^{2}] —**a•vow•ed•ly** (ə vou′id lē), *adv.* —**a•vow′ed•ness,** *n.*

a•vow•ry (ə vou′rē), *n., pl.* **-ries.** *Law.* a plea by a defendant in an action of replevin who admits taking the distrained goods and shows just cause for the taking. [1300–50; ME *avowrie* < OF *avouerie,* equiv. to *avou(er)* to AVOW + *-erie* -RY]

Av•ram (āv′rəm, av′rəm, ä vrôm′), *n.* a male given name, form of **Abram.**

a vues•tra sa•lud (ä vwes′TRä sä lo͞oth′), *Spanish.* to your health.

a•vulse (ə vuls′), *v.t.,* **a•vulsed, a•vuls•ing.** to pull off or tear away forcibly: *to avulse a ligament.* [1755–65; < L *āvulsus,* ptp. of *āvellere* to pluck off, tear away, equiv. to *ā-* A-^{4} + *vul-,* ptp. s. of *vellere* to forcibly pull, pluck + *-sus,* var. of *-tus* ptp. suffix]

a•vul•sion (ə vul′shən), *n.* **1.** a tearing away. **2.** *Law.* the sudden removal of soil by change in a river's course or by a flood, from the land of one owner to that of another. **3.** a part torn off. [1615–25; < L *āvulsiōn-* (s. of *āvulsiō*), equiv. to *āvuls(us)* torn off (see AVULSE) + *-iōn-* -ION]

a•vun•cu•lar (ə vung′kyə lər), *adj.* of, pertaining to, or characteristic of an uncle: *avuncular affection.* [1825–35; < L *avuncul(us)* a mother's brother, equiv. to *av(us)* a forefather + **-ont-* + **-l(os)* dim. suffix (cf. UNCLE) + -AR^{1}] —**a•vun′cu•lar′i•ty,** *n.* —**a•vun′cu•lar•ly,** *adv.*

a•vun•cu•late (ə vung′kyə lit, -lāt′), *n. Anthropol.* a close social relationship between a maternal uncle and his nephew. [1915–20; < L *avuncul(us)* uncle (see AVUNCULAR) + -ATE^{3}]

aw (ô), *interj.* **1.** (used to express protest, disbelief, disgust, or commiseration.) **2.** (used to express sentimental or sugary approval.) [1850–55]

AW, Articles of War.

a.w., **1.** actual weight. **2.** (in shipping) all water. **3.** atomic weight. Also, **aw**

a•wa (ə wô′, ə wä′), *adv. Scot.* away.

AWACS (ā′waks), *n.* a sophisticated detection aircraft, fitted with powerful radar and a computer, capable of simultaneously tracking and plotting large numbers of low-flying aircraft at much greater distances than is possible with ground radar. [1965–70; *A(irborne) W(arning) A(nd) C(ontrol) S(ystem)*]

CONCISE ETYMOLOGY KEY: <, descended or borrowed from; >, whence; b., blend of, blended; c., cognate with; cf., compare; deriv., derivative; equiv., equivalent; imit., imitative; obl., oblique; r., replacing; s., stem; sp., spelling, spelled; resp., respelling, respelled; trans., translation; ?, origin unknown; *, unattested; ‡, probably earlier than. See the full key inside the front cover.

a•wait (ə wāt′), *v.t.* **1.** to wait for; expect; look for: *He is still awaiting an answer.* **2.** to be in store for; be imminent: *A pleasant surprise awaits her in today's mail.* **3.** *Obs.* to lie in wait for. —*v.i.* **4.** to wait, as in expectation. [1200–50; ME *awaiten* < ONF *awaitier,* equiv. to *a-* A-^{5} + *waitier* to WAIT] —**a•wait′er,** *n.*
—**Syn. 1.** See **expect.**

A•wa•ji (ä wä′jē), *n.* an island in Japan, S of Honshu and N of Shikoku. 230 sq. mi. (596 sq. km).

a•wake (ə wāk′), *v.,* **a•woke** or **a•waked, a•woke** or **a•waked** or **a•wo•ken, a•wak•ing,** *adj.* —*v.t., v.i.* **1.** to wake up; rouse from sleep: *I awoke at six with a feeling of dread.* **2.** to rouse to action; become active: *His flagging interest awoke.* **3.** to come or bring to an awareness; become cognizant (often fol. by *to*): *She awoke to the realities of life.* —*adj.* **4.** waking; not sleeping. **5.** vigilant; alert: *They were awake to the danger.* [bef. 1000; ME *awaken,* OE *awacen,* ptp. of *awæcnan;* see A^{1}, WAKEN] —**a•wake′a•ble,** *adj.*

a•wak•en (ə wā′kən), *v.t., v.i.* to awake; waken. [bef. 900; ME *awak(e)nen,* OE *awæcnian* earlier *onwæcnian.* See A-^{1}, WAKEN] —**a•wak′en•a•ble,** *adj.* —**a•wak′en•er,** *n.*

a•wak•en•ing (ə wā′kə ning), *adj.* **1.** rousing; quickening: *an awakening interest in ballet.* —*n.* **2.** the act of awaking from sleep. **3.** a revival of interest or attention. **4.** a recognition, realization, or coming into awareness of something: *a rude awakening to the disagreeable facts.* **5.** a renewal of interest in religion, esp. in a community; a revival. [1585–95; AWAKEN + -ING^{2}, -ING^{1}] —**a•wak′en•ing•ly,** *adv.*

a•ward (ə wôrd′), *v.t.* **1.** to give as due or merited; assign or bestow: *to award prizes.* **2.** to bestow by judicial decree; assign or appoint by deliberate judgment, as in arbitration: *The plaintiff was awarded damages of $100,000.* —*n.* **3.** something awarded, as a payment or medal. **4.** *Law.* **a.** a decision after consideration; a judicial sentence. **b.** the decision of arbitrators on a matter submitted to them. [1250–1300; (v.) ME *awarden* < AF *awarder,* equiv. to *a-* A-^{4} + *warder* << Gmc; cf. OE *weardian* to guard, WARD; (n.) ME < AF, deriv. of *awarder*] —**a•ward′a•bil′i•ty,** *n.* —**a•ward′a•ble,** *adv.* —**a•ward′er,** *n.*

a•ward•ee (ə wôr dē′, ə wôr′dē), *n.* the recipient of an award. [AWARD + -EE]

a•ware (ə wâr′), *adj.* **1.** having knowledge; conscious; cognizant: *aware of danger.* **2.** informed; alert; knowledgeable; sophisticated: *She is one of the most politically aware young women around.* [bef. 1100; ME, var. of *iwar,* OE *gewær* watchful (c. OHG, OS *giwar,* G *gewahr*), equiv. to *ge-* Y- + *wær* WARE^{2}] —**a•ware′ness,** *n.*
—**Syn. 1.** mindful. See **conscious.** —**Ant. 1.** oblivious.

a•wash (ə wosh′, ə wôsh′), *adj., adv.* **1.** *Naut.* **a.** just level with or scarcely above the surface of the water, so that waves break over the top. **b.** overflowing with water, as the upper deck of a ship in a heavy sea. **2.** covered with water. **3.** washing about; tossed about by the waves. **4.** covered, filled, or crowded: *streets awash with shoppers; a garden awash in brilliant colors.* [1825–35; A-^{1} + WASH]

a•way (ə wā′), *adv.* **1.** from this or that place; off: *to go away.* **2.** aside; to another place; in another direction: *to turn your eyes away; to turn away customers* **3.** far; apart: *away back; away from the subject.* **4.** out of one's possession or use: *to give money away.* **5.** out of existence or notice; into extinction: *to fade away; to idle away the morning.* **6.** incessantly or relentlessly; repeatedly: *He kept hammering away.* **7.** without hesitation: *Fire away.* **8. away with, a.** take away: *Away with him!* **b.** go away! leave!: *Away with you!* **9. do away with, a.** to get rid of; abolish; stop. **b.** to kill: *Bluebeard did away with all his wives.* **10. where away?** (of something sighted from a ship) in which direction? where? —*adj.* **11.** absent; gone: *to be away from home.* **12.** distant: *six miles away.* **13.** immediately off and on the way: *The order was given and he was away.* **14.** *Sports.* played in a ball park, arena, or the like, other than the one that is or is assumed to be the center of operations of a team: *winners in their last three away games.* Cf. **home** (def. 16). **15.** *Baseball.* having been put out: *with two away in the top of the seventh.* **16.** *Golf.* **a.** (of a golf ball) lying farthest from the hole. **b.** (of a golfer) having hit such a ball and being required to play first. [bef. 950; ME; OE *aweg,* reduction of *on weg.* See ON, A-^{1}, WAY]

a•way′-go•ing crop′ (ə wā′gō′ing), *Law.* a crop planted by a tenant that matures after the expiration of the tenancy and is rightfully the tenant's to harvest. Also called **waygoing crop.** [1860–65]

AWB, See **air waybill.**

awe (ô), *n., v.,* **awed, aw•ing.** —*n.* **1.** an overwhelming feeling of reverence, admiration, fear, etc., produced by that which is grand, sublime, extremely powerful, or the like: *in awe of God; in awe of great political figures.* **2.** *Archaic.* power to inspire fear or reverence. **3.** *Obs.* fear or dread. —*v.t.* **4.** to inspire with awe. **5.** to influence or restrain by awe. [1250–1300; ME *aghe, awe* < Scand; cf. ON *agi* fear, c. Goth *agis,* OE *ege,* Gk *áchos* pain]
—**Syn. 1.** wonder, veneration. —**Ant. 1.** apathy; contempt.

a•wea•ry (ə wēr′ē), *adj. Literary.* wearied or tired; fatigued. [1545–55; A-^{1} + WEARY]

a•weath•er (ə weth′ər), *adv., adj. Naut.* upon or toward the weather side of a vessel; in the direction of the wind (opposed to *alee*). [1590–1600; A-^{1} + WEATHER]

awed (ôd), *adj.* filled with or expressing awe. [1635–45; AWE + -ED^{2}] —**aw•ed•ly** (ô′id lē, ôd′-), *adv.* —**aw′•ed•ness,** *n.*

a•weigh (ə wā′), *adj. Naut.* (of an anchor) just free of the bottom; atrip: *Anchors aweigh!* [1620–30; A-^{1} + WEIGH^{2}]

awe-in•spir•ing (ô′in spī^{ə}r′ing), *adj.* causing awe; spectacular; magnificent: *an awe-inspiring cathedral; an awe-inspiring sunset.* [1805–15]

awe•less (ô′lis), *adj.* **1.** displaying no awe; unawed. **2.** not to be awed; fearless. **3.** rude; impertinent. Also, **awless.** [bef. 900; ME, OE; see AWE, -LESS] —**awe′less•ness,** *n.*

awe•some (ô′səm), *adj.* **1.** inspiring awe: *an awesome sight.* **2.** showing or characterized by awe. **3.** *Slang.* very impressive: *That new white convertible is totally awesome.* [1590–1600; AWE + -SOME^{1}] —**awe′some•ly,** *adv.* —**awe′some•ness,** *n.*
—**Usage.** See **awful.**

awe-struck (ô′struk′), *adj.* filled with awe. Also, **awe′struck′, awe-strick•en, awe•strick•en** (ô′strik′-ən). [1625–35]

aw•ful (ô′fəl), *adj.* **1.** extremely bad; unpleasant; ugly: *awful paintings; an awful job.* **2.** inspiring fear; dreadful; terrible: *an awful noise.* **3.** solemnly impressive; inspiring awe: *the awful majesty of alpine peaks.* **4.** full of awe; reverential. **5.** extremely dangerous, risky, injurious, etc.: *That was an awful fall she had. He took an awful chance by driving here so fast.* —*adv.* **6.** *Informal.* very; extremely: *He did an awful good job of painting the barn. It's awful hot in here.* [1200–50; ME *a(g)heful, aueful;* see AWE, -FUL; r. OE *egefull* dreadful] —**aw′ful•ness,** *n.*
—**Usage.** Although some object to any use of AWFUL or AWFULLY in any sense not connected with a feeling of awe, both have been used in other senses for several centuries. AWFUL and AWFULLY as adverbial intensifiers —*awful(ly) hot; awful(ly) cold*—appear in the early 19th century, following much the same pattern as *horribly* and *dreadfully.* As an adverb AWFUL is less formal in tone than AWFULLY. In the sense "inspiring awe or fear" AWESOME has largely replaced AWFUL.

aw•ful•ly (ô′fə lē, ôf′lē), *adv.* **1.** very; extremely: *That was awfully nice of you. He's awfully slow.* **2.** in a manner provoking censure, disapproval, or the like: *She behaved awfully all evening.* **3.** *Archaic.* **a.** in a manner inspiring awe: *shouting awfully the dreaded curse.* **b.** in a manner expressing awe: *to stare awfully.* [1350–1400; ME *auefulli;* see AWFUL, -LY]
—**Usage.** See **awful.**

a•while (ə hwīl′, ə wīl′), *adv.* for a short time or period: *Stay awhile.* [bef. 1000; ME; OE *āne hwīle* (dat.); see A^{1}, WHILE]
—**Usage.** The adverb AWHILE is spelled as a single word: *After stopping in Hadley awhile, we drove to Deerfield.* As the object of a preposition, the noun phrase A WHILE is used, especially in edited writing, but the single-word form is becoming increasingly common: *We rested for a while* (or *awhile*).

a•whirl (ə hwûrl′, ə wûrl′), *adj.* rotating rapidly; spinning; whirling (usually used predicatively): *dancers awhirl to the strains of a lively waltz.* [1880–85; A-^{1} + WHIRL]

awk•ward (ôk′wərd), *adj.* **1.** lacking skill or dexterity; clumsy. **2.** lacking grace or ease in movement: *an awkward gesture; an awkward dancer.* **3.** lacking social graces or manners: *a simple, awkward frontiersman.* **4.** not well planned or designed for easy or effective use: *an awkward instrument; an awkward method.* **5.** requiring caution; somewhat hazardous; dangerous: *an awkward turn in the road.* **6.** hard to deal with; difficult; requiring skill, tact, or the like: *an awkward situation; an awkward customer.* **7.** embarrassing or inconvenient; caused by lack of social grace: *an awkward moment* **8.** *Obs.* untoward; perverse. [1300–50; ME, equiv. to *awk(e), auk(e)* backhanded, OE **afoc* (< ON *ǫfugr* turned the wrong way; c. OS, OHG *abuh,* OE *afu(h)lic* wrong, OFF) + *-ward* -WARD] —**awk′ward•ly,** *adv.* —**awk′ward•ness,** *n.*
—**Syn. 1.** unskillful, unhandy, inexpert. —**Ant. 1.** deft, adroit. **2.** graceful.

awk′ward age′, early adolescence. [1890–95]

awl (ôl), *n.* a pointed instrument for piercing small holes in leather, wood, etc. [bef. 900; ME *al, eal, aul,* OE *al, eal, æl;* c. ON *alr;* akin to ME *ēl,* OE *ǣl,* OHG *āla* (G *Ahle*), Skt *ā́rā*]

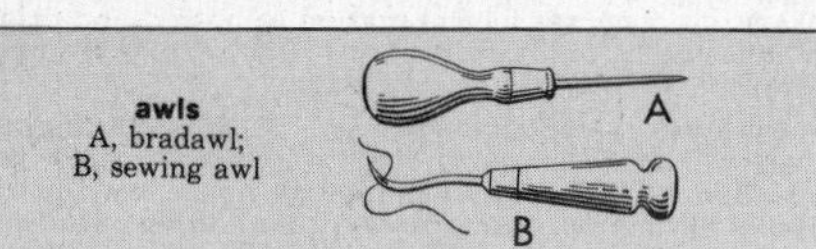

awls
A, bradawl;
B, sewing awl

A.W.L., absent with leave. Also, **a.w.l.**

aw•less (ô′lis), *adj.* aweless. —**aw′less•ness,** *n.*

awl-shaped (ôl′shāpt′), *adj.* **1.** having the shape of an awl. **2.** subulate (def. 2). [1755–65]

awl′ snail′, any tiny, usually white land snail of the family Subulinidae, some introduced species being pests of hothouse flowers.

awl•wort (ôl′wûrt′, -wôrt′), *n.* a small, stemless aquatic plant, *Subularia aquatica,* of the mustard family, having slender, sharp-pointed leaves and minute white flowers. [AWL + WORT^{2}]

aw•mous (ô′məs), *n.* (*used with a plural v.*) *Scot.* almous.

awn (ôn), *n. Bot.* **1.** a bristlelike appendage of a plant, esp. on the glumes of grasses. **2.** such appendages collectively, as those forming the beard of wheat, barley, etc. **3.** any similar bristle. [1250–1300; ME *aw(u)n, agune, agene,* prob. < Scand; cf. ON *ǫgn,* ODan *aghn* husk; r. and c. OE *ægnan;* c. Goth *ahana,* OHG *agana* (G *Agen, Ahne*), D, Fris *agen;* OL *agna* ear of grain, Czech *osina* awn; Gk *ákaina* thorn, bristle, *ákhnē* chaff (< a pre-Hellenic substratum language); < IE **$H_a$ek-* sharp] —**awned,** *adj.* —**awn′less,** *adj.*

awn•er (ô′nər), *n.* a machine for cutting the awns from grain. [1880–85; AWN + -ER^{1}]

awn·ing (ô′ning), *n.* **1.** a rooflike shelter of canvas or other material extending over a doorway, from the top of a window, over a deck, etc., in order to provide protection, as from the sun. **2.** a shelter. [1615–25; orig. uncert.] —**awn′inged,** *adj.*

awn′ing deck′, *Naut.* a weather deck supported on very light scantlings. [1865–70]

awn′ing win′dow, a window frame having one or more sashes hinged at the top and swinging outward.

awn′less brome′grass. See **Hungarian bromegrass.** [AWN + -LESS]

a·woke (ə wōk′), *v.* a pt. and pp. of **awake.**

a·wo·ken (ə wō′kən), *v.* a pp. of **awake.**

AWOL (*pronounced as initials or* ā′wôl, ā′wol), *adj., adv.* **1.** away from military duties without permission, but without the intention of deserting. —*n.* **2.** a soldier or other military person who is absent from duty without leave. **3. go AWOL, a.** to depart from military duty without leave. **b.** to absent oneself without explanation. Also, **awol, A.W.O.L., a.w.o.l.** [1915–20; *A(bsent) W(ith)o(ut) L(eave)*]

A·wo·lo·wo (ä wo͞o′lō wō′), *n.* **O·ba·fe·mi** (ô bä′fā mē), born 1909, Nigerian lawyer and statesman.

a·wry (ə rī′), *adv., adj.* **1.** with a turn or twist to one side; askew: *to glance or look awry.* **2.** away from the expected or proper direction; amiss; wrong: *Our plans went awry.* [1325–75; ME *on wry.* See A-[1], WRY]

aw-shucks (ô′shuks′), *adj. Informal.* characterized by a shy, embarrassed, often provincial manner. [1930–35]

ax (aks), *n., pl.* **ax·es** (ak′siz), *v.,* **axed, ax·ing.** —*n.* **1.** an instrument with a bladed head on a handle or helve, used for hewing, cleaving, chopping, etc. **2.** *Jazz Slang.* any musical instrument. **3. have an ax to grind,** to have a personal or selfish motive: *His interest may be sincere, but I suspect he has an ax to grind.* **4. the ax,** *Informal.* **a.** dismissal from employment: *to get the ax.* **b.** expulsion from school. **c.** rejection by a lover, friend, etc.: *His girlfriend gave him the ax.* **d.** any usually summary removal or curtailment. —*v.t.* **5.** to shape or trim with an ax. **6.** to chop, split, destroy, break open, etc., with an ax: *The firemen had to ax the door to reach the fire.* **7.** *Informal.* to dismiss, restrict, or destroy brutally, as if with an ax: *The main office axed those in the field who didn't meet their quota. Congress axed the budget.* Also, **axe.** [bef. 1000; ME; *ax(e), ex(e),* OE *æx, æces;* akin to Goth *aquizi,* ON *øx, ǫx,* OHG *acc(h)us, a(c)kus* (G *Axt*), MHG pl. *exa* < Gmc **akwiz-, akuz-, aksi-* << **ákəs, áks-;* L *ascia* (< **acsiā*), Gk *axínē;* < IE **ag-s-*] —**ax′like′,** *adj.*

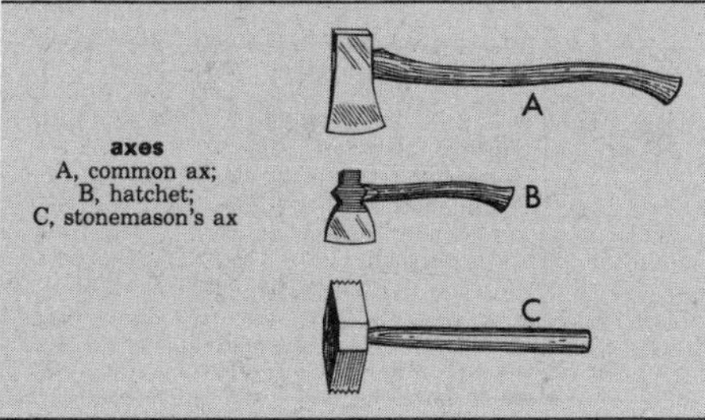

axes
A, common ax;
B, hatchet;
C, stonemason's ax

ax-, var. of **axi-,** esp. before a vowel.

ax., axiom.

Ax·a (ak′sə), *n. Douay Bible.* Achsah.

ax·an·thop·si·a (ak′san thop′sē ə), *n. Ophthalm.* a defect of vision in which the retina fails to respond to yellow. [A-[6] + XANTH(O)- + -OPSIA]

axe (aks), *n., pl.* **ax·es** (ak′siz), *v.,* **axed, ax·ing.** ax.

ax·el (ak′səl), *n. Figure Skating.* a jump performed by a skater leaping from the front outer edge of one skate into the air to make 1½ rotations of the body and landing on the back outer edge of the other skate. [1925–30; after *Axel* Paulsen (1855–1938), Norwegian figure skater, who popularized the maneuver]

Ax·el (ak′səl), *n.* a male given name.

Ax·el Hei·berg (ak′səl hī′bûrg), the largest island belonging to the Sverdrup group in the Canadian Northwest Territories. 15,779 sq. mi. (40,868 sq. km).

Ax·el·rod (ak′səl rod′), *n.* **Julius,** born 1912, U.S. biochemist and pharmacologist: Nobel prize for medicine 1970.

a·xen·ic (ā zen′ik, ā zē′nik), *adj. Biol.* **1.** (of an experimental animal) raised under sterile conditions; germfree. **2.** (of a laboratory culture) uncontaminated. [1940–45; A-[6] + Gk *xenikós* foreign. See XENO-, -IC] —**a·xen′i·cal·ly,** *adv.*

ax·es[1] (ak′sēz), *n.* pl. of **axis**[1].

ax·es[2] (ak′siz), *n.* pl. of **ax** or **axe.**

axi-, a combining form meaning "axis": *axial; axilemma.* Also, **axo-;** *esp. before a vowel,* **ax-.** [comb. form repr. L *axis* axle, wheel; c. Gk *áxōn,* Skt *ákṣas,* Lith *ašis,* OCS *osĭ,* OE *eax*]

ax·i·al (ak′sē əl), *adj.* **1.** of, pertaining to, characterized by, or forming an axis: *an axial relationship.* **2.** situated in or on an axis. [1840–50; AXI- + -AL[1]] —**ax′i·al′i·ty,** *n.* —**ax′i·al·ly,** *adv.*

ax·i·al-flow (ak′sē əl flō′), *adj.* having a fluid flow parallel to an axis of rotation, as in a turbine.

ax′ial skel′eton, *Anat.* the skeleton of the head and trunk. [1870–75]

ax·il (ak′sil), *n. Bot.* the angle between the upper side of a leaf or stem and the supporting stem or branch. [1785–95; < L *axilla* armpit]

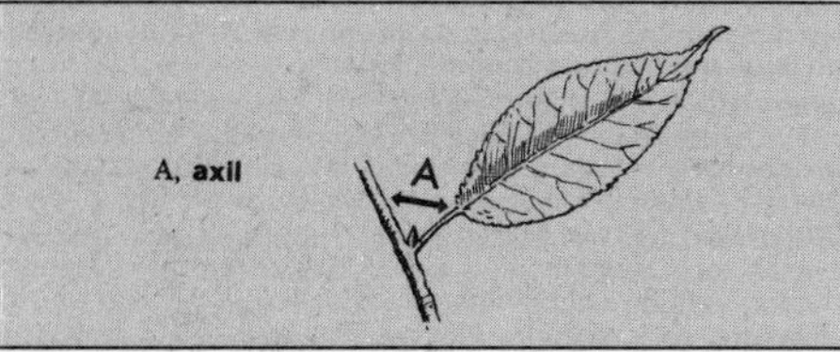

A, axil

ax·ile (ak′sil), *adj. Bot.* in or of an axis. [1835–45; < L *ax(is)* AXIS[1] + -ILE]

ax·i·lem·ma (ak′sə lem′ə), *n., pl.* **-lem·ma·ta** (-lem′ə tə). *Anat.* the membrane surrounding the axon of a nerve fiber. [AXI- + LEMMA[2]]

ax·il·la (ak sil′ə), *n., pl.* **ax·il·lae** (ak sil′ē). **1.** *Anat.* the armpit. **2.** *Ornith.* the corresponding region under the wing of a bird. **3.** *Bot.* an axil. [1610–20; < L]

ax·il·lar (ak′sə lər), *n. Ornith.* an axillary feather. [1535–45; AXILL(A) + -AR[1]]

ax·il·lar·y (ak′sə ler′ē), *adj., n., pl.* **-lar·ies.** —*adj.* **1.** *Anat., Ornith.* pertaining to the axilla. **2.** *Bot.* pertaining to or growing from the axil. —*n.* **3.** *Ornith.* axillar. [1605–15; AXILL(A) + -ARY]

ax′illary bud′, *Bot.* a bud that is borne at the axil of a leaf and is capable of developing into a branch shoot or flower cluster. Also called **lateral bud.** See illus. under **axil.**

ax·i·nite (ak′sə nit′), *n.* a mineral, complex calcium and aluminum borosilicate, usually occurring in thin brown crystals. [1795–1805; < Gk *axín(ē)* AX + -ITE[1]]

ax′iolog′ical eth′ics, the branch of ethics dealing primarily with the relative goodness or value of the motives and end of any action. Cf. **deontological ethics.** [AXIOLOG(Y) + -ICAL]

ax·i·ol·o·gy (ak′sē ol′ə jē), *n.* the branch of philosophy dealing with values, as those of ethics, aesthetics, or religion. [1905–10; < F *axiologie* < Gk *axí(a)* worth, value + *-ologie;* see -O-, -LOGY] —**ax·i·o·log·i·cal** (ak′sē ə loj′i kəl), *adj.* —**ax′i·o·log′i·cal·ly,** *adv.* —**ax′i·ol′o·gist,** *n.*

ax·i·om (ak′sē əm), *n.* **1.** a self-evident truth that requires no proof. **2.** a universally accepted principle or rule. **3.** *Logic, Math.* a proposition that is assumed without proof for the sake of studying the consequences that follow from it. [1475–85; < L *axiōma* < Gk: something worthy, equiv. to *axiō-,* var. s. of *axioûn* to reckon worthy + *-ma* resultative n. suffix]

ax·i·o·mat·ic (ak′sē ə mat′ik), *adj.* **1.** pertaining to or of the nature of an axiom; self-evident; obvious. **2.** aphoristic. Also, **ax′i·o·mat′i·cal.** [1790–1800; < Gk *axiōmatikós,* equiv. to *axiōmat-* (s. of *axíōma* AXIOM) + *-ikos* -IC] —**ax′i·o·mat′i·cal·ly,** *adv.*

ax′iom of choice′, *Math.* the axiom of set theory that given any collection of disjoint sets, a set can be so constructed that it contains one element from each of the given sets. Also called **Zermelo's axiom;** *esp. Brit.,* **multiplicative axiom.**

ax′iom of countabil′ity, *Math.* the property satisfied by a topological space in which the neighborhood system of each point has a base consisting of a countable number of neighborhoods **(first axiom of countability)** or the property satisfied by a topological space that has a base for its topology consisting of a countable number of subsets of the space **(second axiom of countability).**

ax·i·on (ak′sē on′), *n. Physics.* a hypothetical particle having no charge, zero spin, and small mass: postulated in some forms of quantum chromodynamics. [1978; perh. *axi(al current)* + -ON[1]]

ax·is[1] (ak′sis), *n., pl.* **ax·es** (ak′sēz). **1.** the line about which a rotating body, such as the earth, turns. **2.** *Math.* **a.** a central line that bisects a two-dimensional body or figure. **b.** a line about which a three-dimensional body or figure is symmetrical. **3.** *Anat.* **a.** a central or principal structure, about which something turns or is arranged: *the skeletal axis.* **b.** the second cervical vertebra. **4.** *Bot.* the longitudinal support on which organs or parts are arranged; the stem and root; the central line of any body. **5.** *Analytic Geom.* any line used as a fixed reference in conjunction with one or more other references for determining the position of a point or of a series of points forming a curve or a surface. Cf. **x-axis, y-axis. 6.** *Crystall.* See **crystallographic axis. 7.** *Aeron.* any one of three lines defining the attitude of an airplane, one being generally determined by the direction of forward motion and the other two at right angles to it and to each other. **8.** *Fine Arts.* an imaginary line, in a given formal structure, about which a form, area, or plane is organized. **9.** an alliance of two or more nations to coordinate their foreign and military policies, and to draw in with them a group of dependent or supporting powers. **10. the Axis,** (in World War II) Germany, Italy, and Japan, often with Bulgaria, Hungary, and Rumania. **11.** a principal line of development, movement, direction, etc. [1540–50; < L *axis* an axletree, axle, axis. See AXI-] —**ax·ised** (ak′sist), *adj.*

ax·is[2] (ak′sis), *n., pl.* **ax·is·es.** See **axis deer.** [1595–1605; < L *axis* a wild animal of India (Pliny)]

ax′is deer′, an Asian deer, *Cervus (Axis) axis,* of India and Sri Lanka, having a reddish-brown coat spotted with white. Also called **axis, chital, spotted deer.**

ax′is of abscis′sas, *Math.* x-axis (def. 1).

ax′is of or′dinates, *Math.* y-axis (def. 1).

ax′is of revolu′tion, *Math.* an axis in a plane, about which an area is revolved to form a solid of revolution.

ax′is of sym′metry, 1. *Math.* a straight line for which every point on a given curve has corresponding to it another point such that the line connecting the two points is bisected by the given line. **2.** *Crystall.* See **rotation axis.** [1875–80]

ax·i·sym·met·ric (ak′sē si me′trik), *adj.* symmetric about an axis. [1890–95; AXI- + SYMMETRIC] —**ax′i·sym·met′ri·cal·ly,** *adv.*

ax′ job′. *Informal.* See **hatchet job.** [‡1975–1980]

ax·le (ak′səl), *n.* **1.** *Mach.* the pin, bar, shaft, or the like, on which or by means of which a wheel or pair of wheels rotates. **2.** the spindle at either end of an axletree. **3.** an axletree. [bef. 900; ME *axel,* OE *eaxl* shoulder, crossbeam (in *eaxle-gespann*); c. OFris *ax(e)le,* OS *ahsla,* OHG *ahsala* shoulder (G *Achsel*), ON *ǫxl,* L *āla* (< deriv. of **akslā*)] —**ax′led,** *adj.*

ax·le·tree (ak′səl trē′), *n.* a bar, fixed crosswise under an animal-drawn vehicle, with a rounded spindle at each end upon which a wheel rotates. [1250–1300; ME; see AXLE, TREE]

ax·man (aks′mən), *n., pl.* **-men. 1.** a person who wields an ax. **2.** *Informal.* See **hatchet man.** [1665–75 *Amer.;* AX + -MAN]

Ax′min·ster car′pet (aks′min′stər), a machine-made carpet having a cut pile and an intricate design of many colors. [1810–20; named after town in SW England where manufactured]

axo-, var. of **axi-,** esp. before a consonant.

ax·o·lotl (ak′sə lot′l), *n.* any of several salamanders of the genus *Ambystoma* that inhabit lakes and ponds of Mexico and remain in the larval stage as sexually mature adults. [1780–90; < Nahuatl *āxōlōtl,* equiv. to *ā(tl)* water + *xōlōtl* page, male servant]

axolotl,
Ambystoma mexicanum,
length 6 to 12 in.
(15 to 30 cm)

ax·on (ak′son), *n. Cell Biol.* the appendage of the neuron that transmits impulses away from the cell body. Also, **ax·one** (ak′sōn). See diag. under **neuron.** [1835–45; < NL < Gk *áxōn* an axle, axis; c. L *axis*] —**ax·on·al** (ak′sə nl, -son′l), *adj.*

ax·o·neme (ak′sə nēm′), *n. Cell Biol.* the shaft within a flagellum or cilium, containing twenty microtubules arranged as nine doublets and two singlets. Cf. **nine plus two array.** [1900–05; AXO- + *-neme* < Gk *nêma* thread]

ax·o·no·met·ric (ak′sə nō me′trik, -nə-), *adj. Drafting.* designating a method of projection **(ax′onomet′ric projec′tion)** in which a three-dimensional object is represented by a drawing **(ax′onomet′ric draw′ing)** having all axes drawn to exact scale, resulting in the optical distortion of diagonals and curves. Cf. **cabinet** (def. 19), **isometric** (def. 5), **oblique** (def. 13). See illus. under **isometric.** [1905–10; < Gk *áxōn* (see AXON) + -O- + -METRIC]

ax·o·plasm (ak′sə plaz′əm), *n. Cell Biol.* cytoplasm within an axon. [1895–1900; AXO- (as comb. form of AXON) + PLASM] —**ax′o·plas′mic,** *adj.*

ax·seed (aks′sēd′), *n.* See **crown vetch.** [1555–65; AX + SEED]

Ax·um (äk′so͞om), *n.* Aksum.

ay[1] (ā), *adv. Archaic.* ever; always. Also, **aye.** [1150–1200; ME *ei, ai* < Scand; cf. ON *ei,* c. OE *ā* ever]

ay[2] (ā), *interj. Archaic.* (used to express regret or sorrow.) [1300–50; ME]

ay[3] (ī), *adv., n.* aye[1].

A·ya·cu·cho (ä′yä ko͞o′chô), *n.* a city in SW Peru: decisive victory of Bolívar over Spanish troops 1824. 27,900.

a·yah (ä′yə), *n.* (in India) a native maid or nurse. [1775–85; < Hindi *āyā* < Pg *aia* maidservant < L *avia* grandmother, equiv. to *av(us)* grandfather + *-ia* fem. suffix]

a·ya·huas·ca (ä′yə wä′skə), *n.* a woody South American vine, *Banisteriopsis caapi,* of the malpighia family, having bark that is the source of harmine, a hallucinogenic alkaloid used by Amazon Indians. [< AmerSp; further orig. uncert.]

A·ya·na (ə yä′nə), *n.* a female given name: from an African word meaning "beautiful flower."

A·yan·de (ə yän′dā, ä′yän dā′), *n.* a male given name: from a Yoruba word meaning "we gave praises and he came."

a·ya·tol·lah (ä′yə tō′lə), *n.* (among Shi'ites) a title in the religious hierarchy achieved by scholars who have demonstrated highly advanced knowledge of Islamic law and religion. [1975–80; < Pers < Ar *āyat allāh* sign of God; cf. ALLAH]

Ay·de·lotte (ād′l ot′), *n.* **Frank,** 1880–1956, U.S. educator.

aye[1] (ī), *adv.* **1.** yes. —*n.* **2.** an affirmative vote or voter, esp. in British Parliament, corresponding to yea in U.S. Congress. Also, **ay.** [1570–80; earlier sp. *I,* of uncert. orig.]

aye[2] (ā), *adv.* ay[1].

CONCISE PRONUNCIATION KEY: *act, cāpe, dâre, pärt; set, ēqual; if, īce; ox, ōver, ôrder, oil, bo͝ok, bo͞ot, out; up, ûrge; child; sing; shoe; thin, that;* zh as in *treasure.* ə = *a* as in *alone, e* as in *system, i* as in *easily, o* as in *gallop, u* as in *circus;* ᵊ as in *fire* (fīᵊr), *hour* (ouᵊr). l and n can serve as syllabic consonants, as in *cradle* (krād′l), and *button* (but′n). See the full key inside the front cover.

aye-aye (ī′ī′), *n.* a nocturnal lemur, *Daubentonia madagascariensis,* of Madagascar, feeding on insects and fruit, and having rodentlike incisors and long fingers: an endangered species. [1775–85; < F < Malagasy *aiay,* prob. imit. of its cry]

aye-aye,
Daubentonia madagascariensis, head and body 1⅓ ft. (0.4 m); tail 22 in. (55.9 cm)

Ayer (âr), *n.* **Sir A(lfred) J(ules),** born 1910, English philosopher, teacher, and author.

Ayers′ Rock′ (ârz), a conspicuous red monadnock in central Australia, in the SW Northern Territory: tourist attraction. 1143 ft. (348 m) high.

A·ye·sha (ä′ē shä′), *n.* Aisha.

A.Y.H., American Youth Hostels.

a·yin (ä′yin; *Seph. Heb.* ä′yēn), *n.* **1.** the 16th letter of the Hebrew alphabet. **2.** the voiced pharyngeal constrictive consonant represented by this letter and cognate with Arabic ′ain. [1875–80; < Heb *′ayin* lit., eye]

A·yin·de (ə yin′dā, ä′yin dā′), *n.* a male given name: from a Yoruba word meaning "we gave praises and he came."

Ayles·bur·y (ālz′bə rē, -brē), *n.* one of an English breed of white, domestic ducks. [1850–55; named after *Aylesbury,* England]

Ay·ma·ra (ī′mä rä′), *n., pl.* **-ras,** *(esp. collectively)* **-ra** for 1. **1.** a member of an Indian people living in the mountainous regions around Lake Titicaca in Bolivia and Peru. **2.** the language of the Aymara people. [1855–60] —**Ay′ma·ran′,** *adj.*

Ay·mé (e mā′), *n.* **Mar·cel** (mar sel′), 1902–67, French novelist and short-story writer.

′ayn (īn, ān), *n.* ′ain.

a·yous (ä yo͞os′), *n.* the wood of the obeche. [< F: market name for the timber in Cameroon, presumably < a language of the region]

Ayr (âr), *n.* **1.** a seaport in SW Scotland. 40,000. **2.** Ayrshire (def. 2).

ayre (âr), *n. Music.* air[1] (def. 7d).

Ayr·shire (âr′shēr, -shər), *n.* **1.** one of a Scottish breed of hardy dairy cattle having long, curving horns. **2.** Also called **Ayr.** a historic county in SW Scotland.

ayr′ stone′, (âr), a fine-grained stone used for polishing marble and as a whetstone. Also called **snakestone.** [1855–60; named after AYR]

A·yub Khan (ä yo͞ob′ kän′), **Mohammed,** 1908–74, Pakistani army officer and political leader: president 1958–69.

a·yun·ta·mien·to (ä yo͞on′tä myen′tô), *n., pl.* ***-tos*** (-tôs). *Spanish.* **1.** a municipal government. **2.** a town hall or city hall.

A·yur·ve·da (ä′yər vā′də, -vē′-), *n.* the ancient Hindu art of medicine and of prolonging life. [< Skt, equiv. to *āyur-* life, vital power + *veda* knowledge] —**A′yur·ve′dic,** *adj.*

A·yu·the·a (ä yo͞o′thē ä′, -thē ə; *Thai.* ä yo͞o′tē ä), *n.* a city in central Thailand, on the Chao Phraya: former national capital. 40,000. Also, **A·yudh·ya** (ä yo͞od′yä), **A·yut·tha·ya** (ä yo͞o′tä yä).

AZ, Arizona (approved esp. for use with zip code).

az-, var. of **azo-,** esp. before a vowel: *azine.*

az., **1.** azimuth. **2.** azure.

a·zal·ea (ə zāl′yə), *n.* any of numerous shrubs belonging to a particular group (Azalea) of the genus *Rhododendron,* of the heath family, comprising species with handsome flower clusters of various colors, some of which are familiar in cultivation: the group was formerly the botanical genus *Azalea* but is now a horticultural classification. [1750–60; < NL < Gk *azaléa,* n. use of fem. of *azaléos* dry; so named because it grows in dry soil]

a·zan (ä zän′), *n.* (in Islamic countries) the call to prayer proclaimed five times a day by the muezzin. [1850–55; < Ar *adhān* invitation. See MUEZZIN]

A·za·ña (ä sä′nyä, ä thä′-), *n.* **Ma·nuel** (mä nwel′), *(Manuel Azaña y Diez),* 1880–1940, Spanish statesman: prime minister 1931–33, 1936; president 1936–39.

A·zan·de (ə zan′dē), *n., pl.* **-des,** *(esp. collectively)* **-de** for 1. **1.** a member of a people of the Congo-Sudan region of central Africa. **2.** the Adamawa-Eastern language spoken by the Azande. Also called **Zande.**

A·za·ni·a (ə zā′nē ə, ə zān′yə), *n.* the indigenous name applied to South Africa by indigenous black nationalists or liberationists. —**A·za′ni·an,** *n., adj.*

Az·a·ri·ah (az′ə rī′ə), *n.* Uzziah. II Kings 15:1–7.

az·a·thi·o·prine (az′ə thī′ə prēn′), *n. Pharm.* a cytotoxic purine analog, $C_9H_7N_7O_2S$, used as an immunosuppressive in organ transplantations and in rheumatoid arthritis and connective tissue disorders. [1960–65; coinage appar. based on *imidazol,* THIO-, and PURINE, parts of the chemical name]

A·za·zel (ə zā′zəl, az′ə zel′), *n.* **1.** the demon or place in the wilderness to which the scapegoat is released in an atonement ritual. Lev. 16:8, 10, 26. **2.** the scapegoat itself. [< Heb *′ăzāzēl*]

Az·ca·po·tzal·co (äs′kä pô tsäl′kô), *n.* a city in central Mexico: suburb of Mexico City; a cultural center during the pre-Columbian period. 545,513.

a·zed·a·rach (ə zed′ə rak′), *n.* chinaberry. [1745–55; < NL < F *azédarac* << Pers *āzād dirakht* noble tree]

A·ze·glio (ä ze′lyô), *n.* **Mas·si·mo Ta·pa·rel·li** (mäs′sē mô′ tä′pä rel′lē), **Marchese d′,** 1798–1866, Italian statesman and author.

a·ze·o·trope (ə zē′ə trōp′, ā′zē-), *n. Physical Chem.* any liquid mixture having constant minimum and maximum boiling points and distilling off without decomposition and in a fixed ratio, as isopropyl alcohol and water. [1910–15; A-[6] + Gk *zé(ein)* to boil + -O- + -TROPE] —**a·ze·o·trop·ic** (ā′zē ə trop′ik, -trō′pik), *adj.* —**a·ze·ot·ro·py** (ā′zē o′trə pē), **a′ze·ot′ro·pism,** *n.*

Az·er·bai·jan (ä′zər bī jän′, az′ər bī jan′; *Russ.* u zyir bī jän′), *n.* **1.** Also, **Az′er·bai·dzhan′.** Formerly, **Azerbaijan′ So′viet So′cialist Repub′lic.** a republic in Transcaucasia, N of Iran and W of the Caspian Sea. 7,029,000; 33,430 sq. mi. (86,600 sq. km). *Cap.:* Baku. **2.** a region of NW Iran, divided into two provinces in 1938: East Azerbaijan (4,114,084; *Cap.:* Tabriz) and West Azerbaijan (1,971,677; *Cap.:* Orumiyeh).

A·zer·bai·ja·ni (ä′zər bī jä′nē, az′ər bī jan′ē), *n., pl.* **-ja·nis,** *(esp. collectively)* **-ja·ni** for 1, 2. **1.** a native or inhabitant of Azerbaijan. **2.** a member of an Azerbaijani-speaking people of Azerbaijan and of the Iranian provinces of Azerbaijan. **3.** the Turkic language of the Azerbaijani, written with Cyrillic letters in Azerbaijan and with Arabic letters in Iran. Also, **A′zer·bai·ja′ni·an.** [1885–90; AZERBAIJAN + *-i* suffix of membership]

az·ide (az′īd, -id, ā′zīd, ā′zid), *n. Chem.* any compound containing the azido group, as sodium azide, NaN_3. [AZ- + -IDE]

az·i·do (az′i dō′), *adj. Chem.* containing the azido group. [1905–10; AZIDE + -O-]

az′ido group′, *Chem.* the univalent group N_3-, derived from hydrazoic acid. Also called **az′ido rad′ical.**

a·zi·do·thy·mi·dine (ə zī′dō thī′mi dēn′, -zē′-, az′i-), *n. Pharm.* See **AZT.** [AZIDO + THYMIDINE]

A·zi·ki·we (ä′zē kē′wā), *n.* **Nnam·di** (näm′dē), *("Zik"),* born 1904, Nigerian statesman: president 1963–66.

A·zil·ian (ə zēl′yən, -ē ən, ə zil′-), *adj.* of, pertaining to, or characteristic of an early Mesolithic culture of southern France and northern Spain. [1895–1900; named after Mas d′*Azil,* village in Ariège, S France, near where remains of the culture were found; see -IAN]

az·i·muth (az′ə məth), *n.* **1.** *Astron., Navig.* the arc of the horizon measured clockwise from the south point, in astronomy, or from the north point, in navigation, to the point where a vertical circle through a given heavenly body intersects the horizon. **2.** *Survey., Gunnery.* the angle of horizontal deviation, measured clockwise, of a bearing from a standard direction, as from north or south. [1350–1400; ME *azimut* < MF << Ar *as sumūt* the ways (i.e., directions)] —**az·i·muth·al** (az′ə muth′əl), *adj.* —**az′i·muth′al·ly,** *adv.*

azimuth′al equidis′tant projec′tion, *Cartog.* a projection in which the shortest distance between any point and a central point is a straight line, such a line representing a great circle through the central point. [1940–45]

azimuth′al quan′tum num′ber, *Physics.* the quantum number that designates the orbital angular momentum of a particular quantum state of an electron in an atom and that assumes integral values from zero to one less than the value of the principal quantum number. Also called **orbital quantum number.**

az′imuth bar′, a device used in measuring azimuths, consisting of a bar with a sighting vane at each end, pivoted at its center, and rotating in a horizontal plane around the center of a compass.

az′imuth cir′cle, a device for measuring azimuths, consisting of a graduated ring equipped with a sighting vane on each side, which fits concentrically over a compass. [1585–95]

az·ine (az′ēn, -in, ā′zēn, ā′zin), *n. Chem.* any of a group of six-membered heterocyclic compounds containing one or more nitrogen atoms in the ring, the number of nitrogen atoms present being indicated by a prefix, as in diazine or triazine. [1885–90; AZ- + -INE[2]]

az′ine dye′, *Chem.* any of various dyes derived from phenazine, used chiefly for dyeing wood, leather, and textiles. [1890–95]

az·lon (az′lon), *n. Chem.* any of the class of textile fibers derived from such proteins as casein or zein. [AZ- + *-lon,* modeled on NYLON]

az·o (az′ō, ā′zō), *adj. Chem.* containing the azo group. [1875–80; independent use of AZO-]

azo-, a combining form used in the formation of compound words, esp. names of chemical compounds containing nitrogen or the azo group: *azobenzene.* Also, *esp. before a vowel,* **az-.** [< Gk *ázō(os)* without life, equiv. to *a-* A-[6] + *zō-* ZO-]

az·o·ben·zene (az′ō ben′zēn, -ben zēn′, ā′zō-), *n. Chem.* an orange-red, crystalline, water-insoluble powder, $C_{12}H_{10}N_2$, obtained from nitrobenzene by reduction: used chiefly in the manufacture of dyes and as an insecticide. Also called **benzeneazobenzene.** [AZO- + BENZENE]

az′o dye′, *Chem.* any of a large class of dyes containing one or more azo groups. [1880–85]

A·zof (az′ôf, ā′zôf; *Russ.* u zôf′), *n.* **Sea of,** Azov.

az′o group′, *Chem.* the bivalent group −N=N− united to two aromatic groups, as in azobenzene. Also called **azo radical.** [1890–95]

a·zo·ic[1] (ə zō′ik, ā-), *adj. Geol.* (formerly) noting or pertaining to the Precambrian Era, esp. that part formerly believed to precede the first appearance of life; Archean. Cf. **Eozoic.** [1840–50; < Gk *ázō(os)* lifeless (see AZO-) + -IC]

a·zo·ic[2] (a zō′ik), *adj.* of, pertaining to, or characteristic of the azo group. [AZO- + -IC]

azo′ic dye′ (a zō′ik), *Chem.* any of a group of brilliant, long-lasting azo dyes, formed on the fiber by coupling diazotized materials, used chiefly for printing on cotton.

az·o·im·ide (az′ō im′īd, -id, ā′zō-), *n. Chem.* See **hydrazoic acid.** [1890–95; AZO- + IMIDE]

az·ole (az′ōl, ə zōl′), *n. Chem.* any of a group of five-membered heterocyclic compounds containing one or more nitrogen atoms in the ring, the number of nitrogen atoms present being indicated by a prefix, as in diazole. [1895–1900; AZ- + -OLE]

a·zon·al (ā zōn′l), *adj.* **1.** not divided into zones. **2.** (of soil) so young that horizons have not yet developed. [1895–1900; A-[6] + ZONAL]

a·zon·ic (ā zon′ik), *adj.* not confined to any particular zone or region; not local. [1785–95; < Gk *ázōn(os)* not restricted to a ZONE (*a-* A-[6] + *zṓn(ē)* belt + *-os* adj. suffix) + -IC]

az·o·phen·yl·ene (az′ō fen′l ēn′, -fēn′-, ā′zō-), *n. Chem.* phenazine. [AZO- + PHENYLENE]

az′o rad′ical. See **azo group.**

A·zores (ə zôrz′, ə zōrz′, ā′zôrz, ā′zōrz), *n.* (*used with a plural v.*) a group of islands in the N Atlantic, W of Portugal: politically part of Portugal. 336,100; 890 sq. mi. (2305 sq. km). —**A·zo·re·an, A·zo·ri·an** (ə zôr′ē ən, -zōr′-), *adj., n.*

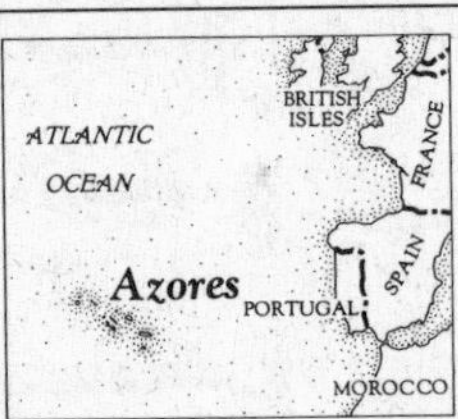

Azores′ high′, *Meteorol.* a subtropical high centered near the Azores.

A·zo·rín (ä′thô rēn′, ä′sô-), *n.* (*José Martínez Ruiz*), 1873–1967, Spanish novelist and critic.

az·ote (az′ōt, ā′zōt, ə zōt′), *n. Chem.* nitrogen. [1785–95; < F < Gk *ázōtos* ungirt, taken to mean lifeless]

az·o·te·mi·a (az′ə tē′mē ə, ā′zə-), *n. Pathol.* the accumulation of abnormally large amounts of nitrogenous waste products in the blood, as in uremic poisoning. [1895–1900; AZOTE + -EMIA] —**az′o·te′mic,** *adj.*

az·oth (az′oth), *n.* **1.** mercury, regarded by alchemists as the assumed first principle of all metals. **2.** the universal remedy of Paracelsus. [1470–80; << Ar *az zā′ūq* the quicksilver]

a·zot·ic (ə zot′ik, ā zot′-), *adj.* of or pertaining to azote; nitric. [1785–95; AZOTE + -IC]

az·o·tize (az′ə tīz′, ā′zə-), *v.t.,* **-tized, -tiz·ing.** to nitrogenize. [1795–1805; AZOTE + -IZE]

a·zo·to·bac·ter (ə zō′tə bak′tər, ā zō′-), *n.* any of several rod-shaped or spherical soil bacteria of the genus *Azotobacter,* important as nitrogen fixers. [1901; < NL; see AZOTE, -O-, -BACTER]

A·zo·tos (ə zō′tos), *n.* Greek name of **Ashdod.**

az·o·tu·ri·a (az′ə to͝or′ē ə, -tyo͝or′-, ā′zə-), *n.* **1.** an elevated level of nitrogenous compounds in the urine. **2.** *Vet. Pathol.* Also called **Monday morning disease.** a disease of horses, esp. draft horses returning to work after several days of inactivity and heavy feeding, characterized by muscle stiffness, paralysis, excessive sweating, and excretion of dark urine. [1830–40; AZOTE + -URIA]

A·zov (az′ôf, ā′zôf; *Russ.* u zôf′), *n.* **Sea of,** a northern arm of the Black Sea connected with the Black Sea by Kerch Strait. ab. 14,500 sq. mi. (37,555 sq. km). See map under **Black Sea.** Also, **Azof.** Russian, **A·zov·sko·ye Mo·re** (u zôf′skə yə mô′ryə).

Az·ra·el (az′rē əl, -rā-), *n.* (in Jewish and Islamic angelology) the angel who separates the soul from the body at the moment of death. Also called **Angel of Death, death angel.**

AZT, *n. Pharm., Trademark.* azidothymidine: an antiviral drug, manufactured from genetic materials in fish sperm or produced synthetically, used in the treatment of AIDS.

CONCISE ETYMOLOGY KEY: <, descended or borrowed from; >, whence; b., blend of, blended; c., cognate with; cf., compare; deriv., derivative; equiv., equivalent; imit., imitative; obl., oblique; r., replacing; s., stem; sp., spelling, spelled; resp., respelling, respelled; trans., translation; ?, origin unknown; *, unattested; ‡, probably earlier than. See the full key inside the front cover.

Az•tec (az′tek), *n.* **1.** a member of a Nahuatl-speaking state in central Mexico that was conquered by Cortés in 1521. **2.** Also called **classical Nahuatl.** the variety of Nahuatl that served as the medium of Aztec civilization, aboriginally written in a chiefly pictographic script. Cf. **Nahuatl** (def. 2). **3.** the Nahuatl language. [1780–90; < Sp *azteca* < Nahuatl *aztēcah,* pl. of *aztēcatl* person from *Aztlān,* the legendary place of origin of the Aztecs] —**Az′tec•an,** *adj.*

Az′tec lil′y. See **Jacobean lily.**

Az′tec mar′igold. See **African marigold.**

Az′tec two′-step, *Slang.* traveler's diarrhea, esp. as experienced by some visitors to Mexico. [1950–55]

A-Z test. See **Aschheim-Zondek test.**

A•zu•chi-Mo•mo•ya•ma (ä′zo͞o chē′mô′mô yä′mä), *n.* a period of Japanese art, 1568–1600, characterized by construction of imposing, elegant castles and small, unadorned teahouses, lavish decorative arts, and bright-colored painting. [after the locations of castles built by two dominant warlords of the period, Oda Nobunaga and Toyotomi Hideyoshi]

A•zue•la (ä swā′lə; *Sp.* ä swe′lä), *n.* **Ma•ria•no** (mä-ryä′nô), 1873–1952, Mexican physician and novelist.

A•zue′ro Penin′sula (ä swâr′ō; *Sp.* ä swe′rô), a peninsula in SW Panama, bordered on the E by the Gulf of Panama.

a•zu′ki bean′ (ə zo͞o′kē). See **adzuki bean.**

a•zu•le•jo (*Sp.* ä′so͞o le′hô, ä′tho͞o-; *Port.* ä′zo͞o le′-zho͝o), *n., pl.* **-jos** (*Sp.* -hôs; *Port.* -zho͝osh). (in Spanish-speaking and Portuguese-speaking countries) a glazed and painted tile used as a wainscot or facing. [1835–45; < Sp: blue tile, deriv. of *azul* blue]

az•ure (azh′ər), *adj.* **1.** of or having a light, purplish shade of blue, like that of a clear and unclouded sky. **2.** *Heraldry.* of the tincture or color blue. —*n.* **3.** the blue of a clear or unclouded sky. **4.** a light, purplish blue. **5.** *Heraldry.* the tincture or color blue. **6.** the clear, cloudless sky. [1275–1325; ME *asure* < AF, OF, ult. alter. of Ar *al lazuwar(d)* (by misdividing the initial *l* together with the article) < Pers *lāzhuward* LAPIS LAZULI]

az•ur•ite (azh′ə rīt′), *n.* **1.** a blue mineral, a hydrous copper carbonate, $Cu_3(CO_3)_2(OH)_2$: an ore of copper. **2.** a gem of moderate value cut from this mineral. [1810–20; AZURE + -ITE[1]]

az•ur•mal•a•chite (azh′ər mal′ə kīt′), *n.* a blue-green ornamental stone consisting of a mixture of azurite and malachite. [AZUR(ITE) + MALACHITE]

A•zu•sa (ə zo͞o′sə), *n.* a city in SW California, near Los Angeles. 29,380.

a•zy•go•spore (ā zī′gə spôr′, -spōr′), *n. Bot., Mycol.* a reproductive cell formed without the fusion of gametes, as in certain algae and fungi. [1885–90; AZYGO(US) + -SPORE]

az•y•gous (az′ə gəs, ā zī′-), *adj. Biol.* not being one of a pair; single. [1640–50; < Gk *ázygos,* equiv. to *a-* A-[6] + *zygós,* deriv. of *zygón* YOKE]

az•yme (az′īm), *n. Western Ch.* unleavened bread used in a Eucharistic service. [1350–1400; < LL *azȳma* (n.), L *azȳmus* (adj.) unleavened < Gk *ázȳmos,* equiv. to *a-* A-[6] + *-zȳmos* (deriv. of *zȳmē* leavening; see ZYME)]

Az-Zar•qa (az zär′kə), *n.* Zarqa.

CONCISE PRONUNCIATION KEY: *act, cāpe, dâre, pärt; set, ēqual; if, īce; ox, ōver, ôrder, oil, bo͝ok, bo͞ot, out; up, ûrge; child; sing; shoe; thin, that;* zh as in *treasure.* ə = *a* as in *alone, e* as in *system, i* as in *easily, o* as in *gallop, u* as in *circus;* ᵊ as in *fire* (fīᵊr), *hour* (ouᵊr). l and n can serve as syllabic consonants, as in *cradle* (krād′l), and *button* (but′n). See the full key inside the front cover.

DEVELOPMENT OF MAJUSCULE								
NORTH SEMITIC	GREEK		ETR.	LATIN		MODERN		
						GOTHIC	ITALIC	ROMAN

B

DEVELOPMENT OF MINUSCULE					
ROMAN CURSIVE	ROMAN UNCIAL	CAROL. MIN	MODERN		
			GOTHIC	ITALIC	ROMAN

The second letter of the English alphabet developed from North Semitic *beth* through Greek *beta* (β, B). The capital (B) goes back to North Semitic *beth* and particularly to Greek B, retained in the Latin monumental script. The minuscule (b) derives from cursive ß, formed by eliminating the upper loop.

B, b (bē), *n., pl.* **B's** or **Bs, b's** or **bs. 1.** the second letter of the English alphabet, a consonant. **2.** any spoken sound represented by the letter *B* or *b,* as in *bid, bauble,* or *daubed.* **3.** something having the shape of a B. **4.** a written or printed representation of the letter *B* or *b.* **5.** a device,.as a printer's type, for reproducing the letter *B* or *b.*

B, 1. *Chess.* bishop. **2.** black. **3.** *Photog.* bulb (def. 8).

B, *Symbol.* **1.** the second in order or in a series. **2.** (*sometimes l.c.*) (in some grading systems) a grade or mark, as in school or college, indicating the quality of a student's work as good or better than average. **3.** (*sometimes l.c.*) (in some school systems) a symbol designating the second semester of a school year. **4.** *Physiol.* a major blood group usually enabling a person whose blood is of this type to donate blood to persons of type B or AB and to receive blood from persons of type O or B. Cf. **ABO system. 5.** *Music.* **a.** the seventh tone in the scale of C major or the second tone in the relative minor scale, A minor. **b.** a string, key, or pipe tuned to this tone. **c.** a written or printed note representing this tone. **d.** (in the fixed system of solmization) the seventh tone of the scale of C major, called *ti.* **e.** the tonality having B as the tonic note. **6.** (*sometimes l.c.*) the medieval Roman numeral for 300. **7.** *Chem.* boron. **8.** a proportional shoe width size, narrower than C and wider than A. **9.** a proportional brassiere cup size, smaller than C and larger than A. **10.** *Physics.* See **magnetic induction. 11.** *Elect.* susceptance. **12.** a designation for a motion picture made on a low budget and meant as the secondary part of a double feature. **13.** a quality rating for a corporate or municipal bond, lower than BB and higher than CCC.

b, 1. *Physics.* **a.** bar; bars. **b.** barn; barns. **2.** black.

B., 1. bachelor. **2.** bacillus. **3.** *Baseball.* base; baseman. **4.** bass. **5.** basso. **6.** bay. **7.** Bible. **8.** bolivar. **9.** boliviano. **10.** book. **11.** born. **12.** breadth. **13.** British. **14.** brother. **15.** brotherhood.

b., 1. bachelor. **2.** bale. **3.** *Baseball.* base; baseman. **4.** bass. **5.** basso. **6.** bay. **7.** billion. **8.** blend of; blended. **9.** book. **10.** born. **11.** breadth. **12.** brother. **13.** brotherhood.

B-, *U.S. Mil.* (in designations of aircraft) bomber: *B-29.*

B-1 (bē′wun′), *n., pl.* **B-1's.** a U.S. long-range bomber, having sweptback wings and a subsonic cruising speed. [1970–75]

B-17 (bē′sev′ən tēn′), *n., pl.* **B-17's.** See **Flying Fortress.** [1940–45]

B-29 (bē′twen′tē nīn′), *n., pl.* **B-29's.** Superfortress. [1940–45]

ba (bä), *n. Egyptian Religion.* an aspect of the soul, represented as a human-headed bird. [vocalization of Egyptian *b'*]

bā (bä), *n.* the second letter of the Arabic alphabet.

BA, See **bank acceptance.**

Ba, *Symbol, Chem.* barium.

ba., 1. bath. **2.** bathroom.

B.A., 1. Bachelor of Arts. [1755–65; < NL *Baccalaureus Artium*] **2.** bastard amber. **3.** batting average. **4.** British Academy. **5.** British America. **6.** British Association (for Advancement of Science). **7.** Buenos Aires.

baa (ba, bä), *v.,* **baaed, baa·ing,** *n.* —*v.i.* **1.** to make the sound of a sheep; bleat. —*n.* **2.** the bleating cry of a sheep. [1580–90; imit.]

B.A.A., Bachelor of Applied Arts.

CONCISE ETYMOLOGY KEY: <, descended or borrowed from; >, whence; b., blend of, blended; c., cognate with; cf., compare; deriv., derivative; equiv., equivalent; imit., imitative; obl., oblique; r., replacing; s., stem; sp., spelling, spelled; resp., respelling, respelled; trans., translation; ?, origin unknown; *, unattested; ‡, probably earlier than. See the full key inside the front cover.

B.A.A.E., Bachelor of Aeronautical and Astronautical Engineering.

baal (bäl), *adv. Australian Slang.* no; not. [Austral Pidgin E < Dharuk *bí-al*]

Ba·al (bā′əl, bāl), *n., pl.* **Ba·al·im** (bā′ə lim, bā′lim). **1.** any of numerous local deities among the ancient Semitic peoples, typifying the productive forces of nature and worshiped with much sensuality. **2.** (*sometimes l.c.*) a false god. [< Heb *ba'al* lord] —**Ba′al·ish,** *adj.*

Baal·bek (bäl′bek, bā′əl-, bāl′-), *n.* a town in E Lebanon: ruins of ancient city; Temple of the Sun. 16,000. Ancient Greek name, **Heliopolis.**

Ba·al·ism (bā′ə liz′əm, bā′liz-), *n.* **1.** the worship of Baal. **2.** idolatry. [1615–25; BAAL + -ISM] —**Ba′al·ist, Ba·al·ite** (bā′ə līt′, bā′līt), *n.* —**Ba′al·is′tic, Ba·al·it·i·cal** (bā′ə lit′i kəl, bā lit′-), *adj.*

baal ko·re (*Seph.* bäl kô RE′; *Ashk.* bäl kō′RĀ), *Hebrew.* an official in the synagogue, as a cantor, who reads the weekly portion of the Torah. [*ba'al qōrē* lit., reading master]

Ba′al Mer′o·dach (mer′ə däk′), Marduk.

Baal·shem (bäl shem′), *n.* a person who works miracles by calling upon the name of God, esp. one of the German and Polish Jews of the 16th–19th centuries considered to be saintly and to possess magical powers. Also, **Balshem.** [< Heb *ba'al shem* lit., master of the name]

Baal Shem-Tov (*Ashk. Heb.* bäl′ shem′tōv′, -tōv′; *Seph. Heb.* bäl′ shem′tôv′, -tôv′), (*Israel ben Eliezer*) (*"BeShT"*), c1700–60, Ukrainian teacher and religious leader: founder of the Hasidic movement of Judaism. Also, **Baal′ Shem′-Tob′.**

Ba·ath (bä′äth), *n.* a socialist party of some Arab countries, esp. Iraq and Syria. Also, **Ba'ath, Ba'th.** [< Ar *ba'ath* lit., renaissance] —**Ba′ath·ism,** *n.* —**Ba′·ath·ist,** *n., adj.*

Bāb (bäb), *n.* abbreviated form of Bab ed-Din.

Bab., Babylon; Babylonia.

ba·ba (bä′bə; *Fr.* bA bA′), *n., pl.* **-bas** (-bəz; *Fr.* -bA′). a spongelike cake leavened with yeast and often containing raisins, baked in a small mold and then usually soaked with a rum syrup. [1820–30; < F < Pol: lit., old woman, peasant woman; the cake was introduced into France by the court of the exiled Polish king Stanislaus I]

ba·ba au rhum (bä′bə ō rum′; *Fr.* bA bA ō RÔM′), *pl.* **ba·bas au rhum** (bä′bəz ō rum′; *Fr.* bA bA ō RÔM′). a baba steeped in rum syrup. [1930–35; < F: baba with rum]

ba·ba gha·nouj (ba′bə gə no͞ozh′), *Middle Eastern Cookery.* a salad of cooked eggplant, olive oil, garlic, etc. [of uncert. orig.]

Ba·bar (bä′bər), *n.* Baber.

ba·bas·su (bä′bə so͞o′), *n.* a palm, *Orbignya barbosiana,* of northeastern Brazil, bearing nuts that yield babassu oil. [1920–25; < Pg *babaçú* < Tupi, equiv. to *ybá* fruit + *guasu* large]

babassu′ oil′, a yellow oil expressed or extracted from babassu nuts, used chiefly in the manufacture of soaps and cosmetics and as a cooking oil. [1955–60]

Bab·bage (bab′ij), *n.* **Charles,** 1792–1871, English mathematician: invented the precursor of the modern computer.

Bab·bit·ry (bab′i trē), *n.* (*often l.c.*) Babbittry.

bab·bitt (bab′it), *n.* **1.** See **Babbitt metal. 2.** a bearing or lining of Babbitt metal. —*adj.* **3.** pertaining to or made of Babbitt metal. —*v.t.* **4.** to line, face, or furnish with Babbitt metal. [1900–05; short for BABBITT METAL]

Bab·bitt (bab′it), *n.* **1. Irving,** 1865–1933, U.S. educator and critic. **2. Milton Byron,** born 1916, U.S. composer. **3.** (*italics*) a novel (1922) by Sinclair Lewis. **4.** (*often l.c.*) a self-satisfied person who conforms readily to conventional, middle-class ideas and ideals, esp. of business and material success; Philistine: from the main character in the novel by Sinclair Lewis.

Bab′bitt met′al, *Metall.* **1.** any of various alloys of tin with smaller amounts of antimony and copper, used as an antifriction lining for bearings. **2.** any of various similar alloys. Also, **bab′bitt met′al, bab′bitt.** [1870–75, *Amer.*; named after Isaac *Babbitt* (1799–1862), American inventor]

Bab·bitt·ry (bab′i trē), *n.* (*often l.c.*) the attitude and behavior of a Babbitt. Also, **Babbitry.** [1925–30; BABBITT + -RY]

bab·ble (bab′əl), *v.,* **-bled, -bling,** *n.* —*v.i.* **1.** to utter sounds or words imperfectly, indistinctly, or without meaning. **2.** to talk idly, irrationally, excessively, or foolishly; chatter or prattle. **3.** to make a continuous, murmuring sound. —*v.t.* **4.** to utter in an incoherent, foolish, or meaningless fashion. **5.** to reveal foolishly or thoughtlessly: *to babble a secret.* —*n.* **6.** inarticulate or imperfect speech. **7.** foolish, meaningless, or incoherent speech; prattle. **8.** a murmuring sound or a confusion of sounds. **9.** babbling (def. 2). **10.** *Telecommunications.* a confused mixture of extraneous sounds in a circuit, resulting from cross talk from other channels. Cf. **cross talk** (def. 1). [1200–50; ME *babelen*; c. ON *babbla,* D *babbelen,* G *pappelen*]
—**Syn. 2.** chitchat, gabble, drivel, blather. **3.** murmur, gurgle, burble.

bab·bler (bab′lər), *n.* **1.** a person or thing that babbles. **2.** any of the birds of the family Timaliidae, many of which have a loud, babbling cry. [1520–30; BABBLE + -ER[1]]

bab·bling (bab′ling), *n.* **1.** foolish or meaningless chatter; prattle: *the constant babbling of idle gossips.* **2.** the random production of meaningless vocal sounds characteristic of infants after about the sixth week. —*adj.* **3.** chattering or prattling aimlessly. [1200–50; ME; see BABBLE, -ING[1], -ING[2]] —**bab′bling·ly,** *adv.*

Bab′cock test′ (bab′kok′), a test for determining the butterfat content of milk and milk products, conducted by adding sulfuric acid to a sample and then centrifuging it in a flask with a calibrated neck in which the liquefied fat collects. [named after Stephen M. *Babcock* (1843–1931), U.S. agricultural chemist]

babe (bāb), *n.* **1.** a baby or child. **2.** an innocent or inexperienced person. **3.** (*usually cap.*) *Southern U.S.* (used, often before the surname, as a familiar name for a boy or man, esp. the youngest of a family.) **4.** *Slang* **a.** *Sometimes Disparaging and Offensive.* a girl or woman, esp. an attractive one. **b.** (*sometimes cap.*) an affectionate or familiar term of address (sometimes offensive when used to strangers, casual acquaintances, subordinates, etc., esp. by a male to a female). **5. babe in the woods,** an innocent, unsuspecting person, esp. one likely to be victimized by others: *Some highly informed people are mere babes in the woods where the stock market is concerned.* Also, **babe in the wood.** [1150–1200; 1915–20 for def. 4; ME; early ME *baban,* prob. nursery word in origin]
—**Syn. 1.** toddler, infant, tot, nursling.

Bab ed-Din (bäb′ ed dēn′), (*the Bab, Ali Muhammad of Shiraz*), 1819–50, a Persian religious leader: founder of Bābī. [< Ar *bāb al-dīn* gate(way) of the faith]

Ba·bel (bā′bəl, bab′əl), *n.* **1.** an ancient city in the land of Shinar in which the building of a tower **(Tower of Babel)** intended to reach heaven was begun and the confusion of the language of the people took place. Gen. 11:4–9. **2.** (*usually l.c.*) a confused mixture of sounds or voices. **3.** (*usually l.c.*) a scene of noise and confusion. [< Heb *Bābhel* Babylon] —**Ba·bel·ic** (bā bel′ik, ba-), *adj.*
—**Syn. 3.** tumult, turmoil, uproar, bedlam, clamor.

Ba·bel (bab′əl; *Russ.* bä′byil), *n.* **I·saak Em·ma·nu·i·lo·vich** (ī′zək; *Russ.* ē säk′ yi mə no͞o yē′lə vyich), 1894–1941, Russian author.

Ba·bel·ism (bā′bə liz′əm, bab′ə-), *n.* (*sometimes l.c.*) a confusion, as of ideas, speech, etc. [1825–35; BABEL + -ISM]

Ba•bel•ize (bā′bə līz′, bab′ə-), *v.t.*, **-ized, -iz•ing.** (*sometimes l.c.*) to make a confusion of (customs, languages, usages, etc.); cause to be mixed or unintelligible; confound. Also, *esp. Brit.*, **Ba′bel•ise′.** [1590–1600; BABEL + -IZE] —**Ba′bel•i•za′tion,** *n.*

Ba•bel•ized (bā′bə līzd′, bab′ə-), *adj.* (*sometimes l.c.*) reduced to complete confusion or meaninglessness. [1590–1600; BABELIZE + -ED[2]]

Bab el Man•deb (bäb′ el män′deb), a strait between NE Africa and the SW tip of the Arabian peninsula, connecting the Red Sea and the Gulf of Aden. 20 mi. (32 km) wide.

Ba•ber (bä′bər), *n.* (*Zahir ed-Din Mohammed*) 1483–1530, founder of the Mogul Empire. Also, **Babar, Babur.**

ba•be•sia (bə bē′zhə, -zhē ə, -zē ə), *n.* any protozoan of the genus *Babesia*, certain species of which are parasitic and pathogenic for warm-blooded animals. [1893; < NL, named after Victor *Babeş* (1854–1926), Rumanian bacteriologist; see -IA]

ba•be•si•o•sis (bə bē′zē ō′sis), *n. Vet. Pathol.* any of several tick-borne diseases of cattle, dogs, horses, sheep, and swine, caused by a babesia protozoan and characterized by fever and languor. Also, **bab•e•si•a•sis** (bab′i sī′ə sis, -zī′-, bā′bə-). Also called **piroplasmosis.** Cf. **tick fever.** [1910–15; < NL; see BABESIA, -OSIS]

Ba•bette (ba bet′), *n.* a female given name, form of **Barbara.**

Ba•beuf (bA bœf′), *n.* **Fran•çois No•ël** (fräN swA′ nō el′), (*Gracchus Babeuf*), 1760–97, French revolutionary. [1840–50]

Bā•bī (bä′bē), *n.* **1.** Also called **Babism.** a Persian religion, originating in the 19th century, now supplanted by Baha'i. **2.** an adherent of Bābī. Also, **Ba′bi.** [1840–50; < Pers, equiv. to *Bāb* (*al-dīn*) BAB ED-DIN + Ar -ī suffix of appurtenance] —**Bab•ite** (bä′bīt), *adj.*

ba•biche (bə bēsh′), *n.* (in the Pacific Northwest) thong, thread, or lacings made of rawhide, gut, or sinew, esp. for making snowshoes. [1800–10; < CanF (*la*) *babiche* < Micmac *a·papi·č* cord, thread, dim. of *a·papi* < Proto-Algonquian **aʔlapa·py*(*i*) (**aʔlapy-* net + *-*a·py-* string)]

ba•bies'-breath (bā′bēz breth′), *n.* baby's-breath.

Ba•bin′ski's re′flex (bə bin′skēz), a reflex extension of the great toe with flexion of the other toes, evoked by stroking the sole of the foot: normal in infants but otherwise denoting central nervous system damage. Also, **Babin′ski re′flex.** Cf. **plantar reflex.** [named after J. F. F. *Babinski* (d. 1932), French neurologist]

bab•i•ru•sa (bab′ə rōō′sə, bä′bə-), *n.* an East Indian swine, *Babyrousa babyrussa*, the male of which has upper canine teeth growing upward through the roof of the mouth and curving toward the eyes, and lower canine teeth growing upward outside the upper jaw. Also, **bab′i•rous′sa, bab′i•rus′sa.** [1690–1700; < Malay, equiv. to *babi* pig + *rusa* deer]

babirusa, *Babyrousa babyrussa,* 2½ ft. (0.8 m) high at shoulder; length 3½ ft. (1.1 m)

Bab•ism (bä′biz əm), *n.* Bābī (def. 1). [1840–50; BAB + -ISM] —**Bab′ist,** *n., adj.*

Ba•bi Yar (bä′bē yär′; *Russ.* bä′byē yär′), a ravine near Kiev, U.S.S.R.: site of German massacre of Jews in World War II.

bab•ka (bäb′kə), *n.* a sweet, spongy yeast cake with raisins, traditionally made in the form of a high cylinder, either solid or with a hole, often glazed, and sometimes flavored with rum. [< Pol, dim. of *baba* BABA]

ba•boo (bä′bōō), *n., pl.* **-boos.** babu.

ba•boon (ba bōōn′ *or, esp. Brit.,* bə-), *n.* **1.** any of various large, terrestrial monkeys of the genus *Papio* and related genera, of Africa and Arabia, having a doglike muzzle, large cheek pouches, and a short tail. **2.** a coarse, ridiculous, or brutish person, esp. one of low intelligence. [1275–1325; ME *baboyne, babewyn* grotesque figure, gargoyle, late ME: baboon (cf. AL *babevynus*) < MF *babouin*, akin to *babine* pendulous lip, deriv. of an expressive base **bab-* grimace] —**ba•boon′ish,** *adj.*

ba•boon•er•y (ba bōō′nə rē *or, esp. Brit.,* bə-), *n., pl.* **-er•ies.** an uncouth, ridiculous, or brutish condition, attitude, or action. [1375–1425; late ME *babwynrie*, equiv. to *bab*(*e*)*wyn* BABOON + *-rie* -ERY]

bab•ra•cot (bab′rə kot′), *n.* a wooden grating used by Indians in South America for roasting and drying food. [of uncert. orig.]

Babs (babz), *n.* a female given name, form of **Barbara.**

Bab•son (bab′sən), *n.* **Roger Ward,** 1875–1967, U.S. statistician and businessman.

ba•bu (bä′bōō), *n.* **1.** a Hindu title of address equivalent to Sir, Mr., or Esquire. **2.** a Hindu gentleman. **3.** a native Indian clerk who writes English. **4.** *Usually Disparaging.* any native Indian having only a limited knowledge of English. Also, **baboo.** [1875–80; < Hindi *bābū*]

ba•bul (bə bōōl′, bä′bōōl), *n.* **1.** any of several leguminous trees of the genus *Acacia* that yield a gum, esp. *A. nilotica*, of tropical Africa. **2.** the gum, pods, or bark of such a tree. [1815–25; < Hindi *babūl* < Pers]

Ba•bur (bä′bər), *n.* Baber.

ba•bush•ka (bə bōōsh′kə, -bōōsh′-), *n.* **1.** a woman's scarf, often triangular, used as a hood with two of the ends tied under the chin. **2.** an elderly Russian woman, esp. an elderly grandmother. [1935–40; < Russ *bábushka* grandmother, equiv. to *báb*(*a*) old woman + *-ushka* dim. suffix]

Ba•bu•yan′ Is′lands (bä′bōō yän′), a group of islands in the Philippines, N of Luzon. 225 sq. mi. (580 sq. km).

ba•by (bā′bē), *n., pl.* **-bies,** *adj., v.,* **-bied, -by•ing.** —*n.* **1.** an infant or very young child. **2.** a newborn or very young animal. **3.** the youngest member of a family, group, etc. **4.** an immature or childish person. **5.** *Informal.* **a.** *Sometimes Disparaging and Offensive.* a girl or woman, esp. an attractive one. **b.** a person of whom one is deeply fond; sweetheart. **c.** (*sometimes cap.*) an affectionate or familiar address (sometimes offensive when used to strangers, casual acquaintances, subordinates, etc., esp. by a male to a female). **d.** a man or boy; chap; fellow: *He's a tough baby to have to deal with.* **e.** an invention, creation, project, or the like that requires one's special attention or expertise or of which one is especially proud. **f.** an object; thing: *Is that car there your baby?* —*adj.* **6.** of or suitable for a baby: *baby clothes.* **7.** of or like a baby; infantile: *baby skin.* **8.** small; comparatively little: *a baby car.* **9.** treating babies: *a baby doctor.* —*v.t.* **10.** to treat like a young child; pamper. **11.** to handle or use with special care; treat gently. [1350–1400; ME; see BABE, -Y[2]] —**ba′by•hood′,** *n.* —**ba′by•ish,** *adj.* —**ba′by•ish•ly,** *adv.* —**ba′by•ish•ness,** *n.* —**ba′by•like′,** *adj.*
—**Syn. 10.** indulge, spoil, humor, coddle.

ba′by beef′, 1. a young beef animal that has been fattened for marketing when 12 to 20 months old. **2.** the meat of a baby beef. [1885–90, *Amer.*]

Ba′by Bell′, one of the seven telephone companies formed after the breakup of the Bell system in 1983. [1985–90]

ba′by blue′, 1. a very light blue. **2. baby blues,** *Informal.* a person's blue eyes: *His charm lies largely in the way he bats his baby blues.* [1885–90, *Amer.*] —**ba′by-blue′,** *adj.*

ba•by-blue-eyes (bā′bē blōō′īz′), *n., pl.* **-eyes.** (*used with a singular or plural v.*) any of several plants of the genus *Nemophila*, of western North America, esp. *N. menziesii*, a low-growing plant having blue, white-centered flowers. [1885–90, *Amer.*; so called from fancied resemblance of its spots to eyes]

ba′by book′, an album for mounting pictures and other memorabilia of a baby and for keeping a record of its growth from infancy.

ba′by boom′, a period of sharp increase in the birthrate, as that in the U.S. following World War II. [1950–55]

ba′by boom′er, a person born during a baby boom, esp. one born in the U.S. between 1946 and 1965. [1970–75; BABY BOOM + -ER[1]]

ba′by car′riage, a conveyance similar to an infant's crib set on four wheels and meant to be pushed. Also called **ba′by bug′gy, carriage.** [1865–70]

ba′by coach′, *Chiefly Eastern Pennsylvania and Chesapeake Bay.* a baby carriage.

ba′by doll′, 1. a doll, esp. one resembling a human baby. **2.** Often, **baby dolls.** Also called **ba′by doll′ night′gown, ba′by doll′ paja′mas.** a garment for women or girls consisting of a hip-length top of delicate fabric often decorated with ruffles, ribbons, or lace, with a matching panty, worn for sleeping. **3.** a short dress styled to resemble this. Also, **ba′by•doll′** (for defs. 2, 3). [1860–65]

ba′by face′, 1. a face having a bland babyish or childish appearance, esp. a plump, small-featured face unmarked by characteristic lines. **2.** a person having such a face. [1705–15] —**ba′by-faced′,** *adj.*

ba′by farm′, *Informal.* **1.** a place that houses and takes care of babies for a fee. **2.** a residence for unwed pregnant girls or women that also arranges adoptions. [1865–70] —**ba′by farm′er.** —**ba′by farm′ing.**

ba′by food′, food, as vegetables, fruits, or meat, puréed or minced for easy ingestion by infants. [1895–1900]

ba′by grand′, the smallest form of the grand piano. Also called **ba′by grand′ pian′o.** [1900–05]

Bab•y•lon (bab′ə lən, -lon′), *n.* **1.** an ancient city of SW Asia, on the Euphrates River, famed for its magnificence and culture: capital of Babylonia and later of the Chaldean empire. **2.** any rich and magnificent city believed to be a place of excessive luxury and wickedness. **3.** a city on S Long Island, in SE New York. 12,388.

Bab•y•lo•ni•a (bab′ə lō′nē ə, -lōn′yə), *n.* an ancient empire in SW Asia, in the lower Euphrates valley: its greatest period was 2800–1750 B.C. *Cap.:* Babylon.

Bab•y•lo•ni•an (bab′ə lō′nē ən, -lōn′yən), *adj.* Also, **Babylonish. 1.** of or pertaining to Babylon or Babylonia. **2.** extremely luxurious. **3.** wicked; sinful. —*n.* **4.** an inhabitant of ancient Babylonia. **5.** the dialect of Akkadian spoken in Babylonia. Cf. **Akkadian** (def. 1). [1555–65; BABYLONI(A) + -AN]

Babylo′nian captiv′ity, 1. the period of the exile of the Jews in Babylonia, 597–538 B.C. **2.** the exile of the popes at Avignon, 1309–77.

Bab•y•lon•ish (bab′ə lon′ish, -lō′nish, bab′ə lō′nish, bab′ə lə nish), *adj.* Babylonian. [1525–35; BABYLON(IA) + -ISH[1]]

ba′by prim′rose, a tender primrose, *Primula forbesii*, native to China and Burma, having white, hairy leaves and rose- or lilac-colored flowers with a yellow center.

ba•by•proof (bā′bē prōōf′), *adj., v.t.* childproof. Also, **ba′by-proof′.** [BABY + -PROOF]

ba•by's-breath (bā′bēz breth′), *n.* a tall plant, *Gypsophila paniculata*, of the pink family, having lance-shaped leaves and numerous small, fragrant, white or pink flowers. Also, **babies'-breath.** [1885–90; so called from its delicate odor and bloom]

ba•by-sit (bā′bē sit′), *v.,* **-sat, -sit•ting.** —*v.i.* **1.** to take charge of a child while the parents are temporarily away. —*v.t.* **2.** to baby-sit for (a child): *We've placed an ad for someone to baby-sit the youngsters in the evening.* **3.** to take watchful responsibility for; tend: *It will be necessary for someone to baby-sit the machine until it is running properly.* Also, **ba′by•sit′.** [1945–50] —**ba′by-sit′ter, ba′by•sit′ter,** *n.*

ba′by split′, *Bowling.* a split in which the two and seven pins or the three and ten pins remain standing.

ba′by spot′, a small spotlight, usually 250–400 watts, used to highlight a specific section of a stage setting or acting area. Also called **ba′by spot′light.**

ba•by's-tears (bā′bēz tērz′), *n., pl.* **-tears.** (*used with a singular or plural v.*) a mosslike plant, *Soleirolia* (or *Helxine*) *soleirolii*, of the nettle family, native to Corsica and Sardinia, having small, roundish leaves and minute flowers. Also, **ba′by-tears′.** Also called **mind-your-own-business.**

ba′by step′, (in the game of giant steps) the shortest step permitted a player, executed by placing the heel of one foot against the toe of the other and drawing the back foot up to the front foot. Cf. **umbrella step.**

ba′by talk′, 1. the speech of children learning to talk, marked by syntactic differences from adult speech and by phonetic modifications like lisping, lalling, omission and substitution of sounds, etc. **2.** a style of speech used by adults in addressing children, pets, or sweethearts, and formed in imitation of the voice and pronunciation of children learning to talk: it is generally characterized in English by the addition of diminutive endings to words, the use of special words and pet names, and the systematic distortion of certain words, as *dolly* for *doll*, *teensy-weensy*, *oo* for *you*, *twain* for *train*, etc. [1830–40]

ba′by tooth′. See **milk tooth.**

BAC, blood-alcohol concentration: the percentage of alcohol in the bloodstream: under the laws of most states, a BAC of 0.10 is the legal definition of intoxication, although a few states use a slightly lower percentage, as 0.08.

Ba•ca•bal (bä′kä bôl′), *n.* a city in NE Brazil. 111,753.

ba•ca•lao (bä′kə lou′, bak′ə-; *Sp.* bä′kä lä′ô), *n., pl.* **-laos** (-louz′; *Sp.* -lä′ôs). *Spanish or Spanish-American Cookery.* **1.** codfish, esp. when dried and salted. **2.** a dish of this, cooked with a tomato sauce, olives, garlic, etc. [1545–55; < Sp *bacal*(*l*)*ao*, prob. < Basque *bakailao*, perh., by metathesis, < Gascon, the presumed source of OF *cabellau*, *cabillau* (F *cabillaud*) fresh codfish, equiv. to Gascon *cabilh*, *cabelh* (dim. of *cap* head; see CHIEF) + a suffix, alluding to the fish's prominent head; though ML (Flanders) *cabellauwus*, the earliest attestation of the form (cf. MD *cab*(*b*)*eliau*, D *kabeljauw*) suggests a non-Rom, N European origin]

Ba•car•di (bə kär′dē), **1.** *Trademark.* a brand of dry rum of the West Indies. —*n.* **2.** a cocktail made with Bacardi rum, grenadine, and lime juice.

Ba•că•u (bä kə′ōō; *Eng.* bə kou′), *n.* a city in E Rumania. 141,981.

B.Acc., Bachelor of Accountancy.

bac•ca (bak′ə), *n., pl.* **bac•cae** (bak′ē). *Bot.* a berry. [< L *bacca* olive, any round fruit, berry]

bac•ca•lau•re•ate (bak′ə lôr′ē it, -lor′-), *n.* **1.** See **bachelor's degree. 2.** a religious service held at an educational institution, usually on the Sunday before commencement day. **3.** See **baccalaureate sermon.** [1615–25; < ML *baccalaureātus*, equiv. to *baccalaure*(*us*) advanced student, bachelor (for *baccalārius* (see BACHELOR), alter. by assoc. with L phrase *bacca laureus* laurel berry) + *-ātus* -ATE[1]]

baccalau′reate ser′mon, a farewell sermon addressed to a graduating class in some U.S. colleges and schools. [1860–65]

bac•ca•rat (bak′ə rä′, bak′ə-; bä′kə rä′, bak′ə-; *Fr.* bA kA rA′), *n.* a gambling game at cards played by a banker and two or more punters who bet against the banker. Also, **bac′ca•ra′.** [1865–70; var. of *baccara* < F < ?]

bac•cate (bak′āt), *adj. Bot.* **1.** berrylike. **2.** bearing berries. [1820–30; < L *bāca*, *bacca* berry + -ATE[1]]

Bac•chae (bak′ē), *n.pl. Class. Myth.* **1.** the female attendants of Bacchus. **2.** the priestesses of Bacchus. **3.** the women who took part in the Bacchanalia. [< L < Gk *Bákkhai*, pl. of *Bákkhē* maenad]

bac•cha•nal (*n.* bä′kə näl′, bak′ə nal′, bak′ə nl; *adj.* bak′ə nl), *n.* **1.** a follower of Bacchus. **2.** a drunken reveler. **3.** an occasion of drunken revelry; orgy. —*adj.* **4.** pertaining to Bacchus; bacchanalian. [1530–40; < L *Bacchānāl*, equiv. to *Bacch*(*us*) + *-ānāl*, prob. as back formation from *Bacchānālia*; see BACCHANALIA]
—**Syn. 3.** saturnalia, debauch, spree, carousal.

Bac•cha•na•li•a (bak′ə nā′lē ə, -nāl′yə), *n., pl.* **-li•a, -li•as. 1.** (*sometimes used with a plural v.*) a festival in honor of Bacchus. Cf. **Dionysia. 2.** (*l.c.*) a drunken feast; orgy. [1625–35; < L equiv. to *Bacch*(*us*) + *-ān*(*us*) -AN + *-ālia*, neut. pl. of *-ālis* -AL[1]; prob. modeled on *volcānālia*. See SATURNALIA] —**bac′cha•na′li•an,** *adj., n.*

bac•chant (bak′ənt, bə kant′, -känt′), *n., pl.* **bac•chants, bac•chan•tes** (bə kan′tēz, -kän′-), *adj.* —*n.* **1.** a priest, priestess, or votary of Bacchus; bacchanal. **2.** a drunken reveler. —*adj.* **3.** inclined to revelry. [1690–1700; < L *bacchant-* (s. of *bacchāns*, prp. of *bacchārī* to revel). See BACCHUS, -ANT] —**bac•chan′tic,** *adj.*

bac•chan•te (bə kan′tē, -kän′-, bə kant′, -känt′), *n.*

CONCISE PRONUNCIATION KEY: act, cāpe, dâre, pärt; set, ēqual; *if*, īce; ox, ōver, ôrder, oil, bo͝ok, bo͞ot, out; up, ûrge; child; sing; shoe; thin, *th*at; zh as in *treasure*. ə = *a* as in *alone*, *e* as in *system*, *i* as in *easily*, *o* as in *gallop*, *u* as in *circus*; ᵊ as in *fire* (fīᵊr), *hour* (ouᵊr). l and n can serve as syllabic consonants, as in *cradle* (krād′l), and *button* (but′n). See the full key inside the front cover.

a female bacchant. Also called **maenad, menad, Thyiad.** [1790–1800; back formation from L *bacchantēs*, fem. pl. of *bacchāns* BACCHANT; pron. with silent *-e* < F *bacchante*, fem. of *bacchant* bacchant]

Bac•chic (bak′ik), *adj.* **1.** of, pertaining to, or honoring Bacchus. **2.** (*l.c.*) riotously or jovially intoxicated; drunken. [1660–70; < L *Bacchicus* < Gk *Bakkhikós.* See BACCHUS, -IC]

bac•chi•us (bə kī′əs, ba-), *n., pl.* **-chi•i** (-kī′ī). *Pros.* a foot of three syllables that in quantitative meter consists of one short syllable followed by two long ones, and that in accentual meter consists of one unstressed syllable followed by two stressed ones. Cf. **antibacchius.** [1580–90; < L < Gk *Bakkheîos* (*poús*) (foot) of BACCHUS]

Bac•chus (bak′əs), *n. Class. Myth.* the god of wine; Dionysus. [< L < Gk *Bákkhos*]

Bac•chyl•i•des (bə kil′i dēz′), *n.* fl. 5th century B.C., Greek poet.

bacci-, a combining form meaning "berry," used in the formation of compound words: *baccivorous.* [< L, comb. form of *bacca, bāca*]

bac•cif•er•ous (bak sif′ər əs), *adj. Bot.* bearing or producing berries. [1650–60; < L *baccifer* (see BACCI-, -FER) + -OUS]

bac•civ•or•ous (bak siv′ər əs), *adj.* feeding on berries. [1655–65; BACCI- + -VOROUS]

bac•cy (bak′ē), *n., pl.* **-cies.** *Older Use.* tobacco. [1825–35; by aphesis and alter. of final schwa to folk regional *-y*]

bach (bach), *Informal.* —*v.* **1. bach it,** to live alone or share living quarters with someone of the same sex, usually doing one's own housework, cooking, laundry, etc. —*n.* **2.** a bachelor. **3.** *New Zealand.* a small weekend or vacation house or shack. [1850–55, *Amer.*; by shortening]

Bach (bäKH), *n.* **1. Jo•hann Se•bas•ti•an** (yō′hän si bas′chən; *Ger.* yō′häŋ zä bäs′tē än′), 1685–1750, German organist and composer. **2.** his sons: **Carl Philipp E•ma•nu•el** (kärl fil′ip i man′yo͞o əl; *Ger.* kärl fē′lip ā mä′no͞o el′), 1714–88; **Johann Chris•ti•an** (kris′chən; *Ger.* KRIS′tē än′), 1735–82; **Johann Chris•toph Frie•drich** (kris′tof frē′drik; *Ger.* KRIS′tôf FRĒ′DRIKH), 1732–95; and **Wil•helm Frie•de•mann** (wil′helm frē′də män′; *Ger.* vil′helm FRĒ′də män′), 1710–84, German organists and composers.

bach•e•lor (bach′ə lər, bach′lər), *n.* **1.** an unmarried man. **2.** a person who has been awarded a bachelor's degree. **3.** a fur seal, esp. a young male, kept from the breeding grounds by the older males. **4.** Also called **bachelor-at-arms.** a young knight who followed the banner of another. **5.** Also called **household knight.** a landless knight. [1250–1300; ME *bacheler* < OF < VL **baccalār(is)* farm hand; akin to LL *baccalāria* piece of land, orig. pl. of **baccalārium* dairy farm, equiv. to **baccālis* of cows (*bacca*, var. of L *vacca* cow + *-ālis* -AL[1]) + *-ārium* place] —**bach′e•lor•like′,** *adj.* —**bach′e•lor•ly,** *adj.*

bach•e•lor-at-arms (bach′ə lər ət ärmz′, bach′lər-), *n., pl.* **bach•e•lors-at-arms.** bachelor (def. 4).

bach′elor chest′, *Eng. Furniture.* a low chest of drawers of the 18th century, having a top inclining to form a writing surface.

bach•e•lor•ette (bach′ə lə ret′, bach′lə-), *n.* an unmarried young woman. [1900–05; BACHELOR + -ETTE]
—**Usage.** See **-ette.**

bach′elor girl′, an unmarried woman, esp. a young one, who supports herself and often lives alone. [1890–95]
—**Usage.** See **girl.**

bach•e•lor•hood (bach′ə lər ho͝od′, bach′lər-), *n.* the state of being a bachelor. Also, **bach′e•lor•dom.** [1825–35; BACHELOR + -HOOD]

bach•e•lor•ism (bach′ə lə riz′əm, bach′lə-), *n.* **1.** state of being a bachelor. **2.** a characteristic or peculiarity of a bachelor: *Excessive tidiness had been added to his bachelorisms.* [1800–10, *Amer.*; BACHELOR + -ISM]

Bach′elor of Arts′, 1. a bachelor's degree in the liberal arts, usually awarded for studies in the social sciences or humanities. **2.** a person having this degree. *Abbr.:* A.B., B.A. [1570–80]

Bach′elor of Sci′ence, 1. a bachelor's degree, usually awarded for studies in natural science, pure science, or technology. **2.** a person having this degree. *Abbr.:* B.S., B.Sc., S.B., Sc.B. [1850–55, *Amer.*]

bach′elor par′ty. See **stag party** (def. 2). [1920–25]

bach•e•lor's (bach′ə lərz, bach′lərz), *n. Informal.* See **bachelor's degree.**

bach•e•lor's-but•ton (bach′ə lərz but′n, bach′lərz-), *n.* any of various plants with round flower heads, esp. the cornflower. [1570–80]

bach′elor's degree′, a degree awarded by a college or university to a person who has completed undergraduate studies. Also called **baccalaureate.**

Bach′ trum′pet, a three-valved trumpet designed especially for playing the high, florid trumpet parts in the works of J. S. Bach and other baroque composers. Cf. **clarino.**

bacill-, a combining form of **bacillus:** *bacillary.*

bac•il•lar•y (bas′ə ler′ē, bə sil′ə rē), *adj.* **1.** Also, **ba•cil•li•form** (bə sil′ə fôrm′). of or like a bacillus; rod-shaped. **2.** *Bacteriol.* characterized by bacilli. Also, **ba•cil•lar** (bə sil′ər, bas′ə lər). [1880–85; BACILL- + -ARY]

bac′illary dys′entery, *Pathol.* shigellosis. [1905–10]

CONCISE ETYMOLOGY KEY: <, descended or borrowed from; >, whence; b., blend of, blended; c., cognate with; cf., compare; deriv., derivative; equiv., equivalent; imit., imitative; obl., oblique; r., replacing; s., stem; sp., spelling, spelled; resp., respelling, respelled; trans., translation; ?, origin unknown; *, unattested; ‡, probably earlier than. See the full key inside the front cover.

bac•il•le•mi•a (bas′ə lē′mē ə), *n. Pathol.* the presence of bacilli in the blood. [BACILL- + -EMIA]

bac•il•lu•ri•a (bas′ə lo͝or′ē ə), *n. Pathol.* the presence of bacilli in the urine. [1880–85; BACILL- + -URIA]

ba•cil•lus (bə sil′əs), *n., pl.* **-cil•li** (-sil′ī). **1.** any rod-shaped or cylindrical bacterium of the genus *Bacillus*, comprising spore-producing bacteria. See diag. under **bacteria. 2.** (formerly) any bacterium. [1880–85; < LL, var. of L *bacillum* (dim. of *baculum*) staff, walking stick]

bacil′lus Cal•mette′-Gué•rin′ (kal met′gā RAN′, -ran′), a weakened strain of the tubercle bacillus, *Mycobacterium bovis*, used in the preparation of BCG vaccine. [named after Albert L. C. *Calmette* (1863–1933) and Camille *Guérin* (1872–1961), French bacteriologists]

Bacil′lus thu•rin•gi•en′sis (tho͝o rin′jē en′sis), a bacterium used in genetically altered form in the biological control of budworms, gypsy moth larvae, Japanese beetles, and other insect pests. *Abbr.:* B.t. [< NL (1915): Thuringian bacillus; so named in reference to its discovery in larvae of Mediterranean flour moths from a mill in Thuringia]

bac•i•tra•cin (bas′i trā′sin), *n. Pharm.* an antibiotic polypeptide derived by the hydrolytic action of *Bacillus subtilis* on protein, primarily used topically in the treatment of superficial infections caused by susceptible Gram-positive organisms. [1940–45; BACI(LLUS) + (Margaret) *Trac*(y) (b. 1936), American child whose tissues were found to contain *Bacillus subtilis* + -IN[2]]

back[1] (bak), *n.* **1.** the rear part of the human body, extending from the neck to the lower end of the spine. **2.** the part of the body of animals corresponding to the human back. **3.** the rear portion of any part of the body: *the back of the head.* **4.** the whole body, with reference to clothing: *the clothes on his back.* **5.** ability for labor; effort; endurance: *He put his back into the task.* **6.** the part opposite to or farthest from the front; the rear part: *the back of a hall.* **7.** the part that forms the rear of any object or structure: *the back of a chair.* **8.** the part that covers the back: *the back of a jacket.* **9.** the spine or backbone: *The fall broke his back.* **10.** any rear part of an object serving to support, protect, etc.: *the back of a binder.* **11.** *Naut., Aeron.* the forward side of a propeller blade (opposed to *face*). **12.** *Aeron.* the top part or upper surface of an aircraft, esp. of its fuselage. **13.** *Bookbinding.* the edge of a book formed where its sections are bound together. **14. the backs,** grounds along the River Cam in back of certain colleges at Cambridge University in England: noted for their great beauty. **15.** *Archit.* extrados. **16.** *Carpentry.* **a.** the upper side of a joist, rafter, handrail, etc. **b.** the area of interior wall between a window stool and the floor. **17.** *Mining.* the roof of a stope or drift. **18.** *Sports.* **a.** a player whose regular position is behind that of players who make initial contact with the opposing team, as behind the forward line in football or nearest the player's own goal in polo. **b.** the position occupied by this player. **19. be flat on one's back, a.** to be helpless or beaten: *He's flat on his back after a long succession of failures.* **b.** to be confined to one's bed because of illness. **20. behind one's back,** in one's absence; without one's knowledge; treacherously; secretly: *I'd rather talk to him about it directly than discuss it behind his back.* **21. break someone's back,** to cause a person to fail, esp. to cause to become bankrupt: *His family's extravagance is breaking his back.* **22. break the back of, a.** to complete the principal or hardest part of (a project, one's work, etc.): *He finally broke the back of the problem.* **b.** to overcome; defeat: *They broke the back of our union.* **23. get off one's back,** *Informal.* to cease to find fault with or to disturb someone: *The fight started when they wouldn't get off my back.* **24. get one's back up,** *Informal.* to become annoyed; take offense: *She gets her back up whenever someone mentions her family's influence.* **25. have one's back to the wall,** to be in a difficult or hopeless situation. **26. in back of,** behind: *He hid in back of the billboard. What could be in back of his strange behavior?* Also, **back of. 27. on one's back,** *Informal.* finding fault with or disturbing someone: *The boss is always on my back about promptness.* **28. pat on the back.** See **pat**[1] (defs. 6, 10). **29. stab in the back.** See **stab** (def. 13). **30. turn one's back on, a.** to forsake or neglect: *He was unable to turn his back on any suffering creature.* **b.** to leave behind, as in anger.
—*v.t.* **31.** to support, as with authority, influence, help, or money (often fol. by *up*): *to back a candidate; to back up a theory with facts.* **32.** to bet on: *to back a horse in the race.* **33.** to cause to move backward (often fol. by *up*): *to back a car.* **34.** to furnish with a back: *to back a book.* **35.** to lie at the back of; form a back or background for: *a beach backed by hills.* **36.** to provide with an accompaniment: *a singer backed by piano and bass.* **37.** to get upon the back of; mount. **38.** to write or print on the back of; endorse; countersign. **39.** *Carpentry.* to attach strips of wood to the upper edge of (a joist or rafter) to bring it to a desired level. **40.** *Naut.* **a.** to alter the position of (a sail) so that the wind will strike the forward face. **b.** to brace (yards) in backing a sail. **c.** to reinforce the hold of (an anchor) by means of a smaller one attached to it and dropped farther away.
—*v.i.* **41.** to go or move backward (often fol. by *up*). **42.** *Naut.* (of wind) to change direction counterclockwise (opposed to *veer*). **43. back and fill, a.** *Naut.* to trim the sails of a boat so that the wind strikes them first on the forward and then on the after side. **b.** to change one's opinion or position; vacillate. **44. back and forth,** *South Midland U.S.* **a.** to go back and forth, as in running errands or visiting: *He spent the day backing and forthing to the post office.* **b.** to work in an aimless or ineffective way; expend effort with little result. **45. back away,** to retreat; withdraw: *They gradually began to back away from their earlier opinion.* **46. back down,** to abandon an argument, opinion, or claim; withdraw; retreat: *He backed down as soon as a member of the audience challenged his assertion.* **47. back off, a.** to back down: *Now that the time for action had arrived, it was too late to back off.* **b.** *Textiles.* to reverse (the spindle) in mule spinning prior to winding on the newly spun length of yarn. **48. back out** or **out of,** to fail to keep an engagement or promise; withdraw from; abandon: *Two entrants have backed out of competing in the marathon. You can't back out now.* **49. back up, a.** to bring (a stream of traffic) to a standstill: *A stalled car backed up traffic for miles.* **b.** *Printing.* to print a sheet again on its other side. **c.** *Printing.* to fill in (the thin copper shell of an electrotype) with metal in order to strengthen it. **d.** to move backward: *Back up into the garage.* **e.** to reinforce: *We backed up the cardboard with slats so it wouldn't fall down.* **f.** to support or confirm: *He backed up my story and they let us go.* **g.** *Computers.* to duplicate (a file or a program) as a precaution against failure. **50. back up for,** *Australian Informal.* to return for more of, as another helping of food. **51. back water, a.** *Naut.* to reverse the direction of a vessel. **b.** to retreat from a position; withdraw an opinion: *I predict that the council will back water on the tax issue.*
—*adj.* **52.** situated at or in the rear: *at the back door; back fence.* **53.** far away or removed from the front or main area, position, or rank; remote: *back settlements.* **54.** belonging to the past: *back files; back issues.* **55.** in arrears; overdue: *back pay.* **56.** coming or going back; moving backward: *back current.* **57.** *Navig.* reciprocal (def. 7). **58.** *Phonet.* (of a speech sound) produced with the tongue articulating in the back part of the mouth, as in either of the sounds of *go.* [bef. 1000; ME *bak*, OE *bæc* back of the body; c. OFris *bek*, OS, ON *bak*; perh. < IE **bhogo-* bending; cf. BACON] —**back′less,** *adj.*
—**Syn. 31.** sustain, abet, favor, assist; countenance, endorse. **41.** retire, retreat, withdraw. **52.** BACK, HIND, POSTERIOR, REAR refer to something situated behind something else. BACK means the opposite of front: *back window.* HIND, and the more formal word POSTERIOR, suggest the rearmost of two or more often similar objects: *hind legs; posterior lobe.* REAR is used of buildings, conveyances, etc., and in military language it is the opposite of fore: *rear end of a truck; rear echelon.* —**Ant. 1, 52.** front.
—**Usage. 26.** Although some object to their use, the phrases IN BACK OF and the shorter—and much older—BACK OF with the meaning "behind" are fully established as standard in American English: *The car was parked (in) back of the house.* Both phrases occur in all types of speech and writing.

back[2] (bak), *adv.* **1.** at, to, or toward the rear; backward: *to step back.* **2.** in or toward the past: *to look back on one's youth; They met in Chicago back in 1976.* **3.** at or toward the original starting point, place, or condition: *to go back to the old neighborhood.* **4.** in direct payment or return: *to pay back a loan; to answer back.* **5.** in a state of restraint or retention: *to hold back the tears; to hold back salary.* **6.** in a reclining position: *to lean back; to lie back.* **7. back and forth,** from side to side; to and fro; from one to the other: *The pendulum of the grandfather clock swung back and forth.* **8. back yonder,** *Chiefly South Midland U.S.* formerly; many years ago: *Back yonder, when I was a boy, things were different.* **9. go back on, a.** to be treacherous or faithless to; betray: *to go back on friends.* **b.** to fail to keep; renege on: *to go back on promises.* [1480–90; aph. var. of ABACK]

back[3] (bak), *n.* **1.** a large tub, vat, or cistern used by dyers, brewers, distillers, etc., to hold liquids. **2.** a broad-beamed ferryboat hauled across a body of water by a rope or chain. [1685–95; < D *bak* tub, trough < LL *bacca* water container; cf. F *bac* ferryboat, punt. See BASIN.]

back•ache (bak′āk′), *n.* a pain, esp. in the lumbar region of the back, usually caused by the strain of a muscle or ligament. [1595–1605; BACK[1] + ACHE]

back-al•ley (bak′al′ē), *adj.* dirty, unprepossessing, sordid, or clandestine: *back-alley morals; back-alley political schemes.* [1860–65, *Amer.*]

back′ an′chor, *Naut.* a small anchor for backing a larger one.

back-and-forth (bak′ən fôrth′, -f ōrth′, -ənd-), *adj.* **1.** backward and forward; side to side; to and fro: *a back-and-forth shuttling of buses to the stadium; the back-and-forth movement of a clock's pendulum.* —*n.* **2.** unresolved argument or discussion. [1605–15]

back′ and to′, *New Eng. and South Atlantic States.* back-and-forth; to and fro.

back•band (bak′band′), *n.* **1.** *Carpentry.* a piece of millwork surrounding the trim at the top and sides of a door or window. **2.** a broad band passing over the back of a horse, for supporting the shafts of a vehicle. [BACK[1] + BAND[2]]

back•bar (bak′bär′), *n.* **1.** *Shipbuilding.* a short length of angle iron fitted over flanges of two angle irons butted together side by side to connect or reinforce them. **2.** a construction of shelves and counter space behind a bar, used for storing bottles, glasses, etc. [BACK[1] + BAR[1]]

Back′ Bay′, a prosperous residential and commercial area of Boston, Massachusetts.

back•beat (bak′bēt′), *n. Popular Music.* a secondary or supplementary beat, as by a jazz drummer. [BACK[1] + BEAT]

back′ bench′, any of the rows of seats occupied by the backbenchers. Cf. **front bench.** [1870–75]

back•bench•er (bak′ben′chər, -ben′-), *n.* any of the members of a legislature, esp. of the House of Commons of Great Britain, but not including the leaders of the parties. [1905–10; BACK BENCH + -ER[1]]

back•bend (bak′bend′), *n.* an acrobatic feat in which one bends backward from a standing position until one's hands touch the floor. [BACK[1] + BEND[1]]

back•bite (bak′bīt′), *v.,* **-bit, -bit•ten** or (*Informal*) **-bit; -bit•ing.** —*v.t.* **1.** to attack the character or reputation of (a person who is not present). —*v.i.* **2.** to speak unfavorably or slanderously of a person who is not present. [1125–75; ME; see BACK[1], BITE] —**back′bit′er,** *n.*
—**Syn. 1.** belittle, disparage, deprecate; slander, libel, defame.

back•blocks (bak′bloks′), *n.* (*used with a plural v.*) *Australian.* the outback: *They live in the backblocks.* [1870–75; BACK[1] + BLOCK + -S[3]]

back•board (bak′bôrd′, -bōrd′), *n.* **1.** a board placed at or forming the back of anything. **2.** *Basketball.* a board or other flat vertical surface to which the basket is attached. [1755–65; BACK[1] + BOARD]

back•bone (bak′bōn′), *n.* **1.** *Anat.* the spinal column; spine. **2.** strength of character; resolution. **3.** something resembling a backbone in appearance, position, or function. **4.** *Bookbinding.* a back or bound edge of a book; spine. **5.** *Naut.* a rope running along the middle of an awning, as a reinforcement and as an object to which a supporting bridle or crowfoot may be attached. **6.** *Naval Archit.* the central fore-and-aft assembly of the keel and keelson, giving longitudinal strength to the bottom of a vessel. [1250–1300; ME *bacbon.* See BACK[1], BONE[1]] **—back′boned′,** *adj.* **—back′bone′less,** *adj.*
—Syn. 2. firmness, decision, fortitude.

back•break•ing (bak′brā′king), *adj.* demanding great effort, endurance, etc.; exhausting: *a backbreaking job.* Also, **back′-break′ing.** [1780–90; BACK[1] + BREAK + -ING[2]] **—back′break′er,** *n.*

back′ burn′er, a condition of low priority or temporary deferment (usually used in the phrase *on the back burner*): *Put other issues on the back burner until after the election.* [1945–50; from the custom in cooking of placing pots not requiring immediate attention toward the rear of the stove]

back•cast (bak′kast′, -käst′), *n.* a short backward and often upward swing of a fishing rod, its line, and its lure in preparation for the cast that immediately follows. [1570–80, for an earlier sense; BACK[2] + CAST[1]]

back•chat (bak′chat′), *n. Informal.* **1.** repartee. **2.** back talk. [1895–1900; BACK[2] + CHAT[1]]

back-check (bak′chek′), *v.i. Ice Hockey.* **1.** to skate back toward one's defensive zone obstructing or impeding the movement or progress of one or more opponents on attack. Cf. **check**[1] (def. 15), **fore-check.** *—v.t.* **2.** to check over or through; review: *Back-check the files to see if the patient's records are there.* [1935–40]

back′ clear′ance, runout (def. 1b).

back′ clip′ping, a word formed by omitting the last part of the form from which it is derived. Also called **hind clipping.** Cf. **apocope, clipped form, fore clipping.**

back-cloth (bak′klôth′, -kloth′), *n., pl.* **-cloths** (-klôthz′, -klôths′, -kloths′). *Chiefly Brit. Theat.* backdrop (def. 1). [1870–75]

back′ coun′try, 1. a sparsely populated rural region remote from a settled area. **2.** *Australian.* a remote, undeveloped part of a large farm or cattle station. [1740–50] **—back′-coun′try,** *adj.*

back•court (bak′kôrt′, -kōrt′), *n.* **1.** *Basketball.* the half of a court in which the basket being defended is located. **2.** *Tennis.* the part of a tennis court between the base line and the line, parallel to the net, that marks the in-bounds limit of a service. Cf. **forecourt** (def. 2). [1765–75; BACK[1] + COURT]

back•court•man (bak′kôrt′mən, -kōrt′-), *n., pl.* **-men.** *Basketball.* guard (def. 17). [1950–55; BACKCOURT + MAN[1]]

back•cross (bak′krôs′, -kros′), *Genetics.* *—v.t.* **1.** to cross (a hybrid of the first generation) with either of its parents. *—n.* **2.** an instance of such crossing. [1900–05; BACK[2] + CROSS]

back•date (bak′dāt′), *v.t.,* **-dat•ed, -dat•ing.** to date earlier than the actual date; predate; antedate: *Backdate the letter so he'll think I wrote it last week.* [1945–50, *Amer.*; BACK[2] + DATE[1]]

back′ dive′, a dive in which the diver stands on the springboard with the back to the water and jumps up, arching backward to land either feetfirst facing the springboard or headfirst facing away from the springboard.

back′ door′, 1. a door at the rear of a house, building, etc. **2.** a secret, furtive, or illicit method, manner, or means. [1520–30]

back•door (bak′dôr′, -dōr′), *adj.* secret; furtive; illicit; indirect. Also, **back′-door′.** [1605–15; adj. use of BACK DOOR]

backdoor′ play′, *Basketball.* an offensive tactic whereby a player breaks away from a defender to receive a pass near the baseline in order to make a quick layup. [1975–80]

back•down (bak′doun′), *n.* a withdrawal from a previously held position, esp. in the face of superior power or upon further consideration. [1860–65, *Amer.*; n. use of v. phrase *back down*]

back•draft (bak′draft′, -dräft′), *n.* an explosive surge in a fire produced by the sudden mixing of air with other combustible gases. [1815–25; BACK[2] + DRAFT]

back•drop (bak′drop′), *n., v.,* **-dropped** or **-dropt, -drop•ping.** *—n.* **1.** Also called, *esp. Brit.,* **back-cloth.** *Theat.* the rear curtain of a stage setting. **2.** the background of an event; setting. **3.** *Gymnastics.* a maneuver in which a trampolinist jumps in the air, lands on the back with the arms and legs pointed upward, and then springs up to a standing position. *—v.t.* **4.** to provide a setting or background for: *A vast mountain range backdrops the broad expanse of lake.* [1910–15, *Amer.*; BACK[1] + DROP]

backed (bakt), *adj.* **1.** having a back, backing, setting, or support (often used in combination): *a low-backed sofa.* **2.** (of fabric) having an extra set of threads in either the warp or the weft to provide added warmth. Cf. **double cloth. 3.** *Photog.* (of a film or plate) coated with a substance for absorbing light and thereby reducing halation. [1350–1400; ME; see BACK[1], -ED[3]]

back′ electromo′tive force′, *Elect.* See **counter electromotive force.** [1890–95]

back•end-to (bak′end′tōō′), *adv. Northern U.S.* in a reversed position; backward. Also, **backside-to, backside-front.** [BACK[1] + END[1]]

back•er (bak′ər), *n.* **1.** a person who supports or aids a person, cause, enterprise, etc. **2.** a person who bets on a competitor in a race or contest. **3.** canvas or other material used for backing. [1535–45; BACK[1] + -ER[1]]
—Syn. 1. supporter, sponsor, guarantor; aide, helper.

back•er-up (bak′ər up′), *n., pl.* **back•ers-up. 1.** a supporter; backer; second. **2.** *Football.* a linebacker. [1920–25; *back up* + -ER[1]]

back•fall (bak′fôl′), *n.* something that falls back. [1670–80; BACK[2] + FALL]

back•field (bak′fēld′), *n. Football.* **1.** (*used with a plural v.*) the members of the team who, on offense, are stationed behind the linemen and, on defense, behind the linebackers. **2.** their positions considered as a unit. **3.** the area where the backs play. [1910–15, *Amer.*; BACK[1] + FIELD]

back•fill (bak′fil′), *n.* **1.** material used for refilling an excavation. *—v.t.* **2.** to refill (an excavation). [1950–55; BACK[2] + FILL]

back•fire (bak′fīᵊr′), *v.,* **-fired, -fir•ing,** *n.* *—v.i.* **1.** (of an internal-combustion engine) to have a loud, premature explosion in the intake manifold. **2.** to bring a result opposite to that which was planned or expected: *The plot backfired.* **3.** to start a fire deliberately in order to check a forest or prairie fire by creating a barren area in advance of it. *—n.* **4.** (in an internal-combustion engine) premature ignition of fuel in the intake manifold. **5.** an explosion coming out of the breech of a firearm. **6.** a fire started intentionally to check the advance of a forest or prairie fire. [1775–85, *Amer.*; BACK[2] + FIRE]
—Syn. 2. miscarry, boomerang; flop, bomb, wash out.

back•fist (bak′fist′), *n.* a karate punch with the back of a clenched hand. [BACK[1] + FIST[1]]

back•fit (bak′fit′), *v.t.,* **-fit** or **-fit•ted, -fit•ting.** to update by providing new or improved equipment or features: *a five-year program of installing new power plants and backfitting existing ones.* [BACK[2] + FIT[1]]

back′flap hinge′ (bak′flap′), *Building Trades.* flap (def. 20a).

back•flash (bak′flash′), *n.* a flashback: *Backflashes of the heroine's childhood fill in gaps in the novel's narrative.* [1930–35; BACK[2] + FLASH]

back•flip (bak′flip′), *n., v.,* **-flipped, -flip•ping.** *—n.* **1.** a backward somersault. **2.** a dive executed by somersaulting backward. **3.** *Informal.* a complete reversal in attitude or policy: *Some committee members did sudden backflips, urging spending cuts instead of expanded programs.* *—v.i.* **4.** to perform a backflip: *She backflipped off a bucking horse.* [1930–35; BACK[2] + FLIP[1]]

back′ float′, *Swimming.* a floating position on one's back with arms extended out to the sides and face upward. [‡1975–80]

back•flow (bak′flō′), *n.* a flow of a liquid opposite to the usual or desired direction. [1880–85; BACK[2] + FLOW]

back′flow valve′. See **backwater valve.**

back′ fo′cus, *Photog.* the distance between the back surface of a lens and the focal plane when the lens is focused at infinity. [1895–1900]

back′ forma′tion, *Ling.* **1.** the analogical creation of one word from another word that appears to be a derived or inflected form of the first by dropping the apparent affix or by modification. **2.** a word so formed, as *typewrite* from *typewriter.* [1885–90]

back′ for′ty, remote, usually uncultivated acreage on a large piece of land, as on a farm or ranch. Also, **back 40.** [appar. because forty acres was a typical size for such a piece of land]

back•gam•mon (bak′gam′ən, bak′gam′-), *n.* **1.** a game for two persons played on a board having two tables or parts, each marked with 12 points, and with both players having 15 pieces that are moved in accordance with throws of the dice. **2.** a victory at this game, esp. one resulting in a tripled score. *—v.t.* **3.** to defeat at backgammon, esp. to win a triple score over. [1635–45; BACK[2] + GAMMON[1]]

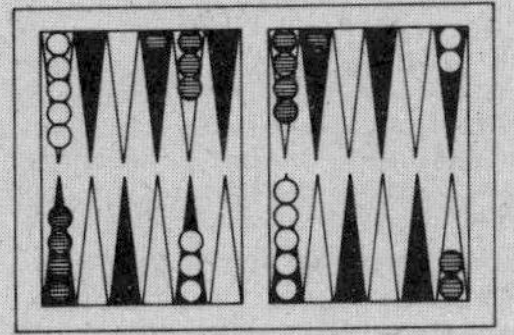

backgammon (def. 1)

back′ gear′, (in a lathe) one of several gears for driving the headstock at various speeds. **—back′geared′,** *adj.*

back•ground (bak′ground′), *n.* **1.** the ground or parts, as of a scene, situated in the rear (opposed to *foreground*). **2.** *Fine Arts.* **a.** the part of a painted or carved surface against which represented objects and forms are perceived or depicted: *a portrait against a purple background.* **b.** the part of an image represented as being at maximum distance from the frontal plane. **3.** one's origin, education, experience, etc., in relation to one's present character, status, etc. **4.** the social, historical, and other antecedents or causes of an event or condition: *the background of the war.* **5.** the complex of physical, cultural, and psychological factors that serves as the environment of an event or experience; the set of conditions against which an occurrence is perceived. **6.** *Physics.* the totality of effects that tend to obscure a phenomenon under investigation and above which the phenomenon must be detected. **7.** *Telecommunications.* (in an electronic device for transmitting or receiving signals) the sum of the effects, as noise or random signals, from which a phenomenon must differentiate itself in character or degree in order to be detected. **8. in** or **into the background,** unobtrusive; inconspicuous; out of sight or notice; in or into obscurity: *He kept his dishonest dealings in the background.* *—adj.* **9.** of, pertaining to, or serving as a background: *background noise.* *—v.t.* **10.** to supply a background to: *The passenger's idle thoughts were backgrounded by the drone of the plane's engines.* **11.** to supply a background of information for: *To background themselves, reporters dug through all available files on the case.* [1665–75; BACK[1] + GROUND[1]]
—Syn. 4. environment, circumstances, upbringing, milieu, element, sphere, medium.

back•ground•er (bak′groun′dər), *n.* **1.** a briefing for the press in which an official, often from government or business, gives background information to clarify particular policies, actions, or newsworthy issues, with the understanding that the official will not be named or quoted directly in any resulting press reports. **2.** any briefing or report for the purpose of providing background information. [1955–60, *Amer.*; BACKGROUND + -ER[1]]

back′ground mu′sic, 1. music, often recorded, intended to provide a soothing background, usually played over loudspeaker systems in public places, as railway stations or restaurants. **2.** music composed specifically to accompany and heighten the mood of a visual production, as a movie. [1925–30]

back′ground projec′tion, the projection from the rear of previously photographed material on a translucent screen, used as background for a television or motion-picture shot. Also called **back projection, rear projection.**

back•hand (bak′hand′), *n.* **1.** a stroke, slap, etc., made with the palm of the hand turned toward the body and the back of the hand turned in the direction of the stroke, slap, etc. **2.** (in tennis, squash, etc.) a stroke made from the side of the body opposite to that of the hand holding the racket, paddle, etc. **3.** handwriting that slopes toward the left. *—adj.* **4.** backhanded. **5.** (in tennis, squash, etc.) of, pertaining to, or noting a stroke made from the side of the body opposite to that of the hand holding the racket, paddle, etc. Cf. **forehand** (def. 1). *—adv.* **6.** with the back of the hand: *He hit him backhand across the face.* **7.** from across the body; backhanded: *She returned the ball backhand on the first serve.* *—v.t.* **8.** to strike with the back of the hand. **9.** to hit, produce, or accomplish with a backhand. **10.** to catch (a ball or the like) backhanded. [1650–60; BACK[2] + HAND]

back•hand•ed (bak′han′did), *adj.* **1.** performed with the hand turned backward, crosswise, or in any oblique direction so that the palm of the hand faces in the direction of the body and the back of the hand faces in the direction of forward movement. **2.** sloping in a downward direction from left to right: *backhanded writing.* **3.** oblique or ambiguous in meaning; indirect; insincere or malicious; wry: *backhanded methods; a backhanded compliment.* **4.** *Ropemaking.* noting a rope in which the yarns and the strands are laid in the same direction, the rope itself being laid in the opposite direction. *—adv.* **5.** with the hand across the body; backhand: *He caught the ball backhanded.* [1790–1800; BACK[2] + HANDED] **—back′hand′ed•ly,** *adv.* **—back′hand′ed•ness,** *n.*

back•hand•er (bak′han′dər), *n.* **1.** a backhanded slap, punch, stroke, or play. **2.** *Brit. Slang.* **a.** a drink served out of turn to a guest as a bottle or decanter is passed around the table during dessert. **b.** a bribe. [1795–1805; BACKHAND + -ER[1]]

back•haul (bak′hôl′), *n.* the return trip of a vehicle, as a truck, transporting cargo or freight, esp. when carrying goods back over all or part of the same route. [BACK[2] + HAUL]

backhoe

back•hoe (bak′hō′), *n.* a hydraulic excavating machine consisting of a tractor having an attached hinged boom, with a bucket with movable jaws on the end of the boom. Also, **back′-hoe′, back′ hoe′.** [1940–45; BACK[1] + HOE]

back•house (bak′hous′), *n., pl.* **-hous•es** (-hou′ziz). **1.** a building behind the main building, often serving a subsidiary purpose. **2.** a privy; outhouse. [1550–60; BACK[1] + HOUSE]

back•ing (bak′ing), *n.* **1.** aid or support of any kind. **2.** supporters or backers collectively. **3.** something that forms the back or is placed at or attached to the back of anything to support, strengthen, or protect it. **4.** *Theat.* a curtain or flat placed behind a window, entrance, or other opening in a stage set to conceal the offstage area. **5.** material for backing a joist or rafter. **6.** a bevel given to the outer and upper edge of a hip rafter. **7.** the musical accompaniment for a soloist; backup. [1590–1600; BACK[1] + -ING[1]]
—Syn. 1. help, assistance, endorsement, sponsorship, patronage, encouragement.

back′ing light′, 1. Also called **back′ing strip′light, back′ing strip′.** *Theat.* a striplight providing diffused illumination for the background of a stage set. **2.** See **backup light.**

back•lash (bak′lash′), *n.* **1.** a sudden, forceful backward movement; recoil. **2.** a strong or violent reaction, as to some social or political change: *a backlash of angry feeling among Southern conservatives within the party.*

3. *Mach.* **a.** the space between the thickness of a gear tooth and the width of the space between teeth in the mating gear, designed to allow for a film of lubricant, binding from heat expansion and eccentricity, or manufacturing inaccuracies. **b.** play or lost motion between loosely fitting machine parts. **4.** *Angling.* a snarled line on a reel, usually caused by a faulty cast. *—v.i.* **5.** to make or undergo a backlash. [1805–15; BACK[2] + LASH[1]]

back•light (bak′līt′), *n., v.,* **-light•ed** or **-lit, -light•ing.** *—n.* **1.** *Motion Pictures, Television.* a light source placed behind an actor, object, or scene to create a highlight that separates the subject from the background. *—v.t.* **2.** to illuminate (something) from behind. [1950–55; BACK[1] + LIGHT[1]]

back•light•ing (bak′lī′ting), *n.* a controlled technique of lighting, used in photography or the theater, in which a light is placed behind or at right angles to an object, person, or scene to produce such effects as depth or separation of subject and background. Also called **rim lighting.** [1950–55; BACK[1] + LIGHTING]

back•lins (bak′linz), *adv. Scot. and North Eng.* backward; back. Also, **back•lings** (bak′lingz). [bef. 1000; ME *bakling*, OE *bæcling* (see BACK[1], -LING[2]) + -S[1]]

back•list (bak′list′), *n.* **1.** the books that a publisher has kept in print over several years, as distinguished from newly issued titles. *—adj.* **2.** Also, **back′list′ed.** placed or maintained on a backlist. *—v.t.* **3.** to place on a backlist. [1945–50; BACK[2] + LIST[1]]

back•lite (bak′līt′), *n.* (in automotive styling) the rear window of a vehicle. [BACK[1] + LITE]

back•load (bak′lōd′), *v.t.* to defer to a later date, as wages, benefits, or costs: *The union agreed to back-load pay raises.* Cf. **front-load.**

back•log (bak′lôg′, -log′), *n., v.,* **-logged, -log•ging.** *—n.* **1.** a reserve or accumulation, as of stock, work, or business: *a backlog of business orders.* **2.** a large log at the back of a hearth to keep up a fire. Cf. **forestick.** *—v.t.* **3.** to hold in reserve, as for future handling or repair. **4.** to enter and acknowledge (an order) for future shipment. *—v.i.* **5.** to accumulate in a backlog: *Orders are starting to backlog faster than we can process them.* [1675–85; BACK[1] + LOG]
—Syn. 1. supply, stock, store, fund, cache, reservoir.

back′ lot′, *Motion Pictures.* an outdoor area, usually adjoining a studio, used for the shooting of exterior scenes. Also, **back′lot′.** [1795–1805, *Amer.*]

back′ mat′ter, *Print.* the parts of a book that appear after the main text, as bibliography, index, and appendixes. Also called **end matter.** Cf. **front matter.** [1945–50]

back′ mold′ing, a molding, as a backband, applied to interior window and door trim to conceal the edge of the wall surface.

back-mu•tate (bak′myōō′tāt), *v.i.,* **-tat•ed, -tat•ing.** *Genetics.* to undergo back mutation. [1960–65]

back′ muta′tion, *Genetics.* a mutation of an existing mutant gene that restores it to its previous form. Also called **reverse mutation.** [1935–40]

back′ nine′, *Golf.* the final nine holes on an eighteen-hole course.

back′ num′ber, **1.** an out-of-date issue of a serial publication. **2.** *Informal.* anything out-of-date. [1805–15, *Amer.*]

back′ o′ beyond′, *Australian Informal.* remote; out-of-the-way; isolated.

back′ of Bourke′ (bûrk), *Australian Informal.* a remote area or place. [1915–20; *Bourke*, a town in far NW New South Wales]

back′ of′fice, any department or office, as a private office or a department of record keeping, that is not usually seen by outsiders.

back′ or′der, *Com.* an order or part of an order waiting to be filled.

back-or•der (bak′ôr′dər), *v.t.* to treat as a back order: *We have to back-order your sofa until the new fabric arrives.*

back•pack (bak′pak′), *n.* **1.** a pack or knapsack, often of canvas or nylon, to be carried on one's back, sometimes supported on a lightweight metal frame strapped to the body. **2.** a piece of equipment designed to be used while being carried on the back. *—v.i.* **3.** to go on a hike, using a backpack: *We went backpacking in the Adirondacks.* *—v.t.* **4.** to place or carry in a backpack or on one's back. [1910–15, *Amer.*; BACK[1] + PACK[1]] **—back′pack′er,** *n.*

back-pad•dle (bak′pad′l), *v.i.,* **-dled, -dling.** to propel a boat by paddling backward, as by using a stroke in the direction of stern to bow.

back-pat•ting (bak′pat′ing), *n.* an act or instance of offering praise or congratulation: *The winners indulged in a certain amount of mutual back-patting.*

back-ped•al (bak′ped′l), *v.i.,* **-aled, -al•ing** or (*esp. Brit.*) **-alled, -al•ling.** **1.** to retard the forward motion by pressing backward on the pedal, esp. of a bicycle with coaster brakes. **2.** to retreat from or reverse one's previous stand on any matter; shift ground: *to back-pedal after severe criticism.* **3.** *Boxing.* to retreat from an opponent, esp. by stepping rapidly backward. [1895–1900]

back′ plas′tering, *Building Trades.* **1.** the introduction of partitions of lath and plaster between the inner and outer surfaces of a stud wall in order to improve the insulating properties of the wall. **2.** parging applied behind the exterior brickwork of a wall in order to exclude moisture and air from the interior of the wall.

back•plate (bak′plāt′), *n.* **1.** *Building Trades.* a wood or metal plate serving as a backing for a structural member. **2.** *Armor.* a piece of plate armor for protecting the back: worn as part of a cuirass. [1650–60; BACK[1] + PLATE[1]]

back′ projec′tion. See **background projection.**

back•rest (bak′rest′), *n.* a support used to rest one's back. [1855–60; BACK[1] + REST[1]]

back′ road′, a little-used secondary road, esp. one through a sparsely populated area. [1780–90, *Amer.*]

back′ room′, **1.** a room located in the rear, esp. one used only by certain people. **2.** a place where powerful or influential persons, esp. politicians, meet to plan secretly or from which they exercise control in an indirect manner: *The candidate for mayor was chosen in the precincts' back rooms.* Also, **back′room′.** [1585–95]

back•rub (bak′rub′), *n.* **1.** therapeutic manipulation of the muscles of the back; massage of the back. **2.** a liniment or anodyne ointment for relieving muscular soreness: *a tube of greaseless backrub.* [BACK[1] + RUB]

back′ run′, **1.** a period during which a particular process, as the flow of materials in manufacturing, is reversed. **2.** *Australian.* a tract of dry land in the public domain used as an auxiliary pasture by owners of adjacent private property.

back•rush (bak′rush′), *n.* the return of water seaward, down the foreshore of a beach, following the uprush of a wave. [BACK[2] + RUSH[1]]

back•saw (bak′sô′), *n. Carpentry.* a short saw with a reinforced back. [1875–80; BACK[1] + SAW[1]]

back•scat•ter (bak′skat′ər), *n. Physics.* the deflection of nuclear particles or of radiation in a scattering process through an angle greater than 90°. Also, **back′•scat′ter•ing.** [1955–60; BACK[2] + SCATTER]

back′ score′, *Curling.* a line at each end of the rink parallel to and equidistant from the foot score and the sweeping score.

back′ scratch′er, **1.** a long-handled device for scratching one's own back. **2.** a person who exchanges favors or services for mutual advantage. Also, **back′-scratch′er, back′scratch′er.** [1785–95] **—back′ scratch′ing.**

back•seat (bak′sēt′), *n.* **1.** a seat at the rear. **2. take a backseat,** to occupy a secondary or inferior position: *Her writing has taken a backseat because of other demands on her time.* [1825–35]

back′seat driv′er, **1.** an automobile passenger who offers the driver unsolicited advice, warnings, criticism, etc., esp. from the backseat. **2.** any person who, by means of criticism, unsolicited advice, or the like, interferes in affairs that are not his or her concern or responsibility. [1925–30] **—back′seat driv′ing.**

back•set (bak′set′), *n.* **1.** *New England, Southern, and South Midland U.S.* **a.** a setback; relapse; reverse. **b.** an eddy or countercurrent. **2.** (on a lock on a door or the like) the horizontal distance between the face through which the bolt passes and the center line of the knob stem or keyhole. [1565–75; BACK[2] + SET]

back′ shaft′, *Mach.* a spindle carrying back gears. [1875–80]

back•shore (bak′shôr′, -shōr′), *n. Geol.* **1.** the zone of the shore or beach above the high-water line, acted upon only by severe storms or exceptionally high tides. **2.** the area immediately adjacent to a sea cliff. **3.** berm (def. 3). [1915–20; BACK[1] + SHORE[1]]

back•side (bak′sīd′), *n.* **1.** the rear or back part or view of an object, person, scene, etc.; that part which is opposite the front. **2.** rump; buttocks. [1350–1400; ME *back syde*; see BACK[1], SIDE[1]; cf. OE *bæce* backside]

back•side-front (bak′sīd′frunt′), *adv.* backend-to.

back•side-to (bak′sīd′tōō′), *adv. Chiefly Northern U.S.* **1.** backend-to. **2.** inside out.

back•sight (bak′sīt′), *n. Survey.* **1.** a sight on a previously occupied instrument station. **2.** (in leveling) the reading on a rod that is held on a point of known elevation, used in computing the elevation of the instrument. [1840–50; BACK[2] + SIGHT]

back•slap (bak′slap′), *v.,* **-slapped, -slap•ping,** *n.* *—v.t.* **1.** to subject to backslapping. *—v.i.* **2.** to engage in backslapping. *—n.* **3.** a hearty slap on the back given as a token of affability or congratulation: *The bridegroom received many a warm handshake and backslap.* [1925–30; BACK[1] + SLAP[1]]

back•slap•ping (bak′slap′ing), *n.* the practice of making a loud and effusive display of friendliness, cordiality, etc., as by slapping persons on the back. [1770–80; BACK[1] + SLAPPING] **—back′slap′per,** *n.*

back•slash (bak′slash′), *n.* a short oblique stroke (\): used in some computer operatng systems to mark the division between a directory and a subdirectory, as in typing a path.

back•slide (bak′slīd′), *v.,* **-slid, -slid** or **-slid•den, -slid•ing,** *n.* *—v.i.* **1.** to relapse into bad habits, sinful behavior, or undesirable activities. *—n.* **2.** an act or instance of backsliding: *a backslide from his early training.* [1575–85; BACK[2] + SLIDE] **—back′slid′er,** *n.*

back•space (bak′spās′), *v.,* **-spaced, -spac•ing,** *n.* *—v.i.* **1.** to shift the carriage or typing element of a typewriter one space backward by depressing a special key. **2.** *Computers.* to move the cursor, printhead, etc., toward the beginning of the data. *—n.* **3.** the space made by backspacing. **4.** Also called **back′spac′er, back′space key′.** the key on a typewriter or computer keyboard used for backspacing. [BACK[2] + SPACE]

back•spin (bak′spin′), *n.* reverse rotation of a ball causing it to bounce or roll backward or stop short. Also called **underspin.** [1905–10; BACK[2] + SPIN]

back•splash (bak′splash′), *n.* paneling, as that attached to the back of a stovetop or to the wall behind a kitchen countertop, to protect against splashed liquids. [1950–55, *Amer.*; BACK[1] + SPLASH]

back•splice (bak′splīs′), *n., v.,* **-spliced, -splic•ing.** *—n.* **1.** a knot for finishing a rope end neatly, beginning with a crown and proceeding in a series of tucks, each strand over the first adjoining strand and under the next, the strands being split in half at each tuck. *—v.t.* **2.** to make a backsplice in (a rope end). [BACK[2] + SPLICE]

back•stab (bak′stab′), *v.t.,* **-stabbed, -stab•bing.** to attempt to discredit (a person) by underhanded means, as innuendo, accusation, or the like. [1920–25; BACK[2] + STAB] **—back′stab′ber,** *n.*

back′ staff′, an obsolete instrument for determining the altitude of the sun by facing away from the sun, sighting upon the horizon, adjusting a cursor until its shadow falls upon the sight through which the horizon appears, and measuring the resulting arc. [1620–30]

back•stage (bak′stāj′), *adv.* **1.** behind the proscenium in a theater, esp. in the wings or dressing rooms. **2.** toward the rear of the stage; upstage. **3.** out of view of the public; in private; behind the scenes: *Many of the deals were made backstage at the convention.* *—adj.* **4.** located or occurring backstage. **5.** of or pertaining to activities unknown to the public. **6.** of or pertaining to the private lives of people in the entertainment industry: *backstage gossip.* *—n.* **7.** *Theat.* a backstage area. [1895–1900; BACK[2] + STAGE]

back′ stairs′, **1.** stairs at the back of a house, as for use by servants. **2.** a means of intrigue. [1620–30]

back•stairs (bak′stârz′), *adj.* **1.** associated or originating with household servants. **2.** secret, underhanded, or scandalous: *backstairs gossip.* Also, **back′stair′.** [1635–45; adj. use of BACK STAIRS]

back•stay[1] (bak′stā′), *n.* **1.** *Mach.* a supporting or checking piece in a mechanism. **2.** *Building Trades.* an anchored tension member, as a cable, permanently or temporarily supporting a compression member, as a tower or pole, subject to a pull above its base from the opposite direction. **3.** a strip of leather at the back of a shoe used for reinforcement and sometimes to connect the quarters. [1860–65; BACK[1] + STAY[2]]

back•stay[2] (bak′stā′), *n. Naut.* any of various shrouds forming part of a vessel's standing rigging and leading aft from masts above a lower mast to the sides or stern of the vessel in order to reinforce the masts against forward pull. [1620–30; BACK[1] + STAY[3]]

back•stitch (bak′stich′), *n.* **1.** stitching or a stitch in which the thread is doubled back on the preceding stitch. *—v.t., v.i.* **2.** to sew by backstitch. [1605–15; BACK[2] + STITCH[1]]

back•stop (bak′stop′), *n., v.,* **-stopped, -stop•ping.** *—n.* **1.** a wall, wire screen, or the like, serving to prevent a ball from going too far beyond the normal playing area. **2.** *Baseball.* the catcher. **3.** a person or thing that serves as a support, safeguard, or reinforcement: *There were technicians on board as backstops to the automated controls.* *—v.i.* **4.** to act as a backstop. *—v.t.* **5.** to act as a backstop to: *The government agreed to backstop companies that invested in oil exploration.* [1810–20; BACK[1] + STOP] **—back′stop′per,** *n.*

back′strap loom′ (bak′strap′), a simple horizontal loom, used esp. in Central and South America, on which one of two beams holding the warp yarn is attached to a strap that passes across the weaver's back. [BACK[1] + STRAP]

back′ street′, a street apart from the main or business area of a town. Cf. **side street.** [1630–40]

back•street (bak′strēt′), *adj.* taking place in secrecy and often illegally: *back-street political maneuvering; back-street drug dealing.* [1895–1900]

back•stretch (bak′strech′), *n.* the straight part of a race track opposite the part leading to the finish line. Cf. **homestretch.** [1830–40; BACK[1] + STRETCH]

back•stroke (bak′strōk′), *n., v.,* **-stroked, -strok•ing.** *—n.* **1.** a backhanded stroke. **2.** *Swimming.* a stroke made while on one's back. **3.** a blow or stroke in return; recoil. *—v.i.* **4.** *Swimming.* to swim the backstroke: *She backstroked across the pool.* [1665–75; BACK[2] + STROKE[1]]

back•strok•er (bak′strō′kər), *n.* a person who swims the backstroke, esp. a member of a competitive swimming team who specializes in the backstroke. [BACKSTROKE + -ER[1]]

back•swept (bak′swept′), *adj.* **1.** slanting backward or away from the front. **2.** *Aeron.* sweptback. [1915–20; BACK[2] + SWEPT]

back•swim•mer (bak′swim′ər), *n.* any of numerous predaceous aquatic hemipterous insects, of the family Notonectidae, that swim on their backs, and may inflict a painful bite if handled. Also called **boat bug.** [1860–65; BACK[1] + SWIMMER]

backswimmer, *Notonecta undulata,* length ½ in. (1.3 cm)

back•swing (bak′swing′), *n. Sports.* the movement of a bat, racket, or the like, toward the back of a player in preparation for the forward movement with which the ball is struck. [1895–1900; BACK[2] + SWING[1]]

back•sword (bak′sôrd′, -sōrd′), *n.* **1.** a sword with only one sharp edge; broadsword. **2.** (formerly) a cudgel having a basket hilt, used in fencing exhibitions. **3.** a backswordman. [1590–1600; BACK[1] + SWORD]

back•sword•man (bak′sôrd′mən, -sōrd′-), *n., pl.* **-men.** a person who uses a backsword. Also, **back•swords•man** (bak′sôrdz′mən, -sōrdz′-). [1590–1600; BACKSWORD + MAN]

CONCISE ETYMOLOGY KEY: <, descended or borrowed from; >, whence; b., blend of, blended; c., cognate with; cf., compare; deriv., derivative; equiv., equivalent; imit., imitative; obl., oblique; r., replacing; s., stem; sp., spelling, spelled; resp., respelling, respelled; trans., translation; ?, origin unknown; *, unattested; ‡, probably earlier than. See the full key inside the front cover.

back′ talk′, an impudent response; impudence. [1855–60] **—Syn.** rudeness, insolence, impertinence, cheek, sass.

back-talk (bak′tôk′), *v.i., v.t.* to answer back. [1855–60]

back′ to back′, **1.** adjacent or contiguous but oppositely oriented; having the backs close together or adjoining: *The seats in the day coach are back to back.* **2.** (of two similar events) following one immediately after the other; in unbroken sequence; consecutively: *After losing all day, he picked winners back to back in the last two races.* **3.** *Stud Poker.* having a pair, consisting of the hole card and the first upcard: *He had aces back to back.* **—back′-to-back′,** *adj.*

back-to-ba•sics (bak′tə bā′siks), *adj.* **1.** stressing simplicity and adherence to fundamental principles: *The movement suggests a back-to-basics approach to living for those whose lives have become complicated.* **2.** emphasizing or based upon the teaching of such basic subjects as reading, arithmetic, grammar, or history in a traditional way.

back•track (bak′trak′), *v.i.* **1.** to return over the same course or route. **2.** to withdraw from an undertaking, position, etc.; reverse a policy. [1715–25, *Amer.;* BACK[2] + TRACK]

back-trail (bak′trāl′), *v.i.* to backtrack. [1905–10]

back•up (bak′up′), *n.* **1.** a person or thing that supports or reinforces another. **2.** a musician or singer or group of musicians or singers accompanying a soloist: *a singer with a three-man backup that plays cello, bass, and guitar.* **3.** an overflow or accumulation due to stoppage, malfunctioning, etc.: *a sewage backup; a backup of cars at the tollbooth.* **4.** a person, plan, device, etc., kept in reserve to serve as a substitute, if needed. **5.** *Computers.* **a.** a copy or duplicate version, esp. of a file, program, or entire computer system, retained for use in the event that the original is in some way rendered unusable. **b.** a procedure to follow in such an event. **6.** *Bowling.* a ball that curves in a direction corresponding to the bowling hand of the bowler. **—adj. 7.** (of a person, plan, device, etc.) held in reserve as a substitute if needed: *a backup driver; a backup generator.* **8.** performing a secondary or supporting function: *A drummer and guitarist are the singer's backup musicians.* [1775–85, *Amer.;* n. use of v. phrase *back up*]

back′up light′, a light at the rear of a motor vehicle that lights as a warning to those behind. Also called **backing light.**

back′ vent′, (in plumbing) a vent situated on the sewer side of a trap.

back′ walk′over, *Gymnastics.* See under **walkover** (def. 4).

back•ward (bak′wərd), *adv.* Also, **back′wards. 1.** toward the back or rear. **2.** with the back foremost. **3.** in the reverse of the usual or right way: *counting backward from 100.* **4.** toward the past: *to look backward over one's earlier mistakes.* **5.** toward a less advanced state; retrogressively: *Since the overthrow of the president the country has moved steadily backward.* **6. backward and forward,** thoroughly: *He knew his lesson backward and forward.* Also, **backwards and forwards.** **—adj. 7.** directed toward the back or past. **8.** reversed; returning: *a backward movement; a backward journey.* **9.** behind in time or progress; late; slow: *a backward learner; a backward country.* **10.** bashful or hesitant; shy: *a backward lover.* [1250–1300; ME *bakwarde.* See BACK[1], -WARD] **—back′ward•ly,** *adv.* **—back′ward•ness,** *n.* **—Syn. 9.** tardy; retarded, underdeveloped. **10.** disinclined; timid, retiring. **—Ant. 1.** forward.

back•ward•a•tion (bak′wər dā′shən), *n.* (on the London stock exchange) the fee paid by a seller of securities to the buyer for the privilege of deferring delivery of purchased securities. [1840–50; BACKWARD + -ATION]

back•wash (bak′wosh′, -wôsh′), *n.* **1.** *Naut.* water thrown backward by the motion of oars, propellers, paddle wheels, etc. **2.** *Aeron.* the portion of the wash of an aircraft that flows to the rear, usually created by the power plant. Cf. **wash** (def. 35). **3.** a condition, usually undesirable, that continues long after the event which caused it. **—v.t. 4.** to affect, as by hitting, rocking, or splashing, with a backwash: *a powerful cutter backwashing the skiers.* **5.** to clean out (a clogged filter) by reversing the flow of fluid: *Backwash the swimming pool's filters regularly.* [1765–75; BACK[2] + WASH] **—back′•wash′er,** *n.* **—Syn. 3.** aftermath, consequence, result, upshot.

back•wa•ter (bak′wô′tər, -wot′ər), *n.* **1.** water held or forced back, as by a dam, flood, or tide. **2.** a place or state of stagnant backwardness: *This area of the country is a backwater that continues to resist progress.* **3.** an isolated, peaceful place. **4.** a stroke executed by pushing a paddle forward, causing a canoe to move backward. [1350–1400; ME *bakwateres;* see BACK[2], WATER]

back′water valve′, a valve for preventing flowing liquid, as sewage, from reversing its direction. Also called **backflow valve.**

back•wind (bak′wind′), *v.t.,* **-wind•ed, -wind•ing.** *Naut.* **1.** to divert wind against the lee side of (a sail) from another sail. **2.** to set (a sail) so that the wind is on what would ordinarily be the lee side, as for turning the bow of a boat away from the wind. **3.** to blanket (another sailing vessel) by spilling wind from the sails of one vessel onto the lee side of the sails of the other. [1895–1900; BACK[2] + WIND[1]]

back•woods (bak′wŏŏdz′), *n.* **1.** (*often used with a singular v.*) wooded or partially uncleared and unsettled districts. **2.** any remote or isolated area. **—adj.** Also, **back′wood′, back′woods′y. 3.** of or pertaining to the backwoods. **4.** unsophisticated; uncouth. [1700–10, *Amer.;* BACK[1] + WOODS] **—Syn. 2.** hinterland, provinces, wilds, woodland; sticks, boondocks, boonies, bush, backwater.

back•woods•man (bak′wŏŏdz′mən), *n., pl.* **-men. 1.** a person living in or coming from the backwoods. **2.** a person of uncouth manners, rustic behavior or speech, etc. **3.** *Brit.* a peer who rarely attends the House of Lords. [1700–10, *Amer.;* BACKWOODS + -MAN]

back•wrap (bak′rap′), *n.* an article of clothing, as a dress, that overlaps and fastens in the back. [1950–55; BACK[1] + WRAP]

back•yard (bak′yärd′), *n.* **1.** the portion of a lot or building site behind a house, structure, or the like, sometimes fenced, walled, etc. **2.** a familiar or nearby area; neighborhood. [1650–60; BACK[1] + YARD[2]]

Ba•co•lod (bä kō′lôd), *n.* a seaport on N Negros, in the central Philippines. 262,415.

ba•con (bā′kən), *n.* **1.** the back and sides of the hog, salted and dried or smoked, usually sliced thin and fried for food. **2.** Also called **white bacon.** *South Midland and Southern U.S.* pork cured in brine; salt pork. **3. bring home the bacon, a.** to provide for material needs; earn a living. **b.** to accomplish a task; be successful or victorious: *Our governor went to Washington to appeal for disaster relief and brought home the bacon—$40 million.* **4. save one's bacon,** *Informal.* to allow one to accomplish a desired end; spare one from injury or loss: *Quick thinking saved our bacon.* [1300–50; ME *bacoun* < AF; OF *bacon* < Gmc **bakōn-* (OHG *bacho* back, ham, bacon) deriv. of **baka-* BACK[1]; cf. MD *bake* bacon]

Ba•con (bā′kən), *n.* **1. Francis** (*Baron Verulam, Viscount St. Albans*), 1561–1626, English essayist, philosopher, and statesman. **2. Francis,** 1910–92, English painter, born in Ireland. **3. Henry,** 1866–1924, U.S. architect. **4. Nathaniel,** 1647–76, American colonist, born in England: leader of a rebellion in Virginia 1676. **5. Roger** (*"The Admirable Doctor"*), 1214?–94?, English philosopher and scientist.

ba•con•burg•er (bā′kən bûr′gər), *n.* a hamburger topped with strips of cooked bacon. [1975–80; BACON + -BURGER]

Ba•co•ni•an (bā kō′nē ən), *adj.* **1.** of or pertaining to the philosopher Francis Bacon or his doctrines. **—n. 2.** an adherent of the Baconian philosophy. [1805–15; BACON + -IAN] **—Ba•co′ni•an•ism, Ba•co•nism** (bā′kə niz′əm), *n.*

Baco′nian meth′od, *Logic.* induction (def. 4a).

Baco′nian the′ory, the theory attributing the authorship of Shakespeare's plays to Francis Bacon. Cf. **Oxford theory.** [1870–75]

Ba′con's Rebel′lion, an unsuccessful uprising by frontiersmen in Virginia in 1676, led by Nathaniel Bacon against the colonial government in Jamestown.

bact., 1. bacterial. **2.** bacteriology. **3.** bacterium.

-bacter, a combining form with the meaning "rod," used primarily in biology to form generic names of bacteria: *aerobacter; arthrobacter.* [< NL, masc n. coined as var. of neut. *bactrum* < Gk *báktron;* see BACTERIUM]

bac•te•re•mi•a (bak′tə rē′mē ə), *n. Pathol.* the presence of bacteria in the blood. [1885–90; BACTER- + -EMIA]

bacteri-, a combining form meaning "bacteria," used in the formation of compound words: *bactericide; bacteriuria.* Also, **bacter-, bacterio-.** [< Gk *baktḗrion* little staff; see BACTERIUM]

bac•te•ri•a (bak tēr′ē ə), *n.pl., sing.* **-te•ri•um** (-tēr′ē-əm). ubiquitous one-celled organisms, spherical, spiral, or rod-shaped and appearing singly or in chains, comprising the Schizomycota, a phylum of the kingdom Monera (in some classification systems the plant class Schizomycetes), various species of which are involved in fermentation, putrefaction, infectious diseases, or nitrogen fixation. [1905–10; < NL < Gk *baktḗria,* pl. of *baktḗrion;* see BACTERIUM] **—bac•te′ri•al,** *adj.* **—bac•te′•ri•al•ly,** *adv.*

bacteria (greatly magnified)
A, cocci (spherical): 1, *Staphylococcus pyogenes aureus;* 2, *Streptococcus pyogenes.* B, bacilli (rod): 3, *Bacillus sporogenes;* 4, *Bacillus proteus;* 5, *Bacillus subtilis;* 6, *Bacillus typhosus.* C, spirilla (spiral): 7, *Vibrio cholerae asiaticae;* 8, *Spirillum undulum;* 9, *Theospirillum;* 10, *Spirochaeta*

bacte′rial can′ker, *Plant Pathol.* a disease of plants, characterized by cankers and usually by exudation of gum, caused by bacteria, as of the genera *Pseudomonas* and *Corynebacterium.*

bacte′rial endocardi′tis, *Pathol.* a bacterial infection of the inner lining of the heart, most often of the heart valves, characterized by fever, enlarged spleen, and heart murmur.

bac•te•ri•cide (bak tēr′ə sīd′), *n. Pharm.* any substance capable of killing bacteria. [1880–85; BACTERI- + -CIDE] **—bac•te′ri•cid′al,** *adj.* **—bac•te′ri•cid′al•ly,** *adv.*

bac•ter•in (bak′tə rin), *n. Immunol.* a vaccine prepared from killed bacteria. [1910–15; BACTER- + -IN[2]]

bacterio-, var. of **bacteri-.**

bac•te•ri•o•chlo•ro•phyll (bak tēr′ē ō klôr′ə fil, -klōr′-), *n. Biochem.* a pale blue-gray form of chlorophyll that is unique to the photosynthetic but anaerobic purple bacteria. [1935–40; BACTERIO- + CHLOROPHYLL]

bac•te•ri•oid (bak tēr′ē oid′), *n.* **1.** bacteroid. **—adj. 2.** Also, **bac•te′ri•oi′dal.** bacteroid.

bacteriol., bacteriology.

bac•te•ri•ol•o•gy (bak tēr′ē ol′ə jē), *n.* a branch of microbiology dealing with the identification, study, and cultivation of bacteria and with their applications in medicine, agriculture, industry, and biotechnology. [1880–85; BACTERIO- + -LOGY] **—bac•te•ri•o•log•i•cal** (bak tēr′ē ə loj′i kəl), **bac•te′ri•o•log′ic,** *adj.* **—bac•te′ri•o•log′i•cal•ly,** *adv.* **—bac•te′ri•ol′o•gist,** *n.*

bac•te•ri•ol•y•sis (bak tēr′ē ol′ə sis), *n.* disintegration or dissolution of bacteria. [1890–95; BACTERIO- + -LYSIS] **—bac•te•ri•o•lyt•ic** (bak tēr′ē ə lit′ik), *n., adj.*

bac•te•ri•o•phage (bak tēr′ē ə fāj′), *n.* any of a group of viruses that infect specific bacteria, usually causing their disintegration or dissolution. Also called **phage.** [1920–25; < F *bactériophage.* See BACTERIO-, -PHAGE] **—bac•te•ri•o•phag•ic** (bak tēr′ē ə faj′ik, -fā′-jik), **bac•te•ri•oph•a•gous** (bak tēr′ē of′ə gəs), *adj.* **—bac•te′ri•oph′a•gy** (bak tēr′ē of′ə jē), *n.*

bac•te•ri•o•rho•dop•sin (bak tēr′ē ō rō dop′sin), *n. Biochem.* a protein complex in the membrane of halobacteria that conducts a unique form of photosynthesis, employing the light-sensitive pigment retinal rather than the chlorophyll used by all other known photosynthetic organisms. [1975–80; BACTERIO- + RHODOPSIN]

bac•te•ri•os•co•py (bak tēr′ē os′kə pē), *n.* the examination of bacteria with a microscope. [BACTERIO- + -SCOPY] **—bac•te•ri•o•scop•ic** (bak tēr′ē ə skop′ik), **bac•te′ri•o•scop′i•cal,** *adj.* **—bac•te′ri•o•scop′i•cal•ly,** *adv.* **—bac•te′ri•os′co•pist,** *n.*

bac•te•ri•o•sta•sis (bak tēr′ē ə stā′sis), *n.* the prevention of the further growth of bacteria. [1910–15; BACTERIO- + STASIS] **—bac•te•ri•o•stat•ic** (bak tēr′ē ə-stat′ik), *adj.* **—bac•te′ri•o•stat′i•cal•ly,** *adv.*

bac•te•ri•o•stat (bak tēr′ē ə stat′), *n.* a substance or preparation that inhibits the further growth of bacteria. [1915–20; BACTERIO- + -STAT]

bac•te•ri•um (bak tēr′ē əm), *n.* sing. of **bacteria.** [1840–50; < NL < Gk *baktḗrion,* dim. of *baktēría* staff; akin to *báktron* stick, L *baculum, bacillum*]

bac•te•ri•u•ri•a (bak tēr′ē yŏŏr′ē ə), *n. Pathol.* the presence of bacteria in the urine. Also, **bac•ter•u•ri•a** (bak′tə rŏŏr′ē ə, -tər yŏŏr′). [1885–90; BACTERI- + -URIA]

bac•te•rize (bak′tə rīz′), *v.t.,* **-rized, -riz•ing.** to change in composition by means of bacteria. Also, *esp. Brit.,* **bac′te•rise′.** [1910–15; BACTER- + -IZE] **—bac′•te•ri•za′tion,** *n.*

bac•te•roid (bak′tə roid′), *n.* **1.** any of the rod-shaped or branched bacteria in the root nodules of nitrogen-fixing plants. **—adj. 2.** Also, **bac′te•roi′dal.** resembling bacteria. Also, **bacterioid.** [1850–55; BACTER- + -OID]

bac•te•roi•des (bak′tə roi′dēz), *n., pl.* **-des.** any of several rod-shaped, anaerobic bacteria of the genus *Bacteroides,* occurring in the alimentary and genitourinary tracts of humans and other mammals, certain species of which are pathogenic. [1919; < NL; see BACTER-, -OID]

Bac•tra (bak′trə), *n.* ancient name of **Balkh.**

Bac•tri•a (bak′trē ə), *n.* an ancient country in W Asia, between the Oxus River and the Hindu Kush Mountains. *Cap.:* Bactra. **—Bac′tri•an,** *adj., n.*

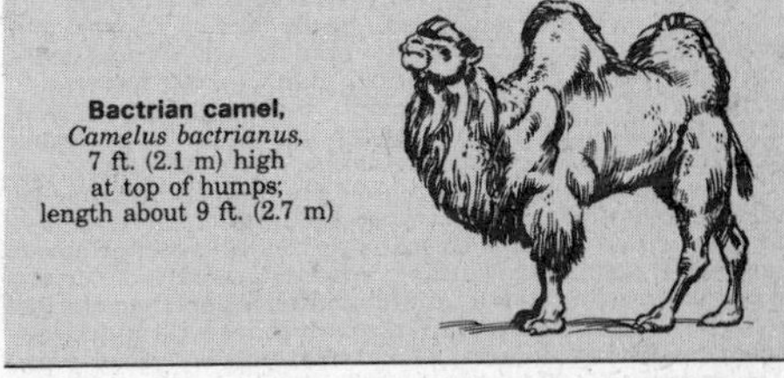

Bactrian camel, *Camelus bactrianus,* 7 ft. (2.1 m) high at top of humps; length about 9 ft. (2.7 m)

Bac′trian cam′el, an Asian camel, *Camelus bactrianus,* having two humps on the back: an endangered species. Cf. **dromedary.** [1600–10]

ba•cu•li•form (bə kyŏŏ′lə fôrm′, bak′yə-), *adj. Biol.* rod-shaped. [< L *bacul(um)* walking stick, staff + -I- + -FORM]

bac•u•line (bak′yə lin, -līn′), *adj.* pertaining to the rod or its use in punishing: *baculine discipline in the classroom.* [1700–10; < L *bacul(um)* walking stick, staff + -INE[1]]

bac•u•lite (bak′yə līt′), *n.* any ammonite of the genus *Baculites,* of the Cretaceous Period, having a straight shell with a spiral tip. [1815–25; < L *bacul(um)* walking stick, staff + -ITE[1]] **—bac•u•lit•ic** (bak′yə lit′ik), *adj.* **—bac′u•loid′,** *n.*

bad[1] (bad), *adj.,* **worse, worst;** (*Slang*) **bad•der, bad•dest** for 36; *n.; adv.* **—adj. 1.** not good in any manner or degree. **2.** having a wicked or evil character; morally reprehensible: *There is no such thing as a bad boy.* **3.** of poor or inferior quality; defective; deficient: *a bad diamond; a bad spark plug.* **4.** inadequate or below standard; not satisfactory for use: *bad heating; Living*

CONCISE PRONUNCIATION KEY: act, cāpe, dâre, pärt; set, ēqual; *if,* ice; ox, ōver, ôrder, oil, bŏŏk, bōōt, out; up, ûrge; child; sing; shoe; thin, *th*at; zh as in *treasure.* ə = *a* as in *alone, e* as in *system, i* as in *easily, o* as in *gallop, u* as in *circus;* ᵊ as in *fire* (fīᵊr), *hour* (ouᵊr). l and n can serve as syllabic consonants, as in *cradle* (krād′l), and *button* (but′n). See the full key inside the front cover.

conditions in some areas are very bad. **5.** inaccurate, incorrect, or faulty: *a bad guess.* **6.** invalid, unsound, or false: *a bad insurance claim; bad judgment.* **7.** causing or liable to cause sickness or ill health; injurious or harmful: *Too much sugar is bad for your teeth.* **8.** suffering from sickness, ill health, pain, or injury; sick; ill: *He felt bad from eating the green apples.* **9.** not healthy or in good physical condition; diseased, decayed, or physically weakened: *A bad heart kept him out of the army.* **10.** tainted, spoiled, or rotten, esp. to the point of being inedible: *The meat is bad because you left it out of the refrigerator too long.* **11.** having a disastrous or detrimental effect, result, or tendency; unfavorable: *The drought is bad for the farmers. His sloppy appearance made a bad impression.* **12.** causing or characterized by discomfort, inconvenience, uneasiness, or annoyance; disagreeable; unpleasant: *I had a bad flight to Chicago.* **13.** easily provoked to anger; irascible: *a bad temper.* **14.** cross, irritable, or surly: *If I don't have my morning coffee, I'm in a bad mood all day.* **15.** more uncomfortable, persistent, painful, or dangerous than usual; severe: *a bad attack of asthma.* **16.** causing or resulting in disaster or severe damage or destruction: *a bad flood.* **17.** regretful, contrite, dejected, or upset: *He felt bad about having to leave the children all alone.* **18.** disobedient, naughty, or misbehaving: *If you're bad at school, you'll go to bed without supper.* **19.** disreputable or dishonorable: *He's getting a bad name from changing jobs so often.* **20.** displaying a lack of skill, talent, proficiency, or judgment: *a bad painting; Bad drivers cause most of the accidents.* **21.** causing distress; unfortunate or unfavorable: *I'm afraid I have bad news for you.* **22.** not suitable or appropriate; disadvantageous or dangerous: *It was a bad day for fishing.* **23.** inclement; considered too stormy, hot, cold, etc.: *We had a bad winter with a lot of snow.* **24.** disagreeable or offensive to the senses: *a bad odor.* **25.** exhibiting a lack of artistic sensitivity: *The room was decorated in bad taste.* **26.** not in keeping with a standard of behavior or conduct; coarse: *bad manners.* **27.** (of a word, speech, or writing) **a.** vulgar, obscene, or blasphemous: *bad language.* **b.** not properly observing rules or customs of grammar, usage, spelling, etc.; incorrect: *He speaks bad English.* **28.** unattractive, esp. because of a lack of pleasing proportions: *She has a bad figure.* **29.** (of the complexion) marred by defects; pockmarked or pimply; blemished: *bad skin.* **30.** not profitable or worth the price paid: *The land was a bad buy.* **31.** *Com.* deemed uncollectible or irrecoverable and treated as a loss: *a bad debt.* **32.** ill-spent; wasted: *Don't throw good money after bad money.* **33.** counterfeit; not genuine: *There was a bad ten-dollar bill in with the change.* **34.** having the character of a villain; villainous: *In the movies the good guys always beat the bad guys.* **35.** *Sports.* failing to land within the in-bounds limits of a court or section of a court; missing the mark; not well aimed. **36.** *Slang.* outstandingly excellent; first-rate: *He's a bad man on drums, and the fans love him.* **37. in a bad way,** in severe trouble or distress. **38. not bad, a.** tolerably good; not without merit: *The dinner wasn't bad, but I've had better.* **b.** not difficult: *Once you know geometry, trigonometry isn't bad.* Also, **not so bad, not too bad. 39. too bad,** unfortunate or disappointing: *It's too bad that he didn't go to college.* —*n.* **40.** that which is bad: *You have to take the bad with the good.* **41.** a bad condition, character, or quality: *His health seemed to go from bad to worse.* **42.** (*used with a plural v.*) evil persons collectively (usually prec. by *the*): *The bad are always stirring up trouble.* **43. go to the bad,** to deteriorate physically or morally; go to ruin: *She wept at seeing her son go to the bad.* **44. in bad,** *Informal.* **a.** in trouble or distress. **b.** in disfavor: *He's in bad with his father-in-law.* **45. to the bad,** in arrears: *He's $100 to the bad on his debt.* —*adv. Informal.* **46.** badly: *He wanted it bad enough to steal it.* **47. bad off,** in poor or distressed condition or circumstances; destitute: *His family has been pretty bad off since he lost his job.* Also, **badly off.** Cf. **well-off.** [1250–1300; ME *badde,* perh. akin to OE *bæddel* hermaphrodite, *bædling* womanish man] —**bad′ness,** *n.*

—**Syn. 2.** depraved, corrupt, base, sinful, criminal, atrocious. BAD, EVIL, ILL, WICKED are closest in meaning in reference to that which is lacking in moral qualities or is actually vicious and reprehensible. BAD is the broadest and simplest term: *a bad man; bad habits.* EVIL applies to that which violates or leads to the violation of moral law: *evil practices.* ILL now appears mainly in certain fixed expressions, with a milder implication than that in evil: *ill will; ill-natured.* WICKED implies willful and determined doing of what is very wrong: *a wicked plan.* **10.** putrefied. **21.** adverse, unlucky, unhappy.

—**Usage.** The adjective BAD meaning "unpleasant, unattractive, unfavorable, spoiled, etc.," is the usual form to follow such copulative verbs as *sound, smell, look,* and *taste: After the rainstorm the water tasted bad. The coach says the locker room smells bad.* After the copulative verb *feel,* the adjective BADLY in reference to physical or emotional states is also used and is standard, although BAD is more common in formal writing: *I feel bad from overeating. She felt badly about her friend's misfortune.*

When the adverbial use is required, BADLY is standard with all verbs: *She reacted badly to the criticism.* BAD as an adverb appears mainly in informal contexts: *I didn't do too bad on the tests. He wants money so bad it hurts.* See also **badly, good.**

bad[2] (bad), *v. Archaic.* a pt. of **bid.**

bad′ ac′tor, 1. a mean, ill-tempered, troublemaking, or evil person. **2.** a vicious animal. **3.** an inveterate criminal. [1940–45]

Ba·da·joz (bä′thä hôth′), *n.* a city in SW Spain. 101,710.

Ba·dakh·shan (bä däкн shän′), *n.* a former province in NE Afghanistan.

CONCISE ETYMOLOGY KEY: <, descended or borrowed from; >, whence; b., blend of, blended; c., cognate with; cf., compare; deriv., derivative; equiv., equivalent; imit., imitative; obl., oblique; r., replacing; s., stem; sp., spelling, spelled; resp., respelling, respelled; trans., translation; ?, origin unknown; *, unattested; ‡, probably earlier than. See the full key inside the front cover.

Ba·da·lo·na (bä′thä lô′nä), *n.* a seaport in NE Spain, near Barcelona. 162,888.

bad′ ap′ple, *Informal.* a discontented, troublemaking, or dishonest person: *In any group of average citizens there are bound to be a few bad apples.* [from the proverb "one bad apple spoils the barrel"]

Ba·da·ri·an (bə där′ē ən), *adj.* of, pertaining to, or belonging to the predynastic culture of Upper Egypt, 4100–3500 B.C., characterized by flint tools, stone axes, and pottery. [1920–25; after *Badari,* village in Upper Egypt, where the pottery was discovered; see -AN]

bad·ass (bad′as′), *Slang* (*vulgar*). —*adj.* Also, **bad′·assed′. 1.** (of a person) difficult to deal with; mean-tempered; touchy. **2.** distinctively tough or powerful; so exceptional as to be intimidating. —*n.* **3.** a mean-tempered troublemaker. [1960–65; BAD[1] + ASS[2]]

Badb (bov), *n. Irish Myth.* a spirit who, delighting in war, incited armies to fight and appeared to warriors about to be defeated.

bad′ blood′, unfriendly or hostile relations; enmity; hostility; animosity: *When the territory was being settled there was bad blood between the farmers and the ranchers.* [1815–25]

bad′ breath′, halitosis.

bad′ con′duct dis′charge, *U.S. Mil.* **1.** a discharge of a person from military service for an offense less serious than one for which a dishonorable discharge is given. **2.** a certificate of such a discharge.

bad·de·ley·ite (bad′l ē it′ bad′lē-), *n.* a mineral, zirconium oxide, ZrO_2, used as a refractory. [1890–95; named after Joseph *Baddeley,* Englishman who first brought specimens to Europe (in 19th century) from Asia; see -ITE[1]]

bad·der (bad′ər), *adj.* **1.** *Slang.* compar. of **bad**[1] (def. 36). **2.** *Nonstandard.* a compar. of **bad**[1].

bad·der·locks (bad′ər loks′), *n.* (*used with a singular v.*) an edible kelp, *Alaria esculenta,* found on the coasts of Europe and the British Isles. [1780–90; perh. BALDER + LOCK[2] + -S[3]; cf. *Balder brae* plant name < ON *Baldro brā* Balder's eyelash]

bad·dest (bad′ist), *adj.* **1.** *Slang.* superl. of **bad**[1] (def. 36). **2.** *Nonstandard.* a superl. of **bad**[1].

bad·die (bad′ē), *n.* a villainous or criminal person. Also, **baddy.** [1935–40, *Amer.*; BAD + -IE]

bad·dish (bad′ish), *adj.* rather bad; not very good. [1745–55; BAD[1] + -ISH[1]]

bad·dy (bad′ē), *n., pl.* **-dies.** baddie.

bade (bad), *v.* a pt. of **bid.**

bad′ egg′, a person who is bad, dishonest, or unreliable; a good-for-nothing: *a bad egg who had served several years in prison.* [1850–55, *Amer.*]

Ba·den (bäd′n), *n.* **1.** a region in SW Germany, formerly a state, now incorporated in Baden-Württemberg. **2.** Baden-Baden.

Ba·den-Ba·den (bäd′n bäd′n), *n.* a city in W Baden-Württemberg, in SW Germany: spa. 48,680.

Ba·den-Pow·ell (bäd′n pō′əl, bad′n pou′əl), *n.* **Robert Stephenson Smyth** (smith), **1st Baron,** 1857–1941, British general who founded the Boy Scouts in 1908 and, with his sister Lady Agnes, the Girl Guides in 1910.

Ba·den-Würt·tem·berg (bäd′n vYRT′əm berK′), *n.* a state in SW Germany: formed 1951. 9,390,900; 13,800 sq. mi. (35,740 sq. km). *Cap.:* Stuttgart.

bad′ faith′, lack of honesty and trust: *Bad faith on the part of both negotiators doomed the talks from the outset.* Cf. **good faith.** —**bad′-faith′,** *adj.*

badge (baj), *n., v.,* **badged, badg·ing.** —*n.* **1.** a special or distinctive mark, token, or device worn as a sign of allegiance, membership, authority, achievement, etc.: *a police badge; a merit badge.* **2.** any emblem, token, or distinctive mark: *He considered a slide rule as the badge of an engineering student.* **3.** a card bearing identifying information, as one's name, symbol or place of employment, or academic affiliation, and often worn pinned to one's clothing. —*v.t.* **4.** to furnish or mark with a badge. [1300–50; ME *bag(g)e* < ?] —**badge′less,** *adj.*
—**Syn. 1.** insignia, shield, seal; hallmark, earmark.

badg·er (baj′ər), *n.* **1.** any of various burrowing, carnivorous mammals of the family Mustelidae, as *Taxidea taxus,* of North America, and *Meles meles,* of Europe and Asia. **2.** the fur of this mammal. **3.** *Australian.* **a.** a wombat. **b.** bandicoot (def. 2). **4.** (*cap.*) a native or inhabitant of Wisconsin (the **Badger State**) (used as a nickname). **5.** a swablike device for cleaning excess mortar from the interiors of newly laid tile drains. —*v.t.* **6.** to harass or urge persistently; pester; nag: *I had to badger him into coming with us.* [1515–25; var. of *badgeard,* perh. BADGE + -ARD, in allusion to white mark or badge on head]
—**Syn. 6.** vex, bedevil, plague, worry, disturb, bait.

American badger, *Taxidea taxus,* head and body 2 ft. (0.6 m); tail 6 in. (15 cm)

badg′er game′, an extortion scheme in which a woman places a man in a compromising position and then victimizes him by demanding money when her male accomplice, pretending to be an outraged husband or relative, enters and threatens violence, scandal, etc. [1895–1900]

badg′er plane′, *Carpentry.* a plane for finishing rabbets or the like. [1875–80]

badg′er skunk′. See **hog-nosed skunk** (def. 1).

Badg′er State′, Wisconsin (used as a nickname).

Bad′ Go′desberg (bät), official name of **Godesberg.**

ba·di·geon (bə dij′ən), *n.* a composition for patching surface defects in carpentry or masonry. [1745–55; < F < ?]

bad·i·nage (bad′n äzh′, bad′n ij), *n., v.,* **-naged, -nag·ing.** —*n.* **1.** light, playful banter or raillery. —*v.t.* **2.** to banter with or tease (someone) playfully. [1650–60; < F, equiv. to *badin(er)* to joke, trifle (v. deriv. of *badin* joker, banterer < OPr: fool; *bad(ar)* to gape (< VL *batāre;* cf. BAY[2]) + *-in* < L *-īnus* -INE[1]) + *-age* -AGE]

bad·lands (bad′landz′), *n.* (*used with a plural v.*) a barren area in which soft rock strata are eroded into varied, fantastic forms. [1850–55, *Amer.*; BAD[1] + LAND + -S[3]; trans. of F *mauvaises terres,* perh. based on expressions in AmerInd languages, alluding to the difficulty in traversing such country]

Bad′ Lands′, a barren, severely eroded region in SW South Dakota and NW Nebraska.

Bad′lands Na′tional Park′, a national park in SW South Dakota: rock formations and animal fossils. 380 sq. mi. (985 sq. km). Formerly (1929–77), **Bad′lands Na′tional Mon′ument.**

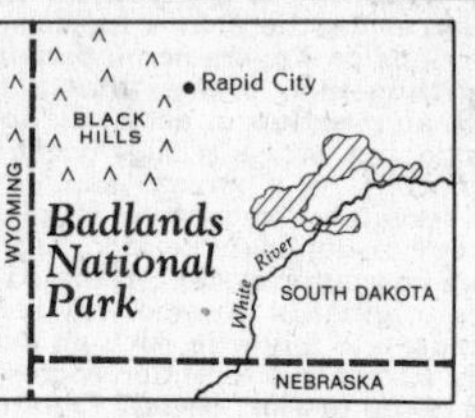

bad·ly (bad′lē), *adv.,* **worse, worst,** *adj.* —*adv.* **1.** in a defective, incorrect, or undesirable way: *The car runs badly.* **2.** in an unsatisfactory, inadequate, or unskilled manner: *a vague, badly written letter; He paints badly.* **3.** unfavorably: *His neighbors spoke badly of him. The weather turned out badly for the cruise.* **4.** in a wicked, evil, or morally or legally wrong way. **5.** in a disobedient, naughty, or ethically or socially wrong way: *He treats his parents badly.* **6.** very much; to a great extent or degree: *a house badly in need of repair; to want something badly.* **7.** severely; direly: *to be injured badly.* **8.** with great distress, resentment, regret, or emotional display: *She took the news of her mother's death badly.* **9. badly off.** See **bad** (def. 47). —*adj.* **10.** in ill health; sick: *He felt badly.* **11.** sorry; regretful: *I feel badly about your reaction to my remark.* **12.** dejected; downcast. [1350–1400; ME *baddeli.* See BAD[1], -LY]
—**Usage.** In the sense "very much," BADLY is fully standard: *He needs help badly.* See also **bad.**

bad′ man′, *Older Use.* **1.** (*sometimes caps.*) the devil. **2.** the bogeyman. [1850–55, *Amer.*]

bad·man (bad′man′), *n., pl.* **-men.** a bandit, outlaw, desperado, etc., esp. in the early history of the western U.S. [1850–55, *Amer.*; BAD[1] + MAN]

bad·min·ton (bad′min tn), *n.* a game played on a rectangular court by two players or two pairs of players equipped with light rackets used to volley a shuttlecock over a high net that divides the court in half. See illus. under **racket.** [1835–45; named after *Badminton,* the country seat of the duke of Beaufort in Gloucestershire, England]

bad-mouth (bad′mouth′ *or, sometimes,* -mouth′), *v.t.,* **-mouthed, -mouth·ing.** *Slang.* to speak critically and often disloyally of; disparage: *Why do you bad-mouth your family so much?* Also, **bad′mouth′.** [1935–40; orig. a curse, spell (the sense recorded in Gullah); cf. Vai (Mande language of Liberia and Sierra Leone) *dà n'à mà* curse, lit., bad mouth] —**bad′-mouth′er,** *n.*

bad′ news′, *Informal.* an annoying, disturbing, unwelcome thing or person; nuisance; troublemaker.

Ba·do·glio (bä dô′lyô), *n.* **Pie·tro** (pye′trô), 1871–1956, Italian general.

bad′ pa′per, *Slang.* a less-than-honorable discharge from military service.

bad′ place′, the, *Midland and Southern U.S.* hell.

Badr (bad′ər), *n.* **Battle of,** *Islam.* a decisive battle in the early days of Islam (A.D. 624), in which Muhammad with about 300 men overcame a force of about 1000 Meccans.

bad′ rap′, *Slang.* See **bum rap.**

bad-tem·pered (bad′tem′pərd), *adj.* cross; cranky; surly; ill-tempered: *a bad-tempered person.* [1920–25]

bad′ trip′, *Slang.* **1.** a mentally or physically horrifying drug-taking experience, as one accompanied by nightmarish hallucinations or by physical pain. **2.** a dismayingly unpleasant experience: *He was so ill-prepared that college was a bad trip for him.* [1965–70]

BAE, 1. Bureau of Agricultural Economics. **2.** Bureau of American Ethnology.

B.A.E., 1. Bachelor of Aeronautical Engineering. **2.** Bachelor of Agricultural Engineering. **3.** Bachelor of Architectural Engineering. **4.** Bachelor of Art Education. **5.** Bachelor of Arts in Education.

B.A.Ed., Bachelor of Arts in Education.

Bae·da (bē′də), *n.* **Saint.** See **Bede, Saint.**

Bae·de·ker (bā′di kər), *n.* **1.** any of the series of guidebooks for travelers issued by the German publisher Karl Baedeker, 1801–59, and his successors. **2.** any guidebook, pamphlet, or the like, containing information useful to travelers: *a Baedeker to the restaurants of the region.*

B.A.E.E., Bachelor of Arts in Elementary Education.

Baeke•land (bāk′land′; *Flem.* bä′kə länt′), *n.* **Le•o Hen•drik** (lē′ō hen′drik; *Flem.* lā′ō hen′drik), 1863–1944, U.S. chemist, born in Belgium: developed Bakelite.

bael (bel, bäl, bīl), *n.* **1.** a spiny citrus tree, *Aegle marmelos,* of India. **2.** the hard-shelled, greenish-yellow, edible fruit of this tree. Also, **bel.** Also called **Bengal quince.** [1610–20; < Hindi *bēl*]

Baer (bâr), *n.* **1. Karl Ernst von** (kärl ûrnst von, fən), 1792–1876, Estonian zoologist and pioneer embryologist. **2. Max,** 1909–59, U.S. boxer: world heavyweight champion 1934.

bae•tyl (bēt′l), *n. Class. Antiq.* a meteorite or stone held sacred or believed to be of divine origin. Also, **bae•tu•lus** (bē′chə ləs, bēt′l əs), **bae•ty•lus** (bēt′l əs). [1850–55; < L *baetulus* < Gk *baítylos* meteoric stone] —**bae•tyl•ic** (bē til′ik), *adj.*

Bae•yer (bā′ər; *Ger.* be′yər), *n.* **(Jo•hann Frie•drich Wil•helm) A•dolf von** (yō′hän frē′drik wil′helm ad′olf von, ā′dolf; *Ger.* yō′hän frē′drikh vil′helm ä′dôlf fən), 1835–1917, German chemist: Nobel prize 1905.

Ba•ez (bī ez′, bī′iz), *n.* **Joan,** born 1941, U.S. folk singer.

baff (baf), *Golf.* —*v.i.* **1.** to strike the ground with a club in making a stroke. —*n.* **2.** a stroke with a club that unduly lofts the ball. [1790–1800; Scots dial., special use of *baff* blow, buffet, prob. ult. of imit. orig.]

Baf•fin (baf′in), *n.* **William,** 1584?–1622, an English navigator who explored arctic North America.

Baf′fin Bay′, a part of the Arctic Ocean between W Greenland and E Baffin Island.

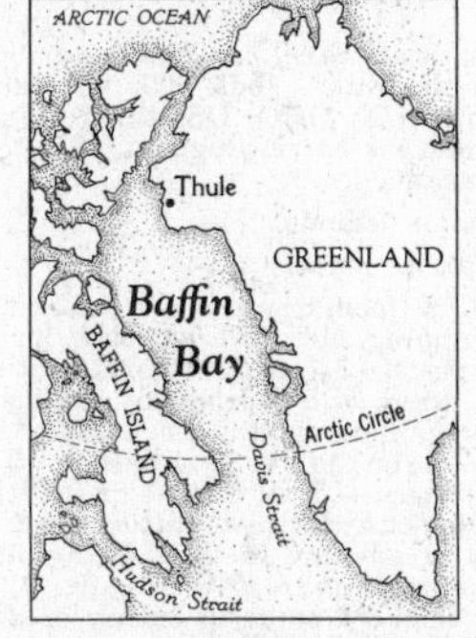

Baf′fin Is′land, a Canadian island in the Arctic Ocean, between Greenland and N Canada. ab. 1000 mi. (1600 km) long; 190,000 sq. mi. (492,000 sq. km). Also called **Baf′fin Land′.**

baf•fle (baf′əl), *v.,* **-fled, -fling,** *n.* —*v.t.* **1.** to confuse, bewilder, or perplex: *He was baffled by the technical language of the instructions.* **2.** to frustrate or confound; thwart by creating confusion or bewilderment. **3.** to check or deflect the movement of (sound, light, fluids, etc.). **4.** to equip with a baffle or baffles. **5.** *Obs.* to cheat; trick. —*v.i.* **6.** to struggle ineffectually, as a ship in a gale. —*n.* **7.** something that balks, checks, or deflects. **8.** an artificial obstruction for checking or deflecting the flow of gases (as in a boiler), sounds (as in the loudspeaker system of a radio or hi-fi set), light (as in a darkroom), etc. **9.** any boxlike enclosure or flat panel for mounting a loudspeaker. [1540–50; 1910–15 for def. 8; perh. < Scots *bauchle* to disgrace, treat with contempt, equiv. to *bauch* (see BAFF) + -LE] —**baf′fle•ment,** *n.* —**baf′fler,** *n.* —**baf′fling,** *adj.* —**baf′fling•ly,** *adv.* —**baf′fling•ness,** *n.*
—**Syn. 1.** See **thwart.**

baf•fle•gab (baf′əl gab′), *n. Slang.* confusing or generally unintelligible jargon; gobbledegook: *an insurance policy written in bafflegab impenetrable to a lay person.* [1950–55; BAFFLE + GAB[1]] —**baf′fle•gab′ber,** *n.*

baf•fle•plate (baf′əl plāt′), *n.* a plate used as a baffle. [1880–85; BAFFLE + PLATE[1]]

baff•y (baf′ē), *n., pl.* **baff•ies.** *Golf.* a short, wooden club with a steep-sloped face, for lofting the ball. Also called **number four wood.** [1885–90; BAFF + -Y[2]]

bag (bag), *n., v.,* **bagged, bag•ging,** *interj.* —*n.* **1.** a container or receptacle of leather, plastic, cloth, paper, etc., capable of being closed at the mouth; pouch. **2.** something resembling or suggesting such a receptacle. **3.** a suitcase or other portable container for carrying articles, as in traveling. **4.** a purse or moneybag. **5.** the amount or quantity a bag can hold. **6.** any of various measures of capacity. **7.** a sac, as in an animal body. **8.** an udder. **9.** *Slang.* a small glassine or cellophane envelope containing a narcotic drug or a mixture of narcotics. **10.** something hanging in a loose, pouchlike manner, as skin or cloth; a baggy part: *He had bags under his eyes from lack of sleep.* **11.** *Baseball.* base[1] (def. 8b). **12.** *Hunting.* the amount of game taken, esp. by one hunter in one hunting trip or over a specified period. **13.** *Slang.* **a.** a person's avocation, hobby, major interest, or obsession: *Jazz isn't my bag.* **b.** a person's mood or frame of mind: *The boss is in a mean bag today.* **c.** an environment, condition, or situation. **14. bags, a.** *Informal.* plenty; much; many (usually fol. by *of*): *bags of time; bags of money.* **b.** *Slang.* trousers. **15. bag and baggage, a.** with all one's personal property: *When they went to collect the rent, they found he had left, bag and baggage.* **b.** completely, totally: *The equipment had disappeared, bag and baggage, without even the slightest trace.* **16. bag of bones,** an emaciated person or animal. **17. bag of tricks,** a supply of expedient resources; stratagems: *Maybe they will finally be honest with us, once they've run through their bag of tricks.* **18. hold the bag,** *Informal.* to be forced to bear the entire blame, responsibility, or loss that was to have been shared: *His accomplices flew to South America on news of the theft and left him holding the bag.* **19. in the bag,** *Informal.* virtually certain; assured; definite: *Her promotion is in the bag. The sale of the house is in the bag.* **20. old bag,** *Slang.* an unattractive, often slatternly woman: *a gossipy old bag.* —*v.i.* **21.** to swell or bulge: *A stiff breeze made the sails bag out.* **22.** to hang loosely like an empty bag: *His socks bagged at the ankles.* **23.** to pack groceries or other items into a bag. —*v.t.* **24.** to cause to swell or bulge; distend: *The wind bagged the curtain.* **25.** to put into a bag. **26.** *Informal.* to kill or catch, as in hunting: *I bagged my first deer when I was a teenager.* **27.** *Theat.* clew (def. 10a). **28. bag school,** *Slang.* to be truant. Also, **bag it.** —*interj.* **29. bags!** *Brit. Slang.* (used to lay first claim to something): *Bags it! Bags, I go first!* [1200–50; 1920–25 for def. 20; ME *bagge* < ON *baggi* pack, bundle] —**bag′like′,** *adj.*
—**Regional Variation. 1.** Although BAG and SACK are both used everywhere throughout the U.S., the more commonly used word in the North Midland U.S. is BAG and in the South Midland is SACK.

B.Ag., Bachelor of Agriculture.

ba•gasse (bə gas′), *n.* **1.** crushed sugar cane or beet refuse from sugar making. **2.** paper made from fibers of bagasse. [1820–30, *Amer.*; < F < AmerSp, Sp *bagazo,* deriv. of *baga* seed capsule of the flax plant (presumably orig. of any fruit) < L *bāca* berry; cf. BAY[4]]

bag•a•telle (bag′ə tel′), *n.* **1.** something of little value or importance; a trifle. **2.** a game played on a board having holes at one end into which balls are to be struck with a cue. **3.** pinball. **4.** a short and light musical composition, typically for the piano. [1630–40; < F < Upper It *bagat(t)ella,* equiv. to *bagatt(a)* small possession (perh. *bag(a)* berry (< L *bāca;* cf BAY[4]) + *-att(a)* dim. suffix) + *-ella* < L *-illa* dim. suffix]

Bag•a•tha (bag′ə thə), *n. Douay Bible.* Bigtha.

Bag•dad (bag′dad, bəg dad′), *n.* Baghdad.

B.Ag.E., Bachelor of Agricultural Engineering.

Bage•hot (baj′ət), *n.* **Walter,** 1826–77, English economist, political journalist, and critic.

ba•gel (bā′gəl), *n.* a leavened, doughnut-shaped, firm-textured roll, with a brownish glazed surface, made of dough first poached and then baked. [1930–35; < Yiddish *beygl;* cf. dial. G *Beugel* < Gmc **baug-* ring (see BEE[2]) + *-*il-* n. suffix]

bag•ful (bag′fo͝ol), *n., pl.* **-fuls. 1.** the contents of or amount held by a bag: *three bagfuls of groceries.* **2.** the quantity required to fill a bag. **3.** a considerable amount: *He has a bagful of clever ideas.* [1275–1325; ME; see BAG, -FUL]
—**Usage.** See **-ful.**

bag•gage (bag′ij), *n.* **1.** trunks, suitcases, etc., used in traveling; luggage. **2.** the portable equipment of an army. **3.** things that encumber one's freedom, progress, development, or adaptability; impediments: *intellectual baggage that keeps one from thinking clearly; neurotic conflicts that arise from struggling with too much emotional baggage.* **4.** *Disparaging and Offensive.* **a.** a woman. **b.** a prostitute or disreputable woman. **5.** *Often Offensive.* a pert, playful young woman or girl. [1400–50; late ME *bagage* < MF, equiv. to OF *bag(ues)* bundles, packs (perh. < ON; see BAG) + *-age* -AGE]

bag′gage car′, a car of a passenger train in which luggage, trunks, etc., are carried. [1825–35, *Amer.*]

bag′gage han′dler, a person employed by a railway, airline, or steamship company to load or unload baggage.

bag•gage•mas•ter (bag′ij mas′tər, -mä′stər), *n.* a person employed, esp. by a railroad, bus company, or steamship line, to take charge of passengers' baggage. [1805–15; BAGGAGE + MASTER]

bag•gat•a•way (bə gat′ə wā′), *n.* a form of lacrosse as played originally by the Ojibwa Indians. [1800–10; < Ojibwa *pa·ka′atowe·* (he) plays lacrosse]

bag•ger (bag′ər), *n.* **1.** a person who packs groceries or other items into bags. **2.** a bag of cloth or plastic attached to a power lawn mower to collect grass as it is cut. [1730–40, for earlier sense; BAG + -ER[1]]

Bag•gie (bag′ē), **1.** *Trademark.* a brand of plastic bag, manufactured in various sizes, as for preserving food or holding trash. —*n.* **2.** (*l.c.*) *Informal.* any small bag or packet. [1780–90; BAG + -IE]

bag•gies (bag′ēz), *n.* (*used with a plural v.*) **1.** loose-fitting swimming trunks, often with a drawstring at the waist, esp. as worn by surfers. **2.** loose-fitting slacks, esp. women's slacks gathered at the waist and tapering toward the ankles. [1960–65; BAG + -Y[2] + -S[3]]

bag•ging (bag′ing), *n.* woven material, as of hemp or jute, for bags. [1725–35; BAG + -ING[1]]

bag•gy (bag′ē), *adj.,* **-gi•er, -gi•est.** baglike; hanging loosely. [1820–30; BAG + -Y[1]] —**bag′gi•ly,** *adv.* —**bag′gi•ness,** *n.*
—**Syn.** droopy, sagging, loose, loose-fitting.

Bagh•dad (bag′dad, bəg dad′), *n.* a city in and the capital of Iraq, in the central part, on the Tigris. 2,800,000. Also, **Bagdad.**

bagh•eer•a (bag ēr′ə), *n.* a crush-resistant velvet made of uncut pile and used in the manufacture of evening wear and wraps.

bagh•la (bug′lä), *n.* an Arabian sailing vessel, having lugsails on two or three masts, a straight, raking stem, and a transom stern. Also, **bag•ga•la** (bug′ə lä′). [< Ar *baghlah* lit., she-mule]

Bāgh•lān (bäg′län), *n.* **1.** a province in N Afghanistan. **2.** a city in and the capital of this province. 110,874.

bag′ job′, *Slang.* illegal entry, esp. as authorized by an agency of the federal government to gather criminal evidence, install listening devices, etc. [1970–75]

bag′ la′dy, 1. a homeless woman who lives and sleeps on city streets or in public places, often keeping all her belongings with her in shopping bags. **2.** bagwoman.

Bag•ley (bag′lē), *n.* **William Chandler,** 1874–1946, U.S. educator and writer.

bag•man (bag′man′ *for 1;* bag′mən *for 2, 3*), *n., pl.* **-men** (-men′ *for 1;* -mən *for 2, 3*). **1.** dishonest official; a person who collects, carries, or distributes illegal payoff money. **2.** *Brit.* a traveling salesman; drummer. **3.** *Australian.* a tramp; swagman. [1525–35, for an earlier lit. sense; BAG + MAN[1]]

bagn•io (ban′yō, bän′-), *n., pl.* **-ios. 1.** a brothel. **2.** (esp. in Italy or Turkey) a bath or bathing house. **3.** *Archaic.* a prison for slaves, esp. in the Orient. [1590–1600; < It *bagno* < L *balneum, balineum* < Gk *balaneîon* bathroom, bath]

Bag•nold (bag′nəld), *n.* **Enid,** 1889–1981, English novelist and playwright.

bag′ of wa′ters, a fluid-filled membranous sac in the pregnant uterus that encloses and cushions the fetus, normally breaking at or just before the time of birth; the amnion. [1880–85]

bag′ of wind′ (wind), windbag.

bag•pipe (bag′pīp′), *n., v.,* **-piped, -pip•ing.** —*n.* **1.** Often, **bagpipes.** a reed instrument consisting of a melody pipe and one or more accompanying drone pipes protruding from a windbag into which the air is blown by the mouth or a bellows. —*v.t.* **2.** *Naut.* to back (a fore-and-aft sail) by hauling the sheet to windward. [1300–50; ME *baggepipe.* See BAG, PIPE[1]] —**bag′•pip′er,** *n.*

bagpipe (def. 1)

B.Agr., Bachelor of Agriculture.

B.Ag.Sc., Bachelor of Agricultural Science.

bag′ ta′ble, a sewing table or worktable having a suspended pouch or bag for holding needlework.

ba•guette (ba get′), *n.* **1.** *Jewelry.* **a.** a rectangular shape given to a small gem, esp. a diamond, by cutting and polishing. **b.** a gem having this shape. **2.** *Archit.* a small convex molding, esp. one of semicircular section. **3.** a long, narrow loaf of French bread. Also, **ba•guet′.** [1720–30; < F < It *bacchetta* little stick, equiv. to *bacch(io)* stick (< L *baculus*) + *-etta* -ETTE]

Ba•gui•o (bä′gē ō′; *Sp.* bä′gyô), *n.* a city on W Luzon, in the N Philippines: summer capital. 119,009; 4961 ft. (1512 m) high.

bag•wig (bag′wig′), *n.* a wig with the back hair enclosed in a fabric bag, much used in the 18th century. [1710–20; BAG + WIG] —**bag′wigged′,** *adj.*

bag•wom•an (bag′wo͝om′ən), *n., pl.* **-wom•en.** a woman who collects, carries, or distributes illegal payoff money. Also called **bag lady.** [1970–75; BAG + -WOMAN]

bag•work (bag′wûrk′), *n. Civ. Engin.* a revetment, consisting of heavy material sewn into bags, for protecting embankments against scour. [BAG + WORK]

bag•worm (bag′wûrm′), *n.* any moth of the family Psychidae in its caterpillar phase, in which it wraps itself in a bag of silk, leaves, etc. [1860–65, *Amer.*; BAG + WORM]

bah (bä, ba), *interj.* (an exclamation of contempt or annoyance): *Bah! Humbug!*

ba•ha•dur (bə hô′do͝or, -hä′-), *n.* (*often cap.*) a title of respect commonly affixed to the names of European officers in Indian documents or in ceremonious mention by Indians: *Jonas Sahib Bahadur.* [1770–80; < Hindi *bahādur* brave, brave person < Pers, prob. < Mongolian; cf. Classical Mongolian *bayatur,* with same sense < Turkic, perh. orig. a Turkic personal name]

Ba•ha•'i (bə hä′ē, -hī′), *n., pl.* **-ha•'is,** *adj.* —*n.* **1.** a religion founded in Iran in 1863 by Husayn 'Alī (called Bahaullah) teaching the essential worth of all religions, the unity of all races, and the equality of the sexes. **2.** an adherent of Baha'i. —*adj.* **3.** of or pertaining to Baha'i or Baha'is. Also, **Ba•ha′i, Ba•hā′ī.** [< Pers < Ar *bahā* (*Allāh*) Bahaullah, lit., splendor (of God) + *-ī* suffix of appurtenance]

Ba•ha•'ism (bə hä′iz əm, -hī′iz-), *n.* the religion of Baha'i. Also, **Ba•ha′ism, Ba•hā′ism.** [BAHA'(I) + -ISM] —**Ba•ha′ist,** *n., adj.*

Ba•ha′ma grass′ (bə hä′mə, -hā′-). See **Bermuda grass.** [1885–90]

Ba•ha•mas (bə hä′məz, -hā′-), *n.* (*used with a plural*

CONCISE PRONUNCIATION KEY: act, cāpe, dâre, pärt; set, ēqual; *if,* īce; ox, ōver, ôrder, oil, bo͝ok, bo͞ot, out; up, ûrge; child; sing; shoe; thin, *that;* zh as in *treasure.* ə = *a* as in *alone, e* as in *system, i* as in *easily, o* as in *gallop, u* as in *circus;* ᵊ as in *fire* (fīᵊr), *hour* (ouᵊr). l and n can serve as syllabic consonants, as in *cradle* (krād′l), and *button* (but′n). See the full key inside the front cover.

v.) **1.** a group of islands in the W Atlantic Ocean, SE of Florida. **2.** an independent country comprising this group: formerly a British colony; gained independence 1973. 210,000; 4404 sq. mi. (11,406 sq. km). *Cap.:* Nassau. Also called **Baha′ma Is′lands.** —**Ba·ha·mi·an** (bə hā′mē ən, -hä′-), *n., adj.*

Ba·ha′sa Indone′sia (bä hä′sə), official name of the Indonesian language. [< Malay: Indonesian language]

Baha′sa Malay′sia, the dialect of Malay used as the official language of Malaysia. Also called **Baha′sa Ma′lay.** [< Malay: Malaysian language]

Ba·hau (bə hou′), *n., pl.* **-haus,** (*esp. collectively*) **-hau.** a member of any of several Dayak tribes of central and eastern Borneo.

Ba·ha·ul·lah (bä hä′ŏŏl lä′), *n.* See **Husayn ′Alī.** Also, **Ba·hā′-u′l·lāh′.**

Ba·ha·wal·pur (bə hä′wəl pŏŏr′, bä′wəl-), *n.* **1.** a state in E Pakistan. 4,652,000; 32,443 sq. mi. (83,000 sq. km). **2.** the capital of this state. 133,956.

Ba·hi·a (bä ē′ə, bə-), *n.* **1.** a coastal state of E Brazil. 9,593,687; 216,130 sq. mi. (559,700 sq. km). *Cap.:* Salvador. **2.** a former name of **Salvador.**

Ba·hí·a Blan·ca (bä ē′ä vläng′kä), a seaport in E Argentina. 220,765.

Ba·hí·a de Co·chi·nos (bä ē′ä the kô chē′nôs), Spanish name of **Bay of Pigs.**

Ba·hi′a grass′ (bə hē′ə), a grass, *Paspalum notatum,* of tropical America, grown in the southern United States for lawns and pasturage. [1925–30; after BAHIA (state)]

Bahr (bär), *n.* **Her·mann** (her′män), 1863–1934, Austrian playwright and critic.

Bah·rain (bä rān′, -rīn′, bə-), *n.* **1.** a sheikdom in the Persian Gulf, consisting of a group of islands: formerly a British protectorate; declared independent 1971. 300,000; 232 sq. mi. (601 sq. km). *Cap.:* Manama. **2.** the largest island in this group: oil fields. 265,000; 213 sq. mi. (552 sq. km). Also, **Bah·rein′.**

Bah·rain·i (bä rā′nē, -rī′-, bə-), *n., pl.* **-rain·is,** *adj.* —*n.* **1.** a native or inhabitant of Bahrain. —*adj.* **2.** of, pertaining to, or characteristic of Bahrain or its people. [BAHRAIN + Ar -*ī* suffix of appurtenance]

baht (bät), *n., pl.* **bahts, baht.** a paper money and monetary unit of Thailand, equal to 100 satangs. [1820–30; < Thai *bà:t,* earlier, a measure of weight, ult. < Pali *pāda* FOOT]

ba·hut (bä′hōōt, -hōōt; bə hōōt′, -hōōt′; *Fr.* bA Y′), *n., pl.* **ba·huts** (bä′hōōts, -hōōts; bə hōōts′, -hōōts′; *Fr.* bA Y′). **1.** a medieval French chest for household goods, originally small and portable. **2.** a dwarf parapet or attic wall, esp. one carrying the wall plates of a church roof. [1830–40; < F, OF *bahu, bahuz,* perh. < Old Low Franconian **baghôdi* cover, protection, equiv. to **bag*-BAG + *-*hôdi* protection, akin to HIDE[1], HUT]

ba·hu·vri·hi (bä′hōō vrē′hē), *n., pl.* **-his.** *Gram.* a compound noun or adjective consisting of two constituents, the first of which is adjectival and describes the person or object denoted by the second, which is nominal: the compound as a whole denotes or describes a person or object having what is denoted by the second element, as *bonehead, heavy-handed, redcoat.* [1840–50; < Skt: lit., having much rice, equiv. to *bahu-* much + *vrīhi* rice; used to name the type of compound word of which it is an example]

bai (bī), *n.* a yellow mist occurring in eastern China and Japan during the spring and fall, caused by dust from the interior of China. [< Japn < MChin, equiv. to Chin *mái* dust storm]

Ba·iae (bä′yē), *n.* an ancient resort city in SW Italy, near Naples: villas of Caesar, Nero, and Pompey.

bai·dar·ka (bī där′kə), *n.* bidarka.

bai·gneuse (be nyœz′), *n., pl.* **-gneuses** (-nyœz′). *Fr. Furniture.* a day bed of the Empire period, having a back sloping and curving to form a rounded head and foot. [< F: lit., bather (fem.)]

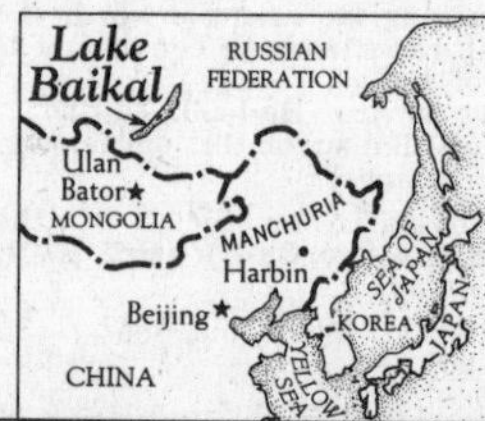

CONCISE ETYMOLOGY KEY: <, descended or borrowed from; >, whence; b., blend of, blended; c., cognate with; cf., compare; deriv., derivative; equiv., equivalent; imit., imitative; obl., oblique; r., replacing; s., stem; sp., spelling, spelled; resp., respelling, respelled; trans., translation; ?, origin unknown; *, unattested; ‡, probably earlier than. See the full key inside the front cover.

Bai·kal (bī käl′), *n.* **Lake,** a lake in the Russian Federation, in S Siberia: the deepest lake in the world. 13,200 sq. mi. (34,188 sq. km); 5714 ft. (1742 m) deep.

bail[1] (bāl), *Law.* —*n.* **1.** property or money given as surety that a person released from custody will return at an appointed time. **2.** the person who agrees to be liable if someone released from custody does not return at an appointed time. **3.** the state of release upon being bailed. **4. go** or **stand bail for,** to provide bail for: *They spent the night in jail because no one would stand bail for them.* **5. jump bail,** to abscond while free on bail: *The suspect jumped bail and is now being sought.* **6. on bail,** released or free as a result of having posted bond: *He was out on bail within 10 hours of his arrest.* —*v.t.* **7.** to grant or obtain the liberty of (a person under arrest) on security given for his or her appearance when required, as in court for trial. **8.** to deliver possession of (goods) for storage, hire, or other special purpose, without transfer of ownership. [1375–1425; late ME *bayle* < AF *bail* custody, charge < OF, n. deriv. of *baillier* to hand over < L *bāiulāre* to serve as porter v. deriv. of *bāiulus* porter, perh. an Imperial L borrowing from Moesia < **ba(r)i̯-* carry (akin to Albanian *m-ba* hold) < **bhor-i̯-;* see BEAR[1]]

bail[2] (bāl), *n.* **1.** the semicircular handle of a kettle or pail. **2.** a hooplike support, as for the canvas cover on a Conestoga wagon. **3.** a metal band or bar equipped with rollers for holding a sheet or sheets of paper against the platen of a printing press, typewriter, etc. Also, **bale.** [1400–50; late ME *beyl,* perh. < ON; cf. ON *beyglast* to become bent, equiv. to *baug(r)* ring (see BEE[2]) + *-*il* n. suffix + -*ast* middle inf. suffix]

bail[3] (bāl), *v.t.* **1.** to dip (water) out of a boat, as with a bucket. **2.** to clear of water by dipping (usually fol. by *out*): *to bail out a boat.* —*v.i.* **3.** to bail water. **4. bail out, a.** to make a parachute jump from an airplane. **b.** to relieve or assist (a person, company, etc.) in an emergency situation, esp. a financial crisis: *The corporation bailed out its failing subsidiary through a series of refinancing operations.* **c.** to give up on or abandon something, as to evade a responsibility: *His partner bailed out before the business failed.* —*n.* **5.** Also, **bail′er.** a bucket, dipper, or other container used for bailing. Also, **bale** (for defs. 1–3). [1425–75; late ME *bayle* < MF *baille* a bucket < VL **bāi(u)la;* akin to L *bāiulus* carrier. See BAIL[1]]

bail[4] (bāl), *n.* **1.** *Cricket.* either of the two small bars or sticks laid across the tops of the stumps which form the wicket. **2.** *Brit., Australian.* a bar, framework, partition, or the like, for confining or separating cows, horses, etc., in a stable. **3. bails,** *Obs.* the wall of an outer court of a feudal castle. —*v.t.* **4. bail up,** *Australian.* **a.** to confine a cow for milking, as in a bail. **b.** to force (one) to surrender or identify oneself or to state one's business. **c.** to waylay or rob (someone). —*interj.* **5. bail up!** *Australian.* (the cry of challenge of a pioneer or person living in the bush.) [1350–1400; ME *baile* < OF < L *bacula,* pl. of *baculum* stick]

bail·a·ble (bā′lə bəl), *adj. Law.* **1.** capable of being set free on bail. **2.** admitting of bail: *a bailable offense.* [1495–1505; BAIL[1] + -ABLE]

bail′ bond′, a formal document that gives bail for someone to be released from custody. [1700–10]

Bai·le Átha Cli·ath (blä klē′ə), Gaelic name of **Dublin.**

bail·ee (bā lē′), *n. Law.* a person to whom personal property is delivered in bailment. [1520–30; BAIL[1] + -EE]

bai·ley (bā′lē), *n., pl.* **-leys.** **1.** the defensive wall surrounding an outer court of a castle. **2.** the courtyard itself. Also, **ballium.** [1250–1300; ME, var. of BAIL[4]]

Bai·ley (bā′lē), *n.* **1. Liberty Hyde,** 1858–1954, U.S. botanist, horticulturist, and writer. **2. Nathan** or **Nathaniel,** died 1742, English lexicographer.

Bai′ley bridge′, a temporary bridge formed of prefabricated, interchangeable, steel truss panels bolted together. [named after Sir Donald Bailey (1901–85), British engineer, its designer]

bail·ie (bā′lē), *n.* **1.** (in Scotland) a municipal officer or magistrate, corresponding to an English alderman. **2.** *Obs.* bailiff. [1250–1300; ME *baillie* < OF *bailli,* var. of *baillif* BAILIFF]

bail·iff (bā′lif), *n.* **1.** an officer, similar to a sheriff or a sheriff's deputy, employed to execute writs and processes, make arrests, keep order in the court, etc. **2.** (in Britain) a person charged with local administrative authority, or the chief magistrate in certain towns. **3.** (esp. in Britain) an overseer of a landed estate or farm. [1250–1300; ME *baillif* < OF, equiv. to *bail* custody (see BAIL[1]) + -*if* -IVE] —**bail′iff·ship′,** *n.*

bail·i·wick (bā′lə wik′), *n.* **1.** the district within which a bailie or bailiff has jurisdiction. **2.** a person's area of skill, knowledge, authority, or work: *to confine suggestions to one's own bailiwick.* [1425–75; late ME, equiv. to *baili-* BAILIE + *wick* WICK[3]]
—**Syn. 2.** domain, department, sphere, territory, turf.

bail·ment (bāl′mənt), *n. Law.* the delivery of personal property returnable to the bailor after being held for some purpose. [1545–55; earlier *bailement* < AF; OF *baillement.* See BAIL[1], -MENT]

bail·or (bā′lər, bā lôr′), *n.* a person who delivers personal property in bailment. [1595–1605; BAIL[1] + -OR[2]]

bail·out (bāl′out′), *n.* **1.** the act of parachuting from an aircraft, esp. to escape a crash, fire, etc. **2.** an instance of coming to the rescue, esp. financially: *a government bailout of a large company.* **3.** an alternative, additional choice, or the like: *If the highway is jammed, you have two side roads as bailouts.* —*adj.* **4.** of, pertaining to, or consisting of means for relieving an emergency situation: *bailout measures for hard-pressed small businesses.* Also, **bail′-out′.** [1950–55; n., adj. use of v phrase *bail out*]

bails·man (bālz′mən), *n., pl.* **-men.** a person who gives bail or acts as surety. [1860–65; BAIL[1] + 's[1] + -MAN]

Bai′ly's beads′ (bā′lēz), spots of light that appear to encircle the moon, resembling a string of luminous beads, visible immediately before and after a total eclipse, caused by the sun's light shining between the mountains on the moon's surface. Cf. **diamond ring effect.** [named after Francis Baily (1774–1844), English astronomer who first described them]

Bain·bridge (bān′brij′), *n.* a city in SW Georgia. 10,553.

bain·ite (bā′nīt), *n. Metall.* an aggregate of iron carbide and ferrite, formed from austenite below the temperature at which pearlite forms and above that at which martensite forms. [1930–35; after Edgar C. Bain (1891–1971), American physicist and metallurgist; see -ITE[1]]

bain-ma·rie (bān′mə rē′; *Fr.* baN mA Rē′), *n., pl.* **bains-ma·rie** (bān′mə rē′; *Fr.* baN mA Rē′). **1.** (in cooking) a receptacle containing hot or boiling water into which other containers are placed to warm or cook the food in them. **2.** *Brit.* a double boiler. [1815–25; < F MF, trans. of ML *balneum Mariae* lit., bath of Mary, reputed to be a Jewish alchemist who devised such a heating technique, and sometimes identified with Moses' sister Miriam]

Bain′gen La′ma (bīn′chen). See **Tashi Lama.**

Bai·ram (bī räm′, bī′räm), *n.* See **′Id al-Adha.** [1590–1600; < Turk *bayram* lit., holiday, festival, prob. ult. < Pers]

Baird′ Moun′tains, a mountain range in NW Alaska forming the west range of the Brooks Range.

baire (bâr), *n. Chiefly Louisiana.* See **mosquito net.** [see BAR[2]]

bairn (bârn; *Scot.* bāRn), *n. Scot. and North Eng.* a child; son or daughter. [bef. 900; ME *bern, barn,* OE *bearn;* c. Goth, ON, OHG, OS, *barn,* OFris *bern,* MD *baren,* Albanian *me barrë* pregnant; akin to Lith *bérnas* boy, fellow, BEAR[1]]

Ba. Is., Bahama Islands.

bai·sa (bī′zä), *n.* baiza.

bait (bāt), *n.* **1.** food, or some substitute, used as a lure in fishing, trapping, etc. **2.** a poisoned lure used in exterminating pests. **3.** an allurement; enticement: *Employees were lured with the bait of annual bonuses.* **4.** an object for pulling molten or liquefied material, as glass, from a vat or the like by adhesion. **5.** *South Midland and Southern U.S.* **a.** a large or sufficient quantity or amount: *He fetched a good bait of wood.* **b.** an excessive quantity or amount. **6.** *Brit. Slang.* food. —*v.t.* **7.** to prepare (a hook or trap) with bait. **8.** to entice by deception or trickery so as to entrap or destroy: *using fake signal lights to bait the ships onto the rocks.* **9.** to attract, tempt, or captivate. **10.** to set dogs upon (an animal) for sport. **11.** to worry, torment, or persecute, esp. with malicious remarks: *a nasty habit of baiting defenseless subordinates.* **12.** to tease: *They love to bait him about his gaudy ties.* **13.** to feed and water (a horse or other animal), esp. during a journey. —*v.i. Archaic.* **14.** to stop for food or refreshment during a journey. **15.** (of a horse or other animal) to take food; feed. [1150–1200; ME *bait, beit* (n.), *baiten* (v.) < ON, prob. reflecting both *beita* to pasture, hunt, chase with dogs or hawks (ult. causative of *bīta* to BITE; cf. BATE[3]) and *beita* fish bait] —**bait′er,** *n.*
—**Syn. 11.** badger, heckle, pester.

bait-and-switch (bāt′n swich′), *adj.* **1.** denoting a deceptive method of selling, by which customers, attracted to a store by sale items, are told either that the advertised bargain item is out of stock or is inferior to a higher-priced item that is available. —*n.* **2.** an act or instance of such practice.

bait′ cast′ing, *Angling.* the act or technique of casting an artificial or natural lure attached to a silk or nylon line wound on a reel having a revolving spool, the rod used being shorter and less flexible than that used in fly casting.

bait·fish (bāt′fish′), *n., pl.* (*esp. collectively*) **-fish,** (*esp. referring to two or more kinds or species*) **-fish·es.** **1.** a small fish that is a source of food for a larger fish: *Fishermen knew the presence of baitfish meant plenty of bass nearby.* **2.** *Angling.* any small fish, as a minnow or shiner, used as bait. [BAIT + FISH]

baith (bāth), *adj., pron. Scot. and North Eng.* both.

bai·za (bī′zä), *n.* a coin and monetary unit of Oman, the 1000th part of a rial omani. Also, **baisa.** [< Ar *bayzah* < Hindi *paisā*]

baize (bāz), *n., v.,* **baized, baiz·ing.** —*n.* **1.** a soft, usually green, woolen or cotton fabric resembling felt, used chiefly for the tops of billiard tables. **2.** an article of this fabric or of a fabric resembling it. —*v.t.* **3.** to line or cover with baize. [1570–80; earlier *bayes* < F *baies* (n.), OF (*estoffes* fabrics) *baies,* fem. pl. of *bai* (adj.) BAY[5]]

Ba·ja Ca·li·for·nia (bä′hä kal′ə fôr′nyə, -fôr′nē ə; *Sp.* bä′hä kä′lē fôr′nyä), a narrow peninsula in NW Mexico between the Gulf of California and the Pacific, forming two territories of Mexico. 1,434,000; 55,634 sq. mi. (144,090 sq. km). *Caps:* Mexicali (Northern Territory) and La Paz (Southern Territory). Also called **Ba′ja, Lower California.**

ba·ja·da (bə hä′də), *n.* an alluvial plain formed at the base of a mountain by the coalescing of several alluvial fans. [1865–70, *Amer.*; < Sp: slope, swoop, orig. fem. ptp. of *bajar* to descend < VL **bassiāre,* deriv. of LL *bassus* short, low]

Baj·er (bī′ər), *n.* **Fred·rik** (fred′rik; *Dan.* fʀith′ʀik), 1837–1922, Danish politician and author: Nobel peace prize 1908.

Ba Jin (bä′ jin′), (*Li Feigan*), born 1904, Chinese writer and novelist.

B.A.Jour., Bachelor of Arts in Journalism.

bake (bāk), *v.*, **baked, bak•ing,** *n.* —*v.t.* **1.** to cook by dry heat in an oven or on heated metal or stones. **2.** to harden by heat: *to bake pottery in a kiln.* **3.** to dry by, or subject to heat: *The sun baked the land.* —*v.i.* **4.** to bake bread, a casserole, etc. **5.** to become baked: *The cake will bake in about half an hour.* **6.** to be subjected to heat: *The lizard baked on the hot rocks.* —*n.* **7.** a social occasion at which the chief food is baked. **8.** *Scot.* cracker (def. 1). [bef. 1000; ME *baken,* OE *bacan,* ptp. *bōc* baked; c. OHG *bahhan,* past *buoh,* ON *baka;* akin to D *bakken,* G *backen,* Gk *phṓgein* to roast; < IE alternating base **bheH*ₒ*g*-, *bhәg*-]

bake•ap•ple (bāk′ap′әl), *n. Canadian Atlantic Provinces.* cloudberry. Also, **bake′ ap′ple, baked-ap•ple** (bākt′ap′әl), **baked′-ap′ple ber′ry.** [1765–75; appar. BAKE (as n. or adj.; cf. BAKEMEAT) + APPLE, said to be so called because its taste resembles that of a roasted apple]

baked′ Alas′ka, a dessert consisting of ice cream on a cake base, placed briefly in a hot oven to brown its topping of meringue. [1905–10, *Amer.*]

baked′ beans′, small white dried beans that have been baked, usually with salt pork, brown sugar or molasses, and seasonings. Also called **Boston baked beans.** [1825–35]

baked′ meat′, bakemeat.

bake•goods (bāk′go͝odz′), *n.* (*used with a singular or plural v.*) baked goods, as bread, cakes, or pies. [1975–80, *Amer.*; BAKE + GOODS, perh. from rapid speech pron. of *baked goods*]

bake•house (bāk′hous′), *n., pl.* **-hous•es** (-hou′ziz). a building or room to bake in; bakery. [1250–1300; ME *bak(e)hous;* see BAKE, HOUSE]

Ba•ke•lite (bā′kә līt′, bāk′līt), *Trademark.* a brand name for any of a series of thermosetting plastics prepared by heating phenol or cresol with formaldehyde and ammonia under pressure: used for radio cabinets, telephone receivers, electric insulators, and molded plastic ware.

bake•meat (bāk′mēt′), *n. Obs.* **1.** pastry; pie. **2.** cooked food, esp. a meat pie. Also, **baked meat.** [1350–1400; ME *bake mete,* OE *bacen mete* baked food. See BAKE, MEAT]

Bake-Off (bāk′ôf′, -of′), *Trademark.* a baking contest in which competitors gather to prepare their specialties for judging. Cf. **cookoff.** [BAKE + -OFF]

bak•er (bā′kәr), *n.* **1.** a person who bakes. **2.** a person who makes and sells bread, cake, etc. **3.** a small portable oven. **4.** (*usually cap.*) a code word used in communications to represent the letter *B.* [bef. 1000; ME *bakere,* OE *bæcere.* See BAKE, -ER¹] —**bak′er•like′,** *adj.*

Ba•ker (bā′kәr), *n.* **1. Sir Benjamin,** 1840–1907, English engineer. **2. George Pierce,** 1866–1935, U.S. critic, author, and professor of drama. **3. Howard H(enry), Jr.,** born 1925, U.S. politician: senator 1967–85. **4. Dame Janet,** born 1933, English mezzo-soprano. **5. Josephine,** 1906–75, French entertainer, born in the U.S. **6. Newton Diehl** (dēl), 1871–1937, U.S. lawyer: Secretary of War 1916–21. **7. Ray Stan•nard** (stan′әrd) ("*David Grayson*"), 1870–1946, U.S. author. **8. Mount,** a mountain in NW Washington, in the Cascade Range: highest peak, 10,750 ft. (3277 m). **9.** a town in central Louisiana. 12,865.

Ba′ker Is′land, an island in the central Pacific near the equator, belonging to the U.S. 1 sq. mi. (2.6 sq. km).

Ba′ker Lake′, a lake in the Northwest Territories, in N Canada. 975 sq. mi. (2525 sq. km).

bak′er's doz′en, a group of 13; a dozen plus one: from the former practice among bakers and other tradespeople of giving 13 items to the dozen as a safeguard against penalties for short weights and measures. [1590–1600]

Ba•kers•field (bā′kәrz fēld′), *n.* a city in S California. 105,611.

bak•er•y (bā′kә rē, bāk′rē), *n., pl.* **-er•ies. 1.** Also called **bake•shop** (bāk′shop′). a baker's shop. **2.** a place where baked goods are made. [1535–45; BAKER + -Y³; now taken as BAKE + -ERY]

bake′ sale′, a sale of homemade, donated baked goods, as by a church or club to raise money.

bake•ware (bāk′wâr′), *n.* heat-resistant dishes, as of glass or pottery, in which food may be baked; ovenware. [1880–85, *Amer.;* BAKE + WARE¹]

Bakh•mut (bäk′mo͞ot, bäкн′-; *Russ.* buкн mo͞ot′), *n.* former name of **Artemovsk.**

bak′ing pow′der, any of various powders used as a substitute for yeast in baking, composed of sodium bicarbonate mixed with an acid substance, as cream of tartar, capable of setting carbon dioxide free when the mixture is moistened, causing the dough to rise. [1840–50]

bak′ing sheet′, a flat metal pan used for baking cookies, bread, etc.

bak′ing so′da. See **sodium bicarbonate.** [1880–85, *Amer.*]

ba•kla•va (bä′klә vä′, bä′klә vä′), *n.* a Near Eastern pastry made of many layers of paper-thin dough with a filling of ground nuts, baked and then drenched in a syrup of honey and sometimes rosewater. Also, **ba•kla•wa** (bä′klә vä′, bä′klә vä′). [1815–25; < Turk]

bak•sheesh (bak′shēsh, bak shēsh′), (in the Near and Middle East) —*n.* **1.** a tip, present, or gratuity. —*v.t., v.i.* **2.** to give a tip. Also, **bak′shish, bak′shis.** [1615–25; < Pers *bakhshish* gift]

Bakst (bäkst), *n.* **Lé•on Ni•ko•la•e•vich** (lyi ôɴ′ nyiku lä′yi vyich), 1866–1924, Russian painter and designer.

Ba•ku (bu ko͞o′), *n.* a city in and the capital of Azerbaijan, in the E part, on the Caspian Sea. 1,022,000; with suburbs, 1,550,000.

Ba•ku•nin (bu ko͞o′nyin), *n.* **Mi•kha•il A•le•ksan•dro•vich** (myi кнu yēl′ u lyi ksän′drә vyich), 1814–76, Russian anarchist and writer.

Ba•kwan•ga (bә kwäng′gә), *n.* former name of **Mbuji-Mayi.**

bal (bal), *n.* Balmoral (def. 2).

BAL, 1. *Chem.* British Anti-Lewisite: dimercaprol. **2.** *Computers.* Basic Assembly Language.

Bal., Baluchistan.

bal., 1. balance. **2.** balancing.

Ba•la (bā′lә), *n. Douay Bible.* Bilhah.

Ba•laam (bā′lәm), *n.* a Mesopotamian diviner who, when commanded by Balak to curse the Israelites, blessed them and uttered favorable prophecies after having been rebuked by the ass he rode. Num. 22–23. —**Ba•laam•ite** (bā′lә mīt′), *n.* —**Ba•laam•it•i•cal** (bā′lә mi t′i kәl), *adj.*

bal•a•cla•va (bal′ә klä′vә), *n.* a close-fitting, knitted cap that covers the head, neck, and tops of the shoulders, worn esp. by mountain climbers, soldiers, skiers, etc. Also called **balacla′va hel′met.** [1880–85; named after BALAKLAVA]

Ba•la•guer (bä′lä gɛr′), *n.* **Joa•quin** (hwä kēn′), (*Joaquin Balaguer y Ricardo*), born 1907, Dominican political leader: president 1960–62, 1966–78, and since 1986.

Ba•lak (bā′lak), *n.* a Moabite king who sent for Balaam to come and curse the Israelites. Num. 22–23. Also, *Douay Bible,* **Ba′lac.**

Bal•a•kla•va (bal′ә klä′vә; *Russ.* bә lu klä′vә), *n.* a seaport in S Crimea, in S Ukraine, on the Black Sea: scene of English cavalry charge against Russians (1854), celebrated in Tennyson's poem *Charge of the Light Brigade.*

Ba•la•ko•vo (bä′lә kō′vә, bә lä′kә vō′; *Russ.* bә lukô′vә), *n.* a city in the W Russian Federation in Europe, SW of Nizhni Novgorod. 152,000.

balalaika

bal•a•lai•ka (bal′ә lī′kә), *n.* a Russian musical instrument having a triangular body and a neck like that of a guitar. [1780–90; < Russ *balalaĭka,* equiv. to *balalaĭ-,* prob. orig. a v. base, akin to *balabólit′, balákat′* chatter, talk nonsense (cf. Russ dial., Ukrainian *balabáĭka* balalaika), expressive derivs. of Slavic **bay-* speak, tell, akin to FATE, -PHASIA + *-ka* n. suffix]

bal•ance (bal′әns), *n., v.,* **-anced, -anc•ing.** —*n.* **1.** a state of equilibrium or equipoise; equal distribution of weight, amount, etc. **2.** something used to produce equilibrium; counterpoise. **3.** mental steadiness or emotional stability; habit of calm behavior, judgment, etc. **4.** a state of bodily equilibrium: *He lost his balance and fell down the stairs.* **5.** an instrument for determining weight, typically by the equilibrium of a bar with a fulcrum at the center, from each end of which is suspended a scale or pan, one holding an object of known weight, and the other holding the object to be weighed. **6.** the remainder or rest: *He carried what he could and left the balance for his brother to bring.* **7.** the power or ability to decide an outcome by throwing one's strength, influence, support, or the like, to one side or the other. **8.** (in winemaking) the degree to which all the attributes of a wine are in harmony, with none either too prominent or deficient. **9.** *Accounting.* **a.** equality between the totals of the two sides of an account. **b.** the difference between the debit total and the credit total of an account. **c.** unpaid difference represented by the excess of debits over credits. **10.** an adjustment of accounts. **11.** the act of balancing; comparison as to weight, amount, importance, etc.; estimate. **12.** preponderating weight: *The balance of the blame is on your side.* **13.** *Fine Arts.* composition or placement of elements of design, as figures, forms, or colors, in such a manner as to produce an aesthetically pleasing or harmoniously integrated whole. **14.** *Dance.* a balancing movement. **15.** Also called **balance wheel.** *Horol.* a wheel that oscillates against the tension of a hairspring to regulate the beats of a watch or clock. **16.** (*cap.*) *Astron., Astrol.* the constellation or sign of Libra; Scales. **17.** *Audio.* (in a stereophonic sound system) the comparative loudness of two speakers, usually set by a control (**balance control**) on the amplifier or receiver. **18. in the balance,** with the outcome in doubt or suspense: *While the jury deliberated, his fate rested in the balance.* **19. on balance,** considering all aspects: *On balance, the new product is doing well.* —*v.t.* **20.** to bring to or hold in equilibrium; poise: *to balance a book on one's head.* **21.** to arrange, adjust, or proportion the parts of symmetrically. **22.** to be equal or proportionate to: *I'm always happy when cash on hand balances expected expenses. One side of an equation must balance the other.* **23.** *Accounting.* **a.** to add up the two sides of (an account) and determine the difference. **b.** to make the necessary entries in (an account) so that the sums of the two sides will be equal. **c.** to settle by paying what remains due on an account; equalize or adjust. **24.** to weigh in a balance. **25.** to estimate the relative weight or importance of; compare: *to balance all the probabilities of a situation.* **26.** to serve as a counterpoise to; counterbalance; offset: *The advantages more than balance the disadvantages.* **27.** *Dance.* to move in rhythm to and from: *to balance one's partner.* —*v.i.* **28.** to have an equality or equivalence in weight, parts, etc.; be in equilibrium: *The account doesn't balance. Do these scales balance?* **29.** *Accounting.* to reckon or adjust accounts. **30.** to waver or hesitate: *He would balance and temporize endlessly before reaching a decision.* **31.** *Dance.* to move forward and backward or in opposite directions. [1250–1300; ME *balaunce* < AF; OF *balance* < VL **balancia,* var. of **bilancia,* equiv. to LL *bilanc-* (s. of *bilanx* with double scales; L *bi-* BI-¹ + *lanx* metal dish, pan of a pair of scales) + *-ia* -IA] —**bal′ance•a•ble,** *adj.*

—**Syn. 3.** poise, composure. **6.** See **remainder. 13.** See **symmetry.**

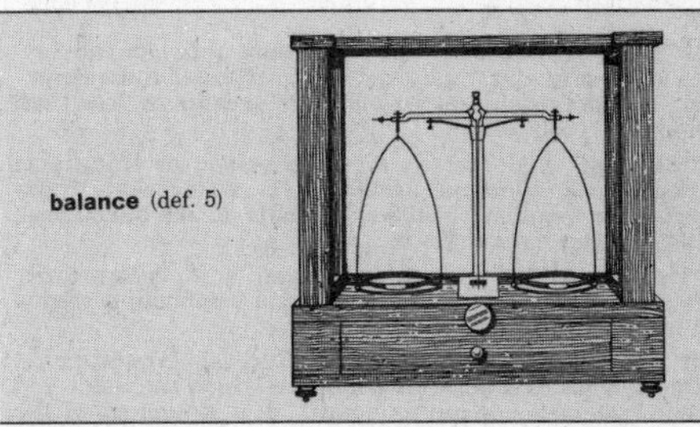
balance (def. 5)

bal•an•cé (bal′әn sā′; *Fr.* bᴀ läɴ sā′), *n., pl.* **-cés** (-sāz′; *Fr.* -sā′). *Ballet.* a swaying step performed in place in which the weight is lightly shifted from one foot to the other, the dancer sinking down on the heel of the foot to which the body is shifting, with flexed knees. [< F, n. use of ptp. of *balancer* to BALANCE, swing, rock]

bal′ance beam′, 1. a narrow wooden rail about 16 ft. (5 m) long and 4 in. (10 cm) wide, set horizontally on upright posts about 4 ft. (1.2 m) from the floor, used for performing feats of balancing and demonstrating gymnastic ability. **2.** a competitive gymnastic event for women in which such an apparatus is used. [1945–50]

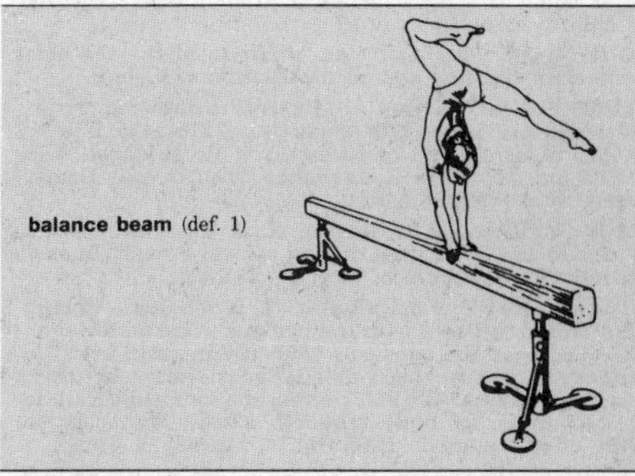
balance beam (def. 1)

bal′ance control′. See under **balance** (def. 17). [1925–30]

bal•anced (bal′әnst), *adj.* **1.** being in harmonious or proper arrangement or adjustment, proportion, etc. **2.** *Football.* pertaining to or noting an offensive line formation having three linemen on each side of the center. Cf. **unbalanced** (def. 5). [1585–95; BALANCE + -ED²]

—**Syn. 1.** fair, equitable, just, impartial, evenhanded.

bal′anced di′et, a diet consisting of the proper quantities and proportions of foods needed to maintain health or growth. [1935–40]

bal′anced fund′, *Finance.* a type of open-end investment company that includes bonds and preferred stocks in its portfolio.

bal′anced line′, *Elect.* a transmission line in which the oppositely directed components are symmetrical with respect to each other and to the ground.

bal′anced rud′der, *Naut.* a rudder so designed that the center of water pressure on the forward face, when turned, lies about halfway along the length, minimizing the turning effort required. [1865–70]

bal′anced sen′tence, a sentence consisting of two or more clauses that are parallel in structure.

bal′anced step′, any of a series of staircase winders so planned that they are nearly as wide at the inside of the stair as the adjacent fliers. Also called **dancing step, dancing winder.**

bal′anced tick′et, *U.S. Politics.* a slate of candidates chosen to appeal to a wide range of voters, esp. by including members of large regional, ethnic, or religious groups. [1955–60]

bal′anced valve′, a valve designed so that pressure-induced forces from the fluid being controlled oppose one another so that resistance to opening and closing the valve is negligible. [1930–35]

bal′ance lug′, *Naut.* a lugsail having a portion of its area forward of the mast and having a long foot, often with a boom.

bal′ance of na′ture, population equilibrium among organisms and their environments resulting from continuous interaction and interdependency. [1905–10]

bal′ance of pay′ments, the difference between a nation's total payments to foreign countries, including movements of capital and gold, investments, tourist spending, etc., and its total receipts from foreign countries. [1835–45]

bal′ance of pow′er, a distribution and opposition of forces among nations such that no single nation is strong enough to assert its will or dominate all the others. [1570–80]

bal′ance of ter′ror, the distribution of nuclear arms among nations such that no nation will initiate an attack for fear of retaliation: *maintaining the balance of terror between the United States and the Soviet Union.* [1955–60]

bal′ance of trade′, the difference between the values of exports and imports of a country, said to be favorable or unfavorable as exports are greater or less than imports. [1660–70]

bal•anc•er (bal′ən sər), *n.* **1.** a person or thing that balances. **2.** *Entomol.* halter[2]. **3.** an acrobat, ropedancer, or tumbler. [1400–50 (earlier in AF surnames); late ME; see BALANCE, -ER[1]]

bal′ance shaft′, a special shaft with eccentrically mounted weights used in an internal-combustion engine to reduce vibrations.

bal′ance sheet′, *Accounting.* **1.** a tabular statement of both sides of a set of accounts in which the debit and credit balances add up as equal. **2.** a statement of the financial position of a business on a specified date. [1830–40]

bal′ance spring′, *Horol.* hairspring. [1880–85]

bal′ance staff′, *Horol.* a pivoted axle or shaft on which the balance is mounted. [1880–85]

bal′ance wheel′, *Horol.* balance (def. 15). [1660–70]

Bal•an•chine (bal′ən chēn′, bal′ən chēn′), *n.* **George,** 1904–83, U.S. choreographer, born in Russia.

bal•a•noid (bal′ə noid′), *adj.* shaped like an acorn. [1865–70; < Gk *balanoeidḗs,* equiv. to *bálan(os)* acorn + *-oeidēs* -OID]

ba•lao (bə lou′), *n., pl.* **-laos.** a halfbeak, *Hemiramphus balao,* of tropical western Atlantic seas. [1850–55; < Puerto Rican Sp *balajú*]

Ba•la•ra•ma (bul′ə rä′mə), *n. Hindu Myth.* the elder brother of Krishna and an incarnation of Vishnu.

bal•as (bal′əs, bā′ləs), *n. Mineral.* a rose-red variety of spinel. Also called **bal′as ru′by.** [1375–1425; late ME < ML *balasius,* var. of *balascius* < Ar *balakhsh,* back formation from Pers *Badakhshān,* district near Samarkand, where gem is found]

Ba•la•shi•kha (bal′ə shē′kə; *Russ.* bə lu shi′KHə), *n.* a city in the W RSFSR, in the central Soviet Union in Europe: a NE suburb of Moscow. 118,000.

ba•la•ta (bə lä′tə, bal′ə tə), *n.* **1.** a nonelastic, rubberlike, water-resistant gum that softens in hot water and is obtained from the latex of a tropical American tree, *Manilkara bidentata:* used chiefly in the manufacture of machinery belts, golf ball covers, and as a substitute for gutta percha. Cf. **bully tree. 2.** a tree, *Mimusops balata,* of Madagascar. [1855–60; < AmerSp < Carib]

Bal•a•ton (bal′ə ton′; *Hung.* bo′lo tôn), *n.* a lake in W Hungary: the largest lake in central Europe. ab. 50 mi. (80 km) long; 230 sq. mi. (596 sq. km). German, **Plattensee.**

ba•laus•tine (bə lô′stin), *adj.* **1.** of or pertaining to the pomegranate. —*n.* **2.** the dried flowers of the pomegranate used in medicines. [1665–75; earlier *balaust(y)* pomegranate flower (< L *balaustium* < Gk *balaústion* in same sense) + -INE[1]; cf. BALUSTER]

Bal•bo (bäl′bô), *n.* **I•ta•lo** (ē′tä lô), 1896–1940, Italian aviator, general, and statesman.

Bal•bo•a (bal bō′ə; *Sp.* bäl bô′ä), *n.* **1. Vas•co Nú•ñez de** (bäs′kô no͞o′nyeth the), 1475?–1517, Spanish adventurer and explorer who discovered the Pacific Ocean in 1513. **2.** a seaport in Panama at the Pacific terminus of the Panama Canal. 2568. **3.** (*l.c.*) a silver coin and monetary unit of Panama, equal to 100 centesimos.

bal•brig•gan (bal brig′ən), *n.* a plain-knit cotton fabric, used esp. in hosiery and underwear. [1855–60; after *Balbriggan,* town in Ireland, where first made]

Bal•bue•na (bäl bwā′nə; *Sp.* bäl bwe′nä), *n.* **Ber•nar•do de** (bər när′dō də; *Sp.* ber när′thô the), 1568–1627, Mexican poet and priest, born in Spain.

Balch (bôlch), *n.* **Emily Greene,** 1867–1961, U.S. economist, sociologist, and author: Nobel peace prize 1946.

bal•che (bäl chā′), *n.* (among the Yucatec Maya) a drink made from the bark of a leguminous tree, *Lonchocarpus violaceus,* which is soaked in honey and water and fermented. Also, **bal•ché′.** [< AmerSp < Yucatec Mayan]

Balch′ Springs′, a town in NE Texas. 13,746.

bal•co•net (bal′kə net′), *n.* a railing or balustrade before a window, giving the effect of a balcony. Also, **bal′•co•nette′.** [1875–80; BALCON(Y) + -ET]

bal•co•ny (bal′kə nē), *n., pl.* **-nies. 1.** a balustraded or railed elevated platform projecting from the wall of a building. **2.** a gallery in a theater. [1610–20; < It *balcone* balcony, floor-length window < Langobardic (cf. OHG *balc(h)o,* acc. sing. *balcon* beam; see BALK); sense extended from the beam over an aperture to the aperture itself] —**bal′co•nied,** *adj.*

CONCISE ETYMOLOGY KEY: <, descended or borrowed from; >, whence; b., blend of, blended; c., cognate with; cf., compare; deriv., derivative; equiv., equivalent; imit., imitative; obl., oblique; r., replacing; s., stem; sp., spelling, spelled; resp., respelling, respelled; trans., translation; ?, origin unknown; *, unattested; ‡, probably earlier than. See the full key inside the front cover.

bald (bôld), *adj.* **1.** having little or no hair on the scalp: *a bald head; a bald person.* **2.** destitute of some natural growth or covering: *a bald mountain.* **3.** lacking detail; bare; plain; unadorned: *a bald prose style.* **4.** open; undisguised: *a bald lie.* **5.** *Zool.* having white on the head: *the bald eagle.* **6.** *Auto.* (of a tire) having the tread completely worn away. —*v.i.* **7.** to become bald. —*n.* **8.** (*often cap.*) *Chiefly South Midland and Southern U.S.* a treeless mountaintop or area near the top: often used as part of a proper name. [1250–1300; ME *ball(e)d,* equiv. to *ball* white spot (cf. Welsh *bal,* Gk *phaliós* having a white spot) + *-ed* -ED[3]] —**bald′ish,** *adj.* —**bald′ly,** *adv.* —**bald′ness,** *n.*
—**Syn. 4.** bare, barefaced, flagrant, patent, utter, outand-out, downright, flat-out.

bal•da•chin (bal′də kin, bôl′-), *n.* **1.** Also, **baudekin.** *Textiles.* a silk brocade interwoven with gold or silver threads, used chiefly for ceremonial purposes. **2.** *Archit.* a permanent ornamental canopy, as above a freestanding altar or throne. **3.** a portable canopy carried in religious processions. Also, **bal•dac•chi•no, bal•da•chi•no** (bal′də kē′nō), **bal′da•quin.** [1250–1300; earlier *baldakin* < ML *baldakinus* < It *baldacchino,* equiv. to *Baldacc(o)* Baghdad (famous as a source of silk brocades) + *-ino* -INE[1]] —**bal′da•chined,** *adj.*

Bal•dad (bal′dad), *n. Douay Bible.* Bildad.

bald′ cy′press, a tree, *Taxodium distichum,* of swampy areas of the southern U.S., having featherlike needles and cone-shaped projections growing up from the roots, yielding a hardwood used in construction, shipbuilding, etc. Also called **southern cypress.** [1700–10, *Amer.*]

bald′ ea′gle, a large, fish-eating eagle, *Haliaeetus leucocephalus,* of the U.S. and Canada, having dark golden-brown back and wings, and white plumage on the head and tail in the adult: some recently endangered populations are now recovering. Cf. **American eagle.** [1680–90, *Amer.*]

bald eagle, *Haliaeetus leucocephalus,* length 2½ ft. (0.8 m); wingspread to 7½ ft. (2.3 m)

Bal•der (bôl′dər), *n. Scand. Myth.* a god, a son of Odin and Frigg and the twin brother of Hod, by whom he was killed. [< ON *Baldr,* c. OE *bealdor* prince, lord; perh. akin to ON *baldr* brave]

bal•der•dash (bôl′dər dash′), *n.* **1.** senseless, stupid, or exaggerated talk or writing; nonsense. **2.** *Obs.* a muddled mixture of liquors. [1590–1600; of obscure orig.]

bald-faced (bôld′fāst′), *adj.* barefaced (def. 2). [1640–50]

bald′-faced hor′net. See under **hornet.** [1860–65, *Amer.*]

bald•head (bôld′hed′), *n.* **1.** a person who has a bald head. **2.** one of a breed of domestic pigeons. [1525–35; BALD + HEAD]

bald•head•ed (bôld′hed′id), *adj.* **1.** having a bald head. **2.** *Naut.* (of a schooner rig) having no topmasts. [1570–80; BALD + -HEADED]

bald•ie (bôl′dē), *n. Informal.* a bald person (often used as a disparaging and offensive or facetious epithet). Also, **baldy.** [1860–65; BALD + -IE]

bald•pate (bôld′pāt′), *n.* **1.** baldhead (def. 1). **2.** the American widgeon, *Anas americana,* having a gray head with a white crown. [1570–80; BALD + PATE] —**bald′•pat′ed,** *adj.* —**bald′pat′ed•ness,** *n.*

bal•dric (bôl′drik), *n.* a belt, sometimes richly ornamented, worn diagonally from shoulder to hip, supporting a sword, horn, etc. Also, **bal′drick.** [1250–1300; ME *bauderik, bawdryk, baudry* < AF *baudré, baldré,* OF *baldrei, baudré,* perh. < Frankish **baltirad* sword belt, equiv. to L *balte(us)* BELT + Gmc **-rad* provision, equipment (cf. OHG *rat*); source of final *-ik* uncert.] —**bal′•dricked,** *adj.*

Bald•win (bôld′win), *n.* **1. James,** 1924–87, U.S. writer. **2. James Mark,** 1861–1934, U.S. psychologist. **3. Lo•am•mi** (lō am′ī), 1740–1807, U.S. civil engineer and developer of the Baldwin apple. **4. Mat•thi•as William** (mə thī′əs), 1795–1866, U.S. inventor, manufacturer, and philanthropist. **5. Roger,** 1884–1981, U.S. advocate of constitutional rights: a founder of the American Civil Liberties Union. **6. Stanley** (*1st Earl Baldwin of Bewdley*), 1867–1947, British statesman: prime minister 1923–24, 1924–29, 1935–37. **7.** a variety of red, or red and yellow, winter apple, grown esp. in the northeast U.S. **8.** a town on S Long Island, in SE New York. 31,630. **9.** a city in W Pennsylvania, near Pittsburgh. 24,598.

Baldwin I, 1058–1118, king of Jerusalem 1100–18: fought in the first crusade.

Bald′win Park′, a city in SW California, near Los Angeles. 50,554.

bald•y (bôl′dē), *n., pl.* **bald•ies.** *Informal.* baldie.

bale[1] (bāl), *n., v.,* **baled, bal•ing.** —*n.* **1.** a large bundle or package prepared for shipping, storage, or sale, esp. one tightly compressed and secured by wires, hoops, cords, or the like, and sometimes having a wrapping or covering: *a bale of cotton; a bale of hay.* **2.** a group of turtles. —*v.t.* **3.** to make or form into bales: *to bale wastepaper for disposal.* [1350–1400; ME < AL *bala,* AF *bale* pack, bale < Frankish **balla;* cf. OHG *balo,* akin to *balla* BALL[1]] —**bale′less,** *adj.* —**bal′er,** *n.*

bale[2] (bāl), *n. Archaic.* **1.** evil; harm; misfortune. **2.** woe; misery; sorrow. [bef. 1000; ME; OE *bealu, balu;* ON *bǫl,* OS *balu,* OHG *balo,* Goth *balw-;* akin to Ru *bol′* pain, OCS *bolŭ* ill]

bale[3] (bāl), *n.* bail[2].

bale[4] (bāl), *v.t., v.i.,* **baled, bal•ing.** bail[3] (defs. 1–3).

Bâle (bäl), *n.* French name of **Basel.**

Bal•e•ar′ic Is′lands (bal′ē ar′ik), a group of islan including Iviza, Majorca, and Minorca, and constitutin a province of Spain in the W Mediterranean Se 558,287; 1936 sq. mi. (5015 sq. km). *Cap.:* Palma. Spanis **Ba•le•a•res** (bä′le ä′RES).

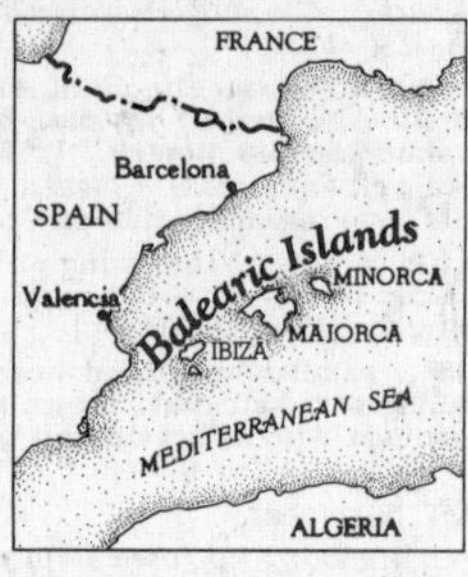

ba•le•bos•te (bä′lə bus′tə, -bôs′-), *n. Informal.* a ca pable, efficient housewife, esp. a traditional Jewish on devoted to maintaining a well-run home. Also, **ba•le bus•te** (bä′lə bus′tə, -bo͞os′-). [< Yiddish *bal(e)bost bal(e)buste* proprietress, housekeeper, housewife, equiv to *bal(e)bos, bal(e)bus* proprietor, owner, master (cf. He *ba'al habayth* master of the house) + *-te* fem. n. suffi (cf. Aram *-ta,* equiv. to *-t* fem. suffix + *-a* definite art cle)]

bale′ cu′bic, *Naut.* the space available in a ship hold for the stowage of general cargo, measured in cubi feet.

ba•leen (bə lēn′), *n.* whalebone (def. 1). [1275–132 ME *balene* (< AF *baleine, beleine*) < L *bal(l)ēna,* var. c *bal(l)aena* whale < an unidentified language, also th source of Gk *phál(l)aina* whale; r. ME *balayn* < MF *ba laine* whale(bone) < L, as above]

baleen′ whale′. See **whalebone whale.** [1870–75]

bale•fire (bāl′fīᵊr′), *n.* **1.** a large fire in the open ai bonfire. **2.** a signal fire; beacon. **3.** the fire of a funera pile. [1250–1300; ME *bal(e)fir,* equiv. to *bale* (< ON *bā* funeral pyre) + *fire* FIRE; r. OE *bǣlfȳr*]

bale•ful (bāl′fəl), *adj.* **1.** full of menacing or malign in fluences; pernicious. **2.** *Obs.* wretched; miserable. [be 1000; ME; OE *bealofull.* See BALE[2], -FUL] —**bale′ful•ly** *adv.* —**bale′ful•ness,** *n.*
—**Syn. 1.** harmful, malign, injurious, detrimental; evi wicked; deadly.

Ba•len•ci•a•ga (bə len′sē ä′gə; *Sp.* bä′len thyä′gä), *n* **Cri•stó•bal** (kri stō′bəl; *Sp.* kRē stô′väl), 1895–197 French fashion designer, born in Spain.

ba•les•tra (bə les′trə), *n. Fencing.* a jump toward th opponent followed immediately by a lunge. [< It: lit crossbow < LL *ballistra,* var. of L *ballista* BALLISTA]

Ba•le•wa (bä′lā wä′), *n.* **Sir A•bu•ba•kar Ta•fa•w** (ä′bo͞o bä′kär tä fä′wä, ä bo͞o′bä kär′), 1912–6 Nigerian statesman: prime minister 1957–66.

Bal•four (bal′fo͝or, -fər), *n.* **Arthur James** (*1st Earl o Balfour*), 1848–1930, British statesman and writer: prim minister 1902–05.

Bal′four Declara′tion, a statement, issued by th British government on November 2, 1917, favoring th establishment in Palestine of a national home for th Jews but without prejudice to the civil and religiou rights of existing non-Jewish communities in Palestine

Ba•li (bä′lē, bal′ē), *n.* **1.** an island in Indonesia, E o Java. 2,247,000; 2147 sq. mi. (5561 sq. km). *Cap.:* Sin garaja. **2.** one of a breed of domesticated banteng cattle *Bos banteng domesticus,* raised for milk and meat and a a work animal.

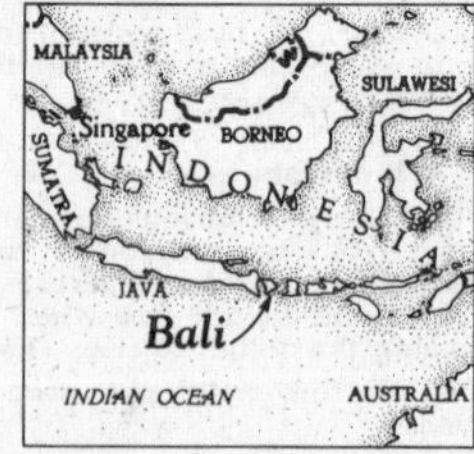

Ba•lik•pa•pan (bä′lik pä′pän), *n.* a seaport on E Bor neo, in central Indonesia. 137,340.

Ba•li•nese (bä′lə nēz′, -nēs′, bal′ə-), *adj., n., pl.* **-nese** —*adj.* **1.** of or pertaining to Bali, its people, or their lan guage. —*n.* **2.** a native or inhabitant of Bali. **3.** th language of Bali, an Indonesian language of the Austro nesian family. [1810–20; < D *Balinees,* equiv. to *Bal* BALI + *-n-* connective + *-ees* -ESE]

Bal•iol (bāl′yəl, bā′lē əl), *n.* **John de,** 1249–1315, kin of Scotland 1292–96.

bal•i•sage (bal′ə säzh′), *n. Mil.* a method of markin a land route with dim lighting so that vehicles can trave at higher speeds in blackout conditions. [< F, equiv. t alis(er) to place beacons, markers, buoys, etc., v. deriv. of *balise* beacon, buoy (< Pg *baliza* < Mozarabic < VL *pālitia;* see PALISADE) + *-age* -AGE]

al·is·tra·ri·a (bal′ə strâr′ē ə), *n., pl.* **-is·tra·ri·ae** -ə strâr′ē ē′). (in a medieval fortification) an opening, usually in the form of a cross, through which a crossbow ould be fired. [1835–45; < ML, fem. of LL *bal(l)is-tārius,* L *ballistārius* pertaining to a BALLISTA (in ML a rossbow), equiv. to *ballist(a)* + *-ārius* -ARY]

alk (bôk), *v.i.* **1.** to stop, as at an obstacle, and refuse o proceed or to do something specified (usually fol. by *at*): *He balked at making the speech.* **2.** (of a horse, mule, etc.) to stop short and stubbornly refuse to go on. **3.** *Baseball.* to commit a balk. *—v.t.* **4.** to place an obstacle in the way of; hinder; thwart: *a sudden reversal hat balked her hopes.* **5.** *Archaic.* to let slip; fail to use: *o balk an opportunity.* *—n.* **6.** a check or hindrance; defeat; disappointment. **7.** a strip of land left unplowed. **8.** a crossbeam in the roof of a house that unites and supports the rafters; tie beam. **9.** any heavy timber used for building purposes. **10.** *Baseball.* an illegal motion by a pitcher while one or more runners are on base, as a pitch in which there is either an insufficient or too long a pause after the windup or stretch, a pretended throw to first or third base or to the batter with one foot on the pitcher's rubber, etc., resulting in a penalty advancing the runner or runners one base. **11.** *Billiards.* any of the eight panels or compartments lying between he cushions of the table and the balklines. **12.** *Obs.* a miss, slip, or failure: *to make a balk.* **13.** **in balk,** inside any of the spaces in back of the balklines on a billiard table. Also, **baulk.** [bef. 900; ME; OE *balca* covering, beam, ridge; c. ON *bǫlkr* bar, partition, D *balk,* OS *balko,* G *Balken,* ON *bjalki* beam, OE *bolca* plank; perh. akin to L *sufflāmen,* Slovene *blazína,* Lith *balžíenas* beam. See BALCONY] **—balk′er,** *n.* **—balk′ing·ly,** *adv.*
—Syn. 4. check, retard, obstruct, impede, prevent.

al·kan (bôl′kən), *adj.* **1.** pertaining to the Balkan States or their inhabitants. **2.** pertaining to the Balkan Peninsula. **3.** pertaining to the Balkan Mountains. *—n.* **4.** **the Balkans.** See **Balkan States.** **—Bal′kan·ite′,** *n., adj.* [1825–35]

al′kan frame′, an overhead frame, fastened to a bed, from which a splinted, fractured leg or arm is suspended and held in traction. [1925–30; so called because first used in the BALKAN MOUNTAINS]

al·kan·ize (bôl′kə nīz′), *v.t.,* **-ized, -iz·ing.** **1.** to divide (a country, territory, etc.) into small, quarrelsome, ineffectual states. **2.** (*often l.c.*) to divide (groups, areas, etc.) into contending and usually ineffectual factions: *a movement to balkanize minority voters.* Also, *esp. Brit.,* **Bal′kan·ise′.** [1915–20; BALKAN + -IZE] **—Bal′kan·i·za′tion,** *n.* **—Bal′kan·ism,** *n.*

al′kan Moun′tains, a mountain range extending from W Bulgaria to the Black Sea: highest peak, 7794 ft. (2370 m).

al′kan Penin′sula, a peninsula in S Europe, S of the Danube River and bordered by the Adriatic, Ionian, Aegean, and Black seas.

al′kan States′, the countries in the Balkan Peninsula: Yugoslavia, Bosnia and Herzegovina, Croatia, Macedonia, Slovenia, Romania, Bulgaria, Albania, Greece, and the European part of Turkey. Also called **the Balkans.**

al′kan War′, **1.** Also called **First Balkan War.** a war (1912–13) in which Bulgaria, Serbia, and Greece opposed Turkey. **2.** Also called **Second Balkan War.** a war (1913) in which Greece, Rumania, and Serbia opposed Bulgaria for the redivision of territory taken from Turkey in the First Balkan War.

al·kar (bäl′kär), *n., pl.* **-kars,** (*esp. collectively*) **-kar** for 1. *n.* **1.** a member of a Sunni Muslim people living mainly in the Kabardino-Balkar Autonomous Republic, closely related to the Karachai. **2.** the Turkic language spoken by the Balkars.

alkh (bälkʜ), *n.* a town in N Afghanistan: capital of ancient Bactria; center of Zoroastrianism. Ancient, **Bactra.** Also called **Wazirabad.**

al·khash (bal kash′, bäl käsh′; *Russ.* bul kʜäsh′), *n.* a salt lake in SE Kazakhstan. ab. 7115 sq. mi. (18,430 sq. km).

alk·line (bôk′līn′), *n.* **1.** *Sports.* (in track events) the starting line. **2.** *Billiards.* **a.** a straight line drawn across the table behind which the cue balls are placed in beginning a game. **b.** any of four lines, each near to and parallel with one side of the cushion, that divide the table into a large central panel or section and eight smaller sections or balks lying between these. **c.** a balk lying inside one of these sections. **d.** balk (def. 11). [1830–40; BALK + LINE[1]]

alk·y (bô′kē), *adj.,* **balk·i·er, balk·i·est.** given to balking; stubborn; obstinate: *a balky mule.* [1840–50; BALK + -Y[1]] **—balk′i·ly,** *adv.* **—balk′i·ness,** *n.*
—Syn. contrary, perverse, headstrong, mulish.

all[1] (bôl), *n.* **1.** a spherical or approximately spherical body or shape; sphere: *He rolled the piece of paper into a ball.* **2.** a round or roundish body, of various sizes and materials, either hollow or solid, for use in games, as baseball, football, tennis, or golf. **3.** a game played with a ball, esp. baseball: *The boys are out playing ball.* **4.** *Baseball.* a pitched ball, not swung at by the batter, that does not pass over home plate between the batter's shoulders and knees. **5.** *Mil.* **a.** a solid, usually spherical projectile for a cannon, rifle, pistol, etc., as distinguished from a shell. **b.** projectiles, esp. bullets, collectively. **6.** any part of a thing, esp. of the human body, that is rounded or protuberant: *the ball of the thumb.* **7.** a round mass of food, as of chopped meat, dough, or candy. **8.** *Slang* (*vulgar*). a testis. **9.** **balls,** *Slang* (*vulgar*). **a.** boldness; courage; brashness. **b.** nonsense (often used as an interjection). **10.** bolus (def. 1). **11.** *Hort.* a compact mass of soil covering the roots of an uprooted tree or other plant. **12.** *Literary.* a planetary or celestial body, esp. the earth. **13.** *Math.* (in a metric space) the set of points whose distance from the zero element is less than, or less than or equal to, a specified number. **14.** **carry the ball,** to assume the responsibility; bear the burden: *You can always count on him to carry the ball in an emergency.* **15.** **keep the ball rolling,** to continue or give renewed vigor to an activity already under way: *When their interest lagged, he tried to keep the ball rolling.* **16.** **on the ball,** **a.** alert and efficient or effective: *If you don't get on the ball, you'll be fired.* **b.** indicating intelligence or ability: *The tests show your students don't have much on the ball. The new manager has a lot on the ball.* **17.** **play ball,** **a.** to begin or continue playing a game. **b.** to start or continue any action. **c.** to work together; cooperate: *union leaders suspected of playing ball with racketeers.* **18.** **run with the ball,** to assume responsibility or work enthusiastically: *If management approves the concept, we'll run with the ball.* **19.** **start the ball rolling,** to put into operation; begin: *The recreation director started the ball rolling by having all the participants introduce themselves.* *—v.t.* **20.** to make into a ball (sometimes fol. by *up*): *The children were balling up snow to make a snowman.* **21.** to wind into balls: *to ball cotton.* **22.** *Slang* (*vulgar*). to have sexual intercourse with. *—v.i.* **23.** to form or gather into a ball: *When the spun sugar balls, the candy has cooked sufficiently.* **24.** *Slang* (*vulgar*). to have sexual intercourse. **25.** **ball the jack,** *Slang.* **a.** to act with speed. **b.** to stake everything on one attempt. **26.** **ball up,** *Slang.* to make or become utterly confused; muddle: *The records had been all balled up by inefficient file clerks.* [1175–1225; ME *bal, balle* < OF < Gmc **ballaz;* cf. ON *bǫllr,* OHG *bal, ballo, balla,* G *Ball,* D *bal;* perh. akin to L *follis* leather bag; see BALLOCK] **—ball′er,** *n.*

ball[2] (bôl), *n.* **1.** a large, usually lavish, formal party featuring social dancing and sometimes given for a particular purpose, as to introduce debutantes or benefit a charitable organization. **2.** *Informal.* a thoroughly good time: *Have a ball on your vacation!* [1625–35; < F *bal,* n. deriv. of *baler* (now *baller*) to dance < LL *ballāre* < Gk (Magna Graecia) *ballízein* to dance]

Ball (bôl), *n.* **1.** **George W(ild·man)** (wīld′mən), born 1909, U.S. lawyer, investment banker, and government official. **2.** **John,** died 1381, English priest: one of the leaders of Wat Tyler's peasants' revolt in 1381.

Bal·la (bäl′lä), *n.* **Gia·co·mo** (jä′kô mô), 1871?–1958, Italian painter.

bal·lad (bal′əd), *n.* **1.** any light, simple song, esp. one of sentimental or romantic character, having two or more stanzas all sung to the same melody. **2.** a simple narrative poem of folk origin, composed in short stanzas and adapted for singing. **3.** any poem written in similar style. **4.** the music for a ballad. **5.** a sentimental or romantic popular song. [1350–1400; ME *balade* < MF < OPr *balada* dance, dancing-song, equiv. to *bal(ar)* to dance (< LL *ballāre;* see BALL[2]) + *-ada* -ADE[1]] **—bal·lad·ic** (bə lad′ik), *adj.* **—bal′lad·like′,** *adj.*

bal·lade (bə läd′, ba-; *Fr.* bᴀ lᴀd′), *n., pl.* **-lades** (-lädz′; *Fr.* -lᴀd′). **1.** a poem consisting commonly of three stanzas having an identical rhyme scheme, followed by an envoy, and having the same last line for each of the stanzas and the envoy. **2.** *Music.* a composition in free style and romantic mood, often for solo piano or for orchestra. [1485–95; < MF, var. of *balade* BALLAD]

bal·lad·eer (bal′ə dēr′), *n.* a person who sings ballads. Also, **bal′lad·ier′.** [1630–40; BALLAD + -EER]

bal·lad·ist (bal′ə dist), *n.* a person who writes, composes, or sings ballads. [1855–60; BALLAD + -IST]

bal·lad·ize (bal′ə dīz′), *v.,* **-ized, -iz·ing.** *—v.t.* **1.** to make (something) into a ballad; write a ballad about. *—v.i.* **2.** to write or compose ballads. Also, *esp. Brit.,* **bal′lad·ise′.** [1590–1600; BALLAD + -IZE]

bal·lad·mon·ger (bal′əd mung′gər, -mong′-), *n.* **1.** a seller of ballads. **2.** an inferior poet. [1590–1600; BALLAD + MONGER] **—bal′lad·mon′ger·ing,** *n.*

Bal′lad of Read′ing Gaol′, The (red′ing), a poem (1898) by Oscar Wilde.

bal′lad op′era, a theater entertainment of 18th-century England, consisting of popular tunes, folk songs, and dialogue. [1770–80]

bal·lad·ry (bal′ə drē), *n.* **1.** ballad poetry. **2.** the composing, playing, or singing of ballads. [1590–1600; BALLAD + -RY]

bal′lad stan′za, *Pros.* a four-line stanza consisting of unrhymed first and third lines in iambic tetrameter and rhymed second and fourth lines in iambic trimeter, often used in ballads. [1930–35]

Bal·lance (bal′əns), *n.* **John,** 1839–93, New Zealand statesman, born in Ireland: prime minister 1891–93.

ball′ and chain′, **1.** a heavy iron ball fastened by a chain to a prisoner's leg. **2.** burdensome restraint: *The steady accumulation of small debts was a ball and chain to his progress.* **3.** *Slang* (*disparaging and offensive*). a man's wife (often used facetiously). [1825–35, *Amer.*]

ball′-and-claw′ foot′ (bôl′ən klô′), *Furniture.* a foot having the form of a bird's claw grasping a ball. Also called **claw-and-ball foot.** [1900–05]

ball′ and ring′, a simplified bead-and-reel turning, used esp. in English and American furniture of the 17th century.

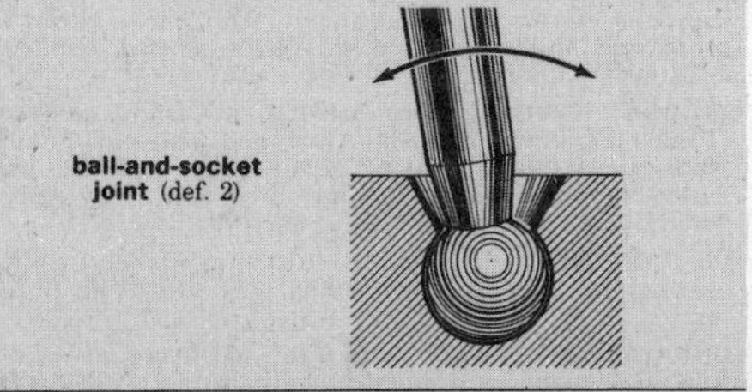
ball-and-socket joint (def. 2)

ball′-and-sock′et joint′ (bôl′ən sok′it), **1.** Also called **enarthrosis.** *Anat., Zool.* a joint in which the rounded end of one bone fits into a cuplike end of the other bone, allowing for relatively free rotary motion, as at the hip or shoulder. **2.** Also called **ball joint.** a similar joint between rods, links, pipes, etc., consisting of a ball-like termination on one part held within a concave, spherical socket on the other. [1660–70]

Bal·la·rat (bal′ə rat′, bal′ə rat′), *n.* a city in S Victoria, in SE Australia. 62,641.

bal·las (bal′əs), *n.* (*used with a singular v.*) *Mineral.* a spherical aggregate of small diamond crystals used for drilling and for various industrial purposes. [appar. var. of BALAS in phrase *balas ruby* spinel ruby, *balas* being taken to mean "spinel"]

bal·last (bal′əst), *n.* **1.** *Naut.* any heavy material carried temporarily or permanently in a vessel to provide desired draft and stability. **2.** *Aeron.* something heavy, as bags of sand, placed in the car of a balloon for control of altitude and, less often, of attitude, or placed in an aircraft to control the position of the center of gravity. **3.** anything that gives mental, moral, or political stability or steadiness: *the ballast of a steady income.* **4.** gravel, broken stone, slag, etc., placed between and under the ties of a railroad to give stability, provide drainage, and distribute loads. **5.** *Elect.* **a.** Also called **ballast resistor.** a device, often a resistor, that maintains the current in a circuit at a constant value by varying its resistance in order to counteract changes in voltage. **b.** a device that maintains the current through a fluorescent or mercury lamp at the desired constant value, sometimes also providing the necessary starting voltage and current. **6.** **in ballast,** *Naut.* carrying only ballast; carrying no cargo. *—v.t.* **7.** to furnish with ballast: *to ballast a ship.* **8.** to give steadiness to; keep steady: *parental responsibilities that ballast a person.* [1520–30; < MLG, perh. ult. < Scand; cf. ODan, OSw *barlast,* equiv. to *bar* BARE[1] + *last* load; see LAST[4]] **—bal′last·er,** *n.* **—bal·last·ic** (bə las′tik), *adj.*

bal′last line′, *Naut.* the level to which a vessel is immersed when in ballast.

bal′last pock′et, *Railroads.* a depression that is formed beneath the ballast layer by penetration of ballast particles into the subgrade and that tends to collect moisture.

bal′last resis′tor, ballast (def. 5a).

bal·la·ta (bə lä′tə), *n., pl.* **-la·te** (-lä′tā). a 14th-century Italian verse form composed of stanzas beginning and ending with a refrain, often set to music and accompanied by dancing. [1755–65; < It < OPr *balada* BALLAD]

ball′ bear′ing, *Mach.* **1.** a bearing consisting of a number of hard balls running in grooves in the surfaces of two concentric rings, one of which is mounted on a rotating or oscillating shaft or the like. **2.** any of the balls so used. [1880–85] **—ball′-bear′ing,** adj.

ball′ boy′, **1.** *Tennis.* an attendant, usually a boy or young man, employed to retrieve balls and supply players with them. **2.** *Baseball.* an attendant, usually a boy or young man, who retrieves foul balls and brings the umpire new balls during the game. [1900–05]

ball-bust·er (bôl′bus′tər), *n. Slang* (*vulgar*). **1.** an arduous, often unpleasant task. **2.** a person who makes great demands on others; taskmaster. Also called **ball-break·er** (bôl′brā′kər).

ball′ cap′. See **baseball cap.**

ball-car·ri·er (bôl′kar′ē ər), *n. Football.* the offensive player having the ball and attempting to gain ground. [1930–35]

ball′ clay′, *Ceram.* a fine dark kaolinic clay that turns white or nearly white when fired, used in the manufacture of a wide variety of ceramic wares in combination with other clays for its exceptional bonding properties and plasticity. [1805–15]

ball′ club′, **1.** a permanent team of professional or amateur players of a ball game, esp. baseball. **2.** a club or similar organization that sponsors and promotes a baseball team. [1825–35]

ball′ cock′, a device for regulating the supply of water in a tank, cistern, or the like, consisting essentially of a valve connected to a hollow floating ball which by its rise or fall shuts or opens the valve. Also, **ball′cock′.** [1780–90]

ball′ control′, *Sports.* a team's ability to maintain possession of the ball on offense. [1925–30]

balled-and-bur·lapped (bôld′n bûr′lapt), *adj. Hort.* of or pertaining to a tree, shrub, or other plant prepared for transplanting by allowing the roots to remain covered by a ball of soil around which canvas or burlap is tied. Cf. **bare-root.**

bal·le·ri·na (bal′ə rē′nə), *n.* **1.** a principal female dancer in a ballet company. Cf. **prima ballerina.** **2.** any female ballet dancer. **3.** a woman's very low-heeled or heelless shoe or slipper, made to resemble a ballet slipper. Cf. **ballet slipper.** [1785–95; < It, fem. of *ballerino* professional dancer, prob. equiv to *baller(ia)* dance (*ball(are)* to dance (< LL; see BALL[2]) + *-eria* < OF; see -ERY) + *-ino* -INE[1]]

bal·let (ba lā′, bal′ā), *n.* **1.** a classical dance form demanding grace and precision and employing formalized steps and gestures set in intricate, flowing patterns to create expression through movement. **2.** a theatrical entertainment in which ballet dancing and music, often with scenery and costumes, combine to tell a story, establish an emotional atmosphere, etc. **3.** an interlude of ballet in an operatic performance. **4.** a company of ballet dancers. **5.** the musical score for a ballet: *the brilliant ballets of Tchaikovsky.* **6.** a dance or balletlike performance: *an ice-skating ballet.* [1660–70; < F, MF < It *balletto,* equiv. to *ball(o)* BALL[2] + *-etto* -ET] —**bal·let·ic** (ba let′ik, bə-), *adj.* —**bal·let′i·cal·ly,** *adv.*

bal·let blanc (*Fr.* bA le bläN′), *pl.* **bal·lets blancs** (*Fr.* bA le bläN′, bläNz′). a ballet in which the ballerinas' skirts are white. [1945–50; < F: lit., white ballet]

ballet′ mas′ter, a man who trains a ballet company. Also called **maître de ballet.** [1755–65]

ballet′ mis′tress, a woman who trains a ballet company. [1835–45]

bal·let·o·mane (ba let′ə män′, bə-), *n.* a ballet enthusiast. [1925–30; back formation from *balletomania;* see BALLET, -O-, -MANIA] —**bal·let′o·ma′ni·a,** *n.*

ballet′ slip′per, 1. a heelless cloth or leather slipper worn by ballet dancers. **2.** a woman's shoe similar in form.

ballet′ suite′, music written for a ballet but suitable or arranged for performance in an orchestral concert. [‡1960–65]

bal·lett (ba let′), *n.* an early 17th-century dancelike vocal composition similar to the madrigal in style. [1585–95; perh. var. of obs. *ballette* (see BALLET, -ETTE)]

ball′ fern′, a feathery fern, *Davallia trichomanoides,* of Malaysia, having rhizomes covered with toothed scales. Also called **squirrel's-foot fern.**

ball·flow·er (bôl′flou′ər), *n. Archit.* a medieval English ornament suggesting a flower of three or four petals enclosing and partly concealing a ball. [1835–45; BALL[1] + FLOWER]

ball′ foot′, *Furniture.* a ball-like turned foot, used esp. in the 16th and 17th centuries. Cf. **bun foot.**

ball′ game′, 1. any game played with a ball, esp. baseball or softball. **2.** *Informal.* a situation and all its attendant circumstances: *Having a new administration in power changes the entire ball game at city hall.* Cf. **new ball game. 3.** *Archaeol.* a ceremonial game of both ritual and sporting significance, played by teams on a ball court in Mesoamerican cultures from the Preclassic period to the Spanish conquest. Also, **ball′game′.** [1840–50, *Amer.*]

ball′ girl′, 1. *Tennis.* an attendant, usually a girl or young woman, employed to retrieve balls and supply players with them. **2.** *Baseball.* an attendant, usually a girl or young women, who retrieves foul balls and brings the umpire new balls during the game. [1925–30]

ball′ han′dling, the control of the ball, as in basketball or soccer, by skillful dribbling and accurate passing.

ball′ hawk′, 1. *Baseball.* an outfielder with outstanding defensive skills, esp. at fielding fly balls. **2.** *Sports.* a defensive player, as in basketball or football, who excels in gaining possession of the ball.

ball′ ice′, floating balls of slushy ice formed at sea.

ball′ in′dicator. See **bank indicator.**

Bal·liol (bāl′yəl, bā′lē əl), *n.* a college of Oxford University, founded before 1268.

bal·lism (bal′iz əm), *n. Pathol.* **1.** a condition characterized by twisting, shaking, and jerking motions. **2.** See **Parkinson's disease.** Also, **bal·lis·mus** (bə liz′məs). [1955–60; < NL *ballismus* < Gk *ballismós* a jumping around, dancing, equiv. to *bállein* to throw + *-ismos* -ISM]

bal·lis·ta (bə lis′tə), *n., pl.* **-tae** (-tē). an ancient military engine for throwing stones or other missiles. [1590–1600; < L, prob. < Gk **ballistás,* dial. var. of **ballistḗs,* equiv. to *bállein* to throw + *-istēs* -IST]

ballista

bal·lis·tic (bə lis′tik), *adj.* **1.** of or pertaining to ballistics. **2.** having its motion determined or describable by the laws of exterior ballistics. [1765–75; BALLIST(A) + -IC] —**bal·lis′ti·cal·ly,** *adv.*

ballis′tic cam′era, a camera for tracking missiles launched at night. [1955–60]

ballis′tic galvanom′eter, *Elect.* a galvanometer used to measure the quantity of electricity in a current of short duration. [1875–80]

ballis′tic mis′sile, *Rocketry.* any missile that, after being launched and possibly guided during takeoff, travels unpowered in a ballistic trajectory. [1950–55]

ballis′tic pen′dulum, *Physics.* a device consisting of a large mass hung from a horizontal bar by two rods, used to measure the velocity of an object, as a bullet, by retaining the object upon impact, its velocity being a function of the displacement of the mass. [1770–80]

bal·lis·tics (bə lis′tiks), *n.* (*usually used with a singular v.*) **1.** the science or study of the motion of projectiles, as bullets, shells, or bombs. **2.** the art or science of designing projectiles for maximum flight performance. [1745–55; see BALLISTIC, -ICS] —**bal·lis·ti·cian** (bal′ə stish′ən), *n.*

CONCISE ETYMOLOGY KEY: <, descended or borrowed from; >, whence; b., blend of, blended; c., cognate with; cf., compare; deriv., derivative; equiv., equivalent; imit., imitative; obl., oblique; r., replacing; s., stem; sp., spelling, spelled; resp., respelling, respelled; trans., translation; ?, origin unknown; *, unattested; ‡, probably earlier than. See the full key inside the front cover.

ballis′tic trajec′tory, the path of an unpowered object, as a missile, moving only under the influence of gravity and possibly atmospheric friction and with its surface providing no significant lift to alter the course of flight.

ballis′tic wind′ (wind), a single wind vector that would have the same net effect on the trajectory of a projectile as the varying winds encountered in flight.

bal·lis·tite (bal′ə stīt′), *n. Chem.* a smokeless powder consisting of nitroglycerine and cellulose nitrate chiefly in a 40 to 60 percent ratio: used as a solid fuel for rockets. [1890–95; formerly a trademark]

bal·lis·to·car·di·o·gram (bə lis′tō kär′dē ə gram′), *n. Med.* the graphic record produced by a ballistocardiograph. [1935–40; BALLIST(IC) + -O- + CARDIOGRAM]

bal·lis·to·car·di·o·graph (bə lis′tō kär′dē ə graf′, -gräf′), *n. Med.* a device that determines cardiac output by recording the movements of the body caused by contraction of the heart and ejection of blood into the aorta. [1935–40; BALLIST(IC) + -O- + CARDIOGRAPH] —**bal·lis·to·car·di·og·ra·phy** (bə lis′tō kär′dē og′rə fē), *n.*

bal·lis·to·spore (bə lis′tə spôr′, -spōr′), *n. Mycol.* a forcibly expelled mature fungal spore. [BALLIST(IC) + -O- + -SPORE]

bal·li·um (bal′ē əm), *n.* bailey. [1790–1800; < ML, Latinized var.]

ball′ joint′. See **ball-and-socket joint** (def. 2).

ball′ light′ning, a rare form of lightning, consisting of a bright, luminous ball that moves rapidly along objects or floats in the air. Also called **globe lightning.** [1855–60]

ball′ mill′, a grinding mill in which the material to be ground is tumbled in a drum with heavy balls of iron, steel, or stone. [1900–05]

bal·locks (bol′əks), *n.pl. Vulgar.* testes. [bef. 1000; ME *ballokes* (pl.), OE *beallucas,* with unclear suffix. See BALL[1]]

ball′ of fire′, a dynamic person capable of or displaying rapid and highly effective thought, action, etc.: *The new manager turned out to be a ball of fire.* [1815–25]

ball′ of wax′, *Informal.* everything, including all details, parts, etc., relating to a particular matter: *He came back from Chicago with the contract for the whole ball of wax.* [1950–55]

bal·lon (*Fr.* bA lôN′), *n. Ballet.* the lightness and grace of movement that make a dancer appear buoyant. Also, **balon.** [1820–30; < F: lit., BALLOON]

bal·lon d'es·sai (bA lôN de se′), *pl.* ***bal·lons d'es·sai*** (bA lôN de se′). *French.* See **trial balloon** (def. 1).

bal·lo·net (bal′ə nā′), *n.* an air or gasbag compartment in a balloon or airship, used to control buoyancy and maintain shape. [1900–05; < F; see BALLOON, -ET]

bal·lon·né (bal′ə nā′; *Fr.* bA lô nā′), *n., pl.* **-nés** (-nāz′; *Fr.* -nā′). *Ballet.* a broad leap with a battement to the front, side, or back. [1770–80; < F: lit., ballooned, i.e. done like a balloon]

bal·loon (bə lo͞on′), *n.* **1.** a bag made of thin rubber or other light material, usually brightly colored, inflated with air or with some lighter-than-air gas and used as a children's plaything or as a decoration. **2.** a bag made of a light material, as silk or plastic, filled with heated air or a gas lighter than air, designed to rise and float in the atmosphere and often having a car or gondola attached below for carrying passengers or scientific instruments. **3.** (in drawings, cartoons, etc.) a balloon-shaped outline enclosing words represented as issuing from the mouth of the speaker. **4.** an ornamental ball at the top of a pillar, pier, or the like. **5.** a large, globular wineglass. **6.** *Chem. Now Rare.* a round-bottomed flask. —*v.i.* **7.** to go up or ride in a balloon. **8.** to swell or puff out like a balloon. **9.** to multiply or increase at a rapid rate: *Membership has ballooned beyond all expectations.* —*v.t.* **10.** to fill with air; inflate or distend (something) like a balloon. —*adj.* **11.** puffed out like a balloon: *balloon sleeves.* **12.** *Finance.* (of a loan, mortgage, or the like) having a payment at the end of the term that is much bigger than previous ones. [1570–80; < Upper It *ballone,* equiv. to *ball(a)* (< Langobardic; see BALL[1]) + *-one* aug. suffix; or < MF *ballon* < Upper It] —**bal·loon′like′,** *adj.*

balloon′ an′gioplasty, *Surg.* a method of opening a clogged or narrowed blood vessel in which a small balloon is introduced into the vessel by means of a catheter and then inflated at the site of blockage.

balloon′ barrage′, a series of moored balloons, usually strung together and hung with cables, for impeding a low-level attack by enemy aircraft. [1915–20]

bal·loon·ber·ry (bə lo͞on′ber′ē), *n., pl.* **-ber·ries.** See **strawberry-raspberry.**

balloon′ chuck′, a lathe chuck having the form of a hollow hemisphere, for enclosing and holding small parts, as balance staffs of watches, so that only their ends are exposed.

balloon′ clock′, a bracket clock of the late 18th century, having a round dial on a short case with concave sides resting on bracket feet.

bal·loon·fish (bə lo͞on′fish′), *n., pl.* **-fish·es,** (*esp. collectively*) **-fish.** a porcupinefish, *Diodon holacanthus,* inhabiting tropical and subtropical waters. [1825–35; BALLOON + FISH]

balloon′ frame′, a wooden building frame composed of machine-sawed scantlings fastened with nails, having studs rising the full height of the frame with the joists nailed to the studs and supported by sills or by ribbons let into the studs. [1850–55, *Amer.*]

bal·loon·ist (bə lo͞o′nist), *n.* a person who ascends in a balloon, esp. as a sport or hobby. [1775–85; BALLOON + -IST]

balloon′ sail′, *Naut.* any light, loose sail, as a jib or spinnaker, used by a yacht in light wind. [1895–1900]

balloon′ seat′, *Furniture.* See **bell seat.**

balloon′ shade′, a window shade that when raised i gathered into a series of puffy festoons created by i verted pleats in the fabric.

balloon′ tire′, a broad tire filled with air at low pre sure for cushioning the shock of uneven surfaces: us on road vehicles such as bicycles and early automobile [1890–95]

balloon′ vine′, a tropical climbing plant, *Cardiospe mum halicacabum,* of the soapberry family, bearing bi bladderlike pods and black seeds with a white, hear shaped spot. [1830–40, *Amer.*]

bal·lot (bal′ət), *n., v.,* **-lot·ed, -lot·ing.** —*n.* **1.** a slip sheet of paper, cardboard, or the like, on which a vot marks his or her vote. **2.** the method of secret voting b means of printed or written ballots or by means of votir machines. **3.** voting in general, or a round of votin *Our candidate was defeated on the third ballot.* **4.** th list of candidates to be voted on: *They succeeded in ge ting her name placed on the ballot.* **5.** the right to vot *to gain the ballot after years of struggle.* **6.** the who number of votes cast or recorded. **7.** a system or th practice of drawing lots: *The assassin would be chosen ballot.* **8.** (formerly) a little ball used in voting. —*v.i.* to vote by ballot: *to ballot against a candidate.* **10.** draw lots: *to ballot for places.* —*v.t.* **11.** to canvass solicit (a group, membership, etc.) for votes: *Membe were balloted on the resolution.* **12.** to select, esp. f military service, by ballot: *Certain age groups will not balloted at this time.* [1540–50; (< MF *ballotte*) < *ballotta* (prob. < Venetian), equiv. to *ball(a)* BALL[1] *-otta* dim. suffix] —**bal′lot·er,** *n.*

bal·lo·tade (bal′ə tād′, -täd′), *n. Dressage.* a mov ment similar to a croupade except that the horse dra in its hind legs so that the iron of the shoes is visib [1720–30; < F *ballottade, balotade,* equiv. to *ballott(e* to move, stir (intrans.), to toss, shake (deriv. of *ballot* OF *balote* little ball < It; see BALLOT) + *-ade* -ADE[1]]

bal′lot box′, 1. a receptacle for voters' ballots. **2.** system or instance of voting by ballot. [1670–80]

bal·lotte·ment (bə lot′mənt), *n. Med.* a physical d agnostic technique used to detect solid objects su rounded by fluid, as abdominal organs or tumors, pe formed by suddenly compressing the fluid with the han causing the solid object to abut against the hand. [183 40; < F: a tossing, equiv. to *ballotte(r)* to move, stir (s BALLOTADE) + *-ment* -MENT]

bal·lot·tine (bal′ə tēn′, bal′ə tēn′; *Fr.* bA lô tēn′), *pl.* **-tines** (-tēnz′, -tēnz′; *Fr.* -tēn′). a kind of galanti made of meat, poultry, or fish that is stuffed and roll and usually served hot. [perh. < F *ballott(é)* toss about (see BALLOTTEMENT) + (GALANT)INE]

ball·park (bôl′pärk′), *n.* **1.** a tract of land where b games, esp. baseball, are played. **2.** a baseball stadiu **3. in the ballpark,** *Informal.* within reasonable, accep able, or expected limits: *The price may go up anot $10, but that's still in the ballpark.* —*adj.* **4.** *Inform* being an approximation, based on an educated gue *Give me a ballpark figure on our total expenses for ne year.* Also, **ball′ park′.** [1895–1900, *Amer.*; BALL[1] PARK]

ball′-peen ham′mer (bôl′pēn′), a hammer having hemispherical peen (**ball′ peen′**) for beating metal. S illus. under **hammer.**

ball·play·er (bôl′plā′ər), *n.* **1.** a person who plays b professionally, esp. baseball. **2.** anyone who plays b [1610–20; BALL[1] + PLAYER]

ball·point (bôl′point′), *n.* a pen in which the point is fine ball bearing that rotates against a supply of sem solid ink in a cartridge. Also called **ball′point pen** [1945–50; BALL[1] + POINT]

ball·room (bôl′ro͞om′, -ro͝om′), *n.* a large room, as a hotel or resort, with a polished floor for dancin [1730–40; BALL[2] + ROOM]

ball′room dance′, any of a variety of social or re reational dances performed by couples, as in a ballroo [1890–95] —**ball′room danc′ing.**

balls·y (bôl′zē), *adj.,* **balls·i·er, balls·i·est.** *Slang* (*us ally vulgar*). boldly aggressive or courageous: *a bal gal who isn't afraid of anyone.* [1955–60; BALLS + -Y cf. -SY] —**balls′i·ness,** *n.*

ball′ turn′ing, *Furniture.* the turning of arms or le on furniture to make them resemble a continuous row balls.

ball·up (bôl′up′), *n. Slang.* a state of confusion; mi up. Also, *esp. Brit.,* **balls-up** (bôlz′up′). [1935–40; n. u of v. phrase *ball up*]

ball′ valve′, *Mach.* **1.** a valve controlling flow b means of a ball pierced with an opening in one directi and fixed to rotate on a spindle at right angles to t opening. **2.** any valve that checks flow by the seating a ball. [1830–40]

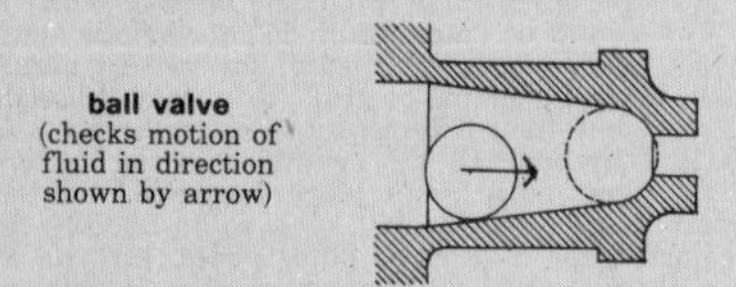
ball valve (checks motion of fluid in direction shown by arrow)

Ball·win (bôl′win), *n.* a town in E Missouri. 12,750.

bal·ly (bal′ē), *adj., adv. Brit. Slang.* damned (euph mism for *bloody*). [1840–50; by alter.]

Bal·ly (bä′lē), *n.* a city in SW West Bengal, in E Indi NW of Calcutta. 262,001.

bal·ly·hoo (*n.* bal′ē ho͞o′; *v.* bal′ē ho͞o′, bal′ē ho͞o′), *pl.* **-hoos,** *v.,* **-hooed, -hoo·ing.** —*n.* **1.** a clamorous a vigorous attempt to win customers or advance a

cause; blatant advertising or publicity. **2.** clamor or outcry. **3.** a halfbeak, *Hemiramphus brasiliensis,* inhabiting both sides of the Atlantic Ocean. **—*v.t., v.i.*** **4.** to advertise or push by ballyhoo. [1830–40, *Amer.*; of uncert. orig.]
—Syn. 1. buildup, hoopla, fanfare; hype.

al•ly•rag (bal′ē rag′), *v.t.,* **-ragged, -rag•ging.** bullyrag.

alm (bäm), *n.* **1.** any of various oily, fragrant, resinous substances, often of medicinal value, exuding from certain plants, esp. tropical trees of the genus *Commiphora.* **2.** a plant or tree yielding such a substance. **3.** any aromatic or fragrant ointment. **4.** aromatic fragrance; sweet odor: *the balm of orange blossoms.* **5.** any of various aromatic plants of the mint family, esp. those of the genus *Melissa,* as *M. officinalis* **(lemon balm),** having ovate lemon-scented leaves used as a seasoning. **6.** anything that heals, soothes, or mitigates pain: *the balm of friendship in troubled times.* [1175–1225; ME *basme, ba(u)me* < AF *basme, bal(s)me, ba(u)me;* OF < L *balsamum* BALSAM; with orthographic *l* pedantically restored] **—balm′like′,** *adj.*
—Syn. 3. salve, unguent, lotion, emollient.

al•ma•caan (bal′mə kan′, -kän′), *n.* a loose-fitting, somewhat flared, single-breasted overcoat, often of tweed and having raglan sleeves, originally worn by men. [1915–20; after *Balmacaan* near Inverness, Scotland]

al•main (bal maɴ′), *n.* **Pierre (A•lex•an•dre)** (pyer a lek säɴ′drᵊ), 1914–82, French fashion designer.

al′mer se′ries (bäl′mər), *Physics.* a series of lines in the visible spectrum of hydrogen. [1960–65; named after J. J. *Balmer* (1825–98), Swiss physicist who derived its formula]

alm-of-Gil•e•ad (bäm′əv gil′ē əd), *n.* **1.** any of several plants of the genus *Commiphora,* esp. *C. opobalsamum* and *C. meccanensis,* which yield a fragrant oleoresin. **2.** Also called **Mecca balsam.** the resin itself, a turbid yellow, green, or brownish-red water-insoluble gluey liquid, used chiefly in perfumery. **3.** a hybrid North American poplar, *Populus gileadensis,* cultivated as a shade tree. [1695–1705]

al•mor•al (bal môr′əl, -mor′əl), *n.* **1.** a colored woolen petticoat, formerly worn under a skirt and draped so that portions of it could be seen. **2.** (*l.c.*) Also called **bal.** an ankle-high shoe, laced in front. **3.** a brimless Scottish cap with a flat top that projects all around the head. Cf. **tam-o'-shanter.** [1855–60; after *Balmoral* Castle in Scotland]

al•mung (bäl′mŏŏng), *n.* (in the *Nibelungenlied*) a sword seized from the Nibelungs by Siegfried. Also, **Balmunc** (bäl′mŏŏngk). Cf. **Gram.**

alm•y (bä′mē), *adj.,* **balm•i•er, balm•i•est. 1.** mild and refreshing; soft; soothing: *balmy weather.* **2.** having the qualities of balm; aromatic; fragrant: *balmy leaves.* **3.** producing balm: *balmy plants; a balmy shrub.* **4.** *Informal.* crazy; foolish; eccentric. [1490–1500; BALM + -Y¹] **—balm′i•ly,** *adv.* **—balm′i•ness,** *n.*
—Syn. 1. fair, gentle, temperate, clement.

al•ne•al (bal′nē əl), *adj.* of or pertaining to baths or bathing. [1635–45; < L *balne(um)* (< Gk *balaneîon* bathing room, bath) + -AL¹]

al•ne•ol•o•gy (bal′nē ol′ə jē), *n. Med.* the science dealing with the therapeutic effects of baths and bathing. [1880–85; *balne-* (see BALNEAL) + -O- + -LOGY] **—bal•ne•o•log•ic** (bal′nē ə loj′ik), **bal′ne•o•log′i•cal,** *adj.* **—bal′ne•ol′o•gist,** *n.*

al•ne•o•ther•a•py (bal′nē ō ther′ə pē), *n.* the treatment of diseases, injuries, and other physical ailments with baths and bathing, esp. in natural mineral waters. [1880–85; *balne-* (see BALNEAL) + -O- + THERAPY]

a•lo•chi (bə lō′chē), *n., pl.* **-chis,** (*esp. collectively*) **-chi.** Baluchi.

a•lon (*Fr.* ba lôɴ′), *n. Ballet.* ballon. [< F]

a•lo•ney (bə lō′nē), *n.* **1.** *Slang.* foolishness; nonsense. **2.** *Informal.* bologna. **—*interj.*** **3.** *Slang.* nonsense. Also, **boloney.** [1915–20, *Amer.*; 1925–30 for def. 2; alter. of BOLOGNA, with substitution of -EY² for final -chwa]

al•op (bal′op), *n.* **1.** Also called **bal′op card′.** a photographic print made on smooth, matte, double-weight paper, used esp. in television advertisements. **2.** *Informal.* balopticon. [by shortening of BALOPTICON]

al•op•ti•con (ba lop′ti kon′, bə-), *n.* a type of stereopticon for projecting images of objects by reflected light. [formerly trademark]

al•sa (bôl′sə, bäl′-), *n.* **1.** a tropical American tree, *Ochroma pyramidale (lagopus),* of the bombax family, yielding an exceedingly light wood used for life preservers, rafts, toy airplanes, etc. **2.** a raft made of balsa wood. **3.** any life raft. [1770–80; < Sp: boat]

al•sam (bôl′səm), *n.* **1.** any of various fragrant exudations from certain trees, esp. trees of the genus *Commiphora,* as balm-of-Gilead. Cf. **balm** (def. 1). **2.** the similar products yielded by the leguminous trees *Myroxylon pereirae* and *M. balsamum,* of South America. Cf. **Peru balsam, tolu. 3.** oleoresin (def. 1). **4.** any of certain transparent turpentines, as Canada balsam. **5.** a plant or tree yielding a balsam. **6.** See **balsam fir. 7.** any of several plants belonging to the genus *Impatiens,* as *I. balsamina,* a common garden annual. Cf. **balsam family. 8.** any aromatic ointment for ceremonial or medicinal use. **9.** any agency that heals, soothes, or restores: *the balsam of understanding and appreciation.* [bef. 1000; ME *balsamum, balsaum,* OE *balzaman* < L *balsamum* < Gk *bálsamon.* See BALM] **—bal•sa•ma•ceous** (bôl′sə mā′shəs), *adj.* **—bal•sam•ic** (bôl sam′ik), *adj.* **—bal′sam•y,** *adj.*

al′sam ap′ple, 1. a climbing Old World tropical vine, *Momordica balsamina,* of the gourd family. **2.** the orange, ovoid, warty fruit of this vine. [1570–80]

al′sam ca•pi′vi (kə pē′vē, -pī′-), copaiba.

bal′sam fam′ily, the plant family Balsaminaceae, typified by succulent stems, alternate, opposite, or whorled simple leaves, and irregular solitary or clustered flowers, including the balsam and jewelweed.

bal′sam fir′, 1. a North American fir, *Abies balsamea,* having dark purplish cones and yielding Canada balsam. **2.** the wood of this tree. **3.** any of certain other firs. [1795–1805, *Amer.*]

bal•sam•if•er•ous (bôl′sə mif′ər əs), *adj.* yielding balsam. [1675–85; BALSAM + -I- + -FEROUS]

bal•sa•mi•na•ceous (bôl′sə mə nā′shəs), *adj.* belonging to the plant family Balsaminaceae. Cf. **balsam family.** [< Gk *balsamín(ē)* garden balsam + -ACEOUS]

bal′sam of fir′. See **Canada balsam.**

bal′sam of Peru′. See **Peru balsam.** [1765–75]

bal′sam of tolu′, tolu. [1665–75]

bal′sam pear′, an Old World tropical vine, *Momordica charantia,* of the gourd family, having yellow flowers and orange-yellow fruit.

bal′sam pop′lar, a North American tree, *Populus balsamifera,* having sticky, resinous buds and shiny ovate leaves. Also called **hackmatack, tacamahac.** [1780–90, *Amer.*]

bal′sam wool′ly a′phid. See under **woolly aphid** (def. 2).

Bal•shem (bäl shem′), *n.* Baalshem.

Balt (bôlt), *n.* a native or inhabitant of Estonia, Latvia, or Lithuania.

Balt., Baltic.

Bal•tas•sar (bal tas′ər), *n. Douay Bible.* Belteshazzar.

bal•te•us (bal′tē əs, bôl′-), *n., pl.* **-te•i** (-tē ī′). **1.** (on an Ionic capital) the horizontal band connecting the volutes on either side. **2.** (in an ancient Roman amphitheater) a horizontal walk dividing upper and lower tiers. [< L: belt, girdle, said by the Romans to be of Etruscan orig.]

Bal•tha•zar (bal thā′zər, -thaz′ər, bôl-, bäl′thə zär′), *n.* **1.** one of the three Magi. **2.** a wine bottle holding 13 qt. (12.3 l). **3.** a male given name.

Bal•tic (bôl′tik), *adj.* **1.** of, near, or on the Baltic Sea. **2.** of or pertaining to the Baltic States. **3.** of or pertaining to a group of languages, as Latvian, Lithuanian, and Old Prussian, that constitute a branch of the Indo-European family. **—*n.*** **4.** the Baltic branch of the Indo-European family of languages.

Bal′tic Sea′, a sea in N Europe, bounded by Denmark, Sweden, Finland, Estonia, Latvia, Lithuania, Poland, and Germany. ab. 160,000 sq. mi. (414,000 sq. km).

Bal′tic States′, Estonia, Latvia, Lithuania, and sometimes Finland.

Bal•ti•more (bôl′tə môr′, -mōr′), *n.* a black nymphalid butterfly, *Melitaea phaeton,* characterized by orange-red, yellow, and white markings, common in those areas of the northeastern U.S. where turtlehead, the food plant of its larvae, is found. [see BALTIMORE ORIOLE]

Bal•ti•more (bôl′tə môr′, -mōr′), *n.* **1. David,** born 1938, U.S. microbiologist: Nobel prize for medicine 1975. **2. Lord.** See **Calvert, Sir George. 3.** a seaport in N Maryland, on an estuary near the Chesapeake Bay. 786,775.

Bal′timore Can′yon, a submarine valley cut into the continental shelf and slope seaward of Chesapeake Bay.

Bal′timore chop′, *Baseball.* a batted ball that takes a high bounce upon hitting the ground on or immediately in front of home plate, often enabling the batter to reach first base safely. [1890–95, *Amer.*]

Bal′timore clip′per, a small, fast American sailing vessel of the early 19th century, having a sharp hull form and two masts with a pronounced rake and carrying a brig or schooner rig. [1815–25, *Amer.*]

Bal′timore heat′er, a stove for heating a lower and upper room, having its fire door in the lower room. [1865–70, *Amer.*]

Bal′timore o′riole, an oriole, *Icterus galbula galbula,* of eastern North America: a subspecies of the northern oriole. [1800–10; earlier *Baltimore (bird);* so named because the black and orange of the male were the colors of Lord BALTIMORE'S livery]

Bal•to-Sla•vic (bôl′tō slä′vik, -slav′ik), *n.* a grouping of Indo-European languages comprising the Baltic and Slavic groups. [1895–1900; *Balto-* (comb. form of BALTIC) + SLAVIC]

Ba•luch (bə lōōch′) *n., pl.* **-luch•es,** (*esp. collectively*) **-luch.** Baluchi.

Ba•lu•chi (bə lōō′chē), *n., pl.* **-chis,** (*esp. collectively*) **-chi** for 1. **1.** a member of a nomadic, primarily Sunni Muslim people of Baluchistan. **2.** the language of the Baluchi, an Iranian language of the Indo-European family. Also, **Balochi, Baluch.** [1610–20; < Pers]

Ba•lu•chi•stan (bə lōō′chə stän′, -stan′, bə lōō′chə stan′), *n.* **1.** an arid mountainous region in S Asia, in SE Iran and SW Pakistan, bordering on the Arabian Sea. **2.** a former territory of W British India, now incorporated into Pakistan.

Balu′chistan States′, a group of three former native states in W British India: now incorporated into Pakistan.

ba•lu•chi•there (bə lōō′chə thēr′), *n.* a hornless rhinoceros of the extinct genus *Baluchitherium* that inhabited central Asia during the Oligocene and early Miocene epochs: the largest land mammal known. [1910–15; < NL *Baluchitherium* genus name, equiv. to *Baluchi-* (see BALUCHISTAN) + *-therium* -THERE]

bal•un (bal′ən), *n. Elect.* a device for converting a balanced line into an unbalanced line and vice versa. [BAL(ANCE) + UN(BALANCE)]

bal•us•ter (bal′ə stər), *n.* **1.** *Archit.* any of a number of closely spaced supports for a railing. **2. balusters,** a balustrade. **3.** any of various symmetrical supports, as furniture legs or spindles, tending to swell toward the bottom or top. [1595–1605; < F, MF *balustre* < It *balaustro* pillar shaped like the calyx of the pomegranate flower, ult. < L *balaustium* < Gk *balaústion* pomegranate flower] **—bal′us•tered,** *adj.*

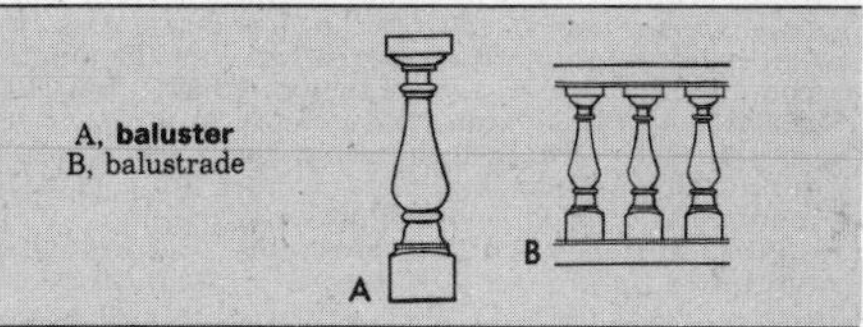

A, **baluster**
B, balustrade

bal′uster meas′ure, an antique liquid measure usually made of pewter, having a concave top on a convex base.

bal′uster stem′, a stem of a drinking glass or the like having a gradual swelling near the top or bottom. [1870–75]

bal•us•trade (bal′ə strād′, bal′ə strād′), *n. Archit.* a railing with supporting balusters. [1635–45; < F *balustre* BALUSTER + *-ade* -ADE¹; cf. Sp *balaustrada,* It *balaustrata*] **—bal′us•trad′ed,** *adj.*

Bal•zac (bôl′zak, bal′-; *Fr.* bal zak′), *n.* **Ho•no•ré de** (on′ə rā′ də; *Fr.* ô nô rā′ də), 1799–1850, French novelist.

bam (bam), *n., v.,* **bammed, bam•ming. —*n.*** **1.** a loud thud, as that produced when two objects strike against each other with force. **—*v.i.*** **2.** to make or emit a bam. [imit.]

B.A.M., 1. Bachelor of Applied Mathematics. **2.** Bachelor of Arts in Music.

Ba•ma•ko (bam′ə kō′; *Fr.* ba ma kō′), *n.* a city in and the capital of Mali: inland port on the Niger River. 380,000.

Bam•ba•ra (bäm bär′ä, -bär′ə), *n.* **1.** a Mande language that is used as a trade language in the upper Niger drainage basin in Africa. **2.** a member of an agricultural, Mande-speaking people of Mali.

Bam•berg (bam′bûrg; *Ger.* bäm′berk), *n.* a city in N Bavaria in south-central West Germany. 73,800.

Bam•bi (bam′bē), *n.* **1.** a familiar name for a baby deer. **2.** a female given name. [from the deer in the children's book of the same name (1923) by Hungarian-born author Felix Salten, pen name of Siegmund Salzmann (1869–1945)]

bam•bi•no (bam bē′nō, bäm-; *It.* bäm bē′nô), *n., pl.* **-nos,** *It.,* **-ni** (-nē). **1.** a small child or baby. **2.** an image of the infant Jesus. [1755–65; < It, equiv. to *bamb(o)* childish (perh. orig. nursery word) + *-ino* dim. suffix]

bam•boc•cia•ta (*It.* bäm′bôt chä′tä), *n., pl.* **-te** (*It.* -te). a genre painting of usually small size produced in Rome in the 17th century. [< It, equiv. to *Bambocci(o)* a nickname of the Dutch painter Pieter van Laer (1592–1645), who popularized such paintings in Rome + *-ata* -ADE¹]

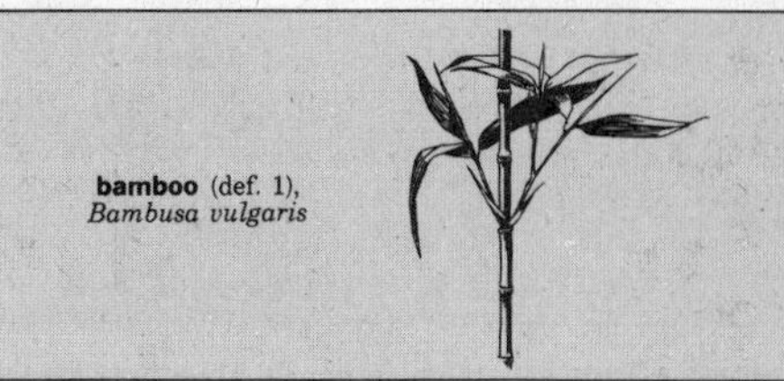
bamboo (def. 1),
Bambusa vulgaris

bam•boo (bam bōō′), *n., pl.* **-boos. 1.** any of the woody or treelike tropical and semitropical grasses of the genera *Bambusa, Phyllostachys, Dendrocalamus,* and allied genera, having woody, usually hollow stems with stalked blades and flowering only after years of growth. **2.** the stem of such a plant, used as a building material and for making furniture, poles, etc. [1590–1600; sp. var. of earlier *bambu* < Malay, appar. < Dravidian; cf. Kannada *bambu, bombu* a large, hollow bam-

CONCISE PRONUNCIATION KEY: act, cāpe, dâre, pärt; set, ēqual; if, īce; ox, ōver, ôrder, oil, bŏŏk, bōōt, out; up, ûrge; child; sing; shoe; thin, *th*at; zh as in *treasure.* ə = *a* as in *alone, e* as in *system, i* as in *easily, o* as in *gallop, u* as in *circus;* ᵊ as in *fire* (fīᵊr), *hour* (ouᵊr). l and n can serve as syllabic consonants, as in *cradle* (krād′l), and *button* (but′n). See the full key inside the front cover.

boo (or directly < Dravidian); r. *bambus* < D *bamboes;* cf. NL *bambūsa*]

bam′boo cur′tain, a political and ideological barrier that impeded relations between Communist Asia, esp. China, and the West from 1949 to 1972. Cf. **iron curtain.**

bamboo′ shoots′, the young shoots produced by the rhizome of a bamboo, used as a vegetable. [1885–90]

bamboo′ turn′ing, *Furniture.* turning of spindles and framing members to simulate the jointing of bamboo.

bamboo′ ware′, a cane-colored Wedgwood stoneware of c1770 imitating bamboo. [1900–05]

bam•boo•zle (bam bo͞o′zəl), *v.,* **-zled, -zling.** —*v.t.* **1.** to deceive or get the better of (someone) by trickery, flattery, or the like; humbug; hoodwink (often fol. by *into*): *They bamboozled us into joining the club.* **2.** to perplex; mystify. —*v.i.* **3.** to practice trickery, deception, cozenage, or the like. [1695–1705; orig. uncert.] —**bam•boo′zle•ment,** *n.* —**bam•boo′zler,** *n.*
—**Syn. 1.** gyp, dupe, trick, cheat, swindle.

B.A.Mus.Ed., Bachelor of Arts in Music Education.

ban[1] (ban), *v.,* **banned, ban•ning,** *n.* —*v.t.* **1.** to prohibit, forbid, or bar; interdict: *to ban nuclear weapons; The dictator banned all newspapers and books that criticized his regime.* **2.** *Archaic.* **a.** to pronounce an ecclesiastical curse upon. **b.** to curse; execrate. —*n.* **3.** the act of prohibiting by law; interdiction. **4.** informal denunciation or prohibition, as by public opinion: *society's ban on racial discrimination.* **5.** *Law.* **a.** a proclamation. **b.** a public condemnation. **6.** *Eccles.* a formal condemnation; excommunication. **7.** a malediction; curse. [bef. 1000; ME *bannen,* OE *bannan* to summon, proclaim; c. ON *banna* to curse (prob. influencing some senses of ME word), OHG *bannan;* akin to L *fārī* to speak, Skt *bhanati* (he) speaks] —**ban′na•ble,** *adj.*
—**Syn. 1.** taboo, outlaw, proscribe. **3.** prohibition, proscription, interdict. **3, 4.** taboo. —**Ant. 1.** allow.

ban[2] (ban), *n.* **1.** a public proclamation or edict. **2. bans,** *Eccles.* banns. **3.** (in the feudal system) **a.** the summoning of the sovereign's vassals for military service. **b.** the body of vassals summoned. [1200–50; ME, aph. var. of *iban,* OE *gebann* proclamation, summons to arms (deriv. of *bannan* BAN[1]), influenced in some senses by OF *ban,* from same Gmc base]

ban[3] (ban, bän), *n.* **1.** (formerly) the governor of Croatia and Slavonia. **2.** *Hist.* a provincial governor of the southern marches of Hungary. [1605–15; < Serbo-Croatian *bân,* contracted from **bojan,* **bajan,* said to be < a Turkic personal name, perh. introduced into the Balkans by the Avars; cf. MGk *bo(e)ános* ban]

ban[4] (bän), *n., pl.* **ba•ni** (bä′nē). a Rumanian coin, the 100th part of a leu. [1960–65; < Rumanian, of uncert. orig., perh. < Serbo-Croatian *bân* BAN[3]]

Ba′nach space′ (bä′näkн, ban′ək), *Math.* a vector space on which a norm is defined that is complete. [1945–50; after Stefan *Banach* (1892–1945), Polish mathematician]

ba•nal (bə nal′, -näl′, bān′l), *adj.* devoid of freshness or originality; hackneyed; trite: *a banal and sophomoric treatment of courage on the frontier.* [1745–55; < F; OF: pertaining to a ban (see BAN[2], -AL[1])] —**ba•nal•i•ty** (bə nal′i tē, bā-), *n.* —**ba•nal′ly,** *adv.*
—**Syn.** See **commonplace.**

ba•nal•ize (bə nal′īz, -nä′līz, bān′l īz′), *v.t.,* **-ized, -iz•ing.** to render or make banal; trivialize: *Television has often been accused of banalizing even the most serious subjects.* Also, *esp. Brit.,* **ba•nal′ise.** [1960–65; BANAL + -IZE]

ba•nan•a (bə nan′ə), *n.* **1.** a tropical plant of the genus *Musa,* certain species of which are cultivated for their nutritious fruit. Cf. **banana family. 2.** the fruit, esp. that of *M. paradisiaca,* with yellow or reddish rind. [1590–1600; < Sp < Pg (perh. via Sp); akin to various words for banana or plantain in WAfr languages (e.g., Wolof, Malinke *banana,* Vai (Mande language of Liberia) *bana*), but ultimate source and direction of borrowing uncert.]

banana plant, *Musa cavendishii,* height 10 to 25 ft. (3.0 m to 7.6 m)

banan′a fam′ily, the plant family Musaceae, characterized by large treelike herbaceous plants of tropical regions, having a trunk formed by spiraling leaf sheaths, and bearing large leaves, flower clusters above leathery red-to-purple bracts, and fleshy fruit in clusters, including the banana and plantain.

Ba•nan•a•land (bə nan′ə land′), *n. Australian Archaic.* Queensland.

banan′a oil′, 1. a sweet-smelling liquid ester, $C_7H_{14}O_2$, a mixture of isomers derived from amyl alcohol and having the characteristic odor of bananas: used chiefly as a paint solvent and in artificial fruit flavors; amyl acetate. **2.** *Slang.* insincere talk; nonsense. [1925–30]

CONCISE ETYMOLOGY KEY: <, descended or borrowed from; >, whence; b., blend of, blended; c., cognate with; cf., compare; deriv., derivative; equiv., equivalent; imit., imitative; obl., oblique; r., replacing; s., stem; sp., spelling, spelled; resp., respelling, respelled; trans., translation; ?, origin unknown; *, unattested; ‡, probably earlier than. See the full key inside the front cover.

banan′a repub′lic, *Usually Disparaging.* any of the small countries in the tropics, esp. in the Western Hemisphere, whose economies are largely dependent on fruit exports, tourism, and foreign investors. [1930–35]

ba•nan•as (bə nan′əz), *adj. Slang.* **1.** crazy; deranged: *All that chatter is driving me bananas.* **2.** wildly enthusiastic: *The crowd went bananas when the music began.* [1965–70, *Amer.*; see BANANA, -S[3]]

banan′a seat′, an elongated bicycle seat that is tapered toward the front and has a gentle upward curve at the back. [1960–65]

banan′a shrub′, a tall Chinese shrub, *Michelia figo,* of the magnolia family, having cream-yellow flowers with a reddish edge and a strong banana odor.

banan′a spi′der, a large, brown and yellow nonvenomous crab spider, *Heteropoda venatoria,* seen on the walls of buildings in the tropics, sometimes transported to other regions in shipments of bananas.

banan′a split′, an elaborate confection, typically consisting of a banana sliced lengthwise, on top of which are placed two or more scoops of ice cream, fruit or other syrup, and a topping of whipped cream, nuts, and a maraschino cherry. [1915–20]

Ba•na•ras (bə när′əs), *n.* a former name of **Varanasi.**

Ban•at (ban′it, bä′nit), *n.* a fertile low-lying region extending through Hungary, Rumania, and Yugoslavia. [< Serbo-Croatian *Bànāt* < ML *Banātus* (*Temesiēnsis*); see BAN[3], -ATE[3]]

ba•nau•sic (bə nô′sik, -zik), *adj.* serving utilitarian purposes only; mechanical; practical: *architecture that was more banausic than inspired.* [1835–45; < Gk *banausikós,* equiv. to *bánaus(os)* artisan + *-ikos* -IC]

Ban•bur•y (ban′ber′ē, -bə rē, -brē, bam′-), *n.* a town in N Oxfordshire, in S England. 29,216.

Ban′bury cake′, a small, oval pastry containing currants, candied peel, honey, spices, etc., usually with three parallel cuts across the top. Also called **Ban′bury bun′.** [1605–15; named after BANBURY, where it was made]

Ban′bury tart′, a tart filled with a lemon-flavored mixture of currants, raisins, or the like.

banc (bangk), *n. Law.* **1.** the seat on which judges sit in court. **2. in banc,** with all the judges of a court present; as a full court: *a hearing in banc.* [1250–1300; ME < OF < Gmc: bench]

ban•co (bang′kō, bäng′-), *n., pl.* **-cos,** *v.* —*n.* **1.** a declaration made by a bettor in certain gambling games, as baccarat and chemin de fer, indicating a bet matching the full amount in the bank, to the exclusion of all previous lower bets: often used as an interjection. —*v.i.* **2.** to make such a declaration. [1745–55; < F < It < Gmc; see BANK[2]]

Ban•croft (ban′krôft, -kroft, bang′-), *n.* **1. George,** 1800–91, U.S. historian and statesman. **2. Hubert Howe,** 1832–1918, U.S. publisher and historian.

Ban′croft Prize′, one of a group of annual awards for literary achievement in American history and biography: administered by Columbia University. [named after G. BANCROFT]

band[1] (band), *n.* **1.** a company of persons or, sometimes, animals or things, joined, acting, or functioning together; aggregation; party; troop: *a band of protesters.* **2.** *Music.* **a.** a group of instrumentalists playing music of a specialized type: *rock band; calypso band; mariachi band.* **b.** a musical group, usually employing brass, percussion, and often woodwind instruments, that plays esp. for marching or open-air performances. **c.** See **big band. d.** See **dance band. 3.** a division of a nomadic tribe; a group of individuals who move and camp together and subsist by hunting and gathering. **4.** a group of persons living outside the law: *a renegade band.* **5. to beat the band,** *Informal.* energetically; abundantly: *It rained all day to beat the band.* —*v.t.* **6.** to unite in a troop, company, or confederacy. —*v.i.* **7.** to unite; confederate (often fol. by *together*): *They banded together to oust the chairman.* [1480–90; < MF *bande* < It *banda;* c. LL *bandum* < Gmc; akin to Goth *bandwa* standard, BAND[2], BAND[3], BEND[1], BOND[1]]
—**Syn. 1.** gang, group; body; set; society, association, assembly. See **company.**

band[2] (band), *n.* **1.** a thin, flat strip of some material for binding, confining, trimming, protecting, etc.: *a band on each bunch of watercress.* **2.** a fillet, belt, or strap: *a band for the hair; a band for connecting pulleys.* **3.** a stripe, as of color or decorative work. **4.** a strip of paper or other material serving as a label: *a cigar band.* **5.** a plain or simply styled ring, without mounted gems or the like: *a thin gold band on his finger.* **6.** (on a long-playing phonograph record) one of a set of grooves in which sound has been recorded, separated from an adjacent set or sets by grooves without recorded sound. **7. bands.** See **Geneva bands. 8.** a flat collar commonly worn by men and women in the 17th century in western Europe. **9.** Also called **frequency band, wave band.** *Radio and Television.* a specific range of frequencies, esp. a set of radio frequencies, as HF, VHF, and UHF. **10.** Also called **energy band.** *Physics.* a closely spaced group of energy levels of electrons in a solid. **11.** *Computers.* one or more tracks or channels on a magnetic drum. **12.** *Dentistry.* a strip of thin metal encircling a tooth, usually for anchoring an orthodontic apparatus. **13.** *Anat., Zool.* a ribbonlike or cordlike structure encircling, binding, or connecting a part or parts. **14.** (in handbound books) one of several cords of hemp or flax handsewn across the back of the collated signatures of a book to provide added strength. —*v.t.* **15.** to mark, decorate, or furnish with a band or bands. [1480–90; < MF; OF *bende* < Gmc; cf. OHG *binta* fillet. See BIND, BAND[1]] —**band′er,** *n.* —**band′less,** *adj.*

band[3] (band), *n. Archaic.* **1.** Usually, **bands.** articles for binding the person or the limbs; shackles; manacles; fetters. **2.** an obligation; bond: *the nuptial bands* [1100–50; late OE < ON *band;* c. OS, OFris *band,* OHG *bant;* akin to Skt *bandha-.* See BAND[1]]

Ban•da (ban′də), *n.* **Hastings Ka•mu•zu** (kä mo͞o′zo͞o), born 1906, Malawi physician, political leader, and public official: 1st president of Malawi 1966–94.

band•age (ban′dij), *n., v.,* **-aged, -ag•ing.** —*n.* **1.** a strip of cloth or other material used to bind up a wound, sore, sprain, etc. **2.** anything used as a band or ligature. —*v.t.* **3.** to bind or cover with a bandage: *to bandage the ankles of a football player to prevent sprains.* —*v.i.* **4.** to put a bandage on a wound, sprain, etc.: *Apply some iodine before you bandage.* [1590–1600; < MF; see BAND[2], -AGE] —**band′ag•er,** *n.*
—**Syn. 1.** dressing, binding, compass.

Band-Aid (band′ād′), **1.** *Trademark.* a brand of adhesive bandage with a gauze pad in the center, used to cover minor abrasions and cuts. —*n.* **2.** (*often l.c.*) *Informal.* a makeshift, limited, or temporary aid or solution that does not satisfy the basic or long-range need: *The proposed reform isn't thorough enough to be more than just a band-aid.* —*adj.* **3.** (*often l.c.*) *Informal.* serving as a makeshift, limited, or temporary aid or solution: *band-aid measures to solve a complex problem.* [1965–70 for defs. 2, 3]

ban•dan•na (ban dan′ə), *n.* **1.** a large, printed handkerchief, typically one with white spots or figures on a red or blue background. **2.** any large scarf for the neck or head. Also, **ban•dan′a.** [1745–55; earlier *bandanno* (second syll. unstressed) < Hindi *bādhnū* tie dyeing] —**ban•dan•naed** (ban dan′əd), *adj.*

Ban•dar Ab•bas (bun′dər ə bäs′), a seaport in S Iran. 605,387.

Ban•dara•nai•ke (bän′drä nī′kē), *n.* **Si•ri•ma•vo** (sē′rē mä′vô), born 1916, Sri Lankan political leader: prime minister of Sri Lanka (Ceylon) 1960–65, 1970–77.

Ban•dar Se•ri Be•ga•wan (bun′dər ser′ē bə gä′wən), a seaport in and the capital of the sultanate of Brunei, on the NW coast of Borneo, in the Malay Archipelago. 36,987.

Ban′da Sea′ (bän′də, ban′-), a sea between Sulawesi (Celebes) and New Guinea, S of the Moluccas and N of Timor.

B and B, 1. *Trademark.* a brand of liqueur combining Benedictine and brandy. **2.** bed-and-breakfast.

B&B, 1. bed-and-breakfast. **2.** See **B and B** (def. 1).

band•box (band′boks′), *n.* **1.** a lightweight box of pasteboard, thin wood, etc., for holding a hat, clerical collars, or other articles of apparel. **2.** an area or structure that is smaller in dimensions or size than the standard: *It's easy to hit home runs out of this bandbox.* [1625–35; BAND[2] + BOX[1]] —**band′box′i•cal,** *adj.* —**band′box′y,** *adj.*

band′ brake′, a brake using a brake band. [1885–90]

B&C, *Insurance.* building and contents. Also, **B and C**

B&D, bondage and discipline: used in reference to sadomasochistic sexual practices. Also, **B and D**

ban•deau (ban dō′, ban′dō), *n., pl.* **-deaux** (-dōz′, -dōz). **1.** a headband, esp. one worn about the forehead. **2.** a narrow brassiere. [1700–10; < F; OF *bandel,* equiv. to *bande* BAND[2] + *-el* < L *-illus* dim. suffix]

band•ed (ban′did), *adj.* **1.** marked or fitted with a band or bands. **2.** *Archit.* (of a column, door architrave, etc.) having the regular flutings, moldings, or the like interrupted at regular intervals by projecting blocks or drums. [1480–90; BAND[2] + -ED[2]]

band′ed ant′eater, an Australian marsupial, *Myrmecobius fasciatus,* feeding on termites and having the body marked with whitish transverse bars: nearly extinct. Also called **numbat.**

band′ed Flor′ida tree′ snail′, a tree-dwelling snail, *Liguus fasciatus,* of Florida and nearby keys, having a long, conical shell in many color variations: now greatly reduced in numbers. Also called **lig snail.**

band′ed pur′ple. See under **purple** (def. 7).

band′ed rat′tlesnake. See **timber rattlesnake** [1815–25]

ban•de•let (ban′dl et′, -dl it, ban′dl et′), *n. Archit.* **1.** a flat molding, broader than a fillet and narrower than a fascia. **2.** annulet (def. 1). Also, **bandlet.** [1640–50; < F *bandelette,* equiv. to OF *bandele* (fem. of *bandel* BANDEAU) + *-ete* -ETTE]

Ban•del•lo (bän del′lô), *n.* **Mat•te•o** (mät te′ô), 1485–1561, Italian ecclesiastic and author.

ban•de•ril•la (ban′də rē′ə, -rēl′yə; *Sp.* bän′de rē′lyä, -yä), *n., pl.* **-ril•las** (-rē′əz, -rēl′yəz; *Sp.* -rē′lyäs, -yäs). an ornamented dart with barbs used by banderilleros for sticking into the neck or shoulder of the bull. [1790–1800; < Sp, equiv. to *bander(a)* BANNER + *-illa* dim. suffix < L]

ban•de•ril•le•ro (ban′də rē âr′ō, -rel yâr′-; *Sp.* bän′de rē lye′rô, -ye′-), *n., pl.* **-ril•le•ros** (-rē âr′ōz, -rel yâr′-; *Sp.* -rē lye′rôs, -ye′-). a matador's assistant who sticks the banderillas into the bull. [1790–1800; < Sp, equiv. to *banderill(a)* BANDERILLA + *-ero* -ARY]

ban•de•role (ban′də rōl′), *n.* **1.** a small flag or streamer fastened to a lance, masthead, etc. **2.** a narrow scroll, usually bearing an inscription. **3.** (esp. in Renaissance architecture) a sculptured band, as on a building, adapted to receive an inscription. Also, **ban′de•rol, ban•drol, ban•drole** (ban′drōl). [1555–65; < MF < It *banderuola,* equiv. to *bandier(a)* BANNER + *-uola* < L *-e-* or *-i-* + *-ola* -OLE[2]]

ban•der•snatch (ban′dər snach′), *n.* **1.** an imaginary wild animal of fierce disposition. **2.** a person of uncouth or unconventional habits, attitudes, etc., esp. one considered a menace, nuisance, or the like. [coined by Lewis Carroll in *Through the Looking Glass* (1871)]

band•file (band′fīl′), *v.t.,* **-filed, -fil•ing.** to file with a file band on a band mill or band saw. [BAND[2] + FILE[2]]

ban·di·coot (ban′di ko͞ot′), *n.* **1.** any of several large East Indian rats of the genus *Nesokia.* **2.** any of several insectivorous and herbivorous marsupials of the family Peramelidae, of Australia and New Guinea: some are endangered. [1780–90; < Telugu *pandi-kokku* pig-rat]

bandicoot (def. 2), *Macrotis lagotis,* head and body 16 in. (41 cm); tail 8 in. (20 cm)

ban·di·do (ban dē′dō), *n., pl.* **-dos.** bandito. [*Amer.;* < Sp < It *bandito.* See BANDIT]

Ban·di·nel·li (bän′dē nel′lē), *n.* **Bac·cio** (bät′chô) or **Bar·to·lom·me·o** (bär′tô lôm me′ô), 1493–1560, Italian sculptor.

band·ing (ban′ding), *n. Furniture.* decorative inlay, as for bordering or paneling a piece, composed of strips of wood contrasting in grain or color with the principal wood of the surface. [1730–40; BAND[2] + -ING[1]]

ban·dit (ban′dit), *n., pl.* **ban·dits** or (*Rare*) **ban·dit·ti** (ban dit′ē). **1.** a robber, esp. a member of a gang or marauding band. **2.** an outlaw or highwayman. **3.** *Informal.* **a.** a person who takes unfair advantage of others, as a merchant who overcharges; swindler; cheat. **b.** a vendor, cab driver, etc., who operates a business or works without a required license or permit, and without observing the usual rules or practices. **4.** *Mil. Informal.* an enemy aircraft, esp. an attacking fighter. **5. make out like a bandit,** *Slang.* to be extremely successful; profit greatly: *The early investors in the company have made out like bandits.* [1585–95; earlier *bandetto,* pl. *banditti* < It *banditi* outlaws, pl. of *bandito* proscribed, ptp. of *bandire* banish, exile, announce publicly < Goth *bandwjan* to make a sign, indicate (cf. BAND[1]) with v. suffix *-ire* < L *-īre*]
—Syn. 1, 2. brigand, desperado.

ban·di·to (ban dē′tō), *n., pl.* **-tos.** (esp. in Mexico and Central America) an outlaw; bandit. Also, **bandido.** [1585–95; < It; see BANDIT (or as pseudo-Sp alter. of BANDIT)]

ban·dit·ry (ban′di trē), *n.* **1.** the activities or practices of bandits. **2.** bandits collectively; banditti. [1920–25; BANDIT + -RY]

Ban·djer·ma·sin (bän′jər mä′sin), *n.* Banjermasin. Also, **Ban′djar·ma′sin.**

Band·ke·ram·ik (bänt′kä rä′mik), *n.* the pottery of the early Neolithic Danubian culture of Europe, having characteristic parallel spiral lines over the body and neck of the gourdlike vessels and dated 5000–4000 B.C. [1920–25; < G; see BAND[2], CERAMIC]

band·lead·er (band′lē′dər), *n.* the leader of a musical band, esp. a dance band. [1890–95; BAND[1] + LEADER]

band·let (band′lit), *n. Archit.* **1.** annulet (def. 1). **2.** bandelet. [1720–30; BAND[2] + -LET]

band·mas·ter (band′mas′tər, -mä′stər), *n.* the conductor of a military band, circus band, etc. [1855–60; BAND[1] + MASTER]

band′ mill′, a powered machine having two pulleys for a saw band or a file band; band saw. [1815–25, *Amer.*]

Ban·doeng (*Du.* bän′do͝ong), *n.* Bandung.

ban·dog (ban′dôg′, -dog′), *n.* any dog, as a mastiff or bloodhound, kept tied or chained. [1250–1300; ME *band-dogge.* See BAND[3], DOG]

ban·do·leer (ban′dl ēr′), *n.* a broad belt worn over the shoulder by soldiers and having a number of small loops or pockets, for holding a cartridge or cartridges. Also, **ban′do·lier′.** [1570–80; earlier *bandollier* < MF *bandoulliere* < Catalan *bandolera,* fem. deriv. of *bandoler* member of a band of men (*bandol* (< Sp *bando* BAND[1]) + *-er* < L *-ārius* -ARY; cf. -EER)] **—ban′do·leered′, ban′do·liered′,** *adj.*

ban·do·line (ban′dl ēn′, -dl in), *n.* a mucilaginous preparation made from quince seeds and used for smoothing, glossing, or waving the hair. [1840–50; < F *bandeau* BANDEAU + *-line* < L *linere* to anoint, smear]

ban·dore (ban dôr′, -dōr′, ban′dôr, -dōr), *n.* an obsolete musical instrument resembling the guitar. Also, **ban·do·ra** (ban dôr′ə, -dōr′ə). Also called **pandora, pandore, pandoura, pandure.** [1560–70; earlier *bandurion* < Sp *bandurria* < L *pandūra* < Gk *pandoûra* three-stringed musical instrument]

band′-pass fil′ter (band′pas′, -päs′), *Elect., Electronics.* a filter that attenuates all frequencies except those of a specific band, which it amplifies. [1920–25]

band′ ra′zor, a safety razor with a replaceable head whose cutting edge is a narrow band of steel that can be wound forward, exposing a new, sharp section.

band′ saw′, *Mach.* a saw consisting of an endless toothed steel band passing over two wheels. [1860–65, *Amer.*]

band·saw (band′sô′), *v.t.,* **-sawed, -sawed** or **-sawn, -saw·ing.** to cut with a band saw. [v. use of BAND SAW]

band′ shell′, a concave, acoustically resonant structure at the back of an outdoor bandstand. [1925–30]

bands·man (bandz′mən), *n., pl.* **-men.** a musician who plays in a band. [1835–45; BAND[1] + 's[1] + -MAN]
—Usage. See **-man.**

band′ spec′trum, *Physics.* an optical spectrum consisting of groups of closely spaced spectral lines, characteristic of molecules. Cf. **continuous spectrum, line spectrum.** [1865–70]

band·stand (band′stand′), *n.* **1.** a platform, often roofed, for outdoor band performances. **2.** a raised platform in a nightclub, restaurant, etc., used by the members of a band or orchestra while performing. [1855–60; BAND[1] + STAND]

band′-tailed pi′geon (band′tāld′), a wild pigeon, *Columba fasciata,* of western North America, having a gray band on its tail. [1815–25, *Amer.*]

Ban·dung (bän′do͞ong, -do͝ong, ban′-), *n.* a city in W Java, in Indonesia. 1,200,000. Dutch, **Bandoeng.**

ban·du·ra (ban do͝or′ə), *n.* a Ukrainian stringed instrument of the lute family. [< Ukrainian *bandúra,* prob. < Pol < It < Gk *pandoûra.* See BANDORE]

ban·dur·ria (ban do͝or′yə), *n.* a Spanish musical instrument of the guitar family with six pairs of double strings. [1835–45; < Sp; see BANDORE]

b and w, 1. (of a motion picture, photograph, drawing, etc.) black and white, as distinguished from color. **2.** a black and white motion picture, photograph, drawing, etc. Also, **B and W, b&w, B&W**

band·wag·on (band′wag′ən), *n.* **1.** a wagon, usually large and ornately decorated, for carrying a musical band while it is playing, as in a circus parade or to a political rally. **2.** a party, cause, movement, etc., that by its mass appeal or strength readily attracts many followers: *After it became apparent that the incumbent would win, everyone decided to jump on the bandwagon.* [1850–55, *Amer.;* BAND[1] + WAGON]

band·width (band′width′, -with′), *n. Telecommunications.* the smallest range of frequencies constituting a band, within which a particular signal can be transmitted without distortion. [1925–30; BAND[2] + WIDTH]

ban·dy (ban′dē), *v.,* **-died, -dy·ing,** *adj., n., pl.* **-dies.** —*v.t.* **1.** to pass from one to another or back and forth; give and take; trade; exchange: *to bandy blows; to bandy words.* **2.** to throw or strike to and fro or from side to side, as a ball in tennis. **3.** to circulate freely: *to bandy gossip.* —*adj.* **4.** (of legs) having a bend or crook outward; bowed: *a new method for correcting bandy legs.* —*n.* **5.** an early form of tennis. **6.** *Chiefly Brit.* (formerly) hockey or shinny. **7.** *Obs.* a hockey or shinny stick. [1570–80; perh. < Sp *bandear* to conduct, bandy, orig. help, serve as member of a band of men. See BAND[1]] **—ban′di·ness,** *n.*
—Syn. 1. reciprocate, interchange, swap, barter.

ban·dy-ban·dy (ban′dē ban′dē), *n., pl.* **-dies.** a small venomous snake, *Vermicella annulata,* inhabiting New South Wales, marked with black and white bands. [1925–30; < Kattang (Australian Aboriginal language spoken between Port Stephens and Port Macquarie, New South Wales) *bandi-bandi*]

ban·dy-leg·ged (ban′dē leg′id, -legd′), *adj.* having crooked legs; bowlegged. [1680–90]

bane (bān), *n.* **1.** a person or thing that ruins or spoils: *Gambling was the bane of his existence.* **2.** a deadly poison (often used in combination, as in the names of poisonous plants): *wolfsbane; henbane.* **3.** death; destruction; ruin. **4.** *Obs.* that which causes death or destroys life: *entrapped and drowned beneath the watery bane.* [bef. 1000; ME; OE *bana* slayer; c. ON *bani* death, murderer, OFris *bona* murder, OS *bano* murderer, OHG *bano* slayer, *bana* death; akin to OE *benn,* Goth *banja* wound]

bane·ber·ry (bān′ber′ē, -bə rē), *n., pl.* **-ries. 1.** any plant belonging to the genus *Actaea,* of the buttercup family, having large compound leaves, spikes of small white flowers, and poisonous red or white berries. **2.** the berry of such a plant. [1745–55; BANE + BERRY]

bane·ful (bān′fəl), *adj.* **1.** destructive; pernicious: *a baneful superstition.* **2.** deadly; poisonous: *baneful herbs.* [1570–80; BANE + -FUL] **—bane′ful·ly,** *adv.* **—bane′ful·ness,** *n.*
—Syn. harmful, noxious; venomous, toxic.

Ba·ner·jea (ban′ər jē′), *n.* **Sir Su·ren·dra·nath** (so͞o-ren′drə nät′), 1848–1925, Indian political leader.

Banff (bamf), *n.* **1.** Also called **Banff·shire** (bamf′-shēr, -shər). a historic county in NE Scotland. **2.** a seaport in this district. 3723. **3.** a resort town in Banff National Park. 3410.

Banff′ Na′tional Park′, a national reserve, 2585 sq. mi. (6695 sq. km), in the Rocky Mountains, in SW Alberta, Canada.

bang[1] (bang), *n.* **1.** a loud, sudden, explosive noise, as the discharge of a gun. **2.** a resounding stroke or blow: *a nasty bang on the head.* **3.** *Informal.* a sudden movement or show of energy: *He started with a bang.* **4.** energy; vitality; spirit: *The bang has gone out of my work.* **5.** *Informal.* sudden or intense pleasure; thrill; excitement: *a big bang out of seeing movies.* **6.** *Slang* (*vulgar*). sexual intercourse. **7.** *Printing and Computer Slang.* an exclamation point. —*v.t.* **8.** to strike or beat resoundingly; pound: *to bang a door.* **9.** to hit or bump painfully: *to bang one's ankle on a chair leg.* **10.** to throw or set down roughly; slam: *He banged the plates on the table.* **11.** *Slang* (*vulgar*). to have sexual intercourse with. —*v.i.* **12.** to strike violently or noisily: *to bang on the door.* **13.** to make a loud, sudden, explosive noise like that of a violent blow: *The guns banged all night.* **14.** *Slang* (*vulgar*). to have sexual intercourse. **15. bang into,** to collide with; bump into: *The truck skidded on the ice and banged into a parked car.* **16. bang up,** to damage: *A passing car banged up our fender.* —*adv.* **17.** suddenly and loudly; abruptly or violently: *She fell bang against the wall.* **18.** directly; precisely; right: *He stood bang in the middle of the flower bed.* **19. bang off,** *Chiefly Brit. Slang.* immediately; right away. **20. bang on,** *Chiefly Brit. Slang.* terrific; marvelous; just right: *That hat is absolutely bang on.* [1540–50; 1930–35 for def. 5; cf. ON *banga* to beat, hammer, LG *bangen* to strike, beat, G dial. *banken;* perh. orig. imit.]
—Syn. 2. smack, clout, box, wallop, sock, bash, cuff.

bang[2] (bang), *n.* **1.** Often, **bangs.** a fringe of hair combed or brushed forward over the forehead. —*v.t.* **2.** to cut (the hair) so as to form a fringe over the forehead. **3.** to dock (the tail of a horse or dog). [1860–65, *Amer.;* short for BANGTAIL]

bang[3] (bang), *n.* bhang.

bang·al·ay (bang al′ē), *n.* See **bastard mahogany.** [1880–85]

Ban·ga·lore (bang′gə lôr′, -lōr′, bang′gə lôr′, -lōr′), *n.* a city in and the capital of Karnataka, in SW India. 1,653,779.

Ban′galore torpe′do, a metal tube filled with explosives and equipped with a firing mechanism, esp. for destroying barbed-wire entanglements, mine fields, etc. [1910–15]

bang·er (bang′ər), *n.* **1.** a person or thing that bangs. **2.** *Brit.* **a.** *Informal.* a sausage. **b.** a firecracker. [1650–60; BANG[1] + -ER[1]]

Bang·ka (bang′kə), *n.* an island in Indonesia, E of Sumatra: tin mines. 4611 sq. mi. (11,942 sq. km). Also, **Banka.**

Bang·kok (bang′kok, bang kok′), *n.* **1.** a seaport in and the capital of Thailand, in the S central part, on the Chao Phraya. 4,000,000. **2.** (*l.c.*) a kind of Siamese straw. **3.** (*l.c.*) a hat woven of strands of this straw.

Ban·gla·desh (bäng′glə desh′, bang′-), *n.* republic in S Asia, N of the Bay of Bengal: a member of the Commonwealth of Nations; a former province of Pakistan. 85,000,000; 54,501 sq. mi. (141,158 sq. km). *Cap.:* Dhaka. Formerly, **East Pakistan.**

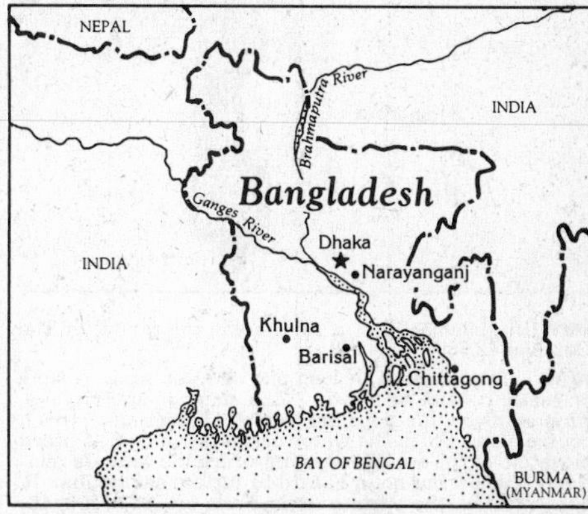

Ban·gla·desh·i (bäng′glə desh′ē, bang′-), *n., pl.* **-desh·is,** *adj.* —*n.* **1.** a native or inhabitant of Bangladesh. —*adj.* **2.** of, pertaining to, or characteristic of Bangladesh or its people. [1970–75; BANGLADESH + *-i* ult. < Ar *-ī* suffix of appurtenance]

ban·gle (bang′gəl), *n.* a rigid, ring-shaped bracelet usually made without a clasp so as to slip over the hand, but sometimes having a hinged opening and a clasp. [1780–90; < Hindi *banglī,* var. of *bangrī* glass ring, armlet] **—ban′gled,** *adj.*

Ban·gor (bang′gôr, -gər), *n.* a seaport in S Maine, on the Penobscot River. 31,643.

Bangs (bangz), *n.* **John Ken·drick** (ken′drik), 1862–1922, U.S. humorist.

Bang's′ disease′ (bangz), *Vet. Pathol.* an infectious disease of cattle caused by a bacterium, *Brucella abortus,* that infects the genital organs and frequently causes spontaneous abortions. [1930–35; named after B.L.F. *Bang* (1848–1932), Danish biologist]

bang·tail (bang′tāl′), *n. Horse Racing Slang.* a racehorse. [1885–90; *bang* cut (nasal var. of *bag* cut < ?) + TAIL[1]. Cf. PIGTAIL]

Ban·gui (*Fr.* bän gē′), *n.* a city in and the capital of the Central African Republic, in the SW part. 350,000.

bang-up (bang′up′), *adj. Informal.* excellent; extraordinary. [1800–10; adj. use of v. phrase *bang up*]

Bang·we·u·lu (bang′wē o͞o′lo͞o), *n.* a shallow lake and swamp in NE Zambia. ab. 150 mi. (240 km) long.

ba·ni (bä′nē), *n.* pl. of **ban[4].**

ban·ia (ban′yə), *n.* banyan (def. 2). Also, **ban·iya** (ban′yə, -ē ə). [1590–1600]

ban·ian (ban′yən), *n.* banyan.

ban·ish (ban′ish), *v.t.* **1.** to expel from or relegate to a country or place by authoritative decree; condemn to exile: *He was banished to Devil's Island.* **2.** to compel to depart; send, drive, or put away: *to banish sorrow.* [1275–1325; ME *banisshen* < AF, OF *baniss-,* long s. of *banir* < Frankish **bannjan* to proclaim, akin to BAN[1]] **—ban′ish·er,** *n.* **—ban′ish·ment,** *n.*
—Syn. 1. exile, expatriate, outlaw; deport.

ban·is·ter (ban′ə stər), *n.* **1.** a baluster. **2.** Sometimes, **banisters.** the balustrade of a staircase. Also, **bannister.** [1660–70; appar. by dissimilation from earlier *barrister,* alter. of BALUSTER, perh. by assoc. with BAR[1]]

ban′ister back′, *Furniture.* a back of a chair or the like, usually having semicircular spindles between the top rail and the cross rail or seat.

Ban·jer·ma·sin (bän′jər mä′sin), *n.* a seaport on the S coast of Borneo, in Indonesia. 281,673. Also, **Ban′jarma′sin, Bandjermasin, Bandjarmasin.**

CONCISE PRONUNCIATION KEY: act, cāpe, dâre, pärt; set, ēqual; *if,* ice; ox, ōver, ôrder, oil, bo͝ok, bo͞ot, out; up, ûrge; child; sing; shoe; thin, *that;* zh as in *treasure.* ə = *a* as in *alone, e* as in *system, i* as in *easily, o* as in *gallop, u* as in *circus;* ᵊ as in *fire* (fīᵊr), *hour* (ouᵊr). l and n can serve as syllabic consonants, as in *cradle* (krād′l), and *button* (but′n). See the full key inside the front cover.

ban•jo (ban′jō), *n., pl.* **-jos, -joes.** a musical instrument of the guitar family, having a circular body covered in front with tightly stretched parchment and played with the fingers or a plectrum. [1730–40; cf. Jamaican E *banja, bonjour, bangil,* Brazilian Pg *banza;* prob. of African orig.; cf. Kimbundu *mbanza* a plucked string instrument] —**ban′jo•ist,** *n.*

banjo

ban′jo clock′, a clock of the early 19th century in the U.S., having a drumlike case for the dial mounted on a narrow, tapering body, with a boxlike bottom containing the pendulum and its weight. [1795–1805, *Amer.*]

banjo clock

Ban′jul (bän′jōōl), *n.* a port in and the capital of The Gambia. 42,689.

bank[1] (bangk), *n.* **1.** a long pile or heap; mass: *a bank of earth; a bank of clouds.* **2.** a slope or acclivity. **3.** *Physical Geog.* the slope immediately bordering a stream course along which the water normally runs. **4.** a broad elevation of the sea floor around which the water is relatively shallow but not a hazard to surface navigation. **5.** *Coal Mining.* the surface around the mouth of a shaft. **6.** Also called **cant, superelevation.** the inclination of the bed of a banked road or railroad. **7.** *Aeron.* the lateral inclination of an aircraft, esp. during a turn. **8.** *Billiards, Pool.* the cushion of the table. —*v.t.* **9.** to border with or like a bank; embank: *banking the river with sandbags at flood stage.* **10.** to form into a bank or heap (usually fol. by *up*): *to bank up the snow.* **11.** to build (a road or railroad track) with an upward slope from the inner edge to the outer edge at a curve. **12.** *Aeron.* to tip or incline (an airplane) laterally. **13.** *Billiards, Pool.* **a.** to drive (a ball) to the cushion. **b.** to pocket (the object ball) by driving it against the bank. **14.** to cover (a fire) with ashes or fuel to make it burn long and slowly. —*v.i.* **15.** to build up in or form banks, as clouds or snow. **16.** *Aeron.* to tip or incline an airplane laterally. **17.** *Horol.* (of a lever or balance) to be halted at either end of its oscillation by striking a pin or the like. **18.** (of a road or railroad track) to slope upward from the inner edge to the outer edge at a curve. [1150–1200; ME *banke,* OE *hōbanca* couch; c. ON *bakki* elevation, hill, Sw *backe,* Dan *bakke* < Gmc **bank-ōn-;* perh. akin to Skt *bhañj-* bend, Lith *bangà* wave; see BANK[3], BENCH] —**Syn. 1.** embankment, mound, ridge, dike. **3.** See **shore**[1].

bank[2] (bangk), *n.* **1.** an institution for receiving, lending, exchanging, and safeguarding money and, in some cases, issuing notes and transacting other financial business. **2.** the office or quarters of such an institution. **3.** *Games.* **a.** the stock or fund of pieces from which the players draw. **b.** the fund of the manager or the dealer. **4.** a special storage place: *a blood bank; a sperm bank.* **5.** a store or reserve. **6.** *Obs.* **a.** a sum of money, esp. as a fund for use in business. **b.** a moneychanger's table, counter, or shop. —*v.i.* **7.** to keep money in or have an account with a bank: *Do you bank at the Village Savings Bank?* **8.** to exercise the functions of a bank or banker. **9.** *Games.* to hold the bank. —*v.t.* **10.** to deposit in a bank: *to bank one's paycheck.* **11. bank on** or **upon,** to count on; depend on: *You can bank on him to hand you a reasonable bill for his services.* [1425–75; late ME < MF *banque* < It *banca* table, counter, moneychanger's table < OHG *bank* BENCH]

bank[3] (bangk), *n.* **1.** an arrangement of objects in a line or in tiers: *a bank of seats; a bank of lights.* **2.** *Music.* a row of keys on an organ. **3.** a row of elevator cars, as in a hotel or high-rise office building. **4.** a bench for rowers in a galley. **5.** a row or tier of oars. **6.** the group of rowers occupying one bench or rowing one oar. **7.** *Print.* **a.** (formerly) a bench on which sheets are placed as printed. **b.** Also called, *esp. Brit.,* **random.** the sloping work surface at the top of a compositor's workbench. **c.** a table or rack on which type material is stored before being made up in forms. **8.** Also called **deck.** *Journalism.* a part of a headline containing one or more lines of type, esp. a part that appears below the main part. **9.** *Elect.* a number of similar devices connected to act together: *a bank of transformers; a bank of resistors.* —*v.t.* **10.** to arrange in a bank: *to bank the seats; to bank the lights.* [1200–50; ME *bank(e)* < OF *banc* bench < Gmc; see BANK[1]]

Ban•ka (bang′kə), *n.* Bangka.

bank•a•ble (bang′kə bəl), *adj.* **1.** acceptable for processing by a bank: *bankable checks and money orders.* **2.** considered powerful, prestigious, or stable enough to ensure profitability: *Without bankable stars the film script aroused no interest.* [1810–20, *Amer.;* BANK[2] + -ABLE] —**bank′a•bil′i•ty,** *n.*

bank′ accept′ance, a draft or bill of exchange that a bank has accepted. *Abbr.:* BA Also called **banker's acceptance.** Cf. **acceptance** (def. 6).

bank′ account′, **1.** an account with a bank. **2.** balance standing to the credit of a depositor at a bank. Also called, *Brit.,* **banking account.** [1790–1800]

bank′-and-turn′ in′dicator (bangk′ən tûrn′), *Aeron.* a flight instrument that combines a bank indicator and turn indicator in a single unit. Also called **turn-and-bank indicator, turn-and-slip indicator.**

bank′ annu′ities, Sometimes, **bank annuity.** consols.

bank′ bal′ance, **1.** balance standing to the credit of a depositor at a bank. **2.** *Finance.* the balance that a bank has in the clearinghouse at a given time.

bank′ barn′, *Chiefly Midland U.S. and Canadian (chiefly Ontario).* a barn built into the side of a hill or with earth banked around it, often a two-story barn thus having a ground-level entrance for each story. [1890–95, *Amer.*]

bank′ bill′, *Chiefly U.S.* a bank note. [1690–1700]

bank•book (bangk′bo͝ok′), *n.* a book held by a depositor in which a bank enters a record of deposits and withdrawals. [1705–15; BANK[2] + BOOK]

bank′ box′. See **safe-deposit box.**

bank′ card′, Also called **bank′ cred′it card′.** a card issued by a bank for credit or identification purposes, as for use in cashing checks or at an automated teller machine. [1965–70]

bank′ check′, **1.** See **cashier's check.** **2.** a check that the holder of a checking account draws on a bank for payment. [1795–1805, *Amer.*]

bank′ clerk′, *Brit.* teller (def. 2). [1820–30]

bank′ depos′it, money placed in a bank against which the depositor can withdraw under prescribed conditions. [1825–35]

bank′ depos′it insur′ance, the protection of bank deposits against the insolvency of banks in the U.S., up to a specified maximum per account that is revised periodically, under special insurance through the Federal Deposit Insurance Corporation.

bank′ dis′count, interest on a loan, deducted in advance from the face value of the note. [1905–10]

bank′ draft′, a draft drawn by one bank on another. Also called **banker's bill.** [1825–35, *Amer.*]

bank•er[1] (bang′kər), *n.* **1.** a person employed by a bank, esp. as an executive or other official. **2.** *Games.* the keeper or holder of the bank. [1525–35; < MF *banquier;* see BANK[2], -ER[2]]

bank•er[2] (bang′kər), *n.* **1.** a vessel employed in cod fishery on the banks off Newfoundland. **2.** a fisherman on such a vessel. **3.** *Australian.* a river near flood level, the water being almost bank high. [1660–70; BANK[1] + -ER[1]]

bank•er[3] (bang′kər), *n.* a bench or table used by masons for dressing stones or bricks. [1670–80; BANK[3] + -ER[1]]

bank•er•ish (bang′kər ish), *adj.* resembling or befitting a banker, esp. in being perceived as reserved and conservative in dress and demeanor: *a model of bankerish decorum.* [BANKER[1] + -ISH[1]]

bank′er's accep′tance. See **bank acceptance.**

bank′er's bill′. See **bank draft.**

bank′er's check′. See **cashier's check.**

bank′ers' hours′, a short working day, esp. one that extends from 9 or 10 A.M. until 2 P.M., the hours during which banks were traditionally open to the public.

bank′ exam′iner, a public official appointed under U.S. state or federal laws to inspect and audit the operations and accounts of banks in the examiner's jurisdiction. [1865–70, *Amer.*]

Bank•head (bangk′hed), *n.* **1. Tal•lu•lah (Brock•man)** (tə lo͞o′lə brok′mən), 1903–68, U.S. actress (daughter of William Brockman Bankhead). **2. William Brockman,** 1874–1940, U.S. politician: Speaker of the House 1936–40.

bank′ hol′iday, **1.** a weekday on which banks are closed by law; legal holiday. **2.** *Brit.* a secular day on which banks are closed, obligations then falling due being performable on the following secular day. [1870–75]

bank′ in′dicator, *Aeron.* a flight instrument that measures the angle of roll about an aircraft's horizontal axis, thereby indicating whether or not the aircraft is skidding or slipping. Also called **ball indicator, slip indicator.** Cf. **bank-and-turn indicator.**

bank•ing (bang′king), *n.* **1.** the business carried on by a bank or a banker. **2.** banking as a profession. [1725–35; BANK[2] + -ING[1]]

bank′ing account′, *Brit.* See **bank account.**

bank′ing pin′, *Horol.* either of two pins for damping or halting the oscillation, in either direction, of a balance or lever.

bank′ing prin′ciple, the principle that bank notes are a form of credit and should be issued freely in order to maintain an elastic currency. Also called **bank′ing doc′trine.** Cf. **currency principle.**

bank′ loan′, an amount of money loaned at interest by a bank to a borrower, usually on collateral security, for a certain period of time.

bank′ mon′ey, checks, drafts, and bank credits other than currency that are the equivalent of money. [1900–05]

bank′ night′, *Informal.* (esp. in the 1930's) an evening when prizes are awarded to members of the audience at a motion-picture theater. [1935–40, *Amer.*]

bank′ note′, a promissory note, payable on demand, issued by an authorized bank and intended to circulate as money. Also, **bank′note′.** [1685–95]

bank′ of is′sue, a bank, as a Federal Reserve Bank, empowered by a government to issue currency. [1930–35]

bank′ pa′per, **1.** drafts, bills, and acceptances payable by banks. **2.** commercial paper that may be discounted in a bank. [1780–90]

bank′ rate′, **1.** the rate of discount fixed by a bank or banks. **2.** *Brit.* the discount charge set by a central bank, as by the Bank of England. [1875–80]

bank•roll (bangk′rōl′), *n.* **1.** money in one's possession; monetary resources. —*v.t.* **2.** *Informal.* to finance; provide funds for: *to bankroll a new play.* [1885–90; BANK[2] + ROLL] —**bank′roll′er,** *n.*

bank•rupt (bangk′rupt, -rəpt), *n.* **1.** *Law.* a person who upon his or her own petition or that of his or her creditors is adjudged insolvent by a court and whose property is administered for and divided among his or her creditors under a bankruptcy law. **2.** any insolvent debtor; a person unable to satisfy any just claims made upon him or her. **3.** a person who is lacking in a particular thing or quality: *a moral bankrupt.* —*adj.* **4.** *Law.* subject to or under legal process because of insolvency; insolvent. **5.** at the end of one's resources; lacking (usually fol. by *of* or *in*): *bankrupt of compassion; bankrupt in good manners.* **6.** pertaining to bankrupts or bankruptcy. —*v.t.* **7.** to make bankrupt: *His embezzlement bankrupted the company.* [1525–35; < ML *banca rupta* bank broken; r. adaptations of It *banca rota* and F *banqueroute* in same sense] —**Syn. 4.** destitute, impoverished.

bank•rupt•cy (bangk′rupt sē, -rəp sē), *n., pl.* **-cies.** **1.** the state of being or becoming bankrupt. **2.** utter ruin, failure, depletion, or the like. [1690–1700; BANKRUPT + -CY]

bank′rupt worm′, a roundworm (genus *Trichostrongylus*) that is an intestinal parasite of birds and mammals, especially devastating to young livestock. [so called because of its destructive effect on farmers' welfare]

Banks (bangks), *n.* **1. Sir Joseph,** 1734–1820, English naturalist. **2. Nathaniel Pren•tiss** (pren′tis), 1816–94, U.S. army officer and politician: Speaker of the House 1856–57.

bank′ shot′, **1.** *Basketball.* a shot into the basket, made by rebounding the ball off the backboard. **2.** *Billiards, Pool.* a shot in which the cue ball or object ball is banked. [1935–40]

bank•si•a (bangk′sē ə), *n.* any Australian shrub or tree of the genus *Banksia,* having alternate leaves and dense, cylindrical flower heads. [1782; < NL; named after Sir Joseph BANKS; see -IA]

bank′sia rose′, a climbing rose, *Rosa banksiae,* native to China, having long, serrated leaves and white or yellow flowers. [1885–90; from the specific name, after Sir Joseph BANKS; see -IA]

bank•side (bangk′sīd′), *n.* the slope of the bank of a stream or river. [1590–1600; BANK[1] + SIDE[1]]

Banks′ Is′land, an island in the W Northwest Territories, in NW Canada. 24,600 sq. mi. (63,700 sq. km).

bank′ state′ment, **1.** a monthly statement of account mailed by a bank to each of its customers with checking or other accounts, recording the banking transactions and current balance during a period and usually including canceled checks. **2.** a statement required to be published periodically by a bank showing its financial status, as assets and liabilities.

bank′ swal′low, a swallow, *Riparia riparia,* of the Northern Hemisphere, that nests in tunnels dug in sand or clay banks. [1645–55]

Ban-Lon (ban′lon′), *Trademark.* a brand of multi-stranded, continuous-filament synthetic yarn modified by crimping to increase bulk.

Ban•ne•ker (ban′i kər), *n.* **Benjamin,** 1731–1806, U.S. mathematician, natural historian, and astronomer.

ban•ner (ban′ər), *n.* **1.** the flag of a country, army, troop, etc. **2.** an ensign or the like bearing some device, motto, or slogan, as one carried in religious processions, political demonstrations, etc. **3.** a flag formerly used as the standard of a sovereign, lord, or knight. **4.** a sign painted on cloth and hung over a street, entrance, etc.: *Banners at the intersection announced the tennis tournament.* **5.** anything regarded or displayed as a symbol of principles. **6.** *Heraldry.* a square flag bearing heraldic devices. **7.** Also called **ban′ner line′, line, screamer, streamer.** *Journalism.* a headline extending across the width of a newspaper page, usually across the top of the front page. **8.** an open streamer with lettering, towed behind an airplane in flight, for advertising purposes. —*adj.* **9.** leading or foremost: *a banner year for crops.* [1200–50; ME *banere* < OF *baniere* < LL *bann(um)* (var. of *bandum* standard < Gmc, cf. Goth *bandwa* sign; see BAND[1]) + OF *-iere* < L *-āria* -ARY] —**ban′nered,** *adj.* —**ban′ner•less,** *adj.* —**ban′ner•like′,** *adj.* —**Syn. 9.** notable, record, winning, red-letter, vintage.

ban′ner cloud′, a plume-shaped cloud extending downwind from an isolated mountain peak. Also called **cloud banner.** Cf. **cap cloud** (def. 1). [1905–10]

ban•ner•et[1] (ban′ər it, -ə ret′), *n.* **1.** *Hist.* a knight who could bring a company of followers into the field under his own banner. **2.** a rank of knighthood; knight banneret. [1250–1300; ME *baneret* < OF, equiv. to *baner(e)* BANNER + *-et* < L *-ātus* -ATE[1]]

ban•ner•et[2] (ban′ə ret′), *n.* a small banner. Also, **ban′ner•ette′.** [1250–1300; ME *banerett* < MF *banerete* little banner. See BANNER, -ETTE]

ban•ner•man (ban′ər mən), *n., pl.* **-men.** a person who carries a flag or banner; standard-bearer. [1400–50; late ME *baner(e)man.* See BANNER, -MAN]
—Usage. See **-man.**

ban•ner•stone (ban′ər stōn′), *n.* a North American prehistoric stone implement in the form of a double-edged ax with a notch or hole, possibly for attaching a handle. [BANNER (from the flaglike shape of the blades) + STONE]

Ban•ning (ban′ing), *n.* a city in S California, near Los Angeles. 14,020.

ban•nis•ter (ban′ə stər), *n.* banister.

Ban•nis•ter (ban′ə stər), *n.* **Sir Roger (Gilbert),** born 1929, English track and field athlete: first to run a mile in less than four minutes.

ban•nock (ban′ək), *n. Scot. and Brit. Cookery.* a flat cake made of oatmeal, barley meal, etc., usually baked on a griddle. [bef. 1000; ME *bannok,* OE *bannuc* morsel < British Celtic; cf. ScotGael *bannach*]

Ban•nock (ban′ək), *n., pl.* **-nocks,** (*esp. collectively*) **-nock** for 1. **1.** a member of a North American Indian people formerly of Idaho and Wyoming who merged with the Shoshone in the 19th century, now living primarily in southeastern Idaho. **2.** the language of the Bannock, belonging to the Shoshonean group of Uto-Aztecan languages.

Ban•nock•burn (ban′ək bûrn′, ban′ək bûrn′), *n.* a village in central Scotland: site of the victory (1314) of the Scots under Robert the Bruce over the English, which assured the independence of Scotland.

banns (banz), *n.* (*used with a plural v.*) *Eccles.* **1.** notice of an intended marriage, given three times in the parish church of each of the betrothed. **2.** any public announcement of a proposed marriage, either verbal or written and made in a church or by church officials. Also, **bans.** [1540–50; var. of *bans,* pl. of BAN[2]]

ba•non (ba non′, -nôɴ′), *n.* a small, round goat cheese from Provence, France, that is dipped in brandy before being wrapped in chestnut leaves. [after *Banon,* a village in SE France (Basses-Alpes)]

ban•quet (bang′kwit), *n., v.,* **-quet•ed, -quet•ing.** —*n.* **1.** a lavish meal; feast. **2.** a ceremonious public dinner, esp. one honoring a person, benefiting a charity, etc. —*v.t.* **3.** to entertain or regale with a banquet: *They banqueted the visiting prime minister in grand style.* —*v.i.* **4.** to have or attend a banquet; feast: *They banqueted on pheasant, wild boar, and three kinds of fish.* [1425–75; < MF < It *banchetto* (*banc(o)* table (see BANK[2]) + *-etto* -ET); r. late ME *banket* < MF] —**ban′•quet•er, ban•que•teer** (bang′kwi tēr′), *n.*
—Syn. 1. See **feast.**

ban′quet room′, a spacious dining room for accommodating banquets, as in a hotel. [1830–40]

ban•quette (bang ket′; *locally* bang′kit *for 3*), *n.* **1.** a long bench with an upholstered seat, esp. one along a wall, as in a restaurant. **2.** an embankment for buttressing the base of a levee and forming a berm. **3.** *Chiefly Coastal Louisiana and East Texas.* a sidewalk, esp. a raised one of bricks or planks. **4.** *Fort.* a platform or step along the inside of a parapet, for soldiers to stand on when firing. **5.** a ledge running across the back of a buffet. **6.** a bench for passengers on top of a stagecoach. [1620–30; < F < Pr *banqueta,* equiv. to *banc* bench (see BANK[3]) + *-eta* -ETTE]

Ban•quo (bang′kwō, -kō), *n.* (in Shakespeare's *Macbeth*) a murdered thane whose ghost appears to Macbeth.

bans (banz), *n.* (*used with a plural v.*) *Eccles.* banns.

ban•shee (ban′shē, ban shē′), *n.* (in Irish folklore) a spirit in the form of a wailing woman who appears to or is heard by members of a family as a sign that one of them is about to die. Also, **ban′shie.** [1765–75; < Ir *bean sidhe* woman of a fairy mound; see SÍDH]

bant (bant), *v.i. Med.* to lose weight by practicing Bantingism. [1860–65; back formation from BANTING]

ban•tam (ban′təm), *n.* **1.** (*often cap.*) a chicken of any of several varieties or breeds characterized by very small size. **2.** a small and feisty or quarrelsome person. —*adj.* **3.** diminutive; tiny: *bantam editions of the classics.* [1740–50; appar. after BANTAM, through which such chickens may have been imported to Europe]
—Syn. 3. miniature, small, petite, wee, pygmy, Lilliputian.

Ban•tam (ban′təm; *Du.* bän täm′), *n.* a village in W Java, in S Indonesia: first Dutch settlement in the East Indies.

ban•tam•weight (ban′təm wāt′), *n.* a boxer or other contestant intermediate in weight between a flyweight and a featherweight, esp. a professional boxer weighing up to 118 pounds. [1880–85; BANTAM + WEIGHT]

Ban′tam work′. See **Coromandel work.** [1745–55]

ban•teng (ban′teng), *n., pl.* **-tengs,** (*esp. collectively*) **-ting.** a wild ox, *Bos banteng* (*javanicus*), of southeastern Asia and the Malay Archipelago, resembling the domestic cow: now greatly reduced in number. Also, **banting** (bän′ting). [< Indonesian Malay *banténg* < Javanese *banṭéng*]

ban•ter (ban′tər), *n.* **1.** an exchange of light, playful, teasing remarks; good-natured raillery. —*v.t.* **2.** to address with banter; chaff. —*v.i.* **3.** to use banter. [1660–70; orig. uncert.] —**ban′ter•er,** *n.* —**ban′ter•ing•ly,** *adv.*
—Syn. 1. badinage, joking, jesting, pleasantry, persiflage. **2.** tease, twit; ridicule, deride, mock.

ban-the-bomb•er (ban′thə bom′ər), *n. Informal.* a person who vigorously advocates banning the development or use of nuclear weapons. [*Amer.; ban the bomb* (a slogan) + -ER[1]]

Ban•thine (ban′thēn, -thin), *Pharm., Trademark.* a brand of methantheline.

Ban•ting (ban′ting), *n.* **1. Sir Frederick Grant,** 1891–1941, Canadian physician: one of the discoverers of insulin; Nobel prize 1923. **2.** (*often l.c.*) Bantingism.

Ban•ting•ism (ban′ting iz′əm), *n.* (*often l.c.*) *Med.* a weight-reduction method based on a diet high in proteins and low in fats and carbohydrates. Also, **Banting.** [1860–65; after W. *Banting* (19th-century London cabinetmaker); see -ISM]

bant•ling (bant′ling), *n.* a very young child. [1585–95; < G *Bänkling* illegitimate child. See BENCH, -LING[1]]

Ban•tu (ban′to͞o), *n., pl.* **-tus,** (*esp. collectively*) **-tu,** *adj.* —*n.* **1.** a member of any of several Negroid peoples forming a linguistically and in some respects culturally interrelated family in central and southern Africa. **2.** a grouping of more than 500 languages of central and southern Africa, as Kikuyu, Swahili, Tswana, and Zulu, all related within a subbranch of the Benue-Congo branch of the Niger-Kordofanian family. —*adj.* **3.** of, pertaining to, or characteristic of Bantu or the Bantu peoples.

Ban•tu•stan (ban′to͞o stan′), *n.* homeland (def. 3).

Ban•ville (bäɴ vēl′), *n.* **Thé•o•dore Faul•lain de** (tā ô dôʀ′ fō laɴ′ də), 1823–91, French poet and dramatist.

ban•yal•la (ban yal′ə), *n.* See **Victorian box.**

ban•yan (ban′yən), *n.* **1.** Also called **ban′yan tree′.** an East Indian fig tree, *Ficus benghalensis,* of the mulberry family, having branches that send out adventitious roots to the ground and sometimes cause the tree to spread over a wide area. **2.** Also, **bania, baniya.** (in India) **a.** a Hindu trader or merchant of a particular caste, the rules of which forbid eating flesh. **b.** a loose shirt, jacket, or gown. Also, **banian.** [1590–1600; < Pg (perh. < Ar) < Gujarati *vāṇiyo* (sing.) or *vāṇiyā* (pl.) member of the merchant caste (cf. Prakrit *vāṇiaya,* Skt *vāṇija* trader); the tree is said to have taken its name from a particular tree of the species near which merchants had built a booth; source of final nasal uncert.]

banyan, *Ficus benghalensis,* height 70 to 100 ft. (21.3 m to 30.5 m)

ban•zai (bän′zī′, bän′-; *Japn.* bän′dzä′ē), *interj.* **1.** (used as a Japanese patriotic cry or joyous shout.) **2.** (used as a Japanese battle cry.) —*adj.* **3.** leading to likely or inevitable death; suicidal: *a banzai attack by Japanese troops in the last days of World War II.* [1890–95; < Japn, equiv. to *ban* ten thousand + *-zai,* comb. form of *sai* years of age (< MChin, akin to Chin *wànsuì,* Korean *manse*)]

bao (bou), *n.* an African board game usually played by moving pebbles along two rows of holes. [< Swahili]

ba•o•bab (bā′ō bab′, bä′ō-, bou′bab), *n.* any large tree belonging to the genus *Adansonia,* of the bombax family, esp. *A. digitata,* which is native to tropical Africa, has an exceedingly thick trunk, and bears a gourdlike fruit. [1630–40; < NL *bahobab,* first cited in a description of the tree's fruit by Italian physician and botanist Prospero Alpini (1553–1616 or 17); orig. obscure]

Bao Dai (bou′ dī′), *n.* (*Nguyen Vinh Thuy*), born 1913, emperor of Annam 1925–45, chief of state of Vietnam 1949–55.

Bao•ding (bou′ding′), *n. Pinyin.* a city in central Hebei province, in NE China. Also, **Paoting.** Formerly, **Qingyuan.**

Bao•ji (bou′jē′), *n. Pinyin.* a city in W Shaanxi province, in central China. 275,000. Also, **Paochi, Paoki.**

Bao•qing (bou′ching′), *n. Pinyin.* former name of **Shaoyang.** Also, **Paoch'ing, Paoking.**

Bao•shan (bou′shän′), *n. Pinyin.* a town in W Yunnan province, in S China, on the Burma Road. Also, **Paoshan.**

bap (bap), *n. Brit.* a soft, flattish bread roll. [1505–15; of obscure orig.]

Bap., Baptist. Also, **Bapt.**

bap., baptized.

B.A.P.C.T., Bachelor of Arts in Practical Christian Training.

B.App.Arts, Bachelor of Applied Arts.

bap•tism (bap′tiz əm), *n.* **1.** *Eccles.* a ceremonial immersion in water, or application of water, as an initiatory rite or sacrament of the Christian church. **2.** any similar ceremony or action of initiation, dedication, etc. **3.** a trying or purifying experience or initiation. **4.** *Christian Science.* purification of thought and character. [1250–1300; ME < LL *baptisma* < Gk *bapt(ízein)* to BAPTIZE + *-isma* -ISM; r. ME *bapteme* < OF < LL, as above] —**bap•tis•mal** (bap tiz′məl), *adj.* —**bap•tis′mal•ly,** *adv.*
—Syn. 2. induction, admittance, introduction.

baptis′mal name′. See **Christian name** (def. 1). [1865–70]

baptis′mal regenera′tion, *Theol.* the doctrine that regeneration and sanctification are received in and through baptism. [1645–55]

bap′tism for the dead′, the baptism of a living person in the place of and for the sake of one who has died unbaptized: now practiced chiefly by Mormons.

bap′tism of fire′, **1.** spiritual sanctification as a gift of the Holy Ghost. **2.** the first time a soldier faces battle. **3.** any severe ordeal that tests one's endurance. [1815–25]

Bap•tist (bap′tist), *n.* **1.** a member of a Christian denomination that baptizes believers by immersion and that is usually Calvinistic in doctrine. **2.** (*l.c.*) a person who baptizes. **3. the Baptist.** See **John the Baptist.** —*adj.* **4.** Also, **Bap•tis′tic.** of or pertaining to Baptists or their doctrines or practices. [1150–1200; ME *baptiste* < OF < LL *baptista* < Gk *baptistḗs,* equiv. to *bapt(izein)* to BAPTIZE + *-istēs* -IST]

Bap•tis•ta (bap tis′tə), *n.* a female given name.

bap•tis•ter•y (bap′tə strē, -tis tə rē), *n., pl.* **-ter•ies.** **1.** a building or a part of a church in which baptism is administered. **2.** (esp. in Baptist churches) a tank for administering baptism by immersion. [1425–75; < LL *baptistērium* < Gk *baptistḗrion* bathing place (see BAPTIST, -ERY); r. late ME *baptizatory* < ML *baptizātōrium*]

bap•tist•ry (bap′tə strē), *n., pl.* **-ries.** baptistery.

bap•tize (bap tīz′, bap′tīz), *v.,* **-tized, -tiz•ing.** —*v.t.* **1.** to immerse in water or sprinkle or pour water on in the Christian rite of baptism: *They baptized the new baby.* **2.** to cleanse spiritually; initiate or dedicate by purifying. **3.** to give a name to at baptism; christen. —*v.i.* **4.** to administer baptism. Also, *esp. Brit.,* **baptise′.** [1250–1300; ME < LL *baptizāre* < Gk *baptízein* to immerse (*báptein*) to bathe + *-izein* -IZE)] —**bap•tiz′a•ble,** *adj.* —**bap•tize′ment,** *n.* —**bap•tiz′er,** *n.*

bar[1] (bär), *n., v.,* **barred, bar•ring,** *prep.* —*n.* **1.** a relatively long, evenly shaped piece of some solid substance, as metal or wood, used as a guard or obstruction or for some mechanical purpose: *the bars of a cage.* **2.** an oblong piece of any solid material: *a bar of soap; a candy bar.* **3.** the amount of material in a bar. **4.** an ingot, lump, or wedge of gold or silver. **5.** a long ridge of sand, gravel, or other material near or slightly above the surface of the water at or near the mouth of a river or harbor entrance, often constituting an obstruction to navigation. **6.** anything that obstructs, hinders, or impedes; obstacle; barrier: *a bar to important legislation.* **7.** a counter or place where beverages, esp. liquors, or light meals are served to customers: *a snack bar; a milk bar.* **8.** a barroom or tavern. **9.** (in a home) a counter, small wagon, or similar piece of furniture for serving food or beverages: *a breakfast bar.* **10.** the legal profession. **11.** the practicing members of the legal profession in a given community. **12.** any tribunal: *the bar of public opinion.* **13.** a band or strip: *a bar of light.* **14.** a railing in a courtroom separating the general public from the part of the room occupied by the judges, jury, attorneys, etc. **15.** a crowbar. **16.** *Music.* **a.** Also called **bar line.** the line marking the division between two measures of music. **b.** See **double bar. c.** the unit of music contained between two bar lines; measure. **17.** *Ballet.* barre. **18.** *Law.* **a.** an objection that nullifies an action or claim. **b.** a stoppage or defeat of an alleged right of action. **19.** *Typography.* a horizontal stroke of a type character, as of an *A, H, t,* and sometimes *e.* **20.** *Archit.* (in tracery) a relatively long and slender upright of stone treated as a colonette or molded. **21.** *Building Trades.* **a.** an iron or steel shape: *I-bar.* **b.** a muntin. **22.** *Mil.* one of a pair of metal or cloth insignia worn by certain commissioned officers. **23. bars,** the transverse ridges on the roof of the mouth of a horse. **24.** a space between the molar and canine teeth of a horse into which the bit is fitted. **25.** (in a bridle) the mouthpiece connecting the cheeks. **26.** bride[2] (def. 1). **27.** *Heraldry.* a horizontal band, narrower than a fess, that crosses the field of an escutcheon. **28.** *Obs.* a gateway capable of being barred. **29. at bar,** *Law.* **a.** before the court and being tried: *a case at bar.* **b.** before all the judges of a court: *a trial at bar.* **30. behind bars,** in jail: *We wanted the criminal behind bars.* —*v.t.* **31.** to equip or fasten with a bar or bars: *Bar the door before retiring for the night.* **32.** to block by or as if by bars: *The police barred the exits in an attempt to prevent the thief's escape.* **33.** to prevent or hinder: *They barred her entrance to the club.* **34.** to exclude or except: *He was barred from membership because of his reputation.* **35.** to mark with bars, stripes, or bands. —*prep.* **36.** except; omitting; but: *bar none.* [1175–1225; ME *barre* < OF < VL **barra* rod of obscure, perh. of pre-L orig.] —**bar′•less,** *adj.* —**bar′ra•ble,** *adj.*
—Syn. 1. rod, pole. **5.** shoal, reef, bank, sand bar. **6.** deterrent, stop. BAR, BARRIER, BARRICADE mean something put in the way of advance. BAR has the general meaning of hindrance or obstruction: *a bar across the doorway.* BARRIER suggests an impediment to progress or a defensive obstruction (natural or artificial): *a trade barrier; a mountain barrier; a road barrier.* A BARRICADE is esp. a pile of articles hastily gathered or a rude earthwork for protection in street fighting: *a barricade of wooden boxes.* **7.** saloon, café; cocktail lounge. **32, 33.** obstruct, deter, impede, barricade. **34.** eliminate.

bar[1] (def. 16a, b) A, single; B, double

bar[2] (bär), *n.* See **mosquito net.** [1770–80; < LaF *bère, baire,* appar. repr. dial. pron. of F *barre* barrier, BAR[1]]

bar[3] (bär), *n. Physics.* **1.** a centimeter-gram-second unit of pressure, equal to one million dynes per square

CONCISE PRONUNCIATION KEY: act, cāpe, dâre, pärt; set, ēqual; if, īce; ox, ōver, ôrder, oil, bo͝ok, bo͞ot, out; up, ûrge; child; sing; shoe; thin, *th*at; zh as in *treasure.* ə = *a* as in *alone, e* as in *system, i* as in *easily, o* as in *gallop, u* as in *circus;* ˘ as in *fire* (fīˀr), *hour* (ouˀr). l and n can serve as syllabic consonants, as in *cradle* (krād′l), and *button* (but′n). See the full key inside the front cover.

centimeter. **2.** (formerly) microbar. *Abbr.:* b [1900–05; < Gk *báros* weight; cf. BAROMETER, ISOBAR]

BAR, See **Browning automatic rifle.**

Bar., *Bible.* Baruch.

bar., **1.** barometer. **2.** barometric. **3.** barrel. **4.** barrister.

B.Ar., Bachelor of Architecture.

Bar•a (bar′ə), *n.* **The•da** (thē′də), (*Theodosia Goodman*), 1890–1955, U.S. actress.

bar•a•bar•a (bär′ə bär′ə), *n.* an Alaskan or north Siberian semisubterranean house built of sod or turf. [1865–70, *Amer.*; < dial. Russ *barabóra;* further orig. uncert.]

Bar•ab•bas (bə rab′əs), *n.* a condemned criminal pardoned by Pilate in order to appease the mob, which demanded that he be freed instead of Jesus. Mark 15:6–11; John 18:40.

Ba•ra•cal•do (bä′rä käl′dô), *n.* a city in N Spain. 108,757.

Ba•ra•co•a (bä′rä kô′ä), *n.* a seaport in E Cuba: oldest town in Cuba; settled 1512. 20,926.

bar•ag•no•sis (bar′ag nō′sis, ba rag′nō-), *n. Pathol.* loss of the ability to estimate or perceive the weight of an object. Cf. **barognosis.** [BAR(O)- + A-⁶ + -GNOSIS]

Bar•ak (bâr′ək, bä′rak), *n.* a military commander who, with Deborah, defeated the Canaanite army under Sisera. Judges 4. Also, *Douay Bible,* **Bar′ac.**

ba•ra•ka (bə rä′kə), *n. Islam.* a spiritual power believed to be possessed by certain persons, objects, tombs, etc. [< Ar *barakah;* cf. Heb *bərākhāh* blessing]

Ba•ra•ka (bə rä′kə), *n.* **I•ma•mu A•mi•ri** (i mä′mo͞o ə mēr′ē), (*Everett LeRoi Jones*), born 1934, U.S. dramatist, poet, and political activist.

bar-and-grill (bär′ən gril′), *n.* a place where food and alcoholic drinks are served to customers; a combined barroom and grillroom.

Ba•ra•nov (bu rä′nəf), *n.* **A•le•ksandr An•dre•ye•vich** (u lyi ksän′dr un drye′yi vyich), 1747–1819, Russian fur trader in Alaska.

Ba•ra•no•vi•chi (bə rä′nə vich′ē; *Russ.* bu rä′nə vyichyi), *n.* a city in central Byelorussia (Belarus), SW of Minsk. 131,000.

Bá•rány (bä′rän′y[ə]), *n.* **Ro•bert** (rō′bert), 1876–1936, Austrian physician: Nobel prize 1914.

bar•a•the•a (bar′ə thē′ə), *n.* a closely woven fabric of silk, rayon, cotton, or wool, having a pebbled surface. [1860–65; orig. obscure]

barb[1] (bärb), *n.* **1.** a point or pointed part projecting backward from a main point, as of a fishhook or arrowhead. See illus. under **fishhook. 2.** an obviously or openly unpleasant or carping remark. **3.** *Bot., Zool.* a hooked or sharp bristle. **4.** *Ornith.* one of the processes attached to the rachis of a feather. See illus. under **feather. 5.** one of a breed of domestic pigeons, similar to the carriers or homers, having a short, broad bill. **6.** any of numerous, small, Old World cyprinid fishes of the genera *Barbus* and *Puntius,* often kept in aquariums. **7.** Usually, **barbs.** *Vet. Pathol.* a small protuberance under the tongue in horses and cattle, esp. when inflamed and swollen. **8.** Also, **barbe.** a linen covering for the throat and breast, formerly worn by women mourners and now only by some nuns. **9.** *Obs.* a beard. —*v.t.* **10.** to furnish with a barb or barbs. [1300–50; ME *barbe* < MF << L *barba* BEARD or beardlike projection]
—**Syn. 1.** spur, spike, prong, barbule; snag, prickle, spicule.

barb[2] (bärb), *n.* one of a breed of horses raised originally in Barbary. [1630–40; < F *barbe,* shortened form of It *barbero* Barbary steed, equiv. to *Barber(ia)* Barbary + *-o* masc. n. suffix]

barb[3] (bärb), *n. Slang.* barbiturate. [by shortening]

bar•ba (bär′bə), *n. Med.* **1.** the beard. **2.** a hair of the head. [< NL, L: BEARD]

bar′ba am•a•ril′la (am′ə ril′ə, -rē′ə), *pl.* **barba amarillas.** fer-de-lance. [< MexSp: lit., yellow beard]

bar•ba•can (bär′bə kən), *n.* barbican.

Bar•ba•dos (bär bā′dōz, -dōs, -dəs), *n.* an island in the E West Indies constituting an independent state in the Commonwealth of Nations: formerly a British colony. 245,000; 166 sq. mi. (430 sq. km). *Cap.:* Bridgetown. —**Bar•ba•di•an** (bär bā′dē ən), *adj., n.*

Barba′dos al′oe, a tropical aloe, *Aloe barbadensis* (or *A. vera*), of the lily family, having clusters of yellow flowers: its juice is used medicinally.

Barba′dos goose′berry, 1. Also called **lemon vine.** a treelike cactus, *Pereskia aculeata,* of tropical America, characterized by broad, elliptical leaves and spiny stems bearing a yellow, edible fruit. **2.** the fruit itself. Also called **blade apple.** [1750–60]

Barba′dos nut′. See **physic nut.**

Barba′dos pride′, 1. Also called **bead tree.** a tropical African and Asian tree, *Adenanthera pavonina,* of the legume family, having feathery foliage and bearing red seeds that are used in beadwork. **2.** Also called **Barba′dos flow′er fence′, dwarf poinciana.** a tropical, prickly shrub, *Caesalpinia pulcherrima,* having orange-yellow flowers with bright red stamens and bearing pods. [1880–85]

Bar•ba•ra (bär′brə, -bər ə), *n.* a female given name: from a Greek word meaning "foreign, exotic."

bar•bar•i•an (bär bâr′ē ən), *n.* **1.** a person in a savage, primitive state; uncivilized person. **2.** a person without culture, refinement, or education; philistine. **3.** (loosely) a foreigner. **4.** (in ancient and medieval periods) **a.** a non-Greek. **b.** a person living outside, esp. north of, the Roman Empire. **c.** a person not living in a Christian country or within a Christian civilization. **5.** (among Italians during the Renaissance) a person of non-Italian origin. —*adj.* **6.** uncivilized; crude; savage. **7.** foreign; alien. [1540–50; < L *barbari(a)* barbarous country (see BARBAROUS, -IA) + -AN] —**bar•bar′i•an•ism,** *n.*
—**Syn. 3.** alien. **6.** rude, primitive, wild, rough, barbaric, coarse, ignorant, uncultivated. BARBARIAN, BARBARIC, BARBAROUS pertain to uncivilized people. BARBARIAN is the general word for anything uncivilized: *a barbarian tribe.* BARBARIC has both unfavorable and mildly favorable connotations, implying crudeness of taste or practice, or conveying an idea of rude magnificence and splendor: *barbaric noise.* BARBAROUS emphasizes the inhumanity and cruelty of barbarian life: *barbarous customs.* —**Ant. 6.** cultivated, civilized.

bar•bar•i•an•ize (bär bâr′ē ə nīz′), *v.t.,* **-ized, -iz•ing.** to make barbarian. Also, *esp. Brit.,* **bar•bar′i•an•ise′.** [1855–60; BARBARIAN + -IZE]

bar•bar•ic (bär bar′ik), *adj.* **1.** without civilizing influences; uncivilized; primitive: *barbaric invaders.* **2.** of, like, or befitting barbarians: *a barbaric empire; barbaric practices.* **3.** crudely rich or splendid: *barbaric decorations.* [1480–90; < L *barbaricus* < Gk *barbarikós.* See BARBAROUS, -IC] —**bar•bar′i•cal•ly,** *adv.*
—**Syn. 1, 3.** See **barbarian.**

bar•ba•rism (bär′bə riz′əm), *n.* **1.** a barbarous or uncivilized state or condition. **2.** a barbarous act; something belonging to or befitting a barbarous condition. **3.** the use in a language of forms or constructions felt by some to be undesirably alien to the established standards of the language. **4.** such a form or construction: *Some people consider "complected" as a barbarism.* [1570–80; < L *barbarismus* < Gk *barbarismós* foreign way of speaking. See BARBAROUS, -ISM]

bar•bar•i•ty (bär bar′i tē), *n., pl.* **-ties. 1.** brutal or inhuman conduct; cruelty. **2.** an act or instance of cruelty or inhumanity. **3.** crudity of style, taste, expression, etc. [1560–70; < L *barbar(us)* (see BARBAROUS) + -ITY]

bar•ba•rize (bär′bə rīz′), *v.,* **-rized, -riz•ing.** —*v.t.* **1.** to make barbarous; brutalize; corrupt: *foreign influences barbarizing the Latin language.* —*v.i.* **2.** to become barbarous; lapse into barbarism. **3.** to use barbarisms in speaking or writing. Also, *esp. Brit.,* **bar′ba•rise′.** [1635–45; partly < Gk *barbarízein,* equiv. to *bárbar(os)* barbarian + *-izein* -IZE; partly BARBAR(OUS) + -IZE] —**bar′ba•ri•za′tion,** *n.*

Bar•ba•ros•sa (bär′bə ros′ə), *n.* **1. Frederick.** See **Frederick I** (def. 1). **2.** the planning and operational code name the Germans gave to their invasion of the Soviet Union (June 22, 1941).

Barbarossa I, (*Aruj*), died 1518, Barbary pirate, born in Greece.

Barbarossa II, (*Khair ed-Din*), c1466–1546, Barbary pirate, born in Greece (brother of Barbarossa I).

bar•ba•rous (bär′bər əs), *adj.* **1.** uncivilized; wild; savage; crude. **2.** savagely cruel or harsh: *The prisoners of war were given barbarous treatment.* **3.** full of harsh sounds; noisy; discordant: *an evening of wild and barbarous music.* **4.** not conforming to classical standards or accepted usage, as language. **5.** foreign; alien. **6.** (among ancient Greeks) designating a person or thing of non-Greek origin. [1400–50; late ME < L *barbarus* < Gk *bárbaros* non-Greek, foreign, barbarian; akin to Skt *barbara* stammering, non-Aryan; see -OUS] —**bar′ba•rous•ly,** *adv.* —**bar′ba•rous•ness,** *n.*
—**Syn. 1.** See **barbarian. 2.** ferocious, inhuman, brutal.

Bar•ba•ry (bär′bə rē), *n.* a region in N Africa, extending from W of Egypt to the Atlantic Ocean and including the former Barbary States.

Bar′bary ape′, a tailless macaque, *Macaca sylvanus,* of mountain ranges in northwestern Africa, now greatly reduced in number: a small, managed colony of unknown origin is maintained on the Rock of Gibraltar. [1870–75]

Bar′bary Coast′, 1. the Mediterranean coastline of the former Barbary States: former pirate refuge. **2.** the waterfront district of San Francisco in the 19th century, notorious for its cheap bars and nightclubs, prostitutes, gambling houses, and high incidence of crime.

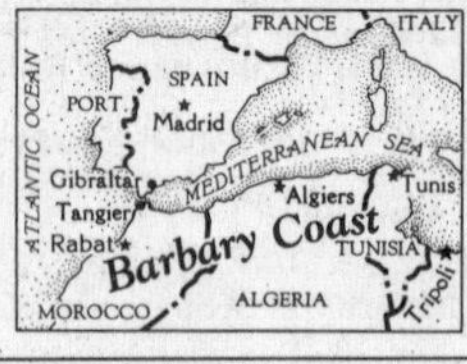

Bar′bary Coast′ Wars′, *U.S. Hist.* wars fought along the coast of North Africa 1801–15 over the harassment of U.S. ships despite the payment of tribute money to the piratical Barbary States. Cf. **Tripolitan War.**

Bar′bary fig′. See **prickly pear.**

Bar′bary sheep′, aoudad. [1895–1900]

Bar′bary States′, the name for Morocco, Algiers, Tunis, and Tripoli when they were centers of corsair activity, c1520–1830.

bar•bas•co (bär bas′kō, -bä′skō), *n., pl.* **-cos. 1.** a shrub or small tree, *Jacquinia barbasco,* of tropical America, the source of a substance used to stun fish so they can be caught easily. **2.** any similar plant yielding a substance that stuns or kills fish. **3.** the fish-stunning or fish-killing substance obtained from these plants. [1855–60; < AmerSp, said to be alter. of *verbasco* mullein < L *verbascum*]

bar•bate (bär′bāt), *adj. Bot., Zool.* tufted or furnished with hairs; bearded. [1850–55; < L *barbātus,* equiv. to *barb(a)* BEARD + *-ātus* -ATE[1]]

barb′ bolt′, a bolt having barbs for resisting pull. Also called **rag bolt.**

barbe (bärb), *n.* **1.** a band or small scarf of lace, worn around the head or neck by women. **2.** barb[1] (def. 8). [see BARB[1]]

bar•be•cue (bär′bi kyo͞o′), *n., v.,* **-cued, -cu•ing.** —*n.* **1.** pieces of beef, fowl, fish, or the like, roasted over an open hearth, esp. when basted in a barbecue sauce. **2.** a framework, as a grill or a spit, or a fireplace for cooking meat or vegetables over an open fire. **3.** a dressed steer, lamb, or other animal, roasted whole. **4.** a meal, usually in the open air and often as a political or social gathering, at which meats are roasted over an open hearth or pit. —*v.t.* **5.** to broil or roast whole or in large pieces over an open fire, on a spit or grill, often seasoning with vinegar, spices, salt, and pepper. **6.** to cook (sliced or diced meat or fish) in a highly seasoned sauce. —*v.i.* **7.** to cook by barbecuing or to entertain at a barbecue: *If the weather's nice, we'll barbecue in the backyard.* Also, **barbeque, bar-b-que.** [1655–65; < Sp *barbacoa* < Arawak (perh. Taino) *barbacoa* a raised frame of sticks] —**bar′be•cu′er,** *n.*

bar′becue sauce′, a piquant sauce often containing vinegar, tomatoes, sugar, and spices, used esp. for basting in barbecuing meat.

barbed (bärbd), *adj.* **1.** having barbs. **2.** calculated to wound; cutting: *a professor noted for his barbed criticisms.* [1520–30; BARB[1] + -ED[3]]

barbed′ tape′. See **concertina wire.**

barbed′ trib′utary, a tributary that joins its mainstream in an upstream direction rather than in the more common downstream direction.

barbed′ wire′, a wire or strand of wires having small pieces of sharply pointed wire twisted around it at short intervals, used chiefly for fencing in livestock, keeping out trespassers, etc. Also called **barbwire.** [1860–65]

bar•bel (bär′bəl), *n.* **1.** a slender, external process on the jaw or other part of the head of certain fishes. **2.** any of various cyprinoid fishes of the genus *Barbus,* esp. *B. barbus,* of European waters. [1400–1450; late ME *barbell* < MF *barbel* (F *barbeau*) < VL **barbellus,* equiv. to LL *barb(us)* a barbel (fish) (akin to L *barba* BEARD) + L *-ellus* -ELLE]

bar•bell (bär′bel′), *n.* an apparatus used in weightlifting, consisting of a bar with replaceable, disk-shaped weights fastened to the ends. [1885–90; BAR[1] + BELL[1]]

bar•bel•late (bär′bə lāt′, bär bel′it, -āt), *adj. Bot., Zool.* having short, stiff hairs. [1840–50; < NL *barbell(a),* dim. of L *barbula* little beard (see BARBULE, -ELLE) + -ATE[1]]

bar•be•que (bär′bi kyo͞o′), *n., v.t., v.i.,* **-qued, -qu•ing.** barbecue.

bar•ber (bär′bər), *n.* **1.** a person whose occupation it is to cut and dress the hair of customers, esp. men, and to shave or trim the beard. **2.** See **frost smoke** (def. 1). —*v.t.* **3.** to trim or dress the hair or beard of. [1275–1325; ME *barbour* < AF; OF *barbeor,* equiv. to *barb(e)* (< L *barba* beard) + *-eor* < L *-ātōr-* -ATOR]

Bar•ber (bär′bər), *n.* **Samuel,** 1910–81, U.S. composer.

Bar•be•ra (bär bâr′ə; *It.* bär be′rä), *n.* **1.** a red wine grape grown primarily in the Piedmont region of Italy and the Central Valley of California. **2.** a dry red wine produced from this grape.

bar′ber chair′, 1. a chair used by barbers, adjustable in height and having an adjustable headrest, back, and footrest. **2.** *Eng. Furniture.* a corner chair having a solid splat extending above the toprail to form a headrest. Also, **bar′ber's chair′.** [1595–1605]

bar′ber col′lege, a school that trains barbers.

bar•ber•ite (bär′bə rīt′), *n.* an alloy of about 88 percent copper, 5 percent nickel, 5 percent tin, and 2 percent silicon, resistant to sea water and sulfuric acid.

Bar′ber of Seville′, The, (Italian, *Il barbiere di Siviglia*), a comic opera (1816) by Gioacchino Rossini based on a comedy (1775) by Beaumarchais.

bar′ber pole′, a pole with red and white spiral stripes symbolizing the barber's former sideline of surgery. Also, **bar′ber's pole′.** [1675–85]

bar•ber•ry (bär′ber′ē, -bə rē), *n., pl.* **-ries. 1.** a shrub of the genus *Berberis,* esp. *B. vulgaris,* having yellow flowers in elongated clusters. Cf. **barberry family. 2.** the red, elongated, acid fruit of this shrub. [1350–1400; ME *barbere* < ML *barbaris* (< Ar *barbāris*), with *-baris* conformed to *bere* BERRY]

bar′berry fam′ily, the plant family Berberidaceae, characterized by shrubs and herbaceous plants having very varied leaves and flowers and fruit in the form of a berry or capsule, and including the barberry, May apple, and Oregon grape.

bar•ber•shop (bär′bər shop′), *n.* **1.** Also called, *esp Brit.,* **bar′ber's shop′.** the place of business of a barber. **2.** the singing of four-part harmony in barbershop style or the music sung in this style. —*adj.* **3.** specializing in the unaccompanied part-singing of popular songs in which four voices move in close, highly chromatic harmony: *a barbershop quartet.* **4.** characteristic of such part-singing. [1570–80; BARBER + SHOP]

bar•ber•shop•per (bär′bər shop′ər), *n.* a member of a barbershop singing group. [BARBERSHOP + -ER[1]]

bar′ber's itch′, *Pathol.* ringworm of the bearded areas of the face and neck, characterized by reddish patches; tinea barbae. [1885–90]

bar•ber-sur•geon (bär′bər sûr′jən), *n.* (formerly) a barber practicing surgery and dentistry. [1675–85]

Bar•ber•ton (bär′bər tən), *n.* a city in NE Ohio 29,751.

bar•bet (bär′bit), *n.* any of several stocky, tropical birds of the family Capitonidae, having a stout bill with

CONCISE ETYMOLOGY KEY: <, descended or borrowed from; >, whence; b., blend of, blended; c., cognate with; cf., compare; deriv., derivative; equiv., equivalent; imit., imitative; obl., oblique; r., replacing; s., stem; sp., spelling, spelled; resp., respelling, respelled; trans., translation; ?, origin unknown; *, unattested; ‡, probably earlier than. See the full key inside the front cover.

bristles at the base. [1745–55; < F << L *barbātus;* see BARBATE]

bar•bette (bär bet′), *n.* **1.** (within a fortification) a platform or mound of earth from which guns may be fired over the parapet instead of through embrasures. **2.** *Navy.* an armored cylinder for protecting the lower part of a turret on a warship. [1765–75; < F, equiv. to *barbe* BEARD + *-ette* -ETTE, prob. from the general metaphorical use of *barbe* for something which protrudes or faces outward]

Bar•bette (bär bet′), *n.* a female given name, form of **Barbara.**

bar•bi•can (bär′bi kən), *n.* **1.** an outwork of a fortified place, as a castle. **2.** a defensive outpost of any sort. Also, **barbacan.** [1250–1300; ME *barbecan, barbican* < OF *barbacane* or ML *barbacana,* perh. << Pers *bālāḥāna* terrace over a roof, upper floor, altered by assoc. with L *barba* BEARD, a beard marking the front or face of a thing]

bar•bi•cel (bär′bə sel′), *n. Ornith.* one of the minute processes fringing the barbules of certain feathers. [1865–70; < NL *barbicella,* equiv. to L *barbi-* (comb. form of *barba* beard) + *-cella* dim. suffix]

Bar•bie (bär′bē), **1.** *Trademark.* a brand of doll representing a slim, shapely young woman, esp. one with blond hair, blue eyes, and fair skin. —*n.* **2.** Also called **Bar′bie doll′.** a person, esp. a young woman, perceived as blandly attractive and vacuous.

Bar•bi•rol•li (bär′bə rō′lē, -rol′ē), *n.* **Sir John,** 1899–1970, English conductor.

bar•bi•tal (bär′bi tôl′, -tal′), *n. Pharm.* a barbiturate compound, $C_8H_{12}N_2O_3$, formerly used as a hypnotic. [1915–20; BARBIT(URIC ACID) + (VERON)AL]

bar•bi•tal•ism (bär′bi tô liz əm, -tal′iz-), *n. Pathol.* barbiturism. [BARBITAL + -ISM]

bar•bi•tone (bär′bi tōn′), *n. Pharm. Chiefly Brit.* barbital. [1910–15; BARBIT(URIC) + -ONE]

bar•bi•tu•rate (bär bich′ər it, -ə rāt′; bär′bi to͝or′it, -āt, -tyo͝or′-), *n. Pharm.* any of a group of barbituric acid derivatives, used in medicine as sedatives and hypnotics. [1925–30; BARBITUR(IC) + -ATE²]

bar•bi•tu•ric (bär′bi to͝or′ik, -tyo͝or′-), *adj. Chem.* of or derived from barbituric acid. [1865–70; < F *barbiturique* < G *Barbitur(säure)* barbituric acid (of obscure orig.) + *-ique* -IC]

bar′bitu′ric ac′id, a white, crystalline, slightly water-soluble powder, $C_4H_4N_2O_3$, used chiefly in the synthesis of barbiturates. Also called **malonylurea.** [1865–70]

bar•bi•tur•ism (bär bich′ə riz′əm), *n. Pathol.* chronic poisoning caused by the excessive use of phenobarbital, secobarbital, or other derivative of barbituric acid. Also, **barbitalism, bar•bi•tu•ism** (bär bich′o͞o iz′əm). [BARBITUR(IC) + -ISM]

Bar′bi•zon School′ (bär′bə zon′), a group of French painters of the mid-19th century whose landscapes and genre paintings depicted peasant life and the quality of natural light on objects. [named after *Barbizon,* village near Paris, where the painters gathered]

barb•less (bärb′lis), *adj.* not equipped with a barb: *barbless fishhooks.* [1880–85; BARB¹ + -LESS]

bar•bo•tine (bär′bə tēn′), *n.* a thin clay paste for making ceramic decorations in low relief. [1860–65; < F, equiv. to *barbot(er)* to dabble, splash about (of a duck, etc.) + *-ine* -INE²]

Bar-B-Q (bär′bi kyo͞o′, -bē-), *n.* barbecue. [playful representation of the phonetics by letter names]

bar-b-que (bär′bi kyo͞o′, -bē-), *n., v.t., v.i.,* **-qued, -quing.** barbecue. [see BAR-B-Q]

bar•bu (bär bo͞o′), *n.* a threadfin, *Polydactylus virginicus,* inhabiting western Atlantic coastal waters. [< F: lit., bearded, having barbels or wattles < LL **barbūtus,* for L *barbātus.* See BARBATE]

Bar•bu•da (bär bo͞o′də), *n.* one of the NE Leeward Islands, in the E West Indies: part of Antigua and Barbuda. 62 sq. mi. (161 sq. km).

bar•bu•do (bär bo͞o′dō), *n., pl.* **-dos.** beardfish. [< Caribbean Sp, Sp: bearded]

bar•bule (bär′byo͞ol), *n.* **1.** a small barb. **2.** any of the small processes fringing the barbs of a feather. [1825–35; < L *barbula.* See BARB¹, -ULE]

Bar•busse (bᴀʀ bʏs′), *n.* **Hen•ri** (äɴ ʀē′), 1873?–1935, French journalist and author.

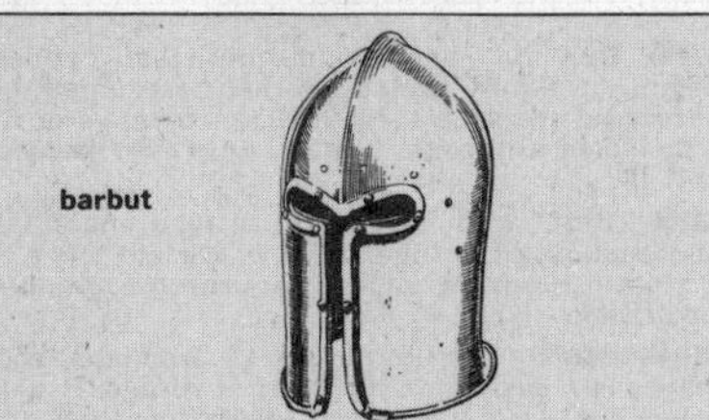
barbut

bar•but (bär′bət), *n.* a steel helmet of the 15th century completely enclosing the head and having a T-shaped face slit: similar in form to the ancient Corinthian bronze helmet. Also, **bar′bute.** [< MF < Pr *barbuta,* fem. of *barbut* lit., bearded; see BARBU]

barb•wire (bärb′wīᵊr′), *n.* See **barbed wire.**

Bar•ca (bär′kə), *n.* **1.** an ancient Carthaginian family to which Hamilcar, Hasdrubal, and Hannibal belonged. **2.** Cyrenaica. —**Bar′can,** *adj.*

bar′ car′, a railroad car equipped with a bar that serves beverages, esp. liquors and beer, and sometimes snacks. [1940–45]

bar•ca•role (bär′kə rōl′), *n.* **1.** a boating song of the Venetian gondoliers. **2.** a piece of music composed in the style of such songs. Also, **bar′ca•rolle′.** [1605–15; < Venetian *barcarola* boatman's song, fem. of *barcarolo,* equiv. to *barcar-* (< LL *barcārius* boatman; see BARK³, -ARY) + *-olo* (<< L *-eolus*)]

bar′ cart′, a small table on wheels, outfitted for serving drinks; a portable bar.

Bar•ce•lo•na (bär′sə lō′nə; *Sp.* bäʀ′the lô′nä), *n.* a seaport in NE Spain, on the Mediterranean. 2,000,000.

Barcelo′na chair′, *Trademark.* a wide, armless chair designed by Ludwig Mies van der Rohe for the International Exposition in Barcelona, Spain, in 1929, having leather-covered cushions on a double X-shaped frame of gently curved bars of stainless steel, the longer bars of each X forming the front legs and back, the shorter bars forming the seat and rear legs.

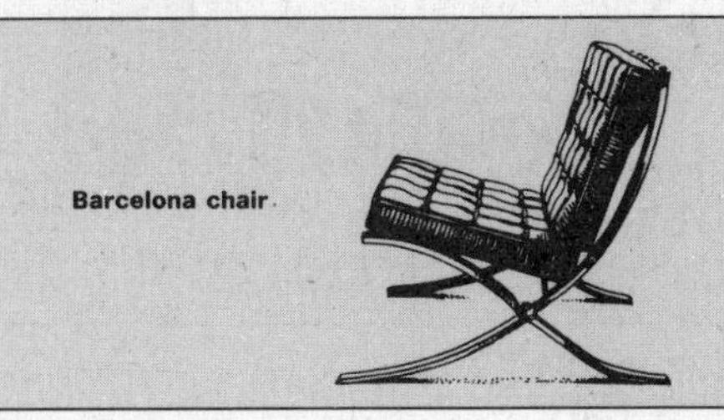
Barcelona chair

B.Arch., Bachelor of Architecture.

bar•chan (bär kän′), *n.* a crescent-shaped sand dune with the convex side in the direction of the wind. [1885–90; < Russ *barkhán,* said to be < Turkic]

bar′ chart′. See **bar graph.** [1920–25]

B.Arch.E., Bachelor of Architectural Engineering.

Bar′ches•ter Tow′ers (bär′ches tər, -chi stər), a novel (1857) by Anthony Trollope.

bar′ clamp′, a clamp having two jaws attached to a bar, one fixed and the other adjustable by means of a screw mechanism. See illus. under **clamp.**

Barc•lay (bärk′lē), *n.* a male given name. Also, **Berkeley.**

Bar•clay de Tol•ly (bər klī′ də tōl′yē; *Russ.* buʀ klī′ dyi tô′lyi), **Prince Mi•kha•il Bog•da•no•vich** (mi kä ēl′ bog dä′nə vich; *Russ.* myi ᴋʜu yēl′ bug dä′nə vyich), 1761–1818, Russian field marshal: commander in chief against Napoleon I in 1812.

Bar Coche•ba (bäʀ′ kôᴋʜ′bä, -vä). See **Bar Kokba.** Also, **Bar′ Coch′ba.**

bar′ code′, a series of lines of varying width, printed; as on a container or product, that can be read by an optical scanner to determine charges for purchases, destinations for letters, etc. Cf. **Universal Product Code.** [1970–75]

bard¹ (bärd), *n.* **1.** (formerly) a person who composed and recited epic or heroic poems, often while playing the harp, lyre, or the like. **2.** one of an ancient Celtic order of composers and reciters of poetry. **3.** any poet. **4. the bard,** William Shakespeare. [1400–50; late ME < Celt; cf. Ir, ScotGael *bard,* Welsh *bardd,* Breton *barz* < IE **gʷʳrs-do-s* singer, akin to Albanian *grisha* (I) invited (to a wedding)] —**bard′ic,** *adj.* —**bard′ish, bard′like′,** *adj.*

bard² (bärd), *n.* **1.** *Armor.* any of various pieces of defensive armor for a horse. **2.** *Cookery.* a thin slice of fat or bacon secured to a roast to prevent its drying out while cooking. —*v.t.* **3.** *Armor.* to caparison with bards. **4.** *Cookery.* to secure thin slices of fat or bacon to (a roast) before cooking. Also, **barde** (for defs. 1, 3). [1470–80; < MF *barde* < Southern It *barda* armor for a horse < Ar *barda′ah* packsaddle < Pers *pardah* covering]

barde (bärd), *n., v.,* **bard•ed, bard•ing.** *Armor.* —*n.* **1.** bard² (def. 1). —*v.t.* **2.** bard² (def. 3).

bar•dee (bär′dē), *n.* bardy².

Bar•deen (bär dēn′), *n.* **John,** 1908–91, U.S. physicist: Nobel prize 1956, 1972.

Bar•deen′-Coo′per-Schrief′fer the′ory (bär-dēn′ko͞op′ər shrī′fər), *Physics.* See **BCS theory.**

bar′ ditch′, *Western U.S.* See **barrow pit.**

Bard′ of A′von, William Shakespeare: so called from his birthplace, Stratford-on-Avon. [1880–1885]

Bar•do•li•no (bär′dl ē′nō; *It.* bäʀ′dô lē′nô), *n.* a dry red wine from the Veneto region of northern Italy.

bard•y¹ (bär′dē), *adj.,* **bard•i•er, bard•i•est.** *Scot.* bold; audacious; defiant. [1780–90; BARD¹ + -Y¹] —**bard′i•ly,** *adv.* —**bard′i•ness,** *n.*

bar•dy² (bär′dē), *n., pl.* **-dies.** a beetle larva of Australia, *Bardistus cibarius,* that bores into plants and is used as food by Aborigines. Also, **bardee.** [1925–30; < Nyungar *bardi*]

bare¹ (bâr), *adj.,* **bar•er, bar•est,** *v.t.,* **bared, bar•ing.** —*adj.* **1.** without covering or clothing; naked; nude: *bare legs.* **2.** without the usual furnishings, contents, etc.: *bare walls.* **3.** open to view; unconcealed; undisguised: *his bare dislike of neckties.* **4.** unadorned; bald; plain: *the bare facts.* **5.** (of cloth) napless or threadbare. **6.** scarcely or just sufficient; mere: *the bare necessities of life.* **7.** *Obs.* with the head uncovered; bareheaded. —*v.t.* **8.** to open to view; reveal or divulge: *to bare one's arms; to bare damaging new facts.* [bef. 900; ME; OE *bær;* c. OFris *ber,* D *baar,* OS, OHG, G *bar,* ON *berr,* Lith *bāsas* barefoot, Russ *bos;* akin to Armenian *bok* naked] —**bar′ish,** *adj.* —**bare′ness,** *n.*

—**Syn. 1.** undressed. **2.** plain, stark, empty, barren. BARE, STARK, BARREN share the sense of lack or absence of something that might be expected. BARE, the least powerful in connotation of the three, means lack of expected or usual coverings, furnishings, or embellishments: *bare floor, feet, head.* STARK implies extreme severity or desolation and resultant bleakness or dreariness: *a stark landscape; a stark, emotionless countenance.* BARREN carries a strong sense of sterility and oppressive dullness: *barren fields; a barren relationship.* **6.** See **mere¹. 8.** uncover, expose. —**Ant. 1.** covered.

bare² (bâr), *v. Archaic.* pt. of **bear.**

Ba•re•a (bə rā′ə; *Sp.* bä ʀe′ä), *n.* **Ar•tu•ro** (är to͝or′ō; *Sp.* äʀ to͞o′ʀô), 1897–1957, Spanish author, critic, lecturer, and broadcaster: in England after 1939.

bare•ass (bâr′as′), *adj., adv. Slang (vulgar).* wearing no clothes; naked. Also, **bare′assed′.** [BARE¹ + ASS²]

bare•back (bâr′bak′), *adv., adj.* with the back of a horse, burro, etc., bare; without a saddle: *to ride bareback; a bareback rider.* Also, **bare′backed′.** [1555–65; BARE¹ + BACK¹]

bare•bel•ly (bâr′bel′ē), *n., pl.* **-lies.** *New Zealand.* a sheep with a defective growth of wool on its belly and legs. [1870–75; BARE¹ + BELLY]

bare•boat (bâr′bōt′), *adj.* providing a boat only, exclusive of crew, stores, fuel, and the like: *a bareboat charter.* [*Amer.;* BARE¹ + BOAT] —**bare′boat′ing,** *n.*

bare•boned (bâr′bōnd′), *adj.* **1.** lean or spare, as a person. **2.** emaciated; gaunt: *bareboned victims of a terrible famine.* [1590–1600; BARE¹ + BONED, from the earlier use *bare-bones* or *bare-bone* a lean person]

bare′ bones′, the irreducible minimum; the most essential components: *Reduce this report to its bare bones. There is nothing left of the town but the bare bones—a couple of stores, a church, and a few houses.* [1910–15] —**bare′-bones′,** *adj.*

bare•faced (bâr′fāst′), *adj.* **1.** with the face uncovered. **2.** shameless; impudent; audacious: *a barefaced lie.* **3.** without concealment or disguise; boldly open: *a barefaced approach.* [1580–90] —**bare•fac•ed•ly** (bâr′fā′sid lē, -fāst′lē), *adv.* —**bare′fac′ed•ness,** *n.*

—**Syn. 2.** brazen, bold, unabashed. **3.** patent, palpable, transparent.

bare•fist•ed (bâr′fis′tid), *adj., adv.* with the fists bare: *a fierce, barefisted fight; to fight barefisted.* [BARE¹ + FISTED]

bare•foot (bâr′fo͝ot′), *adj., adv.* **1.** Also, **bare′foot′•ed.** with the feet bare: *a barefoot boy; to walk barefoot.* **2.** *Carpentry.* (of a post or stud) secured to a sill or the like without mortising. [bef. 1000; ME *barfot,* OE *bærfōt.* See BARE¹, FOOT]

bare′foot doc′tor, (in China) a layperson trained to provide a number of basic health-care services, esp. in rural areas. [1965–70]

ba•rege (bə rezh′), *n.* a sheer fabric constructed in a leno weave of silk warp and cotton or worsted filling, often used to make veils and dresses. Also, **ba•rège′.** [1805–15; after *Barèges,* town in southern France (Hautes-Pyrénées)]

bare•hand•ed (bâr′han′did), *adj., adv.* **1.** with hands uncovered: *He caught the baseball barehanded.* **2.** without tools, weapons, or other means: *foolishly coming barehanded to the besieged city.* [1400–50; late ME *barehandyd.* See BARE¹, HANDED]

bare•head•ed (bâr′hed′id), *adj., adv.* with the head uncovered. Also, **bare′head′.** [1520–30; BARE¹ + HEADED; cf. ME *bareheved, barehed*] —**bare′head′ed•ness,** *n.*

Ba•reil•ly (bə rā′lē), *n.* a city in N central Uttar Pradesh, in N India. 326,127. Also, **Ba•re′li.**

bare•knuck•le (bâr′nuk′əl), *adj.* **1.** (of a prizefight, prizefighter, etc.) without boxing gloves; using the bare fists. **2.** without conventional niceties; rough-and-tumble. —*adv.* **3.** without boxing gloves. **4.** in a rough-and-tumble manner. Also, **bare′knuck′led.** [1920–25; BARE¹ + KNUCKLE]

bare•leg•ged (bâr′leg′id, -legd′), *adj., adv.* with bare legs. [1325–75; ME *barlegged.* See BARE¹, LEGGED]

bare•ly (bâr′lē), *adv.* **1.** only just; scarcely; no more than; almost not: *He had barely enough money to pay for the car.* **2.** without disguise or concealment; openly: *They gave the facts to him barely.* **3.** scantily; meagerly; sparsely. **4.** *Archaic.* merely. [bef. 950; ME; OE *bærlice.* See BARE¹, -LY]

—**Usage. 1.** See **hardly.**

Bar•ents (bar′ənts, bär′-; *Du.* bä′ʀənts), *n.* **Wil•lem** (wil′əm), died 1597, Dutch navigator and explorer.

Bar′ents Sea′, a part of the Arctic Ocean between NE Europe and the islands of Spitzbergen, Franz Josef Land, and Novaya Zemlya.

bare-root (bâr′ro͞ot′, -ro͝ot′), *adj. Hort.* of or pertaining to a tree or shrub prepared for transplanting by having all or most of the soil removed from about its roots. Cf. **balled-and-burlapped.**

bare•sark (bâr′särk), *n.* **1.** *Scand. Legend.* a berserker. —*adv.* **2.** without armor. [1830–40; var. of BERSERK, as if BARE¹ + SARK]

bar•es•the•sia (bar′əs thē′zhə, -zhē ə, -zē ə), *n.* the sense or perception of pressure. [BAR(O)- + ESTHESIA]

bar′ examina′tion, a written examination to determine if one is qualified to practice law in a particular jurisdiction. Also, **bar′ exam′.**

barf (bärf), *v., n. Slang.* vomit. [1955–60; expressive word of uncert. orig.]

barf′ bag′, *Slang.* a disposable paper bag provided by

CONCISE PRONUNCIATION KEY: act, cāpe, dâre, pärt; set, ēqual; if, īce; ox, ōver, ôrder, oil, bo͝ok, bo͞ot, out; up, ûrge; child; sing; shoe; thin, *th*at; zh as in *treasure.* ə = *a* as in *alone, e* as in *system, i* as in *easily, o* as in *gallop, u* as in *circus;* ᵊ as in *fire* (fīᵊr), *hour* (ouᵊr). l and n can serve as syllabic consonants, as in *cradle* (krād′l), and *button* (but′n). See the full key inside the front cover.

airlines for each passenger in the event of air sickness and usually placed in the pocket behind every seat.

bar·fly (bär′flī′), *n., pl.* **-flies.** *Slang.* a person who frequents barrooms. [1905–10, *Amer.*; BAR[1] + FLY[2]]

bar′ foot′, *Furniture.* See **runner foot.**

bar·gain (bär′gən), *n.* **1.** an advantageous purchase, esp. one acquired at less than the usual cost: *The sale offered bargains galore.* **2.** an agreement between parties settling what each shall give and take or perform and receive in a transaction. **3.** such an agreement as affecting one of the parties: *a losing bargain.* **4.** something acquired by bargaining. **5.** *Informal.* an agreeable person, esp. one who causes no trouble or difficulty (usually used in negative constructions): *His boss is no bargain.* **6. in** or **into the bargain,** over and above what has been stipulated; moreover; besides: *The new housekeeper proved to be a fine cook in the bargain.* **7. strike a bargain,** to make a bargain; agree to terms: *They were unable to strike a bargain because the owner's asking price was more than the prospective buyer could afford.* —*v.i.* **8.** to discuss the terms of a bargain; haggle; negotiate. **9.** to come to an agreement; make a bargain: *We bargained on a three-year term.* —*v.t.* **10.** to arrange by bargain; negotiate: *to bargain a new wage increase.* **11.** to anticipate as likely to occur; expect (usually fol. by a clause): *I'll bargain that he's going to give those company directors plenty of trouble.* **12. bargain for,** to anticipate or take into account: *The job turned out to be more than he had bargained for.* **13. bargain on,** to expect or anticipate; count or rely on: *You can't bargain on what she'll do in this situation.* [1300–50; (v.) ME *bargaynen* < AF, OF *bargai(g)ner,* prob. < Frankish **borganjan,* extended form of Gmc **borgan* (cf. OHG *bor(a)gēn* to look after, MHG, G *borgen* to lend, BORROW); (n.) ME *bargayn* < AF, OF *bargai(g)ne, bargain,* n. deriv. of the v.; *o* > *a* in 1st syll. is unexplained] —**bar′gain·a·ble,** *adj.* —**bar′gain·er,** *n.*
—**Syn. 2.** stipulation, arrangement, transaction. See **agreement. 8.** See **trade. 9.** contract, covenant.

bar′gain base′ment, a basement area in some stores where goods are sold at prices lower than usual. [1895–1900]

bar·gain-base·ment (bär′gən bās′mənt), *adj.* **1.** very low-priced. **2.** noticeably lacking in quality; inferior. [1955–60]

bar′gain count′er, a counter or area in a retail store where merchandise is sold at reduced prices. [1885–90]

bar′gaining chip′, something, as a concession or inducement, that can be used in negotiating. [1970–75]

bar′gaining u′nit, a group of employees represented by a union in collective bargaining.

barge (bärj), *n., v.,* **barged, barg·ing.** —*n.* **1.** a capacious, flat-bottomed vessel, usually intended to be pushed or towed, for transporting freight or passengers; lighter. **2.** a vessel of state used in pageants: *elegantly decorated barges on the Grand Canal in Venice.* **3.** *Navy.* a boat reserved for a flag officer. **4.** a boat that is heavier and wider than a shell, often used in racing as a training boat. **5.** *New England. Chiefly Older Use.* a large, horse-drawn coach or, sometimes, a bus. —*v.i.* **6.** to move clumsily; bump into things; collide: *to barge through a crowd.* **7.** to move in the slow, heavy manner of a barge. —*v.t.* **8.** to carry or transport by barge: *Coal and ore had been barged down the Ohio to the Mississippi.* **9. barge in,** to intrude, esp. rudely: *I hated to barge in without an invitation.* **10. barge into, a.** Also, **barge in on.** to force oneself upon, esp. rudely; interfere in: *to barge into a conversation.* **b.** to bump into; collide with: *He started to run away and barged into a passer-by.* [1250–1300; ME < MF, perh. < L **bārica;* see BARK[3]]

barge·board (bärj′bôrd′, -bōrd′), *n.* a board, often carved, hanging from the projecting end of a sloping roof. Also called **vergeboard.** [1825–35; *barge* (of obscure orig.) + BOARD]

barge′ cou′ple, either of the pair of rafters carrying the part of a gable roof that projects beyond the gable wall. [1555–65; see BARGEBOARD]

barge′ course′, 1. tiling on a gable roof beyond the exterior surface of the gable wall. **2.** the tiles or slates placed on and projecting over the raking edges of a gable roof. **3.** a coping of bricks set on edge, arranged transversely. [1660–70; see BARGEBOARD]

bar·gel·lo (bär jel′ō), *n.* **1.** a straight stitch worked in a high and low relief pattern to form a variety of zigzag or oblique designs. **2.** needlepoint work or a design done in such stitches, esp. the traditional needlepoint created by a classic stitch **(Florentine stitch)** done in diagonal lines. [1920–25; allegedly after a set of chairs embroidered with such a stitch in the *Bargello,* a museum in Florence]

barge·man (bärj′mən), *n., pl.* **-men. 1.** one of the crew of a barge. **2.** a person who owns, manages, or captains a barge. Also called, *esp. Brit.,* **bar·gee** (bär jē′). [1400–50, earlier in AL, AF; ME; see BARGE, MAN[1]]

bar′ gem′el, (jem′əl), *pl.* **bars gemels.** *Heraldry.* a charge consisting of two barrulets separated by an area the width of a barrulet. [1600–10]

barge′ spike′, a square spike with a chisel point. Also called **boat spike.** See illus. under **spike.**

barge·stone (bärj′stōn′), *n.* any of several stones forming the sloping edge of a gable. [1825–35; see BARGEBOARD]

bar·ghest (bär′gest), *n.* a legendary doglike goblin believed to portend death or misfortune. [1725–35; appar. BAR(ROW)[2] + *ghest,* OE *gæst,* var. of *gāst* GHOST]

bar′ girl′, 1. a barmaid. **2.** B-girl. **3.** a female prostitute who frequents bars in search of customers. [1855–60]

bar′ graph′, a graph using parallel bars of varying lengths, as to illustrate comparative costs, exports, birthrates, etc. Also called **bar chart.** [1920–25]

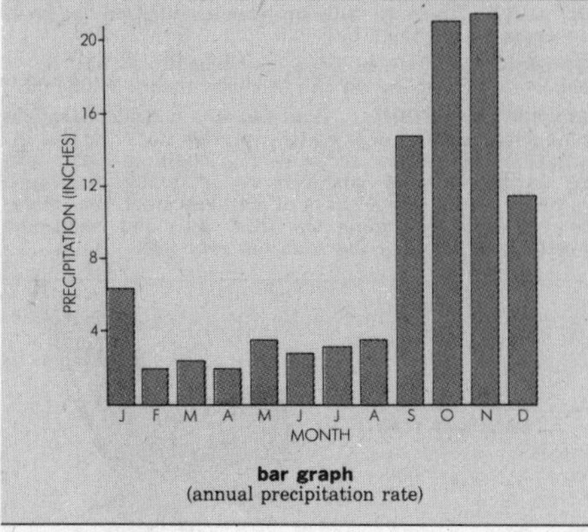

bar graph
(annual precipitation rate)

Bar′ Har′bor, a town on Mount Desert Island, in S Maine: summer resort. 4124.

bar·hop (bär′hop′), *v.i.,* **-hopped, -hop·ping.** *Informal.* to go to a succession of bars or nightclubs, with a brief stay at each. [1945–50; BAR[1] + HOP[1]]

Ba·ri (bär′ē), *n.* a seaport in SE Italy, on the Adriatic. 384,722. Italian, **Bari delle Puglie.**

bar·i·a·tri·cian (bar′ē ə trish′ən), *n.* a physician who specializes in bariatrics. [1965–70; BARIATRIC(S) + -IAN, on the model of PEDIATRICIAN]

bar·i·at·rics (bar′ē a′triks), *n.* (*used with a singular v.*) a branch of medicine that deals with the control and treatment of obesity and allied diseases. [1965–70; < Gk *bár(os)* weight (cf. BARO-) + -IATRICS] —**bar′i·at′ric,** *adj.*

bar·ic[1] (bar′ik), *adj. Chem.* of or containing barium. [1860–65; BAR(IUM) + -IC]

bar·ic[2] (bar′ik), *adj.* of or pertaining to weight, esp. that of the atmosphere. [1880–85; BAR(O)- + -IC]

Ba·ri del·le Pu·glie (bä′rē del′le pōō′lye), Italian name of **Bari.**

ba·ril·la (bə rē′ə, -rēl′yə, -ril′ə), *n.* **1.** either of two European saltworts, *Salsola kali* or *S. soda,* whose ashes yield an impure carbonate of soda. **2.** the alkali obtained from the ashes of these and certain other maritime plants. [1615–25; < Sp *barrilla,* appar. equiv. to *bar(ra)* BAR[1] + *-illa* dim. suffix]

Ba·ri·nas (bä rē′näs), *n.* a city in W Venezuela. 56,329.

Bar·ing (bâr′ing), *n.* **1. Alexander, 1st Baron Ashburton,** 1774–1848, British statesman. **2. Evelyn, 1st Earl of Cromer,** 1841–1917, British statesman and diplomat.

Ba·ri·sal (bur′ə säl′, bar′ə sôl′), *n.* a port city in S Bangladesh, on the Ganges River. 98,127.

barit., *Music.* baritone.

bar·ite (bâr′it, bar′-), *n.* a common mineral, barium sulfate, $BaSO_4$, occurring in white, yellow, or colorless tabular crystals: the principal ore of barium. Also, **barytes.** Also called **heavy spar.** [1780–90; BAR(YTES) + -ITE[1]]

bar·i·tone (bar′i tōn′), *Music.* —*n.* **1.** a male voice or voice part intermediate between tenor and bass. **2.** a singer with such a voice. **3.** a large, valved brass instrument shaped like a trumpet or coiled in oval form, used esp. in military bands. —*adj.* **4.** of or pertaining to a baritone; having the compass of a baritone. Also, **barytone.** [1600–10; < It *baritono* low voice < Gk *barýtonos* deep-sounding. See BARYTONE[2]] —**bar′i·ton′al,** *adj.*

bar′itone clef′, *Music.* an F clef locating F below middle C on the third line of the staff.

bar·i·um (bâr′ē əm, bar′-), *n. Chem.* a whitish, malleable, active, divalent, metallic element, occurring in combination chiefly as barite or as witherite. *Symbol:* Ba; *at. wt.:* 137.34; *at. no.:* 56; *sp. gr.:* 3.5 at 20°C. [1800–10; BAR(YTES) + -IUM]

barium 140, *Chem.* the radioactive isotope of barium having a mass number of 140 and a half-life of 12.8 days, used chiefly as a tracer.

bar′ium bro′mate, *Chem.* colorless, slightly water-soluble, poisonous crystals, $Ba(BrO_3)_2 \cdot H_2O$, used in the preparation of certain bromates.

bar′ium car′bonate, *Chem.* a white, poisonous, water-insoluble powder, $BaCO_3$, used chiefly in the manufacture of rodenticides, paints, and dyes. [1870–75]

bar′ium chlo′ride, *Chem.* a colorless, crystalline, water-soluble, poisonous solid, $BaCl_2 \cdot 2H_2O$, used chiefly in the synthesis of pigments and in the manufacture of rodenticides and pharmaceuticals.

bar′ium chro′mate, *Chem.* a yellow, crystalline compound, $BaCrO_4$, used as a pigment **(barium yellow).**

bar′ium en′ema, *Med.* See under **GI series.** [1925–30]

bar′ium hydrox′ide, *Chem.* baryta (def. 2). Also called **bar′ium hy′drate.**

bar′ium ox′ide, *Chem.* baryta (def. 1). Also called **bar′ium monox′ide, bar′ium protox′ide.**

bar′ium perox′ide, *Chem.* a grayish-white, water-insoluble, poisonous powder, BaO_2, used chiefly in the manufacture of hydrogen peroxide and as a bleaching agent for textiles. Also called **bar′ium diox′ide.**

bar′ium ste′arate, *Chem.* a white, crystalline, water-insoluble solid, $Ba(C_{18}H_{35}O_2)_2$, used chiefly as a waterproofing agent and as a lubricant.

bar′ium sul′fate, *Chem.* a white, crystalline, water-insoluble powder, $BaSO_4$, used chiefly in the synthesis of pigments, as in paints and printing inks, and, because of its radiopacity, for x-ray diagnosis in medicine. [1870–75]

bar′ium sul′fide, *Chem.* a gray or yellowish-green, water-soluble, poisonous powder, BaS, used chiefly as a depilatory and as an intermediate in the synthesis of pigments, esp. lithopone.

bar′ium thiosul′fate, *Chem.* a white, crystalline, water-insoluble, poisonous solid, $BaS_2O_3 \cdot H_2O$, used chiefly in the manufacture of explosives, matches, paints, and varnishes.

bar′ium ti′tanate, *Chem.* a crystalline compound, $BaTiO_3$, used to make ferroelectric ceramics for capacitors and also used in transducers.

bar′ium x′-ray. See **GI series.**

bar′ium yel′low, *Chem.* See under **barium chromate.**

bar′ joist′, a welded steel joist having an open web consisting of a single bent bar running in a zigzag pattern between horizontal upper and lower chords.

bark[1] (bärk), *n.* **1.** the abrupt, harsh, explosive cry of a dog. **2.** a similar sound made by another animal, as a fox. **3.** a short, explosive sound, as of firearms: *the bark of a revolver.* **4.** a brusque order, reply, etc.: *The foreman's bark sent the idlers back to their machines.* **5.** a cough. —*v.i.* **6.** (of a dog or other animal) to utter an abrupt, explosive cry or a series of such cries. **7.** to make a similar sound: *The big guns barked.* **8.** to speak or cry out sharply or gruffly: *a man who barks at his children.* **9.** *Informal.* to advertise a theater performance, carnival sideshow, or the like, by standing at the entrance and calling out to passersby. **10.** to cough. —*v.t.* **11.** to utter in a harsh, shouting tone: *barking orders at her subordinates.* **12. bark at the moon,** to protest in vain: *Telling her that she's misinformed is just barking at the moon.* **13. bark up the wrong tree,** to assail or pursue the wrong person or object; misdirect one's efforts: *If he expects me to get him a job, he's barking up the wrong tree.* [bef. 900; ME *berken,* OE *beorcan;* akin to OE *borcian* to bark, ON *berkja* to bluster, Lith *burgė́ti* to growl, quarrel, Serbo-Croatian *br̀gljati* to murmur] —**bark′less,** *adj.*
—**Syn. 11.** shout, bellow, yell, roar, bawl.

bark[2] (bärk), *n.* **1.** the external covering of the woody stems, branches, and roots of plants, as distinct and separable from the wood itself. **2.** *Tanning.* a mixture of oak and hemlock barks. **3.** candy, usually of chocolate with large pieces of nuts, made in flat sheets. —*v.t.* **4.** to rub off or scrape the skin of, as by bumping into something: *to bark one's shins.* **5.** to remove a circle of bark from; girdle. **6.** to cover, enclose, or encrust with or as if with bark. **7.** to treat with a bark infusion; tan. **8.** to strip the bark from; peel. [1250–1300; ME < ON *bǫrkr* (gen. *barkar*)] —**bark′less,** *adj.*

bark[3] (bärk), *n.* **1.** *Naut.* a sailing vessel having three or more masts, square-rigged on all but the aftermost mast, which is fore-and-aft-rigged. **2.** *Literary.* a boat or sailing vessel. Also, **barque.** [1425–75; late ME *barke* < OF *barque* << LL *barca,* L **bārica, bāris* < Gk *bâris* Egyptian barge < Coptic *barī* barge]

bark[3] (def. 1)

bark′ bee′tle, any of numerous small, cylindrical beetles of the family Scolytidae that nest under the bark of hardwood trees, leaving intricate tracings on the wood. Also called **ambrosia beetle, engraver beetle.** [1860–65]

bark′ cloth′, 1. any cloth, as tapa, made by soaking and pounding the inner bark of certain trees. **2.** a fabric woven to resemble such cloth, used for upholstery, bedcovers, etc.

bar·keep·er (bär′kē′pər), *n.* **1.** a person who owns or manages a bar where alcoholic beverages are sold. **2.** a bartender. Also, **bar′keep′.** [1705–15; BAR[1] + KEEPER]

bark·en·tine (bär′kən tēn′), *n. Naut.* a sailing vessel having three or more masts, square-rigged on the foremast and fore-and-aft-rigged on the other masts. Also, **bark′an·tine′, barquentine, barquantine.** [1685–95, *Amer.*; BARK[3] + (BRIG)ANTINE]

bark·er[1] (bär′kər), *n.* **1.** an animal or person that barks. **2.** a person who stands before a theater, carnival sideshow, or the like, calling out its attractions to passers-by. [1350–1400; ME *berker, berkar.* See BARK[1], -ER[1]]

bark·er[2] (bär′kər), *n.* **1.** a person or thing that removes bark from trees. **2.** a person or thing that prepares bark for tanning. [1375–1425, earlier as surname; late ME. See BARK[2] (v.), -ER[1]]

CONCISE ETYMOLOGY KEY: <, descended or borrowed from; >, whence; b., blend of, blended; c., cognate with; cf., compare; deriv., derivative; equiv., equivalent; imit., imitative; obl., oblique; r., replacing; s., stem; sp., spelling, spelled; resp., respelling, respelled; trans., translation; ?, origin unknown; *, unattested; ‡, probably earlier than. See the full key inside the front cover.

Bark′hau·sen effect′ (bärk′hou′zən, bär′kou′-), *Physics.* the phenomenon of short, sudden changes in the magnetism of a ferromagnetic substance occurring when the intensity of the magnetizing field is continuously altered. [1955–60; named after H. *Barkhausen* (1881–1956), German physicist]

Bar·king (bär′king), *n.* a borough of Greater London, England. 154,200.

bark′ing deer′, muntjac. [1875–80]

bark′ing frog′, a robber frog, *Hylactophryne augusti,* of Texas, New Mexico, and Mexico, having a call like a dog's bark.

Bark·la (bärk′lə), *n.* **Charles Glov·er** (gluv′ər), 1877–1944, English physicist: Nobel prize 1917.

Bark·ley (bärk′lē), *n.* **Al·ben William** (al′bən), 1877–1956, vice president of the U.S. 1949–53.

bark·louse (bärk′lous′), *n., pl.* **-lice** (-līs′). any of numerous insects of the order Psocoptera that live on the bark of trees and other plants. Also, **bark′ louse′.** Cf. **psocid.** [1835–45; *Amer.;* BARK² + LOUSE]

Bar Kok·ba (bär′ kôkh′bä, -vä), **Simon,** died A.D. 135, Hebrew leader of insurrection against the Romans A.D. 132–135. Also, **Bar Cocheba, Bar Cochba, Bar′ Koch′ba.**

bark·y (bär′kē), *adj.,* **bark·i·er, bark·i·est. 1.** consisting of, containing, or covered with bark. **2.** resembling bark. [1580–90; BARK² + -Y¹]

Bar·lach (bär′läk; *Ger.* bär′läkh), *n.* **Ernst Heinrich** (ûrnst hīn′rik; *Ger.* ernst hīn′rikh), 1870–1938, German sculptor and playwright.

bar·ley¹ (bär′lē), *n.* **1.** a widely distributed cereal plant belonging to the genus *Hordeum,* of the grass family, having awned flowers that grow in tightly bunched spikes, with three small additional spikes at each node. **2.** the grain of this plant, used as food and in making beer, ale, and whiskey. [bef. 1000; ME; OE *bærlic* (adj.), equiv. to *bær-* (var. of *bere* barley; akin to ON *barr* barley, Goth *barizeins* made of barley, Serbo-Croatian *brăšno* flour, L *far* emmer; all < European IE **bHₐer-* spike, prickle, perh. akin to BEARD) + *-lic* -LY]

bar·ley² (bär′lē), *n., pl.* **-leys.** *Scot. and North Eng.* a truce or quarter, esp. in children's games; parley. [1805–15; prob. to be identified with Scots *barley, burley, birlie* local customary law (cf. *birleyman* arbiter, *birleycourt* neighborhood court), var. of *birlaw,* ML *birlawe, birelegia, birelag* < ON **býjarlagu,* equiv. to *býjar* gen. sing. of *býr* town (cf. BOWER¹, BYRE) + **lagu* LAW¹; cf. BY-LAW]

bar·ley-bree (bär′lē brē′), *n. Chiefly Scot.* liquor, malt liquor, or the like, esp. whiskey. [1780–90]

bar′ley coal′, anthracite in sizes ranging from more than ³⁄₆₄ in. (1.2 mm) to less than ³⁄₁₆ in. (4.8 mm).

bar·ley·corn (bär′lē kôrn′), *n.* **1.** barley. **2.** a grain of barley. **3.** a measure equal to ⅓ in. (8.5 mm). **4.** Also, **bar′ley corn′.** a type of basket weave that produces an allover geometric pattern. [1375–1425; late ME. See BARLEY¹, CORN¹]

Bar·ley·corn (bär′lē kôrn′), *n.* **John.** See **John Barleycorn.**

bar′ley sack′, *Southwestern U.S. (chiefly California).* a burlap bag.
—**Regional Variation.** See **gunnysack.**

bar′ley stripe′, *Plant Pathol.* a disease of barley, characterized by blighted heads and chlorotic, brown, or frayed stripes on the leaves, caused by a fungus, *Helminthosporium gramineum.*

bar′ley sug′ar, a brittle, amber-colored, transparent candy, formerly boiled in a decoction of barley, consisting of sugar, cream of tartar, and orange or lemon juice, usually twisted into strips or molded into a variety of shapes. Also called **bar′ley can′dy.** [1705–15]

bar′ley wa′ter, a decoction of barley, used esp. in the treatment of diarrhea in infants. [1275–1325]

bar′ line′, *Music.* bar¹ (def. 16a). [1925–30]

bar·low (bär′lō), *n. South Midland and Southern U.S.* a large pocketknife with one blade. Also called **bar′low knife′.** [1770–80, *Amer.;* after a family of Sheffield cutlers named *Barlow,* who are alleged to have produced a knife of this type before 1700]

Bar·low (bär′lō), *n.* **Joel,** 1754–1812, U.S. poet and diplomat.

barm (bärm), *n.* yeast formed on malt liquors while fermenting. [bef. 1000; ME *berme,* OE *beorma;* c. Fris *berme,* G *Bärme,* Sw *bärme;* akin to FERMENT]

bar′ mag′net, a bar-shaped, usually permanent, magnet. [1820–30]

bar·maid (bär′mād′), *n.* a woman who bartends; bartender. [1650–60; BAR¹ + MAID]

bar·man (bär′mən), *n., pl.* **-men.** a man who bartends; bartender. [1650–60; BAR¹ + -MAN]

Bar·me·cid·al (bär′mə sīd′l), *adj.* giving only the illusion of plenty; illusory: *a Barmecidal banquet.* Also, **Barmecide.** [1835–45; BARMECIDE + -AL¹]

Bar·me·cide (bär′mə sīd′), *n.* **1.** a member of a noble Persian family of Baghdad who, according to a tale in *The Arabian Nights' Entertainments,* gave a beggar a pretended feast with empty dishes. —*adj.* **2.** Barmecidal. [< Pers *Barmekī* family name, lit., offspring of *Barmek,* with *-ide* -ID¹ for Pers *-ī* < Ar]

Bar·men (bär′mən), *n.* a former city in W West Germany, now incorporated into Wuppertal.

bar mitz·vah (bär mits′və *or, Ashk. Heb.* bär; *Seph. Heb.* bär′ mēts vä′), (*often caps.*) *Judaism.* **1.** a solemn ceremony held in the synagogue, usually on Saturday morning, to admit as an adult member of the Jewish community a Jewish boy 13 years old who has successfully completed a prescribed course of study in Judaism. **2.** the boy participating in this ceremony. **3.** to administer the ceremony of bar mitzvah to: *Our son was bar mitzvahed at the family synagogue.* Cf. **bat mitzvah.** Also, **bar miz′vah.** [1860–65; < Biblical Aram *bar* son + Heb *miṣwāh* divine law, commandment]

barm·y (bär′mē), *adj.,* **barm·i·er, barm·i·est. 1.** containing or resembling barm; frothy. **2.** *Brit. Slang.* balmy (def. 4). [1525–35; BARM + -Y¹; def. 2 prob. resp. of BALMY by r-less speaker]

barn¹ (bärn), *n.* **1.** a building for storing hay, grain, etc., and often for housing livestock. **2.** a very large garage for buses, trucks, etc.; carbarn. —*v.t.* **3.** to store (hay, grain, etc.) in a barn. [bef. 950; ME *bern,* OE *berern* (*bere* (see BARLEY¹) + *ern, ærn* house, c. OFris *fīaern* cowhouse, OHG *erin,* Goth *razn,* ON *rann* house; cf. RANSACK, REST¹)] —**barn′like′,** *adj.*

barn² (bärn), *n. Physics.* a unit of nuclear cross section, equal to 10^{-24} square centimeter. *Abbr.:* b [1945–50; special use of BARN¹]

Bar·na·bas (bär′nə bəs), *n.* the surname of the Cyprian Levite Joseph, a companion of Paul on his first missionary journey. Acts 4:36, 37.

Bar·na·by (bär′nə bē), *n.* a male given name: from a Hebrew word meaning "son of exhortation."

bar·na·cle¹ (bär′nə kəl), *n.* **1.** any marine crustacean of the subclass Cirripedia, usually having a calcareous shell, being either stalked **(goose barnacle)** and attaching itself to ship bottoms and floating timber, or stalkless **(rock barnacle** or **acorn barnacle)** and attaching itself to rocks, esp. in the intertidal zone. **2.** a person or thing that clings tenaciously. [1580–85; perh. a conflation of *barnacle* BARNACLE GOOSE with Cornish *brennyk,* Ir *báirneach* limpet, Welsh *brenig* limpets, reflecting the folk belief that such geese, whose breeding grounds were unknown, were engendered from rotten ships' planking] —**bar′na·cled,** *adj.*

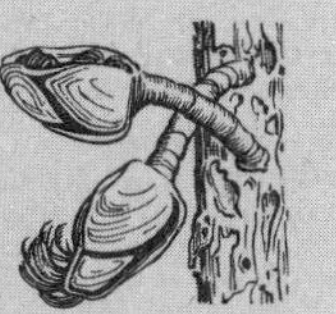

goose barnacle, *Lepas fascicularis,* length of shell 2 in. (5 cm)

bar·na·cle² (bär′nə kəl), *n.* **1.** Usually, **barnacles.** an instrument with two hinged branches for pinching the nose of an unruly horse. **2. barnacles,** *Brit. Dial.* spectacles. [1350–1400; ME *bernacle* bit, dim of *bernac* < OF < ?]

bar′nacle goose′, a wild goose, *Branta leucopsis,* of northern Europe and Greenland. [1760–70; earlier *barnacle,* ME *bernacle;* cf. MF *bernacle,* NL *bernacula,* all deriv. of earlier ME *bernak, bernekke,* AL *bernaca,* OF *bernaque,* of uncert. orig.]

Bar·nard (bär′närd, -nərd *for 1;* bär′nərd *for 2–5*), *n.* **1. Chris·tiaan N(eeth·ling)** (kris′tyän nit′ling), born 1922, South African surgeon: performed first successful human-heart transplant 1967. **2. Frederick Augustus Porter,** 1809–89, U.S. educator and advocate of higher education for women: president of Columbia University 1864–89. **3. George Gray,** 1863–1938, U.S. sculptor. **4. Henry,** 1811–1900, U.S. educator. **5.** a male given name.

Bar·nar·do (bär när′dō, bər-), *n.* **Thomas John,** 1845–1905, English physician, social reformer, and philanthropist, born in Ireland.

Bar′nard's star′ (bär′nərdz), a red dwarf star of magnitude 9.5 in the constellation Ophiuchus, having the largest known proper motion and being the nearest star to earth (5.9 light-years) beyond the Alpha Centauri system. [after Edward E. *Barnard* (1857–1923), American astronomer, its discoverer]

Bar·na·ul (bär′nə o͞ol′; *Russ.* bər nu o͞ol′), *n.* a city in and the capital of the Altai territory in the Russian Federation, on the Ob River, S of Novosibirsk. 602,000.

barn·board (bärn′bôrd′, -bōrd′), *n.* barnwood. [*Amer.;* BARN¹ + BOARD]

barn·burn·er (bärn′bûr′nər), *n.* **1.** *Informal.* something that is highly exciting, impressive, etc.: *The All Stars game was a real barnburner.* **2.** *Chiefly Pennsylvania.* a wooden friction match. **3.** (*cap.*) a member of the progressive faction in the Democratic party in New York State 1845–52. Cf. **Hunker.** [1835–45, *Amer.;* BARN¹ + BURNER; (def. 3) so called with reference to burning down a barn to get rid of rats]

barn′ dance′, 1. a social gathering, originally held in a barn, and including square dances, round dances, and hoedown music. **2.** any party featuring country dances, dress, music, etc. [1890–95, *Amer.*]

barn′-door′ skate′, (bärn′dôr, -dōr′), an Atlantic skate, *Raja laevis,* that grows to a length of 4 ft. (1.2 m) or more.

Bar·net (bär′nit), *n.* a borough of Greater London, England. 302,600.

Bar·nett (bär net′), *n.* a male given name.

Bar·ne·veldt (bär′nə velt′), *n.* **Jan van Ol·den** (yän vän ôl′dən), 1547–1619, Dutch statesman and patriot.

bar·ney (bär′nē), *n., pl.* **-neys. 1.** *Informal.* **a.** an argument. **b.** a prizefight. **c.** a fight or brawl. **d.** a blunder or mistake. **2.** a small locomotive used in mining and logging. **3.** *Motion Picture Slang.* a heavily padded cover for a camera, used to reduce the camera noise so that it will not be picked up by the sound-recording equipment. [1860–65; perh. special uses of BARNEY]

Bar·ney (bär′nē), *n.* a male given name, form of **Bernard.**

barn′ grass′. See **barnyard grass.**

barn·lot (bärn′lot′), *n. Chiefly Midland and Southern U.S.* barnyard. [1735–45, *Amer.;* BARN¹ + LOT]

barn′ owl′, a yellowish-brown and white owl, *Tyto alba,* often inhabiting barns and other buildings. [1665–75]

barn′ rais′ing, (in rural areas) a party, usually providing food, drink, etc., for the purpose of assisting a neighbor to put up a new barn. [1855–60, *Amer.*]

Barns·ley (bärnz′lē), *n.* a city in South Yorkshire, in N England. 224,000.

Barn·sta·ble (bärn′stə bəl), *n.* a city in SE Massachusetts. 30,898.

barn·storm (bärn′stôrm′), *v.i.* **1.** to conduct a campaign or speaking tour in rural areas by making brief stops in many small towns. **2.** *Theat.* to tour small towns to stage theatrical performances. **3.** (of a pilot) to give exhibitions of stunt flying, participate in airplane races, etc., in the course of touring country towns and rural areas. **4.** (of a professional athletic team) to tour an area playing exhibition games after the regular season. —*v.t.* **5.** to tour (various places) as a barnstormer. [1880–85; BARN¹ + STORM] —**barn′storm′er,** *n.*

barn′ swal′low, a common swallow, *Hirundo rustica,* of North America and Eurasia, that nests in barns and similar buildings. [1780–90, *Amer.*]

Bar·num (bär′nəm), *n.* **P(hineas) T(aylor),** 1810–91, U.S. showman who established a circus in 1871.

barn·wood (bärn′wo͝od′), *n.* aged and weathered boards, esp. those salvaged from dismantled barns: *The den was paneled in barnwood.* Also, **barnboard.** [*Amer.;* BARN¹ + WOOD¹]

barn·yard (bärn′yärd′), *n.* **1.** Also called **barnlot.** a yard next to or surrounding a barn. —*adj.* **2.** of, pertaining to, or typical of a barnyard: *barnyard noises; simple paintings of barnyard life.* **3.** indecent; smutty; vulgar: *His barnyard humor made us all blush.* [1505–15; BARN¹ + YARD²]

barn′yard golf′, *Informal* (*facetious*). the game of horseshoes. [1925–30]

barn′yard grass′, a weedy, coarse grass, *Echinochloa crus-galli,* having a spikelike cluster of flowers. Also called **barn grass.** [1835–45, *Amer.*]

barn·yard·ism (bärn′yär diz′əm), *n.* a smutty or indecent word or expression. [*Amer.;* BARNYARD + -ISM]

baro-, a combining form meaning "pressure," used in the formation of compound words: *barograph.* [comb. form of Gk *báros* weight; akin to Skt *guru,* L *gravis,* Goth *kaurus* heavy]

Ba·roc·chio (bä rôk′kyô), *n.* **Gia·co·mo** (jä′kô mô). See **Vignola, Giacomo da.**

bar·o·clin·ic (bar′ə klin′ik), *adj.* of, pertaining to, or having the property of baroclinity. [BAROCLIN(ITY) + -IC]

bar·o·clin·i·ty (bar′ə klin′i tē), *n. Meteorol.* a common state of fluid stratification in which surfaces of constant pressure and others of constant density are not parallel but intersect. Also, **bar·o·cli·nic·i·ty** (bar′ə kli nis′i tē). Cf. **barotropy.** [BARO- + (IN)CLINE + -ITY]

bar·o·co·co (bar′ə kō′kō), *adj.* excessively ornate or fussy in artistic or architectural style. [b. BAROQUE and ROCOCO]

Ba·ro·da (bə rō′də), *n.* **1.** a former state in W India. **2.** a city in E Gujarat state, in W India: former capital of the state of Baroda. 467,422.

bar·og·no·sis (bar′og nō′sis, bar′əg-), *n.* the ability to estimate or perceive differences in the weight of an object. Cf. **baragnosis.** [BARO- + -GNOSIS]

bar·o·gram (bar′ə gram′), *n. Meteorol.* a record traced by a barograph or similar instrument. [1880–85; BARO- + -GRAM¹]

bar·o·graph (bar′ə graf′, -gräf′), *n.* any of several automatic recording barometers, of which the most common is the aneroid barograph. [1860–65; BARO- + -GRAPH] —**bar·o·graph·ic** (bar′ə graf′ik), *adj.*

Ba·ro·ja (bä rô′hä), *n.* **Pí·o** (pē′ô), 1872–1956, Spanish novelist.

Ba·ro·lo (bə rō′lō; *It.* bä rô′lô), *n.* a dry red wine from the Piedmont region of Italy. [1870–75; after *Barolo,* locality where it is produced]

ba·rom·e·ter (bə rom′i tər), *n.* **1.** *Meteorol.* any instrument that measures atmospheric pressure. Cf. **aneroid barometer, mercury barometer. 2.** anything that indicates changes. [1655–65; BARO- + -METER] —**bar·o·met·ric** (bar′ə me′trik), **bar′o·met′ri·cal,** *adj.* —**bar′o·met′ri·cal·ly,** *adv.*

bar′omet′ric er′ror, *Horol.* error of a timepiece due to the fluctuations in density of the atmosphere through which the balance or pendulum moves. [1880–85]

bar′omet′ric gra′dient, *Meteorol.* See **pressure gradient.**

bar′omet′ric pres′sure. See **atmospheric pressure.** [1820–30]

bar′omet′ric switch′, baroswitch.

bar·o·met·ro·graph (bar′ə me′trə graf′, -gräf′), *n.* barograph. [1840–50; BAROMET(E)R + -O- + -GRAPH]

ba·rom·e·try (bə rom′i trē), *n.* the process of measuring atmospheric pressure. [1705–15; BARO- + -METRY]

bar·on (bar′ən), *n.* **1.** a member of the lowest grade of nobility. **2.** (in Britain) **a.** a feudal vassal holding his lands under a direct grant from the king. **b.** a direct descendant of such a vassal or his equal in the nobility. **c.** a member of the House of Lords. **3.** an important financier or industrialist, esp. one with great power in a particular area: *an oil baron.* **4.** a cut of mutton or lamb comprising the two loins, or saddle, and the hind legs. Cf. **baron of beef.** [1200–50; ME < AF, OF < LL *barōn-* (s.

CONCISE PRONUNCIATION KEY: *act, cāpe, dâre, pärt; set, ēqual; if, īce; ox, ōver, ôrder, oil, bo͝ok, bo͞ot, out; up, ûrge; child; sing; shoe; thin, that;* zh *as in treasure.* ə = *a* as in *alone, e* as in *system, i* as in *easily, o* as in *gallop, u* as in *circus;* ᵊ as in *fire* (fīᵊr), *hour* (ouᵊr). l and n can serve as syllabic consonants, as in *cradle* (krād′l), and *button* (but′n). See the full key inside the front cover.

of barō) man < Gmc; sense "cut of beef" perh. by analogy with the fanciful analysis of SIRLOIN as "Sir Loin"]

Ba·ron (bA RÔN′), *n.* **Mi·chel** (mē shel′), (*Michel Boyron*), 1653–1729, French actor.

bar·on·age (bar′ə nij), *n.* **1.** the entire British peerage, including all dukes, marquesses, earls, viscounts, and barons. **2.** Also, **barony.** the dignity or rank of a baron. [1250–1300; ME *barunage* < AF (see BARON, -AGE); r. ME *barnage* < OF]

bar·on·ess (bar′ə nis), *n.* **1.** the wife of a baron. **2.** a woman holding a baronial title in her own right. [1400–50; late ME *baronnesse* < AF, MF (see BARON, -ESS); r. ME *barnesse* < AF, OF]
—Usage. See **-ess.**

bar·on·et (bar′ə nit, bar′ə net′), *n.* a member of a British hereditary order of honor, ranking below the barons and made up of commoners, designated by *Sir* before the name and *Baronet*, usually abbreviated *Bart.*, after: *Sir John Smith, Bart.* [1350–1400; ME; see BARON, -ET] **—bar′o·net′i·cal,** *adj.*

bar·on·et·age (bar′ə nit ij, -net′-), *n.* **1.** baronets collectively. **2.** baronetcy. [1710–20; BARONET + -AGE]

bar·on·et·cy (bar′ə nit sē, -net′), *n., pl.* **-cies.** the rank or dignity of a baronet. [1805–15; BARONET + -CY]

bar·on·et·ize (bar′ə ni tīz′), *v.t.,* **-ized, -iz·ing.** to make (someone) a baronet; confer a baronetcy upon. Also, *esp. Brit.,* **bar′on·et·ise′.** [1855–60; BARONET + -IZE]

ba·rong (bä rông′, -rong′, bə-), *n.* a large, broad-bladed knife or cleaver used by the Moros. [1840–50; appar. Philippine var. of PARANG]

barong′ ta·ga′log (tə gä′ləg, -lôg, tä-), (in the Philippines) a man's long-sleeved formal overblouse, made of fine, sheer fabric, often embroidered. [< Tagalog *baro ng tagalog* lit., Tagalog upper garment]

ba·ro·ni·al (bə rō′nē əl), *adj.* **1.** pertaining to a baron or barony or to the order of barons. **2.** befitting a baron: *living in baronial splendor.* [1760–70; BARONY + -AL[1]]

bar·on·ize (bar′ə nīz′), *v.t.,* **-ized, -iz·ing.** to make or create (someone) a baron; confer the rank of baron upon. Also, *esp. Brit.,* **bar′on·ise′.** [1605–15; BARON + -IZE]

bar′on of beef′, *Chiefly Brit.* a joint of beef consisting of the two sirloins joined at the backbone; double sirloin. Cf. **baron** (def. 4). [1745–55]

Bar′ons' War′, a rebellion of English nobles (1263–67) against King Henry III, undertaken in an effort to curtail royal prerogatives and extend the powers of the nobles.

bar·o·ny (bar′ə nē), *n., pl.* **-nies. 1.** the domain of a baron. **2.** baronage (def. 2). [1250–1300; ME *baronie* < AF, OF. See BARON, -Y[3]]

ba·roque (bə rōk′; *Fr.* bA RÔK′), *adj.* **1.** (*often cap.*) of or pertaining to a style of architecture and art originating in Italy in the early 17th century and variously prevalent in Europe and the New World for a century and a half, characterized by free and sculptural use of the classical orders and ornament, by forms in elevation and plan suggesting movement, and by dramatic effect in which architecture, painting, sculpture, and the decorative arts often worked to combined effect. **2.** (*sometimes cap.*) of or pertaining to the musical period following the Renaissance, extending roughly from 1600 to 1750. **3.** extravagantly ornate, florid, and convoluted in character or style: *the baroque prose of the novel's more lurid passages.* **4.** irregular in shape: *baroque pearls.* **—n. 5.** (*often cap.*) the baroque style or period. **6.** anything extravagantly ornamented, esp. something so ornate as to be in bad taste. **7.** an irregularly shaped pearl. [1755–65; < F < Pg *barroco, barroca* irregularly shaped pearl (of obscure orig.; cf. Sp *berrueco, barrueco* granitic crag, irregular pearl, spherical nodule), prob. conflated with ML *baroco* invented word for a kind of obfuscating syllogism]

baroque′ or′gan, a pipe organ dating from or built to the specifications of the baroque period at the time of J. S. Bach.

bar·o·re·cep·tor (bar′ō ri sep′tər), *n.* a nerve ending, as one of those located in the blood vessels, that responds to changes in pressure. [1950–55; BARO- + RECEPTOR]

bar·o·scope (bar′ə skōp′), *n.* an instrument showing roughly the variations in atmospheric pressure. [1655–65; BARO- + -SCOPE] **—bar·o·scop·ic** (bar′ə skop′ik), **bar′o·scop′i·cal,** *adj.*

bar·o·si·nus·i·tis (bar′ə sī′nə sī′tis), *n. Med.* aerosinusitis. [BARO- + SINUSITIS]

bar·o·switch (bar′ə swich′), *n.* a switch actuated by barometric pressure. Also called **barometric switch.** [BARO- + SWITCH]

bar·o·ther·mo·graph (bar′ə thûr′mə graf′, -gräf′), *n. Meteorol.* an automatic instrument for recording pressure and temperature. [1895–1900; BARO- + THERMOGRAPH]

bar·o·ther·mo·hy·gro·graph (bar′ə thûr′mə hī′grə graf′, -gräf′), *n. Meteorol.* an automatic instrument for recording pressure, temperature, and humidity. [BARO- + THERMO- + HYGROGRAPH]

bar·o·trau·ma (bar′ə trou′mə, -trô′-), *n., pl.* **-ma·ta** (-mə tə), **-mas.** *Pathol.* injury of certain organs, esp. the ear, due to a change in the atmospheric pressure. Cf. **aerotitis media.** [BARO- + TRAUMA]

bar·o·trop·ic (bar′ə trop′ik), *adj.* (of a fluid) having a density that is a function only of pressure. [BARO- + -TROPIC]

ba·rot·ro·py (bə ro′trə pē), *n. Meteorol.* a state of fluid stratification in which surfaces of constant pressure and others of constant density do not intersect but are parallel. Cf. **baroclinity.** [BARO- + -TROPY]

CONCISE ETYMOLOGY KEY: <, descended or borrowed from; >, whence; b., blend of, blended; c., cognate with; cf., compare; deriv., derivative; equiv., equivalent; imit., imitative; obl., oblique; r., replacing; s., stem; sp., spelling, spelled; resp., respelling, respelled; trans., translation; ?, origin unknown; *, unattested; ‡, probably earlier than. See the full key inside the front cover.

Ba·rot·se·land (bə rot′sə land′), *n.* a region in W Zambia. 410,087; 44,920 sq. mi. (116,343 sq. km).

ba·rouche (bə rōōsh′), *n.* a four-wheeled carriage with a high front seat outside for the driver, facing seats inside for two couples, and a calash top over the back seat. [1795–1805; < dial. G *Barutsche* < It *baroccio* < VL **birotium,* equiv. to LL *birot(us)* two-wheeled (see BI-[1], ROTA[1]) + *-ium* -IUM]

barouche

Ba·roz·zi (bä rôt′tsē), *n.* **Gia·co·mo** (jä′kô mô). See **Vignola, Giacomo da.**

bar′ pin′, a long, slender, decorative pin or brooch.

bar′ pit′, *Western U.S.* See **barrow pit.**

barque (bärk), *n.* bark[3].

bar·quen·tine (bär′kən tēn′), *n.* barkentine. Also, **bar′quan·tine′.**

bar·quette (bär ket′), *n.* a small, boat-shaped pastry shell filled with a savory or sweet mixture and served as an hors d'oeuvre or dessert. [< F; see BARQUE, -ETTE]

Bar·qui·si·me·to (bär′kē sē me′tô), *n.* a city in N Venezuela. 421,617.

barr., barrister.

bar·rack[1] (bar′ək), *n.* Usually, **barracks. 1.** a building or group of buildings for lodging soldiers, esp. in garrison. **2.** any large, plain building in which many people are lodged. **—v.t., v.i. 3.** to lodge in barracks. [1680–90; < F *baraque,* MF < Catalan *barraca* hut, of obscure orig.]

bar·rack[2] (bar′ək), *Australian, Brit.* **—v.i. 1.** to shout boisterously for or against a player or team; root or jeer. **—v.t. 2.** to shout for or against. [1885–90; orig. Australian E, perh. < N Ireland dial. *barrack* to BRAG] **—bar′·rack·er,** *n.*

Bar′rack-Room Bal′lads (bar′ək rōōm′, -rŏŏm′), a volume of poems (1892) by Rudyard Kipling, including *Gunga Din, Danny Deever,* and *Mandalay.*

bar′racks bag′, a large bag of heavy cotton, closed with a drawstring, used by military personnel for carrying personal belongings. [1940–45]

bar′racks law′yer, a member of the armed forces who speaks or acts like an authority on military law, regulations, and the rights of service personnel.

bar·ra·coon (bar′ə kōōn′), *n.* (formerly) a place of temporary confinement for slaves or convicts. [1850–55, *Amer.*; < Sp *barracón,* equiv. to *barrac(a)* hut (see BARRACK[1]) + *-on* aug. suffix]

bar·ra·cu·da (bar′ə kōō′də), *n., pl.* (*esp. collectively*) **-da,** (*esp. referring to two or more kinds or species*) **-das** for 1; **-das** for 2. **1.** any of several elongated, predaceous, tropical and subtropical marine fishes of the genus *Sphyraena,* certain species of which are used for food. **2.** *Slang.* a treacherous, greedy person. [1670–80; < AmerSp < ?]

great barracuda, *Sphyraena barracuda,* length 6 ft. (1.8 m)

bar·ra·cu·di·na (bar′ə kōōd′n ə), *n.* any of several slender, large-mouthed, pelagic fishes of the family Paralepididae. [< AmerSp, equiv. to *barracud(a)* BARRACUDA + *-ina* dim. suffix]

Bar·ra de São Fran·cis·co (bäR′Rä di souN′ fRäN-sēs′kōō), a city in SE Brazil, on the São Francisco River. 114,945.

bar·rage (bə räzh′; *esp. Brit.* bar′äzh *for 1, 2, 4, 5;* bär′ij *for 3*), *n., v.,* **-raged, -rag·ing. —n. 1.** *Mil.* a heavy barrier of artillery fire to protect one's own advancing or retreating troops or to stop the advance of enemy troops. **2.** an overwhelming quantity or explosion, as of words, blows, or criticisms: *a barrage of questions.* **3.** *Civ. Engin.* an artificial obstruction in a watercourse to increase the depth of the water, facilitate irrigation, etc. **4.** *Mycol.* an aversion response of sexually incompatible fungus cultures that are growing in proximity, revealed by a persistent growth gap between them. **—v.t. 5.** to subject to a barrage. [1855–60; < F: blocking, barring off, barrier, equiv. to *barr(er)* to BAR[1] + *-age* -AGE; artillery sense by ellipsis from F *tir de barrage* barrier fire]
—Syn. 2. volley, torrent, deluge, burst, storm.

barrage′ balloon′, a balloon or blimp, usually one of several anchored around a military area, city, etc., from which wires or nets are hung as a protection against attacks from low-flying aircraft. [1920–25]

bar·ra·mun·da (bar′ə mun′də), *n., pl.* **-das,** (*esp. collectively*) **-da.** a lungfish, *Neoceratodus forsteri,* of the rivers of Australia. [1870–75; of uncert. orig.]

bar·ra·mun·di (bar′ə mun′dē), *n., pl.* **-dis, -dies,** (*esp. collectively*) **-di.** barramunda.

bar·ran·ca (bə rang′kə; *Sp.* bäR RäNG′kä), *n., pl.* **-cas** (-kəz; *Sp.* -käs). **1.** a steep-walled ravine or gorge. **2.** a gully with steep sides; arroyo. [1685–95; < Sp, var. of *barranco,* of obscure, prob. pre-L orig.]

Bar·ran·ca·ber·me·ja (bäR RäNG′kä veR me′hä), *n.* a city in N Colombia. 106,100.

Bar·ran·qui·lla (bäR′Rän kē′yä), *n.* a seaport in N Colombia, on the Magdalena River. 661,920.

bar·ra·tor (bar′ə tər), *n. Law.* a person who commits barratry. Also, **bar′ra·ter, barretor.** [1350–1400; ME *barettour* brawler, fighter < AF *barretor, barator,* OF *barateor,* equiv. to *barat(er)* to make a disturbance, *baret(er)* to trick, cheat (< VL **prattāre* < Gk *prā́ttein* to do, perform, manage; see PRACTICAL) + *-eor* -ATOR]

bar·ra·try (bar′ə trē), *n. Law.* **1.** fraud by a master or crew at the expense of the owners of the ship or its cargo. **2.** the offense of frequently stirring up lawsuits and quarrels. **3.** the purchase or sale of ecclesiastical preferments or of offices of state. Also, **barretry.** [1400–50; late ME *barratrie* < AF, MF *baraterie* combat, fighting. See BARRATOR, -ERY] **—bar′ra·trous,** *adj.*

Bar·rault (bA RŌ′), *n.* **Jean-Louis** (zhäN lwē′), born 1910, French actor and director.

Barr′ bod′y (bär), a condensed, inactivated X chromosome present in most female mammals in the nuclei of all cells except the germ cells: used, as in sports competitions, to verify that an individual is genetically female. Also called **sex chromatin.** [1960–65; after Murray L. Barr (born 1908), Canadian physician]

barre (bär), *n. Ballet.* a handrail placed at hip height, used by a dancer to maintain balance during practice. Also, **bar.** [1945–50]

bar·ré (bä rā′), *n. Textiles.* **1.** a pattern of stripes or bands of color extending across the warp in woven and knitted fabrics. **2.** a streak in the filling direction when one or more picks are of a color different from that of adjacent picks. [< F: lit., barred, ptp. of *barrer,* deriv. of *barre* BAR[1]]

barred (bärd), *adj.* **1.** provided with one or more bars: *a barred prison window.* **2.** striped; streaked: *barred fabrics.* **3.** *Ornith.* (of feathers) marked with transverse bands of distinctive color. [1300–50; ME; see BAR[1], -ED[3]]

barred i, *Phonet.* **1.** a high central vowel with phonetic quality approximating that of the vowels in *pit, put, putt,* or *pet,* and considered by most phonologists as a phonetic variant of one of these vowels, depending on the context, but by some as an autonomous phoneme in some varieties of English. **2.** the phonetic symbol ɨ.

barred′ owl′, a large owl, *Strix varia,* of eastern North America, having its breast barred and abdomen streaked with dark brown. [1805–15, *Amer.*]

barred′ spi′ral gal′axy, *Astron.* a spiral galaxy whose center has the form of an extended bar.

bar·rel (bar′əl), *n., v.,* **-reled, -rel·ing** or (*esp. Brit.*) **-relled, -rel·ling. —n. 1.** a cylindrical wooden container with slightly bulging sides made of staves hooped together, and with flat, parallel ends. **2.** the quantity that such a vessel of some standard size can hold: for most liquids, 31½ U.S. gallons (119 L); for petroleum, 42 U.S. gallons (159 L); for dry materials, 105 U.S. dry quarts (115 L). *Abbr.:* bbl **3.** any large quantity: *a barrel of fun.* **4.** any container, case, or part similar to a wooden barrel in form. **5.** *Ordn.* the tube of a gun. **6.** *Mach.* the chamber of a pump in which the piston works. **7.** a drum turning on a shaft, as in a weight-driven clock. **8.** *Horol.* the cylindrical case in a watch or clock within which the mainspring is coiled. **9.** *Ornith. Obs.* a calamus or quill. **10.** the trunk of a quadruped, esp. of a horse, cow, etc. **11.** *Naut.* the main portion of a capstan, about which the rope winds, between the drumhead at the top and the pawl rim at the bottom. **12.** a rotating horizontal cylinder in which manufactured objects are coated or polished by tumbling in a suitable substance. **13.** any structure having the form of a barrel vault. **14.** Also called **throat.** *Auto.* a passageway in a carburetor that has the shape of a Venturi tube. **15. over a barrel,** *Informal.* in a helpless, weak, or awkward position; unable to act: *They really had us over a barrel when they foreclosed the mortgage.* **—v.t. 16.** to put or pack in a barrel or barrels. **17.** to finish (metal parts) by tumbling in a barrel. **18.** *Informal.* to force to go or proceed at high speed: *He barreled his car through the dense traffic.* **—v.i. 19.** *Informal.* to travel or drive very fast: *to barrel along the highway.* [1250–1300; ME *barell* < AF *baril,* OF *barril* < VL **barrīculum,* equiv. to **barrīc(a),* perh. deriv. of LL *barra* BAR[1] + L *-ulum* -ULE; cf. ML (ca. 800) *barriclus* small cask]

bar·rel·age (bar′ə lij), *n.* the amount contained in barrels. [1885–90; BARREL + -AGE]

bar·rel-ass (bar′əl as′), *v.i. Slang (vulgar).* to charge headlong; move at high speed. [1955–60]

bar′rel bolt′, a rod-shaped bolt for fastening a door or the like, attached to one side of the door at the edge and sliding into a socket on the frame of the opening. Also called **tower bolt.** [1850–55]

bar′rel cac′tus, any of several large, cylindrical, ribbed, spiny cacti of the genera *Echinocactus* and *Ferocactus.* [1880–85, *Amer.*]

bar′rel chair′, *U.S. Furniture.* an easy chair having a high, semicircular back forming a single upholstered piece with the wings or arms; tub chair. Also called **bar′·rel-back chair′** (bar′əl bak′). [1840–50, *Amer.*]

bar·rel-chest·ed (bar′əl ches′tid), *adj.* having a broad, prominent chest or thorax. [1960–65]

bar′rel cuff′, a single cuff on a tailored sleeve, formed by a band of material and usually fastened by a button.

bar′rel distor′tion, *Optics.* a distortion produced by a lens in which the magnification decreases toward the edge of the field. Cf. **pincushion distortion.** [1885–90]

bar′rel en′gine, an engine having cylinders arranged around and parallel to a shaft, which they rotate by means of the contact of their piston rods with a swash plate or cam on the shaft.

bar•rel•eye (bar′əl ī′), *n., pl.* **-eyes.** any of the bathypelagic fishes of the family Opisthoproctidae, esp. *Macropinna microstoma,* having telescoping eyes. [BARREL + EYE]

bar•rel•fish (bar′əl fish′), *n., pl.* **-fish•es,** (*esp. collectively*) **-fish.** a blackish stromateid fish, *Hyperoglyphe perciformis,* inhabiting New England coastal waters. Also called **black rudderfish.** [1880–85; BARREL + FISH]

bar•rel•ful (bar′əl fo͝ol′), *n., pl.* **-fuls. 1.** the amount that a barrel can hold. **2.** any large quantity: *a barrelful of jokes.* [1350–1400; ME; see BARREL, -FUL]
—Usage. See **-ful.**

bar•rel•head (bar′əl hed′), *n.* **1.** either of the round, flat sections that form the top and bottom of a barrel. **2. on the barrelhead,** in advance or on demand: *They won't deliver the merchandise unless we pay cash on the barrelhead.* [1830–40; BARREL + HEAD]

bar•rel•house (bar′əl hous′), *n., pl.* **-hous•es** (-hou′ziz) for 1. **1.** a cheap saloon, esp. one in New Orleans in the early part of the 20th century: so called from the racks of liquor barrels originally placed along the walls. **2.** a vigorous style of jazz originating in the barrelhouses of New Orleans in the early part of the 20th century. [1880–85, *Amer.*; BARREL + HOUSE]

bar′rel knot′, *Angling.* a knot for fastening together two strands of gut or nylon, as fishing lines or leaders. Also called **blood knot.**

bar′rel or′gan, a musical instrument in which air from a bellows enters a set of pipes by means of pins inserted into a revolving barrel; hand organ. [1765–75]

bar′rel race′, a rodeo event, usually for women, in which a horse and rider must race in a zigzag pattern around three barrels, competing for the fastest time. **—bar′rel rac′ing.**

bar•rel-race (bar′əl rās′), *v.i.,* **-raced, -rac•ing.** to compete in a barrel race. **—bar′rel-rac′er,** *n.*

bar′rel roll′, *Aeron.* a maneuver in which an airplane executes a complete roll by revolving once around its longitudinal axis. [1930–35]

bar•rel-roll (bar′əl rōl′), *v.i. Aeron.* to perform a barrel roll. [1925–30]

bar′rel roof′, 1. a roof or ceiling having a semicylindrical form. **2.** See **barrel vault.**

bar′rel vault′, *Archit.* a vault having the form of a very deep arch. Also called **barrel roof, cradle vault, tunnel vault, wagon roof, wagon vault.** See illus. under **vault.** [1840–50] **—bar′rel-vault′ed,** *adj.*

bar•ren (bar′ən), *adj.* **1.** not producing or incapable of producing offspring; sterile: *a barren woman.* **2.** unproductive; unfruitful: *barren land.* **3.** without capacity to interest or attract: *a barren period in American architecture.* **4.** mentally unproductive; dull; stupid. **5.** not producing results; fruitless: *a barren effort.* **6.** destitute; bereft; lacking (usually fol. by *of*): *barren of tender feelings.* —*n.* **7.** Usually, **barrens.** level or slightly rolling land, usually with a sandy soil and few trees, and relatively infertile. [1200–50; ME *bareyn(e), barayn(e)* < AF *barai(gn)e,* OF *brahaigne* (F *bréhaigne* (of animals) sterile), akin to Sp *breña* scrubby, uncultivated ground, Upper It *barena* land along a lagoon covered by high water; appar < Celtic, cf. Welsh *braenar,* Ir *branar* fallow land, but derivational details unclear] **—bar′ren•ly,** *adv.* **—bar′ren•ness,** *n.*
—Syn. 1. childless, unprolific, infertile. **2.** infertile, depleted, waste. See **bare**[1]. **5.** ineffectual, ineffective.
—Ant. 1–6. fertile.

bar′ren ground′ car′ibou, a migrating caribou of the North American tundra and taiga, having many-branched slender antlers. Also, **Bar′ren Ground′ car′ibou.** [1820–30]

Bar′ren Grounds′, a sparsely inhabited region of tundra in N Canada, esp. in the area W of Hudson Bay. Also called **Bar′ren Lands′.**

bar′ren straw′berry, a low-growing plant, *Waldsteinia fragarioides,* of the rose family, native to north temperate regions, having long stalks with three toothed leaflets and yellow flowers. [1890–95, *Amer.*; so called because the fruit is dry and inedible]

bar•re•ra (bə râr′ə; *Sp.* bär ʀe′rä), *n., pl.* **-re•ras** (-râr′əz; *Sp.* -ʀe′ʀäs). **1.** the wall, usually a red wooden fence, bordering a bullring. **2.** the first row of seats in a bullfight arena. [1920–25; < Sp: barrier, equiv. to *barr(a)* BAR[1] + *-era* << L *-āria* -ARY]

Bar•rès (bᴀ res′), *n.* **Mau•rice** (mō rēs′), 1862–1923, French novelist, writer on politics, and politician.

bar•ret (bar′it), *n.* a small cap, akin to the biretta, worn in the Middle Ages by soldiers and ecclesiastics. [1820–30; < F *barrette,* MF < dial. It *barretta* (It *berretta*) BIRETTA]

bar•re•tor (bar′i tər), *n. Law.* barrator.

bar•re•try (bar′i trē), *n. Law.* barratry.

Bar•rett (bar′it), *n.* **Elizabeth.** See **Browning, Elizabeth Barrett.**

bar•rette (bə ret′), *n.* a clasp for holding a woman's or girl's hair in place. [1900–05; < F; see BAR[1], -ETTE]

bar•ret•ter (bar′et ər, bə ret′-), *n. Electronics.* a form of detector or control device employing a resistor that varies in proportion to its temperature. [1900–05; of uncert. orig.; supposed connection with BARRATOR is unclear]

bar•ri•a•da (bär′ē ä′də, bar′-; *Sp.* bäʀ ʀyä′ᵺä), *n., pl.* **-das** (-dəz; *Sp.* -ᵺäs). a shantytown section on the outskirts of a large city in Latin America. [< AmerSp; Sp: district, quarter, equiv. to *barri(o)* BARRIO + *-ada* -ADE[1]]

bar•ri•cade (bar′i kād′, bar′i kād′), *n., v.,* **-cad•ed, -cad•ing.** —*n.* **1.** a defensive barrier hastily constructed, as in a street, to stop an enemy. **2.** any barrier that obstructs passage. —*v.t.* **3.** to obstruct or block with a barricade: *barricading the streets to prevent an attack.* **4.** to shut in and defend with or as if with a barricade: *The rebels had barricaded themselves in the old city.* [1585–95; < F, equiv. to *barrique* BARREL (< Gascon) + *-ade* -ADE[1]; early barricades in Paris were often composed of barrels] **—bar′ri•cad′er,** *n.*
—Syn. 1. See **bar**[1]. **4.** fortify.

bar•ri•ca•do (bar′i kā′dō), *n., pl.* **-does, -dos,** *v.,* **-doed, -do•ing.** *Archaic.* —*n.* **1.** a barricade. —*v.t.* **2.** to barricade. [1580–90; a pseudo-Sp form of BARRICADE]

Bar•rie (bar′ē), *n.* **1. Sir James M(atthew),** 1860–1937, Scottish novelist, short-story writer, and playwright. **2.** a city in SE Ontario, in S Canada, NW of Toronto. 38,423.

bar•ri•er (bar′ē ər), *n.* **1.** anything built or serving to bar passage, as a railing, fence, or the like: *People may pass through the barrier only when their train is announced.* **2.** any natural bar or obstacle: *a mountain barrier.* **3.** anything that restrains or obstructs progress, access, etc.: *a trade barrier.* **4.** a limit or boundary of any kind: *the barriers of caste.* **5.** *Physical Geog.* an antarctic ice shelf or ice front. **6.** See **barrier beach. 7. barriers,** *Hist.* the palisade or railing surrounding the ground where tourneys and jousts were carried on. **8.** *Archaic.* a fortress or stockade. [1275–1325; ME < MF *barriere* (*barre* BAR[1] + *-iere* < L *-āria* -ARY); r. ME *barrere* < AF < ML *barrera*]
—Syn. 1. palisade, wall. **1–3.** obstruction, hindrance, impediment. See **bar**[1].

bar′rier beach′, a sand ridge that rises slightly above the surface of the sea and runs roughly parallel to the shore, from which it is separated by a lagoon.

bar′rier is′land, a broadened barrier beach, habitable in places, that provides a measure of protection for the mainland, as during hurricanes and tidal waves.

bar′rier reef′, a reef of coral running roughly parallel to the shore and separated from it by a wide, deep lagoon. [1795–1805]

Bar′rier Reef′. See **Great Barrier Reef.**

bar•ring (bär′ing), *prep.* excepting; except for: *Barring accidents, I'll be there.* [1475–85; BAR[1] + -ING[2]]

Bar•ring•ton (bar′ing tən), *n.* a town in E Rhode Island. 16,174.

bar•ri•o (bär′ē ō′, bar′-; *Sp.* bäʀ′ʀyô), *n., pl.* **bar•ri•os** (bär′ē ōz′, bar′-; *Sp.* bäʀ′ʀyôs). **1.** (in Spain and countries colonized by Spain) one of the divisions into which a town or city, together with the contiguous rural territory, is divided. **2.** a part of a large U.S. city, esp. a crowded inner-city area, inhabited chiefly by a Spanish-speaking population. [1890–95; < Sp < Ar *barrī* of open country (*barr* outside, open country + *-ī* adj. suffix)]

Bar•rios (bäʀ′ʀyôs), *n.* **Jus•to Ru•fi•no** (ho͞o′stô ʀo͞o-fē′nô), 1835–85, Guatemalan statesman: president of Guatemala 1873–85.

bar•ris•ter (bar′ə stər), *n. Law.* **1.** (in England) a lawyer who is a member of one of the Inns of Court and who has the privilege of pleading in the higher courts. Cf. **solicitor** (def. 4). **2.** *Informal.* any lawyer. [1535–45; deriv. of BAR[1], perh. after obs. *legister* lawyer or MINISTER] **—bar•ris•te•ri•al** (bar′ə stēr′ē əl), *adj.*

Bar•ron (bar′ən), *n.* **Clarence Walker,** 1855–1928, U.S. financial publisher.

bar•room (bär′ro͞om′, -ro͝om′), *n.* an establishment or room with a bar for the serving of alcoholic beverages. [1790–1800, *Amer.*; BAR[1] + ROOM]

bar′room plant′, aspidistra.

Bar•ros (bäʀ′ro͞osh), **João de** (zhwouɴ də), (*"the Portuguese Livy"*), 1496–1570, Portuguese historian.

bar•row[1] (bar′ō), *n.* **1.** a flat, rectangular frame used for carrying a load, esp. such a frame with projecting shafts at each end for handles; handbarrow. **2.** a wheelbarrow. **3.** *Brit.* a pushcart used by street vendors, esp. by costermongers. [bef. 1000; ME *bar(e)we,* OE *bearwe;* akin to MHG *bere,* BIER, BEAR[1]]

bar•row[2] (bar′ō), *n.* **1.** *Archaeol.* tumulus (def. 1). **2.** *Chiefly Brit.* a hill (sometimes used in combination): *Trentishoe Barrow in North Devon; Whitbarrow in North Lancashire.* [bef. 900; ME *berw, beruh, bargh, berg(h),* OE *beorg* hill, mound; c. OFris, OS, D, OHG *berg* mountain, ON *bjarg, berg* cliff, Armenian *berdz* height, Welsh *bera* heap; akin to Avestan *bərəz-, bərəzant-,* Skt *bṛhánt-* high. See BOROUGH]

bar•row[3] (bar′ō), *n.* a castrated male swine. [bef. 1000; ME *barowe, baru,* OE *bearg;* c. OHG *barug,* ON *bǫrgr.* Cf. BORE[1], whose meaning is close to the semantics of cutting or splitting (referring to castration)]

Bar•row (bar′ō), *n.* **1.** Also called **Bar•row-in-Fur•ness** (bar′ō in fûr′nis). a seaport in Cumbria, in NW England. 73,900. **2. Point,** the N tip of Alaska: the northernmost point of the U.S. **3.** a town in N Alaska, S of Barrow Point: site of a government science-research center. 2207.

bar•row-boy (bar′ō boi′), *n. Brit.* a man or boy who sells wares from a barrow; costermonger. [1935–40]

bar′row pit′, *Western U.S.* a roadside borrow pit dug for drainage purposes. Also called **bar pit, bar ditch.** [appar. in reference to the mound of earth dug from the pit (see BARROW[2]); vars. with *bar* perh. from regional pron. of *barrow*]

Bar′row's gol′deneye. See under **goldeneye** (def. 1). [after Sir John *Barrow* (1764–1848), British traveler and secretary of the admiralty]

Bar•ry (bar′ē), *n.* **1. Sir Charles,** 1795–1860, English architect. **2. John,** 1745–1803, American naval commander in the Revolution. **3. Leonora Marie Kearney** (*"Mother Lake"*), 1849–1930, U.S. labor leader and social activist, born in Ireland. **4. Philip,** 1896–1949, U.S. playwright. **5.** a male given name: from an Irish word meaning "spear."

Bar•ry•more (bar′ə môr′, -mōr′), *n.* **1. Maurice** (*Herbert Blythe*), 1847–1905, U.S. and English actor, born in India. **2.** his children: **Ethel,** 1879–1959, **John,** 1882–1942, and **Lionel,** 1878–1954, U.S. actors.

Bar•sac (bär′sak; *Fr.* bᴀʀ sᴀk′), *n.* **1.** a village and winegrowing district in Gironde, in SW France. **2.** a sweet, white Sauterne from here.

bar′ sin′ister, 1. *Heraldry.* (not in technical use) a bend sinister or a baton. **2.** the proof, condition, or stigma of illegitimate birth. [1815–25]

bar•spoon (bär′spo͞on′), *n.* a long-handled spoon, usually having the capacity of a teaspoon, used for mixing or measuring ingredients for alcoholic drinks. [BAR[1] + SPOON]

bar•stool (bär′sto͞ol′), *n.* a stool or seat, usually high and having a round, cushioned top, of a type often used for seating customers at a bar. [BAR[1] + STOOL]

Bar•stow (bär′stō), *n.* a city in S California. 17,690.

bar′ syr′up. See **simple syrup** (def. 1).

Bart (bärt), *n.* a male given name, form of **Bartholomew, Bartlett,** or **Bartram.**

Bart., Baronet.

bar′ tack′, a close series of stitches crossing a piece of cloth, as in an article of clothing, in order to reinforce it at a point of concentrated strain. [1950–55]

bar-tack (bär′tak′), *v.t., v.i.* to sew or reinforce with bar tack. [1950–55]

bar•tend (bär′tend′), *v.i.* to serve or work as a bartender. [back formation from BARTENDER]

bar•tend•er (bär′ten′dər), *n.* a person who mixes and serves alcoholic drinks at a bar. [1830–40, *Amer.*; BAR[1] + TENDER[3]]

bar•ter (bär′tər), *v.i.* **1.** to trade by exchange of commodities rather than by the use of money. —*v.t.* **2.** to exchange in trade, as one commodity for another. **3.** to bargain away unwisely or dishonorably (usually fol. by *away*): *bartering away his pride for material gain.* —*n.* **4.** the act or practice of bartering. **5.** items or an item for bartering: *We arrived with new barter for the villagers.* [1400–50; late ME, appar. < AF, OF *bareter, barater* (see BARRATOR), with shift of sense] **—bar′ter•er,** *n.*
—Syn. 1, 2. traffic. See **trade.**

Bar′tered Bride′, The, a comic opera (1866) by Bedřich Smetana.

Barth (bärth *for 1;* bärt, bärth *for 2*), *n.* **1. John (Simmons)** (sim′ənz), born 1930, U.S. novelist. **2. Karl,** 1886–1968, Swiss theologian.

Bar•thé (bär tā′), *n.* **Richmond,** born 1901, U.S. sculptor.

Barth•i•an (bär′tē ən, -thē-), *adj.* **1.** of or pertaining to Karl Barth or his theology. —*n.* **2.** a supporter or adherent of Karl Barth or his theology. [1925–30; BARTH + -IAN]

Barth•i•an•ism (bär′tē ə niz′əm, -thē-), *n.* the theological doctrines and principles of Karl Barth and his followers, esp. in reference to neoorthodoxy. [1930–35; BARTHIAN + -ISM]

Bar•thol•di (bär thol′dē, -tol′-; *Fr.* bᴀʀ tôl dē′), *n.* **Fré•dé•ric Au•guste** (fʀā dā ʀēk′ ō gʏst′), 1834–1904, French sculptor who designed the Statue of Liberty.

Bar•tho′lin's gland′ (bär tō′linz, bär′tl inz), *Anat.* either of two small, oval, mucus-secreting glands, one on each side of the base of the vagina. [1920–25; named after Caspar *Bartholin* (1655–1738), Danish anatomist, who described them in 1637]

Bar•thol•o•mew (bär thol′ə myo͞o′), *n.* **1.** one of the 12 apostles: sometimes called Nathanael. Mark 3:18. **2.** a male given name: from a Hebrew word meaning "son of Talmai."

Bartholomew I, (*Dimitrios Archontonis*), born 1940, Archbishop of Constantinople and Ecumenical Patriarch of the Eastern Orthodox Church since 1991.

Bar•thou (bᴀʀ to͞o′), *n.* **(Jean) Louis** (zhäɴ lwē), 1862–1934, French statesman and author.

Bar•ti•ca (bär tē′kə), *n.* a town in N Guyana, on the Essequibo River: river transportation center. 2352.

bar•ti•zan (bär′tə zən, bär′tə zan′), *n. Archit.* a small overhanging turret on a wall or tower. [1325–75; ME alter. of *bertisene,* misspelling of *bretising,* var. of *bratticing.* See BRATTICE, -ING[1]] **—bar•ti•zaned** (bär′tə-zənd, bär′tə zand′), *adj.*

bartizan

Bar•tles•ville (bär′tlz vil′), *n.* a city in NE Oklahoma. 34,568.

Bart•lett (bärt′lit), *n. Hort.* a large, yellow, juicy variety of pear. Also called **Bart′lett pear′.** [1825–35, *Amer.*; so named by Enoch *Bartlett* of Dorchester, Mass.]

Bart•lett (bärt′lit), *n.* **1. John,** 1820–1905, U.S. publisher: compiled *Familiar Quotations.* **2. John Russell,** 1805–86, U.S. editor and bibliographer of early Americana. **3. Josiah,** 1729–95, U.S. physician and statesman. **4. Paul Wayland,** 1865–1925, U.S. sculptor. **5. Robert Abram,** 1875–1946, U.S. arctic explorer, born in Newfoundland. **6. Vernon,** born 1894, English writer. **7.** a

CONCISE PRONUNCIATION KEY: act, cāpe, dâre, pärt; set, ēqual; if, ice; ox, ōver, ôrder, oil, bo͝ok, bo͞ot, out; up, ûrge; child; sing; shoe; thin, that; zh as in *treasure.* ə = *a* as in *alone, e* as in *system, i* as in *easily, o* as in *gallop, u* as in *circus;* ᵊ as in *fire* (fīᵊr), *hour* (ouᵊr). l and n can serve as syllabic consonants, as in *cradle* (krād′l), and *button* (but′n). See the full key inside the front cover.

town in SW Tennessee. 17,170. **8.** a town in NE Illinois. 13,254. **9.** a male given name, form of **Bartholomew.**

Bar·tók (bär′tok, -tôk; *Hung.* bôʀ′tōk), *n.* **Bé·la** (bā′lə; *Hung.* bā′lo), 1881–1945, Hungarian composer.

Bar·tok·i·an (bär tok′ē ən, -tô′kē-), *adj.* characteristic of the music of Béla Bartók: *driving, percussive, Bartokian rhythm.* [Béla BARTÓK + -IAN]

Bar·to·lom·me·o (bär tol′ə mā′ō; *It.* bäʀ′tô lôm me′ô), *n.* **Fra** (frä; *It.* fʀä), (*Baccio della Porta*), 1475–1517, Italian painter.

Bar·to·loz·zi (bäʀ′tô lôt′tsē), *n.* **Fran·ces·co** (fʀän ches′kô), 1725?–1815?, Italian engraver.

Bar·ton (bär′tn), *n.* **1. Clara,** 1821–1912, U.S. philanthropist who organized the American Red Cross in 1881. **2. Derek H(arold) R(ichard),** born 1918, English chemist: Nobel prize 1969. **3. Sir Edmund,** 1849–1920, Australian jurist and statesman: prime minister 1901–03. **4.** a male given name.

Bar·tow (bär′tō), *n.* a city in central Florida. 14,780.

Bar·tram (bär′trəm), *n.* **1. John,** 1699–1777, U.S. botanist. **2.** a male given name.

Bar·tra′mi·an sand′piper (bär trā′mē ən). See **upland sandpiper.** [1805–15, *Amer.*; named after John BARTRAM; see -IAN]

Bar·uch (bâr′ək *for 1;* bə ro͞ok′ *for 2, 3*), *n.* **1.** the amanuensis and friend of Jeremiah and nominal author of the book of Baruch in the Apocrypha. Jer. 32:12. **2. Bernard Man·nes** (man′əs), 1870–1965, U.S. statesman and financier. **3.** a male given name.

Ba·ru·ta (bä ʀo͞o′tä), *n.* a city in N Venezuela: a suburb of Caracas. 121,066.

bar·ware (bär′wâr′), *n.* glassware and other items for preparing and serving alcoholic drinks. [1940–45; BAR[1] + WARE[1]]

bar·wise (bär′wīz′), *adj. Heraldry.* (of a charge or charges) transversely across an escutcheon, in the manner of a bar. Also, **bar·ways** (bär′wāz′). [BAR[1] + -WISE]

bar·y·cen′tric coor′dinate sys′tem (bar′ə sen′trik), *Math.* a coordinate system for an *n*-dimensional Euclidean space in which each point is represented by *n* constants whose sum is 1 and whose product with a given set of linearly independent points equals the point. [< Gk *bary(s)* heavy + -CENTRIC]

bar·ye (bar′ē), *n.* microbar. [< F < Gk *barys* heavy]

Ba·rye (bA ʀē′), *n.* **An·toine Louis** (äN twAN′ lwē), 1795–1875, French sculptor and painter.

bar·y·on (bar′ē on′), *n. Physics.* a proton, neutron, or any elementary particle that decays into a set of particles that includes a proton. Cf. **quark model.** [1950–55; < Gk *bary(s)* heavy + (FERMI)ON] —**bar·y·on·ic** (bar′ē-on′ik), *adj.*

bar′yon num′ber, *Physics.* a quantum number assigned to elementary particles, baryons having baryon number 1, antibaryons −1, and all other observable particles 0; quarks have baryon number ⅓ and antiquarks −⅓. Cf. **conservation of baryon number.**

Ba·rysh·ni·kov (bə rish′ni kôf′, -kof′; *Russ.* bu ʀish′nyi kəf), *n.* **Mi·kha·il** (mi käl′; *Russ.* myi KHU yēl′), born 1948, Soviet ballet dancer, in the U.S. since 1974.

ba·ry·ta (bə rī′tə), *n. Chem.* **1.** Also called **calcined baryta, barium oxide, barium monoxide, barium protoxide.** a white or yellowish-white poisonous solid, BaO, highly reactive with water: used chiefly as a dehydrating agent and in the manufacture of glass. **2.** Also called **caustic baryta, barium hydroxide, barium hydrate.** the hydroxide, hydrated form of this compound, $Ba(OH)_2 \cdot 8H_2O$, used chiefly in the industrial preparation of beet sugar and for refining animal and vegetable oils. [1800–10; < NL, equiv. to *bary-* (< Gk *barys* heavy) + *-ta* (< Gk *-(i)tēs* -ITE[1])] —**ba·ryt·ic** (bə rit′ik), *adj.*

bary′ta wa′ter, *Chem.* an aqueous solution of barium hydroxide, used chiefly as a reagent. [1875–80]

ba·ry·tes (bə rī′tēz), *n. Mineral.* barite. [1780–90; see BARYTA]

ba·ry·to·cal·cite (bə rī′tə kal′sīt), *n.* a mineral, double carbonate of calcium and barium, $CaCO_3 \cdot BaCO_3$, usually found in veins of lead minerals. [BARYT(A) + -O- + CALCITE]

bar·y·ton (bar′i ton′; *Fr.* bA ʀē tôN′), *n., pl.* **-tons** (-tonz′; *Fr.* -tôN′). an 18th-century stringed instrument with six bowed strings and several additional strings that vibrate sympathetically. [< F; see BARITONE]

bar·y·tone[1] (bar′i tōn′), *n., adj. Music.* baritone.

bar·y·tone[2] (bar′i tōn′), *Classical Gk. Gram.* —*adj.* **1.** having the last syllable unaccented. —*n.* **2.** a barytone word. [1820–30; < Gk *barýtonos,* equiv. to *bary(s)* heavy, deep (of sound) + *tónos* TONE]

Bar·zun (bär′zun), *n.* **Jacques (Martin),** born 1907, U.S. historian, educator, and writer, born in France.

B.A.S., **1.** Bachelor of Agricultural Science. **2.** Bachelor of Applied Science.

ba·sad (bā′sad), *adv.* toward the base. [BASE[1] + -AD[3]]

ba·sal (bā′səl, -zəl), *adj.* **1.** of, at, or forming the base. **2.** forming a basis; fundamental; basic. **3.** *Physiol.* **a.** indicating a standard low level of activity of an organism, as during total rest. **b.** of an amount required to maintain this level. **4.** *Med.* serving to induce a preliminary or light anesthesia prior to total anesthetization. **5.** used in elementary instruction; fundamental: *a basal reader.* [1820–30; BASE[1] + -AL[1]] —**ba′sal·ly,** *adv.*

ba′sal bod′y, *Cell Biol.* a cylindrical organelle, within the cytoplasm of flagellated and ciliated cells, that contains microtubules and forms the base of a flagellum or cilium: identical in internal structure to a centriole. [1900–05]

CONCISE ETYMOLOGY KEY: <, descended or borrowed from; >, whence; b., blend of, blended; c., cognate with; cf., compare; deriv., derivative; equiv., equivalent; imit., imitative; obl., oblique; r., replacing; s., stem; sp., spelling, spelled; resp., respelling, respelled; trans., translation; ?, origin unknown; *, unattested; ‡, probably earlier than. See the full key inside the front cover.

ba′sal cell′, *Cell Biol.* any cell situated at the base of a multilayered tissue, as at the lowest layer of the epidermis. [1925–30]

ba′sal cell′ carcino′ma, a common and usually curable skin cancer that arises from epithelial cells and rarely metastasizes: often associated with overexposure to sunlight.

ba′sal conglom′erate, a conglomerate deposited on an erosion surface and constituting the bottom layer of a stratigraphic series. [1895–1900]

ba′sal disk′, *Anat.* the flattened basal surface by which coelenterate polyps attach to the substrate. Also called **pedal disk.**

ba′sal gang′lion, *Anat.* any of several masses of gray matter in each cerebral hemisphere. [1910–15]

ba′sal metabol′ic rate′, *Physiol.* the rate at which energy is expended in a basal condition, calculated as calories per hour per square meter of body surface and compared with a normal standard expressed as the percentage above or below the amount of oxygen normally used at rest, −15 to +5 percent being considered normal. *Abbr.:* BMR [1920–25]

ba′sal metab′olism, *Physiol.* the minimal amount of energy necessary to maintain respiration, circulation, and other vital body functions while fasting and at total rest. [1910–15]

ba′sal ridge′, *Dentistry.* a U-shaped ridge at the base of the posterior surface of the crown of a tooth. Also called **cingulum.**

ba·salt (bə sôlt′, bas′ôlt, bā′sôlt), *n.* the dark, dense igneous rock of a lava flow or minor intrusion, composed essentially of labradorite and pyroxene and often displaying a columnar structure. [1595–1605; < L *basaltēs,* a misreading, in mss. of Pliny, of *basanītēs* < Gk *basanī́tēs (líthos)* touchstone, equiv. to *básan(os)* touchstone (ult. < Egyptian *bḫn(w)* graywacke) + *-ītēs* -ITE[1]] —**ba·sal′tic, ba·sal·tine** (bə sôl′tin, -tīn), *adj.*

ba·salt·ware (bə sôlt′wâr′, bas′ôlt-, bā′sôlt-), *n.* a type of unglazed stoneware, usually black with a dull gloss, developed by Josiah Wedgwood. Also called **ba·sal·tes** (bə sôl′tēz). [BASALT + WARE[1]]

bas·a·nite (bas′ə nīt′, baz′-), *n. Petrog.* a basaltic rock composed chiefly of plagioclase, olivine, and augite. [1745–55; < L *basanītēs;* see BASALT]

B.A.Sc., **1.** Bachelor of Agricultural Science. **2.** Bachelor of Applied Science.

bas·cule (bas′kyo͞ol), *n. Civ. Engin.* a device operating like a balance or seesaw, esp. an arrangement of a movable bridge (**bas′cule bridge′**) by which the rising floor or section is counterbalanced by a weight. [1670–80; F: name for a number of seesawlike mechanical devices, MF *bacule,* n. deriv. of *baculer* to strike on the buttocks (prob. orig., to land on one's buttocks), equiv. to *bas* down (see BASE[2]) + *-culer,* v. deriv. of *cul* rump, buttocks (see CULET); *-s-* by false analysis as *bas(se)* adj. + *cule* taken as a fem. n.]

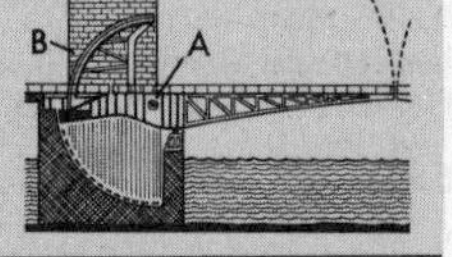

bascule bridge
A, pivot about which bridge swings in rising; B, toothed quadrant engaging with machinery

base[1] (bās), *n., adj., v.,* **based, bas·ing.** —*n.* **1.** the bottom support of anything; that on which a thing stands or rests: *a metal base for the table.* **2.** a fundamental principle or groundwork; foundation; basis: *the base of needed reforms.* **3.** the bottom layer or coating, as of makeup or paint. **4.** *Archit.* **a.** the distinctively treated portion of a column or pier below the shaft or shafts. See diag. under **column. b.** the distinctively treated lowermost portion of any construction, as a monument, exterior wall, etc. **5.** *Bot., Zool.* **a.** the part of an organ nearest its point of attachment. **b.** the point of attachment. **6.** the principal element or ingredient of anything, considered as its fundamental part: *face cream with a lanolin base; paint with a lead base.* **7.** that from which a commencement, as of action or reckoning, is made; a starting point or point of departure. **8.** *Baseball.* **a.** any of the four corners of the diamond, esp. first, second, or third base. Cf. **home plate. b.** a square canvas sack containing sawdust or some other light material, for marking first, second, or third base. **9.** a starting line or point for runners, racing cars, etc. **10.** (in hockey and other games) the goal. **11.** *Mil.* **a.** a fortified or more or less protected area or place from which the operations of an army or an air force proceed. **b.** a supply installation for a large military force. **12.** *Geom.* the line or surface forming the part of a figure that is most nearly horizontal or on which it is supposed to stand. **13.** *Math.* **a.** the number that serves as a starting point for a logarithmic or other numerical system. **b.** a collection of subsets of a topological space having the property that every open set in the given topology can be written as the union of sets of the collection. **c.** a collection of neighborhoods of a point such that every neighborhood of the point contains one from the collection. **d.** a collection of sets of a given filter such that every set in the filter is contained in some set in the collection. **14.** Also called **base line.** *Survey.* See under **triangulation** (def. 1). **15.** *Painting.* **a.** vehicle (def. 10). **b.** Also called **carrier.** inert matter, used in the preparation of lakes, onto which a coloring compound is precipitated. **16.** *Photog.* a thin, flexible layer of cellulose triacetate or similar material that holds the light-sensitive film emulsion and other coatings, esp. on motion-picture film. **17.** *Chem.* **a.** a compound that reacts with an acid to form a salt, as ammonia, calcium hydroxide, or certain nitrogen-containing organic compounds. **b.** the hydroxide of a metal or of an electropositive element or group. **c.** a group or molecule that takes up or accepts protons. **d.** a molecule or ion containing an atom with a free pair of electrons that can be donated to an acid; an electron-pair donor. **e.** any of the purine and pyrimidine compounds found in nucleic acids: the purines adenine and guanine and the pyrimidines cytosine, thymine, and uracil. **18.** *Gram.* the part of a complex word, consisting of one or more morphemes, to which derivational or inflectional affixes may be added, as *want* in *unwanted* or *biolog-* in *biological.* Cf. **root**[1] (def. 11), **stem**[1] (def. 16). **19.** *Ling.* the component of a generative grammar containing the lexicon and phrase-structure rules that generate the deep structure of sentences. **20.** *Electronics.* **a.** an electrode or terminal on a transistor other than the emitter or collector electrodes or terminals. **b.** the part of an incandescent lamp or electron tube that includes the terminals for making electrical connection to a circuit or power supply. **21.** *Stock Exchange.* the level at which a security ceases a decline in price. **22.** *Heraldry.* the lower part of an escutcheon. **23. bases,** *Armor.* a tonlet formed of two shaped steel plates assembled side by side. **24.** *Jewelry.* pavilion (def. 6). **25. get to first base.** See **first base** (def. 2). **26. in base,** *Heraldry.* in the lower part of an escutcheon. **27. off base, a.** *Baseball.* not touching a base: *The pitcher caught him off base and, after a quick throw, he was put out by the second baseman.* **b.** *Informal.* badly mistaken: *The police were way off base when they tried to accuse her of the theft.* **28. on base,** *Baseball.* having reached a base or bases: *Two men are on base.* **29. touch base with,** to make contact with: *They've touched base with every political group on campus.*
—*adj.* **30.** serving as or forming a base: *The walls will need a base coat and two finishing coats.*
—*v.t.* **31.** to make or form a base or foundation for. **32.** to establish, as a fact or conclusion (usually fol. by *on* or *upon*): *He based his assumption of her guilt on the fact that she had no alibi.* **33.** to place or establish on a base or basis; ground; found (usually fol. by *on* or *upon*): *Our plan is based on a rising economy.* **34.** to station, place, or situate (usually fol. by *at* or *on*): *He is based at Fort Benning. The squadron is based on a carrier.*
—*v.i.* **35.** to have a basis; be based (usually fol. by *on* or *upon*): *Fluctuating prices usually base on a fickle public's demand.* **36.** to have or maintain a base: *I believe they had based on Greenland at one time.* [1275–1325; ME (n.) < MF < L *basis* BASIS; cf. PRISONER'S BASE]
—**Syn. 1.** BASE, BASIS, FOUNDATION refer to anything upon which a structure is built and upon which it rests. BASE usually refers to a literal supporting structure: *the base of a statue.* BASIS more often refers to a figurative support: *the basis of a report.* FOUNDATION implies a solid, secure understructure: *the foundation of a skyscraper or a rumor.*

base[2] (bās), *adj.,* **bas·er, bas·est,** *n.* —*adj.* **1.** morally low; without estimable personal qualities; dishonorable; meanspirited; selfish; cowardly. **2.** of little or no value; worthless: *hastily composed of base materials.* **3.** debased or counterfeit: *an attempt to eliminate the base coinage.* **4.** characteristic of or befitting an inferior person or thing. **5.** of illegitimate birth. **6.** not classical or refined: *base language.* **7.** *Old Eng. Law.* held by tenure less than freehold in return for a service viewed as somewhat demeaning to the tenant. **8.** *Archaic.* **a.** of humble origin or station. **b.** of small height. **c.** low in place, position, or degree: *base servitude.* **9.** *Obs.* deep or grave in sound; bass: *the base tones of a piano.* —*n.* **10.** *Music. Obs.* bass[1] (defs. 3, 4). [1350–1400; ME *bas* < OF < LL *bassus* low, short, perh. of Oscan orig.] —**base′ly,** *adv.* —**base′ness,** *n.*
—**Syn. 1.** despicable, contemptible. See **mean**[2]. **2.** poor, inferior, cheap, tawdry. **3.** fake, spurious. **4.** servile, ignoble, abject, slavish, menial.

base·ball (bās′bôl′), *n.* **1.** a game of ball between two nine-player teams played usually for nine innings on a field that has as a focal point a diamond-shaped infield with a home plate and three other bases, 90 ft. (27 m) apart, forming a circuit that must be completed by a base runner in order to score, the central offensive action entailing hitting of a pitched ball with a wooden or metal bat and running of the bases, the winner being the team scoring the most runs. **2.** the ball used in this game, being a sphere approximately 3 in. (7 cm) in diameter with a twine-covered center of cork covered by stitched horsehide. **3.** *Cards.* a variety of five-card or seven-card stud poker in which nines and threes are wild and in which threes and fours dealt face up gain the player either penalties or privileges. [1795–1805; BASE[1] + BALL[1]]

base′ball cap′, a close-fitting cap with a deep visor and usually the name or emblem of a baseball team, worn by baseball players, or by others as casual attire. Also called **ball cap.**

base·ball·er (bās′bô′lər), *n.* a baseball player, esp. a member of a major-league team. [1885–90, *Amer;* BASEBALL + -ER[1]; neologism for *baseball player*]

base′ball glove′, a padded, leather covering for the hand, having a pocket in the area over the palm, webbing between the sections for the thumb and forefinger, and either separate sections for each finger or sections for more than one finger: used by baseball players in the field for catching batted or thrown balls. Cf. **mitt** (def. 1).

base·board (bās′bôrd′, -bōrd′), *n.* **1.** Also called **mopboard, skirt.** a board forming the foot of an interior wall. **2.** a board forming the base of anything. [1850–55, *Amer.*; BASE[1] + BOARD]

base·born (bās′bôrn′), *adj.* **1.** of humble parentage. **2.** born out of wedlock; illegitimate. **3.** having a base character or nature; mean. [1585–95; BASE[2] + BORN]

base′ box′, a unit used in the sale of tin plate, equal to the total area of 112 sheets each measuring 14 by 20 in. (35 by 50 cm), or 31,360 sq. in. (196,000 sq. cm). [1920–25]

base′ bul′lion, *Metall.* smelted lead containing impurities, as gold, silver, or zinc, that are later removed.

base·burn·er (bās′bûr′nər), *n.* a stove or furnace with a self-acting fuel hopper over the fire chamber.

Also, **base′ burn′er, base′-burn′er.** [1870–75, *Amer.*; BASE[1] + BURNER]

base′ camp′, a main encampment providing supplies, shelter, and communications for persons engaged in wide-ranging activities, as exploring, reconnaissance, hunting, or mountain climbing. [1895–1900]

base•coat (bās′kōt′), *n.* **1.** a first coat of a surfacing material, as paint. **2.** any coat of plastering beneath the finish coat. [BASE[1] + COAT]

base′ estate′, *Old Eng. Law.* an estate held from a lord on the condition of performing some service, esp. service of a demeaning nature.

base′ exchange′, *U.S. Air Force.* a department store operated under government supervision at an air base. *Abbr.:* BX [1955–60]

base•heart•ed (bās′här′tid), *adj.* having a low, mean, or contemptible nature or character; meanspirited. [BASE[2] + HEARTED]

base′ hit′, *Baseball.* a fair ball enabling the batter to reach base without the commission of an error in the field or the making of a force-out or fielder's choice on another base runner. [1870–75, *Amer.*]

Ba•sel (bä′zəl), *n.* **1.** a city in and the capital of Basel-Stadt, in NW Switzerland, on the Rhine River. 192,800. **2.** a canton in N Switzerland, divided into two independent areas. Also, **Basle.** French, **Bâle.** Cf. **Basel-Land, Basel-Stadt.**

base•less (bās′lis), *adj.* having no base; without foundation; groundless: *a baseless claim.* [1600–10; BASE[1] + -LESS]

base′ lev′el, *Geol.* the lowest level to which running water can erode the land. [1870–75]

base•line (bās′līn′), *n.* Also, **base′ line′. 1.** *Baseball.* the area between bases within which a base runner must keep when running from one base to another. **2.** *Tennis.* the line at each end of a tennis court, parallel to the net, that marks the in-bounds limit of play. **3.** (in perspective drawing) a horizontal line in the immediate foreground formed by the intersection of the ground plane and the picture plane. **4.** a basic standard or level; guideline: *to establish a baseline for future studies.* **5.** a specific value or values that can serve as a comparison or control. **6.** *Typography.* the imaginary line on which the bottoms of primary letters align. **7.** *Survey.* See under **triangulation** (def. 1). **8.** *Electronics.* a horizontal or vertical line formed on the face of a cathode-ray tube by the sweep of the scanning dot. **9.** *Naval Archit.* a line on the body plan or sheer plan of a hull, representing a horizontal reference plane for vertical dimensions. —*adj.* **10.** basic or essential. [1740–50; BASE[1] + LINE[1]]

base•lin•er (bās′lī′nər), *n. Tennis.* a player who typically plays near the baseline using ground strokes, as distinguished from one who typically goes to the net. [1900–05; BASELINE + -ER[1]]

Ba•sel-Land (bä′zəl länt′), *n.* a demicanton in N Switzerland. 220,500; 165 sq. mi. (425 sq. km). *Cap.:* Liestal.

base′ load′, *Chiefly Brit.* the constant or permanent load on a power supply. [1925–30]

Ba•sel-Stadt (bä′zəl shtät′), *n.* a demicanton in N Switzerland: virtually coextensive with the city of Basel. 215,000; 14 sq. mi. (36 sq. km). *Cap.:* Basel.

base•man (bās′mən), *n., pl.* **-men.** *Baseball.* a first, second, or third baseman. [1855–60, *Amer.*; BASE[1] + -MAN]

base′ map′, an outline map of an area to which specific information is added for any of various purposes.

base•ment (bās′mənt), *n.* **1.** a story of a building, partly or wholly underground. **2.** (in classical and Renaissance architecture) the portion of a building beneath the principal story, treated as a single compositional unit. **3.** the lowermost portion of a structure. **4.** the substructure of a columnar or arched construction. [1720–30; BASE[1] + -MENT]

base′ment com′plex, *Geol.* the undifferentiated assemblage of rock **(base′ment rock′)** underlying the oldest stratified rocks in any region: usually crystalline, metamorphosed, and mostly, but not necessarily, Precambrian in age. [1895–1900]

base′ment mem′brane, *Cell Biol.* a thin, extracellular membrane underlying epithelial tissue. [1840–50]

base′ met′al, 1. any metal other than a precious or noble metal, as copper, lead, zinc, or tin. Cf. **noble metal, precious metal. 2.** the principal metal of an alloy. **3.** the principal metal of a piece underlying a coating of another metal; core.

Ba•sen•ji (bə sen′jē), *n.* one of an African breed of dogs having a chestnut coat with white points and a curled tail, characterized chiefly by their inability to bark. [1930–35; said to be < Lingala *basenji,* pl. of *mosenji* native, inhabitant of the hinterland (or < a cognate Bantu word)]

base′ on balls′, *pl.* **bases on balls.** *Baseball.* the awarding of first base to a batter to whom four balls have been pitched. Also called **walk, pass.** [1890–95]

base′ pair′, *Genetics.* any of the pairs of the hydrogen-bonded purine and pyrimidine bases that form the links between the sugar-phosphate backbones of nucleic acid molecules: the pairs are adenine and thymine in DNA, adenine and uracil in RNA, and guanine and cytosine in both DNA and RNA. [1960–65]

base-pair•ing (bās′pâr′ing), *n. Biotech.* the process of binding separate DNA sequences by base pairs.

base′-pair•ing rules′, *Genetics.* constraints imposed by the molecular structure of DNA and RNA on the formation of hydrogen bonds among the four purine and pyrimidine bases such that adenine pairs with thymine or uracil, and guanine pairs with cytosine.

base′ path′, *Baseball.* the prescribed course for a base runner on the field extending in designated areas between the bases. [1930–35]

base′ pay′, pay received for a given work period, as an hour or week, but not including additional pay, as for overtime work. Also called **base′ sal′ary, base′ wage′.** [1915–20]

base′ pe′riod, a period of time used as a standard of comparison in measuring changes in prices, taxes, income, etc., at other periods of time.

base•plate (bās′plāt′), *n.* **1.** bedplate. **2.** *Dentistry.* **a.** a sheet of plastic material for making trial denture plates. **b.** the portion of a denture in contact with the jaw. **3.** *Metall.* a plate of metal to be clad with another metal. [1875–80; BASE[1] + PLATE[1]]

base′ price′, 1. a price quoted as a base without including additional charges. **2.** a price used as a basis for computing freight charges at a basing point, as for steel.

base′ rate′, the rate of pay per unit of time, as by the hour, or per piece, or for work performed at an established standard rate. Also called **basic rate.** [1920–25]

base′ run′ner, *Baseball.* a player of the team at bat who is on base or is trying to run from one base to another. [1865–70, *Amer.*] —**base′ run′ning.**

ba•ses[1] (bā′sēz), *n.* pl. of **basis.**

bas•es[2] (bā′siz), *n.* pl. of **base**[1].

base′ sta′tion, a unit functioning as a transmitter and receiver of broadcasting or other signals, as in connection with a CB radio or mobile phone.

base′ ten′ant, *Old Eng. Law.* a tenant of a base estate.

base′ u′nit, *Physics.* one of the units, as mass, length, time, or electric current, taken as a basis for a system of units in the sciences. Also called **fundamental unit.**

bash (bash), *v.t.* **1.** to strike with a crushing or smashing blow. **2.** *Chiefly Brit., Canadian.* to hurl harsh verbal abuse at. —*n.* **3.** a crushing blow. **4.** *Informal.* a thoroughly enjoyable, lively party. **5. have a bash (at),** *Brit.* to attempt; make an attempt. **6. on the bash,** *Brit.* working as a prostitute. [1635–45; perh. alter. of PASH[1]] —**bash′er,** *n.*

Ba•shan (bā′shən), *n.* a region in ancient Palestine, E of the Jordan River.

ba•shaw (bə shô′), *n.* **1.** pasha. **2.** a person who is important, imperious, or self-important. [1525–35; < Ar *bāshā* < Turk *pāshā* PASHA]

bash•ful (bash′fəl), *adj.* **1.** uncomfortably diffident and easily embarrassed; shy; timid. **2.** indicative of, accompanied by, or proceeding from bashfulness. [1540–50; (A)BASH + -FUL] —**bash′ful•ly,** *adv.* —**bash′ful•ness,** *n.*

—**Syn. 1.** abashed, modest. See **shy**[1]. —**Ant.** arrogant.

bash•i-ba•zouk (bash′ē bə zo͞ok′), *n.* (formerly) one of a class of irregular mounted troops in the Turkish military service. [1850–55; < Turk *başı-bozuk* civilian, irregular, orig., leaderless, not attached (to a regular military unit), lit., (one) whose head (is) broken]

bash•ing (bash′ing), *n.* **1.** the act of beating, whipping, or thrashing: *a series of unsolved bashings and robberies.* **2.** a decisive defeat. **3.** (used in combination) **a.** unprovoked physical assaults against members of a specified group: *gay-bashing.* **b.** verbal abuse, as of a group or a nation: *feminist-bashing; China bashing.* [1725–35; BASH + -ING[1]]

Bash•kir (bäsh kēr′, bash-; *Russ.* bu shkyēr′), *n., pl.* **-kirs,** (*esp. collectively*) **-kir** for 1. **1.** a member of a people living in the Bashkir Autonomous Republic and adjacent areas. **2.** the Turkic language of the Bashkir, closely related to Tatar.

Bashkir′ Auton′omous Repub′lic, (bäsh kēr′, bash-), an autonomous republic in the Russian Federation in Europe. 3,952,000; 55,430 sq. mi. (143,600 sq. km). *Cap.:* Ufa.

Ba•sho (bä shô′), *n.* (*Basho Matsuo*), 1644?–94, Japanese poet.

ba•si•ate (bā′sē āt′), *v.t., v.i.,* **-at•ed, -at•ing.** *Obs.* to kiss. [1615–25; < L *bāsiātus* (ptp. of *bāsiāre*), equiv. to *bāsi(um)* a kiss + *-ātus* -ATE[1]] —**ba′si•a′tion,** *n.*

ba•sic (bā′sik), *adj.* **1.** of, pertaining to, or forming a base; fundamental: *a basic principle; the basic ingredient.* **2.** *Chem.* **a.** pertaining to, of the nature of, or containing a base. **b.** not having all of the hydroxyls of the base replaced by the acid group, or having the metal or its equivalent united partly to the acid group and partly to oxygen. **c.** alkaline. **3.** *Metall.* noting, pertaining to, or made by a steelmaking process **(basic process)** in which the furnace or converter is lined with a basic or nonsiliceous material, mainly burned magnesite and a small amount of ground basic slag, to remove impurities from the steel. Cf. **acid** (def. 9). **4.** *Geol.* (of a rock) having relatively little silica. **5.** *Mil.* **a.** primary: *basic training.* **b.** of lowest rank: *airman basic.* —*n.* **6.** *Mil.* **a.** See **basic training. b.** a soldier or airman receiving basic training. **7.** Often, **basics.** something that is fundamental or basic; an essential ingredient, principle, procedure, etc.: *to learn the basics of music; to get back to basics.* [1835–45; BASE[1] + -IC]

—**Syn. 1.** elementary, essential, key, primary; basal.

BASIC (bā′sik), *n. Computers.* a widely adopted programming language that uses English words, punctuation marks, and algebraic notation to facilitate communication between the operator or lay user and the computer. [1965–70; *B(eginner's) A(ll-purpose) S(ymbolic) I(nstruction) C(ode)*]

ba•si•cal•ly (bā′sik lē), *adv.* fundamentally. [1900–05; BASIC + -ALLY]

ba′sic anhy′dride, *Chem.* See under **anhydride** (def. 1).

Ba′sic Assem′bly Lan′guage, *Computers.* a specific assembly language. *Abbr.:* BAL

ba′sic dichro′mate, *Chem.* See **bismuth chromate.**

ba′sic dress′, a simple, usually dark dress that may be worn with various accessories or in combination with other garments so that it is suitable for different occasions.

ba′sic dye′, a dye soluble in acid and insoluble in basic solution, consisting mostly of amino or imino compounds of xanthene or triarylmethane: used mainly for inks, carbon paper, and typewriter ribbon. [1890–95]

Ba′sic Eng′lish, a simplified form of English restricted to an 850-word vocabulary and a few rules of grammar, intended esp. as an international auxiliary language and for use in teaching English as a foreign language: devised by Charles Kay Ogden. [1925–30]

ba′sic fuch′sin, fuchsin.

ba•sic•i•ty (bā sis′i tē), *n. Chem.* **1.** the state of being a base. **2.** the power of an acid to react with bases, dependent on the number of replaceable hydrogen atoms of the acid. [1840–50; BASIC + -ITY]

ba′sic lead′ car′bonate (led), *Chem.* ceruse.

ba′sic magen′ta, fuchsin.

ba′sic ox′ygen proc′ess, a high-speed method of steelmaking in which oxygen of high purity is blown through an oxygen lance at high velocity onto the surface of a bath containing steel scrap and molten pig iron within a vessel with a basic lining **(ba′sic ox′ygen fur′nace).**

ba′sic plum′age, *Ornith.* **1.** the plumage assumed by an adult bird at its complete, usually annual, molt. **2.** (in birds having more than one plumage in their cycle of molts) the plumage of the first molt, usually the duller plumage.

ba′sic proc′ess. *Metall.* See under **basic** (def. 3). [1900–05]

ba′sic proposi′tion, protocol (def. 6).

ba′sic rate′. See **base rate.**

ba′sic sal′ary. See **base pay.**

ba′sic salt′, *Chem.* a salt formed by the partial neutralization of a base.

ba′sic slag′, *Metall.* slag formed by the basic process of steelmaking, used as a furnace or converter lining or as a fertilizer. [1885–90]

ba′sic state′ment, protocol (def. 6). [1955–60]

ba′sic steel′, steel produced by the basic process. [1880–85]

ba′sic train′ing, *Mil.* a period following a person's induction into the armed forces devoted to training in basic military comportment, duties, and combat skills.

ba′sic vocab′ulary, *Ling.* the set of lexical items in a language that are most resistant to replacement, referring to the most common and universal elements of human experience, such as parts of the body (*foot, eye*), universal features of the environment (*water, star*), common activities (*eat, sleep*), and the lowest numerals. Also called **core vocabulary.**

ba′sic wage′. See **base pay.**

ba′sic weight′, *Print.* See **basis weight.** Also called **ba′sic sub′stance weight′.**

ba•sid•i•a (bə sid′ē ə), *n.* pl. of **basidium.**

ba•sid•i•o•carp (bə sid′ē ō kärp′), *n. Mycol.* the fruiting body of basidiomycetes that produces the basidia. [BASIDI(UM) + -O- + -CARP]

ba•sid•i•o•my•cete (bə sid′ē ō mī′sēt, -mī sēt′), *n. Mycol.* any of a group of fungi constituting the phylum Basidiomycota of the kingdom Fungi (or, in older classification schemes, the class Basidiomycetes of the kingdom Plantae), characterized by bearing the spores on a basidium, including the smuts, rust, mushrooms, and puffballs. [1895–1900; < NL *Basidiomycetes;* see BASIDIUM, -O-, -MYCETE]

ba•sid•i•o•my•ce•tous (bə sid′ē ō mī sē′təs), *adj.* belonging or pertaining to the basidiomycetes. [BASIDIOMYCETE + -OUS]

ba•sid•i•o•my•co•ta (bə sid′ē ō mī kō′tə), *n.pl. Mycol.* the basidiomycetes considered as belonging to the phylum Basidiomycota of the kingdom Fungi. [< NL; see BASIDIOMYCETE, -OTA]

ba•sid•i•o•spore (bə sid′ē ō spôr′, -spōr′), *n. Mycol.* a spore that is borne by a basidium. [1855–60; BASIDI(UM) + -O- + -SPORE] —**ba•sid•i•os•por•ous** (bə sid′ē os′pər əs, -ē ə spôr′əs, -spōr′-), *adj.*

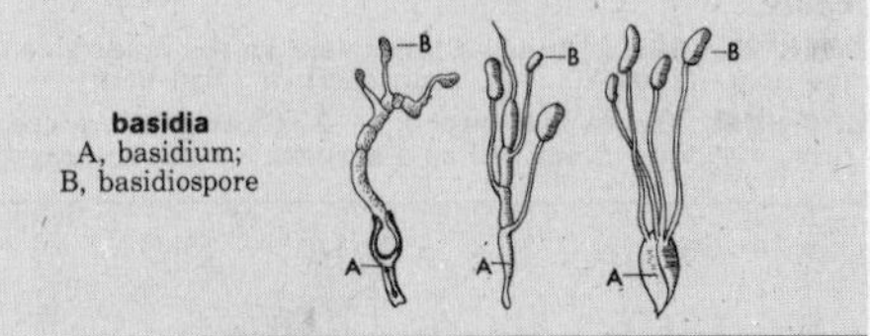

basidia
A, basidium;
B, basidiospore

ba•sid•i•um (bə sid′ē əm), *n., pl.* **-sid•i•a** (-sid′ē ə). *Mycol.* a special form of sporophore, characteristic of basidiomycetous fungi, on which the sexual spores are borne, usually at the tips of slender projections. [1855–60; BAS(IS) + -IDIUM] —**ba•sid′i•al,** *adj.*

Ba•sie (bā′sē), *n.* **William** ("*Count*"), 1904–84, U.S. jazz pianist, bandleader, and composer.

ba•si•fixed (bā′sə fikst′), *adj. Bot.* attached at or near

CONCISE PRONUNCIATION KEY: act, cāpe, dâre, pärt; set, ēqual; if, īce; ox, ōver, ôrder, oil, bo͝ok, bo͞ot, out; up, ûrge; child; sing; shoe; thin, *th*at; zh as in *treasure.* ə = a as in *alone,* e as in *system,* i as in *easily,* o as in *gallop,* u as in *circus;* ə as in *fire* (fīər), *hour* (ouər). l and n can serve as syllabic consonants, as in *cradle* (krād′l), and *button* (but′n). See the full key inside the front cover.

the base, as a leaf to a stem. [1870–75; BASE[1] + -I- + FIXED]

ba·si·fy (bā′sə fī′), *v.t.*, **-fied, -fy·ing.** to raise the pH of (a substance) above 7, thus making it alkaline. [1840–50; BASE[1] + -IFY] **—ba′si·fi·ca′tion,** *n.*

bas·il (baz′əl, bas′-, bā′zəl, -səl), *n.* any of several aromatic herbs belonging to the genus *Ocimum*, of the mint family, as *O. basilicum* **(sweet basil),** having purplish-green ovate leaves used in cooking. [1400–50; late ME *basile* < MF < LL *basilicum* < Gk *basilikón*, neut. of *basilikós* royal. See BASILIC]

Bas·il (baz′əl, bas′-, bā′zəl, -səl), *n.* **1. Saint.** Also, **Basilius.** (*"the Great"*), A.D. 329?–379, bishop of Caesarea in Asia Minor (brother of Saint Gregory of Nyssa). **2.** a male given name: from a Greek word meaning "royal."

Ba·si·lan (bə sē′län), *n.* **1.** an island in the Philippines, SW of Mindanao. 495 sq. mi. (1282 sq. km). **2.** Formerly, **Isabela.** a city on this island. 201,407.

bas·i·lar (bas′ə lər), *adj.* **1.** pertaining to or situated at the base, esp. the base of the skull. **2.** basal. Also, **bas·i·lar·y** (bas′ə ler′ē). [1535–45; < NL *basilāre*, equiv. to ML *bassil(e)* pelvis + *-āre*, neut. of *-āris* -AR[1]]

bas·i·lard (bas′ə lərd), *n.* a medieval dagger having a tapering blade with straight transverse quillons and a T-shaped pommel. [1300–50; ME *bas(e)lard*, ML *basalardus, bassilardus.* See BACILLUS, -ARD]

bas′ilar mem′brane, *Anat.* a supporting membrane, esp. the membrane that supports the organ of Corti in the ear and aids in translating sound vibrations into electrical signals. [1865–70]

Ba·sil·don (bā′zəl dən, baz′əl-), *n.* a town in S Essex, in SE England: designated as a model residential community after World War II. 138,100.

ba·si·lect (bā′zə lekt′, baz′ə-), *n. Ling.* the variety of language in a creole continuum that is most distinct from the acrolect. Cf. **acrolect, mesolect.** [1960–65; *basi-* (as comb. form of BASE[1] or BASIS) + (DIA)LECT] **—ba′si·lec′·tal,** *adj*

Ba·sil·i·an (bə zil′ē ən, -zil′yən, -sil′-), *adj.* **1.** of or pertaining to Saint Basil or to his monastic rule. —*n.* **2.** a monk or nun following the rule of Saint Basil. [1770–80; BASIL + -IAN]

ba·sil·ic (bə sil′ik, -zil′-), *adj.* **1.** kingly; royal. **2.** Also, **basilican, basilical.** of, pertaining to, or like a basilica. [1535–45; < L *basilicus* < Gk *basilikós* royal (*basil(eús)* king + *-ikos* -IC)]

ba·sil·i·ca (bə sil′i kə, -zil′-), *n.* **1.** an early Christian or medieval church of the type built esp. in Italy, characterized by a plan including a nave, two or four side aisles, a semicircular apse, a narthex, and often other features, as a short transept, a number of small semicircular apses terminating the aisles, or an atrium. The interior is characterized by strong horizontality, with little or no attempt at rhythmic accents. All spaces are usually covered with timber roofs or ceilings except for the apse or apses, which are vaulted. **2.** one of the seven main churches of Rome or another Roman Catholic church accorded the same religious privileges. **3.** (in ancient Rome) a large oblong building used as a hall of justice and public meeting place. [1535–45; < L < Gk *basilikḗ* hall, short for *basilikḗ oikía* royal house. See BASILIC]

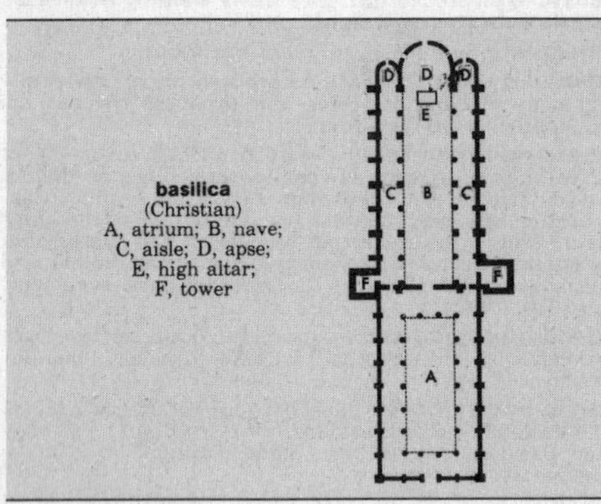

basilica (Christian) A, atrium; B, nave; C, aisle; D, apse; E, high altar; F, tower

ba·sil·i·can (bə sil′i kən, -zil′-), *adj.* basilic (def. 2). Also, **ba·sil′i·cal.**

Ba·si·li·ca·ta (bä zē′lē kä′tä), *n.* Italian name of **Lucania.**

basil′ic vein′, *Anat.* a large vein on the inner side of the arm. [1660–70; < L *vēna basilica* royal vein]

bas·i·lisk (bas′ə lisk, baz′-), *n.* **1.** *Class. Myth.* a creature, variously described as a serpent, lizard, or dragon, said to kill by its breath or look. **2.** any of several tropical American iguanid lizards of the genus *Basiliscus*, noted for their ability to run across the surface of water on their hind legs. [1250–1300; ME < L *basiliscus* < Gk *basilískos* princeling, basilisk, equiv. to *basil(eús)* king + *-iskos* dim. suffix; allegedly so named from a crownlike white spot on its head] **—bas·i·lis·cine** (bas′ə lis′in, -īn, baz′-), **bas′i·lis′can,** *adj.*

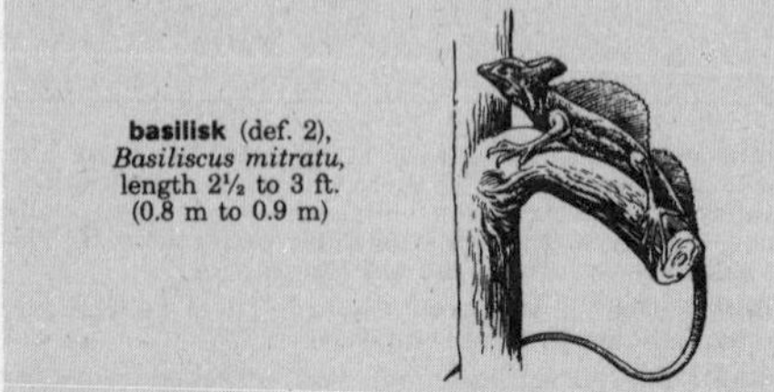
basilisk (def. 2), *Basiliscus mitratu*, length 2½ to 3 ft. (0.8 m to 0.9 m)

CONCISE ETYMOLOGY KEY: <, descended or borrowed from; >, whence; b., blend of, blended; c., cognate with; cf., compare; deriv., derivative; equiv., equivalent; imit., imitative; obl., oblique; r., replacing; s., stem; sp., spelling, spelled; resp., respelling, respelled; trans., translation; ?, origin unknown; *, unattested; ‡, probably earlier than. See the full key inside the front cover.

Ba·sil·i·us (bə sil′ē əs, -zil′-), *n.* **Saint.** See **Basil, Saint.**

bas′il thyme′, a plant, *Acinos thymoides*, of the mint family, having egg-shaped leaves and purplish flowers. [1630–40]

ba·sin (bā′sən), *n.* **1.** a circular container with a greater width than depth, becoming smaller toward the bottom, used chiefly to hold water or other liquid, esp. for washing. **2.** any container of similar shape, as the pan of a balance. **3.** the quantity held by such a container: *We need another basin of water to dilute the mixture.* **4.** a natural or artificial hollow place containing water. **5.** a partially enclosed, sheltered area along a shore, often partly man-made or dredged to a greater depth, where boats may be moored: *a yacht basin.* **6.** *Geol.* an area in which the strata dip from the margins toward a common center. **7.** *Physical Geog.* **a.** a hollow or depression in the earth's surface, wholly or partly surrounded by higher land: *river basin.* **b.** See **drainage basin. 8.** *Bot.* the depression in an apple, pear, or other pome at the end opposite the stem. [1175–1225; ME *bacin* < OF < LL *bac(c)īnum* (*bacc(a)* water vessel, BACK[3] + *-īnum* -INE[1]); perh. further related in Latin to BEAKER] **—ba′sin·al,** *adj.* **—ba′sined,** *adj.* **—ba′sin·like′,** *adj.*

bas·i·net (bas′ə nit, -net′, bas′ə net′), *n. Armor.* **1.** a globular or pointed helmet of the 14th century, often provided with a visor or aventail: evolved from the cervellière. Cf. **great basinet. 2.** a supplementary cap that is worn underneath a helm, as an arming cap. Also, **basnet, bassinet.** [1250–1300; ME *bas(e)net* < MF *bacinet.* See BASIN, -ET]

bas′ing point′, a geographical location from which freight charges are computed by the seller regardless of the point from which the goods are shipped.

ba′sin range′, *Geol.* a mountain range of the type found in the Great Basin region of the western U.S., typically long and narrow and characterized by faulted, tilted blocks of strata.

ba·si·on (bā′sē on′, -zē-), *n. Craniom.* the midpoint of the anterior margin of the foramen magnum. [1875–80; < NL < Gk *bás(is)* (see BASIS) + *-ion* n. suffix]

ba·sip·e·tal (bā sip′i tl), *adj. Bot., Mycol.* growing or moving toward the base of a structure or part. [1865–70; BASI(S) + *-petal* < L *pet(ere)* to seek + -AL[1]; cf. CENTRIPETAL] **—ba·sip′e·tal·ly,** *adv.*

ba·sis (bā′sis), *n., pl.* **-ses** (-sēz). **1.** the bottom or base of anything; the part on which something stands or rests. **2.** anything upon which something is based; fundamental principle; groundwork. **3.** the principal constituent; fundamental ingredient. **4.** a basic fact, amount, standard, etc., used in making computations, reaching conclusions, or the like: *The nurse is paid on an hourly basis. He was chosen on the basis of his college grades.* **5.** *Math.* a set of linearly independent elements of a given vector space having the property that every element of the space can be written as a linear combination of the elements of the set. [1525–35; < L < Gk *básis* step, place one stands on, pedestal, equiv. to *ba-*, base of *baínein* to walk, step (akin to COME) + *-sis* -SIS; cf. BASE[1]] **—Syn. 1, 2.** See **base**[1].

ba′sis of articula′tion, *Phonet.* a configuration of the speech tract that represents the most neutral articulatory configuration for a given language.

ba′sis point′, *Finance.* one hundredth of one percent, as of interest rates, or investment yields. [1965–70]

ba′sis weight′, the weight in pounds of a ream of paper of a basic size, usually 25 × 38 in. (63 × 96 cm) for book stock, 17 × 22 in. (43 × 55 cm) for writing stock, and 20 × 26 in. (50 × 66 cm) for cover stock. Also called **basic weight, basic substance weight.**

bask (bask, bäsk), *v.i.* **1.** to lie in or be exposed to a pleasant warmth: *to bask in the sunshine.* **2.** to enjoy a pleasant situation: *He basked in royal favor.* —*v.t.* **3.** *Obs.* to expose to warmth or heat. [1350–1400; ME < ON *bathask* to bathe oneself, equiv. to *bath-* BATH[1] + *-ask* reflexive suffix]

Bas·ker·ville (bas′kər vil′), *n.* **1. John,** 1706–75, English typographer and manufacturer of lacquered ware. **2.** a style of type.

bas·ket (bas′kit, bä′skit), *n.* **1.** a container made of twigs, rushes, thin strips of wood, or other flexible material woven together. **2.** a container made of pieces of thin veneer, used for packing berries, vegetables, etc. **3.** the amount contained in a basket; a basketful: *to pick a basket of apples.* **4.** anything like a basket in shape or use: *He never empties my wastepaper basket.* **5.** any group of things or different things grouped as a unit; a package; package deal: *You can't buy the single stock; you have to take the basket—all companies, stocks and bonds.* **6.** the car or gondola suspended beneath a balloon, as for carrying passengers or scientific instruments into the atmosphere. **7.** *Basketball.* **a.** an open net suspended from a metal rim attached to the backboard and through which the ball must pass in order for a player to score points. **b.** a score, counting two for a field goal and one for a free throw. **8.** Also called **snow ring.** *Skiing.* a ring strapped to the base of a ski pole to limit penetration of the pole in the snow. **9.** *Slang (vulgar).* the male genitals, esp. when outlined by a tight-fitting garment. [1250–1300; ME *basket(te)* < early Romance **baskauta* (> F dial. *bâchot, bachou* wooden or interwoven vessel, OHG *baskiza* box) < L *bascauda* basin, perh. < British Celtic] **—bas′ket·like′,** *adj.*

bas·ket·ball (bas′kit bôl′, bä′skit-), *n.* **1.** a game played by two teams of usually five players each on a rectangular court having a raised basket or goal at each end, points being scored by tossing the ball through the opponent's basket. **2.** the round, inflated ball, approximately 30 in. (76 cm) in circumference, used in this game. [1890–95, *Amer.*; BASKET + BALL[1]]

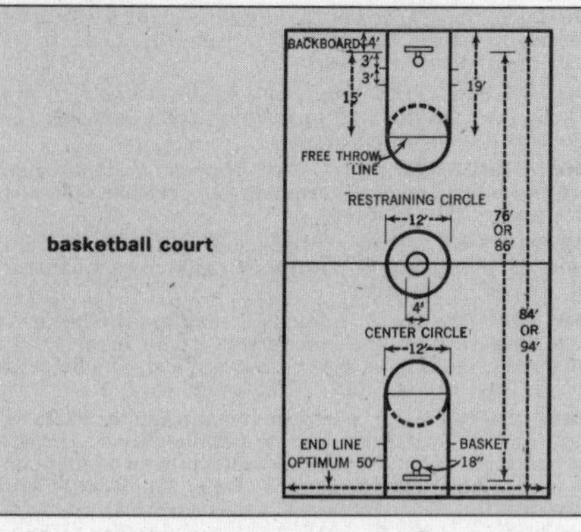

basketball court

bas′ket case′, *Slang.* **1.** (*offensive*) a person who has had all four limbs amputated. **2.** a person who is helpless or incapable of functioning normally, esp. due to overwhelming stress, anxiety, or the like. **3.** anything that is impaired or incapable of functioning: *Right after the war the conquered nation was considered an economic basket case.* [1915–20]

bas′ket chair′, a wicker chair the arms of which are a forward continuation of the back. [1625–35]

bas′ket din′ner, *Chiefly Midland and Southern U.S.* a group social gathering, as of church members, to which participants contribute casseroles or other dishes to share. [1890–95, *Amer.*]

bas′ket fern′, a small, compact fern, *Nephrolepis pectinata*, of tropical America, often grown in hanging baskets. [1940–45]

bas′ket fish′. See **basket star.** [1745–55]

bas′ket flow′er, a composite plant, *Centaurea americana*, of central U.S. to Mexico, having raylike heads of tubular rose-colored flowers, each surrounded by a whorl of bracts making the flower head appear as if it is set in a basket.

bas·ket·ful (bas′kit fo͝ol′, bä′skit-), *n., pl.* **-fuls. 1.** a sufficient quantity to fill a basket; the amount contained in a basket. **2.** any considerable quantity: *a basketful of surprises.* [1565–75; BASKET + -FUL] **—Usage.** See **-ful.**

bas′ket-han′dle arch′ (bas′kit han′dl, bä′skit-), *Archit.* an arch having a symmetrical form drawn from an odd number of radii in excess of one, which increase in length from the springing toward the center. See illus. under **arch.**

bas′ket hilt′, the basketlike hilt of a sword, foil, etc., serving to cover and protect the hand. [1540–50] **—bas′ket-hilt′ed,** *adj.*

Bas′ket Mak′er, 1. an American Indian culture of the southwestern U.S. from 100 B.C. to A.D. 65 that developed in three phases, immediately preceded the Pueblo culture, and was noted for its basketry, agriculture, use of the bow and arrow, and, in its later stages, the building of semisubterranean houses. **2.** an American Indian belonging to the Basket Maker culture. [1895–1900]

bas·ket-of-gold (bas′kit əv gōld′, -gōld′, bä′skit-), *n.* a widely cultivated alyssum, *Aurinia saxatilis* (or *Alyssum saxatile*), of the mustard family, growing in dense clumps and having clusters of small yellow flowers. [1925–30]

bas·ket·ry (bas′ki trē, bä′ski-), *n.* **1.** baskets collectively; basketwork. **2.** the art or process of making baskets. [1850–55; BASKET + -RY]

bas′ket star′, any echinoderm of the class Ophiuroidea, esp. of the genus *Gorgonocephalus*, having long, slender, branching arms. Also called **basket fish.** [1920–25]

bas′ket weave′, a plain weave with two or more yarns woven together in a checkered pattern resembling that of a woven basket. [1920–25]

bas·ket·work (bas′kit wûrk′, bä′skit-), *n.* objects, textiles, etc., made or woven in the manner of a basket; basketry; wickerwork; interwoven work. [1760–70; BASKET + WORK]

Bas·kin (bas′kin), *n.* **Leonard,** born 1922, U.S. sculptor and artist.

bask′ing shark′ (bas′king, bä′sking), a large shark, *Cetorhinus maximus*, of cold and temperate seas, that often swims slowly or floats at the surface. [1760–70]

Basle (bäl), *n.* Basel.

bas mitz·vah (*Ashk. Heb., Eng.* bäs mits′və), (*often caps.*) *Judaism.* See **bat mitzvah.**

bas·net (bas′nit, -net), *n. Armor.* basinet.

ba·son (bā′sən), *n. Anglican Ch.* a basin.

ba·so·phil (bā′sə fil), *n.* **1.** *Biol.* a basophilic cell, tissue, organism, or substance. **2.** *Anat.* a white blood cell having a two-lobed nucleus and basophilic granules in its cytoplasm. —*adj.* **3.** *Biol.* basophilic. Also, **ba·so·phile** (bā′sə fīl′, -fil). [1885–90; BAS(IC DYE) + -O- + -PHIL]

ba·so·phil·i·a (bā′sə fil′ē ə, -fēl′yə), *n. Pathol.* an abnormal increase in the number of basophils in the blood, occurring in some types of leukemia, severe anemia, and other disorders. [1900–05; BASOPHIL + -IA]

ba•so•phil•ic (bā′sə fil′ik), *adj. Biol.* having an affinity for basic stains. Also, **ba•soph•i•lous** (bā sof′ə ləs), **basophil, basophile.** [1890–95; BASOPHIL + -IC]

Ba•sov (bä′səf), *n.* **Ni•ko•lai Gen•na•di•ye•vich** (nyi-ku lī′ gyi nä′dyi yi vyich), born 1922, Russian physicist: Nobel prize 1964.

Basque (bask), *n.* **1.** one of a people of unknown origin inhabiting the western Pyrenees regions in France and Spain. **2.** their language, not known to be related to any other language. **3.** (*l.c.*) a close-fitting bodice, sometimes having an extension that covers the hips. **4.** (*l.c.*) the extension of this bodice or of a doublet. —*adj.* **5.** of or pertaining to the Basques or their language.

Basque′ Prov′inces, a region in N Spain, bordering on the Bay of Biscay.

Basque′ shirt′, a knitted pullover shirt having a crew neck, long or short sleeves, and a pattern of horizontal stripes.

Bas•ra (bus′rə, bäs′rä), *n.* a port in SE Iraq, N of the Persian Gulf. 915,000. Also, **Busra, Busrah.**

bas-re•lief (bä′ri lēf′, bas′-; bä′ri lēf′, bas′-), *n.* relief sculpture in which the figures project slightly from the background. Also called **low relief.** See illus. under **relief**[2]. [1660–70; < F, on the model of It *bassorilievo.* Cf. BASSORILIEVO, BASE[2], RELIEF]

Bas-Rhin (bä RAN′), *n.* a department in NE France. 827,367; 1848 sq. mi. (4785 sq. km). *Cap.:* Strasbourg.

bass[1] (bās), *Music.* —*adj.* **1.** low in pitch; of the lowest pitch or range: *a bass voice; a bass instrument.* **2.** of or pertaining to the lowest part in harmonic music. —*n.* **3.** the bass part. **4.** a bass voice, singer, or instrument. **5.** See **double bass.** [1400–50; late ME, var. of BASE[2] with ss of BASSO] —**bass′ly,** *adv.* —**bass′ness,** *n.* —**bass′y,** *adj.*

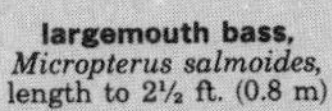
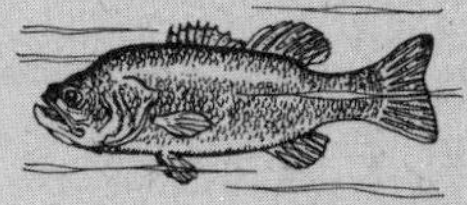
largemouth bass, *Micropterus salmoides,* length to 2½ ft. (0.8 m)

bass[2] (bas), *n., pl.* (*esp. collectively*) **bass,** (*esp. referring to two or more kinds or species*) **bass•es. 1.** any of numerous edible, spiny-finned, freshwater or marine fishes of the families Serranidae and Centrarchidae. **2.** (originally) the European perch, *Perca fluviatilis.* [1375–1425; late ME *bas,* earlier *bærs,* OE *bærs* (with loss of *r* before *s* as in ASS[2], PASSEL, etc.); c. D *baars,* G *Barsch,* OSw *aghborre*]

bass[3] (bas), *n.* **1.** the basswood or linden. **2.** *Bot.* bast. [1685–95; var. of BAST with unexplained loss of *-t*]

Bass (bas), *n.* **Sam,** 1851–78, U.S. outlaw: bank and train robber in the West.

bass•ack•wards (bas′ak′wərdz), *adv., adj. Slang.* assbackwards: used as a euphemism. [1955–60; euphemistic spoonerism as alter. of ASSBACKWARDS]

Bas•sa•no (bə sä′nō; *It.* bäs sä′nô), *n.* **1. Ja•co•po** (yä′kô pô), (*Giacomo da Ponte*), 1510–92, Italian painter. **2.** his sons, **Fran•ces•co** (frän ches′kô), 1549–92; **Giam•bat•tis•ta da Pon•te** (jäm′bät tēs′tä dä pôn′te), 1533–?; **Gi•ro•la•mo da Ponte** (jē RÔ′lä mô), 1566–1621; **Le•an•dro** (le än′dRô), 1557–1623, Italian painters.

bas•sa•risk (bas′ə risk′), *n.* any carnivorous mammal of the genus *Bassariscus,* comprising the cacomistles and ringtails. [< NL *Bassariscus* name of genus, equiv. to Gk *bassár(a)* fox + NL *-iscus* dim. suffix < Gk *-iskos*]

bass-bar (bās′bär′), *n.* a strip of wood glued lengthwise inside the belly of instruments of the violin family, used to spread vibrations over the surface. [1830–40]

bass′ clef′ (bās), *Music.* a symbol placed on the fourth line of a staff to indicate that the fourth line of the staff corresponds to the F next below middle C; F clef. See illus. under **clef.** [1900–05]

bass′ drum′ (bās), the largest and lowest toned of drums, having a cylindrical body and two membrane heads. [1795–1805]

Bas•sein (bə sān′), *n.* a city in SW Burma, near the mouth of the Irrawaddy River. 175,000.

Basses-Alpes (bäs zAlp′), *n.* former name of **Alpes-de-Hautes-Provence.**

Basses-Py•ré•nées (bäs pē RA nā′), *n.* former name of **Pyrénées-Atlantiques.**

basset[1] 14 in. (36 cm) high at shoulder

bas•set[1] (bas′it), *n.* one of a breed of hounds having short legs, long body and ears, and usually a black, tan, and white coat. Also called **bas′set hound′.** [1610–20; < F: n. use of adj. *basset* of low stature (*bass-* low (see BASE[2]) + *-et* attenuating suffix; see -ET)]

bas•set[2] (bas′it), *n., v.,* **-set•ed, -set•ing.** *Geol., Mining.* —*n.* **1.** an outcrop, as of the edges of strata. —*v.i.* **2.** to crop out. [1680–90; appar. < obs. F *basset* low stool, n. use of adj. *basset.* See BASSET[1]]

bas•set[3] (bas′it), *n.* an 18th-century card game similar to faro. [1635–45; < F *bassette* < It *bassetta,* n. use of fem. of *bassetto* somewhat low; so called because the game is played with low cards. See BASSET[1]]

basse-taille (bäs tä′yᵊ), *adj.* of or pertaining to an enameling technique in which transparent enamels are fused over a background carved in low relief, or to a piece, as of jewelry, so enameled. [1895–1900; < F, equiv. to *basse* low (see BASE[2]) + *taille* cutting (see TAIL[2])]

Basse•terre (bäs târ′), *n.* a seaport in and the capital of St. Kitts-Nevis, in the West Indies. 15,897.

Basse-Terre (bäs târ′; *Fr.* bäs teR′), *n.* **1.** a seaport in and the capital of Guadeloupe, in the French West Indies. 15,690. **2.** See under **Guadeloupe.**

bas′set horn′, an alto horn with a soft tone. [1825–35; < G *Bassetthorn* < It *corno di bassetto* horn of a somewhat low range. See CORN[2], BASSET[1]]

bas′set ta′ble, a card table of the early 18th century in England.

bass′ fid′dle (bās). See **double bass.** [1950–55]

bass′ horn′ (bās), **1.** tuba. **2.** an obsolete wind instrument related to the tuba but resembling a bassoon in shape. [1855–60]

bas•si•net (bas′ə net′, bas′ə net′), *n.* **1.** a basket with a hood over one end, for use as a baby's cradle. **2.** a style of perambulator resembling this. **3.** *Armor.* basinet. [1570–80; < F: pan; see BASIN, -ET]

bass•ist (bā′sist), *n.* **1.** a singer with a bass voice. **2.** a player of a bass instrument, esp. of the bass viol. [1865–70; BASS[1] + -IST]

bas•so (bas′ō, bä′sō; *It.* bäs′sô), *n., pl.* **-sos, -si** (-sē). *Music.* a person who sings bass; a bass. [1810–20; < It < LL *bassus.* See BASE[2]]

Bas•so (bas′ō), *n.* **Hamilton,** 1904–64, U.S. journalist and novelist.

bas•so can•tan•te (bas′ō kən tän′tē, -tā, bä′sō; *It.* bäs′sô kän tän′te), *pl.* **bas•si can•tan•ti** (bas′ē kən-tän′tē, bä′sē; *It.* bäs′sē kän tän′tē). *Music.* a bass voice with an upper range that is more developed than that of the basso profundo. [1875–80; < It: lit., singing bass]

bas′so contin′uo, *Music.* continuo. [1665–75]

bas•soon (ba sōōn′, bə-), *n.* a large woodwind instrument of low range, with a doubled tube and a curved metal crook to which a double reed is attached. [1720–30; < F *basson* < It *bassone* (*bass(o)* low (see BASE[2]) + *-one* aug. suffix)] —**bas•soon′ist,** *n.*

bassoon

bas•so pro•fun•do (bas′ō prō fun′dō, -fŏŏn′-, prə-, bä′sō), *pl.* **bas•si pro•fun•di** (bas′ē prō fun′dē, bä′sē). a singer with a bass voice of the lowest range. [1855–60; < It *basso profondo* lit., deep bass. See BASSO, PROFOUND]

bas•so-re•lie•vo (bas′ō ri lē′vō), *n., pl.* **-vos.** bas-relief. [1660–70; < It *basso rilievo* low relief]

bass′ re′flex (bās), a loudspeaker equipped with a baffle having openings designed to improve the reproduction of low-frequency sounds.

bass′ response′ (bās), the response of a loudspeaker or other amplifying device to low-frequency sounds.

bass′ sax′ophone (bās), a large saxophone of low range, usually supported on a stand while being played.

bass′ staff′ (bās), *Music.* a staff marked with a bass clef.

Bass′ Strait′ (bas), a strait between Australia and Tasmania. 80–150 mi. (130–240 km) wide.

bass′ vi′ol (bās), **1.** viola da gamba. **2.** See **double bass.** [1580–90]

bass•wood (bas′wŏŏd′), *n.* **1.** any tree of the genus *Tilia,* esp. *T. americana,* the American linden, having drooping branches and large, toothed, ovate leaves. **2.** the wood of a linden. [1660–70, *Amer.*; BASS[3] + WOOD[1]]

bast (bast), *n.* **1.** *Bot.* phloem. **2.** Also called **bast fiber.** any of several strong, woody fibers, as flax, hemp, ramie, or jute, obtained from phloem tissue and used in the manufacture of woven goods and cordage. [bef. 900; ME; OE *bæst;* c. D, G, ON *bast;* perh. ult. c. L *fascis* bundle. See BASS[3]]

ba•sta (bä′stä), *interj. Italian.* enough; stop.

bas•tard (bas′tərd), *n.* **1.** a person born of unmarried parents; an illegitimate child. **2.** *Slang.* **a.** a vicious, despicable, or thoroughly disliked person: *Some bastard slashed the tires on my car.* **b.** a person, esp. a man: *The poor bastard broke his leg.* **3.** something irregular, inferior, spurious, or unusual. **4.** See **bastard culverin.** —*adj.* **5.** illegitimate in birth. **6.** spurious; not genuine; false: *The architecture was bastard Gothic.* **7.** of abnormal or irregular shape or size; of unusual make or proportions: *bastard quartz; bastard mahogany.* **8.** having the appearance of; resembling in some degree: *a bastard Michelangelo; bastard emeralds.* **9.** *Print.* (of a character) not of the font in which it is used or found. [1250–1300; ME < AF *bastard,* ML *bastardus* (from 11th century), perh. < Gmc (Ingvaeonic) **bāst-,* presumed var. of **bōst-* marriage + OF *-ard* -ARD, taken as signifying the offspring of a polygynous marriage to a woman of lower status, a pagan tradition not sanctioned by the church; cf. OFris *bost* marriage < Gmc **bandstu-,* a n. deriv. of IE **bhendh-* BIND; the traditional explanation of OF *bastard* as deriv. of *fils de bast* "child of a packsaddle" is doubtful on chronological and geographical grounds]
—**Syn. 6.** fake, imitation, imperfect, sham, irregular, phony.

bas′tard am′ber, a color of gelatin commonly used in stage lighting, similar to light amber but having a pinkish cast.

bas′tard cul′verin, *Mil.* a 16th-century cannon, smaller than a culverin, firing a shot of between 5 and 8 lb. (11 and 17.6 kg). Also called **bastard.** [1540–50]

bas′tard eigne′ (ān), *Old Eng. Law.* the first-born illegitimate son of parents whose second son was legitimate. Cf. **mulier puisne.** [1580–90; *eigne* < AF: elder, OF *ainsné* (*ainz* before (< VL **antius,* for L *anteā*) + *ne* born; see NEE)]

bas′tard file′, a file of the commercial grade of coarseness between coarse and second-cut.

bas′tard in′digo, a bushy shrub, *Amorpha fruticosa,* of the legume family, native to North America, having elongated clusters of dull purplish or bluish flowers.

bas•tard•ize (bas′tər dīz′), *v.,* **-ized, iz•ing.** —*v.t.* **1.** to lower in condition or worth; debase: *hybrid works that neither preserve nor bastardize existing art forms.* **2.** to declare or prove (someone) to be a bastard. **3.** *Australian.* to harass or humiliate as part of initiation into a college or regiment. —*v.i.* **4.** to become debased. Also, *esp. Brit.,* **bas′tard•ise′.** [1580–90; BASTARD + -IZE] —**bas′tard•i•za′tion,** *n.*

bas•tard•ly (bas′tərd lē), *adj.* **1.** of no value; worthless. **2.** spurious; counterfeit: *a bastardly version of a text.* **3.** bastard; baseborn. **4.** vicious or despicable. [1545–55; BASTARD + -LY]

bas′tard mahog′any, an Australian tree, *Eucalyptus botryoides,* of the myrtle family, having lance-shaped leaves and furrowed bark. Also called **bangalay.**

bas′tard point′ing, *Masonry.* an imitation of tuck pointing, having a fillet made from the mortar of the joint.

bas′tard rid′ley, ridley (def. 1).

bas•tard•ry (bas′tər drē), *n. Australia and New Zealand.* unpleasant, often aggressive behavior. [1635–45, for earlier sense; BASTARD + -RY]

bas•tard-saw (bas′tərd sô′), *v.t.,* **-sawed, -sawed** or **-sawn, -saw•ing.** plain-saw. [BASTARD + SAW[1]]

bas′tard ti′tle. *Print.* See **half title** (def. 1).

bas′tard toad′flax, any of several low-growing, often parasitic plants of the genus *Comandra,* having alternate leaves and clusters of small whitish flowers.

bas′tard tur′tle, ridley (def. 1).

bas′tard wing′, *Ornith.* alula (def. 1). [1765–75]

bas•tar•dy (bas′tər dē), *n.* **1.** the state or condition of being a bastard; illegitimacy. **2.** the act of begetting a bastard. [1400–50; late ME < AF, OF *bastardie.* See BASTARD, -Y[3]]

baste[1] (bāst), *v.t.,* **bast•ed, bast•ing.** to sew with long, loose stitches, as in temporarily tacking together pieces of a garment while it is being made. [1400–50; late ME *basten* < AF, MF *bastir* to build, baste < Gmc; cf. OHG *bestan* to mend, patch for **bastian* to bring together with bast thread or string (*bast* BAST + *-i-* v. suffix + *-an* inf. suffix)]

baste[2] (bāst), *v.,* **bast•ed, bast•ing,** *n.* —*v.t.* **1.** to moisten (meat or other food) while cooking, with drippings, butter, etc. —*n.* **2.** liquid used to moisten and flavor food during cooking: *a baste of sherry and pan juices.* [1425–75; late ME *basten,* of obscure orig.]

baste[3] (bāst), *v.t.,* **bast•ed, bast•ing. 1.** to beat with a stick; thrash; cudgel. **2.** to denounce or scold vigorously: *an editorial basting the candidate for irresponsible statements.* [1525–35; var. of *baist,* perh. < ON *beysta* to beat, thrash]

bas′tel house′ (bas′tl), (on the Anglo-Scottish border) a partly fortified house, usually with a vaulted ground floor. Also, **bastille house, bastle house.** [1535–45; see BASTILLE]

bast•er[1] (bā′stər), *n. Sewing.* a person or thing that bastes. [1880–85; BASTE[1] + -ER[1]]

bast•er[2] (bā′stər), *n.* **1.** a person who bastes meat or other food. **2.** a large glass, plastic, or metal tube with a rubber bulb at one end and a small opening at the other, to be filled with butter, drippings, etc., for basting food as it is cooking. [1515–25; BASTE[2] + -ER[1]]

bast′ fi′ber, bast (def. 2).

Ba•sti•a (bä stē′ə; *Fr.* bA styA′), *n.* a seaport on the NE coast of Corsica: the former capital of Corsica. 52,000.

Ba•sti•an (bäs′tē än′), *n.* **A•dolf** (ä′dôlf), 1826–1905, German anthropologist.

bas•tide (ba stēd′), *n.* **1.** a medieval fortified town, planned as a whole and built at one time, esp. in southern France, for strategic or commercial purposes. **2.** a small country house in southern France. [1515–25; < MF < OPr *bastida* fortification, n. use of fem. ptp. of *bastir* to build, equiv. to *basti-* (< Gmc; see BASTE[1]) + *-da* < L *-ta* fem. ptp. suffix]

bas•tille (ba stēl′; *Fr.* bAs tē′yᵊ), *n., pl.* **bas•tilles** (ba-stēlz′; *Fr.* bAs tē′yᵊ). **1.** (*cap.*) a fortress in Paris, used as a prison, built in the 14th century and destroyed July 14, 1789. **2.** any prison or jail, esp. one conducted in a tyrannical way. **3.** a fortified tower, as of a castle; a small fortress; citadel. Also, **bas•tile** (ba stēl′). [1350–1400; ME *bastile* < MF, prob. alter. of *bastide* BASTIDE, with *-ile* (< ML, L *-īle* n. suffix of place) r. *-ide;* r. ME *bastel* < OF *basstel,* with *-el* similarly r. *-ide*]

Bastille′ Day′, July 14, a national holiday of the

CONCISE PRONUNCIATION KEY: act, cāpe, dâre, pärt; set, ēqual; if, ice; ox, ōver, ôrder, oil, bŏŏk, bōōt, out; up, ûrge; child; sing; shoe; thin, *th*at; zh as in *treasure.* ə = *a* as in *alone, e* as in *system, i* as in *easily, o* as in *gallop, u* as in *circus;* ᵊ as in *fire* (fīᵊr), *hour* (ouᵊr). l and n can serve as syllabic consonants, as in *cradle* (krād′l), and *button* (but′n). See the full key inside the front cover.

French republic, commemorating the fall of the Bastille in 1789.

bastille′ house′. See **bastel house.**

bas·ti·nade (bas′tə nād′, -näd′), *n., v.t.,* **-nad·ed, -nad·ing.** bastinado.

bas·ti·na·do (bas′tə nā′dō, -nä′dō), *n., pl.* **-does,** *v.,* **-doed, -do·ing.** —*n.* **1.** a mode of punishment consisting of blows with a stick on the soles of the feet or on the buttocks. **2.** a blow or a beating with a stick, cudgel, etc. **3.** a stick or cudgel. —*v.t.* **4.** to beat with a stick, cane, etc., esp. on the soles of the feet or on the buttocks. [1570–80; earlier *bastanado* < Sp *bastonada* (*bastón* stick (see BATON) + *-ada* -ADE[1])]

bast·ing[1] (bā′sting), *n.* **1.** sewing with long, loose stitches to hold material in place until the final sewing. **2. bastings,** the stitches taken or the threads used. [1515–25; BASTE[1] + -ING[1]]

bast·ing[2] (bā′sting), *n.* **1.** the act of moistening food while cooking, esp. with stock or pan juices. **2.** the liquid used in basting. [1520–30; BASTE[2] + -ING[1]]

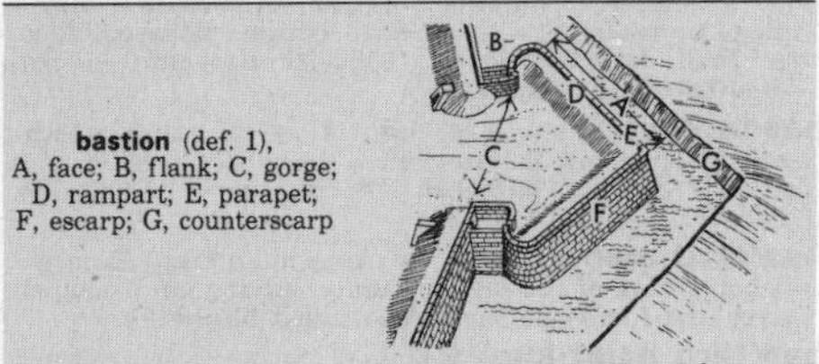

bastion (def. 1), A, face; B, flank; C, gorge; D, rampart; E, parapet; F, escarp; G, counterscarp

bas·tion (bas′chən, -tē ən), *n.* **1.** *Fort.* a projecting portion of a rampart or fortification that forms an irregular pentagon attached at the base to the main work. **2.** a fortified place. **3.** anything seen as preserving or protecting some quality, condition, etc.: *a bastion of solitude; a bastion of democracy.* [1590–1600; < MF < It *bastione,* equiv. to Upper It *bastí(a)* bastion, orig., fortified, built (c. It *bastita,* ptp. of *bastire* to build < Gmc; see BASTE[1]) + *-one* aug. suffix] —**bas·tion·ar·y** (bas′chə ner′ē), *adj.* —**bas′tioned,** *adj.*
—**Syn. 2.** fortress, fort, bulwark, stronghold, citadel.

bas′tle house′ (bas′tl). See **bastel house.**

bast·naes·ite (bast′nə sit′), *n.* a rare-earth mineral, fluorocarbonate of lanthanum and cerium, with a waxy-yellow to reddish-brown color, commonly associated with zinc ores. Also, **bast′näs·ite′.** [named after *Bastnäs,* mine in Sweden; see -ITE[1]]

Bas·togne (ba stōn′; *Fr.* bA stôn′yᵊ), *n.* a town in SE Belgium: in World War II U.S. forces besieged here during German counteroffensive in 1944. 6816.

Bas·trop (bas′trəp), *n.* a city in N Louisiana. 15,527.

Ba·su·to (bə so͞o′to͞o, -tō), *n., pl.* **-tos,** (*esp. collectively*) **-to.** Sotho (def. 3).

Ba·su·to·land (bə so͞o′to͞o land′, -tō-), *n.* former name of **Lesotho.**

bat[1] (bat), *n., v.,* **bat·ted, bat·ting.** —*n.* **1.** *Sports.* **a.** the wooden club used in certain games, as baseball and cricket, to strike the ball. **b.** a racket, esp. one used in badminton or table tennis. **c.** a whip used by a jockey. **d.** the act of using a club or racket in a game. **e.** the right or turn to use a club or racket. **2.** a heavy stick, club, or cudgel. **3.** *Informal.* a blow, as with a bat. **4.** any fragment of brick or hardened clay. **5.** *Masonry.* a brick cut transversely so as to leave one end whole. **6.** *Brit. Slang.* speed; rate of motion or progress, esp. the pace of the stroke or step of a race. **7.** *Slang.* a spree; binge: *to go on a bat.* **8.** *Ceram.* **a.** a sheet of gelatin or glue used in bat printing. **b.** a slab of moist clay. **c.** a ledge or shelf in a kiln. **d.** a slab of plaster for holding a piece being modeled or for absorbing excess water from slip. **9.** batt. **10. at bat,** *Baseball.* **a.** taking one's turn to bat in a game: *at bat with two men in scoring position.* **b.** an instance at bat officially charged to a batter except when the batter is hit by a pitch, receives a base on balls, is interfered with by the catcher, or makes a sacrifice hit or sacrifice fly: *two hits in three at bats.* **11. go to bat for,** *Informal.* to intercede for; vouch for; defend: *to go to bat for a friend.* **12. right off the bat,** *Informal.* at once; without delay: *They asked me to sing right off the bat.* —*v.t.* **13.** to strike or hit with or as if with a bat or club. **14.** *Baseball.* to have a batting average of; hit: *He batted .325 in spring training.* —*v.i.* **15.** *Sports.* **a.** to strike at the ball with the bat. **b.** to take one's turn as a batter. **16.** *Slang.* to rush. **17. bat around, a.** *Slang.* to roam; drift. **b.** *Informal.* to discuss or ponder; debate: *We batted the idea around.* **c.** *Baseball.* to have every player in the lineup take a turn at bat during a single inning. **18. bat in,** *Baseball.* to cause (a run) to be scored by getting a hit: *He batted in two runs with a double to left.* **19. bat out,** to do, write, produce, etc., hurriedly: *I have to bat out a term paper before class.* **20. bat the breeze.** See **breeze**[1] (def. 5). [1175–1225; (n.) ME *bat, bot, batte,* OE *batt,* perh. < Celt; cf. Ir, Scot-Gael *bat, bata* staff, cudgel; (v.) ME *batten,* partly from the n., partly < OF *batre;* see BATTER[1]]
—**Syn. 13.** knock, wallop, swat, smack, sock, slug; clout, clobber.

bat[2] (bat), *n.* **1.** any of numerous flying mammals of the order Chiroptera, of worldwide distribution in tropical and temperate regions, having modified forelimbs that serve as wings and are covered with a membranous skin extending to the hind limbs. **2. blind as a bat,** nearly or completely blind; having very poor vision: *Anyone can tell that he's blind as a bat, but he won't wear glasses.* **3. have bats in one's belfry,** *Informal.* to have crazy ideas; be very peculiar, erratic, or foolish: *If you think you can row across the ocean in that boat, you have bats in your belfry.* [1570–75; appar. < Scand; cf. dial. Sw *natt-batta,* var. of OSw *natt-bakka* night-bat; r. ME *bakke* (< Scand), ME *balke* for **blake* < Scand; cf. dial. Sw *natt-blacka*] —**bat′like′,** *adj.*

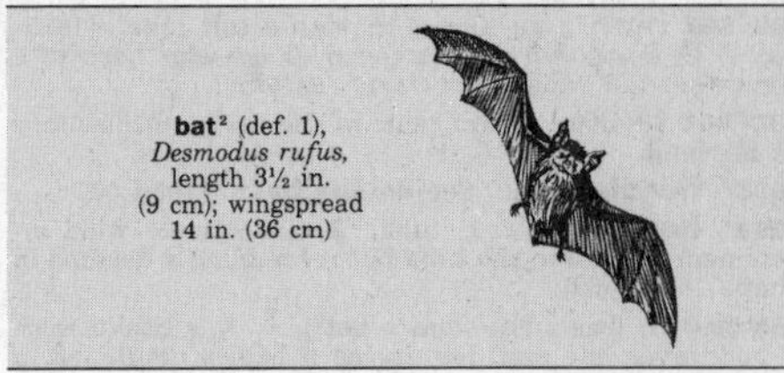
bat[2] (def. 1), *Desmodus rufus,* length 3½ in. (9 cm); wingspread 14 in. (36 cm)

bat[3] (bat), *v.t.,* **bat·ted, bat·ting. 1.** to blink; wink; flutter. **2. not bat an eye,** to show no emotion or surprise; maintain a calm exterior: *The murderer didn't bat an eye when the jury announced its verdict of guilty.* [1605–15; var. of BATE[2]]

bat., 1. battalion. **2.** battery.

Ba·taan (bə tan′, -tän′; *locally* bä′tä än′), *n.* a peninsula on W Luzon, in the Philippines: U.S. troops surrendered to Japanese April 9, 1942. Also, **Ba·taán′.**

Ba·taisk (bu tīsk′), *n.* a city in the SW RSFSR, in the S Soviet Union in Europe, on the Don River. 103,000.

Ba·tak (bə täk′, bä-), *n., pl.* **-taks,** (*esp. collectively*) **-tak** for 1, 2. **1.** a member of a group of people chiefly inhabiting north-central Sumatra. **2.** a member of a group of mountain-dwelling people of northeastern Palawan in the Philippines. **3.** either of the Austronesian languages spoken by the Batak peoples.

Ba·tan·gas (bä täng′gäs), *n.* a seaport on SW Luzon, in the N central Philippines. 143,570.

Ba·tan′ Is′lands (bə tän′, bä-), a group of islands in the N Philippines. 12,091; 76 sq. mi. (197 sq. km). Also called **Ba·ta·nes** (bä tä′nes).

Ba·ta·vi·a (bə tā′vē ə), *n.* **1.** a city in NW New York. 16,703. **2.** a town in NE Illinois. 12,574. **3.** former name of **Jakarta.**

bat′ boy′, *Baseball.* a boy or young man who takes care of the bats and sometimes other equipment of a team. [1920–25, *Amer.*]

batch[1] (bach), *n.* **1.** a quantity or number coming at one time or taken together: *a batch of prisoners.* **2.** the quantity of material prepared or required for one operation: *mixing a batch of concrete.* **3.** the quantity of bread, cookies, dough, or the like, made at one baking. **4.** *Computers.* **a.** a group of jobs, data, or programs treated as a unit for computer processing. **b.** See **batch processing. 5.** *Glassmaking.* **a.** a quantity of raw materials mixed in proper proportions and prepared for fusion into glass. **b.** the material so mixed. —*v.t.* **6.** to combine, mix, or process in a batch. [1400–50; late ME *bache,* akin to *bacan* to BAKE; cf. OE *gebæc,* G *Gebäck* batch]
—**Syn. 1.** group, lot, number, bunch, gang, set, pack, flock, troop.

batch[2] (bach), *v.i., n.* bach. [*tch* to clarify and normalize pron.]

batch′ plant′, a manufacturing plant where concrete is mixed before being transported to a construction site ready to be poured. Also, **batch′ing plant′.** [1940–45]

batch′ proc′essing, *Computers.* a form of data processing in which a number of input jobs are grouped for processing during the same machine run. [1970–75]

bate[1] (bāt), *v.,* **bat·ed, bat·ing.** —*v.t.* **1.** to moderate or restrain: *unable to bate our enthusiasm.* **2.** to lessen or diminish; abate: *setbacks that bated his hopes.* —*v.i.* **3.** to diminish or subside; abate. **4. with bated breath,** with breath drawn in or held because of anticipation or suspense: *We watched with bated breath as the runners approached the finish line.* [1250–1300; ME, aph. var. of ABATE]

bate[2] (bāt), *v.,* **bat·ed, bat·ing,** *n.* —*v.i.* **1.** (of a hawk) to flutter its wings and attempt to escape in a fit of anger or fear. —*n.* **2.** a state of violent anger or fear. [1250–1300; ME *baten* to beat, flap (wings, etc.) < MF *(se) batre* << L *battuere* to beat; cf. ABATE]

bate[3] (bāt), *v.,* **bat·ed, bat·ing,** *n.* —*v.t., v.i.* **1.** *Tanning.* to soak (leather) after liming in an alkaline solution to soften it and remove the lime. —*n.* **2.** the solution used. [1870–75; var. of *beat* to pare off turf, OE *bǣtan* to BAIT; c. Sw *beta* to tan, G *beissen* to macerate]

bat-eared (bat′ērd′), *adj.* (of a dog or other canid) having large, erect ears rounded at the top, resembling those of a bat. [1900–05]

bat′-eared fox′. See **Cape fox.**

ba·teau (ba tō′; *Fr.* bA tō′), *n., pl.* **-teaux** (-tōz′; *Fr.* -tō′). **1.** Also, **batteau.** *Naut.* **a.** *Chiefly Canadian and Southern U.S.* a small, flat-bottomed rowboat used on rivers. **b.** a half-decked, sloop-rigged boat used for fishing on Chesapeake Bay; skipjack. **c.** (in some regions) a scow. **2.** a pontoon of a floating bridge. [1705–15, *Amer.*; < F; OF *batel,* equiv. to *bat* (< OE *bāt* BOAT) + *-el* dim. suffix < L *-ellus;* see -ELLE]

bateau′ neck′. See **boat neck.** Also called **bateau′ neck′line.** [1920–25]

ba·te·leur (bat′l ûr′, bat′l ûr′), *n.* a common African eagle, *Terathopius ecaudatus,* having a very short tail. [1860–65; < F: mountebank, juggler; OF *bastelleur*]

bate′ment light′ (bāt′mənt), a compartment of a window with tracery, the bottom of which is formed by the arched head of a compartment or compartments below. [1400–50; late ME; short for ABATEMENT]

Bates (bāts), *n.* **Katherine Lee,** 1859–1929, U.S. educator and author.

Bates′i·an mim′icry (bāt′sē ən), *Ecol.* the protective resemblance in appearance of a palatable or harmless species, as the viceroy butterfly, to an unpalatable or dangerous species, as the monarch butterfly, that is usually avoided by predators. Cf. **Müllerian mimicry.** [after Henry Walter *Bates* (1825–92), English naturalist, who described such mimicry in 1861; see -IAN]

BATF, Bureau of Alcohol, Tobacco, and Firearms.

bat·fish (bat′fish′), *n., pl.* (*esp. collectively*) **-fish,** (*esp. referring to two or more kinds or species*) **-fish·es. 1.** any of the flat-bodied, marine fishes of the family Ogcocephalidae, as *Ogcocephalus vespertilio,* common in the southern Atlantic coastal waters of the U.S. **2.** a stingray, *Aetobatis californicus,* found off the coast of California. [1900–05; BAT[2] + FISH]

bat·fowl (bat′foul′), *v.i.* to catch birds at night by dazzling them with a light and then capturing them in a net. [1400–50; late ME *batfowlyn.* See BAT[2], FOWL (v.)] —**bat′fowl′er,** *n.*

bat′ girl′, *Baseball.* a girl or young woman who takes care of the bats and sometimes other equipment of a team.

bath[1] (bath, bäth), *n., pl.* **baths** (bat͟hz, bät͟hz, baths, bäths), *v.* —*n.* **1.** a washing or immersion of something, esp. the body, in water, steam, etc., as for cleansing or medical treatment: *I take a bath every day. Give the dog a bath.* **2.** a quantity of water or other liquid used for this purpose: *running a bath.* **3.** a container for water or other cleansing liquid, as a bathtub. **4.** a room equipped for bathing; bathroom: *The house has two baths.* **5.** a building containing rooms or apartments with equipment for bathing; bathhouse. **6.** Often, **baths.** one of the elaborate bathing establishments of the ancients: *the baths of Caracalla.* **7.** Usually, **baths.** a town or resort visited for medical treatment by bathing or the like; spa. **8.** a preparation, as an acid solution, in which something is immersed. **9.** the container for such a preparation. **10.** a device for controlling the temperature of something by the use of a surrounding medium, as sand, water, oil, etc. **11.** *Metall.* **a.** the depressed hearth of a steelmaking furnace. **b.** the molten metal being made into steel in a steelmaking furnace. **12.** the state of being covered by a liquid, as perspiration: *in a bath of sweat.* **13. take a bath,** *Informal.* to suffer a large financial loss: *Many investors are taking a bath on their bond investments.* —*v.t., v.i.* **14.** to wash or soak in a bath. [bef. 900; ME; OE *bæth;* c. OFris *beth,* OS, ON *bath,* G *Bad;* < Gmc **bátha-n* what is warmed, akin to OHG *bājan* (G *bähen*), Sw *basa* to warm; pre-Gmc **bheH-* to warm, ptp. **bhH-to-*] —**bath′less,** *adj.*

bath[2] (bath), *n.* a Hebrew unit of liquid measure, equal to a quantity varying between 10 and 11 U.S. gallons (38 and 42 liters). [< Heb]

Bath (bath, bäth), *n.* **1.** a city in Avon, in SW England: mineral springs. 84,300. **2.** a seaport in SW Maine. 10,246.

Ba'th (bä′äth), *n.* Baath.

Bath′ bun′, a round, sweet bun, usually containing raisins, citron, etc. [1795–1805]

Bath′ chair′, 1. a wheeled and hooded chair, used esp. by invalids. **2.** any wheelchair. Also, **bath′ chair′.** [1815–25]

bathe (bāt͟h), *v.,* **bathed, bath·ing,** *n.* —*v.t.* **1.** to immerse (all or part of the body) in water or some other liquid, for cleansing, refreshment, etc. **2.** to wet; wash. **3.** to moisten or suffuse with any liquid. **4.** to apply water or other liquid to, with a sponge, cloth, etc.: *to bathe a wound.* **5.** to wash over or against, as by the action of the sea, a river, etc.: *incoming tides bathing the coral reef.* **6.** to cover or surround: *a shaft of sunlight bathing the room; a morning fog bathing the city.* —*v.i.* **7.** to take a bath or sunbath. **8.** to swim for pleasure. **9.** to be covered or surrounded as if with water. —*n.* **10.** *Brit.* the act of bathing, esp. in the sea, a lake, or a river; a swimming bath. [bef. 1000; ME *bath(i)en,* OE *bathian,* equiv. to *bæth* BATH[1] + *-ian* inf. suffix]

bath·er (bā′t͟hər), *n.* **1.** a person or thing that bathes. **2. bathers,** (*used with a plural v.*) *Australian Informal.* a bathing suit. [1630–40; BATHE + -ER[1]; cf. -S[3]]

ba·thet·ic (bə thet′ik), *adj.* displaying or characterized by bathos: *the bathetic emotionalism of soap operas.* [1825–35; BATH(os) + -ETIC, on the model of PATHETIC] —**ba·thet′i·cal·ly,** *adv.*

bath·house (bath′hous′, bäth′-), *n., pl.* **-hous·es** (-hou′ziz). **1.** a structure, as at the seaside, containing dressing rooms for bathers. **2.** a building for bathing, sometimes equipped with swimming pools, medical baths, etc. [1695–1705; BATH[1] + HOUSE]

Bath·i·nette (bath′ə net′, bä′thə-), *Trademark.* a folding bathtub for babies, usually of rubberized cloth.

bath′ing beau′ty (bā′t͟hing), an attractive woman in a bathing suit, esp. an entrant in a beauty contest. [1915–20]

bath′ing cap′ (bā′t͟hing), a tight-fitting elastic cap, usually of rubber, worn to keep the hair dry while swimming and bathing. [1865–70]

bath·ing-ma·chine (bā′thing mə shēn′), *n.* a small bathhouse on wheels formerly used as a dressing room and in which bathers could also be transported from the beach to the water. [1765–75]

bath′ing suit′ (bā′thing), a garment worn for swimming. Also called **swimsuit.** [1870–75]

bath′ mat′ (bath, bäth), a mat or washable rug used to stand on when entering or leaving a bath. [1890–95]

bath mitz·vah (bät mits′və, bäs; *Seph. Heb.* bät′ mēts vä′; *Ashk. Heb.* bäs mits′və), (*often caps.*) *Judaism.* See **bat mitzvah.**

batho-, a combining form meaning "depth," used in the formation of compound words: *bathometer.* Also, **bathy-.** [comb. form of Gk *báthos; bathy-,* s. of *bathýs* deep]

bath·o·lith (bath′ə lith), *n. Geol.* a large body of intrusive igneous rock believed to have crystallized at a considerable depth below the earth's surface; pluton. [1900–05; BATHO- + -LITH] —**bath′o·lith′ic,** *adj.*

ba·thom·e·ter (bə thom′i tər), *n. Oceanog.* a device for ascertaining the depth of water. [1870–75; BATHO- + -METER]

ba·thos (bā′thos, -thôs, -thōs), *n.* **1.** a ludicrous descent from the exalted or lofty to the commonplace; anticlimax. **2.** insincere pathos; sentimentality; mawkishness. **3.** triteness or triviality in style. [1630–40; < Gk: depth]
—**Syn. 2.** maudlinness, tearfulness; mush, gush, schmaltz. **3.** insipidity, inanity.

bath·robe (bath′rōb′, bäth′-), *n.* a long, loose, coatlike garment, often tied with a belt of the same material, worn before and after a bath, over sleepwear, or as leisure wear at home. [1900–05, *Amer.*; BATH[1] + ROBE]

bath·room (bath′ro͞om′, -ro͝om′, bäth′-), *n.* **1.** a room equipped for taking a bath or shower. **2.** toilet (def. 2). **3. go to** or **use the bathroom,** to use the toilet; urinate or defecate. [1690–1700; BATH[1] + ROOM]

bath′room tis′sue. See **toilet paper.**

bath′ salts′ (bath, bäth), a preparation used to soften or give a pleasant scent to a bath, as colored, sweet-smelling flakes, crystals, etc. [1905–10]

Bath·she·ba (bath shē′bə, bath′shə-), *n.* **1.** the wife of Uriah and afterward of David: mother of Solomon. II Sam. 11, 12. **2.** a female given name: from a Hebrew phrase meaning "daughter of the oath."

bath′ sheet′ (bath, bäth), an extra-large bath towel, esp. one at least 3 ft. (1 m) wide and 5 ft. (1.5 m) long. [1895–1900]

bath′ sponge′, any of various common sponges, of the family Spongiidae, that have a skeletal network composed of fibers of spongin: collected in the Gulf of Mexico, the Mediterranean, and the Caribbean for their commercial value.

bath′ tow′el (bath, bäth), a large towel used to dry the body after bathing or showering, usually made of heavy, absorbent material. [1860–65]

bath·tub (bath′tub′, bäth′-), *n.* a tub to bathe in, esp. one that is a permanent fixture in a bathroom. [1825–35; BATH[1] + TUB]

bath′tub gin′, *Informal.* homemade gin, esp. gin made illegally during Prohibition. [1920–25]

Bath·urst (bath′ərst), *n.* **1.** former name of **Banjul.** **2.** a town in E New South Wales, in SE Australia. 19,640. **3.** a port on the Gulf of St. Lawrence in NE New Brunswick, in SE Canada: summer resort. 15,705.

bath·wa·ter (bath′wô′tər, -wot′ər, bäth′-), *n.* **1.** water for bathing: *He ran the bathwater while he shaved.* **2. throw out the baby with the bathwater,** to eliminate or reject the good along with the bad. [1910–15; BATH[1] + WATER]

bathy-, var. of **batho-:** *bathysphere.*

bath·y·al (bath′ē əl), *adj. Oceanog.* of or pertaining to the biogeographic region of the ocean bottom between the sublittoral and abyssal zones: from depths of approximately 660 to 13,000 ft. (200 to 4000 m). [1925–30; BATHY- + -AL[1]]

ba·thym·e·try (bə thim′i trē), *n.* **1.** the measurement of the depths of oceans, seas, or other large bodies of water. **2.** the data derived from such measurement, esp. as compiled in a topographic map. [1860–65; BATHY- + -METRY] —**ba·thym′e·ter,** *n.* —**bath·y·met·ric** (bath′ə me′trik), **bath′y·met′ri·cal,** *adj.* —**bath′y·met′ri·cal·ly,** *adv.*

bath·y·pe·lag·ic (bath′ə pə laj′ik), *adj. Oceanog.* pertaining to or living in the bathyal region of an ocean. [1905–10; BATHY- + PELAGIC]

bath·y·scaphe (bath′ə skāf′, -skaf′), *n. Oceanog.* a navigable, submersible vessel for exploring the depths of the ocean, having a separate, overhead chamber filled with gasoline for buoyancy and iron or steel weights for ballast. Also, **bath·y·scaph** (bath′ə skaf′), **bath·y·scape** (bath′ə skāp′). [1947; < F, equiv. to *bathy-* BATHY- + Gk *skáphos* ship; coined by Auguste Piccard]

bath·y·sphere (bath′ə sfēr′), *n. Oceanog.* a spherical diving apparatus from which to study deep-sea life, lowered into the ocean depths by a cable. [1925–30; BATHY- + -SPHERE]

bath·y·ther·mo·gram (bath′ə thûr′mə gram′), *n.* a record made by a bathythermograph. [1955–60; BATHY- + THERMO- + -GRAM[1]]

bath·y·ther·mo·graph (bath′ə thûr′mə graf′, -gräf′), *n. Oceanog.* an instrument that makes a record of the temperature at various depths in the ocean. [1935–40; BATHY- + THERMOGRAPH]

ba·tik (bə tēk′, bat′ik), *n.* **1.** a technique of hand-dyeing fabrics by using wax as a dye repellent to cover parts of a design, dyeing the uncovered fabric with a color or colors, and dissolving the wax in boiling water. **2.** the fabric so decorated. —*v.t.* **3.** to hand-dye (material) using the technique of batik. Also, **battik.** [1875–80; < Javanese *baṭik*]

bat·ing (bā′ting), *prep. Scots.* with the exception of; excluding. [1560–70; aph. var. of *abating.* See ABATE]

Bat·in·ism (bat′n iz′əm), *n. Islam.* a secret movement in Islam, often associated with Isma'ili Shi'ism. [partial trans. of Ar *bāṭiniyyah,* equiv. to *bāṭin* inner, hidden + *-iyyah* abstract n. suffix]

Ba·tis·ta (bə tē′stə; *Sp.* bä tēs′tä), *n.* **Ful·gen·cio** (fo͞ol hen′syô), (*Fulgencio Batista y Zaldívar*), 1901–73, Cuban military leader: dictator of Cuba 1934–40; president 1940–44, 1952–59.

ba·tiste (bə tēst′, ba-), *n.* a fine, often sheer fabric, constructed in either a plain or figured weave and made of any of various natural or synthetic fibers. [1690–1700; < F; MF (*toile de*) *ba(p)tiste,* after *Baptiste* of Cambrai, said to have been first maker]

Bat·lle y Or·dó·ñez (bät′ye ē ôʀ thô′nyes), **Jo·sé** (hô se′), 1856–1929, Uruguayan statesman: president of Uruguay 1903–07, 1911–15.

bat·man (bat′mən), *n., pl.* **-men.** (in the British army) a soldier assigned to an officer as a servant. [1745–55; short for *bat-horse man,* equiv. to *bat* < F *bât* packsaddle (< VL **bastum,* n. deriv. of **bastāre* to carry < LGk **bastân,* re-formation of Gk *bastázein* to lift, carry) + HORSE + MAN[1]]

bat mitz·vah (bät mits′və, bäs; *Seph. Heb.* bät′ mēts-vä′; *Ashk. Heb.* bäs mits′və), (*often caps.*) *Judaism.* **1.** a solemn ceremony, chiefly among Reform and Conservative Jews, that is held in the synagogue on Friday night or Saturday morning to admit formally as an adult member of the Jewish community a girl 12 to 13 years old. **2.** the girl participating in this ceremony. **3.** to administer the ceremony of bat mitzvah to. Also, **bath mitzvah, bas mitzvah.** Cf. **bar mitzvah.** [< Heb *bath miṣwāh* lit., daughter of the divine law]

Bat·na (bat′nə, -na), *n.* a city in NE Algeria. 85,000.

ba·ton (bə ton′, ba-, bat′n), *n.* **1.** *Music.* a wand used by a conductor. **2.** a rod of lightweight metal fitted with a weighted bulb at each end and carried and twirled by a drum major or majorette. **3.** *Track.* a hollow rod of wood, paper, or plastic that is passed during a race from one member of a relay team to the next in a prescribed area. **4.** a staff, club, or truncheon, esp. one serving as a mark of office or authority. **5.** *Heraldry.* **a.** a diminutive of the bend sinister, couped at the extremities: used in England as a mark of bastardy. **b.** a similar diminutive of the ordinary bend. [1540–50; < MF *bâton,* OF *baston* < VL **bastōn-* (s. of **bastō*) stick, club; cf. LL *bastum* staff]
—**Syn. 4.** mace, scepter, crosier, rod, wand; fasces; caduceus.

bâ·ton de com·man·de·ment (*Fr.* bä tôɴ də kô-mäɴ də mäɴ′), an Upper Paleolithic instrument possibly used as a shaft straightener, often made from the main beam of an antler and having one or more perforations through which a shaft could pass. [< F: lit., staff of command; so called because it was originally thought to function as a sign of authority]

Bat·on Rouge (bat′n ro͞ozh′), the capital of Louisiana, in the SE part: a river port on the Mississippi. 219,486.

baton′ twirl′er, a person who twirls a baton in a parade, exhibition, or competition. —**baton′ twirl′ing.**

bat′ print′ing, ornamenting of ceramics by means of an adhesive substance, as linseed oil, transferred onto the ceramic surface from a sheet of glue or gelatin, dusted with color, and fired.

ba·tra·chi·an (bə trā′kē ən), *adj.* **1.** belonging or pertaining to the Batrachia, a former group comprising the amphibians, and sometimes restricted to the salientians. —*n.* **2.** an amphibian, esp. a salientian. [1825–35; < NL *Batrachi(a)* (< Gk *bátrach(os)* frog + NL *-ia* n. suffix (neut. pl.)) + -AN]

ba·trach·o·tox·in (bə trak′ə tok′sin, ba′trə kō-), *n. Pharm.* a venom, $C_{31}H_{42}N_2O_6$, obtained from skin secretions of Colombian frogs of the genus *Pyllobates* and used experimentally in neurology. [1960–65; < Gk *bátrach(os)* frog + -O- + TOXIN]

bat′ ray′, batfish (def. 2). Also called **bat′ sting′ray.**

bats (bats), *adj. Slang.* insane; crazy: *He's gone bats.* [1915–20; see BAT[2], -S[3]]

bats·man (bats′mən), *n., pl.* **-men.** a batter, esp. in cricket. [1750–60; BAT[1] + 'S[1] + MAN[1]] —**bats′man·ship′,** *n.*

batt (bat), *n.* a sheet of matted cotton, wool, or synthetic fibers. Also, **bat.** [1830–40; special use of BAT[1]]

batt., **1.** battalion. **2.** battery.

bat·tail·ous (bat′l əs), *adj. Archaic.* ready for battle; warlike. [1350–1400; ME *batailous* < MF *bataillos.* See BATTLE[1], -OUS]

bat·ta·lia (bə tāl′yə, -täl′-), *n. Obs.* **1.** order of battle. **2.** an armed or arrayed body of troops. [1585–95; < It *battaglia* body of troops, BATTLE[1]]

bat·tal·ion (bə tal′yən), *n.* **1.** *Mil.* a ground force unit composed of a headquarters and two or more companies or similar units. **2.** an army in battle array. **3.** Often, **battalions.** a large number of persons or things; force: *battalions of bureaucrats.* [1580–90; < MF *bataillon* < It *battaglione* large squadron of soldiers, equiv. to *battagli(a)* BATTAGLIA + *-one* aug. suffix]

Bat·ta·ni (bə tä′nē), *n.* **Al-** (al), c850–929, Arab astronomer. Also called **Albategnius.**

bat·teau (ba tō′; *Fr.* bᴀ tō′), *n., pl.* **-teaux** (-tōz′; *Fr.* -tō′). *Naut.* bateau (def. 1).

bat·tel (bat′l), *n., v.,* **-teled, -tel·ing.** *Brit.* —*n.* **1.** an account with or terminal bill from a college of Oxford University for board, kitchen, and buttery expenses. **2. battels,** expenses, bills, and accounts of a student at Oxford, including those for clothing, books, and personal expenses as well as for tuition, lodging, and food. —*v.i.* **3.** to have an account with or to be supplied with food and drink from a college kitchen or buttery at Oxford University. [1700–10; cf. NL *batellae* (1636), *batilli* (1557), prob. to be identified with late ME *batell* (in AL), taken to mean "charge for provisions"; of obscure orig.; kinship with Scots, N England dial. *ba(i)ttle* rich, fattening (of pasture) is dubious] —**bat′tel·er,** *n.*

batte·ment (bat′mənt; *Fr.* bᴀtᵊ mäɴ′), *n., pl.* **-ments** (-mənts; *Fr.* -mäɴ′). *Ballet.* a movement in which the dancer lifts one leg to the front, side, or back, and returns it to the supporting leg. [1820–30; < F, equiv. to *batt(re)* to beat (see BATE[2]) + *-ment* -MENT]

bat·ten[1] (bat′n), *v.i.* **1.** to thrive by feeding; grow fat. **2.** to feed gluttonously or greedily; glut oneself. **3.** to thrive, prosper, or live in luxury, esp. at the expense of others: *robber barons who battened on the poor.* —*v.t.* **4.** to cause to thrive by or as if by feeding; fatten. [1585–95; appar. < ON *batna* to improve; c. Goth *gabatnan* (*bati* change for the better + *-na* inf. suffix). Cf. OE *bet,* Goth *batis,* OHG *baz* better]

bat·ten[2] (bat′n), *n.* **1.** a small board or strip of wood used for various building purposes, as to cover joints between boards, reinforce certain doors, or supply a foundation for lathing. **2.** a transverse iron or steel strip supporting the flooring strips of a metal fire escape. **3.** *Naut.* **a.** a thin strip of wood inserted in a sail to keep it flat. **b.** a thin, flat length of wood or metal used for various purposes, as to hold the tarpaulin covering a hatch in place. **4.** *Shipbuilding.* a flexible strip of wood used for fairing the lines of a hull on the floor of a mold loft. **5.** *Theat.* **a.** Also called **pipe batten.** a length of metal pipe hung from the gridiron, for suspending scenery or equipment, as drops, flats, or lighting units. **b.** a narrow strip of lumber for constructing, reinforcing, or joining flats. **c.** a similar strip attached to a drop to keep it flat or taut. —*v.t.* **6.** to furnish or bolster with battens. **7.** *Naut.* to cover (a hatch) so as to make watertight (usually fol. by *down*). **8.** *Mach.* to secure (work) to a table or bed for a machining operation. **9.** *Building Trades.* to join or assemble (a steel column or the like) with batten plates. **10.** *Theat.* **a.** to suspend (scenery, stage lights, etc.) from a batten. **b.** to fasten a batten to (a flat or drop). [1400–50; late ME *bataunt, batent* finished board < OF *batant,* n. use of ptp. of *batre* to beat; see BATE[2], -ANT] —**bat′ten·er,** *n.*

bat·ten[3] (bat′n), *Textiles.* —*n.* **1.** (in a loom) the swinging frame for holding and positioning the reed. **2.** a part of the lay of a loom. —*v.t.* **3.** to beat (filling yarn) into place with the batten. [1825–35; alter. of F *battant;* see BATTEN[1]]

bat′ten plate′, an iron or steel plate uniting the angles or flanges of a composite girder, column, or strut.

bat·ter[1] (bat′ər), *v.t.* **1.** to beat persistently or hard; pound repeatedly. **2.** to damage by beating or hard usage: *Rough roads had battered the car. High winds were battering the coast.* —*v.i.* **3.** to deal heavy, repeated blows; pound steadily: *continuing to batter at the front door.* —*n.* **4.** *Print.* **a.** a damaged area on the face of type or plate. **b.** the resulting defect in print. [1300–50; ME *bateren,* prob. < MF, OF *batre* to beat (see BATE[2]), with the inf. ending identified with -ER[6]; cf. AF *baterer*]
—**Syn. 1.** belabor, smite, pelt. **2.** bruise, wound; smash, shatter, shiver; destroy, ruin.

bat·ter[2] (bat′ər), *n.* **1.** a mixture of flour, milk or water, eggs, etc., beaten together for use in cookery. —*v.t.* **2.** to coat with batter. [1350–1400; ME *bat(o)ur, bat(e)re,* perh. < AF *bature,* OF *bat(e)ure* act of beating (*bat(re)* to beat (see BATE[2]) + *-eure* < **-ātūra;* see -ATE[2], -URE), reinforced by BATTER[1]]

bat·ter[3] (bat′ər), *n.* a player who swings a bat or whose turn it is to bat, as in baseball or cricket. [1765–75; BAT[1] + -ER[1]]

bat·ter[4] (bat′ər), *Archit.* —*v.i.* **1.** (of the face of a wall or the like) to slope backward and upward. —*n.* **2.** a backward and upward slope of the face of a wall or the like. [1540–50; of obscure orig.]

bat′ter board′, (at a building site) one of a number of boards set horizontally to support strings for outlining the foundation plan of a building.

bat′ter brace′, *Building Trades.* a diagonal brace reinforcing one end of a truss.

bat′ter bread′, *Chiefly Eastern Virginia.* See **spoon bread.** [1895–1900, *Amer.*]

bat·ter·cake (bat′ər kāk′), *n. South Midland and Southern U.S.* pancake (def. 1). [1820–30; BATTER[2] + CAKE]
—**Regional Variation.** See **pancake.**

bat′tered child′ syn′drome, the array of physical injuries exhibited by young children who have been beaten repeatedly or otherwise abused by their parents or guardians. [1960–65]

bat·ter·er (bat′ər ər), *n.* **1.** a person or thing that batters. **2.** a person who inflicts violent physical abuse upon a child, spouse, or other person. [1605–15; BATTER[1] + -ER[1]]

bat·ter-fry (bat′ər frī′), *v.t.,* **-fried, -fry·ing.** to coat with batter and fry in deep fat.

bat·te·rie (bat′ə rē; *Fr.* bᴀtᵊ ʀē′), *n., pl.* **bat·te·ries** (bat′ə rēz; *Fr.* bᴀtᵊ ʀē′). *Ballet.* **1.** a beating together of the calves or feet during a leap. **2.** (in tap dancing) a rapid succession of taps, often compared to drumming or to machine-gun fire. **3.** battery (def. 11). [1705–15; < F; see BATTERY]

bat·te·rie de cui·sine (bᴀtᵊ ʀēdᵊ kwē zēn′), *pl.* **bat-**

CONCISE PRONUNCIATION KEY: *act, cāpe, dâre, pärt; set, ēqual; if, īce; ox, ōver, ôrder, oil, bo͝ok, bo͞ot, out; up, ûrge; child; sing; shoe; thin, that;* zh as in *treasure.* ə = *a* as in *alone, e* as in *system, i* as in *easily, o* as in *gallop, u* as in *circus;* ᵊ as in *fire* (fīᵊr), *hour* (ouᵊr). l and n can serve as syllabic consonants, as in *cradle* (krād′l), and *button* (but′n). See the full key inside the front cover.

te·ries de cui·sine (bat[ə] rēd[ə] kwē zēn′). *French.* kitchen utensils.

bat′tering ram′, 1. an ancient military device with a heavy horizontal ram for battering down walls, gates, etc. 2. any of various similar devices, usually machine-powered, used in demolition, by police and firefighters to force entrance to a building, etc. [1605–15]

bat′ter pile′, *Building Trades.* a pile driven at an angle to the vertical.

bat′ter's box′, *Baseball.* box (def. 16a).

Bat·ter·sea (bat′ər sē), *n.* **1.** a former borough of London, England, now part of Wandsworth, on the Thames. **2.** an enameling technique in which designs are either painted or printed on a white ground fused onto a metal base.

bat·ter·y (bat′ə rē), *n., pl.* **-ter·ies. 1.** *Elect.* **a.** Also called **galvanic battery, voltaic battery.** a combination of two or more cells electrically connected to work together to produce electric energy. **b.** cell (def. 7a). **2.** any large group or series of related things: *a battery of questions.* **3.** *Mil.* **a.** two or more pieces of artillery used for combined action. **b.** a tactical unit of artillery, usually consisting of six guns together with the artillerymen, equipment, etc., required to operate them. **c.** a parapet or fortification equipped with artillery. **4.** a group or series of similar articles, machines, parts, etc. **5.** *Baseball.* the pitcher and catcher considered as a unit. **6.** *Navy.* **a.** (on a warship) a group of guns having the same caliber or used for the same purpose. **b.** the whole armament of a warship. **7.** *Psychol.* a series of tests yielding a single total score, used for measuring aptitude, intelligence, personality, etc. **8.** the act of beating or battering. **9.** *Law.* an unlawful attack upon another person by beating or wounding, or by touching in an offensive manner. **10.** an instrument used in battering. **11.** Also, **batterie.** *Music.* the instruments comprising the percussion section of an orchestra. **12.** any imposing group of persons or things acting or directed in unison: *a battery of experts.* [1525–35; < MF *batterie,* equiv. to *batt(re)* to beat (see BATE[2]) + *-erie* -ERY]

Bat·ter·y (bat′ə rē), *n.* **The,** a park at the S end of Manhattan, in New York City. Also called **Bat′tery Park′.**

bat′tery elim′inator, eliminator (def. 2).

bat′tery jar′, a rather large cylindrical container of heavy glass with an open top, used in laboratories.

Bat·ti·ca·lo·a (but′i kə lō′ə), *n.* a seaport in E Sri Lanka. 24,000.

bat·tik (bə tēk′, bat′ik), *n., v.t.,* batik.

bat·ting (bat′ing), *n.* **1.** the act or manner of using a bat in a game of ball. **2.** cotton, wool, or synthetic fibers in batts or sheets, used as filling for quilts or bedcovers. [1605–15; BAT[1] + -ING[1]]

bat′ting av′erage, 1. *Baseball.* a measure of the batting ability of a player, obtained by dividing the number of base hits by the number of official times at bat and carrying out the result to three decimal places. A player with 100 base hits in 300 times at bat has a batting average of 0.333. **2.** *Informal.* a degree of achievement or accomplishment in any activity. [1865–70, *Amer.*]

bat′ting eye′, *Baseball.* the batter's visual appraisal of balls pitched toward home plate.

bat′ting or′der, *Baseball.* the sequence in which hitters will bat in a given game, determined in advance by the team manager.

bat·tle[1] (bat′l), *n., v.,* **-tled, -tling.** —*n.* **1.** a hostile encounter or engagement between opposing military forces: *the battle of Waterloo.* **2.** participation in such hostile encounters or engagements: *wounds received in battle.* **3.** a fight between two persons or animals: *ordering a trial by battle to settle the dispute.* **4.** any conflict or struggle: *a battle for control of the Senate.* **5.** *Archaic.* a battalion. **6. give** or **do battle,** to enter into conflict; fight: *He was ready to do battle for his beliefs.* —*v.i.* **7.** to engage in battle: *ready to battle with the enemy.* **8.** to work very hard or struggle; strive: *to battle for freedom.* —*v.t.* **9.** to fight (a person, army, cause, etc.): *We battled strong winds and heavy rains in our small boat.* **10.** to force or accomplish by fighting, struggling, etc.: *He battled his way to the top of his profession.* [1250–1300; ME *bataile* < OF < VL **battālia* for LL *battuālia* (neut. pl.) gladiatorial exercises, equiv. to *battu(ere)* to strike (see BATE[2]) + *-ālia,* neut. pl. of *-ālis* -AL[2]] —**bat′tler,** *n.*

—**Syn. 1.** contest, conflict, war. BATTLE, ACTION, SKIRMISH mean a conflict between organized armed forces. A BATTLE is a prolonged and general conflict pursued to a definite decision: *the Battle of the Bulge in World War II.* A SKIRMISH is a slight engagement, often on the periphery of an area of battle: *several minor skirmishes.* An ACTION can be a battle or a skirmish or can refer to actual fighting or combat: *a major military action; action along the border; He saw action in the campaign.* **2.** warfare, combat, fighting. **6.** conflict. **8.** contest.

bat·tle[2] (bat′l), *v.t.,* **-tled, -tling.** *Archaic.* to furnish (a building or wall) with battlements; crenelate. [1300–50; ME *batailen* < MF *bataillier* to provide with *batailles.* See BATTLEMENT]

bat·tle-ax (bat′l aks′), *n.* **1.** a broadax formerly used as a weapon of war. **2.** *Slang.* a domineering, aggressive, sharp-tempered person, esp. a woman. Also, **bat′·tle-axe′.** [1350–1400; ME *batelax*]

Bat′tle-Ax cul′ture, a late Neolithic to Copper Age culture of northern Europe marked esp. by the production of pottery bearing the imprint of cord and by the use of battle-axes as burial accouterments. Also called **Corded culture.** [1945–50]

CONCISE ETYMOLOGY KEY: <, descended or borrowed from; >, whence; b., blend of, blended; c., cognate with; cf., compare; deriv., derivative; equiv., equivalent; imit., imitative; obl., oblique; r., replacing; s., stem; sp., spelling, spelled; resp., respelling, respelled; trans., translation; ?, origin unknown; *, unattested; ‡, probably earlier than. See the full key inside the front cover.

bat′tle clasp′, clasp (def. 4).

Bat′tle Creek′, a city in S Michigan. 35,724.

bat′tle cruis′er, a warship of maximum speed and firepower, but with lighter armor than a battleship. [1910–15]

bat′tle cry′, 1. a cry or shout of troops in battle. **2.** the phrase or slogan used in any contest or campaign. [1805–15]

bat·tle·dore (bat′l dôr′, -dōr′), *n., v.,* **-dored, -dor·ing.** —*n.* **1.** Also called **bat′tledore and shut′tlecock.** a game from which badminton was developed, played since ancient times in India and other Asian countries. **2.** a light racket for striking the shuttlecock in this game. **3.** a 17th- and 18th-century hornbook of wood or cardboard, used as a child's primer. —*v.t., v.i.* **4.** to toss or fly back and forth: *to battledore the plan among one's colleagues.* [1400–50; late ME *batyldo(u)re* washing beetle, equiv. to *batyl* to beat (clothes) in washing (freq. of BAT[1]) + *-dore* dung beetle (BEETLE[1] for BEETLE[2] by way of pun, with allusion to filth on clothes). See DOR[1]]

bat′tle dress′, military field uniform and accouterments, generally camouflaged and stripped of all ornamentation. [1935–40]

bat′tle fatigue′, *Psychiatry.* a posttraumatic stress disorder occurring among soldiers engaged in active combat, characterized by excessive autonomic arousal, psychic numbing, and persistent reliving of traumatic experiences. Also called **combat fatigue, combat neurosis, shell shock.** [1940–45] —**bat′tle-fa·tigued′,** *adj.*

bat·tle·field (bat′l fēld′), *n.* **1.** the field or ground on which a battle is fought. **2.** an area of contention, conflict, or hostile opposition: *During that era the classroom became a battlefield of incompatible ideologies.* Also called **bat·tle·ground** (bat′l ground′). [1805–15; BATTLE[1] + FIELD]

bat·tle·front (bat′l frunt′), *n.* the extreme forward area of a battlefield, where troops are in direct contact with the enemy. [1910–15; BATTLE[1] + FRONT]

bat′tle group′, *U.S. Mil.* a planning or command unit within a division of the army. [1950–55]

bat′tle jack′et, 1. *U.S. Mil.* a close-fitting waist-length woolen jacket with snugly fitting cuffs and waist, formerly worn as part of the service uniform. **2.** any of various adaptations of this jacket in men's and women's sportswear. Also called **combat jacket.**

bat′tle lan′tern, a portable, battery-operated light for emergency use aboard a warship. [1820–30]

bat′tle line′, the line along which warring troops meet. [1805–15]

bat·tle·ment (bat′l mənt), *n.* Often, **battlements.** a parapet or cresting, originally defensive but later usually decorative, consisting of a regular alternation of merlons and crenels; crenelation. Also called **embattlement.** [1275–1325; ME *batelment* < MF *bataille* battlement; see -MENT] —**bat·tle·ment·ed** (bat′l men′tid), *adj.*

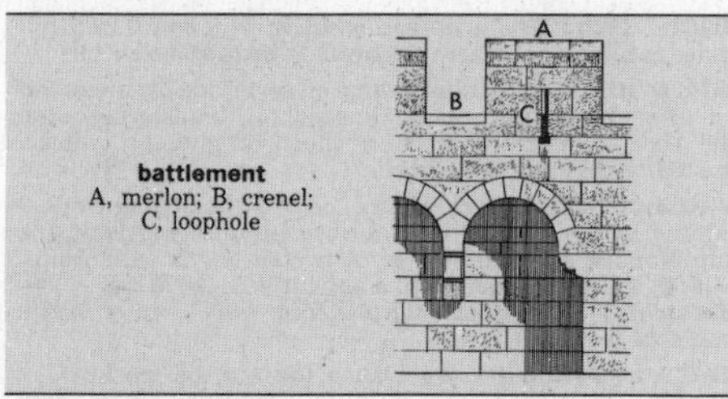

battlement
A, merlon; B, crenel;
C, loophole

Bat′tle of Brit′ain, (in World War II) the series of aerial combats that took place between British and German aircraft during the autumn of 1940 and that included the severe bombardment of British cities.

Bat′tle of the Bulge′. See **Bulge, Battle of the.**

bat′tle plan′, 1. the strategy to be used in a military engagement. **2.** the plan for accomplishing a goal or dealing with a problem or difficult situation: *the President's battle plan for getting his legislation through Congress.*

bat·tle·plane (bat′l plān′), *n.* an airplane designed for combat; warplane. [1910–15; BATTLE[1] + PLANE[1]]

bat′tle roy′al, *pl.* **battles royal. 1.** a fight in which more than two combatants are engaged. **2.** a heated argument: *After a while the discussion turned into a battle royal.* [1665–75]

bat·tle-scarred (bat′l skärd′), *adj.* **1.** bearing scars or damages received in battle: *a battle-scarred warship.* **2.** showing the effects of hard wear or use: *a sale of battle-scarred desks.* [1860–65]

bat·tle·ship (bat′l ship′), *n.* **1.** any of a class of warships that are the most heavily armored and are equipped with the most powerful armament. **2.** See **ship of the line.** [1785–95, *Amer.*; BATTLE[1] + SHIP]

bat′tleship gray′, a subdued bluish gray. [1825–35, *Amer.*] —**bat′tle·ship-gray′,** *adj.*

bat·tle·some (bat′l səm), *adj.* argumentative; quarrelsome. [1875–80; BATTLE[1] + -SOME[1]]

bat′tle star′, *U.S. Mil.* **1.** a small bronze star worn on a campaign ribbon by members of organizations taking part in certain battles or other wartime operations. **2.** a small silver star similarly worn, equivalent to five bronze battle stars.

bat′tle sta′tion, *Mil., Navy.* the place or position that one is assigned to for battle or in an emergency.

bat′tle wag′on, *Informal.* a battleship. [1925–30, *Amer.*]

bat·tle·wor·thy (bat′l wûr′thē), *adj.* capable of engaging in combat; ready for battle: *a decline in the nation's battleworthy forces.* [1885–90; BATTLE[1] + -WORTHY]

bat·tol·o·gize (bə tol′ə jīz′), *v.,* **-gized, -giz·ing.** —*v.t.* **1.** to repeat (a word, phrase, mannerism, etc.) excessively. —*v.i.* **2.** (of writing or speaking) to repeat words, phrases, etc., to an excessive and tiresome degree. Also, *esp. Brit.,* **bat·tol′o·gise′.** [1625–35; BATTOLOG(Y) + -IZE]

bat·tol·o·gy (bə tol′ə jē), *n.* wearisome repetition of words in speaking or writing. [1595–1605; < Gk *battologia* (*bátt(os)* stammerer + *-o-* -O- + *-logia* -LOGY)] —**bat·tol′o·gist,** *n.* —**bat·to·log·i·cal** (bat′l oj′i kəl), *adj.*

bat·tue (ba to͞o′, -tyo͞o′; *Fr.* ba ty′), *n., pl.* **-tues** (-to͞oz′, -tyo͞oz′; *Fr.* -ty′). *Chiefly Brit.* **1.** *Hunting.* **a.** the beating or driving of game from cover toward a stationary hunter. **b.** a hunt or hunting party using this method of securing game. **2.** undiscriminating slaughter of defenseless or unresisting crowds. [1810–20; < F, n. use of fem. of *battu,* ptp. of *battre* < L *battuere* to beat. See BATTUTA, BATTLE[1]]

bat′ turn′, *Air Force Slang.* a sharp and sudden change in an aircraft's heading.

bat·tu·ta (bə to͞o′tə; *It.* bät to͞o′tä), *n., pl.* **-tas, -te** (-tā; *It.* -te). *Music.* **1.** a beat. **2.** a measure. [1810–20; < It, fem. ptp. of *battere* to beat < L *battuere*]

bat·tu·to (bə to͞o′tō), *n., pl.* **-tos.** *Italian Cookery.* soffritto. [< It; masc. of BATTUTA]

bat·ty (bat′ē), *adj.,* **-ti·er, -ti·est.** *Slang.* insane; crazy; eccentric. [BAT[2] + -Y[1]] —**bat′ti·ness,** *n.*

Ba·tu Khan (bä′to͞o kän′), d. 1255, Mongol conqueror: leader of the Golden Horde (grandson of Genghis Khan).

Ba·tu·mi (bä to͞o′mē), *n.* a seaport in and the capital of Adzharistan, in the SW Georgian Republic, on the Black Sea. 124,000. Formerly, **Ba·tum** (bä to͞om′).

ba·tu·que (bə to͞o′kə), *n.* a Brazilian round dance of African origin. [< Pg, of uncert. orig.]

Ba·twa (bä′twä), *n., pl.* **-twas,** (*esp. collectively*) **-twa.** Twa (def. 1).

bat·wing (bat′wing′), *adj.* **1.** formed, shaped, etc., in the manner of a bat's wing or wings. **2.** (of a garment or part of a garment) resembling or conceived of as resembling the wing or wings of a bat, as a loose long sleeve **(bat′wing sleeve′)** having a deep armhole and a tight wrist. [1955–60; BAT[2] + WING]

Bat Yam (bät′ yäm′), a city on the coast of the Mediterranean Sea in W central Israel, S of Tel Aviv. 132,100.

bau·ble (bô′bəl), *n.* **1.** a showy, usually cheap, ornament; trinket; gewgaw. **2.** a jester's scepter. [1275–1325; ME *babel, babulle* < OF *babel, baubel,* derivs. of an expressive base with varying vocalisms; cf. OF *baubelet,* BIBELOT]

Bau·cis (bô′sis), *n. Class. Myth.* an aged Phrygian peasant woman who, with her husband Philemon, offered hospitality to the disguised Zeus and Hermes: they were rewarded by being saved from a flood and changed into trees.

baud (bôd), *n. Telecommunications.* a unit used to measure the speed of signaling or data transfer, equal to the number of pulses or bits per second: *baud rate.* [1925–30; named after J. M. É. *Baudot* (1845–1903), French inventor]

bau·de·kin (bô′dē kin), *n.* baldachin (def. 1). [1350–1400; ME < MF < ML *baldakinus* BALDACHIN]

Bau·de·laire (bōd′l âr′; *Fr.* bōd[ə] lɛʀ′), *n.* **Charles Pierre** (sharl pyer), 1821–67, French poet and critic.

Bau·douin I (*Fr.* bō dwaɴ′), 1930–93, king of the Belgians 1951–93.

Bau·douin de Cour·te·nay (bō dwaɴ′ də ko͝or′tə-nā′), **Jan Ig·na·cy Nie·cis·law** (yän ig nä′tsi nye′tsis-läf′), 1845–1929, Polish linguist: pioneer in modern phonology.

bau·drons (bô′drənz), *n. Scot.* a cat. [1400–50; late ME (Scots) *balderonis;* perh. akin to ME *badde* cat]

Bau·er (bou′ər; *Ger.* bou′əʀ), *n.* **Ge·org** (gā ôʀk′). See **Agricola, Georgius.**

Baugh (bô), *n.* **Samuel Adrian** ("*Slinging Sammy*"), born 1914, U.S. football player and coach.

Bau·haus (bou′hous′), *n.* **1.** a school of design established in Weimar in 1919 by Walter Gropius, moved to Dessau in 1926, and closed in 1933 as a result of Nazi hostility. —*adj.* **2.** of or pertaining to the concepts, ideas, or styles developed at the Bauhaus, characterized chiefly by an emphasis on functional design in architecture and the applied arts. [1920–25; < G, equiv. to *Bau-* build, building + *Haus* house]

bau·hin·i·a (bô hin′ē ə, bō in′-), *n.* any of numerous trees, shrubs, or vines of the genus *Bauhinia,* native to warm regions, having two-lobed leaves and showy, usually white, purple, or reddish flowers, widely planted in southern Florida. [< NL (Linnaeus), named after the brothers Jean *Bauhin* (1541–1612) and Gaspard *Bauhin* (1560–1624), Swiss botanists; see -IA]

Ba·ul (bä′o͝ol), *n.* a member of a nonconformist Bengalese sect having gurus but no dogmas, rituals, religious institutions, or scriptures.

baulk (bôk), *v.i., v.t., n.* balk.

Baum (bôm, bäm *for 1;* boum *for 2*), *n.* **1. L(y·man) Frank** (lī′mən), 1856–1919, U.S. journalist, playwright, and author of children's books. **2. Vicki,** 1888–1960, U.S. novelist, born in Austria.

Bau·mé (bō mā′, bō′mā), *adj.* pertaining to, noting, or calibrated according to a Baumé scale. [1835–45]

Bau·meis·ter (bou′mī′stər), *n.* **Wil·li** (vil′ē), 1889–1955, German painter.

Baumé′ scale′, a scale for use with a hydrometer, calibrated in such manner that the specific gravity of a given liquid may be easily computed. [named after A. *Baumé* (1728–1804), French chemist]

baum′ mar′ten (boum), **1.** the European pine marten. **2.** the fur of this animal. [1875–80; < G *Baum-(marder)* tree marten + MARTEN]

Bau·ru (bou ro͞o′), *n.* a city in E Brazil. 120,178.

bau·son (bô′sən), *n. Archaic.* a badger (applied contemptuously to people). [1275–1325; ME *bausen, bauson* < MF *bausen, bauzan,* var. of *baucent, balcent* BAUSOND]

bau·sond (bô′sənd, bos′ənd), *adj. Brit. Dial.* **1.** (of animals) having white spots on a black or bay background; piebald. **2.** (of horses and cattle) having a white patch or streak on the forehead or having one white foot. [1275–1325; ME *bausand* < MF, OF *bausant, baucent* < VL **balteānus* belted, striped, equiv. to L *balte(us)* BELT + *-ānus* -AN]

Bau·tzen (bou′tsən), *n.* a city in E East Germany, on the Spree River: scene of defeat of Prussian and Russian armies by Napoleon I, 1813. 47,494.

baux·ite (bôk′sīt, bō′zīt), *n.* a rock consisting of aluminum oxides and hydroxides with various impurities: the principal ore of aluminum. [1860–65; named after *Les Baux,* near Arles in S France; see -ITE¹] **—baux·it·ic** (bôk sit′ik, bō zit′-), *adj.*

Bav., **1.** Bavaria. **2.** Bavarian.

Ba·var·i·a (bə vâr′ē ə), *n.* a state in SE Germany: formerly a kingdom. 11,082,600; 27,239 sq. mi. (70,550 sq. km). *Cap.:* Munich. German, **Bayern.**

Ba·var·i·an (bə vâr′ē ən), *adj.* **1.** of or pertaining to Bavaria, its inhabitants, or their dialect. *—n.* **2.** a native or an inhabitant of Bavaria. **3.** the High German speech of Bavaria and Austria. Cf. **Alemannic** (def. 1). [1630–40; BAVARI(A) + -AN]

Bavar′ian cream′, a dessert made with custard, gelatin, and whipped cream. [1875–80]

ba·va·rois (*Fr.* bᴀ vᴀ rwᴀ′), *n. French Cookery.* See **Bavarian cream.** [1840–50; < F: lit., Bavarian]

ba·veux (bᴀ vœ′), *n., pl.* **-veux** (-vœ′). *Canadian French Slang.* a meanspirited know-it-all.

bav·in (bav′in), *n. Brit. Dial. and Newfoundland.* a piece of kindling wood. [1520–30; orig. obscure]

baw·bee (bô bē′, bô′bē), *n.* **1.** an old Scottish bullion coin, originally worth about three halfpence of English coin, later sixpence. **2.** a halfpenny. **3.** anything of little value. [1535–45; named after Alexander Orok, 16th-century mintmaster, laird of Sille*bawby*]

baw·cock (bô′kok′), *n. Archaic.* (used familiarly) a fine fellow. [1590–1600; < F *beau coc* fine cock]

bawd (bôd), *n.* **1.** a woman who maintains a brothel; madam. **2.** a prostitute. **3.** *Archaic.* a procuress. [1325–75; ME *bawde,* n. use of MF *baude,* fem. of *baud* jolly, dissolute < WGmc; cf. OE *bald* BOLD]

bawd·ry (bô′drē), *n.* **1.** *Archaic.* lewdness; obscenity; bawdiness. **2.** *Obs.* **a.** the business of a prostitute. **b.** illicit intercourse; fornication. [1350–1400; ME *bawdery.* See BAWD, -ERY]

bawd·y (bô′dē), *adj.,* **bawd·i·er, bawd·i·est,** *n.* *—adj.* **1.** indecent; lewd; obscene: *another of his bawdy stories.* *—n.* **2.** coarse or indecent talk or writing; bawdry; bawdiness: *a collection of Elizabethan bawdy.* [1505–15; BAWD + -Y¹] **—bawd′i·ly,** *adv.* **—bawd′i·ness,** *n.*
—Syn. **1.** lascivious, salacious, prurient, earthy, risqué, ribald, coarse, licentious, raunchy.

bawd·y·house (bô′dē hous′), *n., pl.* **-hous·es** (-hou′-ziz). a brothel. [1545–55; BAWDY + HOUSE]

bawl (bôl), *v.i.* **1.** to cry or wail lustily. *—v.t.* **2.** to utter or proclaim by outcry; shout out: *to bawl one's dissatisfaction; bawling his senseless ditties to the audience.* **3.** to offer for sale by shouting, as a hawker: *a peddler bawling his wares.* **4.** **bawl out,** *Informal.* to scold vociferously; reprimand or scold vigorously: *Your father will bawl you out when he sees this mess.* *—n.* **5.** a loud shout; outcry. **6.** a period or spell of loud crying or weeping. **7.** *Chiefly Midland and Western U.S.* the noise made by a calf. [1400–50; late ME < ML *baulāre* to bark < Gmc; cf. ON *baula* to low, *baula* cow, perh. a conflation of *belja* (see BELL²) with an old root **bhu-*] **—bawl′er,** *n.*
—Syn. **1.** howl, yowl, squall, roar, bellow.

bawn (bôn), *n. Newfoundland.* **1.** a rocky stretch of foreshore on which caught fish are laid out to dry. **2.** a patch of grassland or meadow near a dwelling. [1530–40; Hiberno-E < Ir *bábhún* (earlier sp. *badhbhdhún, badhún*) enclosure, perh. equiv. to *ba,* pl. of *bó* cow + *dún* fort; see COW¹, TOWN]

Bax (baks), *n.* **Sir Arnold Edward Trevor,** 1883–1953, English composer.

B-ax·is (bē′ak′sis), *n., pl.* **B-ax·es** (bē′ak′sēz). *Crystall.* the horizontal crystallographic axis that is in a right-left position. Cf. **A-axis, C-axis.**

Bax·ter (bak′stər), *n.* **1.** **Richard,** 1615–91, English Puritan preacher, scholar, and writer. **2.** a male given name.

bay¹ (bā), *n.* **1.** a body of water forming an indentation of the shoreline, larger than a cove but smaller than a gulf. **2.** *South Atlantic States.* an arm of a swamp. **3.** a recess of land, partly surrounded by hills. **4.** an arm of a prairie or swamp, extending into woods and partly surrounded by them. [1350–1400; ME *baye* < MF *baie* < ML, LL *bāia,* perh. by back formation from L *Bāiae* name of a spa on the Bay of Naples]
—Syn. **1.** inlet, estuary, sound, firth, bight.

bay² (bā), *n.* **1.** *Archit.* **a.** any of a number of similar major vertical divisions of a large interior, wall, etc.: *The nave is divided into six bays.* **b.** a division of a window between a mullion and an adjoining mullion or jamb. **c.** See **bay window** (def. 1). **2.** *Aeron.* **a.** any portion of an airplane set off by two successive bulkheads or other bracing members. **b.** a compartment in an aircraft: *a bomb bay; an engine bay.* **3.** a compartment, as in a barn for storing hay. **4.** *Naut.* **a.** the deck space between the anchor windlass and the stem of a vessel. **b.** See **sick bay.** [1275–1325; ME < MF *baee* an opening in a wall, n. use of fem. ptp. of *baer* to stand open, gape < VL **batāre*]
—Syn. **3.** alcove, nook, recess, niche; loft, garret.

bay³ (bā), *n.* **1.** a deep, prolonged howl, as of a hound on the scent. **2.** the position or stand of an animal or fugitive that is forced to turn and resist pursuers because it is no longer possible to flee (usually prec. by *at* or *to*): *a stag at bay; to bring an escaped convict to bay.* **3.** the situation of a person or thing that is forced actively to oppose or to succumb to some adverse condition (usually prec. by *at* or *to*). **4.** the situation of being actively opposed by an animal, person, etc., so as to be powerless to act fully (often prec. by *at*). *—v.i.* **5.** to howl, esp. with a deep, prolonged sound, as a hound on the scent. *—v.t.* **6.** to assail with deep, prolonged howling: *a troubled hound baying the moon.* **7.** to bring to or to hold at bay: *A dog bays its quarry.* [1250–1300; ME, aph. var. of *abay* < AF, dial. OF *abai* barking, n. deriv. of *abaier* to bark, from an imit. base **bay-*]
—Syn. **5.** roar, bellow, bark, bell, clamor.

bay⁴ (bā), *n.* **1.** laurel (def. 1). **2.** Also called **bayberry, bay rum tree.** a tropical American shrub, *Pimenta racemosa,* having aromatic leaves that are used in making bay oil and bay rum. **3.** any of various laurellike trees or shrubs. **4.** any of several magnolias. **5.** an honorary garland or crown bestowed for military victory, literary excellence, etc. **6.** **bays,** fame; renown. [1350–1400; ME *bai(e),* OE *beg-* (in *begbēam* lit., berry tree), conflated with MF *baie* < L *bāca, bacca* berry]

bay⁵ (bā), *n.* **1.** reddish brown. **2.** a horse or other animal of reddish-brown color. *—adj.* **3.** (of horses or other animals) having a reddish-brown body. [1300–50; ME < MF *bai* < L *badius;* cf. OIr *buide* yellow]

ba·ya (bä′yə, bä yä′), *n.* a common weaverbird, *Ploceus philippinus,* of India. [< Hindi *ba(i)yā*]

ba·ya·dere (bī′ə dēr′, -der′), *n.* a fabric with horizontal stripes of brilliant colors. [1855–60; < F: a professional female dancer of India < Pg *bailadeira,* fem. of *bailador* dancer (*baila(r)* to dance (see BALL²) + *-dor* < L *-tor* -TOR); appar. in reference to the fabrics worn by such dancers]

Ba·ya·mo (bä yä′mô), *n.* a city in S Cuba. 71,660.

Ba·ya·món (bä′yä môn′), *n.* a city in N Puerto Rico, near San Juan. 205,800.

bay′ ant′ler, the second prong from the base of a stag's antler. See diag. under **antler.** Also called **bes antler, bez antler.** [1860–65; *bay* for *bes, bez,* ME *bes* secondary (< MF < L *bis* BIS¹)]

Ba·yar (bä yär′), *n.* **Ce·lâl** (je läl′), 1884–1986, Turkish statesman: president 1950–60.

Bay·ard (bā′ərd), *n.* **1.** a magical legendary horse in medieval chivalric romances. **2.** a mock-heroic name for any horse. **3.** (*l.c.*) *Archaic.* a bay horse. [1275–1325; ME < MF; see BAY⁵, -ARD]

Ba·yard (bā′ərd; *for 1 also Fr.* bᴀ yᴀʀ′), *n.* **1.** **Pierre Ter·rail** (pyeʀ te ʀᴀ′yᵊ), **Sei·gneur de** (se nyœʀ′ də), (*"the knight without fear and without reproach"*), 1473–1524, heroic French soldier. **2.** any man of heroic courage and unstained honor. **3.** a male given name.

bay·ber·ry (bā′ber′ē, -bə rē), *n., pl.* **-ries.** **1.** any of several often aromatic trees or shrubs of the genus *Myrica,* as *M. pensylvanica,* of northeastern North America, and *M. californica,* of the western U.S. Cf. **wax myrtle.** **2.** the berry of such a plant. **3.** bay⁴ (def. 2). [1570–80; BAY⁴ + BERRY]

Bay′ Cit′y, **1.** a lake port in E Michigan, near the mouth of the Saginaw River. 41,593. **2.** a town in SE Texas. 17,837.

Bay·ern (bī′əʀn), *n.* German name of **Bavaria.**

Bayes·i·an (bā′zē ən, -zhən), *adj. Statistics.* of or pertaining to statistical methods that regard parameters of a population as random variables having known probability distributions. [1960–65; Thomas *Bayes* (1702–61), English mathematician + -IAN]

Bayes′ the′orem (bāz, bā′ziz), *Statistics.* a theorem describing how the conditional probability of each of a set of possible causes, given an observed outcome, can be computed from knowledge of the probability of each cause and of the conditional probability of the outcome, given each cause. [see BAYESIAN]

Ba·yeux′ tap′estry (bā yo͞o′, bä-; *Fr.* bᴀ yœ′), a strip of embroidered linen 231 ft. (70 m) long and 20 in. (50 cm) wide, depicting the Norman conquest of England and dating from c1100. [after *Bayeux,* France, the town in which it was made]

bay′-head bar′ (bā′hed′), a sand bar at the head of a bay.

bay′ ice′, *Oceanog.* smooth sea ice formed in the sheltered waters of an arctic or antarctic bay. [1810–20]

Bay′ Is′lands, a group of islands in the Caribbean Sea, N of Honduras. Spanish, **Islas de la Bahía.**

Bayle (bāl), *n.* **Pierre** (pyeʀ), 1647–1706, French philosopher and critic.

bay′ leaf′, **1.** the dried leaf of the laurel, used in cookery. **2.** the leaf of the bayberry, *Pimenta racemosa,* used in making bay oil and bay rum. [1630–40]

Bay·liss (bā′lis), *n.* **Sir William Mad·dock** (mad′ək), 1860–1924, English physiologist: codiscoverer of secretin.

bay′ lynx′, bobcat. [1775–85, *Amer.*]

bay·o (bä′ō), *n., pl.* **bay·os.** *Chiefly Northern California.* a pinto or chili bean. Also called **bay′o bean′.** [1850–55; presumably < AmerSp *(frijol) bayo* name for a reddish-colored bean; see BAY⁵]

Bay′ of Pigs′, a bay of the Caribbean Sea in SW Cuba: site of attempted invasion of Cuba by anti-Castro forces April 1961. Spanish, **Bahía de Cochinos.**

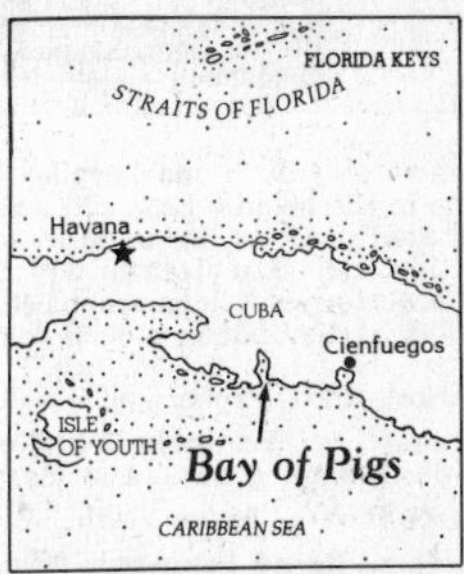

bay′ oil′, a yellow essential oil distilled from the leaves of the tropical American bay, *Pimenta racemosa,* used in the manufacture of perfumes and bay rum.

bay·o·net (bā′ə nit, -net′, bā′ə net′), *n., v.,* **-net·ed** or **-net·ted, -net·ing** or **-net·ting.** *—n.* **1.** a daggerlike steel weapon that is attached to or at the muzzle of a gun and used for stabbing or slashing in hand-to-hand combat. **2.** a pin projecting from the side of an object, as the base of a flashbulb or camera lens, for securing the object in a bayonet socket. *—v.t.* **3.** to kill or wound with a bayonet. [1605–15; < F *baïonnette,* after BAYONNE in France (where the weapon was first made or used); see -ETTE]

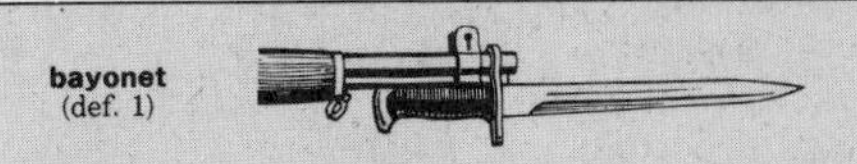
bayonet (def. 1)

bay′onet sock′et, a cylindrical socket having one or more L-shaped slots, the longer side parallel and the shorter side perpendicular to the axis of the socket, along which a knoblike projection on the object slides in such a way that a twist of the object when fully inserted locks it into place. [1890–95]

Ba·yonne (bā yōn′ *for 1;* bᴀ yôn′ *for 2*), *n.* **1.** a seaport in NE New Jersey. 65,047. **2.** a seaport in SW France, near the Bay of Biscay. 44,706.

bay·ou (bī′o͞o, bī′ō), *n., pl.* **-ous.** *Chiefly Lower Mississippi Valley and Gulf States.* **1.** a marshy arm, inlet, or outlet of a lake, river, etc., usually sluggish or stagnant. **2.** any of various other often boggy and slow-moving or still bodies of water. [1710–20, *Amer.;* < LaF, said to be < Choctaw *bayuk* river forming part of a delta]

bay′ pop′lar, the tupelo, *Nyssa aquatica.*

Bay′ Psalm′ Book′, a translation of the Psalms by John Eliot and others: the first book published (1640) in America.

Bay·reuth (bī′roit; *Ger.* bī roit′), *n.* a city in NE Bavaria, in SE Germany: annual music festivals founded by Richard Wagner. 71,848.

bay′ rum′, a fragrant liquid used chiefly as an after-shaving lotion, prepared by distilling the leaves of the tropical American bay, *Pimenta racemosa,* with rum or by mixing oil from the leaves with alcohol, water, and other oils. [1830–40, *Amer.*]

bay′ rum′ tree′, bay⁴ (def. 2).

bay′ salt′, salt derived by evaporating seawater in the sun. [1425–75; late ME]

bay′ scal′lop, **1.** a small scallop, *Pecten irradians,* inhabiting shallow waters and mud flats from southeastern Canada to the Gulf of Mexico, esp. eastern Long Island Sound. **2.** the edible abductor muscle of this scallop, having a sweet and delicate flavor.

Bay′ Shore′, a town on the S shore of Long Island, in SE New York. 10,784.

bay·smelt (bā′smelt′), *n., pl.* **-smelts,** (*esp. collectively*) **-smelt.** topsmelt. [BAY¹ + SMELT²]

Bay′ State′, Massachusetts (used as a nickname). [1780–90, *Amer.*] **—Bay′ Stat′er.**

Bay·town (bā′toun′), *n.* a city in SE Texas, on Galveston Bay. 56,923.

bay′ tree′, **1.** laurel (def. 1). **2.** See **California laurel** (def. 1). [1520–30]

CONCISE PRONUNCIATION KEY: *act, cāpe, dâre, pärt; set, ēqual; if, īce; ox, ōver, ôrder, oil, bo͝ok, bo͞ot, out; up, ûrge; child; sing; shoe; thin, that;* zh as in *treasure.* ə = *a* as in *alone, e* as in *system, i* as in *easily, o* as in *gallop, u* as in *circus;* ᵊ as in *fire* (fīᵊr), *hour* (ouᵊr). l and n can serve as syllabic consonants, as in *cradle* (krād′l), and *button* (but′n). See the full key inside the front cover.

Bay′ Vil′lage, a city in N central Ohio. 17,846.

bay′ win′dow, **1.** an alcove of a room, projecting from an outside wall and having its own windows, esp. one having its own foundations. Cf. **bow window, oriel.** **2.** *Informal.* a large, protruding belly; paunch. [1400–50; late ME]

bay window (def. 1)

ba·zaar (bə zär′), *n.* **1.** a marketplace or shopping quarter, esp. one in the Middle East. **2.** a sale of miscellaneous contributed articles to benefit some charity, cause, organization, etc. **3.** a store in which many kinds of goods are offered for sale; department store. Also, **ba·zar′.** [1590–1600; earlier *bazarro* < It << Pers *bāzār* market]
—Syn. 1. market, mart, exchange.

Ba·zaine (bᴀ zen′), *n.* **Fran·çois A·chille** (fʀäɴ swᴀ′ ᴀ shēl′), 1811–88, French general and marshal.

Baz·a·tha (baz′ə thə), *n. Douay Bible.* Biztha.

Ba·zin (bᴀ zᴀɴ′), *n.* **Re·né Fran·çois Ni·co·las Ma·rie** (rə nā′ fʀäɴ swᴀ′ nē kô lä′ mᴀ ʀē′), 1853–1932, French novelist.

Baz·i·otes (baz′ē ō′tēz), *n.* **William,** 1912–63, U.S. painter.

ba·zoo·ka (bə zo͞o′kə), *n. Mil.* a tube-shaped, portable rocket launcher that fires a rocket capable of penetrating several inches of armor plate, as of a tank or other armored military vehicle. [1930–35, *Amer.*; from its resemblance to a musical instrument so named, invented and played by comedian Bob Burns in the 1930's and 1940's]

bazooka

BB (bē′bē′), *n.* **1.** a size of shot, 0.18 in. (0.46 cm) in diameter, fired from an air rifle or BB gun. **2.** Also called **BB shot.** shot of this size. [1870–75, *Amer.*]

BB, a quality rating for a corporate or municipal bond, lower than BBB and higher than B.

bb., **1.** ball bearing. **2.** *Baseball.* base on balls; bases on balls.

B/B, bottled in bond.

B.B., **1.** bail bond. **2.** Blue Book. **3.** B'nai B'rith. **4.** Bureau of the Budget.

b.b., **1.** bail bond. **2.** baseboard.

B.B.A., **1.** Bachelor of Business Administration. **2.** Big Brothers of America.

B battery, *Electronics.* an electric battery for supplying a constant, positive voltage to the plate of a vacuum tube. Cf. **A battery, C battery.** [1920–25]

BBB, See **Better Business Bureau.**

BBB, a quality rating for a corporate or municipal bond, lower than A and higher than BB.

B.B.C., British Broadcasting Corporation. Also, **BBC**

bbl., *pl.* **bbls.** barrel.

BBQ, barbecue.

BBS, bulletin board system: a computerized facility, accessible by modem, for collecting and relaying electronic messages and software programs. Also called **electronic bulletin board.**

BC, *Scuba Diving.* buoyancy compensator.

bc, **1.** *Music.* basso continuo. **2.** Also, **bcc** blind copy: used as a notation on the carbon copy of a letter or other document sent to a third person without the addressee's knowledge.

B/C, bills for collection.

B.C., **1.** Bachelor of Chemistry. **2.** Bachelor of Commerce. **3.** bass clarinet. **4.** battery commander. **5.** before Christ (used in indicating dates). **6.** British Columbia.
—Usage. 5. The abbreviation B.C. "before Christ" is always placed after a date or century: *Cleopatra lived from 69 to 30* B.C. *The war took place in the first century* B.C. See also **A.D.**

BCA, Boys' Clubs of America.

bcc, blind carbon copy.

CONCISE ETYMOLOGY KEY: <, descended or borrowed from; >, whence; b., blend of, blended; c., cognate with; cf., compare; deriv., derivative; equiv., equivalent; imit., imitative; obl., oblique; r., replacing; s., stem; sp., spelling, spelled; resp., respelling, respelled; trans., translation; ?, origin unknown; *, unattested; ‡, probably earlier than. See the full key inside the front cover.

BCD, **1.** *Mil.* bad conduct discharge. **2.** *Computers.* binary-coded decimal system.

B.C.E., **1.** Bachelor of Chemical Engineering. **2.** Bachelor of Christian Education. **3.** Bachelor of Civil Engineering. **4.** before Christian (or Common) Era.

B cell, *Biol.* **1.** Also called **B lymphocyte.** a type of lymphocyte, developed in bone marrow, that circulates in the blood and lymph and, upon encountering a particular foreign antigen, differentiates into a clone of plasma cells that secrete a specific antibody and a clone of memory cells that make the antibody on subsequent encounters. **2.** Also called **beta cell.** a cell in the islet of Langerhans that produces and secretes insulin. [1970–75; (def. 1) perh. *B(one-derived)*; (def. 2) *B(ursa of Langerhans-derived)*]

B.Cer.E., Bachelor of Ceramic Engineering.

BCG vaccine, *Immunol.* a vaccine made from weakened strains of tubercle bacilli, used to produce immunity against tuberculosis. [1925–30; B(ACILLUS) C(ALMETTE-)G(UÉRIN)]

bch., *pl.* **bchs.** bunch.

B.Ch., Bachelor of Chemistry.

B.Ch.E., Bachelor of Chemical Engineering.

B chromosome, *Genetics.* a type of densely staining chromosome of uncertain biological function, found in many plant and animal species. Also called **accessory chromosome, satellite chromosome.** [1975–80]

B.C.L., Bachelor of Civil Law.

BCNU, *Pharm.* carmustine. [abbrev. of the chemical name *1,3-bis (2-chloroethyl)-1-nitrosourea*]

B complex. See **vitamin B complex.**

B.Com.Sc., Bachelor of Commercial Science.

B.C.P., **1.** Bachelor of City Planning. **2.** See ***Book of Common Prayer.***

B.C.S., **1.** Bachelor of Chemical Science. **2.** Bachelor of Commercial Science.

BC soil, a soil with a profile having a B horizon and a C horizon but no A horizon.

BCS theory, *Physics.* a general quantum theory of superconductivity that describes many properties of superconducting materials. Also called **Bardeen-Cooper-Schrieffer theory.** [after U.S. physicists J. BARDEEN, Leon N. Cooper (born 1930), and John R. Schrieffer (born 1929)]

BD., (in Bahrain) dinar; dinars.

bd., *pl.* **bds.** **1.** board. **2.** bond. **3.** bound. **4.** bundle.

B/D, **1.** bank draft. **2.** bills discounted. **3.** *Accounting.* brought down.

b/d, barrels per day.

B.D., **1.** Bachelor of Divinity. **2.** bank draft. **3.** bills discounted.

B.D.A., **1.** Bachelor of Domestic Arts. **2.** Bachelor of Dramatic Art.

bde, *Mil.* brigade.

bdel·li·um (del′ē əm, -yəm), *n.* **1.** a fragrant gum resin obtained from certain burseraceous plants, as of the genus *Commiphora.* **2.** a plant yielding this resin. **3.** a substance mentioned in the Bible. Gen. 2:12; Num. 11:7. [< L < Gk *bdéllion,* prob. from a Sem word akin to Heb *bedhōlah,* name of a fragrant yellowish gum]

B.Des., Bachelor of Design.

bd. ft., board foot; board feet.

bdl., *pl.* **bdls.** bundle.

bdle., *pl.* **bdles.** bundle

bdrm., bedroom.

B.D.S., Bachelor of Dental Surgery.

b.d.s., (in prescriptions) twice a day. [< L *bis diē sūmendum*]

BDSA, Business and Defense Services Administration.

be (bē; *unstressed* bē, bi), *v.* and *auxiliary v., pres. sing. 1st pers.* **am,** *2nd* **are** or (*Archaic*) **art,** *3rd* **is,** *pres. pl.* **are;** *past sing. 1st pers.* **was,** *2nd* **were** or (*Archaic*) **wast** or **wert,** *3rd* **was,** *past pl.* **were;** *pres. subj.* **be;** *past subj. sing. 1st pers.* **were,** *2nd* **were** or (*Archaic*) **wert,** *3rd* **were;** *past subj. pl.* **were;** *past part.* **been;** *pres. part.* **be·ing.** *—v.i.* **1.** to exist or live: *Shakespeare's "To be or not to be" is the ultimate question.* **2.** to take place; happen; occur: *The wedding was last week.* **3.** to occupy a place or position: *The book is on the table.* **4.** to continue or remain as before: *Let things be.* **5.** to belong; attend; befall: *May good fortune be with you.* **6.** (used as a copula to connect the subject with its predicate adjective, or predicate nominative, in order to describe, identify, or amplify the subject): *Martha is tall. John is president. This is she.* **7.** (used as a copula to introduce or form interrogative or imperative sentences): *Is that right? Be quiet!* *—auxiliary verb.* **8.** (used with the present participle of another verb to form the progressive tense): *I am waiting.* **9.** (used with the present participle or infinitive of the principal verb to indicate future action): *She is visiting there next week. He is to see me today.* **10.** (used with the past participle of another verb to form the passive voice): *The date was fixed. It must be done.* **11.** (used in archaic or literary constructions with some intransitive verbs to form the perfect tense): *He is come. Agamemnon to the wars is gone.* [bef. 900; ME *been,* OE *bēon* (*bēo-* (akin to OFris, OHG *bim,* G *bin,* OS *bium, biom* (I) am, OE, OHG, OS *būan,* ON *būa* reside, L *fui* (I) have been, Gk *phy-* grow, become, OIr *boí* (he) was, Skt *bhávati* (he) becomes, is, Lith *búti* to be, OCS *byti,* Pers *būd* was)) + *-n* inf. suffix. See AM, IS, ARE[1], WAS, WERE]
—Usage. See **me.**

Be, *Symbol, Chem.* beryllium.

be-, a native English prefix formerly used in the formation of verbs: *become, besiege, bedaub, befriend.* [ME, OE, unstressed form of *bī* BY]

Bé., Baumé.

B/E, bill of exchange. Also, **b.e.**

B.E., **1.** Bachelor of Education. **2.** Bachelor of Engineering. **3.** Bank of England. **4.** bill of exchange. **5.** Board of Education.

Bea (bē), *n.* a female given name, form of **Beatrice.**

beach (bēch), *n.* **1.** an expanse of sand or pebbles along a shore. **2.** the part of the shore of an ocean, sea, river, lake, etc., washed by the tide or waves. **3.** the area adjacent to a seashore: *We're vacationing at the beach.* *—v.t.* **4.** *Naut.* to haul or run onto a beach: *We beached the ship to save it.* **5.** to make inoperative or unemployed. [1525–35; of obscure orig.] **—beach′less,** *adj.*
—Syn. 2. coast, seashore, strand, littoral, sands. See **shore**[1]. **5.** ground.

Beach (bēch), *n.* **1. Moses Yale,** 1800–68, U.S. newspaper publisher. **2. Rex El·ling·wood** (el′ing wo͝od′), 1877–1949, U.S. novelist and short-story writer.

beach′ as′ter, a seaside plant, *Erigeron glaucus,* of the temperate western coast of North America, having solitary, violet- or lilac-colored flowers. Also called **seaside daisy.**

beach·bag (bēch′bag′), *n.* a large handbag, sometimes of canvas, used to carry personal items, as a bathing suit, towel, and suntan lotion, to and from a beach. [1930–35; BEACH + BAG]

beach·ball (bēch′bôl′), *n.* a large, light, buoyant ball, used esp. for games at the seashore, swimming pools, etc. [1935–40; BEACH + BALL[1]]

beach′ berm′, berm (def. 3).

beach·boy (bēch′boi′), *n.* a male attendant or swimming instructor at a beach. [1935–40; BEACH + BOY]

beach′ bug′gy. See **dune buggy.**

beach·comb·er (bēch′kō′mər), *n.* **1.** a person who lives by gathering salable articles of jetsam, refuse, etc., from beaches. **2.** a vagrant who lives on the seashore, esp. a nonnative person living in such a way on a South Pacific island. **3.** a long wave rolling in from the ocean onto the beach. [1830–40; BEACH + COMBER]

beach′ crab′, any of various crabs that live on beaches, as the ghost crab. [1905–10]

beach′ drift′, the drifting of sediments, esp. marine sediments, in patterns parallel to the contours of a beach, due to the action of waves and currents. Also called **littoral drift, longshore drift.**

beach·er (bē′chər), *n.* a long, curling wave of the sea. [1920–25; BEACH + -ER[1]]

beach′ face′, the seaward section of a beach exposed to and shaped by the action of waves.

beach′ flea′, any of various small crustaceans, found on beaches, that jump about like fleas. [1835–45, *Amer.*]

beach flea, *Orchestia agilis,* length ½ in. (1.3 cm)

beach·front (bēch′frunt′), *n.* **1.** land fronting on a beach. *—adj.* **2.** located on or adjacent to a beach: *beachfront property.* Also called **shorefront.** [1920–25, *Amer.*; BEACH + FRONT]

beach′ gold′enrod, a composite plant, *Solidago sempervirens,* of eastern and southern North America, having a thick stem and large, branched, one-sided terminal clusters of yellow flowers, flourishing on sea beaches or salt marshes. Also called **seaside goldenrod.**

beach′ grass′, any of several erect, strongly rooted grasses, esp. of the genus *Ammophila,* common on exposed sandy shores and dunes. [1675–85, *Amer.*]

beach·head (bēch′hed′), *n.* **1.** the area that is the first objective of a military force landing on an enemy shore. **2.** a secure initial position that has been gained and can be used for further advancement; foothold: *The company has won a beachhead in the personal computer market.* [1935–40; BEACH + HEAD]

Beach-la-Mar (bēch′lə mär′), *n.* Neo-Melanesian. [alter. of BÊCHE-DE-MER a well-known trade item in the region where this type of pidgin is spoken]

beach·mas·ter (bēch′mas′tər, -mä′stər), *n.* a bull fur seal having its own territory in the breeding grounds. [BEACH + MASTER]

beach′ pea′, either of two plants of the legume family, *Lathyrus japonicus,* of seashores of the North Temperate Zone, or *L. littoralis,* of the temperate western coast of North America, both having oblong leaves and clusters of pealike flowers. [1795–1805, *Amer.*]

beach′ plum′, **1.** a shrub, *Prunus maritima,* of the rose family, of the seashores of northeastern North America, having sharply toothed leaves and white flowers. **2.** the purple or blackish edible fruit of this shrub. [1775–85, *Amer.*]

beach′ ridge′, a long, low ridge, usually one of a series, composed of sand or gravel transported by the waves and currents of a storm surge.

beach′ scarp′, a steep slope or miniature cliff, formed by wave action, fronting the berm on a beach.

beach·side (bēch′sīd′), *adj.* situated on or facing a beach: *a beachside hotel.* [1950–55; BEACH + SIDE[1], on the model of SEASIDE]

beach′ umbrel′la, a large umbrella used to provide shade on sunny beaches, lawns, etc.

beach·wear (bēch′wâr′), *n.* clothing for wear at a beach, swimming pool, etc. [1925–30; BEACH + WEAR]

beach′ worm′wood, a composite plant, *Artemisia stellerana,* having yellow flowers and deeply lobed leaves covered with dense white fuzz. Also called **dusty miller.**

beach·y (bē′chē), *adj.* covered with pebbles or sand. [1590–1600; BEACH + -Y[1]]

bea·con (bē′kən), *n.* **1.** a guiding or warning signal, as a light or fire, esp. one in an elevated position. **2.** a tower or hill used for such purposes. **3.** a lighthouse, signal buoy, etc., on a shore or at a dangerous area at sea to warn and guide vessels. **4.** *Navig.* **a.** See **radio beacon. b.** a radar device at a fixed location that, upon receiving a radar pulse, transmits a reply pulse that enables the original sender to determine his or her position relative to the fixed location. **5.** a person, act, or thing that warns or guides. **6.** a person or thing that illuminates or inspires: *The Bible has been our beacon during this trouble.* —*v.t.* **7.** to serve as a beacon to; warn or guide. **8.** to furnish or mark with beacons: *a ship assigned to beacon the shoals.* —*v.i.* **9.** to serve or shine as a beacon: *A steady light beaconed from the shore.* [bef. 950; ME *beken,* OE *bēacen* sign, signal; c. OFris *bāken,* OS *bōkan,* OHG *bouhhan*] —**bea′con·less,** *adj.*
—**Syn. 1.** beam, buoy, pharos; signal fire; balefire.

Bea·con (bē′kən), *n.* a city in SE New York. 12,937.

bea·con·age (bē′kə nij), *n. Naut.* **1.** a number or system of beacons. **2.** a tax or fee for maintaining beacons. [1600–10; BEACON + -AGE]

Bea·cons·field (bē′kənz fēld′, bek′ənz-), *n.* **1. Earl of.** See **Disraeli, Benjamin. 2.** a city in S Quebec, in E Canada: suburb of Montreal. 19,613.

bead (bēd), *n.* **1.** a small, usually round object of glass, wood, stone, or the like with a hole through it, often strung with others of its kind in necklaces, rosaries, etc. **2. beads, a.** a necklace of beads: *You don't have your beads on this evening.* **b.** a rosary. **c.** *Obs.* devotions; prayers. **3.** any small globular or cylindrical body. **4.** a drop of liquid: *beads of moisture.* **5.** a bubble rising through effervescent liquid. **6.** Usually, **beads.** a mass of such bubbles on the surface of a liquid. **7.** the front sight of a rifle or gun. **8.** a reinforced area of a rubber tire terminating the sidewall and fitting within the rim of a wheel. See illus. under **tire. 9.** *Elect.* a glass, ceramic, or plastic insulator that contains and supports the inner conductor in a coaxial cable. **10.** *Chem.* a globule of borax or some other flux, supported on a platinum wire, in which a small amount of some substance is heated in a flame as a test for its constituents. **11.** *Metall.* the rounded mass of refined metal obtained by cupellation. **12.** *Archit., Furniture.* a small molding having a convex circular section and, usually, a continuous cylindrical surface; astragal. **13.** *Welding.* a continuous deposit of fused metal, either straight **(stringer bead)** or zigzag **(weave bead). 14. count, say,** or **tell one's beads,** to say one's prayers, using rosary beads: *There were a few old women counting their beads in the hushed silence of the chapel.* **15. draw** or **get a bead on,** to take careful aim at: *The marksman drew a bead on his target.* —*v.t.* **16.** to form or cause to form beads or a bead on. **17.** to ornament with beads. **18.** *Carpentry.* to form a bead on (a piece). —*v.i.* **19.** to form beads; form in beads or drops: *perspiration beading on his forehead.* [bef. 900; ME *bede* prayer, prayer bead (where, on a rosary each bead symbolizes a prayer, the word for the notion symbolized was transferred to the designating object), OE *gebed* prayer; akin to BID[1], G *Gebet*] —**bead′like′,** *adj.*
—**Syn. 4.** droplet, globule, blob, dot.

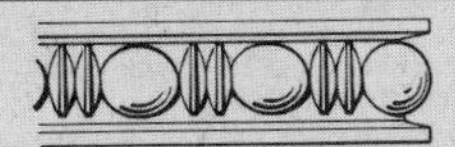
bead and reel

bead′ and reel′, *Archit.* a convex molding having the form of elongated beads alternating with disks placed edge-on, or with spherical beads, or with both. Also called **reel and bead.** [1950–55]

bead·ed (bē′did), *adj.* ornamented with or largely composed of beads: *a beaded handbag.* [1570–80; BEAD + -ED[3]]

bead′ed liz′ard, a large, stout-bodied, venomous lizard, *Heloderma horridum,* inhabiting western Mexico, having black, beadlike scales with yellow to pinkish spots and splotches. Also called **Mexican beaded lizard.**

bead·er (bē′dər), *n. Carpentry.* a tool for forming beads on lumber. [1880–85; BEAD + -ER[1]]

bead·eye (bēd′ī′), *n., pl.* **-eyes.** stonecat. [1880–85; BEAD + EYE]

bead·flush (bēd′flush′), *adj.* (of paneling) having panels flush with their stiles and rails and surrounded with a flush bead. [BEAD + FLUSH[2]]

bead·house (bēd′hous′), *n., pl.* **-hous·es** (-hou′ziz). (formerly) an almshouse in which the residents were required to pray for the founder. Also, **bedehouse.** [1125–75; ME; see BEAD, HOUSE]

bead·ing (bē′ding), *n.* **1.** material composed of or adorned with beads. **2.** narrow, lacelike trimming or edging. **3.** narrow openwork trimming through which ribbon may be run. **4.** *Archit., Furniture.* **a.** a bead molding. **b.** all of the bead moldings in a single design. Also, **beadwork** (for defs. 1, 4). [1855–60; BEAD + -ING[1]]

bea·dle (bēd′l), *n.* **1.** a parish officer having various subordinate duties, as keeping order during services, waiting on the rector, etc. **2.** sexton (def. 2). [bef. 1000; ME *bedel,* dial. (SE) var. of *bidel,* OE *bydel* apparitor, herald (c. G *Büttel*), equiv. to *bud-* (weak s. of *bēodan* to command) + *-il* n. suffix]

Bea·dle (bēd′l), *n.* **George Wells,** born 1903, U.S. biologist and educator: Nobel prize for medicine 1958.

bea·dle·dom (bēd′l dəm), *n.* a stupid or officious display or exercise of authority, as by petty officials. [1855–60; BEADLE + -DOM]

bead′ light′ning, lightning in which the intensity appears to vary along the path and which thus resembles a string of beads. Also called **chain lightning, pearl lightning.** [1900–05]

bead′ mold′ing, *Archit., Furniture.* **1.** bead (def. 12). **2.** See **pearl molding.** [1795–1805]

bead′ plane′, *Carpentry.* a plane for cutting beads. [1855–60]

bead′ plant′, a creeping plant, *Nertera granadensis,* of New Zealand and South America, having leathery leaves and orange-colored, transparent berries. [1875–80]

beads·man (bēdz′mən), *n., pl.* **-men.** *Archaic.* **1.** a person who prays for another as a duty, esp. when paid. **2.** an inmate of a poorhouse; almsman. [1200–50; *bead's man* man of prayer; r. ME *bedeman.* See BEAD, 'S[1], MAN[1]]

beads·wom·an (bēdz′wo͝om′ən), *n., pl.* **-wom·en.** *Archaic.* **1.** a woman who prays for another person as a duty, esp. when paid. **2.** an almswoman. [1325–75; earlier *bedes woman,* r. ME *bedewoman;* see BEAD, 'S[1], WOMAN]

bead′ tree′. See **Barbados pride** (def. 1). [1660–70; so called from its bright scarlet seeds, used for necklaces]

bead·work (bēd′wûrk′), *n.* beading (defs. 1, 4). [1745–55; BEAD + WORK]

bead·y (bē′dē), *adj.,* **bead·i·er, bead·i·est. 1.** beadlike; small, globular, and glittering: *beady eyes.* **2.** covered with or full of beads. [1820–30; BEAD + -Y[1]] —**bead′i·ly,** *adv.* —**bead′i·ness,** *n.*

bead·y-eyed (bē′dē īd′), *adj.* **1.** marked by or having small, glittering eyes, esp. eyes that seem to gleam with malice, avarice, or lechery. **2.** staring with suspicion, skepticism, etc.: *The gambler gave the newcomer a beady-eyed look.* [1870–75]

bea·gle (bē′gəl), *n.* one of a breed of small hounds having long ears, short legs, and a usually black, tan, and white coat. [1490–1500; perh. < MF *beegueule* one who whines insistently, equiv. to *bee,* 3d pers. sing. of *beer* to be open, gape (by-form of *bayer* (see BAY[2]) + *gueule* mouth (of an animal); see GULLET]

beagle
15 in. (38 cm)
high at shoulder

bea·gling (bē′gling), *n. Chiefly Brit.* hunting with beagle hounds. [1815–25; BEAGLE + -ING[1]]

beak (bēk), *n.* **1.** the bill of a bird; neb. **2.** any similar horny mouthpart in other animals, as the turtle or duck-bill. **3.** anything beaklike or ending in a point, as the spout of a pitcher. **4.** *Slang.* a person's nose. **5.** *Entomol.* proboscis (def. 3). **6.** *Bot.* a narrowed or prolonged tip. **7.** *Naut.* (formerly) a metal or metal-sheathed projection from the bow of a warship, used to ram enemy vessels; ram; rostrum. **8.** *Typography.* a serif on the arm of a character, as of a *K.* **9.** Also called **bird's beak.** *Archit.* a pendant molding forming a drip, as on the soffit of a cornice. **10.** *Chiefly Brit. Slang.* **a.** a judge; magistrate. **b.** a schoolmaster. [1175–1225; ME *bec* < OF < L *beccus* < Gaulish] —**beaked** (bēkt, bē′kid), *adj.* —**beak′less,** *adj.* —**beak′like′,** *adj.* —**beak′y,** *adj.*

beak
(def. 7)

beaked′ sal′mon, sandfish (def. 2).

beaked′ whale′, any of several toothed whales of the family Hyperoodontidae (Ziphiidae), inhabiting all oceans and having beaklike jaws. [1875–80]

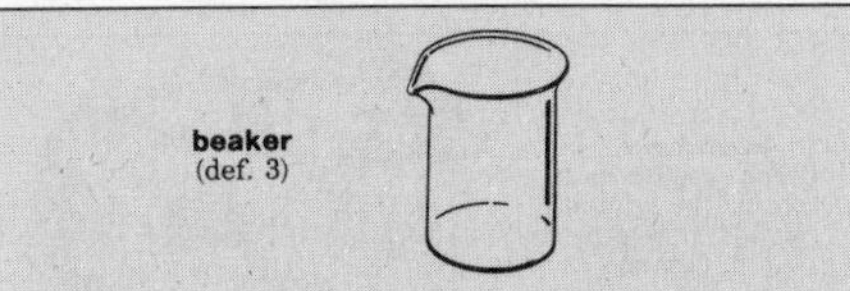
beaker
(def. 3)

beak·er (bē′kər), *n.* **1.** a large drinking cup or glass with a wide mouth. **2.** contents of a beaker: *consuming a beaker of beer at one gulp.* **3.** a flat-bottomed cylindrical container, usually with a pouring lip, esp. one used in a laboratory. —*adj.* **4.** (*cap.*) of or pertaining to the Beaker folk. [1300–50; alter. of ME *biker* < ON *bikarr* < OS *bikeri* (cf. OHG *behhari,* G *Becher,* D *beker*) < L **bic(c)ārium, -ius,* of disputed orig. See PITCHER[1]]

Beak′er folk′ (bē′kər), a late Neolithic to Copper Age people living in Europe, so called in reference to the bell beakers commonly found buried with their dead in barrows. Also called **Beak′er peo′ple.** [1920–25]

beak′ing joint′ (bē′king), *Carpentry.* a straight joint made by several members, as strips of flooring, ending at the same line. [1660–70]

Beal (bel), *n.* a god of the ancient Celts, a personification of the sun.

be-all and end-all (bē′ôl′ ənd end′ôl′), the central and all-important part: *His work was the be-all and end-all of his existence.* [1595–1605]

beam (bēm), *n.* **1.** any of various relatively long pieces of metal, wood, stone, etc., manufactured or shaped esp. for use as rigid members or parts of structures or machines. **2.** *Building Trades.* a horizontal bearing member, as a joist or lintel. **3.** *Engineering.* a rigid member or structure supported at each end, subject to bending stresses from a direction perpendicular to its length. **4.** *Naut.* **a.** a horizontal structural member, usually transverse, for supporting the decks and flats of a vessel. **b.** the extreme width of a vessel. **c.** the shank of an anchor. **5.** *Aeron.* the direction perpendicular to the plane of symmetry of an aircraft and outward from the side. **6.** the widest part. **7.** *Slang.* the measure across both hips or buttocks: *broad in the beam.* **8.** *Mach.* **a.** See **walking beam. b.** (in a loom) a roller or cylinder on which the warp is wound before weaving. **c.** a similar cylinder on which cloth is wound as it is woven. **9.** the crossbar of a balance, from the ends of which the scales or pans are suspended. **10.** a ray of light: *The sun shed its beams upon the vineyard.* **11.** a group of nearly parallel rays. **12.** *Radio, Aeron.* a signal transmitted along a narrow course, used to guide pilots through darkness, bad weather, etc. **13.** *Electronics.* a narrow stream of electrons, as that emitted from the electron gun of a cathode ray tube. **14.** the angle at which a microphone or loudspeaker functions best. **15.** the cone-shaped range of effective use of a microphone or loudspeaker. **16.** *CB Radio Slang.* See **beam antenna. 17.** a gleam; suggestion: *a beam of hope.* **18.** a radiant smile. **19.** the principal stem of the antler of a deer. **20. fly the beam,** *Radio, Aeron.* (of an aircraft) to be guided by a beam. **21. off the beam, a.** not on the course indicated by a radio beam. **b.** *Informal.* wrong; incorrect: *The pollsters were off the beam again for the last presidential election.* **22. on the beam, a.** on the course indicated by a radio beam, as an airplane. **b.** *Naut.* at right angles to the keel. **c.** *Informal.* proceeding well; correct; exact: *Their research is right on the beam and the results should be very valuable.* —*v.t.* **23.** to emit in or as in beams or rays. **24.** *Radio.* to transmit (a signal) in a particular direction. **25.** *Radio and Television.* to direct (a program, commercial message, etc.) to a predetermined audience. —*v.i.* **26.** to emit beams, as of light. **27.** to smile radiantly or happily. **28. beam in,** *CB Radio Slang.* to be received under optimum conditions; be heard loud and clear: *They told me I was really beaming in.* [bef. 900; ME *beem,* OE *bēam* tree, post, ray of light; c. OFris *bām,* OS *bōm,* D *boom,* OHG *boum* (G *Baum*), Goth *bagms,* ON *bathmr* tree; the identity of the consonant which has assimilated itself to the following *m* is unclear, as is the original root; perh. Gmc **bagmaz* < **bargmaz* < IE **bhorgh-mos* growth; see BARROW[2]] —**beam′less,** *adj.* —**beam′like′,** *adj.*
—**Syn. 10.** See **gleam. 23.** See **shine.**

beam′ anten′na, *Radio.* an antenna that transmits its radiation in a particular direction. [1930–35]

beam′ brick′, a face brick for bonding to a concrete lintel poured in place, having a section like a right triangle.

beam′ com′pass, *Drafting.* a compass having adjustable legs, set perpendicular to the paper and sliding along a horizontal bar so as to permit the drawing of large circles. [1775–85]

beam-ends (bēm′endz′), *n.pl.* **1.** *Naut.* the ends of the transverse deck beams of a vessel. **2. on her beam-ends,** *Naut.* heeled so far on one side that the deck is practically vertical: *The schooner was blown over on her beam-ends.* **3. on one's** or **the beam-ends,** *Slang.* in desperate straits, esp. financial straits. Also, **on the beam's ends.** [1765–75]

beam′ fill′, *Building Trades.* material, as concrete, for filling spaces between beams or joists in or on top of a masonry wall. Also, **beam′ fill′ing.** [1350–1400; ME (in AL texts) *bemfyllyng*]

beam·ing (bē′ming), *adj.* **1.** radiant; bright. **2.** smiling brightly; cheerful. [1660–70; BEAM + -ING[2]] —**beam′ing·ly,** *adv.*

beam·ish (bē′mish), *adj.* bright, cheerful, and optimistic. [1520–30; BEAM (n.) + -ISH[1]]

beam′ lights′, (in a theater or other auditorium) spotlights affixed to the ceiling of a stage setting, as distinguished from footlights, border lights, etc. [1520–30, for an earlier sense]

beam′ mill′, *Metalworking.* a rolling mill for roughing a bloom and rolling it into a shape.

Bea·mon (bē′mən), *n.* **Robert** (*Bob*), born 1946, U.S. track-and-field athlete.

beam′-pow·er tube′ (bēm′pou′ər), *Radio.* a vacuum tube in which the stream of electrons flowing to the plate is focused by the action of a set of auxiliary, charged elements, giving an increase in output power.

beam′ reach′, *Naut.* See under **reach** (def. 27).

beam′ sea′, *Naut.* a sea striking the vessel at right angles to its keel. [1880–85]

beam′ split′ter, *Optics, Photog.* a mirror or prism that divides a beam of light into two parts by reflecting a part of the beam, used in camera range finders. [1930–35]

beam′ trawl′, a trawl net whose lateral spread during trawling is maintained by a beam across its mouth. Cf. **otter trawl.**

CONCISE PRONUNCIATION KEY: act, cāpe, dâre, pärt; set, ēqual; if, īce; ox, ōver, ôrder, oil, bo͝ok, bo͞ot, out; up, ûrge; child; sing; shoe; thin, *th*at; zh as in *treasure.* ə = *a* as in *alone, e* as in *system, i* as in *easily, o* as in *gallop, u* as in *circus;* ᵊ as in *fire* (fīᵊr), *hour* (ouᵊr). l and n can serve as syllabic consonants, as in *cradle* (krād′l), and *button* (but′n). See the full key inside the front cover.

beam′ weap′on, a laser-beam or particle-beam weapon. Also called **directed-energy device.**

beam′ wind′ (wind), *Naut.* a wind blowing against a vessel from a direction at right angles to its keel.

beam•y (bē′mē), *adj.,* **beam•i•er, beam•i•est. 1.** emitting beams of or as of light; radiant. **2.** broad in the beam, as a ship. **3.** *Zool.* having antlers, as a stag. [1350–1400; ME *bemy.* See BEAM, -Y[1]] **—beam′i•ly,** *adv.* **—beam′i•ness,** *n.*

bean (bēn), *n.* **1.** the edible nutritious seed of various plants of the legume family, esp. of the genus *Phaseolus.* **2.** a plant producing such seeds. **3.** the pod of such a plant, esp. when immature and eaten as a vegetable. **4.** any of various other beanlike seeds or plants, as the coffee bean. **5.** *Slang.* **a.** a person's head. **b.** a coin or a bank note considered as a coin: *I can't pay for the ticket, I don't have a bean in my jeans.* **6.** *Brit. Informal.* a minimum amount of money: *They've been disinherited and now haven't a bean.* **7. beans,** *Informal.* the slightest amount: *He doesn't know beans about navigation.* **8. full of beans,** *Informal.* **a.** energetic; vigorously active; vital: *He is still full of beans at 95.* **b.** stupid; erroneous; misinformed. **9. spill the beans,** *Informal.* to disclose a secret, either accidentally or imprudently, thereby ruining a surprise or plan: *He spilled the beans, and she knew all about the party in advance.* **—***v.t.* **10.** *Slang.* to hit on the head, esp. with a baseball. **—***interj.* **11. beans,** (used to express disbelief, annoyance, etc.). [bef. 950; ME *bene,* OE *bēan;* c. ON *baun,* OFris *bāne,* D *boon,* OS, OHG *bona* (G *Bohne*), prob. < Gmc **babnō,* c. Russ *bob,* L *faba* < European IE **bhabh-*] **—bean′like′,** *adj.*

Bean (bēn), *n.* **1. Alan L(aVern),** born 1932, U.S. astronaut. **2. Roy** ("*Judge*"), 1825?–1903, U.S. frontiersman and justice of the peace: called himself "the law west of the Pecos."

bean′ a′phid, a small, black aphid, *Aphis fabae,* often found on beans and related plants.

bean•bag (bēn′bag′), *n.* **1.** a small cloth bag filled with dried beans, as for tossing in various children's games. **2.** any such game. **3.** any similar bag used as a cushion or support, as the base for an ashtray, etc. **4.** Also called **bean′bag chair′.** a large, soft, frameless chair resembling a beanbag, typically a clothlike plastic shell, filled with plastic chips, that molds itself readily to the contours of the occupant. [1870–75; BEAN + BAG]

bean′ ball′, *Baseball.* a ball thrown by a pitcher purposely at or near the head of the batter. [1900–05]

bean′ bee′tle. See **Mexican bean beetle.** [1930–35, *Amer.*]

bean′ ca′per, a small tree, *Zygophyllum fabago,* of eastern Mediterranean regions, having flower buds that are used as a substitute for capers. [1590–1600]

bean′ curd′, tofu.

bean•er•y (bē′nə rē), *n., pl.* **-er•ies.** *Informal.* a cheap, usually inferior, restaurant. [1885–90, *Amer.;* BEAN + -ERY]

bean•feast (bēn′fēst′), *n. Chiefly Brit. Slang.* **1.** (formerly) an annual dinner or party given by an employer for employees. **2.** a celebration or festive occasion, esp. when a meal is provided. Also, **bean•fest** (bēn′fest′). [1795–1805; BEAN + FEAST]

bean•ie (bē′nē), *n.* a skullcap, often brightly colored, worn esp. by children and by college freshmen, esp. in the 1940's. [1940–45, *Amer.;* BEAN + -IE]

bean•o[1] (bē′nō), *n.* bingo. [1930–35; b. BEAN and KENO]

bean•o[2] (bē′nō), *n., pl.* **bean•os.** *Chiefly Brit. Slang.* beanfeast. [1885–90; BEAN(FEAST) + -O]

bean•pole (bēn′pōl′), *n.* **1.** a tall pole for a bean plant to climb on. **2.** *Informal.* a tall, lanky person. [1790–1800; BEAN + POLE[1]]

bean′ pot′, a heavy, covered crockery or metal pot, suitable for the slow cooking of beans, stews, etc. [1840–50, *Amer.*]

bean•shoot•er (bēn′sho͞o′tər), *n.* peashooter. [1885–90, *Amer.;* BEAN + SHOOTER]

bean′ shot′, *Metall.* refined copper having a shotlike form from being thrown into water in a molten state.

bean′ sprouts′, the sprouts of newly germinated beans, esp. of mung beans, used as a vegetable. [1920–25]

bean•stalk (bēn′stôk′), *n.* the stem of a bean plant. [1790–1800; BEAN + STALK[1]]

Bean′ Town′, Boston, Mass. (used as a nickname).

bean′ tree′, 1. any of several trees bearing pods resembling those of a bean, as the catalpa and the carob tree. **2.** the laburnum, *Laburnum anagyroides.* [1610–20]

bean′ wee′vil, a seed beetle, *Acanthoscelides obtectus,* the larvae of which live in and feed on growing or stored beans. [1865–70, *Amer.*]

bear[1] (bâr), *v.,* **bore** or (*Archaic*) **bare; borne** or **born; bear•ing.** **—***v.t.* **1.** to hold up; support: *to bear the weight of the roof.* **2.** to hold or remain firm under (a load): *The roof will not bear the strain of his weight.* **3.** to bring forth (young); give birth to: *to bear a child.* **4.** to produce by natural growth: *a tree that bears fruit.* **5.** to hold up under; be capable of: *His claim doesn't bear close examination.* **6.** to press or push against: *The crowd was borne back by the police.* **7.** to hold or carry (oneself, one's body, one's head, etc.): *to bear oneself erectly.* **8.** to conduct (oneself): *to bear oneself bravely.* **9.** to suffer; endure; undergo: *to bear the blame.* **10.** to sustain without yielding or suffering injury; tolerate (usually used in negative constructions, unless qualified): *I can't bear your nagging. I can hardly bear to see her suffering so.* **11.** to be fit for or worthy of: *It doesn't bear repeating.* **12.** to carry; bring: *to bear gifts.* **13.** to carry in the mind or heart: *to bear love; to bear malice.* **14.** to transmit or spread (gossip, tales, etc.). **15.** to render; afford; give: *to bear witness; to bear testimony.* **16.** to lead; guide; take: *They bore him home.* **17.** to have and be entitled to: *to bear title.* **18.** to exhibit; show: *to bear a resemblance.* **19.** to accept or have, as an obligation: *to bear responsibility; to bear the cost.* **20.** to stand in (a relation or ratio); have or show correlatively: *the relation that price bears to profit.* **21.** to possess, as a quality or characteristic; have in or on: *to bear traces; to bear an inscription.* **22.** to have and use; exercise: *to bear authority; to bear sway.* **—***v.i.* **23.** to tend in a course or direction; move; go: *to bear west; to bear left at the fork in the road.* **24.** to be located or situated: *The lighthouse bears due north.* **25.** to bring forth young or fruit: *Next year the tree will bear.* **26. bear down, a.** to press or weigh down. **b.** to strive harder; intensify one's efforts: *We can't hope to finish unless everyone bears down.* **c.** *Naut.* to approach from windward, as a ship: *The cutter was bearing down the channel at twelve knots.* **27. bear down on** or **upon, a.** to press or weigh down on. **b.** to strive toward. **c.** to approach something rapidly. **d.** *Naut.* to approach (another vessel) from windward: *The sloop bore down on us, narrowly missing our stern.* **28. bear off, a.** *Naut.* to keep (a boat) from touching or rubbing against a dock, another boat, etc. **b.** *Naut.* to steer away. **c.** *Backgammon.* to remove the stones from the board after they are all home. **29. bear on** or **upon,** to affect, relate to, or have connection with; be relevant to: *This information may bear on the case.* **30. bear out,** to substantiate; confirm: *The facts bear me out.* **31. bear up,** to endure; face hardship bravely: *It is inspiring to see them bearing up so well.* **32. bear with,** to be patient or forbearing with: *Please bear with me until I finish the story.* **33. bring to bear,** to concentrate on with a specific purpose: *Pressure was brought to bear on those with overdue accounts.* [bef. 900; ME *beren,* OE *beran;* c. OS, OHG *beran,* D *baren,* OFris, ON *bera,* Goth *bairan,* G *(ge)bären,* Russ *berët* (he) takes, Albanian *bie,* Tocharian *pär-,* Phrygian *ab-beret* (he) brings, L *ferre,* OIr *berid* (he) carries, Armenian *berem,* Gk *phérein,* Skt *bhárati,* Avestan *baraiti;* < IE **bher-* (see -FER, -PHORE)]

—Syn. 1. uphold, sustain. **4.** yield. **6.** thrust, drive, force. **10.** brook, abide, suffer. BEAR, STAND, ENDURE refer to supporting the burden of something distressing, irksome, or painful. BEAR and STAND are close synonyms and have a general sense of withstanding: *to bear a disappointment well; to stand a loss.* ENDURE implies continued resistance and patience in bearing through a long time: *to endure torture.*

—Usage. Since the latter part of the 18th century, a distinction has been made between BORN and BORNE as past participles of the verb BEAR[1]. BORNE is the past participle in all senses that do not refer to physical birth: *The wheatfields have borne abundantly this year. Judges have always borne a burden of responsibility.* BORNE is also the participle when the sense is "to bring forth (young)" and the focus is on the mother rather than on the child. In such cases, BORNE is preceded by a form of *have* or followed by *by: Anna had borne a son the previous year. Two children borne by her earlier were already grown.* When the focus is on the offspring or on something brought forth as if by birth, BORN is the standard spelling, and it occurs only in passive constructions: *My friend was born in Ohio. No children have been born at the South Pole. A strange desire was born of the tragic experience.* BORN is also an adjective meaning "by birth," "innate," or "native": *born free; a born troublemaker; Mexican-born.*

bear[2] (bâr), *n., pl.* **bears,** (*esp. collectively*) **bear,** *adj., v.,* **beared, bear•ing.** **—***n.* **1.** any of the plantigrade, carnivorous or omnivorous mammals of the family Ursidae, having massive bodies, coarse heavy fur, relatively short limbs, and almost rudimentary tails. **2.** any of various animals resembling the bear, as the ant bear. **3.** a gruff, burly, clumsy, bad-mannered, or rude person. **4.** a person who believes that market prices, esp. of stocks, will decline (opposed to *bull*). **5.** *Informal.* a person who shows great ability, enthusiasm, stamina, etc.: *a bear for physics.* **6.** (*cap.*) *Astron.* either of two constellations, Ursa Major or Ursa Minor. **7.** *Informal.* a player at cards who rarely bluffs. **8.** (*cap.*) Russia. **9. loaded for bear,** *Informal.* fully prepared and eager to initiate or deal with a fight, confrontation, or trouble: *Keep away from the boss—he's loaded for bear today.* **—***adj.* **10.** having to do with or marked by declining prices, as of stocks: *bear market.* **—***v.t.* **11.** *Stock Exchange.* to force prices down in (a market, stock, etc.). [bef. 1000; ME *be(a)re, beor(e),* OE *bera;* c. Fris *bār,* D *beer,* OHG *bero* (G *Bär*); < Gmc **beran-* lit., the brown one; akin to ON *bjǫrn, bersi;* cf. Lith *bė́ras* brown. Cf. BRUIN] **—bear′like′,** *adj.*

black bear, *Ursus americanus,* 3 ft. (0.9 m) high at shoulder; length 5 ft. (1.5 m)

bear•a•ble (bâr′ə bəl), *adj.* capable of being endured or tolerated; endurable. [1540–50; BEAR[1] + -ABLE] **—bear′a•ble•ness,** *n.* **—bear′a•bly,** *adv.*

bear′ animal′cule, *Zool.* tardigrade (def. 3). [1885–90]

bear•bait•ing (bâr′bā′ting), *n.* the former practice of setting dogs to fight a captive bear. [1250–1300; ME. See BEAR[2], BAITING] **—bear′bait′er,** *n.*

bear•ber•ry (bâr′ber′ē, -bə rē), *n., pl.* **-ries. 1.** any of several prostrate shrubs belonging to the genus *Arctostaphylos,* of the heath family, esp. *A. uva-ursi,* having tonic, astringent leaves and bright-red berries. **2.** cascara. **3.** possum haw (def. 1). **4.** any of several other plants, as some species of cranberry. [1615–25; BEAR[2] + BERRY]

bear•cat (bâr′kat′), *n.* **1.** *Informal.* a person or thing that fights or acts with force or fierceness. **2.** binturong. **3.** a panda, *Ailurus fulgens.* [1885–90; BEAR[2] + CAT[1]]

bear′ claw′, a sweet, almond-flavored breakfast pastry made with yeast dough and shaped in an irregular semicircle resembling a bear's claw. Also called **bear-paw.**

beard (bērd), *n.* **1.** the growth of hair on the face of an adult man, often including a mustache. **2.** *Zool.* a tuft, growth, or part resembling or suggesting a human beard, as the tuft of long hairs on the lower jaw of a goat or the cluster of hairlike feathers at the base of the bill in certain birds. **3.** *Bot.* a tuft or growth of awns or the like, as on wheat or barley. **4.** a barb or catch on an arrow, fishhook, knitting needle, crochet needle, etc. **5.** Also called **bevel neck.** *Print.* **a.** the sloping part of a type that connects the face with the shoulder of the body. **b.** *Brit.* the space on a type between the bottom of the face of an x-high character and the edge of the body, comprising both beard and shoulder. **c.** the cross stroke on the stem of a capital *G.* See diag. under **type.** **—***v.t.* **6.** to seize, pluck, or pull the beard of: *The hoodlums bearded the old man.* **7.** to oppose boldly; defy: *It took courage for the mayor to beard the pressure groups.* **8.** to supply with a beard. [bef. 900; ME *berd,* OE *beard;* c. G *Bart,* D *baard,* LL *Langobardi* Long-beards, name of the Lombards, Crimean Goth *bars,* L *barba* (> Welsh *barf*), Lith *barzdà,* OCS *brada,* Russ *borodá;* European IE **bhₐer-dhā,* perh. akin to BARLEY[1]] **—beard′like′,** *adj.*

—Syn. 7. confront, brave, dare, face, challenge.

Beard (bērd), *n.* **1. Charles Austin,** 1874–1948, and his wife **Mary,** 1876–1958, U.S. historians. **2. Daniel Carter,** 1850–1941, U.S. artist and naturalist: organized the Boy Scouts of America in 1910.

beard•ed (bēr′did), *adj.* **1.** having a beard. **2.** having a hairlike growth or tuft, as certain wheats. **3.** having a barb, as a fishhook. [1350–1400; ME *beerdid.* See BEARD, -ED[3]] **—beard′ed•ness,** *n.*

beard′ed col′lie, one of a British breed of medium-sized herding dogs with a medium-length, shaggy coat, black, blue, brown, or fawn in color. [1875–80]

beard′ed dar′nel, a grass, *Lolium tementulum,* related to rye, having bristles on the seed head and bearing seeds that yield a narcotic poison.

beard′ed seal′, a large gray-to-golden seal, *Erignathus barbatus,* inhabiting the Arctic Ocean and adjacent waters, having square foreflippers and a thick mustache of long bristles on each side of the muzzle.

beard′ed tit′, a small European bird, *Panurus biarmicus,* found in reedy places, the male of which has a tuft of black feathers on each side of the face.

beard′ed vul′ture, lammergeier.

beard•fish (bērd′fish′), *n., pl.* (*esp. collectively*) **-fish,** (*esp. referring to two or more kinds or species*) **-fish•es.** any of several fishes of the family Polymyxiidae, found in the deeper waters of the Atlantic and Pacific oceans, having a pair of long barbels under the chin. Also called **barbudo.** [for *bearded fish*]

beard•less (bērd′lis), *adj.* **1.** having no beard or one shaved close to the skin. **2.** (of a male) very young or immature. [1275–1325; ME; see BEARD, -LESS] **—beard′less•ness,** *n.*

beard′ moss′, any of several green or yellow lichens of the genus *Usnea,* having long, threadlike stems in a tangled mass typically hanging from tree branches, and growing in a wide range of habitats from tropical zones to the Arctic. Also called **old-man's-beard.**

Beards•ley (bērdz′lē), *n.* **Aubrey Vincent,** 1872–98, English illustrator.

beard•tongue (bērd′tung′), *n.* any plant belonging to the genus *Penstemon,* of the figwort family. [1815–25, *Amer.;* BEARD + TONGUE]

beard′ worm′, *Zool.* pogonophoran. [1965–70]

bear•er (bâr′ər), *n.* **1.** a person or thing that carries, upholds, or brings: *dozens of bearers on the safari.* **2.** the person who presents an order for money or goods: *Pay to the bearer.* **3.** a tree or plant that yields fruit or flowers. **4.** the holder of rank or office; incumbent. **5.** pallbearer. **6.** (esp. in India) a native boy or man employed as a personal or household servant. **7.** *Print.* **a.** furniture (def. 4). **b.** one of several strips of metal fitted at the sides of a plate for support during inking and proving. **8.** a joistlike member supporting the floorboards of a scaffold. **9.** *Furniture.* See **bearing rail.** [1250–1300; ME *berere.* See BEAR[1], -ER[1]]

bear′er bond′, a bond not registered in anyone's name and payable to whoever possesses it. Cf. **registered bond.** [1910–15]

bear′ gar′den, 1. a place for keeping or exhibiting bears, esp. (formerly) for bearbaiting. **2.** a place or scene of tumult. [1590–1600]

bear′ grass′, 1. Also called **elk grass.** a tall, western North American plant, *Xerophyllum tenax,* of the lily family, having narrow leaves and a dense, broad cluster of tiny white flowers. **2.** any of several other plants having linear, grasslike leaves, as those of the genera *Nolina* and *Dasylirion.* [1740–50, *Amer.*]

bear′ hug′, 1. a forcefully or heartily tight embrace. **2.** *Wrestling.* a hold in which one contestant locks both arms around the other from the front in order to make the opponent fall backward. [1920–25]

bear-hug (bâr′hug′), *v.t.,* **-hugged, -hug•ging.** to greet with or hold in a bear hug: *eager fans bear-hugging the victorious team.* [1955–60]

bear•ing (bâr′ing), *n.* **1.** the manner in which one conducts or carries oneself, including posture and gestures:

CONCISE ETYMOLOGY KEY: <, descended or borrowed from; >, whence; b., blend of, blended; c., cognate with; cf., compare; deriv., derivative; equiv., equivalent; imit., imitative; obl., oblique; r., replacing; s., stem; sp., spelling, spelled; resp., respelling, respelled; trans., translation; ?, origin unknown; *, unattested; ‡, probably earlier than. See the full key inside the front cover.

a man of dignified bearing. **2.** the act, capability, or period of producing or bringing forth: *a tree past bearing.* **3.** something that is produced; a crop. **4.** the act of enduring or capacity to endure. **5.** reference or relation (usually fol. by *on*): *It has some bearing on the problem.* **6.** *Archit.* **a.** a supporting part of a structure. **b.** the area of contact between a bearing member, as a beam, and a pier, wall, or other underlying support. **7.** *Mach.* the support and guide for a rotating, oscillating, or sliding shaft, pivot, or wheel. **8.** Often, **bearings.** direction or relative position: *The pilot radioed his bearings.* **9.** *Survey.* a horizontal direction expressed in degrees east or west of a true or magnetic north or south direction. **10.** *Heraldry.* any single device on an escutcheon; charge. [1200–50; ME *beryng.* See BEAR[1], -ING[1]]
—Syn. 1. carriage, mien, demeanor, behavior, conduct. See **manner**[1]. **5.** connection, dependency; application. **8.** course, aim.

bear′ing plate′, a heavy metal plate for receiving and distributing concentrated weight, as from a column or one end of a truss.

bear′ing rail′, *Furniture.* a transverse rail carrying a drawer or drawers. Also called **bearer.**

bear′ing rein′, checkrein (def. 1). [1875–80]

bear′ing sword′, a large sword carried for its owner by a squire or servant because of its size.

bear′ing wall′, any of the walls supporting a floor or the roof of a building. [1870–75]

bear•ish (bâr′ish), *adj.* **1.** like a bear; rough, burly, or clumsy. **2.** *Informal.* grumpy, bad-mannered, or rude. **3.** *Com.* **a.** declining or tending toward a decline in prices. **b.** characterized by or reflecting unfavorable prospects for the economy or some aspect of it: *a bearish market.* [1735–45; BEAR[2] + -ISH[1]] **—bear′ish•ly,** *adv.* **—bear′ish•ness,** *n.*

bear′ lead′er, (formerly) a tutor traveling with a wealthy or aristocratic young man. Also, **bear′-lead′er.** [1740–50]

Bé•ar•naise (ber nāz′, bā′ər-; *Fr.* bā AR nez′), *n.* (*sometimes l.c.*) a sauce of egg yolks, shallots, tarragon, butter, vinegar, and sometimes white wine and chopped chervil. Also called **Béarnaise′ sauce′.** [< F, equiv. to *Béarn* district in SW France + *-aise,* fem. of *-ais* -ESE]

bear•paw (bâr′pô′), *n. Chiefly Canadian.* **1.** a small, almost round snowshoe used on steep or rocky terrain. **2.** See **bear claw. 3.** a round horseshoe. [1775–85; BEAR[2] + PAW]

Bear′ Riv′er, a river in NE Utah, SW Wyoming, and SE Idaho, flowing into the Great Salt Lake. 350 mi. (565 km) long.

bear•skin (bâr′skin′), *n.* **1.** the skin or pelt of a bear. **2.** a tall, black fur cap forming part of the dress uniform of a soldier in some armies. [1670–80; BEAR[2] + SKIN]

bear′s-paw (bârz′pô′), *n.* a clam of the genus *Hippopus,* having a ridged, white shell with purplish-red spots.

bear•wood (bâr′wo͝od′), *n.* a buckthorn, *Rhamnus purshiana,* the bark of which yields the drug cascara sagrada. [1865–70, *Amer.*; BEAR[2] + WOOD[1]]

beast (bēst), *n.* **1.** any nonhuman animal, esp. a large, four-footed mammal. **2.** the crude animal nature common to humans and the lower animals: *Hunger brought out the beast in him.* **3.** a cruel, coarse, filthy, or otherwise beastlike person. **4.** a live creature, as distinguished from a plant: *What manner of beast is this?* **5. the beast,** the Antichrist. Rev. 13:18. [1175–1225; ME *be(e)ste* < OF *beste* (F *bête*) < L *bēstia*] **—beast′like′,** *adj.*
—Syn. 1. See **animal. 3.** cad, swine, pig, brute, savage, ogre, monster, barbarian.

beast′ ep′ic, a long verse narrative in which the misadventures of animals satirize human foibles and follies. [1885–90]

beast•ie (bē′stē), *n.* **1.** *Chiefly Literary.* a small animal, esp. one toward which affection is felt. **2.** *Facetious.* an insect; bug. **3.** *Canadian Slang* (*chiefly Alberta*). construction worker. [1775–85; BEAST + -IE]

beast•ings (bē′stingz), *n.* (*used with a singular v.*) beestings.

beast•ly (bēst′lē), *adj.,* **-li•er, -li•est,** *adv.* **—***adj.* **1.** of or like a beast; bestial. **2.** *Informal.* nasty; unpleasant; disagreeable. **—***adv.* **3.** *Chiefly Brit. Informal.* very; exceedingly: *It's beastly cold out.* **4.** *Brit. Informal.* disagreeably; outrageously: *beastly rude.* [1175–1225; ME *beasteliche,* later *be(e)stly.* See BEAST, -LY[1]] **—beast′li•ness,** *n.*
—Syn. 2. abominable, hateful, vile, foul, mean, disgusting.

beast′ of bur′den, an animal used for carrying heavy loads or pulling heavy equipment, as a donkey, mule, or ox. [1795–1805]

beast′ of prey′, a predatory mammal.

beat (bēt), *v.,* **beat, beat•en** or **beat, beat•ing,** *n., adj.* **—***v.t.* **1.** to strike violently or forcefully and repeatedly. **2.** to dash against: *rain beating the trees.* **3.** to flutter, flap, or rotate in or against: *beating the air with its wings.* **4.** to sound, as on a drum: *beating a steady rhythm; to beat a tattoo.* **5.** to stir vigorously: *Beat the egg whites well.* **6.** to break, forge, or make by blows: *to beat their swords into plowshares.* **7.** to produce (an attitude, idea, habit, etc.) by repeated efforts: *I'll beat some sense into him.* **8.** to make (a path) by repeated treading. **9.** to strike (a person or animal) repeatedly and injuriously: *Some of the hoodlums beat their victims viciously before robbing them.* **10.** *Music.* to mark (time) by strokes, as with the hand or a metronome. **11.** *Hunting.* to scour (the forest, grass, or brush), and sometimes make noise, in order to rouse game. **12.** to overcome in a contest; defeat. **13.** to win over in a race: *We beat the English challenger to Bermuda.* **14.** to be superior to: *Making reservations beats waiting in line.* **15.** to be incomprehensible to; baffle: *It beats me how he got the job.* **16.** to defeat or frustrate (a person), as a problem to be solved: *It beats me how to get her to understand.* **17.** to mitigate or offset the effects of: *beating the hot weather; trying to beat the sudden decrease in land values.* **18.** *Slang.* to swindle; cheat (often fol. by *out*): *He beat him out of hundreds of dollars on that deal.* **19.** to escape or avoid (blame or punishment). **20.** *Textiles.* to strike (the loose pick) into its proper place in the woven cloth by beating the loosely deposited filling yarn with the reed. **—***v.i.* **21.** to strike repeated blows; pound. **22.** to throb or pulsate: *His heart began to beat faster.* **23.** to dash; strike (usually fol. by *against* or *on*): *rain beating against the windows.* **24.** to resound under blows, as a drum. **25.** to achieve victory in a contest; win: *Which team do you think will beat?* **26.** to play, as on a drum. **27.** to scour cover for game. **28.** *Physics.* to make a beat or beats. **29.** (of a cooking ingredient) to foam or stiffen as a result of beating or whipping: *This cream won't beat.* **30.** *Naut.* to tack to windward by sailing close-hauled. **31. beat about, a.** to search through; scour: *After beating about for several hours, he turned up the missing papers.* **b.** *Naut.* to tack into the wind. **32. beat all,** *Informal.* to surpass anything of a similar nature, esp. in an astonishing or outrageous way: *The way he came in here and ordered us around beats all!* **33. beat a retreat.** See **retreat** (def. 8). **34. beat around** or **about the bush.** See **bush**[1] (def. 14). **35. beat back,** to force back; compel to withdraw: *to beat back an attacker.* **36. beat down, a.** to bring into subjection; subdue. **b.** *Informal.* to persuade (a seller) to lower the price of something: *His first price was too high, so we tried to beat him down.* **37. beat it,** *Informal.* to depart; go away: *He was pestering me, so I told him to beat it.* **38. beat off, a.** to ward off; repulse: *We had to beat off clouds of mosquitoes.* **b.** *Slang* (*vulgar*). to masturbate. **39. beat out, a.** *Informal.* to defeat; win or be chosen over: *to beat out the competition.* **b.** *Carpentry.* to cut (a mortise). **c.** to produce hurriedly, esp. by writing or typing: *There are three days left to beat out the first draft of the novel.* **d.** *Baseball.* (of a hitter) to make (an infield ground ball or bunt) into a hit: *He beat out a weak grounder to third.* **40. beat the air** or **wind,** to make repeated futile attempts. **41. beat the rap.** See **rap**[1] (def. 16). **42. beat up, a.** Also, **beat up on.** to strike repeatedly so as to cause painful injury; thrash: *A gang of toughs beat him up on the way home from school. In the third round the champion really began to beat up on the challenger.* **b.** *Brit. Informal.* to find or gather; scare up: *I'll beat up some lunch for us while you make out the shopping list.* **—***n.* **43.** a stroke or blow. **44.** the sound made by one or more such blows: *the beat of drums.* **45.** a throb or pulsation: *a pulse of 60 beats per minute.* **46.** the ticking sound made by a clock or watch escapement. **47.** one's assigned or regular path or habitual round: *a policeman's beat.* **48.** *Music.* **a.** the audible, visual, or mental marking of the metrical divisions of music. **b.** a stroke of the hand, baton, etc., marking the time division or an accent for music during performance. **49.** *Theat.* a momentary time unit imagined by an actor in timing actions: *Wait four beats and then pick up the phone.* **50.** *Pros.* the accent stress, or ictus, in a foot or rhythmical unit of poetry. **51.** *Physics.* a pulsation caused by the coincidence of the amplitudes of two oscillations of unequal frequencies, having a frequency equal to the difference between the frequencies of the two oscillations. **52.** *Journalism.* **a.** the reporting of a piece of news in advance, esp. before it is reported by a rival or rivals. Cf. **exclusive** (def. 13), **scoop** (def. 8). **b.** Also called **newsbeat, run.** the particular news source or activity that a reporter is responsible for covering. **53.** a subdivision of a county, as in Mississippi. **54.** (*often cap.*) *Informal.* beatnik. **55. off one's beat,** outside of one's routine, general knowledge, or range of experience: *He protested that nonobjective art was off his beat.* **56. on the beat,** in the correct rhythm or tempo: *By the end of the number they were all finally playing on the beat.* **—***adj.* **57.** *Informal.* exhausted; worn out. **58.** (*often cap.*) of or characteristic of members of the Beat Generation or beatniks. [bef. 900; ME *beten,* OE *bēatan*; c. ON *bauta,* MLG *bōten,* OHG *bōzzan*; akin to MIr *búalaim* I hit, L *fūstis* a stick < **bheud-*] **—beat′a•ble,** *adj.*
—Syn. 1. belabor, batter, drub, maul, baste, pommel, cudgel, buffet, flog. BEAT, HIT, POUND, STRIKE, THRASH refer to the giving of a blow or blows. BEAT implies the giving of repeated blows: *to beat a rug.* To HIT is usually to give a single blow, definitely directed: *to hit a ball.* To POUND is to give heavy and repeated blows, often with the fist: *to pound a nail, the table.* To STRIKE is to give one or more forceful blows suddenly or swiftly: *to strike a gong.* To THRASH implies inflicting repeated blows as punishment, to show superior strength, and the like: *to thrash a child.* **12.** conquer, subdue, vanquish, overpower. **14.** excel, outdo, surpass. **22.** See **pulsate.**

beat•en (bēt′n), *adj.* **1.** formed or shaped by blows; hammered: *a dish of beaten brass.* **2.** much trodden; commonly used: *a beaten path.* **3.** defeated; vanquished; thwarted. **4.** overcome by exhaustion; fatigued by hard work, intense activity, etc. **5.** (of food) whipped up, pounded, pulverized, or the like: *adding three beaten eggs.* **6. off the beaten track** or **path,** novel; uncommon; out of the ordinary: *a tiny shop that was off the beaten track.* [bef. 1100; ME *beten,* OE *bēaten,* ptp. of *bēatan* to BEAT]

beat′en bis′cuit, *Southern U.S.* a hard, unleavened biscuit, made to rise by pounding and folding the dough. [1875–80, *Amer.*]

beat•en•est (bēt′n ist), *adj.* beatinest.

beat•er (bē′tər), *n.* **1.** a person or thing that beats. **2.** an implement or device for beating something: *a rug beater.* **3.** *Hunting.* a person who rouses or drives game from cover. **4.** *Papermaking.* a machine for beating half-stuff to pulp by separating and shortening the fibers to produce a gelatinous mass. **5.** *Textiles.* the reed. **6.** *Newfoundland.* a young seal, usually a month to six weeks old, having completely or almost completely shed its initial white fur. [1400–50; late ME *better.* See BEAT, -ER[1]]

Beat′ Genera′tion, members of the generation that came of age after World War II who, supposedly as a result of disillusionment stemming from the Cold War, espoused forms of mysticism and the relaxation of social and sexual inhibitions. Also, **beat′ genera′tion.** [1950–55; appar. BEAT, though the sense intended by earliest users of the phrase is not clear; the association with BEATITUDE later made by Jack Kerouac is prob. fanciful]

be•a•tif•ic (bē′ə tif′ik), *adj.* **1.** bestowing bliss, blessings, happiness, or the like: *beatific peace.* **2.** blissful; saintly: *a beatific smile.* [1630–40; (< F) < LL *beātificus* making happy, equiv. to *beāt(us)* (ptp. of *beāre; be-* bless + *-āt(us)* -ATE[1]) + *-i-* -I- + *-ficus* -FIC] **—be′a•tif′i•cal•ly,** *adv.*
—Syn. 2. serene, exalted, angelic, rapturous.

be•at•i•fi•ca•tion (bē at′ə fi kā′shən), *n.* **1.** the act of beatifying. **2.** the state of being beatified. **3.** *Rom. Cath. Ch.* the official act of the pope whereby a deceased person is declared to be enjoying the happiness of heaven, and therefore a proper subject of religious honor and public cult in certain places. [1495–1505; < LL *beātificātiōn-* (s. of *beātificātiō*), equiv. to *beātificāt(us)* (ptp. of *beātificāre* to BEATIFY) + *-iōn-* -ION; see -ATE[1]]

be•at•i•fy (bē at′ə fī′), *v.t.,* **-fied, -fy•ing. 1.** to make blissfully happy. **2.** *Rom. Cath. Ch.* to declare (a deceased person) to be among the blessed and thus entitled to specific religious honor. [1525–35; < MF *beatifier* < LL *beātificāre.* See BEATIFIC]

beat•in•est (bēt′n ist), *adj. South Midland and Southern U.S.* most remarkable or unusual: *This is the beatinest town I ever did see.* Also, **beatenest.** [1855–60, *Amer.*; appar. *beatin(g)* (prp. of BEAT) + -EST[1]]

beat•ing (bē′ting), *n.* **1.** the act of a person or thing that beats, as to punish, clean, mix, etc.: *Give the rug a good beating.* **2.** a defeat or reverse; loss; setback: *Several stocks took a beating in the market today.* **3.** pulsation; throbbing: *the beating of her heart.* [1200–50; ME *betynge.* See BEAT, -ING[1]]

beat•ing-up (bē′ting up′), *n.* **1.** a severe thrashing administered for intimidation or revenge. **2.** *Textiles.* the process by which the loose pick is made an integral part of the woven material. [1945–50]

be•at•i•tude (bē at′i to͞od′, -tyo͞od′), *n.* **1.** supreme blessedness; exalted happiness. **2.** (*often cap.*) any of the declarations of blessedness pronounced by Jesus in the Sermon on the Mount. [1375–1425; late ME < L *beātitūdō* perfect happiness, equiv. to *beāti-* (see BEATIFIC) + *-tūdō* -TUDE]

Bea•tles (bēt′lz), *n.* **the,** (*used with a plural v.*) British rock-'n'-roll group (1962–70) including **George Harrison** (born 1943), **John (Winston) Len•non** (len′ən) (1940–80), **Paul (James) Mc•Cart•ney** (mə kärt′nē) (born 1942), and **Rin•go** (ring′gō) **Starr** (*Richard Starkey*) (born 1940).

beat′ man′. See **district man.**

beat•nik (bēt′nik), *n.* **1.** (*sometimes cap.*) a member of the Beat Generation. **2.** a person who rejects or avoids conventional behavior, dress, etc. [1955–60, *Amer.*; BEAT (adj.) (as in BEAT GENERATION) + -NIK]

Bea•ton (bēt′n), *n.* **Sir Cecil (Walter Hardy),** 1904–80, English photographer, writer, and theatrical designer.

beat′ po′ets, any of a number of U.S. poets concentrated in California in the 1950's and noted chiefly for their rejection of poetic as well as social conventions, exemplified through experimental, often informal phrasing and diction and formless verse that attempts to capture spontaneity of thought and feeling. [see BEAT GENERATION]

Be•a•trice (bē′ə tris, bē′tris *for 1, 3;* bē a′tris *for 2; for 1, 3 also It.* be′ä trē′che), *n.* **1.** (in Dante's *Vita Nuova* and *Divine Comedy*) a symbolic figure developed from the person whom Dante first saw as a child and loved as an ideal of womanhood. **2.** a city in SE Nebraska. 12,891. **3.** a female given name: from a Latin word meaning "one who brings joy."

Be•a•trix (bē′ə triks, bē′-), *n.* (*Beatrix Wilhelmina Armgard*), born 1938, queen of the Netherlands since 1980 (daughter of Juliana).

Beat•tie (bē′tē), *n.* **James,** 1735–1803, Scottish poet.

Beat•ty (bē′tē), *n.* **David** (*1st Earl of the North Sea and of Brooksby*), 1871–1936, British admiral.

beat-up (bēt′up′), *adj.* **1.** *Informal.* dilapidated; in poor condition from use: *a beat-up old jalopy.* **—***n.* **2.** the warpwise count of tufts of pile in the warp of carpets. [1935–40; adj., n. use of v. phrase *beat up*]

beau (bō), *n., pl.* **beaus, beaux** (bōz), *v.* **—***n.* **1.** a frequent and attentive male companion. **2.** a male escort for a girl or woman. **3.** a dandy; fop. **—***v.t.* **4.** to escort (a girl or woman), as to a social gathering. [1250–1300; ME < F < L *bellus* beautiful] **—beau′ish,** *adj.*
—Syn. 3. peacock, swell, blade, dude, coxcomb.

Beau′ Brum′mell (brum′əl), **1.** (*George Bryan Brummell*), 1778–1840, an Englishman who set the fashion in men's clothes. **2.** an extremely or excessively well-dressed man; fop; dandy. **3.** a dressing table for men, having a variety of elaborate arrangements of mirrors, candle brackets, etc. (invented in England in the late 18th century). Also, **Beau′ Brum′mel** (for defs. 2, 3).

beau•coup (bō ko͞o′), *adj. Informal* (*usually facetious*). many; numerous; much: *It's a hard job, but it pays beaucoup money.* [1910–15; < F; see BEAU, COUP[1]]

beau′ dol′lar, *South Midland and Southern U.S. Older Use.* a silver dollar. [*beau* perh. to be identified with BEAU, but sense is uncert.]

Beau•fort (bō′fərt), *n.* a male given name.

Beau′fort scale′ (bō′fərt), (no longer in technical use) **1.** a scale of wind forces, described by name and range of velocity, and classified as from force 0 to force 12, or, sometimes, to force 17. **2.** a scale of the states of sea created by winds of these various forces up to and including force 10. [1855–60; named after Sir Francis *Beaufort* (1774–1857), British admiral who devised it]

Beau′fort Sea′ (bō′fərt), a part of the Arctic Ocean, NE of Alaska.

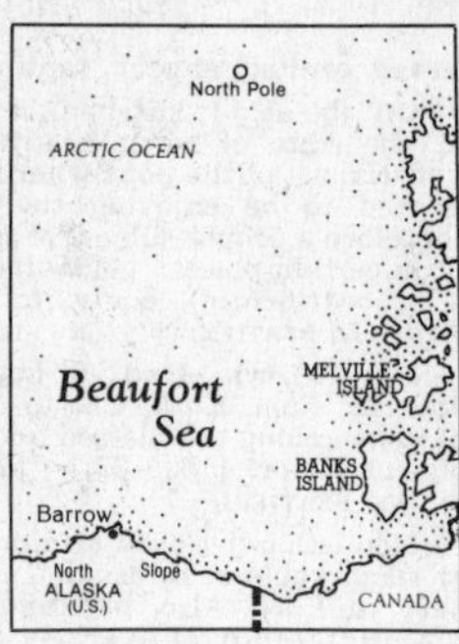

beau geste (bō zhest′), *pl.* ***beaux gestes*** (bō zhest′). *French.* a fine or noble gesture, often futile or only for effect.

beau·greg·o·ry (bō greg′ə rē), *n., pl.* **-ries.** a blue and yellow damselfish, *Pomacentrus leucostictus,* inhabiting shallow waters off Bermuda, Florida, and the West Indies. [1840–50; of obscure orig.]

Beau·har·nais (bō ar ne′), *n.* **1. Eu·gé·nie Hortense de** (œ zhā nē′ ôr täns′ də), 1782–1837, queen of Holland: wife of Louis Bonaparte. **2. Jo·sé·phine de** (zhō zā fēn′ də), 1763–1814, empress of France 1804–09: first wife of Napoleon I.

beau′ ide′al, *pl.* **beaus ideal, beaux ideal** for 1; **beau ideals** for 2. **1.** a conception of perfect beauty. **2.** a model of excellence. [1795–1805; < F *beau idéal* lit., ideal beauty. See BEAU, IDEAL]

Beau·jo·lais (bō′zhə lā′), *n., pl.* **-laises** (-lāz′) for 2. **1.** a wine-growing region in E France, in Rhône department. **2.** a dry, fruity red Burgundy wine from this region that does not age and usually must be drunk within a few months after it is made.

Beau·jo·lais Nou·veau (bō′zhə lā′ no͞o vō′; *Fr.* bō zhô le no͞o vō′), the first Beaujolais wine of the season, usually available for sale within two months after the grapes are harvested. Also called **Beau·jo·lais Pri·meur** (bō′zhə lā′ prē mûr′; *Fr.* bō zhô le prē mœr′).

Beau·mar·chais (bō mar she′), *n.* **Pierre Au·gus·tin Ca·ron de** (pyer ō gy stan′ ka rôn′ də), 1732–99, French dramatist.

beau monde (bō′ mond′; *Fr.* bō mônd′), the fashionable world; high society. [1705–15; < F: lit., fine world. See BEAU, MONDE]

Beau·mont (bō′mont), *n.* **1. Francis,** 1584–1616, English dramatist who collaborated with John Fletcher. **2. William,** 1785–1853, U.S. surgeon. **3.** a city in SE Texas. 118,102. **4.** a male given name.

Beau·port (*Fr.* bō pôr′), *n.* a city in E Quebec, in E Canada: suburb of Quebec, on the St. Lawrence River. 60,447.

Beau·re·gard (bō′ri gärd′; *Fr.* bōrᵊ gar′), *n.* **Pierre Gus·tave Tou·tant** (pyer gy stav′ to͞o tän′), 1818–93, Confederate general in the U.S. Civil War.

beaut (byo͞ot), *n. Informal.* (often used ironically) something or someone beautiful, remarkable, or amazing. [1865–70, *Amer.*; by shortening from BEAUTY]

beau·te·ous (byo͞o′tē əs, -tyəs), *adj. Chiefly Literary.* beautiful. [1400–50; late ME; see BEAUTY, -OUS] **—beau′te·ous·ly,** *adv.* **—beau′te·ous·ness,** *n.*

beau·ti·cian (byo͞o tish′ən), *n.* **1.** a person trained to style and dress the hair; hairdresser. Cf. **esthetician. 2.** a manager or an employee of a beauty parlor. [1920–25, *Amer.*; BEAUT(Y) + -ICIAN]

beau·ti·ful (byo͞o′tə fəl), *adj.* **1.** having beauty; having qualities that give great pleasure or satisfaction to see, hear, think about, etc.; delighting the senses or mind: *a beautiful dress; a beautiful speech.* **2.** excellent of its kind: *a beautiful putt on the seventh hole; The chef served us a beautiful roast of beef.* **3.** wonderful; very pleasing or satisfying. —*n.* **4.** the concept of beauty (usually prec. by *the*). **5.** (*used with a plural v.*) beautiful things or people collectively (usually prec. by *the*): *the good and the beautiful.* **6.** the ideal of beauty (usually prec. by *the*): *to strive to attain the beautiful.* —*interj.* **7.** wonderful; fantastic: *You got two front-row seats? Beautiful!* **8.** extraordinary; incredible: used ironically: *Your car broke down in the middle of the freeway? Beautiful!* [1520–30; BEAUTY + -FUL] **—beau′ti·ful·ly,** *adv.* **—beau′ti·ful·ness,** *n.*
—Syn. 1. comely, seemly, attractive, fair, beauteous. BEAUTIFUL, HANDSOME, LOVELY, PRETTY refer to a pleasing appearance. A person or thing that is BEAUTIFUL has perfection of form, color, etc., or noble and spiritual qualities: *a beautiful landscape, a beautiful woman.* HANDSOME often implies stateliness or pleasing proportion and symmetry: *a handsome man.* That which is LOVELY is beautiful but in a warm and endearing way: *a lovely smile.* PRETTY implies a moderate but noticeable beauty, esp. in that which is small or of minor importance: *a pretty child.* **—Ant. 1.** ugly.

beau′tiful peo′ple, (*often caps.*) wealthy or famous people, often members of the jet set, who mingle in glamorous social circles and who, because of their celebrity, often establish trends or fashions. [1965–70]

beau·ti·fy (byo͞o′tə fī′), *v.t., v.i.,* **-fied, -fy·ing.** to make or become beautiful. [1520–30; BEAUTY + -FY] **—beau·ti·fi·ca·tion** (byo͞o′tə fi kā′shən), *n.* **—beau′ti·fi′er,** *n.*
—Syn. adorn, embellish, enhance; bedeck, array.

beau·ty (byo͞o′tē), *n., pl.* **-ties. 1.** the quality present in a thing or person that gives intense pleasure or deep satisfaction to the mind, whether arising from sensory manifestations (as shape, color, sound, etc.), a meaningful design or pattern, or something else (as a personality in which high spiritual qualities are manifest). **2.** a beautiful person, esp. a woman. **3.** a beautiful thing, as a work of art or a building. **4.** Often, **beauties.** something that is beautiful in nature or in some natural or artificial environment. **5.** an individually pleasing or beautiful quality; grace; charm: *a vivid blue area that is the one real beauty of the painting.* **6.** *Informal.* a particular advantage: *One of the beauties of this medicine is the freedom from aftereffects.* **7.** (usually used ironically) something extraordinary: *My sunburn was a real beauty.* **8.** something excellent of its kind: *My old car was a beauty.* [1225–75; ME *be(a)ute* < OF *beaute;* r. ME *bealte* < OF *beltet* < VL **bellitāt-* (s. of **bellitās*), equiv. to L *bell(us)* fine + *-itāt-* -ITY]
—Syn. 1. loveliness, pulchritude, comeliness, fairness, attractiveness. **2.** belle. **—Ant. 1.** ugliness.

beau·ty·ber·ry (byo͞o′tē ber′ē), *n., pl.* **-ries.** any of various shrubs of the genus *Callicarpa,* of southern North America, as *C. americana,* having clusters of bluish flowers and purple, berrylike fruit. [1920–25, *Amer.*; BEAUTY + BERRY, as trans. of NL *Callicarpa*]

beau·ty-bush (byo͞o′tē bo͝osh′), *n.* a Chinese shrub, *Kolkwitzia amabilis,* of the honeysuckle family, having showy, pinkish flowers and grown as an ornamental. [1925–30]

beau′ty con′test, 1. a competition in which the entrants, usually women, are judged as to physical beauty and sometimes personality and talent, with the winners awarded prizes or titles. **2.** *Informal.* any contest, election, etc., that is decided on the basis of popularity. [1895–1900]

beau′ty par′lor, an establishment for the hairdressing, manicuring, or other cosmetic treatment of women. Also called **beau′ty salon′, beau′ty shop′.** [1905–10, *Amer.*]

beau′ty quark′, *Physics.* See **bottom quark.**

beau′ty sleep′, *Informal.* **1.** sleep before midnight, assumed to be necessary for one's beauty. **2.** any extra sleep. [1855–60]

beau′ty spot′, 1. a tiny, molelike patch worn, usually on the face, as to set off the fairness of the skin. **2.** a mole or other dark mark on the skin. **3.** a place of exceptional scenic or architectural beauty: *Montserrat is the beauty spot of the islands.* [1650–60]

Beau·vais (bō vā′; *Fr.* bō ve′), *n.* a city in and the capital of Oise, in NW France: 13th-century cathedral. 56,725.

Beau·voir (bōv wär′; *Fr.* bō vwar′), *n.* See **de Beauvoir.**

beaux (bōz; *Fr.* bō), *n.* a pl. of **beau.**

Beaux-Arts (bō zär′; *Fr.* bō zar′), *adj.* **1.** noting or pertaining to a style of architecture, popularly associated with the École des Beaux-Arts in Paris, that prevailed in France in the late 19th century and that was adopted in the U.S. and elsewhere c1900, characterized by the free and eclectic use and adaptation of French architectural features of the 16th through 18th centuries combined so as to give a massive, elaborate, and often ostentatious effect, and also by the use of symmetrical plans preferably allowing vast amounts of interior space. **2.** resembling the architecture, architectural precepts, or teaching methods of the Ecole des Beaux-Arts in Paris: often used in a pejorative sense to designate excessive formalism disregarding considerations of structural truth, advanced aesthetic theory, rational planning, or economy. —*n.pl.* **3.** (*l.c.*) the fine arts, as painting or music. [1815–25]

beaux-es·prits (bō zes prē′), *n. French.* pl. of **bel-esprit.**

Beaux′ Strat′agem, The (bōz), a comedy (1707) by George Farquhar.

beaver¹, *Castor canadensis,* head and body 2½ ft. (0.8 m); tail 1 ft. (0.3 m)

bea·ver¹ (bē′vər), *n., pl.* **-vers,** (*esp. collectively*) **-ver** for 1; *v.* —*n.* **1.** a large, amphibious rodent of the genus *Castor,* having sharp incisors, webbed hind feet, and a flattened tail, noted for its ability to dam streams with trees, branches, etc. **2.** the fur of this animal. **3.** a flat, round hat made of beaver fur or a similar fabric. **4.** a tall, cylindrical hat for men, formerly made of beaver and now of a fabric simulating this fur. Cf. **opera hat, silk hat, top hat. 5.** *Informal.* a full beard or a man wearing one. **6.** *Informal.* an exceptionally active or hard-working person. **7.** *Slang (vulgar).* **a.** a woman's pubic area. **b.** *Offensive.* a woman. **8.** *Textiles.* **a.** a cotton cloth with a thick nap, used chiefly in the manufacture of work clothes. **b.** (formerly) a heavy, soft, woolen cloth with a thick nap, made to resemble beaver fur. **9.** (*cap.*) a native or inhabitant of Oregon, the Beaver State (used as a nickname). —*v.i.* **10.** *Brit.* to work very hard or industriously at something (usually fol. by *away*). [bef. 1000; ME *bever,* OE *beofor, befor;* c. G *Biber,* Lith *bebrùs,* L *fiber,* Skt *babhrús* reddish brown, large ichneumon] **—bea′ver·like′, bea′ver·ish,** *adj.*

bea·ver² (bē′vər), *n. Armor.* **1.** a piece of plate armor for covering the lower part of the face and throat, worn esp. with an open helmet, as a sallet or basinet. Cf. **buffe, wrapper** (def. 7). **2.** a piece of plate armor, pivoted at the sides, forming part of a close helmet below the visor or ventail. See diag. under **close helmet.** [1400–50; late ME *bavier, bavour* < MF *baviere* (OF: bib), equiv. to *bave* spit, dribble + *-iere* < L *-āria,* fem. of *-ārius* -ARY; alteration of vowel in the initial syll. is unexplained]

bea·ver·board (bē′vər bôrd′, -bōrd′), *n.* a light, stiff sheeting made of wood fiber and used in building, esp. for partitions or temporary structures. [1905–10, *Amer.*; formerly a trademark]

Bea·ver·brook (bē′vər bro͝ok′), *n.* **William Maxwell Aitken, Lord** (*1st Baron*), 1879–1964, English publisher, born in Canada.

bea′ver cloth′, beaver¹ (def. 8).

Bea·ver·creek (bē′vər krēk′), *n.* a town in SW Ohio. 31,589.

Bea′ver Dam′, a city in SE Wisconsin. 14,149.

bea·ver·ette (bē′və ret′), *n.* rabbit fur dyed to resemble beaver. [1705–15; BEAVER¹ + -ETTE]

Bea′ver Falls′, a city in W Pennsylvania. 12,525.

bea′ver fe′ver, *Western U.S.* giardiasis.

Bea′ver State′, Oregon (used as a nickname).

Bea·ver·ton (bē′vər tən), *n.* a town in NW Oregon. 30,582.

be·bee·rine (bə bēr′ēn, -in, beb′ē ə rēn′), *n. Pharm.* an alkaloid resembling quinine, obtained from the bark of the greenheart and other plants. [1850–55; < G *Bebeerin,* equiv. to *Bebeer(ubaum)* bebeeru tree + *-in* -INE²]

be·bee·ru (bə bēr′o͞o, beb′ē ə ro͞o′), *n.* greenheart (def. 1). [1850–55; < Sp *bibirú* < Carib]

Be·bel (bā′bəl), *n.* **Fer·di·nand Au·gust** (fûr′dn and′ ô′gəst; *Ger.* fer′di nänt′ ou′go͝ost), 1840–1913, German socialist and writer.

be·bop (bē′bop′), *n. Jazz.* bop¹. [1940–45, *Amer.*; prob. from the nonsense syllables typical of scat singing] **—be′bop′per,** *n.*

Beb·ry·ces (be brī′sēz), *n.pl.* the original inhabitants of Bithynia who lost their land to the Mariandyni.

bec., because.

be·calm (bi käm′), *v.t.* **1.** to deprive (a sailing vessel) of the wind necessary to move it; subject to a calm: *The schooner was becalmed in the horse latitudes for two weeks.* **2.** *Archaic.* to calm; pacify. [1550–60; BE- + CALM]

be·came (bi kām′), *v.* pt. of **become.**

bec·ard (bek′ərd, bə kärd′), *n.* any of several passerine birds of the genus *Pachyramphus,* of the American tropics, having large heads and swollen bills, and variously classified with the flycatchers or the cotingas. [< F *bécard, beccard* a merganser with a prominent beak, equiv. to *bec* BEAK + *-ard* -ARD]

be·cause (bi kôz′, -koz′, -kuz′), *conj.* **1.** for the reason that; due to the fact that: *The boy was absent because he was ill.* **2. because of,** by reason of; due to: *Schools were closed because of heavy snowfall.* [1275–1325; ME *bi cause* BY CAUSE]
—Syn. 1. BECAUSE, AS, SINCE, FOR, INASMUCH AS agree in implying a reason for an occurrence or action. BECAUSE introduces a direct reason: *I was sleeping because I was tired.* As and SINCE are so casual as to imply merely circumstances attendant on the main statement: *As* (or *since*) *I was tired, I was sleeping.* The reason, proof, or justification introduced by FOR is like an afterthought or a parenthetical statement: *I was sleeping, for I was tired.* INASMUCH AS implies concession; the main statement is true in view of the circumstances introduced by this conjunction: *Inasmuch as I was tired, it seemed best to sleep.*
—Usage. 1. See **reason.**

bé·cha·mel (bā′shə mel′; *Fr.* bā sha mel′), *n.* a white sauce, sometimes seasoned with onion and nutmeg. Also called **be′chamel sauce′.** [1790–1800; named after Louis, Marquis de *Béchamel* (steward of Louis XIV of France), its originator]

be·chance (bi chans′, -chäns′), *v.i., v.t.* **-chanced, -chanc·ing.** *Archaic.* to befall. [1520–30; from phrase *by chance*]

Bé·char (bā shär′; *Fr.* bā shar′), *n.* a city in W Algeria. 56,563. Formerly, **Colomb-Béchar.**

be·charm (bi chärm′), *v.t.* to charm; bewitch; captivate. [1300–50; ME; see BE-, CHARM]

bêche (besh, bāsh), *n.* a grab for retrieving tools used in drilling a well. [1850–55; < F: spade]

bêche-de-mer (besh′də mâr′, bāsh′-), *n., pl.* **bêch·es-de-mer,** (*esp. collectively*) **bêche-de-mer** for 1. **1.** a trepang. **2.** Often, **Bêche-de-Mer.** Neo-Melanesian. [1805–15; erroneously for F *biche de mer* < Pg *bicho do mar* lit., animal of the sea; cf. BEACH-LA-MAR]

Be·chet (bə shā′), *n.* **Sidney,** 1897–1959, U.S. jazz soprano saxophonist and clarinetist.

Bech·u·a·na (bech′o͞o ä′nə, bek′yo͞o-), *n., pl.* **-nas,** (*esp. collectively*) **-na.** Tswana (def. 1). [1795–1805]

Bech·u·a·na·land (bech′o͞o ä′nə land′, bek′yo͞o-), *n.* former name of **Botswana.**

beck¹ (bek), *n.* **1.** a gesture used to signal, summon, or direct someone. **2. at someone's beck and call,** ready to do someone's bidding; subject to someone's slightest wish: *He has three servants at his beck and call.* **3.**

Chiefly Scot. a bow or curtsy of greeting. —*v.t., v.i.* **4.** *Archaic.* beckon. [1325–75; ME *becken,* short var. of *becnen* to BECKON]

beck[2] (bek), *n. North Eng.* a brook, esp. a swiftly running stream with steep banks. [1250–1300; ME *becc* < Scand; cf. ON *bekkr;* akin to OE *bece,* D *beek,* G *Bach* brook, MIr *bual* flowing water < IE **bhog-lā*]

beck[3] (bek), *v.t. Metalworking.* to form (a billet or the like) into a tire or hoop by rolling or hammering on a mandrel or anvil. [v. use of *beck* (n.), shortening of *beck-iron,* var. of BICK-IRON]

Beck (bek), *n.* **Dave,** born 1894, U.S. labor leader: president of the International Brotherhood of Teamsters 1952–57.

Beck·er (bek′ər), *n.* **1. Carl Lo·tus** (lō′təs), 1873–1945, U.S. historian. **2. George Ferdinand,** 1847–1919, U.S. scientist and mathematician. **3. Howard Paul,** 1899–1960, U.S. sociologist.

beck·et (bek′it), *n. Naut.* **1.** a short length of rope for securing spars, coils of rope, etc., having an eye at one end and a thick knot or a toggle at the other, which is passed through the eye. **2.** a grommet of rope, as one used as a handle or oarlock. **3.** a grommet or eye on a block to which the standing end of a fall can be secured. **4.** a wooden cleat or hook secured to the shrouds of a sailing vessel to hold tacks and sheets not in use. [1760–70; orig. uncert.]

Beck·et (bek′it), *n.* **Saint Thomas à,** 1118?–70, archbishop of Canterbury: murdered because of his opposition to Henry II's policies toward the church.

beck′et bend′, *Naut.* See **sheet bend.** [1895–1900]

Beck·ett (bek′it), *n.* **Samuel,** born 1906, Irish playwright and novelist, living in France: Nobel prize for literature 1969.

Beck·ford (bek′fərd), *n.* **William,** 1759–1844, English writer.

Beck·ley (bek′lē), *n.* a city in SW West Virginia. 20,492.

Beck·mann (bek′män), *n.* **Max** (mäks), 1884–1950, German painter.

Beck·nell (bek′nl), *n.* **William,** c1790–1865, U.S. frontier trader: opened Santa Fe Trail 1822.

beck·on (bek′ən), *v.t., v.i.* **1.** to signal, summon, or direct by a gesture of the head or hand. **2.** to lure; entice. —*n.* **3.** a nod, gesture, etc., that signals, directs, summons, indicates agreement, or the like. [bef. 950; ME *beknen,* OE *gebē(a)cnian,* deriv. of *bēacen* BEACON] —**beck′on·er,** *n.* —**beck′on·ing·ly,** *adv.*
—**Syn. 1.** motion, wave, gesture, bid, nod. **2.** invite, attract, draw, coax, tempt, tantalize, allure, beguile.

Beck·y (bek′ē), *n.* a female given name, form of **Rebecca.**

be·clasp (bi klasp′, -kläsp′), *v.t.* to clasp all around or on all sides. [1600–10; BE- + CLASP]

bec·lo·meth·a·sone (bek′lō meth′ə sōn′, -zōn′), *n. Pharm.* a potent synthetic corticosteroid, $C_{28}H_{37}ClO_7$, prepared as an inhalant in the treatment of bronchial asthma. [1970–75; perh. *be(ta-)* + C(H)LO(RO-) + METH(YL) + *-as-* (< ?) + -ONE]

be·cloud (bi kloud′), *v.t.* **1.** to darken or obscure with clouds. **2.** to make confused: *Angry words beclouded the issue.* [1590–1600; BE- + CLOUD]
—**Syn. 2.** confuse, obscure, befog, obfuscate, muddle.

be·come (bi kum′), *v.,* **be·came, be·come, be·com·ing.** —*v.i.* **1.** to come, change, or grow to be (as specified): *He became tired.* **2.** to come into being. —*v.t.* **3.** to be attractive on; befit in appearance; look well on: *That gown becomes you.* **4.** to be suitable or necessary to the dignity, situation, or responsibility of: *conduct that becomes an officer.* **5. become of,** to happen to; be the fate of: *What will become of him?* [bef. 900; ME *becumen,* OE *becuman* to come about, happen; c. D *bekomen,* G *bekommen,* Goth *biqiman.* See BE-, COME]

be·com·ing (bi kum′ing), *adj.* **1.** that suits or gives a pleasing effect or attractive appearance, as to a person or thing: *a becoming dress; a becoming hairdo.* **2.** suitable; appropriate; proper: *a becoming sentiment.* —*n.* **3.** any process of change. **4.** *Aristotelianism.* any change involving realization of potentialities, as a movement from the lower level of potentiality to the higher level of actuality. [1555–65; BECOME + -ING[1], -ING[2]] —**be·com′ing·ly,** *adv.* —**be·com′ing·ness,** *n.*
—**Syn. 1.** comely. **2.** fitting, meet, fit, apt, right, decorous, congruous, seemly.

Béc·quer (be′kər), *n.* **Gus·ta·vo A·dol·fo** (go͞os tä′vô ä thôl′fô), 1836–70, Spanish poet.

Bec·que·rel (bek′ə rel′; *Fr.* bek[ə] rel′), *n.* **1. A·lex·an·dre Ed·mond** (a lek sän′dr[ə] ed môn′), 1820–91, French physicist (son of Antoine César). **2. An·toine Cé·sar** (än twan′ sä zar′), 1788–1878, French physicist. **3. An·toine Hen·ri** (än twan′ än rē′), 1852–1908, French physicist (son of Alexandre Edmond): Nobel prize 1903.

Becquerel′ effect′, *Physics.* the electromotive force produced by the unequal illumination of two identical electrodes placed in an electrolyte. [named after A. H. BECQUEREL]

Becquerel′ rays′, (formerly) rays emitted by radioactive substances. [named after A. H. BECQUEREL]

be·crip·ple (bi krip′əl), *v.t.,* **-pled, -pling.** to make or cause to become crippled. [BE- + CRIPPLE]

bed (bed), *n., v.,* **bed·ded, bed·ding.** —*n.* **1.** a piece of furniture upon which or within which a person sleeps, rests, or stays when not well. **2.** the mattress and bedclothes together with the bedstead of a bed. **3.** the bedstead alone. **4.** the act of or time for sleeping: *Now for a cup of cocoa and then bed.* **5.** the use of a bed for the night; lodging: *I reserved a bed at the old inn.* **6.** the marital relationship. **7.** any resting place: *making his bed under a tree.* **8.** something resembling a bed in form or position. **9.** a piece or area of ground in a garden or lawn in which plants are grown. **10.** an area in a greenhouse in which plants are grown. **11.** the plants in such areas. **12.** the bottom of a lake, river, sea, or other body of water. **13.** a piece or part forming a foundation or base. **14.** a layer of rock; a stratum. **15.** a foundation surface of earth or rock supporting a track, pavement, or the like: *a gravel bed for the roadway.* **16.** *Building Trades.* **a.** the underside of a stone, brick, slate, tile, etc., laid in position. **b.** the upper side of a stone laid in position. **c.** the layer of mortar in which a brick, stone, etc., is laid. **d.** the natural stratification of a stone: *a stone laid on bed.* **17.** *Furniture.* skirt (def. 6b). **18.** the flat surface in a printing press on which the form of type is laid. **19.** *Transp.* the body or, sometimes, the floor or bottom of a truck or trailer. **20.** *Chem.* a compact mass of a substance functioning in a reaction as a catalyst or reactant. **21.** *Sports.* **a.** the canvas surface of a trampoline. **b.** the smooth, wooden floor of a bowling alley. **c.** the slate surface of a billiard table to which the cloth is fastened. **22.** *Zool.* flesh enveloping the base of a claw, esp. the germinative layer beneath the claw. **23.** Also called **mock, mock mold.** *Shipbuilding.* a shaped steel pattern upon which furnaced plates for the hull of a vessel are hammered to shape. **24.** See **bed and board.** **25. get up on the wrong side of the bed,** to be irritable or bad-tempered from the start of a day: *Never try to reason with him when he's gotten up on the wrong side of the bed.* **26. go to bed, a.** to retire, esp. for the night. **b.** to engage in sexual relations. **27. go to bed with,** to have sexual intercourse with. **28. in bed, a.** beneath the covers of a bed. **b.** engaged in sexual intercourse. **29. jump** or **get into bed with,** to form a close, often temporary, alliance, usually with an unlikely ally: *Industry was charged with jumping into bed with labor on the issue.* **30. make a bed,** to fit a bed with sheets and blankets. **31. make one's bed,** to be responsible for one's own actions and their results: *You've made your bed—now lie in it.* **32. put to bed, a.** to help (a child, invalid, etc.) go to bed. **b.** *Printing.* to lock up (forms) in a press in preparation for printing. **c.** to work on the preparation of (an edition of a newspaper, periodical, etc.) up to the time of going to press. —*v.t.* **33.** to provide with a bed. **34.** to put to bed. **35.** *Hort.* to plant in or as in a bed. **36.** to lay flat. **37.** to place in a bed or layer: *to bed oysters.* **38.** to embed, as in a substance: *bedding the flagstones in concrete.* **39.** to take or accompany to bed for purposes of sexual intercourse. —*v.i.* **40.** to have sleeping accommodations: *He says we can bed there for the night.* **41.** *Geol.* to form a compact layer or stratum. **42.** (of a metal structural part) to lie flat or close against another part. **43.** *Archaic.* to go to bed. **44. bed down, a.** to make a bed for (a person, animal, etc.). **b.** to retire to bed: *They put out the fire and decided to bed down for the night.* [bef. 1000; ME; OE *bedd;* c. OFris, D *bed,* OS *bed(de),* OHG *betti* (G *Bett*), Goth *badi* < Gmc **badja*[n] (neut.); akin to L *fodere* to dig, OCS *bodǫ,* Lith *bedù* I pierce, Welsh *bedd* a grave; presumably a bed was dug out in the ground] —**bed′less,** *adj.* —**bed′like′,** *adj.*
—**Syn. 14.** band, belt, seam, lode.

B.Ed., Bachelor of Education.

be·dab·ble (bi dab′əl), *v.t.,* **-bled, -bling.** to spatter or soil all over: *clothes bedabbled with paint.* [1580–90; BE- + DABBLE]

bed′ and board′, 1. living quarters and meals: *In this school students must pay by the week for bed and board.* **2.** one's home regarded as exemplifying the obligations of marriage: *He said he would not be responsible for her debts after she left his bed and board.* [1400–50; late ME]

bed-and-break·fast (bed′n brek′fəst), *n.* **1.** an accommodation offered by an inn, hotel, or esp. a private home, consisting of a room for the night and breakfast the next morning for one inclusive price. **2.** an inn, hotel, or private home offering such accommodation. *Abbr.:* B&B Also, **bed′ and break′fast.** [1905–10]

be·dash (bi dash′), *v.t.* **1.** to dash or spatter (something) all over: *to bedash a salad with pepper.* **2.** to dash or strike against: *windows bedashed with rain.* **3.** to demolish or ruin; obliterate: *His dreams of glory were quickly bedashed.* [1555–65; BE- + DASH]

be·daub (bi dôb′), *v.t.* **1.** to smear all over; besmear; soil. **2.** to ornament gaudily or excessively. [1545–55; BE- + DAUB]

Be·daux′ sys′tem (bə dō′), a system of payment for work on the basis of the number of points of work done in a given amount of time, each point representing one minute of work on a given job at a normal rate of speed. Also called **Bedaux′ plan′, point system.** [after Charles Eugène *Bedaux* (1887–1944), American industrialist]

be·daz·zle (bi daz′əl), *v.t.,* **-zled, -zling. 1.** to impress forcefully, esp. so as to make oblivious to faults or shortcomings: *Audiences were bedazzled by her charm.* **2.** to dazzle so as to blind or confuse: *The glare of the headlights bedazzled him.* [1590–1600; BE- + DAZZLE] —**be·daz′zle·ment,** *n.* —**be·daz′zling·ly,** *adv.*
—**Syn. 1.** dazzle, astound, overwhelm, flabbergast, enchant, captivate. **2.** daze, bewilder, disconcert, blind, befuddle, fluster.

bed′ board′, a thin, rigid board placed between a mattress and bedspring to give firm support. Also, **bed′·board′.** [1675–85]

bed′ bolt′, a bolt on a bed for attaching a side rail to the head or foot. [1760–70]

bed·bug (bed′bug′), *n.* **1.** a flat, wingless, bloodsucking hemipterous insect, *Cimex lectularius,* that infests houses and esp. beds. **2.** any of several other bloodsucking bugs of the family Cimicidae. Also, **bed′ bug′.** [1800–10; BED + BUG[1]]

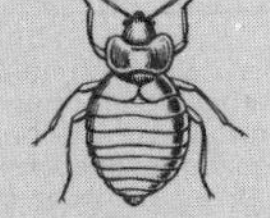

bedbug,
Cimex lectularius,
length ⅛ in. (0.3 cm)

bed′ chair′, an adjustable frame for assisting invalids to sit up in bed. Also called **chair bed.**

bed·cham·ber (bed′chām′bər), *n.* bedroom. [1325–75; ME *bedchaumbre.* See BED, CHAMBER]

bed′ check′, an inspection conducted soon after bedtime or during the night, as in a barracks or dormitory, to determine the presence or absence of persons required by regulation to be in bed. [1925–30]

bed·clothes (bed′klōz′, -klōthz′), *n.pl.* coverings for a bed, as sheets and blankets; bedding. [1350–1400; ME; see BED, CLOTHES]

bed·cloth·ing (bed′klō′thing), *n.* bedclothes; bedding. [1850–55, *Amer.;* BED + CLOTHING]

bed·cov·er (bed′kuv′ər), *n.* a bedspread. [1820–30; BED + COVER]

bed·da·ble (bed′ə bəl), *adj.* willing or easily persuaded to have sexual relations; seduceable: *The director is known for hiring actresses he thinks are beddable.* [1940–45; BED + -ABLE]

bed·ded (bed′id), *adj. Geol.* of or pertaining to rocks that exhibit bedding. [1820–30; BED + -ED[3]]

bed·der (bed′ər), *n.* **1.** bedmaker (def. 1). **2.** Also called **bedding plant.** *Hort.* an ornamental plant that is suitable for planting with other plants in a bed to achieve a desired visual effect. [1605–15; BED + -ER[1]]

bed·ding (bed′ing), *n.* **1.** blankets, sheets, etc., used on a bed; bedclothes. **2.** bedclothes together with a mattress. **3.** litter; straw, etc., as a bed for animals. **4.** *Building Trades.* **a.** a foundation or bottom layer. **b.** a thin layer of putty laid in the rabbet of a window frame or muntin to give a pane of glass an even backing. **5.** *Geol.* arrangement of sedimentary rocks in strata. —*adj.* **6.** *Hort.* of or pertaining to a plant esp. suited to or prepared for planting in an open-air bed for ornamental displays: *bedding hyacinths; bedding begonias.* [bef. 1000; ME, OE; see BED, -ING[1]]

bed′ding plane′, *Geol.* the surface that separates one stratum, layer, or bed of stratified rock from another. [1895–1900]

bed′ding plant′, *Hort.* bedder.

Bed·does (bed′ōz), *n.* **Thomas Lov·ell** (luv′əl), 1803–49, English dramatist and poet.

bed·dy-bye (bed′ē bī′), *n. Baby Talk.* the act of or time for going to bed or sleeping: *One more game and then it's beddy-bye.* [1905–10; BED + -Y[2] + (BYE)-BYE]

Bede (bēd), *n.* **Saint** (*"the Venerable Bede"*), A.D. 673?–735, English monk, historian, and theologian: wrote earliest history of England. Also, **Baeda.**

be·deck (bi dek′), *v.t.* to deck out; adorn, esp. in a showy or gaudy manner. [1560–70; BE- + DECK]
—**Syn.** array, decorate, ornament; beautify, enhance.

bed·e·guar (bed′i gär′), *n.* a gall on roses, esp. the sweetbrier, produced by a gall wasp. Also, **bed′e·gar′.** [1570–80; < MF < Ar < Pers *bād-āwar(d)* windfall, lit., wind-brought]

bede·house (bēd′hous′), *n., pl.* **-hous·es** (-hou′ziz). beadhouse.

be·dev·il (bi dev′əl), *v.t.,* **-iled, -il·ing** or (*esp. Brit.*) **-illed, -il·ling. 1.** to torment or harass maliciously or diabolically, as with doubts, distractions, or worries. **2.** to possess, as with a devil; bewitch. **3.** to cause confusion or doubt in; muddle; confound: *an issue bedeviled by prejudices.* **4.** to beset or hamper continuously: *a new building bedeviled by elevator failures.* [1760–70; BE- + DEVIL] —**be·dev′il·ment,** *n.*

be·dew (bi do͞o′, -dyo͞o′), *v.t.* to wet with or as if with dew. [1300–50; ME *bydewen.* See BE-, DEW]

bed·fast (bed′fast′, -fäst′), *adj. Chiefly Midland and Western U.S.* confined to bed, as by illness or age; bedridden. [1630–40; BED + FAST[1]]

bed·fel·low (bed′fel′ō), *n.* **1.** Also called **bedmate.** a person who shares one's bed. **2.** an associate or collaborator, esp. one who forms a temporary alliance for reasons of expediency: *Politics makes strange bedfellows.* [1400–50; late ME *bedfelow.* See BED, FELLOW]

Bed·ford (bed′fərd), *n.* **1. John of Lancaster, Duke of,** 1389–1435, English regent of France. **2.** a city in N Texas. 20,821. **3.** a city in NE Ohio, near Cleveland. 15,056. **4.** a city in S Indiana. 14,410. **5.** a city in NE Massachusetts. 13,067. **6.** former name of **North Bedfordshire. 7.** Bedfordshire.

Bed′ford cord′, cotton, worsted, rayon, or silk, distinctively woven for a lengthwise, corded effect. [1860–65]

Bed′ford Heights′, a town in N Ohio. 13,214.

Bed·ford·shire (bed′fərd shēr′, -shər), *n.* a county in central England. 489,500; 477 sq. mi. (1235 sq. km). Also called **Bedford, Beds.**

bed·frame (bed′frām′), *n.* the frame of a bed, including the bedrails, headboard, and footboard. [1805–15; BED + FRAME]

be·dight (bi dīt′), *v.t.,* **-dight, -dight** or **-dight·ed, -dight·ing.** *Archaic.* to deck out; array. [1350–1400; ME; see BE-, DIGHT]

be·dim (bi dim′), *v.t.,* **-dimmed, -dim·ming.** to make dim; darken; obscure. [1560–70; BE- + DIM]
—**Syn.** becloud, overcast, shroud; muddle. —**Ant.** illumine, brighten.

Bed·i·vere (bed′ə vēr′), *n.* **Sir,** *Arthurian Legend.* the

CONCISE PRONUNCIATION KEY: act, cāpe, dâre, pärt; set, ēqual; if, īce; ox, ōver, ôrder, oil, bo͝ok, bo͞ot, out; up, ûrge; child; sing; shoe; thin, that; zh as in *treasure.* ə = *a* as in *alone, e* as in *system, i* as in *easily, o* as in *gallop, u* as in *circus;* [ə] as in *fire* (fī[ə]r), *hour* (ou[ə]r). l and n can serve as syllabic consonants, as in *cradle* (krād′l), and *button* (but′n). See the full key inside the front cover.

knight who brought the dying King Arthur to the barge in which the three queens bore him to the Isle of Avalon.

be•di•zen (bi dī′zən, -diz′ən), *v.t.* to dress or adorn in a showy, gaudy, or tasteless manner. [1655–65; BE- + DIZEN] —**be•di′zen•ment,** *n.*

bed′ jack′et, a short jacket worn, usually by a woman, over a nightgown or pajamas, esp. while sitting up in bed. [1910–15]

bed•lam (bed′ləm), *n.* **1.** a scene or state of wild uproar and confusion. **2.** *Archaic.* an insane asylum or madhouse. [a popular name for the Hospital of St. Mary of Bethlehem in London, which served as a lunatic asylum from ca. 1400; cf. ME *Bedleem, Bethleem,* OE *Betleem* BETHLEHEM]
—**Syn. 1.** disorder, tumult, chaos, clamor, turmoil, commotion, pandemonium.

bed•lam•er (bed′lə mər), *n. Newfoundland.* a harp seal, beyond the beater stage but not yet mature. [1760–70; orig. uncert.; alleged to be a folk-etymological alter. of F *bête de la mer* beast of the sea, but cf. Brit. dial. *bedlam* wild, ill-behaved, a troublesome person or animal (developments of BEDLAM)]

bed•lam•ite (bed′lə mīt′), *n.* an insane person; lunatic. [1615–25; BEDLAM + -ITE[1]]

bed•lamp (bed′lamp′), *n.* a lamp at the side or head of a bed. [BED + LAMP]

bed•light (bed′līt′), *n.* a bedlamp. [BED + LIGHT[1]]

bed′ lin′en, sheets and pillowcases. [1805–15]

Bed•ling•ton (bed′ling tən), *n.* **1.** Also called **Bed•ling•ton•shire** (bed′ling tən shēr′, -shər). an urban area in E Northumberland, in N England. 28,167. **2.** See **Bedlington terrier.**

Bed′lington ter′rier, one of an English breed of terriers having a topknot and a thick, fleecy, usually bluish coat, groomed to resemble a lamb. [1865–70; named after BEDLINGTON]

Bedlington terrier
15 in. (38 cm)
high at shoulder

bed′ load′, *Geol.* the sand, gravel, boulders, or other debris transported by rolling or sliding along the bottom of a stream.

Bed′loe's Is′land (bed′lōz), former name of **Liberty Island.** Also, **Bed′loe Is′land.**

bed•mak•er (bed′mā′kər), *n.* **1.** a person who makes up beds. **2.** a person who constructs beds, as a carpenter. [1425–75; late ME; see BED, MAKER] —**bed′mak′•ing,** *n.*

bed•mate (bed′māt′), *n.* **1.** bedfellow (def. 1). **2.** one's husband, wife, or lover. [1575–85; BED + MATE[1]]

bed′ mold′ing, 1. *Archit.* the molding or group of moldings immediately beneath the corona of a cornice. **2.** any molding under a projection. [1695–1705]

bed′ of nails′, a situation of extreme hardship or suffering: *Taking care of her sick brother all these years has been a bed of nails for her.* [1965–70]

bed′ of ros′es, a situation of luxurious ease; a highly agreeable position: *Caring for a houseful of active kids is no bed of roses.* [1800–10]

Bed•ou•in (bed′o͞o in, bed′win), *n., pl.* **-ins,** (*esp. collectively*) **-in,** *adj.* —*n.* **1.** an Arab of the desert, in Asia or Africa; nomadic Arab. **2.** a nomad; wanderer. —*adj.* **3.** of, pertaining to, or characteristic of the Bedouin. Also, **Beduin.** [1350–1400; ME *Bedoyn* < MF *beduyn* < Ar *badawī* desert-dweller (*badw* desert + *-ī* suffix of appurtenance)] —**Bed′ou•in•ism,** *n.*

bed•pad (bed′pad′), *n.* a pad or other protective covering used between the mattress and the bottom sheet of a bed. [BED + PAD[1]]

bed•pan (bed′pan′), *n.* **1.** a shallow toilet pan for use by persons confined to bed. **2.** bedwarmer. [1575–85; BED + PAN[1]]

bed′ place′, a space housing a bed or bedding, esp. one having the form of a cupboard closed with doors or curtains. [1560–70]

bed•plate (bed′plāt′), *n.* a plate, platform, or frame supporting the lighter parts of a machine. Also called **baseplate.** [1840–50; BED + PLATE[1]]

bed•post (bed′pōst′), *n.* **1.** one of the upright supports of a bedstead. **2. bedposts,** *Bowling.* a split in which the seven and ten pins remain standing. [1590–1600; BED + POST[1]]

bed•quilt (bed′kwilt′), *n.* a quilted coverlet. [1755–65; BED + QUILT]

be•drab•ble (bi drab′əl), *v.t.,* **-bled, -bling.** to drench or muddy. [1400–50; late ME; see BE-, DRABBLE]

be•drag•gle (bi drag′əl), *v.t.,* **-gled, -gling.** to make limp and soiled, as with rain or dirt. [1720–30; BE- + DRAGGLE]

bed•rail (bed′rāl′), *n.* a board at the side of a bed connecting the footboard and headboard. [BED + RAIL[1]]

bed′ rest′, 1. a prolonged rest in bed, as in the treatment of an illness. **2.** a device used to support a person sitting up in bed. [1870–75]

bed•rid (bed′rid′), *adj.* **1.** bedridden. **2.** worn-out; exhausted; decrepit. [bef. 1000; ME *bedrede,* OE *bedreda, bedrida,* equiv. to *bed* BED + *-rida* rider, akin to RIDE]

bed•rid•den (bed′rid′n), *adj.* confined to bed because of illness, injury, etc. [1300–50; ME, var. (by confusion with ptp. of RIDE) of BEDRID]

bed•rock (bed′rok′), *n.* **1.** *Geol.* unbroken solid rock, overlaid in most places by soil or rock fragments. **2.** bottom layer; lowest stratum. **3.** any firm foundation or basis: *Technical courses will be founded on a bedrock of sound, general education so as to produce a well-rounded engineer.* **4.** the fundamental principles, as of a teaching, belief, or science: *Let's strip away the cant and get down to bedrock.* —*adj.* **5.** basic; fundamental. [1840–50, *Amer.*; BED + ROCK[1]]

bed•roll (bed′rōl′), *n.* bedding rolled for portability and used esp. for sleeping out-of-doors. [1645–55; BED + ROLL]

bed•room (bed′ro͞om′, -ro͝om′), *n.* **1.** a room furnished and used for sleeping. —*adj.* **2.** concerned mainly with love affairs or sex: *The movie is a typical bedroom comedy.* **3.** sexually inviting; amorous: *bedroom eyes.* **4.** inhabited largely by commuters: *a bedroom community.* [1580–90; BED + ROOM]

bed′room slip′per, a slipper for use within the house, often heelless and backless and with a flexible sole, of leather or any of various fabrics.

bed′room sub′urb. See **dormitory suburb.**

Beds (bedz), *n.* Bedfordshire.

bed•sheet (bed′shēt′), *n.* sheet[1] (def. 1). [BED + SHEET[1]]

bed•side (bed′sīd′), *n.* **1.** the side of a bed, esp. as the place of one attending the sick. —*adj.* **2.** at or for a bedside: *a bedside table.* [1325–75; ME; orig. BED + 's[1] + SIDE[1]]

bed′side man′ner, the attitude, approach, and deportment of a doctor with patients: *He has a reassuring bedside manner.* [1865–70]

bed-sit (bed′sit′), *n. Brit. Slang.* bed-sitter.

bed-sit•ter (bed′sit′ər), *n.* a combination bedroom and sitting room. Also called **bed′-sit′ting room′** (bed′-sit′ing). [1925–30; *bed-sitt(ing room)* + -ER[7]]

bed•sore (bed′sôr′, -sōr′), *n. Pathol.* an ulceration of the skin and subcutaneous tissue caused by poor circulation due to prolonged pressure on body parts, esp. bony protuberances, occurring in bedridden or immobile patients; decubitus ulcer. [1860–65; BED + SORE]

bed•spread (bed′spred′), *n.* an outer covering, usually decorative, for a bed. [1835–45, *Amer.*; BED + SPREAD]

bed•spring (bed′spring′), *n.* a set of springs for the support of a mattress. [1910–15; BED + SPRING]

bed•stand (bed′stand′), *n.* See **night table.** [BED + STAND]

bed•stead (bed′sted′, -stid), *n.* the framework of a bed supporting the springs and a mattress. [1400–50; late ME *bedstede.* See BED, STEAD]

bed′ stone′, the fixed lower member of a pair of millstones. Cf. **runner** (def. 12). [1715–25]

bed•straw (bed′strô′), *n.* a rubiaceous plant, *Galium verum,* or some allied species, formerly used as straw for stuffing mattresses. [1350–1400; late ME; see BED, STRAW]

bed′ ta′ble, 1. an adjustable table or a tray with legs, designed to extend over or rest upon a bed. **2.** See **night table.** [1805–15]

bed•tick (bed′tik′), *n.* tick[3]. [1560–70; BED + TICK[3]]

bed•time (bed′tīm′), *n.* **1.** the time at which a person usually goes to bed: *It's past my bedtime.* **2.** the time at which a person goes to bed on a particular night: *I have to get up early tomorrow so bedtime tonight will be 9 o'clock.* [1200–50; ME; see BED, TIME]

bed′time sto′ry, a story told to a child at bedtime. [1885–90]

bed′ tray′, a meal tray with legs or supports at each end to fit across the lap of a person who is sitting up in bed.

Bed•u•in (bed′o͞o in, bed′win), *n., pl.* **-ins,** (*esp. collectively*) **-in,** *adj.* Bedouin. [1895–1900]

bed•warm•er (bed′wôr′mər), *n.* a long-handled, covered pan containing hot coals, used for warming beds. Also called **bedpan.** [1920–25; BED + WARMER]

bed•wet•ter (bed′wet′ər), *n.* a person, usually a child, who urinates while sleeping, esp. habitually. Also, **bed′-wet′ter.** [1935–40; BED + WET (v.) + -ER[1]]

bed•wet•ting (bed′wet′ing), *n.* urinating in bed, esp. habitually and involuntarily; enuresis. Also, **bed′-wet′•ting.** [1885–90; BED + WET (v.) + -ING[1]]

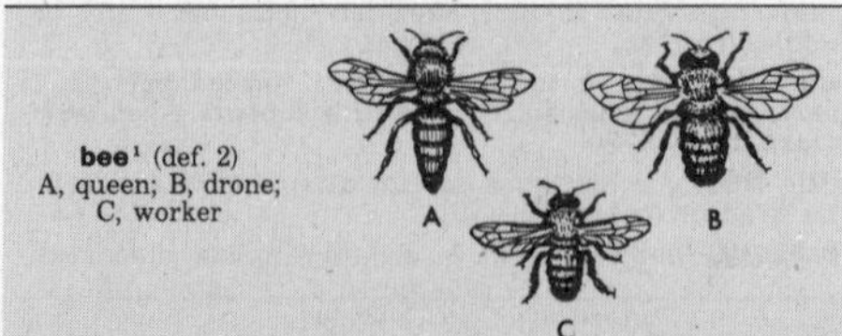

bee[1] (def. 2)
A, queen; B, drone;
C, worker

bee[1] (bē), *n.* **1.** any hymenopterous insect of the superfamily Apoidea, including social and solitary species of several families, as the bumblebees, honeybees, etc. **2.** the common honeybee, *Apis mellifera.* **3.** a community social gathering in order to perform some task, engage in a contest, etc.: *a sewing bee; a spelling bee; a husking bee.* **4. have a bee in one's bonnet, a.** to be obsessed with one idea. **b.** to have eccentric or fanciful ideas or schemes: *Our aunt obviously has a bee in her bonnet, but we're very fond of her.* **5. put the bee on,** *Informal.* to try to obtain money from, as for a loan or donation: *My brother just put the bee on me for another $10.* **6. the bee's knees,** *Older Slang.* (esp. in the 1920's) a person or thing that is wonderful, great, or marvelous: *Her new roadster is simply the bee's knees.* [bef. 1000; ME *be(e);* OE *bīo, bēo;* c. D *bij,* OS *bī, bini,* OHG *bīa, bini* (G *Biene*), ON *bȳ;* with other suffixes, Lith *bitė,* OPruss *bitte,* OCS *bĭchela,* OIr *bech;* **bhi-* is a North European stem with the same distribution as WAX[1], APPLE; *put the bee on* prob. an allusion to STING in sense "dupe, cheat"] —**bee′like′,** *adj.*

bee[2] (bē), *n.* **1.** Also called **bee block.** *Naut.* a piece of hardwood, bolted to the side of a bowsprit, through which to reeve stays. **2.** *Obs.* a metal ring or bracelet. [bef. 1050; ME *beh* ring, OE *bēag, bēah;* c. OFris *bāg,* OS, MLG *bōg,* OHG *boug,* ON *baugr,* Skt *bhoga-;* akin to BOW[1]]

B.E.E., Bachelor of Electrical Engineering.

bee′ balm′, 1. Also called **Oswego tea.** a wildflower, *Monarda didyma,* of the mint family, having thin, lance-shaped leaves and white, salmon, or intensely red flowers, growing along streams in temperate forests and widely cultivated in gardens. **2.** a plant, *Melissa officinalis,* having broad, opposite, serrated leaves and tight clusters of white, lemon-scented flowers that attract bees. [1840–50, *Amer.*]

Bee•be (bē′bē), *n.* **(Charles) William,** 1877–1962, U.S. naturalist, explorer, and writer.

bee′ bee′tle, a European beetle, *Trichodes apiarius,* which sometimes infests beehives.

bee′ bird′, any of several birds, as the bee-eaters, that feed on bees. [1780–90]

bee′ block′, *Naut.* bee[2] (def. 1). [1855–60]

bee•bread (bē′bred′), *n.* a mixture of pollen and honey stored by bees and fed to their young. [bef. 900; ME *be bred,* OE. See BEE[1], BREAD]

beech (bēch), *n.* **1.** any tree of the genus *Fagus,* of temperate regions, having a smooth gray bark and bearing small, edible, triangular nuts. **2.** Also called **beechwood.** the wood of such a tree. **3.** any member of the plant family Fagaceae, characterized by trees and shrubs having alternate, usually toothed or lobed leaves, male flowers in catkins and female flowers either solitary or in clusters and bearing a nut enclosed in a cupule or bur, including the beeches, chestnuts, and oaks. [bef. 900; ME *beche,* OE *bēce* < Gmc **bōkjōn-;* akin to OS, MLG *boke,* D *beuk,* OHG *buohha* (G *Buche*), ON *bōk,* L *fāgus* beech, Doric Gk *phāgós,* Albanian *bung* oak (appar. not akin to BOOK)] —**beech′en,** *adj.* —**beech′y,** *adj.*

Bee•cham (bē′chəm), *n.* **Sir Thomas,** 1879–1961, English conductor and impresario.

beech•drops (bēch′drops′), *n.* (*used with a singular or plural v.*) a low plant, *Epifagus virginiana,* of the broomrape family, without green foliage, parasitic upon the roots of the beech. [1805–15, *Amer.*; BEECH + DROP + -S[3]]

Bee•cher (bē′chər), *n.* **1. Catharine Esther,** 1800–78, U.S. educator: advocated educational rights for women. **2. Edward,** 1803–95, U.S. clergyman, educator, and abolitionist. **3. Henry Ward,** 1813–87, U.S. preacher and writer. **4. Lyman,** 1775–1863, U.S. preacher and theologian (father of Catharine Esther Beecher, Edward Beecher, Harriet Beecher Stowe, and Henry Ward Beecher).

beech′ fern′, either of two ferns, *Thelypteris hexagonoptera,* of eastern North America, or *T. phegopteris,* common in rich, moist woodlands of northern temperate regions.

Beech′ Grove′, a city in central Indiana. 13,196.

beech′ mar′ten. See **stone marten.** [1835–45]

beech′ mast′, the edible nuts of the beech, esp. when lying on the ground. [1570–80]

beech•nut (bēch′nut′), *n.* the small, triangular, edible nut of the beech. [1730–40; BEECH + NUT]

beech•wood (bēch′wo͝od′), *n.* beech (def. 2). [1675–85; BEECH + WOOD[1]]

bee•di (bē′dē), *n., pl.* **-dis.** bidi.

bee-eat•er (bē′ē′tər), *n.* any of several colorful birds of the family Meropidae, of the Old World tropics, that feed on bees and other insects. [1660–70]

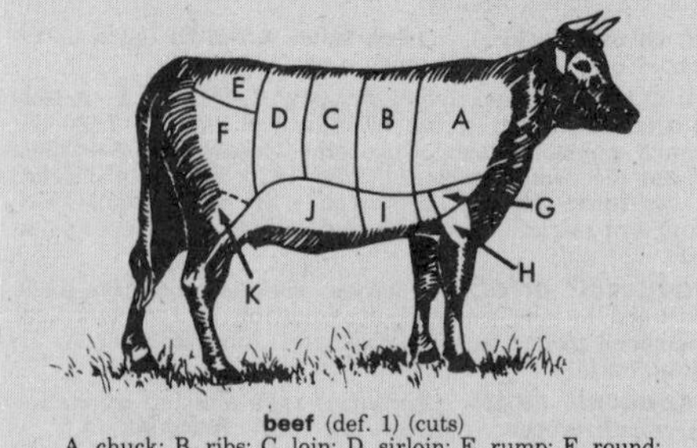

beef (def. 1) (cuts)
A, chuck; B, ribs; C, loin; D, sirloin; E, rump; F, round; G, brisket; H, foreshank; I, plate; J, flank; K, hind shank

beef (bēf), *n., pl.* **beeves** (bēvz) for 2; **beefs** for 4, *v.* —*n.* **1.** the flesh of a cow, steer, or bull raised and killed for its meat. **2.** an adult cow, steer, or bull raised for its meat. **3.** *Informal.* **a.** brawn; muscular strength. **b.** strength; power. **c.** weight, as of a person. **d.** human flesh. **4.** *Slang.* **a.** a complaint. **b.** an argument or dispute. —*v.i.* **5.** *Slang.* to complain; grumble. **6. beef up, a.** to add strength, numbers, force, etc., to; strengthen:

CONCISE ETYMOLOGY KEY: <, descended or borrowed from; >, whence; b., blend of, blended; c., cognate with; cf., compare; deriv., derivative; equiv., equivalent; imit., imitative; obl., oblique; r., replacing; s., stem; sp., spelling, spelled; resp., respelling, respelled; trans., translation; ?, origin unknown; *, unattested; ‡, probably earlier than. See the full key inside the front cover.

During the riots, the nighttime patrol force was beefed up with volunteers. **b.** to increase or add to: *to beef up our fringe benefits.* [1250–1300; 1885–90 for def. 5; ME < AF *beof,* OF *boef* < L *bov-* (s. of *bōs*) ox, cow; akin to cow[1]] —**beef′less,** *adj.*

beef•a•lo (bē′fə lō′), *n., pl.* **-loes, -los,** (*esp. collectively*) **-lo** for 1. **1.** a hybrid animal that is $3/8$ to $3/32$ buffalo, the remaining genetic component being domestic cow, bred for disease resistance and for meat with low fat content. **2.** the meat of such an animal. Also called **cattalo.** [1970–75; b. BEEF and BUFFALO]

beef′ bouil′lon, a broth made either by straining water in which bits of lean beef have been cooked or by dissolving beef extract in hot water. Also called, *esp. Brit.,* **beef tea.**

beef•burg•er (bēf′bûr′gər), *n.* hamburger. [1935–40; BEEF + -BURGER]

beef•cake (bēf′kāk′), *n. Informal.* photographs of nearly nude young men in magazines or the like, posed to display their muscular bodies. [1945–50; BEEF + CAKE, modeled on CHEESECAKE]

beef′ cat′tle, cattle, as Hereford, raised for its edible meat. [1750–60, *Amer.*]

beef•eat•er (bēf′ē′tər), *n.* **1.** a yeoman of the English royal guard or a warder of the Tower of London. **2.** *Informal.* an Englishman. **3.** a person who eats beef. [1600–10; BEEF + EATER]

beefed-up (bēft′up′), *adj.* strengthened or reinforced. [1940–45]

beef′ ex′tract, a soluble paste of beef or beef blood extracts.

bee′ fly′, any of numerous dipterous insects of the family Bombyliidae, some of which resemble bees. [1850–55, *Amer.*]

Beef•mas•ter (bēf′mas′tər, -mä′stər), *n.* one of a breed of fast-growing beef cattle of the western U.S., tolerant of humidity, heat, and insects, developed by crossbreeding Brahman, Hereford, and Shorthorn stock. [BEEF + MASTER]

beef•steak (bēf′stāk′), *n.* a cut of beef for broiling, pan-frying, etc. [1705–15; BEEF + STEAK]

beef′steak bego′nia, an ornamental plant, *Begonia erythrophylla,* having light-pink flowers and nearly round, thick, fleshy leaves that are red on the underside.

beef′steak mush′room, an edible bracket fungus, *Fistulina hepatica,* that grows on trees and can rot the heartwood of living oaks and chestnuts. Also called **beef′steak fun′gus.** [1890–95]

beef′steak toma′to, 1. any of several tomato plant varieties bearing fruit of large size with especially meaty flesh. **2.** the fruit of such a plant.

beef′ stro′ganoff, *Cookery.* stroganoff made with strips of beef. [1940–45]

beef′ tea′, *Chiefly Brit.* See **beef bouillon.**

beef-up (bēf′up′), *n.* an act or instance of strengthening or reinforcing. [n. use of v. phrase *beef up*]

beef′ Wel′lington, a steak fillet covered with pâté de foie gras, then wrapped in pastry and baked. [1960–65; the *Wellington* alluded to is of uncert. identity]

beef•wood (bēf′wo͝od′), *n.* **1.** any of several chiefly Australian trees of the genus *Casuarina,* having feathery branches that lack true foliage leaves. **2.** the hard, reddish wood of any of these trees, used for making furniture. Also called **belah.** [1750–60; BEEF + WOOD[1]]

beef•y (bē′fē), *adj.,* **beef•i•er, beef•i•est. 1.** of or like beef. **2.** brawny; thickset; heavy. **3.** obese. [1735–45; BEEF + -Y[1]] —**beef′i•ly,** *adv.* —**beef′i•ness,** *n.*

bee′ glue′, propolis. [1590–1600]

bee′ gum′, *Southern and South Midland U.S.* **1.** a gum tree, hollowed esp. by decay, in which bees live or from which hives are made. **2.** a beehive. [1810–20, *Amer.*]

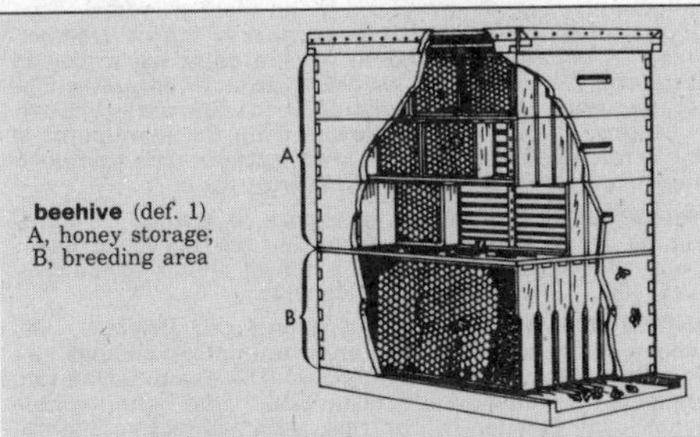

beehive (def. 1)
A, honey storage;
B, breeding area

bee•hive (bē′hīv′), *n.* **1.** a habitation or dwelling-place constructed for bees, usually either dome-shaped or box-shaped. **2.** a natural habitation of bees, as a hollowed-out tree. **3.** a crowded, busy place. **4.** something resembling an artificial beehive in appearance, as a hut or hairdo. **5.** Also called **bee′hive ov′en.** an oven for converting coal into coke, characterized by its dome-shaped roof. [1325–75; ME; see BEE[1], HIVE]

Bee′hive clus′ter, *Astron.* Praesepe.

bee′hive round′, *Mil.* an artillery shell that ejects thousands of naillike metal projectiles on exploding.

Bee′hive State′, Utah (used as a nickname). [1930–35, *Amer.*]

bee′hive tomb′, a type of subterranean tomb of the Mycenaean civilization consisting of a domed chamber entered by a passage through a hillside. [1885–90]

beek (bēk), *Scot. and North Eng.* —*v.t., v.i.* **1.** to bask or warm in the sunshine or before a fireplace, stove, or bonfire. **2.** (of wood) to season by exposure to heat. —*n.* **3.** *Obs.* the act of basking or warming by a fire. [1200–50; ME *beken,* akin to BAKE (perh. < Gmc **bōkjan*)]

bee•keep•er (bē′kē′pər), *n.* a person who raises honeybees; apiculturist. [1810–20; BEE[1] + KEEPER]

bee•keep•ing (bē′kē′ping), *n.* the rearing and breeding of honeybees; apiculture. [1830–40; BEE[1] + KEEPING]

bee′ kil′ler. See **robber fly.**

bee•line (bē′līn′), *n.* a direct route traveled quickly (usually in the phrase *make a beeline for*): *The minute he came home he made a beeline for the refrigerator.* [1820–30, *Amer.*; BEE[1] + LINE[1]]

Be•el•ze•bub (bē el′zə bub′, bēl′zə-), *n.* **1.** the chief devil; Satan. **2.** a devil. **3.** (in Milton's *Paradise Lost*) one of the fallen angels, second only to Satan.

bee′ mar′tin, kingbird. [1795–1805, *Amer.*]

bee′ moth′, a brownish pyralid moth, *Galleria mellonella,* the larvae of which feed on the honeycombs in beehives. Also called **wax moth.** [1820–30, *Amer.*]

been (bin), *v.* pp. of **be.**

beep (bēp), *n.* **1.** a short, relatively high-pitched tone produced by a horn, electronic device, or the like as a signal, summons, or warning. **2.** one of the periodic signals sounded by a beeper. —*v.i.* **3.** to make or emit such a sound: *When the timer beeps, take the cake out of the oven.* —*v.t.* **4.** to sound (a horn, warning signal, etc.): *impatient drivers beeping their horns.* **5.** to announce, warn, summon, etc., by beeping: *The doctor was beeped to call the hospital.* [1925–30; imit.]

beep•er (bē′pər), *n.* **1.** a device that connects into a telephone circuit and transmits a periodic signal as an indication that the conversation over the circuit is being recorded. **2.** a similar device attached to a free-ranging animal as an aid to learning its habits; biotelemeter. **3.** Also called **pager.** a pocket-size electronic device whose signal notifies a person of an important message, sometimes displaying the telephone number to be called. [1945–50; BEEP + -ER[1]]

bee′ plant′, any of various plants frequented by bees as a source of nectar, esp. *Cleome serrulata* or *C. lutea,* of western North America.

beer (bēr), *n.* **1.** an alcoholic beverage made by brewing and fermentation from cereals, usually malted barley, and flavored with hops and the like for a slightly bitter taste. **2.** any of various beverages, whether alcoholic or not, made from roots, molasses or sugar, yeast, etc.: *root beer; ginger beer.* **3.** an individual serving of beer; a glass, can, or bottle of beer: *We'll have three beers.* [bef. 1000; ME *bere,* OE *bēor;* c. OS, OHG *bior,* MLG, MD *bēr,* D, G *Bier* (ON *bjórr,* prob. < OE); of disputed and ambiguous orig.]

Beer (bēr), *n.* **Thomas,** 1889–1940, U.S. author.

beer′ and skit′tles, *Brit.* amusement; pleasure; fun.

beer′ bel′ly, a protuberant belly from or as if from drinking large quantities of beer; potbelly; paunch. [1915–20] —**beer′-bel′lied,** *adj.*

Beer•bohm (bēr′bōm), *n.* **Sir Max,** 1872–1956, English essayist, critic, and caricaturist.

beer′ bust′, *Informal.* a large, usually boisterous party, as for college students, club members, or soldiers, at which beer is the sole or principal beverage and is consumed in large quantities. [1960–65]

beer′ en′gine, *Brit.* See **beer pump.** [1815–25]

beer′ gar′den, an outdoor tavern where beer and other alcoholic beverages are served. [1860–65]

beer′ hall′, a bar, cabaret, or the like, chiefly serving beer and usually offering music, dancing, etc. [1880–85, *Amer.*]

beer•house (bēr′hous′), *n., pl.* **-hous•es** (-hou′ziz). *Brit.* an establishment licensed to serve only liquors fermented from malt, as beer, ale, or the like. [1485–95; BEER + HOUSE]

Beer•naert (*Fr.* beʀ naʀt′; *Eng.* bâr′närt), *n.* **Auguste Ma•rie Fran•çois** (*Fr.* ō gyst′ ma ʀē′ fräɴ swa′), 1829–1912, Belgian statesman: Nobel peace prize 1909.

Beer′ Nuts′, *Trademark.* a brand of tavern nuts.

beer•pull (bēr′po͝ol′), *n.* **1.** the handle of a beer pump. **2.** the pump itself; a beer pump. [1860–65; BEER + PULL]

beer′ pump′, a pump for drawing beer directly from a keg or cask. [1620–30]

Beers (bērz), *n.* **Clifford Whit•ting•ham** (hwit′ing əm, wit′-), 1876–1943, U.S. pioneer in mental hygiene.

Beer•she•ba (bēr shē′bə, bēr′shə-; *Seph. Heb.* bershe′vä), *n.* **1.** a city in Israel, near the N limit of the Negev desert: the southernmost city of ancient Palestine. 109,600. **2. from Dan to Beersheba.** See **Dan** (def. 4).

beer•y (bēr′ē), *adj.,* **beer•i•er, beer•i•est. 1.** of, like, or abounding in beer: *a stale, beery smell.* **2.** affected by or suggestive of beer: *beery exuberance; beery breath.* [1840–50; BEER + -Y[1]] —**beer′i•ness,** *n.*

beest•ings (bē′stingz), *n.* (*used with a singular v.*) the first milk or colostrum of a mammal, esp. a cow, after giving birth. Also, **beastings, biestings.** [bef. 1000; late ME *bestynge,* OE *bȳsting,* equiv. to *bēost* beestings (c. OS, OHG *biost,* G *Biest*) + *-ing* -ING[1]]

bees•wax (bēz′waks′), *n.* **1.** wax[1] (def. 1). —*v.t.* **2.** to rub or treat with beeswax. [1670–80; BEE[1] + 'S[1] + WAX[1]]

bees•wing (bēz′wing′), *n.* a light, flaky deposit found in port and some other bottle-aged wines. [1855–60; BEE[1] + 'S[1] + WING]

beet (bēt), *n.* **1.** any of various biennial plants belonging to the genus *Beta,* of the goosefoot family, esp. *B. vulgaris,* having a fleshy red or white root. Cf. **sugar beet. 2.** the edible root of such a plant. **3.** the leaves of such a plant, served as a salad or cooked vegetable. [bef. 1000; ME *bete,* OE *bēte* < L *bēta*] —**beet′like′,** *adj.*

beet′ ar′myworm, the caterpillar of a noctuid moth, *Laphygma exigua,* a pest of beets, asparagus, corn, cotton, peas, and peppers. Also called **asparagus fern caterpillar.** [1900–05]

Bee•tho•ven (bā′tō vən; *Ger.* bāt′hō fən), *n.* **Ludwig van** (van; *Ger.* fən), 1770–1827, German composer. —**Bee•tho•vi•an** (bā tō′vē ən), **Bee•tho•ve•ni•an** (bā′tō-vē′nē ən, -vēn′yən), *adj.*

bee•tle[1] (bēt′l), *n., v.,* **-tled, -tling.** —*n.* **1.** any of numerous insects of the order Coleoptera, characterized by hard, horny forewings that cover and protect the membranous flight wings. **2.** (loosely) any of various insects resembling the beetle, as a cockroach. —*v.i.* **3.** *Chiefly Brit.* to move quickly; scurry: *He beetled off to catch the train.* [bef. 900; late ME *betylle, bityl,* OE *bitela* (*bitelbiting* (*bit-* BITE + *-el* adj. suffix) + *-a* n. suffix)]

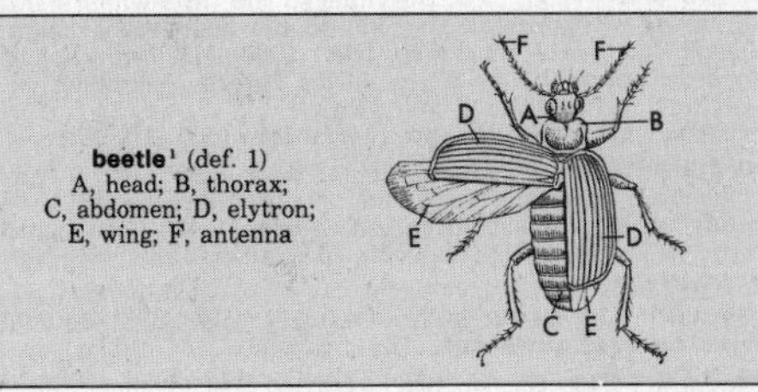

beetle[1] (def. 1)
A, head; B, thorax;
C, abdomen; D, elytron;
E, wing; F, antenna

bee•tle[2] (bēt′l), *n., v.,* **-tled, -tling.** —*n.* **1.** a heavy hammering or ramming instrument, usually of wood, used to drive wedges, force down paving stones, compress loose earth, etc. **2.** any of various wooden instruments for beating linen, mashing potatoes, etc. —*v.t.* **3.** to use a beetle on; drive, ram, beat, or crush with a beetle. **4.** to finish (cloth) with a beetling machine. [bef. 900; ME *betel,* OE *bētl, bȳtel* hammer (c. MLG *bētel* chisel), equiv. to *bē(a)t-* BEAT + *-il* n. suffix] —**bee′tler,** *n.*

bee•tle[3] (bēt′l), *adj., v.,* **-tled, -tling.** —*adj.* **1.** projecting; overhanging: *beetle brows.* —*v.i.* **2.** to project; jut out; overhang: *a cliff that beetles over the sea.* **3.** to hang or tower over in a threatening or menacing manner: *The prospect of bankruptcy beetled over him.* [1325–75; ME; back formation from BEETLE-BROWED]

beet′ leaf′hopper, a leafhopper, *Circulifer tenellus,* of the western U.S., a vector of curly top disease, esp. in beets. [1915–20]

bee•tle-browed (bēt′l broud′), *adj.* **1.** having heavy projecting eyebrows. **2.** scowling or sullen. [1325–75; ME *bitel-browed,* prob. with *bitel* sharp(-edged), OE **bitel* (see BEETLE[1]); see BROW, -ED[3]]

bee•tle•bung (bēt′l bung′), *n.* See **sour gum.**

bee•tle•head (bēt′l hed′), *n.* a stupid person; blockhead. [1570–80; BEETLE[2] + HEAD] —**bee′tle•head′ed,** *adj.*

bee•tle•weed (bēt′l wēd′), *n.* galax. [BEETLE[1] + WEED[1]]

bee′ tree′, a hollow tree used by wild bees as a hive, esp. the basswood or American linden. [1775–85, *Amer.*]

beet•root (bēt′ro͞ot′, -ro͝ot′), *n. Chiefly Brit.* beet (def. 2). [1570–80; BEET + ROOT[1]]

beet′ sug′ar, sugar from the roots of the sugar beet. Cf. **sugar** (def. 1). [1825–35]

beeves (bēvz), *n.* a pl. of **beef.**

Bee•ville (bē′vil), *n.* a city in S Texas. 14,574.

bef., before.

B.E.F., British Expeditionary Force; British Expeditionary Forces.

be•fall (bi fôl′), *v.,* **-fell, -fall•en, -fall•ing.** —*v.i.* **1.** to happen or occur. **2.** *Archaic.* to come, as by right. —*v.t.* **3.** to happen to, esp. by chance or fate. [bef. 900; ME *befallen,* OE *befeallan.* See BE-, FALL (v.)]
—**Syn. 1.** bechance, ensue, betide, materialize, chance.

be•fit (bi fit′), *v.t.,* **-fit•ted, -fit•ting.** to be proper or appropriate for; suit; fit: *His clothes befit the occasion.* [1425–75; late ME; see BE-, FIT[1]]

be•fit•ting (bi fit′ing), *adj.* suitable; proper; becoming: *planned with a befitting sense of majesty.* [1555–65; BEFIT + -ING[2]] —**be•fit′ting•ly,** *adv.* —**be•fit′ting•ness,** *n.*
—**Syn.** appropriate, fitting, apt, seemly. —**Ant.** unsuitable, inappropriate, unbecoming.

be•flag (bi flag′), *v.t.,* **-flagged, -flag•ging.** to cover or deck with flags. [1880–85; BE- + FLAG[1]]

be•flow•ered (bi flou′ərd), *adj.* adorned or decorated with flowers. [1620–30; BE- + FLOWER + -ED[2]]

be•fog (bi fog′, -fôg′), *v.t.,* **-fogged, -fog•ging. 1.** to envelop in fog or obscurity; becloud: *Low-hanging clouds befogged the city.* **2.** to render unclear; confuse by irrelevancies or distractions: *Petty differences befogged the legislators' task.* [1595–1605; BE- + FOG[1]]
—**Syn. 2.** confound, blur, muddle, obfuscate.

be•fool (bi fo͞ol′), *v.t.* **1.** to fool; deceive; dupe. **2.** *Obs.* to treat as a fool; call (someone) a fool. [1350–1400; ME *befolen.* See BE-, FOOL[1]]
—**Syn. 1.** bamboozle, delude, mislead; cheat, swindle.

be•fore (bi fôr′, -fōr′), *prep.* **1.** previous to; earlier or sooner than: *Phone me before noon.* **2.** in front of; ahead of; in advance of: *his shadow advancing before him; She*

CONCISE PRONUNCIATION KEY: *act, cāpe, dâre, pärt; set, ēqual; if, īce; ox, ōver, ôrder, oil, bo͝ok, bo͞ot, out; up, ûrge; child; sing; shoe; thin, that;* zh as in *treasure.* ə = *a* as in *alone, e* as in *system, i* as in *easily, o* as in *gallop, u* as in *circus;* ᵊ as in *fire* (fīᵊr), *hour* (ouᵊr). l and n can serve as syllabic consonants, as in *cradle* (krād′l), and *button* (but′n). See the full key inside the front cover.

stood before the window. **3.** ahead of; in the future of; awaiting: *The golden age is before us.* **4.** in preference to; rather than: *They would die before surrendering.* **5.** in precedence of, as in order or rank: *We put freedom before wealth.* **6.** in the presence or sight of: *to appear before an audience.* **7.** less than; until: used in indicating the exact time: *It's ten before three.* **8.** under the jurisdiction or consideration of: *He was summoned before a magistrate.* **9.** confronted by; in the face of: *Before such wild accusations, he was too stunned to reply.* **10.** in the regard of: *a crime before God and humanity.* **11.** under the overwhelming influence of: *bending before the storm.* **12.** without figuring or deducting: *income before deductions.* —*adv.* **13.** in front; in advance; ahead: *The king entered with macebearers walking before.* **14.** in time preceding; previously: *If we'd known before, we'd have let you know.* **15.** earlier or sooner: *Begin at noon, not before.* —*conj.* **16.** previous to the time when: *Send the telegram before we go.* **17.** sooner than; rather than: *I will die before I submit.* [bef. 1000; ME *beforen,* OE *beforan,* equiv. to *be* BY + *foran* before (*fore* FORE[1] + *-an* adv. suffix)]
—**Ant. 13.** after, behind. **14.** afterward. **15.** later.

be•fore•hand (bi fôr′hand′, -fōr′-), *adv., adj.* in anticipation; in advance; ahead of time: *We should have made reservations beforehand. I hope to be beforehand with my report.* [1175–1225; ME *bifor-hand.* See BEFORE, HAND]

before′ the pres′ent, *Archaeol.* See **B.P.** (def. 3). Also, **before′ pres′ent.**

be•fore•time (bi fôr′tīm′, -fōr′-), *adv. Archaic.* formerly. [1250–1300; ME *bifor time.* See BEFORE, TIME]

be•foul (bi foul′), *v.t.* to make dirty or filthy; soil; defile; sully: *a bird that befouls its own nest.* [1275–1325; ME *bi-foulen.* See BE-, FOUL] —**be•foul′er,** *n.* —**be•foul′ment,** *n.*

be•friend (bi frend′), *v.t.* to make friends or become friendly with; act as a friend to; help; aid: *to befriend the poor and the weak.* [1550–60; BE- + FRIEND]
—**Syn.** assist, comfort, succor; welcome.

be•fud•dle (bi fud′l), *v.t.,* **-dled, -dling. 1.** to confuse, as with glib statements or arguments: *politicians befuddling the public with campaign promises.* **2.** to make stupidly drunk. [1885–90; BE- + FUDDLE] —**be•fud′•dler,** *n.* —**be•fud′dle•ment,** *n.*
—**Syn. 1.** perplex, bewilder, baffle, daze, muddle.

beg[1] (beg), *v.,* **begged, beg•ging.** —*v.t.* **1.** to ask for as a gift, as charity, or as a favor: *to beg alms; to beg forgiveness.* **2.** to ask (someone) to give or do something; implore: *He begged me for mercy. Sit down, I beg you.* **3.** to take for granted without basis or justification: *a statement that begs the very point we're disputing.* **4.** to fail or refuse to come to grips with; avoid; evade: *a report that consistently begs the whole problem.* —*v.i.* **5.** to ask alms or charity; live by asking alms. **6.** to ask humbly or earnestly: *begging for help; begging to differ.* **7.** (of a dog) to sit up, as trained, in a posture of entreaty. **8. beg off,** to request or obtain release from an obligation, promise, etc.: *He had promised to drive us to the recital but begged off at the last minute.* **9. beg the question,** to assume the truth of the very point raised in a question. **10. go begging,** to remain open or available, as a position that is unfilled or an unsold item: *The job went begging for lack of qualified applicants.* [bef. 900; ME *beggen,* by assimilation from OE **bedican,* syncopated var. of *bedecian* to beg; cf. Goth *bidagwa* beggar. See BEAD]
—**Syn. 2.** entreat, pray, beseech, petition. BEG and REQUEST are used in certain conventional formulas, in the sense of *ask.* BEG, once a part of many formal expressions used in letter writing, debate, etc., is now used chiefly in such courteous formulas as *I beg your pardon; The Committee begs to report,* etc. REQUEST, more impersonal and now more formal, is used in giving courteous orders (*You are requested to report*) and in commercial formulas like *to request payment.*

beg[2] (bāg, beg), *n.* bey. [1680–90; << Turkic; see BEY]

beg., **1.** begin. **2.** beginning.

be•gan (bi gan′), *v.* pt. of **begin.**

be•gar (bā′gär), *n. Anglo-Indian.* compulsory labor, as for the repair of bridges or roads. [< Hindi *begār* < Pers]

be•gat (bi gat′), *v. Archaic.* pt. of **beget.**

be•gats (bi gats′), *n.pl. Informal.* genealogical lists, esp. those in the Old Testament. [n. pl. use of BEGAT]

be•gem (bi jem′), *v.t.,* **-gemmed, -gem•ming.** to cover with gems. [1740–50; BE- + GEM]

be•get (bi get′), *v.t.,* **be•got** or (*Archaic*) **be•gat; be•got•ten** or **be•got; be•get•ting. 1.** (esp. of a male parent) to procreate or generate (offspring). **2.** to cause; produce as an effect: *a belief that power begets power.* [bef. 1000; ME *begeten* (see BE-, GET); r. ME *biyeten,* OE *begetan;* c. Goth *bigitan,* OHG *bigezzan*] —**be•get′•ter,** *n.*
—**Syn. 1.** spawn, sire, breed, father. **2.** occasion, engender, effect, generate.

beg•gar (beg′ər), *n.* **1.** a person who begs alms or lives by begging. **2.** a penniless person. **3.** a wretched fellow; rogue: *the surly beggar who collects the rents.* **4.** a child or youngster (usually prec. by *little*): *a sudden urge to hug the little beggar.* —*v.t.* **5.** to reduce to utter poverty; impoverish: *The family had been beggared by the war.* **6.** to cause one's resources of or ability for (description, comparison, etc.) to seem poor or inadequate: *The costume beggars description.* [1175–1225; ME *beggare, beggere.* See BEG[1], -ER[1], -AR[3]] —**beg′gar•hood′,** *n.*

beg•gar•dom (beg′ər dəm), *n.* beggary (def. 2). [1880–85; BEGGAR + -DOM]

CONCISE ETYMOLOGY KEY: <, descended or borrowed from; >, whence; b., blend of, blended; c., cognate with; cf., compare; deriv., derivative; equiv., equivalent; imit., imitative; obl., oblique; r., replacing; s., stem; sp., spelling, spelled; resp., respelling, respelled; trans., translation; ?, origin unknown; *, unattested; ‡, probably earlier than. See the full key inside the front cover.

beg•gar•ly (beg′ər lē), *adj.* **1.** like or befitting a beggar. **2.** meanly inadequate: *How does he manage on such a beggarly salary?* [1520–30; BEGGAR + -LY] —**beg′gar•li•ness,** *n.*

beg•gar-my-neigh•bor (beg′ər mī nā′bər), *n.* beggar-your-neighbor. [1725–35]

beg•gar's-lice (beg′ərz līs′), *n., pl.* **-lice. 1.** (*used with a singular or plural v.*) any of several plants, esp. of the genera *Cynoglossum* and *Hackelia,* having small, prickly fruits that stick to clothing. **2.** (*used with a plural v.*) the fruits or seeds of such a plant. Also, **beg•gar-lice** (beg′ər līs′). [1840–50, *Amer.*]

Beg′gar's Op′era, The, a ballad opera (1728) with text by John Gay and music arranged by John Pepusch.

beg•gar-ticks (beg′ər tiks′), *n., pl.* **-ticks.** (*used with a singular or plural v.*) **1.** any of several composite plants of the genus *Bidens,* having rayless yellow flowers and barbed achenes that cling to clothing. **2.** the achenes of these plants. **3.** any of several other plants having seeds or fruits that cling to clothing, as those of the genus *Desmodium.* Also, **beg′gar's-ticks′.** [1850–55, *Amer.*]

beg•gar•weed (beg′ər wēd′), *n.* **1.** any of various tick trefoils, esp. *Desmodium tortuosum,* grown for forage in subtropical regions. **2.** *Chiefly Brit.* any weed that impoverishes soil. [1875–80; BEGGAR + WEED[1]]

beg•gar•y (beg′ə rē), *n., pl.* **-gar•ies** for 3. **1.** a state or condition of utter poverty. **2.** beggars collectively. **3.** a place lived in or frequented by beggars. [1350–1400; ME *beggerie.* See BEGGAR, -Y[3]]

beg•gar-your-neigh•bor (beg′ər yər nā′bər), *n.* a children's card game for two, played with 52 cards, that is won when a player captures all of the cards. Also called **beggar-my-neighbor.**

Beg•hard (beg′ərd, bə gärd′), *n.* a member of a former lay brotherhood, founded in Flanders in the 13th century, living after the manner of the Beguines. [1650–60; < ML *beghardus,* equiv. to *beg-* (see BEGUINE) + *-hardus* -ARD]

be•gin (bi gin′), *v.,* **be•gan, be•gun, be•gin•ning.** —*v.i.* **1.** to proceed to perform the first or earliest part of some action; commence; start: *The story begins with their marriage.* **2.** to come into existence; arise; originate: *The custom began during the Civil War.* —*v.t.* **3.** to proceed to perform the first or earliest part of (some action): *Begin the job tomorrow.* **4.** to originate; be the originator of: *civic leaders who began the reform movement.* **5.** to succeed to the slightest extent in (fol. by an infinitive): *The money won't even begin to cover expenses.* [bef. 1000; ME *beginnen,* OE *beginnan,* equiv. to *be-* BE- + *-ginnan* to begin, perh. orig. to open, akin to YAWN]
—**Syn. 3.** BEGIN, COMMENCE, INITIATE, START (when followed by noun or gerund) refer to setting into motion or progress something that continues for some time. BEGIN is the common term: *to begin knitting a sweater.* COMMENCE is a more formal word, often suggesting a more prolonged or elaborate beginning: *to commence proceedings in court.* INITIATE implies an active and often ingenious first act in a new field: *to initiate a new procedure.* START means to make a first move or to set out on a course of action: *to start paving a street.* **4.** institute, inaugurate, initiate. —**Ant. 1.** end.

Be•gin (bā′gin), *n.* **Me•na•chem** (mə nä′KHəm), 1913–92, Israeli political leader, born in Poland: prime minister 1977–83; Nobel peace prize 1978.

be•gin•ner (bi gin′ər), *n.* **1.** a person or thing that begins. **2.** a person who has begun a course of instruction or is learning the fundamentals: *swimming for beginners.* **3.** a person who is inexperienced; novice. [1350–1400; ME; see BEGIN, -ER[1]]

begin′ner's luck′, the initial good fortune or success commonly supposed to come to a person who has recently taken up a new pursuit, as a sport or game: *Catching a large trout the first time you go fishing is simply beginner's luck.* [1895–1900]

be•gin•ning (bi gin′ing), *n.* **1.** an act or circumstance of entering upon an action or state: *the beginning of hostilities.* **2.** the point of time or space at which anything begins: *the beginning of the Christian era; the beginning of the route.* **3.** the first part: *the beginning of the book; the beginning of the month.* **4.** Often, **beginnings.** the initial stage or part of anything: *the beginnings of science.* **5.** origin; source; first cause: *A misunderstanding about the rent was the beginning of their quarrel.* —*adj.* **6.** just formed: *a beginning company.* **7.** first; opening: *the beginning chapters of a book.* **8.** basic or introductory: *beginning Spanish.* **9.** learning the fundamentals: *a beginning swimmer.* [1175–1225; ME *beginnung, -ing.* See BEGIN, -ING[1]]
—**Syn. 1.** initiation, inauguration, inception. **2.** start, commencement, outset, onset, arising, emergence.
—**Ant. 1.** ending. **2.** end.

begin′ning rhyme′, the repetition of consonant sounds at the beginning of words; alliteration, as in *The fair breeze blew, the white foam flew.* Also called **head rhyme, initial rhyme.** [1940–45]

be•gird (bi gûrd′), *v.t.,* **-girt** or **-gird•ed, -gird•ing.** to gird about; encompass; surround. [bef. 900; ME *begirden,* OE *begierdan.* See BE-, GIRD[1]]

be•gone (bi gôn′, -gon′), *v.i.* to go away; depart (usually used in the imperative). [1325–75; ME; see BE (impv.), GONE]

be•go•nia (bi gōn′yə, -gō′nē ə), *n.* any tropical plant belonging to the genus *Begonia,* including species cultivated for the handsome, succulent leaves and waxy flowers. [< NL (Linnaeus), named after Michel *Bégon* (1638–1710), French patron of science; see -IA]

be•gor•ra (bi gôr′ə, -gor′ə, bē-), *interj. Irish Eng.* (used as a euphemism for *by God*): *It's a fine day, begorra.* Also, **be•gor′ah, be•gor′rah.** [1830–40]

be•got (bi got′), *v.* pt. and a pp. of **beget.**

be•got•ten (bi got′n), *v.* a pp. of **beget.**

beg-par•don (beg′pär′dn), *n. Australia and New Zealand.* an expression of apology (used esp. in the phrase *with no beg-pardons*). [1905–10]

be•grime (bi grīm′), *v.t.,* **-grimed, -grim•ing.** to make grimy. [1545–55; BE- + GRIME]

be•grudge (bi gruj′), *v.t.,* **-grudged, -grudg•ing. 1.** to envy or resent the pleasure or good fortune of (someone): *She begrudged her friend the award.* **2.** to be reluctant to give, grant, or allow: *She did not begrudge the money spent on her children's education.* [1350–1400; ME *bigrucchen.* See BE-, GRUDGE] —**be•grudg′ing•ly,** *adv.*
—**Syn. 1.** See **envy.**

be•guile (bi gīl′), *v.t.,* **-guiled, -guil•ing. 1.** to influence by trickery, flattery, etc.; mislead; delude. **2.** to take away from by cheating or deceiving (usually fol. by *of*): *to be beguiled of money.* **3.** to charm or divert: *a multitude of attractions to beguile the tourist.* **4.** to pass (time) pleasantly: *beguiling the long afternoon with a good book.* [1175–1225; ME *bigilen.* See BE-, GUILE] —**be•guile′ment,** *n.* —**be•guil′er,** *n.*
—**Syn. 1.** deceive, cheat. **3.** amuse, entertain.

Beg•uin (beg′in; *Fr.* be gaN′), *n.* a Beghard. [back formation from BEGUINE]

be•guine (bə gēn′), *n.* **1.** a dance in bolero rhythm that originated in Martinique. **2.** a modern social dance based on the beguine. **3.** music for either of these dances. [1930–35; < F (West Indies) *béguine,* fem. deriv. of *béguin* BIGGIN[1], trifling love affair]

Beg•uine (beg′ēn, bā′gēn, bə gēn′), *n. Rom. Cath. Ch.* a member of a lay sisterhood, founded in Liège in the 12th century. [1350–1400; ME *begyne* < MF *beguine,* said to be after Lambert (*le*) *Begue* (the stammerer), founder of the order; see -INE[1]]

be•gum[1] (bē′gəm, bā′-), *n.* (in India) a high-ranking Muslim woman, esp. a widow. [1625–35; < Urdu *begam* << Turkic *begim,* appar. a deriv. of *beg.* See BEY]

be•gum[2] (bi gum′), *v.t.,* **-gummed, -gum•ming.** to smear, soil, clog, etc., with or as if with gum or a gummy substance. [BE- + GUM[1]]

be•gun (bi gun′), *v.* pp. of **begin.**

be•half (bi haf′, -häf′), *n.* **1. in** or **on behalf of,** as a representative of or a proxy for: *On behalf of my colleagues, I address you tonight.* **2. in** or **on (someone's) behalf,** in the interest or aid of (someone): *He interceded in my behalf.* [1400–50; late ME; ME *bihalve,* earlier as adv. and prep. with the sense "near(by)," orig. as prep. phrase *bi halve* on one side; see BE-, BY, HALF]

Be•han (bē′ən), *n.* **Bren•dan (Francis)** (bren′dən), 1923–64, Irish playwright.

Be•har (bi här′), *n.* Bihar.

be•have (bi hāv′), *v.,* **-haved, -hav•ing.** —*v.i.* **1.** to act in a particular way; conduct or comport oneself or itself: *The ship behaves well.* **2.** to act properly: *Did the child behave?* **3.** to act or react under given circumstances: *This plastic behaves strangely under extreme heat or cold.* —*v.t.* **4.** to conduct or comport (oneself) in a proper manner: *Sit quietly and behave yourself.* [1400–50; late ME *behaven* (reflexive). See BE-, HAVE]
—**Syn. 1.** perform, acquit oneself, deport oneself.

be•hav•ior (bi hāv′yər), *n.* **1.** manner of behaving or acting. **2.** *Psychol., Animal Behav.* **a.** observable activity in a human or animal. **b.** the aggregate of responses to internal and external stimuli. **c.** a stereotyped, species-specific activity, as a courtship dance or startle reflex. **3.** Often, **behaviors.** a behavior pattern. **4.** the action or reaction of any material under given circumstances: *the behavior of tin under heat.* Also, *esp. Brit.,* **behaviour.** [1375–1425; BEHAVE + *-ior* (on model of *havior,* var. of *havor* < MF (*h*)*avoir* << L *habēre* to have); r. late ME *behavoure, behaver.* See BEHAVE, -OR[1]] —**be•hav′ior•al,** *adj.* —**be•hav′ior•al•ly,** *adv.*
—**Syn. 1.** demeanor, manners; bearing, carriage. BEHAVIOR, CONDUCT, DEPORTMENT, COMPORTMENT refer to one's actions before or toward others, esp. on a particular occasion. BEHAVIOR refers to actions usually measured by commonly accepted standards: *His behavior at the party was childish.* CONDUCT refers to actions viewed collectively, esp. as measured by an ideal standard: *Conduct is judged according to principles of ethics.* DEPORTMENT is behavior related to a code or to an arbitrary standard: *Deportment is guided by rules of etiquette. The teacher gave Susan a mark of B in deportment.* COMPORTMENT is behavior as viewed from the standpoint of one's management of one's own actions: *His comportment was marked by a quiet assurance.*

behav′ioral sci′ence, a science or branch of learning, as psychology or sociology, that derives its concepts from observation of the behavior of living organisms. [1955–60] —**behav′ioral sci′entist.**

be•hav•ior•ism (bi hāv′yə riz′əm), *n. Psychol.* the theory or doctrine that human or animal psychology can be accurately studied only through the examination and analysis of objectively observable and quantifiable behavioral events, in contrast with subjective mental states. [1910–15; BEHAVIOR + -ISM] —**be•hav′ior•ist,** *n., adj.* —**be•hav′ior•is′tic,** *adj.* —**be•hav′ior•is′ti•cal•ly,** *adv.*

behav′ior modifica′tion, *Psychol.* the direct changing of unwanted behavior by means of biofeedback or conditioning. [1970–75]

behav′ior pat′tern, a recurrent way of acting by an individual or group toward a given object or in a given situation. [1955–60]

behav′ior ther′apy, *Psychol.* a form of therapy emphasizing the correction of a person's undesirable behavior through Pavlovian conditioning, aversive therapy, or similar learning techniques. [1955–60]

be•hav•iour (bi hāv′yər), *n. Chiefly Brit.* behavior.
—**Usage.** See **-or[1]**.

be•head (bi hed′), *v.t.* **1.** to cut off the head of; kill or execute by decapitation. **2.** *Geol.* (of a pirate stream) to divert the headwaters of (a river, stream, etc.). [bef. 1000; ME *behe(f)den, beheveden,* OE *beheāfdian.* See BE-, HEAD] —**be•head′al,** *n.* —**be•head′er,** *n.*

be•held (bi held′), *v.* pt. and pp. of **behold.**

be•he•moth (bi hē′məth, bē′ə-), *n.* **1.** an animal, perhaps the hippopotamus, mentioned in Job 40:15–24. **2.** any creature or thing of monstrous size or power: *The army's new tank is a behemoth. The cartel is a behemoth small business owners fear.* [1350–1400; < Heb *bəhēmōth,* an aug. pl. of *bəhēmāh* beast; r. ME *bemoth*]

be•hen•ic (bə hen′ik, -hē′nik), *adj. Chem.* of or derived from behenic acid; docosanoic. [1870–75; *behen,* var. of BEN[2] + -IC]

behen′ic ac′id, *Chem.* a crystalline, saturated fatty acid, $C_{22}H_{44}O_2$, obtained from plant sources, used chiefly in the manufacture of cosmetics, waxes, and plasticizers. [1870–75]

be•hest (bi hest′), *n.* **1.** a command or directive. **2.** an earnest or strongly worded request. [bef. 1000; ME *bihest(e),* OE *behǣs* promise. See BE-, HEST]
—Syn. 1. order, bidding, decree, dictate, mandate.

be•hind (bi hīnd′), *prep.* **1.** at or toward the rear of: *Look behind the house.* **2.** not keeping up with, later than; after: *behind schedule.* **3.** in the state of making less progress than: *We can't afford to fall behind our competitors.* **4.** on the farther side of; beyond: *behind the mountain.* **5.** originating, supporting, or promoting: *Who's behind this program?* **6.** hidden or unrevealed by: *Malice lay behind her smile.* **7.** at the controls of: *behind the wheel of a car.* **—*adv.*** **8.** at or toward the rear; rearward: *to lag behind.* **9.** in a place, state, or stage already passed. **10.** in arrears; behindhand: *to be behind in one's rent.* **11.** slow, as a watch or clock: *more than 20 minutes behind.* **12.** as a cause or often latent feature of: *Behind their harassment lay the traditional fear of foreigners.* **13.** in a situation that exists afterward: *The victim left behind a large family.* **14.** *Archaic.* in reserve; to come: *Greater support is yet behind.* **—*adj.*** **15.** following: *the man behind.* **—*n.*** **16.** *Informal.* the buttocks. [bef. 900; ME *behinde(n),* OE *behindan;* for adv. suffix *-an* cf. BEFORE. See BE-, HIND[1]]
—Syn. 1, 2. BEHIND, AFTER both refer to a position following something else. BEHIND applies primarily to position in space, and suggests that one person or thing is at the back of another; it may also refer to (a fixed) time: *He stood behind the chair. You are behind the appointed time.* AFTER applies primarily to time; when it denotes position in space, it is not used with precision, and refers usually to bodies in motion: *Rest after a hard day's work. They entered the room, one after another.*
—Usage. See **back**[1].

be•hind•hand (bi hīnd′hand′), *adv., adj.* **1.** late; tardy. **2.** behind in progress; backward: *They were never behindhand in following artistic fads.* **3.** in debt or arrears. [1520–30; BEHIND + HAND]

be•hind-the-scenes (bi hīnd′*th*ə sēnz′), *adj.* **1.** happening or conducted out of view of the general public: *The behind-the-scenes preparations made the convention a huge success.* **2.** held or kept privately by or among a few key or influential persons: *behind-the-scenes negotiations.* **3.** occurring backstage: *the behind-the-scenes activities of the stage crew.* [1835–45]

Be•his•tun (bā′hi stōōn′), *n.* a ruined town in W Iran: site of a cliff that bears on its face a cuneiform inscription in Old Persian, Elamite, and Babylonian that provided a key for the decipherment of cuneiform in other languages. Also, **Bisitun, Bisutun.**

Beh•men (bā′mən), *n.* **Ja•kob** (jä′kəb). See **Böhme, Jakob.**

Beh•men•ism (bā′mə niz′əm), *n.* Boehmenism.

Beh•men•ist (bā′mə nist), *n.* Boehmenist. Also, **Beh•men•ite** (bā′mə nīt′).

be•hold (bi hōld′), *v.,* **be•held, be•hold•ing,** *interj.* **—*v.t.*** **1.** to observe; look at; see. **—*interj.*** **2.** look; see: *And, behold, three sentries of the King did appear.* [bef. 900; ME *beholden,* OE *behaldan* to keep. See BE-, HOLD[1]] **—be•hold′a•ble,** *adj.* **—be•hold′er,** *n.*
—Syn. 1. regard, gaze upon, view; watch; discern.

be•hold•en (bi hōl′dən), *adj.* obligated; indebted: *a man beholden to no one.* [1300–50; ME, adj. use of *beholden,* old ptp. of BEHOLD]
—Syn. obliged, bound, grateful, liable.

be•hoof (bi hōōf′), *n., pl.* **-hooves** (hōōvz′). use; advantage; benefit: *The money was spent for his own behoof.* [bef. 1000; ME *behove,* OE *behōf* profit, need; c. D *behoef,* G *Behuf*]

be•hoove (bi hōōv′), *v.,* **-hooved, -hoov•ing.** (chiefly in impersonal use) **—*v.t.*** **1.** to be necessary or proper for, as for moral or ethical considerations; be incumbent on: *It behooves the court to weigh evidence impartially.* **2.** to be worthwhile to, as for personal profit or advantage: *It would behoove you to be nicer to those who could help you.* **—*v.i.*** **3.** *Archaic.* to be needful, proper, or due: *Perseverance is a quality that behooves in a scholar.* [bef. 900; ME *behoven,* OE *behōfian* to need (*behōf* BEHOOF + *-ian* inf. suffix)]
—Syn. 2. benefit, advantage, serve, better, advance; suit, befit, beseem.

be•hove (bi hōv′), *v.t., v.i.,* **-hoved, -hov•ing.** *Chiefly Brit.* behoove.

Beh•rens (bâr′ənz; *Ger.* bā′rəns), *n.* **Pe•ter** (pē′tər; *Ger.* pā′tər), 1868–1940, German architect.

Beh•ring (bā′ring), *n.* **1. E•mil von** (ā′mēl fən), 1854–1917, German physician and bacteriologist: Nobel prize 1901. **2. Vi•tus** (vē′tōōs). See **Bering, Vitus.**

Behr•man (bâr′mən), *n.* **S(amuel) N(athan),** 1893–1973, U.S. playwright and author.

Bei•der•becke (bī′dər bek′), *n.* **Leon Bismarck** ("*Bix*"), 1903–31, U.S. jazz cornetist and composer.

beige (bāzh), *n.* **1.** very light brown, as of undyed wool; light gray with a brownish tinge. **—*adj.*** **2.** of the color beige. [1855–60; < F; OF *bege,* of uncert. orig.]

bei•gnet (ben yā′; *Fr.* be nye′), *n., pl.* **bei•gnets** (ben yāz′; *Fr.* be nye′). **1.** a fritter or doughnut. **2.** *French Cookery.* any fruit, vegetable, seafood, etc., dipped in batter and deep-fried. [1830–35, *Amer.;* < LaF (def. 1), F (def. 2), MF *bignet* pastry filled with fruit or meat, equiv. to *buyne* lit., bruise, lump from a blow (of uncert. orig.; cf. BUNION) + *-et* -ET]

Bei•jing (bā′jing′), *n. Pinyin.* a city in and the capital of the People's Republic of China, in the NE part, in central Hebei province: traditional capital of China. 7,570,000. Also, **Peking, Peiching.** Formerly (1928–49), **Peiping.**

Bei′jing duck′. See **Peking duck.**

Bei•lan′ Pass′ (bā län′), a mountain pass in SE Turkey near Syria. 2395 ft. (730 m).

be•ing (bē′ing), *n.* **1.** the fact of existing; existence (as opposed to nonexistence). **2.** conscious, mortal existence; life: *Our being is as an instantaneous flash of light in the midst of eternal night.* **3.** substance or nature: *of such a being as to arouse fear.* **4.** something that exists: *inanimate beings.* **5.** a living thing: *strange, exotic beings that live in the depths of the sea.* **6.** a human being; person: *the most beautiful being you could imagine.* **7.** (*cap.*) God. **8.** *Philos.* **a.** that which has actuality either materially or in idea. **b.** absolute existence in a complete or perfect state, lacking no essential characteristic; essence. **—*conj.*** **9.** *Nonstandard.* since; because; considering that (often fol. by *as, as how,* or *that*): *Being it's midnight, let's go home. Being as how you cooked supper, I'll do the dishes.* [1250–1300; ME; see BE, -ING[1]]

Bei•ra (bā′rə), *n.* a seaport in central Mozambique. 115,000.

Bei•rut (bā rōōt′, bā′rōōt), *n.* a seaport in and the capital of Lebanon. 702,000. Also, **Beyrouth.**

Be•ja (bā′jə), *n., pl.* **-jas,** (*esp. collectively*) **-ja** for 1. **1.** a member of a group of nomadic, predominantly Muslim peoples of northeastern Sudan. **2.** the Cushitic language of the Beja.

be•jab•bers (bi jab′ərz), *interj.* **1.** (used as a mild oath expressing astonishment, dismay, disbelief, or the like). **—*n.*** **2.** *Informal.* dickens; devil: *The fighter's left uppercut knocked the bejabbers out of his opponent.* Also, **be•ja•bers** (bi jā′bərz). [1815–25; alleged to be euphemistic alter. of *by Jesus*]

Bé•jart (bā zhar′), *n.* **Mau•rice** (mô rēs′), (*Maurice Berger*), born 1927, French ballet dancer and choreographer.

bej•el (bej′əl), *n. Pathol.* a nonvenereal syphilis occurring mainly among children in certain subtropical areas of southern Africa and southeastern Asia, caused by the spirochete strain *Treponema pallidum endemicum.* [1925–30; < Ar *bajl*]

be•je•sus (bi jē′zəs, -jā′-), *interj.* **1.** (used as a mild oath expressing dismay, anger, or the like). **—*n.*** **2.** *Informal.* dickens; devil; deuce: *The conglomerate plans to take that tiny company and expand the bejesus out of it.* [1905–10; alter. of oath *by Jesus*]

be•jew•el (bi jōō′əl), *v.t.,* **-eled, -el•ing** or (*esp. Brit.*) **-elled, -el•ling.** to adorn with or as if with jewels. [1550–60; BE- + JEWEL]

Bé•ké•sy (bā′kə shē; *Hung.* bā′kā shi), *n.* **Ge•org von** (gā′ôrg von; *Hung.* ge′org fôn). See **Von Békésy, Georg.**

bel[1] (bel), *n. Physics.* a unit of power ratio, equal to 10 decibels. [1925–30; named after A. G. BELL]

bel[2] (bel), *n.* bael.

Bel., **1.** Belgian. **2.** Belgic. **3.** Belgium.

Be•la (bā′lə, bel′ə), *n.* a male given name. Hungarian, **Bé•la** (bā′lo).

be•la•bor (bi lā′bər), *v.t.* **1.** to explain, worry about, or work at (something) repeatedly or more than is necessary: *He kept belaboring the point long after we had agreed.* **2.** to assail persistently, as with scorn or ridicule: *a book that belabors the provincialism of his contemporaries.* **3.** to beat vigorously; ply with heavy blows. **4.** *Obs.* to labor at. Also, *esp. Brit.,* **be•la′bour.** [1590–1600; BE- + LABOR]

be•lah (bē′lə), *n.* beefwood. [1860–65; < Wiradjuri *bilärr*]

Bel′ and the Drag′on, a book of the Apocrypha that is included as chapter 14 of Daniel in the Douay Bible.

Be•la•rus (byel′ə rōōs′, bel′-), *n.* official name of **Byelorussia.**

Be•las•co (bə las′kō), *n.* **David,** 1854–1931, U.S. playwright, actor, and producer.

be•lat•ed (bi lā′tid), *adj.* **1.** coming or being after the customary, useful, or expected time: *belated birthday greetings.* **2.** late, delayed, or detained: *We started the meeting without the belated representative.* **3.** *Archaic.* obsolete; old-fashioned; out-of-date: *a belated view of world politics.* **4.** *Archaic.* overtaken by darkness or night. [1610–20; *belate* to delay (BE- + LATE) + -ED[2]] **—be•lat′ed•ly,** *adv.* **—be•lat′ed•ness,** *n.*

Be•lau (bə lou′), *n.* **Republic of,** a group of Pacific islands in the W part of the Caroline group: taken by U.S. forces after severe fighting 1944; formerly a Japanese mandate, then under U.S. trusteeship; gained independence 1981. 13,519; 171 sq. mi. (443 sq. km). Formerly, **Palau Islands.**

be•laud (bi lôd′), *v.t.* to praise excessively. [1840–50; BE- + LAUD] **—be•laud′er,** *n.*

Be•la•ún•de (be′lä ōōn′de), *n.* **Fer•nan•do** (fer nän′dô), (*Fernando Belaúnde Terry*), born 1913?, Peruvian architect and statesman: president 1963–68.

be•lay (bi lā′), *v.,* **-layed, -lay•ing,** *n.* **—*v.t.*** **1.** *Naut.* to fasten (a rope) by winding around a pin or short rod inserted in a holder so that both ends of the rod are clear. **2.** *Mountain Climbing.* **a.** to secure (a person) by attaching to one end of a rope. **b.** to secure (a rope) by attaching to a person or to an object offering stable support. **3.** (used chiefly in the imperative) **a.** to cease (an action); stop. **b.** to ignore (an announcement, order, etc.). **—*v.i.*** **4.** to belay a rope: *Belay on that cleat over there.* **—*n.*** **5.** *Mountain Climbing.* a rock, bush, or other object sturdy enough for a running rope to be passed around it to secure a hold. [bef. 900; ME *beleggen,* OE *belecgan.* See BE-, LAY[1]]

Be•la•ya Tser•kov (bye′lə yə tser′kəf; *Eng.* bel′ə yə tsûr′kôf, -kof), a city in E Ukraine, S of Kiev. 151,000.

belay′ing cleat′, cleat (def. 8). [1860–65]

belay′ing pin′, *Naut.* a short, round bar of metal or wood, inserted in a fife rail or pin rail, to which a rope is belayed. [1830–40]

bel can•to (bel′ kan′tō, -kän′-; *It.* bel kän′tô), *Music.* a smooth, cantabile style of singing. [1890–95; < It: lit., fine singing, equiv. to *bel* (c. BEAU) + *canto* (see CANTO)]

belch (belch), *v.i.* **1.** to eject gas spasmodically and noisily from the stomach through the mouth; eruct. **2.** to emit contents violently, as a gun, geyser, or volcano. **3.** to issue spasmodically; gush forth: *Fire and smoke belched from the dragon's mouth.* **—*v.t.*** **4.** to eject (gas or the like) spasmodically or violently; give forth: *a chimney belching smoke.* **—*n.*** **5.** an instance of belching; eructation. **6.** a violent emittance of flame, smoke, gas, etc. [bef. 1000; ME *belchen,* OE *bealcettan;* c. D *balken, belken* to bray; perhaps extended form akin to BELL[2], BELLOW] **—belch′er,** *n.*

beld (beld), *adj. Scot.* bald; hairless.

bel•dam (bel′dəm, -dam), *n.* **1.** an old woman, esp. an ugly one; hag. **2.** *Obs.* grandmother. Also, **bel•dame** (bel′dəm, -dām′). [1400–50; late ME, equiv. to *bel*grand- (< MF *bel, belle* fine; see BEAU, BELLE) + *dam* mother (see DAM[2])]

be•lea•guer (bi lē′gər), *v.t.* **1.** to surround with military forces. **2.** to surround or beset, as with troubles. [1580–90; BE- + LEAGUER[1]] **—be•lea′guer•er,** *n.*
—Syn. 2. harass, pester, badger, bother, vex, annoy, plague, hector.

be•lec•tion (bi lek′shən), *n. Archit., Furniture.* bolection.

Be•lém (bə lem′; *Port.* be lān′), *n.* a seaport in N Brazil on the Pará River. 949,463. Also called **Pará.**

bel•em•nite (bel′əm nīt′), *n. Paleontol.* a conical fossil, several inches long, consisting of the internal calcareous rod of an extinct animal allied to the cuttlefish; a thunderstone. [1640–50; < F *bélemnite,* equiv. to Gk *bélemn(on)* a dart (n. deriv. from base of *bállein* to throw) + F *-ite* -ITE[1]]

bel-es•prit (bel es prē′), *n., pl.* ***beaux-es•prits*** (bō-zes prē′). *French.* a person of great wit or intellect.

Bel•fast (bel′fast, -fäst, bel fast′, -fäst′), *n.* a seaport in and capital of Northern Ireland, on the E coast. 374,300.

Bel•fort (bel fôr′, bā-), *n.* **1. Ter•ri•toire de** (te rē-twar′ də), a department in E France. 128,125; 235 sq. mi. (610 sq. km). *Cap.:* Belfort. **2.** a fortress city in E France, strategically located on a mountain pass between the Vosges and Jura mountains: siege 1870–71; battle 1944. 57,317.

bel•fry (bel′frē), *n., pl.* **-fries. 1.** a bell tower, either attached to a church or other building or standing apart. **2.** the part of a steeple or other structure in which a bell is hung. **3.** a frame of timberwork that holds or encloses a bell. **4.** *Slang.* head; mind: *a belfry full of curious notions.* **5. have bats in one's belfry.** See **bat**[2] (def. 3). [1225–75; ME *belfray,* appar. b. earlier *berfray* (< MF < Gmc) and ML *belfredus,* dissimilated var. of *berefredus* < Gmc; cf. MHG *ber(c) frit,* equiv. to *berc* defense, protection, refuge (c. OE *gebeorg;* see HARBOR) + *frit* peace, (place of) safety (c. OE *frith*)]

Belg., **1.** Belgian. **2.** Belgium.

bel•ga (bel′gə), *n.* a former Belgian currency unit in foreign exchange, equal to five Belgian francs: in use from 1926 to 1945. [1925–30; < F, D < L *Belga,* sing. of BELGAE]

Bel•gae (bel′jē), *n.* (*used with a plural v.*) an ancient chiefly Celtic people that lived in northern Gaul.

Bel•gaum (bel goum′), *n.* a city in W Karnataka state, in W India. 213,830.

Bel•gian (bel′jən), *n.* **1.** a native or an inhabitant of Belgium. **2.** one of a breed of large, strong draft horses, raised originally in Belgium. **—*adj.*** **3.** of or pertaining to Belgium. [1615–25; BELGI(UM) + -AN]

Bel′gian Con′go, a former name of **Zaire** (def. 1).

Bel′gian en′dive, endive (def. 2).

Bel′gian grif′fon, one of a variety of the Brussels griffon having a black or reddish-brown and black coat.

Bel′gian hare′, one of a breed of domestic rabbits. [1895–1900]

Bel′gian Ma•li•nois (mal′ən wä′), one of a Belgian breed of medium-sized dogs having a short coat, tan to dark brown in color, a black mask, and erect ears, bred originally as a sheepherding dog. [1965–70; < F *malinois* pertaining to MALINES]

CONCISE PRONUNCIATION KEY: act, cāpe, dâre, pärt; set, ēqual; *if,* ice; ox, ōver, ôrder, oil, bŏŏk, bōōt, out; up, ûrge; child; sing; shoe; thin, *th*at; zh as in *treasure.* ə = *a* as in *alone, e* as in *system, i* as in *easily, o* as in *gallop, u* as in *circus;* ᵊ as in *fire* (fīᵊr), *hour* (ouᵊr). l and n can serve as syllabic consonants, as in *cradle* (krād′l), and *button* (but′n). See the full key inside the front cover.

Bel′gian sheep′dog, one of a Belgian breed of medium-sized dogs having a long, straight black coat and erect ears, raised originally for herding sheep. [1925–30]

Bel′gian Ter·vu′ren (ter vyŏŏr′ən, tər-), one of a Belgian breed of medium-sized dogs having a long, straight coat, fawn to mahogany in color, differing from the Belgian sheepdog only in color. [1960–65; *Tervu(e)ren,* a town E of Brussels]

Bel·gic (bel′jik), *adj.* **1.** of or pertaining to the Belgae. **2.** Belgian. [1580–90; < L *belgicus.* See BELGAE, -IC]

Bel·gium (bel′jəm), *n.* a kingdom in W Europe, bordering the North Sea, N of France. 9,813,152; 11,779 sq. mi. (30,508 sq. km). *Cap.:* Brussels. French, **Bel·gique** (bel zhēk′); Flemish, **Bel·gi·ë** (bel′KHē ə).

Bel·go·rod (bel′gə rod′; *Russ.* byel′gə Rət), *n.* a city in the W Russian Federation, NE of Kharkov. 293,000.

Bel·go·rod-Dne·strov·sky (bel′gə rod′ne strôf′skē; *Russ.* byel′gə Rət dnyi strôf′skyə), *n.* a seaport in SW Ukraine, on the Black Sea. 37,000. Rumanian, **Cetatea Alba.** Formerly, **Akkerman.**

Bel·grade (bel′grād, -gräd, -grad, bel grād′, -gräd′, -grad′), *n.* a city in and the capital of Yugoslavia and the republic of Serbia, at the confluence of the Danube and Sava rivers. 1,209,360. Serbo-Croatian, **Beograd.**

Bel·gra·no (bel grä′nō; *Sp.* bel grä′nô), *n.* **Ma·nuel** (mä nwel′), 1770–1820, Argentine general.

Bel·gra·vi·a (bel grā′vē ə), *n.* a fashionable district in London, England, adjoining Hyde Park. —**Bel·gra′vi·an,** *adj.*

Be·li·al (bē′lē əl, bēl′yəl), *n.* **1.** *Theol.* the spirit of evil personified; the devil; Satan. **2.** (in Milton's *Paradise Lost*) one of the fallen angels. [< Heb *bəliyyaʿal,* equiv. to *bəli* without + *yaʿal,* worth, use]

be·lie (bi lī′), *v.t.,* **-lied, -ly·ing. 1.** to show to be false; contradict: *His trembling hands belied his calm voice.* **2.** to misrepresent: *The newspaper belied the facts.* **3.** to act unworthily according to the standards of (a tradition, one's ancestry, one's faith, etc.). **4.** *Archaic.* to lie about; slander. [bef. 1000; ME *belyen,* OE *belēogan.* See BE-, LIE[1]] —**be·li′er,** *n.*
—**Syn. 1.** refute, disprove, controvert, repudiate, confute, gainsay. **1, 2.** See **misrepresent.** —**Ant. 1.** prove, verify, support.

be·lief (bi lēf′), *n.* **1.** something believed; an opinion or conviction: *a belief that the earth is flat.* **2.** confidence in the truth or existence of something not immediately susceptible to rigorous proof: *a statement unworthy of belief.* **3.** confidence; faith; trust: *a child's belief in his parents.* **4.** a religious tenet or tenets; religious creed or faith: *to follow the Christian belief.* [1125–75; earlier *bile(e)ve* (n. use of v.); r. ME *bileave,* equiv. to *bi-* BE- + *leave;* cf. OE *gelēafa* (c. D *geloof,* G *Glaube;* akin to Goth *galaubeins*)]
—**Syn. 1.** view, tenet, conclusion, persuasion. **2.** assurance. BELIEF, CERTAINTY, CONVICTION refer to acceptance of, or confidence in, an alleged fact or body of facts as true or right without positive knowledge or proof. BELIEF is such acceptance in general: *belief in astrology.* CERTAINTY indicates unquestioning belief and positiveness in one's own mind that something is true: *I know this for a certainty.* CONVICTION is settled, profound, or earnest belief that something is right: *a conviction that a decision is just.* **4.** doctrine, dogma.

be·lieve (bi lēv′), *v.,* **-lieved, -liev·ing.** —*v.i.* **1.** to have confidence in the truth, the existence, or the reliability of something, although without absolute proof that one is right in doing so: *Only if one believes in something can one act purposefully.* —*v.t.* **2.** to have confidence or faith in the truth of (a positive assertion, story, etc.); give credence to. **3.** to have confidence in the assertions of (a person). **4.** to have a conviction that (a person or thing) is, has been, or will be engaged in a given action or involved in a given situation: *The fugitive is believed to be headed for the Mexican border.* **5.** to suppose or assume; understand (usually fol. by a noun clause): *I believe that he has left town.* **6. believe in, a.** to be persuaded of the truth or existence of: *to believe in Zoroastrianism; to believe in ghosts.* **b.** to have faith in the reliability, honesty, benevolence, etc., of: *I can help only if you believe in me.* **7. make believe.** See **make** (def. 46). [1150–1200; ME *bileven,* equiv. to *bi-* BE- + *leven,* OE (Anglian) *gelēfan* (c. D *gelooven,* G *glauben,* Goth *galaubjan*)] —**be·liev′a·bil′i·ty, be·liev′a·ble·ness,** *n.* —**be·liev′a·ble,** *adj.* —**be·liev′a·bly,** *adv.* —**be·liev′er,** *n.* —**be·liev′ing·ly,** *adv.*

be·like (bi līk′), *adv. Archaic.* very likely; perhaps; probably. [1525–35; BE- + LIKE[1]]

Be·lin·da (bə lin′də), *n.* a female given name: from an Old Spanish word meaning "beautiful."

Bel·i·sar·i·us (bel′ə sâr′ē əs), *n.* A.D. 505?–565, general of the Eastern Roman Empire.

Be·li·tong (be lē′tong), *n.* Billiton. Also, **Be·li·toeng, Be·li·tung** (be lē′tŏŏng).

be·lit·tle (bi lit′l), *v.t.,* **-tled, -tling.** to regard or portray as less impressive or important than appearances indicate; depreciate; disparage. [1775–85, *Amer.;* BE- + LITTLE] —**be·lit′tle·ment,** *n.* —**be·lit′tler,** *n.*
—**Syn.** minimize, decry, deprecate, deride, scorn, dismiss.

be·live (bi līv′), *adv. Scot.* before long; soon. [1150–1200; ME *bi live* BY LIFE, i.e., with liveliness]

Be·lize (bə lēz′), *n.* **1.** Formerly, **British Honduras.** a parliamentary democracy in N Central America: a former British crown colony; gained independence 1981. 8867 sq. mi. (22,966 sq. km). *Cap.:* Belmopan. **2.** Also called **Belize′ Cit′y.** a seaport in and the main city of Belize. 45,000. **3.** a river flowing NE through Belize to the Gulf of Honduras. 180 mi. (290 km) long. —**Be·li·ze·an** (bə lē′zē ən), *adj., n.*

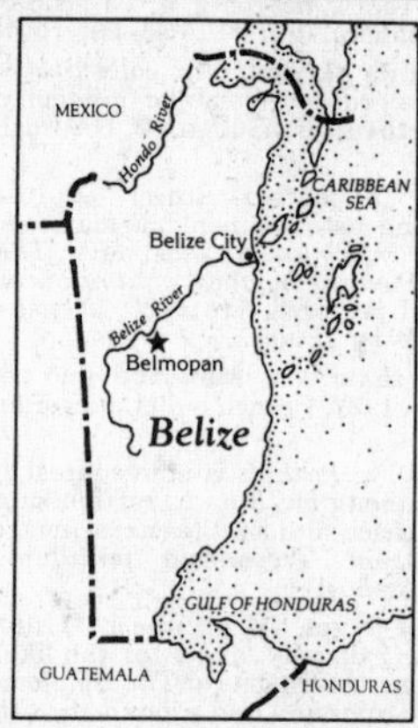

bell[1] (bel), *n.* **1.** a hollow instrument of cast metal, typically cup-shaped with a flaring mouth, suspended from the vertex and rung by the strokes of a clapper, hammer, or the like. **2.** the stroke or sound of such an instrument: *We rose at the bell.* **3.** anything in the form of a bell. **4.** the large end of a funnel, or the end of a pipe, tube, or any musical wind instrument, when its edge is turned out and enlarged. **5.** *Archit.* the underlying part of a foliated capital. **6.** *Naut.* **a.** any of the half-hour units of nautical time rung on the bell of a ship. **b.** each individual ring of the bell, counted with others to reckon the time: *It is now four bells.* **c.** a signal on the telegraph of a large power vessel, made between the navigating officers and the engineer. **7.** *Zool.* umbrella (def. 2). **8.** *Bot.* the bell-shaped corolla of a flower. **9.** *Metall.* a conical lid that seals the top of a blast furnace and lowers to admit a charge. **10. ring a bell,** to evoke a memory, esp. a vague or partial recollection; remind one of something: *His name rings a bell but I can't remember him.* **11. ring the bell,** to provide what is desired; be satisfactory or successful: *This new book rings the bell with teenagers.* **12. saved by the bell, a.** (of a boxer) saved from a knockout by the ringing of a gong signaling the end of a round. **b.** (of any person) spared from anticipated trouble by some extraneous event. **13. with bells on,** *Informal.* eagerly; ready to enjoy oneself: *Just say when, and we'll be there with bells on.* —*v.t.* **14.** to cause to swell or expand like a bell (often fol. by *out*): *Belling out the tubes will permit a freer passage of air.* **15.** to put a bell on. —*v.i.* **16.** to take or have the form of a bell. **17.** *Bot.* to produce bells; be in bell (said of hops when the seed vessels are forming). **18. bell the cat.** See **cat**[1] (def. 15). [bef. 1000; ME, OE *belle;* c. D *bel;* deriv. of BELL[2]] —**bell′-less′,** *adj.*

bell[2] (bel), *v.i., v.t.* **1.** to bellow like a stag in rutting time. **2.** to bay, as a hunting dog. —*n.* **3.** the cry of a rutting stag or hunting dog. [1275–1325; ME *bellen,* OE *bellan* to roar; c. OHG *bellan* (G *bellen* to bark), MD *bellen, belen,* ON *belja;* akin to Lith *balsas* voice, Skt *bhaṣ-* bark, *bhāṣ-* speak. See BELLOW, BELCH]

Bell (bel), *n.* **1. Ac·ton** (ak′tən), pen name of Anne Brontë. **2. Alexander Graham,** 1847–1922, U.S. scientist, born in Scotland: inventor of the telephone. **3. (Arthur) Clive (Howard),** 1881–1964, English critic of literature and art. **4. Cur·rer** (kûr′ər), pen name of Charlotte Brontë. **5. Ellis,** pen name of Emily Brontë. **6. John,** 1797–1869, U.S. political leader: Speaker of the House 1834–35. **7.** a city in SW California, near Los Angeles. 25,450.

Bel·la (bel′ə), *n.* a female given name, form of **Isabella.**

Bel·la·bel·la (bel′ə bel′ə), *n., pl.* **-las,** (*esp. collectively*) **-la** for 1. **1.** a member of a branch of the Kwakiutl Indians inhabiting central coastal British Columbia. **2.** the language of this group, belonging to the Wakashan family. Also, **Bel′la Bel′la.**

Bel·la·coo·la (bel′ə kōō′lə), *n., pl.* **-las,** (*esp. collectively*) **-la** for 1. **1.** a member of a riverine tribe of North American Indians inhabiting an area near the central coast of British Columbia. **2.** the language of this group, belonging to the Salishan family. Also, **Bel′la Coo′la.**

bel·la·don·na (bel′ə don′ə), *n.* **1.** Also called **deadly nightshade.** a poisonous plant, *Atropa belladonna,* of the nightshade family, having purplish-red flowers and black berries. **2.** *Pharm.* a drug from the leaves and root of this plant, containing atropine and related alkaloids: used in medicine to check secretions and spasms, to relieve pain or dizziness, and as a cardiac and respiratory stimulant. [1590–1600; < It *bella donna* lit., fair lady (so called because it is said to have been used by women to dilate the pupils of the eyes and to create an artificial pallor). See BELLE, DONNA]

bel′ladon′na lil′y, amaryllis (def. 2). [1725–35]

Bel·laire (bə lâr′, bel âr′), *n.* a city in SE Texas, within the city limits of Houston. 14,950.

Bel·la·my (bel′ə mē), *n.* **Edward,** 1850–98, U.S. author.

bell′ arch′, a round arch resting on prominent corbels. See illus. under **arch.**

bel·lar·mine (bel′är mēn′, bel′är mēn′, -ər-), *n.* a fat, narrow-necked stoneware bottle of the 16th and 17th centuries, ornamented with a bearded mask. Also called **graybeard, longbeard.** [1710–20; named after Cardinal *Bellarmino* (1542–1621), Italian churchman, the object of the caricature on the bottle]

Bel·la·trix (bə lā′triks), *n. Astron.* a blue-white giant star in the constellation Orion, with apparent magnitude +1.63. [< ML, L *bellātrīx* martial, waging war, equiv. to *bellā(re)* to wage war, (v. deriv. of *bellum* war) + *-trīx* -TRIX; appar. by assoc. with *bellātor* a name for Orion (L: warrior), though precise connection with this star unexplained]

Bel·lay (be lā′), *n.* **Jo·a·chim du** (zhô A kēm′ dY), c1525–60, French poet.

bell′ beak′er, *Archaeol.* a bell-shaped beaker, esp. one associated with the Beaker folk. [1900–05]

bell·bird (bel′bûrd′), *n.* any of several birds having a loud bell-like cry, esp. *Anthornis melanura,* a honey eater of New Zealand, and *Procnias tricarunculata* **(three-wattled bellbird)** of Central America. Also, **bell′ bird′.** [1795–1805; BELL[1] + BIRD]

bell′ book′, *Naut.* a book in which all orders affecting the main engines of a ship are recorded. [so called from the special use of bells on a ship]

bell-bot·tom (bel′bot′əm), *adj.* **1.** Also, **bell′-bot′·tomed.** (of trousers) wide and flaring at the bottoms of the legs. —*n.* **2. bell-bottoms,** (*used with a plural v.*) bell-bottom trousers. [1885–90]

bell·boy (bel′boi′), *n.* a bellhop. [1830–40, *Amer.;* BELL[1] + BOY]

bell′ bu′oy, *Naut.* a buoy having a bell that is rung by the motion of the buoy. [1830–40]

bell′ cap′tain, a hotel employee who supervises the work of bellhops. [1925–30, *Amer.*]

bell′ cow′, a cow, esp. the lead cow of a herd, having a bell attached to a collar around its neck so that the herd can be located easily. [1855–60, *Amer.*]

bell′ crank′, *Mach.* a lever or rocker having two arms meeting at a pivot at a right angle, used for transmitting motion between two parts meeting at an angle. [1880–85] —**bell′-cranked′,** *adj.*

bell′ curve′. See **bell-shaped curve.**

belle (bel), *n.* **1.** a woman or girl admired for her beauty and charm. **2.** the most beautiful, charming, or engaging woman or girl among a number: *the belle of the ball.* [1615–25; < F; OF *bele* < L *bella,* fem. of *bellus* fine, good-looking. See BEAU]

Belle (bel), *n.* a female given name, form of **Bella.**

Bel′leau Wood′ (bel′ō; *Fr.* be lō′), a forest in N France, NW of Château-Thierry: a memorial to the U.S. Marines who won a battle there 1918.

Bel·leek (bə lēk′), *n.* a fragile Irish porcelain with a bright luster. Also called **Belleek′ ware′.** [1865–70; after *Belleek,* town in Northern Ireland where it is made]

Belle Époque, La (lA bel ā pôk′), *French.* the period (1871–1914) between the end of the Franco-Prussian War and the outbreak of World War I, characterized by relative peacefulness in Western Europe and by marked advances and productivity in the arts, literature, technology, etc. [lit., the beautiful epoch]

Belle·fon·taine (bel foun′tn, -fon′-), *n.* a city in W Ohio. 11,888.

Bellefon′taine Neigh′bors, a city in E Missouri. 12,082.

Belle′ Glade′, a city in SE Florida. 16,535.

Belle′ Isle′, Strait of, a strait between Newfoundland and Labrador, Canada. 10–15 mi. (16–24 km) wide.

Bel·ler·o·phon (bə ler′ə fon′), *n. Class. Myth.* a Corinthian hero who, mounted on Pegasus, killed the Chimera. Also, **Bel·ler·o·phon·tes** (bə ler′ə fon′tēz). —**Bel′ler·o·phon′tic,** *adj.*

belles-let·tres (*Fr.* bel le′tRᵊ), *n.pl.* **1.** literature regarded as a fine art, esp. as having a purely aesthetic function. **2.** light and elegant literature, esp. that which is excessively refined, characterized by aestheticism, and minor in subject, substance, or scope. [1700–10; < F lit., fine letters. See BELLE, LETTER[1]] —**bel·let·rist** (bel le′trist), *n.* —**bel·let·ris·tic** (bel′li tris′tik), *adj.*
—**Syn. 1.** See **literature.**

Belle·ville (bel′vil), *n.* **1.** a city in SW Illinois. 42,150. **2.** a city in NE New Jersey. 35,367. **3.** a city in S Ontario, in S Canada. 34,881.

Belle′ville spring′, *Mach.* a spring having the form of a washer or dished disk with an open center, used for cushioning heavy loads with short motion.

CONCISE ETYMOLOGY KEY: <, descended or borrowed from; >, whence; b., blend of, blended; c., cognate with; cf., compare; deriv., derivative; equiv., equivalent; imit., imitative; obl., oblique; r., replacing; s., stem; sp., spelling, spelled; resp., respelling, respelled; trans., translation; ?, origin unknown; *, unattested; ‡, probably earlier than. See the full key inside the front cover.

Belle·vue (bel′vyo͞o), *n.* **1.** a city in E Washington. 73,903. **2.** a town in E Nebraska. 21,813. **3.** a city in SW Pennsylvania. 10,128.

bell·flow·er (bel′flou′ər), *n.* **1.** any of numerous plants of the genus *Campanula,* having usually bell-shaped flowers and including many species cultivated as ornamentals. Cf. **bellflower family.** **2.** any of various other plants having bell-shaped flowers. [1570–80; BELL[1] + FLOWER]

Bell·flow·er (bel′flou′ər), *n.* a city in SW California, near Los Angeles. 53,441.

bell′flower fam′ily, the plant family Campanulaceae, characterized by chiefly herbaceous plants having simple, alternate leaves and solitary or clustered flowers with a bell-shaped, five-lobed, often blue or purple corolla, and including the harebell, Canterbury bells, and balloon flower.

bell′ frog′, any of several tree frogs having a bell-like call. [1680–90]

Bell′ Gar′dens, a town in SW California, near Los Angeles. 34,117.

bell′ glass′. See **bell jar.**

bell·hang·er (bel′hang′ər), *n.* a person who installs and repairs bells and their attachments. [1530–40; BELL[1] + HANGER]

bell′-hang·er's bit′ (bel′hang′ərz), *Carpentry.* a bit for drilling small holes through studs or the like.

bell′ heath′er, a European heath, *Erica cinerea,* having prostrate branches with terminal clusters of red flowers.

bell·hop (bel′hop′), *n., v.,* **-hopped, -hop·ping.** —*n.* **1.** a person who is employed, esp. by a hotel, to carry guests' luggage, run errands, etc. —*v.i.* **2.** Also, **bell′-hop′.** to work as a bellhop. [1895–1900, *Amer.*; BELL[1] + HOP[1]]

bell′ hous′ing, *Auto.* a flared casing that encloses a clutch assembly.

bel·li·cose (bel′i kōs′), *adj.* inclined or eager to fight; aggressively hostile; belligerent; pugnacious. [1400–50; late ME < L *bellicōsus,* equiv. to *bellic(us)* pertaining to war (*bell(um)* war + *-icus* -IC) + *-ōsus* -OSE[1]] —**bel′li·cose′ly,** *adv.* —**bel·li·cos·i·ty** (bel′i kos′i tē), **bel′li·cose′ness,** *n.*

bel·lied (bel′ēd), *adj.* **1.** having a belly, esp. one of a specified kind, size, shape, condition, etc. (usually used in combination): *big-bellied.* **2.** swelled or puffed out: *a bellied sail.* [1425–75; late ME; see BELLY, -ED[3]]

bel·lig·er·ence (bə lij′ər əns), *n.* **1.** a warlike or aggressively hostile nature, condition, or attitude. **2.** an act of carrying on war; warfare. [1805–15; BELLIGER(ENT) + -ENCE]

bel·lig·er·en·cy (bə lij′ər ən sē), *n.* **1.** the position or status as a belligerent; state of being actually engaged in war. **2.** belligerence. [1860–65; BELLIGER(ENT) + -ENCY]

bel·lig·er·ent (bə lij′ər ənt), *adj.* **1.** warlike; given to waging war. **2.** of warlike character; aggressively hostile; bellicose: *a belligerent tone.* **3.** waging war; engaged in war: *a peace treaty between belligerent powers.* **4.** pertaining to war or to those engaged in war: *belligerent rights.* —*n.* **5.** a state or nation at war. **6.** a member of the military forces of such a state. [1570–80; < L *belliger* waging war (*belli-,* comb. form of *bellum* war + *-ger-,* base of *gerere* to conduct) + -ENT; r. *belligerant* < L *belligerant-* (s. of *belligerāns,* prp. of *belligerāre* to wage war; see -ANT)] —**bel·lig′er·ent·ly,** *adv.*
—**Syn. 2.** pugnacious, truculent, combative, quarrelsome, antagonistic, contentious.

bel·ling (bel′ing), *n. Chiefly Midland U.S.* shivaree (def. 1). [1860–65; BELL[1] + -ING[1]]

Bel·ling·ham (bel′ing ham′), *n.* **1.** a seaport in NW Washington. 45,794. **2.** a city in E Massachusetts. 14,300.

Bel·lings·hau·sen (bel′ingz hou′zən), *n.* **Fa·bi·an Gott·lieb von** (fä′bē ən got′lēb von), (*Faddey Faddeyevich Bellingshauzen*), 1778–1852, Russian naval officer and explorer.

Bel·li·ni (bə lē′nē; *It.* bel lē′nē), *n.* **1. Gen·ti·le** (jentē′le), 1427?–1507, Venetian painter (son of Jacopo): teacher of Giorgione and Titian. **2. Gio·van·ni** (jô vän′nē), 1430?–1516, Venetian painter (son of Jacopo). **3. Ja·co·po** (yä′kô pô), 1400?–70, Venetian painter. **4. Vin·cen·zo** (vēn chen′dzô), 1801?–35, Italian composer of opera.

Bel·lin·zo·na (bel′in zō′nə; *It.* bel′lēn tsô′nä), *n.* a town in and the capital of Ticino, in S Switzerland. 17,700.

bell′ jar′, a bell-shaped glass jar or cover for protecting delicate instruments, bric-a-brac, or the like, or for containing gases or a vacuum in chemical experiments. Also called **bell glass.** [1875–80]

bell′ lap′, the final lap in a race of repeated circuits, signaled by the ringing of a bell. [1970–75]

bell·man (bel′mən), *n., pl.* **-men. 1.** a bellhop. **2.** a person who carries or rings a bell, esp. a town crier or watchman. [1350–1400; ME; see BELL[1], -MAN]

Bell·mawr (bel mär′), *n.* a borough in SW New Jersey. 13,721.

bell′ met′al, an alloy of about 80 percent copper and 20 percent tin, sometimes with small amounts of lead and zinc, having low damping qualities and used esp. for bells. [1535–45]

Bell·more (bel′môr, -mōr), *n.* a city on S Long Island, in SE New York. 18,106.

Bel·lo (be′yô), *n.* **1. An·drés** (än dʀes′), 1781–1865, Venezuelan poet, philologist, and educator. **2.** a city in central Colombia. 113,439.

Bel·loc (bel′ək, -ok), *n.* **Hi·laire** (hi lâr′), 1870–1953, English essayist, poet, and satirist, born in France.

Bel·lo Ho·ri·zon·te (*Port.* be′lo͝o ô′ʀi zôɴ′ti). See **Belo Horizonte.**

Bel·lo·na (bə lō′nə), *n.* the ancient Roman goddess of war.

Bel·lot·to (bə lot′ō; *It.* bel lôt′tô), *n.* **Ber·nar·do** (bər när′dō; *It.* beʀ näʀ′dô), (*Canaletto*), 1720–80, Italian painter.

bel·low (bel′ō), *v.i.* **1.** to emit a hollow, loud, animal cry, as a bull or cow. **2.** to roar; bawl: *bellowing with rage.* —*v.t.* **3.** to utter in a loud deep voice: *He bellowed his command across the room.* —*n.* **4.** an act or sound of bellowing. [bef. 1000; ME *belwen,* akin to OE *bylgan* to roar (cf. for the vowel OHG *bullôn*); extended form akin to BELL[2]] —**bel′low·er,** *n.*
—**Syn. 2.** See **cry.**

Bel·low (bel′ō), *n.* **Saul,** born 1915, U.S. novelist, born in Canada: Nobel prize for literature 1976.

bel·lows (bel′ōz, -əz), *n.* (*used with a singular or plural v.*) **1.** a device for producing a strong current of air, consisting of a chamber that can be expanded to draw in air through a valve and contracted to expel it through a tube. **2.** anything resembling or suggesting bellows in form, as the collapsible part of a camera or enlarger. **3.** the lungs. [bef. 900; ME *bel(o)wes* (pl.), OE *belg,* short for *blǣst belg,* pl. *belgas* blast-bag; c. D *blaasbalg,* G *Blasebalg,* ON *belgr.* See BELLY] —**bel′lows·like′,** *adj.*

Bel·lows (bel′ōz), *n.* **George Wesley,** 1882–1925, U.S. painter and lithographer.

bel′lows fish′, snipefish. [1675–85]

bell′ pep′per. See **sweet pepper.** [1700–10]

bell·per·son (bel′pûr′sən), *n.* a bellhop. [BELL(HOP) + -PERSON]
—**Usage.** See **-person.**

bell·pull (bel′po͝ol′), *n.* a handle, cord, or strip of cloth pulled to ring a bell. [1835–45, *Amer.*; BELL[1] + PULL]

Bell′ pur′chase, a tackle consisting of two standing single blocks, two running single blocks, a fall, and a runner, so arranged that it gives a mechanical advantage of six, neglecting friction. Also, **Bell's′ pur′chase.**

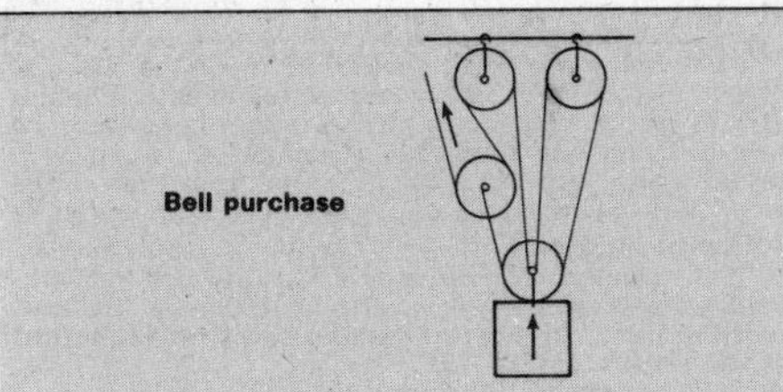
Bell purchase

bell′ push′, a button, as on the front door of a house, that rings a bell when pushed. [1880–85]

bells (belz), *n.* (*used with a plural v.*) *Informal.* bell-bottom (def. 2). [1965–70; by shortening of the full phrase, as in *shorts* from *short pants*]

bells′ and whis′tles, *Informal.* features added to a product; special parts or functions; extras. [1970–75]

bell′ seat′, (on some 18th-century chairs) a seat having an outline resembling that of a bell. Also called **balloon seat.**

bell′-shaped curve′ (bel′shāpt′), *Statistics.* a frequency curve that resembles the outline of a bell, as the normal curve. Also called **bell curve.**

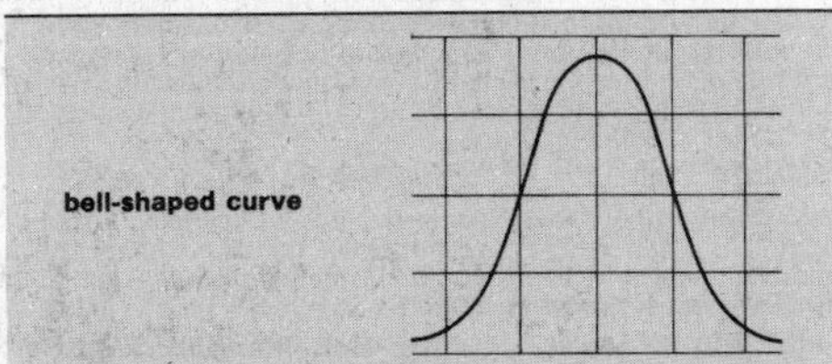
bell-shaped curve

bells′ of Ire′land, a plant, *Molucella laevis,* native to western Asia, having inconspicuous white flowers, each surrounded by an enlarged green calyx. Also called **shellflower.** [1955–60; so called from the bell-like green calyx]

Bell's′ pal′sy, *Pathol.* suddenly occurring paralysis that distorts one side of the face, caused by a lesion of the facial nerve. [1855–60; named after Charles Bell (1774–1842), Scottish anatomist, who first described it]

bell′ toad′. See **tailed frog.**

bell·weth·er (bel′weth′ər), *n.* **1.** a wether or other male sheep that leads the flock, usually bearing a bell. **2.** a person or thing that assumes the leadership or forefront, as of a profession or industry: *Paris is a bellwether of the fashion industry.* **3.** a person or thing that shows the existence or direction of a trend; index. **4.** a person who leads a mob, mutiny, conspiracy, or the like; ringleader. [1400–50; late ME; see BELL[1], WETHER]
—**Syn. 2.** leader, pacesetter, frontrunner, trailblazer.

Bell·wood (bel′wo͝od′), *n.* a city in NE Illinois, near Chicago. 19,811.

bell·wort (bel′wûrt′, -wôrt′), *n.* a plant of the genus *Uvularia,* of the lily family, having a delicate, bell-shaped yellow flower. Also called **merry-bells.** [1775–85; BELL[1] + WORT[2]]

bel·ly (bel′ē), *n., pl.* **-lies,** *v.,* **-lied, -ly·ing.** —*n.* **1.** the front or under part of a vertebrate body from the breastbone to the pelvis, containing the abdominal viscera; the abdomen. **2.** the stomach with its adjuncts. **3.** appetite or capacity for food; gluttony. **4.** the womb. **5.** the inside or interior of anything: *the belly of a ship.* **6.** a protuberant or bulging surface of anything: *the belly of a flask.* **7.** *Anat.* the fleshy part of a muscle. **8.** the front, inner, or under surface or part, as distinguished from the back. **9.** the front surface of a violin or similar instrument. **10.** a bulge on a vertical surface of fresh concrete. **11.** the underpart of the fuselage of an airplane. —*v.t.* **12.** to fill out; swell: *Wind bellied the sails.* —*v.i.* **13.** to swell out: *Sails bellying in the wind.* **14.** to crawl on one's belly: *soldiers bellying through a rice paddy.* **15. belly up to,** *Informal.* **a.** to approach closely, esp. until one is in physical contact: *to belly up to a bar.* **b.** to curry favor from: *Would you have gotten the promotion if you hadn't bellied up to the boss?* **16. go** or **turn belly up,** *Informal.* to come to an end; die; fail: *After years of barely surviving on donations, the neighborhood social club finally went belly up.* [bef. 950; ME *bely,* OE *belig, belg* bag, skin; c. G *Balg,* Goth *balgs,* ON *belgr* sack; akin to Welsh *bol(a), boly,* Ir *bolg* sack, belly, bellows, Serbo-Croatian *blàzina,* Latvian *pabàlsts,* Avestan *barəziš-,* Pers *bālish* cushion] —**bel′ly·like′,** *adj.*

bel·ly·ache (bel′ē āk′), *n., v.,* **-ached, -ach·ing.** —*n.* **1.** *Informal.* a pain in the abdomen or bowels. —*v.i.* **2.** *Informal.* to complain; grumble. [1545–55; BELLY + ACHE] —**bel′ly·ach′er,** *n.*

bel·ly·band (bel′ē band′), *n.* **1.** a band worn about the belly, as of a harnessed horse or of an infant to protect the navel. See illus. under **harness. 2.** a band of paper around a new book, usually printed with information about the book's contents and sometimes used instead of a book jacket. **3.** a band of strong paper, plastic, tape, or the like, placed around a product or package to protect it during shipping, prevent it from opening, etc. [1515–25; BELLY + BAND[2]]

bel·ly·board (bel′ē bôrd′, -bōrd′), *n.* a small surfboard, usually 3–4 ft. (0.9–1.2 m) long, for riding waves on one's belly, sometimes used in conjunction with swim fins. [1960–65; BELLY + BOARD]

bel′ly bust′, *South Midland and Southern U.S.* See **belly flop.** Also, **bel′ly bust′er.** [1885–90]

bel·ly-bust (bel′ē bust′), *v.i. South Midland and Southern U.S.* belly-flop.

bel·ly·but·ton (bel′ē but′n), *n. Informal.* the navel. Also, **bel′ly but′ton.** [1875–80, *Amer.*; BELLY + BUTTON]

bel′lybutton sur′gery. *Informal.* laparoscopy.

bel′ly dance′, an Oriental solo dance, performed by a woman with midriff exposed, emphasizing movements of the pelvis and abdominal muscles. Also called **danse du ventre.** [1895–1900] —**bel′ly danc′er.** —**bel′ly danc′ing.**

bel′ly flop′, *Northern and North Midland U.S.* **1.** an awkward, usually unintentional dive in which the front of the body strikes the water horizontally, the abdomen or chest bearing the brunt of the impact. **2.** a maneuver with a sled in which the sledder runs with the sled to gain momentum and jumps forward to land on top of the sled as it moves through the snow. Also, **bel′ly flop′per.** [1890–95]

bel·ly-flop (bel′ē flop′), *v.i.,* **-flopped, -flop·ping.** *Northern and North Midland U.S.* **1.** to do a belly flop, as in diving or sledding. **2.** to land or throw oneself heavily down on one's belly: *so tired he just belly-flopped on the bed.* [1930–35]

bel·ly·ful (bel′ē fo͝ol′), *n., pl.* **-fuls.** *Informal.* all that a person can tolerate: *I've had a bellyful of your whining.* [1525–35; BELLY + -FUL]

bel′ly girt′, *Chiefly New Eng. and South Atlantic States.* girth[1] (def. 2). Also, **bel′ly girth′.**

bel·ly-helve (bel′ē helv′), *n. Brit. Metalworking.* a triphammer in which the cams act at a point along the helve, partway between the fulcrum and the head. [1880–85]

bel·ly-land (bel′ē land′), *Aeron.* —*v.t.* **1.** (of an aviator) to land (an aircraft) directly on the fuselage, as because of defective landing gear. —*v.i.* **2.** (of an aircraft) to land directly on the fuselage, without using the landing gear. [1940–45]

bel′ly laugh′, a deep, loud, hearty laugh. [1920–25]

bel′ly pan′, a plate enclosing the bottom of an automotive vehicle or the like below the chassis.

bel′ly slam′, *Chiefly Ohio, Pennsylvania, and New York State.* See **belly flop.**

bel·ly-slam (bel′ē slam′), *v.i.,* **-slammed, -slam·ming.** *Chiefly Ohio, Pennsylvania, and New York State.* belly-flop.

bel·ly-wash (bel′ē wosh′, -wôsh′), *n. Slang.* any barely drinkable liquid or beverage, as inferior soda, beer, coffee, or soup.

Bel·mont (bel′mont), *n.* **1. Alva Ert·skin Smith Van·der·bilt** (ûrt′skin), 1853–1933, U.S. women's-rights activist and socialite. **2. August,** 1816–90, U.S. financier, diplomat, and horse-racing enthusiast, born in Germany. **3.** a town in E Massachusetts, near Boston. 26,100. **4.** a city in W California. 24,505.

Bel·mon·te (bel môn′te), *n.* **Juan** (hwän), 1893–1962, Spanish matador.

Bel·mo·pan (bel′mō pan′), *n.* a city in and the capital of Belize, in the central part. 2700.

Bel·oeil (bə lil′; *Fr.* be lœ′yᵊ), *n.* a town in S Quebec, in E Canada. 17,540.

Be·lo Ho·ri·zon·te (be′lo͝o ô′ʀi zôɴ′ti), a city in SE Brazil. 1,814,990. Also, **Bello Horizonte.**

Be·loit (bə loit′), *n.* a city in S Wisconsin. 35,207.

CONCISE PRONUNCIATION KEY: *act, cāpe, dâre, pärt; set, ēqual; if, īce; ox, ōver, ôrder, oil, bo͝ok, bo͞ot, out; up, ûrge; child; sing; shoe; thin, that;* zh as in *treasure.* ə = *a* as in *alone, e* as in *system, i* as in *easily, o* as in *gallop, u* as in *circus;* ᵊ as in *fire* (fīᵊr), *hour* (ouᵊr). l and n can serve as syllabic consonants, as in *cradle* (krād′l), and *button* (but′n). See the full key inside the front cover.

bel·o·man·cy (bel′ə man′sē), *n.* divination using arrows drawn at random from a quiver or other holder. [1640–50; < Gk *bélo(s)* arrow, dart + -MANCY]

be·long (bi lông′, -long′), *v.i.* **1.** to be in the relation of a member, adherent, inhabitant, etc. (usually fol. by *to*): *He belongs to the Knights of Columbus.* **2.** to have the proper qualifications, esp. social qualifications, to be a member of a group: *You don't belong in this club.* **3.** to be proper or due; be properly or appropriately placed, situated, etc.: *Books belong in every home. This belongs on the shelf. He is a statesman who belongs among the great.* **4. belong to, a.** to be the property of: *The book belongs to her.* **b.** to be a part or adjunct of: *That cover belongs to this jar.* [1300–50; ME *belongen,* equiv. to *be-* BE- + *longen* to belong, v. deriv. of *long* (adj.) belonging, OE *gelang* ALONG[1]]

be·long·ing (bi lông′ing, -long′-), *n.* **1.** something that belongs. **2. belongings,** possessions; goods; personal effects. [1595–1605; BELONG + -ING[1]]

be·long·ing·ness (bi lông′ing nis, -long′-), *n.* the quality or state of being an essential or important part of something: *The company has developed social programs to give employees a sense of belongingness.* [1930–35; BELONGING + -NESS]

bel·o·noid (bel′ə noid′), *adj.* needlelike; styloid. [< Gk *belonoeidḗs,* equiv. to *belṓn(ē)* needle (akin to *bélos* arrow, dart) + *-oeidēs* -OID]

Be·lo·rus·sia (byel′ə rush′ə, bel′ə-), *n.* Byelorussia. —**Be′lo·rus′sian,** *adj., n.*

Be·lo·stok (*Russ.* byi lu stôk′), *n.* Bialystok.

be·lote (bə lot′), *n.* a card game for two players, using 32 cards and following the same basic rules as klabberjass, popular in France. Also, **be·lotte′.** [1940–45; < F, of uncert. orig.; the hypothesis that the game was put in its present form by an F. *Belot* is unsubstantiated]

be·lov·ed (bi luv′id, -luvd′), *adj.* **1.** greatly loved; dear to the heart. —*n.* **2.** a person who is greatly loved. [1350–1400; ME *biloved,* ptp. of *biloven* to like, love; see BE-, LOVE, -ED[2]]
—**Syn. 1.** cherished, precious; sweet, darling.

Be·lo·vo (byi lô′və), *n.* a city in the S Russian Federation in Asia. 112,000.

be·low (bi lō′), *adv.* **1.** in or toward a lower place: *Look out below!* **2.** on, in, or toward a lower level, as a lower deck of a ship: *The captain of the ship went below.* **3.** beneath the surface of the water: *Divers were sent below to view the wreck.* **4.** on earth: *the fate of creatures here below.* **5.** in hell or the infernal regions. **6.** at a later point on a page or in a text: *See the illustration below.* Cf. **above** (def. 5). **7.** in a lower rank or grade: *He was demoted to the class below.* **8.** under zero on the temperature scale: *The temperature in Buffalo was ten below this morning.* **9.** *Theat.* downstage. Cf. **above** (def. 8). **10.** *Zool.* on the lower or ventral side. —*prep.* **11.** lower down than: *below the knee.* **12.** lower in rank, degree, amount, rate, etc., than: *below cost; below freezing.* **13.** too low or undignified to be worthy of; beneath: *He considered such an action below his notice.* **14.** *Theat.* downstage of: *There are two chairs below the table.* [1275–1325; ME *bilooghe,* equiv. to *bi-* by (see BE-) + *looghe* LOW[1]]
—**Syn. 11.** BELOW, UNDER, BENEATH indicate position in some way lower than something else. BELOW implies being in a lower plane: *below the horizon, the water line.* UNDER implies being lower in a perpendicular line: *The book is under the chair.* BENEATH may have a meaning similar to BELOW, but more usually denotes being under so as to be covered, overhung, or overtopped: *the pool beneath the falls.*

be·low·decks (bi lō′deks′), *adv. Naut.* within the hull of a vessel: *Fire raged belowdecks.* [BELOW + DECK + -S[1]]

be·low·ground (bi lō′ground′), *adj.* **1.** situated beneath the surface of the earth; subterranean. **2.** no longer living; buried, as in a cemetery (usually used predicatively): *All those who might have known about the incident are now belowground.* [1955–60; BELOW + GROUND[1]]

below′ stairs′, *Chiefly Brit.* (formerly) the basement rooms usually used by servants, as servants' quarters, kitchen, and laundry room.

below′ the line′, *Bridge.* See under **line**[1] (def. 31).

Bel Pa·e·se (bel′ pä ā′zē; *It.* bel′ pä e′ze), *Trademark.* a brand of semisoft, mild Italian cheese.

Bel·sen (bel′zən), *n.* locality in Germany: site of Nazi concentration camp during World War II. Also called **Bergen-Belsen.**

Bel·shaz·zar (bel shaz′ər), *n.* a prince of Babylon, son of Nabonidus and co-regent with him, referred to in the Bible as a king of Babylon and son of Nebuchadnezzar. Dan. 5. [< Heb *Belshaṣṣar* < Akkadian *Bēl-shar-uṣur* may Bel guard the king]

belt (belt), *n.* **1.** a band of flexible material, as leather or cord, for encircling the waist. **2.** any encircling or transverse band, strip, or stripe. **3.** an elongated region having distinctive properties or characteristics: *a belt of cotton plantations.* **4.** *Mach.* an endless flexible band passing about two or more pulleys, used to transmit motion from one pulley to the other or others or to convey materials and objects. **5.** *Mil.* **a.** a cloth strip with loops or a series of metal links with grips, for holding cartridges fed into an automatic gun. **b.** a band of leather or webbing, worn around the waist and used as a support for weapons, ammunition, etc. **6.** a series of armor plates forming part of the hull of a warship. **7.** a broad, flexible strip of rubber, canvas, wood, etc., moved along the surface of a fresh concrete pavement to put a finish on it after it has been floated. **8.** a road, railroad, or the like, encircling an urban center to handle peripheral traffic. **9.** *Slang.* a hard blow or hit. **10.** *Slang.* a shot of liquor, esp. as swallowed in one gulp. **11.** *Auto.* a strip of material used in a type of motor-vehicle tire **(belted tire),** where it is placed between the carcass and the tread for reinforcement. **12. below the belt,** not in accord with the principles of fairness, decency, or good sportsmanship: *criticism that hit below the belt.* **13. tighten one's belt, a.** to undergo hardship patiently. **b.** to curtail one's expenditures; be more frugal: *They were urged to tighten their belts for the war effort.* **14. under one's belt,** *Informal.* **a.** in one's stomach, as food or drink: *With a few Scotches under his belt, he's everyone's friend.* **b.** considered as a matter of successful past experience: *I don't think our lawyer has enough similar cases under his belt.* —*v.t.* **15.** to gird or furnish with a belt. **16.** to surround or mark as if with a belt or band: *Garbage cans were belted with orange paint.* **17.** to fasten on (a sword, gun, etc.) by means of a belt. **18.** to beat with or as if with a belt, strap, etc. **19.** *Slang.* to hit very hard, far, etc.: *You were lucky he didn't belt you in the mouth when you said that. He belted a triple to right field.* **20.** *Informal.* to sing (a song) loudly and energetically (sometimes fol. by *out*): *She can belt out a number with the best of them.* **21.** *Slang.* to drink (a shot of liquor) quickly, esp. in one gulp (sometimes fol. by *down*): *He belted a few and went back out into the cold.* [bef. 1000; ME; OE; cf. OHG *balz;* both < L *balteus;* see BALTEUS] —**belt′less,** *adj.*
—**Syn. 3.** BELT and ZONE agree in their original meaning of a girdle or band. BELT is more used in popular or journalistic writing: *the corn belt.* ZONE tends to be used in technical language: *the Torrid Zone; a parcel-post zone.* **15.** girdle, encircle. **17.** gird (on). **18.** flog, lash.

Bel·tane (bel′tān, -tin), *n.* an ancient Celtic festival observed on May Day in Scotland and Ireland to mark the beginning of summer. [1375–1425; late ME (Scots) < ScotGael *bealltainn,* OIr *bel(l)taine,* perh. equiv. to **bel-* an obscure element, perh. the name of a supernatural person + *tene* fire]

belt′ bag′. See **fanny pack.**

belt′ course′, *Archit.* stringcourse.

belt·ed (bel′tid), *adj.* **1.** having or made with a belt: *a belted dress.* **2.** wearing or girded with a belt, esp. as a mark of distinction: *the belted lords and emissaries.* **3.** marked with a band of color different from that of the rest of the body: *a belted cow.* [1475–85; BELT + -ED[3]]

belt′ed-bi·as tire′ (bel′tid bī′əs), a motor-vehicle tire of the same construction as a bias-ply tire but with an added belt of steel or a strong synthetic material under the tread. Also called **bias-belted tire.** Cf. **belted tire, radial tire.** [1965–70]

belt′ed king′fisher, a grayish-blue, North American kingfisher, *Ceryle alcyon,* having a white breast marked with a grayish-blue band. See illus. under **kingfisher.** [1805–15, *Amer.*]

belt′ed sand′fish, a sea bass, *Serranus subligarius,* inhabiting warm, shallow waters of the western Atlantic Ocean.

belt′ed tire′, *Auto.* See under **belt** (def. 11).

Bel·te·shaz·zar (bel′tə shaz′ər), *n.* the Babylonian name given to Daniel. Dan. 1:7.

belt′ high′way, beltway. [1940–45]

belt·ing (bel′ting), *n.* **1.** material for belts. **2.** belts collectively. **3.** *Informal.* a beating or thrashing. **4.** *Obs.* belt. [1560–70; BELT + -ING[1]]

belt′ line′, **1.** a transportation system partially or wholly surrounding a city, terminal, district, or port. **2.** (in automotive styling) a horizontal boundary dividing the upper and lower parts of a car body, either an actual line of trim or an imaginary line that follows contours of the body. [1890–95, *Amer.*]

belt·line (belt′līn′), *n.* the waistline. [BELT + LINE[1]]

belt·man (belt′mən, -man′), *n., pl.* **-men** (-mən, -men′). **1.** a worker responsible for the inspection, maintenance, and repair of machine belts. **2.** *Australian.* lifeguard. [BELT + MAN[1]]

Belt′ Moun′tains. See **Big Belt Mountains, Little Belt Mountains.**

Bel·ton (bel′tn), *n.* **1.** a town in W Missouri. 12,708. **2.** a town in central Texas. 10,660.

Bel·tra·mi (bel trä′mē; *It.* bel tʀä′mē), *n.* **E·u·ge·nio** (e′o͞o je′nyô), 1835–1900, Italian mathematician.

belt′ sand′er, a sander that uses an endless abrasive belt driven by an electric motor. Cf. **disk sander, orbital sander.**

Belts·ville (belts′vil), *n.* **1.** a town in central Maryland, near Washington, D.C. 12,760. **2.** See **Beltsville small white.**

Belts′ville small′ white′, a small domestic turkey developed by the U.S. Department of Agriculture to fit small ovens when being cooked. Also called **Beltsville.** [1965–70; after *Beltsville,* Md., location of a Department of Agriculture research station where the bird was developed]

Bel·tsy (bel′tsē; *Russ.* byel′tsi), *n.* a city in the NW Moldavian SSR, in the W Soviet Union in Europe, SW of Kiev. 125,000.

belt-tight·en·ing (belt′tīt′n ing), *n.* a curtailment in spending; period of economizing: *The mayor ordered a belt-tightening for all city offices.* [1935–40]

belt·way (belt′wā′), *n.* a highway around the perimeter of an urban area. Also called **belt highway.** [1950–55; BELT + WAY]

be·lu·ga (bə lo͞o′gə), *n.* **1.** Also called **hausen.** a white sturgeon, *Huso huso,* of the Black and Caspian seas, valued as a source of caviar and isinglass. **2.** Also called **white whale.** a cetacean, *Delphinapterus leucas,* of northern seas, that has a rounded head and is white when adult. [1585–95; < Russ *belúga* (now regularly *belúkha* for the cetacean), equiv. to *bél(yĭ)* white + *-uga,* prob. earlier *-ǫga* (cf. Czech *pstruh,* Pol *pstrąg* trout < **pĭstr-* mottled + *-ǫgŭ* a cognate suffix)]

bel·ve·dere (bel′vi dēr′, bel′vi dēr′; *for 3 also It.* bel′ve de′ʀe), *n.* **1.** a building, or architectural feature of a building, designed and situated to look out upon a pleasing scene. **2.** a cigar, shorter and with thinner ends than a corona. **3.** (*cap.*) a palace in Vatican City, Rome, used as an art gallery. [1590–1600; < It: fine view < L *bellus* fine + *vidēre* to see]

Bel·vi·dere (bel′vi dēr′), *n.* a city in N Illinois. 15,176.

Be·ly (bye′lē), *n.* **An·drei** (un dʀyā′), (*Boris Nikolayevich Bugayev*), 1880–1934, Russian writer.

BEM (*sometimes* bem), (in esp. pulp science fiction) bug-eyed monster: an extraterrestrial being, esp. one having a grotesque appearance. [1955–60]

B.E.M., **1.** Bachelor of Engineering of Mines. **2.** British Empire Medal.

be·ma (bē′mə), *n., pl.* **-ma·ta** (-mə tə), **-mas.** **1.** *Eastern Ch.* the enclosed space surrounding the altar; the sanctuary or chancel. **2.** (in a Christian basilica) an open space between the end of the nave arcade and the apse. **3.** bimah. **4.** a platform for public speaking. [1675–85; < Gk *bêma* step, platform, equiv. to *bē-* (verbid s. of *baínein* to step, go; see COME) + *-ma* (n. suffix denoting result of action)]

be·maul (bi môl′), *v.t.* to maul severely. [1610–20; BE- + MAUL]

be·mazed (bi māzd′), *adj. Archaic.* muddled; confused; dazed. [1175–1225; ME *bemazen.* See BE-, MAZE, -ED[2]]

Bem·ba (bem′bə), *n., pl.* **-bas,** (*esp. collectively*) **-ba.** for 1. **1.** a member of a numerous agricultural people of Zambia. **2.** the Bantu language spoken by the Bemba, widely used as a lingua franca in Zambia. [1935–40]

be·mean (bi mēn′), *v.t.,* **-meaned, -mean·ing.** *Archaic.* to make mean; demean; debase (usually used reflexively). [1645–55; BE- + MEAN[2]]

be·med·aled (bi med′ld), *adj.* wearing or adorned with many medals: *a bemedaled general; wearing a bemedaled military blouse.* Also, *esp. Brit.,* **be·med′alled.** [1875–80; BE- + MEDAL + -ED[2]]

Be·mel·mans (bē′məl mənz, bem′əl-), *n.* **Lud·wig** (lud′wig, lo͝od′-), 1898–1962, U.S. humorous satirist and painter; born in Austria: author and illustrator of children's books.

Be·mid·ji (bə mij′ē), *n.* a town in central Minnesota. 10,949.

be·mire (bi mīᵊr′), *v.t.,* **-mired, -mir·ing.** **1.** to soil with mire; dirty or muddy: *bemired clothing.* **2.** to cause (an object or person) to sink in mire: *a bemired wagon.* [1525–35; BE- + MIRE] —**be·mire′ment,** *n.*

be·moan (bi mōn′), *v.t.* **1.** to express distress or grief over; lament: *to bemoan one's fate.* **2.** to regard with regret or disapproval. [bef. 1000; BE- + MOAN; r. *bemene,* ME *bimenen,* OE *bimǣnan* (*bi-* BE- + *mǣnan* to moan)] —**be·moan′ing·ly,** *adv.*

be·mock (bi mok′), *v.t.* to mock or jeer at (something or someone): *to bemock a trusting heart.* [1600–10; BE- + MOCK]

be·mud·dle (bi mud′l), *v.t.,* **-dled, -dling.** to muddle or confuse (someone). [1860–65; BE- + MUDDLE]

be·muse (bi myo͞oz′), *v.t.,* **-mused, -mus·ing.** to bewilder or confuse (someone). [1695–1705; BE- + MUSE] —**be·muse′ment,** *n.*

be·mused (bi myo͞ozd′), *adj.* **1.** bewildered or confused. **2.** lost in thought; preoccupied. [1695–1705; BEMUSE + -ED[2]] —**be·mus·ed·ly** (bi myo͞o′zid lē), *adv.*

ben[1] (ben), *Scot.* —*n.* **1.** the inner or back room of a two-room cottage, esp. when used as a combined parlor and bedroom. —*adv., prep.* **2.** within; inside. —*adj.* **3.** inside; inner. [1400–50; late ME (Scots); as adv., unexplained var. of late ME *bin,* ME *binne,* OE *binnan* (c. OFris *binna,* MD, G *binnen*), equiv. to *bi-* BE- + *innan* within (cf. IN)]

ben[2] (ben), *n.* the seed of a tropical tree, *Moringa pterygosperma,* that yields an oil **(ben oil)** used in manufacturing cosmetics and lubricating delicate machinery. Cf. **horseradish tree.** [1550–60; < Ar *bān*]

ben[3] (ben), *n. Scot., Irish.* a mountain peak; high hill: *Ben Nevis.* [1780–90; < ScotGael, Ir *beann* peak]

ben[4] (ben), *n.* (*often cap.*) son of (used esp. in Hebrew and Arabic names): *Moses ben Maimon.*

Ben (ben), *n.* a male given name, form of **Benjamin.**

Ben·a·dryl (ben′ə dril), *Pharm., Trademark.* a brand of diphenhydramine.

be·name (bi nām′), *v.t.,* **-named; -named, -nempt,** or **-nempt·ed; -nam·ing.** *Obs.* to name; call by name. [bef. 1000; ME; see BE-, NAME; r. OE *benemnan;* akin to G *benennen,* Sw *benämna*]

Be·na·res (bə när′is, -ēz), *n.* a former name of **Varanasi.**

Be·na·ven·te y Mar·tí·nez (be′nä ven′te ē mär tē′neth), **Ja·cin·to** (hä thēn′tô), (*Jacinto Benavente y Martínez*), 1866–1954, Spanish dramatist: Nobel prize 1922.

Ben Bel·la (ben bel′lä, bel′ə), **Ah·med** (ä′med), born 1916, Algerian statesman: premier 1962–65; president 1963–65.

Ben·bow (ben′bō′), *n.* **John,** 1653–1702, English admiral.

Ben·brook (ben′bro͝ok′), *n.* a town in N Texas. 13,579.

bench (bench), *n.* **1.** a long seat for several persons: *a bench in the park.* **2.** a seat occupied by an official, esp. a judge. **3.** such a seat as a symbol of the office and dignity of an individual judge or the judiciary. **4.** the office or dignity of various other officials, or the officials themselves. **5.** *Sports.* **a.** the seat on which the players of a team sit during a game while not playing. **b.** the quality and number of the players of a team who are usually used as substitutes: *A weak bench hurt their chances for the championship.* **6.** *Informal.* See **bench press.** **7.** Also called **workbench.** the strong worktable of a carpenter or other mechanic. **8.** a platform on which animals are placed for exhibition, esp. at a dog show. **9.** a contest or exhibition of dogs; dog show. **10.** *Phys. Geog.* a shelflike area of rock with steep slopes above and below. **11.** *Mining.* a step or working elevation in a mine. **12.** berm (def. 2). **13. on the bench, a.** serving as a judge in a court of law; presiding. **b.** *Sports.* (of a player) not participating in play, either for part or all of a game. —*v.t.* **14.** to furnish with benches. **15.** to seat on a bench or on the bench: *an election that benched him in the district court.* **16.** to place (a show dog or other animal) in exhibition. **17.** to cut away the working faces of (a mine or quarry) in benches. **18.** *Sports.* to remove from a game or keep from participating in a game: *to be benched because of poor hitting.* [bef. 1000; ME, OE *benc;* c. OFris *benk,* OS, D, OHG *bank,* ON *bekkr* < Gmc *bank-i-; see BANK[1]] —**bench′less,** *adj.*

bench′ check′, a test made on an engine or other machine or device in a workshop rather than under field conditions. Also called **bench test.**

bench′ dog′, a dog on exhibit at a dog show before and after competition in the show ring.

bench·er (ben′chər), *n.* **1.** (in England) **a.** a senior member of an Inn of Court. **b.** a member of the House of Commons. **2.** a person who handles an oar; rower. [1525–35; BENCH + -ER[1]]

bench′ hook′, *Carpentry.* a device with a hooklike part fitting over the front edge of a workbench as a means of preventing an object from slipping toward the rear of the bench. [1815–25]

bench′ing i′ron, *Survey.* a triangular, pronged plate driven into the ground to provide a temporary bench mark or turning point.

bench′ jock′ey, *Chiefly Baseball.* a vociferous player, coach, or manager who makes a specialty of baiting or harassing the umpires or opposing players, usually from the bench. [1935–40]

Bench·ley (bench′lē), *n.* **Robert (Charles),** 1889–1945, U.S. humorist, drama critic, and actor.

bench-made (bench′mād′), *adj.* (of articles made of leather, wood, etc.) individually produced and finished, as on a carpenter's bench; custom-made.

bench·man (bench′mən), *n., pl.* **-men.** a person whose job requires sitting at a workbench: *The TV repair shop employs five benchmen.* [1900–05; BENCH + -MAN]

bench′ mark′, **1.** *Survey.* a marked point of known or assumed elevation from which other elevations may be established. *Abbr.:* BM **2.** benchmark. [1835–45]

bench·mark (bench′märk′), *n.* **1.** a standard of excellence, achievement, etc., against which similar things must be measured or judged: *The new hotel is a benchmark in opulence and comfort.* **2.** any standard or reference by which others can be measured or judged: *The current price for crude oil may become the benchmark.* **3.** *Computers.* an established point of reference against which computers or programs can be measured in tests comparing their performance, reliability, etc. —*adj.* **4.** of, pertaining to, or resulting in a benchmark: *benchmark test, benchmark study.* Also **bench mark.** [1835–45; BENCH + MARK[1]]

bench′ press′, **1.** a weightlifting exercise in which one lies supine on a bench and with both hands pushes a barbell or fixed weight upward from chest level to arm's length and then lowers it back to chest level: usually repeated in sets. **2.** one complete repetition of this exercise. **3.** this exercise as an event in weightlifting competition. [1975–80]

bench-press (bench′pres′), *v.t., v.i.* to perform a bench press with (a weight): *He is small but can bench-press more than 400 pounds.*

bench·rest (bench′rest′), *n.* a tablelike support for a target rifle used in target practice. [BENCH + REST[1]]

bench′ screw′, *Carpentry.* a wooden or metal screw rotated by a handle fixed to one end within a threaded block fixed to a workbench: used with various jaws to form a vise. [1815–25]

bench′ show′, a dog show in which the animals of each breed are judged and awarded prizes on the basis of standards established for that breed. [1870–75, *Amer.*]

bench′ stop′, *Carpentry.* a metal device set flush with the top of a workbench and having a portion able to be raised to stop longitudinal movement of an object placed against it. [1880–85]

bench′ ta′ble, *Archit.* a course of masonry forming a bench at the foot of a wall. [1665–75]

bench′ test′. See **bench check.**

bench·warm·er (bench′wôr′mər), *n. Sports.* a substitute who rarely gets to play in a game. Also, **bench′ warm′er, bench′-warm′er.** [1890–95; BENCH + WARMER]

bench′ war′rant, *Law.* a warrant issued or ordered by a judge or court for the apprehension of an offender. [1690–1700]

bench′ work′, work done at a workbench, worktable, etc., as in a factory or laboratory.

bend[1] (bend), *v.,* **bent** or (*Archaic*) **bend·ed; bend·ing,** *n.* —*v.t.* **1.** to force (an object, esp. a long or thin one) from a straight form into a curved or angular one, or from a curved or angular form into some different form: *to bend an iron rod into a hoop.* **2.** to direct or turn in a particular direction: *to bend one's energies to the task.* **3.** to cause to submit or yield: *to bend someone to one's will.* **4.** to modify or relax (restrictions, regulations, etc.) temporarily or in certain circumstances: *to bend the rules.* **5.** to incline mentally (usually fol. by *to* or *toward*): *bending his thoughts back toward his childhood.* **6.** to pull back the string of (a bow or the like) in preparation for shooting. **7.** *Naut.* to fasten. **8.** *Archaic.* to strain or brace tensely (often fol. by *up*). —*v.i.* **9.** to become curved, crooked, or bent: *a bow that bends easily.* **10.** to assume a bent posture; stoop (often fol. by *over*): *to bend as one walks; to bend over and pick up something.* **11.** to turn or incline in a particular direction; be directed: *The road bent toward the south.* **12.** to yield or submit; give in. **13.** to bow in submission or reverence: *bending to one's monarch.* **14.** to direct one's energies: *We bent to our work as the bell sounded.* **15. bend** or **lean** or **fall over backward,** to exert oneself to the utmost; make a serious effort: *They bent over backward to make sure their guests were comfortable.* —*n.* **16.** the act of bending. **17.** something that bends; curve; crook: *a bend in the road; a bend in the curtain rod.* **18.** *Naut.* any of various loops or knots for joining the ends of two ropes or the like, or for joining the end of a rope or the like to some other object. **19. bends,** *Naut.* **a.** thick planking immediately below the waterways of a wooden vessel. **b.** the wales of a vessel. **20. the bends,** aeroembolism (def. 2). **21. around** or **round the bend,** *Slang.* insane; crazy: *These interruptions will send me round the bend!* [bef. 1000; ME *benden* (v.) OE *bendan* to bind, bend (a bow); c. MHG *benden,* ON *benda;* akin to ON *band* band. See BAND[3]] —**bend′a·ble,** *adj.*
—**Syn. 1.** curve, crook, flex, bow. **3.** mold, subdue, influence. **10.** BEND, BOW, STOOP imply taking a bent posture. BEND and BOW are used of the head and upper body; STOOP is used of the body only.

bend[2] (bend), *n.* **1.** *Heraldry.* **a.** a diagonal band extending from the dexter chief of an escutcheon to the sinister base. Cf. **bend sinister. b. in bend,** (of a charge) set diagonally or in a diagonal row. **2.** *Tanning.* half of a trimmed butt or hide. See diag. under **hide.** [bef. 1000; ME: coalescence of OE *bend* band (see BAND[3]) and MF *bende* BAND[2]]

Bend (bend), *n.* a city in central Oregon. 17,263.

Ben′ Day′ proc′ess (ben′ dā′), *Photoengraving.* a technique for producing shading, texture, or tone in line drawings and photographs by overlaying a fine screen or a pattern of dots on the original artwork, on a negative of it, or on the plate before etching. Also, **Ben′day′ proc′ess.** [1910–15; named after *Ben(jamin) Day* (1838–1916), American printer]

bend′ dex′ter, *Heraldry.* the ordinary bend, extending from the dexter chief to the sinister base. [1615–25]

Ben·dec·tin (ben dek′tin), *Pharm., Trademark.* a brand name for a preparation containing the antihistamine doxylamine succinate and a vitamin supplement, formerly prescribed as an antiemetic and antinauseant in the treatment of morning sickness: suspected of causing birth defects and removed from the market.

bend·ed (ben′did), *v. Archaic.* pt. and pp. of **bend.**

bend·er (ben′dər), *n.* **1.** a person or thing that bends, as a pair of pliers or a powered machine. **2.** *Slang.* a drinking spree. **3.** *Baseball Slang.* curve (def. 6a). [1200–50; ME (in surnames); see BEND[1], -ER[1]]

bend·er·board (ben′dər bôrd′, -bōrd′), *n.* pliable, lightweight board used for making concrete patios, in gardens, and as woven fencing: often 4 to 6 in. (10 to 15 cm) wide and ¼ to ½ in. (0.6 to 1.2 cm) thick and made from California redwood. [BENDER + BOARD]

Ben·de·ry (ben der′ē; *Russ.* byin dye′RI), *n.* a city in the E central Moldavia (Moldova), SE of Kishinev. 101,000.

Ben·di·go (ben′di gō′), *n.* a city in central Victoria in SE Australia: gold mining. 52,741.

bend′ing mo′ment, *Physics.* the algebraic sum of the moments about the neutral axis of any cross section of a beam. [1855–60]

bend′ sin′ister, *n. Heraldry.* a diagonal band extending from the sinister chief of an escutcheon to the dexter base: a supposed mark of bastardy. [1615–25]

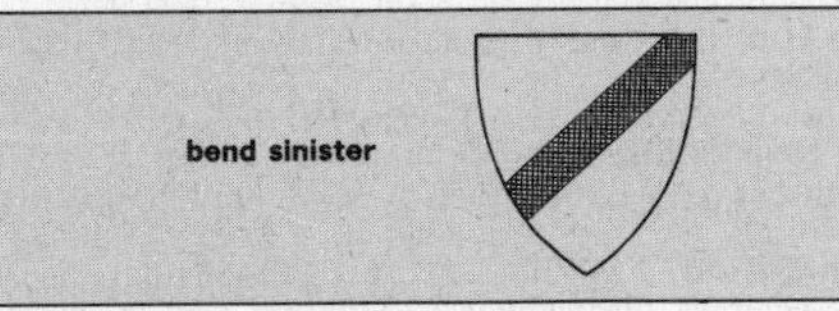
bend sinister

bend·y (ben′dē), *adj.,* **bend·i·er, bend·i·est.** tending to bend; flexible or resilient. [1975–80; BEND[1] + -Y[1]]

bene-, a combining form occurring in loanwords from Latin, where it meant "well": *benediction.* [comb. form of *bene* (adv.) well (< **dwenē*), akin to *bonus* good (< **dwenos*)]

be·neath (bi nēth′, -nēth′), *adv.* **1.** below; in or to a lower place, position, state, or the like. **2.** underneath: *heaven above and the earth beneath.* —*prep.* **3.** below; under: *beneath the same roof.* **4.** farther down than; underneath; lower in place than: *The first drawer beneath the top one.* **5.** lower down on a slope than: *beneath the crest of a hill.* **6.** inferior or less important, as in position, rank, or power: *A captain is beneath a major.* **7.** unworthy of; below the level or dignity of: *to regard others as beneath one; behavior that was beneath contempt.* [bef. 900; ME *benethe,* OE *beneothan,* equiv. to *be-* BE- + *neothan* below, akin to OHG *nidana.* See NETHER]
—**Syn. 3.** See **below.** —**Ant. 1.** above.

Be·ne·ba (bä′nə bä′), *n.* a female day name for Tuesday. See under **day name.**

Ben·e·dic·i·te (ben′i dis′i tē), *n. Eccles.* the canticle beginning in Latin *Benedicite, omnia opera Domini,* and in English "O all ye works of the Lord." [1150–1200; ME < L, impv. 2nd person pl. of *benedīcere* (*bene* BENE- + *dīcere* to speak)]

Ben·e·dick (ben′i dik), *n.* **1.** (in Shakespeare's *Much Ado About Nothing*) the confident bachelor who courts and finally marries Beatrice. **2.** (*l.c.*) benedict.

ben·e·dict (ben′i dikt), *n.* a newly married man, esp. one who has been long a bachelor. [1820–25; erroneous assimilation of BENEDICK to a more familiar name]

Ben·e·dict (ben′i dikt), *n.* **1. Ruth (Fulton),** 1887–1948, U.S. writer and anthropologist. **2. Saint,** A.D. 480?–543?, Italian monk: founded Benedictine order. **3. Stanley Ros·si·ter** (ros′i tər), 1884–1936, U.S. biochemist. **4.** a male given name: from a Latin word meaning "blessed."

Benedict I, died A.D. 579, pope 575–79.

Benedict II, Saint, died A.D. 685, pope 684–85.

Benedict III, died A.D. 858, pope 855–58.

Benedict IV, died A.D. 903, pope 900–03.

Benedict V, died A.D. 966, pope 964.

Benedict VI, died A.D. 974, pope 973–74.

Benedict VII, died A.D. 983, pope 974–83.

Benedict VIII, died 1024, pope 1012–24.

Benedict IX, died 1056?, pope 1032–44; 1045; 1047–48.

Benedict XI, (*Niccolò Boccasini*) 1240–1304, Italian ecclesiastic: pope 1303–04.

Benedict XII, (*Jacques Fournier*) died 1342, French ecclesiastic: pope 1334–42.

Benedict XIII, (*Pietro Francesco Orsini*) 1649–1730, Italian ecclesiastic: pope 1724–30.

Benedict XIV, (*Prospero Lambertini*) 1675–1758, Italian ecclesiastic: pope 1740–58; scholar and patron of the arts.

Benedict XV, (*Giacomo della Chiesa*) 1854–1922, Italian ecclesiastic: pope 1914–22.

Ben·e·dic·tine (ben′i dik′tin, -tēn, -tīn *for 1, 3;* ben′i-dik′tēn *for 2*), *n.* **1.** *Rom. Cath. Ch.* **a.** a member of an order of monks founded at Monte Cassino by St. Benedict about A.D. 530. **b.** a member of any congregation of nuns following the rule of St. Benedict. **2.** a French liqueur originally made by Benedictine monks. —*adj.* **3.** of or pertaining to St. Benedict or the Benedictines. [1620–30; St. BENEDICT + -INE[1]]

ben·e·dic·tion (ben′i dik′shən), *n.* **1.** an utterance of good wishes. **2.** the form of blessing pronounced by an officiating minister, as at the close of divine service. **3.** a ceremony by which things are set aside for sacred uses, as a church, vestments, or bells. **4.** (*usually cap.*) Also called **Benedic′tion of the Bless′ed Sac′rament.** a service consisting of prayers, at least one prescribed hymn, censing of the congregation and the Host, and a blessing of the congregation by moving in the form of a cross the ciborium or monstrance containing the Host. **5.** the advantage conferred by blessing; a mercy or benefit. [1400–50; late ME (< MF) < L *benedictiōn-* (s. of *benedictiō*). See BENEDICTUS, -ION]

ben·e·dic·tion·al (ben′i dik′shə nl), *adj.* **1.** of or pertaining to benediction. —*n.* **2.** Also, **ben·e·dic·tion·a·le** (ben′i dik′shə nä′lē). a book of benedictions. [1835–45; BENEDICTION + -AL[1]]

ben·e·dic·to·ry (ben′i dik′tə rē), *adj.* of, giving, or expressing benediction. [1700–10; < ML *benedictōrius*]

Ben′edict's solu′tion, *Pharm.* a reagent solution containing cupric sulfate, sodium citrate, and sodium carbonate and used to detect glucose in the urine. [named after S. R. BENEDICT]

Ben·e·dic·tus (ben′i dik′təs), *n. Eccles.* **1.** the short canticle or hymn beginning in Latin *Benedictus qui venit in nomine Domini,* and in English "Blessed is he that cometh in the name of the Lord." **2.** the canticle or hymn beginning in Latin *Benedictus Dominus Deus Israel,* and in English "Blessed be the Lord God of Israel." **3.** a musical setting of a Benedictus. [< L: blessed (ptp. of *benedīcere* to commend, bless). See BENE-, DICTUM]

benef., beneficiary.

ben·e·fac·tion (ben′ə fak′shən, ben′ə fak′-), *n.* **1.** an act of conferring a benefit; the doing of good; a good deed: *He is known throughout the region for his many benefactions.* **2.** the benefit conferred; charitable donation: *to solicit benefactions for earthquake victims.* [1655–65; < LL *benefactiōn-* (s. of *benefactiō*), equiv. to L *bene* BENE- + *fact(us)* done (see FACT) + *-iōn-* -ION]

ben·e·fac·tive (ben′ə fak′tiv), *Ling.* —*adj.* **1.** of or pertaining to a linguistic form, case, or semantic role that denotes the person or persons for whom an action is performed, as *for his son* in *He opened the door for his son.* —*n.* **2.** a benefactive form or case. [1940–45; < L *benefact(um)* benefit, good deed (n. use of neut. of *benefactus;* see BENEFACTION) + -IVE]

ben·e·fac·tor (ben′ə fak′tər, ben′ə fak′-), *n.* **1.** a person who confers a benefit; kindly helper. **2.** a person who makes a bequest or endowment, as to an institution. [1425–75; late ME *benefactour* < LL; see BENE-, FACTOR]
—**Syn. 2.** patron, supporter, sponsor, backer, protector.

ben·e·fac·tress (ben′ə fak′tris, ben′ə fak′-), *n.* a woman who confers a benefit, bequest, endowment, or the like. Also, **benefactrix.** [1425–75; late ME *benefactrice;* see BENEFACTOR, -ESS]
—**Usage.** See **-ess.**

ben·e·fac·trix (ben′ə fak′triks, ben′ə fak′-), *n., pl.* **ben·e·fac·trix·es** (ben′ə fak′trik siz, ben′ə fak′-), **ben·e·fac·tri·ces** (ben′ə fak′trə sēz′, -fak tri′sēz). benefactress. [BENEFAC(TOR) + -TRIX]
—**Usage.** See **-trix.**

be·nef·ic (bə nef′ik), *adj.* doing or promoting some good; beneficent: *a benefic truce; a benefic confluence of planets.* [1590–1600; < L *beneficus.* See BENE-, -FIC]

ben·e·fice (ben′ə fis), *n., v.,* **-ficed, -fic·ing.** —*n.* **1.** a position or post granted to an ecclesiastic that guarantees a fixed amount of property or income. **2.** the revenue itself. **3.** the equivalent of a fief in the early Middle

Ages. —*v.t.* **4.** to invest with a benefice or ecclesiastical living. [1300–50; ME < MF < L *beneficium* service, kindness (*benefic(us)* BENEFIC + *-ium* -IUM)]

be·nef·i·cence (bə nef′ə səns), *n.* **1.** the doing of good; active goodness or kindness; charity. **2.** a beneficent act or gift; benefaction. [1425–75; late ME < L *beneficentia;* see BENEFIC, -ENCE]

be·nef·i·cent (bə nef′ə sənt), *adj.* doing good or causing good to be done; conferring benefits; kindly in action or purpose. [1610–20; BENEFIC(ENCE) + -ENT] —**be·nef′i·cent·ly,** *adv.*

ben·e·fi·cial (ben′ə fish′əl), *adj.* **1.** conferring benefit; advantageous; helpful: *the beneficial effect of sunshine.* **2.** *Law.* **a.** helpful in the meeting of needs: *a beneficial association.* **b.** involving the personal enjoyment of proceeds: *a beneficial owner.* [1425–75; late ME < LL *beneficiālis,* equiv. to L *benefici(um)* kindness (see BENEFICE) + *-ālis* -AL[1]] —**ben′e·fi′cial·ly,** *adv.* —**ben′e·fi′cial·ness,** *n.*
—**Syn. 1.** salutary, wholesome, serviceable, useful, favorable, profitable. —**Ant. 1.** harmful.

ben·e·fi·ci·ar·y (ben′ə fish′ē er′ē, -fish′ə rē), *n., pl.* **-ar·ies. 1.** a person or group that receives benefits, profits, or advantages. **2.** a person designated as the recipient of funds or other property under a will, trust, insurance policy, etc. **3.** *Eccles.* the holder of a benefice. [1605–15; < L *beneficiārius,* equiv. to *benefici(um)* BENEFICE + *-ārius* -ARY]

ben·e·fi·ci·ate (ben′ə fish′ē āt′), *v.t.,* **-at·ed, -at·ing.** *Metall.* to treat (ore) to make more suitable for smelting. [1870–75, *Amer.;* < Sp *benefici(ar)* to benefit, profit from (especially mining or farming) (v. deriv. of *beneficio* < L *beneficium;* see BENEFICE) + -ATE[1]] —**ben′e·fi′ci·a′tion,** *n.*

ben·e·fit (ben′ə fit), *n., v.,* **-fit·ed, -fit·ing.** —*n.* **1.** something that is advantageous or good; an advantage: *He explained the benefits of public ownership of the postal system.* **2.** a payment or gift, as one made to help someone or given by a benefit society, insurance company, or public agency: *The company offers its employees a pension plan, free health insurance, and other benefits.* **3.** a theatrical performance or other public entertainment to raise money for a charitable organization or cause. **4.** *Archaic.* an act of kindness; good deed; benefaction. **5. for someone's benefit,** so as to produce a desired effect in another's mind: *He wasn't really angry; that was just an act for his girlfriend's benefit.* —*v.t.* **6.** to do good to; be of service to: *a health program to benefit everyone.* —*v.i.* **7.** to derive benefit or advantage; profit; make improvement: *He has never benefited from all that experience.* [1350–1400; late ME *benefytt, benefett* (n.), alter. (with Latinized first syll.) of ME *b(i)enfet, benefait* < AF *benfet,* MF *bienfait* < L *benefactum* good deed; see BENE-, FACT] —**ben′e·fit·er,** *n.*
—**Syn. 1.** favor, service. See **advantage.**

ben′efit of cler′gy, 1. the rites or sanctions of a church. **2.** formal marriage: *living together without benefit of clergy.* **3.** the privilege claimed by church authorities to try and punish, by an ecclesiastical court, any member of the clergy accused of a serious crime. The privilege was abolished in the U.S. in 1790 and in England in 1827. [1480–90]

ben′efit of the doubt′, a favorable opinion or judgment adopted despite uncertainty. [1840–50]

ben′efit soci′ety, an association of persons to create a fund, either by dues or assessments, for the assistance of members and their families in case of sickness, death, etc. Also called **ben′efit associa′tion.** [1835–45]

Ben·e·lux (ben′l uks′), *n.* **1.** a customs union comprising Belgium, the Netherlands, and Luxembourg, begun January 1, 1948. **2.** Belgium, the Netherlands, and Luxembourg considered together.

Ben·e·mid (ben′ə mid), *Pharm., Trademark.* a brand name for probenecid.

be·nempt (bi nempt′), *v.* a pp. of **bename.** Also, **be·nempt′ed.**

Be·neš (be′nesh), *n.* **Ed·u·ard** (e′dŏŏ ärt′), 1884–1948, Czech patriot and statesman: president of Czechoslovakia 1935–38 and 1945–48.

Be·nét (bi nā′), *n.* **1. Stephen Vincent,** 1898–1943, U.S. poet and novelist. **2.** his brother **William Rose,** 1886–1950, U.S. poet and critic.

Be·ne·ven·to (ben′ə ven′tō; *It.* be′ne ven′tô), *n.* a city in N Campania, in S Italy: monumental arch erected by Trajan. 62,131.

be·nev·o·lence (bə nev′ə ləns), *n.* **1.** desire to do good to others; goodwill; charitableness: *to be filled with benevolence toward one's fellow creatures.* **2.** an act of kindness; a charitable gift. **3.** *Eng. Hist.* a forced contribution to the sovereign. [1350–1400; ME < L *benevolentia.* See BENEVOLENT, -ENCE]
—**Ant. 1.** malevolence.

be·nev·o·lent (bə nev′ə lənt), *adj.* **1.** characterized by or expressing goodwill or kindly feelings: *a benevolent attitude; her benevolent smile.* **2.** desiring to help others; charitable: *gifts from several benevolent alumni.* **3.** intended for benefits rather than profit: *a benevolent institution.* [1425–75; late ME < L *benevolent-* (s. of *benevolēns*) kindhearted (*bene-* BENE- + *vol-* wish (akin to WILL[1]) + *-ent-* -ENT)] —**be·nev′o·lent·ly,** *adv.* —**be·nev′o·lent·ness,** *n.*
—**Syn. 2.** good, kind, humane, generous, liberal, benign, philanthropic, altruistic. —**Ant.** cruel.

Benev′olent and Protec′tive Or′der of Elks′. See under **elk** (def. 4).

Beng., 1. Bengal. **2.** Bengali.

Ben·gal (ben gôl′, -gäl′, beng-; ben′gəl, beng′-), *n.* **1.** a former province in NE India, now divided between India and Bangladesh. Cf. **East Bengal, West Bengal. 2. Bay of,** a part of the Indian Ocean between India and Burma (Myanmar). **3.** a raw silk from Bengal. **4.** a fabric, esp. one made of silk and hair. **5.** a fabric, similar to muslin, with printed stripes.

Ben′gal cat′echu, catechu.

Ben·ga·lee (ben gô′lē, -gä′-, beng-), *n.* a native or inhabitant of Bangladesh. Also, **Bengali.**

Ben·ga·lese (ben′gə lēz′, -lēs′, beng′-), *adj., n., pl.* **-lese.** —*adj.* **1.** of or pertaining to Bengal. —*n.* **2.** a native or inhabitant of Bengal. [1770–80; BENGAL + -ESE]

Ben·ga·li (ben gô′lē, -gä′-, beng-), *n.* **1.** a native or an inhabitant of Bengal. **2.** an Indic language spoken in E India and Bangladesh. **3.** Bengalee. —*adj.* **4.** of or pertaining to Bengal, its inhabitants, or their language; Bengalese.

ben·ga·line (beng′gə lēn′, beng′gə lēn′), *n.* a poplinlike fabric having a crosswise corded effect, woven with coarse yarn in the filling direction. [1880–85; < F; see BENGAL, -INE[2]]

Ben′gal quince′, bael. [1865–70]

Ben′gal rose′. See **China rose** (def. 1).

Beng·bu (bœng′bY′), *n. Pinyin.* a city in N Anhui province, in E China. 400,000. Also, **Pangfou, Pengpu.**

Ben·gha·zi (ben gä′zē, beng-), *n.* a seaport in N Libya: former capital. 325,000. Also, **Ben·ga′si.**

B. Engr., Bachelor of Engineering.

Ben·guel·a (ben gel′ə, -gä′lə, beng-), *n.* a seaport in SW Angola. 50,000.

Benguel′a Cur′rent, a cold ocean current flowing N along the W coast of southern Africa.

Ben-Gu·rion (ben gŏŏr′ē ən; *Seph. Heb.* ben′gōō-RYôn′), *n.* **David,** 1886–1973, Israeli statesman, born in Poland: prime minister of Israel 1948–53, 1955–63.

Ben Hur (ben′ hûr′), a historical novel (1880) by Lew Wallace.

Be·ni (be′nē), *n.* a river flowing NE from W Bolivia to the Madeira River. ab. 600 mi. (965 km) long.

Be·ni·cia (bə nē′shə), *n.* a town in W California. 15,376.

be·night·ed (bi nī′tid), *adj.* **1.** intellectually or morally ignorant; unenlightened: *benighted ages of barbarism and superstition.* **2.** overtaken by darkness or night. [1565–75; *benight* (BE- + NIGHT) + -ED[2]] —**be·night′ed·ly,** *adv.* —**be·night′ed·ness,** *n.*
—**Syn. 1.** backward, primitive, crude, uncultivated.

be·nign (bi nīn′), *adj.* **1.** having a kindly disposition; gracious: *a benign king.* **2.** showing or expressive of gentleness or kindness: *a benign smile.* **3.** favorable; propitious: *a series of benign omens and configurations in the heavens.* **4.** (of weather) salubrious; healthful; pleasant or beneficial. **5.** *Pathol.* not malignant; self-limiting. [1275–1325; ME *benigne* < AF, OF *benigne* (fem.), *benin* (masc.) < L *benignus* kind, generous, equiv. to *beni-,* comb. form of *bonus* good (see BENE-) + *-gnus,* deriv. of the base of *gignere* to beget (see GENITOR, GENUS), hence, perh., "good by nature"; cf. MALIGN] —**be·nign′ly,** *adv.*
—**Syn. 1.** good, kindly, benignant, benevolent, tender, humane, gentle, compassionate. —**Ant. 3.** sinister.

be·nig·nant (bi nig′nənt), *adj.* **1.** kind, esp. to inferiors; gracious: *a benignant sovereign.* **2.** exerting a good influence; beneficial: *the benignant authority of the new president.* **3.** *Pathol.* benign. [1775–85; BENIGN + -ANT, modeled on MALIGNANT] —**be·nig·nan·cy** (bi nig′nən-sē), *n.* —**be·nig′nant·ly,** *adv.*
—**Syn. 1.** benevolent, benign, generous, charitable.

be·nig·ni·ty (bi nig′ni tē), *n., pl.* **-ties. 1.** the quality of being benign; kindness. **2.** *Archaic.* a good deed or favor; an instance of kindness: *benignities born of selfless devotion.* [1325–75; ME *benignite* < MF < L *benignitās.* See BENIGN, -ITY]

Be·ni Ha·san (ben′ē hä′sän), a village in central Egypt, on the Nile, N of Asyut: ancient cliff tombs.

Be·ni Mel·lal (ben′ē me läl′), a city in central Morocco. 130,000.

Be·nin (be nēn′), *n.* **1.** Formerly, **Dahomey.** a republic in W Africa: formerly part of French West Africa; gained independence in 1960. 3,197,000; 44,290 sq. mi. (114,711 sq. km). *Cap.:* Porto Novo. **2. Bight of,** a bay in N Gulf of Guinea in W Africa. **3.** a former native kingdom in W Africa: now incorporated into Nigeria. **4.** a river in S Nigeria, flowing into the Bight of Benin.

Benin′ Cit′y, a city in S Nigeria. 127,000.

Be·ni·nese (bə nē′nēz′, -ēs, ben′ə nēz′, -nēs′), *adj., n., pl.* **-nese.** —*adj.* **1.** of or pertaining to the republic of Benin. —*n.* **2.** a native or inhabitant of Benin. [BENIN + -ESE]

Ben′i·off zone′ (ben′ē ôf′, -of′), *Geol., Oceanog.* a planar seismic zone in oceanic crust along which subduction of lithospheric plates gives rise to frequent earthquakes: marked by oceanic trenches sloping downward at about 45° toward adjacent island arcs or continents. [after Hugo *Benioff* (1899–1968), U.S. geophysicist]

ben·i·son (ben′ə zən, -sən), *n.* benediction. [1250–1300; ME < AF *beneiçon,* MF *beneison* < L *benedictiōn-* BENEDICTION]

Be·ni-Suef (ben′ē swäf′), *n.* a city in NW Egypt on the Nile River. 107,100.

Be·ni·ta (bə nē′tə), *n.* a female given name.

be·ni·to·ite (bə nē′tō īt′), *n.* a rare mineral, barium titanium silicate, $BaTiSi_3O_9$, occurring in blue hexagonal crystals exhibiting dichroism. [1905–10; named after San *Benito* County, California; see -ITE[1]]

ben·ja·min (ben′jə mən), *n.* benzoin[1] (def. 2). [1570–80; alter. (by assoc. with the proper name) of *benjoin,* early form of BENZOIN[1]]

Ben·ja·min (ben′jə mən), *n.* **1.** the youngest son of Jacob and Rachel, and the brother of Joseph. Gen. 35:18. **2.** one of the 12 tribes of ancient Israel traditionally descended from him. **3. Asher,** 1773–1845, U.S. architect and writer. **4. Judah Philip,** 1811–84, Confederate statesman. **5.** a male given name: from a Hebrew word meaning "son of the right."

ben·ja·min-bush (ben′jə mən bŏŏsh′), *n.* spicebush. [1755–65]

Ben·ja·min-Con·stant (baN zhA mAN′ kôN stäN′), *n.* **Jean Jo·seph** (zhäN zhô zef′). See **Constant, Jean Joseph Benjamin.**

Ben·ja·min·ite (ben′jə mə nīt′), *n.* a member of the tribe of Benjamin. Also, **Ben·ja·mite** (ben′jə mīt′). [1605–15; BENJAMIN + -ITE[1]]

Ben Lo·mond (ben lō′mənd), a mountain in central Scotland, in Stirlingshire, on the E shore of Loch Lomond. 3192 ft. (975 m).

ben·ne (ben′ē), *n. Southern U.S., esp. South Carolina, and Bahamian English.* the sesame plant or its seeds. Also, **benny.** [1760–70, *Amer.;* < Wolof, Malinke *bene*]

ben·net (ben′it), *n.* See **herb bennet.** [1225–75; ME (*herbe*) *beneit* < OF (*herbe*) *beneite,* trans. of L (*herba*) *benedicta* blessed (herb) (> OE *benedicte,* OHG *benedicta,* MD *benedictus-kruid*). See BENEDICTUS]

Ben·nett (ben′it), *n.* **1. (Enoch) Arnold,** 1867–1931, English novelist. **2. Floyd,** 1890–1928, U.S. aviator. **3. James Gordon,** 1795–1872, U.S. journalist. **4. Richard Bedford,** 1870–1947, Canadian statesman: prime minister 1930–35. **5. Robert Russell,** 1894–1981, U.S. composer and conductor. **6. William A(ndrew) C(ecil),** 1900–79, Canadian political leader: premier of British Columbia 1952–72. **7.** Also, **Ben′net.** a male given name, form of **Benedict.**

Ben Ne·vis (ben nē′vis, nev′is), a mountain in NW Scotland, in the Grampians: highest peak in Great Britain. 4406 ft. (1345 m).

Ben·ning·ton (ben′ing tən), *n.* a town in SW Vermont: defeat of British by the Green Mountain Boys 1777. 15,815.

Ben·nu (ben′ōō), *n.* Benu.

ben·ny[1] (ben′ē), *n., pl.* **-nies.** *Slang.* **1.** Benzedrine, esp. in tablet form. **2.** any amphetamine tablet. [1950–55, *Amer.;* by alter. and shortening of BENZEDRINE; see -Y[2]]

ben·ny[2] (ben′ē), *n.* benne.

CONCISE ETYMOLOGY KEY: <, descended or borrowed from; >, whence; b., blend of, blended; c., cognate with; cf., compare; deriv., derivative; equiv., equivalent; imit., imitative; obl., oblique; r., replacing; s., stem; sp., spelling, spelled; resp., respelling, respelled; trans., translation; ?, origin unknown; *, unattested; ‡, probably earlier than. See the full key inside the front cover.

Ben•ny (ben′ē), *n.* **1. Jack** (*Benjamin Kubelsky*), 1894–1974, U.S. comedian. **2.** a male given name, form of **Benjamin.**

ben′ oil′. See under **ben**[2]. [1585–95]

Be•noît (bə nwa′), *n.* **Pierre** (pyer) (or **Peter**) **Lé•o•nard Lé•o•pold** (lā ô nar′ lā ô pôld′), 1834–1901, Belgian composer.

Be•noît de Sainte-Maure (bə nwad[a] sant môr′), fl. 12th century, French trouvère.

ben•o•myl (ben′ə mil), *n. Chem.* a toxic compound, $C_{14}H_{18}N_4O_3$, derived from carbamate and benzimidizole, used as a fungicide and miticide. [1965–70; BEN(Z)O- + M(ETH)YL]

Be•no•ni (bə nō′nī, -nē), *n.* a city in the NE of the Republic of South Africa, near Johannesburg: gold mines. 167,000.

Ben•sen•ville (ben′sən vil′), *n.* a town in NE Illinois. 16,124.

ben•su•lide (ben′sə līd′), *n.* a selective preemergence herbicide, $C_{14}H_{24}O_4NPS_3$, used primarily to control crabgrass and broadleaf weeds. [BEN(ZENE) + SUL(FON-AM)IDE]

bent[1] (bent), *adj.* **1.** curved; crooked: *a bent bow; a bent stick.* **2.** determined; set; resolved (usually fol. by *on*): *to be bent on buying a new car.* **3.** *Chiefly Brit. Slang.* **a.** morally crooked; corrupt. **b.** stolen: *bent merchandise.* **c.** homosexual. —*n.* **4.** direction taken, as by one's interests; inclination: *a bent for painting.* **5.** capacity of endurance: *to work at the top of one's bent.* **6.** *Civ. Eng.* a transverse frame, as of a bridge or an aqueduct, designed to support either vertical or horizontal loads. **7.** *Archaic.* bent state or form; curvature. [1525–35; orig. ptp. of BEND[1]]
—**Syn. 1.** bowed, flexed. **2.** fixed. **4.** tendency, propensity, proclivity, predilection, penchant, partiality, leaning, bias.

bent[2] (bent), *n.* **1.** See **bent grass. 2.** a stalk of bent grass. **3.** *Scot., Northern Eng.* (formerly) any stiff grass or sedge. **4.** *Brit. Dial.* a moor; heath; tract of uncultivated, grassy land, used as a pasture or hunting preserve. [1300–50; ME; earlier *benet-, bunet-* (in compounds), OE *beonet-, beonot-* (in place names); c. OHG *binuz* (cf. G *Binse*) rush]

bent′ grass′, any grass of the genus *Agrostis,* esp. the redtop. [1770–80]

Ben•tham (ben′thəm, -təm), *n.* **Jeremy,** 1748–1832, English jurist and philosopher.

Ben•tham•ism (ben′thə miz′əm, -tə-), *n.* the utilitarian philosophy of Jeremy Bentham. [1820–30; BENTHAM + -ISM] —**Ben•tham•ic** (ben tham′ik, -tam′-), *adj.* —**Ben•tham•ite** (ben′thə mīt′, -tə-), *n.*

ben•thic (ben′thik), *adj.* **1.** of or pertaining to a benthos. **2.** of or pertaining to a benthon. Also, **ben′thal, ben•thon•ic** (ben thon′ik). [BENTH(OS) + -IC]

ben•thon (ben′thon), *n.* the aggregate of organisms that live on or in the benthos. [BENTH(OS) + *-on,* extracted from PLANKTON]

ben•thos (ben′thos), *n.* the biogeographic region that includes the bottom of a lake, sea, or ocean, and the littoral and supralittoral zones of the shore. Also called **ben′thic divi′sion, benthon′ic zone′.** [1890–95; < Gk *bénthos* depth (of the sea); akin to BATHOS, BATHY-]

Ben•tinck (ben′tingk), *n.* **William Henry Cavendish, Duke of Portland,** 1738–1809, British statesman: prime minister 1783; 1807–09.

Bent•ley (bent′lē), *n.* **1. Eric (Russell),** born 1916, U.S. critic, editor, and translator; born in England. **2. Phyllis,** born 1894, English novelist. **3. Richard,** 1662–1742, English scholar and critic.

ben•to (ben′tō; *Japn.* ben′tô), *n., pl.* **-tos;** *Japn.* **-to.** *Japanese Cookery.* a meal, usually served in a lacquered or elaborately decorated box that is divided into sections for holding individual portions of food. Also called **obento.** [< Japn *bentō,* prob. < MChin, equiv. to Chin *biàn* manage, provide + *dāng* apply, i.e., provision for an eat-out meal]

Ben•ton (ben′tn), *n.* **1. Thomas Hart** (*"Old Bullion"*), 1782–1858, U.S. political leader. **2.** his grandnephew **Thomas Hart,** 1889–1975, U.S. painter and lithographer. **3.** a city in central Arkansas. 17,437.

Ben′ton Har′bor, a city in SW Michigan, on Lake Michigan. 14,707.

ben•ton•ite (ben′tn īt′), *n. Mineral.* a clay formed by the decomposition of volcanic ash, having the ability to absorb large quantities of water and to expand to several times its normal volume. [1895–1900; named after Fort *Benton,* Montana; see -ITE[1]] —**ben•ton•it•ic** (ben′tn it′ik), *adj.*

bent•wood (bent′wŏŏd′), *n.* **1.** wood steamed and bent for use in furniture. **2.** an article of furniture made of bentwood. —*adj.* **3.** of or pertaining to furniture made principally of pieces of wood of circular or oval section, steamed, bent, and screwed together: *a bentwood rocking chair.* [1860–65; BENT[1] + WOOD[1]]

Ben•u (ben′ōō), *n.* the sacred bird of ancient Egypt, corresponding to the phoenix. Also, **Bennu.** [vocalization of Egyptian *bnw* heron]

Be•nue (bā′nwā), *n.* a river in W Africa, flowing W from Cameroon to the Niger River in Nigeria. 870 mi. (1400 km).

Be•nue-Con•go (bā′nwā kong′gō), *n.* a branch of Niger-Congo that comprises a large number of languages, as Efik, Tiv, and the Bantu languages, spoken in central and southern Africa.

be•numb (bi num′), *v.t.* **1.** to make numb; deprive of sensation: *benumbed by cold.* **2.** to render inactive; deaden or stupefy. [1350–1400; back formation from ME *benomen,* ptp. of *benimen* to take away, OE *beniman;* c. D *benemen,* G *benehmen,* Goth *biniman.* See BE-, NIMBLE, NUMB] —**be•numbed•ness** (bi numd′nis, -num′id-), *n.* —**be•numb′ing•ly,** *adv.* —**be•numb′ment,** *n.*

Ben•xi (bœn′shē′), *n. Pinyin.* a city in E Liaoning province, in NE China. 750,000. Also, **Penchi, Penhsi, Penki.**

Ben Ye•hu•dah (ben′ yə hōō′də), **El•i•ez•er** (el′ē ez′ər), 1858–1922, Jewish scholar, born in Lithuania.

Benz (bents; *Eng.* benz), *n.* **Karl,** 1844–1929, German automotive engineer and manufacturer.

benz-, var. of **benzo-** before a vowel: *benzaldehyde.*

ben•zal (ben′zal), *Chem.* —*adj.* **1.** containing the benzal group. —*n.* **2.** the benzal group. Also, **benzylidene.** [BENZ- + -AL[3]]

ben•zal•ac•e•tone (ben′zal as′i tōn′), *n. Chem.* See **benzylidene acetone.** [BENZAL + ACETONE]

ben′zal chlo′ride, *Chem.* a colorless, oily liquid, $C_7H_6Cl_2$, used chiefly in the synthesis of benzaldehyde, and in the manufacture of dyes. Also called **benzyl dichloride, benzylidene chloride.** [1875–80]

benz•al•de•hyde (ben zal′də hīd′), *n. Chem.* a colorless or yellowish, water-soluble, volatile oil, C_7H_6O, having a bitter, almondlike odor, used chiefly in the organic synthesis of dyes, perfumes, and flavors, and as a solvent; artificial oil of bitter almond. Also called **benzoic aldehyde.** [1865–70; < G; see BENZ-, ALDEHYDE]

ben′zal group′, *Chem.* the bivalent group C_7H_6–, derived from benzaldehyde. Also called **ben′zal rad′i•cal.**

ben•zal•ko′ni•um chlo′ride (ben′zal kō′nē əm), *Chem.* a white or yellowish-white, water-soluble mixture of ammonium chloride derivatives having the structure $C_6H_{10}NRCl$, where R is a mixture of radicals ranging from C_8H_{17}– to $C_{18}H_{37}$–, that occurs as an amorphous powder or in gelatinous lumps: used chiefly as an antiseptic and a disinfectant. [BENZ- + ALK(YL) + (AMM)ONIUM]

ben•za•mine (ben′zə mēn′), *n. Pharm.* eucaine. [BENZ- + AMINE]

benz•an•thra•cene (ben zan′thrə sēn′), *n. Chem.* a carcinogenic aromatic hydrocarbon, $C_{18}H_{12}$, consisting of four fused benzene rings, produced by incomplete combustion of organic matter. [1935–40; BENZ- + ANTHRACENE]

Ben•ze•drine (ben′zi drēn′, -drin), *Pharm., Trademark.* a brand of amphetamine.

ben•zene (ben′zēn, ben zēn′), *n. Chem.* a colorless, volatile, flammable, toxic, slightly water-soluble, liquid, aromatic compound, C_6H_6, obtained chiefly from coal tar: used in the manufacture of commercial and medicinal chemicals, dyes, and as a solvent for resins, fats, or the like. [1825–35; BENZ(OIC ACID) + -ENE]

ben•zene•az•o•ben•zene (ben′zēn az′ō ben′zēn, ben zēn′az ō ben zēn′), *n. Chem.* azobenzene. [BENZENE + AZOBENZENE]

ben′zene•car•box•yl′ic ac′id (ben′zēn kär′bok-sil′ik, ben zēn′kär-), *Chem., Pharm.* See **benzoic acid.** [BENZENE + CARBOXYLIC ACID]

ben′zene hexachlo′ride, *Chem.* See **BHC.** [1880–85]

ben′zene ring′, *Chem.* the graphic representation of the structure of benzene as a hexagon with a carbon atom at each of its points. Each carbon atom is united with an atom of hydrogen, one or more of which may be replaced to form benzene derivatives. Also called **ben′zene nu′cleus.** Cf. **cyclohexane, Kekulé's formula, meta**[2]**, ortho, para**[3]. [1875–80]

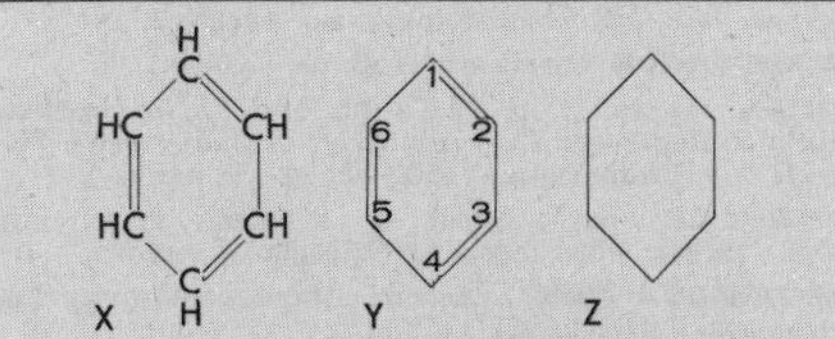

benzene ring (Kekulé's formula)
X, graphic representation; Y, positions numbered for replacement of one or more hydrogen atoms, leading to benzene derivatives; Z, used when cyclohexane is not indicated. Double bonds are assumed

ben′zene se′ries, *Chem.* a series of aromatic hydrocarbons derived from benzene by replacing one or more of the hydrogen atoms with one or more methyl groups. The first three members are benzene, toluene, and xylene.

ben′zene•sul•fon′ic ac′id (ben′zēn sul fon′ik, ben-zēn′-), *Chem.* a fine, needlelike substance, $C_6H_6SO_3$, used chiefly as a catalyst and in the synthesis of phenol, resorcinol, and other organic products. [BENZENE + SULFONIC ACID]

ben•ze•noid (ben′zə noid′), *Chem.* —*adj.* **1.** of, pertaining to, or similar to benzene, esp. with respect to structure. —*n.* **2.** any benzene compound. [1885–90; BENZENE + -OID]

ben•ze•tho′ni•um chlo′ride (ben′zə thō′nē əm), *Chem.* a colorless, water-soluble, crystalline solid, ammonium chloride derivative, $(C_{27}H_{42}O_2N)Cl{\cdot}H_2O$, used chiefly as an antiseptic. [BENZ(YL) + (M)ETH(YL) + (AMM)ONIUM]

ben•zi•dine (ben′zi dēn′, -din), *n. Chem.* a grayish, crystalline, slightly water-soluble, basic compound, $C_{12}H_{12}N_2$, usually derived from nitrobenzene: used chiefly in the synthesis of certain azo dyes, esp. Congo red. [1875–80; BENZ- + -ID[3] + -INE[2]]

ben•zim•id•az•ole (ben′zim i daz′ōl, ben′zə mid′ə-zōl′), *n. Chem.* a colorless crystalline compound, $C_7H_6N_2$, used in organic synthesis. Also called **benzoglyoxaline.** [1925–30; BENZ- + IMIDAZOLE]

ben•zine (ben′zēn, ben zēn′), *n.* a colorless, volatile, flammable, liquid mixture of various hydrocarbons, obtained in the distillation of petroleum, and used in cleaning, dyeing, etc. Also, **ben•zin** (ben′zin). [1850–55; BENZ- + -INE[2]]

benzo-, a combining form used in the names of chemical compounds in which benzene, benzoic acid, or one or more of the phenyl groups is present: *benzocaine.* Also, *esp. before a vowel,* **benz-.** [BENZ(ENE) OR BENZ(OIC) + -O-]

ben•zo•ate (ben′zō āt′, -it), *n. Chem.* a salt or ester of benzoic acid. [1800–10; BENZO- + -ATE[2]]

ben′zoate of so′da, *Chem.* See **sodium benzoate.**

ben•zo•caine (ben′zō kān′), *n. Pharm.* ethyl aminobenzoate; a white, crystalline powder, $C_9H_{11}NO_2$, used as a local anesthetic, usually in ointment form. [1920–25; BENZO- + (CO)CAINE]

ben•zo•di•az•e•pine (ben′zō dī az′ə pēn′, -ā′zə-), *n. Pharm.* any of a family of minor tranquilizers that act against anxiety and convulsions and produce sedation and muscle relaxation. [1965–70; BENZ- + DIAZEP(AM) + -INE[2]]

ben•zo•fu•ran (ben′zō fyŏŏr′an, -fyə ran′), *n. Chem.* coumarone. [1945–50; BENZO- + FURAN]

ben•zo•gly•ox•a•line (ben′zō glī ok′sə lēn′, -lin), *n. Chem.* benzimidazole. [BENZO- + GLYOXALINE]

ben•zo•ic (ben zō′ik), *adj. Chem.* of or derived from benzoin or benzoic acid. [1785–95; BENZO(IN)[1] + -IC]

benzo′ic ac′id, *Chem., Pharm.* a white, crystalline, slightly water-soluble powder, $C_7H_6O_2$, usually derived from benzoin or other balsams, or synthesized from phthalic acid or toluene: used chiefly as a preservative, in the synthesis of dyes, and in medicine as a germicide. Also called **benzenecarboxylic acid, phenylformic acid.** [1785–95]

benzo′ic al′dehyde, *Chem.* benzaldehyde.

ben•zo•in[1] (ben′zō in, -zoin, ben zō′in), *n.* **1.** Also called **gum benjamin, gum benzoin.** a reddish-brown, aromatic balsamic resin occurring in almondlike fragments and having a vanillalike odor, obtained from trees of the genus *Styrax,* esp. *S. benzoin,* of Java, Sumatra, etc.: used in the manufacture of perfume and cosmetics and in medicine internally as an expectorant and externally as an antiseptic. **2.** Also called **benjamin, benjamin-bush.** any plant belonging to the genus *Lindera* (*Benzoin*), of the laurel family, including the spicebush and similar aromatic plants. [1550–60; earlier *benjoin* < MF < Pg *beijoim* and Sp *benjuí* < Ar *lubān jāwī* frankincense of Java (*lu-* prob. constructed as the definite article); *z* of *benzoin* < It *benzoi* << Ar]

ben•zo•in[2] (ben′zō in, -zoin, ben zō′in), *n. Chem.* a white, slightly water-soluble powder, $C_{14}H_{12}O_2$, derived by the condensation of benzaldehyde in the presence of potassium cyanide, and used in organic synthesis. [BENZO- + -IN[2]]

ben•zol (ben′zôl, -zol), *n. Chem.* (no longer in technical use) benzene. [BENZ- + -OL[1]]

ben•zon•a•tate (ben zon′ə tāt′), *n. Pharm.* a nonnarcotic substance, $C_{30}H_{53}NO_{11}$, used as a cough suppressant. [perh. BENZO(IC ACID) + *(no)na(ethylene)* + *-t-* (< ?) + -ATE[2]]

ben•zon•i•trile (ben zon′i tril, ben′zō nī′-), *n. Chem.* a clear, colorless, viscous, poisonous liquid, C_7H_5N, used chiefly as an intermediate in organic synthesis. [BENZO- + NITRILE]

ben•zo•phe•none (ben′zō fi nōn′, -fē′nōn), *n. Chem.* a crystalline, water-insoluble ketone, $C_{13}H_{10}O$, used in organic synthesis. Also called **diphenyl ketone.** [1880–85; BENZO- + PHEN- + -ONE]

ben•zo•py•rene (ben′zō pī′rēn, -pī rēn′), *n. Chem.* a yellow, crystalline aromatic carcinogenic hydrocarbon, $C_{20}H_{12}$, consisting of five fused benzene rings, produced by incomplete combustion of organic material, as coal, petroleum, or tobacco. Also, **benzpyrene.** [1925–30; BENZO- OR BENZ- + PYRENE]

ben•zo•sul•fi•mide (ben′zō sul′fə mīd′), *n. Chem.* saccharin. [BENZO- + SULF- + IMIDE]

ben•zo•tri•chlo•ride (ben′zō trī klôr′īd, -id, -klōr′-), *n. Chem.* a colorless or yellowish liquid, $C_7H_5Cl_3$, used chiefly in the manufacture of dyes. Also called **toluene trichloride.** [BENZO- + TRICHLORIDE]

ben•zo•tri•fluor•ide (ben′zō trī flŏŏr′īd, -flôr′-, -flōr′-), *n. Chem.* a colorless, flammable liquid, $C_7H_5F_3$, used chiefly as an intermediate in the manufacture of dyes and pharmaceuticals, and as a solvent. Also called **toluene trifluoride.** [BENZO- + TRI- + FLUORIDE]

benzoxy-, a combining form used in the names of chemical compounds in which the benzoyl group is present: *benzoxyacetanilide.* [BENZ- + OXY-[2]]

ben•zo•yl (ben′zō il), *Chem.* —*adj.* **1.** containing the benzoyl group. —*n.* **2.** the benzoyl group. [1850–55; BENZO- + -YL]

CONCISE PRONUNCIATION KEY: *act, cāpe, dâre, pärt; set, ēqual; if, īce; ox, ōver, ôrder, oil, bŏŏk, bōōt, out; up, ûrge; child; sing; shoe; thin, that;* zh as in *treasure.* ə = *a* as in *alone, e* as in *system, i* as in *easily, o* as in *gallop, u* as in *circus;* [a] as in *fire* (fī[a]r), *hour* (ou[a]r). l and n can serve as syllabic consonants, as in *cradle* (krād′l), and *button* (but′n). See the full key inside the front cover.

ben•zo•yl•ate (ben′zō ə lāt′, ben zō′-), *v.t.*, **-at•ed, -at•ing.** *Chem.* to introduce the benzoyl group into (an organic compound). [BENZOYL + -ATE[2]] **—ben′zo•yl•a′•tion,** *n.*

ben′zoyl group′, *Chem.* the univalent group C_7H_5O–, derived from benzoic acid. Also called **ben′zoyl rad′ical.**

ben′zoyl perox′ide, *Chem.* a white, crystalline, water-insoluble, explosive solid, $C_{14}H_{10}O_4$, used chiefly as a bleaching agent for flour, fats, oils, and waxes, and as a catalyst in polymerization reactions.

benz•py•rene (benz pī′rēn, benz′pī rēn′), *n. Chem.* benzopyrene.

benz•tro′pine mes′yl•ate (benz trō′pēn mez′ə lāt′, mes′-, mē′zə-, mē′sə-), *n. Pharm.* a synthetic anticholinergic, $C_{21}H_{25}NO{\cdot}CH_4O_3S$, used in the treatment of Parkinson's disease. [*benztropine* appar. as rearrangement of *tropine benzohydryl; mesylate* prob. a contr. of *methanesulfonate*]

Ben-Zvi (ben tsvē′), *n.* **Itz•hak** (yits′hok), 1884?–1963, Israeli statesman, born in Russia: president of Israel 1952–63.

ben•zyl (ben′zil, -zēl), *Chem.* —*adj.* **1.** containing the benzyl group. —*n.* **2.** the benzyl group. [1865–70; BENZ- + -YL] **—ben•zyl′ic,** *adj.*

ben′zyl ac′etate, *Chem.* a colorless liquid, $C_9H_{10}O_2$, having a flowerlike odor: used chiefly for flavoring tobacco and in soaps and cosmetics.

ben′zyl al′cohol, *Chem.* a colorless, faintly aromatic, slightly water-soluble liquid, C_7H_8O, used chiefly as a solvent in the manufacture of perfumes and flavorings, and as an intermediate in the synthesis of benzyl esters and ethers. Also called **phenylcarbinol.**

ben′zyl ben′zoate, *Chem., Pharm.* a colorless, faintly aromatic liquid, $C_{14}H_{12}O_2$, used chiefly as a fixative and solvent in the manufacture of flavorings and perfume and in medicine in the treatment of certain skin conditions. [1915–20]

ben′zyl bu′tyrate, *Chem.* a liquid, $C_{11}H_{14}O_2$, having a fruitlike odor, used as a plasticizer and in flavoring.

ben′zyl chlo′ride, *Chem.* a colorless, corrosive liquid, C_7H_7Cl, used chiefly as an intermediate in the synthesis of benzyl compounds.

ben′zyl dichlo′ride, *Chem.* See **benzal chloride.**

ben′zyl fluor′ide, *Chem.* a colorless liquid, C_7H_7F, used in organic synthesis.

ben′zyl group′, *Chem.* the univalent group C_7H_7–, derived from toluene. Also called **ben′zyl rad′ical.**

ben•zyl•i•dene (ben zil′i dēn′), *adj., n. Chem.* benzal. [BENZYL + -ID[3] + -ENE]

benzyl′idene ac′etone, *Chem.* a colorless, crystalline, water-insoluble solid, $C_{10}H_{10}O$, having a vanillalike odor, used chiefly as a scent in the manufacture of perfume. Also called **benzalacetone, methyl styryl ketone.**

benzyl′idene chlo′ride, *Chem.* See **benzal chloride.**

ben′zyl isoam′yl e′ther, *Chem.* See **isoamyl benzyl ether.**

benzyloxy-, a combining form used in the names of chemical compounds in which the benzyl group is present: *benzyloxyamine.* [BENZYL + OXY-[2]]

ben′zyl thiocy′anate, *Chem.* a colorless, crystalline, water-insoluble solid, C_8H_7NS, used as an insecticide.

Be•o•grad (be′ô gräd), *n.* Serbo-Croatian name of **Belgrade.**

Be•o•wulf (bā′ə wŏŏlf′), *n.* **1.** (*italics*) an English alliterative epic poem, probably written in the early 8th century A.D. **2.** the hero of this poem.

B.E.P., Bachelor of Engineering Physics.

be•paint (bi pānt′), *v.t.* **1.** to cover or smear with paint. **2.** to color or tint: *a face bepainted with excessive makeup.* [1545–55; BE- + PAINT]

Be′ Prepared′, motto of the Boy Scouts of America and of the Girl Scouts of America.

be•queath (bi kwēth′, -kwēth′), *v.t.* **1.** to dispose of (personal property, esp. money) by last will: *She bequeathed her half of the company to her niece.* **2.** to hand down; pass on. **3.** *Obs.* to commit; entrust. [bef. 1000; ME *bequethen,* OE *becwethan* (*be-* BE- + *cwethan* to say (see QUOTH), c. OHG *quedan,* Goth *qithan*)] **—be•queath′a•ble,** *adj.* **—be•queath′al, be•queath′ment,** *n.* **—be•queath′er,** *n.*
—Syn. 1. will, impart, leave, bestow, grant, consign.

be•quest (bi kwest′), *n.* **1.** a disposition in a will. **2.** a legacy: *A small bequest allowed her to live independently.* [1250–1300; ME *biqueste, biquyste,* equiv. to *bi-* BE- + *quiste* will, bequest, OE *-cwis(se)* (with excrescent *t,* as in BEHEST), n. deriv. of *cwethan* to say; on the model of *bequethen* BEQUEATH]

be•ra•chah (*Seph.* brä KHä′; *Ashk.* brô′KHə), *n., pl.* ***-choth, -chot*** (*Seph.* -KHôt′), ***-chos*** (*Ashk.* -KHəz). *Hebrew.* berakhah.

be•ra•kah (*Seph.* brä KHä′; *Ashk.* brô′KHə), *n., pl.* ***-koth, -kot*** (*Seph.* -KHôt′), ***-kos*** (*Ashk.* -KHəz). *Hebrew.* berakhah.

be•ra•khah (*Seph.* brä KHä′; *Ashk.* brô′KHə), *n., pl.* ***-khoth, -khot*** (*Seph.* -KHôt′), ***-khos*** (*Ashk.* -KHəz). *Hebrew.* a blessing or benediction, usually recited according to a traditional formula. Also, ***berakah, berachah.*** [Heb *bərākhāh*]

CONCISE ETYMOLOGY KEY: <, descended or borrowed from; >, whence; b., blend of, blended; c., cognate with; cf., compare; deriv., derivative; equiv., equivalent; imit., imitative; obl., oblique; r., replacing; s., stem; sp., spelling, spelled; resp., respelling, respelled; trans., translation; ?, origin unknown; *, unattested; ‡, probably earlier than. See the full key inside the front cover.

Bé•ran•ger (bā RäN zhā′), *n.* **Pierre Jean de** (pyer zhäN də), 1780–1857, French poet.

Be•rar (bā rär′, ba-), *n.* a former division of the Central Provinces and Berar, in central India: now part of Maharashtra state.

be•ras•cal (bi ras′kəl), *v.t.* to call (someone) a rascal. [1735–45; BE- + RASCAL]

Be•rat (be rät′, ber′ät), *n.* a city in S central Albania. 26,000.

be•rate (bi rāt′), *v.t.*, **-rat•ed, -rat•ing.** to scold; rebuke: *He berated them in public.* [1540–50; BE- + RATE[2]]
—Syn. abuse, vilify, vituperate, objurgate.

Ber•ber (bûr′bər), *n.* **1.** a member of a group of North African tribes living in Barbary and the Sahara. **2.** a subfamily of Afro-Asiatic, consisting of the languages of the Berbers, including Tuareg and Kabyle. —*adj.* **3.** of or pertaining to the Berbers or their language. [1835–45; < Ar *barbar* < Gk *bárbaros;* see BARBAROUS]

Ber•be•ra (bûr′bər ə), *n.* a seaport in Somalia, on the Gulf of Aden: former capital of British Somaliland. 65,000.

ber•ber•i•da•ceous (bûr′bər i dā′shəs), *adj.* belonging to the Berberidaceae, the barberry family of plants. Cf. **barberry family.** [1850–55; < NL *Berberidace(ae)* (*Berberid-,* s. of *Berberis* a genus, the BARBERRY + *-aceae* -ACEAE) + -OUS]

ber•be•rine (bûr′bə rēn′), *n. Pharm.* a white or yellow, crystalline, water-soluble alkaloid, $C_{20}H_{19}NO_5$, derived from barberry or goldenseal, used as an antipyrotic, antibacterial, and stomachic. [1860–65; < NL *Berber(is)* (see BERBERIDACEOUS) + -INE[1]]

Ber•bice (bûr bēs′), *n.* a river in E Guyana, flowing NE to the Atlantic Ocean. ab. 370 mi. (595 km) long.

ber•ceuse (*Fr.* beR sœz′), *n., pl.* **-ceuses** (*Fr.* -sœz′). *Music.* **1.** a cradlesong; lullaby. **2.** a composition for instrument or voice, having a soothing, reflective character. [1875–80; < F, equiv. to *berc(er)* to rock + *-euse* -EUSE]

Berch•ta (*Ger.* beRKH′tä), *n.* Perchta.

Berch•tes•ga•den (beRKH′təs gäd′n), *n.* a town in the SE extremity of Bavaria, in SE West Germany: site of the fortified mountain chalet of Adolf Hitler. 39,800.

Ber•cy (bâr sē′; *Fr.* beR sē′), *n. French Cookery.* a white sauce flavored with white wine, shallots, fish stock, and parsley: usually served with fish. Also called **Bercy′ sauce′.** [after *Bercy,* a district of Paris]

ber•dache (bər dash′), *n.* (in some American Indian tribes) a man who adopts the dress and social roles traditionally assigned to women. [1800–10; < North American F; F *bardache* passive partner in sodomy, boy prostitute < South Italian *bardascia* < Ar *bardaj* slave < Pers *bardah*]

Ber•di•chev (bər dē′chef, -chev; *Russ.* byiR dyē′chyif), *n.* a city in the central Ukraine, in the SW Soviet Union. 82,000.

Ber•dya•ev (bər dyä′yef, -yev; *Russ.* byiR dyä′yif), *n.* **Ni•ko•lai A•le•ksan•dro•vich** (nik′ə lī′ al′ig zan′drə vich, -zän′-; *Russ.* nyi ku lī′ u lyi ksän′drə vyich), 1874–1948, Russian theologian and philosopher: in France after 1922.

Ber•dyansk (bər dyansk′; *Russ.* byiR dyänsk′), *n.* a city in S Ukraine, on the Sea of Azov. 122,000. Formerly, **Osipenko.**

Be•re•a (bə rē′ə), *n.* a city in NE Ohio, near Cleveland. 19,567. **—Be•re′an,** *n.*

be•reave (bi rēv′), *v.t.*, **-reaved** or **-reft, -reav•ing. 1.** to deprive and make desolate, esp. by death (usually fol. by *of*): *Illness bereaved them of their mother.* **2.** to deprive ruthlessly or by force (usually fol. by *of*): *The war bereaved them of their home.* **3.** *Obs.* to take away by violence. [bef. 900; ME *bereven,* OE *berēafian;* c. D *berooven,* G *berauben,* Goth *biraubōn.* See BE-, REAVE[1]] **—be•reave′ment,** *n.* **—be•reav′er,** *n.*

be•reaved (bi rēvd′), *adj.* **1.** (of a person) greatly saddened at being deprived by death of a loved one. —*n.* **2.** a bereaved person or persons (usually prec. by *the*): *to extend condolences to the bereaved.* [1100–50; ME *bireved,* late OE *birēafod* (ptp.); see BEREAVE, -ED[2]]

Ber•e•cyn•ti•a (ber′ə sin′tē ə), *n.* Cybele.

be•reft (bi reft′), *v.* **1.** a pt. and pp. of **bereave.** —*adj.* **2.** deprived: *They are bereft of their senses. He is bereft of all happiness.* [1525–35; BE- + REFT]

Ber•e•ni•ce (ber′ə nī′sē), *n.* a female given name: from a Greek word meaning "bringer of victory."

Ber′eni′ce's Hair′, *Astron.* the constellation Coma Berenices. [1595–1605]

Ber•en•son (ber′ən sən), *n.* **Bernard** or **Bern•hard** (bûr′närd, bûrn′härd), 1865–1959, U.S. art critic, born in Lithuania.

beret

be•ret (bə rā′), *n.* a soft, visorless cap with a close-fitting headband and a wide, round top often with a tab at its center. [1820–30; < F < Gascon *berret,* OPr. *ber(r)et.* See BIRETTA]

ber•et•ta (bə ret′ə), *n.* biretta.

Be•re•zi•na (*Pol.* be′Re zē′nä; *Russ.* byi Ryi zyi nä′), *n.* a river in central Byelorussia (Belarus), flowing SE into the Dnieper River: costly crossing by Napoleon 1812. 350 mi. (565 km) long.

Be•rez•ni•ki (bə rez′ni kē; *Russ.* byi Ryôz′nyi kyē), *n.* a city in the Russian Federation, on the Kama river, near the Ural Mountains. 200,000.

berg (bûrg), *n. Oceanog.* iceberg. [1815–25; by shortening]

Berg (berg; *for 1 also Ger.* beRk), *n.* **1. Al•ban** (äl bän′, äl′bän), 1885–1935, Austrian composer. **2. Patricia Jane** (*Patty*), born 1918, U.S. golfer.

ber•gall (bûr′gôl), *n.* cunner. [1805–15, *Amer.;* < Norw *berggalt* a labrid fish, equiv. to *berg* (see ICEBERG) + *galt* boar]

Ber•ga•ma (bər gä′mə, bûr′gə mə), *n.* **1.** a town in W Turkey in Asia. 24,121. Ancient, **Pergamum. 2.** Bergamo.

ber•ga•mas•ca (*It.* beR′gä mäs′kä), *n., pl.* **-che** (-ke). **1.** a fast dance similar to the tarantella. **2.** the music for this dance. [1580–90; < It, n. use of fem. of *Bergamasco* of Bergama]

Ber•ga•mo (bûr′gə mō′), *n., pl.* **-mos.** a Turkish rug characterized by a long pile, floral or geometric patterns, and red-orange hues. Also, **Bergama, Ber•ga•mee** (bûr′gə mē′), **Ber•ga•mot** (bûr′gə mot′, -mət). [after BERGAMA]

Ber•ga•mo (beR′gä mô), *n.* a city in central Lombardy, in N Italy. 127,390.

ber•ga•mot (bûr′gə mot′, -mət), *n.* **1.** a small citrus tree, *Citrus aurantium bergamia,* having fruit with a rind that yields a fragrant essential oil. **2.** Also called **essence of bergamot.** the oil or essence itself. **3.** any of various plants of the mint family, as *Monarda fistulosa,* yielding an oil resembling essence of bergamot. **4.** a variety of pear. [1610–20; < F *bergamote* < It *bergamotta* < Ottoman Turk; cf. Mod Turk *bey armudlu* lit., bey's pear (*bey* BEY + *armut* pear (< Pers) + *-u* 3d sing. possessive suffix); It form perh. by assoc. with BERGAMO, BERGAMA, with *-otta* as alter. to a familiar suffix; the citrus appar. so called from its resemblance to the pear]

ber′gamot mint′, an aromatic herb, *Mentha piperita citrata,* having a lemonlike odor when crushed. [1855–60]

Ber•gen (bûr′gən; *for 1 also Nor.* beR′gən), *n.* **1.** a city in SW Norway, on the Atlantic Ocean. 213,594. **2.** a male given name.

Ber•gen-Bel•sen (*Ger.* beR′gən bel′zən; *Eng.* bûr′gən bel′sən), *n.* Belsen.

Ber•gen•field (bûr′gən fēld′), *n.* a city in NE New Jersey. 25,568.

Ber•ge•rac (bûr′zhə rak′; *Fr.* beR zhə RAK′), *n.* **Sa•vi•nien Cy•ra•no de** (sav′in yen′ sir′ə nō′ də; *Fr.* SA vē nyaN′ sē RA nô′ də), 1619–55, French soldier, swordsman, and writer: hero of play by Rostand.

ber•gère (bər zhâr′; *Fr.* beR zheR′), *n., pl.* **-gères** (-zhârz′; *Fr.* -zheR′). a chair of the 18th century, having arms with closed spaces between them and the seat. [1755–65; < F: lit., shepherdess, fem. of *berger* shepherd]

ber•ge•rie (beR zhə Rē′), *n., pl.* ***-ries*** (-Rē′). *Canadian French.* a farm, country estate, or other rural retreat maintained by a wealthy owner as a facility for rest and recreation.

Bergh (bûrg), *n.* **Henry,** 1811–88, U.S. social reformer: founder of A.S.P.C.A.

Ber•gi•us (ber′gē əs; *Ger.* beR′gē ŏŏs′), *n.* **Frie•drich** (frē′drik; *Ger.* fRē′dRIKH), 1884–1949, German chemist: Nobel prize 1931.

Ber′gius proc′ess, *Chem.* a method of hydrogenation formerly used with coal to produce an oil similar to petroleum. [after Friedrich BERGIUS]

Berg•man (bûrg′mən), *n.* **1. Ing•mar** (ing′mär), born 1918, Swedish motion-picture director and writer. **2. Ingrid,** 1915–82, Swedish film actress.

berg•schrund (berk′shrŏŏnt), *n.* a crevasse, or series of crevasses, at the upper end of a mountain glacier. [1835–45; < G (*Berg* mountain + *Schrunde* crevice)]

Bergs•ma (bûrgz′mə), *n.* **William,** born 1921, U.S. composer.

Berg•son (bûrg′sən, berg′-; *Fr.* beRg sôN′), *n.* **Hen•ri** (äN Rē′), 1859–1941, French philosopher and writer: Nobel prize for literature 1927. **—Berg•so•ni•an** (bûrg sō′nē ən, berg-), *adj., n.*

Berg•son•ism (bûrg′sə niz′əm, berg′-), *n.* the philosophy of Bergson, emphasizing duration as the central fact of experience and asserting the existence of the élan vital as an original life force essentially governing all organic processes. [1905–10; BERGSON + -ISM]

berg′ wind′ (wind), a foehn blowing coastward from the interior plateau of South Africa. [1900–05]

berg′y bit′ (bûr′gē), a small iceberg, somewhat larger than a growler. [1930–35; BERG + -Y[2]]

be•rhyme (bi rīm′), *v.t.*, **-rhymed, -rhym•ing.** to celebrate in verse. Also, **berime.** [1580–90; BE- + RHYME]

Be•ri•a (ber′ē ə; *Russ.* bye′ryi yə), *n.* **La•vren•ti Pa•vlo•vich** (ləv ren′tē pav lô′vich; *Russ.* lu vRyen′tyē pu vlô′vyich), 1899–1953, Soviet secret-police chief: executed for treason.

be•rib•boned (bi rib′ənd), *adj.* adorned with ribbons. [1825–35; *beribbon* (BE- + RIBBON) + -ED[2]]

ber•i•ber•i (ber′ē ber′ē), *n. Pathol.* a disease of the peripheral nerves caused by a deficiency of vitamin B_1, characterized by pain in and paralysis of the extremities, and severe emaciation or swelling of the body. [1695–1705; < Sinhalese, redupl. of *beri* weakness] **—ber′i•ber′ic,** *adj.*

be•rime (bi rīm′), *v.t.*, **-rimed, -rim•ing.** berhyme. [BE- + RIME[1]]

Ber·ing (bēr′ing, ber′-, bâr′-; *Dan.* bā′ʀing), *n.* **Vi·tus** (vē′to͝os), 1680–1741, Danish navigator: explorer of the N Pacific. Also, **Behring.**

Ber′ing Sea′, a part of the N Pacific, N of the Aleutian Islands. 878,000 sq. mi. (2,274,000 sq. km).

Ber′ing Strait′, a strait between Alaska and the Russian Federation in Asia, connecting the Bering Sea and the Arctic Ocean. 36 mi. (58 km) wide.

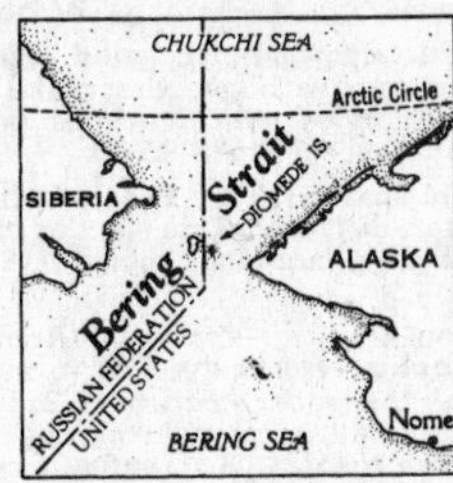

Ber′ing time′. See under **standard time.** Also called **Ber′ing Stand′ard Time′.**

Ber. Is., Bermuda Islands.

Be·rith (*Seph.* brēt; *Ashk.* bʀis; *Eng.* bris, brit), *n. Hebrew.* Brith. [*bərith* lit., covenant]

Berke·le·ian (bûrk′lē ən, bûrk lē′-; *esp. Brit.* bärk′lē-ən, bärk lē′-), *adj.* **1.** pertaining or relating to George Berkeley or his philosophy. —*n.* **2.** an advocate of the philosophy of George Berkeley, esp. its denial of the existence of a material world. [1855–60; George Berkeley + -an] —**Berke′le·ian·ism,** *n.*

Berke·ley (bûrk′lē; *for 2, 3, 6 also Brit.* bärk′lē), *n.* **1. Bus·by** (buz′bē), (*William Berkeley Enos*), 1895–1976, U.S. choreographer and musical-film director. **2. George,** 1685?–1753, Irish bishop and philosopher. **3. Sir William,** 1610–77, British colonial governor of Virginia 1642–76. **4.** a city in W California, on San Francisco Bay. 103,328. **5.** a city in E Missouri, near St. Louis. 16,146. **6.** a male given name.

Berke·ley·ism (bûrk′lē iz′əm; *Brit.* bärk′lē iz′əm), *n.* any philosophical system or doctrine derived from the views of Bishop Berkeley. [1860–65; George Berkeley + -ism]

ber·ke·li·um (bər kē′lē əm), *n. Chem.* a transuranic element. *Symbol:* Bk; *at. no.:* 97; *at. wt.:* 249 (?). [1945–50; named after Berkeley, California, where it was discovered; see -ium]

Berk·ley (bûrk′lē), *n.* a city in SE Michigan, near Detroit. 18,637.

Berk′ner Is′land (bûrk′nər), an island in Antarctica, in the S Weddell Sea, between the Ronne Ice Shelf and the Filchner Ice Shelf.

Berk·shire (bûrk′shēr, -shər; *Brit.* bärk′shēr, -shər), *n.* **1.** Also called **Berks** (bûrks; *Brit.* bärks). a county in S England. 658,300; 485 sq. mi. (1255 sq. km). **2.** one of an English breed of black hogs, having white markings on the feet, face, and tail. **3.** a steam locomotive having a two-wheeled front truck, eight driving wheels, and a four-wheeled rear truck. See table under **Whyte classification.**

Berk′shire Hills′ (bûrk′shēr, -shər), a range of low mountains in W Massachusetts: resort region. Highest peak, Mt. Greylock, 3505 ft. (1070 m). Also called **Berk′·shires.**

ber·ley (bûr′lē), *n. Australian.* chum² (defs. 1, 2). [1870–75; of obscure orig.]

berlin (def. 1)

ber·lin (bər lin′, bûr′lin), *n.* **1.** a large, four-wheeled, closed carriage hung between two perches and having two interior seats. **2.** *Auto.* berline. **3.** (*sometimes cap.*) See **Berlin wool.** [1725–35; after Berlin, Germany; the carriage was allegedly designed about 1670 by an architect of the Elector of Brandenburg]

Ber·lin (bər lin′ *for 1, 2;* bûr′lin *for 3, 4; for 2 also Ger.* beʀ lēn′), *n.* **1. Irving,** born 1888, U.S. songwriter. **2.** the capital of Germany, in the NE part: constitutes a state. 3,121,000; 341 sq. mi. (883 sq. km). Formerly (1948–90) divided into a western zone (**West Berlin**), a part of West Germany; and an eastern zone (**East Berlin**), the capital of East Germany. **3.** a town in central Connecticut. 15,121. **4.** a city in N New Hampshire. 13,084.

ber·line (bər lin′, bûr′lin), *n.* an automobile with the front and rear compartments separated by a glass partition, as some limousines. Also, **berlin.** [< F; see berlin]

Ber·li·ner (bûr′lə nər), *n.* **Emile,** 1851–1929, U.S. inventor, born in Germany.

Ber·lin·er (bûr lin′ər), *n.* a native or resident of Berlin, Germany. [1855–60; Berlin + -er¹]

Ber′lin Wall′, a guarded concrete wall, with minefields and controlled checkpoints, erected across Berlin by East Germany in 1961 and dismantled in 1989.

Ber′lin wool′, a soft woolen yarn for embroidery or knitting. Also called **berlin.** [1840–50; after Berlin, Germany, where such wools were orig. dyed]

Ber·li·oz (ber′lē ōz′; *Fr.* beʀ lyôz′), *n.* **Louis Hec·tor** (lwē ek tôʀ′), 1803–69, French composer.

berm (bûrm), *n.* **1.** Also, **berme.** *Fort.* a horizontal surface between the exterior slope of a rampart and the moat. **2.** Also called **bench.** any level strip of ground at the summit or sides, or along the base, of a slope. **3.** Also called **backshore, beach berm.** a nearly flat back portion of a beach, formed of material deposited by the action of the waves. **4.** *Chiefly Indiana, Ohio, Pennsylvania, and West Virginia.* the bank of a canal or the shoulder of a road. **5.** *Chiefly Alaska.* a mound of snow or dirt, as formed when clearing land. **6.** a bank of earth placed against an exterior wall or walls of a house or other building as protection against extremes of temperature. —*v.t.* **7.** to cover or protect with a berm: *The side walls were bermed to a height of three feet.* [1720–30; < F *berme* < D *berm;* akin to brim¹]

Ber·me·jo (beʀ me′hô), *n.* a river in N Argentina, flowing SE to the Paraguay River. 1000 mi. (1600 km) long.

Ber·mu·da (bər myo͞o′də), *n.* a group of islands in the Atlantic, 580 mi. (935 km) E of North Carolina: a British colony; resort. 53,500; 19 sq. mi. (49 sq. km). *Cap.:* Hamilton. Also, **Ber·mu·das.** —**Ber·mu′dan, Ber·mu·di·an** (bər myo͞o′dē ən), *adj., n.*

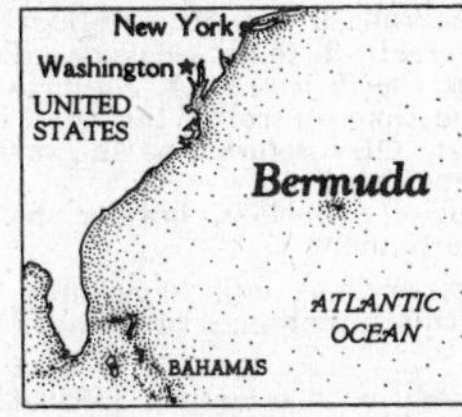

Bermu′da but′tercup, a bulbous plant, *Oxalis pes-caprae,* native to southern Africa, having nodding, yellow flowers.

Bermu′da cut′ter, *Naut.* a marconi-rigged cutter.

Bermu′da grass′, a creeping grass, *Cynodon dactylon,* of southern Europe, grown in the southern U.S. and Bermuda for lawns and pastures. Also called **Bahama grass, scutch grass.** [1800–10, *Amer.*]

Bermu′da high′, *Meteorol.* a subtropical high centered near Bermuda.

Bermu′da lil′y, a lily, *Lilium longiflorum eximium,* having white, funnel-shaped flowers, cultivated esp. as an Easter lily. [1895–1900]

Bermu′da on′ion, any of several mild, flat varieties of onion, grown in Texas and, to some extent, in other parts of the southern U.S. and in Bermuda. [1940–45]

Bermu′da palmet′to, a palm, *Sabal bermudana,* of Bermuda, having small, roundish, black fruit and leaves that are checkered beneath.

Bermu′da pet′rel, cahow.

Bermu′da rig′. See **Marconi rig.** Also, **Bermu′dan rig′, Bermu′dian rig′.** [1850–55]

Ber·mu·das (bər myo͞o′dəz), *n.* **1. the Bermudas.** Bermuda. **2.** (*used with a plural v.*) *Informal.* See **Bermuda shorts.**

Bermu′da shorts′, shorts extending almost to the knee, worn for informal warm-weather dress. [1950–55]

Bermu′da Tri′angle, the triangular area in the Atlantic Ocean bounded by Bermuda, Puerto Rico, and a point near Melbourne, Florida, in which a number of ships and aircraft are purported to have disappeared mysteriously. [1970–75]

Bern (bûrn; Ger. beʀn), *n.* **1.** a city in and the capital of Switzerland, in the W part: capital of Bern canton. 149,800. **2.** a canton in W Switzerland. 992,000; 2658 sq. mi. (6885 sq. km). *Cap.:* Bern. Also, **Berne.**

Ber·na·dette (bûr′nə det′; *Fr.* beʀ nᴀ det′), *n.* **1. Saint.** Also called **Bernadette′ of Lourdes′.** (*Marie Bernarde Soubirous* or *Soubiroux*), 1844–79, French nun. **2.** a female given name: derived from *Bernard.*

Ber·na·dotte (bûr′nə dot′; *Fr.* beʀ nᴀ dôt′), *n.* **Jean Bap·tiste Jules** (zhäɴ bᴀ tēst′ zhyl), 1764–1844, French marshal under Napoleon; as Charles XIV, king of Sweden and Norway 1818–44.

Ber·na·nos (beʀ nᴀ nôs′), *n.* **Georges** (zhôʀzh), 1888–1948, French novelist and pamphleteer.

Ber·nard (beʀ nᴀʀ′ *for 1;* bûr′nərd, bûr närd′ *for 2*), *n.* **1. Claude** (klōd), 1813–78, French physiologist. **2.** a male given name: from Germanic words meaning "bear" and "hardy."

Ber·nard·ine (bûr′nər din, -dēn′), *adj.* **1.** of or pertaining to St. Bernard of Clairvaux. **2.** of or pertaining to the Cistercians. —*n.* **3.** a Cistercian. **4.** Also, **Bernadine** (bûr′nə dēn′). a female given name.

Ber·nard of Clair·vaux (bûr närd′ əv klâr vō′), **Saint** ("*the Mellifluous Doctor*"), 1090–1153, French monk, preacher, and mystical writer.

Berne (bûrn; Fr. beʀn), *n.* Bern.

Ber·nese (bûr′nēz, -nēs, bûr nēz′, -nēs′), *adj., n., pl.* **-nese.** —*adj.* **1.** of or pertaining to Bern or its inhabitants. —*n.* **2.** an inhabitant or native of Bern. [1800–10; Bern + -ese]

Ber′nese Alps′, a mountain range in SW Switzerland, part of the Alps: highest peak, 14,026 ft. (4275 m).

Ber′nese moun′tain dog′, one of a Swiss breed of large, long-haired dogs having a black coat with white and russet-brown or deep-tan markings. [1930–35]

Bern·har·di (beʀn här′dē), *n.* **Frie·drich A. J. von** (fʀē′dʀiᴋʜ fən), 1849–1930, German general.

Bern·hardt (bûrn′härt; *Fr.* beʀ nᴀʀ′), *n.* **Sar·ah** (sâr′ə, sar′ə; *Fr.* sᴀ ʀᴀ′), (*Rosine Bernard*), 1845–1923, French actress.

Ber·nice (bûr nēs′, bûr′nis), *n.* a female given name: from a Greek word meaning "bringer of victory."

Ber·nie (bûr′nē), *n.* a male given name, form of **Bernard.**

Ber·ni·na (bər nē′nə; *It.* beʀ nē′nä), *n.* a mountain in SE Switzerland, in the Rhaetian Alps. 13,295 ft. (4050 m).

Berni′na Pass′, a pass traversing Bernina Mountain, between SE Switzerland and N Italy. 7640 ft. (2330 m) high.

Ber·ni·ni (bər nē′nē; *It.* beʀ nē′nē), *n.* **Gio·van·ni** (jē′ə-vä′nē; *It.* jô vän′nē) or **Gian** (jän) **Lo·ren·zo** (lə ren′zō; *It.* lô ʀen′dzô), 1598–1680, Italian sculptor, architect, and painter. —**Ber·ni·nesque** (bûr′ni nesk′, ber′-), *adj.*

Ber·noul·li (bər no͞o′lē; *Ger.* beʀ no͞o′lē; *Fr.* beʀ no͞o-yē′), *n.* **1. Dan·iel** (dan′yəl; *Ger.* dä′nē el′; *Fr.* dᴀ-nyel′), 1700–82, Swiss physicist and mathematician born in the Netherlands (son of Johann Bernoulli). **2. Ja·kob** (*Ger.* yä′kôp) or **Jacques** (*Fr.* zhäk), 1654–1705, Swiss mathematician and physicist. **3. Jo·hann** (*Ger.* yō′hän) or **Jean** (*Fr.* zhäɴ), 1667–1748, Swiss mathematician (brother of Jakob Bernoulli). Also, **Ber·nouil′li.** —**Ber·noul′li·an,** *adj.*

Bernoul′li distribu′tion, *Statistics.* See **binomial distribution.** [named after Jakob Bernoulli]

Bernoul′li effect′, *Hydraulics.* the decrease in pressure as the velocity of a fluid increases. [named after Jakob Bernoulli]

Bernoul′li equa′tion, **1.** *Hydrodynamics.* See **Bernoulli's theorem** (def. 2). **2.** Also called **Bernoul′li's differen′tial equa′tion.** *Math.* a differential equation of the form $dy/dx + f(x)y = g(x)y^n$, where n is any number other than 0 or 1. [1915–20; (in def. 1) named after Daniel Bernoulli; (in def. 2) named after Jakob Bernoulli]

Bernoul′li's lemnis′cate, *Analyt. Geom.* lemniscate. [named after Jakob Bernoulli]

Bernoul′li's the′orem, **1.** *Statistics.* See **law of averages** (def. 1). **2.** *Hydrodynamics.* an expression of the conservation of energy in streamline flow, stating that the sum of the ratio of the pressure to the mass density, the product of the gravitational constant and the vertical height, and the square of the velocity divided by 2 are constant. [1920–25; (in def. 1) named after Jakob Bernoulli; (in def. 2) named after Daniel Bernoulli]

Bernoul′li tri′als, *Math.* repeated independent experiments having two possible outcomes for each experiment with the probability for each outcome remaining constant throughout the experiments, as tossing a coin several times. [1950–55; named after Jakob Bernoulli]

Bern·stein (bûrn′stīn, -stēn), *n.* **Leonard,** 1918–90, U.S. conductor, composer, and pianist.

Bern·storff (beʀn′shtôʀf), *n.* **Count Jo·hann·Hein·rich** (yō′hän hīn′ʀiᴋʜ), 1862–1939, German diplomat.

ber·ret·ta (bə ret′ə), *n. Rom. Cath. Ch.* biretta.

ber·ried (ber′ēd), *adj.* **1.** covered with or yielding berries. **2.** of or like a berry; baccate. **3.** (of lobsters, crayfish, etc.) having eggs. [1785–95; berry + -ed³]

ber·ry (ber′ē), *n., pl.* **-ries,** *v.,* **-ried, -ry·ing.** —*n.* **1.** any small, usually stoneless, juicy fruit, irrespective of botanical structure, as the huckleberry, strawberry, or hackberry. **2.** *Bot.* a simple fruit having a pulpy pericarp in which the seeds are embedded, as the grape, gooseberry, currant, or tomato. **3.** a dry seed or kernel, as of wheat. **4.** the hip of the rose. **5.** one of the eggs of a lobster, crayfish, etc. **6. the berries,** *Older Slang.* someone or something very attractive or unusual. —*v.i.* **7.** to gather or pick berries: *We went berrying this morning.* **8.** to bear or produce berries. [bef. 1000; ME *berie,* OE *beri(g)e;* c. OS, OHG *beri* (G *Beere*), ON *ber* < Gmc *basjá-;* akin to D *besie,* Goth *-basi* < Gmc *básja-*] —**ber′ry·less,** *adj.* —**ber′ry·like′,** *adj.*

Ber·ry (ber′ē; *for 2 also Fr.* be ʀē′), *n.* **1. Charles Edward Anderson** ("*Chuck*"), born 1926, U.S. rock-'n'-roll singer, musician, and composer. **2.** Also, **Ber′ri.** a former province in central France.

Ber·ry·man (ber′ē mən), *n.* **John,** 1914–72, U.S. poet and critic.

ber′ry spoon′, a small spoon, esp. of the late 18th century, having a perforated bowl. Also called **ber′ry la′dle, sugar sifter.** [1870–75, *Amer.*]

ber·sa·glie·re (ber′səl yâr′ē; *It.* ber′sä lye′ʀe), *n., pl.* **-sa·glie·ri** (-səl yâr′ē; *It.* -sä lye′ʀē). one of a class of riflemen or sharpshooters in the Italian army. [1860–65; < It: lit., marksman, equiv. to *bersagl(io)* target (< OF *bersail; bers(er)* to hunt (perh. < Gmc; cf. MHG *birsen,* G *birschen, pirschen* to hunt) + *-ail* n. suffix) + *-iere* -ary]

CONCISE PRONUNCIATION KEY: act, cāpe, dâre, pärt; set, ēqual; if, īce; ox, ōver, ôrder, oil, bo͝ok, bo͞ot, out; up, ûrge; child; sing; shoe; thin, *th*at; zh as in *treasure.* ə = *a* as in *alone, e* as in *system, i* as in *easily, o* as in *gallop, u* as in *circus;* ᵊ as in *fire* (fīᵊr), *hour* (ouᵊr). l and n can serve as syllabic consonants, as in *cradle* (krād′l), and *button* (but′n). See the full key inside the front cover.

ber·seem (bər sēm′), *n.* a clover, *Trifolium alexandrinum,* of Egypt and Syria, grown for forage in the southwestern U.S. Also called **Egyptian clover.** [1900–05; < dial. Ar *barsīm* < Coptic *bersim,* equiv. to *ebra* seed (< Demotic Egyptian *prt* < Egyptian *ptr*) + *sim* herbs (< Demotic Egyptian *sm* < Egyptian *smw*)]

ber·serk (bər sûrk′, -zûrk′), *adj.* **1.** violently or destructively frenzied; wild; crazed; deranged: *He suddenly went berserk.* —*n.* **2.** (*sometimes cap.*) *Scand. Legend.* Also, **ber·serk′er.** an ancient Norse warrior who fought with frenzied rage in battle, possibly induced by eating hallucinogenic mushrooms. [1865–70; < ON *berserkr,* equiv. to *ber-* (either **ber-,* base of *bjorn* BEAR[2] or *berr* BARE[1]) + *serkr* SARK, shirt, armor] —**ber·serk′ly,** *adv.* —**ber·serk′ness,** *n.*
—**Syn. 1.** violent, mad, maniacal, rabid, demented, lunatic. —**Ant. 1.** rational, calm.

Bert (bûrt), *n.* a male given name, form of **Albert, Bertram, Herbert, Hubert,** etc.

berth (bûrth), *n.* **1.** a shelflike sleeping space, as on a ship, airplane, or railroad car. **2.** *Naut.* **a.** the space allotted to a vessel at anchor or at a wharf. **b.** the distance maintained between a vessel and the shore, another vessel, or any object. **c.** the position or rank of a ship's officer. **d.** the cabin of a ship's officer. **3.** a job; position. **4.** a place, listing, or role: *She clinched a berth on our tennis team.* **5. give a wide berth to,** to shun; remain discreetly away from: *Since his riding accident, he has given a wide berth to skittish horses.* —*v.t.* **6.** *Naut.* **a.** to allot to (a vessel) a certain space at which to anchor or tie up. **b.** to bring to or install in a berth, anchorage, or moorage: *The captain had to berth the ship without the aid of tugboats.* **7.** to provide with a sleeping space, as on a train. —*v.i.* **8.** *Naut.* to come to a dock, anchorage, or moorage. [1615–25; prob. BEAR[1] + -TH[1]]
—**Syn. 4.** spot, slot, position, post, niche, appointment.

ber·tha (bûr′thə), *n.* a collar or trimming, as of lace, worn about the shoulders by women, as over a low-necked waist or dress. [1835–45; named after *Bertha* (d. A.D. 783), wife of Frankish king Pepin the Short; she was famed for her modesty]

Ber·tha (bûr′thə), *n.* a female given name: from a Germanic word meaning "bright."

berth·age (bûr′thij), *n. Naut.* **1.** a place assigned to a vessel for anchoring or tying up. **2.** a charge made for the occupancy of such a place. [1880–85; BERTH + -AGE]

Bert·ie (bûr′tē), *n.* a male or female given name.

Ber·til·lon (bûr′tl on′; *Fr.* ber tē yôN′), *n.* **Al·phonse** (al′fons, -fonz; *Fr.* al fôNs′), 1853–1914, French anthropologist: devised Bertillon system.

Ber′tillon sys′tem, a system of identifying persons, esp. criminals, by a record of individual physical measurements and peculiarities. [1895–1900; named after A. BERTILLON]

Ber·tram (bûr′trəm), *n.* a male given name: from Germanic words meaning "bright" and "raven."

Ber·trand (bûr′trənd; *Fr.* ber träN′), *n.* a male given name, French form of **Bertram.**

ber·trand·ite (bûr′trən dīt′), *n.* a mineral, hydrous beryllium silicate, $Be_4Si_2O_7(OH)_2$, colorless or pale yellow, with a vitreous luster, occurring as tabular or prismatic crystals in pegmatites and hydrothermal veins. [1885–90; < F, after E. *Bertrand,* French mineralogist, who first described it; see -ITE[1]]

Berw., Berwick (def. 1).

Ber·wick (ber′ik *for 1, 2;* bûr′wik *for 3*), *n.* **1.** Also called **Ber·wick·shire** (ber′ik shēr′, -shər), a historic county in SE Scotland. **2.** Berwick-upon-Tweed. **3.** a city in E central Pennsylvania. 12,189.

Ber·wick-up·on-Tweed (ber′ik ə pon′twēd′), *n.* a town in N Northumberland, in N England, on the North Sea at the mouth of the Tweed. 25,700. Also called **Berwick.**

Ber·wyn (bûr′win), *n.* a city in NE Illinois, near Chicago. 46,849.

ber·yl (ber′əl), *n.* a mineral, beryllium aluminum silicate, $Be_3Al_2Si_6O_{18}$, usually green, but also blue, rose, white, and golden, and both opaque and transparent, the latter variety including the gems emerald and aquamarine: the principal ore of beryllium. [1275–1325; ME *beril* (< AF) < LL *bērillus,* L *bēryllus* < Gk *bḗryllos*] —**ber·yl·ine** (ber′ə lin, -līn′), *adj.*

Ber·yl (ber′il), *n.* a female given name.

ber′yl blue′, a light greenish blue. [1880–85]

ber′yl green′, a light bluish green.

be·ryl·li·o·sis (bə ril′ē ō′sis), *n. Pathol.* beryllium poisoning, characterized by the formation of granulomas, primarily affecting the lungs and causing a cough, chest pain, and shortness of breath. [BERYLLI(UM) + -OSIS]

be·ryl·li·um (bə ril′ē əm), *n. Chem.* a steel-gray, bivalent, hard, light, metallic element, the salts of which are sweet: used chiefly in copper alloys for better fatigue endurance, in springs, and in electrical contacts. *Symbol:* Be; *at. wt.:* 9.0122; *at. no.:* 4; *sp. gr.:* 1.8 at 20° C. [1860–65; < L *bēryll(us)* BERYL + -IUM]

beryl′lium cop′per, a copper alloy containing a small amount of beryllium and often some nickel or cobalt, having high strength, hardness, and electrical conductivity.

be·ryl·lon·ite (bə ril′ə nīt′), *n.* a mineral, sodium beryllium phosphate, $NaBePO_4$, occurring in colorless or light-yellow crystals, sometimes used as a gemstone. [1885–90; < Gk *bḗryll(i)on* (*bḗryll(os)* BERYL + -*ion* dim. suffix) + -ITE[1]]

CONCISE ETYMOLOGY KEY: <, descended or borrowed from; >, whence; b., blend of, blended; c., cognate with; cf., compare; deriv., derivative; equiv., equivalent; imit., imitative; obl., oblique; r., replacing; s., stem; sp., spelling, spelled; resp., respelling, respelled; trans., translation; ?, origin unknown; *, unattested; ‡, probably earlier than. See the full key inside the front cover.

Ber·ze·li·us (bər zē′lē əs; *Swed.* ber sā′lē o͝os′), *n.* **Jöns Ja·kob** (yœns yä′kôp), **Baron,** 1779–1848, Swedish chemist.

bes (bās), *n.* beth.

Bes (bes), *n. Egyptian Religion.* the patron deity of music, dancing, and children, represented as a hairy dwarf having a tail and wearing a lion's skin.

B.E.S., Bachelor of Engineering Science.

bes·a·gue (bes′ə gyo͞o′), *n. Armor.* a plate protecting an open area, as at the elbow or armpit. Also called **moton.** [< MF]

Be·san·çon (bə zäN sôN′), *n.* a city in and the capital of Doubs, in E France: Roman ruins. 126,187.

bes·ant (bez′ənt, bə zant′), *n.* bezant.

Bes·ant (bez′ənt *for 1;* bə zant′, *older* bez′ənt *for 2*), *n.* **1. Annie (Wood),** 1847–1933, English theosophist. **2. Sir Walter,** 1836–1901, English novelist.

bes′ ant′ler (bes, bās). See **bay antler.** [1590–1600]

be·screen (bi skrēn′), *v.t.* screen (def. 17). [1585–95; BE- + SCREEN]

be·scrib·ble (bi skrib′əl), *v.t.,* **-bled, -bling.** to scribble all over (something). [1575–85; BE- + SCRIBBLE[1]]

be·seech (bi sēch′), *v.,* **-sought** or **-seeched, -seech·ing.** —*v.t.* **1.** to implore urgently: *They besought him to go at once.* **2.** to beg eagerly for; solicit. —*v.i.* **3.** to make urgent appeal: *Earnestly did I beseech, but to no avail.* [bef. 1100; ME *bisechen,* OE *besēcan.* See BE-, SEEK] —**be·seech′er,** *n.* —**be·seech′ing·ly,** *adv.* —**be·seech′ing·ness,** *n.*
—**Syn. 1.** pray, petition, supplicate, adjure. **1, 2.** entreat, importune.

be·seem (bi sēm′), *Archaic.* —*v.t.* **1.** to be fit for or worthy of; become: *conduct that beseems a gentleman.* —*v.i.* **2.** to be suitable or fitting. [1175–1225; ME *bisemen.* See BE-, SEEM]

Be·sel·e·el (bi sel′ē əl), *n. Douay Bible.* Bezaleel.

be·set (bi set′), *v.t.,* **-set, -set·ting. 1.** to attack on all sides; assail; harass: *to be beset by enemies; beset by difficulties.* **2.** to surround; hem in: *a village beset on all sides by dense forest.* **3.** to set or place upon; bestud: *a gold bracelet beset with jewels.* **4.** *Naut.* to surround (a vessel) by ice, so that control of the helm is lost. [bef. 1000; ME *besetten,* OE *besettan.* See BE-, SET] —**be·set′ment,** *n.* —**be·set′ter,** *n.*
—**Syn. 2.** encircle, enclose, besiege, beleaguer. **3.** stud, decorate, ornament.

be·set·ting (bi set′ing), *adj.* constantly assailing or obsessing, as with temptation: *a besetting sin.* [1540–50; BESET + -ING[2]]

be·show (bi shō′), *n.* a sablefish. [1880–85, *Amer.;* < Makah, c. Nootka *mi·š̓a·wi·ḥ*]

be·shrew (bi shro͞o′), *v.t. Archaic.* to curse; invoke evil upon. [1275–1325; ME *beshrewen.* See BE-, SHREW[1]]

BEShT (besht), *n.* See **Baal Shem-Tov.**

be·side (bi sīd′), *prep.* **1.** by or at the side of; near: *Sit down beside me.* **2.** compared with: *Beside him other writers seem amateurish.* **3.** apart from; not connected with: *beside the point; beside the question.* **4.** besides (defs. 4, 5). **5. beside oneself,** almost out of one's senses from a strong emotion, as from joy, delight, anger, fear, or grief: *He was beside himself with rage when the train left without him.* —*adv.* **6.** along the side of something: *The family rode in the carriage, and the dog ran along beside.* **7.** besides (def. 2). [bef. 1000; ME; earlier *bi-siden,* OE *bī sīdan, be sīdan;* see BE-, SIDE]
—**Usage.** For the prepositional meanings "over and above, in addition to" and "except" BESIDES is preferred, especially in edited writing: *Besides these honors he received a sum of money. We heard no other sound besides the breaking surf.* However, BESIDE sometimes occurs with these meanings as well.

be·sides (bi sīdz′), *adv.* **1.** moreover; furthermore; also: *Besides, I promised her we would come.* **2.** in addition: *There are three elm trees and two maples besides.* **3.** otherwise; else: *They had a roof over their heads but not much besides.* —*prep.* **4.** over and above; in addition to: *Besides a mother he has a sister to support.* **5.** other than; except: *There's no one here besides Bill and me.* [1150–1200; ME; see BESIDE, -S[1]]
—**Syn. 1.** further. BESIDES, MOREOVER both indicate something additional to what has already been stated. BESIDES often suggests that the addition is in the nature of an afterthought: *The bill cannot be paid as yet; besides, the work is not completed.* MOREOVER is more formal and implies that the addition is something particular, emphatic, or important: *I did not like the house; moreover, it was too high-priced.*
—**Usage. 4, 5.** See **beside.**

be·siege (bi sēj′), *v.t.,* **-sieged, -sieg·ing. 1.** to lay siege to. **2.** to crowd around; crowd in upon; surround: *Vacationers besieged the travel office.* **3.** to assail or ply, as with requests or demands. [1250–1300; ME *bysegen.* See BE-, SIEGE] —**be·siege′ment,** *n.* —**be·sieg′er,** *n.* —**be·sieg′ing·ly,** *adv.*
—**Syn. 3.** beset, pester, harass, harry, hound.

be·slob·ber (bi slob′ər), *v.t.* to slobber all over (something): *The child beslobbered his bib.* [1350–1400; ME; see BE-, SLOBBER]

be·smear (bi smēr′), *v.t.* **1.** to smear all over; bedaub. **2.** to sully; defile; soil: *to besmear someone's reputation.* [bef. 1050; ME *bismeren,* OE *besmerian.* See BE-, SMEAR] —**be·smear′er,** *n.*

be·smirch (bi smûrch′), *v.t.* **1.** to soil; tarnish; discolor. **2.** to detract from the honor or luster of: *to besmirch someone's good name.* [1590–1600; BE- + SMIRCH] —**be·smirch′er,** *n.*
—**Syn. 2.** stain, tarnish, soil, blacken, dishonor, discredit, sully, besmear.

be·som (bē′zəm), *n.* **1.** a broom, esp. one of brush or twigs. **2.** broom (def. 2). [bef. 1000; ME *besem,* OE *besma;* c. D *bezem,* G *Besen*]

be′som pock′et, an interior pocket with edging or stitching around the opening.

be·sot (bi sot′), *v.t.,* **-sot·ted, -sot·ting. 1.** to intoxicate or stupefy with drink. **2.** to make stupid or foolish: *a mind besotted with fear and superstition.* **3.** to infatuate; obsess: *He is besotted by her youth and beauty.* [1575–85; BE + SOT] —**be·sot′ted·ly,** *adv.* —**be·sot′ted·ness,** *n.* —**be·sot′ting·ly,** *adv.*

be·sought (bi sôt′), *v.* a pt. and pp. of **beseech.**

be·spake (bi spāk′), *v. Archaic.* pt. of **bespeak.**

be·span·gle (bi spang′gəl), *v.t.,* **-gled, -gling.** to cover or adorn with or as if with spangles; make sparkle brilliantly: *grass bespangled with dewdrops; poetry bespangled with vivid imagery.* [1585–95; BE- + SPANGLE]

be·spat·ter (bi spat′ər), *v.t.* **1.** to soil by spattering; splash with water, dirt, etc. **2.** to slander or libel: *a reputation bespattered by malicious gossip.* [1635–45; BE- + SPATTER]

be·speak (bi spēk′), *v.t.,* **-spoke** or (*Archaic*) **-spake; -spo·ken** or **-spoke; -speak·ing. 1.** to ask for in advance: *to bespeak the reader's patience.* **2.** to reserve beforehand; engage in advance; make arrangements for: *to bespeak a seat in a theater.* **3.** *Literary.* to speak to; address. **4.** to show; indicate: *This bespeaks a kindly heart.* **5.** *Obs.* to foretell; forebode. [bef. 900; ME *bespeken,* OE *besprecan.* See BE-, SPEAK]

be·speck·le (bi spek′əl), *v.t.,* **-led, -ling.** to speckle.

be·spec·ta·cled (bi spek′tə kəld), *adj.* wearing eyeglasses. [1735–45; BE- + SPECTACLED]

be·spoke (bi spōk′), *v.* **1.** a pt. and pp. of **bespeak.** —*adj.* **2.** *Brit.* **a.** (of clothes) made to individual order; custom-made: *a bespoke jacket.* **b.** making or selling such clothes: *a bespoke tailor.* **3.** *Older Use.* engaged to be married; spoken for. [1745–55 for def. 2]

be·spo·ken (bi spōkən), *v.* **1.** a pp. of **bespeak.** —*adj.* **2.** bespoke. [1600–10 for def. 2]

be·spread (bi spred′), *v.t.,* **-spread, -spread·ing.** to spread over (a surface); cover (usually fol. by *with*): *a table bespread with fine linens.* [1350–1400; ME *bespreden.* See BE-, SPREAD]

be·sprent (bi sprent′), *adj. Archaic.* besprinkled; bestrewn. [1325–75; ME *bespre(y)nt,* ptp. of *besprengen,* OE *besprengan,* equiv. to *be-* BE- + *sprengan* to sprinkle, akin to SPRING]

be·sprin·kle (bi spring′kəl), *v.t.,* **-kled, -kling.** to sprinkle (something) all over, as with water or a powder. [1400–50; late ME; see BE-, SPRINKLE]

Bess (bes), *n.* a female given name, form of **Elizabeth.**

Bes·sa·ra·bi·a (bes′ə rā′bē ə), *n.* a region in Moldavia (Moldova), on the W shore of the Black Sea: formerly in Rumania. —**Bes′sa·ra′bi·an,** *adj., n.*

Bes·sel (bes′əl), *n.* **Frie·drich Wil·helm** (frē′drik wil′helm; *Ger.* frē′drikh vil′helm), 1784–1846, German astronomer.

Bes′sel func′tion, *Math.* one of several transcendental functions, usually represented as power series, that are solutions to a group of related differential equations. [1870–75; named after F. W. BESSEL]

Bes′sel meth′od, a method of ascertaining position by the use of a map showing prominent features of the terrain and enabling one to sight through them to obtain a fix. [1935–40; named after F. W. BESSEL]

Bes·se·mer (bes′ə mər), *n.* **1. Sir Henry,** 1813–98, English engineer: inventor of the Bessemer process. **2.** a city in central Alabama. 31,729.

Bes′semer convert′er, the refractory-lined metal container in which steel is produced by the Bessemer process. [1925–30]

Bes′semer proc′ess, *Metall.* a process of producing steel, in which impurities are removed by forcing a blast of air through molten iron. [1855–60; after H. BESSEMER]

Bes′semer steel′, steel made by the Bessemer process. [1870–75]

Bes·sie (bes′ē), *n.* a female given name, form of **Elizabeth.** Also, **Bes′sy.**

best (best), *adj., superl. of* **good** *with* **better** *as compar.* **1.** of the highest quality, excellence, or standing: *the best work; the best students.* **2.** most advantageous, suitable, or desirable: *the best way.* **3.** largest; most: *the best part of a day.* —*adv., superl. of* **well** *with* **better** *as compar.* **4.** most excellently or suitably; with most advantage or success: *an opera role that best suits her voice.* **5.** in or to the highest degree; most fully (usually used in combination): *best-suited; best-known; best-loved.* **6. as best one can,** in the best way possible under the circumstances: *We tried to smooth over the disagreement as best we could.* **7. had best,** would be wisest or most reasonable to; ought to: *You had best phone your mother to tell her where you are going.* —*n.* **8.** something or someone that is best: *They always demand and get the best. The best of us can make mistakes.* **9.** a person's finest clothing: *It's important that you wear your best.* **10.** a person's most agreeable or desirable emotional state (often prec. by *at*). **11.** a person's highest degree of competence, inspiration, etc. (often prec. by *at*). **12.** the highest quality to be found in a given activity or category of things (often prec. by *at*): *cabinetmaking at its best.* **13.** the best effort that a person, group, or thing can make: *Their best fell far short of excellence.* **14.** a person's best wishes or kindest regards: *Please give my best to your father.* **15. all for the best,** for the good as the final result; to an ultimate advantage: *At the time it was hard to realize how it could be all for the best.* Also, **for the best. 16. at best,** under the most favorable circumstances: *You may expect to be treated civilly, at best.* **17. get** or **have the best of, a.** to gain the advantage over. **b.** to defeat; subdue: *His arthritis gets the best of him from time to time.* **18. make the best of,** to cope with in the best way possible: *to make the best of a bad situation.* **19. with the best,** on a par with the most capable: *He can play bridge with the best.* —*v.t.* **20.** to get the better of; defeat; beat: *He easily bested his opponent in hand-to-hand combat. She bested me in the argument.* [bef. 900; ME *beste,* OE *betst, best;* c. D *best,* OHG *bezzist* (G *best*), ON *bezt,* Goth *batists.* See BETTER[1], -EST]

Best (best), *n.* **Charles Herbert,** 1899–1978, Canadian physiologist, born in the U.S.: one of the discoverers of insulin.

best′-ball′ four′some (best′bôl′), *Golf.* a match, scored by holes, between two pairs of players, in which the score of the lower scoring member of each pair is taken as their score for the hole.

best′-ball′ match′, *Golf.* a match, scored by holes, in which one player competing against two or more others must score lower than the lowest scoring opponent to win a hole. [1905–10]

best′ boy′, *Motion Picture and Television Slang.* the first assistant to the head electrician.

best-case (best′kās′), *adj.* being the best result that could be expected under the circumstances: *The best-case scenario shows her winning the nomination easily.* Cf. **worst-case.** [1975–80]

be•stead[1] (bi sted′), *v.t.,* **-stead•ed, -stead•ed** or **-stead, -stead•ing.** to help; assist; serve; avail. [1575–85; BE- + STEAD]

be•stead[2] (bi sted′), *adj. Archaic.* placed or situated, often unfavorably or in difficulty. [1300–50; ME *bisted, bistad,* equiv. to *bi* BE- + *sted,* var. of *stad* placed < ON *staddr,* ptp. of *stethja* to place, deriv. of *stathr* place]

best′-ef′forts sell′ing (best′ef′ərts), a method of underwriting a security whereby a syndicate takes a new issue without any guarantees of sale to the issuer.

bes•tial (bes′chəl, bēs′-), *adj.* **1.** of, pertaining to, or having the form of a beast: *the belief that a person could assume bestial form after death; the bestial signs of the zodiac.* **2.** without reason or intelligence; brutal; inhuman: *bestial treatment of prisoners.* **3.** beastlike in gratifying one's sensual desires; carnal; debased. [1350–1400; ME (< AF) < LL *bēstiālis* (L *bēsti(a)* BEAST + *-ālis* -AL[1])] —**bes′tial•ly,** *adv.*

bes•ti•al•i•ty (bes′chē al′i tē, bēs′-), *n., pl.* **-ties. 1.** brutish or beastly character or behavior; beastliness. **2.** indulgence in beastlike appetites, instincts, impulses, etc. **3.** an instance of bestial character or behavior. **4.** sexual relations between a person and an animal; sodomy. [1350–1400; ME *bestial(i)te* (< AF, MF) < ML *bēstiālitās.* See BESTIAL, -ITY]

bes•tial•ize (bes′chə līz′, bēs′-), *v.t.,* **-ized, -iz•ing.** to make bestial or beastlike: *War bestializes its participants.* Also, *esp. Brit.,* **bes′tial•ise′.** [1675–85; BESTIAL + -IZE]

bes•ti•ar•y (bes′chē er′ē, bēs′-), *n., pl.* **-ar•ies.** a collection of moralized fables, esp. as written in the Middle Ages, about actual or mythical animals. [1615–25; < ML *bēstiārium,* neut. of L *bēstiārius.* See BEAST, -ARY] —**bes•ti•a•rist** (bes′chē ər ist, -chər-, bēs′-), *n.*

best′ in show′, 1. an award to the dog, cat, or other animal judged best of all breeds in a competition. **2.** the animal that wins such an award.

be•stir (bi stûr′), *v.t.,* **-stirred, -stir•ring.** to stir up; rouse to action (often used reflexively): *She bestirred herself at the first light of morning.* [bef. 900; ME *bistiren,* OE *bestyrian* to heap up. See BE-, STIR[1]]

best′ man′, the chief attendant of the bridegroom at a wedding. [1775–85]

be•stow (bi stō′), *v.t.* **1.** to present as a gift; give; confer (usually fol. by *on* or *upon*): *The trophy was bestowed upon the winner.* **2.** to put to some use; apply: *Time spent in study is time well bestowed.* **3.** *Archaic.* **a.** to provide quarters for; house; lodge. **b.** to put; stow; deposit; store. [1275–1325; ME *bestowen.* See BE-, STOW[1]] —**be•stow′al, be•stow′ment,** *n.*
—**Syn. 1.** grant, vouchsafe, award, accord.

be•strad•dle (bi strad′l), *v.t.,* **-dled, -dling.** to bestride. [1800–10; BE- + STRADDLE]

be•strew (bi strōō′), *v.t.,* **-strewed, -strewed** or **-strewn, -strew•ing. 1.** to strew or cover (a surface). **2.** to strew or scatter about. **3.** to lie scattered over. [bef. 1000; ME *bistrewen,* OE *bestrēowian.* See BE-, STREW]

be•stride (bi strīd′), *v.t.,* **-strode** or **-strid, -strid•den** or **-strid, -strid•ing. 1.** to get or be astride of; have or place the legs on both sides of. **2.** to step over or across with long strides. **3.** to stand or tower over; dominate. [bef. 1000; ME *bestriden,* OE *bestrīdan.* See BE-, STRIDE]

be•strow (bi strō′), *v.t.,* **-strowed, -strown** or **-strowed, -strow•ing.** *Archaic.* bestrew.

best•sell•er (best′sel′ər), *n.* **1.** a book that is among those having the largest sales during a given period. **2.** any product that among those of its kind is selling particularly well at a given time: *This car was a bestseller last year.* Also, **best′ sell′er.** [1885–90, *Amer.;* BEST + SELLER] —**best′sell′er•dom,** *n.* —**best′-sell′ing,** *adj.*

be•stud (bi stud′), *v.t.,* **-stud•ded, -stud•ding.** to set with or as if with studs; dot: *an evening sky bestudded with stars.* [1595–1605; BE- + STUD]

bet[1] (bet), *v.,* **bet** or **bet•ted, bet•ting,** *n.* —*v.t.* **1.** to wager with (something or someone). —*v.i.* **2.** to make a wager: *Do you want to bet?* **3. you bet!** *Informal.* of course! surely!: *You bet I'd like to be there!* —*n.* **4.** a pledge of a forfeit risked on some uncertain outcome; wager: *Where do we place our bets?* **5.** that which is pledged: *a two-dollar bet.* **6.** something that is bet on, as a competitor in a sporting event or a number in a lottery: *That horse looks like a good bet.* **7.** an act or instance of betting: *It's a bet, then?* **8.** a person, plan of action, etc., considered as being a good alternative; choice: *Your best bet is to sell your stocks now.* [1585–95; perh. special use of obs. *bet* better, in phrase *the bet* the advantage, i.e., the odds]
—**Syn. 1.** gamble, stake, risk, hazard, venture, chance.

bet[2] (bät; bet), *n.* beth.

bet., between.

be•ta (bā′tə *or, esp. Brit.,* bē′-), *n.* **1.** the second letter of the Greek alphabet (*β*, B). **2.** the consonant sound represented by this letter. **3.** (*cap.*) *Astron.* a star that is usually the second brightest of a constellation: *The second brightest star in Taurus is Beta Tauri.* **4.** *Chem.* **a.** one of the possible positions of an atom or group in a compound. **b.** one of two or more isomeric compounds. **5.** the second of any series, as in chemistry or physics. **6.** Also called **beta coefficient, beta line.** *Stock Exchange.* an arbitrary measure of the volatility of a given stock using an index of the volatility of the market as a whole: *A beta of 1.1 indicates a stock that is 10 percent more volatile than the market.* **7.** (*cap.*) *Trademark.* a brand of tape format for VCR tape, incompatible with other formats. Cf. **VHS. 8.** *Chiefly Brit.* a grade showing that a student is in the middle or second of three scholastic sections in a class. Cf. **alpha** (def. 7), **gamma** (def. 9). [< L < Gk *bêta* < Sem; cf. Heb *bēth* BETH]

be•ta-ad•ren•er•gic (bā′tə ad′rə nûr′jik *or, esp. Brit.,* bē′-), *adj.* of or pertaining to a beta receptor. [1965–70]

be′ta-adrener′gic recep′tor, *Biochem., Physiol.* See **beta receptor.**

be′ta block′er, *Pharm.* any of various substances that interfere with the action of the beta receptors: used primarily to reduce the heart rate or force in the prevention, management, or treatment of angina, hypertension, or arrythmias. Also, **be′ta-block′er.** Cf. **alpha blocker.** —**be′ta-block′ing,** *adj.* [1975–80]

be′ta brass′, an alloy consisting of nearly equal proportions of copper and zinc. [1910–15]

be′ta car′otene, *n. Biochem.* the most abundant of various isomers of carotene, $C_{40}H_{56}$, that can be converted by the body to vitamin A.

be′ta cell′. See **B cell** (def. 2). [1925–30]

be′ta coeffi′cient, *Stock Exchange.* beta (def. 6).

Be′ta Cru′cis, a star of the first magnitude in the constellation Southern Cross. [< NL: Beta of the Cross]

be′ta decay′, *Physics.* a radioactive process in which a beta particle is emitted from the nucleus of an atom, raising the atomic number of the atom by one if the particle is negatively charged, lowering it by one if positively charged. [1930–35]

Be•ta•dine (bā′tə dīn′ *or, esp. Brit.,* bē′-), *Pharm., Trademark.* a brand name for povidone-iodine.

be•ta-en•dor•phin (bā′tə en dôr′fin *or, esp. Brit.,* bē′-), *n.* a potent endorphin released by the anterior pituitary gland in response to pain, trauma, exercise, or other forms of stress. [1975–80]

be′ta func′tion, *Math.* a function of two variables, usually expressed as an improper integral and equal to the quotient of the product of the values of the gamma function at each variable divided by the value of the gamma function at the sum of the variables. [1885–90]

be•ta•ga•lac•to•si•dase (bā′tə gə lak′tə sī′dās, -dāz *or, esp. Brit.,* bē′-), *n. Biochem.* any of a family of enzymes capable of liberating galactose from carbohydrates. [BETA + *galactoside* a glycoside in which the sugar is galactose (< F; see GALACTOSE, -IDE) + -ASE]

be′ta glob′ulin, a blood plasma protein that is separable from other globulins by electrophoresis. [1945–50]

be′ta-in•dole•a•ce′tic ac′id (bā′tə in′dōl ə sē′tik, -ə set′ik *or, esp. Brit.,* bē′-), *Biochem.* See **indoleacetic acid.**

be•ta•ine (bē′tə ēn′, -in; bi tā′ēn, -in), *n. Chem., Pharm.* a colorless, crystalline, water-soluble, sweet-tasting alkaloid, $C_5H_{11}NO_2$, usually obtained from sugar beets or synthesized from glycine, used chiefly in medicine. Also, **be•ta•in** (bē′tə in, bi tā′-). Also called **lycine, oxyneurine, trimethylglycine.** [1875–80; < L *bēta* BEET + -INE[2]]

be′ta i′ron, *Metall.* an allotrope of iron, stable between 768°C and 910°C, similar to alpha iron but nonmagnetic. [1890–95]

be•take (bi tāk′), *v.t.,* **-took, -tak•en, -tak•ing. 1.** to cause to go (usually used reflexively): *She betook herself to town.* **2.** *Archaic.* to resort or have recourse to. [1175–1225; ME *bitaken.* See BE-, TAKE]

be′ta line′, *Stock Exchange.* beta (def. 6).

be•ta•meth•a•sone (bā′tə meth′ə sōn′ *or, esp. Brit.,* bē′-), *n. Pharm.* a synthetic analogue of a glucocorticoid, $C_{22}H_{29}FO_5$, used in various forms in the treatment of inflammation, allergies, and tumors, and for replacement therapy in adrenal insufficiency. [perh. BETA + METH(YL) + *-a-* connective vowel + (HYDROCORTI)SONE, components of the chemical name]

be′ta•meth′yl acro′lein (bā′tə meth′əl, bā′- *or, esp. Brit.,* bē′tə-, bē′-), crotonaldehyde.

be•ta-naph•thol (bā′tə naf′thôl, -thol, -nap′- *or, esp. Brit.,* bē′-), *n. Chem.* naphthol (def. 1). [BETA + NAPHTHOL]

be•ta-naph•thyl•a•mine (bā′tə naf′thə lə mēn′, -nap′- *or, esp. Brit.,* bē′-), *n. Chem.* a white to reddish, crystalline, water-soluble, extremely toxic solid, $C_{10}H_9N$, used chiefly in the manufacture of azo dyes. [BETA + NAPHTHYL + AMINE]

be′ta-naph′thyl group′ (bā′tə naf′thil, -nap′- *or, esp. Brit.,* bē′-), *Chem.* See under **naphthyl.** Also called **be′ta-naph′thyl rad′ical.**

Bet•an•court (bet′n kŏŏr′, -kôr′; *Sp.* be′täng kôrt′), *n.* **Ró•mu•lo** (rom′yə lō′; *Sp.* RÔ′mōō lô′), 1908–81, Venezuelan journalist and political leader: president of Venezuela 1945–48 and 1959–64.

be•ta-ox•i•da•tion (bā′tə ok′si dā′shən *or, esp. Brit.,* bē′-), *n. Biochem.* a process by which fatty acids are degraded, involving oxidation of the beta carbons and removal of successive two-carbon fragments from the fatty acid. [1930–35]

be′ta par′ticle, *Physics.* an electron or positron emitted from an atomic nucleus in a certain type of radioactive decay. [1900–05]

be′ta ray′, *Physics.* a stream of beta particles. [1900–05]

be′ta recep′tor, *Biochem., Physiol.* a site on a cell, as of the heart, that, upon interaction with epinephrine or norepinephrine, controls heartbeat and heart contractability, vasodilation, smooth muscle inhibition, and other physiological processes. Also, **be′ta-re•cep′tor.** Also called **beta-adrenergic receptor.** Cf. **alpha receptor.** [1960–65]

be′ta rhythm′, a pattern of high-frequency brain waves **(beta waves)** observed in normal persons upon sensory stimulation, esp. with light, or when they are engaging in purposeful mental activity. [1935–40; earlier *beta waves,* trans. of G *Betawellen;* see ALPHA RHYTHM]

be′ta test′, 1. *Psychol.* a set of mental tests designed to measure the general intelligence of individuals unable to read and write adequately or at all, used by the U.S. Army in World War I. Cf. **alpha test. 2.** *Computers.* a quality-control technique in which hardware or software is subjected to trial in the environment for which it was designed, usually after debugging by the manufacturer and immediately prior to marketing.

be•ta•tron (bā′tə tron′ *or, esp. Brit.,* bē′-), *n. Physics.* an accelerator in which electrons are accelerated to high energies by an electric field produced by a changing magnetic field. [1940–45; BETA (see BETA PARTICLE) + -TRON]

be′ta waves′. See under **beta rhythm.** [1930–35]

be•ta•zole (bā′tə zōl′), *n. Pharm.* a substance, $C_5H_9N_3$, used in medicine to stimulate gastric secretion. [prob. BETA + (PYRA)ZOLE components of the chemical name]

be•tel (bēt′l), *n.* an East Indian pepper plant, *Piper betle,* the leaves of which are chewed with other ingredients. Also, **be′tel pep′per.** [1545–55; < Pg *bétele, bétere* < Malayalam *veṟṟila* or Tamil *veṟṟilai*]

Be•tel•geuse (bēt′l jōōz′, bet′l jœz′), *n. Astron.* a first-magnitude red supergiant in the constellation Orion. Also, **Be′tel•geux′.** [1790–1800; < F < Ar *bīt al jauzā′* shoulder of the giant (i.e., of Orion)]

be′tel nut′, the astringent kernel of the seed of the betel palm, chewed in many tropical regions in combination with slaked lime and the leaves of the betel plant. Also called **areca nut.** [1675–85]

be′tel palm′, a tropical Asian palm, *Areca catechu,* cultivated in the Old World tropics for its seeds, the kernels of which are chewed in combination with other ingredients. [1870–75]

bête noire (bāt′ nwär′; *Fr.* bet NWAR′), *pl.* **bêtes noires** (bāt′ nwärz′; *Fr.* bet NWAR′). a person or thing especially disliked or dreaded; bane; bugbear. [1835–45; < F: lit., black beast]

beth (bās, bāt; *Seph. Heb.* bet), *n.* **1.** the second letter of the Hebrew alphabet. **2.** either of the consonant sounds represented by this letter. Also, **bet, bes.** [1905–10; < Heb *bēth* lit., house; see BETA]

Beth (beth), *n.* a female given name, form of **Elizabeth.**

be•than•e•chol (be than′i kôl′, -kol′), *n. Pharm.* a substance, $C_7H_{17}ClN_2O_2$, used to treat urinary retention, esp. postoperatively. [perh. *beth-* (b. BETA and METHYL) + -ANE + CHOL(INE); the substance is a urethan of betamethylcholine chloride]

Beth•a•ny (beth′ə nē), *n.* **1.** a village in W Jordan, near Jerusalem, at the foot of the Mount of Olives; occupied by Israel since 1967: home of Lazarus and his sisters, Martha and Mary. John 11:1. 3560. **2.** a city in central Oklahoma. 22,130. **3.** a female given name.

Beth Din (*Seph. Heb.* bet′ dēn′), a Jewish court of law. [< Heb *bēth dīn,* lit., house of law]

Be•the (bā′tə), *n.* **Hans Al•brecht** (hanz ôl′brekt, häns; *Ger.* häns äl′brekht), born 1906, U.S. physicist, born in Alsace: Nobel prize 1967.

beth•el (beth′əl), *n.* **1.** a sacred area or sanctuary. Gen. 28:19. **2.** a church or hostel for sailors. [1610–20; < Heb *bēth ′ēl* house of God]

Beth•el (beth′əl; *for 1 also* beth′el, beth′el′), *n.* **1.** a village in W Jordan, near Jerusalem; occupied by Israel since 1967: dream of Jacob. Gen. 28:19. **2.** a town in SW Connecticut. 16,004.

Beth′el Park′, a city in SW Pennsylvania. 34,755.

Be·thes·da (bə thez′də), *n.* **1.** a pool in Biblical Jerusalem, believed to have healing powers. John 5:2–4. **2.** a city in central Maryland; residential suburb of Washington, D.C. 62,736. **3.** (*l.c.*) a chapel.

Beth Hil·lel (*Seph.* bet′ hē lel′), *Hebrew.* the school of Jewish legal thought and hermeneutics founded in Jerusalem in the 1st century B.C. by the Jewish spiritual leader Hillel and characterized by its systematic use of interpretive principles and a certain flexibility in interpreting the oral and written law. Cf. ***Beth Shammai.*** [*bēth Hillēl* lit., house of Hillel]

be·think (bi thingk′), *v.*, **-thought, -think·ing.** —*v.t.* **1.** to think; consider (used reflexively): *He bethought himself a moment.* **2.** to remind (oneself): *to bethink oneself of family obligations.* **3.** to remember; recall (used reflexively): *She lives in the past now, bethinking herself of happier days.* **4.** to determine; resolve: *Under the circumstances I could not otherwise bethink me.* **5.** *Archaic.* to bear in mind; remember. —*v.i.* **6.** *Archaic.* to consider; meditate. [bef. 1000; ME *bethenken,* OE *bethencan.* See BE-, THINK[1]]

Beth·le·hem (beth′li hem′, -lē əm), *n.* **1.** a town in NW Jordan, near Jerusalem; occupied by Israel since 1967: birthplace of Jesus and David. 15,000. **2.** a city in E Pennsylvania. 70,419.

Beth′lehem sage′, a plant, *Pulmonaria saccharata,* of the borage family, native to Europe, having mottled, white leaves and white or reddish-purple flowers in clusters.

Beth·mann-Holl·weg (bāt′män hôl′väk), *n.* **The·o·bald von** (tā′ō bält′ fən), 1856–1921, German statesman: chancellor 1909–17.

Beth Mid·rash (*Seph.* bet′ mē drāsh′), *Hebrew.* a place where Jews gather to study the Talmud and other religious writings; a small synagogue. [*bēth midhrāsh* lit., house of study]

Beth′nal Green′ (beth′nl), a former borough of London, England, N of the Thames.

be·thought (bi thôt′), *v.* pt. and pp. of **bethink.**

Beth·page (beth pāj′), *n.* a city on S Long Island, in SE New York. 16,840.

Beth·sa·be·e (beth sä′bē ē′), *n. Douay Bible.* Bathsheba.

Beth·sa·i·da (beth sā′i də), *n.* an ancient town in N Israel, near the N shore of the Sea of Galilee.

Beth Sham·mai (*Seph.* bet′ shä mī′), *Hebrew.* the school of Jewish legal thought and hermeneutics founded in Jerusalem in the 1st century B.C. by the Jewish teacher Shammai and characterized by an austere or rigid interpretation of Jewish law and tradition. Cf. ***Beth Hillel.*** [*bēth Shammai* lit., house of Shammai]

Be·thune (bə thyōōn′, -thōōn′), *n.* **Mary Mc·Leod** (mə kloud′), 1875–1955, U.S. educator and civil-rights leader.

be·tide (bi tīd′), *v.*, **-tid·ed, -tid·ing.** —*v.t.* **1.** to happen to; come to; befall: *Woe betide the villain!* —*v.i.* **2.** to happen; come to pass: *Whatever betides, maintain your courage.* [1125–75; ME *betiden.* See BE-, TIDE[2]]

be·times (bi tīmz′), *adv.* **1.** early; in good time: *He was up betimes doing his lessons.* **2.** occasionally; at times. **3.** *Archaic.* within a short time; soon. [1275–1325; ME *bitimes,* equiv. to *bitime* (from phrase *bi time* by time) + -s -s[1]]

bê·tise (be tēz′), *n.* **1.** lack of understanding, perception, or the like; stupidity. **2.** a stupid or foolish act or remark. **3.** something inconsequential or without merit; absurdity; trifle. [1820–30; < F: lit., foolishness, equiv. to *bête* foolish (see BEAST) + *-ise* -ICE]

Bet·je·man (bech′ə mən), *n.* **Sir John,** 1906–84, English poet: poet laureate 1972–84.

be·to·ken (bi tō′kən), *v.t.* **1.** to give evidence of; indicate: *to betoken one's fidelity with a vow; a kiss that betokens one's affection.* **2.** to be or give a token or sign of; portend: *a thunderclap that betokens foul weather; an angry word that betokens hostility.* [1125–75; ME *bitocnen, bitacnen.* See BE-, TOKEN]

bet·o·ny (bet′n ē), *n., pl.* **-nies. 1.** a plant, *Stachys* (formerly *Betonica*) *officinalis,* of the mint family, having hairy leaves and dense spikes of purple flowers, formerly used in medicine and dyeing. **2.** any of various similar plants, esp. of the genus *Pedicularis.* [bef. 1000; late ME; ME *betayny, betanie* < ML *betōnia,* re-formation of L *betōnica* (Pliny), in earlier readings *vettōnica* (*herba*) Vettonic (herb) (*Vettōn*(*ēs*) an Iberian tribe + *-ica,* fem. of *-icus* -IC); cf. ME *beteyne, betoyne* (< AF), OE *bet*(*t*)*onice* (< L)]

be·took (bi tŏŏk′), *v.* pt. of **betake.**

be·tray (bi trā′), *v.t.* **1.** to deliver or expose to an enemy by treachery or disloyalty: *Benedict Arnold betrayed his country.* **2.** to be unfaithful in guarding, maintaining, or fulfilling: *to betray a trust.* **3.** to disappoint the hopes or expectations of; be disloyal to: *to betray one's friends.* **4.** to reveal or disclose in violation of confidence: *to betray a secret.* **5.** to reveal unconsciously (something one would preferably conceal): *Her nervousness betrays her insecurity.* **6.** to show or exhibit; reveal; disclose: *an unfeeling remark that betrays his lack of concern.* **7.** to deceive, misguide, or corrupt: *a young lawyer betrayed by political ambitions into irreparable folly.* **8.** to seduce and desert. [1200–50; ME *bitraien,* equiv. to *bi-* BE- + *traien* < OF *trair* < L *trādere* to betray. See TRAITOR] —**be·tray′al,** *n.* —**be·tray′er,** *n.*
—**Syn. 4.** bare, expose, tell, divulge. **6.** display, manifest, expose, uncover. —**Ant. 4, 6.** hide, conceal.

be·troth (bi trōth′, -trôth′), *v.t.* **1.** to arrange for the marriage of; affiance (usually used in passive constructions): *The couple was betrothed with the approval of both families.* **2.** *Archaic.* to promise to marry. [1275–1325; ME *betrouthe,* var. of *betreuthe* (*be-* BE- + *treuthe* TRUTH; see TROTH)]
—**Syn. 1.** engage, promise, pledge, plight.

be·troth·al (bi trō′thəl, -trô′thəl), *n.* the act or state of being betrothed; engagement. Also, **be·troth′ment.** [1835–45; BETROTH + -AL[2]]

be·trothed (bi trōthd′, -trôtht′), *adj.* **1.** engaged to be married: *She is betrothed to that young lieutenant.* —*n.* **2.** the person to whom one is engaged: *He introduced us to his betrothed.* [1530–40; BETROTH + -ED[2]]

Bet·si·bo·ka (bet′sē bō′kə, -bōō′-), *n.* a river in central Madagascar, flowing NW to the Mozambique Channel. ab. 200 mi. (320 km) long.

Bet·sy (bet′sē), *n.* a female given name, form of **Elizabeth.** Also, **Bet′sey, Bet′si.**

bet·ta (bet′ə), *n.* See **fighting fish.** [1925–30; < NL < ?]

Bet·te (bet′ē, bet), *n.* a female given name, form of **Elizabeth.**

bet·ted (bet′id), *v.* a pt. and pp. of **bet.**

Bet·tel·heim (bet′l hīm′), *n.* **Bruno,** 1903–90, U.S. psychologist, educator, and writer, born in Austria.

Bet·ten·dorf (bet′n dôrf′), *n.* a city in E Iowa. 27,381.

bet·ter[1] (bet′ər), *adj., compar. of* **good** *with* **best** *as superl.* **1.** of superior quality or excellence: *a better coat; a better speech.* **2.** morally superior; more virtuous: *They are no better than thieves.* **3.** of superior suitability, advisability, desirability, acceptableness, etc.; preferable: *a better time for action.* **4.** larger; greater: *the better part of a lifetime.* **5.** improved in health; healthier than before. **6.** completely recovered in health. **7. no better than one should be,** *Disparaging.* morally inferior; immoral or amoral. —*adv., compar. of* **well** *with* **best** *as superl.* **8.** in a more appropriate or acceptable way or manner: *to behave better.* **9.** to a greater degree; more completely or thoroughly: *He knows the way better than we do. I probably know him better than anyone else.* **10.** more: *I walked better than a mile to town.* **11. better off, a.** in better circumstances. **b.** more fortunate; happier: *Because of his asthma, he would be better off in a different climate.* **12. go (someone) one better,** to exceed the effort of; be superior to: *The neighbors went us one better by buying two new cars.* **13. had better,** would be wiser or more well-advised to; ought to: *We had better stay indoors today.* **14. think better of, a.** to reconsider and decide more favorably or wisely regarding: *I was tempted to make a sarcastic retort, but thought better of it.* **b.** to form a higher opinion of. —*v.t.* **15.** to increase the good qualities of; make better; improve: *to better the lot of the suburban commuter.* **16.** to improve upon; surpass; exceed: *We have bettered last year's production record.* **17.** *Cards.* to raise (a previous bid). **18. better oneself,** to improve one's social standing, financial position, or education: *He is going to night school because he wants to better himself.* —*n.* **19.** that which has greater excellence or is preferable or wiser: *the better of two choices.* **20.** Usually, **betters.** those superior to one in wisdom, wealth, etc. **21. for the better,** in a way that is an improvement: *His health changed for the better.* **22. get** or **have the better of, a.** to get an advantage over. **b.** to prevail against. [bef. 900; ME *bettre,* OE *bet*(*t*)(*e*)*ra;* c. OHG *bezziro* (G *besser*), D *beter,* ON *betr,* Goth *batiza,* equiv. to *bat-* (c. OHG *baz* (adv.) better; akin to BOOT[2]) + *-iza* comp. suffix; suggested relation to Skt *bhadrá-* "fortunate" is doubtful. See BEST]
—**Syn. 15.** amend; advance, promote; reform, correct, rectify. See **improve.**

bet·ter[2] (bet′ər), *n.* bettor. [BET + -ER[1]]

Bet′ter Busi′ness Bu′reau, any of a nationwide system of local organizations, supported by business, whose function is to receive and investigate customer complaints of dishonest business practices. *Abbr.:* BBB

bet′ter half′, 1. a person's wife. **2.** a person's husband. [1830–40]

bet·ter·ment (bet′ər mənt), *n.* **1.** the act or process of bettering; improvement. **2.** an improvement of property other than by mere repairs. [1590–1600; BETTER[1] + -MENT]

bet′terment tax′, a tax on real property, for use by a government for the improvement of public property. [1885–90]

bet·ter-off (bet′ər ôf′, -of′), *adj.* being in better circumstances, esp. economically: *Only the better-off nations can afford to send probes into space.* [1860–65]

Bet·ter·ton (bet′ər tən), *n.* **Thomas,** 1635?–1710, English actor and dramatist.

Bet·ti (bet′tē), *n.* **U·go** (ōō′gô), 1892–1953, Italian poet and dramatist.

bet′ting shop′, *Brit.* a licensed bookmaking establishment that takes off-track bets on horse races. [1850–55]

Bet·ti·nus (bet′n əs), *n.* a crater in the third quadrant of the face of the moon: about 60 miles (96 km) in diameter.

bet·tong (bə tông′, -tong′), *n.* any of several marsupials of the genus *Bettongia,* of Australia and nearby regions, comprising the short-nosed rat-kangaroos, characterized by short, rounded ears, long hind feet, and a naked muzzle tip: all four species are endangered. [1830–40; < Dharuk *ba-daŋ*]

bet·tor (bet′ər), *n.* a person who bets. Also, **better.** [1600–10; BET + -OR[2]]

bet·ty (bet′ē), *n., pl.* **-ties.** See **brown betty.** [1915–20, *Amer.*; by shortening]

Bet·ty (bet′ē), *n.* a female given name, form of **Elizabeth.**

Bet′ty lamp′, an Early American lamp, consisting of a shallow, covered basin filled with oil, tallow, etc., providing fuel for a wick housed in a teapotlike spout, and often hung by a hook or suspended from a chain. Also, **bet′ty lamp′.** [1890–95]

bet·u·la·ceous (bech′ŏŏ lā′shəs), *adj.* belonging to the Betulaceae, the birch family of plants. Cf. **birch family.** [< L *betul*(*a*) birch + -ACEOUS]

bet′u·la oil′ (bech′ə lə), *Chem.* See **methyl salicylate.**

be·tween (bi twēn′), *prep.* **1.** in the space separating (two points, objects, etc.): *between New York and Chicago.* **2.** intermediate to, in time, quantity, or degree: *between twelve and one o'clock; between 50 and 60 apples; between pink and red.* **3.** linking; connecting: *air service between cities.* **4.** in portions for each of (two people): *splitting the profits between them.* **5.** among: *sharing the responsibilities between the five of us.* **6.** by the dual or common action or participation of: *Between us, we can finish the job in a couple of hours.* **7.** distinguishing one from the other: *He couldn't see the difference between good and bad.* **8.** in comparing: *no preference between the two wines.* **9.** by the combined effect of. **10.** existing confidentially for: *We'll keep this matter between the two of us.* **11.** involving; concerning: *war between nations; choice between things.* **12.** being felt jointly or reciprocated by: *the love between them.* **13.** by joint possession of: *Between them they own most of this company.* **14.** *Heraldry.* in the midst of, so as to make a symmetrical composition: *a cross argent between four bezants.* **15. between ourselves,** confidentially; in trust. Also, **between you and me, between you, me, and the post (lamppost, gatepost,** etc.). —*n.* **16.** Usually, **betweens.** a short needle with a rounded eye and a sharp point, used for fine hand stitchery in heavy fabric. —*adv.* **17.** in the intervening space or time; in an intermediate position or relation: *two windows with a door between; visits that were far between.* **18. in between, a.** situated in an intermediary area or on a line or imaginary line connecting two points, things, etc. **b.** in the way: *I reached for the ball, but the dog got in between.* [bef. 900; ME *betwene,* OE *betwēonan, betwēonum,* equiv. to *be-* BE- + *twēon-* (c. Goth *tweihn*(*ai*) two each) + *-um* dat. pl. ending] —**be·tween′ness,** *n.*
—**Syn.** See **among.**
—**Usage.** AMONG expresses a relationship when more than two persons or things are involved: *Distrust spread among even his strongest supporters.* BETWEEN is used when only two persons or things are involved: *between you and me; to decide between tea and coffee.* BETWEEN also continues to be used, as it has been throughout its entire history, to express a relationship of persons or things considered individually, no matter how many: *Tossing up coins between three people always takes a little working out. Between holding public office, teaching, and writing, she has little free time.*
Although not generally accepted as good usage, BETWEEN YOU AND I is heard occasionally in the speech of educated persons. By the traditional rules of grammar, when a pronoun is the object of a preposition, that pronoun should be in the objective case: *between you and me; between her and them.* The use of the nominative form (*I, he, she, they,* etc.) arises partly as overcorrection, the reasoning being that if it is correct at the end of a sentence like *It is I,* it must also be correct at the end of the phrase BETWEEN YOU AND . . . . The choice of pronoun also owes something to the tendency for the final pronoun in a compound object to be in the nominative case after a verb: *It was kind of you to invite my wife and I.* This too is not generally regarded as good usage.
The construction BETWEEN EACH (or EVERY) is sometimes objected to on the grounds that BETWEEN calls for a plural or compound object. However, the construction is old and fully standard when the sense indicates that more than one thing is meant: *Spread softened butter between each layer of pastry. There were marigolds peeking between every row of vegetables.* The construction BETWEEN . . . TO is a blend of BETWEEN . . . AND (*between 15 and 25 miles*) and FROM . . . TO (*from 15 to 25 miles*). It occurs occasionally in informal speech but not in formal speech or writing.

be·tween·brain (bi twēn′brān′), *n.* the diencephalon. [1930–35; BETWEEN + BRAIN]

be·tween-deck (bi twēn′dek′), *n. Naut.* See **'tween deck.** [1715–25]

be·tween′-the-lens′ shut′ter (bi twēn′thə lenz′), *Photog.* See **iris shutter.** [1905–10]

be·tween·times (bi twēn′tīmz′), *adv.* between periods of work, activity, etc.: *a part-time teacher who studied law betweentimes.* [1905–10; BETWEEN + TIME + -S[1]]

be·tween·whiles (bi twēn′hwīlz′, -wīlz′), *adv.* betweentimes. [1760–70; BETWEEN + WHILES]

be·twixt (bi twikst′), *prep., adv.* **1.** *Chiefly South Midland and Southern U.S.* between. **2. betwixt and between,** neither the one nor the other; in a middle or unresolved position: *Not wanting to side with either her father or her mother, she was betwixt and between.* [bef. 950; ME *betwix,* OE *betwix, betweox,* equiv. to *be-* BE- + *tweox,* c. OHG *zwiski* two each; akin to G *zwischen* between (prep.)]

Betz (bets), *n.* **Pauline** (*Pauline Betz Addie*), born 1919, U.S. tennis player.

Beu·lah (byōō′lə), *n.* **1.** a name applied to the land of Israel or Jerusalem, possibly as denoting their future prosperity. Isa. 62:4. Cf. **Hephzibah** (def. 2). **2.** See **Land of Beulah. 3.** a female given name. [< Heb *bəʿūlāh* lit., married woman]

beurre blanc (bûr′ blängk′; *Fr.* bœr blän′), *French Cookery.* a reduction sauce of wine vinegar and shallots, cooked with butter and beaten until thick and foamy. [1930–35; < F: lit., white butter]

beurre fondu (bûr′ fon dōō′; *Fr.* bœr fôn dy′), *French Cookery.* melted butter. [< F]

beurre ma·nié (bûr′ män yā′; *Fr.* bœr ma nyā′),

CONCISE ETYMOLOGY KEY: <, descended or borrowed from; >, whence; b., blend of, blended; c., cognate with; cf., compare; deriv., derivative; equiv., equivalent; imit., imitative; obl., oblique; r., replacing; s., stem; sp., spelling, spelled; resp., respelling, respelled; trans., translation; ?, origin unknown; *, unattested; ‡, probably earlier than. See the full key inside the front cover.

French Cookery. butterpaste. [1935–40; < F: lit., kneaded butter]

beurre noir (bûr′ nwär′; *Fr.* bœr NWAR′), *French Cookery.* a sauce of darkly browned butter, sometimes flavored with herbs, vinegar, etc. [1855–60; < F: lit., black butter]

beurre noi·sette (bûr′ nwä zet′; *Fr.* bœr NWA zet′), *French Cookery.* a sauce of butter cooked until golden or nut brown, sometimes flavored with capers, vinegar, herbs, etc. [< F: lit., butter the color of a hazelnut]

Beu·then (boit′n), *n.* German name of **Bytom.**

BeV (bev), *Physics.* billion electron-volts. Also, **Bev, bev**

Bev·an (bev′ən), *n.* **1. A·neu·rin** (ə nī′rən), 1897–1960, British political leader: minister of health 1945–50. **2.** a male given name.

bev·a·tron (bev′ə tron′), *n. Physics.* an accelerator in which protons are raised to energies of several billion electron-volts by modulating the frequency of the accelerating voltage. [1945–50; BEV + *-a-* connective + -TRON]

bev·el (bev′əl), *n., v.,* **-eled, -el·ing** or (*esp. Brit.*) **-elled, -el·ling,** *adj.* —*n.* **1.** the inclination that one line or surface makes with another when not at right angles. **2.** a surface that does not form a right angle with adjacent surfaces. Cf. **chamfer. 3.** (of a lock bolt) the oblique end that hits the strike plate. **4.** (of a lock with a beveled bolt) the side facing in the same direction as the bevel at the end of the bolt. Cf. **regular bevel, reverse bevel. 5.** See **bevel square. 6.** an adjustable instrument for drawing angles or adjusting the surface of work to a particular inclination. **7.** *Print.* beard (def. 5). —*v.t., v.i.* **8.** to cut or slant at a bevel: *to bevel an edge to prevent splintering.* —*adj.* **9.** Also, **beveled;** *esp. Brit.,* **bevelled.** oblique; sloping; slanted. [1555–65; < MF *bevel (F *béveau, biveau*), OF *baivel, equiv. to *baif* with open mouth (*ba(er)* to gape (see BAY[2]) + *-if* -IVE) + *-el* < L *-ellus;* see -ELLE] —**bev′el·er;** *esp. Brit.,* **bev′el·ler,** *n.*

bev′el-faced ham′mer (bev′əl fāst′), a riveting hammer having an oblique face.

bev′el gear′, *Mach.* a gear having teeth cut into a conical surface, usually meshing with a similar gear set at right angles. Cf. **hypoid gear.** [1825–35]

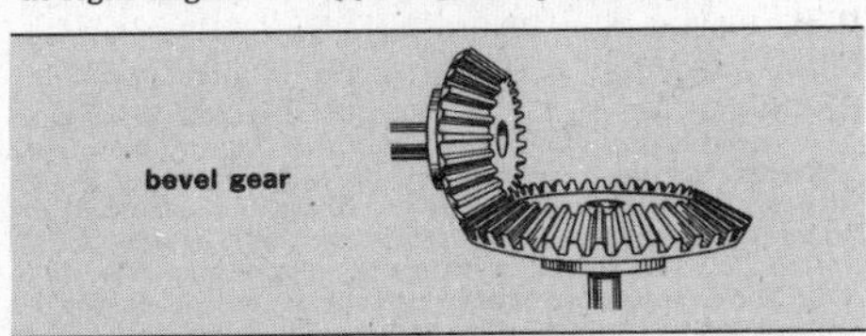

bevel gear

bev′el joint′, *Carpentry.* a miter joint, esp. one in which two pieces meet at other than a right angle. [1815–25]

bev′el sid′ing, *Carpentry.* siding composed of tapered pieces, as clapboards, laid with the thicker lower edge of any piece overlapping the thinner upper edge of the piece below it.

bev′el square′, an adjustable tool used by woodworkers for laying out angles and for testing the accuracy of surfaces worked to a slope. [1605–15]

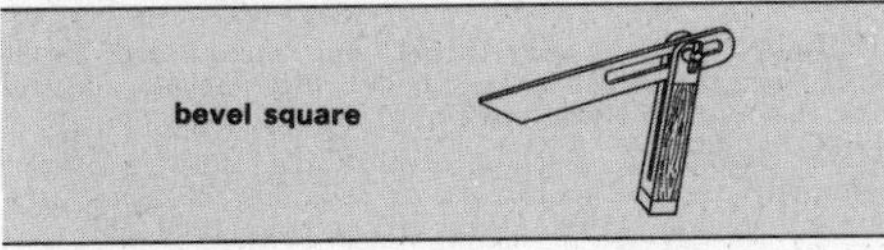

bevel square

bev·er·age (bev′ər ij, bev′rij), *n.* any potable liquid, esp. one other than water, as tea, coffee, beer, or milk: *The price of the meal includes a beverage.* [1250–1300; ME < AF *beverage, bevarage,* equiv. to *be(i)vre* to drink + *-age* -AGE]

bev′erage room′, *Canadian.* a tavern or bar selling only malt liquors. [1935–40]

Bev·er·idge (bev′ər ij, bev′rij), *n.* **1. Albert Jeremiah,** 1862–1927, U.S. senator and historian. **2. Sir William Henry,** 1879–1963, English economist.

Bev′eridge plan′, the plan for comprehensive social insurance, proposed by Sir William Beveridge in Great Britain in 1941.

Bev·er·ly (bev′ər lē), *n.* **1.** a city in NE Massachusetts. 37,655. **2.** Also, **Bev′er·ley.** a female or male given name: from an Old English word meaning "dweller at the beaver meadow."

Bev′erly Hills′, 1. a city in SW California, near Los Angeles. 32,367. **2.** a town in SE Michigan. 11,598.

Bev·in (bev′in), *n.* **Ernest,** 1881–1951, British labor leader: foreign minister 1941–51.

bev·y (bev′ē), *n., pl.* **bev·ies. 1.** a group of birds, as larks or quail, or animals, as roebuck, in close association. **2.** a large group or collection: *a bevy of boisterous sailors.* [1400–50; late ME *bevey,* of obscure orig.]
—Syn. 1. covey, flight; brood. **2.** assembly, company.

BEW, Board of Economic Warfare.

be·wail (bi wāl′), *v.t.* **1.** to express deep sorrow for; lament: *a little child bewailing the loss of her dog.* —*v.i.* **2.** to express grief. [1250–1300; ME; see BE-, WAIL] **—be·wail′ing·ly,** *adv.* **—be·wail′ment,** *n.*
—Syn. 1. bemoan, mourn.

be·ware (bi wâr′), *v.t.* **1.** to be wary, cautious, or careful of (usually used imperatively): *Beware such inconsistency. Beware his waspish wit.* —*v.i.* **2.** to be cautious or careful: *Beware of the dog.* [1150–1200; ME, from phrase of warning *be ware.* See BE, WARE[2]]

be·weep (bi wēp′), *v.t.,* **-wept, -weep·ing.** *Archaic.* to weep over (something): *to beweep one's foolish mistakes.* [bef. 1000; ME *bewepen,* OE *bewēpan.* See BE-, WEEP[1]]

be·whisk·ered (bi hwis′kərd, -wis′-), *adj.* **1.** having whiskers; bearded. **2.** ancient, as a witticism, expression, etc.; passé; hoary: *a bewhiskered catchword of a bygone era.* [1755–65; BE- + WHISKERED]

Bew·ick (byōō′ik), *n.* **Thomas,** 1753–1828, English wood engraver.

Bew′ick's swan′, a tundra swan subspecies, *Cygnus columbianus bewickii,* of Eurasia, having white plumage, black legs, and a yellow patch on a black bill. [1820–30; after T. BEWICK]

be·wigged (bi wigd′), *adj.* wearing a wig. [1765–75; BE- + WIG + -ED[2]]

be·wil·der (bi wil′dər), *v.t.* to confuse or puzzle completely; perplex: *These shifting attitudes bewilder me.* [1675–85; BE- + WILDER (v.)]
—Syn. mystify, nonplus, confuse, daze, confound, stagger, muddle.

be·wil·dered (bi wil′dərd), *adj.* completely puzzled or confused; perplexed. [1675–85; BEWILDER + -ED[2]] **—be·wil′dered·ly,** *adv.* **—be·wil′dered·ness,** *n.*

be·wil·der·ing (bi wil′dər ing), *adj.* extremely confusing: *a bewildering schedule of events.* [1785–95; BEWILDER + -ING[2]] **—be·wil′der·ing·ly,** *adv.*

be·wil·der·ment (bi wil′dər mənt), *n.* **1.** bewildered state. **2.** a confusing maze or tangle, as of objects or conditions: *a bewilderment of smoke, noise, and pushing people.* [1810–20; BEWILDER + -MENT]

be·witch (bi wich′), *v.t.* **1.** to affect by witchcraft or magic; cast a spell over. **2.** to enchant; charm; fascinate. [1175–1225; ME *biwicchen.* See BE-, WITCH] **—be·witch′er,** *n.* **—be·witch′er·y,** *n.* **—be·witch′ing·ness,** *n.* **—be·witch′ment,** *n.*
—Syn. 2. captivate, enrapture, transport.

be·witch·ing (bi wich′ing), *adj.* enchanting; charming; fascinating. [1555–65; BEWITCH + -ING[2]] **—be·witch′ing·ly,** *adv.*

be·wray (bi rā′), *v.t. Archaic.* **1.** to reveal or expose. **2.** to betray. [1250–1300; ME *bewraien,* equiv. to *be-* BE- + *wraien,* OE *wrēgan* to accuse, c. OHG *ruogen* (G *rügen*), Goth *wrohjan*] **—be·wray′er,** *n.*

Bex·ley (beks′lē), *n.* **1.** a borough of Greater London, England. 216,900. **2.** a city in central Ohio. 13,405.

bey (bā), *n., pl.* **beys. 1.** a provincial governor in the Ottoman Empire. **2.** (formerly) a title of respect for Turkish dignitaries. **3.** (formerly) the title of the native ruler of Tunis or Tunisia. Turkish, **beg.** [1590–1600; < Turk, by-form of earlier *beg,* Old Turkic *beg* subordinate chief, head of a clan, perh. < a MChin word akin to Chin *bǎi* hundred (Guangdong dial. *baak*)]

Beyle (bāl), *n.* **Ma·rie Hen·ri** (MA RĒ′ ÄN RĒ′), real name of **Stendhal.**

bey·lic (bā′lik), *n.* the power or jurisdiction of a bey. Also, **bey′lik.** [1725–35; < Turk *beylik,* equiv. to *bey* BEY + *-lik* n. suffix of appurtenance]

Bey·oğ·lu (bā′ə lōō′; *Turk.* bā′ō lōō′), *n.* a modern section of Istanbul, Turkey, N of the Golden Horn: commercial and residential area. Formerly, **Pera.**

be·yond (bē ond′, bi yond′), *prep.* **1.** on, at, or to the farther side of: *Beyond those trees you'll find his house.* **2.** farther on than; more distant than: *beyond the horizon; beyond the sea.* **3.** outside the understanding, limits, or reach of; past: *beyond comprehension; beyond endurance; beyond help.* **4.** superior to; surpassing; above: *wise beyond all others.* **5.** more than; in excess of; over and above: *to stay beyond one's welcome.* —*adv.* **6.** farther on or away: *as far as the house and beyond.* —*n.* **7. the beyond, a.** that which is at a great distance. **b.** Also, **the great beyond.** the afterlife; life after death. [bef. 1000; ME *beyonden,* OE *begeondan.* See BE-, YOND (adv.)] **—be·yond′ness,** *n.*

Bey·routh (bā′rōōt, bā rōōt′), *n.* Beirut.

Be·zal·e·el (bi zal′ē əl), *n.* the chief architect of the tabernacle. Ex. 31:1–11. **—Be·zal·e·el·i·an** (bi zal′ē el′ē ən, bez′ə lē′lē-), *adj.*

bez·ant (bez′ənt, bi zant′), *n.* **1.** Also, **bezzant.** the gold solidus of the Byzantine Empire, widely circulated in the Middle Ages. **2.** Also, **byzant.** (in Romanesque architecture) any of a number of disklike ornaments, similar in form to the classical patera, used esp. on the faces of archivolts. Also, **besant.** [1150–1200; ME *besant* < OF < L *byzantius* (*nummus*) Byzantine (coin)]

bez′ ant′ler (bez, bāz). See **bay antler.** [1590–1600]

bez·el (bez′əl), *n.* **1.** Also, **basil.** the diagonal face at the end of the blade of a chisel, or the like, leading to the edge. **2.** *Jewelry.* **a.** that part of a ring, bracelet, etc., to which gems are attached. **b.** crown (def. 27). **3.** a grooved ring or rim holding a gem, watch crystal, etc., in its setting. **4.** *Auto.* the part of a vehicle's bodywork that surrounds a light. [1605–15; akin to F *biseau* bevel, chamfer]

Bé·ziers (bā zyā′), *n.* a city in S France, SW of Montpellier. 85,677.

be·zique (bə zēk′), *n. Cards.* a game resembling pinochle, originally played with 64 cards and now more commonly with 128 cards and, sometimes, 192 or 256 cards. [1860–65; < F *bésigue, bézigue,* perh. < It *bazzica* a similar game, derived variously from *bazza* trump card, stroke of luck, or *bazzicare* to frequent, haunt]

be·zoar (bē′zôr, -zōr), *n.* **1.** a calculus or concretion found in the stomach or intestines of certain animals, esp. ruminants, formerly reputed to be an effective remedy for poison. **2.** *Obs.* a counterpoison or antidote. [1470–80; earlier *bezear* < ML *bezahar* < Ar *bā(di)zahr* < Pers *pād-zahr* counterpoison; *-o-* < NL]

be·zo·ni·an (bi zō′nē ən), *n. Archaic.* an indigent rascal; scoundrel. [1585–95; obs. *besoni(o)* raw recruit (< It *bisogno* need, needy soldier < ?) + -AN]

Bez·wa·da (bez wä′də), *n.* former name of **Vijayawada.**

bez·zant (bez′ənt, bi zant′), *n.* bezant (def. 1).

bf., *Law.* brief.

B/F, *Accounting.* brought forward.

B.F., 1. Bachelor of Finance. **2.** Bachelor of Forestry.

b.f., *Printing.* boldface. Also, **bf**

B.F.A., Bachelor of Fine Arts.

B.F.A.Mus., Bachelor of Fine Arts in Music.

B.F.S., Bachelor of Foreign Service.

BFT, biofeedback training.

B.F.T., Bachelor of Foreign Trade.

bg., 1. background. **2.** bag.

B.G., 1. Birmingham gauge. **2.** brigadier general. Also, **BG**

B.Gen.Ed., Bachelor of General Education.

bGH, *Biochem., Agric.* See **bovine growth hormone.**

B-girl (bē′gûrl′), *n.* a woman employed by a bar, nightclub, etc., to act as a companion to male customers and induce them to buy drinks. [1935–40, *Amer.;* prob. B(AR)[1] + GIRL]

Bglr., bugler.

BHA, *Chem., Pharm.* butylated hydroxyanisole: the synthetic antioxidant $C_{11}H_{16}O_2$, used to retard rancidity in foods, pharmaceuticals, and other products containing fat or oil. [1945–50]

Bha·bha (bä′bä), *n.* **Ho·mi J(e·han·gir)** (hō′mē jə hän gēr′), 1909–1966, Indian physicist and government official.

Bhad·gaon (bud′goun), *n.* a former name of **Bhaktapur.**

Bha·ga·vad-Gi·ta (bug′ə vəd gē′tä), *n. Hinduism.* a portion of the Mahabharata, having the form of a dialogue between the hero Arjuna and his charioteer, the avatar Krishna, in which a doctrine combining Brahmanical and other elements is evolved. Also called **Gita.** [< Skt: Song of the Blessed One]

bha·jan (buj′ən), *n. Hinduism.* a religious song of praise. [1910–15; < Skt]

bhak·ta (buk′tə), *n.* one who practices bhakti. [1820–30; < Skt: devoted; akin to BHAKTI]

Bhak·ta·pur (buk′tə po͝or′), *n.* a city in E central Nepal, near Katmandu. 104,703. Formerly, **Bhadgaon, Bhatgaon.**

bhak·ti (buk′tē), *n. Hinduism.* **1.** selfless devotion as a means of reaching Brahman. Cf. **jnana, karma** (def. 1). **2.** (*cap.*) a popular religious movement centered around the personal worship of gods, esp. Vishnu and Shiva. Cf. **Saiva, Vaishnava.** [1825–35; < Skt: devotion]

bhak·ti-mar·ga (buk′ti mär′gə), *n. Hinduism.* See under **marga.** [1935–40]

bhang (bang), *n.* **1.** a mild preparation of marijuana made from young leaves and stems of the Indian hemp plant, *Cannabis sativa,* drunk with milk or water as a fermented brew or smoked for its hallucinogenic effects. **2.** a water pipe. Also, **bang.** [1555–65; < Hindi *bhāng* < Skt *bhangā* hemp]

bhan·gi (bung′gē), *n., pl.* **-gis.** *Anglo-Indian.* a Hindu scavenger who belongs to one of the untouchable castes. Also, **bhungi.** [< Hindi *bhaṅgī* lit., user of BHANG]

bhar·al (bûr′əl), *n.* a wild sheep, *Pseudois nahoor,* of Tibet and adjacent mountainous regions, having goatlike horns that curve backward. Also, **burrhel.** Also called **blue sheep.** [1830–40; < Hindi]

Bha·rat (bu′RUT), *n.* Hindi name of the republic of **India.**

Bha·ra·ta Nat·ya (bûr′ə tə nät′yə), a traditional south Indian dance style, formerly performed only by devadasis.

Bhar·tri·ha·ri (bur′tri hur′ē), *n.* A.D. 570?–650?, Indian grammarian and poet.

Bhat·gaon (bud′goun), *n.* a former name of **Bhaktapur.**

Bhat·pa·ra (bät′pär ə), *n.* a city in SW West Bengal, in E India, N of Calcutta. 204,750.

Bhau·na·gar (bou nug′ər), *n.* a seaport in S Gujarat, in W India. 226,072. Also, **Bhav·na·gar** (bäv nug′ər).

Bha·va·bhu·ti (buv′ə bo͞o′tē), *n.* fl. 8th century, Indian dramatist.

Bha·ve (bä′vā), *n.* **Vi·no·ba** (vē nō′bə), 1895–1982, Indian religious leader and mystic.

BHC, *Chem.* benzene hexachloride: the white to yellowish, crystalline, water-soluble, poisonous solid $C_6H_6Cl_6$, used chiefly as an insecticide.

bhd., bulkhead.

bhees·ty (bē′stē), *n., pl.* **-ties.** (in India) a water carrier. Also, **bhees′tie.** [1775–85; < Urdu *bhistī* < Pers *bihishtī* pertaining to paradise, i.e., beautiful, as poetic convention describes cup-bearers (equiv. to *bihisht* paradise + *-i* suffix of appurtenance)]

bhik·shu (bik′sho͞o), *n. Buddhism.* **1.** a monk. **2.** any of the first disciples of Buddha. Also, **bhik·ku** (bik′o͞o). [1805–15; < Skt *bhikṣu* (> Pali *bhikkhu*)]

bhik·shu·ni (bik′sho͞o nē), *n. Buddhism.* a female bhikshu; nun. Also, **bhik·ku·ni** (bik′o͞o nē). [< Skt *bhikṣuṇī* (> Pali *bhikkhunī*)]

Bhil (bēl), *n., pl.* **Bhils,** (*esp. collectively*) **Bhil.** a people inhabiting the hills of west central India. [1815–25]

Bhi·lai (bi lī′), *n.* a city in S Madhya Pradesh, in central India. 174,370.

Bhi·li (bē′lē), *n.* an Indic language of west central India, the language of the Bhil.

B.H.L., **1.** Bachelor of Hebrew Letters. **2.** Bachelor of Hebrew Literature.

Bhn, See **Brinell hardness number.**

Bhoo·dan (bo͞o dän′), *n.* (in India) a socioagricultural movement, started by Vinoba Bhave in 1951, in which village landowners are persuaded to give land to the landless. Also, **Bhu·dan′.**

Bho·pal (bō päl′), *n.* **1.** a former state in central India: now part of Madhya Pradesh state. **2.** a city in and the capital of Madhya Pradesh state, in central India. 392,077.

B horizon, *Geol.* the subsoil in a soil profile. Cf. **A horizon, C horizon.** [1935–40]

bhp, See **brake horsepower.** Also, **BHP, B.H.P., b.hp., b.h.p.**

BHT, *Chem., Pharm.* butylated hydroxytoluene: the antioxidant $C_{15}H_{24}O$, used to retard rancidity in foods, pharmaceuticals, and other products containing fat or oil. [1960–65]

Bhu·mi·bol A·dul·ya·dej (po͞o mē pôn′ ä do͞ol yä′de). See **Rama IX.**

bhun·gi (bung′gē), *n., pl.* **-gis.** bhangi.

bhut (bo͞ot), *n.* (in Indian mythology) a spirit or demon. Also, **bhoot** (bo͞ot). [1775–85; < Hindi *bhūt* < Skt *bhūtā*]

Bhu·tan (bo͞o tän′), *n.* a kingdom in the Himalayas, NE of India: foreign affairs under Indian jurisdiction. 1,100,000; ab. 19,300 sq. mi. (50,000 sq. km). *Cap.:* Thimphu.

Bhu·tan·ese (bo͞ot′n ēz′, -ēs′), *n., pl.* **-ese,** *adj.* —*n.* **1.** a native or inhabitant of Bhutan. **2.** the Tibetan language as spoken in Bhutan. —*adj.* **3.** of, pertaining to, or characteristic of Bhutan, its inhabitants, or their language. [1805–15; BHUTAN + -ESE]

Bhu·ta·ta·tha·ta (bo͞o′tə tə tə tä′), *n. Buddhism.* Tathata. [< Skt; see BHUT, TATHATA]

bi (bī), *adj., n., pl.* **bis, bi's.** *Slang.* bisexual. [by shortening]

Bl, *pl.* **Bl's.** built-in.

Bi, *Symbol, Chem.* bismuth.

bi-[1], a combining form meaning "twice," "two," used in the formation of compound words: *bifacial; bifarious.* Cf. **bin-.** [< L, comb. form of *bis;* see TWICE]
—Usage. All words except *biennial* referring to periods of time and prefixed by BI-[1] are potentially ambiguous. Since BI- can be taken to mean either "twice each" or "every two," a word like *biweekly* can be understood as "twice each week" or "every two weeks." To avoid confusion, it is better to use the prefix SEMI- to mean "twice each" (*semiannual; semimonthly; semiweekly*) or the phrase *twice a* or *twice each* (*twice a month; twice a week; twice each year*), and for the other sense to use the phrase *every two* (*every two months; every two weeks; every two years*).

bi-[2], var. of **bio-,** esp. before a vowel: *biopsy.*

Bi·a (bī′ə), *n.* the ancient Greek personification of force: daughter of Pallas and Styx and sister of Cratus, Nike, and Zelos.

BIA, See **Bureau of Indian Affairs.**

bi·a·ce·tyl (bī′ə sēt′l, -set′l, bī as′i tl), *n. Chem.* a yellow, water-soluble liquid, $C_4H_6O_2$, occurring in butter and in certain essential oils, as bay, and also synthesized: used chiefly to augment the flavor and odor of vinegar, coffee, and other foods. Also, **diacetyl.** [BI-[1] + ACETYL]

Bi·a·fra (bē ä′frə), *n.* **1.** a former secessionist state (1967–70) in SE Nigeria, in W Africa. *Cap.:* Enugu. **2. Bight of,** a wide bay in the E part of the Gulf of Guinea, off the W coast of Africa. **—Bi·a′fran,** *adj., n.*

Bi·ak (bē yäk′), *n.* an island N of Irian Barat, in Indonesia. 948 sq. mi. (2455 sq. km). Also, **Wiak.**

Bia·lik (byä′lik), *n.* **Cha·im Nach·man** (KHī ĕm′ näKH-män′; *Eng.* KHī′im näKH′mən), 1873–1934, Hebrew poet, born in Russia.

bi·a·ly (bē ä′lē, byä′-), *n., pl.* **-lies.** a round, flat, leavened, onion-flavored roll made of white flour, having a depression at the center and a crusty bottom. [1960–65; after BIALYSTOK]

Bia·ly·stok (byä wi′stôk), *n.* a city in E Poland. 196,000. Russian, **Belostok, Byelostok.**

CONCISE ETYMOLOGY KEY: <, descended or borrowed from; >, whence; b., blend of, blended; c., cognate with; cf., compare; deriv., derivative; equiv., equivalent; imit., imitative; obl., oblique; r., replacing; s., stem; sp., spelling, spelled; resp., respelling, respelled; trans., translation; ?, origin unknown; *, unattested; ‡, probably earlier than. See the full key inside the front cover.

Bian·ca (byäng′kä, bē äng′kə), *n.* a female given name: from an Italian word meaning "white."

Bian·co (byäng′kô), *n.* **Mon·te** (môn′te), Italian name of **Mont Blanc.**

bi·an·gu·lar (bī ang′gyə lər), *adj.* having two angles or corners. [BI-[1] + ANGULAR]

bi·an·nu·al (bī an′yo͞o əl), *adj.* **1.** occurring twice a year; semiannual. **2.** occurring every two years; biennial. [1875–80; BI-[1] + ANNUAL] **—bi·an′nu·al·ly,** *adv.*
—Usage. See **bi-**[1].

bi·an·nu·late (bī an′yə lit, -lāt′), *adj. Zool.* having two ringlike bands, as of color. [BI-[1] + ANNULATE]

Biar·ritz (bē′ə rits′; *Fr.* byA RēTS′), *n.* a city in SW France, on the Bay of Biscay: resort. 27,653.

bi·ar·tic·u·late (bī′är tik′yə lit, -lāt′), *adj. Zool.* having two joints, as the antennae of certain insects. Also, **bi′ar·tic′u·lat′ed.** [1810–20; BI-[1] + ARTICULATE]

bi·as (bī′əs), *n., adj., adv., v.,* **bi·ased, bi·as·ing** or (*esp. Brit.*) **bi·assed, bi·as·sing.** —*n.* **1.** an oblique or diagonal line of direction, esp. across a woven fabric. **2.** a particular tendency or inclination, esp. one that prevents unprejudiced consideration of a question; prejudice. **3.** *Statistics.* a systematic as opposed to a random distortion of a statistic as a result of sampling procedure. **4.** *Lawn Bowling.* **a.** a slight bulge or greater weight on one side of the ball or bowl. **b.** the curved course made by such a ball when rolled. **5.** *Electronics.* the application of a steady voltage or current to an active device, as a diode or transistor, to produce a desired mode of operation. **6.** a high-frequency alternating current applied to the recording head of a tape recorder during recording in order to reduce distortion. **7. on the bias, a.** in the diagonal direction of the cloth. **b.** out of line; slanting. —*adj.* **8.** cut, set, folded, etc., diagonally: *This material requires a bias cut.* —*adv.* **9.** in a diagonal manner; obliquely; slantingly: *to cut material bias.* —*v.t.* **10.** to cause partiality or favoritism in (a person); influence, esp. unfairly: *a tearful plea designed to bias the jury.* **11.** *Electronics.* to apply a steady voltage or current to (the input of an active device). [1520–30; < MF *biais* oblique < OPr, prob. < VL **(e)bigassius* < Gk *epikársios* oblique, equiv. to *epi-* EPI- + *-karsios* oblique]
—Syn. 2. predisposition, preconception, predilection, partiality, proclivity; bent, leaning. BIAS, PREJUDICE mean a strong inclination of the mind or a preconceived opinion about something or someone. A BIAS may be favorable or unfavorable: *bias in favor of or against an idea.* PREJUDICE implies a preformed judgment even more unreasoning than BIAS, and usually implies an unfavorable opinion: *prejudice against a race.* **10.** predispose, bend, incline, dispose. **—Ant. 2.** impartiality.

Bi·as (bī′əs), *n.* fl. 570 B.C., Greek philosopher, born in Ionia.

bi′as-belt·ed tire′ (bī′əs bel′tid). See **belted-bias tire.**

bi·ased (bī′əst), *adj.* having or showing bias or prejudice: *They gave us a biased report on immigration trends.* Also, *esp. Brit.,* **bi′assed.** [1605–15; BIAS + -ED[2]] **—bi′ased·ly;** *esp. Brit.,* **bi′assed·ly,** *adv.*

bi′as-ply tire′ (bī′əs plī′), a vehicle tire in which the main plies or cords run across the bead. Also called **cross-ply tire.** See illus. under **tire.** [1970–75]

bi·ath·lete (bī ath′lēt), *n.* a competitor in a biathlon. [1970–75; b. BIATHLON and ATHLETE]

bi·ath·lon (bī ath′lon), *n.* **1.** a contest in which cross-country skiers, carrying rifles, shoot at targets at four stops along a 12.5-mi. (20 km) course. **2.** an athletic contest comprising any two consecutive events. [1955–60; BI-[1] + Gk *âthlon* contest; modeled on DECATHLON]

bi·au·ric·u·lar (bī′ô rik′yə lər), *adj. Anat.* **1.** having two auricles. **2.** pertaining to both ears. [1825–35; BI-[1] + AURICULAR]

bi·au·ric·u·late (bī′ô rik′yə lit, -lāt′), *adj. Biol.* having two auricles or earlike parts. [1825–35; BI-[1] + AURICULATE]

bi·ax·i·al (bī ak′sē əl), *adj.* **1.** having two axes. **2.** *Crystall.* having two optical axes along which double refraction does not occur. [1850–55; BI-[1] + AXIAL] **—bi·ax′i·al′i·ty,** *n.* **—bi·ax′i·al·ly,** *adv.*

bib (bib), *n., v.,* **bibbed, bib·bing.** —*n.* **1.** a piece of cloth, plastic, or paper that covers the chest and is often tied under the chin of a child to protect the clothing while the child is eating. **2.** any similar cloth or part of a garment. **3.** the front part of an apron, overalls, or similar protective garment above the waist. **4.** *Fencing.* a piece of canvas attached to the base of the mask, for protecting the throat. **5.** bibcock. **6. put** or **stick one's bib in,** *Australian Informal.* to interfere. —*v.t., v.i.* **7.** *Archaic.* to tipple; drink. [1275–1325; ME *bibben* to drink < L *bibere*] **—bib′less,** *adj.* **—bib′like′,** *adj.*

Bib., 1. Bible. **2.** Biblical.

bib., (in prescriptions) drink. [< L *bibe*]

bib′ and tuck′er, clothes: *to dress in one's best bib and tucker.* [1740–50]

bi·ba·sic (bī bā′sik), *adj. Chem.* (formerly) dibasic. [1840–50; BI-[1] + BASIC]

bibb (bib), *n.* **1.** *Naut.* any of several brackets or timbers bolted to the hounds of a mast to give additional support to the trestletrees. **2.** *Plumbing.* bibcock. [1770–80; resp. of BIB]

bib·ber (bib′ər), *n.* a steady drinker; tippler (usually used in combination): *winebibber.* [1530–40; BIB + -ER[1]]

Bibb′ let′tuce (bib), a variety of lettuce having a small, somewhat tapering head and tender, light-green leaves. [1960–65; allegedly after a 19th century U.S. grower, though the variety was first introduced about 1890 under the name "Half Century," and the history of its reintroduction as "Bibb" is obscure]

bib·cock (bib′kok′), *n. Plumbing.* a faucet having a nozzle bent downward. Also, **bib, bibb.** [1790–1800; BIB + COCK[1]]

bi·be·lot (bib′lō; *Fr.* bēbə lō′), *n., pl.* **-lots** (-lōz; *Fr.* -lō′). a small object of curiosity, beauty, or rarity. [1870–75; < F, equiv. to *bibel-* (expressive formation akin to BAUBLE) + *-ot* n. suffix]

bi·bi·va·lent (bī′bī vā′lənt, bī biv′ə-), *adj. Chem.* noting an electrolytic compound which splits into two ions, each with a valence of two. [BI-[1] + BIVALENT]

Bibl, Biblical. Also, **Bibl.**

bibl., 1. biblical. **2.** bibliographical. **3.** bibliography.

Bi·ble (bī′bəl), *n.* **1.** the collection of sacred writings of the Christian religion, comprising the Old and New Testaments. See table below. **2.** Also called **Hebrew Scriptures.** the collection of sacred writings of the Jewish religion: known to Christians as the Old Testament. **3.** (*often l.c.*) the sacred writings of any religion. **4.** (*l.c.*) any book, reference work, periodical, etc., accepted as authoritative, informative, or reliable: *He regarded that particular bird book as the birdwatchers' bible.* [1300–50; ME *bible, bibel* < OF *bible* < ML *biblia* (fem. sing.) < Gk, in *tà biblía tà hagía* (Septuagint) the holy books; *biblíon, byblíon* papyrus roll, strip of papyrus, equiv. to *býbl(os)* papyrus (after *Býblos,* a Phoenician port where papyrus was prepared and exported) + *-ion* n. suffix]

Bi′ble Belt′, an area of the U.S., chiefly in the South and Midwest, noted for its religious fundamentalism. [1925–30, *Amer.*]

Bi′ble class′, a class or course of study devoted to the Bible or Biblical subjects, as in a Sunday School. [1815–25, *Amer.*]

Bi′ble pa′per, a very thin, strong, opaque rag paper often used for Bibles, prayer books, dictionaries, and the like. Also called **India paper.** [1925–30]

Bi′ble school′, a school or organized study program primarily devoted to Biblical or religious teaching, as a Sunday school, church study group, etc. [1900–05]

Bi′ble Soci′ety, a Christian organization devoted to the printing and distribution of the Bible.

BOOKS OF THE BIBLE

Old Testament		
Genesis	II Chronicles	Daniel
Exodus	Ezra	Hosea
Leviticus	Nehemiah	Joel
Numbers	Esther	Amos
Deuteronomy	Job	Obadiah
Joshua	Psalms	Jonah
Judges	Proverbs	Micah
Ruth	Ecclesiastes	Nahum
I Samuel	Song of Solomon	Habakkuk
II Samuel	Isaiah	Zephaniah
I Kings	Jeremiah	Haggai
II Kings	Lamentations	Zechariah
I Chronicles	Ezekiel	Malachi
Apocrypha		
I Esdras	(additional parts of Esther)	(additional parts of Daniel)
II Esdras	Wisdom of Solomon	Prayer of Manasses
Tobit	Ecclesiasticus	I Maccabees
Judith	Baruch	II Maccabees
New Testament		
Matthew	Ephesians	Hebrews
Mark	Philippians	James
Luke	Colossians	I Peter
John	I Thessalonians	II Peter
The Acts	II Thessalonians	I John
Romans	I Timothy	II John
I Corinthians	II Timothy	III John
II Corinthians	Titus	Jude
Galatians	Philemon	Revelation

Bi·ble-thump·er (bī′bəl thum′pər), *n. Informal.* an evangelist or other person who quotes the Bible frequently, esp. as a means of exhortation or rebuke. [1920–25] —**Bi′ble-thump′ing,** *adj.*

BiblHeb, Biblical Hebrew.

Bi·bli·a Pau·pe·rum (bib′lē ä pou′pe ro͝om′, bib′lē ə pô′pər əm), any of the picture books illustrating Biblical events and usually containing a short text, used chiefly in the Middle Ages for purposes of religious instruction. [< NL: lit., Bible of poor men]

Bib·li·cal (bib′li kəl), *adj.* **1.** of or in the Bible: *a Biblical name.* **2.** in accord with the Bible. Also, **bib′li·cal.** [1780–90; < ML *biblic(us)* (*bibl(ia)* BIBLE + *-icus* -IC) + -AL[1]] —**Bib′li·cal·ly, bib′li·cal·ly,** *adv.*

Bib′lical Arama′ic, a Semitic language that was the vernacular in Palestine in the time of Christ and in which a few sections of the Old Testament are written.

Bib′lical He′brew, the Hebrew language used in the Old Testament. *Abbr.:* BiblHeb

Bib′lical Lat′in, the form of Latin used in the translation of the Bible and that became current in western Europe at the beginning of the Middle Ages.

Bib·li·cism (bib′lə siz′əm), *n.* literal interpretation of the Bible. [1850–55; BIBLIC(AL) + -ISM]

Bib·li·cist (bib′lə sist), *n.* **1.** a person who interprets the Bible literally. **2.** a Biblical scholar. [1830–40; < ML *biblic(us)* (see BIBLICAL) + -IST] —**Bib′li·cis′tic,** *adj.*

biblio-, a combining form occurring in loanwords from Greek (*bibliography*); on this model, used in the formation of compound words with the meaning "book" (*bibliophile*), and sometimes with the meaning "Bible" (*bibliolatry,* on the model of *idolatry*). [< L < Gk, comb. form of *biblíon;* see BIBLE]

bib·li·o·clast (bib′lē ə klast′), *n.* a person who mutilates or destroys books. [1875–80; BIBLIO- + (ICONO)CLAST] —**bib′li·o·clasm,** *n.*

bib·li·o·film (bib′lē ə film′), *n.* a microfilm used esp. in libraries to photograph the pages of valuable or much-used books. [BIBLIO- + FILM]

bibliog., **1.** bibliographer. **2.** bibliography.

bib·li·og·o·ny (bib′lē og′ə nē), *n.* the art of producing and publishing books. Also called **bib·li·o·gen·e·sis** (bib′lē ō jen′ə sis). [1835–45; BIBLIO- + -GONY]

bib·li·o·graph (bib′lē ə graf′, -gräf′), *v.t.* **1.** to put in a bibliography. **2.** to make a bibliography of. **3.** to provide with a bibliography. [1805–15; back formation from BIBLIOGRAPHY]

bib·li·og·ra·pher (bib′lē og′rə fər), *n.* **1.** an expert in bibliography. **2.** a person who compiles bibliographies. [1650–60; < Gk *bibliográph(os)* book-writer (see BIBLIO-, -GRAPH) + -ER[1]]

bib′liograph′ic control′, *Library Science.* the identification, description, analysis, and classification of books and other materials of communication so that they may be effectively organized, stored, retrieved, and used when needed.

bib′liograph′ic util′ity, *Library Science.* an organization that maintains computerized bibliographic records and offers to its members or customers various products and services related to these records.

bib·li·og·ra·phy (bib′lē og′rə fē), *n., pl.* **-phies. 1.** a complete or selective list of works compiled upon some common principle, as authorship, subject, place of publication, or printer. **2.** a list of source materials that are used or consulted in the preparation of a work or that are referred to in the text. **3.** a branch of library science dealing with the history, physical description, comparison, and classification of books and other works. [1670–80; < Gk *bibliographía.* See BIBLIO-, -GRAPHY] —**bib·li·o·graph·ic** (bib′lē ə graf′ik), **bib′li·o·graph′i·cal,** *adj.* —**bib′li·o·graph′i·cal·ly,** *adv.*

bib·li·o·klept (bib′lē ə klept′), *n.* a person who steals books. [1880–85; BIBLIO- + Gk *kléptēs* thief; see KLEPTOMANIA]

bib·li·ol·a·try (bib′lē ol′ə trē), *n.* **1.** excessive reverence for the Bible as literally interpreted. **2.** extravagant devotion to or dependence upon books. [1755–65; BIBLIO- + -LATRY] —**bib′li·ol′a·ter, bib′li·ol′a·trist,** *n.* —**bib′li·ol′a·trous,** *adj.*

bib·li·ol·o·gy (bib′lē ol′ə jē), *n., pl.* **-gies.** bibliography (def. 3). [1800–10; BIBLIO- + -LOGY] —**bib·li·o·log·i·cal** (bib′lē ə loj′i kəl), *adj.* —**bib′li·ol′o·gist,** *n.*

bib·li·o·man·cy (bib′lē ō man′sē), *n.* divination by means of a book, esp. the Bible, opened at random to some verse or passage, which is then interpreted. [1745–55; BIBLIO- + -MANCY]

bib·li·o·ma·ni·a (bib′lē ō mā′nē ə, -mān′yə), *n.* excessive fondness for acquiring and possessing books. [1725–35; BIBLIO- + -MANIA; r. earlier *bibliomanie* < F] —**bib·li·o·ma·ni·ac** (bib′lē ō mā′nē ak′), *n.* —**bib·li·o·ma·ni·a·cal** (bib′lē ō mə nī′ə kəl), *adj.*

bib·li·op·e·gy (bib′lē op′ə jē), *n.* the art of binding books. [1825–35; BIBLIO- + Gk *pēg-* (s. of *pēgnýnai* to fasten) + -Y[3]] —**bib·li·o·peg·ic** (bib′lē ə pej′ik, -pē′jik), *adj.* —**bib′li·op′e·gist,** *n.* —**bib′li·op′e·gis′tic, bib′li·op′e·gis′ti·cal,** *adj.*

bib·li·o·phage (bib′lē ə fāj′), *n.* an ardent reader; a bookworm. [BIBLIO- + -PHAGE] —**bib·li·oph·a·gous** (bib′lē of′ə gəs), **bib·li·o·phag·ic** (bib′lē ə faj′ik, -fā′jik), *adj.*

bib·li·o·phile (bib′lē ə fīl′, -fil), *n.* a person who loves or collects books, esp. as examples of fine or unusual printing, binding, or the like. Also, **bib·li·oph·i·list** (bib′lē of′ə list). [1815–25; BIBLIO- + -PHILE] —**bib′li·oph′i·lism, bib′li·oph′i·ly,** *n.* —**bib′li·oph′i·lis′tic, bib·li·o·phil·ic** (bib′lē ō fil′ik), *adj.*

bib·li·o·phobe (bib′lē ə fōb′), *n.* a person who hates, fears, or distrusts books. [BIBLIO- + -PHOBE] —**bib′li·o·pho′bi·a,** *n.*

bib·li·o·pole (bib′lē ə pōl′), *n.* a bookseller, esp. a dealer in rare or used books. Also, **bib·li·op·o·list** (bib′lē op′ə list). [1765–75; < L *bibliopōla* < Gk *bibliopṓlēs* (*biblio-* BIBLIO- + *pōl-* (s. of *pōleîsthai* to sell) + *-ēs* agentive suffix)] —**bib·li·o·pol·ic** (bib′lē ə pol′ik), **bib′li·o·pol′i·cal, bib′li·o·po′lar,** *adj.* —**bib′li·o·pol′i·cal·ly,** *adv.* —**bib·li·op·o·lism** (bib′lē op′ə liz′əm), **bib′li·op′o·ly,** *n.* —**bib′li·op′o·lis′tic,** *adj.*

bib·li·o·taph (bib′lē ə taf′, -täf′), *n.* a person who caches or hoards books. Also, **bib′li·o·taphe′.** [1815–25; BIBLIO- + Gk *táphos* burial; see EPITAPH] —**bib′li·o·taph′ic** (bib′lē ə taf′ik), *adj.*

bi·blio·te·ca (bē′vlyô te′kä), *n., pl.* **-cas** (-käs). *Spanish.* a library.

bib·li·o·the·ca (bib′lē ə thē′kə), *n., pl.* **-cas, -cae** (-kē). **1.** a collection of books; a library. **2.** a list of books, esp. a bookseller's catalog. **3.** *Obs.* the Bible. [1820–25; < L: library, collection of books (ML: Bible; cf. OE *bibliothēce* Bible) < Gk *bibliothḗkē.* See BIBLIO-, THECA] —**bib′li·o·the′cal,** *adj.*

bi·bli·o·thèque (bē blē ô tek′; *Eng.* bib′lē ə tek′), *n., pl.* **-thèques** (-tek′; *Eng.* -teks′). *French.* a library.

bib·li·o·ther·a·py (bib′lē ō ther′ə pē), *n. Psychiatry.* the use of reading as an ameliorative adjunct to therapy. [1915–20; BIBLIO- + THERAPY] —**bib·li·o·ther·a·peu·tic** (bib′lē ō ther′ə pyo͞o′tik), *adj.* —**bib′li·o·ther′a·pist,** *n.*

bib·li·ot·ics (bib′lē ot′iks), *n.* (*used with a singular or plural v.*) the analysis of handwriting and documents, esp. for authentication of authorship. [1900–05; < Gk *biblí(on)* (see BIBLE) + -OT(IC) + -ICS] —**bib′li·ot′ic,** *adj.* —**bib·li·o·tist** (bib′lē ə tist), *n.*

Bib·list (bib′list, bī′blist), *n.* **1.** a person who regards the Bible as the only rule of faith. **2.** Biblicist. [1555–65; BIBLE + -IST] —**Bib′lism,** *n.*

bib′ o′veralls, *Chiefly Northern and North Midland U.S.* overalls (def. 3a).

bib·u·lous (bib′yə ləs), *adj.* **1.** fond of or addicted to drink. **2.** absorbent; spongy. [1665–75; < L *bibulus* (*bib(ere)* to drink (c. Skt *pibati* (he) drinks) + *-ulus* -ULOUS)] —**bib′u·lous·ly,** *adv.* —**bib′u·lous·ness, bib·u·los·i·ty** (bib′yə los′i tē), *n.*

bi·cam·er·al (bī kam′ər əl), *adj. Govt.* having two branches, chambers, or houses, as a legislative body. [1825–35; BI-[1] + L *camer(a)* CHAMBER + -AL[1]] —**bi·cam′er·al·ism,** *n.* —**bi·cam′er·al·ist,** *n.*

bi·cap·su·lar (bī kap′sə lər), *adj. Bot.* **1.** divided into two capsules. **2.** having a divided or two-part capsule. [BI-[1] + CAPSULAR]

bi·carb (bī kärb′), *n. Informal.* See **sodium bicarbonate.** [1920–25; by shortening]

bicarb., **1.** bicarbonate. **2.** bicarbonate of soda.

bi·car·bo·nate (bī kär′bə nit, -nāt′), *n. Chem.* a salt of carbonic acid, containing the HCO_3^{-1} group; an acid carbonate, as sodium bicarbonate, $NaHCO_3$. [1810–20; BI-[1] + CARBONATE]

bicar′bonate of so′da, *Chem.* See **sodium bicarbonate.** [1865–70]

bi·cau·date (bī kô′dāt), *adj. Zool.* having two tails or taillike appendages. Also, **bi·cau·dal** (bī kôd′l). [BI-[1] + CAUDATE]

bi·cen·ten·ar·y (bī′ sen ten′ə rē, bī sen′tn er′ē; *esp. Brit.* bī′sen tē′nə rē), *adj., n., pl.* **-ar·ies.** *Chiefly Brit.* bicentennial. [1860–65; BI-[1] + CENTENARY]

bi·cen·ten·ni·al (bī′sen ten′ē əl), *adj.* **1.** pertaining to or in honor of a 200th anniversary: *bicentennial celebration; a bicentennial exposition.* **2.** consisting of or lasting 200 years: *a bicentennial period.* **3.** occurring every 200 years: *the bicentennial return of a comet.* —*n.* **4.** a 200th anniversary: *The United States had its bicentennial in 1976.* **5.** a celebration of such an anniversary. Also, *esp. Brit.,* **bicentenary.** [1880–85; BI-[1] + CENTENNIAL] —**bi′cen·ten′ni·al·ly,** *adv.*
—**Usage.** See **bi-**[1].

bi·cen·tric (bī sen′trik), *adj. Biol.* **1.** (of a taxon) having two centers of evolution. **2.** (of a plant or animal) having two centers of distribution. [1955–60; BI-[1] + -CENTRIC] —**bi·cen′tri·cal·ly,** *adv.*

bi·ceph·a·lous (bī sef′ə ləs), *adj. Bot., Zool.* having two heads. [1795–1805; BI-[1] + -CEPHALOUS]

bi·ceps (bī′seps), *n., pl.* **-ceps·es** (-sep siz), **-ceps.** *Anat.* either of two flexor muscles, one **(biceps brachii)** located in the front of the upper arm and assisting in bending the arm, and the other **(biceps femoris)** located on the back of the thigh and assisting in bending the leg. [1625–35; < L: two-headed, having two parts, equiv. to *bi-* BI-[1] + *-ceps* (s. *-cipit-*), comb. form of *caput* head]

bi′ceps bra′chi·i (brā′kē ī′, -kē ē′, brak′ē ī′, -ē ē′). See under **biceps.** [1855–60: < NL: lit., biceps of (the) arm]

bi′ceps fem′o·ris (fem′ər is). See under **biceps.** [1855–60; < NL: lit., biceps of (the) femur]

Bi·chat (bē shA′), *n.* **Ma·rie Fran·çois Xa·vier** (mA rē′ fräN swA′ gzA vyā′), 1771–1802, French physician.

bich·ir (bich′ər), *n.* any of several primitive freshwater African fishes of the genus *Polypterus* having functional lungs as well as gills. [‡1965–70; < F < dial. Ar *abu shīr*]

bi·chlo·ride (bī klôr′īd, -id, -klōr′-), *n. Chem.* dichloride. [1800–10; BI-[1] + CHLORIDE]

bichlo′ride of mer′cury, *Chem.* See **mercuric chloride.** [1800–10]

Bi·chon Frise (bē′shon frēz′, fri zā′; *Fr.* bē shôN frē-zā′), one of a French-Belgian breed of small dog having a silky, loosely curled, thick white coat, a topknot, dropped ears with long flowing hair, and a tail curved over its back, originally developed in the Mediterranean area. [1965–70; < F: lit., curly *bichon* a breed of lap dog, aph. var. of *barbichon,* dim. of *barbet* a kind of spaniel, ult. deriv. of *barbe* BARB[1]]

Bichon Frise
12 in. (30 cm) high
at the shoulder

bi·chro·mate (bī krō′māt), *n. Chem.* dichromate. [1850–55; BI-[1] + CHROMATE]

bichro′mate proc′ess, any of several methods of photography in which the light-sensitive medium is alkaline bichromate associated with a colloid such as gum, albumen, or gelatin.

bi·chrome (bī′krōm′), *adj.* bicolor. [1920–25; BI-[1] + -CHROME]

bi·cip·i·tal (bī sip′i tl), *adj.* **1.** having two heads; two-headed. **2.** *Anat.* pertaining to the biceps. [1640–50; < L *bicipit-* (s. of *biceps*) BICEPS + -AL[1]]

bick·er[1] (bik′ər), *v.i.* **1.** to engage in petulant or peevish argument; wrangle: *The two were always bickering.* **2.** to run rapidly; move quickly; rush; hurry: *a stream bickering down the valley.* **3.** to flicker; glitter: *The sun bickered through the trees.* —*n.* **4.** an angry, petty dispute or quarrel; contention. [1250–1300; ME *bikeren* < ?] —**bick′er·er,** *n.*
—**Syn. 1.** disagree, squabble, argue, quarrel, haggle, dispute, spar, spat.

bick·er[2] (bik′ər), *n. Scot.* **1.** any wooden dish or bowl, esp. a wooden porridge bowl. **2.** *Obs.* a wooden drinking cup. [1300–50; ME *biker* BEAKER]

bick·i·ron (bik′ī′ərn, bik′ərn), *n.* the tapered end of an anvil. [1660–70; alter. (by assoc. with IRON) of earlier *bickern* for *bycorne* two-horned anvil < L *bicornis* two-horned (see BICORN); meaning perh. influenced by MF *bigorne* in same sense]

bi·coast·al (bī kōs′tl), *adj.* occurring or existing on two coasts, or on both the east and west coasts of the U.S.: *a bicoastal firm with offices in San Francisco and New York.* [BI-[1] + COASTAL] —**bi·coast′al·ism,** *n.*

Bi·col (bē kōl′), *n., pl.* **-cols,** (*esp. collectively*) **-col.** Bikol.

bi·col·lat·er·al (bī′kə lat′ər əl), *adj. Bot.* (of a bundle) having the xylem lined with phloem on both its inner and outer faces. [1880–85; BI-[1] + COLLATERAL] —**bi′col·lat′er·al′i·ty,** *n.*

bi·col·or (bī′kul′ər), *adj.* **1.** Also, **bi′col′ored;** *esp. Brit.,* **bi′col′oured.** having two colors: *a bicolor flower.* —*n.* **2.** a flag divided into two major areas of color. Also, *esp. Brit.,* **bi′col′our.** [1860–65; < L; see BI-[1], COLOR]

bi·com·pact (bī′kəm pakt′), *adj. Math.* compact[1] (def. 7). [BI-[1] + COMPACT[1]]

bi·con·cave (bī kon′kāv, bī′kon kāv′), *adj.* concave on both sides, as a lens. See diag. under **lens.** [1825–35; BI-[1] + CONCAVE] —**bi·con·cav·i·ty** (bī′kən kav′i tē), *n.*

bi·con·di·tion·al (bī′kən dish′ə nl), *adj. Logic.* (of a proposition) asserting that the existence or occurrence of one thing or event depends on, and is dependent on, the existence or occurrence of another, as "A if and only if B." [1935–40; BI-[1] + CONDITIONAL]

bi·cone (bī′kōn′), *n.* an object shaped like two cones with their bases together. [1925–30; BI-[1] + CONE] —**bi·con·i·cal** (bī kon′i kəl), *adj.* —**bi·con′i·cal·ly,** *adv.*

bi·con·ti·nen·tal (bī′kon tn en′tl), *adj.* of, on, or involving two continents: *a bicontinental survey.*

bi·con·vex (bī kon′veks, bī′kon veks′), *adj.* convex on both sides, as a lens. See diag. under **lens.** [1840–50; BI-[1] + CONVEX] —**bi′con·vex′i·ty,** *n.*

bi·corn (bī′kôrn), *adj.* Also, **bi·cor·nate** (bī kôr′nit, -nāt), **bi·cor·nu·ate** (bī kôr′nyo͞o it, -āt′), **bi·cor′nu·ous. 1.** *Bot., Zool.* having two horns or hornlike parts. **2.** shaped like a crescent. —*n.* **3.** bicorne. [1745–55; < L *bicornis,* equiv. to *bi-* BI-[1] + *corn(ū)* HORN + *-is* adj. suffix]

Bi·corn (bī′kôrn), *n.* (in early French and English literature) a mythical animal, usually depicted as a grotesquely fat beast, that existed solely by devouring virtuous husbands. Cf. **Chichivache.** [1375–1425; late ME *Bycorne* < MF < L *bicornis* BICORN]

bi·corne (bī′kôrn), *n.* **1.** a two-cornered cocked hat worn esp. in the 18th and early 19th centuries. **2.** a two-horned animal. Also, **bicorn.** [< F, MF; see BICORN, BICORN]

bi·cor·po·ral (bī kôr′pər əl), *adj.* having two bodies, main divisions, symbols, etc. Also, **bi·cor·po·re·al** (bī′kôr pôr′ē əl, -pōr′-). [1680–90; < L *bicorpor* (*bi-* BI-[1] + *corpor-,* s. of *corpus* body) + -AL[1]]

bi·cul·tur·al (bī kul′chər əl), *adj.* **1.** of, pertaining to, or combining two cultures. **2.** of or pertaining to biculturalism. [1935–40; BI-[1] + CULTURAL]

bi·cul·tur·al·ism (bī kul′chər ə liz′əm), *n.* the presence of two different cultures in the same country or region: *a commission on bilingualism and biculturalism in Canada.* [1950–55; BICULTURAL + -ISM]

bi·cus·pid (bī kus′pid), *adj.* **1.** Also, **bi·cus′pi·date′.** having or terminating in two cusps or points, as certain teeth. —*n.* **2.** premolar (def. 4). [1830–40; BI-[1] + CUSPID]

bicus′pid valve′. See **mitral valve.** [1895–1900]

CONCISE PRONUNCIATION KEY: act, cāpe, dâre, pärt; set, ēqual; if, īce; ox, ōver, ôrder, oil, bo͝ok, bo͞ot, out; up, ûrge; child; sing; shoe; thin, *th*at; zh as in *treasure.* ə = *a* as in *alone, e* as in *system, i* as in *easily, o* as in *gallop, u* as in *circus;* ᵊ as in *fire* (fīᵊr), *hour* (ouᵊr). l and n can serve as syllabic consonants, as in *cradle* (krād′l), and *button* (but′n). See the full key inside the front cover.

bi•cy•cle (bī′si kəl, -sik′əl, -sī′kəl), *n.*, *v.*, **-cled, -cling.** —*n.* **1.** a vehicle with two wheels in tandem, usually propelled by pedals connected to the rear wheel by a chain, and having handlebars for steering and a saddlelike seat. —*v.i.* **2.** to ride a bicycle. —*v.t.* **3.** to ship or transport directly by bicycle or other means. [1865–70; < F; see BI-[1], CYCLE] —**bi′cy•clist, bi′cy•cler,** *n.*

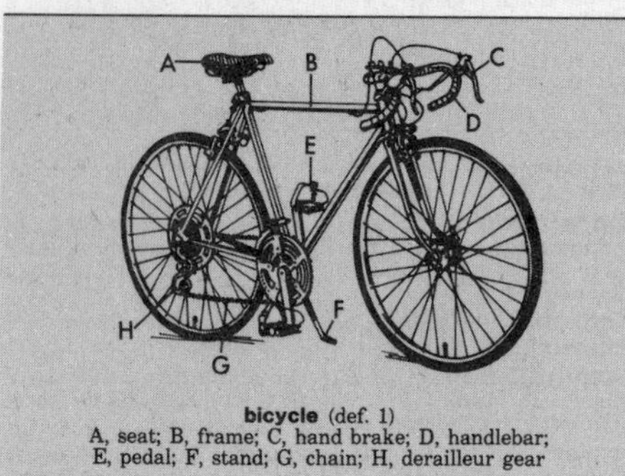

bicycle (def. 1)
A, seat; B, frame; C, hand brake; D, handlebar; E, pedal; F, stand; G, chain; H, derailleur gear

bi′cycle kick′, **1.** an exercise performed by lying on one's back with the hips and legs in the air, supported by the hands, and moving the legs as if pedaling a bicycle. **2.** *Soccer.* a dramatic kick made by a player throwing both feet in the air as a ball is approaching on the fly, while moving the legs with a pedaling motion to kick the ball in the opposite direction to which the player is facing, with the player usually ending up sprawled on the ground. [1960–65]

bi′cycle path′, a path, as one alongside a roadway, for the use of bicyclists. Also called **bike path.** [1970–75]

bi′cycle race′, *Sports.* cycling (def. 2). Also, **bi′•cycle rac′ing.** [1865–70]

bi•cy•clic (bī sī′klik, -sik′lik), *adj.* **1.** consisting of or having two cycles or circles. **2.** *Bot.* in two whorls, as the stamens of a flower. **3.** pertaining to or resembling a bicycle. Also, **bi•cy′cli•cal.** [1875–80; BI-[1] + CYCLIC]

bicy′clic ter′pene, *Chem.* See under **terpene** (def. 2).

bid[1] (bid), *v.*, **bade** or (*Archaic*) **bad** for 1, 2, 5, 6, 8 or **bid** for 3, 4, 7, 9, 10; **bid•den** or **bid** for 1, 2, 5, 6, 8 or **bid** for 3, 4, 7, 9; **bid•ding;** *n.* —*v.t.* **1.** to command; order; direct: *to bid them depart.* **2.** to express (a greeting, farewell, benediction, or wish): *to bid good night.* **3.** *Com.* to offer (a certain sum) as the price one will pay or charge: *They bid $25,000 and got the contract.* **4.** *Cards.* to enter a bid of (a given quantity or suit): *to bid two no-trump.* **5.** to summon by invitation; invite. —*v.i.* **6.** to command; order; direct: *I will do as you bid.* **7.** to make a bid: *She bid at the auction for the old chair.* **8. bid fair.** See **fair**[1] (def. 23). **9. bid in,** *Com.* to overbid all offers for (property) at an auction in order to retain ownership. **10. bid up,** *Com.* to increase the market price of by increasing bids. —*n.* **11.** an act or instance of bidding. **12.** *Cards.* **a.** an offer to make a specified number of points or to take a specified number of tricks. **b.** the amount of such an offer. **c.** the turn of a person to bid. **13.** an invitation: *a bid to join the club.* **14.** an attempt to attain some goal or purpose: *a bid for election.* **15.** Also called **bid price.** *Stock Exchange.* the highest price a prospective buyer is willing to pay for a security at a given moment. [bef. 900; ME *bidden,* OE *biddan* to beg, ask; c. OFris *bidda,* OS *biddian,* OHG *bittan* (G *bitten*), ON *bithja,* Goth *bidjan;* all < Gmc **bidja-* (< IE **bhidh-*) command, akin to Gk *peíthein* to persuade, inspire with trust, E BIDE] —**bid′der,** *n.*
—**Syn. 1.** charge; require, enjoin. **3.** offer, tender, proffer. **11.** offer, proposal; proffer.

bid[2] (bid), *v. Archaic.* pp. of **bide.**

B.I.D., Bachelor of Industrial Design.

b.i.d., (in prescriptions) twice a day. [< L *bis in diē*]

bi•dar•ka (bī där′kə), *n.* a sealskin boat used by Aleuts and southern Alaskan Eskimos. Also, **bi•da•ra** (bī där′ə), **bi•dar•kee** (bī där′kē), **baidarka.** [1825–35; < Russ *baĭdárka,* equiv. to *baĭdár(a)* kind of river craft (appar. akin to *baĭdák* river craft, barge, ORuss *baidakŭ,* *bodakŭ,* of obscure orig.) + *-ka* dim. suffix]

Bi•dault (bē dō′), *n.* **Georges** (zhôrzh), 1899–1983, French statesman.

bid•da•ble (bid′ə bəl), *adj.* **1.** *Cards.* adequate to bid upon: *a biddable suit.* **2.** willing to do what is asked; obedient; tractable; docile: *a biddable child.* **3.** that may be acquired by bidding: *biddable merchandise.* [1820–30; BID[1] + -ABLE] —**bid′da•bil′i•ty, bid′da•ble•ness,** *n.* —**bid′da•bly,** *adv.*

Bid•de•ford (bid′ə fərd), *n.* a city in SW Maine. 19,638.

bid•den (bid′n), *v.* **1.** a pp. of **bid.** —*adj.* **2.** invited.

bid•ding (bid′ing), *n.* **1.** command; summons; invitation: *I went there at his bidding.* **2.** bids collectively, or a period during which bids are made or received: *The bidding began furiously.* **3.** a bid. **4. do someone's bidding,** to submit to someone's orders; perform services for someone: *After he was promoted to vice president at the bank, he expected everyone around him to do his bidding.* [1125–75; ME; see BID[1], -ING[1]]

bid′ding prayer′, **1.** the formal petitionary prayer, said esp. in the Anglican Church immediately before the sermon. **2.** an intercessory prayer for persons living and dead, said in English churches up to about the middle of the 16th century. [1745–55]

Bid•dle (bid′l), *n.* **1. Francis,** 1886–1968, U.S. attorney general 1941–45. **2. John,** 1615–62, English theologian: founder of English Unitarianism. **3. Nicholas,** 1786–1844, U.S. financier.

bid•dy[1] (bid′ē), *n., pl.* **-dies.** *Chiefly New England, South Midland, and Southern U.S.* **1.** a chicken. **2.** a newly hatched chick. [1595–1605; cf. Brit. dial. *biddy* (< ?) with same sense, usually as a call to chickens]

bid•dy[2] (bid′ē), *n., pl.* **-dies. 1.** a fussbudget, esp. a fussy old woman. **2.** a female domestic servant, esp. a cleaning woman. [1700–10; special use of *Biddy,* by-form of BRIDGET]

bide (bīd), *v.*, **bid•ed** or **bode; bid•ed** or (*Archaic*) **bid; bid•ing.** —*v.t.* **1.** *Archaic.* to endure; bear. **2.** *Obs.* to encounter. —*v.i.* **3.** to dwell; abide; wait; remain. **4. bide one's time,** to wait for a favorable opportunity: *He wanted to ask for a raise, but bided his time.* [bef. 900; ME *biden,* OE *bīdan;* c. OFris *bīdia,* OS *bīdan,* OHG *bītan,* ON *bītha,* Goth *beidan,* L *fīdere,* Gk *peíthesthai* to trust, rely < IE **bheidh-;* the meaning appar. developed: have trust > endure > wait > ABIDE > remain] —**bid′er,** *n.*
—**Syn. 3.** stay, linger, tarry.

bi•den•tate (bī den′tāt), *adj. Biol.* having two teeth or toothlike parts or processes. [1750–60; < L *bident-* (s. of *bidēns,* equiv. to *bi-* BI-[1] + *dēns* tooth) + -ATE[1]]

bi•den•tic•u•late (bī′den tik′yə lit, -lāt′), *adj. Zool., Bot.* having two small teeth or toothlike processes. [BI-[1] + DENTICULATE]

bi•det (bē dā′, bi det′), *n.* **1.** a low, basinlike bathroom fixture, usually with spigots, used for bathing the genital and perineal areas. **2.** a small saddle horse. [1620–30; < MF: pony; akin to OF *bider* to trot]

bi•di (bē′dē), *n., pl.* **-dis.** (in India) an inexpensive cigarette, locally produced usually from cut tobacco rolled in leaf. Also, **beedi, biri.** [< Hindi *biḍī* < Skt *vīṭikā* a preparation rolled in betel leaf]

bi•di•a•lec•tal (bī′dī ə lek′təl), *adj.* proficient in or using two dialects of the same language. [1965–70; BI-[1] + DIALECTAL, on the model of BILINGUAL] —**bi′di•a•lec′tal•ism, bi•di′a•lect•ism,** *n.* —**bi′di•a•lec′tal•ist,** *n.* —**bi′di•a•lec′tal•ly,** *adv.*

bi•di•rec•tion•al (bī′di rek′shə nl, -dī-), *adj.* capable of reacting or functioning in two, usually opposite, directions. [1940–45; BI-[1] + DIRECTIONAL] —**bi′di•rec′tion•al′i•ty,** *n.* —**bi′di•rec′tion•al•ly,** *adv.*

bi•don•ville (*Fr.* bē dôɴ vēl′), *n., pl.* **-villes** (*Fr.* -vēl′). (esp. in France and North Africa) an impoverished shantytown on the outskirts of a city. [1950–55; < F, equiv. to *bidon* metal drum, can (for oil, etc.) (earlier, five-pint wooden jug; of uncert. orig.) + *-ville,* comb. form, in placenames, of *ville* city < L *vīlla* VILLA; metal cans are often used as building materials in such towns]

bid′ price′, *Stock Exchange.* bid[1] (def. 15).

bid-up (bid′up′), *n.* **1.** the act or an instance of increasing the price of something by forcing the bidding upward. **2.** the amount of such increase: *a bid-up of 100 percent in the last year.* [1860–65; n. use of v. phrase *bid up*]

B.I.E., Bachelor of Industrial Engineering.

Bie•der•mei•er (bē′dər mī′ər), *adj.* noting or pertaining to a style of furnishings common in German-speaking areas in the early to middle 19th century, generally existing as a simplification of the French Directoire and Empire styles, usually executed in fruitwood with much use of matched veneers, and often displaying architectural motifs. [named after Gottlieb *Biedermeier,* imaginary author of poems actually composed by various writers and published in German magazine *Fliegende Blätter* from 1855 on]

Biedermeier cabinet

Biel (bēl), *n.* **Lake.** See **Bienne, Lake of.**

bield (bēld), *n. Scot.* a shelter; refuge. [1400–50; late ME (Scots) *beld(e), beild,* appar. to be identified with ME *beild* courage, power, aid, OE *bieldo* boldness; akin to Goth *balthei* confidence. See BOLD]

Bie•le•feld (bē′lə felt′), *n.* a city in NW Germany. 315,000.

Bie•ler•see (bē′lər zā′), *n.* German name of Lake of Bienne.

Biel•sko-Bia•ła (byel′skô byä′lä, -byä′wä), *n.* a city in S Poland. 116,100. German, **Bie•litz** (bē′lits).

bien en•ten•du (bya näɴ täɴ dʏ′), *French.* naturally; of course. [lit., well understood]

Bienne (byen), *n.* **Lake of,** a lake in NW Switzerland: traces of prehistoric lake dwellings. 16 sq. mi. (41 sq. km). Also called **Lake Biel.** German, **Bielersee.**

bi•en•ni•al (bī en′ē əl), *adj.* **1.** happening every two years: *biennial games.* **2.** lasting or enduring for two years: *a biennial life cycle.* **3.** *Bot.* completing its normal term of life in two years, flowering and fruiting the second year, as beets or winter wheat. —*n.* **4.** any event occurring once in two years. **5.** *Bot.* a biennial plant. Also, **biyearly** (for defs. 1, 2). [1615–25; BIENNI(UM) + -AL[1]] —**bi•en′ni•al•ly,** *adv.*
—**Usage.** See **bi-**[1].

bi•en•ni•um (bī en′ē əm), *n., pl.* **-en•ni•ums, -en•ni•a** (-en′ē ə). a period of two years. [1895–1900; < L, equiv. to *bi-* BI-[1] + *-enn-* (comb. form of *annus* year) + *-ium* -IUM]

bien•ve•nu (byaɴ və nʏ′), *adj. French.* welcome. [lit., well arrived]

bien•ve•nue (byaɴ və nʏ′), *French.* —*adj.* **1.** welcome (used when addressing or referring to a woman). —*n.* **2.** a welcome; kindly greeting or reception.

Bien•ville (byaɴ vēl′), *n.* **Jean Bap•tiste Le Moyne** (zhäɴ ba tēst′ lə mwan′), **Sieur de** (syœr də), 1680–1768, French governor of Louisiana.

bier (bēr), *n.* **1.** a frame or stand on which a corpse or the coffin containing it is laid before burial. **2.** such a stand together with the corpse or coffin. [bef. 900; ME *bere,* OE *bēr, bǣr(e);* c. OHG *bāra* (G *Bahre*), D, Dan *baar,* Sw *bår;* sp. influenced by F *bière;* akin to BEAR[1], BARROW[1]]

Bierce (bērs), *n.* **Ambrose (Gwin•nett)** (gwi net′), 1842–1914?, U.S. journalist and short-story writer.

bier•kä•se (bēr′kā′zə), *n.* a semisoft, strong white cow's-milk cheese that originated in Germany, and is eaten esp. with beer. Also, **Bier′kä′se.** [< G, equiv. to *Bier* BEER + *Käse* CHEESE[1]]

Bier•stadt (bēr′stat; *Ger.* bēʀ′shtät), *n.* **Al•bert** (al′bərt; *Ger.* äl′bɛʀt), 1830–1902, U.S. painter, born in Germany.

bier•stu•be (bēr′shtōō bə), *n., pl.* **-bes, -ben** (-bən). a tavern or café offering German or German-style atmosphere, décor, food, beer, etc. [1905–10; < G, equiv. to *Bier* BEER + *Stube* room; see STOVE[1]]

biest•ings (bē′stingz), *n.* (*used with a singular v.*) beestings.

bi•fa•cial (bī fā′shəl), *adj.* **1.** having two faces or fronts. **2.** *Archaeol.* having the opposite surfaces alike, as some tools. [1880–85; BI-[1] + FACIAL] —**bi•fa′cial•ly,** *adv.*

bi•far•i•ous (bī fâr′ē əs), *adj. Bot.* in two vertical rows. [1650–60; < LL *bifārius* twofold, double, deriv. (see -IOUS) of L *bifāriam* (adv.) in two parts or places, equiv. to *bi-* BI-[1] + *-fāriam* (perh. deriv. of **fās* utterance, thus orig. "having two expressions"; see INFANT); cf. MULTIFARIOUS] —**bi•far′i•ous•ly,** *adv.*

biff[1] (bif), *Slang.* —*n.* **1.** a blow; punch. —*v.t.* **2.** to hit; punch. [1840–50, *Amer.*; perh. imit.]

biff[2] (bif), *n.* biffy.

bif•fin (bif′in), *n.* a deep-red cooking apple native to Britain. [1785–95; var. of *beefing* (so called from color of beef); see -ING[3]]

bif•fy (bif′ē), *n., pl.* **-fies.** *Chiefly Upper Midwest and Canadian Slang.* a toilet or privy. Also, **biff.** [orig. obscure]

bi•fid (bī′fid), *adj.* separated or cleft into two equal parts or lobes. [1655–65; < L *bifidus,* equiv. to *bi-* BI-[1] + *fid-* (var. s. of *findere* to split; akin to BITE) + *-us* adj. suffix] —**bi•fid′i•ty,** *n.* —**bi′fid•ly,** *adv.*

bi•fi•lar (bī fī′lər), *adj.* furnished or fitted with two filaments or threads. [1830–40; BI-[1] + L *fīl(um)* (see FILE[1]) + -AR[1]] —**bi•fi′lar•ly,** *adv.*

bi•flag•el•late (bī flaj′ə lāt′, -lit), *adj. Zool.* having two flagella. [1855–60; BI-[1] + FLAGELLATE]

bi•flex (bī′fleks), *adj.* bent at two places. [BI-[1] + *-flex* < L *flexus;* see FLEX]

bi•fluor•ide (bī flŏŏr′id, -flôr′-, -flōr′-), *n. Chem.* an acid salt of hydrofluoric acid containing the group HF_2^-, as ammonium bifluoride, NH_4HF_2. [BI-[1] + FLUORIDE]

bi•fo•cal (bī fō′kəl, bī′fō′-), *adj.* **1.** *Chiefly Optics.* having two foci. **2.** (of an eyeglass or contact lens) having two portions, one for near and one for far vision. —*n.* **3. bifocals,** bifocal eyeglasses or contact lenses. [1885–90, *Amer.*; BI-[1] + FOCAL]

bi•fold (bī′fōld′), *adj.* capable of being folded into two parts, as with leaves that are hinged together: *a bifold door; bifold shutters.* Also, **bi′fold′ing.** [BI-[1] + -FOLD]

bi•fo•li•ate (bī fō′lē it, -āt′), *adj.* having two leaves. [1830–40; BI-[1] + FOLIATE]

bi•fo•li•o•late (bī fō′lē ə lāt′, -lit), *adj. Bot.* having two leaflets. [1825–35; BI-[1] + FOLIOLATE]

bi•fo•rate (bī fôr′āt, -fōr′-, bī′fə rāt′, bif′ə-), *adj. Biol.* having two pores or perforations. [1835–45; BI-[1] + L *forātus* perforated, ptp. of *forāre* to bore]

bi•forked (bī′fôrkt′), *adj.* bifurcate (def. 2). [1570–80; BI-[1] + FORKED]

bi•form (bī′fôrm′), *adj.* having or combining two forms, as a centaur or mermaid. Also, **bi′formed′.** [1810–20; < L *biformis,* equiv. to *bi-* BI-[1] + *form(a)* FORM + *-is* adj. suffix] —**bi•for′mi•ty,** *n.*

Bif•rost (biv′rost), *n. Scand. Myth.* the rainbow bridge of the gods from Asgard to earth. [< ON *Bifrǫst,* equiv. to *bif-* (root of *bifa,* c. OE *bifian* to shake) + *rǫst,* c. OHG *rasta* stretch of road]

bi•func•tion•al (bī fungk′shə nl), *adj.* **1.** having or serving two functions. **2.** *Chem.* having or involving two functional groups. [1935–40; BI-[1] + FUNCTIONAL]

bi•fur•cate (*v., adj.* bī′fər kāt′, bī fûr′kāt; *adj. also* bī′fər kit, bī fûr′-), *v.*, **-cat•ed, -cat•ing,** *adj.* —*v.t., v.i.* **1.** to divide or fork into two branches. —*adj.* **2.** divided into two branches. [1605–15; < ML *bifurcātus,* ptp. of *bifurcāre* (*bi-* BI-[1] + *furc(a)* FORK + *-ātus* -ATE[1])] —**bi•fur•cate•ly** (bī′fər kāt′lē; bī fûr′kāt lē, -kit-), *adv.* —**bi′fur•ca′tion,** *n.*

big[1] (big), *adj.*, **big•ger, big•gest,** *adv.*, *n.* —*adj.* **1.** large, as in size, height, width, or amount: *a big house; a*

CONCISE ETYMOLOGY KEY: <, descended or borrowed from; >, whence; b., blend of, blended; c., cognate with; cf., compare; deriv., derivative; equiv., equivalent; imit., imitative; obl., oblique; r., replacing; s., stem; sp., spelling, spelled; resp., respelling, respelled; trans., translation; ?, origin unknown; *, unattested; ‡, probably earlier than. See the full key inside the front cover.

big quantity. **2.** of major concern, importance, gravity, or the like: *a big problem.* **3.** outstanding for a specified quality: *a big liar; a big success.* **4.** important, as in influence, standing, or wealth: *a big man in his field.* **5.** grown-up; mature: *big enough to know better.* **6.** elder: *my big sister.* **7.** doing business or conducted on a large scale; major in size or importance: *big government.* **8.** consisting of the largest or most influential companies in an industry: *Big steel wants to lower prices, but the smaller mills don't.* **9.** *Informal.* known or used widely; popular: *Nouvelle cuisine became big in the 1970's.* **10.** magnanimous; generous; kindly: *big enough to forgive.* **11.** boastful; pompous; pretentious; haughty: *a big talker.* **12.** loud; orotund: *a big voice.* **13.** (of clothing or a clothing design) made of or distinguished by voluminous fabric that is loosely or softly shaped and fitted: *a big shirt; the big look.* **14.** (of a wine) having more than average flavor, body, and alcoholic content. **15.** filled; brimming: *eyes big with tears.* **16.** *Chiefly South Midland and Southern U.S.* pregnant. **17.** *Obs.* very strong; powerful. **18. be big on,** to have a special liking or enthusiasm for: *Mother is big on family get-togethers.* **19. big with child.** See **great** (def. 17). —*adv.* **20.** *Informal.* boastfully; pretentiously: *to act big; to talk big.* **21.** *Informal.* with great success; successfully: *to go over big.* —*n.* **22. the bigs,** *Sports Slang.* the highest level of professional competition, as the major leagues in baseball. [1250–1300; ME *big(ge)* < ?] —**big′gish,** *adj.* —**big′ly,** *adv.*
—**Syn. 1.** huge, immense; bulky, massive; capacious, voluminous; extensive. See **great. 4.** consequential. **15.** overflowing, flooded. —**Ant. 1.** little.

big[2] (big), *v.t.,* **bigged, big·ging.** *Brit. Dial.* to build. Also, **bigg.** [1150–1200; ME *biggen* orig., to inhabit < ON *byggja* to inhabit, c. OE *bū(i)an,* G *bauen*]

big[3] (big), *n. Scot. and North Eng.* bigg[1].

bi·ga (bē′gä, -gə, bī′-), *n., pl.* **-gae** (-gē, -jē, -gī). *Class. Antiq.* a two-wheeled chariot drawn by two horses harnessed abreast. Cf. **quadriga, triga.** [1840–50; < L *biga, bigae,* for **biiuga* (*bi-* BI-[1] + *iug(um)* YOKE + *-a* fem. nom. sing. ending)]

big·a·mist (big′ə mist), *n.* a person who commits bigamy. [1625–35; BIGAM(Y) + -IST] —**big′a·mis′tic,** *adj.* —**big′a·mis′ti·cal·ly,** *adv.*

big·a·mous (big′ə məs), *adj.* **1.** having two wives or husbands at the same time; guilty of bigamy. **2.** involving bigamy. [1860–65; < LL *bigamus,* equiv. to *bi-* BI-[1] + Gk *-gamos* -GAMOUS] —**big′a·mous·ly,** *adv.*

big·a·my (big′ə mē), *n., pl.* **-mies. 1.** *Law.* the crime of marrying while one has a wife or husband still living, from whom no valid divorce has been effected. **2.** *Eccles.* any violation of canon law concerning marital status that would disqualify a person from receiving holy orders or from retaining or surpassing an ecclesiastical rank. [1200–50; ME *bigamie* < ML *bigamia* (LL *bigam(us)* BIGAMOUS + L *-ia* -Y[3])]

Big′ Ap′ple, the, *Informal.* New York City. [1925–30; promulgated as a tourist slogan during the 1970's; perh. reuse of earlier "the Apple" (New York City in jazz musicians' argot) with *Big* as in BIG CHEESE, BIG TIME, etc.]

big·a·rade (big′ə räd′, bē′gə räd′; *Fr.* bē GA RAD′), *n., pl.* **-rades** (-rädz′, -rädz′; *Fr.* -RAD′). —*n.* **1.** a Seville or bitter orange. —*adj.* **2.** *French Cookery.* (of a sauce) prepared with bitter oranges: *duck bigarade.* [1695–1705; < F: bitter orange < Pr *bigarrado,* deriv. of *bigarrar* to variegate; see BIGARREAU]

big·ar·reau (big′ə rō′, big′ə rō′), *n.* a large, heart-shaped variety of sweet cherry, having firm flesh. [1620–30; < F, equiv. to *bigarr(é)* variegated (ptp. of *bigarrer,* perh. *bi(s)* twice (see BIS[1]) + *-garrer,* v. deriv. of MF *garre* of two colors; of obscure orig.) + *-eau* n. suffix (earlier *-el* < L *-ellus*)]

big′ band′, a jazz or dance band that is the size of an orchestra. Cf. **combo.** [1925–30]

Big′ Band′ mu′sic, swing[2] (def. 1).

big′ bang′ the′ory, *Astron.* a theory that deduces a cataclysmic birth of the universe **(big′ bang′)** from the observed expansion of the universe, cosmic background radiation, abundance of the elements, and the laws of physics. Also called **big′-bang′ mod′el.** Cf. **steady state theory.** [1950–55]

big′ beat′, (*sometimes caps.*) *Slang.* rhythmic popular music, esp. rock-'n'-roll, notable for its prominent and persistent beat.

Big′ Belt′ Moun′tains, a range of the Rocky Mountains, in W Montana.

Big′ Ben′, the bell in the clock tower of the Houses of Parliament in London, England. [1890–95]

Big′ Bend′ Na′tional Park′, a national park in W Texas, on the Rio Grande. 1080 sq. mi. (2800 sq. km).

Big′ Ber′tha, *Informal.* a large, long-range German cannon used during World War I.

Big′ Board′, (*sometimes l.c.*) *Informal.* the New York Stock Exchange. [1920–25, *Amer.*]

big-boned (big′bōnd′), *adj.* having a bone structure that is massive in contrast with the surrounding flesh. [1600–10]

Big′ Boy′, an articulated steam locomotive having a four-wheeled front truck, one section of eight driving wheels, a second section of eight driving wheels, and a four-wheeled rear truck. See table under **Whyte classification.**

big′ broth′er, 1. an elder brother. **2.** (*sometimes caps.*) a man who individually or as a member of an organized group undertakes to sponsor or assist a boy in need of help or guidance. **3.** (*usually caps.*) the head of a totalitarian regime that keeps its citizens under close surveillance. **4.** (*usually caps.*) the aggregate of officials and policy makers of a powerful and pervasive state. **5.** *CB Radio Slang.* a police officer or police car. [1860–65; 1949 for defs. 3 and 4, the epithet of a dictator in G. Orwell's novel *1984*]

Big′ Broth′er·ism (bruth′ə riz′əm), paternalistic authoritarianism that seeks to supply the needs and regulate the conduct of people. [1950–55; BIG BROTHER + -ISM]

big′ brown′ bat′. See under **brown bat.**

big′ bucks′, *Slang.* a large amount of money.

big′ busi′ness, 1. large business, commercial, and financial firms taken collectively, esp. when considered as a group having shared attitudes and goals and exercising control over economic policy, politics, etc. **2.** any large organization of a noncommercial nature resembling this. **3.** any large business enterprise. [1900–05, *Amer.*]

Big C, *Slang.* cancer. Also, **big C.** [1970–75]

big′ casi′no, (in the game of casino) the ten of diamonds.

big′ cheese′, *Older Slang.* an influential or important person: *Who's the big cheese around here?* [1885–90; see CHEESE[3]]

big′-cone pine′ (big′kōn′). See **Coulter pine.** [1905–10, *Amer.*]

Big D, *Informal.* Dallas, Texas.

big′ dad′dy, (*often caps.*) *Informal.* **1.** a man regarded as the paternalistic head of a family. **2.** the founder or a leading member of a company, organization, movement, etc.: *the big daddy of soil conservation.* **3.** the federal government: *to thank big daddy for the tax cut.* **4.** *Chiefly Southern U.S.* grandfather. [1950–55]

big′ deal′, *Slang.* **1.** an important or impressive person or thing: *to make a big deal out of nothing; I hear he's a big deal on Wall Street now.* **2.** (used ironically as an interjection to indicate that one considers something to be unimportant or unimpressive): *So you're the mayor's cousin—big deal!* [1945–50]

Big′ Di′omede. See under **Diomede Islands.**

Big′ Dip′per, *Astron.* the group of seven bright stars in Ursa Major resembling a dipper in outline. Also called **Dipper.** [1865–70]

bi·gem·i·ny (bī jem′ə nē), *n. Med.* the occurrence of premature atrial or ventricular heartbeats in pairs. [1920–25; < LL *bigemin(us)* double (equiv. to L *bi-* BI-[1] + *geminus* twin) + -Y[3]] —**bi·gem′i·nal,** *adj.*

big′ enchila′da. See **enchilada** (def. 2). [1970–75; on the pattern of such expressions as BIG CHEESE, BIG WHEEL, etc.]

big′ end′, *Mach.* the end of a connecting rod or piston rod that is attached to a crankpin. [1905–10]

bi·gen·er (bī′jē nər, -jə-), *n.* a bigeneric hybrid, as certain orchids. [1825–35; < L: hybrid, equiv. to *bi-* BI-[1] + *gener-* (s. of *genus*) GENUS]

bi·ge·ner·ic (bī′jə ner′ik), *adj.* of, pertaining to, or involving two genera. [1880–85; BI-[1] + GENERIC]

big·eye (big′ī′), *n., pl.* (*esp. collectively*) **-eye,** (*esp. referring to two or more kinds or species*) **-eyes.** any of several silver and red fishes of the family Priacanthidae, found in the warm waters of the Pacific Ocean and in the West Indies, having a short, flattened body and large eyes. [1885–90; BIG[1] + EYE]

big′eye scad′, a carangid fish, *Selar crumenophthalmus,* of tropical seas and Atlantic coastal waters of the U.S., having prominent eyes and commonly used as bait. Also called **goggle-eye.**

Big′ Five′, *Hist.* **1.** the United States, Great Britain, France, Italy, and Japan during World War I and at the Paris Peace Conference in 1919. **2.** (after World War II) the United States, Great Britain, the Soviet Union, China, and France.

Big′ Foot′, a very large, hairy, humanoid creature reputed to inhabit wilderness areas of the U.S. and Canada, esp. the Pacific Northwest. Also, **Big′foot′.** Also called **Sasquatch.** Cf. **Abominable Snowman.** [1960–65; so called from the size of its alleged footprints]

bigg[1] (big), *n. Scot. and North Eng.* four-rowed barley. Also, **big.** [1400–50; late ME *big, bigge* < ON *bygg* barley, c. OE *bēow*]

bigg[2] (big), *v.t.* big[2].

big′ game′, 1. large wild animals, esp. when hunted for sport. **2.** large fish, as tuna and marlin, when sought by deep-sea anglers. **3.** a major objective, esp. one that involves risk. [1860–65]

big·ge·ty (big′i tē), *adj. Chiefly South Midland and Southern U.S.* biggity.

big·gie (big′ē), *n. Slang.* **1.** an important, influential, or prominent person; big shot; bigwig. **2.** something that is very large, important, impressive, or successful: *a merger of two corporate biggies; a movie that was this year's box-office biggie.* [1930–35; BIG[1] + -IE]

big·gin[1] (big′in), *n. Archaic.* **1.** a close-fitting cap worn esp. by children in the 16th and 17th centuries. **2.** a soft cap worn while sleeping; nightcap. [1520–30; < MF *beguin* kind of hood or cap, orig. one worn by a BEGUINE]

big·gin[2] (big′in), *n.* a coffeepot, usually silver, having a separate container in which the coffee is immersed while being boiled. [after *Biggin,* the name of its early 19th-century inventor]

big·ging (big′in), *n. Scot. and North Eng.* a building, esp. one's home. [1200–50; ME *biging.* See BIG[2], -ING[1]]

big·gish (big′ish), *adj.* rather or fairly big. [1620–30; BIG[1] + -ISH[1]]

big·gi·ty (big′i tē), *adj. Chiefly South Midland and Southern U.S.* conceited or self-important. Also, **biggety.** [1875–80; BIG[1] + *-ity* suffix of unclear orig., perh. containing -Y[1]; cf. UPPITY]

Biggs (bigz), *n.* **E(dward George) Pow·er** (pou′ər), 1906–77, English organist in the U.S.

big′ gun′, *Slang.* an influential or important person or thing: *He's a big gun in science.*

big·gy (big′ē), *n., pl.* **-gies.** *Slang.* biggie. [1930–35, *Amer.*; BIG[1] + -Y[2]]

big·head (big′hed′, -hed′), *n.* **1.** *Informal.* an excessive estimate of one's importance; conceit. **2.** *Vet. Pathol.* **a.** an inflammatory swelling of the tissues of the head of sheep, caused by the anaerobic bacillus *Clostridium novyi.* **b.** enlargement of the head and jawbones of horses resulting from nutritional hyperthyroidism. [1795–1805, *Amer.*; BIG[1] + HEAD] —**big′head′ed,** *adj.* —**big′head′ed·ness,** *n.*

big-heart·ed (big′här′tid), *adj.* generous; kind. [1865–70] —**big′heart′ed·ly,** *adv.* —**big′heart′ed·ness,** *n.*
—**Syn.** unstinting, openhanded, benevolent, bountiful.

big′ hook′, *Railroad Slang.* See **wrecking crane.**

big·horn (big′hôrn′), *n., pl.* **-horns,** (*esp. collectively*) **-horn.** a wild sheep, *Ovis canadensis,* of the Rocky Mountains, with large, curving horns. Also called **cimarron, Rocky Mountain bighorn, Rocky Mountain sheep.** [1775–85, *Amer.*; BIG[1] + HORN]

bighorn,
Ovis canadensis,
3½ ft. (1.1 m) high
at shoulder; horns to
3½ ft. (1.1 m);
length to 5½ ft. (1.7 m)

Big·horn (big′hôrn′), *n.* a river flowing from central Wyoming to the Yellowstone River in S Montana. 336 mi. (540 km) long.

Big′horn Moun′tains, a mountain range in N Wyoming, part of the Rocky Mountains. Highest peak, Cloud Peak, 13,165 ft. (4013 m). Also called **Big′horns′.**

big′ house′, *Slang.* a penitentiary (usually prec. by *the*). [1815–25]

bight (bīt), *n.* **1.** the middle part of a rope, as distinguished from the ends. **2.** the loop or bent part of a rope, as distinguished from the ends. **3.** a bend or curve in the shore of a sea or river. **4.** a body of water bounded by such a bend. **5.** a bay or gulf. —*v.t.* **6.** to fasten with a bight of rope. [bef. 1000; ME *byght,* OE *byht* bend, bay; c. D *bocht,* G *Bucht;* akin to BOW[1]]

big′ ide′a, *Informal.* **1.** any plan or proposal that is grandiose, impractical, and usually unsolicited: *You're always coming around here with your big ideas.* **2.** purpose; intention; aim: *What's the big idea of shouting at me?* [1920–25, *Amer.*]

big′ Ike′, *Chiefly South Midland and Southern U.S. Disparaging.* a self-important person. [1900–05, *Amer.*]

big′ la′bor, large labor unions collectively.

big′ lau′rel, *South Midland U.S.* the rhododendron. [1800–10, *Amer.*]

big′leaf ma′ple (big′lēf′), a tree, *Acer macrophyllum,* of western North America, having large, deeply lobed leaves and fragrant yellow flowers in drooping clusters. Also called **Oregon maple.** [1900–05, *Amer.*; BIG[1] + LEAF]

big′ league′, 1. *Sports.* See **major league. 2.** Often, **big leagues.** *Informal.* the area of greatest competition, highest achievement or rewards, etc.: *He's a local politician who isn't ready for the big league.* [1895–1900]

big-league (big′lēg′), *adj.* **1.** *Sports.* of or belonging to a major league: *a big-league pitcher.* **2.** *Informal.* among the largest, foremost, etc., of its kind: *the big-league steel companies.* [1895–1900; adj. use of BIG LEAGUE]

big-lea·guer (big′lē′gər), *n.* **1.** *Sports.* a player in a major league. **2.** *Informal.* a person who belongs to or works for a big-league organization. [1895–1900, *Amer.*; BIG LEAGUE + -ER[1]]

big′-leaved magno′lia (big′lēvd′). See **evergreen magnolia.**

big′ lie′, a false statement of outrageous magnitude employed as a propaganda measure in the belief that a lesser falsehood would not be credible. [1945–50]

big′ ma′ma, (*often caps.*) *Informal.* **1.** a man's sweetheart, girlfriend, or wife. **2.** a woman regarded as the head of a family. **3.** the female founder or a leading female member of a company, organization, movement, etc. **4.** *Chiefly Southern U.S.* grandmother. [1950–55]

big·mouth (big′mouth′), *n., pl.* **-mouths** (-mouthz′, -mouths′) for 1; (*esp. collectively*) **-mouth,** (*esp. referring to two or more kinds or species*) **-mouths** for 2. **1.** a loud, talkative person, esp. one who lacks discretion. **2.** any of several fishes having an unusually large mouth. [1885–90, *Amer.*; BIG[1] + MOUTH]

big·mouthed (big′moutht′, -mouthd′), *adj.* **1.** having a very large mouth. **2.** very talkative; loud-mouthed. [BIG[1] + MOUTH + -ED[3]]

big′mouth buf′falofish, a buffalofish, *Ictiobus cyprinellus,* found in central North America, characterized by a large mouth.

Big′ Mud′dy, a nickname of the Missouri River.

Big′ Mud′dy Riv′er, a river in SW Illinois, flowing SW into the Mississippi. ab. 120 mi. (195 km) long. [1815–25, *Amer.*]

big′ name′, a person who has a preeminent public reputation in a specified field: *He's a big name in education.* [1930–35, *Amer.*]

big-name (big′nām′), *adj.* **1.** having a widespread public reputation as a leader in a specified field; famous: *a big-name doctor; a big-name actress.* **2.** of, pertaining to, or composed of a big-name person or persons. [1925–30, *Amer.*]

big·ness (big′nis), *n.* **1.** the fact or condition of being large in size, extent, amount, etc. **2.** *Chiefly New Eng.* size. [1485–95; BIG[1] + -NESS]

big·no·ni·a (big nō′nē ə), *n.* **1.** any chiefly tropical American climbing shrub of the genus *Bignonia,* cultivated for its showy, trumpet-shaped flowers. **2.** any member of the plant family Bignoniaceae, characterized by trees, shrubs, and woody vines having opposite leaves, showy, bisexual, tubular flowers, and often large, gourdlike or capsular fruit with flat, winged seeds, and including the bignonia, catalpa, princess tree, and trumpet creeper. [1690–1700; < NL, named after Abbé *Bignon* (librarian of Louis XIV of France); see -IA]

big·no·ni·a·ceous (big nō′nē ā′shəs), *adj.* belonging to the plant family Bignoniaceae. Cf. **bignonia** (def. 2). [< NL *Bignoniace(ae)* (see BIGNONIA, -ACEAE) + -OUS]

Big O, *Slang.* orgasm.

big′ one′, *Slang.* a one-thousand-dollar bill or the sum of one thousand dollars. [1955–60]

big·ot (big′ət), *n.* a person who is utterly intolerant of any differing creed, belief, or opinion. [1590–1600; < MF (OF: derogatory name applied by the French to the Normans), perh. < OE *bī God* by God]

big·ot·ed (big′ə tid), *adj.* utterly intolerant of any creed, belief, or opinion that differs from one's own. [1635–45; BIGOT + -ED[3]] **—big′ot·ed·ly,** *adv.*
—Syn. See **intolerant.**

big·ot·ry (big′ə trē), *n., pl.* **-ries. 1.** stubborn and complete intolerance of any creed, belief, or opinion that differs from one's own. **2.** the actions, beliefs, prejudices, etc., of a bigot. [1665–75; BIGOT + -RY, formation parallel to F *bigoterie*]
—Syn. 1. narrow-mindedness, bias, discrimination.

big′ pic′ture, a broad, overall view or perspective of an issue or problem.

Big′ Rap′ids, a town in central Michigan. 14,361.

big′ road′, *Chiefly South Midland and Southern U.S.* a main road or highway.

big′ shot′, *Informal.* an important or influential person. [1905–10]

big′ sis′ter, 1. an elder sister. **2.** (*sometimes caps.*) a woman who individually or as a member of an organized group undertakes to sponsor or assist a girl in need of help or guidance. **3.** (*sometimes caps.*) a young woman in the junior or senior class in college who advises a young woman in the freshman class on studies, social activities, etc., often as a part of a sorority program.

big′ skate′. See under **skate**[2].

Big′ Spring′, a city in W Texas. 24,804.

big′ stick′, force, esp. political or military, used by a government as a means of influence. [1895–1900, *Amer.*]

big′ talk′, *Informal.* exaggeration; bragging. [1855–60, *Amer.*]

Big·tha (big′thə), *n.* one of the seven eunuchs who served in the court of King Ahasuerus. Esther 1:10.

big-tick·et (big′tik′it), *adj.* costing a great deal; expensive: *fur coats and other big-ticket items.* [1940–45]

big′ time′, 1. *Informal.* the highest or most important level in any profession or occupation: *She's a talented violinist, but she's not ready for the big time.* **2.** *Slang.* a very good time. **3.** *Theat.* (in vaudeville) any highly successful circuit of theaters that produces two performances daily. **—big′-time′,** *adj.* **—big′-tim′er,** *n.* [1860–65, *Amer.*]

big′ toe′, the first, innermost, largest digit of the foot. [1885–90]

big′ top′, 1. the largest or main tent of a circus. **2.** a circus. [1890–95, *Amer.*]

big′ tree′, a large coniferous tree, *Sequoiadendron giganteum* (formerly *Sequoia gigantea*), of California, often reaching 300 ft. (91 m) in height, having reddish-brown bark, scalelike blue-green leaves, and bearing large elliptical cones. Also called **giant sequoia.** Cf. **sequoia.** [1850–55, *Amer.*]

big′ wheel′, *Informal.* an influential or important person: *a big wheel in business.* [1905–10]

big·wig (big′wig′), *n. Informal.* an important person, esp. an official: *senators and other political bigwigs.* [1725–35; rhyming compound from phrase *big wig,* i.e., person important enough to wear such a wig] **—big′·wigged′,** *adj.* **—big·wig·ged·ness** (big′wig′id nis), *n.*

Bi·har (bē här′), *n.* **1.** a state in NE India. 62,700,000; 67,164 sq. mi. (173,955 sq. km). *Cap.:* Patna. **2.** a city in the central part of this state. 100,052. Also, **Behar.**

Bihar′ and O·ris′sa (ô ris′ə, ō ris′ə), a former province of NE India: now divided into the states of Bihar and Orissa.

Bi·ha·ri (bi här′ē), *n.* **1.** a native or inhabitant of Bihar. **2.** the Indic language of Bihar. [1880–85]

bi·hour·ly (bī ouᵊr′lē, -ou′ər-), *adj.* occurring every two hours. [BI-[1] + HOURLY]

CONCISE ETYMOLOGY KEY: <, descended or borrowed from; >, whence; b., blend of, blended; c., cognate with; cf., compare; deriv., derivative; equiv., equivalent; imit., imitative; obl., oblique; r., replacing; s., stem; sp., spelling, spelled; resp., respelling, respelled; trans., translation; ?, origin unknown; *, unattested; ‡, probably earlier than. See the full key inside the front cover.

Bih·zad (bē′zäd), *n.* **Ka·mal ad-Din** (kä′mäl äd dēn′), c1440–c1527, Persian painter and calligrapher.

Biisk (byēsk), *n.* Bisk.

Bi′ja·gos Is′lands (bē′zhä gôsh′, bē′zhä gôsh′), a group of islands in Guinea-Bissau, W of the mainland.

bi·jec·tion (bī jek′shən), *n. Math.* a map or function that is one-to-one and onto. [1965–70; BI-[1] + *-jection,* as in PROJECTION]

bi·jou (bē′zhōō, bē zhōō′), *n., pl.* **-joux** (-zhōōz, -zhōōz′). **1.** a jewel. **2.** something small, delicate, and exquisitely wrought. [1660–70; < F < Breton *bizou* (jeweled) ring, deriv. of *biz* finger; c. Cornish *bisou* finger-ring, deriv. of *bis* finger]

bi·jou·te·rie (bē zhōō′tə rē), *n.* jewelry. [1805–15; < F, equiv. to *bijou* BIJOU + *-terie,* extended form of *-erie* -ERY]

bi·ju·gate (bī′jŏŏ gāt′, -git, bī jōō′gāt, -git), *adj. Bot.* (of leaves) having two pairs of leaflets or pinnae. Also, **bi·ju·gous** (bī′jŏŏ gəs, bī jōō′gəs). [1715–25; BI-[1] + JUGATE]

Bi·ka·ner (bē′kə nēr′, -ner′, bik′ə-), *n.* **1.** a former native state of NW India: now incorporated into Rajasthan state. **2.** a city in NW Rajasthan. 188,598.

bike[1] (bīk), *n., v.,* **biked, bik·ing.** **—***n.* **1.** *Informal.* **a.** a bicycle. **b.** a motorbike. **c.** a motorcycle. **2.** *Harness Racing.* a sulky with tires like those of a bicycle. **3. get off one's bike,** *Australian Informal.* to lose control of oneself or become angry. **—***v.i.* **4.** to ride a bike: *I bike to work.* [1880–85, *Amer.*; alter. of BICYCLE]

bike[2] (bīk), *n. Scot. and North Eng.* **1.** a colony, nest, or swarm of wild bees, wasps, or hornets. **2.** a teeming crowd; swarm of people. [1250–1300; ME, equiv. to *bi bee (< ON *bý* BEE[1]) + *yeke, OE *gēoc* help, safety]

bike′ path′. See **bicycle path.**

bik·er (bī′kər), *n.* **1.** a person who rides a bicycle, motorcycle, or motorbike, esp. in competition or as a hobby. **2.** *Informal.* a member of a motorcycle gang. [1880–85; BIKE[1] + -ER[1]]

bike·way (bīk′wā′), *n.* See **bicycle path.** [1960–65; BIKE[1] + WAY]

Bi·ki·la (bi kē′lə), *n.* **A·be·be** (ä bā′bā), 1932–73, Ethiopian track-and-field athlete.

bi·ki·ni (bi kē′nē), *n., pl.* **-nis. 1.** a very brief, close-fitting, two-piece bathing suit for women or girls. **2.** a very brief, close-fitting pair of bathing trunks for men or boys. **3.** Often, **bikinis.** underwear briefs that are fitted low on the hip or below it. [1945–50; < F, appar. named after BIKINI]

Bi·ki·ni (bi kē′nē), *n.* an atoll in the N Pacific, in the Marshall Islands: atomic bomb tests 1946. 3 sq. mi. (8 sq. km).

biki′ni cut′, a horizontal surgical incision in the lower abdomen, often used for a hysterectomy or a Cesarean delivery, so called because it leaves a less noticeable scar than does a vertical incision.

Bi·kol (bē kōl′), *n., pl.* **-kols,** (*esp. collectively*) **-kol. 1.** a member of a Malayan people in SE Luzon and the nearby Philippines: converted to Christianity early in the Spanish conquest. **2.** the Austronesian language of the Bikol people. Also, **Bicol.**

bi·la·bi·al (bī lā′bē əl), *Phonet.* **—***adj.* **1.** produced with the lips close together or touching: the lips touch at one phase of the production of the bilabial consonants *p, b,* and *m;* they do not for the bilabial *w.* **—***n.* **2.** a bilabial speech sound. [1860–65; BI-[1] + LABIAL]

bi·la·bi·ate (bī lā′bē it, -āt′), *adj. Bot.* two-lipped, as a corolla. See illus. under **corolla.** [1785–95; BI-[1] + LABIATE]

bi·lat·er·al (bī lat′ər əl), *adj.* **1.** pertaining to, involving, or affecting two or both sides, factions, parties, or the like: *a bilateral agreement; bilateral sponsorship.* **2.** located on opposite sides of an axis; two-sided, esp. when of equal size, value, etc. **3.** *Biol.* pertaining to the right and left sides of a structure, plane, etc. **4.** *Chiefly Law.* (of a contract) binding the parties to reciprocal obligations. **5.** through both parents equally: *bilateral affiliation.* Cf. **unilateral** (def. 7). **—***n.* **6.** *Informal.* a bilateral agreement, esp. regarding international trade. [1765–75; BI-[1] + LATERAL] **—bi·lat′er·al·ism, bi·lat′er·al·ness,** *n.* **—bi·lat′er·al·ly,** *adv.*

bilat′eral sym′metry, *Biol.* a basic body plan in which the left and right sides of the organism can be divided into approximate mirror images of each other along the midline. Cf. **radial symmetry.** [1850–55]

bi·lay·er (bī′lā′ər), *n. Biochem.* a structure composed of two molecular layers, esp. of phospholipids in cellular membranes. [1960–65; BI-[1] + LAYER]

Bil·ba·o (bil bou′; *Sp.* bēl bä′ô), *n.* **1.** a seaport in N Spain, near the Bay of Biscay. 450,000. **2.** *U.S. Furniture.* a mirror of the late 18th century, originally imported from Spain, having a frame partly or wholly of marble and a gilt openwork cresting.

bil·ber·ry (bil′ber′ē, -bə rē), *n., pl.* **-ries.** the fruit of several shrubby species of the genus *Vaccinium.* [1570–80; obs. *bil* (< Scand; cf. Dan *bölle* bilberry) + BERRY]

bil·bo[1] (bil′bō), *n., pl.* **-boes.** Usually, **bilboes.** a long iron bar or bolt with sliding shackles and a lock, formerly attached to the ankles of prisoners. [1550–60; earlier *bilbow* < ?]

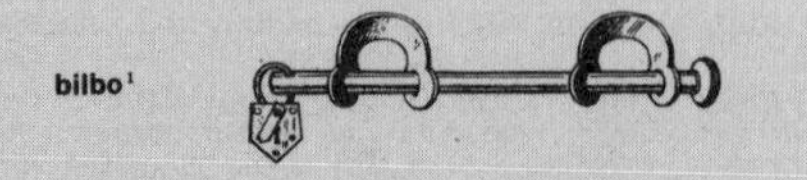

bil·bo[2] (bil′bō), *n., pl.* **-boes.** *Archaic.* a finely tempered sword. [1585–95; short for *Bilboa blade* sword made in *Bilboa* (var. of BILBAO)]

Bil·bo (bil′bō), *n.* **Theodore Gil·more** (gil′môr, -mōr), 1877–1947, U.S. Southern populist politician: senator 1935–47.

bil·by (bil′bē), *n., pl.* **-bies.** See **rabbit bandicoot.** Also, **bil′bi.** [1900–05; < Yuwaalaraay (Australian Aboriginal language of N New South Wales) *bilbi*]

Bil·dad (bil′dad), *n.* a friend of Job. Job 2:11.

Bil·dungs·ro·man (bil′dŏŏngz rō män′; *Ger.* bĕl′dŏŏngks rô män′), *n., pl.* **-mans,** *Ger.* **-ma·ne** (-mä′nə). a type of novel concerned with the education, development, and maturing of a young protagonist. [1905–10; < G, equiv. to *Bildung* formation + *-s* n. ending in compounds + *Roman* novel]

bile (bīl), *n.* **1.** *Physiol.* a bitter, alkaline, yellow or greenish liquid, secreted by the liver, that aids in absorption and digestion, esp. of fats. **2.** ill temper; peevishness. **3.** *Old Physiol.* either of two humors associated with anger and gloominess. Cf. **black bile, yellow bile.** [1655–65; < F < L *bīlis*]

bile′ ac′id, *Physiol.* any of various steroid acids, produced in the liver and stored with bile, that emulsify fats during digestion. Cf. **bile salt.** [1880–85]

bi·lec·tion (bī lek′shən), *n.* bolection.

bile′ duct′, *Anat.* a large duct that transports bile from the liver to the duodenum, having in humans and many other vertebrates a side branch to a gallbladder for bile storage. [1765–75]

bile′ salt′, *Physiol.* a product of a bile acid and a base, functioning as an emulsifier of lipids and fatty acids for absorption in the duodenum. [1880–85]

bile·stone (bīl′stōn′), *n.* gallstone. [BILE + STONE]

bi-lev·el (bī lev′əl), *adj.* **1.** having two levels of space, as a railroad passenger car with two tiers of seats. **2.** (esp. of a house) split-level. **—***n.* **3.** a bi-level house, vehicle, etc.: *The family moved from a bungalow into a bi-level.* [1955–60]

bilge (bilj), *n., v.,* **bilged, bilg·ing.** **—***n.* **1.** *Naut.* **a.** either of the rounded areas that form the transition between the bottom and the sides on the exterior of a hull. **b.** Also, **bilges.** (in a hull with a double bottom) an enclosed area between frames at each side of the floors, where seepage collects. **c.** Also called **bilge well.** a well into which seepage drains to be pumped away. **d.** Also called **bilge water.** seepage accumulated in bilges. **2.** *Slang.* See **bilge water** (def. 2). **3.** the widest circumference or belly of a cask. **—***v.i.* **4.** *Naut.* **a.** to leak in the bilge. **b.** (of white paint) to turn yellow. **5.** to bulge or swell out. **—***v.t.* **6.** *Naut.* to damage (a hull bottom) so as to create an entry for seawater. [1505–15; perh. var. of BULGE]

bilge′ board′, *Naut.* a board lowered from the bilge of a sailing vessel to serve as a keel.

bilge′ keel′, *Naut.* either of two keellike projections extending lengthwise along a ship's bilge, one on each side, to retard rolling. Also called **bilge′ piece′.** [1840–50]

bilge′ pump′, *Naut.* a pump for removing water from a bilge. [1865–70]

bilge′ wa′ter, 1. *Naut.* bilge (def. 1d). **2.** Also called **bilge.** *Slang.* foolish, worthless, or offensive talk or ideas; nonsense; rubbish. [1700–10]

bilge′ well′, *Naut.* bilge (def. 1c).

bilg·y (bil′jē), *adj.,* **bilg·i·er, bilg·i·est.** *Naut.* smelling like bilge water. [1875–80; BILGE + -Y[1]]

Bil·hah (bil′hə), *n.* the mother of Dan and Naphtali. Gen. 30:1–8.

bil·har·zi·a (bil här′zē ə), *n.* schistosome. [1880–85]

bil·har·zi·a·sis (bil′här zī′ə sis), *n. Pathol.* schistosomiasis. Also, **bil·har·zi·o·sis** (bil här′zē ō′sis). [1885–90; < NL *Bilharz(ia)* the genus of trematode worms causing the disease (after German physician Theodor *Bilharz* (1825–62), who discovered the genus in 1852) + -IASIS]

bil·i·ar·y (bil′ē er′ē bil′yə rē), *adj.* **1.** *Physiol.* **a.** of bile. **b.** conveying bile: *a biliary duct.* **2.** *Archaic.* bilious. [1725–35; perh. < F *biliaire;* see BILE, -AIRE, -ARY]

bil′iary cal′culus, *Pathol.* gallstone.

bi·lin·e·ar (bī lin′ē ər), *adj. Math.* **1.** of, pertaining to, or having reference to two lines: *bilinear coordinates.* **2.** of the first degree in each of two variables, as an equation. [1850–55; BI-[1] + LINEAR]

bilin′ear form′, *Math.* a function or functional of two variables that is linear with respect to each variable when the other variable is held fixed. [1965–70]

bilin′ear transforma′tion, *Math.* See **Möbius transformation.** [1935–40]

bi·lin·e·ate (bī lin′ē it′, -āt′), *adj. Zool.* marked with two usually parallel lines. Also, **bi·lin′e·at′ed.** [BI-[1] + LINEATE]

bi·lin·gual (bī ling′gwəl *or, Can.,* -ling′gyōō əl), *adj.* **1.** able to speak two languages with the facility of a native speaker. **2.** spoken, written, or containing similar information in two different languages: *a bilingual dictionary; Public notices at the embassy are bilingual.* **3.** of, involving, or using two languages: *a bilingual community; bilingual schools.* **—***n.* **4.** a bilingual person. [1835–45; < L *bilingu(is)* (*bi-* BI-[1] + *lingu-,* s. of *lingua* tongue + *-is* adj. suffix) + -AL[1]] **—bi·lin′gual·ly,** *adv.*

bilin′gual educa′tion, schooling in which those not fluent in the standard or national language are taught in their own language. [1970–75]

bi·lin·gual·ism (bī ling′gwə liz′əm *or, Can.,* -ling′gyōō ə-), *n.* **1.** the ability to speak two languages fluently. **2.** the habitual use of two languages. **3.** *Canadian.* a government-supported program encouraging all citizens to acquire a knowledge of both English and French. Also, **bi·lin·gual·i·ty** (bī′ling gwal′i tē *or, Can.,* -ling gyōō al′-). [1870–75; BILINGUAL + -ISM]

bil·ious (bil′yəs), *adj.* **1.** *Physiol., Pathol.* pertaining to bile or to an excess secretion of bile. **2.** *Pathol.* suffering from, caused by, or attended by trouble with the bile or

liver. **3.** peevish; irritable; cranky. **4.** extremely unpleasant or distasteful: *a long scarf of bright, bilious green.* [1535–45; < L *biliōsus.* See BILE, -OUS] —**bil′ious·ly,** *adv.* —**bil′ious·ness,** *n.*
—**Syn. 3.** grumpy, crabby, cross, grouchy, dyspeptic.

bil·i·ru·bin (bil′ə ro͞o′bin, bil′ə ro͞o′bin), *n. Biochem.* a reddish bile pigment, $C_{33}H_{36}O_6N_4$, resulting from the degradation of heme by reticuloendothelial cells in the liver: a high level in the blood produces the yellow skin symptomatic of jaundice. [< G *Bilirubin* (1864), equiv. to L *bīli(s)* BILE + *rub(er)* red + G *-in* -IN²]

bi·lit·er·al (bī lit′ər əl), *adj.* **1.** using or consisting of two letters. **2.** (of Semitic roots) having two consonants. [1780–90; BI-¹ + LITERAL] —**bi·lit′er·al·ism,** *n.*

bi·lit·er·ate (bī lit′ər it), *adj.* **1.** able to read and write in two languages. —*n.* **2.** a person who is biliterate. [BI-¹ + LITERATE, on the model of BILINGUAL]

bi·lith (bī′lith), *n.* a prehistoric structure consisting of a horizontal stone slab supported by an upright stone. Also, **bi·lith·on** (bī lith′on). [BI-¹ + -LITH]

bil·i·ver·din (bil′ə vûr′din), *n. Biochem.* a dark-green bile pigment, $C_{33}H_{34}O_6N_4$, formed as a breakdown product of hemoglobin and converted in humans to bilirubin. [< G *Biliverdin* (1840) < L *bīli(s)* BILE + *verd-* green (as in F *verdir* to make green; see VERDURE) + *-in* -IN²]

bilk (bilk), *v.t.* **1.** to defraud; cheat: *He bilked the government of almost a million dollars.* **2.** to evade payment of (a debt). **3.** to frustrate: *a career bilked by poor health.* **4.** to escape from; elude: *to bilk one's pursuers.* —*n.* **5.** a cheat; swindler. **6.** a trick; fraud; deceit. [1625–35; of obscure orig.] —**bilk′er,** *n.*
—**Syn. 1.** swindle, trick, dupe, fleece, rook.

bill¹ (bil), *n.* **1.** a statement of money owed for goods or services supplied: *He paid the hotel bill when he checked out.* **2.** a piece of paper money worth a specified amount: *a ten-dollar bill.* **3.** *Govt.* a form or draft of a proposed statute presented to a legislature, but not yet enacted or passed and made law. **4.** See **bill of exchange. 5.** a written or printed public notice or advertisement. **6.** any written paper containing a statement of particulars: *a bill of expenditures.* **7.** *Law.* a written statement, usually of complaint, presented to a court. **8.** *Slang.* one hundred dollars: *The job pays five bills a week.* **9.** playbill. **10.** entertainment scheduled for presentation; program. **11.** *Obs.* **a.** a promissory note. **b.** a written and sealed document. **c.** a written, formal petition. **12. fill the bill,** to fulfill the purpose or need well: *As a sprightly situation comedy this show fills the bill.* —*v.t.* **13.** to charge for by bill; send a bill to: *The store will bill me.* **14.** to enter (charges) in a bill; make a bill or list of: *to bill goods.* **15.** to advertise by bill or public notice: *A new actor was billed for this week.* **16.** to schedule on a program: *The management billed the play for two weeks.* [1300–50; ME *bille* < AF < AL *billa* for LL *bulla* BULL²] —**bill′er,** *n.*
—**Syn. 1.** reckoning, invoice, statement. **5.** bulletin, handbill, poster, placard, announcement, circular, throwaway, flyer, broadside.

bill² (bil), *n.* **1.** the parts of a bird's jaws that are covered with a horny or leathery sheath; beak. See diag. under **bird. 2.** the visor of a cap or other head covering. **3.** a beaklike promontory or headland. —*v.i.* **4.** to join bills or beaks, as doves. **5. bill and coo,** to kiss or fondle and whisper endearments, as lovers: *My sister and her boyfriend were billing and cooing on the porch.* [bef. 1000; ME *bile, bille,* OE *bile* beak, trunk; akin to BILL³]

bill³ (bil), *n.* **1.** a medieval shafted weapon having at its head a hooklike cutting blade with a beak at the back. **2.** Also called **billman.** a person armed with a bill. **3.** Also called **billhook.** a sharp, hooked instrument used for pruning, cutting, etc. **4.** Also called **pea.** *Naut.* the extremity of a fluke of an anchor. See diag. under **anchor.** [bef. 1000; ME *bil,* OE *bill* sword; c. OHG *bil* pickax]

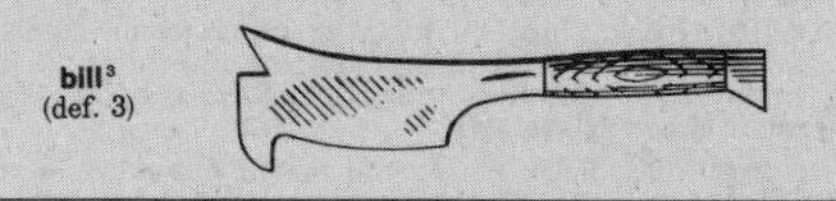
bill³ (def. 3)

bill⁴ (bil), *n. Brit. Dial.* the cry of the bittern. [1780–90; akin to BELL², BELLOW]

Bill (bil), *n.* a male given name, form of **William.**

bill·a·ble (bil′ə bəl), *adj.* **1.** that may or should be billed: *Attorneys put in hundreds of billable hours on the case.* —*n.* **2.** an active customer account. [1570–80; BILL¹ + -ABLE]

bil·la·bong (bil′ə bông′, -bong′), *n. Australian.* **1.** a branch of a river flowing away from the main stream but leading to no other body of water; a blind or dead-end channel. **2.** a creek bed holding water only in the rainy season; a dried-up watercourse. **3.** a stagnant backwater or slough formed by receding floodwater. [1830–40; < Wiradjuri *bilabaŋ* creek that runs only during the rainy season, equiv. to *bila* river + *baŋ* poss. suffix]

bill·ber·gi·a (bil bûr′jē ə, -jə), *n.* any bromeliad of the tropical American genus *Billbergia,* having stiff leaves and flowers with showy, variously colored bracts. [1821; < NL, named after Gustaf Johan Billberg (1772–1844), Swedish botanist; see -IA]

bill·board¹ (bil′bôrd′, -bōrd′), *n.* **1.** a flat surface or board, usually outdoors, on which large advertisements or notices are posted. —*v.t.* **2.** to place, advertise, proclaim, etc., on or as if on a billboard: *The movie was billboarded as the year's biggest hit.* [1850–55, *Amer.*; BILL¹ + BOARD]

bill·board² (bil′bôrd′, -bōrd′), *n. Naut.* See **anchor bed.** [1855–60; BILL³ + BOARD]

bill′ bro′ker, a money dealer who buys, sells, discounts, or negotiates bills of exchange or promissory notes. [1825–35, *Amer.*]

bill·bug (bil′bug′), *n.* any of several weevils, esp. of the genera *Calendra* and *Sitophilus,* that feed on various grasses. [1860–65, *Amer.*; BILL² + BUG¹]

billed (bild), *adj.* having a bill or beak, esp. one of a specified kind, shape, color, etc. (usually used in combination): *a yellow-billed magpie.* [1350–1400; ME; see BILL², -ED³]

Bille·ric·a (bil rik′ə, bel′ə-, bil′ri kə), *n.* a city in NE Massachusetts. 36,727.

bil·let¹ (bil′it), *n., v.,* **-let·ed, -let·ing.** —*n.* **1.** lodging for a soldier, student, etc., as in a private home or nonmilitary public building. **2.** *Mil.* an official order, written or verbal, directing the person to whom it is addressed to provide such lodging. **3.** a place assigned, as a bunk, berth, or the like, to a member of a ship's crew. **4.** job; position; appointment. **5.** *Archaic.* a written note, short letter, or the like. —*v.t.* **6.** *Mil.* to direct (a soldier) by ticket, note, or verbal order, where to lodge. **7.** to provide lodging for; quarter: *We arranged with the townspeople to billet the students.* —*v.i.* **8.** to obtain lodging; stay: *They billeted in youth hostels.* [1375–1425; late ME *bylet, billett* official register < AF *billette,* OF *bullette,* equiv. to *bulle* BILL¹ + *-ette* -ETTE] —**bil′let·er,** *n.*

bil·let² (bil′it), *n.* **1.** a small chunk of wood; a short section of a log, esp. one cut for fuel. **2.** *Metalworking.* a comparatively narrow, generally square, bar of steel, esp. one rolled or forged from an ingot; a narrow bloom. **3.** an iron or steel slab upon concrete, serving as a footing to a column. **4.** *Archit.* any of a series of closely spaced cylindrical objects, often in several rows, used as ornaments in a hollow molding or cornice. **5.** a strap that passes through a buckle, as to connect the ends of a girth. **6.** a pocket or loop for securing the end of a strap that has been buckled. **7.** thumbpiece. **8.** *Heraldry.* a small, rectangular figure with the longer sides generally vertical, said to represent a block of wood. [1400–50; late ME *bylet, bel(l)et* < AF, MF *billette,* equiv. to *bille* log, tree trunk (< Gaulish **bilia* tree trunk; cf. OIr *bile* landmark tree) + *-ette* -ETTE]

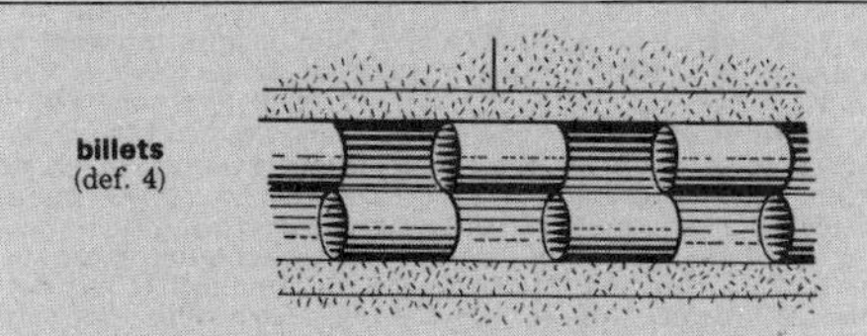
billets (def. 4)

bil·let-doux (bil′ā do͞o′, bil′ē-; *Fr.* bē yā do͞o′), *n., pl.* **bil·lets-doux** (bil′ā do͞oz′, bil′ē-; *Fr.* bē yā do͞o′). a love letter. [1665–75; < F: lit., sweet note. See BILLET¹, DOUCE]

bil·let·head (bil′it hed′), *n. Naut.* a carved ornamental scroll or volute terminating a stem or cutwater at its upper end in place of a figurehead. Also called **scroll-head.** [1830–40; BILLET² + HEAD]

bil·let·y (bil′i tē), *adj. Heraldry.* semé of billets: *azure, billety or.* [1565–75; < F *billeté;* see BILLET², -EE]

bill·fish (bil′fish′), *n., pl.* (*esp. collectively*) **-fish,** (*esp. referring to two or more kinds or species*) **-fish·es.** any of various fishes having a long, sharp bill or snout, as a gar, needlefish, or saury. [1775–85, *Amer.*; BILL² + FISH]

bill·fold (bil′fōld′), *n.* **1.** a thin, flat, folding case, often of leather, for carrying paper money in the pocket and with fewer compartments than a wallet. **2.** wallet (def. 1). Also called, *esp. Brit.,* **notecase.** [1890–95, *Amer.*; BILL¹ + FOLD¹]

bill·fold·er (bil′fōl′dər), *n. Chiefly South Midland and Southern U.S.* billfold. [1895–1900; see BILLFOLD, -ER¹]

bill·head (bil′hed′), *n.* **1.** a sheet of paper with a printed heading, usually giving one's name and address, on which a statement of money due is rendered. **2.** the heading itself. **3.** a printed form for itemized statements. [1835–45; BILL¹ + HEAD]

bill·hook (bil′ho͝ok′), *n.* bill³ (def. 3). [1605–15; BILL³ + HOOK]

bil·liard (bil′yərd), *adj.* **1.** of or used in billiards. —*n.* **2.** carom (def. 1). [1630–40; < F *billard* cue, equiv. to *bille* stick (see BILLET²) + *-ard* -ARD]

bil′liard ball′, one of the balls used in the game of billiards. [1630–40]

bil′liard par′lor, poolroom (def. 1). [1905–10, *Amer.*]

bil′liard room′, a room in a house, club, etc., where billiards is played. [1695–1705]

bil·liards (bil′yərdz), *n.* (*used with a singular v.*) any of several games played with hard balls of ivory or of a similar material that are driven with a cue on a cloth-covered table enclosed by a raised rim of rubber, esp. a game played with a cue ball and two object balls on a table without pockets. Cf. **pool²** (def. 8). [1585–95; pl. of BILLIARD] —**bil′liard·ist,** *n.*

bil′liard ta′ble, an oblong table with a slate surface covered by a cloth and enclosed by a raised rim of vulcanized rubber, for use in playing billiards. [1635–45]

Bil·li Bi (bil′ē bē′, bē′), *n.* a rich soup of mussels, cream, shallots, and white wine. Also, **bil′li-bi′.** [< F, perh. < E *Billy B.,* of uncert. identitiy]

Bil·lie (bil′ē), *n.* **1.** a male given name, form of **William. 2.** a female given name.

bill·ing (bil′ing), *n.* **1.** the relative position in which a performer or act is listed on handbills, posters, etc.: *A star usually receives billing above the title of the play.* **2.** advertising; publicity: *The show was a sellout weeks ahead of the opening because of advance billing.* **3.** the amount of business done by a firm, esp. an advertising agency, within a specified period of time. **4.** an act or instance of preparing or sending out a bill or invoice. **5.** the total amount of the cost of goods or services billed to a customer, usually covering purchases made or services rendered within a specified period of time. [1870–75; BILL¹ + -ING¹]

bill′ing cy′cle, the schedule of recurrent times in any regular system of preparing or sending bills.

bill′ing machine′, a business machine used to itemize and total customer accounts, produce bills, post account records, etc. [1905–10]

Bil·lings (bil′ingz), *n.* **1. Josh,** pen name of Henry Wheeler Shaw. **2.** a city in S Montana. 66,798.

bil·lings·gate (bil′ingz gāt′ *or, esp. Brit.,* -git), *n.* coarsely or vulgarly abusive language. [1645–55; orig. the kind of speech often heard at *Billingsgate,* a London fish market at the gate of the same name]
—**Syn.** vituperation, vilification, invective, scurrility, vulgarity.

bil·lion (bil′yən), *n., pl.* **-lions,** (*as after a numeral*) **-lion,** *adj.* —*n.* **1.** a cardinal number represented in the U.S. by 1 followed by 9 zeros, and in Great Britain by 1 followed by 12 zeros. **2.** a very large number: *I've told you so billions of times.* —*adj.* **3.** equal in number to a billion. [1680–90; < F, equiv. to *b(i)-* BI-¹ + *-illion,* as in *million*] —**bil′lionth,** *adj., n.*

bil·lion·aire (bil′yə nâr′, bil′yə nâr′), *n.* a person who has assets worth a billion or more dollars, francs, pounds, or the like. [1855–60, *Amer.*; BILLION + -AIRE, on the model of MILLIONAIRE]

Bil·li·ton (bi lē′ton), *n.* an island in Indonesia, between Borneo and Sumatra. 100,000; 1866 sq. mi. (4833 sq. km). Also, **Belitong, Belitoeng, Belitung.**

bill·man (bil′mən), *n., pl.* **-men.** bill³ (def. 2). [1520–30; BILL³ + -MAN]

bill′ of attain′der, an act of legislature finding a person guilty of treason or felony without trial.

bill′ of en′try, an account of imported or exported goods kept at a custom house.

bill′ of exchange′, a written authorization or order to pay a specified sum of money to a specified person. [1570–80]

bill′ of fare′, **1.** a list of foods that are served; menu. **2.** the program of entertainment, as at a theater. [1630–40]

bill′ of goods′, **1.** a quantity or consignment of salable items, as an order, shipment, etc. **2.** *Informal.* a misrepresented, fraudulent, or defective article. **3. sell someone a bill of goods,** to defraud or deceive someone: *He sold me a bill of goods about that used car.* [1925–30]

bill′ of health′, **1.** a certificate, carried by a ship, attesting to the presence or absence of infectious diseases among the ship's crew and at the port from which it has come. **2. clean bill of health,** an attestation of fitness or qualification; a commendation: *The investigating committee gave him a clean bill of health.* [1635–45]

bill′ of indict′ment, *Law.* a written accusation submitted to a grand jury for its decision.

bill′ of lad′ing, a written receipt given by a carrier for goods accepted for transportation. *Abbr.:* b.l., B.L., b/l, B/L [1590–1600]

bill′ of partic′ulars, *Law.* **1.** a formal statement prepared by a plaintiff or a defendant itemizing a claim or counterclaim in a suit. **2.** an itemized statement prepared by the prosecution and informing the accused of the charges in a criminal case. [1855–60]

Bill′ of Rights′, **1.** a formal statement of the fundamental rights of the people of the United States, incorporated in the Constitution as Amendments 1–10, and in all state constitutions. **2.** (*sometimes l.c.*) a similar statement of the fundamental rights of the people of any nation. **3.** (*sometimes l.c.*) a statement of the rights belonging to or sought by any group: *Our student bill of rights would include the right to dress as we please.* **4.** an English statute of 1689 confirming, with minor changes, the Declaration of Rights, declaring the rights and liberties of the subjects and settling the succession in William III and Mary II.

bill′ of sale′, a document transferring title in personal property from seller to buyer. *Abbr.:* b.s., B.S., b/s [1600–10]

bil·lon (bil′ən), *n.* **1.** an alloy used in coinage, consisting of gold or silver with a larger amount of base metal. **2.** an alloy of silver with copper or the like, used for coins of small denomination. **3.** any coin struck from such an alloy. [1720–30; < F: debased metal, orig. ingot, equiv. to MF *bille* log (see BILLET²) + *-on* n. suffix]

bil·low (bil′ō), *n.* **1.** a great wave or surge of the sea. **2.** any surging mass: *billows of smoke.* —*v.i.* **3.** to rise or roll in or like billows; surge. **4.** to swell out, puff up, etc., as by the action of wind: *flags billowing in the breeze.* —*v.t.* **5.** to make rise, surge, swell, or the like: *A sudden wind billowed the tent alarmingly.* [1545–55; < ON *bylgja* wave, c. MLG *bulge;* akin to OE *gebylgan* to anger, provoke]
—**Syn. 1.** swell, breaker, crest, roller, whitecap.

bil′low cloud′, *Meteorol.* a cloud consisting of broad, parallel bands oriented perpendicularly to the wind. Also called **undulatus.**

bil·low·y (bil′ō ē), *adj.,* **-low·i·er, -low·i·est.** characterized by or full of billows; surging: *a rough, billowy sea.* [1605–15; BILLOW + -Y¹] —**bil′low·i·ness,** *n.*

bill·post·er (bil′pō′stər), *n.* a person who posts bills and advertisements. Also called **bill·stick·er** (bil′stik′ər). [1860–65; BILL¹ + POSTER] —**bill′post′ing, bill′·stick′ing,** *n.*

bil·ly (bil′ē), *n., pl.* **-lies. 1.** Also called **billy club.** a police officer's club or baton. **2.** a heavy wooden stick used as a weapon; cudgel. **3.** *Scot. Dial.* comrade. **4.** Also called **bil·ly·can** (bil′ē kan′). *Australian.* any con-

CONCISE PRONUNCIATION KEY: act, cāpe, dâre, pärt; set, ēqual; *if,* īce; ox, ōver, ôrder, oil, bo͝ok, bo͞ot, out; up, ûrge; child; sing; shoe; thin, *th*at; zh as in *treasure.* ə = *a* as in *alone, e* as in *system, i* as in *easily, o* as in *gallop, u* as in *circus;* ᵊ as in *fire* (fīᵊr), *hour* (ouᵊr). l and n can serve as syllabic consonants, as in *cradle* (krād′l), and *button* (but′n). See the full key inside the front cover.

tainer in which water may be carried and boiled over a campfire, ranging from a makeshift tin can to a special earthenware kettle; any pot or kettle in which tea is boiled over a campfire. **5.** *Textiles* (in Great Britain) a roving machine. [perh. all independently derived generic uses of BILLY (male name); for Australian sense cf. Scots dial. *billy-pot* cooking pot]

Bil•ly (bil′ē), *n.* **1.** a male given name, form of **William. 2.** Also, **Bil′lye.** a female given name.

Bil′ly Budd′ (bud), a novella (1924) by Herman Melville.

bil′ly club′, billy (def. 1). [1945–50]

bil•ly•cock (bil′ē kok′), *n. Chiefly Brit. Informal.* a derby or a hat resembling it. Also called **bil′lycock hat′.** [1715–25; alter. of *bullycocked* (*hat*); see BULLY[1], COCKED]

bil′ly goat′, 1. a male goat. **2.** *Informal.* goat (def. 6).

Bil′ly the Kid′, 1. (*William H. Bonney*) 1859–81, U.S. outlaw. **2.** (*italics*) a ballet (1938) choreographed by Eugene Loring, with musical score by Aaron Copland.

bi•lo•bate (bī lō′bāt), *adj.* consisting of or divided into two lobes. Also, **bi•lo′bat•ed, bi•lobed** (bī′lōbd′). [1785–95; BI-[1] + LOBATE]

bi•lo•ca•tion (bī′lō kā′shən), *n.* the state of being or the ability to be in two places at the same time. [1855–60; BI-[1] + LOCATION]

bi•loc•u•lar (bī lok′yə lər), *adj. Biol.* divided into two chambers or containing two compartments internally. Also, **bi•loc•u•late** (bī lok′yə lit, -lāt′). [1775–85; BI-[1] + LOCULAR]

Bi•lox•i (bi lok′sē, -luk′-), *n.* a city in SE Mississippi, on the Gulf of Mexico. 49,311.

bil•sted (bil′sted), *n.* the liquidambar tree. [1755–65, *Amer.*; orig. uncert.]

bil•tong (bil′tông′ -tong′), *n.* (in South Africa) strips of lean meat dried in the open air. [1805–15; < Afrik, equiv. to *bil* rump + *tong* TONGUE]

bi•mac•u•late (bī mak′yə lit), *adj. Zool.* marked with two spots. Also, **bi•mac•u•lat•ed** (bī mak′yə lā′tid). [1760–70; BI-[1] + MACULATE]

bi•mah (bē′mə, bim′ə, bē mä′), *n.* a platform in a synagogue holding the reading table used when chanting or reading portions of the Torah and the Prophets. Also, **bema, bi′ma.** Also called **almemar.** [(< Yiddish *bime*) < Heb *bīmāh* < Gk *bêma* BEMA]

bi•mane (bī′mān), *n.* a bimanous animal. [1825–35; BI-[1] + *-mane* (< L *manus* hand)]

bim•a•nous (bim′ə nəs, bī mā′-), *adj. Zool.* having two hands, esp. as distinct from feet. Also, **bim•a•nal** (bim′ə nl, bī mān′l). [1825–35; < NL *biman(a)* (*animalia*) two-handed (animals) + -OUS. See BIMANE]

bi•man•u•al (bī man′yo͞o əl), *adj.* involving or requiring the use of both hands. [1870–75; BI-[1] + MANUAL] **—bi•man′u•al•ly,** *adv.*

bim•bette (bim bet′), *n.* bimbo (def. 3).

bim•bo (bim′bō), *n., pl.* **-bos, -boes.** *Slang.* **1.** a foolish, stupid, or inept person. **2.** a man or fellow, often a disreputable or contemptible one. **3.** *Disparaging and Offensive.* an attractive but stupid young woman, esp. one with loose morals. [1915–20, *Amer.*; perh. < It *bimbo* baby]

bi•men•sal (bī men′səl), *adj. Obs.* occurring once in two months; bimonthly. [1670–80; BI-[1] + MENSAL[1]]
—Usage. See **bi-**[1].

bi•mes•ter (bī mes′tər, bī′mes-), *n.* a two-month period. [< L *bimē(n)stris* of a bimester, equiv. to *bi-* BI-[1] + *mē(n)s-* (s. of *mēnsis*) month + *-tris* adj. suffix]

bi•mes•tri•al (bī mes′trē əl), *adj.* **1.** occurring every two months; bimonthly. **2.** lasting two months. [1840–50; < L *bimē(n)stris* BIMESTER + -AL[1]]

bi•met•al (bī met′l), *n.* **1.** a material made by the bonding of two sheets or strips of different metals, each metal having a different coefficient of thermal expansion. **—***adj.* **2.** bimetallic. [1920–25; BI-[1] + METAL, or as back formation from BIMETALLIC]

bi•me•tal•lic (bī′mə tal′ik), *adj.* **1.** *Metall.* **a.** made or consisting of two metals. **b.** of or pertaining to a bimetal. **2.** pertaining to bimetallism. **3.** *Engraving.* (of an offset plate) consisting of a face layer of chromium, stainless steel, or chemically prepared aluminum over a layer of copper. Also, **bimetal.** [1875–80; < F *bimétallique.* See BI-[1], METALLIC]

bi•met•al•lism (bī met′l iz′əm), *n.* **1.** the use of two metals, ordinarily gold and silver, at a fixed relative value, as the monetary standard. **2.** the doctrine or policies supporting such a standard. [1875–80; BI-[1] + METAL + -ISM] **—bi•met′al•list,** *n.* **—bi•met′al•lis′tic,** *adj.*

bi•mil•le•nar•y (bī mil′ə ner′ē), *adj., n., pl.* **-nar•ies.** **—***adj.* **1.** of or pertaining to a bimillennium. **—***n.* **2.** bimillennium. Also, **bi•mil•len•ni•al** (bī′mi len′ē əl). [1840–50; BI-[1] + MILLENARY]

bi•mil•len•ni•um (bī′mi len′ē əm), *n., pl.* **-len•ni•ums, -len•ni•a** (-len′ē ə). **1.** a period of two thousand years. **2.** a two thousandth anniversary. Also, **bimillenary, bimillennial.** [BI-[1] + MILLENNIUM]

Bim′i•ni Is′lands (bim′ə nē), a group of small islands in the W Bahamas: resort center; supposed site of the Fountain of Youth for which Ponce de León searched. 1503; 9 sq. mi. (23 sq. km). Also called **Bim′i•nis.**

bi•mod•al (bī mōd′l), *adj.* **1.** having or providing two modes, methods, systems, etc. **2.** *Statistics.* (of a distribution) having or occurring with two modes. Cf. **unimodal. 3.** *Transp.* pertaining to or suitable for transportation involving the use of two forms of carrier, as truck and rail. Cf. **intermodal.** [1900–05; BI-[1] + MODAL] **—bi′mo•dal′i•ty,** *n.*

bi•mo•lec•u•lar (bī′mə lek′yə lər), *adj. Chem.* having or involving two molecules. [1895–1900; BI-[1] + MOLECULAR] **—bi′mo•lec′u•lar•ly,** *adv.*

bi•month•ly (bī munth′lē), *adj., n., pl.* **-lies,** *adv.* **—***adj.* **1.** occurring every two months. **2.** occurring twice a month; semimonthly. **—***n.* **3.** a bimonthly publication. **—***adv.* **4.** every two months: *Next year we plan six field trips to take place bimonthly.* **5.** twice a month; semimonthly. [1840–50; BI-[1] + MONTHLY]
—Usage. See **bi-**[1].

bi•mor•phe•mic (bī′môr fē′mik), *adj.* containing two morphemes, as the words *waited* and *dogs.* [1940–45; BI-[1] + MORPHEME + -IC]

bi•mo•tor (bī′mō′tər), *n.* an airplane or other vehicle that has two engines. [BI-[1] + MOTOR]

bi•mo•tored (bī mō′tərd), *adj.* having two engines. [BI-[1] + MOTORED]

bin (bin), *n., v.,* **binned, bin•ning.** **—***n.* **1.** a box or enclosed place for storing grain, coal, or the like. **—***v.t.* **2.** to store in a bin. [bef. 950; ME *binne,* OE *binn(e)* crib, perh. < Celt; cf. Welsh *benn* cart]

bin-, a combining form meaning "two," "two at a time," used in the formation of compound words: *binary; binocular.* Cf. **bi-**[1]. [comb. form of L *bīnī* two each, by twos]

bi•nal (bīn′l), *adj.* double; twofold. [1650–60; < NL *bīnālis* twin, double. See BIN-, -AL[1]]

bi•nar•i•ty (bī nar′i tē, -nâr′-), *n. Ling.* a principle of analysis requiring that a linguistic system, as a phonological, case, or semantic system, be represented as a set of binary oppositions. Also, **bi•nar•ism** (bī′nə riz′əm). [BINAR(Y) + -ITY]

bi•na•ry (bī′nə rē, -ner ē), *adj., n., pl.* **-ries.** **—***adj.* **1.** consisting of, indicating, or involving two. **2.** *Math.* **a.** of or pertaining to a system of numerical notation to the base 2, in which each place of a number, expressed as 0 or 1, corresponds to a power of 2. The decimal number 58 appears as 111010 in binary notation, since $58 = 1 \times 2^5 + 1 \times 2^4 + 1 \times 2^3 + 0 \times 2^2 + 1 \times 2^1 + 0 \times 2^0$. **b.** of or pertaining to the digits or numbers used in binary notation. **c.** of or pertaining to a binary system. **d.** (of an operation) assigning a third quantity to two given quantities, as in the addition of two numbers. **3.** *Chem.* noting a compound containing only two elements or groups, as sodium chloride, methyl bromide, or methyl hydroxide. **4.** *Metall.* (of an alloy) having two principal constituents. **—***n.* **5.** a whole composed of two. **6.** *Astron.* See **binary star. 7.** Also called **bi′nary num′ber.** *Math.* a number expressed in the binary system of notation. [1350–1400; ME < LL *bīnārius,* equiv. to *bīn(ī)* (see BIN-) + *-ārius* -ARY]

bi′nary cell′, *Computers.* an electronic element that can assume either of two stable states and is capable of storing a binary digit.

bi′nary code′, *Computers.* a system of representing letters, numbers, or other characters, using binary notation.

bi′na•ry-cod•ed dec′imal sys′tem (bī′nə rē kō′did, -ner ē-), a numerical system in which each decimal digit is represented by a unique collection of binary digits, not necessarily the same as those used in binary notation. *Abbr.:* BCD

bi′nary col′or. See **secondary color.** [1875–80]

bi′nary dig′it, *Math., Computers.* **1.** either of the digits 0 or 1 when used in the binary number system. **2.** bit[3] (def. 1). [1945–50]

bi′nary fis′sion, *Biol.* fission into two organisms approximately equal in size. Cf. **multiple fission.** [1895–1900]

bi′nary form′, a basic musical form having two closely related sections. [1870–75]

bi′nary opera′tion, a mathematical operation in which two elements are combined to yield a single result: *Addition and multiplication are binary operations on the set of real numbers.* Cf. **ternary operation, unary operation.** [1930–35]

bi′nary opposi′tion, *Ling.* a relation between the members of a pair of linguistic items, as a pair of distinctive features, such that one is the absence of the other, as voicelessness and voice, or that one is at the opposite pole from the other, as stridency and mellowness. [1950–55]

bi′nary pul′sar, *Astron.* a pulsar in a binary system.

bi′nary star′, *Astron.* a system of two stars that revolve about their common center of mass. Also called **binary, binary system.** [1875–80]

bi′nary sys′tem, 1. a system involving only two elements, as 0 and 1 or yes and no. **2.** *Math.* a system of counting or measurement whose units are powers of two. Cf. **binary** (def. 2a). **3.** *Astron.* See **binary star.** Also called **dyadic system** (for defs. 1, 2). [1825–35]

bi•nate (bī′nāt), *adj. Bot.* produced or borne in pairs; double. [1800–10; < NL *bīnātus,* appar. extracted from LL *combīnātus* yoked together. See BIN-, -ATE[1]] **—bi′•nate•ly,** *adv.*

binate leaf

bi•na•tion (bī nā′shən), *n.* celebration of Mass twice on the same day by the same priest. [< NL *bīnātiōn-* (s. of *bīnātiō*), equiv. to L *bīn(ī)* BIN- + *-ātiōn-* -ATION]

bi•na•tion•al (bī nash′ə nl), *adj.* of or pertaining to two nations. [1885–90; BI-[1] + NATIONAL]

bin•au•ral (bī nôr′əl, bin ôr′əl), *adj.* **1.** having two ears. **2.** of, with, or for both ears: *binaural hearing; a binaural stethoscope.* **3.** (of sound) recorded through two separate microphones and transmitted through two separate channels to produce a stereophonic effect. [1875–80; BIN- + AURAL[2]]

Bin•chois (*Fr.* baN shwa′), *n.* **Gil•les** (*Du.* KHil′əs; *Fr.* zhēl) or **E•gi•di•us** (*Du.* ā KHē′dē o͝os′), c1400–60, Flemish composer.

bind (bīnd), *v.,* **bound, bind•ing,** *n.* **—***v.t.* **1.** to fasten or secure with a band or bond. **2.** to encircle with a band or ligature: *She bound her hair with a ribbon.* **3.** to swathe or bandage (often fol. by *up*): *to bind up one's wounds.* **4.** to fasten around; fix in place by girding: *They bound his hands behind him.* **5.** to tie up (anything, as sheaves of grain). **6.** to cause to cohere: *Ice bound the soil.* **7.** to unite by any legal or moral tie: *to be bound by a contract.* **8.** to hold to a particular state, place, employment, etc.: *Business kept him bound to the city.* **9.** to place under obligation or compulsion (usually used passively): *We are bound by good sense to obey the country's laws.* **10.** *Law.* to put under legal obligation, as to keep the peace or appear as a witness (often fol. by *over*): *This action binds them to keep the peace. He was bound over to the grand jury.* **11.** to make compulsory or obligatory: *to bind the order with a deposit.* **12.** to fasten or secure within a cover, as a book: *They will bind the new book in leather.* **13.** to cover the edge of, as for protection or ornament: *to bind a carpet.* **14.** (of clothing) to chafe or restrict (the wearer): *This shirt binds me under the arms.* **15.** *Med.* to hinder or restrain (the bowels) from their natural operations; constipate. **16.** to indenture as an apprentice (often fol. by *out*): *In his youth his father bound him to a blacksmith.* **—***v.i.* **17.** to become compact or solid; cohere. **18.** to be obligatory: *an obligation that binds.* **19.** to chafe or restrict, as poorly fitting garments. **20.** to stick fast, as a drill in a hole. **21.** *Falconry.* (of a hawk) to grapple or grasp prey firmly in flight. **22. bind off,** *Textiles.* to loop (one stitch) over another in making an edge on knitted fabric. **—***n.* **23.** the act or process of binding; the state or instance of being bound. **24.** something that binds. **25.** *Music.* a tie, slur, or brace. **26.** *Falconry.* the act of binding. **27.** *Informal.* a difficult situation or predicament: *This schedule has us in a bind.* [bef. 1000; ME *binden* (v.), OE *bindan;* c. OHG *bintan,* ON *binda,* Goth *bindan,* Skt *bandhati* (he) binds] **—bind′a•ble,** *adj.*
—Syn. 1. gird, attach, tie. **2.** confine, restrain. **9.** engage, oblige, obligate. **—Ant. 1.** untie.

B.Ind.Ed., Bachelor of Industrial Education.

bind•er (bīn′dər), *n.* **1.** a person or thing that binds. **2.** a detachable cover, resembling the cover of a notebook or book, with clasps or rings for holding loose papers together: *a three-ring binder.* **3.** a person who binds books; a bookbinder. **4.** *Insurance.* an agreement by which property or liability coverage is granted pending issuance of a policy. **5.** *Agric.* **a.** an attachment to a harvester or reaper for binding the cut grain. **b.** Also called **self-binder.** a machine that cuts and binds grain. **6.** *Chem.* any substance that causes the components of a mixture to cohere. **7.** *Painting.* a vehicle in which pigment is suspended. **8.** (in powder metallurgy) a substance for holding compacted metal powder together while it is being sintered. **9.** *Building Trades.* **a.** a stone, as a perpend, for bonding masonry. **b.** a girder supporting the ends of two sets of floor joists. **c.** a material for holding loose material together, as in a macadamized road. **d.** stirrup (def. 5). **10.** *Brit., Australian Slang.* a large quantity, esp. of food. [bef. 1000; ME, OE; see BIND, -ER[1]]

bind′er twine′, a strong, coarse twine, as of sisal, used esp. in binding sheaves of grain and bales of hay. Also, **bind′er's twine′.** [1885–90]

bind•er•y (bīn′də rē, -drē), *n., pl.* **-er•ies.** a place where books are bound. [1800–10, *Amer.*; BIND + -ERY]

bind•heim•ite (bint′hī mīt′), *n.* a mineral, hydrous antimonate of lead, resulting from the alteration of lead antimony ores. [named after J. J. *Bindheim* (d. 1825), German chemist; see -ITE[1]]

bind•ing (bīn′ding), *n.* **1.** the act of fastening, securing, uniting, or the like. **2.** anything that binds. **3.** the covering within which the leaves of a book are bound. **4.** a strip of material that protects or decorates the edge of a tablecloth, rug, etc. **5.** *Skiing.* a mechanical device on a ski, usually made of metal, that fastens the boot securely to the ski. **—***adj.* **6.** that binds; restrictive. **7.** having power to bind or oblige; obligatory: *a binding promise.* [1200–50; ME; see BIND, -ING[1], -ING[2]] **—bind′•ing•ly,** *adv.* **—bind′ing•ness,** *n.*

bind′ing en′ergy, *Physics.* **1.** Also called **separation energy.** the energy required to decompose a molecule, atom, or nucleus into its constituent particles, equal to the energy equivalent of the mass defect. **2.** the energy required to separate a single particle or group of particles from a molecule, atom, or nucleus. Cf. **mass defect.** [1930–35]

bind′ing post′, one of several metal pegs or rods, fitted into a loose-leaf binder, for holding sheets with prepunched holes.

bind′ing raft′er, a timber for supporting rafters between their extremities, as a purlin. [1835–45]

bind′ing strake′, *Shipbuilding.* a very strong, heavy strake of planking, esp. one next to a sheer strake.

bin•dle (bin′dl), *n. Slang.* a bundle, usually of bedding and other possessions, carried by a hobo. [1895–1900; prob. akin to BUNDLE; uncert. if < dial. source or < G *Bündel*]

bin′dle stiff′, *Slang.* a hobo. [1900–05]

bind•weed (bīnd′wēd′), *n.* any of various twining or vinelike plants, esp. certain species of the genera *Convolvulus* and *Calystegia.* [1540–50; BIND + WEED[1]]

bine (bīn), *n.* **1.** a twining plant stem, as of the hop. **2.** any bindweed. **3.** woodbine (defs. 1, 2). [1720–30; var. of BIND]

CONCISE ETYMOLOGY KEY: <, descended or borrowed from; >, whence; b., blend of, blended; c., cognate with; cf., compare; deriv., derivative; equiv., equivalent; imit., imitative; obl., oblique; r., replacing; s., stem; sp., spelling, spelled; resp., respelling, respelled; trans., translation; ?, origin unknown; *, unattested; ‡, probably earlier than. See the full key inside the front cover.

Bi•net (bi nā′; *Fr.* bē ne′), *n.* **Al•fred** (al′frid; *Fr.* al-fred′), 1857–1911, French psychologist: co-deviser of the Binet-Simon scale.

Bi•net′-Si′mon scale′ (bi nā′sī′mən; *Fr.* bē ne sē-môN′), *Psychol.* a test for determining the relative development of intelligence, consisting of a series of questions and tasks graded with reference to the ability of the normal child to deal with them at successive age levels. Also called **Binet′-Si′mon test′, Binet′ scale′, Binet′ test′.** Cf. **Stanford-Binet test.** [1920–25]

bing[1] (bing), *n. Brit. Dial.* a heap or pile. [1275–1325; ME < ON *bingr* bunk, bin]

bing[2] (bing), *v.i. Obs.* to go. [1560–70; orig. uncert.]

Bing (bing), *n.* a variety of dark red or blackish sweet cherry. Also called **Bing′ cher′ry.** [1920–25, *Amer.*]

Bing (bing), *n.* **1. Sir Rudolf,** born 1902, English opera impresario born in Austria; in the U.S. since 1949. **2.** a male given name.

binge (binj), *n., v.,* **binged, bing•ing.** *Informal.* —*n.* **1.** a period or bout, usually brief, of excessive indulgence, as in eating, drinking alcoholic beverages, etc.; spree. —*v.i.* **2.** to have a binge: *to binge on junk food.* [1850–55; dial. (Lincolnshire) *binge* to soak < ?] —**bing′er,** *n.* —**Syn. 1.** bender, blast, jag, tear, bust, toot; orgy.

Bing•en (bing′ən), *n.* a town in W West Germany, on the Rhine River: whirlpool; tourist center. 24,500.

binge′-purge′ syn′drome (binj′pûrj′), bulimia.

Bing•ham (bing′əm), *n.* **George Caleb,** 1811–79, U.S. painter.

Bing•ham•ton (bing′əm tən), *n.* a city in S New York, on the Susquehanna River. 55,860.

bing•hi (bing′ī), *n., pl.* **-his.** (*sometimes cap.*) *Australian Slang.* an Aborigine. [1930–35; < Dyangadi (Australian Aboriginal language of Macleay River valley, E New South Wales) *biŋay* elder brother]

bin•gle[1] (bing′gəl), *n. Baseball Slang.* See **base hit.** [1900–05, *Amer.*; perh. B(AT)[1] + (S)INGLE]

bin•gle[2] (bing′gəl), *n. Australian Informal.* a collision, esp. an automobile accident. [perh. expressive alter. of BANG[1]; cf. -LE]

bin•go (bing′gō), *n.* (*sometimes cap.*) a form of lotto in which balls or slips, each with a number and one of the letters B, I, N, G, or O, are drawn at random and players cover the corresponding numbers printed on their cards, the winner being the first to cover five numbers in any row or diagonal. [1935–40; appar. alter. of BEANO[1]]

bin′go card′, a prepaid postcard inserted in a magazine by its publisher to enable a reader to order free information about advertised products. [1985–90; so called from the series of coded numbers on such cards, appar. suggesting the cards used in bingo]

Bing Xin (bing′ shin′), (*Xie Wanying*), born 1900, Chinese writer.

bin•gy (bing′ē), *n., pl.* **-gies.** *Australian.* belly. [1850–55; < Dharuk *bi-ndi*]

Binh Dinh (bin′ din′), former name of **An Nhon.** Also, **Binh′dinh′.**

bin•na•cle[1] (bin′ə kəl), *n. Naut.* a stand or enclosure of wood or nonmagnetic metal for supporting and housing a compass. [1615–25; BIN + (*bitt*)*acle* (late ME *bitakille*) < Pg *bitacola* < L *habitāculum* lodge, equiv. to *habitā-* (see INHABIT) + *-culum* -CULE[2]]

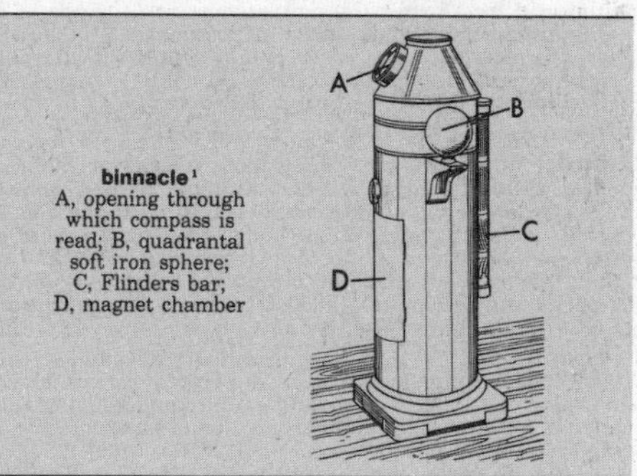

binnacle[1]
A, opening through which compass is read; B, quadrantal soft iron sphere; C, Flinders bar; D, magnet chamber

bin•na•cle[2] (bin′ə kəl), *New York State Older Use.* a side branch of a river. [1855–60, *Amer.*; prob. folk-etymological sp. of New York D **binnekil,* equiv. to D *binne(n)* inner, interior (see BEN[1]) + *kil* channel; see KILL[2]]

bin•o•cle[1] (bin′ə kəl), *n.* binocular (def. 1). [1690–1700; < F < L *bīn(ī)* BIN- + *oculus* eye]

bi•no•cle[2] (bī′nuk əl), *n.* a card game of the bezique family that is played by two persons with a 48-card pack, the lowest card of which is nine. [see PINOCHLE]

bin•oc•u•lar (bə nok′yə lər, bī-), *n.* **1.** Usually, **binoculars.** Also called **prism binoculars.** an optical device, providing good depth effect, for use with both eyes, consisting of two small telescopes fitted together side by side, each telescope having two prisms between the eyepiece and objective for erecting the image. —*adj.* **2.** involving both eyes: *binocular vision.* [1705–15; BIN- + OCULAR] —**bin•oc′u•lar′i•ty,** *n.*

binoc′ular fu′sion, *Ophthalm.* fusion (def. 5a).

bi•no•mi•al (bī nō′mē əl), *n.* **1.** *Algebra.* an expression that is a sum or difference of two terms, as $3x + 2y$ and $x^2 - 4x$. **2.** *Zool., Bot.* a taxonomic name consisting of a generic and a specific term, used to designate species. —*adj.* **3.** *Algebra.* consisting of or pertaining to two terms or a binomial. **4.** *Zool., Bot.* consisting of or characterized by binomials. [1550–60; < LL *binōmi(us)* having two names (cf. L *binōminis*) + -AL[1]. See BI-[1], NOMINAL] —**bi•no′mi•al•ism,** *n.* —**bi•no′mi•al•ly,** *adv.*

bino′mial coeffi′cient, *Math.* any one of the coefficients of the variables in an expanded binomial series. Cf. **binomial theorem.** [1885–90]

bino′mial distribu′tion, *Statistics.* a distribution giving the probability of obtaining a specified number of successes in a finite set of independent trials in which the probability of a success remains the same from trial to trial. Also called **Bernoulli distribution.** [1910–15]

bino′mial law′, *Genetics.* See **Hardy-Weinberg law.**

bino′mial no′menclature, *Zool., Bot.* a system of nomenclature in which each species is given a unique name that consists of a generic and a specific term. [1875–80]

bino′mial se′ries, *Math.* an infinite series obtained by expanding a binomial raised to a power that is not a positive integer. Cf. **binomial theorem.** [1965–70]

bino′mial the′orem, *Math.* the theorem giving the expansion of a binomial raised to any power. [1865–70]

bi•nor•mal (bī′nôr′məl, bī nôr′-), *n. Geom.* the normal to a curve, lying perpendicular to the osculating plane at a given point on the curve. [1840–50; BI-[1] + NORMAL]

bi•nox•a•late (bī nok′sə lāt′, -lit), *n. Chem.* an acid containing the group HC_2O_4–, as ammonium binoxalate, $C_2H_5NO_4{\cdot}H_2O$. [1800–10; BIN- + OXALATE]

bint (bint), *n. Brit. Slang* (*disparaging and offensive*). a woman or girl. [1850–55; < Ar: girl, daughter]

bin•tu•rong (bin to͝or′ông, -ong), *n.* an arboreal civet, *Arctictis binturong,* of Asia, having a long, prehensile tail. Also called **bearcat.** [< Malay *binturung, binturun, benturung*]

bi•nu•cle•ate (bī no͞o′klē it, -āt′, -nyo͞o′-), *adj. Cell Biol.* having two nuclei. Also, **bi•nu′cle•ar, bi•nu′cle•at′ed.** [1880–85; BI-[1] + NUCLEATE]

bi•o (bī′ō), *n., pl.* **bi•os,** *adj. Informal.* —*n.* **1.** biography. **2.** biology. —*adj.* **3.** biographical. **4.** biological: *a bio control service using praying mantises to reduce the population of garden pests.* [1945–50; by shortening; as adj., independent use of BIO-, taken as a free form]

bio-, a combining form meaning "life" occurring in loanwords from Greek (*biography*); on this model, used in the formation of compound words (*bioluminescence*). Also, *esp. before a vowel,* **bi-.** [comb. form of Gk *bíos* life; akin to L *vīvus* living, Skt *jīvas.* See QUICK]

bi•o•ac•cu•mu•la•tion (bī′ō ə kyo͞o′myə lā′shən), *n.* See **biological accumulation.** —**bi′o•ac•cu′mu•la′tive,** *adj.*

bi•o•a•cous•tics (bī′ō ə ko͞o′stiks *or, esp. Brit.,* -ə kou′-), *n.* (*used with a singular v.*) the science of sounds produced by or affecting living organisms, as for communication or echolocation. [1955–60; BIO- + ACOUSTICS] —**bi′o•a•cous′ti•cal,** *adj.*

bi•o•ac•tiv•i•ty (bī′ō ak tiv′i tē), *n.* any effect on, interaction with, or response from living tissue. [1970–75; BIO- + ACTIVITY] —**bi′o•ac′tive,** *adj.*

bi•o•as•say (*n.* bī′ō ə sā′, -as′ā; *v.* bī′ō ə sā′), *n., v.,* **-sayed, -say•ing.** —*n.* **1.** determination of the biological activity or potency of a substance, as a vitamin or hormone, by testing its effect on the growth of an organism. —*v.t.* **2.** to subject to a bioassay. [1910–15; BIO(LOGICAL) + ASSAY]

bi•o•as•tro•nau•tics (bī′ō as′trə nô′tiks), *n.* (*used with a singular v.*) the science dealing with the effects of space travel on life. [1955–60; BIO- + ASTRONAUTICS] —**bi′o•as′tro•nau′tic, bi′o•as′tro•nau′ti•cal,** *adj.*

bi•o•au•tog•ra•phy (bī′ō ô tog′rə fē), *n. Biochem.* an analytical technique in which organic compounds are separated by chromatography and identified by studying their effects on microorganisms. [BIO- + AUTOGRAPHY] —**bi•o•au•to•graph** (bī′ō ô′tə graf′, -gräf′), *n.* —**bi′o•au′to•graph′ic,** *adj.*

bi•o•a•vail•a•bil•i•ty (bī′ō ə vā′lə bil′i tē), *n. Biochem.* the extent to which a nutrient or medication can be used by the body. [1965–70; BIO- + AVAILABILITY] —**bi′o•a•vail′a•ble,** *adj.*

bi•o•be•hav•ior•al (bī′ō bi hāv′yər əl), *adj.* of or pertaining to the application of biological methods and ideas to the study of behavior in an attempt to understand emotions and reactions in terms of brain and physiological function. [1980–85; BIO- + BEHAVIORAL]

bi′obehav′ioral sci′ence, any of the various branches of the life sciences, as neurobiology, neurochemistry, or neuroendocrinology, that deal with biological aspects of behavior. [1980–85]

bi•o•bib•li•og•ra•phy (bī′ō bib′lē og′rə fē), *n., pl.* **-phies.** a bibliography containing biographical sketches of the authors listed. [1955–60; BIO- + BIBLIOGRAPHY] —**bi′o•bib′li•og′ra•pher,** *n.* —**bi•o•bib•li•o•graph•ic** (bī′ō bib′lē ə graf′ik), **bi′o•bib′li•o•graph′i•cal,** *adj.*

Bí•o-Bí•o (bē′ô bē′ô), *n.* a river in central Chile, flowing NW from the Andes to the Pacific at Concepción. ab. 240 mi. (384 km) long.

bi•o•cat•a•lyst (bī′ō kat′l ist), *n. Biochem.* enzyme. [1930–35; BIO- + CATALYST]

bi•oc•el•late (bī os′ə lāt′, bī′ō sel′it), *adj. Zool., Bot.* marked with two ocelli or eyelike parts. [1840–50; BI-[1] + OCELLATE]

bi•o•ce•nol•o•gy (bī′ō si nol′ə jē), *n.* the branch of biology dealing with the study of biological communities and the interactions among their members. Also, **bi′o•coe•nol′o•gy.** [1930–35; BIOCEN(OSIS) + -O- + -LOGY]

bi•o•ce•no•sis (bī′ō si nō′sis), *n., pl.* **-ses** (-sēz). *Ecol.* a self-sufficient community of naturally occurring organisms occupying and interacting within a specific biotope. Also, **bi′o•coe•no′sis.** [trans. of G *Biocönose* (1877), equiv. to *bio-* BIO- + *-cönose* < Gk *koínōsis* mingling (*koinō-,* verbid s. of *koinoûn* to make common (v. deriv. of *koinós* common; see CENO-[2]) + *-sis* -SIS)]

bi•o•cen•tric (bī′ō sen′trik), *adj.* centered in life; having life as its principal fact. [1885–90; BIO- + -CENTRIC]

bi′ochem′ical ox′ygen demand′, the oxygen required by aerobic organisms, as those in sewage, for metabolism. *Abbr.:* BOD Also called **biological oxygen demand.** [1925–30]

bi•o•chem•is•try (bī′ō kem′ə strē), *n.* **1.** the science dealing with the chemistry of living matter. **2.** the chemistry of living matter. [1880–85; BIO- + CHEMISTRY] —**bi•o•chem•i•cal** (bī′ō kem′i kəl), *adj., n.* —**bi′o•chem′ic,** *adj.* —**bi′o•chem′i•cal•ly,** *adv.* —**bi′o•chem′ist,** *n.*

bi•o•chip (bī′ō chip′), *n.* an experimental integrated circuit composed of biochemical substances or organic molecules. [1980–85]

bi•o•cide (bī′ə sīd′), *n.* any chemical that destroys life by poisoning, esp. a pesticide, herbicide, or fungicide. [1945–50; BIO- + -CIDE] —**bi′o•cid′al,** *adj.*

bi•o•clean (bī′ō klēn′), *adj.* free or almost free from harmful microorganisms. [BIO- + CLEAN]

bi•o•cli•mat•ic (bī′ō klī mat′ik), *adj.* of or pertaining to the effects of climate on living organisms. [1915–20; BIO- + CLIMATIC]

bi•o•cli•ma•tol•o•gy (bī′ō klī′mə tol′ə jē), *n.* the study of the effects of climate on the biological processes of living organisms. [1920–25; BIO- + CLIMATOLOGY] —**bi•o•cli•ma•to•log•i•cal** (bī′ō klī′mə tl oj′i kəl), *adj.* —**bi′o•cli′ma•to•log′i•cal•ly,** *adv.* —**bi′o•cli′ma•tol′o•gist,** *n.*

bi•o•com•pat•i•bil•i•ty (bī′ō kəm pat′ə bil′i tē), *n.* the capability of coexistence with living tissues or organisms without causing harm: *Artificial joint adhesives must have biocompatibility with bone and muscle.* [1975–80; BIO- + COMPATIBILITY] —**bi′o•com•pat′i•ble,** *adj.*

bi•o•con•tain•ment (bī′ō kən tān′mənt), *n.* the confinement, as by sealed-off chambers, of materials that are harmful or potentially harmful to life. [BIO- + CONTAINMENT]

bi•o•con•trol (bī′ō kən trōl′), *n.* See **biological control.** [BIO- + CONTROL]

bi•o•con•ver•sion (bī′ō kən vûr′zhən, -shən), *n.* the conversion of biomass to usable energy, as by burning solid fuel for heat, by fermenting plant matter to produce liquid fuel, as ethanol, or by the bacterial decomposition of organic waste to produce methane. [1955–60; BIO- + CONVERSION]

bi•o•cor•ro•sion (bī′ō kə rō′zhən), *n.* corrosion caused by or enhanced by bacteria or other microorganisms; biologically induced corrosion. [BIO- + CORROSION]

bi•o•cy•ber•net•ics (bī′ō sī′bər net′iks), *n. Biol.* (*used with a singular v.*) the application of mathematical theory to communication and control in living organisms, esp. regarding physiological feedback mechanisms and central nervous system control. [1965–70; BIO- + CYBERNETICS] —**bi′o•cy′ber•net′ic,** *adj.* —**bi′o•cy′ber•net′i•cist, bi•o•cy•ber•ne•ti•cian** (bī′ō sī′bər ni tish′ən), *n.*

bi•o•de•grad•a•ble (bī′ō di grā′də bəl), *adj.* capable of decaying through the action of living organisms: *biodegradable paper; biodegradable detergent.* [1960–65; BIO- + DEGRADE + -ABLE] —**bi′o•de•grad′a•bil′i•ty,** *n.*

bi•o•de•grade (bī′ō di grād′), *v.i.,* **-grad•ed, -grad•ing.** to decay and become absorbed by the environment: *toys that will biodegrade when they're discarded.* [1970–75; back formation from BIODEGRADABLE] —**bi•o•deg•ra•da•tion** (bī′ō deg′rə dā′shən), *n.*

bi•o•de•te•ri•o•ra•tion (bī′ō di tēr′ē ə rā′shən), *n.* biodegradation. [1960–65; BIO- + DETERIORATION]

bi•o•dra•ma (bī′ō drä′mə, -dram′ə), *n. Television.* a drama based on the life of an actual person or persons. [BIO- (in sense "biographical") + DRAMA]

bi•o•dy•nam•ics (bī′ō di nam′iks, -di-), *n.* (*used with a singular v.*) the branch of biology dealing with energy or the activity of living organisms (opposed to *biostatics*). [BIO- + DYNAMICS] —**bi′o•dy•nam′ic,** *adj.*

bi•o•e•col•o•gy (bī′ō i kol′ə jē), *n.* the study of the interrelations among living organisms in their natural environment; ecology. [1920–25; BIO- + ECOLOGY] —**bi•o•ec•o•log•ic** (bī′ō ek′ə loj′ik, -ē′kə-), **bi′o•ec′o•log′i•cal,** *adj.* —**bi′o•ec′o•log′i•cal•ly,** *adv.* —**bi′o•e•col′o•gist,** *n.*

bi•o•e•lec•tric (bī′ō i lek′trik), *adj.* of or pertaining to electric phenomena occurring in living organisms. Also, **bi′o•e•lec′tri•cal.** [1915–20; BIO- + ELECTRIC] —**bi•o•e•lec•tric•i•ty** (bī′ō i lek tris′i tē, -ē′lek-), *n.*

bi•o•e•lec•tro•gen•e•sis (bī′ō i lek′trō jen′ə sis), *n.* the production of electricity by organisms. [BIO- + ELECTRO- + GENESIS] —**bi•o•e•lec•tro•ge•net•ic** (bī′ō i-lek′trō jə net′ik), *adj.* —**bi′o•e•lec′tro•ge•net′i•cal•ly,** *adv.*

bi•o•e•lec•tron•ics (bī′ō i lek tron′iks, -ē′lek-), *n.* (*used with a singular v.*) **1.** *Biol.* the study of electron transfer reactions as they occur in biological systems. **2.** *Med.* the application of electronic devices to living organisms for clinical testing, diagnosis, and therapy. [BIO- + ELECTRONICS] —**bi′o•e•lec•tron′ic,** *adj.*

bi•o•en•er•get•ics (bī′ō en′ər jet′iks), *n.* (*used with a singular v.*) **1.** *Biochem.* the study of energy transformation in living systems. **2.** *Psychol.* a school of therapy that seeks to relieve stress and concomitant muscular tension through respiratory exercises, physical movement, improvement in body image, and free expression of ideas. [1910–15; BIO- + ENERGETICS]

bi•o•en•er•gy (bī′ō en′ər jē), *n.* energy derived from biofuel. [1975–80; BIO- + ENERGY]

CONCISE PRONUNCIATION KEY: act, cāpe, dâre, pärt; set, ēqual; if, īce; ox, ōver, ôrder, oil, bo͝ok, bo͞ot, out; up, ûrge; child; sing; shoe; thin, *th*at; zh as in *treasure.* ə = *a* as in *alone, e* as in *system, i* as in *easily, o* as in *gallop, u* as in *circus;* ᵊ as in *fire* (fīᵊr), *hour* (ouᵊr). l and n can serve as syllabic consonants, as in *cradle* (krād′l), and *button* (but′n). See the full key inside the front cover.

bi•o•en•gi•neer•ing (bī′ō en′jə nēr′ing), *n.* **1.** Also called **biomedical engineering.** the application of engineering principles and techniques to problems in medicine and biology, as the design and production of artificial limbs and organs. **2.** the branch of engineering that deals with applications of biological processes to the manufacture of products, as the use of fermentation to produce beer. [1960–65; BIO- + ENGINEERING] —**bi′o•en′gi•neer′,** *n.*

bi•o•en•vi•ron•men•tal (bī′ō en vī′rən men′tl, -vī′ərn-), *adj. Ecol.* pertaining to the environment of living organisms: *Bioenvironmental engineers seek to reduce air and water pollution.* [1960–65; BIO- + ENVIRONMENTAL]

bi•o•e•quiv•a•lence (bī′ō i kwiv′ə ləns), *n. Pharm.* the condition in which different formulations of the same drug or chemical are equally absorbed when taken into the body. Also, **bi′o•e•quiv′a•len•cy.** [BIO- + EQUIVALENCE] —**bi′o•e•quiv′a•lent,** *adj.*

bi•o•eth•ics (bī′ō eth′iks), *n.* (*used with a singular v.*) a field of study concerned with the ethics and philosophical implications of certain biological and medical procedures, technologies, and treatments, as organ transplants, genetic engineering, and care of the terminally ill. [1970–75; BIO- + ETHICS] —**bi′o•eth′i•cal,** *adj.* —**bi•o•eth•i•cist** (bī′ō eth′ə sist), *n.*

bi•o•feed•back (bī′ō fēd′bak′), *n.* **1.** a method of learning to control one's bodily functions by monitoring one's own brain waves, blood pressure, degree of muscle tension, etc. **2.** the feedback thus obtained. [1970–75; BIO- + FEEDBACK]

bi•o•fla•vo•noid (bī′ō flā′və noid′), *n. Biochem.* any of a group of water-soluble yellow compounds, present in citrus fruits, rose hips, and other plants, that in mammals maintain the resistance of capillary walls to permeation and change of pressure. Also called **citrin, vitamin P.** [1950–55; BIO- + *flavonoid* any derivative of flavone (FLAVONE + -OID)]

bi•o•fog (bī′ō fog′, -fôg′), *n. Meteorol.* a fog, resembling steam fog, produced by the contact of very cold air with the warmth and moisture issuing from animal or human bodies. [BIO- + FOG[1]]

bi•o•fu•el (bī′ō fyōō′əl), *n.* fuel, as wood or ethanol, derived from biomass. [1970–75; BIO- + FUEL]

bi•og (bī′og), *n. Informal.* biography. Also, **bio.** [1940–45; by shortening]

biog., **1.** biographer. **2.** biographical. **3.** biography.

bi•o•gas (bī′ō gas′), *n.* any gas fuel derived from the decay of organic matter, as the mixture of methane and carbon dioxide produced by the bacterial decomposition of sewage, manure, garbage, or plant crops. Also, **bi′o-gas′.** [1970–75; BIO- + GAS]

bi•o•gas•i•fi•ca•tion (bī′ō gas′ə fi kā′shən), *n.* the conversion of organic matter into biogas. [1970–75; BIO- + GASIFICATION]

bi•o•gen (bī′ə jən, -jen′), *n. Biochem.* a hypothetical protein molecule, large and unstable, once assumed to be basic to fundamental biological processes. [1895–1900; BIO- + -GEN]

bi•o•gen•e•sis (bī′ō jen′ə sis), *n.* the production of living organisms from other living organisms. Also, **bi•og•e•ny** (bī oj′ə nē). [BIO- + GENESIS, coined by T.H. Huxley in 1870] —**bi•o•ge•net•ic** (bī′ō jə net′ik), **bi′o•ge•net′i•cal, bi•og′e•nous,** *adj.* —**bi′o•ge•net′i•cal•ly,** *adv.*

bi•o•ge•net•ics (bī′ō jə net′iks), *n.* (*used with a singular v.*) See **genetic engineering.** [BIO- + GENETICS] —**bi′o•ge•net′ic,** *adj.* —**bi′o•ge•net′i•cist,** *n.*

bi•o•gen•ic (bī′ō jen′ik), *adj.* **1.** resulting from the activity of living organisms, as fermentation. **2.** necessary for the life process, as food and water. [1875–80; BIO- + -GENIC]

bi•o•ge•o•chem•is•try (bī′ō jē′ō kem′ə strē), *n.* the science dealing with the relationship between the geochemistry of a given region and its flora and fauna, including the circulation of such elements as carbon and nitrogen between the environment and the cells of living organisms. [1935–40; BIO- + GEOCHEMISTRY] —**bi•o•ge•o•chem•i•cal** (bī′ō jē′ō kem′i kəl), *adj.*

bi•o•ge•og•ra•phy (bī′ō jē og′rə fē), *n. Ecol.* the study of the geographical distribution of living things. [1890–95; BIO- + GEOGRAPHY] —**bi′o•ge•og′ra•pher,** *n.* —**bi•o•ge•o•graph•ic** (bī′ō jē′ə graf′ik), **bi′o•ge′o•graph′i•cal,** *adj.* —**bi′o•ge′o•graph′i•cal•ly,** *adv.*

bi•og•ra•phee (bī og′rə fē′, bē-), *n.* the subject of a biography; the person whose life is described in a biography. [1835–45; BIOGRAPH(Y) + -EE]

bi•og•ra•pher (bī og′rə fər, bē-), *n.* a writer of someone's biography. [1705–15; BIOGRAPH(Y) + -ER[1]]

bi•o•graph•i•cal (bī′ə graf′i kəl), *adj.* **1.** of or pertaining to a person's life: *He's gathering biographical data for his book on Milton.* **2.** pertaining to or containing biography: *a biographical dictionary.* Also, **bi′o•graph′ic.** [1730–40; BIOGRAPH(Y) + -ICAL] —**bi′o•graph′i•cal•ly,** *adv.*

bi•og•ra•phy (bī og′rə fē, bē-), *n., pl.* **-phies.** **1.** a written account of another person's life: *the biography of Byron by Marchand.* **2.** an account in biographical form of an organization, society, theater, animal, etc. **3.** such writings collectively. **4.** the writing of biography as an occupation or field of endeavor. [1675–85; < Gk *biographía.* See BIO-, -GRAPHY]

bi•o•haz•ard (bī′ō haz′ərd), *n.* **1.** a pathogen, esp. one used in or produced by biological research. **2.** the health risk posed by the possible release of such a pathogen into the environment. [BIO- + HAZARD] —**bi′o•haz′ard•ous,** *adj.*

bi•o•herm (bī′ō hûrm′), *n. Geol.* a carbonate rock formation, in the form of an ancient reef or hummock, consisting of the fossilized remains of corals, algae, mollusks, and other sedentary marine life, and commonly surrounded by rock of a different lithology. [1925–30; BIO- + *-herm* < Gk *hérma* sunken rock, reef] —**bi′o•her′mal,** *adj.*

bi•o•in•or•gan•ic (bī′ō in′ôr gan′ik), *adj. Biochem.* pertaining to the biological activity of metal complexes and nonmetal compounds based on elements other than carbon (contrasted with *bioorganic*). [1970–75; BIO- + INORGANIC]

bi•o•in•stru•men•ta•tion (bī′ō in′strə men tā′shən), *n.* **1.** the use of sensors and other instruments to record and transmit physiological data from persons or other living things, as in space flight. **2.** such instruments collectively. [1960–65; BIO- + INSTRUMENTATION]

bi•o•ki•net•ics (bī′ō ki net′iks, -kī-), *n.* (*used with a singular v.*) *Biol., Med.* the study of movements of or within organisms. [BIO- + KINETICS]

Bi•o•ko (bē ō′kō), *n.* an island in the Bight of Biafra, near the W coast of Africa: a province of Equatorial Guinea. 80,000; ab. 800 sq. mi. (2072 sq. km). Formerly, **Fernando Po, Macías Nguema Biyogo.**

biol., **1.** biological. **2.** biologist. **3.** biology.

bi•o•lin•guis•tics (bī′ō ling gwis′tiks), *n.* (*used with a singular v.*) *Ling.* the study of language functions as they relate to or derive from the biological characteristics of an organism. [BIO- + LINGUISTICS]

bi•o•log•i•cal (bī′ə loj′i kəl), *adj.* **1.** pertaining to biology. **2.** of or pertaining to the products and operations of applied biology: *a biological test.* —*n.* **3.** *Pharm.* any substance, as a serum or vaccine, derived from animal products or other biological sources and used to treat or prevent disease. Also, **bi′o•log′ic.** [1855–60; BIOLOG(Y) + -ICAL] —**bi′o•log′i•cal•ly,** *adv.*

biolog′ical accumula′tion, the accumulation within living organisms of toxic substances occurring in the environment. Also called **bioaccumulation.** Cf. **biological magnification.**

biolog′ical child′, any child conceived rather than adopted by a specified parent, and therefore carrying genes from the parent.

biolog′ical clock′, *Physiol.* an innate mechanism of the body that regulates its rhythmic and periodic cycles, as that of sleeping and waking. [1950–55]

biolog′ical control′, the control of pests by interference with their ecological status, as by introducing a natural enemy or a pathogen into the environment. Also called **biocontrol.** [1920–25]

biolog′ical engineer′ing, bioengineering. [1965–70]

biolog′ical magnifica′tion, the increasing concentration of toxic substances within each successive link in the food chain. Also called **biomagnification.** Cf. **biological accumulation.**

biolog′ical ox′ygen demand′. See **biochemical oxygen demand.** [1940–45]

biolog′ical par′ent, a parent who has conceived (**biolog′ical moth′er**) or sired (**biolog′ical fath′er**) rather than adopted a child and whose genes are therefore transmitted to the child. Also called **birth parent.**

biolog′ical psychi′atry, a school of psychiatric thought concerned with the medical treatment of mental disorders, esp. through medication, and emphasizing the relationship between behavior and brain function and the search for physical causes of mental illness. —**biological psychiatrist.**

biolog′ical rhythm′, *Physiol.* biorhythm.

biolog′ical val′ue, the nutritional effectiveness of the protein in a given food, expressed as the percentage used by the body of either the total protein consumed or the digestible protein available. [1920–25]

biolog′ical war′fare, warfare that makes use of bacteria, viruses, toxins, etc., to disable or destroy people, domestic animals, and food crops. *Abbr.:* B.W. Also called **biowarfare, germ warfare.** [1945–50]

bi•o•log•ics (bī′ə loj′iks), *n.* (*used with a plural v.*) commercial products derived from biotechnology.

bi•ol•o•gism (bī ol′ə jiz′əm), *n.* the use or emphasis of biological principles or methods in explaining human, esp. social, behavior. [1850–55; BIOLOG(Y) + -ISM]

bi•ol•o•gist (bī ol′ə jist), *n.* a specialist in biology. [1805–15; BIOLOG(Y) + -IST]

bi•ol•o•gy (bī ol′ə jē), *n.* **1.** the science of life or living matter in all its forms and phenomena, esp. with reference to origin, growth, reproduction, structure, and behavior. **2.** the living organisms of a region: *the biology of Pennsylvania.* **3.** the biological phenomena characteristic of an organism or a group of organisms: *the biology of a worm.* [1805–15; < G *Biologie.* See BIO-, -LOGY]

bi•o•lu•mi•nes•cence (bī′ō lōō′mə nes′əns), *n.* the production of light by living organisms. [1915–20; BIO- + LUMINESCENCE] —**bi′o•lu′mi•nes′cent,** *adj.*

bi•ol•y•sis (bī ol′ə sis), *n. Biol.* disintegration of organic matter through the biochemical action of living organisms, as bacteria. [1895–1900; < NL; see BIO-, -LYSIS]

bi•o•lyt•ic (bī′ə lit′ik), *adj.* able to destroy life. [BIO(LYSIS) + -LYTIC]

bi•o•mag•net•ism (bī′ō mag′ni tiz′əm), *n.* See **animal magnetism.** [BIO- + MAGNETISM] —**bi•o•mag•net•ic** (bī′ō mag net′ik), *adj.*

bi•o•mag•ni•fi•ca•tion (bī′ō mag′nə fi kā′shən), *n.* See **biological magnification.** [1970–75; BIO- + MAGNIFICATION]

bi•o•mag•ni•fy (bī′ō mag′nə fī′), *v.i.,* **-fied, -fy•ing.** to undergo biological magnification. [1970–75; back formation from BIOMAGNIFICATION; see -FY]

bi•o•mass (bī′ō mas′), *n.* **1.** *Ecol.* the amount of living matter in a given habitat, expressed either as the weight of organisms per unit area or as the volume of organisms per unit volume of habitat. **2.** *Energy.* organic matter, esp. plant matter, that can be converted to fuel and is therefore regarded as a potential energy source. [1930–35; BIO- + MASS]

bi•o•ma•te•ri•al (bī′ō mə tēr′ē əl, bī′ō mə tēr′-), *n.* a synthetic material, usually a plastic, suitable for implanting in a living body to repair damaged or diseased parts. [1965–70; BIO- + MATERIAL]

bi•o•math•e•mat•ics (bī′ō math′ə mat′iks), *n.* (*used with a singular v.*) *Biol.* the application of mathematical methods to the study of living organisms. [1920–25; BIO- + MATHEMATICS] —**bi′o•math′e•mat′i•cal,** *adj.* —**bi•o•math•e•ma•ti•cian** (bī′ō math′ə mə tish′ən), *n.*

bi•ome (bī′ōm), *n. Ecol.* a complex biotic community characterized by distinctive plant and animal species and maintained under the climatic conditions of the region, esp. such a community that has developed to climax. [1915–20; BI-[2] + *-ome* -OMA]

bi•o•me•chan•ics (bī′ō mi kan′iks), *n.* (*used with a singular v.*) **1.** *Med.* **a.** the study of the action of external and internal forces on the living body, esp. on the skeletal system. **b.** the development of prostheses. **2.** *Biol.* the study of the mechanical nature of biological processes, as heart action and muscle movement. [1930–35; BIO- + MECHANICS] —**bi′o•me•chan′i•cal,** *adj.* —**bi′o•me•chan′i•cal•ly,** *adv.*

biomed′ical engineer′ing, bioengineering (def. 1). [1965–70]

bi•o•med•i•cine (bī′ō med′ə sin), *n.* **1.** the application of the natural sciences, esp. the biological and physiological sciences, to clinical medicine. **2.** the science concerned with the effects of the environment on the human body, esp. environments associated with space travel. [1945–50; BIO- + MEDICINE] —**bi′o•med′i•cal,** *adj.*

bi•o•me•te•or•ol•o•gy (bī′ō mē′tē ə rol′ə jē), *n.* the scientific study of the effects of natural or artificial atmospheric conditions, as temperature and humidity, on living organisms. [1945–50; BIO- + METEOROLOGY] —**bi•o•me•te•or•o•log•i•cal** (bī′ō mē′tē ər ə loj′i kəl), *adj.* —**bi′o•me′te•or•ol′o•gist,** *n.*

bi•om•e•ter (bī om′i tər), *n.* an instrument for measuring the amount of carbon dioxide given off by an organism, tissue, etc. [1860–65; BIO- + -METER]

bi•o•me•tri•cian (bī′ō mi trish′ən, bī om′i-), *n.* a person skilled in biometrics. Also, **bi•o•met•ri•cist** (bī′ō-me′trə sist). [1900–05; BIOMETRIC(S) + -IAN]

bi•o•met•rics (bī′ə me′triks), *n.* (*used with a singular v.*) **1.** *Biol., Statistics.* biostatistics. **2.** biometry (def. 1). [1900–05; BIOMETR(Y) + -ICS] —**bi′o•met′ric, bi′o•met′ri•cal,** *adj.* —**bi′o•met′ri•cal•ly,** *adv.*

bi•om•e•try (bī om′i trē), *n.* **1.** the calculation of the probable duration of human life. **2.** biometrics (def. 1). [1825–35; BIO- + -METRY]

bi•o•mod•el•ing (bī′ō mod′l ing), *n.* the mathematical modeling of biological reactions. [BIO- + MODELING]

bi•o•morph (bī′ō môrf′), *n.* a painted, drawn, or sculptured free form or design suggestive in shape of a living organism, esp. an ameba or protozoan: *The paintings of Joan Miró are often notable for their playful, bright-colored biomorphs.* [1890–95; BIO- + -MORPH] —**bi′o•mor′phic,** *adj.* —**bi′o•mor′phism,** *n.*

Bi•on (bī′on), *n.* fl. c100 B.C., Greek pastoral poet.

bi•on•ic (bī on′ik), *adj.* **1.** utilizing electronic devices and mechanical parts to assist humans in performing difficult, dangerous, or intricate tasks, as by supplementing or duplicating parts of the body: *The scientist used a bionic arm to examine the radioactive material.* **2.** *Informal.* having superhuman strength or capacity. **3.** of or pertaining to bionics. [1955–60; BIO- + (ELECTRO)NIC; cf. BIONICS] —**bi•on′i•cal•ly,** *adv.*

bi•on•ics (bī on′iks), *n.* (*used with a singular v.*) the study of how humans and animals perform certain tasks and solve certain problems, and of the application of the findings to the design of electronic devices and mechanical parts. [1955–60; BIO(LOGY) + (ELECTRO)NICS]

bi•o•nom•ics (bī′ə nom′iks), *n.* (*used with a singular v.*) ecology (def. 1). [1885–90; BIO- + *-nomics,* prob. on the model of ECONOMICS; see -NOMY, -ICS] —**bi′o•nom′ic, bi′o•nom′i•cal,** *adj.* —**bi′o•nom′i•cal•ly,** *adv.* —**bi•on•o•mist** (bī on′ə mist), *n.*

bi•on•o•my (bī on′ə mē), *n.* **1.** physiology. **2.** ecology. [BIO- + -NOMY]

bi•o•or•gan•ic (bī′ō ôr gan′ik), *adj. Biochem.* pertaining to the composition and biological activity of carbon-based compounds, esp. those of laboratory rather than biogenic origin (contrasted with *bioinorganic*). [1970–75; BIO- + ORGANIC]

bi•o•phys•ics (bī′ō fiz′iks), *n.* (*used with a singular v.*) the branch of biology that applies the methods of physics to the study of biological structures and processes. [1890–95; BIO- + PHYSICS] —**bi•o•phys•i•cal** (bī′ō fiz′i-kəl), *adj.* —**bi′o•phys′i•cal•ly,** *adv.* —**bi•o•phys•i•cist** (bī′ō fiz′ə sist), *n.*

bi•o•plas•tic (bī′ō plas′tik), *n.* plastic suitable for use as a biomaterial. [1980–85; BIO- + PLASTIC]

bi•o•pol•y•mer (bī′ō pol′ə mər), *n. Biotech.* **1.** any polymeric chemical manufactured by a living organism, as proteins and polysaccharides. **2.** such a chemical prepared by laboratory synthesis. [1960–65; BIO- + POLYMER]

bi•o•proc•ess (bī′ō pros′es *or, esp. Brit.,* -prō′ses), *Biotech.* —*n.* **1.** a method or operation of preparing a

CONCISE ETYMOLOGY KEY: <, descended or borrowed from; >, whence; b., blend of, blended; c., cognate with; cf., compare; deriv., derivative; equiv., equivalent; imit., imitative; obl., oblique; r., replacing; s., stem; sp., spelling, spelled; resp., respelling, respelled; trans., translation; ?, origin unknown; *, unattested; ‡, probably earlier than. See the full key inside the front cover.

biological material, esp. a product of genetic engineering, for commercial use. —*v.t.* **2.** to treat or prepare through bioprocess. —*adj.* **3.** noting, pertaining to, or involving a bioprocess: *bioprocess technology.* [1975–80; BIO- + PROCESS]

bi•op•sy (bī′op sē), *n., pl.* **-sies,** *v.,* **-sied, -sy•ing.** *Med.* —*n.* **1.** the removal for diagnostic study of a piece of tissue from a living body. **2.** a specimen obtained from a biopsy. —*v.t.* **3.** to remove (living tissue) for diagnostic evaluation. [1890–95; BI-[2] + -OPSY[1]]

bi•o•psy•chic (bī′ō sī′kik), *adj. Psychol.* of, pertaining to, or comprising psychological and biological phenomena. Also, **bi′o•psy′chi•cal.** [BIO- + PSYCHIC]

bi•o•psy•chol•o•gy (bī′ō sī kol′ə jē), *n.* a field of psychology that deals with the effects of biological factors on behavior. [BIO- + PSYCHOLOGY] —**bi′o•psy•chol′o•gist,** *n.*

bi•o•re•ac•tor (bī′ō rē ak′tər), *n. Biotech.* a fermentation vat for the production of living organisms, as bacteria or yeast, used in industrial processes such as waste recycling or in the manufacture of drugs or other products. [1970–75; BIO- + REACTOR]

bi•o•re•gion (bī′ō rē′jən), *n.* a place, locale, or area that constitutes a natural ecological community. [1980–85; BIO- + REGION] —**bi′o•re′gion•al,** *adj.*

bi•o•re•search (bī′ō ri sûrch′, -rē′sûrch), *n.* **1.** the investigation of the nature of living organisms; biological research. **2.** biotechnology. [BIO- + RESEARCH]

bi•o•rhythm (bī′ō rith′əm), *n. Physiol.* an innate periodicity in an organism's physiological processes, as sleep and wake cycles. [1960–65; BIO- + RHYTHM] —**bi′o•rhyth′mic,** *adj.* —**bi•o•rhyth•mic•i•ty** (bī′ō rith mis′i tē), *n.* —**bi′o•rhyth′mist, bi′o•rhyth′mi•cist,** *n.*

bi•o•rhyth•mics (bī′ō rith′miks), *n.* (*used with a singular v.*) the study of biorhythms. [see BIORHYTHMIC, -ICS]

BIOS (bī′ōs), *n.* computer firmware that directs many basic functions of the operating system, as booting and keyboard control. [*B(asic) I(nput)/O(utput) S(ystem)*]

bi•o•safe•ty (bī′ō sāf′tē), *n.* the maintenance of safe conditions in biological research to prevent harm to workers, nonlaboratory organisms, or the environment. [1975–80; BIO- + SAFETY]

bi•o•sci•ence (bī′ō sī′əns), *n.* any science that deals with the biological aspects of living organisms. [1960–65; BIO- + SCIENCE] —**bi•o•sci•en•tif•ic** (bī′ō sī′ən tif′ik), *adj.* —**bi′o•sci′en•tist,** *n.*

bi•o•scope (bī′ə skōp′), *n.* an early form of motion-picture projector, used about 1900. [1895–1900; BIO- + -SCOPE]

bi•os•co•py (bī os′kə pē), *n., pl.* **-pies.** *Med.* examination of a body to discover whether or not it is alive. [BIO- + -SCOPY] —**bi•o•scop•ic** (bī′ə skop′ik), *adj.*

bi•o•sen•sor (bī′ō sen′sər, -sôr, bī′ō sen′-), *n.* a device that senses and transmits information about a biological process, as blood pressure, of an individual under observation. [BIO- + SENSOR]

-biosis, a combining form meaning "mode of life," used in the formation of compound words: *aerobiosis; parabiosis.* [< Gk *bíōsis,* equiv. to *biō-,* verbid s. of *bioûn* to live + *-sis* -SIS; cf. ANABIOSIS, SYMBIOSIS, on which subsequent coinages were prob. modeled]

bi•o•so•cial (bī′ō sō′shəl), *adj.* **1.** of, pertaining to, or entailing the interaction or combination of social and biological factors. **2.** *Sociol.* of, pertaining to, or characteristic of the theories of or phenomena studied in biosociology. **3.** of or pertaining to social phenomena that are affected by biological factors. Also, **bi•o•so•ci•o•log•i•cal** (bī′ō sō′sē ə loj′i kəl, -shē-). [1890–95; BIO- + SOCIAL] —**bi′o•so′cial•ly,** *adv.*

bi•o•so•ci•ol•o•gy (bī′ō sō′sē ol′ə jē, -shē-), *n.* the study of the evolution of social forms and the development of social behavior in terms analogous to or correlated with biological studies. [1890–95; BIO- + SOCIOLOGY]

bi•o•spe•le•ol•o•gy (bī′ō spē′lē ol′ə jē), *n.* the study of organisms that live in caves. [1945–50; BIO- + SPELEOLOGY] —**bi•o•spe•le•o•log•i•cal** (bī′ō spē′lē ə loj′i kəl), *adj.* —**bi′o•spe′le•ol′o•gist,** *n.*

bi•o•sphere (bī′ə sfēr′), *n.* **1.** the part of the earth's crust, waters, and atmosphere that supports life. **2.** the ecosystem comprising the entire earth and the living organisms that inhabit it. [1895–1900; < G *Biosphäre;* see BIO-, -SPHERE] —**bi•o•spher•ic** (bī′ə sfer′ik), *adj.*

bi•o•stat•ics (bī′ō stat′iks), *n.* (*used with a singular v.*) the branch of biology dealing with the structure of organisms in relation to their functions (opposed to *biodynamics*). [1870–75; BIO- + STATICS] —**bi′o•stat′ic,** *adj.*

bi•o•sta•tis•tics (bī′ō stə tis′tiks), *n.* (*used with a singular v.*) the application of statistics to biological and medical data. [1945–50; BIO- + STATISTICS] —**bi•o•stat•is•ti•cian** (bī′ō stat′ə stish′ən), *n.*

bi•o•stra•tig•ra•phy (bī′ō strə tig′rə fē), *n.* a branch of geology dealing with the differentiation of sedimentary rock units on the basis of the fossils they contain. [BIO- + STRATIGRAPHY] —**bi•o•strat•i•graph•ic** (bī′ō strat′i graf′ik), *adj.*

bi•o•strome (bī′ə strōm′), *n. Geol.* a bedded, blanketlike sedimentary deposit of organic origin built by marine organisms and including shell beds, flat reefs, and corals. [1930–35; BIO- + Gk *strôma* layer, bed; see STROMA] —**bi′o•stro′mal,** *adj.*

bi•o•syn•the•sis (bī′ō sin′thə sis), *n. Biochem.* **1.** the formation of chemical compounds by a living organism. **2.** the laboratory preparation of biological molecules by the use of reagents or catalysts derived from natural substances and modeled on a series of reactions occurring in a living organism. [1925–30; BIO- + SYNTHESIS]

bi•o•syn•thet•ic (bī′ō sin thet′ik), *adj. Biochem.* **1.** of or pertaining to biosynthesis. **2.** of or pertaining to a substance produced by a biosynthetic process. [1945–50; BIO- + SYNTHETIC]

bi•o•ta (bī ō′tə), *n. Ecol.* the animals, plants, fungi, etc., of a region or period. [1900–05; < NL < Gk *biotḗ* life]

bi•o•tech (bī′ō tek′), *n. Informal.* biotechnology.

biotech., biotechnology.

bi•o•tech•nol•o•gy (bī′ō tek nol′ə jē), *n.* the use of living organisms or other biological systems in the manufacture of drugs or other products or for environmental management, as in waste recycling: includes the use of bioreactors in manufacturing, microorganisms to degrade oil slicks or organic waste, genetically engineered bacteria to produce human hormones, and monoclonal antibodies to identify antigens. Cf. **human engineering.** [1940–45; BIO- + TECHNOLOGY] —**bi•o•tech•ni•cal** (bī′ō-tek′ni kəl), **bi•o•tech•no•log•i•cal** (bī′ō tek′nl oj′i kəl), *adj.* —**bi′o•tech′no•log′i•cal•ly,** *adv.* —**bi′o•tech•nol′o•gist,** *n.*

bi•o•te•lem•e•try (bī′ō tə lem′i trē), *n.* the tracking of a free-ranging animal, or the monitoring of one or more of its physiological conditions, by means of electronic equipment that receives signals from a radio transmitter or similar device attached to or embedded in the animal. [1960–65; BIO- + TELEMETRY] —**bi′o•te•lem′e•ter,** *n.* —**bi•o•tel•e•met•ric** (bī′ō tel′ə me′trik), *adj.* —**bi′o•tel′e•met′ri•cal•ly,** *adv.*

bi•ot•ic (bī ot′ik), *adj.* pertaining to life. Also, **bi•ot′i•cal.** [1590–1600; < Gk *biōtikós* of, pertaining to life, equiv. to *biō-,* verbid s. of *bioûn* to live + *-tikos* -TIC]

biot′ic poten′tial, the capacity of a population of organisms to increase in numbers under optimum environmental conditions. [1930–35]

bi•o•tin (bī′ə tin), *n. Biochem.* a crystalline, water-soluble vitamin, $C_{10}H_{16}O_3N_2S$, of the vitamin B complex, that is present in all living cells and functions as a growth factor and as a catalyst in carboxylation reactions. Also called **vitamin H.** [1935–40; < G *Biotin* < Gk *biotḗ* life + *-in* -IN[2]]

bi•o•tite (bī′ə tīt′), *n.* a very common mineral of the mica group, occurring in black, dark-brown, or dark-green sheets and flakes: an important constituent of igneous and metamorphic rocks. [1860–65; named after J. B. *Biot* (1774–1862), French mineralogist and mathematician; see -ITE[1]] —**bi•o•tit•ic** (bī′ə tit′ik), *adj.*

bi•o•tope (bī′ə tōp′), *n. Ecol.* a portion of a habitat characterized by uniformity in climate and distribution of biotic and abiotic components, as a tidal pool or a forest canopy. [1925–30; < G *Biotop,* equiv. to *bio-* BIO- + Gk *tópos* place]

bi•o•trans•for•ma•tion (bī′ō trans′fər mā′shən), *n.* the series of chemical changes occurring in a compound, esp. a drug, as a result of enzymatic or other activity by a living organism. [1950–55; BIO- + TRANSFORMATION]

bi•o•tron (bī′ə tron′), *n. Biol.* a controlled laboratory environment designed to provide uniform experimental conditions with the aim of producing uniform organisms for use in experiments. [1970–75; BIO- + -TRON]

Bi′ot-Sa•vart′ law′ (bē′ō sə vär′, byō′-), *Physics.* the law that the magnetic induction near a long, straight conductor, as wire, varies inversely as the distance from the conductor and directly as the intensity of the current in the conductor. [named after J. B. *Biot* (see BIOTITE) and Felix *Savart* (1791–1841), French physician and physicist]

bi•o•type (bī′ə tīp′), *n. Genetics.* **1.** a group of organisms having the same genotype. **2.** a distinguishing feature of the genotype. [1905–10; BIO- + -TYPE] —**bi•o•typ•ic** (bī′ə tip′ik), *adj.*

bi•o•var (bī′ə vär′), *n. Bacteriol.* a group of microorganisms, usually bacteria, that have identical genetic but different biochemical or physiological characters. [BIO- + VAR(IANT); cf. CULTIVAR]

bi•o•war•fare (bī′ō wôr′fâr′), *n.* See **biological warfare.** [1965–70; BIO- + WARFARE]

bi•pack (bī′pak′), *n. Photog.* two separate films, each having an emulsion layer sensitive to a different color, held together with their emulsion layers facing for simultaneous exposure through the back of one. [1920–25; BI-[1] + PACK[1]]

bi•pa•ren•tal (bī′pə ren′tl), *adj.* pertaining to or having traits or characteristics that stem from both parents. [1895–1900; BI-[1] + PARENTAL] —**bi′pa•ren′tal•ly,** *adv.*

bi•pa•ri•e•tal (bī′pə rī′i tl), *adj. Craniom.* of or pertaining to both parietal bones, esp. in their being determinants in measurements of the breadth of the skull. [1855–60; BI-[1] + PARIETAL]

bip•a•rous (bip′ər əs), *adj.* **1.** *Zool.* bringing forth offspring in pairs. **2.** *Bot.* bearing two branches or axes. [1725–35; BI-[1] + -PAROUS]

bi•par•ti•san (bī pär′tə zən), *adj.* representing, characterized by, or including members from two parties or factions: *Government leaders hope to achieve a bipartisan foreign policy.* [1905–10; BI-[1] + PARTISAN[1]] —**bi•par′ti•san•ism,** *n.* —**bi•par′ti•san•ship′,** *n.*

bi•par•tite (bī pär′tīt), *adj.* **1.** divided into or consisting of two parts. **2.** *Law.* being in two corresponding parts: *a bipartite contract.* **3.** shared by two; joint: *a bipartite pact; bipartite rule.* **4.** *Bot.* divided into two parts nearly to the base, as a leaf. [1500–10; < L *bipartītus* divided into two parts, bisected (ptp. of *bipartīre*). See BI-[1], PART, -ITE[2]] —**bi•par′tite•ly,** *adv.* —**bi•par•ti•tion** (bī′pär tish′ən), *n.*

bi•par•ty (bī′pär′tē), *adj.* representing two distinct parties: *a biparty committee.* [1895–1900; BI-[1] + PARTY]

bi•pec•ti•nate (bī pek′tə nāt′), *adj. Zool., Bot.* having both margins toothed like a comb, as the antennae of certain moths. Also, **bi•pec′ti•nat′ed.** [1830–40; BI-[1] + PECTINATE]

bi•ped (bī′ped), *Zool.* —*n.* **1.** a two-footed animal. —*adj.* **2.** having two feet. [1640–50; < L *biped-* (s. of *bipēs*) two-footed. See BI-[1], -PED]

bi•ped•al (bī′ped′l, -pi dl, bī ped′l), *adj.* biped. [1600–10; BI-[1] + PEDAL (adj.)] —**bi•ped′al•ly,** *adv.*

bi•ped•al•ism (bī ped′l iz′əm), *n.* the condition of being two-footed or of using two feet for standing and walking. Also, **bi•pe•dal•i•ty** (bī′pi dal′i tē). [1905–10; BIPEDAL + -ISM]

bi•pet•al•ous (bī pet′l əs), *adj. Bot.* having two petals. [BI-[1] + PETALOUS]

bi•pha•sic (bī fā′zik), *adj.* **1.** having two phases. **2.** *Bot.* having a gametophytic and a sporophytic phase. [1905–10; BI- + PHASE + -IC]

bi•phen•yl (bī fen′l, -fēn′l), *n. Chem.* a water-insoluble, pleasant-smelling, colorless powder or white scales, $C_{12}H_{10}$, composed of two phenyl groups, from which benzidine dyes are derived: used chiefly as a heat-transfer agent and in organic synthesis. Also called **diphenyl, phenylbenzene.** [1920–25; BI-[1] + PHENYL]

Bi•phet•a•mine (bī fet′ə mēn′, -min), *Pharm., Trademark.* a brand name for a preparation containing a mixture of two isomers of amphetamine.

bi•pin•nar•i•a (bī′pi nâr′ē ə), *n., pl.* **-nar•i•ae** (-nâr′ē-ē′), **-nar•i•as.** the free-swimming, bilaterally symmetrical larva of certain starfishes. [< NL; see BI-[1], PINNA, -ARIA]

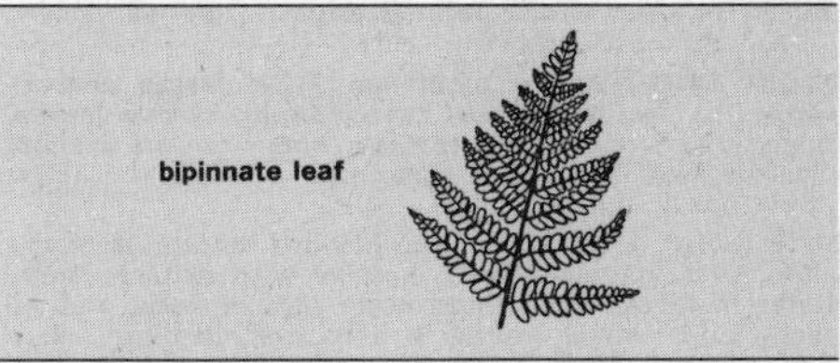

bi•pin•nate (bī pin′āt), *adj. Bot.* pinnate, as a leaf, with the divisions also pinnate. [1785–95; < NL *bipinnātus.* See BI-[1], PINNATE] —**bi•pin′nate•ly,** *adv.*

bi•plane (bī′plān′), *n.* an airplane with two sets of wings, one above and usually slightly forward of the other. [1870–75; BI-[1] + (AIR)PLANE]

bi•pod (bī′pod), *n.* a two-legged support, as for an automatic rifle. [1935–40; BI-[1] + -POD]

bi•po•lar (bī pō′lər), *adj.* **1.** having two poles, as the earth. **2.** of, pertaining to, or found at both polar regions. **3.** characterized by opposite extremes, as two conflicting political philosophies. **4.** *Electronics.* of or pertaining to a transistor that uses both positive and negative charge carriers. [1800–10; BI-[1] + POLAR] —**bi′po•lar′i•ty,** *n.* —**bi•po′lar•i•za′tion,** *n.*

bipo′lar disor′der, *Psychiatry.* an affective disorder characterized by periods of mania alternating with periods of depression, usually interspersed with relatively long intervals of normal mood. Formerly, **manic-depressive illness.**

bip•py (bip′ē), *n., pl.* **-pies.** *Slang.* an unspecified part of the anatomy (usually used in the phrase *You bet your (sweet) bippy).* [nonce word of uncert. orig.]

bi•prism (bī′priz′əm), *n. Optics.* a triangular prism with an apex angle slightly less than 180°: when illuminated by a point source of light it produces two overlapping beams that form an interference pattern on a screen. Also called **Fresnel biprism.** [1880–85; BI-[1] + PRISM]

bi•pro•pel•lant (bī′prə pel′ənt), *n. Rocketry.* a missile or rocket propellant, composed of fuel and oxidizer, the components of which are kept in separate compartments prior to combustion. [1945–50; BI-[1] + PROPELLANT]

bi•pyr•a•mid (bī pir′ə mid), *n. Crystall.* a form symmetrical about a plane dividing it into two pyramids. Also called **dipyramid.** [BI-[1] + PYRAMID] —**bi•py•ram•i•dal** (bī′pi ram′i dl), *adj.*

bi•quad•rate (bī kwod′rāt, -rit), *n. Math.* the fourth power. Also, **biquadratic.** [1700–10; BI-[1] + QUADRATE]

bi•quad•rat•ic (bī′kwo drat′ik), *Math.* —*adj.* **1.** involving the fourth, but no higher, power of the unknown or variable. —*n.* **2.** quartic (def. 2). **3.** biquadrate. [1655–65; BI-[1] + QUADRATIC]

bi•quar•ter•ly (bī kwôr′tər lē), *adj.* occurring twice in each quarter of a year. [1880–85; BI-[1] + QUARTERLY]

bi•ra•cial (bī rā′shəl), *adj.* consisting of, representing, or combining members of two separate races: *a biracial committee on neighborhood problems.* [1920–25; BI-[1] + RACIAL] —**bi•ra′cial•ism,** *n.*

bi•ra•di•al (bī rā′dē əl), *adj. Biol.* having both bilateral and radial symmetry, as ctenophores. [1905–10; BI-[1] + RADIAL]

bi•rad•i•cal (bī rad′i kəl), *n. Chem.* diradical. [BI-[1] + RADICAL]

bi•ra•mous (bī rā′məs), *adj. Biol.* consisting of or divided into two branches: *a biramous appendage.* Also, **bi•ra•mose** (bī rā′mōs, bī′rə mōs′). [1875–80; BI-[1] + RAMOUS]

Bi•rat•na•gar (bi rät′nug ər), *n.* a city in SE Nepal. 44,938.

birch (bûrch), *n.* **1.** any tree or shrub of the genus *Betula,* comprising species with a smooth, laminated outer bark and close-grained wood. Cf. **birch family. 2.** the wood itself. **3.** a birch rod, or a bundle of birch twigs, used esp. for whipping. —*adj.* **4.** birchen. —*v.t.* **5.** to beat or punish with or as if with a birch: *The young ruffians were birched soundly by their teacher.* [bef. 900; ME *birche,* OE *birce;* c. OHG *birka* (G *Birke*); akin to Skt *bhūrja* kind of birch]

birch′ beer′, a carbonated or fermented drink containing an extract from the bark of the birch tree. Cf. **root beer.** [1880–85, *Amer.*]

birch•en (bûr′chən), *adj.* **1.** of or pertaining to birch. **2.** made or consisting of birch: *birchen furniture.* [1400–50; late ME; see BIRCH, -EN[2]]

Birch•er (bûr′chər), *n.* a member, advocate, or follower of the John Birch Society and its principles. Also, **Birch′ite.** Also called **John Bircher.** [1960–65, *Amer.;* (JOHN) BIRCH (SOCIETY) + -ER[1]]

birch′ fam′ily, the plant family Betulaceae, characterized by deciduous trees having simple serrate leaves, male flowers in drooping catkins, female flowers in short clusters, and one-seeded nuts, and including the alder, birch, hazel, and hornbeam.

bird (bûrd), *n.* **1.** any warm-blooded vertebrate of the class Aves, having a body covered with feathers, forelimbs modified into wings, scaly legs, a beak, and no teeth, and bearing young in a hard-shelled egg. **2.** a fowl or game bird. **3.** *Sports.* **a.** See **clay pigeon. b.** a shuttlecock. **4.** *Slang.* a person, esp. one having some peculiarity: *He's a queer bird.* **5.** *Informal.* an aircraft, spacecraft, or guided missile. **6.** *Cookery.* a thin piece of meat, poultry, or fish rolled around a stuffing and braised: *veal birds.* **7.** *Southern U.S.* (in hunting) a bobwhite. **8.** *Chiefly Brit. Slang.* a girl or young woman. **9.** *Archaic.* the young of any fowl. **10. a little bird,** *Informal.* a secret source of information: *A little bird told me that today is your birthday.* **11. bird in the hand,** a thing possessed in fact as opposed to a thing about which one speculates: *A bird in the hand is worth two in the bush.* Also, **bird in hand. 12. birds of a feather,** people with interests, opinions, or backgrounds in common: *Birds of a feather flock together.* **13. eat like a bird,** to eat sparingly: *She couldn't understand why she failed to lose weight when she was, as she said, eating like a bird.* **14. for the birds,** *Slang.* useless or worthless; not to be taken seriously: *Their opinions on art are for the birds. That pep rally is for the birds.* **15. kill two birds with one stone,** to achieve two aims with a single effort: *She killed two birds with one stone by shopping and visiting the museum on the same trip.* **16. the bird,** *Slang.* **a.** disapproval, as of a performance, by hissing, booing, etc.: *He got the bird when he came out on stage.* **b.** scoffing or ridicule: *He was trying to be serious, but we all gave him the bird.* **c.** an obscene gesture of contempt made by raising the middle finger. **17. the birds and the bees,** basic information about sex and reproduction: *It was time to talk to the boy about the birds and the bees.* —*v.i.* **18.** to catch or shoot birds. **19.** to bird-watch. [bef. 900; ME *byrd, bryd,* OE *brid(d)* young bird, chick] —**bird′less,** *adj.*

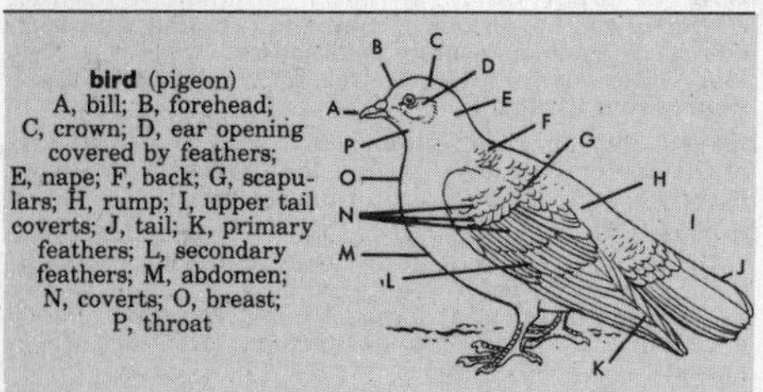

bird (pigeon) A, bill; B, forehead; C, crown; D, ear opening covered by feathers; E, nape; F, back; G, scapulars; H, rump; I, upper tail coverts; J, tail; K, primary feathers; L, secondary feathers; M, abdomen; N, coverts; O, breast; P, throat

bird′ band′, a band put on a bird's leg to identify it for observations about its range, behavior, longevity, migration patterns, etc. Also called, *Brit.,* **bird ring.** [1935–40, *Amer.*] —**bird′ band′er.** —**bird′ band′ing.**

bird•bath (bûrd′bath′, -bäth′), *n., pl.* **-baths** (-bathz′, -bäthz′, -baths′, -bäths′). a basin or tublike garden ornament for birds to drink from or bathe in. [1890–95; BIRD + BATH[1]]

bird•brain (bûrd′brān′), *n. Slang.* a stupid, foolish, or scatterbrained person. [1920–25; BIRD + BRAIN] —**bird′brained′, bird′-brained′,** *adj.*

bird•cage (bûrd′kāj′), *n.* **1.** a cage for confining birds. **2.** something that resembles a birdcage in form. **3.** *Slang.* the airspace over an airport, together with the airplanes in it. [1480–90; BIRD + CAGE]

bird′cage clock′. See **lantern clock.** [1950–55]

bird′ call′, 1. a sound made by a bird. **2.** a sound imitating that of a bird. **3.** a device used to imitate the sound of a bird. Also, **bird′call′.** [1615–25]

bird′ cher′ry, 1. any of several species of cherry, esp. *Prunus padus* **(European bird cherry),** of Europe and Asia, and *P. pensylvanica* **(pin cherry),** of the U.S. **2.** the fruit of any such tree, for which birds have a particular liking. [1590–1600]

CONCISE ETYMOLOGY KEY: <, descended or borrowed from; >, whence; b., blend of, blended; c., cognate with; cf., compare; deriv., derivative; equiv., equivalent; imit., imitative; obl., oblique; r., replacing; s., stem; sp., spelling, spelled; resp., respelling, respelled; trans., translation; ?, origin unknown; *, unattested; ‡, probably earlier than. See the full key inside the front cover.

bird′ colo′nel, *U.S. Mil. Slang.* See **chicken colonel.** [1945–50]

bird′ dis′mount, Hecht (def. 1).

bird′ dog′, 1. one of any of various breeds of dogs trained to hunt or retrieve birds. **2.** *Informal.* a person hired to locate special items or people, esp. a talent scout who seeks out promising athletes. **3.** *Slang.* a person who steals another person's date. [1885–90, *Amer.*]

bird-dog (bûrd′dôg′, -dog′), *v.,* **-dogged, -dog•ging.** —*v.t. Informal.* **1.** to follow, watch carefully, or investigate. **2.** to seek out. —*v.i.* **3.** *Informal.* to follow or watch carefully. **4.** *Slang.* to steal or attempt to steal another person's date. [v. use of BIRD DOG]

bird•er (bûr′dər), *n.* **1.** a person who raises birds. **2.** See **bird watcher.** [1475–85 for earlier sense "bird-catcher"; 1820–30 for def. 1; BIRD + -ER[1]]

bird′ farm′, *Slang.* an aircraft carrier. [1955–60]

bird′-foot•ed di′nosaur (bûrd′fo͝ot′id), theropod.

bird′ grass′, 1. a grass, *Poa trivialis,* grown in temperate regions of North America largely for lawns and turf. **2.** the knotgrass, *Polygonum aviculare.* [1775–85, *Amer.*]

bird•house (bûrd′hous′), *n., pl.* **-hous•es** (-hou′ziz). **1.** a box, usually fashioned to resemble a house, for birds to live in. **2.** an aviary. [1865–70, *Amer.;* BIRD + HOUSE]

bird•ie (bûr′dē), *n., v.,* **bird•ied, bird•ie•ing.** —*n.* **1.** a small bird. **2.** *Golf.* a score of one stroke under par on a hole. **3.** a shuttlecock. —*v.t.* **4.** *Golf.* to make a birdie on (a hole). [1785–95; BIRD + -IE]

bird•ing (bûr′ding), *n.* the identification and observation of wild birds in their natural habitat as a recreation; bird-watching. [1560–70 for earlier sense "hunting birds"; BIRD + -ING[1]]

bird•like (bûrd′līk′), *adj.* having the appearance or characteristics of a bird, as quickness, lightness, fragility, etc.: *birdlike gestures.* [1580–90; BIRD + -LIKE]

bird•lime (bûrd′līm′), *n., v.,* **-limed, -lim•ing.** —*n.* **1.** a sticky material prepared from holly, mistletoe, or other plants, and smeared on twigs to catch small birds that light on it. —*v.t.* **2.** to smear with birdlime. **3.** to catch or capture, as with birdlime: *to be birdlimed by flattery.* [1400–50; late ME *brydelyme.* See BIRD, LIME[1]]

bird′ louse′. See under **louse** (def. 2). [1820–30]

bird•man (bûrd′man′, -mən), *n., pl.* **-men** (-men′, -mən). **1.** an ornithologist. **2.** a bird watcher. **3.** a person who keeps or tends birds. **4.** a person who hunts birds for food or sport; fowler. **5.** *Informal.* aviator. [1690–1700; BIRD + MAN[1]]

bird′ of ill′ o′men, a person who brings bad news.

bird′ of par′adise, any of several passerine birds of the family Paradisaeidae, of New Guinea and adjacent islands, the males of which have ornate, colorful plumage. [1600–10]

bird-of-par•a•dise (bûrd′əv par′ə dīs′, -dīz′), *n., pl.* **birds-of-paradise. 1.** Also called **bird′-of-par′adise flow′er.** any of several plants of the genus *Strelitzia,* native to southern Africa, esp. *S. reginae,* having a large, showy orange and blue inflorescence. **2.** a small tree or shrub, *Caesalpinia (Poinciana) gilliesii,* native to South America, having featherlike leaves and showy yellow flowers with red stamens. [1880–85]

Bird′ of Par′adise, *Astron.* the constellation Apus. [1650–60]

bird′ of pas′sage, 1. a bird that migrates seasonally. **2.** a transient or migratory person. [1785–95]

bird′ of peace′, a dove.

bird′ of prey′, any of numerous predacious, flesh-eating birds, as the eagles, hawks, kites, vultures, falcons, and owls, having a sharp, downwardly curved beak, talons, and, usually, soaring flight. [1350–1400; ME]

bird′ pep′per, a variety of pepper, *Capsicum anuum glabriusculum,* with small, elongated berries. [1780–90]

bird′ plague′. See **avian influenza.**

bird′ ring′, *Brit.* See **bird band.** —**bird′ ring′er.** —**bird′ ring′ing.**

Birds, The, a comedy (414 B.C.) by Aristophanes.

bird′s′ beak′, *Archit.* beak (def. 9). [1860–65]

bird•seed (bûrd′sēd′), *n.* **1.** any seed or mixture of seeds used for feeding birds. **2.** the seed of a grass, *Phalaris canariensis,* used as food for birds. [1830–40; BIRD + SEED]

Birds•eye (bûrdz′ī′), *n.* **Clarence,** 1886–1956, U.S. inventor and businessman: developer of food-freezing process.

bird's-eye (bûrdz′ī′), *adj., n., pl.* **-eyes.** —*adj.* **1.** seen from above, as by a bird in flight; panoramic: *a bird's-eye view of the city.* **2.** omitting many details; hasty; superficial; general: *a bird's-eye view of ancient history.* **3.** having spots or markings resembling birds' eyes: *bird's-eye tweed.* —*n.* **4.** any of various plants having small, round, bright-colored flowers, as a primrose, *Primula farinosa,* or a speedwell, *Veronica chamaedrys.* **5.** *Textiles.* **a.** a woven, allover pattern on fabrics, characterized chiefly by small diamond shapes resembling the eye of a bird. **b.** a fabric having this pattern, esp. a cotton used for diapers or a linen used for toweling. [1590–1600; BIRD + 'S[1] + EYE]

bird's′-eye ma′ple, a cut of sugar maple wood used esp. for veneers, having a wavy grain with many dark, circular markings. [1785–95]

bird's′-eye prim′rose, a hardy primrose, *Primula farinosa,* of alpine regions of Europe and Asia, having small, lilac-colored flowers with yellow throat and eye. [1810–20]

bird's′-foot tre′foil (bûrdz′fo͝ot′), **1.** a plant, *Lotus corniculatus,* of the legume family, the pods of which spread like a crow's foot, grown for forage. **2.** any similar plant of the same genus. [1825–35]

bird's′-foot vi′olet, a violet, *Viola pedata,* of the eastern and midwestern U.S., having single flowers with a yellow center, two purple upper petals, and three lavender lower petals: the state flower of Wisconsin. [1830–40, *Amer.*]

bird′ shot′, small-sized shot used for shooting birds. [1620–30]

bird's′ mouth′, *Carpentry.* a right-angled notch cut in the underside of a rafter for fitting over a longitudinal member, as a wall plate. [1815–25]

bird's′ nest′, 1. nest (def. 1). **2.** *Angling.* backlash (def. 4). [1590–1600]

bird's′-nest fern′ (bûrdz′nest′), a tropical fern, *Asplenium nidus,* having fronds arranged in clumps resembling a bird's nest. [1855–60]

bird's′-nest fun′gus, any fungus of the order Nidulariales, having fruiting bodies that resemble a bird's nest containing eggs.

bird's′-nest soup′, a Chinese soup made from the mucilaginous lining of the nests of the Asiatic swift. [1870–75]

bird•song (bûrd′sông′, -song′), *n.* the singing or calling of birds, esp. songbirds. [BIRD + SONG]

bird′-voiced tree′ frog′ (bûrd′voist′), a frog, *Hyla avivoca,* of the southern U.S., having a birdlike, whistling call.

bird′ walk′, an excursion, usually undertaken as a group with an expert leader, for observing and studying birds in their natural habitat.

bird-watch (bûrd′woch′), *v.i.* to identify wild birds and observe their actions and habits in their natural habitat as a recreation. Also, **bird′watch′.** [1945–50; back formation from BIRD WATCHER]

bird′ watch′er, a person who identifies and observes birds in their natural habitat as a recreation. [1900–05]

bi•rec•tan•gu•lar (bī′rek tang′gyə lər), *adj. Geom.* having two right angles. [BI-[1] + RECTANGULAR]

bi•re•frin•gence (bī′ri frin′jəns), *n. Optics.* See **double refraction.** [1885–90; BI-[1] + REFRINGENCE] —**bi′re•frin′gent,** *adj.*

bi•reme (bī′rēm), *n. Naut.* a galley having two banks or tiers of oars. [1590–1600; < L *birēmis* two-oared, having two banks of oars (*bi-* BI-[1] + *rēm(us)* oar + *-is* adj. suffix)]

bi•ret•ta (bə ret′ə), *n.* a stiff square cap with three or four upright projecting pieces extending from the center of the top to the edge, worn by ecclesiastics. Also, **berretta, birretta.** [1590–1600; < It *berretta,* fem. var. of *berretto* < OPr *berret* < ML *birrettum* cap, equiv. to LL *birr(us)* BIRRUS + *-ettum* -ET; appar. by the development: hooded cloak > hood > cap; cf. ML (ca. 800) *byrrus* short hood (*cuculla brevis*)]

biretta

bi•ri (bēr′ē), *n., pl.* **-ris.** bidi.

birk (bûrk; *Scot.* birk), *n., adj., v.t. Scot. and North Eng.* birch. [bef. 900; ME *byrk,* OE *birc,* by-form of *birce* BIRCH]

birk•en (bûr′kən; *Scot.* bir′kən), *adj. Scot. and North Eng.* birchen; birch. [1250–1300; ME; see BIRK, -EN[2]]

Bir•ken•head (bûr′kən hed′), *n.* a seaport in Merseyside metropolitan county, in W England, on the Mersey River opposite Liverpool. 135,750.

Bir•ket Ka•run (bir′kit kə ro͞on′), a lake in N Egypt. 25 mi. (40 km) long; ab. 5 mi. (8 km) wide; 90 sq. mi. (233 sq. km). Also, **Bir′ket Qâ•run′.**

bir•kie (bûr′kē; *Scot.* bir′kē), *n. Scot.* an aggressive, independent man. [1715–25; of uncert. orig.]

birl (bûrl), *v.t.* **1.** *Chiefly Northern U.S. Lumbering.* to cause (a floating log) to rotate rapidly by treading upon it. **2.** *Brit.* to spin or cause to rotate. —*v.i.* **3.** *Chiefly Northern U.S. Lumbering.* to cause a floating log to rotate rapidly by treading on it. **4.** *Brit.* **a.** to move or rotate rapidly. **b.** *Informal.* to spend money freely. **c.** *Informal.* to gamble. —*n.* **5.** *Brit. Informal.* an attempt; a gamble. [1715–25; perh. b. BIRR[1] and WHIRL, influenced, in some senses, by BIRLE] —**birl′er,** *n.*

birle (bûrl; *Scot.* birl), *v.,* **birled, birl•ing.** *Chiefly Scot.* —*v.t.* **1.** to pour (a drink) or pour a drink for. —*v.i.* **2.** to drink deeply; carouse. [bef. 1000; ME *birlen,* OE *byrelian,* deriv. of *byrele* butler; akin to BEAR[1]]

birl•ing (bûr′ling), *n. Chiefly Northern U.S.* a game played by lumberjacks, in which each tries to balance longest on a floating log while rotating the log with the feet. [BIRL + -ING[1]]

Bir•ming•ham (bûr′ming əm *for 1;* bûr′ming ham′ *for 2, 3*), *n.* **1.** a city in West Midlands, in central England. 1,084,600. **2.** a city in central Alabama. 284,413. **3.** a city in SE Michigan, near Detroit. 21,689.

bir•ne (bir′nə), *n.* boule[1] (def. 1). [< G: lit., pear]

Bi•ro•bi•dzhan (bir′ō bi jän′), *n.* a city in and the capital of the Jewish Autonomous Region, in E Siberia, in the SE Russian Federation in Asia, W of Khabarovsk. 82,000. Also, **Bi′ro•bi•jan′.**

bi•ro•ta (bi rot′ə), *n. Rom. Antiq.* a two-wheeled cart, usually drawn by three mules, used for transporting commercial goods and one or two passengers. [< L, n.

use of fem. of *birotus* two-wheeled, equiv. to *bi-* BI-[1] + *rot(a)* wheel + *-us* adj. suffix]

birr[1] (bûr), *n.* **1.** force; energy; vigor. **2.** emphasis in statement, speech, etc. **3.** a whirring sound. —*v.i.* **4.** to move with or make a whirring sound. [1275–1325; ME *bire, bur,* OE *byre* strong wind; c. Icel *byrr* favorable wind; akin to BEAR[1]]

birr[2] (bēr), *n., pl.* **birr.** a paper money, silver coin, and monetary unit of Ethiopia, equal to 100 cents: replaced the Ethiopian dollar in 1976.

bir•ret•ta (bə ret′ə), *n.* biretta.

bir•rus (bir′əs), *n., pl.* **bir•ri** (bir′ī). a hooded cloak of coarse wool, a common article of apparel in the later Roman Empire. Also, **byrrus.** [< LL, perh. < Celtic *birros short (> Welsh *byrr,* MIr *berr*); for sense cf. SHIRT]

birse (bûrs; *Scot.* birs), *n. Scot.* **1.** a short hair of the beard or body; a bristle. **2.** anger; rage. [bef. 900; OE *byrst;* c. OHG *borst, burst,* ON *burst.* See BRISTLE]

birth (bûrth), *n.* **1.** an act or instance of being born: *the day of his birth.* **2.** the act or process of bearing or bringing forth offspring; childbirth; parturition: *a difficult birth.* **3.** lineage; extraction; descent: *of Grecian birth.* **4.** high or noble lineage: *to be foolishly vain about one's birth.* **5.** natural heritage: *a musician by birth.* **6.** any coming into existence; origin; beginning: *the birth of an idea.* **7.** *Archaic.* something that is born. **8. give birth to, a.** to bear (a child). **b.** to initiate; originate: *Her hobby gave birth to a successful business.* —*v.t. Chiefly South Midland and Southern U.S.* **9.** to give birth to. **10.** to assist in giving birth; act as midwife for. [1150–1200; ME *byrthe* < Scand; cf. OSw *byrth;* c. OE *gebyrd,* OHG *giburt,* Goth *gabaurths*]
—**Syn. 3.** parentage, ancestry, line, blood, family, race. **6.** start, commencement, inception, genesis; launching, inauguration.

birth′ canal′, the passage through which the young of mammals pass during birth, formed by the cervix, vagina, and vulva.

birth′ certif′icate, an official form recording the birth of a baby and containing pertinent data, as name, sex, date, place, and parents. [1895–1900]

birth′ control′, regulation of the number of children born through the deliberate control or prevention of conception. Cf. **family planning** (def. 1). [1914, *Amer.*]

birth′-con•trol pill′ (bûrth′kən trōl′), an oral contraceptive for women, containing the hormones estrogen and progesterone or progesterone alone, that inhibits ovulation, fertilization, or implantation of a fertilized ovum, causing temporary infertility. [1955–60]

birth•day (bûrth′dā′), *n.* **1.** the anniversary of a birth. **2.** the day of a person's birth. **3.** a day marking or commemorating the origin, founding, or beginning of something. **4.** the festivities or celebration marking such a day or anniversary. [1350–1400; ME; see BIRTH, DAY]

birth′day suit′, bare skin; nakedness: *They were sunbathing in their birthday suits.* [1745–55]

birth′ de′fect, *Pathol.* any physical, mental, or biochemical abnormality present at birth. Also called **congenital defect.**

birth•ing (bûr′thing), *n.* an act or instance of giving birth, esp. by natural childbirth. [1925–30]

birth′ing room′, a section of a hospital or an outpatient facility set aside and equipped for childbirth and usually simulating a home environment in which family members or friends may be present during the delivery.

birth•mark (bûrth′märk′), *n.* a minor disfigurement or blemish on a person's skin at birth; nevus. [1570–80; BIRTH + MARK[1]]

birth′ name′, the surname given a person at birth.

birth•night (bûrth′nīt′), *n.* **1.** the night of a person's birth, esp. a birthday celebration for royalty. **2.** the anniversary of such a date. **3.** the celebration of a royal birthday. [1620–30; BIRTH + NIGHT]

Birth′ of a Na′tion, The, an American film (1915), directed by D. W. Griffith.

birth′ pangs′, **1.** pains associated with the process of childbirth. **2.** *Informal.* the hardships and difficulties accompanying a major innovation, change, or new venture. [1885–90]

birth′ par′ent. See **biological parent.** Also, **birth′•par′ent.**

birth•place (bûrth′plās′), *n.* place of birth or origin. [1600–10; BIRTH + PLACE]

birth•rate (bûrth′rāt′), *n.* the proportion of births to the total population in a place in a given time, usually expressed as a quantity per 1000 of population. [1855–60; BIRTH + RATE[1]]

birth•right (bûrth′rīt′), *n.* any right or privilege to which a person is entitled by birth: *Democracy maintains that freedom is a birthright.* [1525–35; BIRTH + RIGHT]

birth•root (bûrth′ro͞ot′, -ro͝ot′), *n.* **1.** Also called **birthwort, purple trillium.** a trillium, *Trillium erectum,* the roots of which were formerly used in medicine as an astringent. **2.** any of certain other species of trillium. [1815–25; BIRTH + ROOT[1]]

birth•stone (bûrth′stōn′), *n.* a precious or semiprecious stone traditionally associated with a particular month or sign of the zodiac and believed to attract good fortune. See table in next column. [1905–10; BIRTH + STONE]

birth•stool (bûrth′sto͞ol′), *n.* a specially shaped seat formerly used in childbirth. [1620–30; BIRTH + STOOL]

birth′ trau′ma, *Psychoanal.* an emotional shock caused by being born. [1925–30]

birth•weight (bûrth′wāt′), *n.* the weight of an infant at birth. [BIRTH + WEIGHT]

birth•wort (bûrth′wûrt′, -wôrt′), *n.* **1.** any of various plants of the genus *Aristolochia,* esp. *A. clematitis,* an Old World species reputed to facilitate childbirth. Cf. **birthwort family. 2.** any of various other plants believed to aid childbirth. **3.** birthroot. [1545–55; BIRTH + WORT[2]]

birth′wort fam′ily, the plant family Aristolochiaceae, typified by mostly tropical woody vines and herbaceous plants, having alternate, heart-shaped leaves and flowers lacking true petals but having petallike sepals, and including the birthwort and wild ginger.

bis[1] (bis), *adv.* **1.** twice. **2.** again (used interjectionally as an enthusiastic call for the repetition of a musical performance). [1810–20; < It < L; OL *duis* TWICE]

bis[2] (bis), *n.* a sheer, often embroidered linen, used in the manufacture of altar cloths. Also, **bisso.** [1350–1400; ME < L *byssus* BYSSUS]

B.I.S., **1.** Bank for International Settlements. **2.** British Information Services.

Bi•sa•yan (bi sī′ən), *n., pl.* **-yans,** (*esp. collectively*) **-yan.** Visayan.

Bi•sa•yas (bē sä′yäs), *n.pl.* Spanish name of the **Visayan Islands.**

Bis•cay (bis′kā, -kē), *n.* **Bay of,** a bay of the Atlantic between W France and N Spain.

bis′cay green′ (bis′kā, -kē), a yellowish green. [1955–60]

Bis′cayne Bay′ (bis′kān, bis kān′), an inlet of the Atlantic Ocean, on the SE coast of Florida, separating the cities of Miami and Miami Beach.

bis•cot•to (bē skôt′tô; *Eng.* bi skot′ō), *n., pl.* ***bis•cot•ti*** (bē skôt′tē; *Eng.* bi skot′ē). *Italian.* a cookie or cracker.

bis•cuit (bis′kit), *n.* **1.** a kind of bread in small, soft cakes, raised with baking powder or soda, or sometimes with yeast. **2.** *Chiefly Brit.* **a.** a dry and crisp or hard bread in thin, flat cakes, made without yeast or other raising agent; a cracker. **b.** a cookie. **3.** a pale-brown color. **4.** Also called **bisque.** *Ceram.* unglazed earthenware or porcelain after firing. **5.** Also called **preform.** a piece of plastic or the like, prepared for pressing into a phonograph record. —*adj.* **6.** having the color biscuit. [1300–50; ME *bysquyte* < MF *biscuit* (ML *biscoctus*), var. of *bescuit* seamen's bread, lit., twice cooked, equiv. to *bes* BIS[1] + *cuit,* ptp. of *cuire* < L *coquere* to COOK[1]] —**bis′•cuit•like′,** *adj.*

bis•cuit (bēs kwē′), *n. French.* a cookie or cracker.

bis′cuit bread′, *Chiefly South Midland and Southern U.S.* biscuits or a biscuit: *I like biscuit bread more than corn bread for supper.* [1400–50; late ME]

bis•cuit-fired (bis′kit fī°rd′), *adj.* (of a ceramic object) fired to harden the body.

bis′cuit torto′ni (bis′kit, bis′kwē), an individual portion of tortoni, frozen and served in a small cup, often topped with ground almonds.

bis′cuit ware′, bisque[3] (def. 2).

bi•sect (*v.* bī sekt′, bī′sekt; *n.* bī′sekt), *v.t.* **1.** to cut or divide into two equal or nearly equal parts. **2.** *Geom.* to cut or divide into two equal parts: *to bisect an angle.* **3.** to intersect or cross: *the spot where the railroad tracks bisect the highway.* —*v.i.* **4.** to split into two, as a road; fork: *There's a charming old inn just before the road bisects.* —*n.* **5.** Also called **split.** *Philately.* a portion of a stamp, usually half, used for payment of a proportionate amount of the face value of the whole stamp. [1640–50; BI-[1] + -SECT] —**bi•sec′tion,** *n.* —**bi•sec′tion•al,** *adj.* —**bi•sec′tion•al•ly,** *adv.*

bi•sec•tor (bī sek′tər, bī′sek-), *n. Geom.* a line or plane that bisects an angle or line segment. [1860–65; BISECT + -OR[2]]

bi•sec•trix (bī sek′triks), *n., pl.* **bi•sec•tri•ces** (bī′sek-trī′sēz). **1.** *Crystall.* an imaginary line bisecting either the acute angle **(acute bisectrix)** or the obtuse angle **(obtuse bisectrix)** of the optic axes of a biaxial crystal. **2.** *Geom.* a bisector. [1850–55; BISEC(T) + -TRIX]

bi•sel•li•um (bī sel′ē əm), *n., pl.* **-sel•li•a** (-sel′ē ə). an ancient Roman seat of honor for two persons. [< L, equiv. to *bi-* BI-[1] + *sell(a)* seat (c. SETTLE[2]) + *-ium* -IUM]

bi•se•ri•al (bī sēr′ē əl), *adj. Statistics.* of or pertaining to the correlation between two sets of measurements, one set of which is limited to one of two values. [1830–40; BI-[1] + SERIAL] —**bi•se′ri•al•ly,** *adv.*

bi•ser•rate (bī ser′āt, -it), *adj. Bot.* notched like a saw, with the teeth also notched; doubly serrate. [1825–35; BI-[1] + SERRATE]

bi•sex•u•al (bī sek′sho͞o əl), *adj.* **1.** *Biol.* **a.** of both sexes. **b.** combining male and female organs in one individual; hermaphroditic. **2.** sexually responsive to both sexes; ambisexual. —*n.* **3.** *Biol.* an animal or plant that has the reproductive organs of both sexes. **4.** a person sexually responsive to both sexes; ambisexual. [1815–25; BI-[1] + SEXUAL] —**bi′sex•u•al′i•ty, bi•sex′u•al•ism** *n.* —**bi•sex′u•al•ly,** *adv.*

BIRTHSTONES

Month	Birthstone
January	Garnet
February	Amethyst
March	Aquamarine or Bloodstone
April	Diamond
May	Emerald
June	Pearl, Alexandrite, or Moonstone
July	Ruby
August	Peridot or Sardonyx
September	Sapphire
October	Opal or Tourmaline
November	Topaz
December	Turquoise or Zircon

Bish•kek (bish kek′), *n.* the capital of Kirghizia (Kyrgyzstan), in the N part. 616,000. formerly, **Pishpek** (until 1926), **Frunze** (1926–91).

Bisho (bē′shō), *n.* a town in and the capital of Ciskei, SE Africa.

bish•op (bish′əp), *n., v.,* **-oped, -op•ing.** —*n.* **1.** a person who supervises a number of local churches or a diocese, being in the Greek, Roman Catholic, Anglican, and other churches a member of the highest order of the ministry. **2.** a spiritual supervisor, overseer, or the like. **3.** *Chess.* one of two pieces of the same color that may be moved any unobstructed distance diagonally, one on white squares and the other on black. **4.** a hot drink made of port wine, oranges, cloves, etc. **5.** Also called **bish′op bird′.** any of several colorful African weaverbirds of the genus *Euplectes,* often kept as pets. —*v.t.* **6.** to appoint to the office of bishop. [bef. 900; ME; OE *bisc(e)op* < VL **ebiscopus,* for LL *episcopus* < Gk *epískopos* overseer, equiv. to *epi-* EPI- + *skopós* watcher; see SCOPE] —**bish′op•less,** *adj.* —**bish′op•like′,** *adj.*

Bish•op (bish′əp), *n.* **1. Elizabeth,** 1911–79, U.S. poet. **2. Hazel** (*Gladys*), born 1906, U.S. chemist and businesswoman. **3. John Peale,** 1892–1944, U.S. poet and essayist. **4. Morris** (*Gilbert*), 1893–1973, U.S. humorist, poet, and biographer. **5. William Avery** (*"Billy"*), 1894–1956, Canadian aviator: helped to establish Canadian air force.

bish•op•ric (bish′əp rik), *n.* the see, diocese, or office of a bishop. [bef. 900; ME *bisshoprike,* OE *biscoprīce,* equiv. to *biscop* BISHOP + *rīce* realm; see RICH]

Bish′ops' Bi′ble, an English translation of the Bible made under the direction of Matthew Parker and published in 1568: the recognized translation of the Bible in England until the Authorized (King James) Version of 1611. [so called because a number of the scholars who worked on the translation were Anglican bishops]

bish•op's-cap (bish′əps kap′), *n.* miterwort (def. 1). [1830–40, *Amer.*]

Bish′op's Hat′field, Hatfield.

Bish′op's ring′, *Meteorol.* a reddish-brown corona occasionally seen around the sun, caused by volcanic dust in the atmosphere. [after Sereno E. *Bishop* (1827–1909), U.S. missionary in Hawaii, who described such rings, resulting from the explosion of Krakatoa, in 1883]

bish•op's-weed (bish′əps wēd′), *n.* goutweed. [1605–15]

bish′op vi′olet, a reddish purple. —**bish′op-vi′o•let,** *adj.*

Bi•si•tun (bē′si to͞on′), *n.* Behistun.

bisk (bisk), *n.* bisque[1].

Bisk (byēsk), *n.* a city in the S Russian Federation in Asia, near the Ob River, SE of Barnaul. 231,000. Also, **Biisk, Biysk.**

Bis•kra (bis′krä), *n.* a town and oasis in NE Algeria, in the Sahara. 59,000.

bis•ma•nol (bis′mə nôl′, -nol′), *n. Metall.* a highly ferromagnetic alloy of bismuth and manganese, having a high degree of magnetic force. [BIS(MUTH) + MAN(GANESE) + -OL[1]]

Bis•marck (biz′märk; *for 1 also Ger.* bis′märk), *n.* **1. Ot•to von** (ot′ō von; *Ger.* ô′tō fən), 1815–98, German statesman: first chancellor of modern German Empire 1871–90. **2.** a city in and the capital of North Dakota, in the central part. 44,485. **3.** (*often l.c.*) **a.** *Chiefly Northern U.S.* a jelly doughnut. **b.** *Chiefly Midland U.S.* a fried cruller.

Bis′marck Archipel′ago, a group of islands in Papua New Guinea, in the W central Pacific Ocean, including the Admiralty Islands, New Britain, New Ireland, and adjacent islands. ab. 23,000 sq. mi. (59,570 sq. km).

Bis′marck her′ring, salted fillet and roe of herring, pickled in vinegar, white wine, and spices, served cold, often as an hors d'oeuvre. [1930–35]

Bis•marck•i•an (biz mär′kē ən), *adj.* of, pertaining to, or resembling Otto von Bismarck, esp. in respect to his aggressiveness in politics and diplomacy. [1865–70; BISMARCK + -IAN] —**Bis•marck′i•an•ism,** *n.*

bis•mil•lah (bis mil′ə), *interj. Arabic.* in the name of Allah.

bis•muth (biz′məth), *n. Chem.* a brittle, grayish-white, red-tinged, metallic element used in the manufacture of fusible alloys and in medicine. *Symbol:* Bi; *at. wt.:* 208.980; *at. no.:* 83. [1660–70; earlier *bismutum* < NL *bisemūtum,* Latinized form of G *Wissmuth* (now *Wismut*) < ?] —**bis′muth•al,** *adj.*

bis′muth chro′mate, *Chem.* an orange-red, amorphous, water-insoluble powder, $Bi_2O_3 \cdot 2CrO_3$, used chiefly as a pigment in paints. Also called **basic dichromate.**

bis•mu•thic (biz myo͞o′thik, -muth′ik, biz′mə thik), *adj. Chem.* of or containing bismuth, esp. in the pentavalent state. [1790–1800; BISMUTH + -IC]

bis•muth•ine (biz′mə thēn′, -thin), *n. Chem.* **1.** an unstable hydride of bismuth, BiH_3, analogous to arsine and stibine. **2.** any derivative of this compound in which the hydrogen atoms are replaced by one or more organic groups. [BISMUTH + -INE[2]]

bis•muth•in•ite (biz muth′ə nīt′, biz′mə thə-), *n.* a mineral, bismuth sulfide, Bi_2S_3, occurring in lead-gray masses: an ore of bismuth. Also called **bis′muth glance′.** [BISMUTHINE + -ITE[1]]

bis·muth·ous (biz′mə thəs), *adj. Chem.* containing trivalent bismuth. [1880–85; BISMUTH + -OUS]

bis′muth oxychlo′ride, *Chem.* a white, crystalline, water-insoluble powder, BiOCl, used chiefly in the manufacture of pigments, face powders, and artificial pearls.

bis·muth·yl (biz′mə thil), *n. Chem.* the univalent group BiO^+, occurring in certain bismuth salts, as bismuth oxychloride, BiOCl. [BISMUTH + -YL]

bis·mut·ite (biz′mə tīt′), *n.* a mineral, bismuth carbonate, resulting from the alteration of bismuth minerals: a minor source of bismuth. [< G *Bismutit,* equiv. to *Bismut* BISMUTH + *-it* -ITE[1]]

bis·na·ga (bis nä′gə), *n.* any of several thorny cactuses of the genera *Echinocactus, Ferocactus,* and *Astrophytum* of the southwestern U.S. Also, **biznaga.** [1835–45, *Amer.*; < MexSp *biznaga,* (prob. by assoc. with *biznaga* parsnip) r. earlier *vitznauac* < Nahuatl *huitznāhuac,* equiv. to *huitz(tli)* thorn + *-nāhua-* vicinity + -*c(o)* locative suffix]

bison, *Bison bison,* 7 ft. (2.1 m) high at shoulder; head and body 10½ ft. (3.2 m); tail 1½ ft. (0.5 m)

bi·son (bī′sən, -zən), *n., pl.* **-son.** **1.** Also called **American bison, American buffalo.** a North American, oxlike ruminant, *Bison bison,* having a large head and high, humped shoulders: formerly common in North America, its small remaining population in isolated western areas of the U.S. and Canada is now protected. **2.** Also called **wisent.** a related animal, *Bison bonasus,* of Europe, less shaggy and slightly larger than the American bison: now greatly reduced in number. Cf. **buffalo.** [1350–1400; ME *bisontes* (pl.) < L (nom. sing. *bisōn*) < Gmc; cf. OHG *wisunt,* OE *wesend,* ON *visundr*] **—bi·son·tine** (bī′sən tīn′, -zən-), *adj.*

bi·sphe·noid (bī sfē′noid), *n. Crystall.* a tetrahedral form, each edge of which is bisected by the perpendicular bisecting the edge that does not intersect it. Also called **disphenoid.** [BI-[1] + SPHENOID]

bisque[1] (bisk), *n.* **1.** a thick cream soup, esp. of puréed shellfish or vegetables. **2.** ice cream made with powdered macaroons or nuts. Also, **bisk.** [1640–50; < F, of uncert. orig.]

bisque[2] (bisk), *n. Sports.* a point, extra turn, or the like, as in court tennis or croquet. [1605–15; < F, earlier *biscaye,* of uncert. orig.]

bisque[3] (bisk), *n.* **1.** biscuit (def. 4). **2.** Also called **biscuit ware.** vitreous china that is left unglazed. **3.** pinkish-tan. *—adj.* **4.** having the color bisque. [1655–65; short for BISCUIT]

Bis·sau (bi sou′), *n.* a seaport in and the capital of Guinea-Bissau, in the W part. 75,000. Also, **Bis·são** (bē-soun′).

bis·sex·tile (bī seks′til, -tīl, bi-), *adj.* **1.** containing or noting the extra day of leap year: *The years 1980 and 1984 were both bissextile.* *—n.* **2.** See **leap year.** [1585–95; < LL *bi(s)sextilis (annus)* leap year, equiv. to *bissext(us)* BISSEXTUS + *-ilis* -ILE]

bis·sex·tus (bī seks′təs, bi-), *n.* February 29th: the extra day added to the Julian calendar every fourth year (except those evenly divisible by 400) to compensate for the approximately six hours a year by which the common year of 365 days falls short of the solar year. [< LL *bissextus (diēs)* intercalary (day); see BIS[1], SEXT; so called because the 6th day before the Calends of March (Feb. 24th) appeared twice every leap year]

bis·so (bis′ō), *n.* bis[2].

bis·so·na·ta (bis′ə nä′tə, -nā′-), *n.* a coarse, dark woolen cloth constructed in plain weave, used in the manufacture of clerical vestments. [of uncert. orig.]

bi·sta·ble (bī stā′bəl), *adj.* (of an electric or electronic circuit) having two stable states. [1945–50; BI-[1] + STABLE[2]]

bi·state (bī′stāt′), *adj.* **1.** of, pertaining to, or involving two states, esp. of the U.S.: *a bistate water commission.* **2.** of, pertaining to, or involving the area where two states adjoin: *Three million people work in the bistate area.* [1915–20, *Amer.*; BI-[1] + STATE]

bis·ter (bis′tər), *n.* bistre. **—bis′tered,** *adj.*

bis·tort (bis′tôrt), *n.* **1.** Also called **snakeweed.** a European plant, *Polygonum bistorta,* of the buckwheat family, having a twisted root, which is sometimes used as an astringent. **2.** any of several related plants, as *P. viviparum* **(alpine bistort).** [1570–80; < ML *bistorta* twice twisted. See BIS[1], TORT]

bis·tou·ry (bis′tə rē), *n., pl.* **-ries.** a long, narrow surgical knife. [1745–50; < F *bistouri,* MF *bistorin* < Upper It *bistorino,* for It *pistorino* pertaining to PISTOIA, a city famous for its cutlery]

bis·tre (bis′tər), *n.* **1.** a brown pigment extracted from the soot of wood, often used in pen and wash drawings. **2.** a yellowish to dark-brown color. Also, **bister.** [1720–30; < F, MF, of obscure orig.] **—bis′tred,** *adj.*

bis·tro (bis′trō; *Fr.* bē strō′), *n., pl.* **bis·tros** (bis′trōz; *Fr.* bē strō′). **1.** a small, modest, European-style restaurant or café. **2.** a small nightclub or restaurant. [1920–25; < F *bistro(t),* orig. argot, first attested in the sense "proprietor of a tavern" (1884); of obscure orig.]

CONCISE ETYMOLOGY KEY: <, descended or borrowed from; >, whence; b., blend of, blended; c., cognate with; cf., compare; deriv., derivative; equiv., equivalent; imit., imitative; obl., oblique; r., replacing; s., stem; sp., spelling, spelled; resp., respelling, respelled; trans., translation; ?, origin unknown; *, unattested; ‡, probably earlier than. See the full key inside the front cover.

bi·sul·cate (bī sul′kāt), *adj.* **1.** with two grooves. **2.** cloven-hoofed. [1825–35; < L *bisulc(us)* two-furrowed, cloven (see BI-[1], SULCUS) + -ATE[1]]

bi·sul·fate (bī sul′fāt), *n. Chem.* a salt of sulfuric acid, containing the HSO_4^- group; an acid sulfate; a hydrogen sulfate, as sodium bisulfate, $NaHSO_4$. Also, **bi·sul′phate.** [1860–65; BI-[1] + SULFATE]

bi·sul·fide (bī sul′fīd, -fid), *n. Chem.* a disulfide. Also, **bi·sul′phide.** [1860–65; BI-[1] + SULFIDE]

bi·sul·fite (bī sul′fīt), *n. Chem.* a salt of sulfurous acid, containing the HSO_3^- group; an acid sulfite; a hydrogen sulfite, as sodium bisulfite, $NaHSO_3$. Also, **bi·sul′phite.** [1885–90; BI-[1] + SULFITE]

Bi·su·tun (bē′sə to͞on′), *n.* Behistun.

bi·swing (bī′swing′), *adj.* **1.** (of a garment) made with a deep pleat starting at the back waistline or belt and extending up to the shoulder on each side, to avoid constriction when the wearer's arms are extended. *—n.* **2.** a garment made with such pleats at the back, esp. a jacket. [1965–70]

bit[1] (bit), *n., v.,* **bit·ted, bit·ting.** *—n.* **1.** *Mach.* **a.** a removable drilling or boring tool for use in a brace, drill press, or the like. **b.** a removable boring head used on certain kinds of drills, as a rock drill. **c.** a device for drilling oil wells or the like, consisting of a horizontally rotating blade or an assembly of rotating toothed wheels. **2.** the mouthpiece of a bridle, having fittings at each end to which the reins are fastened. See illus. under **harness.** **3.** anything that curbs or restrains. **4.** the blade or iron of a carpenter's plane. **5.** the cutting part of an ax or hatchet. **6.** the wide portion at the end of an ordinary key that moves the bolt. **7. take the bit in** or **between one's teeth,** to cast off control; willfully go one's own way: *He took the bit in his teeth and acted against his parents' wishes.* *—v.t.* **8.** to put a bit in the mouth of (a horse). **9.** to curb or restrain with, or as with, a bit. **10.** to grind a bit on (a key). [bef. 900; ME *bite,* OE: action of biting; c. G *Biss,* ON *bit.* See BITE] **—bit′less,** *adj.*

bits (def. 1a) A, auger bit; B, straight shank drill bit

bit[2] (bit), *n.* **1.** a small piece or quantity of anything: *a bit of string.* **2.** a short time: *Wait a bit.* **3.** *Informal.* an amount equivalent to 12½ U.S. cents (used only in even multiples): *two bits; six bits.* **4.** an act, performance, or routine: *She's doing the Camille bit, pretending to be near collapse.* **5.** a stereotypic or habitual set of behaviors, attitudes, or styles associated with an individual, role, situation, etc.: *the whole Wall Street bit.* **6.** Also called **bit part.** a very small role, as in a play or motion picture, containing few or no lines. Cf. **walk-on** (def. 1). **7.** any small coin: *a threepenny bit.* **8.** a Spanish or Mexican silver real worth 12½ cents, formerly current in parts of the U.S. **9. a bit,** rather or somewhat; a little: *a bit sleepy.* **10. a bit much,** somewhat overdone or beyond tolerability. **11. bit by bit,** by degrees; gradually: *saving money bit by bit.* **12. do one's bit,** to contribute one's share to an effort: *They all did their bit during the war.* **13. every bit,** quite; just: *every bit as good.* [bef. 1000; ME *bite,* OE *bita* bit, morsel; c. G *Bissen,* ON *biti.* See BITE]
—Syn. 1. particle, speck, grain, mite; whit, iota, jot; scrap, fragment.

bit[3] (bit), *n. Computers.* **1.** Also called **binary digit.** a single, basic unit of information, used in connection with computers and information theory. **2.** baud. [1945–50; B(INARY) + (DIG)IT]

bit[4] (bit), *v.* pt. and a pp. of **bite.**

B.I.T., Bachelor of Industrial Technology.

bi·tar·trate (bī tär′trāt), *n. Chem.* a tartrate in which only one of the two acidic hydrogen atoms of tartaric acid is replaced by a metal or positive group; an acid tartrate; a hydrogen tartrate, as sodium bitartrate. [1875–80; BI-[1] + TARTRATE]

bit·brace (bit′brās′), *n. Mach., Carpentry.* brace (def. 3). [BIT[1] + BRACE]

bitch (bich), *n.* **1.** a female dog. **2.** a female of canines generally. **3.** *Slang.* **a.** a malicious, unpleasant, selfish person, esp. a woman. **b.** a lewd woman. **4.** *Slang.* **a.** a complaint. **b.** anything difficult or unpleasant: *The test was a bitch.* **c.** anything memorable, esp. something exceptionally good: *That last big party he threw was a real bitch.* *—v.i.* **5.** *Slang.* to complain; gripe: *They bitched about the service, then about the bill.* *—v.t.* **6.** *Slang.* to spoil; bungle (sometimes fol. by *up*): *He bitched the job completely. You really bitched up this math problem.* [bef. 1000; ME *bicche,* OE *bicce;* c. ON *bikkja*]

bitch·en (bich′ən), *adj. Slang.* marvelous; wonderful. Also, **bitch′in′.** [BITCH + *-en, -in′* informal or dial. var. of -ING[2] (here forming nonparticipial adj.)]

bitch·er·y (bich′ə rē), *n.* behavior characteristic of a bitch. [1525–35; BITCH + -ERY]

bitch′ god′dess, worldly or material success personified as a goddess, esp. one requiring sacrifice and being essentially destructive: *He went to New York to worship the bitch goddess.* [1905–10]

bitch·y (bich′ē), *adj.,* **bitch·i·er, bitch·i·est.** *Slang.* characteristic of a bitch; spiteful; malicious. [1925–30; BITCH + -Y[1]] **—bitch′i·ly,** *adv.* **—bitch′i·ness,** *n.*
—Syn. hateful, mean, vicious, malevolent, invidious.

bite (bīt), *v.,* **bit, bit·ten** or **bit, bit·ing,** *n.* *—v.t.* **1.** to cut, wound, or tear with the teeth: *She bit the apple greedily. The lion bit his trainer.* **2.** to grip or hold with the teeth: *Stop biting your lip!* **3.** to sting, as does an insect. **4.** to cause to smart or sting: *an icy wind that bit our faces.* **5.** to sever with the teeth (often fol. by *off*): *Don't bite your nails. The child bit off a large piece of the candy bar.* **6.** to start to eat (often fol. by *into*): *She bit into her steak.* **7.** to clamp the teeth firmly on or around (often fol. by *on*): *He bit hard on the stick while they removed the bullet from his leg.* **8.** *Informal.* **a.** to take advantage of; cheat; deceive: *I got bitten in a mail-order swindle.* **b.** to annoy or upset; anger: *What's biting you, sorehead?* **9.** to eat into or corrode, as does an acid. **10.** to cut or pierce with, or as with, a weapon: *The sword split his helmet and bit him fatally.* **11.** *Etching.* to etch with acid (a copper or other surface) in such parts as are left bare of a protective coating. **12.** to take firm hold or act effectively on: *We need a clamp to bite the wood while the glue dries.* **13.** *Archaic.* to make a decided impression on; affect. *—v.i.* **14.** to press the teeth into something; attack with the jaws, bill, sting, etc.; snap: *Does your parrot bite?* **15.** *Angling.* (of fish) to take bait: *The fish aren't biting today.* **16.** to accept an offer or suggestion, esp. one intended to trick or deceive: *I knew it was a mistake, but I bit anyway.* **17.** *Informal.* to admit defeat in guessing: *I'll bite, who is it?* **18.** to act effectively; grip; hold: *This wood is so dry the screws don't bite.* **19. bite off more than one can chew,** to attempt something that exceeds one's capacity: *In trying to build a house by himself, he bit off more than he could chew.* **20. bite someone's head off,** to respond with anger or impatience to someone's question or comment: *He'll bite your head off if you ask for anything.* **21. bite the bullet.** See **bullet** (def. 6). **22. bite the dust.** See **dust** (def. 14). **23. bite the hand that feeds one,** to repay kindness with malice or injury: *When he berates his boss, he is biting the hand that feeds him.* *—n.* **24.** an act of biting. **25.** a wound made by biting: *a deep bite.* **26.** a cutting, stinging, or nipping effect: *the bite of an icy wind; the bite of whiskey on the tongue.* **27.** a piece bitten off: *Chew each bite carefully.* **28.** a small meal. **29.** a portion severed from the whole: *the government's weekly bite of my paycheck.* **30.** a morsel of food: *not a bite to eat.* **31.** the occlusion of one's teeth: *The dentist said I had a good bite.* **32.** *Mach.* **a.** the catch or hold that one object or one part of a mechanical apparatus has on another. **b.** a surface brought into contact to obtain a hold or grip, as in a lathe chuck or similar device. **c.** the amount of material that a mechanical shovel or the like can carry at one time. **33.** sharpness; incisiveness; effectiveness: *The bite of his story is spoiled by his slovenly style.* **34.** the roughness of the surface of a file. **35.** *Metalworking.* the maximum angle, measured from the center of a roll in a rolling mill, between a perpendicular and a line to the point of contact where a given object to be rolled will enter between the rolls. **36. put the bite on,** *Slang.* **a.** to solicit or attempt to borrow money or something of value from. **b.** to press for money, as in extortion: *They found out about his prison record and began to put the bite on him.* [bef. 1000; ME *biten,* OE *bītan;* c. OHG *bīzan* (G *beissen*), Goth *beitan,* ON *bīta;* akin to L *findere* to split] **—bit′a·ble, bite′a·ble,** *adj.*
—Syn. 1. gnaw, chew, nip. **27.** mouthful, morsel, taste; scrap, crumb, dab. **28.** snack, nosh.

bite·plate (bīt′plāt′), *n. Orthodontics.* a removable appliance worn in the mouth to separate the jaws so that some of the teeth will gradually shift upward or downward. Also, **bite′ plate′.** [BITE + PLATE[1]]

bit·er (bī′tər), *n.* **1.** a person or animal that bites, esp. habitually or viciously: *That dog is a biter.* **2.** *Chiefly Chesapeake Bay.* the larger claw of a crab. **3.** *Obs.* a cheat; swindler; fraud. [1250–1300; ME; see BITE, -ER[1]]

bite-size (bīt′sīz′), *adj.* **1.** small enough to fit in the mouth or be consumed in one or two bites: *bite-size candies.* **2.** very small. **3.** quickly or easily comprehended, resolved, etc.: *bite-size problems.* Also, **bite′-sized′.**

bite·wing (bīt′wing′), *n. Dentistry.* a holder for x-ray film with a projecting fin that is held between the teeth so as to show the crowns of the upper and lower teeth in one picture. [1935–40; BITE + WING]

bit′ gauge′, *Carpentry.* a device for stopping a bit when it has reached a desired depth. Also called **bit stop.**

Bi·thyn·i·a (bi thin′ē ə), *n.* an ancient state in NW Asia Minor. **—Bi·thyn′i·an,** *adj., n.*

bit·ing (bī′ting), *adj.* **1.** nipping; smarting; keen: *biting cold; a biting sensation on the tongue.* **2.** cutting; sarcastic: *a biting remark.* [1250–1300; ME *bitynge.* See BITE, -ING[2]] **—bit′ing·ly,** *adv.* **—bit′ing·ness,** *n.*
—Syn. 2. incisive, trenchant; caustic, mordant, scathing, lacerating.

bit′ing house′fly. See **stable fly.**

bit′ing louse′. See under **louse** (def. 2). [1895–1900]

bit′ing midge′, punkie. [1940–45]

bit′ key′, a key having a wing bit for moving a lever-like tumbler of a lock.

bit′ map′, a piece of text, a drawing, etc., represented, as on a computer display, by the activation of certain dots in a rectangular matrix of dots. **—bit′-mapped′,** *adj.*

Bi·to·la (bē′tô lä), *n.* a city in S Macedonia. 137,636. Serbo-Croatian, **Bi·tolj** (bē′tôl yə). Turkish, **Monastir.**

bi·ton·al (bī tōn′l), *adj. Music.* marked by or using bitonality. [BI-[1] + TONAL]

bi·to·nal·i·ty (bī′tō nal′i tē), *n., pl.* **-ties.** *Music.* the simultaneous occurrence of two tonalities in a composition. [1925–30; BI-[1] + TONALITY]

bit′ part′, bit[2] (def. 6). [1925–30]

bit′ play′er, an actor having a very small speaking part in a play, motion picture, etc. [1935–40]

bit·ser (bit′sər), *n. Australian Informal.* a mongrel dog. [1905–10; perh. BIT[2] + -S[3] + -ER[1]]

bit·stock (bit′stok′), *n. Mach., Carpentry.* brace (def. 3). [1880–85; BIT[1] + STOCK]

bit′ stop′, *Carpentry.* See **bit gauge.**

bit·sy (bit′sē), *adj.,* **-si·er, -si·est.** *Informal.* tiny; itty-bitty. [1900–05; BIT + -SY]

bitt (bit), *Naut.* —*n.* **1.** Also called **bollard.** a strong post of wood or iron projecting, usually in pairs, above the deck of a ship, used for securing cables, lines for towing, etc. —*v.t.* **2.** to wrap (a cable) around a bitt to secure it. [ME, perh. < D or LG; cf. D, LG *beting,* in same sense, akin to MHG *bizze* wooden peg, ON *biti* crossbeam]

bit·ten (bit′n), *v.* a pp. of **bite.**

bit·ter (bit′ər), *adj.,* **-er, -est,** *n., v., adv.* —*adj.* **1.** having a harsh, disagreeably acrid taste, like that of aspirin, quinine, wormwood, or aloes. **2.** producing one of the four basic taste sensations; not sour, sweet, or salt. **3.** hard to bear; grievous; distressful: *a bitter sorrow.* **4.** causing pain; piercing; stinging: *a bitter chill.* **5.** characterized by intense antagonism or hostility: *bitter hatred.* **6.** hard to admit or accept: *a bitter lesson.* **7.** resentful or cynical: *bitter words.* —*n.* **8.** that which is bitter; bitterness: *Learn to take the bitter with the sweet.* **9.** *Brit.* a very dry ale having a strong taste of hops. —*v.t.* **10.** to make bitter: *herbs employed to bitter vermouth.* —*adv.* **11.** extremely; very; exceedingly: *a bitter cold night.* [bef. 1000; ME, OE *biter;* c. G *bitter,* ON *bitr,* Goth *baitrs;* akin to BITE] —**bit′ter·ish,** *adj.* —**bit′ter·ly,** *adv.* —**bit′ter·ness,** *n.*
—**Syn. 1.** acrid, biting, distasteful. **3.** distressing, poignant, painful. **4.** biting, nipping. **5.** fierce, cruel, ruthless, relentless. **7.** acrimonious, caustic, sardonic, scornful.

bit′ter al′mond. See under **almond** (def. 1).

bit′ter al′mond oil′, *Chem.* See **almond oil** (def. 2).

bit′ter ap′ple, colocynth (defs. 1, 2). [1860–65]

bit′ter cassa′va. See under **cassava** (def. 1).

bit′ter cress′, any plant belonging to the genus *Cardamine,* of the mustard family, having usually pinnate leaves and clusters of white, pink, or purple flowers. [1885–90]

bit′ter dock′. See under **dock**[4] (def. 1).

bit·ter end (bit′ər end′ *for 1;* bit′ər end′ *for 2*), **1.** the conclusion of a difficult or unpleasant situation; the last or furthest extremity: *Despite the unpleasant scenes in the movie, she insisted on staying until the bitter end.* **2.** *Naut.* **a.** the inboard end of an anchor chain or cable, secured in the chain locker of a vessel. **b.** the end of any chain or cable. [1620–30 in form *bitters end;* prob. BITT + ER[1], later taken as BITTER]

bit·ter·end·er (bit′ər en′dər), *n.* a person who persists until the bitter end without compromising or yielding; diehard. [1840–50, *Amer.;* BITTER END + -ER[1]]

bit′ter herb′, 1. an Old World herb, *Centaurium erythraea,* used dried in medicine as a tonic. **2.** the turtlehead, *Chelone glabra,* used in medicine as a tonic, cathartic, and anthelmintic. **3.** *Judaism.* an herb that tastes bitter, as horseradish, traditionally eaten at the Seder, and serving as a reminder of the Israelites' slavery in Egypt.

bit′ter lake′, a salt lake containing in solution a high concentration of sulfates, carbonates, and chlorides. [1880–85]

Bit′ter Lakes′, two lakes in NE Egypt, forming part of the Suez Canal. [1835–45]

bit·ter·ling (bit′ər ling), *n.* a cyprinid fish, *Rhodeus sericeus,* found in central and eastern Europe, the female of which has a long, bright yellow or red ovipositor to deposit eggs in the mantle cavity of mussels. [1875–80; < G, equiv. to *bitter* BITTER + *-ling* -LING[1]]

bit·tern[1] (bit′ərn), *n.* **1.** any of several tawny brown herons that inhabit reedy marshes, as *Botaurus lentiginosus* **(American bittern),** of North America, and *B. stellaris,* of Europe. **2.** any of several small herons of the genus *Ixobrychus,* as *I. exilis* **(least bittern),** of temperate and tropical North and South America. [1510–20; *bitter, bittor* bittern + *-n* (perh. by assoc. with HERON), ME *bito(u)r, butur, boto(u)r* < AF *bytore,* AF, OF *butor* < VL **būtitaurus,* equiv. to **būti-,* perh. to be identified with L *būteō* a species of hawk (see BUTEO) + L *taurus* bull (cited by Pliny as a name for a bird emitting a bellowing sound)]

American bittern,
Botaurus lentiginosus,
length 2½ ft. (0.8 m);
wingspread 3 ft. (0.9 m)

bit·tern[2] (bit′ərn), *n. Chem.* a bitter solution remaining in salt making after the salt has crystallized out of seawater or brine, used as a source of bromides, iodides, and certain other salts. [1675–85; var. of *bittering;* see BITTER, -ING[1]]

bit·ter·nut (bit′ər nut′), *n.* a hickory, *Carya cordiformis,* of the eastern and southern U.S., bearing a smooth, gray, bitter seed. [1800–10, *Amer.;* BITTER + NUT]

bit′ter or′ange. See under **orange** (def. 2). [1820–30, *Amer.*]

bit′ter pill′, a distressing experience or result that is hard to accept (often in the expression *a bitter pill to swallow*): *Being passed over for promotion was a bitter pill to swallow.*

bit′ter prin′ciple, *Chem.* any of several hundred natural compounds, usually of vegetable origin, having a bitter taste, and not admitting of any chemical classification. [1930–35]

bit·ter·root (bit′ər ro͞ot′, -ro͝ot′), *n.* a plant, *Lewisia rediviva,* of the purslane family, having pink flowers and fleshy roots that are edible when young: the state flower of Montana. Also, **bit′ter root′.** [1825–35, *Amer.;* BITTER + ROOT[1]]

Bit′terroot Range′, a mountain range on the boundary between Idaho and Montana, a part of the Rocky Mountains: highest peak, ab. 10,000 ft. (3050 m). Also, **Bit′ter Root′ Range′.**

bit′ter rot′, *Plant Pathol.* a disease of apples, grapes, and other fruit, characterized by cankers on the branches or twigs and bitter, rotted fruit, caused by any of several fungi. [1860–65, *Amer.*]

bit·ters (bit′ərz), *n.* (*used with a plural v.*) **1.** a liquid, often an alcoholic liquor, in which bitter herbs or roots have steeped, used as a flavoring, esp. in mixed drinks, or as a tonic. **2.** *Pharm.* **a.** a liquid, usually alcoholic, impregnated with a bitter medicine, as gentian or quassia, used to increase the appetite or as a tonic. **b.** bitter medicinal substances in general, as quinine. [1705–15; BITTER + -S[3]]

bit·ter·sweet (*adj.* bit′ər swēt′, bit′ər swēt′; *n.* bit′ər swēt′), *adj.* **1.** both bitter and sweet to the taste: *bittersweet chocolate.* **2.** both pleasant and painful or regretful: *a bittersweet memory.* —*n.* **3.** Also called **woody nightshade.** a climbing or trailing plant, *Solanum dulcamara,* of the nightshade family, having small, violet, star-shaped flowers with a protruding yellow center and scarlet berries. **4.** Also called **climbing bittersweet.** any climbing plant of the genus *Celastrus,* bearing orange capsules opening to expose red-coated seeds, esp. *C. scandens.* **5.** pleasure mingled with pain or regret: *the bittersweet of parting.* [1350–1400; ME; see BITTER, SWEET] —**bit′ter·sweet′ly,** *adv.* —**bit′ter·sweet′ness,** *n.*

bit·ter·weed (bit′ər wēd′), *n.* **1.** any of various plants containing a bitter principle, as those of the genus *Picris.* **2.** a sneezeweed, *Helenium amarum.* [1810–20, *Amer.;* BITTER + WEED[1]]

bit·ter·wood (bit′ər wo͝od′), *n.* **1.** any of various chiefly tropical trees having wood with a bitter taste, as *Vatairea lundelii* or *Simarouba glauca.* **2.** quassia. [BITTER + WOOD[1]]

bit·ter·wort (bit′ər wûrt′, -wôrt′), *n.* See **yellow gentian.** [1590–1600; BITTER + WORT[2]]

bit·ting (bit′ing), *n.* one of the indentations on the bit of a key. [BIT[1] + -ING[1]]

bit·tock (bit′ək), *n. Chiefly Scot.* a little bit. [1795–1805; BIT[2] + -OCK]

bit·ty (bit′ē), *adj.,* **-ti·er, -ti·est. 1.** *Informal.* tiny; itty-bitty: *a little bitty town.* **2.** *Chiefly Brit.* containing or consisting of small bits or pieces; fragmentary. [1890–95; BIT + -Y[1]] —**bit′ti·ness,** *n.*

bi·tu·men (bī to͞o′mən, -tyo͞o′-, bi-, bich′o͞o-), *n.* **1.** any of various natural substances, as asphalt, maltha, or gilsonite, consisting mainly of hydrocarbons. **2.** (formerly) an asphalt of Asia Minor used as cement and mortar. [1425–75; late ME *bithumen* < L *bitūmen*] —**bi·tu·mi·noid** (bī to͞o′mə noid′, -tyo͞o′-, bi-), *adj.*

bi·tu·mi·nize (bī to͞o′mə nīz′, -tyo͞o′-, bi-), *v.t.,* **-nized, -niz·ing.** to convert into or treat with bitumen. Also, *esp. Brit.,* **bi·tu′mi·nise′.** [1745–55; < L *bitūmin-* (s. of *bitūmen*) BITUMEN + -IZE] —**bi·tu′mi·ni·za′tion,** *n.*

bi·tu·mi·nous (bī to͞o′mə nəs, -tyo͞o′-, bi-), *adj.* resembling or containing bitumen: *bituminous shale.* [1610–20; < L *bitūminōsus,* equiv. to *bitūmin-* (s. of *bitūmen*) BITUMEN + *-ōsus* -OUS]

bitu′minous coal′, a mineral coal that contains volatile hydrocarbons and tarry matter and burns with a yellow, smoky flame; soft coal. [1875–80]

bi·u·nique (bī′yo͞o nēk′), *adj. Math., Ling.* one-to-one. [1945–50; BI-[1] + UNIQUE] —**bi′u·nique′ly,** *adv.*

bi·u·nique·ness (bī′yo͞o nēk′nis), *n. Ling.* a principle providing for a one-to-one correspondence between the phonemic and phonetic levels of analysis. [1970–75; BIUNIQUE + -NESS]

bi·u·ret (bī′yə ret′, bī′yə ret′), *n. Chem.* a white crystalline substance, $C_2H_5O_2N_3 \cdot H_2O$, soluble in water and alcohol, used for the identification of urea, from which it is formed on heating. Also called **allophanamide, carbamylurea.** [< G *Biuret* (1847); see BI-[1], UREA, -URET]

bi·va·lent (bī vā′lənt, biv′ə-), *adj.* **1.** *Chem.* **a.** having a valence of two. **b.** having two valences, as aluminum with valences of two and three. **2.** *Genetics.* pertaining to associations of two homologous chromosomes. —*n.* **3.** *Genetics.* a pair of bivalent chromosomes, esp. when pairing during meiosis. [1865–70; BI-[1] + -VALENT] —**bi·va·lence** (bī vā′ləns, biv′ə ləns), **bi·va′len·cy,** *n.*

bi·valve (bī′valv′), *n.* **1.** Also called **lamellibranch.** *Zool.* any mollusk, as the oyster, clam, scallop, or mussel, of the class Bivalvia, having two shells hinged together, a soft body, and lamellate gills. —*adj.* **2.** *Bot.* having two valves, as a seedcase. **3.** *Zool.* having two shells, usually united by a hinge. **4.** having two similar parts hinged together. [1670–80; BI-[1] + VALVE] —**bi·val·vu·lar** (bī val′vyə lər), *adj.*

bi·vane (bī′vān′), *n.* a sensitive vane that measures both the horizontal and vertical components of wind direction. [BI-[1] + VANE]

bi·var·i·ate (bī vâr′ē it, -āt′), *adj. Statistics.* of, relating to, or having two variates. [1915–20; BI-[1] + VARIATE]

bi·vi·nyl (bī vīn′l), *n. Chem.* butadiene. [BI-[1] + VINYL]

bi·vol·tine (bī vōl′tēn, -tn), *adj. Entomol.* producing two broods in one year, as certain silkworm moths. [< F *bivoltin.* See BI-[1], VOLTA, -INE[1]]

biv·ou·ac (biv′o͞o ak′, biv′wak), *n., v.,* **-acked, -ack·ing.** —*n.* **1.** a military encampment made with tents or improvised shelters, usually without shelter or protection from enemy fire. **2.** the place used for such an encampment. —*v.i.* **3.** to rest or assemble in such an area; encamp. [1700–10; < F < Swiss G *biwacht* auxiliary patrol, equiv. to *bī-* BY- + *wacht* patrol, WATCH]

Bi·wa (bē′wä), *n.* **Lake,** the largest lake in Japan, on Honshu, near Kyoto. 260 sq. mi. (673 sq. km). Also called **Omi.**

bi·week·ly (bī wēk′lē), *adj., n., pl.* **-lies,** *adv.* —*adj.* **1.** occurring every two weeks. **2.** occurring twice a week; semiweekly. —*n.* **3.** a periodical issued every other week. —*adv.* **4.** every two weeks. **5.** twice a week. [1880–85; BI-[1] + WEEKLY]
—**Usage.** See **bi-**[1].

bi·year·ly (bī yēr′lē), *adj.* **1.** biennial (defs. 1, 2). —*adv.* **2.** biennially; biannually. **3.** twice yearly. [1875–80; BI-[1] + YEARLY]
—**Usage.** See **bi-**[1].

Biysk (byēsk), *n.* Bisk.

biz (biz), *n. Informal.* business: *How's the used car biz these days? Her brother's in show biz.* [1855–60, *Amer.;* by shortening and resp.]

bi·zarre (bi zär′), *adj.* markedly unusual in appearance, style, or general character and often involving incongruous or unexpected elements; outrageously or whimsically strange; odd: *bizarre clothing; bizarre behavior.* [1640–50; < F < It *bizzarro* lively, capricious, eccentric, first attested (ca. 1300) in sense "irascible"; of disputed orig.] —**bi·zarre′ly,** *adv.* —**bi·zarre′ness,** *n.*
—**Syn.** weird, freakish, grotesque, ludicrous. See **fantastic.**

Bi·zer·te (bi zûr′tə; *Fr.* bē zert′), *n.* a seaport in N Tunisia. 62,000. Also, **Bi·zer·ta** (bi zûr′tə; *Sp.* bē therʹtä, -ser′-). Ancient, **Hippo Zarytus.**

Bi·zet (bē zā′), *n.* **Georges** (zhôrzh), (*Alexandre César Léopold*), 1838–75, French composer, esp. of opera.

biz·na·ga (bis nä′gə), *n.* bisnaga.

bi·zon·al (bī zōn′l), *adj.* of or pertaining to two zones in an area: *a bizonal territory.* [1945–50; see BI-[1], ZONE, -AL[1]; in political use, from the post–World War II occupation zones in Germany]

bi·zone (bī′zōn′), *n.* two combined zones. [prob. back formation from BIZONAL]

Biz·tha (biz′thə), *n.* one of the seven eunuchs who served in the court of King Ahasuerus. Esther 1:10.

B.J., Bachelor of Journalism.

Bjoer·ling (byœr′ling), *n.* **Jus·si** (yo͞os′ē), 1911–60, Swedish tenor. Also, **Björ′ling.**

Björn·son (byûrn′sən; *Norw.* byœrn′so͞on), *n.* **Björn·stjer·ne** (byœrn′styer′nə), 1832–1910, Norwegian poet, novelist, and playwright: Nobel prize 1903.

Bk, *Symbol, Chem.* berkelium.

bk, *Baseball.* balk.

bk., 1. bank. **2.** book.

bkbndr., bookbinder.

bkcy., *Law.* bankruptcy.

bkg., 1. banking. **2.** bookkeeping. **3.** breakage.

bkgd., background.

bklr., *Printing.* black letter.

bkpg., bookkeeping.

bkpr., bookkeeper.

bkpt., bankrupt.

bks., 1. banks. **2.** barracks. **3.** books.

bkt., 1. basket. **2.** bracket.

bl., 1. bale; bales. **2.** barrel; barrels. **3.** black. **4.** block. **5.** blue.

b/l, *Com.* See **bill of lading.** Also, **B/L**

B.L., 1. Bachelor of Laws. **2.** Bachelor of Letters. **3.** See **bill of lading.**

b.l., 1. See **bill of lading. 2.** *Ordn.* breech loading.

B.L.A., 1. Bachelor of Landscape Architecture. **2.** Bachelor of Liberal Arts. **3.** Black Liberation Army.

blab (blab), *v.,* **blabbed, blab·bing,** *n. Informal.* —*v.t.* **1.** to reveal indiscreetly and thoughtlessly: *They blabbed my confidences to everyone.* —*v.i.* **2.** to talk or chatter indiscreetly or thoughtlessly: *Don't confide in him, because he blabs. She blabbed so much I couldn't hear the concert.* —*n.* **3.** idle, indiscreet chattering. **4.** a person who blabs; blabbermouth. Also, **blab·ber** (blab′ər). [1325–75; ME *blabbe* (n.), perh. back formation from *blaberen* to blabber; c. ON *blabbra,* G *plappern*]

blab·ber·mouth (blab′ər mouth′), *n., pl.* **-mouths** (-mouthz′, -mouths′). a person who talks too much, esp. indiscreetly. [1935–40, *Amer.;* BLABBER + MOUTH]
—**Syn.** gossip, gossipmonger, busybody, talebearer, bigmouth, tattler.

black (blak), *adj.,* **-er, -est,** *n., v., adv.* —*adj.* **1.** lacking hue and brightness; absorbing light without reflecting any of the rays composing it. **2.** characterized by absence of light; enveloped in darkness: *a black night.* **3.** (*sometimes cap.*) **a.** pertaining or belonging to any of the various populations characterized by dark skin pigmentation, specifically the dark-skinned peoples of Africa, Oceania, and Australia. **b.** African-American. **4.** soiled or stained with dirt: *That shirt was black within an hour.* **5.** gloomy; pessimistic; dismal: *a black outlook.* **6.** deliberately; harmful; inexcusable: *a black lie.* **7.** boding ill; sullen or hostile; threatening: *black words; black looks.* **8.** (of coffee or tea) without milk or cream. **9.** without any moral quality or goodness; evil; wicked: *His black heart has concocted yet another black deed.* **10.** indicating censure, disgrace, or liability to punishment: *a black mark on one's record.* **11.** marked by disaster or misfortune: *black areas of drought; Black Friday.* **12.** wearing black or dark clothing or armor: *the black prince.* **13.** based on the grotesque, morbid, or unpleasant aspects of life: *black comedy; black humor.* **14.** (of a check mark, flag, etc.) done or written in black to indicate, as on a list, that which is undesirable, sub-

CONCISE PRONUNCIATION KEY: act, cāpe, dâre, pärt; set, ēqual; *if,* īce; ox, ōver, ôrder, oil, bo͝ok, bo͞ot, out; up, ûrge; child; sing; shoe; thin, *th*at; zh as in *treasure.* ə = *a* as in *alone,* *e* as in *system,* *i* as in *easily,* *o* as in *gallop,* *u* as in *circus;* ə as in *fire* (fīər), *hour* (ouər). l and n can serve as syllabic consonants, as in *cradle* (krād′l), and *button* (but′n). See the full key inside the front cover.

standard, potentially dangerous, etc.: *Pilots put a black flag next to the ten most dangerous airports.* **15.** illegal or underground: *The black economy pays no taxes.* **16.** showing a profit; not showing any losses: *the first black quarter in two years.* **17.** deliberately false or intentionally misleading: *black propaganda.* **18.** *Brit.* boycotted, as certain goods or products by a trade union. **19.** (of steel) in the form in which it comes from the rolling mill or forge; unfinished. **20. black or white,** completely either one way or another, without any intermediate state. —*n.* **21.** the color at one extreme end of the scale of grays, opposite to white, absorbing all light incident upon it. Cf. **white** (def. 20). **22.** (*sometimes cap.*) **a.** a member of any of various dark-skinned peoples, esp. those of Africa, Oceania, and Australia. **b.** an African-American. **23.** black clothing, esp. as a sign of mourning: *He wore black at the funeral.* **24.** *Chess, Checkers.* the dark-colored men or pieces or squares. **25.** black pigment: *lamp black.* **26.** *Slang.* See **black beauty. 27.** a horse or other animal that is entirely black. **28. black and white, a.** print or writing: *I want that agreement in black and white.* **b.** a monochromatic picture done with black and white only. **c.** a chocolate soda containing vanilla ice cream. **29. in the black,** operating at a profit or being out of debt (opposed to *in the red*): *New production methods put the company in the black.* —*v.t.* **30.** to make black; put black on; blacken. **31.** *Brit.* to boycott or ban. **32.** to polish (shoes, boots, etc.) with blacking. —*v.i.* **33.** to become black; take on a black color; blacken. **34. black out, a.** to lose consciousness: *He blacked out at the sight of blood.* **b.** to erase, obliterate, or suppress: *News reports were blacked out.* **c.** to forget everything relating to a particular event, person, etc.: *When it came to his war experiences he blacked out completely.* **d.** *Theat.* to extinguish all of the stage lights. **e.** to make or become inoperable: *to black out the radio broadcasts from the U.S.* **f.** *Mil.* to obscure by concealing all light in defense against air raids. **g.** *Radio and Television.* to impose a broadcast blackout on (an area). **h.** to withdraw or cancel (a special fare, sale, discount, etc.) for a designated period: *The special air fare discount will be blacked out by the airlines over the holiday weekend.* —*adv.* **35.** (of coffee or tea) served without milk or cream. [bef. 900; ME *blak,* OE *blæc;* c. OHG *blah-;* akin to ON *blakkr* black, *blek* ink] —**black′ish,** *adj.* —**black′ish·ly,** *adv.* —**black′ish·ness,** *n.*

—**Syn. 1.** dark, dusky; sooty, inky; swart, swarthy; sable, ebony. **4.** dirty, dingy. **5.** sad, depressing, somber, doleful, mournful, funereal. **7.** disastrous, calamitous. **9.** sinful, inhuman, fiendish, devilish, infernal, monstrous; atrocious, horrible; nefarious, treacherous, traitorous, villainous. —**Ant. 1.** white. **4.** clean. **5.** hopeful, cheerful.

—**Usage. 3, 22.** BLACK, COLORED, and NEGRO have all been used to describe or name the dark-skinned African peoples or their descendants. COLORED, now somewhat old-fashioned, is often offensive. In the late 1950's BLACK began to replace NEGRO and today is the most widely used term. Common as an adjective (*black woman, man, American, people,* etc.), BLACK is also used as a noun, especially in the plural. Like other terms referring to skin color (*white, yellow*), BLACK is usually not capitalized, except in proper names or titles (*Black Muslim; Black English*). By the close of the 1980's AFRICAN-AMERICAN, patterned after the earlier AFRO-AMERICAN and widely used by leaders in the American black community, had begun to supplant BLACK in both print and speech, especially as a term of self-reference.

Black (blak), *n.* **1. Hugo Lafayette,** 1886–1971, U.S. political official: associate justice of the U.S. Supreme Court 1937–71. **2. Joseph,** 1728–99, Scottish physician and chemist. **3. Shirley Temple.** See **Temple, Shirley.**

black′ aca′cia, a tall Australian tree, *Acacia melanoxylon,* of the legume family, having cream-yellow flowers and yielding a very light wood.

black·a·cre (blak′ā′kər), *n.* an arbitrary name for a piece of land used for purposes of supposition in legal argument or the like (often distinguished from *whiteacre*). [1620–30; BLACK + ACRE]

black′ al′der, 1. Also called **winterberry.** a holly, *Ilex verticillata,* of eastern and midwestern North America, bearing red fruit that remains through early winter. **2.** a European alder, *Alnus glutinosa,* having a dark-gray bark and sticky foliage. [1795–1805, *Amer.*]

black·a·moor (blak′ə mo͝or′), *n. Now Usually Offensive.* **1.** a black person. **2.** any dark-skinned person. [1540–50; unexplained var. of phrase *black Moor*]

black-and-blue (blak′ən blo͞o′), *adj.* discolored, as by bruising; exhibiting ecchymosis: *a black-and-blue mark on my knee.* [1300–50; ME]

Black′ and Tan′, 1. Usually, **Black and Tans.** an armed force of about 6000 soldiers sent by the British government to Ireland in June, 1920, to suppress revolutionary activity: so called from the colors of their uniform. **2.** a member of this force. **3.** (*l.c.*) a drink made of equal parts of ale and stout or porter. **4.** (*l.c.*) a black-and-tan dog. [1880–85 for def. 4]

black-and-tan (blak′ən tan′), *adj.* **1.** (of a dog) of a black color with tan markings above the eyes and on the muzzle, chest, legs, feet, and breech. **2.** *Informal.* composed of or frequented by both blacks and whites: *a black-and-tan musical revue of the 1920's.* [1855–60]

black′ and tan′ coon′hound, one of an American breed of large, powerful hound dogs having a short, dense, black coat with tan markings above the eyes and on the muzzle, chest, legs, feet, and breech, and low-set, drooping ears, used for hunting raccoons, opossums, and other larger game. [1945–50]

black′ and white′, black (def. 28).

black-and-white (blak′ən hwīt′, -wīt′), *adj.* **1.** displaying only black and white tones; without color, as a picture or chart: *a black-and-white photograph.* **2.** partly black and partly white; made up of separate areas or design elements of black and white: *black-and-white shoes.* **3.** of, pertaining to, or constituting a two-valued system, as of logic or morality; absolute: *To those who think in black-and-white terms, a person must be either entirely good or entirely bad.* [1590–1600]

CONCISE ETYMOLOGY KEY: <, descended or borrowed from; >, whence; b., blend of, blended; c., cognate with; cf., compare; deriv., derivative; equiv., equivalent; imit., imitative; obl., oblique; r., replacing; s., stem; sp., spelling, spelled; resp., respelling, respelled; trans., translation; ?, origin unknown; *, unattested; ‡, probably earlier than. See the full key inside the front cover.

Black′ An′gus. See **Aberdeen Angus.**

black′ arm′, *Plant Pathol.* a type or phase of bacterial blight of cotton, characterized by black, elongated lesions on the stem and branches, caused by a bacterium, *Xanthomonas malvacearum.* [1905–10]

black′ art′, witchcraft; magic. [1580–90]

black-a-vised (blak′ə vīst′, -vīzd′), *adj.* dark-complexioned. Also, **black-a-viced** (blak′ə vīst′). [1750–60; Scots *blackaviced,* equiv. to *black a vice* (one) black of face (BLACK + A[3] + obs. *vice* < MF *vis;* see VISAGE) + -ED[3]]

black′-backed gull′ (blak′bakt′), any of several white gulls, as *Larus marinus* **(great black-backed gull),** having a black back and wings. [1770–80]

black′back floun′der (blak′bak′). See under **lemon sole.**

black-bag (blak′bag′), *adj. Informal.* of, pertaining to, or distributing money for expenses that has been diverted from the regular budget: *Black-bag funds have paid for much overseas travel by the military.*

black′-bag′ job′, *Informal.* surreptitious or illegal entry or activity by government agents seeking incriminating evidence. [1970–75, *Amer.*]

black·ball (blak′bôl′), *v.t.* **1.** to vote against (a candidate, applicant, etc.). **2.** to exclude socially; ostracize: *The whole town blackballed them.* **3.** to reject (a candidate) by placing a blackball in the ballot box. —*n.* **4.** a negative vote, esp. in deciding on an applicant or candidate. **5.** a black ball placed in a ballot box signifying a negative vote. [1760–70; BLACK + BALL[1]] —**black′·ball′er,** *n.*

—**Syn. 2.** boycott, ban, debar, snub, cut.

black′ bal′sam. See **Peru balsam.** [1880–85, *Amer.*]

black′ ba·sal′tes (bə sôl′tēz), basaltware.

black′ bass′ (bas), any freshwater American game fish of the genus *Micropterus.* Cf. **largemouth bass, smallmouth bass.** [1805–15]

black·bead (blak′bēd′), *n.* cat's-claw (def. 1). [BLACK + BEAD]

black′ bear′, a medium-sized North American bear, *Ursus* (*Euarctos*) *americanus,* relatively common in uninhabited mountainous areas, ranging from light brown to black with a straight brown muzzle: northern populations may be gray to near-white. See illus. under **bear.**

Black·beard (blak′bērd′), *n.* pseudonym of Edward Teach.

black′ beau′ty, *Slang.* a Biphetamine capsule.

black·bee·tle (blak′bēt′l), *n.* See **oriental cockroach.** [BLACK + BEETLE[1]]

black′-bel·lied plov′er (blak′bel′ēd), a large plover, *Pluvialis squatarola,* of both the New and Old Worlds, having black underparts when in nuptial plumage. [1805–15, *Amer.*]

black′bel·ly rose′fish (blak′bel′ē), a reddish scorpionfish, *Helicolenus dactylopterus,* inhabiting the deep waters of the western Atlantic Ocean. [BLACK + BELLY]

black belt (blak′ belt′ *for 1, 2;* blak′ belt′, belt′ *for 3, 4*), **1.** (*caps.*) a narrow belt of dark-colored, calcareous soils in central Alabama and Mississippi highly adapted to agriculture, esp. the growing of cotton. **2.** the area of a city or region inhabited primarily by blacks. **3.** *Martial Arts.* **a.** a black cloth waistband conferred upon a participant in one of the martial arts, as judo or karate, to indicate a degree of expertise of the highest rank. **b.** a person who has obtained such rank. **c.** the rank itself. Cf. **brown belt, white belt. 4.** a person proficient in some particular skill or endeavor; expert. [1865–70] —**black′-belt′,** *adj.*

black·ber·ry (blak′ber′ē, -bə rē), *n., pl.* **-ries. 1.** the fruit, black or very dark purple when ripe, of certain species of the genus *Rubus.* **2.** the plant itself. [bef. 1000; ME *blakeberie,* OE *blaceberie.* See BLACK, BERRY] —**black′ber′ry·like′,** *adj.*

black′berry lil′y, a perennial iris, *Belamcanda chinensis,* having globose seeds resembling blackberries and orange, lilylike flowers with red spots.

black′ bile′, one of the four elemental bodily humors of medieval physiology, regarded as causing gloominess. [1790–1800]

black′-billed cuck′oo (blak′bild′), a black-billed North American cuckoo, *Coccyzus erythropthalmus,* that, unlike most cuckoos, constructs its own nest and rears its own young. [1905–10, *Amer.*]

black′-billed mag′pie. See under **magpie** (def. 1). [1865–70, *Amer.*]

black′ bind′weed, 1. a weedy twining vine, *Polygonum convolvulus,* native to Europe and widely naturalized in North America. **2.** See **black bryony.**

black′ birch′. See **sweet birch.** [1665–75, *Amer.*]

black·bird (blak′bûrd′), *n.* **1.** a common European thrush, *Turdus merula,* the male of which is black with a yellow bill. **2.** any of several American birds of the family Icteridae, having black plumage. Cf. **crow blackbird, red-winged blackbird, rusty blackbird. 3.** any of several other unrelated birds having black plumage in either or both sexes. **4.** (formerly) a person, esp. a Kanaka, who was kidnapped and sold abroad, usually in Australia, as a slave. —*v.t.* **5.** to kidnap (a person), as in blackbirding. —*v.i.* **6.** to engage in blackbirding. [1480–90; earlier *blacke bride.* See BLACK, BIRD]

black·bird·er (blak′bûr′dər), *n.* (formerly) a person or ship illegally engaged in the slave trade, esp. in the Pacific. [1880–85; BLACKBIRD + -ER[1]]

black·bird·ing (blak′bûr′ding), *n.* (formerly) the act or practice of kidnapping persons, esp. Kanakas, and selling them abroad as slaves. [1870–75; BLACKBIRD + -ING[1]]

black′ bliz′zard, *Chiefly Oklahoma and Texas.* a dust storm.

black·board (blak′bôrd′, -bōrd′), *n.* a sheet of smooth, hard material, esp. dark slate, used in schools, lecture rooms, etc., for writing or drawing on with chalk. Also called **chalkboard.** Cf. **greenboard.** [1815–25; BLACK + BOARD]

black′board jun′gle, *Informal.* a school or school system characterized by lack of discipline and by juvenile delinquency. [on the model of ASPHALT JUNGLE; popularized by the novel of the same name (1954) by American author Evan Hunter (b. 1926)]

black·bod·y (blak′bod′ē), *n., pl.* **-bod·ies.** *Physics.* a hypothetical body that absorbs without reflection all of the electromagnetic radiation incident on its surface. Also called **perfect radiator.** [1700–10]

black′ book′, 1. a book of names of people liable to censure or punishment. **2. in someone's black books,** in disfavor with someone. [1470–80]

black′ bot′tom, an American dance, popular in the late 1920's, marked by emphatic, sinuous movements of the hips. [1910–15, *Amer.*]

black′ bot′tom pie′, a rich pie with a rum- or whiskey-flavored chocolate filling, often with a crust of crushed graham crackers or gingersnaps, and topped with whipped cream.

black′ box′, 1. any unit that forms part of an electronic circuit and that has its function, but not its components, specified. **2.** any comparatively small, usually black, box containing a secret, mysterious, or complex mechanical or electronic device. **3.** *Aeron.* an electronic device, such as a flight recorder, that can be removed from an aircraft as a single package. **4.** *Auto.* a device in an electronic ignition system that generates electrical pulses. [1940–45]

black′ bread′, a coarse-grained dark bread, often sour and made from whole-grain rye flour.

black′ bry′ony, a twining Old World vine, *Tamus communis,* having heart-shaped leaves, small greenish flowers, and scarlet berries. Also called **black bindweed.**

black·buck (blak′buk′), *n.* a blackish-brown antelope, *Antilope cervicapra,* of India. Also, **black′ buck′.**

blackbuck, *Antilope cervicapra,* 2½ ft. (0.8 m) high at shoulder; horns 2 ft. (0.6 m); length 4 ft. (1.2 m)

black′ buf′falo, a buffalofish, *Ictiobus niger,* of the Great Lakes and Mississippi River drainage systems south to Mexico. Also called **rooter.** [1835–45, *Amer.*]

black′ bull′head, a common freshwater catfish, *Ictalurus melas,* of North America, considered by some to be a food delicacy.

Black·burn (blak′bərn), *n.* **1.** a city in central Lancashire, in NW England. 142,200. **2. Mount,** a mountain in SE Alaska, in the Wrangel Mountains. 16,140 ft. (4920 m).

Black·burn′i·an war′bler (blak bûr′nē ən), a black-and-white North American wood warbler, *Dendroica fusca,* having an orange throat and an orange and black head. [1775–85, *Amer.*; named after Mrs. Hugh *Blackburn,* 18th-century Englishwoman; see -IAN]

black′ but′ter. See **beurre noir.** [1800–10]

Black′ Can′yon, a canyon of the Colorado River between Arizona and Nevada: site of Boulder Dam.

black·cap (blak′kap′), *n.* **1.** any of several birds having the top of the head black, as the chickadee and certain warblers, esp. the Old World blackcap, *Sylvia atricapilla.* **2.** the black raspberry plant or fruit. [1650–60; BLACK + CAP[1]]

black′-capped chick′adee (blak′kapt′). See under **chickadee.** [1870–75, *Amer.*]

black′ car′penter ant′, a large, black ant, *Camponotus pennsylvanicus,* that lives in damp wood in nature or in houses, where it can cause considerable damage by boring or tunneling.

black′ car′pet bee′tle. See under **carpet beetle.**

black′ chaff′, *Plant Pathol.* a disease of wheat, characterized by dark, elongated stripes on the chaff, caused by a bacterium, *Xanthomonas translucens undulosum.*

black′ cher′ry, 1. a North American cherry, *Prunus serotina,* having drooping clusters of fragrant white flowers and bearing a black, sour, edible fruit. **2.** the fruit itself. **3.** the hard, reddish-brown wood of this tree, used for making furniture. [1720–30, *Amer.*]

black′ choke′berry. See under **chokeberry** (def. 1).

black·cock (blak′kok′), *n.* the male of the black grouse. [1400–50; late ME; see BLACK, COCK[1]]

black·cod (blak′kod′), *n., pl.* **-cods,** (*esp. collectively*) **-cod.** sablefish. [BLACK + COD[1]]

Black′ Code′, *U.S. Hist.* (in the ex-Confederate states) any code of law that defined and esp. limited the rights of former slaves after the Civil War. Cf. **Jim Crow Law.**

black′ co′hosh, 1. See under **cohosh.** 2. See **black snakeroot.** [1820–30, *Amer.*]

black′ com′edy, comedy that employs morbid, gloomy, grotesque, or calamitous situations in its plot. [1965–70]

black′ cop′per, *Metall.* a regulus of 95-percent-pure copper, produced in a blast furnace by smelting oxidized copper ores.

black′ cos′mos, a garden plant, *Cosmos diversifolius,* of Mexico, having small, dahlialike tubers and solitary flower heads with red disk flowers and velvety, dark-red or purplish ray flowers.

Black′ Coun′try, a district in the English Midlands, around Birmingham: so called from the soot and grime produced by the many local industries.

black′ crap′pie. See under **crappie.** [1925–30]

black′-crowned night′ her′on (blak′kround′). See under **night heron.** [1835–45, *Amer.*]

black′ cur′rant, 1. the small, round, blackish, edible fruit of a widely cultivated shrub, *Ribes nigrum,* of the saxifrage family. 2. the shrub itself.

black•damp (blak′damp′), *n. Mining.* chokedamp. [1830–40; BLACK + DAMP]

Black′ Death′, a form of bubonic plague that spread over Europe in the 14th century and killed an estimated quarter of the population. [1815–25]

black′ dia′mond, 1. carbonado[1]. 2. **black diamonds,** coal. [1910–15]

black′ disease′, *Vet. Pathol.* an acute, usually fatal disease of sheep caused by general intoxication from *Clostridium novyi,* an anaerobic organism that multiplies in parts of the liver damaged by the common liver fluke. [1910–15]

black′ dog′, *Informal.* melancholy; despondency; the blues: *The black dog is over him.* [1700–10]

black′ duck′, any of several ducks having dusky or black plumage, as *Anas rubripes,* of the northeastern U.S. and Canada. [1630–40]

black′ dwarf′, *Astron.* See under **white dwarf.**

black•en (blak′ən), *v.t.* 1. to make black; darken. 2. to speak evil of; defame: *to blacken a person's reputation.* —*v.i.* 3. to grow or become black. [1250–1300; ME; see BLACK, -EN[1]] —**black′en•er,** *n.*
—**Syn.** 2. denigrate, smear, slander, vilify, libel, traduce, calumniate.

black•ened (blak′ənd), *adj.* (esp. of fish) coated with spices and sautéed quickly over high heat so that the outside chars.

Black′ Eng′lish, 1. Also called **Afro-American English.** a dialect of American English characterized by pronunciations, syntactic structures, and vocabulary associated with and used by some North American blacks and exhibiting a wide variety and range of forms varying in the extent to which they differ from standard English. 2. any of a variety of dialects of English or English-based pidgins and creoles associated with and used by black people. Also, **black′ Eng′lish.**

Black•ett (blak′it), *n.* **Patrick Maynard Stuart,** 1897–1974, English physicist: Nobel prize 1948.

black′ eye′, 1. discoloration of the skin around the eye, resulting from a blow, bruise, etc. 2. a mark of shame, dishonor, etc.: *These slums are a black eye to our town.* 3. damaged reputation: *Your behavior will give the family a black eye.* [1595–1605]

black′-eyed pea′ (blak′īd′), cowpea. [1720–30]

black′-eyed Su′san, any of a number of composite plants having daisylike flowers with a dark center disk and usually yellow ray flowers, esp. *Rudbeckia hirta:* the state flower of Maryland. [1890–95, *Amer.*]

black•face (blak′fās′), *n.* 1. *Theat.* a. an entertainer, esp. one in a minstrel show, made up in the role of a black. b. the makeup, as burnt cork, used in this role: *They performed in blackface.* 2. *Print.* a heavy-faced type. [1695–1705; BLACK + FACE]

black•fel•low (blak′fel′ō), *n. Usually Offensive.* an Aborigine of Australia. [1730–40; BLACK + FELLOW]

black′fellow's bread′, the edible portion of a species of pore fungus, *Polyporus mylittae,* that occurs in Australia. [1920–25]

black-fig•ure (blak′fig′yər), *adj.* pertaining to or designating a style of vase painting developed in Greece in the 7th and 6th centuries B.C., chiefly characterized by silhouetted figures painted in black slip on a red clay body, details incised into the design, and a two-dimensional structure of form and space. Also, **black′fig′•ured.** Cf. **red-figure.** [1890–95]

black•fin (blak′fin′), *n.* a cisco, *Coregonus nigripinnis,* found in the Great Lakes. Also called **black′fin cis′co.** [1870–75, *Amer.*; BLACK + FIN]

black•fire (blak′fīər′), *n. Plant Pathol.* a disease of tobacco, characterized by angular, dark lesions on the leaves, caused by a bacterium, *Pseudomonas angulata.* [BLACK + FIRE]

black•fish (blak′fish′), *n., pl.* (esp. collectively) **-fish,** (esp. referring to two or more kinds or species) **-fish•es.** 1. any of various dark-colored fishes, as the tautog, *Tautoga onitis,* or the sea bass, *Centropristes striatus.* 2. a small, freshwater food fish, *Dallia pectoralis,* found in Alaska and Siberia, noted for its ability to survive frozen in ice. 3. See **black whale.** [1680–90, *Amer.*; BLACK + FISH]

black′ flag′, 1. a pirate flag, usually of black cloth with a white skull and crossbones on it; Jolly Roger. 2. a flag having two yellow and two black squares, signifying the letter *L* in the International Code of Signals: formerly so called when used by itself to indicate the presence of cholera on board a vessel. 3. a signal given to an automobile racing driver to stop, usually because the car may have a dangerous problem that requires inspection. Also called **blackjack** (for defs. 1, 2). [1585–95]

black′ flux′, *Metall.* a reducing flux consisting of finely divided carbon and potassium carbonate.

black′ fly′, any of the minute, black gnats of the dipterous family Simuliidae, having aquatic larvae. Also called **buffalo gnat.** [1600–10]

black′ fog′, (in Cape Cod, Mass.) a dense fog.

Black•foot (blak′fŏŏt′), *n., pl.* **-feet,** (esp. collectively) **-foot,** *adj.* —*n.* 1. a member of a North American tribe of Indians of Algonquian stock. 2. the Algonquian language of the Blackfeet. —*adj.* 3. of or pertaining to the Blackfeet. [1785–95; trans. of Blackfoot *siksika*]

Black•foot (blak′fŏŏt′), *n.* a town in SE Idaho. 10,065.

black′-foot•ed fer′ret (blak′fŏŏt′id), a weasellike polecat, *Mustela nigripes,* of prairie regions of the U.S., having a yellowish-brown body with the tip of the tail and legs black: an endangered species. See illus. under **ferret.** [1880–85, *Amer.*]

Black′ For′est, a wooded mountain region in SW Germany. Highest peak, Feldberg, 4905 ft. (1495 m). German, **Schwarzwald.**

Black′ For′est cake′, *German Cookery.* a rich chocolate cake, sometimes kirsch-flavored, with a cream filling, containing and often decorated with candied or sour cherries.

black′ fox′, a red fox in a color phase in which its fur is mostly black. [1595–1605, *Amer.*]

Black′ Fri′ar, a Dominican friar: so called from the distinctive black mantle worn by the order. [1400–50; late ME]

black′ frost′, intense cold without hoarfrost, causing vegetation to turn black. Cf. **frost** (def. 2). [1700–10]

black′ gang′, the crew working in a stokehold of a ship. [1915–20]

black′ gnat′, *Angling.* a type of artificial fly, used chiefly for trout and salmon.

black′ gold′, petroleum. [1905–10]

black′ gram′. See under **gram**[2].

black′ grouse′, a large grouse, *Lyrurus tetrix,* of Europe and western Asia, the male of which is black, the female mottled gray and brown. [1820–30]

black•guard (blag′ärd, -ərd, blak′gärd′), *n.* 1. a low, contemptible person; scoundrel. 2. *Obs.* a. a group of menial workers in the kitchen of a large household. b. the servants of an army. c. camp followers. —*v.t.* 3. to revile in scurrilous language. [1525–35; BLACK + GUARD; original sense obscure] —**black′guard•ism,** *n.* —**black′guard•ly,** *adv.*
—**Syn.** 1. scamp, rascal, rapscallion, rogue, devil, villain. 3. berate, vilify.

black′ guil′lemot. See under **guillemot** (def. 1). [1760–70]

black′ gum′. See **sour gum.**

Black′ Hand′, 1. Italian, ***La Mano Nera.*** any of various secret criminal groups organized in Italy and operating in the U.S. in the late 19th and early 20th centuries, practicing blackmail and violence. 2. an anarchistic society in Spain, suppressed in 1883. 3. a nationalistic society in Serbia, suppressed in 1914. —**Black′•hand′er,** *n.*

black′ hat′, *Informal.* 1. a villain, as in a cowboy movie; bad guy. Cf. **white hat.** 2. **wear** or **put on a black hat,** to behave villainously.

black′ haw′, sheepberry. [1700–10, *Amer.*]

Black′ Hawk′, 1767–1838, American Indian chief of the Sauk tribe: leader of Sauk and Fox Indians in the Black Hawk War.

Black′ Hawk′ War′, a war fought in northern Illinois and present-day southern Wisconsin, 1831–32, in which U.S. regulars and militia with Indian allies defeated the Sauk and Fox Indians, led by Chief Black Hawk, attempting to recover lost hunting grounds.

black•head (blak′hed′), *n.* 1. a small, black-tipped, fatty mass in a skin follicle, esp. of the face; comedo. 2. any of several birds having a black head, as the greater scaup, *Aythya marila.* 3. Also called **enterohepatitis.** *Vet. Pathol.* a malignant, infectious disease of turkeys, chickens, and many wild birds, caused by a protozoan parasite, *Histomonas meleagridas,* attacking esp. the intestines and liver, and often characterized by a darkening of the skin on the head. [1650–60; BLACK + HEAD]

black′-head•ed fire′worm (blak′hed′id). See under **fireworm** (def. 1).

black′-headed gull′, any of several gulls having a dusky or black head, as *Larus ribidundus* of northern Europe and Asia. [1865–70]

black•heart (blak′härt′), *n.* 1. *Plant Pathol.* a nonparasitic disease of plants, as of potatoes and various trees, in which internal plant tissues blacken, usually as a result of extremes in temperature. 2. *Hort.* a. a heart cherry having a dark skin. b. the tree bearing this fruit. [1700–10; BLACK + HEART]

black-heart•ed (blak′här′tid), *adj.* disposed to doing or wishing evil; malevolent; malicious. [1840–50] —**black′-heart′ed•ly,** *adv.* —**black′-heart′ed•ness,** *n.*

Black′ Hills′, a group of mountains in W South Dakota and NE Wyoming. Highest peak, Harney Peak, 7242 ft. (2205 m).

black′ hole′, *Astron.* a theoretical massive object, formed at the beginning of the universe or by the gravitational collapse of a star exploding as a supernova, whose gravitational field is so intense that no electromagnetic radiation can escape.

Black′ Hole′, 1. Also called **Black′ Hole′ of Cal•cut′ta.** a small prison cell in Fort William, Calcutta, in which, in 1756, Indians are said to have imprisoned 146 Europeans, only 23 of whom were alive the following morning. 2. (*l.c.*) any usually wretched place of imprisonment or confinement.

black′ huck′leberry, a low eastern North American shrub, *Gaylussacia baccata,* of the heath family, having yellowish leaves with resinous dots on the underside, clustered orange-red flowers, and shiny, black, edible fruit. Also called **highbush huckleberry.** [1840–50, *Amer.*]

black′ hu′mor, a form of humor that regards human suffering as absurd rather than pitiable, or that considers human existence as ironic and pointless but somehow comic. [1965–70]

black′ ice′, 1. a thin sheet of ice, as on a road surface, usually caused by freezing mist and creating hazardous driving conditions. 2. *Oceanog.* sea ice that is clear enough to show the color of the water underneath. [1820–30, *Amer.*]

black•ing (blak′ing), *n.* any preparation for producing a black coating or finish, as on shoes or stoves. [1590–1600; BLACK + -ING[1]]

black•jack (blak′jak′), *n.* 1. a short, leather-covered club, consisting of a heavy head on a flexible handle, used as a weapon. 2. *Cards.* a. twenty-one (def. 4). b. Also called **natural.** (in twenty-one) an ace together with a ten or a face card as the first two cards dealt. c. a variety of twenty-one in which any player can become dealer. 3. See **black flag** (defs. 1, 2). 4. a small oak, *Quercus marilandica,* of the eastern U.S., having a nearly black bark and a wood of little value except for fuel. 5. a large drinking cup or jug for beer, ale, etc., originally made of leather coated externally with tar. Cf. **bombard** (def. 7). 6. caramel or burnt sugar for coloring spirits, vinegar, coffee, etc. 7. *Mineral.* a dark, iron-rich variety of sphalerite. —*v.t.* 8. to strike or beat with a blackjack. 9. to compel by threat. [1505–15; BLACK + JACK[1]]

leather blackjacks
(17th century)

black′ kite′, an Old World kite, *Milvus migrans,* having dark brown plumage and a forked tail, and feeding chiefly on carrion.

black′ knot′, *Plant Pathol.* a disease of plants, esp. of plums and cherries, characterized by black knotlike overgrowths on the branches, twigs, etc., caused by a fungus, *Dibotryon morbosa.* [1835–45, *Amer.*]

black′ land′, a black, clayey soil. Also, **black•land** (blak′land′, -lənd). Cf. **vertisol.** [1795–1805]

black′ lead′ (led), *Mineral.* graphite; plumbago. [1575–85]

black•leg (blak′leg′), *n., v.,* **-legged, -leg•ging.** —*n.* 1. Also called **black quarter, symptomatic anthrax.** *Vet. Pathol.* an infectious, often fatal disease of cattle and sheep, caused by the soil bacterium *Clostridium chauvoei* and characterized by painful, gaseous swellings in the muscles, usually of the upper parts of the legs. 2. *Plant Pathol.* a. a disease of cabbage and other cruciferous plants, characterized by dry, black lesions on the base of the stem, caused by a fungus, *Phoma lingam.* b. a disease of potatoes, characterized by wet, black lesions on the base of the stem, caused by a bacterium, *Erwinia atroseptica.* 3. a swindler, esp. in racing or gambling. 4. *Brit. Informal.* a strikebreaker; scab. —*v.t. Brit. Informal.* 5. to replace (a worker) who is on strike. 6. to refuse to support (a union, union workers, or a strike). 7. to betray or deceive (a person or cause). —*v.i.* 8. *Brit. Informal.* to return to work before a strike is settled. [1715–25; BLACK + LEG; orig. of nonliteral senses unclear; cf. JACKLEG]

black′ let′ter, *Print.* a heavy-faced type in a style like that of early European hand lettering and the earliest printed books.

This is a sample of black letter

Also called **text.** [1630–40] —**black′-let′ter,** *adj.*

black′-let′ter day′ (blak′let′ər), an unlucky or tragic day. [1750–60]

black′ light′, invisible infrared or ultraviolet light. [1925–30]

black′-light′ trap′ (blak′līt′), a trap for insects that uses ultraviolet light as an attractant.

black′ liq′uor, (in making wood pulp for paper) the liquor that remains after digestion. Cf. **white liquor.**

black•list (blak′list′), *n.* 1. a list of persons under sus-

CONCISE PRONUNCIATION KEY: act, cāpe, dâre, pärt; set, ēqual; if, īce; ox, ōver, ôrder, oil, bŏŏk, bōōt, out; up, ûrge; child; sing; shoe; thin, *th*at; zh as in *treasure.* ə = *a* as in *alone, e* as in *system, i* as in *easily, o* as in *gallop, u* as in *circus;* ᵊ as in *fire* (fīᵊr), *hour* (ouᵊr). l and n can serve as syllabic consonants, as in *cradle* (krād′l), and *button* (but′n). See the full key inside the front cover.

picion, disfavor, censure, etc.: *His record as an anarchist put him on the government's blacklist.* **2.** a list privately exchanged among employers, containing the names of persons to be barred from employment because of untrustworthiness or for holding opinions considered undesirable. **3.** a list drawn up by a labor union, containing the names of employers to be boycotted for unfair labor practices. —*v.t.* **4.** to put (a person, group, company, etc.) on a blacklist. [1610–20; BLACK + LIST[1]] —**Syn. 4.** blackball, bar, debar, proscribe, ban, shun, ostracize.

black′ lo′cust, 1. Also called **false acacia, yellow locust.** a North American tree, *Robinia pseudoacacia,* of the legume family, having pinnate leaves and clusters of fragrant white flowers. **2.** See **honey locust.** [1780–90, *Amer.*]

black′ lung′, pneumoconiosis of coal miners, caused by coal dust; anthracosis. [1905–10]

black•ly (blak′lē), *adv.* **1.** darkly; gloomily. **2.** wickedly: *a plot blackly contrived to wreak vengeance.* **3.** angrily: *blackly refusing to yield to reason.* [1555–65; BLACK + -LY]

black′ mag′ic, magic used for evil purposes; witchcraft; sorcery.

black•mail (blak′māl′), *n.* **1.** any payment extorted by intimidation, as by threats of injurious revelations or accusations. **2.** the extortion of such payment: *He confessed rather than suffer the dishonor of blackmail.* **3.** a tribute formerly exacted in the north of England and in Scotland by freebooting chiefs for protection from pillage. —*v.t.* **4.** to extort money from (a person) by the use of threats. **5.** to force or coerce into a particular action, statement, etc.: *The strikers claimed they were blackmailed into signing the new contract.* [1545–55; BLACK + MAIL[3]] —**black′mail′er,** *n.*

black′ ma′ple, a tree, *Acer saccharum nigrum,* of eastern and central North America, having furrowed, blackish bark and yellow-green flowers. [1810–20, *Amer.*]

black′ mar′gate (mär′git), *Ichthyol.* a grayish grunt, *Anisotremus surinamensis,* of the Atlantic Ocean from Florida to Brazil. Also called **pompon.**

Black′ Ma•ri′a (mə rī′ə). See **patrol wagon.** [1840–50, *Amer.*]

black′ mark′, an indication of failure or censure: *His chronic lateness is a black mark against him.* [1835–45]

black′ mar′ket, 1. the illicit buying and selling of goods in violation of legal price controls, rationing, etc. **2.** a place where such activity is carried on. [1930–35]

black-mar•ket (blak′mär′kit), *v.i.* **1.** to black-marketeer. —*v.t.* **2.** to sell (something) in the black market. [1930–35; v. use of BLACK MARKET]

black-mar•ke•teer (blak′mär′ki tēr′), *v.i.* to sell articles in the black market. [1940–45; BLACK MARKET + -EER] —**black′ marketeer′, black′ mar′keter.**

Black′ Mass′, 1. a blasphemous ceremony mocking the Christian Mass, esp. one by an alleged worshiper of Satan. **2.** a Requiem Mass. Also, **black′ mass′.** [1890–95]

black′ mea′sles, *Pathol.* a severe form of measles characterized by dark, hemorrhagic eruptions. Also called **hemorrhagic measles.**

black′ mercu′ric sul′fide, *Chem.* See under **mercuric sulfide.**

black′ mold′. See **bread mold.**

black′ mol′ly, a jet-black molly, a color form esp. of *Poecilia latipinna* or *P. sphenops,* popular as an aquarium fish.

black′ mon′ey, income earned surreptitiously or illegally, usually in cash, and not reported to the government so as to avoid paying taxes on it. [1965–70]

Black′ Monk′, a Benedictine monk (so called from the black habit worn by the order). Also, **black′ monk′.** [1250–1300; ME]

Black•more (blak′môr, -mōr), *n.* **Richard Dodd•ridge** (dod′rij), 1825–1900, English novelist.

Black′ Moun′tains, a mountain range in W North Carolina, part of the Appalachian Mountains. Highest peak, Mount Mitchell, 6684 ft. (2035 m).

black′ mul′berry. See under **mulberry** (def. 2). [1695–1705]

Black•mun (blak′mən), *n.* **Harry A(ndrew),** born 1908, U.S. jurist: associate justice of the U.S. Supreme Court 1970–94.

Black•mur (blak′mər), *n.* **R(ichard) P(almer),** 1904–65, U.S. critic and poet.

Black′ Mus′lim, a member of the Nation of Islam. [1955–60, *Amer.*]

black′ mus′tard. See under **mustard** (def. 2). [1775–85]

black′ na′tionalism, (*often caps.*) a social and political movement advocating the separation of blacks and whites and self-government for black people. [1965–70] —**black′ na′tionalist.**

black•ness (blak′nis), *n.* **1.** the quality or state of being black. **2.** the quality or state of being a black person. **3.** Negritude. [1300–50; ME; see BLACK, -NESS]

black′ nick′el ox′ide, *Chem.* See **nickelic oxide.**

black′ night′shade, a common weed, *Solanum nigrum,* of the nightshade family, having poisonous leaves, white flowers, and black edible berries. [1810–20]

CONCISE ETYMOLOGY KEY: <, descended or borrowed from; >, whence; b., blend of, blended; c., cognate with; cf., compare; deriv., derivative; equiv., equivalent; imit., imitative; obl., oblique; r., replacing; s., stem; sp., spelling, spelled; resp., respelling, respelled; trans., translation; ?, origin unknown; *, unattested; ‡, probably earlier than. See the full key inside the front cover.

black′ oak′, 1. any of several oak trees, as *Quercus velutina,* characterized by a blackish bark. **2.** the hard, durable wood of such a tree, used for making furniture, floors, etc. [1625–35, *Amer.*]

black′ ol′ive, a tropical American tree, *Bucida buceras,* having leathery leaves and greenish-yellow flowers.

black′ o′pal, *Mineral.* a dark variety of opal having the characteristic opaline play of color.

black•out (blak′out′), *n.* **1.** the extinguishing or concealment of all visible lights in a city, military post, etc., usually as a precaution against air raids. **2.** a period during a massive power failure when the lack of electricity for illumination results in utter darkness except from emergency sources, as candles. **3.** *Theat.* **a.** the extinguishing of all stage lights, as in closing a vaudeville skit or separating the scenes of a play. **b.** Also called **black′•out skit′.** a skit ending in a blackout. **4.** *Pathol.* **a.** temporary loss of consciousness or vision: *She suffered a blackout from the blow on the head.* **b.** a period of total memory loss, as one induced by an accident or prolonged alcoholic drinking: *The patient cannot account for the bizarre things he did during his blackout.* **5.** a brief, passing lapse of memory: *An actor may have an occasional blackout and forget a line or two.* **6.** complete stoppage of a communications medium, as by a strike, catastrophe, electrical storm, etc.: *a newspaper blackout; a radio blackout.* **7.** a stoppage, suppression, or obliteration: *a news blackout.* **8.** a period during which a special sales offer, fare rate, or other bargain is not available: *The airline's discount on fares does not apply during the Christmas week blackout.* **9.** *Radio and Television.* a prohibition that is imposed on the broadcasting of an event and has the purpose of encouraging or ensuring ticket sales. [1910–15; n. use of v. phrase *black out*]

Black′ Pan′ther, a member of a militant black American organization (**Black′ Pan′ther par′ty**) active esp. in the late 1960's and early 1970's, formed to work for the advancement of the rights of blacks, often by radical means. Also called **Panther.** [1960–65, *Amer.*]

black•patch (blak′pach′), *n. Plant Pathol.* a disease of red and white clover, caused by an unidentified fungus and characterized by brown or blackish lesions on the plant. [BLACK + PATCH]

black′ pep′per, a hot, sharp condiment prepared from the dried berries of a tropical vine, *Piper nigrum.*

black′ perch′, a livebearing surfperch, *Embiotoca jacksoni,* occurring in abundance along the coast of California, having brownish-black scales often tinged with blue or yellow and a thick, reddish mouth.

black′ pew′ter, *Metall.* pewter composed of 60 percent tin and 40 percent lead.

black′ pit′, *Plant Pathol.* a disease of lemons, characterized by dark brown, sunken spots on the skin of the fruit, caused by a bacterium, *Xanthomonas syringae.*

Black′ Plague′. See **Great Plague.**

black•plate (blak′plāt′), *n. Metall.* **1.** cold-rolled sheet steel before pickling or cleaning. **2.** sheet steel coated with a lacquer or enamel. [1855–60; BLACK + PLATE[1]]

black′poll war′bler (blak′pōl′), a North American warbler, *Dendroica striata,* the adult male of which has the top of the head black. Also called **black′poll′.** [1775–85, *Amer.*; BLACK + POLL[1]]

Black•pool (blak′po͞ol′), *n.* a seaport in W Lancashire, in NW England: resort. 147,000.

Black′ Pope′, *Archaic.* the head of the Jesuit order (so called from the power he once possessed and from the black habit worn by the order). [1875–80]

black′ pop′lar, 1. a poplar, *Populus nigra,* characterized by spreading branches, triangular leaves, and a gray bark. **2.** the light, soft wood of this tree, used for making doors, window frames, etc. [1720–30]

black′ pow′der, an explosive powder consisting of saltpeter, sulfur, and charcoal, used chiefly in old guns fired for sport, in fireworks, and for spotting charges in practice bombs; black gunpowder.

black′ pow′er, (*often caps.*) the political and economic power of black Americans as a group, esp. such power used for achieving racial equality. [1965–70, *Amer.*]

Black′ Prince′. See **Edward** (def. 1).

black′ pud′ding, 1. *Brit. and Southern U.S.* See **blood sausage. 2.** a dark dessert pudding made with flour, baking soda, eggs, and molasses. [1560–70]

black′ quar′ter, *Vet. Pathol.* blackleg (def. 1). [1825–35]

black′ rac′er, blacksnake (def. 1). [1840–50]

black′ rasp′berry, 1. the edible fruit of a prickly North American clambering shrub, *Rubus occidentalis,* resembling a raspberry in form and a blackberry in color. **2.** the plant itself. Also called **blackcap.** [1775–85, *Amer.*]

black′ rat′, an Old World rat, *Rattus rattus,* now common in the southern U.S., having a black or brown body with grayish or white underparts. [1765–75]

Black′ Ren′aissance. See **Harlem Renaissance.**

black′ ring′, *Plant Pathol.* a disease of grasses, characterized by black rings surrounding the stems and blighted seeds, caused by a fungus, *Balansia strangulans.*

Black′ Rod′, 1. (in England) an official of the Order of the Garter and chief ceremonial usher of the House of Lords: so called from the rod carried as the symbol of office. **2.** a similar official in British colonial and Commonwealth legislatures. [1625–35]

black′ root′ rot′, *Plant Pathol.* **1.** any of several diseases of plants characterized by black or brown lesions on the root. **2.** a common disease of the apple caused by the fungus *Xylaria mali.* **3.** a disease of tobacco caused by the fungus *Thielaviopsis basicola* and characterized by retarded growth and wilting. [1905–10]

black′ rot′, *Plant Pathol.* any of several diseases of fruits and vegetables, characterized by black discoloration and decay of affected parts, caused by fungi, as *Guignardia bidwellii,* or bacteria, as *Xanthomonas campestris.* [1840–50, *Amer.*]

black′ rud′derfish, barrelfish.

black′ ruff′, a large, blackish, pelagic fish, *Centrolophus niger,* of the Atlantic Ocean, chiefly along the coast of Europe.

Black′ Rus′sian, a drink made from one part coffee liqueur and two parts vodka, served over ice.

black′ rust′, *Plant Pathol.* any of several diseases of plants caused by rusts and characterized by black discoloration resulting from the fungal teliospores. [1780–90, *Amer.*]

black′ sage′, a shrubby Californian plant, *Salvia mellifera,* of the mint family, having an interrupted spike of lavender-blue or white flowers. [1875–80, *Amer.*]

Blacks•burg (blaks′bûrg), *n.* a town in SW Virginia. 30,638.

black′ sco′ter, a scoter of Eurasia and North America, *Melanitta nigra,* the adult male of which is black.

Black′ Sea′, a sea between Europe and Asia, bordered by Turkey, Rumania, Bulgaria, Ukraine, Georgia, and the Russian Federation. 164,000 sq. mi. (424,760 sq. km). Also called **Euxine Sea.** Ancient, **Pontus Euxinus.**

black′ sea′ bass′ (bas), a bluish, black-striped sea bass, *Centropristes striata,* abundant off the coast of eastern North America: a valuable food fish. [1835–45, *Amer.*]

black′ sele′nium, *Chem.* an allotropic form of selenium occurring as a black, amorphous, water-insoluble, light-sensitive powder: used chiefly in photoelectric cells.

black′ shank′, *Plant Pathol.* a disease of tobacco, characterized by wilting and by decayed, blackened roots and stems, caused by a fungus, *Phytophthora parasitica nicotianae.*

black′ sheep′, 1. a sheep with black fleece. **2.** a person who causes shame or embarrassment because of deviation from the accepted standards of his or her group. [1785–95]

Black′ Shirt′, a member of a fascist organization, esp. the Italian Fascist militia, wearing a black shirt as part of the uniform. [1920–25]

black′ skim′mer, a black and white New World skimmer, *Rynchops nigra,* having a bill with a reddish-orange base. [1805–15, *Amer.*]

black•smith (blak′smith′), *n.* **1.** a person who makes horseshoes and shoes horses. **2.** a person who forges objects of iron. **3.** a blackish damselfish, *Chromis punctipinnis,* inhabiting coastal waters off southern California. [1250–1300; ME; see BLACK (in reference to iron or black metal), SMITH[1]; cf. WHITESMITH]

black•smith•ing (blak′smith′ing), *n.* the work of a blacksmith. [1820–30; BLACKSMITH + -ING[1]]

black•snake (blak′snāk′), *n.* **1.** Also called **black racer.** a blackish racer, *Coluber constrictor* subspecies, of the eastern U.S., that grows to a length of 6 ft. (1.8 m). **2.** any of various other snakes of a black or very dark color. **3.** a heavy, tapering, flexible whip of braided cowhide or the like. Also, **black′ snake′.** [1625–35, *Amer.*; BLACK + SNAKE]

black′ snake′root, a tall bugbane, *Cimicifuga racemosa,* of the buttercup family, of eastern North America, having thin, tapering, toothed or deeply cut leaflets and branched clusters of small, white flowers. Also called **black cohosh.** [1690–1700, *Amer.*]

black spot (blak′ spot′ *for 1;* blak′ spot′ *for 2*), **1.** *Plant Pathol.* a disease of plants, characterized by black spots on the fruit and foliage, twig lesions, defoliation, and rotting, caused by any of several fungi, as *Diplocarpon rosae,* or bacteria. **2.** *Brit.* **a.** a hazardous place in a road where accidents frequently occur. **b.** a dangerous area or place. Also, **black′spot′.** [1885–90]

black′ spruce′, 1. a spruce, *Picea mariana,* of North America, having bluish-green leaves and grayish-brown bark. **2.** the light, soft wood of this tree. [1755–65, *Amer.*]

black′ squir′rel, a fox squirrel or gray squirrel in that color phase in which the fur is black. [1595–1605, *Amer.*]

black′ stem′, *Plant Pathol.* a disease of plants, characterized by blackened stems and defoliation, caused by any of several fungi, as *Ascochyta imperfecta* or *Mycosphaerella lethalis.*

Black•stone (blak′stōn′; *for 1 also* blak′stən), *n.* **1. Sir William,** 1723–80, English jurist and writer on law. **2.** a river in S Massachusetts, flowing SE across NE Rhode Island to Pawtucket. ab. 40 mi. (64 km) long.

black′strap molas′ses (blak′strap′), molasses remaining after maximum extraction of sugar from the raw product, used chiefly as a constituent of cattle feed and as a source of ethyl alcohol. [1915–20, *Amer.*; BLACK + STRAP]

Black′ Stream′. See **Japan Current.**

black′ stud′ies, a program of studies in black history and culture offered by a school or college, often including Afro-American history and black literature. Also called **Afro-American studies.** [1965–70]

Black′ Stump′, *Australian.* an imaginary spot marking the supposed limits of civilization: *beyond the Black Stump.* [1925–30]

black′ suck′er, a hog sucker, *Hypentelium nigricans,* of eastern U.S. streams. [1830–40, *Amer.*]

black′ swal′lowtail. See under **swallowtail** (def. 2).

black′ swal′lowwort. See under **swallowwort** (def. 2).

black′-tailed deer′ (blak′tāld′), a variety of mule deer, *Odocoileus hemionus columbianus,* of the western slope of the Rocky Mountains, having a tail that is black above. Also, **black′tail deer′** (blak′tāl′). Also called **black′tail′.** [1800–10, *Amer.*]

black′ tea′, a tea that has been allowed to wither and ferment under controlled conditions before being subjected to a heating process that stops fermentation and turns the leaves black. Cf. **green tea.** [1780–90]

black•thorn (blak′thôrn′), *n.* **1.** a shrub or tree of the genus *Crataegus,* as *C. calpodendron.* **2.** a walking stick made of a blackthorn tree or shrub. **3.** Also called **sloe.** a much-branched, thorny, Old World shrub, *Prunus spinosa,* having white flowers and small plumlike fruits. **4.** See **pear haw.** [1350–1400; ME *blak thorn.* See BLACK, THORN]

black′ tie′, **1.** a black bow tie, worn with a dinner jacket. **2.** semiformal evening wear for men (distinguished from *white tie*). [1855–60]

black-tie (blak′tī′), *adj.* requiring that guests wear semiformal attire, esp. that men wear black bow ties with tuxedos or dinner jackets: *a black-tie dance.* Cf. **white-tie.** [1930–35]

black′tip shark′ (blak′tip′), a widely distributed sand shark, *Charcharinus limbatus,* having fins that appear to have been dipped in ink, inhabiting shallow waters of warm seas.

black′ ti′ti. See under **titi**[2].

black•tongue (blak′tung′), *n. Vet. Pathol.* canine pellagra. [1825–35, *Amer.*; BLACK + TONGUE]

black•top (blak′top′), *n., adj., v.,* **-topped, -top•ping.** —*n.* **1.** a bituminous substance, usually asphalt, for paving roads, parking lots, playgrounds, etc. **2.** a road covered with blacktop. —*adj.* **3.** pertaining to or surfaced with blacktop: *a blacktop driveway.* —*v.t.* **4.** to pave with blacktop. [1930–35, *Amer.*; BLACK + TOP[1]]

black′ vel′vet, a cocktail made with stout and champagne. [1925–30]

Black′ Vol′ta, a river in W Africa, in Ghana: the upper branch of the Volta River. ab. 500 mi. (800 km) long.

black′ vul′ture, **1.** Also called **carrion crow.** an American vulture, *Coragyps atratus,* having a black, bald head and black plumage. **2.** any of several Old World vultures, esp. *Aegypius monachus,* of southern Europe, Asia, and North Africa. [1785–95]

Black′wall hitch′ (blak′wôl′), a hitch made with a rope over a hook so that it holds fast when pulled but is loose otherwise. See illus. under **knot.** [1860–65; named after *Blackwall,* a London shipyard]

black′ wal′nut, **1.** a tree, *Juglans nigra,* of North America, having pinnate leaves and dark-brown bark and bearing an edible nut covered by a thick green or brown husk. **2.** the nut of this tree. **3.** the wood of this tree, valued in furniture-making. [1605–15, *Amer.*]

Black′ Watch′, **1.** a regiment of Scottish infantry in the British army (so called from the dark colors in their tartan). **2.** the plaid pattern of their tartan.

black′ wa′ter, wastewater from toilets, garbage disposal, and industrial processes. Cf. **gray water.**

black•wa•ter (blak′wô′tər, -wot′ər), *n. Pathol.* **1.** any of several human or animal diseases characterized by the production of dark urine as a result of the rapid breakdown of red blood cells. **2.** See **blackwater fever.** [1790–1800; BLACK + WATER]

black′water fe′ver, *Pathol.* a severe form of malaria characterized by kidney damage and hemoglobinuria resulting in urine that is dark red or black. [1880–85]

black′ wat′tle, a tree, *Acacia mearnsii,* native to Australia and Tasmania, having bark used in tanning.

black•weed (blak′wēd′), *n.* the common ragweed. [BLACK + WEED[1]]

Black•well (blak′wəl, -wel′), *n.* **1. Antoinette Louisa (Brown),** 1825–1921, U.S. clergywoman, abolitionist, and women's-rights activist. **2. Elizabeth,** 1821–1910, U.S. physician, born in England: first woman physician in the U.S. **3. Henry Brown,** 1825?–1909, U.S. editor, abolitionist, and suffragist, born in England (husband of Lucy Stone).

Black′wells Is′land (blak′welz′, -wəlz), a former name of **Roosevelt Island.**

black′ whale′, a black, dolphinlike whale, *Globicephala melaena,* of the North Atlantic. Also called **blackfish.**

black′ wid′ow, a venomous spider, *Latrodectus mactans,* widely distributed in the U.S., the female of which is jet-black with an hourglass-shaped red mark on the underside of its abdomen. [1910–15]

black′ witch′. See under **witch moth.**

Black•wood (blak′wo͝od′), *n.* **William,** 1776–1834, English publisher.

black′ work′, **1.** work for which a person is paid in cash, with the transaction not recorded or reported, so as to avoid paying income tax on the amount earned. **2.** blackwork.

black•work (blak′wûrk′), *n.* embroidery done with black, usually silk, thread on white fabric, esp. linen. Also, **black work.** [BLACK + WORK]

blad (blad), *n. Advertising Informal.* a flier or other promotional material distributed by a company to sell a product. [1930–35; perh. BL(URB) + AD]

blad•der (blad′ər), *n.* **1.** *Anat., Zool.* **a.** a membranous sac or organ serving as a receptacle for a fluid or air. **b.** See **urinary bladder.** **2.** *Pathol.* a vesicle, blister, cyst, etc., filled with fluid or air. **3.** *Bot.* an air-filled sac or float, as in certain seaweeds. **4.** something resembling a bladder, as the inflatable lining of a football or basketball. **5.** an air-filled sac, usually made to resemble a club, used for beatings in low comedy, vaudeville, or the like. [bef. 900; ME; OE *blǣddre, blǣdre* bladder, blister, pimple; c. ON *blāthra,* dial. D *bladder,* G *Blatter;* akin to BLOW[2]] —**blad′der•less,** *adj.* —**blad′der•like′,** *adj.*

blad′der cam′pion, a European campion, *Silene vulgaris* (or *S. cucubalus*), of the pink family, having white flowers with an inflated calyx. [1755–65]

blad′der fern′, any of several ferns of the genus *Cystopteris,* having pinnate leaves and growing in rocky areas. [1820–30; so called from the bladderlike indusium]

blad′der kelp′, any of several species of giant kelp bearing prominent flotation bladders.

blad•der•nose (blad′ər nōz′), *n.* See **hooded seal.** [BLADDER + NOSE]

blad•der•nut (blad′ər nut′), *n.* **1.** the bladderlike fruit capsule of any shrub or small tree of the genus *Staphylea,* as *S. trifolia,* of the eastern U.S. **2.** the shrub itself. [BLADDER + NUT]

blad•der•pod (blad′ər pod′), *n.* **1.** any of several plants belonging to the genera *Alyssoides* and *Lesquerella,* of the mustard family, having inflated seed pods. **2.** See **poison bean** (def. 1). [1855–60; BLADDER + POD[1], so called from its full shape]

blad′der worm′, the bladderlike, encysted larva of a tapeworm; a cysticercus or hydatid. [1855–60]

blad•der•wort (blad′ər wûrt′, -wôrt′), *n.* any of various plants of the genus *Utricularia,* including aquatic, terrestrial, and epiphytic forms throughout the world. [1805–15; BLADDER + WORT[2]]

blad′der wrack′, a common seaweed, *Fucus vesiculosus,* found in cold marine waters, having narrow brownish fronds with air-filled vesicles.

blad•der•y (blad′ə rē), *adj.* **1.** like or resembling a bladder. **2.** inflated. [1785–95; BLADDER + -Y[1]]

blade (blād), *n.* **1.** the flat cutting part of a sword, knife, etc. **2.** a sword, rapier, or the like. **3.** a similar part, as of a mechanism, used for clearing, wiping, scraping, etc.: *the blade of a windshield wiper; the blade of a bulldozer.* **4.** the arm of a propeller or other similar rotary mechanism, as an electric fan or turbine. **5.** *Bot.* **a.** the leaf of a plant, esp. of a grass or cereal. **b.** the broad part of a leaf, as distinguished from the stalk or petiole. See illus. under **leaf.** **6.** the metal part of an ice skate that comes into contact with the ice. **7.** a thin, flat part of something, as of an oar or a bone: *shoulder blade.* **8.** a dashing, swaggering, or jaunty young man: *a gay blade from the nearby city.* **9.** a swordsman. **10.** *Phonet.* **a.** the foremost and most readily flexible portion of the tongue, including the tip and implying the upper and lower surfaces and edges. **b.** the upper surface of the tongue directly behind the tip, lying beneath the alveolar ridge when the tongue is in a resting position. **11.** the elongated hind part of a fowl's single comb. [bef. 1000; ME; OE *blæd* blade of grass; c. D *blad,* ON *blath,* G *Blatt;* akin to BLOW[3]] —**blade′less,** *adj.*

blade′ ap′ple. See **Barbados gooseberry.**

blade•bone (blād′bōn′), *n.* the scapula, or shoulder blade. [1670–80; BLADE + BONE[1]]

blad•ed (blā′did), *adj.* **1.** having a blade or blades (often used in combination): *a single-bladed leaf.* **2.** *Crystall.* of or pertaining to a thin, flat form suggestive of knife blades: *bladed arsenopyrite.* [1570–80; BLADE + -ED[3]]

blade•let (blād′lit), *n.* a small, blade-shaped, sometimes retouched piece of stone used as the cutting edge of a weapon or tool by late Stone Age peoples. Also, **blade′lette.** Also called **microblade.** [1855–60; BLADE + -LET]

blad•ing (blā′ding), *n.* the act of skating on in-line skates. [1985–90; < (ROLLER)BLAD(E) + -ING] —**blad′•er,** *n.*

blae (blā, blē), *adj. Scot. and North Eng.* bluish-black; blue-gray. [1150–1200; ME (north) *bla* < ON *blā* blackish blue; see BLUE]

blae•ber•ry (blā′ber′ē, -bə rē), *n., pl.* **-ries.** *Scot. and North Eng.* whortleberry. [1375–1425; late ME (north) *blaberie.* See BLAE, BERRY]

Blaeu (blou), *n.* **Wil•lem Jans•zoon** (vil′əm yän′sən, -sōn), 1571–1638, Dutch cartographer, geographer, astronomer, and mathematician. Also, **Blaeuw, Blaew.**

Bla•gon•ra•vov (blä′gən rä′vôf, -vof; *Russ.* blə gunrä′vəf), *n.* **A•na•to•li Ar•ka•dye•vich** (an′ə tō′lē; *Russ.* u nu tô′lyĕ ur kä′dyi vyich), 1894–1975, Russian scientist.

Bla•go•ve•shchensk (blä′gə vesh′ensk, -chensk; *Russ.* blə gu vye′shchyinsk), *n.* a city in the SE Russian Federation in Asia, on the Amur River. 172,000.

blah (blä), *Slang.* —*n.* **1.** nonsense; rubbish: *What they say is blah.* **2. the blahs,** a feeling of physical uneasiness, general discomfort, or mild depression; malaise: *After the long weekend many workers had the Monday-morning blahs.* —*adj.* **3.** insipid; dull; uninteresting. [1915–20; imit.]
—**Syn. 1.** bunkum, humbug, hooey, eyewash, twaddle.

blah-blah-blah (blä′blä′blä′), *n. Slang.* meaningless chatter; idle gossip: *the blah-blah-blah of gossip columnists.* Also, **blah′-blah′.** [1920–25, *Amer.*; redupl. of BLAH]

blain (blān), *n.* an inflammatory swelling or sore. [bef. 1000; ME *blein(e),* OE *blegene.* See CHILBLAIN]

Blaine (blān), *n.* **1. James Gil•les•pie** (gi les′pē), 1830–93, U.S. statesman. **2.** a town in E Minnesota. 28,558.

Blain•ville (*Fr.* blaɴ vēl′), *n.* a town in S Quebec, in E Canada, near Montreal. 14,682.

Blair (blâr), *n.* a male or female given name. Also, **Blaire.**

Blais (blā), *n.* **Ma•rie-Claire** (mə rē′klâr′), born 1939, Canadian poet and novelist.

Blaise (blāz; *Fr.* blez), *n.* a male given name.

Blake (blāk), *n.* **1. Hector** (*"Toe"*), born 1912, Canadian ice hockey player and coach. **2. James Hubert** (*"Eubie"*), 1883–1983, U.S. jazz pianist and composer. **3. Robert,** 1599–1657, British admiral. **4. William,** 1757–1827, English poet, engraver, and painter. **5.** a male or female given name.

blam•a•ble (blā′mə bəl), *adj.* deserving blame; censurable. Also, **blameable.** [1350–1400; ME; see BLAME, -ABLE] —**blam′a•bly,** *adv.*

blame (blām), *v.,* **blamed, blam•ing,** *n.* —*v.t.* **1.** to hold responsible; find fault with; censure: *I don't blame you for leaving him.* **2.** to place the responsibility for (a fault, error, etc.) (usually fol. by *on*): *I blame the accident on her.* **3.** *Informal.* blast; damn (used as a mild curse): *Blame the rotten luck.* **4. to blame,** at fault; censurable: *I am to blame for his lateness.* —*n.* **5.** an act of attributing fault; censure; reproof: *The judge said he found nothing to justify blame in the accident.* **6.** responsibility for anything deserving of censure: *We must all share the blame for this deplorable condition.* [1150–1200; (v.) ME *blamen* < AF, OF *blasmer* < VL **blastēmāre,* for LL *blasphēmāre* to BLASPHEME; (n.) ME < AF, OF *bla(s)me,* deriv. of the v.] —**blam′er,** *n.*
—**Syn. 1, 2.** reproach, reprove, reprehend, criticize. BLAME, CENSURE, CONDEMN imply finding fault with someone or something. To BLAME is to hold accountable for, and disapprove because of, some error, mistake, omission, neglect, or the like: *Whom do you blame for the disaster?* The verb CENSURE differs from the noun in connoting scolding or rebuking even more than adverse criticism: *to censure one for extravagance.* To CONDEMN is to express an adverse (esp. legal) judgment, without recourse: *to condemn conduct, a building, a person to death.* **5.** reprehension, condemnation, stricture, reproach, animadversion. **6.** guilt, culpability, fault, sin.
—**Usage.** Some speakers avoid BLAME ON as informal (*He blamed the fight on me*), preferring BLAME alone (*He blamed me*) or BLAME FOR (*He blamed me for it*). Since all three forms occur with equal frequency in educated usage, they may all be considered equally acceptable.

blame•a•ble (blā′mə bəl), *adj.* blamable. —**blame′a•bly,** *adv.*

blamed (blāmd), *Informal.* —*adj.* **1.** confounded: *The blamed car won't start.* —*adv.* **2.** confoundedly; excessively: *It's blamed cold out tonight.* [1825–35; BLAME + -ED[2]]

blame•ful (blām′fəl), *adj.* **1.** deserving blame; blameworthy: *blameful neglect.* **2.** *Archaic.* imputing blame; accusing. [1350–1400; ME; see BLAME, -FUL] —**blame′•ful•ly,** *adv.* —**blame′ful•ness,** *n.*

blame•less (blām′lis), *adj.* free from or not deserving blame; guiltless: *a blameless child.* [1350–1400; ME; see BLAME, -LESS] —**blame′less•ly,** *adv.* —**blame′less•ness,** *n.*
—**Syn.** irreproachable. See **innocent.** —**Ant.** guilty.

blame•wor•thy (blām′wûr′thē), *adj.* deserving blame; blameful: *a blameworthy administration.* [1350–1400; ME; see BLAME, WORTHY] —**blame′wor′thi•ness,** *n.*

blanc (blangk; *Fr.* bläɴ), *n., pl.* **blancs** (blangks; *Fr.* bläɴ). **1.** a silver coin of France of the 14th–18th centuries, debased in later years. **2.** an Anglo-Gallic copy of this coin, issued by Henry VI. **3.** *French Cookery.* a liquid for poaching meat, fish, or vegetables, often containing wine, herbs, and vegetables; court-bouillon. [< F, OF: white; see BLANK]

Blanc (bläɴ), *n.* **1. Jean Jo•seph Charles Louis** (zhäɴ zhô zef′ sharl lwē), 1811–82, French socialist and historian. **2. Mont.** See **Mont Blanc** (def. 1).

Blan′ca Peak′ (blang′kə), a mountain in S Colorado: highest peak in the Sangre de Cristo Range. 14,390 ft. (4385 m).

blanc de blancs (blängk′ də blängk′; *Fr.* bläɴ də bläɴ′), **1.** a type of champagne made entirely from the white grape Pinot Blanc. **2.** a white table wine, sometimes sparkling, made entirely from white grapes. Also, **blanc′ de blanc′.** [< F: lit., white from whites]

blanc fixe (blängk′ fēks′, blangk′ fiks′; *Fr.* bläɴ fēks′), barium sulfate used as a white pigment in paints. [1865–70; < F: lit., fixed white. See FIX, BLANK]

blanch[1] (blanch, blänch), *v.t.* **1.** to whiten by removing color; bleach: *Workers were blanching linen in the sun.* **2.** *Cookery.* **a.** to scald briefly and then drain, as peaches or almonds to facilitate removal of skins, or as rice or macaroni to separate the grains or strands. **b.** to scald or parboil (meat or vegetables) so as to whiten, remove the odor, prepare for cooking by other means, etc. **3.** *Hort.* (of the stems or leaves of plants, as celery or lettuce) to whiten or prevent from becoming green by excluding light. **4.** *Metall.* **a.** to give a white luster to (metals), as by means of acids. **b.** to coat (sheet metal) with tin. **5.** to

make pale, as with sickness or fear: *The long illness had blanched her cheeks of their natural color.* —*v.i.* **6.** to become white; turn pale: *The very thought of going made him blanch.* [1300–50; ME *bla(u)nchen* < AF, MF *blanchir* to whiten, deriv. of *blanc, blanche* white; see BLANK] —**blanch′er,** *n.*
—**Syn. 1.** See **whiten.**

blanch[2] (blanch, blänch), *v.t.* to force back or to one side; head off, as a deer or other quarry. [1565–75; var. of BLENCH[1]]

Blanche (blanch, blänch), *n.* a female given name: ultimately from a Germanic word meaning "white."

blanc·mange (blə mänj′, -mänzh′), *n.* **1.** a sweet pudding prepared with almond milk and gelatin and flavored with rum or kirsch. **2.** a sweet, white pudding made with milk and cornstarch and flavored with vanilla. [1350–1400; apocopated var. of ME *blancmanger* < MF: lit., white eating. See BLANK, MANGER]

Blan·co-Fom·bo·na (bläng′kô fôm bô′nä), *n.* **Ru·fi·no** (ro͞o fē′nô), 1874–1944, Venezuelan author.

bland (bland), *adj.,* **-er, -est. 1.** pleasantly gentle or agreeable: *a bland, affable manner.* **2.** soothing or balmy, as air: *a bland southern breeze.* **3.** nonirritating, as food or medicines: *a bland diet.* **4.** not highly flavored; mild; tasteless: *a bland sauce.* **5.** lacking in special interest, liveliness, individuality, etc.; insipid; dull: *a bland young man; a bland situation comedy.* **6.** unemotional, indifferent, or casual: *his bland acknowledgment of guilt.* [1590–1600; < L *blandus* of a smooth tongue, pleasant, soothing] —**bland′ly,** *adv.* —**bland′·ness,** *n.*
—**Syn. 1.** affable, mild, amiable; suave, urbane. **2, 3.** soft, mild. —**Ant. 1.** cruel; boorish. **2.** harsh. **3.** irritating.

Bland (bland), *n.* **James A(llen),** 1854–1911, U.S. songwriter and minstrel performer.

Bland′-Al′li·son Act′ (bland′al′ə sən), *U.S. Hist.* an act of Congress (1878) requiring the federal government to purchase at the market price from two to four million dollars' worth of silver monthly for conversion into silver dollars containing 16 times more silver per coin than gold in dollar coins of gold.

B.Land.Arch., Bachelor of Landscape Architecture.

blan·dish (blan′dish), *v.t.* **1.** to coax or influence by gentle flattery; cajole: *They blandished the guard into letting them through the gate.* —*v.i.* **2.** to use flattery or cajolery. [1350–1400; ME *blandisshen* < AF, MF *blandiss-,* long s. of *blandir* < L *blandiri* to soothe, flatter. See BLAND, -ISH[2]] —**blan′dish·er,** *n.* —**blan′·dish·ing·ly,** *adv.*

blan·dish·ment (blan′dish mənt), *n.* Often, **blandishments.** something, as an action or speech, that tends to flatter, coax, entice, etc.: *Our blandishments left him unmoved. We succumbed to the blandishments of tropical living.* [1585–95; BLANDISH + -MENT]
—**Syn.** flattery, cajolery, wheedling, ingratiation, fawning, blarney.

blank (blangk), *adj.,* **-er, -est,** *n., v.* —*adj.* **1.** (of paper or other writing surface) having no marks; not written or printed on: *a blank sheet of paper.* **2.** not filled in, as a printed form: *a blank check.* **3.** unrelieved or unbroken by ornament, opening, decoration, etc.: *a blank wall.* **4.** lacking some usual or completing feature: *a blank roll of film.* **5.** (of a recording medium) containing no previously recorded information: *a blank videocassette; a blank floppy disk.* Cf. **prerecorded. 6.** void of interest, variety, results, etc.: *She sometimes occupied her blank days reading detective stories.* **7.** showing no attention, interest, or emotion: *a blank expression on his face.* **8.** disconcerted; nonplussed; speechless: *He looked blank when I asked him why he applied for the job.* **9.** complete; utter; unmitigated: *blank stupidity.* **10.** *Archaic.* white; pale; colorless. —*n.* **11.** a place where something is lacking; an empty space: *a blank in one's memory.* **12.** a space in a printed form, test, etc., to be filled in: *Write your name in the blank.* **13.** a printed form containing such spaces: *Have you filled out one of these blanks?* **14.** a dash put in place of an omitted letter, series of letters, etc., esp. to avoid writing a word considered profane or obscene. **15.** *Metalworking.* a piece of metal ready to be drawn, pressed, or machined into a finished object. **16.** *Archery.* the bull's-eye. **17.** the object toward which anything is directed; aim; target. **18.** See **blank cartridge. 19. draw a blank, a.** to fail in an attempt; be unsuccessful: *We've drawn a blank in the investigation.* **b.** to fail to comprehend or be unable to recollect: *He asked me their phone number and I drew a blank.* —*v.t.* **20.** to cross out or delete, esp. in order to invalidate or void (usually fol. by *out*): *to blank out an entry.* **21.** *Informal.* to keep (an opponent) from scoring in a game. **22.** *Metalworking.* to stamp or punch out of flat stock, as with a die. [1300–50; ME (n. and adj.) < AF, F *blanc* (adj.) < Gmc; cf. OE *blanca* white horse, OHG *blanch* bright, white] —**blank′ness,** *n.*
—**Syn. 1–4.** See **empty. 8.** dumfounded, confused, astounded. **9.** pure, simple, unadulterated; perfect, absolute, unqualified. **11.** void, vacancy, emptiness; gap, lacuna, hiatus.

blank·book (blangk′bo͝ok′ *for 1;* blangk′bo͝ok′ *for 2*), *n.* **1.** a book containing blank pages, as a notebook or sketchbook. **2.** a book or pad of blank forms, as printed blanks for receipts or reports. [1705–15, *Amer.*; BLANK + BOOK]

blank′ car′tridge, *Ordn.* a cartridge containing powder only, without a bullet. [1820–30]

blank′ check′, 1. a bank check bearing a signature but no stated amount. **2.** unrestricted authority; a free hand: *He was given a blank check in the choice of personnel for the new department.* [1885–90]

CONCISE ETYMOLOGY KEY: <, descended or borrowed from; >, whence; b., blend of, blended; c., cognate with; cf., compare; deriv., derivative; equiv., equivalent; imit., imitative; obl., oblique; r., replacing; s., stem; sp., spelling, spelled; resp., respelling, respelled; trans., translation; ?, origin unknown; *, unattested; ‡, probably earlier than. See the full key inside the front cover.

blank′ endorse′ment, an endorsement on a check or note naming no payee, and therefore payable to bearer. Also called **endorsement in blank.**

blan·ket (blang′kit), *n.* **1.** a large, rectangular piece of soft fabric, often with bound edges, used esp. for warmth as a bed covering. **2.** a similar piece of fabric used as a covering for a horse, dog, etc. **3.** the chief garment traditionally worn by some American Indians. **4.** any extended covering or layer: *a blanket of snow.* **5.** *Print.* **a.** (in a press for offset printing) the rubber-covered cylinder to which an inked impression is transferred from the plate for transfer directly to the paper. **b.** (in a press for letterpress printing) the resilient covering on the cylinder against which the paper is pressed in printing. **6.** a thick roll or strip of material for thermal insulation. **7. born on the wrong side of the blanket,** born out of wedlock. —*v.t.* **8.** to cover with or as with a blanket: *wild flowers blanketing the hillside.* **9.** to obscure or obstruct; interfere with; overpower (usually fol. by *out*): *An electrical storm blanketed out the radio program.* **10.** to toss (someone) in a blanket, as in fraternity hazing. **11.** *Naut.* (of a vessel) to take wind from the sails of (another vessel) by passing closely to windward. —*adj.* **12.** covering or intended to cover a large group or class of things, conditions, situations, etc.: *a blanket proposal; a blanket indictment.* [1250–1300; ME < AF, OF, equiv. to *blanc* white (see BLANK) + *-et* -ET] —**blan′·ket·less,** *adj.* —**blan′ket·like′,** *adj.*
—**Syn. 4.** cover, coat, mantle, overlay, coating.

blan′ket chest′, *Furniture.* a chest, with or without drawers, having a rectangular space under a lifting lid or top, used for storing blankets, bedding, or clothing.

blan·ket-flow·er (blang′kit flou′ər), *n.* any composite plant of the genus *Gaillardia,* having showy heads of yellow or red flowers. [1875–80; BLANKET + FLOWER]

blan·ket·ing (blang′ki ting), *n.* **1.** blankets: *The blanketing was too warm.* **2.** *Radio.* the effect of a signal from a powerful transmitter that interferes with or prevents the reception of other signals. [1570–80; BLANKET + -ING[1]]

blan′ket roll′, 1. a blanket or sleeping bag rolled into a cylindrical pack for easy carrying and outdoor use by hikers, soldiers, cowboys, etc., often with cooking utensils, food, and personal articles carried inside. **2.** a method of cheating at craps whereby the dice are thrown on a blanket, rug, or other soft surface so that they roll only in a forward direction, making it impossible for the four side numbers to appear face up. [1890–95]

blan′ket sheet′, a newspaper of larger than average size, common in the mid 19th century. [1830–40, *Amer.*]

blan′ket stitch′, a basic sewing stitch in which widely spaced, interlocking loops, or purls, are formed, used for cutwork, as a decorative finish for edges, etc. [1875–80]

blan·ket-stitch (blang′kit stich′), *v.t., v.i.* to sew using a blanket stitch. [1955–60; v. use of BLANKET STITCH]

blan′ket toss′, a game in which a person is repeatedly tossed into the air and caught on an open blanket by a group of people who hold the blanket at its edges and stretch and relax it for each toss and catch.

blank·e·ty-blank (blang′ki tē blangk′), *adj., adv. Informal.* damned; darned (used to imply an omission of an unprintable or unspeakable word): *The blankety-blank motor stalled again.* [1885–90; after the practice of leaving blank spaces to represent profanity, as *G-- d---* for *God damn*]

blank·ly (blangk′lē), *adv.* **1.** without expression or understanding: *She stared blankly at her inquisitors.* **2.** in every respect; totally; fully: *He blankly denied ever saying such a thing.* [1815–25; BLANK + -LY]

blank′ shell′, a shotgun shell containing powder but no shot.

blank′ tape′, magnetic tape that has no recorded sound or image, as an unused or erased tape.

blank′ verse′, unrhymed verse, esp. the unrhymed iambic pentameter most frequently used in English dramatic, epic, and reflective verse. [1580–90]

blank′ wall′, an impassable barricade or obstacle; a situation in which further progress is impossible: *Attempts to get information by questioning the neighbors ran into a blank wall.*

blan·quette (bläng ket′, blän-), *n.* a ragout of lamb, veal, or chicken, prepared in a velouté sauce, usually garnished with croutons or small onions and mushrooms. [1740–50; < F; see BLANK, -ETTE]

blan·qui·llo (bläng kēl′yō; *Sp.* bläng kē′lyô, -kē′yô), *n., pl.* (*esp. collectively*) **-qui·llo,** (*esp. referring to two or more kinds or species*) **-qui·llos** (-kēl′yōz; *Sp.*-kē′lyôs, -kē′yôs). any of several game fishes of the genus *Caulolatilus,* related to the tilefishes. [< Sp. equiv. to *blanc(o)* white (see BLANK) + *-illo* < L *-illus* dim. suffix]

Blan·tyre (blan tīər′), *n.* a city in S Malawi: includes the former town of Limbe. 228,520.

blare (blâr), *v.,* **blared, blar·ing,** *n.* —*v.i.* **1.** to emit a loud, raucous sound: *The trumpets blared as the procession got under way.* —*v.t.* **2.** to sound loudly; proclaim noisily: *We sat there horrified as the radio blared the awful news.* —*n.* **3.** a loud, raucous noise: *The blare of the band made conversation impossible.* **4.** glaring intensity of light or color: *A blare of sunlight flooded the room as she opened the shutters.* **5.** fanfare; flourish; ostentation; flamboyance: *a new breakfast cereal proclaimed with all the blare of a Hollywood spectacle.* **6.** *Eastern New Eng.* the bawl of a calf. [1400–50; late ME *bleren;* akin to MD *blaren,* MLG *blarren,* MHG *blerren* (G *plärren*)]
—**Syn. 1, 3.** blast, bellow, roar, clang, clamor; screech, honk.

blar·ney (blär′nē), *n., v.,* **-neyed, -ney·ing.** —*n.* **1.** flattering or wheedling talk; cajolery. **2.** deceptive or misleading talk; nonsense; hooey: *a lot of blarney about why he was broke.* —*v.t., v.i.* **3.** to flatter or wheedle; use blarney: *He blarneys his boss with the most shameless compliments.* [1760–70; after the hamlet *Blarney,* in Ireland; see BLARNEY STONE]

Blar′ney stone′, a stone in Blarney Castle near Cork, Ireland, said to impart skill in flattery to anyone who kisses it.

Blas·co I·bá·ñez (blä′skô ē vä′nyeth, -nyes), **Vi·cen·te** (bē then′te, -sen′-), 1867–1928, Spanish novelist, journalist, and politician.

bla·sé (blä zā′, blä′zā; *Fr.* blä zā′), *adj.* indifferent to or bored with life; unimpressed, as or as if from an excess of worldly pleasures. [1810–20; < F, ptp. of *blaser* to cloy, sicken from surfeit, perh. < D *blasen* to blow; see BLAST]
—**Syn.** apathetic, jaded, cloyed, sated, glutted, surfeited, world-weary.

blas·pheme (blas fēm′, blas′fēm), *v.,* **-phemed, -phem·ing.** —*v.t.* **1.** to speak impiously or irreverently of (God or sacred things). **2.** to speak evil of; slander; abuse. —*v.i.* **3.** to speak irreverently of God or sacred things; utter impieties. [1300–50; ME (< AF) < LL *blasphēmāre* < Gk *blasphēmeîn* to speak profanely, deriv. of *blásphēmos* BLASPHEMOUS] —**blas·phem·er** (blas fē′mər, blas′fē-, -fə-), *n.*
—**Syn. 1.** See **curse.**

blas·phe·mous (blas′fə məs), *adj.* uttering, containing, or exhibiting blasphemy; irreverent; profane. [1525–35; < LL *blasphēmus* < Gk *blásphēmos* defaming, speaking evil, equiv. to *blá(p)s(is)* harm, evil (*blab-* harm + *-sis* -SIS; cf. *bláptein* to harm) + *-phēmos* speaking, deriv. of *phḗmē* speech; see -OUS] —**blas′phe·mous·ly,** *adv.* —**blas′phe·mous·ness,** *n.*
—**Syn.** sacrilegious, impious, irreligious; apostate, iconoclastic.

blas·phe·my (blas′fə mē), *n., pl.* **-mies. 1.** impious utterance or action concerning God or sacred things. **2.** *Judaism.* **a.** an act of cursing or reviling God. **b.** pronunciation of the Tetragrammaton (YHVH) in the original, now forbidden manner instead of using a substitute pronunciation such as *Adonai.* **3.** *Theol.* the crime of assuming to oneself the rights or qualities of God. **4.** irreverent behavior toward anything held sacred, priceless, etc.: *He uttered blasphemies against life itself.* [1175–1225; ME *blasphemie* < LL *blasphēmia* < Gk. See BLASPHEMOUS, -Y[3]]
—**Syn. 1.** profanity, cursing, swearing; sacrilege, impiety.

blast (blast, bläst), *n.* **1.** a sudden and violent gust of wind: *Wintry blasts chilled us to the marrow.* **2.** the blowing of a trumpet, whistle, etc.: *One blast of the siren was enough to clear the street.* **3.** a loud, sudden sound or noise: *The radio let out an awful blast before I could turn it off.* **4.** a forcible stream of air from the mouth, bellows, or the like. **5.** *Mach.* **a.** air forced into a furnace by a blower to increase the rate of combustion. **b.** a jet of steam directed up a smokestack, as of a steam locomotive, to increase draft. **c.** a draft thus increased. **6.** a forceful or explosive throw, hit, etc.: *a blast down the third-base line.* **7.** *Slang.* **a.** a party or riotously good time: *Did we have a blast last night!* **b.** something that gives great pleasure or enjoyment; thrill; treat: *My new electronic game is a blast.* **8.** a vigorous outburst of criticism; attack. **9.** See **blast wave. 10.** *Mining, Civ. Engin.* the charge of dynamite or other explosive used at one firing in blasting operations. **11.** the act of exploding; explosion: *Some say the blast was in the next county.* **12.** any pernicious or destructive influence, esp. on animals or plants; a blight. **13.** the sudden death of buds, flowers, or young fruit. **14. at full blast,** at maximum capacity; at or with full volume or speed: *The factory is going at full blast.* Also, **full blast.** —*v.t.* **15.** to make a loud noise on; blow (a trumpet, automobile horn, etc.): *He blasted his horn irritably at every car in his way.* **16.** to cause to shrivel or wither; blight. **17.** to affect with any pernicious influence; ruin; destroy: *Failure in the exam blasted her hopes for college. It was an indiscretion that blasted his good reputation.* **18.** to break up or dislodge (a tree stump, rock, etc.): *Their explosives were inadequate to blast the granite.* **19.** to make, form, open up, etc., by blasting: *to blast a tunnel through a mountain.* **20.** to show to be false, unreliable, etc.; discredit: *His facts soundly blasted the new evidence.* **21.** *Informal.* to curse; damn (usually fol. by *it* or an object): *Blast it, there's the phone again! Blast the time, we've got to finish this work.* **22.** to censure or criticize vigorously; denounce: *In his campaign speech he really blasts the other party.* **23.** to hit or propel with great force: *He blasted a homer that tied the game. They were blasted into outer space.* **24.** to shoot: *The terrorists blasted him down.* —*v.i.* **25.** to produce a loud, blaring sound: *The trumpets blasted as the overture began. His voice blasted until the microphone was turned down.* **26.** to shoot: *He whipped out his revolver and started blasting.* **27.** *Slang.* to take narcotics. **28. blast off, a.** (of a rocket) to leave a launch pad under its own power. **b.** (of an astronaut) to travel aloft in a rocket. [bef. 1000; 1955–60 for def. 7a; ME (n. and v.); OE *blǣst* (n.) a blowing; akin to ON *blāstr,* OHG *blāst* (deriv. of *blāsan,* c. Goth *ufblēsan,* ON *blāsa*). See BLOW[2]] —**blast′er,** *n.* —**blast′y,** *adj.*
—**Syn. 1.** squall, gale, blow, storm. See **wind**[1]. **2.** blare, screech. **11.** discharge, outburst. **17.** annihilate.

-blast, var. of **blasto-** as final element of a compound word: *ectoblast.*

blast′ cell′, *Biol.* any undifferentiated or immature cell. [1950–55]

blast·ed (blas′tid, blä′stid), *adj.* **1.** withered; shriveled; blighted; ruined. **2.** damned; confounded: *This blasted pen leaked all over my shirt.* [1545–55; BLAST (v.) + -ED[2]]

blas·te·ma (bla stē′mə), *n., pl.* **-mas, -ma·ta** (-mə tə). *Embryol.* an aggregation of cells in an early embryo, capable of differentiation into specialized tissue and organs. [1840–50; < NL < Gk *blástēma* (*blastē-* verbid s.

of *blasteîn* to sprout + *-ma* n. suffix denoting result of action)] —**blas·te′mal, blas·te·mat·ic** (blas′tə mat′ik), **blas·te·mic** (bla stē′mik, -stem′ik), *adj.*

blast′ fur′nace, a large vertical furnace for smelting iron from ore, using coke as fuel: designed so as to direct a continuous blast of air through the fuel in order to obtain a high rate of combustion. [1700–10]

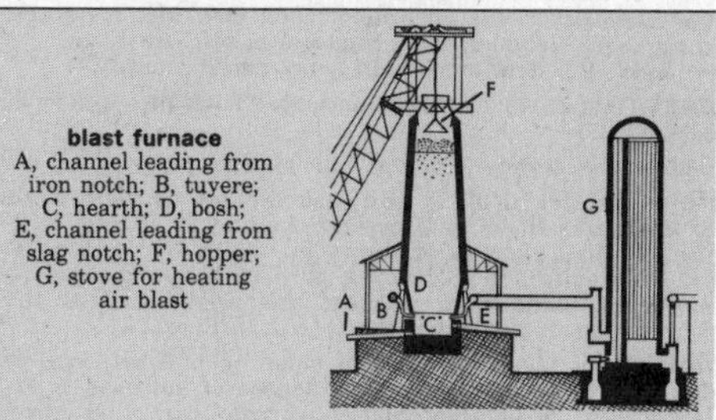

blast furnace
A, channel leading from iron notch; B, tuyere; C, hearth; D, bosh; E, channel leading from slag notch; F, hopper; G, stove for heating air blast

-blastic, a combining form meaning "having a given type or number of buds, cells, or cell layers," or "undergoing a given type of development," as specified by the initial element: *holoblastic.* [see BLASTO-, -IC]

blast′ing gel′atin, a type of plastic dynamite containing about 7 percent of a cellulose nitrate, used chiefly in underwater work.

blast′ing pow′der, a form of gunpowder made with sodium nitrate instead of saltpeter, used chiefly for blasting rock, ore, etc. [1865–70]

blast′ lamp′, a torch or lamp, as a blowtorch or a lamp for lampworking, in which the flame is fed by an air or oxygen blast. [1880–85]

blasto-, a combining form meaning "bud, sprout," "embryo," "formative cells or cell layer," used in the formation of compound words: *blastosphere.* Also, **-blast.** [< Gk, comb. form of *blastós* a bud, sprout]

blas·to·coel (blas′tə sēl′), *n. Embryol.* the cavity of a blastula, arising in the course of cleavage. Also, **blas′to·coele′.** Also called **segmentation cavity.** [1875–80; BLASTO- + -COEL] —**blas′to·coel′ic,** *adj.*

blas·to·cyst (blas′tə sist), *n. Embryol.* the blastula of the mammalian embryo, consisting of an inner cell mass, a cavity, and an outer layer, the trophoblast. [1885–90; BLASTO- + -CYST]

blas·to·derm (blas′tə dûrm′), *n. Embryol.* **1.** the primitive layer of cells that results from the segmentation of the ovum. **2.** the layer of cells forming the wall of the blastula, and in most vertebrates enclosing a cavity or a yolk mass. [1855–60; BLASTO- + -DERM] —**blas′to·der′mic, blas′to·der·mat′ic,** *adj.*

blas·to·disk (blas′tə disk′), *n. Embryol.* the blastula that forms as a flattened sphere on top of the yolk in the yolk-laden eggs of birds and reptiles. Also, **blas′to·disc′.** [1885–90; BLASTO- + DISK]

blast·off (blast′ôf′, -of′, bläst′-), *n. Aerospace.* the launching of a rocket, guided missile, or spacecraft. [1950–55; n. use of v. phrase *blast off*]

blas·to·gen·e·sis (blas′tə jen′ə sis), *n. Biol.* **1.** reproduction by budding. **2.** the theory of the transmission of hereditary characters by germ plasm. [1885–90; BLASTO- + -GENESIS]

blas·to·ma (bla stō′mə), *n., pl.* **-mas, -ma·ta** (-mə tə). *Pathol.* a tumor originating from undifferentiated embryonic cells and having little or no connective tissue. [BLAST- + -OMA]

blas·to·mere (blas′tə mēr′), *n. Embryol.* any cell produced during cleavage. [1875–80; BLASTO- + -MERE] —**blas·to·mer·ic** (blas′tə mer′ik, -mēr′-), *adj.*

blas·to·my·cete (blas′tə mī′sēt, -mī sēt′), *n.* any yeastlike fungus of the genus *Blastomyces,* all members of which are pathogenic to humans and other animals. [1895–1900; back formation from NL *Blastomycetes,* pl. of *Blastomyces* genus name; see BLASTO-, -MYCETES]

blas·to·my·co·sis (blas′tō mī kō′sis), *n. Pathol.* any of several diseases caused by certain yeastlike fungi, esp. blastomycetes. [1895–1900; < NL; see BLASTO-, MYCOSIS] —**blas·to·my·cot·ic** (blas′tō mī kot′ik), *adj.*

blas·to·pore (blas′tə pôr′, -pōr′), *n. Embryol.* the opening of an archenteron. [1875–80; BLASTO- + *-pore* passage; see PORE[2]] —**blas·to·por·ic** (blas′tə pôr′ik, -por′-), **blas·to·po·ral** (blas′tə pôr′əl, -pōr′-), *adj.*

blas·to·sphere (blas′tə sfēr′), *n. Embryol.* a blastula, esp. a blastocyst. [BLASTO- + -SPHERE]

blas·to·spore (blas′tə spôr′, -spōr′), *n. Bot.* a fungal spore that arises by budding. [1920–25; BLASTO- + -SPORE]

blas·to·style (blas′tə stīl′), *n. Zool.* the central rodlike portion of a gonangium, upon which buds that develop into medusae are formed. [BLASTO- + STYLE] —**blas′to·sty′lar,** *adj.*

blas·tu·la (blas′chə lə), *n., pl.* **-las, -lae** (-lē′). *Embryol.* the early developmental stage of an animal, following the morula stage and consisting of a single, spherical layer of cells enclosing a hollow, central cavity. Cf. **blastocyst.** [1885–90; < NL < Gk *blast(ós)* bud, sprout + NL *-ula* -ULE] —**blas′tu·lar,** *adj.* —**blas·tu·la·tion** (blas′chə lā′shən), *n.*

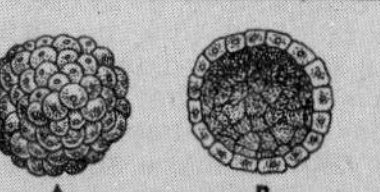

blastula
A, exterior view
B, cross section

blast′ wave′, a violent propagating disturbance, produced by an explosion in air, that consists of an abrupt rise in pressure followed by a drop in pressure to or below atmospheric pressure. Also, **blast.** Cf. **shock wave.** [1935–40]

blat (blat), *v.,* **blat·ted, blat·ting,** *n. Chiefly Northeastern U.S. and Great Lakes.* —*v.i.* **1.** bleat. **2.** to make a loud or raucous noise. —*v.t* **3.** to utter loudly and indiscreetly; blurt. —*n.* **4.** bleat (def. 4). [1840–50; perh. expressive var. of BLEAT; cf. BLATE[2]]

bla·tant (blāt′nt), *adj.* **1.** brazenly obvious; flagrant: *a blatant error in simple addition; a blatant lie.* **2.** offensively noisy or loud; clamorous: *blatant radios.* **3.** tastelessly conspicuous: *the blatant colors of the dress.* [coined by Spenser in 1596; cf. L *blatīre* to babble, prate, *blaterāre* to talk foolishly, babble] —**bla′tan·cy,** *n.* —**bla′tant·ly,** *adv.*
—**Syn. 1.** unmistakable, overt, undeniable, obtrusive.
—**Ant. 1.** subtle, hidden, inconspicuous.

blate[1] (blāt), *adj. Chiefly Scot.* bashful; shy. [bef. 1000; OE *blāt* livid, pallid, (of a sound) low (not found in ME)] —**blate′ly,** *adv.* —**blate′ness,** *n.*

blate[2] (blāt), *v.,* **blat·ed, blat·ing,** *n. Chiefly South Midland and Southern U.S.* —*v.i.* **1.** bleat. —*n.* **2.** bleat (def. 4). [1855–60; perh. dial. var. of BLEAT (cf. GREAT)]

blath·er (blath′ər), *n.* **1.** foolish, voluble talk: *His speech was full of the most amazing blather.* —*v.i., v.t.* **2.** to talk or utter foolishly; blither; babble: *The poor thing blathered for hours about the intricacies of his psyche.* Also, **blether.** [ME; ON *blathra* to chatter, blabber] —**blath′er·er,** *n.*

blath·er·skite (blath′ər skīt′), *n.* **1.** a person given to voluble, empty talk. **2.** nonsense; blather. [1640–50; BLATHER + *skite* SKATE[3]]

blat·ter (blat′ər), *v.i.* **1.** to chatter volubly. —*v.t.* **2.** to utter volubly. —*n.* **3.** the act or sound of blattering. [1545–55; < L *blaterāre* to prate, babble; use and spelling prob. altered by association with other expressive verbs ending in -ER[6]] —**blat′ter·er,** *n.*

blau·bok (blou′bok′), *n., pl.* **-boks,** (*esp. collectively*) **-bok.** a bluish antelope, *Hippotragus leucophaeus,* of southern Africa, having backward curving horns: now extinct. [< Afrik < D *blauwbok,* equiv. to *blauw* BLUE + *bok* BUCK[1]]

Blau·e Rei·ter (blou′ə rī′tər), *German.* a group of artists active in Germany, esp. in or near Munich, during the early 20th century, whose works were characterized by the use of Fauve color and forms distorted for structural or emotive purposes. Also called **Blue Rider School.**

Bla·vat·sky (blə vat′skē), *n.* **Madame** (*Elena Petrovna Blavatskaya, nee Hahn*), 1831–91, Russian theosophist.

blaw (blô), *v.i., v.t. Scot. and North Eng.* blow[2].

blaze[1] (blāz), *n., v.,* **blazed, blaz·ing.** —*n.* **1.** a bright flame or fire: *the welcome blaze of the hearth.* **2.** a bright, hot gleam or glow: *the blaze of day.* **3.** a sparkling brightness: *a blaze of jewels.* **4.** a sudden, intense outburst, as of fire, passion, or fury: *to unleash a blaze of pent-up emotions; a blaze of glory.* **5. blazes,** *Informal.* hell: *Go to blazes!* —*v.i.* **6.** to burn brightly (sometimes fol. by *away, up, forth*): *The bonfire blazed away for hours. The dry wood blazed up at the touch of a match.* **7.** to shine like flame (sometimes fol. by *forth*): *Their faces blazed with enthusiasm.* **8.** to burn with intense feeling or passion (sometimes fol. by *up*): *He blazed up at the insult.* **9.** to shoot steadily or continuously (usually fol. by *away*): *The contestants blazed away at the clay pigeons.* **10.** to be brilliantly conspicuous. [bef. 1000; ME, OE *blase* torch, flame; c. MHG *blas* torch]
—**Syn. 1.** See **flame.**

blaze[2] (blāz), *n., v.,* **blazed, blaz·ing.** —*n.* **1.** a spot or mark made on a tree, as by painting or notching or by chipping away a piece of the bark, to indicate a trail or boundary. **2.** a white area down the center of the face of a horse, cow, etc. —*v.t.* **3.** to mark with blazes: *to blaze a trail.* **4.** to lead in forming or finding (a new method, course, etc.): *His research in rocketry blazed the way for space travel.* [1655–65; akin to ON *blesi,* D *bles,* G *Blässe* white mark on a beast's face, and to G *blass* pale]

blaze[3] (blāz), *v.t.,* **blazed, blaz·ing.** **1.** to make known; proclaim; publish: *Headlines blazed the shocking news.* **2.** *Obs.* to blow, as from a trumpet. [1350–1400; ME *blasen* < MD; c. ON *blāsa* to blow. See BLAST]

blaz·er (blā′zər), *n.* **1.** something that blazes or shines brightly. **2.** a sports jacket, usually a solid color or striped, having metal buttons and sometimes an insignia on the breast pocket, as one worn by a member of a club, school, or the like. **3.** a small cooking apparatus using as its source of heat a spirit lamp, hot coals, etc., used esp. for preparing food at the table or outdoors. [1400–50; late ME; see BLAZE[1], -ER[1]]

blaz·ing (blā′zing), *adj.* **1.** burning brightly and with great heat, force, etc. **2.** of tremendous intensity or fervor: *a performance of blazing ferocity.* [1350–1400; ME; see BLAZE[1], -ING[2]] —**blaz′ing·ly,** *adv.*

blaz′ing star′, **1.** any of certain plants with showy flower clusters, as *Chamaelirium luteum,* of the lily family, or the composite plant *Liatris spicata.* **2.** a plant, *Mentzelia laevicaulis,* of the western U.S., having large, light-yellow flowers with many conspicuous stamens.

bla·zon (blā′zən), *v.t.* **1.** to set forth conspicuously or publicly; display; proclaim: *The pickets blazoned their grievances on placards.* **2.** to adorn or embellish, esp. brilliantly or showily. **3.** to describe in heraldic terminology. **4.** to depict (heraldic arms or the like) in proper form and color. —*n.* **5.** an escutcheon; coat of arms. **6.** the heraldic description of armorial bearings. **7.** conspicuous display. [1275–1325; ME *blaso(u)n* < AF, OF *blason* buckler, of obscure orig.] —**bla′zon·er,** *n.* —**bla′zon·ment,** *n.*

bla·zon·ry (blā′zən rē), *n.* **1.** brilliant decoration or display: *The wedding had all the blazonry of a coronation.* **2.** *Heraldry.* **a.** the act or technique of describing coats of arms. **b.** a coat, or coats, of arms. [1615–25; BLAZON + -RY]

bldg., building.

Bldg.E., Building Engineer.

bldr., builder.

-ble, var. of **-able** (*soluble*); occurring first in words of Latin origin that came into English through French, later in words taken directly from Latin. [ME < OF < L *-bilem,* acc. of *-bilis* (masc. and fem.) or < *-bile* (neut.) adj. suffix]

B.L.E., Brotherhood of Locomotive Engineers.

bleach (blēch), *v.t.* **1.** to make whiter or lighter in color, as by exposure to sunlight or a chemical agent; remove the color from. **2.** *Photog.* to convert (the silver image of a negative or print) to a silver halide, either to remove the image or to change its tone. —*v.i.* **3.** to become whiter or lighter in color. —*n.* **4.** a bleaching agent. **5.** degree of paleness achieved in bleaching. **6.** an act of bleaching. [bef. 1050; ME *blechen,* OE *blǣcean,* deriv. of *blāc* pale; c. ON *bleikja,* OHG *bleichēn*] —**bleach′a·ble,** *adj.* —**bleach′a·bil′i·ty,** *n.*
—**Syn. 1.** See **whiten.**

bleach·er (blē′chər), *n.* **1.** Usually, **bleachers.** a typically roofless section of inexpensive and unreserved seats in tiers, esp. at an open-air athletic stadium. **2.** a person or thing that bleaches. **3.** a container, as a vat or tank, used in bleaching. [1540–50; 1885–90 for def. 1; BLEACH + -ER[1]]

bleach·er·ite (blē′chə rīt′), *n.* a spectator seated in the bleachers. [1895–1900, *Amer.*; BLEACHER(S) + -ITE[1]]

bleach·er·y (blē′chə rē), *n., pl.* **-er·ies.** a place or establishment where bleaching is carried on. [1705–15, *Amer.*; BLEACH + -ERY]

bleach′ing pow′der, *Chem.* a white powder that decomposes on contact with water and has the characteristic odor of gaseous chlorine: regarded, when dry, as a mixed calcium hypochlorite-chloride, used as a commercial bleach for wood pulp, textiles, oils, and soaps, and in laundering as a decolorizer and disinfectant. Also called **chloride of lime, chlorinated lime, calcium oxychloride.** [1850–55]

bleak[1] (blēk), *adj.,* **-er, -est.** **1.** bare, desolate, and often windswept: *a bleak plain.* **2.** cold and piercing; raw: *a bleak wind.* **3.** without hope or encouragement; depressing; dreary: *a bleak future.* [1300–50; ME *bleke* pale, b. variants *bleche* (OE *blǣc*) and *blake* (OE *blāc*); both c. ON *bleikr,* G *bleich;* akin to BLEACH] —**bleak′ish,** *adj.* —**bleak′ly,** *adv.* —**bleak′ness,** *n.*
—**Syn. 3.** See **austere.**

bleak[2] (blēk), *n.* a European freshwater fish, *Alburnus alburnus,* having scales with a silvery pigment that is used in the production of artificial pearls. [1400–50; late ME *bleke,* n. use of *bleke* pale; see BLEAK[1]]

Bleak′ House′, a novel (1852) by Charles Dickens.

blear (blēr), *v.t.* **1.** to make dim, as with tears or inflammation: *a biting wind that bleared the vision.* —*adj.* **2.** (of the eyes) dim from tears. **3.** dim; indistinct. —*n.* **4.** a blur; cloudiness; dimness: *She was concerned about the recent blear in her vision.* [1250–1300; ME *bleri, blere* (v.), *blere* (adj.) < ?] —**blear·ed·ness** (blēr′id nis), *n.*

blear·y (blēr′ē), *adj.,* **blear·i·er, blear·i·est.** **1.** (of the eyes or sight) blurred or dimmed, as from sleep or weariness. **2.** indistinct; unclear: *The day begins with a bleary view of one's world.* **3.** fatigued; worn-out. [1350–1400; ME *blery.* See BLEAR (adj.), -Y[1]] —**blear′i·ly,** *adv.* —**blear′i·ness,** *n.*

blear·y-eyed (blēr′ē īd′), *adj.* **1.** having bleary eyes. **2.** dull of perception; shortsighted. Also, **blear′-eyed′.** [1350–1400; ME]

bleat (blēt), *v.i.* **1.** to utter the cry of a sheep, goat, or calf or a sound resembling such a cry. —*v.t.* **2.** to give forth with or as if with a bleat: *He bleated his objections in a helpless rage.* **3.** to babble; prate. —*n.* **4.** the cry of a sheep, goat, or calf. **5.** any similar sound: *the bleat of distant horns.* **6.** foolish, complaining talk; babble: *I listened to their inane bleat all evening.* [bef. 1000; ME *bleten,* OE *blǣtan;* c. D *blaten,* OHG *blāzen;* akin to L *flēre* to weep] —**bleat′er,** *n.* —**bleat′ing·ly,** *adv.*

ble·aunt (blē′ənt), *n.* a short tunic or blouse, worn in the Middle Ages. [1275–1325; ME *bleaunt, blihand* < AF *blia(u)nt, bliaut,* OF *blialt,* akin to OPr *blidal, blizal;* of uncert. orig.]

bleb (bleb), *n.* **1.** *Med.* a blister or vesicle. **2.** a bubble. [1600–10; akin to BLOB, BLUBBER] —**bleb′by,** *adj.*

bleed (blēd), *v.,* **bled** (bled), **bleed·ing,** *n., adj.* —*v.i.* **1.** to lose blood from the vascular system, either internally into the body or externally through a natural orifice or break in the skin: *to bleed from the mouth.* **2.** (of injured tissue, excrescences, etc.) to exude blood: *a wart that is bleeding.* **3.** (of a plant) to exude sap, resin, etc., from a wound. **4.** (of dye or paint) to run or become diffused: *All the colors bled when the dress was washed.* **5.** (of a liquid) to ooze or flow out. **6.** to feel pity, sorrow, or anguish: *My heart bleeds for you. A nation bleeds for its dead heroes.* **7.** to suffer wounds or death, as in battle: *The soldiers bled for the cause.* **8.** (of a broadcast signal) to interfere with another signal: *CB transmissions bleeding over into walkie-talkies.* **9.** *Print.* (of printed matter) to run off the edges of a page, either by

CONCISE PRONUNCIATION KEY: act, cāpe, dâre, pärt; set, ēqual; if, īce; ox, ōver, ôrder, oil, bo͝ok, bo͞ot, out; up, ûrge; child; sing; shoe; thin, *th*at; zh as in *treasure.* ə = *a* as in *alone, e* as in *system, i* as in *easily, o* as in *gallop, u* as in *circus;* ᵊ as in *fire* (fīᵊr), *hour* (ouᵊr). l and n can serve as syllabic consonants, as in *cradle* (krād′l), and *button* (but′n). See the full key inside the front cover.

design or through mutilation caused by too close trimming. **10.** *Slang.* to pay out money, as when overcharged or threatened with extortion. **11.** *Metall.* (of a cooling ingot or casting) to have molten metal force its way through the solidified exterior because of internal gas pressure. —*v.t.* **12.** to cause to lose blood, esp. surgically: *Doctors no longer bleed their patients to reduce fever.* **13.** to lose or emit (blood or sap). **14.** to drain or draw sap, water, electricity, etc., from (something): *to bleed a pipeline of excess air.* **15.** to remove trapped air from (as an automotive brake system) by opening a bleeder valve. **16.** to obtain an excessive amount from; extort money from. **17.** *Print.* **a.** to permit (printed illustrations or ornamentation) to run off the page or sheet. **b.** to trim the margin of (a book or sheet) so closely as to mutilate the text or illustration. **18. bleed off,** to draw or extract: *to bleed off sap from a maple tree; to bleed off static electricity.* **19. bleed white.** See **white** (def. 19). —*n.* **20.** *Print.* **a.** a sheet or page margin trimmed so as to mutilate the text or illustration. **b.** a part thus trimmed off. **21.** *Med.* an instance of bleeding; hemorrhage: *an intracranial bleed.* —*adj.* **22.** *Print.* characterized by bleeding: *a bleed page.* [bef. 1000; ME *bleden,* OE *blēdan,* deriv. of *blōd* BLOOD]

bleed·er (blē′dər), *n.* **1.** a person who bleeds abnormally because of low clotting rate; hemophiliac. **2.** a person or animal that bleeds easily, esp. an athlete or racehorse. **3.** a person who draws blood from a sick person; phlebotomist. **4.** *Slang.* a person who drains another of money, resources, etc.; parasite or usurer. **5.** *Metall.* an ingot or casting from which some metal has escaped. **6.** Also called **bleed′er resis′tor.** *Elect.* a resistor that is connected across a power supply for voltage regulation and to dissipate the charge remaining in capacitors when the power is discontinued. **7.** Also called **bleed′er valve′.** a valve or opening for draining a tank, tubing, etc. **8.** *Brit. Slang.* **a.** a despicable person. **b.** a person, esp. a man; fellow. [1780–90; BLEED + -ER[1]]

bleed′er tile′, a terra-cotta pipe for conveying water from a drainage tile to a sewer or drain. Also called **bleed′er pipe′.**

bleed·ing (blē′ding), *n.* **1.** the act, fact, or process of losing blood or having blood flow. **2.** the act or process of drawing blood from a person, esp. surgically; bloodletting. **3.** the extension of color beyond an edge or border, esp. so as to combine with a contiguous color or to affect an adjacent area. —*adj.* **4.** sending forth blood: *a bleeding sore.* **5.** feeling, expressing, or characterized by extreme or excessive anguish and compassion. **6.** *Brit. Slang.* (used as an intensifier): *bleeding fool.* —*adv.* **7.** *Brit. Slang.* (used as an intensifier): *a bleeding silly idea.* [1175–1225; ME (n. and adj.); see BLEED, -ING[1], -ING[2]]

bleed′ing heart′, **1.** any of various plants belonging to the genus *Dicentra,* of the fumitory family, esp. *D. spectabilis,* a common garden plant having long, one-sided clusters of rose or red heart-shaped flowers. **2.** a person who makes an ostentatious or excessive display of pity or concern for others. [1685–95] —**bleed′·ing-heart′,** *adj.*

bleep (blēp),*n.* **1.** a brief, constant beeping sound, usually of a high pitch and generated by an electronic device. **2.** such an electronic sound used to replace a censored word or phrase, as on a television broadcast. **3.** Also, **blip.** (used as a euphemism to indicate the omission or deletion of an obscenity or other objectionable word). —*v.i.* **4.** (of an electronic device) to emit a series of bleeps as an audible signal, summons, or warning. —*v.t.* **5.** Also, **blip.** to censor (an obscene, vulgar, or other objectionable word or phrase) from a radio or television broadcast by deleting from the audio signal, leaving a gap or an electronic tone: *The word was bleeped out of the comedian's routine.* [1950–55; perh. imit.]

bleep·ing (blē′ping), *adj.* (used as a substitute word for one regarded as objectionable): *Get that bleeping cat out of here!* Also, **blipping.** [1975–80; BLEEP + -ING[2]]

blel·lum (blel′əm), *n. Scot. Obs.* an idle, indiscreet talker. [1780–90; orig. uncert.]

blem·ish (blem′ish), *v.t.* **1.** to destroy or diminish the perfection of: *The book is blemished by those long, ineffective descriptions.* —*n.* **2.** a mark that detracts from appearance, as a pimple or a scar. **3.** a defect or flaw; stain; blight: *a blemish on his record.* [1275–1325; ME (v.) < AF, MF *blemiss-,* long s. of *ble(s)mir* to make livid, perh. < Old Low Franconian **blesmjan;* see BLAZE[2]] —**blem′ish·er,** *n.*
—**Syn. 1.** stain, sully, spot, tarnish, taint; injure, mar, damage, impair, deface. **3.** blot, spot, speck, taint. See **defect.** —**Ant. 1.** purify, repair.

blench[1] (blench), *v.i.* to shrink; flinch; quail: *an unsteady eye that blenched under another's gaze.* [bef. 1000; ME *blenchen,* OE *blencan;* c. ON *blekkja,* MHG *blenken*] —**blench′er,** *n.* —**blench′ing·ly,** *adv.*
—**Syn.** See **wince.**

blench[2] (blench), *v.t., v.i.* to make or become pale or white; blanch. [1805–15; var. of BLANCH[1]]

blend (blend), *v.,* **blend·ed** or **blent, blend·ing,** *n.* —*v.t.* **1.** to mix smoothly and inseparably together: *to blend the ingredients in a recipe.* **2.** to mix (various sorts or grades) in order to obtain a particular kind or quality: *Blend a little red paint with the blue paint.* **3.** to prepare by such mixture: *This tea is blended by mixing chamomile with pekoe.* **4.** to pronounce (an utterance) as a combined sequence of sounds. —*v.i.* **5.** to mix or intermingle smoothly and inseparably: *I can't get the eggs and cream to blend.* **6.** to fit or relate harmoniously; accord; go: *The brown sofa did not blend with the purple wall.* **7.** to have no perceptible separation: *Sea and sky seemed to blend.* —*n.* **8.** an act or manner of blending: *tea of our own blend.* **9.** a mixture or kind produced by blending: *a special blend of rye and wheat flours.* **10.** *Ling.* a word made by putting together parts of other words, as *motel,* made from *motor* and *hotel, brunch,* from *breakfast* and *lunch,* or *guesstimate,* from *guess* and *estimate.* **11.** a sequence of two or more consonant sounds within a syllable, as the *bl* in *blend;* consonant cluster. [1250–1300; ME *blenden,* OE *blendan* to mix, for *blandan;* c. ON *blanda,* OHG *blantan* to mix]
—**Syn. 1.** compound. See **mix. 1, 5.** mingle, commingle, combine, amalgamate, unite. **5.** coalesce. **8, 9.** combination, amalgamation. —**Ant. 1, 5.** separate.

blende (blend), *n. Mineral.* **1.** sphalerite; zinc sulfide. **2.** any of certain other sulfides. [1675–85; < G; cf. MHG *blenden* to make blind, deceive; so called because it often looks deceptively like galena]

blend′ed fam′ily, a family composed of a couple and their children from previous marriages. [1980–85]

blend′ed whis′key, whiskey that is a blend of two or more whiskeys, or of whiskey and neutral spirits, and that contains at least 20 percent of 100-proof straight whiskey by volume after blending. [1935–40]

blend·er (blen′dər), *n.* **1.** a person or thing that blends. **2.** an electric culinary grinding and mixing appliance, consisting of a container with propellerlike blades at the bottom that are whirled by a high-speed motor to purée, chop, or mix foods. **3.** See **pastry blender.** [1870–75; BLEND + -ER[1]]

blend′ing inher′itance, *Genetics.* inheritance in which contrasting parental characters appear as a blend in the offspring. Cf. **particulate inheritance.** [1920–25]

Blen·heim (blen′əm), *n.* village in S Germany, on the Danube: famous victory of the Duke of Marlborough over the French, 1704. German, **Blindheim.**

Blen′heim span′iel, one of a breed of toy spaniels having a short head and long ears. [1830–40; named after *Blenheim,* country house of Duke of Marlborough in Oxfordshire, England]

blen·ni·oid (blen′ē oid′), *adj.* **1.** resembling a blenny. **2.** of or pertaining to the blennies. [1860–65; BLENNY + -OID]

blen·ny (blen′ē), *n., pl.* **-nies.** any of several fishes of the family Blenniidae and related families, esp. of the genus *Blennius,* having a long, tapering body and small pelvic fins inserted before the pectoral fins. [1745–55; < L *blennius* a kind of fish < Gk *blénnos* slime, mucus; so called from its slimy coating]

blent (blent), *v.* a pt. and pp. of **blend.**

ble·o·my·cin (blē′ə mī′sin), *n. Pharm.* a cytotoxic antibiotic, $C_{55}H_{84}N_{17}O_{21}S_3$, derived from the fermentation product of the bacterium *Streptomyces verticillus,* used in the management of certain epithelial cell and testicular carcinomas and malignant lymphomas. [1965–70; appar. alter. of *phleomycin,* an antibiotic derived earlier from the same source; initial elements *phleo-, bleo-* unexplained by originators; see -MYCIN]

blephar-, a combining form meaning "eyelid," used in the formation of compound words: *blepharitis.* Also, *esp. before a consonant,* **blepharo-.** [< Gk *blephar-,* comb. form of *blépharon*]

bleph·a·ri·tis (blef′ə rī′tis), *n. Pathol.* inflammation of the eyelids. [BLEPHAR- + -ITIS] —**bleph·a·rit·ic** (blef′ə rit′ik), *adj.*

bleph·a·ro·plas·ty (blef′ər ə plas′tē), *n., pl.* **-ties.** plastic surgery of the eyelid, used to remove epicanthic folds, sagging tissue, or wrinkles around the eyes or to repair injury to the eyelid. [1960–65; BLEPHARO- + -PLASTY]

bleph·a·ro·spasm (blef′ər ə spaz′əm), *n. Pathol.* spasmodic winking. [1870–75; BLEPHARO- + SPASM]

Blé·riot (blā ryō′; *Eng.* blâr′ē ō′), *n.* **Louis** (lwē), 1872–1936, French aviator, pioneer aeronautical engineer, and inventor.

bles·bok (bles′bok′), *n., pl.* **-boks,** (*esp. collectively*) **-bok.** a large antelope, *Damaliscus albifrons,* of southern Africa, having a blaze on the face. Also, **blesbuck.** [1815–25; < Afrik, equiv. to D *bles* BLAZE[2] + *bok* BUCK[1]]

bles·buck (bles′buk′), *n., pl.* **-bucks,** (*esp. collectively*) **-buck.** blesbok.

bless (bles), *v.t.,* **blessed** or **blest, bless·ing. 1.** to consecrate or sanctify by a religious rite; make or pronounce holy. **2.** to request of God the bestowal of divine favor on: *Bless this house.* **3.** to bestow good of any kind upon: *a nation blessed with peace.* **4.** to extol as holy; glorify: *Bless the name of the Lord.* **5.** to protect or guard from evil (usually used interjectionally): *Bless you! Bless your innocent little heart!* **6.** to condemn or curse: *I'll be blessed if I can see your reasoning. Bless me if it isn't my old friend!* **7.** to make the sign of the cross over or upon: *The Pope blessed the multitude.* [bef. 950; ME *blessen,* OE *blētsian, blēdsian* to consecrate, orig. with blood, earlier **blōdisōian* (*blōd* BLOOD + *-isō-* derivational suffix + *-ian* v. suffix)] —**bless′er,** *n.* —**bless′·ing·ly,** *adv.*
—**Syn. 1.** exalt, hallow, glorify, magnify, beatify.

bless·ed (bles′id; *esp. for 3,* 7 blest), *adj.* **1.** consecrated; sacred; holy; sanctified: *the Blessed Sacrament.* **2.** worthy of adoration, reverence, or worship: *the Blessed Trinity.* **3.** divinely or supremely favored; fortunate: *to be blessed with a strong, healthy body; blessed with an ability to find friends.* **4.** blissfully happy or contented. **5.** *Rom. Cath. Ch.* beatified. **6.** bringing happiness and thankfulness: *the blessed assurance of a steady income.* **7.** *Informal.* damned: *I'm blessed if I know.* **8.** *Informal.* (used as an intensifier): *every blessed cent.* Also, **blest.** [1125–75; ME; see BLESS, -ED[2]] —**bless′ed·ly,** *adv.* —**bless′ed·ness,** *n.*

bless′ed event′, the birth of a child.

Bless′ed Sac′rament, *Eccles.* the consecrated Host. [1550–60]

Bless′ed Trin′ity, Trinity (def. 1).

Bless′ed Vir′gin, the Virgin Mary.

bless·ing (bles′ing), *n.* **1.** the act or words of a person who blesses. **2.** a special favor, mercy, or benefit: *the blessings of liberty.* **3.** a favor or gift bestowed by God, thereby bringing happiness. **4.** the invoking of God's favor upon a person: *The son was denied his father's blessing.* **5.** praise; devotion; worship, esp. grace said before a meal: *The children took turns reciting the blessing.* **6.** approval or good wishes: *The proposed law had the blessing of the governor.* [bef. 900; ME *blessinge, -unge,* OE *bletsung, bledsung.* See BLESS, -ING[1]]
—**Syn. 2.** advantage, boon, gain, profit, bounty.

blest (blest), *v.* **1.** a pt. and pp. of **bless.** —*adj.* **2.** blessed.

bleth·er (bleth′ər), *n., v.i., v.t.* blather.

ble·til·la (bli til′ə), *n.* any of several terrestrial orchids of the genus *Bletilla,* of eastern Asia, as *B. striata,* having terminal clusters of showy purple or white flowers. [< NL, equiv. to *Blet(ia)* a similar genus (named in honor of Louis *Blet,* botanist and apothecary at the Spanish court in 1794; see -IA) + L *-illa* -ILLA]

blet·ting (blet′ing), *n.* the ripening of fruit, esp. of fruit stored until the desired degree of softness is attained. [< F *blet* (fem. *blette*) overripe (var. of OF *blece,* adj. deriv. of *blecier* to bruise < Old Low Franconian **blettian*) + -ING[1]]

bleu′ cheese′ (blo͞o). See **blue cheese.** [1955–60; F *bleu* for BLUE because certain highly prized blue cheeses come from France]

bleu-de-roi (*Fr.* blœdᵊ RWA′), *n.* the bright enamel blue color characteristic of Sèvres ware. Also called **bleu roy·al** (*Fr.* blœ RWA yAl′; *Eng.* blo͞o′ roi′əl, roi al′). [1840–50; < F: lit., king's blue]

Bleu·ler (bloi′lər), *n.* **Eu·gen** (oi gān′), 1857–1939, Swiss psychiatrist and neurologist.

blew (blo͞o), *v.* **1.** pt. of **blow**[2]. **2.** pt. of **blow**[3].

blew·it (blo͞o′it), *n.* an edible pale-bluish mushroom, *Tricholoma personatum.* Also, **bluette, blew′its, blew′·itt.** Also called **blue-leg.** [1820–30; prob. BLUE + -ET]

Bli·da (blē′dä), *n.* a city in N Algeria. 99,238.

Bligh (blī), *n.* **William,** 1754–1817, British naval officer: captain of H.M.S. *Bounty,* the crew of which mutinied 1789.

blight (blīt), *n.* **1.** *Plant Pathol.* **a.** the rapid and extensive discoloration, wilting, and death of plant tissues. **b.** a disease so characterized. **2.** any cause of impairment, destruction, ruin, or frustration: *Extravagance was the blight of the family.* **3.** the state or result of being blighted or deteriorated; dilapidation; decay: *urban blight.* —*v.t.* **4.** to cause to wither or decay; blast: *Frost blighted the crops.* **5.** to destroy; ruin; frustrate: *Illness blighted his hopes.* —*v.i.* **6.** to suffer blight. [1605–15; of uncert. orig.] —**blight′ing·ly,** *adv.*
—**Syn. 2.** curse, plague, scourge, bane.

blight·er (blī′tər), *n. Brit. Slang.* **1.** a contemptible, worthless person, esp. a man; scoundrel or rascal. **2.** a chap; bloke. [1815–25; BLIGHT + -ER[1]]

blight·y (blī′tē), *n., pl.* **blight·ies.** *Brit. Slang.* **1.** (*often cap.*) England as one's native land; England as home: *We're sailing for old Blighty tomorrow.* **2.** a wound or furlough permitting a soldier to be sent back to England from the front. **3.** military leave. [1885–90; < Hindi *bilāyatī* the country (i.e., Great Britain), var. of *wilāyatī* VILAYET]

bli·mey (blī′mē), *interj. Brit. Informal.* (used to express surprise or excitement.) Also, **bli′my.** [1885–90; orig. reduced form of *blind me,* as ellipsis from *God blind me;* cf. GORBLIMEY]

blimp (blimp), *n.* **1.** a small, nonrigid airship or dirigible, esp. one used chiefly for observation. **2.** *Slang.* a fat person. [1915–20; of uncert. orig.]

Blimp (blimp), (*sometimes l.c.*) See **Colonel Blimp.** [1930–35]

blimp·ish (blim′pish), *adj.* (*sometimes cap.*) pompously reactionary: *the blimpish attitudes of the old colonialists.* [1935–40; COLONEL BLIMP + -ISH[1]] —**blimp′ish·ly,** *adv.* —**blimp′ish·ness,** *n.*

blin (blin), *n. Russian Cookery.* sing. of **blini.** [1885–90; < Russ; ORuss *blinŭ,* by dissimilation from *mlinŭ,* n. deriv. from base of Russ *molót'* to grind, *mél'nitsa* mill; cf. MILL[1]]

blind (blīnd), *adj.,* **-er, -est,** *v., n., adv.* —*adj.* **1.** unable to see; lacking the sense of sight; sightless: *a blind man.* **2.** unwilling or unable to perceive or understand: *They were blind to their children's faults. He was blind to all arguments.* **3.** not characterized or determined by reason or control: *blind tenacity; blind chance.* **4.** not having or based on reason or intelligence; absolute and unquestioning: *She had blind faith in his fidelity.* **5.** lacking all consciousness or awareness: *a blind stupor.* **6.** drunk. **7.** hard to see or understand: *blind reasoning.* **8.** hidden from immediate view, esp. from oncoming motorists: *a blind corner.* **9.** of concealed or undisclosed identity; sponsored anonymously: *a blind ad signed only with a box number.* **10.** having no outlets; closed at one end: *a blind passage; a blind mountain pass.* **11.** *Archit.* (of an archway, arcade, etc.) having no windows, passageways, or the like. **12.** dense enough to form a screen: *a blind hedge of privet.* **13.** done without seeing; by instruments alone: *blind flying.* **14.** made without some prior knowledge: *a blind purchase; a blind lead in a card game.* **15.** of or pertaining to an experimental design that prevents investigators or subjects from knowing the hypotheses or conditions being tested. **16.** of, pertaining to, or for blind persons. **17.** *Bookbinding.* (of a design, title, or the like) impressed into the cover or spine of a book by a die without ink or foil. **18.** *Cookery.* (of pastry shells) baked or fried without the filling. **19.** (of a rivet or other fastener) made so that the end inserted, though inaccessible, can be headed or spread. —*v.t.* **20.** to make sightless permanently, temporarily, or momentarily, as by injuring, dazzling, bandaging the eyes, etc.: *The explosion blinded him. We were blinded*

by the bright lights. **21.** to make obscure or dark: *The room was blinded by heavy curtains.* **22.** to deprive of discernment, reason, or judgment: *a resentment that blinds his good sense.* **23.** to outshine; eclipse: *a radiance that doth blind the sun.* —*n.* **24.** something that obstructs vision, as a blinker for a horse. **25.** a window covering having horizontal or vertical slats that can be drawn out of the way, often with the angle of the slats adjustable to admit varying amounts of light. **26.** See **Venetian blind.** **27.** *Chiefly Midland U.S. and Brit.* See **window shade.** **28.** a lightly built structure of brush or other growths, esp. one in which hunters conceal themselves. **29.** an activity, organization, or the like for concealing or masking action or purpose; subterfuge: *The store was just a blind for their gambling operation.* **30.** a decoy. **31.** *Slang.* a bout of excessive drinking; drunken spree. **32.** *Poker.* a compulsory bet made without prior knowledge of one's hand. **33.** (*used with a plural v.*) persons who lack the sense of sight (usually preceded by *the*): *The blind are said to have an acute sense of hearing.* —*adv.* **34.** into a stupor; to the degree at which consciousness is lost: *He drank himself blind.* **35.** without the ability to see clearly; lacking visibility; blindly: *They were driving blind through the snowstorm.* **36.** without guidance or forethought: *They were working blind and couldn't anticipate the effects of their actions.* **37.** to an extreme or absolute degree; completely: *The confidence men cheated her blind.* [bef. 1000; (adj.) ME *blind,* OE; c. Goth *blinds,* ON *blindr,* G, D *blind* (< Gmc **blindaz,* perh. akin to BLEND; original sense uncert.); (v.) ME *blinden,* deriv. of the adj.] —**blind′ing·ly,** *adv.* —**blind′ness,** *n.*
—**Syn. 1.** BLIND, STONE-BLIND, PURBLIND mean unable to see. BLIND means unable to see with the physical eyes. STONE-BLIND emphasizes complete blindness. PURBLIND refers to weakened vision, literally or figuratively. **4.** irrational, uncritical, rash, thoughtless, unreasoning. **8.** concealed. **25.** See **curtain. 28.** hiding place, ambush. —**Ant. 1.** seeing. **2.** receptive. **4.** rational.
—**Regional Variation. 27.** See **window shade.**

blind′ al′ley, 1. a road, alley, etc., that is open at only one end. **2.** a position or situation offering no hope of progress or improvement: *That line of reasoning will only lead you up another blind alley.* [1575–85]

blind′ cas′ing, *Building Trades.* (in a box window frame) a rough framework to which the trim is secured.

blind·cat (blīnd′kat′), *n.* any of several catfishes, as *Satan eurystomus* (**widemouth blindcat**) of Texas, that inhabit underground streams and have undeveloped eyes and unpigmented skin. [BLIND + CAT¹]

blind′ cop′y, a copy of a letter or the like, the original of which bears no evidence that the copy was sent to some other person.

blind′ date′, 1. a social appointment or date arranged, usually by a third person, between two people who have not met. **2.** either of the participants in such an arrangement. [1920–25, *Amer.*]

blind′ door′, a door having louvers permitting circulation of air. [1880–85, *Amer.*]

blind-em·boss (blīnd′em bôs′, -bos′), *v.t. Bookbinding.* blind-stamp.

blind·er (blīn′dər), *n.* **1.** a person or thing that blinds. **2.** a blinker for a horse. **3.** *Brit. Informal.* a spectacular shot or action in sports, esp. soccer: *He played a blinder.* [1580–90; BLIND + -ER¹]

blind·fish (blīnd′fish′), *n., pl.* **-fish·es,** (*esp. collectively*) **-fish.** cavefish. [1835–45, *Amer.*; BLIND + FISH]

blind′ flange′, a disk for closing the end of a pipe, having holes for bolting it to a flange.

blind′ floor′, subfloor.

blind·fold (blīnd′fōld′), *v.t.* **1.** to prevent or occlude sight by covering (the eyes) with a cloth, bandage, or the like; cover the eyes of. **2.** to impair the awareness or clear thinking of: *Don't let their hospitality blindfold you to the true purpose of their invitation.* —*n.* **3.** a cloth or bandage put before the eyes to prevent seeing. —*adj.* **4.** with the eyes covered: *a blindfold test.* **5.** rash; unthinking: *a blindfold denunciation before knowing the facts.* [1520–30; alter., by assoc. with FOLD¹, of *blindfell* to cover the eyes, strike blind, ME *blindfellen;* see BLIND, FELL²]

blind′ gut′, the cecum. [1585–95]

Blind·heim (blint′hīm′), *n.* German name of **Blenheim.**

blind′ hole′, *Golf.* a hole whose green cannot be seen by the approaching golfer because of trees or other obstructions. [1895–1900]

blind·ing (blīn′ding), *n.* a layer of sand or fine gravel for filling the gaps in the surfaces of a road or pavement, as one of crushed and compacted stone. [1350–1400; ME; see BLIND, -ING¹]

blind·ly (blīnd′lē), *adv.* **1.** in a blind manner: *We felt our way blindly through the black tunnel.* **2.** without understanding, reservation, or objection; unthinkingly: *They followed their leaders blindly.* **3.** without continuation: *The passage ended blindly 50 feet away.* [bef. 900; ME; OE *blindlice;* see BLIND, -LY]

blind·man's buff (blīnd′manz′ buf′), a game in which a blindfolded player tries to catch and identify one of the other players. Also called **blind′man's bluff′.** [1580–90]

blind′ man's′ rule′, a carpenter's rule having large numbers to permit its reading in dim light.

blind′ pig′, *Chiefly Inland North and Pacific States.* See **blind tiger.** [1865–70, *Amer.*]

blind′ roll′er, *Oceanog.* a long ocean swell that rises almost to breaking as it passes over shoals. [1885–90]

blind′ sal′amander, any of several North American salamanders, esp. of the genera *Typhlotriton, Typhlomolge,* and *Haideotriton,* that inhabit underground streams or deep wells and have undeveloped eyes and scant pigmentation.

blind′ seed′, *Plant Pathol.* a disease of ryegrass, characterized by shriveled, soft seeds, caused by a fungus, *Phialea temulenta.* [1935–40]

blind′ side′, 1. the part of one's field of vision, as to the side and rear, where one is unable to see approaching objects. **2.** the side opposite that toward which a person is looking. [1600–10]

blind·side (blīnd′sīd′), *v.t.,* **-sid·ed, -sid·ing. 1.** *Sports.* to tackle, hit, or attack (an opponent) from the blind side: *The quarterback was blindsided and had the ball knocked out of his hand.* **2.** *Informal.* to attack critically where a person is vulnerable, uninformed, etc.: *The president was blindsided by the press on the latest tax bill.* [1970–75; v. use of n. phrase BLIND SIDE]

blind·sight (blīnd′sīt′), *n.* the ability of a blind person to sense accurately a light source or other visual stimulus even though unable to see it consciously. [BLIND + SIGHT]

blind′ snake′, any of numerous wormlike, burrowing snakes of the families Typhlopidae, Leptotyphlopidae, and Anomalepididae, most of which have vestigial eyes. Also called **worm snake.**

blind′ spot′, 1. *Anat.* a small area on the retina that is insensitive to light due to the interruption, where the optic nerve joins the retina, of the normal pattern of light-sensitive rods and cones. See diag. under **eye. 2.** an area or subject about which one is uninformed, prejudiced, or unappreciative: *I confess that operettas are my blind spot.* **3.** *Radio.* an area in which signals are weak and their reception poor. **4.** Also called **dead spot.** any part of an auditorium, arena, or the like, in which a person is unable to see or hear satisfactorily. **5.** an area to the side and slightly behind a driver's field of vision that is not reflected in the vehicle's rearview mirror. [1860–65]

blind′ stag′gers, *Vet. Pathol.* **1.** stagger (def. 13). **2.** *Informal.* a condition of staggering and dizziness, esp. as the result of drunkenness. [1775–85, *Amer.*]

blind-stamp (blīnd′stamp′), *v.t. Bookbinding.* to emboss or impress (the cover or spine of a book) without using ink or foil. Also, **blind-emboss.** Cf. **blind** (def. 17). [1905–10]

blind·sto·ry (blīnd′stôr′ē, -stōr′ē), *n., pl.* **-ries.** *Archit.* a story, or major horizontal division of a wall, having no exterior windows or other major openings. [1510–20; BLIND + STORY²]

blind′ ti′ger, *Chiefly Midland and Southern U.S.* an illegal saloon. [1855–60, *Amer.*; perh. so called because exhibitions of natural curiosities served as fronts for such places]

blind′ trust′, a trust in which a trustee controls the financial investments of a public official, without the beneficiary's knowledge of how his or her affairs are administered, in order to avoid conflict of interest. [1965–70]

blind·worm (blīnd′wûrm′), *n.* **1.** a limbless European lizard, *Anguis fragilis,* related to the glass lizards. **2.** a caecilian, *Ichthyophis glutinosus,* of Sri Lanka, that coils around its eggs. [1425–75; late ME; see BLIND, WORM; so called because the eyes are very small]

blin·i (blin′ē, blē′nē), *n.pl., sing.* **blin.** *Russian Cookery.* pancakes made with yeast and either white or buckwheat flour and traditionally served during Shrovetide with caviar and sour cream. Also, **blin′is, bliny.** [< Russ *blíny,* pl. of *blin* BLIN]

blink (blingk), *v.i.* **1.** to open and close the eye, esp. involuntarily; wink rapidly and repeatedly. **2.** to look with winking or half-shut eyes: *I blinked at the harsh morning light.* **3.** to be startled, surprised, or dismayed (usually fol. by *at*): *She blinked at his sudden fury.* **4.** to look evasively or with indifference; ignore (often fol. by *at*): *to blink at another's eccentricities.* **5.** to shine unsteadily, dimly, or intermittently; twinkle: *The light on the buoy blinked in the distance.* —*v.t.* **6.** to open and close (the eye or eyes), usually rapidly and repeatedly; wink: *She blinked her eyes in an effort to wake up.* **7.** to cause (something) to blink: *We blinked the flashlight frantically, but there was no response.* **8.** to ignore deliberately; evade; shirk. —*n.* **9.** an act of blinking: *The faithful blink of the lighthouse.* **10.** a gleam; glimmer: *There was not a blink of light anywhere.* **11.** *Chiefly Scot.* a glance or glimpse. **12.** *Meteorol.* **a.** iceblink. **b.** snowblink. **13. on the blink,** not in proper working order; in need of repair: *The washing machine is on the blink again.* [1250–1300; ME *blinken* (v.), var. of *blenken* to BLENCH¹; c. D, G *blinken*]
—**Syn. 1.** See **wink¹. 8.** overlook, disregard, avoid, condone. **9.** wink, flicker, twinkle, flutter.

blink′ compar′ator, an optical instrument used to detect small differences in two photographs of the same field or object by viewing them alternately, switching rapidly from one to the other. [1925–30]

blink·er (bling′kər), *n.* **1.** a device for flashing light signals. **2.** a light that flashes intermittently, esp. one that serves as a traffic signal. **3.** either of two leather flaps on a bridle, to prevent a horse from seeing sideways; a blinder. See illus. under **harness.** —*v.t.* **4.** to put blinkers on. [1630–40; BLINK + -ER¹]

blink·ing (bling′king), *adj., adv. Chiefly Brit.* (used as an intensifier): *He's a blinking idiot.* [1910–15; BLINK + -ING²] —**blink′ing·ly,** *adv.*

blink·y (bling′kē), *adj.,* **blink·i·er, blink·i·est.** *Midland U.S.* (of milk) sour. [BLINK (in the sense "to turn sour"; cf. Brit. dial. blink to bewitch, turn (milk, beer) sour by witchcraft) + -Y¹]

blintze (blints, blint′sə), *n. Jewish Cookery.* a thin pancake folded or rolled around a filling, as of cheese or fruit, and fried or baked. Also, **blintz** (blints). [1900–05; < Yiddish *blintse;* cf. Byelorussian *blints-,* s. of *blinéts,* dim. of *blin* pancake; see BLIN]

blin·y (blin′ē, blē′nē), *n.pl., sing.* **blin.** blini.

blip (blip), *n., v.,* **blipped, blip·ping.** —*n.* **1.** Also called **pip.** *Electronics.* **a.** a spot of light on a radar screen indicating the position of a plane, submarine, or other object. **b.** (loosely) any small spot of light on a display screen. **2.** a brief upturn, as in revenue or income: *The midwinter blip was no cause for optimism among store owners.* **3.** anything small, as in amount or number: *a blip of light; Those opposed were merely a blip in the opinion polls.* **4.** bleep (def. 3). **5.** *Slang.* a nickel; five cents. **6.** *Motion Pictures.* a mark of synchronization on a sound track. **7.** a small or brief interruption, as in the continuity of a motion-picture film or the supply of light or electricity: *There were blips in the TV film where the commercials had been edited out.* —*v.i.* **8.** *Informal.* to move or proceed in short, irregular, jerking movements: *The stock market has blipped one point higher this week.* —*v.t.* **9.** bleep (def. 5). [1890–95, for an earlier sense; sound symbolism, with *p* for brevity and abrupt end of the impulse; *bl-* perh. from BLINK]

blip·ping (blip′ing), *adj.* bleeping.

bliss (blis), *n.* **1.** supreme happiness; utter joy or contentment: *wedded bliss.* **2.** *Theol.* the joy of heaven. **3.** heaven; paradise: *the road to eternal bliss.* **4.** *Archaic.* a cause of great joy or happiness. —*v.t., v.i.* **5.** *Slang.* **bliss out, a.** to experience bliss or euphoria: *Just give them some bean sprouts and a little tofu and they bliss out.* **b.** to cause to become blissful or euphoric: *a recording guaranteed to bliss out every Mozart fan.* [bef. 1000; ME *blisse,* OE *bliss, bliths,* equiv. to *blīthe* BLITHE + *-s* suffix] —**bliss′less,** *adj.*
—**Syn. 1.** See **happiness.** —**Ant. 1.** misery.

Bliss (blis), *n.* **1. Sir Arthur (Edward Drummond),** 1891–1975, English composer. **2. Tas·ker** (tas′kər) **Howard,** 1853–1930, U.S. general.

bliss·ful (blis′fəl), *adj.* full of, abounding in, enjoying, or conferring bliss. [1175–1225; ME; see BLISS, -FUL; r. OE *blissig*] —**bliss′ful·ly,** *adv.* —**bliss′ful·ness,** *n.*

blis·ter (blis′tər), *n.* **1.** a thin vesicle on the skin, containing watery matter or serum, as from a burn or other injury. **2.** any similar swelling, as an air bubble in a coat of paint. **3.** a relatively large bubble occurring in glass during blowing. **4.** *Mil.* a transparent bulge or dome on the fuselage of an airplane, usually for mounting a gun. **5.** *Photog.* a bubble of air formed where the emulsion has separated from the base of a film, as because of defective processing. **6.** a dome or skylight on a building. **7.** the moving bubble in a spirit level. **8.** a small blisterlike covering of plastic, usually affixed to a piece of cardboard and containing a small item, as a pen, bolt, or medicinal tablet. —*v.t.* **9.** to raise a blister or blisters on: *These new shoes blistered my feet.* **10.** to criticize or rebuke severely: *The boss blistered his assistant in front of the whole office.* **11.** to beat or thrash; punish severely. —*v.i.* **12.** to form or rise as a blister or blisters; become blistered. [1250–1300; ME *blister, blester* < ON *blǣstri,* dat. of *blāstr* swelling. See BLAST, BLOW²]

blis′ter bee′tle, any of various beetles of the family Meloidae, many of which produce a secretion capable of blistering the skin. [1810–20]

blis′ter cop′per, *Metall.* a matte of from 96 to 99 percent copper, having a blistered surface after smelting because of gases generated during solidification. [1860–65]

blis′ter gas′, *Chemical Warfare.* a poison gas that burns or blisters the tissues of the body; vesicant. [1935–40]

blis·ter·ing (blis′tər ing), *adj.* **1.** causing a blister or blisters. **2.** (esp. of sunlight, heat, etc.) very severe or intense. **3.** very fast or rapid: *a blistering pace.* —*n.* **4.** the act or an instance of forming a blister or blisters. **5.** a series or group of blisters, as on a painted surface. [1555–65; BLISTER + -ING²] —**blis′ter·ing·ly,** *adv.*

blis′ter pack′, a package consisting of a clear plastic overlay affixed to a cardboard backing for protecting and displaying a product: *a blister pack of four flashlight batteries.* Also called **blis′ter pack′age, bubble card, bubble pack.** [1950–55; from the shape of the plastic]

blis′ter rust′, *Plant Pathol.* a disease, esp. of white pines, characterized by cankers and in the spring by blisters on the stems, caused by a rust fungus of the genus *Cronartium.* [1915–20]

blis′ter steel′, *Metall.* steel produced from wrought iron by cementation in covered pots, having a blistered appearance because of the gases generated during the process. [1830–40]

blis·ter·y (blis′tə rē), *adj.* having blisters, as paint or glass. [1735–45; BLISTER + -Y¹]

B.Lit., Bachelor of Literature.

blite (blīt), *n.* **1.** See **sea blite. 2.** See **strawberry blite.** [1375–1425; late ME < L *blitum* < Gk *blíton*]

blithe (blīth, blīth), *adj.,* **blith·er, blith·est. 1.** joyous, merry, or gay in disposition; glad; cheerful: *Everyone loved her for her blithe spirit.* **2.** without thought or regard; carefree; heedless: *a blithe indifference to anyone's feelings.* [bef. 1000; ME; OE *blīthe;* c. ON *blīthr,* OHG *blīdi,* Goth *bleiths*] —**blithe′ful,** *adj.* —**blithe′ful·ly,** *adv.* —**blithe′ly,** *adv.* —**blithe′ness,** *n.*
—**Syn. 1.** happy, mirthful, sprightly, light-hearted, buoyant, joyful, blithesome. —**Ant. 1.** joyless.

Blithe (blīth, blīth), *n.* a female given name.

blith·er (blith′ər), *v.i.* to talk foolishly; blather: *He's blithering about some problem of his.* [1865–70; var. of BLATHER]

blithe·some (blīth′səm, blīth′-), *adj.* lighthearted; merry; cheerful: *a blithesome nature.* [1715–25; BLITHE + -SOME¹] —**blithe′some·ly,** *adv.* —**blithe′some·ness,** *n.*

B.Litt., Bachelor of Letters.

CONCISE PRONUNCIATION KEY: act, cāpe, dâre, pärt; set, ēqual; *if,* ice; ox, ōver, ôrder, oil, bŏŏk, bōōt, out; up, ûrge; child; sing; shoe; thin, *that;* zh as in *treasure.* ə = *a* as in *alone, e* as in *system, i* as in *easily, o* as in *gallop, u* as in *circus;* ᵊ as in *fire* (fīᵊr), *hour* (ouᵊr). l and n can serve as syllabic consonants, as in *cradle* (krād′l), and *button* (but′n). See the full key inside the front cover.

blitz (blits), *n.* **1.** *Mil.* **a.** an overwhelming all-out attack, esp. a swift ground attack using armored units and air support. **b.** an intensive aerial bombing. **2.** any swift, vigorous attack, barrage, or defeat: *a blitz of commercials every few minutes.* **3.** *Football.* act or instance of charging directly for (the passer) as soon as the ball is snapped; red-dogging. **4.** bingo. —*v.t.* **5.** to attack or defeat with or as if with a blitz: *The town was blitzed mercilessly by enemy planes. The visitors really blitzed the home team.* **6.** to destroy; demolish: *His last-minute refusal blitzed all our plans.* —*v.i.* **7.** *Football.* to charge directly and immediately at the passer; red-dog. **8.** to move in the manner of a blitz: *a car that will blitz through rough terrain.* [1935–40; shortening of BLITZKRIEG] —**blitz′er,** *n.*

blitz′ can′, *Mil.* See **jerry can** (def. 1).

blitzed (blitst), *adj. Slang.* **1.** drunk or stoned. **2.** extremely tired. Also, **blitzed-out** (blitst′out′). [BLITZ + -ED[2]]

blitz·krieg (blits′krēg′), *n., v.t.* blitz (defs. 1, 2, 5). [1935–40; < G, equiv. to *Blitz* lightning + *Krieg* war]

Blitz·stein (blits′stīn), *n.* **Marc,** 1905–64, U.S. composer.

Blix·en (blik′sən), *n.* **Karen.** See **Dinesen, Isak.**

bliz·zard (bliz′ərd), *n.* **1.** *Meteorol.* **a.** a storm with dry, driving snow, strong winds, and intense cold. **b.** a heavy and prolonged snowstorm covering a wide area. **2.** an inordinately large amount all at one time; avalanche: *a blizzard of Christmas cards.* —*v.i.* **3.** to snow as a blizzard: *Looks as though it's going to blizzard tonight.* [1820–30, *Amer.*; earlier: violent blow, shot; cf. Brit. dial. (Midlands) *blizzer, blizzom* blaze, flash, anything that blinds momentarily; prob. expressive formations with components of BLAST, BLAZE[1], BLUSTER, etc.] —**bliz′zard·y, bliz′zard·ly,** *adj.*

blk., **1.** black. **2.** block. **3.** bulk.

B.LL., Bachelor of Laws.

BLM, Bureau of Land Management. Also, **B.L.M.**

bloat (blōt), *v.t.* **1.** to expand or distend, as with air, water, etc.; cause to swell: *Overeating bloated their bellies.* **2.** to puff up; make vain or conceited: *The promotion has bloated his ego to an alarming degree.* **3.** to cure (fishes) as bloaters. —*v.i.* **4.** to become swollen; be puffed out or dilated: *The carcass started to bloat.* —*n.* **5.** Also called **hoven.** *Vet. Pathol.* (in cattle, sheep, and horses) a distention of the rumen or paunch or of the large colon by gases of fermentation, caused by eating ravenously of green forage, esp. legumes. **6.** a person or thing that is bloated. **7.** bloater (defs. 1, 2). [1250–1300; earlier *bloat* (adj.) soft, puffy, ME *blout* < ON *blautr* wet, soft]
—**Syn. 1.** swell, inflate, enlarge, balloon.

bloat·ed (blō′tid), *adj.* **1.** swollen; puffed up; overlarge. **2.** excessively vain; conceited. **3.** excessively fat; obese. [1655–65; BLOAT + -ED[2]] —**bloat′ed·ness,** *n.*

bloat·er (blō′tər), *n.* **1.** a herring cured by being salted and briefly smoked and dried. **2.** a mackerel similarly cured. **3.** a freshwater cisco, *Coregonus hoyi,* found in the Great Lakes. [1825–35; *bloat* (adj.) + -ER[1]]

blob (blob), *n., v.,* **blobbed, blob·bing.** —*n.* **1.** a globule of liquid; bubble. **2.** a small lump, drop, splotch, or daub: *A blob of paint marred the surface.* **3.** an object, esp. a large one, having no distinct shape or definition: *a blob on the horizon.* **4.** a dull, slow-witted, and uninteresting person. —*v.t.* **5.** to mark or splotch with blobs. [1400–50; late ME; appar. expressive formation]

bloc (blok), *n.* **1.** a group of persons, businesses, etc., united for a particular purpose. **2.** a group of legislators, usually of both major political parties, who vote together for some particular interest: *the farm bloc.* **3.** a group of nations that share common interests and usually act in concert in international affairs: *the Soviet bloc.* [1900–05; < F; see BLOCK]
—**Syn.** coalition.

Bloch (blok), *n.* **1. Ernest,** 1880–1959, Swiss composer, in the U.S. after 1916. **2. Felix,** 1905–83, Swiss physicist in the U.S.: Nobel prize 1952. **3. Konrad E.,** born 1912, U.S. biochemist, born in Germany: Nobel prize for medicine 1964.

block (blok), *n.* **1.** a solid mass of wood, stone, etc., usually with one or more flat or approximately flat faces. **2.** a hollow masonry building unit of cement, terra cotta, etc.: *a wall made of concrete blocks.* **3.** one of a set of cube-shaped pieces of wood, plastic, or the like, used as a child's toy in building. **4.** a mold or piece on which something is shaped or kept in shape: *a hat block.* **5.** a piece of wood used in the art of making woodcuts or wood engravings. **6.** *Print.* the base on which a plate is mounted to make it type-high. **7.** a projection left on a squared stone to provide a means of lifting it. **8.** a short length of plank serving as a bridging, as between joists. **9.** a stump or wooden structure on which a condemned person is beheaded: *Mary Stuart went bravely to the block.* **10.** See **auction block. 11.** *Mach.* a part enclosing one or more freely rotating, grooved pulleys, about which ropes or chains pass to form a hoisting or hauling tackle. **12.** an obstacle, obstruction, or hindrance: *His stubbornness is a block to all my efforts.* **13.** the state or condition of being obstructed; blockage: *The traffic block lasted several hours.* **14.** *Pathol.* **a.** an obstruction, as of a nerve. **b.** See **heart block. 15.** *Sports.* a hindering of an opponent's actions. **16.** a quantity, portion, or section taken as a unit or dealt with at one time: *a large block of theater tickets.* **17.** a small section of a city, town, etc., enclosed by neighboring and intersecting streets: *She lives on my block.* **18.** the length of one side of such a section: *We walked two blocks over.* **19.** *Chiefly Brit.* a large building divided into separate apartments, offices, shops, etc. **20.** a large number of bonds or shares of stock sold together as a single unit. **21.** *Computers.* **a.** a group of data stored as a unit on an external storage medium and handled as a unit by the computer for input or output: *This file has 20 records per block.* **b.** a section of storage locations in a computer allocated to a particular set of instructions or data. **c.** a group of consecutive machine words organized as a unit and guiding a particular computer operation, esp. with reference to input and output. **d.** (on a flow chart) a symbol representing an operation, device, or instruction in a computer program. **22.** *Railroads.* any of the short lengths into which a track is divided for signaling purposes. **23.** *Philately.* a group of four or more unseparated stamps, not in a strip. **24.** *Slang.* a person's head. **25.** *Glassmaking.* a wooden or metal cup for blocking a gather. **26.** an obstruction or stoppage in mental processes or speech, esp. when related to stress, emotional conflict, etc. **27.** See **writer's block. 28.** *Geol.* **a.** any large, angular mass of solid rock. **b.** See **fault block. 29.** (in Canada) a wild or remote area of land that has not yet been surveyed: *the Peace River block.* **30.** *Auto.* See **cylinder block. 31.** *Falconry.* a low perch to which a falcon is tethered outdoors. **32. put** or **go on the block,** to offer or be offered for sale at auction: *to put family heirlooms on the block.* —*v.t.* **33.** to obstruct (someone or something) by placing obstacles in the way (sometimes fol. by *up*): *to block one's exit; to block up a passage.* **34.** to fit with blocks; mount on a block. **35.** to shape or prepare on or with a block: *to block a hat; to block a sweater.* **36.** to join (the ends of boards or the like) by fastening to a block of wood. **37.** *Theat.* **a.** Also, **block out.** to plan or work out the movement of performers in a play, pageant, etc.: *Tomorrow we'll block act one.* **b.** to draw a floor plan on (a stage) in order to indicate placement of scenery, stage property, etc. **38.** *Pathol., Physiol.* to stop the passage of impulses in (a nerve). **39.** *Computers.* to group (contiguous data) together so as to allow to be read or written in a single operation. **40.** *Sports.* to hinder or bar the actions or movements of (an opposing player), esp. legitimately. **41.** *Glassmaking.* **a.** to shape (a molten gather) in a wet cup of wood or metal. **b.** to plunge a block of wood into (molten glass) to aid in refining the glass. **42.** *Metalworking.* to give (a forging) a rough form before finishing. **43.** *Electronics.* to apply a high negative bias to the grid of (a vacuum tube), for reducing the plate current to zero. —*v.i.* **44.** to act so as to obstruct an opponent, as in football, hockey, and basketball: *He doesn't get many baskets, but he sure can block.* **45.** *Theat.* to block a play, act, scene, stage, etc.: *The director will block tomorrow.* **46.** to suffer a block. **47. block out, a.** block (def. 36a). **b.** *Basketball.* to box out. **48. block in** or **out,** to sketch or outline roughly or generally, without details: *She blocked out a color scheme for the interiors.* [1275–1325; ME *blok* log, stump (< MF *bloc*) < MD *blok;* perh. akin to BALK] —**block′a·ble,** *adj.*
—**Syn. 12.** impediment, blockade, barrier, stoppage, jam. **33.** close, blockade, impede; hinder, deter, stop.

CONCISE ETYMOLOGY KEY: <, descended or borrowed from; >, whence; b., blend of, blended; c., cognate with; cf., compare; deriv., derivative; equiv., equivalent; imit., imitative; obl., oblique; r., replacing; s., stem; sp., spelling, spelled; resp., respelling, respelled; trans., translation; ?, origin unknown; *, unattested; ‡, probably earlier than. See the full key inside the front cover.

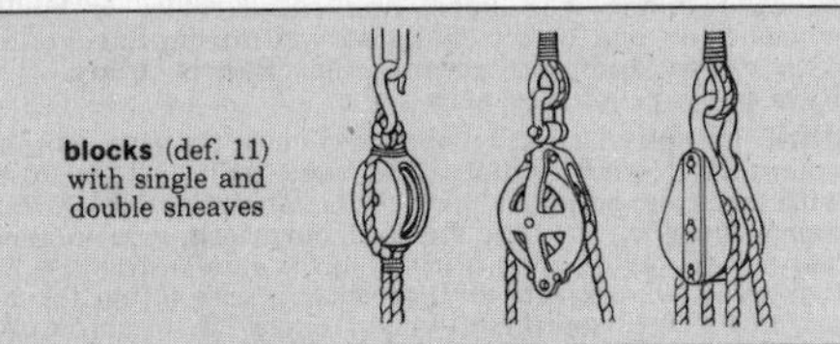

blocks (def. 11) with single and double sheaves

Block (blok), *n.* **Herbert Lawrence** ("*Herblock*"), born 1909, U.S. cartoonist.

block·ade (blo kād′), *n., v.,* **-ad·ed, -ad·ing.** —*n.* **1.** the isolating, closing off, or surrounding of a place, as a port, harbor, or city, by hostile ships or troops to prevent entrance or exit. **2.** any obstruction of passage or progress: *We had difficulty in getting through the blockade of bodyguards.* **3.** *Pathol.* interruption or inhibition of a normal physiological signal, as a nerve impulse or a heart muscle-contraction impulse. —*v.t.* **4.** to subject to a blockade. [1670–80; BLOCK (v.) + -ADE[1]] —**block·ad′er,** *n.*
—**Syn. 1.** See **siege.**

block·ade-run·ner (blo kād′run′ər), *n.* a ship or person that passes through a blockade. [1860–65] —**block·ade′-run′ning,** *n.*

block·age (blok′ij), *n.* **1.** an act of blocking. **2.** the state of being blocked; an obstructed condition: *the blockage of the streets by heavy snows.* **3.** something that blocks; obstruction. [1870–75; BLOCK + -AGE]

block′ and tack′le, the ropes or chains and blocks used in a hoisting tackle. [1830–40]

block′ associa′tion, an association of residents of a city block who work together to maintain a safe and attractive neighborhood. Also called **block′ club′, block organization.** [1970–75]

block′ book′ing, a practice among motion-picture distributors of contracting with an exhibitor to show a predetermined series of films. [1920–25]

block·bust (blok′bust′), *v.t., v.i.* to subject or be subjected to blockbusting: *Developers blockbusted in order to buy up the entire area.* [*Amer.*; by back formation from BLOCKBUSTER or BLOCKBUSTING]

block·bust·er (blok′bus′tər), *n.* **1.** an aerial bomb containing high explosives and weighing from four to eight tons, used as a large-scale demolition bomb. **2.** a motion picture, novel, etc., esp. one lavishly produced, that has or is expected to have wide popular appeal or financial success. **3.** something or someone that is forcefully or overwhelmingly impressive, effective, or influential: *The campaign was a blockbuster.* **4.** a real-estate speculator who practices blockbusting. [1940–45; BLOCK + BUSTER]

block·bust·ing (blok′bus′ting), *n.* the profiteering practice by unscrupulous real-estate agents or speculators of reselling or renting homes that they obtain by inducing panic selling at prices below value, esp. by exploiting racial prejudices. [1940–45; BLOCK + BUST[2] + -ING[1]]

block′ cap′ital, a sans-serif letter with lines of uniform weight. Cf. **block letter.** [1900–05]

block′ cav′ing, *Mining.* a method of mining a large block of ore by systematically undercutting so the ore will cave. Cf. **cave** (def. 5a).

block′ chord′, a two-handed chord played usually in the middle range of the piano with the left hand duplicating or complementing the right-hand notes.

block′ coal′, bituminous coal that breaks into large lumps or cubical blocks. [1870–75, *Amer.*]

block′ coeffi′cient, *Naval Archit.* the ratio of the immersed volume of a vessel to the product of its immersed draft, length, and beam. Also called **coefficient of fineness.** [1900–05]

block′ di′agram, **1.** a chart or diagram using labeled blocks connected by straight lines to represent the relationship of parts or phases, as the steps in a data-processing application. Cf. **flow chart** (def. 2). **2.** *Geol.* a perspective representation of the geology of an area showing surface contours and generally including two vertical cross sections. [1920–25]

block·er (blok′ər), *n.* **1.** a person or thing that blocks. **2.** *Football.* a player whose assignment or special skill is blocking. **3.** *Biochem.* a substance that inhibits the physiological action of another substance, as the beta blocker propranolol that interferes with neurotransmitters in the sympathetic nervous system. [1200–50; ME see BLOCK, -ER[1]]

block′ fault′ing, *Geol.* the process by which tensional forces in the earth's crust cause large bodies of rock to founder. Cf. **fault block.** [1920–25]

block·flö·te (*Ger.* blôk′flœ′tə), *n., pl.* **-flö·ten** (*Ger.* -flœt′n). *Music.* a recorder. Also, **block·flute** (blok′-flōōt′). [< G *Blockflöte,* equiv. to *Block* BLOCK + *Flöte* FLUTE]

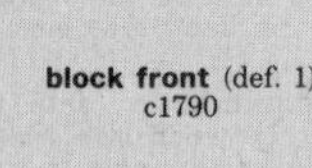

block front (def. 1) c1790

block front (blok′ frunt′ *for 1;* blok′ frunt′ *for 2*) **1.** *Furniture.* a front of a desk, chest of drawers, etc., of the third quarter of the 18th century, having three vertical divisions of equal width, a sunken one between raised ones, all divided by flat areas to which they are connected by curves, often with a shell motif forming a rounded termination to each section. **2.** the frontage of a block, esp. in a city or town. Also, **block′front′** —**block′-front′,** *adj.*

block′ grant′, a consolidated grant of federal funds formerly allocated for specific programs, that a state or local government may use at its discretion for such programs as education or urban development. [1895–1900]

block·head (blok′hed′), *n.* **1.** a stupid, doltish person dunce. **2.** *Obs.* a piece of wood in the shape of a head used as a block for hats or wigs. [1540–50; BLOCK + HEAD] —**block′head′ed,** *adj.* —**block′head′ed·ly** *adv.* —**block′head′ed·ness,** *n.* —**block′head′ism,** *n.*
—**Syn. 1.** fool, nitwit, dolt, dullard, ignoramus, booby.

block′ heat′er, an electrically operated immersion heater fitted either to enter the water hose or the water jacket surrounding the cylinder block of a motor to warm the coolant in cold weather.

block′ house′, *Stock Exchange.* a firm that specializes in block trades.

block·house (blok′hous′), *n., pl.* **-hous·es** (hou′ziz) **1.** *Mil.* a fortified structure with ports or loopholes through which defenders may direct gunfire. **2.** Also called **garrison house.** (formerly) a building, usually of hewn timber and with a projecting upper story, having loopholes for musketry. **3.** a house built of squared logs **4.** *Rocketry.* a structure near a launching site for rockets, generally made of heavily reinforced concrete, for housing and protecting personnel, electronic controls and auxiliary apparatus before and during launching operations. [1505–15; < MD *blochuus,* equiv. to *blo* BLOCK + *huus* HOUSE]

block·ing (blok′ing), *n. Carpentry.* a number of small pieces of wood for filling interstices, or for spacing, joining, or reinforcing members. [1575–85; BLOCK + -ING[1]]

block′ing an′tibody, *Immunol.* an antibody that partly combines with an antigen and interferes with cell-mediated immunity, thereby preventing an allergic reaction. Also called **block′ing fac′tor.**

block′ing capac′itor, *Electronics.* a capacitor used for stopping the passage of direct current from one circuit to another while allowing alternating current to pass. Also called **coupling capacitor.**

block·ish (blok′ish), *adj.* like a block; dull; stupid [1540–50; BLOCK + -ISH[1]] —**block′ish·ly,** *adv* —**block′ish·ness,** *n.*

Block′ Is′land, an island off the coast of and a part of Rhode Island, at the E entrance to Long Island Sound.

block′ la′va, *Geol.* basaltic lava in the form of a chaotic assemblage of angular blocks; aa. [1910–15]

lock′ let′ter, 1. *Print.* a sans-serif typeface or letter, usually compressed and having tight curves.

This is a sample of block letter

2. a simple, hand-printed capital letter. [1905–10]

lock′ line′, a rope or chain running through the blocks of a tackle.

lock′ mast′, *Naut.* a short mast from the head of which a lateen yard is suspended.

lock′ moun′tain, *Geol.* a mountain formed by the uplift of blocks of the earth's crust. [1895–1900]

lock′ organiza′tion. See **block association.**

lock′ par′ty, an outdoor festival, usually held in a closed-off city street, often to raise money for a local organization or for a block association.

lock′ plane′, *Carpentry.* a small plane for cutting across the grain. [1880–85]

lock′ print′, *Fine Arts.* a design printed by means of one or more blocks of wood or metal. [1810–20]

lock′ sig′nal, a fixed railroad signal governing the movements of trains entering and using a given section of track. [1880–85] **—block′ sig′naling.**

lock′ sys′tem, *Railroads.* 1. a series of consecutive blocks. Cf. **block** (def. 22). 2. a system of blocks and block signals for controlling train movements. [1860–65]

lock′ tin′, pure tin.

lock′ trade′, the purchase and sale of blocks of securities through brokers, sometimes not members of an exchange, who negotiate between buyers and sellers. **—block′ trad′er.**

ock•y (blok′ē), *adj.*, **block•i•er, block•i•est.** 1. heavily built; solid; stocky. 2. marked by blocks or patches of unequally distributed light and shade, as in a photograph. [1870–75; BLOCK + -Y[1]]

loc-vote (blok′vōt′), *v.i.*, **-vot•ed, -vot•ing.** to vote in or as a bloc: *Party conservatives can be counted on to bloc-vote.*

loem•fon•tein (blo͞om′fon tān′), *n.* a city in and the capital of the Orange Free State, in the central Republic of South Africa. 182,000.

lois (blwA), *n.* a city in and the capital of Loire-et-Cher, in central France, on the Loire River: historic castle. 51,950.

lok (blok; *Russ.* blôk), *n.* **A•le•xan•der A•le•xan•dro•vich** (al′ig zan′dər al′ig zan′drə vich, -zän′drə-, -zän′dər; *Russ.* u lyi ksändʀ′ u lyi ksän′dʀə vyich), 1880–1921, Russian poet.

loke (blōk), *n. Chiefly Brit. Informal.* man; fellow; guy. [1850–55; orig. uncert.]

lond (blond), *adj.*, **-er, -est,** *n.* **—***adj.* 1. (of hair, skin, etc.) light-colored: *the child's soft blond curls.* 2. (of a person) having light-colored hair and skin. 3. (of furniture wood) light in tone. **—***n.* 4. a blond person. 5. silk lace, originally unbleached but now often dyed any of various colors, esp. white or black. [1475–85; < MF *blonde* blond, light brown, fem. of *blond* < Gmc; akin to OE *blondenfeax* grayhaired, L *flāvus* yellow (see FLAVO-)] **—blond′ness,** *n.* **—blond′ish,** *adj.*

—Usage. See **blonde.**

londe (blond), *adj.* 1. (of a woman or girl) having fair hair and usually fair skin and light eyes. **—***n.* 2. a woman or girl having this coloration. [see BLOND] **—blonde′ness,** *n.*

—Usage. The spelling BLONDE is still widely used for the noun that specifies a woman or girl with fair hair: *The blonde with the baby in her arms is my anthropology professor.* Some people object to this as an unnecessary distinction, preferring BLOND for all persons: *My sister is thinking of becoming a blond for a while.* As an adjective, the word is more usually spelled BLOND in reference to either sex (*an energetic blond girl; two blond sons*), although the form BLONDE is occasionally still used of a female: *the blonde model and her escort.* The spelling BLOND is almost always used for the adjective describing hair, complexion, etc.: *His daughter has blond hair and hazel eyes.*

lon•del (blôn del′), *n.* **Fran•çois** (fräN swA′), (*Sieur des Croisettes*), 1618–86, French architect.

lond•ie (blon′dē), *n.* 1. *Informal.* a blond person: *All the children were blondies.* 2. a dessert confection resembling a brownie but made with butterscotch flavoring in place of chocolate. [BLOND + -IE]

lond•ing (blon′ding), *n.* the act or method of dyeing or tinting hair blond: *true-to-life blondings that defy detection.* [1960–65; BLOND + -ING[1]]

lood (blud), *n.* 1. the fluid that circulates in the principal vascular system of human beings and other vertebrates, in humans consisting of plasma in which the red blood cells, white blood cells, and platelets are suspended. 2. the vital principle; life: *The excitement had got into the very blood of the nation.* 3. a person or group regarded as a source of energy, vitality, or vigor: *It's time we got some new blood in this company.* 4. one of the four elemental bodily humors of medieval physiology, regarded as causing cheerfulness. 5. bloodshed; gore; slaughter; murder: *to avenge the blood of his father.* 6. the juice or sap of plants: *the blood of the grape.* 7. temperament; state of mind: *a person of hot blood.* 8. physical nature of human beings: *the frailty of our blood.* 9. *Chiefly Brit.* a high-spirited dandy; an adventuresome youth: *the young bloods of Cambridge.* 10. a profligate or rake. 11. physical and cultural extraction: *It was a trait that seemed to be in their blood.* 12. royal extraction: *a prince of the blood.* 13. descent from a common ancestor; ancestry; lineage: *related by blood.* 14. recorded and respected ancestry; purebred breeding. 15. *Slang.* a black person, esp. a man. 16. **get** or **have one's blood up,** to become or be enraged or impassioned: *Injustice of any sort always gets my blood up.* 17. **have someone's blood on one's head** or **hands,** to be to blame for someone's affliction or death: *Though a criminal, he had no blood on his hands.* 18. **in cold blood,** deliberately; ruthlessly: *The dictator, in cold blood, ordered the execution of all his political enemies.* 19. **make one's blood boil,** to inspire resentment, anger, or indignation: *Such carelessness makes my blood boil.* 20. **make one's blood run cold,** to fill with terror; frighten: *The dark, deserted street in that unfamiliar neighborhood made her blood run cold.* 21. **sweat blood.** See **sweat** (def. 24). 22. **taste blood,** to experience a new sensation, usually a violent or destructive one, and acquire an appetite for it: *Once the team had tasted blood, there was no preventing them from winning by a wide margin.* **—***v.t.* 23. *Hunting.* to give (hounds) a first sight or taste of blood. Cf. **flesh** (def. 17). 24. to stain with blood. [bef. 1000; ME *blo(o)d,* OE *blōd;* c. OFris, OS *blōd,* OHG *bluot* (G *Blut*), ON *blōth,* Goth *bloth* < Gmc **blōdaⁿ*, an old neuter adj. meaning "spurting" that accompanied the lost IE noun **HesHr* (> Hittite *eshar*) blood; akin to BLOOM[1]; for the meaning cf. SPURT and SPROUT] **—blood′like′,** *adj.*

—Syn. 13. kinship, stock, family.

blood-and-guts (blud′n guts′), *adj.* 1. dealing with or depicting war or violence, esp. in a lurid manner: *a blood-and-guts movie.* 2. concerned with fundamental needs, problems, values, etc.: *The blood-and-guts issues will determine the election.*

blood′ and thun′der, sensationalism, violence, or exaggerated melodrama: *a movie full of blood and thunder.* [1855–60]

blood′ bank′, 1. a place where blood or blood plasma is collected, processed, stored, and distributed. 2. such a supply of blood or blood plasma. [1935–40]

blood•bath (blud′bath′, -bäth′), *n., pl.* **-baths** (-baṫhz′, -bäṫhz′, -baths′, -bäths′). 1. a ruthless slaughter of a great number of people; massacre. 2. *Informal.* a period of disastrous loss or reversal: *A few mutual funds performed well in the general bloodbath of the stock market.* 3. a widespread dismissal or purge, as of employees. Also, **blood′ bath′.** [1865–70; BLOOD + BATH[1]]

blood′ boost′ing, *Sports Med.* See **blood doping.**

blood′-brain′ bar′rier (blud′brān′), *Physiol.* a layer of tightly packed cells that make up the walls of brain capillaries and prevent substances in the blood from diffusing freely into the brain: passage across the cell membranes is determined by solubility in the lipid bilayer or recognition by a transport molecule. [1940–45]

blood′ broth′er, 1. a person's brother by birth. 2. a male person bound to another by ties of great friendship. 3. something usually associated with or thought to exist inseparably from another thing, quality, circumstance, etc.: *Humility is often the blood brother of patience.* 4. a male established in a close relationship with another male through the performance of a specific ritual, as the commingling of blood. [1350–1400; ME] **—blood′ broth′erhood.**

blood′ cell′, any of the cellular elements of the blood, as white blood cells or red blood cells. Also called **blood′ cor′puscle.** [1840–50]

blood′ count′, the count of the number of red and white blood cells and platelets in a specific volume of blood. [1895–1900]

blood•cur•dler (blud′kûr′dlər), *n.* something causing great fright or horror: *a bloodcurdler of a mystery novel.* [1885–90; BLOOD + CURDLE + -ER[1]]

blood•cur•dling (blud′kûrd′ling, -kûr′dl ing), *adj.* arousing terror; horrifying: *a bloodcurdling scream.* [1930–35; BLOOD + CURDLE + -ING[2]] **—blood′cur′dling•ly,** *adv.*

blood′ dop′ing, *Sports Med.* a procedure in which an athlete is injected with his or her own blood or the blood of a family member prior to competition, purportedly increasing the blood's oxygen-carrying capacity owing to the addition of red blood cells. Also called **blood packing, blood boosting.**

blood•ed (blud′id), *adj.* 1. having blood of a specified kind (used in combination): *warm-blooded animals.* 2. (of horses, cattle, etc.) derived from ancestors of good blood; having a good pedigree. [1200–50; ME; see BLOOD, -ED[3]]

blood′ feud′, feud[1] (def. 1). [1855–60]

blood•fin (blud′fin′), *n.* a South American characin fish, *Aphyocharax rubropinnis,* having a silvery body and bright red fins: popular in home aquariums. [BLOOD + FIN]

blood•flow•er (blud′flou′ər), *n.* a showy milkweed, *Asclepias curassavica,* of tropical America, having brilliant orange-red flowers and smooth fruit. [BLOOD + FLOWER]

blood′ fluke′, a schistosome. [1870–75]

blood′ group′, *Med.* any of various classes into which human blood can be divided according to immunological compatibility, based on the presence or absence of specific antigens on red blood cells. Also called **blood type.** Cf. **ABO system, Rh factor.** [1915–20]

blood′ group′ing. See **blood typing.** [1915–20]

blood•guilt•y (blud′gil′tē), *adj.* guilty of murder or bloodshed. [1590–1600; BLOOD(SHED) + GUILTY] **—blood′guilt′, blood′guilt′i•ness,** *n.*

blood′ heat′, the normal temperature of human blood, being about 98.6°F (37°C). [1805–15]

blood•hound (blud′hound′), *n.* 1. one of a breed of medium- to large-sized dogs, usually having a black-and-tan coat, very long ears, loose skin, and an acute sense of smell: used chiefly for following human scents. 2. a person who is a steadfast pursuer. [1300–50; ME *blod-hound.* See BLOOD, HOUND[1]]

bloodhound
26 in. (66 cm)
high at shoulder

blood•ing (blud′ing), *n. Chiefly Brit.* (in fox hunting) an informal initiation ceremony in which the face of a novice is smeared with the blood of the first fox that person has seen killed. [1590–1600; BLOOD + -ING[1]]

blood′ knot′, *Angling.* See **barrel knot.** [1900–05]

blood•less (blud′lis), *adj.* 1. without blood: *bloodless surgery.* 2. very pale: *a bloodless face.* 3. free from bloodshed; accomplished without bloodshed: *a bloodless victory; a bloodless coup.* 4. spiritless; without vigor, zest, or energy: *a dull, insipid, bloodless young man.* 5. without emotion or feeling; cold-hearted: *bloodless data.* [1175–1225; ME *blodles,* OE *blōdlēas.* See BLOOD, -LESS] **—blood′less•ly,** *adv.* **—blood′less•ness,** *n.*

Blood′less Revolu′tion. See **English Revolution.**

blood•let•ting (blud′let′ing), *n.* 1. the act or practice of letting blood by opening a vein; phlebotomy. 2. bloodshed or slaughter. 3. bloodbath. 4. *Informal.* severe cutbacks or reduction in personnel, appropriations, etc.: *The company went through a period of bloodletting in the 1970's.* [1175–1225; ME *blod letunge.* See BLOOD, LET[1], -ING[1]] **—blood′let′ter,** *n.*

blood′ lev′el, the amount of a substance, as cholesterol, alcohol, or triglycerides, circulating in the bloodstream: often expressed as a percent or in milligrams or micrograms per deciliter of blood.

blood′ lil′y, any of various bulbous plants of the genus *Haemanthus,* native to Africa, having clusters of red or white flowers.

blood•line (blud′līn′), *n.* (usually of animals) the line of descent; pedigree; strain. [1905–10; BLOOD + LINE[1]]

blood′ meal′, the dried blood of animals used as a fertilizer, diet supplement for livestock, or deer repellent. [1885–90]

blood•mo•bile (blud′mə bēl′), *n.* a small truck with medical equipment for receiving blood donations. [1945–50; BLOOD + -MOBILE]

blood′ mon′ey, 1. a fee paid to a hired murderer. 2. compensation paid to the next of kin of a slain person. 3. money obtained ruthlessly and at a cost of suffering to others. 4. money paid to an informer in order to cause somebody to be arrested, convicted, or esp. executed.

blood•noun (blud′noun′), *n. South Atlantic States (chiefly South Carolina).* a bullfrog, esp. *Rana catesbeiana.* Also, **bloody noun.** [1910–15; of uncert. orig.]

blood′ or′ange, any of various sweet oranges having a dark-red pulp. [1850–55]

blood′ pack′ing, *Sports Med.* See **blood doping.**

blood′ plas′ma, the plasma or liquid portion of human blood. [1905–10]

blood′ plate′let, any of numerous, minute, protoplasmic bodies in mammalian blood that aid in coagulation. [1895–1900]

blood′ poi′soning, *Pathol.* invasion of the blood by toxic matter or microorganisms, characterized by chills, sweating, fever, and prostration; toxemia; septicemia; pyemia. [1860–65]

blood′ pres′sure, *Physiol.* the pressure of the blood against the inner walls of the blood vessels, varying in different parts of the body during different phases of contraction of the heart and under different conditions of health, exertion, etc. *Abbr.:* BP Cf. **diastolic, systolic.** [1870–75]

blood′ pud′ding. *South Midland and Southern U.S.* See **blood sausage.** [1575–85]

blood′ purge′, the mass execution, esp. by a government, of persons considered guilty of treason or sedition. [1930–35]

blood-red (blud′red′), *adj.* 1. of the deep-red color of blood: *a fiery, blood-red sunset.* 2. red with blood: *The blood-red banner symbolized the army's defeat.* [1250–1300; ME]

blood′ rela′tion, one related by birth. Also, **blood′ rel′ative.** [1700–10]

blood•root (blud′ro͞ot′, -ro͝ot′), *n.* a North American plant, *Sanguinaria canadensis,* of the poppy family, having a red root and root sap and a solitary white flower. [1570–80; BLOOD + ROOT[1]]

blood′ roy′al, all persons related by birth to a hereditary monarch, taken collectively; the royal kin: *a prince of the blood royal.* [1595–1605]

blood′ sau′sage, a dark sausage with a high content of blood, esp. one made with diced pork fat, pork blood, chopped onion, etc., usually stuffed in casings and cooked by broiling, frying, or boiling. Also called **black pudding.** [1865–70]

blood′ se′rum, serum (def. 1). [1905–10]

blood•shed (blud′shed′), *n.* 1. destruction of life, as in war or murder; slaughter. 2. the shedding of blood by injury, wound, etc. Also, **blood′shed′ding.** [BLOOD + SHED[2]]

CONCISE PRONUNCIATION KEY: act, cāpe, dâre, pärt; set, ēqual; *if, ice;* ox, ōver, ôrder, oil, bo͝ok, bo͞ot, out; up, ûrge; child; sing; shoe; thin, ṫhat; zh as in *treasure.* ə = a as in *alone,* e as in *system,* i as in *easily,* o as in *gallop,* u as in *circus;* ᵊ as in *fire* (fīᵊr), *hour* (ouᵊr). l and n can serve as syllabic consonants, as in *cradle* (krād′l), and *button* (but′n). See the full key inside the front cover.

blood•shot (blud′shot′), *adj.* (of the eyes) red because of dilated blood vessels. [1545–55; apocopated var. of *blood-shotten.* See BLOOD, SHOTTEN]

blood′ spav′in, *Vet. Pathol.* See under **spavin** (def. 1).

blood′ sport′, any sport involving killing or the shedding of blood, as bullfighting, cockfighting, or hunting. [1890–95]

blood•stain (blud′stān′), *n.* a spot or stain made by blood. [1810–20; back formation from BLOODSTAINED]

blood•stained (blud′stānd′), *adj.* **1.** stained with blood: *a bloodstained knife.* **2.** guilty of murder, slaughter, or bloodshed. [1590–1600; BLOOD + *stained;* see STAIN, -ED[2]]

blood•stock (blud′stok′), *n.* racehorses of Thoroughbred breeding, taken as a whole. [1820–30; BLOOD + STOCK]

blood•stone (blud′stōn′), *n.* a greenish variety of chalcedony with small bloodlike spots of red jasper scattered through it. Also called **heliotrope.** [1545–55; BLOOD + STONE]

blood•stream (blud′strēm′), *n.* the blood flowing through a circulatory system. [1870–75; BLOOD + STREAM]

blood•suck•er (blud′suk′ər), *n.* **1.** any animal that sucks blood, esp. a leech. **2.** an extortioner or usurer. **3.** sponger (def. 2). [1350–1400; ME; see BLOOD, SUCKER] —**blood′suck′ing,** *adj.*

blood′ sug′ar, 1. glucose in the blood. **2.** the quantity or percentage of glucose in the blood. [1925–30]

blood′ test′, a test of a sample of blood to determine blood group, presence of infection or other pathological condition, parentage, etc. [1910–15]

blood•thirst•y (blud′thûr′stē), *adj.* **1.** eager to shed blood; murderous: *to capture a bloodthirsty criminal.* **2.** enjoying or encouraging bloodshed or violence, esp. as a spectator or clamorous partisan: *the bloodthirsty urgings of the fight fans.* [1525–35; BLOOD + THIRSTY] —**blood′thirst′i•ly,** *adv.* —**blood′thirst′i•ness,** *n.*
—**Syn. 1.** homicidal, savage, brutal, bloody; merciless, pitiless.

blood′ transfu′sion, the injection of blood from one person or animal into the bloodstream of another. [1875–80]

blood′ type′. See **blood group.** [1930–35]

blood′ typ′ing, *Physiol.* the process of classifying blood into blood groups, based on laboratory tests to reveal the presence or absence of particular antigens on the surface of red blood cells. Also called **blood grouping.** [1925–30]

blood′ ves′sel, any of the vessels, as arteries, veins, or capillaries, through which the blood circulates. [1685–95]

blood•wood (blud′wo͝od′), *n.* **1.** any of several Australian trees of the genus *Eucalyptus,* as *E. gummifera* or *E. ptychocarpa,* having rough, scaly bark. **2.** an African tree, *Pterocarpus angolensis,* having reddish wood. **3.** the wood of any of these trees. [1715–25; BLOOD + WOOD; so called from the color of the sap or wood]

blood•worm (blud′wûrm′), *n.* **1.** any of several red or red-blooded annelid worms, esp. various earthworms. **2.** the freshwater larva of midges. [1735–45; BLOOD + WORM]

blood•wort (blud′wûrt′, -wôrt′), *n.* **1.** the redroot, *Lachnanthes caroliana.* **2.** any of various plants having red roots, markings, juices, etc. **3.** bloodroot. [1200–50; ME *blodwurt.* See BLOOD, WORT[2]]

blood•y (blud′ē), *adj.,* **blood•i•er, blood•i•est,** *v.,* **blood•ied, blood•y•ing,** *adv.* —*adj.* **1.** stained or covered with blood: *a bloody handkerchief.* **2.** bleeding: *a bloody nose.* **3.** characterized by bloodshed: *bloody battle; a bloody rule.* **4.** inclined to bloodshed; bloodthirsty: *a bloody dictator.* **5.** of, pertaining to, or resembling blood; containing or composed of blood: *bloody tissue.* **6.** *Slang.* (used as an intensifier): *a bloody shame; a bloody nuisance.* —*v.t.* **7.** to stain or smear with blood. **8.** to cause to bleed, as by a blow or accident: *to bloody someone's nose.* —*adv.* **9.** *Slang.* (used as an intensifier): *bloody awful; bloody wonderful.* [bef. 1000; ME *blody,* OE *blōdig.* See BLOOD, -Y[1]] —**blood′i•ly,** *adv.* —**blood′i•ness,** *n.*
—**Syn. 1–3.** sanguinary, ensanguined, gory. **4.** murderous, homicidal; savage, brutal, ferocious; cruel, inhuman, ruthless.

blood′y butch′ers. See **red trillium.**

Blood′y Cae′sar, a Bloody Mary made with a combination of clam juice and tomato juice.

blood′y flux′, dysentery. [1350–1400; ME]

Blood′y Mar′y, 1. a mixed drink made principally with vodka and tomato juice. **2.** See **Mary I.** [1955–60]

blood•y-mind•ed (blud′ē mīn′did), *adj.* **1.** disposed to violence or bloodshed; bloodthirsty; sanguinary: *bloody-minded anarchists.* **2.** *Chiefly Brit.* unreasonably stubborn or cantankerous. [1575–85] —**blood′y-mind′ed•ness,** *n.*

blood′y noun′, *South Atlantic states (chiefly South Carolina).* bloodnoun.

blood′y shirt′, 1. a bloodstained shirt used to incite a mob to vengeance. **2.** any symbol used for this purpose. [1870–75]

bloo•ey (blo͞o′ē), *adj. Slang.* **1.** out of order; faulty. **2. go blooey,** to go totally out of commission; break down completely: *If the generator fails, the whole system will go blooey.* Also, **bloo′ie.** [orig. uncert.]

CONCISE ETYMOLOGY KEY: <, descended or borrowed from; >, whence; b., blend of, blended; c., cognate with; cf., compare; deriv., derivative; equiv., equivalent; imit., imitative; obl., oblique; r., replacing; s., stem; sp., spelling, spelled; resp., respelling, respelled; trans., translation; ?, origin unknown; *, unattested; ‡, probably earlier than. See the full key inside the front cover.

bloom[1] (blo͞om), *n.* **1.** the flower of a plant. **2.** flowers collectively: *the bloom of the cherry tree.* **3.** state of having the buds opened: *The gardens are all in bloom.* **4.** a flourishing, healthy condition; the time or period of greatest beauty, artistry, etc.: *the bloom of youth; the bloom of Romanticism.* **5.** a glow or flush on the cheek indicative of youth and health: *a serious illness that destroyed her bloom.* **6.** the glossy, healthy appearance of the coat of an animal. **7.** a moist, lustrous appearance indicating freshness in fish. **8.** redness or a fresh appearance on the surface of meat. **9.** *Bot.* a whitish powdery deposit or coating, as on the surface of certain fruits and leaves: *the bloom of the grape.* **10.** any similar surface coating or appearance: *the bloom of newly minted coins.* **11.** any of certain minerals occurring as powdery coatings on rocks or other minerals. **12.** Also called **chill.** a clouded or dull area on a varnished or lacquered surface. **13.** the sudden development of conspicuous masses of organisms, as algae on the surface of a lake. **14.** *Television.* image spread produced by excessive exposure of highlights in a television image. **15. take the bloom off,** to remove the enjoyment or ultimate satisfaction from; dampen the enthusiasm over: *The coach's illness took the bloom off the team's victory.* —*v.i.* **16.** to produce or yield blossoms. **17.** to flourish or thrive: *a recurrent fad that blooms from time to time.* **18.** to be in or achieve a state of healthful beauty and vigor: *a sickly child who suddenly bloomed; a small talent that somehow bloomed into major artistry.* **19.** to glow with warmth or with a warm color. —*v.t.* **20.** to cause to yield blossoms. **21.** to make bloom or cause to flourish: *a happiness that blooms the cheek.* **22.** to invest with luster or beauty: *an industry that blooms one's talents.* **23.** to cause a cloudy area on (something shiny); dampen; chill: *Their breath bloomed the frosty pane.* **24.** *Optics.* to coat (a lens) with an antireflection material. [1150–1200; (n.) ME *blom, blome* < ON *blōm, blōmi;* c. Goth *blōma* lily, G *Blume* flower; akin to BLOW[3]; (v.) ME *blomen,* deriv. of the n.] —**bloom′less,** *adj.*
—**Syn. 1.** blossom. **3.** efflorescence. **4.** freshness, glow, flush; vigor, prime. **16, 17.** effloresce.

bloom[2] (blo͞om), *Metalworking.* —*n.* **1.** a piece of steel, square or slightly oblong in section, reduced from an ingot to dimensions suitable for further rolling. **2.** a large lump of iron and slag, of pasty consistency when hot, produced in a puddling furnace or bloomery and hammered into wrought iron. —*v.t.* **3.** to make (an ingot) into a bloom. [bef. 1000; repr. AL, AF *blomes* (pl.), OE *blōma* mass of iron; perh. akin to BLOOM[1]]

bloo•mer[1] (blo͞o′mər), *n.* **1.** a costume for women, advocated about 1850 by Amelia Jenks Bloomer, consisting of a short skirt, loose trousers gathered and buttoned at the ankle, and often a coat and a wide hat. **2. bloomers,** *(used with a plural v.)* **a.** loose trousers gathered at the knee, formerly worn by women as part of a gymnasium, riding, or other sports outfit. **b.** women's underpants of similar, but less bulky, design. **c.** the trousers of a bloomer costume. **d.** any of various women's garments with full-cut legs gathered at the bottom edge. —*adj.* **3.** (of a woman's garment) having full-cut legs gathered at the bottom edge: *bloomer shorts.* [1850–55, *Amer.*; named after A.J. BLOOMER]

bloom•er[2] (blo͞o′mər), *n.* **1.** a plant that blooms: *a night bloomer.* **2.** a person who develops skills, abilities, interests, etc., commensurate with his or her capacities: *a quiet, methodical child who became a late bloomer.* [1720–30; BLOOM[1] + -ER[1]]

bloom•er[3] (blo͞o′mər), *n.* a foolish mistake; blunder. [1885–90; BLOOM(ING) (as euphemism for BLOODY) + -ER[1]]

Bloo•mer (blo͞o′mər), *n.* **Amelia Jenks** (jengks), 1818–94, U.S. social reformer and women's-rights leader.

bloom•er•y (blo͞o′mə rē), *n., pl.* **-er•ies.** *Metalworking.* a hearth for smelting iron in blooms of pasty consistency by means of charcoal. [1575–85; BLOOM[2] + -ERY]

Bloom•field (blo͞om′fēld′), *n.* **1. Leonard,** 1887–1949, U.S. linguist and educator. **2.** a city in NE New Jersey. 47,792. **3.** a town in N Connecticut. 18,608.

Bloom•field•i•an (blo͞om fēl′dē ən), *adj.* **1.** *Ling.* influenced by, resembling, or deriving from the linguistic theory and the methods of linguistic analysis advocated by Leonard Bloomfield, characterized esp. by emphasis on the classification of overt formal features. —*n.* **2.** a Bloomfieldian linguist. [BLOOMFIELD + -IAN]

bloom•ing (blo͞o′ming), *adj.* **1.** in bloom; flowering; blossoming. **2.** glowing, as with youthful vigor and freshness: *blooming cheeks.* **3.** flourishing; prospering: *a blooming business.* **4.** *Chiefly Brit. Slang.* (used as an intensifier): *He's got his blooming nerve.* —*adv.* **5.** *Chiefly Brit. Slang.* (used as an intensifier): *not blooming likely.* [1350–1400; ME; see BLOOM[1], -ING[2]; as intensifier, a euphemism for BLOODY, by phonetic similarity] —**bloom′ing•ly,** *adv.* —**bloom′ing•ness,** *n.*

Bloom•ing•dale (blo͞o′ming dāl′), *n.* a town in NE Illinois. 12,659.

bloom′ing mill′, *Metalworking.* a mill for rolling ingots into blooms.

bloom′ing oil′, an oil used as a lubricant in fine sandpapering.

Bloo•ming•ton (blo͞o′ming tən), *n.* **1.** a city in SE Minnesota. 81,831. **2.** a city in S Indiana. 51,646. **3.** a city in central Illinois. 44,189.

Blooms•burg (blo͞omz′bûrg), *n.* a city in E central Pennsylvania. 11,717.

Blooms•bur•y (blo͞omz′bə rē, -brē), *n.* **1.** a residential and academic district in London, N of the Thames and Charing Cross. Artists, writers, and students living there have given it a reputation as an intellectual center. —*adj.* **2.** of or pertaining to a group of artists and writers who flourished in the early decades of the 20th century and were associated with the Bloomsbury section of London. **3.** of, pertaining to, following, or imitating the cultural and intellectual pursuits, interests, or opinions characteristic of this group.

bloom•y (blo͞o′mē), *adj.,* **bloom•i•er, bloom•i•est. 1.** covered with blossoms; in full flower. **2.** *Bot.* having a bloom, as fruit. [1585–95; BLOOM[1] + -Y[1]]

bloop (blo͞op), *Informal.* —*v.t.* **1.** to ruin; botch: *to bloop an easy catch.* **2.** to hit a blooper in baseball. —*n.* **3.** a clumsy mistake. **4.** blooper (def. 3). [1925–30; earlier, a high-pitched sound produced by interference in a radio signal; expressive coinage]

bloop•er (blo͞o′pər), *n.* **1.** *Informal.* an embarrassing mistake, as one spoken over the radio or TV. **2.** *Radio.* a receiving set that generates from its antenna radio-frequency signals that interfere with other nearby receivers. **3.** Also, **bloop.** *Baseball.* **a.** Also called **looper.** a fly ball that carries just beyond the infield. **b.** a pitched ball with backspin, describing a high arc in flight. [1925–30; BLOOP + -ER[1], orig. in reference to a radio receiver that emits bloops]
—**Syn. 1.** error, blunder, slip, gaffe, goof.

blos•som (blos′əm), *n. Bot.* **1.** the flower of a plant, esp. of one producing an edible fruit. **2.** the state of flowering: *The apple tree is in blossom.* —*v.i.* **3.** *Bot.* to produce or yield blossoms. **4.** to flourish; develop (often fol. by *into* or *out*): *a writer of commercial jingles who blossomed out into an important composer.* **5.** (of a parachute) to open. [bef. 900; (n.) ME *blosme, blossem,* OE *blōstm(a), blōsma* flower; c. MD *bloesem,* MLG *blosem, blossem;* (v.) ME *blosmen,* OE *blōstmian,* deriv. of the n. See BLOOM[1], BLOW[3]] —**blos′som•less,** *adj.* —**blos′som•y,** *adj.*
—**Syn. 4.** thrive, bloom, burgeon, sprout.

Blos•som (blos′əm), *n.* a female given name.

blos′som-end rot′ (blos′əm end′), *Plant Pathol.* a disease of tomato and pepper caused by a deficiency of calcium, characterized by decay at the blossom end of the fruit.

blot[1] (blot), *n., v.,* **blot•ted, blot•ting.** —*n.* **1.** a spot or stain, esp. of ink on paper. **2.** a blemish on a person's character or reputation: *He had been haunted by a blot on his past.* **3.** *Archaic.* an erasure or obliteration, as in a writing. —*v.t.* **4.** to spot, stain, soil, or the like. **5.** to darken; make dim; obscure or eclipse (usually fol. by *out*): *We watched as the moon blotted out the sun.* **6.** to dry with absorbent paper or the like: *to blot the wet pane.* **7.** to remove with absorbent paper or the like. —*v.i.* **8.** to make a blot; spread ink, dye, etc., in a stain: *The more slowly I write, the more this pen blots.* **9.** to become blotted or stained: *This paper blots too easily.* **10.** *Chem.* to transfer an array of separated components of a mixture to a chemically treated paper for analysis. Cf. **gel, gel electrophoresis. 11. blot out, a.** to make indistinguishable; obliterate: *to blot out a name from the record.* **b.** to wipe out completely; destroy: *Whole cities were blotted out by bombs.* [1275–1325; (n.) ME *blotte,* akin to ON *blettr* blot, spot, stain; (v.) late ME *blotten,* deriv. of the n.] —**blot′less,** *adj.* —**blot′ting•ly,** *adv.* —**blot′ty,** *adj.*
—**Syn. 1.** blotch, ink stain. **2.** stain, taint, dishonor, disgrace, spot. **4.** sully, disfigure. **5.** obliterate, efface, erase, expunge. **7.** absorb.

blot[2] (blot), *n.* **1.** *Backgammon.* an exposed piece liable to be taken or forfeited. **2.** *Archaic.* an exposed or weak point, as in an argument or course of action. [1590–1600 < LG *blat,* akin to *bloot* bare, exposed, unprotected; c. D *bloot,* G *bloss* bare]

blotch (bloch), *n.* **1.** a large, irregular spot or blot. **2.** *Plant Pathol.* **a.** a diseased, discolored spot or area on a plant. **b.** a disease so characterized, usually accompanied by cankers and lesions. **3.** a skin eruption; blemish —*v.t.* **4.** to mark with blotches; blot, spot, or blur: *The floor of the forest was blotched with cool, dark moss* —*adj.* **5.** *Textiles.* of or pertaining to blotch printing, or to the colored ground produced by this process. [1595–1605; perh. b. BLOT[1] + BOTCH[2]]
—**Syn. 1.** splotch, mark, blemish, stain.

blotch′ print′ing, a fabric-printing method in which the ground color is transferred from the cylinder and the motif retains the original hue of the cloth.

blotch•y (bloch′ē), *adj.,* **blotch•i•er, blotch•i•est. 1** having blotches: *a blotchy complexion.* **2.** resembling a blotch. [1815–25; BLOTCH + -Y[1]] —**blotch′i•ly,** *adv.*

blot•ter (blot′ər), *n.* **1.** a piece of blotting paper used to absorb excess ink, to protect a desk top, etc. **2.** a book in which transactions or events, as sales or arrests, are recorded as they occur: *a police blotter.* **3.** *Mach.* a soft washer of blotting paper or felt for cushioning a brittle object against shock or pressure or for increasing the friction or contact area between two surfaces. [1585–95; 1887 for def. 2; BLOT[1] + -ER[1]]

blot′ting pa′per, a soft, absorbent, unsized paper used esp. to dry the ink on a piece of writing. [1510–20]

blot•to (blot′ō), *adj. Slang.* very drunk; so drunk as to be unconscious or not know what one is doing. [1915–20; BLOT[1] (v.) + -O]

blouse (blous, blouz), *n., v.,* **bloused, blous•ing.** —*n.* **1.** a usually lightweight, loose-fitting garment for women and children, covering the body from the neck or shoulders more or less to the waistline, with or without a collar and sleeves, worn inside or outside a skirt, slacks etc. **2.** a single-breasted, semifitted military jacket. **3.** a loose outer garment, reaching to the hip or thigh, or below the knee, and sometimes belted. Cf. **smock frock** —*v.i.* **4.** to puff out in a drooping fullness, as a blouse above a fitted waistband. —*v.t.* **5.** to dispose the material of a garment in loose folds, as trouser legs over the tops of boots. [1820–30; < F, perh. from the phrase **vêtement de laine blouse* garment of short (i.e., uncarded, pure) wool; cf. Pr (*lano*) *blouso* pure (wool) < OHG *blōz* naked, c. OE *bleat* poor, miserable] —**blouse′like′,** *adj.*

blous•on (blou′son, -zon, blo͞o zōn′, blo͞o′zon), *n.* **1.** a woman's outer garment having a drawstring, belt, or similar closing, at or below the waist, which causes it to blouse. —*adj.* **2.** of or pertaining to such a garment, the style it exemplifies, or something considered to resemble this style, as a hairdo: *a blouson dress; the blouson effec* *a blouson bob.* [1900–05; < F, equiv. to *blouse* BLOUSE + *-on* n. suffix]

blous•y (blou′zē), *adj.*, **blous•i•er, blous•i•est.** blowzy. —**blous′i•ly,** *adv.*

blow[1] (blō), *n.* **1.** a sudden, hard stroke with a hand, fist, or weapon: *a blow to the head.* **2.** a sudden shock, calamity, reversal, etc.: *His wife's death was a terrible blow to him.* **3.** a sudden attack or drastic action: *The invaders struck a blow to the south.* **4. at one blow,** with a single act: *He became wealthy and famous at one blow.* Also, **at a blow. 5. come to blows,** to begin to fight, esp. to engage in physical combat: *They came to blows over the referee's ruling.* **6. strike a blow,** to hit. **7. strike a blow for,** to further or advance the cause of: *to strike a blow for civil rights.* **8. without striking a blow,** without a battle or contest: *The military coup was accomplished without striking a blow.* [1425–75; late ME *blaw,* northern form repr. later *blowe;* akin to OHG *bliuwan,* Goth *bliggwan* to beat]

—Syn. 1. buffet, thump, thwack, rap, slap, cuff, box, beat, knock. **1, 2.** BLOW, STROKE, HIT, SLAP refer to a sudden or forceful impact, but differ in their literal and figurative uses. BLOW emphasizes the violence of the impact and, figuratively, adverse fortune: *a blow from a hammer; a blow to one's hopes.* STROKE emphasizes movement as well as impact; it indicates precision or, figuratively, either good fortune or sudden or unexpected pain or misfortune: *the stroke of a piston; a stroke of luck, of lightning; a paralytic stroke.* HIT, in its current uses, emphasizes the successful result of a literal or figurative blow, impact, or impression, for example in baseball, social life, the theater: *a two-base hit; to make a hit with someone; a smash hit.* SLAP, a blow with the open hand or with something flat, emphasizes the instrument with which the blow is delivered and, often, the resulting sound; figuratively, it connotes an unfriendly or sarcastic statement, action, or attitude: *Her coldness was like a slap in the face; the slap of a beaver's tail on the water.*

blow[2] (blō), *v.*, **blew, blown, blow•ing,** *n.* —*v.i.* **1.** (of the wind or air) to be in motion. **2.** to move along, carried by or as by the wind: *Dust seemed to blow through every crack in the house.* **3.** to produce or emit a current of air, as with the mouth or a bellows: *Blow on your hands to warm them.* **4.** (of a horn, trumpet, etc.) to give out sound. **5.** to make a blowing sound; whistle: *The siren blew just as we rounded the corner.* **6.** (of horses) to breathe hard or quickly; pant. **7.** *Informal.* to boast; brag: *He kept blowing about his medals.* **8.** *Zool.* (of a whale) to spout. **9.** (of a fuse, light bulb, vacuum tube, tire, etc.) to burst, melt, stop functioning, or be destroyed by exploding, overloading, etc. (often fol. by *out*): *A fuse blew just as we sat down to dinner. The rear tire blew out.* **10.** to burst from internal pressure: *Poorly sealed cans will often blow.* **11.** *Slang.* to leave; depart. —*v.t.* **12.** to drive by means of a current of air: *A sudden breeze blew the smoke into the house.* **13.** to spread or make widely known: *Growing panic blew the rumor about.* **14.** to drive a current of air upon. **15.** to clear or empty by forcing air through: *Try blowing your nose.* **16.** to shape (glass, smoke, etc.) with a current of air: *to blow smoke rings.* **17.** to cause to sound, as by a current of air: *Blow your horn at the next crossing.* **18.** *Jazz.* to play (a musical instrument of any kind). **19.** to cause to explode (often fol. by *up, to bits,* etc.): *A mine blew the ship to bits.* **20.** to burst, melt, burn out, or destroy by exploding, overloading, etc. (often fol. by *out*): *to blow a tire; blow a fuse.* **21.** to destroy; demolish (usually fol. by *down, over,* etc.): *The windstorm blew down his house.* **22.** *Informal.* **a.** to spend money on. **b.** to squander; spend quickly: *He blew a fortune on racing cars.* **c.** to waste; lose: *The team blew the lead by making a bad play.* **23.** *Informal.* to mishandle, ruin, botch; make a mess of; bungle: *With one stupid mistake he blew the whole project. It was your last chance and you blew it!* **24.** *Slang.* to damn: *Blow the cost!* **25.** to put (a horse) out of breath by fatigue. **26.** *Slang.* to depart from: *to blow town.* **27.** *Slang (vulgar).* to perform fellatio on. **28.** *Slang.* to smoke (marijuana or other drugs). **29. blow away,** *Slang.* **a.** to kill, esp. by gunfire: *The gang threatened to blow away anyone who talked to the police.* **b.** to defeat decisively; trounce: *She blew her opponent away in three straight sets.* **c.** to overwhelm with emotion, astonishment, etc.: *Good poetry just blows me away.* **30. blow down,** *Metall.* to suspend working of (a blast furnace) by smelting the existing charge with a diminishing blast. **31. blow hot and cold,** to favor something at first and reject it later on; waver; vacillate: *His enthusiasm for the job blows hot and cold.* **32. blow in,** **a.** *Slang.* to arrive at a place, esp. unexpectedly: *My uncle just blew in from Sacramento.* **b.** *Metall.* to begin operations in (a blast furnace). **33. blow off, a.** to allow steam to be released. **b.** *Informal.* to reduce or release tension, as by loud talking. **34. blow one's cool,** *Slang.* to lose one's composure; become angry, frantic, or flustered. **35. blow one's cover.** See **cover** (def. 53). **36. blow one's lines,** *Theat.* to forget or make an error in a speaking part or stage directions. **37. blow one's mind.** See **mind** (def. 20). **38. blow one's stack.** See **stack** (def. 17). **39. blow one's top.** See **top**[1] (def. 21). **40. blow out, a.** to become extinguished: *The candles blew out at once.* **b.** to lose force or cease: *The storm has blown itself out.* **c.** (of an oil or gas well) to lose oil or gas uncontrollably. **d.** *Metall.* to blow down and clean (a blast furnace) in order to shut down. **41. blow over, a.** to pass away; subside: *The storm blew over in five minutes.* **b.** to be forgotten: *The scandal will eventually blow over.* **42. blow up, a.** to come into being: *A storm suddenly blew up.* **b.** to explode: *The ship blew up.* **c.** to cause to explode: *to blow up a bridge.* **d.** to exaggerate; enlarge: *He blew up his own role in his account of the project.* **e.** *Informal.* to lose one's temper: *When he heard she had quit school, he blew up.* **f.** to fill with air; inflate: *to blow up a tire.* **g.** *Photog.* to make an enlarged reproduction of. **h.** *Math.* (of a function) to become infinite. —*n.* **43.** a blast of air or wind: *to clean machinery with a blow.* **44.** *Informal.* a violent windstorm, gale, hurricane, or the like: *one of the worst blows we ever had around here.* **45.** an act of producing a blast of air, as in playing a wind instrument: *a few discordant blows by the bugler.* **46.** *Metall.* **a.** a blast of air forced through a converter, as in the production of steel or copper. **b.** the stage of the production process during which this blast is used. **47.** *Civ. Engin.* boil[1] (def. 15). **48.** *Slang.* cocaine. [bef. 1000; ME *blowen* (v.), OE *blāwan;* c. L *flāre* to blow]

blow[3] (blō), *n.*, *v.*, **blew, blown, blow•ing.** —*n.* **1.** a yield or display of blossoms: *the lilac's lavender blows.* **2.** a display of anything bright or brilliant: *a rich, full blow of color.* **3.** state of blossoming; a flowering: *a border of tulips in full blow.* —*v.i., v.t.* **4.** *Archaic.* to blossom or cause to blossom. [bef. 1000; ME *blowen* (v.), OE *blōwan;* akin to G *blühen* to bloom, L *flōs* FLOWER]

blow•ball (blō′bôl′), *n.* the downy head or pappus of the dandelion, salsify, etc. [1660–70; BLOW[2] + BALL[1]]

blow-by (blō′bī′), *n., pl.* **-bies.** *Auto.* **1.** leakage of the air-fuel mixture or of combustion gases between a piston and the cylinder wall into the crankcase of an automobile. **2.** a device, fitted to a crankcase, for conducting such gases back to the cylinders for combustion. Also, **blow′by′.** [1930–35; n. use of v. phrase *blow by*]

blow-by-blow (blō′bī blō′), *adj.* **1.** precisely detailed; describing every minute detail and step: *a blow-by-blow account of the tennis match; a blow-by-blow report on the wedding ceremony.* —*n.* **2.** a blow-by-blow account. [1930–35, *Amer.*]

blow-comb (blō′kōm′), *n.* a small, usually hand-held electrical appliance combining a comb and blow-dryer, permitting one to style the hair while drying it. Also, **blow′ comb′.**

blow•down (blō′doun′), *n.* **1.** *Auto.* a procedure for measuring the compression within an engine to identify certain mechanical defects, such as worn piston rings. **2.** a tree or stand of timber that has been blown down by the wind. [1880–85 for earlier sense; n. use of v. phrase *blow down*]

blow-dry (blō′drī′), *v.*, **-dried, -dry•ing,** *n., pl.* **-drys.** —*v.t.* **1.** to dry or style (shampooed or wet hair) with a blow-dryer or blow-comb. —*n.* **2.** an act or instance of blow-drying: *a wash, cut, and blow-dry.* [1965–70; back formation from BLOW-DRYER]

blow-dry•er (blō′drī′ər), *n.* a small, usually hand-held electrical appliance that dries hair by emitting a stream of heated air. Cf. **blow-comb.** [1965–70; perh. b. DRYER and v. phrase *blow dry,* i.e., blow until dry]

blowed (blōd), *v. Nonstandard.* a pt. and pp. of **blow**[2].

blow•er (blō′ər), *n.* **1.** a person or thing that blows. **2.** a machine for supplying air at a moderate pressure, as to supply forced drafts or supercharge and scavenge diesel engines. **3.** snowblower. **4.** *Mining.* a jet of firedamp issuing from a crevice. **5.** *Slang.* a braggart. **6.** supercharger. **7.** *Chiefly Brit. Slang.* a telephone. [bef. 900; ME; OE. See BLOW[2], -ER[1]]

blow•fish (blō′fish′), *n., pl.* (*esp. collectively*) **-fish,** (*esp. referring to two or more kinds or species*) **-fish•es.** puffer (def. 2). [1890–95; BLOW[2] + FISH]

blow′ fly′, any of numerous dipterous insects of the family Calliphoridae that deposit their eggs or larvae on carrion, excrement, etc., or in wounds of living animals. Also, **blow′fly′.** [1815–25]

blow•gun (blō′gun′), *n.* a pipe or tube through which darts or other missiles are blown by the breath. Also called **blowtube.** [1800–10, *Amer.;* BLOW[2] + GUN[1]]

blow-hard (blō′härd′), *n. Slang.* an exceptionally boastful and talkative person. [1850–55, *Amer.*]

blow•hole (blō′hōl′), *n.* **1.** an air or gas vent, esp. one to carry off fumes from a tunnel, underground passage, etc. **2.** either of two nostrils or spiracles, or a single one, at the top of the head in whales and other cetaceans, through which they breathe. **3.** a hole in the ice to which whales or seals come to breathe. **4.** *Metall.* a defect in a casting or ingot caused by the escape of gas. **5.** *Geol.* a hole in a sea cliff or coastal terrace through which columns of spray are jetted upward. [1685–95; BLOW[2] + HOLE]

blow•ing (blō′ing), *n.* **1.** the sound of any vapor or gas issuing from a vent under pressure. **2.** *Metall.* a disturbance caused by gas or steam blowing through molten metal. **3.** Also called **blow molding.** a method of producing hollowware by injecting air under pressure into a molten mass, as of glass or plastic, and shaping the material within a mold. [bef. 1000; ME, OE; see BLOW[2], -ING[1]]

blow•i•ron (blō′ī′ərn), *n.* blowpipe (def. 2). [BLOW[2] + IRON]

blow′ job′, *Slang (vulgar).* an act or instance of fellatio.

blow′ mold′, a hinged mold for shaping molten glass during blowing.

blow′ mold′ing, blowing (def. 3).

blown[1] (blōn), *adj.* **1.** inflated; swollen; expanded: *a blown stomach.* **2.** destroyed, melted, inoperative, misshapen, ruined, or spoiled: *to replace a blown fuse; to dispose of blown canned goods.* **3.** being out of breath. **4.** flyblown. **5.** formed by blowing: *blown glass.* **6.** *Automotive Slang.* **a.** (of an engine) supercharged. **b.** (of a cylinder) destroyed or severely damaged under mechanical stress. [ptp. of BLOW[2]]

blown[2] (blōn), *adj. Hort.* fully expanded or opened, as a flower. [ptp. of BLOW[3]]

blown-mold•ed (blōn′mōl′did), *adj.* (of plastic hollowware) made by blowing and shaping in a mold; mold-blown. Also, **blow′-mold′ed, blown′-mold′.** Cf. **free-blown.**

blown-up (blōn′up′), *adj.* **1.** (of a picture, photograph, image, etc.) enlarged. **2.** damaged or destroyed by demolition, explosion, etc.: *blown-up bridges.* **3.** (of a ball, balloon, etc.) inflated. **4.** overexpanded; unduly large: *a blown-up sense of importance.* [1860–65]

blow•off (blō′ôf′, -of′), *n.* **1.** a current of escaping surplus steam, water, etc.: *The safety valve released a violent blowoff from the furnace.* **2.** a device that permits and channels such a current. **3.** *Slang.* a person who brags or boasts; a blow-hard. **4.** a temporary, sudden surge, as in prices: *The Federal Reserve Board's credit tightening could cause a blowoff in interest rates.* [1830–40; n. use of v. phrase *blow off*]

blow•out (blō′out′), *n.* **1.** a sudden bursting or rupture of an automobile tire. **2.** a sudden or violent escape of air, steam, or the like. **3.** a hollow formed in a region of shifting sands or light soil by the action of the wind. **4.** an uncontrollable escape of oil, gas, or water from a well. **5.** *Aeron.* flame-out. **6.** *Slang.* a lavish party or entertainment. [1815–25; n. use of v. phrase *blow out*]

blow•pipe (blō′pīp′), *n.* **1.** a tube through which a stream of air or gas is forced into a flame to concentrate and increase its heating action. **2.** Also called **blowiron, blowtube.** *Glass Blowing.* a long metal pipe used to gather and blow the molten glass in making hollowware. **3.** blowgun. **4.** *Med.* an instrument used to observe or clean a cavity. [1675–85; BLOW[2] + PIPE[1]]

blows•y (blou′zē), *adj.*, **blows•i•er, blows•i•est.** blowzy. —**blows′i•ly,** *adv.*

blow•torch (blō′tôrch′), *n.* **1.** a small portable apparatus that gives an extremely hot gasoline flame intensified by a blast, used esp. in metalworking. —*v.t.* **2.** to weld, burn, or ignite with or as with a blowtorch. [1905–10; BLOW[2] + TORCH]

blowtorch (def. 1)

blow•tube (blō′to͞ob′, -tyo͞ob′), *n.* **1.** blowgun. **2.** blowpipe (def. 2). [1870–75; BLOW[2] + TUBE]

blow•up (blō′up′), *n.* **1.** an explosion. **2.** a violent argument, outburst of temper, or the like, esp. one resulting in estrangement. **3.** Also, **blow′-up′.** an enlargement of a photograph. [1800–10; n. use of v. phrase *blow up*]

blow•y (blō′ē), *adj.*, **blow•i•er, blow•i•est. 1.** windy: *a chill, blowy day.* **2.** easily blown about: *flimsy, blowy curtain material.* [1820–30; BLOW[2] + -Y[1]] —**blow′i•ness,** *n.*

blowzed (blouzd), *adj.* blowzy.

blowz•y (blou′zē), *adj.*, **blowz•i•er, blowz•i•est. 1.** having a coarse, ruddy complexion. **2.** disheveled in appearance; unkempt. Also, **blowsy, blowzed, blowsed** (blouzd), **blousy.** [1760–70; obs. *blowze* wench (< ?) + -Y[1]] —**blowz′i•ly,** *adv.*

BLS, Bureau of Labor Statistics.

bls., **1.** bales. **2.** barrels.

B.L.S., **1.** Bachelor of Library Science. **2.** Bureau of Labor Statistics.

BLT, *pl.* **BLTs.** a bacon, lettuce, and tomato sandwich. Also, **B.L.T.** [1950–55]

blub (blub), *n.* a swelling of fresh plasterwork. [1550–60; var. of BLOB]

blub•ber (blub′ər), *n.* **1.** *Zool.* the fat layer between the skin and muscle of whales and other cetaceans, from which oil is made. **2.** excess body fat. **3.** an act of weeping noisily and without restraint. —*v.i.* **4.** to weep noisily and without restraint: *Stop blubbering and tell me what's wrong.* —*v.t.* **5.** to say, esp. incoherently, while weeping: *The child seemed to be blubbering something about a lost ring.* **6.** to contort or disfigure (the features) with weeping. —*adj.* **7.** disfigured with blubbering; blubbery: *She dried her blubber eyes.* **8.** fatty; swollen; puffed out (usually used in combination): *thick, blubber lips; blubber-faced.* [1250–1300; ME *bluber* bubble, bubbling water, entrails, whale oil; appar. imit.] —**blub′ber•er,** *n.* —**blub′ber•ing•ly,** *adv.*

blub•ber•head (blub′ər hed′), *n. Slang.* a stupid, inept person; blockhead. [1850–55; BLUBBER + HEAD]

blub•ber•y (blub′ə rē), *adj.* **1.** abounding in or resembling blubber; fat. **2.** puffy; swollen: *blubbery lips.* [1785–95; BLUBBER + -Y[1]]

blu•cher (blo͞o′kər, -chər), *n.* **1.** a strong, leather half boot. **2.** a shoe having the vamp and tongue made of one piece and overlapped by the quarters, which lace across the instep. [1825–35; named after G. L. von BLÜCHER]

Blü•cher (blo͞o′kər, -chər; *Ger.* blʏ′ᴋʜəʀ), *n.* **Geb•hart Le•be•recht von** (gep′härt lā′bə ʀeᴋʜt′ fən), 1742–1819, Prussian field marshal.

bludge (bluj), *v.*, **bludged, bludg•ing,** *n. Australian.* —*v.t.* **1.** to shirk. **2.** to impose on (someone). —*n.* **3.** an easy task. [1915–20; false analysis of BLUDGEON (v.) gives phrase *bludge on* to impose on; back formation from BLUDGEON (n.) gives *bludge* (v.) to use a bludgeon, whence *bludger* bully, esp. a harlot's bully, pimp, hence shirker, whence *bludge* (v.) to shirk] —**bludg′er,** *n.*

bludg•eon (bluj′ən), *n.* **1.** a short, heavy club with one end weighted, or thicker and heavier than the other. —*v.t.* **2.** to strike or knock down with a bludgeon. **3.** to force into something; coerce; bully: *The boss finally bludgeoned him into accepting responsibility.* [1720–30;

CONCISE PRONUNCIATION KEY: *act, cāpe, dâre, pärt; set, ēqual; if, īce; ox, ōver, ôrder, oil, bo͝ok, bo͞ot, out; up, ûrge; child; sing; shoe; thin, that;* zh as in *treasure.* ə = *a* as in *alone, e* as in *system, i* as in *easily, o* as in *gallop, u* as in *circus;* ᵊ as in *fire* (fīᵊr), *hour* (ouᵊr). l and n can serve as syllabic consonants, as in *cradle* (krād′l), and *button* (but′n). See the full key inside the front cover.

orig. uncert.] —**bludg′eon·er, bludg·eon·eer** (bluj′ə nēr′), *n.*

blue (blo͞o), *n., adj.,* **blu·er, blu·est,** *v.,* **blued, blu·ing** or **blue·ing.** —*n.* **1.** the pure color of a clear sky; the primary color between green and violet in the visible spectrum, an effect of light with a wavelength between 450 and 500 nm. **2.** bluing. **3.** something having a blue color: *Place the blue next to the red.* **4.** a person who wears blue or is a member of a group characterized by some blue symbol: *Tomorrow the blues will play the browns.* **5.** (*often cap.*) a member of the Union army in the American Civil War or the army itself. Cf. **gray** (def. 13). **6.** bluestocking. **7.** See **blue ribbon** (def. 1). **8.** any of several blue-winged butterflies of the family Lycaenidae. **9.** *Print.* blueline. **10. the blue, a.** the sky. **b.** the sea. **c.** the remote distance: *They've vanished into the blue somewhere.* **11. out of the blue,** suddenly and unexpectedly: *The inheritance came out of the blue as a stroke of good fortune.* —*adj.* **12.** of the color of blue: *a blue tie.* **13.** (*cap.*) of or pertaining to the Union army in the American Civil War. **14.** (of the skin) discolored by cold, contusion, fear, or vascular collapse. **15.** depressed in spirits; dejected; melancholy: *She felt blue about not being chosen for the team.* **16.** holding or offering little hope; dismal; bleak: *a blue outlook.* **17.** characterized by or stemming from rigid morals or religion: *statutes that were blue and unrealistic.* **18.** marked by blasphemy: *The air was blue with oaths.* **19.** (of an animal's pelage) grayish-blue. **20.** indecent; somewhat obscene; risqué: *a blue joke or film.* **21. blue in the face,** exhausted and speechless, as from excessive anger, physical strain, etc.: *I reminded him about it till I was blue in the face.* —*v.t.* **22.** to make blue; dye a blue color. **23.** to tinge with bluing: *Don't blue your clothes till the second rinse.* —*v.i.* **24.** to become or turn blue. [1250–1300; ME *blewe* < AF *blew, bl(i)u, bl(i)ef* blue, livid, discolored, OF *blo, blau* (F *bleu*) < Gmc **blǣwaz;* cf. OE *blǣwen,* contr. of *blǣhǣwen* deep blue, perse (see BLAE, HUE), OFris *blāw,* MD *blā(u),* OHG *blāo* (G *blau*), ON *blár*] —**blue′ly,** *adv.* —**blue′ness,** *n.*
—**Syn. 1.** azure, cerulean, sapphire. **15.** despondent, unhappy, morose, doleful, dispirited, sad, glum, downcast. **16.** gloomy, dispiriting. **17.** righteous, puritanical, moral, severe, prudish. —**Ant. 15.** happy.

blue′ alert′, (in military or civilian defense) an alert following the first, or yellow, alert, in which air attack seems probable. Cf. **red alert, white alert, yellow alert.**

blue′ an′gel, *Slang.* See **blue heaven.**

Blue′ Ar′my, *Canadian* (*chiefly Winnipeg, Calgary, and Vancouver*). an organization maintaining a directory of tradesmen and checking on the quality of the service they provide.

blue′ asbes′tos, *Mineral.* crocidolite.

blue′ ba′by, *Pathol.* an infant born with cyanosis resulting from a congenital heart or lung defect. [1900–05]

blue′back salm′on (blo͞o′bak′). See **sockeye salmon.** [1525–35]

blue·bead (blo͞o′bēd′), *n.* See **corn lily** (def. 2). [BLUE + BEAD; so called from its beadlike blue berries]

Blue·beard (blo͞o′bērd′), *n.* **1.** a fairy-tale character whose seventh wife found the bodies of her predecessors in a room she had been forbidden to enter. **2.** any man alleged to have murdered a number of his wives or other women. —**Blue′beard′ism,** *n.*

blue·beat (blo͞o′bēt′), *n.* ska. [BLUE + BEAT; cf. BLUES[1]]

blue·bell (blo͞o′bel′), *n.* **1.** any of numerous plants of the bellflower family, having blue, bell-shaped flowers, as a bellflower or harebell. **2.** Also called **wood hyacinth.** an Old World plant, *Endymion non-scriptus,* of the lily family, having blue, bell-shaped flowers. **3.** any of various other plants having blue flowers, as those of the genus *Mertensia.* [1570–80; BLUE + BELL[1]] —**blue′-belled′,** *adj.*

blue·ber·ry (blo͞o′ber′ē, -bə rē), *n., pl.* **-ries. 1.** the edible, usually bluish berry of various shrubs belonging to the genus *Vaccinium,* of the heath family. **2.** any of these shrubs. [1700–10; BLUE + BERRY]

blue·bill (blo͞o′bil′), *n.* the scaup duck. [1805–15, *Amer.*; BLUE + BILL[2]]

bluebird, *Sialia sialis,* length 7 in. (18 cm)

blue·bird (blo͞o′bûrd′), *n.* **1.** any of several small North American songbirds of the genus *Sialia,* having predominantly blue plumage, as the eastern *S. sialis,* which has a blue back and a reddish-brown breast. **2.** See **fairy bluebird. 3.** (*usually cap.*) a member of Camp Fire, Inc., who is between the ages of six and eight. [1680–90; BLUE + BIRD]

blue-black (blo͞o′blak′), *adj.* black with bluish highlights. [1815–25] —**blue′-black′ness,** *n.*

blue blood (blo͞o′ blud′ *for 1;* blo͞o′ blud′ *for 2*), **1.** an aristocrat, noble, or member of a socially prominent family. **2.** aristocratic, noble, or socially prominent lineage or relatives: *They boasted a lineage of pure blue blood.* [1825–35; trans. of Sp *sangre azul.* See SANGUINE, AZURE] —**blue′-blood′ed,** *adj.*

blue·blos·som (blo͞o′blos′əm), *n.* a shrub, *Ceanothus thyrsiflorus,* of the buckthorn family, abundant in the western U.S., having finely toothed oblong leaves and lilaclike clusters of blue flowers. Also called **blue myrtle.** [BLUE + BLOSSOM]

blue·bon·net (blo͞o′bon′it), *n.* **1.** the cornflower, *Centaurea cyanus.* **2.** a blue-flowered lupine, esp. *Lupinus subcarnosus,* having spikes of light blue flowers with a white or yellow spot: the state flower of Texas. **3.** a broad, flat cap of blue wool, formerly worn in Scotland. **4.** a Scottish soldier who wore such a cap. **5.** any Scot. Also called **blue·cap** (blo͞o′kap′). [1675–85; BLUE + BONNET]

blue′ book′, 1. a register or directory of socially prominent persons. **2.** any register or directory, as of major companies or officials. **3.** a blank book used in taking college examinations, usually with a blue cover. **4.** a British parliamentary or other publication bound in a blue cover. **5.** (*caps.*) *Trademark.* a reference manual listing the current market value of used cars by model and year of manufacture. **6.** a similar manual listing the market value of other items, appliances, etc. Also, **blue′book′.**

blue·bot·tle (blo͞o′bot′l), *n.* **1.** cornflower (def. 1). **2.** a composite plant, *Centaurea cyanus,* having narrow leaves and blue flower heads. **3.** See **bluebottle fly. 4.** *Chiefly Australian.* Portuguese man-of-war. [1545–55; BLUE + BOTTLE[1]]

blue′bottle fly′, any of several iridescent blue blow flies, esp. those of the genus *Calliphora,* some of which are parasitic on domestic animals. [1710–20]

blue′-breast·ed quail′ (blo͞o′bres′tid), a small, brightly colored quail, *Coturnix chinensis,* of southern Asia and Australia, widely kept as a cage bird. Also called **button quail.**

blue′ bull′, nilgai.

blue′ cat′fish, a large freshwater catfish, *Ictalurus furcatus,* that is a popular food fish in the states of the Mississippi River valley. Also, **blue′ cat′.** Also called **blue′ chan′nel cat′, blue′ chan′nel cat′fish.** [1825–35, *Amer.*]

blue′ cheese′, a rich cheese in which the internal mold manifests itself in blue veins: made in France esp. from sheep's milk and elsewhere also from cow's milk and goat's milk. Also, **bleu cheese.** [1920–25]

blue′ chip′, 1. *Chiefly Poker.* a blue-colored chip of high value. **2.** a common stock issued by a major company that has financial strength, stability against fluctuations, and a good record of dividend payments: regarded as a low-risk investment. **3.** a secure and valuable item or property held in reserve: *The airfield was a blue chip in the struggle for military supremacy.* [1900–05, *Amer.*]

blue-chip (blo͞o′chip′), *adj.* **1.** of, pertaining to, or constituting a blue chip. **2.** having outstanding or exemplary qualities within a specified category; leading: *a group of blue-chip scientists; blue-chip stock.* [1930–35]

blue·coat (blo͞o′kōt′), *n.* **1.** a person who wears a blue coat or uniform. **2.** a police officer. **3.** a soldier in the U.S. Army in earlier times. [1585–95; BLUE + COAT] —**blue′coat′ed,** *adj.*

blue′ co′hosh. See under **cohosh.** [1815–25, *Amer.*]

blue-col·lar (blo͞o′kol′ər), *adj.* **1.** of or pertaining to wage-earning workers who wear work clothes or other specialized clothing on the job, as mechanics, longshoremen, and miners. Cf. **white-collar.** —*n.* **2.** a blue-collar worker. [1945–50]

blue′ comb′, *Vet. Pathol.* a disease of birds resembling Bright's disease in humans affecting esp. domestic fowl, characterized by fever, sunken eyes, and shriveling of the skin of the wattles, shanks, and comb. Also called **x-disease.** [1940–45]

blue′ cop′peras, *Chem.* See **blue vitriol.**

blue′ cor′al, any coral of the genus *Heliopora,* having brown polyps and a blue skeleton, found in the Indo-Pacific region.

blue′ crab′, an edible crab, *Callinectes sapidus,* having a dark green body and bluish legs, found along the Atlantic and Gulf coasts of North America. [1880–85, *Amer.*]

blue′ crane′, the great blue heron. [1775–85, *Amer.*]

Blue′ Cross′ and Blue′ Shield′, *Trademark.* a nonprofit organization that offers its members health insurance covering hospitalization, surgical, and medical expenses.

blue-curls (blo͞o′kûrlz′), *n., pl.* **-curls. 1.** (*used with a singular or plural v.*) any of several plants belonging to the genus *Trichostema,* of the mint family, having blue to pink or, rarely, white flowers with long, curved filaments. **2.** selfheal (def. 1). Also, **blue′ curls′.** [1810–20, *Amer.*]

blue′ dai′sy, a bushy, composite shrub, *Felicia amelloides,* of southern Africa, having solitary, daisylike flowers with yellow disks and blue rays, grown as an ornamental. Also called **blue marguerite.** [1590–1600]

blue′ dan′delion, chicory (def. 1).

blue′ dawn′-flower, a tropical American vine, *Ipomoea acuminata,* of the morning glory family, having large, funnel-shaped flowers that turn from blue to pink.

blue′ dev′il, *Slang.* See **blue heaven.**

blue′ dev′ils, 1. low spirits; depression. **2.** See **delirium tremens.** [1780–90]

blue′ dicks′ (diks), a plant, *Dichelostemma pulchellum,* of the amaryllis family, common on the western coast of the U.S., having headlike clusters of blue flowers.

blue′ dog′wood, a shrub or small tree, *Cornus alternifolia,* of eastern North America, having clusters of white flowers and bluish fruit.

blue-eyed (blo͞o′īd′), *adj.* **1.** having blue eyes. **2.** having or representing childlike innocence. [1600–10]

blue′-eyed grass′, any of numerous plants belonging to the genus *Sisyrinchium,* of the iris family, having grasslike leaves and small, usually blue, flowers. [1775–85]

blue′-eyed Mar′y, a North American plant, *Collinsia verna,* of the figwort family, having long-stalked flowers with the upper lip white or purple and the lower lip blue. Also called **innocence.** [1890–95, *Amer.*]

blue′ false′ in′digo, a North American plant, *Baptisia australis,* of the legume family, having wedge-shaped leaflets and blue, clustered flowers. Also called **rattle-bush.**

Blue·field (blo͞o′fēld′), *n.* a city in SW West Virginia. 16,060.

Blue·fields (blo͞o′fēldz′), *n.* a seaport in E Nicaragua. 17,706.

blue′fin tu′na (blo͞o′fin′), a large tuna, *Thunnus thynnus,* common in temperate seas. See illus. under **tuna.** [1920–25; BLUE + FIN]

blue·fish (blo͞o′fish′), *n., pl.* (*esp. collectively*) **-fish,** (*esp. referring to two or more kinds or species*) **-fish·es. 1.** a predaceous, marine, bluish or greenish food fish, *Pomatomus saltatrix,* inhabiting Atlantic coastal waters of North and South America. **2.** any of various fishes, usually of a bluish color. [1615–25, *Amer.*; BLUE + FISH]

blue′ flag′, any North American plant of the genus *Iris,* esp. *I. versicolor:* the state flower of Tennessee. [1775–85, *Amer.*]

blue′ flash′. *Meteorol.* See **green flash.**

blue′ flu′, absenteeism among police officers or firefighters who claim to be ill but are in fact absent to support union contract demands or negotiations: so called from the officers' blue uniforms. [1965–70]

blue′ fox′, 1. a bluish-gray winter color phase of the Arctic fox, *Alopex lagopus.* **2.** the Arctic fox in summer pelage. **3.** the blue fur of this animal. **4.** any white fox fur dyed blue. [1860–65]

blue′ gas′, *Chem.* See **water gas.** [1900–05]

blue′ gi′ant, *Astron.* any of the large, bright stars having surface temperatures of about 20,000 K and diameters that are often ten times that of the sun.

blue·gill (blo͞o′gil′), *n.* a freshwater sunfish, *Lepomis macrochirus,* of the Mississippi River valley, used for food. [1880–85, *Amer.*; BLUE + GILL[1]]

blue′ goose′, a dark color phase of the snow goose, *Chen caerulescens,* of North America. [1870–75, *Amer.*]

blue′ gra′ma. See under **grama.** [1870–75, *Amer.*]

blue·grass (blo͞o′gras′, -gräs′), *n.* **1.** any grass of the genus *Poa,* as the Kentucky bluegrass, *P. pratensis,* having dense tufts of bluish-green blades and creeping rhizomes. **2.** country music that is polyphonic in character and is played on unamplified stringed instruments, with emphasis esp. on the solo banjo. **3. the Bluegrass.** See **Bluegrass Region.** [1745–55, *Amer.*; BLUE + GRASS]

Blue′grass Re′gion, a region in central Kentucky, famous for its horse farms and fields of bluegrass.

Blue′grass State′, Kentucky (used as a nickname). [1885–90, *Amer.*]

blue-green (blo͞o′grēn′), *n.* a color about midway between blue and green in the spectrum. [1850–55]

blue′-green al′gae, *Biol.* a widely distributed group of predominantly photosynthetic prokaryotic organisms of the subkingdom Cyanophyta, resembling phototrophic bacteria, occurring singly or in colonies in diverse habitats: some species can fix atmospheric nitrogen. Also called **cyanobacteria.** [1895–1900]

blue′ gros′beak, a grosbeak, *Guiraca caerulea,* of the U.S., Mexico, and Central America, the male of which is blue with two rusty bars on each wing. [1720–30, *Amer.*]

blue′ grouse′, a dull gray grouse, *Dendragapus obscurus,* of western North America, the male of which has a yellow or orange comb. Also called **dusky grouse, sooty grouse.** [1855–60, *Amer.*]

blue′ gum′, eucalyptus. [1795–1805]

blue·head (blo͞o′hed′), *n.* a wrasse, *Thalassoma bifasciatum,* of Atlantic seas, the adult male of which has a brilliant purplish-blue head. [BLUE + HEAD]

blue′-head·ed vir′eo (blo͞o′hed′id). See **solitary vireo.**

blue′ heav′en, *Slang.* a blue capsule or tablet containing the barbiturate amobarbital or its derivative. Also called **blue angel, blue devil.**

blue′ huck′leberry, tangleberry. [1880–85, *Amer.*]

blue′ ice′, *Geol.* the oldest and densest ice in a glacier, distinguished by a pale-blue color.

blue·ing (blo͞o′ing), *n. Chem.* bluing.

blue·ish (blo͞o′ish), *adj.* bluish.

Blue′ Is′land, a city in NE Illinois, near Chicago. 21,855.

blue′ jack′. See **coho salmon.**

blue·jack (blo͞o′jak′), *n.* a small oak, *Quercus incana,* of the southern U.S., having crooked branches and blue-green leaves. Also called **blue′jack oak′.** [1855–60, *Amer.*; BLUE + JACK[1], modeled after BLACKJACK; so called from the bluish look of the leaves]

blue·jack·et (blo͞o′jak′it), *n.* a sailor, esp. in the U.S or British navies. [1820–30; BLUE + JACKET]

blue′ jas′mine, a southern U.S. shrubby vine, *Clematis crispa,* of the buttercup family, having solitary, bell-shaped, blue or bluish-purple to pink flowers and bearing fruit with silky appendages. Also called **curly clematis.**

blue′ jay′, a common, crested jay, *Cyanocitta cristata,* of eastern North America, having a bright blue back and a gray breast. [1700–10, *Amer.*]

blue′ jeans′, close-fitting trousers made of blue denim or denimlike fabric, having pockets and seams often reinforced with rivets, and worn originally as work pants but now also as casual attire by persons of all ages. Cf. **jean** (def. 2), **Levi's.** [1850–55]

blue′ law′, any puritanical law that forbids certain practices, esp. drinking or working on Sunday, dancing, etc. Cf. **sumptuary law.** [1775–85, *Amer.*]

blue-leg (blo͞o′leg′), *n.* blewit.

blue′ line′, *Ice Hockey.* either of two lines of the color blue that are parallel to and equidistant from the goal lines and divide the rink into three zones of equal size. Also called **zone line.** Cf. **end zone** (def. 2), **neutral zone.** [1925–30]

blue·line (blo͞o′līn′), *n. Print.* a print made on light-sensitive paper and used as a proof for checking the position of stripped-up negatives or positives and copy prior to platemaking. Also, **blue.** [BLUE + LINE[1]]

blue′ lips′, a plant, *Collinsia grandiflora,* of the figwort family, of western central North America, having short-stalked flowers with the upper lip purple or white and the lower lip blue or violet.

blue′ lo′tus, 1. See under **Egyptian lotus** (def. 1). **2.** a water lily, *Nymphaea stellata,* of India, having pale-blue flowers.

blue′ marguerite′. See **blue daisy.**

blue′ mar′lin, a large marlin, *Makaira nigricans,* occurring worldwide in warm and temperate seas, highly prized in sportfishing and as a food fish.

blue′ mass′, *Pharm.* **1.** Also called **mercury mass.** a preparation of metallic mercury and other ingredients, used for making blue pills. **2.** See **blue pill** (def. 1). [1850–55, *Amer.*]

blue′ mel′ilot, a European plant, *Trigonella caerulea,* of the legume family, having long-stalked clusters of blue and white flowers.

blue′ mock′ingbird. See under **mockingbird** (def. 2).

blue′ mold′, 1. Also called **green mold.** any fungus of the genus *Penicillium,* which forms a bluish-green, furry coating on foodstuffs inoculated by its spores. **2.** *Plant Pathol.* **a.** a disease of plants, characterized by necrosis of leaves or fruit and the growth of bluish or grayish mold on affected parts, caused by any of several fungi, as of the genus *Penicillium* or *Peronospora tabacina.* **b.** See **downy mildew** (def. 2). [1655–65]

blue′ Mon′day, a Monday regarded as a depressing workday in contrast to the pleasant relaxation of the weekend.

blue′ moon′, moon (def. 9). [1815–25]

Blue′ Moun′tains, a range of low mountains in NE Oregon and SE Washington.

blue′ mud′, *Geol., Oceanog.* a deep-sea sediment of fine silt and clay that derives its bluish color from organic material and iron sulfide. [1830–40, *Amer.*]

blue′ myr′tle, blueblossom. [1880–85, *Amer.*]

blue·ness (blo͞o′nis), *n.* the quality or state of being blue. [1485–95; BLUE + -NESS]

Blue′ Nile′, a river in E Africa, flowing NNW from Lake Tana in Ethiopia into the Nile at Khartoum: a tributary of the Nile. ab. 950 mi. (1530 km) long. Cf. **Nile.**

blue′ north′er, *Oklahoma and Texas.* a cold north wind that brings rapidly falling temperatures. Also called **blue whistler.** [1870–75, *Amer.*]

blue·nose (blo͞o′nōz′), *n.* **1.** a puritanical person; prude. **2.** (*cap.*) Also, **Blue′ Nose′.** *Canadian.* an inhabitant of the Maritime Provinces, esp. of Nova Scotia. **3.** *Naut. Slang.* **a.** a sailing vessel of Nova Scotia. **b.** a seaman on such a vessel. [1780–85 (def. 2, 3); 1925–30, *Amer.* (def. 1); BLUE + NOSE; (def. 1) cf. BLUE LAW, etc.; (def. 2, 3) orig. a derisive name for a person residing in Nova Scotia before the Loyalists' arrival; allegedly so called from a variety of potato with a bluish tip, though there is no certain evidence for this or any of various other explanations of the name]

blue′ note′, *Jazz.* a flatted note, esp. the third or the seventh degree of the scale, recurring frequently in blues and jazz as a characteristic feature. [1925–30]

blue′ on′yx. *Jewelry.* See **German lapis.**

blue-pen·cil (blo͞o′pen′səl), *v.t.,* **-ciled, -cil·ing** or (*esp. Brit.*) **-cilled, -cil·ling.** to alter, abridge, or cancel with or as with a pencil that has blue lead, as in editing a manuscript. [1885–90]

blue′ pe′ter, *Naut.* a blue flag with a white square in the center, designating the letter *P* in the International Code of Signals, flown by a vessel in port to indicate its imminent departure. [1815–25]

blue′ phlox′, a plant, *Phlox divaricata,* of eastern North America, having creeping, rooting stems and mauve flowers. Also called **wild sweet william.**

blue′ pike′, a variety of the walleye, *Strizostedion vitreum glaucum,* inhabiting the Great Lakes. Also called **blue pickerel, blue′ pike′perch, blue walleye.** [1835–45]

blue′ pill′, *Pharm.* a pill of blue mass, used in medicine chiefly as a cathartic. Also called **mercury mass.** [1785–95]

blue′ plate′, 1. a plate, often decorated with a blue willow pattern, divided by ridges into sections for holding apart several kinds of food. **2.** Also called **blue′ plate′ spe′cial.** a specially priced main course, as of meat and vegetables, listed as an item on a menu, esp. in an inexpensive restaurant. [1940–45]

blue′ point′, a Siamese cat having a light-colored body and darker, bluish-gray points. [1940–45]

blue·point (blo͞o′point′), *n.* a small oyster, esp. one from the oyster beds near Blue Point, Long Island, usually served raw on the half shell or in a cocktail. [1780–90, *Amer.*]

blue′ point′er, a large shark, *Isuropsis mako,* having a blue-colored back and pointed snout, found in Australian waters where it is prized for sportfishing. [1880–85]

blue·print (blo͞o′print′), *n.* **1.** a process of photographic printing, used chiefly in copying architectural and mechanical drawings, which produces a white line on a blue background. **2.** a print made by this process. **3.** a detailed outline or plan of action: *a blueprint for success.* —*v.t.* **4.** to make a blueprint of or for. [1885–90; BLUE + PRINT] —**blue′print′er,** *n.*

blue·print·ing (blo͞o′prin′ting), *n. Automotive Slang.* the procedure of improving the performance of an engine by dismantling and then rebuilding the reciprocating parts so that they meet exact tolerances. [1815–25, for literal sense; BLUEPRINT + -ING[1]]

blue′ rac′er, a bluish racer, *Coluber constrictor flaviventris,* of Ohio to eastern Iowa. [1885–90, *Amer.*]

blue-red (blo͞o′red′), *n.* a color about midway between blue and red in the spectrum; purplish.

blue′ rib′bon, 1. the highest award or distinction, as the first prize in a contest: *His entry at the state fair won a blue ribbon.* **2.** a blue ribbon worn as a badge of honor, esp. by members of the Order of the Garter of the British knighthood. **3.** (*caps.*) Also, *Brit.,* **Blue′ Rib′·band.** (formerly) a prize awarded to an ocean liner making the fastest recorded trip across the Atlantic Ocean between Ambrose Lightship and Bishop Rock. **4.** a badge used by some temperance organizations to indicate a pledge of abstinence from alcohol. [1645–55]

blue-rib·bon (blo͞o′rib′ən), *adj.* of superior quality or prominence; first-rate; specially selected: *a blue-ribbon committee of fund-raisers.* [1925–30; adj. use of BLUE RIBBON]

blue′-ribbon ju′ry, a jury composed of persons having more than ordinary education and presumably exceptional intelligence and perceptiveness, selected by the court on the motion of plaintiff or defendant to try cases of unusual complexity or importance. Also called **special jury.** [1935–40, *Amer.*]

Blue′ Rid′er School′. See ***Blaue Reiter.***

Blue′ Ridge′, a mountain range extending SW from N Virginia to N Georgia: part of the Appalachian Mountains. Also called **Blue′ Ridge′ Moun′tains.**

blue-rinse (blo͞o′rins′), *adj.* of, for, or composed mostly of elderly women: *the blue-rinse matinee audience.* [1975–80; so called from the bluish tinge produced by certain rinses used on gray hair]

blue′ rock′fish, a bluish-black rockfish, *Sebastodes mystinus,* inhabiting Pacific coastal waters of North America. Also called **priestfish.**

blue′ run′ner, a carangid food fish, *Caranx crysos,* of the Atlantic Ocean.

blues[1] (blo͞oz), *n.* **1. the blues,** (*used with a plural v.*) depressed spirits; despondency; melancholy: *This rainy spell is giving me the blues.* **2.** (*used with a singular v.*) *Jazz.* **a.** a song, originating with American blacks, that is marked by the frequent occurrence of blue notes, and that takes the basic form, customarily improvised upon in performance, of a 12-bar chorus consisting of a 3-line stanza with the second line repeating the first. **b.** the genre constituting such songs. [1800–10, *Amer.*; cf. BLUE DEVILS] —**blues′y,** *adj.*

blues[2] (blo͞oz), *n.* (*used with a plural v.*) **1.** any of various blue military uniforms worn by members of the U.S. armed services: *dress blues.* **2.** a blue uniform for work; blue work clothes: *a doctor in surgical blues.* **3.** *Informal.* police. [see BLUE, -S[3]]

blue′ shark′, a slender, pelagic shark, *Prionace glauca,* that is indigo blue above, shading to white below. Also called **great blue shark.** [1665–75]

blue′ sheep′, bharal.

Blue′ Shield′. See **Blue Cross and Blue Shield.**

blue·shift (blo͞o′shift′), *n. Astron.* a shift toward shorter wavelengths of the spectral lines of a celestial object, caused by the motion of the object toward the observer. Also, **blue′ shift′.** [1950–55; BLUE + SHIFT]

blue-sky (blo͞o′skī′), *adj.* **1.** fanciful; impractical: *blue-sky ideas.* **2.** (esp. of securities) having dubious value; not financially sound: *a blue-sky stock.* [1890–95]

blue′-sky′ law′, a law regulating the sale of securities, real estate, etc., esp. such a law designed to prevent the promotion of fraudulent stocks. [1910–15, *Amer.*]

blues·man (blo͞oz′mən, -man′), *n., pl.* **-men** (-mən, -men′). a musician who sings or plays blues. [1965–70; BLUES[1] + -MAN]

blue′ spire′a, a grayish, hairy, eastern Asian shrub, *Caryopteris incana,* of the verbena family, having clusters of showy, blue or bluish-purple flowers.

Blue′ Springs′, a town in W Missouri. 25,927.

blue′ spruce′, a spruce, *Picea pungens,* of western North America, having bluish-green leaves, grown as an ornamental: the state tree of Colorado and Utah. Also called **Colorado blue spruce, Colorado spruce.** [1880–85, *Amer.*]

blues-rock (blo͞oz′rok′), *n.* a blend of rock-'n'-roll and blues. [1970–75]

blue′ stain′, *Plant Pathol.* a serious fungal disease of certain trees that reduces the economic value of the timber, caused by various species of the genus *Ceratocystis.*

blue′ stel′lar ob′ject, *Astron.* any of a class of blue celestial objects, at one time thought to be stars, that do not emit appreciable radio waves. *Abbr.:* BSO

blue′ stem′, *Plant Pathol.* a disease of raspberries and blackberries, characterized by blue discoloration of the stem, wilting, and discoloration and decay of the roots, caused by a fungus, *Verticillium alboatrum.*

blue·stem (blo͞o′stem′), *n.* **1.** any of several prairie grasses of the genus *Andropogon,* having bluish leaf sheaths, now grown in the western U.S. for forage. **2.** See **dwarf palmetto.** [1850–55, *Amer.*; BLUE + STEM[1]]

blue·stock·ing (blo͞o′stok′ing), *n.* **1.** a woman with considerable scholarly, literary, or intellectual ability or interest. **2.** a member of a mid-18th-century London literary circle. [1675–85; so called from the informal attire, esp. blue woolen instead of black silk stockings, worn by some women of the group (def. 2)] —**blue′stock′ing·ism,** *n.*

blue·stone (blo͞o′stōn′), *n.* a bluish, argillaceous sandstone used for building purposes, flagging, etc. [1645–55; BLUE + STONE]

blue′ strag′gler, *Astron.* one of a small group of blue stars within a cluster that falls near the main sequence even though other stars of its color have evolved off the main sequence. [1965–70]

blue′ streak′, 1. something moving very fast: *They traveled like a blue streak through Italy.* **2.** continuous, rapid, or interminable speech: *to talk a blue streak.* [1820–30, *Amer.*]

blue′ suc′cory, a composite garden plant, *Catananche caerulea,* of southern Europe, having very hairy leaves and blue flower heads, used by the ancients as a love potion. Also called **Cupid's-dart.**

blue′ swim′mer, an edible Australian crab, *Portunus pelagicus.*

blu·et (blo͞o′it), *n.* **1.** Usually, **bluets.** Also called **innocence, Quaker-ladies.** any of several North American plants of the genus *Houstonia* (or *Hedyotis*), of the madder family, esp. *H. caerulea,* a low-growing plant having four-petaled blue and white flowers. **2.** any of various other plants having blue flowers. [1400–50; late ME *blewet, blewed,* var. of ME *bloweth, blowed* (see BLUE, BLAE); suffix perh. OE *-et,* as in THICKET]

blue′ this′tle, blueweed (def. 1).

blue′throat pike′blenny (blo͞o′thrōt′). See under **pikeblenny.** [1870–75; BLUE + THROAT]

blue·tick (blo͞o′tik′), *n.* an American hound having a usually black, tan, and white coat flecked with black, used in hunting foxes and raccoons. [BLUE + TICK[1]]

blue′ tit′, an Old World titmouse, *Parus caeruleus,* having a cobalt-blue crown. [1835–45]

blue·tongue (blo͞o′tung′), *n. Vet. Pathol.* a viral disease of sheep and sometimes cattle, transmitted by biting insects and characterized by high fever, excessive salivation, swelling of the face and tongue, and cyanosis of the tongue. Also called **catarrhal fever.** [1860–65; BLUE + TONGUE]

blue′-tongued liz′ard (blo͞o′tungd′), a large Australian lizard, *Tiliqua scincoides,* characterized by having a cobalt-blue tongue.

blu·ette (blo͞o′it), *n.* blewit.

blue′ vel′vet, *Slang.* a mixture of paregoric and Pyribenzamine taken by vein as an illicit drug.

blue′ ver′diter. See under **verditer.**

blue′ vit′riol, *Chem., Mineral.* a salt, copper sulfate, $CuSO_4 \cdot 5H_2O$, occurring naturally as large transparent, deep-blue triclinic crystals, appearing in its anhydrous state as a white powder: used chiefly as a mordant, insecticide, fungicide, and in engraving. Also called **blue copperas, chalcanthite, cupric sulfate.** [1760–70]

blue′ wall′eye. See **blue pike.**

blue-wa·ter (blo͞o′wô′tər, -wot′ər), *adj.* designed to operate on and range over the open sea; oceangoing: *a bluewater navy that can be dispatched throughout the world, far from its home base.* [1900–05]

blue′ wa′vey. See under **wavey.**

blue·weed (blo͞o′wēd′), *n.* **1.** Also called **blue thistle.** a bristly weed, *Echium vulgare,* of the borage family, having showy blue flowers, a native of Europe naturalized in the U.S. **2.** chicory (def. 1). [1835–45; BLUE + WEED[1]]

blue′ whale′, a migratory baleen whale, *Balaenoptera musculus,* mostly of oceans and seas in the Southern Hemisphere, growing to a length of 100 ft. (30.5 m) and having a furrowed, slate-blue skin mottled with lighter spots, in some seas acquiring a yellowish coating of diatoms on the underside: the largest mammal ever known, it is now endangered. Also called **sulfur-bottom.** [1850–55]

blue′ whis′tler, *Oklahoma and Texas.* See **blue norther.** [1835–45, *Amer.*]

blue′-winged teal′ (blo͞o′wingd′), a small duck, *Anas discors,* inhabiting ponds and rivers of North America, having a dull-brown mottled body and grayish-blue patches on the wings. [1630–40]

blue·wood (blo͞o′wo͝od′), *n.* a shrub or small tree, *Condalia obovata,* of the buckthorn family, of western Texas and northern Mexico, often forming dense chaparral. [1880–85, *Amer.*; BLUE + WOOD[1]]

blue′ wood′ as′ter, a composite plant, *Aster cordifolius,* of North America, having heart-shaped leaves and pale-blue flowers.

blue·y (blo͞o′ē), *n., pl.* **blue·ys.** *Australian.* **1.** swag[2] (def. 2). **2.** a legal summons. [1795–1805; BLUE + -Y[2]; (def. 1) so called because usu. wrapped in a blue blanket; (def. 2) so called from its blue binder]

bluff[1] (bluf), *adj.,* **-er, -est,** *n.* —*adj.* **1.** good-naturedly direct, blunt, or frank; heartily outspoken: *a big, bluff, generous man.* **2.** presenting a bold and

nearly perpendicular front, as a coastline: *a bluff, precipitous headland.* **3.** *Naut.* (of the bow of a vessel) having a full, blunt form. —*n.* **4.** a cliff, headland, or hill with a broad, steep face. **5.** *North Dakota, Wisconsin, and the Canadian Prairie Provinces.* a clump or grove of trees on a prairie or other generally treeless area. [1620–30; perh. < MLG *blaff* smooth, even, or < MD *blaf* broad, flat] —**bluff′ly,** *adv.* —**bluff′ness,** *n.*
—**Syn. 1.** forthright, open, honest; rough, crude. See **blunt. 2.** abrupt, steep. —**Ant. 1.** subtle.

bluff[2] (bluf), *v.t.* **1.** to mislead by a display of strength, self-confidence, or the like: *He bluffed me into believing that he was a doctor.* **2.** to gain by bluffing: *He bluffed his way into the job.* **3.** *Poker.* to deceive by a show of confidence in the strength of one's cards. —*v.i.* **4.** to mislead someone by presenting a bold, strong, or self-confident front: *That open face makes it impossible for him to bluff.* —*n.* **5.** an act or instance or the practice of bluffing: *Her pathetic story was all a bluff to get money from us. His assertive manner is mostly bluff.* **6.** a person who bluffs; bluffer: *That big bluff doesn't have a nickel to his name.* **7. call someone's bluff,** to expose a person's deception; challenge someone to carry out a threat: *He always said he would quit, so we finally called his bluff.* [1665–75; perh. < LG *bluffen* to bluster, frighten; akin to MD *bluffen* to make a trick at cards] —**bluff′a·ble,** *adj.* —**bluff′er,** *n.*
—**Syn. 1.** deceive, fool, dupe, delude, hoodwink.

blu·ing (blo͞o′ing), *n. Chem.* a substance, as indigo, used to whiten clothes or give them a bluish tinge. Also, **blueing.** [1660–70; BLUE + -ING[1]]

blu·ish (blo͞o′ish), *adj.* somewhat blue. Also, **blueish.** [1350–1400; ME; see BLUE, -ISH[1]] —**blu′ish·ness,** *n.*

Blum (blo͞om), *n.* **Lé·on** (lē′on; *Fr.* lā ôN′), 1872–1950, French statesman, journalist, and Socialist Party leader: premier of France 1936–37, 1938, 1946–47.

Blum·berg (blum′bûrg), *n.* **Baruch S(amuel),** born 1925, U.S. physician: Nobel prize 1976.

blun·der (blun′dər), *n.* **1.** a gross, stupid, or careless mistake: *That's your second blunder.* —*v.i.* **2.** to move or act blindly, stupidly, or without direction or steady guidance: *Without my glasses I blundered into the wrong room.* **3.** to make a gross or stupid mistake, esp. through carelessness or mental confusion: *Just pray that he doesn't blunder again and get the names wrong.* —*v.t.* **4.** to bungle; botch: *Several of the accounts were blundered by that new assistant.* **5.** to utter thoughtlessly; blurt out: *He blundered his surprise at their winning the award.* [1350–1400; ME *blunderen blondren,* (v.) < ON *blunda* shut one's eyes, nap; cf. Norw dial. *blundra*] —**blun′der·er,** *n.* —**blun′der·ing·ly,** *adv.*
—**Syn. 1.** error. See **mistake.**

blun·der·buss (blun′dər bus′), *n.* **1.** a short musket of wide bore with expanded muzzle to scatter shot, bullets, or slugs at close range. **2.** an insensitive, blundering person. [1645–55; < D *donderbus* (equiv. to *donder* THUNDER + *bus* gun, BOX[1]) with *donder* replaced by BLUNDER. See HARQUEBUS]

blun·der·head (blun′dər hed′), *n. Informal.* a blunderer; nincompoop. [1690–1700; BLUNDER + HEAD]

blunge (blunj), *v.t.,* **blunged, blung·ing.** to mix (clay or the like) with water, so as to form a liquid suspension. [1820–30; b. BLEND and PLUNGE]

blung·er (blun′jər), *n.* **1.** a large container with rotating arms for mechanical mixing of clay with water. **2.** a person who blunges. [1820–30; BLUNGE + -ER[1]]

blunt (blunt), *adj.,* **-er, -est,** *v., n.* —*adj.* **1.** having an obtuse, thick, or dull edge or point; rounded; not sharp: *a blunt pencil.* **2.** abrupt in address or manner: *a blunt, ill-timed question.* **3.** slow in perception or understanding; obtuse: *His isolation has made him blunt about the feelings of others.* —*v.t.* **4.** to make blunt; hebetate: *He blunted the knife by using it to cut rope.* **5.** to weaken or impair the force, keenness, or susceptibility of: *to blunt the imagination.* —*v.i.* **6.** to become blunt. —*n.* **7.** something blunt, as a small-game arrow, a short sewing needle, or a short, thick cigar. [1150–1200; ME; perh. akin to BLIND] —**blunt′ly,** *adv.* —**blunt′ness,** *n.*
—**Syn. 1.** See **dull. 2.** short, gruff, rough, rude, uncivil, impolite. BLUNT, BLUFF, BRUSQUE, CURT characterize manners and speech. BLUNT suggests lack of polish and of regard for the feelings of others: *blunt and tactless.* BLUFF implies an unintentional roughness together with so much good-natured heartiness that others rarely take offense: *a bluff sea captain.* BRUSQUE connotes sharpness and abruptness of speech or manner: *a brusque denial.* CURT applies esp. to disconcertingly concise language: *a curt reply.* **3.** dimwitted, thick, stolid. **4.** dull.

blur (blûr), *v.,* **blurred, blur·ring,** *n.* —*v.t.* **1.** to obscure or sully (something) by smearing or with a smeary substance: *The windows were blurred with soot.* **2.** to obscure by making confused in form or outline; make indistinct: *The fog blurred the outline of the car.* **3.** to dim the perception or susceptibility of; make dull or insensible: *The blow on the head blurred his senses.* —*v.i.* **4.** to become indistinct: *Everything blurred as she ran.* **5.** to make blurs. —*n.* **6.** a smudge or smear that obscures: *a blur of smoke.* **7.** a blurred condition; indistinctness: *They could see nothing in the foggy blur.* **8.** something seen indistinctly: *The ship appeared as a blur against the horizon.* [1540–50; akin to BLEAR] —**blur·red·ly** (blûr′id lē, blûrd′-), *adv.* —**blur′red·ness,** *n.* —**blur′ring·ly,** *adv.*
—**Syn. 2.** cloud, dim, darken, veil, mask.

blurb (blûrb), *n.* **1.** a brief advertisement or announcement, esp. a laudatory one: *She wrote a good blurb for her friend's novel.* —*v.t.* **2.** to advertise or praise in the manner of a blurb. [1910–15, *Amer.*; allegedly coined by F. G. Burgess] —**blurb′ist,** *n.*

CONCISE ETYMOLOGY KEY: <, descended or borrowed from; >, whence; b., blend of, blended; c., cognate with; cf., compare; deriv., derivative; equiv., equivalent; imit., imitative; obl., oblique; r., replacing; s., stem; sp., spelling, spelled; resp., respelling, respelled; trans., translation; ?, origin unknown; *, unattested; ‡, probably earlier than. See the full key inside the front cover.

blur·ry (blûr′ē), *adj.* **-ri·er, -ri·est.** blurred; indistinct. [BLUR + -Y[1]] —**blur′ri·ly,** *adv.* —**blur′ri·ness,** *n.*

blurt (blûrt), *v.t.* **1.** to utter suddenly or inadvertently; divulge impulsively or unadvisedly (usually fol. by *out*): *He blurted out the hiding place of the spy.* —*n.* **2.** an abrupt utterance. [1565–75; appar. imit.]

blush (blush), *v.i.* **1.** to redden, as from embarrassment or shame: *He blushed when they called him a conquering hero.* **2.** to feel shame or embarrassment (often fol. by *at* or *for*): *Your behavior makes me blush for your poor mother.* **3.** (of the sky, flowers, etc.) to become rosy. **4.** (of new house paint or lacquer) to become cloudy or dull through moisture or excessive evaporation of solvents. —*v.t.* **5.** to make red; flush. **6.** to make known by a blush: *She could not help blushing the truth.* —*n.* **7.** a reddening, as of the face. **8.** rosy or pinkish tinge. **9.** blusher (def. 2). **10. at first blush,** without previous knowledge or adequate consideration; at first glance: *At first blush, the solution to the problem seemed simple.* [1275–1325; (v.) ME *bluschen,* OE *blyscan* to redden; akin to OE *blysa,* ON *blys,* MLG *blus* torch, *bloschen* to blaze; (n.) ME *blusch, blisch,* deriv. of the v.] —**blush′ful,** *adj.* —**blush′ful·ly,** *adv.* —**blush′ful·ness,** *n.* —**blush′ing·ly,** *adv.* —**blush′less,** *adj.*
—**Syn. 1.** flush, color. —**Ant. 1.** pale, blanch.

blush·er (blush′ər), *n.* **1.** a person who blushes. **2.** Also called **blush, blush-on.** a cosmetic similar to rouge, used to add color to the cheeks. **3.** an edible mushroom, *Amanita rubescens,* that turns from yellow to red when touched. [1655–65; BLUSH + -ER[1]]

blush-on (blush′on′, -ôn′), *n.* blusher (def. 2). [b. BLUSH and v. phrase *brush on*]

blush′ wine′, a pale pink wine resembling white wine in taste, made from red grapes by removing the skins from the must before fermentation is completed. [1980–85]

blus·ter (blus′tər), *v.i.* **1.** to roar and be tumultuous, as wind. **2.** to be loud, noisy, or swaggering; utter loud, empty menaces or protests: *He blusters about revenge but does nothing.* —*v.t.* **3.** to force or accomplish by blustering: *He blustered his way through the crowd.* —*n.* **4.** boisterous noise and violence: *the bluster of the streets.* **5.** noisy, empty threats or protests; inflated talk: *bluff and bluster.* [1520–30; perh. < LG *blustern, blüstern* to blow violently; cf. ON *blāstr* blowing, hissing] —**blus′ter·er,** *n.* —**blus′ter·ing·ly,** *adv.* —**blus′ter·y, blus′ter·ous,** *adj.* —**blus′ter·ous·ly,** *adv.*
—**Syn. 2.** rant, brag, boast, gloat. **3.** threaten, storm, bully.

blvd., boulevard.

Bly (blī), *n.* **Nellie** (*Elizabeth Cochrane Seaman*), 1867–1922, U.S. journalist and social reformer.

B lymphocyte, *Immun.* See **B cell.** Also, **B-lymphocyte.** [1970–75]

blype (blīp), *n. Scot.* a thin skin or membrane, esp. a small piece of skin. [1780–90; orig. uncert.]

Blythe (blīth, blīth), *n.* a female given name. Also, **Blithe.**

Blythe·ville (blīth′vil), *n.* a city in NE Arkansas. 24,314.

BM, 1. basal metabolism. **2.** *Survey.* bench mark. **3.** *Informal.* bowel movement.

B.M., 1. Bachelor of Medicine. **2.** Bachelor of Music. **3.** British Museum.

B.Mar.E., Bachelor of Marine Engineering.

B.M.E., 1. Bachelor of Mechanical Engineering. **2.** Bachelor of Mining Engineering. **3.** Bachelor of Music Education.

B.M.Ed., Bachelor of Music Education.

B meson, *Physics.* a meson composed of a bottom quark and an up or down antiquark or of a bottom antiquark and an up or down quark. Also called **B particle.**

B.Met., Bachelor of Metallurgy.

B.Met.E., Bachelor of Metallurgical Engineering.

BMEWS (bē myo͞oz′), *n. U.S. Mil.* Ballistic Missile Early Warning System.

B.Mgt.E., Bachelor of Management Engineering.

B.Min.E., Bachelor of Mining Engineering.

BMOC, big man on campus. Also, **B.M.O.C.**

B-mov·ie (bē′mo͞o′vē), *n.* a low-budget movie made esp. to accompany a major feature film on a double bill. Also called **B-picture.**

BMR, basal metabolic rate.

B.M.S., Bachelor of Marine Science.

B.M.T., Bachelor of Medical Technology.

B.Mus., Bachelor of Music.

B.M.V., Blessed Mary the Virgin. [< L *Beāta Maria Virgō*]

BMX, bicycle motocross.

Bn., 1. Baron. **2.** Also, **bn.** Battalion.

B.N., Bachelor of Nursing.

BNA, British North America. Also, **B.N.A.**

B'nai B'rith (bə nā′ brith′), an international Jewish organization, founded in New York City in 1843, which institutes and administers programs designed to promote the social, educational, and cultural betterment of Jews and of the public at large. [< Heb *bənē bərith* sons of the covenant]

BND, West Germany's national intelligence service. [< G, for *Bundesnachrichtendienst*]

B.N.S., Bachelor of Naval Science.

B/o, *Accounting.* brought over.

B.O., 1. Board of Ordnance. **2.** *Informal.* body odor. **3.** *Theat.* box office.

b.o., 1. back order. **2.** box office. **3.** branch office. **4.** broker's order. **5.** buyer's option.

bo·a (bō′ə), *n., pl.* **bo·as. 1.** any of several nonvenomous, chiefly tropical constrictors of the family Boidae, having vestigial hind limbs at the base of the tail. **2.** a scarf or stole of feathers, fur, or fabric. [1350–1400; ME < L: water adder]

Bo·ab·dil (bō′əb dil; *Sp.* bô′äb thēl′), *n.* (*abu-Abdallah*) ("*El Chico*"), died 1533?, last Moorish king of Granada 1482–83, 1486–92.

bo′a constric′tor, 1. a snake, *Constrictor (Boa) constrictor,* of tropical America, noted for its large size and its ability to suffocate a prey by coiling around it. **2.** any large snake of the boa family, as the python or anaconda. [1800–10]

boa constrictor, *Constrictor constrictor,* length 10 ft. (3 m)

Bo·ad·i·ce·a (bō ad′ə sē′ə), *n.* died A.D. 62, queen of the Iceni: leader of an unsuccessful revolt against the Romans in Britain.

Bo·a·ner·ges (bō′ə nûr′jēz), *n.* **1.** a surname given by Jesus to James and John. Mark 3:17. **2.** (*used with a singular v.*) a vociferous preacher or orator. [< LL < Gk *Boanergés* << Heb *bənē reghesh* sons of thunder]

boar (bôr, bōr), *n.* **1.** the uncastrated male swine. **2.** See **wild boar.** —*adj.* **3.** *South Midland and Southern U.S.* (of animals) male, esp. full-grown: *a boar cat.* [bef. 1000; ME *boor,* OE *bār*; c. D *beer,* OHG *bēr* < WGmc **baira-,* perh. akin to Welsh *baedd*]

board (bôrd, bōrd), *n.* **1.** a piece of wood sawed thin, and of considerable length and breadth compared with the thickness. **2.** a flat slab of wood or other material for some specific purpose: *a cutting board.* **3.** a sheet of wood, cardboard, paper, etc., with or without markings, for some special use, as a checkerboard or chessboard. **4. boards, a.** *Theat.* the stage: *The play will go on the boards next week.* **b.** the wooden fence surrounding the playing area of an ice-hockey rink. **c.** a racing course made of wood, used esp. in track meets held indoors: *his first time running on boards.* **5.** *Bookbinding.* stiff cardboard or other material covered with paper, cloth, or the like to form the covers for a book. **6.** *Building Trades.* composition material made in large sheets, as plasterboard or corkboard. **7.** a table, esp. to serve food on. **8.** daily meals, esp. as provided for pay: *room and board.* **9.** an official group of persons who direct or supervise some activity: *a board of directors.* **10.** *Naut.* **a.** the side of a ship. **b.** one leg, or tack, of the course of a ship beating to windward. **11.** *Railroads.* a fixed signal or permanent sign regulating traffic. **12.** a flat surface, as a wall or an object of rectangular shape, on which something is posted, as notices or stock-market quotations: *a bulletin board.* **13.** surfboard. **14.** *Computers.* **a.** Also called **card, circuit board.** a piece of fiberglass or other material upon which chips can be mounted to perform specific functions. **b.** plugboard (def. 2). **15.** *Electronics.* See **circuit board** (def. 2). **16.** a switchboard. **17.** *Australian.* **a.** the area of a woolshed where shearing is done. **b.** a crew of shearers working in a particular woolshed. **c.** sheep about to be sheared. **18.** *Obs.* the edge, border, or side of anything. **19. across the board, a.** *Racing.* betting on a horse or dog to finish first, second, or third, so that any result where a selection wins, places, or shows enables the bettor to collect. **b.** applying to or affecting every person, class, group, etc. **20. go by the board, a.** to go over the ship's side. **b.** to be destroyed, neglected, or forgotten: *All his devoted labor went by the board.* **21. on board, a.** on or in a ship, plane, or other vehicle: *There were several movie stars on board traveling incognito.* **b.** *Baseball.* on base: *There were two men on board as the next batter came up.* **c.** present and functioning as a member of a team or organization. Also, **aboard. 22. on the boards,** in the theatrical profession. **23. tread the boards.** See **tread** (def. 11). —*v.t.* **24.** to cover or close with boards (often fol. by *up* or *over*): *to board up a house; to board over a well.* **25.** to furnish with meals, or with meals and lodging, esp. for pay: *They boarded him for $50 a week.* **26.** to go on board of or enter (a ship, train, etc.). **27.** to allow on board: *We will be boarding passengers in approximately ten minutes.* **28.** to come up alongside (a ship), as to attack or to go on board: *The pirate ship boarded the clipper.* **29.** *Obs.* to approach; accost. —*v.i.* **30.** to take one's meals, or be supplied with food and lodging at a fixed price: *Several of us board at the same rooming house.* **31.** *Ice Hockey.* to hit an opposing player with a board check. [bef. 900; ME, OE *bord* board, table, shield; c. D *boord* board, bord plate, G *Bort,* ON *borth,* Goth *-baurd*] —**board′a·ble,** *adj.* —**board′like′,** *adj.*

board′ and bat′ten, *Carpentry.* a siding consisting of wide boards or of sheets of plywood set vertically with butt joints covered by battens. See illus. under **siding.** [1900–05]

board′ chair′man. See **chairman of the board.**

board′ check′, *Ice Hockey.* a body check in which the opponent is thrown against the wooden wall enclosing the rink. Cf. **check**[1] (def. 42). [1935–40]

board·er (bôr′dər, bōr′-), *n.* **1.** a person, esp. a lodger, who is supplied with regular meals. **2.** a member of a boarding party. [1520–30; BOARD + -ER[1]]

board′er ba′by, an infant or young child who is abandoned or orphaned and left in a hospital for lack of a foster home. [1975–80]

board′ foot′, *Building Trades.* a unit of measure equal to the cubic contents of a piece of lumber one foot square and one inch thick, used in measuring logs and lumber. *Abbr.:* bd. ft. [1895–1900, *Amer.*]

board′ game′, 1. a game, as checkers or chess, requiring the moving of pieces from one section of a board to another. **2.** any game played on a board. [1930–35]

board·ing (bôr′ding, bōr′-), *n.* **1.** wooden boards collectively. **2.** a structure of boards, as in a fence or a floor. **3.** the act of a person who boards a ship, train, airplane, or the like: *an uneventful boarding.* [1525–35; BOARD + -ING[1]]

board·ing·house (bôr′ding hous′, bōr′-), *n., pl.* **-hous·es** (-hou′ziz). a house at which board or board and lodging may be obtained for payment. Also, **board′·ing house′.** [1720–30]

board′ing par′ty, a group of persons who board a vessel, esp. to attack, seize, or search it. [1880–85]

board′ing pass′, a pass that authorizes a passenger to board an aircraft and is issued after one's ticket has been purchased or collected. [1965–70]

board′ing ramp′, ramp (def. 5).

board′ing school′, a school at which the pupils receive board and lodging during the school term (distinguished from *day school*). [1670–80]

board′ meas′ure, *Building Trades.* a system of cubic measure in which the unit is the board foot. [1650–60]

board′ of commis′sioners, the administrative body of a county in many U.S. states, esp. in the South and the West, having from two to seven elected members. Cf. **board of supervisors.**

board′ of educa′tion, 1. a board having control over a school system. **2.** an appointive or elective body that directs and administers chiefly the primary and secondary public schools in a town, city, county, or state.

board′ of elec′tions, *U.S. Politics.* a bipartisan board appointed usually by local authorities and charged with control of elections and voting procedure. Also called **election board.**

board′ of es′timate, a special organ of a municipal government, as of New York City, composed of the mayor, the president of the city council, and the controller, and charged with approving the city's budget and fiscal matters.

board′ of health′, a government department concerned with public health.

board′ of su′pervisors, the governing body of a county in many U.S. states, esp. in the Midwest and the East, consisting of from 15 to 100 members elected from towns, townships, cities, or wards. Cf. **board of commissioners.**

board′ of trade′, 1. an association of business people. **2. Board of Trade,** (in England) the national ministry that supervises and encourages commerce and industry. [1770–80]

board′ of trustees′, an appointed or elective board that supervises the affairs of a public or private organization: *the board of trustees of the university; the art museum's board of trustees.* [1800–10]

board·room (bôrd′ro͞om′, -ro͝om′, bōrd′-), *n.* **1.** a room set aside for meetings of a board, as of a corporation. **2.** a room in a broker's office where stock-market quotations are listed on a board or by other means. Also, **board′ room′.** [1880–85, *Amer.*; BOARD + ROOM]

board′ rule′, *Building Trades.* a measuring device having scales for finding the cubic contents of a board without calculation. [1840–50, *Amer.*]

board·sail·ing (bôrd′sā′ling, bōrd′-), *n.* the sport of sailing a boat that has no cockpit, as in windsurfing. [1980–85]

board′ side′, the broad side of a piece of lumber.

board·walk (bôrd′wôk′, bōrd′-), *n.* **1.** a promenade made of wooden boards, usually along a beach or shore. **2.** any walk made of boards or planks. [1870–75, *Amer.*; BOARD + WALK]

boar·fish (bôr′fish′, bōr′-), *n., pl.* (*esp. collectively*) **-fish,** (*esp. referring to two or more kinds or species*) **-fish·es.** any of several fishes having a projecting snout, esp. a small, spiny-rayed fish, *Capros aper,* of European waters. [1830–40; BOAR + FISH]

boar·hound (bôr′hound′, bōr′-), *n.* any of various large dogs, esp. a Great Dane, used originally for hunting wild boars. [1880–85; BOAR + HOUND[1]]

boar·ish (bôr′ish, bōr′-), *adj.* of or like a boar; swinish. [1540–50; BOAR + -ISH[1]] **—boar′ish·ly,** *adv.* **—boar′ish·ness,** *n.*

boart (bôrt), *n. Mineral.* bort.

Bo·as (bō′az), *n.* **Franz** (fränts), 1858–1942, U.S. anthropologist, born in Germany.

boast[1] (bōst), *v.i.* **1.** to speak with exaggeration and excessive pride, esp. about oneself. **2.** to speak with pride (often fol. by *of*): *He boasted of his family's wealth.* —*v.t.* **3.** to speak of with excessive pride or vanity: *He boasts himself a genius.* **4.** to be proud in the possession of: *The town boasts a new school.* —*n.* **5.** a thing boasted of; a cause for pride: *Talent is his boast. It is her boast that she has never betrayed a friend.* **6.** exaggerated or objectionable speech; bragging: *empty boasts and threats.* [1250–1300; ME *bost* (n.), *bosten* (v.), of uncert. orig.] **—boast′ing·ly,** *adv.* **—boast′less,** *adj.*

—Syn. 1, 2. BOAST, BRAG imply vocal self-praise or claims to superiority over others. BOAST usually refers to a particular ability, possession, etc., that may be one of such kind as to justify a good deal of pride: *He boasts of his ability as a singer.* BRAG, a more colloquial term, usually suggests a more ostentatious and exaggerated boasting but less well-founded: *He brags loudly of his marksmanship.*

boast[2] (bōst), *v.t. Masonry.* to dress or shape (stone) roughly. [1815–25; of uncert. orig.]

boast·er[1] (bō′stər), *n.* a person who boasts or brags. [1275–1325; ME; see BOAST[1], -ER[1]]

boast·er[2] (bō′stər), *n. Masonry.* a chisel for boasting stone. [1875–80; BOAST[2] + -ER[1]]

boast·ful (bōst′fəl), *adj.* given to or characterized by boasting. [1275–1325; ME *bostful.* See BOAST[1], -FUL] **—boast′ful·ly,** *adv.* **—boast′ful·ness,** *n.*

—Syn. conceited, cocky, pompous, cocksure, vainglorious, egotistical.

boat (bōt), *n.* **1.** a vessel for transport by water, constructed to provide buoyancy by excluding water and shaped to give stability and permit propulsion. **2.** a small ship, generally for specialized use: *a fishing boat.* **3.** a small vessel carried for use by a large one, as a lifeboat: *to lower the boats.* **4.** a ship. **5.** a vessel of any size built for navigation on a river or other inland body of water. **6.** a serving dish resembling a boat: *a gravy boat; a celery boat.* **7.** *Eccles.* a container for holding incense before it is placed in the censer. **8. in the same boat,** in the same circumstances; faced with the same problems: *The new recruits were all in the same boat.* **9. miss the boat,** *Informal.* **a.** to fail to take advantage of an opportunity: *He missed the boat when he applied too late to get into college.* **b.** to miss the point of; fail to understand: *I missed the boat on that explanation.* **10. rock the boat.** See **rock[2]** (def. 12). —*v.i.* **11.** to go in a boat: *We boated down the Thames.* —*v.t.* **12.** to transport in a boat: *They boated us across the bay.* **13.** to remove (an oar) from the water and place athwartships. Cf. **ship** (def. 11). [bef. 900; ME *boot* (n.), OE *bāt;* c. ON *beit*] **—boat′a·ble,** *adj.* **—boat′less,** *adj.*

boat·age (bō′tij), *n. Naut.* **1.** the act of hauling by boat. **2.** a charge for such hauling. [1605–15; BOAT + -AGE]

boat′ bed′. See **sleigh bed.**

boat·bill (bōt′bil′), *n.* a wading bird, *Cochlearius cochlearius,* of tropical America, related to the herons, having a broad bill resembling an inverted boat. Also called **boat′-billed her′on** (bōt′bild′). [1770–80; BOAT + BILL[2]]

boat′ bug′, 1. See **water boatman. 2.** backswimmer.

boat·build·er (bōt′bil′dər), *n.* a person who builds boats. [1670–80; BOAT + BUILDER]

boat′ deck′, *Naut.* a superstructure deck on which most of the lifeboats of a ship are stowed. [1925–30]

boat·el (bō tel′), *n.* a waterside hotel with dock space for persons who travel by boat. Also, **botel.** [1955–60; BOAT + (HOT)EL]

boat·er (bō′tər), *n.* **1.** a person who boats, esp. for pleasure. **2.** a stiff straw hat with a shallow, flat-topped crown, ribbon band, and straight brim. [1595–1605; BOAT + -ER[1]]

boat′ hook′, a hook mounted at the end of a pole, used to pull or push boats toward or away from a landing, to pick up a mooring, etc. [1605–15]

boat·house (bōt′hous′), *n., pl.* **-hous·es** (-hou′ziz). a building or shed, usually built partly over water, for sheltering a boat or boats. [1715–25; BOAT + HOUSE]

boat·ing (bō′ting), *n.* **1.** the use of boats, esp. for pleasure: *He enjoyed boating and swimming.* —*adj.* **2.** of or pertaining to boats: *boating clothes.* [1600–10; BOAT + -ING[1], -ING[2]]

boat·lift (bōt′lift′), *n.* an operation in which large numbers of people or vast quantities of supplies are transported by ships or boats in an emergency. [BOAT + LIFT, perh. modeled on AIRLIFT]

boat′ lil′y, Moses-in-the-cradle.

boat·load (bōt′lōd′), *n.* the cargo that a vessel carries or is capable of carrying. [1670–80; BOAT + LOAD]

boat·man (bōt′mən), *n., pl.* **-men. 1.** a person skilled in the use of small craft. **2.** a person who sells, rents, or works on boats. Also, **boatsman.** [1505–15; BOAT + -MAN]

boat·man·ship (bōt′mən ship′), *n.* boatsmanship.

boat′ nail′, a nail with a convex head and a chisel point. See illus. under **nail.**

boat′ neck′, a wide, high neckline that follows the curve of the collarbone and ends in points on the shoulder seams. Also called **boat′ neck′line, bateau neck, bateau neckline.** [1955–60]

boat′ patch′, *Building Trades.* an oval patch for plywood, terminating in a point at each end.

boat′ peo′ple, refugees who have fled a country by boat, usually without sufficient provisions, navigational aids, or a set destination, esp. those who left Indochina by sea as a result of the fall of South Vietnam in 1975. [1975–80]

boat·slip (bōt′slip′), *n.* a docking place for a boat, as between wharves. [BOAT + SLIP[1]]

boats·man (bōts′mən), *n., pl.* **-men.** boatman.

boats·man·ship (bōts′mən ship′), *n.* seamanship as applied to boats, esp. rowboats and motorboats. Also, **boatmanship.** [1805–15; BOATS(MAN) + -MANSHIP]

boat′ spike′. See **barge spike.**

boat·swain (bō′sən; *spelling pron.* bōt′swān′), *n.* a warrant officer on a warship, or a petty officer on a merchant vessel, in charge of rigging, anchors, cables, etc. Also, **bo's'n, bosun.** [1400–50; late ME *bote-swayn.* See BOAT, SWAIN]

boat′swain bird′, tropicbird. Also, **boat′swain·bird′.** [1865–70]

boat′swain's chair′, a seat composed of a plank suspended in a horizontal position from ropes, used by painters and other persons who work on the exteriors of buildings, ships, etc., while seated at a considerable height. [1875–80]

boat′swain's pipe′, a high-pitched whistle used by a boatswain for giving signals. Also called **boat′swain's call′.**

boat′ tail′, *Auto.* a body style in which the rear end of the vehicle tapers to a point or a cone.

boat′-tailed grack′le (bōt′tāld′), a large grackle, *Quiscalus major,* of the southeastern U.S., that folds its tail into a shape resembling the keel of a boat. [1830–40, *Amer.*]

boat′ train′, a train scheduled to carry passengers to or from a landing point: *The boat train to Paris was waiting at Cherbourg.* [1880–85]

boat·wright (bōt′rīt′), *n.* a craftsman who builds wooden boats. [1400–50; late ME; see BOAT, WRIGHT]

boat·yard (bōt′yärd′), *n.* a yard or waterside location at which boats, small craft, and the like are built, maintained, docked, etc. Cf. **shipyard.** [1795–1805, *Amer.*; BOAT + YARD[2]]

Bo·az (bō′az), *n.* husband of Ruth. Ruth 2–4.

bob[1] (bob), *n., v.,* **bobbed, bob·bing.** —*n.* **1.** a short, jerky motion: *a bob of the head.* —*v.t.* **2.** to move quickly down and up: *to bob the head.* **3.** to indicate with such a motion: *to bob a greeting.* —*v.i.* **4.** to make a jerky motion with the head or body. **5.** to move about with jerky, usually rising and falling motions: *The ball bobbed upon the waves.* **6. bob up,** to emerge or appear, esp. unexpectedly: *A familiar face bobbed up in the crowd.* [1400–50; late ME *bobben.* See BOB[2]]

bob[2] (bob), *n., v.,* **bobbed, bob·bing.** —*n.* **1.** a style of short haircut for women and children. **2.** a docked horse's tail. **3.** a dangling or terminal object, as the weight on a pendulum or a plumb line. **4.** a short, simple line in a verse or song, esp. a short refrain or coda. **5.** *Angling.* **a.** a knot of worms, rags, etc., on a string. **b.** a float for a fishing line. **6.** a bobsled or bob skate. **7.** *Scot.* a bunch, cluster, or wad, esp. a small bouquet of flowers. **8.** *Obs.* See **walking beam.** —*v.t.* **9.** to cut short; dock: *They bobbed their hair to be in style.* —*v.i.* **10.** to try to snatch floating or dangling objects with the teeth: *to bob for apples.* **11.** *Angling.* to fish with a bob. [1300–50; ME *bobbe* (n.) spray, cluster, bunch (of leaves, flowers, fruit, etc.); of uncert. orig.]

bob[3] (bob), *n., v.,* **bobbed, bob·bing.** —*n.* **1.** a tap; light blow. **2.** a polishing wheel of leather, felt, or the like. —*v.t.* **3.** to tap; strike lightly. [1350–1400; ME *bobben* to strike, beat, perh. imit. See BOP[2]]

bob[4] (bob), *n., pl.* **bob.** *Brit. Informal.* a shilling. [1780–90; perh. from BOB]

Bob (bob), *n.* a male given name, form of **Robert.**

Bo·ba·di·lla (bō′vä thē′lyä, -thē′yä), *n.* **Fran·cis·co de** (frän thēs′kô the, -sēs′-), died 1502, Spanish colonial governor in the West Indies: sent Columbus back to Spain in chains.

bob·ber[1] (bob′ər), *n.* **1.** a person or thing that bobs. **2.** a fishing bob. [1830–40; BOB[1] + -ER[1]]

bob·ber[2] (bob′ər), *n.* a member of a bobsled team. [1900–05; BOB[2] + -ER[1]]

bob·ber·y (bob′ə rē), *n., pl.* **-ber·ies.** a disturbance; brawl. [1810–20; < Hindi *bāp re* O father!]

Bob·bie (bob′ē), *n.* **1.** a male given name, form of **Robert. 2.** a female given name.

bob·bin (bob′in), *n.* **1.** a reel, cylinder, or spool upon which yarn or thread is wound, as used in spinning, machine sewing, lacemaking, etc. **2.** *Elect.* **a.** a spoollike form around which a coil of insulated wire is wound to provide an inductance. **b.** the coil itself. [1520–30; < MF *bobine* hank of thread, perh. *bob-* an expressive base akin to BOB[2] + *-ine* -INE[2]]

bob′bin and fly′ frame′, a roving machine used in the final stages of converting spun cotton fiber into yarn.

Bob′bin and Joan′, the European arum, *Arum maculatum.*

bob·bi·net (bob′ə net′), *n.* a net of hexagonal mesh, made on a lace machine. [1805–15; BOBBI(N) + NET[1]]

bob·bing (bob′ing), *n. Radar.* the effect on a radarscope of the fluctuation of a radar echo because of alternating interference and reinforcement of the reflected waves. [BOB[1] + -ING[1]]

bob′bin lace′, lace made by hand with bobbins of thread, the thread being twisted around pins stuck into a pattern placed on a pad. Also called **pillow lace.**

bob′bin turn′ing, turning of furniture legs, stretchers, etc., to resemble a continuous row of bobbins.

bob·ble (bob′əl), *n., v.,* **-bled, -bling.** —*n.* **1.** a repeated, jerky movement; bob. **2.** a momentary fumbling or juggling of a batted or thrown baseball. **3.** an error; mistake. **4.** a small ball of fabric usually used decoratively, as in a fringe or other trimming: *a sweater with a line of bobbles up the sleeves.* —*v.t.* **5.** to juggle or fumble (a batted or thrown baseball) momentarily, usually resulting in an error. [1805–15; BOB[1] + -LE; (def. 4) perh. new formation with BOB[2]]

Bobb′sey twins′ (bob′zē), two people who are often together or seem to resemble each other, as in appearance or actions: *We called them the Bobbsey twins, because they always had the same opinions.* [from the central characters in a series of children's books by Laura Lee Hope, pen name of a literary syndicate; some of the books are attributed to U.S. author Lillian C. Garis (1873–1954)]

bob·by (bob′ē), *n., pl.* **-bies.** *Brit. Informal.* a policeman. [1835–45; special use of *Bobby,* for Sir *Robert* Peel, who set up the Metropolitan Police system of London in 1828]

Bob·by (bob′ē), *n.* **1.** a male given name, form of **Robert. 2.** a female given name.

bob′by calf′, *Brit., Australian.* a calf no more than a week old that is sent to be slaughtered. [1925–30; *bob* (as in BOB VEAL) + -Y[2]]

bob′by daz′zler, *Brit. and Australian Slang.* a person or thing that is outstanding or excellent. [1865–70; appar. generic use of BOBBY]

CONCISE PRONUNCIATION KEY: act, cāpe, dâre, pärt; set, ēqual; *if,* īce; ox, ōver, ôrder, oil, bo͝ok, bo͞ot, out; up, ûrge; child; sing; shoe; thin, *that;* zh as in *treasure.* ə = *a* as in *alone, e* as in *system, i* as in *easily, o* as in *gallop, u* as in *circus;* ᵊ as in *fire* (fīᵊr), *hour* (ouᵊr). l and n can serve as syllabic consonants, as in *cradle* (krād′l), and *button* (but′n). See the full key inside the front cover.

bob′by pin′, a flat, springlike metal hairpin having the prongs held close together by tension. [1935–40, *Amer.*; perh. BOBBY (proper name), by assoc. with *bobbed* hair (see BOB[2]), in which such pins are used]

bob•by•socks (bob′ē soks′), *n.pl.* **1.** socks that reach above the ankle and are sometimes folded down to the ankle. —*adj.* **2.** indicating or associated with the wearing of bobbysocks; adolescent: *strictly a bobbysocks crowd; the bobbysocks generation.* Also, **bob′by•sox′, bob′by socks′, bob′by sox′.** Also, **bob′sox′.** [1940–45, *Amer.*; *bobby* (for *bobbed,* altered by assoc. with BOBBY PIN) + SOCKS[1]]

bob•by•sox•er (bob′ē sok′sər), *n.* an adolescent girl, esp. during the 1940's, following youthful fads and fashions. Also, **bob′by sox′er, bob′by-sox′er.** [1940–45, *Amer.*; BOBBYSOCKS + -ER[1]]

bob•cat (bob′kat′), *n., pl.* **-cats,** (*esp. collectively*) **-cat.** a North American wildcat, *Lynx rufus,* ranging from southern Canada to central Mexico, having a brownish coat with black spots. Also called **bay lynx.** [1885–90, *Amer.*; BOB(TAIL) + CAT[1]]

bo•bèche (bō besh′), *n.* a slightly cupped ring placed over the socket of a candleholder to catch the drippings of a candle. [1895–1900; < F, of uncert. orig.; *bob-* perh. akin to the base of *bobine* BOBBIN]

Bo•bi•gny (bô bē nyē′), *n.* a city in and the capital of Seine-St-Denis department, in N France, NE of Paris. 43,125.

Bo•bo-Diou•las•so (bō′bō dyōō las′ō), *n.* a city in W Burkina Faso. 102,059.

bob•o•link (bob′ə lingk′), *n.* a common North American songbird, *Dolichonyx oryzivorus,* that winters in South America. [1765–75, *Amer.*; short for *Bob o' Lincoln,* the bird's call as heard by speakers of English]

bobolink, *Dolichonyx oryzivorus,* length 7 in. (18 cm)

Bo•bruisk (bə brōō′isk; *Russ.* bu brōō′isk), *n.* a city in SE Byelorussia (Belarus), in Europe, SE of Minsk. 192,000.

bob•run (bob′run′), *n.* an ice-covered course for bobsledding consisting of a chute with high walls, banked turns, and straightaways. [BOB(SLED) + RUN]

bob′ skate′, an ice skate with two parallel blades. [BOB(SLED) + SKATE[1]]

bob•sled (bob′sled′), *n., v.,* **-sled•ded, -sled•ding.** —*n.* **1.** a sled having two pairs of runners, a brake, and a steering wheel or other mechanism that enables the front rider to direct the sled down a steeply banked run or chute. **2.** a sled formed of two short sleds coupled one behind the other. **3.** either of the sleds thus coupled. —*v.i.* **4.** to ride on a bobsled. [1830–40, *Amer.*; BOB[2] + SLED] —**bob′sled′der,** *n.*

bob•sled•ding (bob′sled′ing), *n.* the sport of coasting or competing in races on a bobsled. [1830–40; BOBSLED + -ING[1]]

bob•sleigh (bob′slā′), *n., v.i. Chiefly Brit.* bobsled.

bob•stay (bob′stā′), *n. Naut.* a rope, chain, or rod from the outer end of the bowsprit to the cutwater. [1750–60; BOB[1] + STAY[3]]

bob•tail (bob′tāl′), *n.* **1.** a short or docked tail. **2.** an animal with such a tail. —*adj.* **3.** Also, **bob′tailed′.** having a bobtail. **4.** cut short; docked; cropped. **5.** shorter or briefer than usual; abbreviated: *Several legislative items must be dropped from the current bobtail session of Congress.* —*v.t.* **6.** to cut short the tail of; dock, often by cutting a muscle in a horse's tail to make it stand erect. [1535–45; BOB[2] + TAIL[1]]

bob′ veal′, the flesh of an unborn or newborn calf, used for food. [1850–55, *Amer.*; dial. (Cornwall) *bob* young calf (from its uncertain, staggering movements; see BOB[1])]

bob•white (bob′hwīt′, -wīt′), *n.* any of several American quail of the genus *Colinus,* esp. *C. virginianus* **(northern bobwhite),** having mottled reddish-brown, black, and white plumage. See illus. under **quail.** [1805–15, *Amer.*; from its cry, as heard by speakers of English]

bob′ wire′. See **barbed wire.** [1925–30, *Amer.*; by folk etymology]

bo•cac•cio (bə kä′chō, -chē ō′, bō-), *n., pl.* **-cios.** a large, brown, big-mouthed rockfish, *Sebastes paucispinis,* of California coastal waters. [1885–90; < It *boccaccio* ugly mouth, equiv. to *bocc(a)* mouth (< L *bucca*) + *-accio* pejorative suffix, appar. r. an AmerSp fish name of like formation; cf. Sp *bocacha* big mouth]

bo•cage (bō käzh′), *n. Fine Arts.* a decorative motif of trees, branches, or foliage, as in a tapestry or a ceramic figure group. [1635–45; < F; OF *boscage* BOSCAGE]

Bo•ca Ra•ton (bō′kə rə tōn′), a city in SE Florida. 49,505.

Boc•cac•ci•o (bō kä′chē ō′, -chō, bə-; *It.* bôk kät′chô), *n.* **Gio•van•ni** (jē′ə vä′nē; *It.* jô vän′nē), 1313–75, Italian writer: author of the *Decameron.*

CONCISE ETYMOLOGY KEY: <, descended or borrowed from; >, whence; b., blend of, blended; c., cognate with; cf., compare; deriv., derivative; equiv., equivalent; imit., imitative; obl., oblique; r., replacing; s., stem; sp., spelling, spelled; resp., respelling, respelled; trans., translation; ?, origin unknown; *, unattested; ‡, probably earlier than. See the full key inside the front cover.

Boc•che•ri•ni (bok′ə rē′nē, bō′kə-; *It.* bôk′ke rē′nē), *n.* **Lu•i•gi** (lōō ē′jē), 1743–1805, Italian composer.

boc•cie (boch′ē), *n.* an Italian variety of lawn bowling played on a dirt court that is shorter and narrower than the rink of a bowling green. Also, **boc•ci** (boch′ē; *It.* bôt′chē), **boc•ce** (boch′ē; *It.* bôt′che), **boc•cia** (boch′ə; *It.* bôt′chä). [1900–05; < It *bocce* bowls, pl. of *boccia* ball < VL **bottia* round body]

Boc•cio•ni (bo chō′nē; *It.* bôt chô′nē), *n.* **Um•ber•to** (ōōm ber′tô), 1882–1916, Italian painter and sculptor.

Boche (bosh, bôsh), *n., pl.* **Boche, Boches** (bosh, bôsh). *Disparaging.* a German, esp. a German soldier in World War I. Also, **boche.** [1885–90; < F, aph. var. of *Alboche* German, equiv. to *al(lemand)* German + *(ca)boche* blockhead, head of a nail]

Bo•chum (bō′khōōm), *n.* a city in central North Rhine-Westphalia, in W West Germany. 413,400.

bock′ beer′ (bok), a strong, dark beer typically brewed in the fall and aged through the winter for consumption the following spring. Also called **bock.** [1855–60; < G *Bock, Bockbier* lit., buck beer, perh. by misdivision of *Eimbecker Bier* (as if *ein Bockbier* one Bockbier) beer of Eimbeck in Lower Saxony, Germany]

Bocks•car (boks′kär′), *n.* the U.S. B-29 bomber that dropped the atom bomb on Nagasaki, Japan, on Aug. 9, 1945. Also, ***Bock's′ Car′.***

bo•cor (bō kôr′), *n.* a malevolent voodoo priest of Haiti. [< Haitian Creole *boco(r)* sorcerer, one who practices magic]

bod (bod), *n. Informal.* **1.** body: *You've got to have a great bod to look good in that bathing suit.* **2.** *Chiefly Brit.* person: *We need a few more bods to help with the extra work.* [1780–90; short for BODY]

BOD, biochemical oxygen demand.

bo•da•cious (bō dā′shəs), *adj. South Midland and Southern U.S.* **1.** thorough; blatant; unmistakable: *a bodacious gossip.* **2.** remarkable; outstanding: *a bodacious story.* **3.** audacious; bold or brazen. [1835–45; prob. to be identified with dial. (Devon, Cornwall) *bo(w)ldacious* brazen, impudent, b. BOLD and AUDACIOUS] —**bo•da′cious•ly,** *adv.*

Bo•danz•ky (bō dänts′kē), *n.* **Ar•tur** (är′tōōr), 1877–1939, Austrian opera director and orchestra conductor: in the U.S. after 1915.

bode[1] (bōd), *v.,* **bod•ed, bod•ing.** —*v.t.* **1.** to be an omen of; portend: *The news bodes evil days for him.* **2.** *Archaic.* to announce beforehand; predict. —*v.i.* **3.** to portend: *The news bodes well for him.* [bef. 1000; ME *boden,* OE *bodian* to announce, foretell (c. ON *botha*), deriv. of *boda* messenger, c. G *Bote,* ON *bothi*]

bode[2] (bōd), *v.* a pt. of **bide.**

bo•de•ga (bō dā′gə; *Sp.* bô the′gä), *n., pl.* **-gas** (-gəz; *Sp.* -gäs). **1.** (esp. among Spanish-speaking Americans) a grocery store. **2.** a wineshop. **3.** a warehouse for storing or aging wine. [< AmerSp, Sp < L *apothēca* storehouse; see APOTHECARY]

bode•ment (bōd′mənt), *n.* **1.** a foreboding or omen; presentiment. **2.** a prophecy or prediction. [1595–1605; BODE[1] + -MENT]

Bo•den•heim (bōd′n hīm′), *n.* **Maxwell,** 1892–1954, U.S. poet and novelist.

Bo•den•see (bōd′n zā′), *n.* German name of Lake Constance.

Bo′de's law′ (bō′dəz), *Astron.* a numerical scheme that gives the approximate distance from the sun of the seven inner planets but fails for Neptune and Pluto. Also called **Titius-Bode law.** [1825–35; after Johann E. *Bode* (1747–1826), German astronomer, though prob. first formulated by Johann D. *Titius* (Tietz) (1729–96)]

bodg•ie (boj′ē), *n. Australian.* a juvenile delinquent; youthful troublemaker. [1950–55; perh. dial. (Yorkshire) *bodge* clumsy worker (see BOTCH) + -IE; cf. *bodger* inferior, worthless]

Bod•go Ge•gen (bōd′gō gā′gān), a former Buddhist leader of the Mongols.

bo•dhi (bō′dē), *n. Buddhism.* supreme knowledge or enlightenment. [< Pali, Skt]

Bo•dhi•dhar•ma (bō′di dur′mə), *n.* died A.D. c530, Indian Buddhist philosopher and missionary: founder of Ch'an in China, which was later called Zen in Japan.

Bo•dhi•satt•va (bō′də sut′və), *n. Buddhism.* a person who has attained prajna, or Enlightenment, but who postpones Nirvana in order to help others to attain Enlightenment: individual Bodhisattvas are the subjects of devotion in certain sects and are often represented in painting and sculpture. Cf. **Arhat.** [1820–30; < Pali, Skt]

bo′dhi tree′. See **bo tree.**

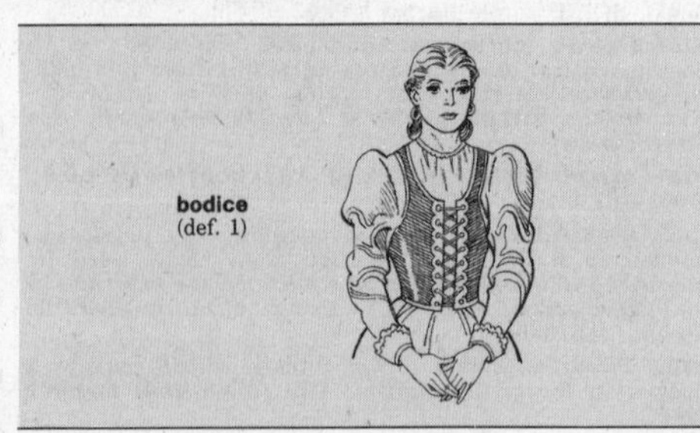

bodice (def. 1)

bod•ice (bod′is), *n.* **1.** a usually fitted vest or wide, lace-up girdle worn by women over a dress or blouse, esp. a cross-laced, sleeveless outer garment covering the waist and bust, common in peasant dress. **2.** the part of a woman's dress covering the body between the neck or shoulders and the waist. Cf. **waist** (def. 4). **3.** *Obs.* stays or a corset. [1560–70; *bodies,* pl. of BODY]

bod′ice rip′per, *Informal.* a modern Gothic novel or historical romance, usually in paperback format, featuring at least one passionate love scene, characteristically one in which the heroine vainly resists submitting to the villain or hero. Also called **bod′ice bust′er.**

bod•ied (bod′ēd), *adj.* having a body of a specific kind (used in combination): *a flat-bodied fish; a wide-bodied car.* [BODY + -ED[3]]

bod•i•less (bod′ē lis, -i lis), *adj.* having no body or material form; incorporeal; disembodied. [1350–1400; ME *bodiles.* See BODY, -LESS] —**bod′i•less•ness,** *n.*

bod•i•ly (bod′l ē), *adj.* **1.** of or pertaining to the body. **2.** corporeal or material, as contrasted with spiritual or mental. —*adv.* **3.** as a physical entity; as a complete physical unit: *The tornado picked him up bodily and threw him against the wall.* **4.** in person: *You have to appear bodily at the box office in order to have your reservation confirmed.* [1250–1300; ME *bodylich.* See BODY, -LY]
—**Syn. 2.** See **physical.**

bod•ing (bō′ding), *n.* **1.** a foreboding; omen. —*adj.* **2.** foreboding; ominous. [bef. 1000; (n.) ME; OE *bodunge* announcement (see BODE[1], -ING[1]); (adj.) BODE[1] + -ING[2]] —**bod′ing•ly,** *adv.*

bod•kin (bod′kin), *n.* **1.** a small, pointed instrument for making holes in cloth, leather, etc. **2.** a long pin-shaped instrument used by women to fasten up the hair. **3.** a blunt, needlelike instrument for drawing tape, cord, etc., through a loop, hem, or the like. **4.** *Obs.* a small dagger; stiletto. [1350–1400; ME *badeken, bo(i)dekyn,* of uncert. orig.]

Bod•lei•an (bod lē′ən, bod′lē-), *n.* **1.** the library of Oxford University, reestablished by Sir Thomas Bodley, 1545–1613, English diplomat and scholar. —*adj.* **2.** of, pertaining to, or belonging to this library. [after Sir Thomas *Bodley;* see -AN]

Bod•ley (bod′lē), *n.* **George Frederick,** 1827–1907, English architect.

Bod•ö (bōō′dœ, bō-), *n.* a seaport in W Norway. 31,096.

Bo•do•ni (bə dō′nē; *for 1 also It.* bô dô′nē), *n.* **1. Giam•bat•tis•ta** (jäm′bät tēs′tä), 1740–1813, Italian painter and printer. **2.** *Print.* a style of type based on a design by G. Bodoni.

Bod•var Bjar•ki (bôth′vär byär′kē), *Scand. Legend.* the greatest of Rolf Kraki's heroes, often fighting in the likeness of a bear: probably identical with Beowulf. [< ON *Bǫthvar,* equiv. to *bǫth* battle + *herr* master; *Bjarki,* ult. dim. from base of *bjǫrn* BEAR[2]]

bod•y (bod′ē), *n., pl.* **bod•ies,** *v.,* **bod•ied, bod•y•ing,** *adj.* —*n.* **1.** the physical structure and material substance of an animal or plant, living or dead. **2.** a corpse; carcass. **3.** the trunk or main mass of a thing: *the body of a tree.* **4.** *Anat., Zool.* the physical structure of a human being or animal, not including the head, limbs, and tail; trunk; torso. **5.** *Archit.* the principal mass of a building. **6.** the section of a vehicle, usually in the shape of a box, cylindrical container, or platform, in or on which passengers or the load is carried. **7.** *Naut.* the hull of a ship. **8.** *Aeron.* the fuselage of a plane. **9.** *Print.* the shank of a type, supporting the face. See diag. under **type. 10.** *Geom.* a figure having the three dimensions of length, breadth, and thickness; a solid. **11.** *Physics.* a mass, esp. one considered as a whole. **12.** the major portion of an army, population, etc.: *The body of the American people favors the president's policy.* **13.** the principal part of a speech or document, minus introduction, conclusion, indexes, etc. **14.** a person: *She's a quiet sort of body.* **15.** *Law.* the physical person of an individual. **16.** a collective group: *student body; corporate body.* **17.** *Astron.* an object in space, as a planet or star. **18.** a separate physical mass or quantity, esp. as distinguished from other masses or quantities. **19.** consistency or density; richness; substance: *This wine has good body. Wool has more body than rayon.* **20.** the part of a dress that covers the trunk or the part of the trunk above the waist. **21.** *Ceram.* the basic material of which a ceramic article is made. **22. in a body,** as a group; together; collectively: *We left the party in a body.* **23. keep body and soul together,** to support oneself; maintain life: *Few writers can make enough to keep body and soul together without another occupation.* —*v.t.* **24.** to invest with or as with a body. **25.** to represent in bodily form (usually fol. by *forth*). —*adj.* **26.** of or pertaining to the body; bodily. **27.** of or pertaining to the main reading matter of a book, article, etc., as opposed to headings, illustrations, or the like. [bef. 900; ME; OE *bodig;* akin to OHG *botah*]
—**Syn. 1, 2.** BODY, CARCASS, CORPSE, CADAVER agree in referring to a physical organism, usually human or animal. BODY refers to the material organism of an individual, human or animal, either living or dead: *the muscles in a horse's body; the body of a victim (human or animal).* CARCASS refers only to the dead body of an animal, unless applied humorously or contemptuously to the human body: *a sheep's carcass; Save your carcass.* CORPSE refers only to the dead body of a human being: *preparing a corpse for burial.* CADAVER refers to a dead body, usually a corpse, particularly one used for scientific study: *dissection of cadavers in anatomy classes.* **3.** substance, bulk. **12.** mass, group, throng, multitude; bulk, preponderance, majority. —**Ant. 12.** handful, scattering, few.

bod′y art′, an artistic practice or style of the 1960's and 1970's developing from conceptual art and performance art and utilizing the artist's body as both the subject and object in such experimentation as decoration, wax casts, and even mutilation. [1970–75] —**bod′y art′ist.**

bod′y bag′, a large bag made of heavy material and used to transport a dead body, as from a battlefield to a place of burial or from the scene of a death to a city morgue.

bod′y blow′, *Boxing.* **1.** a blow driven to the opponent's body between the breastbone and the navel. **2.** any action that causes severe damage, losses, etc.: *Our business received a body blow in the recession.* [1785–95]

bod′y bol′ster, *Railroads.* the lower transverse member of a car body to which the body center plate is attached. Cf. **truck bolster.**

bod′y Brus′sels. See under **Brussels carpet.**

bod·y·build·er (bod′ē bil′dər), *n.* a person who practices bodybuilding. Also, **bod′y-build′er.** [1965–70; BODYBUILD(ING) + -ER[1]]

bod·y·build·ing (bod′ē bil′ding), *n.* the act or practice of exercising, lifting weights, etc., so as to develop the muscles of the body. Also, **bod′y-build′ing, bod′y build′ing.** [1900–05; from the v. phrase *build (up one's) body;* see -ING[1]]

bod·y-cen·tered (bod′ē sen′tərd), *adj. Crystall.* (of a crystal structure) having lattice points at the centers of the unit cells. Cf. **face-centered.** [1920–25]

bod′y cen′ter plate′, *Railroads.* See under **center plate.**

bod′y check′, *Ice Hockey.* an obstructing or impeding with the body of the movement or progress of an opponent. Cf. **check**[1] (def. 42). [1890–95]

bod·y·check (bod′ē chek′), *v.t., v.i. Ice Hockey.* to give (an opponent) a body check. [1905–10; v. use of BODY CHECK]

bod′y cor′porate, *Law.* a person, association, or group of persons legally incorporated; corporation. [1490–1500]

bod′y count′, the number of soldiers killed in a specific period or in a particular military action: *The daily body count increased as the war went on.* [1965–70]

bod′y drop′, a judo throw executed by grabbing the opponent as one is turning one's back and then extending a leg to pull the opponent down over it. [1945–50]

bod′y Eng′lish, *Sports.* a twisting of the body by a player as if to help a ball already hit, rolled, or kicked to travel in the desired direction. [1905–10]

bod·y·guard (bod′ē gärd′), *n.* **1.** a person or group of persons employed to guard an individual, as a high official, from bodily harm. **2.** a retinue; escort. —*v.t., v.i.* **3.** to provide with or act as a bodyguard. [1725–35; BODY + GUARD]

bod′y im′age, an intellectual or idealized image of what one's body is or should be like that is sometimes misconceived in such mental disorders as anorexia nervosa. [1930–35]

bod′y lan′guage, nonverbal, usually unconscious, communication through the use of postures, gestures, facial expressions, and the like. Cf. **kinesics, paralanguage, proxemics.** [1925–30]

bod′y louse′. See under **louse** (def. 1). [1565–75]

bod′y mechan′ics, (*used with a singular or plural v.*) a set of exercises designed to develop an individual's coordination, grace, and stamina. [1965–70]

bod′y mike′, a small, wireless microphone worn inconspicuously by an actor, singer, or other performer to amplify the voice without inhibiting mobility. [1970–75]

bod·y-mike (bod′ē mīk′), *v.t.,* **-miked, -mik·ing.** to equip with a body mike: *The star was body-miked, but he was still inaudible.* [1970–75]

Bod′y of Christ′, **1.** the community of believers of which Christ is the head. I Cor. 12:27. **2.** the consecrated bread of the Eucharist.

bod′y plan′, **1.** *Biol.* the basic shape of members of an animal phylum; the general structure each individual organism assumes as it develops. Cf. **bilateral symmetry, radial symmetry. 2.** *Naval Archit.* a diagrammatic elevation of a hull, consisting of an end view of the bow on one side of the center line and an end view of the stern on the other side, marked with water lines, diagonals, bow or buttock lines, stations, and sometimes details of the hull. Cf. **half-breadth plan, sheer plan.** [1840–50]

bod′y pol′itic, *Political Science.* a people regarded as a political body under an organized government. [1425–75; late ME *bodi politik*]

bod′y post′, *Naut.* sternpost.

bod′y press′, a hold in which a wrestler places full body weight on a supine opponent in trying to pin the opponent's shoulders to the mat.

bod′y rhythm′, biorhythm.

bod′y rub′, massage.

bod·y-search (bod′ē sûrch′), *v.t.* to search all parts of the body of: *Police ordered the suspects to strip and then body-searched them for hidden caches of narcotics.*

body·shell (bod′ē shel′), *n.* the outer shell of an automobile body, excluding doors, window glass, interior fittings, and all mechanical components. [BODY + SHELL]

bod′y shirt′, **1.** a close-fitting shirt or blouse having a shape and seams that follow the contours of the body. **2.** such a garment with a sewn-in or snap crotch, esp. a woman's leotard or combination shirt and panty with a snap crotch. [1965–70]

bod′y shop′, **1.** a factory or machine shop in which bodies for vehicles, as automobiles, trucks, or the like, are manufactured, repaired, etc. **2.** *Slang.* **a.** an employment agency, school, or the like that provides large numbers of workers, trainees, recent graduates, etc., to fill entry-level jobs. **b.** a gym, health club, or the like where people may exercise, do bodybuilding, etc. **c.** a singles bar. [1950–55]

bod′y slam′, a wrestling throw in which an opponent is lifted and hurled to the mat, landing on his or her back.

bod′y snatch′er, **1.** a person who steals corpses; graverobber. **2.** *Slang.* an agency that recruits executives working for one company to fill top management positions in another. [1805–15]

bod′y snatch′ing, the act or practice of robbing a grave to obtain a cadaver for dissection. [1825–35]

bod′y stock′ing, a close-fitting, one-piece garment made of knitted or stretch material and usually covering the feet, legs, trunk, and arms, worn as an exercise costume or under other clothing. [1960–65, *Amer.*]

bod·y·suit (bod′ē so͞ot′), *n.* a close-fitting, one-piece, usually sleeved garment for the torso, having a snap crotch. Also, **bod′y suit′.** Cf. **body shirt, leotard.** [1965–70; BODY + SUIT]

bod·y-surf (bod′ē sûrf′), *v.i.* to ride a cresting wave toward the shore by lying face down in the water with the arms stretched forward in the direction of the wave. [1940–45] —**bod′y-surf′er,** *n.*

bod′y track′, the tracks of a railroad yard used for switching or sorting cars.

bod′y type′, *Print.* type used in the main text of printed matter, generally less than 14 points. Cf. **display type.** [1895–1900]

bod′y wave′, **1.** *Geol.* a transverse or longitudinal earthquake wave that travels through the interior of the earth (distinguished from *surface wave*). **2.** a permanent with little or no curl, designed to give fullness and body to the hair and to make it more manageable.

bod·y·wear (bod′ē wâr′), *n.* close-fitting clothing, as leotards or bodysuits, made of lightweight, usually stretch fabrics and worn for exercising, dancing, or leisure activity. [BODY + WEAR]

bod·y·work (bod′ē wûrk′), *n.* **1.** the work involved in making or repairing automobile or other vehicle bodies. **2.** the body of an automobile or other vehicle, esp. with regard to the details or the quality of its construction. [1905–10; BODY + WORK]

Bo·ece (bō ēs′), *n.* Boethius.

Boeh·me (bā′mə, bō′-; *Ger.* bœ′mə), *n.* **Ja·kob** (*Ger.* yä′kôp). See **Böhme, Jakob.**

Boeh·men·ism (bā′mə niz′əm, bō′-), *n.* the mystical doctrines or conceptions of Jakob Böhme. Also, **Behmenism.** [1650–60; J. BOEHME + -*n* (as in BEHMEN) + -ISM]

Boeh·men·ist (bā′mə nist, bō′-), *n.* a supporter or adherent of Boehmenism. Also, **Behmenist, Boeh′men·ite′, Behmenite, Boeh′mist.** [1645–55; J. BOEHME + -*n* (as in BEHMEN) + -IST]

Boehm·i·an (bā′mē ən, bō′-), *adj.* of or pertaining to Boehmenism. [J. BOEHME + -IAN]

boehm·ite (bā′mīt, bō′-), *n.* a mineral, hydrous aluminum oxide, AlO(OH), a major component of bauxite. [1925–30; < G *Böhmit,* named after J. *Böhm,* 20th-century German scientist; see -ITE[1]]

Boehm′ sys′tem (bām, bōm), a system of improved fingering and keying for the flute and clarinet, invented by the German musician Theobald Boehm (1794–1881). [1900–05]

Boe·o·tia (bē ō′shə), *n.* a district in ancient Greece, NW of Athens. *Cap.:* Thebes.

Boe·o·tian (bē ō′shən), *adj.* **1.** of or pertaining to Boeotia or its inhabitants. **2.** dull; obtuse; without cultural refinement. —*n.* **3.** a native or inhabitant of Boeotia. **4.** a dull, obtuse person; Philistine. [1590–1600; BOEOTI(A) + -AN]

Boe·o·tus (bē ō′təs), *n. Class. Myth.* a son of Arne and Poseidon, and ancestor of the Boeotians.

Boer (bôr, bōr, bo͝or; *Du.* bo͞or), *n.* **1.** a South African of Dutch extraction. —*adj.* **2.** of or pertaining to the Boers. [1825–35; < Afrik < D: peasant, farmer. See BOOR]

Boer′ War′, **1.** a war in which Great Britain fought against the Transvaal and Orange Free State, 1899–1902. **2.** a war between Great Britain and the Transvaal, 1880–81.

Bo·e·thi·us (bō ē′thē əs), *n.* **A·ni·ci·us Man·li·us Sev·e·ri·nus** (ə nish′ē əs man′lē əs sev′ə rī′nəs), A.D. 475?–525?, Roman philosopher and statesman. Also, **Bo·e·tius** (bō ē′shəs). Also called **Boece.** —**Bo·e′thi·an,** *adj.*

boeuf bour·gui·gnon (bœf bo͞or gē nyôN′), *French Cookery.* beef cubes cooked in red wine with mushrooms, onions, and bacon. Also called **boeuf à la bour·gui·gnonne** (bœf A lA bo͞or gē nyôn′). [< F: lit., Burgundian beef; see BOURGUIGNON]

boff (bof), *Slang.* —*n.* **1.** *Theat.* **a.** a box-office hit. **b.** a joke or humorous line producing hearty laughter. **2.** a loud hearty laugh; belly laugh. —*v.t.* **3.** to cause to be overcome with laughter. **4.** to hit; strike. [cf. BOFFO]

bof·fin (bof′in), *n. Brit. Slang.* a scientist or technical expert. [1940–45; orig. uncert.]

bof·fo (bof′ō), *n., pl.* **-fos,** *adj. Slang.* —*n.* **1.** boff. —*adj.* **2.** highly effective or successful: *He gave a boffo performance as Cyrano.* Also, **boff·o·la** (bo fō′lə). [perh. alter. of BUFFO or BOUFFE]

Bo′fors gun′ (bō′fôrz, -fôrs), **1.** a 40-millimeter automatic gun used chiefly as an antiaircraft weapon. **2.** two such guns mounted and fired together as one unit. [1935–40; named after *Bofors,* Sweden, where first made]

bog[1] (bog, bôg), *n., v.,* **bogged, bog·ging.** —*n.* **1.** wet, spongy ground with soil composed mainly of decayed vegetable matter. **2.** an area or stretch of such ground. —*v.t., v.i.* **3.** to sink in or as if in a bog (often fol. by *down*): *We were bogged down by overwork.* **4. bog in,** *Australian Slang.* to eat heartily and ravenously. [1495–1505; < Ir or ScotGael *bogach* soft ground (*bog* soft + *-ach* n. suffix); (def. 4) perh. a different word] —**bog′gish,** *adj.*

bog[2] (bog, bôg), *n.* Usually, **bogs.** *Brit. Slang.* a lavatory; bathroom. [1780–90; prob. shortening of *bog-house;* cf. *bog* to defecate, *boggard* (16th century) privy, of obscure orig.]

Bo·ga·lu·sa (bō′gə lo͞o′sə), *n.* a city in SE Louisiana. 16,976.

bo·gan (bō′gən), *n. Northern Maine and Canadian* (*chiefly Maritimes and Northern New Brunswick*). **1.** a backwater, usually narrow and tranquil. **2.** any narrow stretch of water. [1895–1900; appar. shortening of POKELOGAN, perh. conflated with BOG[1]; cf. LOGAN]

Bo·gan (bō gan′, bō′gən), *n.* **Louise,** 1897–1970, U.S. poet.

Bo·gart (bō′gärt), *n.* **Humphrey (DeForest)** ("*Bogey*"), 1900–57, U.S. motion-picture actor.

bog′ as′phodel, any of several plants of the genus *Narthecium,* of the lily family; having yellowish flowers and growing in boggy places. [1880–85]

bog·bean (bog′bēn′, bôg′-), *n.* See **buck bean.** [1785–95; BOG[1] + BEAN]

bo·gey[1] (bō′gē; *for 2 also* bo͝og′ē, bo͞o′gē), *n., pl.* **-geys,** *v.,* **-geyed, -gey·ing.** —*n.* **1.** *Golf.* **a.** a score of one stroke over par on a hole. **b.** par (def. 4). **2.** bogy[1] (defs. 1–3). **3.** Also, **bogy, bogie.** *Mil.* an unidentified aircraft or missile, esp. one detected as a blip on a radar screen. **4.** bogie[1]. —*v.t.* **5.** *Golf.* to make a bogey on (a hole): *Arnold Palmer bogeyed the 18th hole.* [1890–95; sp. var. of BOGY]

bo·gey[2] (bō′gē), *n., pl.* **-geys,** *v.,* **-geyed, -gey·ing.** *Australian.* —*n.* **1.** a swim; bathe. —*v.i.* **2.** to swim; bathe. [< Dharuk, equiv. to *bu-* bathe + *-gi* past tense marker]

bo·gey-hole (bō′gē hōl′), *n. Australian.* a swimming hole.

bo·gey·man (bo͝og′ē man′, bō′gē-, bo͞o′-), *n., pl.* **-men.** an imaginary evil character of supernatural powers, esp. a mythical hobgoblin supposed to carry off naughty children. Also, **bogyman, boogerman, boogeyman, boogieman.** [1885–90; BOGEY (var. of BOGY[1]) + MAN[1]]

bog·gle[1] (bog′əl), *v.,* **-gled, -gling,** *n.* —*v.t.* **1.** to overwhelm or bewilder, as with the magnitude, complexity, or abnormality of: *The speed of light boggles the mind.* **2.** to bungle; botch. —*v.i.* **3.** to hesitate or waver because of scruples, fear, etc. **4.** to start or jump with fear, alarm, or surprise; shrink; shy. **5.** to bungle awkwardly. **6.** to be overwhelmed or bewildered. —*n.* **7.** an act of shying or taking alarm. **8.** a scruple; demur; hesitation. **9.** bungle; botch. [1590–1600; perh. from BOGGLE[2]] —**bog′gling·ly,** *adv.*

bog·gle[2] (bog′əl), *n.* bogle.

bog·gler (bog′lər), *n.* something, as an amazing fact, puzzle, or riddle, that astounds or defeats: *The puzzle was a real boggler.* [1600–10; BOGGLE[1] + -ER[1]]

bog·gy (bog′ē, bô′gē), *adj.,* **-gi·er, -gi·est.** **1.** containing or full of bogs: *It was difficult walking through the boggy terrain.* **2.** wet and spongy: *The ground is boggy under foot.* [1580–90; BOG[1] + -Y[1]] —**bog′gi·ness,** *n.*

Bo·ghaz·köy (bō′gäz kœ′ē, -koi′, bō′äz-), *n.* a village in N central Turkey: site of the ancient Hittite city of Hattusas. Also, **Bo′gaz·köy′, Bo·ghaz·keu·i** (bō′gäz-kœ′ē).

bog′head coal′ (bog′hed′), compact bituminous coal that burns brightly and yields large quantities of tar and oil upon distillation. [1935–40; named after *Boghead,* Scotland]

bog′ hole′, *Phys. Geog.* a land-surface depression occupied by waterlogged soil and spongy vegetative material that cannot bear the weight of large animals. [1780–90]

bo·gie[1] (bō′gē), *n.* **1.** *Auto.* (on a truck) a rear-wheel assembly composed of four wheels on two axles, either or both driving axles, so mounted as to support the rear of the truck body jointly. **2.** *Railroads.* (in Britain) a truck that rotates about a central pivot under a locomotive or car. **3.** *Brit.* **a.** any low, strong, four-wheeled cart or truck, as one used by masons to move stones. **b.** truck[1] (def. 4). Also, **bogey, bogy.** [1810–20; orig. uncert.]

bo·gie[2] (bō′gē, bo͝og′ē, bo͞o′gē), *n.* bogy[1].

bo·gie[3] (bō′gē), *n. Mil.* bogey[1] (def. 3).

bog′-i·ron ore′ (bog′ī′ərn, bôg′-), *Mineral.* a deposit of impure limonite formed in low, wet areas. Also called **bog′ ore′.** [1780–90]

bo·gle (bō′gəl, bog′əl), *n.* a bogy; specter. Also, **boggle.** [1495–1505; *bog* (var. of BUG bugbear) + -LE]

bog′ moss′. See **peat moss.** [1775–85]

bog′ myr′tle. See **sweet gale.** [1880–85]

bog′ oak′, oak or other wood preserved in peat bogs. Also called **bogwood.** [1855–60]

Bog·o·mil (bog′ə mil), *n.* a member of a dualistic sect, flourishing chiefly in Bulgaria in the Middle Ages, that rejected most of the Old Testament and was strongly anticlerical in polity. Also, **Bog·o·mile** (bog′ə mīl′). [1840–45; < MGk *Bogómilos,* from the name of a 10th cent. Bulgarian priest alleged to have founded the sect, in later South Slavic sources *Bogomilŭ* (a calque of Gk *Theóphilos;* see THEO-, -PHILE)] —**Bog′o·mil′i·an,** *adj.* —**Bog′o·mil·ism,** *n.*

bo·gong (bō′gông, -gong), *n.* a dark-colored Australian moth, *Agrostis infusa,* used by Aborigines as food. [1830–35; earlier *bugong,* perh. < Ngayawung (Austral Aboriginal language of the lower Murray River, New South Wales) *buguŋ*]

Bo·gor (bō′gôr), *n.* a city on W Java, in Indonesia. 195,882. Former Dutch name, **Buitenzorg.**

Bo·go·rodsk (bog′ə rotsk′; *Russ.* bə gu rôtsk′), *n.* former name of **Noginsk.**

Bo·go·tá (bō′gə tä′, bō′gə tä′; *Sp.* bô′gô tä′), *n.* a city in and the capital of Colombia, in the central part. 2,855,065.

CONCISE PRONUNCIATION KEY: act, cāpe, dâre, pärt; set, ēqual; if, īce; ox, ōver, ôrder, oil, bo͝ok, bo͞ot, out; up, ûrge; child; sing; shoe; thin, *th*at; zh as in *treasure*. ə = *a* as in *alone*, *e* as in *system*, *i* as in *easily*, *o* as in *gallop*, *u* as in *circus*; ᵊ as in *fire* (fīᵊr), *hour* (ouᵊr). l and n can serve as syllabic consonants, as in *cradle* (krād′l), and *button* (but′n). See the full key inside the front cover.

bog′ rose′mar·y, either of two low-growing shrubs, *Andromeda glaucophylla* or *A. polifolia,* of the heath family, having narrow evergreen leaves and clusters of pink or white flowers.

bog′ spav′in, *Vet. Pathol.* See under **spavin** (def. 1). [1625–35]

bog·trot·ter (bog′trot′ər, bôg′-), *n.* **1.** a person who lives among bogs. **2.** *Disparaging.* a rural native or inhabitant of Ireland. [1675–85; BOG[1] + TROTTER]

bog′ tur′tle, a small turtle, *Clemmys muhlenbergi,* inhabiting swamps and slow, muddy-bottomed streams in scattered areas from New York to North Carolina.

bogue[1] (bōg), *n. Gulf States.* a bayou, stream, or waterway. [1805–15; (< LaF) < Choctaw *bok* creek, stream, river]

bogue[2] (bōg), *v.i.,* **bogued, bogu·ing.** *Naut.* (of a sailing vessel) to tend to fall off from the wind. [perh. akin to dial. *bog* to move off]

bo·gus (bō′gəs), *adj.* **1.** not genuine; counterfeit; spurious; sham. —*n.* **2.** *Print., Journalism.* matter set, by union requirement, by a compositor and later discarded, duplicating the text of an advertisement for which a plate has been supplied or type set by another publisher. [1825–30, *Amer.*; orig. an apparatus for coining false money; perh. akin to BOGY[1]]
—Syn. 1. fraudulent, pseudo, fake, phony.

bog·wood (bog′wŏŏd′, bôg′-), *n.* See **bog oak.** [1820–30; BOG[1] + WOOD[1]]

bo·gy[1] (bō′gē; *for 1, 2 also* bŏŏg′ē, bōō′gē), *n., pl.* **-gies. 1.** a hobgoblin; evil spirit. **2.** anything that haunts, frightens, annoys, or harasses. **3.** something that functions as a real or imagined barrier that must be overcome, bettered, etc.: *Fear is the major bogy of novice mountain climbers. A speed of 40 knots is a bogy for motorboats.* **4.** *Mil.* bogey[1] (def. 3). Also, **bogey** (for defs 1–3); **bogie.** [1830–40; *bog,* var. of BUG (n.) + -Y[2]]

bo·gy[2] (bō′gē), *n., pl.* **-gies.** bogie[1].

bo·gy·man (bŏŏg′ē man′, bō′gē-, bōō′-), *n., pl.* **-men.** bogeyman. [1885–90; BOGY[1] + MAN[1]]

Bo·hai (bô′hī′), *n. Pinyin.* an arm of the Yellow Sea in NE China. Also, **Pohai.** Formerly, **Gulf of Chihli.**

Bo·hea (bō hē′), *n.* an inferior grade of black tea. [1695–1705; < dial. Chin (Fujian) *Bu-i,* mountains on the border of Fujian and Jiangxi provinces, where the tea is grown]

Bo·he·mi·a (bō hē′mē ə), *n.* **1.** Czech, **Čechy.** a region in the W Czech Republic: formerly a kingdom in central Europe; under Hapsburg rule 1526–1918. 20,101 sq. mi. (52,060 sq. km). **2.** (*often l.c.*) a district inhabited by persons, typically artists, writers, and intellectuals, whose way of life, dress, etc., are generally unconventional or avant-garde. **3.** (*often l.c.*) the social circles where such behavior is prevalent.

Bo·he·mi·a-Mo·ra·vi·a (bō hē′mē ə mô rā′vē ə, -mō-, -mə-), *n.* a former German protectorate including Bohemia and Moravia, 1939–45.

Bo·he·mi·an (bō hē′mē ən), *n.* **1.** a native or inhabitant of Bohemia. **2.** (*usually l.c.*) a person, as an artist or writer, who lives and acts free of regard for conventional rules and practices. **3.** the Czech language, esp. as spoken in Bohemia. **4.** a Gypsy. —*adj.* **5.** of or pertaining to Bohemia, its people, or their language. **6.** (*usually l.c.*) pertaining to or characteristic of the unconventional life of a bohemian. **7.** living a wandering or vagabond life, as a Gypsy. [1570–80; BOHEMI(A) + -AN] —**Bo·he′·mi·an·ism,** *n.*

Bohe′mian Breth′ren, a Christian denomination formed in Bohemia in 1467 from various Hussite groups, reorganized in 1722 as the Moravian Church.

Bohe′mian For′est, a wooded mountain range in central Europe, on the boundary between the SW Czech Republic and SE Germany. Highest peak, Arber, 4780 ft. (1455 m). German, **Böhmerwald.**

Bohe′mian wax′wing. See under **waxwing.** [1835–45]

Boh·len (bō′lin), *n.* **Charles Eus·tis** (yōō′stis), (*"Chip"*) 1904–74, U.S. diplomat.

Böhm (bœm), *n.* **1. Do·mi·ni·kus** (dō mē′nē kŏŏs′), 1880–1955, German architect. **2. Ja·kob** (yä′kôp). See **Böhme, Jakob. 3. Karl,** 1894–1981, Austrian opera conductor.

Böh·me (bā′mə, bō′-; *Ger.* bœ′mə), *n.* **Ja·kob** (yä′kôp), 1575–1624, German theosophist and mystic. Also, **Behmen, Boehme, Böhm.**

Böh·mer·wald (bœ′mər vält′), *n.* German name of **Bohemian Forest.**

Bo·hol (bô hôl′), *n.* an island in the S central Philippines. 806,013; 1492 sq. mi. (3864 sq. km).

Bohr (bôr, bōr; *Dan.* bōr), *n.* **1. Aa·ge Niels** (ô′gə nels), born 1922, Danish physicist: Nobel prize 1975 (son of Niels Bohr). **2. Niels Hen·rik Dav·id** (nels hen′rēk dav′id), 1885–1962, Danish physicist: Nobel prize 1922.

Bohr′ at′om. *Physics.* See under **Bohr theory.** [1920–25; after N. BOHR]

Bohr′ mag′neton, *Physics.* a unit that is used to indicate the magnetic moment of the electron structure in an atom, equal to 9.27×10^{-21} erg/gauss. Also called **electronic Bohr magneton.** [1920–25; after N. BOHR]

Bohr′ ra′dius, *Physics.* (in the Bohr atom) the radius of the electron orbit having the lowest energy. Also called **atomic unit of length.** [1955–60; after N. BOHR]

Bohr′ the′ory, *Physics.* a theory of atomic structure in which the hydrogen atom (**Bohr atom**) is assumed to consist of a proton as nucleus, with a single electron moving in distinct circular orbits around it, each orbit corresponding to a specific quantized energy state: the theory was extended to other atoms. [1920–25; after N. BOHR]

bo·hunk (bō′hungk′), *n.* **1.** *Slang (disparaging and offensive).* an unskilled or semiskilled foreign-born laborer, esp. from east central or southeastern Europe. Cf. **hunky**[2]. **2.** a rough, stupid person. [1900–05, *Amer.*; BO(HEMIAN) + HUNG(ARIAN), with devoicing of the *g*]

Bo·iar·do (boi är′dō; *It.* bô yär′dô), *n.* **Mat·te·o Ma·ri·a** (mä tā′ō mə rē′ə; *It.* mät te′ô mä rē′ä), 1434–94, Italian poet. Also, **Bojardo.**

Boi·el·dieu (bwa el dyœ′), *n.* **Fran·çois A·dri·en** (frän swa′ a drē an′), 1775–1834, French composer.

boil[1] (boil), *v.i.* **1.** to change from a liquid to a gaseous state, producing bubbles of gas that rise to the surface of the liquid, agitating it as they rise. **2.** to reach or be brought to the boiling point: *When the water boils, add the meat and cabbage.* **3.** to be in an agitated or violent state: *The sea boiled in the storm.* **4.** to be deeply stirred or upset. **5.** to contain, or be contained in, a liquid that boils: *The kettle is boiling. The vegetables are boiling.* —*v.t.* **6.** to cause to boil or to bring to the boiling point: *Boil two cups of water.* **7.** to cook (something) in boiling water: *to boil eggs.* **8.** to separate (sugar, salt, etc.) from a solution containing it by boiling off the liquid. **9. boil down, a.** to reduce the quantity of by boiling off liquid. **b.** to shorten; abridge. **c.** to be simplifiable or summarizable as; lead to the conclusion that; point: *It all boils down to a clear case of murder.* **10. boil off,** *Textiles.* **a.** to degum (silk). **b.** to remove (sizing, wax, impurities, or the like) from a fabric by subjecting it to a hot scouring solution. Also, **boil out. 11. boil over, a.** to overflow while boiling or as if while boiling; burst forth; erupt. **b.** to be unable to repress anger, excitement, etc.: *Any mention of the incident makes her boil over.* —*n.* **12.** the act or an instance of boiling. **13.** the state or condition of boiling: *He brought a kettle of water to a boil.* **14.** an area of agitated, swirling, bubbling water, as part of a rapids. **15.** Also called **blow.** *Civ. Engin.* an unwanted flow of water and solid matter into an excavation, due to excessive outside water pressure. [1250–1300; ME *boillen* < AF, OF *boillir* < L *bullire* to bubble, effervesce, boil, v. deriv. of *bulla* bubble]
—Syn. 3. foam, churn, froth. **4.** rage. BOIL, SEETHE, SIMMER, STEW are used figuratively to refer to agitated states of emotion. To BOIL suggests the state of being very hot with anger or rage: *Rage made his blood boil.* To SEETHE is to be deeply stirred, violently agitated, or greatly excited: *A mind seething with conflicting ideas.* To SIMMER means to be on the point of bursting out or boiling over: *to simmer with curiosity, with anger.* To STEW is to worry, to be in a restless state of anxiety and excitement: *to stew about (or over) one's troubles.*

boil[2] (boil), *n. Pathol.* a painful, circumscribed inflammation of the skin or a hair follicle, having a dead, suppurating inner core: usually caused by a staphylococcal infection. Also called **furuncle.** [bef. 1000; ME *bile, bule,* OE *bȳle;* c. G *Beule* boil, hump, akin to ON *beyla* hump, swelling]

boil·a·ble (boi′lə bəl), *adj.* **1.** suitable or recommended for boiling: *a diet of vegetables, rice, and other boilable foods.* **2.** (of sealed plastic bags or pouches) leakproof and immersible in boiling water so as to cook or heat the contents: *dinner entrées in boilable bags that are slit open and emptied for serving.* [1880–85; BOIL[1] + -ABLE]

Boi·leau-Des·pré·aux (bwa lō′de prā ō′), *n.* **Ni·co·las** (nē kô lä′), 1636–1711, French critic and poet.

boiled (boild), *adj. Slang.* drunk. [1795–1805; BOIL[1] + -ED[2]]

boiled′ din′ner, *Northern and North Midland U.S.* a meal of meat and vegetables, as of corned beef, cabbage, and potatoes, prepared by boiling. Also called **New England boiled dinner.** [1795–1805, *Amer.*]

boiled′ dress′ing, a cooked salad dressing thickened with egg yolks and often containing mustard.

boiled′ oil′, *Chem.* any oil, as linseed oil, heated together with driers to improve its drying properties. [1855–60]

boiled′ shirt′, a formal or semiformal dress shirt with a starched front. [1850–55, *Amer.*]

boiled′ sweet′, *Brit.* See **hard candy.**

boil·er (boi′lər), *n.* **1.** a closed vessel or arrangement of vessels and tubes, together with a furnace or other heat source, in which steam or other vapor is generated from water to drive turbines or engines, supply heat, process certain materials, etc. Cf. **fire-tube boiler, water-tube boiler. 2.** a vessel, as a kettle, for boiling or heating. **3.** *Brit.* a large tub in which laundry is boiled or sterilized. **4.** a tank in which water is heated and stored, as for supplying hot water. [1530–40; BOIL[1] + -ER[1]] —**boil′er·less,** *adj.*

boil′er horse′power, a unit of measurement of the ability of a boiler to evaporate water, usually given as the ability to evaporate 34½ lb. (15.6 kg) of water an hour, into dry saturated steam from and at 212°F (100°C).

boil·er·mak·er (boi′lər mā′kər), *n.* **1.** a person employed to make and repair boilers or other heavy metal items. **2.** whiskey with beer as a chaser. [1860–65; BOILER + MAKER]

boil·er·plate (boi′lər plāt′), *n.* **1.** plating of iron or steel for making the shells of boilers, covering the hulls of ships, etc. **2.** *Journalism.* **a.** syndicated or ready-to-print copy, used esp. by weekly newspapers. **b.** trite, hackneyed writing. **3.** the detailed standard wording of a contract, warranty, etc. **4.** *Informal.* phrases or units of text used repeatedly, as in correspondence produced by a word-processing system. **5.** frozen, crusty, hard-packed snow, often with icy patches. Also, **boil′er plate′.** [1855–60]

boil′er room′, 1. a room in a building, ship, etc., that houses one or more steam boilers. **2.** *Slang.* **a.** a place where illicit brokers engage in high-pressure selling, over the telephone, of securities of a highly speculative nature or of dubious value. **b.** any room or business where salespeople, bill collectors, solicitors for charitable donations, etc., conduct an intensive telephone campaign, esp. in a fast-talking or intimidating manner. —**boil′·er-room′,** *adj.*

boil′er suit′, *Chiefly Brit.* coveralls. Also, **boil′er·suit′.** [1925–30]

boil-in-bag (boil′in bag′), *adj.* of or being a prepared, often frozen, food sealed and sold in a plastic bag that is immersed in boiling water until the contents are cooked or heated for serving.

boil·ing (boi′ling), *adj.* **1.** having reached the boiling point; steaming or bubbling up under the action of heat: *boiling water.* **2.** fiercely churning or swirling: *the boiling seas.* **3.** (of anger, rage, etc.) intense; fierce; heated. —*adv.* **4.** to an extreme extent; very: *August is usually boiling hot; boiling mad.* [1250–1300; ME. See BOIL[1], -ING[2]] —**boil′ing·ly,** *adv.*

boil′ing point′, 1. *Physics, Chem.* the temperature at which the vapor pressure of a liquid is equal to the pressure of the atmosphere on the liquid, equal to 212°F (100°C) for water at sea level. *Abbr.:* b.p. **2.** the point beyond which one becomes angry, outraged, or agitated. **3.** the point at which matters reach a crisis. [1765–75]

boil-off (boil′ôf′, -of′), *n.* **1.** *Rocketry.* any vapor loss from the oxidizer or fuel in a rocket during countdown. **2.** Also called **boil·ing-off** (boi′ling ôf′, -of′). *Textiles.* **a.** the process of degumming silk. **b.** the process of removing sizing, wax, impurities, etc., from fabric by scouring. [1955–60; n. use of v. phrase *boil off*]

boil-o·ver (boil′ō′vər), *n. Australian and New Zealand Slang.* an unexpected result. [n. use of v. phrase *boil over*]

boil·o·ver (boil′ō′vər), *n.* the act or fact of boiling over: *an automatic burner control that eliminates boilovers.* [n. use of v. phrase *boil over*]

Bois·bri·and (*Fr.* bwä brē än′), *n.* a town in S Quebec, in E Canada, near Montreal. 13,471.

bois brû·lé (bwä′ brōō lā′; *Fr.* bwä bry lā′), *pl.* **bois brû·lés** (bwä′ brōō lāz′; *Fr.* bwä bry lā′), *Canadian.* métis (def. 2). [< F: lit., burnt wood]

bois d'arc (bō′ därk′), *pl.* **bois d'arcs, bois d'arc.** *Louisiana French.* See **Osage orange** (def. 1). [1795–1805, *Amer.*; < LaF: lit., bow wood]

Bois de Bou·logne (bwä′ də bōō lōn′; *Fr.* bwäd[a] bōō lôn′y[a]), a park W of Paris, France. 2095 acres (850 hectares).

bois′ de rose′ oil′ (bwä). See **rosewood oil.** [1930–35; < F *bois de rose* rosewood]

bois de vache (bwä′ də vash′), dried buffalo dung, used as fuel by Canadian and U.S. fur trappers in the 18th and 19th centuries. [1835–45, *Amer.*; < Prairie CanF: lit., buffalo wood (*vache* buffalo, F: cow)]

Boi·se (boi′zē *or, esp. locally,* -sē), *n.* a city in and the capital of Idaho, in the SW part: built on the site of an army post on the Oregon Trail. 102,451.

boi·se·rie (bwä zə rē′), *n.* sculptured paneling, esp. that of French architecture in the 18th century. [1825–35; < F: wainscot, equiv. to *bois* wood + *-erie* -ERY]

Bois-le-Duc (bwä lə dyk′), *n.* French name of **'s Hertogenbosch.**

bois·ter·ous (boi′stər əs, -strəs), *adj.* **1.** rough and noisy; noisily jolly or rowdy; clamorous; unrestrained: *the sound of boisterous laughter.* **2.** (of waves, weather, wind, etc.) rough and stormy. **3.** *Obs.* rough and massive. [1425–75; late ME *boistrous,* var. of ME *boistous* crude, strong, fierce, gross; of obscure orig.] —**bois′ter·ous·ly,** *adv.* —**bois′ter·ous·ness,** *n.*
—Syn. 1. uproarious, obstreperous, roistering, loud, vociferous, impetuous. **1, 2.** tempestuous, tumultuous, turbulent, violent, wild. **—Ant. 1, 2.** calm, serene.

boîte (bwät; *Fr.* bwat), *n., pl.* **boîtes** (bwäts; *Fr.* bwat). a nightclub; cabaret. [< F: box; OF *boiste* < VL **buxita,* for LL *buxida,* formation based on L *pyxis* box (see PYX), s. *pyxid-,* conflated with *buxus* BOX[3]]

boîte de nuit (bwat də nwē′), *pl.* ***boîtes de nuit*** (bwat də nwē′). *French.* boîte.

Bo·i·to (boi′tō; *It.* bô′ē tô), *n.* **Ar·ri·go** (ə rē′gō; *It.* är rē′gô), 1842–1918, Italian opera composer, poet, and novelist.

Bo·jar·do (boi är′dō; *It.* bô yär′dô), *n.* **Mat·te·o Ma·ri·a** (mä tā′ō mə rē′ə; *It.* mät te′ô mä rē′ä). See **Boiardo, Matteo Maria.**

Boj·er (boi′ər), *n.* **Jo·han** (yō′hän; *Nor.* yō hän′, yōō-), 1872–1959, Norwegian novelist and playwright.

Bo Ju·yi (*Chin.* bô′ jy′yē′), *Pinyin.* See **Po Chü-i.**

Bok (bok), *n.* **Edward William,** 1863–1930, U.S. editor and writer, born in the Netherlands.

bok choy (bok′ choi′), **1.** an Asian plant, *Brassica rapa chinensis,* of the mustard family, having a loose cluster of edible, dark-green leaves on white stalks. **2.** the leaves and stalks of this plant cooked as a vegetable or eaten raw in salads. Also, **bok′-choy′, pak-choi, pak-choi.** [< Chin dial. (Guangdong) *baahk-chōi,* akin to Chin *báicài* lit., white vegetable]

Bok′ glob′ule (bok), *Astron.* a dense spherical cloud of gas and dust in interstellar space that absorbs light from stars. Also called **globule.** [1975–80; after Bart J. Bok (b. 1906), American astronomer]

Bo·kha·ra (bō kär′ə; *Russ.* bōō khä′rə), *n.* Bukhara. —**Bo·kha′ran,** *adj.*

Bokha′ra clo′ver. See **white melilot.** [1865–70, *Amer.*]

CONCISE ETYMOLOGY KEY: <, descended or borrowed from; >, whence; b., blend of, blended; c., cognate with; cf., compare; deriv., derivative; equiv., equivalent; imit., imitative; obl., oblique; r., replacing; s., stem; sp., spelling, spelled; resp., respelling, respelled; trans., translation; ?, origin unknown; *, unattested; ‡, probably earlier than. See the full key inside the front cover.

Bokha′ra rug′, a Turkoman rug having a tan or red background and decorated with varied octagon patterns. Also, **Bukhara rug.**

Bok•mål (bŏŏk′môl), *n.* a literary form of Norwegian, derived from the Danish writing of urban Norwegians: one of the two official forms of written Norwegian. Also called **Dano-Norwegian, Riksmål.** Cf. **Nynorsk.** [1935–40; < Norw: book language]

Boks•burg (boks′bûrg), *n.* a city in Transvaal, NE South Africa. 104,745.

Bol., Bolivia.

bol., (in prescriptions) bolus.

bo•la (bō′lə), *n., pl.* **-las** (-ləz). **1.** Also, **bolas.** a weapon consisting of two or more heavy balls secured to the ends of one or more strong cords, hurled by the Indians and gauchos of southern South America to entangle the legs of cattle and other animals. **2.** See **bolo tie.** [1835–45; < Sp: ball < OPr < L *bulla* bubble, knob; see BOIL[1]]

Bo•lan′ Pass′ (bō län′), a mountain pass in W Pakistan. ab. 60 mi. (97 km) long.

bo•lar (bō′lər), *adj.* of or pertaining to bole or clay. [1670–80; BOLE[2] + -AR[1]]

bo•las (bō′ləs), *n., pl.* **bo•las** (bō′ləz), **bo•las•es** (bō′lə-siz). (*used with a singular v.*) bola (def. 1).

bo′la tie′. See **bolo tie.** Also called **bola.**

bold (bōld), *adj.,* **-er, -est. 1.** not hesitating or fearful in the face of actual or possible danger or rebuff; courageous and daring: *a bold hero.* **2.** not hesitating to break the rules of propriety; forward; impudent: *He apologized for being so bold as to speak to the emperor.* **3.** necessitating courage and daring; challenging: *a bold adventure.* **4.** beyond the usual limits of conventional thought or action; imaginative: *Einstein was a bold mathematician. a difficult problem needing a bold answer.* **5.** striking or conspicuous to the eye; flashy; showy: *a bold pattern.* **6.** steep; abrupt: *a bold promontory.* **7.** *Naut.* deep enough to be navigable close to the shore: *bold waters.* **8.** *Print.* typeset in boldface. **9.** *Obs.* trusting; assured. **10. make bold,** to presume or venture; dare: *I made bold to offer my suggestion.* [bef. 1000; ME *bald, bold,* OE *b(e)ald;* c. OS, OHG *bald,* D *boud* bold, ON *ballr* dire < Gmc **bál-tha-z;* akin to Welsh *balch* proud, Ir *balc* strong < **bal-ko-*] **—bold′•ly,** *adv.* **—bold′ness,** *n.*
—Syn. 1. fearless, adventurous, brave, valiant, intrepid, valorous, dauntless. **2.** BOLD, BRAZEN, FORWARD, PRESUMPTUOUS may refer to manners in a derogatory way. BOLD suggests impudence, shamelessness, and immodesty: *a bold stare.* BRAZEN suggests the same, together with a defiant manner: *a brazen liar.* FORWARD implies making oneself unduly prominent or bringing oneself to notice with too much assurance. PRESUMPTUOUS implies overconfidence, effrontery, taking too much for granted. **—Ant. 2.** modest.

Bol•den (bōl′dən), *n.* **Charles** (*"Buddy"*), 1868?–1931, U.S. cornet player: early pioneer in jazz.

bold•face (bōld′fās′), *n., adj., v.,* **-faced, -fac•ing.** *Print.* **—n. 1.** type or print that has thick, heavy lines, used for emphasis, headings, etc.

This is a sample of boldface

—*adj.* **2.** typeset or printed in boldface. —*v.t.* **3.** to mark (copy) to be set in boldface. Cf. **lightface.** [1685–95; BOLD + FACE]

bold-faced (bōld′fāst′), *adj.* **1.** impudent; brazen: *He had the bold-faced effrontery to ask for a raise.* **2.** *Print.* (of type) having thick, heavy lines. [1585–95] **—bold-fac•ed•ly** (bōld′fā′sid lē, -fāst′-), *adv.* **—bold′-fac′ed•ness,** *n.*

bold•heart•ed (bōld′här′tid), *adj.* courageous or daring; intrepid. [BOLD + HEARTED] **—bold′heart′ed•ly,** *adv.* **—bold′heart′ed•ness,** *n.*

bol•do (bol′dō), *n., pl.* **-dos.** a Chilean evergreen tree, *Peumus boldus,* cultivated in California for its aromatic foliage. [1710–20; < AmerSp < Araucanian *voldo*]

bole[1] (bōl), *n. Bot.* the stem or trunk of a tree. [1275–1325; ME < ON *bolr* trunk (of a tree), torso; see BULWARK]

bole[2] (bōl), *n.* **1.** any of a variety of soft, unctuous clays of various colors, used as pigments. **2.** a medium reddish-brown color made from such clay. Also, **bolus.** [1350–1400; ME *bol* < LL *bōlus* lump; see BOLUS]

bo•lec•tion (bō lek′shən), *n. Archit., Furniture.* a raised molding, esp. one having flat edges and a raised center, for framing a panel, doorway, fireplace, etc. Also, **bilection.** [1700–10; orig. uncert.] **—bo•lec′tioned,** *adj.*

bo•le•ro (bə lâr′ō, bō-), *n., pl.* **-le•ros. 1.** a lively Spanish dance in triple meter. **2.** the music for this dance. **3.** a jacket ending above or at the waistline, with or without collar, lapel, and sleeves, worn open in front. [1780–90; < Sp]

bo•le′tic ac′id (bō lē′tik), *Chem.* See **fumaric acid.** [1810–20; BOLET(US) + -IC]

bo•le•tus (bō lē′təs), *n., pl.* **-tus•es, -ti** (-tī). any mushroomlike fungus of the genus *Boletus,* having an easily separable layer of tubes on the underside of the cap or pileus. [1595–1605; < NL; L *bōlētus* a mushroom]

Bol•eyn (bŏŏl′in, bŏŏ lin′), *n.* **Anne,** 1507–36, second wife of Henry VIII of England: mother of Queen Elizabeth I.

bo•lide (bō′līd, -lid), *n. Astron.* a large, brilliant meteor, esp. one that explodes; fireball. [1850–55; < F < Gk *bolid-* (s. of *bolís*) missile]

bo•lil•lo (bə lē′ō; *Sp.* bô lē′yô), *n., pl.* **-lil•los** (-lē′ōz; *Sp.* -lē′yôs). *Mexican Cookery.* **1.** a crusty hard roll with a soft center. **2.** a sandwich made with this roll. [< Sp, equiv. to *boll(o)* bun, roll (with gender change < L *bulla* bubble, knob; cf. BOLA, BOIL[1]) + *-illo* dim. suffix]

Bol•ing•broke (bol′ing brŏŏk′; *older* bŏŏl′-), *n.* **1.** See **Henry IV** (def. 2). **2. Henry St. John** (sin′jən), **1st Viscount,** 1678–1751, British statesman, writer, and orator.

Bo•ling•brook (bō′ling brŏŏk′), *n.* a city in NE Illinois. 37,261.

bo•li•ta (bə lē′tə, bō-), *n.* a form of numbers pool. [< Cuban Sp: lit., little ball (prob. after the balls used to choose lottery winners), equiv. to Sp *bol(a)* ball (see BOLA) + *-ita* dim. suffix]

bol•i•var (bol′ə vər, bə lē′vär; *Sp.* bô lē′vär), *n., pl.* **bol•i•vars,** *Sp.* ***bo•li•va•res*** (bô′lē vä′res). a coin and monetary unit of Venezuela, equal to 100 centimos. *Abbr.:* B. [1880–85; < AmerSp, after S. BOLÍVAR]

Bol•í•var (bol′ə vər, bə lē′vär; *Sp.* bô lē′vär), *n.* **Si•món** (sī′mən; *Sp.* sē môn′), (*"El Libertador"*), 1783–1830, Venezuelan statesman: leader of revolt of South American colonies against Spanish rule.

Bo•liv•i•a (bə liv′ē ə, bō-; *Sp.* bô lē′vyä), *n.* **1.** a republic in W South America. 5,633,800; 404,388 sq. mi. (1,047,370 sq. km). *Caps.:* La Paz and Sucre. **2.** (*often l.c.*) a twill fabric made of cut pile with lines either in the warp direction or on the bias. **—Bo•liv′i•an,** *adj., n.*

bo•li•via•no (bə liv′ē ä′nō, bō-; *Sp.* bô′lē vyä′nô), *n., pl.* **-nos** (-nōz; *Sp.* -nôs). a former silver or bronze coin, paper money, and monetary unit of Bolivia, equal to 100 centavos: replaced by the peso boliviano in 1963. [1870–75; < Sp; see BOLIVIA, -AN]

bol•ix (bol′iks), *v.t., n.* bollix.

boll (bōl), *n. Bot.* a rounded seed vessel or pod of a plant, as of flax or cotton. [1400–50; late ME *bolle,* perh. < MD *bolle* (D *bol*), though formally identical with BOWL[1]]

Böll (bœl), *n.* **Hein•rich (The•o•dor)** (hīn′rikh tā′ô-dōr′), 1917–85, German novelist and short-story writer: Nobel prize 1972.

Bol•land (bol′ənd; *Fr.* bô län′; *Flemish* bol′änt), *n.* **Jean de** (*Fr.* zhän də) or **Jo•han van** (*Flemish.* yō hän′ vän) or **John,** 1596–1665, Belgian Jesuit hagiographer. Also, **Bol•lan•dus** (bō lan′dəs).

Bol•land•ist (bol′ən dist), *n.* any of the editors of the *Acta Sanctorum.* [1745–55; after Jean de BOLLAND; see -IST]

bol•lard (bol′ərd), *n.* **1.** *Naut.* **a.** a thick, low post, usually of iron or steel, mounted on a wharf or the like, to which mooring lines from vessels are attached. **b.** a small post to which lines are attached. **c.** bitt (def. 1). **2.** *Brit.* one of a series of short posts for excluding or diverting motor vehicles from a road, lawn, or the like. [1835–45; BOLE[1] + -ARD]

bol•lix (bol′iks), *v.t. Informal.* **1.** to do (something) badly; bungle (often fol. by *up*): *His interference bollixed up the whole deal.* **—n. 2.** a confused bungle. Also, **bolix, bol′lox.** [1930–35; var. of BALLOCKS]

bol•locks (bol′əks), *n.* **1.** (*used with a plural v.*) *Vulgar.* ballocks. **2.** (*used with a singular or plural v.*) *Brit. Vulgar.* rubbish; nonsense; claptrap (often used interjectionally). [1735–45; var. of BALLOCKS]

boll′ wee′vil, 1. a snout beetle, *Anthonomus grandis,* that attacks the bolls of cotton. **2.** *Informal.* (esp. in the U.S. Congress) a Southern Democrat with conservative views who often votes with the Republicans as part of a Southern or conservative power bloc. [1890–95, *Amer.*]

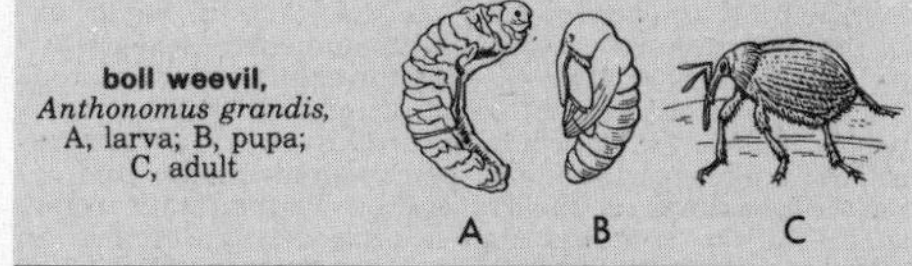

boll weevil, *Anthonomus grandis,* A, larva; B, pupa; C, adult

boll•worm (bōl′wûrm′), *n.* **1.** See **pink bollworm. 2.** See **corn earworm.** [1840–50, *Amer.;* BOLL + WORM]

bo•lo[1] (bō′lō), *n., pl.* **-los.** a large, heavy, single-edged knife or machete for hacking, used in the Philippines and by the U.S. Army. [1900–05; < Philippine Sp; further orig. uncert.]

bo•lo[2] (bō′lō), *n., pl.* **-los,** *v.,* **-loed, -lo•ing.** *U.S. Mil. Slang.* **—n. 1.** a soldier who does not meet the minimum standards of marksmanship. **—***v.i.* **2.** to fail to meet the minimum standards of marksmanship. [1915–20; said to be after *Bolo* Pascha (d. 1918), German agent in France during World War I]

bo•lo[3] (bō′lō), *n.* See **bolo tie.**

bo•lo•gna (bə lō′nē, -nə, -lōn′yə), *n.* a large seasoned sausage made of finely ground meat, usually beef and pork, that has been cooked and smoked. Also called **bolo′gna sau′sage.** [1555–65; after BOLOGNA, Italy]

Bo•lo•gna (bə lōn′yə; *It.* bô lô′nyä), *n.* **1. Gio•van•ni da** (jē′ə vä′nē də; *It.* jô vän′nē dä), (*Jean de Boulogne, Giambologna*), c1525–1608, Italian sculptor, born in France. **2.** a city in N Italy. 484,406.

Bo•lo•gnese (bō′lə nēz′, -nēs′, -lən yēz′, -yēs′; *for 2 also* bō′lən yāz′, -yä′zē *or, It.,* bô′lô nye′ze), *adj., n., pl.* **-gnese.** **—***adj.* **1.** of or pertaining to Bologna or its inhabitants. **2.** *Italian Cookery.* served with a cream sauce typically containing prosciutto, ground beef, and cheese. **3.** *Fine Arts.* noting a style or manner of painting developed in Bologna during the late 16th century by the Carracci, characterized chiefly by forms and colors derived from the Roman high renaissance and from the Venetians. **—***n.* **4.** a native or inhabitant of Bologna. [1750–60; < It; see BOLOGNA, -ESE]

bo•lom•e•ter (bō lom′i tər, bə-), *n. Physics.* a device for measuring minute amounts of radiant energy by determining the changes of resistance in an electric conductor caused by changes in its temperature. [1880–85; < Gk *bol(ḗ)* ray + -o- + -METER] **—bo•lo•met•ric** (bō′lə me′trik), *adj.* **—bo′lo•met′ri•cal•ly,** *adv.*

bo′lomet′ric mag′nitude, *Astron.* the magnitude of a star derived either from the total energy that it radiates at all wavelengths or from the total energy of those of its wavelengths that are received on earth.

bo•lo•ney (bə lō′nē), *n.* baloney. [1895–1900, *Amer.*]

bo′lo tie′, a necktie of thin cord fastened in front with an ornamental clasp or other device. Also, **bola tie.** Also called **bolo, bola.** [1960–65; *bolo,* appar. an error for BOLA, after the tie's resemblance to a bola]

Bol•she•vik (bōl′shə vik, bol′-; *Russ.* bəl shi vyēk′), *n., pl.* **-viks, -vik•i** (-vik′ē, -vē′kē; *Russ.* -vyi kyē′). **1.** (in Russia) **a.** a member of the more radical majority of the Social Democratic party, 1903–17, advocating immediate and forceful seizure of power by the proletariat. **b.** (since 1918) a member of the Russian Communist party. **2.** (loosely) a member of the Communist party, esp. outside of the Soviet Union. **3.** *Derogatory.* an extreme political radical; revolutionary or anarchist. Also, **bol′she•vik.** [1915–20; < Russ *bol'shevík,* equiv. to *ból'sh(iĭ)* larger, greater (comp. of *bol'shóĭ* large; cf. *bol'shinstvó* majority) + *-evik,* var. of *-ovik* n. suffix; cf. MENSHEVIK]

Bol•she•vism (bōl′shə viz′əm, bol′-), *n.* **1.** the doctrines, methods, or procedure of the Bolsheviks. **2.** (*sometimes l.c.*) the principles or practices of ultraradical socialists or political ultraradicals generally. Also, **bol′•she•vism, Bol•she•vik•ism, bol•she•vik•ism** (bōl′shə vi-kiz′əm, bol′-). [1915–20; BOLSHEV(IK) + -ISM]

Bol•she•vist (bōl′shə vist, bol′-), *n.* **1.** a follower or advocate of the doctrines or methods of the Bolsheviks. **2.** (*sometimes l.c.*) an ultraradical socialist; any political ultraradical. **—***adj.* **3.** Bolshevistic. [1915–20; BOLSHE-V(IK) + -IST]

Bol•she•vis•tic (bōl′shə vis′tik, bol′-), *adj.* of, pertaining to, or characteristic of Bolshevists or Bolshevism. Also, **bol′she•vis′tic.** [1915–20; BOLSHEVIST + -IC] **—Bol′she•vis′ti•cal•ly, bol′she•vis′ti•cal•ly,** *adv.*

Bol•she•vize (bōl′shə vīz′, bol′-), *v.,* **-vized, -viz•ing.** **—***v.t.* **1.** to bring under the influence or domination of Bolshevists; render Bolshevik or Bolshevistic. **—***v.i.* **2.** to become Bolshevik or Bolshevistic; act like a Bolshevik. Also, **bol′she•vize′;** *esp. Brit.,* **Bol′she•vise′.** [1915–20; BOLSHEV(IST) + -IZE] **—Bol′she•vi•za′tion,** *n.*

Bol•shie (bōl′shē, bol′-), *n. Slang.* **1.** Bolshevik. **2.** Bolshevist. [1915–20; BOLSH(EVIK) + -IE]

Bol′shoi Ballet′ (bōl′shoi, bol′-), a ballet company founded in Moscow in 1776.

Bol•shy (bōl′shē, bol′-), *n., pl.* **-shies.** *Slang.* **1.** Bolshevik. **2.** Bolshevist. [1915–20; see BOLSHIE, -Y[2]]

bol•son (bōl sōn′), *n.* a desert valley, the level of which has been raised by aggradation, usually draining into a playa. [1830–40, *Amer.;* < Sp; big purse, equiv. to *bols(a)* purse (< LL *bursa;* see BURSA) + *-ón* aug. suffix]

bol•ster (bōl′stər), *n.* **1.** a long, often cylindrical, cushion or pillow for a bed, sofa, etc. **2.** anything resembling this in form or in use as a support. **3.** any pillow, cushion, or pad. **4.** *Naut.* **a.** Also called **bol′ster plate′.** a circular casting on the side of a vessel, through which an anchor chain passes. **b.** a timber used as a temporary support. **c.** a beam for holding lines or rigging without chafing. **d.** a bag filled with buoyant material, fitted into a small boat. **5.** *Metalworking.* an anvillike support for the lower die of a drop forge. **6.** *Masonry.* **a.** a timber or the like connecting two ribs of a centering. **b.** a chisel with a blade splayed toward the edge, used for cutting bricks. **7.** *Carpentry.* a horizontal timber on a post for lessening the free span of a beam. **8.** a structural member on which one end of a bridge truss rests. **—***v.t.* **9.** to support with or as with a pillow or cushion. **10.** to add to, support, or uphold (sometimes fol. by *up*): *They bolstered their morale by singing. He bolstered up his claim with new evidence.* [bef. 1000; ME *bolstre* (n.), OE *bolster;* c. ON *bolstr,* D *bolster,* G *Polster*] **—bol′ster•er,** *n.*
—Syn. 1. See **cushion. 10.** strengthen, sustain, aid, reinforce, fortify.

bolt[1] (bōlt), *n.* **1.** a movable bar or rod that when slid into a socket fastens a door, gate, etc. **2.** the part of a lock that is shot from and drawn back into the case, as by the action of the key. **3.** any of several types of strong fastening rods, pins, or screws, usually threaded to receive a nut. **4.** a sudden dash, run, flight, or escape. **5.** a sudden desertion from a meeting, political party, social movement, etc. **6.** a length of woven goods, esp. as it comes on a roll from the loom. **7.** a roll of wallpaper. **8.** *Bookbinding.* the three edges of a folded sheet that must be cut so that the leaves can be opened. **9.** a rod,

bar, or plate that closes the breech of a breechloading rifle, esp. a sliding rod or bar that shoves a cartridge into the firing chamber as it closes the breech. **10.** a jet of water, molten glass, etc. **11.** an arrow, esp. a short, heavy one for a crossbow. **12.** a shaft of lightning; thunderbolt. **13.** a length of timber to be cut into smaller pieces. **14.** a slice from a log, as a short, round piece of wood used for a chopping block. **15. bolt from the blue,** a sudden and entirely unforeseen event: *His decision to leave college was a bolt from the blue for his parents.* Also, **bolt out of the blue. 16. shoot one's bolt,** *Informal.* to make an exhaustive effort or expenditure: *The lawyer shot his bolt the first day of the trial and had little to say thereafter.* —*v.t.* **17.** to fasten with or as with a bolt. **18.** to discontinue support of or participation in; break with: *to bolt a political party.* **19.** to shoot or discharge (a missile), as from a crossbow or catapult. **20.** to utter hastily; say impulsively; blurt out. **21.** to swallow (one's food or drink) hurriedly: *She bolted her breakfast and ran to school.* **22.** to make (cloth, wallpaper, etc.) into bolts. **23.** *Fox Hunting.* (of hounds) to force (a fox) into the open. —*v.i.* **24.** to make a sudden, swift dash, run, flight, or escape; spring away suddenly: *The rabbit bolted into its burrow.* **25.** to break away, as from one's political party. **26.** to eat hurriedly or without chewing. **27.** *Hort.* to produce flowers or seeds prematurely. —*adv.* **28.** *Archaic.* with sudden meeting or collision; suddenly. **29. bolt upright,** stiffly upright; rigidly straight: *The explosive sound caused him to sit bolt upright in his chair.* [bef. 1000; ME (n., v., and adv.), OE (n.), c. D *bout,* G *Bolz*] —**bolt′er,** *n.* —**bolt′less,** *adj.* —**bolt′like′,** *adj.*
—**Syn. 24.** dash, rush, run, fly, speed, scoot, flee, bound.

bolts (def. 3)
A, carriage bolt;
B, machine bolt;
C, stove bolt

bolt[2] (bōlt), *v.t.* **1.** to sift through a cloth or sieve. **2.** to examine or search into, as if by sifting. [1150–1200; ME *bulten* < OF *bul(e)ter,* metathetic var. of **buteler* < Gmc; cf. MHG *biuteln* to sift, deriv. of *biutel,* OHG *būtil* bag, whence G *Beutel*] —**bolt′er,** *n.*

bolt-ac·tion (bōlt′ak′shən), *adj.* (of a rifle) equipped with a manually operated sliding bolt. [1870–75]

bolt′ boat′, a boat suitable for use in rough seas.

bol·tel (bōl′təl), *n. Archit.* **1.** Also, **boutel, boutell, bowtel, bowtell.** a convex molding, as a torus or ovolo. **2.** Also, **bottle.** a curved fractable. [1425–75; late ME *boltell,* equiv. to *bolt* BOLT[1] + *-ell* n. suffix]

bolt·head (bōlt′hed′), *n.* **1.** the head of a bolt. **2.** *Chem.* (formerly) a matrass. [1425–75; late ME; see BOLT[1], HEAD]

bolt-hole (bōlt′hōl′), *n.* **1.** a hole in the ground, protected opening in bushes, etc., into which an animal can flee when pursued or frightened. **2.** a place or avenue of escape or refuge: *The remote mountain village was a safe bolt-hole for refugees during the war.* [1830–40]

bolt′ing cloth′, a sturdy fabric, usually of fine silk or nylon mesh, used chiefly in serigraphy, embroidery, and as a foundation fabric for wigs. [1275–1325; ME]

Bol·ton (bōl′tn), *n.* a borough in Greater Manchester, in NW England. 263,300.

bol·to·ni·a (bōl tō′nē ə), *n.* any of several composite plants of the genus *Boltonia,* of the U.S., having blue, purple, or white asterlike flower heads. [< NL (1788); after James *Bolton,* 18th-century English botanist; see -IA]

bolt·rope (bōlt′rōp′), *n.* **1.** *Naut.* a rope or the cordage sewn on the edges of a sail to strengthen it. **2.** a superior grade of rope. Also, **bolt′ rope′.** [1620–30; BOLT[1] + ROPE]

Boltz·mann (bôlts′män′; *Eng.* bōlts′mən), *n.* **Ludwig** (lo͝od′viKH, lo͞ot′-), 1844–1906, Austrian physicist.

Boltz′mann con′stant, *Physics.* the ratio of the universal gas constant to Avogadro's number, equal to 1.3803×10^{-16} erg per degree C. *Symbol:* k Also, **Boltz′·mann's con′stant.** [1905–10; after L. BOLTZMANN]

bo·lus (bō′ləs), *n., pl.* **-lus·es. 1.** *Pharm., Vet. Med.* a round mass of medicinal material, larger than an ordinary pill. *Abbr.:* bol. **2.** a soft, roundish mass or lump, esp. of chewed food. **3.** bole[2]. [1595–1605; < LL *bōlus* clod of earth < Gk *bôlos* clod, lump; see BOLE[2]]

Bo·lyai (bô′lyoi), *n.* **Já·nos** (yä′nôsh), 1802–60, Hungarian mathematician.

Bol·za·no (bōl zä′nō, bōlt sä′-; *for 2 also It.* bôl tsä′nô), *n.* **1. Bern·hard** (berN′härt), 1781–1848, Austrian mathematician and theologian. **2.** German, **Bozen.** a city in NE Italy. 106,857.

Bol·za′no-Wei′er·strass the′orem (bōl zä′nō-vī′ər shträs′, -sträs′, bōlt sä′-), *Math.* the theorem that every bounded set with an infinite number of elements contains at least one accumulation point. [named after B. BOLZANO and K. *Weierstrass* (1815–97), German mathematician]

Bo·ma (bō′mə), *n.* a city in W Zaire, on the Zaire (Congo) River. 79,000.

Bo·marc (bō′märk), *n. U.S. Mil.* a winged, surface-to-air interceptor missile. [1960–65; *Bo(eing)* + *M(ichigan) A(eronautical) R(esearch) C(enter)*]

bomb (bom), *n.* **1.** *Mil.* a projectile, formerly usually spherical, filled with a bursting charge and exploded by means of a fuze, by impact, or otherwise, now generally designed to be dropped from an aircraft. **2.** any similar missile or explosive device used as a weapon, to disperse crowds, etc.: *a time bomb; a smoke bomb.* **3.** Also called **volcanic bomb.** *Geol.* a rough spherical or ellipsoidal mass of lava, ejected from a volcano and hardened while falling. **4.** See **aerosol bomb. 5.** *Football.* a long forward pass, esp. one to a teammate who scores a touchdown. **6.** *Slang.* **a.** an absolute failure; fiasco: *The play was a bomb and closed after two performances.* **b.** *Chiefly Brit.* an overwhelming success: *The novel is selling like a bomb.* **7.** *Jazz.* a sudden, unexpected accent or rhythmic figure played by a drummer during a performance. **8.** a lead or lead-lined container for transporting and storing radioactive materials. **9. the bomb, a.** See **atomic bomb. b.** nuclear weapons collectively. **10.** *Computers.* a spectacular program or system failure. **11.** *Slang.* a powerful automobile or other vehicle. —*v.t.* **12.** to hurl bombs at or drop bombs upon, as from an airplane; bombard: *The enemy planes bombed the city.* **13.** to explode by means of a bomb or explosive. **14.** *Computers.* to deliberately cause (a computer system) to fail with a program written for the purpose. —*v.i.* **15.** to hurl or drop bombs. **16.** to explode a bomb or bombs. **17.** *Slang.* to be or make a complete failure, esp. to fail to please or gain an audience; flop (sometimes fol. by *out*): *His last play bombed on Broadway. The business bombed out with a $25,000 debt.* **18.** (of a computer program or system) to fail spectacularly. **19.** *Informal.* to move very quickly: *They came bombing through here on their motorcycles at 2 A.M.* [1580–90; 1960–65 for def. 17; earlier *bom(b)e* < Sp *bomba (de fuego)* ball (of fire), akin to *bombo* drum < L *bombus* a booming sound < Gk *bómbos*] —**bomb′able,** *adj.*

bom·ba·ceous (bom′bə kā′shəs), *adj.* belonging to the Bombacaceae, the bombax family of plants. Cf. **bombax family.** [1860–65; < NL *Bombacace(ae)* name of the family (see BOMBAX FAMILY, -ACEAE) + -OUS]

bom·bard (*v.* bom bärd′, bəm-; *n.* bom′bärd), *v.t.* **1.** to attack or batter with artillery fire. **2.** to attack with bombs. **3.** to assail vigorously: *to bombard the speaker with questions.* **4.** *Physics.* to direct high energy particles or radiations against: *to bombard a nucleus.* —*n.* **5.** the earliest kind of cannon, originally throwing stone balls. **6.** *Naut.* See **bomb ketch. 7.** an English leather tankard of the 18th century and earlier, similar to but larger than a blackjack. **8.** *Obs.* a leather jug. [1400–50; late ME (n.) < ML *bombarda* stone-throwing engine (L *bomb(us)* booming noise (see BOMB) + *-arda* -ARD)] —**bom·bard′er,** *n.* —**bom·bard′ment,** *n.*
—**Syn. 3.** beset, harass, hound, besiege.

bom·bar·dier (bom′bər dēr′, -bə-), *n.* **1.** *Mil.* the member of a bombing plane crew who operates the bombsight and bomb-release mechanism. **2.** *Hist.* artilleryman. [1550–60; < MF; see BOMBARD, -IER[2]]

Bom·bar·dier (bom′bər dēr′, -bə-, bom′bär dyā′), *Trademark, Canadian.* a snowmobilelike vehicle driven by an internal-combustion engine, equipped with caterpillar tracks at the rear, steered by skis at the front, and designed for travel over snow. [1945–50; after Canadian inventor and industrialist Armand *Bombardier* (d. 1964), who designed it]

bombardier′ bee′tle, any ground beetle of the genus *Brachinus,* which ejects a puff of volatile fluid from its abdomen with a popping sound when disturbed. [1795–1805]

bom·bar·don (bom′bər dən, bom bär′dn), *n.* **1.** a bass reed stop on a pipe organ. **2.** a large, deep-toned, valved, brass wind instrument resembling a tuba. [1855–60; < It *bombardone* wind instrument, equiv. to *bombard(o)* an oboelike instrument, orig., mortar (see BOMBARD) + *-one* aug. suffix]

bom·ba·sine (bom′bə zēn′, -sēn′; bom′bə zēn′, -sēn′), *n.* bombazine.

bom·bast (bom′bast), *n.* **1.** speech too pompous for an occasion; pretentious words. **2.** *Obs.* cotton or other material used to stuff garments; padding. —*adj.* **3.** *Obs.* bombastic. [1560–70; earlier *bombace* padding < MF < ML *bombācem,* acc. of *bombāx;* see BOMBAX FAMILY]

bom·bas·tic (bom bas′tik), *adj.* (of speech, writing, etc.) high-sounding; high-flown; inflated; pretentious. Also, **bom·bas′ti·cal.** [1695–1705; BOMBAST + -IC] —**bom·bas′ti·cal·ly,** *adv.*
—**Syn.** pompous, grandiloquent, turgid, florid, grandiose. BOMBASTIC, FLOWERY, PRETENTIOUS, VERBOSE all describe a use or a user of language more elaborate than is justified by or appropriate to the content being expressed. BOMBASTIC suggests language with a theatricality or staginess of style far too powerful or declamatory for the meaning or sentiment being expressed: *a bombastic sermon on the evils of cardplaying.* FLOWERY describes language filled with extravagant images and ornate expressions: *a flowery eulogy.* PRETENTIOUS refers specifically to language that is purposely inflated in an effort to impress: *a pretentious essay designed to demonstrate one's sophistication.* VERBOSE characterizes utterances or speakers that use more words than necessary to express an idea: *a verbose speech, speaker.*

bom′bax fam′ily (bom′baks), the plant family Bombacaceae, typified by tropical deciduous trees having palmate leaves, large and often showy solitary or clustered flowers, and dry fruit with a woolly pulp, and including the baobab and silk-cotton tree. [< NL (Linnaeus): the silk-cotton tree genus; ML: silk, cotton, alter. of L *bombȳx* silkworm, silk < Gk *bómbyx* silkworm; see BOMBYCID]

Bom·bay (bom bā′), *n.* **1.** a seaport in and the capital of Maharashtra, in W India, on the Arabian Sea. 5,970,575. **2.** a former state in W India: divided in 1960 into the Gujarat and Maharashtra states.

Bom′bay duck′, 1. a small lizardfish, *Harpadon nehereus,* inhabiting river mouths and estuaries of Asia. **2.** (in India) the flesh of this fish, impregnated with asafetida, dried, salted, and used as a condiment or relish, esp. with curry. Also called **bummalo.** [1665–75]

Bom′bay hemp′, sunn.

bom·ba·zine (bom′bə zēn′, bom′bə zēn′), *n.* a twill fabric constructed of a silk or rayon warp and worsted filling, often dyed black for mourning wear. Also, **bombasine, bom′ba·zeen′.** [1545–55; earlier *bombasin* < MF < ML *bombasinum,* var. of *bombȳcinum,* n. use of neut. of L *bombȳcinus* silken < Gk *bombýkinos,* equiv. to *bombyk-,* s. of *bómbyx* silkworm + *-inos* -INE[1]]

bomb′ bay′, *Aeron., Mil.* (in the fuselage of a bomber) the compartment in which bombs are carried and from which they are dropped. [1915–20]

bombe (bom, bomb; *Fr.* bôNb), *n., pl.* **bombes** (bomz, bombz; *Fr.* bôNb). a round or melon-shaped frozen mold made from a combination of ice creams, mousses, or ices. [1890–95; < F: lit., BOMB, from its shape]

bom·bé (bom bā′; *Fr.* bôN bā′), *adj. Furniture.* curving or swelling outward. Also, **bombed.** Cf. **swell front.** [1900–05; < F: lit., rounded like a bomb (*bombe* BOMB + *-é* adj. suffix < L *-ātus* -ATE[1])]

bombé desk

bombed (bomd), *adj. Slang.* **1.** completely intoxicated; drunk. **2.** completely under the influence of drugs; high. [1935–40; BOMB + -ED[2]]

bombed-out (bomd′out′), *adj.* destroyed or severely damaged by or as by bombing: *a bombed-out village; a bombed-out economy.* [1915–20]

bomb·er (bom′ər), *n.* **1.** *Mil.* an airplane equipped to carry and drop bombs. **2.** a person who drops or sets bombs, esp. as an act of terrorism or sabotage. **3.** See **bomber jacket.** [1910–15; BOMB + -ER[1]]

bomb′er jack′et, a jacket, often made of leather with ribbed trim, resembling those worn by World War II bomber crews.

bom·bi·lla (bôm bē′yä, -lyä), *n., pl.* ***-llas*** (-yäs, -lyäs). *Spanish.* a tube or drinking straw with a strainer at one end, esp. for drinking maté. [1865–70]

bom·bi·nate (bom′bə nāt′), *v.i.,* **-nat·ed, -nat·ing.** to make a humming or buzzing noise. [1875–80; < NL *bombinātus,* ptp. of *bombināre,* appar. coined by Rabelais on basis of L *bombilāre* to hum, buzz < Gk *bombyliázein,* deriv. of *bómbos;* see BOMB] —**bom′bi·na′·tion,** *n.*

bomb′ing run′. See **bomb run.** [1940–45]

bomb′ ketch′, *Naut.* a ketch-rigged vessel of the 17th and 18th centuries, carrying heavy mortars for firing bombs. Also called **bombard, mortar ketch.** [1685–95]

bomb′ lance′, a harpoon fitted with an explosive head. [1900–05]

bomb·let (bom′lit), *n.* any of numerous explosive, incendiary, or fragmentation bombs packed into a larger bomb or canister that releases or scatters them to explode separately. [BOMB + -LET]

bomb·load (bom′lōd′), *n.* the total load of bombs carried by an airplane, usually expressed in terms of their total weight. [BOMB + LOAD]

bom·bor·a (bom bôr′ə), *n. Australian.* **1.** a hidden reef of rocks. **2.** a dangerous eddy over such a reef. [1930–35; perh. < Dharuk *bumbora* name of a current off Dobroyde Head, Port Jackson]

bom·bous (bom′bəs), *adj. Entomol.* convex; spherical. [1705–15; BOMB + -OUS]

bomb·proof (bom′pro͞of′), *adj.* **1.** strong enough to resist the impact and explosive force of bombs or shells: *a bombproof shelter.* —*v.t.* **2.** to make bombproof. [1695–1705; BOMB + -PROOF]

bomb′ rack′, a device for carrying bombs in or under the fuselage of an aircraft. [1915–20]

bomb′ run′, the part of a bombing mission between the sighting of the target or its identification by electronic instruments and the release of the bombs. Also, **bombing run.** [1940–45]

bomb·shell (bom′shel′), *n.* **1.** a bomb. **2.** something or someone having a sudden and sensational effect: *The news of his resignation was a bombshell.* [1700–10; 1925–30 for def. 2; BOMB + SHELL]

bomb′ shel′ter, a room or area, usually underground, especially reinforced against the effects of bombs, used as a shelter during an air raid. Cf. **air-raid shelter.** [1935–40]

bomb·sight (bom′sīt′), *n. Mil.* (in an aircraft) an instrument for aiming bombs at a target, esp. a device that can assume complete control of the aircraft during a bombing run, can automatically compensate for speed, winds, etc., and can guide the release of bombs for maximum accuracy in striking the target. [1915–20; BOMB + SIGHT]

bomb′ squad′, a squad or force of police officers or others trained to disarm bombs and other explosive devices.

bom•by•cid (bom′bə sid), *n.* **1.** a moth of the family Bombycidae, comprising a single species, *Bombyx mori,* the Chinese silkworm moth. —*adj.* **2.** belonging or pertaining to the family Bombycidae. [< NL *Bombycidae,* equiv. to L *bombȳc-* (s. of *bombȳx* silkworm < Gk *bómbyx*) + *-idae* -ID[2]]

Bo•mu (bō′mo͞o), *n.* a river in central Africa, forming part of the boundary between Zaire and the Central African Republic, flowing N and W into the Uele River to form the Ubangi River. ab. 500 mi. (805 km) long. Also, **Mbomu.**

Bon (bon; *Fr.* bôN), *n.* **Cape,** a cape on the NE coast of Tunisia: surrender of the German African forces, May 12, 1943. Also called **Ras Addar.**

Bon (bôn), *n.* an annual festival of the Japanese Buddhists, welcoming ancestral spirits to household altars. Also called **Feast of Lanterns.** [< Japn, orig. *Urabon* < Chin version of Skt *ullambana* lit., hanging upside down (a metaphor for the suffering brought on by physical desires)]

Bön (bœn), *n.* a shamanistic Tibetan sect, absorbed by the first Buddhist sects of the 7th century and later.

Bo•na (bō′nə, -nä), *n.* Bône.

bo•na•ci (bō′nə sē′), *n., pl.* (*esp. collectively*) **-ci,** (*esp. referring to two or more kinds or species*) **-cis.** any of several edible serranid fishes, as *Mycteroperca bonaci.* [< Sp *bonasí* a fish]

Bo•na De•a (bō′nə dē′ə, dā′ə), an ancient Roman goddess of chastity and fertility. Also called **Fauna.** [< L: lit., (the) Good Goddess]

Bon•a•dox•in (bon′ə dok′sin), *Pharm., Trademark.* a brand of meclizine.

bo•na fide (bō′nə fīd′, bon′ə; bō′nə fī′dē), **1.** made, done, presented, etc., in good faith; without deception or fraud: *a bona fide statement of intent to sell.* **2.** authentic; true: *a bona fide sample of Lincoln's handwriting.* Also, **bona′-fide′.** [1935–45; < L *bonā fidē*]
—**Syn. 1.** honest, sincere; lawful, legal. **2.** genuine.
—**Ant.** spurious, deceitful, false.

bo•na fi•des (bō′nä fē′des; *Eng.* bō′nə fī′dēz *or, esp. for 2,* bō′nə fīdz′, bon′ə), **1.** (*italics*) *Latin.* (*used with a singular v.*) good faith; absence of fraud or deceit; the state of being exactly as claims or appearances indicate: *The bona fides of this contract is open to question.* Cf. ***mala fides.*** **2.** (*sometimes italics*) (*used with a plural v.*) the official papers, documents, or other items that prove authenticity, legitimacy, etc., as of a person or enterprise; credentials: *All our bona fides are on file with the SEC.*
—**Usage.** BONA FIDES is originally a Latin phrase meaning "good faith." FIDES is singular in Latin and has been used as such in English. At least partially because its *-es* ending makes BONA FIDES look and sound like a plural, it has developed the plural sense "credentials." This plural use, although criticized by some usage guides, has been increasing in recent decades in all varieties of speech and writing.

Bon•aire (bô nâr′), *n.* an island in the E Netherlands Antilles, in the S West Indies. 9137; 95 sq. mi. (245 sq. km).

bon a•mi (bô nA mē′), *pl.* ***bons a•mis*** (bôN zA mē′). *French.* **1.** a good friend. **2.** a sweetheart or lover.

bo•nan•za (bə nan′zə, bō-), *n.* **1.** a rich mass of ore, as found in mining. **2.** a source of great and sudden wealth or luck; a spectacular windfall: *The play proved to be a bonanza for its lucky backers.* [1835–45, *Amer.*; < Sp: lit., smooth sea (hence, good luck, rich vein of ore), nasalized var. of ML *bonacia,* equiv. to L *bon(us)* good + *(mal)acia* calm sea < Gk *malakía* softness (*malak(ós)* soft + *-ia* -IA)]

Bo•na•parte (bō′nə pärt′; *Fr.* bô nA pART′), *n.* **1. Jé•rôme** (jə rōm′; *Fr.* zhā RŌM′), 1784–1860, king of Westphalia 1807 (brother of Napoleon I). **2. Jo•seph** (jō′zəf, -səf; *Fr.* zhō zef′), 1768–1844, king of Naples 1806–08; king of Spain 1808–13 (brother of Napoleon I). **3. Lou•is** (lo͞o′ē; *Fr.* lwē; *Du.* lo͞o ē′), 1778–1846, king of Holland 1806–10 (brother of Napoleon I). **4. Lou•is Na•po•lé•on** (lo͞o′ē nə pō′lē ən; *Fr.* lwē nA pô lā ôN′). See **Napoleon III. 5. Lu•cien** (lo͞o′shən; *Fr.* lʏ syaN′), 1775–1840, prince of Canino, a principality in Italy (brother of Napoleon I). **6. Napoléon.** See **Napoleon I. 7. Napoléon.** See **Napoleon II.** Italian, **Buonaparte.** —**Bo′na•par′•te•an,** *adj.*

Bo•na•part•ist (bō′nə pär′tist), *n.* an adherent of the Bonapartes or their policies. [1805–15; earlier *Buonapartist.* See BONAPARTE, -IST] —**Bo′na•part′ism,** *n.*

bon ap•pé•tit (bô nA pā tē′), *French.* (I wish you) a hearty appetite.

bo•na va•can•ti•a (bō′nä vä kän′tē ä; *Eng.* bō′nə və kan′tē ə), *Law.* property without an apparent owner or claimant. [1750–60; < L]

Bon•a•ven•tu•ra (bon′ə ven cho͝or′ə; *It.* bô′nä ventoo′rä), *n.* See **Bonaventure, Saint.**

bon•a•ven•ture (bon′ə ven′chər, bon′ə ven′-), *n. Naut.* a mast fitted with a lateen sail (**bonaventure miz′zen**) or lugsail, situated behind the mizzenmast at or near the stern, used in the 16th and early 17th centuries. [1490–1500; < It *buonaventura* lit., good luck. See BONUS, VENTURE]

Bon•a•ven•ture (bon′ə ven′cher, bon′ə ven′-), *n.* **Saint** ("*the Seraphic Doctor*"), 1221–74, Italian scholastic theologian. Also, **Bonaventura.**

bon•a•vist (bon′ə vist), *n.* See **hyacinth bean.** [1690–1700; < It *buonavista* good sight. See BONUS, VISTA]

bon•bon (bon′bon′; *Fr.* bôN bôN′), *n., pl.* **-bons** (-bonz′; *Fr.* -bôN′). **1.** a fondant, fruit, or nut center dipped in fondant or chocolate; a chocolate. **2.** a piece of confectionery; candy. [1790–1800; < F: lit., good-good; a repetitive compound, orig. nursery word]

bon•bon•nière (bon′bə nēr′, -nyâr′; *Fr.* bôN bônyeR′), *n., pl.* **-nières** (-nērz′, -nyârz′; *Fr.* -nyeR′). **1.** a person or store that makes or sells candies. **2.** a box or dish for candies. [1810–20; < F]

bonce (bons), *n. Brit. Slang.* head; skull. [1860–65; perh. to be identified with *bonce* a large playing marble, perh. repr. dial. pron. of BOUNCE; cf. dial. (Yorkshire) *bouncer* large earthenware marble]

bond[1] (bond), *n.* **1.** something that binds, fastens, confines, or holds together. **2.** a cord, rope, band, or ligament. **3.** something that binds a person or persons to a certain circumstance or line of behavior: *the bond of matrimony.* **4.** something, as an agreement or friendship, that unites individuals or peoples into a group; covenant: *the bond between nations.* **5.** binding security; firm assurance: *My word is my bond.* **6.** a sealed instrument under which a person, corporation, or government guarantees to pay a stated sum of money on or before a specified day. **7.** any written obligation under seal. **8.** *Law.* a written promise of a surety. **9.** *Govt.* the state of dutiable goods stored without payment of duties or taxes until withdrawn: *goods in bond.* **10.** Also called **bonded whiskey.** a whiskey that has been aged at least four years in a bonded warehouse before bottling. **11.** *Finance.* a certificate of ownership of a specified portion of a debt due to be paid by a government or corporation to an individual holder and usually bearing a fixed rate of interest. **12.** *Insurance.* **a.** a surety agreement. **b.** the money deposited, or the promissory arrangement entered into, under any such agreement. **13.** a substance that causes particles to adhere; binder. **14.** adhesion between two substances or objects, as concrete and reinforcing strands. **15.** Also called **chemical bond.** *Chem.* the attraction between atoms in a molecule or crystalline structure. Cf. **coordinate bond, covalent bond, electrovalent bond, hydrogen bond, metallic bond. 16.** See **bond paper. 17.** *Masonry.* **a.** any of various arrangements of bricks, stones, etc., having a regular pattern and intended to increase the strength or enhance the appearance of a construction. **b.** the overlap of bricks, stones, etc., in a construction so as to increase its strength. **18.** *Elect.* an electric conductor placed between adjacent metal parts within a structure, as in a railroad track, aircraft, or house, to prevent the accumulation of static electricity. **19.** *Obs.* bondsman[1]. —*v.t.* **20.** to put (goods, an employee, official, etc.) on or under bond: *The company refused to bond a former criminal.* **21.** to connect or bind. **22.** *Finance.* to place a bonded debt on or secure a debt by bonds; mortgage. **23.** to join (two materials). **24.** *Masonry.* to lay (bricks, stones, etc.) so as to produce a strong construction. **25.** *Elect.* to provide with a bond: *to bond a railroad track.* **26.** to establish a close emotional relationship to or with (another): *the special period when a mother bonds to her infant.* —*v.i.* **27.** to hold together or cohere, from or as from being bonded, as bricks in a wall or particles in a mass. **28.** *Psychol., Animal Behav.* to establish a bonding. [1175–1225; ME (n.); var. of BAND[3]] —**bond′a•ble,** *adj.* —**bond′a•bil′i•ty,** *n.* —**bond′er,** *n.* —**bond′less,** *adj.*
—**Syn. 1.** bonds, chains, fetters. **3.** BOND, LINK, TIE agree in referring to a force or influence that unites people. BOND, however, usually emphasizes the strong and enduring quality of affection, whereas TIE may refer more esp. to duty, obligation, or responsibility: *bonds of memory; Blessed be the tie that binds; family ties.* A LINK is a definite connection, though a slighter one; it may indicate affection or merely some traceable influence or desultory communication: *a close link between friends.*

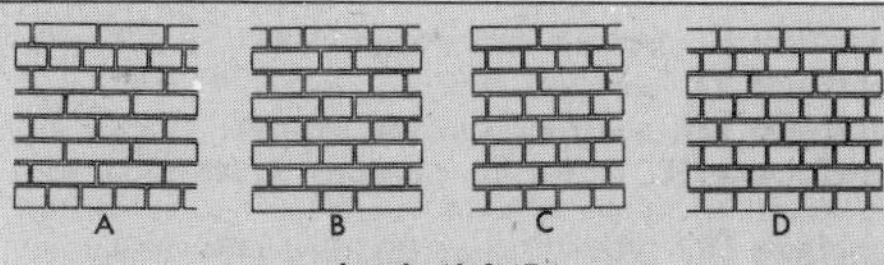

bonds (def. 17a)
A, American bond; B, Flemish bond; C, English bond; D, English cross bond

bond[2] (bond), *Obs.* —*n.* **1.** a serf or slave. —*adj.* **2.** in serfdom or slavery. [bef. 1050; ME *bonde,* OE *bonda* < ON *bōndi* HUSBANDMAN, contr. of **bōande,* var. of *būande,* c. OE *būend* dweller, equiv. to *bū(an)* to dwell (see BOOR) + *-end* n. suffix, as in FIEND, FRIEND]

Bond (bond), *n.* **1. Carrie** (nee **Jacobs**), 1862–1946, U.S. songwriter and author. **2. Julian,** born 1940, U.S. civil-rights leader and politician.

bond•age (bon′dij), *n.* **1.** slavery or involuntary servitude; serfdom. **2.** the state of being bound by or subjected to some external power or control. **3.** the state or practice of being physically restrained, as by being tied up, chained, or put in handcuffs, for sexual gratification. **4.** *Early Eng. Law.* personal subjection to the control of a superior; villeinage. [1250–1300; ME < AL *bondagium.* See BOND[2], -AGE]
—**Syn. 1.** captivity, restraint; prison. See **slavery. 2.** thralldom, captivity, confinement, imprisonment.

bond•ed (bon′did), *adj.* **1.** secured by or consisting of bonds: *bonded debt.* **2.** placed in bond: *bonded goods.* **3.** *Textiles.* made of two layers of the same fabric or of a fabric and a lining material attached to each other by a chemical process or adhesive: *bonded wool.* [1590–1600; BOND[1] + -ED[3]]

bond′ed ware′house, a warehouse for goods held in bond by the government. [1840–50]

bond′ed whis′key, bond[1] (def. 10).

bond•er•ize (bon′də rīz′), *v.t.,* **-ized, -iz•ing.** to coat (steel) with an anticorrosive phosphate solution, usually in preparation for the application of paint, enamel, or lacquer. Also, *esp. Brit.,* **bond′er•ise′.** [1935–40; back formation from *Bonderized,* a trademark, prob. equiv. to BOND[1] + -ER[1] + -IZE + -ED[2]]

bond•hold•er (bond′hōl′dər), *n.* a holder of a bond or bonds issued by a government or corporation. [1815–25; BOND[1] + HOLDER] —**bond′hold′ing,** *adj., n.*

bond′ immuniza′tion, immunization (def. 2).

bond•ing (bon′ding), *n.* **1.** *Psychol., Animal Behav.* **a.** a relationship that usually begins at the time of birth between a parent and offspring and that establishes the basis for an ongoing mutual attachment. **b.** the establishment of a pair bond. **2.** a close friendship that develops between adults, often as a result of intense experiences, as those shared in military combat. **3.** *Dentistry.* a technique or procedure for restoring the discolored or damaged surface of a tooth by coating it with a highly durable resinous material that adheres to the existing enamel. [1670–80, for earlier sense; BOND[1] + -ING[1]]

bond•maid (bond′mād′), *n.* **1.** a female slave. **2.** a woman bound to service without wages. [1520–30; BOND[2] + MAID]

bond•man (bond′mən), *n., pl.* **-men. 1.** a male slave. **2.** a man bound to service without wages. **3.** *Old Eng. Law.* a villein or other unfree tenant. Also, **bondsman.** [1200–50; ME *bonde man.* See BOND[2], MAN[1]]

bond′ pa′per, a superior variety of paper usually with high cotton fiber content, esp. used for stationery. Also called **bond.** [1875–80]

bond′ serv′ant, 1. a person who serves in bondage; slave. **2.** a person bound to service without wages. Also, **bond′-serv′ant.** [1525–35]

bond•slave (bond′slāv′), *n.* a person held in bondage. [1555–65; BOND[2] + SLAVE]

bonds•man[1] (bondz′mən), *n., pl.* **-men.** *Law.* a person who by bond becomes surety for another. [1725–35; *bond's man* man of the bond, i.e., its signer; see BOND[1], 'S[1], MAN[1]]

bonds•man[2] (bondz′mən), *n., pl.* **-men.** bondman. [1250–1300; ME *bondesman.* See BOND[2], 'S[1], MAN[1]]

bond•stone (bond′stōn′), *n.* a stone, as a perpend, for bonding facing masonry to a masonry backing. [1835–45; BOND[1] + STONE]

bonds•wom•an[1] (bondz′wo͝om′ən), *n., pl.* **-wom•en.** *Law.* a woman who is bound or who by bond becomes surety for another. [1605–15; *bond's woman* woman of the bond, i.e., its signer; see BONDSMAN[1], WOMAN]

bonds•wom•an[2] (bondz′wo͝om′ən), *n., pl.* **-wom•en.** bondwoman. [BOND[2] + 'S[1] + WOMAN]

bon•duc (bon′duk), *n.* a semitropical tree, *Caesalpinia bonducella,* of the legume family, the decorative seeds of which are used for jewelry and rosaries. [‡1940–45; < F < Ar *bunduq* hazelnut << Gk *Pontikòn* (*káryon*) hazelnut, lit., Pontic nut]

bond•wom•an (bond′wo͝om′ən), *n., pl.* **-wom•en.** a female slave. [1350–1400; ME *bonde womman.* See BOND[2], WOMAN]

bone (bōn), *n., v.,* **boned, bon•ing,** *adv.* —*n.* **1.** *Anat., Zool.* **a.** one of the structures composing the skeleton of a vertebrate. **b.** the hard connective tissue forming the substance of the skeleton of most vertebrates, composed of a collagen-rich organic matrix impregnated with calcium, phosphate, and other minerals. **2.** such a structure from an edible animal, usually with meat adhering to it, as an article of food: *Pea soup should be made with a ham bone.* **3.** any of various similarly hard or structural animal substances, as ivory or whalebone. **4.** something made of or resembling such a substance. **5.** a small concession, intended to pacify or quiet; a conciliatory bribe or gift: *The administration threw the student protesters a couple of bones, but refused to make any basic changes in the curriculum or requirements.* **6. bones, a.** the skeleton. **b.** a body: *Let his bones rest in peace.* **c.** *Games Slang.* dice. **d.** (*cap.*) See **Mr. Bones. e.** a simple rhythm instrument consisting of two sometimes curved bars or short strips of bone, ivory, wood, or the like, held between the fingers of one hand and clacked together. **7.** the color of bone; ivory or off-white. **8.** a flat strip of whalebone or other material for stiffening corsets, petticoats, etc.; stay. **9.** *Games Slang.* a domino. **10. feel in one's bones,** to think or feel intuitively: *She felt in her bones that it was going to be a momentous day.* **11. have a bone to pick with someone,** to have cause to disagree or argue with someone: *The teacher had a bone to pick with him because his homework paper was identical with his neighbor's.* **12. make no bones about, a.** to deal with in a direct manner; act or speak openly: *He makes no bones about his dislike of modern music.* **b.** to have no fear of or objection to. **13. to the bone, a.** to the essentials; to the minimum: *The government cut social service programs to the bone.* **b.** to an extreme degree; thoroughly: *chilled to the bone.* —*v.t.* **14.** to remove the bones from: *to bone a turkey.* **15.** to put whalebone or another stiffener into (clothing). **16.** *Agric.* to put bone meal into (feed, fertilizer, etc.). **17. bone up,** *Informal.* to study intensely; cram: *We're going to have to bone up for the exam.* —*adv.* **18.** completely; absolutely: *bone tired.* [bef. 900; ME *bo(o)n,* OE *bān;* c. OFris, OS *bēn,* D *been* bone, ON *bein* bone, leg, G *Bein* leg (*-bein* bone, in compounds); < Gmc **bainan* (neut.), prob. orig. ptp. (cf. OIr *benaid* (he) hews), meaning "lopped off," from butchering of animals; orig. in phrase **bainan astan* lopped-off bone or branch (hence, "leg," as a branch of the body); r. **astan* bone < IE **Host-* (> L *os(s),* Albanian *asht,* Avestan *ast-,* Hittite *hast-ai*), which fell together in Gmc with **astaz* branch (> G *Ast*) < IE **osdos* (> Gk *ózos,* Armenian *ost*)]

Bône (bōn), *n.* former name of **Annaba.**

bone′ ash′, a white ash obtained by calcining bones, used as a fertilizer and in the making of bone china. Also called **bone′ earth′.** [1615–25]

CONCISE PRONUNCIATION KEY: act, cāpe, dâre, pärt; set, ēqual; *if,* īce; ox, ōver, ôrder, oil, bo͝ok, bo͞ot, out; up, ûrge; child; sing; shoe; thin, *th*at; zh as in *treasure.* ə = *a* as in *alone, e* as in *system, i* as in *easily, o* as in *gallop, u* as in *circus;* ᵊ as in *fire* (fīᵊr), *hour* (ouᵊr). l and n can serve as syllabic consonants, as in *cradle* (krād′l), and *button* (but′n). See the full key inside the front cover.

bone•black (bōn′blak′), *n.* a black, carbonaceous substance obtained by calcining bones in closed vessels, used as a black pigment, a decolorizing agent, etc. Also, **bone′ black′.** [1805–15; BONE[1] + BLACK]

bone′ cell′, *Biol.* a cell found in bone in any of its functional states; an osteoblast, osteoclast, or osteocyte. [1830–40]

bone′ chi′na, a fine, naturally white china made with bone ash. Also called **bone porcelain.** [1900–05]

bone′ conduc′tion, *Med.* the transmission of sound vibrations to the internal ear through the cranial bones (opposed to *air conduction*).

bone-crush•ing (bōn′krush′ing), *adj.* **1.** powerful or constricting enough to crush one's bones: *a bone-crushing handshake.* **2.** extremely painful, troublesome, costly, etc.: *a bone-crushing mortgage.* [1670–80]

boned (bōnd), *adj.* **1.** having a particular kind of bone or bony structure (used in combination): *beautifully boned; raw-boned; small-boned.* **2.** having the bones taken out; cooked or served with the bones removed: *boned chicken; boned veal.* **3.** braced or supported with stays, as a corset. **4.** fertilized with bone: *boned land.* [1250–1300; ME; see BONE[1], -ED[3]]

bone-dry (bōn′drī′), *adj.* **1.** very dry. **2.** very thirsty. **3.** *Slang.* dry (def. 17). **4.** *Ceram.* (of clay) thoroughly dried. [1815–25]

bone′ earth′. See **bone ash.** [1850–55]

bone′ fel′on, *Chiefly Southern U.S.* felon[2].

bone•fish (bōn′fish′), *n., pl.* **-fish•es,** (*esp. collectively*) **-fish.** a marine game fish, *Albula vulpes,* found in shallow tropical waters, having a skeleton composed of numerous small, fine bones. Also called **ladyfish.** [1725–35, *Amer.*; BONE[1] + FISH]

bone•head (bōn′hed′), *Slang.* —*n.* **1.** a foolish or stupid person; blockhead. —*adj.* **2.** being of, by, or for a stupid or unthinking person: *a bonehead mistake.* [1905–10, *Amer.*; BONE[1] + HEAD] —**bone′head′ed,** *adj.* —**bone′head′ed•ness,** *n.*

bone′ mar′row, marrow[1] (def. 1).

bone′-mar•row trans′plant (bōn′mar′ō), *Surg.* a technique in which a small amount of bone marrow is withdrawn by a syringe from a donor's pelvic bone and injected into a patient whose ability to make new blood cells has been impaired by a disease, as anemia or cancer, or by exposure to radiation.

bone′ meal′, *Agric.* bones ground to a coarse powder, used as fertilizer or feed. Also, **bone′meal′.** [1840–50, *Amer.*]

bone′ of conten′tion, a subject, cause, or focal point of a dispute: *The terms of the old man's will were a bone of contention to his survivors.* [1705–15]

bone′ oil′, a fetid, tarry liquid obtained in the dry distillation of bone.

bone′ por′celain. See **bone china.** [1880–85]

bon•er[1] (bō′nər), *n.* a person or thing that bones. [1895–1900; BONE[1] + -ER[1]]

bon•er[2] (bō′nər), *n.* a foolish and obvious blunder; stupid mistake. [1910–15, *Amer.*; BONE(HEAD) + -ER[1]]

bone•set (bōn′set′), *n.* any composite plant of the genus *Eupatorium,* esp. *E. perfoliatum,* of North America, having white flowers in a flat-topped cluster. Also called **thoroughwort.** [1810–20, *Amer.*; BONE[1] + SET (v.), so named (by hyperbole) because supposed to have healing properties]

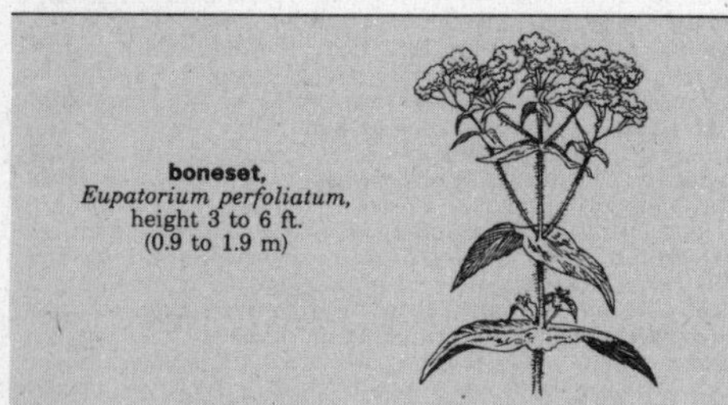

boneset, *Eupatorium perfoliatum,* height 3 to 6 ft. (0.9 to 1.9 m)

bone•set•ter (bōn′set′ər), *n.* a person who treats or sets fractures, broken or dislocated bones, or the like, esp. one who is not a regular physician or surgeon; healer. [1425–75; late ME; see BONE[1], SETTER]

bone′ shak′er, *Slang.* **1.** an early-model bicycle, esp. one with hard rubber tires. **2.** any uncomfortable vehicle. **3.** a rough ride in a vehicle.

bone′ spav′in, *Vet. Pathol.* See under **spavin** (def. 1).

bone′ tur′quoise, fossil bone or ivory that has been colored naturally or artificially so as to resemble turquoise. Also called **fossil turquoise, odontolite.**

bone•yard (bōn′yärd′), *n.* **1.** *Slang.* a cemetery. **2.** *Slang.* an area where old or discarded cars, ships, planes, etc., are collected prior to being broken up for scrap or otherwise disposed of. **3.** Also called **stock.** *Dominoes.* the bank, consisting of the remaining dominoes after each person has made an initial draw. **4.** a place or area where the bones of wild animals accumulate or are collected. [1850–55, *Amer.*; BONE[1] + YARD[2]]

bon•fire (bon′fīᵊr′), *n.* **1.** a large fire built in the open air, for warmth, entertainment, or celebration, to burn leaves, garbage, etc., or as a signal. **2.** any fire built in the open. [1375–1425; late ME *bone fire,* i.e., a fire with bones for fuel]

CONCISE ETYMOLOGY KEY: <, descended or borrowed from; >, whence; b., blend of, blended; c., cognate with; cf., compare; deriv., derivative; equiv., equivalent; imit., imitative; obl., oblique; r., replacing; s., stem; sp., spelling, spelled; resp., respelling, respelled; trans., translation; ?, origin unknown; *, unattested; ‡, probably earlier than. See the full key inside the front cover.

bong[1] (bong, bông), *n.* **1.** a dull, resonant sound, as of a large bell. —*v.i.* **2.** to produce this sound: *The church bell bonged promptly at noon.* [1855–60; imit.]

bong[2] (bong, bông), *n.* a type of hookah or water pipe for smoking marijuana or other drugs. [of uncert. orig.]

bon•go[1] (bong′gō, bông′-), *n., pl.* **-gos,** (*esp. collectively*) **-go.** a reddish-brown antelope, *Taurotragus eurycerus,* of the forests of tropical Africa, having white stripes and large, spirally twisted horns. [1860–65; prob. < a Bantu language; cf. Lingala *mongu* an antelope]

bongo[1], *Taurotragus eurycerus,* 4 ft. (1.2 m) high at shoulder

bon•go[2] (bong′gō, bông′-), *n., pl.* **-gos, -goes.** one of a pair of small tuned drums, played by beating with the fingers. Also called **bon′go drum′.** [1915–20, *Amer.*; < AmerSp *bongó*] —**bon′go•ist,** *n.*

bon gré, mal gré (bôɴ′ grā′ mal′ grā′), *French.* whether willing or not; willy-nilly.

Bon•heur (bo nûr′; *Fr.* bô nœr′), *n.* **Ro•sa** (rō′zə; *Fr.* rô zȧ′), (*Maria Rosalie Bonheur*), 1822–99, French painter.

bon•heur-du-jour (bə nûr′do͞o zho͝or′, -dyo͞o-, -də-; *Fr.* bô nœr dy zho͞or′), *n., pl.* **bon•heurs-du-jour** (bə nûr′do͞o zho͝or′, -dyo͞o-, -də-; *Fr.* bô nœr dy-zho͞or′). *French Furniture.* a delicate fall-front desk of the late 18th and early 19th centuries. [1875–80; < F: lit., happiness of the day, from the favor it found in its time]

bon•ho•mie (bon′ə mē′, bon′ə mē′; *Fr.* bô nô mē′), *n.* frank and simple good-heartedness; a good-natured manner; friendliness; geniality. [1795–1805; < F, equiv. to *bonhomme* good-natured man (see BOON[2], HOMO) + -ie -Y[3]] —**bon•ho•mous** (bon′ə məs), *adj.*

Bon•homme Rich•ard (bon′əm rich′ərd; *Fr.* bô nôm rē shȧr′), the flagship of John Paul Jones.

Bon•i•face (bon′ə fās′, -fis; *for 4 also Fr.* bô nē fȧs′), *n.* **1.** **Saint** (*Wynfrith*), A.D. 680?–755?, English monk who became a missionary in Germany. **2.** a jovial innkeeper in George Farquhar's *The Beaux' Stratagem.* **3.** (*l.c.*) any landlord or innkeeper. **4.** a male given name: from a Latin word meaning "doer of good."

Boniface I, Saint, died A.D. 422, pope 418–422.

Boniface II, pope A.D. 530–532.

Boniface III, pope A.D. 607.

Boniface IV, Saint, pope A.D. 608–615.

Boniface V, died A.D. 625, pope 619–625.

Boniface VI, pope A.D. 896.

Boniface VII, antipope A.D. 974, 984–985.

Boniface VIII, (*Benedetto Caetani*) c1235–1303, Italian ecclesiastic: pope 1294–1303.

Boniface IX, (*Pietro Tomacelli*) died 1404, Italian ecclesiastic: pope 1389–1404.

bon′ing knife′, a small kitchen knife having a narrow blade for boning meat or fish.

Bon•ing•ton (bon′ing tən), *n.* **Richard Parkes** (pärks), 1801–28, English painter.

Bo′nin Is′lands (bō′nin), a group of islands in the N Pacific, SE of and belonging to Japan: under U.S. administration 1945–68. 40 sq. mi. (104 sq. km). Japanese, **Ogasawara Jima.**

Bo•ni•ta (bə nē′tə, bō-), *n.* a female given name.

bo•ni•to (bə nē′tō), *n., pl.* (*esp. collectively*) **-to,** (*esp. referring to two or more kinds or species*) **-tos. 1.** any mackerellike fish of the genus *Sarda,* as *S. sarda,* of the Atlantic Ocean. **2.** any of several related species, as the skipjack, *Euthynnus pelamis.* [1590–1600; < Sp < Ar *bainīth*]

bon•jour (bôɴ zho͞or′), *interj. French.* good day; good morning; hello.

bonk (bongk), *v.t., v.i. Slang.* to hit, strike, collide, etc.: *to get bonked on the head; cars bonking into each other.* [perh. var. of BONG[1]]

bon•kers (bong′kərz), *adj. Slang.* mentally unbalanced; mad; crazy. [1945–50; of uncert. orig.; for final element, cf. -ERS]

bon mar•ché (bôɴ mar shā′), *pl.* ***bons mar•chés*** (bôɴ mar shā′). *French.* a bargain. [lit., good market]

bon mot (bon′ mō′; *Fr.* bôɴ mō′), *pl.* **bons mots** (bon′ mōz′; *Fr.* bôɴ mō′). a witty remark or comment; clever saying; witticism. [1725–35; < F: lit., good word; see BOON[2], MOTTO]

Bonn (bon; *Ger.* bôn), *n.* a city in W Germany, on the Rhine: seat of the government; former capital of West Germany. 291,400.

Bon•nard (bô nȧr′), *n.* **Pierre** (pyer), 1867–1947, French painter.

Bon•naz (bə naz′), *n.* (*sometimes l.c.*) embroidery made by machine. [1880–85; named after J. *Bonnaz,* 19th-century French inventor]

bonne (bôn), *n., pl.* ***bonnes*** (bôn). *French.* **1.** a maidservant. **2.** a child's nurse. [lit., good (fem.)]

bonne a•mie (bô nȧ mē′), *pl.* ***bonnes a•mies*** (bôn zȧ-mē′). *French.* **1.** a good female friend. **2.** a female sweetheart or lover.

bonne bouche (bôn bo͞osh′), *pl.* ***bonnes bouches*** (bôn bo͞osh′). *French.* **1.** a tidbit. **2.** an elegant treat: *The special wine was a* bonne bouche. [lit., good mouth]

bonne femme (bôn fȧm′), *French Cookery.* prepared in simple style, as in a cream sauce containing mushrooms: *fillet of sole bonne femme.* [1815–25; < F *à la bonne femme* lit., in the manner of a good housewife]

bonne foi (bôn fwȧ′), *French.* sincerity. [lit., good faith]

bonne nuit (bôn nwē′), *French.* good night.

bon•net (bon′it), *n.* **1.** a hat, usually tying under the chin and often framing the face, formerly much worn by women but now worn mostly by children. **2.** *Informal.* any hat worn by women. **3.** *Chiefly Scot.* a man's or boy's cap. **4.** a bonnetlike headdress: *an Indian war bonnet.* **5.** any of various hoods, covers, or protective devices. **6.** a cowl, hood, or wind cap for a fireplace or chimney, to stabilize the draft. **7.** the part of a valve casing through which the stem passes and that forms a guide and seal for the stem. **8.** a chamber at the top of a hot-air furnace from which the leaders emerge. **9.** *Chiefly Brit.* an automobile hood. **10.** *Naut.* a supplementary piece of canvas laced to the foot of a fore-and-aft sail, esp. a jib, in light winds. —*v.t.* **11.** to put a bonnet on. [1375–1425; late ME *bonet* < MF; OF *bonet* material from which hats are made, perh. < Old Low Franconian **bunni* something bound (< Gmc **bund-,* n. deriv. of **bind-* BIND; cf. BUNDLE), with *-et* -ET; cf. LL *abonnis, obbonis* ribbon forming part of a headdress < Gmc, with a prefix corresponding to MHG *obe-* ABOVE] —**bon′net•less,** *adj.* —**bon′net•like′,** *adj.*

Bon•net (bô ne′), *n.* **Georges** (zhôrzh), 1889–1973, French statesman.

bon′net glass′, monteith (def. 2).

bon•net•head (bon′it hed′), *n.* a hammerhead shark, *Sphyrna tiburo,* found in shallow waters from Brazil to Massachusetts, having a spade-shaped head. Also called **bonnet shark, shovelhead.** [1875–80, *Amer.*; BONNET + HEAD]

bonne•tière (bun tyâr′; *Fr.* bôn tyer′), *n., pl.* **-tières** (-tyârz′; *Fr.* -tyer′). *French Furniture.* a tall, narrow wardrobe of the 18th century, found esp. in Normandy and Brittany. [< F: lit., hosier]

bon′net mon′key, a long-tailed South Indian macaque, *Macaca radiata,* having a gray-brown coat and a caplike thatch of hair at the top of its head. Also called **bon′net macaque′.**

bon•net rouge (bô ne ro͞ozh′), *pl.* ***bon•nets rouges*** (bô ne ro͞ozh′). *French.* **1.** a red liberty cap, worn by extremists during the French Revolution. **2.** an extremist or radical.

bon′net shark′, bonnethead.

bon′net top′, *U.S. Furniture.* a top to a secretary, highboy, etc., following in outline a broken pediment on the front. Cf. **dome top, hooded top.**

bonnet top of highboy

Bon•ne•ville (bon′ə vil′), *n.* **Lake,** a prehistoric lake in Utah, E Nevada, and S Idaho: Great Salt Lake is its remnant. 350 mi. (564 km) long.

Bon′neville Flats′, an area of salt flats in the W part of Great Salt Lake Desert, in NW Utah: site of automobile speed tests. Also called **Bon′neville Salt′ Flats′.**

Bon•nie (bon′ē), *n.* a female given name: from the Latin word meaning "good." Also, **Bon′ny.**

bon•ny (bon′ē), *adj.,* **-ni•er, -ni•est,** *adv., n.* —*adj.* **1.** *Chiefly Scot.* pleasing to the eye; handsome; pretty. **2.** *Brit. Dial.* **a.** (of people) healthy, sweet, and lively. **b.** (of places) placid; tranquil. **c.** pleasing; agreeable; good. —*adv.* **3.** *Brit. Dial.* pleasingly; agreeably; very well. —*n.* **4.** *Scot. and North Eng. Archaic.* a pretty girl or young woman. Also, **bon′nie.** [1425–75; late ME (Scots) *bonie,* perh. < OF *bon* good + *-ie* -Y[1], perh. by analogy with *jolie* JOLLY] —**bon′ni•ly,** *adv.* —**bon′ni•ness,** *n.*

bon•ny•clab•ber (bon′ē klab′ər), *n. Northern and Midland U.S.* clabber (def. 1). Also, **bon•ny•clap•per** (bon′ē klap′ər). [1625–35; < Ir *bainne clabair* lit., milk of the clapper (i.e., of the churn lid or dasher)]
—**Regional Variation.** See **clabber.**

bo•no•bo (bə nō′bō), *n., pl.* **-bos.** See **pygmy chimpanzee.**

Bo•non•ci•ni (bô′nôn chē′nē), *n.* **Gio•van•ni Ma•ri•a** (jô vän′nē mä rē′ä), 1640–78, and his sons **Giovanni Bat•ti•sta** (bät tē′stä), 1670–1747, and **Marc An•to•nio** (märk än tô′nyô), 1675–1726, Italian composers. Also, **Buononcini.**

Bön•pa (bön pä′), *n.* a member of the Bön sect.

bon•sai (bon sī′, -zī′, bōn-, bon′sī, bōn′-), *n., pl.* **-sai. 1.** a tree or shrub that has been dwarfed, as by pruning the roots and pinching, and is grown in a pot or other container and trained to produce a desired shape or effect. **2.** the art or hobby of developing and growing such a plant or plants. [1945–50; < Japn *bon-sai* tray planting < MChin, equiv. to Chin *pén* tray + *zāi* plant, shoot]

bon•soir (bôN SWAR′), *interj. French.* good evening; good night.

bon•spiel (bon′spēl′), *n.* a competition or meet in curling at which teams from several clubs or districts compete with one another. [1555–65; Scots dial., perh. < D or LG; cf. D *spel* game, play (MD, c. OHG *spil,* G *Spiel*); identity of first element uncert.]

bon•te•bok (bon′tē bok′), *n., pl.* **-boks,** (*esp. collectively*) **-bok.** a purplish-red antelope, *Damaliscus dorcas,* of southern Africa, having a white face and rump: now nearly extinct. [1780–90; < Afrik, equiv. to *bont* piebald (<< ML *punctus* dotted; see POINT) + *bok* BUCK[1]]

bontebok, *Damaliscus dorcas,* 3½ ft. (1.1 m) high at shoulder; horns 15 in. (38 cm); head and body 5 ft. (1.5 m); tail 1 ft. (0.3 m)

bon•te•buck (bon′tē buk′), *n., pl.* **-bucks,** (*esp. collectively*) **-buck.** bontebok.

Bon•tem•pel•li (bôn′tem pel′lē), *n.* **Mas•si•mo** (mäs′sē mô), 1878–1960, Italian novelist.

Bon•toc (bon tok′), *n., pl.* **-tocs,** (*esp. collectively*) **-toc.** Bontok.

Bon•tok (bon tok′), *n., pl.* **-toks,** (*esp. collectively*) **-tok.** a member of a people who inhabit northern Luzon in the Philippines.

bon ton (bon′ ton′; *Fr.* bôN tôN′), **1.** good or elegant form or style. **2.** something regarded as fashionably correct: *The bon ton in this circle is to dress well and know influential people.* **3.** fashionable society. [1765–75; < F: lit., good tone. See BOON[2], TONE]

bo•nus (bō′nəs), *n., pl.* **-nus•es. 1.** something given or paid over and above what is due. **2.** a sum of money granted or given to an employee, a returned soldier, etc., in addition to regular pay, usually in appreciation for work done, length of service, accumulated favors, etc. **3.** something free, as an extra dividend, given by a corporation to a purchaser of its securities. **4.** a premium paid for a loan, contract, etc. **5.** something extra or additional given freely: *Every purchaser of a pound of tea received a strainer as a bonus.* [1765–75; < L: good]
—**Syn. 1.** reward, honorarium, gift. **2.** BONUS, BOUNTY, PREMIUM refer to something extra beyond a stipulated payment. A BONUS is a gift to reward performance, paid either by a private employer or by a government: *a bonus based on salary; a soldiers' bonus.* A BOUNTY is a public aid or reward offered to stimulate interest in a specific purpose or undertaking and to encourage performance: *a bounty for killing wolves.* A PREMIUM is usually something additional given as an inducement to buy, produce, or the like: *a premium received with a magazine subscription.*

Bo′nus Ar′my, *U.S. Hist.* a group of 12,000 World War I veterans who massed in Washington, D.C., the summer of 1932 to induce Congress to appropriate moneys for the payment of bonus certificates granted in 1924.

bo′nus ba′by, an athlete who is paid a substantial bonus to sign his or her first professional contract.

Bo′nus Even′tus, the ancient Roman god of agricultural prosperity. Also called **Eventus.**

bon vi•vant (bon′ vē vänt′; *Fr.* bôN vē väN′), *pl.* **bons vi•vants** (bon′ vē vänts′; *Fr.* bôN vē väN′). a person who lives luxuriously and enjoys good food and drink. [< F]

bon vo•yage (bon′ voi äzh′; *Fr.* bôN VWA YAZH′), (have a) pleasant trip. [1490–1500; < F: lit., good journey. See BOON[2], VOYAGE]

bonx•ie (bongk′sē), *n.* skua (def. 1). [1765–75; of uncert. orig.; final element is appar. -SY]

bon•y (bō′nē), *adj.,* **bon•i•er, bon•i•est. 1.** of or like bone. **2.** full of bones. **3.** having prominent bones; big-boned. **4.** skinny; emaciated. [1350–1400; ME *boni.* See BONE[1], -Y[1]] —**bon′i•ness,** *n.*

bon′y fish′, any fish of the class Osteichthyes, characterized by gill covers, an air bladder, and a skeleton composed of bone in addition to cartilage. [1805–15, *Amer.*]

bon′y lab′yrinth, *Anat.* See under **labyrinth** (def. 6a).

bon•y•tail (bō′nē tāl′), *n.* a fish, *Gila elegans,* found in the Colorado River, having flaring fins and a thin caudal peduncle. [BONY + TAIL[1]]

bonze (bonz), *n.* a Buddhist monk, esp. of Japan or China. [1580–90; < MF < Pg *bonzo* or NL *bonzius* < Japn *bonsō, bonzō* ordinary priest (*bon-* ordinary + *sō* priest < MChin, equiv. to Chin *fán-sēng*); or < dial. Japn *bonzu* for *bōzu* priest]

bon•zer (bon′zər), *adj. Australian.* remarkable; wonderful. [1900–05; orig. uncert.]

boo[1] (bo͞o), *interj., n., pl.* **boos,** *v.,* **booed, boo•ing.** —*interj.* **1.** (used to express contempt or disapprobation or to startle or frighten). —*n.* **2.** an exclamation of contempt or disapproval: *a loud boo from the bleachers.* —*v.i.* **3.** to cry *boo* in derision. —*v.t.* **4.** to show disapproval of by booing. [1810–20; expressive formation]

boo[2] (bo͞o, bō), *n. Slang.* marijuana. Also called **boo grass.** [1955–60; of uncert. orig.]

boob[1] (bo͞ob), *Slang.* —*n.* **1.** a stupid person; fool; dunce. **2.** *Brit.* a blunder; mistake. —*v.i.* **3.** *Brit.* to blunder. [1905–10, *Amer.*; back formation from BOOBY[1]]

boob[2] (bo͞ob), *n. Slang* (*sometimes vulgar*). a female breast. [1945–50; appar. back formation from BOOBY[2]]

boob•ie (bo͝ob′ē), *n.* bube.

boob•oi•sie (bo͞o′bwä zē′), *n.* a segment of the general public composed of uneducated, uncultured persons. [b. BOOB[1] and BOURGEOISIE; coined by H.L. Mencken in 1922]

boo-boo (bo͞o′bo͞o′), *n., pl.* **-boos.** *Slang.* **1.** a stupid or silly mistake; blunder. **2.** a minor injury. [1950–55, *Amer.*; baby talk]

boo•book (bo͞o′bo͝ok, -bo͞ok), *n.* a small, reddish-brown spotted owl, *Ninox boobook,* native to Australia and New Zealand. [1795–1805; < Dharuk *bokbok* (imit.)]

boob′ tube′, *Informal.* **1.** television. **2.** a television set. [1965–70; rhyming coinage, from the notion that television programming is foolish, induces foolishness, or is watched by foolish people]

boo•by[1] (bo͞o′bē), *n., pl.* **-bies. 1.** a stupid person; dunce. **2.** a gannet of the genus *Sula,* having a bright bill, bright feet, or both: some are endangered. [1590–1600; earlier *pooby,* appar. b. *poop* to befool (now obs.) and BABY; (def. 2) perh. by association with Sp *bobo* < L *balbus* stuttering] —**boo′by•ish,** *adj.*

boob•y[2] (bo͞ob′ē), *n., pl.* **boob•ies.** *Slang* (*sometimes vulgar*). a female breast. [1930–35, *Amer.*; prob. var. of earlier BUBBY]

boo′by hatch′, 1. *Naut.* **a.** a small hatch giving access to a ladder from the weather deck of a vessel to the interior of the hull. **b.** a small companion secured over a deck opening. **c.** a hoodlike hatch cover having a sliding top. **2.** *Slang.* **a.** an insane asylum. **b.** jail. [1830–40]

boo′by prize′, a prize given in good-natured ridicule to the worst player or team in a game or contest. [1885–90]

boo′by trap′, 1. a hidden bomb or mine so placed that it will be set off by an unsuspecting person through such means as moving an apparently harmless object. **2.** any hidden trap set for an unsuspecting person. [1840–50]

boo•by-trap (bo͞o′bē trap′), *v.t.,* **-trapped, -trap•ping.** to set with or as if with a booby trap; attach a booby trap to or in. [1940–45]

boo•dle (bo͞od′l), *n., v.,* **-dled, -dling.** *Slang.* —*n.* **1.** the lot, pack, or crowd: *Send the whole boodle back to the factory.* **2.** a large quantity of something, esp. money: *He's worth a boodle.* **3.** a bribe or other illicit payment, esp. to or from a politician; graft. **4.** stolen goods; loot; booty; swag. **5. kit and boodle.** See **kit**[1] (def. 8). —*v.i.* **6.** to obtain money dishonestly, as by bribery or swindling. [1615–25, *Amer.*; < D *boedel* property] —**boo′dler,** *n.*

boog•er (bo͝og′ər), *n.* **1.** *Informal.* any person or thing: *That shark was a mean-looking booger. Paddle the little booger and send him home.* **2.** *Slang.* a piece of dried mucus in or from the nose. **3.** bogeyman. **4.** *Chiefly South Midland and Southern U.S.* any ghost, hobgoblin, or other frightening apparition. [1865–70; perh. var. of Brit. dial. *boggard* goblin, bogy; in senses of defs. 1 and 2 conflated with BUGGER[1]]

boog•er•man (bo͝og′ər man′, bo͞o′gər-), *n., pl.* **-men.** *South Midland and Southern U.S.* bogeyman. [b. BOOGER and BOGEYMAN]

boog•ey•man (bo͝og′ē man′, bo͞o′gē-), *n., pl.* **-men.** bogeyman. [1840–50; var. of BOGYMAN]

boog•ie (bo͝og′ē, bo͞o′gē), *n., v.,* **-ied, -ie•ing.** —*n.* **1.** *Slang* (*disparaging and offensive*). a black. **2.** boogie-woogie. **3.** a lively form of rock 'n' roll, based on the blues. —*v.i.* **4.** to dance energetically, esp. to rock music. **5.** *Slang.* (often fol. by *on down*) to go. [1920–25, *Amer.*; of uncert. orig.]

Boog′ie Board′, *Trademark.* a small, flexible plastic surfboard.

boog•ie•man (bo͝og′ē man′, bo͞o′gē-), *n., pl.* **-men.** bogeyman.

boog•ie-woog•ie (bo͝og′ē wo͝og′ē, bo͞o′gē wo͞o′gē), *n. Jazz.* a form of instrumental blues, esp. for piano, using melodic variations over a constantly repeated bass figure. Also called **boogie.** [1925–30, *Amer.*; rhyming compound perh. based on BOOGIE]

boo′ grass′, boo[2].

boo•hoo (bo͞o′ho͞o′), *v.,* **-hooed, -hoo•ing,** *n., pl.* **-hoos.** *Informal.* —*v.i.* **1.** to weep noisily; blubber. —*n.* **2.** the sound of noisy weeping. [1515–25; rhyming compound based on BOO]

boo′jum tree′ (bo͞o′jəm), a tree, *Idria columnaris,* native to Baja California, having spreading spiny branches, deciduous leaves, and yellow flowers. Also called **cirio.** [1960–65; after the *boojum,* an imaginary creature invented by Lewis Carroll in the poem *The Hunting of the Snark* (1876)]

book (bo͝ok), *n.* **1.** a written or printed work of fiction or nonfiction, usually on sheets of paper fastened or bound together within covers. **2.** a number of sheets of blank or ruled paper bound together for writing, recording business transactions, etc. **3.** a division of a literary work, esp. one of the larger divisions. **4. the Book,** the Bible. **5.** *Music.* the text or libretto of an opera, operetta, or musical. **6. books.** See **book of account. 7.** *Jazz.* the total repertoire of a band. **8.** a script or story for a play. **9.** a record of bets, as on a horse race. **10.** *Cards.* the number of basic tricks or cards that must be taken before any trick or card counts in the score. **11.** a set or packet of tickets, checks, stamps, matches, etc., bound together like a book. **12.** anything that serves for the recording of facts or events: *The petrified tree was a book of Nature.* **13.** *Sports.* a collection of facts and information about the usual playing habits, weaknesses, methods, etc., of an opposing team or player, esp. in baseball: *The White Sox book on Mickey Mantle cautioned pitchers to keep the ball fast and high.* **14.** *Stock Exchange.* **a.** the customers served by each registered representative in a brokerage house. **b.** a loose-leaf binder kept by a specialist to record orders to buy and sell stock at specified prices. **15.** a pile or package of leaves, as of tobacco. **16.** *Mineral.* a thick block or crystal of mica. **17.** a magazine: used esp. in magazine publishing. **18.** See **book value. 19.** *Slang.* bookmaker (def. 1). **20. bring to book,** to call to account; bring to justice: *Someday he will be brought to book for his misdeeds.* **21. by the book,** according to the correct or established form; in the usual manner: *an unimaginative individual who does everything by the book.* **22. close the books,** to balance accounts at the end of an accounting period; settle accounts. **23. cook the books,** *Informal.* See **cook** (def. 10). **24. in one's bad books,** out of favor; disliked by someone: *He's in the boss's bad books.* **25. in one's book,** in one's personal judgment or opinion: *In my book, he's not to be trusted.* **26. in one's good books,** in favor; liked by someone. **27. like a book,** completely; thoroughly: *She knew the area like a book.* **28. make book, a.** to accept or place the bets of others, as on horse races, esp. as a business. **b.** to wager; bet: *You can make book on it that he won't arrive in time.* **29. off the books,** done or performed for cash or without keeping full business records: esp. as a way to avoid paying income tax, employment benefits, etc.: *Much of his work as a night watchman is done off the books.* **30. one for the book** or **books,** a noteworthy incident; something extraordinary: *The daring rescue was one for the book.* **31. on the books,** entered in a list or record: *He claims to have graduated from Harvard, but his name is not on the books.* **32. the book, a.** a set of rules, conventions, or standards: *The solution was not according to the book but it served the purpose.* **b.** the telephone book: *I've looked him up, but he's not in the book.* **33. throw the book at,** *Informal.* **a.** to sentence (an offender, lawbreaker, etc.) to the maximum penalties for all charges against that person. **b.** to punish or chide severely. **34. without book, a.** from memory. **b.** without authority: *to punish without book.* **35. write the book,** to be the prototype, originator, leader, etc., of: *So far as investment banking is concerned, they wrote the book.* —*v.t.* **36.** to enter in a book or list; record; register. **37.** to reserve or make a reservation for (a hotel room, passage on a ship, etc.): *We booked a table at our favorite restaurant.* **38.** to register or list (a person) for a place, transportation, appointment, etc.: *The travel agent booked us for next week's cruise.* **39.** to engage for one or more performances. **40.** to enter an official charge against (an arrested suspect) on a police register. **41.** to act as a bookmaker for (a bettor, bet, or sum of money): *The Philadelphia syndicate books 25 million dollars a year on horse racing.* —*v.i.* **42.** to register one's name. **43.** to engage a place, services, etc. **44.** *Slang.* **a.** to study hard, as a student before an exam: *He left the party early to book.* **b.** to leave; depart: *I'm bored with this party, let's book.* **c.** to work as a bookmaker: *He started a restaurant with money he got from booking.* **45. book in,** to sign in, as at a job. **46. book out,** to sign out, as at a job. **47. book up,** to sell out in advance: *The hotel is booked up for the Christmas holidays.* —*adj.* **48.** of or pertaining to a book or books: *the book department; a book salesman.* **49.** derived or learned from or based on books: *a book knowledge of sailing.* **50.** shown by a book of account: *The firm's book profit was $53,680.* [bef. 900; ME, OE *bōc;* c. D *boek,* ON *bōk,* G *Buch;* akin to Goth *boka* letter (of the alphabet) and not of known relation to BEECH, as is often assumed] —**book′less,** *adj.* —**book′like′,** *adj.*
—**Syn. 39.** reserve, schedule, bill, slate, program.
—**Ant. 39.** cancel.

book′ bag′, a bag or satchel used esp. by a student for carrying books. Also, **book′bag′.**

book•bind•er (bo͝ok′bīn′dər), *n.* a person or company whose business or work is the binding of books. [1300–50; ME *bok-bindere;* see BOOK, BINDER[1]]

book•bind•er•y (bo͝ok′bīn′də rē), *n., pl.* **-er•ies.** bindery. [1805–15, *Amer.*; BOOKBINDER + -RY]

book•bind•ing (bo͝ok′bīn′ding), *n.* the process or art of binding books. [1765–75; BOOK + BINDING]

book′ burn′ing, the destruction of writings of which the subject, the view of the author, or the like is considered politically or socially objectionable: used as a means of censorship or oppression. [1890–95]

book•case (bo͝ok′kās′), *n.* a set of shelves for books. [1720–30; BOOK + CASE[2]]

book′ club′, 1. a company or other organization that sells books to its subscribers, often at a discount and usually through the mail. **2.** a club organized for the discussion and reviewing of books. Also called, *esp. Brit.,* **book society.** [1785–95]

book•craft (bo͝ok′kraft′, -kräft′), *n. Archaic.* literary skill; authorship. [bef. 900; OE *bōccræft* (not recorded in ME). See BOOK, CRAFT]

book•end (bo͝ok′end′), *n.* a support placed at the end of a row of books to hold them upright, usually used in pairs. [1905–10; BOOK + END[1]]

book•er (bo͝ok′ər), *n.* See **booking agent.**

book′ gill′, the gill of a horseshoe crab, composed of numerous membranous structures arranged like the leaves of a closed book. [1895–1900]

book•ie (bo͝ok′ē), *n.* bookmaker (def. 1). [1880–85; BOOK(MAKER) + -IE]

book•ing (bo͝ok′ing), *n.* **1.** a contract, engagement, or scheduled performance of a professional entertainer. **2.**

CONCISE PRONUNCIATION KEY: act, cāpe, dâre, pärt; set, ēqual; *if,* īce; ox, ōver, ôrder, oil, bo͝ok, bo͞ot, out; up, ûrge; child; sing; shoe; thin, *th*at; zh as in *treasure.* ə = *a* as in *alone, e* as in *system, i* as in *easily, o* as in *gallop, u* as in *circus;* ᵊ as in *fire* (fīᵊr), *hour* (ouᵊr). l and n can serve as syllabic consonants, as in *cradle* (krād′l), and *button* (but′n). See the full key inside the front cover.

reservation (def. 5). **3.** the act of a person who books. [1635–45; BOOK + -ING[1]]

book′ing a′gent, an agent who makes bookings, as reservations for travel or the theater or engagements for performers, for clients.

book′ing clerk′, **1.** a person who sells tickets, as for a train or plane. **2.** a person who arranges and lists passage for persons, baggage, and goods. [1830–40]

book′ing of′fice, *Brit.* a ticket office, esp. one in a railway station. [1830–40]

book•ish (bo͝ok′ish), *adj.* **1.** given or devoted to reading or study. **2.** more acquainted with books than with real life. **3.** of or pertaining to books; literary. **4.** stilted; pedantic. [1560–70; BOOK + -ISH[1]] —**book′ish•ly,** *adv.* —**book′ish•ness,** *n.*
—**Syn. 4.** academic, scholastic.

book′ jack′et, a removable paper cover, usually illustrated, for protecting the binding of a book and usually giving information about the book and the author. [1925–30]

book•keep•ing (bo͝ok′kē′ping), *n.* the work or skill of keeping account books or systematic records of money transactions (distinguished from *accounting*). [1680–90; BOOK + KEEPING] —**book′keep′er,** *n.*

book′ learn′ing, **1.** knowledge acquired by reading books, as distinguished from that obtained through observation and experience. **2.** formal education: *She thought that common sense was just as important as book learning.* [1580–90] —**book-learn•ed** (bo͝ok′lûr′nid, -lûrnd′), *adj.*

book•let (bo͝ok′lit), *n.* a little book, esp. one with paper covers; pamphlet. [1855–60; BOOK + -LET]

book′let pane′, *Philately.* any of a number of panes or small pages of postage stamps, stapled together into a booklet for the convenience of users.

book′ list′, a list of books, esp. a list of recommended or required readings. [1935–40]

book′ lore′. See **book learning.** [bef. 1000; ME, OE]

book•louse (bo͝ok′lous′), *n., pl.* **-lice** (-līs′). any of numerous minute, wingless insects of the order Psocoptera, often living among books or papers. Also, **book′ louse′.** [1865–70; BOOK + LOUSE]

book•lov•er (bo͝ok′luv′ər), *n.* a person who enjoys reading books. [1860–65; BOOK + LOVER]

book′ lung′, the respiratory organ of a spider, scorpion, or other arachnid, composed of thin, membranous structures arranged like the leaves of a book. [1895–1900]

book•mak•er (bo͝ok′mā′kər), *n.* **1.** a person who makes a business of accepting the bets of others on the outcome of sports contests, esp. of horse races. **2.** a person who makes books. [1375–1425; late ME *bokmakere.* See BOOK, MAKER] —**book′mak′ing,** *n., adj.*

book•man (bo͝ok′mən, -man′), *n., pl.* **-men** (-mən, -men′). **1.** a studious or learned man; scholar. **2.** a person whose occupation is selling or publishing books. [1575–85; BOOK + -MAN]

book•mark (bo͝ok′märk′), *n.* **1.** a ribbon or other marker placed between the pages of a book to mark a place. **2.** a bookplate. [1860–65; BOOK + MARK[1]]

book′ match′, a match in or from a matchbook. [1935–40]

book•mo•bile (bo͝ok′mə bēl′, -mō-), *n.* an automobile, small truck, or trailer constructed to carry books and serve as a traveling library, as for communities where libraries are not accessible. [1935–40; BOOK + -MOBILE]

book′ of account′, **1.** any journal, ledger, and supporting vouchers included in a system of accounts. **2. books of account,** the original records and books used in recording business transactions.

Book′ of Books′, the Bible.

Book′ of Chang′es. See ***I Ching.***

Book′ of Com′mon Prayer′, the service book of the Church of England, essentially adopted but changed in details by other churches of the Anglican communion.

book′ of hours′, a book containing the prescribed order of prayers, readings from Scripture, and rites for the canonical hours. Also, **Book′ of Hours′.**

Book′ of Kells′ (kelz), an illuminated manuscript (A.D. c800) in the Hiberno-Saxon style.

Book′ of Mor′mon, a sacred book of the Mormon Church, believed by Mormons to be an abridgment by a prophet **(Mormon)** of a record of certain ancient peoples in America, written on golden plates, and discovered and translated (1827–30) by Joseph Smith.

Book′ of Odes′, a collection of 305 poems compiled in the 6th century B.C. by Confucius. Chinese, ***Shih Ching, Shih King.***

book′ of orig′inal en′try, *Bookkeeping.* **1.** a book in which transactions are recorded before being transferred into a ledger. **2.** journal (def. 5a, b).

Book′ of the Dead′, a collection of ancient Egyptian papyrus books, many with elaborate illustrations, each containing prayers, hymns, incantations, and formulas for the behavior of the souls of the dead.

book•pa•per (bo͝ok′pā′pər), *n.* the paper used in printing books, esp. when of superior quality. [BOOK + PAPER]

book•plate (bo͝ok′plāt′), *n.* a label bearing the owner's name and often a design, coat of arms, or the like, for pasting on the front end paper of a book. [1785–95; BOOK + PLATE[1]]

CONCISE ETYMOLOGY KEY: <, descended or borrowed from; >, whence; b., blend of, blended; c., cognate with; cf., compare; deriv., derivative; equiv., equivalent; imit., imitative; obl., oblique; r., replacing; s., stem; sp., spelling, spelled; resp., respelling, respelled; trans., translation; ?, origin unknown; *, unattested; ‡, probably earlier than. See the full key inside the front cover.

book•rack (bo͝ok′rak′), *n.* **1.** a support for an open book. **2.** a rack for holding books. [1880–85; BOOK + RACK[1]]

book•rest (bo͝ok′rest′), *n.* a support for an open book, usually holding it at a slight angle. [1865–70; BOOK + REST[1]]

book′ review′, **1.** a critical description, evaluation, or analysis of a book, esp. one published in a newspaper or magazine. **2.** a section or page of a newspaper or magazine devoted to such material. [1860–65] —**book′ review′er.** —**book′ review′ing.**

book′ scor′pion, pseudoscorpion.

book•sell•er (bo͝ok′sel′ər), *n.* the owner or proprietor of a bookstore. [1520–30; BOOK + SELLER] —**book′•sell′ing,** *n.*

book′ share′, a share of a mutual fund credited to the account of a shareholder without the physical issuance of a certificate evidencing ownership. Also called **uncertificated share.**

book•shelf (bo͝ok′shelf′), *n., pl.* **-shelves.** a shelf for holding books, esp. one of several shelves in a bookcase. [1810–20; BOOK + SHELF]

book′ soci′ety, *Chiefly Brit.* See **book club.** [1805–15]

book•stack (bo͝ok′stak′), *n.* Usually, **bookstacks.** stack (def. 4). [1895–1900; BOOK + STACK]

book•stall (bo͝ok′stôl′), *n.* **1.** a stand, booth, or stall at which books are sold, usually secondhand. **2.** *Brit.* a newsstand. [1790–1800; BOOK + STALL[1]]

book•stand (bo͝ok′stand′), *n.* **1.** a bookrack. **2.** a bookstall. [1800–10; BOOK + STAND]

book•store (bo͝ok′stôr′, -stōr′), *n.* a store where books are sold. Also called **book•shop** (bo͝ok′shop′). [1755–65, *Amer.*; BOOK + STORE]

book′ tile′, a flat, cellular roofing tile having two parallel edges one of which is convex and the other concave, so that a number may be fit together edge to edge between rafters, joists, etc.

book′ val′ue, **1.** the value of a business, property, etc., as stated in a book of accounts (distinguished from *market value*). **2.** total assets minus all liabilities; net worth. [1895–1900]

book•work (bo͝ok′wûrk′), *n.* **1.** work or research that requires studying or reading, as distinguished from laboratory experimentation or the like. **2.** bookkeeping or other paperwork necessary to the running of a business. **3.** *Print.* work on books or pamphlets, as distinguished from work on newspapers. Also, **book′-work′.** [1840–50; BOOK + WORK; cf. OE *bōcweorc* study, independently formed from same elements]

book•worm (bo͝ok′wûrm′), *n.* **1.** a person devoted to reading or studying. **2.** any of various insects that feed on books, esp. a booklouse. [1590–1600; BOOK + WORM]

Boole (bo͞ol), *n.* **George,** 1815–64, English mathematician and logician.

Bool′e•an al′gebra (bo͞o′lē ən), **1.** *Logic.* a deductive logical system, usually applied to classes, in which, under the operations of intersection and symmetric difference, classes are treated as algebraic quantities. **2.** *Math.* a ring with a multiplicative identity in which every element is an idempotent. [1885–90; named after G. BOOLE; see -AN]

Bool′ean opera′tion, *Computers.* any operation in which each of the operands and the result take one of two values. [1960–65]

Bool′ean ring′, *Math.* a nonempty collection of sets having the properties that the union of two sets of the collection is a set in the collection and that the relative complement of each set with respect to any other set is in the collection. Cf. **algebra of sets.** [1935–40; named after G. BOOLE; see -AN]

Bool′ean sum′, *Math.* See **symmetric difference.** [1960–65; named after G. BOOLE; see -AN]

Boole's′ inequal′ity, *Math.* the theorem that the probability of several events occurring is less than or equal to the sum of the probabilities of each event occurring. [named after G. BOOLE]

boom[1] (bo͞om), *v.i.* **1.** to make a deep, prolonged, resonant sound. **2.** to move with a resounding rush or great impetus. **3.** to progress, grow, or flourish vigorously, as a business or a city: *Her business is booming since she enlarged the store.* —*v.t.* **4.** to give forth with a booming sound (often fol. by *out*): *The clock boomed out nine.* **5.** to boost; campaign for vigorously: *His followers are booming George for mayor.* —*n.* **6.** a deep, prolonged, resonant sound. **7.** the resonant cry of a bird or animal. **8.** a buzzing, humming, or droning, as of a bee or beetle. **9.** a rapid increase in price, development, numbers, etc.: *a boom in housing construction.* **10.** a period of rapid economic growth, prosperity, high wages and prices, and relatively full employment. **11.** a rise in popularity, as of a political candidate. —*adj.* **12.** caused by or characteristic of a boom: *boom prices.* [1400–50; 1910–15 for def. 10; late ME *bombon, bummyn* to buzz; c. D *bommen,* G *bummen,* orig. imit.] —**boom′ing•ly,** *adv.*
—**Syn. 3.** prosper, thrive, develop.

boom[2] (bo͞om), *n.* **1.** *Naut.* any of various more or less horizontal spars or poles for extending the feet of sails, esp. fore-and-aft sails, for handling cargo, suspending mooring lines alongside a vessel, pushing a vessel away from wharves, etc. **2.** *Aeron.* **a.** an outrigger used on certain aircraft for connecting the tail surfaces to the fuselage. **b.** a maneuverable and retractable pipe on a tanker aircraft for refueling another aircraft in flight. **c.** chord[1] (def. 4). **3.** a chain, cable, series of connected floating timbers, or the like, serving to obstruct navigation, confine floating timber, etc. **4.** the area thus shut off. **5.** *Mach.* a spar or beam projecting from the mast of a derrick for supporting or guiding the weights to be lifted. **6.** (on a motion-picture or television stage) a spar or beam on a mobile crane for holding or manipulating a microphone or camera. **7. lower the boom,** to take decisive punitive action: *The government has lowered the boom on tax evaders.* —*v.t.* **8.** to extend or position, as a sail (usually fol. by *out* or *off*). **9.** to manipulate (an object) by or as by means of a crane or derrick. —*v.i.* **10.** to sail at full speed. [1635–45; < D: tree, pole, BEAM] —**boom′less,** *adj.*

boom-and-bust (bo͞om′ən bust′), *adj.* characteristic of a period of economic prosperity followed by a depression. Also, **boom-or-bust.** [1940–45]

boom′ box′, box (def. 20b). [‡1980–85]

boom•er (bo͞o′mər), *n.* **1.** a person or thing that booms. **2.** a person who settles in areas or towns that are booming. **3.** *Informal.* See **baby boomer.** **4.** *Informal.* a wandering or migratory worker; hobo. **5.** a period of sudden and decisive economic growth: *July was a boomer for the retail trade.* **6.** *Informal.* a person, fad, etc., that enjoys a brief popularity or financial success: *A new group of boomers made this season's hit record.* **7.** an enthusiastic supporter; booster: *The boomers tell us our town can double its size.* **8.** *Australian.* a fully grown male kangaroo, esp. a large one. [1820–30; BOOM[1] + -ER[1]]

boo•mer•ang (bo͞o′mə rang′), *n.* **1.** a bent or curved piece of tough wood used by the Australian Aborigines as a throwing club, one form of which can be thrown so as to return to the thrower. **2.** something, as a scheme or argument, that does injury to the originator. **3.** *Theat.* **a.** a mobile platform, adjustable to different levels, for painting scenery. **b.** a batten, usually suspended vertically in the wings, for holding lighting units. —*v.i.* **4.** to come back or return, as a boomerang. **5.** to cause harm to the originator; backfire. [1820–30; < Dharuk *bumarin^y*]

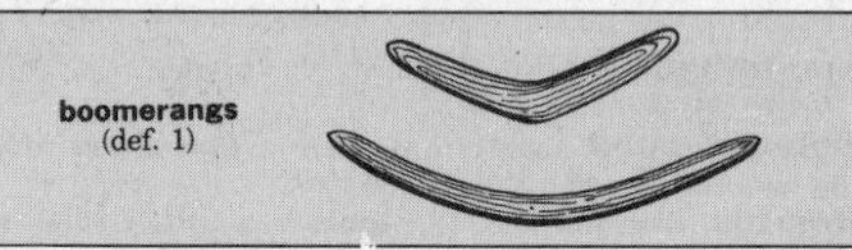
boomerangs (def. 1)

Boom′er State′, Oklahoma (used as a nickname).

boom•ie (bo͞o′mē), *n. Canadian Slang.* a person who was an adolescent in the 1960's. [(BABY) BOOM + -IE]

boom•kin (bo͞om′kin), *n. Naut.* bumpkin[2]. [See BUMPKIN[2]]

boom•let (bo͞om′lit), *n.* a brief increase, as in business activity or political popularity. [1875–80, *Amer.*; BOOM[1] + -LET]

boom-or-bust (bo͞om′ər bust′), *adj.* boom-and-bust.

boom′ shot′, *Motion Pictures, Television.* a shot taken by a camera on a boom.

boom•slang (bo͞om′släng, -slang), *n.* a venomous, tree-dwelling snake, *Dispholidus typus,* of tropical and southern Africa, having black to greenish scales. [1785–95; < Afrik, equiv. to *boom* tree (see BOOM[2], BEAM) + *slang* snake]

boom′ town′, a town that has grown very rapidly as a result of sudden prosperity. Also, **boom′town′.** [1895–1900]

boom•y (bo͞o′mē), *adj.,* **boom•i•er, boom•i•est.** **1.** excessively resonant: *a loudspeaker with a boomy sound in the lower register.* **2.** affected by, characterized by, or indicative of an economic boom. [1925–30; BOOM[1] + -Y[1]]

boon[1] (bo͞on), *n.* **1.** something to be thankful for; blessing; benefit. **2.** something that is asked; a favor sought. [1125–75; ME *bone* < ON *bōn* prayer; c. OE *bēn*] —**boon′less,** *adj.*

boon[2] (bo͞on), *adj.* **1.** jolly; jovial; convivial: *boon companions.* **2.** *Archaic.* kindly; gracious; bounteous. [1275–1325; ME *bone* < MF < L *bonus* good]

boon[3] (bo͞on), *n. Textiles.* the ligneous waste product obtained by braking and scutching flax. Also called **shive, shove.** [1350–1400; ME (north) *bone;* cf. OE *bune* reed]

boon•dock•er (bo͞on′dok′ər), *n. Slang.* See **combat boot.** [1950–55, *Amer.*; BOONDOCK(S) + -ER[1]]

boon•docks (bo͞on′doks′), *n.* (*used with a plural v.*) **1.** an uninhabited area with thick natural vegetation, as a backwoods or marsh (usually prec. by *the*). **2.** a remote rural area (usually prec. by *the*): *The company moved to a small town out in the boondocks.* [1940–45, *Amer.*; < Tagalog *bundok* mountain + -s[3] (in locative derivations such as *the sticks, the dumps,* etc.)]
—**Syn. 2.** back country, backwoods, provinces; boonies, sticks.

boon•dog•gle (bo͞on′dog′əl, -dô′gəl), *n., v.,* **-gled, -gling.** —*n.* **1.** a product of simple manual skill, as a plaited leather cord for the neck or a knife sheath, made typically by a camper or a scout. **2.** work of little or no value done merely to keep or look busy. **3.** a project funded by the federal government out of political favoritism that is of no real value to the community or the nation. —*v.t.* **4.** to deceive or attempt to deceive: *to boondoggle investors into a low-interest scheme.* —*v.i.* **5.** to do work of little or no practical value merely to keep or look busy. [1930–35, *Amer.*; said to have been coined by R. H. Link, American scoutmaster, as name for def. 1] —**boon′dog′gler,** *n.*

Boone (bo͞on), *n.* **1. Daniel,** 1734–1820, American pioneer, esp. in Kentucky. **2.** a city in central Iowa. 12,602. **3.** a town in NW North Carolina. 10,191.

boong (bo͝ong, bo͞o′ong), *n. Australian Informal* (*disparaging*). **1.** a native of New Guinea. **2.** an Aborigine. [1940–45; of obscure orig.]

boon•ga•ry (bo͝ong′gə rē), *n., pl.* **-ries.** a small, tree-dwelling kangaroo, *Dendrolagus lumholtzi,* inhabiting northeastern Queensland. Also called **Lumholtz's kangaroo.** [1885–90; < Warrgamay (Austral Aboriginal language spoken on the lower Herbert River, Queensland) *bulŋgarri*]

boon•ies (bo͞o′nēz), *n.* (*used with a plural v.*) *Informal.* boondocks. [see BOONDOCKS, -IE]

boor (bo͝or), *n.* **1.** a churlish, rude, or unmannerly person. **2.** a country bumpkin; rustic; yokel. **3.** peasant. **4.** Boer. [1545–55; < D *boer* or LG *būr* (c. G *Bauer* farmer), deriv. of Gmc **bū-* to dwell, build, cultivate; see -ER[1]; cf. BOND[2]]
—Syn. 1. lout, oaf, boob, churl, philistine, vulgarian.

boor•ish (bo͝or′ish), *adj.* of or like a boor; unmannered; crude; insensitive. [1555–65; BOOR + -ISH[1]] **—boor′ish•ly,** *adv.* **—boor′ish•ness,** *n.*
—Syn. coarse, uncouth, loutish, churlish. BOORISH, OAFISH, RUDE, UNCOUTH all describe persons, acts, manners, or mannerisms that violate in some way the generally accepted canons of polite, considerate behavior. BOORISH, originally referring to behavior characteristic of an unlettered rustic or peasant, now implies a coarse and blatant lack of sensitivity to the feelings or values of others: *a boorish refusal to acknowledge greetings.* OAFISH suggests slow-witted, loutlike, clumsy behavior: *oafish table manners.* RUDE has the widest scope of meaning of these words; it suggests either purposefully impudent discourtesy or, less frequently, a rough crudity of appearance or manner: *a rude remark; a rude thatched hut.* UNCOUTH stresses most strongly in modern use a lack of good manners, whether arising from ignorance or brashness: *uncouth laughter; an uncouth way of staring at strangers.* **—Ant.** refined.

boost (bo͞ost), *v.t.* **1.** to lift or raise by pushing from behind or below. **2.** to advance or aid by speaking well of; promote: *She always boosts her hometown.* **3.** to increase; raise: *to boost prices; to boost the horsepower of the car by 20 percent.* **4.** *Slang.* to steal, esp. to shoplift: *Two typewriters were boosted from the office last night.* —*v.i.* **5.** *Slang.* to engage in stealing, esp. shoplifting. —*n.* **6.** an upward shove or raise; lift. **7.** an increase; rise: *There's been a tremendous boost in food prices.* **8.** an act, remark, or the like, that helps one's progress, morale, efforts, etc.: *His pep talk was the boost our team needed.* [1805–15, *Amer.*; perh. Scots dial. *boose* (var. of *pouss* PUSH) + (HOI)ST]
—Syn. 7. hike, growth, upsurge, upswing, uptick.

boost•er (bo͞o′stər), *n.* **1.** a person or thing that boosts, esp. an energetic and enthusiastic supporter. **2.** *Elect.* a device connected in series with a current for increasing or decreasing the nominal circuit voltage. **3.** *Railroads.* any machine, device, phenomenon, etc., that helps to move a train, as a tailwind, downgrade, roller bearings, or esp. a helper locomotive. **4.** *Mil.* an explosive more powerful than a primer, for ensuring the detonation of the main charge of a shell. **5.** *Rocketry.* **a.** a rocket engine used as the principal source of thrust in the takeoff of a rocket or missile. **b.** the first stage containing this engine and its fuel supply, which may or may not be detached from the rocket when the fuel has been consumed. **6.** *Med.* Also called **boost′er dose′, boost′er shot′.** a dose of an immunizing substance given to maintain or renew the effect of a previous one. **7.** *Pharm.* a chemical compound, medicinal substance, or the like, that serves as a synergist. **8.** a radio-frequency amplifier for connecting between a radio or television antenna and the receiving set to intensify the received signal. **9.** an auxiliary pump, used in a pipeline or other system, to add to or maintain a prevailing amount of pressure or vacuum. **10.** *Slang.* a shoplifter or petty thief. [1885–90, *Amer.*; BOOST + -ER[1]] **—boost′er•ish,** *adj.*

boost′er ca′ble, *Auto.* either of a pair of electric cables having clamps at each end and used for starting the engine of a vehicle whose battery is dead. Also called **jumper cable, jumper.**

boost•er•ism (bo͞o′stə riz′əm), *n.* the action or policy of enthusiastically promoting something, as a city, product, or way of life: *boosterism about the latest world's fair.* [1910–15; BOOSTER + -ISM]

boost′er seat′, a padded seat that can be placed on a chair seat, for seating a child at the proper height, as at a table or in a barber chair.

boost-start (bo͞ost′stärt′), *v.t. Auto.* jump-start.

boot[1] (bo͞ot), *n.* **1.** a covering of leather, rubber, or the like, for the foot and all or part of the leg. **2.** *Chiefly Brit.* any shoe or outer foot covering reaching to the ankle. **3.** an overshoe, esp. one of rubber or other waterproof material. **4.** an instrument of torture for the leg, consisting of a kind of vise extending from the knee to the ankle, tightened around the leg by means of screws. **5.** any sheathlike protective covering: *a boot for a weak automobile tire.* **6.** a protective covering for the foot and part of the leg of a horse. **7.** a protecting cover or apron for the driver's seat of an open vehicle. **8.** the receptacle or place into which the top of a convertible car fits when lowered. **9.** a cloth covering for this receptacle or place. **10.** *Brit.* the trunk of an automobile. **11.** a rubber covering for the connection between each spark-plug terminal and ignition cable in an automotive ignition system. **12.** Also called **Denver boot.** a metal device attached to the wheel of a parked car so that it cannot be driven away until a fine is paid or the owner reports to the police: used by police to catch scofflaws. **13.** *U.S. Navy, Marines.* a recruit. **14.** *Music.* the box that holds the reed in the reed pipe of an organ. **15.** a kick. **16.** *Slang.* a dismissal; discharge: *They gave him the boot for coming in late.* **17.** *Informal.* a sensation of pleasure or amusement: *Watching that young skater win a gold medal gave me a real boot.* **18.** *Baseball.* a fumble of a ball batted on the ground, usually to the infield. **19. bet your boots,** to be sure or certain: *You can bet your boots that I'll be there!* **20. die with one's boots on, a.** to die while actively engaged in one's work, profession, etc. **b.** to die fighting, esp. in battle, or in some worthy cause. Also, *esp. Brit.,* **die in one's boots. 21. get a boot,** *Informal.* to derive keen enjoyment: *I really got a boot out of his ridiculous stories.* —*v.t.* **22.** to kick; drive by kicking: *The boy booted a tin can down the street.* **23.** *Football.* to kick. **24.** *Baseball.* to fumble (a ground ball). **25.** to put boots on; equip or provide with boots. **26.** Also, **bootstrap.** *Computers.* **a.** to start (a computer) by loading the operating system. **b.** to start (a program) by loading the first few instructions, which will then bring in the rest. **27.** *Slang.* to dismiss; discharge: *They booted him out of school for not studying.* **28.** to attach a Denver boot to: *Police will boot any car with unpaid fines.* **29.** to torture with the boot. [1275–1325; ME *bote* < AF, OF; of uncert. orig.]

boot[2] (bo͞ot), *n.* **1.** *Archaic.* something given into the bargain. **2.** *Obs.* **a.** advantage. **b.** remedy; relief; help. **3. to boot,** in addition; besides: *We received an extra week's pay to boot.* —*v.i., v.t.* **4.** *Archaic.* to be of profit, advantage, or avail (to): *It boots thee not to complain.* [bef. 1000; ME *bote,* OE *bōt* advantage; c. D *boete,* G *Busse,* ON *bōt,* Goth *bota;* see BET, BETTER[1]]

boot[3] (bo͞ot), *n. Archaic.* booty; spoil; plunder. [1585–95; special use of BOOT[2] by assoc. with BOOTY]

boot•black (bo͞ot′blak′), *n.* a person who shines shoes and boots for a living. [1810–20, *Amer.*; BOOT[1] + BLACK]

boot′ camp′, *U.S. Navy, Marines.* a camp for training recruits. [1940–45, *Amer.*]

boot•ed (bo͞o′tid), *adj.* **1.** equipped with or wearing boots. **2.** *Ornith.* (of the tarsus of certain birds) covered with a continuous horny, bootlike sheath. [1545–55; BOOT[1] + -ED[3]]

boot•ee (bo͞o tē′ *or, esp. for 1, 3* bo͞o′tē), *n.* **1.** Also, **bootie.** a baby's socklike shoe, usually knitted or crocheted, and calf-length or shorter. **2.** any boot having a short leg. **3.** bootie (def. 1). [1790–1800, *Amer.*; BOOT[1] + *-ee,* perh. as pseudo-F sp. of -Y[2] (-IE)]

boot•er•y (bo͞o′tə rē), *n., pl.* **-er•ies.** a store selling boots, shoes, etc. [1915–20, *Amer.*; BOOT[1] + -ERY]

Bo•ö•tes (bō ō′tēz), *n., gen.* **-tis** (-tis). *Astron.* the Herdsman, a northern constellation between Ursa Major and Serpens, containing the bright star Arcturus. [1650–60; < L < Gk *Boṓtēs* lit., ox-driver]

booth (bo͞oth), *n., pl.* **booths** (bo͞othz, bo͞oths). **1.** a stall, compartment, or light structure for the sale of goods or for display purposes, as at a market, exhibition, or fair. **2.** a small compartment or boxlike room for a specific use by one occupant: *a telephone booth; a projection booth.* **3.** a small, temporary structure used by voters at elections. **4.** a partly enclosed compartment or partitioned area, as in a restaurant or music store, equipped for a specific use by one or more persons. **5.** a temporary structure of any material, as boughs, canvas, or boards, used esp. for shelter; shed. [1150–1200; ME *bōthe* < ON *būth* (cf. ODan *bōth* booth); c. G *Bude*]

Booth (bo͞oth; *Brit.* bo͞oth), *n.* **1. Bal•ling•ton** (bal′ing-tən), 1859–1940, founder of the Volunteers of America 1896 (son of William Booth). **2. Edwin Thomas,** 1833–93, U.S. actor (brother of John Wilkes Booth). **3. Evangeline Co•ry** (kôr′ē, kōr′ē), 1865?–1950, general of the Salvation Army 1934–39 (daughter of William Booth). **4. John Wilkes,** 1838–65, U.S. actor: assassin of Abraham Lincoln (brother of Edwin Thomas Booth). **5. Junius Brutus,** 1796–1852, English actor (father of Edwin and John Booth). **6. William** (*"General Booth"*), 1829–1912, English religious leader: founder of the Salvation Army 1865. **7. William Bram•well** (bram′wel′, -wəl), 1856–1929, general of the Salvation Army (son of William Booth). **8.** a male given name.

boot•heel (bo͞ot′hēl′), *n.* (*sometimes cap.*) an area of SE Missouri where the Missouri-Arkansas border dips southward forming a rectangular-shaped extension of the state. [BOOT[1] + HEEL[1]; so called from the shape on the map; cf. PANHANDLE]

Boo•thi•a (bo͞o′thē ə), *n.* **1.** a peninsula in N Canada: the northernmost part of the mainland of North America; former location of the north magnetic pole. **2. Gulf of,** a gulf between this peninsula and Baffin Island.

boot′ hill′, *Western U.S.* a cemetery of a frontier settlement, esp. one in which gunfighters were buried. [1900–05, *Amer.*]

boot′ hook′, one of a pair of L-shaped metal hooks fixed to a handle, for drawing on a boot by inserting it through a bootstrap. [1800–10]

boot•ie (bo͞o′tē), *n.* **1.** Also, **bootee.** a usually soft, sometimes disposable sock or bootlike covering for the foot or shoe, as for informal wear, warmth, or protection: *quilted booties for après-ski; germfree, throwaway booties for surgical teams.* **2.** bootee (def. 1). [1790–1800; BOOT[1] + -IE]

boot•ing (bo͞o′ting), *n.* the practice of dealing with scofflaws by attaching a boot to the wheel of a car, immobilizing it until its owner reports to the police or pays delinquent fines. [BOOT[1] + -ING[1]]

boot•jack (bo͞ot′jak′), *n.* **1.** a yokelike device for catching the heel of a boot, as a riding boot, to aid in removing it. **2.** a notch or molding for the same purpose, cut into a piece of furniture. [1835–45; BOOT[1] + JACK[1]]

boot•lace (bo͞ot′lās′), *n.* **1.** a long, strong lace used to fasten a boot. **2.** *Brit.* a shoelace. [1930–35; BOOT[1] + LACE]

boot′lace worm′, a brownish-black, ribbonlike nemertean, *Lineus longissimus.*

Boo•tle (bo͞ot′l), *n.* a city in Merseyside metropolitan county, in W England, on the Mersey estuary. 74,208.

boot•leg (bo͞ot′leg′), *n., v.,* **-legged, -leg•ging,** *adj.* —*n.* **1.** alcoholic liquor unlawfully made, sold, or transported, without registration or payment of taxes. **2.** the part of a boot that covers the leg. **3.** something, as a recording, made, reproduced, or sold illegally or without authorization: *a flurry of bootlegs to cash in on the rock star's death.* —*v.t.* **4.** to deal in (liquor or other goods) unlawfully. —*v.i.* **5.** to make, transport, or sell something, esp. liquor, illegally or without registration or payment of taxes. —*adj.* **6.** made, sold, or transported unlawfully. **7.** illegal or clandestine. **8.** of or pertaining to bootlegging. [1625–35, *Amer.*; BOOT[1] + LEG; secondary senses arose from practice of hiding a liquor bottle in the leg of one's boot] **—boot′leg′ger,** *n.*

boot•legged (bo͞ot′legd′), *adj.* bootleg. [see BOOTLEG, -ED[3]]

boot′leg play′, *Football.* a play in which the quarterback pretends to hand the ball to a teammate, hides it by placing it next to his hip, and runs with it.

boot•less (bo͞ot′lis), *adj.* without result, gain, or advantage; unavailing; useless. [bef. 1000; ME *bot(e)les,* OE *bōtlēas* unpardonable. See BOOT[2], -LESS] **—boot′•less•ly,** *adv.* **—boot′less•ness,** *n.*

boot•lick (bo͞ot′lik′), *v.t.* **1.** to seek the favor or goodwill of in a servile, degraded way; toady to. —*v.i.* **2.** to be a toady. [1835–45, *Amer.*; BOOT[1] + LICK] **—boot′•lick′er,** *n.*
—Syn. 1, 2. flatter, fawn; apple-polish.

boots (bo͞ots), *n., pl.* **boots.** *Brit.* a servant, as at a hotel, who blacks or polishes shoes and boots. [1615–25; pl. of BOOT[1]; see -S[3]]

boots′ and sad′dles, *U.S. Army.* a cavalry bugle call for mounted drill or formation.

boot•strap (bo͞ot′strap′), *n., adj., v.,* **-strapped, -strap•ping.** —*n.* **1.** a loop of leather or cloth sewn at the top rear, or sometimes on each side, of a boot to facilitate pulling it on. **2.** a means of advancing oneself or accomplishing something: *He used his business experience as a bootstrap to win voters.* **3. pull oneself up by one's bootstraps,** to help oneself without the aid of others; use one's resources: *I admire him for pulling himself up by his own bootstraps.* —*adj.* **4.** relying entirely on one's efforts and resources: *The business was a bootstrap operation for the first ten years.* **5.** self-generating or self-sustaining: *a bootstrap process.* —*v.t.* **6.** *Computers.* boot[1] (def. 26). **7.** to help (oneself) without the aid of others: *She spent years bootstrapping herself through college.* [1890–95; BOOT[1] + STRAP]

boot•top•ping (bo͞ot′top′ing), *n. Naut.* **1.** the area between the water lines of a ship when fully loaded and when unloaded. **2.** a distinctive band of paint covering this area. Also called **boot•top** (bo͞ot′top′). [1760–70; BOOT[1] + TOPPING]

boot′ tree′, a device of wood, metal, or plastic, inserted in a boot or shoe when it is not being worn, to preserve the shape. [1760–70]

boo•ty (bo͞o′tē), *n., pl.* **-ties. 1.** spoil taken from an enemy in war; plunder; pillage. **2.** something that is seized by violence and robbery. **3.** any prize or gain. [1425–75; late ME *botye,* var. of *buty* < MLG *bute* booty (orig. a sharing of the spoils); c. ON *býti* exchange, barter; *oo* of BOOT[2]] **—boo′ty•less,** *adj.*
—Syn. 1–3. spoils, loot, gain, takings, winnings, swag.

booze (bo͞oz), *n., v.,* **boozed, booz•ing.** *Informal.* —*n.* **1.** any alcoholic beverage; whiskey. **2.** a drinking bout or spree. —*v.i.* **3.** to drink alcohol, esp. to excess: *He continued to booze until his health finally gave out.* **4. booze it up,** to drink heavily and persistently. [1610–20; resp. of BOUSE[2], reflecting one of its pron. variants] **—booz′er,** *n.*

boozed-up (bo͞ozd′up′), *adj.* drunk; intoxicated. [1855–60; BOOZE + -ED[2]]

booze•hound (bo͞oz′hound′), *Informal. n.* a boozer. [1925–30; BOOZE + HOUND[1]]

booze-up (bo͞oz′up′), *n. Chiefly Brit.* a drinking spree. [1895–1900]

booz•y (bo͞o′zē), *adj.,* **booz•i•er, booz•i•est. 1.** drunken; intoxicated. **2.** addicted to liquor. [1520–30; BOOZE + -Y[1]] **—booz′i•ly,** *adv.* **—booz′i•ness,** *n.*

bop[1] (bop), *n., v.,* **bopped, bop•ping.** —*n.* **1.** Also called **bebop.** early modern jazz developed in the early 1940's and characterized by often dissonant triadic and chromatic chords, fast tempos and eccentric rhythms, intricate melodic lines punctuated by pop-tune phrases, and emphasizing the inventiveness of soloists. Cf. **cool jazz, hard bop, modern jazz, progressive jazz.** —*v.i.* **2.** *Slang.* to move, go, or proceed (often fol. by *on down*): *Let's bop on down to the party.* [1945–50, *Amer.*; (BE)BOP]

bop[2] (bop), *v.,* **bopped, bop•ping,** *n. Slang.* —*v.t.* **1.** to strike, as with the fist or a stick; hit. —*n.* **2.** a blow. [1935–40; var. of BOB[3]]

bo-peep (bō pēp′), *n.* peekaboo. [1520–30; *bo* (var. of BOO) + PEEP[1]]

Bo•phu•that•swa•na (bō′po͞o tät swä′nə), *n.* a self-governing Bantu territory of South Africa, consisting of several landlocked areas, along the NE part: granted independence in 1977 by South Africa, but not recognized by any other country as an independent state. 2,600,000; 16,988 sq. mi. (44,000 sq. km). *Cap.:* Mmabatho.

Bopp (bop; *Ger.* bôp), *n.* **Franz,** 1791–1867, German philologist.

bop•per (bop′ər), *n.* **1.** a musician who specializes in bop. **2.** a fan of bop. **3.** teenybopper. **4.** *Slang.* a hip, self-assured person. Also, **bop•ster** (bop′stər) (for defs. 1, 2). [BOP[1] + -ER[1]]

BOQ, *U.S. Mil.* bachelor officers' quarters.

bor-, var. of **boro-** esp. before a vowel.

bor., borough.

bo•ra[1] (bôr′ə, bōr′ə), *n. Meteorol.* (on the Adriatic coasts) a violent, dry, cold wind blowing from the north or northeast. [1860–65; < Upper It, var. of It *borea* BOREAS]

bo•ra[2] (bôr′ə, bōr′ə), *n. Australian.* an initiation rite of the Aborigines in which boys are accepted into the tribe as men. [1865–70; < Kamilaroi *būru* initiation rite, initiation belt]

Bo•ra Bo•ra (bôr′ə bôr′ə; bōr′ə bōr′ə), an island in the Society Islands, in the S Pacific, NW of Tahiti. ab. 2000; 15 sq. mi. (39 sq. km).

CONCISE PRONUNCIATION KEY: act, cāpe, dâre, pärt; set, ēqual; if, īce; ox, ōver, ôrder, oil, bo͝ok, bo͞ot, out; up, ûrge; child; sing; shoe; thin, *th*at; zh as in *treasure.* ə = *a* as in *alone, e* as in *system, i* as in *easily, o* as in *gallop, u* as in *circus;* ᵊ as in *fire* (fīᵊr), *hour* (ouᵊr). l and n can serve as syllabic consonants, as in *cradle* (krād′l), and *button* (but′n). See the full key inside the front cover.

bo·rac·ic (bə ras′ik, bô-, bō-), *adj. Chem.* boric. [1795–1805; *borac-* (s. of BORAX[1]) + -IC]

bo·ra·cite (bôr′ə sīt′, bōr′-), *n.* a strongly pyroelectric mineral, a borate and chloride of magnesium, $Mg_6Cl_2B_{14}O_{26}$, occurring in white or colorless cubic crystals or fine-grained masses. [1800–10; *borac-* (s. of BORAX[1]) + -ITE[1]]

bor·age (bôr′ij, bor′-, bûr′-), *n.* **1.** a plant, *Borago officinalis,* native to southern Europe, having hairy leaves and stems, used medicinally and in salads. Cf. **borage family. 2.** any of various allied or similar plants. [1250–1300; ME *burage* < AF *borage, bo(u)rache,* MF *bourage* < VL **burrāgō* (LL *burra* hair stuffing + *-gō* n. suffix)]

bor′age fam′ily, any member of the plant family Boraginaceae, typified by herbaceous plants, shrubs, and trees having simple, alternate, hairy leaves and usually blue, five-lobed flowers in a cluster that uncoils as they bloom, including borage, bugloss, and forget-me-not.

bo·rag·i·na·ceous (bə raj′ə nā′shəs, bô-, bō-), *adj.* belonging to the plant family Boraginaceae. Cf. **borage family.** [< NL *Boraginace(ae)* family name (*Boragin-,* s. of *Borago* genus name; see BORAGE + *-aceae* -ACEAE) + -OUS]

Bo·rah (bôr′ə, bōr′ə), *n.* **William Edgar,** 1865–1940, U.S. senator from Idaho 1906–40.

bor·ak (bôr′ək, bor′-), *n. Australian.* ridicule. [1835–45; < Wathawurrung (Austral Aboriginal language spoken around Geelong, Victoria) *borak* no]

bor·al (bôr′al, -əl, bōr′-), *n. Pharm.* a compound of an aluminum tartrate and borate, used chiefly as an astringent and antiseptic. [BOR(ATE) + AL(UMINUM)]

bo·rane (bôr′ān, bōr′-), *n. Chem.* any of the compounds, both neutral and anionic, of boron and hydrogen with formulas ranging from B_2H_6 to $B_{20}H_{16}$. Also called **boron hydride.** [< G *Boran* (1916); see BORON, -ANE]

Bo·rås (bo͞o RÔS′), *n.* a city in S Sweden, near Göteborg. 102,129.

bo·ras·ca (bə ras′kə), *n.* (esp. in the Mediterranean) a squall, usually accompanied by thunder and lightning. Also, **bo·ras·co** (bə ras′kō), **bo·rasque** (bə rask′). [1680–90; < It *bor(r)asca,* equiv. to *borr-* (<< Gk *borrâs,* Attic var. of *boréas* north wind) + *-asca* (n. suffix; perh. of pre-L orig.); r. *borasque* < MF]

bo·rate (*n.* bôr′āt, -it, bōr′-; *v.* bôr′āt, bōr′-), *n., v.,* **-rat·ed, -rat·ing.** *Chem.* —*n.* **1.** a salt or ester of boric acid. **2.** (loosely) a salt or ester of any acid containing boron. —*v.t.* **3.** to treat with borate, boric acid, or borax. [1810–20; BOR- + -ATE[2]]

bo·rax[1] (bôr′aks, -əks, bōr′-), *n., pl.* **bo·rax·es, bo·ra·ces** (bôr′ə sēz′, bōr′-). a white, water-soluble powder or crystals, hydrated sodium borate, $Na_2B_4O_7 \cdot 10H_2O$, occurring naturally or obtained from naturally occurring borates; tincal: used as a flux, cleansing agent, in the manufacture of glass, porcelain, and enamel, and in tanning. Also called **sodium borate, sodium pyroborate, sodium tetraborate.** [1350–1400; < ML << dial. Ar *būraq* < MPers *būrag;* r. ME *boras* < MF < ML *borax*]

bo·rax[2] (bôr′aks, -əks, bōr′-), *n.* cheap, showy, poorly made merchandise, esp. cheaply built furniture of an undistinguished or heterogeneous style. [1940–45, *Amer.;* of uncert. orig.]

bo′rax bead′, *Chem.* a bead of fused borax, used in chemical analysis for the identification of certain metal oxides.

bo′rax pentahy′drate, *Chem.* a white, crystalline, water-soluble solid, $Na_2B_4O_7 \cdot 5H_2O$, used chiefly for killing weeds, as a water softener, and as a disinfectant and deodorizing agent.

bo·ra·zine (bôr′ə zēn′, bōr′-), *n. Chem.* a colorless liquid, $B_3N_3H_6$, that hydrolyzes with water to form boron hydrides. It is the inorganic analogue of benzene with similar physical properties. Also, **bo·ra·zole** (bôr′ə zōl′, bōr′-). [BOR- + AZINE]

Bo·ra·zon (bôr′ə zon′, bōr′-), *Chem. Trademark.* a brand name for a cubic, diamondlike, extremely hard form of boron nitride, obtained at high temperatures and pressures: used as an abrasive and grinding agent.

bor·bo·ryg·mus (bôr′bə rig′məs), *n., pl.* **-mi** (-mī). *Physiol.* a rumbling or gurgling sound caused by the movement of gas in the intestines. [1710–20; < NL < Gk *borborygmós* intestinal rumbling]

Bor·deaux (bôr dō′), *n.* **1.** a seaport in and the capital of Gironde, in SW France, on the Garonne River. 226,281. **2.** any of various wines produced in the region surrounding Bordeaux, esp. claret. **3.** See **Bordeaux mixture.**

Bordeaux′ mix′ture, *Hort.* a fungicide consisting of a mixture of copper sulfate, lime, and water. [1890–95; free trans. of F *bouillie bordelaise.* See BOIL[1], BORDELAISE]

bor·del (bôr′dl), *n. Archaic.* a brothel. [1275–1325; ME < AF, OF, equiv. to *borde* wooden hut (< Gmc; akin to BOARD) + *-el* < L *-ellus* dim. suffix]

Bor·de·lais (bôr′dl ā′; *Fr.* bôʀ də le′), *n.* a wine-growing region in SW France, in Gironde.

Bor·de·laise (bôr′dl āz′; *Fr.* bôʀ də lez′), *n.* a brown sauce flavored with red wine and shallots and garnished with poached marrow and parsley. Also called **Bordelaise′ sauce′.** [< F, fem. of *bordelais* of Bordeaux, equiv. to *Bordel-* Bordeaux + *-ais* -ESE]

bor·del·lo (bôr del′ō), *n., pl.* **-los.** a brothel. [1590–1600; < It < OF *bordel* BORDEL]

Bor·den (bôr′dn), *n.* **1. Gail,** 1801–74, U.S. inventor: developed technique for condensing milk. **2. Lizzie (Andrew),** 1860–1927, defendant in U.S. 1893 trial: acquitted of ax murder of father and stepmother. **3. Sir Robert Laird** (lârd), 1854–1937, Canadian statesman: prime minister 1911–20.

bor·der (bôr′dər), *n.* **1.** the part or edge of a surface or area that forms its outer boundary. **2.** the line that separates one country, state, province, etc., from another; frontier line: *You cannot cross the border without a visa.* **3.** the district or region that lies along the boundary line of another. **4.** the frontier of civilization. **5. the border, a.** the border between the U.S. and Mexico, esp. along the Rio Grande. **b.** (in the British Isles) the region along the boundary between England and Scotland. **6.** brink; verge. **7.** an ornamental strip or design around the edge of a printed page, a drawing, etc. **8.** an ornamental design or piece of ornamental trimming around the edge of a fabric, rug, garment, article of furniture, etc. **9.** *Hort.* **a.** a long, narrow bed planted with flowers, shrubs, or trees. **b.** a strip of ground in which plants are grown, enclosing an area in a garden or running along the edge of a walk or driveway. **c.** the plants growing in such a strip: *a border of tulips along the path.* **10.** *Theat.* **a.** a narrow curtain or strip of painted canvas hung above the stage, masking the flies and lighting units, and forming the top of the stage set. **b.** See **border light.** —*v.t.* **11.** to make a border around; adorn with a border. **12.** to form a border or boundary to. **13.** to lie on the border of; adjoin. —*v.i.* **14.** to form or constitute a border; be next to: *California borders on the Pacific Ocean.* **15.** to approach closely in character; verge: *The situation borders on tragedy.* [1325–75; ME *bordure* < AF, OF, equiv. to *bord(er)* to border (deriv. of *bord* ship's side, edge < Gmc; see BOARD) + *-ure* -URE] —**bor′dered,** *adj.* —**bor′der·less,** *adj.*
—**Syn. 1.** rim, periphery, verge. See **edge. 2.** See **boundary.**

Bor′der col′lie, one of a breed of herding dogs, developed in the border area between Scotland and England, having a harsh, wavy coat, usually black with white around the neck, chest, face, feet, and the tip of the tail, used for both sheep and cattle herding. [1940–45]

bor·de·reau (bôr′də rō′; *Fr.* bôʀ də ʀō′), *n., pl.* **-reaux** (-rōz′; *Fr.* -ʀō′). a detailed memorandum, esp. one in which documents are listed. [1895–1900; < F, equiv. to *bord* edge (see BORDER) + *-ereau;* see -REL]

bor·der·er (bôr′dər ər), *n.* a person who dwells on or near the border of a country, region, etc. [1485–95; BORDER + -ER[1]]

bor·der·land (bôr′dər land′), *n.* **1.** land forming a border or frontier. **2.** an uncertain, intermediate district, space, or condition. [1805–15; BORDER + LAND]

bor′der light′, *Theat.* a striplight hung upstage of a border, for lighting the stage. Also, **bor′der·light′.**

bor′der line′, boundary line; frontier. [1865–70]

bor·der·line (bôr′dər līn′), *adj.* **1.** on or near a border or boundary. **2.** uncertain; indeterminate; debatable: *not an alcoholic, but a borderline case.* **3.** not quite meeting accepted, expected, or average standards. **4.** approaching bad taste or obscenity: *He made several borderline remarks that offended them.* —*n.* **5.** a person suffering from borderline personality. [1865–70; BORDER + LINE[1]]
—**Syn. 3.** marginal, problematic, uncertain, doubtful.

bor′derline personal′ity, *Psychiatry.* a personality disorder characterized by instability in many areas, as mood, identity, self-image, and behavior, and often manifested by impulsive actions, suicide attempts, inappropriate anger, or depression.

Bor·ders (bôr′dərz), *n.* a region in SE Scotland. 99,409; 1804 sq. mi. (4671 sq. km).

Bor′der States′, 1. *U.S. Hist.* the slave states of Delaware, Maryland, Kentucky, and Missouri, which refused to secede from the Union in 1860–61. **2.** the U.S. states touching the Canadian border. **3.** certain countries of central and northern Europe that border on the Soviet Union and formerly belonged to the Russian Empire: Finland, Poland (prior to 1940), Estonia, Latvia, and Lithuania.

bor′der tax′, a tax system for imports and exports, esp. one that compensates for internal taxes in Common Market countries by levying fees or paying rebates.

Bor′der ter′rier, one of a British breed of small terriers having a dense, wiry coat ranging in color from red to pale yellow, sometimes being gray and tan, or blue and tan. [1890–95]

Bor·det (bôr dā′; *Fr.* bôʀ de′), *n.* **Jules Jean Baptiste Vin·cent** (zhyl zhän ʙᴀ tēst′ vᴀɴ säɴ′), 1870–1961, Belgian physiologist and bacteriologist: Nobel prize for medicine 1919.

bor·dure (bôr′jər), *n. Heraldry.* the area adjacent to the outer edges of an escutcheon. [1300–50; ME; see BORDER]

bore[1] (bôr, bōr), *v.,* **bored, bor·ing,** *n.* —*v.t.* **1.** to pierce (a solid substance) with some rotary cutting instrument. **2.** to make (a hole) by drilling with such an instrument. **3.** to form, make, or construct (a tunnel, mine, well, passage, etc.) by hollowing out, cutting through, or removing a core of material: *to bore a tunnel through the Alps; to bore an oil well 3000 feet deep.* **4.** *Mach.* to enlarge (a hole) to a precise diameter with a cutting tool within the hole, by rotating either the tool or the work. **5.** to force (an opening), as through a crowd, by persistent forward thrusting (usually fol. by *through* or *into*); force or make (a passage). —*v.i.* **6.** to make a hole in a solid substance with a rotary cutting instrument. **7.** *Mach.* to enlarge a hole to a precise diameter. **8.** (of a substance) to admit of being bored: *Certain types of steel do not bore well.* —*n.* **9.** a hole made or enlarged by boring. **10.** the inside diameter of a hole, tube, or hollow cylindrical object or device, such as a bushing or bearing, engine cylinder, or the barrel of a gun. [bef. 900; ME *boren,* OE *borian;* c. D *boren,* G *bohren,* L *forāre*] —**bore′a·ble, bor′a·ble,** *adj.*
—**Syn. 1.** perforate, drill. **10.** caliber.

bore[2] (bôr, bōr), *v.,* **bored, bor·ing,** *n.* —*v.t.* **1.** to weary by dullness, tedious repetition, unwelcome attentions, etc.: *The long speech bored me.* —*n.* **2.** a dull, tiresome, or uncongenial person. **3.** a cause of ennui or petty annoyance: *repetitious tasks that are a bore to do.* [1760–70; of uncert. orig.]
—**Syn. 1.** fatigue, tire, annoy. —**Ant. 1.** amuse; thrill, enrapture.

bore[3] (bôr, bōr), *n.* an abrupt rise of tidal water moving rapidly inland from the mouth of an estuary. Also called **tidal bore.** [1275–1325; ME *bare* < ON *bāra* wave]

bore[4] (bôr, bōr), *v.* pt. of **bear**[1].

bo·re·al (bôr′ē əl, bōr′-), *adj.* **1.** of or pertaining to the north wind. **2.** of or pertaining to the north. **3.** (*sometimes cap.*) pertaining to Boreas. [1425–75; late ME *boriall* < LL *boreālis* northern (L *bore(ās)* BOREAS + *-ālis* -AL[1])]

Bo·re·as (bôr′ē əs, bōr′-), *n.* the ancient Greek personification of the north wind. Cf. **Aquilo.**

bore·cole (bôr′kōl′, bōr′-), *n.* kale (def. 1). [1705–15; < D *boerenkool* lit., farmer's cabbage; equiv. to *boer* (see BOOR) + *-en-* connective + *kool* COLE]

bore·dom (bôr′dəm, bōr′-), *n.* the state of being bored; tedium; ennui. [1850–55; BORE[2] + -DOM]
—**Syn.** dullness, doldrums, weariness. —**Ant.** excitement, diversion, amusement.

bore·hole (bôr′hōl′, bōr′-), *n. Mining.* a hole drilled in the earth, as for the purpose of extracting a core, releasing gas, oil, water, etc. [1700–10; BORE[1] + HOLE]

Bo·rel (bô rel′, bə-; *Fr.* bô ʀel′), *n.* **Fé·lix É·douard É·mile** (fā lēks′ ā dwᴀʀ′ ā mēl′), 1871–1956, French mathematician.

Bo·rel′-Le·besgue′ the′orem (bô rel′lə beg′, bə-), *Math.* See **Heine-Borel theorem.** [1950–55; named after F.E.E. BOREL and H. LEBESGUE]

Bo·rel·li (bô rel′ē, bə-; *It.* bô ʀel′lē), *n.* **Gio·van·ni Al·fon·so** (jō vä′nē al fon′sō, -zō, jē′ə-; *It.* jô vän′nē äl fôn′zô), 1608–79, Italian astronomer, physicist, and physiologist.

bor·er (bôr′ər, bōr′-), *n.* **1.** a person or thing that bores or pierces. **2.** *Mach.* a tool used for boring; auger. **3.** *Zool.* **a.** any of several insects that bore into trees, fruits, etc., esp. a beetle that bores into the woody part of plants. **b.** any of various mollusks, worms, etc., that bore into wood, stone, coral, or shells. **4.** a marsipobranch fish, as a hagfish, that bores into other fishes to feed on their flesh. [1275–1325; ME; see BORE[1], -ER[1]]

bore·scope (bôr′skōp′, bōr′-), *n. Optics.* an instrument using optical fibers for the visual inspection of narrow cavities, as the bore of a gun. [1955–60; BORE[1] + -SCOPE]

bore·sight (bôr′sīt′, bōr′-), *v.t.* to verify the alignment of the sights and bore of (a firearm). [back formation from *boresighting;* see BORE[1], SIGHT, -ING[1]]

bore·some (bôr′səm, bōr′-), *adj.* tedious; dull; wearisome; boring. [1865–70; BORE[2] + -SOME[1]]

Borg (bôrg), *n.* **Björn** (byôrn), born 1956, Swedish tennis player.

Bor·ger (bôr′gər), *n.* a city in N Texas. 15,837.

Bor·ger·hout (*Flemish.* bôʀ′ᴋʜəʀ hout′), *n.* a city in N Belgium, near Antwerp. 46,794.

Bor·ges (bôr′hes), *n.* **Jor·ge Luis** (hôʀ′he lwēs), 1899–1986, Argentine poet, short-story writer, and philosophical essayist.

Bor·ghe·se (bôʀ ge′ze; *Eng.* bôr gā′zē, -zā), *n.* a member of a noble Italian family, originally from Siena, that was important in Italian politics and society from the 16th to the early 19th century.

Borg·hild (bôrg′hild′), *n.* (in the *Volsunga Saga*) the first wife of Sigmund: she poisons Sinfiotli in revenge for his killing of her brother.

Bor·gia (bôr′jə, -zhə; *It.* bôʀ′jä), *n.* **1. Ce·sa·re** (che′zä ʀe), 1476?–1507, Italian cardinal, military leader, and politician. **2. Lu·cre·zia** (lo͞o krē′shə, -zhə; *It.* lo͞o kʀe′tsyä), (*Duchess of Ferrara*), 1480–1519, sister and political pawn of Cesare Borgia: patron of the arts. **3.** their father, **Ro·dri·go** (ʀô dʀē′gô). See **Alexander VI.**

Bor·glum (bôr′gləm), *n.* **John Gut·zon** (gut′sən), 1867–1941, and his brother **Solon Hannibal,** 1868–1922, U.S. sculptors.

bo·ric (bôr′ik, bōr′-), *adj. Chem.* of or containing boron; boracic. [1860–65; BOR- + -IC]

bo′ric ac′id, 1. Also called **orthoboric acid.** *Chem., Pharm.* a white, crystalline acid, H_3BO_3, occurring in nature or prepared from borax: used chiefly in the manufacture of ceramics, cements, glass, and enamels, for fireproofing, and in medicine in aqueous solution as a mild antiseptic. **2.** *Chem.* any of a group of acids containing boron. [1865–70]

bo′ric ox′ide, *Chem.* a colorless crystalline compound, B_2O_3, used in metallurgy and chemical analysis. Also called **bo′ric anhy′dride, boron oxide.**

bo·ride (bôr′īd, bōr′-), *n. Chem.* a compound consisting of two elements of which boron is the more electronegative one. [1860–65; BOR- + -IDE]

bor·ing[1] (bôr′ing, bōr′-), *n.* **1.** *Mach.* **a.** the act or process of making or enlarging a hole. **b.** the hole so made. **2.** *Geol.* a cylindrical sample of earth strata obtained by boring a vertical hole. **3. borings,** the chips, fragments, or dust produced in boring. [1400–50; late ME; see BORE[1], -ING[1]]

bor·ing[2] (bôr′ing, bōr′-), *adj.* causing or marked by boredom: *a boring discussion; to have a boring time.* [1835–45; BORE[2] + -ING[2]] —**bor′ing·ly,** *adv.* —**bor′·ing·ness,** *n.*
—**Syn.** dull, tiresome, tedious.

bor′ing bar′, *Metalworking.* a bar holding a tool for boring a cylinder or the like. [1835–45]

bor′ing machine′, *Metalworking.* a machine for bor-

CONCISE ETYMOLOGY KEY: <, descended or borrowed from; >, whence; b., blend of, blended; c., cognate with; cf., compare; deriv., derivative; equiv., equivalent; imit., imitative; obl., oblique; r., replacing; s., stem; sp., spelling, spelled; resp., respelling, respelled; trans., translation; ?, origin unknown; *, unattested; ‡, probably earlier than. See the full key inside the front cover.

ing holes in which the cutter is rotated, usually about a horizontal axis.

bor′ing mill′, *Metalworking.* a machine for boring large holes in heavy work, having a table on which the work rotates while the hole is bored vertically. [1825–35]

Bo·ris (bôr′is, bōr′-, bor′-; *Russ.* bu ʀyēs′), *n.* a male given name.

Boris III, 1894–1943, king of Bulgaria 1918–43.

Bo·ris Go·du·nov (bôr′is god′n ôf′, -of′, go͝od′-, bōr′-; bor′-; *Russ.* bu ʀyēs′ gə do͞o nôf′), **1.** a play (1825) by Pushkin. **2.** an opera (1874) by Modest Moussorgsky, based on Pushkin's drama. Also, **Bo′ris Go′·dou·nov′, Bo′ris Go′du·noff′.**

Bo·ri·sov (bə rē′səf, -səv; *Russ.* bu ʀyē′səf), *n.* a city in NE Byelorussia, in the W central Soviet Union in Europe, NE of Minsk. 112,000.

Bor·laug (bôr′lôg, -log), *n.* **Norman Ernest,** born 1914, U.S. agronomist: Nobel peace prize 1970.

Bor·man (bôr′mən), *n.* **Frank,** born 1928, U.S. astronaut.

Bor·mann (bôr′mən; *Ger.* bôʀ′män), *n.* **Mar·tin Lud·wig** (mär′tn lud′wig, lo͝od′-; *Ger.* mäʀ′tēn lo͞ot′vɪᴋʜ, lo͞od′-), 1900–45, German Nazi official.

born (bôrn), *adj.* **1.** brought forth by birth. **2.** possessing from birth the quality, circumstances, or character stated: *a born musician; a born fool.* **3.** native to the locale stated; immigrated to the present place from the locale stated: *a German-born scientist; a Chicago-born New Yorker.* **4. born yesterday,** naive; inexperienced: *You can't fool me with that old trick—I wasn't born yesterday.* —*v.* **5.** a pp. of **bear**[1]. [bef. 1000; ME; OE *boren* (ptp. of *beran* to ʙᴇᴀʀ[1]), equiv. to *bor-* ptp. s. + *-en* -ᴇɴ[3]] —**Usage.** See **bear**[1].

Born (bôrn), *n.* **Max,** 1882–1970, German physicist: Nobel prize 1954.

born-a·gain (bôrn′ə gen′ *or, esp. Brit.,* -ə gān′), *adj.* **1.** committed or recommitted to religious faith through an intensely religious experience: *a born-again Christian.* **2.** reactivated or revitalized: *a born-again conservatism in American politics.* **3.** enthusiastically committed: *a born-again jogger.* —*n.* **4.** a person who is characterized by a newfound faith or enthusiasm. [1965–70]

borne[1] (bôrn, bōrn), *v.* a pp. of **bear**[1]. —**Usage.** See **bear**[1].

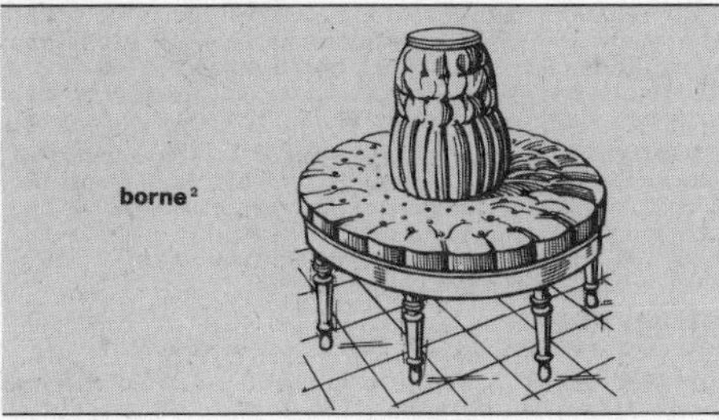

borne[2]

borne[2] (bōrn, bôrn), *n.* a circular sofa having a conical or cylindrical back piece at the center. [< F: pillar; see ʙᴏᴜʀɴ[2]]

Bor·ne·o (bôr′nē ō′), *n.* an island in the Malay Archipelago, politically divided among Indonesia, Malaysia, and the British-protected sultanate of Brunei. 6,000,000; 290,000 sq. mi. (750,000 sq. km). —**Bor′ne·an,** *adj., n.*

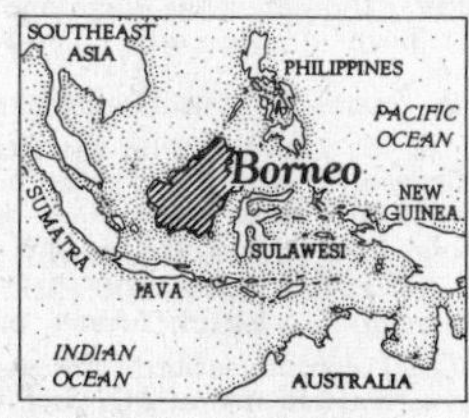

bor·ne·ol (bôr′nē ôl′, -ol′), *n. Chem.* a white, translucent, lumpy, very slightly water-soluble, solid terpene alcohol, $C_{10}H_{18}O$, occurring in various isomeric forms, having a burning, mintlike taste, obtained from the trunk of a tree, *Dryobalanops aromatica,* or by the reduction of camphor: used in the form of its esters in the manufacture of synthetic camphor and in perfumery. Also called **Bor′neo cam′phor, bornyl alcohol, camphol, Malayan camphor, Sumatra camphor.** [1875–80; Bᴏʀɴᴇ(ᴏ) + -ᴏʟ[1]]

Born·holm (bôʀɴ′hôlm′; *Eng.* bôrn′hōm, -hōlm), *n.* a Danish island in the Baltic Sea, S of Sweden. 47,126; 227 sq. mi. (588 sq. km).

born·ite (bôr′nīt), *n.* a common mineral and important ore of copper, copper iron sulfide, Cu_5FeS_4, occurring in masses, of brownish color when first exposed to the air; peacock ore. [1850–55; named after I. von *Born* (1742–91), Austrian mineralogist; see -ɪᴛᴇ[1]] —**born·it·ic** (bôr-nit′ik), *adj.*

Bor·nu (bôr′no͞o), *n.* a former sultanate in Africa, SW of Lake Chad: now largely a province in Nigeria.

bor′nyl ac′etate (bôr′nl, -nil), *Chem.* a colorless liquid, $C_{12}H_{20}O_2$, having a piny, camphorlike odor, used chiefly as a scent in the manufacture of perfume, and as a plasticizer. [ʙᴏʀɴ(ᴇᴏʟ) + -ʏʟ]

bor′nyl al′cohol, *Chem.* borneol.

bor′nyl for′mate, *Chem.* a liquid, $C_{11}H_{18}O_2$, having a piny odor, used chiefly as a scent in the manufacture of soaps and disinfectants.

boro-, a combining form used in the names of chemical compounds in which boron is present: *borofluoride.* Also, *esp. before a vowel,* **bor-.**

Bo·ro·din (bôr′ə dēn′, bor′-; *Russ.* bə ʀu dyēn′), *n.* **A·le·ksan·dr Por·fi·re·vich** (al′ig zan′dər pôr fēr′ə-vich, -zän′-; *Russ.* u lyi ksändʀ′ puʀ fyē′ʀyi vyich), 1833–87, Russian composer and chemist.

Bo·ro·di·no (bôr′ə dē′nō, bor′-; *Russ.* bə ʀə dyi nô′), *n.* a village in the W Russian Federation, 70 mi. (113 km) W of Moscow: Napoleon's victory here made possible the capture of Moscow, 1812.

bo·ro·glyc·er·ide (bôr′ə glis′ə rīd′, -ər id, bōr′-), *n. Chem.* any compound containing boric acid and glycerol, used chiefly as an antiseptic. [1880–85; ʙᴏʀᴏ- + ɢʟʏᴄᴇʀɪᴅᴇ]

bo·ro·hy·dride (bôr′ə hī′drīd, -drid, bōr′-), *n. Chem.* any of the class of compounds containing the group BH_4-, as sodium borohydride, used chiefly as reducing agents. [1935–40; ʙᴏʀᴏ- + ʜʏᴅʀɪᴅᴇ]

bo·ron (bôr′on, bōr′-), *n. Chem.* a nonmetallic element occurring naturally only in combination, as in borax or boric acid, and obtained in either an amorphous or a crystalline form when reduced from its compounds. *Symbol:* B; *at. wt.:* 10.811; *at. no.:* 5. [1805–15; ʙᴏʀ(ᴀx[1]) + (ᴄᴀʀʙ)ᴏɴ] —**bo·ron·ic** (bō ron′ik, bô-, bə-), *adj.*

bo′ron car′bide, *Chem.* a black, crystalline, extremely hard, water-insoluble solid, B_4C, used chiefly as a moderator in nuclear reactors, as an abrasive, and as a refractory.

bo′ron hy′dride, *Chem.* borane. [1875–80]

bo′ron ni′tride, *Chem.* a white powder, BN, formed by heating boron in nitrogen. In its ordinary form, it has a structure of stacked layers of hexagonal rings, very similar to that of graphite, and is used as a refractory electrical insulator. Cf. **Borazon.**

bo′ron ox′ide, *Chem.* See **boric oxide.**

bo·ro·sil·i·cate (bôr′ə sil′i kit, -kāt′, bōr′-), *n. Chem.* a salt of boric and silicic acids. [1810–20; ʙᴏʀᴏ- + sɪʟɪ-ᴄᴀᴛᴇ]

borosil′icate glass′, a glass containing 5 percent or more of B_2O_3, highly resistant to heat and shock, used esp. in making cookware and chemical glassware. [1930–35]

bo′ro·si·lic′ic ac′id (bôr′ō si lis′ik, bōr′-, bôr′-, bōr′-), *Chem.* any of several hypothetical acids that form borosilicates. [ʙᴏʀᴏ- + sɪʟɪᴄɪᴄ ᴀᴄɪᴅ]

bor·ough (bûr′ō, bur′ō), *n.* **1.** (in certain states of the U.S.) an incorporated municipality smaller than a city. **2.** one of the five administrative divisions of New York City. **3.** *Brit.* **a.** an urban community incorporated by royal charter, similar to an incorporated city or municipality in the U.S. **b.** a town, area, or constituency represented by a Member of Parliament. **c.** (formerly) a fortified town organized as and having some of the powers of an independent country. **4.** (in Alaska) an administrative division similar to a county in other states. [bef. 900; ME *burw(e), borwg(h), borogh, bur(u)g, bur(u)gh, burgh* town, OE *burg* fortified town; c. ON *borg,* OS, D *burg,* G *Burg* castle, Goth *baurgs* city; MIr *brí, brig,* Welsh, Breton *bre* hill, Avestan *barəz-* height; akin to Armenian *bardzr,* Hittite *parkus* high. See ʙᴀʀʀᴏᴡ[2].]

bor·ough-Eng·lish (bûr′ō ing′glish *or, often,* -lish, bur′-), *n.* (formerly, in some parts of England) a custom by which the youngest son inherited the entire estate upon the death of his father. [1300–50; ME]

bor′ough hall′, a building housing the administrative offices of a borough. [1935–40]

bor·rel·i·a (bə rel′ē ə, -rel′yə, -rē′lē ə, -rēl′yə), *n. Bacteriol.* any of several spiral, parasitic bacteria of the genus *Borrelia,* certain species of which are pathogenic for humans, other mammals, or birds. [< NL (1907), named after Amédée Borrel (d. 1936); see -ɪᴀ]

Bor·ro·mi·ni (bôr′ə mē′nē, bor′-; *It.* bôʀ′ʀô mē′nē), *n.* **Fran·ces·co** (fran ches′kō; *It.* fʀän ches′kô), 1599–1667, Italian architect and sculptor.

bor·row (bor′ō, bôr′ō), *v.t.* **1.** to take or obtain with the promise to return the same or an equivalent: *Our neighbor borrowed my lawn mower.* **2.** to use, appropriate, or introduce from another source or from a foreign source: *to borrow an idea from the opposition; to borrow a word from French.* **3.** *Arith.* (in subtraction) to take from one denomination and add to the next lower. —*v.i.* **4.** to borrow something: *Don't borrow unless you intend to repay.* **5.** *Naut.* **a.** to sail close to the wind; luff. **b.** to sail close to the shore. **6.** *Golf.* to putt on other than a direct line from the lie of the ball to the hole, to compensate for the incline or roll of the green. **7. borrow trouble,** to do something that is unnecessary and may cause future harm or inconvenience. [bef. 900; ME *borowen,* OE *borgian* to borrow, lend, deriv. of *borg* a pledge; akin to D *borg* a pledge, *borgen* to charge, give credit, G *Borg* credit, *borgen* to take on credit] —**bor′row·a·ble,** *adj.* —**bor′row·er,** *n.*
—**Syn. 2.** acquire, take, get; copy, pirate, plagiarize.

Bor·row (bor′ō, bôr′ō), *n.* **George,** 1803–81, English traveler, writer, and student of languages, esp. Romany. —**Bor·ro·vi·an** (bə rō′vē ən), *adj., n.*

bor′rowed time′, an uncertain, usually limited period of time extending beyond or postponing the occurrence of something inevitable. [1895–1900]

bor′rower's card′. See **library card.**

bor·row·ing (bor′ō ing, bôr′-), *n.* **1.** the act of one who borrows. **2.** the process by which something, as a word or custom, is adopted or absorbed. **3.** the result of such a process; something borrowed, as a foreign word or phrase or a custom. [1350–1400; ME; see ʙᴏʀʀᴏᴡ, -ɪɴɢ[1]]

bor′row pit′, *Civ. Engin.* a pit from which construction material, as sand or gravel, is taken for use as fill at another location. [1890–95]

Bors (bôrz), *n.* **Sir,** *Arthurian Romance.* **1.** Also, **Sir Bors de Gan·is** (də gan′is). a knight of the Round Table, nephew of Lancelot. **2.** a natural son of King Arthur.

borscht (bôrsht), *n.* any of various eastern European soups made with beets, cabbage, potatoes, or other vegetables and served hot or chilled, often with sour cream. Also, **borsch** (bôrsh), **borshch** (bôrsh, bôrshch). [1880–85; < Yiddish *borsht;* cf. Ukrainian, Byelorussian, Russ *borshch* soup with red beets as ingredient; or directly < East Slavic]

borscht′ cir′cuit, (*sometimes caps.*) the hotels of the predominantly Jewish resort area in the Catskill Mountains, many of them offering nightclub or cabaret entertainment. Also called **borscht′ belt′.** [1935–40; so called, facetiously, from the quantities of borscht consumed there]

bor·stal (bôr′stəl), *n.* (in England) a school for delinquent boys that provides therapy and vocational training. Also, **bor′stal institu′tion.** [1900–05; named after *Borstal,* village in Kent, England]

bort (bôrt), *n.* low-quality diamond, in granular aggregate or small fragments, valuable only in crushed or powdered form, esp. for industrial use as an abrasive. Also, **boart, bortz** (bôrts). Cf. **ballas, carbonado**[2]. [1615–25; appar. metathetic var. of **brot* (OE *gebrot* fragment); akin to ME *brotel* brittle, ON *brot* fragment] —**bort′y,** *adj.*

bor·zoi (bôr′zoi), *n., pl.* **-zois.** any of a breed of tall, slender dogs having long, silky hair, raised originally in Russia for hunting wolves. Also called **Russian wolfhound.** [1885–90; < Russ *borzói* orig., swift, fast; c. Czech *brzý,* Serbo-Croatian *bȑz* swift, Pol *bardzo* very]

borzoi
2½ ft. (.8 m) high at shoulder

Bo·san·quet (bō′zən ket′, -kit), *n.* **Bernard,** 1848–1923, English philosopher and writer.

Bosc (bosk), *n.* a large, greenish-yellow variety of pear.

bos·cage (bos′kij), *n.* a mass of trees or shrubs; wood, grove, or thicket. Also, **boskage.** [1350–1400; ME *boskage* < MF *boscage.* See ʙᴏsᴋ, -ᴀɢᴇ]

Bosch (bosh; *Ger., Sp.* bôsh; *Du.* bôs), *n.* **1. Carl** or **Karl,** 1874–1940, German chemist: Nobel prize 1931. **2. Hi·e·ro·ny·mus** (hī′ə ron′ə məs; *Du.* hē′ʀ ʀō′nē mœs), (*Hieronymus van Aeken*), 1450?–1516, Dutch painter. **3. Juan** (hwän), (*Juan Bosch Gaviño*), born 1909, Dominican writer and political leader: president 1963.

bosch·vark (bosh′värk′), *n.* See **bush pig.** [1825–35; < Afrik *bos,* earlier *bosch* forest, ʙᴜsʜ[1] + *vark* pig; cf. ᴀᴀʀᴅᴠᴀʀᴋ]

Bose (bōs), *n.* **Sir Ja·ga·dis Chan·dre** (jə gə dēs′ chun′drə), 1858–1937, Indian physicist and plant physiologist.

Bose′-Ein′stein statis′tics (bōs′īn′stīn), *Physics.* quantum statistics for particles not obeying the exclusion principle, based on the assumption that in a given physical system consisting of indistinguishable particles and regions all distinguishable arrangements of the particles have equal probability. [1925–30; named after S. N. *Bose* (see ʙᴏsᴏɴ) and Albert Eɪɴsᴛᴇɪɴ]

bosh[1] (bosh), *n.* absurd or foolish talk; nonsense. [1830–35; < Turk *boş* empty; popularized from its use in the novel *Ayesha* (1834) by British author James J. Morier (1780–1849)]

bosh[2] (bosh), *n. Metall.* the section of a blast furnace between the hearth and the stack, having the form of a frustum of an inverted cone. See diag. under **blast furnace.** [1670–80; prob. < G; akin to G *böschen* to slope, *Böschung* slope, scarp]

bosk (bosk), *n.* a small wood or thicket, esp. of bushes. [1250–1300; ME *boske,* var. of *busk(e)* < ON *buskr* ʙᴜsʜ[1]]

bos·kage (bos′kij), *n.* boscage.

bos·ker (bos′kər), *adj. Australian Slang.* very good; excellent. [1905–10; of obscure orig.]

bos·ket (bos′kit), *n.* a grove; thicket. Also, **bosquet.** [1730–40; earlier *bosquet* < F < It *boschetto,* equiv. to *bosc(o)* wood (see ʙᴜsʜ[1]) + *-etto* -ᴇᴛ]

Bos′kop man′ (bos′kop), the undated cranial remains of a possible *Homo sapiens* found in the Transvaal of South Africa. [after a locale in the Transvaal, where the remains were found in 1913]

bos·ko·poid (bos′kə poid′), *adj.* of, pertaining to, or characteristic of Boskop man. [Bᴏsᴋᴏᴘ (ᴍᴀɴ) + -ᴏɪᴅ]

bosk·y (bos′kē), *adj.,* **bosk·i·er, bosk·i·est. 1.** covered with bushes, shrubs, and small trees; woody. **2.** shady. [1585–95; ʙᴏsᴋ + -ʏ[1]] —**bosk′i·ness,** *n.*

bo's'n (bō′sən), *n.* boatswain.

Bos•ni•a (boz′nē ə), *n.* a historic region in SE Europe: a former Turkish province; a part of Austria-Hungary (1879–1918); now part of Bosnia and Herzegovina. —**Bos′ni•an,** *adj.*

Bos′nia and Herzegovi′na, a republic in S Europe: formerly (1945–92) a constituent republic of Yugoslavia. 4,355,000; 19,741 sq. mi. (51,129 sq. km). *Cap.:* Sarajevo.

bos•om (bo͝oz′əm, bo͞o′zəm), *n.* **1.** the breast of a human being. **2.** the breasts of a woman. **3.** the part of a garment that covers the breast. **4.** the breast, conceived of as the center of feelings or emotions. **5.** something likened to the human breast: *the bosom of the earth.* **6.** a state of enclosing intimacy; warm closeness: *the bosom of the family.* —*adj.* **7.** of, pertaining to, or worn on or over the bosom. **8.** intimate or confidential: *a bosom friend.* —*v.t.* **9.** to take to the bosom; embrace; cherish. **10.** to hide from view; conceal. [bef. 1000; ME; OE *bōs(u)m;* c. D *boesem,* G *Busen*]
—**Syn. 4.** heart, affection. **8.** close, cherished, dear.

bos•omed (bo͝oz′əmd, bo͞o′zəmd), *adj.* **1.** having a specified type of bosom (usually used in combination): *a full-bosomed garment; the green-bosomed earth.* **2.** concealed or secreted in the bosom. [1640–50; BOSOM + -ED[3]]

bos•om•y (bo͝oz′ə mē, bo͞o′zə-), *adj.* (of a woman) having a large or prominent bosom. [1925–30; BOSOM + -Y[1]]

bo•son (bō′son), *n. Physics.* any particle that obeys Bose-Einstein statistics: bosons have integral spins: 0, 1, 2, . . . Cf. **fermion.** [1945–50; named after S. N. *Bose* (1894–1974), Indian physicist; see -ON[1]]

Bos•po•rus (bos′pər əs), *n.* a strait connecting the Black Sea and the Sea of Marmara. 18 mi. (29 km) long. Also, **Bos•pho•rus** (bos′fər əs). Cf. **Dardanelles.** —**Bos′po•ran, Bos•po•ran•ic** (bos′pə ran′ik), **Bos•po•ri•an** (bo spôr′ē ən, -spōr′-), *adj.*

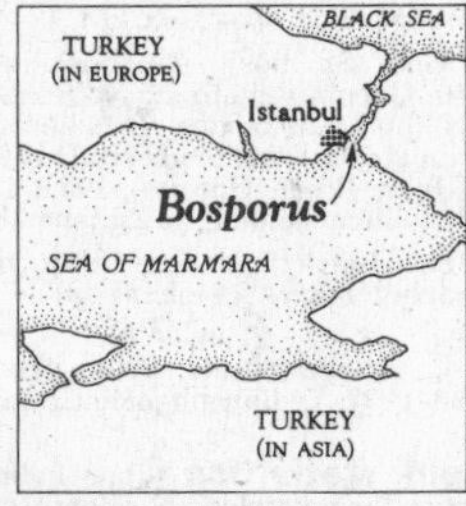

bos•quet (bos′kit), *n.* bosket.

boss[1] (bôs, bos), *n.* **1.** a person who employs or superintends workers; manager. **2.** a politician who controls the party organization, as in a particular district. **3.** a person who makes decisions, exercises authority, dominates, etc.: *My grandfather was the boss in his family.* —*v.t.* **4.** to be master of or over; manage; direct; control. **5.** to order about, esp. in an arrogant manner. —*v.i.* **6.** to be boss. **7.** to be too domineering and authoritative. —*adj.* **8.** chief; master. **9.** *Slang.* first-rate. [1640–50, *Amer.;* < D *baas* master, foreman]
—**Syn. 1.** supervisor, head, foreman, chief, superintendent, administrator, overseer.

boss[2] (bôs, bos), *n.* **1.** *Bot., Zool.* a protuberance or roundish excrescence on the body or on some organ of an animal or plant. **2.** *Geol.* a knoblike mass of rock, esp. an outcrop of igneous or metamorphic rock. **3.** an ornamental protuberance of metal, ivory, etc.; stud. **4.** *Archit.* **a.** an ornamental, knoblike projection, as a carved keystone at the intersection of ogives. **b.** a stone roughly formed and set in place for later carving. **5.** *Bookbinding.* one of several pieces of brass or other metal inset into the cover of a book to protect the corners or edges or for decoration. **6.** *Mach.* a small projection on a casting or forging. **7.** *Naut.* a projecting part in a ship's hull, or in one frame of a hull, fitting around a propeller shaft. —*v.t.* **8.** to ornament with bosses. **9.** to emboss. **10.** (in plumbing) to hammer (sheet metal, as lead) to conform to an irregular surface. [1250–1300; ME *boce* < AF: lump, growth, boil; OF < VL **bottia,* of uncert. orig.]

boss[3] (bos, bôs), *n.* a familiar name for a calf or cow. [1790–1800, *Amer.;* cf. dial. (SW England) *borse, boss, buss* six-month-old calf]

CONCISE ETYMOLOGY KEY: <, descended or borrowed from; >, whence; b., blend of, blended; c., cognate with; cf., compare; deriv., derivative; equiv., equivalent; imit., imitative; obl., oblique; r., replacing; s., stem; sp., spelling, spelled; resp., respelling, respelled; trans., translation; ?, origin unknown; *, unattested; ‡, probably earlier than. See the full key inside the front cover.

boss[4] (bos), *adj. Scot.* hollow; empty. [1505–15; of obscure orig.]

bos•sage (bô′sij, bos′ij), *n. Masonry.* **1.** stonework blocked out for later carving. **2.** stonework, as rusticated ashlar, having faces projecting beyond the mortar joints. [1695–1705; < F, equiv. to *bosse* BOSS[2] + *-age* -AGE]

bos•sa no•va (bos′ə nō′və, bô′sə), **1.** jazz-influenced music of Brazilian origin, rhythmically related to the samba. **2.** a dance performed to this music. [1960–65; < Pg: lit., new tendency, leaning]

boss′ cock′y, *Australian Slang.* **1.** (formerly) a farmer employing laborers. **2.** a boss, esp. an officious one. [1895–1900; COCKY[2] in derivative sense "small farmer"]

boss•dom (bôs′dəm, bos′-), *n.* **1.** the status, influence, or power of a boss, esp. a political boss. **2.** bossism. [1885–90; BOSS[1] + -DOM]

boss•eyed (bôs′id′, bos′-), *adj. Brit. Informal.* cross-eyed. [1855–60; perh. BOSS[2] + EYED]

Bos′sier Cit′y (bō′zhər), a city in NW Louisiana. 49,969.

boss•ism (bô′siz əm, bos′iz-), *n.* control by bosses, esp. political bosses. [1880–85, *Amer.;* BOSS[1] + -ISM]

boss•man (bôs′man′, bos′-), *n., pl.* **-men.** *Informal.* a leader or boss. [1930–35; BOSS[1] + MAN[1]]

Bos•suet (bô swe′), *n.* **Jacques Bé•ni•gne** (zhäk bā nēn′y[ə]), 1627–1704, French bishop, writer, and orator.

boss•y[1] (bô′sē, bos′ē), *adj.,* **boss•i•er, boss•i•est.** given to ordering people about; overly authoritative; domineering. [1880–85, *Amer.;* BOSS[1] + -Y[1]] —**boss′i•ly,** *adv.* —**boss′i•ness,** *n.*
—**Syn.** highhanded, officious, dictational; overbearing, abrasive.

boss•y[2] (bô′sē, bos′ē), *adj.* **boss•i•er, boss•i•est.** studded with bosses. [1535–45; BOSS[2] + -Y[1]]

bos•sy[3] (bos′ē, bô′sē), *n., pl.* **-sies.** a familiar name for a cow or calf. [1835–45, *Amer.;* BOSS[3] + -Y[2]]

Bos•ton (bô′stən, bos′tən), *n.* **1.** a seaport in and the capital of Massachusetts, in the E part. 562,994. **2.** (*l.c.*) a variety of whist, popular in the early 19th century, played by four persons with two packs of cards. **3.** (*usually l.c.*) a social dance that is a modification of the waltz.

Bos′ton bag′, a two-handled bag for carrying books, papers, etc. [1920–25, *Amer.*]

Bos′ton baked′ beans′. See **baked beans.** [1850–55, *Amer.*]

Bos′ton brown′ bread′, a dark-brown steamed bread made of cornmeal and rye meal or graham or wheat flour sweetened with molasses. [1855–60, *Amer.*]

Bos′ton bull′. See **Boston terrier.**

Bos′ton cream′ pie′, a two-layer cake with a thick filling of cream or custard between the layers, often having a chocolate icing on top. [1860–65, *Amer.*]

Bos′ton fern′, a variety of sword fern, *Nephrolepis exaltata bostoniensis,* having long, narrow, drooping fronds. [1895–1900]

Bos•to•ni•an (bô stō′nē ən, bo stō′-), *adj.* **1.** of, pertaining to, or typical of Boston, Mass., or its residents: *a Bostonian childhood; Bostonian reserve.* —*n.* **2.** a native or inhabitant of Boston, Mass. [1675–85; BOSTON + -IAN]

Bostonians, The, a novel (1886) by Henry James.

Bos′ton i′vy, a climbing woody vine, *Parthenocissus tricuspidata,* of the grape family, native to eastern Asia and grown in North America as a wall covering. Also called **Japanese ivy.** [1895–1900]

Bos′ton let′tuce, a cultivated variety of lettuce having a rounded head of soft, crumpled leaves, used for salads.

Bos′ton mar′riage, (esp. in 19th-century New England) an intimate friendship between two women often maintaining a household together.

Bos′ton Mas′sacre, *Amer. Hist.* a riot in Boston (March 5, 1770) arising from the resentment of Boston colonists toward British troops quartered in the city, in which the troops fired on the mob and killed several persons.

Bos′ton rock′er, an American wooden rocking chair having a solid, curved seat, often painted or grained, a spindle back, narrow rockers, and usually gilt designs stenciled on the crest rail. [1855–60]

Bos′ton states′, *Canadian* (*chiefly the Maritime Provinces*). the New England states, esp. Maine and Massachusetts.

Bos′ton Tea′ Par′ty, *Amer. Hist.* a raid on three British ships in Boston Harbor (December 16, 1773) in which Boston colonists, disguised as Indians, threw the contents of several hundred chests of tea into the harbor as a protest against British taxes on tea and against the monopoly granted the East India Company. [1825–35, *Amer.*]

Boston terrier
14 in. (36 cm)
high at shoulder

Bos′ton ter′rier, one of an American breed of small, pug-faced, short-haired dogs having erect ears, a short tail, and a brindled or black coat with white markings. Also called **Boston bull.** [1890–95, *Amer.*]

bo•sun (bō′sən), *n.* boatswain. [1865–70]

bo′sun bird′, tropicbird. Also, **bo′sun•bird′.**

Bos•wash (bôs′wosh′, -wôsh′, bos′-), *n. Informal.* the heavily populated area extending from Boston to Washington and including New York City, Philadelphia, and Baltimore. [BOS(TON) + WASH(INGTON)]

Bos•well (boz′wel′, -wəl), *n.* **1. James,** 1740–95, Scottish author: biographer of Samuel Johnson. **2.** any devoted biographer of a specific person. —**Bos•well•i•an** (boz wel′ē ən), *adj.*

bos•well•ize (boz′wə līz′), *v.,* **-ized, -iz•ing.** —*v.t.* **1.** to write an account of in the detailed manner of Boswell. —*v.i.* **2.** to write in the detailed manner of Boswell. Also, **Bos′well•ize′;** *esp. Brit.,* **bos′well•ise′, Bos′well•ise′.** [1830–40; BOSWELL + -IZE] —**bos′well•ism, Bos′well•ism,** *n.*

Bos′worth Field′ (boz′wərth), a battlefield in central England, near Leicester, where Richard III was defeated and slain by the future Henry VII in 1485.

bot[1] (bot), *n.* the larva of a botfly. Also, **bott.** [1425–75; late ME; akin to D *bot,* Fris dial. *botten* (pl.); further orig. obscure]

bot[2] (bot), *n. Australian Slang.* a person who cadges; scrounger. [1915–20; perh. shortening of BOTFLY]

bot., **1.** botanical. **2.** botanist. **3.** botany. **4.** bottle.

B.O.T., Board of Trade.

bo•ta (bō′tə; *Sp.* bô′tä), *n., pl.* **-tas** (-təz; *Sp.* -täs). **1.** Also called **bo′ta bag′.** a wine bag of Spain made of untanned goatskin and usually holding 1–2 liters (1.1–2.2 qt.). **2.** a wine barrel of Spain holding 500 liters (132 U.S. gallons). [< Sp < LL *butta, buttis* cask; see BUTT[4]]

bo•tan•i•cal (bə tan′i kəl), *adj.* **1.** Also, **bo•tan′ic.** of, pertaining to, made from, or containing plants: *botanical survey; botanical drugs.* —*n.* **2.** *Pharm.* a drug made from part of a plant, as from roots, leaves, bark, or berries. [1650–60; *botanic* (< ML *botanicus* < Gk *botanikós* of plants, equiv. to *botán(ē)* herb + *-ikos* -IC) + -AL[1]] —**bo•tan′i•cal•ly,** *adv.*

botan′ical gar′den, a garden for the exhibition and scientific study of collected, growing plants, usually in association with greenhouses, herbariums, laboratories, etc. Also called **botan′ic gar′den.** [1775–85]

bot•a•nist (bot′n ist), *n.* a specialist in botany. [1675–85; *botan(ism)* botany (< Gk *botanismós,* equiv. to *botán(ē)* plant + *-ismos* -ISM) + -IST]

bot•a•nize (bot′n īz′), *v.,* **-nized, -niz•ing.** —*v.i.* **1.** to study plants or plant life. **2.** to collect plants for scientific study. —*v.t.* **3.** to explore botanically; study the plant life of. Also, *esp. Brit.,* **bot′a•nise′.** [1760–70; < NL *botanizāre* < Gk *botanízein* to gather plants. See BOTANIST, -IZE] —**bot′a•niz′er,** *n.*

bot•a•ny (bot′n ē), *n., pl.* **-nies.** **1.** the science of plants; the branch of biology that deals with plant life. **2.** the plant life of a region: *the botany of Alaska.* **3.** the biology of a plant or plant group: *the botany of deciduous trees.* **4.** (*sometimes cap.*) See **Botany wool.** [1690–1700; *botan(ic)* (see BOTANICAL) + -Y[3]]

Bot′any Bay′, a bay on the SE coast of Australia, near Sydney: site of early British penal colony.

Bot′any wool′, a fine wool obtained from merino sheep. Also called **botany.** [1880–85]

botch[1] (boch), *v.t.* **1.** to spoil by poor work; bungle (often fol. by *up*): *He botched up the job thoroughly.* **2.** to do or say in a bungling manner. **3.** to mend or patch in a clumsy manner. —*n.* **4.** a clumsy or poor piece of work; mess; bungle: *He made a complete botch of his first attempt at baking.* **5.** a clumsily added part or patch. **6.** a disorderly or confused combination; conglomeration. [1350–1400; ME *bocchen* to patch up; perh. to be identified with *bocchen* to swell up, bulge (v. deriv. of *bocche* BOTCH[2]), though sense development unclear] —**botch•ed•ly** (boch′id lē), *adv.* —**botch′er,** *n.* —**botch′er•y,** *n.*
—**Syn. 1.** ruin, mismanage; muff, butcher, flub.

botch[2] (boch), *n.* **1.** a swelling on the skin; a boil. **2.** an eruptive disease. [1350–1400; ME *bocche* < OF *boche,* dial. var. of *boce* BOSS[2]]

botch•y (boch′ē), *adj.,* **botch•i•er, botch•i•est.** poorly made or done; bungled. [1350–1400; ME; see BOTCH[1], -Y[1]] —**botch′i•ly,** *adv.* —**botch′i•ness,** *n.*

bote (bōt), *n. Law.* compensation, such as for injury to person or honor. [learned use of ME *bote* BOOT[2]]

bo•tel (bō tel′), *n.* boatel.

bot•fly (bot′flī′), *n., pl.* **-flies.** any of several flies of the families Oestridae, Gasterophilidae, and Cuterebridae, the larvae of which are parasitic in the skin or other parts of various mammals. Also, **bot′ fly′.** [1810–20; BOT + FLY[2]]

both (bōth), *adj.* **1.** one and the other; two together: *He met both sisters. Both performances were canceled.* —*pron.* **2.** the one as well as the other: *Both of us were going to the party.* —*conj.* **3.** alike; equally: *He is both ready and willing.* [1125–75; ME *bothe, bathe,* influenced by Scand (cf. ON *bāthir* both; c. G, D *beide,* Goth *ba tho skipa* both (the) ships, OHG *bêde* < **bai thai*); r. ME *bo, ba,* OE *bā;* c. Goth *bai;* akin to L *ambō,* Gk *ámphō,* Lith *abù,* Skt *ubháu*]

Bo•tha (bō′tə), *n.* **1. Lou•is** (lo͞o ē′), 1862–1919, South African general and statesman. **2. Pie•ter Willem** (pē′tər), born 1916, South African political leader: prime minister 1978–84; state president since 1984.

Bo•the (bō′tə), *n.* **Wal•ther** (väl′tər), 1891–1957, German physicist: Nobel prize 1954.

both•er (both′ər), *v.t.* **1.** to give trouble to; annoy; pester; worry: *His baby sister bothered him for candy.* **2.** to bewilder; confuse: *His inability to understand the joke bothered him.* —*v.i.* **3.** to take the trouble; trouble or inconvenience oneself: *Don't bother to call. He has no time to bother with trifles.* —*n.* **4.** something troublesome, burdensome, or annoying: *Doing the laundry every week can be a terrible bother.* **5.** effort, work, or worry: *Gardening takes more bother than it's worth.* **6.** a worried or perplexed state: *Don't get into such a bother about small matters.* **7.** someone or something that bothers or annoys: *My cousin is a perpetual bother to me.* —*interj.* **8.** *Chiefly Brit.* (used to express mild irritation.) [1710–20; orig. Hiberno-E; prob. by hypercorrection from *bodder,* an alternate early form; orig. obscure] —**Syn. 1.** harass, vex, irritate; molest, disturb. BOTHER, ANNOY, PLAGUE, TEASE imply persistent interference with one's comfort or peace of mind. BOTHER suggests causing trouble or weariness or repeatedly interrupting in the midst of pressing duties. To ANNOY is to vex or irritate by bothering. PLAGUE is a strong word, connoting unremitting annoyance and harassment. To TEASE is to pester, as by long-continued whining and begging.

both•er•a•tion (bot͟h′ə rā′shən), *interj.* **1.** (used as an exclamation indicating vexation or annoyance.) —*n.* **2.** the act or state of bothering or the state of being bothered. [1790–1800; BOTHER + -ATION]

both•er•some (bot͟h′ər səm), *adj.* causing annoyance or worry; troublesome. [1825–35; BOTHER + -SOME[1]] —**Syn.** annoying, irritating, irksome, vexing, vexatious, galling.

Both•ni•a (both′nē ə), *n.* **Gulf of,** an arm of the Baltic Sea, extending N between Sweden and Finland. ab. 400 mi. (645 km) long. —**Both′ni•an,** *adj., n.* —**Both′nic,** *adj.*

Both•well (both′wel′, -wəl, bot͟h′-), *n.* **James Hepburn** (hep′bûrn *or, esp. Brit.,* heb′ərn), **Earl of,** 1536?–78, third husband of Mary, Queen of Scots.

both•y (both′ē, bô′thē), *n., pl.* **both•ies.** *Scot.* a hut or small cottage. [1560–70; prob. < ScotGael *bothan* hut, with -y[2] r. *-an*]

Bot•kin (bot′kin), *n.* **Benjamin Albert,** 1901–75, U.S. folklorist, editor, and essayist.

bot•o•née (bot′n ā′, bot′n ā′), *adj. Heraldry.* (of a cross) having arms terminating in the form of a trefoil: *cross botonée.* See illus. under **cross.** Also, **bot′on•née′, bot•o•ny, bot•on•ny** (bot′n ē). [1565–75; < MF: covered with buds, equiv. to *boton* bud, BUTTON + *-ée;* see -EE]

bo′ tree′ (bō), the pipal, or sacred fig tree, *Ficus religiosa,* of India, under which the founder of Buddhism is reputed to have attained the Enlightenment that constituted him the Buddha. Also called **bodhi tree.** [1860–65; partial trans. of Sinhalese *bogaha,* equiv. to *bo* (< Pali *bodhi* < Skt; see BODHISATTVA) + *gaha* tree]

bot•ry•oi•dal (bo′trē oid′l), *adj. Mineral.* having the form of a bunch of grapes: *botryoidal hematite.* Also, **bot′ry•oid′, botryose.** [1810–20; < Gk *botryoeid(ēs)* shaped like a bunch of grapes (*bótry(s)* bunch of grapes + *-oeidēs* -OID) + -AL[1]] —**bot′ry•oi′dal•ly,** *adv.*

bot•ry•o•my•co•sis (bo′trē ō mī kō′sis), *n. Vet. Pathol.* a disease of horses and other domestic animals, often occurring after castration, usually caused by *Staphylococcus aureus* and characterized by the formation of granulomatous masses. [< Gk *botryo-* (comb. form of *bótrys* bunch of grapes) + MYCOSIS] —**bot•ry•o•my•cot•ic** (bo′trē ō mī kot′ik), *adj.*

bot•ry•ose (bo′trē ōs′), *adj.* **1.** *Mineral.* botryoidal. **2.** racemose. [< Gk *bótry(s)* bunch of grapes + -OSE[1]]

bo•try•tis (bō trī′tis), *n.* **1.** any imperfect fungus of the genus *Botrytis,* having the conidia in grapelike bunches: a major cause of plant disease. **2.** See **noble rot.** [< NL (1832) < Gk *bótry(s)* bunch of grapes + NL *-(i)tis* -ITIS]

botry′tis rot′, *Plant Pathol.* a disease of many plants caused by fungi of the genus *Botrytis,* characterized by leaf blight, a tan-gray moldlike surface growth, and the rotting of stems and storage organs. Cf. **noble rot.**

bots (bots), *n.* (*used with a plural v.*) *Vet. Pathol.* a disease affecting various mammals, esp. horses, caused by the attachment of the parasitic larvae of botflies to the stomach of the host. [1780–90; pl. of BOT[1]; see -S[3]]

Bot•sa•res (*Gk.* bô′tsä rēs), *n.* **Mar•kos** (*Gk.* mär′kôs). See **Bozzaris, Marco.**

Bot•swa•na (bot swä′nə), *n.* a republic in S Africa: formerly a British protectorate; gained independence 1966; member of the Commonwealth of Nations. 800,000; 275,000 sq. mi. (712,250 sq. km). *Cap.:* Gaborone. Formerly, **Bechuanaland.**

bott[1] (bot), *n.* bot.

bott[2] (bot), *n. Metall.* a conical knob, mounted on a rod, for stopping temporarily the flow of molten metal or slag from a blast furnace or cupola. [1875–80; perh. special use of dial. *bot* (now obs.) iron tool for marking sheep, itself special use of ME *botte* (var. of BAT[1]) shepherd's crook]

bot•te•ga (bō tā′gə, bə-; *It.* bôt te′gä), *n., pl.* **-te•gas, -te•ghe** (-tā′gē; *It.* -te′ge). the studio of a master artist, in which lesser artists, apprentices, or students learn by participating in the work. [1895–1900; < It: lit., shop < L *apothēca;* see APOTHECARY]

Bött•ger (bœt′gər), *n.* **Jo•hann Frie•drich** (yō′hän frē′drikh), 1682–1719, German chemist.

Bot•ti•cel•li (bot′i chel′ē; *It.* bôt′tē chel′lē), *n.* **Sandro** (san′drō, sän′-; *It.* sän′drô), (*Alessandro di Mariano dei Filipepi*), 1444?–1510, Italian painter. —**Bot′ti•cel′li•an,** *adj.*

bot•tle[1] (bot′l), *n., v.,* **-tled, -tling.** —*n.* **1.** a portable container for holding liquids, characteristically having a neck and mouth and made of glass or plastic. **2.** the contents of such a container; as much as such a container contains: *a bottle of wine.* **3.** bottled cow's milk, milk formulas, or substitute mixtures given to infants instead of mother's milk: *raised on the bottle.* **4. hit the bottle,** *Slang.* to drink alcohol to excess often or habitually. **5. the bottle,** intoxicating beverages; liquor: *He became addicted to the bottle.* —*v.t.* **6.** to put into or seal in a bottle: *to bottle grape juice.* **7.** *Brit.* to preserve (fruit or vegetables) by heating to a sufficient temperature and then sealing in a jar. **8. bottle up, a.** to repress, control, or restrain: *He kept all of his anger bottled up inside him.* **b.** to enclose or entrap: *Traffic was bottled up in the tunnel.* [1325–75; ME *botel* < AF; OF *bo(u)teille* < ML *butticula,* equiv. to LL *butti(s)* BUTT[4] + *-cula* -CULE[1]] —**bot′tle•like′,** *adj.*

bot•tle[2] (bot′l), *n. Archit.* boltel (def. 2).

bot′tle ba′by, an infant fed by bottle from birth, as distinguished from one who is breast-fed. [1890–95]

bot′tle bill′, a legislative bill that requires the charging of a refundable deposit on certain beverage bottles and cans, to encourage the return of these containers for recycling while at the same time reducing littering.

bot•tle•brush (bot′l brush′), *n. Bot.* any of various trees or shrubs of the myrtle family, esp. of the genera *Callistemon* and *Melaleuca,* native to Australia and adjacent areas, having spikes of flowers with numerous conspicuous stamens. [1705–15; BOTTLE[1] + BRUSH[1]; so called from the resemblance of the flower spike to a brush used for cleaning bottles, with bristles on all sides of a central stem]

bot′tlebrush grass′, a North American grass, *Hystrix patula,* having loose flower spikes with long awns. [1835–45]

bot′tle cap′, a device for closing or sealing a bottle, esp. a metal cover with a cork gasket fitting tightly over the mouth of a glass or plastic bottle, held in place by crimping the edge of the cap over the lip or flange of the bottle. [1925–30, *Amer.*]

bot′tle club′, a club serving drinks to members who have reserved or purchased their own bottles of liquor. [1940–45]

bot′tled gas′, 1. gas stored in portable cylinders under pressure. **2.** See **liquefied petroleum gas.** [1925–30]

bot′tled in bond′, (of a straight whiskey or brandy) bottled at 100 proof after aging at least four years and being stored untaxed under U.S. government supervision until released for sale by the manufacturer.

bot′tled wa′ter, drinking water, often spring water, sometimes carbonated, sealed in bottles and usually certified as pure.

bot•tle-feed (bot′l fēd′), *v.t.,* **-fed, -feed•ing. 1.** to nurse or feed (an infant or young animal) with milk or other nourishment from a nursing bottle. **2.** to nurture or teach with exaggerated care: *We had to bottle-feed the new salesman on how to make door-to-door calls.* [1860–65]

bot′tle fern′. See **brittle fern.**

bot•tle•ful (bot′l fo͝ol′), *n., pl.* **-fuls.** the amount that a bottle can hold: *drinking soda by the bottleful.* [1860–65; BOTTLE[1] + -FUL]

bot′tle gen′tian. See **closed gentian.** [1905–10, *Amer.*]

bot′tle glass′, glass of a deep green or amber color. [1620–30] —**bot′tle-glass′,** *adj.*

bot′tle gourd′. See under **gourd** (def. 1). [1860–65]

bot′tle green′, a deep green. [1810–20] —**bot′tle-green′,** *adj.*

bot•tle•head (bot′l hed′), *n.* bottlenose (def. 2). [1645–55; BOTTLE[1] + HEAD]

bot′tle imp′. See **Cartesian diver.** [1815–25]

bot•tle•neck (bot′l nek′), *n.* **1.** a narrow entrance or passageway. **2.** a place or stage in a process at which progress is impeded. **3.** Also called **slide guitar.** a method of guitar playing that produces a gliding sound by pressing a metal bar or glass tube against the strings. —*v.t.* **4.** to hamper or confine by or as if by a bottleneck. —*v.i.* **5.** to become hindered by or as if by a bottleneck. [1895–1900; BOTTLE[1] + NECK]

bot•tle•nose (bot′l nōz′), *n.* **1.** See **bottle-nosed dolphin. 2.** See **bottle-nosed whale.** [1540–50; BOTTLE[1] + NOSE] —**bot′tle-nosed′, bot′tle•nosed′,** *adj.*

bot′tle-nosed dol′phin, any of several dolphins of the genus *Tursiops,* common in North Atlantic and Mediterranean waters, having a rounded forehead and well-defined beak. See illus. under **dolphin.** Also, **bot′tlenose dol′phin, bot′tlenosed dol′phin.** Also called **bottlenose.**

bot′tle-nosed whale′, any of various beaked whales of the family Hyperoodontidae, characterized by a bulbous forehead, esp. *Hyperoodon ampullatus* of the North Atlantic. Also, **bot′tlenose whale′, bot′tlenosed whale′.** Also called **bottlenose.**

bot′tle par′ty, a party at which guests contribute their own liquor. [1925–30]

bot•tler[1] (bot′l ər), *n.* a person, thing, or company that bottles. [BOTTLE[1] + -ER[1]]

bot•tler[2] (bot′lər), *n. Australian and New Zealand Slang.* a person or thing that is excellent or excites admiration. [orig. obscure; the final *-er* (appar. -ER[1]) is shared by a number of synonymous expressive words, the earliest of which is perh. BONZER]

bot′tle shop′, a store that sells wines, liquor, etc., by the bottle; liquor store. [1925–30]

bot′tle tree′, any of several trees of the genus *Brachychiton,* native to Australia, characterized by a bottle-shaped swelling of the trunk, as *B. rupestris* **(narrow-leaved bottle tree)** or *B. australis* **(broad-leaved bottle tree).** [1840–50]

bot′tle turn′ing, *Furniture.* the turning of the legs of chairs, tables, etc., in manufacturing to give certain sections an ornamental, bottlelike form.

bot•tle•wash•er (bot′l wosh′ər, -wô′shər), *n.* **1.** a person or machine that washes bottles. **2. chief cook and bottlewasher,** a person who does a wide variety of routine, sometimes menial, tasks: *He's not just sales manager, he's the chief cook and bottlewasher in this firm.* Also, **bot′tle-wash′er.** [1860–65; BOTTLE[1] + WASHER]

bot′tom (bot′əm), *n.* **1.** the lowest or deepest part of anything, as distinguished from the top: *the bottom of a hill; the bottom of a page.* **2.** the under or lower side; underside: *the bottom of a typewriter.* **3.** the ground under any body of water: *the bottom of the sea.* **4.** Usually, **bottoms.** Also called **bottom land.** *Phys. Geog.* low alluvial land next to a river. **5.** *Naut.* **a.** the part of a hull between the bilges, including the keel. **b.** the part of a hull that is immersed at all times. **c.** the cargo space in a vessel. **d.** a cargo vessel. **6.** the seat of a chair. **7.** *Informal.* the buttocks; rump. **8.** the fundamental part; basic aspect. **9. bottoms,** (*used with a plural v.*) the trousers of a pair of pajamas. **10.** the working part of a plow, comprising the plowshare, landside, and moldboard. **11.** the cause; origin; basis: *Try getting to the bottom of the problem.* **12.** *Baseball.* **a.** the second half of an inning. **b.** the last three players in the batting order. **13.** lowest limit, esp. of dignity, status, or rank: *When people sink that low, they're bound to reach the bottom soon.* **14.** Usually, **bottoms.** *Chem.* the heaviest, least volatile fraction of petroleum, left behind in distillation after more volatile fractions are driven off. **15. at bottom,** in reality; fundamentally: *They knew at bottom that they were only deceiving themselves.* Also, **at the bottom. 16. bottoms up,** (used interjectionally to urge the downing of one's drink). —*v.t.* **17.** to furnish with a bottom. **18.** to base or found (usually fol. by *on* or *upon*). **19.** to discover the full meaning of (something); fathom. **20.** to bring (a submarine) to rest on the ocean floor: *They had to bottom the sub until the enemy cruisers had passed by.* —*v.i.* **21.** to be based; rest. **22.** to strike against the bottom or end; reach the bottom. **23.** (of an automotive vehicle) to sink vertically, as when bouncing after passing over a bump, so that the suspension reaches the lower limit of its motion: *The car bottomed too easily on the bumpy road.* **24. bottom out,** to reach the lowest state or level: *The declining securities market finally bottomed out and began to rise.* —*adj.* **25.** of or pertaining to the bottom or a bottom. **26.** located on or at the bottom: *I want the bottom book in the stack.* **27.** lowest: *bottom prices.* **28.** living near or on the bottom: *A flounder is a bottom fish.* **29.** fundamental: *the bottom cause.* **30. bet one's bottom dollar, a.** to wager the last of one's money or resources. **b.** to be positive or assured: *You can bet your bottom dollar that something will prevent us from leaving on time.* [bef. 1000; ME *botme,* OE *botm;* akin to ON *botn,* D *bodem,* G *Boden,* L *fundus,* Gk *pythmḗn,* Skt *budhná*] —**Syn. 1.** base, foot. **8, 11.** foundation, groundwork.

bot′tom bolt′, a bolt at the bottom of a door or the like, sliding into a socket in the floor or sill and equipped with a device for keeping it raised when the door is not fastened.

bot′tom dog′, underdog. [1880–85; by analogy with TOP DOG]

bot′tom drawer′ (drôr), *Brit.* any drawer used for a hope chest. [1885–90]

bot′tom fish′, any of certain fishes that live at or near the bottom of a body of water, as certain of the cod and related species, the flatfishes, and catfishes. Also called **ground fish.**

bot•tom-fish (bot′əm fish′), *v.i.* to fish with a weighted line for fish that feed close to the bottom. Also, **ground-fish.** [1840–50]

bot′tom gear′, *Brit.* low[1] (def. 47).

bot′tom grass′, any grass that grows on bottoms or lowlands.

bot′tom heat′, *Hort.* heat artificially applied to a container in which plants are grown in order to induce their germination, rooting, or growth. [1880–85]

bot′tom ice′. See **anchor ice.** [1720–30, *Amer.*]

bot′tom la′dy, *Slang.* **1.** a pimp's most reliable prostitute. **2.** a female pimp. **3.** the madam of a brothel. Also called **bottom woman.**

bot′tom land′, *Phys. Geog.* bottom (def. 4). [1720–30, *Amer.*]

bot•tom•less (bot′əm lis), *adj.* **1.** lacking a bottom. **2.** immeasurably deep. **3.** unfathomable; mysterious: *a bottomless problem.* **4.** without bounds; unlimited: *He seems to have a bottomless supply of money.* **5.** without basis, cause, or reason: *a bottomless accusation.* **6.** nude or nearly nude below as well as above the waist: *bottomless dancers.* **7.** featuring bottomless entertainers: *a bottomless club.* [1275–1325; ME *botomles.* See BOTTOM, -LESS; defs. 5, 6 on the model of TOPLESS] —**bot′tom•less•ly,** *adv.* —**bot′tom•less•ness,** *n.* —**Syn. 4.** boundless, infinite, inexhaustible.

bot′tomless pit′, 1. hell (def. 1). **2.** something that drains all one's energy or resources. [1525–35]

bot′tom line′, 1. the last line of a financial statement, used for showing net profit or loss. **2.** net profit or loss. **3.** the deciding or crucial factor. **4.** the ultimate result; outcome. [1965–70] —**bot′tom-line′,** *adj.*

bot•tom-lin•er (bot′əm lī′nər), *n.* a person, as an executive, accountant, or stockholder, who puts the net profits of a business ahead of all other considerations. [BOTTOM LINE + -ER[1]]

bot•tom•most (bot′əm mōst′ *or, esp. Brit,* -məst), *adj.* **1.** of, pertaining to, or situated at the bottom. **2.** (of one of a series) farthest down; lowest. **3.** bottom. [1860–65; BOTTOM + -MOST]

bot•tom-of-the-line (bot′əm əv t͟hə līn′), *adj.* being the cheapest item of its kind made by a manufacturer; produced as inexpensively as possible (opposed to *top-of-the-line*): *bottom-of-the-line merchandise that has no warranty.*

CONCISE PRONUNCIATION KEY: *act, cāpe, dâre, pärt; set, ēqual; if, īce; ox, ōver, ôrder, oil, bo͝ok, bo͞ot, out; up, ûrge; child; sing; shoe; thin, t͟hat;* zh as in *treasure.* ə = *a* as in *alone, e* as in *system, i* as in *easily, o* as in *gallop, u* as in *circus;* ᵊ as in *fire* (fīᵊr), *hour* (ouᵊr). l and n can serve as syllabic consonants, as in *cradle* (krād′l), and *button* (but′n). See the full key inside the front cover.

bot′tom quark′, *Physics.* the quark having electric charge −⅓ times the elementary charge and bottom quantum number −1. It is more massive than the up, down, strange, and charmed quarks. Also called **beauty quark, b quark, b-quark.** [1975–80]

bot′tom round′, a cut of beef taken from outside the round, which is below the rump and above the upper leg. Cf. **top round.** [1920–25]

bot•tom•ry (bot′əm rē), *n., pl.* **-ries.** *Marine Law.* a contract, of the nature of a mortgage, by which the owner of a ship borrows money to make a voyage, pledging the ship as security. [1615–25; modeled on D *bodemerij,* equiv. to *bodem* BOTTOM + *-erij* -RY]

bot′tom time′, *Scuba Diving.* the total time, in minutes, from the beginning of a descent to the beginning of an ascent.

bot•tom-up (bot′əm up′), *adj.* of, pertaining to, or originating with the common people, nonprofessionals, or the lower ranks of an organization: *The five-day workweek was a bottom-up movement some business leaders and politicians finally supported.*

bot′tom-up′ pro′gramming, *Computers.* a programming technique in which lower-level modules are developed before higher-level modules are (opposed to *top-down programming*).

bot′tom wom′an, *Slang.* See **bottom lady.**

bot′tom yeast′, a yeast whose cells, in the manufacture of wine and lager beer, fall to the bottom as a sediment. Also called **sediment yeast.** [1905–10]

Bot•trop (bôt′rôp), *n.* a city in W West Germany, in the Ruhr region. 100,800.

Botts′ dots′ (bots), *Slang.* small, protruding, reflecting ceramic tiles used on some roads instead of painted lines to mark lanes. [after Elbert D. Botts (born 1893), U.S. chemist, who developed them]

bot•u•lin (boch′ə lin), *n.* the toxin formed by botulinus and causing botulism. [1885–90; < L *botul(us)* (see BOTULISM) + -IN[2]]

bot•u•li•nus (boch′ə lī′nəs), *n., pl.* **-nus•es.** a soil bacterium, *Clostridium botulinum,* that thrives and forms botulin under anaerobic conditions. Also, **bot•u•li•num** (boch′ə lī′nəm). [1895–1900; < NL: the former specific name, equiv. to L *botul(us)* a sausage (see BOTULISM) + *-inus* -INE[2]] —**bot′u•li′nal,** *adj.*

bot•u•lism (boch′ə liz′əm), *n. Pathol.* a sometimes fatal disease of the nervous system acquired from spoiled foods in which botulin is present, esp. improperly canned or marinated foods. [1875–80; < G *Botulismus,* equiv. to L *botul(us)* sausage (a source of botulin toxin) + *-ismus* -ISM]

Bot•vin•nik (bot vē′nik, -vin′ik; *Russ.* but vyē′nyik), *n.* **Mi•kha•il (Moi•se•e•vich)** (mi kä ēl′ moi sā′yə vich; *Russ.* myi khu yēl′ mī sye′yi vyich), born 1911, Russian chess master.

Boua•ké (bwä kā′, bwä′kā), *n.* a city in central Ivory Coast. 200,000.

Bouar (bwär), *n.* a city in the W Central African Republic. 51,000.

bou•bou (bo͞o′bo͞o), *n.* a long, loose-fitting, brightly colored garment worn by both sexes in parts of Africa. Also, **bubu.** [1960–65; < F < Malinke *bubu*]

Bou•chard (bo͞o shar′), *n.* **(Louis) Hen•ri** (lwē äN rē′), 1875–1960, French sculptor.

bouche (bo͞osh), *n. Armor.* a curved indentation in an upper corner of a jousting shield, serving as a lance rest: used from the 14th to the 17th century. [< F phrase *à bouche* lit., with (a) mouth, said of a notched shield. See BOUCHÉE]

Bou•ché (bo͞o shā′), *n.* **Louis,** 1896–1969, U.S. painter.

bou•chée (bo͞o shā′), *n.* a small patty shell of puff pastry, used esp. for hot hors d'oeuvres. [1840–50; < F: lit., a mouthful, equiv. to *bouche* mouth (< L *bucca*) + *-ée* < L *-āta* -ATE[1]]

Bou•cher (bo͞o shā′), *n.* **Fran•çois** (fräN swa′), 1703–70, French painter.

Bou•cher de Crève•coeur de Perthes (bo͞o shā′ də krev kœr′ də pert′), **Jacques** (zhäk), 1788–1868, French archaeologist and writer.

Bou•cher•ville (bo͞o′shər vil′; *Fr.* bo͞o sher vēl′), *n.* a town in S Quebec, in E Canada, near Montreal, on the St. Lawrence. 29,704.

Bouches-du-Rhône (bo͞osh dy rōn′), *n.* a department in SE France. 1,632,974; 2026 sq. mi. (5245 sq. km). *Cap.:* Marseilles.

bou•chon (bo͞o shon′; *Fr.* bo͞o shôN′), *n., pl.* **-chons** (-shonz′; *Fr.* -shôN′). *Furniture.* a supplementary, baize-covered top set in the center of a bouillotte table. [1880–85; < F: stopper, deriv. of OF *bouche* sheaf]

Bou•ci•cault (bo͞o′sē kôlt′, -kō′), *n.* **Di•on** (dī′on, -ən), 1822–90, Irish playwright and actor, in the U.S. after 1853.

bou•clé (bo͞o klā′), *n.* **1.** yarn with loops producing a rough, nubby appearance on woven or knitted fabrics. **2.** a fabric made of this yarn. Also, **bou•cle′.** [1890–95; < F: lit., curled; see BUCKLE]

bou•deuse (bo͞o dœz′), *n.* a sofa or settee, usually upholstered, having two seats with a common backrest between them. [< F, n. use of *boudeuse* sulky, sullen (*boud(er)* to sulk, be sullen + *-euse* -EUSE]

Bou•dic•ca (bo͞o dik′ə), *n.* Boadicea.

bou•din (bo͞o daN′), *n., pl.* **-dins** (-daN′; *Eng.* -danz′). *French Cookery.* a blood sausage **(boudin noir)** or sometimes a white sausage **(boudin blanc),** made of chicken, pork, or veal. [1795–1805, *Amer.;* < LaF, F: sausage; OF, of obscure orig.]

bou•din blanc (*Fr.* bo͞o daN bläN′). See under **boudin.** [< F: white sausage]

bou•din noir (*Fr.* bo͞o daN nwar′). See under **boudin.** [< F: black sausage]

bou•doir (bo͞o′dwär, -dwôr), *n.* a woman's bedroom or private sitting room. [1775–85; < F: lit., a sulking place (*boud(er)* to sulk + *-oir* -ORY[2])]

bouf•fant (bo͞o fänt′, bo͞o′fänt; *Fr.* bo͞o fäN′), *adj.* **1.** puffed out; full: *a bouffant skirt.* —*n.* **2.** a woman's hair style in which the hair is teased to give an overall puffed-out appearance and often combed to frame the face. [1875–80; < F: lit., swelling (*bouff(er)* to swell + *-ant* -ANT)] —**bouf•fan•cy** (bo͞o′fən sē), *n.*

bouffe (bo͞of), *n. Music.* See **opéra bouffe.** [< F < It *buffa,* fem. of *buffo* comic; see BUFFOON]

Bou•gain•ville (bo͞o gaN vēl′ *for 1;* bo͞o′gən vil′, bō′-, *Fr.* bo͞o gaN vēl′ *for 2*), *n.* **1. Louis An•toine de** (lwē äN twan′ də), 1729–1811, French navigator. **2.** the largest of the Solomon Islands, in the W Pacific Ocean: part of Papua New Guinea. 78,000; 4080 sq. mi. (10,567 sq. km).

bou•gain•vil•le•a (bo͞o′gən vil′ē ə, -vil′yə, bō′-), *n.* any of several shrubs or vines of the genus *Bougainvillea,* native to South America, having small flowers with showy, variously colored bracts, and often cultivated in warm regions. [1789; < NL, named after L. A. de BOUGAINVILLE]

bough (bou), *n.* a branch of a tree, esp. one of the larger or main branches. [bef. 1000; ME *bogh,* OE *bōg, bōh* shoulder, bough; c. ON *bōgr,* D *boeg,* G *Bug,* Gk *pêchys,* Skt *bāhu*] —**bough′less,** *adj.*
—**Syn. 1.** See **branch.**

boughed (boud), *adj.* **1.** having a bough or boughs (usually used in combination): *golden-boughed elms.* **2.** covered or shaded with boughs: *a boughed retreat in the woods.* [1350–1400; ME; see BOUGH, -ED[3]]

bough•pot (bou′pot′), *n.* a large vase or pot for cut flowers or small branches. Also, **bowpot.** [1575–85; BOUGH + POT[1]]

bought (bôt), *v.* **1.** pt. and pp. of **buy.** —*adj.* **2.** *South Midland and Southern U.S.* store-bought.

bought•en (bôt′n), *adj. Northern and North Midland U.S. Nonstandard.* store-bought. [1785–95; BOUGHT + -EN[3]]

bou•gie (bo͞o′jē, -zhē, bo͞o zhē′), *n.* **1.** *Med.* **a.** a slender, flexible instrument introduced into passages of the body, esp. the urethra, for dilating, examining, medicating, etc. **b.** a suppository. **2.** a wax candle. [1745–55; < F, after *Bougie* (< Ar *Bujāyah*), town in Algeria, center of the wax trade]

Bou•gue•reau (bo͞og[ə] rō′), *n.* **A•dolphe Wil•liam** (a dôlf′ vēl yam′), 1825–1905, French painter.

bouil•la•baisse (bo͞ol′yə bās′, bo͞ol′yə bās′; *Fr.* bo͞o-ya bes′), *n.* a soup or stew containing several kinds of fish and often shellfish, usually combined with olive oil, tomatoes, and saffron. [1850–55; < F < Pr *boui-abaisso,* taken as either "boil it, then lower the heat," or "when it boils, lower the heat"; *boui* 2d sing. impv. or 3d sing. pres. of *bouie* to BOIL[1]; *abaisso* 2d sing. impv. of *abaissa* to lower; see ABASE]

bouil•lon (bo͝ol′yon, -yən; *Fr.* bo͞o yôN′), *n.* a clear, usually seasoned broth made by straining water in which beef, chicken, etc., has been cooked, or by dissolving a commercially prepared bouillon cube or cubes in hot water. [1650–60; < F, equiv. to *bouill(ir)* to BOIL[1] + *-on* n. suffix]

bouil′lon cube′, a small compressed cube of dehydrated beef, chicken, or vegetable stock. [1930–35]

bouil′lon cup′, a small, bowl-shaped vessel, with two handles, in which bouillon is served.

bouil′lon spoon′, a spoon with a round bowl, smaller than a soup spoon.

bouil•lotte′ lamp′ (bo͞o yot′), *Fr. Furniture.* a table lamp of the 18th century, having two or three adjustable candle brackets and a common shade sliding on a central shaft. [from its use on a BOUILLOTTE TABLE]

bouillotte′ ta′ble, *Fr. Furniture.* a small round table of the 18th century, having around its top a gallery within which a bouchon could be set for the playing of card games. [< F *bouillotte* card game, equiv. to *bouill(ir)* to BOIL[1] + *-otte* n. suffix]

Bou•lan•ger (bo͞o′län jā′; *Fr.* bo͞o läN zhā′), *n.* **1. Georges Er•nest Jean Ma•rie** (zhôrzh er nest′ zhäN ma rē′), 1837–91, French general and politician. **2. Na•dia (Ju•liette)** (nä′dē ə jo͞o′lē et′; *Fr.* na dya′ zhy-lyet′), 1887–1979, French musician and teacher.

bou•lan•ge•rie (bo͞o laNzh[ə] rē′), *n., pl.* ***-ries*** (-rē′). *French.* a bakery that specializes in baking and selling bread.

bou•lan•ger•ite (bo͞o lan′jə rīt′), *n.* a bluish lead-gray mineral, lead antimony sulfide, $Pb_5Sb_4S_{11}$, a minor ore of lead. [named after C. L. *Boulanger* (1810–49), French mining engineer; see -ITE[1]]

Bou•lan•gism (bo͞o lan′jiz əm), *n.* the doctrines of militarism and reprisals against Germany, advocated, esp. in the 1880's, by the French general Boulanger. [1885–90; < F *boulangisme.* See G. E. J. M. BOULANGER, -ISM] —**Bou•lan′gist,** *n.*

boul•der (bōl′dər), *n.* a detached and rounded or worn rock, esp. a large one. Also, **bowlder.** [1610–20; short for *boulder stone;* ME *bulderston* < Scand; cf. dial. Sw *bullersten* big stone (in a stream), equiv. to *buller* rumbling noise (< OSw *bulder*) + *sten* STONE] —**boul′•dered,** *adj.* —**boul′der•y,** *adj.*

Boul•der (bōl′dər), *n.* a city in N Colorado. 76,685.

Boul′der Can′yon, a canyon of the Colorado River between Arizona and Nevada, above Boulder Dam.

boul′der clay′, *Geol.* a glacial deposit consisting chiefly of unstratified clay with embedded boulders. [1855–60]

Boul′der Dam′, a dam on the Colorado River, on the boundary between SE Nevada and NW Arizona. 726 ft. (221 m) high; 1244 ft. (379 m) long. Official name, **Hoover Dam.**

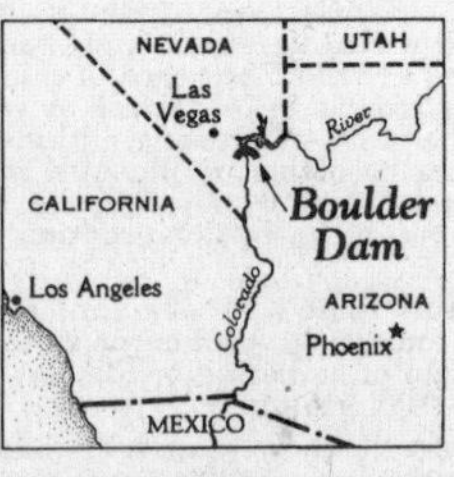

boul•der•ing (bōl′dər ing), *n.* pavement made with small boulders. Also, **bowldering.** [1875–80; *boulder* to pave with BOULDER(S) + -ING[1]]

boul′der rasp′berry. See **Rocky Mountain flowering raspberry.**

boule[1] (bo͞ol), *n.* **1.** Also called **birne.** a cylindrical lump of material for synthetic gems, made by the Verneuil process. **2.** a metal ball, usually made out of steel, used in pétanque. **3.** Sometimes, **boules.** pétanque. [1915–20; < F: lit., a ball; see BOWL[2]]

boule[2] (bo͞ol), *n.* (*often cap.*) *Furniture.* buhl. Also called **boule•work** (bo͞ol′wûrk′).

Bou•le (bo͞o′lē, bo͞o lā′), *n.* **1.** the legislative assembly of modern Greece. **2.** (*sometimes l.c.*) a state legislative, advisory, or administrative council in ancient Greece. [1840–50; < Gk: a council, body of chosen ones]

bou•leu•te•ri•on (bo͞o′lo͞o tēr′ē on′, bo͞ol′yo͞o-), *n., pl.* **-te•ri•a** (-tēr′ē ə). a council chamber in ancient Greece. [< Gk, equiv. to *bouleú(ein)* to deliberate + *-tērion* n. suffix of place]

boul•e•vard (bo͝ol′ə värd′, bo͞o′lə-), *n.* **1.** a broad avenue in a city, usually having areas at the sides or center for trees, grass, or flowers. **2.** *Upper Midwest.* a strip of lawn between a sidewalk and the curb. [1765–75; < F, MF (orig. Picard, Walloon): rampart, avenue built on the site of a razed rampart < MD *bol(le)werc;* see BULWARK]
—**Syn.** See **street.**

bou•le•var•dier (bo͝ol′ə vär dēr′, bo͞o′lə-; *Fr.* bo͞ol[ə]-var dyā′), *n., pl.* **-diers** (-dērz′; *Fr.* -dyā′). **1.** a person who frequents the most fashionable Parisian locales. **2.** See **bon vivant.** [1875–80; < F; see BOULEVARD, -IER[2]]

bou•le•ver•se•ment (bo͞ol[ə] vers mäN′), *n. French.* an overturning; convulsion; turmoil.

Bou•lez (bo͞o lez′), *n.* **Pierre** (pē âr′; *Fr.* pyer), born 1925, French composer and conductor.

bou•lim•i•a (bo͞o lim′ē ə, -lē′mē ə, bə-), *n. Med.* bulimia.

boulle (bo͞ol), *n.* (*often cap.*) *Furniture.* buhl. Also called **boulle•work** (bo͞ol′wûrk′).

Bou•logne (bo͞o lōn′, -loin′, bə-; *Fr.* bo͞o lôn′y[ə]), *n.* a seaport in N France, on the English Channel. 49,284. Also called **Bou•logne-sur-Mer** (bo͞o lôn′y[ə] syr mer′).

Bou•logne Bil•lan•court (bo͞o lôn′y[ə] bē yäN ko͞or′), a suburb of Paris, in N France. 103,948. Also called **Bou•logne-sur-Seine** (bo͞o lôn′y[ə] syr sen′).

Boult (bōlt), *n.* **Sir Adrian Cedric,** 1889–1983, English conductor.

boul•ter (bōl′tər), *n.* a long, stout fishing line with several hooks attached. [1595–1605; orig. uncert.]

Bou•me•dienne (bo͞o′mə dyen′, -dē en′), *n.* **Hou•a•ri** (o͞o är′ē), (*Mohammed Boukharouba*), 1925?–78, Algerian military and political leader: president 1965–78.

boun (boun, bo͞on), *v.t., v.i. Archaic.* to prepare; make ready. [ME; see BOUND[4]]

bounce (bouns), *v.,* **bounced, bounc•ing,** *n., adv.* —*v.i.* **1.** to spring back from a surface in a lively manner: *The ball bounced off the wall.* **2.** to strike the ground or other surface, and rebound: *The ball bounced once before he caught it.* **3.** to move or walk in a lively, exuberant, or energetic manner: *She bounced into the room.* **4.** to move along in a lively manner, repeatedly striking the surface below and rebounding: *The box bounced down the stairs.* **5.** to move about or enter or leave noisily or angrily (fol. by *around, about, out, out of, into,* etc.): *He bounced out of the room in a huff.* **6.** (of a check or the like) to fail to be honored by the bank against which it was drawn, due to lack of sufficient funds. —*v.t.* **7.** to cause to bound and rebound: *to bounce a ball; to bounce a child on one's knee; to bounce a signal off a satellite.* **8.** to refuse payment on (a check) because of insufficient funds: *The bank bounced my rent check.* **9.** to give (a bad check) as payment: *That's the first time anyone bounced a check on me.* **10.** *Slang.* to eject, expel, or dismiss summarily or forcibly. **11. bounce back,** to recover quickly: *After losing the first game of the double-header, the team bounced back to win the second.* —*n.* **12.** a bound or rebound: *to catch a ball on the first bounce.* **13.** a sudden spring or leap: *In one bounce he was at the door.* **14.** ability to rebound; resilience: *This tennis ball has no more bounce.* **15.** vitality; energy; liveliness: *There is bounce in his step. This soda water has more bounce to it.* **16.** the fluctuation in magnitude of target echoes on a radarscope. **17.** *Slang.* a dismissal, rejection, or expulsion: *He's gotten the bounce from three different jobs.* —*adv.* **18.** with a bounce; suddenly. [1175–1225; ME *buncin, bounsen,* var. of *bunkin,* appar. c. D *bonken* to thump, belabor, *bonzen* to knock, bump] —**bounce′a•ble,** *adj.* —**bounce′a•bly,** *adv.*

—Syn. 15. animation, vivacity, life, spirit, pep, vigor, zip.

bounce•back (bouns′bak′), *n.* the act or an instance of bouncing back, recovering, or recuperating: *Fall sales have experienced a tremendous bounceback.* Also, **bounce′-back′.** [n. use of v. phrase *bounce back*]

bounced′ flash′, *Photog.* a flash bounced off a reflective surface, as a ceiling or wall, to illuminate a subject indirectly.

bounce′ flash′, *Photog.* a flash lamp designed to produce a bounced flash. [1950–55]

bounce′ light′, *Photog.* **1.** Also, **bounce′ light′ing.** light that is bounced off a reflective surface onto the subject in order to achieve a softer lighting effect. **2.** any arrangement of a light source and reflective surface used to provide such light.

bounc•er (boun′sər), *n.* **1.** a person or thing that bounces. **2.** a person who is employed at a bar, nightclub, etc., to eject disorderly persons. **3.** something large of its kind. [1755–65; BOUNCE + -ER[1]]

bounc•ing (boun′sing), *adj.* **1.** stout, strong, or vigorous: *a bouncing baby boy.* **2.** exaggerated; big; hearty; noisy. [1570–80; BOUNCE + -ING[2]] **—bounc′ing•ly,** *adv.*

bounc′ing Bet′ (bet), soapwort. Also, **bounc′ing Bess′** (bes). [1880–85]

bounc•y (boun′sē), *adj.,* **bounc•i•er, bounc•i•est. 1.** tending characteristically to bounce or bounce well: *An old tennis ball is not as bouncy as a new one.* **2.** resilient: *a thick carpet that is bouncy underfoot.* **3.** animated; lively: *a bouncy personality.* [1920–25; BOUNCE + -Y[1]] **—bounc′i•ly,** *adv.*

bound[1] (bound), *v.* **1.** pt. and pp. of **bind.** *—adj.* **2.** tied; in bonds: *a bound prisoner.* **3.** made fast as if by a band or bond: *She is bound to her family.* **4.** secured within a cover, as a book. **5.** under a legal or moral obligation: *He is bound by the terms of the contract.* **6.** destined; sure; certain: *It is bound to happen.* **7.** determined or resolved: *He is bound to go.* **8.** *Pathol.* constipated. **9.** *Math.* (of a vector) having a specified initial point as well as magnitude and direction. Cf. **free** (def. 31). **10.** held with another element, substance, or material in chemical or physical union. **11.** (of a linguistic form) occurring only in combination with other forms, as most affixes. Cf. **free** (def. 34). **12. bound up in** or **with, a.** inseparably connected with. **b.** devoted or attached to: *She is bound up in her teaching.* [ptp. and past tense of BIND] **—bound′ness,** *n.*
—Syn. 5. liable, obligated, obliged, compelled.

bound[2] (bound), *v.i.* **1.** to move by leaps; leap; jump; spring: *The colt bounded through the meadow.* **2.** to rebound, as a ball; bounce: *The ball bounded against the wall.* *—n.* **3.** a leap onward or upward; jump. **4.** a rebound; bounce. [1545–55; < MF *bond* a leap, *bondir* to leap, orig. resound << VL **bombitīre* for **bombitāre* to buzz, whiz (L *bomb(us)* (see BOMB) + *-it-* intensive suffix + *-ā-* thematic vowel + *-re* inf. suffix)] **—bound′ing•ly,** *adv.*
—Syn. 1. See **skip**[1].

bound[3] (bound), *n.* **1.** Usually, **bounds.** limit or boundary: *the bounds of space and time; within the bounds of his estate; within the bounds of reason.* **2.** something that limits, confines, or restrains. **3. bounds, a.** territories on or near a boundary. **b.** land within boundary lines. **4.** *Math.* a number greater than or equal to, or less than or equal to, all the numbers in a given set. Cf. **greatest lower bound, least upper bound, lower bound, upper bound. 5. out of bounds, a.** beyond the official boundaries, prescribed limits, or restricted area: *The ball bounced out of bounds.* **b.** forbidden; prohibited: *The park is out of bounds to students.* *—v.t.* **6.** to limit by or as if by bounds; keep within limits or confines. **7.** to form the boundary or limit of. **8.** to name or list the boundaries of. *—v.i.* **9.** to abut. [1175–1225; ME *bunde* < AF; OF *bone, bonde,* var. of *bodne* < ML *budina,* of uncert. orig.; cf. BOURN[2]] **—bound′a•ble,** *adj.*
—Syn. 1. border, frontier, confine.

bound[4] (bound), *adj.* **1.** going or intending to go; on the way to; destined (usually fol. by *for*): *The train is bound for Denver.* **2.** *Archaic.* prepared; ready. [1150–1200; ME *b(o)un* ready < ON *būinn,* ptp. of *būa* to get ready]

-bound[1], a combining form of **bound**[1]: *snowbound.*

-bound[2], a combining form of **bound**[4]: *eastbound.*

bound•a•ry (boun′də rē, -drē), *n., pl.* **-ries. 1.** something that indicates bounds or limits; a limiting or bounding line. **2.** Also called **frontier.** *Math.* the collection of all points of a given set having the property that every neighborhood of each point contains points in the set and in the complement of the set. **3.** *Cricket.* a hit in which the ball reaches or crosses the boundary line of the field on one or more bounces, counting four runs for the batsman. Cf. **six** (def. 5). [1620–30; BOUND[3] + -ARY]
—Syn. 1. BOUNDARY, BORDER, FRONTIER share the sense of that which divides one entity or political unit from another. BOUNDARY, in reference to a country, city, state, territory, or the like, most often designates a line on a map: *boundaries are shown in red.* Occasionally, it also refers to a physical feature that marks the agreed-upon line separating two political units: *The Niagara River forms part of the boundary between the United States and Canada.* BORDER is more often used than BOUNDARY in direct reference to a political dividing line; it may also refer to the region (of, for instance, a country) adjoining the actual line of demarcation: *crossing the Mexican border; border towns along the Rio Grande.* FRONTIER may refer to a political dividing line: *crossed the Spanish frontier on Tuesday.* It may also denote or describe the portion of a country adjoining its border with another country (*towns in the Polish frontier*) or, especially in North America, the most remote settled or occupied parts of a country: *the frontier towns of the Great Plains.* FRONTIER, especially in the plural, also refers to the most advanced or newest activities in an area of knowledge or practice: *the frontiers of nuclear medicine.*

bound′ary condi′tion, *Math.* a stated restriction, usually in the form of an equation, that limits the possible solutions to a differential equation.

bound′ary lay′er, *Physics.* the portion of a fluid flowing past a body that is in the immediate vicinity of the body and that has a reduced flow due to the forces of adhesion and viscosity. [1920–25]

bound′ary line′, 1. boundary (def. 1). **2.** See **partition line.** [1695–1705]

bound′ary rid′er, *n. Australian.* a ranch hand who patrols the boundary of a sheep or cattle station in order to watch the stock, repair fences, etc. [1860–65]

bound′ary val′ue prob′lem, *Math.* any of a series of problems occurring in the solution of a differential equation with boundary conditions.

bound′ charge′, *Elect.* See **polarization charge.**

bound•ed (boun′did), *adj.* **1.** having bounds or limits. **2.** *Math.* **a.** (of a function) having a range with an upper bound and a lower bound. **b.** (of a sequence) having the absolute value of each term less than or equal to some specified positive number. **c.** (of the variation of a function) having the variation less than a positive number. [1590–1600; BOUND[3] + -ED[2]] **—bound′ed•ly,** *adv.* **—bound′ed•ness,** *n.*

bound•en (boun′dən), *adj.* **1.** obligatory; compulsory: *one's bounden duty.* **2.** *Archaic.* under obligation; obliged. [1250–1300; ME, var. of BOUND[1]]

bound•er (boun′dər), *n.* **1.** an obtrusive, ill-bred man. **2.** a person or thing that bounds. [1535–45; BOUND[2] + -ER[1]]

bound′ form′, a linguistic form that never occurs by itself but always as part of some larger construction, as *-ed* in *seated.* Cf. **free form** (def. 2).

bound•less (bound′lis), *adj.* having no bounds; infinite or vast; unlimited: *His boundless energy amazed his friends.* [1585–95; BOUND[3] + -LESS] **—bound′less•ly,** *adv.* **—bound′less•ness,** *n.*
—Syn. limitless, endless, unbounded, inexhaustible, illimitable.

bound′ var′iable, *Logic.* (in the functional calculus) a variable occurring in a quantifier and in a sentential function within the scope of the quantifier. Cf. **free variable.**

boun•te•ous (boun′tē əs), *adj.* **1.** giving or disposed to give freely; generous; liberal. **2.** freely bestowed; plentiful; abundant. [1325–75; late ME (*bounte* BOUNTY + *-ous*); r. ME *bountevous* < MF *bontive* (*bonte* BOUNTY + *-ive,* fem. of *-if* -IVE) + -OUS] **—boun′te•ous•ly,** *adv.* **—boun′te•ous•ness,** *n.*

boun•tied (boun′tēd), *adj.* **1.** offering a bounty. **2.** rewarded with a bounty. [1780–90; BOUNTY + -ED[3]]

boun•ti•ful (boun′tə fəl), *adj.* **1.** liberal in bestowing gifts, favors, or bounties; munificent; generous. **2.** abundant; ample: *a bountiful supply.* [1500–10; BOUNTY + -FUL] **—boun′ti•ful•ly,** *adv.* **—boun′ti•ful•ness,** *n.*
—Syn. 1. See **generous. 2.** See **plentiful.**

Boun•ti•ful (boun′tə fəl), *n.* a city in N Utah, near Salt Lake City. 32,877.

boun•ty (boun′tē), *n., pl.* **-ties. 1.** a premium or reward, esp. one offered by a government: *There was a bounty on his head. Some states offer a bounty for dead coyotes.* **2.** a generous gift. **3.** generosity in giving. [1200–50; ME *b(o)unte* < AF, OF *bonte,* OF *bontet* < L *bonitāt-* (s. of *bonitās*) goodness. See BOON[2], -ITY] **—boun′ty•less,** *adj.*
—Syn. 1. See **bonus. 2.** present, benefaction. **3.** munificence, liberality, charity, beneficence.

boun′ty hunt′er, 1. a person who hunts outlaws or wild animals for the bounty offered for capturing or killing them. **2.** a person who seeks a reward for recovering valuable property. **3.** *Slang.* a salesman or agent who works for a fee or commission. [1955–60]

bou•quet (bō kā′, bo͞o- *for 1, 2;* bo͞o kā′ *or, occas.,* bō- *for 3*), *n.* **1.** a bunch of flowers; nosegay. **2.** a compliment: *The drama critics greeted her performance with bouquets.* **3.** the characteristic aroma of wines, liqueurs, etc. [1710–20; < F: bunch, orig. thicket, grove; OF *bosquet,* equiv. to *bosc* wood (< Gmc; see BOSK, BUSH[1]) + *-et* -ET]
—Syn. 3. scent, odor, fragrance, perfume, nose.

bou•quet gar•ni (bō kā′ gär nē′, bo͞o-; *Fr.* bo͞o ke gar nē′), *pl.* **bou•quets gar•nis** (bō kāz′ gär nē′, bo͞o-; *Fr.* bo͞o ke gar nē′). a small bundle of herbs, as thyme, parsley, bay leaf, and the like, often tied in a cheesecloth bag and used for flavoring soups, stews, etc. [1850–55; < F; see BOUQUET, GARNISH]

bouquet′ lark′spur. See **Siberian larkspur.**

Bour•bon (bo͝or′bən, bôr′-, bōr′- *or, Fr.,* bo͞or bôn′ *for 1–3;* bûr′bən *for 4 or occas. for 3*), *n.* **1.** a member of a French royal family that ruled in France 1589–1792, Spain 1700–1931, and Naples 1735–1806, 1815–60. **2. Charles** (sharl), (*"Constable de Bourbon"*), 1490–1527, French general. **3.** a person who is extremely conservative or reactionary. **4.** (*l.c.*) Also called **bour′bon whis′key.** a straight whiskey distilled from a mash having 51 percent or more corn: originally the corn whiskey produced in Bourbon County, Kentucky.

Bour•bon•ism (bo͝or′bə niz′əm *or, occas.,* bûr′-), *n.* **1.** adherence to the ideas and system of government practiced by the Bourbons. **2.** extreme conservatism, esp. in politics. [1875–80, *Amer.;* BOURBON + -ISM] **—Bour•bo•ni•an** (bo͝or bō′nē ən *or, occas.,* bûr-), **Bour•bon•ic** (bo͝or bon′ik *or, occas.,* bûr-), *adj.* **—Bour′bon•ist,** *n.*

Bour•bon•nais (bo͝or′bō nā′, bər bō′nis), *n.* a town in NE Illinois. 13,280.

bour′bon rose′, a hybrid rose, *Rosa borboniana,* having dark, carmine-colored flowers, cultivated in many horticultural varieties. [1835–45]

bour•don (bo͝or′dn, bôr′-, bōr′-), *n. Music.* **1. a.** the drone pipe of a bagpipe. **b.** the drone string of a stringed instrument. **2.** a low-pitched tone; bass. **3.** a pipe organ stop of very low pitch. **4.** the bell in a carillon having the lowest pitch. [1350–1400; ME < MF; see BURDEN[2]]

Bour′don-tube gauge′ (bo͝or′dn to͞ob′, -tyo͞ob′, bôr′-, bōr′-, bo͝or dôN′-), *Chem.* an instrument for measuring the pressure of gases or liquids, consisting of a semicircular or coiled, flexible metal tube attached to a gauge that records the degree to which the tube is straightened by the pressure of the gas or liquid inside. [1900–05; named after E. Bourdon, 19th-century French inventor]

bourg (bo͝org; *Fr.* bo͞oR), *n., pl.* **bourgs** (bo͝orgz; *Fr.* bo͞oR). **1.** a town. **2.** a French market town. [1400–50; late ME < AF << LL *burgus* < Gmc; see BOROUGH]

bour•geois[1] (bo͝or zhwä′, bo͝or′zhwä; *Fr.* bo͞or zhwa′), *n., pl.* **-geois,** *adj.* *—n.* **1.** a member of the middle class. **2.** a person whose political, economic, and social opinions are believed to be determined mainly by concern for property values and conventional respectability. **3.** a shopkeeper or merchant. *—adj.* **4.** belonging to, characteristic of, or consisting of the middle class. **5.** conventional; middle-class. **6.** dominated or characterized by materialistic pursuits or concerns. [1555–65; < MF; OF *borgeis* BURGESS]

bour•geois[2] (bər jois′), *n. Print.* a size of type approximately 9-point, between brevier and long primer. [1815–25; perh. from a printer so named]

Bour•geois (bo͝or zhwä′, bo͝or′zhwä; *Fr.* bo͞oR zhwa′), *n.* **Lé•on Vic•tor Au•guste** (lā ôN′ vēk tôr′ ō gyst′), 1851–1925, French statesman: Nobel peace prize 1920.

bour•geoise (bo͝or′zhwäz, bo͝or zhwäz′; *Fr.* bo͞oR-zhwaz′), *n., pl.* **-geois•es** (-zhwä ziz, -zhwä′-; *Fr.* -zhwaz′). **1.** a female member of the bourgeoisie. **2.** bourgeoisie (def. 1). [1755–65; < F; fem. of BOURGEOIS]

bour•geoi•sie (bo͝or′zhwä zē′; *Fr.* bo͞oR zhwa zē′), *n.* **1.** the bourgeois class. **2.** (in Marxist theory) the class that, in contrast to the proletariat or wage-earning class, is primarily concerned with property values. [1700–10; < F; see BOURGEOIS[1], -Y[3]]

bour•geon (bûr′jən), *n., v.i., v.t.* burgeon.

Bourges (bo͞oRzh), *n.* a city in and the capital of Cher, in central France: cathedral. 80,379.

Bour•get (bo͝or zhā′; *Fr.* bo͞oR zhe′), *n.* **Paul** (pôl), 1852–1935, French novelist and critic.

Bour•gogne (bo͞oR gôn′yə), *n.* French name of **Burgundy.**

Bour•gui•ba (bo͝or gē′bə), *n.* **Ha•bib ben A•li** (hä′bēb ben ä′lē), born 1903, leader in Tunisian independence movements: president of Tunisia 1957–87.

bour•gui•gnon (bo͝or′gēn yun′; *Fr.* bo͞oR gē nyôN′), *n.* *French Cookery.* Burgundy (def. 7). [1915–20; < F, masc. adj.: of Burgundy]

Bour•gui•gnonne (bo͝or′gēn yôn′, -yōn′, -yun′; *Fr.* bo͞oR gē nyôn′), *n.* Burgundy (def. 5). Also called **Bourguignonne′ sauce′.** [1915–20; < F, fem. of BOURGUIGNON]

Bourke-White (bûrk′hwīt′, -wīt′), *n.* **Margaret,** 1906–71, U.S. photographer and author.

bour•kha (bo͝or′kə), *n.* burka.

bourn[1] (bôrn, bōrn), *n. Scot. and North Eng.* burn[2]. Also, **bourne.**

bourn[2] (bôrn, bōrn, bo͝orn), *n. Archaic.* **1.** a bound; limit. **2.** destination; goal. **3.** realm; domain. [1515–25; earlier *borne* < MF, OF, orig. a Picard form of *bodne;* see BOUND[3]] **—bourn′less,** *adj.*

Bourne (bôrn, bōrn), *n.* a city in SE Massachusetts. 13,874.

Bourne•mouth (bo͝orn′məth, bôrn′-, bōrn′-), *n.* a city in Dorset in S England: seashore resort. 146,400.

bour•non•ite (bôr′nə nīt′, bōr′-, bo͝or′-), *n. Mineral.* a sulfide of lead, antimony, and copper, $PbCuSbS_3$, occurring in gray to black crystals or granular masses. Also called **cogwheel ore.** [1795–1805; named after Count J. L. de *Bournon* (d. 1825), French mineralogist; see -ITE[1]]

Bour•non•ville (bo͝or′nən vil′; *Fr.* bo͞oR nôN vēl′), *n.* **Au•guste** (*Fr.* ō gyst′), 1805–79, Danish ballet dancer and choreographer.

bour•rée (bo͞o rā′; *Fr.* bo͞o Rā′), *n., pl.* **-rées** (-rāz′; *Fr.* -Rā′). **1.** an old French and Spanish dance, somewhat like a gavotte. **2.** the music for it. [1700–10; < F: lit., bundle of brushwood, orig., the twigs with which the bundle was stuffed (the dance may once have been done around brushwood bonfires); n. use of ptp. (fem.) of *bourrer* to stuff, fill, v. deriv. of *bourre* hair, fluff < LL *burra* wool, coarse fabric]

bourse (bo͝ors), *n.* a stock exchange, esp. the stock exchange of certain European cities. [1835–45; < F: lit., purse; see BURSA]

bour•tree (bo͝or′trē′), *n.* See **European elder.** [1400–50; late ME *burtre,* equiv. to *bur* (of uncert. orig.) + *tre* TREE]

bouse[1] (bous, bouz), *v.t.,* **boused, bous•ing.** *Naut.* to haul with tackle. Also, **bowse.** [1585–95; of uncert. orig.]

bouse[2] (bo͞oz, bouz), *n., v.,* **boused, bous•ing.** *—n.* **1.** liquor or drink. **2.** a drinking bout; carouse. *—v.t., v.i.* **3.** to drink, esp. to excess. Also, **bowse.** [1250–1300; ME *bous* strong drink < MD *būsen* drink to excess; cf. BOOZE]

bou•sou•ki (bo͞o zo͞o′kē), *n., pl.* **-kis, -ki•a** (-kē ə). bouzouki.

CONCISE PRONUNCIATION KEY: act, cāpe, dâre, pärt; set, ēqual; *if,* ice; ox, ōver, ôrder, oil, bo͝ok, bo͞ot, out; up, ûrge; child; sing; shoe; thin, *that;* zh as in *treasure.* ə = *a* as in *alone, e* as in *system, i* as in *easily, o* as in *gallop, u* as in *circus;* ə as in *fire* (fīər), *hour* (ouər). l and n can serve as syllabic consonants, as in *cradle* (krād′l), and *button* (but′n). See the full key inside the front cover.

bou·stro·phe·don (bo͞o′strə fēd′n, -fē′don, bou′-), *n.* an ancient method of writing in which the lines run alternately from right to left and from left to right. [1775–85; < Gk *boustrophēdón* lit., like ox-turning (in plowing), equiv. to *bou-* (s. of *boûs*) ox + *-strophē-* (see STROPHE) + *-don* adv. suffix]

bous·y (bo͞o′zē, bou′-), *adj.* intoxicated; drunk; boozy. [1520–30; BOUSE² + -Y¹]

bout (bout), *n.* **1.** a contest or trial of strength, as of boxing. **2.** period; session; spell: *a bout of illness.* **3.** a turn at work or any action. **4.** a going and returning across a field, as in mowing or reaping. [1535–45; var. of obs. *bought* bend, turn, deriv. of *bow* BOW¹; see BIGHT] —**Syn. 1.** match, fray, encounter.

bou·tel (bōt′l), *n.* boltel (def. 1). Also, **bou′tell.**

bou·tique (bo͞o tēk′), *n.* **1.** a small shop or a small specialty department within a larger store, esp. one that sells fashionable clothes and accessories or a special selection of other merchandise. **2.** any small, exclusive business offering customized service: *Our advertising is handled by a new Madison Avenue boutique.* **3.** *Informal.* a small business, department, etc., specializing in one aspect of a larger industry: *one of Wall Street's leading research boutiques.* —*adj.* **4.** of, designating, or characteristic of a small, exclusive producer or business: *one of California's best boutique wineries.* [1760–70; < F, MF, prob. < OPr *botica, botiga* (with LGk *ē* > *i*) < Gk *apothḗkē*; see APOTHECARY, BOTTEGA]

bou·ton·niere (bo͞ot′n ēr′, bo͞o′tən yâr′), *n.* a flower or small bouquet worn, usually by a man, in the buttonhole of a lapel. [1875–80; < F *boutonnière* buttonhole (*bouton* BUTTON + *-ière* suffix for things that facilitate the use of that denoted by the stem < L *-āria* -ARY]

bouts-ri·més (bo͞o′rē māz′, *Fr.* bo͞o Rē mā′), *n.pl. Pros.* **1.** words or word endings forming a set of rhymes to be used in a given order in the writing of verses. **2.** verses using such a set of rhymes. [1705–15; < F, equiv. to *bouts* ends (see BUTT²) + *rimés* rhymed (see RHYME)]

bou·var·di·a (bo͞o vär′dē ə), *n.* any tropical shrub belonging to the genus *Bouvardia,* of the madder family, having cymes of red, yellow, or white tubular flowers. [1805; < NL; named after Charles *Bouvard* (d. 1658), French physician; see -IA]

Bou·vier des Flan·dres (bo͞o vyā′ də flan′dərz; *Fr.* bo͞o vyā dā fläɴ′dʀᵊ), *pl.* **Bou·viers des Flan·dres** (bo͞o-vyāz′ də flan′dərz; *Fr.* bo͞o vyā dā fläɴ′dʀᵊ). one of a Belgian breed of dogs having eyebrows, a mustache and a beard, and a rough, wiry, tousled coat ranging in color from fawn to pepper-and-salt, gray, brindle, or black. [1930–35; < F: lit., cowherd of Flanders, from their use with cattle]

bou·zou·ki (bo͞o zo͞o′kē), *n., pl.* **-kis, -ki·a** (-kē ə). *n.* a long-necked, fretted lute of modern Greece. Also, **bousouki, buzuki.** [1950–55; < ModGk *mpouzoúki;* Turk *bozuk* (broken, ruined, depraved; cf. BASHI-BAZOUK) or *büzük* (constricted, puckered) adduced as sources, but sense development is obscure]

bo·va·rism (bō′və riz′əm), *n.* an exaggerated, esp. glamorized, estimate of oneself; conceit. [1900–05; < F *bovaryisme,* after Emma *Bovary,* a character in Flaubert's novel *Madame Bovary* (1857); see -ISM] —**bo′va·rist,** *n.* —**bo′va·ris′tic,** *adj.*

bo·vate (bō′vāt), *n.* an old English unit of land area measurement equivalent to one-eighth of a carucate. [1680–90; < ML *bovāta,* equiv. to L *bov-* (s. of *bōs*) cow + *-āta* -ATE¹]

Bo·vet (bō vā′, -vet′), *n.* **Daniel,** 1907–92, Italian pharmacologist, born in Switzerland: Nobel prize for medicine 1957.

bo·vid (bō′vid), *Zool.* —*adj.* **1.** of or pertaining to the Bovidae, comprising the hollow-horned ruminants, as oxen, antelopes, sheep, and goats. —*n.* **2.** any bovid animal. [< NL *Bovidae,* equiv. to *Bov-,* s. of *Bos* a genus, including domestic cattle (L *bōs* ox, bull, akin to COW¹) + *-idae* -ID²]

bo·vine (bō′vīn, -vin, -vēn), *adj.* **1.** of or pertaining to the subfamily Bovinae, which includes cattle, buffalo, and kudus. **2.** oxlike; cowlike. **3.** stolid; dull. —*n.* **4.** a bovine animal. [1810–20; < LL *bovīnus* of, pertaining to oxen or cows, equiv. to L *bov-* (s. of *bōs*) ox + *-īnus* -INE¹] —**bo′vine·ly,** *adv.* —**bo·vin·i·ty** (bō vin′i tē), *n.*

bo′vine growth′ hor′mone, 1. a growth hormone of cattle that regulates growth and milk production in cows. **2.** the same hormone, harvested in large quantities from genetically engineered bacteria for daily injection into dairy cows to increase milk production. *Abbr.:* bGH Also called **bo′vine somatotro′pin.**

bo′vine trichomoni′asis, *Vet. Pathol.* trichomoniasis (def. 3a).

bov·ver (bov′ər), *n. Brit. Slang.* troublemaking or rowdiness by street gang youths. [1965–70; repr. Cockney pron. of BOTHER (n.), prob. orig. as a euphemism]

bow¹ (bou), *v.i.* **1.** to bend the knee or body or incline the head, as in reverence, submission, salutation, recognition, or acknowledgment. **2.** to yield; submit: *to bow to the inevitable.* **3.** to bend or curve downward; stoop: *the pines bowed low.* —*v.t.* **4.** to bend or incline (the knee, body, or head) in worship, submission, respect, civility, agreement, etc.: *He bowed his head to the crowd.* **5.** to cause to submit; subdue; crush. **6.** to cause to stoop or incline: *Age had bowed his head.* **7.** to express by a bow: *to bow one's thanks.* **8.** to usher (someone) with a bow (usually fol. by *in, out,* etc.): *They were bowed in by the footman.* **9.** to cause to bend; make curved or crooked. **10. bow and scrape,** to be excessively polite or deferential. **11. bow out,** to resign a position or withdraw from a job, competition, obligation, etc.: *He bowed out after two terms as governor.* —*n.* **12.** an inclination of the head or body in salutation, assent, thanks, reverence, respect, submission, etc. **13. make one's bow,** to appear publicly for the first time, as a performer, politician, etc.: *The young pianist made her bow last night to an appreciative audience.* **14. take a bow,** to step forward or stand up in order to receive recognition, applause, etc.: *The conductor had the soloists take a bow.* [bef. 900; ME *bowen* (v.), OE *būgan;* c. D *buigen;* akin to G *biegen,* Goth *biugan,* ON *buga,* etc.] —**bowed′ness,** *n.* —**bow′ing·ly,** *adv.*
—**Syn. 1.** See **bend¹. 2.** surrender, accede, defer, acquiesce, comply, capitulate.

CONCISE ETYMOLOGY KEY: <, descended or borrowed from; >, whence; b., blend of, blended; c., cognate with; cf., compare; deriv., derivative; equiv., equivalent; imit., imitative; obl., oblique; r., replacing; s., stem; sp., spelling, spelled; resp., respelling, respelled; trans., translation; ?, origin unknown; *, unattested; ‡, probably earlier than. See the full key inside the front cover.

bow² (bō), *n.* **1.** a flexible strip of wood or other material, bent by a string stretched between its ends, for shooting arrows: *He drew the bow and sent the arrow to its target.* **2.** an instrument resembling this, used for various purposes, as rotating a drill or spindle, or loosening entangled or matted fibers. **3.** a bend or curve. **4.** Also called **bowknot.** a looped knot composed of two or more loops and two ends, as for tying together the ends of a ribbon or string. **5.** any separate piece of looped, knotted, or shaped gathering of ribbon, cloth, paper, etc., used as a decoration, as on a package, dress, or the like. **6.** a long rod, originally curved but now nearly straight, with horsehairs stretched from one end to the other, used for playing on a musical instrument of the violin and viol families. **7.** a single movement of such a device over the strings of a violin, viol, or the like. **8.** See **bow tie. 9.** something curved or arc-shaped. **10.** a saddlebow. **11.** an archer; bowman: *He is the best bow in the county.* **12.** temple² (def. 3). **13.** a U-shaped piece for placing under an animal's neck to hold a yoke. **14.** *Building Trades.* a flexible rod used for laying out large curves. **15.** the part of a key grasped by the fingers. **16.** the loop on the stem of a watch by which the watch is attached to a chain or the like. **17.** a rainbow. —*adj.* **18.** curved outward at the center; bent: *bow legs.* —*v.t., v.i.* **19.** to bend into the form of a bow; curve. **20.** *Music.* to perform by means of a bow upon a stringed instrument. **21.** *Textiles Obs.* to loosen by passing a vibrating bow among entangled fibers. [bef. 1000; ME *bowe* (n.), OE *boga;* c. D *boog,* G *Bogen,* ON *bogi;* akin to BOW¹] —**bowed′ness,** *n.* —**bow′less,** *adj.* —**bow′like′,** *adj.*

bow³ (bou), *n.* **1.** *Naut., Aeron.* **a.** the forward end of a vessel or airship. **b.** either side of this forward end, esp. with reference to the direction of a distant object: *a mooring two points off the port bow.* **2. bows,** *Naut.* the exterior of the forward end of a vessel, esp. one in which the hull slopes back on both sides of the stem. **3.** the foremost oar in rowing a boat. **4.** Also called **bowman, bow oar.** the person who pulls that oar. **5. bows on,** (of a ship) with the bow foremost: *The vessel approached us bows on.* **6. bows under,** (of a ship) shipping water at the bow: *The ship was bows under during most of the storm.* **7. on the bow,** *Naut.* within 45° to the heading of the vessel. —*adj.* **8.** of or pertaining to the bow of a ship. [1620–30; < LG *boog* (n.) or D *boeg* or Dan *bov;* see BOUGH]

Bow (bō), *n.* **Clara,** 1905–65, U.S. film actress: known as the "It Girl."

bow′ back′ (bō), a chair back formed of a single length of wood bent into a horseshoe form and fitted to a seat or arm rail, with spindles or slats as a filling. Also called **hoop back, loop back.**

Bow′ bells′ (bō), the bells of Bow church, in the East End district of London: traditionally, a true Cockney is born and raised within the sound of Bow bells. [1590–1600]

bow′ com′pass (bō), any of several types of compasses having the legs joined by a bow-shaped piece. [1790–1800]

Bow·ditch (bou′dich), *n.* **1. Nathaniel,** 1773–1838, U.S. mathematician, astronomer, and navigator. **2.** a handbook of navigation, *American Practical Navigator,* originally prepared by N. Bowditch and published since 1802 in a series of editions.

bow′ divid′er (bō), a bow compass, each leg of which terminates in a needle, used to transfer measurements from one area of a drawing to another.

bowd·ler·ize (bōd′lə rīz′, boud′-), *v.t.,* **-ized, -iz·ing.** to expurgate (a written work) by removing or modifying passages considered vulgar or objectionable. Also, *esp. Brit.,* **bowd′ler·ise′.** [1830–40; after Thomas *Bowdler* (1754–1825), English editor of an expurgated edition of Shakespeare] —**bowd′ler·ism,** *n.* —**bowd′ler·i·za′tion,** *n.* —**bowd′ler·iz′er,** *n.*

bow·el (bou′əl, boul), *n., v.,* **-eled, -el·ing** or (*esp. Brit.*) **-elled, -el·ling.** —*n.* **1.** *Anat.* **a.** Usually, **bowels.** the intestine. **b.** a part of the intestine. **2. bowels, a.** the inward or interior parts: *the bowels of the earth.* **b.** *Archaic.* feelings of pity or compassion. —*v.t.* **3.** to disembowel. [1250–1300; ME *b(o)uel* < OF < L *botellus* little sausage (*bot(ulus)* sausage + *-ellus* -ELLE)] —**bow′el·less,** *adj.*

Bow·ell (bō′əl), *n.* **Sir Mackenzie,** 1823–1917, Canadian statesman, born in England: prime minister 1894–96.

bow′el move′ment, 1. the evacuation of the bowels; defecation. **2.** excrement from the bowels; feces.

Bow·en (bō′ən), *n.* **1. Catherine (Sho·ber) Drink·er** (shō′bər dring′kər), 1897–1973, U.S. biographer and essayist. **2. Elizabeth (Dorothea Cole),** 1899–1973, Anglo-Irish novelist and short-story writer.

bow·en·ite (bō′ə nīt′), *n. Mineral.* a compact and dense variety of green serpentine resembling jade. [1840–50; named after G. T. *Bowen,* 19th-century American geologist; see -ITE¹]

bow·er¹ (bou′ər), *n.* **1.** a leafy shelter or recess; arbor. **2.** a rustic dwelling; cottage. **3.** a lady's boudoir in a medieval castle. —*v.t.* **4.** to enclose in or as in a bower; embower. [bef. 900; ME *bour,* OE *būr* chamber; c. ON *būr* pantry, G *Bauer* birdcage; akin to NEIGHBOR] —**bow′er·like′,** *adj.*

bow·er² (bou′ər), *n. Naut.* an anchor carried at a ship's bow. Also called **bow′er an′chor.** [1645–55; BOW³ + -ER¹]

bow·er³ (bou′ər), *n.* a person or thing that bows or bends. [1590–1600; BOW¹ + -ER¹]

bow·er⁴ (bō′ər), *n. Music.* a musician, as a violinist, who performs with a bow on a stringed instrument. [1400–50; late ME; see BOW², -ER¹]

bow·er·bird (bou′ər bûrd′), *n.* any of several oscine birds of the family Ptilonorhynchidae, of Australia, New Guinea, and adjacent islands, the males of which build bowerlike, decorated structures to attract the females. [1840–50; BOWER¹ + BIRD]

Bow·ers (bou′ərz), *n.* **Claude Ger·nade** (zhər näd′), 1878–1958, U.S. diplomat and historian.

bow·er·y¹ (bou′ə rē), *adj.* containing bowers; leafy; shady: *a bowery maze.* [1695–1705; BOWER¹ + -Y¹]

bow·er·y² (bou′ə rē, bou′rē), *n., pl.* **-er·ies. 1.** (among the Dutch settlers of New York) a farm or country seat. **2. the Bowery,** a street and area in New York City, historically noted for its cheap hotels and saloons and peopled by the destitute and homeless. [1640–50, *Amer.;* < D *bouwerij* farm, equiv. to *bouw* cultivation + *-erij* -ERY]

bow·fin (bō′fin′), *n.* a carnivorous ganoid fish, *Amia calva,* found in sluggish fresh waters of eastern North America. Also called **grindle.** [1835–45, *Amer.;* BOW² + FIN]

bow′ front′ (bō), *Furniture.* See **swell front.** [1920–25]

bow·grace (bou′grās′), *n. Naut.* a fender or pad used to protect the bows of a vessel from ice. [BOW³ + GRACE; perh. by folk etym. < F *bonnegrace* protecting brim on a hat]

bow′ hand′ (bō), **1.** *Archery.* the hand that holds the bow, the left hand for right-handed people. **2.** *Music.* the hand that draws the bow. [1580–90]

bow·head (bō′hed′), *n.* a whalebone whale, *Balaena mysticetus,* of northern seas, having an enormous head and mouth: an endangered species. See illus. under **whale.** Also called **Greenland whale.** [1885–90; BOW² + HEAD]

bow·hunt·ing (bō′hun′ting), *n.* the sport of hunting with a bow and arrows. [‡1970–75; BOW² + HUNTING] —**bow′hunt′er,** *n.*

Bow·ie (bō′ē, bo͞o′ē *for 1, 2;* bo͞o′ē *for 3*), *n.* **1. James,** 1799–1836, U.S. soldier and pioneer. **2. William,** 1872–1940, U.S. geodesist. **3.** a city in W Maryland. 33,695.

bow′ie knife′ (bō′ē, bo͞o′ē), a heavy sheath knife having a long, single-edged blade. [1830–40, *Amer.;* named after James BOWIE, for whom the knife was designed, either by James or his brother Rezin P. Bowie (1793–1841)]

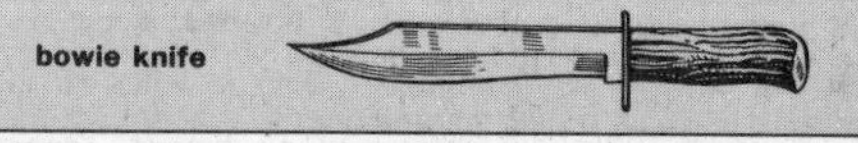

Bow′ie State′, Arkansas (used as a nickname).

bow·ing (bō′ing), *n.* **1.** the act or art of playing a stringed instrument with a bow. **2.** the individual way of using the bow in playing a stringed instrument, including the way in which the musician approaches the music emotionally, the articulation of individual notes, and the manner in which the notes of a passage are grouped together. [1830–40; BOW² + -ING¹]

bow·i·ron (bō′ī′ərn), *n.* (on the car of a sidewalk elevator) a metal arch for parting the cellar doors as the elevator rises. [1875–80]

bow·knot (bō′not′), *n.* bow² (def. 4). [1540–50; BOW² + KNOT¹]

bowl¹ (bōl), *n.* **1.** a rather deep, round dish or basin, used chiefly for holding liquids, food, etc. **2.** the contents of a bowl: *a bowl of tomato soup.* **3.** a rounded, cuplike, hollow part: *the bowl of a pipe.* **4.** a large drinking cup. **5.** festive drinking; conviviality. **6.** any bowl-shaped depression or formation. **7.** an edifice with tiers of seats forming sides like those of a bowl, having the arena at the bottom; stadium. **8.** Also called **bowl game.** a football game played after the regular season by teams selected by the sponsors of the game, usually as representing the best from a region of the country: *the Rose Bowl.* **9.** *Typography.* a curved or semicircular line of a character, as of *a, d, b,* etc. —*v.t.* **10.** to give (a floor) a gentle inclination on all sides toward some area, as a stage or platform. [bef. 950; ME *bolle,* OE *bolla;* c. ON *bolli.* See BOLL] —**bowl′like′,** *adj.*

bowl² (bōl), *n.* **1.** one of the balls, having little or no bias, used in playing ninepins or tenpins. **2.** one of the biased or weighted balls used in lawn bowling. **3. bowls,** (*used with a singular v.*) See **lawn bowling. 4.** a delivery of the ball in bowling or lawn bowling. **5.** (formerly) a rotating cylindrical part in a machine, as one to reduce friction. —*v.i.* **6.** to play at bowling or bowls; participate in or have a game or games of bowling. **7.** to roll a bowl or ball. **8.** to move along smoothly and rapidly. **9.** *Cricket.* to deliver the ball to be played by the batsman. —*v.t.* **10.** to roll or trundle, as a ball or hoop. **11.** to attain by bowling: *He bowls a good game. She usually bowls a 120 game, but today she bowled 180.* **12.** to knock or strike, as by the ball in bowling (usually fol. by *over* or *down*). **13.** to carry or convey, as in a wheeled vehicle. **14.** *Cricket.* to eliminate (a batsman) by bowling (usually fol. by *out*): *He was bowled for a duck. He was bowled out for a duck.* **15. bowl over,** to surprise greatly: *We were bowled over by the news.*

[1375–1425; late ME *bowle,* var. of *boule* < MF < L *bulla* bubble, knob; cf. BOIL[1], BOLA]

bowl·der (bōl′dər), *n.* boulder.

bowl·der·ing (bōl′dər ing), *n.* bouldering.

bow·leg (bō′leg′), *n. Pathol.* **1.** outward curvature of the legs causing a separation of the knees when the ankles are close or in contact. **2.** a leg so curved. [1545–55; BOW[2] + LEG] —**bow·leg·ged** (bō′leg′id, bō′legd′), *adj.* —**bow·leg·ged·ness** (bō′leg′id nis), *n.*

bowl·er[1] (bō′lər), *n.* **1.** a person who bowls, esp. a participant in a bowling game, as candlepins or tenpins. **2.** *Cricket.* the player who throws the ball to be played by the batsman. [1490–1500; BOWL[2] + -ER[1]]

bowl·er[2] (bō′lər), *n. Chiefly Brit.* derby (def. 5). [1860–65; BOWL[1] + -ER[1]]

Bowles (bōlz), *n.* **1. Chester,** 1901–86, U.S. statesman and author: special adviser on Afro-Asian and Latin-American affairs; ambassador to India 1951–53, 1963–69. **2. Paul (Frederic),** born 1910?, U.S. novelist and composer. **3. Samuel,** 1826–78, U.S. journalist.

bowl·ful (bōl′fo͝ol), *n., pl.* **-fuls.** as much as a bowl can hold: *He ate two bowlfuls of soup.* [1605–15; BOWL[1] + -FUL]

bowl′ game′, bowl[1] (def. 8). [1915–20]

bow·line (bō′lin, -līn′), *n.* **1.** Also called **bow′line knot′.** a knot used to make a nonslipping loop on the end of a rope. See illus. under **knot. 2.** *Naut.* a rope made fast to the weather leech of a square sail, for keeping the sail as flat as possible when close-hauled. **3. on a bowline,** *Naut.* sailing close-hauled. **4. on an easy bowline,** *Naut.* close-hauled with sails well filled. [1275–1325; ME *bouline,* equiv. to *bou-* (perh. *boue* BOW[2]) + *line* LINE[1]]

bowl·ing (bō′ling), *n.* **1.** any of several games in which players standing at one end of an alley or green roll balls at standing objects or toward a mark at the other end, esp. a game in which a heavy ball is rolled from one end of a wooden alley at wooden pins set up at the opposite end. Cf. **boccie, candlepin** (def. 2), **duckpin** (def. 2), **lawn bowling, ninepin** (def. 2), **tenpin** (def. 2). **2.** the game of bowls. **3.** an act or instance of playing or participating in any such game: *Bowling is a pleasant way to exercise.* [1525–35; BOWL[2] + -ING[1]]

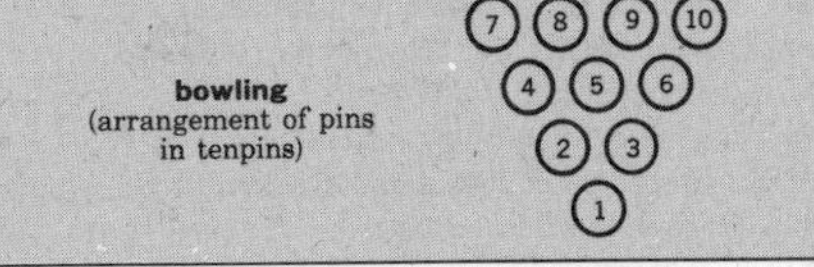

bowling
(arrangement of pins in tenpins)

bowl′ing al′ley, **1.** a long, narrow wooden lane or alley, for the game of tenpins. **2.** a building or enclosed area containing a number of such lanes or alleys. [1545–55]

bowl′ing bag′, a bag for carrying a bowling ball and often bowling shoes or other equipment.

bowl′ing ball′, a round, heavy ball for bowling, usually made of hard rubber or plastic, with holes drilled into it for the bowler's thumb and two fingers.

bowl′ing crease′, *Cricket.* either of two lines, each with a wicket set lengthwise at the center, marking the limit of a bowler's approach in delivering the ball to the opposite wicket. [1745–55]

bowl′ing green′, a level, closely mowed green for lawn bowling. [1640–50]

Bowl′ing Green′, **1.** a city in S Kentucky. 40,450. **2.** a city in NW Ohio. 25,728. **3.** a small open area near the S tip of Manhattan in New York City, at the foot of Broadway.

bowl′ing on the green′. See **lawn bowling.**

bow·man[1] (bō′mən), *n., pl.* **-men.** an archer. [1250–1300; ME; see BOW[2], -MAN]

bow·man[2] (bou′mən), *n., pl.* **-men.** bow[3] (def. 4). [1820–30; BOW[3] + -MAN]

Bow′man's cap′sule (bō′mənz), *Anat.* a membranous, double-walled capsule surrounding a glomerulus of a nephron. Cf. **Malpighian corpuscle.** [1880–85; named after Sir William *Bowman* (1816–92), English surgeon]

bow′man's root′ (bō′mənz), an eastern U.S. plant, *Gillenia trifoliata,* of the rose family, having terminal clusters of white flowers. Also called **false ipecac, Indian physic.** [1805–15, *Amer.*; by folk etym. from *beaumont root,* from proper name *Beaumont*]

bow′ net′ (bō), a clam-shaped net for trapping hawks, set open and baited with a pigeon, and closed upon the hawk by means of a trigger sprung from a blind.

bow′ oar′ (bou), bow[3] (def. 4). [1850–55]

bow·pot (bou′pot′), *n.* boughpot.

bow·rid·er (bou′rī′dər), *n.* a motorboat with an open bow provided with seating. [BOW[3] + RIDER]

bow′ rud′der (bou), (in canoeing) a technique in which a paddler in the bow holds the paddle at an angle from the side of the bow, using it as a rudder to steer.

bow′ saw′ (bō), a saw having a narrow blade held at both ends by a bowed handle. [1670–80]

bowse[1] (bous, bouz), *v.t.,* **bowsed, bows·ing.** *Naut.* bouse[1].

bowse[2] (bo͞oz, bouz), *n., v.t., v.i.,* **bowsed, bows·ing.** bouse[2].

bow·ser (bou′zər), *n. Australian and New Zealand.* a gasoline pump at a filling station. [1930–35; said to be after S.F. Bowser and Co., a Sydney manufacturer of gasoline and oil storage systems]

bow′ser bag′ (bou′zər), *Informal.* See **doggie bag.** [after *Bowser,* a traditional name for a dog]

Bow′ser boat′ (bou′sər, -zər), *Trademark.* a small boat having gasoline tanks for refueling seaplanes.

bow′ shock′ (bou), *Astron.* the shock front along which the solar wind encounters a planet's magnetic field. [1945–50]

bow·shot (bō′shot′), *n.* the distance a bow sends an arrow. [1250–1300; ME; see BOW[2], SHOT[1]]

bow·sprit (bou′sprit, bō′-), *n. Naut.* a spar projecting from the upper end of the bow of a sailing vessel, for holding the tacks of various jibs or stays and often supporting a jib boom. [1300–50; ME *bouspret* < MLG *bōchsprēt* (c. D *boegspriet*) (*bōch* BOW[3] + *sprēt* pole, c. OE *sprēot*)]

Bow′ Street′ (bō), a street in London, England: location of a metropolitan police court.

bow·string (bō′string′), *n., v.,* **-stringed** or **-strung, -string·ing.** —*n.* **1.** the string of an archer's bow. **2.** a string, typically of horsehair, for the bow of an instrument of the violin and viol families. **3.** (esp. in the Ottoman Empire) a similar string for killing people by strangulation. —*v.t.* **4.** to strangle with a bowstring or any string or band. [1350–1400; ME *bowe streng.* See BOW[2], STRING]

bow′string hemp′, any of various fibrous plants of the genus *Sansevieria,* of Asia and Africa, having stiff, erect, variegated or mottled leaves, cultivated in the U.S. as an ornamental. [1865–70]

bow′string truss′, a structural truss consisting of a curved top chord meeting a bottom chord at each end.

bow·tel (bōt′l), *n.* boltel (def. 1). Also, **bow′tell.**

bow′ thrust′er (bou), a propeller located in a ship's bow to provide added maneuverability, as when docking. [1965–70]

bow′ tie′ (bō), **1.** a small necktie tied in a bow at the collar. **2.** a sweet roll or Danish pastry having a shape similar to that of a bow tie or butterfly. [1910–15]

bow′ trol′ley (bō), *Railroads.* See under **trolley** (def. 4). [1900–05]

bow′ wave′ (bou), **1.** the wave generated on either side of a vessel's bow by its forward movement through the water. **2.** a type of shock wave formed in front of a body moving at supersonic speed. [1875–80]

bow′ win′dow (bō), a rounded bay window. [1745–55] —**bow′-win′dowed,** *adj.*

bow·wood (bō′wo͝od′), *n.* See **Osage orange** (def. 1). [1800–10, *Amer.*; BOW[2] + WOOD[1]; so called because it was used to make archery bows]

bow·wow (bou′wou′, -wou′), *n.* **1.** the bark of a dog. **2.** an imitation of this. **3.** *Chiefly Baby Talk.* a dog. [1570–80; rhyming compound; imit.]

bow·yer (bō′yər), *n.* a maker or seller of archers' bows. [1150–1200; ME *bogiere, bouwyer, bouer;* see BOW[2], -YER]

box[1] (boks), *n.* **1.** a container, case, or receptacle, usually rectangular, of wood, metal, cardboard, etc., and often with a lid or removable cover. **2.** the quantity contained in a box: *She bought a box of candy as a gift.* **3.** *Chiefly Brit.* a gift or present: *a Christmas box.* **4.** See **post-office box. 5.** a compartment or section in a public place, shut or railed off for the accommodation of a small number of people, esp. in a theater, opera house, sports stadium, etc. **6.** a small enclosure or area in a courtroom, for witnesses or the jury. **7.** a small shelter: *a sentry's box.* **8.** *Brit.* **a.** a small house, cabin, or cottage, as for use while hunting: *a shooting box.* **b.** a telephone booth. **c.** a wardrobe trunk. **9.** See **box stall. 10.** the driver's seat on a coach. **11.** the section of a wagon in which passengers or parcels are carried. **12.** *Auto.* the section of a truck in which cargo is carried. **13. the box,** *Informal.* television: *Are there any good shows on the box tonight?* **14.** part of a page of a newspaper or periodical set off in some manner, as by lines, a border, or white space. **15.** any enclosing, protective case or housing, sometimes including its contents: *a gear box; a fire-alarm box.* **16.** *Baseball.* **a.** either of two marked spaces, one on each side of the plate, in which the batter stands. **b.** either of two marked spaces, one outside of first base and the other outside of third, where the coaches stand. **c.** the pitcher's mound. **d.** the marked space where the catcher stands. **17.** a difficult situation; predicament. **18.** *Agric.* a bowl or pit cut in the side of a tree for collecting sap. **19.** *Jazz Slang.* **a.** a stringed instrument, as a guitar. **b.** a piano. **20.** *Informal.* **a.** a phonograph. **b.** a large, powerful portable radio or combination radio and cassette player. **c.** a computer. **21.** *Slang (vulgar).* **a.** the vulva or vagina. **b.** basket (def. 9). **22. out of the box,** *Australian Slang.* remarkable or exceptional; extraordinary. —*v.t.* **23.** to put into a box: *She boxed the glassware before the movers came.* **24.** to enclose or confine as in a box (often fol. by *in* or *up*). **25.** to furnish with a box. **26.** to form into a box or the shape of a box. **27.** to block so as to keep from passing or achieving better position (often fol. by *in*): *The Ferrari was boxed in by two other cars on the tenth lap.* **28.** to group together for consideration as one unit: *to box bills in the legislature.* **29.** *Building Trades.* to enclose or conceal (a building or structure) as with boarding. **30.** *Agric.* to make a hole or cut in (a tree) for sap to collect. **31.** to mix (paint, varnish, or the like) by pouring from one container to another and back again. **32.** *Australian.* **a.** to mix groups of sheep that should be kept separated. **b.** to confuse someone or something. **33. box out,** *Basketball.* to position oneself between an opposing player and the basket to hinder the opposing player from rebounding or tipping in a shot; block out. [bef. 1000; ME, OE, prob. < LL *buxis,* a reshaping of L *pyxis;* see BOÎTE] —**box′like′,** *adj.*

box[2] (boks), *n.* **1.** a blow, as with the hand or fist: *He gave the boy a box on his ear.* —*v.t.* **2.** to strike with the hand or fist, esp. on the ear. **3.** to fight against (someone) in a boxing match. —*v.i.* **4.** to fight with the fists; participate in a boxing match; spar. **5.** to be a professional or experienced prizefighter or boxer: *He has boxed since he was 16.* [1300–50; ME *box* a blow, *boxen* to beat, of uncert. orig.]

box[3] (boks), *n.* **1.** an evergreen shrub or small tree of the genus *Buxus,* esp. *B. sempervirens,* having shiny, elliptic, dark-green leaves, used for ornamental borders, hedges, etc., and yielding a hard, durable wood. **2.** the wood itself. Cf. **boxwood** (defs. 1, 2). **3.** any of various other shrubs or trees, esp. species of eucalyptus. [bef. 950; ME, OE < L *buxus* boxwood < Gk *pýxos*]

box[4] (boks), *v.t.* **1.** *Naut.* to boxhaul (often fol. by *off*). **2.** *Meteorol.* to fly around the center of a storm in a boxlike pattern in order to gather meteorological data: *to box a storm.* **3. box the compass,** *Naut.* to recite all of the points of the compass in a clockwise order. [1745–55; prob. < Sp *bojar* to sail around, earlier *boxar,* perh. < Catalan *vogir* to (cause to) turn << L *volvere* (see REVOLVE); influenced by BOX[1]]

box·ball (boks′bôl′), *n.* a game played between two players on two adjoining squares or sections of a sidewalk or a playground, in which a ball is hit back and forth between the players, each defending a square, the object being to prevent a fair ball from bouncing twice before hitting it back into the opponent's square. [BOX[1] + BALL[1]]

box′ beam′, a beam or girder built up from shapes and having a hollow, rectangular cross section. Also called **box girder.**

box′ bed′, **1.** a bed completely enclosed so as to resemble a box. **2.** a bed that folds up in the form of a box. [1795–1805]

box·ber·ry (boks′ber′ē, -bə rē), *n., pl.* **-ries. 1.** the checkerberry. **2.** the partridgeberry. [1700–10, *Amer.*; BOX[3] + BERRY]

box·board (boks′bôrd′, -bōrd′), *n.* cardboard used for making cartons. [1835–45, *Amer.*; BOX[1] + BOARD]

box′ bolt′, a rod-shaped bolt of rectangular section for fastening a door or the like, attached to the inside of the door at the edge and sliding into a socket on the frame. [1955–60]

box·boy (boks′boi′), *n.* a clerk who packs groceries into cartons, esp. at a supermarket, as for delivery or carrying out to a customer's car. [BOX[1] + BOY]

box′ calf′, a chrome-tanned calfskin with square markings produced by graining. [1900–05, *Amer.*; allegedly after Joseph Box, a London bootmaker]

box′ cam′era, a simple, boxlike camera, without bellows, sometimes allowing for adjustment of lens opening but usually not of shutter speed. [1835–45]

box′ can′yon, a canyon with steep side walls terminating headwards in a vertical cliff. [1870–75, *Amer.*]

box·car (boks′kär′), *n.* **1.** *Railroads.* a completely enclosed freight car. **2. boxcars,** a pair of sixes on the first throw of the dice in the game of craps. —*adj.* **3.** *Informal.* extremely or disproportionately large: *The business had boxcar profits during its first year.* [1855–60, *Amer.*; BOX[1] + CAR[1]]

box′ coat′, **1.** an outer coat with a straight, unfitted back. **2.** a heavy overcoat worn by coachmen. [1815–25]

box′ col′umn, a hollow wooden column, as for a porch, usually having a rectangular cross section.

box′ cor′nice, *Carpentry.* a hollow cornice of boards and moldings nailed to rafters and lookouts. Also, **boxed′ cor′nice.** Also called **closed cornice.**

box′ el′der, a North American maple, *Acer negundo,* having light gray-brown bark, pinnate, coarsely toothed leaves, and dry, winged fruit, cultivated as a shade tree, and yielding a light, soft wood used in making furniture, woodenware, etc. [1780–90, *Amer.*]

box·er (bok′sər), *n.* **1.** a person who fights as a sport, usually with gloved fists, according to set rules; prizefighter; pugilist. **2.** one of a German breed of medium-sized, stocky, short-haired, pug-faced dogs having a brindled or tan coat with white markings. **3.** a person or thing that packs items into boxes. **4. boxers.** See **boxer shorts.** [1735–45; BOX[2] + -ER[1]]

Box·er (bok′sər), *n.* a member of a Chinese secret society that carried on an unsuccessful uprising, 1898–1900 (**Box′er Rebel′lion**), principally against foreigners, culminating in a siege of foreign legations in Peking that was put down by an international expeditionary force. [trans. of Chin *yìhé juǎn* Righteous Harmony Fist, name of the militant policy of the *yìhé tuán* Righteous Harmony Group]

box′er shorts′, men's loose-fitting undershorts with an elastic waistband. Also called **boxers.** [1945–50]

box·er-style (bok′sər stīl′), *adj.* cut or fashioned in the style of boxer shorts: *men's boxer-style bathing suits.*

box·fish (boks′fish′), *n., pl.* **-fish·es,** (*esp. collectively*) **-fish.** trunkfish. [1830–40; BOX[1] + FISH]

box′ frame′, **1.** *Archit.* a monolithic reinforced-concrete structure having walls and floors in the form of slabs. **2.** *Building Trades.* a window frame with pockets for sash weights. [1875–80]

box·ful (boks′fo͝ol), *n., pl.* **-fuls.** as much as a box can hold: *a boxful of cornflakes.* [1840–50; BOX[1] + -FUL] —**Usage.** See **-ful.**

box′ gird′er. See **box beam.** [1860–65]

box′ gut′ter, a gutter set into the slope of a roof above the cornice. [1875–80]

box·haul (boks′hôl′), *v.t. Naut.* to put (a square-rigged sailing vessel) on a new tack by bracing the head yards aback and backing onto the new heading. [1760–70; BOX[1] (v.) + HAUL]

box·head (boks′hed′), *n. Print.* a heading, usually at

CONCISE PRONUNCIATION KEY: act, cāpe, dâre, pärt; set, ēqual; if, ice; ox, ōver, ôrder, oil, bo͝ok, bo͞ot, out; up, ûrge; child; sing; shoe; thin, *th*at; zh as in *treasure.* ə = *a* as in *alone, e* as in *system, i* as in *easily, o* as in *gallop, u* as in *circus;* ᵊ as in *fire* (fīᵊr), *hour* (ouᵊr). l and n can serve as syllabic consonants, as in *cradle* (krād′l), and *button* (but′n). See the full key inside the front cover.

the top of a page, newspaper column, or column of figures, enclosed in a box formed by rules. [1905–10; BOX[1] + HEAD]

box•hold•er (boks′hōl′dər), *n.* **1.** a person who has rented or subscribed for a box, as at a theatrical performance, sporting event, or the like. **2.** a person entitled to receive mail in a specific post-office box. [BOX[1] + HOLDER]

box′ huck′leberry, a nearly prostrate evergreen huckleberry shrub, *Gaylussacia brachycera,* of central to eastern North America, having short clusters of white or pink flowers and blue fruit. Also called **juniper berry.** [1905–10, *Amer.*]

box•ing[1] (bok′sing), *n.* **1.** the material used to make boxes or casings. **2.** a boxlike enclosure; casing. **3.** an act or instance of putting into or furnishing with a box. [1510–20; BOX[1] + -ING[1]]

box•ing[2] (bok′sing), *n.* the act, technique, or profession of fighting with the fists, with or without boxing gloves. [1705–15; BOX[2] + -ING[1]]

Box′ing Day′, (in Britain) the first weekday after Christmas, when Christmas gifts or boxes are given to employees, letter carriers, etc. [1825–35]

box′ing glove′, one of a pair of heavily padded leather mittens laced on the palm side of the wrist and hand, worn by boxers in a match or in training for a match. [1870–75]

box′ing ring′, an enclosed area for a boxing match, usually marked off in the form of a square by posts and ropes, and having a padded floor.

box′ i′ron, a flatiron that is heated by putting hot coals or a piece of hot metal in its boxlike holder. [1735–45]

box′ keel′, *Naut.* a keel in the form of a box beam and having internal space for pipes, ballast, etc.

box′ kite′, a tailless kite consisting of two or more light, box-shaped frames joined together, covered except at the ends and around the middle. [1895–1900]

box′ lacrosse′, a form of lacrosse played indoors, usually on a hockey rink with a wooden floor, between two teams of six players.

box′ loom′, a loom with a number of shuttle boxes on one or both sides of the lay, enabling the weaver to use a variety of colors in the filling direction. [1905–10]

box′ lunch′, a lunch or light meal packed in a cardboard box or similar container: *Each student was given a box lunch to eat on the bus.* [1945–50]

box′ nail′, a nail having a long shank, smooth or barbed, with a sharp point and a flat head.

box′ of′fice, **1.** the office of a theater, stadium, or the like, at which tickets are sold. **2.** *Theat.* **a.** receipts from a play or other entertainment. **b.** entertainment popular enough to attract paying audiences and make a profit: *This show will be good box office.* [1780–90]

box-of•fice (boks′ô′fis, -of′is), *adj.* of or pertaining to the box office or to the business and commercial aspects of the theater: *a box-office window; box-office receipts; a box-office attraction.* [1805–15; adj. use of BOX OFFICE]

box′ pleat′, a double pleat, with the material folded under at each side. Also called **box′ plait′.** [1880–85]

box′ plot′, *Statistics.* a graphic representation of a distribution by a rectangle, the ends of which mark the maximum and minimum values, and in which the median and first and third quartiles are marked by lines parallel to the ends.

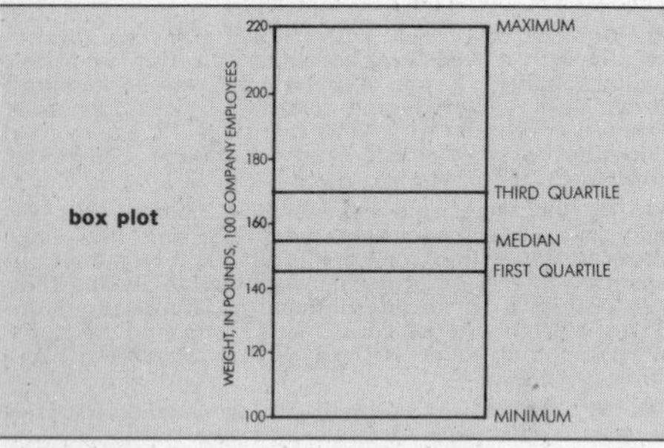

box plot

box′ room′, *Brit.* a storage room, esp. one for trunks, suitcases, etc. [1925–30]

box′ score′, *Sports.* a record of the play of a game, esp. a baseball or basketball game, in which, on separate sides of the record, the players on each team are listed in a column by name and position, with additional rows of columns, each headed by the abbreviation of the type of information to be given for each player. [1910–15, *Amer.*]

box′ seat′, a seat in a box at the theater, opera, etc. [1830–40]

box′ set′, *Theat.* a boxlike stage set consisting of flats that form the back wall, side walls, and often the ceiling, painted to represent the interior of a room. Also called, *esp. Brit.,* **box′ scene′.** [1885–90]

box′ sill′, *Carpentry.* a sill for a building frame, composed of a plate resting on the basement wall and a joist or header at the outer edge of the plate, as well as a soleplate for the studs resting either directly on the joists or on the rough flooring. Cf. **L sill.**

CONCISE ETYMOLOGY KEY: <, descended or borrowed from; >, whence; b., blend of, blended; c., cognate with; cf., compare; deriv., derivative; equiv., equivalent; imit., imitative; obl., oblique; r., replacing; s., stem; sp., spelling, spelled; resp., respelling, respelled; trans., translation; ?, origin unknown; *, unattested; ‡, probably earlier than. See the full key inside the front cover.

box′ so′cial, a social event, usually to raise funds, at which individually prepared and contributed box lunches or dinners are auctioned off to the participants, the highest bidder in each case often having the privilege of sharing the meal with its preparer. [1925–30, *Amer.*]

box′ spring′, an upholstered bedspring composed of a number of helical springs, each in a cylindrical cloth pocket. [1890–95]

box′ stall′, a room-sized stall, usually square, for a horse or other large animal. Cf. **straight stall.** [1880–85, *Amer.*]

box′ sta′ple, (on a doorpost) a socket for holding the end of a lock bolt when the door is closed. [1875–80]

box′ stoop′, a high stoop reached by a flight or flights of steps alongside the building front.

box′ store′, a retail store that sells a limited assortment of basic grocery items, often, as at a warehouse, displayed in their original cartons in order to lower costs and prices.

box′ stretch′er, *Furniture.* a heavy rectangular stretcher connecting successive legs of a table, chair, etc.

box•thorn (boks′thôrn′), *n.* See **matrimony vine.** [1670–80; BOX[3] + THORN]

box′ tur′tle, any of several chiefly terrestrial turtles of the genus *Terrapene,* of North America, having a hinged plastron that can be tightly shut to enclose and protect the body. Also called **box′ tor′toise.** See illus. under **turtle.** [1795–1805, *Amer.*]

box•wood (boks′wŏŏd′), *n.* **1.** the hard, fine-grained, compact wood of the box shrub or tree, used for wood-engravers' blocks, musical instruments, etc. **2.** the tree or shrub itself. Cf. **box**[3]. [1645–55; BOX[3] + WOOD[1]]

box′ wrench′, a wrench having ends that surround the nut or head of a bolt. See illus. under **wrench.**

box•y (bok′sē), *adj.,* **box•i•er, box•i•est.** like or resembling a box, esp. in shape: *a boxy little house.* [1860–65; BOX[1] + -Y[1]] —**box′i•ness,** *n.*

boy (boi), *n.* **1.** a male child, from birth to full growth, esp. one less than 18 years of age. **2.** a young man who lacks maturity, judgment, etc. **3.** *Informal.* a grown man, esp. when referred to familiarly: *He liked to play poker with the boys.* **4.** a son: *Sam's oldest boy is helping him in the business.* **5.** a male who is from or native to a given place. **6. boys,** (*used with a singular or plural v.*) **a.** a range of sizes from 8 to 20 in garments made for boys. **b.** a garment in this size range. **c.** the department or section of a store where these garments are sold. **7. boys,** military personnel, esp. combat soldiers: *Support the boys overseas.* **8.** *Disparaging and Offensive.* a man considered by the speaker to be inferior in race, nationality, or occupational status. **9.** a young male servant; page. **10.** *Offensive.* (in India, China, Japan, etc.) a native male servant, working as a butler, waiter, houseboy, etc. **11.** *Naut.* an apprentice seaman or fisherman. —*interj.* **12.** an exclamation of wonder, approval, etc., or of displeasure or contempt. [1250–1300; ME *boy(e),* perh. after OE *Bōia* man's name; c. Fris *boi* young man; akin to OE *bōfa,* ON *bōfi,* OHG *Buobo* man's name (G *Bube* knave, (dial.) boy, lad)]

bo•yar (bō yär′, boi′ər), *n.* **1.** *Russian Hist.* a member of the old nobility of Russia, before Peter the Great made rank dependent on state service. **2.** a member of a former privileged class in Rumania. Also, **bo•yard** (bō yärd′, boi′ərd). [1585–95; earlier *boiaren* < Russ *boyárin,* akin to OCS *bolyarinŭ* (translating Gk *megistán* man of high status), Bulg *bolyár(in);* of disputed orig.] —**bo•yar′ism, bo•yard′ism,** *n.*

boy•chik (boi′chik), *n. Slang.* a boy or young man. Also, **boy′chick.** [1960–65; BOY + Yiddish *-chik* dim. suffix of Slavic orig.]

boy•cott (boi′kot), *v.t.* **1.** to combine in abstaining from, or preventing dealings with, as a means of intimidation or coercion: *to boycott a store.* **2.** to abstain from buying or using: *to boycott foreign products.* —*n.* **3.** the practice of boycotting. **4.** an instance of boycotting. [after Charles C. *Boycott* (1832–97), English estate manager in Ireland, against whom nonviolent coercive tactics were used in 1880] —**boy′cott•er,** *n.*

Boyd (boid), *n.* a male given name: from a Gaelic word meaning "light."

Boyd′ Orr′ (ôr), **John** (*1st Baron Boyd Orr of Brechin Mearns*), 1880–1971, Scottish nutritionist and writer: Nobel peace prize 1949.

Boy•er (bwa yā′), *n.* **Jean Pierre** (zhän pyer), 1776–1850, Haitian political leader: president 1818–43.

boy•friend (boi′frend′), *n.* **1.** a frequent or favorite male companion; beau. **2.** a male friend. **3.** a male lover. [1895–1900; BOY + FRIEND]

boy•hood (boi′hŏŏd), *n.* **1.** the state or period of being a boy: *Boyhood is a happy time of life.* **2.** boys collectively: *the boyhood of America.* [1735–45; BOY + -HOOD]

boy•ish (boi′ish), *adj.* of or befitting a boy; engagingly youthful or innocent: *a boyish grin.* [1540–50; BOY + -ISH[1]] —**boy′ish•ly,** *adv.* —**boy′ish•ness,** *n.*

boy•la (boi′lə), *n. Australian.* a witch doctor; sorcerer. Also called **koradji, coraji.** [1860–65; < Nyungar *boil-ya*]

Boyle (boil), *n.* **1. Kay,** born 1903, U.S. novelist, short-story writer, and poet. **2. Robert,** 1627–91, English chemist and physicist.

Boyle's′ law′, *Thermodynam.* the principle that, for relatively low pressures, the pressure of an ideal gas kept at constant temperature varies inversely with the volume of the gas. Also called **Mariotte's law.** Cf. **Gay-Lussac's law.** [named after R. BOYLE]

Boyne (boin), *n.* a river in E Ireland: William III defeated James II near here 1690. 70 mi. (110 km) long.

Boyn′ton Beach′ (boin′tn), a city in SE Florida. 35,624.

boy•o (boi′ō), *n., pl.* **boy•os.** *Irish Eng., Australian Informal.* boy; lad. Also, **boy′-o.** [1865–70; BOY + -O]

boy′ scout′, **1.** (*sometimes caps.*) a member of an organization of boys (**Boy′ Scouts′**), founded in England in 1908 by Lieut. Gen. Sir Robert S. S. Baden-Powell, that seeks to develop certain skills in its members, as well as character, self-reliance, and usefulness to others. **2.** a member of any similar society elsewhere. **3.** *Sometimes Disparaging.* a person whose good deeds, idealism, etc., exceed normal expectations. [1905–10]

boy•sen•ber•ry (boi′zən ber′ē, -sən-), *n., pl.* **-ries.** a blackberrylike fruit with a flavor similar to that of raspberries, developed by crossing various plants of the genus *Rubus.* [1930–35; named after R. *Boysen,* 20th-century American botanist, who bred it]

boy′ toy′, **1.** *Slang (disparaging).* a young man noted for his good looks and sexual prowess, esp. one who maintains relationships with older, more powerful persons. **2.** a female sex object. [1985–90]

boy′ won′der, a young man whose skills or accomplishments are precocious. [1960–65; perh. fashioned on G *Wunderkind*]

Boz (boz), *n.* pen name of Charles Dickens.

Boz•ca•a•da (bōz′jä ä dä′, -jä dä′), *n.* Tenedos.

Boze•man (bōz′mən), *n.* a city in S Montana. 21,645.

Bo•zen (bō′tsən), *n.* German name of **Bolzano** (def. 2).

bo•zo (bō′zō), *n., pl.* **-zos.** *Slang.* **1.** a fellow, esp. a big, strong, stupid fellow. **2.** a rude, obnoxious, or annoying person: *Two bozos tried to cut in ahead of us in the supermarket line.* [1915–20, *Amer.;* of uncert. orig.]

Boz•za•ris (bō zar′is, -zär′-), *n.* **Mar•co** (mär′kō), 1788?–1823, Greek patriot. Also, **Botsares.**

BP, **1.** beautiful people; beautiful person. **2.** See **B.P.** (def. 4). **3.** See **blood pressure.**

bp., **1.** baptized. **2.** birthplace. **3.** bishop.

B/P, *Com.* bills payable.

B.P., **1.** Bachelor of Pharmacy. **2.** Bachelor of Philosophy. **3.** *Finance.* See **basis point. 4.** *Archaeol.* before the present: (in radiocarbon dating) in a specified amount of time or at a specified point in time before A.D. 1950: *between 2 and 3 million years* B.P.; *human groups living in cities by 5000* B.P. **5.** *Com.* bills payable.

b.p., **1.** *Finance.* See **basis point. 2.** below proof. **3.** *Com.* bills payable. **4.** *Physics, Chem.* See **boiling point.**

B.P.A., Bachelor of Professional Arts.

B particle, *Physics.* See **B meson.** [1965–70]

BPD, barrels per day. Also, **B.P.D.**

B.P.E., Bachelor of Physical Education.

B.Pet.E., Bachelor of Petroleum Engineering.

B.P.H., Bachelor of Public Health.

B.Ph., Bachelor of Philosophy.

B.Pharm., Bachelor of Pharmacy.

B.Phil., Bachelor of Philosophy.

BPI, **1.** Also, **bpi** *Computers.* **a.** bits per inch. **b.** bytes per inch. **2.** Bureau of Public Inquiries.

B-pic•ture (bē′pik′chər), *n.* B-movie. [1950–55]

bpl., birthplace.

B.P.O.E., Benevolent and Protective Order of Elks. See under **elk** (def. 4).

B power supply, *Electronics.* See **B supply.**

bps, *Computers.* bits per second. Also, **BPS**

b quark, *Physics.* See **bottom quark.** Also, **b-quark.**

BR, *Real Estate.* bedroom.

Br, *Symbol, Chem.* bromine.

Br., **1.** brick. **2.** Britain. **3.** British.

br., **1.** bedroom. **2.** branch. **3.** brass. **4.** brig. **5.** bronze. **6.** brother. **7.** brown.

b.r., *Com.* bills receivable. Also, **B.R., B/R**

bra (brä), *n.* **1.** brassiere. **2.** *Automotive Slang.* a removable cover for the front end of an automobile to protect it from road debris. [by shortening]

Brab•an•çon (brab′ən son′, brə ban′sən), *n.* one of a variety of the Brussels griffon having a short, smooth coat. [< F: lit., a native of BRABANT]

Bra•bant (brə bant′, brä′bənt; *Du.* brä′bänt; *Fr.* bra-bän′), *n.* **1.** a former duchy in W Europe, now divided between the Netherlands and Belgium. See map under **Agincourt. 2.** a province in central Belgium. 2,220,088; 1268 sq. mi. (3285 sq. km). *Cap.:* Brussels. —**Bra•bant•ine** (brə ban′tin, -tīn), *adj.*

brab•ble (brab′əl), *v.,* **-bled, -bling,** *n. Obs.* —*v.i.* **1.** to argue stubbornly about trifles; wrangle. —*n.* **2.** noisy, quarrelsome chatter. [1490–1500; < D *brabbelen* to quarrel, jabber] —**brab′ble•ment,** *n.* —**brab′bler,** *n.*

Brab•ham (brab′əm), *n.* **Sir John Arthur** (*"Jack"*), born 1926, Australian racing-car driver.

brac•cio (brä′chō, -chē ō′), *n., pl.* **brac•cia** (brä′chə, -chē ə). an old Italian unit of length, usually about 26 or 27 in. (66 or 68 cm), but varying between 18 and 28 in. (46 and 71 cm). [1750–60; < It: lit., an arm < L *bracchium;* see BRACE]

brace (brās), *n., v.,* **braced, brac•ing.** —*n.* **1.** something that holds parts together or in place, as a clasp or clamp. **2.** anything that imparts rigidity or steadiness. **3.** Also called **bitbrace, bitstock.** *Mach.* a device for holding and turning a bit for boring or drilling. **4.** *Building Trades.* a piece of timber, metal, etc., for supporting or positioning another piece or portion of a framework. **5.** *Naut.* (on a square-rigged ship) a rope by which a yard is swung about and secured horizontally. **6.** *Music.* leather loops sliding upon the tightening cords of a drum to change their tension and the drum's pitch. **7.** Often, **braces.** *Dentistry.* a round or flat metal wire placed against the surfaces of the teeth for straightening irregularly arranged teeth. **8.** *Med.* an appliance for supporting a weak joint or joints. **9. braces,** *Chiefly*

Brit. suspender (def. 1). **10.** a pair; couple: *a brace of grouse.* **11.** *Printing.* **a.** one of two characters { or } used to enclose words or lines to be considered together. **b.** bracket (def. 7). **12.** *Music.* connected staves. **13.** a protective band covering the wrist or lower part of the arm, esp. a bracer. **14.** *Mil.* a position of attention with exaggeratedly stiff posture. —*v.t.* **15.** to furnish, fasten, or strengthen with or as if with a brace. **16.** to fix firmly; make steady; secure against pressure or impact: *He braces himself when the ship rolls. Brace yourself for some bad news.* **17.** to make tight; increase the tension of. **18.** to act as a stimulant to. **19.** *Naut.* to swing or turn around (the yards of a ship) by means of the braces. **20.** *Mil.* to order (a subordinate) to assume and maintain a brace. —*v.i.* **21.** *Mil.* to assume a brace. **22. brace in,** *Naut.* to brace (the yards of a square-rigged vessel) more nearly athwartships, as for running free. **23. brace up,** *Informal.* to summon up one's courage; become resolute: *She choked back her tears and braced up.* [1300–50; (n.) ME < AF, OF: pair of arms < L *brā(c)chia* pl. (taken as fem. sing.) of *brā(c)chium* arm (< Gk; see BRACHIUM); (v.) in part ME *bracen* (< AF *bracier,* deriv. of *brace;* cf. EMBRACE[1]), in part. deriv. of the n.]
—Syn. 1. vise. **4.** stay, prop, strut. **10.** See **pair. 15.** support, fortify, prop. **17.** tauten, tense. **18.** fortify.

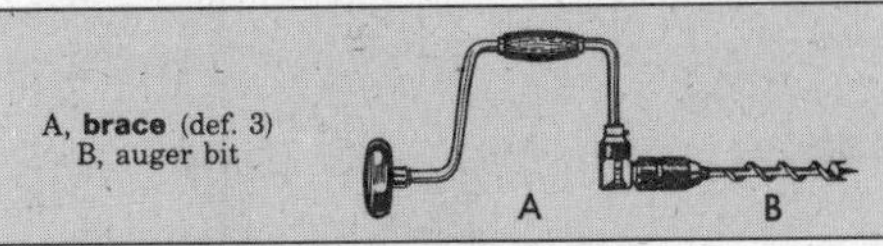

A, **brace** (def. 3)
B, auger bit

braced′ arch′, an arch of steel, timber, etc., having a trusslike framework maintaining rigidity under a variety of eccentric loads: a true arch because it is fixed or tied at both sides of the base. Cf. **arched truss.**

braced′ frame′, *Carpentry.* a building frame employing a heavy, braced framework of solid girts mortised into solid posts the full height of the frame, with studs one story high filling the interstices. Also called **full frame.**

brace′ jack′, *Theat.* a triangular piece of wood used for propping up scenery from behind.

brace•let (brās′lit), *n.* **1.** an ornamental band or circlet for the wrist or arm or, sometimes, for the ankle. **2. bracelets,** *Slang.* a pair of handcuffs. **3.** *Furniture.* collar (def. 13). [1400–50; late ME < MF; OF *bracel* (< L *brāchiāle,* n. use of neut. of *brāchiālis* BRACHIAL) + *-et* -ET] **—brace′let•ed,** *adj.*

brace′ mold′ing, *Archit.* keel[1] (def. 6).

brac•er[1] (brā′sər), *n.* **1.** a person or thing that braces, binds, or makes firm. **2.** *Informal.* a stimulating drink, esp. one of liquor. [1570–80; BRACE + -ER[1]]

brac•er[2] (brā′sər), *n. Archery.* a guard or band worn over the wrist of the bow hand to protect it from the snap of the bowstring. [1350–1400; ME < AF; OF *braceure,* equiv. to *brace* arm (see BRACE (n.)) + *-ure* -URE]

bra•ce•ro (brə sâr′ō; *Sp.* brä se′rô), *n., pl.* **-ce•ros** (-sâr′ōz; *Sp.* -se′rôs). a Mexican laborer admitted legally into the U.S. for a short period to perform seasonal, usually agricultural, labor. [1915–20; < Sp: laborer, lit., one who swings his arms. See BRACE, -ARY]

brace′ root′. See **prop root.** [1890–95]

brace′ ta′ble, *Carpentry.* a table giving the lengths of the hypotenuses of right isosceles triangles of varying sizes: used esp. for calculating the lengths of diagonal braces.

brachi-, var. of **brachio-** before a vowel.

bra•chi•al (brā′kē əl, brak′ē-), *Anat., Zool.* —*adj.* **1.** belonging to the arm, foreleg, wing, pectoral fin, or other forelimb of a vertebrate. **2.** belonging to the upper part of such a member, from the shoulder to the elbow. **3.** armlike, as an appendage. —*n.* **4.** a brachial part or structure. [1570–80; < L *brāchiālis* of, belonging to the arm. See BRACHI-, -AL[1]]

bra•chi•al•gi•a (brā′kē al′jē ə, -jə, brak′ē-), *n. Pathol.* pain in the nerves of the upper arm. [BRACHI- + -ALGIA]

bra′chial plex′us, *Anat.* a network of nerves in the armpits and neck, innervating the shoulders, arms, and hands. [1855–60]

bra•chi•ate (*adj.* brā′kē it, -āt′, brak′ē-; *v.* brā′kē āt′, brak′ē-), *adj., v.,* **-at•ed, -at•ing.** —*adj.* **1.** *Bot.* having widely spreading branches in alternate pairs. **2.** *Zool.* having arms. —*v.i.* **3.** to progress by means of brachiation. [1825–35; < L *brāchiātus* with branches like arms. See BRACHI-, -ATE[1]]

bra•chi•a•tion (brā′kē ā′shən, brak′ē-), *n. Zool.* locomotion accomplished by swinging by the arms from one hold to another. [BRACHIATE + -ION]

bra•chi•a•tor (brā′kē ā′tər, brak′ē-), *n.* an animal that can progress by means of brachiation, as a gibbon. [BRACHIATE + -OR[2]]

brachio-, a combining form meaning "arm," "upper arm," used in the formation of compound words: *brachiopod.* Also, *esp. before a vowel,* **brachi-.** [comb. form repr. L *brāchium* and Gk *brachíōn*]

bra′chi•o•ce•phal′ic ar′tery (brā′kē ō sə fal′ik, brak′ē-, brā′kē-, brak′ē-), *Anat.* a major artery, arising from the arch of the aorta, that supplies blood to the right arm and the head. [1830–40; BRACHIO- + CEPHALIC]

bra′chiocephal′ic vein′, *Anat.* either of two major veins, formed by the merger of the subclavian and internal jugular veins, that drain blood from the head and arms. [1850–55]

bra•chi•o•pod (brā′kē ə pod′, brak′ē-), *n.* **1.** any mollusklike, marine animal of the phylum Brachiopoda, having a dorsal and ventral shell; a lamp shell. —*adj.* **2.** Also, **bra•chi•op•o•dous** (brā′kē op′ə dəs, brak′ē). belonging or pertaining to the Brachiopoda. [1830–40; < NL *Brachiopoda.* See BRACHIO-, -POD]

bra•chi•o•saur (brā′kē ə sôr′, brak′ē-), *n.* a huge sauropod dinosaur of the genus *Brachiosaurus,* having a small head with nostrils on a knob above the eyes, long forelegs, and a sloping, massive body, and reaching a length of about 80 ft. (24 m). [< NL *Brachiosaurus* (1903); see BRACHIO-, -SAUR; so named in allusion to the unusual length of the humerus relative to the femur]

bra•chis•to•chrone (brə kis′tə krōn′), *n. Mech.* the curve between two points that in the shortest time by a body moving under an external force without friction; the curve of quickest descent. [1765–75; < Gk *bráchisto(s)* shortest (superl. of *brachýs* BRACHY-) + *chrónos* time] **—bra•chis•to•chron•ic** (brə kis′tə kron′ik), **bra•chis•toch•ro•nous** (brā′kə stok′rə nəs, brak′ə-), *adj.*

bra•chi•um (brā′kē əm, brak′ē-), *n., pl.* **bra•chi•a** (brā′kē ə, brak′ē ə). **1.** *Anat.* the part of the arm from the shoulder to the elbow. **2.** the corresponding part of any limb, as in the wing of a bird. **3.** an armlike part or process. [1725–35; < NL; L *brāc(c)hium* the arm; cf. Gk *brachíōn,* formally the comp. of *brachýs* short]

brachy-, a learned borrowing from Greek meaning "short," used in the formation of compound words: *brachycerous.* [< Gk, comb. form of *brachýs*]

brach•y•ce•phal•ic (brak′ē sə fal′ik), *adj. Cephalom.* short-headed; having a cephalic index of 81.0–85.4. Also, **brach•y•ceph•a•lous** (brak′ē sef′ə ləs). [1840–50; BRACHY- + -CEPHALIC] **—brach•y•ceph•a•ly** (brak′ē-sef′ə lē), **brach′y•ceph′a•lism,** *n.*

bra•chyc•er•ous (brə kis′ər əs), *adj. Entomol.* having short antennae. [1870–75; BRACHY- + Gk *kér(as)* a horn + -OUS]

brach•y•cra•nic (brak′ē krā′nik), *adj. Craniom.* having a cranial index of 81.0–85.4. [BRACHY- + CRAN(I-O)- + -IC]

brach•y•dac•tyl•i•a (brak′ē dak til′ē ə), *n. Med.* abnormal shortness of the fingers and toes. Also, **brach•y•dac•ty•ly** (brak′ē dak′tl ē). [1880–85; < NL; see BRACHY-, -DACTYL, -IA] **—brach′y•dac•tyl′ic, brach′y•dac′ty•lous,** *adj.*

brach•y•dome (brak′i dōm′), *n. Crystall.* a dome the faces of which are parallel to the shorter lateral axis. Cf. **macrodome.** [1865–70; BRACHY- + DOME]

bra•chyl•o•gy (brə kil′ə jē), *n., pl.* **-gies.** brevity of diction; concise or abridged form of expression. [1615–25; < Gk *brachylogía* brevity in speech. See BRACHY-, -LOGY]

bra•chyp•ter•ous (brə kip′tər əs), *adj. Zool., Ornith.* having short wings. [1835–45; BRACHY- + -PTEROUS]

brach•y•sto•ma•tous (brak′ē stom′ə təs, -stō′mə-), *adj.* having a short proboscis, as certain insects. [BRACHY- + STOMATOUS]

brach•y•ur•an (brak′ē yŏŏr′ən), *adj.* **1.** belonging or pertaining to the suborder Brachyura, comprising the true crabs. —*n.* **2.** a brachyuran crustacean. [1875–80; BRACHYUR(OUS) + -AN]

brach•y•ur•ous (brak′ē yŏŏr′əs), *adj. Zool.* short-tailed, as a crab (opposed to *macrurous*). [1820–30; < NL *Brachyura* name of the group. See BRACHY-, -UROUS]

brac•ing (brā′sing), *adj.* **1.** strengthening; invigorating: *This mountain air is bracing.* **2.** of, pertaining to, or serving as a brace. —*n.* **3.** a brace. **4.** braces collectively: *The bracing on this scaffold is weak.* **5.** material, as timber, used for braces. [1475–85; BRACE (v.) + -ING[1], -ING[2]] **—brac′ing•ly,** *adv.* **—brac′ing•ness,** *n.*
—Syn. 1. stimulating, revivifying, energizing.

bra•ci•o•la (brä′chē ō′lə, brä chō′-; *It.* brä chô′lä), *n., pl.* **-las, -le** (-lā; *It.* -le). *Italian Cookery.* a flat piece of veal or beef rolled around a filling and baked in stock and wine. [1940–45; < It: slice of meat roasted over coals, equiv. to *brac(e)* hot coal, ember (earlier *bracia, bragia* < Gmc; see BRAISE) + *-iola* n. suffix]

brack•en (brak′ən), *n.* **1.** a large fern or brake, esp. *Pteridium aquilinum.* **2.** a cluster or thicket of such ferns; an area overgrown with ferns and shrubs. [1275–1325; ME *braken* < Scand; cf. Sw *bräken* fern, Norw *brake* juniper] **—brack′ened,** *adj.*

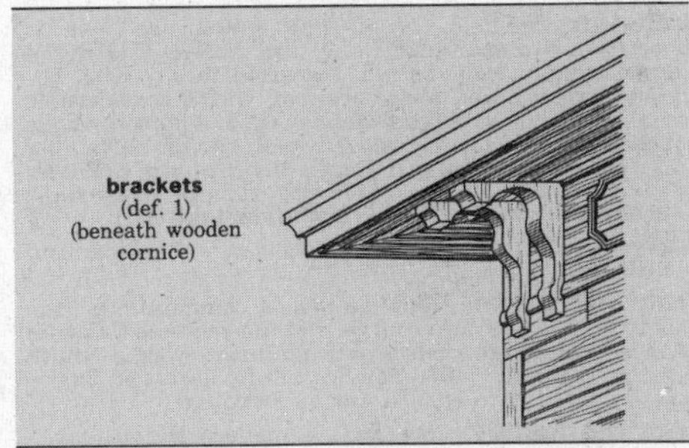
brackets (def. 1)
(beneath wooden cornice)

brack•et (brak′it), *n.* **1.** a support, as of metal or wood, projecting from a wall or the like to hold or bear the weight of a shelf, part of a cornice, etc. **2.** a shelf or shelves so supported. **3.** Also called **square bracket.** one of two marks [or] used in writing or printing to enclose parenthetical matter, interpolations, etc. **4.** *Math.* **a. brackets,** parentheses of various forms indicating that the enclosed quantity is to be treated as a unit. **b.** (loosely) vinculum (def. 2). **c.** *Informal.* an expression or formula between a pair of brackets. **5.** a grouping of people based on the amount of their income: *the low-income bracket.* **6.** a class; grouping; classification: *She travels in a different social bracket.* **7.** *Archit.* **a.** any horizontally projecting support for an overhanging weight, as a corbel, cantilever, or console. **b.** any of a series of fancifully shaped false consoles beneath an ornamental cornice. **8.** (on a staircase) an ornamental piece filling the angle between a riser and its tread. **9.** *Shipbuilding.* **a.** a flat plate, usually triangular with a flange on one edge, used to unite and reinforce the junction between two flat members or surfaces meeting at an angle. **b.** any member for reinforcing the angle between two members or surfaces. **10.** a projecting fixture for gas or electricity. **11.** *Gunnery.* range or elevation producing both shorts and overs on a target. —*v.t.* **12.** to furnish with or support by a bracket or brackets. **13.** to place within brackets; couple with a brace. **14.** to associate, mention, or class together: *Gossip columnists often bracket them together, so a wedding may be imminent.* **15.** *Gunnery.* to place (shots) both beyond and short of a target. **16.** *Photog.* to take (additional shots) at exposure levels above and below the estimated correct exposure. [1570–80; earlier also *brag(g)et* (in architecture); of obscure orig.]

brack′et clock′, a small clock designed to be placed on a bracket or shelf. [1890–95]

brack′et creep′, the gradual movement of a wage earner into a higher federal income-tax bracket as a result of wage increases intended to help offset inflation.

brack′eted blen′ny, gunnel[1].

brack′et foot′, *Furniture.* a corner foot of a chest or the like joining the sides in a concave line.

bracket feet

brack′et fun′gus, the leathery, corky, or woody, shelflike basidiocarp of certain wood-rotting fungi that form on tree trunks, lumber, etc.; conk. [1895–1900]

brack•et•ing (brak′i ting), *n.* **1.** a series of brackets. **2.** framework for supporting a cove, cornice, plaster ceiling ornament, etc. [1815–25; BRACKET + -ING[1]]

brack′et saw′, *Carpentry.* a handsaw for cutting curved forms.

Brack′ett se′ries (brak′it), *Physics.* a series of lines in the infrared spectrum of hydrogen. [after Frederick S. Brackett (born 1896), U.S. physicist]

brack•ish (brak′ish), *adj.* **1.** slightly salt; having a salty or briny flavor. **2.** distasteful; unpleasant. [1530–40; < D *brak* salty + -ISH[1]] **—brack′ish•ness,** *n.*

Brack•nell (brak′nl), *n.* a town in E Berkshire, in S England. 71,400.

brac•o•nid (brak′ə nid), *n.* **1.** any of numerous wasps of the family Braconidae, the larvae of which are parasitic on aphids and on the larvae of moths, butterflies, beetles, etc. —*adj.* **2.** belonging or pertaining to the family Braconidae. [1890–95; < NL *Braconidae,* equiv. to *Bracon* a genus (irreg. < Gk *brachýs* short; see BRACHY-) + *-idae* -ID[2])]

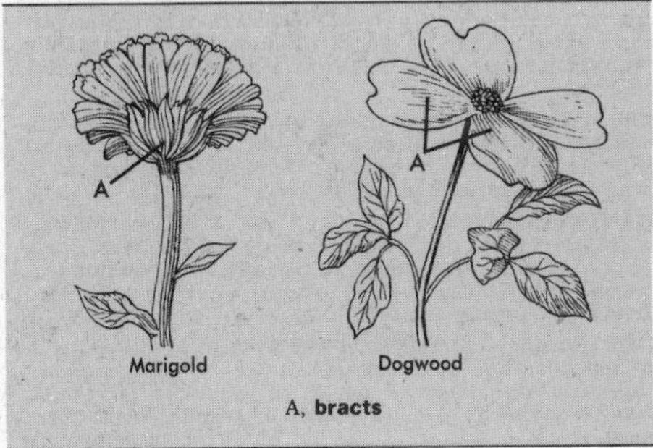

A, **bracts**

bract (brakt), *n. Bot.* a specialized leaf or leaflike part, usually situated at the base of a flower or inflorescence. [1760–70; earlier *bractea* < L: a thin plate of metal] **—brac•te•al** (brak′tē əl), *adj.* **—bract′ed,** *adj.* **—bract′less,** *adj.*

brac•te•ate (brak′tē it, -āt′), *adj.* **1.** Also, **brac•te•ose** (brak′tē ōs′). *Bot.* having bracts. —*n.* **2.** a thin coin, struck only on one face, the pattern of which shows through on the reverse face. [1835–45; < NL *bracteātus.* See BRACT, -ATE[1]]

brac•te•o•late (brak′tē ə lit, -lāt′, brak tē′-), *adj. Bot.* having bracteoles. [1820–30; < NL *bracteolātus,* equiv. to *bracteol(a)* BRACTEOLE + *-ātus* -ATE[1]]

brac•te•ole (brak′tē ōl′), *n. Bot.* a small or secondary bract, as on a pedicel. Also, **bract•let** (brakt′lit). [1820–30; < NL *bracteola,* equiv. to L *bracte(a)* a thin plate of metal, gold leaf + *-ola* -OLE[1]]

brad (brad), *n., v.,* **brad•ded, brad•ding.** —*n.* **1.** a slender wire nail having either a small, deep head or a projection to one side of the head end. See illus. under **nail.** —*v.t.* **2.** to fasten with brads. [1425–75; late ME *brad,* dial. var. of ME *brod(d)* sprout, shoot, nail < ON *broddr,* c. OE *brord* spike (see BRAIRD)]

Brad (brad), *n.* a male given name.

brad•awl (brad′ôl′), *n. Carpentry.* an awl for making small holes in wood for brads. See illus. under **awl.** [1815–25; BRAD + AWL]

Brad•bur•y (brad′bə rē), *n.* **Ray (Douglas),** born 1920, U.S. science-fiction writer.

CONCISE PRONUNCIATION KEY: *act, cāpe, dâre, pärt; set, ēqual; if, īce; ox, ōver, ôrder, oil, bŏŏk, bo͞ot, out; up, ûrge; child; sing; shoe; thin, that;* zh *as in treasure.* ə = *a* as in *alone, e* as in *system, i* as in *easily, o* as in *gallop, u* as in *circus;* ᵊ as in *fire* (fīᵊr), *hour* (ouᵊr). l and n can serve as syllabic consonants, as in *cradle* (krād′l), and *button* (but′n). See the full key inside the front cover.

brad•ded (brad′id), *adj.* having brads. [1785–95; BRAD + -ED[3]]

Brad•dock (brad′ək), *n.* **1. Edward,** 1695–1755, British general in America. **2.** a city in SW Pennsylvania, near Pittsburgh: the site of General Braddock's defeat by the French and Indians 1755. 5634.

Brad′dock Hills′, a town in SE Pennsylvania. 12,189.

Bra•den•ton (brād′n tən), *n.* a city in W Florida. 30,170.

Brad•ford (brad′fərd), *n.* **1. Gamaliel,** 1863–1932, U.S. biographer and novelist. **2. Roark** (rôrk, rōrk), 1896–1948, U.S. novelist and short-story writer. **3. William,** 1590–1657, Pilgrim settler: second governor of Plymouth Colony 1621–56. **4. William,** 1663–1752, American printer, born in England. **5.** a city in West Yorkshire, in N England. 460,600. **6.** a city in N Pennsylvania. 11,211. **7.** Braford. **8.** a male given name.

Brad′ford spin′ning, a wool-spinning method in which the fibers are oiled prior to combing and subsequently spun into worsted yarn. Also called **Brad′ford sys′tem.** [after BRADFORD, England]

Brad•ley (brad′lē), *n.* **1. Bill** (*William Warren*), born 1943, U.S. politician: senator from New Jersey since 1979. **2. Francis Herbert,** 1846–1924, English philosopher. **3. Henry,** 1845–1923, English lexicographer and philologist. **4. Omar Nelson,** 1893–1981, U.S. general: Chief of Staff 1948–49; chairman of the Joint Chiefs of Staff 1949–53. **5. Thomas** (*Tom*), born 1917, U.S. politician: mayor of Los Angeles since 1973. **6.** a town in NE Illinois. 11,008. **7.** a male given name.

Brad′ley Fight′ing Ve′hicle, a 25-ton, tracked U.S. armored personnel carrier of the 1980's, designed to carry nine soldiers into battle and armed with a 25mm rapid-fire cannon, a machine gun, and an antitank missile launcher. [named after O. N. BRADLEY]

brad•sot (brad′sət), *n. Vet. Pathol.* braxy (def. 1). [< Dan; cf. ON *brātha-sōtt* sudden illness, plague (*brāth* haste + *sōtt* illness; c. OE *suht*)]

Brad•street (brad′strēt′), *n.* **1. Anne (Dudley),** 1612?–72, American poet. **2.** her husband, **Simon,** 1603–97, governor of the Massachusetts colony 1679–86, 1689–92.

Bra•dy (brā′dē), *n.* **1. James Buchanan** ("*Diamond Jim*"), 1856–1917, U.S. financier, noted for conspicuously extravagant living. **2. Mathew B.,** 1823?–96, U.S. photographer, esp. of the Civil War. **3.** a male given name.

brady-, a combining form meaning "slow," used in the formation of compound words: *bradytelic.* [< Gk, comb. form of *bradýs* slow, heavy]

brad•y•car•di•a (brad′i kär′dē ə), *n. Med.* a slow heartbeat rate, usually less than 60 beats per minute. [1885–90; BRADY- + -CARDIA] —**brad′y•car′dic,** *adj.*

brad•y•kin•in (brad′i kin′in, -kī′nin), *n. Biochem.* a peptide hormone that dilates peripheral blood vessels and increases capillary permeability. [1945–50; BRADY- + -KININ]

brad•y•tel•ic (brad′i tel′ik), *adj. Biol.* of or pertaining to evolution at a rate slower than the standard for a given group of plants or animals. Cf. **horotelic, tachytelic.** [BRADY- + TELIC] —**brad•y•tel•y** (brad′i-tel′ē), *n.*

brae (brā, brē; *Scot.* brɑ, brɛ), *n. Scot. and North Eng.* a slope; declivity; hillside. [1300–50; ME *bra* < ON *brā* brow, c. OE *brēaw* eyebrow, eyelid, OHG *brāwa* (G *Braue*); for semantic development, cf. BROW]

Bra•ford (brā′fərd, brä′-), *n.* one of a breed of beef cattle, developed in the southwestern U.S. from Brahman and Hereford stock, especially well adapted to sparse grazing and a hot, humid environment. Also, **Bradford.** [BRA(HMAN) + (HERE)FORD]

brag (brag), *v.,* **bragged, brag•ging,** *n., adj.* —*v.i.* **1.** to use boastful language; boast: *He bragged endlessly about his high score.* —*v.t.* **2.** to boast of: *He bragged that he had won.* —*n.* **3.** a boast or vaunt. **4.** a thing to boast of. **5.** a boaster. **6.** an old English card game similar to poker. —*adj.* **7.** *Archaic.* unusually fine; first-rate. [1350–1400; ME *brag* (n.) ostentation, arrogance, *braggen* (v.); of obscure orig.] —**brag′ging•ly,** *adv.* —**brag′less,** *adj.*
—**Syn. 1.** See **boast**[1]. —**Ant. 2.** depreciate.

Bra•ga (brɑ′gə), *n.* a city in N Portugal: an ecclesiastical center. 48,735.

Brag•don (brag′dən), *n.* **Claude,** 1866–1946, U.S. architect, stage designer, and author.

Bragg (brag), *n.* **1. Brax•ton** (brak′stən), 1817–76, Confederate general in the U.S. Civil War. **2. Sir William Henry,** 1862–1942, and his son, **Sir William Lawrence,** 1890–1971, English physicists: Nobel prize winners 1915.

brag•ga•do•ci•o (brag′ə dō′shē ō′), *n., pl.* **-ci•os. 1.** empty boasting; bragging. **2.** a boasting person; braggart. [after *Braggadocchio,* boastful character in Spenser's *Faerie Queene* (1590), appar. a pseudo-It coinage based on BRAG] —**brag′ga•do′ci•an,** *adj.*

brag•gart (brag′ərt), *n.* **1.** a person who does a lot of bragging. —*adj.* **2.** bragging; boastful. [1570–80; BRAG + -ART] —**brag′gart•ism,** *n.* —**brag′gart•ly,** *adv.*
—**Syn.** bragger, boaster; blow-hard.

brag•ger (brag′ər), *n.* **1.** a person who brags. **2.** *Cards.* **a.** (in some forms of brag) the jack of clubs or nine of diamonds. **b.** (in other forms of brag) any jack or nine. **c.** the first bettor in a game of brag. [1350–1400; ME; see BRAG, -ER[1]]

Bragg′ scat′tering, *Physics.* the diffraction phenomenon exhibited by a crystal bombarded with x-rays in such a way that each plane of the crystal lattice acts as a reflector **(Bragg′ reflec′tor).** Also called **Bragg′ reflec′tion.** [see BRAGG'S LAW]

Bragg's′ law′, *Physics.* the law that the intensity of a crystal reflection of an x-ray is a function of the angle **(Bragg′ an′gle)** that is the complement of the angle of incidence of the x-ray. [1910–15; named after Sir W. H. and Sir W. L. BRAGG]

Bra•gi (brä′gē), *n. Scand. Myth.* the god of poetry and eloquence, son of Odin, husband of Idun: may be an apotheosis of the 9th-century poet Bragi Boddason. [< ON; cf. OE *brego* prince, ON *bragr* poetic art; perh. akin to Skt *bráhma* BRAHMA]

Brahe (brä, brä′hē; *Dan.* brɑ′ɛ), *n.* **Ty•cho** (tē′kō; *Dan.* tʏ′kō), 1546–1601, Danish astronomer.

Brah•ma (brä′mə), *n. Hinduism.* **1.** Brahman (def. 2). **2.** (in later Hinduism) "the Creator," the first member of the Trimurti, with Vishnu the Preserver and Shiva the Destroyer. [1775–85; < Skt *brahma,* nom. sing. of *brahman*]

Brah•ma (brä′mə, brā′-), *n.* one of a breed of large Asian chickens, having feathered legs and small wings and tail. [1850–55; short for *Brahmaputra fowl,* so called because brought to England from a town on that river]

Brah•ma (brä′mə, brā′-), *n.* a Brahman bull, steer, or cow. [1935–40; alter. of BRAHMAN]

brah•ma•cha•ri (brä′mə chär′ē), *n. Hinduism.* **1.** a student of the Vedas, esp. one committed to brahmacharya. **2.** a celibate. Also, **brah•ma•cā•rin** (brä′mə-chär′in). [< Skt *brahmacārin*]

brah•ma•char•ya (brä′mə chär′yə), *n. Hinduism.* the stage of life of the student, entailing study of the Vedas and complete celibacy, usually lasting for twelve years. Also, **brah′ma•cār′ya.** [< Skt *brahmacarya*]

Brah•ma•jna•na (brä′mə jə nä′nə), *n. Hinduism.* jnana. [< Skt; see BRAHMA, JNANA]

Brah•ma•lo•ka (brä′mə lō′kə), *n. Hinduism.* the highest part of Kamaloka, where refined souls exist in blissful contemplation of Brahma. [< Skt *brahma* BRAHMA + *loka* world, c. L *lūcus* sacred grove]

Brah•man (brä′mən), *n., pl.* **-mans.** *Hinduism.* **1.** Also, **Brahmin.** a member of the highest, or priestly, class among the Hindus. Cf. **Kshatriya, Shudra, Vaisya. 2.** Also, **Brahma.** the impersonal supreme being, the primal source and ultimate goal of all beings, with which Atman, when enlightened, knows itself to be identical. [1475–85; < Skt *brāhmaṇa* (def. 1), *brahman* (def. 2)] —**Brah•man•ic** (brä man′ik), **Brah•man′i•cal,** *adj.*

Brah•man (brā′mən, brä′-), *n.* any of several breeds of Indian cattle, esp. a grayish, heat-resistant American breed raised chiefly in the Gulf States. [1935–40; special use of BRAHMAN priest]

Brah•ma•na (brä′mə nə), *n. Hinduism.* one of a class of prose pieces dealing with Vedic rituals and sacrifices. Cf. **Veda.** [< Skt *brāhmaṇa*]

Brah•ma•ni (brä′mə nē), *n., pl.* **-nis.** a woman of the Brahman class. Also, **Brah′ma•nee.** [1785–95; < Skt, fem. of *brāhmaṇa* BRAHMAN]

Brah•man•ism (brä′mə niz′əm), *n.* **1.** the religious and social system of the Brahmans and orthodox Hindus, characterized by the caste system and diversified pantheism. **2.** the Hinduism of the Vedas, Brahmanas, and Upanishads. Also, **Brahminism.** [1810–20; BRAHMAN + -ISM] —**Brah′man•ist,** *n.*

Brah•ma•pu•tra (brä′mə po͞o′trə), *n.* a river in S Asia, flowing from S Tibet through NE India and joining the Ganges River in Bangladesh. ab. 1700 mi. (2700 km) long.

Brah′ma Samaj′. See **Brahmo Samaj.**

Brah′ma Viha′ra, *Buddhism.* vihara (def. 3).

Brah•mi (brä′mē), *n.* a script of India that was probably adapted from the Aramaic alphabet about the 7th century B.C., and from which most of the later Indian scripts developed. [1890–95; < Skt, equiv. to *brahm-* (see BRAHMAN) + *-i* as in HINDI, etc.]

Brah•min (brä′min), *n., pl.* **-min, -mins,** *adj.* —*n.* **1.** *Hinduism.* Brahman (def. 1). **2.** (esp. in New England) a person usually from an old, respected family who, because of wealth and social position, wields considerable social, economic, and political power. **3.** a person who is intellectually or socially aloof. —*adj.* **4.** of, pertaining to, or characteristic of a Brahmin: *the Brahmin attitudes of a true aristocrat.* [1475–85; var. of BRAHMAN] —**Brah•min•ic** (brä min′ik), **Brah•min′i•cal,** *adj.*

Brah•min•ism (brä′mə niz′əm), *n.* Brahmanism. —**Brah′min•ist,** *n.*

Brah′mi•ny kite′ (brä′mə nē), a common kite, *Haliastur indus,* of southern Asia and the southwest Pacific islands, having reddish-brown plumage with a white head and breast. [1880–85; *Brahminy,* deriv. of BRAHMIN, by analogy to such words as BENGALI]

Brah′mo Samaj′ (brä′mō), a modern Hindu movement advocating a monotheistic religion based on the Upanishads, and social and educational reforms according to Western principles. Also, **Brahma Samaj.** [< Bengali *brāhma samāj* assembly of Brahma]

Brahms (brämz; *Ger.* brɑms), *n.* **Jo•han•nes** (yō hä′-nəs), 1833–97, German composer. —**Brahms′i•an,** *adj.* —**Brahms′ite,** *n.*

Bra•hu•i (brä ho͞o′ē), *n.* **1.** a member of a nomadic people of Baluchistan. **2.** the Dravidian language spoken by the Brahui.

braid (brād), *v.t.* **1.** to weave together strips or strands of; plait: *to braid the hair.* **2.** to form by such weaving: *to braid a rope.* **3.** to bind or confine (the hair) with a band, ribbon, etc. **4.** to trim with braid, as a garment. —*n.* **5.** a braided length or plait, esp. of hair. **6.** a hair style formed by interweaving three or more strands of hair. **7.** a narrow, ropelike band formed by plaiting or weaving together several strands of silk, cotton, or other material, used as trimming for garments, drapery, etc. **8.** a band, ribbon, etc., for binding or confining the hair. [bef. 950; ME *braiden, breiden* (v.), OE *bregdan* to move quickly, move to and fro, weave; c. ON *bregtha,* D *breien*] —**braid′er,** *n.*

braid•ing (brā′ding), *n.* **1.** braids collectively. **2.** braided work. [1400–50; late ME. See BRAID[1], -ING[1]]

brail (brāl), *n.* **1.** *Naut.* any of several horizontal lines fastened to the edge of a fore-and-aft sail or lateen sail, for gathering in the sail. **2.** a leather binding for a hawk's wings, to prohibit flight. —*v.t.* **3.** *Naut.* **a.** to gather or haul in (a sail) by means of brails (usually fol. by *up*). **b.** to transfer (fish) from a net to the hold of a ship. **4.** to bind (the wings of a bird) in order to prevent it from flying. [1400–50; late ME, var. of *brayell* < AF *braiel;* OF < ML *brācāle* breechbelt, n. use of neut. of *brācālis,* equiv. to L *brāc(ae)* trousers (< Gaulish) + *-ālis* -AL[1]]

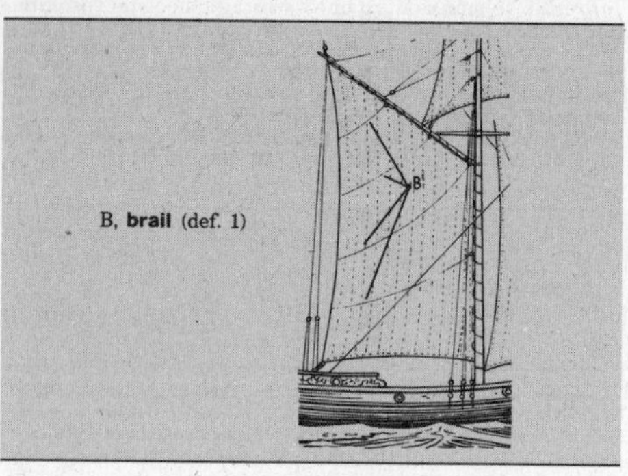

B, **brail** (def. 1)

Bră•i•la (brə ē′lä), *n.* a port in E Rumania, on the Danube River. 203,983.

Braille (brāl), *n., v.,* **Brailled, Braill•ing.** —*n.* **1. Louis** (lo͞o′is, lo͞o′ē; *Fr.* lwē), 1809–52, French teacher of the blind. **2.** a system of writing or printing, devised by L. Braille for use by the blind, in which combinations of tangible dots or points are used to represent letters, characters, etc., that are read by touch. —*v.t.* **3.** to write or transliterate in Braille characters. Also, **braille** (for defs. 2, 3). [1850–55]

Braille•writ•er (brāl′rī′tər), *n.* (*sometimes l.c.*) a machine, similar to a typewriter, for writing texts in Braille. [1940–45; BRAILLE + (TYPE)WRITER]

Braill•ist (brā′list), *n.* **1.** an expert at writing Braille. **2.** a person whose vocation is the writing of Braille. Also, **braill′ist.** [1905–10; BRAILLE + -IST]

Brai•low•sky (brī lôf′skē, brā-, -lof′-; *Russ.* brɪ lôf′-skyē), *n.* **A•le•xan•der** (al′ig zan′dər, -zän′-; *Russ.* u lyi ksän′drɐ), 1896–1976, Russian pianist.

brain (brān), *n.* **1.** *Anat., Zool.* the part of the central nervous system enclosed in the cranium of humans and other vertebrates, consisting of a soft, convoluted mass of gray and white matter and serving to control and coordinate the mental and physical actions. **2.** *Zool.* (in many invertebrates) a part of the nervous system more or less corresponding to the brain of vertebrates. **3.** Sometimes, **brains.** (*used with a plural v.*) understanding; intellectual power; intelligence. **4.** the brain as the center of thought, understanding, etc.; mind; intellect. **5. brains,** *Slang.* a member of a group who is regarded as its intellectual leader or planner: *The junior partner is the brains of the firm.* **6.** *Informal.* a very intelligent or brilliant person. **7.** *Informal.* **a.** the controlling or guiding mechanism in a computer, robot, pacemaker, etc. **b.** the part of a computer system for coordination or guidance, as of a missile. **8. beat one's brains out,** *Informal.* to try very hard to understand and work out a problem, remember something, etc.: *She beat her brains out studying for the exam.* **9. have something on the brain,** to have an obsession; be occupied with: *Lately I seem to have food on the brain.* **10. pick someone's brains,** to obtain information by questioning another person rather than by seeking it independently: *He refused to prepare for the exam but counted on being able to pick his roommate's brains.* —*v.t.* **11.** to smash the skull of. **12.** *Slang.* to hit or bang (someone) on the head. [bef. 1000; ME; OE *bræg(e)n, bregen;* c. LG *brägen,* D *brein*] —**brain′like′,** *adj.*
—**Syn. 3.** sense; capacity. See **mind.**

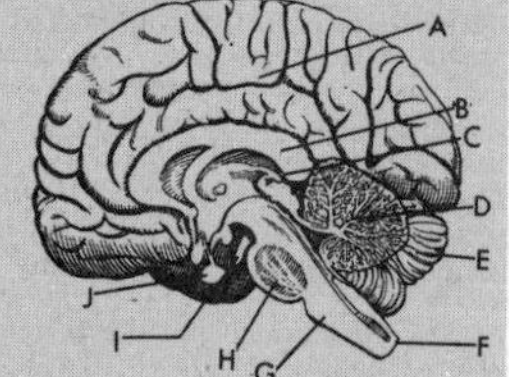

human brain (cross section) A, cerebrum; B, corpus callosum; C, pineal gland; D, vermis; E, cerebellum; F, spinal cord; G, medulla oblongata; H, pons; I, oculomotor nerve; J, pituitary gland

brain•case (brān′kās′), *n.* cranium (def. 2). Also, **brain′ case′.** [1735–45; BRAIN + CASE[2]]

brain′ cell′, *Anat.* a neuron in the brain.

brain•child (brān′chīld′), *n., pl.* **-chil•dren.** a product of one's creative work or thought. Also, **brain′-child′, brain′ child′.** [1880–85; BRAIN + CHILD]

brain′ cor′al, any of several reef-building corals of the genus *Meandrina,* having a highly convoluted and furrowed surface. [1700–10]

brain′ dam′age, *Pathol.* injury or harm, congenital or acquired, to the tissues of the brain resulting from

CONCISE ETYMOLOGY KEY: <, descended or borrowed from; >, whence; b., blend of, blended; c., cognate with; cf., compare; deriv., derivative; equiv., equivalent; imit., imitative; obl., oblique; r., replacing; s., stem; sp., spelling, spelled; resp., respelling, respelled; trans., translation; ?, origin unknown; *, unattested; ‡, probably earlier than. See the full key inside the front cover.

inadequate oxygen supply, trauma, or other cause. —**brain′-dam′aged,** *adj.* —**brain′ dam′aged.**

brain′ death′, complete cessation of brain function as evidenced by absence of brain-wave activity on an electroencephalogram: sometimes used as a legal definition of death. [1965–70] —**brain-dead** (brān′ded′), *adj.* —**brain′ dead′.**

brain′ drain′, a loss of trained professional personnel to another company, nation, etc., that offers greater opportunity. Also, **brain′-drain′.** [1960–65]

brained (brānd), *adj.* having a particular type of brain (used in combination): *small-brained dinosaurs.* [1400–50; late ME; see BRAIN, -ED[3]]

Brai′nerd (brā′nərd), *n.* a city in central Minnesota. 11,489.

brain·fag (brān′fag′), *n. Informal.* prolonged mental fatigue. [1850–55; BRAIN + FAG[1]]

brain′ fe′ver. See **cerebrospinal meningitis.** [1825–35]

brain′ gain′, an increase in the number of highly trained, foreign-born professionals entering a country to live and work where greater opportunities are offered. [1965–70; modeled on BRAIN DRAIN]

brain·ish (brā′nish), *adj. Archaic.* headstrong; impetuous. [1520–30; BRAIN + -ISH[1]]

brain·less (brān′lis), *adj.* mentally weak; foolish; witless; stupid. [1400–50; late ME *braynles.* See BRAIN, -LESS] —**brain′less·ly,** *adv.* —**brain′less·ness,** *n.*

brain·pan (brān′pan′), *n.* the skull or cranium. [bef. 1000; ME *brayn panne,* OE *brægenpanne.* See BRAIN, PAN[1]]

brain-pick·ing (brān′pik′ing), *n. Informal.* the act of obtaining information or ideas by questioning another person. [1950–55; from the v. phrase *pick someone's brains;* see -ING[1]] —**brain′-pick′er,** *n.*

brain·pow·er (brān′pou′ər), *n.* **1.** intellectual capacity; mental ability. **2.** people with superior mental abilities: *an emergency medical conference of all available brainpower.* [1875–80; BRAIN + POWER]

brain′ scan′, *Med.* a scintigram of the brain, used to estimate cerebral blood flow and to detect brain tumors.

brain·sick (brān′sik′), *adj.* insane; crazy; mad. [bef. 1000; ME *brain-seke,* OE *brægensēoc.* See BRAIN, SICK[1]] —**brain′sick′ly,** *adv.* —**brain′sick′ness,** *n.*

brain·stem (brān′stem′), *n.* the portion of the brain that is continuous with the spinal cord and comprises the medulla oblongata, pons, midbrain, and parts of the hypothalamus, functioning in the control of reflexes and such essential internal mechanisms as respiration and heartbeat. Also, **brain′ stem′.** [1875–80; BRAIN + STEM[1]]

brain·storm (brān′stôrm′), *n.* **1. a.** a sudden impulse, idea, etc. **b.** a fit of mental confusion or excitement. **2.** brainstorming. —*adj.* **3.** of or pertaining to brainstorming. —*v.i.* **4.** to conduct or practice brainstorming. —*v.t.* **5.** to subject (a problem) to brainstorming. [1890–95; BRAIN + STORM; orig. a severe mental disturbance] —**brain′storm′er,** *n.*

brain·storm·ing (brān′stôr′ming), *n.* a conference technique of solving specific problems, amassing information, stimulating creative thinking, developing new ideas, etc., by unrestrained and spontaneous participation in discussion. [1955–60; BRAINSTORM + -ING[1]]

Brains′ Trust′, (*sometimes l.c.*) *Brit.* **1.** See **brain trust. 2.** a panel of experts on radio or television, giving impromptu answers to selected questions from the listening audience.

brain·teas·er (brān′tē′zər), *n.* a puzzle or problem whose solution requires great ingenuity. [1920–25; BRAIN + TEASE + ER[1]]

Brain·tree (brān′trē′), *n.* a town in E Massachusetts, near Boston. 36,337.

brain′ trust′, a group of experts from various fields who serve as unofficial consultants on matters of policy and strategy. Also, *Brit.,* **Brains Trust.** [1905–10, *Amer.*]

brain-trust (brān′trust′), *v.t.* to serve as a brain trust or a brain truster for: *They have brain-trusted many major corporations.*

brain′ trust′er, a member of a brain trust; an important but usually unofficial adviser. [1930–35; BRAIN TRUST + -ER[1]]

brain·wash (brān′wosh′, -wôsh′), *v.t.* **1.** to cause (someone) to undergo brainwashing. —*n.* **2.** the process of brainwashing. **3.** a subjection to brainwashing. Also, **brain′-wash′, brain′ wash′.** [1950–55; back formation from BRAINWASHING] —**brain′wash′er,** *n.*

brain·wash·ing (brān′wosh′ing, -wô′shing), *n.* **1.** a method for systematically changing attitudes or altering beliefs, originated in totalitarian countries, esp. through the use of torture, drugs, or psychological-stress techniques. **2.** any method of controlled systematic indoctrination, esp. one based on repetition or confusion: *brainwashing by TV commercials.* **3.** an instance of subjecting or being subjected to such techniques: *efforts to halt the brainwashing of captive audiences.* Also, **brain′-wash′ing, brain′ wash′ing.** [1945–50; BRAIN + WASHING]

brain′ wave′, **1.** Usually, **brain waves.** *Med.* electrical potentials or impulses given off by brain tissue. Cf. **alpha rhythm, beta rhythm, delta rhythm. 2.** *Informal.* a sudden idea or inspiration; brainstorm. [1865–70]

brain·work (brān′wûrk′), *n.* **1.** work or effort consisting principally or largely of mental activity, thought, imagination, etc., as opposed to physical or manual work. **2.** the effort of thought, reasoning, planning, or the like; ordered or directed thinking: *Solving problems is a form of brainwork.* [1835–45; BRAIN + WORK]

brain·y (brā′nē), *adj.,* **brain·i·er, brain·i·est.** *Informal.* intelligent; clever; intellectual. [1835–45; BRAIN + -Y[1]] —**brain′i·ly,** *adv.* —**brain′i·ness,** *n.*

braird (brârd), *Chiefly Scot. n.* **1.** the first sprouts or shoots of grass, corn, or other crops; new growth. —*v.i.* **2.** (of a crop or a seed) to sprout; appear above the ground. [1400–50; late ME *breird,* var. of *brerd* a sprout, to sprout, OE *brerd* edge, top; akin to BRAD]

braise (brāz), *v.t.,* **braised, brais·ing.** to cook (meat, fish, or vegetables) by sautéeing in fat and then simmering slowly in very little liquid. [1760–70; < F *braiser,* deriv. of *braise* live coals < Gmc; akin to Sw *brasa* pyre, fire, whence *brasa* to roast, c. Dan *brase*]

brake[1] (brāk), *n., v.,* **braked, brak·ing.** —*n.* **1.** a device for slowing or stopping a vehicle or other moving mechanism by the absorption or transfer of the energy of momentum, usually by means of friction. **2. brakes,** the drums, shoes, tubes, levers, etc., making up such a device on a vehicle. **3.** anything that has a slowing or stopping effect. **4.** Also called **brakeman.** a member of a bobsled team who operates the brake. **5.** Also called **breaker.** a tool or machine for breaking up flax or hemp, to separate the fiber. **6.** Also called **press brake.** a machine for bending sheet metal to a desired shape. **7.** *Obs.* an old instrument of torture. —*v.t.* **8.** to slow or stop by means of or as if by means of a brake. **9.** to furnish with brakes. **10.** to process (flax or hemp) by crushing it in a brake. —*v.i.* **11.** to use or run a brake. **12.** to stop or slow upon being braked. **13.** to run a hoisting machine. [1400–50; late ME < MD, MLG; akin to BREAK] —**brake′less,** *adj.*
—**Syn. 8.** halt, arrest, stay, restrain; curb, curtail.

brake[2] (brāk), *n.* a place overgrown with bushes, brambles, or cane. [1400–50; late ME (in phrase *brake of fern* thicket of fern) < MLG *brake* thicket]

brake[3] (brāk), *n.* any of several large or coarse ferns, esp. the bracken, *Pteridium aquilinum.* [1275–1325; ME *brake,* prob. by back formation from *braken* BRACKEN, taken as pl.]

brake[4] (brāk), *v. Archaic.* pt. of **break.**

brake·age (brā′kij), *n.* **1.** the action of a brake or set of brakes, as in stopping a vehicle. **2.** brakes collectively. [1860–65; BRAKE[1] + -AGE]

brake′ band′, a flexible strap, usually of steel, lined with a friction-producing material and tightened against a brake drum to produce a braking action.

brake′ drum′, a narrow metal cylinder, fixed to a rotating shaft or wheel, against which brake shoes or brake bands act. [1895–1900]

brake′ fade′, *Auto.* a gradual loss of braking power resulting from decreased friction between the lining and the drum or disc of the brake and usually caused by overheating. Also called **fade.**

brake′ flu′id, *Auto.* the fluid used in a brake system to transmit pressure from the brake pedal to the pistons at each wheel, producing the braking action.

brake′ horse′power, the horsepower made available by an engine or turbine for driving machinery other than itself, as measured by a dynamometer.

brake′ lin′ing, the material, usually asbestos combined with other materials, used as the friction-producing element of a brake. [1920–25]

brake·man (brāk′mən), *n., pl.* **-men. 1.** a railroad worker who assists the conductor in the operation of a train. **2.** brake[1] (def. 4). [1825–35; BRAKE[1] + -MAN]

brake′ ped′al, *Auto.* the pedal used by the driver of a vehicle to operate the brakes.

brak·er (brā′kər), *n. Shipbuilding.* mask (def. 19). [BRAKE[1] + -ER[1]]

brake′ shoe′, **1.** a rigid plate, usually of steel in the shape of an arc of a cylinder, coated on the outside of its curved surface with a friction-producing material and tightened against the inside of a brake drum to produce a braking action. **2.** (on a bicycle) one of two metal blocks holding rubber pads that, when the hand brake is activated, press against the rotating wheel to produce a braking action. Cf. **caliper** (def. 6). Also called **shoe.** [1870–75, *Amer.*]

brake-van (brāk′van′), *n. Brit.* the caboose of a railway train. [1880–85]

brake′ wheel′, (in a windmill) a bevel gearwheel rotating with the wind shaft. [1870–75, *Amer.*]

Brak·pan (brak′pan′), *n.* a city in the NE Republic of South Africa, near Johannesburg. 113,115.

Brale (brāl), *Trademark.* a brand of conoidal diamond or diamond-pointed tool, having convexly curved sides meeting at an angle of 120°, used as an indenter in testing the hardness of metals.

bra·less (brä′lis), *adj.* wearing no bra. [1965–70; BRA + -LESS] —**bra′less·ness,** *n.*

Bram (bram), *n.* a male given name.

Bram·ah (bram′ə, brä′mə), *n.* **Joseph,** 1748–1814, English engineer and inventor.

Bra·man·te (brə män′tā; *It.* brä män′te), *n.* **Do·na·to d'A·gno·lo** (dô nä′tô dä′nyô lô), 1444–1514, Italian architect and painter.

bram·ble (bram′bəl), *n., v.,* **-bled, -bling.** —*n.* **1.** any prickly shrub belonging to the genus *Rubus,* of the rose family. **2.** *Brit.* the common blackberry. **3.** any rough, prickly shrub, as the dog rose. —*v.i.* **4.** *Brit.* to look for and gather wild blackberries; pick blackberries from the vine. [bef. 1000; ME; OE *bræmbel,* var. of *bræmel,* equiv. to *bræm-* (c. D *braam* BROOM) + *-el* n. suffix]

bram·bling (bram′bling), *n.* an Old World finch, *Fringilla montifringilla,* the male of which is black and white with a reddish-brown breast. [1560–70; earlier *bramlin* (*bram-* (var. of BROOM) + *-lin* -LING[1]); akin to G *Brämling*]

bram·bly (bram′blē), *adj.,* **-bli·er, -bli·est.** having or resembling brambles. [1575–85; BRAMBLE + -Y[1]]

Bramp·ton (bramp′tən), *n.* a city in SE Ontario, in S Canada, near Toronto. 149,030.

Bram·well (bram′wel, -wəl), *n.* a male given name.

bran (bran), *n., v.,* **branned, bran·ning.** —*n.* **1.** the partly ground husk of wheat or other grain, separated from flour meal by sifting. —*v.t.* **2.** to soak or boil in bran water, as in the tanning of hides. [1250–1300; ME < AF, OF *bran, bren,* of uncert. orig.] —**bran′ner,** *n.*

Bran (bran), *n.* **1.** *Welsh Legend.* a king of Britain and the brother of Manawydan and Branwen: his head was buried at London as a magical defense against invasion. He was sometimes regarded as a sea god or Christian saint. **2.** a male given name, form of **Brandon.**

branch (branch, bränch), *n.* **1.** a division or subdivision of the stem or axis of a tree, shrub, or other plant. **2.** a limb, offshoot, or ramification of any main stem: *the branches of a deer's antlers.* **3.** any member or part of a body or system; a section or subdivision: *the various branches of learning.* **4.** a local operating division of a business, library, or the like. **5.** a line of family descent stemming from a particular ancestor, as distinguished from some other line or lines from the same stock; a division of a family. **6.** a tributary stream or any stream that is not a large river or a bayou. **7.** *Chiefly South Midland and Southern U.S.* See **branch water** (def. 2). **8.** *Ling.* (in the classification of related languages within a family) a category of a lower order than a subfamily and of a higher order than a subbranch or a group, as the Germanic branch of Indo-European. Cf. **group** (def. 4a). **9.** *Computers.* a point in a computer program where the computer selects one of two or more instructions to execute, according to some criterion. **10.** *Naut.* a warrant or license permitting a pilot to navigate in certain waters. —*v.i.* **11.** to put forth branches; spread in branches. **12.** to divide into separate parts or subdivisions; diverge: *The main road branches off to the left.* **13.** to expand or extend, as business activities: *The bank has plans to branch throughout the state.* —*v.t.* **14.** to divide into branches or sections. **15.** to adorn with needlework; decorate with embroidery, as in textile fabrics. **16. branch out,** to expand or extend, as business activities, pursuits, interests, etc.: *The business is branching out into computers.* [1250–1300; ME *bra(u)nche* < AF; OF *branche* < LL *branca* paw, of uncert. orig.] —**branch′less,** *adj.* —**branch′like′,** *adj.*
—**Syn. 1.** offshoot, shoot. BRANCH, BOUGH, LIMB refer to divisions of a tree. BRANCH is general, meaning either a large or a small division. BOUGH refers only to the larger branches: *a bough loaded with apples.* A LIMB is a large primary division of a tree trunk or of a bough: *to climb out on a limb.* **12.** ramify, subdivide.

branch′ cut′, *Math.* a method for selecting a single-valued function on a subset of the domain of a multiple-valued function of a complex variable.

branched′ chain′, *Chem.* an open chain of atoms, usually carbon, with one or more side chains attached to it. Cf. **straight chain.** [1900–05]

branched′ polyeth′ylene. See **low-density polyethylene.**

branchi-, var. of **branchio-** before a vowel.

bran·chi·a (brang′kē ə), *n., pl.* **-chi·ae** (-kē ē′). *Zool.* a gill. [1350–1400; ME < Gk: gills, pl. of *bránchion* fin]

bran·chi·al (brang′kē əl), *adj.* of or pertaining to gills or to the homologous, embryonic parts in animals without gills. [1795–1805; BRANCHI- + -AL[1]]

bran′chial arch′, **1.** *Zool.* one of a series of bony or cartilaginous arches on each side of the pharynx that support the gills of fishes and aquatic amphibians; gill bar. **2.** *Embryol.* one of a series of archlike mesodermal thickenings of the body wall in the pharyngeal region of the embryo of amphibians, reptiles, birds, and mammals. Also called **gill arch, visceral arch.** [1870–75]

bran′chial cleft′, *Zool.* one of a series of slitlike openings in the walls of the pharynx between the branchial arches of fishes and aquatic amphibians through which water passes from the pharynx to the exterior. Also called **visceral cleft.**

bran′chial groove′, *Embryol.* one of a series of rudimentary depressions on the surface of the embryo between adjacent branchial arches, homologous to the branchial clefts of gill-breathing ancestral forms. Also called **visceral groove.**

bran′chial pouch′, *Embryol.* one of a series of rudimentary outcroppings of the inner pharyngeal wall, corresponding to the branchial grooves on the surface. Also called **gill pouch, pharyngeal pouch.**

bran·chi·ate (brang′kē it, -āt′), *adj. Zool.* having gills. [1865–70; BRANCHI- + -ATE[1]]

bran·chi·form (brang′kə fôrm′), *adj.* shaped like a gill. [1835–45; BRANCHI- + -FORM]

branchio-, a combining form meaning "gills," used in the formation of compound words: *branchiopod.* Also, *esp. before a vowel,* **branchi-.** [comb. form repr. Gk *bránchia* BRANCHIA]

bran·chi·op·neus·tic (brang′kē op no͞o′stik, -nyo͞o′-), *adj. Entomol.* breathing by means of gills, as certain aquatic insect larvae. [BRANCHIO- + Gk *pneustikós,* equiv. to *pneus-* (verbid s. of *pneîn* to breathe) + *-tikos* -TIC]

bran·chi·o·pod (brang′kē ə pod′), *n.* **1.** any crustacean of the class (or subclass) Branchiopoda, having flattened, footlike appendages that bear respiratory organs. —*adj.* **2.** Also, **bran·chi·op·o·dous** (brang′kē op′ə dəs). belonging or pertaining to the Branchiopoda. [1820–30; < NL *Branchiopoda.* See BRANCHIO-, -POD]

bran·chi·os·te·gal (brang′kē os′ti gəl), *Ichthyol.* —*n.* **1.** Also called **branchios′tegal ray′.** one of the long, curved bones just below the operculum, supporting the gill membranes. —*adj.* **2.** of or pertaining to the branchiostegals. [1740–50; BRANCHIO- + STEG(O)- + -AL[1]]

bran•chi•os•te•gous (brang′kē os′ti gəs), *adj. Ichthyol.* **1.** branchiostegal. **2.** having covered gills. [1760–70; BRANCHIO- + STEG(O)- + -OUS]

branch•let (branch′lit, bränch′-), *n.* a small branch or a subdivision of a branch. [1725–35; BRANCH + -LET]

branch′ line′, a rail line, directly or indirectly connected with a main line, having its own stations and service. [1840–50]

branch′ point′, **1.** *Elect.* a point in an electric network at which three or more conductors meet. **2.** *Math.* a point such that analytic continuation of a given function of a complex variable in a small neighborhood of the point produces a different functional value at the point. [1875–80]

Bran•chus (brang′kəs), *n. Class. Myth.* a son of Apollo, given the power of augury by his father.

branch′ wa′ter, **1.** water in or from a branch, creek, stream, etc.; pure, natural water. **2.** Also called **branch.** *Chiefly South Midland and Southern U.S.* (in a drink, highball, etc.) plain water as distinguished from soda water, ginger ale, or the like; ordinary water. [1840–50]

branch′ wilt′, *Plant Pathol.* a disease of walnut trees, characterized by sudden wilting of the leaves, and cankers and discoloration of the bark and branches, caused by a fungus, *Hendersonula toruloidea.*

Bran•cu•si (bräng ko͞o′zē, brang-; *Rum.* bʀäng-ko͞osh′), *n.* **Con•stan•tin** (kon′stən tin; *Rum.* kon′stän-tēn′), 1876–1957, Rumanian sculptor.

brand (brand), *n.* **1.** kind, grade, or make, as indicated by a stamp, trademark, or the like: *the best brand of coffee.* **2.** a mark made by burning or otherwise, to indicate kind, grade, make, ownership, etc. **3.** a mark formerly put upon criminals with a hot iron. **4.** any mark of disgrace; stigma. **5.** See **branding iron. 6.** a kind or variety of something distinguished by some distinctive characteristic: *The movie was filled with slapstick—a brand of humor he did not find funny.* **7.** a burning or partly burned piece of wood. **8.** *Archaic.* a sword. —*v.t.* **9.** to label or mark with or as if with a brand. **10.** to mark with disgrace or infamy; stigmatize. **11.** to impress indelibly: *The plane crash was branded on her mind.* [bef. 950; ME, OE: burning, a burning piece of wood, torch, sword; c. D *brand,* G *Brand,* ON *brandr;* akin to BURN[1]] —**brand′er,** *n.* —**brand′less,** *adj.*
—**Syn. 4.** stain, spot, blot, taint.

Brand (brand), *n.* **1. Oscar,** born 1920, U.S. folk singer, born in Canada. **2.** a male given name.

brand•ed (bran′did), *adj.* **1.** marked with a branding iron to show ownership: *branded cattle.* **2.** *Com.* carrying the brand or trademark of a manufacturer: *branded merchandise.* [1645–55; BRAND + -ED[3]]

Bran•deis (bran′dīs), *n.* **Louis Dem•bitz** (dem′bits), 1856–1941, U.S. lawyer and writer: associate justice of the U.S. Supreme Court 1916–39.

Bran•den•burg (bran′dən bûrg′; *Ger.* brän′dən-bo͝orк′), *n.* **1.** a state in NE central Germany. 2,700,000; 10,039 sq. mi. (26,000 sq. km). *Cap.:* Potsdam. **2.** a city in NE Germany. 95,203. —**Bran′den•burg′er,** *n.*

bran•der (bran′dər), *v.t. Building Trades.* **1.** to apply furring to (a surface). —*v.i.* **2.** to apply furring. [1865–70; back formation from BRANDERING]

bran•der•ing (bran′dər ing), *n.* furring (def. 4b). [1865–70; perh. *brander* gridiron (ME *brandire,* equiv. to *brand(en)* to BRAND + *ire* IRON) + -ING[1]]

Bran•des (brän′des), *n.* **Ge•org Mor•ris** (ge ōrg′ mō′-ris), (*Georg Morris Cohen*), 1842–1927, Danish historian and literary critic.

bran•died (bran′dēd), *adj.* flavored, soaked in, or treated with brandy. [1825–35; BRANDY + -ED[3]]

brand′ing i′ron, a long-handled metal rod with a stamp at one end, used for branding livestock, esp. cattle, with a registered or recognized symbol or character to indicate ownership. Also called **brand.** [1400–50; late ME]

bran•dish (bran′dish), *v.t.* **1.** to shake or wave, as a weapon; flourish: *Brandishing his sword, he rode into battle.* —*n.* **2.** a flourish or waving, as of a weapon. [1275–1325; ME *bra(u)ndisshen* < AF, MF *brandiss-* (long s. of *brandir,* deriv. of *brand* sword < Gmc). See BRAND, -ISH[2]] —**bran′dish•er,** *n.*
—**Syn. 1.** swing, flaunt, wield, display.

brand•ling (brand′ling), *n.* a small, reddish-brown earthworm, *Eisenia foetida,* having yellow markings, found chiefly in manure piles and used as bait. [1645–55; BRAND + -LING[1]]

brand′ name′, **1.** a word, name, symbol, etc., esp. one legally registered as a trademark, used by a manufacturer or merchant to identify its products distinctively from others of the same type and usually prominently displayed on its goods, in advertising, etc. **2.** a product, line of products, or service bearing a widely known brand name. **3.** *Informal.* a person who is notable or famous, esp. in a particular field: *The reception was replete with brand names from politics and the arts.* [1920–25]

brand-name (brand′nām′), *adj.* **1.** having or being a brand name: *nationally known brand-name food products.* **2.** *Informal.* widely familiar; well-known: *Several brand-name personalities will be performing at the benefit.* [1920–25]

brand-new (bran′no͞o′, -nyo͞o′, brand′-), *adj.* entirely new. [1560–70] —**brand′-new′ness,** *n.*

Bran•do (bran′dō), *n.* **Marlon,** born 1924, U.S. actor.

Bran•don (bran′dən), *n.* **1.** a city in SW Manitoba, in S central Canada. 34,901. **2.** a male given name.

CONCISE ETYMOLOGY KEY: <, descended or borrowed from; >, whence; b., blend of, blended; c., cognate with; cf., compare; deriv., derivative; equiv., equivalent; imit., imitative; obl., oblique; r., replacing; s., stem; sp., spelling, spelled; resp., respelling, respelled; trans., translation; ?, origin unknown; *, unattested; ‡, probably earlier than. See the full key inside the front cover.

bran•dreth (bran′drith), *n.* **1.** a wooden fence around a well. **2.** an iron tripod or trivet placed over a fire. **3.** any similar support or framework. Also, **bran′drith.** [1350–1400; ME < ON *brandreith* grate, equiv. to *brand* BRAND + *reith* vehicle (c. ROAD, RAID); r. OE *brandrād* trivet and *brandrida* fire-grate]

Brandt (brant; *Ger.* bʀänt), *n.* **Wil•ly** (wil′ē; *Ger.* vil′ē), 1913–92, German political leader: chancellor 1969–74; Nobel peace prize 1971.

Brand X (eks), **1.** (in advertising) a competing brand or product not referred to by name but implied to be of inferior quality. **2.** an unknown or little-known brand name or a product bearing it. **3.** any item that one chooses not to refer to by name, esp. when used as a basis of comparison. [1965–70]

bran•dy (bran′dē), *n., pl.* **-dies,** *v.,* **-died, -dy•ing.** —*n.* **1.** a spirit distilled from wine or from the fermented juice of grapes or of apples, peaches, plums, etc. —*v.t.* **2.** to mix, flavor, or preserve with brandy. [1615–25; short for *brandywine* < D *brandewijn* burnt (i.e., distilled) wine]

bran′dy alexan′der. See under **alexander.**

bran′dy mint′, peppermint.

bran′dy snif′ter, snifter (def. 1).

Bran•dy•wine (bran′dē wīn′), *n.* a creek in SE Pennsylvania and N Delaware: British defeat of the Americans 1777.

Bran•ford (bran′fərd), *n.* a town in S Connecticut. 23,363.

bran•gle (brang′gəl), *n., v.,* **-gled, -gling.** *Brit. Archaic.* —*n.* **1.** a squabble. —*v.i.* **2.** to dispute in a noisy or angry manner; squabble. [1545–55; perh. var. of BRANLE]

Bran•gus (brang′gəs), *n., pl.* **-gus•es.** one of an American breed of cattle developed from Brahman and Aberdeen Angus stock, bred to withstand a hot climate. [BRA(HMAN) + (ABERDEEN A)NGUS]

branks (brangks), *n.* (*used with a plural v.*) a device consisting of a headpiece with a flat, iron bit to restrain the tongue, formerly used to punish scolds. [1585–95; perh. to be identified with ME *bernak* bridle, snaffle; see BARNACLE[2]]

bran•le (bran′l), *n.* **1.** a lively 16th- and 17th-century round dance originating in France. **2.** the music for this dance. [1575–85; < MF, deriv. of *branler* to shake, swing (prob. from the phrase *branler une danse*), OF *bran(s)ler* to move (a limb, the head), contr. of *brandeler* to shake, equiv. to *brand(ir)* to BRANDISH + *-eler* suffix of expressive verbs < VL *-*illāre*]

bran•ni•gan (bran′i gən), *n.* **1.** a carouse. **2.** a squabble; brawl. [1925–30; prob. from proper name]

bran•ny (bran′ē), *adj.,* **-ni•er, -ni•est.** of, containing, or like bran. [1525–35; BRAN + -Y[1]]

brant (brant), *n., pl.* **brants,** (*esp. collectively*) **brant.** any of several species of small, dark-colored geese of the genus *Branta,* esp. *B. bernicla,* breeding in high northern latitudes and migrating south in the autumn. Also called **brant′ goose′;** *esp. Brit.,* **brent, brent goose.** [1535–45; short for *brantgoose, brentgoose;* akin to ON *brandgās,* G *Brandgans*]

Brant (brant), *n.* **1. Joseph** (*Thayendanegea*), 1742–1807, Mohawk Indian chief who fought on the side of the British in the American Revolution. **2.** a male given name.

Brant•ford (brant′fərd), *n.* a city in S Ontario, in SE Canada, near Lake Erie. 66,950.

Bran•ting (bran′ting, brän′-), *n.* **Karl Hjal•mar** (kärl yäl′mär), 1860–1925, Swedish statesman: prime minister 1920, 1921–23, 1924–25; Nobel peace prize 1921.

Bran•wen (bran′wen), *n. Welsh Legend.* a sister of Bran: her son, by Matholwych, was killed by Evnissyen.

Braque (bräk; *Fr.* bʀak), *n.* **Georges** (jôrj; *Fr.* zhôʀzh), 1882–1963, French painter.

brash (brash), *adj.,* **-er, -est,** *n.* —*adj.* Also, **brashy. 1.** impertinent; impudent; tactless: *a brash young man.* **2.** hasty; rash; impetuous. **3.** energetic or highly spirited, esp. in an irreverent way; zesty: *a brash new musical.* **4.** (used esp. of wood) brittle. —*n.* **5.** a pile or stack of loose fragments or debris, as of rocks or hedge clippings. **6.** See **brash ice. 7.** *Pathol.* heartburn (def. 1). **8.** *Scot. and North Eng. Dial.* **a.** a sudden shower or burst of rain. **b.** any sudden, minor sickness or indisposition, esp. of the digestive tract. **c.** an assault; attack. [1400–50; (n.) late ME *brass(c)he* a slap, crash, perh. b. *brok(e)* (OE *broc* breach, fragment, sickness; akin to BREAK) and *dasch* smashing blow; see DASH[1]; (adj.) in sense "brittle," deriv. of n.; in sense "hasty" by confusion with RASH[1]] —**brash′ly,** *adv.* —**brash′ness,** *n.*
—**Syn. 2.** reckless, overhasty, imprudent, foolhardy, precipitate. —**Ant. 2.** cautious, wary, prudent, careful.

brash′ ice′, small, floating fragments of sea ice or river ice. Also called **brash.**

brash•y (brash′ē), *adj.,* **brash•i•er, brash•i•est. 1.** brash. **2.** *Scot. and North Eng. Dial.* showery. [1795–1805; BRASH + -Y[1]] —**brash′i•ness,** *n.*

bra•sier (brā′zhər), *n.* brazier.

Bra•sil (*Port.* bʀə zēl′; *Sp.* bʀä sēl′), *n.* Brazil.

bra•sil•e•in (brə zil′ē in), *n. Chem.* brazilein.

Bra•síl•ia (brə zil′yə; *Port.* bʀä zēl′yə), *n.* a city in and the capital of Brazil, on the central plateau. 411,505. See map in previous column.

bras•i•lin (braz′ə lin), *n. Chem.* brazilin.

Bra•șov (bʀä shôv′), *n.* a city in central Rumania. 299,172. Formerly, **Stalin.** Hungarian, **Brassó.** German, **Kronstadt.**

brass (bras, bräs), *n.* **1.** any of various metal alloys consisting mainly of copper and zinc. **2.** a utensil, ornament, or other article made of such an alloy. **3.** *Music.* **a.** See **brass instrument. b.** brass instruments collectively in a band or orchestra. **4.** metallic yellow; lemon, amber, or reddish yellow. **5.** *Informal.* **a.** high-ranking military officers. **b.** any very important officials. **6.** *Informal.* excessive self-assurance; impudence; effrontery. **7.** *Mach.* a replaceable semicylindrical shell, usually of bronze, used with another such to line a bearing; a half bushing. See diag. under **exploded view. 8.** *Brit.* a memorial tablet or plaque, often incised with an effigy, coat of arms, or the like. **9.** *Furniture.* any piece of ornamental or functional hardware, as a drawer pull, made of brass. **10.** *Brit. Slang.* money. —*adj.* **11.** of, made of, or pertaining to brass. **12.** composed for or using musical instruments made of brass. **13.** having the color brass. [bef. 1000; 1945–50 for def. 5; ME *bras,* OE *bræs;* c. OFris *bres* copper, MLG *bras* metal] —**brass′ish,** *adj.*
—**Syn. 6.** cheek, nerve, brashness, gall, chutzpa.

brass•age (bras′ij, brä′sij), *n.* a charge to cover the costs of coining money. [1800–10; < F (*droit de*) *brassage* the stirring of molten metals prior to casting, equiv. to *brass(er)* to stir (melted metal), lit., to brew (see BRASSERIE) + *-age* -AGE]

bras•sard (bras′ärd, brə särd′), *n.* **1.** a decorative cloth band, often braided or tasseled, worn around the upper arm, as by military personnel to signify a particular group, regiment, etc. **2.** Also, **brassart** (bras′ärt, brə särt′). a piece of plate armor for the arm. [1820–30; < F, equiv. to *bras* arm (see BRACE) + *-ard* -ARD]

brass′ band′, *Music.* a band made up principally of brass wind instruments. [1825–35]

brass•bound (bras′bound′, bräs′-), *adj.* **1.** having a frame or reinforcements strengthened or made rigid by brass, bronze, etc., as a trunk or chest. **2.** rigid; inflexible: *brassbound regulations.* **3.** impudent; brazen: *brassbound presumption.* [1900–05; BRASS + -BOUND[1]]

brass-col•lar (bras′kol′ər, bräs′-), *adj. Informal.* unwaveringly faithful to a political party; voting the straight ticket: *a brass-collar Democrat.* [1950–55, *Amer.*]

bras•se•rie (bras′ə rē′; *Fr.* bʀasᵊ ʀē′), *n., pl.* **-ries** (-rēz′; *Fr.* -ʀē′). an unpretentious restaurant, tavern, or the like, that serves drinks, esp. beer, and simple or hearty food. [1860–65; < F: lit., brewery; MF, equiv. to *brass(er)* to brew (< Gallo-L **braciāre,* deriv. of **bracmalt* < Gaulish; cf. Welsh *brag,* MIr *mraich, braich* malt) + *-erie* -ERY]

brass•ey (bras′ē, brä′sē), *n., pl.* **-eys.** *Golf.* brassie.

brass′ hat′, *Slang.* a person in a high position, esp. a top-ranking army or navy officer. [1890–95]

bras•si•ca (bras′i kə), *n.* any plant belonging to the genus *Brassica,* of the mustard family, including many economically important vegetables, as cabbage, kale, broccoli, cauliflower, turnip, and mustard. [1825–35; < NL, L: cabbage]

bras•si•ca•ceous (bras′i kā′shəs), *adj.* belonging to the plant family Brassicaceae, an alternative name for the plant family Cruciferae. Cf. **mustard family.** [< NL *Brassicace(ae)* family name (see BRASSICA, -ACEAE) + -OUS]

brass•ie (bras′ē, brä′sē), *n. Golf.* a club with a wooden head, the brass-plated face of which has more slope than a driver but less than a spoon, for hitting long, low drives on the fairway. Also, **brassy, brassey.** Also called **number two wood.** [1885–90; BRASS + -IE]

bras•siere (brə zēr′), *n.* a woman's undergarment for supporting the breasts. Also, **bras•sière′.** Also called **bra.** [1910–15; < F *brassière* bodice worn as an undergarment to support the breasts (now obs. in this sense), MF *bracieres* camisole, OF: armor for the arms, equiv. to *bras* arm (see BRACE) + *-ière,* suffix added to body part nouns, the resultant deriv. denoting an article for that part < L *-āria* -ARY]

brass′ in′strument, a musical wind instrument of brass or other metal with a cup-shaped mouthpiece, as the trombone, tuba, French horn, trumpet, or cornet. Also called **brass′ wind′.** [1850–55]

brass′ knuck′les, a band of metal with four holes that fits over the upper fingers and that is gripped when a fist is made, used for increasing the effect of a blow with the fist. [1850–55, *Amer.*]

Bras•só (bʀosh′shô), *n.* Hungarian name of **Brașov.**

brass′ ring′, *Informal.* **1.** wealth, success, or a prestigious position considered as a goal or prize: *Few of those who reach for the brass ring of the Presidency achieve it.* **2.** the opportunity to try for such a prize. [from the practice of picking a ring from a box while riding a merry-go-round: whoever selected a brass ring received a free ride]

brass-rub•bing (bras′rub′ing, bräs′-), *n.* **1.** an antiquarian's technique for copying designs from incised brass memorial slabs and the like. **2.** a copy made by brass-rubbing. Cf. **rubbing** (def. 2). [1885–90]

brass′ tacks′, *Informal.* the most fundamental considerations; essentials; realities (usually used in the phrase *get down to brass tacks*). [1895–1900]

brass•ware (bras′wâr′, bräs′-), *n.* articles made of brass. [BRASS + WARE[1]]

brass•y[1] (bras′ē, brä′sē), *adj.,* **brass•i•er, brass•i•est. 1.** made of or covered with brass. **2.** resembling brass, as in color. **3.** harsh and metallic: *brassy tones.* **4.** bra-

zen; bold; loud. **5.** noisy; clamorous: *a big, brassy night-club.* [1570–80; BRASS + -Y[1]] **—brass′i·ly,** *adv.* **—brass′i·ness,** *n.*
—Syn. 4. insolent, saucy, forward, cheeky, brash. **—Ant. 4.** modest, shy, retiring.

brass·y[2] (bras′ē, brä′sē), *n., pl.* **brass·ies.** *Golf.* brassie.

brat (brat), *n.* a child, esp. an annoying, spoiled, or impolite child (usually used in contempt or irritation). [1495–1505; perh. transferred use of *brat* rag, OE *bratt* cloak < Celt; cf. Ir *brat* mantle, cloak] **—brat′tish,** *adj.*

Bra·ti·sla·va (brat′ə slä′və, brä′tə-; *Czech.* brä′tyi-slä vä), *n.* the capital of Slovakia, in the SW part, on the Danube River: a former capital of Hungary. 435,000. Hungarian, **Pozsony.** German, **Pressburg.**

Bratsk (brätsk), *n.* a city in the S central Russian Federation in Asia, on the Angara River. 249,000.

Brat·tain (brat′n), *n.* **Walter Hou·ser** (hou′zər), born 1902, U.S. physicist: Nobel prize 1956.

brat·tice (brat′is), *n., v.,* **-ticed, -tic·ing.** **—***n.* **1.** a partition or lining, as of planks or cloth, forming an air passage in a mine. **2.** (in medieval architecture) any temporary wooden fortification, esp. at the top of a wall. [1300–50; ME *brutaske, bretage, bretice* < AF *bretaske, bretage,* AF, OF *bretesche* wooden parapet on a fortress < ML (9th century) *brittisca,* appar. a Latinized form of OE *Bryttisc* BRITISH (or a new formation in ML), on the presumption that such parapets were introduced from Britain]

brat·tle (brat′l), *n., v.,* **-tled, -tling.** **—***n.* **1.** a clattering noise. **—***v.i.* **2.** to scamper noisily. [1495–1505; imit; see RATTLE[1]]

Brat·tle·bor·o (brat′l bûr′ō, -bur′ō), *n.* a town in SE Vermont. 11,886.

brat·ty (brat′ē), *adj.,* **-ti·er, -ti·est.** characteristic of or resembling a brat; impudent; ill-mannered: *bratty remarks; bratty tricks.* [BRAT + -Y[1]]

brat·wurst (brat′wûrst, -wŏŏrst, brät′-; *Ger.* brät′-vŏŏrsht′), *n.* a sausage made of pork, spices, and herbs, sometimes without a casing, usually served sautéed or broiled. [1910–15; < G, equiv. to *brat(en)* to roast, bake + *Wurst* sausage]

Brau·del (brō del′), *n.* **Fer·nand** (fer nän′), 1902–85, French historian.

Braun (broun; *Ger.* broun), *n.* **1. E·va** (ē′və; *Ger.* ā′vä), 1912–45, mistress of Adolf Hitler. **2. Karl Fer·di·nand** (kärl fûr′dn and′; *Ger.* kärl fer′dē nänt′), 1850–1918, German physicist and specialist in wireless telegraphy: Nobel prize in physics 1909. **3. Wern·her von** (vâr′nər von, vûr′-, wûr′-; *Ger.* ver′nər fən), 1912–77, German rocket engineer, in U.S. after 1945.

braun·ite (brou′nit), *n.* an ore of manganese, $3Mn_2O_3 \cdot MnSiO_3$. [1830–40; named after A. E. *Braun* (1809–56), German official; see -ITE[1]]

Braun·schweig (broun′shvīk′), *n.* German name of **Brunswick.**

Braun·schwei·ger (broun′shwī′gər; *Ger.* broun′-shvī′gər), *n.* (*sometimes l.c.*) a soft, spiced liver sausage, usually smoked. [1925–30; < G; see BRAUNSCHWEIG, -ER[1]]

bra·va (brä′vä, brä vä′), *interj., n., pl.* **-vas.** **—***interj.* **1.** (used in praising a female performer). **—***n.* **2.** a shout of "brava!" [1875–80; < It, fem. of *bravo* BRAVO]

bra·va·do (brə vä′dō), *n., pl.* **-does, -dos.** a pretentious, swaggering display of courage. [1575–85; < Sp *bravada* (now *bravata* < It), equiv. to *brav(o)* BRAVE + *-ada* -ADE[1]]
—Syn. brag, bluster, bombast, braggadocio. See **courage.**

Bra′vais lat′tice (brav′ä, brə vä′), *Crystall.* lattice (def. 4). [named after Auguste *Bravais* (d. 1863), French physicist]

brave (brāv), *adj.,* **brav·er, brav·est,** *n., v.,* **braved, brav·ing.** **—***adj.* **1.** possessing or exhibiting courage or courageous endurance. **2.** making a fine appearance. **3.** *Archaic.* excellent; fine; admirable. **—***n.* **4.** a brave person. **5.** a warrior, esp. among North American Indian tribes. **6.** *Obs.* **a.** a bully. **b.** a boast or challenge. **—***v.t.* **7.** to meet or face courageously: *to brave misfortunes.* **8.** to defy; challenge; dare. **9.** *Obs.* to make splendid. **—***v.i.* **10.** *Obs.* to boast; brag. [1475–85; < MF < Sp *bravo* (> It) < VL **brabus* for L *barbarus* BARBAROUS] **—brave′ly,** *adv.* **—brave′ness,** *n.*
—Syn. 1. bold, intrepid, daring, dauntless, heroic. BRAVE, COURAGEOUS, VALIANT, FEARLESS, GALLANT refer to confident bearing in the face of difficulties or dangers. BRAVE is the most comprehensive: it is especially used of that confident fortitude or daring that actively faces and endures anything threatening. COURAGEOUS implies a higher or nobler kind of bravery, esp. as resulting from an inborn quality of mind or spirit that faces or endures perils or difficulties without fear and even with enthusiasm. VALIANT implies a correspondence between an inner courageousness and external deeds, particularly of physical strength or endurance. FEARLESS implies unflinching spirit and coolness in the face of danger. GALLANT implies a chivalrous, impetuous, or dashing bravery. **—Ant. 1.** cowardly.

Brave′ New′ World′, a novel (1932) by Aldous Huxley.

brav·er·y (brā′və rē, brāv′rē), *n., pl.* **-er·ies. 1.** brave spirit or conduct; courage; valor. **2.** showiness; splendor; magnificence. [1540–50; prob. < It *braveria,* equiv. to *brav(are)* to brave + *-eria* -ERY]
—Syn. 1. intrepidity, fearlessness, boldness, daring, prowess, heroism, pluck, spirit, audacity, nerve, mettle, spunk. See **courage.** **—Ant. 1.** cowardice.

brave′ west′ winds′, *Naut., Meteorol.* the strong west and west-northwest winds blowing between latitudes 40° S and 60° S.

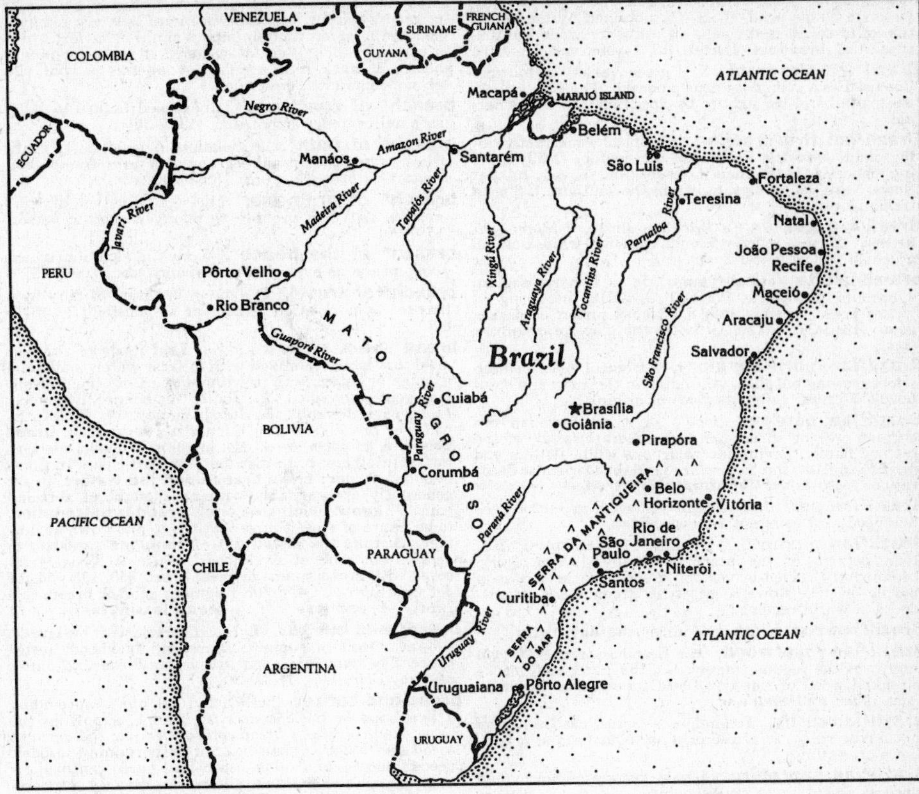

bra·vis·si·mo (brä vis′ə mō′; *It.* brä vēs′sē mô), *interj.* (used to express the highest praise to a performer). [1755–65; < It, equiv. to *brav(o)* BRAVO + *-issimo* superl. suffix]

bra·vo (brä′vō; *for 1, 2, 5 also* brä vō′), *interj., n., pl.* **-vos** for 2, **-vos** or **-voes** for 3, *v.,* **-voed, -vo·ing.** **—***interj.* **1.** (used in praising a performer). **—***n.* **2.** a shout of "bravo!" **3.** a daring bandit, assassin, or murderer, esp. one hired to steal or murder for another. **4.** a word used in communications to represent the letter *B.* **—***v.i.* **5.** to shout "bravo!" [1755–65; < It; see BRAVE]

bra·vu·ra (brə vyŏŏr′ə, -vŏŏr′ə; *It.* brä vōō′rä), *n., pl.* **-ras, -re** (*It.* -re), *adj.* **—***n.* **1.** *Music.* a florid passage or piece requiring great skill and spirit in the performer. **2.** a display of daring; brilliant performance. **—***adj.* **3.** *Music.* spirited; florid; brilliant (applied chiefly to vocal but occasionally to instrumental compositions). [1780–90; < It: spirit, dash. See BRAVE, -URE]

braw (brô, brä), *adj. Scot. and North Eng.* **1.** fine or fine-looking; excellent. **2.** finely dressed; dressed in a splendid or gaudy fashion. [1555–65; var. of BRAVE] **—braw′ly, braw′lie, braw·lis, braw·lys** (brô′lis, brä′-), *adv.*

brawl (brôl), *n.* **1.** a noisy quarrel, squabble, or fight. **2.** a bubbling or roaring noise; a clamor. **3.** *Slang.* a large, noisy party. **—***v.i.* **4.** to quarrel angrily and noisily; wrangle. **5.** to make a bubbling or roaring noise, as water flowing over a rocky bed. [1350–1400; (v.) ME *brawlen, brallen* to raise a clamor, quarrel, boast; of uncert. orig.; (n.) ME *braule, brall,* deriv. of the n.] **—brawl′er,** *n.* **—brawl′y,** *adj.*
—Syn. 1. wrangle, row, tumult, affray, altercation, rumpus. See **disorder. 4.** squabble, fight, bicker, row.

Braw·ley (brô′lē), *n.* a city in S California. 14,946.

brawn (brôn), *n.* **1.** strong, well-developed muscles. **2.** muscular strength. **3.** *Chiefly Brit.* **a.** a boar's or swine's flesh, esp. when boiled and pickled. **b.** headcheese. [1275–1325; ME *brawne* < OF *braon* slice of flesh (Pr *bradon*) < Gmc; cf. G *Braten* joint of meat, akin to OE *brǣd* flesh]
—Syn. 2. brawniness, robustness, muscle, sturdiness, might, power.

brawn·y (brô′nē), *adj.,* **brawn·i·er, brawn·i·est.** muscular; strong. [1375–1425; late ME; see BRAWN, -Y[1]] **—brawn′i·ly,** *adv.* **—brawn′i·ness,** *n.*
—Syn. burly, robust, strapping. **—Ant.** weak, slight, frail.

brax·y (brak′sē), *Vet. Pathol.* **—***n.* **1.** Also called **bradsot.** an acute inflammatory disease of the intestines of sheep, caused by a bacterium, *Clostridium septicum.* **—***adj.* **2.** affected with braxy. [1775–85; back formation from *braxes* (*brax* for *bracks* (pl. of *brack,* OE *brǣc* rheum; akin to BREAK) + *-es* pl. ending)]

bray[1] (brā), *n.* **1.** the loud, harsh cry of a donkey. **2.** any similar loud, harsh sound. **—***v.i.* **3.** to utter a loud and harsh cry, as a donkey. **4.** to make a loud, harsh, disagreeable sound. **—***v.t.* **5.** to utter with a loud, harsh sound, like a donkey. [1250–1300; ME *brayen* < OF *braire* to cry out (c. ML *bragīre* to neigh) < Celtic; cf. OIr *braigid* (he) breaks wind]

bray[2] (brā), *v.t.* **1.** to pound or crush fine, as in a mortar. **2.** *Print.* to thin (ink) on a slate before placing on the ink plate of a press. [1350–1400; ME *brayen* < AF *bra(i)er,* OF *broier* < Gmc; see BREAK]

bray·er (brā′ər), *n. Print.* a small roller for inking type by hand, usually for making a proof. [1680–90; BRAY[2] + -ER[1]]

Braz., 1. Brazil. **2.** Brazilian.

bra·za (brä′thä, -sä), *n., pl.* **-zas** (-thäs, -säs). a unit of length in some Spanish-speaking countries, representing the reach of outspread arms, officially 5.48 U.S. ft. (1.67 m) in Spain and 5.68 U.S. ft. (1.73 m) in Argentina. [< Sp < L *brāchia* arms (neut. pl.), taken as fem. sing.; see BRACE]

braze[1] (brāz), *v.t.,* **brazed, braz·ing. 1.** to make of brass. **2.** to cover or ornament with or as if with brass. **3.** to make brasslike. [bef. 1000; ME *brasen,* OE *bræsian;* see BRASS]

braze[2] (brāz), *v.t.,* **brazed, braz·ing.** *Metall.* to unite (metal objects) at high temperatures by applying any of various nonferrous solders. [1575–85; < F *braser* to solder (MF), burn (OF) < Gmc; cf. Sw *brasa,* Dan *brase* to roast; see BRAISE] **—braz′er,** *n.*

Braz·el·ton (braz′əl tən), *n.* Brazelton behavioral scale: a test widely used to evaluate infants' responses to environmental stimuli. Also called **Neonatal Behavioral Assessment Scale.** [after T. Berry *Brazelton* (born 1918), U.S. physician, who devised it]

bra·zen (brā′zən), *adj.* **1.** shameless or impudent: *brazen presumption.* **2.** made of brass. **3.** like brass, as in sound, color, or strength. **—***v.t.* **4.** to make brazen or bold. **5. brazen out** or **through,** to face boldly or shamelessly: *He prefers to brazen it out rather than admit defeat.* [bef. 1000; ME *brasen* (adj.), OE *bræsen* of BRASS] **—bra′zen·ly,** *adv.* **—bra′zen·ness,** *n.*
—Syn. 1, 3. brassy. **1.** insolent, defiant. See **bold.**

bra·zen-faced (brā′zən fāst′), *adj.* openly shameless; impudent. [1565–75] **—bra·zen-fac·ed·ly** (brā′zən fā′sid lē, -fāst′-), *adv.*

bra′zen law′ of wag′es, *Econ.* See **iron law of wages.**

bra·zier[1] (brā′zhər), *n.* **1.** a metal receptacle for holding live coals or other fuel, as for heating a room. **2.** a simple cooking device consisting of a container of live coals covered by a grill or thin metal top upon which the food, usually meat, is placed. Also, **brasier.** [1680–90; earlier *brasier* < F. See BRAISE, -ER[2]]

bra·zier[2] (brā′zhər), *n.* a person who makes articles of brass. Also, **brasier.** [1275–1325; ME *brasier,* equiv. to OE *bræsi(an)* to work in brass + *-er* -ER[1]]

bra·zil (brə zil′), *n.* brazilwood. [1350–1400; ME *brasile* < ML < It < Sp *brasil,* deriv. of *brasa* live coal (the wood being red in color) < Gmc; see BRAISE]

Bra·zil (brə zil′), *n.* a republic in South America. 121,075,669; 3,286,170 sq. mi. (8,511,180 sq. km). *Cap.:* Brasília. Portuguese and Spanish, **Brasil.** Official name, **Federative Republic of Brazil.** See map at top of page. **—Bra·zil·ian** (brə zil′yən), *adj., n.*

Brazil′ Cur′rent, a warm current in the Atlantic Ocean flowing SE along the E coast of Brazil.

bra•zil•e•in (brə zil′ē in), *n. Chem.* a red, crystalline, water-insoluble solid, $C_{16}H_{12}O_5$, obtained by the oxidation of brazilin: used chiefly as a dye for wood and textiles. Also, **brasilein.** [BRAZIL(IN) + *-ein,* var. of -IN[2]]

Brazil′ian em′erald, 1. a green variety of tourmaline used as a gem: not a true emerald. **2.** a pale yellowish-green beryl too light to be classified as a true emerald.

Brazil′ian fire′cracker, a tropical American twining plant, *Manettia inflata,* of the madder family, having opposite, lance-shaped leaves and a red, tubular flower with yellow tips, grown in the southern U.S. as a trellis plant.

Brazil′ian gua′va, a Brazilian shrub, *Psidium guineense,* of the myrtle family, having white-fleshed, greenish-yellow, bitter fruit.

bra•zil•ian•ite (brə zil′yə nīt′), *n.* a mineral, sodium aluminum phosphate, $Na_2Al_6P_4O_{16}(OH)_8$, occurring in yellow-green crystals with a vitreous luster: used as a gem. [1810–20; BRAZILIAN (after the place of origin) + -ITE[1]]

Brazil′ian morn′ing glory, a tropical vine, *Ipomoea setosa,* having purplish, stiff hairs on the stem and rose-purple flowers. [after its place of origin]

Brazil′ian pep′per tree′, a small Brazilian evergreen tree or shrub, *Schinus terebinthifolius,* of the cashew family, having inconspicuous white flowers and bright red fruit: the berries are used for Christmas decorations. Also called **Christmasberry tree.**

Brazil′ian per′idot, a light yellowish-green tourmaline used as a gem: not a true peridot.

Brazil′ian plume′, a tropical American plant, *Justicia carnea,* of the acanthus family, having hairy, prominently veined leaves and a short, dense cluster of purple or pink flowers, grown in greenhouses or outdoors in warm regions.

Brazil′ian rhat′any. See under **rhatany** (def. 1).

Brazil′ian rose′wood, 1. a Brazilian tree, *Dalbergia nigra,* of the legume family. **2.** the hard, red, black-streaked wood of this tree, used for making furniture. Also called **palisander.**

Brazil′ian ru′by, 1. a light-rose spinel used as a gem: not a true ruby. **2.** a rose or pink topaz used as a gem: not a true ruby.

Brazil′ian sap′phire, a blue variety of tourmaline used as a gem: not a true sapphire.

braz•i•lin (braz′ə lin, brə zil′in), *n. Chem.* a yellow, water-soluble, needlelike, crystalline solid, $C_{16}H_{14}O_5$, obtained from brazil and sappanwood: used as a dye and an indicator. Also, **brasilin.** [1860–65; BRAZIL + -IN[2]]

Brazil′ nut′, the three-sided, hard-shelled edible seed of the tree *Bertholletia excelsa* and related species, of South America. [1820–30]

bra•zil•wood (brə zil′wo͝od′), *n.* **1.** any of several tropical trees of the genus *Caesalpinia,* as *C. echinata,* having wood from which a red dye is obtained. **2.** the wood of such a tree. [1550–60; BRAZIL + WOOD[1]]

braz′ing al′loy. See **hard solder.**

braz′ing met′al, a nonferrous metal, as copper, zinc, or nickel, or an alloy, as hard solder, used for brazing together pieces of metal.

Bra•zos (brä′zōs; *locally* braz′əs, brä′zəs), *n.* a river flowing SE from N Texas to the Gulf of Mexico. 870 mi. (1400 km) long.

Braz•za (*Fr.* BRA ZA′), *n.* **Pierre Paul Fran•çois Ca•mille Sa•vor•gnan de** (pyer pôl fräN swa′ ka mē′y[ə] sa vôr nyäN′ də), 1852–1905, French explorer in Africa, born in Italy.

Braz•za•ville (braz′ə vil′, brä′zə-; *Fr.* BRA ZA vēl′), *n.* a port in and the capital of the People's Republic of the Congo, in the S part, on the Congo (Zaire) River: former capital of French Equatorial Africa. 290,000.

B.R.C.A., Brotherhood of Railway Carmen of America.

B.R.C.S., British Red Cross Society.

B.R.E., Bachelor of Religious Education.

Bre•a (brā′ə), *n.* a town in S California. 27,913.

breach (brēch), *n.* **1.** the act or a result of breaking; break or rupture. **2.** an infraction or violation, as of a law, trust, faith, or promise. **3.** a gap made in a wall, fortification, line of soldiers, etc.; rift; fissure. **4.** a severance of friendly relations. **5.** the leap of a whale above the surface of the water. **6.** *Archaic.* the breaking of waves; the dashing of surf. **7.** *Obs.* wound[1]. —*v.t.* **8.** to make a breach or opening in. **9.** to break or act contrary to (a law, promise, etc.). —*v.i.* **10.** (of a whale) to leap partly or completely out of the water, head first, and land on the back or belly with a resounding splash. [bef. 1000; ME *breche,* OE *bræc* breaking; see BREAK] —**breach′er,** *n.*

—**Syn. 1.** fracture. **2.** BREACH, INFRACTION, VIOLATION, TRANSGRESSION all denote in some way the breaking of a rule or law or the upsetting of a normal and desired state. BREACH is used infrequently in reference to laws or rules, more often in connection with desirable conditions or states of affairs: *a breach of the peace, of good manners, of courtesy.* INFRACTION most often refers to clearly formulated rules or laws: *an infraction of the criminal code, of university regulations, of a labor contract.* VIOLATION, a stronger term than either of the preceding two, often suggests intentional, even forceful or aggressive, refusal to obey the law or to respect the rights of others: *repeated violations of parking regulations; a human rights violation.* TRANSGRESSION, with its root sense of "a stepping across (of a boundary of some sort)," applies to any behavior that exceeds the limits imposed by a law, especially a moral law, a commandment, or an order; it often implies sinful behavior: *a serious transgression of social customs, of God's commandments.* **3.** crack, rent, opening. **4.** alienation, split, rift, schism, separation; dissension.

breach′ of con′tract, unexcused failure to fulfill one's duties under a contract. [1825–35]

breach′ of faith′, a violation of good faith, confidence, or trust; betrayal: *To abandon your friends now would be a breach of faith.* [1630–40]

breach′ of prom′ise, *Law.* a violation of one's promise, esp. of a promise to marry a specific person. [1580–90]

breach′ of the peace′, *Law.* a violation of the public peace, as by a riot, disturbance, etc. [1665–75]

breach′ of trust′, 1. *Law.* a violation of duty by a trustee. **2.** a violation of duty or responsibility. [1875–80]

bread (bred), *n.* **1.** a kind of food made of flour or meal that has been mixed with milk or water, made into a dough or batter, with or without yeast or other leavening agent, and baked. **2.** food or sustenance; livelihood: *to earn one's bread.* **3.** *Slang.* money. **4.** *Eccles.* the wafer or bread used in a Eucharistic service. **5. break bread, a.** to eat a meal, esp. in companionable association with others. **b.** to distribute or participate in Communion. **6. cast one's bread upon the waters,** to act generously or charitably with no thought of personal gain. **7. know which side one's bread is buttered on,** to be aware of those things that are to one's own advantage. **8. take the bread out of someone's mouth,** to deprive someone of livelihood. —*v.t.* **9.** *Cookery.* to cover with breadcrumbs or meal. [bef. 950; 1950–55 for def. 3; ME *breed,* OE *brēad* fragment, morsel, bread; c. G *Brot*] —**bread′less,** *adj.* —**bread′less•ness,** *n.*

bread′ and but′ter, 1. bread spread with butter. **2.** a basic means of support; source of livelihood; sustenance: *The automobile industry is the bread and butter of many Detroiters.* [1620–30]

bread-and-but•ter (bred′n but′ər), *adj.* **1.** providing a livelihood or basic source of income; supplying the basic needs of life: *a bread-and-butter job; the agency's bread-and-butter account.* **2.** of or pertaining to basic needs: *housing and other bread-and-butter political issues.* **3.** basic or everyday; staple; routine. **4.** expressing thanks for hospitality: *a bread-and-butter letter.* [1720–30; adj. use of n. phrase *bread and butter*]

bread′-and-but′ter mod′el, *Naval Archit.* a wooden hull model carved from a number of horizontal planks glued together to represent the outlines of the various decks.

bread′-and-but′ter pick′le, an unpeeled slice of cucumber marinated in salt water and boiled with vinegar, celery seed, spices, and brown sugar.

bread′ and cir′cuses, something, as extravagant entertainment, offered as an expedient means of pacifying discontent or diverting attention from a source of grievance. [1910–15; trans. of L *pānis et circēnsēs;* from a remark by the Roman satirist Juvenal on the limited desires of the Roman populace]

bread•bas•ket (bred′bas′kit, -bä′skit), *n.* **1.** a basket or similar container for bread or rolls. **2.** an agricultural area that provides large amounts of food, esp. grain, to other areas. **3.** *Slang.* a person's stomach or abdomen. —*adj.* **4.** of, pertaining to, or characteristic of a geographical breadbasket: *Iowa is a breadbasket state.* [1545–55; BREAD + BASKET]

bread•board (bred′bôrd′, -bōrd′), *n.* **1.** a slab of wood on which dough is kneaded and bread is sliced. **2.** *Electronics.* a circuit assembled on an insulating surface, often with solderless contacts, in which components can easily be replaced for circuit alteration and experimentation. —*v.t.* **3.** *Electronics.* to construct (an experimental circuit) for the purpose of feasibility tests. [1855–60; BREAD + BOARD]

bread•box (bred′boks′), *n.* an airtight, or nearly airtight, boxlike container, as of metal or plastic, for storing bread and other baked goods to keep them fresh. [BREAD + BOX]

bread•crumb (bred′krum′), *n.* a crumb of bread, either dried or soft. [1760–70; BREAD + CRUMB]

bread′ flour′, wheat flour from which a large part of the starch has been removed, thus increasing the proportion of gluten. Also called **gluten flour.**

bread•fruit (bred′fro͞ot′), *n.* **1.** a large, round, starchy fruit borne by a tree, *Artocarpus altilis,* of the mulberry family, native to the Pacific islands, used, baked or roasted, for food. **2.** the tree bearing this fruit. [1690–1700; BREAD + FRUIT]

breadfruit, *Artocarpus altilis,* fruit, diam. 5 in. (13 cm)

bread′ knife′, a knife designed or suitable for slicing bread, as one having a wavy or saw-toothed blade. [1860–65]

bread′ line′, a group of needy persons waiting in line for free food to be distributed by a government agency or charitable organization. [1825–35]

bread′ mold′, any fungus of the family Mucoraceae, esp. *Rhizopus nigricans,* that forms a black, furry coating on foodstuffs. Also called **black mold.** [1920–25]

bread•nut (bred′nut′), *n.* the round, yellow or brown fruit of the ramon, *Brosimum alicastrum,* of the mulberry family, used, roasted or boiled, as a substitute for bread in the West Indies. [1750–60; BREAD + NUT]

bread•root (bred′ro͞ot′, -ro͝ot′), *n.* the edible starchy root of *Psoralea esculenta,* a leguminous plant of central North America. Also called **Indian breadroot, pomme blanche, prairie turnip.** [1820–30, *Amer.*; BREAD + ROOT[1]]

bread•stick (bred′stik′), *n. Cookery.* a slender, sticklike piece of crisp bread, served with soups, salads, etc. [1905–10; BREAD + STICK[1]]

bread•stuff (bred′stuf′), *n.* **1.** grain, flour, or meal for making bread. **2.** any kind of bread. [1785–95, *Amer.*; BREAD + STUFF]

breadth (bredth, bretth, breth), *n.* **1.** the measure of the second largest dimension of a plane or solid figure; width. **2.** an extent or piece of something of definite or full width or as measured by its width: *a breadth of cloth.* **3.** freedom from narrowness or restraint; liberality: *a person with great breadth of view.* **4.** size in general; extent. **5.** *Art.* a broad or general effect due to subordination of details or nonessentials. [1515–25; earlier *bredeth,* equiv. to *brede* breadth (ME; OE *brǣdu,* equiv. to *brǣd-,* mutated var. of *brād* BROAD + *-u* n. suffix) + -TH[1]; akin to G *Breite,* Goth *braidei*] —**breadth′less,** *adj.*

—**Syn. 3.** latitude, impartiality, open-mindedness. **4.** scope, range, reach, compass, span.

breadth•ways (bredth′wāz′, bretth′-, breth′-), *adv.* in the direction of the breadth. Also, **breadth•wise** (bredth′wīz′, bretth′-, breth′-). [1670–80; BREADTH + -WAYS]

bread•win•ner (bred′win′ər), *n.* a person who earns a livelihood, esp. one who also supports dependents. [1810–20; BREAD + WINNER] —**bread′win′ning,** *n., adj.*

break (brāk), *v.,* **broke** or (*Archaic*) **brake; bro•ken** or (*Archaic*) **broke; break•ing;** *n.* —*v.t.* **1.** to smash, split, or divide into parts violently; reduce to pieces or fragments: *He broke a vase.* **2.** to infringe, ignore, or act contrary to (a law, rule, promise, etc.): *She broke her promise.* **3.** to dissolve or annul (often fol. by *off*): *to break off friendly relations with another country.* **4.** to fracture a bone of (some part of the body): *He broke his leg.* **5.** to lacerate; wound: *to break the skin.* **6.** to destroy or interrupt the regularity, uniformity, continuity, or arrangement of; interrupt: *The bleating of a foghorn broke the silence. The troops broke formation.* **7.** to put an end to; overcome; stop: *His touchdown run broke the tie. She found it hard to break the cigarette habit.* **8.** to discover the system, key, method, etc., for decoding or deciphering (a cryptogram), esp. by the methods of cryptanalysis. **9.** to remove a part from (a set or collection): *She had to break the set to sell me the two red ones I wanted.* **10.** to exchange for or divide into smaller units or components: *She broke a dollar bill into change. The prism broke the light into all the colors of the rainbow.* **11.** to make a way through; penetrate: *The stone broke the surface of the water.* **12.** *Law.* **a.** to open or force one's way into (a dwelling, store, etc.). **b.** to contest (a will) successfully by judicial action. **13.** to make one's way out of, esp. by force: *to break jail.* **14.** to better (a given score or record): *He never broke 200 in bowling or 80 in golf.* **15.** to disclose or divulge personally in speech or writing: *He broke the good news to her at dinner.* **16.** to solve: *The police needed only a week to break that case.* **17.** to rupture (a blood vessel): *She almost broke a blood vessel from laughing so hard.* **18.** to disable or destroy by or as if by shattering or crushing: *to break a watch.* **19.** to cause (a blister, boil, or the like) to burst, as by puncturing: *She broke the blister with a needle.* **20.** to ruin financially; make bankrupt: *They threatened to break him if he didn't stop discounting their products.* **21.** to overcome or wear down the spirit, strength, or resistance of; to cause to yield, esp. under pressure, torture, or the like: *They broke him by the threat of blackmail.* **22.** to dismiss or reduce in rank. **23.** to impair or weaken the power, effect, or intensity of: *His arm broke the blow.* **24.** to train to obedience; tame: *to break a horse.* **25.** to train away from a habit or practice (usually fol. by *of*). **26.** *Elect.* to render (a circuit) incomplete; stop the flow of (a current). **27.** *Journalism.* **a.** to release (a story) for publication or airing on radio or television: *They will break the story tomorrow.* **b.** to continue (a story or article) on another page, esp. when the page is not the following one. **28.** *Pool.* to cause (racked billiard balls) to scatter by striking with the cue ball. **29.** *Sports.* **a.** (of a pitcher, bowler, etc.) to hurl (a ball) in such a way as to cause it to change direction after leaving the hand: *He broke a curve over the plate for a strike.* **b.** (in tennis and other racket games) to score frequently or win against (an opponent's serve). **30.** *Naut.* to unfurl (a flag) suddenly by an easily released knot. **31.** to prove the falsity or show the lack of logic of: *The FBI broke his alibi by proving he knew how to shoot a pistol.* **32.** to begin or initiate (a plan or campaign), esp. with much publicity: *They were going to break the sales campaign with a parade in April.* **33.** to open the breech or action of (a shotgun, rifle, or revolver), as by snapping open the hinge between the barrel and the butt.

—*v.i.* **34.** to shatter, burst, or become broken; separate into parts or fragments, esp. suddenly and violently: *The glass broke on the floor.* **35.** to become suddenly discontinuous or interrupted; stop abruptly: *She pulled too hard and the string broke.* **36.** to become detached, separated, or disassociated (usually fol. by *away, off,* or *from*): *The knob broke off in his hand.* **37.** to become inoperative or to malfunction, as through wear or damage: *The television set broke this afternoon.* **38.** to begin suddenly or violently or change abruptly into something else: *War broke over Europe.* **39.** to begin uttering a sound or series of sounds or to be uttered suddenly: *She*

CONCISE ETYMOLOGY KEY: <, descended or borrowed from; >, whence; b., blend of, blended; c., cognate with; cf., compare; deriv., derivative; equiv., equivalent; imit., imitative; obl., oblique; r., replacing; s., stem; sp., spelling, spelled; resp., respelling, respelled; trans., translation; ?, origin unknown; *, unattested; ‡, probably earlier than. See the full key inside the front cover.

broke into song. When they entered, a cheer broke from the audience. **40.** to express or start to express an emotion or mood: *His face broke into a smile.* **41.** to free oneself or escape suddenly, as from restraint or dependency (often fol. by *away*): *He broke away from the arresting officer. She finally broke away from her parents and got an apartment of her own.* **42.** to run or dash toward something suddenly (usually fol. by *for*): *The pass receiver broke for the goal line.* **43.** to force a way (usually fol. by *in, into,* or *through*): *The hunters broke through the underbrush.* **44.** to burst or rupture: *A blood vessel broke in his nose. The blister broke when he pricked it.* **45.** to interrupt or halt an activity (usually fol. by *in, into, forth,* or *from*): *Don't break in on the conversation. Let's break for lunch.* **46.** to appear or arrive suddenly (usually fol. by *in, into,* or *out*): *A deer broke into the clearing. A rash broke out on her arm.* **47.** to dawn: *The day broke hot and sultry.* **48.** to begin violently and suddenly: *The storm broke.* **49.** (of a storm, foul weather, etc.) to cease: *The weather broke after a week, and we were able to sail for home.* **50.** to part the surface of water, as a jumping fish or surfacing submarine. **51.** to give way or fail, as health, strength, or spirit; collapse: *After years of hardship and worry, his health broke.* **52.** to yield or submit to pressure, torture, or the like: *He broke under questioning.* **53.** (of the heart) to be overwhelmed with sorrow: *Her heart broke when he told her that he no longer loved her.* **54.** (of the voice or a musical instrument) to change harshly from one register or pitch to another: *After his voice broke, he could no longer sing soprano parts.* **55.** (of the voice) to cease, waver, or change tone abruptly, esp. from emotional strain: *His voice broke when he mentioned her name.* **56.** (of value or prices) to drop sharply and considerably. **57.** to disperse or collapse by colliding with something: *The waves broke on the shore.* **58.** to break dance. **59.** (of a horse in a harness race) to fail to keep to a trot or pace, as by starting to gallop. **60.** *Bot.* to mutate; sport. **61.** *Ling.* to undergo breaking. **62.** *Billiards, Pool.* to make a break; take the first turn in a game. **63.** *Sports.* (of a pitched or bowled ball) to change direction: *The ball broke over the plate.* **64.** *Horse Racing, Track.* to leave the starting point: *The horses broke fast from the gate.* **65.** *Boxing.* to step back or separate from a clinch: *The fighters fell into a clinch and broke on the referee's order.* **66.** to take place; occur. **67.** *Journalism.* to become known, published, or aired: *The story broke in the morning papers.* **68.** *Hort.* to produce flowers or leaves. **69. break away, a.** to leave or escape, esp. suddenly or hurriedly. **b.** to sever connections or allegiance, as to tradition or a political group. **c.** to start prematurely: *The horse broke away from the starting gate.* **70. break back,** *Tennis.* to win a game served by an opponent immediately after the opponent has done so against one's own serve. **71. break bulk,** *Naut.* to remove a cargo wholly or in part. **72. break camp,** to pack up tents and equipment and resume a journey or march: *They broke camp at dawn and proceeded toward the mountains.* **73. break down, a.** to become ineffective. **b.** to lose control; weaken: *He broke down and wept at the sad news.* **c.** to have a physical or mental collapse. **d.** to cease to function: *The car broke down.* **e.** to itemize: *to break down a hotel bill into daily charges.* **f.** *Chem.* to separate (a compound) into its constituent molecules. **g.** *Elect.* (of an insulator) to fail, as when subjected to excessively high voltage, permitting a current to pass. **h.** to decompose. **i.** to analyze. **j.** to classify. **k.** to separate into constituent parts: *to break down a beef carcass into basic cuts.* **74. break even,** to finish a business transaction, period of gambling, series of games, etc., with no loss or gain: *He played poker all night and broke even.* **75. break ground, a.** to begin construction, esp. of a building or group of buildings: *to break ground for a new housing development.* **b.** *Naut.* to free an anchor from the bottom; break out. **76. break in, a.** to enter by force or craft: *Someone broke in and made off with all the furniture.* **b.** to train or instruct; initiate: *The boss is breaking in a new assistant.* **c.** to begin to wear or use in order to make comfortable: *These shoes haven't been broken in.* **d.** to interrupt: *He broke in with a ridiculous objection.* **e.** to run (new machinery) initially under reduced load and speed, until any stiffness of motion has departed and all parts are ready to operate under normal service conditions; run in; wear in. **77. break in on** or **upon,** to enter with force upon or accidentally interrupt; intrude upon: *The visitor opened the wrong door and broke in on a private conference.* **78. break into, a.** to interpose; interrupt: *He broke into the conversation at a crucial moment.* **b.** to begin some activity. **c.** to be admitted into; enter, as a business or profession: *It is difficult to break into the theater.* **d.** to enter by force: *They broke into the store and stole the safe.* **79. break it down,** *Australian Slang.* **a.** stop it; calm down. **b.** (used as an exclamation of disbelief) that can't be true! **80. break off, a.** to sever by breaking. **b.** to stop suddenly; discontinue: *to break off a conversation; to break off relations with one's neighbors.* **81. break one's heart.** See **heart** (def. 19). **82. break out, a.** to begin abruptly; arise: *An epidemic broke out.* **b.** *Pathol.* (of certain diseases) to appear in eruptions. **c.** (of a person) to manifest a skin eruption. **d.** to prepare for use: *to break out the parachutes.* **e.** to take out of (storage, concealment, etc.) for consumption: *to break out one's best wine.* **f.** *Naut.* to dislodge (the anchor) from the bottom. **g.** to escape; flee: *He spent three years in prison before he broke out.* **h.** to separate into categories or list specific items: *to break out gift ideas according to price range; The report breaks out quarterly profits and losses.* **83. break service,** *Tennis.* to win a game served by one's opponent. **84. break sheer,** *Naut.* (of an anchored vessel) to drift into such a position as to risk fouling the anchor or anchor cable. Cf. **sheer**[2] (def. 6). **85. break step.** See **step** (def. 20). **86. break up, a.** to separate; scatter. **b.** to put an end to; discontinue. **c.** to divide or become divided into pieces. **d.** to dissolve. **e.** to disrupt; upset: *Television commercials during a dramatic presentation break up the continuity of effect.* **f.** (of a personal relationship) to end: *to break up a friendship; Their marriage broke up last year.* **g.** to end a personal relationship: *Bob and Mary broke up last month.* **h.** to be or cause to be overcome with laughter: *The comedian told several jokes that broke up the audience.* **87. break wind.** See **wind**[1] (def. 21). **88. break with, a.** to sever relations with; separate from: *to break with one's family.* **b.** to depart from; repudiate: *to break with tradition.*

—*n.* **89.** an act or instance of breaking; disruption or separation of parts; fracture; rupture: *There was a break in the window.* **90.** an opening made by breaking; gap: *The break in the wall had not been repaired.* **91.** a rush away from a place; an attempt to escape: *a break for freedom.* **92.** a sudden dash or rush, as toward something: *When the rain lessened, I made a break for home.* **93.** a suspension of or sudden rupture in friendly relations. **94.** an interruption of continuity; departure from or rupture with: *Abstract painters made a break with the traditions of the past.* **95.** an abrupt or marked change, as in sound or direction, or a brief pause: *They noticed a curious break in his voice.* **96.** *Informal.* **a.** an opportunity or stroke of fortune, esp. a lucky one. **b.** a chance to improve one's lot, esp. one unlooked for or undeserved. **97. the breaks,** *Informal.* the way things happen; fate: *Sorry to hear about your bad luck, but I guess those are the breaks.* **98.** a brief rest, as from work: *The actors took a ten-minute break from rehearsal.* **99.** *Radio, Television.* a brief, scheduled interruption of a program or broadcasting period for the announcement of advertising or station identification. **100.** *Pros.* a pause or caesura. **101.** *Jazz.* a solo passage, usually of from 2 to 12 bars, during which the rest of the instruments are silent. **102.** *Music.* the point in the scale where the quality of voice of one register changes to that of another, as from chest to head. **103.** See **break dancing. 104.** a sharp and considerable drop in the prices of stock issues. **105.** *Elect.* an opening or discontinuity in a circuit. **106.** *Print.* **a.** one or more blank lines between two paragraphs. **b. breaks.** See **suspension points. 107.** the place, after a letter, where a word is or may be divided at the end of a line. **108.** a collapse of health, strength, or spirit; breakdown. **109.** *Informal.* an indiscreet or awkward remark or action; social blunder; faux pas. **110.** *Billiards, Pool.* a series of successful strokes; run. **111.** *Pool.* the opening play, in which the cue ball is shot to scatter the balls. **112.** *Sports.* a change in direction of a pitched or bowled ball. **113.** *Horse Racing, Track.* the start of a race. **114.** (in harness racing) an act or instance of a horse's changing from a trot or pace into a gallop or other step. **115.** *Bowling.* a failure to knock down all ten pins in a single frame. **116.** *Boxing.* an act or instance of stepping back or separating from a clinch: *a clean break.* **117.** any of several stages in the grinding of grain in which the bran is separated from the kernel. **118.** *Bot.* a sport. **119.** *Journalism.* the point at the bottom of a column where a printed story is carried over to another column or page. **120.** *Naut.* the place at which a superstructure, deckhouse, or the like, rises from the main deck of a vessel. **121. breaks,** *Phys. Geog.* an area dissected by small ravines and gullies. **122.** *Mining.* a fault or offset, as in a vein or bed of ore. [bef. 900; ME *breken,* OE *brecan;* c. D *breken,* G *brechen,* Goth *brikan;* akin to L *frangere;* see FRAGILE] —**break′a•ble,** *adj.* —**break′a•ble•ness,** *n.* —**break′•a•bly,** *adv.* —**break′less,** *adj.*

—**Syn. 1.** fracture, splinter, shiver. BREAK, CRUSH, SHATTER, SMASH mean to reduce to parts, violently or by force. BREAK means to divide by means of a blow, a collision, a pull, or the like: *to break a chair, a leg, a strap.* To CRUSH is to subject to (usually heavy or violent) pressure so as to press out of shape or reduce to shapelessness or to small particles: *to crush a beetle.* To SHATTER is to break in such a way as to cause the pieces to fly in many directions: *to shatter a light globe.* To SMASH is to break noisily and suddenly into many pieces: *to smash a glass.* **2.** disobey, contravene. **6.** disrupt. **14.** surpass, beat. **22.** demote. **34.** fragment, smash. **89.** rent, tear, rip, rift, split; breach, fissure, crack. **94.** stop, hiatus, lacuna, pause, caesura. —**Ant. 1.** repair.

break•age (brā′kij), *n.* **1.** the act of breaking; state of being broken. **2.** the amount or quantity of things broken: *There was a great deal of breakage in that shipment of glassware.* **3.** an allowance or compensation for the loss or damage of articles broken in transit or in use. **4.** the money accrued by a racetrack from calculating the payoff to winning pari-mutuel bettors only in multiples of dimes for each dollar bet. [1805–15; BREAK + -AGE]

break′ and en′try. See **breaking and entering.**

break•a•way (brāk′ə wā′), *n.* **1.** an act or instance of breaking away; secession; separation: *the breakaway of two provinces from a state.* **2.** a departure or break from routine or tradition: *a three-day breakaway in the Bahamas.* **3.** a person or thing that breaks away. **4.** an object, as a theatrical prop, constructed so that it breaks or falls apart easily, esp. upon impact. **5.** *Ice Hockey.* a sudden rush down the ice by a player or players in an attempt to score a goal, after breaking clear of defending opponents. **6.** *Football.* a run by an offensive player breaking through the defense for a long gain. **7.** *Basketball.* See **fast break. 8.** *Chiefly Australian.* **a.** a stampede. **b.** an animal that breaks away from the herd or flock. —*adj.* **9.** of, pertaining to, or being that which separates or secedes: *the breakaway faction of the Socialist party.* **10.** departing from routine or tradition. **11.** constructed of such lightweight material or in such a way as to shatter or come apart easily: *breakaway highway signposts; Build a breakaway set for the barroom brawl.* **12.** (of theatrical costumes) constructed so as to be quickly removable, as by a performer playing several roles. [1885–95; n., adj. use of v. phrase *break away*]

break′bone fe′ver (brāk′bōn′), *Pathol.* dengue. [1860–65; BREAK + BONE, so called because it makes the bones ache as if breaking at the joints]

break-bulk (brāk′bulk′), *adj. Transp.* **1.** of or pertaining to packaged cargo, usually manufactured goods, that is marked for individual consignees and has to be loaded and unloaded piece by piece at each point of transfer. Cf. **bulk**[1] (def. 3), **containerization. 2.** of or pertaining to the small, conventional cargo ships designed to hold such cargo. Cf. **containership.** [1615–25]

break′ dance′, to perform break dancing. Also, **break.**

break′ danc′ing, a style of acrobatic dancing originating in the mid-1970's, often performed to rap music usually by teenage males in the streets, and characterized by intricate footwork, pantomime, spinning headstands, tumbling, and elaborate improvised virtuosic movements. Also, **break′danc′ing.** Also called **break, breaking.** [sense of BREAK unclear; cf. BREAKDOWN (def. 6)] —**break′ danc′er.**

break•down (brāk′doun′), *n.* **1.** a breaking down, wearing out, or sudden loss of ability to function efficiently, as of a machine. **2.** a loss of mental or physical health; collapse. Cf. **nervous breakdown. 3.** an analysis or classification of something; division into parts, categories, processes, etc. **4.** *Chem.* **a.** decomposition. **b.** analysis (def. 7). **5.** *Elect.* an electric discharge passing through faulty insulation or other material used to separate circuits or passing between electrodes in a vacuum or gas-filled tube. **6.** a noisy, lively folk dance. [1825–35; n. use of v. phrase *break down*]

break′down volt′age, *Elect.* the minimum applied voltage that would cause a given insulator or electrode to break down. Cf. **dielectric strength.** [1910–15]

break•er[1] (brā′kər), *n.* **1.** a person or thing that breaks. **2.** a wave that breaks or dashes into foam. **3.** *CB Radio Slang.* a person who indicates a wish to transmit a message, as by breaking in on a channel. **4.** Also called **break′er strip′.** *Auto.* a strip of fabric under the tread of a pneumatic tire casing, designed to protect the carcass. **5.** *Textiles.* **a.** brake[1] (def. 4). **b.** a machine that separates the fiber from foreign matter in preparation for the carding process. **6.** Also called **prairie breaker.** a plow with a long, low moldboard for turning virgin land. **7.** *Elect.* See **circuit breaker. 8.** *Mining.* **a.** a building where coal delivered from a mine is broken up and sorted. **b.** a machine that reduces large lumps of coal or ore to a size that can be accommodated by a conveyor belt. **9.** a break dancer. —*interj.* **10.** *CB Radio Slang.* (used to announce that a person is about to transmit a message or question on a channel, esp. one already in use.) [1125–75; ME; see BREAK, -ER[1]]
—**Syn. 2.** See **wave.**

break•er[2] (brā′kər), *n. Naut.* a small water cask for use in a boat. [1825–35; said to be alter. of Sp *bareca,* var. of *barrica* small keg]

break′er card′, the first card in the carding process, used to open the raw stock and to convert it into sliver form. Cf. **finisher card, intermediate card.** [1870–75]

break′er•less igni′tion (brā′kər lis), *Auto.* See **electronic ignition.**

break′er point′, *Auto., Elect.* point (def. 43a).

break′er strip′, *Auto.* breaker[1] (def. 4).

break-e•ven (brāk′ē′vən), *adj.* **1.** having income exactly equal to expenditure, thus showing neither profit nor loss. —*n.* **2.** See **break-even point. 3.** *Energy.* the stage at which a fission or fusion reaction becomes self-sustaining. Also, **break′e′ven.** [1935–40, *Amer.*]

break′-e′ven point′, the point at which the income from sale of a product or service equals the invested costs, resulting in neither profit nor loss; the stage at which income equals expenditure. [1935–40, *Amer.*]

break•fast (brek′fəst), *n.* **1.** the first meal of the day; morning meal: *A hearty breakfast was served at 7* A.M. **2.** the food eaten at the first meal of the day: *a breakfast of bacon and eggs.* —*v.i.* **3.** to eat breakfast: *He breakfasted on bacon and eggs.* —*v.t.* **4.** to supply with breakfast: *We breakfasted the author in the finest restaurant.* [1425–75; late ME *brekfast.* See BREAK, FAST[2]] —**break′fast•er,** *n.* —**break′fast•less,** *adj.*

break′fast food′, a cold or hot cereal eaten chiefly for breakfast. [1895–1900, *Amer.*]

break•front (brāk′frunt′), *adj.* **1.** (of a cabinet, bookcase, etc.) having a central section extending forward from those at either side. —*n.* **2.** a cabinet or the like having such a front. [1925–30; BREAK + FRONT]

break-in (brāk′in′), *n.* **1.** an illegal entry into a home, car, office, etc. **2.** See **break-in period.** [1855–60; n. use of v. phrase *break in*]

break•ing[1] (brā′king), *n. Phonol.* the change of a pure vowel to a diphthong, esp. in certain environments, as, in Old English, the change of a vowel to a diphthong under the influence of a following consonant or combination of consonants, as the change of *-a-* to *-ea-* and of *-e-* to *-eo-* before preconsonantal *r* or *l* and before *h,* as in *earm* "arm" developed from *arm,* and *eorthe* "earth" from *erthe.* Also called **vowel fracture.** [1870–75; trans. of G *Brechung;* see BREAK, -ING[1]]

break•ing[2] (brā′king), *n.* See **break dancing.** [by ellipsis]

break′ing and en′tering, *Criminal Law.* forcible entry into the home or office of another. [1790–1800]

break′ing point′, 1. the point at which a person, object, structure, etc., collapses under stress. **2.** the point at which a situation or condition becomes critical. [1895–1900]

break′-in pe′riod (brāk′in′), a period during which certain restrictions or moderation in operating should be followed, as the avoidance of high speed, rapid acceleration, or severe braking for a new automobile. Also called **break-in.**

break•neck (brāk′nek′), *adj.* reckless or dangerous, esp. because of excessive speed; hazardous: *He raced through the streets at breakneck speed.* [1555–65; BREAK + NECK]

break′ of day′, dawn; daybreak.

break·out (brāk′out′), *n.* **1.** an escape, often with the use of force, as from a prison or mental institution. **2.** an appearance or manifestation, as of a disease, that is sudden and often widespread; outbreak. **3.** an itemization; breakdown: *a hotel bill with a breakout of each service offered.* **4.** an instance of surpassing any previous achievement: *a breakout in gold prices.* **5.** the act or process of removing and disassembling equipment that has been used in drilling a well. —*adj.* **6.** of or constituting a sudden increase, advance, or unexpected success: *The director has finally scored with a breakout movie.* [1810–20; n. use of v. phrase *break out*]

break·o·ver (brāk′ō′vər), *n.* jump (def. 59). [n. use of v. phrase *break over*]

break′ point′, *Tennis.* a situation in which the receiving side, holding the advantage, can win the game by winning the next point.

break·point (brāk′point′), *n.* a convenient point at which to make a change, interruption, etc. [BREAK + POINT]

break·through (brāk′thro͞o′), *n.* **1.** a military movement or advance all the way through and beyond an enemy's front-line defense. **2.** an act or instance of removing or surpassing an obstruction or restriction; the overcoming of a stalemate: *The president reported a breakthrough in the treaty negotiations.* **3.** any significant or sudden advance, development, achievement, or increase, as in scientific knowledge or diplomacy, that removes a barrier to progress: *The jet engine was a major breakthrough in air transport.* —*adj.* **4.** constituting a breakthrough: *engineered with breakthrough technology; Critics called it a breakthrough film.* [1915–20; n. use of v. phrase *break through*]

break·time (brāk′tīm′), *n.* the time at or during which a break is taken from work or other activity. [BREAK + TIME]

break·up (brāk′up′), *n.* **1.** disintegration; disruption; dispersal. **2.** the ending of a personal, esp. a romantic, relationship. **3.** (in Alaska and Canada) **a.** the melting and loosening of ice in rivers and harbors during the early spring. **b.** the first day on which such ice is soft or dispersed enough to permit ships to use the waterways. **4.** *Informal.* an act or instance of being convulsed with laughter. **5.** temporary distortion in a televised picture. [1785–95; n. use of v. phrase *break up*]

break·wa·ter (brāk′wô′tər, -wot′ər), *n.* a barrier that breaks the force of waves, as before a harbor. [1715–25; BREAK + WATER]

break·weath·er (brāk′weth′ər), *n. Australian.* any makeshift shelter. [BREAK + WEATHER]

bream[1] (brim, brēm), *n., pl.* (*esp. collectively*) **bream,** (*esp. referring to two or more kinds or species*) **breams.** **1.** any of various freshwater fishes of the genus *Abramis,* as *A. brama,* of Europe, with a compressed, deep body and silvery scales. **2.** any of various related and similar fishes. **3.** any of several porgies, as the sea bream, *Archosargus rhomboidalis.* **4.** any of several freshwater sunfishes of the genus *Lepomis.* [1350–1400; ME *breme* < AF; OF *bresme, braisme* < Old Low Franconian **brahsima;* cf. OHG *brahsema,* D *brasem*]

bream[2] (brēm), *v.t. Naut.* to clean (a ship's bottom) by applying burning furze, reeds, etc., to soften the pitch and loosen adherent matter. [1620–30; < MD *brem(e)* furze]

Bream (brēm), *n.* **Julian (Alexander),** born 1933, English guitarist and lutanist.

breast (brest), *n.* **1.** *Anat., Zool.* (in bipeds) the outer, front part of the thorax, or the front part of the body from the neck to the abdomen; chest. **2.** *Zool.* the corresponding part in quadrupeds. **3.** either of the pair of mammae occurring on the chest in humans and having a discrete areola around the nipple, esp. the mammae of the female after puberty, which are enlarged and softened by hormonally influenced mammary-gland development and fat deposition and which secrete milk after the birth of a child: the breasts of males normally remain rudimentary. **4.** the part of a garment that covers the chest. **5.** the bosom conceived of as the center of emotion: *What anger lay in his breast when he made that speech?* **6.** a projection from a wall, as part of a chimney. **7.** any surface or part resembling or likened to the human breast. **8.** *Mining.* the face or heading at which the work is going on. **9.** *Metall.* **a.** the front of an openhearth furnace. **b.** the clay surrounding the taphole of a cupola. **10.** *Naut.* **a.** See **breast line. b.** a rounded bow. **11. beat one's breast,** to display one's grief, remorse, etc., in a loud and demonstrative manner. **12. make a clean breast of,** to confess everything (of which one is guilty): *You'll feel better if you make a clean breast of it.* —*v.t.* **13.** to meet or oppose boldly; confront: *As a controversial public figure he has breasted much hostile criticism.* **14.** to contend with or advance against: *The ship breasted the turbulent seas.* **15.** to climb or climb over (a mountain, obstacle, etc.). **16.** to overcome, succeed against. **17.** to come alongside or abreast of. **18. breast in,** *Naut.* to bind (an object, as a boatswain's chair) securely under a projection, as the flare of a bow. **19. breast off,** *Naut.* **a.** to thrust (a vessel) sideways from a wharf. **b.** to keep (a vessel) away from a wharf by means of timbers. [bef. 1000; ME *brest,* OE *brēost;* c. ON *brjóst;* akin to G *Brust,* Goth *brusts,* D *borst*] —**breast′·less,** *adj.*

breast′ beam′, **1.** a horizontal bar, located at the front of a loom, over which the woven material is passed on its way to the cloth roll. **2.** *Archit.* breastsummer. [1780–90]

breast-beat·ing (brest′bē′ting), *n.* **1.** a loud and demonstrative display of grief, remorse, or the like: *The authorities indulged in a great deal of breast-beating about traffic accidents but failed to pass new driving laws.* —*adj.* **2.** characterized by or involving breast-beating. [1950–55] —**breast′-beat′er,** *n.*

breast·bone (brest′bōn′), *n.* the sternum. [bef. 1000; ME *brust-bon,* OE *brēostbān.* See BREAST, BONE[1]]

breast′ drill′, a geared drill that can be braced against the chest for additional leverage. [1860–65]

breast·ed (bres′tid), *adj.* **1.** having a breast. **2.** having a specified kind of breast (usually used in combination): *narrow-breasted.* [1275–1300; ME; see BREAST, -ED[3]]

Breas·ted (bres′tid), *n.* **James Henry,** 1865–1935, U.S. archaeologist and historian of ancient Egypt.

breast-feed (brest′fēd′), *v.t.,* **-fed, -feed·ing.** to nurse (a baby) at the breast; suckle. [1900–05]

breast·ing (bres′ting), *n.* a piece of leather or other material for covering the heel breast of a shoe. [BREAST + -ING[1]]

breast′ line′, *Naut.* a mooring line securing a ship to that part of a pier alongside it. Also called **breast, breast′ fast′.**

breast·pin (brest′pin′), *n.* a pin worn on the breast or at the throat; brooch. [1825–35; BREAST + PIN]

breast·plate (brest′plāt′), *n.* **1.** a piece of plate armor partially or completely covering the front of the torso: used by itself or as part of a cuirass. See diag. under **armor. 2.** the part of the harness that runs across the chest of a saddle horse. **3.** *Judaism.* **a.** a square, richly embroidered vestment ornamented with 12 precious stones, each inscribed with the name of one of the 12 tribes of Israel, secured to the ephod of the high priest and worn on the chest. Ex. 28:15–28. **b.** a rectangular ornament, typically of silver, suspended by a chain over the front of a scroll of the Torah. **4.** a plate opposite the chuck end of a breast drill against which the operator's chest is placed. [1350–1400; ME *brestplate.* See BREAST, PLATE[1]]

breast·plow (brest′plou′), *n. Agric.* a cultivator moved forward by a person pressing the chest against a crossbar. Also, *esp. Brit.,* **breast′plough′.** [1715–25; BREAST + PLOW]

breast·stroke (brest′strōk′, bres′-), *n., v.,* **-stroked, -strok·ing.** —*n.* **1.** *Swimming.* a stroke, made in the prone position, in which both hands move simultaneously forward, outward, and rearward from in front of the chest while the legs move in a frog kick. —*v.i.* **2.** to swim using the breaststroke. [1865–70; BREAST + STROKE[1]] —**breast′strok′er,** *n.*

breast·sum·mer (bres′sum′ər, brest′-, bres′ə mər), *n. Archit.* a horizontal beam supporting an exterior wall over an opening, as a shop window. Also called **breast beam.** [1605–15; BREAST + SUMMER[2]]

breast′ tim′ber, *Building Trades.* wale[1] (def. 5).

breast′ wall′. See **retaining wall.**

breast′ wheel′, a waterwheel onto which the propelling water is fed at the height of a horizontal axle. [1750–60]

breast·work (brest′wûrk′), *n. Fort.* a defensive work, usually breast high. [1635–45; BREAST + WORK]

breath (breth), *n.* **1.** the air inhaled and exhaled in respiration. **2.** respiration, esp. as necessary to life. **3.** life; vitality. **4.** the ability to breathe easily and normally: *She stopped to regain her breath.* **5.** time to breathe; pause or respite: *Give him a little breath.* **6.** a single inhalation or respiration: *He took a deep breath.* **7.** the brief time required for a single respiration; a moment or instant: *They gave it to her and took it away all in a breath.* **8.** a slight suggestion, hint, or whisper: *The breath of slander never touched her.* **9.** a light current of air. **10.** *Phonet.* **a.** the air drawn into or expelled from the lungs to provide the generative source for most speech sounds. **b.** the audible expiration generating voiceless speech sounds, as (p), (k), (sh), etc. **11.** moisture emitted in respiration, esp. when condensed and visible. **12.** a trivial circumstance; trifle. **13.** an odorous exhalation, or the air impregnated by it. **14.** *Obs.* exhalation or vapor. **15. below** or **under one's breath,** in a low voice or whisper; sotto voce: *He protested under his breath because he was afraid to speak up.* **16. catch one's breath,** to pause or rest before continuing an activity or beginning a new one; resume regular breathing: *Let me catch my breath before I begin anything new.* **17. in the same breath,** at virtually the same time; almost simultaneously: *She lost her temper and apologized in the same breath.* **18. out of breath,** exhausted or gasping for breath, in consequence of an effort; breathless: *After climbing to the top of the tower, we were so out of breath that we had to sit down.* **19. save one's breath,** to avoid futile talk or discussion: *We were told to save our breath because the matter had already been decided.* **20. take away one's breath,** to make one as if breathless with astonishment; surprise; stun: *The sheer beauty of the sea took away my breath.* Also, **take one's breath away.** [bef. 900; ME *breth, breeth,* OE *brǣth* smell, exhalation; akin to G *Brodem* vapor, steam] —**Syn. 3.** spirit, animation, vigor, force.

breath·a·ble (brē′thə bəl), *adj.* **1.** able or fit to be breathed: *filters to make the air more breathable.* **2.** allowing the passage of air and moisture: *a breathable fabric.* [1725–35; BREATHE + -ABLE] —**breath′a·bil′i·ty, breath′a·ble·ness,** *n.*

Breath·a·lyz·er (breth′ə lī′zər), *Trademark.* a brand of breath analyzer.

breath′ an′alyzer, an instrument consisting of a small bag or tube filled with chemically treated crystals, into which a sample of a motorist's breath is taken as a test for intoxication.

breathe (brēth), *v.,* **breathed** (brēthd), **breath·ing.** —*v.i.* **1.** to take air, oxygen, etc., into the lungs and expel it; inhale and exhale; respire. **2.** (in speech) to control the outgoing breath in producing voice and speech sounds. **3.** to pause, as for breath; take rest: *How about giving me a chance to breathe?* **4.** to move gently or blow lightly, as air. **5.** to live; exist: *Hardly a man breathes who has not known great sorrow.* **6.** to be redolent of. **7.** (of a material) to allow air and moisture to pass through easily: *The jacket is comfortable because the fabric breathes.* **8.** (of the skin) to absorb oxygen and give off perspiration. **9.** (of a wine) to be exposed to air after being uncorked, in order to develop flavor and bouquet. —*v.t.* **10.** to inhale and exhale in respiration. **11.** to exhale: *Dragons breathe fire.* **12.** to inject as if by breathing; infuse: *She breathed life into the party.* **13.** to give utterance to; whisper. **14.** to express; manifest. **15.** to allow to rest or recover breath: *to breathe a horse.* **16.** to deprive of breath; tire; exhaust. **17.** to cause to pant; exercise. **18. breathe down someone's neck, a.** to be close to someone in pursuit; menace; threaten: *Police from four states were breathing down his neck.* **b.** to watch someone closely so as to supervise or control: *If everyone keeps breathing down my neck, how can I get my work done?* **19. breathe freely,** to have relief from anxiety, tension, or pressure: *Now that the crisis was over, he could breathe freely.* Also, **breathe easily, breathe easy. 20. breathe one's last,** to die: *He breathed his last and was buried in the churchyard.* **21. not breathe a word** or **syllable,** to maintain secrecy; keep a matter confidential: *I'll tell you if you promise not to breathe a word.* [1250–1300; ME *brethen,* deriv. of BREATH]
—**Syn. 14.** utter, tell, murmur, voice; reveal, divulge.

breathed (brètht, brēthd), *adj. Phonet.* **1.** not phonated; unvoiced; voiceless. **2.** utilizing the breath exclusively in the production of a speech sound. [1875–80; BREATH + -ED[3] or BREATHE + -ED[2]]

breath·er (brē′thər), *n.* **1.** a pause, as for breath. **2.** vigorous exercise that causes heavy breathing. **3.** a person who breathes. **4.** a vent in a container or covering, as in a casing for machinery or in a storage tank, to equalize interior and exterior pressure, permit entry of air, escape of fumes, or the like. **5.** a device for providing air from the atmosphere to submerged or otherwise sealed-off persons, internal-combustion engines, etc.: *the snorkel breather of a submarine.* [1350–1400; ME *brethere.* See BREATHE, -ER[1]]
—**Syn. 1.** rest, break, time-out, recess, intermission.

breath′ group′, *Phonet.* a sequence of sounds articulated in the course of a single exhalation; an utterance or part of an utterance produced between pauses for breath. [1875–80]

breath·ing (brē′thing), *n.* **1.** the act of a person or other animal that breathes; respiration. **2.** a single breath. **3.** the short time required for a single breath. **4.** a pause, as for breath. **5.** utterance or words. **6.** a gentle moving or blowing, as of wind. **7.** *Class. Gk. Gram.* **a.** the manner of articulating the beginning of a word written with an initial vowel sign, with or without aspiration before the vowel. **b.** one of the two symbols used to indicate this. Cf. **rough breathing, smooth breathing.** [1350–1400; ME *brethynge.* See BREATHE, -ING[1]] —**breath′ing·ly,** *adv.*

breath′ing space′, **1.** Also called **breath′ing spell′.** an opportunity to rest or think. **2.** sufficient space in which to move, work, etc.: *The train was so crowded that there was hardly breathing space.* [1640–50]

breath·less (breth′lis), *adj.* **1.** without breath or breathing with difficulty; gasping; panting: *We were breathless after the steep climb.* **2.** with the breath held, as in suspense, astonishment, fear, or the like: *breathless listeners of the mystery story.* **3.** causing loss of breath, as from excitement, anticipation, or tension: *a breathless ride.* **4.** dead; lifeless. **5.** motionless or still, as air without a breeze: *a breathless summer day.* [1350–1400; ME *brethles.* See BREATH, -LESS] —**breath′less·ly,** *adv.* —**breath′less·ness,** *n.*

breath·tak·ing (breth′tā′king), *adj.* thrillingly beautiful, remarkable, astonishing, exciting, or the like: *a breathtaking performance.* [1875–80; BREATH + TAKE + -ING[2]] —**breath′tak′ing·ly,** *adv.*

breath′ test′, a test by breath analyzer. [1965–70]

breath·y (breth′ē), *adj.,* **breath·i·er, breath·i·est.** (of the voice) characterized by audible or excessive emission of breath. [1520–30; BREATH + -Y[1]] —**breath′i·ness,** *n.*

B. Rec., bills receivable. Also, **b. rec.**

brec·ci·a (brech′ē ə, bresh′-), *n. Petrol.* rock composed of angular fragments of older rocks melded together. [1765–75; < It < Gmc; cf. OHG *brecha* breaking]

brec·ci·ate (brech′ē āt′, bresh′-), *v.t.,* **-at·ed, -at·ing.** *Petrol.* to form as breccia. [1765–75; BRECCI(A) + -ATE[1]] —**brec·ci·a·tion** (brech′ē ā′shən, bresh′-), *n.*

Brecht (brekt; *Ger.* BREKHT), *n.* **Ber·tolt** (beʀ′tôlt), 1898–1956, German dramatist and poet. —**Brecht′i·an,** *adj.*

Breck·in·ridge (brek′ən rij′), *n.* **John Cabell,** 1821–75, vice president of the U.S. 1857–61: Confederate general in the American Civil War.

Breck·nock·shire (brek′nək shēr′, -shər, -nok-), *n.* a historic county in S Wales, now part of Powys, Gwent, and Mid Glamorgan.

Brecks·ville (breks′vil), *n.* a town in N Ohio. 10,132.

bred (bred), *v.* pt. and pp. of **breed.**

Bre·da (brā dä′), *n.* a city in the S Netherlands. 118,086.

brede (brēd), *n. Archaic.* **1.** something braided or en-

CONCISE ETYMOLOGY KEY: <, descended or borrowed from; >, whence; b., blend of, blended; c., cognate with; cf., compare; deriv., derivative; equiv., equivalent; imit., imitative; obl., oblique; r., replacing; s., stem; sp., spelling, spelled; resp., respelling, respelled; trans., translation; ?, origin unknown; *, unattested; ‡, probably earlier than. See the full key inside the front cover.

twined, esp. a plait of hair; braid. **2.** braiding or embroidery. [archaic sp. of BRAID, given a new pron. in accord with modern sp. conventions]

bred-in-the-bone (bred′n *th*ə bōn′), *adj.* **1.** firmly instilled or established as if by heredity: *the bred-in-the-bone integrity of the school's headmaster.* **2.** deeply committed or resolved; unwavering: *a bred-in-the-bone believer in civil rights.* [from the proverb "What is bred in the bone will not come out of the flesh," first recorded in England (in Latin) ca. 1290, widespread in various versions since the 15th cent.]

breech (*n.* brēch; *v.* brēch, brich), *n.* **1.** the lower, rear part of the trunk of the body; buttocks. **2.** the hinder or lower part of anything. **3.** *Ordn.* the rear part of the bore of a gun, esp. the opening and associated mechanism that permits insertion of a projectile. **4.** *Mach.* the end of a block or pulley farthest from the supporting hook or eye. **5.** *Naut.* the outside angle of a knee in the frame of a ship. —*v.t.* **6.** *Ordn.* to fit or furnish (a gun) with a breech. **7.** to clothe with breeches. [bef. 1000; ME *breeche,* OE *brēc,* pl. of *brōc;* c. ON *brōk,* OHG *bruoh*]

breech′ ba′by, *Obstet.* a baby whose buttocks or feet are presented first during the birth process. [1965–70]

breech′ birth′. See **breech delivery.**

breech•block (brēch′blok′), *n. Ordn.* a movable piece of metal for closing the breech in certain firearms. Also, **breech′-block′.** [1880–85; BREECH + BLOCK]

breech•cloth (brēch′klôth′, -kloth′), *n., pl.* **-cloths** (-klô*th*z′, -klo*th*z′, -klôths′, -kloths′). a cloth worn about the breech and loins; loincloth. Also, **breech•clout** (brēch′klout′). [1785–95, *Amer.*; BREECH + CLOTH]

breech′ deliv′ery, *Obstet.* the delivery of an infant with the feet or buttocks appearing first. [1880–85]

breech•es (brich′iz), *n.* (*used with a plural v.*) **1.** Also called **knee breeches.** knee-length trousers, often having ornamental buckles or elaborate decoration at or near the bottoms, commonly worn by men and boys in the 17th, 18th, and early 19th centuries. **2.** See **riding breeches. 3.** *Informal.* trousers. **4. too big for one's breeches,** asserting oneself beyond one's authority or ability. [1125–75; ME, pl. of BREECH]

breech′es bu′oy, *Naut.* a rescue device consisting of a life buoy from which is suspended a canvas sling, similar in form to a pair of breeches, in which shipwrecked or disabled persons are hauled from a vessel to the shore or to another vessel by means of a rope and pulley between them. [1875–80]

breeches buoy

breech′es part′, *Theat.* a male role played by an actress. [1860–65]

breech•ing (brich′ing, brē′ching), *n.* **1.** the part of a harness that passes around the haunches of a horse. See illus. under **harness. 2.** a smoke pipe connecting one or more boilers with a chimney. **3.** *Navy.* (formerly) a strong rope fastened to a ship's side for securing a gun or checking its recoil. [1505–15; BREECH + -ING[1]]

breech•less (brēch′lis), *adj.* **1.** *Ordn.* without a breech. Cf. **muzzleloader. 2.** without breeches or trousers. [1350–1400; ME *breklesse.* See BREECH, -LESS]

breech•load•er (brēch′lō′dər), *n.* a firearm loaded at the breech. [1855–60; BREECH + LOADER]

breech•load•ing (brēch′lō′ding), *adj.* loaded at the breech. [1855–60; BREECH + LOADING]

breed (brēd), *v.,* **bred, breed•ing,** *n.* —*v.t.* **1.** to produce (offspring); procreate; engender. **2.** to produce by mating; propagate sexually; reproduce: *Ten mice were bred in the laboratory.* **3.** *Hort.* **a.** to cause to reproduce by controlled pollination. **b.** to improve by controlled pollination and selection. **4.** to raise (cattle, sheep, etc.): *He breeds longhorns on the ranch.* **5.** to cause or be the source of; engender; give rise to: *Dirt breeds disease. Stagnant water breeds mosquitoes.* **6.** to develop by training or education; bring up; rear: *He was born and bred a gentleman.* **7.** *Energy.* to produce more fissile nuclear fuel than is consumed in a reactor. **8.** to impregnate; mate: *Breed a strong mare with a fast stallion and hope for a Derby winner.* —*v.i.* **9.** to produce offspring: *Many animals breed in the spring.* **10.** to be engendered or produced; grow; develop: *Bacteria will not breed in alcohol.* **11.** to cause the birth of young, as in raising stock. **12.** to be pregnant. —*n.* **13.** *Genetics.* a relatively homogenous group of animals within a species, developed and maintained by humans. **14.** lineage; stock; strain: *She comes from a fine breed of people.* **15.** sort; kind; group: *Scholars are a quiet breed.* **16.** *Offensive.* half-breed (def. 2). [bef. 1000; ME *breden,* OE *brēdan* to nourish (c. OHG *bruotan,* G *brüten*); n. use from 16th century] —**breed′a•ble,** *adj.*
—**Syn. 1, 2.** beget, bear, generate. **5.** promote, occasion, foster, produce, induce, develop. **14.** family, pedigree, line.

breed•er (brē′dər), *n.* **1.** an animal, plant, or person that produces offspring or reproduces: *hens that are good breeders.* **2.** a person who raises animals or plants primarily for breeding purposes. **3.** Also called **breed′•er reac′tor.** *Energy.* a nuclear reactor in which more fissile material is produced than is consumed. [1525–35; BREED + -ER[1]]

breed•ing (brē′ding), *n.* **1.** the producing of offspring. **2.** the improvement or development of breeds of livestock, as by selective mating and hybridization. **3.** *Hort.* the production of new forms by selection, crossing, and hybridizing. **4.** training; nurture: *He is a man of good breeding.* **5.** the result of upbringing or training as shown in behavior and manners; manners, esp. good manners: *You can tell when a person has breeding.* **6.** *Energy.* the production in a nuclear reactor of more fissile material than is consumed. [1250–1300; ME; see BREED, -ING[1]]

breed′ing ground′, **1.** a place where animals breed or to which they return to breed. **2.** an environment suitable for or fostering the development of an idea, thing, etc.: *a breeding ground for violence.* [1930–35]

breed′ing plum′age. See **nuptial plumage.**

breed′ of cat′, *Informal.* type; sort; variety: *The new airplane is a completely different breed of cat from any that has been designed before.*

Breed's′ Hill′ (brēdz), a hill adjoining Bunker Hill, where the Battle of Bunker Hill was actually fought.

breeks (brēks, briks), *n.* (*used with a plural v.*) *Scot. and North Eng.* breeches; trousers.

breen (brēn), *n.* **1.** a deep brownish green. —*adj.* **2.** of a deep brownish green. [b. BROWN and GREEN]

breeze[1] (brēz), *n., v.,* **breezed, breez•ing.** —*n.* **1.** a wind or current of air, esp. a light or moderate one. **2.** a wind of 4–31 mph (2–14 m/sec). **3.** *Informal.* an easy task; something done or carried on without difficulty: *Finding people to join in the adventure was a breeze.* **4.** *Chiefly Brit. Informal.* a disturbance or quarrel. **5. shoot** or **bat the breeze,** *Slang.* **a.** to converse aimlessly; chat. **b.** to talk nonsense or exaggerate the truth: *He likes to shoot the breeze, so don't take everything he says seriously.* —*v.i.* **6.** (of the wind) to blow a breeze (usually used impersonally with *it* as subject): *It breezed from the west all day.* **7.** to move in a self-confident or jaunty manner: *She breezed up to the police officer and asked for directions.* **8.** *Informal.* to proceed quickly and easily; move rapidly without intense effort (often fol. by *along, into,* or *through*): *He breezed through the task. The car breezed along the highway.* —*v.t.* **9.** to cause to move in an easy or effortless manner, esp. at less than full speed: *The boy breezed the horse around the track.* **10. breeze in,** *Slang.* **a.** to win effortlessly: *He breezed in with an election plurality of 200,000.* **b.** Also, **breeze into** or **out.** to move or act with a casual or careless attitude: *He breezed out without paying attention to anyone.* **11. breeze up,** *Atlantic States.* to become windy. [1555–65; earlier *brize, brise* north or northeast wind; cf. D *bries,* East Fris *brîse,* F *brize,* Sp, Pg, Catalan *brisa,* It *brezza;* orig. and path of transmission disputed] —**breeze′less,** *adj.* —**breeze′like′,** *adj.*
—**Syn. 1.** See **wind[1].**

breeze[2] (brēz), *n.* **1.** cinders, ash, or dust from coal, coke, or charcoal. **2.** concrete, brick, or cinder block in which such materials form a component. [1720–30; var. of dial. *brays* < F *braise* live coals, cinders; see BRAZE[2]]

breeze′ block′, *Brit.* a cinder block. [1920–25]

breeze•way (brēz′wā′), *n.* a porch or roofed passageway open on the sides, for connecting two buildings, as a house and a garage. [1930–35, *Amer.*; BREEZE[1] + WAY]

breez•y (brē′zē), *adj.,* **breez•i•er, breez•i•est. 1.** abounding in breezes; windy. **2.** fresh; sprightly: *His breezy manner was half his charm.* [1710–20; BREEZE[1] + -Y[1]] —**breez′i•ly,** *adv.* —**breez′i•ness,** *n.*
—**Syn. 2.** carefree, lighthearted, buoyant, lively, jaunty, easygoing.

Bre•genz (brā′gents), *n.* a city in W Austria, on Lake Constance. 24,683.

breg•ma (breg′mə), *n., pl.* **-ma•ta** (-mə tə). *Craniom.* the junction point of the sagittal and coronal sutures of the skull. [1570–80; < Gk: front of the head] —**breg•mat•ic** (breg mat′ik), **breg•mate** (breg′māt), *adj.*

brei (brī), *n. Microbiology.* a suspension of finely divided tissue in an isotonic medium, used chiefly as a culture for certain viruses. [< G: mush; akin to OE *brīg, brīw* soup]

Brei′dha Fjord′ (brā′*th*ä), an inlet of Denmark Strait on the NW coast of Iceland.

bre•loque (brə lōk′), *n.* a charm or trinket, esp. one attached to a watch chain. [1855–60; < F]

Brem•en (brem′ən; *Ger.* brā′mən), *n.* **1.** a state in NW Germany. 654,000; 156 sq. mi. (405 sq. km). **2.** a port in and the capital of this state, on the Weser River: formerly a member of the Hanseatic League. 522,000.

Brem•er•ha•ven (brem′ər hä′vən; *Ger.* brā′mər hä′fən), *n.* a seaport in NW Germany, at the mouth of the Weser River. 132,200. Formerly, **Wesermünde.**

Brem•er•ton (brem′ər tən), *n.* a city in W Washington, on Puget Sound: navy yard. 36,208.

brems•strah•lung (brem′shträ′ləng), *n. Physics.* radiation emitted by a charged particle when accelerating, as x-rays emitted by an electron that is scattered by a nucleus. [1940–45; < G, equiv. to *Brems(e)* brake + *Strahlung* radiation]

Bren•da (bren′də), *n.* a female given name: from a Germanic word meaning "flame" or "sword."

Bren′ gun′ (bren), a .303-caliber, gas-operated, air-cooled, clip-fed submachine gun. Also, **bren′ gun′.** Also called **Bren, bren.** [1935–40; *Br(no),* Moravia + *En(field),* England, towns of manufacture]

Bren•ham (bren′əm), *n.* a town in central Texas. 10,966.

Bren•nan (bren′ən), *n.* **William Joseph, Jr.,** born 1906, U.S. lawyer and jurist: associate justice of the U.S. Supreme Court 1956–90.

Bren′ner Pass′ (bren′ər), a mountain pass in the Alps, on the border between Italy and Austria. 4494 ft. (1370 m) high.

brent (brent), *n. Chiefly Brit.* brant. Also called **brent′ goose′.**

Brent (brent), *n.* **1.** a borough of Greater London, England. 262,800. **2.** a male given name.

Bren•ta•no (bren tä′nō), *n.* **Franz,** 1838–1917, German philosopher and psychologist.

Brent•wood (brent′wo͝od′), *n.* **1.** a town on central Long Island, in SE New York. 44,321. **2.** a city in SW Pennsylvania. 11,907.

br'er (brûr, brâr; *Sou. dial.* bûr), *n. Chiefly Southern U.S.* brother. [1875–80, *Amer.*]

Bres (bres), *n. Irish Legend.* a Fomorian king of Ireland, whose unpopular rule led to the expulsion of the Fomorians by the Tuatha De Danann. Also, **Bress.**

Bre•scia (brē′shä), *n.* a city in central Lombardy, in N Italy. 215,260. —**Bre•scian** (bresh′ən), *adj.*

Bresh•kov•sky (bresh kôf′skē, -kof′-), *n.* **Catherine,** 1844–1934, Russian revolutionary of noble birth: called "the little grandmother of the Russian Revolution."

Bres•lau (brez′lou; *Ger.* brɛs′lou), *n.* German name of **Wrocław.**

Brest (brest; *for 2 also Russ.* bryest), *n.* **1.** a seaport in the W extremity of France: German submarine base in World War II; surrendered to Allies September 1944. 172,176. **2.** Formerly, **Brest Litovsk.** a city in SW Byelorussia (Belarus), on the Bug River: formerly in Poland; German-Russian peace treaty 1918. 238,000.

Brest Li•tovsk (brest′ li tôfsk′; *Russ.* bryest′ lyi-tôfsk′), former name (until 1921) of **Brest.** Polish, **Brześć nad Bugiem.**

Bre•tagne (brə tan′yᵊ), *n.* French name of **Brittany.**

bre•telle (bri tel′), *n.* one of a pair of ornamental suspenderlike shoulder straps that attach to the waistband at the front and back of a garment. [1855–60; < F, OF < OHG *brittila* (pl.) BRIDLE]

breth•ren (bre*th*′rin), *n.pl.* **1.** fellow members. **2.** *Archaic.* brothers.
—**Syn. 1, 2.** See **brother.**

Bret•on (bret′n; *Fr.* brə tôn′), *n.* **1.** a native or inhabitant of Brittany. **2.** Also called **Armorican, Armoric.** the Celtic language of Brittany. **3.** (*often l.c.*) a round hat for women, with a flat crown and a turned-up brim. —*adj.* **4.** pertaining to Brittany, the Bretons, or their language. [1815–20; < F *breton;* r. *Britain, Brit(t)on, Breton* used for both this sense and the sense of BRITON]

Bre•ton (brə tôn′), *n.* **1. An•dré** (än drā′), 1896–1966, French poet, essayist, and critic. **2. Jules A•dolphe** (zhyl a dôlf′), 1827–1906, French painter.

Bret′on lace′, a net lace with a design embroidered in heavy, often colored, thread.

Brett (bret), *n.* a male or female given name. Also, **Bret.**

Bret′ton Woods′ Con′ference (bret′n), an international conference called at Bretton Woods, N.H., in July 1944 to deal with international monetary and financial problems: resulted in the creation of the International Monetary Fund and the World Bank.

bre•tyl•i•um (brə til′ē əm), *n. Pharm.* a substance, $C_{18}H_{24}BrNO_3S$, used to treat acute ventricular arrhythmias and suppress ventricular fibrillation. [presumably *br(omobenzyl)* + *(dim)et(h)yl(ammon)ium,* two of its chemical components]

Breu•er (broi′ər), *n.* **1. Jo•sef** (yō′zef), 1842–1925, Austrian neurologist: pioneer in psychoanalytic techniques. **2. Mar•cel La•jos** (mär sel′ lo′yôsh; *Eng.* mär-sel′), 1902–81, Hungarian architect and furniture designer, in the U.S. after 1937.

Breu′er chair′, **1.** See **Cesca chair. 2.** See **Wassily chair.** [after M. L. BREUER, their designer]

Breu•ghel (broi′gəl, bro͞o′-; *Flemish.* brœ′gəl), *n.* **1. Pie•ter the Elder** (pē′tər; *Flemish.* pē′tər), ("*Peasant Breughel*"), c1525–69, Flemish genre and landscape painter. **2.** his sons, **Jan** (yän), ("*Velvet Breughel*"), 1568–1625, and **Pieter the Younger** ("*Hell Breughel*"), 1564–1637?, Flemish painters. Also, **Breu′gel, Brueghel, Bruegel.**

brev., **1.** brevet. **2.** brevier.

breve (brēv, brev), *n.* **1.** a mark (˘) over a vowel to show that it is short, or to indicate a specific pronunciation, as ŭ in (kŭt) *cut.* **2.** *Law.* **a.** an initial writ. **b.** a writ, as one issued by a court of law. **3.** *Music.* **a.** the longest modern note, equivalent to two semibreves or whole notes. See illus. under **note. b.** Also, **brevis.** a note in medieval mensural notation equal to one-half or one-third of a longa. **4.** *Pros.* a mark (˘) over a syllable to show that it is not stressed. [1250–1300; ME < ML, L *breve,* neut. of *brevis* short; see BRIEF]

bre•vet (brə vet′, brev′it), *n., v.,* **-vet•ted, -vet•ting** or **-vet•ed, -vet•ing.** —*n.* **1.** a commission promoting a military officer to a higher rank without increase of pay and with limited exercise of the higher rank, often granted as an honor immediately before retirement. —*v.t.* **2.** to appoint, promote, or honor by brevet. [1325–75; ME < AF; OF *brievet.* See BRIEF, -ET]

brevi-, a combining form meaning "short," used in the formation of compound words: *brevirostrate.* [< L, comb. form of *brevis;* akin to Gk *brachýs*]

bre•vi•ar•y (brē′vē er′ē, brev′ē-), *n., pl.* **-ar•ies. 1.** *Rom. Cath. Ch.* a book containing all the daily psalms, hymns, prayers, lessons, etc., necessary for reciting the office. **2.** a book of daily prayers and readings in some other churches. [1540–50; < L *breviārium* an abridgment. See BREVI-, -ARY]

brev•i•cau•date (brev′i kô′dāt), *adj. Zool.* having a short tail. [BREVI- + CAUDATE]

bre•vier (brə vēr′), *n. Print.* a size of type approximately 8-point, between minion and bourgeois. [1590–1600; < G: lit., BREVIARY; so called from use in printing breviaries]

brev•i•pen•nate (brev′ə pen′āt), *adj. Ornith.* having short wings; brachypterous. [BREVI- + PENNATE]

brev•i•ros•trate (brev′ə ros′trāt), *adj. Ornith.* having a short beak or bill. [BREVI- + ROSTRATE]

brev•i•ty (brev′i tē), *n.* **1.** shortness of time or duration; briefness: *the brevity of human life.* **2.** the quality of expressing much in few words; terseness: *Brevity is the soul of wit.* [1500–10; < AF *brevite,* OF *brievete.* See BRIEF, -ITY]
—**Syn. 2.** compactness, succinctness, pithiness. BREVITY, CONCISENESS refer to the use of few words in speaking. BREVITY emphasizes the short duration of speech: *reduced to extreme brevity.* CONCISENESS emphasizes compactness of expression: *clear in spite of great conciseness.* —**Ant. 1, 2.** length.

brew (bro͞o), *v.t.* **1.** to make (beer, ale, etc.) by steeping, boiling, and fermenting malt and hops. **2.** to make or prepare (a beverage, as tea) by mixing, steeping, soaking, or boiling a solid in water. **3.** to concoct, mix, or cook (a beverage or food, esp. one containing unmeasured or unusual ingredients): *She brewed a pot of soup from the leftovers.* **4.** to contrive, plan, or bring about: *to brew mischief.* —*v.i.* **5.** to make a fermented alcoholic malt beverage, as beer or ale. **6.** to boil, steep, soak, or cook: *Wait until the tea brews.* **7. be brewing,** to be forming or gathering; be in preparation: *Trouble was brewing.* —*n.* **8.** a quantity brewed in a single process. **9.** a particular brewing or variety of malt liquor. **10.** a hot beverage made by cooking a solid in water, esp. tea or coffee. **11.** any concoction, esp. a liquid produced by a mixture of unusual ingredients: *a witches' brew.* **12.** *Informal.* **a.** beer or ale. **b.** an individual serving of beer or ale: *Let's have a few brews after the game.* [bef. 900; ME *brewen,* OE *brēowan;* akin to D *brouwen,* G *brauen,* ON *brugga*] —**brew′er,** *n.*
—**Syn. 4.** concoct, scheme, plot, devise, hatch, cook up.

brew•age (bro͞o′ij), *n.* a fermented liquor brewed from malt. [1535–45; BREW + -AGE; modeled on BEVERAGE]

Brew′er's black′bird (bro͞o′ərz), a blackbird, *Euphagus cyanocephalus,* of the U.S., the male of which has greenish-black plumage with a purplish-black head. [1855–60, *Amer.;* named after Thomas M. Brewer (1814–80), American ornithologist]

Brew′er's mole′. See **hairy-tailed mole.** [see BREWER'S BLACKBIRD]

brew′er's yeast′, a yeast, as of the genus *Saccharomyces,* suitable for use as a ferment in the manufacture of wine and beer. [1915–20]

brew•er•y (bro͞o′ə rē, bro͝or′ē), *n., pl.* **-er•ies.** a building or establishment for brewing beer or other malt liquors, esp. the building where the brewing is done. [1650–60; BREW + -ERY]

brew•house (bro͞o′hous′), *n., pl.* **-hous•es** (-hou′ziz). brewery. [1325–75; ME; see BREW, HOUSE]

brew•ing (bro͞o′ing), *n.* **1.** the act of a person who brews. **2.** the process of being brewed. **3.** the occupation or business of producing beer, ale, etc. **4.** a quantity or batch brewed in a single process or at one time. [1350–1400; ME; see BREW, -ING[1]]

brew•is (bro͞o′is, bro͞oz), *n. Newfoundland.* **1.** hard bread soaked in water and then boiled. **2.** such bread, with pieces of fish added, served as a meal. [1520–30; earlier *brewz, brewes,* appar. b. *bree* broth, juice (ME *bre,* OE **brēo,* var. of *briw;* cf. BREI) and *browes,* ME *broys* broth, soup < OF *broez* (nom.), *broet* (acc.), equiv. to *bro* (< OHG *brod* BROTH) + *-et* -ET]

brew•mas•ter (bro͞o′mas′tər, -mä′stər), *n.* the supervisor of the brewing processes in a brewery. [BREW + MASTER]

brew•pub (bro͞o′pub′), *n.* a bar serving beer brewed at a small microbrewery on the premises. [1985–90]

brew•ski (bro͞o′skē), *n., pl.* **-skis.** *Slang.* brew (def. 12). [1980–1985]

Brew•ster (bro͞o′stər), *n.* **1. William,** 1560?–1644, Pilgrim settler: leader of the colonists at Plymouth. **2.** a male given name.

Brew′ster chair′, a chair of 17th-century New England having heavy turned uprights with vertical turned spindles filling in the back, the space beneath the arms, and the spaces between the legs. Cf. **Carver chair.** [1920–25, *Amer.;* named after W. BREWSTER]

Brew′ster's law′, *Optics.* the law that light will receive maximum polarization from a reflecting surface when it is incident to the surface at an angle **(angle of polarization** or **polarizing angle)** having a tangent equal to the index of refraction of the surface. [named after Sir David *Brewster* (1781–1868), Scottish physicist]

Brezh•nev (brezh′nef; *Russ.* bʀye′zhnyif), *n.* **Le•o•nid Il•yich** (lā′ə nid il′yich; *Russ.* lyi u nyēt′ ē lyēch′), 1906–82, Russian political leader: first secretary of the Soviet Communist party 1964–66; general secretary 1966–82; president of the Soviet Union 1960–64; 1977–82.

Brezh′nev Doc′trine, the doctrine expounded by Leonid Brezhnev in November 1968 affirming the right of the Soviet Union to intervene in the affairs of Communist countries to strengthen Communism.

Bri•an (brī′ən), *n.* a male given name.

Bri•an Bo•ru (brī′ən bô rō′, -ro͞o′, brēn′), 926–1014, king of Ireland 1002–14. Also, **Bri•an Bo•ramha, Bri•an Bo•raimhe, Bri•an Bo•roimhe, Bri•an Bo•rumha** (*all pronounced* brī′ən bô rō′, -ro͞o′, brēn′).

Bri•and (brē änd′; *Fr.* bʀē äɴ′), *n.* **A•ri•stide** (ar′ə-stēd′; *Fr.* a ʀē stēd′), 1862–1932, French statesman: minister of France 11 times; Nobel peace prize 1926.

bri•ar[1] (brī′ər), *n.* brier[1]. —**bri′ar•y,** *adj.*

bri•ar[2] (brī′ər), *n.* brier[2].

Bri•ard (brē är′, -ärd′), *n.* one of a French breed of dogs having a long, slightly wavy coat, raised originally for herding sheep. [1930–35; < F; see BRIE, -ARD]

bri•ar•root (brī′ər ro͞ot′, -ro͝ot′), *n.* brierroot.

bri•ar•wood (brī′ər wo͝od′), *n.* brierwood.

bribe (brīb), *n., v.,* **bribed, brib•ing.** —*n.* **1.** money or any other valuable consideration given or promised with a view to corrupting the behavior of a person, esp. in that person's performance as an athlete, public official, etc.: *The motorist offered the arresting officer a bribe to let him go.* **2.** anything given or serving to persuade or induce: *The children were given candy as a bribe to be good.* —*v.t.* **3.** to give or promise a bribe to: *They bribed the reporter to forget about what he had seen.* **4.** to influence or corrupt by a bribe: *The judge was too honest to be bribed.* —*v.i.* **5.** to give a bribe; practice bribery. [1350–1400; ME < MF: remnant of food given as alms, said to be < an expressive base **bri(m)b-* denoting something small] —**brib′a•ble, bribe′a•ble,** *adj.* —**brib′a•bil′i•ty, bribe′a•bil′i•ty,** *n.* —**brib•ee′,** *n.* —**brib′er,** *n.*

brib•er•y (brī′bə rē), *n., pl.* **-er•ies.** the act or practice of giving or accepting a bribe: *Bribery of a public official is a felony.* [1350–1400; ME *briberie* theft < MF: begging. See BRIBE, -ERY]

bric-a-brac (brik′ə brak′), *n.* (*used with a singular or plural v.*) miscellaneous small articles collected for their antiquarian, sentimental, decorative, or other interest. Also, **bric′-à-brac′.** [1830–40; < F, MF: lit., at random, without rhyme or reason; gradational compound from elements of obscure orig.]
—**Syn.** trinkets, gimcracks, knickknacks, gewgaws.

Brice (brīs), *n.* **1. Fanny** (*Fannie Borach*), 1891–1951, U.S. singer and comedian. **2.** a male given name.

brick (brik), *n.* **1.** a block of clay hardened by drying in the sun or burning in a kiln, and used for building, paving, etc.: traditionally, in the U.S., a rectangle 2¼ × 3¾ × 8 in. (5.7 × 9.5 × 20.3 cm), red, brown, or yellow in color. **2.** such blocks collectively. **3.** the material of which such blocks are made. **4.** any block or bar having a similar size and shape: *a gold brick; an ice-cream brick.* **5.** the length of a brick as a measure of thickness, as of a wall: *one and a half bricks thick.* **6.** *Informal.* an admirably good or generous person. **7. drop a brick,** to make a social gaffe or blunder, esp. an indiscreet remark. **8. hit the bricks, a.** to walk the streets, esp. as an unemployed or homeless person. **b.** to go on strike: *With contract talks stalled, workers are threatening to hit the bricks.* Also, **take to the bricks. 9. make bricks without straw, a.** to plan or act on a false premise or unrealistic basis. **b.** to create something that will not last: *To form governments without the consent of the people is to make bricks without straw.* **c.** to perform a task despite the lack of necessary materials. —*v.t.* **10.** to pave, line, wall, fill, or build with brick. —*adj.* **11.** made of, constructed with, or resembling bricks. [1400–50; late ME *brike* < MD *bricke;* akin to BREAK] —**brick′like′, brick′ish,** *adj.*

brick•bat (brik′bat′), *n.* **1.** a piece of broken brick, esp. one used as a missile. **2.** any rocklike missile. **3.** an unkind or unfavorable remark; caustic criticism: *a new play greeted with brickbats.* [1555–65; BRICK + BAT[1]]

brick′ cheese′, a semisoft, sweet-tasting American cheese, made from the whole milk of cows and produced in brick form. [1875–80, *Amer.*]

brick•field (brik′fēld′), *n. Brit.* brickyard. [1795–1805; BRICK + FIELD]

brick•kiln (brik′kil′, -kiln′), *n.* a kiln or furnace in which bricks are baked or burned. [1475–85; BRICK + KILN]

brick•lay•ing (brik′lā′ing), *n.* the act or occupation of laying bricks in construction. [1475–85; BRICK + LAYING] —**brick′lay′er,** *n.*

brick•le (brik′əl), *adj. Midland and Southern U.S.* easily broken; brittle. [bef. 1000; Brit. dial., Scots; late ME *bryckell,* OE *-brycel* tending to break, equiv. to *bryc-* (mutated ptp. s. of *brecan* to BREAK) + *-el* adj. suffix] —**brick′le•ness,** *n.*

brick•mak•ing (brik′mā′king), *n.* the act, process, or occupation of making bricks. [1695–1705; BRICK + MAKING] —**brick′mak′er,** *n.*

brick′ red′, yellowish or brownish red. [1800–10] —**brick′-red′,** *adj.*

brick•top (brik′top′), *n. Informal.* **1.** a person having red or reddish-brown hair. **2.** hair of this color. [1840–50, *Amer.;* BRICK + TOP[1], from the typical color of bricks]

brick•work (brik′wûrk′), *n.* brick construction, as contrasted with that using other materials. [1570–80; BRICK + WORK]

brick•y (brik′ē), *adj.,* **brick•i•er, brick•i•est.** constructed of, made of, or resembling bricks. [1590–1600; BRICK + -Y[1]]

brick•yard (brik′yärd′), *n.* a place where bricks are made, stored, or sold. [1725–35, *Amer.;* BRICK + YARD[2]]

bri•cole (bri kōl′, brik′əl), *n.* **1.** *Billiards.* a shot in which the cue ball strikes a cushion after touching the object ball and before hitting the carom ball. **2.** an indirect action or unexpected stroke. [1515–25; earlier, rebound off a court wall (in tennis), catapult < MF < It *briccola,* prob., with suffix substitution, < Langobardic **brihhil-* that which breaks; cf. MHG *brechel-,* deriv. of *brechen* to BREAK]

brid•al (brīd′l), *adj.* **1.** of, for, or pertaining to a bride or a wedding: *a bridal gown.* —*n.* **2.** a wedding. **3.** *Archaic.* a wedding feast. [bef. 1100; ME *bridale* wedding feast, OE *brȳdealu,* equiv. to *brȳd* BRIDE[1] + *ealu* ALE, i.e., ale-drinking; now taken as BRIDE[1] + -AL[1]]

Brid•al•veil (brīd′l vāl′), *n.* a waterfall in Yosemite National Park, California. 620 ft. (189 m) high. Also called **Brid′alveil Fall′.**

brid′al wreath′, any of several shrubs belonging to the genus *Spiraea,* of the rose family, esp. *S. prunifolia,* having finely toothed ovate leaves and sprays of small white flowers. [1885–90]

bride[1] (brīd), *n.* a newly married woman or a woman about to be married. [bef. 1000; ME; OE *brȳd;* c. D *bruid,* G *Braut,* ON *brūthr,* Goth *brūths*] —**bride′less,** *adj.* —**bride′like′,** *adj.*

bride[2] (brīd; *Fr.* bʀed), *n.* **1.** Also called **bar, leg, tie.** a connection consisting of a thread or a number of threads for joining various solid parts of a design in needlepoint lace. **2.** an ornamental bonnet string. [1865–70; < F: bonnet-string, bridle, OF < Gmc; see BRIDLE]

Bride (brīd), *n.* **Saint.** See **Brigid, Saint.**

bride•groom (brīd′gro͞om′, -gro͝om′), *n.* a newly married man or a man about to be married. [bef. 1000; late ME (Scots) *brydgrome,* alter. of ME *bridegome,* OE *brȳdguma* (*brȳd* BRIDE[1] + *guma* man, c. L *homō*), with final element conformed to GROOM]

bride′ price′, (in some nonindustrial societies) the money or goods given to the family of a bride by the bridegroom or his family. Also, **bride′-price′.** Also called **bride•wealth** (brīd′welth′). [1875–80]

brides•maid (brīdz′mād′), *n.* **1.** a young woman who attends the bride at a wedding ceremony. **2.** *Informal.* a person, group, etc., that is in a secondary position, never quite attains a goal, etc.: *Bridesmaids for 12 seasons, the Eagles finally won the championship.* [1545–55; BRIDE[1] + 'S[1] + MAID]

bride•well (brīd′wel′, -wəl), *n. Brit.* a prison. [1545–55; after a prison that formerly stood near the church of St. Bride in London]

Brid•ey (brī′dē), *n.* a female given name, form of **Bridget.**

bridge[1] (brij), *n., v.,* **bridged, bridg•ing.** —*n.* **1.** a structure spanning and providing passage over a river, chasm, road, or the like. **2.** a connecting, transitional, or intermediate route or phase between two adjacent elements, activities, conditions, or the like: *Working at the hospital was a bridge between medical school and private practice.* **3.** *Naut.* **a.** a raised transverse platform from which a power vessel is navigated: often includes a pilot house and a chart house. **b.** any of various other raised platforms from which the navigation or docking of a vessel is supervised. **c.** a bridge house or bridge superstructure. **d.** a raised walkway running fore-and-aft. **4.** *Anat.* the ridge or upper line of the nose. **5.** *Dentistry.* an artificial replacement, fixed or removable, of a missing tooth or teeth, supported by natural teeth or roots adjacent to the space. **6.** *Music.* **a.** a thin, fixed wedge or support raising the strings of a musical instrument above the sounding board. **b.** a transitional, modulatory passage connecting sections of a composition or movement. **c.** (in jazz and popular music) the contrasting third group of eight bars in a thirty-two-bar chorus; channel; release. **7.** Also, **bridge passage.** a passage in a literary work or a scene in a play serving as a movement between two other passages or scenes of greater importance. **8.** *Ophthalm.* the part of a pair of eyeglasses that joins the two lenses and rests on the bridge or sides of the nose. **9.** Also called **bridge circuit.** *Elect.* a two-branch network, including a measuring device, as a galvanometer, in which the unknown resistance, capacitance, inductance, or impedance of one component can be measured by balancing the voltage in each branch and computing the unknown value from the known values of the other components. Cf. **Wheatstone bridge. 10.** *Railroads.* a gantry over a track or tracks for supporting waterspouts, signals, etc. **11.** *Building Trades.* a scaffold built over a sidewalk alongside a construction or demolition site to protect pedestrians and motor traffic from falling materials. **12.** *Metall.* **a.** a ridge or wall-like projection of fire brick or the like, at each end of the hearth in a metallurgical furnace. **b.** any layer of partially fused or densely compacted material preventing the proper gravitational movement of molten material, as in a blast furnace or cupola, or the proper compacting of metal powder in a mold. **13.** (in a twist drill) the conoid area between the flutes at the drilling end. **14.** *Billiards, Pool.* **a.** the arch formed by the hand and fingers to support and guide the striking end of a cue. **b.** a notched piece of wood with a long handle, used to support the striking end of the cue when the hand cannot do so comfortably; rest. **15.** transitional music, commentary, dialogue, or the like, between two parts of a radio or television program. **16.** *Theat.* **a.** a gallery or platform that can be raised or lowered over a stage and is used by technicians, stagehands, etc., for painting scenery **(paint bridge),** arranging and supporting lights **(light bridge),** or the like. **b.** *Brit.* a part of the floor of

a stage that can be raised or lowered. **17.** *Horol.* a partial plate, supported at both ends, holding bearings on the side opposite the dial. Cf. **cock**[1] (def. 10). **18.** *Chem.* a valence bond illustrating the connection of two parts of a molecule. **19.** a support or prop, usually timber, for the roof of a mine, cave, etc. **20.** any arch or rooflike figure formed by acrobats, dancers, etc., as by joining and raising hands. **21. burn one's bridges (behind one),** to eliminate all possibilities of retreat; make one's decision irrevocable: *She burned her bridges when she walked out angrily.* —*v.t.* **22.** to make a bridge or passage over; span: *The road bridged the river.* **23.** to join by or as if by a bridge: *a fallen tree bridging the two porches.* **24.** to make (a way) by a bridge. —*v.i.* **25.** *Foundry.* (of molten metal) to form layers or areas heterogeneous either in material or in degree of hardness. [bef. 1000; ME *brigge,* OE *brycg;* c. D *brug,* G *Brücke;* akin to ON *bryggja* pier] —**bridge′a·ble,** *adj.* —**bridge′less,** *adj.* —**bridge′like′,** *adj.*
—**Syn. 22.** traverse, cross, vault. **23.** link, connect.

bridge[2] (brij), *n. Cards.* a game derived from whist in which one partnership plays to fulfill a certain declaration against an opposing partnership acting as defenders. Cf. **auction bridge, contract** (def. 5). [1885–90; earlier also sp. *britch, biritch;* of obscure orig; perh. < Turk *bir* one + *üç* three (one hand being exposed while the other three are concealed), but such a name for the game is not attested in Turkey or the Near East, from where it is alleged to have been introduced into Europe]

bridge·board (brij′bôrd′, -bōrd′), *n.* a notched board serving as a string or carriage for a stair. [1875–80; BRIDGE[1] + BOARD]

bridge′ chair′, a lightweight folding chair, often part of a set of matching chairs and bridge table.

bridge′ cir′cuit, *Elect.* bridge[1] (def. 9). [1930–35]

bridge′ cloth′, a tablecloth for a bridge table. [1905–10]

bridge′ deck′, *Naut.* **1.** a deck on top of a bridge house; flying bridge. **2.** the first deck in a bridge house. **3.** the deck from which a vessel is usually operated; the location of the pilot house.

bridge′ fi′nancing, interim or emergency financing through a short- or medium-term loan **(bridge loan).**

bridge′ flut′ing, (on the stem of a drinking glass) flutes or facets continuing onto the underside of the bowl.

bridge·head (brij′hed′), *n.* **1.** a position held or to be gained on the enemy side of a river, defile, or other obstacle, to cover the crossing of friendly troops. **2.** any position gained that can be used as a foothold for further advancement; beachhead. **3.** a defensive work covering or protecting the end of a bridge toward the enemy. [1805–15; BRIDGE[1] + HEAD]

bridge′ house′, *Naut.* a deckhouse including a bridge or bridges for navigation. [1350–1400; ME]

bridge′ lamp′, a floor lamp, esp. one having the light source on an arm so hinged as to be horizontally adjustable. [1925–30, *Amer.*]

bridge′ loan′, 1. See under **bridge financing. 2.** See **swing loan.**

bridge·man (brij′mən), *n., pl.* **-men. 1.** a person who works on a bridge or on the construction of bridges. **2.** a person who manages the loading and unloading of ferries at a landing dock. [1640–50; BRIDGE[1] + -MAN]
—**Usage.** See **-man.**

Bridge′ of San′ Lu′is Rey′, The (san′ lo͞o′is rā′, lo͞o ēs′), a novel (1927) by Thornton Wilder.

Bridge′ of Sighs′, a bridge in Venice across which prisoners were formerly led for trial in the ducal palace.

bridge′ pas′sage, bridge (def. 7). [1925–30]

Bridge·port (brij′pôrt′, -pōrt′), *n.* a seaport in SW Connecticut, on Long Island Sound. 142,546.

Bridg·es (brij′iz), *n.* **1. Calvin Black·man** (blak′mən), 1889–1938, U.S. geneticist. **2. Harry (Alfred Bryant Ren·ton)** (ren′tn), 1900–90, U.S. labor leader, born in Australia. **3. Robert (Seymour),** 1884–1930, English poet and essayist: poet laureate 1913–30.

Bridg·et (brij′it), *n.* **1. Saint.** See **Brigid, Saint. 2.** a female given name.

bridge′ ta′ble, a square card table with folding legs. [1900–05]

Bridge·ton (brij′tən), *n.* **1.** a city in SW New Jersey. 18,795. **2.** a town in E Missouri. 18,445.

Bridge·town (brij′toun′), *n.* a seaport on and the capital of Barbados, on the SW coast. 8789.

bridge·tree (brij′trē′), *n.* a beam supporting the shaft on which an upper millstone rotates. [1610–20; BRIDGE[1] + TREE]

Bridge′ View′, a town in NE Illinois. 14,155.

bridge·wall (brij′wôl′), *n.* (in a furnace or boiler) a transverse baffle that serves to deflect products of combustion. [BRIDGE[1] + WALL]

Bridge·wa·ter (brij′wô′tər, -wot′ər), *n.* a town in E Massachusetts. 17,202.

bridge·work (brij′wûrk′), *n.* **1.** *Dentistry.* **a.** a dental bridge. **b.** dental bridges collectively. **c.** any of several different types of dental bridges. **2.** *Civ. Engin.* the art or process of bridge building. [1880–85; BRIDGE[1] + WORK]

bridg·ing (brij′ing), *n. Building Trades.* a brace or an arrangement of braces fixed between floor or roof joists to keep them in place. [1830–40; BRIDGE[1] + -ING[1]]

bridg′ing shot′, *Motion Pictures.* a shot inserted in a film to indicate the passage of time between two scenes, as of a series of newspaper headlines or calendar pages being torn off.

Bridg·man (brij′mən), *n.* **Percy Williams,** 1882–1961, U.S. physicist: Nobel prize 1946.

Brid·ie (brī′dē), *n.* a female given name, form of **Bridget.**

bri·dle (brīd′l), *n., v.,* **-dled, -dling.** —*n.* **1.** part of the tack or harness of a horse, consisting usually of a headstall, bit, and reins. **2.** anything that restrains or curbs: *His common sense is a bridle to his quick temper.* **3.** *Mach.* a link, flange, or other attachment for limiting the movement of any part of a machine. **4.** *Naut.* a rope or chain secured at both ends to an object to be held, lifted, or towed, and itself held or lifted by a rope or chain secured at its center. **5.** a raising up of the head, as in disdain. —*v.t.* **6.** to put a bridle on. **7.** to control or hold back; restrain; curb. —*v.i.* **8.** to draw up the head and draw in the chin, as in disdain or resentment. [bef. 900; ME *bridel,* OE *brīdel* for *brigdels,* equiv. to *brigd-* (var. s. of *bregdan* to BRAID[1]) + *-els* n. suffix; akin to D *breidel,* OHG *brittel*] —**bri′dle·less,** *adj.* —**bri′dler,** *n.*
—**Syn. 2.** governor. **2, 7.** check. **7.** govern, constrain, inhibit, restrict, limit. **8.** bristle.

bri′dle hand′, (of a horseback rider) the hand, usually the left hand, that holds both reins or both pairs of reins, leaving the other hand free to manage a whip, crop, lariat, or the like. [1570–80]

bri′dle joint′, *Carpentry.* a heading joint in which the end of one member, notched to form two parallel tenons, is fitted into two gains cut into the edges of a second member.

bri′dle path′, a wide path for riding horses. [1805–15]

bri·dle·wise (brīd′l wīz′), *adj.* (of a horse) obedient to a touch of the reins on the neck, without pressure of the bit on the mouth. [1820–30, *Amer.*; BRIDLE + WISE[1]]

bri·doon (bri do͞on′, bri-), *n.* a snaffle when used with a curb on a full bridle. [1745–55; < F, MF *bridon,* equiv. to *bride* bridle (see BRIDE[2]) + *-on* n. suffix]

Brie (brē), *n.* a salted, white, soft cheese, ripened with bacterial action, originating in Brie. [1840–50]

Brie (bʀē), *n.* a region in NE France, between the Seine and the Marne.

brief (brēf), *adj.,* **-er, -est,** *n., v.* —*adj.* **1.** lasting or taking a short time; of short duration: *a brief walk; a brief stay in the country.* **2.** using few words; concise; succinct: *a brief report on weather conditions.* **3.** abrupt or curt. **4.** scanty: *a brief bathing suit.* —*n.* **5.** a short and concise statement or written item. **6.** an outline, the form of which is determined by set rules, of all the possible arguments and information on one side of a controversy: *a debater's brief.* **7.** *Law.* **a.** a writ summoning one to answer to any action. **b.** a memorandum of points of fact or of law for use in conducting a case. **c.** a written argument submitted to a court. **d.** (in England) the material relevant to a case, delivered by a solicitor to the barrister who tries the case. **8.** an outline, summary, or synopsis, as of a book. **9. briefs,** (*used with a plural v.*) close-fitting, legless underpants with an elastic waistband. **10.** briefing. **11.** *Rom. Cath. Ch.* a papal letter less formal than a bull, sealed with the pope's signet ring or stamped with the device borne on this ring. **12.** *Theat. Brit.* a free ticket; pass. **13.** *Obs.* a letter. **14. hold a brief for,** to support or defend by argument; endorse. **15. in brief,** in a few words; in short: *The supervisor outlined in brief the duties of the new assistant.* —*v.t.* **16.** to make an abstract or summary of. **17.** to instruct by a brief or briefing: *They brief all the agents before assigning them.* **18.** *Law.* to retain as advocate in a suit. [1250–1300; ME *bref* < AF, OF < L *brevis* short; see BREVE] —**brief′er,** *n.* —**brief′ness,** *n.*
—**Syn. 1.** short-lived, fleeting, transitory, ephemeral, transient. See **short. 2.** terse, compact, pithy, condensed. **5.** outline, précis, epitome, abstract. See **summary. 16.** summarize, outline.

brief·case (brēf′kās′), *n.* a flat, rectangular case with a handle, often of leather, for carrying books, papers, etc. [1925–30; BRIEF (n.) + CASE[2]]

brief·ing (brē′fing), *n.* **1.** *Mil.* a short, factual oral summary of the details of a current or projected military operation given to the participants or observers. **2.** any set of concise instructions or a summary of events. [1860–65; BRIEF + -ING[1]]

brief·less (brēf′lis), *adj.* **1.** having no brief. **2.** having no clients, as a lawyer. [1815–25; BRIEF (n.) + -LESS] —**brief′less·ly,** *adv.* —**brief′less·ness,** *n.*

brief·ly (brēf′lē), *adv.* **1.** for a short duration: *He stopped over briefly in Chicago.* **2.** in a few words: *Let me explain briefly.* **3.** in a brief manner; quickly or brusquely: *She nodded briefly and began to speak.* [1250–1300; ME; see BRIEF, -LY]

brief′ of ti′tle. See **abstract of title.**

Bri·enz (brē ents′), *n.* **Lake of,** a lake in SE Bern canton in Switzerland. 11.5 sq. mi. (30 sq. km). German, **Bri·enz·er See** (brē en′tsəʀ zā′).

bri·er[1] (brī′ər), *n.* **1.** a prickly plant or shrub, esp. the sweetbrier or a greenbrier. **2.** a tangled mass of prickly plants. **3.** a thorny stem or twig. Also, **briar.** [bef. 1000; ME *brer,* OE *brǣr, brēr;* akin to BRAMBLE] —**bri′er·y,** *adj.*

bri·er[2] (brī′ər), *n.* **1.** the white heath, *Erica arborea,* of France and Corsica, the woody root of which is used for making tobacco pipes. **2.** a pipe made of brierroot. Also, **briar.** [1865–70; earlier *bruyer* < F *bruyère,* OF < Gallo-Latin **brūcāria* field of heather, equiv to **brūc-* heather (< Gaulish, perh. **broiko-* (with early L change of *oi* > *ū*) < Celtic **wroiko-* > OIr *froech,* Welsh *grug*) + L *-āria* -ARY; cf. early ML *brucus, brugaria;* see -ER[2], -AR[2]]

bri·er[3] (brī′ər), *n. Usually Disparaging.* (chiefly in Ohio, Kentucky, and Tennessee) a rustic or hillbilly, esp. one from Appalachia. [shortening of *brier hopper*]

bri·er·root (brī′ər ro͞ot′, -ro͝ot′), *n.* **1.** the root wood of the brier. **2.** certain other woods from which tobacco pipes are made. **3.** a pipe made of brierroot. Also, **briarroot.** [1865–70; BRIER[2] + ROOT[1]]

bri·er·wood (brī′ər wo͝od′), *n.* brierroot. Also, **briarwood.** [1865–70; BRIER[2] + WOOD[1]]

Bri·eux (bʀē œ′), *n.* **Eu·gène** (œ zhen′), 1858–1932, French playwright, journalist, and editor.

brig (brig), *n.* **1.** *Naut.* **a.** a two-masted vessel square-rigged on both masts. **b.** (formerly, in the U.S. Navy) an armed brig-rigged or brigantine-rigged vessel. **c.** the compartment of a ship where prisoners are confined. **2.** a place of confinement or detention, esp. in the U.S. Navy or Marines; guardhouse. [1705–15; short for BRIGANTINE]

Brig., 1. brigade. **2.** brigadier.

bri·gade (bri gād′), *n., v.,* **-gad·ed, -gad·ing.** —*n.* **1.** a military unit having its own headquarters and consisting of two or more regiments, squadrons, groups, or battalions. **2.** a large body of troops. **3.** a group of individuals organized for a particular purpose: *a fire brigade; a rescue brigade.* **4.** See **bucket brigade. 5.** *Hist.* a convoy of canoes, sleds, wagons, or pack animals, esp. as used to supply trappers in the 18th- and 19th-century Canadian and U.S. fur trade. —*v.t.* **6.** to form into a brigade. **7.** to group together. [1630–40; < F < OIt *brigata* company of soldiers, orig. group, band, equiv. to *brig(are)* prob. to associate (with), be together (obs. sense) (see BRIGAND) + *-ata* -ADE[1]]

brig·a·dier (brig′ə dēr′), *n.* **1.** *Brit. Mil.* a rank between colonel and major general. **2.** *U.S. Army Informal.* a brigadier general. **3.** *Hist.* a noncommissioned rank in the Napoleonic armies. [1670–80; < F: officer commanding a brigade; see BRIGADE, -IER[2]] —**brig′a·dier′ship,** *n.*

brig′adier gen′eral, *pl.* **brigadier generals.** *U.S. Army.* an officer of the rank between colonel and major general. [1680–90]

brig·and (brig′ənd), *n.* a bandit, esp. one of a band of robbers in mountain or forest regions. [1350–1400; var. of ME *briga(u)nt* < MF *brigand* < OIt *brigante* companion, member of an armed company, equiv. to *brig(are)* to treat, deal (with), make war (deriv. of *briga* trouble, strife; of uncert. orig.) + *-ante* -ANT] —**brig′and·age,** *n.* —**brig′and·ish,** *adj.* —**brig′and·ish·ly,** *adv.*
—**Syn.** outlaw, highwayman, desperado, cutthroat.

brig·an·dine (brig′ən dēn′, -dīn′), *n. Armor.* a flexible body armor of overlapping steel plates with an exterior covering of linen, velvet, leather, etc. [1425–75; late ME *brigandyn* < MF *brigandine.* See BRIGAND, -INE[2]]

brig·an·tine (brig′ən tēn′, -tīn′), *n. Naut.* **1.** a two-masted sailing vessel, square-rigged on the foremast and having a fore-and-aft mainsail with square upper sails. **2.** See **hermaphrodite brig.** [1515–25; < ML *brigantinus* or OIt *brigantino,* orig., armed escort ship (see BRIGAND, -INE[2]); r. *brigandyn* < MF *brigandin*]

Brig. Gen., brigadier general.

Briggs (brigz), *n.* **Henry,** 1561–1630, English mathematician.

Briggs′i·an log′arithm (brig′zē ən), *Math.* See **common logarithm.** Also **Briggs′ log′arithm.** [named after H. BRIGGS; see -IAN]

Brig·ham (brig′əm), *n.* a male given name.

Brig′ham Cit′y, a city in N Utah. 15,596.

bright (brīt), *adj.,* **-er, -est,** *n., adv.,* **-er, -est.** —*adj.* **1.** radiating or reflecting light; luminous; shining: *The bright coins shone in the gloom.* **2.** filled with light: *The room was bright with sunshine.* **3.** vivid or brilliant: *a bright red dress; bright passages of prose.* **4.** quick-witted or intelligent: *They gave promotions to bright employees.* **5.** clever or witty, as a remark: *Bright comments enlivened the conversation.* **6.** animated; lively; cheerful: *a bright and happy child; a bird's bright song.* **7.** characterized by happiness or gladness: *All the world seems bright and gay.* **8.** favorable or auspicious: *bright prospects for the future.* **9.** radiant or splendid: *the bright pageantry of court.* **10.** illustrious or glorious, as an era: *the bright days of the Renaissance.* **11.** clear or translucent, as liquid: *The bright water trickled through his fingers.* **12.** having a glossy, glazed, or polished finish. **13.** intensely clear and vibrant in tone or quality; clear and sharp in sound: *a bright singing voice.*

CONCISE PRONUNCIATION KEY: act, cāpe, dâre, pärt; set, ēqual; *if,* ice; ox, ōver, ôrder, oil, bo͝ok, bo͞ot, out; up, ûrge; child; sing; shoe; thin, *th*at; zh as in *treasure.* ə = *a* as in *alone, e* as in *system, i* as in *easily, o* as in *gallop, u* as in *circus;* ᵊ as in *fire* (fīᵊr), *hour* (ouᵊr). l and n can serve as syllabic consonants, as in *cradle* (krād′l), and *button* (but′n). See the full key inside the front cover.

—*n.* **14. brights, a.** the automobile or truck headlights used for driving at night or under conditions of decreased visibility. **b.** the brighter level of intensity of these lights, usually deflected upward by switching on a bulb in the headlamp that strikes the lens at a different angle. **15.** flue-cured, light-hued tobacco. **16.** an artist's paintbrush having short, square-edged bristles. **17.** *Archaic.* brightness; splendor. —*adv.* **18.** in a bright manner; brightly. [bef. 1000; ME; OE *breht, beorht;* c. Goth *bairht(s),* OS *ber(a)ht,* OHG *beraht,* ON *bjartr;* Welsh *berth* splendid (< **berkto-*); akin to L *flagrāre* to blaze (see FLAGRANT), Albanian (*i*) *bardhë* white, Skt *bhrājate(it)* shines] —**bright′ish,** *adj.* —**bright′ly,** *adv.*

—**Syn. 1.** refulgent, effulgent, lustrous, lucent, beaming, lambent. BRIGHT, BRILLIANT, RADIANT, SHINING refer to that which gives forth, is filled with, or reflects light. BRIGHT suggests the general idea: *bright flare, stars, mirror.* BRILLIANT implies a strong, unusual, or sparkling brightness, often changeful or varied and too strong to be agreeable: *brilliant sunlight.* RADIANT implies the pouring forth of steady rays of light, esp. as are agreeable to the eyes: *a radiant face.* SHINING implies giving forth or reflecting a strong or steady light: *shining eyes.* **4.** keen, discerning, sharp, sharp-witted, ingenious, clever. **8.** promising, encouraging. —**Ant. 1.** dull, dim.

Bright (brīt), *n.* **1. John,** 1811–89, British statesman and economist. **2. Richard,** 1789–1858, English physician.

bright′ coal′, coal consisting of alternating layers of clarain and vitrain.

bright·en (brīt′n), *v.i., v.t.* to become or make bright or brighter. [1250–1300; ME *brightnen.* See BRIGHT, -EN[1]]
—**Syn.** lighten; cheer, gladden, lift, hearten, perk up.
—**Ant.** darken; deject, sadden.

bright·en·er (brīt′n ər), *n.* **1.** a person or thing that brightens. **2.** a chemical or other agent used to increase brightness, as one added to toothpaste or detergent to intensify the cleansing or bleaching process. [1790–1800; BRIGHTEN + -ER[1]]

bright-eyed (brīt′īd′), *adj.* **1.** having bright eyes. **2.** alertly eager. **3. bright-eyed and bushy-tailed,** alertly eager; full of energy and enthusiasm: *Get a good night's sleep so you'll be bright-eyed and bushy-tailed in the morning.* [1585–95]

bright-field (brīt′fēld′), *adj. Micros.* of or pertaining to the illuminated region about the object of a microscope.

bright′-line spec′trum (brīt′līn′), *Physical Chem.* the spectrum of an incandescent substance appearing on a spectrogram as one or more bright lines against a dark background. [1885–90; BRIGHT + LINE[1]]

bright·ness (brīt′nis), *n.* **1.** the quality of being bright. **2.** *Optics.* the luminance of a body, apart from its hue or saturation, that an observer uses to determine the comparative luminance of another body. Pure white has the maximum brightness, and pure black the minimum brightness. [bef. 950; ME *brihtnes,* OE *beorhtnes.* See BRIGHT, -NESS]

Bright·on (brīt′n), *n.* **1.** a city in East Sussex, in SE England: seashore resort. 159,000. **2.** a city near Melbourne in S Victoria, in SE Australia. 40,617. **3.** a town in central Colorado. 12,773.

Bright's′ disease′, *Pathol.* a disease characterized by albuminuria and heightened blood pressure. [1825–35; named after R. BRIGHT]

bright′ wool′, the wool of sheep raised east of the Mississippi River. Cf. **territory wool.** [so called from its shade]

bright·work (brīt′wûrk′), *n.* **1.** polished metal parts, as on a ship or automobile. **2.** *Naut.* all plain or varnished woodwork that is kept scoured on a vessel. [1835–45, *Amer.;* BRIGHT + WORK]

Brig·id (brij′id; *esp. for 1 also* brē′id), *n.* **1. Saint.** Also, **Bride.** A.D. 453–523, Irish abbess: a patron saint of Ireland. **2.** a female given name.

Brig·it (brij′it; *esp. for 1, 2 also* brē′it), *n.* **1.** *Irish Myth.* a goddess of fire, fertility, agriculture, household arts, and wisdom, later associated with St. Brigid. **2. Saint.** See **Brigid, Saint. 3.** a female given name.

Bri·gitte (brē zhēt′; *Eng.* bri zhēt′), *n.* a female given name, French form of **Bridget.**

brig·sail (brig′sāl′; *Naut.* brig′səl), *n. Naut.* a large gaffsail on the mainmast or trysail mast of a brig. [BRIG[1] + SAIL]

brill (bril), *n., pl.* **brills,** (*esp. collectively*) **brill.** a European flatfish, *Scophthalmus rhombus,* closely related to the turbot. [1475–85; of uncert. orig.]

Brill (bril), *n.* **A(braham) A(rden),** 1874–1948, U.S. psychoanalyst and author, born in Austria.

Bril·lat-Sa·va·rin (brē yȧ sȧ vȧ raN′), *n.* **Anthelme** (äN telm′), 1755–1826, French jurist, writer, and gastronome.

bril·liance (bril′yəns), *n.* **1.** great brightness; luster: *the brilliance of a fine diamond.* **2.** excellence or distinction; conspicuous talent, mental ability, etc. **3.** splendor, elegance, or magnificence: *the brilliance of the court of Louis XIV.* **4.** *Optics.* that luminance of a body consisting of its saturation and brightness. [1745–55; BRILLI(ANT) + -ANCE]
—**Syn. 1.** radiance, effulgence, refulgence. **2.** illustriousness, preeminence; genius. —**Ant. 1, 2.** dullness.

bril·lian·cy (bril′yən sē), *n., pl.* **-cies** for 1. **1.** an instance of brilliance: *the brilliancies of Congreve's wit.* **2.** brilliance. [1740–50; BRILLI(ANT) + -ANCY]

bril·liant (bril′yənt), *adj.* **1.** shining brightly; sparkling; glittering; lustrous: *the brilliant lights of the city.* **2.** distinguished; illustrious: *a brilliant performance by a young pianist.* **3.** having or showing great intelligence, talent, quality, etc.: *a brilliant technician.* **4.** strong and clear in tone; vivid; bright: *brilliant blues and greens; the brilliant sound of the trumpets.* **5.** splendid or magnificent: *a brilliant social event.* —*n.* **6.** *Jewelry.* a gem, esp. a diamond, having any of several varieties of the brilliant cut. **7.** *Print.* a size of type about 3½-point. [1675–85; < F *brillant* shining, prp. of *briller* < It *brillare* to glitter (perh. deriv. of an expressive root); see -ANT] —**bril′liant·ly,** *adv.* —**bril′liant·ness,** *n.*
—**Syn. 1.** See **bright.**

bril′liant cut′, *Jewelry.* a cut intended to enhance the brilliance of a gem with the least possible sacrifice of weight, characterized by a form resembling two pyramids set base to base, truncated so as to give a broad table and a very small culet, and having from 18 to 104 facets, 58 being typical. [1705–15] —**bril′liant-cut′,** *adj.*

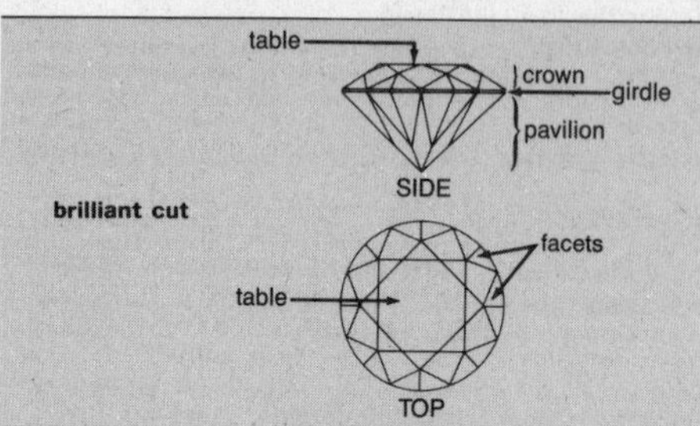

bril·lian·tine (bril′yən tēn′), *n.* **1.** an oily preparation used to make the hair lustrous. **2.** a dress fabric resembling alpaca. [1870–75, *Amer.;* < F *brillantine.* See BRILLIANT, -INE[2]] —**bril′lian·tined′,** *adj.*

Bril·lo (bril′ō), **1.** *Trademark.* a brand of scouring pad of fine, intermeshed steel wool impregnated with cleanser. —*adj.* **2.** (*l.c.*) resembling a Brillo pad, as in wiriness: *a brillo mop of hair.*

Brill's′ disease′, *Pathol.* a relatively mild form of typhus. [named after N. E. *Brill* (1859–1925), American physician]

brim[1] (brim), *n., v.,* **brimmed, brim·ming.** —*n.* **1.** the upper edge of anything hollow; rim; brink: *the brim of a cup.* **2.** a projecting edge: *the brim of a hat.* **3.** margin. —*v.i.* **4.** to be full to the brim. —*v.t.* **5.** to fill to the brim. [1175–1225; ME *brimme* brink, rim (earlier, shore, bank); appar. akin to MHG *brem* (G *Bräme*), ON *barmr* rim, edge] —**brim′less,** *adj.* —**brim′ming·ly,** *adv.*
—**Syn. 1.** See **rim.**

brim[2] (brim), *n., pl.* (*esp. collectively*) **brim,** (*esp. referring to two or more kinds or species*) **brims.** *Southern U.S.* bream[1] (def. 4).

brim·ful (brim′fo͝ol′), *adj.* full to the brim. Also, **brim′full′.** [1520–30; BRIM[1] + -FUL] —**brim′ful′ly,** *adv.* —**brim′ful′ness, brim′full′ness,** *n.*

brim·mer (brim′ər), *n.* a cup, glass, or bowl full to the brim. [1645–55; BRIM[1] + -ER[1]]

brim·stone (brim′stōn′), *n.* **1.** sulfur. **2.** a virago; shrew. [bef. 1150; ME *brinston,* etc., late OE *brynstān.* See BURN[1], STONE] —**brim′ston′y,** *adj.*

brind·ed (brin′did), *adj. Archaic.* brindled. [earlier *brended,* ME *brend, brind* lit., burnt, ptp. of *brennen* BURN[1]]

Brin·di·si (brin′də zē′; *It.* brEn′dē zē), *n.* an Adriatic seaport in SE Apulia, in SE Italy: important Roman city and naval station. 87,420. Ancient, **Brundisium.**

brin·dle (brin′dl), *n.* **1.** a brindled coloring. **2.** a brindled animal. —*adj.* **3.** brindled. [1670–80; back formation from BRINDLED]

brin·dled (brin′dld), *adj.* gray or tawny with darker streaks or spots. [1670–80; alter. of BRINDED, with *-le* perh. from GRIZZLED, SPECKLED, etc.]

brine (brīn), *n., v.,* **brined, brin·ing.** —*n.* **1.** water saturated or strongly impregnated with salt. **2.** a salt and water solution for pickling. **3.** the sea or ocean. **4.** the water of the sea. **5.** *Chem.* any saline solution. —*v.t.* **6.** to treat with or steep in brine. [bef. 1000; ME; OE *brȳne;* c. D *brijn*] —**brine′less,** *adj.* —**brin′er,** *n.* —**brin′ish,** *adj.* —**brin′ish·ness,** *n.*

Brinell′ hard′ness num′ber, *Metall.* a rating obtained from a test (**Brinell′ test′**) to determine the hardness of a metal by pressing a steel ball of a standard size into the metal using a standard force. Also called **Brinell′ num′ber.** *Abbr.:* Bhn [named after J.A. *Brinell* (1849–1925), Swedish engineer]

brine′ shrimp′, a small crustacean, *Artemia salina,* of the order Anostraca, common to saline lakes, including Great Salt Lake in Utah. [1830–40]

bring (bring), *v.t.,* **brought, bring·ing. 1.** to carry, convey, conduct, or cause (someone or something) to come with, to, or toward the speaker: *Bring the suitcase to my house. He brought his brother to my office.* **2.** to cause to come to or toward oneself; attract: *Her scream brought the police. He brought honor to his family by his heroism.* **3.** to cause to occur or exist: *The medication brought instant relief.* **4.** to cause to come into a particular position, state, or effect: *to bring the car to a stop.* **5.** to cause to appear or occur in the mind; evoke or recall: *The letter brought her memories of youth.* **6.** to persuade, convince, compel, or induce: *She couldn't bring herself to sell the painting.* **7.** to sell for; fetch: *These lamps will bring a good price.* **8.** *Law.* to commence: *to bring an action for damages.* **9. bring about,** to accomplish; cause: *Land reform brought about a great change in the lives of the common people.* **10. bring around** or **round, a.** to convince of a belief or opinion; persuade: *I think we can bring him around to agreeing with the plan.* **b.** to restore to consciousness, as after a faint. **c.** to bring as a visitor: *They brought around a new employee this morning.* **11. bring down, a.** to injure, capture, or kill: *He brought down several ducks on his last hunting trip.* **b.** to lessen; reduce: *I won't buy that lamp unless they bring down the price.* **c.** *Slang.* to cause to be in low spirits; depress: *The bad news brought him down.* **12. bring forth, a.** to give birth to; deliver; bear: *to bring forth a son.* **b.** to give rise to; introduce: *to bring forth a proposal for reducing costs.* **13. bring forward, a.** to bring to view; show. **b.** to present for consideration; adduce: *to bring forward an opinion.* **14. bring in, a.** to yield, as profits or income: *My part-time job doesn't bring in much, but I enjoy it.* **b.** to present officially; submit: *The jury brought in its verdict.* **c.** to cause to operate or yield: *They brought in a gusher on his property.* **d.** to present for consideration, approval, etc.; introduce: *She brought in six new members last month.* **15. bring off,** to accomplish, carry out, or achieve (something): *He brought off his speech with ease.* **16. bring on, a.** to cause to happen or exist; bring about: *This incident will surely bring on a crisis.* **b.** to introduce; cause to appear: *Bring on the clowns.* **17. bring out, a.** to expose; reveal. **b.** to make noticeable or conspicuous in a contrast. **c.** to publish, as a book or play. **d.** to introduce officially into society: *to bring out a debutante.* **18. bring to, a.** to bring back to consciousness; revive. **b.** *Naut.* to head (a vessel) close to or into the wind so as to halt. **19. bring up, a.** to care for during childhood; rear. **b.** to introduce or mention for attention, discussion, action, or consideration. **c.** to vomit. **d.** to stop or cause to stop quickly: *to bring up a car at the curb.* **e.** *Naut.* (of a vessel) to cause to halt, as by lowering an anchor or running aground; fetch up. [bef. 950; ME *bringen,* OE *bringan;* c. D *brengen,* G *bringen,* Goth *briggan*] —**bring′er,** *n.*
—**Syn. 1.** transport; lead, guide. BRING, FETCH, TAKE imply conveying or conducting in relation to the place where the speaker is. To BRING is simply to convey or conduct: *Bring it to me. I'm permitted to bring my dog here with me.* It is the opposite of TAKE, which means to convey or conduct away from the place where the speaker is: *Bring it back here. Take it back there.* FETCH means to go, get, and bring back: *Fetch me that bottle.*

bring·down (bring′doun′), *n. Informal.* **1.** a disappointment or disillusionment; letdown: *It was quite a bringdown to find myself running last in the mayoral race.* **2.** anything, as a cutting remark or critical action, that causes depression or deflates one's ego; a put-down. [1940–45; n. use of v. phrase *bring down;* modeled on LETDOWN and causative of COMEDOWN]

brink (bringk), *n.* **1.** the edge or margin of a steep place or of land bordering water. **2.** any extreme edge; verge. **3.** a crucial or critical point, esp. of a situation or state beyond which success or catastrophe occurs: *We were on the brink of war.* [1250–1300; ME *brink* < ON (Dan) *brink,* c. MLG *brink* edge, hillside, ON *brekka* slope, hill] —**brink′less,** *adj.*

brink·man (bringk′mən), *n., pl.* **-men.** a person who is skilled in or practices brinkmanship. Also, **brinks′man.** [1955–60; back formation from BRINKMANSHIP]

brink·man·ship (bringk′mən ship′), *n.* the technique or practice of maneuvering a dangerous situation to the limits of tolerance or safety in order to secure the greatest advantage, esp. by creating diplomatic crises. Also, **brinks·man·ship** (bringks′mən ship′). [1955–60; BRINK + -MANSHIP, with *brink(s)-* by analogy with SPORTSMANSHIP, etc.]

brin·y[1] (brī′nē), *adj.,* **brin·i·er, brin·i·est.** of or like brine; salty: *a briny taste.* [1600–10; BRINE + -Y[1]] —**brin′i·ness,** *n.*

brin·y[2] (brī′nē), *n.* ocean. [1825–35; BRINE + -Y[2]]

bri·o (brē′ō; *It.* brE′ô), *n.* vigor; vivacity. [1725–35; < It < Sp *brío* energy, determination < Celtic **brigos;* cf. OIr *brig* (fem.) power, strength, force, Middle Welsh *bri* (masc.) honor, dignity, authority]

bri·oche (brē′ōsh, -osh; *Fr.* brE ôsh′), *n., pl.* **-och·es** (-ō shiz, -osh iz; *Fr.* -ôsh′). a light, sweet bun or roll made with eggs, yeast, and butter. [1820–30; < F, MF (Norman dial.), equiv. to *bri(er)* to knead (< Gmc; see BREAK) + *-oche* n. suffix]

bri·o·lette (brē′ə let′; *Fr.* brE ô let′), *n., pl.* **-lettes** (-lets′; *Fr.* -let′). any pear-shaped gem having its entire surface cut with triangular facets. [1860–65; < F, var. of *brillolette,* itself alter. (by assoc. with *brillant* diamond) of *brignolette* lit., little dried plum (facetious coinage), equiv. to *brignole* (after *Brignoles* in Provence, where the plums are dried) + *-ette* -ETTE]

bri·o·ny (brī′ə nē), *n., pl.* **-nies.** bryony.

bri·quet (bri ket′), *n., v.t.,* **-quet·ted, -quet·ting.** briquette.

Bri·quet's′ syn′drome (bri kāz′). See **somatization disorder.** [named after Pierre *Briquet* (1796–1881), French physician, who described it in 1859]

bri·quette (bri ket′), *n., v.,* **-quett·ed, -quett·ing.** —*n.* **1.** a small block of compressed coal dust or charcoal used for fuel, esp. in barbecuing. **2.** a molded block of any material. —*v.t.* **3.** to mold into briquettes. [1880–85; < F; see BRICK, -ETTE]

Bris (*Ashk.* bris; *Eng.* bris), *n. Hebrew.* Brith.

bri·sance (bri zäns′; *Fr.* brE zäNs′), *n.* the shattering effect of a high explosive. [1910–15; < F, equiv. to *bris(er)* to break (< Celt; akin to Ir *brisim* (I) break) + *-ance* -ANCE] —**bri·sant** (bri zänt′; *Fr.* brE zäN′), *adj.*

Bris·bane (briz′bān, -bən), *n.* **1. Arthur,** 1864–1936, U.S. journalist. **2.** a seaport in and the capital of Queensland, in E Australia. 942,836.

Bris′bane box′, a broad-leaved evergreen tree, *Tristania conferta,* native to Australia, having a deciduous outer bark. [after BRISBANE, Australia]

bri·sé (brē zā′; *Fr.* brE zā′), *n., pl.* **-sés** (-zāz′; *Fr.* -zā′). a ballet movement in which the dancer jumps off one foot, beats the legs together, and lands on both feet.

[1780–90; < F: lit., broken, ptp. of *briser* to break; see BRISANCE]

brise-bise (brēz′bēz′), *n.* a short curtain, often of lace, hung on the lower section of a window. [1910–15; < F: lit., (it) breaks (the) wind (*brise* 3d sing. pres. of *briser* to break; *bise* north wind)]

brise-so·leil (brēz′sō lā′), *n.* a screen, usually louvered, placed on the outside of a building to shield the windows from direct sunlight. [1940–45; < F: lit., (it) breaks (the) sun (*brise* 3d sing. pres. of *briser* to break; *soleil* sun)]

Bri·sing·a·men (brē′sing ä men′, brē′sēn gä′men), *n. Scand. Myth.* the magic necklace worn by Freya. [< ON: necklace of the *Brisings,* akin to OE *Brōsinga mene;* see MANE]

brisk (brisk), *adj.,* **-er, -est,** *v.* —*adj.* **1.** quick and active; lively: *brisk trading; a brisk walk.* **2.** sharp and stimulating: *brisk weather; brisk wind.* **3.** (of liquors) effervescing vigorously: *brisk cider.* **4.** abrupt; curt: *I was surprised by her rather brisk tone.* —*v.t., v.i.* **5.** to make or become brisk; liven (often fol. by *up*). [1580–90; of uncert. orig.] —**brisk′ly,** *adv.* —**brisk′ness,** *n.* —**Syn. 1.** spry, energetic, alert. —**Ant. 1.** languid.

bris·ket (bris′kit), *n.* **1.** the breast of an animal, or the part of the breast lying next to the ribs. **2.** a cut of meat, esp. beef, from this part. See diag. under **beef.** [1300–50; ME *brusket,* perh. < ON *brjōsk* cartilage]

bris·ling (briz′ling, bris′-), *n.* sprat (def. 1). [1900–05; < Norw; akin to obs. Dan *bretling,* G *Brätling, Breitling*]

bris·tle (bris′əl), *n., v.,* **-tled, -tling.** —*n.* **1.** one of the short, stiff, coarse hairs of certain animals, esp. hogs, used extensively in making brushes. **2.** anything resembling these hairs. —*v.i.* **3.** to stand or rise stiffly, like bristles. **4.** to erect the bristles, as an irritated animal (often fol. by *up*): *The hog bristled up.* **5.** to become rigid with anger or irritation: *The man bristled when I asked him to move.* **6.** to be thickly set or filled with something suggestive of bristles: *The plain bristled with bayonets. The project bristled with difficulties.* **7.** to be visibly roused or stirred (usually fol. by *up*). —*v.t.* **8.** to erect like bristles: *The rooster bristled his crest.* **9.** to furnish with a bristle or bristles. **10.** to make bristly. [bef. 1000; ME *bristel,* equiv. to *brist* (OE *byrst* bristle, c. G *Borste,* ON *burst*) + *-el* dim. suffix] —**bris′tle·less,** *adj.* —**bris′tle·like′,** *adj.*

bris·tle·bird (bris′əl bûrd′), *n.* any of various Australian warblers of the genus *Dasyornis.* [1820–30; BRISTLE + BIRD]

bris′tlecone pine′, a pine, *Pinus aristata,* of the southwestern U.S., bearing short needles crowded into long, thick bundles and cones having scales tipped with a slender, curved spine. Also called **hickory pine.** [1890–95, *Amer.;* BRISTLE + CONE]

bris·tle·mouth (bris′əl mouth′), *n., pl.* (*esp. collectively*) **-mouth,** (*esp. referring to two or more kinds or species*) **-mouths** (-mouthz′, -mouths′). any of several small, deep-sea fishes of the family Gonostomatidae, having numerous sharp, slender teeth covering the jaws. [BRISTLE + MOUTH]

bris·tle·tail (bris′əl tāl′), *n.* any of various wingless insects of the order Thysanura, having long, bristlelike, caudal appendages, comprising the firebrats, silverfish, and machilids. [1700–10; BRISTLE + TAIL[1]]

bris′tle-thighed cur′lew (bris′əl thīd′), an Alaskan curlew, *Numenius tahitiensis,* that winters in Polynesia, having bristlelike feathers on its thighs.

bris·tly (bris′lē), *adj.,* **-tli·er, -tli·est. 1.** covered or rough with bristles. **2.** like or resembling bristles. **3.** easily antagonized; irascible: *a bristly person with few friends.* [1585–95; BRISTLE + -Y[1]] —**bris′tli·ness,** *n.*

bris′tly sarsaparil′la, a coarse plant, *Aralia hispida,* of the ginseng family, of eastern North America, having a loose cluster of small, greenish flowers and black fruit. [1860–65]

Bris·tol (bris′tl), *n.* **1.** a seaport in Avon, in SW England, on the Avon River near its confluence with the Severn estuary. 420,100. **2.** a city in central Connecticut. 57,370. **3.** a city in NE Tennessee, contiguous with but politically independent of Bristol, Virginia. 23,986. **4.** a town in E Rhode Island. 20,128. **5.** a city in SW Virginia. 19,042. **6.** a town in SE Pennsylvania, on the Delaware River. 10,876. **7.** Bristol, Tennessee, and Bristol, Virginia, considered as a unit.

Bris′tol board′, a fine, smooth pasteboard that is sometimes glazed. [1800–10]

Bris′tol Chan′nel, an inlet of the Atlantic, between S Wales and SW England, extending to the mouth of the Severn estuary. 85 mi. (137 km) long.

Bris′tol fash′ion, in good order; trim: *shipshape and Bristol fashion.* [1830–40; after BRISTOL, England]

brit (brit), *n.* **1.** the group of small marine animals forming the food of whalebone whales. **2.** the young of herring and sprat. Also, **britt.** [1595–1605; perh. < Cornish *brȳthel* mackerel; akin to Old Cornish *brȳth,* Welsh *brith* speckled]

Brit (brit), *n. Informal.* Briton (def. 1). [1900–05; by shortening]

Brit., 1. Britain. **2.** British.

Brit·ain (brit′n), *n.* **1.** See **Great Britain. 2.** Britannia (def. 1).

Bri·tan·ni·a (bri tan′ē ə, -tan′yə), *n.* **1.** the ancient Roman name of the island of Great Britain, esp. the S part where the early Roman provinces were. **2.** the British Empire. **3.** *Chiefly Literary.* **a.** Great Britain. **b.** the United Kingdom of Great Britain and Ireland. **4.** the figure of a seated woman with trident and helmet used as a symbolic representation of Great Britain and the British Empire.

Britan′nia met′al, a white alloy of tin, antimony, and copper in varying proportions, sometimes with small amounts of zinc, lead, and bismuth, used for tableware and as an antifriction material. Also, **britan′nia met′al.** [1810–20]

Bri·tan·nic (bri tan′ik), *adj.* **1.** of Britain; British: *Her Britannic Majesty.* **2.** Brythonic. —*n.* **3.** Brythonic. [1635–45; < L *Britannicus.* See BRITANNIA, -IC]

britch·es (brich′iz), *n.* (*used with a plural v.*) breeches. [1880–85]

Brith (*Seph.* brĕt; *Ashk.* bris; *Eng.* bris, brit), *n. Hebrew.* the Jewish rite of circumcising a male child eight days after his birth. Also, **Berith, Brit, Bris.** Cf. **Brith Milah.** [*bərīth* lit., covenant]

Brith Mi·lah (*Seph.* brĕt′ mē lä′; *Ashk.* bris mē′lə, bris′ mē lô′), *Hebrew.* the covenant between God and Abraham with respect to circumcision. Cf. **Brith.** [*bərīth milāh* lit., covenant of circumcision]

Brit·i·cism (brit′ə siz′əm), *n.* a word, idiom, or phrase characteristic of or restricted to British English, esp. as compared with American English, as *lift* compared with *elevator* or *in hospital* with *in the hospital.* Also, **Britishism.** [1865–70, *Amer.;* BRITISH + -ISM, with *-ic* for *-ish* on the model of GALLICISM, etc.]

Brit·ish (brit′ish), *adj.* **1.** of or pertaining to Great Britain or its inhabitants. **2.** used esp. by natives or inhabitants of Great Britain: *In this dictionary, "Brit." is an abbreviation for "British usage."* —*n.* **3.** the people native to or inhabiting Great Britain. **4.** See **British English. 5.** the Celtic language of the ancient Britons. [bef. 900; ME *Brittische,* OE *Bryttisc,* equiv. to *Brytt(as)* Britons + *-isc* -ISH[1]; see BRITON] —**Brit′ish·ly,** *adv.* —**Brit′ish·ness,** *n.*

Brit′ish Amer′ica. See **British North America.**

Brit′ish Antarc′tic Ter′ritory, a British colony in the S Atlantic, comprising the South Shetland Islands, the South Orkney Islands, and Graham Land: formerly dependencies of the Falkland Islands.

Brit′ish Anti-Lew′isite, *Chem.* dimercaprol.

Brit′ish Broad′casting Corpora′tion, the noncommercial British radio and television broadcasting company. *Abbr.:* BBC, B.B.C.

Brit′ish Cameroons′, Cameroons (def. 2).

Brit′ish Colum′bia, a province in W Canada on the Pacific coast. 2,406,212; 366,255 sq. mi. (948,600 sq. km). *Cap.:* Victoria. —**Brit′ish Colum′bian.**

Brit′ish Com′monwealth of Na′tions, former name of the **Commonwealth of Nations.** Also called **Brit′ish Com′monwealth.**

Brit′ish dol′lar, any of several coins formerly issued by the British Empire for use in certain territories, as the Straits dollar or the Hong Kong dollar.

Brit′ish East′ Af′rica, a comprehensive term for the former British territories of Kenya, Uganda, and Tanzania.

Brit′ish Em′pire, a former collective term for the territories under the leadership or control of the British crown, including those in the Commonwealth of Nations and their colonies, protectorates, dependencies, and trusteeships. [1595–1605]

Brit′ish Eng′lish, the English language as spoken and written in Great Britain, esp. in southern England. Also called **British.** [1865–70]

Brit·ish·er (brit′i shər), *n.* a native or inhabitant of Britain. [1820–30, *Amer.;* BRITISH + -ER[1]]

Brit′ish gal′lon, *Chiefly Brit.* See **Imperial gallon.**

Brit′ish Guia′na, former name of **Guyana.**

Brit′ish gum′, *Chem.* dextrin. [1855–60]

Brit′ish Hondu′ras, former name of **Belize** (def. 1). —**Brit′ish Hondu′ran.**

Brit′ish In′dia, a part of India, comprising 17 provinces, that prior to 1947 was subject to British law: now divided among India, Pakistan, and Bangladesh.

Brit′ish In′dian O′cean Ter′ritory, a British colony in the Indian Ocean, consisting of the Chagos Archipelago. 76 sq. mi. (177 sq. km). *Cap.:* Diego Garcia.

Brit′ish Isles′, a group of islands in W Europe: Great Britain, Ireland, the Isle of Man, and adjacent small islands. 53,978,538; 120,592 sq. mi. (312,300 sq. km).

Brit·ish·ism (brit′i shiz′əm), *n.* **1.** Briticism. **2.** any custom, manner, characteristic, or quality peculiar to or associated with the British people. **3.** the aggregate of such qualities regarded as characteristic of a British person: *His cool reserve is just part of his Britishism.* [1880–85; BRITISH + -ISM]

Brit′ish Le′gion, (in Britain) a national social club for veterans of the armed forces. Cf. **American Legion.**

British Library, the national library of Great Britain: part of the British Museum until 1973.

Brit′ish Malay′a, a comprehensive term for the former British possessions on the Malay Peninsula and the Malay Archipelago: now part of Malaysia.

Brit′ish Muse′um, a national depository and museum in London, England, housing important collections in archaeology, art, and natural history.

Brit′ish North′ Amer′ica, 1. Canada. **2.** all parts of the Commonwealth of Nations in or near North America.

Brit′ish North′ Bor′neo, former name of **Sabah.**

Brit′ish Soma′liland, a former British protectorate in E Africa, on the Gulf of Aden: now the N part of Somalia. Former official name, **Somaliland Protectorate.** Cf. **Somalia.**

Brit′ish ther′mal u′nit, *Physics.* the amount of heat required to raise the temperature of 1 lb. (0.4 kg) of water 1°F. *Abbr.:* Btu, BTU, B.t.u., B.T.U., B.th.u. [1875–80]

Brit′ish Vir′gin Is′lands, a British colony comprising several small islands (largest, Tortola) in the West Indies, E of Puerto Rico. 10,500; 67 sq. mi. (174 sq. km). *Cap.:* Road Town.

Brit′ish warm′, a double-breasted overcoat of military cut.

Brit′ish West′ Af′rica, a former comprehensive term for The Gambia, Ghana, Nigeria, Sierra Leone, Togo, and Cameroon.

Brit′ish West′ In′dies, a term formerly used for the possessions of Great Britain in the West Indies. Cf. **West Indies** (def. 2).

Brit·on (brit′n), *n.* **1.** a native or inhabitant of Great Britain, esp. of England. **2.** one of the Celtic people formerly occupying the southern part of the island of Britain. [1250–1300; < ML *Britōn-* (s. of *Britō*); r. ME *Breton* < OF < LL *Brittōnēs* Britons]

britt (brit), *n., pl.* (*esp. collectively*) **britt,** (*esp. referring to two or more kinds or species*) **britts. 1.** a turbot of northeastern Atlantic seas. **2.** brit. [see BRIT]

Brit·ta·ny (brit′n ē), *n.* a region in NW France, on a peninsula between the English Channel and the Bay of Biscay: a former duchy and province. French, **Bretagne.**

brit′tany blue′, a medium greenish blue. Also, **Brit′·tany blue′.** —**brit′ta·ny-blue′,** *adj.*

Brit′tany span′iel, one of a French breed of large spaniels developed as a game pointer, having a reddish-brown and white or orange and white coat. [1930–35]

Brit·ten (brit′n), *n.* **(Edward) Benjamin,** 1913–76, English composer and pianist.

brit·tle (brit′l), *adj.,* **-tler, -tlest,** *n., v.,* **-tled, -tling.** —*adj.* **1.** having hardness and rigidity but little tensile strength; breaking readily with a comparatively smooth fracture, as glass. **2.** easily damaged or destroyed; fragile; frail: *a brittle marriage.* **3.** lacking warmth, sensitivity, or compassion; aloof; self-centered: *a self-possessed, cool, and rather brittle person.* **4.** having a sharp, tense quality: *a brittle tone of voice.* **5.** unstable or impermanent; evanescent. —*n.* **6.** a confection of melted sugar, usually with nuts, brittle when cooled: *peanut brittle.* —*v.i.* **7.** to be or become brittle; crumble. [1350–1400; ME *britel,* equiv. to *brit-* (akin to OE *brysten* fragment) + *-el* adj. suffix] —**brit′tle·ness,** *n.* —**Syn. 1.** fragile. See **frail[1].**

brit·tle·bush (brit′l bo͝osh′), *n.* any of several composite plants of the genus *Encelia,* of desert regions of the southwestern U.S. and Mexico, having alternate leaves and yellow ray flowers with a yellow or purple center. [1905–10, *Amer.;* BRITTLE + BUSH[1], so called from the texture of its leaves]

brit′tle fern′, a fern, *Cystopteris fragilis,* of rocky, wooded areas throughout North America, having grayish-green fronds and brittle stalks. Also called **bottle fern.**

brit′tle star′, any echinoderm of the class Ophiuroidea, having the body composed of a central, rounded disk from which radiate long, slender, fragile arms. Also, **brit′tle·star′.** Also called **serpent star.** [1835–45]

Brit·ton (brit′n), *n.* **Nathaniel Lord,** 1859–1934, U.S. botanist.

Brit·ton·ic (bri ton′ik), *adj.* Brythonic. [< LL *Brittōn(ēs)* (see BRITON) + -IC]

Brix′ scale′, *Chem.* a graduated scale, used on a hydrometer, that indicates the weight of sugar per volume of solution at a given temperature. [1895–1900; named after A. F. W. *Brix*, 19th-century German inventor]

Br′no (bʀ′nô; *Eng.* bûr′nō), *n.* a city in S Moravia, in the SE Czech Republic: former capital of Moravia. 390,000. German, **Brünn.**

Br′no chair′, an armchair designed by Ludwig Mies van der Rohe in 1930, having a cantilevered frame of chromium-plated or stainless steel composed of two interlocking parts, one forming the legs and arms and the other the seat and back frame, with the back and seat lightly upholstered and usually covered with leather. [orig. created for a house in Brno designed by Mies]

bro (brō, bru), *n., pl.* **bros.** *Slang.* **1.** brother. **2.** friend; pal; buddy. [1830–40; reduced form of BROTHER]

bro., *pl.* **bros.** brother. Also, **Bro.**

broach (brōch), *n.* **1.** *Mach.* an elongated, tapered, serrated cutting tool for shaping and enlarging holes. **2.** a spit for roasting meat. **3.** a gimlet for tapping casks. **4.** (in a lock) a pin receiving the barrel of a key. **5.** Also, **broach′ spire′.** *Archit.* an octagonal spire rising directly from a tower without any intervening feature. **6.** *Masonry.* a pointed tool for the rough dressing of stone. **7.** brooch. —*v.t.* **8.** to enlarge and finish with a broach. **9.** to mention or suggest for the first time: *to broach a subject.* **10.** to draw (beer, liquor, etc.), as by tapping: *to broach beer from a keg.* **11.** to tap or pierce. **12.** *Masonry.* to shape or dress (a block of stone). —*v.i.* **13.** *Naut.* (of a sailing vessel) to veer to windward. **14.** to break the surface of water; rise from the sea, as a fish or a submarine. [1175–1225; (n.) ME *broche* < AF, OF < VL **brocca* spike, horn, tap of a cask (ML *broca*), n. use of fem. of L adj. *brocc(h)us* projecting (said of teeth); (v.) ME *brochen* < OF *broch(i)er,* deriv. of the n.] —**broach′er,** *n.*
—**Syn. 8.** introduce, propose, bring up, submit, advance.

broad (brôd), *adj.,* **-er, -est,** *adv., n.* —*adj.* **1.** of great breadth: *The river was too broad to swim across.* **2.** measured from side to side: *The desk was three feet broad.* **3.** of great extent; large: *the broad expanse of ocean.* **4.** widely diffused; open; full: *We awoke to broad daylight.* **5.** not limited or narrow; of extensive range or scope: *A modern doctor must have a broad knowledge of medicine.* **6.** liberal; tolerant: *A broad interpretation of the law tempers justice with mercy.* **7.** main or general: *the broad outlines of a subject.* **8.** plain or clear: *Her remark was a broad hint of her feelings.* **9.** bold; plain-spoken. **10.** indelicate; indecent: *He smirked at the broad joke.* **11.** (of conversation) rough; countrified. **12.** unconfined; free; unrestrained: *It was a hilarious evening of broad mirth.* **13.** (of pronunciation) strongly dialectal: *He wore kilts and had a broad Scots accent.* **14.** *Phonet.* (of a transcription) using one basic symbol to represent each phoneme. **15. broad a,** the *a*-sound (ä) when used in lieu of the more common *a*-sound (a) in such words as *half, can't,* and *laugh.* **16. broad on the beam,** *Naut.* bearing 90° to the heading of a vessel. **17. broad on the bow,** *Naut.* bearing 45° to the heading of a vessel. **18. broad on the quarter,** *Naut.* bearing 135° to the heading of a vessel. —*adv.* **19.** fully: *He was broad awake.* —*n.* **20.** the broad part of anything. **21.** *Slang.* **a.** *Usually Offensive.* a woman. **b.** a promiscuous woman. **22.** Often, **broads.** *Motion Pictures, Television.* an incandescent or fluorescent lamp used as a general source of light in a studio. **23.** a gold coin of England and Scotland, issued by James I and Charles I and equal to 20 shillings. Cf. **carolus, jacobus.** [bef. 1000; ME *bro(o)d,* OE *brād;* c. D *breed,* G *breit,* ON *breithr,* Goth *braiths*] —**broad′ish,** *adj.* —**broad′ly,** *adv.*
—**Syn. 1.** See **wide. 3.** extensive, ample, vast. **5.** liberal, open. **10.** gross. —**Ant. 1.** narrow.

Broad (brôd), *n.* **C(harlie) D(unbar),** 1887–1971, English philosopher.

broad′ ar′row, 1. a mark in the shape of a broad arrowhead, placed upon British government property. **2.** *Archery.* an arrow having an expanded head. **3.** *Heraldry.* pheon. [1350–1400; ME *brod arwe*]

broad arrow (def. 1)

broad·ax (brôd′aks′), *n., pl.* **-ax·es** (-ak′siz). **1.** an ax for hewing timber. **2.** an ax with a broad head, used as a battle-ax. Also, **broad′axe′.** [bef. 1000; ME *brodax,* OE *brādæx.* See BROAD, AX]

broad·band (brôd′band′), *adj.* *Telecommunications.* of, pertaining to, or responsive to a continuous, wide range of frequencies. Cf. **sharp** (def. 23). [1900–05; BROAD + BAND[2]]

broad-based (brôd′bāst′), *adj.* involving participation or support by a broad spectrum of things or people: *The senator had a broad-based campaign.* [*broad base* + -ED[3]]

broad′ bean′. See **fava bean.** [1775–85]

broad·bill (brôd′bil′), *n.* **1.** any of several small, often brightly colored passerine birds of the family Eurylaimidae, of the Old World tropics, having a broad, flattened bill. **2.** any of various birds with a broad bill, as the scaup duck, shoveler, and spoonbill. [1625–35; BROAD + BILL[2]]

broad·brim (brôd′brim′), *n.* **1.** a hat with a broad brim, as that worn by Quakers. **2.** (*cap.*) *Slang.* a Quaker. [1680–90; BROAD + BRIM[1]]

broad-brush (brôd′brush′), *adj.* characterized by sweeping comprehensiveness with little attention to details: *a broad-brush approach to reform.* [1965–70]

broad·cast (brôd′kast′, -käst′), *v.,* **-cast** or **-cast·ed, -cast·ing,** *n., adj., adv.* —*v.t.* **1.** to transmit (programs) from a radio or television station. **2.** to speak, perform, sponsor, or present on a radio or television program: *The President will broadcast his message on all stations tonight.* **3.** to cast or scatter abroad over an area, as seed in sowing. **4.** to spread widely; disseminate: *She broadcast the good news all over town.* **5.** to indicate unwittingly to another (one's next action); telegraph: *He broadcast his punch and the other man was able to parry it.* —*v.i.* **6.** to transmit programs or signals from a radio or television station. **7.** to make something known widely; disseminate something. **8.** to speak, perform, sponsor, or present all or part of a radio or television program: *The Boston Symphony Orchestra broadcasts every Saturday on our local station.* —*n.* **9.** something that is broadcast. **10.** a single radio or television program. **11.** the broadcasting of radio or television messages, speeches, etc. **12.** a single period of broadcasting. **13.** a method of sowing by scattering seed. —*adj.* **14.** (of programs) transmitted from a radio or television station. **15.** of or pertaining to broadcasting. **16.** cast abroad or all over an area, as seed scattered widely. —*adv.* **17.** so as to reach the greatest number of people by radio or television: *The vital news was sent broadcast to inform the entire nation.* **18.** so as to be cast abroad over an area: *seed sown broadcast.* [1760–70; orig., BROAD (adv.) + *cast,* ptp. of CAST[1]]

broad·cast·er (brôd′kas′tər, -kä′stər), *n.* **1.** a person or thing that broadcasts. **2.** a person or organization, as a network or station, that broadcasts radio or television programs. [1920–25; BROADCAST + -ER[1]]

broad·cast·ing (brôd′kas′ting, -kä′sting), *n.* **1.** the act of transmitting speech, music, visual images, etc., as by radio or television. **2.** radio or television as a business or profession: *She's training for a career in broadcasting.* [1920–25; BROADCAST + -ING[1]]

broad′cast jour′nalism, journalism as practiced in radio and television. [1965–70] —**broad′cast jour′·nalist.**

Broad′ Church′, pertaining or belonging to a party in the Anglican Church emphasizing a liberal interpretation of ritual. Cf. **High Church, Low Church.** —**Broad′ Church′man.**

broad·cloth (brôd′klôth′, -kloth′), *n.* *Textiles.* **1.** a closely woven dress-goods fabric of cotton, rayon, silk, or a mixture of these fibers, having a soft, mercerized finish and resembling poplin. **2.** a woolen or worsted fabric constructed in a plain or twill weave, having a compact texture and lustrous finish. **3.** any fabric woven on a wide loom. [1400–50; late ME *brode clothe.* See BROAD, CLOTH]

broad·en (brôd′n), *v.i., v.t.* to become or make broad. [1720–30; BROAD + -EN[1]]
—**Syn.** extend, expand, enlarge, widen; enlighten, inform, educate; sophisticate.

broad·faced (brôd′fāst′), *adj.* having a broad, wide face. [1600–10]

broad′ gauge′, *Railroads.* See under **gauge** (def. 13). Also, *esp. in technical use,* **broad′ gage′.** [1835–45]

broad-gauge (brôd′gāj′), *adj.* **1.** *Railroads.* of or pertaining to equipment designed for a railroad having track of a broad gauge: *broad-gauge rolling stock.* **2.** of wide scope, application, or experience: *broad-gauge efforts to improve the health of our citizens.* Also, **broad-gauged.** [1835–45, for an earlier sense]

broad′ glass′. See **cylinder glass.** [1670–80]

broad′ hatch′et, a hatchet with a broad cutting edge. Also called **hand ax.**

broad·head (brôd′hed′), *n.* **1.** a flat, triangular, steel arrowhead with sharp edges. **2.** an arrow having such an arrowhead. [BROAD + HEAD]

broad′ jump′, *Track.* See **long jump.** [1870–1875]

broad-jump (brôd′jump′), *v.i.* *Track.* long-jump.

broad′ jump′er, *Track.* See **long jumper.**

broad·leaf (brôd′lēf′), *n., pl.* **-leaves** (-lēvz′), *adj.* —*n.* **1.** any of several cigar tobaccos having broad leaves. —*adj.* **2.** broad-leaved. [1750–60; back formation from *broadleafed.* See BROAD, LEAF, -ED[3]]

broad-leaved (brôd′lēvd′), *adj.* *Bot.* of or pertaining to plants having broad or relatively broad leaves, rather than needles. Also, **broadleaf, broadleafed, broad-leafed** (brôd′lēft′). [1545–55]

broad′-leaved bot′tle tree′. See under **bottle tree.**

broad′-leaved ma′ple, a maple, *Acer macrophyllum,* of western North America, characterized by dark green, thickened leaves that may reach 12 in. (30 cm) or more in width. [1885–90, *Amer.*]

broad·loom (brôd′lo͞om′), *adj.* **1.** of or pertaining to rugs or carpets woven on a wide loom. —*n.* **2.** See **broadloom carpet.** [1920–25; BROAD + LOOM[1]]

broad′loom car′pet, any carpet woven on a wide loom and not having seams, esp. one wider than 54 in. (137 cm). [1920–25]

broad-mind·ed (brôd′mīn′did), *adj.* free from prejudice or bigotry; unbiased; liberal; tolerant. [1590–1600] —**broad′-mind′ed·ly,** *adv.* —**broad′-mind′ed·ness,** *n.*
—**Syn.** open-minded, catholic, flexible; permissive. —**Ant.** narrow-minded, biased, bigoted, intolerant.

broad·ness (brôd′nis), *n.* the state or character of being broad: *the broadness of the ship; the broadness of his jokes.* [1350–1400; ME; see BROAD, -NESS]

broad′ reach′, *Naut.* See under **reach** (def. 27).

Broads (brôdz), *n.* **The,** (*used with a plural v.*) a low-lying region in E England, in Norfolk and Suffolk: bogs and marshy lakes.

broad′ seal′, the official seal of a country or state. [1530–40]

broad·side (brôd′sīd′), *n., adv., v.,* **-sid·ed, -sid·ing.** —*n.* **1.** the whole side of a ship above the water line, from the bow to the quarter. **2.** *Navy.* **a.** all the guns that can be fired from one side of a warship. **b.** a simultaneous discharge of all the guns on one side of a warship. **3.** any strong or comprehensive attack, as by criticism. **4.** Also called **broad·sheet** (brôd′shēt′). **a.** a sheet of paper printed on one or both sides, as for distribution or posting. **b.** any printed advertising circular. **5.** any broad surface or side, as of a house. **6.** Also called **broad′side bal′lad.** a song, chiefly in 16th- and 17th-century England, written on a topical subject, printed on broadsides, and sung in public, as on a street corner, by a professional balladeer. —*adv.* **7.** with the side, esp. with the broader side, facing toward a given point or object: *The truck hit the fence broadside.* **8.** in a wide-ranging manner; at random: *to attack the President's policies broadside.* —*v.i.* **9.** to proceed or go broadside. **10.** to fire a broadside or broadsides. —*v.t.* **11.** to collide with or run into the side of (a vehicle, object, person, etc.): *We got broadsided on the freeway.* **12.** to make concerted verbal attacks on: *The President was broadsided by the opposition.* [1565–75; BROAD + SIDE[1]]

broad-spec·trum (brôd′spek′trəm), *adj.* **1.** *Pharm.* noting an antibiotic effective against a wide range of organisms. **2.** having a wide range of uses. [1950–55]

broad·sword (brôd′sôrd′, -sōrd′), *n.* a sword having a straight, broad, flat blade. [bef. 1000; ME *brood swerd,* OE *brād sweord.* See BROAD, SWORD]

broad·tail (brôd′tāl′), *n.* the wavy, moirélike fur or pelt of a young or stillborn Karakul lamb. Cf. **Karakul** (def. 1), **Persian lamb** (def. 2). [1890–95; BROAD + TAIL[1]]

broa·dus (brō′dəs), *n., pl.* **-dus·es.** *Coastal South Carolina and Georgia.* something given as a bonus; lagniappe. Also, **brotus.** [1905–10; akin to Jamaican, Guyanan E *braata* (appar. < AmerSp *barata* bargain, ult. deriv. of Sp (now obs.) *baratar* to negotiate, barter; see BARRATOR, BARTER); orig. of vowel and final *s* uncert.]

Broad′view Heights′, a town in N Ohio. 10,920.

Broad·way (brôd′wā′), *n.* **1.** a street in New York City, famous for its theaters, restaurants, and bright lights. **2.** the theater district located on or near this street, esp. as the center of the professional or commercial theater in the U.S. —*adj.* **3.** (of a play, theatrical performance, etc.) pertaining to, suitable for, or produced in the commercial theater, esp. on Broadway: *a Broadway show.* **4.** acting or working on Broadway: *a Broadway producer; a Broadway star.* **5.** characteristic of or frequenting the theater district on Broadway. **6.** garish; tawdry. —**Broad′way·ite′,** *n.*

broad·wife (brôd′wīf′), *n., pl.* **-wives.** *U.S. Hist.* a female slave whose husband was owned by another master. [BROAD (adv.: far) + WIFE]

broad′-winged hawk′ (brôd′wingd′), an American hawk, *Buteo platypterus,* dark brown above and white barred with rufous below. [1805–15, *Amer.*]

brob (brob), *n.* a wedge-shaped spike for securing an end of a timber butting against the side of another. [1870–75; of uncert. orig.]

Brob·ding·nag (brob′ding nag′), *n.* the region in Swift's *Gulliver's Travels* where everything was of enormous size.

Brob·ding·nag·i·an (brob′ding nag′ē ən), *adj.* **1.** of huge size; gigantic; tremendous. —*n.* **2.** an inhabitant of Brobdingnag. **3.** a being of tremendous size; giant. [BROBDINGNAG + -IAN]

Bro·ca (brō′kə; *Fr.* bʀô ka′), *n.* **Paul** (pôl), 1824–80, French surgeon and anthropologist.

bro·cade (brō kād′), *n., v.,* **-cad·ed, -cad·ing.** —*n.* **1.** fabric woven with an elaborate design, esp. one having a raised overall pattern. —*v.t.* **2.** to weave with a raised design or figure. [1555–65; earlier *brocado* < Sp < It *broccato* embossed (fabric), ptp. of *broccare,* deriv. of *brocco* twisted thread, shoot < LL; see BROACH]

Bro′ca's apha′sia, *Pathol.* a type of aphasia caused by a lesion in Broca's area of the brain, characterized by misarticulated speech and lack of grammatical morphemes. Also called **motor aphasia.** [1955–60; after P. BROCA]

Bro′ca's ar′ea, *Anat.* a cerebral area, usually in the left inferior frontal gyrus, associated with the movements necessary for speech production. Also called **Bro′·ca's gy′rus, Bro′ca's convolu′tion.** [1900–05; after P. BROCA]

broc·a·tel (brok′ə tel′, brō′kə-), *n.* **1.** a brocade in which the design is woven in high relief. **2.** an ornamental marble with variegated coloring, found esp. in Italy and Spain. Also, **broc′a·telle′.** [1660–70; < F *brocatelle,* late MF *brocatel* < It *broccatello,* equiv. to *broccat(o)* (see BROCADE) + *-ello* dim. suffix]

broc·co·li (brok′ə lē, brok′lē), *n.* a form of a cultivated cruciferous plant, *Brassica oleracea botrytis,* whose leafy stalks and clusters of usually green buds are eaten as a vegetable. Cf. **cauliflower.** [1690–1700; < It, pl. of *broccolo,* equiv. to *brocc(o)* sprout (< LL; see BROACH) + *-olo* dim. suffix]

broc′coli rabe′ (räb), a plant, *Brassica rapa ruvo,* of which the slightly bitter, dark-green leaves and clustered flower buds are eaten as a vegetable. Also, **broc′·coli raab′** (räb), **broc′coli rab′** (räb). Also called **Italian turnip, raab, turnip broccoli.** [perh. alter. of It *broccoli di rapa* flowering tops of the turnip]

broch (*Scot.* brokh, brukh), *n.* a circular stone tower built around the beginning of the Christian era, having an inner and an outer wall, found on the Orkney Islands, Shetland Islands, the Hebrides, and the mainland of Scotland. [1645–55; Scots, metathetic var. of BURGH]

bro·chan·tite (brō shan′tīt), *n.* a mineral, hydrous

CONCISE ETYMOLOGY KEY: <, descended or borrowed from; >, whence; b., blend of, blended; c., cognate with; cf., compare; deriv., derivative; equiv., equivalent; imit., imitative; obl., oblique; r., replacing; s., stem; sp., spelling, spelled; resp., respelling, respelled; trans., translation; ?, origin unknown; *, unattested; ‡, probably earlier than. See the full key inside the front cover.

copper sulfate, $Cu_4(OH)_6SO_4$, occurring in green fibrous masses and similar in physical properties to antlerite: formerly a major ore of copper. [1860–65; named after A. *Brochant* de Villiers (1773–1840), French mineralogist; see -ITE[1]]

broche (brōsh), *n.* (in weaving tapestries) a device on which the filling yarn is wound, used as a shuttle in passing through the shed of the loom to deposit the yarn. [1880–85; < F: spindle, a pointed instrument; see BROACH]

bro·ché (brō shā′; *Fr.* bʀô shā′), *adj., n., pl.* **-chés** (-shāz′; *Fr.* -shā′). —*adj.* **1.** woven with a pattern; brocaded. —*n.* **2.** a pinstripe woven in the warp direction of fabric used in the manufacture of clothing. [1470–80; < F, ptp. of *brocher* to emboss (linen), weave (cloth) with a figure. See BROACH, BROCADE]

bro·chette (brō shet′; *Fr.* bʀô shet′), *n., pl.* **-chettes** (-shets′; *Fr.* -shet′). **1.** a skewer, for use in cookery. **2. en brochette** (en, on; *Fr.* äɴ), on a small spit or skewer: *lamb cubes en brochette.* [1705–10; < F; OF *brochete.* See BROACH, -ETTE]

bro·chure (brō sho͝or′, -shûr′), *n.* a pamphlet or leaflet. [1755–65; < F, deriv. of *brocher* to stitch (a book). See BROACH, -URE]

brock (brok), *n.* a European badger. [bef. 1000; ME *brok,* OE *broc* badger < Celt; cf. Ir, ScotGael *broc,* Welsh *broch*]

brock·age (brok′ij), *n. Numis.* a defect or fault imposed on a coin during its minting. [1875–80; *brock* fragment (ME *brok,* OE *broc;* akin to BREAK) + -AGE]

Brock·en (brok′ən; *Ger.* bʀôk′ən), *n.* a mountain in N central Germany: the highest peak in the Harz Mountains. 3745 ft. (1140 m).

Brock′en bow′ (bō), anticorona. [so called from frequent observation of the phenomenon by individuals standing on the BROCKEN at sunset]

Brock′en spec′ter, an optical phenomenon sometimes occurring at high altitudes when the image of an observer placed between the sun and a cloud is projected on the cloud as a greatly magnified shadow. [1920–25; see BROCKEN BOW]

brock·et (brok′it), *n.* **1.** any of several small, red, South American deer of the genus *Mazama,* having short, unbranched antlers. **2.** the male red deer in the second year, with the first growth of straight horns. [1375–1425; late ME *broket* < AF *broquet,* equiv. to *broque* horn (ML *broca;* see BROACH) + *-et* -ET]

Brock·ton (brok′tən), *n.* a city in E Massachusetts. 95,172.

Brock·ville (brok′vil), *n.* a city in SE Ontario, in S Canada. 19,896.

Bro·cot′ escape′ment (brə kō′, brō′kō), *Horol.* a type of anchor escapement. [named after Achille *Brocot* (d. 1878), French horologist]

Brod·er·ick (brod′ər ik, brod′rik), *n.* a male given name.

bro·de·rie an·glaise (brō′də rē′ äng glāz′, -glez′; *Fr.* bʀôdᵊ ʀē äɴ glez′), fine white needlework done on fine cloth, typically on eyelet. Also, **broderie′ Anglaise′.** Also called **Madeira embroidery.** [1850–55; < F: lit., English embroidery]

bro·di·ae·a (brō′dē ē′ə), *n.* any of several plants belonging to the genus *Brodiaea,* of the amaryllis family, native to western North America, having grasslike basal leaves and clusters of usually purplish flowers. [< NL (1810), named after James *Brodie* (1744–1824), Scottish botanist; see -AEA]

bro·die (brō′dē), *n.* (*sometimes cap.*) *Slang.* **1.** a suicidal or daredevil leap; wild dive: *to do a brodie from a high ledge.* **2.** a complete failure; flop. **3.** a severe vehicular skid. **4.** a sharp reversal in a vehicle's direction by sudden application of the brakes and wrenching of the steering wheel. [after Steve *Brodie,* who claimed that he jumped from the Brooklyn Bridge in 1886]

bro·gan (brō′gən), *n.* a heavy, sturdy shoe, esp. an ankle-high work shoe. [< Ir *brógán,* dim. of *bróg* shoe; see BROGUE[2]]

Bro·glie (brō glē′, brō′glē, broi; *Fr.* bʀô glē′), *n.* **Louis Vic·tor de** (lwē vēk tôʀ′ də). See **de Broglie, Louis Victor.**

brogue[1] (brōg), *n.* **1.** an Irish accent in the pronunciation of English. **2.** any strong regional accent. [1680–90; perh. special use of BROGUE[2]] —**bro′guer·y,** *n.*

brogue[2] (brōg), *n.* **1.** a durable, comfortable, low-heeled shoe, often having decorative perforations and a wing tip. **2.** a coarse, usually untanned leather shoe once worn in Ireland and Scotland. **3.** brogan. [1580–90; < Ir *brōg* shoe, OIr *brōce;* c. L. *brācae* trousers < Gaulish; see BREECH]

brogue[3] (brōg), *n. Scot.* a fraud; trick; prank. [1530–40; of uncert. orig.]

broi·der (broi′dər), *v.t.* to embroider. [1400–50; late ME, var. of *browder,* ME *broide(n), browde(n)* (ptp., taken as inf. of BRAID[1]) + -ER[6]] —**broi′der·er,** *n.* —**broi′der·y,** *n.*

broil[1] (broil), *v.t.* **1.** to cook by direct heat, as on a gridiron over the heat or in an oven under the heat; grill: *to broil a steak.* **2.** to scorch; make very hot. —*v.i.* **3.** to be subjected to great heat; become broiled. **4.** to burn with impatience, annoyance, etc. —*n.* **5.** the act or state of broiling; state of being broiled. **6.** something broiled, esp. meat: *She ordered a beef broil and salad.* [1300–50; ME *brulen, brolyn, broillen* < AF *broill(i)er, broil(l)er,* OF *brusler, brul(l)er* to burn (F *brûler*), a conflation of the verbs represented by OF *bruir* to burn (< Frankish **brōjan;* cf. MHG *brü(ej)en,* G *brühen* to scald) and *usler* < L *ustulāre* to scorch] —**broil′ing·ly,** *adv.*

broil[2] (broil), *n.* **1.** an angry quarrel or struggle; disturbance; tumult: *a violent broil over who was at fault.* —*v.i.* **2.** to quarrel; brawl. [1400–50; late ME *broylen* to present in disorder, quarrel < AF, OF *broiller* to jumble together < Gallo-Rom **brodiculāre,* equiv. to **brod-* (< Gmc; see BROTH, BREWIS) + LL *-iculāre* v. suffix] —**broil′ing·ly,** *adv.*

broil·er (broi′lər), *n.* **1.** any device for broiling meat or fish; a grate, pan, or compartment in a stove for broiling. **2.** a young chicken suitable for broiling. [1350–1400; ME; see BROIL[1], -ER[1]]

bro·kage (brō′kij), *n. Archaic.* brokerage. [1350–1400; ME < AF *brocage;* see BROKER, -AGE]

broke (brōk), *v.* **1.** a pt. of **break. 2.** *Nonstandard.* a pp. of **break. 3.** *Archaic.* a pp. of **break.** —*adj.* **4.** without money; penniless. **5.** bankrupt. **6. go broke, a.** to become destitute of money or possessions. **b.** to go bankrupt: *In that business people are forever going broke.* **7. go for broke,** to exert oneself or employ one's resources to the utmost. —*n.* **8.** *Papermaking.* paper unfit for sale; paper that is to be repulped. **9. brokes,** wool of poor quality taken from the neck and belly of sheep. [1655–65 (adj.); 1875–80 (n.)]
—**Syn. 4, 5.** insolvent, destitute, impoverished.

bro·ken (brō′kən), *v.* **1.** pp. of **break.** —*adj.* **2.** reduced to fragments; fragmented. **3.** ruptured; torn; fractured. **4.** not functioning properly; out of working order. **5.** *Meteorol.* (of sky cover) being more than half, but not totally, covered by clouds. Cf. **scattered** (def. 4). **6.** changing direction abruptly: *The fox ran in a broken line.* **7.** fragmentary or incomplete: *a broken ton of coal weighing 1,500 pounds.* **8.** infringed or violated: *A broken promise is a betrayal of trust.* **9.** interrupted, disrupted, or disconnected: *After the phone call he returned to his broken sleep.* **10.** weakened in strength, spirit, etc.: *His broken health was due to alcoholism.* **11.** tamed, trained, or reduced to submission: *The horse was broken to the saddle.* **12.** imperfectly spoken, as language: *She still speaks broken English.* **13.** spoken in a halting or fragmentary manner, as under emotional strain: *He uttered a few broken words of sorrow.* **14.** disunited or divided: *Divorce results in broken families.* **15.** not smooth; rough or irregular: *We left the plains and rode through broken country.* **16.** ruined; bankrupt: *the broken fortunes of his family.* **17.** *Papermaking, Print.* a quantity of paper of less than 500 or 1000 sheets. —**bro′ken·ly,** *adv.* —**bro′ken·ness,** *n.*

Bro′ken Ar′row, a town in NE Oklahoma. 35,761.

bro·ken-check (brō′kən chek′), *n. Textiles.* a check pattern in which the rectangular shapes are slightly irregular.

bro′ken chord′, *Music.* arpeggio.

bro′ken coal′, anthracite in pieces ranging from 4 to 2½ in. (11 to 6.5 cm) in extreme dimension; the largest commercial size, larger than egg coal.

bro·ken-down (brō′kən doun′), *adj.* **1.** shattered or collapsed, as with age; infirm. **2.** having given way with use or age; out of working order: *a broken-down chair.* [1810–20]

bro′ken field′. See **open field.** [1895–1900, *Amer.*]

bro·ken-field (brō′kən fēld′), *adj. Football.* performed, as by a ball-carrier, in a wide-open area covered by few defensive players, as opposed to the heavily trafficked area near the line of scrimmage. [1920–25, *Amer.*]

bro′ken heart′, despair; disillusionment; devastating sorrow, esp. from disappointment in love. [1825–35]

bro′ken·heart′ed (brō′kən här′tid), *adj.* burdened with great sorrow, grief, or disappointment. [1520–30] —**bro′ken·heart′ed·ly,** *adv.* —**bro′ken·heart′ed·ness,** *n.*
—**Syn.** heartsick, heartbroken, despondent, dejected.

Bro′ken Hill′, 1. a city in W New South Wales, in SE Australia: mining center. 26,913. **2.** former name of **Kabwe.**

bro′ken ice′, *Oceanog.* sea ice that covers from 50 to 80 percent of the surface of water in any particular area.

bro′ken line′, 1. a discontinuous line or series of line segments, as a series of dashes, or a figure made up of line segments meeting at oblique angles. **2.** a highway marking consisting of a series of disconnected line segments painted between lanes of a roadway, indicating that crossing from one to the other is permissible.

bro′ken lot′. See **odd lot.**

bro′ken ped′iment, *Archit.* a pediment, as over a doorway or window, having its raking cornice interrupted at the crown or apex. See illus. under **pediment.**

bro′ken play′, *Football.* an improvised offensive play that results when the originally planned play has failed to be executed properly.

bro′ken twill′ weave′, a twill weave in which the direction of the diagonal produced by the weft threads is reversed after no more than two passages of the weft.

bro′ken wa′ter, *Oceanog.* a patch of water whose surface is rippled or choppy, usually surrounded by relatively calm water.

bro′ken wind′ (wind), *Vet. Pathol.* heave (def. 26). [1745–55] —**bro′ken-wind′ed,** *adj.*

bro·ker (brō′kər), *n.* **1.** an agent who buys or sells for a principal on a commission basis without having title to the property. **2.** a person who functions as an intermediary between two or more parties in negotiating agreements, bargains, or the like. **3.** stockbroker. —*v.t.* **4.** to act as a broker for: *to broker the sale of a house.* —*v.i.* **5.** to act as a broker. [1350–1400; ME *broco(u)r* < AF *broco(u)r, abrocour* middleman, wine merchant; cf. OPr *abrocador,* perh. based on Sp *alboroque* gift or drink concluding a transaction (< Ar *al-burūk* the gift, gratuity), with *-ador* < L *-ātōr-* -ATOR] —**bro′ker·ship′,** *n.*

bro·ker·age (brō′kər ij), *n.* **1.** Also, **bro′ker·ing.** the business of a broker. **2.** the commission of a broker. [1425–75; late ME; see BROKER, -AGE]

bro′kered conven′tion, *U.S. Politics.* a party convention in which many delegates are pledged to favorite sons who use their blocs of votes to bargain with leading candidates who lack a majority of delegate support. Cf. **open convention.**

brol·ga (brol′gə), *n.* a large Australian crane, *Grus rubicunda,* with silvery-gray plumage and a red patch on the head, noted for its elaborate courtship dance. Also called **native companion.** [1895–1900; < Kamilaroi or Yuwaalaraay (Australian Aboriginal language spoken near Lightning Ridge, N New South Wales) *burralga*]

brol·ly (brol′ē), *n., pl.* **-lies.** *Brit. Informal.* an umbrella. [1870–75; alter. of (UM)BRELL(A) + -Y[2]]

brom-, *Chem.* var. of **bromo-** before a vowel.

bro·mal (brō′mal), *n. Pharm.* an oily, colorless liquid, CBr_3CHO, used in medicine chiefly as an anodyne and hypnotic. Also called **tribromoacetaldehyde.** [1870–75; BROM- + -AL[3]]

bro·mate (brō′māt), *n., v.,* **-mat·ed, -mat·ing.** *Chem.* —*n.* **1.** a salt of bromic acid. —*v.t.* **2.** to treat with bromine; brominate. [1830–40; BROM(IC) + -ATE[2]]

bro·ma·ti·um (brō mā′shē əm, -shəm), *n., pl.* **-ti·a** (-shē ə, -shə). any of the swollen hyphal tips of certain fungi, on which ants can feed. [(< NL) < Gk *brōmátion,* equiv. to *brōmat-,* s. of *brôma* food, meat + *-ion* dim. suffix]

Brom·berg (brom′bûrg; *Ger.* bʀôm′beʀk), *n.* German name of **Bydgoszcz.**

brome·grass (brōm′gras′, -gräs′), *n.* any of numerous grasses of the genus *Bromus,* having flat blades and open clusters of flower spikelets. Also called **brome** (brōm), **chess.** [1750–60; < NL *Brom(us)* genus name (< Gk *brómos* oats) + GRASS]

bro·me·lain (brō′mə lən, -lān′), *n. Biochem.* an enzyme, found in pineapple, that breaks down protein and is used as a meat tenderizer. Cf. **papain.** [1890–95; appar. *bromel(in)* an earlier name for the enzyme (*Bromel(ia)* a genus that formerly included the pineapple (see BROMELIAD) + -IN[2]) + (PAP)AIN]

bro·me·li·ad (brō mē′lē ad′), *n.* any of numerous, usually epiphytic tropical American plants, having long, stiff leaves and showy flowers, and including the pineapple, Spanish moss, and many species grown as houseplants or ornamentals. [1865–70; < NL *Bromeli(a)*, the type genus of the family (named after Olaus *Bromelius* (1639–1705), Swedish botanist; see -IA) + -AD[1]] —**bro·me·li·a·ceous** (brō mē′lē ā′shəs), *adj.*

brom·e·o·sin (brō mē′ə sin), *n. Chem.* eosin (def. 1). [BROM- + EOSIN]

Brom·field (brom′fēld′), *n.* **Louis,** 1896–1956, U.S. novelist.

brom·hi·dro·sis (brō′mi drō′sis, brōm′hi-), *n. Med.* the secretion of foul-smelling sweat. Also, **bromidrosis.** Also called **osmidrosis.** [1865–70; BROM- + HIDROSIS]

bro·mic (brō′mik), *adj. Chem.* containing pentavalent bromine. [1820–30; BROM- + -IC]

bro′mic ac′id, *Chem.* an acid, $HBrO_3$, stable only in very dilute solutions, usually produced by the reaction of barium bromate with sulfuric acid: used chiefly as an oxidizing agent in the manufacture of dyes and pharmaceuticals. [1820–30]

bro·mide (brō′mīd *or, for 1,* brō′mid), *n.* **1.** *Chem.* **a.** a salt of hydrobromic acid consisting of two elements, one of which is bromine, as sodium bromide, NaBr. **b.** a compound containing bromine, as methyl bromide. **2.** *Pharm.* potassium bromide, known to produce central nervous system depression, formerly used as a sedative. **3.** a platitude or trite saying. **4.** a person who is platitudinous and boring. [1830–40; BROM- + -IDE; in defs. 3, 4 from use of some bromides as sedatives]

bro′mide pa′per, *Photog.* a fast printing paper coated with an emulsion of silver bromide: used mostly for enlargements. [1880–85]

bro·mid·ic (brō mid′ik), *adj.* pertaining or proper to a platitude; being a bromide; trite. [1905–10, *Amer.;* BROMIDE + -IC] —**bro·mid′i·cal·ly,** *adv.*

bro·mi·dro·sis (brō′mi drō′sis), *n. Med.* bromhidrosis.

bro·min·ate (brō′mə nāt′), *v.t.,* **-at·ed, -at·ing.** *Chem.* to treat or combine with bromine; bromate. [1870–75; BROMINE + -ATE[1]] —**bro′mi·na′tion,** *n.*

bro·mine (brō′mēn, -min), *n. Chem.* an element that is a dark-reddish, fuming, toxic liquid and a member of the halogen family: obtained from natural brines and ocean water, and used chiefly in the manufacture of gasoline antiknock compounds, pharmaceuticals, and dyes. *Symbol:* Br; *at. wt.:* 79.909; *at. no.:* 35; *sp. gr.:* 3.119 at 20°C. [1827; < F *brome* bromine (< Gk *brômos* stench) + -INE[2]]

bro′mine pentafluor′ide, *Chem.* a colorless, corrosive liquid, BrF_5, used as an oxidizer in liquid rocket propellants.

bro·mism (brō′miz əm), *n. Pathol.* a condition due to excessive use of bromides and characterized by skin eruptions. Also, **bro·min·ism** (brō′mə niz′əm). [1865–70; BROM(IDE) + -ISM]

bro·mize (brō′mīz), *v.t.,* **-mized, -miz·ing.** *Chem.* to treat or combine with bromine or a bromide. Also, *esp. Brit.,* **bro′mise.** [1850–55; BROM- + -IZE] —**bro′mi·za′tion,** *n.* —**bro′miz·er,** *n.*

Brom·ley (brom′lē, brum′-), *n.* a borough of Greater London, England. 294,900.

bromo-, a combining form used in the names of chemical compounds in which bromine is present: *bromobenzene.* Also, *esp. before a vowel,* **brom-.**

bro•mo•ac•e•tone (brō′mō as′i tōn′), *n. Chem.* a colorless and highly toxic liquid, $CH_2BrCOCH_3$, used as a lachrymatory compound in tear gas and chemical warfare gas. [BROMO- + ACETONE]

bro•mo•chlo•ro•meth•ane (brō′mə klôr′ə meth′ān, -klōr′-), *n. Chem.* chlorobromomethane. [BROMO- + CHLOROMETHANE]

bro•mo•crip•tine (brō′mə krip′tēn), *n. Pharm.* an ergot derivative, $C_{32}H_{40}BrN_5O_5$, that inhibits prolactin and growth hormone secretions and stimulates dopamine production in the brain, used to prevent postpartum lactation and in the treatments of acromegaly and Parkinson's disease. [1975–80; shortening and alter. of *bromoergocryptine,* equiv. to BROMO- + *ergocryptine* < G *Ergokryptin* an alkaloid derivative of ergotoxine (*ergo-* ERGO-[2] + Gk *krypt(ós)* hidden + *-in* -IN[2]; perh. so called because the independent nature of the derivative was not initially recognized)]

bro•mo•form (brō′mə fôrm′), *n. Chem.* a colorless, heavy liquid, $CHBr_3$, used chiefly as an intermediate in organic synthesis. [1870–75; BROMO- + (CHLORO)FORM]

bro•moil (brō′moil), *n. Photog.* an offset reproduction produced by the bromoil process. [1905–10; BROM- + OIL]

bro′moil proc′ess, *Photog.* a process for making an offset reproduction by first making a photographic print on paper with a silver bromide emulsion, wetting it, and then using it as a lithographic plate, the lighter parts of the emulsion tending to repel the oil base of the ink and the darker parts tending to hold it. [1905–10]

bro•mo•meth•ane (brō′mə meth′ān), *n. Chem.* See **methyl bromide.** [BROMO- + METHANE]

bro•mo•u•ra•cil (brō′mō yo͝or′ə sil), *n. Biochem.* a uracil derivative, $C_4H_3N_2O_2Br$, that pairs with adenine and sometimes with guanine during phage and bacterial DNA synthesis. [1955–60; BROMO- + URACIL]

brom•phen•ir•am•ine (brōm′fə nēr′ə mēn′, -min), *n. Pharm.* a substance, $C_{16}H_{19}BrN_2$, used as an antihistamine in the management of various allergies, as hay fever. [presumably coined from contr. of the component names *bromophenyl, pyridinepropanamine;* see BROMO-, PHENYL, PYRIDINE, PROPANE, -AMINE]

Bromp′ton mix′ture, (bromp′tən), *Pharm.* an analgesic mixture, usually containing morphine and cocaine and sometimes other narcotic substances in an alcohol solution, administered primarily to advanced cancer patients. Also, **Bromp′ton's mix′ture.** Also called **Bromp′ton cock′tail, Bromp′ton's cock′tail.** [1975–80; after *Brompton* Hospital, London, where the mixture was developed]

bronc (brongk), *n.* bronco: *to bust a bronc.* [1890–95; by shortening]

bronch-, var. of **broncho-** before a vowel.

bron•chi (brong′kē, -kī), *n. Anat.* pl. of **bronchus.**

bron•chi•a (brong′kē ə), *n. Anat.* (*used with a plural v.*) the ramifications or branches of the bronchi. [1665–75; < LL < Gk, pl. of *brónchion,* equiv. to *brónch(os)* windpipe + *-ion* dim. suffix]

bron•chi•al (brong′kē əl), *adj. Anat.* pertaining to the bronchia or bronchi. [1725–35; BRONCHI(A) + -AL[1]] —**bron′chi•al•ly,** *adv.*

bron′chial asth′ma, *Pathol.* asthma. [1880–85]

bron′chial pneumo′nia, *Pathol.* bronchopneumonia.

bron′chial tube′, a bronchus or any of its ramifications or branches. [1840–50]

bron•chi•ec•ta•sis (brong′kē ek′tə sis), *n. Pathol.* a diseased condition in which a bronchus or the bronchi are distended, characterized by paroxysmal coughing and copious expectoration of sputum. [1875–80; *bronchi-,* comb. form of BRONCHIA + ECTASIS] —**bron•chi•ec•tat•ic** (brong′kē ek tat′ik), *adj.*

bron•chi•ole (brong′kē ōl′), *n. Anat.* a small branch of a bronchus. [1865–70; < NL *bronchiolum,* equiv. to *bronchi(a)* BRONCHIA + *-olum* -OLE[1]] —**bron•chi•o•lar** (brong′kē ō′lər, brong kī′ə-), *adj.*

bron•chi•tis (brong kī′tis), *n. Pathol.* acute or chronic inflammation of the membrane lining of the bronchial tubes, caused by respiratory infection or exposure to bronchial irritants, as cigarette smoke. [1812; < NL; see BRONCH-, -ITIS] —**bron•chit•ic** (brong kit′ik), *adj.*

bron•cho (brong′kō), *n., pl.* **-chos.** bronco.

broncho-, a combining form representing **bronchus** or **bronchia** in compound words: *bronchopneumonia.* Also, *esp. before a vowel,* **bronch-.**

bron•cho•can•di•di•a•sis (brong′kō kan′di dī′ə sis), *n., pl.* **-ses** (-sēz′). See under **candidiasis.** [BRONCHO- + CANDIDIASIS]

bron•cho•cele (brong′kə sēl′), *n. Pathol.* **1.** dilatation of a bronchus. **2.** a goiter, esp. a cystic goiter. [1650–60; < Gk *bronchokḗlē.* See BRONCHO-, -CELE[1]]

bron•cho•di•la•tor (brong′kō dī lā′tər, -di-), *n.* a substance that acts to dilate constricted bronchial tubes to aid breathing, used esp. for relief of asthma. [1900–05; BRONCHO- + DILATOR]

bron•chog•ra•phy (brong kog′rə fē), *n., pl.* **-phies.** x-ray examination of the tracheobronchial tree after intrabronchial administration of a radiopaque material. [BRONCHO- + -GRAPHY] —**bron•cho•graph•ic** (brong′kə graf′ik), *adj.*

bron•cho•pneu•mo•nia (brong′kō no͞o mōn′yə, -mō′nē ə, -nyo͞o-), *n. Pathol.* a form of pneumonia centering on bronchial passages. Also called **bronchial pneumonia.** [1855–60; BRONCHO- + PNEUMONIA] —**bron•cho•pneu•mon•ic** (brong′kō no͞o mon′ik, -nyo͞o-), *adj.*

bron•chor•rha•gi•a (brong′kə rā′jē ə), *n. Pathol. Obs.* hemorrhage from the bronchial tubes. [BRONCHO- + -RRHAGIA]

bron•cho•scope (brong′kə skōp′), *n. Med.* a lighted, flexible tubular instrument that is inserted into the trachea for diagnosis and for removing inhaled objects. [1895–1900; BRONCHO- + -SCOPE] —**bron•cho•scop•ic** (brong′kə skop′ik), *adj.* —**bron•chos•co•pist** (brong-kos′kə pist), *n.*

bron•chos•co•py (brong kos′kə pē), *n., pl.* **-pies.** an examination by means of a bronchoscope. [1900–10; BRONCHO- + -SCOPY]

bron•cho•spasm (brong′kə spaz′əm), *n.* spasmodic contraction of the muscular lining of the bronchi, as in asthma, causing difficulty in breathing. [1900–05; BRONCHO- + SPASM]

bron•chus (brong′kəs), *n., pl.* **-chi** (-kē, -kī). *Anat.* either of the two main branches of the trachea. See diag. under **lung.** [1700–10; < NL < Gk *brónchos* windpipe]

bron•co (brong′kō), *n., pl.* **-cos.** a range pony or mustang of the western U.S., esp. one that is not broken or is imperfectly broken. Also, **bronc, broncho.** [1865–70, *Amer.*; < MexSp, short for Sp *potro bronco* untamed colt (in MexSp: wild horse, half-tamed horse); *bronco,* appar. nasalized var. of L *broccus;* see BROACH]

bron•co•bust•er (brong′kō bus′tər), *n.* a person who breaks broncos to the saddle. [1885–90, *Amer.*; BRONCO + BUSTER] —**bron′co•bust′ing,** *n.*

Bron•të (bron′tē), *n.* **1. Anne** ("*Acton Bell*"), 1820–49, English novelist. **2.** her sister **Charlotte** ("*Currer Bell*"), 1816–55, English novelist. **3.** her sister **Emily Jane** ("*Ellis Bell*"), 1818–48, English novelist.

bron•tide (bron′tīd), *n.* a rumbling noise heard occasionally in some parts of the world, probably caused by seismic activity. [appar. < Gk *bront(ḗ)* thunder + *-ide* (perh. for -ID[1])]

bron•to•saur (bron′tə sôr′), *n.* a huge sauropod dinosaur of the genus *Apatosaurus* (formerly *Brontosaurus*) and closely related genera, of the Jurassic Period, having a massive body, a small head and long neck, and thick columnar limbs, and ranging up to 77 ft. (23.5 m) in length. [see BRONTOSAURUS]

brontosaur, *Apatosaurus excelsus,* height 14 ft. (4.3 m); length 70 ft. (21.3 m)

bron•to•sau•rus (bron′tə sôr′əs), *n., pl.* **-sau•rus•es, -sau•ri** (-sôr′ī). brontosaur. [< NL (1879), equiv. to Gk *bronto-* (comb. form of *brontḗ* thunder) + *saûros* -SAURUS]

Bronx (brongks), *n.* **1. the,** a borough of New York City, N of Manhattan. 1,168,972; 43.4 sq. mi. (112 sq. km). **2.** a cocktail of gin, sweet and dry vermouth, and orange juice. —**Bronx′ite,** *n.*

Bronx′ cheer′, a loud, abrasive, spluttering noise made with the lips and tongue to express contempt. Also called **raspberry.** Cf. **bird** (def. 12). [1925–30, *Amer.*]

bronze (bronz), *n., v.,* **bronzed, bronz•ing,** *adj.* —*n.* **1.** *Metall.* **a.** any of various alloys consisting essentially of copper and tin, the tin content not exceeding 11 percent. **b.** any of various other alloys having a large copper content. **2.** a metallic brownish color. **3.** a work of art, as a statue, statuette, bust, or medal, composed of bronze. **4.** *Numis.* a coin made of bronze, esp. one from the Roman Empire. —*v.t.* **5.** to give the appearance or color of bronze to. **6.** to make brown, as by exposure to the sun: *The sun bronzed his face.* **7.** *Print.* **a.** to apply a fine metallic powder to (the ink of a printed surface) in order to create a glossy effect. **b.** to apply a fine metallic powder to (areas of a reproduction proof on acetate) in order to increase opacity. —*adj.* **8.** having the color bronze. [1730–40; < F < It, of obscure orig.] —**bronz′•y, bronze′like′,** *adj.*

Bronze′ Age′, 1. a period in the history of humankind, following the Stone Age and preceding the Iron Age, during which bronze weapons and implements were used. **2.** (*l.c.*) *Class. Myth.* the third of the four ages of the human race, marked by war and violence; regarded as inferior to the silver age but superior to the following iron age. [1860–65]

bronzed′ grack′le, the western subspecies of the common grackle, *Quiscalus quiscula versicolor,* having bronzy, iridescent plumage. [1890–95, *Amer.*]

bronze′ diabe′tes, *Pathol.* hemochromatosis. Also, **bronzed′ diabe′tes.** [1885–90]

bronze′ doré′, ormolu (def. 2).

bronze′ med′al, a medal, traditionally of bronze or bronze in color, awarded to a person or team finishing third in a competition, meet, or tournament. Cf. **gold medal, silver medal.** —**bronze′ med′alist.**

bronz•er (bron′zər), *n.* a cosmetic ointment used to give the skin a tanned look. [BRONZE (v.) + -ER[1]]

Bronze′ Star′, a U.S. military decoration awarded for heroism or achievement in military operations other than those involving aerial flights. Also called **Bronze′ Star′ Med′al.**

Bron•zi•no (brôn dzē′nô), *n.* **A•gno•lo (di Co•si•mo di Ma•ria•no)** (ä′nyô lô dē kô′zē mô dē mä ryä′nô), 1502–72, Italian painter.

bronz•ite (bron′zīt), *n.* a greenish-brown or black mineral with a bronzelike luster, an orthorhombic pyroxene, $(Mg,Fe)_2(Si_2O_6)$, intermediate in composition between enstatite and hypersthene. [1810–20; BRONZE + -ITE[1]; so called from its sheen]

brooch (brōch, bro͞och), *n.* a clasp or ornament having a pin at the back for passing through the clothing and a catch for securing the point of the pin. Also, **broach.** [1175–1225; ME *broche* BROACH, differentiated in sp. since ca. 1600]

brood (bro͞od), *n.* **1.** a number of young produced or hatched at one time; a family of offspring or young. **2.** a breed, species, group, or kind: *The museum exhibited a brood of monumental sculptures.* —*v.t.* **3.** to sit upon (eggs) to hatch, as a bird; incubate. **4.** (of a bird) to warm, protect, or cover (young) with the wings or body. **5.** to think or worry persistently or moodily about; ponder: *He brooded the problem.* —*v.i.* **6.** to sit upon eggs to be hatched, as a bird. **7.** to dwell on a subject or to meditate with morbid persistence (usually fol. by *over* or *on*). **8. brood above** or **over,** to cover, loom, or seem to fill the atmosphere or scene: *The haunted house on the hill brooded above the village.* —*adj.* **9.** kept for breeding: *a brood hen.* [bef. 1000; ME; OE *brōd;* c. D *broed,* G *Brut.* See BREED] —**brood′less,** *adj.*
—**Syn. 1.** BROOD, LITTER refer to young creatures. BROOD is esp. applied to the young of fowls and birds hatched from eggs at one time and raised under their mother's care: *a brood of young turkeys.* LITTER is applied to a group of young animals brought forth at a birth: *a litter of kittens or pups.* **2.** line, stock, strain.

brood′ bitch′, a female dog used for breeding.

brood′ bud′, *Bot.* **1.** bulbil. **2.** soredium. **3.** gemma.

brood•er (bro͞o′dər), *n.* **1.** a device or structure for the rearing of young chickens or other birds. **2.** a person or animal that broods. [1590–1600; BROOD + -ER[1]]

brood•ing (bro͞o′ding), *adj.* **1.** preoccupied with depressing, morbid, or painful memories or thoughts: *a brooding frame of mind.* **2.** cast in subdued light so as to convey a somewhat threatening atmosphere: *Dusk fell on the brooding hills.* [1810–20 for def. 1; 1640–50 for def. 2; BROOD + -ING[2]] —**brood′ing•ly,** *adv.*

brood•mare (bro͞od′mâr′), *n.* a mare used for breeding. [1875–80; BROOD + MARE[1]]

brood′ par′asite, a young bird hatched and reared by birds of a different species as a result of brood parasitism.

brood′ par′asitism, a form of social parasitism practiced by certain birds, as cuckoos and cowbirds, in which eggs are laid in the nests of other birds, causing them to be hatched and the young reared by the hosts, often at the cost of the hosts' own young.

brood′ patch′. See **incubation patch.**

brood•y (bro͞o′dē), *adj.,* **brood•i•er, brood•i•est. 1.** moody; gloomy. **2.** inclined to sit on eggs: *a broody hen.* [1505–15; BROOD + -Y[1]] —**brood′i•ness,** *n.*

brook[1] (bro͝ok), *n.* a small, natural stream of fresh water. [bef. 900; ME; OE *brōc* stream; c. D *broek,* G *Bruch* marsh] —**brook′less,** *adj.* —**brook′like′,** *adj.*

brook[2] (bro͝ok), *v.t.* to bear; suffer; tolerate: *I will brook no interference.* [bef. 900; ME *brouken,* OE *brūcan;* c. D *bruiken,* G *brauchen;* akin to Goth *brukjan,* L *fruī* to enjoy] —**brook′a•ble,** *adj.*
—**Syn.** take, stand, endure, abide, stomach.

Brooke (bro͝ok), *n.* **1. Sir James,** 1803–68, British soldier and adventurer: rajah of Sarawak. **2. Rupert,** 1887–1915, English poet.

Brook′ Farm′, a farm in West Roxbury, Massachusetts, where an experimental cooperative community was established from 1841 to 1847.

Brook•field (bro͝ok′fēld′), *n.* **1.** a city in SE Wisconsin, near Milwaukee. 34,035. **2.** a city in NE Illinois, near Chicago. 19,395. **3.** a town in SW Connecticut. 12,872.

Brook•ha•ven (bro͝ok hā′vən), *n.* a town in SW Mississippi. 10,800.

brook•ie (bro͝ok′ē), *n.* the brook trout of eastern North America. [BROOK[1] + -IE]

Brook•ings (bro͝ok′ingz), *n.* **1. Robert Som•ers** (sum′ərz), 1850–1932, U.S. merchant and philanthropist. **2.** a city in E South Dakota. 14,951.

brook•ite (bro͝ok′īt), *n. Mineral.* a brown, red, or black mineral, titanium dioxide, TiO_2, trimorphous with rutile and anatase. [1875–80; named after H. J. *Brooke* (1771–1857), English mineralogist; see -ITE[1]]

brook•let (bro͝ok′lit), *n.* a small brook. [1805–15; BROOK[1] + -LET]

brook•lime (bro͝ok′līm′), *n.* any of various speedwells found along brooks, in marshes, etc., as *Veronica americana* **(American brooklime),** a creeping plant having leafy stems and loose clusters of small blue flowers. [1400–50; late ME *brokelemke,* equiv. to *broke* BROOK[1] + *lemke,* OE *hleomoce* speedwell, c. MLG *lōmeke*]

Brook•line (bro͝ok′līn′), *n.* a town in E Massachusetts, near Boston. 55,062.

Brook•lyn (bro͝ok′lin), *n.* **1.** a borough of New York City, on W Long Island. 2,230,936; 76.4 sq. mi. (198 sq. km). **2.** a city in NE Ohio. 12,342. —**Brook•lyn•ite** (bro͝ok′lə nīt′), *n.*

Brook′lyn Bridge′, a suspension bridge over the East River, in New York City, connecting Manhattan and Brooklyn: built 1867–84. 5989 ft. (1825 m) long.

Brook′lyn Cen′ter, a city in SE Minnesota, near Minneapolis. 31,230.

Brook•lyn•ese (bro͝ok′lə nēz′, -nēs′, bro͝ok′lə nēz′, -nēs′), *n.* the speech, esp. the pronunciation, thought to be characteristic of a person coming from New York City, esp. Brooklyn. [1945–50; BROOKLYN + -ESE]

Brook′lyn Park′, a town in central Minnesota. 43,332.

Brook′ Park′, a city in NE Ohio. 26,195.

Brooks (bro͝oks), *n.* **1. Gwendolyn,** born 1917, U.S. poet and novelist. **2. Phillips,** 1835–93, U.S. Protestant Episcopal bishop and pulpit orator. **3. Van Wyck** (van

CONCISE ETYMOLOGY KEY: <, descended or borrowed from; >, whence; b., blend of, blended; c., cognate with; cf., compare; deriv., derivative; equiv., equivalent; imit., imitative; obl., oblique; r., replacing; s., stem; sp., spelling, spelled; resp., respelling, respelled; trans., translation; ?, origin unknown; *, unattested; ‡, probably earlier than. See the full key inside the front cover.

wik′), 1886–1963, U.S. author and critic. **4.** a male given name.

Brooks′ Range′, a mountain range in N Alaska, forming a watershed between the Yukon River and the Arctic Ocean: highest peak, 9239 ft. (2815 m).

brook′ trout′, **1.** Also called **speckled trout.** a common trout, *Salvelinus fontinalis,* of eastern North America. See illus. under **trout. 2.** See **brown trout.** [1830–40, *Amer.*]

brook•y (bro͝ok′ē), *adj.,* **brook•i•er, brook•i•est.** abounding in brooks. [1750–60; BROOK[1] + -Y[1]]

broom (bro͞om, bro͝om), *n.* **1.** an implement for sweeping, consisting of a brush of straw or stiff strands of synthetic material bound tightly to the end of a long handle. **2.** any shrubby plant belonging to the genus *Genista* or the genus *Cytisus,* of the legume family, esp. *C. scoparius,* common in Western Europe on uncultivated ground and having long, slender branches bearing yellow flowers. **3.** *Building Trades.* the crushed and spread part at the head of a wooden pile after driving. —*v.t.* **4.** to sweep: *Broom the porch.* **5.** to splinter or fray mechanically. **6.** to crush and spread the top of (a piling, tent peg, etc.) by pounding or driving with a hammer or the like. **7.** to brush (freshly poured concrete) with a broom to give a nonskid surface, as to walks or driveways. —*v.i.* **8.** (of a piling, tent peg, etc.) to be crushed and spread at the top from being driven. [bef. 1000; ME *brome,* OE *brōm;* c. D *braam* bramble, G *Bram* broom]
—**Pronunciation.** BROOM and ROOM occur with the vowel (o͞o) of *fool* or (o͝o) of *book.* The first is the more common. The pronunciation with the (o͝o) of *book* is found in New England, eastern Virginia, and South Carolina and Georgia alongside the (o͞o) pronunciation. Farther west the (o͞o) pronunciation is more common, though the pronunciation with the vowel of *brook* occurs everywhere with no marked regional or social pattern. Both pronunciations occur in British standard and folk speech. The pronunciation with (o͝o) predominates in the eastern counties, (o͞o) everywhere else. London lies on the boundary between the two types, and it is thus not surprising that (o͝o) is found in the United States in the coastal areas that had long and close contact with England.

broom•ball (bro͞om′bôl′, bro͝om′-), *n.* a game similar to ice hockey, usually played on a rink, in which the players, often not wearing skates, use brooms instead of hockey sticks to shoot a volleyball into the opponent's goal. [1935–40; BROOM + BALL[1]]

broom′ board′, *Canadian (chiefly the Maritime Provinces).* baseboard (def. 1).

broom•corn (bro͞om′kôrn′, bro͝om′-), *n.* any of several varieties of sorghum having a long, stiff-branched panicle used in the manufacture of brooms. [1775–85, *Amer.;* BROOM + CORN[1]]

Broom•field (bro͞om′fēld′), *n.* a city in N central Colorado. 20,730.

broom•rape (bro͞om′rāp′, bro͝om′-), *n.* any of various parasitic plants, esp. of the genus *Orobanche,* living on the roots of broom and other plants. Cf. **broomrape family.** [1570–80; partial trans. of ML *rāpum genistae* tuber of the broom plant]

broom′rape fam′ily, *adj.* the plant family Orobanchaceae, characterized by scaly, leafless herbaceous plants that are parasitic on the roots of other plants and have irregular flowers and many-seeded capsular fruit, and including beechdrops, broomrape, and squawroot.

broom•stick (bro͞om′stik′, bro͝om′-), *n.* the long slender handle of a broom. [1675–85; BROOM + STICK[1]]

broom′stick skirt′, a full, gathered or pleated skirt that has characteristic tiny creases obtained by wetting the skirt and winding it around a broomstick to dry.

broom•y (bro͞o′mē), *adj.,* **broom•i•er, broom•i•est.** covered with or abounding in broom: *a golden broomy expanse along the trail.* [1640–50; BROOM + -Y[1]]

bros., brothers. Also, **Bros.**

brose (brōz), *n. Scot.* a porridge made by stirring boiling liquid into oatmeal or other meal. [1400–50; late ME *broys* < OF *broez;* see BREWIS] —**bros′y,** *adj.*

Bros•sard (brô särd′; *Fr.* BRÔ SAR′), *n.* a town in S Quebec, in E Canada: suburb of Montreal. 52,232.

broth (brôth, broth), *n.* **1.** thin soup of concentrated meat or fish stock. **2.** water that has been boiled with meat, fish, vegetables, or barley. **3.** *Bacteriol.* a liquid medium containing nutrients suitable for culturing microorganisms. **4. broth of a boy,** a sturdy youth. [bef. 1000; ME, OE; c. ON *broth,* OHG *brod;* akin to BREW] —**broth′y,** *adj.*

broth•el (broth′əl, broth′-, brô′thəl, -thəl), *n.* a house of prostitution. [1350–1400 for earlier sense; short for *brothel-house* whore-house; ME *brothel* harlot, orig. worthless person, equiv. to *broth-* (ptp. s. of *brethen,* OE *brēothan* to decay, degenerate) + *-el* n. suffix] —**broth′el•like′,** *adj.*

broth•er (bruth′ər *or, for 9,* bruth′ûr′), *n., pl.* **brothers,** *(Archaic)* **brethren;** *interj.* —*n.* **1.** a male offspring having both parents in common with another offspring; a male sibling. **2.** Also called **half brother.** a male offspring having only one parent in common with another offspring. **3.** a stepbrother. **4.** a male numbered among the same kinship group, nationality, race, profession, etc., as another; an associate; a fellow member, fellow countryman, fellow man, etc.: *a fraternity brother.* **5.** *Eccles.* **a.** *(often cap.)* a male numbered among the lay members of a religious organization that has a priesthood. **b.** a man who devotes himself to the duties of a religious order without taking holy orders, or while preparing for holy orders. **6. brothers,** all members of a particular race, or of the human race in general: *All men are brothers.* **7.** *Slang.* fellow; buddy: *Brother, can you spare a dime?* **8.** *Informal.* a black man; soul brother. —*interj.* **9.** *Slang.* (used to express disappointment, disgust, or surprise). [bef. 1000; ME; OE *brōthor;* c. D *broeder,* G *Bruder,* ON *brōthir,* Goth *brothar,* Skt *bhrātṛ,* Gk *phrātēr,* L *frāter,* OIr *bráthair,* OCS *bratrŭ*] —**broth′er•less,** *adj.* —**broth′er•like′,** *adj.*
—**Syn. 1.** BROTHERS, BRETHREN are plurals of *brother.* BROTHERS are kinsmen, sons of the same parents: *My mother lives with my brothers.* BRETHREN, now archaic in the foregoing sense, is used of male members of a congregation or of a fraternal organization: *The brethren will meet at the church.*

broth•er•hood (bruth′ər ho͝od′), *n.* **1.** the condition or quality of being a brother or brothers. **2.** the quality of being brotherly; fellowship. **3.** a fraternal or trade organization. **4.** all those engaged in a particular trade or profession or sharing a common interest or quality. **5.** the belief that all people should act with warmth and equality toward one another, regardless of differences in race, creed, nationality, etc. [1250–1300; ME *brithirhod* (see BROTHER, -HOOD); r. early ME *brotherhede;* see -HEAD]

broth•er-in-law (bruth′ər in lô′), *n., pl.* **brothers-in-law. 1.** the brother of one's husband or wife. **2.** the husband of one's sister. **3.** the husband of one's wife's or husband's sister. [1250–1300; ME]

Broth′er Jon′athan, *Brit. Archaic.* a male native or resident of the United States.

broth•er•ly (bruth′ər lē), *adj.* **1.** of, like, or befitting a brother; affectionate and loyal; fraternal: *brotherly love.* —*adv.* **2.** as a brother; fraternally. [bef. 1000; ME; OE *brōthorlīc.* See BROTHER, -LY] —**broth′er•li•ness,** *n.*

Broth′er of the Chris′tian Schools′, *Rom. Cath. Ch.* **1.** a member of a congregation of brothers, founded in France in 1684 for the education of the poor. **2.** Also, **Irish Christian Brother.** a member of a congregation of teaching brothers, founded in Ireland in 1802. Also called **Christian Brother.**

Broth′ers Kar•a•maz′ov, The (kar′ə mä′zôf, -zof, -maz′ôf, -of), a novel (1880) by Dostoevsky.

brot•u•la (broch′ə lə), *n.* any of several chiefly deep-sea fishes of the family Brotulidae. [< NL *Brotula* genus name < AmerSp *brótula* kind of fish, lit., little bud, equiv. to *brot(ón)* bud + *-ula* -ULE]

bro•tus (brō′təs), *n., pl.* **-tus•es.** *Coastal South Carolina and Georgia.* broadus.

brough (*Scot.* BROKH, BRUKH), *n. Obs.* broch.

brougham (def. 1)

brough•am (bro͞o′əm, bro͞om, brō′əm), *n.* **1.** a four-wheeled, boxlike, closed carriage for two or four persons, having the driver's perch outside. **2.** *Auto.* **a.** (formerly) a limousine having an open driver's compartment. **b.** an early type of automobile resembling a coupé, often powered by an electric motor. [1850–55; named after Lord *Brougham* (1778–1868), English statesman]

brought (brôt), *v.* pt. and pp. of **bring.**

brought-on (brôt′on′, -ôn′), *adj. Chiefly South Midland U.S.* **1.** made or bought outside the community, as a commercially manufactured product. **2.** (of a person) not belonging to the community; outside: *They hired themselves a brought-on man from Michigan.*

brou•ha•ha (bro͞o′hä hä′, bro͞o′hä hä′, bro͞o hä′hä), *n.* **1.** excited public interest, discussion, or the like, as the clamor attending some sensational event; hullabaloo: *The brouhaha followed disclosures of graft at City Hall.* **2.** an episode involving excitement, confusion, turmoil, etc., esp. a broil over a minor or ridiculous cause: *A brouhaha by the baseball players resulted in three black eyes.* [1885–90; < F, orig. *brou, ha, ha!* exclamation used by characters repr. the devil in the 16th-cent. drama; perh. < Heb, distortion of the recited phrase *bārūkh habbā* (*beshēm ădhōnai*) "blessed is he who comes (in the name of the Lord)" (Ps. 118:26)]

Broun (bro͞on), *n.* **(Matthew) Heywood (Campbell),** 1888–1939, U.S. journalist, essayist, and novelist.

Brou•wer (brou′ər; *Flemish, Du.* BROU′wər), *n.* **1. A•dri•aen** (ä′drē än′), 1606?–38, Flemish painter. **2. Luit•zen Eg•ber•tus Jan** (loit′sən EKH BER′təs yän), 1881–1966, Dutch mathematician and philosopher.

Brou′wer fixed′-point′ the′orem (brou′ər fikst′point′), *Math.* the theorem that for any continuous transformation of a circle into itself, including its boundary, there is at least one point that is mapped to itself. [named after L. E. J. BROUWER]

brow (brou), *n.* **1.** *Anat.* the ridge over the eye. **2.** the hair growing on that ridge; eyebrow. **3.** the forehead: *He wore his hat low over his brow.* **4.** a person's countenance or mien. **5.** the edge of a steep place: *She looked down over the brow of the hill.* **6.** gangplank. [bef. 1000; ME *browe,* OE *brū;* akin to ON *brūn,* Skt *bhrūs*]

brow′ ant′ler, the first prong from the base of a stag's antler. See diag. under **antler.** [1590–1600]

brow•beat (brou′bēt′), *v.t.,* **-beat, -beat•en, -beat•ing.** to intimidate by overbearing looks or words; bully: *They browbeat him into agreeing.* [1575–85; BROW + BEAT] —**brow′beat′er,** *n.*
—**Syn.** cow, badger, tyrannize, harass, coerce.

Brow•der (brou′dər), *n.* **Earl Russell,** 1891–1973, U.S. Communist party leader 1930–45.

browed (broud), *adj.* having a brow of a specified kind (usually used in combination): *a shaggy-browed brute.* [1425–75; late ME; see BROW, -ED[3]]

brown (broun), *n., adj.,* **-er, -est,** *v.* —*n.* **1.** a dark tertiary color with a yellowish or reddish hue. **2.** a person whose skin has a dusky or light-brown pigmentation. —*adj.* **3.** of the color brown. **4.** (of animals) having skin, fur, hair, or feathers of that color. **5.** sunburned or tanned. **6.** (of persons) having the skin naturally pigmented a brown color. **7. do it up brown,** *Informal.* to do thoroughly: *When they entertain, they really do it up brown.* —*v.t., v.i.* **8.** to make or become brown. **9.** to fry, sauté, or scorch slightly in cooking: *to brown onions before adding them to the stew. The potatoes browned in the pan.* **10. browned off,** *Slang.* angry; fed up. **11. brown out,** to subject to a brownout: *The power failure browned out the southern half of the state.* [bef. 1000; ME; OE *brūn;* c. D *bruin,* G *braun,* ON *brūnn;* akin to Lith *brúnas* brown] —**brown′ish, brown′y,** *adj.* —**brown′ness,** *n.*

Brown (broun), *n.* **1. Charles Brock•den** (brok′dən), 1771–1810, U.S. novelist. **2. Edmund Gerald, Jr.** (*Jerry*), born 1938, U.S. politician: governor of California 1975–83. **3. James Nathaniel** (*Jimmy*), born 1936, U.S. football player and actor. **4. John** ("*Old Brown of Osawatomie*"), 1800–59, U.S. abolitionist: leader of the attack at Harpers Ferry, where he was captured, tried for treason, and hanged. **5. Olympia,** 1835–1926, U.S. women's-rights activist and Universalist minister: first American woman ordained by a major church. **6. Robert,** 1773–1858, Scottish botanist.

brown′ al′ga, an alga of the class Phaeophyceae, usually brown owing to the presence of brown pigments in addition to the chlorophyll. [1900–05]

brown-and-serve (broun′ən sûrv′), *adj.* (of baked or cooked packaged foods) requiring only a brief period of browning, as in an oven, before being ready to serve: *brown-and-serve rolls.*

brown-bag (broun′bag′), *v.,* **-bagged, -bag•ging,** *adj.* —*v.t.* **1.** to bring (one's own liquor) to a restaurant or club, esp. one that has no liquor license. **2.** to bring (one's lunch) to work or elsewhere, usually in a small brown paper bag. —*v.i.* **3.** to carry one's lunch in a brown paper bag. **4. brown-bag it,** to bring one's lunch to work or elsewhere, esp. in a brown paper bag. —*adj.* **5.** brought to work, usually in a small brown paper bag: *a brown-bag lunch.* —**brown′-bag′ger,** *n.*

brown′ bat′, any of several small to medium-sized common bats of the genera *Myotis* and *Eptesicus,* found worldwide in caves, trees, and buildings, including *M. lucifugus* **(little brown bat)** and *E. fuscus* **(big brown bat),** a widespread North American species.

brown′ bear′, any of several medium-sized to large bears of the species *Ursus arctos,* inhabiting North America and Eurasia in dwindling populations, characterized by an upturned muzzle and a hump high on the back and ranging from light tan to near black; formerly considered three distinct species and often still referred to as such: *U. horribilis,* the grizzly bear; *U. middendorffi,* the Kodiak bear; and *U. arctos,* comprising European and Asian brown bears. [1775–85]

brown bear, *Ursus arctos,* 3 to 3½ ft. (0.9 m to 1 m) high at shoulder; length 6 to 8½ ft. (1.8 m to 2.6 m)

brown′ belt′, *Martial Arts.* **1.** a brown cloth waistband conferred upon a participant in one of the martial arts, as judo or karate, to indicate an intermediate rank. **2.** a person who has attained this rank. **3.** the rank itself. Cf. **black belt** (def. 3), **white belt.** [1965–70]

brown′ bent′, a common grass, *Agrostis canina,* of North America, used for lawns and putting greens because its blades can be clipped very short without injury to the plant. Also called **velvet bent.** [1860–65; so called from its dark tufts]

brown′ bet′ty, a baked dessert made of apples or other fruit, bread crumbs, sugar, butter, spice, etc. [1860–65, *Amer.*]

brown′ bread′, **1.** any bread made of flour darker in color than bolted wheat flour, esp. graham or whole wheat bread. **2.** See **Boston brown bread.** [1350–1400; ME]

brown′ bull′head, a freshwater catfish, *Ictalurus nebulosus,* of eastern North America, having an olive to brown body with dark markings on the sides.

brown′ but′ter. See **beurre noir.**

brown′ can′ker, *Plant Pathol.* a fungous disease of roses, characterized by leaf and flower lesions, stem cankers surrounded by a reddish-purple border, and dieback. [1825–35]

brown′ coat′, arriccio. [1800–10, *Amer.*]

brown′ creep′er. See under **creeper** (def. 6).

Brown′ Deer′, a town in SE Wisconsin. 12,921.

brown′ dwarf′, *Astron.* a cold, dark star that is too small to initiate the nuclear reactions that generate heat and light.

Browne (broun), *n.* **1. Charles Far•rer** (far′ər), ("*Artemus Ward*"), 1834–67, U.S. humorist. **2. Sir Thomas,** 1605–82, English physician and author.

brown′-eyed Su′san (broun′īd′), a composite plant, *Rudbeckia triloba,* of the southeastern U.S., having a single flower with yellow rays darkening to an orange or brown at the base and a brownish-black disk. [1905–10, *Amer.*]

brown′ fat′, brownish-yellow adipose tissue in the upper back, or interscapular, region of many mammals, most conspicuously in hibernating species, composed of numerous innervated fat cells that can produce heat during cold stress; thermogenic tissue. [1950–55]

Brown•field (broun′fēld′), *n.* a city in NW Texas. 10,387.

brown′ goods′, **1.** electronic machines, as television sets, stereos, and audio or video recorders, that are often finished in brown. **2.** brown-color liquors, as whiskey, bourbon, and brandy.

brown′ hack′le, *Angling.* an artificial fly having a peacock herl body, golden tag and tail, and brown hackle.

brown′ heart′, *Plant Pathol.* a brown discoloration of the flesh of stored apples, resulting from high concentrations of carbon dioxide. [1920–25]

brown′ hye′na, a hyena, *Hyaena brunnea,* of southern Africa, having a blackish-gray coat: its dwindling population is now protected. Also called **strand wolf.**

Brown′i•an move′ment (brou′nē ən), *Physics.* the irregular motion of small particles suspended in a liquid or a gas, caused by the bombardment of the particles by molecules of the medium: first observed by Robert Brown in 1827. Also called **Brown′ian mo′tion.** [1870–75; *Brown* + -IAN]

brown•ie (brou′nē), *n.* **1.** a tiny, fanciful, good-natured brown elf who secretly helps at night with household chores. **2.** a small, chewy, cakelike cookie, usually made with chocolate and containing nuts. **3.** *Australian.* a bread with currants, baked in a camp oven. **4.** (*sometimes cap.*) a member of the junior division of the Girl Scouts or the Girl Guides, being a girl in the 1st, 2nd, or 3rd grade and usually between 6 and 8 years old. [1505–15; BROWN + -IE; in folkloric sense, orig. Scots]
—**Syn. 1.** See **fairy.**

Brown′ie point′, *Informal.* a credit toward advancement or good standing gained esp. by currying favor. [1960–65; from the point system based on good behavior and performance used by Brownies for advancement]

Brown•ing (brou′ning), *n.* **1. Elizabeth Bar•rett** (bar′it), 1806–61, English poet. **2. John Moses,** 1855–1926, U.S. designer of firearms. **3. Robert,** 1812–89, English poet (husband of Elizabeth Barrett Browning).

Brown′ing au′tomatic ri′fle, an air-cooled, fully automatic rifle capable of firing 200 to 350 rounds per minute. *Abbr.:* BAR [1900–05; named after J. M. BROWNING]

brown′ lung′, *Pathol.* a debilitating lung disease resembling emphysema, occurring among textile workers from inhalation of cotton dust. Also called **byssinosis.**

brown-nose (broun′nōz′), *v.,* **-nosed, -nos•ing,** *n.* *Slang.* —*v.i.* **1.** to curry favor; behave obsequiously. —*v.t.* **2.** to seek favors from (a person) in an obsequious manner; fawn over. —*n.* **3.** Also, **brown′-nos′er.** a toady; sycophant. Cf. **ass-kissing.** [1935–40; BROWN + NOSE]

brown•out (broun′out′), *n.* **1.** the elimination of some or reduction of all electric lights of a city, esp. as a precaution against attack in time of war. **2.** any curtailment of electric power, as by a severe storm. [1940–45; BROWN + OUT, on the model of BLACKOUT]

brown•print (broun′print′), *n.* a process of photographic reproduction using a mixture of iron and silver salts to produce a white image on a sepia ground. [BROWN + PRINT, on the model of BLUEPRINT]

brown′ rat′. See **Norway rat.** [1820–30]

brown′ rec′luse spi′der, a small, pale-brown, venomous North American spider, *Loxosceles reclusa,* distinguished by a violin-shaped marking near the head, found outdoors in rock niches or indoors in drawers or dark corners: its bite may cause deep skin ulcers that are occasionally fatal. Also called **fiddleback spider, violin spider.** [1960–65]

brown′ rice′, rice from which the bran layers and germs have not been removed by polishing. [1915–20]

brown′ rot′, *Plant Pathol.* any plant disease, esp. of apples, peaches, plums, and cherries, characterized by browning and decay of tissues, caused by various fungi and bacteria. [1890–95]

brown′ sauce′, a simple sauce made from reduced meat stock; espagnole. Also called **sauce espagnole.**

brown•shirt (broun′shûrt′), *n.* (*often cap.*) **1.** a Nazi. **2.** a Nazi storm trooper. [1930–35; BROWN + SHIRT so called from the color of the shirt worn as part of the uniform]

brown′ soils′, a zonal group of soils with a brown surface horizon, developed on cool to temperate grasslands. Cf. **mollisol.**

brown′ spot′, *Plant Pathol.* a disease of many plants, characterized by irregular, brownish lesions on the fruit and foliage and by stem cankers, caused by any of several fungi, as *Ceratophorum setosum* or *Cephalosporium apii.*

brown′ stem′ rot′, *Plant Pathol.* a disease of soybeans, characterized by brown discoloration and decay of internal tissues of the stem and leaf, caused by a fungus, *Cephalosporium gregatum.*

brown•stone (broun′stōn′), *n.* **1.** a reddish-brown sandstone, used extensively as a building material. **2.** Also called **brown′stone front′.** a building, esp. a row house, fronted with this stone. —*adj.* **3.** *Archaic.* belonging or pertaining to the well-to-do class. [1830–40; BROWN + STONE]

CONCISE ETYMOLOGY KEY: <, descended or borrowed from; >, whence; b., blend of, blended; c., cognate with; cf., compare; deriv., derivative; equiv., equivalent; imit., imitative; obl., oblique; r., replacing; s., stem; sp., spelling, spelled; resp., respelling, respelled; trans., translation; ?, origin unknown; *, unattested; ‡, probably earlier than. See the full key inside the front cover.

brown•ston•er (broun′stō′nər), *n.* a person who lives in or owns a brownstone house. [BROWNSTONE + -ER[1]]

brown′ stud′y, deep, serious absorption in thought: *Lost in a brown study, she was oblivious to the noise.* [1525–35]

brown′ sug′ar, **1.** unrefined or partially refined sugar that retains some molasses. **2.** a commercial product consisting of white, refined sugar to which molasses has been added. **3.** *Slang.* brownish-colored heroin manufactured illicitly in Mexico. [1695–1705]

Browns•ville (brounz′vil), *n.* a seaport in S Texas, near the mouth of the Rio Grande. 84,997.

Brown′ Swiss′, one of a breed of brownish dairy cattle raised originally in Switzerland. [1900–05]

brown′-tail moth′ (broun′tāl′), a white moth, *Nygmia phaerrhoea,* having a brown tuft at the end of the abdomen, the larvae of which feed on the foliage of various shade and fruit trees. Also called **brown′tail′.** [1775–85]

brown′ thrash′er, a common large songbird, *Toxostoma rufum,* of the eastern U.S., having reddish-brown plumage. Also called **brown′ thrush′.** [1800–10, *Amer.*]

brown′ trout′, a common trout, *Salmo trutta,* of northern European streams. [1885–90]

Brown•wood (broun′wo͝od′), *n.* a city in central Texas. 19,203.

brow•ridge (brou′rij′), *n. Anat.* the bony prominence above the eye. Also, **brow′ ridge′.** Also called **supraorbital ridge, superciliary ridge.** [1895–1900; BROW + RIDGE]

brows•a•ble (brou′zə bəl), *adj.* enabling or encouraging one to browse: *a browsable book; a browsable store.* [BROWSE + -ABLE]

browse (brouz), *v.,* **browsed, brows•ing,** *n.* —*v.t.* **1.** to eat, nibble at, or feed on (leaves, tender shoots, or other soft vegetation). **2.** to graze; pasture on. **3.** to look through or glance at casually: *He's browsing the shelves for something to read.* —*v.i.* **4.** to feed on or nibble at foliage, lichen, berries, etc. **5.** to graze. **6.** to glance at random through a book, magazine, etc. **7.** to look leisurely at goods displayed for sale, as in a store. —*n.* **8.** tender shoots or twigs of shrubs and trees as food for cattle, deer, etc. **9.** an act or instance of browsing. [1400–50; late ME *browsen,* perh. a v. deriv. of AF *broz,* pl. of *brot* shoot, new growth, OF *brost* < Old Low Franconian **brust* bud, n. deriv. of **brustjan;* cf. OS *brustian* to come into bud] —**brows′er,** *n.*
—**Syn. 3.** scan, skim, examine, peruse, check.

Broz (*Serbo-Croatian.* brôz), *n.* **Jo•sip** (yô′sip). See **Tito, Marshal.**

brr (bûr), *interj.* (used to express sensations of cold).

Br. Som., British Somaliland.

B.R.T., Brotherhood of Railroad Trainmen.

Bru•ant (bʀʏ äɴ′), *n.* **Li•bé•ral** (lē bā ʀal′), c1635–1697, French architect.

Bru•beck (bro͞o′bek), *n.* **David Warren** (*Dave*), born 1920, U.S. jazz pianist and composer.

Bruce (bro͞os), *n.* **1. Blanche Kelso,** 1841–98, U.S. politician: first black to serve a full term as U.S. senator 1875–81. **2. Sir David,** 1855–1931, Australian physician. **3. Robert.** See **Robert I** (def. 2). **4. Stanley Melbourne** (*1st Viscount Bruce of Melbourne*), 1883–1967, Australian statesman: prime minister 1923–29. **5.** a male given name: from a Norman family name.

bru•cel•la (bro͞o sel′ə), *n., pl.* **-cel•lae** (-sel′ē), **-cel•las.** *Bacteriol.* any of several rod-shaped, aerobic bacteria of the genus *Brucella,* certain species of which, as *B. melitensis,* are pathogenic for humans and other animals. [1920; < NL; after D. BRUCE; see -ELLA]

bru•cel•lo•sis (bro͞o′sə lō′sis), *n. Pathol., Vet. Pathol.* infection with bacteria of the *Brucella* genus, frequently causing spontaneous abortions in animals and remittent fever in humans. Also called **undulant fever, Malta fever, Mediterranean fever, Rock fever.** [1925–30; BRUCELL(A) + -OSIS]

Bruch (bro͝ok; *Ger.* bro͝okh), *n.* **Max** (maks; *Ger.* mäks), 1838–1920, German composer and conductor.

bru•cine (bro͞o′sēn, -sin), *n. Chem.* a white, crystalline, bitter, slightly water-soluble, very poisonous alkaloid, $C_{23}H_{26}N_2O_4$, obtained from the nux vomica tree *Strychnos nux-vomica,* and from other species of the same genus, resembling but not as powerful as strychnine in its pharmacological action: used chiefly in the denaturation of alcohol. [1815–25; named after J. *Bruce* (1730–94), Scottish explorer; see -INE[2]]

bru•cite (bro͞o′sīt), *n.* a mineral, magnesium hydroxide, $Mg(OH)_2$, occurring in tabular, foliated crystals: used in magnesia refractories. [1865–70; named after A. *Bruce* (1777–1818), American mineralogist; see -ITE[1]]

Bruck•ner (bro͝ok′nər, bruk′-; *Ger.* bro͝ok′nəʀ), *n.* **Anton** (an′tən, -ton, -tōn; *Ger.* än′tôn), 1824–96, Austrian composer and organist.

Brue•ghel (broi′gəl, bro͞o′-; *Flemish* bʀœ′gəl), *n.* Breughel. Also, **Brue′gel.**

Bru•ges (bro͞o′jiz, bro͞ozh; *Fr.* bʀʏzh), *n.* a city in NW Belgium: connected by canal with its seaport, Zeebrugge. 119,718. Flemish, **Brug•ge** (bʀœкн′ə).

Brug•mann (bro͝og′mən; *Ger.* bro͝ok′män), *n.* **(Friedrich) Karl** (frē′drik kärl; *Ger.* fʀē′dʀiкн kärl), 1849–1919. German philologist.

Bruhn (bro͞on), *n.* **Erik** (*Belton Evers*), 1928–86, Danish ballet dancer.

bru•in (bro͞o′in), *n.* a bear, esp. a European brown bear. [1475–85; < MD *bruyn, bruun* lit., the brown one, name of the bear in the fable of Reynard the Fox]

bruise (bro͞oz), *v.,* **bruised, bruis•ing,** *n.* —*v.t.* **1.** to injure by striking or pressing, without breaking the skin: *The blow bruised his arm. Her pinching bruised the peaches.* **2.** to injure or hurt slightly, as with an insult or unkind remark: *to bruise a person's feelings.* **3.** to crush (drugs or food) by beating or pounding. **4.** *Metalworking.* to injure the surface of (an ingot or finished object) by collision. —*v.i.* **5.** to develop or bear a discolored spot on the skin as the result of a blow, fall, etc. **6.** to become injured slightly: *His feelings bruise easily.* —*n.* **7.** an injury due to bruising; contusion. [bef. 900; ME *bro(o)sen, bres(s)en, bris(s)en, bruisen,* repr. OE *brȳsan, brēsan* and AF *bruser,* OF *bruisier,* akin to *briser* to break; see BRISANCE]

bruis•er (bro͞o′zər), *n. Informal.* a strong, tough person: *The football player was over six feet tall and weighed 285 pounds—a real bruiser.* [1580–90; BRUISE + -ER[1]]

bruit (bro͞ot), *v.t.* **1.** to voice abroad; rumor (used chiefly in the passive and often fol. by *about*): *The report was bruited through the village.* —*n.* **2.** *Med.* any generally abnormal sound or murmur heard on auscultation. **3.** *Archaic.* rumor; report. **4.** *Archaic.* noise; din; clamor. [1400–50; late ME (n.) < AF, OF, n. use of ptp. of *bruire* to roar < VL **brūgere,* a conflation of L *rūgire* to bellow and VL **bragere;* see BRAY[1]] —**bruit′er,** *n.*

bru•lé (bro͞o lā′, bro͞o′lē; *Fr.* bʀʏ lā′), *n., pl.* **-lés** (-lāz′, -lēz; *Fr.* -lā′). **1.** (in the Pacific Northwest) an area of forest destroyed by fire. **2.** *Canadian.* land covered with rocks or scrub growth. Also, **bru•lée′.** [1785–95, *Amer.;* < F: burnt, ptp. of *brûler;* see BROIL[1]]

Bru•lé (bro͞o lā′), *n., pl.* **-lés,** (*esp. collectively*) **-lé.** *n.* a member of a North American Indian people belonging to the Teton branch of the Dakota.

Bru•maire (bʀʏ meʀ′), *n.* (in the French Revolutionary calendar) the second month of the year, extending from October 22 to November 20. [< F, equiv. to *brume* BRUME + *-aire* -ARY]

bru•mal (bro͞o′məl), *adj.* wintry. [1505–15; < L *brūmālis* of, pertaining to winter. See BRUME, -AL[1]]

brum•by (brum′bē), *n., pl.* **-bies.** *Australian.* a wild horse. [1875–80; orig. obscure]

brume (bro͞om), *n.* mist; fog. [1800–10; < F: fog < Pr *bruma* < L *brūma* winter, orig. winter solstice, contr. of **brevima* (*diēs*) shortest (day); see BREVE] —**bru•mous** (bro͞o′məs), *adj.*

brum•ma•gem (brum′ə jəm), *adj.* **1.** showy but inferior and worthless. —*n.* **2.** a showy but inferior and worthless thing. [1630–40; local var. of BIRMINGHAM, England (cf. *Bromwichham, Bromecham* (17th century), ME *Burmingeham*); orig. in allusion to counterfeit coins produced there in the 17th cent.]

Brum•mell (brum′əl), *n.* **George Bryan II.** See **Beau Brummell.**

brunch (brunch), *n.* **1.** a meal that serves as both breakfast and lunch. —*v.i.* **2.** to eat brunch: *They brunch at 11:00 on Sunday.* [1895–1900; BR(EAKFAST) + (L)UNCH] —**brunch′er,** *n.*

brunch′ coat′, a knee-length housecoat. [1940–45]

Brun•dis•i•um (brun diz′ē əm, -dizh′ē-), *n.* ancient name of **Brindisi.**

Bru•nei (bro͞o nī′, -nā′), *n.* a sultanate under British protection on the NW coast of Borneo: formerly a British protectorate; gained independence 1984. 235,000; 2220 sq. mi. (5750 sq. km). *Cap.:* Bandar Seri Begawan. Official name, **Brunei′ Da•rus•sa•lam** (dä′ro͞o sä läm′). —**Bru•nei′an,** *adj., n.*

Bru•nel (bro͞o nel′), *n.* **1. Is•am•bard Kingdom** (iz′əm bärd′), 1806–59, English civil engineer and naval architect. **2.** his father, **Sir Marc Isambard,** 1769–1849, English civil engineer, born in France: chief engineer of New York City 1793–99.

Bru•nel•les•chi (bro͞on′l es′kē; *It.* bro͞o′nel les′kē), *n.* **Fi•lip•po** (fi lip′ō; *It.* fē lēp′pô), 1377?–1446, Italian architect. Also, **Bru•nel•les•co** (bro͞on′l es′kō; *It.* bro͞o′nel-les′kô).

bru•net (bro͞o net′), *adj.* **1.** (esp. of a male) brunette. —*n.* **2.** a person, usually a male, with dark hair and, often, dark eyes and darkish or olive skin. [1885–90; < F, equiv. to *brun* BROWN + *-et* -ET] —**bru•net′ness,** *n.*

Bru•ne•tière (bʀʏnᵊ tyeʀ′), *n.* **Fer•di•nand** (feʀ dē-näɴ′), 1849–1906, French literary critic.

bru•nette (bro͞o net′), *adj.* **1.** (of hair, eyes, skin, etc.) of a dark color or tone. **2.** (of a person) having dark hair and, often, dark eyes and darkish or olive skin. —*n.* **3.** a person, esp. a female, with such coloration. [1705–15; < F; fem. of BRUNET] —**bru•nette′ness,** *n.*

brun•fel•si•a (bro͝on fel′zē ə), *n.* any of various shrubs or small trees belonging to the genus *Brunfelsia,* of the nightshade family, native to tropical America, having white or purple tubular or bell-shaped flowers. [< NL (Linnaeus), named in honor of Otto *Brunfels* (ca. 1488–1534), German humanist scholar and pioneer botanist; see -IA]

Brun•hild (bro͝on′hilt, -hild, bro͞on′-), *n.* (in the *Nibelungenlied*) a queen of Isenland and the bride of Gunther, for whom she was won by Siegfried: corresponds to Brynhild in Scandinavian legends. Also, **Brun•hil•de** (bro͝on hil′də), **Brünnhilde.**

bru•ni•zem (bro͞o′nə zem′), *n.* one of the great soil groups of a classification system no longer in general use; would be equivalent to a suborder of the mollisol group. [1950–55; < LL *brūn(us)* brown (< Gmc; see BROWN) + -I- + (CHERNO)ZEM]

Brünn (bʀʏn), *n.* German name of **Brno.**

Brun•ner (bro͝on′ər), *n.* **E•mil** (ā′mēl), 1889–1966, Swiss Protestant theologian.

Brun′ner's gland′, any of the glands in the submucosal layer of the duodenum, secreting an alkaline fluid into the small intestine. [after Swiss anatomist Johann Conrad *Brunner* (1653–1727), who described them in 1687]

Brünn·hil·de (bro͝on hil′də; *Ger.* BRYN′hil′də), *n.* **1.** the heroine of Wagner's *Ring of the Nibelungs.* Cf. **Siegfried. 2.** Brunhild.

Bru·no (bro͞o′nō; *for 1, 3 also It.* BRO͞O′nô), *n.* **1. Gior·da·no** (jôr dä′nō), 1548?–1600, Italian philosopher. **2. Saint,** c1030–1101, German ecclesiastical writer: founder of the Carthusian order. **3.** a male given name: from a Germanic word meaning "brown."

Bruns·wick (brunz′wik), *n.* **1.** a former state of Germany: now part of Lower Saxony in Germany. **2.** a city in Lower Saxony, in N central Germany. 247,800. **3.** a town in NE Ohio. 27,689. **4.** a city in SE Georgia. 17,605. **5.** a town in SW Maine. 17,366. German, **Braunschweig** (for defs. 1, 2).

Bruns′wick stew′, **1.** (esp. in Virginia, Maryland, etc.) a stew of rabbit or squirrel meat cooked with onions and other vegetables. **2.** a similar dish made with chicken. [1855–60; after *Brunswick* Co., Virginia, where it originated]

brunt (brunt), *n.* the main force or impact, as of an attack or blow: *His arm took the brunt of the blow.* [1275–1325; ME; perh. orig. sexual assault; akin to ON *brundr,* G *Brunft* heat, ruttish state, OE *brunetha* heat, itching; c. OHG *bronado.* See BURN¹]
—Syn. thrust, stress, burden.

Bru·sa (*Turk.* BRO͞O sä′), *n.* Bursa.

brush¹ (brush), *n.* **1.** an implement consisting of bristles, hair, or the like, set in or attached to a handle, used for painting, cleaning, polishing, grooming, etc. **2.** one of a pair of devices consisting of long, thin handles with wire bristles attached, used in jazz or dance bands for keeping a soft, rhythmic beat on the trap drums or the cymbals. **3.** the bushy tail of an animal, esp. of a fox. **4.** *Elect.* **a.** a conductor, often made of carbon or copper or a combination of the two, serving to maintain electric contact between stationary and moving parts of a machine, generator, or other apparatus. **b.** See **brush discharge. 5.** a feathery or hairy tuft or tassel, as on the tip of a kernel of grain or on a man's hat. **6.** an act or instance of brushing; application of a brush. **7.** a light, stroking touch. **8.** a brief encounter: *He has already had one brush with the law.* **9.** a close approach, esp. to something undesirable or harmful: *a brush with disaster.* **10. get the brush,** to be rejected or rebuffed: *She greeted Jim effusively, but I got the brush.* **11. give the brush,** to ignore, rebuff, etc.: *If you're still angry with him, give him the brush.* —*v.t.* **12.** to sweep, paint, clean, polish, etc., with a brush. **13.** to touch lightly in passing; pass lightly over: *His lips brushed her ear.* **14.** to remove by brushing or by lightly passing over: *His hand brushed a speck of lint from his coat.* —*v.i.* **15.** to move or skim with a slight contact. **16. brush aside,** to disregard; ignore: *Our complaints were simply brushed aside.* **17. brush off,** to rebuff; send away: *She had never been brushed off so rudely before.* **18. brush up on,** to revive, review, or resume (studies, a skill, etc.): *She's thinking of brushing up on her tennis.* Also, **brush up.** [1350–1400; (n.) ME *brusshe,* prob. to be identified with BRUSH², if orig. sense was implement made from twigs, etc., culled from brushwood; (v.) ME *brushen* to hasten, rush, prob. < OF *brosser* to travel (through brush), v. deriv. of *broce* (see BRUSH²)] **—brush′a·ble,** *adj.* **—brush′er,** *n.* **—brush′like′,** *adj.*
—Syn. 8. engagement, action, skirmish. See **struggle.**

brush² (brush), *n.* **1.** a dense growth of bushes, shrubs, etc.; scrub; thicket. **2.** a pile or covering of lopped or broken branches; brushwood. **3.** bushes and low trees growing in thick profusion, esp. close to the ground. **4.** Also called **brushland.** land or an area covered with thickly growing bushes and low trees. **5.** backwoods; a sparsely settled wooded region. [1350–1400; ME *brusshe* < MF *broisse,* OF *broce* underbrush (cf. AF *brousson* wood, *brusseie* heath), perh. < VL **bruscia* excrescences, deriv. of L *bruscum* knot or excrescence on a maple tree] **—brush′i·ness,** *n.*

Brush (brush), *n.* **Katharine,** 1902–52, U.S. novelist and short-story writer.

brush·back (brush′bak′), *n. Baseball.* a fastball thrown high and inside to force the batter away from the plate, often to intimidate. [1950–55; n. use of v. phrase *brush back*]

brush′ bor′der, *Anat.* a dense array of microvilli projecting from the surface of certain epithelial tissues, as the lining of the intestinal tract. [1900–05]

brush′ broom′, **1.** *Northeastern U.S.* a whisk broom. **2.** *South Midland and Southern U.S.* a large broom made of bound twigs or husks and used for outdoor sweeping. [1860–65, *Amer.*]

brush′ cut′, a short haircut in which the hairs stand up like a brush.

brush′ dis′charge, *Elect.* a type of corona discharge that takes place between two electrodes at atmospheric pressure, characterized by long, branched, luminous streamers of ionized particles. [1840–50]

brushed (brusht), *adj.* having a nap raised or a surface produced by a brushing process: *brushed cotton.* [1425–75; late ME; see BRUSH¹, -ED²]

brush′ fire′, **1.** a fire in an area of bushes, shrubs, or brush, as distinct from a forest fire. **2.** any small but persistent problem, as within a large organization, a department of a government, or between nations: *border skirmishes and other international brush fires.* [1770–80, *Amer.*]

brush-fire (brush′fīər′), *adj.* limited in scope, area, or importance, as some labor disputes or local skirmishes. Also, **brush′fire′.** [1945–50]

brush′-foot·ed but′terfly (brush′fo͝ot′id), any of several butterflies of the family Nymphalidae, including the fritillaries, mourning cloaks, anglewings, and commas, characterized by reduced, nonfunctional forelegs. Also called **four-footed butterfly.**

brush·land (brush′land′), *n.* brush² (def. 4). [1850–55; BRUSH² + -LAND]

brush·less¹ (brush′lis), *adj.* requiring no brush to use or apply: *brushless shaving cream.* [1930–35; BRUSH¹ + -LESS] **—brush′less·ness,** *n.*

brush·less² (brush′lis), *adj.* clear or cleared of brush: *a brushless plain.* [1830–40; BRUSH² + -LESS] **—brush′·less·ness,** *n.*

brush-off (brush′ôf′, -of′), *n.* a refusal to talk or listen to someone; abrupt or final dismissal or rebuff. [1945–50, *Amer.*; n. use of v. phrase *brush off*]

brush-on (brush′on′, -ôn′), *adj.* **1.** fit to be applied with a brush: *a brush-on paint remover.* —*n.* **2.** a substance that can be applied with a brush: *The varnish dries more quickly than most brush-ons.* [adj., n. use of v. phrase *brush on*]

brush·pop·per (brush′pop′ər), *n. Western U.S.* a cowboy, esp. one who works in the brush. [1925–30, *Amer.*; BRUSH² + POPPER]

brush′ tur′key, megapode. [1840–50]

brush·up (brush′up′), *n.* **1.** the act or process of reviewing a subject, technique, or the like, for the purpose of renewing the memory, skill, etc.: *He gave his Spanish a brushup before his trip to Mexico.* **2.** the act or process of eliminating or repairing minor flaws: *He gave the collection a final brushup before putting it on display.* [1895–1900; n. use of v. phrase *brush up*]

brush·wood (brush′wo͝od′), *n.* **1.** the wood of branches that have been cut or broken off. **2.** a pile or covering of such branches. **3.** a growth or thicket of densely growing small trees and shrubs. [1630–40; BRUSH² + WOOD¹]

brush·work (brush′wûrk′), *n.* **1.** the use of a brush as a tool, as in painting. **2.** *Fine Arts.* the surface quality of a painting produced by the distribution of pigment with a brush. **3.** work for which a brush is used, as painting. [1865–70; BRUSH¹ + WORK]

brush·y¹ (brush′ē), *adj.,* **brush·i·er, brush·i·est.** resembling a brush, esp. in roughness or shagginess. [1680–90; BRUSH¹ + -Y¹]

brush·y² (brush′ē), *adj.,* **brush·i·er, brush·i·est.** covered or overgrown with brush or brushwood. [1650–60; BRUSH² + -Y¹] **—brush′i·ness,** *n.*

brusque (brusk; *esp. Brit.* bro͝osk), *adj.* abrupt in manner; blunt; rough: *A brusque welcome greeted his unexpected return.* Also, **brusk.** [1595–1605; < MF < It *brusco* rough, tart, special use of *brusco* (n.) butcher's broom < LL *brūscum,* for L *rūscus, rūscum,* perh. conflated with VL **brūcus* heather (see BRIER²)] **—brusque′ly,** *adv.* **—brusque′ness,** *n.*
—Syn. unceremonious, short, curt. See **blunt.**

Brus·sels (brus′əlz), *n.* a city in and the capital of Belgium, in the central part, with suburbs 1,050,787. Flemish, **Brus·sel** (BRYS′əl); French, **Bruxelles.**

Brus′sels car′pet, a carpet made with three-ply or four-ply worsted yarn drawn up in uncut loops to form a pattern over the entire surface **(body Brussels),** or made of worsted or woolen yarns on which a pattern is printed **(tapestry Brussels).** [1790–1800]

Brus′sels grif′fon, one of a Belgian breed of toy dogs having a thick, wiry, reddish-brown coat. [1935–40]

Brus′sels lace′, **1.** a fine handmade lace in a floral pattern outlined with raised cordonnet, originally made in the area of Brussels. **2.** a modern machine-made net lace on which floral designs are appliquéd. [1740–50]

Brus′sels sprout′, Usually, **Brussels sprouts. 1.** a plant, *Brassica oleracea gemmifera,* having small, cabbagelike heads or buds along the stalk, eaten as a vegetable. **2. Brussels sprouts.** any of the heads or buds, eaten as a vegetable. [1790–1800]

Brussels sprout, *Brassica oleracea*

brut (bro͞ot; *Fr.* BRYT), *adj.* (of wine, esp. champagne) very dry. [1890–95; < F: raw; see BRUTE²]

Brut (bro͞ot), *n.* any of a number of partly legendary, partly historical chronicles dealing with early English history, written during the Middle Ages and usually beginning with Brutus, the mythic and eponymous ancestor of the country. [1300–50; ME < OF < ML *Brūtus*]

bru·tal (bro͞ot′l), *adj.* **1.** savage; cruel; inhuman: *a brutal attack on the village.* **2.** crude; coarse: *brutal language.* **3.** harsh; ferocious: *brutal criticism; brutal weather.* **4.** taxing, demanding, or exhausting: *They're having a brutal time making ends meet.* **5.** irrational; unreasoning. **6.** of or pertaining to lower animals. [1425–75; late ME (< MF) < ML *brūtālis.* See BRUTE¹, -AL¹] **—bru′tal·ly,** *adv.*
—Syn. 1. ferocious, brutish, barbarous. See **cruel. 2.** gross, rude, rough, uncivil. **6.** bestial, beastly, animal.
—Ant. 1. kind. **6.** human.

bru·tal·ism (bro͞ot′l iz′əm), *n.* (in modern architecture) the aesthetic use of basic building processes with no apparent concern for visual amenity. [1795–1805, for literal sense; BRUTAL + -ISM; in reference to architecture first used by British architects Alison Smithson (b. 1928) and Peter Smithson (b. 1923) in 1953] **—bru′tal·ist,** *n., adj.*

bru·tal·i·ty (bro͞o tal′i tē), *n., pl.* **-ties. 1.** the quality of being brutal; cruelty; savagery. **2.** a brutal act or practice. [1540–50; BRUTAL + -ITY]

bru·tal·ize (bro͞ot′l īz′), *v.t.* **-ized, -iz·ing. 1.** to make brutal. **2.** to treat (someone) with brutality. Also, *esp. Brit.,* **bru′tal·ise′.** [1695–1705; BRUTAL + -IZE] **—bru′·tal·i·za′tion,** *n.*

brute¹ (bro͞ot), *n.* **1.** a nonhuman creature; beast. **2.** a brutal, insensitive, or crude person. **3.** the animal qualities, desires, etc., of humankind: *Father felt that rough games brought out the brute in us.* —*adj.* **4.** animal; not human. **5.** not characterized by intelligence or reason; irrational. **6.** characteristic of animals; of brutal character or quality. **7.** savage; cruel: *brute force.* **8.** carnal; sensual. [1375–1425; late ME < MF < L *brūtus* heavy, devoid of feeling, irrational] **—brute′like′,** *adj.* **—brute′ly,** *adv.* **—brute′ness,** *n.*
—Syn. 1. See **animal.**

brute² (bro͞ot), *v.t.,* **brut·ed, brut·ing.** to shape (a diamond) by rubbing with another diamond or a diamond chip. [back formation from *bruting* a rough hewing (of a diamond), partial trans. of F *brutage* lit., a roughing, equiv. to *brut* rough, raw (see BRUTE¹) + *-age* -AGE]

brut·ish (bro͞o′tish), *adj.* **1.** brutal; cruel. **2.** gross; coarse. **3.** carnal; sensual. **4.** uncivilized. **5.** bestial; like an animal. [1485–95; BRUTE¹ + -ISH¹] **—brut′ish·ly,** *adv.* **—brut′ish·ness,** *n.*

Bru·tus (bro͞o′təs), *n.* **Marcus Jun·ius** (jo͞on′yəs), 85?–42 B.C., Roman provincial administrator: one of the assassins of Julius Caesar.

Brux·elles (*Fr.* BRY sel′, BRYK-), *n.* Brussels.

brux·ism (bruk′siz əm), *n. Pathol.* See **teeth grinding.** [1935–40; < Gk **brȳx(is)* a gnashing of teeth (*brȳk-(ein)* to gnash, bite + *-sis* -SIS) + -ISM]

Bry·an (brī′ən), *n.* **1. William Jen·nings** (jen′ingz), 1860–1925, U.S. political leader. **2.** a city in E Texas. 44,337. **3.** a male given name.

Bry′an-Cha·mor′ro Trea′ty (brī′ən chä môr′ō), a treaty (1914) between the U.S. and Nicaragua by which the U.S. secured exclusive rights to build a canal across Nicaragua, to connect the Atlantic and Pacific.

Bry·ansk (brē änsk′; *Russ.* BRYänsk), *n.* a city in the W Russian Federation, on the Desna River, SW of Moscow. 445,000.

Bry·ant (brī′ənt), *n.* **1. Grid·ley** (grid′lē), 1789–1867, U.S. engineer and inventor. **2. William Cullen,** 1794–1878, U.S. poet and journalist. **3.** a male given name.

Bryce (brīs), *n.* **James, 1st Viscount,** 1838–1922, British diplomat, historian, and jurist: born in Ireland.

Bryce′ Can′yon Na′tional Park′, a national park in SW Utah: rock formations.

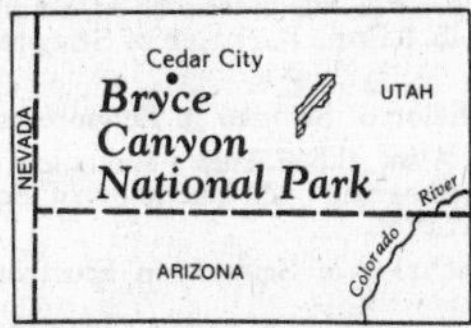

Bryn·hild (brin′hild), *n. Scand. Legend.* a Valkyrie and the wife of Gunnar, for whom she was won by Sigurd: corresponds to Brunhild in the *Nibelungenlied.*

bryn·za (brin′zə), *n.* (in Eastern Europe and Asia Minor) a crumbly, sharp cheese made from sheep's milk and cured. Also, **brynd·za** (brind′zə). [< Rumanian *brînză* cheese < an indigenous language of uncert. identity, perh. akin to pre-Roman Albanian]

bryo-, a combining form meaning "moss, liverwort," used in the formation of compound words: *bryology.* [comb. form repr. Gk *brýon* moss]

bry·ol·o·gy (brī ol′ə jē), *n.* the branch of botany dealing with bryophytes. [1860–65; BRYO- + -LOGY] **—bry·o·log·i·cal** (brī′ə loj′i kəl), *adj.* **—bry·ol′o·gist,** *n.*

bry·o·ny (brī′ə nē), *n., pl.* **-nies.** any Old World vine or climbing plant belonging to the genus *Bryonia,* of the gourd family, yielding acrid juice having emetic and purgative properties. Also, **briony.** [bef. 1000; ME *brionie,* OE *bryōnia* < L < Gk: a wild vine]

bry·o·phyl·lum (brī′ə fil′əm), *n.* any of various kalanchoes, as *Kalanchoe pinnata,* that characteristically bear plantlets along the leaf margins. [< NL (1805), orig. a genus name, equiv. to *bryo-* BRYO- + Gk *phýllon* leaf]

bry·o·phyte (brī′ə fīt′), *n. Bot.* any of the Bryophyta, a phylum of nonvascular plants comprising the true mosses and liverworts. [1875–80; < NL *Bryophyta* name of the group; see BRYO-, -PHYTE] **—bry·o·phyt·ic** (brī′ə-fit′ik), *adj.*

Bry·o·zo·a (brī′ə zō′ə), *n.* a phylum of invertebrates comprising about 4000 marine and freshwater species of bryozoans. Cf. **Ectoprocta, Entoprocta.** [1840–50; < NL; see BRYO-, -ZOA]

bry·o·zo·an (brī′ə zō′ən), *adj.* **1.** belonging or pertaining to the Bryozoa. —*n.* **2.** Also called **moss animal.** any sessile marine or freshwater animal of the phylum Bryozoa, forming branching, encrusting, or gelatinous mosslike colonies of many small polyps, each having a circular or horseshoe-shaped ridge bearing ciliated tentacles, occurring on algae or on shelled objects. Cf. **ectoproct, entoproct.** [1870–75; BRYOZO(A) + -AN]

Bryth•on (brith′ən, -on), *n.* **1.** a member of the Brythonic-speaking Celts. **2.** a Briton. [1880–85; < Welsh; see BRITON]

Bry•thon•ic (bri thon′ik), *adj.* **1.** of or belonging to P-Celtic. —*n.* **2.** P-Celtic, esp. that part either spoken in Britain, as Welsh and Cornish, or descended from the P-Celtic speech of Britain, as Breton. Also, **Britannic, Brittonic.** [1880–85; BRYTHON + -IC]

Brześć nad B•u•giem (bzheshch′ näd bo͞o′gyem). Polish name of **Brest Litovsk.**

BS, *Slang (sometimes vulgar).* bullshit.

b/s, 1. bags. **2.** bales. **3.** See **bill of sale.**

B.S., 1. See **Bachelor of Science. 2.** Bachelor of Surgery. **3.** See **bill of sale. 4.** *Slang (sometimes vulgar).* bullshit.

b.s., 1. balance sheet. **2.** See **bill of sale. 3.** *Slang (sometimes vulgar).* bullshit.

B.S.A., 1. Also, **B.S. Agr.** Bachelor of Science in Agriculture. **2.** Bachelor of Scientific Agriculture. **3.** Boy Scouts of America.

B.S.A.A., Bachelor of Science in Applied Arts.

B.S.Adv., Bachelor of Science in Advertising.

B.S.A.E., 1. Also, **B.S.Ae.Eng.** Bachelor of Science in Aeronautical Engineering. **2.** Also, **B.S.Ag.E.** Bachelor of Science in Agricultural Engineering. **3.** Also, **B.S.Arch.E., B.S.Arch.Eng.** Bachelor of Science in Architectural Engineering.

B.S.Arch., Bachelor of Science in Architecture.

B.S.Art.Ed., Bachelor of Science in Art Education.

B.S.B.A., Bachelor of Science in Business Administration.

B.S.Bus., Bachelor of Science in Business.

B.S.Bus.Mgt., Bachelor of Science in Business Management.

B.Sc., See **Bachelor of Science.**

B.S.C., Bachelor of Science in Commerce.

B.S.C.E., Bachelor of Science in Civil Engineering.

B.S.Ch., Bachelor of Science in Chemistry.

B.S.Ch.E., Bachelor of Science in Chemical Engineering.

B.Sch.Music, Bachelor of School Music.

B school, *Informal.* business school. Also, **B-school.**

B.S.Com., Bachelor of Science in Communications.

B.S.C.P., Brotherhood of Sleeping Car Porters.

B.S.D., Bachelor of Science in Design. Also, **B.S.Des.**

B.S.D.Hyg., Bachelor of Science in Dental Hygiene.

B.S.E., 1. Also, **B.S.Ed.** Bachelor of Science in Education. **2.** Also, **B.S.Eng.** Bachelor of Science in Engineering.

B.S.Ec., Bachelor of Science in Economics.

B.S.E.E., 1. Also, **B.S.E.Engr.** Bachelor of Science in Electrical Engineering. **2.** Bachelor of Science in Elementary Education.

B.S.El.E., Bachelor of Science in Electronic Engineering.

B.S.E.M., Bachelor of Science in Engineering of Mines.

B.S.E.P., Bachelor of Science in Engineering Physics.

B.S.E.S., Bachelor of Science in Engineering Sciences.

B.S.F., Bachelor of Science in Forestry. Also, **B.S.For.**

B.S.F.M., Bachelor of Science in Forest Management.

B.S.F.Mgt., Bachelor of Science in Fisheries Management.

B.S.F.S., Bachelor of Science in Foreign Service.

B.S.F.T., Bachelor of Science in Fuel Technology.

B.S.G.E., Bachelor of Science in General Engineering. Also, **B.S.Gen.Ed.**

B.S.G.Mgt., Bachelor of Science in Game Management.

bsh., bushel; bushels.

B.S.H.A., Bachelor of Science in Hospital Administration.

B.S.H.E., Bachelor of Science in Home Economics. Also, **B.S.H.Ec.**

B.S.H.Ed., Bachelor of Science in Health Education.

B.S.Hyg., Bachelor of Science in Hygiene.

B.S.I.E., 1. Also, **B.S.Ind.Ed.** Bachelor of Science in Industrial Education. **2.** Also, **B.S.Ind.Engr.** Bachelor of Science in Industrial Engineering.

B.S.Ind.Mgt., Bachelor of Science in Industrial Management.

B.S.I.R., Bachelor of Science in Industrial Relations.

B.S.I.T., Bachelor of Science in Industrial Technology.

B.S.J., Bachelor of Science in Journalism.

bskt., basket.

Bs/L, bills of lading.

B.S.L., 1. Bachelor of Sacred Literature. **2.** Bachelor of Science in Law. **3.** Bachelor of Science in Linguistics.

B.S.L.A. and Nurs., Bachelor of Science in Liberal Arts and Nursing.

B.S.Lab.Rel., Bachelor of Science in Labor Relations.

B.S.L.Arch., Bachelor of Science in Landscape Architecture.

CONCISE ETYMOLOGY KEY: <, descended or borrowed from; >, whence; b., blend of, blended; c., cognate with; cf., compare; deriv., derivative; equiv., equivalent; imit., imitative; obl., oblique; r., replacing; s., stem; sp., spelling, spelled; resp., respelling, respelled; trans., translation; ?, origin unknown; *, unattested; ‡, probably earlier than. See the full key inside the front cover.

B.S.L.M., Bachelor of Science in Landscape Management.

B.S.L.S., Bachelor of Science in Library Science.

B.S.M., 1. Bachelor of Sacred Music. **2.** Bachelor of Science in Medicine. **3.** Bachelor of Science in Music.

B.S.M.E., 1. Bachelor of Science in Mechanical Engineering. **2.** Bachelor of Science in Mining Engineering. **3.** Also, **B.S.Mus.Ed.** Bachelor of Science in Music Education.

B.S.Met., Bachelor of Science in Metallurgy.

B.S.Met.E., Bachelor of Science in Metallurgical Engineering.

Bsmt, basement.

B.S.M.T., Bachelor of Science in Medical Technology. Also, **B.S.Med.Tech.**

B.S.N., Bachelor of Science in Nursing.

B.S.N.A., Bachelor of Science in Nursing Administration.

BSO, *Astron.* See **blue stellar object.**

B.S.Orn.Hort., Bachelor of Science in Ornamental Horticulture.

B.S.O.T., Bachelor of Science in Occupational Therapy.

B.S.P., Bachelor of Science in Pharmacy. Also, **B.S.Phar., B.S.Pharm.**

B.S.P.A., Bachelor of Science in Public Administration.

B.S.P.E., Bachelor of Science in Physical Education.

B.S.P.H., Bachelor of Science in Public Health.

B.S.P.H.N., Bachelor of Science in Public Health Nursing.

B.S.P.T., Bachelor of Science in Physical Therapy.

B.S.Radio-TV., Bachelor of Science in Radio and Television.

B.S.Ret., Bachelor of Science in Retailing.

B.S.R.T., Bachelor of Science in Radiological Technology.

B.S.S., 1. Bachelor of Secretarial Science. **2.** Bachelor of Social Science.

B.S.S.A., Bachelor of Science in Secretarial Administration.

B.S.S.E., Bachelor of Science in Secondary Education.

B.S.S.S., 1. Bachelor of Science in Secretarial Studies. **2.** Bachelor of Science in Social Science.

B.S.T.&I.E., Bachelor of Science in Trade and Industrial Education.

B star, *Astron.* a massive, relatively hot, blue to white star, as Rigel or Spica, having a surface temperature between 10,000 and 30,000 K and with an absorption spectrum dominated by the Balmer series of hydrogen with lines of neutral helium present. Cf. **spectral type.**

B.S.Trans., Bachelor of Science in Transportation.

B supply, *Electronics.* a battery or other source of power for supplying a constant positive voltage to the plate of a vacuum tube. Cf. **A supply, C supply.**

Bt., Baronet.

bt., 1. boat. **2.** bought.

B.T., Bachelor of Theology.

B.t., See **Bacillus thuringiensis.**

B.T.Ch., Bachelor of Textile Chemistry.

B.T.E., Bachelor of Textile Engineering.

bth, bathroom.

B.Th., Bachelor of Theology.

btl., bottle.

btry., battery.

B.T.U., *Physics.* British thermal unit; British thermal units. Also, **BTU, B.t.u., B.th.u., Btu**

bu., 1. bureau. **2.** bushel; bushels.

bub (bub), *n. Slang.* (used as an often insolent term of address) brother; buddy. [1830–40, *Amer.*; perh. < G *Bub*, short for *Bube* boy]

bu•bal (byo͞o′bəl), *n.* a hartebeest, *Alcelaphus boselaphus*, of northern Africa. Also, **bu•ba•lis** (byo͞o′bə lis). [1350–1400; ME: aurochs, antelope < L *būbalus* < Gk *boúbalos* a kind of gazelle or buffalo]

bu•ba•line (byo͞o′bə līn′, -lin), *adj.* **1.** (of antelopes) resembling or like the bubal, as the hartebeests or blesbok. **2.** pertaining to or resembling the true buffaloes. [1820–30; < L *būbalinus.* See BUBAL, -INE[1]]

bub•ba (bub′ə), *n., pl.* **-bas. 1.** *Chiefly Southern U.S.* brother. **2.** *Slang.* an uneducated Southern white male; good old boy; redneck. [1860–65]

bub•ble (bub′əl), *n., v.,* **-bled, -bling.** —*n.* **1.** a nearly spherical body of gas contained in a liquid. **2.** a small globule of gas in a thin liquid envelope. **3.** a globule of air or gas, or a globular vacuum, contained in a solid. **4.** anything that lacks firmness, substance, or permanence; an illusion or delusion. **5.** an inflated speculation, esp. if fraudulent: *The real-estate bubble ruined many investors.* **6.** the act or sound of bubbling. **7.** a spherical or nearly spherical canopy or shelter; dome: *A network of radar bubbles stretches across northern Canada.* **8.** a domelike structure, usually of inflated plastic, used to enclose a swimming pool, tennis court, etc. **9.** *Informal.* a protected, exempt, or unique area, industry, etc.: *The oasis is a bubble of green in the middle of the desert.* **10.** an area that can be defended, protected, patrolled, etc., or that comes under one's jurisdiction: *The carrier fleet's bubble includes the Hawaiian Islands.* **11.** a sudden, small, temporary change or divergence from a trend: *In May there was a bubble in car sales, with three percent more being sold than last year.* —*v.i.* **12.** to form, produce, or release bubbles; effervesce. **13.** to flow or spout with a gurgling noise; gurgle. **14.** to boil. **15.** to speak, move, issue forth, or exist in a lively, sparkling manner; exude cheer: *The play bubbled with songs and dances.* **16.** to seethe or stir, as with excitement: *His mind bubbles with plans and schemes.* —*v.t.* **17.** to cause to bubble; make bubbles in. **18.** *Archaic.* to cheat; deceive; swindle. **19. bubble over,** to become lively: *The last time I saw her she was bubbling over with enthusiasm.* [1350–1400; ME *bobel* (n.); c. MD *bobbel*, MLG *bubbele*, Sw *bubbla*] —**bub′ble•less,** *adj.* —**bub′ble•like′,** *adj.* —**bub′bling•ly,** *adv.*

bub′ble and squeak′, *Brit.* a dish of meat, usually beef, and cabbage fried or boiled together. [1765–75]

bub′ble bath′, 1. a crystal, powder, or liquid preparation that foams in, scents, and softens bathwater. **2.** a bath with such a preparation added to the water. [1945–50]

bub′ble bowl′, a spherical, usually clear glass vessel with a wide circular top opening, used as a vase, esp. for displaying a single floating blossom. [1935–40, *Amer.*]

bub′ble card′. See **blister pack.** [1975–80]

bub′ble cham′ber, *Physics.* an apparatus for determining the movements of charged particles, consisting of a chamber containing a superheated transparent liquid that, by boiling and producing bubbles in the path of an ionizing particle, indicates the path of the particle. Cf. **cloud chamber.** [1950–55]

bub′ble dance′, a solo dance by a nude or nearly nude woman, as in a burlesque show, using one or more balloons for covering. Cf. **fan dance.** [1935–40, *Amer.*] —**bub′ble danc′er.**

bub•ble•gum (bub′əl gum′), *n.* **1.** a type of chewing gum that can be blown into large bubbles through the lips. **2.** *Slang.* light rock-'n'-roll music characterized by simple, repetitive phrasing and lyrics. [1935–40; BUBBLE + GUM]

bub•ble•gum•mer (bub′əl gum′ər), *n. Slang.* a young teenager; adolescent. [BUBBLEGUM + -ER[1]]

bub•ble•head (bub′əl hed′), *n. Slang.* a stupid or foolish person; dolt. [1950–55; BUBBLE + HEAD] —**bub′•ble•head′ed,** *adj.*

bub′ble mem′ory, *Computers.* a storage medium employing tiny, movable, bubble-shaped magnetized areas within a magnetic material to represent data bits. [1970–75]

bub′ble pack′. See **blister pack.**

bub•bler (bub′lər), *n.* **1.** a drinking fountain that spouts water. **2.** *Chem.* any device for bubbling gas through a liquid. [1710–20; BUBBLE + -ER[1]]

bub•ble•top (bub′əl top′), *n.* **1.** a transparent dome, usually made of plastic or bulletproof glass, that serves as the roof or part of the roof of an automotive vehicle. **2.** a vehicle having such a dome: *The old van was converted into a bubbletop.* —*adj.* **3.** fitted with such a dome: *a bubbletop limousine.* Also, **bub′ble-top′.** [1965–70; BUBBLE + TOP[1]]

bub′ble wrap′, a clear, bubble-filled plastic material used esp. for cushioning breakable objects during shipment.

bub•bly (bub′lē), *adj.,* **-bli•er, -bli•est,** *n., pl.* **-blies.** —*adj.* **1.** full of, producing, or characterized by bubbles. **2.** lively; effervescent; enthusiastic: *the bubbly spirit of those early movie musicals.* —*n.* **3.** *Informal.* champagne (defs. 1, 2). [1590–1600; BUBBLE + -Y[1]] —**bub′bli•ness,** *n.*

bub•by (bo͞o′bē, bo͝ob′ē, bub′ē), *n., pl.* **-bies.** *Slang.* a female breast. [1680–90; perh. imit. of baby's cry or of sucking sound; see -Y[2]]

Bu•ber (bo͞o′bər), *n.* **Martin,** 1878–1965, Jewish philosopher, theologian, and scholar of Hasidism: born in Austria, in Israel from 1938.

bu•bo (byo͞o′bō, bo͞o′-), *n., pl.* **-boes.** *Pathol.* an inflammatory swelling of a lymphatic gland, esp. in the groin or armpit. [1350–1400; ME < LL < Gk *boubṓn* lit., groin] —**bu′boed,** *adj.*

bu•bon•ic (byo͞o bon′ik, bo͞o-), *adj. Pathol.* **1.** of or pertaining to a bubo. **2.** accompanied by or affected with buboes. [1870–75; < LL *būbōn-* (s. of *būbō*) BUBO + -IC]

bubon′ic plague′, *Pathol.* a serious, sometimes fatal, infection with the bacterial toxin *Yersinia pestis*, transmitted by fleas from infected rodents and characterized by high fever, weakness, and the formation of buboes, esp. in the groin and armpits. Cf. **Black Death.** [1885–90]

bu•bon•o•cele (byo͞o bon′ə sēl′, bo͞o-), *n. Pathol.* an inguinal hernia, esp. one in which the protrusion of the intestine is limited to the region of the groin. [1605–15; < Gk *boubōno-*, comb. form of *boubṓn* groin + -CELE[1]]

bu•bu (bo͞o′bo͞o), *n.* boubou.

Bu•ca•ra•man•ga (bo͞o′kä rä mäng′gä), *n.* a city in N Colombia. 340,783.

buc•cal (buk′əl), *adj. Anat.* **1.** of or pertaining to the cheek. **2.** pertaining to the sides of the mouth or to the mouth; oral. **3.** *Dentistry.* directed toward the cheek. Cf. **distal** (def. 2), **mesial** (def. 2). [1825–35; (< F) < L *bucc(a)* (see BUCCO-) + -AL[1]] —**buc′cal•ly,** *adv.*

buc•ca•neer (buk′ə nēr′), *n.* **1.** any of the piratical adventurers who raided Spanish colonies and ships along the American coast in the second half of the 17th century. **2.** any pirate. [1655–65; < F *boucanier*, lit., barbecuer, equiv. to *boucan* barbecue (< Tupi, var. of *mukém*) + *-ier* -EER] —**buc′ca•neer′ish,** *adj.*

buc•ca•ro (bo͞o kär′ō), *n.* unglazed pottery. [see BUCCHERO]

buc•che•ro (bo͞o′kə rō′, bo͝ok′ə-), *n., pl.* **-ros.** an Etruscan black ceramic ware, often ornamented with incised geometrical patterns or figures carved in relief. [1885–90; < It < Sp *búcaro* < Pg: clay vessel, earlier *púcaro* < Mozarabic < L *pōculum* goblet. See POTION, -CULE[2]]

buc•ci•na•tor (buk′sə nā′tər), *n. Anat.* a thin, flat muscle lining the cheek, the action of which contracts and compresses the cheek. [1665–75; < NL; L *buccinātor, būcinātor* trumpeter, equiv. to *būcinā(re)* to signal on a trumpet (v. deriv. of *būcina* curved trumpet or horn) + *-tor* -TOR] —**buc·ci·na·to·ry** (buk′sə nə tôr′ē, -tōr′ē, buk′sə nā′tə rē), *adj.*

bucco-, a combining form meaning "cheek," "mouth," used in the formation of compound words: *buccolingual.* [< L *bucc(a)* lower cheek, jaw, mouth + -O-]

buc·co·lin·gual (buk′ə ling′gwəl *or, Can.,* -ling′gyoo-əl), *adj. Anat.* of or pertaining to the cheek and tongue. [BUCCO- + LINGUAL]

Bu·ceph·a·lus (byoo sef′ə ləs), *n.* the horse used by Alexander the Great on most of his military campaigns.

Buch·an (buk′ən; *Scot.* bukн′ən), *n.* **John** (*Baron Tweedsmuir*), 1875–1940, Scottish novelist and historian: governor general of Canada 1935–40.

Bu·chan·an (byoo kan′ən, bə-), *n.* **James,** 1791–1868, 15th president of the U.S. 1857–61.

Bu·cha·rest (bōō′kə rest′, byōō′-), *n.* a city in and the capital of Rumania, in the S part. 1,832,015. Rumanian, **București.**

Bu·chen·wald (bōō′kən wôld′, bŏŏk′ən-; *Ger.* bōōкн′ən vält′), *n.* site of a former Nazi concentration camp in central Germany, near Weimar.

Buch·man·ism (bŏŏk′mə niz′əm, buk′-), *n.* the principles or the international movement of Moral Re-Armament or of the Oxford Group, or belief in or adherence to them. [1925–30; Frank N. D. *Buchman* (1879–1961), U.S. religious leader; see -ISM] —**Buch·man·ite** (bŏŏk′mə-nit′, buk′-), *n.*

bu·chu (bōō′kōō, byōō′kyōō), *n.* any of several southern African citrus shrubs of the genus *Agathosma* or the genus *Diosma*, esp. *A. betulina, A. crenulata,* or *D. ericoides,* whose leaves yield a dark-colored oil formerly used as a urinary antiseptic and mild diuretic. [1725–35; < Afrik (now sp. *boegoe*) < Khoikhoi, first attested as *boggoa* (1668)]

buck[1] (buk), *n.* **1.** the male of the deer, antelope, rabbit, hare, sheep, or goat. **2.** the male of certain other animals, as the shad. **3.** an impetuous, dashing, or spirited man or youth. **4.** *Often Disparaging.* a male American Indian or black. **5.** buckskin. **6. bucks,** casual oxford shoes made of buckskin, often in white or a neutral color. —*adj.* **7.** *Mil.* of the lowest of several ranks involving the same principal designation, hence subject to promotion within the rank: *buck private; buck sergeant.* [bef. 1000; ME *bukke,* OE *bucca* he-goat, *bucc* male deer; c. D *bok,* G *Bock,* ON *bukkr;* def. 5, 6 by shortening; *buck private* (from ca. 1870) perh. as extension of general sense "male," i.e., having no status other than being male]

buck[2] (buk), *v.i.* **1.** (of a saddle or pack animal) to leap with arched back and come down with head low and forelegs stiff, in order to dislodge a rider or pack. **2.** *Informal.* to resist or oppose obstinately; object strongly: *The mayor bucked at the school board's suggestion.* **3.** (of a vehicle, motor, or the like) to operate unevenly; move by jerks and bounces. —*v.t.* **4.** to throw or attempt to throw (a rider or pack) by bucking. **5.** to force a way through or proceed against (an obstacle): *The plane bucked a strong headwind.* **6.** to strike with the head; butt. **7.** to resist or oppose obstinately; object strongly to. **8.** *Football.* (of a ball-carrier) to charge into (the opponent's line). **9.** to gamble, play, or take a risk against: *He was bucking the odds when he bought that failing business.* **10.** to press a reinforcing device against (the force of a rivet) in order to absorb vibration and increase expansion. **11. buck for,** to strive for a promotion or some other advantage: *to buck for a raise.* **12. buck up,** to make or become more cheerful, vigorous, etc.: *She knew that with a change of scene she would soon buck up.* —*n.* **13.** an act of bucking. [1855–60; verbal use of BUCK[1], influenced in some senses by BUCK[3]]

buck[3] (buk), *n.* **1.** a sawhorse. **2.** *Gymnastics.* a cylindrical, leather-covered block mounted in a horizontal position on a single vertical post set in a steel frame, for use chiefly in vaulting. **3.** any of various heavy frames, racks, or jigs used to support materials or partially assembled items during manufacture, as in airplane assembly plants. **4.** Also called **door buck.** a doorframe of wood or metal set in a partition, esp. one of light masonry, to support door hinges, hardware, finish work, etc. —*v.t.* **5.** to split or saw (logs, felled trees, etc.). **6. buck in,** *Survey., Optical Tooling.* to set up an instrument in line with two marks. [1855–60; short for SAWBUCK]

buck[4] (buk), *n.* **1.** *Poker.* any object in the pot that reminds the winner of some privilege or obligation when his or her turn to deal next comes. **2. pass the buck,** to shift responsibility or blame to another person: *Never one to admit error, he passed the buck to his subordinates.* —*v.t.* **3.** to pass (something) along to another, esp. as a means of avoiding responsibility or blame: *He bucked the letter on to the assistant vice president to answer.* [1860–65; short for *buckhorn knife,* an object which served this function]

buck[5] (buk), *Brit. Dial.* —*n.* **1.** lye used for washing clothes. **2.** clothes washed in lye. —*v.t.* **3.** to wash or bleach (clothes) in lye. [1350–1400; ME *bouken* (v.); cf. MLG *buken, büken* to steep in lye, MHG *būchen, bruchen*]

buck[6] (buk), *v.i., n. Anglo-Indian.* bukh.

buck[7] (buk), *adv. Informal.* completely; stark: *buck naked.* [1925–30, *Amer.*; of obscure orig.]

buck[8] (buk), *n. Slang.* a dollar. [1855–60, *Amer.*; perh. BUCK[1] in sense "buckskin"; deerskins were used by Indians and frontiersmen as a unit of exchange in transactions with merchants]

Buck (buk), *n.* **1. Pearl (Sy·den·strick·er)** (sīd′n-strik′ər), 1892–1973, U.S. novelist: Nobel prize 1938. **2.** a male given name.

buck′ and wing′, a tap dance derived in style from black and Irish clog dances, marked esp. by vigorous hopping, flinging of the legs, and clicking of the heels. [1890–95, *Amer.*]

buck·a·roo (buk′ə rōō′, buk′ə rōō′), *n., pl.* **-roos. 1.** *Western U.S.* a cowboy, esp. a broncobuster. **2.** *Older Slang.* fellow; guy. [1820–30, *Amer.*; earlier *bakhara, baccaro, bucharo* < Sp *vaquero,* equiv. to *vac(a)* cow (< L *vacca*) + *-ero* < L *-ārius* -ARY; perh. influenced by BUCKRA; later prob. reanalyzed as BUCK[1] + -EROO]

buck′ bean′, a bog plant, *Menyanthes trifoliata,* of the gentian family, having narrow clusters of white or pink flowers. Also called **bogbean, marsh trefoil.** [1570–80; earlier *buckes bean,* trans. of D *boksboon*]

buck·board (buk′bôrd′, -bōrd′), *n.* a light, four-wheeled carriage in which a long elastic board or lattice frame is used in place of body and springs. [1830–40, *Amer.*; obs. *buck* body, holder (see BUCKET) + BOARD]

buckboard

bucked (bukt), *adj. Brit. Informal.* happy; elated. [1905–10; BUCK[2] + -ED[2]]

buck·er[1] (buk′ər), *n.* **1.** a horse that bucks. **2.** a person who bucks rivets. **3.** a person employed to carry, shovel, lift, or load coal, farm produce, etc. [1880–85, *Amer.*; BUCK[2] + -ER[1]]

buck·er[2] (buk′ər), *n. Canadian.* (in lumbering) a person who saws felled trees into shorter, more easily hauled lengths. [1905–10; *buck* to cut wood with a bucksaw + -ER[1]]

buck·et (buk′it), *n., v.,* **-et·ed, -et·ing.** —*n.* **1.** a deep, cylindrical vessel, usually of metal, plastic, or wood, with a flat bottom and a semicircular bail, for collecting, carrying, or holding water, sand, fruit, etc.; pail. **2.** anything resembling or suggesting this. **3.** *Mach.* **a.** any of the scoops attached to or forming the endless chain in certain types of conveyors or elevators. **b.** the scoop or clamshell of a steam shovel, power shovel, or dredge. **c.** a vane or blade of a waterwheel, paddle wheel, water turbine, or the like. **4.** (in a dam) a concave surface at the foot of a spillway for deflecting the downward flow of water. **5.** a bucketful: *a bucket of sand.* **6.** *Basketball.* **a.** *Informal.* See **field goal. b.** the part of the keyhole extending from the foul line to the end line. **7.** See **bucket seat. 8.** *Bowling.* a leave of the two, four, five, and eight pins, or the three, five, six, and nine pins. See illus. under **bowling. 9. drop in the bucket,** a small, usually inadequate amount in relation to what is needed or requested: *The grant for research was just a drop in the bucket.* **10. drop the bucket on,** *Australian Slang.* to implicate, incriminate, or expose. **11. kick the bucket,** *Slang.* to die: *His children were greedily waiting for him to kick the bucket.* —*v.t.* **12.** to lift, carry, or handle in a bucket (often fol. by *up* or *out*). **13.** *Chiefly Brit.* to ride (a horse) fast and without concern for tiring it. **14.** to handle (orders, transactions, etc.) in or as if in a bucket shop. —*v.i.* **15.** *Informal.* to move or drive fast; hurry. [1250–1300; ME *buket* < AF < OE *bucc* (var. of *būc* vessel, belly; c. G *Bauch*) + OF *-et* -ET]
—**Regional Variation.** Though both BUCKET and PAIL are used throughout the entire U.S., PAIL has its greatest use in the Northern U.S., and BUCKET is more commonly used elsewhere, esp. in the Midland and Southern U.S.

buck′et bench′. See **water bench.**

buck′et brigade′, 1. a line of persons formed to extinguish a fire by passing on buckets of water quickly from a distant source. **2.** any group of persons who cooperate to help cope with an emergency. [1910–15]

buck′et convey′or, *Mach.* a conveyor consisting of an endless chain with a series of buckets attached at regular intervals, used for moving ore, gravel, grain, or other bulk materials.

buck·et·ful (buk′it fŏŏl′), *n., pl.* **-fuls.** the amount that a bucket can hold: *a bucketful of water.* [1555–65; BUCKET + -FUL]
—**Usage.** See **-ful.**

buck′et seat′, an individual seat with a rounded or contoured back, as in some automobiles and airplanes, often made to fold forward. Also called **bucket.** [1905–10]

buck′et shop′, 1. *Stock Exchange.* an unsound, unethical, or overly aggressive brokerage house. **2.** *Slang.* any shady commercial agency, as one dealing in illegally priced theater tickets. [1870–75, *Amer.*; orig. a cheap drinking establishment, allegedly so called because liquor was mixed or sold in buckets]

buck·eye (buk′ī′), *n., pl.* **-eyes. 1.** any of various trees or shrubs of the genus *Aesculus,* as *A. glabra* **(Ohio buckeye),** having palmate leaves, gray, scaly bark, and bell-shaped greenish-yellow flowers in upright clusters: the state tree of Ohio. **2.** the brown nut of any of these trees. **3.** (*cap.*) a native or inhabitant of Ohio (used as a nickname). **4.** a butterfly, *Precis lavinia,* having dark-brown wings with purple or red eyespots. [1755–65, *Amer.*; BUCK[1] stag + EYE, orig. used to designate def. 1, in allusion to the look of the seed]

Buck′eye State′, Ohio (used as a nickname).

buck′ fe′ver, 1. nervous excitement of an inexperienced hunter upon the approach of game. **2.** any nervous excitement preceding a new experience. [1835–45, *Amer.*]

buck·hound (buk′hound′), *n.* a hound trained to hunt bucks and other game. [1520–30; BUCK[1] + HOUND[1]]

Buck·ing·ham (buk′ing əm, -ham′), *n.* **1. George Villiers, 1st Duke of,** 1592–1628, English courtier, politician, and military leader: lord high admiral 1617. **2.** his son, **George Villiers, 2nd Duke of,** 1628–87, English courtier and author. **3.** Buckinghamshire.

Buck′ingham Pal′ace, 1. a residence of the British sovereigns since 1837, in London, England: built 1703. **2.** the reigning British monarch or the royal family: *Buckingham Palace has denied the rumor.*

Buck·ing·ham·shire (buk′ing əm shēr′, -shər), *n.* a county in S England. 501,800; 294 sq. mi. (761 sq. km). Also called **Buckingham, Bucks.**

buck·ish (buk′ish), *adj.* impetuous; dashing. [1505–15; BUCK[1] + -ISH[1]] —**buck′ish·ly,** *adv.* —**buck′ish·ness,** *n.*

buck·jump (buk′jump′), *v.i.* (of a horse) to buck. [1840–50; BUCK[2] + JUMP]

buck·jump·er (buk′jum′pər), *n.* a horse that bucks habitually, esp. such a horse kept for use in rodeos. [1840–50; BUCKJUMP + -ER[1]]

buck·le (buk′əl), *n., v.,* **-led, -ling.** —*n.* **1.** a clasp consisting of a rectangular or curved rim with one or more movable tongues, fixed to one end of a belt or strap, used for fastening to the other end of the same strap or to another strap. **2.** any similar contrivance used for such purposes. **3.** an ornament of metal, beads, etc., of similar appearance. **4.** a bend, bulge, or kink, as in a board or saw blade. —*v.t.* **5.** to fasten with a buckle or buckles: *Buckle your seat belt.* **6.** to shrivel, by applying heat or pressure; bend; curl. **7.** to prepare (oneself) for action; apply (oneself) vigorously to something. **8.** to bend, warp, or cause to give way suddenly, as with heat or pressure. —*v.i.* **9.** to close or fasten with a buckle: *Grandmother always wore shoes that buckled.* **10.** to prepare oneself or apply oneself: *The student buckled to the lesson.* **11.** to bend, warp, bulge, or collapse: *The bridge buckled in the storm.* **12.** to yield, surrender, or give way to another (often fol. by *under*): *She refused to take the medicine, but buckled under when the doctor told her to.* **13. buckle down,** to set to work with vigor; concentrate on one's work: *He was by nature a daydreamer and found it hard to buckle down.* **14. buckle up,** to fasten one's belt, seat belt, or buckles: *She won't start the car until we've all buckled up.* [1300–50; ME *bocle* < AF *bo(u)cle, bucle* < L *buc(c)ula* cheekpiece (of a helmet), strip of wood, etc., resembling a cheekpiece, equiv. to *bucc(a)* cheek + *-ula* -ULE] —**buck′le·less,** *adj.*
—**Syn. 8.** sag, bulge, twist; crumple, collapse.

buck·ler (buk′lər), *n.* **1.** a round shield held by a grip and sometimes having straps through which the arm is passed. **2.** any means of defense; protection. —*v.t.* **3.** to be a shield to; support; defend. [1250–1300; ME *bokeler* < AF, MF *bocler,* equiv. to *bocle* BOSS[2] + *-er* -ER[2]]

Buck′ley's chance′, *Australian.* no chance at all or only a slim hope. Also called **Buck′ley's and none′, Buck′ley's hope′.** [1870–75; orig. obscure]

buck·min·ster·ful·ler·ene (buk′min stər fŏŏl′ə-rēn′), *n.* the form of fullerene having sixty carbon atoms. [1985; see FULLERENE]

buck′ moth′, a saturniid moth, *Hemileuca maia,* having delicate, grayish wings with a white band. [1885–90, *Amer.*]

Buck·ner (buk′nər), *n.* **1. Simon Bol·i·var** (bol′ə vər), 1823–1914, U.S. Confederate general and politician. **2.** his son, **Simon Bolivar, Jr.,** 1886–1945, U.S. general.

buck·o (buk′ō), *n., pl.* **buck·oes. 1.** *Chiefly Irish Eng.* young fellow; chap; young companion. **2.** *Brit. Slang.* a swaggering fellow. [1880–85; BUCK[1] + -O]

buck′ pass′er, *Informal.* a person who avoids responsibility by shifting it to another, esp. unjustly or improperly. [1930–35] —**buck′-pass′ing,** *n.*

buck·ra (buk′rə), *n. Southern U.S. (chiefly South Atlantic States).* a white man (often used disparagingly). [1685–90; creole word, perh. < Efik *m̀bakára* white man]

buck·ram (buk′rəm), *n., v.,* **-ramed, -ram·ing.** —*n.* **1.** a stiff cotton fabric for interlinings, book bindings, etc. **2.** stiffness of manner; extreme preciseness or formality. —*v.t.* **3.** to strengthen with buckram. **4.** *Archaic.* to give a false appearance of importance, value, or strength to. [1175–1225; ME *bukeram* < MHG *buckeram* or OIt *bucherame,* said to be named after BUKHARA, once noted for textiles]

Bucks (buks), *n.* Buckinghamshire.

bucksaw

buck·saw (buk′sô′), *n.* a saw having a blade set across an upright frame or bow, used with both hands in cutting wood on a sawhorse. [1855–60, *Amer.*; BUCK[3] + SAW[1]]

buck·shee (buk′shē, buk′shē′), *Chiefly Brit. Slang.* —*n.* **1.** a gift, gratuity, or small bribe. **2.** an extra ration or portion. —*adj.* **3.** free of charge; gratuitous. [1915–20; var. of BAKSHEESH]

buck•shot (buk′shot′), *n.* a large size of lead shot used in shotgun shells for hunting game, as pheasants or ducks. [1400–50; late ME; see BUCK¹, SHOT¹]

buck•skin (buk′skin′), *n.* **1.** the skin of a buck or deer. **2.** a strong, soft, yellowish or grayish leather, originally prepared from deerskins, now usually from sheepskins. **3. buckskins,** breeches or shoes made of buckskin. **4.** a stiff, firm, starched cotton cloth with a smooth surface and napped back. **5.** a sturdy wool fabric constructed in satin weave, napped and cropped short to provide a smooth finish, and used in the manufacture of outer garments. **6.** a person, esp. a backwoodsman, dressed in buckskin. **7.** a horse the color of buckskin. —*adj.* **8.** made of buckskin: *buckskin gloves.* **9.** having the color of buckskin; yellowish or grayish. [1400–50; late ME; see BUCK¹, SKIN]

buck′ slip′, *Informal.* a paper attached to and showing the destination and source of an interoffice memorandum, file, or the like. Also called **buck′ sheet′.**

buck•stay (buk′stā′), *n.* a beam held by stays to the exterior of a masonry wall, as that of a furnace or boiler, to keep the adjacent areas of the wall from being forced outward. [BUCK³ + STAY²]

buck•tail (buk′tāl′), *n. Angling.* an artificial fly made of hairs of or like those of the tail of a deer. [1910–15; BUCK¹ + TAIL¹]

buck•thorn (buk′thôrn′), *n.* **1.** any of several, sometimes thorny trees or shrubs belonging to the genus *Rhamnus,* esp. *R. frangula,* the bark of which is used in medicine. Cf. **buckthorn family. 2.** a tree or shrub belonging to the genus *Bumelia,* of the sapodilla family, esp. *B. lycioides,* a thorny tree having elliptic leaves and large clusters of white flowers, common in the southern and part of the central U.S. [1570–80; BUCK¹ + THORN, rendering NL *cervi spina*]

buck′thorn fam′ily, the plant family Rhamnaceae, characterized by shrubs and trees having alternate, simple leaves, clusters of small flowers, and fruit in the form of a drupe or capsule, and including the buckthorn, cascara, and New Jersey tea.

buck•tooth (buk′to͞oth′), *n., pl.* **-teeth** (-tēth′). a projecting tooth, esp. an upper front tooth. [1745–55; BUCK¹ + TOOTH] —**buck′toothed′,** *adj.*

buck•wheat (buk′hwēt′, -wēt′), *n.* **1.** a plant, esp. *Fagopyrum esculentum,* cultivated for its triangular seeds, which are used as a feed for animals or made into a flour for human consumption, as in pancakes or cereal. Cf. **buckwheat family. 2.** the seeds of this plant. **3.** Also, **buck′wheat flour′.** flour made from seeds of buckwheat. —*adj.* **4.** made with buckwheat flour: *buckwheat pancakes.* [1540–50; obs. *buck*(OE *bōc* BEECH) + WHEAT; cf. D *boekweit,* G *Buchweizen;* so called because its seeds resemble beechnuts] —**buck′wheat′like′,** *adj.*

buck′wheat cake′, a pancake made of buckwheat flour. [1740–50, *Amer.*]

buck′wheat coal′, anthracite in sizes ranging from ⁹⁄₁₆ to ⁵⁄₁₆ in. (14 to 8 mm). [1880–85, *Amer.*]

buck′wheat fam′ily, the plant family Polygonaceae, characterized by herbaceous plants, vines, shrubs, and trees having stems with swollen joints, simple leaves, small, petalless flowers, and fruit in the form of an achene, and including the buckwheat, dock, knotweed, rhubarb, sea grape, and smartweed.

buck′wheat note′. See **shape note.** [1850–55; prob. so called because of the note's fancied resemblance to buckwheat kernels]

bu•col•ic (byo͞o kol′ik), *adj.* Also, **bu•col′i•cal. 1.** of or pertaining to shepherds; pastoral. **2.** of, pertaining to, or suggesting an idyllic rural life. —*n.* **3.** a pastoral poem. **4.** *Archaic.* a farmer; shepherd; rustic. [1525–35; < L *būcolicus* < Gk *boukolikós* rustic, equiv. to *boukó-l*(*os*) herdsman (*bou-,* s. of *boûs* ox + *-kolos* keeper + *-ikos* -IC] —**bu•col′i•cal•ly,** *adv.*
—**Syn. 2, 3.** georgic.

Bu•col•ics (byo͞o kol′iks), *n.* Eclogues.

Bu•co•vi•na (bo͞o′kə vē′nə; *Rum.* bo͞o kô vē′nä), *n.* a region in E central Europe, formerly a district in N Rumania: now divided between Rumania and Ukraine. 4031 sq. mi. (10,440 sq. km). Also, **Bukovina.**

bu•cra•ni•um (byo͞o krā′nē əm), *n., pl.* **-ni•a** (-nē ə). (in classical architecture) an ornament, esp. on a frieze, having the form of the skull of an ox. Also, **bu•crane** (byo͞o krān′). [1850–55; < LL *būcrānium* < Gk *bou-krā́ni*(*on*) an ox-head, equiv. to Gk *bou-* (s. of *boûs*) ox + *krānion* CRANIUM]

Bu•cu•reşti (bo͞o ko͞o resht′), *n.* Rumanian name of **Bucharest.**

Bu•cy•rus (byo͞o sī′rəs), *n.* a city in N central Ohio. 13,433.

CONCISE ETYMOLOGY KEY: <, descended or borrowed from; >, whence; b., blend of, blended; c., cognate with; cf., compare; deriv., derivative; equiv., equivalent; imit., imitative; obl., oblique; r., replacing; s., stem; sp., spelling, spelled; resp., respelling, respelled; trans., translation; ?, origin unknown; *, unattested; ‡, probably earlier than. See the full key inside the front cover.

bud¹ (bud), *n., v.,* **bud•ded, bud•ding.** —*n.* **1.** *Bot.* **a.** a small axillary or terminal protuberance on a plant, containing rudimentary foliage **(leaf bud),** the rudimentary inflorescence **(flower bud),** or both **(mixed bud). b.** an undeveloped or rudimentary stem or branch of a plant. **2.** *Zool.* (in certain animals of low organization) a prominence that develops into a new individual, sometimes permanently attached to the parent and sometimes becoming detached; gemma. **3.** *Mycol.* a small, rounded outgrowth produced from a fungus spore or cell by a process of asexual reproduction, eventually separating from the parent cell as a new individual: commonly produced by yeast and a few other fungi. **4.** *Anat.* any small rounded part. **5.** an immature or undeveloped person or thing. **6. in the bud,** in an immature or undeveloped state: *a Shakespeare in the bud.* Also, **in bud. 7. nip in the bud,** to stop (something) in the beginning of its development: *The rebellion was nipped in the bud.* —*v.i.* **8.** to put forth or produce buds. **9.** to begin to develop. **10.** to be in an early stage of development. —*v.t.* **11.** to cause to bud. **12.** *Hort.* to graft by inserting a single bud into the stock. [1350–1400; ME *budde* bud, spray, pod; akin to G *Hagebutte* hip, ON *budda* purse, dial. Sw *bodd* head, D *buidel* bag, purse, MLG *buddich* swollen] —**bud′der,** *n.* —**bud′less,** *adj.* —**bud′like′,** *adj.*

leaf buds
of the elm

bud² (bud), *n.* brother; buddy (used in informal address, as to one's brother or to a man or boy whose name is not known to the speaker). [1850–55, *Amer.*; back formation from BUDDY]

Bud (bud), *n.* a male given name. Also, **Budd.**

Bu•da (bo͞o′də; *Hung.* bo͞o′do), *n.* See under **Budapest.**

Bu•da•pest (bo͞o′də pest′, bo͞o′də pest′; *Hung.* bo͞o′do-pesht′), *n.* a city in and the capital of Hungary, in the central part, on the Danube River: formed 1873 from two cities on the W bank of the Danube **(Buda** and **Obuda)** and one on the E bank **(Pest).** 2,070,966.

Bud•dha (bo͞o′də, bo͝od′ə), *n.* **1.** Also called **Butsu, Gautama, Gautama Buddha.** (*Prince Siddhāttha* or *Siddhartha*) 566?–c480 B.C., Indian religious leader: founder of Buddhism. **2.** any of a series of teachers in Buddhism, of whom Gautama was the last, who bring enlightenment and wisdom. **3.** (*sometimes l.c.*) *Buddhism.* a person who has attained full prajna, or enlightenment; Arhat. [1675–85; < Skt: awakened (*budh-* awaken, notice, understand + *-ta* ptp. suffix)]

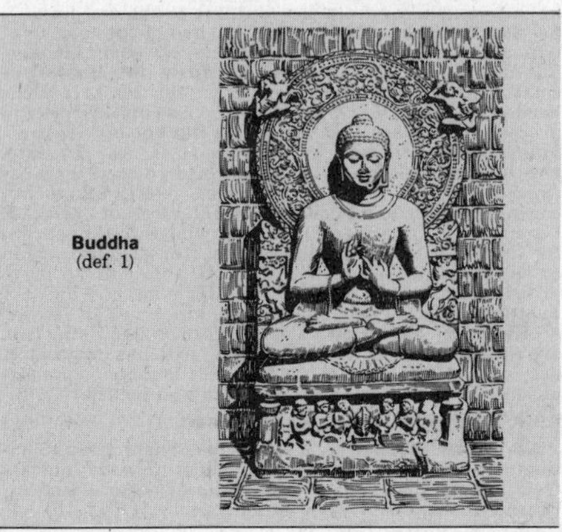
Buddha
(def. 1)

Bud•dha•hood (bo͞o′də ho͝od′, bo͝od′ə-), *n.* the attainment of enlightenment as a Buddha. [1830–40; BUDDHA + -HOOD]

Buddh Ga•ya (bo͝od′ gə yä′), a village in central Bihar, in NE India: site of tree under which Siddhartha became the Buddha.

bud•dhi (bo͞o′dē, bo͝od′ē), *n. Hinduism, Buddhism.* intellect, seen as an intuitive faculty giving increased spiritual awareness. [< Skt; cf. *bodhati* (he) awakes]

Bud•dhism (bo͞o′diz əm, bo͝od′iz-), *n.* a religion, originated in India by Buddha (Gautama) and later spreading to China, Burma, Japan, Tibet, and parts of southeast Asia, holding that life is full of suffering caused by desire and that the way to end this suffering is through enlightenment that enables one to halt the endless sequence of births and deaths to which one is otherwise subject. Cf. **Eightfold Path, Four Noble Truths, Hinayana, Mahayana.** [BUDDH(A) + -ISM] —**Bud′dhist,** *n., adj.* —**Bud•dhis′tic, Bud•dhis′ti•cal,** *adj.* —**Bud•dhis′ti•cal•ly,** *adv.*

Bud•dhol•o•gy (bo͞o dol′ə jē, bo͞o-), *n.* the study of Buddha and of Buddhahood. [BUDDH(A) + -O- + -LOGY]

bud•dle (bud′l, bo͝od′l), *n., v.,* **-dled, -dling.** *Mining.* —*n.* **1.** a shallow trough in which metalliferous ore is separated from gangue by means of running water. —*v.t.* **2.** to wash (ore) in a buddle. [1525–35; of uncert. orig.] —**bud′dler,** *n.*

bud•dle•ia (bud lē′ə, bud′lē ə), *n.* any shrub belonging to the genus *Buddleia,* of the logania family, having opposite, lance-shaped leaves and clusters of flowers, comprising the butterfly bushes. [< NL (Linnaeus), named after Adam *Buddle* (d. 1715), English botanist; see -IA]

bud•dy (bud′ē), *n., pl.* **-dies,** *v.,* **-died, -dy•ing.** *Informal.* —*n.* **1.** comrade or chum (often used as a term of address). **2.** bud². —*v.i.* **3.** to be a companion; be friendly or on intimate terms. **4. buddy up, a.** to become friendly; be on friendly or intimate terms. **b.** to work closely together: *to buddy up with a student from another high school.* **5. buddy up to,** to become friendly with or curry the favor of: *He was buddying up to the political bosses.* [1840–50, *Amer.*; perh. reduced form of BROTHER]

Bud•dy (bud′ē), *n.* a male given name.

bud•dy-bud•dy (bud′ē bud′ē), *adj. Informal.* **1.** very friendly; intimate. **2.** associated for greedy or conniving purposes. [1960–65]

bud′dy seat′, 1. a seat on a motorcycle or moped for the driver and a passenger sitting one behind the other. **2.** a motorcycle sidecar.

bud′dy sys′tem, 1. (in swimming and scuba diving) the practice of pairing swimmers, each being responsible for the other's safety. **2.** any arrangement whereby two or more persons, teams, etc., watch out for each other, as with mountain climbers. [1940–45]

Bu•dën•ny (bo͞o den′ē; *Russ.* bo͞o dyô′nē), *n.* **Se•mën Mi•khai•lo•vich** (syi myôn′ myi KHī′lə vyich), 1883–1973, Russian general in 1917 revolution and World War II.

budge¹ (buj), *v.,* **budged, budg•ing.** (often used negatively) —*v.i.* **1.** to move slightly; begin to move: *He stepped on the gas but the car didn't budge.* **2.** to change one's opinion or stated position; yield: *Once her father had said "no," he wouldn't budge.* —*v.t.* **3.** to cause to move; begin to move: *It took three of them to budge the rock.* **4.** to cause (someone) to reconsider or change an opinion, decision, or stated position: *They couldn't budge the lawyer.* [1580–90; < AF, MF *bouger* to stir < VL **bullicāre* to bubble, freq. of L *bullīre;* see BOIL¹] —**budg′er,** *n.*
—**Syn. 4.** persuade, induce, move, sway, convince.

budge² (buj), *n.* **1.** a fur made from lambskin with the wool dressed outward, used esp. as an inexpensive trimming on academic or official gowns. —*adj.* **2.** made from, trimmed, or lined with budge. **3.** *Obs.* pompous; solemn. [1350–1400; ME *bugee,* perh. akin to BUDGET]

Budge (buj), *n.* **(John) Donald,** born 1915, U.S. tennis player.

budg•er•ee (buj′ə rē), *adj. Australian.* **1.** good; fine. **2.** pretty. [< Austral Pidgin E < Dharuk *bú-ja-ri*]

budg•er•i•gar (buj′ə rē gär′, -ər i-), an Australian parakeet, *Melopsittacus undulatus,* having greenish plumage with black and yellow markings, bred as a pet in a variety of colors. Also, **budg•er•ee•gah, budg•er•y•gah** (buj′ə rē gä′). Also called **shell parakeet.** [1840–50; perh. misrepresentation of Kamilaroi or Yuwaalaraay (Austral Aboriginal language of N New South Wales) *gijirrigā* (perh. *gijirr* yellow or small + *gā* head)]

budg•et (buj′it), *n., adj., v.,* **-et•ed, -et•ing.** —*n.* **1.** an estimate, often itemized, of expected income and expense for a given period in the future. **2.** a plan of operations based on such an estimate. **3.** an itemized allotment of funds, time, etc., for a given period. **4.** the total sum of money set aside or needed for a purpose: *the construction budget.* **5.** a limited stock or supply of something: *his budget of goodwill.* **6.** *Obs.* a small bag; pouch. —*adj.* **7.** reasonably or cheaply priced: *budget dresses.* —*v.t.* **8.** to plan allotment of (funds, time, etc.). **9.** to deal with (specific funds) in a budget. —*v.i.* **10.** to subsist on or live within a budget. [1400–50; late ME *bowgett* (< MF *bougette* (*bouge* bag (< L *bulga;* see BULGE) + *-ette* -ETTE)] —**budg•et•ar•y** (buj′i ter′ē), *adj.* —**budg′et•er,** *n.*

budg•et•eer (buj′i tēr′), a person, esp. a government or business official, who prepares a budget. [1835–45; BUDGET + -EER]

budg′et plan′. See **installment plan.**

budg′et resolu′tion, a resolution adopted by both houses of the U.S. Congress setting forth, reaffirming, or revising the budget for the U.S. government for a fiscal year. [1975–80]

budg•ie (buj′ē), *n.* budgerigar. [1935–40; BUDG(ERIGAR) + -IE]

bud′ muta′tion, a variation produced by a genetic alteration in the bud such that the seeds produced by the resulting growth perpetuate the change in succeeding generations.

bud′ scale′, scale¹ (def. 3a). [1875–80]

bud′ sport′, a sport resulting from a bud mutation or bud variation. [1895–1900]

bud′ stick′, *Hort.* a shoot of a plant from which buds are cut for the propagation of that plant.

bud′ varia′tion, any variation in a bud due to changes in either its genetic composition or environment or both such that the resulting flower, fruit, or shoot differs from others of the same plant or species.

Bud•weis (bo͝ot′vīs), *n.* German name of **České Budějovice.**

bud•wood (bud′wo͝od′), *Hort.* a shoot of a plant bearing buds suitable for bud grafting. [BUD¹ + WOOD¹]

bud•worm (bud′wûrm′), *n.* any of several lepidopterous larvae, esp. the spruce budworm, that attack the buds of plants. [1840–50, *Amer.*; BUD¹ + WORM]

Bu•ell (byo͞o′əl), *n.* **Don Car•los** (kär′lōs), 1818–98, Union general in the U.S. Civil War.

Bue′na Park′ (bwā′nə, byo͞o′-), a city in SW California. 64,165.

bue•nas no•ches (bwe′näs nô′ches), *Spanish.* good night.

Bue•na•ven•tu•ra (bwā′nə ven to͝or′ə, -tyo͝or′ə; *Sp.* bwe′nä ven to͞o′Rä), *n.* a seaport in W Colombia. 115,770.

Bue•na Vis•ta (bwe′nä vēs′tä), a village in NE Mexico, near Saltillo: American victory in battle (1847) during the Mexican War.

bue•no (bwe′nô), *interj. Spanish.* good; all right.

Bue•nos Ai•res (bwā′nəs īᵊr′iz, bō′nəs; *Sp.* bwe′nôs ī′ʀes), a seaport in and the capital of Argentina, in the E part, on the Río de la Plata. 9,927,404.

bue•nos dí•as (bwe′nôs thē′äs), *Spanish.* good morning; good day.

Buer′ger's disease′ (bûr′gərz), *Pathol.* an inflammatory and obliterative disease of the blood vessels of the legs and feet causing numbness and tingling, often leading to phlebitis and gangrene: most common in cigarette smokers. [named after Leo *Buerger* (1879–1943), U.S. physician, who described it in 1908]

bu•fa•di•en•o•lide (byōō′fə dī en′l īd′), *n. Biochem.* any of a family of steroid lactones, occurring in toad venom and squill, that possess cardiac-stimulating and antitumor activity. [1965–70; from *bufa-20, 22-dienolide* a chemical component of such lactones; cf. L *būfō* toad]

buff[1] (buf), *n.* **1.** a soft, thick, light-yellow leather with a napped surface, originally made from buffalo skin but later also from other skins, used for making belts, pouches, etc. **2.** a brownish-yellow color; tan. **3.** a buff stick or buff wheel. **4.** a devotee or well-informed student of some activity or subject: *Civil War buffs avidly read the new biography of Grant.* **5.** *Informal.* the bare skin: *in the buff.* **6.** Also called **buffcoat.** a thick, short coat of buffalo leather, worn esp. by English soldiers and American colonists in the 17th century. **7.** *Informal.* a buffalo. —*adj.* **8.** having the color of buff. **9.** made of buff leather. **10.** *Slang.* physically attractive; muscular. —*v.t.* **11.** to clean or polish (metal) or give a grainless finish of high luster to (plated surfaces) with or as if with a buff stick or buff wheel. **12.** to polish or shine, esp. with a buffer: *to buff shoes.* **13.** to dye or stain in a buff color. [1545–55; 1900–05 for def. 4; earlier *buffe* wild ox, back formation from *buffle* < MF < LL *būfalus;* see BUFFALO; (def. 4) orig. a person enthusiastic about firefighting and firefighters, allegedly after the buff uniforms once worn by volunteer firefighters in New York City] —**buff′a•bil′i•ty,** *n.* —**buff′a•ble,** *adj.*
—**Syn. 10.** burnish, shine.

buff[2] (buf), *v.t.* **1.** to reduce or deaden the force of; act as a buffer. —*n.* **2.** *Chiefly Brit. Dial.* a blow; slap. [1375–1425; late ME *buffe,* back formation from BUFFET[1]]

buff[3] (buf), *n.* buffe.

buf•fa (bōō′fə; *It.* bōōf′fä), *n., pl.* **-fe** (-fā; *It.* -fe). **1.** a woman who sings comic roles in opera. **2.** See **opera buffa.** [< It; fem. of BUFFO]

buf•fa•lo (buf′ə lō′), *n., pl.* **-loes, -los,** (*esp. collectively*) **-lo,** *v.,* **-loed, -lo•ing.** —*n.* **1.** any of several large wild oxen of the family Bovidae. Cf. **bison, Cape buffalo, water buffalo. 2.** See **buffalo robe. 3.** a buffalofish. **4.** a shuffling tap-dance step. —*v.t. Informal.* **5.** to puzzle or baffle; confuse; mystify: *He was buffaloed by the problem.* **6.** to impress or intimidate by a display of power, importance, etc.: *The older boys buffaloed him.* [1535–45, *Amer.;* earlier *bufalo* < Pg (now *bufaro*) < LL *būfalus,* var. of L *būbalus* BUBAL]

Buf•fa•lo (buf′ə lō′), *n.* a port in W New York, on Lake Erie. 357,870.

buf′falo ber′ry, 1. either of two North American shrubs, *Shepherdia argentea* or *S. canadensis,* having silvery, oblong leaves and bearing edible yellow or red berries. **2.** the fruit itself. [1795–1805, *Amer.*]

Buf′falo Bill′. See **Cody, William Frederick.**

buf′falo bird′, a cowbird, *Molothrus ater,* of North America. [1855–60]

buf′falo car′pet bee′tle. See under **carpet beetle.** Also called **buf•fa•lo•bug** (buf′ə lō bug′), **buf′falo bug′, buf′falo moth′.**

buf′falo chips′, *Informal.* the dried dung of buffalo used as fuel, esp. by early settlers on the western plains. [1830–40, *Amer.*]

buf′falo cloth′, a heavyweight woolen fabric constructed in twill weave and having a shaggy pile.

buf′falo cur′rant, an ornamental shrub, *Ribes odoratum,* of the central U.S., having showy, drooping clusters of fragrant yellow flowers and edible black fruit. [1860–65, *Amer.;* so called from its growth in a region where there were buffalo]

buf•fa•lo•fish (buf′ə lō′fish′), *n., pl.* (*esp. collectively*) **-fish,** (*esp. referring to two or more kinds or species*) **-fish•es.** any of several large, carplike, North American, freshwater fishes of the genus *Ictiobus,* of the sucker family. [1760–70, *Amer.;* BUFFALO + FISH]

buf′falo gnat′. See **black fly.** [1815–25, *Amer.*]

buf′falo grass′, 1. a short grass, *Buchloë dactyloides,* having gray-green blades, prevalent on the dry plains east of the Rocky Mountains. **2.** See **St. Augustine grass. 3.** any of several short, tufted grasses that do not form continuous sod. [1775–85, *Amer.*]

Buf′falo Grove′, a city in NE Illinois. 22,230.

Buf′falo In′dian. See **Plains Indian.**

buf′falo plaid′, a plaid with large blocks formed by the intersection of two different-color yarns, typically red and black. [1945–50]

buf′falo robe′, the prepared skin of an American bison, with the hair left on, used as a lap robe, rug, or blanket. [1675–85, *Amer.*]

buf′falo sol′dier, (formerly, esp. among American Indians) a black soldier. [1870–75; *Amer.;* from the kinky hair, thought by the Indians to resemble that of a buffalo]

buff•coat (buf′kōt′), *n.* buff[1] (def. 6). [1625–35]

buffe (buf), *n. Armor.* plate armor for the lower part of the face and the throat, used with a burgonet. Also, **buff.** [1590–1600; < MF < It *buffa,* prob. special use of *buffa* puff of breath, hard breath; see BUFFOON]

buff•er[1] (buf′ər), *n.* **1.** an apparatus at the end of a railroad car, railroad track, etc., for absorbing shock during coupling, collisions, etc. **2.** any device, material, or apparatus used as a shield, cushion, or bumper, esp. on machinery. **3.** any intermediate or intervening shield or device reducing the danger of interaction between two machines, chemicals, electronic components, etc. **4.** a person or thing that shields and protects against annoyance, harm, hostile forces, etc., or that lessens the impact of a shock or reversal. **5.** any reserve moneys, negotiable securities, legal procedures, etc., that protect a person, organization, or country against financial ruin. **6.** See **buffer state. 7.** *Ecol.* an animal population that becomes the prey of a predator that usually feeds on a different species. **8.** *Computers.* a storage device for temporarily holding data until the computer is ready to receive or process the data, as when a receiving unit has an operating speed lower than that of the unit feeding data to it. **9.** *Electronics.* a circuit with a single output activated by one or more of several inputs. **10.** *Chem.* **a.** any substance or mixture of compounds that, added to a solution, is capable of neutralizing both acids and bases without appreciably changing the original acidity or alkalinity of the solution. **b.** Also called **buff′er solu′tion.** a solution containing such a substance. —*v.t.* **11.** *Chem.* to treat with a buffer. **12.** to cushion, shield, or protect. **13.** to lessen the adverse effect of; ease: *The drug buffered his pain.* [1825–35; BUFF[2] + -ER[1]]

buff•er[2] (buf′ər), *n.* **1.** a device for polishing or buffing, as a buff stick or buff wheel. **2.** a worker who uses such a device. [1850–55; BUFF[1] + -ER[1]]

buff•er[3] (buf′ər), *n. Brit. Slang.* **1.** a foolish or incompetent person. **2.** a fellow; man. **3.** a chief boatswain's mate in the British navy. [1680–90; orig. uncert.]

buff′er state′, a nation lying between potentially hostile larger nations. [1880–85]

buff′er zone′, 1. a neutral zone or area between two potentially hostile nations, designed to prevent any overt acts of aggression. **2.** any area serving to mitigate or neutralize potential conflict. [1905–10]

buf•fet[1] (buf′it), *n., v.,* **-fet•ed, -fet•ing.** —*n.* **1.** a blow, as with the hand or fist. **2.** a violent shock or concussion. —*v.t.* **3.** to strike, as with the hand or fist. **4.** to strike against or push repeatedly: *The wind buffeted the house.* **5.** to contend against; battle. —*v.i.* **6.** to struggle with blows of hand or fist. **7.** to force one's way by a fight, struggle, etc. [1175–1225; ME < OF *buffe* a blow + *-et* -ET] —**buf′fet•er,** *n.*
—**Syn. 3.** slap, cuff, box, hit, sock, wallop.

buf•fet[2] (bə fā′, bōō- *or, esp. for adj.,* bōō′fā; *Brit.* buf′it), *n.* **1.** a sideboard or cabinet for holding china, table linen, etc. **2.** a meal laid out on a table or sideboard so that guests may serve themselves. **3.** a counter, bar, or the like, for lunch or refreshments. **4.** a restaurant containing such a counter or bar. —*adj.* **5.** consisting of food, refreshments, etc., laid out on tables or buffets from which guests or customers serve themselves: *a buffet supper; buffet service.* [1710–20; < F, OF, of obscure orig.]

buffet′ car′, *Railroads.* a car having facilities for preparing and serving light meals. [1885–90, *Amer.*]

buff′ing wheel′. See **buff wheel.**

buf•fle•head (buf′əl hed′), *n.* a small North American duck, *Bucephala albeola,* the male of which has bushy head plumage. [1855–60, *Amer.; buffle* (see BUFF[1]) + HEAD] —**buf′fle•head′ed,** *adj.*

buf•fo (bōō′fō; *It.* bōōf′fô), *n., pl.* **-fi** (-fē), **-fos.** *Music.* **1.** (in opera) a comedy part, usually bass. **2.** a male opera singer who specializes in comic roles. [1755–65; < It: ridiculous, comic actor who takes comic parts; back formation from *buffone* BUFFOON]

Buf•fon (bʏ fôɴ′), *n.* **Georges Louis Le•clerc** (zhôʀzh lwē lə kler′), **Comte de,** 1707–88, French naturalist.

buf•foon (bə fōōn′), *n.* **1.** a person who amuses others by tricks, jokes, odd gestures and postures, etc. **2.** a person given to coarse or undignified joking. [1540–50; earlier *buffon* < F < It *buffone,* equiv. to *buff-* (expressive base; cf. *buffa* puff of breath, *buffare* to puff, puff up one's checks) + *-one* agent suffix << L *-ō,* acc. *-ōnem*] —**buf•foon•er•y** (bə fōō′nə rē), *n.* —**buf•foon′ish,** *adj.*
—**Syn. 1.** jester, clown, fool. **2.** boor.

buff′ stick′, a small stick covered with leather or the like, used in polishing. [1880–85]

buff′ top′, *Jewelry.* a very low, almost flat, cabochon cut.

buff′ wheel′, a wheel for buffing, consisting of a number of leather or canvas disks. Also, **buffing wheel.**

buff•y (buf′ē), *adj.* buff-colored. [BUFF[1] + -Y[1]]

buff′y coat′, *Biochem.* a yellowish-white layer consisting of leukocytes that, upon centrifugation of blood, covers the red blood cells. [1790–1800]

bu•fo•ten•ine (byōō′fə ten′ēn, -in), *n. Pharm.* a hallucinogenic bufotoxin derivative, $C_{12}H_{16}N_2O$, used experimentally for its digitalislike action on the heart. Also, **bu•fo•ten•in** (byōō′fə ten′in). [1900–05; < L *būfo* toad + *-ten* (perh. < Gk *tén(ōn)* sinew, tendon) + -INE[2]]

bu•fo•tox•in (byōō′fə tok′sin), *n. Pharm.* a toxin obtained from the skin glands of the European toad, *Bufa vulgaris.* [< NL, L *būfo* toad + TOXIN]

bug[1] (bug), *n., v.,* **bugged, bug•ging.** —*n.* **1.** Also called **true bug, hemipteran, hemipteron.** a hemipterous insect. **2.** (loosely) any insect or insectlike invertebrate. **3.** *Informal.* any microorganism, esp. a virus: *He was laid up for a week by an intestinal bug.* **4.** *Informal.* a defect or imperfection, as in a mechanical device, computer program, or plan; glitch: *The test flight discovered the bugs in the new plane.* **5.** *Informal.* **a.** a person who has a great enthusiasm for something; fan or hobbyist: *a hi-fi bug.* **b.** a craze or obsession: *He's got the sports-car bug.* **6.** *Informal.* **a.** a hidden microphone or other electronic eavesdropping device. **b.** any of various small mechanical or electrical gadgets, as one to influence a gambling device, give warning of an intruder, or indicate location. **7.** a mark, as an asterisk, that indicates a particular item, level, etc. **8.** *Horse Racing.* the five-pound weight allowance that can be claimed by an apprentice jockey. **9.** a telegraph key that automatically transmits a series of dots when moved to one side and one dash when moved to the other. **10.** *Poker Slang.* a joker that can be used only as an ace or as a wild card to fill a straight or a flush. **11.** *Print.* a label printed on certain matter to indicate that it was produced by a union shop. **12.** any of various fishing plugs resembling an insect. **13.** *Chiefly Brit.* a bedbug. **14. put a bug in someone's ear,** to give someone a subtle suggestion; hint: *We put a bug in his ear about a new gymnasium.* —*v.t. Informal.* **15.** to install a secret listening device in (a room, building, etc.) or on (a telephone or other device): *The phone had been bugged.* **16.** to bother; annoy; pester: *She's bugging him to get her into show business.* **17. bug off,** *Slang.* to leave or depart, esp. rapidly: *I can't help you, so bug off.* **18. bug out,** *Slang.* to flee in panic; show panic or alarm. [1615–25; 1885–90 for def. 4; 1910–15 for def. 5a; 1915–20 for def. 15; 1945–50 for def. 16; earlier *bugge* beetle, appar. alter. of ME *budde,* OE *-budda* beetle; sense "leave" obscurely related to other senses and perh. of distinct orig.]
—**Syn. 16.** nag, badger, harass, plague, needle.

bug[2] (bug), *n. Obs.* a bogy; hobgoblin. [1350–1400; ME *bugge* scarecrow, demon, perh. < Welsh *bwg* ghost]

Bug (bug; *Pol., Russ.* bōōk), *n.* **1.** a river in E central Europe, rising in W Ukraine and forming part of the boundary between Poland and Ukraine, flowing NW to the Vistula River in Poland. 450 mi. (725 km) long. **2.** a river in SW Ukraine flowing SE to the Dnieper estuary. ab. 530 mi. (850 km) long.

bug•a•boo (bug′ə bōō′), *n., pl.* **-boos.** something that causes fear or worry; bugbear; bogy. [1730–40; earlier *buggybow.* See BOGY, BOO]

bu•ga•ku (bōō gä′kōō), *n.* a classical Japanese dance of Chinese origin, originally designed as entertainment for the imperial palace: performed exclusively by men, who serve as both dancers and musicians. [< Japn < MChin, equiv. to Chin *wǔ* dance + *yuè* music; cf. GAGAKU]

bug•a•loo (bōōg′ə lōō′, bōō′gə-), *n., pl.* **-loos.** a fast dance of Afro-American origin, performed by couples and characterized by dancing apart and moving the body in short, quick movements. [of obscure orig.]

Bu•ga•yev (*Russ.* bōō gä′yif), *n.* **Bo•ris Ni•ko•la•ye•vich** (bôr′is nik′ə lī′ə vich, bōr′-, bor′-; *Russ.* bu ʀyes′ nyi ku lä′yi vyich). See **Bely, Andrei.**

bug•bane (bug′bān′), *n.* any of several tall, erect plants belonging to the genus *Cimicifuga,* of the buttercup family, as *C. americana,* of the eastern U.S., having loose, elongated clusters of white flowers. [1795–1805; BUG[1] + BANE; so called because it supposedly repels insects]

bug•bear (bug′bâr′), *n.* **1.** any source, real or imaginary, of needless fright or fear. **2.** a persistent problem or source of annoyance. **3.** *Folklore.* a goblin that eats up naughty children. [1570–80; BUG[2] + BEAR[2]]

bug•boy (bug′boi′), *n. Horse Racing Slang.* an apprentice jockey. [BUG[1] (weight allowance) + BOY]

bug•eye (bug′ī′), *n., pl.* **-eyes.** *Naut.* a ketch-rigged sailing vessel used on Chesapeake Bay. [1880–85, *Amer.;* BUG[1] + EYE, after the former practice of painting a large eye on each bow]

bug-eyed (bug′īd′), *adj.* with bulging eyes, as from surprise or wonderment; astonished. [1920–25, *Amer.;* BUG[1] + EYED]

bug•ger[1] (bug′ər, bōōg′-), *n.* **1.** *Informal.* a fellow or lad (used affectionately or abusively): *a cute little bugger.* **2.** *Informal.* any object or thing. **3.** *Often Vulgar.* a sodomite. **4.** *Chiefly Brit. Slang.* **a.** a despicable or contemptible person, esp. a man. **b.** an annoying or troublesome thing, situation, etc. —*v.t.* **5.** *Often Vulgar.* to sodomize. **6.** *Slang.* damn: *Bugger the cost—I want the best.* **7.** *Chiefly Brit. Slang.* to trick, deceive, or take advantage of. **8. bugger up,** *Chiefly Brit. Slang.* to ruin; spoil; botch. —*v.i.* **9. bugger off,** *Chiefly Brit. Slang.* to depart; bug off. [1300–50; ME *bougre* < AF *bugre* < ML *Bulgarus* heretic, lit., Bulgarian, by assoc. of the Balkans with heretical sects such as the Bogomils and their alleged deviant sexual practices; def. 1 perh. by reanalysis as BUG[1] or BUG[2] + -ER[1] (cf. BOOGER)]

bug•ger[2] (bug′ər), *n.* a person who installs a hidden listening device. [1965–70; BUG[1] + -ER[1]]

bug•ger-all (bug′ər ôl′, bōōg′-), *n. Chiefly Brit. Slang.* absolutely nothing; nothing at all: *Those reckless investments left him with bugger-all.* [1935–40; n. use of the exclamation *bugger all!*]

bug•ger•y (bug′ə rē, bōōg′-), *n. Often Vulgar.* sodomy. [1300–50; ME *bugerie* heresy; see BUGGER[1], -Y[3]]

Bug′gin's turn′ (bug′inz), *Brit.* promotion by seniority or rotation rather than merit. [1900–05; identity of the original Buggin or Buggins is obscure]

bug•gy[1] (bug′ē), *n., pl.* **-gies. 1.** a light, four-wheeled, horse-drawn carriage with a single seat and a transverse spring. **2.** (in India) a light, two-wheeled carriage with a folding top. **3.** See **baby carriage. 4.** *Older Slang.* an automobile, esp. an old or dilapidated one. **5.** a small

CONCISE PRONUNCIATION KEY: *act, cāpe, dâre, pärt; set, ēqual; if, īce; ox, ōver, ôrder, oil, bŏŏk, bōōt, out; up, ûrge; child; sing; shoe; thin, that;* zh as in *treasure.* ə = *a* as in *alone, e* as in *system, i* as in *easily, o* as in *gallop, u* as in *circus;* ᵊ as in *fire* (fīᵊr), *hour* (ouᵊr). l and n can serve as syllabic consonants, as in *cradle* (krād′l), and *button* (but′n). See the full key inside the front cover.

wagon or truck for transporting heavy materials, as coal in a mine or freshly mixed concrete at a construction site, for short distances. **6.** *Metall.* a car, as for transporting ingots or charges for open-hearth furnaces. **7.** any of various small vehicles adapted for use on a given terrain, as on sand beaches or swamps. **8.** *Brit.* a light, two-wheeled, open carriage. [1765–75; of obscure orig.]

bug·gy[2] (bug′ē), *adj.*, **-gi·er, -gi·est. 1.** infested with bugs. **2.** *Slang.* crazy; insane; peculiar. [1705–15; BUG[1] + -Y[1]] **—bug′gi·ness,** *n.*

bug·house (bug′hous′), *n., pl.* **-hous·es** (-hou′ziz), *adj. Slang.* **—n. 1.** an insane asylum. **—adj. 2.** insane; crazy. [1890–95, *Amer.*; BUG[1] (cf. BUGGY[2], BUGS) + HOUSE]

Bug′house Square′, *Informal.* any intersection or park mall in a big city where political zealots, agitators, folk evangelists, etc., congregate to argue and make soapbox speeches. [1920–25, *Amer.*]

Bug·i·nese (bug′ə nēz′, -nēs′), *n., pl.* **-nese** for 1. **1.** a member of a Muslim people inhabiting the southern part of Sulawesi. **2.** the Austronesian language spoken by these people. [< D *Boeginees* (with *-nees* on the model of *Balinees, Javanees,* etc.) < Malay *Bugis,* prob. orig. the Makassarese name of this ethnic group]

bug-juice (bug′jo͞os′), *n. Slang.* **1.** an alcoholic beverage, esp. of an inferior quality. **2.** an unusual or concocted drink. [1865–70, *Amer.*]

bu·gle[1] (byo͞o′gəl), *n., v.,* **-gled, -gling. —n. 1.** a brass wind instrument resembling a cornet and sometimes having keys or valves, used typically for sounding military signals. **—v.i. 2.** to sound a bugle. **3.** (of bull elks) to utter a rutting call. **—v.t. 4.** to call by or with a bugle: *to bugle reveille.* [1250–1300; ME *bugle* (*horn*) instrument made of an ox horn < AF, OF < L *būculus* bullock, young ox, equiv. to *bū-* var. s. of *bōs* ox + *-culus* -CLE[1]] **—bu′gler,** *n.*

bugle[1] (def. 1)

bu·gle[2] (byo͞o′gəl), *n.* ajuga. [1225–75; ME < OF < ML *bugula* a kind of plant]

bu·gle[3] (byo͞o′gəl), *n.* **1.** Also called **bu′gle bead′.** a tubular glass bead used for ornamenting dresses. **—adj. 2.** Also, **bu′gled.** ornamented with bugles. [1570–80; of obscure orig.]

bu·gle·weed (byo͞o′gəl wēd′), *n.* **1.** a plant belonging to the genus *Lycopus,* of the mint family, esp. *L. virginicus,* reputed to have medicinal properties. **2.** ajuga. [1855–60; BUGLE[2] + WEED[1]]

bu·gloss (byo͞o′glos, -glôs), *n.* any of various Old World, boraginaceous herbs, as *Anchusa officinalis,* having rough leaves, used in medicine, and *Lycopsis arvensis,* a bristly, blue-flowered herb. [1350–1400; ME *buglossa* < ML, for L *būglōssos* < Gk, equiv. to *bou-,* s. of *boûs* ox + *-glōssos* -tongued, adj. deriv. of *glôssa* tongue]

bu·gong (bo͞o′gông, -gong), *n.* bogong.

bug·out (bug′out′), *n.* **1.** *Mil. Slang.* a hasty retreat from combat, esp. in defiance of orders. **2.** *Slang.* a person who absents himself or herself from duties or obligations. [1950–55; n. use of v. phrase *bug out* leave]

bugs (bugz), *adj. Slang.* crazy; insane. [1920–25; see BUG[1], -S[3]]

bug·sha (bo͝og′shä, bug′-), *n.* buqsha. Also, **bug′shah.**

buhl (bo͞ol), *n.* (*often cap.*) elaborate inlaid work of woods, metals, tortoiseshell, ivory, etc. Also, **boule, boulle.** Also called **buhl·work** (bo͞ol′wûrk′), **boulework, boullework.** [1815–25; from Germanized form of F *boulle* or *boule,* named after A. C. Boulle or Boule (1642–1732), French cabinetmaker]

buhr (bûr), *n.* **1.** burr[1] (def. 1). **2.** burr[4]. **3.** burstone.

buhr·stone (bûr′stōn′), *n.* burstone.

build (bild), *v.,* **built** or (*Archaic*) **build·ed; build·ing;** *n.* **—v.t. 1.** to construct (esp. something complex) by assembling and joining parts or materials: *to build a house.* **2.** to establish, increase, or strengthen (often fol. by *up*): *to build a business; to build up one's hopes.* **3.** to mold, form, or create: *to build boys into men.* **4.** to base; found: *a relationship built on trust.* **5.** *Games.* **a.** to make (words) from letters. **b.** to assemble (cards) according to number, suit, etc., as in melding. **—v.i. 6.** to engage in the art, practice, or business of building. **7.** to form or construct a plan, system of thought, etc. (usually fol. by *on* or *upon*): *He built on the philosophies of the past.* **8.** to increase or develop toward a maximum, as of intensity, tempo, or magnitude (often fol. by *up*): *The drama builds steadily toward a climax.* **9. build in** or **into,** to build or incorporate as part of something else: *to build in bookcases between the windows; an allowance for travel expenses built into the budget.* **10. build up, a.** to develop or increase: *to build up a bank account.* **b.** to strengthen. **c.** to prepare in stages. **d.** to fill in with houses; develop into an urban area. **e.** to praise or flatter. **—n. 11.** the physical structure, esp. of a person; physique; figure: *He had a strong build.* **12.** the manner or form of construction: *The house was of modern build.* **13.** *Masonry.* **a.** a vertical joint. **b.** the vertical dimension of a stone laid on its bed. [bef. 1150; ME *bilden,* OE *byldan,* deriv. of *bold,* var. of *botl* dwelling, house] **—build′a·ble,** *adj.*

CONCISE ETYMOLOGY KEY: <, descended or borrowed from; >, whence; b., blend of, blended; c., cognate with; cf., compare; deriv., derivative; equiv., equivalent; imit., imitative; obl., oblique; r., replacing; s., stem; sp., spelling, spelled; resp., respelling, respelled; trans., translation; ?, origin unknown; *, unattested; ‡, probably earlier than. See the full key inside the front cover.

build-down (bild′doun′), *n.* a process for reducing armaments, esp. the number of nuclear weapons held by the U.S. and the U.S.S.R., by eliminating several older weapons for each new one that is deployed. [1980–85; by analogy with BUILDUP]

build·er (bil′dər), *n.* **1.** a person who builds. **2.** a person who constructs buildings under contract or as a speculation. **3.** a substance, as an abrasive or filler, added to soaps or other cleaning agents to increase their effectiveness. [1350–1400; ME *bildere.* See BUILD, -ER[1]]

build′er's knot′, *Naut.* See **clove hitch.**

build·ing (bil′ding), *n.* **1.** a relatively permanent enclosed construction over a plot of land, having a roof and usually windows and often more than one level, used for any of a wide variety of activities, as living, entertaining, or manufacturing. **2.** anything built or constructed. **3.** the act, business, or practice of constructing houses, office buildings, etc. [1250–1300; ME *byldinge.* See BUILD, -ING[1]] **—build′ing·less,** *adj.*
—Syn. 1. BUILDING, EDIFICE, STRUCTURE refer to something built. BUILDING and STRUCTURE may apply to either a finished or an unfinished product of construction, and carry no implications as to size or condition. EDIFICE is a more formal word and narrower in application, referring to a completed structure, and usually a large and imposing one. BUILDING generally connotes a useful purpose (houses, schools, business offices, etc.); STRUCTURE suggests the planning and constructive process.

build′ing and loan′ associa′tion. See **savings and loan association.**

build′ing block′, 1. block (def. 2). **2.** one of a set of cube-shaped blocks used by children to make simple constructions. **3.** a basic element or component: *the building blocks of proteins.* [1840–50]

build′ing code′. See under **code** (def. 3).

build′ing line′, (on a building lot) a line within, or coinciding with, the property line, beyond which it is illegal to build.

build′ing pa′per, heavy paper used esp. in the construction of frame buildings to block drafts, for insulation, etc. [1870–75, *Amer.*]

build′ing per′mit, an official certificate of permission issued by local authorities to a builder to construct, enlarge, or alter a building.

build′ing sick′ness. See **sick building syndrome.**

build′ing soci′ety, *Brit.* See **savings and loan association.** [1840–50]

build′ing trades′, those trades, as carpentry, masonry, and plastering, that are primarily concerned with the construction and finishing of buildings. [1885–90]

build·up (bild′up′), *n.* **1.** a building up, as of military forces; increase in amount or number. **2.** a process of growth; strengthening; development: *the buildup of heavy industry.* **3.** an accumulation, as of a particular type of material: *a buildup of salt deposits.* **4.** an increase, as in potential, intensity, or pressure: *A buildup of suspense began halfway through the movie.* **5.** a progressive or sequential development: *the buildup of helium atoms from hydrogen.* **6.** praise or publicity designed to enhance a reputation or popularize someone or something: *The studio spent $100,000 on the new star's buildup.* **7.** a process of preparation designed to make possible the achievement of an ultimate objective: *a lengthy buildup to a sales pitch.* **8.** encouragement; a psychological lift: *Every time I need a buildup, I look at her picture.* Also, **build′-up′.** [1925–30, *Amer.*; n. use of v. phrase *build up*]

built (bilt), *v.* **1.** pt. and pp. of **build. —adj. 2.** *Informal.* **a.** of sound or sturdy construction: *These cars are really built.* **b.** having a good physique or figure: *That lifeguard is really built!* **3.** *Naut.* noting any member or part of a vessel assembled from pieces: *built frame; built spar.*

built-in (bilt′in′), *adj.* **1.** built so as to be an integral and permanent part of a larger construction: *The wall has a built-in bookcase.* **2.** existing as a natural or characteristic part of something; inherent: *a built-in contempt for daydreaming.* **—n. 3.** a built-in piece of furniture or appliance. **4.** an additional feature or capability, as of a machine or a service: *a car with power steering, power brakes, and other built-ins.* [1895–1900]

built′-in obsoles′cence. See **planned obsolescence.**

built-up (bilt′up′), *adj.* **1.** built by the fastening together of several parts or enlarged by the addition of layers: *This shoe has a built-up heel.* **2.** (of an area) filled in with houses, as an urban region. [1820–30]

built′-up mast′, *Naut.* See **made mast.**

built′-up roof′, a usually flat or slightly sloped roof that is covered with a special material applied in sealed, waterproof layers.

Bui·ten·zorg (boit′n zôrkh′, bœit′-), *n.* former Dutch name of **Bogor.**

Bu·jum·bu·ra (bo͞o′jo͝om bo͝or′ə), *n.* a port in and the capital of Burundi, in the W part, on Lake Tanganyika. 160,000. Formerly, **Usumbura.**

Bu·ka·vu (bo͞o kä′vo͞o), *n.* a city in E Zaire. 180,633. Formerly, **Costermansville.**

bukh (bo͝ok), *Anglo-Indian.* **—v.i. 1.** to prate or brag. **—n. 2.** small talk; prattle; bragging. Also, **buck.** [< Hindi *bak* talk]

Bu·kha·ra (bo͝o kär′ə, bo͞o-; *Russ.* bo͞o khä′rə), *n.* **1.** a city in S central Uzbekistan, W of Samarkand. 220,000. **2.** a former khanate in SW Asia: now incorporated into Uzbekistan. Also, **Bokhara.**

Bukha′ra rug′. See **Bokhara rug.**

Bu·kha·rin (bo͞o khä′rin), *n.* **Ni·ko·lai I·va·no·vich** (nyi ku lī′ ē vä′nə vyich), 1888–1938, Russian editor, writer, and Communist leader.

Bu·ko·vi·na (bo͞o′kə vē′nə; *Rum.* bo͞o kô vē′nä), *n.* Bucovina.

Bul (bo͞ol), *n. Chiefly Biblical.* a month equivalent to Heshvan of the modern Jewish calendar. I Kings 6:38.

bul., bulletin.

Bu·la·wa·yo (bo͞o′lə wā′yō, -wä′-), *n.* a city in SW Zimbabwe: mining center. 318,000.

bulb (bulb), *n.* **1.** *Bot.* **a.** a usually subterranean and often globular bud having fleshy leaves emergent at the top and a stem reduced to a flat disk, rooting from the underside, as in the onion and lily. **b.** a plant growing from such a bud. **2.** any round, enlarged part, esp. at the end of a cylindrical object: *the bulb of a thermometer.* **3.** *Elect.* **a.** the glass housing, in which a partial vacuum has been established, that contains the filament of an incandescent electric lamp. **b.** an incandescent or fluorescent electric lamp. **4.** *Anat.* any of various small, bulb-shaped structures or protuberances: *olfactory bulb; bulb of urethra.* **5.** See **medulla oblongata. 6.** *Building Trades.* a rounded thickening at the toe of an angle iron or tee. **7.** *Naut.* a cylindrical or spherical prominence at the forefoot of certain vessels. **8.** *Photog.* a shutter setting in which the shutter remains open as long as the shutter release is depressed. *Symbol:* B [1560–70; < L *bulbus* < Gk *bolbós* onion, bulbous plant] **—bulbed,** *adj.* **—bulb′less,** *adj.*

bulb (def. 7)

bul·bar (bul′bər, -bär), *adj.* of or pertaining to a bulb, esp. to the medulla oblongata. [1875–80; BULB + -AR[1]]

bul·bif·er·ous (bul bif′ər əs), *adj.* producing bulbs. [1800–10; < NL *bulbifer* (see BULB, -I-, -FER) + -OUS]

bul·bil (bul′bil), *n.* **1.** *Bot.* Also, **bul·bel** (bul′bəl, -bel). bulblet. **2.** *Mycol.* a rounded mass of fungus cells resembling a sclerotium but of simpler organization, most commonly produced by certain basidiomycetes. [1825–35; < NL *bulbillus,* equiv. to L *bulb*(*us*) BULB + *-illus* dim. suffix]

bulb′ keel′, *Naut.* a narrow keel having a swelling weight of lead or iron at the bottom. [1890–95]

bulb·let (bulb′lit), *n. Bot.* a small bulb or bulblike structure, esp. one growing in the axils of leaves, as in the tiger lily, or replacing flowers, as in the onion. Also called **bulbil.** [1835–45; BULB + -LET]

bul·bo·u·re·thral (bul′bō yo͞o rē′thrəl), *adj. Anat., Zool.* of or pertaining to the rounded mass of tissue surrounding the urethra at the root of the penis. [BULB + -O- + URETHRAL]

bulboure′thral gland′, *Anat., Zool.* See **Cowper's gland.**

bul·bous (bul′bəs), *adj.* **1.** bulb-shaped; bulging. **2.** having or growing from bulbs. Also, **bul·ba·ceous** (bul bā′shəs). [1570–80; < L *bulbōsus.* See BULB, -OUS] **—bul′bous·ly,** *adv.*

bul′bous but′tercup, a European buttercup, *Ranunculus bulbosus,* having yellow flowers in irregular branching clusters: a common weed in North America. Also called **bul′bous crow′foot.**

bul·bul (bo͝ol′bo͝ol), *n.* **1.** a songbird often mentioned in Persian poetry, regarded as being a nightingale. **2.** any of several oscine birds of the family Pycnonotidae, of the Old World tropics. [1775–85; < Pers]

Bul·finch (bo͝ol′finch′), *n.* **1. Charles,** 1763–1844, U.S. architect. **2.** his son, **Thomas,** 1796–1867, U.S. author and mythologist.

Bulg., 1. Bulgaria. **2.** Bulgarian. Also, **Bulg**

Bul·ga·nin (bo͝ol gä′nin, -gan′in; *Russ.* bo͞ol gä′nyin), *n.* **Ni·ko·lai A·le·ksan·dro·vich** (nik′ə lī′ al′ik san′drə vich, -sän′-; *Russ.* nyi ku lyī′ u lyi ksän′drə vyich), 1895–1975, Soviet political leader: premier 1955–58.

Bul·gar (bul′gər, bo͝ol′gär), *n.* Bulgarian (def. 1).

Bul·gar·i·a (bul gâr′ē ə, bo͝ol-), *n.* a republic in SE Europe. 8,761,000; 42,800 sq. mi. (110,850 sq. km). *Cap.:* Sofia.

Bul·gar·i·an (bul gâr′ē ən, bo͝ol-), *n.* **1.** Also, **Bulgar.** a native or inhabitant of Bulgaria. **2.** a Slavic language, the language of Bulgaria. *Abbr.:* Bulg., Bulg **—adj. 3.** of or pertaining to Bulgaria, its people, or their language. [1545–55; BULGARI(A) + -AN]

bulge (bulj), *n., v.,* **bulged, bulg·ing.** —*n.* **1.** a rounded projection, bend, or protruding part; protuberance; hump: *a bulge in a wall.* **2.** any sudden increase, as of numbers, sales, or prices: *the bulge in profits.* **3.** a rising in small waves on the surface of a body of water, caused by the action of a fish or fishes in pursuit of food underwater. —*v.i.* **4.** to swell or bend outward; be protuberant. **5.** to be filled to capacity: *The box bulged with cookies.* —*v.t.* **6.** to make protuberant; cause to swell. [1200–50; ME: bag, hump < OF < L *bulga* bag < Celt; cf. Ir *bolg* bag] —**bulg′ing·ly,** *adv.*
—**Syn. 4.** protrude, project, stick out.
—**Pronunciation.** See **bulk**[1].

Bulge (bulj), *n.* **Battle of the,** the final major German counteroffensive in World War II, begun December 16, 1944, and thrusting deep into Allied territory in N and E Belgium: repulsed January 1945.

bulg·er (bul′jər), *n. Golf.* a wood having a convex face, now rarely used. [1825–35; BULGE + -ER[1]]

bul·gur (bul′gər, bo͝ol′-), *n.* a form of wheat that has been parboiled, cracked, and dried. [1925–30; < Turk (< Ar *burghul, burghūl*) < Pers]

bulg·y (bul′jē), *adj.,* **bulg·i·er, bulg·i·est.** tending to bulge; having a bulge: *a bulgy envelope.* [1840–50; BULGE + -Y[1]] —**bulg′i·ness,** *n.*

-bulia, *Chiefly Psychiatry.* a combining form meaning "will," used in the formation of compound words: *abulia.* [< NL < Gk *-boulia,* equiv. to *boul(ḗ)* will + *-ia* -IA]

bu·lim·a·rex·i·a (byo͞o lim′ə rek′sē ə, -lē′mə-, bo͞o-, bə-), *n. Psychiatry.* a syndrome in which the symptoms of both bulimia and anorexia nervosa are present, characterized by distorted body image, excessive weight loss, and use of forced vomiting to compensate for periods of binge eating. [1975–80; BULIM(IA) + (AN)OREXIA, with *-o-* resp. as *-a-*] —**bu·lim′a·rex′ic,** *adj., n.*

bu·lim·i·a (byo͞o lim′ē ə, -lē′mē ə, bo͞o-, bə-), *n.* **1.** Also called **hyperphagia.** *Pathol.* abnormally voracious appetite or unnaturally constant hunger. **2.** Also called **binge-purge syndrome, bulim′ia ner·vo′sa** (nûr vō′-sə). *Psychiatry.* a habitual disturbance in eating behavior mostly affecting young women of normal weight, characterized by frequent episodes of grossly excessive food intake followed by self-induced vomiting to avert weight gain. Cf. **anorexia nervosa.** Also, **boulimia.** [1350–1400; ME < NL < Gk *boulimía* extreme hunger, equiv. to *bou-* intensive prefix (deriv. of *bou-,* s. of *boûs* OX) + *lim(ós)* hunger + *-ia* -IA]

bu·lim·ic (byo͞o lim′ik, -lē′mik, bo͞o-, bə-), *adj.* **1.** pertaining to, resembling, or affected by bulimia. —*n.* **2.** a person suffering from bulimia. Also, **bu·lim·i·ac** (byo͞o lim′ē ak′, -lē′mē-, bo͞o-, bə-). [1850–55; *bulim(y)* earlier form of BULIMIA + -IC, or BULIM(A) + -AC]

bulk[1] (bulk), *n.* **1.** magnitude in three dimensions: *a ship of great bulk.* **2.** the greater part; main mass or body: *The bulk of the debt was paid.* **3.** goods or cargo not in packages or boxes, usually transported in large volume, as grain, coal, or petroleum. **4.** fiber (def. 9). **5.** (of paper, cardboard, yarn, etc.) thickness, esp. in relation to weight. **6.** the body of a living creature. **7.** See **bulk mail. 8. in bulk, a.** unpackaged: *Fresh orange juice is shipped from Florida in bulk.* **b.** in large quantities: *Those who buy in bulk receive a discount.* —*adj.* **9.** being or traded in bulk: *bulk grain.* —*v.i.* **10.** to increase in size; expand; swell. **11.** to be of or give the appearance of great weight, size, or importance: *The problem bulks large in his mind.* **12.** (of paper, cardboard, yarn, etc.) to be of or to acquire a specific thickness, esp. in relation to weight. **13.** to gather, form, or mix into a cohesive or uniform mass. —*v.t.* **14.** to cause to swell, grow, or increase in weight or thickness. **15.** to gather, bring together, or mix. **16. bulk up,** to increase the bulk of, esp. by increasing the thickness of: *Adding four chapters will bulk up the book.* [1400–50; late ME *bolke* heap, cargo, hold < ON *bulki* cargo, ship's hold]
—**Syn. 1.** See **size**[1].
—**Pronunciation.** BULK and BULGE most often are pronounced with the vowel (u) of *buck.* In South Midland and Southern U.S. the (o͝o) of *book* and *bull* commonly occurs among all speakers. Standard British speech has only (u). Both types exist in British regional speech, and both were brought to the colonies, where each came to predominate in a different area and was carried west by migration.

bulk[2] (bulk), *n. Archit.* a structure, as a stall, projecting from the front of a building. [1350–1400; ME: stall; appar. special use of BULK[1]]

bulk′ car′rier, a single-decked ship designed to carry dry cargoes, as grain or coal, in bulk form. [1955–60]

bulk·er (bul′kər), *Naut. Informal.* See **bulk carrier.** [1875–80; BULK + -ER[1]]

bulk·head (bulk′hed′), *n.* **1.** *Naut.* any of various wall-like constructions inside a vessel, as for forming watertight compartments, subdividing space, or strengthening the structure. **2.** *Aeron.* a transverse partition or reinforcing frame in the body of an airplane. **3.** *Civ. Engin.* **a.** a partition built in a subterranean passage to prevent the passage of air, water, or mud. **b.** a retaining structure of timber, steel, or reinforced concrete, used for shore protection and in harbor works. **4.** *Building Trades.* **a.** a horizontal or inclined outside door over a stairway leading to a cellar. **b.** a boxlike structure, as on a roof, covering a stairwell or other opening. [1490–1500; BULK[2] + HEAD] —**bulk′head′ed,** *adj.*

bulk′head deck′, *Naut.* the uppermost continuous deck in the hull of a vessel, forming watertight compartments with the main transverse bulkheads.

bulk·head·ing (bulk′hed′ing), *n.* the construction of bulkheads; bulkheads in general. [BULKHEAD + -ING[1]]

bulk′ mail′, a category of mail for mailing large numbers of identical printed items to individual addressees at less than first-class rates, as circulars or bulletins.

bulk-mail (bulk′māl′), *v.t.* to mail as bulk mail.

bulk′ mod′ulus, *Physics.* a coefficient of elasticity of a substance, expressing the ratio between a pressure that acts to change the volume of the substance and the fractional change in volume produced. [1905–10]

bulk·y (bul′kē), *adj.,* **bulk·i·er, bulk·i·est. 1.** of relatively large and cumbersome bulk or size. **2.** (of a fabric or yarn) thick; lofty. **3.** (of a garment) made of thick, resilient fabric or yarn: *a bulky sweater.* [1665–75; BULK[1] + -Y[1]] —**bulk′i·ly,** *adv.* —**bulk′i·ness,** *n.*
—**Syn. 1.** massive, ponderous, unwieldy, clumsy.

bull[1] (bo͝ol), *n.* **1.** the male of a bovine animal, esp. of the genus *Bos,* with sexual organs intact and capable of reproduction. **2.** the male of certain other animals, as the elephant and moose. **3.** a large, solidly built person. **4.** a person who believes that market prices, esp. of stocks, will increase (opposed to *bear*). **5.** (*cap.*) *Astron., Astrol.* the constellation or sign of Taurus. **6.** a bulldog. **7.** *Slang.* a police officer. **8. bull in a china shop,** an awkward or clumsy person. **9. take the bull by the horns,** to attack a difficult or risky problem fearlessly. —*adj.* **10.** male. **11.** of, pertaining to, or resembling a bull, as in strength. **12.** having to do with or marked by a continuous trend of rising prices, as of stocks: *a bull market.* —*v.t.* **13.** *Stock Exchange.* to attempt to raise the price of. **14.** to speculate in, in expectation of a rise in price. **15.** to force; shove: *to bull one's way through a crowd.* **16.** *Naut.* to ram (a buoy). [1150–1200; ME *bule,* OE *bula;* akin to ON *boli;* see BULLOCK] —**bull′-like′,** *adj.*

bull[2] (bo͝ol), *n.* **1.** a bulla or seal. **2.** *Rom. Cath. Ch.* a formal papal document having a bulla attached. [1250–1300; ME *bulle* < AF < ML *bulla* seal, sealed document; see BULLA]

bull[3] (bo͝ol), *n. Slang.* **1.** exaggerations; lies; nonsense. **2. shoot the bull,** to talk aimlessly: *We just sat around shooting the bull.* [1620–30; < ML *bulla* play, game, jest, perh. special use of L *bulla* bubble; now generally taken as a euphemistic shortening of BULLSHIT]

Bull (bo͝ol), *n.* **John.** See **John Bull.**

Bull (bo͝ol), *n.* **O·le (Bor·ne·mann)** (ō′lə bôr′nə män′), 1810–80, Norwegian violinist and composer.

Bull., bulletin.

bul·la (bo͝ol′ə, bul′ə), *n., pl.* **bul·lae** (bo͝ol′ē, bul′ē). **1.** a seal attached to an official document, as a papal bull. **2.** an ancient Roman pendant, consisting of a rounded box containing an amulet. **3.** *Pathol.* a large vesicle. **4.** *Zool.* a blisterlike or bubblelike prominence of a bone, as that of the tympanic bone in the skull of certain mammals. [1840–50; < L: bubble, also stud, boss, knob (whence ML *bulla* official seal)]

bul·lace (bo͝ol′is), *n.* **1.** the damson. **2.** the muscadine. [1300–50; ME *bolaz;* akin to ML *bolluca,* F *beloce*]

bull′ ant′. See **bulldog ant.** [1895–1900]

bul·lar·i·um (bo͝o lâr′ē əm), *n., pl.* **-lar·i·a** (-lâr′ē ə). a collection of papal bulls. [< ML, equiv. to *bull(a)* BULL[2] + *-ārium* -ARY]

bul·la·ry (bo͝ol′ə rē), *n., pl.* **-ries.** bullarium.

bul·late (bo͝ol′āt, -it, bul′-), *adj.* **1.** having the surface covered with irregular and slight elevations, giving a blistered appearance. **2.** *Anat.* inflated; vaulted. [1810–20; < L *bullātus.* See BULLA, -ATE[1]]

bull·bait·ing (bo͝ol′bā′ting), *n.* the action or sport of setting dogs upon a bull in a pen or arena. [1570–80; BULL[1] + BAITING]

bull-bar (bo͝ol′bär′), *n. Australian.* a metal frame attached to the front of a vehicle to prevent damage in case of a collision with stray animals on outback roads.

bull·bat (bo͝ol′bat′), *n.* nighthawk (def. 1). [1830–40, *Amer.;* said to be so called from the noise it makes when flying. See BULL[1], BAT[2]]

bull′ bay′, 1. See **evergreen magnolia. 2.** See **red bay.** [1880–85, *Amer.*]

bull′ block′, *Metalworking.* a machine for drawing wire in which the wire is pulled through the dies by a power-operated drum.

bull·boat (bo͝ol′bōt′), *n.* a lightweight, shallow-draft boat made of hides stretched over a wooden frame and used by Plains Indians. [1825–35, *Amer.;* BULL[1] + BOAT]

bull·bri·er (bo͝ol′brī′ər), *n.* catbrier. [1850–55, *Amer.;* BULL[1] + BRIER[1]]

bull·buck·er (bo͝ol′buk′ər), *n. Canadian.* (in lumbering) a foreman who supervises fallers and buckers. [1945–50; BULL[1] + BUCKER[2]]

bull′ chain′, *Lumbering.* a chain for dragging logs to a sawmill. Also called **jack ladder.**

bulldog (def. 1) 13 in. (33 cm) high at shoulder

bull·dog (bo͝ol′dôg′, -dog′), *n., adj., v.,* **-dogged, -dog·ging.** —*n.* **1.** one of an English breed of medium-sized, short-haired, muscular dogs with prominent, undershot jaws, usually having a white and tan or brindled coat, raised originally for bullbaiting. **2.** *Informal.* a stubbornly persistent person. **3.** a short-barreled revolver of large caliber. **4.** *Metall.* slag from a puddling furnace. **5.** an assistant to the proctor at Oxford and Cambridge universities. —*adj.* **6.** like or characteristic of a bulldog or of a bulldog's jaws: *bulldog obstinacy.* —*v.t.* **7.** to attack in the manner of a bulldog. **8.** *Western U.S.* to throw (a calf, steer, etc.) to the ground by seizing the horns and twisting the head. [1490–1500; BULL[1] + DOG] —**bull′dog′ged·ness,** *n.* —**bull′dog′ger,** *n.*

bull′dog ant′, any of several aggressive ants of the genus *Myrmecia,* mostly of Australia and Tasmania, capable of inflicting a painful and potentially dangerous sting. Also called **bull ant, jumper ant.** [1850–55]

bull′dog clip′, a spring clamp with long, narrow jaws, for holding papers together. [1940–45]

bull′dog edi′tion, the earliest daily edition of a newspaper. [1925–30, *Amer.*]

bull·doze (bo͝ol′dōz′), *v.,* **-dozed, -doz·ing.** —*v.t.* **1.** to clear, level, or reshape the contours of (land) by or as if by using a bulldozer: *to bulldoze a building site.* **2.** to clear away by or as if by using a bulldozer: *to bulldoze trees from a site.* **3.** to coerce or intimidate, as with threats. —*v.i.* **4.** to use a bulldozer: *To clear this rubble away we may have to bulldoze.* **5.** to advance or force one's way in the manner of a bulldozer. [1875–80, *Amer.;* orig. uncert.; the notion that it represents a v. use of *bull dose,* i.e., a dose fit for a bull, is prob. specious; defs. 1, 2, 4, 5 are back formations from BULLDOZER tractor]
—**Syn. 3.** browbeat, cow, bully, hector; tyrannize.

bull·doz·er (bo͝ol′dō′zər), *n.* **1.** a large, powerful tractor having a vertical blade at the front end for moving earth, tree stumps, rocks, etc. **2.** a person who intimidates or coerces. [1875–80, *Amer.;* 1925–30 for def. 1; BULLDOZE + -ER[1]]

bulldozer (def. 1)

bull′ dust′, *Australian Slang.* nonsense; bull. [1940–45]

bull′ dyke′, *Slang (disparaging).* a lesbian who is notably masculine or assertive in manner or appearance. [1925–30]

bul·let (bo͝ol′it), *n., v.,* **-let·ed, -let·ing.** —*n.* **1.** a small metal projectile, part of a cartridge, for firing from small arms. See diag. under **cartridge. 2.** a cartridge. **3.** a small ball. **4.** *Print.* a heavy dot for marking paragraphs or otherwise calling attention to or itemizing particular sections of text, esp. in display advertising. **5.** *Cards.* an ace. **6. bite the bullet,** to force oneself to perform a painful, difficult task or to endure an unpleasant situation: *We'll just have to bite the bullet and pay higher taxes.* —*v.i.* **7.** to move swiftly. [1550–60; < MF *boullette,* equiv. to *boulle* ball (see BOWL[2]) + *-ette* -ETTE] —**bul′let·less,** *adj.* —**bul′let·like′,** *adj.*

bul·let·head (bo͝ol′it hed′), *n.* **1.** a head considered similar in shape to a bullet, as that of a person with a high, domelike forehead and cranium and short hair. **2.** a person having such a head. **3.** an obstinate or stupid person. [1680–90; BULLET + HEAD]

bul·le·tin (bo͝ol′i tn, -tin), *n., v.,* **-tined, -tin·ing.** —*n.* **1.** a brief account or statement, as of news or events, issued for the information of the public. **2.** *Journalism.* **a.** a brief, prominently featured newspaper account, based upon information received just before the edition went to press. **b.** a similar brief account broadcast over radio or television pending further information. **3.** a pamphlet or monograph summarizing the past achievements, existing conditions, and future plans of a corporation, educational institution, government agency, etc., esp. one cataloging the classes taught at a college or university. **4.** an official, special, or scholarly periodical, as of a learned society. —*v.t.* **5.** to make known by a bulletin. [1645–55; < F, perh. < It *bullettino,* equiv. to *bullett(a)* (*bulla* BULL[2] + *-etta* -ETTE) + *-ino* -INE[2]]

bul′letin board′, 1. a board for the posting of bulletins, notices, announcements, etc. **2.** *Computers.* See **BBS.** [1825–35, *Amer.*]

bul·let·proof (bo͝ol′it pro͞of′), *adj.* **1.** (of vehicles, glass, clothing, etc.) capable of resisting or absorbing the impact of a bullet. **2.** *Informal.* safe from failure; without errors or shortcomings and beyond criticism: *a bulletproof system; a bulletproof budget.* —*v.t.* **3.** to make (something) bulletproof. [1855–60; BULLET + -PROOF]

bul′let train′, a high-speed passenger train, as on certain routes in Japan. [1965–70]

bul′let tree′. See **bully tree.**

bul′let wood′, the wood of a bully tree. [1835–45]

bull′ fid′dle. *Informal.* See **double bass.** [1875–80, *Amer.*] —**bull′ fid′dler.**

bull·fight (bo͝ol′fīt′), *n.* a traditional Spanish, Portuguese, or Latin American spectacle in which a bull is fought by a matador, assisted by banderilleros and picadors, in a prescribed way in an arena and is usually killed. [1745–55; BULL[1] + FIGHT] —**bull′fight′ing,** *n.*

bull·fight·er (bo͝ol′fī′tər), *n.* a person who participates in a bullfight, esp. a matador. [1840–50; BULL[1] + FIGHTER]

bull·finch[1] (bo͝ol′finch′), *n.* **1.** a European finch, *Pyrrhula pyrrhula,* often kept as a pet, the male of which has a black, white, and bluish-gray back and a rosy breast.

2. any of several related or similar birds. [1560–70; BULL[1] (perh. in sense "bull-necked") + FINCH]

bull•finch[2] (bo͝ol′finch′), *n.* a hedge high enough to impede mounted hunters. [1825–35; of uncert. orig.]

bull′ float′, a machine for giving the final surfacing to an area of concrete, as on a road.

bull•frog (bo͝ol′frog′, -frôg′), *n.* a large frog, esp. the North American *Rana catesbeiana,* having a deep voice. [1690–1700, *Amer.*; BULL[1] + FROG[1]; so called from its size and voice]

bull′ gear′, *Mach.* See **bull wheel.**

bull′ gun′, a target rifle with a heavy barrel.

bull•head (bo͝ol′hed′), *n.* **1.** any of several North American, freshwater catfishes of the genus *Ictalurus,* having a rounded or truncate caudal fin. **2.** any of several other fishes, as the freshwater sculpins of the genus *Cottus,* esp. those species having a hornlike spine on each side of the head. **3.** an obstinate or stupid person. [1665–75, *Amer.*; BULL[1] + HEAD]

bull•head•ed (bo͝ol′hed′id), *adj.* obstinately opinionated, esp. in refusing to consider alternatives; stubborn. [1810–20; BULL[1] + HEAD + -ED[3]] —**bull′head′ed•ly,** *adv.* —**bull′head′ed•ness,** *n.*

bull′ head′er, *Masonry.* **1.** Also called **bullnose header.** a brick having one of the edges across its width rounded for laying as a header in a sill or the like. **2.** a brick laid on edge as a header, as in a rowlock. Cf. **bull stretcher.**

bull•horn (bo͝ol′hôrn′), *n.* a directional, high-powered, electrical loudspeaker or megaphone. Also, **bull′ horn′.** [1950–55; BULL[1] + HORN]

bul•lion (bo͝ol′yən), *n.* **1.** gold or silver considered in mass rather than in value. **2.** gold or silver in the form of bars or ingots. **3.** Also called **bul′lion fringe′.** a thick trimming of cord covered with gold or silver thread, for decorating uniforms. **4.** embroidery or lace worked with gold wire or gold or silver cords. [1300–50; ME: melted mass of gold or silver < AL *bulliōn-* (s. of *bulliō*) in same sense (< AF *bullion* mint), lit., a boiling, equiv. to *bull(īre)* to bubble, BOIL[1] + *-iōn-* -ION] —**bul′lion•less,** *adj.*

bul•lion•ist (bo͝ol′yə nist), *n.* a person who advocates a system in which currency is directly convertible to gold or silver. [1805–15; BULLION + -IST] —**bul′lion•ism,** *n.*

bull•ish (bo͝ol′ish), *adj.* **1.** like a bull. **2.** obstinate or stupid. **3.** *Com.* **a.** rising in prices. **b.** characterized by favorable economic prospects. **c.** *Informal.* regarding a particular investment as potentially profitable (often fol. by *on*): *We're still bullish on treasury bonds.* **4.** hopeful; optimistic. [1560–70; BULL[1] + -ISH[1]] —**bull′ish•ly,** *adv.* —**bull′ish•ness,** *n.*

Bul•litt (bo͝ol′it), *n.* **William C(hristian),** 1891–1967, U.S. diplomat and journalist.

bull•mas•tiff (bo͝ol′mas′tif, -mä′stif), *n.* one of an English breed of dogs having a short, fawn or brindled coat, produced by crossing the bulldog and the mastiff. Also, **bull′-mas′tiff, bull′ mas′tiff.** [1870–75; BULL(DOG) + MASTIFF]

Bull′ Moose′, a member of the Progressive party under the leadership of Theodore Roosevelt. Also called **Bull′ Moos′er** (mo͞o′sər). [1910–15, *Amer.*]

bull•neck (bo͝ol′nek′), *n.* **1.** the leather made from the hide of a bull's neck. **2.** the name applied to various ducks, including the ring-necked duck, the ruddy duck, and the canvasback. [BULL[1] + NECK]

bull-necked (bo͝ol′nekt′), *adj.* having a short, thick neck. Also, **bull′necked′.** [1350–1400; ME]

bull′ nose′, **1.** *Vet. Pathol.* a disease of swine caused by bacterial infection of the tissues of the snout causing gross malformation and frequently serious blocking of the nasal passages. **2.** bullnose. [1880–85, *Amer.*]

bull•nose (bo͝ol′nōz′), *n.* **1.** Also, **bull's nose.** *Archit.* **a.** a rounded or obtuse exterior angle, as the corner made by two walls. **b.** a structural member, as a brick, used in forming such an angle. **2.** Also called **bull′nose step′.** a step having semicircular or quadrantal ends. [1835–45; BULL[1] + NOSE]

bull-nosed bow (bo͝ol′nōzd′ bou′), *Naut.* a bow having a bulbous forefoot.

bull′nose head′er, *Masonry.* See **bull header** (def. 1).

bull′nose stretch′er, *Masonry.* See **bull stretcher** (def. 1).

bul•lock (bo͝ol′ək), *n.* **1.** a castrated bull; steer. **2.** a young bull. [bef. 1000; ME *bullok,* OE *bulluc.* See BULL[1], -OCK]

bul•lock's-heart (bo͝ol′əks härt′), *n.* the large, edible fruit of a tropical American tree, *Annona reticulata.* Also, **bul′lock heart′.** [1865–70; so called from its size, color, and shape]

Bul′lock's o′riole (bo͝ol′əks), a common oriole, *Icterus galbula bullockii,* of western North America: a subspecies of the northern oriole. [1855–60, *Amer.*; named after William *Bullock,* 19th-century English naturalist]

bul•lock•y (bo͝ol′ə kē), *n., pl.* **-lock•ies** for 1, *adj.* —*n.* *Australian.* **1.** a bullock driver. **2.** the coarse language thought to be typical of a bullock driver. —*adj.* **3.** *Australian.* pertaining to driving bullocks or managing cattle. **4.** resembling a bullock. [1880–85; BULLOCK + -Y[1], subsequently nominalized]

bull′ of the woods′, the foreman of a logging operation. [1915–20]

CONCISE ETYMOLOGY KEY: <, descended or borrowed from; >, whence; b., blend of, blended; c., cognate with; cf., compare; deriv., derivative; equiv., equivalent; imit., imitative; obl., oblique; r., replacing; s., stem; sp., spelling, spelled; resp., respelling, respelled; trans., translation; ?, origin unknown; *, unattested; ‡, probably earlier than. See the full key inside the front cover.

bul•lous (bul′əs), *adj. Pathol.* pertaining to, similar to, or characterized by bullae. [1895–1900; BULL(A) + -OUS]

bull′ pen′, **1.** *Baseball.* **a.** a place where relief pitchers warm up during a game. **b.** the relief pitchers on a team. **2.** *Informal.* **a.** a large cell or room, usually next to the courtroom, where prisoners are temporarily held. **b.** a large room in an office occupied by many employees. **3.** any temporary or crowded quarters, as sleeping quarters in a lumber camp. **4.** a pen for a bull or bulls. Also, **bull′pen′.** [1800–10, *Amer.* for def. 4; 1920–25 for def. 1]

bull•pout (bo͝ol′pout′), *n.* See **horned pout.** [1815–25, *Amer.*; BULL(HEAD) + POUT[2]]

bull′ rid′ing, a rodeo event in which a contestant tries to ride a bucking bull for eight seconds, with one hand holding a rope tied to a band around the bull's chest.

bull•ring (bo͝ol′ring′), *n.* an arena for a bullfight. [1600–10; BULL[1] + RING[1]]

bull-roar•er (bo͝ol′rôr′ər, -rōr′-), *n.* a wooden slat that produces a roaring sound when whirled around one's head on the end of a string or thong, used by some peoples of the world in religious ceremonies and by others as a toy. Also called **thunderstick.** [1880–85]

bull′ rope′, *Naut.* any of various ropes for holding objects to prevent them from rubbing against or striking other objects. [1880–85]

Bull′ Run′, a creek in NE Virginia: two important battles of the Civil War were fought near here, 1861 and 1862, both resulting in defeat for the Union forces. See map under **Antietam.**

bull′ ses′sion, *Informal.* an informal, spontaneous discussion. [1915–20]

bull's-eye (bo͝olz′ī′), *n., pl.* **-eyes.** **1.** the circular spot, usually black or outlined in black, at the center of a target marked with concentric circles and used in target practice. **2.** a shot that hits this. **3.** the center or central area of a military target, as of a town or factory, in a bombing raid. **4.** a missile that strikes the central area of a target. **5.** the coordinates or instance of aiming and firing a missile that results in its hitting the center of a target. **6.** *Informal.* **a.** any statement or act that is precisely to the point or achieves a desired result directly. **b.** something that is decisive or crucial; crux. **7.** a small circular opening or window. **8.** a thick disk or lenslike piece of glass inserted in a roof, ship's deck, etc., to admit light. **9.** *Optics.* a lens of short focal length. **10.** a lantern equipped with a lens of this sort. **11.** *Naut.* an oval or circular wooden block having a groove around it and a hole in the center, through which to reeve a rope. **12.** *Meteorol.* (formerly) the eye of a storm. **13.** a large, round piece of peppermint-flavored hard candy. [1680–90] —**bull's′-eyed′,** *adj.*

bull's′-eye mir′ror, a circular, convex, ornamental mirror.

bull's′-eye rot′, *Plant Pathol.* a disease of apples and pears, characterized by sunken, eyelike spots on the fruit and twig cankers, caused by any of several fungi, esp. of the genus *Neofabraea.*

bull's′-eye win′dow, bull's-eye (def. 7). [1925–30]

bull′ shark′, a requiem shark, *Carcharhinus leucas,* inhabiting shallow waters from North Carolina to Brazil. Also called **cub shark.**

bull•shit (bo͝ol′shit′), *n., v.,* **-shit•ted** or **-shit, -shit•ting,** *interj. Slang (vulgar).* —*n.* **1.** nonsense, lies, or exaggeration. —*v.t.* **2.** to lie or exaggerate to. —*v.i.* **3.** to speak lies or nonsense. —*interj.* **4.** (used esp. to express disagreement.) [1910–15; BULL[1] (perh. reinforced by BULL[3]) + SHIT] —**bull′shit′ter,** *n.*

bull•shot (bo͝ol′shot′), *n.* a cocktail of vodka and beef bouillon or consommé. [1960–65; BULL[1] + SHOT[1]]

bull•snake (bo͝ol′snāk′), *n.* any of several large North American constrictors of the genus *Pituophis,* as the gopher snake and pine snake, that feed chiefly upon small rodents. Also, **bull′ snake′.** [1775–85, *Amer.*; BULL[1] + SNAKE]

bull's′ nose′, bullnose (def. 1). [1835–45]

bull′ stretch′er, *Masonry.* **1.** Also called **bullnose stretcher.** a brick having one of the edges along its length rounded for laying as a stretcher in a sill or the like. **2.** a brick laid on edge as a stretcher. Cf. **bull header.**

bull′ ter′rier, *n.* one of an English breed of medium-sized, short-haired dogs having a white, brindled, or tan and white coat, produced by crossing the bulldog and the terrier. Also, **bull′ter′ri•er.** [1840–50; BULL(DOG) + TERRIER[1]]

bull terrier, white variety, 18 in. (46 cm) high at shoulder

bull′ this′tle, a tall, spiny thistle, *Cirsium vulgare,* having heads of pink to purple flowers: a common weed in North America. [1860–65]

bull′ tongue′, a plow having a vertical moldboard, used in cultivating cotton. [1825–35, *Amer.*]

bull′ trout′. See **Dolly Varden.** [1645–55]

bull•whack•er (bo͝ol′hwak′ər, -wak′-), *n. Western U.S.* (esp. in the early 19th century) the driver of a team of oxen. [1855–60, *Amer.*; BULL[1] + WHACKER]

bull′ wheel′, *Mach.* any large driving gear among smaller gears. Also called **bull gear.** [1820–30, *Amer.*]

bull•whip (bo͝ol′hwip′, -wip′), *n.* a rawhide whip having a short handle and a long, plaited lash. Also, **bull′-whip′.** Also called **bull-whack** (bo͝ol′hwak′, -wak′). [1850–55, *Amer.*; BULL[1] + WHIP]

bul•ly[1] (bo͝ol′ē), *n., pl.* **-lies,** *v.,* **-lied, -ly•ing,** *adj., interj.* —*n.* **1.** a blustering, quarrelsome, overbearing person who habitually badgers and intimidates smaller or weaker people. **2.** *Archaic.* a man hired to do violence. **3.** *Obs.* a pimp; procurer. **4.** *Obs.* good friend; good fellow. **5.** *Obs.* sweetheart; darling. —*v.t.* **6.** to act the bully toward; intimidate; domineer. —*v.i.* **7.** to be loudly arrogant and overbearing. —*adj.* **8.** *Informal.* fine; excellent; very good. **9.** dashing; jovial; high-spirited. —*interj.* **10.** *Informal.* good! well done! [1530–40; < MD *boele* lover] —**bul′ly•a•ble,** *adj.*
—**Syn. 6.** cow, browbeat, coerce; terrorize, tyrannize.

bul•ly[2] (bo͝ol′ē), *n.* See **bully beef.** [1865–70; < F *bouilli,* short for *boeuf bouilli* boiled meat. See BOIL[1], BEEF]

bul•ly[3] (bo͝ol′ē), *n., pl.* **-lies.** **1.** *Soccer.* a desperate, freewheeling scramble for the ball by a number of players, usually in the goal area. **2.** *Field Hockey.* a method of putting the ball into play in which two opponents, facing each other, tap their sticks on the ground near the ball and then make contact with each other's sticks over the ball three times, after which each tries to gain possession of the ball. [1860–65; of obscure orig.]

bul′ly beef′, canned or pickled beef. [1865–70]

bul•ly•boy (bo͝ol′ē boi′), *n.* a ruffian or hired hoodlum, esp. one working for or associated with a political group. [1600–10; BULLY[1] + BOY]

bul•ly•rag (bo͝ol′ē rag′), *v.t.,* **-ragged, -rag•ging.** to bully; harass: *to bullyrag fraternity plebs.* Also, **ballyrag.** [1780–90; earlier *ballarag,* of obscure orig.] —**bul′ly•rag′ger,** *n.*

bul′ly tree′, any of various tropical American trees, as *Manilkara bidentata,* of the sapodilla family, that yield the gum balata. Also called **bullet tree.** [1650–60; *bully,* alter. of BALATA]

Bü•low (bʏ′lō), *n.* **1. Prince Bern•hard von** (beʀn′härt fən), 1849–1929, chancellor of Germany 1900–09. **2. Hans (Gu•i•do, Frei•herr) von** (häns go͞o ē′dō, frī′heʀ′ fən), 1830–94, German pianist and conductor.

bul•rush (bo͝ol′rush′), *n.* **1.** (in Biblical use) the papyrus, *Cyperus papyrus.* **2.** any of various rushes of the genera *Scirpus* and *Typha.* [1400–50; late ME *bulrish* papyrus, prob. BULL[1] + *rish* RUSH[2]]

Bult•mann (bo͝olt′män′), *n.* **Ru•dolf** (ro͞o′dôlf), 1884–1976, German theologian.

bul•wark (bo͝ol′wərk, -wôrk, bul′-), *n.* **1.** a wall of earth or other material built for defense; rampart. **2.** any protection against external danger, injury, or annoyance: *The new dam was a bulwark against future floods.* **3.** any person or thing giving strong support or encouragement in time of need, danger, or doubt: *Religion was his bulwark.* **4.** Usually, **bulwarks.** *Naut.* a solid wall enclosing the perimeter of a weather or main deck for the protection of persons or objects on deck. —*v.t.* **5.** to fortify or protect with a bulwark; secure by or as if by a fortification. [1375–1425; late ME *bulwerk,* prob. < MD *bolwerc,* equiv. to *bol(l)e* BOLE[1] + *werk* WORK (n.); cf. BOULEVARD]
—**Syn. 3.** support, buttress, mainstay.

Bul•wer (bo͝ol′wər), *n.* **Sir Henry** (*William Henry Lytton Earle Bulwer; Baron Dalling and Bulwer*), 1801–72, British diplomat and author.

Bul•wer-Lyt•ton (bo͝ol′wər lit′n), *n.* **1st Baron.** See **Lytton, Edward George.**

bum[1] (bum), *n., v.,* **bummed, bum•ming,** *adj.,* **bum•mer, bum•mest.** —*n.* **1.** a person who avoids work and sponges on others; loafer; idler. **2.** a tramp, hobo, or derelict. **3.** *Informal.* an enthusiast of a specific sport or recreational activity, esp. one who gives it priority over work, family life, etc.: *a ski bum; a tennis bum.* **4.** *Informal.* an incompetent person. **5.** a drunken orgy; debauch. **6. on the bum,** *Informal.* **a.** living or traveling as or in a manner suggesting that of a hobo or tramp. **b.** in a state of disrepair or disorder: *The oven is on the bum again.* —*v.t.* **7.** *Informal.* to borrow without expectation of returning; get for nothing; cadge: *He's always bumming cigarettes from me.* **8.** *Slang.* to ruin or spoil: *The weather bummed our whole weekend.* —*v.i.* **9.** to sponge on others for a living; lead an idle or dissolute life. **10.** to live as a hobo. **11. bum around,** *Informal.* to travel, wander, or spend one's time aimlessly: *We bummed around for a couple of hours after work.* **12. bum (someone) out,** *Slang.* to disappoint, upset, or annoy: *It really bummed me out that she could have helped and didn't.* —*adj. Slang.* **13.** of poor, wretched, or miserable quality; worthless. **14.** disappointing; unpleasant. **15.** erroneous or ill-advised; misleading: *That tip on the stock market was a bum steer.* **16.** lame: *a bum leg.* [1860–65, *Amer.*; perh. shortening of or back formation from BUMMER[1]; adj. senses of unclear relation to sense "loafer" and perh. of distinct orig.]
—**Syn. 2.** vagabond, vagrant.

bum[2] (bum), *n. Chiefly Brit. Slang.* the buttocks; rump. [1350–1400; ME *bom;* of uncert. orig.]

bum[3] (bum), *n. Mil. Slang.* **1.** a reproduction of a document made with copying equipment. **2.** a bag into which classified waste is put in preparation for destruction. [perh. as shortening of BUMF or *bumfodder;* def. 2 presumably as shortening of *bum bag*]

bum•bail•iff (bum′bā′lif), *n. Brit. Disparaging.* a bailiff or underbailiff employed in serving writs, making arrests, etc. [1595–1605; BUM[2] + BAILIFF]

bum•ber•shoot (bum′bər sho͞ot′), *n. Informal (often facetious).* an umbrella. [1915–20; *bumber-,* appar. expressive alter. of UMBRELLA + *-shoot,* resp. of *-chute* in PARACHUTE]

bum•ble[1] (bum′bəl), *v.,* **-bled, -bling,** *n.* —*v.i.* **1.** to bungle or blunder awkwardly; muddle: *He somehow bumbled through two years of college.* **2.** to stumble or stagger. **3.** to speak in a low, stuttering, halting manner; mumble. —*v.t.* **4.** to do (something) clumsily; botch.

—*n.* **5.** an awkward blunder. [1525–35; perh. b. BUNGLE and STUMBLE] —**bum′bler,** *n.*

bum·ble[2] (bum′bəl), *v.i.,* **-bled, -bling.** to make a buzzing, humming sound, as a bee. [1350–1400; ME *bomblen,* freq. of *bomben* to boom, buzz; imit.]

bum·ble·bee (bum′bəl bē′), *n.* any of several large, hairy social bees of the family Apidae. Also, **bum′ble bee′.** [1520–30; BUMBLE[2] + BEE[1]]

bumblebee (queen), *Bombus americanorum,* length ³/₄ in. (1.9 cm)

bum·ble·bee·fish (bum′bəl bē′ fish′), *n., pl.* **-fish·es,** (*esp. collectively*) **-fish.** any of several gobies of the genus *Brachygobius,* inhabiting waters of the Malay Archipelago and having brown and yellow bands on the body that resemble the markings of a bumblebee. [BUMBLEBEE + FISH]

bum·ble·foot (bum′bəl fo͝ot′), *n. Vet. Pathol.* a swelling, sometimes purulent, of the ball of the foot in fowl. [1860–65; BUMBLE[1] + FOOT]

bum·ble·head·ed (bum′bəl hed′id), *adj.* clumsy, plodding, or foolish: *He stumbled through the talk in his bumbleheaded way.* [*bumblehead* (see BUMBLE[1], HEAD) + -ED[3]] —**bum′ble·head′ed·ness,** *n.*

bum·ble·pup·py (bum′bəl pup′ē), *n.* a game of whist played carelessly or contrary to rules and conventions. [1795–1805; BUMBLE[1] + PUPPY]

bum·bling (bum′bling), *adj.* **1.** liable to make awkward blunders: *a bumbling mechanic.* **2.** clumsily incompetent or ineffectual: *bumbling diplomacy.* —*n.* **3.** the act or practice of making blunders: *The bumbling of their officers cost them the battle.* [1525–35; BUMBLE[1] + -ING[2]] —**bum′bling·ly,** *adv.*

bum·boat (bum′bōt′), *n. Naut.* a boat used in peddling provisions and small wares among vessels lying in port or offshore. [1665–75; prob. partial trans. of D *bomschuit* a small fishing boat, perh. contr. of *bodemschuit(je)* lit., bottom-boat]

bumf (bumf), *n. Brit.* **1.** *Slang.* toilet paper. **2.** memoranda, official notices, or the like. [1885–90; short for *bumfodder.* See BUM[2], FODDER[1]]

bum·fuz·zled (bum fuz′əld), *adj. Chiefly South Midland and Southern U.S.* baffled; befuddled; confused. [1900–05; *bum-* (expressive prefix, perh. to be identified with the initial syll. of BAMBOOZLE) + *fuzzle* to confuse (perh. expressive alter. of FUDDLE) + -ED[2]]

bum·ma·lo (bum′ə lō′), *n., pl.* **-los.** See **bombay duck.** [1665–75; earlier *bumbelow* < Marathi *bombila,* inflected case-form of *bombil*]

bum·mer[1] (bum′ər), *n. Slang.* a person who bums. [1850–55, *Amer.*; prob. < G *Bummler,* deriv. with *-er* -ER[1] of *bummeln* to take a stroll, dawdle, loiter (expressive v. of uncert. orig.)]

bum·mer[2] (bum′ər), *n. Slang.* **1.** the unpleasant aftermath of taking narcotic drugs, esp. frightening hallucinations or unpleasant physical sensations. **2.** any unpleasant or disappointing experience: *That concert was a real bummer.* [1965–70; appar. BUM[1] (adj. sense) + -ER[1]]

bump (bump), *v.t.* **1.** to come more or less violently in contact with; collide with; strike: *His car bumped a truck.* **2.** to cause to strike or collide: *He bumped the car against a tree.* **3.** to dislodge or displace by the force of collision. **4.** *Informal.* to dislodge; to appropriate the privileges of: *When the general found there were no additional seats on the plane, he bumped a major. The airline bumped me from the flight.* **5.** to demote, promote, or dismiss: *He was bumped from his job.* **6.** *Informal.* to force upward; raise: *Demand from abroad bumped the price of corn.* **7.** *Poker.* raise (def. 24). —*v.i.* **8.** to come in contact or collide with (often fol. by *against* or *into*): *She bumped into me.* **9.** to bounce along; proceed in a series of jolts: *The old car bumped down the road.* **10.** to dance by thrusting the pelvis forward abruptly, in a provocative manner, esp. to the accompaniment of an accented musical beat. Cf. **grind** (def. 13). **11.** to boil with violent jolts caused by the sudden eruption of large bubbles through the surface. **12. bump into,** *Informal.* to meet by chance: *I bumped into an old friend yesterday.* **13. bump off,** *Slang.* to kill, esp. to murder: *They bumped him off because he knew too much.* —*n.* **14.** an act or instance of bumping; collision; blow. **15.** the shock of a blow or collision. **16.** a swelling or contusion from a blow. **17.** a small area raised above the level of the surrounding surface; protuberance: *He tripped over a bump on a road.* **18.** *Informal.* a promotion or demotion; transfer to a higher or lower level: *He got a bump to vice president of the company.* **19.** *Informal.* an increase in amount, esp. of salary or a wager: *He asked the boss for a ten-dollar bump.* **20.** *Aeron.* a rapidly rising current of air that gives an airplane a severe upward thrust. **21.** a dance movement in which the pelvis is abruptly thrust forward in a provocative manner, esp. to the accompaniment of an accented musical beat. Cf. **grind** (def. 20). **22.** *Mining.* crump (def. 6). [1560–70; imit.] —**bump′ing·ly,** *adv.*

bump·er[1] (bum′pər), *n.* **1.** a person or thing that bumps. **2.** a metal guard, usually horizontal, for protecting the front or rear of an automobile, truck, etc. **3.** any protective rim, guard, pad, or disk for absorbing shock and preventing damage from bumping, as a rubber-tipped doorstop or an old tire on the side of a boat. **4.** a cup or glass filled to the brim, as with beer. **5.** *Informal.* something unusually large. **6.** a person who molds bricks by hand. **7.** *Foundry.* a machine for ramming sand into a mold. **8.** a carangid fish, *Chlorosombrus chrysurus,* of southern U.S. and Cuban coastal seas. **9.** *Television Slang.* a brief announcement about a news story to be covered later in the programming. —*adj.* **10.** unusually abundant: *Bumper crops reaped a big profit for local farmers.* —*v.t.* **11.** to fill to the brim. [1750–60; BUMP + -ER[1]]

bump·er[2] (bum′pər), *n. Australian Slang.* the unconsumed end of a cigarette; cigarette butt. [1915–20; expressive coinage, perh. b. BUTT[1] and STUMP + -ER[1]]

bump′er car′, (in an amusement park) a small, carlike electric vehicle with an encircling rubber bumper that one maneuvers around an enclosed arena while purposely bumping other vehicles. [1945–50]

bump′er guard′, either of two vertical crosspieces attached to a bumper of a motor vehicle to prevent it from locking bumpers with another vehicle.

bump′er jack′, a jack for lifting a motor vehicle by the bumper.

bump′er pool′, a pool game played on a small, often octagonally shaped table with two pockets, having strategically placed cushioned pegs on the playing surface, usually necessitating bank shots to sink balls. [‡1975–80]

bump′er stick′er, an adhesive-backed strip of paper for sticking onto the rear bumper of an automobile, usually bearing a tourist advertisement, slogan, joke, etc.

bump·er-to-bump·er (bum′pər tə bum′pər), *adj.* **1.** marked by a long line of cars moving slowly or with many stops and starts, one behind the other: *bumper-to-bumper traffic.* **2.** *Informal.* following one another in profusion: *bumper-to-bumper worries.* [1935–40]

bump·kin[1] (bump′kin), *n.* an awkward, simple rustic; yokel. [1560–70; < MD *bommekijn* little barrel, equiv. to *boom* BEAM + *-kijn* -KIN] —**bump′kin·ish, bump′·kin·ly,** *adj.*

—**Syn.** clod, boor, hillbilly, hayseed, rube, hick, yahoo.

bump·kin[2] (bump′kin), *n. Naut.* a beam or spar projecting outward from the hull of a vessel, for extending a sail, securing blocks, etc. Also, **boomkin.** [1625–35; < MD *boom* BOOM[2], BEAM + -KIN]

bump·off (bump′ôf′, -of′), *n. Slang.* murder. [1905–10, *Amer.*; n. use of v. phrase *bump off*]

bump·tious (bump′shəs), *adj.* offensively self-assertive: *a bumptious young upstart.* [1795–1805; BUMP + (FRAC)TIOUS] —**bump′tious·ly,** *adv.* —**bump′tious·ness,** *n.*

—**Syn.** pushy, forward, cocky, cheeky, brash.

bump·y (bum′pē), *adj.,* **bump·i·er, bump·i·est. 1.** of uneven surface; full of bumps: *a bumpy road.* **2.** full of jolts: *a bumpy ride.* **3.** causing jolts: *Bumpy air shook the airplane.* **4.** having many difficulties or failures; full of ups and downs: *He had a rather bumpy career before he settled down in his present job.* [1860–65; BUMP + -Y[1]] —**bump′i·ly,** *adv.* —**bump′i·ness,** *n.*

bum′ rap′, *Slang.* **1.** an unjust accusation, verdict, or punishment: *He was sent to prison on a bum rap.* **2.** an adverse opinion or judgment considered undeserved or unjust: *The review was a bum rap, but I liked the play.*

bum-rush (bum′rush′), *v.t. Slang.* to force one's way into; crash: *to bum-rush a rap concert.* [1985–90]

bum's′ rush′, *Slang.* **1.** forcible and swift ejection from a place: *The noisy boys were given the bum's rush.* **2.** any rude or abrupt dismissal. [1920–25]

bun[1] (bun), *n.* **1.** any of a wide variety of variously shaped bread rolls, usually leavened and slightly sweetened or plain, sometimes containing spices, dried currants, etc. **2.** hair gathered into a round coil or knot at the nape of the neck or on top of the head in certain coiffures. **3. buns,** *Slang.* the buttocks. [1325–75; ME *bunne,* of obscure orig.]

bun[2] (bun), *n.* **have a bun on,** *Slang.* to be intoxicated: *Everyone at the party seemed to have a bun on.* [1900–05; of uncert. orig.]

BUN, blood urea nitrogen: the concentration of nitrogen in the blood in the form of urea, indicating kidney function.

Bu·na (bo͞o′nə, byo͞o′-), *Trademark.* a brand of synthetic rubber made by polymerizing or copolymerizing butadiene with another material, as acrylonitrile, styrene, or sodium.

bunch (bunch), *n.* **1.** a connected group; cluster: *a bunch of grapes.* **2.** a group of things: *a bunch of papers.* **3.** *Informal.* a group of people: *They're a fine bunch of students.* **4.** a knob; lump; protuberance. —*v.t.* **5.** to group together; make a bunch of. —*v.i.* **6.** to gather into a cluster; gather together. **7.** (of fabric or clothing) to gather into folds (often fol. by *up*). [1275–1325; ME *bunche;* of uncert. orig.]

—**Syn. 1, 2.** lot, batch. See **bundle.**

bunch·ber·ry (bunch′ber′ē, -bə rē), *n., pl.* **-ries.** a dwarf dogwood, *Cornus canadensis,* bearing dense clusters of bright-red berries. Also called **crackerberry.** [1835–45; BUNCH + BERRY]

Bunche (bunch), *n.* **Ralph (Johnson),** 1904–71, U.S. diplomat: at the United Nations 1946–71; Nobel peace prize 1950.

bunch′er res′onator (bun′chər), *Electronics.* See under **Klystron.** [BUNCH + -ER[1]]

bunch·flow·er (bunch′flou′ər), *n.* **1.** a stout North American plant, *Melanthium virginicum,* of the lily family, having grasslike leaves and an open cluster of small greenish flowers. **2.** any other plant of the same genus. [1810–20, *Amer.*; BUNCH + FLOWER]

bunch′ grass′, any of various grasses in different regions of North America, growing in distinct clumps. [1830–40, *Amer.*]

bunch′ light′, a light consisting of a group of small light bulbs mounted in a reflecting box.

bunch′ pink′. See **sweet william.** [1855–60]

bunch·y (bun′chē), *adj.,* **bunch·i·er, bunch·i·est. 1.** having bunches. **2.** bulging or protuberant. [1350–1400; ME; see BUNCH, -Y[1]] —**bunch′i·ly,** *adv.* —**bunch′i·ness,** *n.*

bun·co (bung′kō), *n., pl.* **-cos,** *v.,* **-coed, -co·ing.** *Informal.* bunko.

bun·combe (bung′kəm), *n.* bunkum.

bund (bund), *n.* (in Asian countries) an embankment or an embanked quay, often providing a promenade. [1805–15; < Hindi *band* < Pers: dam, levee; akin to BIND, BOND[1]]

Bund (bo͝ond, bund; *Ger.* bo͝ont), *n., pl.* **Bunds,** *Ger.* **Bün·de** (byn′də). **1.** a short form of "German-American Volksbund," a pro-Nazi organization in the U.S. during the 1930's and 1940's. **2.** (*often l.c.*) an alliance or league, esp. a political society. [< G: association, league] —**Bund′ist,** *n.*

Bun·del·khand (bo͝on′dl kund′, -KHund′), *n.* a former group of native states in central India, now part of Madhya Pradesh.

Bun·des·rat (bo͝on′dəs rät′; *Ger.* bo͝on′dəs rät′), *n.* **1.** the upper house of the federal legislature of West Germany. **2.** the federal council of Switzerland and of Austria. [1870–75; < G, equiv. to *Bundes,* gen. of *Bund* federation + *Rat* council]

Bun·des·tag (bo͝on′dəs täg′; *Ger.* bo͝on′dəs täk′), *n.* the lower house of the federal legislature of West Germany. [1875–80; < G: federal assembly, equiv. to *Bundes,* gen. of *Bund* federation + *-tag,* deriv. of *tagen* to meet, assemble; see DIET[2]]

Bun·des·wehr (bo͝on′dəs vâr′; *Ger.* bo͝on′dəs vār′), *n.* the armed forces of West Germany. [< G, equiv. to *Bundes,* gen. of *Bund* federation + *Wehr* defense]

bun·dle (bun′dl), *n., v.,* **-dled, -dling.** —*n.* **1.** several objects or a quantity of material gathered or bound together: *a bundle of hay.* **2.** an item, group, or quantity wrapped for carrying; package. **3.** a number of things considered together: *a bundle of ideas.* **4.** *Slang.* a great deal of money: *He made a bundle in the market.* **5.** *Bot.* an aggregation of strands of specialized conductive and mechanical tissues. **6.** Also called **bundle of isoglosses.** *Dialect Geog.* a group of close isoglosses running in approximately the same direction, esp. when taken as evidence of an important dialect division. **7.** *Anat., Zool.* an aggregation of fibers, as of nerves or muscles. **8. drop one's bundle,** *Australian and New Zealand Slang.* to lose confidence or hope. —*v.t.* **9.** to tie together or wrap in a bundle: *Bundle the newspapers for the trash man.* **10.** to send away hurriedly or unceremoniously (usually fol. by *off, out,* etc.): *They bundled her off to the country.* **11.** to offer or supply (related products or services) in a single transaction at one all-inclusive price. —*v.i.* **12.** to leave hurriedly or unceremoniously (usually fol. by *off, out,* etc.): *They indignantly bundled out of the meeting.* **13.** (esp. of sweethearts during courtship in early New England) to lie in the same bed while fully clothed, as for privacy and warmth in a house where an entire family shared one room with a fireplace. **14. bundle up,** to dress warmly or snugly: *A blizzard was raging but the children were all bundled up.* [1350–1400; ME *bundel* < MD *bundel, bondel;* akin to BIND] —**bun′dler,** *n.*

—**Syn. 1.** BUNDLE, BUNCH refer to a number of things or an amount of something fastened or bound together. BUNDLE implies a close binding or grouping together, and often refers to a wrapped package: *a bundle of laundry, of dry goods.* A BUNCH is a number of things, usually all of the same kind, fastened together: *a bunch of roses, of keys.* **2.** parcel, pack, packet.

bun′dle bug′gy, a shopping cart, usually one owned by the shopper rather than one provided by the store.

bun·dled (bun′dld), *adj. Computers.* (of hardware or software) sold together, as a package, rather than separately. [BUNDLE + -ED[2]]

bun′dle of His′ (his), *Anat.* See **atrioventricular bundle.** [after Wilhelm *His* (1863–1934), Swiss physician]

bun′dle of i′soglosses, bundle (def. 6).

bun′dle of nerves′, a person who is extremely nervous. [1935–40]

Bundt′ cake′ (bunt, bo͝ont), a ring-shaped cake baked in a tube pan with fluted sides. [after *Bundt,* trademark name of a brand of tube pans]

bun·dy (bun′dē), *n., pl.* **-dies.** *Australian.* a time clock. [1930–35; said to be after W. H. *Bundy,* an Australian manufacturer of time clocks]

bun′ foot′, *Furniture.* a foot having the form of a slightly flattened ball. Cf. **ball foot.** [1900–05]

bun foot

bung[1] (bung), *n.* **1.** a stopper for the opening of a cask. **2.** a bunghole. —*v.t.* **3.** to close with or as if with a bung; cork; plug (often fol. by *up*). [1400–50; late ME *bunge* < MD *bonge* stopper]

bung[2] (bung), *adj. Australian.* **1.** out of order; broken; unusable. **2.** bankrupt. **3.** *Slang.* dead. [1840–50; perh.

CONCISE PRONUNCIATION KEY: act, cāpe, dâre, pärt; set, ēqual; *if,* ice; ox, ōver, ôrder, oil, bo͝ok, bo͞ot, out; up, ûrge; child; sing; shoe; thin, *th*at; zh as in *treasure.* ə = *a* as in *alone, e* as in *system, i* as in *easily, o* as in *gallop, u* as in *circus;* ᵊ as in *fire* (fīᵊr), *hour* (ouᵊr). l and n can serve as syllabic consonants, as in *cradle* (krād′l), and *button* (but′n). See the full key inside the front cover.

< Waga (Australian Aboriginal language spoken around Kingaroy, S Queensland) *bongī* dead]

bung[3] (bung), *v.t.* **1.** to beat; bruise; maul (often fol. by *up*). **2.** *Brit. Slang.* to throw or shove carelessly or violently; sling. [1815–25; orig. Scots var. of BANG[1]]

bun·ga·loid (bung′gə loid′), *adj.* **1.** of, pertaining to, or characteristic of the style or appearance of a bungalow. **2.** (of a town or neighborhood) characterized by having bungalows. [1925–30; BUNGAL(OW) + -OID]

bun·ga·low (bung′gə lō′), *n.* **1.** a cottage of one story. **2.** (in India) a one-storied thatched or tiled house, usually surrounded by a veranda. **3.** (in the U.S.) a derivation of the Indian house type, popular esp. during the first quarter of the 20th century, usually having one and a half stories, a widely bracketed gable roof, and a multiwindowed dormer. [1670–80; < Hindi *banglā* lit., of Bengal]

bun·gee (bun′jē), *n.* **1.** *Aeron.* any of certain springs or elastic tension devices, as the springs attached to movable controls of aircraft to facilitate their manipulation. **2.** See **bungee cord.** [orig. uncert.]

bun′gee cord′, an elasticized cord, typically with a hook at each end, used chiefly as a fastener. Also called **bungee, shock cord.**

bun′gee jump′ing, the sport of jumping off a high structure to which one is attached by bungee cords, so that the body springs back just short of hitting the ground or water. [1975–80]

bung·er (bung′ər), *n. Australian.* a firecracker. [perh. BUNG[3] + -ER[1]]

bung·hole (bung′hōl′), *n.* a hole in a cask through which it is filled. [1565–75; BUNG[1] + HOLE]

bun·gle (bung′gəl), *v.,* **-gled, -gling,** *n.* —*v.t.* **1.** to do clumsily and awkwardly; botch: *He bungled the job.* —*v.i.* **2.** to perform or work clumsily or inadequately. —*n.* **3.** a bungling performance. **4.** that which has been done clumsily or inadequately. [1520–30; of uncert. orig.] —**bun′gler,** *n.* —**bun′gling·ly,** *adv.*
—**Syn. 1.** mismanage, muddle, spoil, ruin; foul up.

bun·gle·some (bung′gəl səm), *adj.* clumsy or awkward. [1885–90, *Amer.*; BUNGLE + -SOME[1]]

bung·start·er (bung′stär′tər), *n.* a mallet for loosening or removing the bung of a cask. [BUNG[1] + STARTER]

Bu·nin (bo͞o′nyin), *n.* **I·van A·le·kse·e·vich** (ē vän′ u lyi ksye′yi vyich), 1870–1953, Russian poet and novelist: Nobel prize 1933.

bun·ion (bun′yən), *n. Podiatry.* inflammation of the synovial bursa of the great toe, usually resulting in enlargement of the joint and lateral displacement of the toe. [1710–20; perh. alter. of *bunny* (obs.) lump, swelling, late ME *bony,* prob. alter. of OF *buigne, buyne* (F *beigne*) swelling, of Gmc orig.; cf. BEIGNET]

bun·ion·ette (bun′yə net′), *n. Podiatry.* a bunionlike enlargement of the joint of the little toe, usually caused by pressure from tight shoes. Also called **tailor's bunion.** [BUNION + -ETTE]

bunk[1] (bungk), *n.* **1.** a built-in platform bed, as on a ship. **2.** *Informal.* any bed. **3.** a cabin used for sleeping quarters, as in a summer camp; bunkhouse. **4.** a trough for feeding cattle. —*v.i.* **5.** *Informal.* to occupy a bunk or any sleeping quarters: *Joe and Bill bunked together at camp.* —*v.t.* **6.** to provide with a place to sleep. [1750–60; back formation from BUNKER]

bunk[2] (bungk), *n. Informal.* humbug; nonsense. [1895–1900, *Amer.*; short for BUNKUM]
—**Syn.** baloney, rot, hogwash, applesauce, bull, hooey.

bunk[3] (bungk), *v.i., v.t.* to bump. [perh. expressive alter. of BUMP]

bunk[4] (bungk), *Brit. Slang.* —*v.t.* **1.** to absent oneself from: *to bunk a history class.* —*v.i.* **2.** to run off or away; flee. —*n.* **3. do a bunk,** to leave hastily, esp. under suspicious circumstances; run away. [1865–70; perh. special use of BUNK[1]]

bunk′ bed′, 1. a piece of furniture consisting of two single platformlike beds connected one above the other. **2.** either of these two beds. [1950–55]

bun·ker (bung′kər), *n.* **1.** a large bin or receptacle; a fixed chest or box: *a coal bunker.* **2.** a fortification set mostly below the surface of the ground with overhead protection provided by logs and earth or by concrete and fitted with openings through which guns may be fired. **3.** *Golf.* any obstacle, as a sand trap or mound of dirt, constituting a hazard. —*v.t.* **4.** *Naut.* **a.** to provide fuel for (a vessel). **b.** to convey (bulk cargo except grain) from a vessel to an adjacent storehouse. **5.** *Golf.* to hit (a ball) into a bunker. **6.** to equip with or as if with bunkers: *to bunker an army's defenses.* [1750–60; earlier *bonkar* (Scots) box, chest, serving also as a seat, of obscure orig.]

bun·ker·age (bung′kər ij, bungk′rij), *n. Naut.* the act of bunkering a vessel. [BUNKER + -AGE]

Bun′ker Hill′, (bung′kər), a hill in Charlestown, Mass.: the first major battle of the American Revolution, known as the Battle of Bunker Hill, was fought on adjoining Breed's Hill on June 17, 1775.

bun′ker oil′, *Naut.* oil taken on board a tanker as fuel, as distinguished from the oil carried as cargo.

bunk·house (bungk′hous′), *n., pl.* **-hous·es** (-hou′ziz). a rough building, often with bunk beds, used for sleeping quarters, as for ranch hands, migratory workers, or campers. [1875–80, *Amer.*; BUNK[1] + HOUSE]

bunk·ie (bung′kē), *n. Slang.* bunkmate. [1855–60, *Amer.*; BUNK[1] + -IE]

bunk·mate (bungk′māt′), *n.* a person who shares sleeping quarters with another, esp. one who sleeps in a neighboring bed. [1875–80, *Amer.*; BUNK[1] + MATE[1]]

CONCISE ETYMOLOGY KEY: <, descended or borrowed from; >, whence; b., blend of, blended; c., cognate with; cf., compare; deriv., derivative; equiv., equivalent; imit., imitative; obl., oblique; r., replacing; s., stem; sp., spelling, spelled; resp., respelling, respelled; trans., translation; ?, origin unknown; *, unattested; ‡, probably earlier than. See the full key inside the front cover.

bun·ko (bung′kō), *n., pl.* **-kos,** *v.,* **-koed, -ko·ing.** *Informal.* —*n.* **1.** a swindle in which a person is cheated at gambling, persuaded to buy a nonexistent, unsalable, or worthless object, or otherwise victimized. **2.** any misrepresentation. —*v.t.* **3.** to victimize by a bunko. Also, **bunco.** [1880–85; shortened form of BUNKUM; cf. -O]

bun′ko steer′er, *Informal.* a swindler, esp. a person who lures another to a gambling game to be cheated. [1870–75, *Amer.*]

bun·kum (bung′kəm), *n.* **1.** insincere speechmaking by a politician intended merely to please local constituents. **2.** insincere talk; claptrap; humbug. Also, **buncombe.** [*Amer.*; after speech in 16th Congress, 1819–21, by F. Walker, who said he was bound to speak for *Buncombe* (N.C. county in district he represented)]

bunn (bun), *n. Obs.* bun[1] (def. 1).

bun·ny (bun′ē), *n., pl.* **-nies,** *adj.* —*n.* **1.** *Informal.* a rabbit, esp. a small or young one. **2.** *Slang (sometimes disparaging and offensive).* a pretty, appealing, or alluring young woman, often one ostensibly engaged in a sport or similar activity: *beach bunny.* **3.** *Chiefly Brit.* a squirrel. **4.** *Australian and New Zealand Slang.* a person imposed upon or made a fool of; victim. —*adj.* **5.** designed for or used by beginners in skiing: *a bunny slope.* [1600–10, *Amer.*; dial. *bun* (tail of a) hare or rabbit, in Scots: buttocks (< ScotGael *bun* bottom) + -Y[2]]

bun′ny hug′, a ballroom dance popular in the U.S. in the early 20th century and characterized by a syncopated rhythm. [1910–15]

bu·no·dont (byo͞o′nə dont′), *adj.* having molar teeth with crowns in the form of rounded or conical cusps. Cf. **lophodont.** [1870–75; < Gk *boun(ós)* hill + -ODONT]

bun·ra·ku (bo͝on rä′ko͞o), *n.* (*sometimes cap.*) a form of Japanese puppet theater in which puppeteers, dressed in black and visible to the audience, manipulate large puppets to the accompaniment of a chanted narration and musical instruments. [1915–30; < Japn, from the *Bunraku(-za),* an Osaka theater of 1789–1801, lit., literature enjoyment (theater) < MChin, equiv. to Chin *wén* + *lè*]

Bun·sen (bun′sən; *Ger.* bo͝on′zən), *n.* **Rob·ert Wil·helm** (rob′ərt wil′helm; *Ger.* rō′bert vil′helm), 1811–99, German chemist.

Bun′sen burn′er, a type of gas burner, commonly used in chemical laboratories, with which a very hot, practically nonluminous flame is obtained by allowing air to enter at the base and mix with the gas. [1865–70; named after R. W. BUNSEN]

Bunsen burner

bunt[1] (bunt), *v.t.* **1.** (of a goat or calf) to push with the horns or head; butt. **2.** *Baseball.* to bat (a pitched ball) very gently so that it rolls into the infield close to home plate, usually by holding the bat loosely in hands spread apart and allowing the ball to bounce off it. —*v.i.* **3.** to push (something) with the horns or head. **4.** *Baseball.* to bunt a ball. —*n.* **5.** a push with the head or horns; butt. **6.** *Baseball.* **a.** the act of bunting. **b.** a bunted ball. [1760–70; orig. Brit. dial. (Central and S England): push, strike; of obscure orig.] —**bunt′er,** *n.*

bunt[2] (bunt), *n.* **1.** *Naut.* the middle part of a square sail. **2.** the bagging part of a fishing net or bagging middle area of various cloth objects. [1575–85; orig. uncert.]

bunt[3] (bunt), *n. Plant Pathol.* a smut disease of wheat in which the kernels are replaced by the black, foul-smelling spores of fungi of the genus *Tilletia.* Also called **stinking smut.** [1595–1605; earlier, puffball; of uncert. orig.] —**bunt′ed,** *adj.*

bun·ting[1] (bun′ting), *n.* **1.** a coarse, open fabric of worsted or cotton for flags, signals, etc. **2.** patriotic and festive decorations made from such cloth, or from paper, usually in the form of draperies, wide streamers, etc., in the colors of the national flag. **3.** flags, esp. a vessel's flags, collectively. [1735–45; perh. orig. "sifting cloth," hence *bunt* to sift (ME *bonten*) + -ING[1]]

bun·ting[2] (bun′ting), *n.* any of several small, chiefly seed-eating birds of the genera *Emberiza, Passerina,* and *Plectrophenax.* Cf. **indigo bunting, reed bunting, snow bunting.** [1250–1300; ME < ?]

bun·ting[3] (bun′ting), *n.* a hooded sleeping garment for infants. Also called **sleeper.** [1920–25; special use of BUNTING[1]]

bunt·line (bunt′lin, -līn′), *n. Naut.* one of the ropes attached to the foot of a square sail to haul it up to the yard for furling. [1620–30; BUNT[2] + LINE[1]]

bun·ton (bun′tn), *n. Mining.* one of a number of struts reinforcing the walls of a shaft and dividing it into vertical compartments. Also called **divider.** [1625–35; earlier *bunting* squared timber, of obscure orig.]

bunt′ or′der, a dominance hierarchy seen in herds of cattle, established and maintained by bunting.

Bu·ñuel (bo͞on wel′; *Sp.* bo͞o nywel′), *n.* **Luis** (lwēs), 1900–83, Spanish film director.

bu·ñu·e·lo (bo͞on′yo͞o ā′lō; *Sp.* bo͞o nywe′lô), *n., pl.* **-los** (-lōz; *Sp.* -lôs). *Mexican Cookery.* a thin, round, fried pastry, often dusted with cinnamon sugar. [< MexSp; Sp: doughnut, fritter; cf. Catalan *bunyol* bun, *bony* lump, bulge; akin to the Rom base of BUNION, BEIGNET]

bun·ya-bun·ya (bun′yə bun′yə), *n.* an evergreen tree, *Araucaria bidwilli,* of Australia, having stiff, sharp, glossy needles in distinct rows, grown as an ornamental in warm regions. [1835–45; < Wiradjuri *bun'a*]

Bun·yan (bun′yən), *n.* **1. John,** 1628–88, English preacher: author of *The Pilgrim's Progress.* **2. Paul.** See **Paul Bunyan.**

Bun·yan·esque (bun′yə nesk′), *adj.* **1.** of or pertaining to the legends about Paul Bunyan. **2.** of immense size or stature, as ascribed to Paul Bunyan or to the other characters, exploits, etc., in the legends about him. **3.** noting, pertaining to, or suggesting the allegorical style of John Bunyan. [1950–55; BUNYAN + -ESQUE]

bun·yip (bun′yip), *Australian.* —*n.* **1.** a mythical creature of Aboriginal legend said to inhabit water and watercourses. **2.** an impostor. —*adj.* **3.** counterfeit; phony. [1840–50; < Wergaia (Australian Aboriginal language of the Wimmera area, Victoria) *banib*]

buo·na not·te (bwô′nä nôt′te), *Italian.* good night.

Buo·na·par·te (*It.* bwô′nä pär′te), *n.* Bonaparte.

Buo·nar·ro·ti (*It.* bwô′när rô′tē), *n.* Michelangelo.

buo·na se·ra (bwô′nä se′rä), *Italian.* good evening.

buon′ fres′co (bwôn), fresco (def. 1). [< It: lit., good fresco]

buon gior·no (bwôn′ jôr′nô), *Italian.* good morning; good day.

Buo·non·ci·ni (*It.* bwô′nôn chē′nē), *n.* Bononcini.

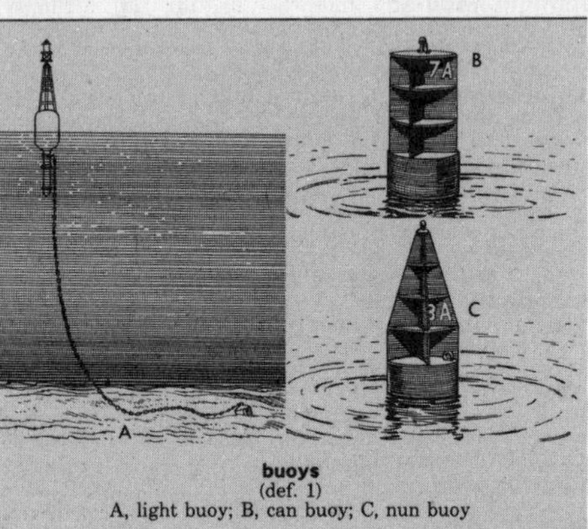

buoys
(def. 1)
A, light buoy; B, can buoy; C, nun buoy

bu·oy (bo͞o′ē, boi), *n.* **1.** *Naut.* a distinctively shaped and marked float, sometimes carrying a signal or signals, anchored to mark a channel, anchorage, navigational hazard, etc., or to provide a mooring place away from the shore. **2.** a life buoy. —*v.t.* **3.** to keep afloat or support by or as if by a life buoy; keep from sinking (often fol. by *up*): *The life jacket buoyed her up until help arrived.* **4.** *Naut.* to mark with a buoy or buoys. **5.** to sustain or encourage (often fol. by *up*): *Her courage was buoyed by the doctor's assurances.* —*v.i.* **6.** to float or rise by reason of lightness. [1425–75; late ME *boye* a float < MF **boie, boue(e)* < Gmc; akin to BEACON]
—**Syn. 5.** lift, uplift, boost, lighten; maintain, nurture.

bu·oy·age (bo͞o′ē ij, boi′ij), *n. Naut.* **1.** a system of buoys. **2.** the provision of buoys. **3.** a fee for the use of a mooring buoy. [1850–55; BUOY + -AGE]

buoy·an·cy (boi′ən sē, bo͞o′yən sē), *n.* **1.** the power to float or rise in a fluid; relative lightness. **2.** the power of supporting a body so that it floats; upward pressure exerted by the fluid in which a body is immersed. **3.** lightness or resilience of spirit; cheerfulness. Also, **buoy′ance.** [1705–15; BUOY(ANT) + -ANCY]

buoy′ancy com′pensator, *Scuba Diving.* an inflatable vest used to control one's buoyancy underwater or to rest at the surface, usually having a connecting hose for inflation or deflation by mouth and a CO_2 cartridge for rapid, emergency inflation. Also called **BC, buoy′ancy control′ device′.**

buoy·ant (boi′ənt, bo͞o′yənt), *adj.* **1.** tending to float in a fluid. **2.** capable of keeping a body afloat, as a liquid. **3.** not easily depressed; cheerful. **4.** cheering or invigorating. [1570–80; BUOY + -ANT] —**buoy′ant·ly,** *adv.*
—**Syn. 3.** happy, lighthearted, breezy, jaunty, sunny.

buoy′ant force′, *Physics.* See under **Archimedes' principle.** Also called **buoy′ancy force′.**

bu′oy boat′, a boat used in whaling for holding and towing the whales killed during a hunt.

bu·piv·a·caine (byo͞o piv′ə kān′), *n. Pharm.* a white, crystalline powder, $C_{18}H_{28}N_2O$, used as a local anesthetic. [perh. BU(TYL) + *pi(pecoloxylidide)* its chemical components + *-vacaine,* irreg. for (NO)VOCAINE; see PROCAINE]

Bup·py (bup′ē), *n., pl.* **-pies.** a young, upwardly mobile black professional. Also, **Bup′pie.** [1980–85, *Amer.*; *b(lack) u(rban) p(rofessional),* on the model of YUPPIE]

bu·pres·tid (byo͞o pres′tid), *n.* any beetle of the family Buprestidae, comprising wood-boring beetles of a metallic luster. [1350–1400; ME < NL *Buprestidae* name of the family, equiv. to L *būprēst(is)* venomous beetle (< Gk *boúprēstis,* lit. ox-sweller) + *-idae* -ID[2]]

buq·sha (bo͝ok′shä, buk′-), *n.* (formerly) an aluminum-copper coin and monetary unit of the Yemen Arab Republic, the 40th part of a riyal. Also, **bugsha, bugshah.** [< Ar *buqshah,* Bedouin Ar *bugsha*]

bur[1] (bûr), *n., v.,* **burred, bur·ring.** —*n.* **1.** a rough, prickly case around the seeds of certain plants, as the chestnut or burdock. **2.** any bur-bearing plant. **3.** something that adheres like a bur. **4.** *Mach.* burr[1] (defs. 1, 3). **5.** *Dentistry.* a rotary cutting tool usually of steel or other hard metal shaped into a shank and a head, for removing carious material from teeth and preparing cavities for filling. **6.** *Surg.* a cutting tool resembling that of a dentist, used for the excavation of bone. —*v.t.* **7.** to extract or remove burs from. [1300–50; ME *burre,* appar. c. Dan *burre,* Norw, Sw *borre* bur]

bur[2] (bûr), *n.* burr[2].

Bur., Burma.

bur., bureau.

Bu·ra·ku·min (bo͝or′ə ko͞o′min), *n.pl.* (in Japan) the members of a large social minority who have traditionally been considered outcasts. [1965–70; < Japn, equiv. to *buraku* settlement, ghetto (< MChin, equiv. to Chin *bùluò* (or *bùlào*) settlement, village) + *-min* people (< MChin, equiv. to Chin *mín*)]

Bu·raq (bo͝o räk′), *n. Islam.* the legendary beast, a winged horse with the face of a woman and the tail of a peacock, on which Muhammad ascended to heaven.

burb (bûrb), *n. Slang.* suburb. [by shortening]

Bur·bage (bûr′bij), *n.* **Richard,** 1567?–1619, English actor and associate of Shakespeare.

Bur·bank (bûr′bangk′), *n.* **1. Luther,** 1849–1926, U.S. horticulturist and plant breeder. **2.** a city in SW California. 84,625. **3.** a town in central Illinois. 28,462.

Bur·ber·ry (bûr′bə rē, -ber′ē), *Trademark.* **1.** a brand of raincoat made of a waterproof, mercerized cotton fabric. **2.** any of various fabrics used in clothing, esp. in coats.

Bur·bidge (bûr′bij), *n.* **(Eleanor) Margaret (Peachey)** (pē′chē), born 1919, U.S. astronomer, born in England.

bur·ble (bûr′bəl), *v.,* **-bled, -bling,** *n.* —*v.i.* **1.** to make a bubbling sound; bubble. **2.** to speak in an excited manner; babble. —*n.* **3.** a bubbling or gentle flow. **4.** an excited flow of speech. **5.** *Aeron.* the breakdown of smooth airflow around a wing at a high angle of attack. [1275–1325; ME; perh. var. of BUBBLE] —**bur′bler,** *n.* —**bur′bly,** *adv.*

bur·bot (bûr′bət), *n., pl.* **-bots,** (*esp. collectively*) **-bot.** a freshwater cod, *Lota lota,* of Europe, Asia, and North America, having an elongated body and a barbel on the chin. [1425–75; late ME < MF *bourbotte,* var. of *bourbete,* deriv. of *bourbeter* to wallow in mud, equiv. to *bourbe* mud + *-t-* freq. suffix + *-er* inf. ending]

Burch·field (bûrch′fēld′), *n.* **Charles Ephraim,** 1893–1967, U.S. painter.

Burck·hardt (bûrk′härt; *Ger.* bo͝ork′härt′), *n.* **Ja·kob** (yä′kôp), 1818–97, Swiss historian.

bur′ clo′ver, any of several Eurasian legumes of the genus *Medicago,* as *M. hispida,* having yellow flowers and prickly, coiled, black pods, naturalized in North America. [1865–70, *Amer.*]

bur′ cu′cumber, 1. a climbing vine, *Sicyos angulatus,* of the gourd family, of eastern and midwestern North America, having leaves with pointed lobes, small white or greenish flowers, and clusters of prickly fruits. **2.** the fruit of this plant.

burd (bûrd), *n. Chiefly Scot.* a young lady; maiden. [1175–1225; ME *burde* lady, perh. repr. OE *byrde* well born]

bur·den[1] (bûr′dn), *n.* **1.** that which is carried; load: *a horse's burden of rider and pack.* **2.** that which is borne with difficulty; obligation; onus: *the burden of leadership.* **3.** *Naut.* **a.** the weight of a ship's cargo. **b.** the carrying capacity of a ship. **4.** *Mining.* overburden (def. 3). **5.** *Metall.* the minerals charged into a blast furnace or steelmaking furnace. **6.** *Accounting.* overhead (def. 6). —*v.t.* **7.** to load heavily. **8.** to load oppressively; trouble. [bef. 1000; ME, var. of *burthen,* OE *byrthen;* akin to G *Bürde,* Goth *baurthei;* see BEAR[1]] —**bur′den·er,** *n.* —**bur′den·less,** *adj.*

—**Syn. 1.** See **load. 2.** weight, encumbrance, impediment. **8.** weigh down, saddle, try, afflict, perturb, plague, grieve, vex.

bur·den[2] (bûr′dn), *n.* **1.** the main point, message, or idea. **2.** *Music.* the refrain or recurring chorus of a song. [1275–1325; ME *bordoun, burdoun* < OF *bourdon* droning sound, instrument making such a sound]

—**Syn. 1.** substance, core, crux, nucleus, essence.

bur·dened (bûr′dnd), *adj. Navig.* (of a vessel) required to yield to a vessel having the right of way. Cf. **privileged** (def. 5). [BURDEN[1] + -ED[2]]

bur′den of proof′, 1. *Chiefly Law.* the obligation to offer evidence that the court or jury could reasonably believe, in support of a contention, failing which the case will be lost. **2.** the obligation to establish a contention as fact by evoking evidence of its probable truth. [1585–95]

bur·den·some (bûr′dn səm), *adj.* **1.** oppressively heavy; onerous. **2.** distressing; troublesome. **3.** *Naut.* having a full hull form, as a merchant vessel built for capacity rather than speed. [1570–80; BURDEN[1] + -SOME[1]] —**bur′den·some·ly,** *adv.* —**bur′den·some·ness,** *n.*

bur·dock (bûr′dok), *n.* a composite plant of the genus *Arctium,* esp. *A. lappa,* a coarse, broad-leaved weed bearing prickly heads of burs that stick to the clothing. [1590–1600; BUR[1] + DOCK[4]]

bu·reau (byo͝or′ō), *n., pl.* **bu·reaus, bu·reaux** (byo͝or′ōz). **1.** a chest of drawers, often with a mirror at the top. **2.** a division of a government department or an independent administrative unit. **3.** an office for collecting or distributing news or information, coordinating work, or performing specified services; agency: *a travel bureau; a news bureau.* **4.** *Chiefly Brit.* a desk or writing table with drawers for papers. [1710–20; < F: desk, office, orig. a kind of cloth (used to cover desks, etc.), AF, OF *burel,* equiv. to *bur-* (prob. < **būra,* var. of LL *burra* wool, fluff; cf. BOURRÉE) + *-el* n. suffix]

bu·reauc·ra·cy (byo͝o rok′rə sē), *n., pl.* **-cies. 1.** government by many bureaus, administrators, and petty officials. **2.** the body of officials and administrators, esp. of a government or government department. **3.** excessive multiplication of, and concentration of power in, administrative bureaus or administrators. **4.** administration characterized by excessive red tape and routine. [1810–20; BUREAU + -CRACY, modeled on F *bureaucratie*]

bu·reau·crat (byo͝or′ə krat′), *n.* **1.** an official of a bureaucracy. **2.** an official who works by fixed routine without exercising intelligent judgment. [1835–45; < F *bureaucrate.* See BUREAU, -CRAT] —**bu·reau·crat·ism** (byo͝or′ə krat iz′əm, byo͝o rok′rə tiz′-), *n.*

bu·reau·crat·ese (byo͝or′ə kra tēz′, -tēs′, byo͝o rok′-rə-), *n.* a style of language, used esp. by bureaucrats, that is full of circumlocutions, euphemisms, buzzwords, abstractions, etc. [BUREAUCRAT + -ESE]

bu·reau·crat·ic (byo͝or′ə krat′ik), *adj.* of, pertaining to, or characteristic of a bureaucrat or a bureaucracy; arbitrary and routine. [1830–40; < F *bureaucratique.* See BUREAUCRAT, -IC] —**bu′reau·crat′i·cal·ly,** *adv.*

bu·reauc·ra·tize (byo͝o rok′rə tīz′), *v.t.,* **-tized, -tiz·ing. 1.** to divide an administrative agency or office into bureaus. **2.** to increase the number of government or business bureaus. **3.** to cause to become bureaucratic or to resemble a bureaucracy: *to bureaucratize a city's social services.* Also, *esp. Brit.,* **bu·reauc′ra·tise′.** [1890–95; < F *bureaucratiser.* See BUREAUCRAT, -IZE] —**bu·reauc′ra·ti·za′tion,** *n.*

bu·reau de change (bʏ rōd[ə] shäɴzh′), *pl.* ***bu·reaux de change*** (bʏ rōd[ə] shäɴzh′). *French.* an office where money can be exchanged.

Bu′reau of Cus′toms, former name of the **United States Customs Service.**

Bu′reau of In′dian Affairs′, *U.S. Govt.* a division of the Department of the Interior that administers federal programs benefiting Native American peoples. *Abbr.:* BIA

Bu′reau of Inter′nal Rev′enue, former name of the **Internal Revenue Service.**

Bu′reau of Land′ Man′agement, *U.S. Govt.* a division of the Department of the Interior that manages public lands and resources. *Abbr.:* BLM, B.L.M.

Bu′reau of Mines′, *U.S. Govt.* a division of the Department of the Interior, created in 1910, that studies the nation's mineral resources and inspects mines.

Bu′reau of the Bud′get, former name of the Office of Management and Budget. See **OMB.**

Bu′reau of the Cen′sus, *U.S. Govt.* the division of the Department of Commerce that gathers, tabulates, and correlates census statistics.

bu·re·lé (bo͝or′ə lā′), *n. Philately.* the netlike pattern of colored lines or dots forming the background design of certain postage stamps. Also, **bu·re·lage** (bo͝or′ə läzh′). [< F, OF, equiv. to *burel* spoke, ray, bar + *-é* -ATE[1]]

bu·rette (byo͝o ret′), *n. Chem.* a graduated glass tube, commonly having a stopcock at the bottom, used for accurately measuring or measuring out small quantities of liquid. Also, **bu·ret′.** [1475–85; < F: cruet, *burette* (OF *biurete*), equiv. to *buire* ewer, flagon (perh. < Frankish **būrja* receptacle, akin to Gmc **būr-* hut; see BOWER[1]) + *-ette* -ETTE]

burg (bûrg), *n.* **1.** *Informal.* a city or town. **2.** *Hist.* a fortified town. [1745–55; var. of BURGH]

bur·ga (bo͝or′gə), *n.* burka.

bur·gage (bûr′gij), *n. Law.* **1.** (in England) a tenure whereby burgesses or townspeople held lands or tenements of the king or other lord, usually for a fixed money rent. **2.** (in Scotland) tenure directly from the crown of property in royal burghs in return for the service of watching and warding. [1250–1300; ME *borgage* < AF *borgage, burgage* or AL *burgāgium;* see BURGH, -AGE]

Bur·gas (bo͝or gäs′), *n.* a seaport in E Bulgaria, on the Black Sea. 144,000.

bur·gee (bûr′jē, bûr jē′), *n.* a triangular flag or one having a shallow, angular indentation in the fly, forming two tails, used as an identification flag, esp. by yachts. [1840–50; perh. shortening of **burgee's flag,* by reanalysis of **burgess flag, burgess* translating F *bourgeois* in sense "owner" (of a ship)]

Bur·gen·land (*Ger.* bo͝or′gən länt′), *n.* a province in E Austria, bordering Hungary. 272,274; 1530 sq. mi. (3960 sq. km). *Cap.:* Eisenstadt.

bur·geon (bûr′jən), *v.i.* **1.** to grow or develop quickly; flourish: *The town burgeoned into a city. He burgeoned into a fine actor.* **2.** to begin to grow, as a bud; put forth buds, shoots, etc., as a plant (often fol. by *out, forth*). —*v.t.* **3.** to put forth, as buds. —*n.* **4.** a bud; sprout. Also, **bourgeon.** [1275–1325; (n.) ME *burjon, burion;* shoot, bud < AF *burjun, burg(e)on;* OF *burjon* < VL **burriōne(m),* acc. of **burriō,* deriv. of LL *burra* wool, fluff (cf. BOURRÉE, BUREAU), presumably from the down covering certain buds; (v.) ME *burg(e)onen, borgen* < AF, OF, deriv. of the n.]

—**Syn. 1.** bloom, blossom, mushroom, expand.

—**Usage.** The two senses of BURGEON, "to bud" (*The maples are burgeoning*) and "to grow or flourish" (*The suburbs around the city have been burgeoning under the impact of commercial growth*), date from the 14th century. Today the sense "to grow or flourish" is the more common. Occasionally, objections are raised to the use of this sense, perhaps because of its popularity in journalistic writing.

burg·er (bûr′gər), *n.* a hamburger. [1935–40, *Amer.;* extracted from HAMBURGER by false analysis as HAM[1] + *burger*]

Bur·ger (bûr′gər), *n.* **Warren Earl,** born 1907, U.S. jurist: Chief Justice of the U.S. 1969–86.

-burger, a combining form extracted from **hamburger,** occurring in compounds the initial element of which denotes a special garnish for a hamburger or a substitute ingredient for the meat patty: *baconburger; cheeseburger; fishburger.*

bur·gess (bûr′jis), *n.* **1.** *Amer. Hist.* a representative in the popular branch of the colonial legislature of Virginia or Maryland. **2.** (formerly) a representative of a borough in the British Parliament. **3.** *Rare.* an inhabitant of an English borough. [1175–1225; ME *burgeis* < AF, OF, equiv. to *burg* city (< Gmc) + *-eis* < L *-ēnsis* -ENSIS; cf. -ESE]

Bur·gess (bûr′jis), *n.* **1. (Frank) Ge·lett** (jə let′), 1866–1951, U.S. illustrator and humorist. **2. Thornton Waldo,** 1874–1965, U.S. author, esp. of children's books. **3.** a male given name.

burgh (bûrg; *Scot.* bur′ō, bur′ə), *n.* **1.** (in Scotland) an incorporated town having its own charter and some degree of political independence from the surrounding area. **2.** *Archaic.* borough. [1350–1400; late ME (Scots); see BOROUGH; cf. BROCH] —**burgh·al** (bûr′gəl), *adj.*

burgh·er (bûr′gər), *n.* an inhabitant of a town, esp. a member of the middle class; citizen. [1560–70; < MD < MHG *burger,* equiv. to *burg* BOROUGH + *-er* -ER[1]] —**burgh′er·ship′,** *n.*

bur′ gher′kin, gherkin (def. 2).

Burgh·ley (bûr′lē), *n.* **1st Baron.** See **Cecil, William.**

bur·glar (bûr′glər), *n.* a person who commits burglary. [1225–75; ME < AF *burgler* (cf. AL *burg(u)lātor*), perh. < OF **borgl(er)* to plunder, pillage (< Gallo-Rom **būriculāre,* equiv. to **būric(āre)* (Old Low Franconian **būrj(an)* to dart at, pounce upon + VL **-icāre* v. suffix; cf. OF *burgier* to strike, hit) + *-ulāre* v. suffix) + AF *-er* -ER[2]; see -AR[2]]

bur′glar alarm′, an automatic device for giving an alarm when a window, door, safe, etc., is opened or tampered with, as by a burglar. [1830–40]

bur·glar·i·ous (bər glâr′ē əs), *adj.* pertaining to or involving burglary. [1760–70; BURGLAR + -IOUS] —**bur·glar′i·ous·ly,** *adv.*

bur·glar·ize (bûr′glə rīz′), *v.,* **-ized, -iz·ing.** —*v.t.* **1.** to break into and steal from: *Thieves burglarized the warehouse.* —*v.i.* **2.** to commit burglary. Also, *esp. Brit.,* **bur′glar·ise′.** [1870–75, *Amer.;* BURGLAR + -IZE]

bur·glar·proof (bûr′glər pro͞of′), *adj.* **1.** safeguarded or secure against burglary. —*v.t.* **2.** to make burglarproof: *to burglarproof one's home.* [1855–60; BURGLAR + -PROOF]

bur·gla·ry (bûr′glə rē), *n., pl.* **-ries.** *Crim. Law.* the felony of breaking into and entering the house of another at night with intent to steal, extended by statute to cover the breaking into and entering of any of various buildings, by night or day. [1150–1200; ME < AF *burglarie;* see BURGLAR, -Y[3]]

bur·gle (bûr′gəl), *v.t., v.i.,* **-gled, -gling.** to burglarize. [1870–75; back formation from BURGLAR]

bur·go·mas·ter (bûr′gə mas′tər, -mä′stər), *n.* the chief magistrate of a municipal town of Holland, Flanders, Germany, or Austria. [1585–95; < D *burgemeester,* equiv. to *burg* BOROUGH + *meester* MASTER, c. G *Bürgermeister* major] —**bur′go·mas′ter·ship′,** *n.*

bur·go·net (bûr′gə net′, -nit, bûr′gə net′), *n. Armor.* an open helmet, usually having a peak and hinged cheek pieces, and often accompanied by a buffe. [1590–1600; MF *burgon* of Burgundy (< MF *Bourgogne* Burgundy) + -ET, modeled on MF *bourguignotte*]

bur·goo (bûr′go͞o, bûr go͞o′), *n., pl.* **-goos** for 2b. **1.** a thick oatmeal gruel, esp. as eaten by sailors. **2.** *Chiefly Kentucky and Tennessee.* **a.** a thick, highly seasoned soup or stew, usually made of chicken or small game and corn, tomatoes, and onions. **b.** a picnic or other gathering at which burgoo is served. [1735–45; perh. ult. < Ar *burghul, burghūl* cracked wheat (see BULGUR), though immediate source is uncert.]

Bur·gos (bo͞or′gôs), *n.* a city in N Spain: Gothic cathedral. 119,915.

Bur·goyne (bər goin′), *n.* **John,** 1722–92, British general and dramatist: surrendered at Saratoga in American Revolutionary War.

bur·grave (bûr′grāv), *n. German Hist.* **1.** the appointed head of a fortress. **2.** the hereditary governor of a castle or town. [1540–50; < G *Burggraf,* equiv. to *Burg* castle, town + *Graf* count]

Bur·gun·di·an (bər gun′dē ən), *adj.* **1.** of or pertaining to Burgundy or its people. —*n.* **2.** a native or inhabitant of Burgundy. [1570–80; BURGUNDY + -AN]

Bur·gun·dy (bûr′gən dē), *n., pl.* **-dies** for 2, 3, 5, *adj.* —*n.* **1.** French, **Bourgogne.** a region in central France: a former kingdom, duchy, and province. **2.** wine, of many varieties, red and white, mostly still, full, and dry,

CONCISE PRONUNCIATION KEY: act, cāpe, dâre, pärt; set, ēqual; if, īce; ox, ōver, ôrder, oil, bo͝ok, bo͞ot, out; up, ûrge; child; sing; shoe; thin, *th*at; zh as in *treasure.* ə = *a* as in *alone, e* as in *system, i* as in *easily, o* as in *gallop, u* as in *circus;* [ə] as in *fire* (fī[ə]r), *hour* (ou[ə]r). l and n can serve as syllabic consonants, as in *cradle* (krād′l), and *button* (but′n). See the full key inside the front cover.

produced in the Burgundy region. **3.** (*often l.c.*) red wine with similar characteristics made elsewhere. **4.** (*l.c.*) a grayish red-brown to dark blackish-purple color. **5.** Also called **Bur′gundy sauce′.** a sauce made with red wine and thickened with an espagnole sauce or kneaded butter, served with eggs, meat, fish, or poultry. —*adj.* **6.** (*l.c.*) having the color burgundy.

Bur′gundy tre′foil, alfalfa. [1825–35; so called from its rich color]

Bu•ri (bŏŏr′ē), *n. Scand. Myth.* the first of the gods, revealed when the cow Audhumla licked away the salty ice that covered him. [< ON, prob. deriv. of *bera* to BEAR[1]]

bur•i•al (ber′ē əl), *n.* **1.** the act or ceremony of burying. **2.** the place of burying; grave. [1200–50; BURY + -AL[2]; r. ME *buriel,* back formation from OE *byrgels* burial place, equiv. to *byrg(an)* to BURY + *-els* n. suffix; cf. RIDDLE[1]]

bur′ial ground′, a tract of land for burial of the dead; a cemetery, often a small or primitive one. [1795–1805]

bur′ial mound′, a mound built over a grave or graves. Cf. **barrow**[2] (def. 1). [1850–55]

Bur•iat (bŏŏr yät′, bŏŏr′ē ät′; *Russ.* boo RYÄT′), *n.* Buryat.

Buriat′ Auton′omous Repub′lic. See **Buryat Autonomous Republic.**

bur•i•er (ber′ē ər), *n.* a person, animal, or thing that buries. [BURY + -ER[1]]

bu•rin (byŏŏr′in, bûr′-), *n.* **1.** a tempered steel rod, with a lozenge-shaped point and a rounded handle, used for engraving furrows in metal. **2.** a similar tool used by marble workers. **3.** a prehistoric pointed or chisellike flint tool. [1655–65; < F < It *burino* (now *bulino*) graving tool, equiv. to *bur-* (perh. < Gmc; see BORE[1]) + *-ino* -INE[2]]

burin (def. 1)

bur•ka (bŏŏr′kə), *n.* a loose garment covering the entire body and having a veiled opening for the eyes, worn by Muslim women. Also, **bourkha, bur′kha, burga.** [1830–40; < Urdu *burqaʿ* < dial. Ar *burqaʿ*]

Burk•bur•nett (bûrk′bər net′), *n.* a town in N Texas. 10,668.

burke (bûrk), *v.t.,* **burked, burk•ing. 1.** to murder, as by suffocation, leaving no or few marks of violence. **2.** to suppress or get rid of by some indirect maneuver. [after W. *Burke,* hanged in 1829 in Edinburgh for murders of this kind] —**burk′er, burk•ite** (bûr′kīt), *n.*

Burke (bûrk), *n.* **1. Billie** (*Mary William Ethelbert Appleton Burke*), 1886–1970, U.S. actress. **2. Edmund,** 1729–97, Irish statesman, orator, and writer. **3. Kenneth Du•va** (do͞o vä′), born 1897, U.S. literary critic.

Bur•ki•na Fa•so (bər kē′nə fä′sō), a republic in W Africa: formerly part of French West Africa. 6,774,000; 106,111 sq. mi. (274,827 sq. km). *Cap.:* Ouagadougou. Formerly, **Upper Volta.**

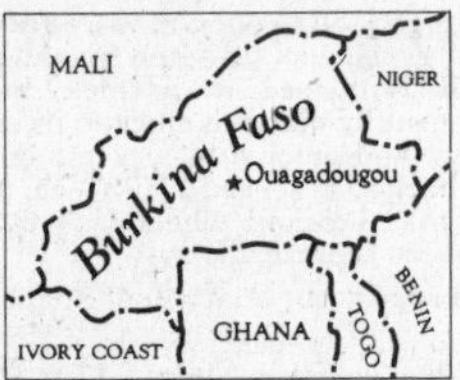

Bur′kitt's lympho′ma (bûr′kits), *Pathol.* a type of poorly differentiated malignant lymphoma, mainly afflicting children in central Africa, characterized by a large, bone-destroying lesion of the jaw, an abdominal mass, or more diffuse disease: believed to be associated with Epstein-Barr virus. [named after Denis Parsons *Burkitt* (b. 1911), Irish physician, who identified the malignancy in Uganda in 1957]

burl (bûrl), *n.* **1.** a small knot or lump in wool, thread, or cloth. **2.** a dome-shaped growth on the trunk of a tree; a wartlike structure sometimes 2 ft. (0.6 m) across and 1 ft. (0.3 m) or more in height, sliced to make veneer. —*v.t.* **3.** to remove burls from (cloth) in finishing. [1400–50; late ME *burle* << OF; akin to ML *burla* bunch, sheaf, LL *burra* wool, fluff] —**burl′er,** *n.*

bur•la•de•ro (bûr′lə dâr′ō, bŏŏr′-; *Sp.* bōōr′lä the′rô), *n., pl.* **-de•ros** (-dâr′ōz; *Sp.* -the′rôs). a wooden panel, located a short distance from and parallel to the bullring wall, behind which a bullfighter can seek protection from a bull. [1935–40; < Sp, equiv. to *burlad(o),* ptp. of *burlar* to ridicule (deriv. of *burla* ridicule, joke, perh. < LL *burra* trifle, lit., wool, fluff) + *-ero* << L *-ārium* -ARY]

bur•lap (bûr′lap), *n., v.,* **-lapped, -lap•ping.** —*n.* **1.** a plain-woven, coarse fabric of jute, hemp, or the like; gunny. **2.** a lightweight fabric made in imitation of this. —*v.t.* **3.** to wrap with burlap: *to burlap and tie a newly dug tree.* [1685–95; earlier *borelap,* equiv. to *bore(l)* coarse cloth (see BUREAU) + LAP[1]]

bur•le•cue (bûr′lə kyo͞o′), *n. Slang* (*now often facetious*). burlesque (def. 3). [1945–50; by alter.]

CONCISE ETYMOLOGY KEY: <, descended or borrowed from; >, whence; b., blend of, blended; c., cognate with; cf., compare; deriv., derivative; equiv., equivalent; imit., imitative; obl., oblique; r., replacing; s., stem; sp., spelling, spelled; resp., respelling, respelled; trans., translation; ?, origin unknown; *, unattested; ‡, probably earlier than. See the full key inside the front cover.

burled (bûrld), *adj.* having burls that produce a distorted grain: *burled lumber.* [1920–25; BURL + -ED[3]]

Bur•leigh (bûr′lē), *n.* **1. 1st Baron.** See **Cecil, William. 2. Henry Thack•er** (thak′ər), 1866–1949, U.S. singer: arranger of spirituals. **3.** a male given name: from Old English words meaning "hill" and "field."

Bur•le•son (bûr′lə sən), *n.* a city in N Texas. 11,734.

bur•lesque (bər lesk′), *n., adj., v.,* **-lesqued, -lesquing.** —*n.* **1.** an artistic composition, esp. literary or dramatic, that, for the sake of laughter, vulgarizes lofty material or treats ordinary material with mock dignity. **2.** any ludicrous parody or grotesque caricature. **3.** Also, **burlesk′.** a humorous and provocative stage show featuring slapstick humor, comic skits, bawdy songs, striptease acts, and a scantily clad female chorus. —*adj.* **4.** involving ludicrous or mocking treatment of a solemn subject. **5.** of, pertaining to, or like stage-show burlesque. —*v.t.* **6.** to make ridiculous by mocking representation. —*v.i.* **7.** to use caricature. [1650–60; < F < It *burlesco,* equiv. to *burl(a)* jest (perh. < Sp; cf. BURLADERO) + *-esco* -ESQUE] —**bur•lesque′ly,** *adv.* —**bur•lesqu′er,** *n.*
—**Syn. 1.** satire, lampoon, farce. BURLESQUE, CARICATURE, PARODY, TRAVESTY refer to the literary or dramatic forms that imitate serious works or subjects to achieve a humorous or satiric purpose. The characteristic device of BURLESQUE is mockery of both high and low through association with their opposites: *a burlesque of high and low life.* CARICATURE, usually associated with visual arts or with visual effects in literary works, implies exaggeration of characteristic details: *The caricature emphasized his nose.* PARODY achieves its humor through application of the manner or technique, usually of a well-known writer, to unaccustomed subjects: *a parody by Swift.* TRAVESTY implies a grotesque form of burlesque: *characters so changed as to produce a travesty.*

bur•let•ta (bər let′ə), *n. Theat.* (in the 18th and 19th centuries) a musical drama containing rhymed lyrics and resembling comic opera or a comic play containing songs. [1740–50; < It, equiv. to *burl(a)* jest (see BURLESQUE) + *-etta* -ETTE]

bur•ley[1] (bûr′lē), *n., pl.* **-leys.** (*often cap.*) an American tobacco with thin leaves and light color, grown esp. in Kentucky and nearby regions, used mostly in cigarettes. [1880–85, *Amer.*; appar. from proper name]

bur•ley[2] (bûr′lē), *n., pl.* **-leys.** *Informal.* a burlesque show. [cf. BURLECUE, BURLEYCUE]

Bur•ley (bûr′lē), *n.* a male given name.

bur•ley•cue (bûr′lē kyo͞o′), *n. Slang* (*now often facetious*). burlesque (def. 3). [see BURLECUE]

Bur•lin•game (bûr′lin gām′, -ling gām′), *n.* **1. Anson** (an′sən), 1820–70, U.S. diplomat. **2.** a city in W California, S of San Francisco. 26,173.

Bur•ling•ton (bûr′ling tən), *n.* **1.** a city in S Ontario, in S Canada, on Lake Ontario. 114,853. **2.** a city in NW Vermont, on Lake Champlain. 37,712. **3.** a city in N North Carolina. 37,266. **4.** a city in SE Iowa, on the Mississippi River. 29,529. **5.** a city in NE Massachusetts. 23,486. **6.** a city in S central New Jersey. 10,246.

burl•wood (bûrl′wŏŏd′), *n.* wood taken or cut from a burl. [BURL + WOOD[1]]

bur•ly (bûr′lē), *adj.,* **-li•er, -li•est. 1.** large in bodily size; stout; sturdy. **2.** bluff; brusque. [1250–1300; ME *borli, burli,* OE *borlīce* (adv.) excellently, equiv. to *bor(a)* ruler + *-līce* -LY] —**bur′li•ly,** *adv.* —**bur′li•ness,** *n.*
—**Syn. 1.** strapping, stocky, brawny, thickset, beefy, hefty. —**Ant. 1.** puny, weak, frail.

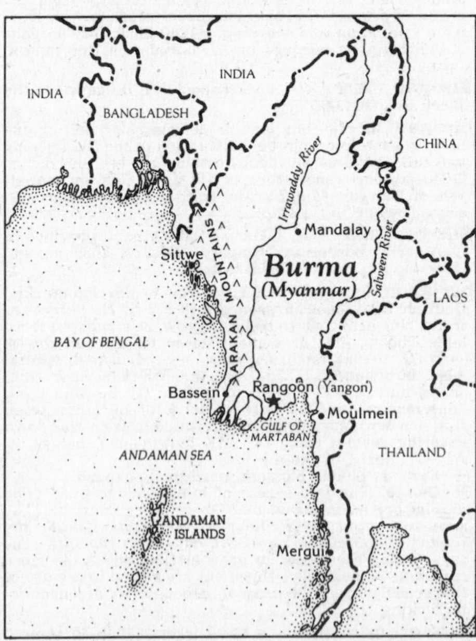

Bur•ma (bûr′mə), *n.* a republic in SE Asia, on the Bay of Bengal. 30,834,000; 261,789 sq. mi. (678,034 sq. km). *Cap.:* Rangoon (Yangon). Official name, **Union of Myanmar.**

Bur•man (bûr′mən), *n., pl.* **-mans,** *adj.* **1.** a member of the dominant ethnic group of Burma, living mainly in the lowlands of the Irrawaddy and Chindwin River drainages and the S panhandle. **2.** Burmese (def. 1). —**adj. 3.** of or pertaining to the Burmans as an ethnic group. **4.** Burmese (def. 4). [1790–1800; BURM(A) + -AN]

bur′ mar′igold, any of various composite plants of the genus *Bidens,* esp. those having conspicuous yellow flowers. [1810–20, *Amer.*]

Bur′ma Road′, a road extending from Lashio, Burma, to Chungking, China: used during World War II to supply Allied military forces in China. [1935–40]

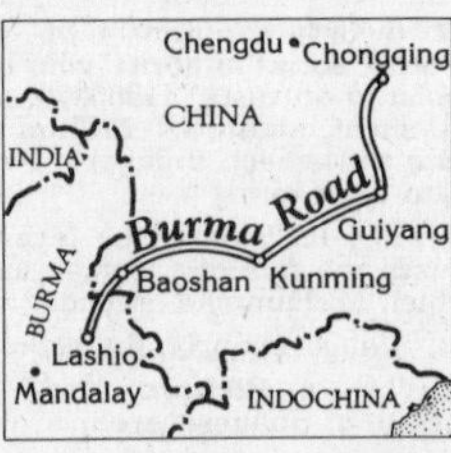

Bur•mese (bər mēz′, -mēs′), *n., pl.* **-mese,** *adj.* —*n.* **1.** a native or inhabitant of Burma. **2.** Burman (def. 1). **3.** the Tibeto-Burman language of the Burman ethnic group: the official language of Burma. —*adj.* **4.** of or pertaining to Burma, its inhabitants, or the language Burmese. **5.** Burman (def. 3). [1815–25; BURM(A) + -ESE]

Bur′mese cat′, one of a breed of short-haired domestic cats closely resembling a Siamese, with a compact body and long tail, but having a rounder head, sable-brown coat, and yellow eyes. [1935–40]

Burmese cat

Bur′mese glass′, an American art glass of the late 19th century, ranging from greenish-yellow to pink.

Bur′mese jade′, *Jewelry.* jadeite of the finest quality: a true jade. Also, **Bur′ma jade′.**

burn[1] (bûrn), *v.,* **burned** or **burnt, burn•ing,** *n.* —*v.i.* **1.** to undergo rapid combustion or consume fuel in such a way as to give off heat, gases, and, usually, light; be on fire: *The fire burned in the grate.* **2.** (of a fireplace, furnace, etc.) to contain a fire. **3.** to feel heat or a physiologically similar sensation; feel pain from or as if from a fire: *The wound burned and throbbed.* **4.** to give off light or to glow brightly: *The lights in the house burned all night.* **5.** to give off heat or be hot: *The pavement burned in the noon sun.* **6.** to produce pain or a stinging sensation similar to that of fire; cause to smart: *The whiskey burned in his throat.* **7.** *Games.* to be extremely close to finding a concealed object or guessing an answer. **8.** to feel extreme anger: *When she said I was rude, I really burned.* **9.** to feel strong emotion or passion: *He burned with desire.* **10.** *Chem.* **a.** to undergo combustion, either fast or slow; oxidize. **b.** to undergo fission or fusion. **11.** to become charred or overcooked by heat: *The steak burned around the edges.* **12.** to receive a sunburn: *She burns easily and has to stay in the shade.* **13.** to be damned: *You may burn for that sin.* **14.** *Slang.* to die in an electric chair: *The murderer was sentenced to burn.* **15.** to be engraved by or as if by burning: *His words burned into her heart.*
—*v.t.* **16.** to cause to undergo combustion or be consumed partly or wholly by fire. **17.** to use as fuel or as a source of light: *He burned coal to heat the house.* **18.** to cause to feel the sensation of heat. **19.** to overcook or char: *I almost burned the roast.* **20.** to sunburn. **21.** to injure, endanger, or damage with or as if with fire: *Look out, you'll burn yourself!* **22.** to execute by burning: *The heretic was burned at the stake.* **23.** to subject to fire or treat with heat as a process of manufacturing. **24.** to produce with or as if with fire: *She burned a hole in her dress.* **25.** to cause sharp pain or a stinging sensation: *The iodine burned his cut.* **26.** to consume rapidly, esp. to squander: *He burned energy as if he never heard of resting.* **27.** *Slang.* to suffer losses or be disillusioned in business or social relationships: *She was burned by that phony stock deal.* **28.** *Slang.* to cheat or rob. **29.** *Chem.* to cause to undergo combustion; oxidize. **30.** to damage through excessive friction, as in grinding or machining; scorch. **31.** *Metall.* to oxidize (a steel ingot), as with a flame. **32.** *Brit.* to scald (a wine, esp. sherry) in an iron container over a fire. **33.** *Cards.* to put (a played or rejected card) face up at the bottom of the pack. **34.** *Slang.* to disclose the identity of (an undercover agent, law officer, etc.): *to burn a narcotics detective.* **35. burn down,** to burn to the ground: *That barn was struck by lightning and burned down.* **36. burn in,** *Photog.* (in printing) to expose (one part of an image) to more light by masking the other parts in order to darken and give greater detail to the unmasked area. Also, **print in.** Cf. **dodge** (def. 2). **37. burn off,** (of morning mist) to be dissipated by the warmth of the rising sun. **38. burn on,** to weld lead with lead. **39. burn one's bridges (behind one).** See **bridge** (def. 21). **40. burn oneself out,** to exhaust one's energy, ideas, etc., through overwork or intemperance: *They feared that he would burn himself out or break down.* **41. burn one up,** *Informal.* to incite to anger: *That attitude burns me up.* **42. burn out, a.** to cease functioning because something has been exhausted or burned up, as fuel or a filament: *Our light bulbs burned out.* **b.** to deprive of a place to live, work, etc., by reason of fire: *They were burned out and had to live with relatives.* **c.** to wear out; exhaust; be worn out; become exhausted. **43. burn the** or **one's candle at both ends,** to be excessively active or immoderate, as by leading an active social life by night and a busy work life by day: *You can't burn the candle at both ends and hold onto a job.* **44. burn the midnight oil,** to work, study,

etc., until late at night: *to burn the midnight oil before final exams.* **45. burn up, a.** to burn completely or utterly: *The papers burned up in a minute.* **b.** *Informal.* to become angry: *He burns up at the mention of her name.* —*n.* **46.** a burned place or area: *a burn where fire had ripped through the forest.* **47.** *Pathol.* an injury usually caused by heat but also by abnormal cold, chemicals, poison gas, electricity, or lightning, and characterized by a painful reddening and swelling of the epidermis **(first-degree burn),** damage extending into the dermis, usually with blistering **(second-degree burn),** or destruction of the epidermis and dermis extending into the deeper tissue with loss of pain receptors **(third-degree burn). 48.** See **slow burn. 49.** the process or an instance of burning or baking, as in brickmaking. **50.** a forest or brush fire. **51.** the firing of a rocket engine. **52.** *Slang.* a swindle. [bef. 900; ME *bernen, brennen,* OE *beornan* (intrans.), (c. Goth, OHG *brinnan*), and OE *bærnan* (transit.), (c. Goth *brannjan,* OHG *brennen*)] —**burn′a·ble,** *adj.*

—**Syn. 1.** flame. **3.** tingle, glow. **16.** char, toast, brown, tan. BURN, SCORCH, SEAR, SINGE refer to the effect of fire or heat. To BURN is to consume, wholly or in part, by contact with fire or excessive heat: *to burn leaves.* SCORCH implies superficial or slight burning, resulting in a change of color or in injury to the texture because of shriveling or curling: *to scorch a dress while ironing.* SEAR refers esp. to the drying or hardening caused by heat: *to sear a roast of meat.* SINGE applies esp. to a superficial burning that takes off ends or projections: *to singe hair; singe the pinfeathers from a chicken.*

burn^2 (bûrn), *n. Scot. and North Eng.* a brook or rivulet. Also, **bourn, bourne.** [bef. 900; ME *burne, bourne,* OE *burna, brunna* brook; c. Goth *brunna,* D *born, bron,* G *Brunnen,* ON *brunnr* spring]

burn′ bag′, a special bag into which discarded secret or sensitive documents are placed for burning.

burned-out (bûrnd′out′), *adj.* **1.** consumed; rendered unserviceable or ineffectual by maximum use: *a burned-out tube.* **2.** exhausted or made listless through overwork, stress, or intemperance. **3.** deprived of one's regular place to live, work, etc., by a destructive fire. Also, **burnt-out.** [1805–15]

Burne-Jones (bûrn′jōnz′), *n.* **Sir Edward Co·ley** (kō′lē), 1833–98, English painter and designer.

burn·er (bûr′nər), *n.* **1.** a person or thing that burns. **2.** that part of a gas fixture, lamp, etc., from which flame issues or in which it is produced. **3.** any apparatus or receptacle in which fuel or refuse is burned. [1350–1400; ME *brenner.* See BURN^1, -ER^1]

bur·net (bər net′, bûr′nit), *n.* any of several plants belonging to the genera *Sanguisorba* and *Poterium,* of the rose family, having pinnate leaves and dense heads of small flowers. [1225–75; ME < MF *burnete,* var. of *brunete* (see BRUNET); so called from its hue]

Bur·net (bər net′, bûr′nit), *n.* **Sir (Frank) Mac·far·lane** (mək fär′lən), 1899–1985, Australian physician: Nobel prize for physiology 1960.

burnet′ rose′. See **Scotch rose.** [1880–85]

Bur·nett (bər net′), *n.* **Frances Hodg·son** (hoj′sən), 1849–1924, U.S. novelist, born in England.

Bur·ney (bûr′nē), *n.* **1. Charles,** 1726–1814, English organist, composer, and music historian. **2.** his daughter, **Frances** or **Fanny** (*Madame D'Arblay*), 1752–1840, English novelist and diarist.

burn·ing (bûr′ning), *adj.* **1.** aflame; on fire. **2.** very hot; simmering: *The water was burning.* **3.** very bright; glowing: *She wore a burning red bathing suit.* **4.** caused by or as if by fire, a burn, or heat: *He had a burning sensation in his throat.* **5.** intense; passionate: *a burning desire.* **6.** urgent or crucial: *a burning question.* —*n.* **7.** the state, process, sensation, or effect of being on fire, burned, or subjected to intense heat. **8.** the baking of ceramic products to develop hardness and other properties. **9.** the heating or the calcining of certain ores and rocks as a preliminary stage in various industrial processes. [bef. 1000; ME *brenning* (n., adj.), OE *byrnende* (adj.). See BURN^1, -ING^1, -ING^2] —**burn′ing·ly,** *adv.*

burn′ing bush′, 1. *Bible.* a bush that "burned with fire and . . . was not consumed," from which an angel spoke to Moses. (Ex. 3:2). **2.** Also called **firebush, summer cypress.** a shrubby plant, *Kochia scoparia,* of the goosefoot family, having dense, feathery foliage that turns red in fall. **3.** any of various plants of the genus *Euonymus* having bright red foliage in autumn. [1775–85 as a plant name]

burn′ing ghat′, a platform at the top of a riverside ghat where Hindus cremate their dead. [1875–80]

burn′ing glass′, a converging lens used to produce heat or ignite substances by focusing the sun's rays. Also called **sunglass.** [1560–70]

bur·nish (bûr′nish), *v.t.* **1.** to polish (a surface) by friction. **2.** to make smooth and bright. **3.** *Engraving.* to flatten and enlarge the dots of (a halftone) by rubbing with a tool. —*n.* **4.** gloss; brightness; luster: *the burnish of brass andirons.* [1275–1325; ME *burnissh* < AF *burniss-,* MF *bruniss-* (long s. of *burnir, brunir* to darken, polish), equiv. to *brun-* BROWN + *-iss-* -ISH^2] —**bur′·nish·a·ble,** *adj.* —**bur′nish·ment,** *n.*

—**Syn. 1.** buff, shine.

bur·nish·er (bûr′ni shər), *n.* **1.** a person who burnishes. **2.** a tool, usually with a smooth, slightly convex head, used for polishing, as in dentistry. [1400–50; late ME *burnessher.* See BURNISH, -ER^2]

Burn·ley (bûrn′lē), *n.* a city in E Lancashire, in NW England. 92,700.

bur·noose (bər nōōs′, bûr′nōōs), *n.* **1.** a hooded mantle or cloak, as that worn by Arabs. **2.** a similar garment worn by women at various periods in Europe and the United States. Also, **bur·nous′.** [1685–95; < F *burnous* < dial. Ar *burnūs* < Gk *bírros* < LL *birrus* BIRRUS] —**bur·noosed′, bur·noused′,** *adj.*

burnoose (def. 1)

burn·out (bûrn′out′), *n.* **1.** a fire that is totally destructive of something. **2.** Also, **burn′-out′.** fatigue, frustration, or apathy resulting from prolonged stress, overwork, or intense activity. **3.** *Rocketry.* **a.** the termination of effective combustion in a rocket engine, due to exhaustion of propellant. **b.** the end of the powered portion of a rocket's flight. **4.** *Elect.* the breakdown of a lamp, motor, or other electrical device due to the heat created by the current flowing through it. [1900–05; n. use of v. phrase *burn out*]

Burns (bûrnz), *n.* **1. Arthur F(rank),** born 1904, U.S. economist, born in Austria: chairman of the Federal Reserve Board 1970–78. **2. George** (*Nathan Birnbaum*), born 1896, U.S. comedian (partner and husband of Gracie Allen). **3. Robert,** 1759–96, Scottish poet. **4. Tommy** (*Noah Brusso*), 1881–1955, U.S. boxer: world heavyweight champion 1906–08.

Burn·side (bûrn′sīd′), *n.* **Ambrose Everett,** 1824–81, Union general in the American Civil War.

burn·sides (bûrn′sīdz′), *n.pl.* full whiskers and a mustache worn with the chin clean-shaven. [1870–75, *Amer.*; named after Gen. A. E. BURNSIDE]

burnsides

Burns·ville (bûrnz′vil), *n.* a city in SE Minnesota. 35,674.

burnt (bûrnt), *v.* **1.** a pt. and pp. of **burn.** —*adj.* **2.** *Fine Arts.* **a.** of or showing earth pigments that have been calcined and changed to a deeper and warmer color: *burnt ocher.* **b.** of or showing colors having a deeper or grayer hue than is usually associated with them: *burnt orange; burnt rose.*

burnt′ al′mond. Often, **burnt almonds.** roasted sweet almond. [1840–50]

burnt′ lime′, lime^1 (def. 1).

burnt′ of′fering, an offering burnt upon an altar in sacrifice to a deity. [1350–1400; ME]

burnt-out (bûrnt′out′), *adj.* burned-out.

burnt′ sien′na, 1. See under **sienna** (def. 1). **2.** an intense dark reddish-brown color. [1835–45]

burnt′ um′ber. See under **umber** (def. 1).

burn·up (bûrn′up′), *n.* the nuclear fuel consumed in a reactor, often measured as a percentage of the atoms of fuel that have undergone fission. [n. use of the v. phrase *burn up*]

bur′ oak′, an oak tree, *Quercus macrocarpa,* of eastern North America, having shiny, dark-green leaves, light-gray deeply ridged bark, and very large acorns with a fringed cup, yielding a hard, durable wood: the state tree of Illinois. [1805–15, *Amer.*]

burp (bûrp), *Informal.* —*n.* **1.** a belch; eructation. —*v.i.* **2.** to belch; eruct. —*v.t.* **3.** to cause (a baby) to belch by patting its back, esp. to relieve flatulence after feeding. [1930–35, *Amer.*; imit.] —**burp′less,** *adj.*

burp′ gun′, *Mil.* See **machine pistol.** [1940–45, *Amer.*]

burp·y (bûr′pē), *adj.,* **burp·i·er, burp·i·est.** *Informal.* **1.** belching, tending to belch, or feeling like belching: *Carbonated beverages make me burpy.* **2.** causing one to belch: *burpy foods.* [BURP + -Y^1] —**burp′i·ness,** *n.*

burr^1 (bûr), *n.* **1.** Also, **buhr.** a protruding, ragged edge raised on the surface of metal during drilling, shearing, punching, or engraving. **2.** a rough or irregular protuberance on any object, as on a tree. **3.** a small, hand-held, power-driven milling cutter, used by machinists and die makers for deepening, widening, or undercutting small recesses. **4.** a lump of brick fused or warped in firing. —*v.t.* **5.** to form a rough point or edge on. **6.** deburr. Also, **bur** (for defs. 1, 3). [1605–15; sp. var. of BUR^1]

burr^2 (bûr), *n.* **1.** a washer placed at the head of a rivet. **2.** a blank punched out of a piece of sheet metal. Also, **bur.** [1375–1425; late ME *burrewez* (pl.), *buruhe* circle, var. of *brough* round tower; see BROCH]

burr^3 (bûr), *n.* **1.** a pronunciation of the *r*-sound as a uvular trill, as in certain Northern English dialects. **2.** a pronunciation of the *r*-sound as an alveolar flap or trill, as in Scottish English. **3.** any pronunciation popularly considered rough or nonurban. **4.** a whirring noise. —*v.i.* **5.** to speak with a burr. **6.** to speak roughly, indistinctly, or inarticulately. **7.** to make a whirring sound. —*v.t.* **8.** to pronounce (words, sounds, etc.) with a burr. [1750–60; appar. both imit. and associative, the sound being thought of as rough like a bur]

burr^4 (bûr), *n.* burstone. Also, **buhr.** [1250–1300; ME *burre,* prob. so called from its roughness]

Burr (bûr), *n.* **Aaron,** 1756–1836, vice president of the U.S. 1801–05.

burr′ cut′, *Slang.* See **crew cut.** Also called **burr′ hair′cut.**

burred (bûrd), *adj.* **1.** prickly or rough in texture. **2.** having a bur or burs. [1905–10; BUR^1 + -ED^2]

bur′ reed′, any plant of the genus *Sparganium,* having ribbony leaves and bearing burlike fruit. [1590–1600]

burr·fish (bûr′fish′), *n., pl.* **-fish·es,** (*esp. referring to two or more kinds or species*) **-fish.** any of several porcupinefishes of the genus *Chilomycterus,* covered with short, immovable spines. [so called from its spines; see BURR^1, FISH]

bur·rhel (bûr′əl), *n.* bharal.

Bur·rill·ville (bûr′əl vil′), *n.* a town in N Rhode Island. 13,164.

bur·ri·to (bə rē′tō; *Sp.* bōōr rē′tô), *n., pl.* **-tos** (-tōz; *Sp.* -tôs). *Mexican Cookery.* a tortilla folded over a filling, as of ground beef, grated cheese, or refried beans. [1940–45; < MexSp (Guerrero): stuffed taco, Sp: young donkey, foal, equiv. to *burr(o)* BURRO + *-ito* dim. suffix]

bur·ro (bûr′ō, bōōr′ō, bur′ō), *n., pl.* **-ros. 1.** a small donkey, esp. one used as a pack animal in the southwestern U.S. **2.** any donkey. [1790–1800; < Sp < Pg, back formation from *burrico* ass < VL **burriccus* for LL *burricus* pony]

bur′ro's tail′, a succulent Mexican plant, *Sedum morganianum,* of the stonecrop family, bearing small, rose-colored flowers and long, hanging, nearly cylindrical stems with closely packed whitish-green leaves. Also called **donkey's tail, horse's tail, lamb's tail.**

Bur·roughs (bûr′ōz, bur′-), *n.* **1. Edgar Rice,** 1875–1950, U.S. novelist and short-story writer. **2. John,** 1837–1921, U.S. naturalist and essayist. **3. William Seward,** 1855–98, U.S. inventor of the adding machine. **4.** his grandson **William S(eward),** born 1914, U.S. novelist.

bur·row (bûr′ō, bur′ō), *n.* **1.** a hole or tunnel in the ground made by a rabbit, fox, or similar animal for habitation and refuge. **2.** a place of retreat; shelter or refuge. —*v.i.* **3.** to make a hole or passage in, into, or under something. **4.** to lodge in a burrow. **5.** to hide. **6.** to proceed by or as if by digging. —*v.t.* **7.** to put a burrow into (a hill, mountainside, etc.). **8.** to hide (oneself), as in a burrow. **9.** to make by or as if by burrowing: *We burrowed our way through the crowd.* [1325–75; ME *borow,* earlier *burh,* appar. gradational var. of late ME *beri* burrow, var. of earlier *berg* refuge, OE *gebeorg,* deriv. of *beorgan* to protect; akin to OE *burgen* grave, i.e., place of protection for a body; see BURY] —**bur′row·er,** *n.*

bur′rowing blen′ny, graveldiver.

bur′rowing owl′, a long-legged terrestrial owl, *Athene cunicularia,* of North and South America, that digs a nesting burrow in open prairie land. [1810–20, *Amer.*]

burr·stone (bûr′stōn′), *n.* burstone.

bur·ry^1 (bûr′ē), *adj.,* **-ri·er, -ri·est.** full of or covered with burs; burlike. [1400–50; late ME; see BUR^1, -Y^1]

bur·ry^2 (bûr′ē), *adj.,* **-ri·er, -ri·est.** characterized by or spoken with a burr. [1865–70; BURR^3 + -Y^1]

bur·sa (bûr′sə), *n., pl.* **-sae** (-sē), **-sas.** *Anat., Zool.* a pouch, sac, or vesicle, esp. a sac containing synovia, to facilitate motion, as between a tendon and a bone. [1795–1805; < NL, LL *bursa* a bag, pouch, purse < Gk *býrsa* a skin, hide] —**bur′sal,** *adj.* —**bur·sate** (bûr′sāt), *adj.*

Bur·sa (bōōr sä′), *n.* a city in NW Turkey in Asia: a former capital of the Ottoman Empire. 346,084. Also, **Brusa.**

bur′sa of Fabri′cius, *Ornith.* a lymphoid gland of the cloaca in birds, believed to function in disease resistance, and closing or disappearing as the bird ages. [after Hieronymus *Fabricius* ab Aquapendente (1537–1619), Italian anatomist, who discovered it]

bur·sar (bûr′sər, -sär), *n.* **1.** a treasurer or business officer, esp. of a college or university. **2.** (in the Middle Ages) a university student. **3.** *Chiefly Scot.* a student attending a university on a scholarship. [1400–50; < ML *bursārius* a purse-keeper, treasurer (see BURSA, -AR^2); r. late ME *bouser,* var. of *bourser* < AF; OF *borsier*]

bur·sar·i·al (bər sâr′ē əl), *adj.* of, pertaining to, or paid to or by a bursar or a bursary. [1860–65; BURSAR + -IAL]

bur·sa·ry (bûr′sə rē), *n., pl.* **-ries. 1.** *Eccles.* the treasury of a monastery. **2.** *Brit.* a college scholarship. [1530–40; < ML *bursāria* treasurer's room, deriv. of *bursārius* a treasurer. See BURSAR, -Y^3]

Bur·schen·schaft (bōōr′shən shäft′), *n., pl.* ***-schaf·ten*** (-shäf′tən). *German.* (at German universities) any of certain associations of students formed to promote patriotism, Christian conduct, and liberal ideas but now primarily social fraternities.

burse (bûrs), *n.* **1.** a pouch or case for some special purpose. **2.** (in Scotland) **a.** a fund to provide allowances for students. **b.** an allowance so provided. **3.** *Eccles.* a case or receptacle for a corporal. [1250–1300; ME < AF < LL *bursa* purse; see BURSA]

bur·seed (bûr′sēd′), *n.* a stickseed, *Lappula echinata,* introduced into North America from Europe. [1840–50, *Amer.*; BUR[1] + SEED]

bur•si•form (bûr′sə fôrm′), *adj. Anat., Zool.* pouch-shaped; saccate. [1830–40; < NL *bursiformis.* See BURSA, -I-, -FORM]

bur•si•tis (bər sī′tis), *n. Pathol.* inflammation of a bursa. [1855–60; < NL; see BURSA, -ITIS]

burst (bûrst), *v.,* **burst** or, often, **burst•ed, burst•ing,** *n.* —*v.i.* **1.** to break, break open, or fly apart with sudden violence: *The bitter cold caused the pipes to burst.* **2.** to issue forth suddenly and forcibly, as from confinement or through an obstacle: *Oil burst to the surface. He burst through the doorway.* **3.** to give sudden expression to or as if to emotion: *to burst into applause; to burst into tears.* **4.** to be extremely full, as if ready to break open: *The house was bursting with people.* **5.** to appear suddenly; become visible, audible, evident, etc., all at once: *The sun burst through the clouds.* —*v.t.* **6.** to cause to break or break open suddenly and violently: *He burst the balloon.* **7.** to cause or suffer the rupture of: *to burst a blood vessel.* **8.** to separate (the parts of a multipart stationery form consisting of interleaved paper and carbon paper). **9. burst at the seams,** to be filled to or beyond normal capacity: *This room will be bursting at the seams when all the guests arrive.* —*n.* **10.** an act or instance of bursting. **11.** a sudden, intense display, as of activity, energy, or effort: *The car passed us with a burst of speed.* **12.** a sudden expression or manifestation, as of emotion: *a burst of affection.* **13.** a sudden and violent issuing forth: *a burst of steam from the pipe.* **14.** *Mil.* **a.** the explosion of a projectile, esp. in a specified place: *an air burst.* **b.** a rapid sequence of shots fired by one pull on the trigger of an automatic weapon: *A burst from the machine gun shattered all the windows.* **15.** the result of bursting; breach; gap: *a burst in the dike.* **16.** a sudden appearance or opening to view. [bef. 1000; ME *bersten, bursten,* OE *berstan* (past. pl. *burston*), c. OHG *brestan* (G *bersten*), ON *bresta;* akin to BREAK]
—**Syn. 1.** crack, explode. **6.** rend, tear. **11.** spurt. **12, 13.** outbreak.
—**Usage.** See **bust**[2].

burst•er (bûr′stər), *n.* **1.** a person or thing that bursts. **2.** *Astron.* See **x-ray burster.** [1850–55; BURST + -ER[1]]

burst′ing point′, 1. the point at which normal capacity is exceeded. **2.** a stage of emotion at which self-control is lost. [1900–05]

burst′ing strength′, 1. the capacity of a thing or substance to resist change when under pressure. **2.** the pressure required to break down the resistance of a substance.

bur•stone (bûr′stōn′), *n.* **1.** any of various siliceous rocks used for millstones. **2.** a millstone of such material. Also, **buhrstone, burrstone.** Also called **buhr, burr.** [BUR(R)[4] + STONE]

Burt (bûrt), *n.* **1. William Austin,** 1792–1858, U.S. surveyor and inventor. **2.** a male given name, form of **Albert, Herbert, Bertram, Burton.**

bur•then (bûr′thən), *n., v.t. Archaic.* burden[1]. —**bur′•then•some,** *adj.*

bur•ton[1] (bûr′tn), *n. Naut.* **1.** any of various small tackles for use on shipboard. **2.** See **Spanish burton.** [1695–1705; prob. by metathesis from *Breton (takles), Brytton (takles)* (late 15th cent.); see BRETON, BRITON]

bur•ton[2] (bûr′tn), *n.* **go for a burton,** *Brit. Slang.* **1.** to be lost, missing, or destroyed. **2.** to die. [1940–45; orig. disputed]

Bur•ton (bûr′tn), *n.* **1. Harold Hitz** (hits), 1888–1964, associate justice of the U.S. Supreme Court 1945–58. **2. Sir Richard Francis,** 1821–90, English explorer, Orientalist, and writer. **3. Robert** (*"Democritus Junior"*), 1577–1640, English clergyman and author. **4.** a town in central Michigan. 29,976. **5.** a male given name.

Bur•ton-up•on-Trent (bûr′tn ə pon′trent′, -ə pôn′-), *n.* a city in E Staffordshire, in central England. 50,175.

Bu•run•di (bo͝o ro͞on′dē), *n.* a republic in central Africa, E of Zaire: formerly the S part of the Belgian trust territory of Ruanda-Urundi; gained independence on July 1, 1962. 4,000,000; 10,747 sq. mi. (27,834 sq. km). *Cap.:* Bujumbura. —**Bu•run′di•an,** *adj., n.*

Bu•ru•sha•ski (bo͝or′ə shä′skē), *n.* a language of NW Kashmir, not known to be related to any other language.

bur•weed (bûr′wēd′), *n.* any of various plants bearing a burlike fruit, as the cocklebur and burdock. [1775–85; BUR[1] + WEED[1]]

bur•y (ber′ē), *v.,* **bur•ied, bur•y•ing,** *n., pl.* **bur•ies.** —*v.t.* **1.** to put in the ground and cover with earth: *The pirates buried the chest on the island.* **2.** to put (a corpse) in the ground or a vault, or into the sea, often with ceremony: *They buried the sailor with full military honors.* **3.** to plunge in deeply; cause to sink in: *to bury an arrow in a target.* **4.** to cover in order to conceal from sight: *She buried the card in the deck.* **5.** to immerse (oneself): *He buried himself in his work.* **6.** to put out of one's mind: *to bury an insult.* **7.** to consign to obscurity; cause to appear insignificant by assigning to an unimportant location, position, etc.: *Her name was buried in small print at the end of the book.* **8. bury one's head in the sand,** to avoid reality; ignore the facts of a situation: *You cannot continue to bury your head in the sand—you must learn to face facts.* **9. bury the hatchet,** to become reconciled or reunited. —*n.* **10.** *Naut.* housing[1] (def. 8a, b). [bef. 1000; ME *berien, buryen,* OE *byrgan* to bury, conceal; akin to OE *beorgan* to hide, protect, preserve; c. D, G *bergen,* Goth *bairgan,* ON *bjarga*]
—**Syn. 2.** inter, entomb, inhume. **4.** hide, secrete. —**Ant. 2.** disinter, exhume. **4.** uncover.

CONCISE ETYMOLOGY KEY: <, descended or borrowed from; >, whence; b., blend of, blended; c., cognate with; cf., compare; deriv., derivative; equiv., equivalent; imit., imitative; obl., oblique; r., replacing; s., stem; sp., spelling, spelled; resp., respelling, respelled; trans., translation; ?, origin unknown; *, unattested; ‡, probably earlier than. See the full key inside the front cover.

Bur•yat (bo͝or yät′, bo͝or′ē ät′; *Russ.* bo͞o ʀyät′), *adj., n., pl.* **-yats,** (*esp. collectively*) **-yat.** —*adj.* **1.** of or pertaining to the Buryat Autonomous Republic, its people, or their language. —*n.* **2.** a member of any of the Mongol people in the Buryat Republic. **3.** the Mongolian language of the Buryat.

Bur•yat′ Auton′omous Repub′lic, an autonomous republic in the Russian Federation in Asia, E of Lake Baikal. 1,042,000; ab. 135,650 sq. mi. (351,300 sq. km). *Cap.:* Ulan Ude. Also, **Buriat Autonomous Republic.**

bur′ying bee′tle, any of various carrion beetles that bury the carcasses of small animals, esp. rodents, in which their eggs have been deposited. [1795–1805]

bur′ying ground′, a burial ground. [1705–15]

Bur•y St. Ed•munds (ber′ē sānt ed′məndz, -sənt-), a city in W Suffolk, in E England: medieval shrine. 25,629.

bus[1] (bus), *n., pl.* **bus•es, bus•ses,** *v.,* **bused** or **bussed, bus•ing** or **bus•sing.** —*n.* **1.** a large motor vehicle, having a long body, equipped with seats or benches for passengers, usually operating as part of a scheduled service; omnibus. **2.** a similar horse-drawn vehicle. **3.** a passenger automobile or airplane used in a manner resembling that of a bus. **4.** any vehicle operated to transport children to school. **5.** a low, movable filing cabinet. **6.** *Elect.* Also called **bus′ bar′, bus•bar** (bus′bär′). a heavy conductor, often made of copper in the shape of a bar, used to collect, carry, and distribute powerful electric currents, as those produced by generators. **7.** *Computers.* a circuit that connects the CPU with other devices in a computer. —*v.t.* **8.** to convey or transport by bus: *to bus the tourists to another hotel.* **9.** to transport (pupils) to school by bus, esp. as a means of achieving racial integration. —*v.i.* **10.** to travel on or by means of a bus: *We bused to New York on a theater trip.* [1825–35; short for OMNIBUS; (def. 6) short for *omnibus bar*]

bus[2] (bus), *v.i., v.t.,* **bused** or **bussed, bus•ing** or **bus•sing.** to work or act as a busboy or busgirl: *She bused for her meals during her student days.* [1830–40; back formation from BUSBOY]

bus., business.

bus•boy (bus′boi′), *n.* a waiter's helper in a restaurant or other public dining room. Also, **bus′ boy′.** [1910–15, *Amer.*; *bus-* short for *omnibus* waiter's helper (see OMNIBUS) + BOY]

bus•by (buz′bē), *n., pl.* **-bies. 1.** a tall fur hat with a baglike ornament hanging from the top over the right side. **2.** the bearskin hat worn by certain British guardsmen. [1755–65; orig., a bushy wig; of obscure orig.]

busby (def. 2)

Busch (bo͝osh), *n.* **Fritz** (frits), 1890–1951, German conductor.

bus•girl (bus′gûrl′), *n.* a girl or woman who works as a waiter's helper. Also, **bus′ girl′.** [1940–45, *Amer.*; BUS(BOY) + GIRL]

bush[1] (bo͝osh), *n.* **1.** a low plant with many branches that arise from or near the ground. **2.** a small cluster of shrubs appearing as a single plant. **3.** something resembling or suggesting this, as a thick, shaggy head of hair. **4.** Also called **bush lot.** *Canadian.* a small, wooded lot, esp. a farm lot with trees left standing to provide firewood, fence posts, etc. **5.** the tail of a fox; brush. **6.** *Geog.* a stretch of uncultivated land covered with mixed plant growth, bushy vegetation, trees, etc. **7.** a large uncleared area thickly covered with mixed plant growth, trees, etc., as a jungle. **8.** a large, sparsely populated area most of which is uncleared, as areas of Australia and Alaska. **9.** a tree branch hung as a sign before a tavern or vintner's shop. **10.** any tavern sign. **11.** *Slang (vulgar).* pubic hair. **12.** *Archaic.* a wineshop. **13. beat around** or **about the bush,** to avoid coming to the point; delay in approaching a subject directly: *Stop beating around the bush and tell me what you want.* **14. beat the bushes,** to scout or search for persons or things far and wide: *beating the bushes for engineers.* **15. go bush,** *Australian.* **a.** to flee or escape into the bush. **b.** *Slang.* to become wild. —*v.i.* **16.** to be or become bushy; branch or spread as or like a bush. —*v.t.* **17.** to cover, protect, support, or mark with a bush or bushes. —*adj.* **18.** bush-league. [bef. 1000; ME *busshe,* OE *busc* (in place-names); c. D *bos* wood, G *Busch,* ON *buskr* bush] —**bush′less,** *adj.* —**bush′like′,** *adj.*

bush[2] (bo͝osh), *n.* **1.** a lining of metal or the like set into an orifice to guard against wearing by friction, erosion, etc. **2.** a bushing. —*v.t.* **3.** to furnish with a bush; line with metal. [1560–70; < MD *bussche;* see BOX[1]]

Bush (bo͝osh), *n.* **1. George (Herbert Walker),** born 1924, U.S. politician: vice president 1981–89; 41st president of the U.S. 1989–93. **2. Van•ne•var** (və nē′vär, -vər), 1890–1974, U.S. electrical engineer: education and research administrator.

bush., bushel; bushels.

bush′ ba′by, any of several nocturnal, lemurlike primates of the genus *Galago,* native to African forests, with large ears and eyes, long and slender fingers and toes, thick woolly fur, and a large, bushy tail. Also called **galago.** [1900–05]

bush′ bas′il. See under **basil.** [1590–1600]

bush′ bean′, a variety of the common edible bean, *Phaseolus vulgaris humilis,* characterized by its bushy growth. [1815–25, *Amer.*]

bush•beat•er (bo͝osh′bē′tər), *n.* a person who conducts a thorough search to recruit talented people, as for an athletic team. [1800–10, *Amer.*; BUSH[1] + BEATER] —**bush′beat′ing,** *n.*

bush′ broom′, an evergreen St.-John's-wort, *Hypericum prolificum,* common from New York to Iowa and southward, having yellow flowers in terminal clusters.

bush•buck (bo͝osh′buk′), *n., pl.* **-bucks,** (*esp. collectively*) **-buck.** a large African antelope, *Tragelaphus scriptus,* of wooded and bushy regions, having a reddish body streaked or spotted with white. Also called **guib.** Cf. **harnessed antelope.** [1850–55; < Afrik *bosbok,* earlier *boschbok,* equiv. to *bos* BUSH[1] + *bok* BUCK[1]]

bush′ clo′ver, any of several plants or shrubs belonging to the genus *Lespedeza,* of the legume family, having pinnately trifoliate leaves and heads of pink, purple, cream, or white flowers. [1810–20, *Amer.*]

bush′ coat′. See **bush jacket.**

bush•craft (bo͝osh′kraft′, -kräft′), *n. Australian.* skill in anything pertaining to bush country, as in finding one's way, hunting, or finding water. [1870–75; BUSH[1] + CRAFT]

bushed (bo͝osht), *adj.* **1.** overgrown with bushes. **2.** *Informal.* exhausted; tired out: *After all that exercise, I'm bushed.* **3.** *Canadian Informal.* mentally unbalanced as a result of prolonged residence in a sparsely inhabited region. **4.** *Australian and New Zealand Slang.* unable to find one's direction; lost; confused. [1485–95; BUSH[1] + -ED[2], -ED[3]]

bush•el[1] (bo͝osh′əl), *n.* **1.** a unit of dry measure containing 4 pecks, equivalent in the U.S. (and formerly in England) to 2150.42 cubic inches or 35.24 liters (**Winchester bushel**), and in Great Britain to 2219.36 cubic inches or 36.38 liters (**Imperial bushel**). *Abbr.:* bu., bush. **2.** a container of this capacity. **3.** a unit of weight equal to the weight of a bushel of a given commodity. **4.** a large, unspecified amount or number: *a bushel of kisses.* [1250–1300; ME *bu(i)sshel* < MF *boissel,* equiv. to *boisse* unit of measure (< Gaulish **bostia;* cf. MIr *bas, bos* palm of the hand, handbreadth) + *-el* n. suffix]

bush•el[2] (bo͝osh′əl), *v.t.,* **-eled, -el•ing** or (*esp. Brit.*) **-elled, el•ling.** to alter or repair (a garment). [1875–80, *Amer.*; < G *bosseln* to patch < F *bosseler* to emboss; see BOSS[2]] —**bush′el•er;** *esp. Brit.,* **bush′el•ler,** *n.*

bush•el•bas•ket (bo͝osh′əl bas′kət, -bä′skit), *n.* a basket capable of holding one bushel. [1520–30; BUSHEL[1] + BASKET]

bush′eled i′ron, 1. heterogeneous iron made from scrap iron and steel. **2.** wrought iron of high quality made from selected pieces cut from various muck bars. [1825–35]

bush•el•ful (bo͝osh′əl fo͝ol′), *n., pl.* **-fuls.** an amount equal to the capacity of a bushel. [1400–50; late ME; see BUSHEL[1], -FUL]
—**Usage.** See **-ful.**

bush•el•man (bo͝osh′əl mən, -man′), *n., pl.* **-men** (-mən, -men′). a person who alters or repairs garments; busheler. [1840–50; BUSHEL[2] + MAN[1]]

bush•er (bo͝osh′ər), *n. Baseball Slang.* See **bush leaguer** (def. 1). [1910–15, *Amer.*; BUSH (LEAGUE) + -ER[1]]

bush•fire (bo͝osh′fīᵊr′), *n.* an uncontrolled fire in the trees and bushes of scrubland. [1865–70; BUSH[1] + FIRE]

bush•ham•mer (bo͝osh′ham′ər), *n. Masonry.* a hammer for dressing stone, having one or two square faces composed of a number of pyramidal points. Also, **bush′ ham′mer.** [1880–85; < G *Bosshammer,* equiv. to obs. *boss(en)* to BEAT + *hammer* HAMMER]

bush′ hog′, 1. a device, pulled behind a tractor, having one or more blades spinning parallel to the ground and attached radially to a central axis, used for cutting vegetation and clearing land. **2.** bush-hog.

bush-hog (bo͝osh′hôg′, -hog′), *v.t.,* **-hogged, -hog•ging.** to clear (land) by using a bush hog.

bush′ hon′eysuckle, any of several shrubs of the genus *Diervilla,* of eastern North America, having clusters of yellowish flowers. [1810–20, *Amer.*]

bush′ hook′, *Dial.* a tool with a curved blade and long handle used to cut bushes and undergrowth. [1805–15, *Amer.*]

bush′ huck′leberry, a huckleberry shrub, *Gaylussacia dumosa,* having sticky, hairy twigs, white or pink flowers, and tasteless but edible black fruit. [1840–50, *Amer.*]

Bu•shi•do (bo͞o′shē dô′), *n.* (in feudal Japan) the code of the samurai, stressing unquestioning loyalty and obedience and valuing honor above life. Also, **bu′shi•do.** [1895–1900; < Japn *bushidō,* equiv. to *bushi* warrior (< MChin, equiv. to Chin *wǔ* military + *shì* gentleman) + *dō* way (< MChin; see JUDO)]

bush•i•ness (bo͝osh′ē nis), *n.* a bushy state or form. [1720–30; BUSHY + -NESS]

bush•ing (bo͝osh′ing), *n.* **1.** *Elect.* a lining for a hole, intended to insulate and protect from abrasion one or more conductors that pass through it. **2.** *Mach.* **a.** a replaceable thin tube or sleeve, usually of bronze, mounted in a case or housing as a bearing. **b.** a replaceable hardened steel tube used as a guide for various tools or parts, as a drill or valve rod. [1785–95; BUSH[2] + -ING[1]]

Bu•shire (bo͞o shēr′), *n.* a seaport in SW Iran, on the Persian Gulf. 40,000.

bush′ jack′et, a belted, hip-length, shirtlike jacket, usually with four patch pockets and a notched collar, adapted from the hunting coat customarily worn in the African bush. Also called **bush coat, bush shirt, safari jacket.** [1935–40]

bush·land (bŏŏsh′land′), *n. Chiefly Canadian.* heavily forested, lightly settled land. [1835–45; BUSH¹ + LAND]

bush′ league′, *Baseball.* See **minor league.** [1905–10, *Amer.*]

bush-league (bŏŏsh′lēg′), *adj.* inferior or amateurish; mediocre: *a bush-league theatrical performance.* [1905–10, *Amer.*]

bush′ lea′guer, 1. Also called **busher.** *Baseball.* **a.** a player in a minor league. **b.** an incompetent player, as one who behaves or plays as if he or she belonged in a minor league. **2.** a person who performs at an inferior level or in an inferior manner. [1905–10, *Amer.*]

bush·line (bŏŏsh′līn′), *n. Canadian.* an airline that flies over sparsely inhabited territory to serve isolated settlements. [BUSH¹ + (AIR)LINE]

bush′ lot′, *Canadian.* bush¹ (def. 4). [1685–95]

bush·man (bŏŏsh′mən), *n., pl.* **-men. 1.** a woodsman. **2.** *Australian.* a pioneer; dweller in the bush. **3.** (*cap.*) San. [1775–85; BUSH¹ + MAN¹, modeled on Afrik *boschjesman* lit., man of the bush]

Bush·man (bŏŏsh′mən), *n.* **Francis X(avier),** 1883–1966, U.S. film actor.

bush·mas·ter (bŏŏsh′mas′tər, -mä′stər), *n.* a pit viper, *Lachesis muta,* of tropical America, that grows to a length of 12 ft. (3.6 m). [1820–30; BUSH¹ + MASTER]

Bush·nell (bŏŏsh′nl), *n.* **David,** 1742?–1824, U.S. inventor: pioneered in submarine construction.

bush′ parole′, *Slang.* an escape from prison. [1915–20]

bush′ pig′, a wild swine, *Potamochaerus porcus,* of southern and eastern Africa, having white facial markings. Also called **boschvark.** [1830–40]

bush′ pi′lot, a pilot who flies small aircraft over rugged terrain or unsettled regions to serve remote areas inaccessible to or off the route of larger planes: *Bush pilots brought supplies to the Alaskan village once a week.* [1935–40]

bush′ pop′py. See **tree poppy.** [1865–70]

bush·rang·er (bŏŏsh′rān′jər), *n.* **1.** a person who lives in the bush or woods. **2.** *Australian.* **a.** a person who lives by robbing travelers and isolated homesteads in the bush. **b.** a person who drives a hard, and sometimes dishonest, bargain. [1810–20; BUSH¹ + RANGER] **—bush′rang′ing,** *n.*

bush′ road′, *Canadian.* a rough road cut through forested land usually to serve a lumbering, mining, or other commercial company. [1820–30]

bush′ shirt′, 1. See **bush jacket. 2.** a shirt resembling a bush jacket; safari shirt. [1905–10]

bush′ tel′egraph, 1. any system of communication in which the natives of a jungle or bush region transmit news rapidly, as by runners, drum codes, or smoke signals. **2.** *Australian.* **a.** any chain of communications by which criminals, originally bushrangers, are warned of police movements. **b.** *Slang.* rumor; the grapevine. [1875–80]

bush′ tit′, any of several North American titmice of the genus *Psaltriparus,* which construct long, pendent nests. [1880–85, *Amer.*]

bush·wa (bŏŏsh′wä, -wô), *n.* rubbishy nonsense; baloney; bull: *You'll hear a lot of boring bushwa about his mechanical skill.* Also, **bush′wah.** [1915–20; perh. repr. BOURGEOIS¹, from its use in political rhetoric, the actual sense being lost; taken as euphemism for BULLSHIT]

bush·whack (bŏŏsh′hwak′, -wak′), *v.i.* **1.** to make one's way through woods by cutting at undergrowth, branches, etc. **2.** to travel through woods. **3.** to pull a boat upstream from on board by grasping bushes, rocks, etc., on the shore. **4.** to fight as a bushwhacker or guerrilla in the bush. *—v.t.* **5.** to fight as a bushwhacker; ambush. **6.** to defeat, esp. by surprise or in an underhanded way: *They bushwhacked our high school team when they used college players.* [1830–40, *Amer.*; back formation from BUSHWHACKER]

bush·whack·er (bŏŏsh′hwak′ər, -wak′ər), *n.* **1.** a person or thing that bushwhacks. **2.** (in the American Civil War) a guerrilla, esp. a Confederate. **3.** any guerrilla or outlaw. **4.** *Australian Slang.* an unsophisticated person; hick. [1800–10, *Amer.*; BUSH¹ + WHACKER] **—bush′whack′ing,** *n.*

bush·y (bŏŏsh′ē), *adj.,* **bush·i·er, bush·i·est. 1.** resembling a bush; thick and shaggy: *bushy whiskers.* **2.** full of or overgrown with bushes. [1350–1400; ME *bushi.* See BUSH¹, -Y¹] **—bush′i·ly,** *adv.*

bush·y-tailed (bŏŏsh′ē tāld′), *adj.* See **bright-eyed** (def. 3). [1865–70]

bus·i·ly (biz′ə lē), *adv.* in a busy manner; actively. [1175–1225; ME *bisiliche.* See BUSY, -LY]

busi·ness (biz′nis), *n.* **1.** an occupation, profession, or trade: *His business is poultry farming.* **2.** the purchase and sale of goods in an attempt to make a profit. **3.** a person, partnership, or corporation engaged in commerce, manufacturing, or a service; profit-seeking enterprise or concern. **4.** volume of trade; patronage: *Most of the store's business comes from local families.* **5.** a building or site where commercial work is carried on, as a factory, store, or office; place of work: *His business is on the corner of Broadway and Elm Street.* **6.** that with which a person is principally and seriously concerned: *Words are a writer's business.* **7.** something with which a person is rightfully concerned: *What they are doing is none of my business.* **8.** affair; project: *We were exasperated by the whole business.* **9.** an assignment or task; chore: *It's your business to wash the dishes now.* **10.** Also called **piece of business, stage business.** *Theat.* a movement or gesture, esp. a minor one, used by an actor to give expressiveness, drama, detail, etc., to a scene or to help portray a character. **11.** excrement: used as a euphemism. **12. business is business,** profit has precedence over personal considerations: *He is reluctant to fire his friend, but business is business.* **13. do one's business,** (usually of an animal or child) to defecate or urinate: *housebreaking a puppy to do his business outdoors.* **14. get down to business,** to apply oneself to serious matters; concentrate on work: *They finally got down to business and signed the contract.* **15. give someone the business,** *Informal.* **a.** to make difficulties for someone; treat harshly: *Instead of a straight answer they give him the business with a needless runaround.* **b.** to scold severely; give a tongue-lashing to: *The passengers will give the bus driver the business if he keeps driving so recklessly.* **16. have no business,** to have no right: *You have no business coming into this house.* **17. mean business,** to propose to take action or be serious in intent; be in earnest: *By the fire in his eye we knew that he meant business.* **18. mind one's own business,** to refrain from meddling in the affairs of others: *When he inquired about the noise coming from the neighbor's apartment, he was told to mind his own business.* *—adj.* **19.** of, noting, or pertaining to business, its organization, or its procedures. **20.** containing, suitable for, or welcoming business or commerce: *New York is a good business town.* [bef. 950; ME; OE *bisignes.* See BUSY, -NESS]
—Syn. 1. calling, vocation, employment. See **occupation. 2.** commerce, trade, traffic. **3.** company, firm.
—Pronunciation. See **isn't.**

busi′ness administra′tion, a program of studies at the university level offering courses on general business theory, management, and practices. [1905–10]

busi′ness a′gent, a paid union official who represents a local and its membership in dealing with an employer. [1840–50]

busi′ness card′, a small card on which is printed, typically, a person's name, job title, firm, business address, and telephone number. [1830–40]

busi′ness case′, a briefcase or attaché case.

busi′ness class′, a class of accommodations on an airliner, usually just below first class. Also called **executive class.**

busi′ness col′lege, a school for training students in the clerical aspects of business and commerce, as in typing or bookkeeping. [1860–65, *Amer.*]

busi′ness cy′cle, a recurrent fluctuation in the total business activity of a country. [1920–25]

busi′ness dou′ble, *Bridge.* a double made to increase the penalty points earned when a player believes the opponents cannot make their bid. Also called **penalty double.** Cf. **informatory double.**

busi′ness educa′tion, 1. education for general knowledge of business practices. **2.** training in specific skills useful in business, such as typing and shorthand.

busi′ness end′, the front part or end of a tool, weapon, etc., with which the work is done or from which a missile is ejected, as opposed to the handle or butt: *the business end of a revolver; the business end of a screwdriver.* [1875–80]

busi′ness Eng′lish, English in business usage, esp. the styles and forms of business correspondence.

busi′ness en′velope, a postal envelope for standard-size business letters 8½ × 11 in. (20 × 28 cm), measuring about 4½ × 9 in. (11 × 23 cm).

busi·ness·like (biz′nis līk′), *adj.* **1.** conforming to, attending to, or characteristic of business. **2.** efficient, practical, or realistic. **3.** capable but unenthusiastic. [1785–95; BUSINESS + -LIKE]

busi′ness machine′, a machine for expediting clerical work, as a tabulator or adding machine.

busi·ness·man (biz′nis man′), *n., pl.* **-men.** a man regularly employed in business, esp. a white-collar worker, executive, or owner. [1705–15; BUSINESS + MAN¹]

busi′nessman's hol′iday. See **busman's holiday.**

busi′ness park′, 1. See **office park. 2.** See **industrial park.**

busi·ness·peo·ple (biz′nis pē′pəl), *n.pl.* businesspersons collectively.

busi·ness·per·son (biz′nis pûr′sən), *n.* a person regularly employed in business, esp. a white-collar worker, executive, or owner. [1970–75, *Amer.*; BUSINESS(MAN) + -PERSON]
—Usage. See **-person.**

busi′ness reply′, a form of mail, as a postcard, letter, or envelope, usually sent as an enclosure, and which can be mailed back by respondents without their having to pay postage.

busi′ness suit′, a suit, esp. one of conservative cut and color. Cf. **suit** (defs. 2, 3). [1865–70, *Amer.*]

busi′ness un′ionism, the trade-union philosophy and activity that concentrates on the improvement of wages, hours, working conditions, etc., rather than on the general reform of the capitalistic system.

busi·ness·wom·an (biz′nis wŏŏm′ən), *n., pl.* **-wom·en.** a woman regularly employed in business, esp. a white-collar worker, executive, or owner. [1835–45, *Amer.*; BUSINESS + -WOMAN]

bus·ing (bus′ing), *n.* the transporting of public-school students by bus to schools outside their neighborhoods, esp. as a means of achieving racial balance. Also, **bus′·sing.** [1885–90; BUS¹ (v.) + -ING¹, spelled irreg. with single *s,* perh. to avoid association with BUSS¹]

busk (busk), *v.i.* **1.** *Chiefly Brit.* to entertain by dancing, singing, or reciting on the street or in a public place. **2.** *Canadian.* to make a showy or noisy appeal. [1850–55; perh., if earlier sense was "to make a living by entertaining," < Polari < It *buscare* to procure < Sp *buscar* to look for, seek (of disputed orig.)] **—busk′er,** *n.*

bus·kin (bus′kin), *n.* **1.** a thick-soled, laced boot or half boot. **2.** Also called **cothurnus.** the high, thick-soled shoe worn by ancient Greek and Roman tragedians. **3. buskins,** stockings decorated with gold thread worn by a bishop at a Pontifical Mass. **4.** tragic drama; tragedy. Cf. **sock**¹ (def. 3). **5.** the art of acting, esp. tragic acting. **6.** a woman's low-cut shoe with elastic gores at the sides of the instep, popular in the early 20th century. [1495–1505; prob. alter. of MF *bro(u)sequin,* of uncert. orig.]

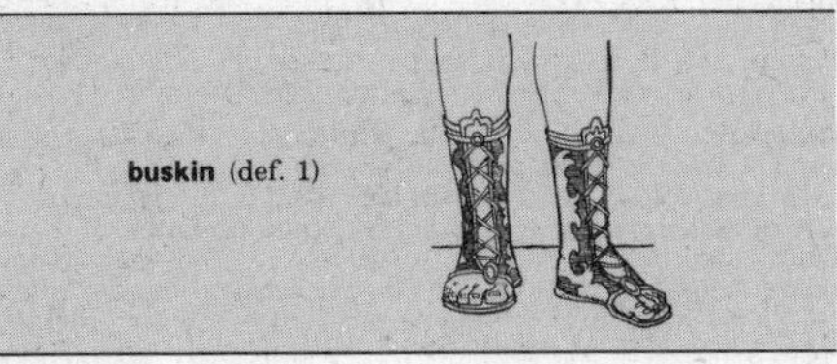
buskin (def. 1)

bus·kined (bus′kind), *adj.* **1.** wearing buskins. **2.** resembling or pertaining to tragic drama. [1580–90; BUSKIN + -ED³]

bus′ line′, 1. the route of a bus or buses. **2.** a company that owns and operates buses.

bus·load (bus′lōd′), *n.* an amount or number as great as a bus can hold. [BUS¹ + LOAD]

bus·man (bus′mən), *n., pl.* **-men.** a person who operates a bus. [1850–55; BUS¹ + -MAN]

bus′man's hol′iday, a vacation or day off from work spent in an activity closely resembling one's work, as a bus driver taking a long drive. [1890–95]

Bu·so·ni (byŏŏ sō′nē; *It.* bōō zô′nē), *n.* **Fer·ruc·cio (Ben·ve·nu·to)** (feʀ ʀōōt′chô ben′ve nōō′tô), 1866–1924, Italian composer and pianist.

Bus·ra (bus′rə), *n.* Basra. Also, **Bus′rah.**

buss (bus), *n., v.t., v.i.* kiss. [1560–70; perh. b. obs. *bass* kiss and obs. *cuss* kiss (c. G *Kuss;* r. ME, OE *coss* (c. ON *koss*))]

bus·ses (bus′iz), *n.* a plural of **bus¹.**

bust¹ (bust), *n.* **1.** a sculptured, painted, drawn, or engraved representation of the upper part of the human figure, esp. a portrait sculpture showing only the head and shoulders of the subject. **2.** the chest or breast, esp. a woman's bosom. [1685–95; < F *buste* < It *busto,* prob. < L *būstum* grave mound, tomb, lit., funeral pyre, ashes; presumably by assoc. with the busts erected over graves]

bust² (bust), *v.i.* **1.** *Informal.* **a.** to burst. **b.** to go bankrupt. **c.** to collapse from the strain of making a supreme effort: *She was determined to make straight A's or bust.* **2.** *Cards.* **a.** *Draw Poker.* to fail to make a flush or straight by one card. **b.** *Blackjack.* to draw cards exceeding the count of 21. *—v.t.* **3.** *Informal.* **a.** to burst. **b.** to bankrupt; ruin financially. **4.** to demote, esp. in military rank or grade: *He was busted from sergeant to private three times.* **5.** to tame; break: *to bust a bronco.* **6.** *Slang.* **a.** to place under arrest: *The gang was busted and put away on narcotics charges.* **b.** to subject to a police raid: *The bar has been busted three times for selling drinks to minors.* **7.** *Informal.* **a.** to hit. **b.** to break; fracture: *She fell and busted her arm.* **8. bust ass,** *Slang (vulgar).* to fight with the fists; strike or thrash another. **9. bust on,** *Slang.* **a.** to attack physically; beat up. **b.** to criticize or reprimand harshly. **c.** to make fun of or laugh at; mock. **d.** to inform on. **10. bust one's ass,** *Slang (vulgar).* to make an extreme effort; exert oneself. **11. bust up,** *Informal.* **a.** to break up; separate: *Sam and his wife busted up a year ago.* **b.** to damage or destroy: *Soldiers got in a fight and busted up the bar.* *—n.* **12.** a failure. **13.** *Informal.* a hit; sock; punch: *He got a bust in the nose before he could put up his hands.* **14.** a sudden decline in the economic conditions of a country, marked by an extreme drop in stock-market prices, business activity, and employment; depression. **15.** *Slang.* **a.** an arrest. **b.** a police raid. **16.** *Informal.* a drinking spree; binge. **17.** *Cards.* **a.** a very weak hand. **b.** *Bridge.* a hand lacking the potential to take a single trick. *—adj.* **18.** *Informal.* bankrupt; broke. [1755–65; var. of BURST, by loss of *r* before *s,* as in ASS², BASS², PASSEL, etc.]
—Usage. Historically BUST is derived from a dialect pronunciation of BURST and is related to it much as *cuss* is related to *curse.* BUST is both a noun and a verb and has a wide range of meanings for both uses. Many are slang or informal. A few, as "a decline in economic conditions, depression," are standard.

Bus·ta·man·te (bŏŏs′tə män′tā; *for 1 also Sp.* bōōs′-tä män′te), *n.* **1. A·nas·ta·sio** (ä′näs tä′syô), 1780–1853, Mexican military and political leader: president 1830–32, 1837–41. **2. Sir (William) Alexander,** 1884–1977, Jamaican political leader: prime minister 1962–67.

bus·tard (bus′tərd), *n.* any of several large, chiefly terrestrial and ground-running birds of the family Otididae, of the Old World and Australia, related to the cranes. [1425–75; late ME, appar. b. MF *bistarde* (OIt *bistarda*) and MF *oustarde,* both < L *avis tarda* (Pliny) lit., slow bird, though *tarda* may be a non-L word, taken erroneously as fem. of *tardus*]

bus′tard quail′. See **button quail.**

bus·tee (bus′tē), *n. India.* **1.** a small settlement; village. **2.** a slum. Also, **bus′ti.** [1880–85; < Hindi *bastī,* akin to *basnā* to dwell]

bust·er (bus′tər), *n. Informal.* **1.** a person who breaks up something: *crime busters.* **2.** something that is very big or unusual for its kind. **3.** a loud, uproarious reveler. **4.** a frolic; spree. **5.** (*cap.*) (used as a familiar term of address to a man or boy who is an object to the speaker's annoyance or anger): *Look, Buster, you're standing in my way!* [1825–35, *Amer.*; BUST² + -ER¹]

Bus·ter (bus′tər), *n.* a male given name.

CONCISE PRONUNCIATION KEY: *act, cāpe, dâre, pärt; set, ēqual; if, īce; ox, ōver, ôrder, oil, bŏŏk, bōōt, out; up, ûrge; child; sing; shoe; thin, that;* zh as in *treasure.* ə = *a* as in *alone, e* as in *system, i* as in *easily, o* as in *gallop, u* as in *circus;* ᵊ as in *fire* (fīᵊr), *hour* (ouᵊr). l and n can serve as syllabic consonants, as in *cradle* (krād′l), and *button* (but′n). See the full key inside the front cover.

Bus′ter Brown′ col′lar, a medium-sized, starched collar with rounded edges, lying flat on the shoulders, worn by women and girls. [after *Buster Brown,* a comic-strip boy drawn by Richard F. Outcault (1863–1928), U.S. cartoonist]

bus·tier (bo͞os tyā′), *n.* a woman's close-fitting, sleeveless, strapless top, often elasticized, usually having boning or facing to give it shape, and worn as a blouse. [< F, orig. an undergarment so tailored; see BUST[1], -IER[2]]

bus·tle[1] (bus′əl), *v.,* **-tled, -tling,** *n.* —*v.i.* **1.** to move or act with a great show of energy (often fol. by *about*): *He bustled about cooking breakfast.* **2.** to abound or teem with something; display an abundance of something; teem (often fol. by *with*): *The office bustled with people and activity.* —*v.t.* **3.** to cause to bustle; hustle. —*n.* **4.** thriving or energetic activity; stir; ferment. [1615–25; ME *bustelen* to hurry aimlessly along, perh. akin to ON *busla* to splash about, bustle] —**bus′tler,** *n.* —**bus′tling·ly,** *adv.*
—**Syn. 4.** ado, flurry, agitation, fuss.

bus·tle[2] (bus′əl), *n.* **1.** fullness around or below the waist of a dress, as added by a peplum, bows, ruffles, etc. **2.** a pad, cushion, or framework formerly worn under the back of a woman's skirt to expand, support, and display the full cut and drape of a dress. [1780–90; orig. uncert.] —**bus′tled,** *adj.*

bus′tle pipe′, *Metall.* (in a blast furnace) an annular pipe distributing hot air to the tuyères.

bust·line (bust′līn′), *n.* **1.** the outline or shape of a woman's bust. **2.** the part of a garment covering the breasts: *a dress with a fitted bustline.* [1935–40; BUST[1] + LINE[1]]

bust-up (bust′up′), *n. Informal.* **1.** a separation or dissolution, as of a marriage or a close friendship. **2.** a large party, esp. a noisy one. **3.** *Chiefly Brit.* a quarrel; disturbance; punch-up. [1840–50; n. use of v. phrase *bust up*]

bust·y (bus′tē), *adj.,* **bust·i·er, bust·i·est.** *Informal.* (of a woman) having a large bust; bosomy. [1940–45; BUST[1] + -Y[1]] —**bust′i·ness,** *n.*

bu·sul·fan (byo͞o sul′fən), *n. Pharm.* a potent cytotoxic substance, $C_6H_{14}O_6S_2$, used in the treatment of chronic myeloid leukemia. [1955–60; *bu(tanediol dimethane) sulf(onate)* its chemical name + *-an* perh. orig. var. of -ANE]

bus·way (bus′wā′), *n.* a highway, or lane of a highway, set aside for the exclusive use of buses, esp. during peak traffic hours. [1960–65, *Amer.*; BUS + WAY[1]]

bus·y (biz′ē), *adj.,* **bus·i·er, bus·i·est,** *v.,* **bus·ied, bus·y·ing.** —*adj.* **1.** actively and attentively engaged in work or a pastime: *busy with her work.* **2.** not at leisure; otherwise engaged: *He couldn't see any visitors because he was busy.* **3.** full of or characterized by activity: *a busy life.* **4.** (of a telephone line) in use by a party or parties and not immediately accessible. **5.** officious; meddlesome; prying. **6.** ornate, disparate, or clashing in design or colors; cluttered with small, unharmonious details; fussy: *The rug is too busy for this room.* —*v.t.* **7.** to keep occupied; make or keep busy: *In summer, he busied himself keeping the lawn in order.* [bef. 1000; ME *busi, bisi,* OE *bysig, bisig;* c. MLG, MD *besich,* D *bezig*]
—**Syn. 1.** assiduous, hard-working. BUSY, DILIGENT, INDUSTRIOUS imply active or earnest effort to accomplish something, or a habitual attitude of such earnestness. BUSY means actively employed, temporarily or habitually: *a busy official.* DILIGENT suggests earnest and constant effort or application, and usually connotes fondness for, or enjoyment of, what one is doing: *a diligent student.* INDUSTRIOUS often implies a habitual characteristic of steady and zealous application, often with a definite goal: *an industrious clerk working for promotion.* **2.** occupied, employed, working. —**Ant. 1.** indolent. **2.** unoccupied.

bus·y·bod·y (biz′ē bod′ē), *n., pl.* **-bod·ies.** a person who pries into or meddles in the affairs of others. [1520–30; BUSY + BODY]
—**Syn.** snoop, pry, meddler, Nosy Parker; gossip, blabbermouth.

bus·y·ness (biz′ē nis), *n.* **1.** the quality or condition of being busy. **2.** lively but meaningless activity. [1840–50; BUSY + -NESS]

bus′y sig′nal, *Teleph.* a regular succession of buzzing tones transmitted to a caller to indicate that the circuit serving the number is blocked or in use, rapid repetition indicating that the network is blocked and normal repetition that the telephone being called is in use. [1890–95]

bus·y·work (biz′ē wûrk′), *n.* work assigned for the sake of looking or keeping busy. [1840–50; BUSY + WORK]

but[1] (but; *unstressed* bət), *conj.* **1.** on the contrary; yet: *My brother went, but I did not.* **2.** except; save: *She was so overcome with grief she could do nothing but weep.* **3.** unless; if not; except that (fol. by a clause, often with *that* expressed): *Nothing would do but that I should come in.* **4.** without the circumstance that: *It never rains but it pours.* **5.** otherwise than: *There is no hope but by prayer.* **6.** that (used esp. after *doubt, deny,* etc., with a negative): *I don't doubt but he will do it.* **7.** who not; that not: *No leaders worthy of the name ever existed but they were optimists.* **8.** (used as an intensifier to introduce an exclamatory expression): *But she's beautiful!* **9.** *Informal.* than: *It no sooner started raining but it stopped.* **10. but what.** See **what** (def. 31). —*prep.* **11.** with the exception of; except; save: *No one replied but me.* —*adv.* **12.** only; just: *There is but one God.* **13. but for,** except for; were it not for: *But for the excessive humidity, it might have been a pleasant day.* —*n.* **14. buts,** reservations or objections: *You'll do as you're told, no buts about it.* [bef. 900; ME *buten,* OE *būtan* for phrase *be ūtan* on the outside, without. See BY, OUT]
—**Syn. 1.** BUT, HOWEVER, NEVERTHELESS, STILL, YET are words implying opposition (with a possible concession). BUT marks an opposition or contrast, though in a casual way: *We are going, but we shall return.* HOWEVER indicates a less marked opposition, but displays a second consideration to be compared with the first: *We are going; however ("notice this also"), we shall return.* NEVERTHELESS implies a concession, something which should not be forgotten in making a summing up: *We are going; nevertheless ("do not forget that"), we shall return.* STILL implies that in spite of a preceding concession, something must be considered as possible or even inevitable: *We have to go on foot; still ("it is probable and possible that"), we'll get there.* YET implies that in spite of a preceding concession, there is still a chance for a different outcome: *We are going; yet ("in spite of all, some day"), we shall return.* **2.** See **except**[1].
—**Usage. 1.** BUT, like *and,* is a common transitional word and often begins sentences. When it is used in the middle of a sentence as a coordinating conjunction like *and* or *so,* it is not followed by a comma unless the comma is one of a pair setting off a parenthetical expression: *His political affiliations make no difference, but his lack of ethics does. The cast is nearly complete, but, our efforts notwithstanding, we lack a star.* See also **and, so**[1].
2, 11. When BUT is understood as a conjunction and the pronoun following it is understood as the subject of an incompletely expressed clause, the pronoun is in the subjective case: *Everyone lost faith in the plan but she (did not lose faith).* In virtually identical contexts, when BUT is understood as a preposition, the pronoun following it is in the objective case: *Everyone lost faith but her.* The prepositional use is more common. However, when prepositional BUT and its following pronoun occur near the beginning of a sentence, the subjective case often appears: *Everyone but she lost faith in the plan.* See also **doubt, than.**

but[2] (but), *n. Scot.* **1.** the outer or front room of a house; the outer or front apartment in an apartment house. **2.** the kitchen of a two-room dwelling, esp. of a cottage. [1715–25; n. use of BUT[1] (adv.) outside, outside the house]

but[3] (but), butt[5].

bu·ta·bar′bi·tal so′dium (byo͞o′tə bär′bi tôl′, -tal′), *Pharm.* a barbiturate, $C_{10}H_{15}N_2NaO_3$, used as a sedative and hypnotic. Also called **sodium butabarbital.** [based on the names of the chemical components BUTYL and BARBITURIC ACID]

bu·ta·di·ene (byo͞o′tə dī′ēn, -dī ēn′), *n. Chem.* a colorless, flammable gas, C_4H_6, soluble in alcohol but not in water, usually derived from butane or butene: used chiefly in the manufacture of rubber and paint, and in organic synthesis. Also called **bivinyl, vinylethylene.** [1895–1900; BUTA(NE) + DI-[1] + -ENE]

bu·tane (byo͞o′tān, byo͞o tān′), *n. Chem.* a colorless, flammable gas, C_4H_{10}, a saturated aliphatic existing in two isometric forms: used chiefly in the manufacture of rubber and as fuel. [1870–75; BUT(YL) + -ANE]

bu′ta·no′ic ac′id (byo͞ot′n ō′ik, byo͞ot′-), *Chem.* See **butyric acid.**

bu·ta·nol (byo͞ot′n ôl′, -ol′), *n. Chem.* See **butyl alcohol.** [1890–95; BUTANE + -OL[1]]

bu·ta·none (byo͞ot′n ōn′), *n. Chem.* See **methyl ethyl ketone.** [1900–05; BUTANE + -ONE]

Bu·ta·zol·i·din (byo͞o′tə zol′i din), *Pharm., Trademark.* a brand of phenylbutazone.

butch (bo͝och), *n.* **1.** See **butch haircut. 2.** *Slang.* a lesbian, esp. one notably masculine in manner or appearance. —*adj.* **3.** *Slang.* **a.** (of a girl or woman) having traits of personality, dress, behavior, or appearance usually associated with males. **b.** (of a male) decidedly or exaggeratedly masculine in manner or appearance. [1940–45; appar. from the proper name]

Butch (bo͝och), *n.* a male given name.

butch·er (bo͝och′ər), *n.* **1.** a retail or wholesale dealer in meat. **2.** a person who slaughters certain animals, or who dresses the flesh of animals, fish, or poultry, for food or market. **3.** a person guilty of brutal or indiscriminate slaughter or murder. **4.** a vendor who hawks newspapers, candy, beverages, etc., as on a train, at a stadium, etc. —*v.t.* **5.** to slaughter or dress (animals, fish, or poultry) for market. **6.** to kill indiscriminately or brutally. **7.** to bungle; botch: *to butcher a job.* [1250–1300; ME *bocher* < AF; OF *bo(u)chier,* equiv. to *bo(u)c* he-goat (< Gaulish **bucco-;* cf. OIr *boc,* Welsh *bwch;* akin to BUCK[1]) + *-ier* -IER[2] (see -ER[2])] —**butch′er·er,** *n.*
—**Syn. 3.** killer, cutthroat. **5, 6.** See **slaughter.**

butch·er·bird (bo͝och′ər bûrd′), *n.* **1.** any of various shrikes of the genus *Lanius,* which impale their prey upon thorns. **2.** any of several large, carnivorous birds of the genus *Cracticus,* of Australia and New Guinea, having shrikelike habits. [1660–70; BUTCHER + BIRD]

butch′er block′, 1. a slab of wood resembling that used for a butcher's chopping block, formed by bonding or gluing together thick laminated strips of unpainted wood, usually maple or oak, in alternating light and dark shades to produce a striped pattern. **2.** a material, as vinyl, made to resemble butcher block in color and pattern. [1835–45] —**butch′er-block′,** *adj.*

butch′er knife′, a large, very sharp knife for cutting or trimming meat. [1705–15, *Amer.*]

butch′er lin′en, a strong, heavy fabric made of rayon or rayon and cotton with a linen finish, constructed in plain weave. Also called **butch′er ray′on.**

butch·er·ly (bo͝och′ər lē), *adj.* like, or characteristic of, a butcher. [1505–15; BUTCHER + -LY] —**butch′er·li·ness,** *n.*

butch′er pa′per, heavy, moisture-resistant paper, as used for wrapping meat.

butch·er's-broom (bo͝och′ərz bro͞om′, -bro͝om′), *n.* a shrubby European evergreen, *Ruscus aculeatus,* of the lily family: used for making brooms. [1555–65]

butch′er shop′, a shop in which meat, poultry, and sometimes fish are sold. [1895–1900, *Amer.*]

butch′er's saw′, a type of hacksaw used esp. by butchers for cutting through meat and bones. See illus. under **saw.**

butch·er·y (bo͝och′ə rē), *n., pl.* **-er·ies. 1.** a slaughterhouse. **2.** brutal or wanton slaughter of animals or humans; carnage. **3.** the trade or business of a butcher. **4.** the act of bungling or botching. [1300–50; ME *bocherie* < AF, MF *boucherie.* See BUTCHER, -Y[3]]

butch′ hair′cut, 1. a short haircut for men, similar to a crew cut. **2.** a haircut for women in which the hair is cropped relatively short. Also called **butch.**

butch·y (bo͝och′ē), *adj.,* **butch·i·er, butch·i·est.** *Slang.* butch. [BUTCH + -Y[1]]

bute (byo͞ot), *n. Slang.* phenylbutazone. [1965–70; by shortening]

Bute (byo͞ot), *n.* **1.** Also, **Bute·shire** (byo͞ot′shēr, -shər). a historic county in SW Scotland, composed of three islands in the Firth of Clyde. **2.** an island in the Firth of Clyde, in SW Scotland: part of the county Bute. 7733; 50 sq. mi. (130 sq. km).

Bu·te·nandt (bo͞ot′n änt′), *n.* **A·dolf Frie·drich Jo·hann** (ä′dôlf frē′drikh yō′hän), born 1903, German chemist: declined 1939 Nobel prize on the demand of the Nazi government.

bu·tene (byo͞o′tēn), *n. Chem.* butylene (def. 1). [BU-T(YL) + -ENE]

bu·te·o (byo͞o′tē ō′), *n., pl.* **-te·os.** any of several buzzards or hawks of the genus *Buteo.* [1905–10; < NL; L *būteō* a kind of hawk or falcon] —**bu·te·o·nine** (byo͞o′tē ō nīn′, -nin, byo͞o tē′-), *adj., n.*

but·ler (but′lər), *n.* **1.** the chief male servant of a household, usually in charge of serving food, the care of silverware, etc. **2.** a male servant having charge of the wines and liquors. [1250–1300; ME *buteler* < AF *butuiller,* OF *bouteillier;* see BOTTLE[1], -ER[2], -IER[2]] —**but′ler·like′,** *adj.* —**but′ler·ship′,** *n.*

But·ler (but′lər), *n.* **1. Benjamin Franklin,** 1818–93, U.S. politician and a Union general in the Civil War. **2. Joseph,** 1692–1752, English bishop, theologian, and author. **3. Nicholas Murray,** 1862–1947, U.S. educator: president of Columbia University 1902–45; Nobel peace prize 1931. **4. Pierce,** 1866–1939, U.S. jurist: associate justice of the U.S. Supreme Court 1923–39. **5. Samuel,** 1612–80, English poet. **6. Samuel,** 1835–1902, English novelist, essayist, and satirist. **7. Smedley Dar·ling·ton** (smed′lē där′ling tən), 1881–1940, U.S. Marine Corps general. **8.** a city in W Pennsylvania. 17,026.

but·ler·age (but′lər ij), *n. Old Eng. Law.* the privilege allowed the king's butler to take a certain quantity of every cask of wine imported by an alien. Cf. **prisage.** [1485–95; BUTLER + -AGE]

but′ler's pan′try, a service room between a kitchen and dining room, typically equipped with counters, a sink, and storage space for china and silver. [1810–20]

but′ler's side′board, a sideboard, often with a fall front, having on its top a china cabinet with glazed doors.

but′ler's ta′ble, a small table, usually used as a coffee table, with a removable or fixed butler's tray for a top.

but′ler's tray′, a rectangular tray, usually of mahogany or similar wood, with hinged sides that may be folded down to form a flat oval.

but·ler·y (but′lə rē), *n., pl.* **-ler·ies.** a butler's room or pantry; buttery. [1250–1300; ME *botelerie.* See BUTLER, -Y[3]]

bu·tor·pha·nol (byo͞o tôr′fə nôl′, -nol′), *n. Pharm.* a narcotic analgesic, $C_{21}H_{29}NO_2$, administered by injection to treat moderate to severe pain. [as contr. of the chemical name *17-(cyclobutylmethyl)morphinan-3,14-diol*]

but·su (bo͞ot′so͞o, bo͞ot′-; *Japn.* bo͞o′tso͞o), *n., pl.* **-su** for 1. **1.** a representation of the Buddha. **2.** (*cap.*) Buddha (def. 1). [< Japn, ult. < MChin (equiv. to Chin *fó* Buddha) < Skt *buddha* BUDDHA]

butt[1] (but), *n.* **1.** the end or extremity of anything, esp. the thicker, larger, or blunt end considered as a bottom, base, support, or handle, as of a log, fishing rod, or pistol. **2.** an end that is not used or consumed; remnant: *a cigar butt.* **3.** a lean cut of pork shoulder. **4.** *Slang.* the buttocks. **5.** *Slang.* a cigarette. [1400–50; late ME *butt* (thick) end, buttock, OE *butt* tree stump (in place names); akin to Sw *but* stump, Dan *but* stubby; cf. BUTTOCK]

butt[2] (but), *n.* **1.** a person or thing that is an object of wit, ridicule, sarcasm, contempt, etc. **2.** a target. **3.** (on a rifle range) **a.** a wall of earth located behind the targets to prevent bullets from scattering over a large area. **b. butts,** a wall behind which targets can be safely lowered, scored, and raised during firing practice. **4.** See **butt hinge. 5.** *Obs.* a goal; limit. —*v.i.* **6.** to have an end or projection on; be adjacent to; abut. —*v.t.* **7.** to position or fasten an end (of something). **8.** to place or join the ends (of two things) together; set end-to-end. [1350–1400; ME < MF *but* target, goal, prob. << ON *bútr* BUTT[1], from the use of a wooden block or stump as a target in archery, etc.]
—**Syn. 1.** victim, target, mark, dupe, gull, laughingstock, prey, pigeon, patsy.

butt[3] (but), *v.t.* **1.** to strike or push with the head or horns. —*v.i.* **2.** to strike or push something or at something with the head or horns. **3.** to project. **4.** *Mach.* (of wheels in a gear train) to strike one another instead

CONCISE ETYMOLOGY KEY: <, descended or borrowed from; >, whence; b., blend of, blended; c., cognate with; cf., compare; deriv., derivative; equiv., equivalent; imit., imitative; obl., oblique; r., replacing; s., stem; sp., spelling, spelled; resp., respelling, respelled; trans., translation; ?, origin unknown; *, unattested; ‡, probably earlier than. See the full key inside the front cover.

of meshing. **5. butt in,** to meddle in the affairs or intrude in the conversation of others; interfere: *It was none of his concern, so he didn't butt in.* **6. butt out,** to stop meddling in the affairs or intruding in the conversation of others: *Nobody asked her opinion, so she butted out.* —*n.* **7.** a push or blow with the head or horns. [1150–1200; ME *butten* < AF *buter,* OF *boter* to thrust, strike < Gmc; cf. MD *botten* to strike, sprout]

butt[4] (but), *n.* **1.** a large cask for wine, beer, or ale. **2.** any cask or barrel. **3.** any of various units of capacity, usually considered equal to two hogsheads. [1350–1400; ME *bote* < AF *bo(u)t(e);* MF < OPr *bota* < LL *butta, buttis,* akin to Gk *boût(t)is*]

butt[5] (but), any of several flatfishes, esp. the halibut. Also, **but.** [1250–1300; ME *butte;* c. Sw *butta* turbot, G *Butt* brill, turbot, flounder, D *bot* flounder]

but·tals (but′lz), *n.pl. Law.* abuttal (def. 1b).

butt′ chis′el, any woodworking chisel having a blade less than 4 in. (10 cm) long.

butte (byo͞ot), *n. Western U.S. and Canada.* an isolated hill or mountain rising abruptly above the surrounding land. [1650–60, *Amer.;* < North American F; F: low hill, OF: landmark, target, appar. fem. deriv. of *but* BUTT[2]]

Butte (byo͞ot), *n.* a city in SW Montana: mining center. 37,205.

butt′ end′, butt[1] (defs. 1, 2). [1950–55]

but·ter (but′ər), *n.* **1.** the fatty portion of milk, separating as a soft whitish or yellowish solid when milk or cream is agitated or churned. **2.** this substance, processed for cooking and table use. **3.** any of various other soft spreads for bread: *apple butter; peanut butter.* **4.** any of various substances of butterlike consistency, as various metallic chlorides, and certain vegetable oils solid at ordinary temperatures. —*v.t.* **5.** to put butter on or in; spread or grease with butter. **6.** to apply a liquefied bonding material to (a piece or area), as mortar to a course of bricks. **7.** *Metalworking.* to cover (edges to be welded together) with a preliminary surface of the weld metal. **8. butter up,** *Informal.* to flatter someone in order to gain a favor: *He suspected that they were buttering him up when everyone suddenly started being nice to him.* [bef. 1000; ME; OE *butere* < L *būtȳrum* < Gk *boútȳron*] —**but′ter·less,** *adj.* —**but′ter·like′,** *adj.*

but′ter-and-egg′ man′ (but′ər ən eg′), *Older Slang.* a prosperous businessman from a small town or a farmer who spends his money ostentatiously on visits to a big city. [1920–25, *Amer.*]

but·ter-and-eggs (but′ər ən egz′), *n., pl.* **but·ter-and-eggs.** (*used with a singular or plural v.*) any of certain plants whose flowers are of two shades of yellow, as the toadflax, *Linaria vulgaris.* [1770–80]

but·ter·ball (but′ər bôl′), *n.* **1.** *Northeastern U.S.* the bufflehead. **2.** *Informal.* a chubby person. **3.** an individual serving of butter shaped into a small sphere. [1930–35; BUTTER + BALL[1]]

but′ter bean′, **1.** a variety of small-seeded lima bean, *Phaseolus lunatus,* grown in the southern U.S. **2.** *Midland and Southern U.S.* any type of lima bean. Also, **but′ter·bean′.** [1810–20]

but·ter·bread (but′ər bred′), *n. Chiefly Pennsylvania.* bread spread with butter. [1905–10; a calque of the PaG equivalent of G *Butterbrot;* see BUTTER, BREAD]

but′ter brick′le, an ice-cream flavor, usually vanilla or butterscotch, containing crunchy bits of butterscotch candy.

but·ter·bur (but′ər bûr′), *n.* any of several composite plants of the genus *Petasites,* having large, woolly leaves said to have been used to wrap butter. [1540–50; BUTTER + BUR[1]]

but′ter clam′, a large edible clam, *Saxidomus nuttalli,* of the west coast of North America. Also called **Washington clam, money shell.** [1935–40]

but′ter cook′ie, *Cookery.* a plain cookie whose chief ingredients are butter, flour, and sugar.

but·ter·cream (but′ər krēm′), *n.* **1.** a vanilla-flavored cake frosting or filling made principally of softened butter and powdered sugar. **2.** a similar mixture used as a filling for bonbons or to flavor ice cream. [1950–55; BUTTER + CREAM]

but·ter·cup (but′ər kup′), *n.* any of numerous plants of the genus *Ranunculus,* having glossy yellow flowers and deeply cut leaves. [1505–15; BUTTER + CUP, from color and shape of flower]

but′tercup fam′ily, the plant family Ranunculaceae, typified by mostly herbaceous plants having usually alternate leaves, multistaminate flowers sometimes lacking petals but with colorful sepals, and including the anemone, buttercup, clematis, columbine, delphinium, and monkshood.

but′tercup squash′, a small, usually dark-green squash that is a variety of *Cucurbita maxima,* having sweet orange flesh.

but·ter·fat (but′ər fat′), *n.* butter; milk fat; a mixture of glycerides, mainly butyrin, olein, and palmitin. [1885–90; BUTTER + FAT]

but·ter·fin·gers (but′ər fing′gərz), *n., pl.* **-gers.** (*used with a singular v.*) a person who frequently drops things; clumsy person. [1830–40; BUTTER + FINGER + -S[3]] —**but′ter·fin′gered,** *adj.*

but·ter·fish (but′ər fish′), *n., pl.* (*esp. collectively*) **-fish,** (*esp. referring to two or more kinds or species*) **-fish·es.** **1.** a small, flattened, marine food fish, *Peprilus triacanthus,* of Atlantic coastal waters of the U.S., having very small scales and smooth skin. **2.** the rock gunnel. See under **gunnel**[1]. [1665–75; BUTTER + FISH]

but·ter·fly (but′ər flī′), *n., pl.* **-flies,** *v.,* **-flied, -fly·ing,** *adj.* —*n.* **1.** any of numerous diurnal insects of the order Lepidoptera, characterized by clubbed antennae, a slender body, and large, broad, often conspicuously marked wings. **2.** a person who flits aimlessly from one interest or group to another: *a social butterfly.* **3. butterflies,** (*used with a plural v.*) *Informal.* a queasy feeling, as from nervousness, excitement, etc. **4.** a racing breaststroke, using a dolphin kick, in which the swimmer brings both arms out of the water in forward, circular motions. **5.** *Carpentry.* See **butterfly wedge.** **6.** *Sculpture.* an X-shaped support attached to an armature. **7.** one of the swinging brackets of a butterfly table. **8.** *Motion Pictures.* a screen of scrim, gauze, or similar material, for diffusing light. —*v.t.* **9.** *Cookery.* to slit open and spread apart to resemble the spread wings of a butterfly. —*adj.* Also, **butterflied.** **10.** *Cookery.* split open and spread apart to resemble a butterfly: *butterfly shrimp.* [bef. 1000; ME *boterflye,* OE *buttorflēoge.* See BUTTER, FLY[2]] —**but′ter·fly′like,** *adj., adv.*

but′terfly bomb′, *Mil.* a small, aerial, antipersonnel bomb with two folding wings that revolve, slowing the rate of descent and arming the fuze. [1940–45]

but′terfly bush′, any tropical shrub belonging to the genus *Buddleia,* of the logania family, having clusters of showy lilac, white, or yellow flowers. [1930–35]

but′terfly chair′, a sling chair in which a canvas or leather sling is suspended from a metal frame by its corners, forming a wide back and seat in a shape resembling the outstretched wings of a butterfly. [1950–55]

but′terfly clo′sure, an adhesive bandage resembling the shape of a butterfly's outstretched wings, used for closing minor cuts.

but′terfly damp′er, a damper, as in a flue, that rotates about a central axis across its face.

but′terfly effect′, a cumulatively large effect that a very small natural force may produce over a period of time. [1980–85; so called from the notion that the fluttering of a butterfly's wings may set off currents that will grow into a large storm]

but·ter·fly·fish (but′ər flī′fish′), *n., pl.* (*esp. collectively*) **-fish·es,** (*esp. referring to two or more kinds or species*) **-fish.** **1.** any tropical marine fish of the family Chaetodontidae, having large, broad fins or brilliant coloration, or both. **2.** See **flying gurnard.** **3.** a blenny, *Blennius ocellaris,* of Europe. [1730–40; BUTTERFLY + FISH]

but′terfly flow′er, **1.** Also called **Jerusalem date.** a shrub or small tree, *Bauhinia monandra,* of French Guiana, having clusters of pink, purple-streaked flowers. **2.** schizanthus. [1880–85]

but′terfly net′, a conical net of fine mesh held open by a round rim to which a long handle is attached, used for collecting butterflies and other insects. [1820–30]

but′terfly nut′. See **wing nut.** [1735–45, *Amer.*]

but′terfly or′chid, **1.** an epiphytic South American orchid, *Oncidium papilio,* having large yellow and reddish-brown flowers. **2.** either of two terrestrial Old World orchids, *Habenaria chlorantha* or *H. bifolia,* having long clusters of greenish-white flowers. [1590–1600]

but′terfly pea′, any of several leguminous plants of the genus *Clitoria,* as *C. mariana,* of North America, having pale-blue flowers. [1855–60, *Amer.*]

but′terfly roof′, a roof having more than one slope, each descending inward from the eaves.

but′ter·fly-shell clam′ (but′ər flī shel′), coquina.

but′terfly ta′ble, a small occasional table, usually having a round or oval top, with drop leaves supported by swinging brackets pivoted to the stretchers and to the underside of the top.

but′terfly valve′, **1.** a clack valve having two flaps with a common hinge. **2.** a valve, as the throttle valve in a carburetor, that swings about a central axis across its face. [1860–65]

but′terfly wedge′, *Carpentry.* a wooden fastening in the form of a double dovetail for joining two boards at their edges. Also called **butterfly.**

but′terfly weed′, **1.** Also called **orange milkweed.** a North American milkweed, *Asclepias tuberosa,* having clusters of bright orange flowers. **2.** an erect North American plant, *Gaura coccinea,* of the evening primrose family, having wandlike spikes of white to pink flowers turning red with age. [1810–20, *Amer.*]

but′ter knife′, a small knife with a dull blade, for cutting, serving, or spreading butter. [1840–50]

but·ter·milk (but′ər milk′), *n.* **1.** the more or less acidulous liquid remaining after butter has been separated from milk or cream. **2.** a similar liquid made from whole or skim milk with the addition of a bacterial culture. [1520–30; BUTTER + MILK]

but′termilk sky′, a cloudy sky resembling the mottled or clabbered appearance of buttermilk.

but′ter mus′lin, *Chiefly Brit.* cheesecloth. [1900–05]

but·ter·nut (but′ər nut′), *n.* **1.** Also called **white walnut.** the edible oily nut of an American tree, *Juglans cinerea,* of the walnut family. **2.** the tree itself. **3.** the light-brown wood of this tree, used for making furniture. **4.** the light-brown color resulting from a dye made from this tree. **5.** *U.S. Hist.* a Confederate soldier or partisan, esp. one whose uniform was dyed with an extract from this tree. **6.** See **souari nut.** [1735–45, *Amer.;* so called from the nut's oiliness]

but′ternut squash′, **1.** a yellowish winter squash having sweet, orange-colored flesh. **2.** the plant bearing this fruit.

but′ter of ar′senic. See **arsenic trichloride.**

but·ter·paste (but′ər pāst′), *n.* a mixture of flour and butter kneaded together, used as a thickening for sauces. Also called **kneaded butter.** [BUTTER + PASTE]

but′ter sauce′, a sauce made of melted butter, often diluted with water, sometimes thickened with flour or egg yolk, or both, and seasoned with lemon juice. [1895–1900, *Amer.*]

but·ter·scotch (but′ər skoch′), *n.* **1.** a flavor produced in puddings, frostings, etc., by combining brown sugar, vanilla extract, and butter with other ingredients. **2.** a hard, brittle taffy made with butter, brown sugar, etc. **3.** a golden brown color. —*adj.* **4.** having the flavor of butterscotch. [1850–55; earlier also *butterscot;* the 2d element of the compound is unexplained]

but′ter spread′er, a small knife with a wide, flat blade, as for spreading butter on bread or rolls.

but′ter tree′, any of several tropical trees of the sapodilla family, having seeds that yield a butterlike oil. [1820–30]

but·ter·weed (but′ər wēd′), *n.* **1.** any wild plant having conspicuously yellow flowers or leaves. **2.** the horseweed. **3.** a ragwort (*Senecio jacobaea*) or groundsel (*S. vulgaris*), both having yellow ray flowers. [1885–90; BUTTER + WEED[1]]

but·ter·wort (but′ər wûrt′, -wôrt′), *n.* any small, carnivorous plant of the genus *Pinguicula,* having leaves that secrete a viscid substance in which small insects are caught. [1590–1600; BUTTER + WORT[2]]

but·ter·y[1] (but′ə rē), *adj.* **1.** like, containing, or spread with butter. **2.** resembling butter, as in smoothness or softness of texture: *a vest of buttery leather.* **3.** grossly flattering; smarmy. [1350–1400; ME *buttry.* See BUTTER, -Y[1]] —**but′ter·i·ness,** *n.*

but·ter·y[2] (but′ə rē, bu′trē), *n., pl.* **-ter·ies.** **1.** *Chiefly New Eng.* a room or rooms in which the provisions, wines, and liquors of a household are kept; pantry; larder. **2.** a room in colleges, esp. at Oxford and Cambridge universities, from which articles of food and drink are sold or dispensed to the students. [1350–1400; ME *boterie* < AF, prob. equiv. to *bote* BUTT[4] + *-erie* -ERY]

butt′ hinge′, a hinge for a door or the like, secured to the butting surfaces rather than to the adjacent sides of the door and its frame. Cf. **flap** (def. 20a). See illus. under **hinge.** [1780–90]

but·tie (but′ē), *n. Brit. Dial.* butty.

but·ting (but′ing), *n.* a boundary; limit. [1545–55; BUTT[3] + -ING[1]]

butt·in·sky (but in′skē), *n., pl.* **-skies.** *Slang.* a person who interferes in the affairs of others; meddler. Also, **butt·in′ski.** [1900–05, *Amer.; butt in* intrude + *-sky,* extracted from Slavic surnames]

butt′ joint′, *Building Trades.* a joint formed by two pieces of wood or metal united end to end without overlapping. [1815–25]

but·tle (but′l), *v.i.,* **-tled, -tling.** *Slang.* to work or serve as a butler. [1865–70; back formation from BUTLER]

but·tock (but′ək), *n.* **1.** Usually, **buttocks. a.** (in humans) either of the two fleshy protuberances forming the lower and back part of the trunk. **b.** (in animals) the rump. **2.** Sometimes, **buttocks.** *Naut.* the aftermost portion of a hull above the water line and in front of the rudder, merging with the run below the water line. [bef. 1000; ME *buttok,* OE *buttuc.* See BUTT[1], -OCK] —**but′·tocked,** *adj.*

but·ton (but′n), *n.* **1.** a small disk, knob, or the like for sewing or otherwise attaching to an article, as of clothing, serving as a fastening when passed through a buttonhole or loop. **2.** anything resembling a button, esp. in being small and round, as any of various candies, ornaments, tags, identification badges, reflectors, markers, etc. **3.** a badge or emblem bearing a name, slogan, identifying figure, etc., for wear on the lapel, dress, etc.: *campaign buttons.* **4.** any small knob or disk pressed to activate an electric circuit, release a spring, or otherwise operate or open a machine, small door, toy, etc. **5.** *Bot.* a bud or other protuberant part of a plant. **6.** *Mycol.* **a.** a young or undeveloped mushroom. **b.** any protuberant part of a fungus. **7.** *Zool.* any of various small parts or structures resembling a button, as the rattle at the tip of the tail in a very young rattlesnake. **8.** *Boxing. Informal.* the point of the chin. **9.** Also called **turn button.** a fastener for a door, window, etc., having two arms and rotating on a pivot that is attached to the frame. **10.** *Metall.* (in assaying) a small globule or lump of metal at the bottom of a crucible after fusion. **11.** *Fencing.* the protective, blunting knob fixed to the point of a foil. **12.** *Horol.* crown (def. 19). **13. have all one's buttons,** *Informal.* to be mentally competent, alert, and sane; have all one's wits: *At 106 she still has all her buttons.* **14. on the button,** *Informal.* exactly as desired, expected, specified, etc.: *The prediction for snow was right on the button.* —*v.t.* **15.** to fasten with a button or buttons: *She quickly buttoned her coat.* **16.** to insert (a button) in a buttonhole or loop: *He buttoned the top button of his shirt.* **17.** to provide (something) with a button or buttons. —*v.i.* **18.** to be capable of being buttoned: *This coat buttons, but that one zips.* **19. button up,** *Informal.* **a.** Also, **button one's lip.** to become or keep silent. **b.** to fasten securely; close up. **c.** to fasten fully or put on, esp. an outer garment: *Button up before going out.* **d.** to complete successfully; finish: *The report is all buttoned up.* [1275–1325; ME *boto(u)n* < AF: rosehip, bud, button, stud; MF *boton,* equiv. to *boter* to BUTT[3] + *-on* n. suffix] —**but′ton·er,** *n.* —**but′ton·like′,** *adj.*

But·ton (but′n), *n.* **Richard Tot·ten** (tot′n), (*Dick*), born 1929, U.S. figure skater.

but·ton·bush (but′n bo͝osh′), *n.* a North American shrub, *Cephalanthus occidentalis,* of the madder family, having globular flower heads. [1625–35; BUTTON + BUSH[1]]

but·ton-down (but′n doun′), *adj.* **1.** (of a shirt collar) having buttonholes so it can be buttoned to the body of the shirt. **2.** (of a shirt) having a button-down collar. **3.**

CONCISE PRONUNCIATION KEY: act, cāpe, dâre, pärt; set, ēqual; *if,* īce; ox, ōver, ôrder, oil, bo͝ok, bo͞ot, out; up, ûrge; child; sing; shoe; thin, *that;* zh as in *treasure.* ə = *a* as in *alone, e* as in *system, i* as in *easily, o* as in *gallop, u* as in *circus;* ᵊ as in *fire* (fīᵊr), *hour* (ouᵊr). l and n can serve as syllabic consonants, as in *cradle* (krād′l), and *button* (but′n). See the full key inside the front cover.

(esp. of attitudes, opinions, etc.) extremely conventional; unimaginative. Also, **but′toned-down′.** [1930–35, *Amer.*]

but′ton ear′, a dog's ear that folds forward completely. [1880–85] —**but′ton-eared′,** *adj.*

but·toned-up (but′nd up′), *adj.* **1.** carefully planned, operated, supervised, etc.: *one of the most buttoned-up companies in the business.* **2.** conservative, as in professional style or manner: *Employers are looking for buttoned-up types.* [1935–40]

but·ton·hole (but′n hōl′), *n., v.,* **-holed, -hol·ing.** —*n.* **1.** the hole, slit, or loop through which a button is passed and by which it is secured. **2.** *Chiefly Brit.* a boutonniere. **3.** *Surg.* a short, straight incision through the wall of a cavity or a canal. —*v.t.* **4.** to sew with a buttonhole stitch. **5.** to make buttonholes in. **6.** to hold by the buttonhole or otherwise abruptly detain (someone) in conversation: *The reporter tried to buttonhole the mayor for a statement on the bus strike.* [1555–65; BUTTON + HOLE] —**but′ton·hol′er,** *n.*

but′tonhole stitch′, *Sewing.* a looped stitch used to strengthen the edge of material and keep it from raveling, as around a buttonhole. Also called **close stitch.** [1885–90]

but·ton·hook (but′n ho͝ok′), *n.* a small, usually metal hook for pulling buttons through buttonholes, as on gloves, dresses, etc. [1865–70; BUTTON + HOOK]

but·ton·less (but′n lis), *adj.* having no button or buttons. [1645–55; BUTTON + -LESS]

but′ton man′, *Slang.* soldier (def. 5). [1970–75]

but′ton man′grove, a tropical tree, *Conocarpus erectus,* having small, reddish, conelike fruits and bark used in tanning.

but·ton·mold (but′n mōld′), *n.* a small disk or knob of wood, metal, plastic, etc., to be covered with fabric to form an ornamental button. [BUTTON + MOLD[1]]

but′ton quail′, 1. any of several birds of the family Turnicidae, of warmer parts of the Old World, resembling but not related to the true quail. Also called **bustard quail, hemipode. 2.** the blue-breasted quail, *Coturnix chinensis.* [1880–85]

but·tons (but′nz), *n.* (*used with a singular v.*) *Chiefly Brit.* a bellboy or page in a hotel. [1840–50; so called from the many buttons of his uniform]

but′ton snake′root, 1. any composite plant of the genus *Liatris,* having narrow, alternate leaves and spikelike heads of rose-purple flowers. **2.** an eryngo, *Eryngium yuccifolium,* of the southeastern U.S., having bristly leaves and whitish flowers. [1765–75, *Amer.*]

but·ton·wood (but′n wo͝od′), *n. Chiefly Eastern New Eng.* sycamore (def. 1). [1665–75, *Amer.*; BUTTON + WOOD[1]]

but·ton·y (but′n ē), *adj.* **1.** like a button. **2.** having many buttons. [1590–1600; BUTTON + -Y[1]]

butt′ plate′, a protective plate on the butt end of a gunstock, usually of metal.

but·tress (bu′tris), *n.* **1.** any external prop or support built to steady a structure by opposing its outward thrusts, esp. a projecting support built into or against the outside of a masonry wall. **2.** any prop or support. **3.** a thing shaped like a buttress, as a tree trunk with a widening base. **4.** a bony or horny protuberance, esp. on a horse's hoof. —*v.t.* **5.** to support by a buttress; prop up. **6.** to give encouragement or support to (a person, plan, etc.). [1350–1400; ME *butres* << OF (*arc*) *boterez* thrusting (arch) nom. sing. of *boteret* (acc.), equiv. to *boter-* abutment (perh. < Gmc; see BUTT[3]) + *-et* -ET] —**but′tress·less,** *adj.* —**but′tress·like′,** *adj.*
—**Syn. 6.** encourage, hearten, support, inspirit, brace, back up, reinforce, shore up.

A, **buttress**
B, flying buttress

butts′ and bounds′, *Law.* the boundary lines of a piece of land, as used in deeds, titles, etc. [1550–60; *butts* ends (see BUTT[2]); *bounds* sides (see BOUND[3])]

butt′ shaft′, a blunt or barbless arrow. [1580–90]

butt·stock (but′stok′), *n.* the part of the stock located behind the breech mechanism of a firearm. Also, **butt′-stock′.** [1905–10; BUTT[1] + STOCK]

butt·strap (but′strap′), *n., v.,* **-strapped, -strap·ping.** —*n.* **1.** (in metal construction) a plate which overlaps and fastens two pieces butted together. —*v.t.* **2.** to unite with a buttstrap or buttstraps. [1865–70; BUTT[1] + STRAP]

butt′ stroke′, a blow struck with the butt of a rifle, as in close combat.

butt′ weld′, a weld between two pieces of metal butted together with the abutted ends shortened and thickened and fused together under heat. [1860–65]

but·ty[1] (but′ē), *n., pl.* **-ties.** *Brit. Dial.* **1.** a slice of bread and butter. **2.** a sandwich. Also, **buttie.** [1850–55; BUTT(ER) + -Y[2]]

but·ty[2] (but′ē), *n., pl.* **-ties.** *Brit. Dial.* a fellow worker or friend, esp. in a coal mine. Also, **buttie.** [1780–90; orig. obscure]

Bu·tu·an (bə to͞o′än), *n.* a city in the Philippines, on NE Mindanao. 112,489.

Bu·tung (bo͞o′to͝ong), *n.* an island of Indonesia, SE of Celebes Island. 100 mi. (161 km) long.

bu·tut (bo͞o′to͞ot), *n., pl.* **-tut, -tuts.** a bronze coin of The Gambia, the 100th part of a dalasi.

bu·tyl (byo͞o′til, byo͞ot′l), *adj. Chem.* containing a butyl group. [1865–70; BUT(YRIC) + -YL]

Bu·tyl (byo͞o′til, byo͞ot′l), *Trademark.* a brand of synthetic rubber prepared by polymerization of butylene containing little butadiene, particularly useful for inner tubes of automobile tires because of its leakproof qualities.

bu′tyl ac′etate, *Chem.* a colorless, fragrant, flammable liquid ester, $C_6H_{12}O_2$, used as a solvent for varnishes and lacquers.

bu′tyl al′cohol, *Chem.* any of four flammable, isomeric, liquid alcohols having the formula C_4H_9OH, used as solvents and in organic synthesis. Also called **butanol.** [1865–70]

bu′tyl al′dehyde, *Chem.* butyraldehyde. [1865–70]

bu·tyl·ate (byo͞ot′l āt′), *v.t.,* **-at·ed, -at·ing.** to introduce one or more butyl groups into (a compound). [BUTYL + -ATE[1]] —**bu′tyl·a′tion,** *n.*

bu′tylated hy·drox·y·an′i·sole (hī drok′sē an′ə sōl′), *Chem., Pharm.* See **BHA.** [1945–50; HYDROXY- + ANISOLE]

bu′tylated hy·drox·y·tol′u·ene (hī drok′sē tol′yo͞o ēn′), *Chem., Pharm.* See **BHT.** [1960–65; HYDROXY- + TOLUENE]

bu·tyl·ene (byo͞ot′l ēn′), *Chem.* —*n.* **1.** Also, **butene.** any of three isomeric, gaseous hydrocarbons having the formula C_4H_8, of the alkene series. —*adj.* **2.** containing the butylene group. [1875–80; BUTYL + -ENE]

bu′tylene group′, *Chem.* any of four bivalent isomeric groups having the formula $-C_4H_8-$. Also called **bu′tylene rad′ical.**

bu′tyl group′, *Chem.* any of four univalent isomeric groups having the formula C_4H_9-. Also called **bu′tyl rad′ical.**

bu′tyl ni′trite, *Chem.* a volatile liquid, $C_4H_9NO_2$, the vapor of which can cause headache and vasodilation, used as an active ingredient in some household deodorizers, and misused by inhalation to prolong the sensation of orgasm. Also called **isobutyl nitrite.** [1975–80]

bu·tyr·a·ceous (byo͞o′tə rā′shəs), *adj.* of the nature of, resembling, or containing butter. [1660–70; < L *būtȳr(um)* BUTTER + -ACEOUS]

bu·tyr·al (byo͞o′tə ral′, -tər əl), *n. Chem.* any acetal of butyraldehyde. [1885–90; BUTYRAL(DEHYDE)]

bu·tyr·al·de·hyde (byo͞o′tə ral′də hīd′), *n. Chem.* a clear, colorless, flammable liquid, C_4H_8O, used chiefly as an intermediate in the manufacture of resins and rubber cement. Also called **butyl aldehyde.** [1885–90; BUTYR(IC) + ALDEHYDE]

bu·tyr·ate (byo͞o′tə rāt′), *n. Chem.* a salt or ester of butyric acid. [1870–75; BUTYR(IC ACID) + -ATE[2]]

bu·tyr·ic (byo͞o tir′ik), *adj. Chem.* pertaining to or derived from butyric acid. [1820–30; < L *būtȳr(um)* BUTTER + -IC] —**bu·tyr′i·cal·ly,** *adv.*

butyr′ic ac′id, *Chem.* either of two isomeric acids having the formula $C_4H_8O_2$, esp. a rancid liquid occurring chiefly in spoiled butter, whose esters are used as flavorings. Also called **butanoic acid.** [1820–30]

bu·tyr·in (byo͞o′tər in), *n. Chem.* a colorless, liquid ester present in butter, formed from glycerin and butyric acid. [1820–30; BUTYR(IC) + (GLYCER)IN]

bu·ty·ro·phe·none (byo͞o tir′ō fə nōn′), *n. Pharm.* any of a class of antipsychotics, as haloperidol, used to relieve symptoms of schizophrenia, acute psychosis, or other severe psychiatric disorders. [1940–45; BUTYR(IC) + -O- + PHEN- + -ONE]

bu·tyr·yl (byo͞o′tər il), *adj. Chem.* containing the butyryl group. [1865–70; BUTYR(IC) + -YL]

bu′tyryl group′, *Chem.* the univalent group C_4H_7O-. Also called **bu′tyryl rad′ical.**

bux·om (buk′səm), *adj.* **1.** (of a woman) full-bosomed. **2.** (of a woman) healthy, plump, cheerful, and lively. [1125–75; ME, earlier *buhsum* pliant, equiv. to OE *būh* (var. s. of *būgan* to BOW[1]) + *-sum* -SOME[1]] —**bux′om·ly,** *adv.* —**bux′om·ness,** *n.*

Bux·te·hu·de (bo͝ok′stə ho͞o′də), *n.* **Die·trich** (dē′trikH), 1637–1707, Danish organist and composer, in Germany after 1668.

buy (bī), *v.,* **bought, buy·ing,** *n.* —*v.t.* **1.** to acquire the possession of, or the right to, by paying or promising to pay an equivalent, esp. in money; purchase. **2.** to acquire by exchange or concession: *to buy favor with flattery.* **3.** to hire or obtain the services of: *The Yankees bought a new center fielder.* **4.** to bribe: *Most public officials cannot be bought.* **5.** to be the monetary or purchasing equivalent of: *Ten dollars buys less than it used to.* **6.** *Chiefly Theol.* to redeem; ransom. **7.** *Cards.* to draw or be dealt (a card): *He bought an ace.* **8.** *Informal.* **a.** to accept or believe: *I don't buy that explanation.* **b.** to be deceived by: *He bought the whole story.* —*v.i.* **9.** to be or become a purchaser. **10. buy down,** to lower or reduce (the mortgage interest rate) by means of a buy-down. **11. buy in, a.** to buy a supply of; accumulate a stock of. **b.** to buy back one's own possession at an auction. **c.** to undertake a buy-in. Also, **buy into. 12. buy into,** to purchase a share, interest, or membership in: *They tried to buy into the club but were not accepted.* **13. buy it,** *Slang.* to get killed: *He bought it at Dunkirk.* **14. buy off,** to get rid of (a claim, opposition, etc.) by payment; purchase the noninterference of; bribe: *The corrupt official bought off those who might expose him.* **15. buy out,** to secure all of (an owner or partner's) share or interest in an enterprise: *She bought out an established pharmacist.* **16. buy up,** to buy as much as one can of something or as much as is offered for sale: *He bought up the last of the strawberries at the fruit market.* —*n.* **17.** an act or instance of buying. **18.** something bought or to be bought; purchase: *That coat was a sensible buy.* **19.** a bargain: *The couch was a real buy.* [bef. 1000; ME *byen,* var. of *byggen, buggen,* OE *bycgan*; c. OS *buggjan,* Goth *bugjan* to buy, ON *byggja* to lend, rent] —**buy′a·ble,** *adj.*
—**Syn. 1.** BUY, PURCHASE imply obtaining or acquiring property or goods for a price. BUY is the common and informal word, applying to any such transaction: *to buy a house, vegetables at the market.* PURCHASE is more formal and may connote buying on a larger scale, in a finer store, and the like: *to purchase a year's supplies.* —**Ant. 1.** sell.

buy·back (bī′bak′), *n.* **1.** the buying of something that one previously sold. **2.** any arrangement to take back something as a condition of a sale, as by a supplier who agrees to purchase its customer's goods. **3.** Also called **stock buyback.** a repurchase by a company of its own stock in the open market, as for investment purposes or for use in future corporate acquisitions. Also, **buy′-back′.** [1960–65; n. use of the v. phrase *buy back*]

buy′ boat′, a boat sent out by a dealer to purchase the catches of fishing vessels.

buy-down (bī′doun′), *n.* a subsidy for a long-term mortgage offered by a third party, as a builder or developer, to lower interest rates for a buyer in the early years of the loan.

buy·er (bī′ər), *n.* **1.** a person who buys; purchaser. **2.** a purchasing agent, as for a department or chain store. [1150–1200; ME *beger, bier.* See BUY, -ER[1]]

buy′ers' infla′tion. See **demand-pull inflation.**

buy′ers' mar′ket, a market in which goods and services are plentiful and prices relatively low. Cf. **sellers' market.** [1925–30]

buy′ers' strike′, an attempt on the part of consumers to lower price levels by boycotting retailers or certain types of goods.

buy-in (bī′in′), *n.* **1.** an act or instance of buying in. **2.** the deliberate submission of a false bid, too low to be met, in order to win a contract. **3.** *Poker.* the chips purchased by a player from the banker, occasionally a set amount required to enter a specific competition or game. [n. use of v. phrase *buy in*]

buy′ing pow′er. See **purchasing power** (def. 1).

buy·off (bī′ôf′, -of′), *n. Informal.* an act or instance of buying off; payment or bribe: *The increased retirement benefit was a buyoff for employees who wanted salary increases.* [n. use of v. phrase *buy off*]

buy·out (bī′out′), *n.* an act or instance of buying out, esp. of buying all or a controlling percentage of the shares in a company. [1970–75]

Buys′-Bal·lot's′ law′ (bīs′bə lots′), *Meteorol.* the law stating that if one stands with one's back to the wind, in the Northern Hemisphere the atmospheric pressure will be lower on one's left and in the Southern Hemisphere it will be lower on one's right: descriptive of the relationship of horizontal winds to atmospheric pressure. [named after C. H. D. *Buys-Ballot* (1817–90), Dutch meteorologist]

buy·up (bī′up′), *n.* an act or instance of buying up: *a spectacular buyup of the city's most valuable real estate.* [n. use of v. phrase *buy up*]

bu·zu·ki (bo͝o zo͞o′kē), *n., pl.* **-kis, -ki·a** (-kē ə). bouzouki.

buzz[1] (buz), *n.* **1.** a low, vibrating, humming sound, as of bees, machinery, or people talking. **2.** a rumor or report. **3.** *Informal.* a phone call: *When I find out, I'll give you a buzz.* **4.** *Slang.* **a.** a feeling of intense enthusiasm, excitement, or exhilaration: *I got a terrific buzz from those Pacific sunsets.* **b.** a feeling of slight intoxication. **5. have** or **get a buzz on,** *Slang.* to be slightly intoxicated: *After a few beers they all had a buzz on.* —*v.i.* **6.** to make a low, vibrating, humming sound. **7.** to speak or murmur with such a sound. **8.** to be filled with the sound of buzzing or whispering: *The room buzzed.* **9.** to whisper; gossip: *Everyone is buzzing about the scandal.* **10.** to move busily from place to place. **11.** *Slang.* to go; leave (usually fol. by *off* or *along*): *I'll buzz along now. Tell him to buzz off and leave me alone.* —*v.t.* **12.** to make a buzzing sound with: *The fly buzzed its wings.* **13.** to tell or spread (a rumor, gossip, etc.) secretively. **14.** to signal or summon with a buzzer: *He buzzed his secretary.* **15.** *Informal.* to make a phone call to. **16.** *Aeron.* **a.** to fly a plane very low over: *to buzz a field.* **b.** to signal or greet (someone) by flying a plane low and slowing the motor spasmodically. [1350–1400; ME *busse*; imit.] —**buzz′ing·ly,** *adv.*

buzz[2] (buz), *n. Slang.* a man's very short haircut; crew cut. [orig. uncert.]

buz·zard[1] (buz′ərd), *n.* **1.** any of several broad-winged, soaring hawks of the genus *Buteo* and allied genera, esp. *B. buteo,* of Europe. **2.** any of several New World vultures of the family Cathartidae, esp. the turkey vulture. **3.** *Slang.* a contemptible or cantankerous person (often prec. by *old*): *That old buzzard has lived in the same shack for twenty years.* —*adj.* **4.** *Obs.* senseless; stupid. [1250–1300; ME *busard* < OF, var. of *buisard,* equiv. to *buis(on)* buzzard (< L *būteōn-,* s. of *būteō* kind of hawk) + *-ard* -ARD] —**buz′zard·like′,** *adj.* —**buz′zard·ly,** *adj., adv.*

buz·zard[2] (buz′ərd), *n. Brit. Dial.* any of various noc-

CONCISE ETYMOLOGY KEY: <, descended or borrowed from; >, whence; b., blend of, blended; c., cognate with; cf., compare; deriv., derivative; equiv., equivalent; imit., imitative; obl., oblique; r., replacing; s., stem; sp., spelling, spelled; resp., respelling, respelled; trans., translation; ?, origin unknown; *, unattested; ‡, probably earlier than. See the full key inside the front cover.

urnal buzzing insects, as cockchafers. [1645–55; BUZZ[1] + -ARD]

uz′zard's Bay′, an inlet of the Atlantic, in SE Massachusetts. 30 mi. (48 km) long.

uzz′ bomb′, *Mil.* a type of self-steering aerial bomb, launched from large land-based rocket platforms: used by the Germans in World War II, esp. over England. [1940–45]

uzz•er (buz′ər), *n.* **1.** a person or thing that buzzes. **2.** a signaling apparatus similar to an electric bell but without hammer or gong, producing a buzzing sound by the vibration of an armature. [1600–10; BUZZ[1] + -ER[1]]

uzz′ saw′, a power-operated circular saw, so named because of the noise it makes. [1855–60, *Amer.*]

uzz•wig (buz′wig′), *n.* **1.** a large, bushy wig. **2.** a person wearing such a wig. **3.** a person of consequence. Also, **buzz′ wig′**. [1810–20; *buzz* bushy wig (prob. shortening of BUSBY) + WIG]

uzz•word (buz′wûrd′), *n.* a word or phrase, often sounding authoritative or technical, that is a vogue term in a particular profession, field of study, popular culture, etc. [1965–70; BUZZ[1] + WORD]

.V., **1.** Blessed Virgin. [< L *Beāta Virgō*] **2.** farewell. [< L *bene valē*]

.v., book value.

.V.A., Bachelor of Vocational Agriculture.

.V.D., *Trademark.* a brand of men's underwear. Also, **BVD's**

.V.E., Bachelor of Vocational Education.

.V.M., Blessed Virgin Mary. [< L *Beāta Virgō Marīa*]

vt., **1.** brevet. **2.** brevetted.

W, **1.** bacteriological warfare. **2.** See **biological warfare. 3.** (in television, motion pictures, photography, etc.) black and white, as opposed to color.

wa•na (bwä′nə), *n.* (in Africa) master; boss. [1875–80; < Swahili < Ar *abūnā* our father]

WC, Board of War Communications.

.W.I., British West Indies.

x, See **base exchange.** Also, **BX**

x., *pl.* **bxs.** box.

X cable, *Elect.* a cable consisting of wires contained in a flexible metal tubing, used chiefly in wiring buildings and in supplying electric power to equipment.

y[1] (bī), *prep., adv., adj., n., pl.* **byes.** —*prep.* **1.** near to or next to: *a home by a lake.* **2.** over the surface of, through the medium of, along, or using as a route: *He came by the highway. She arrived by air.* **3.** on, as a means of conveyance: *They arrived by ship.* **4.** to and beyond the vicinity of; past: *He went by the church.* **5.** within the extent or period of; during: *by day; by night.* **6.** not later than; at or before: *I usually finish work by five o'clock.* **7.** to the extent or amount of: *The new tug is larger than the old one by a great deal. He's taller than his sister by three inches.* **8.** from the opinion, evidence, or authority of: *By his own account he was in Chicago at the time. I know him by sight.* **9.** according to; in conformity with: *This is a bad movie by any standards.* **10.** with (something) at stake; on: *to swear by all that is sacred.* **11.** through the agency, efficacy, work, participation, or authority of: *The book was published by Random House.* **12.** from the hand, mind, invention, or creativity of: *She read a poem by Emily Dickinson. The phonograph was invented by Thomas Edison.* **13.** in consequence, as a result, or on the basis of: *We met by chance. We won the game by forfeit.* **14.** accompanied with or in the atmosphere of: *Lovers walk by moonlight.* **15.** in treatment or support of; for: *He did well by his children.* **16.** after; next after, as of the same items in a series: *piece by piece; little by little.* **17.** (in multiplication) taken the number of times as that specified by the second number, or multiplier: *Multiply 18 by 57.* **18.** (in measuring shapes) having an adjoining side of, as a width relative to a length: *a room 10 feet by 12 feet.* **19.** (in division) separated into the number of equal parts as that specified by the second number, or divisor: *Divide 99 by 33.* **20.** in terms or amounts of; in measuring units of: *Apples are sold by the bushel. I'm paid by the week.* **21.** begot or born of: *Eve had two sons by Adam.* **22.** (of quadrupeds) having as a sire: *Equipoise II by Equipoise.* **23.** *Navig.* (as used in the names of the 16 smallest points on the compass) one point toward the east, west, north, or south of N, NE, E, SE, S, SW, W, or NW, respectively: *He sailed NE by N from Pago Pago.* **24.** into, at, or to: *Come by my office this afternoon.* —*adv.* **25.** near; in the immediate vicinity; at hand: *The school is close by.* **26.** to and beyond a point near something; past: *The car drove by.* **27.** aside; away: *Put your work by for the moment. Over the years, she laid by enough money to retire.* **28.** over; past: *in times gone by.* **29. by and by,** in a short time; before long; presently: *The clouds will disappear by and by.* **30. by and large,** in general; on the whole: *By and large, there is much to be said for the new system.* **31. by me, a.** (in bridge and other bidding card games) a declaration that the speaker is passing. **b.** (in poker) a declaration that the speaker is checking: *Is my pair of tens still high? By me.* —*adj.* Also, **bye. 32.** situated to one side: *They came down a by passage.* **33.** secondary, incidental: *It was only a by comment.* —*n.* **34.** bye[1]. **35. by the by.** See **bye**[1] (def. 5). [bef. 900; ME; OE *bī*; c. D *bij*, OHG *bī* (G *bei*), Goth *bi.* See BE-]

—**Syn. 11.** BY, THROUGH, WITH indicate agency or means of getting something done or accomplished. BY is regularly used to denote the agent (person or force) in passive constructions: *It is done by many; destroyed by fire.* It also indicates means: *Send it by airmail.* WITH denotes the instrument (usually consciously) employed by an agent: *He cut it with the scissors.* THROUGH designates particularly immediate agency or instrumentality or reason or motive: *through outside aid; to yield through fear; wounded through carelessness.*

by[2] *interj.* good-bye: *By now, come again sometime!* Also, **bye.** [by shortening]

by-, a combining form of **by**[1]: *by-product; bystander; byway.* Also, **bye-.**

by-and-by (bī′ən bī′), *n.* the future: *to meet in the sweet by-and-by.* [1300–50; ME *bi and bi* one by one, at once. See BY[1]]

by•bid•der (bī′bid′ər), *n.* a person employed to bid at an auction in order to raise the prices for the auctioneer or seller. [1875–80; BY- + BIDDER] —**by′-bid′ding,** *n.*

Byb•los (bib′ləs), *n.* an ancient Phoenician seaport near the modern city of Beirut, Lebanon: chief port for the export of papyrus: site now partially excavated.

by-blow (bī′blō′), *n.* **1.** an incidental or accidental blow. **2.** Also, **bye-blow.** an illegitimate child; bastard. [1585–95; BY- + BLOW[1]]

by′ crack′y, *Informal (older use).* (an exclamation used to express surprise or to emphasize a comment): *A fine day, by cracky!*

Byd•goszcz (bid′gôshch), *n.* a city in N Poland. 323,000. German, **Bromberg.**

bye[1] (bī), *n.* Also, **by. 1.** *Sports.* in a tournament, the preferential status of a player or team not paired with a competitor in an early round and thus automatically advanced to play in the next round: *The top three seeded players received byes in the first round.* **2.** *Golf.* the holes of a stipulated course still unplayed after the match is finished. **3.** *Cricket.* a run made on a ball not struck by the batsman. **4.** something subsidiary, secondary, or out of the way. **5. by the bye,** by the way; incidentally: *By the bye, how do you spell your name?* Also, **by the by.** —*adj.* **6.** by[1]. [1710–20; var. sp. of BY[1] in its n. sense "side way"]

bye[2] (bī), *interj.* by[2].

bye-, var. of **by-**: *bye-election.*

bye-blow (bī′blō′), *n.* by-blow (def. 2).

bye-bye (*interj.* bī′bī′; *n., adv.* bī′bī′), *interj.* **1.** *Informal.* good-bye. —*n.* **2.** *Baby Talk.* sleep. —*adv.* **3. go bye-bye,** *Baby Talk.* **a.** to leave; depart; go out. **b.** to go to sleep; go to bed. [1700–10; appar. orig. nursery phrase used to lull a child to sleep, later construed as reduplicative form of BY[2], short for GOOD-BYE]

bye•law (bī′lô′), *n.* bylaw.

by-e•lec•tion (bī′i lek′shən), *n.* a special election, not held at the time of a general election, to fill a vacancy in Parliament. Also, **bye′-e•lec′tion.** [1875–80; BY- + ELECTION]

Bye•lo•rus•sia (byel′ō rush′ə, bel′ō-), *n.* **1.** Official name, **Belarus.** Formerly, **White Russian Soviet Socialist Republic, Byelorus′sian So′viet So′cialist Repub′lic.** a republic in E Europe, N of Ukraine: formerly a part of the Soviet Union. 10,200,000; 80,154 sq. mi. (207,600 sq. km). *Cap.:* Minsk. **2.** a region in the W part of former czarist Russia. Also, **Belorussia.** Also called **White Russia.**

Bye•lo•rus•sian (byel′ō rush′ən, bel′ō-), *adj.* **1.** of or pertaining to Byelorussia, its people, or their language. —*n.* **2.** a native or inhabitant of Byelorussia. **3.** an East Slavic language, spoken by the inhabitants of Byelorussia and written in the Cyrillic alphabet. Cf. **Slavic** (def. 1). Also, **Belorussian.** [BYELORUSSI(A) + -AN]

Bye•lo•stok (byi lu stôk′), *n.* Russian name of **Bialystok.**

by-form (bī′fôrm′), *n. Ling.* a closely related and sometimes less frequent form, as *spelt* for *spelled;* variant. [1885–90]

by•gone (bī′gôn′, -gon′), *adj.* **1.** past; gone by; earlier; former: *The faded photograph brought memories of bygone days.* —*n.* **2.** Usually, **bygones.** that which is past: *Let's not talk of bygones.* **3. let bygones be bygones,** to decide to forget past disagreements; become reconciled: *Let's let bygones be bygones and be friends again.* [1375–1425; late ME (north) *by-gane;* see GONE, BY[1]]

by•lane (bī′lān′), *n.* a secondary road or lane. [1580–90; BY- + LANE[1]]

by•law (bī′lô′), *n.* **1.** a standing rule governing the regulation of a corporation's or society's internal affairs. **2.** a subsidiary law. **3.** *Brit.* an ordinance of a municipality or community. Also, **byelaw.** [1325–75; BY- + LAW[1]; r. ME *bilawe*, equiv. to *by* town (< Scand; cf. Dan *by*) + *lawe* law]

by•line (bī′līn′), *n., v.,* **-lined, -lin•ing.** *Journalism.* —*n.* **1.** a printed line accompanying a news story, article, or the like, giving the author's name. —*v.t.* **2.** to accompany with a byline: *Was the newspaper report bylined or was it anonymous?* Also, **by′-line′.** [1925–30, *Amer.*; BY- + LINE[1]]

by•lin•er (bī′lī′nər), *n.* a writer important enough to merit a byline. [1940–45, *Amer.*; BYLINE + -ER[1]]

by-name (bī′nām′), *n.* **1.** a secondary name; cognomen; surname. **2.** a nickname. Also, **by′name′.** [1325–75; ME]

Byng (bing), *n.* **Julian Hed•worth George** (hed′wərth), (*Viscount Byng of Vimy*), 1862–1935, English general: governor general of Canada 1921–26.

BYOB, bring your own bottle, as of liquor or wine: often included in an invitation to indicate that the host will not provide liquor. Also, **BYO.** [1970–75]

by•pass (bī′pas′, -päs′), *n., v.,* **-passed** or (*Rare*) **-past; -passed** or **-past; -pass•ing.** —*n.* **1.** a road enabling motorists to avoid a city or other heavy traffic points or to drive around an obstruction. **2.** a secondary pipe or other channel connected with a main passage, as for conducting a liquid or gas around a fixture, pipe, or appliance. **3.** *Elect.* shunt (def. 9). **4.** a surgical procedure in which a diseased or obstructed hollow organ is temporarily or permanently circumvented. Cf. **coronary bypass, gastric bypass, heart-lung machine, intestinal bypass.** —*v.t.* **5.** to avoid (an obstruction, city, etc.) by following a bypass. **6.** to cause (fluid or gas) to follow a secondary pipe or bypass. **7.** to neglect to consult or to ignore the opinion or decision of: *He bypassed the foreman and took his grievance straight to the owner.* Also, **by′-pass′.** [1840–50; appar. back formation from *by-passage;* see BY[1] (adj.), PASSAGE[1]] —**by′pass′er, by′-pass′er,** *n.*

by′pass capac′itor, *Elect.* a capacitor that provides a path for alternating current around a specified element in a circuit. Also called **by′pass condens′er.**

by•past (bī′past′, -päst′), *adj.* **1.** bygone; earlier; former; past. —*v.* **2.** a pp. of **bypass. 3.** *Rare.* a pt. of **bypass.** [1375–1425; late ME (adj.); see BY[1] (adv.), PAST]

by•path (bī′path′, -päth′), *n., pl.* **-paths** (-pathz′, -päthz′, -paths′, -päths′). a private path or an indirect or secondary course or means; byway. Also, **by′path′.** [1325–75; ME *bi path.* See BY[1] (adj.), PATH]

by-play (bī′plā′), *n.* an action or speech carried on to the side while the main action proceeds, esp. on the stage. Also, **by′play′.** [1805–15]

by-plot (bī′plot′), *n.* subplot. [1570–80]

by-prod•uct (bī′prod′əkt), *n.* **1.** a secondary or incidental product, as in a process of manufacture. **2.** the result of another action, often unforeseen or unintended. [1900–05]

Byrd (bûrd), *n.* **1. Richard Evelyn,** 1888–1957, rear admiral in U.S. Navy: polar explorer. **2. Robert C(arlyle),** born 1917, U.S. politician: senator since 1959. **3. William,** c1540–1623, English composer and organist.

Byrd′ Land′, a part of Antarctica, SE of the Ross Sea: discovered and explored by Adm. Richard E. Byrd. Formerly, **Marie Byrd Land.**

byre (bīᵊr), *n. Brit.* a cow shed. [bef. 800; ME, OE: barn, shed, var. of *būr* hut. See BOWER[1]]

byre-man (bīᵊr′mən), *n., pl.* **-men.** *Brit.* a man who raises or tends cows. [1805–15]

Byr•gi•us (bėr′gē əs), *n.* a crater in the third quadrant of the face of the moon: about 40 miles (64 km) in diameter.

Byrne (bûrn), *n.* **Donn** (don). See **Donn-Byrne, Brian Oswald.**

Byrnes (bûrnz), *n.* **1. James Francis,** 1879–1972, U.S. statesman and jurist: Secretary of State 1945–47. **2. Joseph Wellington,** 1869–1936, U.S. lawyer: Speaker of the House 1935–36.

byr•nie (bûr′nē), *n. Armor.* a coat of mail; hauberk. [1325–75; ME *byrny*, Scot var. of *brynie, brinie* < ON *brynja*, c. OE *byrne* coat of mail, OHG *brunnia*]

by-road (bī′rōd′), *n.* a side road. Also, **by′road′.** [1665–75; BY- + ROAD]

By•ron (bī′rən), *n.* **1. George Gordon, Lord** (*6th Baron Byron*), 1788–1824, English poet. **2.** a male given name.

By•ron•ic (bī ron′ik), *adj.* **1.** of or pertaining to Lord Byron. **2.** possessing the characteristics of Byron or his poetry, esp. romanticism, melancholy, and melodramatic energy. [1815–25; BYRON + -IC] —**By•ron′i•cal•ly,** *adv.* —**By•ron•ism** (bī′rə niz′əm), *n.*

byr•rus (bir′əs), *n., pl.* **byr•ri** (bir′ī). birrus.

bys•si•no•sis (bis′ə nō′sis), *n. Pathol.* See **brown lung.** [1885–90; < Gk *býssin(os)* fine flax, linen (equiv. to *býss(os)* BYSSUS + *-inos* -INE[1]) + -OSIS]

bys•sus (bis′əs), *n., pl.* **bys•sus•es, bys•si** (bis′ī). **1.** *Zool.* a collection of silky filaments by which certain mollusks attach themselves to rocks. **2.** an ancient cloth, thought to be of linen, cotton, or silk. [1350–1400; ME < L < Gk *býssos* a fine cotton or linen < Sem; cf. Heb *būṣ*] —**bys•sa•ceous** (bi sā′shəs), **bys′soid,** *adj.* —**bys′sal,** *adj.*

by•stand•er (bī′stan′dər), *n.* a person present but not involved; chance spectator; onlooker. [1610–20; BY- + STANDER]
—**Syn.** observer, viewer, passerby, witness; rubberneck, sidewalk superintendent.

by-street (bī′strēt′), *n.* a side street or a private or obscure street; byway. Also, **by′street′.** [1665–75; BY- + STREET]

by-talk (bī′tôk′), *n.* incidental conversation; small talk; chitchat. [1555–65; BY- + TALK]

byte (bīt), *n. Computers.* **1.** adjacent bits, usually eight, processed by a computer as a unit. **2.** the combination of bits used to represent a particular letter, number, or special character. [1959; orig. uncert.]

By•tom (bī′tôm), *n.* a city in S Poland. 234,000. German, **Beuthen.**

CONCISE PRONUNCIATION KEY: act, cāpe, dâre, pärt; set, ēqual; if, īce; ox, ōver, ôrder, oil, bŏŏk, bōōt, out; up, ûrge; child; sing; shoe; thin, *th*at; zh as in *treasure.* ə = a as in *alone,* e as in *system,* i as in *easily,* o as in *gallop,* u as in *circus;* ᵊ as in *fire* (fīᵊr), *hour* (ouᵊr). l and n can serve as syllabic consonants, as in *cradle* (krād′l), and *button* (but′n). See the full key inside the front cover.

by•town•ite (bī tou′nīt), *n.* a blue to dark-gray mineral near the anorthite end of the plagioclase feldspar group. [1865–70; named after *Bytown* (old name of Ottawa, Canada), where first found; see -ITE[1]]

by•way (bī′wā′), *n.* **1.** a secluded, private, or obscure road. **2.** a subsidiary or obscure field of research, endeavor, etc. [1300–50; ME *bywey.* See BY[1] (adj.), WAY]

by•word (bī′wûrd′), *n.* **1.** a word or phrase associated with some person or thing; a characteristic expression, typical greeting, or the like. **2.** a word or phrase used proverbially; common saying; proverb. **3.** an object of general reproach, derision, scorn, etc.: *His crimes will make him a byword through the ages.* **4.** an epithet, often of scorn. [bef. 1050; ME *biworde,* OE *biwyrde.* See BY (adj.), WORD]
—Syn. 1. slogan, motto. **2.** maxim, apothegm, aphorism, saw, adage.

by-work (bī′wûrk′), *n.* work done in addition to one's regular work, as in intervals of leisure. [1580–90; BY- + WORK]

by-your-leave (bī′yər lēv′), *n.* an apology for not having sought permission. [1910–15]

Byz., Byzantine.

CONCISE ETYMOLOGY KEY: <, descended or borrowed from; >, whence; b., blend of, blended; c., cognate with; cf., compare; deriv., derivative; equiv., equivalent; imit., imitative; obl., oblique; r., replacing; s., stem; sp., spelling, spelled; resp., respelling, respelled; trans., translation; ?, origin unknown; *, unattested; ‡, probably earlier than. See the full key inside the front cover.

byz•ant (biz′ənt, bi zant′), *n.* bezant (def. 2).

Byz•an•tine (biz′ən tēn′, -tīn′, bī′zən-, bi zan′tin), *adj.* **1.** of or pertaining to Byzantium. **2.** of or pertaining to the Byzantine Empire. **3.** noting or pertaining to the architecture of the Byzantine Empire and to architecture influenced by or imitating it: characterized by masonry construction, round arches, impost blocks, low domes on pendentives, the presence of fine, spiky foliage patterns in low relief on stone capitals and moldings, and the use of frescoes, mosaics, and revetments of fine stone to cover whole interiors. **4.** *Fine Arts.* pertaining to or designating the style of the fine or decorative arts developed and elaborated in the Byzantine Empire and its provinces: characterized chiefly by an ecclesiastically prescribed iconography, highly formal structure, severe confinement of pictorial space to a shallow depth, and the use of rich, often sumptuous color. **5.** (*sometimes l.c.*) complex or intricate: *a deal requiring Byzantine financing.* **6.** (*sometimes l.c.*) characterized by elaborate scheming and intrigue, esp. for the gaining of political power or favor: *Byzantine methods for holding on to his chairmanship.* **7.** of or pertaining to the Byzantine Church. **—***n.* **8.** a native or inhabitant of Byzantium. [1590–1600; < LL *Bȳzantīnus* of BYZANTIUM; see -INE[1]]

Byz′antine chant′, *Music.* liturgical plainsong identified with the Eastern Orthodox Church and dating from the Byzantine Empire.

Byz′antine Church′. See **Orthodox Church** (def. 1).

Byz′antine Em′pire, the Eastern Roman Empire after the fall of the Western Empire in A.D. 476. *Cap.:* Constantinople.

Byz′antine rite′. See **Greek rite.**

By•zan•tin•ism (biz′ən tē niz′əm, -tī-, bī′zən-, bi zan′tə-), *n. Eastern Ch.* caesaropapism, esp. before the Great Schism of 1054. [1850–55; BYZANTINE + -ISM]

By•zan•tin•ist (biz′ən tē nist, -tī-, bī′zən-, bi zan′tə-), *n.* an authority on or student of Byzantine history and culture. [1890–95; BYZANTINE + -IST]

By•zan•ti•um (bi zan′shē əm, -tē əm), *n.* an ancient Greek city on the Bosporus and the Sea of Marmara: Constantine I rebuilt it and renamed it Constantinople A.D. 330. Cf. **Istanbul.**

By•zas (bī′zəs), *n.* a son of Poseidon and the eponymous founder of Byzantium.

Bz., benzene.

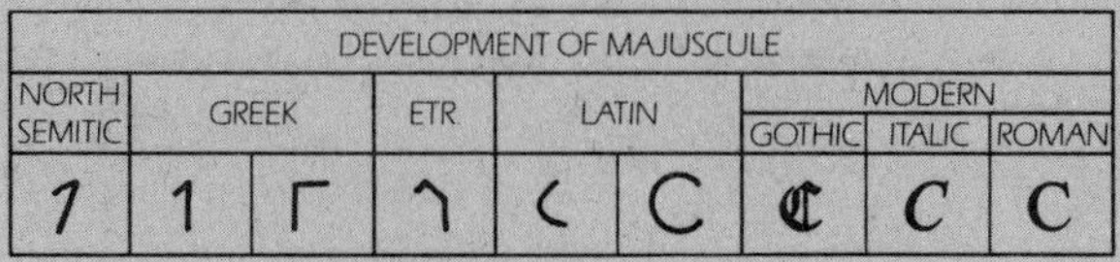

DEVELOPMENT OF MAJUSCULE								
NORTH SEMITIC	GREEK		ETR	LATIN		MODERN		
						GOTHIC	ITALIC	ROMAN
7	1	Γ	٦	‹	C	ℭ	*C*	C

DEVELOPMENT OF MINUSCULE					
ROMAN CURSIVE	ROMAN UNCIAL	CAROL. MIN.	MODERN		
			GOTHIC	ITALIC	ROMAN
‹	c	c	𝔠	*c*	c

The third letter of the English alphabet developed from North Semitic *ghimel* and Greek *gamma* through the Etruscans, in whose language there was no meaningful distinction between the *g*-sound and the *k*-sound and who used C for both. In Latin, C, pronounced like English K, was used mainly before A and O, and retained this sound when introduced into Britain. The capital and minuscule, which assumed their present form in Latin, were originally angular and faced to the left, as in North Semitic *ghimel* and early Greek *gamma* (Γ).

C, c (sē), *n., pl.* **C's** or **Cs, c's** or **cs. 1.** the third letter of the English alphabet, a consonant. **2.** any spoken sound represented by the letter *C* or *c,* as in *cat, race,* or *circle.* **3.** something having the shape of a C. **4.** a written or printed representation of the letter *C* or *c.* **5.** a device, as a printer's type, for reproducing the letter *C* or *c.*

C, 1. cocaine. **2.** *Gram.* complement. **3.** consonant. **4.** coulomb. **5.** county (used with a number to designate a county road): *C55.*

C, *Symbol.* **1.** the third in order or in a series. **2.** (*sometimes l.c.*) (in some grading systems) a grade or mark, as in school or college, indicating the quality of a student's work as fair or average. **3.** *Music.* **a.** the first tone, or keynote, in the scale of C major or the third tone in the relative minor scale, A minor. **b.** a string, key, or pipe tuned to this tone. **c.** a written or printed note representing this tone. **d.** (in the fixed system of solmization) the first tone of the scale of C major, called *do.* **e.** the tonality having C as the tonic note. **f.** a symbol indicating quadruple time and appearing after the clef sign on a musical staff. **4.** (*sometimes l.c.*) the Roman numeral for 100. **5.** Celsius. **6.** centigrade. **7.** *Elect.* **a.** capacitance. **b.** a battery size for 1.5 volt dry cells: diameter, 1 in. (2.5 cm); length, 1.9 in. (4.8 cm). **8.** *Chem.* carbon. **9.** *Physics.* **a.** charge conjugation. **b.** charm[1] (def. 9). **10.** *Biochem.* **a.** cysteine. **b.** cytosine. **11.** Also, **C-note.** *Slang.* a hundred-dollar bill. **12.** a proportional shoe width size, narrower than D and wider than B. **13.** a proportional brassiere cup size, smaller than D and larger than B. **14.** the lowest quality rating for a corporate or municipal bond. **15.** *Computers.* a high-level programming language often used in conjunction with UNIX and offering a degree of low-level machine control.

c, 1. calorie. **2.** *Optics.* candle; candles. **3.** (with a year) about: *c1775.* [< L *circā, circiter, circum*] **4.** *Physics, Chem.* curie; curies. **5.** cycle; cycles.

c, *Symbol.* **1.** *Optics, Physics.* the velocity of light in a vacuum: approximately 186,000 miles per second or 299,793 kilometers per second. **2.** *Acoustics, Physics.* the velocity of sound.

c̄, (in prescriptions) with. [< L *cum*]

C., 1. Calorie. **2.** Cape. **3.** Catholic. **4.** Celsius. **5.** Celtic. **6.** Centigrade. **7.** College. **8.** (in Costa Rica and El Salvador) colon; colons. **9.** Congress. **10.** Conservative.

C-, *U.S. Mil.* (in designations of transport aircraft) cargo: *C-54; C-124.*

c., 1. calorie. **2.** *Optics.* candle; candles. **3.** carat. **4.** carbon. **5.** carton. **6.** case. **7.** *Baseball.* catcher. **8.** cathode. **9.** cent; cents. **10.** centavo. **11.** *Football.* center. **12.** centigrade. **13.** centime. **14.** centimeter. **15.** century. **16.** chairman; chairperson. **17.** chapter. **18.** chief. **19.** child. **20.** church. **21.** (with a year) about: *c. 1775.* [< L *circā, circiter, circum*] **22.** cirrus. **23.** city. **24.** cloudy. **25.** cognate. **26.** color. **27.** gallon. [< L *congius*] **28.** copper. **29.** copyright. **30.** corps. **31.** cubic. **32.** (in prescriptions) with. [< L *cum*] **33.** cycle; cycles.

ca' (kä, kô), *v.t., v.i. Scot.* to call, as to call an animal toward one; urge forward by calling. [var. of CALL]

CA, 1. California (approved esp. for use with zip code). **2.** chronological age.

Ca, *Symbol, Chem.* calcium.

ca-, var. of **ker-.**

ca., 1. cathode. **2.** centiare. **3.** Also, **ca** (with a year) about: *ca. 476 B.C.* [(def. 3) < L *circā*]

C.A., 1. Central America. **2.** See **chartered accountant. 3.** *Accounting.* chief accountant. **4.** Coast Artillery. **5.** commercial agent. **6.** consular agent. **7.** controller of accounts. **8.** See **current assets.**

C/A, 1. capital account. **2.** cash account. **3.** credit account. **4.** current account.

CAA, Civil Aeronautics Administration: reorganized into the Federal Aviation Administration. Also, **C.A.A.**

cab[1] (kab), *n., v.,* **cabbed, cab·bing.** —*n.* **1.** a taxicab. **2.** any of various horse-drawn vehicles, as a hansom or brougham, esp. one for public hire. **3.** the covered or enclosed part of a locomotive, truck, crane, etc., where the operator sits. **4.** the glass-enclosed area of an airport control tower in which the controllers are stationed. —*v.i.* **5.** to ride in a taxicab or horse-drawn cab: *They cabbed to the theater.* [1640–50; short for CABRIOLET] —**Syn. 1., 2.** hack, hackney, jitney.

cab[2] (kab), *n.* an ancient Hebrew measure equal to about two quarts. Also, **kab.** [1525–35; < Heb *qabh*]

cab[3] (kab), *n. Chiefly Brit.* cabbage[2] (def. 1b).

CAB, See **Civil Aeronautics Board.** Also, **C.A.B.**

ca·bal (kə bal′), *n., v.,* **-balled, -bal·ling.** —*n.* **1.** a small group of secret plotters, as against a government or person in authority. **2.** the plots and schemes of such a group; intrigue. **3.** a clique, as in artistic, literary, or theatrical circles. —*v.i.* **4.** to form a cabal; intrigue; conspire; plot. [1610–20, for an earlier sense; earlier *cabbal* < ML *cabbala.* See CABALA] —**ca·bal′ler,** *n.*
—**Syn. 1.** junta, faction, band, league, ring. **2.** See **conspiracy.**

cab·a·la (kab′ə lə, kə bä′-), *n.* **1.** a system of esoteric theosophy and theurgy developed by rabbis, reaching its peak about the 12th and 13th centuries, and influencing certain medieval and Renaissance Christian thinkers. It was based on a mystical method of interpreting Scripture by which initiates claimed to penetrate sacred mysteries. Among its central doctrines are, all creation is an emanation from the Deity and the soul exists from eternity. **2.** any occult or secret doctrine or science. Also, **cabbala, kabala, kabbala.** [1515–25; < ML *cab(b)ala* < Heb *qabbālāh* tradition, lit., something received, i.e., handed down]

ca·ba·let·ta (kab′ə let′ə, kä′bə-; *It.* kä′bä let′tä), *n., pl.* **-let·tas, -let·te** (-let′ā; *It.* -let′te). a short, operatic aria of simple form and style. [1835–45; < It, alter. of *coboletta* stanza, dim. of *cob(b)ola, cobla* stanza, couplet < OPr *cobla* < L *cōpula* bond; see COPULA]

cab·a·lism (kab′ə liz′əm), *n.* **1.** the principles or doctrines of the cabala. **2.** an interpretation of something according to the doctrines of the cabala. **3.** any mystic or occult doctrine; mysticism; occultism. **4.** extreme traditionalism in theological conception or interpretation. **5.** obfuscation or obscurantism, esp. resulting from an excessively recondite vocabulary: *the cabalism of some modern literary criticism.* [1580–90; CABAL(A) + -ISM]

cab·a·list[1] (kab′ə list), *n.* **1.** a student of or expert in the cabala. **2.** a person who is well-versed or highly skilled in obscure or esoteric matters. [1525–35; < ML *cabbalista,* equiv. to *cabbala* CABALA + L *-ista* -IST]

cab·a·list[2] (kab′ə list), *n.* a member of a cabal. [1635–45; perh. < F *cabaliste.* See CABAL, -IST]

cab·a·lis·tic (kab′ə lis′tik), *adj.* **1.** of or pertaining to the cabala. **2.** mystic; occult. **3.** of or marked by cabalism. Also, **cab′a·lis′ti·cal.** [1615–25; CABAL + -ISTIC] —**cab′a·lis′ti·cal·ly,** *adv.*
—**Syn. 2.** obscure, mysterious, arcane, dark.

Ca·ba·llé (kä′bä yā′, -bäl yā′; *Sp.* kä′vä lye′, -ye′), *n.* **Mont·ser·rat** (mônt′sə rät′; *Sp.* môn′seʀ ʀät′), born 1933, Spanish soprano.

ca·bal·le·ro (kab′əl yâr′ō, kab′ə lâr′ō; *Sp.* kä′vä-lye′ʀô, -ye′-), *n., pl.* **ca·bal·le·ros** (kab′əl yâr′ōz, kab′-ə lâr′ōz; *Sp.* kä′vä lye′ʀôs, -ye′-). **1.** a Spanish gentleman. **2.** *Southwestern U.S.* **a.** a horseman. **b.** a woman's escort or admirer; cavalier. [1740–50; < Sp < LL *caballārius* groom; see CAVALIER]

ca·ban·a (kə ban′ə, -ban′yə, -bä′nə, -bän′yə), *n.* **1.** a small cabin or tentlike structure for use as a bathhouse, esp. on a beach or by a swimming pool. **2.** a cabin or cottage. Also, **ca·ba·ña** (*Sp.* kä vä′nyä). [1830–40; < Sp *cabaña;* see CABIN]

Ca·ba·na·tuan (kä′vä nä twän′), *n.* a city on central Luzon, in the N Philippines. 138,298.

ca·bane (kə ban′), *n. Aeron.* a mastlike structure on some early airplanes, used for supporting the wing. [1910–15; < F; see CABIN]

cab·a·ret (kab′ə rā′ *for 1–4, 6, 7;* kab′ə ret′ *for 5*), *n., v.,* **-reted** (-rād′), **-ret·ing** (-rā′ing). —*n.* **1.** a restaurant providing food, drink, music, a dance floor, and often a floor show. **2.** a café that serves food and drink and offers entertainment often of an improvisatory, satirical, and topical nature. **3.** a floor show consisting of such entertainment: *The cover charge includes dinner and a cabaret.* **4.** a form of theatrical entertainment, consisting mainly of political satire in the form of skits, songs, and improvisations: *an actress whose credits include cabaret, TV, and dinner theater.* **5.** a decoratively painted porcelain coffee or tea service with tray, produced esp. in the 18th century. **6.** *Archaic.* a shop selling wines and liquors. —*v.i.* **7.** to attend or frequent cabarets. [1625–35; < F: tap-room, MF dial. (Picard or Walloon) < MD, denasalized var. of *cambret, cameret* < Picard *camberete* small room (c. F *chambrette;* see CHAMBER, -ETTE)]
—**Syn. 2.** nightclub, supper club, club.

cabaret′ tax′, a tax levied on entertainment, dancing, floor shows, etc., at places where liquor is served, as at cabarets and nightclubs. Cf. **amusement tax.**

cab·bage[1] (kab′ij), *n.* **1.** any of several cultivated varieties of a plant, *Brassica oleracea capitata,* of the mustard family, having a short stem and leaves formed into a compact, edible head. **2.** the head or leaves of this plant, eaten cooked or raw. **3.** *Slang.* money, esp. paper money. **4.** *Chiefly Brit. Informal.* **a.** a stupid, dull, or spiritless person. **b.** a mentally impaired person who is unable to live independently; vegetable. [1350–1400; ME *caboche, caboge, cabage* head of cabbage < dial. OF (Picardy, Normandy) lit., head, noggin, equiv. to *ca-* formative in expressive words, of uncert. orig. + *boche;* see BOSS[2], BOTCH[2]] —**cab′bage·like′,** *adj.*

cab·bage[2] (kab′ij), *n., v.,* **-baged, -bag·ing.** —*n.* **1.** *Chiefly Brit.* **a.** cloth scraps that remain after a garment has been cut from a fabric and that by custom the tailor may claim. **b.** Also called **cab.** such scraps used for reprocessing. —*v.t., v.i.* **2.** to steal; pilfer: *He cabbaged whole yards of cloth.* [1615–25; earlier *carbage* shred, piece of cloth, appar. var. of GARBAGE wheat straw chopped small (obs. sense)]

cab′bage a′phid, a small, blue aphid, *Brevicoryne brassicae,* that feeds on cabbage and related plants.

cab′bage bug′. See **harlequin bug.** [1865–70, *Amer.*]

cab′bage but′terfly, any white or chiefly white butterfly of the family Pieridae, as *Pieris rapae,* the larvae of which feed on the leaves of cabbages and other related plants. [1810–20]

cab·bage·head (kab′ij hed′), *n.* **1.** cabbage[1] (def. 2). **2.** *Informal.* a stupid person; dolt. [1675–85; CABBAGE[1] + HEAD]

cab′bage loop′er, the larva of a noctuid moth, *Trichoplusia ni,* common throughout the U.S. and Canada, that feeds on a wide variety of vegetable crops, esp. cabbage and lettuce. [1900–05]

cab′bage moth′. See **diamondback moth.** [1840–50]

cab′bage palm′, 1. any of several palms, esp. those of the genus *Euterpe,* having terminal leaf buds that are eaten as a vegetable or in salads. **2.** See **cabbage tree** (def. 2). [1765–75]

cab′bage palmet′to, a fan palm, *Sabal palmetto,* of the southeastern U.S.: the state tree of Florida and South Carolina. [1795–1805, *Amer.*]

cab′bage rose′, a rose, *Rosa centifolia,* having large and fragrant pink flowers, cultivated in many varieties. [1755–65]

cab•bage•town (kab′ij toun′), *n. Canadian.* a depressed or dilapidated urban area, esp. a city slum. [after *Cabbagetown,* a depressed area of Toronto, allegedly so called because its inhabitants' diet consisted mainly of cabbage]

cab′bage tree′, **1.** any tropical tree or treelike plant having leaves or edible shoots suggestive of cabbage. **2.** an Australian palm tree of the genus *Livistona,* esp. *L. australis.* [1715–25]

cab′bage-tree hat′ (kab′ij trē′), *Australian.* a broad-brimmed hat made from cabbage-tree leaves. [1875–80]

cab•bage•worm (kab′ij wûrm′), *n.* a caterpillar, esp. of the genus *Pieris,* that feeds on cabbages. [1680–90; CABBAGE[1] + WORM]

cab•bag•y (kab′i jē), *adj.* **1.** having the characteristics of the cabbage as in odor, taste, or color; cabbagelike. **2.** resembling or suggestive of a cabbage, as in shape. [1860–65; CABBAGE + -Y[1]]

cab•ba•la (kab′ə lə, kə bä′-), *n.* cabala. **—cab′ba•lism,** *n.* **—cab′ba•list,** *n.* **—cab′ba•lis′tic, cab′ba•lis′ti•cal,** *adj.* **—cab′ba•lis′ti•cal•ly,** *adv.*

cab•ble (kab′əl), *v.t.,* **-bled, -bling.** *Metall.* to cut up (iron or steel bars) for fagoting. [1840–50; var. of SCABBLE]

cab•by (kab′ē), *n., pl.* **-bies.** *Informal.* a cabdriver. Also, **cab′bie.** [1855–60; CAB(DRIVER) + -Y[2]]

cab•driv•er (kab′drī′vər), *n.* a driver of a taxicab or horse-drawn carriage. [1835–45; CAB[1] + DRIVER]

Cabe (kāb), *n.* a male given name, form of **McCabe.**

Ca•bei•ri (kə bī′rī), *n.* Cabiri.

Cab•ell (kab′əl), *n.* **James Branch,** 1879–1958, U.S. novelist, essayist, and critic.

ca•ber (kā′bər), *n. Scot.* a pole or beam, esp. one thrown as a trial of strength. [1505–15; < ScotGael *cabar* pole]

Ca•ber•net Sau•vi•gnon (kab′ər nā′ sō′vin yōN′; *Fr.* kA ber nā sō vē nyôN′), **1.** a premium red grape used in winemaking, esp. in the Bordeaux region of France and in northern California. **2.** a dry red wine made from this grape. Also called **Ca′ber•net′.** [< F *cabernet* variety of red grape < Médoc dial., also *carbenet, carmenet; sauvignon,* MF *sarvinien* name applied regionally to various grape varieties; both words of obscure orig.]

Ca•bet (kA be′), *n.* **Étienne** (ā tyen′), 1788–1856, French socialist who established a utopian community in the U.S. (in Illinois) called Icaria: became U.S. citizen 1854.

Ca•be•za de Va•ca (kä ve′thä the vä′kä, -ve′sä), **Ál•var Nú•ñez** (äl′vär nōō′nyeth, -nyes), c1490–1557?, Spanish explorer in the Americas.

cab•e•zon (kab′ə zon′; *Sp.* kä′ve sôn′), *n., pl.* **-zo•nes** (-zō′nāz; *Sp.* -sô′nes), **-zons:** any of several large-headed fishes, esp. a sculpin, *Scorpaenichthys marmoratus,* of Pacific coastal waters of North America. Also, **cab•e•zone** (kab′ə zōn′, kab′ə zōn′). [< Sp, equiv. to *cabez(a)* head (< VL **capitia,* deriv. of L *caput* head) + *-on* aug. suffix]

ca•bil•do (kä vēl′dô; *Eng.* kə bil′dō), *n., pl.* **-dos** (-thôs; *Eng.* -dōz). *Spanish.* **1.** the chapter house of a cathedral. **2.** a town council, esp. in Latin America. **3.** a town hall in colonial Spanish America.

Ca•bi•mas (kä vē′mäs), *n.* a city in NW Venezuela, on the E coast of Lake Maracaibo. 122,239.

cab•in (kab′in), *n.* **1.** a small house or cottage, usually of simple design and construction: *He was born in a cabin built of rough logs.* **2.** an enclosed space for more or less temporary occupancy, as the living quarters in a trailer or the passenger space in a cable car. **3.** the enclosed space for the pilot, cargo, or esp. passengers in an air or space vehicle. **4.** an apartment or room in a ship, as for passengers. **5.** See **cabin class. 6.** (in a naval vessel) living accommodations for officers. *—adv.* **7.** in cabin-class accommodations or by cabin-class conveyance: *to travel cabin.* *—v.i.* **8.** to live in a cabin: *They cabin in the woods on holidays.* *—v.t.* **9.** to confine; enclose tightly; cramp. [1325–75; ME *cabane* < MF < OPr *cabana* < LL *capanna* (Isidore of Seville), of uncert., perh. pre-L orig.; sp. with *i* perh. by influence of F *cabine* (see CABINET)]
—Syn. 1. cot, shanty, shack, cottage. **6.** quarters, compartment.

cab′in attend′ant, **1.** See **flight attendant. 2.** a cabin steward on a passenger or cruise ship.

cab′in boy′, a boy employed as a servant for the officers and passengers on a ship. [1720–30]

cab′in class′, the class of accommodations on a passenger ship less costly and luxurious than first class but more so than tourist class. Cf. **second class** (def. 1). [1925–30] **—cab′in-class′,** *adj., adv.*

cab′in court′, *Older Use.* a roadside motel having cabins.

cab′in cruis′er, a power-driven pleasure boat having a cabin equipped for sleeping, cooking, and the like. [1920–25]

CONCISE ETYMOLOGY KEY: <, descended or borrowed from; >, whence; b., blend of, blended; c., cognate with; cf., compare; deriv., derivative; equiv., equivalent; imit., imitative; obl., oblique; r., replacing; s., stem; sp., spelling, spelled; resp., respelling, respelled; trans., translation; ?, origin unknown; *, unattested; ‡, probably earlier than. See the full key inside the front cover.

Ca•bin•da (kə bēn′də), *n.* **1.** an exclave of Angola, on the W coast of Africa. 81,265; 2807 sq. mi. (7270 sq. km). **2.** a seaport in and the capital of this exclave, on the Congo (Zaire) River. 30,000.

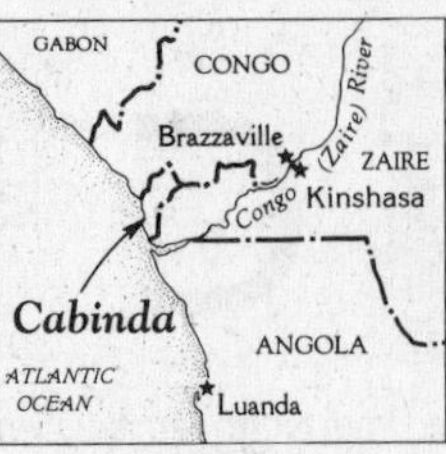

cab′in deck′, the deck above the weather deck in the bridge house of a ship. [‡1960–65]

cab•i•net (kab′ə nit), *n.* **1.** a piece of furniture with shelves, drawers, etc., for holding or displaying items: *a curio cabinet; a file cabinet.* **2.** a wall cupboard used for storage, as of kitchen utensils or toilet articles: *a kitchen cabinet; a medicine cabinet.* **3.** a piece of furniture containing a radio or television set, usually standing on the floor and often having a record player or a place for phonograph records. **4.** (*often cap.*) a council advising a president, sovereign, etc., esp. the group of ministers or executives responsible for the government of a nation. **5.** (*often cap.*) (in the U.S.) an advisory body to the president, consisting of the heads of the 13 executive departments of the federal government. **6.** a small case with compartments for valuables or other small objects. **7.** a small chamber or booth for special use, esp. a shower stall. **8.** a private room. **9.** a room set aside for the exhibition of small works of art or objets d'art. **10.** Also called **cabinet wine.** a dry white wine produced in Germany from fully matured grapes without the addition of extra sugar. **11.** *New Eng.* (*chiefly Rhode Island and Southern Massachusetts*). a milk shake made with ice cream. **12.** *Archaic.* a small room. **13.** *Obs.* a small cabin. *—adj.* **14.** pertaining to a political cabinet: *a cabinet meeting.* **15.** private; confidential; secret. **16.** pertaining to a private room. **17.** of suitable value, beauty, or size for a private room, small display case, etc.: *a cabinet edition of Milton.* **18.** of, pertaining to, or used by a cabinetmaker or in cabinetmaking. **19.** *Drafting.* designating a method of projection **(cab′inet projec′tion)** in which a three-dimensional object is represented by a drawing **(cab′inet draw′ing)** having all vertical and horizontal lines drawn to exact scale, with oblique lines reduced to about half scale so as to offset the appearance of distortion. Cf. **axonometric, isometric** (def. 5), **oblique** (def. 13). See illus. under **isometric.** [1540–50; < MF, equiv. to *cabine* hut, room on a ship (of uncert. orig., but frequently alleged to be alter. of *cabane* CABIN) + *-et* -ET]
—Syn. 4. advisers, ministry, counselors.

CABINET OF THE UNITED STATES

Department of	Abbrev.	Created in
Agriculture	USDA	1889
Commerce	DOC	1913
Defense	DOD	1949
Education	ED	1979
Energy	DOE	1977
Health and Human Services*	HHS	1979*
Housing and Urban Development	HUD	1965
The Interior	DOI	1849
Justice	DOJ	1870
Labor	DOL	1913
State	DOS	1789
Transportation	DOT	1966
The Treasury	TD	1789

*Originally created in 1953 as the Department of Health, Education, and Welfare (HEW).

cab•i•net•eer (kab′ə ni tēr′), *n.* (*sometimes cap.*) a member of a governmental cabinet. [1830–40; CABINET + -EER]

cab′inet gov′ernment. See **parliamentary government.** Also, **Cab′inet gov′ernment.** [1865–70]

cab•i•net•mak•er (kab′ə nit mā′kər), *n.* a person who makes fine furniture and other woodwork. [1675–85; CABINET + MAKER]

cab•i•net•mak•ing (kab′ə nit mā′king), *n.* **1.** the manufacture of fine furniture and other woodwork. **2.** the occupation or craft of a cabinetmaker. [1805–15; CABINET + MAKING]

cab′inet min′ister, a member of a governmental cabinet, as in Great Britain. [1800–10]

cab′inet pic′ture, a small easel painting, usually under 3 ft. (0.9 m) in width and formerly exhibited in a cabinet or special room. [1815–25]

cab′inet pud′ding, a bread or cake pudding baked in a mold placed in a pan of hot water, usually filled with candied fruit, raisins, and currants, and often served hot with a fruit sauce. [1815–25]

cab•i•net•ry (kab′ə ni trē), *n.* cabinetwork. [CABINET + -RY]

cab′inet scrap′er, a scraper used in preparing a wood surface for sanding.

cab′inet wine′, cabinet (def. 10).

cab•i•net•wood (kab′ə nit wŏŏd′), *n.* any wood suitable for use in cabinetwork. [CABINET + WOOD[1]]

cab•i•net•work (kab′ə nit wûrk′), *n.* **1.** fine furniture or other woodwork. **2.** cabinetmaking. [1725–35, *Amer.;* CABINET + WORK] **—cab′i•net•work′er,** *n.*

cab′in fe′ver, a state characterized by anxiety, restlessness, and boredom, arising from a prolonged stay in a remote or confined place. [1915–20, *Amer.*]

cab′in hook′, a hook and eye for fastening a cabinet door or the like.

Ca•bi•ri (kə bī′rī, -rē), *n.* (*used with a plural v.*) a group of gods, probably of Eastern origin, worshiped in mysteries in various parts of ancient Greece, the cult centers being at Samothrace and Thebes. Also, **Cabeiri, Kabeiri.** **—Ca•bi•re•an** (kab′ə rē′ən), **Ca•bir•i•an** (kə bir′ē ən), **Ca•bir•ic** (kə bir′ik), **Cab•i•rit•ic** (kab′ə-rit′ik), *adj.*

ca•ble (kā′bəl), *n., v.,* **-bled, -bling.** *—n.* **1.** a heavy, strong rope. **2.** a very strong rope made of strands of metal wire, as used to support cable cars or suspension bridges. **3.** a cord of metal wire used to operate or pull a mechanism. **4.** *Naut.* **a.** a thick hawser made of rope, strands of metal wire, or chain. **b.** See **cable's length. 5.** *Elect.* an insulated electrical conductor, often in strands, or a combination of electrical conductors insulated from one another. **6.** cablegram. **7.** See **cable television. 8.** cable-stitch. **9.** *Archit.* one of a number of reedings set into the flutes of a column or pilaster. *—v.t.* **10.** to send (a message) by cable. **11.** to send a cablegram to. **12.** to fasten with a cable. **13.** to furnish with a cable. **14.** to join (cities, parts of a country, etc.) by means of a cable television network: *The state will be completely cabled in a few years.* *—v.i.* **15.** to send a message by cable. **16.** to cable-stitch. [1175–1225; ME, prob. < ONF **cable* < LL *capulum* lasso; cf. L *capulāre* to rope, halter (cattle), akin to *capere* to take] **—ca′ble•like′,** *adj.*

Ca•ble (kā′bəl), *n.* **George Washington,** 1844–1925, U.S. novelist and short-story writer.

ca′ble bend′, **1.** a knot or clinch for attaching a cable to an anchor or mooring post. **2.** a short line for forming a loop in a cable to secure it to an anchor.

ca′ble bu′oy, a buoy marking or supporting part of a submerged cable. [1760–70]

ca′ble car′, a vehicle, usually enclosed, used on a cable railway or tramway. Also, **ca′ble-car′.** [1870–75]

ca•ble•cast (kā′bəl kast′, -käst′), *n., adj., v.,* **-cast** or **-cast•ed, -cast•ing.** *—n.* **1.** a television program broadcast via cable television. *—adj.* **2.** (of television programs) broadcast via cable: *a cablecast news program.* *—v.t., v.i.* **3.** to broadcast via cable television. [1965–70; CABLE + (BROAD)CAST] **—ca′ble•cast′er,** *n.*

ca′ble crane′, cableway.

ca•ble•gram (kā′bəl gram′), *n.* a telegram sent by underwater cable. [1865–70; CABLE + (TELE)GRAM]

ca•ble•laid (kā′bəl lād′), *adj.* **1.** noting a rope formed of three plain-laid ropes twisted together in a left-handed direction; hawser-laid. **2.** noting a rope formed of three backhanded ropes twisted together in a right-handed direction. [1715–25; CABLE + LAID]

ca′ble length′. See **cable's length.**

ca′ble mold′ing, a molding in the form of a rope. [1855–60]

ca•ble•pho•to (kā′bəl fō′tō), *n.* a photographic image transmitted via cable, esp. for use by newspapers or in police work. [CABLE + PHOTO]

ca′ble rail′way, a railway on which the cars are pulled by a moving cable under the roadway. [1885–90]

ca•ble-read•y (kā′bəl red′ē), *adj.* (of a television or VCR) able to receive cable television directly, without the need for special reception or decoding equipment. [1980–85]

ca′ble release′, *Photog.* a device consisting of a flexible wire that is pressed at one end to trip a shutter mechanism on a camera. [1955–60]

ca′ble's length′, a nautical unit of length equivalent to 720 feet (219 meters) in the U.S. Navy and 608 feet (185 meters) in the British Navy. Also, **cable length.** Also called **cable.** [1545–55]

ca•ble-stitch (kā′bəl stich′), *n.* **1.** a series of stitches used in knitting to produce a cable effect. **2.** the pattern produced by a cable-stitch. *—v.i.* **3.** to produce such a stitch or pattern. [1885–90]

ca•blet (kā′blit), *n.* a small cable, esp. a cablelaid rope under 10 in. (25 cm) in circumference. [CABLE + -ET]

ca′ble tel′evision, a system of broadcasting television programming to private subscribers by means of coaxial cable. Also called **cable TV, pay cable.**

ca′ble tram′way, tramway (def. 4). [1885–90]

ca•ble•vi•sion (kā′bəl vizh′ən), *n.* See **cable television.** [1970–75; CABLE + (TELE)VISION]

ca•ble•way (kā′bəl wā′), *n.* a system for hoisting and hauling bulk materials, consisting of a cable or pair of cables suspended between two towers, on which travels a carriage from which a bucket is suspended: used in heavy construction work, in storage plants, etc. Also called **cable crane.** [1895–1900; CABLE + WAY]

ca•bling (kā′bling), *n. Archit.* **1.** decoration with cable moldings. **2.** reedings set into the flutes of a column or pilaster. [1745–55; CABLE + -ING[1]]

cab•man (kab′mən), *n., pl.* **-men.** cabdriver. [1825–35; CAB[1] + -MAN]

ca•bob (kə bob′), *n.* kabob.

ca•boched (kə bosht′), *adj.* caboshed. Also, **ca•bo•ché** (kab′ə shā′).

cab•o•chon (kab′ə shon′; *Fr.* kA bô shôN′), *n., pl.* **-chons** (-shonz′; *Fr.* -shôN′), *adv.* *—n.* **1.** a precious stone of convex hemispherical or oval form, polished but not cut into facets. **2.** an ornamental motif resembling this, either concave or convex and often surrounded by ornately carved leaf patterns, used on furniture of the 18th century. —*adv.* **3.** in the form of a cabochon: *a turquoise cut cabochon.* —*adj.* **4.** being cut cabochon: *cabochon gems.* [1570–80; < MF, equiv. to *caboche* head (see CABBAGE[1]) + *-on* dim. suffix]

ca•bo•clo (kə bô′klo͞o, -klō, -bō′-; *Port.* kə bô′klo͝o), *n., pl.* **-clos** (-klo͞oz, -klōz; *Port.* -klo͝osh). a Brazilian of Indian or mixed Indian and white ancestry. [1810–20; < Pg < Tupi *caboco, caboculo, caboclo*]

ca•boo•dle (kə bo͞od′l), *n. Informal.* **1.** the lot, pack, or crowd: *I have no use for the whole caboodle.* **2. kit and caboodle.** See **kit**[1] (def. 8). [1840–50, *Amer.*; perh. CA- + BOODLE]

ca•boose (kə bo͞os′), *n.* **1.** a car on a freight train, used chiefly as the crew's quarters and usually attached to the rear of the train. **2.** *Brit.* a kitchen on the deck of a ship; galley. **3.** *Slang.* the buttocks. [1740–50; < early modern D *cabūse* (D *kabuis*) ship's galley, storeroom; cf. LG *kabuus, kabüse,* MLG *kabuse* booth, shed; further orig. uncert.]

Ca•bo Ro•jo (kä′bō rō′hō; *Sp.* kä′vô rô′hô), a city in SW Puerto Rico. 10,292.

ca•boshed (kə bosht′), *adj. Heraldry.* (of an animal, as a deer) shown facing forward without a neck: *a stag's head caboshed.* Also, **ca•bossed** (kə bost′), **cabouched, caboché.** [1565–75; var. of *cabouched,* ptp. of ME *caboche* to behead (a deer) < AF *cabocher,* deriv. of *caboche* head; see CABBAGE[1]]

Cab•ot (kab′ət), *n.* **1. John** (*Giovanni Caboto*), c1450–98?, Italian navigator in the service of England: discoverer of North American mainland 1497. **2. Richard Clarke,** 1868–1939, U.S. physician and writer on medical ethics. **3. Sebastian,** 1474?–1557, English navigator and explorer (son of John Cabot). **4.** a male given name.

cab•o•tage (kab′ə tij, kab′ə täzh′), *n.* **1.** navigation or trade along the coast. **2.** *Aviation.* the legal restriction to domestic carriers of air transport between points within a country's borders. [1825–35; < F, deriv. of *caboter* to sail coastwise, v. deriv. of MF *cabo* < Sp *cabo* headland, CAPE[2]; see -AGE]

Cab′ot Strait′, a channel in Canada, connecting the Gulf of St. Lawrence with the Atlantic Ocean. 68 mi. (109 km) wide.

cab-o•ver (kab′ō′vər), *n.* **1.** a truck tractor or other vehicle in which the cab is located over the engine. **2.** a camper in which the body extends forward over the cab of the truck on which it is mounted. —*adj.* **3.** pertaining to such a vehicle or camper. **4.** pertaining to the part of a camper that extends over the cab. Also, **cab′o′ver.**

Ca•bral (kə bräl′), *n.* **Pe•dro Ál•va•res** (pe′dro͝o ôl′və rəsh), c1460–c1520, Portuguese navigator.

Ca•bre•ra (*Sp.* kä vre′rä), *n.* **Ma•nuel Es•tra•da** (*Sp.* män wel′ es trä′thä). See **Estrada Cabrera, Manuel.**

ca•bret•ta (kə bret′ə), *n.* a leather made from the skins of sheep that grow hair rather than wool, tougher than other sheepskins and used chiefly for gloves and shoes. [1915–20; < Pg or Sp *cabr(a)* she-goat (< L *capra*) + It *-etta,* for -ETTE, as in LEATHERETTE, etc.]

ca•bril•la (kə bril′ə), *n.* any of several sea basses, esp. *Epinephelus analogus,* of tropical eastern Pacific seas. [1855–60; < Sp: prawn, equiv. to *cabr(a)* she-goat (< L *capra*) + *-illa* dim. suffix]

Ca•bri•ni (kə brē′nē; *It.* kä brē′nē), *n.* **Saint Frances Xavier** ("*Mother Cabrini*"), 1850–1917, U.S. nun, born in Italy; founder of the Missionary Sisters of the Sacred Heart of Jesus.

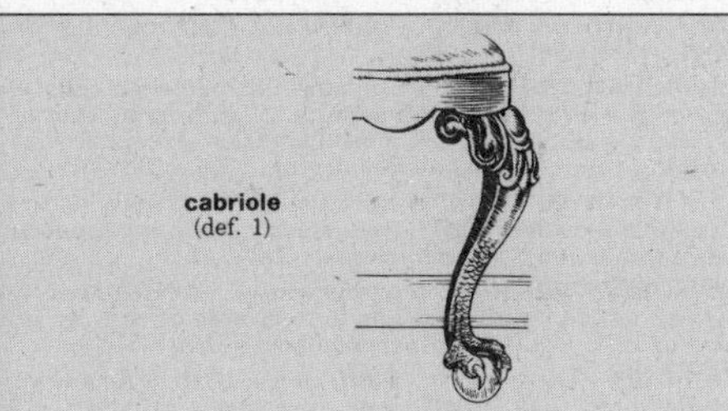
cabriole (def. 1)

cab•ri•ole (kab′rē ōl′; *Fr.* ka brē ôl′), *n., pl.* **-oles** (-ōlz′; *Fr.* -ôl′). **1.** *Furniture.* a curved, tapering leg curving outward at the top and inward farther down so as to end in a round pad, the semblance of an animal's paw, or some other feature: used esp. in the first half of the 18th century. **2.** *Ballet.* a leap in which one leg is raised in the air and the other is brought up to beat against it. [1775–85; < F: leap, caper; so called because modeled on leg of a capering animal (see CAPRIOLE); *b* by influence of *cabri* kid (<< OPr) and kindred words]

cab•ri•o•let (kab′rē ə lā′), *n.* **1.** a light, two-wheeled, one-horse carriage with a folding top, capable of seating two persons. **2.** an automobile resembling a coupe but with a folding top. [1760–70; < F: lit., little caper; so called from its light movement. See CABRIOLE, -ET]

cabriolet (def. 1)

ca•bri•to (kə brē′tō; *Sp.* kä vrē′tô), *n. Mexican Cookery.* the meat of a young goat. [< Sp: kid, equiv. to *cabr(o)* goat (<< L *caper*) + *-ito* dim. suffix]

cab•stand (kab′stand′), *n.* a place where cabs may wait to be hired. [1855–60; CAB[1] + STAND]

ca•bu•ya (kə bo͞o′yə; *Sp.* kä vo͞o′yä), *n., pl.* **-yas** (-yəz; *Sp.* -yäs). See **Mauritius hemp.** [< Sp < Taino]

C.A.C., Coast Artillery Corps.

ca•ca (kä′kä′), *n. Baby Talk.* excrement; feces.

ca′can•ny (kä kan′ē, kô-), *n. Brit. Slang.* a deliberate reduction of working speed and production by workers, to express their discontent. [1895–1900; lit., drive gently; see CA′, CANNY]

ca•ca•o (kə kä′ō, -kā′ō), *n., pl.* **-ca•os. 1.** a small tropical American evergreen tree, *Theobroma cacao,* cultivated for its seeds, the source of cocoa, chocolate, etc. **2.** Also, **cocoa.** the fruit or seeds of this tree. [1545–55; < Sp < Nahuatl *cacahuatl* cacao seeds]

caca′o bean′, a seed of the cacao tree. Also, **cocoa bean.** [1830–40]

caca′o but′ter. See **cocoa butter.** [1545–55]

cac•cia (kä′chə; *It.* kät′chä), *n., pl.* **-ce** (-chā; *It.* -che), **-cias.** a 14th-century Italian vocal form for two voices in canon plus an independent tenor, with a text describing the hunt or the cries and noises of village life. [< It: lit., a hunt; see CATCH, CHASE[1]]

cac•cia•to•re (kä′chə tôr′ē, -tōr′ē), *adj. Italian Cookery.* prepared with or containing tomatoes, mushrooms, herbs, and other seasonings: *chicken cacciatore.* Also, **cac•cia•to•ra** (kä′chə tôr′ə, -tōr′ə). [1940–45; short for It *alla cacciatora* in the manner of hunters; *cacciatora,* fem. deriv. of *cacciatore* hunter, equiv. to *cacci(a)* CACCIA + *-atore* -ATOR]

Cac•ci•ni (kät chē′nē), *n.* **Giu•lio** (jo͞o′lyô), c1546–1618, Italian singer and composer.

cach•a•lot (kash′ə lot′, -lō′), *n.* See **sperm whale.** [1740–50; < F << Pg *cacholote,* equiv. to *cachol(a)* pate, noggin (of obscure orig.) + *-ote* aug. suffix]

cache (kash), *n., v.,* **cached, cach•ing.** —*n.* **1.** a hiding place, esp. one in the ground, for ammunition, food, treasures, etc.: *She hid her jewelry in a little cache in the cellar.* **2.** anything so hidden: *The enemy never found our cache of food.* **3.** *Alaska and Northern Canada.* a small shed elevated on poles above the reach of animals and used for storing food, equipment, etc. —*v.t.* **4.** to put in a cache; conceal; hide. [1585–95; < F, n. deriv. of *cacher* to hide < VL **coācticāre* to stow away, orig. to pack together, equiv. to L *coāct(us)* collected (ptp. of *cōgere;* see COACTIVE) + *-icā-* formative v. suffix + *-re* inf. ending]
—**Syn. 2.** hoard, stockpile, reserve, store. **4.** secrete.

ca•chec•tin (kə kek′tin), *n. Biochem., Immunol.* a protein that is released by activated macrophages as an immune system defense and, when the defense is overwhelmed, is a cause of cachexia or toxic shock: in humans, identical with tumor necrosis factor. [< Gk *kachékt(ikós)* unwell (see CACHEXIA, -TIC) + -IN[2]]

cache•pot (kash′pot′, -pō′), *n.* an ornamental container, usually of china or tole, for holding and concealing a flowerpot. [1870–75; < F: lit., (it) hides (the) pot; see CACHE, POT[1]]

cache′ stor′age, *Computers.* a small, very fast but not addressable memory used on some computers for executing instructions.

ca•chet (ka shā′, kash′ā; *Fr.* ka she′), *n., pl.* **ca•chets** (ka shāz′, kash′āz; *Fr.* ka she′). **1.** an official seal, as on a letter or document. **2.** a distinguishing mark or feature; stamp: *Courtesy is the cachet of good breeding.* **3.** a sign or expression of approval, esp. from a person who has a great deal of prestige. **4.** superior status; prestige: *The job has a certain cachet.* **5.** *Pharm.* a hollow wafer for enclosing an ill-tasting medicine. **6.** *Philately.* a firm name, slogan, or design stamped or printed on an envelope or folded letter. [1630–40; < F: lit., something compressed to a small size, equiv. to *cache* CACHE + *-et* -ET]

Ca•cheu (*Port.* kä′she o͞o), *n.* a port in NW Guinea-Bissau. 134,108.

ca•chex•i•a (kə kek′sē ə), *n. Pathol.* general ill health with emaciation, usually occurring in association with cancer or a chronic infectious disease. Also, **ca•chex•y** (kə kek′sē) [1535–45; < LL < Gk, equiv. to *kak(ós)* bad + *héx(is)* condition (*hek-,* var. s. of *échein* to have + *-sis* -SIS) + *-ia* -IA] —**ca•chec•tic** (kə kek′tik), **ca•chec′ti•cal, ca•chex′ic,** *adj.*

cach•in•nate (kak′ə nāt′), *v.i.,* **-nat•ed, -nat•ing.** to laugh loudly or immoderately. [1815–25; < L *cachinnātus* (ptp. of *cachinnāre* to laugh aloud, laugh immoderately), equiv. to *cachinn-* laugh aloud + *-ātus* -ATE[1]] —**cach′in•na′tion,** *n.* —**cach′in•na′tor,** *n.* —**cach•in•na•to•ry** (kak′ə nə tôr′ē, -tōr′ē, kə kin′ə-), *adj.*

Ca•cho•ei•ro do I•ta•pe•mi•rim (kä′shō ā′ro͝o do͞o ē′tä pe′mi rēn′), a city in SE Brazil. 110,301.

ca•chou (kə sho͞o′, ka-, kash′o͞o), *n.* **1.** catechu. **2.** a pill or lozenge for sweetening the breath. [1700–10; < F < Pg *cachu* < Malay; see CATECHU]

ca•chu•cha (kə cho͞o′chə; *Sp.* kä cho͞o′chä), *n., pl.* **-chas** (-chəz; *Sp.* -chäs). **1.** an Andalusian dance resembling the bolero. **2.** the music for this dance. [1830–40; < Sp: perh. lit., fragment; of obscure orig.]

ca•cim•bo (kə sim′bō), *n., pl.* **-bos.** a heavy mist or drizzle that occurs in the Congo basin area, often accompanied by onshore winds. [< Pg, said to be from Kimbundu]

ca•cique (kə sēk′), *n.* **1.** a chief of an Indian clan or tribe in Mexico and the West Indies. **2.** (in Spain and Latin America) a political boss on a local level. **3.** (in the Philippines) a prominent landowner. **4.** any of several black and red or black and yellow orioles of the American tropics that construct long, pendent nests. [1545–55; < Sp < Taino (Hispaniola)]

cack (kak), *n.* a soft-soled, heelless shoe for infants. [1890–95; of obscure orig.]

cack•le (kak′əl), *v.,* **-led, -ling,** *n.* —*v.i.* **1.** to utter a shrill, broken sound or cry, as of a hen. **2.** to laugh in a shrill, broken manner. **3.** to chatter noisily; prattle. —*v.t.* **4.** to utter with cackles; express by cackling: *They cackled their disapproval.* —*n.* **5.** the act or sound of cackling. **6.** chatter; idle talk. [1175–1225; ME *cakelen;* c. D *kakelen,* LG *kakeln,* Sw *kackla*] —**cack′ler,** *n.*

cack•le•ber•ry (kak′əl ber′ē), *n., pl.* **-ries.** *Facetious.* a hen's egg used for food. [1915–20; CACKLE + BERRY]

caco-, a combining form meaning "bad," occurring in loanwords from Greek (*cacodemon*); on this model, used in the formation of compound words (*cacogenics*). [< Gk, comb. form of *kakós*]

cac•o•de•mon (kak′ə dē′mən), *n.* an evil spirit; devil; demon. Also, **cac′o•dae′mon.** [1585–95; < Gk *kakodaímōn* having an evil genius, ill-fated. See CACO-, DEMON] —**cac•o•de•mon•ic, cac•o•dae•mon•ic** (kak′ə di mon′ik), **cac•o•de•mo•ni•ac, cac•o•dae•mo•ni•ac** (kak′ə di mō′nē ak′), *adj.*

cac•o•dyl (kak′ə dil), —*adj.* **1.** containing the cacodyl group. —*n.* **2.** an oily, slightly water-soluble, poisonous liquid compound composed of two cacodyl groups, $(CH_3)_2As-As(CH_3)_2$, that has a vile, garliclike odor and that undergoes spontaneous combustion in dry air. [1840–50; < Gk *kakṓd(ēs)* ill-smelling (*kak(o)-* CACO- + *-ōd-* smell + *-ēs* adj. suffix) + -YL]

cac•o•dyl•ate (kak′ə dil′āt), *n.* a salt of cacodylic acid. [1905–1910; CACODYL(IC) + -ATE[2]]

cac′odyl group′, the univalent group $(CH_3)_2As-$, derived from arsine. Also called **cac′odyl rad′ical.**

cac•o•dyl•ic (kak′ə dil′ik), *adj.* of, pertaining to, or characteristic of the cacodyl group. [1840–50; CACODYL + -IC]

cac′odyl′ic ac′id, a colorless, crystalline, deliquescent, poisonous solid, $(CH_3)_2AsOOH$, used chiefly in the manufacture of dyes and as an herbicide. [1840–50]

cac•o•ë•thes (kak′ō ē′thēz), *n.* an irresistible urge; mania. Also, **cac′o•e′thes.** [1555–65; < L < Gk *kakóēthes,* neut. (used as n.) of *kakoḗthēs* malignant, lit., of bad character; see CACO-, ETHOS]

cac•o•gen•ics (kak′ə jen′iks), *n.* (*used with a singular v.*) dysgenics. [1915–20; CACO- + (EU)GENICS] —**cac′o•gen′ic,** *adj.*

ca•cog•ra•phy (kə kog′rə fē), *n.* **1.** bad handwriting; poor penmanship. **2.** incorrect spelling. [1570–80; CACO- + -GRAPHY] —**ca•cog′ra•pher,** *n.* —**cac•o•graph•ic** (kak′ə graf′ik), **cac′o•graph′i•cal,** *adj.*

ca•col•o•gy (ka kol′ə jē, kə-), *n.* defectively produced speech; socially unacceptable diction. [1615–25; CACO- + -LOGY]

cac•o•mis•tle (kak′ə mis′əl), *n.* **1.** Also, **cac•o•mix•le** (kak′ə mis′əl, -mik′səl). Also called **bassarisk, ringtail, coon cat.** a carnivorous animal, *Bassariscus astutus,* of Mexico and the southwestern U.S., related to the raccoon but smaller, with a sharper snout and longer tail. **2.** See **civet cat.** [1865–70, *Amer.*; < MexSp *cacomiztle, cacomixtle* < Nahuatl *tlahcomiztli,* equiv. to *tlahco-* half, middle + *miztli* cougar]

cacomistle, *Bassariscus astutus,* head and body 1 ft. (0.3 m); tail 1½ ft. (0.46 m)

cac•o•nym (kak′ə nim), *n.* a name, esp. a taxonomic name, that is considered linguistically undesirable. [1885–90; CAC(O)- + -ONYM]

ca•coph•o•nous (kə kof′ə nəs), *adj.* having a harsh or discordant sound. [1790–1800; < Gk *kakóphōnos.* See CACO-, -PHONE, -OUS] —**ca•coph′o•nous•ly,** *adv.*
—**Syn.** dissonant, strident, grating, raucous.

ca•coph•o•ny (kə kof′ə nē), *n., pl.* **-nies. 1.** harsh discordance of sound; dissonance: *a cacophony of hoots, cackles, and wails.* **2.** a discordant and meaningless mixture of sounds: *the cacophony produced by city traffic at midday.* **3.** *Music.* frequent use of discords of a harshness and relationship difficult to understand. [1650–60; < NL *cacophonia* < Gk *kakophōnía.* See CACO-, -PHONY] —**cac•o•phon•ic** (kak′ə fon′ik), *adj.*

cac•que•teuse (kak′ə to͞oz′; *Fr.* kakᵊ tœz′), *n., pl.* **-teus•es** (-to͞o′ziz; *Fr.* -tœz′). a narrow, upright armchair of 16th-century France, having widely splayed arms and a very narrow back. Also, **caqueteuse, caquetoire.** [< F, equiv. to *caquet(er)* to chatter + *-euse* -EUSE]

cac•ta•ceous (kak tā′shəs), *adj.* belonging to the Cactaceae, the cactus family of plants. [1850–55; < NL *Cactace(ae)* name of the family (see CACTUS, -ACEAE) + -OUS]

cac•tus (kak′təs), *n., pl.* **-ti** (-tī), **-tus•es, -tus.** any of numerous succulent plants of the family Cactaceae, of

CONCISE PRONUNCIATION KEY: act, cāpe, dâre, pärt; set, ēqual; *if,* īce; ox, ōver, ôrder, oil, bo͝ok, bo͞ot, out; up, ûrge; child; sing; shoe; thin, *that;* zh as in *treasure.* ə = *a* as in *alone, e* as in *system, i* as in *easily, o* as in *gallop, u* as in *circus;* ᵊ as in *fire* (fīᵊr), *hour* (ouᵊr). l and n can serve as syllabic consonants, as in *cradle* (krād′l), and *button* (but′n). See the full key inside the front cover.

warm, arid regions of the New World, having fleshy, leafless, usually spiny stems, and typically having solitary, showy flowers. [1600–10; < L < Gk *káktos* cardoon] **—cac′tus·like′, cac′toid,** *adj.*

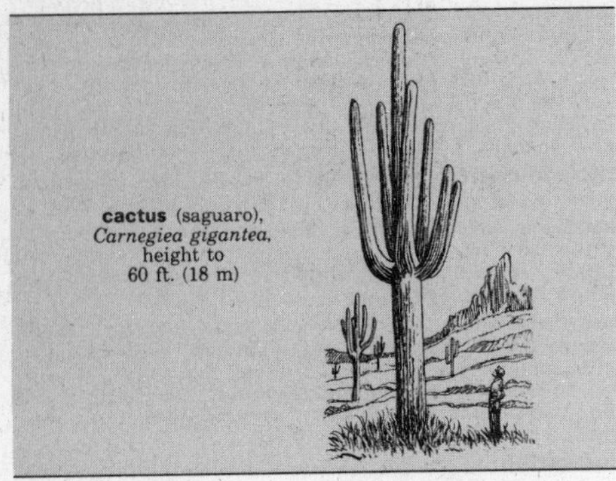

cactus (saguaro), *Carnegiea gigantea,* height to 60 ft. (18 m)

cac′tus dahl′ia, any of several varieties of dahlia having large flower heads with numerous rays incurved to a quill-like form. [1880–85]

cac′tus gera′nium, a plant, *Pelargonium echinatum,* of the geranium family, native to southern Africa, having prickly stipules and white or reddish flowers.

cac′tus moth′, a moth, *Cactoblastis cactorum,* native to South America and introduced into Australia to control prickly pear cactus, on which the larvae feed.

cac′tus wren′, any American wren of the genus *Campylorhynchus,* of arid regions, esp. *C. brunneicapillus,* of the southwestern U.S. and Mexico. [1865–70, *Amer.*]

ca·cu·mi·nal (kə kyo͞o′mə nl), *Phonet.* *—adj.* **1.** pronounced with the tip of the tongue curled back toward or against the hard palate; retroflex; cerebral. *—n.* **2.** a cacuminal sound. [1860–65; < L *cacūmin-* (s. of *cacūmen*) top, tip + -AL[1]]

cad (kad), *n.* **1.** an ill-bred man, esp. one who behaves in a dishonorable or irresponsible way toward women. **2.** *Brit. Archaic.* **a.** a local town boy or youth, as contrasted with a university or public school student. **b.** a servant at a university or public school. [1780–90; short for CADDIE (def. 2)]
—Syn. 1. bounder, rotter, rascal, rogue; heel.

CAD (kad), *n.* computer-aided design.

ca·das·tral (kə das′trəl), *adj.* **1.** *Survey.* (of a map or survey) showing or including boundaries, property lines, etc. **2.** of or pertaining to a cadastre. [1855–60; < F; see CADASTRE, -AL[1]] **—ca·das′tral·ly,** *adv.*

ca·das·tre (kə das′tər), *n.* an official register of the ownership, extent, and value of real property in a given area, used as a basis of taxation. Also, **ca·das′ter.** [1795–1805; < F < Pr *cadastro* < It *catastro,* earlier (Venetian) *catastico* < LGk *katástichon* register, deriv. of phrase *katà stíchon* by line; see CATA-, STICH]

ca·dav·er (kə dav′ər), *n.* a dead body, esp. a human body to be dissected; corpse. [1350–1400; ME < L *cadāver* dead body, corpse; akin to *cadere* to fall, perish (see DECAY, CHANCE)] **—ca·dav′er·ic,** *adj.*
—Syn. See **body.**

ca·dav·er·ine (kə dav′ə rēn′), *n. Biochem.* a colorless, viscous, toxic ptomaine, $C_5H_{14}N_2$, having an offensive odor, formed by the action of bacilli on meat, fish, and other protein: used in polymerization and biological research. Also called **pentamethylenediamine.** [1885–90; CADAVER + -INE[2]]

ca·dav·er·ous (kə dav′ər əs), *adj.* **1.** of or like a corpse. **2.** pale; ghastly. **3.** haggard and thin. [1620–30; < L *cadāverōsus* like a corpse. See CADAVER, -OUS] **—ca·dav′er·ous·ly,** *adv.* **—ca·dav′er·ous·ness,** *n.*

Cad·bur·y (kad′ber ē, -bə rē), *n.* a Neolithic and Iron Age site in Somerset, England, traditionally the Camelot of King Arthur.

CAD/CAM (kad′kam′), *n.* computer-aided design and computer-aided manufacturing; the combination of CAD and CAM. [1980–85]

cad·dice[1] (kad′is), *n.* caddis[1]. **—cad′diced,** *adj.*

cad·dice[2] (kad′is), *n.* caddisworm.

cad·dice·fly (kad′is flī′), *n., pl.* **-flies.** caddisfly.

cad·die (kad′ē), *n., v.,* **-died, -dy·ing.** *—n.* **1.** *Golf.* a person hired to carry a player's clubs, find the ball, etc. **2.** a person who runs errands, does odd jobs, etc. **3.** See **caddie cart. 4.** any rigidly structured, wheeled device for carrying or moving around heavy objects: *a luggage caddie.* *—v.i.* **5.** to work as a caddie. Also, **caddy.** [1625–35; earlier *cadee,* var. of *cadet* < F; see CADET]

cad′die cart′, a small two-wheeled cart used by golfers to carry their clubs. Also called **golf cart.** [1960–65]

cad·dis[1] (kad′is), *n.* a kind of woolen braid, ribbon, or tape. Also, **caddice.** [1570–80; prob. < MF *cadis* kind of woolen cloth < OPr < Catalon *cadirs,* of obscure orig; ME *cadace, cadas* material for padding doublets (< AF) is appar. a distinct word] **—cad′dised,** *adj.*

cad·dis[2] (kad′is), *n.* caddisworm. [by shortening]

CONCISE ETYMOLOGY KEY: <, descended or borrowed from; >, whence; b., blend of, blended; c., cognate with; cf., compare; deriv., derivative; equiv., equivalent; imit., imitative; obl., oblique; r., replacing; s., stem; sp., spelling, spelled; resp., respelling, respelled; trans., translation; ?, origin unknown; *, unattested; ‡, probably earlier than. See the full key inside the front cover.

cad·dis·fly (kad′is flī′), *n., pl.* **-flies.** any of numerous aquatic insects constituting the order Trichoptera, having two pairs of membranous, often hairy wings and superficially resembling moths. Also, **caddicefly.** Cf. **caddisworm.** See illus. in next column. [1780–90; see CADDISWORM, FLY[2]]

cad·dish (kad′ish), *adj.* of or like a cad; dishonorable; ungentlemanly: *caddish behavior.* [1865–70; CAD + -ISH[1]] **—cad′dish·ly,** *adv.* **—cad′dish·ness,** *n.*

cad·dis·worm (kad′is wûrm′), *n.* the aquatic larva of a caddisfly, having an armored head and a pair of abdominal hooks, and typically living in a case built from sand or plant debris. Also called **caddis, caddice, strawworm.** [1615–25; *caddis* (perh. pl., taken as sing., of *caddy,* dim. of *cad* larva, ghost) + WORM]

Cad·do (kad′ō), *n., pl.* **-dos,** (*esp. collectively*) **-do** for 1. **1.** a member of any of several North American Indian tribes formerly located in Arkansas, Louisiana, and eastern Texas, and now living in Oklahoma. **2.** the Caddoan language of the Caddo. [< Caddo *kaduhdá·čuʔ* the name of a band]

Cad·do·an (kad′ō ən), *n.* a family of North American Indian languages spoken in the upper Missouri valley in North Dakota, in the Platte valley in Nebraska, in southwestern Arkansas, and in neighboring parts of Oklahoma, Texas, and Louisiana. [CADDO + -AN]

cad·dy[1] (kad′ē), *n., pl.* **-dies. 1.** a container, rack, or other device for holding, organizing, or storing items: *a pencil caddy; a bedspread caddy.* **2.** *Chiefly Brit.* See **tea caddy.** [1785–95; see TEA CADDY]

cad·dy[2] (kad′ē), *n., pl.* **-dies,** *v.i.,* **-died, -dy·ing.** caddie.

cad′dy spoon′, a small spoon used in taking tea from a storage caddy. [1925–30]

cade[1] (kād), *n.* a juniper, *Juniperus oxycedrus,* of the Mediterranean area, whose wood on destructive distillation yields an oily liquid (**oil of cade**), used in treating skin diseases. Cf. **juniper tar.** [1565–75; < MF < Pr; akin to LL *catanum;* perh. orig. a plant name in a substratum language of the Alps and Pyrenees]

cade[2] (kād), *adj. Eastern New Eng. and Brit.* (of the young of animals) abandoned or left by the mother and raised by humans: *a cade lamb.* [1425–75; late ME *cad(e),* of obscure orig.]

-cade, a combining form extracted from *cavalcade,* used with the meaning "procession" in the formation of compound words: *motorcade; tractorcade.*

ca·delle (kə del′), *n.* a small, blackish beetle, *Tenebroides mauritanicus,* that feeds, as both larva and adult, on stored grain and on other insects. [1860–65; < F < Pr *cadello* < L *catellus, catella* puppy, equiv. to *cat(ulus)* young of an animal + *-ellus, -ella* dim. suffix]

ca·dence (kād′ns), *n., v.,* **-denced, -denc·ing.** *—n.* Also, **cadency. 1.** rhythmic flow of a sequence of sounds or words: *the cadence of language.* **2.** (in free verse) a rhythmic pattern that is nonmetrically structured. **3.** the beat, rate, or measure of any rhythmic movement: *The chorus line danced in rapid cadence.* **4.** the flow or rhythm of events, esp. the pattern in which something is experienced: *the frenetic cadence of modern life.* **5.** a slight falling in pitch of the voice in speaking or reading, as at the end of a declarative sentence. **6.** the general modulation of the voice. **7.** *Music.* a sequence of notes or chords that indicates the momentary or complete end of a composition, section, phrase, etc. *—v.t.* **8.** to make rhythmical. [1350–1400; ME < MF < It *cadenza;* see CADENZA]
—Syn. 3. tempo, pulse, rhythm, meter.

ca·denced (kād′nst), *adj.* having or marked by a rhythmical cadence: *the cadenced steps of marching troops.* [1780–90; CADENCE + -ED[3]]

ca·den·cy (kād′n sē), *n., pl.* **-cies.** cadence (defs. 1–7). [1620–30; CAD(ENCE) + -ENCY]

ca·dent (kād′nt), *adj.* **1.** having cadence. **2.** *Archaic.* falling. [1580–90; < L *cadent-,* (s. of *cadēns* falling, prp. of *cadere*), equiv. to *cad-* fall + *-ent-* -ENT]

ca′dent house′, *Astrol.* any of the four houses that precede the angles: the third, sixth, ninth, and twelfth houses, which correspond, respectively, to neighborhood and relatives, work and health, philosophy and foreign travel, and secret matters and service to others. Cf. **angular house, succedent house.** [1665–75]

ca·den·tial (kā den′shəl), *adj.* of, pertaining to, or constituting a musical cadence. [1875–80; see CADENCE, -IAL; modeled on *substance, substantial*]

ca·den·za (kə den′zə), *n. Music.* an elaborate flourish or showy solo passage, sometimes improvised, introduced near the end of an aria or a movement of a concerto. [1745–55; < It < VL **cadentia* a falling, equiv. to L *cad(ere)* to fall + *-entia* -ENCY; cf. CHANCE]

ca·det (kə det′), *n.* **1.** a student in a national service academy or private military school or on a training ship. **2.** a student in training for service as a commissioned officer in the U.S. Army, Air Force, or Coast Guard. Cf. **midshipman** (def. 1). **3.** a trainee in a business or profession. **4.** a younger son or brother. **5.** the youngest son. **6.** (formerly) a gentleman, usually a younger son, who entered the army to prepare for a subsequent commission. **7.** Also called **cadet′ blue′.** a grayish to strong blue color. **8.** Also called **cadet′ gray′.** a bluish-gray to purplish-blue color. **9.** *Slang.* a pimp. [1600–10; < F < Gascon *capdet* chief, captain (referring to the younger sons of noble families); cf. OPr *capdel* headman < L *capitellum* lit., small head; see CAPITAL[2]] **—ca·det′ship,** *n.*

Ca·det (kə det′), *n. Russ. Hist.* a member of the former Constitutional Democratic party. [< Russ *kadét,* equiv. to *ka* + *de* (the letter names of *k, d,* repr. *konstitutsiónnyĭ demokrát* Constitutional Democrat) + *-t* from *kadét* (now obs.) CADET]

cadet′ cloth′, a heavy woolen cloth of double-cloth construction and bluish-gray color, used esp. for uniforms at military schools. [1875–80, *Amer.*]

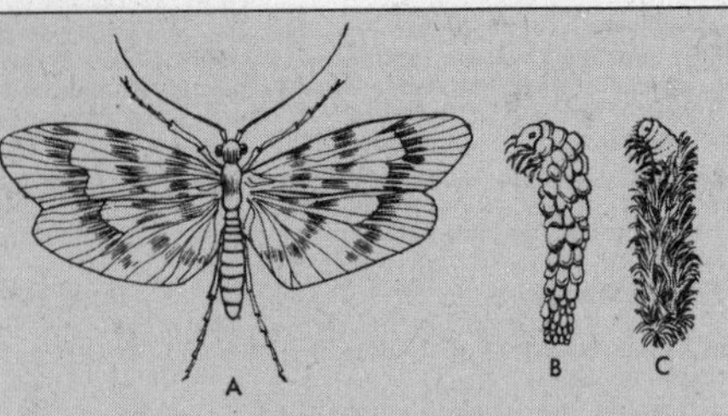

caddisfly and larvae
A, caddisfly; B, larva in case formed of small stones; C, larva in case formed of grass roots

ca·dette (kə det′), *n.* **1.** (*cap.*) Also called **Cadette′ scout′.** a member of the Girl Scouts from 12 through 14 years of age. **2.** *Australian.* a female government employee, esp. a woman appointed to civil service. [1670–80; CAD(ET) + -ETTE]

cadge[1] (kaj), *v.,* **cadged, cadg·ing.** *—v.t.* **1.** to obtain by imposing on another's generosity or friendship. **2.** to borrow without intent to repay. **3.** to beg or obtain by begging. *—v.i.* **4.** to ask, expect, or encourage another person to pay for or provide one's drinks, meals, etc. **5.** to beg. [1275–1325; perh. to be identified with ME *caggen* to tie, of uncert. orig.] **—cadg′er,** *n.*

cadge[2] (kaj), *n. Falconry.* a frame on which hawks are carried to the field. [1605–15; appar. var. of CAGE]

cadg·y (kaj′ē), *adj. Scot.* **1.** cheerful; merry. **2.** amorous; wanton. **3.** (of animals) in rut. [1715–25; of uncert. orig.] **—cadg′i·ly,** *adv.* **—cadg′i·ness,** *n.*

ca·di (kä′dē, kā′-), *n., pl.* **-dis.** qadi.

Cad·il·lac (kad′l ak′; *for 1 also Fr.* KA dē YAK′), *n.* **1. An·toine de la Mothe** (äN TWAN′ də lA môt′), 1657?–1730, French colonial governor in North America: founder of Detroit. **2.** a city in NW Michigan. 10,199.

Ca·diz (kä′dēs), *n.* a city in the Philippines, on N Negros. 129,632.

Cá·diz (kə diz′, kā′diz; *Sp.* kä′thēth, -thēs), *n.* a seaport in SW Spain, on a bay of the Atlantic (**Gulf′ of Cá′·diz**). 135,743.

Cad·me·an (kad mē′ən), *adj.* of, pertaining to, or like Cadmus. [1595–1605; < L *Cadmē(us)* (< Gk *Kadmeîos* of CADMUS) + -AN]

Cadme′an vic′tory, a victory attained at as great a loss to the victor as to the vanquished. Cf. **Pyrrhic victory.** [1595–1605]

cad·mi·um (kad′mē əm), *n.* a white, ductile divalent metallic element resembling tin, used in plating and in making certain alloys. *Symbol:* Cd; *at. wt.:* 112.41; *at. no.:* 48; *sp. gr.* 8.6 at 20°C. [1815–25; < NL, equiv. to L *cadm(ia)* calamine (orig. *Cadmēa terra* < Gk *Kadmeía gê* CADMEAN earth) + *-ium* -IUM] **—cad′mic,** *adj.*

cad′mium bronze′, an alloy of copper with about 1 percent cadmium.

cad′mium cell′, *Elect.* a cell with mercury and cadmium electrodes in a cadmium sulfate electrolyte, used to supply an accurate voltage for electronic measurements. Cf. **Weston cell.** [1905–10]

cad′mium green′, a pigment used in painting, consisting of a mixture of hydrated oxide of chromium with cadmium sulfide, and characterized by its strong green color and slow drying rate. [1930–35]

cad′mium or′ange, a yellow color approaching orange. [1890–95]

cad′mium red′, a pigment used in painting, consisting of the sulfide and the selinide of cadmium, characterized by its strong red or reddish color, excellent film-forming properties, and slow drying rate. [1885–90]

cad′mium sul′fide, a light yellow or orange, water-insoluble powder, CdS, used chiefly as a pigment in paints, inks, and ceramic glazes. [1870–75]

cad′mium yel′low, a pigment used in painting, consisting of cadmium sulfide and characterized by its strong yellow color and permanence. [1870–75]

Cad·mus (kad′məs), *n.* **Paul,** born 1904, U.S. painter and etcher.

Cad·mus (kad′məs), *n. Class. Myth.* a Phoenician prince who introduced writing to the Greeks and who founded the city of Thebes in the company of five warriors. Cf. **Sparti.**

Ca·dog′an tea′pot (kə dug′ən), a lidless teapot that is made from or in imitation of an inverted Chinese wine pot and is filled through the bottom. [perh. named after the 1st Earl of *Cadogan* (d. 1726)]

ca·dre (kad′rē, kä′drā), *n.* **1.** *Mil.* the key group of officers and enlisted personnel necessary to establish and train a new military unit. **2.** a group of trained or otherwise qualified personnel capable of forming, training, or leading an expanded organization, as a religious or political faction, or a skilled work force: *They hoped to form a cadre of veteran party members.* **3.** (esp. in Communist countries) a cell of trained and devoted workers. **4.** a member of a cadre; a person qualified to serve in a cadre. **5.** a framework, outline, or scheme. [1905–10; < F: frame, border, bounds, cadre (metaphorically, the cadre being the framework into which temporary personnel are fit) < It *quadro* < L *quadrum* square; see QUADRI-]

ca·dre·man (kad′rē mən, -man′, kä′drā-), *n., pl.* **-men** (-mən, -men′). **1.** an officer or enlisted person in a military cadre. **2.** a member of a political cadre. [CADRE + -MAN]

ca·du·ce·us (kə do͞o′sē əs, -syo͞os, -shəs, -dyo͞o′-), *n., pl.* **-ce·i** (-sē ī′). **1.** *Class. Myth.* the staff carried by Mercury as messenger of the gods. **2.** a representation of this staff used as an emblem of the medical profession and as the insignia of the U.S. Army Medical Corps. Cf. **staff of Aesculapius.** [1585–95; < L, var. of *cādūceum* < Gk (Doric) *kārȳkeion* herald's staff, equiv. to *kārȳk-* (s. of *kârȳx*) herald + *-eion,* neut. of *-eios* adj. suffix] —**ca·du′ce·an,** *adj.*

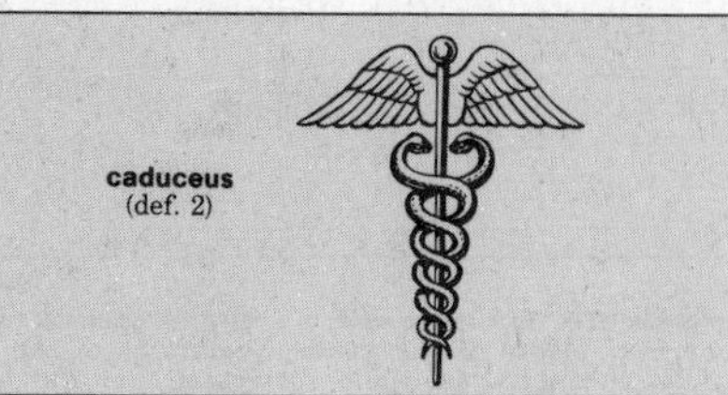
caduceus (def. 2)

ca·du·ci·ty (kə do͞o′si tē, -dyo͞o′-), *n.* **1.** the infirmity or weakness of old age; senility. **2.** frailty; transitoriness: *the caducity of life.* [1760–1770; < F *caducité,* equiv. to *caduc* CADUCOUS + *-ité* -ITY]

ca·du·cous (kə do͞o′kəs, -dyo͞o′-), *adj.* **1.** *Bot.* dropping off very early, as leaves. **2.** *Zool.* subject to shedding. **3.** transitory; perishable. [1675–85; < L *cadūcus* unsteady, perishable, equiv. to *cad(ere)* to fall + *-ūcus* adj. suffix; see -OUS]

Cad·wal·la·der (kad wol′ə dər), *n.* a male given name.

CAE, computer-aided engineering.

cae·cil·i·an (sē sil′ē ən), *n.* **1.** Also called **blindworm.** a legless, wormlike tropical amphibian of the order Gymnophiona (formerly Apoda), spending most of its life underground and usually almost blind. —*adj.* **2.** pertaining to or characteristic of a caecilian. [1875–80; < L *caecili(a)* blindworm + -AN]

cae·cum (sē′kəm), *n., pl.* **-ca** (-kə). cecum. —**cae′·cal,** *adj.* —**cae′cal·ly,** *adv.*

Cæd·mon (kad′mən), *n.* fl. A.D. c670, Anglo-Saxon religious poet.

Cae·li·an (sē′lē ən), *n.* the southeastern hill of the seven hills of ancient Rome.

Cae·lum (sē′ləm), *n., gen.* **-li** (-lī, -lē). *Astron.* the Sculptor's Tool, or Chisel, a small southern constellation between Columba and Eridanus. [< L: engraving tool]

Caen (kän; *Fr.* kän), *n.* a city and the capital of Calvados, in NW France, SW of Le Havre: many Norman buildings destroyed 1944. 122,794.

caeno-, var. of **ceno-**[1]: *Caenozoic.*

Caen′ stone′, a cream-colored limestone quarried near Caen, France, for use in building. [1375–1425; late ME]

cae·o·ma (sē ō′mə), *n.* (in fungi) an aecium in which the spores are formed in chains and not enclosed in a peridium. [< Gk *kaí(ein)* to burn + -OMA; so named because of its rust color]

Caer·e·mo·ni·a·le E·pis·co·por·um (cher′e mô′nē-ä′le e pes′kô pôr′o͝om), *Rom. Cath. Ch.* the liturgical book, used by bishops, containing regulations and prescriptions that are authoritative in matters not covered in the missal or other service books. [LL: ceremonial of bishops]

Caer·le·on (kär lē′ən), *n.* a town in Gwent, in SE Wales: site of ancient Roman fortress, a supposed seat of King Arthur's court. 6235.

Caer·nar·von (kär när′vən), *n.* **1.** a seaport in W Gwynedd, in NW Wales, on Menai Strait: 13th-century castle of Edward II. 9253. **2.** Caernarvonshire. Also, **Carnarvon.**

Caer·nar·von·shire (kär när′vən shēr′, -shər), *n.* a historic county in Gwynedd, in NW Wales. Also, **Carnarvonshire.** Also called **Caernarvon, Carnarvon.**

Caer·phil·ly (kär fil′ē), *n.* a mild, white, crumbly, medium-hard cheese, originally made in Wales. Also called **Caerphil′ly cheese′.** [after *Caerphilly* (Welsh *Caerffili*), town in S Wales where it was orig. made]

Cae·sar (sē′zər), *n.* **1. Ga·ius** (gā′əs) (or **Ca·ius**) (kā′-əs) **Julius,** c100–44 B.C., Roman general, statesman, and historian. **2.** a title of the Roman emperors from Augustus to Hadrian, and later of the heirs presumptive. **3.** any emperor. **4.** a tyrant or dictator. **5.** any temporal ruler; the civil authority. Matt. 22:21. **6.** a male given name: from a Roman family name.

Cae′sar and Cleopa′tra, a comedy (1898) by G. B. Shaw.

Caes·a·re·a (sē′zə rē′ə, ses′ə-, sez′ə-), *n.* **1.** an ancient seaport in NW Israel: Roman capital of Palestine. **2.** ancient name of **Kayseri.**

Cae·sar·e·an (si zâr′ē ən), *adj.* **1.** pertaining to Caesar or the Caesars: *a Caesarean conquest.* —*n.* **2.** (*sometimes l.c.*) Cesarean. Also, **Cae·sar′i·an.** [1520–30; < L *Caesare(us)* of CAESAR + -AN]

Cae·sar·ism (sē′zə riz′əm), *n.* absolute government; imperialism. [1595–1605; CAESAR + -ISM] —**Cae′sar·ist,** *n., adj.*

cae·sa·ro·pap·ism (sē′zə rō pā′piz əm), *n.* **1.** the possession of supreme authority over church and state by one person, often by a secular ruler. **2.** the supremacy of the state over the church in ecclesiastical matters. [1885–90; CAESAR + -O- + PAPISM] —**cae′sa·ro·pap′·ist,** *n., adj.*

Cae′sar sal′ad, a salad of romaine lettuce tossed with an olive oil dressing, a coddled or raw egg, garlic, and grated cheese and topped with croutons and sometimes anchovies. [1945–50; allegedly after a restaurant named *Caesar's* in Tijuana, Mexico]

cae·si·um (sē′zē əm), *n. Chem.* cesium.

caes·pi·tose (ses′pi tōs′), *adj.* cespitose. —**caes′pi·tose′ly,** *adv.*

cae·su·ra (si zho͝or′ə, -zo͝or′ə, siz yo͝or′ə), *n., pl.* **cae·su·ras, cae·su·rae** (si zho͝or′ē, -zo͝or′ē, siz yo͝or′ē). **1.** *Pros.* a break, esp. a sense pause, usually near the middle of a verse, and marked in scansion by a double vertical line, as in *know then thyself* ‖ *presume not God to scan.* **2.** *Class. Pros.* a division made by the ending of a word within a foot, or sometimes at the end of a foot, esp. in certain recognized places near the middle of a verse. **3.** any break, pause, or interruption. Also, **cesura.** [1550–60; < L, equiv. to *caes(us)* cut (ptp. of *caedere*) (*caed-* cut + *-tus* ptp. suffix) + *-ūra* -URE] —**cae·su′ral, cae·su′ric,** *adj.*

C.A.F., **1.** cost and freight. **2.** cost, assurance, and freight. Also, **c.a.f.**

ca·fé (ka fā′, kə- *or, esp. for 4, Fr.* ka fā′), *n., pl.* **-fés** (-fāz′; *Fr.* -fā′). **1.** a restaurant, often with an enclosed or outdoor section extending onto the sidewalk. **2.** a restaurant, usually small and unpretentious. **3.** a barroom, cabaret, or nightclub. **4.** coffee. Also, **ca·fe′.** [1780–90; < F: lit., COFFEE]
—**Syn. 1, 2.** coffeehouse, bistro, lunchroom, tearoom.

CAFE (ka fā′, kə-), *n.* a U.S. federally mandated standard of average minimum miles-per-gallon fuel consumption for all the cars produced by an automobile manufacturer in a given year. [*C(orporate) A(verage) F(uel) E(conomy)*]

ca·fé au lait (kaf′ā ō lā′, ka fā′, kə-; *Fr.* ka fā ō le′), **1.** hot coffee served with an equal amount of hot or scalded milk. **2.** a light brown color. [1755–65; < F: lit., coffee with milk]

ca·fé brû·lot (kaf′ā bro͞o lō′, ka fā′, kə-; *Fr.* ka fā bry lō′), black coffee flavored with sugar, lemon and orange rinds, cloves, cinnamon, and brandy, ignited and allowed to flame briefly. [< F: burnt brandy coffee]

café′ car′, a railroad car, part of which is used as a diner and part as a lounge, smoker, etc. [1895–1900, *Amer.*]

ca·fé chan·tant (kaf′ā shän tän′, ka fā′, kə-; *Fr.* ka fā shän tän′), *pl.* **ca·fés chan·tants** (kaf′ā shän-tänz′, ka fā′, kə-; *Fr.* ka fā shän tän′). an intimate cabaret offering sophisticated musical entertainment. [1850–55; < F: lit., musical café, café where concerts are held]

ca·fé con le·che (kaf′ā kon lech′ā, ka fā′, kə-; *Sp.* kä fe′ kôn le′che), **1.** strong, black coffee mixed with hot milk. **2.** a light brown color. [< Sp: coffee with milk]

ca·fé crème (ka fā krem′), *French.* coffee with cream.

café′ cur′tain, a short curtain suspended directly downward from a series of rings sliding on a horizontal rod so as to cover the lower and sometimes upper portions of a window.

ca·fé fil·tre (ka fā fēl′trᵊ), *French.* coffee made by pouring hot water through ground coffee placed in a filtering device.

ca·fé noir (ka fā nwar′), *French.* black coffee. Also called ***ca·fé na·ture*** (ka fā na tyr′).

ca·fé roy·ale (kaf′ā roi al′, ka fā′, kə-; *Fr.* ka fā rwa yal′), black coffee, to which cognac, lemon peel, sugar, and sometimes cinnamon have been added. Also called **coffee royal.** [< F: royal coffee]

ca′fé soci′ety, socialites who regularly frequent fashionable nightclubs, resorts, etc. [1935–40]

caf·e·te·ri·a (kaf′i tēr′ē ə), *n.* **1.** a restaurant in which patrons wait on themselves, carrying their food to tables from counters where it is displayed and served. **2.** a lunchroom or dining hall, as in a factory, office, or school, where food is served from counters or dispensed from vending machines or where food brought from home may be eaten. [1830–40, *Amer.*; < AmerSp *cafetería* café, equiv. to Sp *cafeter(a)* coffeemaker (< F *caf(f)etière*; *café* COFFEE + *-ière,* fem. of *-ier* -IER[2]; *t* appar. by analogy with words such as *bouquetière* flower seller, from bases ending in *t*) + *-ía* -IA]

cafete′ria plan′, a fringe-benefit plan under which employees may choose from among various benefits those that best fit their needs up to a specified dollar value. [1985–90]

caf·e·to·ri·um (kaf′i tôr′ē əm, -tōr′-), *n.* a large room, esp. in a school, that functions both as a cafeteria and an auditorium. [1950–55; b. CAFETERIA and AUDITORIUM]

caf·fein·at·ed (kaf′ə nā′tid), *adj.* containing caffeine: *a caffeinated soft drink.* [CAFFEINE + -ATE[1] + -ED[2]]

caf·feine (ka fēn′, kaf′ēn, kaf′ē in), *n. Chem., Pharm.* a white, crystalline, bitter alkaloid, $C_8H_{10}N_4O_2$, usually derived from coffee or tea: used in medicine chiefly as a nervous system stimulant. Also, **caf·fein′.** [1820–30; < F *caféine,* equiv. to *café* COFFEE + *-ine* -INE[2]] —**caf·fein·ic** (ka fē′nik, kaf′ē in′ik), *adj.*

caf·fein·ism (ka fē′niz əm, kaf′ē niz′-, kaf′ē ə-), *n.* chronic toxicity caused by excessive intake of caffeine, characterized by anxiety, irritability, palpitations, insomnia, and digestive disturbances. [CAFFEINE + -ISM]

caf·fè lat·te (kaf′ā lat′ä, lä′tä, ka fā′, kə-; *It.* kä fe′ lät′te), *Italian.* coffee served with an equal amount of hot milk.

ca·fo·ne (kä fô′ne), *n., pl.* **-ni** (-nē). *Italian.* an uncouth person; lowlife.

caf·tan (kaf′tan, kaf tan′), *n.* **1.** a long garment having long sleeves and tied at the waist by a girdle, worn under a coat in the Middle East. **2.** a long, full, usually collarless robe with wide sleeves that is worn at home for lounging or entertaining or at the beach as a cover-up. Also, **kaftan.** [1585–95; < Russ *kaftán* < Turk < Pers *qaftān*] —**caf′taned,** *adj.*

Ca·ga·yan de O·ro (*Sp.* kä′gä yän′ de ô′rô), a city in the Philippines, on NW Mindanao. 227,312.

cage (kāj), *n., v.,* **caged, cag·ing.** —*n.* **1.** a boxlike enclosure having wires, bars, or the like, for confining and displaying birds or animals. **2.** anything that confines or imprisons; prison. **3.** something resembling a cage in structure, as for a cashier or bank teller. **4.** the car or enclosed platform of an elevator. **5.** *Mining.* an enclosed platform for raising and lowering people and cars in a mine shaft. **6.** any skeleton framework. **7.** *Baseball.* a movable backstop for use mainly in batting practice. **8.** a frame with a net attached to it, forming the goal in ice hockey and field hockey. **9.** *Basketball Older Use.* the basket. **10.** a loose, sheer or lacy overdress worn with a slip or a close-fitting dress. **11.** *Ordn.* a steel framework for supporting guns. **12.** *Mach.* retainer[1] (def. 3). —*v.t.* **13.** to put or confine in or as if in a cage. **14.** *Sports.* to shoot (as a puck) into a cage so as to score a goal. [1175–1225; ME < OF < L *cavea* birdcage, equiv. to *cav(us)* hollow + *-ea,* fem. of *-eus* adj. suffix] —**cage′less,** *adj.* —**cage′like′,** *adj.*

Cage (kāj), *n.* **John,** 1912–92, U.S. composer.

cage′ bird′, a bird that is commonly kept in a cage as a pet. [1620–30]

cage·ling (kāj′ling), *n.* a bird that is kept in a cage. [1855–60; CAGE + -LING[1]]

cag·er (kā′jər), *n.* **1.** *Informal.* a basketball player. **2.** *Mining.* a machine for putting cars on or off a cage. [1910–15; CAGE + -ER[1]]

cag·ey (kā′jē), *adj.,* **cag·i·er, cag·i·est.** cautious, wary, or shrewd: *a cagey reply to the probing question.* Also, **cagy.** [1890–95, *Amer.*; CAGE + -Y[1]] —**cag′i·ly,** *adv.* —**cag′i·ness, cag′ey·ness,** *n.*
—**Syn.** careful, prudent, leery, chary. —**Ant.** open, forthright.

cage′ zone′ melt′ing, zone melting of a square bar of the material to be purified, done so that the impurities are concentrated at the corners.

Ca·glia·ri (käl′yə rē; *It.* kä′lyä rē′), *n.* **1. Pa·o·lo** (pä′ô lô). See **Veronese, Paolo. 2.** a seaport in S Sardinia. 236,931.

Ca·glios·tro (kal yō′strō; *It.* kä lyôs′trô), *n.* **Count A·les·san·dro di** (ä′les sän′drô dē), (*Giuseppe Balsamo*), 1743–95, Italian adventurer and impostor.

Cag·ney (kag′nē), *n.* **James,** 1899–1986, U.S. film actor.

Ca·gou·lard (kag′o͝o lär′, kag′o͝o lär′; *Fr.* ka go͞o-lär′), *n., pl.* **-lards** (-lärz′, -lärz′; *Fr.* -lär′). a member of a secret French organization, active 1932–40, that conspired to overthrow the Third Republic. [< F, equiv. to *cagoule* hood (see COWL) + *-ard* -ARD]

C.A.G.S., Certificate of Advanced Graduate Study.

Ca·guas (kä′gwäs), *n.* a city in E central Puerto Rico. 87,214.

cag·y (kā′jē), *adj.,* **cag·i·er, cag·i·est.** cagey.

ca·hier (ka yā′, kä-; *Fr.* ka yā′), *n., pl.* **-hiers** (-yāz′; *Fr.* -yā′). **1.** *Bookbinding.* a number of sheets of paper or leaves of a book placed together, as for binding. **2.** a report of the proceedings of any body: *A cahier of the committee was presented to the legislature.* **3.** (*italics*) *French.* **a.** notebook; exercise book; journal. **b.** paperback book. [1835–45; < F; MF *quaer* gathering (of sheets of a book); see QUIRE]

ca·hill (kä′hil, kā′-), *n. Angling.* an artificial fly having a quill body, golden tag, tan-spotted wings and tail, and gray hackle. [perh. named after its inventor]

Ca·ho·ki·a (kə hō′kē ə), *n.* a city in SW Illinois. 18,904.

Caho′kia Mounds′, a group of very large prehistoric Indian earthworks in southwestern Illinois, consisting of mounds with flat tops that supported temples and other structures of mud and thatch.

ca·hoot (kə ho͞ot′), *n. Informal.* **1. go cahoots,** to share equally; become partners: *They went cahoots in the establishment of the store.* Also, **go in cahoot with, go in cahoots. 2. in cahoot** or **cahoots, a.** in partnership; in league. **b.** in conspiracy: *in cahoots with the enemy.* [1820–30, *Amer.*; perh. < F *cahute* cabin, hut, equiv. to *ca(bane)* CABIN + *hutte* HUT]

ca·how (kə hou′), *n.* a rare petrel, *Pterodroma cahow,* of islets off Bermuda, until recently thought to have become extinct. Also called **Bermuda petrel.** [1605–15; imit.]

Ca·huil·la (kə wē′ə), *n., pl.* **-las,** (*esp. collectively*) **-la. 1.** a member of a North American Indian people of southern California. **2.** the Uto-Aztecan language of the Cahuilla.

CAI, computer-assisted instruction. [1965–70]

Cai·a·phas (kā′ə fəs, kī′-), *n.* a high priest of the Jews who presided over the assembly that condemned Jesus to death. Matt. 26.

Cai′cos Is′lands (kī′kōs). See **Turks and Caicos Islands.**

ca·id (kä ēth′, kīth), *n.* **1.** (in North Africa) a Muslim tribal chief, judge, or senior official. **2.** a Berber chieftain. **3.** an alcaide. Also, **qaid.** [1855–60; (< F) < Ar *qā'id.* See ALCAIDE]

cai·man (kā′mən), *n., pl.* **-mans.** any of several tropical American crocodilians of the genus *Caiman* and allied genera: some are endangered. Also, **cayman.** [1570–80; < Sp *caimán* < Carib]

cai′man liz′ard, a crocodilelike lizard, *Dracaena guianensis,* of South America, having powerful jaws for crushing the snails and mussels upon which it feeds.

cain (kān), *n. Scot. and Irish Eng.* rent paid in kind, esp. a percentage of a farm crop. [ME (Scots) *cane* < ScotGael; cf. OIr *cáin* statute, law, rent]

Cain (kān), *n.* **1.** the first son of Adam and Eve, who murdered his brother Abel. Gen. 4. **2.** a murderer. **3.** **raise Cain,** *Slang.* **a.** become angry or violent: *He'll raise Cain when he finds out I lost his watch.* **b.** to behave in a boisterous manner; cause a disturbance: *The students raised Cain while the teacher was out.* —**Cain′ism,** *n.* —**Cain·it·ic** (kā nit′ik), *adj.*

Caine (kān), *n.* **(Sir Thomas Henry) Hall,** 1853–1931, English novelist.

Cain·gang (kīn′gang′), *n., pl.* **-gangs,** (*esp. collectively*) **-gang. 1.** a member of an Indian people of southern Brazil. **2.** a group of languages spoken by the Caingang, constituting a branch of the Ge family of languages. Also, **Kaingang.**

Cain·ite (kā′nīt), *n.* a member of a Gnostic sect that exalted Cain and regarded the God of the Old Testament as responsible for evil. [< ML *Caīnita* (see CAIN, -ITE[1]; cf. LL *Caiānus* with same sense)]

caino-, var. of **ceno-**[1]: *Cainozoic.*

Cai·no·zo·ic (kī′nə zō′ik, kā′-), *adj., n. Geol.* Cenozoic.

ca·ïque (kä ēk′), *n.* **1.** a single-masted sailing vessel used on the eastern Mediterranean Sea, having a sprit mainsail, a square topsail, and two or more other sails. **2.** a long, narrow rowboat used on the Bosporus. Also, **ca·ique′.** [1615–25; < F < It *caicco* < Turk *kayık;* r. *caik* < Turk *kayık*]

ça i·ra (SA′ ē RA′), *French.* it will go on.

caird (kârd; *Scot.* kārd), *n. Scot.* **1.** a traveling tinker, esp. a gypsy. **2.** a wandering tramp or vagrant. [1655–65; < ScotGael *ceard* tinker; akin to L *cerdō* workman, Gk *kerdṓ* cunning one]

Caird′ Coast′, a coastal region in Antarctica, E of the Weddell Sea, 23° to 29° W longitude.

Cai·rene (kī′rēn, kī rēn′), *adj.* **1.** (*sometimes l.c.*) of or pertaining to Cairo, Egypt. —*n.* **2.** a native or resident of Cairo, Egypt. [1835–45; CAIR(O) + -ENE]

cairn (kârn), *n.* a heap of stones set up as a landmark, monument, tombstone, etc. Also, **carn.** [1525–35; earlier *carn* < ScotGael: pile of stones; perh. akin to HORN] —**cairned,** *adj.* —**cairn′y,** *adj.*

cairn·gorm (kârn′gôrm′), *n.* See **smoky quartz.** Also called **Cairn′gorm stone′.** [1785–95; short for *Cairngorm stone,* i.e., stone from Scottish mountain so named]

Cairns (kârnz), *n.* a seaport in NE Australia. 48,557.

cairn′ ter′rier, one of a Scottish breed of small, short-legged terriers having a rough coat of any of several solid colors except white. [1905–10; said to be so called because they are found in areas abounding in cairns]

Cai·ro (kī′rō), *n.* a city in and the capital of Egypt, in the N part on the E bank of the Nile. 5,517,000.

cais·son (kā′sən, -son), *n.* **1.** a structure used in underwater work, consisting of an airtight chamber, open at the bottom and containing air under sufficient pressure to exclude the water. **2.** a boatlike structure used as a gate for a dock or the like. **3.** *Naut.* **a.** Also called **camel, pontoon.** a float for raising a sunken vessel, sunk beside the vessel, made fast to it, and then pumped out to make it buoyant. **b.** a watertight structure built against a damaged area of a hull to render the hull watertight; cofferdam. **4.** a two-wheeled wagon, used for carrying artillery ammunition. **5.** an ammunition chest. **6.** a wooden chest containing bombs or explosives, used formerly as a mine. **7.** *Archit.* coffer (def. 4). [1695–1705; < F, MF < OPr, equiv. to *caissa* box (see CASE[2]) + *-on* aug. suffix] —**cais′soned,** *adj.*

cais′son disease′, aeroembolism (def. 2). [1880–85, *Amer.*]

Caith·ness (kāth′nes, kāth nes′), *n.* a historic county in NE Scotland.

cai·tiff (kā′tif), *Archaic.* —*n.* **1.** a base, despicable person. —*adj.* **2.** base; despicable. [1250–1300; ME *caitif* < AF < L *captīvus* CAPTIVE]

Cait·lin (kāt′lin), *n.* a female given name, Irish form of **Cathleen, Kathleen.**

Ca·ius (kā′əs), *n.* **Saint,** died A.D. 296, pope 283–296. Also, **Gaius.**

Ca·jan (kā′jən), *n., pl.* **-jans,** (*esp. collectively*) **-jan** for 2. **1.** a member of a group of people living in parts of the South, esp. Alabama, whose ancestry is a mixture of white, black, and possibly Indian. **2.** Cajun. [see CAJUN]

caj·e·put (kaj′ə pət, -po͝ot′), *n.* a tree, *Melaleuca leucadendron,* of the myrtle family, native to Australia and New Guinea, having papery bark and yielding a greenish, aromatic oil (**caj′eput oil′**) used in medicine and perfumes. Also, **caj′a·put, caj′u·put.** Also called **paperbark.** [< NL *cajuputi* < D *kajoe-poetih(-olie)* < Malay *kayu putih* the cajeput tree (*kayu* white + *putih* tree)]

caj·e·put·ol (kaj′ə pə tôl′, -tol′), *n. Chem.* cineole. Also, **caj′u·put·ol′.** [CAJEPUT + -OL[2]]

ca·jole (kə jōl′), *v.t., v.i.,* **-joled, -jol·ing.** to persuade by flattery or promises; wheedle; coax. [1635–45; < F *cajoler* to cajole or chatter like a jaybird, appar. deriv. of **cajole* birdcage (< LL *caveola* < L *cave(a)* CAGE + *-ola* OLE[1]) + *-er* inf. suffix] —**ca·jole′ment,** *n.* —**ca·jol′er,** *n.* —**ca·jol′ing·ly,** *adv.*

ca·jol·er·y (kə jō′lə rē), *n., pl.* **-er·ies.** persuasion by flattery or promises; wheedling; coaxing. [1640–50; < F *cajolerie.* See CAJOLE, -ERY]

Ca·jun (kā′jən), *n.* **1.** a member of a group of people with an enduring cultural tradition whose French Catholic ancestors established permanent communities in Louisiana and Maine after being expelled from Acadia in the late 18th century. **2.** the French dialect of the Cajuns. —*adj.* **3.** of, pertaining to, or characteristic of Cajuns, esp. those of Louisiana: *Cajun cooking.* Also, **Cajan.** [1875–80; aph. var. of ACADIAN; cf. *Injun* for INDIAN]

cake (kāk), *n., v.,* **caked, cak·ing.** —*n.* **1.** a sweet, baked, breadlike food, made with or without shortening, and usually containing flour, sugar, baking powder or soda, eggs, and liquid flavoring. **2.** a flat, thin mass of bread, esp. unleavened bread. **3.** pancake; griddlecake. **4.** a shaped or molded mass of other food: *a fish cake.* **5.** a shaped or compressed mass: *a cake of soap; a cake of ice.* **6.** *Animal Husb.* a compacted block of soybeans, cottonseeds, or linseeds from which the oil has been pressed, usually used as a feed or feed supplement for cattle. **7.** **a piece of cake,** *Informal.* something easily done: *She thought her first solo flight was a piece of cake.* **8.** **take the cake,** *Informal.* **a.** to surpass all others, esp. in some undesirable quality; be extraordinary or unusual: *His arrogance takes the cake.* **b.** to win first prize. —*v.t.* **9.** to form into a crust or compact mass. —*v.i.* **10.** to become formed into a crust or compact mass. [1200–50; ME < ON *kaka;* akin to ME *kechel* little cake, G *Kuchen;* see COOKIE] —**cak′y, cak′ey,** *adj.* —**Syn. 10.** harden, solidify, dry, congeal.

caked′ breast′, *Pathol.* a painful hardening of one or more lobules of a lactating breast, caused by stagnation of milk in the secreting ducts and accumulation of blood in the expanded veins; stagnation mastitis.

cake′ eat′er, *Older Slang.* **1.** a ladies' man. **2.** an effeminate lover of ease and pleasure. [1920–25]

cake′ flour′, finely ground wheat flour.

cake′ make′up, face makeup in the form of a cake, usually applied with a damp sponge.

cakes′ and ale′, the good things of life; material pleasures: *Their thoughts were only of cakes and ale.*

cake·walk (kāk′wôk′), *n.* **1.** (formerly) a promenade or march, of black American origin, in which the couples with the most intricate or eccentric steps received cakes as prizes. **2.** a dance with a strutting step based on this promenade. **3.** music for this dance. **4.** *Informal.* something easy, sure, or certain. —*v.i.* **5.** to walk or dance in or as if in a cakewalk. [1860–65; CAKE + WALK] —**cake′walk′er,** *n.*

cak·ra (chuk′rə), *n. Yoga.* any of the points of spiritual power located along the body, usually given as six in number. The points are personified by gods and can be released through the proper exercises. Also, **chakra.** [< Skt: lit., wheel]

cak·ra·var·tin (chuk′rə vär′tin), *n.* (in Indian philosophy, politics, etc.) an ideal, universal, enlightened ruler, under whom the world exists in justice and peace. Also, **chakravartin.** [< Skt]

Cal (kal), *n.* a male given name, form of **Calvin.**

Cal, kilocalorie.

cal, calorie (def. 1a).

Cal., California.

cal., **1.** calendar. **2.** caliber. **3.** calorie (def. 1a).

ca·la·ba (kə lä′bə), *n.* **1.** a tree, *Calophyllum brasiliense,* of the West Indies and Central and South America, having leathery leaves and fragrant white flowers. **2.** the reddish wood of this tree. Also called **Maria, Santa Maria.** [1745–55; < AmerSp]

Cal·a·bar (kal′ə bär′, kal′ə bär′), *n.* **1.** a river in SE Nigeria. ab. 70 mi. (113 km) long. **2.** a seaport near the mouth of this river. 187,000.

Cal′abar bean′, the violently poisonous seed of an African climbing plant, *Physostigma venenosum,* of the legume family, the active principle of which is physostigmine. Also called **ordeal bean.** [1875–80; named after CALABAR, Nigeria]

cal·a·bash (kal′ə bash′), *n.* **1.** any of various gourds, esp. the bottle gourd, *Lagenaria siceraria.* **2.** a tropical American tree, *Crescentia cujete,* of the bignonia family, bearing large, gourdlike fruit. **3.** any of several other plants having gourdlike fruit. **4.** the fruit of any of these plants. **5.** the dried, hollowed-out shell of any of these fruits, used as a container or utensil. **6.** a bottle, kettle, ladle, etc., made from such a shell. **7.** a tobacco pipe with a large bowl made from a calabash and usually having a curved stem. **8.** a gourd used as a rattle, drum, etc. [1590–1600; < MF *calabasse* < Sp *calabaza* < Catalan *carabaça,* perh. < Ar *qar'ah yābisah* gourd (that is) dry]

ca·la·ba·za, (kal′ə bä′zə, kä′lə-; *Sp.* kä′lä vä′sä), *n., pl.* **-zas** (-zəz; *Sp.* -säs). a calabash.

cal·a·ba·zil·la (kal′ə bə zē′ə), *n.* a prostrate vine, *Cucurbita foetidissima,* of the gourd family, native to southwestern North America, having yellow flowers, round, inedible green and yellow fruit, and an unpleasant odor. Also called **mock orange, Missouri gourd, wild pumpkin.** [1880–85, *Amer.*; < MexSp *calabacilla* < Sp: squirting cucumber, dim. of *calabaza;* see CALABASH]

cal·a·boose (kal′ə bo͞os′, kal′ə bo͞os′), *n. Slang.* jail; prison; lockup. [1785–95, *Amer.*; (< North American F) < Sp *calabozo* dungeon, of obscure orig.]

cal·a·bra·sel·la (kal′ə brə zel′ə), *n.* a card game for three persons that is played with a 40-card pack made by removing the eights, nines, and tens from a regular 52-card pack. [< It *calabresella,* equiv. to *calabres(e)* (*Calabr(iā)* CALABRIA + *-ese* -ESE) + *-ella* dim. suffix (< L)]

Ca·la·bri·a (kə lā′brē ə; *It.* kä lä′bryä), *n.* **1.** a region in S Italy. 2,048,901. 5828 sq. mi. (15,100 sq. km). *Cap.:* Reggio Calabria. **2.** an ancient district at the extreme SE part of the Italian peninsula. —**Ca·la′bri·an,** *n., adj.*

ca·la·di·um (kə lā′dē əm), *n.* any of several tropical American plants of the genus *Caladium,* of the arum family, cultivated for their variegated, colorful leaves. [1835–45; < NL: orig. coined as genus name for taro on basis of Malay *kəladi* (sp. *keladi*) araceous plant; see -IUM]

Ca·lah (kā′lə), *n.* Biblical name of **Kalakh.**

Cal·ais (kal′ā, ka lā′, kal′is; *Fr.* KA le′), *n.* a seaport in N France, on the Strait of Dover: the French port nearest England. 79,369.

Ca·la·is (kə lā′is), *n. Class. Myth.* the winged son of Boreas the north wind. As Argonauts he and his brother Zetes chased away the Harpies. Also, **Kalais.**

Ca·lak·mul (kä′läk mo͞ol′), *n.* a ruined Mayan city in SE Mexico.

Ca·la·ma (kä lä′mä), *n.* a city in N Chile. 26,166.

cal·a·man·co (kal′ə mang′kō), *n., pl.* **-cos** for 2. **1.** a glossy woolen fabric checkered or brocaded in the warp so that the pattern shows on one side only, much used in the 18th century. **2.** a garment made from this fabric. Also, **calimanco.** [1585–95; of obscure orig.]

cal·a·man·der (kal′ə man′dər), *n.* the hard, mottled brown and black wood of any of several trees of the genus *Diospyros,* used for cabinetwork. [1795–1805; perh. metathetic var. of COROMANDEL]

ca·la·ma·ri (kal′ə mär′ē, kä′lə-; *It.* kä′lä mä′RE), *n. Italian Cookery.* squid. [< It, pl. of *calamaro, calamaio,* (for *pesce calamaio*) < LL *calamārium* inkhorn, pen case (referring to the ink ejected by the squid), L *calamārius* pertaining to a pen; see CALAMUS, -ARY]

cal·a·mar·y (kal′ə mer′ē, -mə rē), *n., pl.* **-mar·ies.** a squid, esp. of the genus *Loligo.* Also, **cal·a·mar** (kal′ə-mär′). [1560–70; appar. < L *calamārius* (see CALAMARI), though the metaphor may be dependent on a popular form such as It *calamaro*]

Ca·la·mian′ Is′lands (kä′lä myän′), a group of about 100 islands in the SW Philippines. 600 sq. mi. (1554 sq. km). Largest island, Busuanga.

cal·a·mine (kal′ə mīn′, -min), *n.* **1.** a pink, water-insoluble powder consisting of zinc oxide and about 0.5 percent ferric oxide, used in ointments, lotions, or the like, for the treatment of inflammatory conditions of the skin. **2.** *Mineral.* hemimorphite. **3.** *Chiefly Brit.* smithsonite (def. 1). [1595–1605; < ML *calamīna,* unexplained alter. of L *cadmia* CADMIUM; see -INE[1]]

cal′amine brass′, an alloy of zinc carbonate and copper, formerly used to imitate gold.

cal·a·mint (kal′ə mint), *n.* any of several aromatic plants belonging to the genus *Calamintha* (or *Satureja*) of the mint family, having simple, opposite leaves and drooping clusters of flowers. Also called **basil thyme.** [1225–75; alter. (by assoc. with MINT[2]) of ME *calament* < ML *calamentum,* L *calamintha* < Gk *kalaminthē*]

cal·a·mite (kal′ə mīt′), *n.* any fossil plant of the genus *Calamites* and related genera of the Carboniferous Period, resembling oversized horsetails and constituting much of the coal used as fuel. [1745–55; < NL *Calamites* the genus name, L *calamitēs* < Gk *kalamítēs* reedlike. See CALAMUS, -ITE[1]] —**cal·a·mi·te·an** (kal′ə-mī′tē ən), *adj.* —**ca·lam·i·toid** (kə lam′i toid′), *adj.*

ca·lam·i·tous (kə lam′i təs), *adj.* causing or involving calamity; disastrous: *a calamitous defeat.* [1535–45; CALAMIT(Y) + -OUS] —**ca·lam′i·tous·ly,** *adv.* —**ca·lam′i·tous·ness,** *n.*
—**Syn.** catastrophic, ruinous, devastating. —**Ant.** beneficial, advantageous.

ca·lam·i·ty (kə lam′i tē), *n., pl.* **-ties. 1.** a great misfortune or disaster, as a flood or serious injury. **2.** grievous affliction; adversity; misery: *the calamity of war.* [1375–1425; late ME *calamite* < MF < L *calamitāt-* (s. of *calamitās*), perh. akin to *incolumitās* safety]
—**Syn. 1.** reverse, blow, catastrophe, cataclysm; mischance, mishap. See **disaster.**

Calam′ity Jane′, (*Martha Jane Canary Burke*) 1852?–1903, U.S. frontier markswoman.

cal·a·mon·din (kal′ə mun′dən), *n.* **1.** a small citrus tree, *Citrofortunella mitis,* of the Philippines. **2.** the small, tart, tangerinelike fruit of this tree. [1925–35; < Tagalog *kalamunding*]

cal·a·mus (kal′ə məs), *n., pl.* **-mi** (-mī′). **1.** the sweet flag, *Acorus calamus.* **2.** its aromatic root. **3.** any of various tropical Asian palms of the genus *Calamus,* some of which are a source of rattan. **4.** the hollow base of a feather; a quill. See illus. under **feather.** [1350–1400; ME < L < Gk *kálamos* reed, stalk]

ca·lan·do (kä län′dō), *Music.* —*adj.* **1.** becoming slower and softer; dying away. —*adv.* **2.** in a slower, softer manner. [‡1850–55; < It: slackening < L *calandum,* ger. of *calāre* to let down < Gk *chalân* to loosen, slacken]

ca·lan·the (kə lan′thē), *n.* any of various tropical and subtropical orchids of the genus *Calanthe,* having racemes of white, reddish, or yellow flowers. [< NL]

Ca·la·pan (kä′lä pän′), *n.* a seaport on NE Mindoro, in the central Philippines. 67,370.

ca·lash (kə lash′), *n.* **1.** Also, **calèche.** a light vehicle

CONCISE ETYMOLOGY KEY: <, descended or borrowed from; >, whence; b., blend of, blended; c., cognate with; cf., compare; deriv., derivative; equiv., equivalent; imit., imitative; obl., oblique; r., replacing; s., stem; sp., spelling, spelled; resp., respelling, respelled; trans., translation; ?, origin unknown; *, unattested; ‡, probably earlier than. See the full key inside the front cover.

pulled by one or two horses, seating two to four passengers, and having two or four wheels, a seat for a driver on a splashboard, and sometimes a folding top. **2.** a folding top of a carriage. **3.** calèche (def. 1). **4.** a bonnet that folds back like the top of a calash, worn by women in the 18th century. [1660–70; < F *calèche* < G *Kalesche* < Czech *kolesa* carriage, lit., wheels; see WHEEL]

calash (def. 1)

cal•a•the•a (kal′ə thē′ə), *n.* any of various tropical American plants of the genus *Calathea,* some of which have colorful, variegated leaves and are often cultivated as houseplants. [< NL; see KALATHOS, -EA]

cal•a•thi•form (kal′ə thə fôrm′, kə lath′ə-), *adj.* cup-shaped; concave. [1875–80; *calathi-* (comb. form of CALATHUS) + -FORM]

cal•a•thus (kal′ə thəs), *n., pl.* **-thi** (-thī′). kalathos. [< L < Gk *kálathos*]

cal•a•ver•ite (kal′ə vâr′īt), *n.* a silver-white mineral, gold telluride, $AuTe_2$, containing a little silver: an ore of gold. [1865–70, *Amer.*; *Calaver(as),* county in California where first found + -ITE[1]]

Cal•ba•yog (käl bä′yôg), *n.* a city in the Philippines, on NW Samar. 106,719.

calc (kalk), *n. Informal.* a calculator, esp. a small portable one. [by shortening]

calc-, 1. a combining form of **calcareous:** *calc-tufa.* **2.** var. of **calci-** before a vowel: *calcic.* [< G *Kalk* lime < L *calc-* (s. of *calx*) lime, limestone; see CALX, CHALK]

calc., calculate.

cal•ca•ne•um (kal kā′nē əm), *n., pl.* **-ne•a** (-nē ə). calcaneus. [1745–55; short for L *(os) calcāneum* (bone) of the heel, equiv. to *calc-* (s. of *calx*) heel + *-āneum,* neut. of *-āneus;* see -AN, -EOUS]

cal•ca•ne•us (kal kā′nē əs), *n., pl.* **-ne•i** (-nē ī′). **1.** *Anat.* the largest tarsal bone, forming the prominence of the heel. **2.** *Zool.* the corresponding bone in other vertebrates. Also, **calcaneum.** Also called **heel bone.** [1920–25; < LL: heel, n. use of *calcāneus* of the heel; see CALCANEUM] —**cal•ca′ne•al, cal•ca′ne•an,** *adj.*

cal•car[1] (kal′kär), *n., pl.* **cal•car•i•a** (kal kâr′ē ə). *Biol.* a spur or spurlike process. [< L: spur, equiv. to *calc-,* s. of *calx* heel, CALX + *-ar,* shortening of *-āre,* neut. of *-āris* -AR[1]]

cal•car[2] (kal′kär), *n., pl.* **cal•car•i•a** (kal kâr′ē ə). *Glassmaking.* a reverberatory furnace for preparing frit. [1655–65; < It *calcara* < LL *calcāria* lime-kiln, equiv. to L *calc-* lime (see CHALK) + *-āria* -ARY]

cal•ca•rate (kal′kə rāt′), *adj. Biol.* having a calcar or calcaria; spurred. Also, **cal′ca•rat′ed.** [1820–30; CALCAR[1] + -ATE[1]]

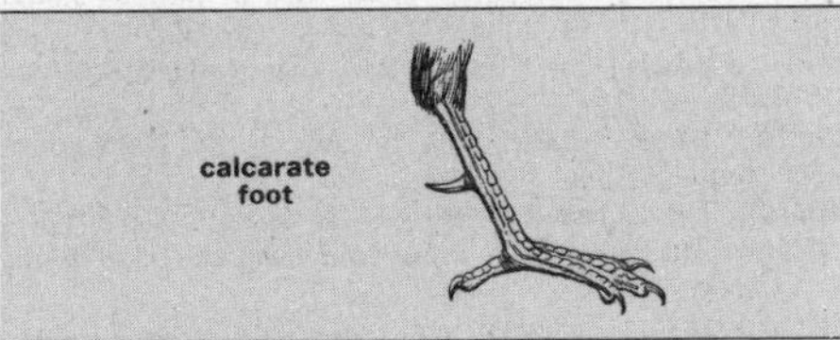
calcarate foot

cal•car•e•ous (kal kâr′ē əs), *adj.* of, containing, or like calcium carbonate; chalky: *calcareous earth.* [1670–80; var. of *calcarious* < L *calcārius* of lime; see CALX, -ARIOUS] —**cal•car′e•ous•ly,** *adv.* —**cal•car′e•ous•ness,** *n.*

calcar′eous tu′fa, tufa (def. 1). [1810–20]

cal•ca•rif•er•ous (kal′kə rif′ər əs), *adj. Biol.* bearing a spur or spurs. [1850–55; < L *calcar* CALCAR[1] + -I- + -FEROUS]

calced (kalst), *adj.* (chiefly of members of certain religious orders) wearing shoes; shod. Cf. **discalced.** [1880–85; < L *calc(eus)* shoe + -ED[3]]

cal•ce•o•lar•i•a (kal′sē ə lâr′ē ə), *n.* any plant of the genus *Calceolaria,* of the figwort family, various species of which are cultivated for their slipperlike flowers. [1840–50; < NL, equiv. to L *calceol(us)* small shoe (*calce(us)* shoe + *-olus* -OLE[1]) + *-āria* -ARIA]

cal•ce•o•late (kal′sē ə lāt′), *adj. Bot.* having the form of a shoe or slipper, as the labellum of certain orchids. [1860–65; < L *calceol(us)* a small shoe (*calce(us)* a shoe + *-olus* -OLE[1]) + -ATE[1]]

cal•ces (kal′sēz), *n.* a pl. of **calx.**

calci-, a combining form of **calcium,** used with the meaning "calcium salt" or "calcite" in the formation of compound words: *calciferous.* Also, *esp. before a vowel,* **calc-.** [< L *calc-* (s. of *calx* lime; see CHALK) + -I-]

cal•cic (kal′sik), *adj.* pertaining to or containing lime or calcium. [1870–75; CALC- + -IC]

cal•ci•cole (kal′si kōl′), *n.* any plant capable of thriving in calcareous soil. Also called **calciphile.** [1880–85; back formation from *calcicolous* growing in limy earth. See CALCI-, -COLOUS] —**cal•cic•o•lous** (kal sik′ə ləs), *adj.*

cal•cif•er•ol (kal sif′ə rôl′, -rol′), *n. Biochem.* a fat-soluble, crystalline, unsaturated alcohol, $C_{28}H_{43}OH$, occurring in milk, fish-liver oils, etc., produced by ultraviolet irradiation of ergosterol, and used as a dietary supplement, as in fortified milk. Also called **vitamin D_2.** [1930–35; CALCIF(EROUS) + (ERGOST)EROL]

cal•cif•er•ous (kal sif′ər əs), *adj.* **1.** forming salts of calcium, esp. calcium carbonate. **2.** containing calcium carbonate. [1790–1800; CALCI- + -FEROUS]

cal•cif•ic (kal sif′ik), *adj. Zool., Anat.* making or converting into salt of lime or chalk. [1860–65; CALCI- + -FIC]

cal•ci•fi•ca•tion (kal′sə fi kā′shən), *n.* **1.** a changing into lime. **2.** *Physiol.* the deposition of lime or insoluble salts of calcium and magnesium, as in a tissue. **3.** *Anat., Geol.* a calcified formation. **4.** a soil process in which the surface soil is supplied with calcium in such a way that the soil colloids are always close to saturation. **5.** a hardening or solidifying; rigidity: *As the conflict developed, there was an increasing calcification of attitudes on both sides.* [1840–50; CALCIFIC + -ATION]

cal•ci•fuge (kal′sə fyōōj′), *n.* any plant incapable of thriving in calcareous soil. Also, **calciphobe.** [1880–85; CALCI- + -FUGE] —**cal•cif•u•gous** (kal sif′yə gəs), *adj.*

cal•ci•fy (kal′sə fī′), *v.t., v.i.,* **-fied, -fy•ing. 1.** *Physiol.* to make or become calcareous or bony; harden by the deposit of calcium salts. **2.** *Geol.* to harden by deposition of calcium carbonate. **3.** to make or become rigid or intransigent, as in a political position. [1830–40; CALCI- + -FY]

cal•ci•mine (kal′sə mīn′, -min), *n., v.,* **-mined, -min•ing.** —*n.* **1.** a white or tinted wash for walls, ceilings, etc. —*v.t.* **2.** to wash or cover with calcimine. Also, **kalsomine.** [1860–65; CALCI- + (KALSO)MINE] —**cal′ci•min′er,** *n.*

cal•cine (kal′sīn, -sin), *v.,* **-cined, -cin•ing,** *n.* —*v.t.* **1.** to convert into calx by heating or burning. **2.** to frit. —*v.i.* **3.** to be converted into calx by heating or burning. —*n.* **4.** material resulting from calcination; calx. [1350–1400; ME < ML *calcināre* to heat, orig. used by alchemists] —**cal•cin•a•ble** (kal′sə nə bəl), *adj.* —**cal•ci•na•tion** (kal′sə nā′shən), *n.* —**cal•ci•na•tor** (kal′sə nā′tər), *n.* —**cal•cin•a•to•ry** (kal sin′ə tôr′ē, -tōr′ē, kal′sin ə-), *adj., n.*

cal′cined bar′y′ta, *Chem.* baryta (def. 1).

cal•cin•er (kal sī′nər, kal′sī-), *n.* **1.** a person or thing that calcines. **2.** an industrial furnace that processes material by calcination. [1700–10; CALCINE + -ER[1]]

cal•ci•no•sis (kal′sə nō′sis), *n. Pathol.* an abnormal condition characterized by the deposit of calcium salts in various tissues of the body. [1925–30; perh. CALCINE or *calcin(ate)* (erroneously taken as synonymous with CALCIFY) + -OSIS]

cal•ci•phile (kal′sə fīl′), *n.* calcicole. [1930–35; CALCI- + -PHILE] —**cal•ci•phil•ic** (kal′sə fil′ik), **cal•ciph•i•lous** (kal sif′ə ləs), *adj.*

cal•ci•phobe (kal′sə fōb′), *n.* calcifuge. [CALCI- + -PHOBE] —**cal′ci•pho′bic, cal•ciph•o•bous** (kal sif′ə bəs), *adj.*

cal•cite (kal′sīt), *n.* one of the commonest minerals, calcium carbonate, $CaCO_3$, found in a great variety of crystalline forms: a major constituent of limestone, marble, and chalk; calc-spar. [1840–50; CALC- + -ITE[1]] —**cal•cit•ic** (kal sit′ik), *adj.*

cal•ci•to•nin (kal′si tō′nin), *n. Biochem.* a polypeptide hormone that participates in the regulation of calcium levels in vertebrates by inhibiting loss of calcium from bone to the blood. [1960–65; CALCI- + TONE + -IN[2]]

cal•cit•ri•ol (kal si′trē ôl′, -ol′), *n.* **1.** *Biochem.* a vitamin D compound, $C_{27}H_{44}O_3$, occurring in humans as a hormone derived from cholesterol, that acts in the regulation and absorption of calcium. **2.** *Pharm.* a preparation of this compound, used in the treatment of osteoporosis and bone fracture. [1975–80; appar. CALCI(UM) + TRIOL]

cal•ci•um (kal′sē əm), *n. Chem., Biol.* a silver-white divalent metal, occurring combined in limestone, chalk, gypsum, etc., occurring also in vertebrates and other animals, as a component of bone, skeletal mass, shell, etc., and as a necessary element in nerve conduction, heartbeat, muscle contraction, and many other physiological functions. *Symbol:* Ca; *at. wt.:* 40.08; *at. no.:* 20; *sp. gr.:* 1.55 at 20°C. [1800–10; CALC- + -IUM]

cal′cium ar′senate, a white, slightly water-soluble, poisonous powder, $Ca_3(AsO_4)_2$, used as an insecticide and as a germicide.

cal′cium block′er, *Pharm.* any of a group of drugs that prevent the influx of calcium into excitable tissues such as smooth muscle of the heart or arterioles, used in the treatment of angina, hypertension, and certain arrhythmias. Also called **cal′cium chan′nel block′er.**

cal′cium car′bide, a grayish-black, lumpy, crystalline powder, CaC_2, usually derived from coke or anthracite by reaction with limestone or quicklime: used chiefly for the generation of acetylene, which it yields upon decomposing in water. Also called **carbide.** [1885–90]

cal′cium car′bonate, a white, crystalline, water-insoluble, tasteless powder, $CaCO_3$, occurring in nature in various forms, as calcite, chalk, and limestone: used chiefly in dentifrices and polishes and in the manufacture of lime and cement. [1870–75]

cal′cium chlo′ride, a white, lumpy, deliquescent solid, $CaCl_2$, usually derived from calcium carbonate by reaction with hydrochloric acid, or as a by-product of various commercial processes: used chiefly as a drying agent and preservative and for preventing dust. [1880–85]

cal′cium cyan′amide, a gray-black, often lumpy powder, $CaCN_2$, unstable in water, obtained by heating calcium carbide and nitrogen; cyanamide: used chiefly as a fertilizer, herbicide, and intermediate in the synthesis of nitrogen compounds. [1905–10]

cal′cium fluor′ide, a white, crystalline compound, CaF_2, insoluble in water, occurring in nature as the mineral fluorite: used as a flux in metallurgy and as a decay preventive in dentifrices.

cal′cium glu′conate, a white, tasteless, water-soluble powder, $CaC_{12}H_{22}O_{14}$, used as a dietary supplement to provide calcium. [1880–85; GLUCON(IC ACID) + -ATE[2]]

cal′cium hydrox′ide. See **slaked lime.** Also called **cal′cium hy′drate.** [1885–90]

cal′cium hypochlo′rite, a white, crystalline compound, $Ca(OCl)_2$, used as a disinfectant and bleaching agent. [1885–90]

cal′cium light′, a brilliant white light produced by heating lime to incandescence in an oxyhydrogen or other hot flame; limelight. Also called **oxycalcium light.** [1860–65]

cal′cium met•a•sil′i•cate (met′ə sil′i kit, -kāt′), a white powder, $CaSiO_3$, insoluble in water, used as an antacid and as a filler for paper.

cal′cium ni′trate, a white, deliquescent solid, $Ca(NO_3)_2$, used chiefly in the manufacture of fertilizers, fireworks, matches, and explosives. Also called **Norwegian saltpeter.**

cal′cium ox′alate, a white, crystalline powder, CaC_2O_4, insoluble in water, used in making oxalic acid.

cal′cium ox′ide, lime[1] (def. 1).

cal′cium oxychlo′ride. See **bleaching powder.**

cal′cium perman′ganate, a violet, crystalline, deliquescent solid, $Ca(MnO_4)_2{\cdot}4H_2O$, used chiefly as a disinfectant and deodorizer.

cal′cium phos′phate, any of several phosphates of calcium occurring naturally in some rocks and in animal bones, used as a fertilizer and food additive as well as in baking powder and dentifrices. [1865–70]

cal′cium pro′pionate, a white, water-soluble powder, $CaC_6H_{10}O_4$, used in bakery products to inhibit the growth of fungi.

cal′cium sil′icate, any of the silicates of calcium: calcium metasilicate, dicalcium silicate, and tricalcium silicate. Cf. **wollastonite.** [1885–90]

cal′cium sul′fide, a yellow to light-gray, slightly water-soluble powder, CaS, having the odor of rotten eggs when moist: used chiefly in the preparation of luminous paint, hydrogen sulfide, and as a depilatory in cosmetics.

calc-sin•ter (kalk′sin′tər), *n. Mineral.* travertine. [1815–25; < G *Kalksinter.* See CALC-, SINTER]

calc-spar (kalk′spär′), *n.* calcite. Also, **calc′spar′.** [1815–25; < Sw *kalkspat* calc-spar; *t* > *r* by assoc. with SPAR[3]; see CALC-]

calc-tu•fa (kalk′tōō′fə, -tyōō′-), *n.* tufa (def. 1). Also, **calc-tuff** (kalk′tuf′). [1815–25; CALC- + TUFA]

cal•cu•la•ble (kal′kyə lə bəl), *adj.* **1.** determinable by calculation; ascertainable: *This map was designed so that distances by road are easily calculable.* **2.** that can be counted on; reliable. [1725–35; CALCUL(ATE) + -ABLE] —**cal′cu•la•bil′i•ty,** *n.* —**cal′cu•la•bly,** *adv.*

cal•cu•late (kal′kyə lāt′), *v.,* **-lat•ed, -lat•ing.** —*v.t.* **1.** to determine or ascertain by mathematical methods; compute: *to calculate the velocity of light.* **2.** to determine by reasoning, common sense, or practical experience; estimate; evaluate; gauge. **3.** to make suitable or fit for a purpose; adapt (usually used passively and with an infinitive): *His remarks were calculated to inspire our confidence.* **4.** *Chiefly Northern U.S.* **a.** to think; guess. **b.** to intend; plan. —*v.i.* **5.** to make a computation or form an estimate. **6.** to count or rely (usually fol. by *on* or *upon*): *They calculated on good weather.* [1560–70; < LL *calculātus* reckoned (ptp. of *calculāre*), equiv. to *calculus* pebble (see CALCULUS) + *-ātus* -ATE[1]]
—**Syn. 1.** count, figure, cast. **3.** design, plan, intend, mean.

cal•cu•lat•ed (kal′kyə lā′tid), *adj.* **1.** arrived at or determined by mathematical calculation; ascertained mathematically. **2.** carefully thought out or planned: *a calculated effort.* [1715–25; CALCULATE + -ED[2]] —**cal′•cu•lat′ed•ly,** *adv.* —**cal′cu•lat′ed•ness,** *n.*

cal′culated risk′, a chance of failure, the probability of which is estimated before some action is undertaken.

cal•cu•lat•ing (kal′kyə lā′ting), *adj.* **1.** capable of or made for performing calculations, esp. arithmetical calculations: *a calculating machine.* **2.** shrewd; cautious: *a wise and calculating lawyer.* **3.** selfishly scheming: *a cold and calculating dictator.* [1800–10; CALCULATE + -ING[2]] —**cal′cu•lat′ing•ly,** *adv.*
—**Syn. 3.** designing.

cal′culating machine′, calculator (def. 2). [1700–10]

cal•cu•la•tion (kal′kyə lā′shən), *n.* **1.** the act or process of calculating; computation. **2.** the result or product of calculating: *His calculations agree with ours.* **3.** an estimate based on the known facts; forecast: *Her calculation of the building costs proved quite accurate.* **4.** forethought; prior or careful planning. **5.** scheming selfishness. [1350–1400; ME < LL *calculātiōn-* (s. of *calculātiō* reckoning). See CALCULATE, -ION] —**cal•cu•la•tive** (kal′kyə lā′tiv, -lə tiv), **cal′cu•la′tion•al, cal•cu•la•to•ry** (kal′kyə lə tôr′ē, -tōr′ē), *adj.*
—**Syn. 1.** figuring, reckoning. **3.** estimation. **4.** circumspection, caution, wariness. See **prudence.**

cal•cu•la•tor (kal′kyə lā′tər), *n.* **1.** a person who calculates or computes. **2.** Also called **calculating machine.** a small electronic or mechanical device that performs calculations, requiring manual action for each individual operation. **3.** a person who operates such a machine. **4.** a set of tables that facilitates calculation. [1375–1425; late ME < L; see CALCULATE, -TOR]

CONCISE PRONUNCIATION KEY: act, cāpe, dâre, pärt; set, ēqual; *if,* īce; ox, ōver, ôrder, oil, bŏŏk, bōōt, out; up, ûrge; child; sing; shoe; thin, *th*at; zh as in *treasure.* ə = *a* as in *alone, e* as in *system, i* as in *easily, o* as in *gallop, u* as in *circus;* ə as in *fire* (fīə r), *hour* (ouə r). l and n can serve as syllabic consonants, as in *cradle* (krād′l), and *button* (but′n). See the full key inside the front cover.

cal•cu•lous (kal′kyə ləs), *adj. Pathol.* characterized by the presence of calculus, or stone. [1400–50; late ME *calculose,* full of stones < L *calculōsus,* equiv. to *calcu-l(us)* small stone (see CALCULUS) + *-ōsus* -OUS]

cal•cu•lus (kal′kyə ləs), *n., pl.* **-li** (-lī′), **-lus•es.** **1.** *Math.* a method of calculation, esp. one of several highly systematic methods of treating problems by a special system of algebraic notations, as differential or integral calculus. **2.** *Pathol.* a stone, or concretion, formed in the gallbladder, kidneys, or other parts of the body. **3.** Also called **tartar.** *Dentistry.* a hard, yellowish to brownish-black deposit on teeth formed largely through the mineralization of dead bacteria in dental plaques by the calcium salts in salivary secretions and subgingival transudates. [1610–20; < L: pebble, small stone (used in reckoning), equiv. to *calc-* (s. of *calx* stone) + *-ulus* -ULE]

cal′culus of fi′nite dif′ferences, the branch of mathematics dealing with the application of techniques similar to those of differential and integral calculus to discrete rather than continuous quantities.

cal′culus of pleas′ure. See **hedonic calculus.**

cal′culus of varia′tions, the branch of mathematics that deals with the problem of finding a curve or surface that maximizes or minimizes a given expression, usually with several restrictions placed on the desired curve. [1830–40]

Cal•cut•ta (kal kut′ə), *n.* **1.** a seaport in and the capital of West Bengal state, in E India, on the Hooghly River: former capital of British India. 7,031,382. **2.** (*sometimes l.c.*) Also called **Calcut′ta pool′.** a form of betting pool for a competition or tournament, as golf or auto racing, in which gamblers bid for participating contestants in an auction, the proceeds from which are put into a pool for distribution, according to a prearranged scale of percentages, to those who selected winners.

cal•dar•i•um (kal dâr′ē əm), *n., pl.* **-dar•i•a** (-dâr′ē ə). (in an ancient Roman bath) a room having a hot bath. [1745–55; < L: n. use of neut. of *caldārius* of warming, equiv. to *cal(i)d(us)* warm (*cal(ēre)* to be warm + *-idus* -ID[4]) + *-ārius* -ARY; see -IUM, -ARIUM]

Cal′de•cott award′ (kôl′di kət), an annual award in the U.S. for an outstanding illustrated juvenile book. [named after Randolph *Caldecott* (1846–86), English illustrator]

Cal•der (kôl′dər), *n.* **Alexander,** 1898–1976, U.S. sculptor; originator of mobiles.

cal•de•ra (kal der′ə, kôl-), *n.* a large, basinlike depression resulting from the explosion or collapse of the center of a volcano. [1860–65; < Sp *Caldera,* name of a crater on Canary Islands, lit., cauldron < LL *caldāria,* n. use of fem. of *caldārius* of warming; see CALDARIUM]

Cal•de•rón de la Bar•ca (käl′də rōn′ del′ə bär′kə; *Sp.* käl′de RÔN′ de lä bäR′kä), **Pe•dro** (pā′drō, ped′rō; *Sp.* pe′thRô), 1600–81, Spanish dramatist and poet.

cal•dron (kôl′drən), *n.* cauldron.

Cald•well (kôld′wel, -wəl), *n.* **1. Erskine,** born 1903, U.S. novelist. **2. Sarah,** born 1924, U.S. conductor and opera producer. **3.** a city in W Idaho. 17,699.

Ca•leb (kā′ləb), *n.* **1.** a Hebrew leader, sent as a spy into the land of Canaan. Num. 13:6. **2.** a male given name: from a Hebrew word meaning "dog."

Ca•leb•ite (kā′lə bīt′), *n.* **1.** a member of a tribe descended from Caleb. —*adj.* **2.** of or pertaining to the Calebites. [CALEB + -ITE[1]]

ca•lèche (*Fr.* KA lesh′; *Eng.* kə lesh′), *n., pl.* **-lèches** (*Fr.* -lesh′; *Eng.* -lesh′əz). **1.** Also, **calash.** (esp. in Quebec, Canada) a type of calash pulled by a single horse, seating two passengers and having two wheels and a folding top. **2.** calash (def. 1). [1660–70; < F; see CALASH]

Cal•e•don (kal′i dən), *n.* a town in SE Ontario, in S Canada, near Toronto. 26,645.

Cal•e•do•ni•a (kal′i dō′nē ə), *n.* **1.** *Chiefly Literary.* Scotland. **2.** a female given name.

Cal•e•do•ni•an (kal′i dō′nē ən), *n.* **1.** a native or inhabitant of Caledonia. —*adj.* **2.** of or pertaining to Caledonia. [1900–05; CALEDONI(A) + -AN]

Caledo′nian Canal′, a canal in N Scotland, extending NE from the Atlantic to the North Sea. 60½ mi. (97 km) long.

calef., (in prescriptions) warmed. [< L *calefactus*]

cal•e•fa•cient (kal′ə fā′shənt), *n.* **1.** *Med.* a substance, as mustard, that produces a sensation of heat when applied to the body. —*adj.* **2.** heating; warming. [1655–65; < L *calefacient-* (s. of *calefaciēns,* prp. of *calefacere* to make warm), equiv. to *cale-* warm (s. of *calēre* to be warm) + *-facient-* -FACIENT]

cal•e•fac•tion (kal′ə fak′shən), *n.* **1.** the act of heating. **2.** a heated state. [1540–50; < L *calefactiōn-* (s. of *calefactiō*) a making warm, equiv. to *cale-* warm (s. of *calēre* to be warm) + *factiōn-* a making; see FACTION] —**cal′e•fac′tive,** *adj.*

cal•e•fac•to•ry (kal′ə fak′tə rē, -fak′trē), *adj., n., pl.* **-ries.** —*adj.* **1.** serving to heat. —*n.* **2.** a heated parlor or sitting room in a monastery. [1530–40; < LL *calefactōrius* having a warming or heating power, equiv. to L *calefac(ere)* to make warm (see CALEFACIENT) + *-tōrius* -TORY[1]]

cal•en•dar (kal′ən dər), *n.* **1.** a table or register with the days of each month and week in a year: *He marked the date on his calendar.* **2.** any of various systems of reckoning time, esp. with reference to the beginning, length, and divisions of the year. Cf. **Chinese calendar, Gregorian calendar, Hindu calendar, Jewish calendar, Julian calendar, Muslim calendar. 3.** a list or register, esp. one arranged chronologically, as of appointments, work to be done, or cases to be tried in a court. **4.** a list, in the order to be considered, of bills, resolutions, etc., brought before a legislative body. **5.** *Obs.* a guide or example. —*v.t.* **6.** to enter in a calendar; register. Also, **kalendar.** [1175–1225; ME *calender* < AF < L *calendārium* account book, equiv. to *Calend(ae)* CALENDS (when debts were due) + *-ārium* -ARY; see -AR[2]] —**ca•len•dri•cal** (kə len′dri kəl), **ca•len′dric, cal•en•dar•i•al** (kal′ən dâr′ē əl), **cal′en•dar′i•an, cal′en•dar′ic,** *adj.*
—**Syn. 3.** diary, schedule, program.

cal′endar art′, a type of sentimental, picturesque, or sexually titillating picture used on some calendars.

cal′endar clock′, a clock that indicates date of the month, day of the week, etc., as well as the time, and sometimes indicates the phases of the moon and other periodical data. [1880–85]

cal′endar day′, the period from one midnight to the following midnight. [1840–50]

cal′endar month′, month (def. 1). [1780–90]

cal′endar watch′, a watch that indicates date of the month, day of the week, etc., as well as the time.

cal′endar year′. See under **year** (def. 1).

cal•en•der (kal′ən dər), *n.* **1.** a machine in which cloth, paper, or the like, is smoothed, glazed, etc., by pressing between rotating cylinders. **2.** a machine for impregnating fabric with rubber, as in the manufacture of automobile tires. —*v.t.* **3.** to press in a calender. [1505–15; < MF *calandre,* by vowel assimilation < *colandre < VL *colendra, for L *cylindrus* CYLINDER; cf. ME *calendrer* (< AF) as name of occupation] —**cal′en•der•er,** *n.*

Cal•en•der (kal′ən dər), *n.* qalandar.

cal•ends (kal′əndz), *n.* (*usually used with a plural v.*) the first day of the month in the ancient Roman calendar, from which the days of the preceding month were counted backward to the ides. Also, **kalends.** [1325–75; ME *kalendes,* alter. (with native pl. suffix) of L *kalendae,* perh. equiv. to *cal-* (base of *calāre* to proclaim) + *-end-* formative suffix (perh. for **-and-*) + *-ae* pl. ending]

ca•len•du•la (kə len′jə lə), *n.* **1.** Also called **pot marigold.** a composite plant, *Calendula officinalis,* widely cultivated for its showy, many-rayed orange or yellow flower heads. **2.** the dried florets of this plant, sometimes used medicinally. **3.** any other plant of the genus *Calendula.* [1870–75; < ML, equiv. to L *calend(ae)* CALENDS + *-ula* -ULE]

cal•en•ture (kal′ən chər, -cho͝or′), *n. Pathol.* a violent fever with delirium, affecting persons in the tropics. [1585–95; earlier *calentura* < Sp: fever, equiv. to *calent(ar)* to heat (< L *calent-,* s. of *calēns,* prp. of *calēre* to be hot) + *-ura* -URE] —**cal′en•tu′ral, cal′en•tu′rish,** *adj.*

ca•le•sa (*Sp.* kä le′sä), *n.* (in the Philippines) a small, two-wheeled calash. [< Sp < F *calèche* CALÈCHE]

ca•les•cent (kə les′ənt), *adj.* growing warm; increasing in heat. [1795–1805; < L *calēscent-* (s. of *calēscēns* becoming warm, prp. of *calēscere*), equiv. to *cal-* (s. of *calēre* to be warm) + *-ēscent-* -ESCENT] —**ca•les′cence,** *n.*

Ca•lex•i•co (kə lek′si kō′), *n.* a town in S California. 14,412.

calf[1] (kaf, käf), *n., pl.* **calves** (kavz, kävz). **1.** the young of the domestic cow or other bovine animal. **2.** the young of certain other mammals, as the elephant, seal, and whale. **3.** calfskin leather. **4.** *Informal.* an awkward, silly boy or man. **5.** a mass of ice detached from a glacier, iceberg, or floe. **6. in calf,** (of a cow or other animal having calves) pregnant. **7. kill the fatted calf,** to prepare an elaborate feast in welcome or celebration. [bef. 900; ME; OE *cealf, calf;* c. OS *kalf,* ON *kalfr,* OHG *kalb*] —**calf′less,** *adj.* —**calf′like′,** *adj.*

calf[2] (kaf, käf), *n., pl.* **calves** (kavz, kävz). the fleshy part of the back of the human leg below the knee. [1275–1325; ME < ON *kalfi;* akin to CALF[1]]

calf′ love′. See **puppy love.** [1815–25]

calf′ rop′ing, a timed rodeo event in which a mounted rider chases and lassos a calf, dismounts, and throws the calf to the ground, tying three of the animal's legs with a short length of rope. [1905–10, *Amer.*]

calf′s′-foot jel′ly (kavz′fo͝ot′, kävz′-, kafs′-, käfs′-), jelly made from the stock of boiled calves' feet. [1765–75]

calf•skin (kaf′skin′, käf′-), *n.* **1.** the skin or hide of a calf. **2.** leather made from this skin. [1580–90; CALF[1] + SKIN]

calf's′ tongue′, *Archit.* a molding having pendent, tonguelike members in relief against a flat or molded surface.

Cal•ga•ry (kal′gə rē), *n.* a city in S Alberta, in SW Canada. 469,917.

Cal′gary red′eye, *Canadian* (*chiefly Alberta*). a drink consisting of a mixture of beer and tomato juice.

Cal•gon (kal′gon), *Trademark.* a brand of sodium phosphate glass (**sodium hexametaphosphate**), soluble in water: used as a water-softening agent.

Cal•houn (kal ho͞on′, kəl-), *n.* **John Caldwell,** 1782–1850, vice president of the U.S. 1825–32.

Ca•li (kä′lē), *n.* a city in SW Colombia. 898,253.

Cal•i•ban (kal′ə ban′), *n.* the ugly, beastlike slave of Prospero in Shakespeare's *The Tempest.*

cal•i•ber (kal′ə bər), *n.* **1.** the diameter of something of circular section, esp. that of the inside of a tube: *a pipe of three-inch caliber.* **2.** *Ordn.* the diameter of the bore of a gun taken as a unit of measurement. **3.** degree of capacity or competence; ability: *a mathematician of high caliber.* **4.** degree of merit or excellence; quality: *the high moral caliber of the era.* Also, *esp. Brit.,* **cal′i•bre.** [1560–70; var. of *calibre* < MF << Ar *qālib* mold, last < Gk *kālópous* shoe last, equiv. to *kāla-* comb. form of *kâlon* wood + *poús* foot (see -POD)] —**cal′i•bered;** *esp. Brit.,* **cal′i•bred,** *adj.*
—**Syn. 4.** worth, distinction.

cal•i•brate (kal′ə brāt′), *v.t.,* **-brat•ed, -brat•ing. 1.** to determine, check, or rectify the graduation of (any instrument giving quantitative measurements). **2.** to divide or mark with gradations, graduations, or other indexes of degree, quantity, etc., as on a thermometer, measuring cup, or the like. **3.** to determine the correct range for (an artillery gun, mortar, etc.) by observing where the fired projectile hits. **4.** to plan or devise (something) carefully so as to have a precise use, application, appeal, etc.: *a sales strategy calibrated to rich investors.* [1860–65; CALIBER + -ATE[1]] —**cal′i•bra′tion,** *n.* —**cal′i•bra′tor, cal′i•brat′er,** *n.*

cal•i•ces (kal′ə sēz′), *n.* pl. of **calix.**

ca•li•che (kə lē′chē), *n. Geol.* **1.** a surface deposit consisting of sand or clay impregnated with crystalline salts such as sodium nitrate or sodium chloride. **2.** a zone of calcium carbonate or other carbonates in soils of semiarid regions. Cf. **duricrust, hardpan.** [1855–60; < Sp: flake of lime, equiv. to *cal* lime (< L *calc-;* see CHALK) + *-iche* n. suffix]

cal•i•cle (kal′i kəl), *n.* **1.** a cuplike depression or formation, as in corals. **2.** *Bot., Zool.* calyculus. [1840–50; < L *caliculus* small cup, equiv. to *calic-* (s. of *calix;* see CALIX) cup + *-ulus* -ULE]

cal•i•co (kal′i kō′), *n., pl.* **-coes, -cos,** *adj.* —*n.* **1.** a plain-woven cotton cloth printed with a figured pattern, usually on one side. **2.** *Brit.* plain white cotton cloth. **3.** an animal having a spotted or particolored coat. **4.** *Obs.* a figured cotton cloth from India. —*adj.* **5.** made of calico. **6.** resembling printed calico; spotted or mottled. [1495–1505; short for *Calico cloth,* var. of *Calicut cloth,* named after city in India which orig. exported it]

cal•i•co•back (kal′i kō bak′), *n.* See **harlequin bug.** [1870–75, *Amer.*]

cal′ico bass′ (bas), the black crappie. See under **crappie.** [1880–85, *Amer.*]

cal′ico bug′. See **harlequin bug.** [1885–90, *Amer.*]

cal′ico bush′. See **mountain laurel.** [1805–15, *Amer.*]

cal′ico cat′, a domestic cat, esp. a female one, of variegated black, yellow, and white coloring. Also called **tortoise-shell cat.**

cal′ico clam′, any marine bivalve mollusk of the genus *Macrocallista,* esp. *M. nimbosa,* having a smooth, thick, rounded shell marked with violet-brown or lilac spots or streaks.

cal′ico crab′. See **lady crab.**

MONTHS OF PRINCIPAL CALENDARS

Gregorian		Jewish		Muslim	
Month	Number of Days	Month	Number of Days	Month	Number of Days
January	31	Tishri[1]	30	Moharram	30
February	28	Heshvan	29	Safar	29
(in leap years:	29)	(in some years:	30)		
March	31	Kislev	29	Rabi I	30
		(in some years:	30)		
April	30	Tevet	29	Rabi II	29
May	31	Shevat	30	Jumada I	30
June	30	Adar[2]	29	Jumada II	29
		(in leap years:	30)		
July	31	Nisan[3]	30	Rajab	30
August	31	Iyar	29	Shaban	29
September	30	Sivan	30	Ramadan	30
October	31	Tammuz	29	Shawwal	29
November	30	Av	30	Dhu 'l-Qa'da	30
December	31	Elul	29	Dhu 'l-hijjah	29
				(in leap years:	30)

[1]The beginning of the civil year, corresponding to September-October.
[2]In leap years Adar is followed by the intercalary month of Veadar or Adar Sheni, having 29 days.
[3]The beginning of the ecclesiastical year, corresponding to March-April.

CONCISE ETYMOLOGY KEY: <, descended or borrowed from; >, whence; b., blend of, blended; c., cognate with; cf., compare; deriv., derivative; equiv., equivalent; imit., imitative; obl., oblique; r., replacing; s., stem; sp., spelling, spelled; resp., respelling, respelled; trans., translation; ?, origin unknown; *, unattested; ‡, probably earlier than. See the full key inside the front cover.

cal•i•coed (kal′i kōd′), *adj.* dressed in calico. [CALICO + -ED[3]]

cal′ico flow′er, a Brazilian woody vine, *Aristolochia elegans,* of the birthwort family, having large, solitary, white-spotted, purple flowers. [1795–1805, *Amer.*]

ca•lic•u•lus (kə lik′yə ləs), *n., pl.* **-li** (-lī′). calyculus (def. 1).

Cal•i•cut (kal′i kut′), *n.* former name of **Kozhikode.**

cal•i•duct (kal′i dukt′), *n.* a pipe or duct for conveying a heating medium, as hot air or steam. [1645–55; < L *cali(dus)* warm + DUCT, modeled on AQUEDUCT]

ca•lif (kā′lif, kal′if), *n.* caliph.

Calif., California.

cal•if•ate (kal′ə fāt′, -fit, kā′lə-), *n.* caliphate.

Cal•i•for•nia (kal′ə fôrn′yə, -fôr′nē ə), *n.* **1.** a state in the W United States, on the Pacific coast. 23,668,562; 158,693 sq. mi. (411,015 sq. km). *Cap.:* Sacramento. *Abbr.:* CA (for use with zip code), Cal., Calif. **2. Gulf of,** an arm of the Pacific Ocean, extending NW between the coast of W Mexico and the peninsula of Lower California. ab. 750 mi. (1207 km) long; 62,600 sq. mi. (162,100 sq. km). **—Cal′i•for′nian,** *adj., n.*

Califor′nia barracu′da. See **Pacific barracuda.**

Cal′ifor′nia blue′bell, 1. either of two plants, *Phacelia campanularia* or *P. minor,* of southern California, having ovate leaves and bell-shaped blue or purple flowers. **2.** a plant, *Campanula prenanthoides,* of California and Oregon, having clusters of pale-blue flowers.

Cal′ifor′nia con′dor. See under **condor** (def. 1). [1825–35]

Cal′ifor′nia Cur′rent, a cold current originating in the northern part of the Pacific Ocean, flowing SE along the coast of W North America.

Cal′ifor′nia fan′ palm′, a tall fan palm, *Washingtonia filifera,* of California, having a shaggy skirt of withered leaves near the top of the trunk. [1895–1900, *Amer.*]

Cal′ifor′nia fuch′sia, fuchsia (def. 2).

Califor′nia gold′ fern′, an evergreen fern, *Pityrogramma triangularis,* growing from British Columbia to California, having the underside of the leaves covered with a deep yellow, powderlike substance.

Cal′ifor′nia gull′, a large gull, *Larus californicus,* of the western U.S.

Cal′ifor′nia job′ case′, *Print.* a job case having sufficient spaces to contain both uppercase and lowercase letters and 37 additional characters of foundry type. Cf. **case**[2] (def. 8).

Cal′ifor′nia lau′rel, 1. Also called **bay tree.** a tree, *Umbellularia californica,* of the laurel family, native to the western coast of the U.S., having aromatic leaves and umbels of yellowish-green flowers. **2.** the hard, golden-brown wood of this tree, used for making furniture and decorative objects. Also called **myrtle, Oregon myrtle, pepperwood.** [1870–75, *Amer.*]

Califor′nia live′ oak′, an evergreen oak, *Quercus agrifolia,* of the western coast of the U.S., having leathery leaves and a short, stout trunk. Also called **coast live oak.**

Cal′ifor′nia mink′. See **civet cat.**

Cal′ifor′nia nut′meg, a tall, pungently aromatic California evergreen tree, *Torreya californica,* of the yew family, having a fissured, gray-brown bark and small, purple-streaked, green fruit. [1905–10, *Amer.*]

Cal′ifor′nia oak′worm. See under **oakworm.**

Cal′ifor′nia pop′py, a plant, *Eschscholtzia californica,* of the poppy family, having feathery bluish foliage and showy, orange-yellow flowers: the state flower of California. [1890–95, *Amer.*]

Cal′ifor′nia priv′et, a privet, *Ligustrum ovalifolium,* of the olive family, native to Japan, having glossy, oval leaves and long clusters of white flowers, widely used for hedges in the U.S.

Cal′ifor′nia quail′, a quail, *Callipepla californica,* of the western coast of the U.S., having grayish-brown plumage with black, white, and chestnut markings. [1825–35, *Amer.*]

Cal′ifor′nia rose′, a cultivated variety of a bindweed, *Calystegia hederacea,* having showy, double, rose-colored flowers.

Cal′ifor′nia rose′bay. See **coast rhododendron.** [1910–15, *Amer.*]

Cal′ifor′nia sea′ li′on. See under **sea lion** (def. 1).

cal•i•for•nite (kal′ə fôr′nīt), *n.* See **vesuvianite jade.** [1900–05; CALIFORN(IA) (where it is found) + -ITE[1]]

cal•i•for•ni•um (kal′ə fôr′nē əm), *n. Chem.* a transuranic element. *Symbol:* Cf; *at. no.:* 98. [1945–50; named after the University of CALIFORNIA where it was discovered; see -IUM]

ca•lig•i•nous (kə lij′ə nəs), *adj. Archaic.* misty; dim; dark. [1540–50; < L *cālīginōsus* misty, equiv. to *cālīgin-* (s. of *cālīgō*) mist + *-ōsus* -OUS] **—ca•lig•i•nos•i•ty** (kə lij′ə nos′i tē), **ca•lig′i•nous•ness,** *n.* **—ca•lig′i•nous•ly,** *adv.*

Ca•lig•u•la (kə lig′yə lə), *n.* (*Gaius Caesar*), A.D. 12–41, emperor of Rome 37–41.

cal•i•man•co (kal′ə mang′kō), *n., pl.* **-cos.** calamanco.

cal•i•pash (kal′ə pash′, kal′ə pash′), *n.* the part of a turtle next to the upper shield, consisting of a greenish gelatinous substance, considered a delicacy. Also, **callipash.** Cf. **calipee.** [1680–90; of obscure orig.]

cal•i•pee (kal′ə pē′, kal′ə pē′), *n.* the part of a turtle next to the lower shield, consisting of a yellowish gelatinous substance, considered a delicacy. Cf. **calipash.** [1650–60; of obscure orig.]

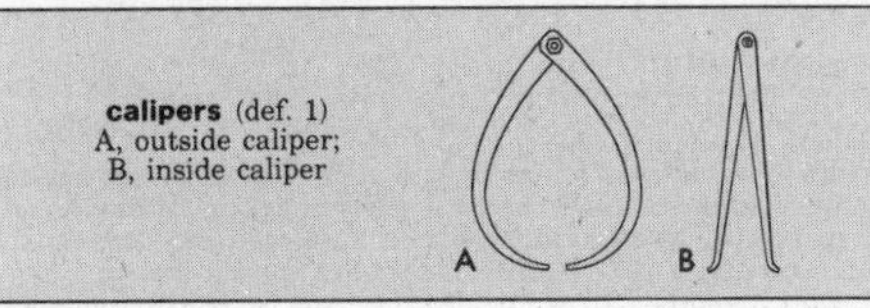

calipers (def. 1)
A, outside caliper;
B, inside caliper

cal•i•per (kal′ə pər), *n.* **1.** Usually, **calipers.** an instrument for measuring thicknesses and internal or external diameters inaccessible to a scale, consisting usually of a pair of adjustable pivoted legs. **2.** any of various calibrated instruments for measuring thicknesses or distances between surfaces, usually having a screwed or sliding adjustable piece. Cf. **vernier caliper. 3.** thickness or depth, as of paper or a tree. **4.** Usually, **calipers.** the pincers of an earwig. **5.** *Auto.* the part of a disc-brake assembly that straddles the disc and presses the brake pads against it. See illus. under **disc brake. 6.** a similar part used with a hand brake on a bicycle. *—v.t.* **7.** to measure with calipers. *—v.i.* **8.** to use calipers. Also, **calliper.** [1580–90; presumably var. of CALIBER]

cal′iper rule′, a caliper with one jaw fixed to or integral with a graduated straight bar on which the other jaw slides.

ca•liph (kā′lif, kal′if), *n.* **1.** a spiritual leader of Islam, claiming succession from Muhammad. **2.** any of the former Muslim rulers of Baghdad (until 1258) and of the Ottoman Empire (from 1571 until 1924). Also, **calif, kalif, kaliph, khalif.** [1350–1400; ME *caliphe, califfe* < MF < ML *calipha* < Ar *khalīf(a)* successor (of Muhammad), deriv. of *khalafa* succeed] **—cal•iph•al** (kal′ə fəl, kā′lə-), *adj.*

cal•iph•ate (kal′ə fāt′, -fit, kā′lə-), *n.* the rank, jurisdiction, or government of a caliph. Also, **califate, kalifate, khalifate.** [1725–35; CALIPH + -ATE[3]]

Ca•lip•pus (kə lip′əs), *n.* Callippus.

cal•i•sa•ya (kal′ə sā′yə), *n.* the medicinal bark of the tree *Cinchona calisaya.* [1830–40; < NL, after *Calisaya,* name of the Bolivian Indian who told the whites about the medicinal values of cinchona bark]

cal•is•then•ics (kal′əs then′iks), *n.* **1.** (*used with a plural v.*) gymnastic exercises designed to develop physical health and vigor, usually performed with little or no special apparatus. **2.** (*used with a singular v.*) the art, practice, or a session of such exercises. Also, **callisthenics.** [1840–50; *cali-* (var. of CALLI-) + Gk *sthén(os)* strength + -ICS] **—cal′is•then′ic, cal′is•then′i•cal,** *adj.*

ca•lix (kā′liks, kal′iks), *n., pl.* **cal•i•ces** (kal′i sēz′). cup. [< L; see CHALICE]

Ca•lix•tine (kə lik′stīn, -stēn), *n.* a member of a body of Hussites in the 15th century holding that the chalice as well as the bread should be received by the laity in the Eucharist. Also, **Ca•lix•tin** (kə lik′stin). Also called **Utraquist.** [< ML *Calixtinus,* equiv. to *calix* cup + *-tinus* adj. suffix; see VESPERTINE]

Ca•lix•tus I (kə lik′stəs), **Saint,** A.D. c160–222, Italian ecclesiastic: pope 218–222. Also, **Callistus I.**

Calixtus II, died 1124, French ecclesiastic: pope 1119–24. Also, **Callistus II.**

Calixtus III, (*Alfonso de Borja* or *Alfonso Borgia*) 1378–1458, Spanish ecclesiastic: pope 1455–58. Also, **Callistus III.**

calk[1] (kôk), *v.t., n.* caulk.

calk[2] (kôk), *n.* **1.** Also, **calkin.** a projection on a horseshoe to prevent slipping on ice, pavement, etc. See illus. under **horseshoe. 2.** Also, **calker.** a similar device on the heel or sole of a shoe to prevent slipping. *—v.t.* **3.** to provide with calks. **4.** to injure with a calk. [1580–90; perh. a back formation from CALKIN, taken as a verb *calk* + *-in* prp. suffix (ME *-inde*), confused with -ING[2]]

calk•er[1] (kô′kər), *n.* caulker.

calk•er[2] (kô′kər), *n.* calk[2] (def. 2). [CALK[2] + -ER[1]]

cal•kin (kô′kin, kal′-), *n.* calk[2] (def. 1). [1400–50; late ME *kakun* < MD *calcoen* hoof < OF (Walloon) *calcain* < L *calcāneum* heel; see CALCANEUM]

call (kôl), *v.t.* **1.** to cry out in a loud voice; shout: *He called her name to see if she was home.* **2.** to command or request to come; summon: *to call a dog; to call a cab; to call a witness.* **3.** to ask or invite to come: *Will you call the family to dinner?* **4.** to communicate or try to communicate with by telephone: *Call me when you arrive.* **5.** to rouse from sleep, as by a call; waken: *Call me at eight o'clock.* **6.** to read over (a roll or a list) in a loud voice. **7.** to convoke or convene: *to call Congress into session.* **8.** to announce authoritatively; proclaim: *to call a halt.* **9.** to order into effect; establish: *to call a strike.* **10.** to schedule: *to call a rehearsal.* **11.** to summon by or as if by divine command: *He felt called to the ministry.* **12.** to summon to an office, duty, etc.: *His country called him to the colors.* **13.** to cause to come; bring: *to call to mind; to call into existence.* **14.** to bring under consideration or discussion: *The judge called the case to court.* **15.** to attract or lure (birds or animals) by imitating characteristic sounds. **16.** to direct or attract (attention): *He called his roommate's attention to the mess.* **17.** to name or address (someone) as: *His parents named him James, but the boys call him Jim.* **18.** to designate as something specified: *He called me a liar.* **19.** to think of as something specified; consider; estimate: *I call that a mean remark.* **20.** to demand of (someone) that he or she fulfill a promise, furnish evidence for a statement, etc.: *They called him on his story.* **21.** to criticize adversely; express disapproval of; censure: *She called him on his vulgar language.* **22.** to demand payment or fulfillment of (a loan). **23.** to demand presentation of (bonds) for redemption. **24.** to forecast correctly: *He has called the outcome of the last three elections.* **25.** *Sports.* (of an official) **a.** to pronounce a judgment on (a shot, pitch, batter, etc.): *The umpire called the pitch a strike.* **b.** to put an end to (a contest) because of inclement weather, poor field conditions, etc.: *A sudden downpour forced the umpire to call the game.* **26.** *Pool.* to name (the ball) one intends to drive into a particular pocket. **27.** (in a computer program) to transfer control of to a procedure or subroutine. **28.** *Cards.* **a.** to demand (a card). **b.** to demand the display of a hand by (a player). **c.** *Poker.* to equal (a bet) or equal the bet made by (the preceding bettor) in a round. **d.** *Bridge.* to signal one's partner for a lead of (a certain card or suit). *—v.i.* **29.** to speak loudly, as to attract attention; shout; cry: *She called to the children.* **30.** to make a short visit; stop at a place on some errand or business: *She called at the store for the package.* **31.** to telephone or try to telephone a person: *He promised to call at noon.* **32.** *Cards.* **a.** to demand a card. **b.** to demand a showing of hands. **c.** *Poker.* to equal a bet. **d.** *Bridge.* to bid or pass. **33.** (of a bird or animal) to utter its characteristic cry. **34. call away,** to cause to leave or go; summon: *A death in the family called him away.* **35. call back, a.** to summon or bring back; recall: *He called back the messenger. The actor was called back for a second audition.* **b.** to revoke; retract: *to call back an accusation.* **36. call down, a.** to request or pray for; invoke: *to call down the wrath of God.* **b.** to reprimand; scold: *The boss called us down for lateness.* **37. call for, a.** to go or come to get; pick up; fetch. **b.** to request; summon. **c.** to require; demand; need: *The occasion calls for a cool head.* **38. call forth,** to summon into action; bring into existence: *to call forth her courage and resolve.* **39. call in, a.** to call for payment; collect. **b.** to withdraw from circulation: *to call in gold certificates.* **c.** to call upon for consultation; ask for help: *Two specialists were called in to assist in the operation.* **d.** to inform or report by telephone: *Did he call in his decision this morning?* **e.** to participate in a radio or television program by telephone. **40. call in** or **into question.** See **question** (def. 12). **41. call in sick.** See **sick**[1] (def. 13). **42. call off, a.** to distract; take away: *Please call off your dog.* **b.** to cancel (something) that had been planned for a certain date: *The performance was called off because of rain.* **43. call on** or **upon, a.** to ask; appeal to: *They called on him to represent them.* **b.** to visit for a short time: *to call on friends.* **44. call out, a.** to speak in a loud voice; shout. **b.** to summon into service or action: *Call out the militia!* **c.** to bring out; elicit: *The emergency called out her hidden abilities.* **d.** to direct attention to with a callout: *to call out each detail in an illustration.* **e.** *Informal.* to challenge to a fight. **45. call to order.** See **order** (def. 38). **46. call up, a.** to bring forward for consideration or discussion. **b.** to cause to remember; evoke. **c.** to communicate or try to communicate with by telephone. **d.** to summon for action or service: *A large number of Army reservists were called up.* **e.** *Computers.* to summon (information) from a computer system for display on a video screen: *She called up the full text.* *—n.* **47.** a cry or shout. **48.** the cry or vocal sound of a bird or other animal. **49.** an instrument for imitating this cry and attracting or luring an animal: *He bought a duck call.* **50.** an act or instance of telephoning: *She went into a telephone booth to place her call.* **51.** a short visit: *to make a call on someone.* **52.** a summons or signal sounded by a bugle, bell, etc.: *We live so close to the fort that we can hear the bugle calls.* **53.** a summons, invitation, or bidding: *The students gathered at the call of the dean.* **54.** a calling of a roll; roll call. **55.** the fascination or appeal of a given place, vocation, etc.: *the call of the sea.* **56.** a mystic experience of divine appointment to a vocation or service: *He had a call to become a minister.* **57.** a request or invitation to become pastor of a church, a professor in a university, etc. **58.** a need or occasion: *He had no call to say such outrageous things.* **59.** a demand or claim: *to make a call on a person's time.* **60.** a demand for payment of an obligation, esp. where payment is at the option of the creditor. **61.** *Cards.* **a.** a demand for a card or a showing of hands. **b.** *Poker.* an equaling of the preceding bet. **c.** *Bridge.* a bid or pass. **62.** *Sports.* a judgment or decision by an umpire, a referee, or other official of a contest, as on a shot, pitch, or batter: *The referees were making one bad call after another.* **63.** *Theat.* **a.** a notice of rehearsal posted by the stage manager. **b.** See **act call. c.** See **curtain call. 64.** *Dancing.* a figure or direction in square dancing, announced to the dancers by the caller. **65.** Also called **call option.** *Finance.* an option that gives the right to buy a fixed amount of a particular stock at a predetermined price within a given period of time, purchased by a person who believes the price will rise. Cf. **put** (def. 47). **66.** *Fox Hunting.* any of several cries, or

sounds made on a horn by the hunter to encourage the hounds. **67. on call, a.** payable or subject to return without advance notice. **b.** readily available for summoning upon short notice. **68. take a call,** to acknowledge the applause of the audience after a performance by appearing for a bow or a curtain call. **69. within call,** within distance or range of being spoken to or summoned: *Please stay within call.* [1200–50; late ME *callen,* prob. < ON *kalla* to call out, conflated with OE (West Saxon) *ceallian* to shout; c. MD *kallen* to talk, OHG *kallôn* to shout, akin to OE *-calla* herald, Ir *gall* swan, OCS *glasŭ* voice]
—Syn. 2, 3, 12. CALL, INVITE, SUMMON imply requesting the presence or attendance of someone at a particular place. CALL is the general word: *to call a meeting.* To INVITE is to ask someone courteously to come as a guest, a participant, etc., leaving the person free to refuse: *to invite guests to a concert; to invite them to contribute to a fund.* SUMMON implies sending for someone, using authority or formality in making the request and (theoretically) not leaving the person free to refuse: *to summon a witness, members of a committee, etc.*

cal·la (kal′ə), *n.* **1.** Also called **cal′la lil′y, arum lily.** any of several plants belonging to the genus *Zantedeschia,* of the arum family, esp. *Z. aethiopica,* having arrow-shaped leaves and a large white spathe enclosing a yellow spike. **2.** a related plant, *Calla palustris,* of cold marshes of Europe and North America, having heart-shaped leaves. [< NL (Linnaeus)]

call·a·ble (kô′lə bəl), *adj.* **1.** capable of being called. **2.** subject to redemption prior to maturity, as a corporate bond. **3.** subject to payment on demand, as money loaned. [1820–30; CALL + -ABLE]

Cal·la·ghan (kal′ə han′ *or, esp. Brit.,* -hən, -gən), *n.* **1. (Leonard) James,** born 1912, British political leader: prime minister 1976–79. **2. Morley Edward,** 1903–90, Canadian novelist.

cal·la·loo (kal′ə lo͞o′, kal′ə lo͞o′), *n. Southern Cookery.* a thick soup of crabmeat, greens, and various seasonings. [1695–1700; cf. Jamaican E *calalu* any of a variety of greens used as an ingredient in soup < AmerSp *calalú,* Pg *carurú,* said to be < Tupi *caárurú* thick leaf]

cal·lant (kä′lənt), *n. Chiefly Scot.* a lad; boy. Also, **cal·lan** (kä′lən). [1710–20; < D *kalant* fellow, chap, customer < ONF *caland* customer]

Ca·llao (kä you′), *n.* a seaport in W Peru, near Lima. 296,721.

Cal·las (kal′əs), *n.* **Maria Men·e·ghi·ni** (men′i gē′nē), 1923–77, U.S. soprano.

cal·la·thump (kal′ə thump′), *n. Chiefly Northeastern U.S.* a shivaree; callithump. **—cal′la·thump′i·an,** *n., adj.*

call·back (kôl′bak′), *n.* **1.** an act of calling back. **2.** a summoning of workers back to work after a layoff. **3.** a summoning of an employee back to work after working hours, as for emergency business. **4.** a request to a performer who has auditioned for a role, booking, or the like to return for another audition. **5.** recall (def. 12). **6.** a return telephone call. *—adj.* **7.** of or pertaining to such a call: *Please leave a callback number.* Also, **call′-back′.** [1925–30; n. use of v. phrase *call back*]

call-board (kôl′bôrd′, -bōrd′), *n.* a bulletin board, as in a theater, on which notices are posted announcing rehearsals, changes in the cast, etc. [1875–80, *Amer.*]

call′ box′, 1. an outdoor telephone or signal box for calling the police or fire department. **2.** *Brit.* a public telephone booth. **3.** a post-office box for mail that can be picked up only by a renter in person. [1880–85]

call·boy (kôl′boi′), *n.* **1.** a boy or man who summons actors, as from their dressing rooms, shortly before they are due to go on stage. **2.** a bellhop. **3.** Also, **call′ boy′.** a male prostitute who arranges appointments with clients by telephone. **4.** Also, **call′-boy′, call′ boy′.** *Railroads Slang.* a railroad employee responsible for ensuring that members of a train crew are on hand for their regular runs and for notifying them of an extra run. [1835–45; CALL + BOY]

called′ strike′, *Baseball.* a pitch not swung at by a batter but ruled a strike by the umpire. [1885–90, *Amer.*]

call·er[1] (kô′lər), *n.* **1.** a person or thing that calls. **2.** a person who makes a short visit. **3.** *Dancing.* a person who directs the movements of dancers, as at a hoedown or square dance, by calling out the successive figures as the music plays. [1400–50; late ME. See CALL, -ER[1]]
—Syn. 2. See **visitor.**

cal·ler[2] (kal′ər, kä′lər), *adj. Scot. and North Eng.* **1.** (of fruit, fish, vegetables, etc.) fresh; recently picked or caught. **2.** refreshing. [1325–75; ME, north. var. of *calver* fresh, alive (said of fish) < ?]

call·er ID (kô′lər), a telephone service that allows a subscriber to identify a caller before answering by displaying the caller's telephone number on a small screen. [1985–1990]

Ca·lles (kä′yes), *n.* **Plu·tar·co E·li·as** (plo͞o tär′kô e lē′äs), 1877–1945, Mexican general and statesman: president of Mexico 1924–28.

call′ for′warding, a telephone service feature whereby, when a customer chooses, all calls coming in to one number are automatically rerouted to another, designated number.

call′ girl′, 1. a female prostitute with whom an appointment can be made by telephone, usually to meet at the client's address. **2.** (formerly) a prostitute available to be called on at a brothel. [1930–35, *Amer.*]

call′ house′, 1. a house or apartment used by prostitutes for arranging or keeping assignations. **2.** a place at which call girls await telephone calls from customers. [1915–20]

calli-, a combining form meaning "beautiful," occurring in loanwords from Greek (*calligraphy*); on this model, used in the formation of compound words (*callisthenics*). [< Gk *kalli-* comb. form of *kállos* beauty, akin to *kalós* beautiful, fair]

CONCISE ETYMOLOGY KEY: <, descended or borrowed from; >, whence; b., blend of, blended; c., cognate with; cf., compare; deriv., derivative; equiv., equivalent; imit., imitative; obl., oblique; r., replacing; s., stem; sp., spelling, spelled; resp., respelling, respelled; trans., translation; ?, origin unknown; *, unattested; ‡, probably earlier than. See the full key inside the front cover.

Cal·lic·ra·tes (kə lik′rə tēz′), *n.* fl. mid-5th century B.C., Greek architect who together with Ictinus designed the Parthenon.

cal·li·graph (kal′i graf′, -gräf′), *v.t.* to produce by means of calligraphy: *The love letter was calligraphed in a delicate hand.* [1880–85; back formation from CALLIGRAPHY; see CALLI-, -GRAPH]

cal·lig·ra·phy (kə lig′rə fē), *n.* **1.** fancy penmanship, esp. highly decorative handwriting, as with a great many flourishes: *She appreciated the calligraphy of the 18th century.* **2.** handwriting; penmanship. **3.** the art of writing beautifully: *He studied calligraphy when he was a young man.* **4.** a script, usually cursive, although sometimes angular, produced chiefly by brush, esp. Chinese, Japanese, or Arabic writing of high aesthetic value. **5.** *Fine Arts.* line or a group of lines either derived from or resembling letter forms and characterized by qualities usually associated with cursive writing, esp. that produced with a brush or pen. [1605–15; < Gk *kalligraphía* beautiful writing. See CALLI-, -GRAPHY] **—cal·lig′ra·pher, cal·lig′ra·phist,** *n.* **—cal·li·graph·ic** (kal′i graf′ik), **cal′li·graph′i·cal,** *adj.* **—cal′li·graph′i·cal·ly,** *adv.*

Cal·lim·a·chus (kə lim′ə kəs), *n.* c310–c240 B.C., Greek poet, grammarian, and critic.

call-in (kôl′in′), *Radio and Television.* *—n.* **1.** a program in which listeners or viewers phone in comments or questions to the host or a person being interviewed. **2.** a live telephone conversation intended for broadcasting between a program's host and a person being interviewed. *—adj.* **3.** of, pertaining to, or featuring such phone calls or conversations: *a call-in program.* [1960–65; n. use of v. phrase *call in*]

call·ing (kô′ling), *n.* **1.** the act of a person or thing that calls. **2.** vocation, profession, or trade: *What is your calling?* **3.** a call or summons: *He had a calling to join the church.* **4.** a strong impulse or inclination: *She did it in response to an inner calling.* **5.** a convocation: *the calling of Congress.* [1200–50; ME; see CALL, -ING[1]]
—Syn. 2. mission, province, forte, specialty, field.

call′ing card′, 1. Also called **card, visiting card.** a small card with the name and often the address of a person or of a couple, for presenting when making a business or social call, for enclosing in gifts, etc. **2.** *Informal.* any mark, sign, or characteristic by which someone or something can be recognized. [1895–1900, *Amer.*]

call′-in pay′, payment made to employees who report for work and find there is no work for them to do. Also called **reporting pay.**

cal·li·o·pe (kə lī′ə pē; *for 1 also* kal′ē ōp′), *n.* **1.** Also called **steam organ.** a musical instrument consisting of a set of harsh-sounding steam whistles that are activated by a keyboard. **2.** (*cap.*) Also, **Kalliope.** *Class. Myth.* the Muse of heroic poetry. [1855–60, *Amer.*; < L < Gk *Kalliópē,* equiv. to *kalli-* CALLI- + *op-* (s. of *óps*) voice + *-ē* fem. ending]

cal·li·o·pe·an (kə lī′ə pē′ən), *adj.* resembling a calliope in sound; piercingly loud: *a calliopean voice.* [1855–60, *Amer.*; CALLIOPE + -AN]

cal·li·op·sis (kal′ē op′sis), *n.* any of several species of coreopsis, esp. *Coreopsis tinctoria,* a widely cultivated garden plant. [CALLI- + -OPSIS]

cal·li·pash (kal′ə pash′, kal′ə pash′), *n.* calipash.

cal·li·per (kal′ə pər), *n., v.t.* caliper.

Cal·lip′pic cy′cle (kə lip′ik), *Astron.* a period equal to four Metonic cycles less one day, proposed by Callippus to correct the Metonic cycle. [1690–1700]

Cal·lip·pus (kə lip′əs), *n.* fl. 4th century B.C., Greek astronomer. Also, **Calippus, Cal·lip′us.**

cal·li·pyg·i·an (kal′ə pij′ē ən), *adj.* having well-shaped buttocks. Also, **cal·li·py·gous** (kal′ə pī′gəs). [1640–50; < Gk *kallipýg(os)* with beautiful buttocks; referring to a statue of Aphrodite (*kalli-* CALLI- + *pyg(ḗ)* rump + *-os* adj. suffix) + -IAN]

Cal·lis·the·nes (kə lis′thə nēz′), *n.* c360–327 B.C., Greek philosopher: chronicled Alexander the Great's conquests.

cal·lis·then·ics (kal′əs then′iks), *n.* (*used with a singular or plural v.*) calisthenics. **—cal′lis·then′ic,** *adj.*

Cal·lis·to (kə lis′tō), *n.* **1.** Also, **Kallisto.** *Class. Myth.* a nymph attendant on Artemis, punished for a love affair with Zeus by being changed into a bear and then transformed into stars as the constellation Ursa Major. **2.** *Astron.* a large natural satellite of the planet Jupiter.

Cal·lis·tus I (kə lis′təs). See **Calixtus I.**

Callistus II. See **Calixtus II.**

Callistus III. See **Calixtus III.**

cal·li·thump (kal′ə thump′), *n. Chiefly Northeastern U.S.* **1.** a shivaree. **2.** *Midwestern U.S.* Also called **cal′lithump parade′.** a children's mummer's parade, as on the Fourth of July, with prizes for the best costumes. Also, **callathump.** [1855–60, *Amer.*; cf. earlier *callithumpian band* assembly of noisemakers on New Year's Eve, Brit. dial. *gallithumpians* disturbers of order at Parliamentary elections, prob. equiv. to dial. *gally* to frighten (as in *gallicrow* scarecrow; akin to OE *agælwan* to scare) + THUMP + -IAN] **—cal′li·thump′i·an,** *adj., n.*

call′ let′ters, letters of the alphabet or such letters in combination with numbers for identifying a radio or television station, an amateur radio transmitting device, or the like. Also called **call sign.** [1910–15]

call′ loan′, a loan repayable on demand. Also called **demand loan.** Cf. **time loan.** [1850–55]

call′ mar′ket, the market for lending call money. [1870–75]

call′ mon′ey, money lent by banks, as to brokerage firms, on which repayment may be demanded at any time.

call′ num′ber, *Library Science.* a number, letter, symbol, or combination of these, indicating the specific location of a work in a library, esp. the combination of the classification symbol and the designation for the author. [1875–80, *Amer.*]

call′ of na′ture, *Informal.* a need to urinate or defecate. [1850–55]

cal·lop (kal′əp), *n.* See **golden perch.** [1920–25]

call′ op′tion, *Finance.* call (def. 65).

cal·lo·sal (ka lō′səl), *adj.* of or pertaining to the corpus callosum. [1865–70; < NL *callōs(um)* (n. use of L *callōsus* CALLOSE) + -AL[1]]

cal·lose (kal′ōs), *adj.* **1.** having thickened or hardened spots, as a leaf. *—n.* **2.** callus (def. 2). [1860–65; < L *callōsus;* see CALLOUS, -OSE[1]]

cal·los·i·ty (kə los′i tē), *n., pl.* **-ties. 1.** a callous condition. **2.** *Bot.* a hardened or thickened part of a plant. **3.** *Pathol.* callus (def. 1a). [1375–1425; late ME *calosite* < LL *callōsitās,* equiv. to *callōs(us)* CALLOUS + *-itās* -ITY]

Cal·lot (kᴀ lō′), *n.* **Jacques** (zhäk), 1592?–1635, French engraver and etcher.

cal·lous (kal′əs), *adj.* **1.** made hard; hardened. **2.** insensitive; indifferent; unsympathetic: *They have a callous attitude toward the sufferings of others.* **3.** having a callus; indurated, as parts of the skin exposed to friction. *—v.t., v.i.* **4.** to make or become hard or callous. [1375–1425; late ME < L *callōsus* hard-skinned, tough, equiv. to *call(um)* tough skin, any hard substance + *-ōsus* -OUS] **—cal′lous·ly,** *adv.* **—cal′lous·ness,** *n.*
—Syn. 1. hard. **2.** inured, insensible. See **hard.**

call-out (kôl′out′), *n.* **1.** an act or instance of calling out. **2.** an order to report for emergency or special work, esp. at an unusual time or place. **3.** a letter, number, or other device for identifying or calling attention to a particular part of an illustration. **4.** a challenge to a duel. [1885–90; n. use of v. phrase *call out*]

cal·low (kal′ō), *adj.* **1.** immature or inexperienced: *a callow youth.* **2.** (of a young bird) featherless; unfledged. *—n.* **3.** a recently hatched worker ant. [bef. 1000; ME, OE *calu* bald; c. D *kaal,* G *kahl* bald, OCS *golŭ* bare] **—cal′low·ness,** *n.*
—Syn. 1. untried, green, raw; naive, puerile, jejune.
—Ant. 1. mature, adult, experienced.

Cal·lo·way (kal′ə wā′), *n.* **Cab(ell),** born 1907, U.S. jazz bandleader and singer.

call′ rate′, interest charge on call loans.

call′ sign′. See **call letters.** [1915–20]

call′ slip′, a printed form filled in by a library patron to request the use of a particular book. [1880–85, *Amer.*]

call′ to arms′, a command to report for active military duty. [1840–50]

call′ to quar′ters, a bugle call summoning soldiers to their quarters. [1915–20]

call-up (kôl′up′), *n.* **1.** an order to report for active military service. **2.** the number of persons drafted during a specific period of time: *The November call-up was set at 15,000.* **3.** a call or urging to service. [1625–35; n. use of v. phrase *call up*]

cal·lus (kal′əs), *n., pl.* **-lus·es,** *v.,* **-lused, -lus·ing.** *—n.* **1.** *Pathol., Physiol.* **a.** a hardened or thickened part of the skin; a callosity. **b.** a new growth of osseous matter at the ends of a fractured bone, serving to unite them. **2.** Also, **callose.** *Bot.* **a.** the tissue that forms over the wounds of plants, protecting the inner tissues and causing healing. **b.** a deposit on the perforated area of a sieve tube. **c.** (in grasses) a tough swelling at the base of a lemma or palea. *—v.i.* **3.** to form a callus. *—v.t.* **4.** to produce a callus or calluses on: *Heavy work callused his hands.* [1555–65; < L *callus,* masc. var. of *callum;* see CALLOUS]

call′ wait′ing, a telephone service feature whereby a person engaged in a telephone call is notified by a tone that a second call is being made to the same number, and is able to talk to either party while keeping the other on hold. Cf. **hold button.**

calm (käm; *older* kam; *spelling pron.* kälm), *adj.,* **-er, -est,** *n., v.* *—adj.* **1.** without rough motion; still or nearly still: *a calm sea.* **2.** not windy or stormy: *a calm day.* **3.** free from excitement or passion; tranquil: *a calm face; a calm manner.* *—n.* **4.** freedom from motion or disturbance; stillness. **5.** *Meteorol.* wind speed of less than 1 mph (0.447 m/sec). **6.** freedom from agitation, excitement, or passion; tranquillity; serenity: *She faced the crisis with complete calm.* *—v.t.* **7.** to make calm: *He calmed the excited dog.* *—v.i.* **8.** to become calm (usually fol. by *down*). [1350–1400; (n., adj.) ME *calm(e)* < It *calma* (n.), *calmo* (adj.) < LL *cauma* summer heat (with *l* perh. from L *calēre* to be hot) < Gk *kaûma* (s. *kaumat-*) burning heat; akin to *kaíein* to burn (see CAUSTIC); (v.) ME *calmen* < It *calmare,* deriv. of the n.] **—calm′ing·ly,** *adv.* **—calm′ly,** *adv.* **—calm′ness,** *n.*
—Syn. 1. quiet, motionless. **3.** placid, peaceful, serene, self-possessed. CALM, COLLECTED, COMPOSED, COOL imply the absence of agitation. CALM implies an unruffled state, esp. under disturbing conditions: *calm in a crisis.* COLLECTED implies complete inner command of oneself, usually as the result of an effort: *He remained collected in spite of the excitement.* One who is COMPOSED has or has gained dignified self-possession: *pale but composed.* COOL implies clarity of judgment along with apparent absence of strong feeling or excitement, esp. in circumstances of danger or strain: *so cool that he seemed calm.* **7.** still, quiet, tranquilize; allay, assuage, mollify, soothe, soften. **—Ant. 2.** tempestuous. **3.** agitated.

calm·a·tive (kä′mə tiv, kal′mə-), *Med.* *—adj.* **1.** having a sedative effect. *—n.* **2.** a calmative agent. [1865–70; CALM + -ATIVE]

cal•mod•u•lin (kal moj′ə lin), *n. Biochem.* a calcium-binding protein occurring in many tissues and participating in the regulation of many biochemical and physiological processes. [1975–80; CAL(CIUM) + MODUL(ATE) + -IN²]

calm•y (kä′mē), *adj.*, **calm•i•er, calm•i•est.** *Archaic.* calm. [1570–80; CALM + -Y¹]

ca•ló (kə lō′; *Sp.* kä lô′), *n.* **1.** a variety of Spanish influenced by Mexican underworld argot with a large admixture of English words, spoken esp. by young Mexican-Americans in cities of the southwestern U.S. **2.** (*often cap.*) a language spoken by Spanish Gypsies. [< Sp]

cal•o•chor•tus (kal′ə kôr′təs), *n., pl.* **-tus•es.** any plant of the genus *Calochortus,* of the lily family, as the mariposa lily and the sego lily. [1813; < NL < Gk *kal(ós)* beautiful + *-o-* -O- + *chórtos* grass, fodder, orig. farmyard; see COHORT, GARTH, YARD²]

cal•o•mel (kal′ə mel′, -məl), *n. Pharm.* a white, tasteless powder, Hg_2Cl_2, used chiefly as a purgative and fungicide. Also called **mercurous chloride.** [1670–80; < NL *calomelas* coined from Gk *kaló(s)* fair + *mélas* black; allegedly so called because its original preparation involved turning black powder into white]

cal′omel elec′trode, *Physical Chem.* a reference electrode consisting of calomel, mercury, and a solution of potassium chloride.

Ca•lo•o•can (kal′ə ō′kän; *Sp.* kä′lô ô′kän), *n.* a city in the Philippines, on SW Luzon. 467,816.

cal•o•re•cep•tor (kal′ō ri sep′tər), *n. Physiol.* a receptor stimulated by heat. [b. L *calor* heat and RECEPTOR]

cal•o•res•cence (kal′ə res′əns), *n. Physics.* incandescence caused by absorption of radiation having a frequency below that of visible light. [1855–65; < L *calor* heat + -ESCENCE] —**cal′o•res′cent,** *adj.*

calori-, a combining form meaning "heat," used in the formation of compound words: *calorimeter.* [< L, comb. form repr. *calor;* see -I-]

ca•lor•ic (kə lôr′ik, -lor′-), *adj.* **1.** of or pertaining to calories: *the caloric content of food.* **2.** of or pertaining to heat. **3.** (of engines) driven by heat. **4.** high in calories: *a caloric meal.* —*n.* **5.** heat. **6.** *Archaic.* a hypothetical fluid whose presence in matter was thought to determine its thermal state. [1785–95; < F *calorique,* equiv. to *calor-* (< L *calor* heat) + *-ique* -IC] —**ca•lor′i•cal•ly,** *adv.* —**cal•o•ric•i•ty** (kal′ə ris′i tē), *n.*

cal•o•rie (kal′ə rē), *n.* **1.** *Thermodynam.* **a.** Also called **gram calorie, small calorie.** an amount of heat exactly equal to 4.1840 joules. *Abbr.:* cal **b.** (*usually cap.*) kilocalorie. *Abbr.:* Cal **2.** *Physiol.* **a.** a unit equal to the kilocalorie, used to express the heat output of an organism and the fuel or energy value of food. **b.** a quantity of food capable of producing such an amount of energy. Also, **calory.** [1800–10; < F, equiv. to *calor-* (< L *calor* heat) + *-ie* -Y³]

ca•lor•i•fa•cient (kə lôr′ə fā′shənt, -lor′-, kal′ər ə-), *adj.* (of foods) producing heat. [1850–55; CALORI- + -FACIENT]

cal•o•rif•ic (kal′ə rif′ik), *adj.* pertaining to conversion into heat. [1675–85; < LL *calōrificus* causing warmth, warming, equiv. to *calōri-* (s. of *calor* heat) + *-ficus* -FIC] —**cal′o•rif′i•cal•ly,** *adv.*

cal′orif′ic val′ue, the amount of heat released by a unit weight or unit volume of a substance during complete combustion. Also called **cal′orif′ic pow′er.**

cal•o•rim•e•ter (kal′ə rim′i tər), *n.* an apparatus for measuring quantities of heat. [1785–95; CALORI- + -METER]

cal•o•rim•e•try (kal′ə rim′i trē), *n.* the measurement of heat. [1855–60; CALORI- + -METRY] —**cal•o•ri•met•ric** (kal′ər ə me′trik, kə lôr′-, -lor′-), **cal′o•ri•met′ri•cal,** *adj.* —**cal′o•ri•met′ri•cal•ly,** *adv.*

cal•o•rize (kal′ə riz′), *v.t.,* **-rized, -riz•ing.** to alloy (carbon steel or alloy steel) by impregnation with aluminum. Also, *esp. Brit.,* **cal′o•rise′.** [< L *calor* heat + -IZE] —**cal′o•riz′er,** *n.*

cal•o•ry (kal′ə rē), *n., pl.* **-ries.** calorie.

ca•lotte (kə lot′), *n.* **1.** zucchetto. **2.** skullcap (def. 1). [1625–35; < F, MF: skullcap, perh. equiv. to OF *cale* ribbon for the hair, kind of hat (perh. from *escale* shell (see SCALE¹) taken as a deverbal form with *es-* EX¹) + *-otte* dim. suffix]

cal•o•type (kal′ə tīp′), *n.* **1.** an early negative-positive photographic process, patented by William Henry Talbot in 1841, in which a paper negative is produced and then used to make a positive contact print in sunlight. **2.** a print made by this process. Also called **Talbotype.** [1835–45; < Gk *kalo-* (comb. form of *kalós* beautiful) + -TYPE]

cal•o•yer (kal′ə yər, kə loi′ər), *n.* a monk of the Eastern Church. [1605–15; < MF *caloyer* < ModGk *kalógeros* venerable, equiv. to *kaló(s)* beautiful + *-gēros* old (*gêr(as)* old age + *-os* adj. suffix)]

cal•pac (kal′pak), *n.* a large black cap of sheepskin or other heavy material, worn by Armenians, Turks, etc. Also, **cal′pack.** [1805–15; < Turk *kalpak*]

Cal•pe (kal′pē), *n.* ancient name of the Rock of Gibraltar.

Cal•pur•ni•a (kal pûr′nē ə), *n.* fl. 1st century B.C., third wife of Julius Caesar 59–44. Cf. **Cornelia** (def. 2), **Pompeia.**

calque (kalk), *n., v.,* **calqued, cal•quing.** *Ling.* —*n.* **1.** a loan translation, esp. one resulting from bilingual interference in which the internal structure of a borrowed word or phrase is maintained but its morphemes are replaced by those of the native language, as German *halbinsel* for *peninsula.* **2.** loanshift. —*v.t.* **3.** to form (a word or phrase) through the process of loan translation. [1655–65; < F, n. deriv. of *calquer* to copy, base on < It *calcare* to trace over, tread < L: to trample]

Cal•ta•nis•set•ta (kal′tə nə set′ə; *It.* käl′tä nēs set′tä), *n.* a city in central Sicily: cathedral; Norman monastery. 60,617.

cal•trop (kal′trəp), *n.* **1.** any of several plants having spiny heads or fruit, as those of the genera *Tribulus* and *Kallstroemia,* or the star thistle, *Centaurea calcitrapa.* **2.** an iron ball with four projecting spikes so disposed that when the ball is on the ground one of them always points upward: used to obstruct the passage of cavalry, armored vehicles, etc. Also, **cal•throp** (kal′thrəp), **cal′•trap.** [bef. 1000; ME *calketrappe,* OE *calcatrippe, coltetræppe,* equiv. to *calce-* (< L *calci-,* s. of *calx* spur, heel) + *træppe* TRAP¹]

caltrop (def. 2)

cal′trop fam′ily, the plant family Zygophyllaceae, typified by tropical herbaceous plants and shrubs having pinnate leaves, solitary or paired regular flowers, and fruit in the form of a capsule, and including the creosote bush, lignum vitae, and puncture vine.

cal•u•met (kal′yə met′, kal′yə met′), *n.* a long-stemmed, ornamented tobacco pipe used by North American Indians on ceremonial occasions, esp. in token of peace. Also called **peace pipe.** [1710–20; < F, orig. dial. (Norman, Picard): pipe stem, a by-form of F *chalumeau* CHALUMEAU, with suffix altered to *-et* -ET]

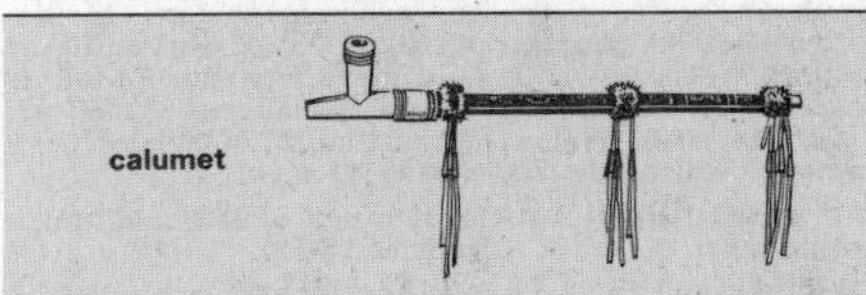
calumet

Cal′u•met Cit′y (kal′yə mit), a city in NE Illinois, near Chicago. 39,673.

ca•lum•ni•ate (kə lum′nē āt′), *v.t.,* **-at•ed, -at•ing.** to make false and malicious statements about; slander. [1545–55; < L *calumniātus* (ptp. of *calumniārī* to accuse falsely, trick), equiv. to *calumni(a)* CALUMNY + *-ātus* -ATE¹] —**ca•lum′ni•a′tion,** *n.* —**ca•lum′ni•a′tor,** *n.*

ca•lum•ni•ous (kə lum′nē əs), *adj.* of, involving, or using calumny; slanderous; defamatory. Also, **ca•lum•ni•a•to•ry** (kə lum′nē ə tôr′ē, -tōr′ē). [1480–90; < L *calumniōsus* full of tricks or artifices, equiv. to *calumni(a)* CALUMNY + *-ōsus* -OUS] —**ca•lum′ni•ous•ly,** *adv.*

cal•um•ny (kal′əm nē), *n., pl.* **-nies.** **1.** a false and malicious statement designed to injure the reputation of someone or something: *The speech was considered a calumny of the administration.* **2.** the act of uttering calumnies; slander; defamation. [1400–50; late ME < L *calumnia,* equiv. to *calumn-,* perh. orig. a middle participle of *calvī* to deceive + *-ia* -Y³)]
—**Syn. 2.** libel, vilification, calumniation, derogation.

cal•u•tron (kal′yə tron′), *n. Physics.* a device for separating isotopes by atomic mass, operating in a manner similar to a mass spectrograph. [1940–45, *Amer.*; *Cal(ifornia) U(niversity)* + -TRON]

Cal•va•dos (kal′və dōs′, -dos′, kal′və dōs′, -dos′; *for 1 also Fr.* KAL VA dôs′), *n.* **1.** a department in NW France. 560,967; 2198 sq. mi. (5693 sq. km). *Cap.:* Caen. **2.** (*sometimes l.c.*) a dry apple brandy made from apple cider in Normandy.

cal•var•i•um (kal vâr′ē əm), *n., pl.* **-var•i•a** (-vâr′ē ə). the dome of the skull. [1880–85; < NL, neut. var. of L *calvāria* skull, equiv. to *calv(us)* bald + *-āria* -ARY; cf. late ME *calvaria* (< L), *calvair* (< MF)]

Cal•va•ry (kal′və rē), *n., pl.* **-ries** for 2, 3. **1.** Golgotha, the place where Jesus was crucified. Luke 23:33. **2.** (*often l.c.*) a sculptured representation of the Crucifixion, usually erected in the open air. **3.** (*l.c.*) an experience or occasion of extreme suffering, esp. mental suffering. [< LL *Calvāria* Calvary < L *calvāria* a skull, used to translate Gk *kraníon* CRANIUM, itself a trans. of the Aramaic name; see GOLGOTHA]
—**Pronunciation.** See **irrelevant.**

Cal′vary cross′. See **cross of Calvary.** [1670–80]

calve (kav, käv), *v.,* **calved, calv•ing.** —*v.i.* **1.** to give birth to a calf: *The cow is expected to calve tomorrow.* **2.** (of a glacier, an iceberg, etc.) to break up or splinter so as to produce a detached piece. —*v.t.* **3.** to give birth to (a calf). **4.** (of a glacier, an iceberg, etc.) to break off or detach (a piece): *The glacier calved an iceberg.* [bef. 1000; ME *calven,* OE (Anglian) **calfian,* deriv. of *calf* CALF¹; c. OE (West Saxon) *cealfian*]

Cal•vert (kal′vərt), *n.* **1. Charles** (*3rd Baron Baltimore*), 1637–1715, English colonial administrator in America: governor (1661–75) and proprietor (1675–89) of Maryland (grandson of George Calvert). **2. Sir George** (*1st Baron Baltimore*), c1580–1632, British statesman: founder of the colony of Maryland. **3.** his son, **Leonard,** 1606–47, first colonial governor of Maryland 1634–47.

calves (kavz, kävz), *n.* pl. of **calf.**

Cal•vin (kal′vin), *n.* **1. John** (*Jean Chauvin* or *Caulvin*), 1509–64, French theologian and reformer in Switzerland: leader in the Protestant Reformation. **2. Melvin,** born 1911, U.S. chemist: Nobel prize 1961. **3.** a male given name: from a Latin word meaning "bald."

Cal•vin•ism (kal′və niz′əm), *n.* **1.** the doctrines and teachings of John Calvin or his followers, emphasizing predestination, the sovereignty of God, the supreme authority of the Scriptures, and the irresistibility of grace. Cf. **Arminianism.** **2.** adherence to these doctrines. [1560–70; CALVIN + -ISM] —**Cal′vin•ist,** *n., adj.* —**Cal′vin•is′tic,** *adj.* —**Cal•vin•is′ti•cal•ly,** *adv.*

cal•vi•ti•es (kal vish′ē ēz′), *n.* baldness. [1615–25; < L *calvitiēs* baldness, equiv. to *calv(us)* bald + *-itiēs* abstract n. suffix]

cal•vous (kal′vəs), *adj.* lacking all or most of the hair on the head; bald. [see CALVUS, -OUS]

cal•vus (kal′vəs), *adj. Meteorol.* (of a cumulonimbus cloud) having its upper portion changing from a rounded, cumuliform shape to a diffuse, whitish, cirriform mass with vertical striations. [< NL, L: lit., bald]

calx (kalks), *n., pl.* **calx•es, cal•ces** (kal′sēz). **1.** the oxide or ashy substance that remains after metals, minerals, etc., have been thoroughly roasted or burned. **2.** lime¹ (def. 1). [1350–1400; late ME < L: lime; r. ME *cals* < OF < L]

cal•y•ces (kal′ə sēz′, kā′lə-), *n.* a pl. of **calyx.**

ca•lyc•i•form (kə lis′ə fôrm′), *adj.* shaped like a calyx. [1825–35; < L *calyci-* (s. of *calyx* CALYX) + -FORM]

cal•y•cine (kal′ə sin, -sīn′), *adj.* pertaining to or resembling a calyx. Also, **ca•lyc•i•nal** (kə lis′ə nl). [1810–20; < L *calyc-* (s. of *calyx* CALYX) + -INE¹]

ca•lyc•u•late (kə lik′yə lit, -lāt′), *adj. Bot.* **1.** of or resembling a calyculus. **2.** having a calyculus. [1680–90; CALYCUL(US) + -ATE¹]

ca•lyc•u•lus (kə lik′yə ləs), *n., pl.* **-li** (-lī′). **1.** *Zool.* Also, **caliculus.** a structure shaped like a cup. **2.** *Bot.* a set of bracts resembling an outer calyx. Also called **cal•y•cle** (kal′i kəl). [< L, equiv. to *calyc-* (s. of *calyx* CALYX) + *-ulus* -ULE]

Cal•y•don (kal′i don′), *n.* an ancient city in W Greece, in Aetolia. —**Cal•y•do•ni•an** (kal′i dō′nē ən, -dōn′yən), *adj.*

Calydo′nian hunt′, *Class. Myth.* the pursuit by Meleager, Atalanta, and others of a savage boar (**Calydo′nian boar′**) sent by Artemis to lay waste to Calydon.

Ca•lyp•so (kə lip′sō), *n., pl.* **-sos,** *v.* —*n.* **1.** Also, **Kalypso.** *Class. Myth.* a sea nymph who detained Odysseus on the island of Ogygia for seven years. **2.** (*l.c.*) Also called **fairy-slipper.** a terrestrial orchid, *Calypso bulbosa,* of the Northern Hemisphere, having a single variegated purple, yellow, and white flower. **3.** (*l.c.*) a musical style of West Indian origin, influenced by jazz, usually having topical, often improvised, lyrics. —*v.i.* **4.** (*l.c.*) to sing or dance to calypso. [the name of the musical style is of obscure orig. and perh. only copies the sp. of *Calypso* the sea nymph] —**ca•lyp•so•ni•an** (kə lip-sō′nē ən, kal′ip-), *n., adj.*

ca•lyp•tra (kə lip′trə), *n. Bot.* **1.** Also called **cap.** a hood or hoodlike part, as the lid of the capsule in mosses. **2.** a root cap. [1745–55; < NL < Gk *kalýptra* veil, covering, equiv. to *kalýp(tein)* to veil, cover + *-tra* n. suffix] —**ca•lyp•trate** (kə lip′trāt), *adj.*

ca•lyp•tro•gen (kə lip′trə jən), *n. Bot.* the histogen layer that develops into the root cap. [1880–85; *calyptro-* (comb. form of CALYPTRA) + -GEN]

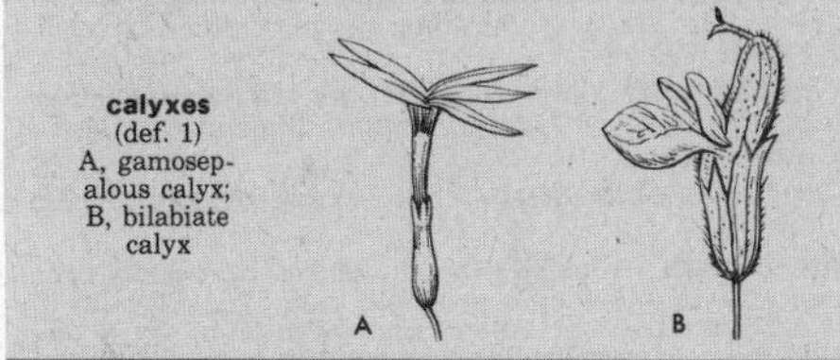

calyxes (def. 1) A, gamosepalous calyx; B, bilabiate calyx

ca•lyx (kā′liks, kal′iks), *n., pl.* **ca•lyx•es, cal•y•ces** (kal′ə sēz′, kā′lə-). **1.** *Bot.* the outermost group of floral parts; the sepals. **2.** *Anat., Zool.* a cuplike part. [1665–75; < L < Gk *kályx* husk, covering, akin to *kalýptein* to veil, cover] —**cal•y•cate** (kal′i kāt′), *adj.*

cal•zo•ne (kal zō′nā, -nē, -zōn′; *It.* käl zô′ne), *n. Italian Cookery.* a turnover made of pizza dough, usually containing cheese, prosciutto, and herbs or garlic and either baked or fried. [1945–50; < It: lit., trouser leg (*calzoni* (pl.) trousers), masc. aug. of *calza* stocking < VL **calcea,* for L *calceus* shoe, deriv. of *calx* heel]

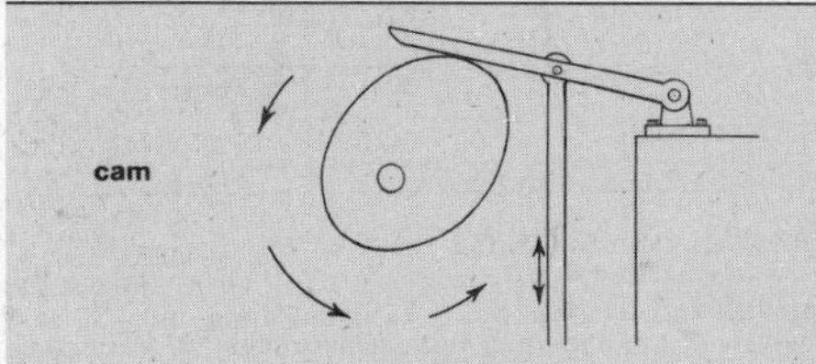
cam

cam (kam), *n., v.,* **cammed, cam•ming.** —*n.* **1.** *Mach.* a disk or cylinder having an irregular form such that its motion, usually rotary, gives to a part or parts in contact with it a specific rocking or reciprocating motion. **2.** *Auto. Slang.* camshaft. —*v.t.* **3.** to provide (a machine part or mechanism) with a cam or cams. [< D or LG *kam, kamm.* See COMB¹]

Cam (kam), *n.* a river in E England flowing NE by Cambridge, into the Ouse River. 40 mi. (64 km) long. Also called **Granta.**

CONCISE PRONUNCIATION KEY: *act, cāpe, dâre, pärt; set, ēqual; if, ice; ox, ōver, ôrder, oil, bo͝ok, bo͞ot, out; up, ûrge; child; sing; shoe; thin, that;* zh as in *treasure.* ə = *a* as in *alone, e* as in *system, i* as in *easily, o* as in *gallop, u* as in *circus;* ᵊ as in *fire* (fīᵊr), *hour* (ouᵊr). l and n can serve as syllabic consonants, as in *cradle* (krād′l), and *button* (but′n). See the full key inside the front cover.

CAM (kam), *n.* computer-aided manufacturing. [1965–70]

Cam., Cambridge.

cam•a•ca (kam′ə kə), *n.* a heavy fabric of silk or mixed fibers, much used in the Middle Ages. Also, **cam′•a•ka, camoca.** [1325–75; ME < ML *camoca* < Ar or Pers *kamkha, kimkha*]

Ca•ma•cho (kä mä′chô), *n.* **Ma•nuel Á•vi•la** (mä-nwel′ ä′vē lä′). See **Ávila Camacho, Manuel.**

Ca•ma•güey (kam′ə gwā′; *Sp.* kä′mä gwā′), *n.* a city in central Cuba. 197,720.

ca•mail (kə māl′), *n.* aventail (def. 1). [1660–70; < F < OPr *capmalh,* equiv. to *cap* head (see CHIEF) + *malh* MAIL²] **—ca•mailed′,** *adj.*

ca•ma•ra•de•rie (kä′mə rä′də rē, -rad′ə-, kam′ə-), *n.* comradeship; good-fellowship. [1830–40; < F, equiv. to *camarade* COMRADE + *-erie* -ERY]
—Syn. conviviality, bonhomie, brotherhood.

cam•a•ra•saur (kam′ər ə sôr′), *n.* a plant-eating sauropod dinosaur of the genus *Camarasaurus* and closely related genera, having a small head, long neck, and short forelimbs, and reaching a length of 40 ft. (12.2 m); until 1981 the type specimen of *Brontosaurus excelcus* was wrongly reconstructed with a *Camarasaurus* skull. [< NL *Camarasaurus* (1877), irreg. < Gk *kamára* space enclosed by an arch, vault (cf. CHAMBER) + *-saurus* -SAUR]

cam•a•ril•la (kam′ə ril′ə; *Sp.* kä′mä rē′lyä, -yä), *n., pl.* **-ril•las** (-ril′əz; *Sp.* -rē′lyäs, -yäs). a group of unofficial or private advisers to a person of authority, esp. a group much given to intrigues and secret plots; cabal; clique. [1830–40; < Sp, equiv. to *camar(a)* room (< L *camera;* see CHAMBER) + *-illa* dim. suffix < L]

Cam•a•ril•lo (kam′ə ril′ō), *n.* a city in SW California. 37,732.

cam•ass (kam′əs), *n.* **1.** any of several plants of the genus *Camassia,* of the lily family, esp. *C. quamash,* of western North America, having long clusters of blue to white flowers and edible bulbs. **2.** See **death camass.** Also, **cam′as.** [1795–1805, *Amer.;* < Chinook Jargon *qamaš, qawaš* < Nootka *qawaš-, qawi-* salmonberry, any berry or small fruit]

ca•mau•ro (kə mou′rō), *n., pl.* **-ros.** *Rom. Cath. Ch.* a crimson velvet cap trimmed with ermine, worn by the pope on nonliturgical occasions. [< It; cf. ML *camaurum;* orig. uncert.]

Camb., Cambridge.

cam•ber (kam′bər), *v.t., v.i.* **1.** to arch slightly; bend or curve upward in the middle. **—***n.* **2.** a slight arching, upward curve, or convexity, as of the deck of a ship. **3.** a slightly arching piece of timber. **4.** *Aeron.* the rise of the curve of an airfoil, usually expressed as the ratio of the rise to the length of the chord of the airfoil. **5.** *Auto.* the outward or inward tilt of a wheel, called positive when the top tilts outward and negative when it tilts inward, measured as the angle, in degrees, between the vertical and a plane through the circumference of the tire. [1610–20; < MF (north) *cambre* bent < L *camur* hooked, curved]

cam′ber piece′, a centering for a flat arch, slightly crowned to allow for settling of the arch. Also called **cam′ber slip′.**

Cam•ber•well (kam′bər wel′, -wəl), *n.* a former residential borough of Greater London, England, now part of Southwark.

Cam′berwell beau′ty. See **mourning cloak.** [1840–50]

cam•bi•a•ta (kam′bē ä′tə), *n. Music.* a melodic ornamental tone following a principal tone by a skip, usually of a third above or below, and progressing by a step. Also called **changing tone, changing note.** Cf. **échappée.** [< It: short for *nota cambiata* changed note; *cambiata,* fem. ptp. of *cambiare* to CHANGE]

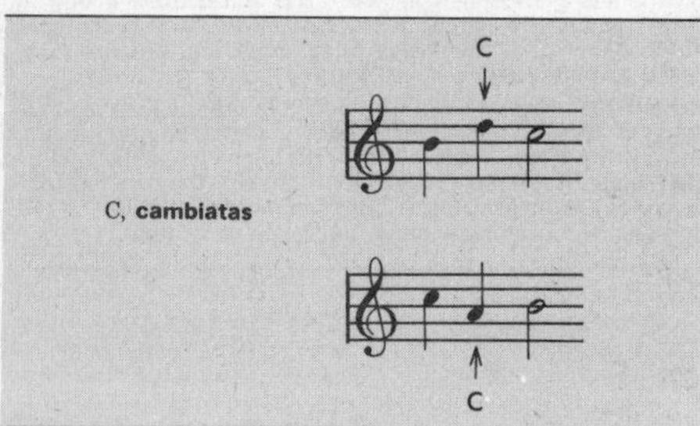

C, **cambiatas**

cam•bio (käm′byô; *Eng.* kam′bē ō′), *n. Spanish.* a currency exchange.

cam•bist (kam′bist), *n.* **1.** a dealer in bills of exchange. **2.** an expert in foreign exchange. **3.** a manual giving the moneys, weights, and measures of different countries, with their equivalents. [1800–10; < F *cambiste* < It *cambista.* See CAMBIUM, -IST] **—cam′bist•ry,** *n.*

cam•bi•um (kam′bē əm), *n., pl.* **-bi•ums, -bi•a** (-bē ə). *Bot.* a layer of delicate meristematic tissue between the inner bark or phloem and the wood or xylem, which produces new phloem on the outside and new xylem on the inside in stems, roots, etc., originating all secondary growth in plants and forming the annual rings of wood. [1665–75; < LL: an exchange, barter; akin to L *cambiāre* to exchange] **—cam′bi•al,** *adj.*

CONCISE ETYMOLOGY KEY: <, descended or borrowed from; >, whence; b., blend of, blended; c., cognate with; cf., compare; deriv., derivative; equiv., equivalent; imit., imitative; obl., oblique; r., replacing; s., stem; sp., spelling, spelled; resp., respelling, respelled; trans., translation; ?, origin unknown; *, unattested; ‡, probably earlier than. See the full key inside the front cover.

Cam•bo•di•a (kam bō′dē ə), *n.* a republic in SE Asia: formerly part of French Indochina. 8,110,000; 69,866 sq. mi. (180,953 sq. km). *Cap.:* Phnom Penh. Formerly, **People's Republic of Kampuchea, Khmer Republic.**

Cam•bo•di•an (kam bō′dē ən), *adj.* **1.** of, pertaining to, or characteristic of Cambodia, its people, or its culture. **—***n.* **2.** a native or inhabitant of Cambodia. **3.** Khmer (def. 2). [1760–70; CAMBODI(A) + -AN]

cam•bo•gi•a (kam bō′jē ə), *n.* gamboge (def. 1).

Cam•brai (kän bre′), *n.* a city in N France: battles 1917, 1918. 41,109.

cam•brel (kam′brəl), *n. Brit. Dial.* gambrel.

Cam•bri•a (kam′brē ə), *n.* medieval name of **Wales.**

Cam•bri•an (kam′brē ən), *adj.* **1.** *Geol.* noting or pertaining to a period of the Paleozoic Era, occurring from 570 million to 500 million years ago, when algae and marine invertebrates were the predominant form of life. See table under **geologic time. 2.** of or pertaining to Cambria; Welsh. **—***n.* **3.** *Geol.* the Cambrian Period or System. **4.** a native of Cambria; Welshman. [1580–90; < ML *Cambri(a)* Wales, Latinization of MWelsh *Cymry* Wales, lit. Welshmen (see CYMRY) + -AN]

Cam′brian Moun′tains, a range of low mountains running north to south in central Wales.

cam•bric (kām′brik), *n.* a thin, plain cotton or linen fabric of fine close weave, usually white. [1520–30; earlier *cameryk,* after *Kameryk,* D name of CAMBRAI]

cam′bric tea′, a mixture of hot water and milk, with sugar and, often, weak tea. [1885–90, *Amer.*]

Cam•bridge (kām′brij), *n.* **1.** a city in Cambridgeshire, in E England: famous university founded in 12th century. 103,900. **2.** a city in E Massachusetts, near Boston. 95,322. **3.** Cambridgeshire. **4.** a city in SE Ontario, in S Canada. 77,183. **5.** a city in E Ohio. 13,573.

Cam•bridge•shire (kām′brij shēr′, -shər), *n.* a county in E England. 536,000; 1316 sq. mi. (3410 sq. km). Also called **Cambridge.**

Cam•by•ses (kam bī′sēz), *n.* died 522 B.C., king of Persia 529–522 (son of Cyrus the Great).

cam•cord•er (kam′kôr′dər), *n. Television.* a lightweight hand-held television camera with an incorporated VCR, forming a compact self-contained unit. [CAM(ERA) + (RE)CORDER]

Cam•den (kam′dən), *n.* **1.** a borough of Greater London, England. 192,800. **2.** a port in SW New Jersey, on the Delaware River opposite Philadelphia. 84,910. **3.** a city in SW Arkansas. 15,356.

came¹ (kām), *v.* pt. of **come.**

came² (kām), *n.* a slender, grooved bar of lead for holding together the pieces of glass in windows of latticework or stained glass. See illus. under **quarrel².** Also called **ribbon.** [1680–90; special use of *came* ridge; see KAME, COMB¹]

cam•el (kam′əl), *n.* **1.** either of two large, humped, ruminant quadrupeds of the genus *Camelus,* of the Old World. Cf. **Bactrian camel, dromedary. 2.** a color ranging from yellowish tan to yellowish brown. **3.** Also called **camel spin.** *Skating.* a spin done in an arabesque position. **4.** *Naut.* **a.** Also called **pontoon.** a float for lifting a deeply laden vessel sufficiently to allow it to cross an area of shallow water. **b.** a float serving as a fender between a vessel and a pier or the like. **c.** caisson (def. 3a). [bef. 950; ME, OE < L *camēlus* < Gk *kámēlos* < Sem; cf. Heb *gāmāl*] **—cam′el•like′,** *adj.*

cam•el•back (kam′əl bak′), *n.* **1.** the back of a camel: *They traveled through the desert on camelback.* **2.** a curved back of a sofa or chair, having a central rising section between two lower sections. **—***adj.* **3.** having a shape resembling the humped back of a camel. **—***adv.* **4.** on camelback: *to ride camelback.* [CAMEL + BACK¹]

cam′elback truss′. See **crescent truss.**

cam′el crick′et. See **cave cricket.** [1855–60, *Amer.;* so called from its humpbacked appearance]

cam•el•eer (kam′ə lēr′), *n.* **1.** a camel driver. **2.** a soldier mounted on a camel. [1800–10; CAMEL + -EER]

cam′el grass′, a grass, *Cymbopogon schoenanthus,* of southern Asia and northern Africa, having fragrant foliage. Also called **cam′el hay′.** [1875–80]

cam•el•hair (kam′əl hâr′), *n.* **1.** See **camel's hair. —***adj.* **2.** camel's-hair. [1350–1400; ME *camel har;* see CAMEL, HAIR]

ca•mel•lia (kə mēl′yə, -mē′lē ə), *n.* any of several shrubs of the genus *Camellia,* esp. *C. japonica,* native to Asia, having glossy evergreen leaves and white, pink, red, or variegated roselike flowers. [1745–55; named after G. J. *Camellus* (1661–1706), Jesuit missionary, who brought it to Europe; see -IA]

ca•mel•o•pard (kə mel′ə pärd′), *n. Archaic.* a giraffe. [1350–1400; ME < ML *camēlopardus,* for L *camēlopardālis* < Gk *kamēlopárdalis* giraffe, equiv. to *kámēlo(s)* CAMEL + *pardalis* PARD]

Ca•mel•o•par•da•lis (kə mel′ə pär′dl is, kam′ə lō-), *n., gen.* **-lis.** *Astron.* the Giraffe, a northern constellation between Ursa Major and Perseus.

Cam•e•lot (kam′ə lot′), *n.* **1.** the legendary site of King Arthur's palace and court, possibly near Exeter, England. **2.** any idyllic place or period, esp. one of great happiness. **3.** the glamorous ambience of Washington, D.C., during the administration of President John F. Kennedy, 1961–63. **—Cam′e•lot′i•an,** *adj.*

cam′el's hair′, 1. the hair of the camel, used esp. for cloth, painters' brushes, and Oriental rugs. **2.** a soft cloth made of this hair, or of a substitute, usually yellowish tan to yellowish brown in color. Also, **camelhair.**

cam•el's-hair (kam′əlz hâr′), *adj.* made of camel's hair.

cam′el spin′, camel (def. 3).

Cam•em•bert (kam′əm bâr′; *Fr.* ka män ber′), *n.* a mellow, soft cheese, the center of which is creamy and of a golden cream color, made from cow's milk. Also called **Cam′embert cheese′.** [1875–80; named after *Camembert,* village in Normandy where it was first marketed]

Ca•me•nae (kə mē′nē), *n.pl., sing.* **-na** (-nə). *Rom. Relig.* four wise and prophetic deities or fountain nymphs: Carmenta, Egeria, Antevorta, and Postvorta; later identified with the Greek Muses.

cam•e•o (kam′ē ō′), *n., pl.* **cam•e•os. 1.** a technique of engraving upon a gem or other stone, as onyx, in such a way that an underlying stone of one color is exposed as a background for a low-relief design of another color. **2.** a gem or other stone so engraved. **3.** a literary sketch, small dramatic scene, or the like, that effectively presents or depicts its subject. **4.** Also called **cam′eo role′.** a minor part played by a prominent performer in a single scene of a motion picture or a television play. [1375–1425; < It *cam(m)eo* < OF *camaieu,* of uncert. orig.; r. late ME *camew, cameu* < OF]

cam′eo glass′, an ornamental glass in which two layers, often blue and opaque white, have been cased, and on which the design has been treated in the manner of a cameo. [1875–80]

cam′eo ware′, jasper¹ (def. 2).

cam•er•a (kam′ər ə, kam′rə), *n., pl.* **-er•as** for 1, 2, **-er•ae** (-ə rē′, -rē), for 3, *adj.* **—***n.* **1.** a boxlike device for holding a film or plate sensitive to light, having an aperture controlled by a shutter that, when opened, admits light enabling an object to be focused, usually by means of a lens, on the film or plate, thereby producing a photographic image. **2.** (in a television transmitting apparatus) the device in which the picture to be televised is formed before it is changed into electric impulses. **3.** a judge's private office. **4. in camera, a.** *Law.* in the privacy of a judge's chambers. **b.** privately. **5. off camera,** out of the range of a television or movie camera. **6. on camera,** being filmed or televised by a live camera: *Be sure to look alert when you are on camera.* **—***adj.* **7.** *Print.* camera-ready. [1700–10; < L *camera* vaulted room, vault < Gk *kamára* vault; see CHAMBER]

cam•er•al (kam′ər əl, kam′rəl), *adj.* **1.** of or pertaining to a judicial or legislative chamber or the privacy of such a chamber. **2.** cameralistic. [1755–65; < ML *camerālis,* equiv. to *camer(a)* treasury, governmental chamber + *-ālis* -AL¹; see CHAMBER]

cam•er•a•list (kam′ər ə list, kam′rə-), *n.* any of the mercantilist economists or public servants in Europe in the 17th and 18th centuries who held that the economic power of a nation can be enhanced by increasing its monetary wealth, as by the accumulation of bullion. [< G *Kameralist* < NL *cameralista,* equiv. to ML *camerāl(is)* (see CAMERAL) + *-ista* -IST] **—cam′er•a•lism′,** *n.*

cam•er•a•lis•tic (kam′ər ə lis′tik, kam′rə-), *adj.* **1.** of or pertaining to public finance. **2.** of or pertaining to cameralism. **—***n.* **3. cameralistics,** (*usually used with a singular v.*) the science of public finance. [1755–65; < G *kameralistisch,* equiv. to *Kameralist* CAMERALIST + *-isch* -ISH¹ (replaced by -IC)]

cam′era lu′ci•da (lo͞o′si də), an optical instrument, often attached to the eyepiece of a microscope, by which the image of an external object is projected on a sheet of paper or the like for tracing. [1660–70; < NL: bright chamber; see CAMERA, LUCID]

cam•er•a•man (kam′ər ə man′, -mən, kam′rə-), *n., pl.* **-men** (-men′, -mən). a person who operates a camera, esp. a movie or television camera. [1900–05; CAMERA + MAN¹]
—Usage. See **-man.**

cam′era ob•scu′ra (ob skyo͝or′ə), a darkened boxlike device in which images of external objects, received through an aperture, as with a convex lens, are exhibited in their natural colors on a surface arranged to receive them: used for sketching, exhibition purposes, etc. [1660–70; < NL: dark chamber; see CAMERA, OBSCURE]

cam•er•a•per•son (kam′ər ə pûr′sən, kam′rə-), *n.* a person who operates a camera, esp. a movie or TV camera. [CAMERA(MAN) + -PERSON]
—Usage. See **-person.**

cam•er•a-read•y (kam′ər ə red′ē, kam′rə-), *adj. Print.* (of text or illustrations) ready to be photographed. Also, **camera.**

cam•er•a-shy (kam′ər ə shī′, kam′rə-), *adj.* unwilling or afraid to be photographed or filmed. [1920–25]

cam′era tube′, *Television.* a cathode-ray tube that converts an optical image projected on its light-sensitive receptor surface into an electrical signal by a scanning process: used in television cameras. Also called **pickup tube.** Cf. **image tube.**

cam•er•a•wom•an (kam′ər ə wo͝om′ən, kam′rə-), *n., pl.* **-wom•en.** a woman who operates a camera, esp. a movie or TV camera. [CAMERA(MAN) + -WOMAN]
—Usage. See **-woman.**

cam•er•len•go (kam′ər leng′gō), *n., pl.* **-gos.** *Rom. Cath. Ch.* the cardinal appointed treasurer of the Holy See, who, upon the death of the pope, presides over the conclave that elects the new pope. [1615–25; < It *camerlingo* < Gmc; akin to OHG *chamarlinc* CHAMBERLAIN]

Cam·er·on (kam′ər ən, kam′rən), *n.* **1. Julia Margaret,** 1815–79, English photographer, born in India. **2. Richard,** 1648?–80, Scottish Covenanter. —**Cam·er·o·ni·an** (kam′ə rō′nē ən, -rōn′yən), *adj., n.*

Cam·e·roon (kam′ə ro͞on′), *n.* **1.** Also, **Cameroun.** Official name, **United Republic of Cameroon.** an independent republic in W Africa: formed 1960 by the French trusteeship of Cameroun; Southern Cameroons incorporated as a self-governing province 1961. 6,600,000; 183,350 sq. mi. (474,877 sq. km). *Cap.:* Yaoundé. **2.** an active volcano in W Cameroon: highest peak on the coast of W Africa. 13,370 ft. (4075 m). —**Cam′e·roon′i·an,** *adj., n.*

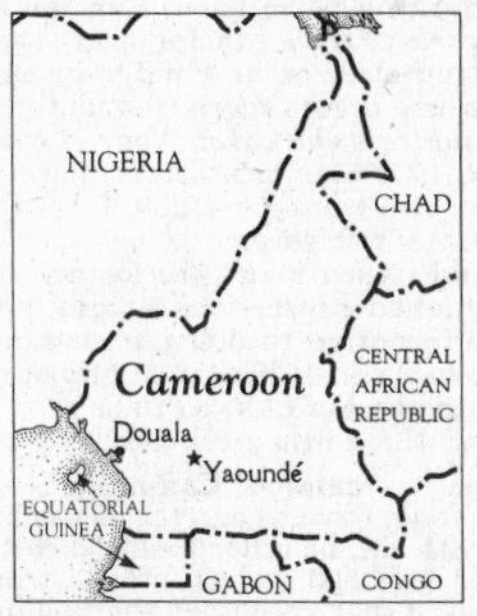

Cam·e·roons (kam′ə ro͞onz′), *n.* (*used with a singular v.*) **1.** German, **Kamerun.** a region in W Africa: a German protectorate 1884–1919; divided in 1919 into British and French mandates. **2.** Also called **British Cameroons.** the NW part of this region: a British mandate 1919–46 and trusteeship 1946–61; by a 1961 plebiscite the S part **(Southern Cameroons)** joined the United Republic of Cameroon and the N part **(Northern Cameroons)** joined Nigeria. —**Cam′e·roon′i·an,** *adj., n.*

Came·roun (kam ro͞on′; *Fr.* kam ro͞on′), *n.* **1.** Cameroon (def. 1). **2.** Also called **French Cameroons.** a former French mandate (1919–46) and trusteeship (1946–60) in W Africa: independence 1960: now part of the United Republic of Cameroon.

cam·i·knick·ers (kam′ə nik′ərz), *n.* (*used with a plural v.*) *Brit.* a woman's one-piece fitted undergarment combining a camisole and knickers. [1910–15; CAMI(SOLE) + KNICKERS]

Ca·mil·la (kə mil′ə), *n.* **1.** *Rom. Legend.* a woman warrior who fought on the side of Turnus against Aeneas. **2.** Also, **Ca·mil′a, Ca·mile, Ca·mille** (kə mēl′). a female given name.

ca·mi·no re·al (kä mē′nô re äl′), *pl.* ***ca·mi·nos re·a·les*** (kä mē′nôs re ä′les). *Spanish.* a main road; highway. [lit., royal road]

cam·i·on (kam′ē ən; *Fr.* ka myôn′), *n., pl.* **cam·i·ons** (kam′ē ənz; *Fr.* ka myôn′). **1.** a strongly built cart or wagon for transporting heavy loads; dray. **2.** a truck, as for military supplies. [1880–85; < F < ?]

cam·i·sa·do (kam′ə sā′dō, -sä′-), *n., pl.* **-dos.** *Archaic.* a military attack made at night. Also, **cam·i·sade** (kam′i sād′, -säd′). [1540–50; < Sp *camisada* (now obs.), equiv. to *camis(a)* shirt (see CHEMISE) + *-ada* -ADE[1]; so called because participants in such attacks would wear shirts over their armor to aid in recognition]

Cam·i·sard (kam′ə zärd′, kam′ə zärd′; *Fr.* ka mē-zar′), *n.* any French Protestant, living in the region of the Cévennes Mountains, who carried on a revolt against Louis XIV in the early part of the 18th century. [1695–1705; < F, equiv. to *camis-* (< Pr *camisa* shirt; see CHEMISE) + *-ard* -ARD]

ca·mise (kə mēz′, -mēs′), *n.* a lightweight, loose-fitting shirt or smock with long sleeves. [1805–15; < Ar *qamīṣ* < LL *camisa,* var. of *camisia* shirt; see CHEMISE]

cam·i·sole (kam′ə sōl′), *n.* **1.** a short garment worn underneath a sheer bodice to conceal the underwear. **2.** a woman's negligee jacket. **3.** a sleeved jacket or jersey once worn by men. **4.** a straitjacket with long sleeves. [1810–20; < F < Pr *camisola;* equiv. to *camis(a)* (< LL *camisa* shirt; see CHEMISE) + *-ola* -ULE]

cam·let (kam′lit), *n., v.,* **-let·ted, -let·ting.** —*n.* **1.** a durable, waterproof cloth, esp. for outerwear. **2.** apparel made of this material. **3.** a rich fabric of medieval Asia believed to have been made of camel's hair or angora wool. —*v.t.* **4.** to decorate (fabric, book edges, etc.) with a colorful, marbled design. [1350–1400; ME *camelet* < MF, perh. < Ar *khamlah* kind of plush fabric, akin to *khaml* nap, pile]

Cam·maerts (kä′märts), *n.* **É·mile** (ā mēl′), 1878–1953, Belgian poet.

cam·o·ca (kam′ə kə), *n.* camaca.

Ca·mo·ëns (kam′ō ens′), *n.* **Lu·ís Vaz de** (lo͞o ēsh′ väzh də), 1524?–80, Portuguese poet. Also, **Ca·mões** (kə moiɴsh′).

cam·o·mile (kam′ə mil′, -mēl′), *n.* chamomile.

Ca·mor·ra (kə môr′ə, -mor′ə; *It.* kä môr′rä), *n.* **1.** a secret society of Naples, Italy, first publicly known about 1820, that developed into a powerful political organization and was later associated with blackmail, robbery, etc., until its destruction in 1911. **2.** (*l.c.*) any similar society or group. [1860–65; < It < Sp: dispute, quarrel (of uncert. orig.)] —**Ca·mor′rism,** *n.*

Ca·mor·ris·ta (*It.* kä′môr rēs′tä), *n., pl.* **-ti** (*It.* -tē). **1.** a member of the Camorra of Italy. **2.** (*l.c.*) a member of a society or group resembling the Camorra. Also, **Ca·mor·rist** (kə môr′ist, -mor′-). [1860–65; < It.; see CAMORRA, -IST]

cam·ou·flage (kam′ə fläzh′), *n., adj., v.,* **-flaged, -flag·ing.** —*n.* **1.** the act, means, or result of obscuring things to deceive an enemy, as by painting or screening objects so that they are lost to view in the background, or by making up objects that have from a distance the appearance of fortifications, guns, roads, etc. **2.** concealment by some means that alters or obscures the appearance: *Drab plumage provides the bird with camouflage against predators.* **3.** a device or stratagem used for concealment: *His loud laughter is really camouflage for his basic shyness.* **4.** clothing made of fabric with a mottled design, usually in shades of green and brown, similar to that used in military camouflage. —*adj.* **5.** (of fabric or clothing) made with or having a mottled design similar to that used on military camouflage: *a camouflage T-shirt.* —*v.t.* **6.** to disguise, hide, or deceive by means of camouflage: *to camouflage ships by painting them gray.* —*v.i.* **7.** to use camouflage. [1915–20; < F, equiv. to *camoufl(er)* to disguise (prob. a v. deriv. of *camouflet;* see CAMOUFLET) + *-age* -AGE] —**cam′ou·flage′a·ble,** *adj.* —**cam′ou·flag′er,** *n.* —**cam′ou·flag′ic,** *adj.*
—**Syn. 3.** mask, blind, front, cover.

ca·mou·flet (kam′ə flā′, kam′ə flā′), *n.* **1.** an underground explosion of a bomb or mine that does not break the surface, but leaves an enclosed cavity of gas and smoke. **2.** the pocket formed by such an explosion. **3.** the bomb or mine so exploded and causing such a pocket. [1830–40; < F: lit., smoke blown in someone's face as a practical joke, MF *chault moufflet,* equiv. to *chault* hot (< L *calidus*) + *moufflet* presumably "puff, breath"; cf. Walloon dial. *moufler* to puff up the cheeks; 1st syll. prob. conformed to the expressive formative *ca-* (see CABBAGE[1])]

camp[1] (kamp), *n.* **1.** a place where an army or other group of persons or an individual is lodged in a tent or tents or other temporary means of shelter. **2.** such tents or shelters collectively: *The regiment transported its camp in trucks.* **3.** the persons so sheltered: *The camp slept through the storm.* **4.** the act of camping out: *Camp is far more pleasant in summer than in winter.* **5.** any temporary structure, as a tent or cabin, used on an outing or vacation. **6.** a group of troops, workers, etc., camping and moving together. **7.** army life. **8.** a group of people favoring the same ideals, doctrines, etc.: *Most American voters are divided into two camps, Republicans and Democrats.* **9.** any position in which ideals, doctrines, etc., are strongly entrenched: *After considering the other side's argument, he changed camps.* **10.** a recreation area in the country, equipped with extensive facilities for sports. **11.** See **day camp. 12.** See **summer camp.** —*v.i.* **13.** to establish or pitch a camp: *The army camped in the valley.* **14.** to live temporarily in or as if in a camp or outdoors, usually for recreation (often fol. by *out*): *They camped by the stream for a week.* **15.** to reside or lodge somewhere temporarily or irregularly, esp. in an apartment, room, etc.: *They camped in our apartment whenever they came to town.* **16.** to settle down securely and comfortably; become ensconced: *The kids camped on our porch until the rain stopped.* **17.** to take up a position stubbornly: *They camped in front of the president's office.* —*v.t.* **18.** to put or station (troops) in a camp; shelter. [1520–30; < MF *can, camp,* orig. dial. (Normandy, Picardy) or < OPr < It *campo* < L *campus* field; cf. OE *campe, compe* battle, battlefield (c. G *Kampf* struggle) < Gmc < L]

camp[2] (kamp), *n.* **1.** something that provides sophisticated, knowing amusement, as by virtue of its being artlessly mannered or stylized, self-consciously artificial and extravagant, or teasingly ingenuous and sentimental. **2.** a person who adopts a teasing, theatrical manner, esp. for the amusement of others. —*v.i.* **3.** Also, **camp it up.** to speak or behave in a coquettishly playful or extravagantly theatrical manner. —*adj.* **4.** campy: *camp Hollywood musicals of the 1940's.* [1905–10; perh. dial. *camp* impetuous, uncouth person (see KEMP[1]); hence, slightly objectionable, effeminate, homosexual; in some senses prob. special use of CAMP[1] brothel, meeting place of male homosexuals]

Camp (kamp), *n.* **Walter Chaun·cey** (chôn′sē, chän′-), 1859–1925, U.S. football coach and author.

cAMP (kamp), *n. Biochem.* See **cyclic AMP.**

Cam·pa·gna (kam pän′yə, kəm-; *It.* käm pä′nyä), *n., pl.* **-pa·gne** (-pän′yā; *It.* -pä′nye) for 2. **1.** a low plain surrounding the city of Rome, Italy. **2.** (*l.c.*) any flat open plain; champaign. [< It; see CAMPAIGN]

cam·paign (kam pān′), *n.* **1.** *Mil.* **a.** military operations for a specific objective. **b.** *Obs.* the military operations of an army in the field for one season. **2.** a systematic course of aggressive activities for some specific purpose: *a sales campaign.* **3.** the competition by rival political candidates and organizations for public office. —*v.i.* **4.** to serve in or go on a campaign: *He planned to campaign for the candidate. He campaigned in France.* —*v.t.* **5.** to race (a horse, boat, car, etc.) in a number or series of competitions. [1620–30; < F *campagne* < It *campagna* < LL *campānia* level district, equiv. to L *camp(us)* field + *-ān(us)* -AN + *-ia* -IA] —**cam·paign′er,** *n.*
—**Syn. 2.** drive, effort, push, offensive.

campaign′ but′ton, a disk-shaped pin worn by a supporter of a political candidate, usually bearing the name of the candidate and often a slogan or the candidate's picture. [1895–1900, *Amer.*]

campaign′ chest′, 1. money collected and set aside for use in a campaign, as of a political one; a campaign fund. **2.** a low chest of drawers having handles at each side for lifting.

campaign′ fund′, money for a campaign, as of a political candidate, usually acquired through contributions by supporters. [1900–05, *Amer.*]

campaign′ fur′niture, furniture, as chests or desks, having metal hinges on the corners and handles on the sides. [from the original use of such furniture by soldiers on campaign]

campaign′ hat′, 1. a felt hat with a broad, stiff brim and four dents in the crown, formerly worn by personnel in the U.S. Army and Marine Corps. **2.** a hat resembling this, worn as part of a uniform by forest rangers, state troopers, boy scouts, and other groups.

campaign′ med′al, *Mil.* See **service medal.**

campaign′ rib′bon, a distinctively colored ribbon, either on a small, narrow bar or in the form of a strip, representing a military campaign participated in by the wearer.

Cam·pa·ni·a (kam pā′nē ə, -pān′yə; *It.* käm pä′nyä), *n.* a region in SW Italy. 5,346,828; 5214 sq. mi. (13,505 sq. km). *Cap.:* Naples. —**Cam·pa′ni·an,** *adj., n.*

cam·pa·ni·le (kam′pə nē′lē, -nēl′; *It.* käm′pä nē′le), *n., pl.* **-ni·les, -ni·li** (-nē′lē). a bell tower, esp. one freestanding from the body of a church. [1630–40; < It, equiv. to *campan(a)* bell (< LL, prob. n. use of L *Campāna,* fem. sing. or neut. pl. of *Campānus* of Campania, reputed to be a source of high-quality bronze casting in antiquity) + *-ile* locative suffix (< L *-ile*)]

campanile

cam·pa·nol·o·gy (kam′pə nol′ə jē), *n.* the principles or art of making bells, bell ringing, etc. [1670–80; < NL *campanologia,* equiv. to LL *campān(a)* bell (see CAMPANILE) + NL *-ologia* (see -O-, -LOGY)] —**cam·pa·no·log·i·cal** (kam′pə nl oj′i kəl), *adj.* —**cam′pa·no·log′i·cal·ly,** *adv.* —**cam′pa·nol′o·gist, cam′pa·nol′o·ger,** *n.*

cam·pan·u·la (kam pan′yə lə), *n.* any plant of the genus *Campanula,* comprising the bellflowers. [1655–65; < NL, equiv. to LL *campān(a)* bell (see CAMPANILE) + L *-ula* -ULE]

cam·pan·u·la·ceous (kam pan′yə lā′shəs), *adj.* belonging to the Campanulaceae, the bellflower family of plants. Cf. **bellflower family.** [1820–30; < NL *Campanulace(ae)* name of the family (see CAMPANULA, -ACEAE) + -OUS]

cam·pan·u·late (kam pan′yə lit, -lāt′), *adj.* bell-shaped, as a corolla. [1660–70; < NL *campānulātus.* See CAMPANULA, -ATE[1]]

camp′ bed′, a light folding cot or bed. [1680–90]

Camp·bell (kam′bəl, kam′əl), *n.* **1. Alexander,** 1788–1866, U.S. religious leader, born in Ireland: cofounder with his father, Thomas, of the Disciples of Christ Church. **2. Col·en** (kol′ən, kō′lən) or **Colin,** died 1729, Scottish architect and author. **3. Colin** (*Baron Clyde*), 1792–1863, Scottish general. **4. Sir John,** 1779–1861, English jurist and writer: Lord Chancellor of England 1859–61. **5. Sir Malcolm,** 1885–1948, English automobile and speedboat racer. **6. Mrs. Patrick** (*Beatrice Stella Tanner*), 1865–1940, English actress. **7. Thomas,** 1763–1854, Irish religious leader, in the U.S. after 1807: cofounder with his son, Alexander, of the Disciples of Christ Church. **8. Thomas,** 1777–1844, Scottish poet and editor. **9.** a city in W California. 27,067. **10.** a city in NE Ohio. 11,619.

Camp·bell-Ban·ner·man (kam′bəl ban′ər mən, kam′əl-), *n.* **Sir Henry,** 1836–1908, British statesman, born in Ireland: prime minister 1905–08.

Camp·bell·ism (kam′bə liz′əm, kam′ə-), *n.* the practices and principles of the Disciples of Christ. [1835–45, *Amer.*; A. CAMPBELL + -ISM]

Camp·bell·ite (kam′bə lit′, kam′ə-), *n. Sometimes Offensive.* a member of the Disciples of Christ. [1820–30, *Amer.*; A. CAMPBELL + -ITE[1]]

Camp·bel·town (kam′bəl toun′), *n.* a seaport on the Kintyre peninsula, in SW Scotland: resort. 5961.

camp′ car′, *Railroads.* See **outfit car.**

camp′ chair′, a light folding chair, usually with a canvas seat and back. [1880–85]

camp·craft (kamp′kraft′, -kräft′), *n.* the art of outdoor camping. [1885–90; CAMP[1] + CRAFT]

Camp′ Da′vid (dā′vid), an area, closed to the public, in Catoctin Mountain Park in N central Maryland: presidential retreat with guests' quarters and conference facilities.

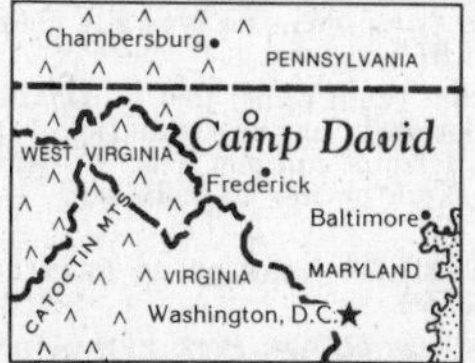

CONCISE PRONUNCIATION KEY: *act, cāpe, dâre, pärt; set, ēqual; if, īce; ox, ōver, ôrder, oil, bo͝ok, bo͞ot, out; up, ûrge; child; sing; shoe; thin, that;* zh as in *treasure.* ə = *a* as in *alone, e* as in *system, i* as in *easily, o* as in *gallop, u* as in *circus;* ᵊ as in *fire* (fīᵊr), *hour* (ouᵊr). l and n can serve as syllabic consonants, as in *cradle* (krād′l), and *button* (but′n). See the full key inside the front cover.

Camp′ Da′vid Accords′, a peace treaty between Israel and Egypt issuing from talks at Camp David between Egyptian President Sadat, Israeli Prime Minister Begin, and the host, U.S. President Carter: signed in 1979.

Cam·pe·che (käm pe′che), *n.* **1.** a state in SE Mexico, on the peninsula of Yucatán. 337,000; 19,672 sq. mi. (50,950 sq. km). **2.** a seaport in and the capital of this state. 69,506. **3. Gulf of,** the SW part of the Gulf of Mexico.

camp·er (kam′pər), *n.* **1.** a person who camps out for recreation, esp. in the wilderness. **2.** a person who attends a summer camp or day camp. **3.** Also called **pickup camper, truck camper.** a trucklike vehicle, van, or trailer that is fitted or suitable for recreational camping, or a pickup truck on which a structure fitted for camping is mounted. —*v.i.* **4.** to travel and live in a vehicular camper: *We're going to camper for two weeks during our vacation.* [1625–35; 1960–65 for def. 3; CAMP[1] + -ER[1]]

cam′per·nelle jon′quil (kam′pər nel′, kam′pər-nel′), a narcissus, *Narcissus odorus,* of the amaryllis family, having clusters of two to four fragrant yellow flowers. [prob. from proper name *Campernelle*]

camp·er·ship (kam′pər ship′), *n.* financial aid given to a needy youngster to attend summer camp. [1945–50; CAMPER + (SCHOLAR)SHIP]

camp′er truck′, a pickup truck having a camper mounted on the truck body. Also, **camp′er-truck′.**

cam·pe·si·no (käm′pe sē′nô; *Eng.* kam′pə sē′nō), *n., pl.* ***-nos*** (-nôs; *Eng.* -nōz). *Spanish.* (in Latin America) a peasant or farmer.

cam·pes·tral (kam pes′trəl), *adj.* of or pertaining to fields or open country. [1730–40; < L *campestr(is)* flat, equiv. to *camp(us)* field + *-estris* adj. suffix) + -AL[1]]

camp·fire (kamp′fīᵊr′), *n.* **1.** an outdoor fire for warmth or cooking, as at a camp. **2.** a gathering around such a fire. **3.** a reunion of soldiers, scouts, etc. [1665–75; CAMP[1] + FIRE]

Camp′ Fire′, a U.S. organization for girls and boys that emphasizes the building of character and good citizenship through work, health, and love; originally founded for girls **(Camp′ Fire′ girls′)** in 1910, it is now open to both boys and girls **(Camp′ Fire′ mem′bers).**

camp′ fol′lower, 1. a civilian not officially connected with a military unit, esp. a prostitute, who follows or settles near an army camp. **2.** a person who sympathizes with or espouses the aims of a group without belonging to it. [1800–10]

camp·ground (kamp′ground′), *n.* a place for a camp or for a camp meeting. [1795–1805, *Amer.*; CAMP[1] + GROUND[1]]

cam·phene (kam′fēn, kam fēn′), *n.* a colorless, crystalline, water-insoluble substance, $C_{10}H_{16}$, occurring in turpentine and many other essential oils, prepared from pinene: used chiefly as an intermediate in the manufacture of synthetic camphor. [1835–45; < NL *camph(ora)* CAMPHOR + -ENE]

cam·phol (kam′fəl, -fôl, -fōl), *n. Chem.* borneol. [1860–65; < NL *camph(ora)* CAMPHOR + -OL[1]]

cam·phor (kam′fər), *n. Chem., Pharm.* **1.** a whitish, translucent, crystalline, pleasant-odored terpene ketone, $C_{10}H_{16}O$, obtained from the camphor tree, used chiefly in the manufacture of celluloid and in medicine as a counter-irritant for infections and in the treatment of pain and itching. **2.** any substance having medicinal or aromatic characteristics similar to those of camphor. [1275–1325; < ML, NL *camphora* << Ar *kāfūr* < Malay *kapur* chalk, lime, camphor; r. ME *caumfre* < AF < ML] —**cam·phor·a·ceous** (kam′fə rā′shəs), *adj.* —**cam·phor·ic** (kam fôr′ik, -for′-), *adj.*

cam·phor·ate (kam′fə rāt′), *v.t.,* **-at·ed, -at·ing.** to impregnate with camphor. [1635–45; < ML *camphorātus,* equiv. to *camphor(a)* CAMPHOR + *-ātus* -ATE[1]]

cam′phorated oil′, *Pharm.* a solution of one part camphor oil in four parts cottonseed oil used as a counterirritant. Also called **cam′phor lin′iment.**

cam′phor ball′. See **moth ball** (def. 1). [1585–95]

cam′phor ice′, a cosmetic preparation composed of camphor, spermaceti, white beeswax, and a vegetable oil and used chiefly in the treatment of mild skin eruptions. [1880–85, *Amer.*]

cam′phor oil′, a colorless liquid obtained from the wood of the camphor tree by distillation and separation from the solid camphor, used in varnish, soaps, and shoe polish, and in medicine chiefly as a rubefacient. [1830–40]

cam′phor tree′, a tree, *Cinnamomum camphora,* of the laurel family, grown in eastern Asia and yielding camphor. [1600–10]

cam·phor·weed (kam′fər wēd′), *n.* vinegarweed. [1910–15, *Amer.*; CAMPHOR + WEED[1]]

Cam·pi·gnian (kam pēn′yən), *adj.* of or pertaining to a Mesolithic and Neolithic technological facies characterized by picks and tranchets. [1920–25; < F *campignien,* after Le *Campigny,* the type site (Seine-Maritime, France); see -AN]

cam·pim·e·ter (kam pim′i tər), *n. Ophthalm.* an instrument for determining the visual field. [1875–80; < L *campi-* (comb. form of *campus* field) + -METER] —**cam·pi·met·ri·cal** (kam′pə me′tri kəl), *adj.* —**cam·pim′e·try,** *n.*

Cam·pi·na Gran·de (käɴ pē′nə grɐɴ′də), a city in NE Brazil. 163,006.

Cam·pi·nas (kam pē′nəs; *Port.* käɴ pē′nəs), *n.* a city in SE Brazil, NNW of São Paulo. 328,629.

cam·pi·on (kam′pē ən), *n.* any of several plants of the genera *Lychnis* and *Silene,* having white, pink, or reddish flowers. [1570–80; special use of *campion,* old var. (< AF) of CHAMPION; cf. Gk (*lychnis*) *stephanōmatikós* (lychnis) for making garlands, with which the winners of games were crowned]

Cam·pi·on (kam′pē ən), *n.* **Thomas,** 1567–1620, English songwriter and poet.

Camp′ Lejeune′, a U.S. Marine Corps base in SE North Carolina SE of Jacksonville on Onslow Bay.

camp′ meet′ing, a religious gathering held in a tent or in the open air. [1790–1800]

cam·po (kam′pō, käm′-), *n., pl.* **-pos.** (in South America) an extensive, nearly level grassland plain. [1605–15; < Sp < L *campus* field]

Cam·po·bel·lo (kam′pə bel′ō), *n.* an island in SE Canada, in New Brunswick province.

cam·po·de·an (kam pō′dē ən), *n.* a campodeid. [< Gk *kámp(ē)* caterpillar + *-ōdēs* -ODE + -AN]

cam·po·de·id (kam pō′dē id), *n.* **1.** any eyeless, wingless, primitive insect of the family Campodeidae, having two long, many-segmented appendages at the rear of its abdomen. —*adj.* **2.** belonging or pertaining to the family Campodeidae. [< NL *Campodeidae* name of the family, equiv. to *Campode(a)* name of the genus (< Gk *kámp(ē)* caterpillar + NL *-odea* -ODE[1]) + *-idae* -ID[2]]

Cam·po For·mio (käm′pô fôʀ′myô), a village in Friuli-Venezia Giulia, in NE Italy, NW of Trieste: treaty between Austria and France 1797. 4495. Modern, **Cam·po·for·mi·do** (käm′pô fôʀ′mē dô).

Cam·po Gran·de (käɴ′pŏŏ grɐɴ′də), a city in SW Brazil. 297,632.

cam·pong (käm′pông, -pong, käm pông′, -pong′), *n.* kampong.

camp·o·ree (kam′pə rē′), *n.* a small camp gathering of boy scouts or girl scouts, usually from a region or district (distinguished from *jamboree*). [b. CAMP[1] and JAMBOREE]

Cam·pos (käɴ′pŏŏs), *n.* a city in E Brazil, near Rio de Janeiro. 153,310.

cam·po san·to (käm′pô sän′tô), *pl. It.* ***cam·pi san·ti*** (käm′pē sän′tē), *Sp.* ***cam·pos san·tos*** (käm′pôs sän′-tôs). *Italian, Spanish.* a cemetery. [lit., holy field]

camp·out (kamp′out′), *n.* a camping out of a group. Also, **camp′-out′.** [1875–80, *Amer.*; n. use of v. phrase *camp out*]

Camp′ Pen′dleton, a U.S. Marine Corps base in SW California on the Gulf of Santa Catalina.

camp′ rob′ber, *Chiefly Northern U.S. and Western Canada.* See **gray jay.** [1885–90; so called from its habit of pilfering food from campsites]

camp·shed (kamp′shed′), *v.t.,* **-shed, -shed·ding.** to line (the bank of a river) with campshot. [1880–85; var. of CAMPSHOT]

camp′ shirt′, a short-sleeved shirt or blouse with a notched collar and usually two breast pockets.

camp·shot (kamp′shot′), *n.* a facing of planks and piles placed along the bank of a river to prevent erosion. Also called **camp′shed′ding, camp′sheet′ing.** [1685–95; orig. uncert.]

camp·site (kamp′sīt′), *n.* a place used or suitable for camping. Also, **camp′-site′.** [1905–10, *Amer.*; CAMP[1] + SITE]

Camp′ Springs′, a city in central Maryland, near Washington, D.C. 16,118.

camp·stool (kamp′stōōl′), *n.* a lightweight folding stool, esp. for use in camping. [1855–60; CAMP[1] + STOOL]

camp′ stove′, a portable stove used for cooking or heating, esp. outdoors. [1860–65, *Amer.*]

camp·ton·ite (kamp′tə nīt′), *n.* a lamprophyric rock occurring in dikes and composed of labradorite, pyroxene, sodic hornblende and olivine. [< G (1887), named after *Campton,* New Hampshire; see -ITE]

cam·pus (kam′pəs), *n., pl.* **-pus·es. 1.** the grounds, often including the buildings, of a college, university, or school. **2.** a college or university: *The large influx of older students radically changed many campuses throughout the country.* **3.** a division of a university that has its own grounds, buildings, and faculty but is administratively joined to the rest of the university. **4.** the world of higher education: *Foundation grants have had a marked effect on the character of the American campus.* **5.** a large, usually suburban, landscaped business or industrial site. [1765–75, *Amer.*; < L: flat place, field, plain]

camp·y (kam′pē), *adj.,* **camp·i·er, camp·i·est.** of, pertaining to, or characterized by camp: *a campy send-up of romantic operetta.* [1955–60; CAMP[2] + -Y[1]] —**camp′i·ly,** *adv.* —**camp′i·ness,** *n.*

Cam·rose (kam′rōz′), *n.* a city in central Alberta, in W Canada, near Edmonton. 12,570.

cam·shaft (kam′shaft′, -shäft′), *n.* a shaft bearing integral cams. [1875–80; CAM + SHAFT]

Ca·mus (ka my′; *Eng.* ka mōō′), *n.* **Al·bert** (al beʀ′), 1913–60, French novelist, short-story writer, playwright, and essayist: Nobel prize 1957.

cam′ wheel′, a wheel, with an off-center axis or irregular shape, that functions as a cam. [1860–65]

can[1] (kan; *unstressed* kən), *auxiliary v.* and *v., pres. sing. 1st pers.* **can,** *2nd* **can** or (*Archaic*) **canst,** *3rd* **can,** *pres. pl.* **can;** *past sing. 1st pers.* **could,** *2nd* **could** or (*Archaic*) **couldst,** *3rd* **could,** *past pl.* **could.** *For auxiliary v.: imperative, infinitive, and participles lacking. For v. (Obs.): imperative* **can;** *infinitive* **can;** *past part.* **could;** *pres. part.* **cun·ning.** —*auxiliary verb.* **1.** to be able to; have the ability, power, or skill to: *She can solve the problem easily, I'm sure.* **2.** to know how to: *He can play chess, although he's not particularly good at it.* **3.** to have the power or means to: *A dictator can impose his will on the people.* **4.** to have the right or qualifications to: *He can change whatever he wishes in the script.* **5.** may; have permission to: *Can I speak to you for a moment?* **6.** to have the possibility: *A coin can land on either side.* —*v.t., v.i.* **7.** *Obs.* to know. [bef. 900; ME, OE, pres. ind. sing. 1st, 3rd person of *cunnan* to know, know how; c. G, ON, Goth *kann;* see KEN, KNOW]

—**Usage.** CAN[1] and MAY[1] are frequently but not always interchangeable in senses indicating possibility: *A power failure can* (or *may*) *occur at any time.* Despite the insistence by some that CAN means only "to be able" and MAY means "to be permitted," both are regularly used in seeking or granting permission: *Can* (or *May*) *I borrow your tape recorder? You can* (or *may*) *use it tomorrow.* Sentences using CAN occur chiefly in spoken English. MAY in this sense occurs more frequently in formal contexts: *May I address the court, Your Honor?* In negative constructions, CAN'T or CANNOT is more common than MAY NOT: *You can't have it today. I need it myself.* The contraction MAYN'T is rare.

CAN BUT and CANNOT BUT are formal and now somewhat old-fashioned expressions suggesting that there is no possible alternative to doing something. CAN BUT is equivalent to CAN ONLY: *We can but do our best.* CANNOT BUT is the equivalent of CANNOT HELP BUT: *We cannot but protest against these injustices.* See also **cannot, help.**

can[2] (kan), *n., v.,* **canned, can·ning.** —*n.* **1.** a sealed container for food, beverages, etc., as of aluminum, sheet iron coated with tin, or other metal: *a can of soup.* **2.** a receptacle for garbage, ashes, etc.: *a trash can.* **3.** a bucket, pail, or other container for holding or carrying liquids: *water can.* **4.** a drinking cup; tankard. **5.** a metal or plastic container for holding film on cores or reels. **6.** *Slang* (*usually vulgar*). toilet; bathroom. **7.** *Slang.* jail: *He's been in the can for a week.* **8.** *Slang* (*sometimes vulgar*). buttocks. **9.** *Mil. Slang.* **a.** a depth charge. **b.** a destroyer. **10. carry the can,** *Brit. and Canadian Slang.* to take the responsibility. **11. in the can,** recorded on film; completed: *The movie is in the can and ready for release.* —*v.t.* **12.** to preserve by sealing in a can, jar, etc. **13.** *Slang.* to dismiss; fire. **14.** *Slang.* to throw (something) away. **15.** *Slang.* to put a stop to: *Can that noise!* **16.** to record, as on film or tape. [bef. 1000; ME, OE *canne,* c. G *Kanne,* ON *kanna,* all perh. < WGmc; cf. LL *canna* small vessel]

Can., 1. Canada. **2.** Canadian.

can., 1. canceled. **2.** canon. **3.** canto.

Ca·na (kā′nə), *n.* an ancient town in N Israel, in Galilee: scene of Jesus' first miracle. John 2:1, 11.

Ca·naan (kā′nən), *n.* **1.** the ancient region lying between the Jordan, the Dead Sea, and the Mediterranean: the land promised by God to Abraham. Gen. 12:5–10. **2.** Biblical name of **Palestine. 3.** any land of promise. **4.** a descendant of Ham, the son of Noah. Gen. 10. [< Heb *Kena'an*]

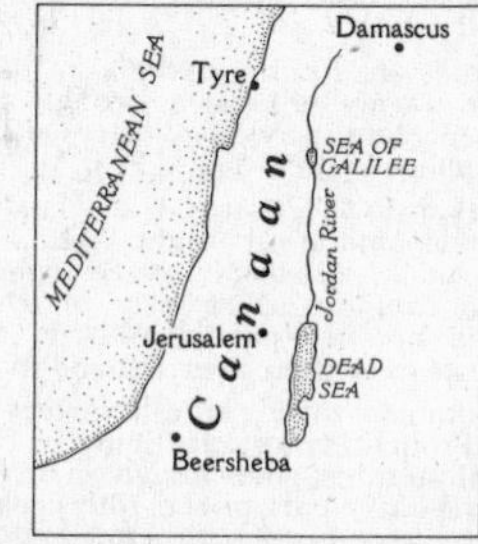

Ca·naan·ite (kā′nə nīt′), *n.* **1.** a member of a Semitic people that inhabited parts of ancient Palestine and were conquered by the Israelites and largely absorbed by them. **2.** a group of Semitic languages, including Hebrew and Phoenician, spoken chiefly in ancient Palestine and Syria. —*adj.* **3.** of, pertaining to, or characteristic of Canaan, the Canaanites, or the Canaanite group of languages. [1350–1400; ME << Gk *Kananítēs;* see CANAAN, -ITE[1]] —**Ca·naan·it·ish** (kā′nə nī′tish), **Ca·naan·it·ic** (kā′nə nit′ik), *adj.*

Can·a·ce (kan′ə sē′), *n. Class. Myth.* a daughter of Aeolus who committed suicide at her father's command because of her incestuous relations with her brother Macareus.

Canad., Canadian.

ca·ña·da (kən yä′də, -yad′ə), *n. Chiefly Western U.S.* **1.** a dry riverbed. **2.** a small, deep canyon. [1840–50; < Sp, equiv. to *cañ(a)* CANE + *-ada* n. suffix]

Can·a·da (kan′ə də), *n.* a nation in N North America: a member of the Commonwealth of Nations. 23,110,000; 3,690,410 sq. mi. (9,558,160 sq. km). *Cap.:* Ottawa. See map on next page.

Can′ada Act′, the act of the British parliament of 1962 that transferred to the Canadian federal government complete control over the constitution of Canada.

Can′ada bal′sam, a pale yellow or greenish, slightly fluorescent, clear, viscous, bitter-tasting, water-insoluble liquid, having a pleasant, aromatic, pinelike odor, and solidifying on exposure to air: obtained from the balsam fir, *Abies balsamea,* and used chiefly for mounting objects on microscope slides, in the manufacture of fine lacquers, and as a cement for lenses. Also called **Canada turpentine, balsam of fir.** [1810–20, *Amer.*]

Can′ada blue′grass, a Eurasian grass, *Poa compressa,* naturalized in North America, having creeping rootstocks and bluish-green leaves. Also called **wire grass.** [1900–05, *Amer.*]

Can′ada Day′, a Canadian national holiday celebrated on July 1, in commemoration of the formation of

CONCISE ETYMOLOGY KEY: <, descended or borrowed from; >, whence; b., blend of, blended; c., cognate with; cf., compare; deriv., derivative; equiv., equivalent; imit., imitative; obl., oblique; r., replacing; s., stem; sp., spelling, spelled; resp., respelling, respelled; trans., translation; ?, origin unknown; *, unattested; ‡, probably earlier than. See the full key inside the front cover.

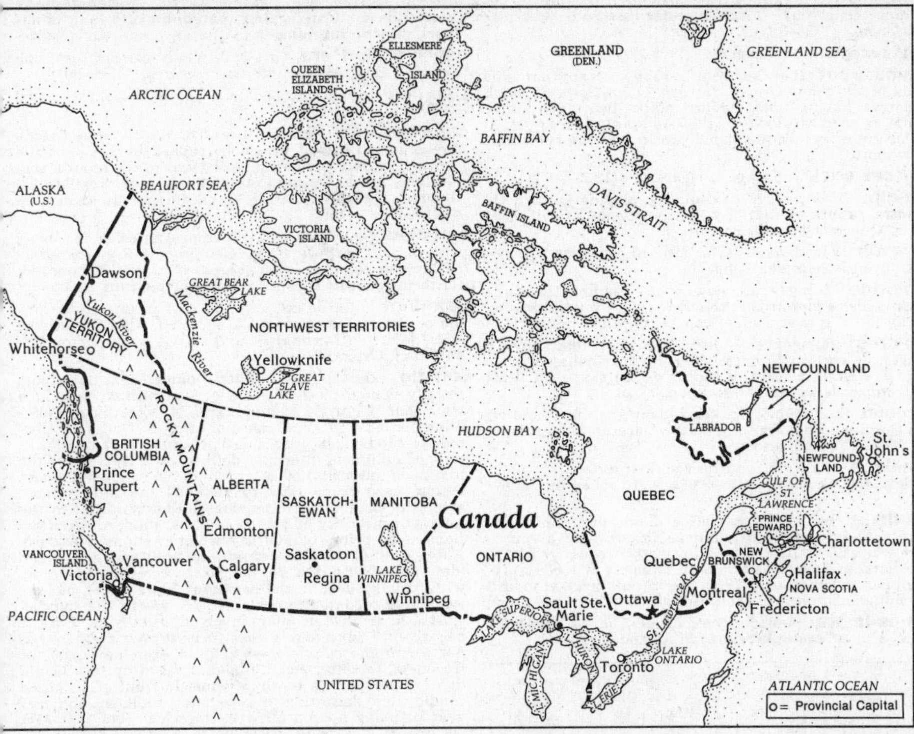

the Dominion on July 1, 1867. Formerly, until 1982, **Dominion Day.**

Can′ada goose′, a common wild goose, *Branta canadensis,* of North America. See illus. under **goose.** Also, **Canadian goose.** [1725–35]

Can′ada hem′lock. See **eastern hemlock.**

Can′ada jay′. See **gray jay.** [1805–15, *Amer.*]

Can′ada lil′y. a plant, *Lilium canadense,* of eastern North America, having large, nodding, yellow or orange flowers with dark spots. Also called **meadow lily.** [1905–10, *Amer.*]

Can′ada lynx′. See under **lynx.** [1830–40, *Amer.*]

Can′ada may′flower. See **wild lily-of-the-valley.** [1930–35, *Amer.*]

Can′ada moon′seed, a vine, *Menispermum canadense,* of eastern North America, having variable leaves and black, grapelike fruit. Also called **yellow parilla.**

Can′ada this′tle, an Old World plant, *Cirsium arvense,* having small purple or white flower heads, now a troublesome weed in North America. [1790–1800, *Amer.*]

Can′ada tur′pentine. See **Canada balsam.**

Ca•na•di•an (kə nā′dē ən), *adj.* **1.** of Canada or its people. —*n.* **2.** a native or inhabitant of Canada. [1560–70; CANAD(A) + -IAN; cf. F *canadien*]

Cana′dian ba′con, bacon made from a boned strip of pork loin. [1935–40]

Cana′dian Broad′casting Corpora′tion, the noncommercial Canadian radio and television broadcasting company that provides programming in both English and French. *Abbr.:* CBC, C.B.C.

Cana′dian Eng′lish, the English language in any of the varieties spoken in Canada.

Cana′dian foot′ball, a game similar to American football but played on a field 165 yd. by 65 yd. (151 m by 59 m) by two teams of 12 players each. Also called **rouge.**

Cana′dian French′, French spoken as a native language in Canada, esp. in Quebec province, by descendants of the settlers of New France. *Abbr.:* CanF

Cana′dian goose′. See **Canada goose.**

Cana′dian hem′lock. See **eastern hemlock.**

Ca•na•di•an•ism (kə nā′dē ə niz′əm), *n.* **1.** allegiance to or pride in Canada and its institutions. **2.** a custom, trait, or thing distinctive of Canada or its citizens. **3.** an English word, idiom, phrase, or pronunciation that originated or is distinctively used in Canada. [1870–75; CANADIAN + -ISM]

Ca•na•di•an•ize (kə nā′dē ə nīz′), *v.t.* **-ized, -iz•ing.** to make Canadian in character. Also, *esp. Brit.,* **Ca•na′•di•an•ise′.** [1820–1830; CANADIAN + -IZE] —**Ca•na′di•an•i•za′tion,** *n.*

Cana′dian Le′gion, a national social club for veterans of the Canadian armed services.

Cana′dian Riv′er, a river flowing E from the Rocky Mountains in NE New Mexico to the Arkansas River in E Oklahoma. 906 mi. (1460 km) long.

Cana′dian Shield′, *Geol.* the extensive region making up much of northern and central Canada underlain by Precambrian rocks that have been eroded to produce a low shieldlike profile. [1920–25]

Cana′dian sol′dier, *Chiefly Northern U.S.* the mayfly.

Cana′dian whis′ky, a rye whiskey made entirely from cereal grain.

ca•nai•gre (kə nī′grē), *n.* a plant, *Rumex hymenosepalus,* of the buckwheat family, found from Oklahoma to California, having clustered, tuberous roots that yield tannin. [1875–80, *Amer.*; < MexSp]

ca•naille (kə nāl′; *Fr.* KA nä′yᵊ), *n.* riffraff; rabble. [1670–80; < F < It *canaglia* pack of dogs, equiv. to *can(e)* dog (< L *canis*) + *-aglia* collective suffix]

ca•nal (kə nal′), *n., v.,* **-nalled** or **-naled, -nal•ling** or **-nal•ing.** —*n.* **1.** an artificial waterway for navigation, irrigation, etc. **2.** a long narrow arm of the sea penetrating far inland. **3.** a tubular passage or cavity for food, air, etc., esp. in an animal or plant; a duct. **4.** channel; watercourse. **5.** *Astron.* one of the long, narrow, dark lines on the surface of the planet Mars, as seen telescopically from the earth. —*v.t.* **6.** to make a canal through. [1400–50; late ME: waterpipe, tubular passage < L *canālis,* perh. equiv. to *can(na)* reed, pipe (see CANE) + *-ālis* -AL[1]; def. 5 a mistranslation of It *canali* channels, term used by G. V. Schiaparelli]

Ca•na•let•to (kan′l et′ō; *It.* kä′nä let′tô), *n.* **1. Anto•nio** (än tô′nyô), (*Canale*), 1697–1768, Italian painter. **2.** See **Bellotto, Bernardo.**

can•a•lic•u•lus (kan′l ik′yə ləs), *n., pl.* **-li** (-lī′). *Anat., Zool.* a small canal or tubular passage, as in bone. [1555–65; < L, equiv. to *canāli(s)* CANAL + *-culus* -CULE[1]] —**can′a•lic′u•lar, can•a•lic•u•late** (kan′l ik′yə lit, -yə lāt′), **can′a•lic′u•lat′ed,** *adj.* —**can•a•lic•u•la•tion** (kan′l ik′yə lā′shən), *n.*

ca•nal•i•za•tion (kə nal′ə zā′shən, kan′l-), *n.* **1.** the formation of canals; the act of canalizing. **2.** *Biol.* the development of an organism along relatively predictable pathways despite abnormality or injury. [1840–50; CANALIZE + -ATION]

can•al•ize (kan′l īz′, kə nal′īz), *v.t.,* **-ized, -iz•ing. 1.** to make a canal or canals through. **2.** to convert into a canal. **3.** to divide (a stream) into reaches with locks or dams, usually to maintain navigable depths. **4.** to divert into certain channels; give a certain direction to or provide a certain outlet for. Also, *esp. Brit.,* **can′al•ise′.** [1850–55; CANAL + -IZE]

ca•nal•ler (kə nal′ər, -nô′lər), *n.* **1.** a freight boat built for use on canals. **2.** a worker on a canal boat, esp. one that formerly plied the Erie Canal. [1860–65; CANAL + -ER[1]]

canal′ ray′, *Physics.* See **positive ray.** [1900–05]

Canal′ Zone′, a zone in central Panama, crossing the Isthmus of Panama on both sides of the Panama Canal: governed by the U.S. from 1903 until 1979, when most of the zone was returned to Panama, for its eventual control of the entire zone by 2000; ab. 10 mi. (16 km) wide; excludes the cities of Panama and Colón. 44,650; 553 sq. mi. (1432 sq. km). *Abbr.:* CZ (for use with zip code), C. Z.

Can•an•dai•gua (kan′ən dā′gwə), *n.* a town in central New York. 10,419.

Ca•na•ne•a (kan′ə nē′ə, -nā′ə; *Sp.* kä′nä ne′ä), *n.* a city in N Mexico: copper mining and smelting. 21,824. —**Can′a•ne′an,** *n.*

can•a•pé (kan′ə pē, -pā′; *Fr.* KA NA pā′), *n., pl.* **-pés** (-pēz, -pāz′; *Fr.* -pā′). **1.** a thin piece of bread or toast or a cracker spread or topped with cheese, caviar, anchovies, or other savory food. **2.** *Furniture.* a sofa of 18th-century France, made in any of several forms, often with matching chairs. **3.** *Bridge.* a style of bidding in which short suits are bid before long ones. [1885–90; < F: lit., a covering or netting, orig. for a bed (see CANOPY), by extension for a piece of bread]

Ca•na•ra (kə när′ə, kä′nər ə), *n.* Kanara.

ca•nard (kə närd′; *Fr.* KA NAR′), *n., pl.* **-nards** (-närdz′; *Fr.* -NAR′). **1.** a false or baseless, usually derogatory story, report, or rumor. **2.** *Cookery.* a duck intended or used for food. **3.** *Aeron.* **a.** an airplane that has its horizontal stabilizer and elevators located forward of the wing. **b.** Also called **canard′ wing′.** one of two small lifting wings located in front of the main wings. **c.** an early airplane having a pusher engine with the rudder and elevator assembly in front of the wings. [1840–50; < F: lit., duck; OF *quanart* drake, orig. cackler, equiv. to *can(er)* to cackle (of expressive orig.) + *-art* -ART, as in *mallart* drake; see MALLARD]

Ca•na•rese (kä′nə rēz′, -rēs′, kan′ə-), *adj., n., pl.* **-rese.** Kanarese.

Canar′ies Cur′rent, an ocean current of the North Atlantic flowing southward past Spain and North Africa.

ca•nar•y (kə nâr′ē), *n., pl.* **-nar•ies,** *adj.* —*n.* **1.** any of several Old World finches of the genus *Serinus,* esp. *S. canaria* **(common canary),** native to the Canary Islands and often kept as a pet, in the wild being greenish with brown streaks above and yellow below and in domesticated varieties usually bright yellow or pale yellow. **2.** Also called **canary yellow.** a light, clear yellow color. **3.** *Slang.* informer (def. 1). **4.** *Slang.* a female singer, esp. with a dance band. **5.** a sweet white wine of the Canary Islands, resembling sherry. **6.** a yellow diamond. —*adj.* **7.** having the color canary. [1585–95; < Sp (*Isla*) *Canaria* < L *Canāria* (*insula*) Dog (Island), equiv. to *can(is)* dog + *-āria,* fem. of *-ārius* -ARY]

ca•nar′y•bird flow′er (kə nâr′ē bûrd′), a nasturtium, *Tropaeolum peregrinum,* of Peru, having round, deeply lobed leaves and yellow flowers. Also called **canar′ybird vine′.** [1815–25; CANARY + BIRD]

canar′y grass′, any of various grasses of the genus *Phalaris,* as *P. canariensis,* native to the Canary Islands, bearing seed used as food for cage birds, or *P. arundinacea* **(reed canary grass),** used throughout the Northern Hemisphere as fodder. [1660–70]

Canar′y Is′lands, a group of mountainous islands in the Atlantic Ocean, near the NW coast of Africa, comprising two provinces of Spain. 1,138,801; 2894 sq. mi. (7495 sq. km). Also called **Ca•nar′ies.** —**Ca•nar′i•an,** *adj., n.*

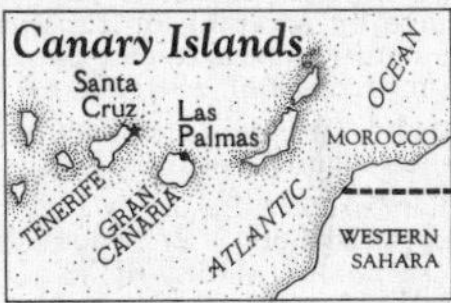

canar′y seed′, birdseed. [1590–1600]

canar′y yel′low, canary (def. 2). [1860–65]

ca•nas•ta (kə nas′tə), *n. Cards.* a variety of rummy in which the main object is to meld sets of seven or more cards. [1945–50; < Sp: lit., basket, appar. var. of *canastro* < Gk *kánastron* wicker basket (see CANISTER)]

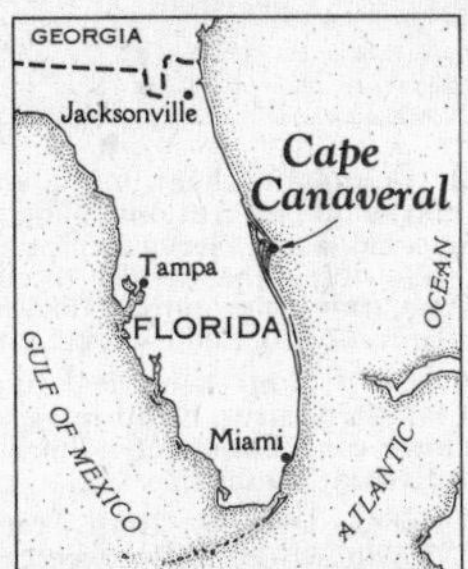

Ca•nav•er•al (kə nav′ər əl), *n.* **Cape,** a cape on an island in E Florida: site of John F. Kennedy Space Center. Formerly (1963–73), **Cape Kennedy.**

Can•ber•ra (kan′ber ə, -bər ə), *n.* a city in and the capital of Australia, in the SE part, in the Australian Capital Territory. 219,331 (with suburbs).

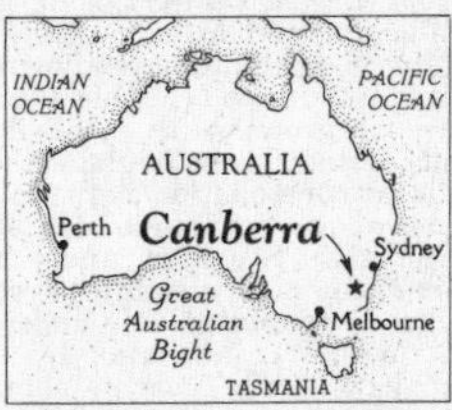

can′ bu′oy, a cylindrical, unlighted buoy used as a channel marker. See illus. under **buoy.** Cf. **nun buoy.** [1620–30]

Can•by (kan′bē), *n.* **Henry Sei•del** (sīd′l), 1878–1961, U.S. author and critic.

CONCISE PRONUNCIATION KEY: act, cāpe, dâre, pärt; set, ēqual; *if,* īce; ox, ōver, ôrder, oil, bŏŏk, bōōt, out; up, ûrge; child; sing; shoe; thin, *th*at; zh as in *treasure.* ə = *a* as in *alone,* *e* as in *system,* *i* as in *easily,* *o* as in *gallop,* *u* as in *circus;* ᵊ as in *fire* (fīᵊr), *hour* (ouᵊr). l and n can serve as syllabic consonants, as in *cradle* (krād′l), and *button* (but′n). See the full key inside the front cover.

canc., **1.** cancel. **2.** canceled. **3.** cancellation.

can•can (kan′kan′), *n.* a lively high kicking dance that came into vogue about 1830 in Paris and after 1844 was used as an exhibition dance. [1840–50; < F, repetitive compound (based on *can*) said to be nursery var. of *canard* duck; see CANARD]

can•cel (kan′səl), *v.,* **-celed, -cel•ing** or (*esp. Brit.*) **-celled, -cel•ling,** *n.* —*v.t.* **1.** to make void; revoke; annul: *to cancel a reservation.* **2.** to decide or announce that a planned event will not take place; call off: *to cancel a meeting.* **3.** to mark or perforate (a postage stamp, admission ticket, etc.) so as to render invalid for reuse. **4.** to neutralize; counterbalance; compensate for: *His sincere apology canceled his sarcastic remark.* **5.** *Accounting.* **a.** to close (an account) by crediting or paying all outstanding charges: *He plans to cancel his account at the department store.* **b.** to eliminate or offset (a debit, credit, etc.) with an entry for an equal amount on the opposite side of a ledger, as when a payment is received on a debt. **6.** *Math.* to eliminate by striking out a factor common to both the denominator and numerator of a fraction, equivalent terms on opposite sides of an equation, etc. **7.** to cross out (words, letters, etc.) by drawing a line over the item. **8.** *Print.* to omit. —*v.i.* **9.** to counterbalance or compensate for one another; become neutralized (often fol. by *out*): *The pros and cons cancel out.* **10.** *Math.* (of factors common to both the denominator and numerator of a fraction, certain terms on opposite sides of an equation, etc.) to be equivalent; to allow cancellation. —*n.* **11.** an act of canceling. **12.** *Print., Bookbinding.* **a.** omission. **b.** a replacement for an omitted part. [1350–1400; ME *cancellen* < ML *cancellāre* to cross out, L: to make like a lattice, deriv. of *cancellī* grating, pl. of *cancellus;* see CANCELLUS] —**can′cel•a•ble;** *esp. Brit.,* **can′cel•la•ble,** *adj.* —**can′•cel•er;** *esp. Brit.,* **can′cel•ler,** *n.*
—**Syn. 1.** countermand, rescind. **3, 7.** CANCEL, DELETE, ERASE, OBLITERATE indicate that something is no longer to be considered usable or in force. To CANCEL is to cross something out by stamping a mark over it, drawing lines through it, or the like: *to cancel a stamp, a word.* To DELETE is to cross something out from written matter or from matter to be printed, often in accordance with a printer's or proofreader's symbol indicating the material is to be omitted: *to delete part of a line.* To ERASE is to remove by scraping or rubbing: *to erase a capital letter.* To OBLITERATE is to blot out entirely, so as to remove all sign or trace of: *to obliterate a record.*

can′celed check′, a check that has been redeemed by a bank and then usually returned to the issuer.

can•cel•late (kan′sə lāt′, -lit), *adj.* **1.** *Anat.* of spongy or porous structure, as bone. **2.** reticulate. Also, **can•cel•lat•ed** (kan′sə lā′tid). [1655–65; < L *cancellātus.* See CANCEL, -ATE[1]]

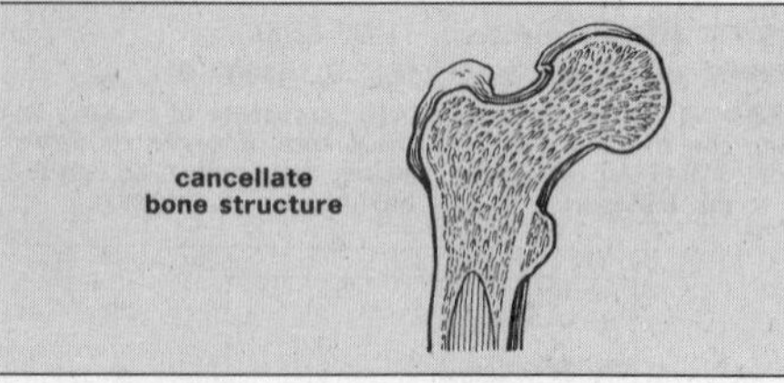
cancellate bone structure

can•cel•la•tion (kan′sə lā′shən), *n.* **1.** an act of canceling. **2.** the marks or perforations made in canceling. **3.** something canceled, as a reservation for a hotel room, airplane ticket, allowing someone else to obtain the accommodation. Also, **can′cel•a′tion.** [1525–35; < L *cancellātiōn-* (s. of *cancellātiō*). See CANCELLATE, -ION]

cancella′tion law′, a mathematical rule pertaining to certain algebraic structures, as an integral domain or a field, that allows cancellation of a nonzero common factor of two equivalent quantities.

can•cel•lous (kan′sə ləs), *adj. Anat.* cancellate (def. 1). [1830–40; < L *cancell(us)* lattice (see CANCELLUS) + -OUS]

can•cel•lus (kan sel′əs), *n., pl.* **-cel•li** (-sel′ī, -sel′ē). *Archit.* **1.** (in an early Christian basilica) one of a row of bars separating the clergy and sometimes the choir from the congregation. **2.** (in an ancient Roman basilica) one of a row of bars separating the court personnel from the spectators. **3. cancelli,** a screen of such bars. [< L, equiv. to *canc(ri)* grating (pl. of *cancer,* appar. dissimilated form of *carcer* prison) + *-ellus* dim. suffix]

can•cer (kan′sər), *n., gen.* **Can•cri** (kang′krē) for 3. **1.** *Pathol.* **a.** a malignant and invasive growth or tumor, esp. one originating in epithelium, tending to recur after excision and to metastasize to other sites. **b.** any disease characterized by such growths. **2.** any evil condition or thing that spreads destructively; blight. **3.** (*cap.*) *Astron.* the Crab, a zodiacal constellation between Gemini and Leo. **4.** (*cap.*) *Astrol.* **a.** the fourth sign of the zodiac: the cardinal water sign. See illus. under **zodiac. b.** a person born under this sign, usually between June 21 and July 22. **5.** (*cap.*) **tropic of.** See under **tropic** (def. 1a). [1350–1400; ME < L: lit., crab; L s. *cancr-,* dissimilated from **carcr-,* with **carc-r-* akin to Gk *karkínos,* Skt *karkata* crab; see CANKER] —**can′cer•ous,** *adj.* —**can′cered,** *adj.* —**can′cer•ous•ly,** *adv.* —**can′cer•ous•ness,** *n.*
—**Syn. 2.** sickness, evil, plague, scourge.

can•cer•ate (kan′sə rāt′), *v.i.,* **-at•ed, -at•ing.** to become cancerous; develop into cancer. [1680–90; < LL *cancerātus* cancerous. See CANCER, -ATE[1]]

CONCISE ETYMOLOGY KEY: <, descended or borrowed from; >, whence; b., blend of, blended; c., cognate with; cf., compare; deriv., derivative; equiv., equivalent; imit., imitative; obl., oblique; r., replacing; s., stem; sp., spelling, spelled; resp., respelling, respelled; trans., translation; ?, origin unknown; *, unattested; ‡, probably earlier than. See the full key inside the front cover.

can•cer•a•tion (kan′sə rā′shən), *n.* the state of becoming cancerous. Also, **can•cer•i•za•tion** (kan′sər i zā′shən). [1725–35; CANCERATE + -ION]

can′cer gene′, oncogene. [1975–80]

can•cer•root (kan′sər ro͞ot′, -ro͝ot′), *n.* any parasitic plant of the genus *Orobanche,* esp. *O. uniflora,* of North America, having pale, leafless stalks bearing a single white or purplish flower. [1705–15; CANCER + ROOT[1]; so called from its folk-medicinal use in treating cancerous growths]

can′cer stick′, *Slang.* a cigarette. [1965–70]

can•cha (kän′chə), *n.* a court for playing jai alai. Cf. **frontis, rebote** (def. 1). [< Sp: court, sports field, cockpit < Quechua *kancha* corral]

can•ción (kän thyôn′, -syôn′), *n., pl.* ***-cio•nes*** (-thyô′nes, -syô′-). *Spanish.* song.

can•crine (kang′krin), *adj. Pros.* reading the same backwards as forwards: *a cancrine line.* Cf. **palindrome.** [1745–55; < L *cancr-* (s. of *cancer*) CANCER + -INE[1]]

can•croid (kang′kroid), *adj.* **1.** *Pathol.* resembling a cancer, as certain tumors. **2.** *Zool.* resembling a crab. —*n.* **3.** *Pathol.* a form of cancer of the skin. [1820–30; < L *cancr-* (s. of *cancer*) CANCER + -OID]

Can•cún (kan ko͞on′; *Sp.* käng ko͞on′), *n.* an island off NE Quintana Roo territory, on the Yucatán Peninsula, in SE Mexico: beach resort.

Can•dace (kan′dis, kan′də sē′, kan dā′sē), *n.* a female given name: from a Greek word meaning "glowing."

can•de•la (kan dē′lə), *n. Optics.* a unit of luminous intensity, defined as the luminous intensity of a source that emits monochromatic radiation of frequency 540 × 10[12] hertz and that has a radiant intensity of 1/683 watt/steradian: adopted in 1979 as the international standard of luminous intensity. *Abbr.:* Cd [1945–50; < L: CANDLE]

can•de•la•bra (kan′dl ä′brə, -dl ā′-), *n., pl.* **-bras** for 2. **1.** a pl. of **candelabrum. 2.** a candelabrum.

candelabrum

can•de•la•brum (kan′dl ä′brəm, -dl ā′-), *n., pl.* **-bra** (-brə), **-brums.** an ornamental branched holder for more than one candle. [1805–15; < L *candēlābrum* candlestick, equiv. to *candēl(a)* CANDLE + *-abrum,* var. (after stems with an *-l-*) of *-bulum* suffix of instruments; *-ā-* by analogy with deverbal derivatives]

can•de•li•lla (kan′dl ē′ə), *n.* a shrub, *Euphorbia antisyphilitica,* of the southwestern U.S. and Mexico, that is the source of a wax (**candeli′lla wax′**) having various commercial uses. [1935–40; < AmerSp; Sp: small candle, equiv. to *candel(a)* CANDLE + *-illa* dim. suffix]

can•dent (kan′dənt), *adj.* glowing with heat; being at a white heat. [1570–80; < L *candent-* (s. of *candēns,* prp. of *candēre* to be shining white), equiv. to *cand-* bright (see CANDID) + *-ent-* -ENT]

can•des•cent (kan des′ənt), *adj.* glowing; incandescent. [1815–25; < L *candēscent-* (s. of *candēscēns,* prp. of *candēscere* to become bright), equiv. to *cand-* bright (see CANDID) + *-ēscent-* -ESCENT] —**can•des′cence,** *n.* —**can•des′cent•ly,** *adv.*

C. & F., *Com.* cost and freight.

C&I, **1.** commerce and industry. **2.** commercial and industrial.

Can•di•a (kan′dē ə), *n.* **1.** Greek, **Herakleion.** a seaport in N Crete. 77,506. **2.** Crete.

Can•dice (kan′dis, kan′də sē′), *n.* a female given name.

can•did (kan′did), *adj.* **1.** frank; outspoken; open and sincere: *a candid critic.* **2.** free from reservation, disguise, or subterfuge; straightforward: *a candid opinion.* **3.** informal; unposed: *a candid photo.* **4.** honest; impartial: *a candid mind.* **5.** *Archaic.* white. **6.** *Archaic.* clear; pure. —*n.* **7.** an unposed photograph. [1620–30; (< F *candide*) < L *candidus* shining white, equiv. to *cand(ēre)* to be shining white (akin to INCENSE) + *-idus* -ID[4]] —**can′did•ly,** *adv.* —**can′did•ness,** *n.*
—**Syn. 1.** ingenuous, naive, plain. See **frank.**

can•di•da (kan′di də), *n.* any of the yeastlike fungi constituting the genus *Candida,* members of which may cause athlete's foot, vaginitis, thrush, or other infections. Cf. **candidiasis.** [1923; < NL; L: fem. of *candidus* bright, light; see CANDID]

Can•di•da (kan′di də), *n.* a female given name.

Can•di•da (kan′di də), *n.* a comedy (1898) by G. B. Shaw.

can•di•date (*n.* kan′di dāt′, -dit; *v.* kan′di dāt′), *n., v.,* **-dat•ed, -dat•ing.** —*n.* **1.** a person who seeks an office, honor, etc.: *a candidate for governor.* **2.** a person who is selected by others as a contestant for an office, honor, etc. **3.** a person who is deserving of or seems destined for a certain end or fate: *Such a reckless spender is a candidate for the poorhouse.* **4.** a student studying for a degree: *Candidates for the B.A. will have to meet certain minimum requirements.* —*v.i.* **5.** to become a candidate for service as a new minister of a church; preach before a congregation that is seeking a new minister. [1605–15; < L *candidātus* clothed in white (adj.), candidate for office (n., in reference to the white togas worn by those seeking office). See CANDID, -ATE[1]] —**can•di•da•cy** (kan′di də sē); *Chiefly Brit.,* **can•di•da•ture** (kan′di də chər), **can′di•date•ship′,** *n.*

can′did cam′era, a small, handy camera, esp. one having a fast lens for informal pictures. [1925–30]

Can•dide (*Fr.* käN dēd′), *n.* a philosophical novel (1759) by Voltaire.

can•di•di•a•sis (kan′di dī′ə sis), *n., pl.* **-ses** (-sēz′). any of a variety of infections caused by fungi of the genus *Candida,* occurring most often in the mouth, respiratory tract (**bronchocandidiasis**), or vagina. Cf. **thrush**[2]. [1945–50; < NL *Candid(a)* genus name (see CANDIDA) + -IASIS]

can•died (kan′dēd), *adj.* **1.** impregnated or incrusted with or as if with sugar: *candied ginger.* **2.** prepared by cooking in sugar or syrup: *candied yams.* **3.** honeyed; flattering: *candied words.* [1590–1600; CANDY + -ED[3]]

Can•di•ot (kan′dē ot′), *adj.* **1.** of or pertaining to Candia or Crete; Cretan. —*n.* **2.** a Cretan. Also, **Can•di•ote** (kan′dē ōt′). [CANDI(A) + *-ot(e)* < Gk *-ōtēs* personal n. suffix; cf. CYPRIOT]

can•dle (kan′dl), *n., v.,* **-dled, -dling.** —*n.* **1.** a long, usually slender piece of tallow or wax with an embedded wick that is burned to give light. **2.** something resembling a candle in appearance or use. **3.** *Optics.* **a.** (formerly) candela. **b.** Also called **international candle.** a unit of luminous intensity, defined as a fraction of the luminous intensity of a group of 45 carbon-filament lamps: used from 1909 to 1948 as the international standard. **c.** a unit of luminous intensity, equal to the luminous intensity of a wax candle of standard specifications: used prior to 1909 as the international standard. *Abbr.:* c., c **4. burn the candle at both ends.** See **burn** (def. 43). **5. hold a candle to,** to compare favorably with (usually used in the negative): *She's smart, but she can't hold a candle to her sister.* **6. worth the candle,** worth the trouble or effort involved (usually used in the negative): *Trying to win them over to your viewpoint is not worth the candle.* —*v.t.* **7.** to examine (eggs) for freshness, fertility, etc., by holding them up to a bright light. **8.** to hold (a bottle of wine) in front of a lighted candle while decanting so as to detect sediment and prevent its being poured off with the wine. [bef. 900; ME, OE *candel* < L *candēla,* equiv. to *cand(ēre)* to shine + *-ēla* deverbal n. suffix; see CANDID] —**can′dler,** *n.*

can•dle•beam (kan′dl bēm′), *n.* a medieval chandelier formed of crossed timbers. [1400–50; late ME. See CANDLE, BEAM]

can•dle•ber•ry (kan′dl ber′ē), *n., pl.* **-ries. 1.** any of several species of wax myrtle. **2.** the fruit of any of these plants. **3.** candlenut. [1730–40, *Amer.;* CANDLE + BERRY]

can•dle•fish (kan′dl fish′), *n., pl.* (*esp. collectively*) **-fish,** (*esp. referring to two or more kinds or species*) **-fish•es. 1.** Also called **eulachon.** a small, edible, smeltlike fish, *Thaleichthys pacificus,* of northwestern coastal waters of North America, being so oily that when dried it can be used as a candle. **2.** sablefish. [1880–85; CANDLE + FISH]

can•dle•hold•er (kan′dl hōl′dər), *n.* a holder for a candle; candlestick. [1585–95; CANDLE + HOLDER]

can•dle•light (kan′dl līt′), *n.* **1.** the light of a candle. **2.** a dim artificial light. **3.** twilight; dusk. [bef. 1000; ME *candel-liht,* OE *candel-lēoht.* See CANDLE, LIGHT[1]]

can•dle•lit (kan′dl lit′), *adj.* lit by candles. [CANDLE + LIT[1]]

Can•dle•mas (kan′dl məs, -mas′), *n.* a church festival, February 2, in honor of the presentation of the infant Jesus in the Temple and the purification of the Virgin Mary: candles are blessed on this day. Also called **Can′dlemas Day′.** [bef. 1050; ME *candelmasse,* OE *candelmæsse.* See CANDLE, -MAS]

can•dle•nut (kan′dl nut′), *n.* **1.** the oily fruit or nut of a southeastern Asian tree, *Aleurites moluccana,* of the spurge family, the kernels of which when strung together are used locally as candles. **2.** the tree itself. Also called **candleberry.** [1850–55; CANDLE + NUT]

can•dle•pin (kan′dl pin′), *n.* **1.** a bowling pin that is almost cylindrical and can be set up on either end, used in a game resembling tenpins. **2. candlepins,** (*used with a singular v.*) the game played with such pins. [1900–05; CANDLE + PIN]

can•dle•pow•er (kan′dl pou′ər), *n. Optics.* (formerly) a measure of luminous intensity expressed in candles. Also, **cand′le pow′er.** [1875–80; CANDLE + POWER]

can•dle•snuff•er (kan′dl snuf′ər), *n.* Usually, **candlesnuffers.** a scissorlike instrument for removing the snuff of candles, tapers, etc., usually with a small box for catching the trimmed wick. Also called **snuffer.** Cf. **extinguisher** (def. 3). [1545–55; CANDLE + SNUFFER[2]]

candlesnuffer

can•dle•stand (kan′dl stand′), *n.* a slender stand or table, often with a tripod base, for holding a candlestick or candelabrum. [1820–30, *Amer.;* CANDLE + STAND]

can•dle•stick (kan′dl stik′), *n.* a device having a socket or a spike for holding a candle. [bef. 1000; ME *candelstikke,* OE *candelsticca.* See CANDLE, STICK[1]]

can•dle•wick (kan′dl wik′), *n.* **1.** the wick of a candle. **2.** Also, **can′dle•wick′ing.** *Textiles.* **a.** Also called **can′dlewick yarn′.** loosely twisted yarn, usually of cotton, used for making candlewick fabric. **b.** the process of making candlewick fabric. **c.** the design made by this process. —*adj.* **3.** (of a fabric) having small, short bunches of wicking tufted to form a design: *a candlewick* bedspread of unbleached muslin. [bef. 1000; ME *candelweke,* OE *candelwēoc.* See CANDLE, WICK[1]]

can•dle•wood (kan′dl wo͝od′), *n.* **1.** any resinous wood used for torches or as a substitute for candles. **2.** any of various trees or shrubs yielding such wood. [1625–35, *Amer.;* CANDLE + WOOD[1]; so called because it burns brightly]

can-do (kan′do͞o′), *adj. Informal.* **1.** marked by purposefulness and efficiency: *a can-do executive.* —*n.* **2.** the quality of being efficient and enthusiastic. [1900–05]

Can•dolle (käɴ dôl′), *n.* **Au•gus•tin Py•rame de** (ō gys taɴ′ pē ʀam′ də), 1778–1841, Swiss botanist.

can•dor (kan′dər), *n.* **1.** the state or quality of being frank, open, and sincere in speech or expression; candidness: *The candor of the speech impressed the audience.* **2.** freedom from bias; fairness; impartiality: *to consider an issue with candor.* **3.** *Obs.* kindliness. **4.** *Obs.* purity. Also, *esp. Brit.,* **can′dour.** [1350–1400 (for sense "extreme whiteness"); ME < L: radiance, whiteness; see CANDID, -OR[1]]
—**Syn. 2.** openness, frankness, honesty, truthfulness.

c&sc, *Print.* capitals and small capitals.

C and W, country-and-western. [1955–60]

can•dy (kan′dē), *n., pl.* **-dies,** *v.,* **-died, -dy•ing.** —*n.* **1.** any of a variety of confections made with sugar, syrup, etc., often combined with chocolate, fruit, nuts, etc. **2.** a single piece of such a confection. **3.** *Slang.* cocaine. —*v.t.* **4.** to cook in sugar or syrup, as sweet potatoes or carrots. **5.** to cook in heavy syrup until transparent, as fruit, fruit peel, or ginger. **6.** to reduce (sugar, syrup, etc.) to a crystalline form, usually by boiling down. **7.** to coat with sugar: *to candy dates.* **8.** to make sweet, palatable, or agreeable. —*v.i.* **9.** to become covered with sugar. **10.** to crystallize into sugar. [1225–75; ME *candi, sugre candi* candied sugar < MF *sucre candi; candi* << Ar *qandī* < Pers *qandi* sugar < Skt *khaṇḍakaḥ* sugar candy] —**can′dy•like′,** *adj.*

Can•dy (kan′dē), *n.* a female given name.

can′dy ap′ple, an apple with a candy coating esp. of taffy and often on a stick inserted in the center.

can′dy ass′, *Slang (vulgar).* a timid or cowardly person; sissy. Also, **can′dy•ass′.**

can•dy-ass (kan′dē as′), *adj. Slang (vulgar).* timid or cowardly; sissified. Also, **can′dy-assed′.**

can′dy corn′, a small candy shaped and colored to look like a kernel of corn.

can′dy floss′, *Brit.* **1.** See **cotton candy. 2.** something that is attractive but inconsequential. [1950–55]

Can•dy•gram (kan′dē gram′), *Trademark.* candy that can be ordered by wire for delivery with an accompanying message, as on the recipient's birthday or anniversary.

can′dy pull′, a social gathering at which taffy or molasses candy is made. [1835–45]

can′dy stripe′, a pattern of bright stripes of one color against a plain background, used chiefly in fabrics. [1935–40]

can•dy-striped (kan′dē strīpt′), *adj.* having a design in candy stripe. [1890–95]

can′dy strip′er, *Informal.* a person, often a teenager, who works as a volunteer in a hospital. [1960–65; so called from the red and white striped uniform often worn]

can•dy•tuft (kan′dē tuft′), *n.* a plant of the genus *Iberis,* of the mustard family, esp. *I. umbellata,* an ornamental plant with tufted pink, violet, purple, or red flowers, originally from the island of Crete. [1570–80; *Candy* (var. of CANDIA) + TUFT]

cane (kān), *n., v.,* **caned, can•ing.** —*n.* **1.** a stick or short staff used to assist one in walking; walking stick. **2.** a long, hollow or pithy, jointed woody stem, as that of bamboo, rattan, sugar cane, and certain palms. **3.** a plant having such a stem. **4.** split rattan woven or interlaced for chair seats, wickerwork, etc. **5.** any of several tall bamboolike grasses, esp. of the genus *Arundinaria,* as *A. gigantea* **(cane reed, large cane, giant cane,** or **southern cane)** and *A. tecta* **(small cane** or **switch cane),** of the southern U.S. **6.** the stem of a raspberry or blackberry. **7.** See **sugar cane. 8.** a rod used for flogging. **9.** a slender cylinder or rod, as of sealing wax or glass. —*v.t.* **10.** to flog with a cane. **11.** to furnish or make with cane: *to cane chairs.* [1350–1400; ME < MF < L *canna* < Gk *kánna* < Sem; cf. Akkadian *qanū,* Heb *qāneh* reed] —**cane′like′,** *adj.* —**can′y,** *adj.*

Ca•ne•a (kə nē′ə), *n.* a seaport on and the capital of Crete, on the W part. 40,564. Greek, **Khania.**

cane•brake (kān′brāk′), *n.* a thicket of canes. [1765–75, *Amer.;* CANE + BRAKE[2]]

cane′ chair′, a chair, the back and seat of which are made of interlaced strips of cane. [1690–1700]

cane•cut•ter (kān′kut′ər), *n.* any of several species of large cottontails inhabiting swamps or marshes. Also, **cane′ cut′ter.** Also called **swamp rabbit.** [1835–45, *Amer.,* for earlier sense; CANE + CUTTER]

cane′ gall′, *Plant Pathol.* a disease of blackberries, characterized by rough, warty outgrowths on the canes, caused by a bacterium, *Agrobacterium rubi.*

ca•nel•la (kə nel′ə), *n.* the cinnamonlike bark of a West Indian tree, *Canella winterana,* used as a condiment and in medicine. [1685–95; < NL, ML: cinnamon, equiv. to L *can(na)* CANE + *-ella* dim. suffix]

can•er (kā′nər), *n.* a person who works with cane, esp. one who produces canework for chairs. [1865–70; CANE + -ER[1]]

cane′ reed′. See under **cane** (def. 5).

ca•nes•cent (kə nes′ənt), *adj.* covered with whitish or grayish pubescence, as certain plants. [1840–50; < L *cānēscent-* s. of *cānēscēns,* prp. of *cānēscere* to grow gray, equiv. to *cān(us)* gray + *-ēscent-* -ESCENT] —**ca•nes′cence,** *n.*

cane′ sug′ar, sugar obtained from sugar cane, identical with that obtained from the sugar beet. Cf. **sugar** (def. 1). [1850–55]

Ca•nes Ve•nat•i•ci (kā′nēz və nat′ə sī′), *gen.* **Ca•num Ve•nat•i•co•rum** (kā′nəm və nat′i kôr′əm, -kōr′-). *Astron.* the Hunting Dogs, a small northern constellation south of Ursa Major. [< L]

cane•ware (kān′wâr′), *n.* a tan unglazed stoneware developed by Wedgwood. [1875–80; CANE + WARE[1]]

cane•work (kān′wûrk′), *n.* strips of cane that are interlaced and used in cane chairs or the like. [1855–60; CANE + WORK]

CanF, Canadian French.

can•field (kan′fēld′), *n. Cards.* a game of solitaire often adapted to gambling purposes. [1910–15; named after R. A. *Canfield* (1855–1914), American gambler, inventor of the game]

Can•field (kan′fēld′), *n.* **Dorothy.** See **Fisher, Dorothy Canfield.**

can•ful (kan′fo͝ol), *n., pl.* **-fuls.** the amount that a can will hold. [1695–1705; CAN[2] + -FUL]
—**Usage.** See **-ful.**

ca•nic′o•la fe′ver (kə nik′ə lə), *Pathol.* an acute febrile disease of humans and dogs, characterized by inflammation of the stomach and intestines and by jaundice: caused by a spirochete, *Leptospira canicola.* Cf. **canine leptospirosis, leptospirosis.** [1940–45; < NL, after the specific epithet of the spirochete, lit., dwelling in dogs, equiv. to L *cani(s)* dog + *-cola,* fem. of *-colus* -COLOUS]

ca•nic•u•lar (kə nik′yə lər), *adj. Astron.* pertaining to the rising of the Dog Star or to the star itself. [ME, late OE < LL *caniculāris* of Sirius, equiv. to L *Canicul(a)* Sirius (*cani(s)* dog + *-cula* -CULE[1]) + *-āris* -AR[1]]

can•id (kan′id, kā′nid), *n.* any animal of the dog family Canidae, including the wolves, jackals, hyenas, coyotes, foxes, and domestic dogs. [1885–90; < NL *Canidae,* equiv. to *Can(is)* a genus, including the dog and wolf (L: dog) + *-idae* -ID[2]]

can•i•kin (kan′i kin), *n.* cannikin.

ca•nine (kā′nīn), *adj.* **1.** of or like a dog; pertaining to or characteristic of dogs: *canine loyalty.* **2.** *Anat., Zool.* of or pertaining to the four pointed teeth, esp. prominent in dogs, situated one on each side of each jaw, next to the incisors. —*n.* **3.** a canid. **4.** a dog. **5.** a canine tooth; cuspid. See illus. under **tooth.** [1350–1400; ME *canine* canine tooth (< MF) < L *canīnus,* equiv. to *can(is)* dog + *-inus* -INE[1]] —**ca•nin•i•ty** (kā nin′i tē), *n.*

ca′nine distem′per, *Vet. Pathol.* distemper[1] (def. 1a).

ca′nine leptospiro′sis, *Vet. Pathol.* an often fatal intestinal disease in dogs, caused by any of several spirochetes of the genus *Leptospira.* Also called **ca′nine ty′phus, Stuttgart disease, Stuttgart's disease.** Cf. **canicola fever, leptospirosis.**

ca′nine tooth′, canine (def. 2). [1600–10]

can•ing (kā′ning), *n.* **1.** the act of providing chairs or the like with seats made of woven cane. **2.** woven cane for seats of chairs or the like. **3.** a beating with a cane. [1705–15; CANE + -ING[1]]

Ca•nis Ma•jor (kā′nis mā′jər), *gen.* **Ca•nis Ma•jo•ris** (kā′nis mə jôr′is, -jōr′-). *Astron.* the Great Dog, a southern constellation between Puppis and Orion, containing Sirius, the Dog Star, the brightest of the stars. [< L: larger dog]

Ca•nis Mi•nor (kā′nis mī′nər), *gen.* **Ca•nis Mi•no•ris** (kā′nis mi nôr′is, -nōr′-). *Astron.* the Little or Lesser Dog, a small southern constellation west of Orion and south of Gemini, containing the bright star Procyon. [< L: smaller dog]

can•is•ter (kan′ə stər), *n.* **1.** a small box or jar, often one of a kitchen set, for holding tea, coffee, flour, and sugar. **2.** Also called **can′ister shot′.** See **case shot. 3.** the part of a gas mask containing the neutralizing substances through which poisoned air is filtered. [1670–80; < L *canistrum* wicker basket < Gk *kánastron,* deriv. of *kánna* reed (see CANE), with *-astron,* var. of *-tron* suffix of instrument (prob. from v. derivs., as *stégastron* covering, from *stegázein* to cover)]

can•ker (kang′kər), *n.* **1.** a gangrenous or ulcerous sore, esp. in the mouth. **2.** a disease affecting horses' feet, usually the soles, characterized by a foul-smelling exudate. **3.** a defined area of diseased tissue, esp. in woody stems. **4.** something that corrodes, corrupts, destroys, or irritates. **5.** Also called **can′ker rose′.** *Brit. Dial.* See **dog rose.** —*v.t.* **6.** to infect with canker. **7.** to corrupt; destroy slowly. —*v.i.* **8.** to become infected with or as if with canker. [bef. 1000; ME; OE *cancer* < L *cancer;* see CANCER]
—**Syn. 4.** blight, cancer, scourge.

can•kered (kang′kərd), *adj.* **1.** morally corrupt. **2.** bad-tempered. **3.** (of plants) **a.** destroyed or having portions destroyed by the feeding of a cankerworm. **b.** having a cankerous part; infected with a canker. **4.** ulcerated. [1375–1425; late ME; see CANKER, -ED[3]] —**can′kered•ly,** *adv.* —**can′kered•ness,** *n.*

can•ker•ous (kang′kər əs), *adj.* **1.** resembling canker. **2.** causing canker. [1535–45; CANKER + -OUS]

can′ker sore′, *Pathol.* an ulceration of a mucous membrane, esp. of the mouth. [1905–10]

can•ker•worm (kang′kər wûrm′), *n.* the striped, green caterpillar of any of several geometrid moths: a foliage pest of various fruit and shade trees, as *Paleacrita vernata* **(spring cankerworm)** and *Alsophila pometaria* **(fall cankerworm).** See illus. under **geometrid.** [1520–30; CANKER + WORM]

Can•lit (kan′lit′), *n. Canadian Informal.* literature, usually in English, written by Canadians or written in or about Canada. [*Can(adian) lit(erature)*]

can•na (kan′ə), *n.* any of various tropical plants of the genus *Canna,* cultivated for their large, usually brightly colored leaves and showy flowers. [1655–65; < NL, L: reed; see CANE]

can•na•bin (kan′ə bin), *n.* a biologically active resin extracted from Indian hemp. [< L *cannab(is)* HEMP + -IN[2]]

can•nab•i•noid (kə nab′ə noid′, kan′ə bə-), *n.* any of the chemical compounds that are the active principles of marijuana. [1965–70; CANNABIN + -OID]

can•nab•i•nol (kə nab′ə nôl′, -nol′, kan′ə bə-), *n.* the parent compound of tetrahydrocannabinol, the active principle of marijuana. [1895–1900; CANNABIN + -OL]

can•na•bis (kan′ə bis), *n.* **1.** the hemp plant, *Cannabis sativa.* **2.** the flowering tops of the plant. **3.** any of the various parts of the plant from which hashish, marijuana, bhang, and similar mildly euphorogenic and hallucinogenic drugs are prepared. [1790–1800; < NL, L: hemp < Gk *kánnabis;* c. HEMP] —**can′na•bic,** *adj.*

Can•nae (kan′ē), *n.* an ancient town in SE Italy: Hannibal defeated the Romans here 216 B.C.

Can•na•nore (kan′ə nôr′, -nōr′), *n.* a port in N Kerala, in SW India, on the Arabian Sea. 55,111. Also, **Kananur.**

canned (kand), *adj.* **1.** preserved in a can or jar: *canned peaches.* **2.** *Informal.* recorded: *canned music.* **3.** *Informal.* prepared in advance: *a canned speech.* **4.** *Slang.* drunk. [1855–60; CAN[2] + -ED[2]]

canned′ heat′, fuel packaged to be used in small cans for heating, as with chafing dishes or in portable stoves. [1915–20, *Amer.*]

can′nel coal′ (kan′l), an oily, compact coal, burning readily and brightly. Also called **can′nel.** [1530–40; *cannel* from CANDLE (dial. form)]

can•nel•lo•ni (kan′l ō′nē; *It.* kän′nel lô′nē), *n. pl.* tubular or rolled pieces of pasta, usually filled with a mixture of meat or poultry and often cheese and baked in a cream or tomato sauce. Also, **can•ne•lons** (kan′l onz′). [1835–45; < It, pl. of *cannellone,* equiv. to *cannell(o)* tube (deriv. of *canna;* see CANE) + *-one* aug. suffix]

can•ner (kan′ər), *n.* **1.** a person who cans meat, fruit, etc., for preservation. **2.** an animal yielding meat of poor quality, suitable only for canning. [1865–70, *Amer.;* CAN[2] + -ER[1]]

can•ner•y (kan′ə rē), *n., pl.* **-ner•ies.** a factory where foodstuffs, as meat, fish, or fruit are canned. [1865–70, *Amer.;* CAN[2] + -ERY]

Cannes (kan, kanz; *Fr.* kaɴ), *n.* a city in SE France, on the Mediterranean Sea: resort; annual film festival. 71,080.

can•ne•tille (kan′i tēl′; *Fr.* kaɴ tē′yᵊ), *n.* a gold or silver thread with a spiral twist, formerly much used in embroidery. [< Sp *cañatillo,* dim of *cañuto* pipe, tube (< Mozarabic) < VL **cannūtus,* equiv. to L *cann(a)* CANE + VL *-*ūtus* for L *-ātus* -ATE[1]]

can•ni•bal (kan′ə bəl), *n.* **1.** a person who eats human flesh, esp. for magical or religious purposes, as among certain tribal peoples. **2.** any animal that eats its own kind. —*adj.* **3.** pertaining to or characteristic of a cannibal. **4.** given to cannibalism. [1545–55; < Sp *caníbal,* var. of *caríbal,* equiv. to *canib-, carib-* (< Arawak) + *-al* -AL[1]; from the belief that the Caribs of the West Indies ate human flesh] —**can′ni•bal•ly,** *adv.*

can•ni•bal•ism (kan′ə bə liz′əm), *n.* **1.** the eating of human flesh by another human being. **2.** the eating of the flesh of an animal by another animal of its own kind. **3.** the ceremonial eating of human flesh or parts of the human body for magical or religious purposes, as to acquire the power or skill of a person recently killed. **4.** the act of pecking flesh from a live fowl by a member of the same flock. **5.** the removal of parts, equipment, assets, or employees from one product, item, or business in order to use them in another. **6.** the acquisition and absorption of smaller companies by a large corporation or conglomerate. [1790–1800; CANNIBAL + -ISM] —**can′ni•bal•is′tic,** *adj.* —**can′ni•bal•is′ti•cal•ly,** *adv.*

can•ni•bal•ize (kan′ə bə līz′), *v.,* **-ized, -iz•ing.** —*v.t.* **1.** to subject to cannibalism. **2.** to remove parts, equipment, assets, employees, etc., from (an item, product, or business) in order to use them in another: *to cannibalize old airplanes for replacement parts.* **3.** to cut into; cause to become reduced; diminish: *New products introduced in the next six months will cannibalize sales from established lines.* —*v.i.* **4.** to act cannibalistically; practice cannibalism. Also, *esp. Brit.,* **can′ni•bal•ise′.** [1940–45; CANNIBAL + -IZE] —**can′ni•bal•i•za′tion,** *n.*

can•ni•kin (kan′i kin), *n.* **1.** a small can or drinking cup. **2.** a small wooden bucket. Also, **canikin.** [1560–70; < MD *cannekijn* little can, equiv. to *canne* CAN[2] + *-kijn* -KIN]

can•ning (kan′ing), *n.* the act, process, or business of preserving cooked food by sealing in cans or jars. [1870–75, *Amer.;* CAN[2] + -ING[1]]

Can•ning (kan′ing), *n.* **1. Charles John, 1st Earl,** 1812–62, British statesman: governor general of India 1856–62. **2.** his father, **George,** 1770–1827, British statesman: prime minister 1827. **3. Sir Stratford.** See **Stratford de Redcliffe, 1st Viscount.**

Can•niz•za•ro (kan′ə zär′ō; *It.* kän′nēd dzär′rô), *n.* **Sta•nis•la•o** (stä′nēz lä′ô), 1826–1910, Italian chemist.

can•no•li (kə nō′lē; *It.* kän nô′lē), *n.pl. Italian Cookery.* tubular pastry shells stuffed with a sweetened filling of whipped ricotta and often containing nuts, citron, or bits of chocolate. [1940–45; < It, pl. of *cannolo,* deriv. of *canna* reed, CANE; cf. CANNELLONI]

can·non (kan′ən), *n., pl.* **-nons,** (*esp. collectively*) **-non,** *v.* **—n. 1.** a mounted gun for firing heavy projectiles; a gun, howitzer, or mortar. **2.** *Brit. Mach.* quill (def. 10). **3.** *Armor.* a cylindrical or semicylindrical piece of plate armor for the upper arm or forearm; a vambrace or rerebrace. **4.** Also called **cannon bit, canon bit.** a round bit for a horse. **5.** the part of a bit that is in the horse's mouth. **6.** (on a bell) the metal loop by which a bell is hung. **7.** *Zool.* **a.** See **cannon bone. b.** the part of the leg in which the cannon bone is situated. See diag. under **horse. 8.** *Brit.* a carom in billiards. **9.** *Underworld Slang.* a pickpocket. **—v.i. 10.** to discharge cannon. **11.** *Brit.* to make a carom in billiards. [1375–1425 (earlier in AL, AF); late ME *canon* < MF < It *cannone,* equiv. to *cann(a)* tube (< L; see CANE) + *-one* aug. suffix]

Can·non (kan′ən), *n.* **1. Annie Jump** (jump), 1863–1941, U.S. astronomer. **2. Joseph Gur·ney** (gûr′nē), ("*Uncle Joe*"), 1836–1926, U.S. politician and legislator.

can·non·ade (kan′ə nād′), *n., v.,* **-ad·ed, -ad·ing. —n. 1.** a continued discharge of cannon, esp. during an attack. **2.** an attack, as of invective or censure, suggestive of cannon fire; barrage. **—v.t. 3.** to attack continuously with or as if with cannon **—v.i. 4.** to discharge like continuous cannon fire. [1645–55; < F *canonnade* < It *cannonata,* equiv. to *cannon(e)* CANNON + *-ata* -ADE[1]]

can·non·ball (kan′ən bôl′), *n.* Also, **can′non ball′. 1.** a missile, usually round and made of iron or steel, designed to be fired from a cannon. **2.** *Tennis.* a served ball that travels with great speed and describes little or no arc in flight. **3.** anything that moves with great speed, as an express train. **—adj. 4.** made from a curled-up position with the arms pressing the knees against one's chest: *a cannonball dive.* **5.** moving at great speed: *a train known as a cannonball express.* [1655–65; CANNON + BALL[1]]

can′non bone′, *Zool.* the greatly developed middle metacarpal or metatarsal bone of hoofed quadruped mammals, extending from the hock to the fetlock. [1825–35; CANNON in obs. sense "tube"]

can·non·eer (kan′ə nēr′), *n.* an artilleryman. [1555–65; < MF *canonnier.* See CANNON, -EER] **—can′non·eer′ing,** *n.*

can′non fod′der, soldiers, esp. infantrymen, who run the greatest risk of being wounded or killed in warfare. [1890–95]

can·non·ry (kan′ən rē), *n., pl.* **-ries. 1.** a discharge of artillery. **2.** artillery (def. 1). [1830–40; CANNON + -RY]

can·not (kan′ot, ka not′, kə-), *v.* **1.** a form of *can not.* **2. cannot but,** have no alternative but to: *We cannot but choose otherwise.* [1350–1400; ME]
—Usage. CANNOT is sometimes also spelled CAN NOT. The one-word spelling is by far the more common: *Interest rates simply cannot continue at their present level.* The contraction CAN'T is most common in speech and informal writing. See also **can**[1].

can·nu·la (kan′yə lə), *n., pl.* **-las, -lae** (-lē′). *Surg.* a metal tube for insertion into the body to draw off fluid or to introduce medication. Also, **canula.** [1675–85; < NL, L: small reed, equiv. to *cann(a)* CANE + *-ula* -ULE] **—can′nu·la′tion,** *n.*

can·nu·lar (kan′yə lər), *adj.* shaped like a cannula; tubular. Also, **can·nu·late** (kan′yə lāt′, -lit), **canular, canulate.** [1815–25; CANNUL(A) + -AR[1]]

can·ny (kan′ē), *adj.,* **-ni·er, -ni·est,** *adv.* **—adj. 1.** careful; cautious; prudent: *a canny reply.* **2.** astute; shrewd; knowing; sagacious: *a canny negotiator.* **3.** skilled; expert. **4.** frugal; thrifty: *a canny housewife.* **5.** *Scot.* **a.** safe to deal with, invest in, or work at (usually used with a negative). **b.** gentle; careful; steady. **c.** snug; cozy; comfortable. **d.** pleasing; attractive. **e.** *Archaic.* having supernatural or occult powers. **—adv.** Also, **can′ni·ly. 6.** in a canny manner. **7.** *Scot.* carefully; cautiously. [1630–40; CAN[1] + -Y[1]] **—can′ni·ness,** *n.*

Ca·no·as (kə nō′əs; *Port.* kä nô′äs), *n.* a city in SE Brazil, N of Pôrto Alegre. 148,798.

ca·noe (kə no͞o′), *n., v.,* **-noed, -noe·ing. —n. 1.** any of various slender, open boats, tapering to a point at both ends, propelled by paddles or sometimes sails and traditionally formed of light framework covered with bark, skins, or canvas, or formed from a dug-out or burned-out log or logs, and now usually made of aluminum, fiberglass, etc. **2.** any of various small, primitive light boats. **3. paddle one's own canoe,** *Informal.* **a.** to handle one's own affairs; manage independently. **b.** to mind one's own business. **—v.i. 4.** to paddle a canoe. **5.** to go in a canoe. **—v.t. 6.** to transport or carry by canoe. [1545–55; < F < Sp *canoa* < Arawak; r. *canoa* < Sp] **—ca·noe′ist,** *n.*

canoe (def. 1)

canoe′ birch′. See **paper birch.** [1800–10, *Amer.*]

canoe′ sla′lom, a competitive event in which a canoeist maneuvers through a slalom course, usually in white water. [1970–75]

CONCISE ETYMOLOGY KEY: <, descended or borrowed from; >, whence; b., blend of, blended; c., cognate with; cf., compare; deriv., derivative; equiv., equivalent; imit., imitative; obl., oblique; r., replacing; s., stem; sp., spelling, spelled; resp., respelling, respelled; trans., translation; ?, origin unknown; *, unattested; ‡, probably earlier than. See the full key inside the front cover.

can′ of worms′, *Informal.* a source of many unpredictable or unexpected problems: *Buying a company we know nothing about would be opening up a whole new can of worms.* [1965–70]

can·o·la (kan′l ə), *n.* a variety of rapeseed that contains reduced levels of erucic acid, making its oil palatable for human consumption, and reduced levels of a toxic glucosin, making its meal desirable as a livestock feed. [of unexplained orig.]

can·on[1] (kan′ən), *n.* **1.** an ecclesiastical rule or law enacted by a council or other competent authority and, in the Roman Catholic Church, approved by the pope. **2.** the body of ecclesiastical law. **3.** the body of rules, principles, or standards accepted as axiomatic and universally binding in a field of study or art: *the neoclassical canon.* **4.** a fundamental principle or general rule: *the canons of good behavior.* **5.** a standard; criterion: *the canons of taste.* **6.** the books of the Bible recognized by any Christian church as genuine and inspired. **7.** any officially recognized set of sacred books. **8.** any comprehensive list of books within a field. **9.** the works of an author that have been accepted as authentic: *There are 37 plays in the Shakespeare canon.* Cf. **apocrypha** (def. 3). **10.** a catalog or list, as of the saints acknowledged by the Church. **11.** *Liturgy.* the part of the Mass between the Sanctus and the Communion. **12.** *Eastern Ch.* a liturgical sequence sung at matins, usually consisting of nine odes arranged in a fixed pattern. **13.** *Music.* consistent, note-for-note imitation of one melodic line by another, in which the second line starts after the first. **14.** *Print.* a 48-point type. [bef. 900; ME, OE < L < Gk *kanṓn* measuring rod, rule, akin to *kánna* CANE] **—can′on·like′,** *adj.*
—Syn. 3, 4, 5. See **principle.**

can·on[2] (kan′ən), *n.* **1.** one of a body of dignitaries or prebendaries attached to a cathedral or a collegiate church; a member of the chapter of a cathedral or a collegiate church. **2.** *Rom. Cath. Ch.* one of the members (**canons regular**) of certain religious orders. [1150–1200; ME; back formation from OE *canōnic* (one) under rule < ML *canōnicus,* L: of or under rule < Gk *kanonikós.* See CANON[1], -IC]

ca·ñon (kan′yən), *n.* canyon.

Ca·non·chet (kə non′chet, -chit), *n.* (*Nanuntenoo*), died 1676, Narragansett leader: executed by colonists.

Can′on Cit′y (kan′yən), a town in central Colorado. 13,037.

can·on·ess (kan′ə nis), *n.* a member of a Christian community of women living under a rule but not under a vow. [1675–85; CANON[2] + -ESS]
—Usage. See **-ess.**

ca·non·i·cal (kə non′i kəl), *adj.* Also, **ca·non′ic. 1.** pertaining to, established by, or conforming to a canon or canons. **2.** included in the canon of the Bible. **3.** authorized; recognized; accepted: *canonical works.* **4.** *Math.* (of an equation, coordinate, etc.) in simplest or standard form. **5.** following the pattern of a musical canon. **6.** *Ling.* (of a form or pattern) characteristic, general or basic: *the canonical form of the past tense; a canonical syllable pattern.* **—n. 7. canonicals,** garments prescribed by canon law for clergy when officiating. [1150–1200; ME (< AF) < ML *canōnicālis,* equiv. to *canōnic(us)* (see CANON[2]) + *-ālis* -AL[1]] **—ca·non′i·cal·ly,** *adv.*

canon′ical age′, *Eccles.* the age specified by canon law when a person becomes eligible to participate in a certain rite or hold a certain office.

canon′ical hour′, *Eccles.* any of certain periods of the day set apart for prayer and devotion: these are matins and lauds, prime, tierce, sext, nones, vespers, and compline. [1400–50; late ME]

can·on·ic·i·ty (kan′ə nis′i tē), *n.* the quality of being canonical. [1790–1800; < L *canōnic(us)* according to rule (see CANON[2]) + -ITY]

Ca·non·i·cus (kə non′i kəs), *n.* c1565–1647, Narragansett leader: yielded Rhode Island to Roger Williams 1636.

can·on·ist (kan′ə nist), *n.* a person who is a specialist in canon law. [1350–1400; ME. See CANON[1], -IST] **—can′on·is′tic, can′on·is′ti·cal,** *adj.*

can·on·ize (kan′ə nīz′), *v.t.,* **-ized, -iz·ing. 1.** *Eccles.* to place in the canon of saints. **2.** to glorify. **3.** to make canonical; place or include within a canon, esp. of scriptural works: *They canonized the Song of Solomon after much controversy.* **4.** to consider or treat as sacrosanct or holy: *They canonized his many verbal foibles and made them gospel.* **5.** to sanction or approve authoritatively, esp. ecclesiastically. **6.** *Archaic.* to deify. Also, *esp. Brit.,* **can′on·ise′.** [1350–1400; ME. See CANON[1], -IZE] **—can′on·i·za′tion,** *n.* **—can′on·iz′er,** *n.*

can′on law′, the body of codified ecclesiastical law, esp. of the Roman Catholic Church as promulgated in ecclesiastical councils and by the pope. [1300–50; ME] **—can′on law′yer.**

can·on·ry (kan′ən rē), *n., pl.* **-ries.** the office or benefice of a canon. [1475–85; CANON[2] + -RY]

Can·ons·burg (kan′ənz bûrg′), *n.* a city in SW Pennsylvania. 10,459.

can·on·ship (kan′ən ship′), *n.* the position or office of canon; canonry. [1525–35; CANON[2] + -SHIP]

can′ons reg′ular. See under **canon**[2] (def. 2). [1350–1400; ME]

ca·noo·dle (kə no͞od′l), *v.t., v.i.,* **-dled, -dling.** *Slang.* caress, fondle, or pet amorously. [1855–60; perh. CA(RESS) + NOODLE[2]] **—ca·noo′dler,** *n.*

can′ o′pener, a manual device or small electric appliance for opening cans. [1865–70]

Ca·no·pic (kə nō′pik, -nop′ik), *adj.* pertaining to Canopus. [1875–80; < L *Canōpicus* of CANOPUS; see -IC]

cano′pic jar′, a jar used in ancient Egypt to contain the entrails of an embalmed body. Also, **Cano′pic jar′.** Also called **cano′pic vase′.** [1890–95]

Ca·no·pus (kə nō′pəs), *n.* **1.** *Astron.* a first-magnitude star in the constellation Carina: the second brightest star in the heavens. **2.** an ancient seacoast city in Lower Egypt, 15 mi. (24 km) E of Alexandria.

can·o·py (kan′ə pē), *n., pl.* **-pies,** *v.,* **-pied, -py·ing. —n. 1.** a covering, usually of fabric, supported on poles or suspended above a bed, throne, exalted personage, or sacred object. **2.** an overhanging projection or covering, as a long canvas awning stretching from the doorway of a building to a curb. **3.** an ornamental, rooflike projection or covering. **4.** Also called **crown canopy, crown cover.** the cover formed by the leafy upper branches of the trees in a forest. **5.** the sky. **6.** the part of a parachute that opens up and fills with air, usually made of nylon or silk. **7.** the transparent cover over the cockpit of an airplane. **—v.t. 8.** to cover with or as with a canopy: *Branches canopied the road.* [1350–1400; ME *canope* < ML *canōpēum,* var. of L *cōnōpēum* mosquito net < Gk *kōnōpeîon* bed with net to keep gnats off, equiv. to *kōnōp(s)* gnat + *-eion,* neut. of *-eios* adj. suffix]

ca·no·rous (kə nôr′əs, -nōr′-), *adj.* melodious; musical. [1640–50; < L *canōrus,* equiv. to *canōr-* (s. of *canor* song, equiv. to *can(ere)* to sing + *-or* -OR[1]) + *-us* -OUS] **—ca·no′rous·ly,** *adv.* **—ca·no′rous·ness,** *n.*

Ca·nos·sa (kə nos′ə; *It.* kä nôs′sä), *n.* **1.** a ruined castle in N Italy: scene of the penance of Emperor Henry IV of the Holy Roman Empire before Pope Gregory VII in 1077. **2. go to Canossa,** to humble oneself.

ca·no·tier (kan′ə tyā′), *n.* a fabric constructed in a twill weave, used in the manufacture of yachting clothes. [< F: boatman, equiv. to *canot* open boat (earlier *canoe* < Sp *canoa* CANOE, conformed to the F suffix *-ot*) + *-ier* -IER[2]]

Ca·no·va (kə nō′və; *It.* kä nô′vä), *n.* **An·to·nio** (än tô′nyô), 1757–1822, Italian sculptor.

Can·ro·bert (kän rô bεr′), *n.* **Fran·çois Cer·tain** (fräN swa′ sεr taN′), 1809–95, French marshal.

Can·so (kan′sō), *n.* **1. Cape,** a cape in SE Canada, the NE extremity of Nova Scotia. **2. Strait of,** Also called **Gut of Canso.** a channel in SE Canada that separates mainland Nova Scotia from Cape Breton Island, flowing NW from the Atlantic Ocean to Northumberland Strait. ab. 17 mi. (27 km) long and 1 mi. (1.6 km) wide.

canst (kanst), *v. Archaic.* 2nd pers. sing. pres. of **can.**

cant[1] (kant), *n.* **1.** insincere, esp. conventional expressions of enthusiasm for high ideals, goodness, or piety. **2.** the private language of the underworld. **3.** the phraseology peculiar to a particular class, party, profession, etc.: *the cant of the fashion industry.* **4.** whining or singsong speech, esp. of beggars. **—v.i. 5.** to talk hypocritically. **6.** to speak in the whining or singsong tone of a beggar; beg. [1495–1505; < L base *cant-* in *cantus* song, *canticus* singsong, etc., whence OE *cantere* singer, *cantic* song; see CHANT] **—cant′ing·ly,** *adv.*
—Syn. 1. hypocrisy, sham, pretense, humbug.

cant[2] (kant), *n.* **1.** a salient angle. **2.** a sudden movement that tilts or overturns a thing. **3.** a slanting or tilted position. **4.** an oblique line or surface, as one formed by cutting off the corner of a square of cube. **5.** an oblique or slanting face of anything. **6.** *Civ. Engin.* bank[1] (def. 6). **7.** a sudden pitch or toss. **8.** Also called **flitch.** a partly trimmed log. **—adj. 9.** oblique or slanting. **—v.t. 10.** to bevel; form an oblique surface upon. **11.** to put in an oblique position; tilt; tip. **12.** to throw with a sudden jerk. **—v.i. 13.** to take or have an inclined position; tilt; turn. [1325–75; ME: side, border < AF *cant,* OF *chant* < a Rom base **cantu(m)* with the related senses "rim, border" and "angle corner," prob. < Celtic; cf. L *cant(h)us* iron tire (< Celtic), Welsh *cant* periphery, rim, felloe; prob. not akin to Gk *kanthós* corner of the eye; cf. CANTEEN, CANTLE, CANTON] **—cant′ic,** *adj.*

cant[3] (känt), *adj. Scot. and North Eng.* hearty; merry. [1250–1300; ME < LG *kant* merry, bold]

can't (kant, känt), contraction of *cannot.*
—Usage. See **can**[1]**, cannot, contraction.**

Cant., **1.** Canterbury. **2.** Cantonese.

Cantab., Cantabrigian.

can·ta·bi·le (kän tä′bi lā′, -bē-, kən-; *It.* kän tä′bē-le′), *Music.* **—adj. 1.** songlike and flowing in style. **—adv. 2.** in a cantabile manner. [1720–30; < It < LL *cantābilis* worth singing, equiv. to L *cantā(re)* to sing (see CANT[1]) + *-bilis* -BLE]

Can·ta·brig·i·an (kan′tə brij′ē ən), *adj.* **1.** of Cambridge, England, or Cambridge University. **2.** of Cambridge, Mass., or Harvard University. **—n. 3.** a native or inhabitant of Cambridge, England or Cambridge, Mass. **4.** a student at or graduate of Cambridge University or Harvard University. [1610–20; < ML *Cantabrigi(a)* Cambridge + -AN]

Can·tal (käN tal′), *n.* a department in S central France. 166,549. 2231 sq. mi. (5780 sq. km). *Cap.:* Aurillac.

can·ta·la (kan tä′lə), *n.* **1.** a cordage fiber obtained from the leaves of a tropical plant, *Agave cantala.* **2.** the plant itself. Also called **maguey.** [1910–15; < NL, the species name (orig. *cantula*), appar. < Skt *kaṇṭala* a mimosa genus]

can·ta·le·ver (kan′tl ē′vər, -ev′ər), *n., v.i., v.t.* cantilever. Also, **can·ta·li·ver** (kan′tl ē′vər).

can·ta·loupe (kan′tl ōp′), *n.* **1.** a variety of melon, *Cucumis melo cantalupensis,* of the gourd family, having a hard scaly or warty rind, grown in Europe, Asia, and the United States. **2.** a muskmelon having a reticulated rind and pale-orange flesh. Also, **can′ta·loup′.** [1730–40; < F, allegedly after *Cantaluppi,* a papal estate near Rome where cultivation of this melon is said to have begun in Europe, though a comparable It word is not attested until much later than the F word, and *Cantaloup,* a village in Languedoc, has also been proposed as the source]

can·tan·ker·ous (kan tang′kər əs), *adj.* disagreeable to deal with; contentious; peevish: *a cantankerous, argumentative man.* [1765–75; perh. var. of earlier **conten-*

kerous, reflecting CONTENTIOUS, RANCOROUS] **—can·tan′ker·ous·ly,** *adv.* **—can·tan′ker·ous·ness,** *n.*

can·tar (kan tär′), *n. Pros.* a poem consisting of four-line stanzas, each line having eight syllables. [< Sp: song, poem (n. use of v. inf.) < L *cantāre* to sing]

can·ta·ta (kən tä′tə), *n.* **1.** a choral composition, either sacred and resembling a short oratorio or secular, as a lyric drama set to music but not to be acted. **2.** a metrical narrative set to recitative or alternate recitative and air, usually for a single voice accompanied by one or more instruments. [1715–25; < It, equiv. to *cant(are)* to sing (see CANT[1]) + *-ata* -ATE[1]]

can·ta·tri·ce (kan′tə trē′chā, -trēs′; *It.* kän′tä trē′-che; *Fr.* käN tA trēs′), *n., pl.* **-tri·ces** (-trē′chāz, -trē′-səz; *Fr.* -trēs′), **-tri·ci** (-trē′chē; *It.* -trē′chē). a professional female singer esp. of opera. [(< F) < It < LL *cantātric-,* s. of *cantātrix* female singer; see CANTOR, -TRIX]

cant′ dog′ (kant). See **cant hook.**

can·teen (kan tēn′), *n.* **1.** a small container used esp. by soldiers and hikers for carrying water or other liquids. **2.** a general store and cafeteria at a military base. **3.** a place where free entertainment is provided for military personnel. **4.** a place, as in a factory, school, or summer camp, where refreshments and sometimes personal supplies are sold. **5.** a recreation center or social club, esp. for teenagers. **6.** a place set up to dispense food during an emergency. **7.** a snack bar. **8.** *Brit.* a box or chest for cutlery and other table utensils. [1730–40; < F *cantine* < It *cantina* cellar, perh. deriv. of *canto* corner (see CANT[2]) with *-ina* -INE[1]]

can·ter[1] (kan′tər), *n.* **1.** an easy gallop. *—v.t., v.i.* **2.** to move or ride at a canter. [1745–55; short for *Canterbury* to ride at a pace like that of Canterbury pilgrims]

cant·er[2] (kan′tər), *n.* a person who is much given to the use of cant. [1870–75; CANT[1] + -ER[1]]

can·ter·bur·y (kan′tər ber′ē, -bə rē), *n., pl.* **-buries.** **1.** a stand having sections for holding magazines, sheet music, or loose papers. **2.** a supper tray with partitions for cutlery and plates. [1840–50; after CANTERBURY, England]

Can·ter·bur·y (kan′tər ber′ē, -bə rē *or, esp. Brit.,* -brē), *n.* **1.** a city in E Kent, in SE England: cathedral; early ecclesiastical center of England. 115,600. **2.** a municipality in E New South Wales, in SE Australia: a part of Sydney. 115,100. **—Can·ter·bu·ri·an** (kan′tər-byŏŏr′ē ən), *adj.*

Can′terbury bells′, *(used with a singular or plural v.)* a plant, *Campanula medium,* cultivated for its showy, bell-shaped violet-blue, pink, or white flowers in loose clusters. [1570–80]

Can′terbury Tales′, The, an uncompleted sequence of tales by Chaucer, written for the most part after 1387.

cant′ frame′, **1.** any of several frames bracketed aft of the transom of a ship and inclined slightly to the fore-and-aft direction. **2.** any transverse frame not perpendicular to the fore-and-aft midship line. [1825–35]

can·thar·i·des (kan thar′i dēz′), *n.pl., sing.* **can·thar·is** (kan thar′is). **1.** See **Spanish fly** (def. 1). **2.** **cantharis.** See **Spanish fly** (def. 2). [1350–1400; ME < L, pl. of *cantharis* < Gk *kantharís* blister fly]

can·tha·rus (kan′thər əs), *n., pl.* **-tha·ri** (-thə rī′). kantharos. [< L < Gk *kántharos*]

Can-Tho (kun′tō′), *n.* a town in S Vietnam, on the Mekong River. 182,424.

cant hook

cant′ hook′ (kant), a wooden lever with a movable iron hook and a blunt, often toothed tip near the lower end, used chiefly for grasping and canting, or turning over logs. Also called **cant dog.** [1840–50]

can·thus (kan′thəs), *n., pl.* **-thi** (-thī). *Anat.* the angle or corner on each side of the eye, formed by the junction of the upper and lower lids. [1640–50; < NL, L < Gk *kanthós;* cf. CANT[2]] **—can′thal,** *adj.*

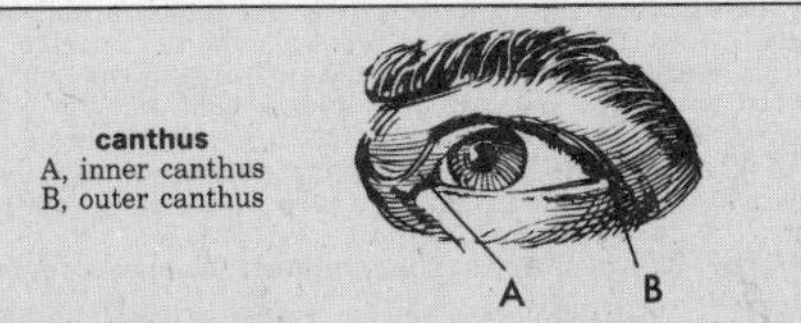

canthus
A, inner canthus
B, outer canthus

can·ti·cle (kan′ti kəl), *n.* **1.** one of the nonmetrical hymns or chants, chiefly from the Bible, used in church services. **2.** a song, poem, or hymn esp. of praise. [1175–1225; ME (< OF) < L *canticulum,* equiv. to *cantic(um)* song (see CANTICUM) + *-ulum* -ULE]

Can′ticle of Can′ticles, *Douay Bible.* See **Song of Solomon, The.**

can·ti·cum (kan′ti kəm), *n., pl.* **-ti·ca** (-ti kə). part of an ancient Roman drama chanted or sung and accompanied by music. Cf. **diverbium.** [< L, equiv. to *cant(us)* song (see CANTO, CHANT) + *-icum* n. suffix; cf. -IC]

Can·ti·gny (käN tē nyē′), *n.* a village in N France, S of Amiens: first major battle of U.S. forces in World War I, May 1918.

can·ti·le·na (kan′tl ē′nə), *n.* a simple, lyric, melodic passage for voice or instrument. [1730–40; < It < L *cantilēna* refrain, perh. by dissimilation from **cantilēla,* deriv. of *cantus* song; see CANT[1]]

can·ti·le·ver (kan′tl ē′vər, -ev′ər), *n.* **1.** any rigid structural member projecting from a vertical support, esp. one in which the projection is great in relation to the depth, so that the upper part is in tension and the lower part in compression. **2.** *Building Trades, Civ. Engin.* any rigid construction extending horizontally well beyond its vertical support, used as a structural element of a bridge (**can′tilever bridge′**), building foundation, etc. **3.** *Aeron.* a form of wing construction in which no external bracing is used. **4.** *Archit.* a bracket for supporting a balcony, cornice, etc. *—v.i.* **5.** to project in the manner of a cantilever. *—v.t.* **6.** to construct in the manner of a cantilever. Also, **cantalever, cantaliver.** [1660–70; perh. CANT[2] + -I- + LEVER]

can′tilever founda′tion, a building foundation supporting its load partly or wholly upon cantilevers.

can·til·late (kan′tl āt′), *v.t.,* **-lat·ed, -lat·ing.** to chant; intone. [1860–65; < LL *cantillātus* sung low, hummed (ptp. of *cantillāre*), equiv. to *cant-* sing (see CANT[1]) + *-ill-* dim. suffix + *-ātus* -ATE[1]] **—can′til·la′·tion,** *n.*

Can·til·lon (käN tē yôN′), *n.* **Ri·chard** (rē shAR′; *Eng.* rich′ərd), c1680–1734, French economist, born in Ireland.

can·ti·na (kan tē′nə; *Sp.* kän tē′nä), *n., pl.* **-nas** (-nəz; *Sp.* -näs). *Southwestern U.S.* a saloon; bar. [1835–45, *Amer.;* < Sp < It; see CANTEEN]

cant·ing (kan′ting), *adj.* affectedly or hypocritically pious or righteous: *a canting social reformer.* [1560–70; CANT[1] + -ING[2]]

can·tle (kan′tl), *n.* **1.** the hind part of a saddle, usually curved upward. See illus. under **saddle. 2.** a corner; piece; portion: *a cantle of land.* [1275–1325; ME *cantel* (< AF) < ML *cantellus,* equiv. to L *cant(us)* (see CANT[2]) + *-ellus* dim. suffix]

can·tling (kant′ling), *n.* a layer of burnt brick lying directly over a clamp of bricks being fired. [1610–20; CANTLE + -ING[1]]

can·to (kan′tō), *n., pl.* **-tos.** one of the main or larger divisions of a long poem. [1580–90; < It < L *cant(us)* singing, song, equiv. to *can(ere)* to sing + *-tus* suffix of v. action; cf. CANT[1], CHANT]

can·ton (kan′tn, -ton, kan ton′ *for 1–7;* kan ton′, -tōn′ or, *esp. Brit.,* -tōōn′ *for 8*), *n.* **1.** a small territorial district, esp. one of the states of the Swiss confederation. **2.** (in a department of France) a division of an arrondissement. **3.** *Heraldry.* a square area in the dexter chief, or right-hand corner, of an escutcheon, often distinctively treated: a diminutive of the dexter chief quarter. **4.** *Archit.* a pilaster or similar feature projecting from the corner of a building. **5.** *Obs.* a division, part, or portion of anything. *—v.t.* **6.** to divide into parts or portions. **7.** to divide into cantons or territorial districts. **8.** to allot quarters to (soldiers, troops, etc.). [1525–35; < MF < OPr, deriv. of *can* side, edge (see CANT[2])] **—can′·ton·al,** *adj.* **—can′ton·al·ism,** *n.*

Can·ton (kan ton′, kan′ton *for 1;* kan′tn *for 2–5*), *n.* **1.** Also called **Kwangchow, Guangzhou, Kuangchou.** *Older Spelling.* a seaport in and the capital of Guangdong province, in SE China, on the Zhu Jiang. 3,000,000. **2.** a city in NE Ohio: location of the football Hall of Fame. 94,730. **3.** a city in E Massachusetts. 18,182. **4.** a city in W central Illinois. 14,626. **5.** a town in central Mississippi. 11,116.

Can′ton crepe′, a thin, light, silk or rayon crepe with a finely wrinkled surface, heavier in texture than crepe de Chine. [1860–65; named after CANTON, China]

Can′ton enam′el, Chinese enamelware similar to Limoges. [1905–10; after CANTON, China]

Can·ton·ese (kan′tn ēz′, -ēs′), *n., pl.* **-ese,** *adj. —n.* **1.** a Chinese language spoken in Canton, the surrounding area of southern China, and Hong Kong. **2.** a native or inhabitant of Canton, China. *—adj.* **3.** pertaining to Canton, China, its inhabitants, or their language. [1855–60; CANTON + -ESE]

Can′ton flan′nel, a plain-weave or twill-weave cotton fabric with a long, fleecy nap usually on one side only, used for sportswear, undergarments, backings and linings, etc. [1880–85; after CANTON, China]

can′ton gin′ger, preserved or crystallized ginger of fine quality. [after CANTON, China]

can·ton·ize (kan′tn īz′, -tə nīz′, kan ton′īz), *v.t.,* **-ized, -iz·ing.** canton (def. 7). Also, *esp. Brit.,* **can′ton·ise′.** [1595–1605; CANTON + -IZE] **—can′ton·i·za′tion,** *n.*

Can′ton lin′en. See **grass cloth.**

can·ton·ment (kan ton′mənt, -tōn′-; *esp. Brit.* kan-tōōn′mənt), *n.* **1.** a camp, usually of large size, where men are trained for military service. **2.** military quarters. **3.** the winter quarters of an army. [1750–60; < F *cantonnement,* equiv. to *cantonne(r)* to quarter troops (see CANTON) + *-ment* -MENT]

Can·ton′ Riv′er (kan ton′). See **Zhu Jiang.**

can·tor (kan′tər, -tôr), *n.* **1.** the religious official of a synagogue who conducts the liturgical portion of a service and sings or chants the prayers and parts of prayers designed to be performed as solos. **2.** an official whose duty is to lead the singing in a cathedral or in a collegiate or parish church; a precentor. [1530–40; < L: singer, equiv. to *can(ere)* to sing + *-tor* -TOR]

Can·tor (kan′tər; Ger. kän′tôR), *n.* **Ge·org** (gā ôRk′), 1845–1918, German mathematician, born in Russia.

can·to·ri·al (kan tôr′ē əl, -tōr′-), *adj.* **1.** of or pertaining to a cantor. **2.** cantoris. [1785–95; CANTOR + -IAL]

can·to·ris (kan tôr′is, -tōr′-), *adj.* of or pertaining to the gospel or liturgical north side of a church (opposed to *decani*). Also, **cantorial.** [1635–45; < L, gen. of *cantor* CANTOR]

Can′tor set′, *Math.* the set obtained from the closed interval from 0 to 1 by removing the middle third from the interval, then the middle third from each of the two remaining sets, and continuing the process indefinitely. Also called **Can′tor ter′nary set′.** [after G. CANTOR]

can·trip (kän′trip), *n.* **1.** *Chiefly Scot.* a magic spell; trick by sorcery. **2.** *Chiefly Brit.* artful shamming meant to deceive. [1710–20; appar. dissimilated var. of OE *calcatrippe;* see CALTROP]

cant′ strip′ (kant), an inclined or beveled strip of wood, for changing the pitch of a roof slope or for rounding out the angle between a flat roof and an adjoining parapet.

can·tus (kan′təs), *n., pl.* **-tus.** See **cantus firmus.** [1580–90; < L; see CANTO]

can·tus fir·mus (kan′təs fûr′məs), **1.** the ancient traditional unisonal plainchant of the Christian Church, having its form set and its use prescribed by ecclesiastical tradition. **2.** *Music.* a fixed melody to which other voices are added, typically in polyphonic treatment. [1840–50; < ML: lit., firm song]

cant·y (kan′tē, kän′-), *adj. Chiefly Scot.* cheerful; lively. [1715–25; < LG *kantig* lively; akin to CANT[3]] **—cant′i·ly,** *adv.* **—cant′i·ness,** *n.*

Ca·nuck (kə nuk′), *n. Slang (sometimes offensive).* a Canadian, esp. a French Canadian. [1825–35; perh. ult. to be identified with *kanaka* Hawaiian, South Sea islander (< Hawaiian; see KANAKA), if the word once identified both French Canadians and such islanders, who both were employed in the Pacific Northwest fur trade; later reanalyzed as CAN(ADIAN) + a suffix]

ca·nu·la (kan′yə lə), *n., pl.* **-las, -lae** (-lē′). *Surg.* cannula.

ca·nu·lar (kan′yə lər), *adj.* cannular. Also, **can·u·late** (kan′yə lāt′, -lit).

Ca·nute (kə nōōt′, -nyōōt′), *n.* A.D. 994?–1035, Danish king of England 1017–35; of Denmark 1018–35; and of Norway 1028–35. Also, **Cnut, Knut.**

can·vas (kan′vəs), *n.* **1.** a closely woven, heavy cloth of cotton, hemp, or linen, used for tents, sails, etc. **2.** a piece of this or similar material on which a painting is made. **3.** a painting on canvas. **4.** a tent, or tents collectively. **5.** sailcloth. **6.** sails collectively. **7.** any fabric of linen, cotton, or hemp of a coarse loose weave used as a foundation for embroidery stitches, interlining, etc. **8.** the floor of a boxing ring traditionally consisting of a canvas covering stretched over a mat. **9. under canvas, a.** *Naut.* with set sails. **b.** in tents; in the field: *the troops under canvas.* [1225–75; ME *canevas* < AF, ONF < VL **cannabāceus* (n. use of adj.), equiv. to L *cannab(is)* HEMP + *-āceus* -ACEOUS] **—can′vas·like′,** *adj.*

can·vas·back (kan′vəs bak′), *n., pl.* **-backs,** *(esp. collectively)* **-back.** a North American wild duck, *Aythya valisineria,* the male of which has a whitish back and a reddish-brown head and neck. [1595–1605, *Amer.;* after the canvaslike color of its back]

can·vass (kan′vəs), *v.t.* **1.** to solicit votes, subscriptions, opinions, or the like from. **2.** to examine carefully; investigate by inquiry; discuss; debate. *—v.i.* **3.** to solicit votes, opinions, or the like. *—n.* **4.** a soliciting of votes, orders, or the like. **5.** a campaign for election to government office. **6.** close inspection; scrutiny. [1500–10; orig. sp. var. of CANVAS, as a v.; sense "discuss" appar. development of the earlier senses "toss in a canvas sheet," "harshly criticize"; sense "solicit votes" obscurely derived] **—can′vass·er,** *n.*
—Syn. 2. analyze, scrutinize, explore.

can·yon (kan′yən), *n.* a deep valley with steep sides, often with a stream flowing through it. Also, **cañon.** [1835–45, *Amer.;* < AmerSp, Sp *cañón* a long tube, a hollow, equiv. to *cañ(a)* tube (< L *canna* CANE) + *-on* aug. suffix]
—Syn. gorge, gully, ravine, pass, gap, arroyo, coulee.

Can·yon (kan′yən), *n.* a town in N Texas. 10,724.

Can′yon·lands Na′tional Park′ (kan′yən landz′), a national park in SE Utah, at the junction of the Colorado and Green rivers: site of geologic interest. 527 sq. mi. (1366 sq. km).

can′yon wind′ (wind), **1.** a nocturnal, down-canyon flow of air caused by the cooling of the canyon walls. Cf. **valley wind. 2.** a wind modified in direction and speed by being forced to blow through a canyon or gorge.

can·zo·na (kan zō′nə; *It.* kän tsô′nä), *n., pl.* **-ne** (-nā; *It.* -ne). canzone.

can·zo·ne (kan zō′nē; *It.* kän tsô′ne). *n., pl.* **-nes, -ni** (-nē), **1.** a variety of lyric poetry in the Italian style, of Provençal origin, that closely resembles the madrigal. **2.** a poem in which each word that appears at the end of a line of the first stanza appears again at the end of one of the lines in each of the following stanzas. Also, **canzona.** [1580–90; < It < L *cantiōnem,* acc. sing. of *cantiō* song; see CANTO, -ION]

can·zo·net (kan′zə net′), *n.* an early polyphonic song of dancelike character. [1585–95; < It *canzonetta.* See CANZONE, -ETTE]

Cao·da·ism (kou dī′iz əm), *n.* an eclectic religion, originated in Cochin-China in 1926, combining Buddhist, Taoist, and Confucianist elements and influenced to some extent by Christianity. [1935–40; < Vietnamese *cao đài* + -ISM]

caou·tchouc (kou′chŏŏk, kou chŏŏk′), *n.* **1.** rubber[1] (def. 1). **2.** pure rubber. [1765–75; < F < Sp *cauchuc* (now obs.), prob. ult. < an Indian language of lowland tropical South America]

Cao Yu (tsou′ yōō′), (*Wan Jiabao*), born 1910, Chinese playwright.

CONCISE PRONUNCIATION KEY: act, cāpe, dâre, pärt; set, ēqual; *if,* īce; ox, ōver, ôrder, oil, bŏŏk, bōōt, out; up, ûrge; child; sing; shoe; thin, *that;* zh as in *treasure.* ə = *a* as in *alone, e* as in *system, i* as in *easily, o* as in *gallop, u* as in *circus;* ° as in *fire* (fī°r), *hour* (ou°r). l and n can serve as syllabic consonants, as in *cradle* (krād′l), and *button* (but′n). See the full key inside the front cover.

cap[1] (kap), *n., v.,* **capped, cap·ping.** —*n.* **1.** a close-fitting covering for the head, usually of soft supple material and having no visor or brim. **2.** a brimless head covering with a visor, as a baseball cap. **3.** mobcap. **4.** a headdress denoting rank, occupation, religious order, or the like: *a nurse's cap.* **5.** mortarboard (def. 2). **6.** *Math.* the symbol ∩, used to indicate the intersection of two sets. Cf. **intersection** (def. 3a). **7.** anything resembling or suggestive of a covering for the head in shape, use, or position: *a cap on a bottle.* **8.** summit; top; acme. **9.** a maximum limit, as one set by law or agreement on prices, wages, spending, etc., during a certain period of time; ceiling: *a 9 percent cap on pay increases for this year.* **10.** *Mycol.* the pileus of a mushroom. **11.** *Bot.* calyptra (def. 1). **12.** *Mining.* a short, horizontal beam at the top of a prop for supporting part of a roof. **13.** a percussion cap. **14.** *Brit. Sports.* a selection for a representative team, usually for a national squad. **15.** a noise-making device for toy pistols, made of a small quantity of explosive wrapped in paper or other thin material. **16.** *Naut.* a fitting of metal placed over the head of a spar, as a mast or bowsprit, and having a collar for securing an additional spar. **17.** a new tread applied to a worn pneumatic tire. **18.** *Archit.* a capital. **19.** *Carpentry.* a metal plate placed over the iron of a plane to break the shavings as they rise. **20.** *Fox Hunting.* See **capping fee. 21.** *Chiefly Brit. Slang.* a contraceptive diaphragm. **22. cap in hand,** humbly; in supplication: *He went to his father cap in hand and begged his forgiveness.* **23. set one's cap for,** to pursue as being a potential mate. —*v.t.* **24.** to provide or cover with or as if with a cap. **25.** to complete. **26.** follow up with something as good or better; surpass; outdo: *to cap one joke with another.* **27.** to serve as a cap, covering, or top to; overlie. **28.** to put a maximum limit on (prices, wages, spending, etc.). **29.** *Brit. Sports.* to select (a player) for a representative team. —*v.i.* **30.** *Fox Hunting.* to hunt with a hunting club of which one is not a member, on payment of a capping fee. [bef. 1000; ME *cappe,* OE *cæppe* < LL *cappa* hooded cloak, cap; cf. CAPE] —**cap′less,** *adj.*

cap[2] (kap), *n., v.,* **capped, cap·ping.** —*n.* **1.** a capital letter. **2.** Usually, **caps.** uppercase: *Please set the underlined in caps.* —*v.t.* **3.** to write or print in capital letters, or make an initial letter a capital; capitalize. [1895–1900; by shortening]

cap[3] (kap), *n. Slang.* a capsule, esp. of a narcotic drug. [by shortening of CAPSULE]

CAP, 1. See **Civil Air Patrol. 2.** Common Agricultural Policy: a coordinated system established in 1960 by the European Economic Community for stabilizing prices of farm products of its member countries. **3.** computer-aided publishing. **4.** *Stock Exchange.* convertible adjustable preferred (stock). Also, **C.A.P.** (for defs. 1, 2, 4).

cap., 1. capacity. **2.** (in prescriptions) let the patient take. [< L *capiat*] **3.** capital. **4.** capitalize. **5.** capitalized. **6.** capital letter. **7.** chapter. [< L *capitulum, caput*] **8.** foolscap.

ca·pa (kä′pə), *n.* the red cloak of a bullfighter, used chiefly in attracting the attention of the bull and guiding the course of its attack. [1780–90; < Sp < LL *cappa;* see CAPE[1]]

Cap·a (kap′ə), *n.* **Robert** (*Andrei Friedmann*), 1913–54, U.S. photographer, born in Hungary.

ca·pa·bil·i·ty (kā′pə bil′i tē), *n., pl.* **-ties. 1.** the quality of being capable; capacity; ability: *His capability was unquestionable.* **2.** the ability to undergo or be affected by a given treatment or action: *the capability of glass in resisting heat.* **3.** Usually, **capabilities.** qualities, abilities, features, etc., that can be used or developed; potential: *Though dilapidated, the house has great capabilities.* [1580–90; (< MF *capabilité*) < LL *capābili(s)* CAPABLE + -TY[2]]

Ca·pa·blan·ca (kap′ə blang′kə; *Sp.* kä′pä vläng′kä), *n.* **Jo·sé Ra·oul** (hō se′ rä o͞ol′), 1888–1942, Cuban chess master.

ca·pa·ble (kā′pə bəl), *adj.* **1.** having power and ability; efficient; competent: *a capable instructor.* **2. capable of, a.** having the ability or capacity for: *a man capable of judging art.* **b.** open to the influence or effect of; susceptible of: *a situation capable of improvement.* **c.** predisposed to; inclined to: *capable of murder.* [1555–65; < LL *capābilis* roomy, appar. equiv. to *cap(āx)* roomy + *-ābilis* ABLE; see CAPACITY] —**ca′pa·ble·ness,** *n.* —**ca′pa·bly,** *adv.*
—**Syn. 1.** skillful, ingenious, accomplished. See **able.**

ca·pa·cious (kə pā′shəs), *adj.* capable of holding much; spacious or roomy: *a capacious storage bin.* [1605–15; CAPACI(TY) + -OUS] —**ca·pa′cious·ly,** *adv.* —**ca·pa′cious·ness,** *n.*
—**Syn.** ample, large. —**Ant.** confining.

ca·pac·i·tance (kə pas′i təns), *n. Elect.* **1.** the ratio of an impressed charge on a conductor to the corresponding change in potential. **2.** the ratio of the charge on either conductor of a capacitor to the potential difference between the conductors. **3.** the property of being able to collect a charge of electricity. *Symbol:* C [1905–10; CAPACIT(Y) + -ANCE]

ca·pac·i·tate (kə pas′i tāt′), *v.t.,* **-tat·ed, -tat·ing.** to make capable; enable. [1645–55; CAPACIT(Y) + -ATE[1]] —**ca·pac′i·ta′tion,** *n.*

ca·pac·i·tive (kə pas′i tiv), *adj. Elect.* pertaining to capacitance. [1915–20; CAPACIT(Y) + -IVE] —**ca·pac′i·tive·ly,** *adv.*

capac′itive cou′pling, *Elect.* the connection of two or more circuits by means of a capacitor. [1940–45]

CONCISE ETYMOLOGY KEY: <, descended or borrowed from; >, whence; b., blend of, blended; c., cognate with; cf., compare; deriv., derivative; equiv., equivalent; imit., imitative; obl., oblique; r., replacing; s., stem; sp., spelling, spelled; resp., respelling, respelled; trans., translation; ?, origin unknown; *, unattested; ‡, probably earlier than. See the full key inside the front cover.

capac′itive react′ance, *Elect.* the opposition of capacitance to alternating current, equal to the reciprocal of the product of the angular frequency of the current times the capacitance. *Symbol:* X_C Cf. **inductive reactance.**

ca·pac·i·tor (kə pas′i tər), *n. Elect.* a device for accumulating and holding a charge of electricity, consisting of two equally charged conducting surfaces having opposite signs and separated by a dielectric. Also called **condenser.** [1925–30; CAPACIT(Y) + -OR[2]]

ca·pac·i·ty (kə pas′i tē), *n., pl.* **-ties,** *adj.* —*n.* **1.** the ability to receive or contain: *This hotel has a large capacity.* **2.** the maximum amount or number that can be received or contained; cubic contents; volume: *The inn is filled to capacity. The gasoline tank has a capacity of 20 gallons.* **3.** power of receiving impressions, knowledge, etc.; mental ability: *the capacity to learn calculus.* **4.** actual or potential ability to perform, yield, or withstand: *He has a capacity for hard work. The capacity of the oil well was 150 barrels a day. She has the capacity to go two days without sleep.* **5.** quality or state of being susceptible to a given treatment or action: *Steel has a high capacity to withstand pressure.* **6.** position; function; role: *He served in the capacity of legal adviser.* **7.** legal qualification. **8.** *Elect.* **a.** capacitance. **b.** maximum possible output. —*adj.* **9.** reaching maximum capacity: *a capacity audience; a capacity crowd.* [1375–1425; late ME *capacite* < MF < L *capācitāt-* (s. of *capācitās*), equiv. to *capāci-,* s. of *capāx* roomy (*cap(ere)* to hold + *-āci-* adj. suffix) + *-tāt-* -TY[2]]
—**Syn. 2.** dimensions, amplitude. **3.** endowment, talent, gifts. **4.** aptitude, adequacy, competence, capability.

cap′ and bells′, a fool's cap hung with bells. [1880–85]

cap′ and gown′, a ceremonial mortarboard and gown worn by faculty, students, etc., as at commencement. Cf. **academic costume.** [1855–60]

Ca·pa·ne·us (kə pā′nē əs, kap′ə no͞os′, -nyo͞os′), *n. Class. Myth.* one of the Seven against Thebes, who was destroyed by Zeus for blasphemy.

cap-a-pie (kap′ə pē′), *adv.* from head to foot. Also, **cap′-à-pie′.** [1515–25; < MF *de cap a pe* from head to foot < OPr < L *dē capite ad pedem*]

ca·par·i·son (kə par′ə sən), *n.* **1.** a decorative covering for a horse or for the tack or harness of a horse; trappings. **2.** rich and sumptuous clothing or equipment. —*v.t.* **3.** to cover with a caparison. **4.** to dress richly; deck. [1585–95; < MF *caparasson* (now *caparaçon*) < OSp *caparazón,* akin to *capa* CAPE[1]]

ca·pa·taz (kä′pä täth′, -täs′; *Eng.* kap′ə täz′), *n., pl.* ***-ta·ces*** (-tä′thes, -ses; *Eng.* -tä′siz). *Spanish.* a foreman or supervisor.

cap′ cloud′, 1. a stationary cloud directly above an isolated mountain peak. Cf. **banner cloud, crest cloud. 2.** pileus (def. 3). Also called **cloud cap.**

Cap-de-la-Ma·de·leine (*Fr.* kap də la mad^e len′), *n.* a city in S Quebec, in E Canada, near Three Rivers, on the St. Lawrence. 32,626.

cape[1] (kāp), *n., v.,* **caped, cap·ing.** —*n.* **1.** a sleeveless garment of various lengths, fastened around the neck and falling loosely from the shoulders, worn separately or attached to a coat or other outer garment. **2.** the capa of a bullfighter. —*v.t.* **3.** (of a matador or capeador during a bullfight) to induce and guide the charge of (a bull) by flourishing a capa. [1350–1400; ME (north); OE *-cāp* (see COPE[2]), reinforced in 16th century by Sp *capa* < LL *cappa* hooded cloak, COPE[2]] —**caped,** *adj.*

cape[2] (kāp), *n., v.,* **caped, cap·ing,** *adj.* —*n.* **1.** a piece of land jutting into the sea or some other large body of water. **2. the Cape. a.** *Northeastern U.S.* See **Cape Cod. b.** See **Cape of Good Hope. 3.** capeskin. —*v.i.* **4.** *Naut.* (of a ship) to have good steering qualities. —*adj.* **5.** (*cap.*) pertaining to the Cape of Good Hope or to South Africa: *a Cape diamond.* [1350–1400; ME *cap* < MF < OPr < VL **capum* for L *caput* head]
—**Syn. 1.** point, promontory, headland, spit.

ca·pe·a·dor (kä′pē ə dôr′; *Sp.* kä pe ä thôr′), *n., pl.* **-dors,** *Sp.* ***-do·res*** (-thô′res). a person who assists a matador by harassing or distracting the bull with a red cape, or capa. [1905–10; < Sp, equiv. to *cape(ar)* to bait with a cape (v. deriv. of *capa* CAPE[1]) + *-ador* -ATOR]

Cape′ Bret′on (brit′n, bret′n), an island forming the NE part of Nova Scotia, in SE Canada. 42,969; 3970 sq. mi. (10,280 sq. km). Also called **Cape′ Bret′on Is′land.**

Cape′ buf′falo, a large black buffalo, *Syncerus caffer,* of southern Africa, having horns that meet at the base forming a helmetlike structure over the forehead. [1885–90]

Cape′ Canav′eral. See **Canaveral, Cape.**

Cape′ Coast′, a seaport in S Ghana, on the Gulf of Guinea, 75 mi. (121 km) SW of Accra. 51,764. Formerly, **Cape′ Coast′ Cas′tle.**

Cape′ Cod′, 1. a sandy peninsula in SE Massachusetts between Cape Cod Bay and the Atlantic Ocean: many resort towns. **2.** a style of cottage developed mainly on Cape Cod, Massachusetts, in the 18th and early 19th centuries, typically a rectangular one- or one-and-a-half story wooden cottage covered by a gable roof and having a central chimney.

Cape′ Cod′ Bay′, a part of Massachusetts Bay, enclosed by the Cape Cod peninsula.

Cape′ Cod′ Canal′, a canal in SE Massachusetts, connecting Buzzards Bay and Cape Cod Bay. 8 mi. (13 km) long.

Cape′ Cod′ light′er, a device for lighting a fire, as in a fireplace, consisting of a lump of nonflammable material on a metal rod, that is soaked in kerosene or the like and lighted with a match.

cape′ col′lar, a soft, wide, circular collar that covers the shoulders and the upper arms like a cape.

Cape′ Col′ony, former name of **Cape of Good Hope.**

Cape′ Col′ored, a South African of mixed European and African or Malayan ancestry. [1895–1900]

Cape′ Cor′al, a city in SE Florida. 32,103.

Cape′ craw′fish, an edible South African spiny lobster, *Jasus lalandii.* Also, **Cape′ cray′fish.**

Cape′ Dutch′, Afrikaans. [1820–30]

Cape′ fox′, a fox, *Vulpes chama,* inhabiting dry areas of southern Africa and having large pointed ears, silvery gray coat, and a bushy tail with a black tip. Also called **bat-eared fox, asse.**

Cape′ Gi·rar′deau (jə rär′dō), a city in SE Missouri, on the Mississippi River. 34,361.

cape′ goose′berry, a tropical American plant, *Physalis peruviana,* of the nightshade family, having heart-shaped, hairy leaves, purple-throated pale yellow flowers, and edible, yellow berries enclosed in an inflated calyx. [1825–35]

Cape′ Horn′, a headland on a small island at the S extremity of South America: belongs to Chile.

Cape′ Horn′ Cur′rent, the part of the Antarctic Circumpolar Current flowing E at Cape Horn.

Cape′ Horn′ fe′ver, *Naut. Slang.* illness feigned by malingerers. [1840–50]

Cape′ jas′mine, the common gardenia, *Gardenia jasminoides.*

Ča·pek (chä′pek), *n.* **Ka·rel** (kâr′əl, kar′-, kär′-; *Czech.* kä′rel), 1890–1938, Czech playwright, novelist, and producer.

cape·let (kāp′lit), *n.* a short cape usually covering just the shoulders. [1910–15; CAPE[1] + -LET]

cap·e·lin (kap′ə lin), *n.* either of two small fishes of the smelt family, *Mallotus villosus,* of coastal North American waters, or *M. catervarius,* of the North Pacific. Also, **caplin.** [1610–20, *Amer.*; < MF *capelan* < OPr: codfish, lit., CHAPLAIN]

cap·e·line (kap′ə lēn′, -lin), *n.* **1.** *Armor.* an iron skullcap worn by medieval archers. **2.** *Heraldry.* a representation of a hood, sometimes used as a mantling. Also, **cap′el·line′.** [1425–75; late ME < MF < early It *cappellina,* equiv. to *capell(o)* (< LL *cappellus,* deriv. of *cappa* hood; see CAP[1]) + *-ina* -INE[1]]

Ca·pel·la (kə pel′ə), *n. Astron.* a first-magnitude star in the constellation Auriga. [1675–85; < L: lit., she-goat, equiv. to *cap(ra)* she-goat + *-ella* dim. suffix]

ca·pel·li d'an·ge·lo (kə pel′ē dan′jə lō′; *It.* kä pel′lē dän′je lō′), *Italian Cookery.* See **angel hair.** [< It: angel hair]

Cape′ mar′igold, any composite plant of the genus *Dimorphotheca,* having variously colored, daisylike flowers. Also called **African daisy.**

Cape′ May′ war′bler, a North American wood warbler, *Dendroica tigrina,* olive-green striped with black on the wings and back and yellow striped with black on the breast. [1805–15; after CAPE MAY, New Jersey]

Cape′ of Good′ Hope′, 1. a cape in S Africa, in the SW Republic of South Africa. **2.** Also called **Cape′ Prov′ince.** Formerly, **Cape Colony.** a province in the Republic of South Africa. 6,731,820; 277,169 sq. mi. (717,868 sq. km). *Cap.:* Cape Town.

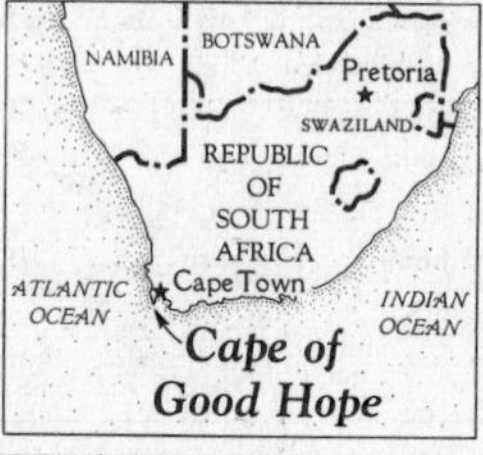

Cape′ pond′weed, an aquatic plant, *Aponogeton distachyus,* of the Cape of Good Hope, having floating leaves and tiny, fragrant white flowers. Also called **water hawthorn.**

Cape′ prim′rose, streptocarpus.

ca·per[1] (kā′pər), *v.i.* **1.** to leap or skip about in a sprightly manner; prance; frisk; gambol. —*n.* **2.** a playful leap or skip. **3.** a prank or trick; harebrained escapade. **4.** a frivolous, carefree episode or activity. **5.** *Slang.* a criminal or illegal act, as a burglary or robbery. **6. cut a caper.** See **cut** (def. 44a). [1585–95; fig. use of L *caper* he-goat (c. OE *hæfer,* ON *hafr,* OIr *caera* sheep < a West IE term **kap-(e)ro-* for a domesticated smaller animal); for the meaning, compare DOG (v.)] —**ca′per·er,** *n.* —**ca′per·ing·ly,** *adv.*
—**Syn. 3.** stunt, antic, shenanigans. **4.** spree, frolic.

ca·per[2] (kā′pər), *n.* **1.** a spiny shrub, *Capparis spinosa,* of Mediterranean regions, having roundish leaves and solitary white flowers. **2.** its flower bud, which is pickled and used for garnish or seasoning. Cf. **caper family.** [1350–1400; back formation from *capers* (taken for pl.), ME *caperes* < L *capparis* < Gk *kápparis*]

cap·er·cail·lie (kap′ər kāl′yē), *n.* a large grouse, *Tetrao urogallus,* of Eurasian forests. Also, **cap·er·cail·zie** (kap′ər kāl′yē, -kāl′zē). [1530–40; < ScotGael *capull coille* (by dissimilation), lit., horse of the woods; for first element, cf. ME *capel* horse, ON *kapall* nag, from the same source (prob. Celtic) as L *caballus* horse; sp. *lz* is early typographical rendering of manuscript sp. *l* + yogh letter (repr. palatal *l*); cf. parallel sp. of surnames *Mackenzie, Menzies*]

ca′per fam′ily, the plant family Capparidaceae (or Capparaceae), characterized by herbaceous plants, shrubs, and trees having alternate, simple, or palmate leaves, irregular flowers with four petals, and fruit in the form of elongated capsules or berries, including the caper and cleome.

Ca·per·na·um (kə pûr′nā əm, -nē-), *n.* an ancient site in N Israel, on the Sea of Galilee: center of Jesus' ministry in Galilee.

ca′per spurge′. See **gopher plant.**

Cape′ Sa′ble sea′side spar′row. See under **seaside sparrow.** [after Cape Sable, the SW tip of Florida, where the race was discovered in 1918]

cape·skin (kāp′skin′), *n.* a firm, washable leather used esp. for gloves, originally made from the skin of goats from the Cape of Good Hope, but now from hairy lambskin or sheepskin. [1910–15; CAPE[2] + SKIN]

Cape′ Sou′nion. See **Sounion, Cape.**

Ca·pet (kā′pit, kap′it; *Fr.* KA pe′), *n.* **Hugh** or *Fr.* **Hugues** (YG), A.D. 938?–996, king of France 987–996.

Ca·pe·tian (kə pē′shən), *adj.* **1.** of or pertaining to the French dynasty that ruled France A.D. 987–1328 in the direct line, and in collateral branches, as the Valois and Bourbons, until 1848 (except 1795–1814). —*n.* **2.** a member of this dynasty. [1830–40; Hugh CAPET + -IAN, modeled on F *capétien*]

Cape′ Town′, a seaport in and the legislative capital of the Republic of South Africa, in the SW part: also capital of Cape of Good Hope province. 1,108,000. Also, **Cape′town′.** Afrikaans, **Kaapstad.** —**Cape·to·ni·an** (kāp tō′nē ən), *n.*

ca·pette (kā pet′), *n.* caponette. [CAP(ON) + -ETTE]

Cape′ Verde′ (vûrd), a republic consisting of a group of islands (**Cape′ Verde′ Is′lands**) in the Atlantic, W of Senegal in W Africa: formerly an overseas territory of Portugal; gained independence in 1975. 360,000; 1557 sq. mi. (4033 sq. km). *Cap.:* Praia. —**Cape′ Ver′de·an** (vûr′dē ən), *n.*

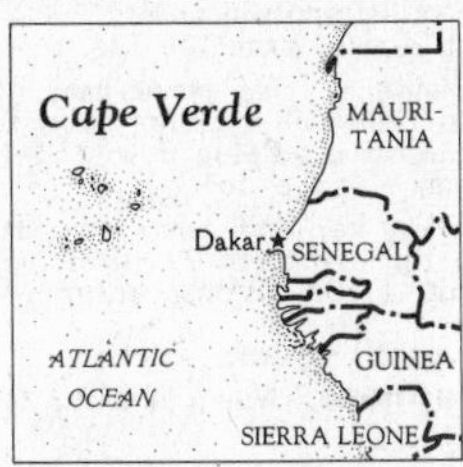

cape·weed (kāp′wēd′), *n.* a low-growing, creeping plant, *Arctotheca calendulacea,* used as a ground cover in warm climates. [1875–80; CAPE[2] (after the CAPE OF GOOD HOPE, where the plant is native) + WEED[1]]

cape′ work′, the skillful practice of a bullfighter in using a cape to maneuver a bull. [1925–30]

Cape′ York′ Penin′sula, a peninsula in NE Australia, in N Queensland, between the Gulf of Carpentaria and the Coral Sea.

cap·ful (kap′fo͝ol), *n., pl.* **-fuls.** the amount that a cap will hold. [1710–20; CAP[1] + -FUL]
—**Usage.** See **-ful.**

cap′ gun′. See **cap pistol.** [1930–35, *Amer.*]

caph (käf, kôf), *n.* kaph.

Cap-Ha·i·tien (*Fr.* KAP A ē syaN′, -tyaN′), *n.* a seaport in N Haiti. 50,000.

ca·pi·as (kā′pē əs, kap′ē-), *n. Law.* a writ commanding an officer to take a specified person into custody. [1400–50; late ME < L: lit., you are to take, subj. 2nd person sing. of *capere*]

cap·i·ba·ra (kap′ə bär′ə), *n.* capybara.

cap·il·la·ceous (kap′ə lā′shəs), *adj.* **1.** hairlike. **2.** capillary. [1725–35; < L *capillāceus* hairy, equiv. to *capill(us)* hair + *-āceus* -ACEOUS]

cap·il·lar·i·ty (kap′ə lar′i tē), *n.* Also called **cap′·illary ac′tion, cap′illary attrac′tion.** *Physics.* a manifestation of surface tension by which the portion of the surface of a liquid coming in contact with a solid is elevated or depressed, depending on the adhesive or cohesive properties of the liquid. [1820–30; CAPILLARY + -TY[2]]

cap·il·lar·y (kap′ə ler′ē), *adj., n., pl.* **-lar·ies.** —*adj.* **1.** pertaining to or occurring in or as if in a tube of fine bore. **2.** resembling a strand of hair; hairlike. **3.** *Physics.* **a.** pertaining to capillarity. **b.** of or pertaining to the apparent attraction or repulsion between a liquid and a solid, observed in capillarity. **4.** *Anat.* pertaining to a capillary or capillaries. —*n.* **5.** *Anat.* one of the minute blood vessels between the terminations of the arteries and the beginnings of the veins. **6.** Also called **cap′·illary tube′.** a tube with a small bore. [1570–80; *capil-l(ar)* (obs., < L *capillāris* pertaining to hair, equiv. to *capill(us)* hair + *-āris* -AR[1]) + -ARY]

cap·il·la·tus (kap′ə lā′təs), *adj.* (of a cumulonimbus cloud) having a cirriform upper portion that resembles an anvil or a disorderly mass of hair. [< L *capillātus* having hair; see CAPILLARY, -ATE[1]]

ca·pi·ta (kap′i tə), *n.* pl. of **caput.**

cap·i·tal[1] (kap′i tl), *n.* **1.** the city or town that is the official seat of government in a country, state, etc.: *Tokyo is the capital of Japan.* **2.** a city regarded as being of special eminence in some field of activity: *New York is the dance capital of the world.* **3.** See **capital letter.** **4.** the wealth, whether in money or property, owned or employed in business by an individual, firm, corporation, etc. **5.** an accumulated stock of such wealth. **6.** any form of wealth employed or capable of being employed in the production of more wealth. **7.** *Accounting.* **a.** assets remaining after deduction of liabilities; the net worth of a business. **b.** the ownership interest in a business. **8.** any source of profit, advantage, power, etc.; asset: *His indefatigable drive is his greatest capital.* **9.** capitalists as a group or class (distinguished from *labor*): *High taxation has reduced the spending power of capital.* —*adj.* **10.** pertaining to financial capital: *capital stock.* **11.** principal; highly important: *This guide offers suggestions of capital interest to travelers.* **12.** chief, esp. as being the official seat of government of a country, state, etc.: *the capital city of France.* **13.** excellent or first-rate: *a capital hotel; a capital fellow.* **14.** See **capital letter.** **15.** involving the loss of life: *capital punishment.* **16.** punishable by death: *a capital crime; a capital offender.* **17.** fatal; extremely serious: *a capital error.* [1175–1225; ME; (adj.) (< AF) < L *capitālis* of the head (*capit-*, s. of *caput* head, + *-ālis* -AL[1]); (n.) (< ML *capitāle* wealth, n. use of neut. of *capitālis* (adj.)] —**cap′i·tal·ness,** *n.*
—**Syn. 4.** principal, investment, assets, stock. **11.** prime, primary, first. The adjectives CAPITAL, CHIEF, MAJOR, PRINCIPAL apply to a main or leading representative of a kind. CAPITAL may mean larger or more prominent; it may also suggest preeminence or excellence: *capital letter, idea, virtue,* etc. CHIEF means leading, highest in office or power: *the chief clerk.* MAJOR may refer to greatness of importance, number, or quantity: *a major operation, the major part of a population.* PRINCIPAL refers to most distinguished, influential, or foremost: *principal officer.* —**Ant. 11.** trivial, minor.
—**Usage.** The noun CAPITAL[1] refers to a city or town that is the seat of government; to a capital letter as opposed to a lowercase letter; and to wealth or resources. The noun CAPITOL refers primarily to the building in Washington, D.C., in which Congress sits or to similar buildings used by state legislatures.

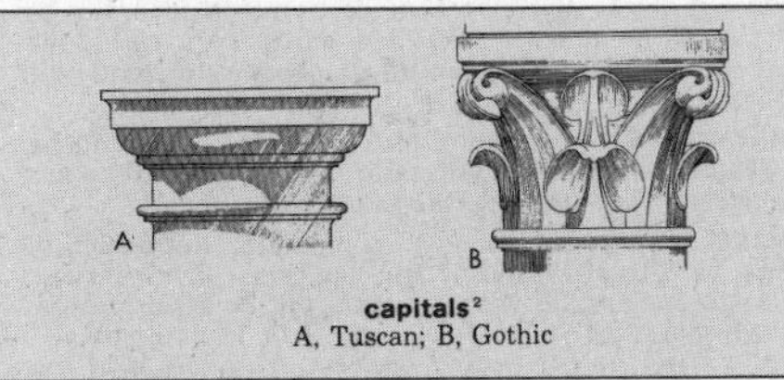

capitals[2]
A, Tuscan; B, Gothic

cap·i·tal[2] (kap′i tl), *n. Archit.* the distinctively treated upper end of a column, pier, or the like. [1250–1300; ME *capitale* head (n. use of neut. of L adj.) for L *capitellum,* equiv. to *capit-* (s. of *caput*) head + *-ellum* dim. suffix]

cap′ital account′, **1.** a business account stating the owner's or shareholder's interest in the assets. **2. capital accounts,** *Accounting.* accounts showing the net worth in a business enterprise. [1890–95]

cap′ital as′set. See **fixed asset.** [1920–25]

cap′ital bud′get, a statement of proposed financial expenditures, esp. for schools, parks, and other municipal facilities, and often including a plan for financing.

cap′ital expen′diture, *Accounting, Finance.* an addition to the value of fixed assets, as by the purchase of a new building. [1895–1900]

cap′ital gain′, profit from the sale of assets, as bonds or real estate. [1920–25]

cap′ital goods′, *Econ.* machines and tools used in the production of other goods (contrasted with *consumer goods*). [1895–1900]

cap·i·tal-in·ten·sive (kap′i tl in ten′siv), *adj.* requiring or using a very large amount of capital relative to the need for or use of labor. Cf. **labor-intensive.** [1955–60]

cap′ital invest′ment, (in a business) the total funds invested in an enterprise.

cap·i·tal·ism (kap′i tl iz′əm), *n.* an economic system in which investment in and ownership of the means of production, distribution, and exchange of wealth is made and maintained chiefly by private individuals or corporations, esp. as contrasted to cooperatively or state-owned means of wealth. [1850–55; CAPITAL[1] + -ISM]

cap·i·tal·ist (kap′i tl ist), *n.* **1.** a person who has capital, esp. extensive capital, invested in business enterprises. **2.** an advocate of capitalism. **3.** a very wealthy person. [1785–95; CAPITAL[1] + -IST]

cap·i·tal·is·tic (kap′i tl is′tik), *adj.* pertaining to capital or capitalists; founded on or believing in capitalism: *a capitalistic system.* [1870–75, *Amer.*; CAPITALIST + -IC] —**cap′i·tal·is′ti·cal·ly,** *adv.*

cap·i·tal·i·za·tion (kap′i tl ə zā′shən), *n.* **1.** the act or process of capitalizing. **2.** the authorized or outstanding stocks and bonds of a corporation. **3.** *Accounting.* **a.** the total investment of the owner or owners in a business enterprise. **b.** the total corporate liability. **c.** the total arrived at after addition of liabilities. **4.** conversion into stocks or bonds. **5.** the act of computing the present value of future periodical payments. [1855–60; CAPITALIZE + -ATION]

cap·i·tal·ize (kap′i tl īz′), *v.,* **-ized, -iz·ing.** —*v.t.* **1.** to write or print in capital letters or with an initial capital. **2.** to authorize a certain amount of stocks and bonds in the corporate charter of: *to capitalize a corporation.* **3.** to issue stock as a dividend, thereby capitalizing retained earnings, or as settlement of an unpaid arrearage of preferred dividends. **4.** *Accounting.* to set up (expenditures) as business assets in the books of account instead of treating as expense. **5.** to supply with capital. **6.** to estimate the value of (a stock or an enterprise). —*v.i.* **7.** to take advantage of; turn something to one's advantage (often fol. by *on*): *to capitalize on one's opportunities.* Also, *esp. Brit.,* **cap′i·tal·ise′.** [1755–65, *Amer.*; CAPITAL[1] + -IZE] —**cap′i·tal·iz′a·ble,** *adj.* —**cap′i·tal·iz′er,** *n.*
—**Syn. 7.** profit by, exploit, utilize.

cap′ital let′ter, a letter of the alphabet that usually differs from its corresponding lowercase letter in form and height, as *A, B, Q,* and *R* as distinguished from *a, b, q,* and *r*: used as the initial letter of a proper name, the first word of a sentence, etc. Also called **capital.**

cap′ital lev′y, a tax based on capital, as distinguished from a tax on income. [1915–20]

cap′ital loss′, loss from the sale of assets, as of bonds or real estate. [1920–25]

cap·i·tal·ly (kap′i tl ē), *adv.* **1.** excellently; very well. **2.** in a manner involving capital punishment. [1600–10; CAPITAL[1] + -LY]

cap′ital out′lay, a capital expenditure.

cap′ital pun′ishment, punishment by death for a crime; death penalty. [1575–85]

cap′ital ship′, one of a class of the largest warships; a battleship, battle cruiser, or aircraft carrier. [1680–90]

cap′ital sins′. See **deadly sins.**

cap′ital stock′, **1.** the total stock authorized or issued by a corporation. **2.** the book value of the outstanding shares of a corporation, including retained earnings and amounts paid in by stockholders. [1890–95]

cap′ital struc′ture, the apportionment of all the financial resources of a business, in equity, bonds, etc.

cap′ital sum′, *Insurance.* the maximum amount collectable for accidental death or for some major disabling injury, as one resulting in the loss of an eye, leg, or arm. Also called **principal sum.**

cap′ital sur′plus, the surplus of a business, exclusive of its earned surplus.

ca·pi·tas·ti (kä′pē täs′tē, -pə-), *n.* a pl. of **capotasto.**

cap·i·tate (kap′i tāt′), *adj.* **1.** *Bot.* forming or shaped like a head or dense cluster. **2.** *Biol.* having an enlarged or swollen, headlike termination. [1655–65; < L *capitātus* headed, equiv. to *capit-* (s. of *caput*) head + *-ātus* -ATE[1]]

cap′itate bone′, *Anat.* the largest and central bone of the carpus, articulating with the second, third, and fourth metacarpal bones.

cap·i·ta·tion (kap′i tā′shən), *n.* **1.** a numbering or assessing by the head. **2.** a poll tax. **3.** a fee or payment of a uniform amount for each person. [1605–15; (< F) < LL *capitātiōn-* (s. of *capitātiō*), equiv. to L *capit-* (s. of *caput*) head + *-ātiōn* -ATION] —**cap′i·ta′tive,** *adj.*

Cap·i·tol (kap′i tl), *n.* **1.** the building in Washington, D.C., used by the Congress of the U.S. for its sessions. **2.** (*often l.c.*) a building occupied by a state legislature. **3.** the ancient temple of Jupiter at Rome, on the Capitoline. **4.** the Capitoline. [1690–1700, *Amer.*; < L *capitōlium* temple of Jupiter on Capitoline hill, Rome, taken to be a derivative of *caput* head; r. ME *capitolie* < ONF]
—**Usage.** See **capital**[1].

Cap′itol Hill′, **1.** the small hill in Washington, D.C., on which the Capitol stands. **2.** *Informal.* the U.S. Congress. Also called **the Hill.**

Cap·i·to·line (kap′i tl īn′), *adj.* **1.** of or pertaining to the Capitoline or to the ancient temple of Jupiter that stood on this hill. —*n.* **2.** one of the seven hills on which ancient Rome was built. [1610–20; < L *Capitōlīnus.* See CAPITOL, -INE[1]]

Cap′itol Reef′ Na′tional Park′, a national park in S central Utah: cliff dwellings and fossils. 397 sq. mi. (1028 sq. km).

ca·pit·u·lar (kə pich′ə lər), *n.* **1.** a member of an ecclesiastical chapter. **2. capitulars,** the laws or statutes of a chapter or of an ecclesiastical council. —*adj.* **3.** *Bot.* capitate. **4.** pertaining to an ecclesiastical or other chapter. [1605–15; < ML *capitulāris,* equiv. to *capitul(um)* chapter (lit., small head; see CAPITULUM) + *-āris* -AR[1]] —**ca·pit′u·lar·ly,** *adv.*

ca·pit·u·lar·y (kə pich′ə ler′ē), *adj., n., pl.* **-lar·ies.** —*adj.* **1.** pertaining to a chapter, esp. to an ecclesiastical one. —*n.* **2.** a member of a chapter, esp. of an ecclesiastical one. **3.** Often, **capitularies.** an ordinance or law of a Frankish sovereign. [1640–50; < LL *capitulārius,* equiv. to *capitul(um)* (see CAPITULAR) + L *-ārius* -ARY]

ca·pit·u·late (kə pich′ə lāt′), *v.i.,* **-lat·ed, -lat·ing.** **1.** to surrender unconditionally or on stipulated terms. **2.** to give up resistance: *He finally capitulated and agreed to do the job my way.* [1570–80; < ML *capitulātus* (ptp. of *capitulāre* to draw up in sections), equiv. to *capitul(um)* section (lit., small head; see CAPITULUM) + *-ātus* -ATE[1]] —**ca·pit′u·lant,** *n.* —**ca·pit′u·la′tor,** *n.*
—**Syn. 2.** yield, acquiesce, accede, give in.

ca·pit·u·la·tion (kə pich′ə lā′shən), *n.* **1.** the act of capitulating. **2.** the document containing the terms of a surrender. **3.** a list of the headings or main divisions of a subject; a summary or enumeration. **4.** Often, **capitulations.** a treaty or agreement by which subjects of one country residing or traveling in another are extended extraterritorial rights or special privileges, esp. such a treaty between a European country and the former Ottoman rulers of Turkey. [1525–35; < ML *capitulātiōn-* (s. of *capitulātiō*). See CAPITULATE, -ION] —**ca·pit·u·la·to·ry** (kə pich′ə lə tôr′ē, -tōr′ē), *adj.*

ca·pit·u·la·tion·ism (kə pich′ə lā′shə niz′əm), *n.* advocacy or approval of capitulation. [1955–60; CAPITULATION + -ISM] —**ca·pit′u·la′tion·ist,** *n.*

ca·pit·u·lum (kə pich′ə ləm), *n., pl.* **-la** (-lə). *Biol.* any globose or knoblike part, as a flower head or the head of a bone. [1715–25; < L, equiv. to *capit-* (s. of *caput*) head + *-ulum,* neut. of *-ulus* -ULE]

ca·piz (kə pēz′, ka-), *n.* **1.** a small marine bivalve of the genus *Placuna,* esp. *P. placenta,* common in Philippine coastal waters and some other parts of the Pacific

CONCISE PRONUNCIATION KEY: act, cāpe, dâre, pärt; set, ēqual; *if,* ice; ox, ōver, ôrder, oil, bo͝ok, bo͞ot, out; up, ûrge; child; sing; shoe; thin, that; zh as in *treasure.* ə = *a* as in *alone, e* as in *system, i* as in *easily, o* as in *gallop, u* as in *circus;* ᵊ as in *fire* (fīᵊr), *hour* (ouᵊr). l and n can serve as syllabic consonants, as in *cradle* (krād′l), and *button* (but′n). See the full key inside the front cover.

Ocean. **2.** Also called **windowpane shell, windowglass shell.** the squarish, translucent inner shell of *Placuna* used in making lamps, windowpane, and decorative objects. [of unexplained orig.]

cap′ jib′, *Naut.* a jib set on a stay to a bowsprit cap.

Cap•let (kap′lit), *Pharm., Trademark.* an oval-shaped tablet that is coated to facilitate swallowing.

cap•lin (kap′lin), *n.* capelin.

cap. moll., (in prescriptions) soft capsule. [< L *capsula mollis*]

cap′n (kap′m), *n.* captain.

ca•po[1] (kä′pō), *n., pl.* **-pos.** **1.** any of various devices for a guitar, lute, banjo, etc., that when clamped or screwed down across the strings at a given fret will raise each string a corresponding number of half tones. **2.** the nut of a guitar, lute, banjo, etc. Also called **capotasto.** [1875–80; < It, shortening of *capotasto* CAPOTASTO]

ca•po[2] (kä′pō, kap′ō), *n., pl.* **-pos.** the chief of a branch of the Mafia. [1960–65; < It: head, leader < VL **capum* for L *caput;* cf. CHIEF]

ca•pon (kā′pon, -pən), *n.* a cockerel castrated to improve the flesh for use as food. [bef. 1000; ME; OE *capun* < L *capōn-* (s. of *capō*) castrated cock; akin to Gk *kóptein* to cut, OCS *skopiti* to castrate]

Ca•pone (kə pōn′), *n.* **Al(phonse)** ("*Scarface*"), 1899–1947, U.S. gangster and Prohibition-era bootlegger, probably born in Italy.

ca•pon•ette (kā′pə net′), *n.,* a capon produced by the administration of a synthetic sex hormone. Also called **capette.** [CAPON + -ETTE]

ca•pon•ize (kā′pə nīz′), *v.t.,* **-ized, -iz•ing.** to castrate (a fowl). Also, *esp. Brit.,* **ca′pon•ise′.** [1645–55; CAPON + -IZE] **—ca′pon•i•za′tion,** *n.* **—ca′pon•iz′er,** *n.*

cap•o•ral[1] (kap′ər əl, kap′ə ral′), *n.* a variety of tobacco. [1840–50; short for F *tabac du caporal* tobacco of the CORPORAL[2]]

cap•o•ral[2] (kap′ə ral′), *n. Southwestern U.S.* an overseer, esp. of a cattle ranch. [1590–1600; < Sp: chief, manager < It; see CORPORAL[2]]

ca•po•re•gime (kä′pō rə zhēm′, kap′ō-), *n.* the second in command to a capo; Mafia lieutenant. [1970–75; < It, lit. head of the regime; see CAPO[2], REGIME]

Cap•o•ret•to (kap′ə ret′ō; *It.* kä′pô ret′tô), *n.* Italian name of **Kobarid.**

ca•pot[1] (kə pot′, -pō′), *n. Cards.* the taking by one player of all the tricks of a deal, as in piquet. [1640–50; < F (n. and adj.), designating or describing the player who has no tricks, after *faire capot* (nautical) to capsize]

ca•pot[2] (kə pō′; *Fr.* ka pō′), *n., pl.* **-pots** (-pōz′; *Fr.* -pō′). capote.

ca•po•tas•to (kä′pō täs′tō, -pə-), *n., pl.* **ca•po•tas•tos, ca•pi•tas•ti** (kä′pē täs′tē, -pə-). capo[1] [< It, equiv. to *capo* head (see CAPO[2]) + *tasto* finger board, fret, lit., touch, feel, n. deriv. of *tastare* to touch lightly, perh. < VL **taxitare,* for L *taxāre,* freq. of L *tangere* to touch]

ca•pote (kə pōt′; *Fr.* ka pôt′), *n., pl.* **-potes** (-pōts′; *Fr.* -pôt′). **1.** a long cloak with a hood. **2.** a close-fitting, caplike bonnet worn by women and children in the mid-Victorian period. **3.** a bullfighter's cape; capa. **4.** an adjustable top or hood of a vehicle, as a buggy. Also, **capot.** [1790–1800, *Amer.;* < F, equiv. to *cape* (< Sp *capa* CAPE[1]) + *-ote,* fem. of *-ot* dim. suffix]

Ca•po•te (kə pō′tē), *n.* **Truman,** 1924–84, U.S. novelist, short-story writer, and playwright.

Capp (kap), *n.* **Al** (*Alfred Gerald Caplin*), 1909–79, U.S. comic-strip artist: creator of "Li'l Abner."

Cap•pa•do•cia (kap′ə dō′shə), *n.* an ancient country in E Asia Minor: it became a Roman province in A.D. 17. **—Cap′pa•do′cian,** *adj., n.*

cap•pa ma•gna (kä′pə mä′nyə, kap′ə mag′nə), *Eccles.* a ceremonial cloak having a long train and a silk or fur-lined hood, worn by cardinals, bishops, and certain other dignitaries. [< ML: great cope]

cap•pa•ri•da•ceous (kap′ə ri dā′shəs), *adj.* belonging to the Capparidaceae (or Capparaceae), the caper family of plants. Cf. **caper family.** [1865–70; < NL *Capparidace(ae)* name of the family (*Cappar(is)* genus name (see CAPER[2]) + *-id-* -ID[2] + *-ace(ae)* -ACEAE) + -OUS]

capped′ el′bow, *Vet. Pathol.* See **shoe boil.**

capped′ hock′, *Vet. Pathol.* any swelling, inflammatory or otherwise, on the point of the hock of horses. [1825–35]

capped′ pawn′, *Chess.* a pawn that has been singled out or marked by a strong player as the one with which he or she intends to effect checkmate in giving a weaker opponent odds.

cap•pel•let•ti (kap′ə let′ē; *It.* käp′pel let′tē), *n.* (*used with a singular v.*) small pieces of pasta filled with meat or cheese. [1940–45; < It, pl. of *cappelletto* little hat, dim. of *capello* hat; see CAPELINE]

cap•per (kap′ər), *n.* **1.** a person or thing that caps. **2.** Also called **topper.** something that completes or adds to what has preceded it: *The capper was that we didn't know each other after all.* **3.** *Slang.* an informer, esp. for gamblers. **4.** *Slang.* a by-bidder at an auction. [1350–1400 (for sense "cap maker"); 1580–90 (for def. 1); ME; see CAP[1], -ER[1]]

cap•ping (kap′ing), *n. Mining.* overburden (def. 3). [CAP[1] + -ING[1]]

cap′ping fee′, *Fox Hunting.* a fee paid for a day of hunting with an association of hunters of which one is not a member. Also called **cap.**

cap′ pis′tol, a toy gun using caps to imitate the sound of a real pistol. Also called **cap gun.** [1915–20, *Amer.*]

cap•puc•ci•no (kap′o͝o chē′nō, kä′po͝o-; *It.* käp′po͞ot-chē′nô), *n.* a hot beverage consisting of espresso coffee and steamed milk, often served with powdered cinnamon and topped with whipped cream. [1945–50; < It: lit., CAPUCHIN, so called from a fancied resemblance of the drink's color to the color of a Capuchin habit]

Cap•ra (kap′rə), *n.* **Frank,** 1897–1991, U.S. film director and producer, born in Italy.

cap•re•o•late (kap′rē ə lāt′, kə prē′-), *adj. Biol.* having or resembling tendrils. [1730–40; < L *capreol(us)* roe deer, vine-tendril (appar. from the tendrillike shape of the deer's horn; see CAPRIOLE) + -ATE[1]]

Ca•pri (kä′prē, kap′rē, kə prē′), *n.* an island in W Italy, in the Bay of Naples: grottoes; resort. 5½ sq. mi. (14 sq. km).

capri-, a combining form meaning "goat," occurring in loanwords from Latin (*Capricorn*); used in the formation of compound words (*caprifoliaceous*). [< L, comb. form of *caper* goat; see CAPER[1]]

cap′ric ac′id (kap′rik), a white crystalline organic acid with an unpleasant odor, $C_{10}H_{20}O_2$, found as a glyceride in goat fat: the esters are used in perfumes and flavors. Also called **decanoic acid, decoic acid, decylic acid.** [1830–40; < L *capr-,* s. of *caper* goat (see CAPER[1]) + -IC]

ca•pric•ci•o (kə prē′chē ō′; *It.* kä prēt′chô), *n., pl.* **-ci•os, -ci** (-chē). **1.** *Music.* a composition in a free, irregular style. **2.** a caper; prank. **3.** a whim; caprice. [1595–1605; < It, perh. a shortening of *caporiccio* head with bristling hair]

ca•pric•ci•o•so (kə prē′chē ō′sō; *It.* kä′prēt chô′sô), *adj. Music.* capricious; fantastic in style. [< It, equiv. to *capricci(o)* CAPRICE + *-oso* -OUS]

ca•price (kə prēs′), *n.* **1.** a sudden, unpredictable change, as of one's mind or the weather. **2.** a tendency to change one's mind without apparent or adequate motive; whimsicality; capriciousness: *With the caprice of a despotic king, he alternated between kindness and cruelty.* **3.** *Music.* capriccio (def. 1). [1660–70; < F < It; see CAPRICCIO]
—Syn. 1. vagary, notion, whim, fancy.

ca•pri•cious (kə prish′əs, -prē′shəs), *adj.* **1.** subject to, led by, or indicative of caprice or whim; erratic: *He's such a capricious boss I never know how he'll react.* **2.** *Obs.* fanciful or witty. [1585–95; < It *capriccioso* CAPRICCIOSO] **—ca•pri′cious•ly,** *adv.* **—ca•pri′cious•ness,** *n.*
—Syn. 1. variable, flighty, mercurial. See **fickle.**
—Ant. 1. steady, constant, consistent.

Cap•ri•corn (kap′ri kôrn′), *n.* **1.** *Astron.* the Goat, a zodiacal constellation between Sagittarius and Aquarius. **2.** *Astrol.* **a.** the tenth sign of the zodiac: the cardinal earth sign. See illus. under **zodiac. b.** a person born under this sign, usually between December 22nd and January 19th. **3. tropic of.** See under **tropic** (def. 1a). Also, **Capricornus** (for defs. 1, 2). [1350–1400; ME *Capricorne* < L *Capricornus* (trans. of Gk *aigókerōs* goat-horned), equiv. to *capri-* CAPRI- + *corn(u)* HORN + *-us* adj. suffix]

Cap•ri•cor•nus (kap′ri kôr′nəs), *n., gen.* **-ni** (-nī). Capricorn (defs. 1, 2). [< L]

cap•ri•fig (kap′rə fig′), *n.* **1.** the wild fig, *Ficus carica,* bearing an inedible fruit used in pollination of the edible fig. **2.** the fruit itself. [1350–1400; ME < L *caprificus* the wild fig tree, lit., the goat-fig, equiv. to *capri-* CAPRI + *ficus* FIG[1]]

cap•ri•fo•li•a•ceous (kap′rə fō′lē ā′shəs), *adj.* belonging to the Caprifoliaceae, the honeysuckle family of plants. Cf. **honeysuckle family.** [1850–55; < NL *Caprifoliace(ae)* honeysuckle family (*Caprifoli(um)* genus of honeysuckle (ML, equiv. to L *capri-* CAPRI- + *folium* leaf) + NL *-aceae* -ACEAE) + -OUS]

cap•rine (kap′rīn, -rin), *adj.* of or pertaining to goats. [1375–1425; late ME < L *caprīnus;* see CAPER[1], -INE[1]]

cap•ri•ole (kap′rē ōl′), *n., v.,* **-oled, -ol•ing.** —*n.* **1.** a caper or leap. **2.** *Manège.* a movement in which the horse jumps up with its forelegs well drawn in, kicks out with its hind legs in a horizontal position in the air, and then lands again on the same spot. —*v.i.* **3.** to execute a capriole. [1570–80; < MF < It *capriola,* n. deriv. of *capriolare* to leap, caper, v. deriv. of *capri(u)olo* roebuck < L *capreolus,* equiv. to *capre(a)* roe deer (deriv. of *caper* male goat; cf. CAPER[1]) + *-olus* -OLE[1]]

Cap•ri•ote (kap′rē ōt′, -ət), *n.* a native or inhabitant of Capri. [< F *capriote,* on the model of *cypriote* CYPRIOT, *candiote,* etc., with Gk *-(i)ōtēs* personal n. suffix]

Capri′ pants′, women's casual trousers with a tapered leg that end above the ankle and a vertical slit at the outside bottom edge. [1955–60; after CAPRI]

Ca•pris (kə prēz′), *n.* (*used with a plural v.*) See **Capri pants.**

Ca•pri′vi Strip′ (kə prē′vē), a strip of land in NE Namibia that extends E between Botswana on the S and Angola and Zambia on the N to the Zambezi River. 280 mi. (450 km) long, 20–65 mi. (32–105 km) wide.

cap•ro•ate (kap′rō āt′), *n.* a salt or ester of caproic acid. [CAPRO(IC ACID) + -ATE[2]]

cap′ rock′, *Geol.* **1.** a mass of anhydrite, gypsum, or limestone immediately above the salt of a salt dome. **2.** an impervious stratum overlying an oil- or gas-bearing structure. Also, **cap′rock′.** [1865–70, *Amer.*]

ca•pro′ic ac′id (kə prō′ik), an oily, colorless or yellow liquid, $C_6H_{12}O_2$, with an odor like limburger cheese, usually obtained from fatty animal tissue or coconut oil, or synthesized: used chiefly in the manufacture of flavoring agents. Also called **hexanoic acid.** [1830–40; alter. of CAPRIC ACID]

cap•ro•lac•tam (kap′rō lak′tam), *n.* a white, water-soluble compound, $C_6H_{11}NO$, used to produce a type of nylon. [1940–45; CAPRO(IC) + LACTAM]

ca•pryl•ic (kə pril′ik, ka-), *adj.* of or pertaining to an animal odor: *the caprylic odor of a barn.* [1835–45; CAPR(IC ACID) + -YL + -IC]

capryl′ic ac′id, an oily organic acid, $C_8H_{16}O_2$, with an unpleasant odor found as a glyceride in goat and other animal fats, and used in perfumes and dyes. Also called **octanoic acid.** [1835–45]

caps., **1.** capital letters. **2.** (in prescriptions) a capsule. [(def. 2) < L *capsula*]

cap•sa•i•cin (kap sā′ə sin), *n.* a colorless, crystalline, bitter compound, $C_{18}H_{27}NO_3$, present in capsicum. [1885–90; earlier *capsicine,* equiv. to CAPSIC(UM) + -INE[2]; refashioned with *capsa-* (< L: box) for *caps-* and -IN[2] for -INE[2]]

cap′ screw′, a fastener for machine parts, threaded along the whole length of its shank and held by threads tapped in the hole in which it is screwed. Cf. **machine bolt, machine screw.** [1880–85]

Cap•si•an (kap′sē ən), *adj. Archaeol.* of or designating an Epipaleolithic culture of northwestern Africa, characterized by the use of geometric microlithic tools. [1910–15; < F *capsien,* equiv. to *Caps(a),* L name of Gafsa, town in Tunisia near which tools of the culture were discovered + *-ien* -IAN]

cap•si•cum (kap′si kəm), *n.* **1.** any plant of the genus *Capsicum,* of the nightshade family, as *C. annuum,* the common pepper of the garden, occurring in many varieties. **2.** the fruit of such a plant or some preparation of it, used as a condiment and intestinal stimulant. [1655–65; < NL, equiv. to L *caps(a)* CASE[2] + *-icum,* neut. of *-icus* -IC]

cap•sid[1] (kap′sid), *n.* the coiled or polyhedral structure, composed of proteins, that encloses the nucleic acid of a virus. Also called **protein coat.** [1960–65; < F *capside,* equiv. to L *caps(a)* CASE[2] + *-ide* -ID[1]]

cap•sid[2] (kap′sid), *n.* See **plant bug.** [< NL *Capsidae,* equiv. to *Caps(us)* a genus (said to have been formed on Gk *kápsis* a gulping down; *káp(tein)* to gulp down + *-sis* -SIS) + *-idae* -ID[2]]

cap•size (kap′sīz, kap sīz′), *v.i., v.t.* **-sized, -siz•ing.** to turn bottom up; overturn: *The boat capsized. They capsized the boat.* [1780–90; orig. uncert.] **—cap′siz•a•ble,** *adj.*
—Syn. See **upset. —Ant.** right.

cap′sizing mo′ment, *Naval Archit.* See **upsetting moment.**

cap′ sleeve′, a short sleeve designed to cover the shoulder and the top of the arm, with little or no extension under the arm. [1925–30]

cap•so•mere (kap′sə mēr′), *n.* any of the protein subunits of a capsid. [1960–65; < F *capsomère;* see CAPSID[1], -O-, -MERE]

cap′ spin′ning, a spinning process in which woolen yarn is twisted and wound onto a revolving bobbin located within a stationary cap, much used in the Bradford spinning process. [1910–15]

cap•stan (kap′stən, -stan), *n.* **1.** any of various windlasses, rotated in a horizontal plane by hand or machinery, for winding in ropes, cables, etc. **2.** a rotating spindle or shaft, powered by an electric motor, that transports magnetic tape past the heads of a tape recorder at a constant speed. [1350–1400; ME < MF *cabestan(t)* < OPr *cabestan,* var. of *cabestran,* presumably prp. of **cabest(r)ar,* a v. deriv. of *cabestre* halter < L *capistrum*]

capstan (def. 1)

cap′stan bar′, a long lever for turning a capstan by hand. [1620–30]

cap′stan ta′ble. See **drum table.** [1925–30]

cap•stone (kap′stōn′), *n.* **1.** a finishing stone of a structure. **2.** the crowning achievement, point, element, or event. [1350–1400; ME. See CAP[1], STONE]

cap•su•lar (kap′sə lər, -syo͝o-), *adj.* of, in, or like a capsule. [1670–80; < NL *capsulāris.* See CAPSULE, -AR[1]]

cap•su•late (kap′sə lāt′, -lit, -syo͝o-), *adj.* enclosed in or formed into a capsule. Also, **cap′su•lat′ed.** [1660–70; < NL *capsulātus.* See CAPSULE, -ATE[1]] **—cap′su•la′tion,** *n.*

cap•sule (kap′səl, -so͞ol, -syo͞ol), *n., v.,* **-suled, -sul•ing,** *adj.* —*n.* **1.** *Pharm.* a gelatinous case enclosing a dose of medicine. **2.** *Biol.* **a.** a membranous sac or integument. **b.** either of two strata of white matter in the cerebrum. **c.** the sporangium of various spore-producing organisms, as ferns, mosses, algae, and fungi. **3.** *Bot.* a dry dehiscent fruit, composed of two or more carpels. **4.** a small case, envelope, or covering. **5.** Also called **space capsule.** *Aerospace.* a sealed cabin, container, or vehicle in which a person or animal can ride in flight in space or at very high altitudes within the earth's atmosphere. **6.** *Aviation.* a similar cabin in a military aircraft, which can be ejected from the aircraft in an emergency. **7.** a thin metal covering for the mouth of a corked bottle. **8.** a concise report; brief outline: *An appendix to the book contains biographical capsules of the contributors.* —*v.t.* **9.** to furnish with or enclose in or as if in a capsule; en-

CONCISE ETYMOLOGY KEY: <, descended or borrowed from; >, whence; b., blend of, blended; c., cognate with; cf., compare; deriv., derivative; equiv., equivalent; imit., imitative; obl., oblique; r., replacing; s., stem; sp., spelling, spelled; resp., respelling, respelled; trans., translation; ?, origin unknown; *, unattested; ‡, probably earlier than. See the full key inside the front cover.

capsulate. **10.** to capsulize. —*adj.* **11.** small and compact. **12.** short and concise; brief and summarized: *a capsule report.* [1645–55; 1950–55 for def. 5; (< F) < L *capsula,* equiv. to *caps(a)* box (see CASE²) + *-ula* -ULE]

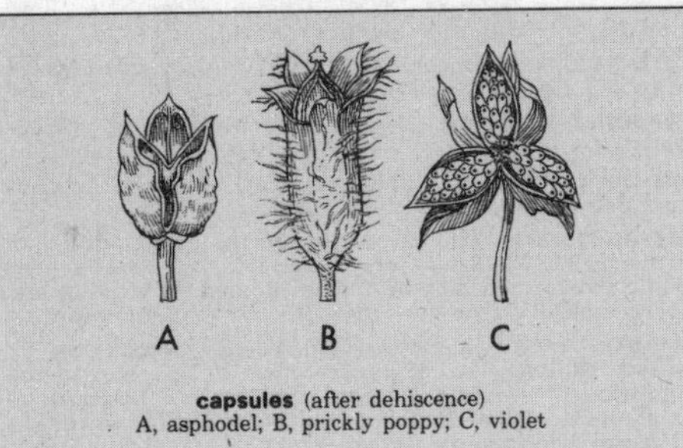

capsules (after dehiscence)
A, asphodel; B, prickly poppy; C, violet

cap•sul•ize (kap′sə līz′, -syŏŏ-), *v.t.,* **-ized, -iz•ing.** to summarize or make very concise; capsule. Also, *esp. Brit.,* **cap′sul•ise′.** [1945–50; CAPSULE + -IZE] —**cap′•sul•i•za′tion,** *n.*

capt., *Mil.* captain. Also, **CPT**

cap•tain (kap′tən, -tin), *n.* **1.** a person who is at the head of or in authority over others; chief; leader. **2.** an officer ranking in most armies above a first lieutenant and below a major. **3.** an officer in the U.S. Navy ranking above a commander and below a rear admiral or a commodore. **4.** a military leader. **5.** an officer in the police department, ranking above a lieutenant and usually below an inspector. **6.** an officer of the fire department, usually in command of a company, ranking above a lieutenant and below a chief or assistant chief. **7.** the commander of a merchant vessel. Cf. **staff captain. 8.** the pilot of an airplane. **9.** a local official in a political party responsible for organizing votes on a ward or precinct level. **10.** *Sports.* the field leader of a team: *The captain of the home team elected to receive on the kickoff.* **11.** a person of great power and influence, esp. based on economic wealth. **12.** headwaiter. **13.** See **bell captain. 14.** *South Midland and Southern U.S.* an unofficial title of respect for a man (sometimes used humorously or ironically). —*v.t.* **15.** to lead or command as a captain. [1325–75; ME *capitain* < AF *capitain, captayn* < LL *capitāneus* chief, equiv. to *capit-* (s. of *caput*) head + *-ān(us)* -AN + *-eus* -EOUS]

cap•tain•cy (kap′tən sē), *n., pl.* **-cies** for 2. **1.** the office or rank of a captain. **2.** a district or area administered by a captain. **3.** the ability of a captain; captainship. [1810–20; CAPTAIN + -CY]

Cap′tain Jack′, (*Kintpuash*), 1837?–73, Modoc leader.

cap′tain of in′dustry, the head of a large business firm, esp. of an industrial complex. [1835–45]

cap′tain's bed′, a bed consisting of a shallow box with drawers in the side and a mattress on top.

cap′tain's chair′, a chair having a rounded back formed by a heavy rail resting upon vertical spindles and coming forward to form the arms. [1945–50]

Cap′tains Coura′geous, a novel (1897) by Rudyard Kipling.

cap•tain•ship (kap′tən ship′), *n.* **1.** captaincy. **2.** the ability or skill of a military captain; leadership or generalship. [1400–50; late ME. See CAPTAIN, -SHIP]

cap′tain's mast′, a session at which the captain of a naval ship hears and acts on the cases of enlisted personnel charged with committing offenses. [1940–45]

cap•tan (kap′tan, -tən), *n.* a powder, $C_9H_8Cl_3NO_2S$, of white to cream color, used as a fungicide on vegetables, fruits, and flowers. [1950–55; shortening of MERCAPTAN]

cap•tion (kap′shən), *n.* **1.** a title or explanation for a picture or illustration, esp. in a magazine. **2.** a heading or title, as of a chapter, article, or page. **3.** *Motion Pictures, Television.* the title of a scene, the text of a speech, etc., superimposed on the film and projected onto the screen. **4.** *Law.* the heading of a legal document stating the time, place, etc., of execution or performance. —*v.t.* **5.** to supply a caption or captions for; entitle: *to caption a photograph.* [1350–1400; ME *capcio(u)n* seizure < L *captiōn-* (s. of *captiō*), equiv. to *capt(us)* taken (see CAPTIVE) + *-iōn-* -ION] —**cap′tion•less,** *adj.*

cap•tious (kap′shəs), *adj.* **1.** apt to notice and make much of trivial faults or defects; faultfinding; difficult to please. **2.** proceeding from a faultfinding or caviling disposition: *He could never praise without adding a captious remark.* **3.** apt or designed to ensnare or perplex, esp. in argument: *captious questions.* [1350–1400; ME *capcious* < L *captiōsus* sophistical, equiv. to *capti(ō)* a taking, hence, sophism (see CAPTION) + *-ōsus* -OUS] —**cap′tious•ly,** *adv.* —**cap′tious•ness,** *n.*
—**Syn. 1.** carping, nitpicking, niggling, picky, testy.

cap•ti•vate (kap′tə vāt′), *v.t.,* **-vat•ed, -vat•ing. 1.** to attract and hold the attention or interest of, as by beauty or excellence; enchant: *Her blue eyes and red hair captivated him.* **2.** *Obs.* to capture; subjugate. [1520–30; < LL *captivātus* (ptp. of *captivāre* to take captive), equiv. to L *captīv(us)* CAPTIVE + *-ātus* -ATE¹] —**cap′ti•vat′•ing•ly,** *adv.* —**cap′ti•va′tion,** *n.* —**cap′ti•va′tive,** *adj.* —**cap′ti•va′tor,** *n.*
—**Syn. 1.** fascinate, bewitch, charm. **2.** subdue.

cap•tive (kap′tiv), *n.* **1.** a prisoner. **2.** a person who is enslaved or dominated; slave: *He is the captive of his own fears.* —*adj.* **3.** made or held prisoner, esp. in war: *captive troops.* **4.** kept in confinement or restraint: *captive animals.* **5.** enslaved by love, beauty, etc.; captivated: *her captive beau.* **6.** of or pertaining to a captive. **7.** managed as an affiliate or subsidiary of a corporation and operated almost exclusively for the use or needs of the parent corporation rather than independently for the general public: *a captive shop; a captive mine.* [1300–50; ME (< MF) < L *captīvus,* equiv. to *capt-(us)* taken (ptp. of *capere* to take) + *-īvus* -IVE]

cap•tiv•i•ty (kap tiv′i tē), *n., pl.* **-ties. 1.** the state or period of being held, imprisoned, enslaved, or confined. **2.** (*cap.*) See **Babylonian captivity.** [1275–1325; ME *captivite* (< OF) < L *captīvitās.* See CAPTIVE, -ITY]
—**Syn. 1.** bondage, servitude, slavery, thralldom, subjection; imprisonment, confinement, incarceration.
—**Ant. 1.** freedom.

cap•to•pril (kap′tə pril), *n. Pharm.* a white to whitish crystalline powder, $C_9H_{15}NO_3S$, used as an antihypertensive. [prob. by contr. and resp. of *mercaptopropanoyl* a chemical component]

cap•tor (kap′tər), *n.* a person who has captured a person or thing. [1640–50; < LL, equiv. to *cap(ere)* to take + *-tor* -TOR]

cap•ture (kap′chər), *v.,* **-tured, -tur•ing,** *n.* —*v.t.* **1.** to take by force or stratagem; take prisoner; seize: *The police captured the burglar.* **2.** to gain control of or exert influence over: *an ad that captured our attention; a TV show that captured 30% of the prime-time audience.* **3.** to take possession of, as in a game or contest: *to capture a pawn in chess.* **4.** to represent or record in lasting form: *The movie succeeded in capturing the atmosphere of Berlin in the 1930's.* **5.** *Computers.* **a.** to enter (data) into a computer for processing or storage. **b.** to record (data) in preparation for such entry. —*n.* **6.** the act of capturing. **7.** the thing or person captured. **8.** *Physics.* the process in which an atomic or nuclear system acquires an additional particle. **9.** *Crystall.* substitution in a crystal lattice of a trace element for an element of lower valence. [1535–45; < MF < L *captūra,* equiv. to *capt(us)* taken (ptp. of *capere* to take) + *-ūra* -URE] —**cap′tur•a•ble,** *adj.* —**cap′tur•er,** *n.*
—**Syn. 1.** catch, arrest, snare, apprehend, grab, nab. **6.** seizure, arrest, apprehension. —**Ant. 1, 6.** release.

Cap•u•a (kap′yŏŏ ə; *It.* kä′pwä), *n.* a town in NW Campania, in S Italy, N of Naples. 17,581.

ca•puche (kə pŏŏsh′, -pŏŏch′), *n.* a hood or cowl, esp. the long, pointed cowl of the Capuchins. [1590–1600; < MF < It *cappuccio,* equiv. to *capp(a)* cloak (see CAP¹) + *-uccio* aug. suffix] —**ca•puched′,** *adj.*

cap•u•chin (kap′yŏŏ chin, -shin), *n.* **1.** a Central and South American monkey, *Cebus capucinus,* having a prehensile tail and hair on the head resembling a cowl. **2.** any monkey of the genus *Cebus.* **3.** a hooded cloak for women. **4.** (*cap.*) Also called **Friar Minor Capuchin.** *Rom. Cath. Ch.* a friar belonging to the branch of the Franciscan order that observes vows of poverty and austerity. Cf. **Friar Minor, Friar Minor Conventual.** Also called **ringtail monkey** (for defs. 1, 2). [1590–1600; < MF < It *cappuccino,* equiv. to *cappucc(io)* CAPUCHE + *-ino* -INE¹]

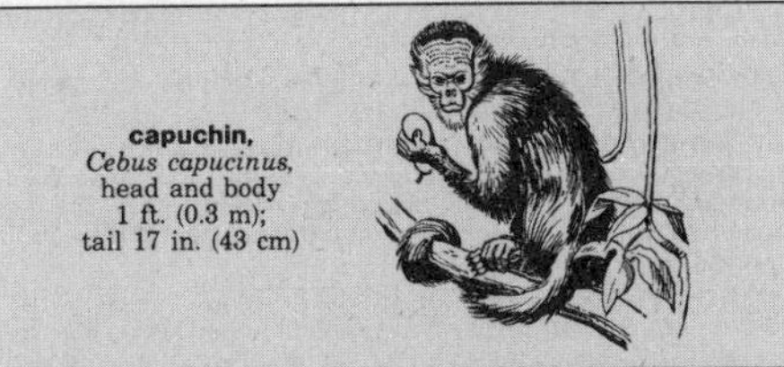

capuchin,
Cebus capucinus,
head and body
1 ft. (0.3 m);
tail 17 in. (43 cm)

Cap•u•let (kap′yə let′, -lit), *n.* (in Shakespeare's *Romeo and Juliet*) the family name of Juliet. Cf. **Montague** (def. 1).

ca•put (kā′pət, kap′ət), *n., pl.* **ca•pi•ta** (kap′i tə). *Anat.* any head or headlike expansion on a structure, as on a bone. [1640–50; < L: head]

cap•y•ba•ra (kap′ə bär′ə), *n.* a South American tailless rodent, *Hydrochaeris hydrochaeris,* living along the banks of rivers and lakes, having partly webbed feet: the largest living rodent. Also, **capibara.** [1765–75; < NL < Pg *capibara* < Tupi]

capybara,
Hydrochaeris hydrochaeris,
about 2 ft. (0.6 m)
high at shoulder;
length 3 to 4 ft.
(0.9 to 1.2 m)

caque•teuse (kak′i tŏŏz′; *Fr.* KAKᵊ TŒZ′), *n., pl.* **-teuses** (-tŏŏ′ziz; *Fr.* -TŒZ′). *Furniture.* cacqueteuse.

caque•toire (kak′i twär′; *Fr.* KAKᵊ TWÄR′), *n., pl.* **-toires** (-twärz′; *Fr.* -TWÄR′). *Furniture.* cacqueteuse. [< F; see CACQUETEUSE, -ORY²]

car¹ (kär), *n.* **1.** an automobile. **2.** a vehicle running on rails, as a streetcar or railroad car. **3.** the part of an elevator, balloon, modern airship, etc., that carries the passengers, freight, etc. **4.** *Brit. Dial.* any wheeled vehicle, as a farm cart or wagon. **5.** *Literary.* a chariot, as of war or triumph. **6.** *Archaic.* cart; carriage. [1350–1400; ME *carre* < AF < LL *carra* (fem. sing.), L *carra,* neut. pl. of *carrum,* var. of *carrus* < Celt.; cf. OIr *carr* wheeled vehicle] —**car′less,** *adj.*

car² (kär), *adj. Chiefly Scot.* **1.** left-handed. **2.** sinister. [1375–1425; ME (Scots) < ScotGael *cearr*]

CAR, computer-assisted retrieval. [1980–85]

car., carat; carats.

Car•a (kar′ə), *n.* a female given name: from an Italian word meaning "dear one."

ca•ra•ba•o (kär′ə bä′ō), *n., pl.* **-ba•os.** (in the Philippines) the water buffalo. [1895–1900; < Philippine Sp < Bisayan *karabáw*]

car•a•bi•neer (kär′ə bə nēr′), *n.* carbineer. Also, **car′a•bi•nier′.**

car•a•bi•ner (kar′ə bē′nər), *n.* a D-shaped ring with a spring catch on one side, used for fastening ropes in mountaineering. Also, **karabiner.** [1915–20; < Austrian G *Karabiner,* shortening of G *Karabinerhaken* carbine hook, equiv. to *Karabiner* (< F *carabine* CARBINE + G *-er* -ER¹) + *Haken* HOOK; it was originally used to fasten carbines to bandoleers]

ca•ra•bi•ne•ro (kä′RÄ vē ne′RÔ; *Eng.* kar′ə bə nâr′ō), *n., pl.* ***-ne•ros*** (-ne′RÔS; *Eng.* -nâr′ōz). *Spanish.* **1.** an officer of the revenue service. **2.** a frontier guard. **3.** carbineer. **4.** (in the Philippines) a coast-guard officer. [1835–45]

ca•ra•bi•nie•re (kä′RÄ bē nye′RE; *Eng.* kar′ə bin-yâr′ē), *n., pl.* ***-bi•nie•ri*** (-bē nye′RĒ; *Eng.* -bin yâr′ē). *Italian.* **1.** a member of the Italian national police force, organized as a military unit and charged with maintaining public security and order as well as assisting local police. **2.** carbineer.

car•a•cal (kar′ə kal′), *n.* **1.** a slender, catlike mammal, *Lynx caracal,* with a reddish-brown coat and long tufted ears, inhabiting northern Africa and India. **2.** the fur of this animal. [1750–60; < F, appar. Buffon's adaption of Turk *karakulak* lynx (*kara* black + *kulak* ear)]

Car•a•cal•la (kar′ə kal′ə), *n.* (*Marcus Aurelius Antoninus Bassianus*) A.D. 188–217, Roman emperor 211–217.

ca•ra•ca•ra (kär′ə kär′ə, kar′ə kar′ə), *n.* any of certain long-legged birds of prey of the falcon family, of the southern U.S. and Central and South America that feed on carrion. [1830–40; < Sp or Pg < Tupi; imit. of its cry]

Ca•ra•cas (kə rä′kəs; *Sp.* kä RÄ′käs), *n.* a city in and the capital of Venezuela, in the N part. 1,035,499.

car•ack (kar′ək), *n. Naut.* carrack.

car•a•col (kar′ə kol′), *n., v.i.,* **-colled, -col•ling.** caracole. [< Sp] —**car′a•col′ler,** *n.*

car•a•cole (kar′ə kōl′), *n., v.,* **-coled, -col•ing.** —*n.* **1.** a half turn executed by a horse and rider. **2.** *Rare.* a winding staircase. —*v.i.* **3.** to execute caracoles; wheel. [1650–60; < F < Sp *caracol* snail, spiral shell or stair, turning movement (of a horse)] —**car′a•col′er,** *n.*

Ca•rac•ta•cus (kə rak′tə kəs), *n.* fl. A.D. c50, British chieftain who opposed the Romans. Also, **Ca•rad•oc** (kə rad′ək).

car•a•cul (kar′ə kəl), *n.* Karakul.

ca•rafe (kə raf′, -räf′), *n.* a wide-mouthed glass or metal bottle with a lip or spout, for holding and serving beverages. [1780–90; < F < It *caraff(a)* < Sp *garrafa,* perh. < dial. Ar *gharrāfah* dipper, drinking vessel]

car•a•ga•na (kar′ə gä′nə, -gā′-), *n.* any Asiatic tree or shrub of the genus *Caragana,* of the pea family, having pinnately compound leaves and mostly yellow flowers, used as hedge plants in the U.S., esp. in cold regions. [< NL, perh. directly < Mongolian *karayana* Siberian pea tree < Turkic]

ca•ram•ba (kä RÄm′bä), *interj. Spanish.* (used as an exclamation of astonishment, dismay, or anger.)

ca•ram•bo•la (kar′əm bō′lə), *n.* **1.** a tree, *Averrhoa carambola,* native to southeastern Asia, bearing deeply ridged, yellow-brown, edible fruit. **2.** Also called **star fruit.** the fruit itself. [1590–1600; < Pg < Marathi *karambal*]

car•a•mel (kar′ə məl, -mel′, kär′məl), *n.* **1.** a liquid made by cooking sugar until it changes color, used for coloring and flavoring food. **2.** a kind of chewy candy, commonly in small blocks, made from sugar, butter, milk, etc. **3.** a yellowish brown or tan color. [1715–25; < F < Sp or Pg *caramelo* < LL *calamellus* little reed (by dissimilation), equiv. to *calam(us)* reed (see CALAMUS) + *-ellus* dim. suffix; meaning changed by assoc. with ML *cannamella, canna mellis,* etc., sugar cane, equiv. to L *canna* CANE + *mel* honey (gen. *mellis*)]

car•a•mel•ize (kar′ə mə līz′, kär′mə-), *v.t., v.i.,* **-ized, -iz•ing.** to convert or be converted into caramel. Also, *esp. Brit.,* **car′a•mel•ise′.** [1720–30; CARAMEL + -IZE] —**car′a•mel•i•za′tion,** *n.*

ca•ran•gid (kə ran′jid), *n.* **1.** any of numerous fishes of the family Carangidae, comprising the jacks, scads, pompanos, and cavallas. —*adj.* **2.** belonging or pertaining to the family Carangidae. [1885–90; < NL *Carangidae,* equiv. to *Carang-* (s. of *Caranx* a genus; see CARANGOID) + *-idae* -ID²]

ca•ran•goid (kə rang′goid), *adj.* **1.** resembling a fish of the family Carangidae; carangid. —*n.* **2.** a carangoid fish. [1860–65; < NL *Carang-* (s. of *Caranx*) genus name, a pseudo-Gk form + -OID]

ca•ra•pa (kə rap′ə), *n.* **1.** a South American tree, *Carapa guianensis,* of the mahogany family. **2.** the light, reddish-brown wood of this tree, used for making furniture. Also called **andiroba, crabwood.** [1860–65; < NL << Carib: oil]

car•a•pace (kar′ə pās′), *n.* a bony or chitinous shield, test, or shell covering some or all of the dorsal part of an animal, as of a turtle. [1830–40; < F < Sp *carapacho,* of obscure orig.] —**car′a•paced′,** *adj.* —**car•a•pa•cial** (kar′ə pā′shəl), *adj.*

car•at (kar′ət), *n.* **1.** a unit of weight in gemstones, 200 milligrams (about 3 grains of troy or avoirdupois weight). *Abbr.:* c., ct. **2.** karat. [1545–55; < ML *carratus* (used by alchemists) < Ar *qīrāṭ* weight of 4 grains < Gk *kerátion* carob bean, weight of 3⅓ grains, lit., little horn, equiv. to *kerat-* (s. of *kéras*) horn + *-ion* dim. suffix]

Ca•ra•tin•ga (kä′RÄ tēN′gə), *n.* a city in E Brazil. 123,344.

CONCISE PRONUNCIATION KEY: *act, cāpe, dâre, pärt; set, ēqual; if, īce; ox, ōver, ôrder, oil, bŏŏk, bōōt, out; up, ûrge; child; sing; shoe; thin,* that; *zh as in treasure.* ə = *a* as in *alone, e* as in *system, i* as in *easily, o* as in *gallop, u* as in *circus;* ᵊ as in *fire* (fīᵊr), *hour* (ouᵊr). l and n can serve as syllabic consonants, as in *cradle* (krād′l), and *button* (but′n). See the full key inside the front cover.

Ca·ra·vag·gio (kar′ə vä′jō; *It.* kä′Rä väd′jô), *n.* **Mi·chel·an·ge·lo Me·ri·si da** (mī′kəl an′jə lō′ mə rē′zē dä, mik′əl-; *It.* mē′kel än′je lô me Rē′zē dä), c1565–1609?, Italian painter.

car·a·van (kar′ə van′), *n., v.,* **-vaned** or **-vanned, -van·ing** or **-van·ning.** —*n.* **1.** a group of travelers, as merchants or pilgrims, journeying together for safety in passing through deserts, hostile territory, etc. **2.** any group traveling in or as if in a caravan and using a specific mode of transportation, as pack animals or motor vehicles: *a caravan of trucks; a camel caravan.* **3.** a large covered vehicle for conveying passengers, goods, a sideshow, etc.; van. **4.** *Chiefly Brit.* a house on wheels; trailer. —*v.t.* **5.** to carry in or as if in a caravan: *Trucks caravaned food and medical supplies to the flood's survivors.* —*v.i.* **6.** to travel in or as if in a caravan: *They caravaned through Egypt.* [1590–1600; earlier *carovan* < It *carovana* < Pers *kārwān*] —**car′a·van′ist,** *n.*
—**Syn. 1.** parade, procession, train, cavalcade, band.

car·a·van·ner (kar′ə van′ər), *n.* **1.** Also, **car·a·van·eer** (kar′ə va nēr′). **a.** a leader of a caravan. **b.** a person who travels or lives in a caravan. **2.** *Chiefly Brit.* a person who travels or lives in a house trailer. Also, **car′a·van′er.** [1890–95; CARAVAN + -ER[1]]

car·a·van·sa·ry (kar′ə van′sə rē), *n., pl.* **-ries. 1.** (in the Near East) an inn, usually with a large courtyard, for the overnight accommodation of caravans. **2.** any large inn or hotel. Also, **car·a·van·se·rai** (kar′ə van′sə rī′, -rā′). [1590–1600; < F *caravanserai* < Pers *kārwānsarāy,* equiv. to *kārwān* CARAVAN + *sarāy* mansion, inn] —**car·a·van·se·ri·al** (kar′ə van sēr′ē əl), *adj.*

car·a·vel (kar′ə vel′), *n.* a small Spanish or Portuguese sailing vessel of the Middle Ages and later, usually lateen-rigged on two or three masts. Also, **carvel.** [1520–30; < MF *car(a)velle* < Pg *caravela,* equiv. to *cárav(o)* kind of ship (< LL *carabus* a small wicker boat < Gk *kárabos* skiff, crayfish) + *-ela* dim. suffix]

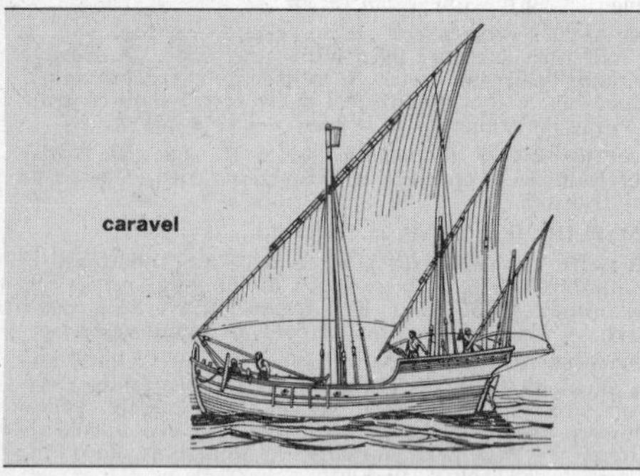
caravel

car·a·way (kar′ə wā′), *n.* **1.** a plant, *Carum carvi,* of the parsley family, native to Europe, having finely divided leaves and umbels of white or pinkish flowers. **2.** Also called **car′away seed′.** the aromatic seedlike fruit of this plant, used in cooking and medicine. [1325–75; ME *car(a)wai,* var. of *carwy* < ML *carui* < Ar *karawiyā* << Gk *káron* caraway]

carb[1] (kärb), *n. Informal.* a carburetor. [1950–55; by shortening]

carb[2] (kärb), *Slang.* —*n.* **1.** carbohydrate. —*v.i.* **2.** to eat large quantities of carbohydrates before a major physical exertion in order to store up energy (usually fol. by *up*): *Some marathon runners carb up on spaghetti the night before a race.* [by shortening of CARBOHYDRATE]

carb-, var. of **carbo-** before a vowel: *carbazole.*

car·ba·chol (kär′bə kôl′, -kol′), *n.* a white or slightly yellow crystalline compound, $C_6H_{15}ClN_2O_2$, soluble in water and alcohol: used in ophthalmology. Also called **carbamylchloride choline, carbocholine, choline chloride carbamate.** [CARBA(MYLCHLORIDE) CHOL(INE)]

car·ba·mate (kär′bə māt′, kär bam′āt), *n.* a salt or ester of carbamic acid. [1860–65; CARBAM(IC) + -ATE[2]]

car·ba·maz·e·pine (kär′bə maz′ə pēn′), *n. Pharm.* a white to whitish toxic powder, $C_{15}H_{12}N_2O$, used as an analgesic in the treatment of trigeminal neuralgia and as an anticonvulsant. [*carbam(oyl)* + *azepine,* components of the chemical name]

car·bam·ic (kär bam′ik), *adj.* of or derived from carbamic acid. [1860–65; CARB- + AM(IDE) + -IC]

carbam′ic ac′id, a hypothetical chemical compound, NH_3CO_2, known only in the form of its salts, as ammonium carbamate, or its esters, as urethan. [1860–65]

car·ba·mide (kär′bə mīd′, -mid, kär bam′īd, -id), *n.* urea. [1860–65; CARB- + AMIDE]

car·bam·i·dine (kär bam′i dēn′, -din), *n.* guanidine. [CARB- + AMIDINE]

car·ba·myl (kär′bə mil), *n.* the radical H_2NCO-. [CARBAM(IC) + -YL]

car′ba·myl·chlo′ride cho′line (kär′bə mil klôr′īd, -id, -klōr′-, kär′-), carbachol. [CARBAMYL + CHLORIDE]

car·ba·myl·u·re·a (kär′bə mil yŏŏ rē′ə, -yŏŏr′ē ə), *n.* biuret. [CARBAMYL + UREA]

car·ba·nil (kär′bə nil), *n.* See **phenyl isocyanate.** [CARB- + ANIL]

car·ban·i·on (kär ban′ī′ən, -on), *n.* an organic ion containing a negatively charged carbon atom (opposed to *carbonium ion*). [1933; CARB- + ANION]

CONCISE ETYMOLOGY KEY: <, descended or borrowed from; >, whence; b., blend of, blended; c., cognate with; cf., compare; deriv., derivative; equiv., equivalent; imit., imitative; obl., oblique; r., replacing; s., stem; sp., spelling, spelled; resp., respelling, respelled; trans., translation; ?, origin unknown; *, unattested; ‡, probably earlier than. See the full key inside the front cover.

car·barn (kär′bärn′), *n.* a large building for the housing and maintenance of streetcars, railroad cars, or buses. [1865–70; CAR[1] + BARN]

car·ba·ryl (kär′bə ril), *n.* a colorless, crystalline solid, $C_{12}H_{11}NO_2$, moderately soluble in acetone, slightly soluble in water, less toxic than DDT, used as a contact insecticide and parasiticide. [1960–65; b. CARBAMATE and ARYL]

car·ba·zole (kär′bə zōl′), *n.* a white, crystalline, water-insoluble compound, $C_{12}H_9N$, usually found along with anthracene in coal tar, or synthesized: used chiefly in the manufacture of dyes. [1885–90; CARB- + AZ- + -OLE]

carb′a·zot′ic ac′id (kär′bə zot′ik, -zō′tik, kär′-). See **picric acid.** [CARB- + AZOTIC]

car′ bed′, a small, legless, basketlike portable bed for an infant, esp. for use in a car. [1950–55]

car·bene (kär′bēn), *n.* the radical CH_2 and its derivatives. [CARB- + -ENE]

car·ben·i·cil·lin (kär′ben ə sil′in), *n. Pharm.* a semisynthetic penicillin, $C_{17}H_{16}N_2Na_2O_6S$, used against certain bacteria, esp. those involved in urinary tract infections. [1965–70; CARB- + (P)ENICILLIN]

car·bide (kär′bīd, -bid), *n.* **1.** a compound of carbon with a more electropositive element or group. **2.** See **calcium carbide. 3.** a very hard mixture of sintered carbides of various heavy metals, esp. tungsten carbide, used for cutting edges and dies. [1860–65; CARB- + -IDE]

car·bine (kär′bēn, -bīn), *n.* **1.** a light, gas-operated semiautomatic rifle. **2.** (formerly) a short rifle used in the cavalry. [1595–1605; earlier *carabine* < MF: small harquebus, weapon borne by a *carabin* a lightly armed cavalryman, compared with *(e)scarabin* gravedigger for plague victims (< Pr, akin to F *escarbot* cockchafer, dung beetle << L *scarabaeus* SCARAB), though semantic change is unclear]

car·bi·neer (kär′bə nēr′), *n.* (formerly) a soldier armed with a carbine. Also, **carabineer, carabinier.** [1795–1805; earlier *carabineer;* see CARBINE, -EER]

car·bi·nol (kär′bə nôl′, -nol′), *n.* **1.** See **methyl alcohol. 2.** an alcohol derived from methyl alcohol. [1860–70; < G *Karbinol,* equiv. to *Karbin* methyl (*karb-* CARB- + *-in* -IN[2]) + *-ol* -OL[1]]

Car·bi·tol (kär′bi tôl′, -tol′), *Chem., Trademark.* any of a group of solvents consisting of ethers of diethylene glycol and their derivatives.

car·bo (kär′bō), *n., pl.* **-bos.** *Informal.* **1.** carbohydrate. **2.** a food having a high carbohydrate content. [by shortening; cf. -O]

carbo-, a combining form used in the names of chemical compounds in which carbon is present: *carbohydrate.* Also, *esp. before a vowel,* **carb-.**

car·bo·cho·line (kär′bō kō′lēn, -kol′ēn), *n.* carbachol. [CARBO- + CHOLINE]

car′bo·cy′clic com′pound (kär′bə sī′klik, -sik′lik, kär′-), any of a group of organic chemical compounds in which all the atoms composing the ring are carbon atoms, as benzene or cyclopropane. [1895–1900; CARBO- + CYCLIC]

car·bo·hy·drase (kär′bō hī′drās, -drāz, -bə-), *n. Biochem.* any of numerous enzymes that catalyze the hydrolysis of disaccharides, polysaccharides, and glycosides. [CARBO- + HYDRASE]

car·bo·hy·drate (kär′bō hī′drāt, -bə-), *n.* any of a class of organic compounds that are polyhydroxy aldehydes or polyhydroxy ketones, or change to such substances on simple chemical transformations, as hydrolysis, oxidation, or reduction, and that form the supporting tissues of plants and are important food for animals and people. [1865–70; CARBO- + HYDRATE]

carbohy′drate load′ing, the practice of eating high amounts of carbohydrates, sometimes after a period of low carbohydrate intake, for several days immediately before competing in an athletic event, esp. a marathon, in order to store glycogen in the body, thereby providing greater reserves of energy.

car·bo·lat·ed (kär′bə lā′tid), *adj.* containing carbolic acid. [1880–85; CARBOL(IC) + -ATE[1] + -ED[2]]

car·bol·ic (kär bol′ik), *adj.* of or derived from carbolic acid. [1860–65; *carbol-* (CARB- + -OL[2]) + -IC]

carbol′ic ac′id, phenol (def. 1).

car·bo·lize (kär′bə līz′), *v.t.,* **-lized, -liz·ing.** phenolate (def. 2). Also, *esp. Brit.,* **car′bo·lise′.** [1865–70; CARBOL(IC) + -IZE]

car·bo·load·ing (kär′bō lō′ding), *n. Informal.* carbohydrate loading.

Car·bo·loy (kär′bə loi′), *Trademark.* a brand of tungsten carbide compound used for dies, cutting tools, and wearing surfaces.

car′ bomb′, 1. a bomb placed in a vehicle and wired to explode when the ignition is started, by remote control, or by a timing device. **2.** a vehicle containing explosives detonated by remote control or a timing device. [1970–75]

car·bon (kär′bən), *n.* **1.** *Chem.* a widely distributed element that forms organic compounds in combination with hydrogen, oxygen, etc., and that occurs in a pure state as diamond and graphite, and in an impure state as charcoal. *Symbol:* C; *at. wt.:* 12.011; *at. no.:* 6; *sp. gr.:* (of diamond) 3.51 at 20°C; (of graphite) 2.26 at 20°C. **2.** See **carbon copy. 3.** a sheet of carbon paper. **4.** *Elect.* **a.** the carbon rod through which current is conducted between the electrode holder and the arc in carbon arc lighting or welding. **b.** the rod or plate, composed in part of carbon, used in batteries. [1780–90; < F *carbone,* coinage based on L *carbōn-* (s. of *carbō*) charcoal] —**car′bon·less,** *adj.*

carbon 12, the isotopic carbon atom that comprises 99 percent of naturally occurring carbon, and that since 1961 has been used as the standard for atomic weight by representing a unit of 12.00000. Also, **car·bon-12** (kär′bən twelv′). [1940–45]

carbon 13, the stable isotope of carbon having an atomic mass number 13, used as a tracer. Also, **car·bon-13** (kär′bən thûr tēn′). [1940–45]

carbon 14, radiocarbon (def. 1). Also, **car·bon-14** (kär′bən fôr tēn′, -fōr-). [1935–40]

carbon-14 dating. See **radiocarbon dating.** [1955–60]

car·bo·na·ceous (kär′bə nā′shəs), *adj.* of, like, or containing carbon. [1785–95; CARBON + -ACEOUS]

car·bo·na·do[1] (kär′bə nā′dō), *n., pl.* **-dos, -does.** a massive, black variety of diamond, found chiefly near São Salvador, Brazil, and formerly used for drilling and other cutting purposes. [1850–55; < Pg: CARBONATE]

car·bo·na·do[2] (kär′bə nā′dō), *n., pl.* **-does, -dos,** *v.,* **-doed, -do·ing.** —*n.* **1.** a piece of meat, fish, etc., scored and broiled. —*v.t.* **2.** to score and broil. **3.** *Archaic.* to slash; hack. [1580–90; < Sp *carbonada,* equiv. to *carbón* charcoal (see CARBON) + *-ada* -ADE]

car·bo·na·ra (kär′bə när′ə; *It.* kär′bô nä′Rä), *n., Italian Cookery.* a sauce or dressing for spaghetti, usually containing minced prosciutto or pancetta, egg yolks, and grated cheese. [1960–65; < dial. It (*alla*) *carbonara* lit., in the manner of the charcoal pit (cf. LL *carbonaria* brazier; see CARBONARI); perh. in reference to the use of leftover grilled meat in the sauce]

car′bon arc′, an electric arc between two carbon electrodes, used mainly for lighting, as in an arc light for a motion-picture projector, or for intense heating, as in the cutting and welding of metals. [1905–10]

Car·bo·na·ri (kär′bə när′ē; *It.* kär′bô nä′Rē), *n.pl., sing.* **-na·ro** (-när′ō; *It.* -nä′Rô). *Europ. Hist.* the members of a secret political society in the early part of the 19th century, active in Italy, France, and Spain. [1815–25; < It, pl. of *carbonaro* charcoal burner < L *carbōnār(ius),* equiv. to *carbōn-* (s. of *carbō*) charcoal + *-ārius* -ARY] —**Car′bo·na′rism,** *n.* —**Car′bo·na′rist,** *n., adj.*

car·bon·a·ta·tion (kär′bə nə tā′shən), *n.* saturation or reaction with carbon dioxide. [1885–90; CARBONATE + -ATION]

car·bon·ate (*n.* kär′bə nāt′, -nit; *v.* kär′bə nāt′), *n., v.,* **-at·ed, -at·ing.** —*n.* **1.** a salt or ester of carbonic acid. —*v.t.* **2.** to form into a carbonate. **3.** to charge or impregnate with carbon dioxide: *carbonated drinks.* **4.** to make sprightly; enliven. [1785–95; CARBON(IC ACID) + -ATE[2], later taken as -ATE[1]] —**car′bon·a′tor,** *n.*

car·bon·a·tion (kär′bə nā′shən), *n.* **1.** saturation with carbon dioxide, as in making soda water. **2.** reaction with carbon dioxide to remove lime, as in sugar refining. **3.** carbonization. [1650–60; CARBONATE + -ION]

car·bon·a·tite (kär bon′ə tīt′), *n.* a calcitic or dolomitic carbonate rock emplaced as an igneous intrusion. [CARBONATE + -ITE[1]]

car′bon bisul′fide. See **carbon disulfide.**

car′bon black′, any of various finely divided forms of amorphous carbon prepared by the partial combustion of hydrocarbons, as of natural gas, or by charring wood, bones, or other plant or animal tissues: used in pigments, as reinforcing agents in the manufacture of rubber products, and as clarifying or filtering agents. [1885–90]

car′bon cop′y, 1. a duplicate of anything written or typed, made by using carbon paper. **2.** a near or exact duplicate of a given person or thing; replica. [1890–95]

car′bon cy′cle, 1. *Ecol.* the circulation of carbon atoms in the biosphere as a result of photosynthetic conversion of carbon dioxide into complex organic compounds by plants, which are consumed by other organisms: the carbon returns to the atmosphere in the form of carbon dioxide as a result of respiration, decay by fungi, bacteria, etc., and combustion of fossil fuels. **2.** *Astrophysics.* a cycle of nuclear transformations in the interiors of the stars by means of which hydrogen is gradually converted into helium with the release of nuclear energy. [1910–15]

Car·bon·dale (kär′bən dāl′), *n.* **1.** a city in SW Illinois. 27,194. **2.** a city in NE Pennsylvania, near Scranton: coal-mining center. 11,255.

car·bon-date (kär′bən dāt′), *v.t.,* **-dat·ed, -dat·ing.** to estimate the age of (an object of plant or animal origin) by radiocarbon dating. [1965–70]

car′bon dat′ing. See **radiocarbon dating.** [1950–55]

car′bon diox′ide, a colorless, odorless, incombustible gas, CO_2, present in the atmosphere and formed during respiration, usually obtained from coal, coke, or natural gas by combustion, from carbohydrates by fermentation, by reaction of acid with limestone or other carbonates, or naturally from springs: used extensively in industry as dry ice, or carbon dioxide snow, in carbonated beverages, fire extinguishers, etc. Also called **carbonic-acid gas, carbonic anhydride.** [1870–75]

car′bon disul′fide, a clear, colorless or faintly yellow, poisonous, flammable liquid, CS_2, used chiefly in the manufacture of cellophane, viscose rayon, and pesticides and as a solvent for fats, resins, and rubber. Also called **carbon bisulfide.** [1865–70]

car′bon fi′ber, a strong, stiff, thin fiber of nearly pure carbon, made by subjecting various organic raw materials to high temperatures, combined with synthetic resins to produce a strong, lightweight material used in construction of aircraft and spacecraft.

car′bon hexachlo′ride, hexachloroethane.

car·bon·ic (kär bon′ik), *adj.* containing tetravalent carbon, as carbonic acid, H_2CO_3. [1785–95; CARBON + -IC]

carbon′ic ac′id, the acid, H_2CO_3, formed when carbon dioxide dissolves in water, known in the form of its salts and esters, the carbonates. [1785–95]

car·bon′ic-ac′id gas′ (kär bon′ik as′id). See **car-**

bon dioxide. Also called **carbon′ic anhy′dride.** [1875–80]

carbon′ic an·hy′drase (an hī′drās, -drāz), *Biochem.* an enzyme that catalyzes the reversible combination of carbon dioxide with water in red blood cells. [1835–45; ANHYDR- + -ASE]

Car·bon·if·er·ous (kär′bə nif′ər əs), *Geol.* —*adj.* **1.** noting or pertaining to a period of the Paleozoic Era, including the Pennsylvanian and Mississippian periods as epochs, occurring from 345 million to 280 million years ago. See table under **geologic time. 2.** (*l.c.*) producing carbon or coal. —*n.* **3.** the Carboniferous Period or System. [1790–1800; < L *carbōn-* (s. of *carbō*) coal + -I- + -FEROUS]

car·bo′ni·um i′on (kär bō′nē əm), an organic ion containing a positively charged carbon atom (opposed to *carbanion*). [CARBON + -IUM]

car·bon·i·za·tion (kär′bə nə zā′shən), *n.* **1.** formation of carbon from organic matter. **2.** coal distillation, as in coke ovens. [1795–1805; CARBONIZE + -ATION]

car·bon·ize (kär′bə nīz′), *v.*, **-ized, -iz·ing.** —*v.t.* **1.** to char (organic matter) until it forms carbon. **2.** to coat or enrich with carbon. —*v.i.* **3.** to become carbonized. Also, *esp. Brit.*, **car′bon·ise′.** [1800–10; CARBON + -IZE] —**car′bon·iz′a·ble,** *adj.* —**car′bon·iz′er,** *n.*

car′bon monox′ide, a colorless, odorless, poisonous gas, CO, that burns with a pale-blue flame, produced when carbon burns with insufficient air: used chiefly in organic synthesis, metallurgy, and in the preparation of metal carbonyls, as nickel carbonyl. [1870–75]

car·bon·nade (kär′bə näd′; *Fr.* KAR bô NAD′), *n., pl.* **-nades** (-nädz′; *Fr.* -NAD′). *Belgian Cookery.* a thick stew of beef, onions, herbs, etc., cooked in beer. [1875–80; < F *carbon(n)ade* lit., meat grilled over hot coals, MF < Pr *carbonada* or It *carbonata;* see CARBONADO[2]]

car·bon·ous (kär′bə nəs), *adj.* of, containing, or derived from carbon. [1785–95; CARBON + -OUS]

car′bon oxychlo′ride, phosgene.

car′bon pa′per, 1. paper faced with a preparation of carbon or other material, used between two sheets of plain paper in order to reproduce on the lower sheet that which is written or typed on the upper. **2.** Also called **carbon tissue.** a paper for making photographs by the carbon process. [1875–80]

car′bon proc′ess, a method of making photographic prints by the use of a pigment, as carbon, contained in sensitized gelatin. [1875–80]

car′bon star′, *Astron.* a relatively cool, red giant having a spectrum with strong bands of carbon compounds. Also called **C star.** Cf. **spectral type.**

car′bon steel′, steel owing its properties principally to its carbon content; ordinary, unalloyed steel. [1900–05]

car′bon tetrachlo′ride, a colorless, nonflammable, vaporous, toxic liquid, CCl_4, usually produced by the reaction of chlorine with carbon disulfide, methane, or other carbon-containing compounds: used mainly as a refrigerant, fire extinguisher, cleaning fluid, solvent, and insecticide. Also called **tetrachloromethane, perchloromethane.** [1900–05]

car′bon tis′sue. See **carbon paper** (def. 2).

car·bon·yl (kär′bə nil), *adj.* **1.** containing the carbonyl group. —*n.* **2.** a compound containing metal combined with carbon monoxide, as nickel carbonyl, $Ni(CO)_4$. [1865–70; CARBON + -YL]

car·bon·y·late (kär bon′l āt′), *v.t.*, **-lat·ed, -lat·ing.** to introduce the carbonyl group into (an organic compound). [CARBONYL + -ATE[1]] —**car·bon′yl·a′tion,** *n.*

car′bonyl chlo′ride, phosgene. [1865–70]

car′bonyl group′, the bivalent radical CO, occurring in acids, ketones, aldehydes, and their derivatives.

car·bon·yl·ic (kär′bə nil′ik), *adj.* of, pertaining to, or characteristic of the carbonyl group. [CARBONYL + -IC]

car·bo·rane (kär′bə rān′), *n.* any of the crystalline compounds obtained by the substitution of carbon for boron in borane. [b. CARBON and BORANE]

Car·bo·run·dum (kär′bə run′dəm), *Trademark.* any of various abrasives or refractories of silicon carbide, fused alumina, and other materials.

car·box·yl (kär bok′sil), *adj.* containing the carboxyl group. [1865–70; CARB- + OX(YGEN) + -YL] —**car′box·yl′ic,** *adj.*

car·box·yl·ase (kär bok′sə lās′, -lāz′), *n. Biochem.* decarboxylase. [< G (1911); see CARBOXYL, -ASE]

car·box·yl·ate (kär bok′sə lāt′), *v.*, **-at·ed, -at·ing,** *n.* —*v.t.* **1.** to introduce the carboxyl group into (an organic compound). —*n.* **2.** a salt or ester of a carboxylic acid. [1925–30; CARBOXYL + -ATE[2]]

car·box·yl·a·tion (kär bok′sə lā′shən), *n.* the process of carboxylating. [CARBOXYL + -ATION]

carbox′yl group′, the univalent radical COOH, present in and characteristic of organic acids. [1875–80]

car′boxyl′ic ac′id, *Chem.* any organic acid containing one or more carboxyl groups. [1900–05; CARBOXYL + -IC]

car·box·y·meth·yl·cel·lu·lose (kär bok′sē meth′əl-sel′yə lōs′), *n.* a white, water-soluble polymer derived from cellulose, used as a coating and sizing for paper and textiles, a stabilizer for various foods, and an appetite suppressor. Also called **cellulose gum.** [1945–50; CARB- + OXY- + METHYL + CELLULOSE]

car·box·y·pep·ti·dase (kär bok′sē pep′ti dās′, -dāz′), *n. Biochem.* any of several digestive enzymes that catalyze the removal of an amino acid from the end of a peptide chain having a free carbonyl group. Cf. **aminopeptidase.** [CARB- + OXY- + PEPTIDASE]

car·boy (kär′boi), *n.* a large glass bottle protected by basketwork or a wooden box, used esp. for holding corrosive liquids. [1705–15; < Pers *qarāba(h)* < Ar *qarrābah* big jug] —**car′boyed,** *adj.*

car′bro proc′ess (kär′brō), *Photog.* a process for making carbon or pigment prints on bromide paper without exposure to light. [CAR(BON) + BRO(MIDE)]

car·bun·cle (kär′bung kəl), *n.* **1.** *Pathol.* a painful circumscribed inflammation of the subcutaneous tissue, resulting in suppuration and sloughing, and having a tendency to spread somewhat like a boil, but more serious in its effects. **2.** a gemstone, esp. a garnet, cut with a convex back and a cabochon surface. **3.** Also called **London brown.** a dark grayish, red-brown color. **4.** *Obs.* any rounded red gem. —*adj.* **5.** having the color carbuncle. [1150–1200; ME < AF < L *carbunculus* kind of precious stone, tumor, lit., live coal, equiv. to *carbōn-* (s. of *carbō*) burning charcoal + *-culus* -CULE[1], appar. assimilated to derivates from short-vowel stems; cf. HOMUNCULUS]

car·bun·cled (kär′bung kəld), *adj.* **1.** infected with a carbuncle. **2.** having a carbuncle as its stone: *a carbuncled ring.* [1570–80; CARBUNCLE + -ED[3]]

car·bun·cu·lar (kär bung′kyə lər), *adj.* of, pertaining to, or resembling a carbuncle, esp. having a carbuncle or a red and inflamed area. [1730–40; < L *carbuncul(us)* (see CARBUNCLE) + -AR[1]]

car·bu·rate (kär′bə rāt′, -byə-), *v.t.*, **-rat·ed, -rat·ing.** carburet. [CARBUR(ET) + -ATE[1]]

car·bu·ret (kär′bə rāt′, -byə-, -byə ret′), *v.t.*, **-ret·ed, -ret·ing** or (*esp. Brit.*) **-ret·ted, -ret·ting.** to combine or mix with carbon or hydrocarbons. [1865–70; CARB- + -URET]

car·bu·ret·ant (kär′bə rāt′nt, -ret′-, -byə-), *n.* any substance for carbureting air or a gas. [CARBURET + -ANT]

car·bu·re·tion (kär′bə rā′shən, -byə-, -byə resh′ən), *n.* (in an internal-combustion engine) the process of producing a mixture of air and fuel in the correct proportion for engine combustion. Also, **car·bu·ra·tion** (kär′bə rā′shən, -byə-) [CARBURET + -ION]

car·bu·re·tor (kär′bə rā′tər, -byə-), *n.* a device for mixing vaporized fuel with air to produce a combustible or explosive mixture, as for an internal-combustion engine. Also, **car′bu·ra′tor, car′bu·ret′er;** *esp. Brit.*, **car·bu·ret·tor, car·bu·ret·ter** (kär′byə ret′ər). [1860–65; CARBURET + -OR[2]]

car·bu·rize (kär′bə rīz′, -byə-), *v.t.*, **-rized, -riz·ing.** **1.** to cause to unite with carbon. **2.** to carburet. Also, *esp. Brit.*, **car′bu·rise′.** [1880–90; CARBUR(ET) + -IZE] —**car′bu·ri·za′tion,** *n.* —**car′bu·riz′er,** *n.*

car·byl·a·mine (kär′bil ə mēn′, -am′in), *n. Chem.* (formerly) isocyanide. [1875–80; CARB- + -YL + AMINE]

car·ca·jou (kär′kə jo͞o′, -zho͞o′), *n.* wolverine (def. 1). [1695–1705; < CanF < Montagnais *kwa·hkwa·če·w,* c. Cree *kwi·hkwaha·ke·w;* cf. QUICKHATCH]

car·ca·net (kär′kə net′, -nit), *n.* a woman's ornamental circlet for the hair, often of gold decorated with jewels or pearls. [1520–30; *carcan* choker < MF, equiv. to *carc-* throat (< Gmc) + *-an* ring (< L *ānus*) + -ET]

car′ card′, 1. a sheet of cardboard bearing an advertising message for display, as in subway cars, buses, and trains. **2.** cardboard coated on one side only.

Car·cas (kär′kəs), *n.* one of the seven eunuchs who served in the court of King Ahasuerus. Esther 1:10.

car·case (kär′kəs), *n., v.t.,* **-cased, -cas·ing.** carcass.

car·cass (kär′kəs), *n.* **1.** the dead body of an animal. **2.** *Slang.* the body of a human being, whether living or dead. **3.** the body of a slaughtered animal after removal of the offal. **4.** anything from which life and power are gone: *The mining town, now a mere carcass, is a reminder of a past era.* **5.** an unfinished framework or skeleton, as of a house or ship. **6.** the body of a furniture piece designed for storage, as a chest of drawers or wardrobe, without the drawers, doors, hardware, etc. **7.** the inner body of a pneumatic tire, resisting by its tensile strength the pressure of the air within the tire, and protected by the tread and other parts. —*v.t.* **8.** to erect the framework for (a building, ship, etc.). Also, **carcase.** [1250–1300; < MF *carcasse* < It *carcassa;* r. ME *carkeis, carkois* < AF, corresponding to ML *carcosium;* ult. orig. obscure] —**car′cass·less,** *adj.*
—**Syn. 1.** See **body.**

Car·cas·sonne (KAR KA sôn′), *n.* a city in and the capital of Aude, in S France: medieval fortifications. 44,623.

Car·chem·ish (kär′kə mish, kär kē′-), *n.* an ancient city in S Turkey, on the upper Euphrates: important city in the Mitanni kingdom; later the capital of the Hittite empire. Also, **Charchemish.**

carcino- a combining form meaning "cancer," used in the formation of compound words: *carcinogen.* [< Gk, comb. form repr. *karkínos* crab, ulcerous sore; cf. CANCER]

car·cin·o·gen (kär sin′ə jən, -jen′, kär′sə nə jen′, -nō-), *n. Pathol.* any substance or agent that tends to produce a cancer. [1935–40; CARCINO- + -GEN] —**car·cin·o·gen·ic** (kär′sə nə jen′ik, -nō-), *adj.* —**car·ci·no·ge·nic·i·ty** (kär′sə nō jə nis′i tē), *n.*

car·ci·no·gen·e·sis (kär′sə nə jen′ə sis, -nō-), *n. Pathol.* the development of a cancer. [1925–30; CARCINO- + -GENESIS]

car·ci·noid (kär′sə noid′), *n. Pathol.* a small, yellowish amino-acid and peptide-secreting tumor usually found in the gastrointestinal tract and lung. [1925–30; CARCIN(O)- + -OID]

car′cinoid syn′drome, *Pathol.* the systemic effects, including flushing, palpitations, diarrhea, and cramps, resulting from increased blood levels of serotonin secreted by a carcinoid. Also called **car·ci·noi·do·sis** (kär′sə noi dō′sis).

car·ci·no·ma (kär′sə nō′mə), *n., pl.* **-mas, -ma·ta** (-mə tə). *Pathol.* a malignant and invasive epithelial tumor that spreads by metastasis and often recurs after excision; cancer. [1715–25; < L: ulcer, tumor < Gk *karkínōma;* see CARCINO-, -OMA] —**car′ci·no′ma·toid′,** *adj.* —**car′ci·no′ma·tous,** *adj.*

car·ci·no·ma·to·sis (kär′sə nō mə tō′sis), *n. Pathol.* a condition marked by the production of an overwhelming number of carcinomas throughout the body. [1900–05; < L *carcinōmat-* (s. of *carcinōma*) CARCINOMA + -OSIS]

car·ci·no·sar·co·ma (kär′sə nō sär kō′mə), *n., pl.* **-mas, -ma·ta** (-mə tə). *Pathol.* a malignant tumor composed of both carcinomatous and sarcomatous elements. Also called **sarcocarcinoma.** [1925–30; < NL; see CARCINO-, SARCOMA]

car′ coat′, a hip-length overcoat or jacket originally designed to be worn while driving a car. [1960–65]

card[1] (kärd), *n.* **1.** a usually rectangular piece of stiff paper, thin pasteboard, or plastic for various uses, as to write information on or printed as a means of identifying the holder: *a 3″ × 5″ file card; a membership card.* **2.** one of a set of thin pieces of cardboard with spots, figures, etc., used in playing various games; playing card. **3. cards,** (*usually used with a singular v.*) **a.** a game or games played with such a set. **b.** the playing of such a game: *to win at cards.* **c.** *Casino.* the winning of 27 cards or more. **d.** *Whist.* tricks won in excess of six. **4.** Also called **greeting card.** a piece of paper or thin cardboard, usually folded, printed with a message of holiday greeting, congratulations, or other sentiment, often with an illustration or decorations, for mailing to a person on an appropriate occasion. **5.** something useful in attaining an objective, as a course of action or position of strength, comparable to a high card held in a game: *If negotiation fails, we still have another card to play.* **6.** postcard. **7.** See **calling card** (def. 1). **8.** *Com.* **a.** See **credit card. b.** See **bank card. 9.** a program of the events at races, boxing matches, etc. **10.** scorecard. **11.** a menu or wine list. **12.** See **compass card. 13.** *Computers.* **a.** See **punch card. b.** board (def. 14a). **14.** See **trading card. 15.** *Informal.* **a.** a person who is amusing or facetious. **b.** any person, esp. one with some indicated characteristic: *a queer card.* **16. in** or **on the cards,** impending or likely; probable: *A reorganization is in the cards.* **17. play one's cards right,** to act cleverly, sensibly, or cautiously: *If you play your cards right, you may get mentioned in her will.* **18. put one's cards on the table,** to be completely straightforward and open; conceal nothing: *He always believed in putting his cards on the table.* —*v.t.* **19.** to provide with a card. **20.** to fasten on a card. **21.** to write, list, etc., on cards. **22.** *Slang.* to examine the identity card or papers of: *The bartender was carding all youthful customers to be sure they were of legal drinking age.* [1350–1400; ME *carde,* unexplained var. of CARTE]

card[2] (kärd), *n.* Also called **carding machine. 1.** a machine for combing and paralleling fibers of cotton, flax, wool, etc., prior to spinning to remove short, undesirable fibers and produce a sliver. **2.** a similar implement for raising the nap on cloth. —*v.t.* **3.** to dress (wool or the like) with a card. **4. card out,** *Print.* to add extra space between lines of text, so as to fill out a page or column or give the text a better appearance. [1325–75; ME *carde* < MF: lit., teasel head < LL *cardus* thistle, var. of L *carduus*] —**card′er,** *n.*

Card., Cardinal.

car·da·mom (kär′də məm), *n.* **1.** the aromatic seed capsules of a tropical Asian plant, *Elettaria cardamomum,* of the ginger family, used as a spice or condiment and in medicine. **2.** the plant itself. **3.** a related plant, *Amomum compactum,* or its seeds, used as a substitute for true cardamom. Also, **car·da·mon** (kär′də-mən), **car′da·mum.** [1350–1400; ME (< MF) < L *cardamōmum* < Gk *kardámōmon,* b. *kárdamon* cress and *ámōmon* a spice plant]

Car′damom Moun′tains, a mountain range in SE India, part of the Western Ghats. Highest peaks over 4500 ft. (1370 m). Also called **Car′damom Hills′.**

Car′dan joint′ (kär′dan), *Mach.* a universal joint consisting of a crosslike piece, opposite ends of which rotate within the forked end of each of the two shafts connected. [1900–05; named after G. *Cardano* (1501–76), Italian mathematician, its inventor]

card·board (kärd′bôrd′, -bōrd′), *n.* **1.** a thin, stiff pasteboard, used for signs, boxes, etc. —*adj.* **2.** resembling cardboard, esp. in flimsiness: *an apartment with cardboard walls.* **3.** not fully lifelike; shallow; two-dimensional: *a play with cardboard characters.* [1840–50; CARD[1] + BOARD]

card-car·ry·ing (kärd′kar′ē ing), *adj.* **1.** admittedly belonging to a group or party: *a card-carrying Communist.* **2.** *Often Facetious.* dedicated to an ideal, profession, or interest: *a card-carrying humanist.* [1945–50]

card′ cat′alog, a file of cards of uniform size arranged in some definite order and listing the items in the collection of a library or group of libraries, each card typically identifying a single item. [1850–55, *Amer.*]

card′ cloth′ing, a very sturdy fabric with a leather or rubber fillet imbedded with wire teeth for disentangling and cleaning textile fibers, used to cover the rollers or flats of a carding machine.

card′ count′er, *Blackjack.* a casino player who memorizes or records which cards have been played in previous hands in order to calculate the odds on receiving winning cards or combinations from those remaining to be dealt, the practice often being held as illegal.

card-cut (kärd′kut′), *adj.* having a fretwork pattern in low relief: *card-cut woodwork.*

Cár·de·nas (kär′th̶e näs′), *n.* **1. Lá·za·ro** (lä′sä rô′), 1895–1970, Mexican general and political reformer: president 1934–40. **2.** a seaport in NW Cuba. 55,209.

card•hold•er (kärd′hōl′dər), *n.* **1.** a registered member of an organization, esp. of a union or a political party, who has been issued a card in evidence of membership. **2.** a person who has a borrower's card from a library. **3.** a person to whom a credit card or bank card is issued. **4.** (on a typewriter) either of a pair of devices able to be raised to hold stiff objects, as envelopes or cards, in place for typing. [1650–60; CARD¹ + HOLDER]

cardi-, var. of **cardio-** before a vowel: *cardialgia.*

car•di•a (kär′dē ə), *n., pl.* **-di•ae** (-dē ē′), **-di•as.** *Anat.* an opening that connects the esophagus and the upper part of the stomach. [1775–85; < NL < Gk *kardia* a medical term for this opening, lit., HEART; perh. so called because the opening is on the same side of the body as the heart]

-cardia, a combining form occurring in compounds that denote an anomalous or undesirable action or position of the heart, as specified by the initial element: *dextrocardia; tachycardia.* [perh. orig. repr. Gk *kardia* HEART, though coincidence with the abstract n. suffix -IA has influenced sense]

car•di•ac (kär′dē ak′), *adj.* **1.** of or pertaining to the heart: *cardiac disease.* **2.** of or pertaining to the esophageal portion of the stomach. —*n.* **3.** *Med.* a cardiac remedy. **4.** a person suffering from heart disease. [1400–50; late ME (< MF *cardiaque*) < L *cardiacus* < Gk *kardiakós,* equiv. to *kardí(a)* HEART + *-akos* -AC]

car′diac arrest′, *Pathol.* abrupt cessation of heartbeat. [1955–60]

car′diac cy′cle, one complete heartbeat, consisting of one contraction and relaxation of the heart.

car′diac gly′coside, *Pharm.* any of a group of drugs used to stimulate the heart in cases of heart failure, obtained from a number of plants, as the foxglove, squill, or yellow oleander. Also, **car′diac glu′coside.**

car′diac mus′cle, *Anat.* **1.** a specialized form of striated muscle occurring in the hearts of vertebrates. **2.** the myocardium. [1900–05]

car′diac neuro′sis, *Pathol.* an anxiety reaction characterized by quick fatigue, shortness of breath, rapid heartbeat, dizziness, and other cardiac symptoms, but not caused by disease of the heart. Also called **effort syndrome, irritable heart, neurocirculatory asthenia, soldier's heart.**

car′diac out′put, blood volume in liters pumped by the left ventricle of the heart per minute.

car′diac tamponade′, *Pathol.* tamponade (def. 2).

car•di•al•gi•a (kär′dē al′jē ə, -jə), *n. Pathol.* **1.** heartburn (def. 1). **2.** cardiodynia. [1645–55; CARDI- + -ALGIA]

car•di•ec•to•my (kär′dē ek′tə mē), *n. Surg.* **1.** excision of the heart. **2.** excision of the cardiac section of the stomach. [CARDI- + -ECTOMY]

Car•diff (kär′dif), *n.* a seaport in South Glamorgan, in SE Wales. 284,000.

car•di•gan (kär′di gən), *n.* a usually collarless knitted sweater or jacket that opens down the front. Also called **car′digan sweat′er, car′digan jack′et.** [1865–70; named after J. T. Brudnell, 7th Earl of *Cardigan* (1797–1868), British cavalryman of Crimean War fame]

Car•di•gan (kär′di gən), *n.* **1.** Cardiganshire. **2.** one of a variety of Welsh corgi having a long tail. Cf. **Pembroke** (def. 3). See illus. under **Welsh corgi.**

Car′digan Bay′, an inlet of St. George's Channel, on the W coast of Wales.

Car•di•gan•shire (kär′di gən shēr′, -shər), *n.* a historic county in Dyfed, in W Wales. Also called **Cardigan.**

cardinal (def. 4), *Cardinalis cardinalis,* length 8½ in. (22 cm)

car•di•nal (kär′dn l), *adj.* **1.** of prime importance; chief; principal: *of cardinal significance.* **2.** of the color cardinal. —*n.* **3.** *Rom. Cath. Ch.* a high ecclesiastic appointed by the pope to the College of Cardinals and ranking above every other ecclesiastic but the pope. **4.** Also called **cardinal grosbeak.** a crested grosbeak, *Cardinalis cardinalis,* of North America, the male of which is bright red. **5.** any of various similar birds. **6.** a deep, rich red color. **7.** a woman's short cloak with a hood, originally made of scarlet cloth and popularly worn in the 18th century. **8.** See **cardinal number.** [bef. 1150; ME, OE < L *cardinālis,* equiv. to *cardin-* (s. of *cardō*) hinge, hence, something on which other things hinge + *-ālis* -AL¹] —**car′di•nal•ly,** *adv.* —**car′di•nal•ship′,** *n.*

car•di•nal•ate (kär′dn l āt′), *n. Rom. Cath. Ch.* **1.** the body of cardinals. **2.** the office, rank, or dignity of a cardinal. [1635–45; CARDINAL + -ATE³]

car•di•nal•fish (kär′dn l fish′), *n., pl.* (*esp. collectively*) **-fish,** (*esp. referring to two or more kinds or species*) **-fish•es.** any of the perchlike fishes of the family Apogonidae, many species of which are bright red with black markings. [CARDINAL + FISH]

car′dinal flow′er, a North American plant, *Lobelia cardinalis,* with showy red tubular flowers in an elongated cluster. Also called **scarlet lobelia.** [1620–30, *Amer.*; so called from its color]

CONCISE ETYMOLOGY KEY: <, descended or borrowed from; >, whence; b., blend of, blended; c., cognate with; cf., compare; deriv., derivative; equiv., equivalent; imit., imitative; obl., oblique; r., replacing; s., stem; sp., spelling, spelled; resp., respelling, respelled; trans., translation; ?, origin unknown; *, unattested; ‡, probably earlier than. See the full key inside the front cover.

car′dinal gros′beak, cardinal (def. 4). [1795–1805]

car•di•nal•i•ty (kär′dn al′i tē), *n., pl.* **-ties.** *Math.* (of a set) the cardinal number indicating the number of elements in the set. [1930–35; CARDINAL + -ITY]

car′dinal num′ber, 1. Also called **car′dinal nu′meral.** any of the numbers that express amount, as *one, two, three,* etc. (distinguished from *ordinal number*). **2.** Also called **potency, power.** *Math.* a number or symbol analogous to the number of elements in a finite set, being identical for two sets that can be placed into one-to-one correspondence: *The cardinal number of the set* $a_1, a_2, \ldots a_n$ *is n.* [1585–95]

car′dinal points′, the four chief directions of the compass; the north, south, east, and west points. [1540–50]

car′dinal sign′, *Astrol.* any of the four astrological signs, Aries, Cancer, Libra, or Capricorn, that begin at the equinoxes and solstices, thus marking the beginning of the seasons: characterized by the attribute of strong initiative. Cf. **quadruplicity.** [1350–1400; ME]

car′dinal sys′tem, a system of coding navigational aids by shape, color, and number, according to their positions relative to navigational hazards. Cf. **lateral system.**

car′dinal tet′ra, a small, brilliantly colored red and blue characin fish, *Paracheirodon axelrodi,* native to tropical forest streams in Brazil and Colombia: a popular aquarium fish.

car′dinal trait′, *Psychol.* a basic and dominant characteristic, as greed or ambition, that, according to a theory developed by psychologist Gordon Allport (1936), controls the behavior of many people.

car′dinal vir′tue, 1. anything considered to be an important or characteristic virtue: *Tenacity is his cardinal virtue.* **2. cardinal virtues,** *Ancient Philos.* justice, prudence, temperance, and fortitude. [1300–50; ME]

car′dinal vow′el, *Phonet.* **1.** any one of eight primary, purportedly invariant, sustained vowel sounds that constitute a reference set for describing the vowel inventory of a language. **2.** any one of the eight or more supplementary or secondary cardinal vowels. [1920–25]

card′ in′dex, a file or catalog consisting of cards on which information has been entered so that desired items or data can be readily found. [1840–50, *Amer.*]

card•ing (kär′ding), *n.* the process in which fibers, as cotton, worsted, or wool, are manipulated into sliver form prior to spinning. [1425–75; late ME. See CARD², -ING¹]

card′ing machine′, card² (defs. 1, 2). [1780–90]

cardio-, a combining form meaning "heart," used in the formation of compound words: *cardiogram.* Also, *esp. before a vowel,* **cardi-.** [< Gk *kardio-,* comb. form of *kardía*]

car•di•o•ac•cel•er•a•tor (kär′dē ō ak sel′ə rā′tər), *n. Pharm.* a substance that increases the heart rate. [CARDIO- + ACCELERATOR]

car•di•o•ac•tive (kär′dē ō ak′tiv), *adj. Pharm.* of or pertaining to a drug or other substance affecting the function of the heart. [CARDIO- + ACTIVE]

car•di•o•dyn•i•a (kär′dē ō din′ē ə), *n. Pathol.* pain in the heart region. Also called **cardialgia.** [CARDI- + Gk *odýn(ē)* pain + *-ia* -IA]

car•di•o•gen•ic (kär′dē ə jen′ik), *adj.* **1.** originating in the heart. **2.** *Pathol.* caused by a disorder of the heart. [1920–25; CARDIO- + -GENIC]

car′diogen′ic shock′, a type of shock caused by decreased cardiac output despite adequate blood volume, owing to a disease of the heart itself, as myocardial infarction, or any other factor that interferes with the filling or emptying of the heart. Cf. **hypovolemic shock.**

car•di•o•gram (kär′dē ə gram′), *n.* electrocardiogram. [1875–80; CARDIO- + -GRAM¹]

car•di•o•graph (kär′dē ə graf′, -gräf′), *n.* electrocardiograph. [1865–70; CARDIO- + -GRAPH] —**car•di•o•graph•ic** (kär′dē ə graf′ik), *adj.* —**car•di•og•ra•phy** (kär′dē og′rə fē), *n.*

car•di•oid (kär′dē oid′), *n. Math.* a somewhat heart-shaped curve, being the path of a point on a circle that rolls externally, without slipping, on another equal circle. Equation: $r = a\,(1 - \cos A)$. [1745–55; < Gk *kardioeidḗs* heart-shaped. See CARDI-, -OID]

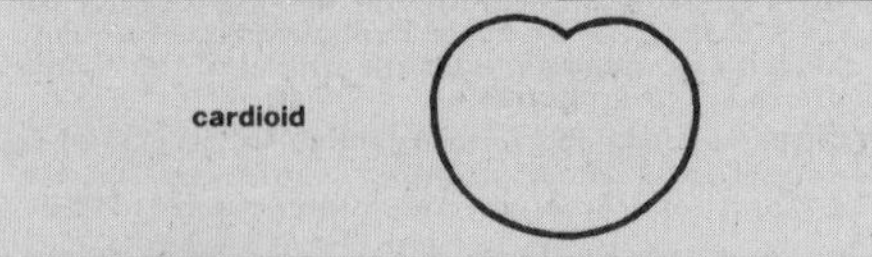

cardioid

car•di•o•lip•in (kär′dē ō lip′in), *n. Biochem.* a lipid purified from bovine heart and used as an antigen for reacting with reagin, the Wassermann antibody, in the Wassermann diagnostic test for syphilis. [1942; CARDIO- + LIP(ID) + -IN²]

car•di•ol•o•gy (kär′dē ol′ə jē), *n.* the study of the heart and its functions in health and disease. [1840–50; CARDIO- + -LOGY] —**car•di•o•log•ic** (kär′dē ə loj′ik), **car′di•o•log′i•cal,** *adj.* —**car′di•ol′o•gist,** *n.*

car•di•o•meg•a•ly (kär′dē ō meg′ə lē), *n. Pathol.* abnormal enlargement of the heart. Also, **car•di•o•me•ga•li•a** (kär′dē ō mə gā′lē ə, -gāl′yə). [CARDIO- + *-megaly* < NL *megalia*; see MEGALO-, -Y³]

car•di•o•my•op•a•thy (kär′dē ō mī op′ə thē), *n. Pathol.* any disease of the heart muscle, leading to decreased function: usually of unknown cause. [1960–65; CARDIO- + MYOPATHY]

car•di•op•a•thy (kär′dē op′ə thē), *n. Pathol.* any disease or disorder of the heart. [1880–85; CARDIO- + -PATHY]

car•di•o•ple•gi•a (kär′dē ō plē′jē ə, -jə), *n.* the temporary arresting of the heartbeat during cardiac surgery by any of various methods, esp. by injection of chemical substances. [CARDIO- + -PLEGIA]

car•di•o•pul•mo•nar•y (kär′dē ō pul′mə ner′ē, -pŏŏl′-), *adj.* of, pertaining to, or affecting the heart and lungs: *cardiopulmonary laboratory.* [1880–85; CARDIO- + PULMONARY]

cardiopul′monary resuscita′tion, emergency procedure for reviving heart and lung function, involving special physical techniques and often the use of electrical and mechanical equipment. *Abbr.:* CPR [1970–75]

car•di•o•res•pi•ra•to•ry (kär′dē ō res′pər ə tôr′ē, -tōr′ē, -ri spīᵊr′ə-), *adj.* of, pertaining to, or affecting the heart and respiratory system. [1890–95; CARDIO- + RESPIRATORY]

car•di•o•spasm (kär′dē ə spaz′əm), *n. Pathol.* failure of the muscle fibers at the lower end of the esophagus to relax, resulting in swallowing difficulty and regurgitation. [1895–1900; CARDIO- + SPASM]

car•di•o•ta•chom•e•ter (kär′dē ō ta kom′i tər, -tə-), *n.* an instrument for measuring the heart rate. [1925–30; CARDIO- + TACHOMETER]

car•di•o•ton•ic (kär′dē ō ton′ik), *Med.* —*adj.* **1.** having a tonic effect on the action of the heart. —*n.* **2.** a cardiotonic substance. [1935–40; CARDIO- + TONIC]

car•di•o•vas•cu•lar (kär′dē ō vas′kyə lər), *adj. Anat.* of, pertaining to, or affecting the heart and blood vessels. [1875–80; CARDIO- + VASCULAR]

cardiovas′cular condi′tioning, enhancement of heart and circulatory function produced by regular vigorous aerobic exercise, as jogging, swimming, or cycling.

car•di•o•ver•sion (kär′dē ō vûr′zhən, -shən), *n. Med.* restoring the rhythm of the heart to normal by applying direct-current electrical shock. [1970–75; CARDIO- + (RE)VERSION]

car•di•tis (kär dī′tis), *n. Pathol.* inflammation of the pericardium, myocardium, or endocardium, separately or in combination. [1775–85; < NL; see CARDI-, -ITIS] —**car•dit•ic** (kär dit′ik), *adj.*

-cardium, a combining form occurring in compounds that denote tissue or organs associated with the heart, as specified by the initial element: *myocardium; pericardium.* [prob. generalized from PERICARDIUM]

card-key (kärd′kē′), *n., pl.* **-keys.** a small plastic card with magnetic coding that is read electronically when inserted into a scanner and used in place of a key to open locks, hotel doors, etc.

car•doon (kär dōōn′), *n.* a composite plant, *Cynara cardunculus,* of the Mediterranean area, having a root and leafstalks eaten as a vegetable. Also, **car•don** (kär-dōn′). [1605–15; < MF *cardon* < OPr < ML *cardōn-,* s. of *cardō,* for L *card(u)us* thistle, cardoon]

Car•do•zo (kär dō′zō), *n.* **Benjamin Nathan,** 1870–1938, associate justice of the U.S. Supreme Court 1932–38.

card•play•er (kärd′plā′ər), *n.* a person who plays cards. [1580–90; CARD¹ + PLAYER]

card′ punch′. See **key punch** (def. 1).

card•room¹ (kärd′rōōm′, -rŏŏm′), *n.* **1.** a room equipped for playing cards: *The club has a big cardroom.* **2.** (in some U.S. states or cities) a commercial gambling establishment licensed to conduct card games, usually poker, only. [1750–60; CARD¹ + ROOM]

card•room² (kärd′rōōm′, -rŏŏm′), *n.* a room for carding wool. [CARD² + ROOM]

card′ shark′, 1. an expert cardplayer. **2.** cardsharp.

card•sharp (kärd′shärp′), *n.* a person, esp. a professional gambler, who cheats at card games. Also, **card′•sharp′er.** [1855–60, *Amer.*; CARD¹ + SHARP] —**card′•sharp′ing,** *n.*

card•stock (kärd′stok′), *n.* paper stock stiff enough for the printing of business cards and similar uses. [CARD¹ + STOCK]

card′ ta′ble, a small, light table, usually with folding legs, used mainly for card games. [1705–15]

Car•duc•ci (kär dōō′chē; *It.* kär dōōt′chē), *n.* **Gio•suè** (jō swe′), ("*Enotrio Romano*"), 1835–1907, Italian poet and critic: Nobel prize 1906.

car•du•e•line (kär′jōō ē′lin), *adj.* **1.** of or pertaining to the passerine subfamily Carduelinae, including the goldfinches, siskins, canaries and crossbills. —*n.* **2.** any bird of the subfamily Carduelinae. [< NL *Carduelinae,* equiv. to *Carduel(is)* genus name (L: goldfinch, deriv. of *carduus* thistle) + *-inae* -INAE]

care (kâr), *n., v.,* **cared, car•ing.** —*n.* **1.** a state of mind in which one is troubled; worry, anxiety, or concern: *He was never free from care.* **2.** a cause or object of worry, anxiety, concern, etc.: *Their son has always been a great care to them.* **3.** serious attention; solicitude; heed; caution: *She devotes great care to her work.* **4.** protection; charge: *He is under the care of a doctor.* **5.** temporary keeping, as for the benefit of or until claimed by the owner: *He left his valuables in the care of friends. Address my mail in care of the American Embassy.* **6.** grief; suffering; sorrow. **7. take care, a.** to be alert; be careful: *Take care that you don't fall on the ice!* **b.** take care of yourself; goodbye: used as an expression of parting. **8. take care of, a.** to watch over; be responsible for: *to take care of an invalid.* **b.** to act on; deal with; attend to: *to take care of paying a bill.* —*v.i.* **9.** to be concerned or solicitous; have thought or regard. **10.** to be concerned or have a special preference (usually used in negative constructions): *I don't care if I do.* **11.** to make provision or look out (usually fol. by *for*): *Will you care for the children while I am away?* **12.** to have an inclination, liking, fondness, or affection (usually fol. by *for*): *Would you care for dessert? I don't care for him very much.* —*v.t.* **13.** to feel concern about: *He doesn't care what others say.* **14.** to wish; desire; like: *Would you care to dance?* **15. couldn't care less,** could not care less; be completely unconcerned: *I couldn't care less* whether she goes to the party or not. Also, **could care less.** [bef. 900; (n.) ME; OE *caru, cearu,* c. Goth *kara,* OHG *chara* lament; (v.) ME *caren,* OE *cearian, carian*] **—car′er,** *n.*

—Syn. 1. See **concern. 3.** To take CARE, PAINS, TROUBLE (to do something) implies watchful, conscientious effort to do something exactly right. To take CARE implies the performance of one particular detail: *She took care to close the cover before striking the match.* To take PAINS suggests a sustained carefulness, an effort to see that nothing is overlooked but that every small detail receives attention: *to take pains with fine embroidery.* To take TROUBLE implies an effort that requires a considerable amount of activity and exertion: *to take the trouble to make suitable arrangements.*

—Usage. 15. COULDN'T CARE LESS, a phrase used to express indifference, is sometimes heard as COULD CARE LESS, which ought to mean the opposite but is intended to be synonymous with the former phrase. Both versions are common mainly in informal speech.

CARE (kâr), *n.* a private organization for the collection of funds, goods, etc., for distribution to the needy in foreign countries. Also, **Care** [*C(ooperative for) A(merican) R(elief) E(verywhere)*]

ca•reen (kə rēn′), *v.i.* **1.** (of a vehicle) to lean, sway, or tip to one side while in motion: *The car careened around the corner.* **2.** (of a ship) to heel over or list. **3.** career (def. 7). **4.** *South Midland U.S.* to lean or bend away from the vertical position: *The barn was careening a little.* **—*v.t. Naut.*** **5.** to cause (a ship) to lie over on a side, as for repairs or cleaning; heave down. **6.** to clean or repair (a ship lying on its side for the purpose). **7.** to cause (a ship) to heel over or list, as by the force of a beam wind. **—*n.*** **8.** a careening. **9.** *Naut.* the position of a careened ship. [1585–95 for def. 9; < MF *carine* < L *carīna* keel, nutshell; akin to Gk *káryon* nut] **—ca•reen′er,** *n.*

ca•reer (kə rēr′), *n.* **1.** an occupation or profession, esp. one requiring special training, followed as one's lifework: *He sought a career as a lawyer.* **2.** a person's progress or general course of action through life or through a phase of life, as in some profession or undertaking: *His career as a soldier ended with the armistice.* **3.** success in a profession, occupation, etc. **4.** a course, esp. a swift one. **5.** speed, esp. full speed: *The horse stumbled in full career.* **6.** *Archaic.* a charge at full speed. **—*v.i.*** **7.** to run or move rapidly along; go at full speed. **—*adj.*** **8.** having or following a career; professional: *a career diplomat.* [1525–35; < MF *carriere* < OPr *carriera* lit., road < LL *carrāria (via)* vehicular (road), equiv. to L *carr(us)* wagon (see CAR[1] + *-āria,* fem. of *-ārius* -ARY]

—Syn. 2. vocation, calling, work, lifework, livelihood.

ca•reer•ism (kə rēr′iz əm), *n.* devotion to a successful career, often at the expense of one's personal life, ethics, etc. [1930–35; CAREER + -ISM]

ca•reer•ist (kə rēr′ist), *n.* **1.** a person who follows a career. **2.** a person who pursues a policy or attitude of careerism. [1905–10; CAREER + -IST]

career′ wom′an, a woman who has a profession or a business career. Also, **ca•reer′wom′an.** [1935–40, *Amer.*]

care•free (kâr′frē′), *adj.* **1.** without anxiety or worry. **2.** requiring little care: *carefree fabrics.* [1785–95; CARE + FREE] **—care′free′ness,** *n.*

—Syn. 1. lighthearted, joyous, elated, cheerful, gleeful, blithe.

care•ful (kâr′fəl), *adj.* **1.** cautious in one's actions: *Be careful when you cross the street.* **2.** taking pains in one's work; exact; thorough: *a careful typist.* **3.** (of things) done or performed with accuracy or caution: *careful research.* **4.** solicitously mindful (usually fol. by *of, about,* or *in*): *careful of the rights of others; careful about one's behavior; careful in speech.* **5.** *Archaic.* **a.** troubled. **b.** attended with anxiety. [bef. 1000; ME; OE *carful, cearful.* See CARE, -FUL] **—care′ful•ly,** *adv.* **—care′ful•ness,** *n.*

—Syn. 1. watchful, guarded, chary, circumspect. CAREFUL, CAUTIOUS, DISCREET, WARY imply a watchful guarding against something. CAREFUL implies guarding against mistakes, by paying strict and close attention to details, and, often, trying to use good judgment: *He was careful to distinguish between them.* CAUTIOUS implies a fear of some unfavorable situation and investigation before coming to conclusions: *cautious about investments.* DISCREET implies being prudent in speech and action and being trustworthy as a confidant: *discreet in manner, in keeping secrets.* WARY implies a vigilant lookout for a danger suspected or feared: *wary of polite strangers.* **2.** meticulous, discerning. **2, 3.** See **painstaking. 3.** conscientious. **4.** thoughtful, concerned, solicitous, attentive, heedful, regardful. **—Ant. 1–4.** careless.

care•giv•er (kâr′giv′ər), *n.* **1.** a person who cares for someone who is sick or disabled. **2.** an adult who cares for an infant or child. [1980–85; CARE + GIVER]

care′ la′bel, a label attached to a garment or fabric giving the manufacturer's instructions for its care and cleaning. [1965–70]

care•less (kâr′lis), *adj.* **1.** not paying enough attention to what one does: *a careless typist.* **2.** not exact, accurate, or thorough: *careless work.* **3.** done or said heedlessly or negligently; unconsidered: *a careless remark.* **4.** not caring or troubling; having no care or concern; unconcerned (usually fol. by *of, about,* or *in*): *careless of the rights of others; careless about one's behavior; careless in speech.* **5.** possessed or caused without effort or art; unstudied: *careless beauty.* **6.** *Archaic.* free from anxiety. [bef. 1000; ME; OE *carlēas.* See CARE, -LESS] **—care′less•ly,** *adv.* **—care′less•ness,** *n.*

—Syn. 1. inattentive, incautious, unwary, indiscreet, reckless. **2.** inaccurate, negligent. **3.** unthoughtful, unmindful. **4.** thoughtless, forgetful; inconsiderate. **—Ant. 1–4.** careful.

Car•en (kar′ən), *n.* a female given name.

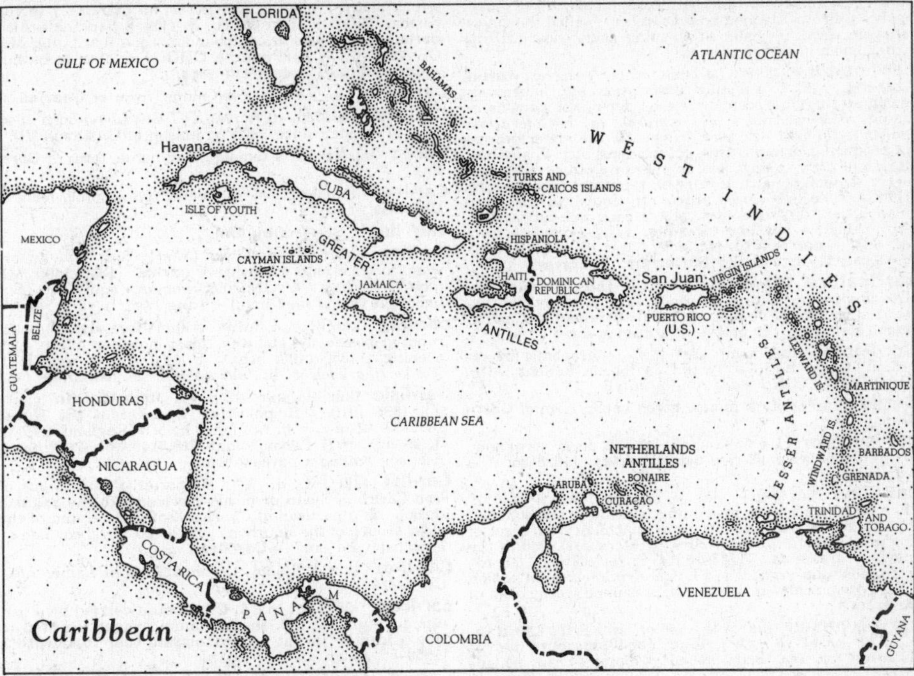

care′ pack′age, **1.** Also **CARE′ pack′age.** a package containing food, clothing, or other items sent as necessities to the needy. **2.** a gift of treats to relatives or friends, esp. of items not readily available to them: *She sends monthly care packages of homemade cookies to her son at college.* [from the aid packages distributed by CARE]

ca•ress (kə res′), *n.* **1.** an act or gesture expressing affection, as an embrace or kiss, esp. a light stroking or touching. **—*v.t.*** **2.** to touch or pat gently to show affection. **3.** to touch, stroke, etc., lightly, as if in affection: *The breeze caressed the trees.* **4.** to treat with favor, kindness, etc. [1605–15; < F *caresse* < It *carezza* < VL **caritia,* equiv. to L *cār(us)* dear + *-itia* suffix of abstract nouns; cf. CHARITY] **—ca•ress′a•ble,** *adj.* **—ca•ress′er,** *n.* **—ca•ress′ing•ly,** *adv.*

—Syn. 1. pat, fondling, hug.

ca•ress•ive (kə res′iv), *adj.* **1.** of the nature of or resembling a caress: *caressive words; a caressive breeze.* **2.** characterized by or given to caresses. [1795–1805; CARESS + -IVE] **—ca•ress′ive•ly,** *adv.*

car•et (kar′it), *n.* a mark (‸) made in written or printed matter to show the place where something is to be inserted. [1700–10; < L *caret* (there) is lacking or wanting, 3rd pers. sing. pres. ind. of *carēre* to be without]

care•tak•er (kâr′tā′kər), *n.* **1.** a person who is in charge of the maintenance of a building, estate, etc.; superintendent. **2.** a person or group that temporarily performs the duties of an office. **3.** *Brit.* a janitor. **4.** a person who takes care of another. **—*adj.*** **5.** involving the temporary performance of the duties of an office: *a caretaker government.* [1855–60; CARE + TAKER] **—care′tak′ing,** *n.*

Ca•rew (kə rōō′; *sometimes* kâr′ōō), *n.* **1. Thomas,** 1598?–1639?, English poet. **2.** a male given name.

care•worn (kâr′wôrn′, -wōrn′), *adj.* showing signs of care or worry; fatigued by trouble or anxiety; haggard: *a careworn old woman.* [1820–30; CARE + WORN]

car•ex (kâr′eks, kar′-), *n.* any sedge of the genus *Carex.* [< NL (Linnaeus); L *cārex* sedge]

Car•ey (kâr′ē, kar′ē), *n.* male given name, form of **Carew.**

car•fare (kär′fâr′), *n.* the amount charged for a ride on a subway, streetcar, bus, etc. [1865–70, *Amer.*; CAR[1] + FARE]

car•ful (kär′fŏŏl), *n., pl.* **-fuls.** the largest number or amount that a car can hold. [1825–35; CAR[1] + -FUL]

—Usage. See **-ful.**

car•go (kär′gō), *n., pl.* **-goes, -gos. 1.** the lading or freight of a ship, airplane, etc. **2.** load. [1640–50; < Sp: a load, n. deriv. of *cargar* to load < LL *carricāre;* see CHARGE]

—Syn. 1. See **freight. 2.** burden.

car′go bay′, the large central area of the space shuttle orbiter's fuselage in which payloads and their support equipment are carried. Also called **payload bay.** Cf. **bay**[2] (def. 2a).

car′go cult′, (*sometimes caps.*) any of various native religious cults of a millenarian and messianic character located in the southwestern Pacific islands, holding that spirits will bring large cargoes of modern goods for distribution among its adherents. **—car′go cult′ist.** [1945–50]

car′go lin′er, a cargo ship that sails regularly between designated ports according to a published schedule. Also, **car′go•lin′er.** Cf. **tramp** (def. 19).

car′go pock′et, a large patch pocket, usually pleated at the sides and often having a flap. [1970–75]

car•hop (kär′hop′), *n., v.,* **-hopped, -hop•ping.** **—*n.*** **1.** a person who serves customers in their cars at a drive-in restaurant. **—*v.i.*** **2.** to work as a carhop. [1935–40; CAR[1] + (BELL)HOP]

Car•i•a (kâr′ē ə), *n.* an ancient district in SW Asia Minor.

car•i•am•a (kar′ē am′ə), *n.* seriema. [< NL < Pg]

Car•i•an (kâr′ē ən), *n.* **1.** a native or inhabitant of Caria. **2.** the extinct language of Caria, not known to be related to any other language, written in a script derived from the Greek alphabet. **—*adj.*** **3.** of or pertaining to Caria. **4.** of or pertaining to the Carians or their language. [1600–10; CARI(A) + -AN]

Ca•rí•as An•di•no (kä rē′äs än dē′nô), **Ti•bur•cio** (tē vōōr′syô), 1876–1968, Honduran lawyer, soldier, and statesman: president 1933–49.

Car•ib (kar′ib), *n., pl.* **-ibs,** (*esp. collectively*) **-ib.** for 1. **1.** a member of a group of Indian peoples formerly dominant through the Lesser Antilles, now found in small numbers in a few areas of the West Indies and in parts of Central America and northeastern South America. **2.** the family of languages spoken by the Caribs. [1545–55; < Sp *caribe* < Arawak]

Car•ib•be•an (kar′ə bē′ən, kə rib′ē-), *adj.* **1.** pertaining to the Caribs, the Lesser Antilles, or the Caribbean Sea and its islands. **—*n.*** **2.** a Carib. **3.** See **Caribbean Sea. 4. the,** *Informal.* the islands and countries of the Caribbean Sea collectively. See map above.

Car′ibbe′an Cur′rent, an ocean current flowing westward through the Caribbean Sea.

Car′ibbe′an Plate′, *Geol.* a major tectonic division of the earth's crust, encompassing the Central American portion of North America, the Caribbean Sea, and the islands of Cuba, Jamaica, Hispaniola, and Puerto Rico, as well as the Leeward and Windward Islands; bordered north and south by the North and South American Plates and west by the Cocos Plate.

Car′ibbe′an Sea′, a part of the Atlantic Ocean bounded by Central America, the West Indies, and South America. ab. 750,000 sq. mi. (1,943,000 sq. km); greatest known depth 22,788 ft. (6946 m). Also called **Caribbean.**

ca•ri•be (kə rē′bē; *Sp.* kä rē′ve), *n., pl.* **-bes** (-bēz; *Sp.* -ves). piranha. [1865–70; < Sp: cannibal, CARIB]

Car•i•bees (kar′ə bēz′), *n.* See under **Antilles.**

Car′i•boo Moun′tains (kar′ə bōō′), a mountain range in SW Canada, in E central British Columbia, part of the Rocky Mountains: highest peak, ab. 11,750 ft. (3580 m).

car•i•bou (kar′ə bōō′), *n., pl.* **-bous,** (*esp. collectively*) **-bou.** any of several large, North American deer of the genus *Rangifer,* related to the reindeer of the Old World. [1665–75, *Amer.*; < CanF *caribou,* r. earlier E *caribo,*

caribou, *Rangifer tarandus,* about 4 ft. (1.2 m) high at shoulder; length 6 ft. (1.8 m)

CONCISE PRONUNCIATION KEY: *act, cāpe, dâre, pärt; set, ēqual; if, īce; ox, ōver, ôrder, oil, bŏŏk, bōōt, out; up, ûrge; child; sing; shoe; thin,* **th**at; *zh as in treasure.* ə = *a* as in *alone, e* as in *system, i* as in *easily, o* as in *gallop, u* as in *circus;* ᵊ as in *fire* (fīᵊr), *hour* (ouᵊr). l and n can serve as syllabic consonants, as in *cradle* (krād′l), and *button* (but′n). See the full key inside the front cover.

both < Micmac *γalipu* deriv. (agent n.) of *γalipi-* shovel snow < Proto-Algonquian **maka·lipi-;* called the snow-shoveler from its habit of scraping aside snow with its front hoofs in search of food]

car·i·ca·ture (kar′i kə chər, -cho͝or′), *n., v.,* **-tured, -tur·ing.** —*n.* **1.** a picture, description, etc., ludicrously exaggerating the peculiarities or defects of persons or things: *His caricature of the mayor in this morning's paper is the best he's ever drawn.* **2.** the art or process of producing such pictures, descriptions, etc. **3.** any imitation or copy so distorted or inferior as to be ludicrous. —*v.t.* **4.** to make a caricature of; represent in caricature. [1740–50; earlier *caricatura* < It, equiv. to *caricat(o)* loaded, i.e., distorted (ptp. of *caricare;* see CHARGE) + *-ura* -URE] —**car′i·ca·tur·a·ble,** *adj.* —**car′i·ca·tur′·al,** *adj.* —**car′i·ca·tur·ist,** *n.*
—**Syn. 1.** cartoon. See **burlesque. 3.** travesty.

car′icature plant′, a tropical Old World shrub, *Graptophyllum pictum,* of the acanthus family, characterized by purple or red tubular flowers and leaf markings resembling the profile of a human face.

Car·i·com (kar′i kom′, kâr′-), *n.* an economic association formed in 1974 by ten Caribbean nations. Also, **CARICOM** [*Cari(bbean) com(munity)*]

Car·ie (kar′ē), *n.* a female given name, form of **Caroline.**

car·ies (kâr′ēz, -ē ēz′), *n., pl.* **-ies. 1.** decay, as of bone or of plant tissue. **2.** See **dental caries.** [1625–35; < L *cariēs* decay]

car·il·lon (kar′ə lon′, -lən *or, esp. Brit.,* kə ril′yən), *n.* **1.** a set of stationary bells hung in a tower and sounded by manual or pedal action, or by machinery. **2.** a set of horizontal metal plates, struck by hammers, used in the modern orchestra. [1765–75; < F: set of bells, OF *car(e)ignon, quarregnon* < VL **quadriniōn-,* re-formation of LL *quaterniōn-* QUATERNION; presumably orig. a set of four bells]

car·il·lon·neur (kar′ə lə nûr′ *or, esp. Brit.,* kə ril′yə nər; *Fr.* KA RĒ YÔ NŒR′), *n., pl.* **car·il·lon·neurs** (kar′ə lə nûrz′ *or, esp. Brit.,* kə ril′yə nərz; *Fr.* KA RĒ YÔ NŒR′). a person who plays a carillon. [1765–75; < F: see CARILLON, -EUR]

Car·in (kar′in), *n.* a female given name.

ca·ri·na (kə rī′nə, -rē′-), *n., pl.* **-nas, -nae** (-nē). **1.** *Zool.* a keellike part or ridge, esp. a ridge of bone on the ventral side of the sternum of birds. **2.** *Bot.* the two conjoined lower petals of a pea or bean flower that enclose the stamen and style. See illus. under **papilionaceous.** [1695–1705; < L: keel; cf. CAREEN] —**ca·ri′·nal,** *adj.*

Ca·ri·na (kə rī′nə *for 1;* kə rē′nə, -rī′- *for 2*), *n., gen.* **-nae** (-nē) for 1. **1.** *Astron.* the Keel, a southern constellation, containing the bright star, Canopus: one of the constellations into which Argo is divided. **2.** a female given name, form of **Carin.** [1695–1705]

car·i·nate (kar′ə nāt′, -nit), *adj. Zool., Bot.* formed with a carina; keellike. Also, **car′i·nat′ed.** [1775–85; < L *carinātus,* equiv. to *carin(a)* keel + *-ātus* -ATE[1]] —**car′i·na′tion,** *n.*

Ca·rin·thi·a (kə rin′thē ə), *n.* a province in S Austria. 536,727; 3681 sq. mi. (9535 sq. km). *Cap.:* Klagenfurt. —**Ca·rin′thi·an,** *adj.*

ca·rin·u·la (kə rin′yə lə), *n. Zool., Bot.* a small carina. Also, **car·i·nule** (kar′ə no͞ol′, -nyo͞ol′). [< NL, equiv. to *carin(a)* CARINA + *-ula* -ULE] —**ca·rin·u·late** (kə rin′yə lāt′, -lit), *adj.*

car·i·o·ca (kar′ē ō′kə), *n.* **1.** a modification of the samba. **2.** the music for this dance. [1930–35; after CARIOCA]

Car·i·o·ca (kar′ē ō′kə; *Port.* kä′RE ô′kə), *n.* a native of Rio de Janeiro. [1820–30; < Brazilian Pg < Tupi, equiv. to *cari* white + *oca* house or *boca* descendant of]

car·i·o·gen·ic (kâr′ē ə jen′ik), *adj.* conducive to the production or promotion of dental caries: *the cariogenic factors in sweets.* [CARI(ES) + -O- + -GENIC] —**car·i·o·ge·nic·i·ty** (kâr′ē ō jə nis′i tē), *n.*

car·i·ole (kar′ē ōl′), *n.* **1.** a small, open, two-wheeled vehicle. **2.** a covered cart. **3.** a light, open sleigh pulled by horses or dogs, esp. one used in French Canada. Also, **carriole.** [1760–70; < F *carriole* < OPr *carriola,* equiv. to *carri* carriage (< LL *carrium,* for L *carrus;* see CAR[1]) + *-ola* -OLE[1]]

car·i·ous (kâr′ē əs), *adj.* having caries, as teeth; decayed. [1520–30; < L *cariōsus* decayed, rotten, equiv. to *cari(ēs)* CARIES + *-ōsus* -OUS] —**car·i·os·i·ty** (kâr′ē os′i tē), **car′i·ous·ness,** *n.*

car·i·sop·ro·dol (kar′ə sop′rə dôl′, -dol′), *n. Pharm.* a crystalline, water-soluble powder, $C_{12}H_{24}N_2O_4$, used as a muscle relaxant. Also called **isopropyl meprobamate.** [CAR(BAMATE) + ISOPRO(PYL) + D(I)-[1] + -OL[1]]

ca·ri·tas (kä′RI täs′; *Eng.* kar′i tas′), *n. Latin.* charity. —**car·i·ta·tive** (kar′i tā′tiv, -tə tiv), *adj.*

car·i·tive (kar′i tiv), *adj.* (in certain inflected languages, esp. of the Caucasian group) abessive. [1855–60; < L *carit(us)* devoid of, without (ptp. of *carēre* not to have, to want) + -IVE]

car·jack·ing (kar′jak′ing), *n.* the forcible stealing of a vehicle from a motorist. —**car′jack′er,** *n.*

cark (kärk), *Archaic.* —*n.* **1.** care or worry. —*v.t., v.i.* **2.** to worry. [1250–1300; ME *carken* to be anxious, OE *becarcian,* appar. deriv. of *car-* (base of *caru* CARE) + *-k* suffix]

cark·ing (kär′king), *adj. Archaic.* distressful. [1300–50 (for ger.); 1555–65 (for current sense); ME; see CARK, -ING[2]]

carl (kärl), *n.* **1.** *Scot.* **a.** a strong, robust fellow, esp. a strong manual laborer. **b.** a miser; an extremely thrifty person. **2.** *Archaic.* a churl. **3.** *Obs.* a bondman. Also, **carle.** [bef. 1000 (in compounds; see HOUSECARL); ME; OE *-carl* < ON *karl* man; c. OHG *karl;* akin to CHURL] —**carl′ish,** *adj.* —**carl′ish·ness,** *n.*

CONCISE ETYMOLOGY KEY: <, descended or borrowed from; >, whence; b., blend of, blended; c., cognate with; cf., compare; deriv., derivative; equiv., equivalent; imit., imitative; obl., oblique; r., replacing; s., stem; sp., spelling, spelled; resp., respelling, respelled; trans., translation; ?, origin unknown; *, unattested; ‡, probably earlier than. See the full key inside the front cover.

Carl (kärl), *n.* a male given name, form of **Charles.**

Carl XVI Gustaf, (*Charles XVI Gustavus*) born 1946, king of Sweden since 1973 (grandson of Gustavus VI).

Car·la (kär′lə), *n.* a female given name, form of **Caroline.**

Car·leen (kär lēn′), *n.* a female given name, form of **Caroline.**

car′ line′. See **trolley line.**

car·line (kär′lin, ker′-), *n. Chiefly Scot.* **1.** an old woman. **2.** a hag; witch. Also, **carlin.** [1350–1400; ME (north) *kerling* < ON: old woman, equiv. to *kerl* (mutated var. of *karl* man) + *-ing* -ING[1]]

car·ling (kär′ling), *n. Naut.* a short fore-and-aft beam running beside a hatchway, mast hole, or other deck opening. [1350–1400; ME < F *carlingue* < Scand; cf. Icel *kerling* keelson, lit., old woman; see CARLINE]

Car·lisle (kär līl′, kär′līl), *n.* **1. John Grif·fin** (grif′in), 1835–1910, U.S. politician: Speaker of the House 1883–89. **2.** a city in Cumbria, in NW England. 99,700. **3.** a city in S Pennsylvania. 18,314. **4.** *Angling.* a fishhook having a narrow bend.

Car·list (kär′list), *n.* **1.** a supporter of the claims of Don Carlos of Spain or of his successors to the Spanish throne. **2.** a partisan of Charles X of France, and of the elder branch of the Bourbons. [1820–30; < Sp *carlista* or F *carliste;* see -IST] —**Car′lism,** *n.*

Car·li·ta (kär lē′tə), *n.* a female given name. Also, **Car·le′ta.**

car·load (kär′lōd′), *n.* **1.** the amount carried by a car, esp. a freight car. **2.** the minimum weight required to ship a load by rail at a discount rate (**car′load rate′**). [1850–55, *Amer.;* CAR[1] + LOAD]

Car·los (kär′lōs, -ləs; *Sp.* kär′lôs), *n.* **1. Don** (don; *Sp.* dôn), (*Carlos María Isidro de Borbón*), 1788–1855, pretender to the Spanish throne. **2.** a male given name.

Car·los de Aus·tri·a (kär′lôs the ous′tRē ä′), **Don** (dôn), 1545–68, eldest son of Philip II of Spain: died during imprisonment for conspiracy against his father.

Car·lo·ta (kär lô′tä), *n.* 1840–1927, wife of Maximilian: empress of Mexico 1864–67 (daughter of Leopold I of Belgium). English, **Charlotte.**

Car·lot·ta (kär lot′ə; *It.* kär lôt′tä), *n.* a female given name, Italian form of **Charlotte.**

Car·lo·vin·gi·an (kär′lə vin′jē ən), *adj., n.* Carolingian.

Car·low (kär′lō), *n.* a county in Leinster, in the SE Republic of Ireland. 39,814; 346 sq. mi. (896 sq. km). *Co. seat:* Carlow.

Carls·bad (kärlz′bad), *n.* **1.** a town in S California. 35,490. **2.** a city in SE New Mexico. 25,496. **3.** former name of **Karlovy Vary.**

Carls′bad Cav′erns, a series of limestone caverns, near Carlsbad, New Mexico. 68 sq. mi. (177 sq. km).

Carls′bad Cav′erns Na′tional Park′, a national park in SE New Mexico: site of Carlsbad Caverns. 71 sq. mi. (184 sq. km).

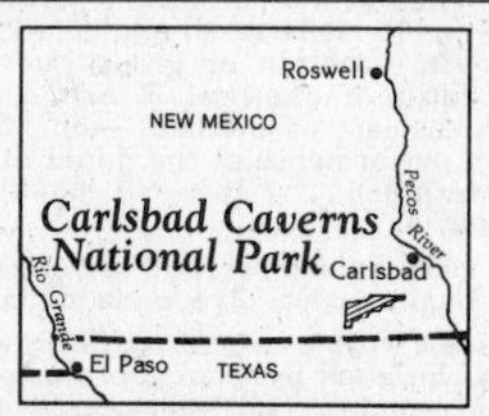

Carls′bad Decrees′, resolutions adopted by ministers of nine German states at a meeting called at Carlsbad in 1819 by Prince Metternich: aim was the suppression of revolutionary activities esp. in the universities.

Carl·son (kärl′sən), *n.* **1. An·ton Julius** (an′tōn, -ton), 1875–1956, U.S. physiologist, born in Sweden. **2. Chester Floyd,** 1906–68, U.S. inventor of xerographic copying process. **3. Evans For·dyce** (fôr′dīs, fōr′-), 1896–1947, U.S. Marine Corps general in World War II.

Carls·son (kärl′sən), *n.* **Ing·var** (ing′vär), born 1934, Swedish political leader: prime minister 1986–91.

Carl·ton (kärl′tən), *n.* a male given name.

Carl′ton ta′ble, an English writing table of c1800, having curved rear corners and a top with drawers surmounted by a U-shaped section of drawers and cabinets, topped by a brass or ormolu gallery surrounding three sides of the writing area. Also called **Carl′ton House′ desk′, Carl′ton House′ ta′ble.** [named after *Carlton* House, the London mansion it was first made for]

Car·lyle (kär līl′), *n.* **1. Thomas,** 1795–1881, Scottish essayist and historian. **2.** a male given name.

car·ma·gnole (kär′mən yōl′; *Fr.* KAR MA nyôl′), *n., pl.* **-ma·gnoles** (-mən yōlz′; *Fr.* -MA nyôl′). **1.** a dance and song popular during the French Revolution. **2.** a man's loose jacket with wide lapels and metal buttons, worn during the French Revolution. **3.** the costume of the French revolutionists, consisting chiefly of this jacket, black pantaloons, and a red liberty cap. [1790–1800; < F, after the name of a ceremonial jacket worn by peasants of Dauphiné and Savoy, named after *Carmagnola,* town in Piedmont, Italy]

car·mak·er (kär′mā′kər), *n.* a manufacturer of automobiles. [1950–55; CAR[1] + MAKER]

car·man (kär′mən), *n., pl.* **-men.** one of the crew of a streetcar or the like, as the motorman. [1570–80, in sense "person driving a cart"; CAR[1] + -MAN]

Car·man (kär′mən), *n.* **(William) Bliss,** 1861–1929, Canadian poet and journalist in the U.S.

Car·ma·ni·a (kär mā′nē ə), *n.* a province of the ancient Persian empire, on the Gulf of Oman.

Car·mar·then (kär mär′thən), *n.* **1.** a seaport in Dyfed, in S Wales. 49,900. **2.** Carmarthenshire.

Car·mar·then·shire (kär mär′thən shēr′, -shər), *n.* a historic county in Dyfed, in S Wales.

Car·me (kär′mē), *n. Astron.* a small natural satellite of the planet Jupiter.

Car·mel (kär′məl, kär mel′ *for 1, 4;* kär′məl *for 2;* kär mel′ *for 3*), *n.* **1. Mount,** a mountain range in NW Israel, near the Mediterranean coast. Highest point, 1818 ft. (554 m). 14 mi. (23 km) long. **2.** a town in central Indiana. 18,272. **3.** Also called **Car·mel-by-the-Sea** (kär-mel′bī′thə sē′). a town in W California, on the Pacific Ocean: artists' colony and resort. 4707. **4.** a female given name: from a Hebrew word meaning "garden."

Car·mel·a (kär mel′ə), *n.* a female given name, form of **Carmel.** Also, **Car·mel′la.**

Car·mel·ite (kär′mə līt′), *n.* **1.** a mendicant friar belonging to a religious order founded at Mt. Carmel, Palestine, in the 12th century. **2.** a nun belonging to this order. —*adj.* **3.** of or pertaining to Carmelites or their order. [1400–50; late ME < ML *Carmelīta,* named after CARMEL, first seat of the order; see -ITE[1]]

Car·men (kär′mən; *Sp.* kär′men), *n.* **1.** See **Ciudad del Carmen. 2.** a male or female given name: from a Latin word meaning "song."

Car·men (kär′mən; *Fr.* KAR men′), *n.* an opera (1875) by Georges Bizet.

Car·mi·chael (kär′mī kəl), *n.* **1. Hoag·land Howard** (hōg′lənd), (*"Hoagy"*), 1899–1981, U.S. songwriter and musician. **2. Stoke·ly** (stōk′lē), born 1941, U.S. civil-rights leader, born in Trinidad: chairman of the Student Nonviolent Coordinating Committee 1966–67. **3.** a town in central California, near Sacramento. 43,108.

car·min·a·tive (kär min′ə tiv, kär′mə nā′tiv), *n.* **1.** a drug causing expulsion of gas from the stomach or bowel. —*adj.* **2.** expelling gas from the body; relieving flatulence. [1645–55; < LL *carmināt(us),* ptp. of *carmināre* to purify (L: to card (wool), v. deriv. of *carmen* (attested only in LL) comb for carding wool) + -IVE]

car·mine (kär′min, -mīn), *n.* **1.** a crimson or purplish-red color. **2.** a crimson pigment obtained from cochineal. [1705–15; < F *carmin* (color), *carmine* (pigment), OF; cf. ML *carminium,* perh. b. *carmesīnum* (see CRIMSON) and *minium* MINIUM]

car·mus·tine (kär′mə stēn′), *n. Pharm.* a toxic nitrosourea, $C_5H_9Cl_2N_3O_2$, used in the treatment of a wide range of tumors. Also called **BCNU.**

carn (kärn), *n.* cairn.

Car·nac (kär′nak; *Fr.* KAR NAK′), *n.* a commune in SW Morbihan, in NW France, SE of Lorient: megalithic monuments. 3681. —**Car·na·cian** (kär nā′shən), *adj.*

car·nage (kär′nij), *n.* **1.** the slaughter of a great number of people, as in battle; butchery; massacre. **2.** *Archaic.* dead bodies, as of those slain in battle. [1590–1600; < MF < It *carnaggio* < ML *carnāticum* payment or offering in meat, equiv. to L *carn-* (s. of *carō*) flesh + *-āticum* -AGE]

car·nal (kär′nl), *adj.* **1.** pertaining to or characterized by the flesh or the body, its passions and appetites; sensual: *carnal pleasures.* **2.** not spiritual; merely human; temporal; worldly: *a man of secular, rather carnal, leanings.* [1350–1400; ME < L *carnālis,* equiv. to *carn-* (s. of *carō*) flesh + *-ālis* -AL[1]] —**car·nal′i·ty, car′nal·ness, car′nal·ism,** *n.* —**car′nal·ly,** *adv.*
—**Syn. 1.** CARNAL, SENSUAL, FLESHLY, ANIMAL all refer to bodily rather than rational or spiritual aspects of humans. CARNAL, although it may refer to the body as opposed to the spirit, often refers to sexual needs or urges: *carnal cravings, attractions, satisfactions.* SENSUAL implies a suggestion of eroticism: *sensual eyes; a sensual dance;* it may also refer to experience of the senses: *a sensual delight.* FLESHLY may refer to any physical need or appetite, sex as well as hunger and thirst: *the fleshly sin of gluttony; fleshly yearnings.* ANIMAL refers to sexual appetites in a censorious way only; it may also describe pleasing or admirable physical characteristics or appearance: *animal lust; to move with animal grace.* **2.** earthly, natural.

car′nal abuse′, 1. *Law.* any lascivious contact with the sexual organs of a child by an adult, esp. without sexual intercourse. **2.** rape, esp. of a young girl.

car′nal knowl′edge, *Chiefly Law.* sexual intercourse.

car·nall·ite (kär′nl īt′), *n. Mineral.* a white hydrous chloride of potassium and magnesium, $KMgCl_3 \cdot 6H_2O$, used chiefly as a source of potassium and magnesium. [1875–85; named after R. von *Carnall* (1804–74), German mining official; see -ITE[1]]

Car·nap (kär′nap), *n.* **Rudolf P.,** 1891–1970, U.S. philosopher, born in Germany.

Car·nar·von (kär när′vən), *n.* **1.** Caernarvon. **2.** Also, **Car·nar·von·shire** (kär när′vən shēr′, -shər). Caernarvonshire.

car·nas·si·al (kär nas′ē əl), *Zool.* —*adj.* **1.** (of teeth) adapted for shearing flesh. —*n.* **2.** a carnassial tooth, esp. the last upper premolar or the first lower molar tooth of certain carnivores. [1840–50; < F *carnassi(er)* flesh-eating (< Pr, equiv. to *carnasse* aug. deriv. of *carn* flesh, meat (< L *carn-,* s. of *carō*) + *-ier* -ARY) + -AL[1]]

Car·nat·ic (kär nat′ik), *n.* a historically important region on the SE coast of India: now in Madras state.

car•na•tion (kär nā′shən), *n.* **1.** any of numerous cultivated varieties of the clove pink, *Dianthus caryophyllus,* having long-stalked, fragrant, usually double flowers in a variety of colors: the state flower of Ohio. **2.** pink; light red. **3.** *Obs.* the color of flesh. —*adj.* **4.** having the color carnation. [1525–35; < LL *carnātiōn-* (s. of *carnātiō*) fleshlikeness, hence flesh-color, equiv. to L *carn-* (s. of *carō*) flesh + *-ātiōn-* -ATION]

car•nau•ba (kär nou′bə, -nô′-, -no͞o′-), *n.* **1.** a palm, *Copernicia prunifera,* of Brazil, having palmate leaves covered with wax. **2.** Also called **carnau′ba wax′.** the hard, lustrous wax obtained from the leaves of this tree, used as a polish or floor wax. [1850–55; < Brazilian Pg < Tupi *karana'iwa*]

Car•né (kär nā′; *Fr.* KAR nā′), *n.* **Mar•cel** (mär sel′; *Fr.* MAR sel′), born 1909, French film director.

Car•ne•a•des (kär nē′ə dēz′), *n.* 214?–129? B.C., Greek philosopher.

Car•ne•gie (kär′ni gē *or, for 1, 3,* kär nā′gē, -neg′ē), *n.* **1. Andrew,** 1835–1919, U.S. steel manufacturer and philanthropist, born in Scotland. **2. Dale,** 1888–1955, U.S. author and teacher of self-improvement techniques. **3.** a city in SW Pennsylvania. 10,099.

Car′negie u′nit, *Educ.* a standardized unit of measurement for evaluating courses in secondary schools in terms of college entrance requirements, representing one year's study in any subject, that subject having been taught for a minimum of 120 classroom hours to qualify. [after the *Carnegie* Foundation for the Advancement of Teaching, where it was developed]

car•nel•ian (kär nēl′yən), *n.* a red or reddish variety of chalcedony, used in jewelry. Also, **cornelian.** [1685–95; var. (with *a* of CARNATION) of *cornelian,* ME *cornel(ine)* (< MF, prob. equiv. to OF *cornele* cornel cherry + *-ine* -INE[1]) + -IAN]

car•ne•ous (kär′nē əs), *adj.* fleshlike; flesh-colored. [1570–80; < LL *carneus,* equiv. to L *carn-* (s. of *carō*) flesh + *-eus* -EOUS]

car•net (kär nā′; *Fr.* KAR ne′), *n., pl.* **-nets** (-nāz′; *Fr.* -ne′). a customs document allowing an automobile to be driven at no cost across international borders. [1895–1900; < F: notebook, book of tickets; MF *quernet,* equiv. to *quern-* (cf. *quaer* (with loss of *n*) group of four sheets; see CAHIER) + *-et* -ET]

car•ney (kär′nē), *n., pl.* **-neys,** *adj.* carny.

Car′nic Alps′ (kär′nik), a mountain range in S Austria and N Italy, part of the E Alps. Highest peak, Kellerwand, 9217 ft. (2809 m).

car•nif•er•ous (kär nif′ər əs), *adj.* bearing flesh. [1835–45; < L *carni-* (comb. form of *carō* flesh) + -FEROUS]

car•ni•fi•ca•tion (kär′nə fi kā′shən), *n. Pathol.* the conversion of tissue into flesh or a fleshlike substance, as of lung tissue into fibrous tissue as a result of pneumonia. [1725–35; CARNI(FY) + -FICATION]

car•ni•fy (kär′nə fī′), *v.,* **-fied, -fy•ing.** —*v.t.* **1.** to form or turn into flesh. —*v.i.* **2.** *Pathol.* to undergo carnification. [1630–40; < L *carni-* (comb. form of *carō* flesh) + -FY]

Car•ni•o•la (kär′nē ō′lə, kärn yō′-), *n.* a former duchy and crown land of Austria: now in Slovenia. —**Car′ni•o′lan,** *adj.*

car•ni•tas (kär nē′təz; *Sp.* kär nē′täs), *n.pl. Mexican Cookery.* small or shredded pieces of crisp roast pork, eaten as a snack, used as a filling for burritos, etc. [< MexSp, pl. of *carnita,* equiv. to Sp *carn(e)* meat (< L *carnem,* acc. of *carō* flesh, meat) + *-ita* dim. suffix]

car•ni•tine (kär′ni tēn′), *n. Biochem.* a dipolar compound that occurs in muscle and liver and is involved in the transport of fatty acids across the inner mitochondrial membrane. [1920–25; < G *Carnitin,* equiv. to L *carni-* (comb. form of *carō,* gen. *carnis* meat, flesh) + *-tin* appar. arbitrarily chosen suffix (cf. -IN[2], -INE[2]); so called because it was first isolated in meat extract]

car•ni•val (kär′nə vəl), *n.* **1.** a traveling amusement show, having sideshows, rides, etc. **2.** any merrymaking, revelry, or festival, as a program of sports or entertainment: *a winter carnival.* **3.** the season immediately preceding Lent, often observed with merrymaking; Shrovetide. [1540–50; < It *carnevale,* OIt *carnelevare* taking meat away, equiv. to *carne* flesh (< L *carnem,* acc. of *caro*) + *levare* < L *levāre* to lift] —**car′ni•val•esque′, car′ni•val•like′,** *adj.*
—**Syn. 2.** fair, celebration, fete, holiday.

car′nival glass′, a colorful iridescent pressed glassware popular in the U.S. in the early 20th century.

Car•niv•o•ra (kär niv′ər ə), *n.* the order comprising the carnivores. [1820–30; < NL; L: neut. pl. of *carnivorus;* see CARNIVOROUS]

car•ni•vore (kär′nə vôr′, -vōr′), *n.* **1.** an animal that eats flesh. **2.** a flesh-eating mammal of the order Carnivora, comprising the dogs, cats, bears, seals, and weasels. **3.** an insectivorous plant. [1850–55; < L *carnivorus* CARNIVOROUS] —**car•niv•o•ral** (kär niv′ər əl), *adj.*

car•niv•o•rous (kär niv′ər əs), *adj.* **1.** flesh-eating: *A dog is a carnivorous animal.* **2.** of the carnivores. [1640–50; < L *carnivorus,* equiv. to *carni-* (comb. form of *carō* flesh) + *-vorus* -VOROUS] —**car•niv′o•rism,** *n.* —**car•niv′o•rous•ly,** *adv.* —**car•niv′o•rous•ness,** *n.*
—**Syn. 1.** meat-eating, predatory, predacious.

car•nose (kär′nōs), *adj.* of or pertaining to flesh; fleshy. Also, **carnous.** [1555–65; < L *carnōsus* fleshy, equiv. to *carn-* (s. of *carō*) flesh + *-ōsus* -OSE[1]] —**car•nos•i•ty** (kär nos′i tē), *n.*

Car•not (kär nō′; *Fr.* KAR nō′), *n.* **1. La•zare Ni•co•las Mar•gue•rite** (LA ZAR′ nē kô lä′ MAR gə RēT′), 1753–1823, French general and statesman. **2. (Ma•rie Fran•çois) Sa•di** (mə rē′ fran swä′ sad′ē; *Fr.* MA Rē′ FRÄN SWA′ SA dē′), 1837–94, French statesman: president of the Republic 1887–94. **3. Ni•co•las Lé•o•nard Sa•di** (nik′ə ləs len′ərd sad′ē; *Fr.* nē kô lä′ lā ô NAR′ SA dē′), 1796–1832, French physicist: pioneer in the field of thermodynamics.

Carnot′ cy′cle, *Thermodynam.* an ideal cycle of reversible engine operations in which a substance at one temperature is compressed adiabatically to a second temperature, expanded isothermally at the second temperature, expanded adiabatically from the second temperature to the first temperature, and compressed isothermally at the first temperature. [after N. L. S. CARNOT]

Carnot′ en′gine, *Thermodynam.* an engine using a Carnot cycle of operations.

car•no•tite (kär′nə tīt′), *n. Mineral.* a yellow, earthy, hydrous potassium uranium vanadate: an ore of uranium. [1895–1900; named after A. *Carnot* (d. 1920), French mining official; see -ITE[1]]

Carnot′ refrig′erator, *Thermodynam.* a device operating on the Carnot cycle in which the first temperature is higher than the second.

Carnot's′ the′orem, *Thermodynam.* the principle that no engine operating between two given temperatures can be more efficient than a Carnot engine operating between the same temperatures.

car•nous (kär′nəs), *adj.* carnose.

car•ny (kär′nē), *n., pl.* **-nies,** *adj. Informal.* —*n.* **1.** a person employed by a carnival. **2.** carnival (def. 1). —*adj.* **3.** of or pertaining to carnivals: *carny slang.* Also, **carney.** [1930–35; CARN(IVAL) + -Y[2]]

car•ob (kar′əb), *n.* **1.** a Mediterranean tree, *Ceratonia siliqua,* of the legume family, bearing long, leathery pods containing hard seeds and sweet, edible pulp. **2.** Also called **St. John's-bread, algarroba, locust bean.** the pod of this tree, the source of various foodstuffs, including a substitute for chocolate, as well as substances having several industrial uses, and sometimes used as food for animals. **3.** a powder made from the ground pods and seeds of this tree and used in cooking, esp. as a substitute for chocolate. [1540–50; < MF *carobe* < ML *carrūbium* < Ar *kharrūb* bean-pods, carobs]

ca•roche (kə rōch′, -rōsh′), *n.* (in the 17th century) a luxurious or stately coach or carriage. [1585–95; < MF < It *carroccio,* equiv. to *carr(o)* wheeled conveyance (see CAR[1]) + *-occio* pejorative suffix]

car•ol (kar′əl), *n., v.,* **-oled, -ol•ing** or (*esp. Brit.*) **-olled, -ol•ling.** —*n.* **1.** a song, esp. of joy. **2.** a Christmas song or hymn. **3.** a seat in a bay window or oriel. **4.** a compartment in a cloister, similar to a carrel. **5.** a kind of circular dance. —*v.i.* **6.** to sing Christmas songs or hymns, esp. in a group performing in a public place or going from house to house. **7.** to sing, esp. in a lively, joyous manner; warble. —*v.t.* **8.** to sing joyously. **9.** to praise or celebrate in song. [1250–1300; ME *carole* ring, circle (of stones), enclosed place for study (see CARREL), ringdance with song (hence, song) < AF *carole,* OF **corole* (cf. OPr *corola*), appar. < L *corolla* garland (see COROLLA), conflated with L *choraula* < Gk *choraúlēs* piper for choral dance, equiv. to *chor(ós)* CHORUS + *-aulēs,* deriv. of *aulós* pipe] —**car′ol•er;** *esp. Brit.,* **car′ol•ler,** *n.*

Car•ol (kar′əl), *n.* a male or female given name.

Carol., Carolingian.

Car•ol II (kar′əl; *Rum.* kä′Rôl), 1893–1953, king of Rumania 1930–40.

Car•o•la (kar′ə lə), *n.* a female given name, form of **Carol.**

Car′ol Cit′y (kar′əl), a town in SE Florida, near Miami. 47,349.

Car•ole (kar′əl), *n.* a female given name.

Car•o•le•an (kar′ə lē′ən), *adj.* characteristic of the time of Charles I and II of England: *a Carolean costume.* [1645–55; < ML *Carolae(us)* (*Carol(us)* Charles + L *-aeus* adj. suffix) + -AN]

Car•o•li•na (kar′ə lī′nə; *for 3 also Sp.* kä′Rô lē′nä), *n.* **1.** a former English colony on the Atlantic coast of North America: officially divided into North Carolina and South Carolina in 1729. **2.** North Carolina or South Carolina. **3.** a city in NE Puerto Rico, SE of San Juan. 147,835. **4.** Also called **the Car′o•li′nas.** North Carolina and South Carolina.

Car′oli′na all′spice, an aromatic shrub, *Calycanthus floridus,* of the southern U.S., having hairy, ovate leaves and purplish-brown flowers. Also called **sweet shrub.** [1780–90, *Amer.*]

Car′oli′na bay′, any of the shallow, usually marshy, oval depressions found in the coastal plains of the eastern U.S. that are heavily forested and have rich soil.

Car′oli′na chick′adee, a chickadee, *Parus carolinensis,* of the southeastern U.S., resembling but smaller than the black-capped chickadee.

Car′oli′na jes′samine, a vine, *Gelsemium sempervirens,* of the southern U.S. and Central America, of the logania family, having glossy, lance-shaped leaves and fragrant yellow flowers: the state flower of South Carolina. Also, **Car′oli′na jas′mine.** Also called **yellow jasmine.** [1825–35, *Amer.*]

Car′oli′na lil′y, a bulbous lily, *Lilium michauxii,* of the southeastern U.S., having large, spotted, orange-red flowers with recurved petals.

Car′oli′na moon′seed, a twining woody vine, *Cocculus carolinus,* of the southeastern U.S., having inconspicuous flowers and showy, red fruit. [1775–85, *Amer.*]

Car′oli′na par′akeet, an extinct New World parakeet, *Conuropsis carolinensis,* that ranged into the northern U.S., having yellowish-green plumage with an orange-yellow head. [1840–50, *Amer.*]

Car′oli′na rail′, sora. [1825–35, *Amer.*]

Car′oli′na wren′, a large wren, *Thryothorus ludovicianus,* of the U.S., having a musical call. [1800–10, *Amer.*]

Car•o•line (kar′ə līn′, -lin), *adj.* of or pertaining to Charles, esp. Charles I and Charles II of England or their times. Also, **Carolinian.** [1645–55; < ML *Carolīnus,* equiv. to *Carol(us)* Charles + *-inus* INE[1]]

Car•o•line (kar′ə lin, -līn′), *n.* a female given name.

Car′oline Is′lands, a group of more than 500 islands in the Pacific, E of the Philippines: formerly a Japanese mandate; now under U.S. trusteeship. 525 sq. mi. (1360 sq. km).

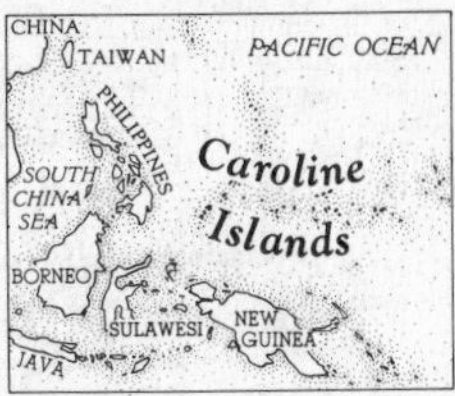

Car•o•lin•gi•an (kar′ə lin′jē ən), *adj.* **1.** of or pertaining to the Frankish dynasty that reigned in France A.D. 751–987, first under Charlemagne, and in Germany until A.D. 911. **2.** pertaining to or designating the arts, script, or culture of the Carolingian period, chiefly characterized by a revival of the forms of classical antiquity modified by ecclesiastical requirements: *Carolingian renaissance.* —*n.* **3.** a member of the Carolingian dynasty. *Abbr.:* Carol. Also, **Carlovingian, Carolinian.** [1880–85; re-formation of earlier *Carlovingian* (conformed to ML *Carolus Magnus* Charlemagne) < F *carlovingien,* equiv. to ML *Car(o)l(us)* + F *-ovingien,* extracted from *mérovingien* MEROVINGIAN]

Car•o•lin•i•an (kar′ə lin′ē ən), *adj.* **1.** of or pertaining to North Carolina or South Carolina or both. —*n.* **2.** a native or inhabitant of North Carolina or of South Carolina. [1695–1705; CAROLIN(A) + -IAN]

Car•o•lin•i•an (kar′ə lin′ē ən), *adj.* **1.** Carolingian. **2.** Caroline. —*n.* **3.** Carolingian. [< ML *Carolin(us)* CAROLINE + -IAN]

Car′ol Stream′, a town in NE Illinois. 15,472.

car•o•lus (kar′ə ləs), *n., pl.* **-lus•es, -li** (-lī′). any of various coins issued under monarchs named Charles, esp. the broad of Charles I of England. [1680–90; < ML: Latinized form of *Charles* or *Karl*]

Car•o•lyn (kar′ə lin), *n.* a female given name.

car•om (kar′əm), *n.* **1.** *Billiards, Pool.* a shot in which the cue ball hits two balls in succession. **2.** any strike and rebound, as a ball striking a wall and glancing off. —*v.i.* **3.** to make a carom. **4.** to strike and rebound. Also, **carrom.** [1770–80; by false analysis of *carambole* (taken as *carom ball*) < F < Sp *carambola,* special use of fruit name; see CARAMBOLA]

car′om ball′, *Billiards, Pool.* the ball struck by the cue ball in rebounding off the object ball. Cf. **object ball** (def. 1). [1770–80]

Ca′ro's ac′id (kär′ōz), *Chem.* See **persulfuric acid** (def. 1). [named after Heinrich Caro (1834–1910), German chemist]

car•o•tene (kar′ə tēn′), *n.* any of three yellow or orange fat-soluble pigments having the formula $C_{40}H_{56}$, found in many plants, esp. carrots, and transformed to vitamin A in the liver; provitamin A. Also, **carotin.** [1860–65; < LL *carōt(a)* CARROT + -ENE]

ca•rot•e•noid (kə rot′n oid′), *Biochem.* —*n.* **1.** any of a group of red and yellow pigments, chemically similar to carotene, contained in animal fat and some plants. —*adj.* **2.** similar to carotene. **3.** pertaining to carotenoids. Also, **ca•rot′i•noid′.** [1910–15; CAROTENE + -OID]

Ca•roth•ers (kə ruth′ərz), *n.* **Wallace Hume,** 1896–1937, U.S. chemist: associated with the invention of synthetic nylon material.

ca•rot•id (kə rot′id), *Anat.* —*n.* **1.** Also called **carot′id ar′tery.** either of the two large arteries, one on each side of the head, that carry blood to the head and that divide into an external branch supplying the neck, face, and other external parts, and an internal branch supplying the brain, eye, and other internal parts. —*adj.* **2.** pertaining to a carotid artery. [1660–70; < Gk *karōtídes* neck arteries, equiv. to *karōt(ikós)* soporific (*kár(os)* stupor + *-ōtikos* -OTIC) + *-ides* -ID[1]; so called by Galen, who found that their compression causes stupor] —**ca•rot′id•al,** *adj.*

carot′id bod′y, *Anat.* a small mass of cells and nerve endings adjacent to the carotid sinus that, in response to chemical changes in the blood, adjusts the respiratory rate. Also called **carot′id gland′.** [1935–40]

carot′id si′nus, *Anat.* specialized nerve end organs producing a slight dilatation of the carotid artery where it branches into the external and internal carotid arteries, responding to changes in blood pressure by mediating changes in the heartbeat rate. [1940–45]

car•o•tin (kar′ə tin), *n.* carotene.

ca•rous•al (kə rou′zəl), *n.* a noisy or drunken feast or social gathering; revelry. [1755–65; CAROUSE + -AL[2]]

ca•rouse (kə rouz′), *v.,* **-roused, -rous•ing,** *n.* —*v.i.* **1.** to engage in a drunken revel: *They caroused all night.* **2.** to drink deeply and frequently. —*n.* **3.** carousal. [1550–60; var. of *garouse* < G *gar aus* (*trinken*) (to drink) fully out, i.e. drain the cup; cf. MF *carous* < dial. G *gar ūs*] —**ca•rous′er,** *n.* —**ca•rous′ing•ly,** *adv.*
—**Syn. 1.** revel, celebrate, drink; live it up.

car•ou•sel (kar′ə sel′, kar′ə sel′), *n.* **1.** merry-go-

CONCISE PRONUNCIATION KEY: *act, cāpe, dâre, pärt; set, ēqual; if, īce; ox, ōver, ôrder, oil, bo͝ok, bo͞ot, out; up, ûrge; child; sing; shoe; thin, that;* zh as in *treasure.* ə = *a* as in *alone, e* as in *system, i* as in *easily, o* as in *gallop, u* as in *circus;* ᵊ as in *fire* (fīᵊr), *hour* (ouᵊr). l and n can serve as syllabic consonants, as in *cradle* (krād′l), and *button* (but′n). See the full key inside the front cover.

round (def. 1). **2.** a continuously revolving belt, track or other device on which items are placed for later retrieval: *a baggage carousel at an airport.* [1640–50; < F: kind of tournament < It *carosello* kind of ball game < Neapolitan dial. *carusello* game played with clay balls, clay ball, lit., little head, equiv. to *carus(o)* shorn head (perh. based on the Gk s. *kors-* shave) + *-ello* dim. suffix]

carousel (def. 2)

Car·ou·sel (kar′ə sel′, kar′ə sel′), *Trademark.* a circular tray in which photographic transparencies are held on a projector and from which they are lowered through slots for projection as the tray is rotated.

carp[1] (kärp), *v.i.* **1.** to find fault or complain querulously or unreasonably; be niggling in criticizing; cavil: *to carp at minor errors.* —*n.* **2.** a peevish complaint. [1200–50; ME *carpen* to speak, prate < ON *karpa* to brag, wrangle] —**carp′er,** *n.*
—**Syn. 1.** criticize, deprecate, condemn, censure.

carp[2] (kärp), *n., pl.* (*esp. collectively*) **carp,** (*esp. referring to two or more kinds or species*) **carps. 1.** a large freshwater cyprinid fish, *Cyprinus carpio,* native to Asia but widely introduced in tropical and temperate waters: an important food fish in many countries. **2.** any of various other fishes of the family Cyprinidae. [1350–1400; ME *carpe* < MF < MD or MLG *karpe;* c. OHG *karpfo*]

-carp, a combining form occurring in compounds that denote a part of a fruit or fruiting body: *endocarp.* [< NL *-carpium* < Gk *-karpion,* deriv. of *karpós* fruit]

carp., carpentry.

car·pac·cio (kär pä′chō, -chē ō′), *n.* an appetizer of thinly sliced raw beef served with a vinaigrette or other piquant sauce. [after V. CARPACCIO; said to have been introduced under this name c1961 at Harry's Bar, a Venetian restaurant]

Car·pac·cio (kär pät′chô), *n.* **Vit·to·re** (vēt tô′re), c1450–1525, Italian painter.

car·pal (kär′pəl), *Anat.* —*adj.* **1.** pertaining to the carpus: *the carpal joint.* —*n.* **2.** a carpale. [1735–45; < NL *carpālis.* See CARPUS, -AL[1]]

car·pa·le (kär pā′lē), *n., pl.* **-li·a** (-lē ə). *Anat.* any of the bones of the wrist. Also, **carpal.** [< NL, neut. of *carpālis* CARPAL]

car′pal tun′nel syn′drome, *Pathol.* a disorder of the wrist and hand characterized by pain, tingling, and muscular weakness, caused by pressure on the median nerve in the wrist area and often associated with trauma, rheumatoid arthritis, or edema of pregnancy.

car′ park′, *Chiefly Brit.* a parking lot. [1930–35]

Car·pa′thi·an Moun′tains (kär pā′thē ən), a mountain range in central Europe, extending from N Slovakia to central Rumania. Highest peak, Gerlachovka, 8737 ft. (2663 m). Also called **Car·pa′thi·ans.**

Car·pa·tho-U·kraine (kär pä′thō yo͞o krān′), *n.* a region in W Ukraine: ceded by Czechoslovakia in 1945. Cf. **Ruthenia.**

Car·peaux (kär pō′; *Fr.* kar pō′), *n.* **Jean Bap·tiste** (zhän ba tēst′), 1827–75, French sculptor.

car·pe di·em (kär′pe dē′em; *Eng.* kär′pē dī′əm, kär′pā dē′əm), *Latin.* seize the day; enjoy the present, as opposed to placing all hope in the future.

car·pel (kär′pəl), *n. Bot.* a simple pistil, or a single member of a compound pistil. [1810–20; < NL *carpellum,* equiv. to Gk *karp(ós)* fruit + L *-ellum* dim. suffix] —**car·pel·lar·y** (kär′pə ler′ē), *adj.*

car·pel·late (kär′pə lāt′), *adj. Bot.* having carpels. [< NL *carpellatus.* See CARPEL, -ATE[1]]

Car·pen·tar·i·a (kär′pən târ′ē ə), *n.* **Gulf of,** a gulf on the coast of N Australia. ab. 480 mi. (775 km) long; ab. 300 mi. (485 km) wide.

car·pen·ter (kär′pən tər), *n.* **1.** a person who builds or repairs wooden structures, as houses, scaffolds, or shelving. —*v.i.* **2.** to do carpenter's work. —*v.t.* **3.** to make by carpentry. **4.** to construct (a plot, scene, article, or the like) in a mechanical or unoriginal fashion. [1275–1325; ME < AF < LL *carpentārius* wainwright, equiv. to L *carpent(um)* two-wheeled carriage (< Celt; cf. OIr *carpad* chariot) + *-ārius* -ARY; see -ER[2]]

Car·pen·ter (kär′pən tər), *n.* **1. John Alden,** 1876–1951, U.S. composer. **2. (Malcolm) Scott,** born 1925, U.S. astronaut and oceanographer.

car′penter ant′, a black or brown ant of the genus *Camponotus* that nests in the wood of decaying or dead trees in which it bores tunnels for depositing its eggs. [1880–85]

car′penter bee′, any of several solitary bees of the family Apidae that nest in solid wood, boring tunnels in which to deposit their eggs. [1830–40]

car′penter goth′ic, (*sometimes caps.*) a style of Victorian Gothic architecture adapted to the resources of contemporary woodworking tools and machinery.

CONCISE ETYMOLOGY KEY: <, descended or borrowed from; >, whence; b., blend of, blended; c., cognate with; cf., compare; deriv., derivative; equiv., equivalent; imit., imitative; obl., oblique; r., replacing; s., stem; sp., spelling, spelled; resp., respelling, respelled; trans., translation; ?, origin unknown; *, unattested; ‡, probably earlier than. See the full key inside the front cover.

car·pen·ter·ing (kär′pən tər ing), *n.* the trade or work of a carpenter. [1830–40; CARPENTER + -ING[1]]

Car·pen·ters·ville (kär′pən tərz vil′), *n.* a city in NE Illinois, near Chicago. 23,272.

car·pen·ter·worm (kär′pən tər wûrm′), *n.* the larva of the carpenterworm moth. [CARPENTER + WORM]

car′penterworm moth′, any moth of the family Cossidae, as *Prionoxystus robiniae* of the U.S. and southern Canada, whose larvae bore into the trunks and branches of oaks, locusts, and other trees. Also called **car′penter moth′.**

car·pen·try (kär′pən trē), *n.* **1.** the trade of a carpenter: *He earned his living at carpentry.* **2.** the work produced by a carpenter. **3.** the way in which something, esp. a work of literature, is structured. [1350–1400; ME *carpentrie* < ONF < L *carpentāria* (*fabrica*) carriage-maker's (workshop). See CARPENTER, -Y[3]]

car·pet (kär′pit), *n.* **1.** a heavy fabric, commonly of wool or nylon, for covering floors. **2.** a covering of this material. **3.** any relatively soft surface or covering like a carpet: *They walked on the carpet of grass.* **4. on the carpet, a.** before an authority or superior for an accounting of one's actions or a reprimand: *He was called on the carpet again for his carelessness.* **b.** *Chiefly Brit.* under consideration or discussion. **5.** any of a number of airborne electronic devices for jamming radar. **6.** a system of such devices. —*v.t.* **7.** to cover or furnish with or as with a carpet. **8.** *Chiefly Brit.* to reprimand. [1300–50; ME *carpete* cloth covering for a table, floor, bed, etc. < MF *carpite* or ML *carpita* < It *carpita* woolen bedspread < VL **carpita,* ptp. of *carpire,* for L *carpere* to pluck, card (wool)] —**car′pet·less,** *adj.*

car·pet·bag (kär′pit bag′), *n., v.,* **-bagged, -bag·ging.** —*n.* **1.** a bag for traveling, esp. one made of carpeting. —*v.i.* **2.** to journey with little luggage. **3.** to act as a carpetbagger. [1820–30; CARPET + BAG]

car·pet·bag·ger (kär′pit bag′ər), *n.* **1.** *U.S. Hist.* a Northerner who went to the South after the Civil War and became active in Republican politics, esp. so as to profiteer from the unsettled social and political conditions of the area during Reconstruction. **2.** any opportunistic or exploitive outsider. [1865–70, *Amer.;* CARPETBAG + -ER[1]; so called because they came South carrying their belongings in carpetbags] —**car′pet·bag′ger·y,** *n.*

car′pet bee′tle, any of several small beetles of the family Dermestidae, the larvae of which are household pests, feeding on rugs and other woolen fabrics, esp. *Anthrenus scrophulariae* **(buffalo carpet beetle)** and *Attagenus piceus* **(black carpet beetle).** Also called **car′pet bug′.** [1885–90]

car′pet grass′, either of two grasses, *Axonopus affinis* or *A. compressus,* native to tropical and subtropical America. [1900–05, *Amer.*]

car·pet·ing (kär′pi ting), *n.* **1.** material for carpets. **2.** carpets in general. [1750–60; CARPET + -ING[1]]

car′pet moth′, a clothes moth, *Trichophaga tapetzella,* the larvae of which infest carpets and other woolen articles. Also called **tapestry moth.** [1855–60]

car′pet shark′, any shark of the family Orectolobidae, found in tropical Indo-Pacific waters, having mottled skin and fleshy lobes along the sides of the head. [1925–30]

car′pet slip′per, a house slipper, esp. one for men, made of carpet material. [1850–55]

car′pet snake′, a large, nonvenomous Australian python, *Morelia spilotes variegata,* having a variegated pattern on its back, often used to control rats and mice in barns and silos. [1860–65]

car′pet sweep′er, a pushable, long-handled implement for removing dirt, lint, etc., from rugs and carpets, consisting of a metal case enclosing one or more brushes that rotate. [1855–60, *Amer.*]

car′pet tack′, a flat-headed tack used esp. to tack down carpets.

car′pet tile′, a tile made of carpeting material that is used for flooring.

car·pet·weed (kär′pit wēd′), *n.* a North American prostrate weed, *Mollugo verticillata,* having whorled leaves and small, whitish flowers. [1775–85, *Amer.* CARPET + WEED[1]]

car·phol·o·gy (kär fol′ə jē), *n. Pathol.* floccillation. [1850–55; < NL *carphologia;* LL: fumbling, plucking at straws, blankets < Gk *karphología,* equiv. to *kárpho(s)* twig, straw, piece of wood + *-logia* collection; see -LOGY]

car·pi (kär′pī), *n.* pl. of **carpus.**

-carpic, a combination of **-carp** and **-ic** used in the formation of adjectives from stems in **-carp:** *endocarpic.*

carp·ing (kär′ping), *adj.* **1.** characterized by fussy or petulant faultfinding; querulous: *carping criticism.* —*n.* **2.** petty faultfinding. [1275–1325; ME (n.); see CARP[1], -ING[2], -ING[1]] —**carp′ing·ly,** *adv.*

Car·pin·te·ri·a (kär′pin tə rē′ə), *n.* a town in SW California. 10,835.

Car·po (kär′pō), *n.* an ancient Greek goddess of summer fruit, considered by Athenians as one of the Horae.

carpo-[1], a combining form meaning "fruit," "fruiting body," used in the formation of compound words: *carpophore; carpogonium.* [< Gk *karpo-,* comb. form of *karpós* fruit]

carpo-[2], a combining form meaning "wrist," used in the formation of compound words: *carpometacarpal.* [< Gk *karpós* wrist]

car·po·go·ni·um (kär′pə gō′nē əm), *n., pl.* **-ni·a** (-nē ə). the one-celled female sex organ of some red algae, that, when fertilized, gives rise to the carpospores. [1880–85; CARPO-[1] + -GONIUM] —**car′po·go′ni·al,** *adj.*

car·pol·o·gy (kär pol′ə jē), *n.* the branch of botany dealing with fruits and seeds. [1800–10; CARPO-[1] + -LOGY]

car·po·met·a·car·pal (kär′pə met′ə kär′pəl, -met′ə-kär′-), *adj.* **1.** *Anat.* of or pertaining to the carpus and the metacarpus. **2.** *Ornith.* of or pertaining to the carpometacarpus. [1830–40; CARPO-[2] + METACARPAL]

car·po·met·a·car·pus (kär′pə met′ə kär′pəs, -met′-ə kär′-), *n., pl.* **-pi** (-pī). *Ornith.* **1.** the bone of a bird's wing formed by fusion of the carpal and metacarpal bones. **2.** the part of the wing supported by this bone. [CARPO-[2] + METACARPUS]

car·pool (kär′po͞ol′), *n.* Also, **car′ pool′. 1.** Also, **car′pool′ing, car′ pool′ing.** an arrangement among a group of automobile owners by which each owner in turn drives the others or their children to and from a designated place. **2.** those included in such an arrangement. —*v.i.* **3.** Also, **car′-pool′.** to form or participate in a carpool. [1940–45; CAR[1] + POOL[2]]

car·pool·er (kär′po͞o′lər), *n.* a member of a carpool. Also, **car′ pool′er.** [CARPOOL + -ER[1]]

car·poph·a·gous (kär pof′ə gəs), *adj.* fruit-eating. [1830–40; CARPO-[1] + -PHAGOUS]

car·po·phore (kär′pə fôr′, -fōr′), *n. Bot.* **1.** a slender prolongation of the floral axis, bearing the carpels of some compound fruits, as in many plants of the parsley family. **2.** *Mycol.* the fruiting body of the higher fungi. [1865–70; CARPO-[1] + -PHORE]

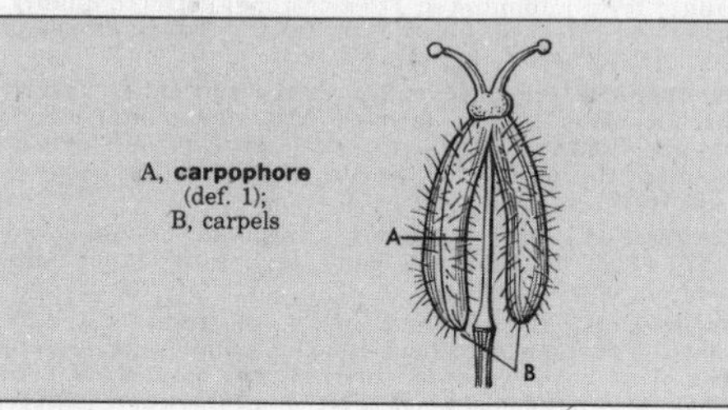

A, **carpophore** (def. 1);
B, carpels

Car·poph·o·rus (kär pof′ər əs), *n. Class. Myth.* an epithet of both Demeter and her daughter, Persephone, meaning "fruit-bearer."

car·port (kär′pôrt′, -pōrt′), *n.* a roofed, wall-less shed, usually projecting from the side of a building, used as a shelter for an automobile. [1935–40, *Amer.;* CAR[1] + PORT[1]]

car·po·spore (kär′pə spôr′, -spōr′), *n.* a nonmotile spore of the red algae. [1880–85; CARPO-[1] + SPORE] —**car·po·spor·ic** (kär′pə spôr′ik, -spor′-), **car·pos·po·rous** (kär pos′pər əs), *adj.*

car·po·stome (kär′pə stōm′), *n.* the opening in the cystocarp of certain red algae through which the spores are discharged. [CARPO-[1] + -STOME]

-carpous, a combining form meaning "fruited," "having fruit, fruiting bodies, or carpels of a given sort," as specified by the initial element: *apocarpous.* [< Gk *-karpos,* adj. deriv. of *karpós* fruit; see -OUS]

carp·suck·er (kärp′suk′ər), *n.* any of several freshwater suckers of the genus *Carpiodes,* as the quillback and the river carpsucker. [CARP[2] + SUCKER]

car·pus (kär′pəs), *n., pl.* **-pi** (-pī). *Anat.* **1.** the part of the upper extremity between the hand and the forearm; wrist. **2.** the wrist bones collectively; the group of bones between the bones of the hand and the radius. See diag. under **skeleton.** [1670–80; < NL < Gk *karpós* wrist]

Carr (kär), *n.* **John Dickson,** 1906–77, U.S. mystery writer.

Car·rac·ci (kə rä′chē; *It.* kär rät′chē), *n.* **1. A·go·sti·no** (ä′gô stē′nô), 1557–1602, and his brother, **An·ni·ba·le** (än nē′bä le), 1560–1609, Italian painters. **2.** their cousin, **Lu·do·vi·co** (lo͞o′dô vē′kô), 1555–1619, Italian painter.

car·rack (kar′ək), *n.* a merchant vessel having various rigs, used esp. by Mediterranean countries in the 15th and 16th centuries; galleon. Also, **carack.** [1350–1400; ME *carrake* < MF *carraque* < Sp *carraca,* perh. back formation from Ar *qarāqir* (pl. of *qurqūr* ship of burden < Gk *kérkouros*), the *-ir* being taken as pl. ending]

car·ra·geen (kar′ə gēn′), *n.* See **Irish moss.** Also, **car′ra·gheen′.** [1825–35; named after *Carrageen* in SE Ireland]

car·ra·gee·nan (kar′ə gē′nən), *n.* a colloidal substance extracted from seaweed, chiefly used as an emulsifying and stabilizing ingredient in foods, cosmetics, and pharmaceuticals. Also, **car′ra·gee′nin.** [CARRAGEEN + *-an* suffix of chemical compounds, here synonymous with -IN[2]]

Car·ran·za (kə ran′zə; *Sp.* kär rän′sä), *n.* **Ve·nus·tia·no** (be′no͞os tyä′nô), 1859–1920, Mexican revolutionary and political leader: president 1915–20.

Car·ra·ra (kə rär′ə; *It.* kär rä′rä), *n.* a city in NW Tuscany, in NW Italy. 70,125. —**Car·ra′ran,** *n., adj.*

Carra′ra mar′ble, a white or blue-gray marble quarried at Carrara, Italy. [1785–95]

car·re·four (kar′ə fo͝or′, kar′ə fo͝or′), *n.* **1.** a crossroads; road junction. **2.** a public square, plaza; marketplace. [1475–85; < F; earlier *quarefour,* MF *quarrefour* < LL *quadrifurcum,* neut. of *quadrifurcus* with four forks, equiv. to *quadri-* QUADRI- + *-furcus* -forked, adj. deriv. of *furcus, furca* FORK]

car·rel (kar′əl), *n.* **1.** Also called **cubicle, stall.** a small recess or enclosed area in a library stack, designed for individual study or reading. **2.** a table or desk with three sides extending above the writing surface to serve as partitions, designed for individual study, as in a library. Also, **car′rell.** [1585–95; var. sp. of CAROL enclosure]

Car•rel (kə rel′, kar′əl; *Fr.* KA REL′), *n.* **A•lex•is** (ə lek′sis; *Fr.* A lek sē′), 1873–1944, French surgeon and biologist, in U.S. 1905–39: Nobel prize 1912.

Car•re•ra (kə râr′ə; *Sp.* kär RE′rä), *n.* **Jo•sé Mi•guel de** (hô se′ mē gel′ de), 1785–1821, Chilean revolutionary and political leader: dictator 1811–13.

Car•rère (kə râr′), *n.* **John Merven,** 1858–1911, U.S. architect.

car•ret•a (kə ret′ə), *n. Southwestern U.S.* a simple two-wheeled oxcart. [1835–45; *Amer.;* < AmerSp, Sp, equiv. to *carr(o)* cart, CAR[1] + *-eta* n. suffix (cf. -ETTE)]

car•riage (kar′ij; *for 9 also* kar′ē ij), *n.* **1.** a wheeled vehicle for conveying persons, as one drawn by horses and designed for comfort and elegance. **2.** See **baby carriage.** **3.** *Brit.* a railway passenger coach. **4.** a wheeled support, as for a cannon. **5.** a movable part, as of a machine, designed for carrying something. **6.** manner of carrying the head and body; bearing: *the carriage of a soldier.* **7.** Also called **carriage piece, horse.** an inclined beam, as a string, supporting the steps of a stair. **8.** the act of transporting; conveyance: *the expenses of carriage.* **9.** the price or cost of transportation. **10.** (in a typewriter) the moving part carrying the platen and its associated parts, usually set in motion to carry the paper across the point where the print element or type bars strike. **11.** management; administration. [1150–1200; ME *cariage* < AF, ONF, equiv. to *cari(er)* to CARRY + *-age* -AGE]
—**Syn. 1.** cart, car, wagon. **6.** mien, comportment, demeanor, air.

car′riage bolt′, a round-headed bolt for timber, threaded along part of its shank, inserted into holes already drilled. See illus. under **bolt.**

car′riage dog′, Dalmatian (def. 3) [1815–25]

car′riage horse′, a horse trained and groomed to draw carriages. [1590–1600]

car′riage house′. See **coach house.** [1755–65, *Amer.*]

car′riage piece′, carriage (def. 7).

car′riage return′, **1.** (on a typewriter) the key or mechanism that causes the next character typed to appear at the left margin and on a new line. **2.** *Computers.* the symbol, command, or key **(return)** that causes the printer to be positioned or the cursor to be displayed at the left margin.

car′riage trade′, wealthy patrons of a store, restaurant, theater, etc.; elite clientele. [1710–20]

car•riage•way (kar′ij wā′), *n. Brit.* a road or lane of a road for use by automobiles. [1790–1800; CARRIAGE + WAY[1]]

car′rick bend′, (kar′ik), a knot or bend for joining the ends of two ropes. See illus. under **knot.** [1810–20; perh. to be identified with ME *carryk,* var. of *carrake* CARRACK]

Car•rie (kar′ē), *n.* a female given name, form of **Caroline.**

car•ri•er (kar′ē ər), *n.* **1.** a person or thing that carries. **2.** an employee of the post office who carries mail. **3.** a person who delivers newspapers, magazines, etc., on a particular route. **4.** *Transp.* **a.** an individual or company, as a railroad or steamship line, engaged in transporting passengers or goods for profit. **b.** See **common carrier.** **5.** *Insurance.* a company that acts or functions as an underwriter or insurer. **6.** a frame, usually of metal, attached to a vehicle for carrying skis, luggage, etc., as on top of an automobile or station wagon; rack. **7.** See **aircraft carrier.** **8.** *Immunol.* an individual harboring specific pathogenic organisms who, though often immune to the agent harbored, may transmit the disease to others. **9.** *Genetics.* **a.** an individual possessing an unexpressed, recessive trait. **b.** the bearer of a defective gene. **10.** Also called **car′rier wave′.** *Radio.* the wave whose amplitude, frequency, or phase is to be varied or modulated to transmit a signal. **11.** *Mach.* a mechanism by which something is carried or moved. **12.** *Chem.* a catalytic agent that brings about a transfer of an element or group of atoms from one compound to another. **13.** Also called **charge carrier.** *Physics.* any of the mobile electrons or holes in a metal or semiconductor that enable it to conduct electrical charge. **14.** *Physical Chem.* a usually inactive substance that acts as a vehicle for an active substance. **15.** See **carrier pigeon.** **16.** *Painting.* base[1] (def. 15b). [1350–1400; ME; see CARRY, -ER[1]]

Car•rière (KA RYER′), *n.* **Eu•gène** (œ zhen′), 1849–1906, French painter and lithographer.

car•ri•er-free (kar′ē ər frē′), *adj. Chem.* (of a radioactive isotope) capable of functioning as a tracer without the use of a carrier.

car′rier pig′eon, **1.** one of a breed of domestic pigeons having a large wattle around the base of the beak. **2.** a homing pigeon trained to carry messages. [1640–50]

car•ri•ole (kar′ē ōl′), *n.* cariole.

car•ri•on (kar′ē ən), *n.* **1.** dead and putrefying flesh. **2.** rottenness; anything vile. —*adj.* **3.** feeding on carrion. [1175–1225; ME *caroyne, careyn, carion* < AF *careine,* OF *charo(i)gne* < VL **caronia,* equiv. to L *carun-* (see CARUNCLE) + *-ia* -Y[3]]

car′rion bee′tle, any of the beetles of the family Silphidae that feed on and deposit their eggs in carrion. [1810–20]

car′rion crow′, **1.** a European crow, *Corvus corone,* that feeds on carrion. **2.** See **black vulture** (def. 1). [1520–30]

car′rion flow′er, **1.** any of several North American climbing plants of the genus *Smilax,* esp. *S. herbacea,* having small white flowers with an odor of carrion. **2.** Also called **starfish flower.** any of various succulent plants of the genus *Stapelia,* of southern Africa, having spotted or variegated flowers often with a fetid odor. [1830–40, *Amer.*]

car•ritch (kär′ich), *n. Scot.* a catechism. [1755–65; back formation from *carritches* (taken as pl.), Scots var. of *catechise* (now dial.) < F *catéchèse* << Gk *katḗchēsis* CATECHESIS; for *t* > *rr,* cf. PORRIDGE]

Car•roll (kar′əl), *n.* **1. Charles,** 1737–1832, American patriot and legislator. **2. Lewis,** pen name of Charles Lutwidge Dodgson. **3.** Also, **Car′rol.** a male or female given name.

Car•roll•ton (kar′əl tən), *n.* **1.** a town in N Texas. 40,591. **2.** a city in W Georgia. 14,078.

car•rom (kar′əm), *n., v.i.* carom.

car•ro•ma•ta (kar′ə mä′tə; *Sp.* kär′RÔ mä′tä), *n., pl.* **-tas** (-təz; *Sp.* -täs). (in the Philippines) a light, two-wheeled covered vehicle, usually drawn by one horse. [< Sp *carromato* < It *carromatto* cart, equiv. to *carro* (< L *carrus;* see CAR[1]) + *matto* stupid, drunk (referring to the cart's motion)]

car′ron oil′ (kar′ən), *Pharm.* a liniment containing limewater and linseed oil, used in medicine chiefly for burns. Also called **lime liniment.** [1880–85; named after *Carron,* Scotland, where it was used for treatment of ironworks laborers]

car•rot (kar′ət), *n.* **1.** a plant, *Daucus carota,* of the parsley family, having pinnately decompound leaves and umbels of small white or yellow flowers, in its wild form a widespread, familiar weed, and in cultivation valued for its edible root. **2.** the nutritious, orange to yellow root of this plant, eaten raw or cooked. **3.** something hoped for or promised as a lure or incentive: *To boost productivity, leaders hinted at the carrot of subsidized housing for the workers.* Cf. **stick[1]** (def. 8). —*v.t.* **4.** to treat (furs) with mercuric nitrate preparatory to felting. [1525–35; < MF *carotte* < LL *carōta* < Gk *karōtón,* deriv. of *kárē* head, with suffix as in *kephalōtón* onion, deriv. of *kephalḗ* head]

car•rot-top (kar′ət top′), *n. Slang.* a person who has red hair.

car•rot•y (kar′ə tē), *adj.* like a carrot, as in color, flavor, or shape. [1690–1700; CARROT + -Y[1]]

car•rou•sel (kar′ə sel′, -zel′; kar′ə sel′, -zel′), *n.* carousel.

car•ry (kar′ē), *v.,* **-ried, -ry•ing.** *n., pl.* **-ries.** —*v.t.* **1.** to take or support from one place to another; convey; transport: *He carried her for a mile in his arms. This elevator cannot carry more than ten people.* **2.** to wear, hold, or have around one: *He carries his knife in his pocket. He carries a cane.* **3.** to contain or be capable of containing; hold: *The suitcase will carry enough clothes for a week.* **4.** to serve as an agency or medium for the transmission of: *The wind carried the sound. He carried the message to me.* **5.** to be the means of conveying or transporting (something or someone): *The wind carried the balloon out of sight.* **6.** to be pregnant with: *His wife is carrying twins.* **7.** to put ahead to a subsequent time, page, etc., or to a higher authority; continue or transfer: *to carry a case to a higher court; to carry a footnote to a new page.* **8.** to bear the weight, burden, etc., of; sustain: *These piers once carried an arch.* **9.** to take (a leading or guiding part), as in singing; bear or sustain (a part or melody). **10.** to hold (the body, head, etc.) in a certain manner: *She carries her head high.* **11.** to behave or comport (oneself): *She carries herself with decorum.* **12.** to take the initiative in (a contest): *The Giants carried the game to the Browns.* **13.** to secure the adoption of (a motion or bill). **14.** to get a plurality or majority of electoral votes in (a district). **15.** to extend or continue in a given direction or to a certain point: *to carry the war into enemy territory.* **16.** to bring, impart, hear, transmit, or communicate news, a message, etc. **17.** to lead or influence by emotional or intellectual appeal: *The actor carried his audience with him.* **18.** to bear the major burden of (a group, performance, etc.) by superior talent, determination, etc.: *The star carried the whole play.* **19.** to serve as a conduit for: *This pipe carries water to the house.* **20.** to have as an attribute, property, consequence, etc.; presume or entail: *Violation carries a penalty of five years in prison.* **21.** to support or give validity to (a related claim, argument, etc.): *One decision carries another.* **22.** *Com.* **a.** to keep on hand or in stock. **b.** to keep on the account books. **23.** to bear as a crop: *This land will not carry corn.* **24.** to sustain or support: *Our grain supply will carry the cattle through the winter. This money will carry us for about a week.* **25.** to be enrolled for or to undertake as an amount of work: *New students are advised not to carry more than 16 credits.* **26.** *Golf.* to advance beyond or go by (an object or expanse) with one stroke. **27.** *Ice Hockey.* to cause (a puck) to move forward along the ice and in one's control by a series of light, short taps with the stick. **28.** *Hunting.* to retain and pursue (a scent). **29.** (in addition) to transfer (a number) from one denomination to the succeeding one. **30.** to have as a maximum working pressure: *This boiler carries 190 pounds per square inch.* —*v.i.* **31.** to act as a bearer or conductor. **32.** to have or exert propelling force. **33.** to be transmitted, propelled, or sustained: *My voice carries farther than his.* **34.** (of a horse) to bear the head in a particular manner while in action: *The horse carries well.* **35. carry all before one,** to be highly successful: *In his academic and social life he carried all before him.* **36. carry a tune,** to sing a melody accurately or on key. **37. carry away, a.** to influence greatly or unreasonably, esp. emotionally; excite; transport: *The spectators were carried away by the appeal to their patriotism.* **b.** *Naut.* (of the wind or sea) to dislodge or send overboard. **c.** *Naut.* (of a vessel) to lose (an object or objects) through breakage. **d.** *Naut.* (of a rope or chain) to break under strain. **38. carry back,** *Accounting.* to apply (an unused credit or operating loss) to the net income of a prior period in order to reduce the tax for that period. **39. carry forward, a.** to make progress with. **b.** *Bookkeeping.* to transfer (an amount) to the next page, column, or book. **c.** *Accounting.* to apply (an unused credit or operating loss) to the net income of a succeeding period in order to reduce the tax for that period. **40. carry it off,** *Informal.* to succeed in an action, endeavor, or scheme. **41. carry off, a.** to win (a prize, honor, etc.). **b.** to cause the death of: *The Black Plague in the Middle Ages carried off more than one-fourth of the population of Europe.* **42. carry on, a.** to manage; conduct. **b.** to continue without stopping: *Rescue operations were carried on in spite of the storm.* **c.** to continue to live, work, etc., despite a setback or tragedy; persevere. **d.** *Informal.* to behave in an agitated, foolish, or indiscreet manner. **e.** to misbehave or be disruptive; act up. **f.** *Naut.* to proceed under excessive sail for the weather conditions. **43. carry out, a.** to put into operation; execute: *He doesn't have the funds to carry out his design.* **b.** to effect or accomplish; complete: *They carried out their plan without incident.* **44. carry over, a.** to hold until a later time; postpone. **b.** to be left; remain. **c.** *Bookkeeping.* to transfer (an amount) to the next page, column, or book. **d.** *Accounting.* to apply (an unused credit or operating loss) to the net income of a succeeding period in order to reduce the tax for that period. **e.** to extend from one activity or time to another: *He does not carry over his business ethics into his personal relationships.* **45. carry the can.** See **can[2]** (def. 10). **46. carry the day,** to win the contest or be triumphant; prevail. *The Republicans carried the day.* **47. carry through, a.** to accomplish; complete. **b.** to support or help through a difficult situation. **c.** to continue or be prevalent in; persist: *a theme that carried through all his writing.* **48. carry too far,** to exceed the limits of; go to excess with: *She is carrying her crusading too far.*
—*n.* **49.** range, as of a gun. **50.** *Golf.* the distance a stroked ball travels. **51.** land that separates navigable waters and over which a canoe or boat must be carried; portage. **52.** a carrying. [1275–1325; ME *carien* < AF *carier* < LL *carricāre,* appar. var. of **carrūcāre,* deriv. of L *carrūca* traveling carriage < Celt; see CAR[1]]
—**car′ri•a•ble, car′ry•a•ble,** *adj.*
—**Syn. 1.** CARRY, CONVEY, TRANSPORT, TRANSMIT imply taking or sending something from one place to another. CARRY means to take by means of the hands, a vehicle, etc.: *to carry a book; The boat carried a heavy load.* CONVEY means to take by means of a nonhuman carrier: *The wheat was conveyed to market by train.* However, news, information, etc., can be CONVEYED by a human carrier: *The secretary conveyed the message.* TRANSPORT means to carry or convey goods, now usually by vehicle or vessel: *to transport milk to customers.* TRANSMIT implies sending or transferring messages or hereditary tendencies: *to transmit a telegram.* **8.** support. **14.** gain, secure.

Car•ry (kar′ē), *n.* **1.** a male given name, form of **Carew.** **2.** a female given name, form of **Caroline.**

car•ry•all[1] (kar′ē ôl′), *n.* a large bag, basket, etc., esp. a large, lightweight piece of luggage with soft sides. [1830–40; n. use of v. phrase *carry all*]

car•ry•all[2] (kar′ē ôl′), *n.* **1.** a four-wheeled covered carriage having seats for four persons, usually drawn by one horse. **2.** a passenger automobile or bus having two facing benches running the length of the body. [1705–15, *Amer.*; alter. of CARIOLE by folk etym.]

car•ry•back (kar′ē bak′), *n.* (in U.S. income-tax law) a special provision allowing part of a net loss or of an unused credit in a given year to be apportioned over one or two preceding years, chiefly in order to ease the tax burden. Cf. **carry•forward** (def. 2). [1940–45; n. use of v. phrase *carry back*]

car•ry•cot (kar′ē kot′), *n. Brit.* a portable bassinet. [1940–45; CARRY + COT[1]]

car•ry•for•ward (kar′ē fôr′wərd), *n.* **1.** carry-over. **2.** (in U.S. income-tax law) a special provision allowing part of a net loss or of an unused credit in a given year to be apportioned over one or two subsequent years, chiefly in order to ease the tax burden. Cf. **carry•back.** [1895–1900; n. use of v. phrase *carry forward*]

car•ry-in (kar′ē in′), *adj.* **1.** intended for or available to customers who bring in appliances to the seller or a repair store for repair or servicing: *carry-in service; a carry-in store for personal computers.* **2.** *North Central U.S.* of, pertaining to, or for a social gathering at which guests are to bring their own food: *A carry-in dinner will precede the lecture.* —*n.* **3.** an appliance or machine, as a television set or a personal computer, portable enough to be taken to a store for repair. **4.** Also called **car′ry-in din′ner, car′ry-in sup′per.** *North Central U.S.* a carry-in meal; potluck dinner. [adj. or n. use of v. phrase *carry in*]

car′rying capac′ity, *Ecol.* the maximum, equilibrium number of organisms of a particular species that can be supported indefinitely in a given environment. *Abbr.:* K [1880–85]

car′rying charge′, **1.** a charge made for carrying an account, usually computed as a percentage of the principal owed. **2.** cost incurred while an asset is unproductive. [1890–95, *Amer.*]

car•ry•ing-on (kar′ē ing on′, -ôn′), *n., pl.* **car•ry•ings-on.** *Informal.* **1.** irresponsible, irritating, self-indulgent, or overwrought behavior: *The baby-sitter was exhausted from the child's noisy carrying-on.* **2.** improper or immoral behavior. [1855–60]

car′rying place′, portage (def. 3).

car′ry light′, *Mil.* a searchlight used to illuminate a target while it is tracked and fired upon.

car•ry-on (kar′ē on′, -ôn′), *adj.* **1.** of a size and shape suitable for being carried onto and stowed in the passenger compartment of an airplane: *carry-on luggage.* —*n.* **2.** a piece of carry-on luggage. [1950–55; adj., n. use of v. phrase *carry on*]

car•ry-out (kar′ē out′), *n., adj.* takeout (defs. 2, 3). Also, **car′ry-out′.** [1965–70, *Amer.*; adj. use of v. phrase *carry out*]

car•ry-o•ver (kar′ē ō′vər), *n.* **1.** that which is carried over, postponed, or extended to a later time, account, etc.

2. *Bookkeeping.* the total of one page of an account carried forward to the next. 3. carryforward (def. 2). [1735–45; n. use of v. phrase *carry over*]

carse (kärs, kers), *n. Scot.* bottom land. [1325–75; ME *cars, kerss,* equiv. to *ker* marsh (< ON *kjarr* marshy grove; cf. Sw *kärr* marsh) + *-ss,* north var. of -ISH[1]]

car′ seat′, 1. a removable seat designed to hold a small child safely while riding in an automobile and that usually attaches to a standard seat with hooks or straps. 2. a removable cushion or pad for a driver or passenger to sit on while traveling by automobile, to give extra height or comfort.

car·sick (kär′sik′), *adj.* ill with carsickness. [1905–10; CAR[1] + SICK[1]]

car·sick·ness (kär′sik′nis), *n.* a feeling of nausea and dizziness, sometimes accompanied by vomiting, as a result of the motion of the car in which one is traveling. Cf. **motion sickness.** [1905–10; CARSICK + -NESS]

Car·son (kär′sən), *n.* 1. **Christopher** (*"Kit"*), 1809–68, U.S. frontiersman and scout. 2. **Sir Edward Henry** (*Baron Carson*), 1854–1935, Irish public official. 3. **Johnny,** born 1925, U.S. television entertainer. 4. **Rachel Louise,** 1907–1964, U.S. marine biologist and author. 5. a city in SW California. 81,221. 6. a male or female given name.

Car′son Cit′y, a town in and the capital of Nevada, in the W part. 32,022.

Car·stensz (kär′stənz), *n.* **Mount.** See **Puncak Jaya.**

cart (kärt), *n.* 1. a heavy two-wheeled vehicle, commonly without springs, drawn by mules, oxen, or the like, used for the conveyance of heavy goods. 2. a light two-wheeled vehicle with springs, drawn by a horse or pony. 3. any small vehicle pushed or pulled by hand. 4. *Obs.* a chariot. 5. **on the water cart,** *Brit.* See **wagon** (def. 12). 6. **put the cart before the horse,** to do or place things in improper order; be illogical. —*v.t.* 7. to haul or convey in or as if in a cart or truck: *to cart garbage to the dump.* —*v.i.* 8. to drive a cart. 9. **cart off** or **away,** to transport or take away in an unceremonious manner: *The police came and carted him off to jail.* [bef. 900; ME *cart(e),* OE *cræt* (by metathesis); c. ON *kartr* cart] —**cart′a·ble,** *adj.* —**cart′er,** *n.*

cart·age (kär′tij), *n.* the act or cost of carting. [1275–1325; ME; see CART, -AGE]

Car·ta·ge·na (kär′tə jē′nə; *Sp.* kär′tä he′nä), *n.* 1. a seaport in SE Spain. 146,904. 2. a seaport in N Colombia. 292,512.

carte (kärt; *Fr.* KART), *n., pl.* **cartes** (kärts; *Fr.* KART). 1. (*italics*) *French.* menu; bill of fare. Cf. **à la carte.** 2. a playing card. 3. *Archaic.* a map or chart. [bef. 1150; ME, OE: writing paper, document, letter < L *charta* < Gk *chártēs* sheet of papyrus]

Carte (kärt), *n.* **Richard d'Oy·ly** (doi′lē). See **D'Oyly Carte, Richard.**

carte blanche (kärt′ blanch′, blänch′; *Fr.* KART bläNsh′), *pl.* **cartes blanches** (kärts′ blanch′, blänch′; *Fr.* KART bläNsh′). 1. unconditional authority; full discretionary power. 2. a sheet of paper that is blank except for a signature and given by the signer to another person to write in what he or she pleases. 3. *Cards.* a hand having no face card but with a special scoring value, as in piquet. [1645–55; < F: lit., blank document; see CARTE, BLANK]

carte du jour (kärt′ də zhŏŏr′, dōō, dyōō; *Fr.* KART dY zhōōR′), *pl.* **cartes du jour** (kärts′ də zhŏŏr′, dōō, dyōō; *Fr.* KART dY zhōōR′). menu (def. 1). [1935–40; < F: menu of the day]

car·tel (kär tel′), *n.* 1. an international syndicate, combine, or trust formed esp. to regulate prices and output in some field of business. 2. a coalition of political or special-interest groups having a common cause, as to encourage the passage of a certain law. 3. a written agreement between belligerents, esp. for the exchange of prisoners. 4. a written challenge to a duel. [1550–60; < MF < It *cartello* letter of defiance, poster, equiv. to *cart(a)* CARTE + *-ello* dim. suffix] —**car·tel′ism,** *n.* —**Syn.** 1. monopoly, merger, combination.

car·tel·ist (kär tel′ist), *n.* 1. a member of a cartel or an advocate of cartelization. —*adj.* 2. Also, **car·tel·is·tic** (kär′tl is′tik, -te lis′-). of, pertaining to, or characteristic of a cartel. 3. characterized by or advocating cartelization. [1670–80; CARTEL + -IST]

car·tel·ize (kär tel′iz, kär′tl iz′), *v.i., v.t.,* **-ized, -iz·ing.** to organize into a business cartel. Also, *esp. Brit.,* **car·tel′ise.** [1925–30; CARTEL + -IZE] —**car′tel·i·za′·tion,** *n.* —**car·tel′iz·er,** *n.*

Car·ter (kär′tər), *n.* 1. **Bennett Lester** (*Benny*), born 1907, U.S. jazz saxophonist and composer. 2. **Don(ald James),** born 1926, U.S. bowler. 3. **Elliott (Cook, Jr.),** born 1908, U.S. composer. 4. **Hod·ding** (hod′ing), 1907–72, U.S. journalist and publisher. 5. **Howard,** 1873–1939, English Egyptologist. 6. **James Earl, Jr.** (*Jimmy*), born 1924, 39th president of the U.S. 1977–81. 7. **Mrs. Leslie** (*Caroline Louise Dudley*), 1862–1937, U.S. actress. 8. **May·belle** (mā′bel′), (*"Mother Maybelle Carter"*), 1909–78, U.S. country-and-western singer and guitarist. 9. **Nick,** pen name of authors who wrote detective-story series in which Nick Carter, created by John R. Coryell, is the main character. 10. a male given name.

Car·ter·et (kär′tər it *or, for 2,* kär′tə ret′), *n.* 1. **John, Earl of Granville,** 1690–1763, British statesman and orator. 2. a city in NE New Jersey. 20,598.

Car·te·sian (kär tē′zhən), *adj.* 1. of or pertaining to Descartes, his mathematical methods, or his philosophy, esp. with regard to its emphasis on logical analysis and its mechanistic interpretation of physical nature. —*n.* 2. a follower of Cartesian thought. [1650–60; < NL *Cartesiānus,* equiv. to *Cartesi(us)* (Latinization of DESCARTES) + *-ānus* -AN] —**Carte′sian·ism,** *n.*

Carte′sian coor′dinates, *Math.* a system of coordinates for locating a point on a plane (**Carte′sian plane′**) by its distance from each of two intersecting lines, or in space by its distance from each of three planes intersecting at a point. [1885–90]

Carte′sian div′er, a glass vessel partially filled with water and covered with an airtight membrane, containing a hollow object that is open at the bottom and contains just enough air to allow it to float. Pressing on the membrane compresses the air in the vessel and forces water into the object, causing it to sink; releasing the membrane causes it to rise. Also called **Carte′sian dev′il, bottle imp.**

Carte′sian doubt′, *Philos.* willful suspension of all interpretations of experience that are not absolutely certain: used as a method of deriving, by elimination of such uncertainties, axioms upon which to base theories.

Carte′sian prod′uct, *Math.* the collection of all ordered pairs of two given sets such that the first elements of the pairs are chosen from one set and the second elements from the other set: this procedure generalizes to an infinite number of sets. [1955–60]

Carte′sian space′, *Math.* See **Euclidean space.**

Car·thage (kär′thij), *n.* 1. an ancient city-state in N Africa, near modern Tunis: founded by the Phoenicians in the middle of the 9th century B.C.; destroyed in 146 B.C. in the last of the Punic Wars. 2. a town in central Missouri. 11,104. —**Car·tha·gin·i·an** (kär′thə jin′ē ən), *adj., n.*

Carthagin′ian peace′, 1. the treaty by which Rome reduced Carthage to the status of a puppet state in 201 B.C. 2. any brutal peace treaty demanding total subjugation of the defeated side.

cart′ horse′, a strong horse bred to draw heavy loads; draft horse. [1350–1400; ME]

Car·thu·sian (kär thōō′zhən), *Rom. Cath. Ch.* —*n.* 1. a member of a monastic order founded by St. Bruno in 1086 near Grenoble, France. —*adj.* 2. pertaining to the Carthusians. [1520–30; < ML *Cartusiānus,* by metathesis from *Catursiānus,* after *Catursiānī* (*montēs*) district in Dauphiné where the order was founded]

Car·tier (kär′tē ā′; *Fr.* KAR tyā′), *n.* 1. **Sir George É·tienne** (zhôrzh ā tyen′), 1814–73, Canadian political leader: prime minister 1857–62, defense minister 1867–73. 2. **Jacques** (zhäk), 1491–1557, French navigator and explorer of Canada: discovered the St. Lawrence River.

Car·tier-Bres·son (KAR tyā bre sôN′), *n.* **Hen·ri** (äN rē′), born 1908, French photographer.

car·ti·lage (kär′tl ij, kärt′lij), *n. Anat., Zool.* 1. a firm, elastic, flexible type of connective tissue of a translucent whitish or yellowish color; gristle. 2. a part or structure composed of cartilage. [1350–1400; ME (< MF) < L *cartilāgō* gristle]

car′tilage bone′, a bone that develops from cartilage. Cf. **membrane bone.**

car·ti·lag·i·nous (kär′tl aj′ə nəs), *adj.* 1. of or resembling cartilage. 2. having a skeleton composed either entirely or mainly of cartilage, as vertebrates of the class Chondrichthyes, which includes the sharks, rays, and skates. [1375–1425; late ME < L *cartilāginōsus,* equiv. to *cartilāgin-* (s. of *cartilāgō*) CARTILAGE + *-ōsus* -OUS]

cart·load (kärt′lōd′), *n.* the amount a cart can hold. [1250–1300; ME. See CART, LOAD]

car·to·gram (kär′tə gram′), *n.* a diagrammatic presentation in highly abstracted or simplified form, commonly of statistical data, on a map base or distorted map base. [1885–90; < F *cartogramme.* See CARTE, -O-, -GRAM[1]]

car·tog·ra·phy (kär tog′rə fē), *n.* the production of maps, including construction of projections, design, compilation, drafting, and reproduction. [1855–60; < L *c(h)art(a)* CARTE + -O- + -GRAPHY] —**car·to·graph** (kär′tə graf′, -gräf′), *n.* —**car·tog′ra·pher,** *n.* —**car·to·graph·ic** (kär′tə graf′ik), **car′to·graph′i·cal,** *adj.* —**car′to·graph′i·cal·ly,** *adv.*

car·ton (kär′tn), *n.* 1. a cardboard or plastic box used typically for storage or shipping. 2. the amount a carton can hold. 3. the contents of a carton. 4. a cardboardlike substance consisting of chewed plant material often mixed with soil, made by certain insects for building nests. —*v.t.* 5. to pack in a carton: *to carton eggs for supermarket sales.* —*v.i.* 6. to make or form cardboard sheets into cartons. [1780–90; < F < It *cartone* pasteboard; see CARTOON]

car·ton·nier (kär′tn yā′; *Fr.* KAR tô nyā′), *n., pl.* **-ton·niers** (-tn yāz′; *Fr.* -tô nyā′). *Fr. Furniture.* an ornamental box for papers, usually for placing on a desk. Also called **serre-papier.** [< F; see CARTON, -IER[2]]

car·ton-pierre (*Fr.* KAR tôN pyeR′), *n.* papier-mâché decorated in imitation of wood, stone, or metal, and chiefly used for ornamental statuary or decorative motifs. [1840–50; < F: stone cardboard]

car·toon (kär tōōn′), *n.* 1. a sketch or drawing, usually humorous, as in a newspaper or periodical, symbolizing, satirizing, or caricaturing some action, subject, or person of popular interest. 2. See **comic strip.** 3. See **animated cartoon.** 4. *Fine Arts.* a full-scale design for a picture, ornamental motif or pattern, or the like, to be transferred to a fresco, tapestry, etc. —*adj.* 5. resembling a cartoon or caricature: *The novel is full of predictable, cartoon characters, never believable as real people.* —*v.t.* 6. to represent by a cartoon. —*v.i.* 7. to draw cartoons. [1665–75; < It *cartone* pasteboard, stout paper, a drawing on such paper, equiv. to *cart(a)* paper (see CARTE) + *-one* aug. suffix] —**car·toon′ish,** *adj.* —**car·toon′ist,** *n.*

car·top (kär′top′), *adj.* of a size and shape suitable for carrying on the top of an automobile. Also, **car′top′pa·ble.** [1945–50; CAR[1] + TOP[1]]

car·top·per (kär′top′ər), *n.* a small, open boat that can be carried atop an automobile. [CAR[1] + TOP[1] + -ER[1]]

car·touche (kär tōōsh′), *n.* 1. *Archit.* a rounded, convex surface, usually surrounded with carved ornamental scrollwork, for receiving a painted or low-relief decoration, as an escutcheon. 2. an oval or oblong figure, as on ancient Egyptian monuments, enclosing characters that represent the name of a sovereign. 3. the case containing the inflammable materials in certain fireworks. 4. cartridge (def. 1). 5. a box for cartridges. Also, **car·touch′.** [1605–15; < MF < It *cartoccio,* equiv. to *cart(a)* paper (see CARTE[2]) + *-occio* aug. suffix]

car·tridge (kär′trij), *n.* 1. Also called **cartouche.** a cylindrical case of pasteboard, metal, or the like, for holding a complete charge of powder, and often also the bullet or the shot for a rifle, machine gun, or other small arm. 2. a case containing any explosive charge, as for blasting. 3. any small container for powder, liquid, or gas, made for ready insertion into some device or mechanism: *an ink cartridge for a pen.* 4. Also called **magazine.** *Photog.* a lightproof metal or plastic container for a roll of film, usually containing both the supply and take-up spools, as well as a pressure plate, for rapid loading without the necessity of threading the film. 5. *Audio.* pickup (def. 8). 6. a flat, compact container enclosing an endless loop of audiotape, operated by inserting into a slot in a player. [1570–80; earlier *cartage, cartrage,* alter. of CARTOUCHE]

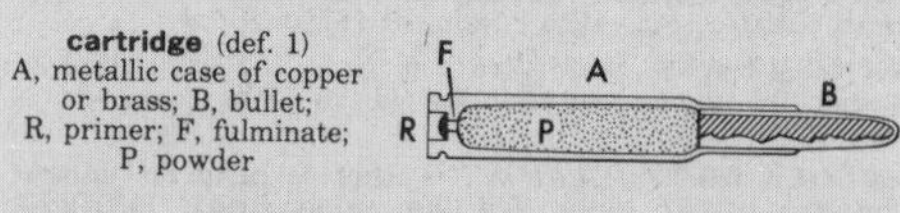

cartridge (def. 1)
A, metallic case of copper or brass; B, bullet; R, primer; F, fulminate; P, powder

car′tridge belt′, a belt of leather or webbing with loops for carrying cartridges or pockets for clips of cartridges. [1870–75]

car′tridge brass′, brass composed of about 70 percent copper and 30 percent zinc.

car′tridge clip′, a metal frame or container holding cartridges for a magazine rifle or automatic pistol.

car·tu·lar·y (kär′chōō ler′ē), *n., pl.* **-lar·ies.** chartulary.

cart·wheel (kärt′hwēl′, -wēl′), *n.* 1. the wheel of a cart. 2. an acrobatic feat in which a person starts from a standing position, with arms extended, and wheels the body sideways, landing first on the hands and then on the feet and usually repeating this in a series. 3. *Slang.* any large coin, esp. a U.S. silver dollar. 4. *Slang.* an amphetamine tablet. —*v.i.* 5. to roll forward end over end: *The skier took a sudden spill and cartwheeled down the slope.* [1350–1400; ME; see CART, WHEEL] —**cart′·wheel′er,** *n.*

Cart·wright (kärt′rīt′), *n.* 1. **Edmund,** 1743–1822, English clergyman: inventor of the power-driven loom. 2. his brother, **John,** 1740–1824, English parliamentary reformer.

Ca·rua·ru (kär′wə rōō′; *Port.* kä′RWä Rōō′), *n.* a city in E Brazil, W of Recife. 101,006.

car·u·cate (kar′ŏŏ kāt′, -yŏŏ-), *n.* an old English unit of land-area measurement, varying from 60 to 160 acres. [1375–1425; late ME < ML *carrūcāta,* equiv. to *car(r)ūc(a)* plow, plow team (L: traveling carriage, with the sense "wheeled plow" in Gaul (>F *charru* plow); akin to L *carrus* four-wheeled Gaulish wagon; see CAR[1]) + *-āta* -ATE[1]] —**car′u·cat′ed,** *adj.*

car·un·cle (kar′ung kəl, kə rung′-), *n.* 1. *Bot.* a protuberance at or surrounding the hilum of a seed. 2. *Zool.* a fleshy excrescence, as on the head of a bird; a fowl's comb. 3. *Anat.* a small, fleshy growth. [1605–15; earlier *caruncula* < L: small piece of flesh, dim. of *carō* (gen. *carnis*) flesh; for suffix, see CARBUNCLE] —**ca·run·cu·lar** (kə rung′kyə lər), **ca·run′cu·lous,** *adj.*

ca·run·cu·late (kə rung′kyə lit, -lāt′), *adj.* having a caruncle. Also, **ca·run′cu·lat′ed.** [1825–35; < NL *carunculātus.* See CARUNCLE, -ATE[1]]

Ca·rú·pa·no (kä Rōō′pä nô), *n.* a seaport in N Venezuela. 46,155.

Ca·ru·so (kə rōō′sō; *It.* kä Rōō′zô), *n.* **En·ri·co** (en rē′kō; *It.* en Rē′kô), 1873–1921, Italian operatic tenor.

car·va·crol (kär′və krōl′, -krol′), *n.* a colorless, thick, oily liquid, $C_{10}H_{14}O$, having a mintlike odor: used chiefly as a disinfectant, as a fungicide, and as a scent in the manufacture of perfume. [1850–55; < ML *caru(i)* CARAWAY + L *acr-* (s. of *acer* sharp; see ACRID) + -OL[1]]

carve (kärv), *v.,* **carved, carv·ing.** —*v.t.* 1. to cut (a solid material) so as to form something: *to carve a piece of pine.* 2. to form from a solid material by cutting: *to carve a statue out of stone.* 3. to cut into slices or pieces, as a roast of meat. 4. to decorate with designs or figures cut on the surface: *The top of the box was beautifully carved with figures of lions and unicorns.* 5. to cut (a

CONCISE ETYMOLOGY KEY: <, descended or borrowed from; >, whence; b., blend of, blended; c., cognate with; cf., compare; deriv., derivative; equiv., equivalent; imit., imitative; obl., oblique; r., replacing; s., stem; sp., spelling, spelled; resp., respelling, respelled; trans., translation; ?, origin unknown; *, unattested; ‡, probably earlier than. See the full key inside the front cover.

design, figures, etc.) on a surface: *Figures of lions and unicorns were carved on the top of the box.* **6.** to make or create for oneself (often fol. by *out*): *He carved out a career in business.* **—*v.i.*** **7.** to carve figures, designs, etc. **8.** to cut meat. [bef. 1000; ME *kerven,* OE *ceorfan* to cut; c. MLG *kerven,* G *kerben,* Gk *gráphein* to mark, write; see GRAPH] **—carv′er,** *n.*

car•vel (kär′vəl), *n.* caravel. [late ME *carvile* < D *karveel* CARAVEL]

car•vel-built (kär′vəl bilt′), *adj.* (of a ship's hull) formed of planks laid close on the frames so as to present a smooth exterior. Cf. **clinker-built** (def. 2). [1790–1800]

carv•en (kär′vən), *adj. Archaic.* carved. [See CARVE, -EN[3]; r. ME *corven,* OE *corfen* (ptp.)]

Car•ver (kär′vər), *n.* **1. George Washington,** 1864?–1943, U.S. botanist and chemist. **2. John,** 1575?–1621, Pilgrim leader: first governor of Plymouth Colony 1620–21.

Car′ver chair′, a chair of 17th-century New England, having a frame formed entirely of turned pieces, a back filled with several spindles, and no spindles between the arms and the seat. Cf. **Brewster chair.** [1900–05; named after John CARVER, who owned one of this kind]

carv•er•y (kär′və rē), *n., pl.* **-er•ies. 1.** a restaurant, hotel dining room, etc., that specializes in roasted meats and poultry carved to the diner's request. **2.** the selection of roasted meats and poultry provided. [CARVE + -ERY]

carv•ing (kär′ving), *n.* **1.** the act of fashioning or producing by cutting into or shaping solid material, as wood. **2.** a carved design or figure. [See CARVE, -ING[1]]

carv′ing fork′, a fork used in carving meat, commonly having two long tines and, at the base of the handle, a projection on which to rest the forefinger and thumb. [1670–80]

carv′ing knife′, a large, sharp knife for carving or slicing meat. [1400–50; late ME]

car′ wash′, 1. a place or structure having special equipment for washing automobiles. **2.** the washing of an automobile: *The service station is offering free car washes to draw customers.* Also, **car′wash′.** [1955–60]

Car•y (kâr′ē, kar′ē), *n.* **1. Alice,** 1820–71, U.S. poet (sister of Phoebe Cary). **2. (Arthur) Joyce (Lu•nel)** (lo͞o nel′), 1888–1957, English novelist. **3. Henry Francis,** 1772–1844, British writer and translator. **4. Phoebe,** 1824–71, U.S. poet (sister of Alice Cary). **5.** a town in central North Carolina. 21,612. **6.** a male given name. **7.** a female given name, form of **Caroline.**

car•y•at•id (kar′ē at′id), *n., pl.* **-ids, -i•des** (-i dēz′). *Archit.* a sculptured female figure used as a column. Cf. **atlas** (def. 5). [1555–65; < L *Caryātides* (sing. *Caryātis*) < Gk *Karyátides* columns shaped like women, lit., women of *Karyai,* Laconia] **—car′y•at′i•dal,** *adj.*

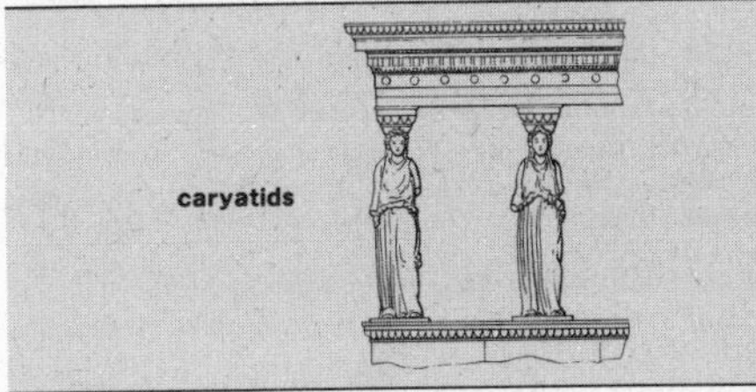
caryatids

Car•yl (kar′əl), *n.* a male or female given name.

Car•yn (kar′in), *n.* a female given name.

caryo-, var. of **karyo-.**

car•y•o•phyl•la•ceous (kar′ē ō fə lā′shəs), *adj.* belonging to the Caryophyllaceae, the pink family of plants. Cf. **pink family.** [1825–35; < NL *Caryophyllace(ae)* the family (*Caryophyll(us)* a genus < Gk *karyóphyllon* clove tree (see CARYO-, -PHYLL) + -ACEAE) + -OUS]

car•y•op•sis (kar′ē op′sis) *n., pl.* **-ses** (-sēz), **-si•des** (-si dēz′). *Bot.* a small, one-celled, one-seeded, dry indehiscent fruit with the pericarp adherent to the seed coat, the typical fruit of grasses and grains. [1820–30; CARY(O)- + -OPSIS]

C.A.S., Certificate of Advanced Studies.

ca•sa (kä′sə, -sä), *n. Southwestern U.S.* a house. [1835–45, *Amer.*; < Sp < L: hut, cabin]

ca•sa•ba (kə sä′bə), *n.* a variety of the winter melon, *Cucumis melo inodorus,* having a wrinkled, yellow rind and sweet, juicy, greenish flesh. Also, **cassaba.** Also called **casa′ba mel′on.** [1885–90, *Amer.*; named after *Kassaba* (now Turgutlu), town near Izmir, Turkey, which exported it]

Ca•sa•bian•ca (ka za byäN ka′), *n.* **Louis de** (lwē də), c1755–98, French naval officer.

Cas•a•blan•ca (kas′ə blang′kə, kä′sə bläng′kə), *n.* a seaport in NW Morocco: wartime conference of Roosevelt and Churchill, January, 1943. 2,139,204.

Ca•sa•de•sus (kä′sə dā′səs; *Fr.* ka sadᵊ sys′), *n.* **Robert** (rob′ərt; *Fr.* rô ber′), 1899–1972, French pianist and composer.

Ca•sa Gran•de (kä′sä grän′dā, -dē, -sə-), **1.** a national monument in S Arizona, near the Gila River: ruins of a prehistoric culture. **2.** a town in central Arizona. 14,971.

Ca•sals (kə salz′, -sälz′, kä sälz′; *Sp.* kä säls′), *n.* **Pablo** (pä′blō; *Sp.* pä′vlô), 1876–1973, Spanish cellist, conductor, and composer; in France after 1936; in Puerto Rico after 1956.

Cas•a•no•va (kaz′ə nō′və, kas′-; *It.* kä′sä nô′vä), *n.* **1. Gio•van•ni Ja•co•po** (jô vän′nē yä′kô pô), 1725–98, Italian adventurer and writer. **2.** a man with a reputation for having many amorous adventures; rake; Don Juan. **—Cas•a•no•van•ic** (kaz′ə nō van′ik, kas′-), *adj.*

ca•saque (ka zak′), *n., pl.* **-saques** (-zak′). *French.* a loose-fitting blouse for women.

Ca•sas (kä′säs), *n.* **Bar•to•lo•mé de las** (bär′tô lô me′ the läs). See **Las Casas, Bartolomé de.**

Ca•sau•bon (kə sô′bən; *Fr.* ka zō bôN′), *n.* **I•saac** (ī′zək; *Fr.* ē zak′), 1559–1614, French classical scholar.

Cas•bah (kaz′bə, -bä, käz′-), *n.* Kasbah.

cas•ca•bel (kas′kə bel′), *n.* a knoblike projection at the rear of the breech of a muzzleloading cannon. [1630–40; < Sp: little round bell, rattle < OPr *cascavel,* akin to ML **cascabellus,* equiv. to VL **cascab(us)* (var. of L *caccabus* pot) + L *-ellus* dim. suffix]

cas•cade (kas kād′), *n., v.,* **-cad•ed, -cad•ing.** **—*n.*** **1.** a waterfall descending over a steep, rocky surface. **2.** a series of shallow or steplike waterfalls, either natural or artificial. **3.** anything that resembles a waterfall, esp. in seeming to flow or fall in abundance: *a cascade of roses covering the wall.* **4.** (in a drain or sewer) a chain of steps for dissipating the momentum of falling water in a steep place in order to maintain a steady rate of flow. **5.** an arrangement of a lightweight fabric in folds falling one over another in random or zigzag fashion. **6.** a type of firework resembling a waterfall in effect. **7.** *Chem.* a series of vessels, from each of which a fluid successively overflows to the next, thus presenting a large absorbing surface, as to a gas. **8.** *Elect.* an arrangement of component devices, as electrolytic cells, each of which feeds into the next in succession. **9.** *Biochem.* a series of reactions catalyzed by enzymes that are activated sequentially by successive products of the reactions, resulting in an amplification of the initial response. **—*v.i.*** **10.** to fall in or like a cascade. **—*v.t.*** **11.** to cause to fall in a cascade. **12.** *Elect.* to arrange (components) in a cascade. [1635–45; < F < It *cascata,* equiv. to *casc(are)* to fall (< VL **cāsicāre,* equiv. to *cās(us)* fallen (ptp. of *cadere*) + *-icā-* formative v. suffix + *-re* inf. ending) + *-ata* -ADE[1]] **—cas•cad′er,** *n.*

cascade′ par′ticle, *Physics.* the least massive member of the xi particle family. Also called **cascade′ hy′peron.**

Cascade′ Range′, a mountain range extending from N California to W Canada: highest peak, Mt. Rainier, 14,408 ft. (4322 m). Also called **the Cascades.**

cas•car•a (kas kâr′ə), *n.* a buckthorn, *Rhamnus purshiana,* of the Pacific coast of the U.S., having finely toothed leaves and flowers in umbels and yielding cascara sagrada. Also called **cascar′a buck′thorn, bearberry, chittamwood.** [1875–80, *Amer.*; < Sp *cáscara* bark, perh. akin to *cascar* to crack << VL **quassicāre,* equiv. to L *quass(āre)* to shatter (see QUASH) + *-icā-* formative v. suffix + *-re* inf. ending]

cascar′a sa•gra′da (sə grä′də, -grä′-, -grad′ə), **1.** cascara. **2.** the bark of the cascara, used as a cathartic or laxative. [1880–85; < Sp: lit., sacred bark]

cas•ca•ril•la (kas′kə ril′ə), *n.* **1.** Also called **cascaril′la bark′.** the bitter, aromatic bark of a West Indian shrub, *Croton eluteria,* of the spurge family, used as a tonic. **2.** the shrub itself. [1870–75; < Sp, equiv. to *cascar(a)* bark (see CASCARA) + *-illa* < L *-illa* dim. suffix]

Cas′co Bay′ (kas′kō), a bay in SW Maine.

case[1] (kās), *n.* **1.** an instance of the occurrence, existence, etc., of something: *Sailing in such a storm was a case of poor judgment.* **2.** the actual state of things: *That is not the case.* **3.** a question or problem of moral conduct; matter: *a case of conscience.* **4.** situation; circumstance; plight: *Mine is a sad case.* **5.** a person or thing whose plight or situation calls for attention: *This family is a hardship case.* **6.** a specific occurrence or matter requiring discussion, decision, or investigation, as by officials or law-enforcement authorities: *The police studied the case of the missing jewels.* **7.** a stated argument used to support a viewpoint: *He presented a strong case against the proposed law.* **8.** an instance of disease, injury, etc., requiring medical or surgical attention or treatment; individual affliction: *She had a severe case of chicken pox.* **9.** a medical or surgical patient. **10.** *Law.* **a.** a suit or action at law; cause. **b.** a set of facts giving rise to a legal claim, or to a defense to a legal claim. **11.** *Gram.* **a.** a category in the inflection of nouns, pronouns, and adjectives, noting the syntactic relation of these words to other words in the sentence, indicated by the form or the position of the words. **b.** a set of such categories in a particular language. **c.** the meaning of or the meaning typical of such a category. **d.** such categories or their meanings collectively. **12.** *Informal.* a peculiar or unusual person: *He's a case.* **13. get off someone's case,** *Slang.* to stop bothering or criticizing someone or interfering in someone's affairs: *I've had enough of your advice, so just get off my case.* **14. get** or **be on someone's case,** *Slang.* to bother or nag someone; meddle in someone's affairs: *Her brother is always on her case about getting married. Why do you keep getting on my case?* **15. have a case on,** *Slang.* to be infatuated with: *He had a case on the girl next door.* **16. in any case,** regardless of circumstances; be that as it may; anyhow: *In any case, there won't be any necessity for you to come along.* **17. in case,** if it should happen that; if: *In case I am late, don't wait to start dinner.* **18. in case of,** in the event of; if there should be: *In case of an error in judgment, the group leader will be held responsible.* **19. in no case,** under no condition; never: *He should in no case be allowed to get up until he has completely recovered from his illness.* [before 1150; ME *ca(a)s* < AF, OF *cas* < L *cāsus* fall, accident, event, grammatical case (trans. of Gk *ptôsis*), equiv. to *cad(ere)* to fall + *-tus* suffix of v. action; cf. OE *cāsus* grammatical case] **—case′less,** *adj.* **—case′less•ly,** *adv.*

—Syn. 1. CASE, INSTANCE, EXAMPLE, ILLUSTRATION suggest the existence or occurrence of a particular thing representative of its type. CASE and INSTANCE are closely allied in meaning, as are EXAMPLE and ILLUSTRATION. CASE is a general word, meaning a fact, occurrence, or situation typical of a class: *a case of assault and battery.* An INSTANCE is a concrete factual case which is adduced to explain a general idea: *an instance of a brawl in which an assault occurred.* An EXAMPLE is one typical case, usually from many similar ones, used to make clear or explain the working of a principle (what may be expected of any others of the group): *This boy is an example of the effect of strict discipline.* An ILLUSTRATION exemplifies a theory or principle similarly, except that the choice may be purely hypothetical: *The work of Seeing Eye dogs is an illustration of what is thought to be intelligence in animals.*

case[2] (kās), *n., v.,* **cased, cas•ing.** **—*n.*** **1.** an often small or portable container for enclosing something, as for carrying or safekeeping; receptacle: *a jewel case.* **2.** a sheath or outer covering: *a knife case.* **3.** a box with its contents: *a case of ginger ale.* **4.** the amount contained in a box or other container: *There are a dozen bottles to a case.* **5.** a pair or couple; brace: *a case of pistols.* **6.** a surrounding frame or framework, as of a door. **7.** *Bookbinding.* a completed book cover ready to be fitted to form the binding of a book. **8.** *Print.* a tray of wood, metal, or plastic, divided into compartments for holding types for the use of a compositor and usually arranged in a set of two, the upper **(upper case)** for capital letters and often auxiliary types, the lower **(lower case)** for small letters and often auxiliary types, now generally replaced by the California job case. Cf. **news case. 9.** a cavity in the skull of a sperm whale, containing an oil from which spermaceti is obtained. **10.** Also called **case card.** *Cards.* the last card of a suit or denomination that remains after the other cards have been played: *a case heart; the case jack.* **11.** *Faro.* casebox. **12.** *Southeastern U.S. (chiefly South Carolina).* a coin of a particular denomination, as opposed to the same amount in change: *a case quarter.* **13.** *Metall.* the hard outer part of a piece of casehardened steel. **—*v.t.*** **14.** to put or enclose in a case; cover with a case. **15.** *Slang.* to examine or survey (a house, bank, etc.) in planning a crime (sometimes fol. by *out*): *They cased the joint and decided to pull the job on Sunday.* **16.** to fuse a layer of glass onto (glass of a contrasting color or of different properties). **17.** to cover (a surface of a wall, well, shaft, etc.) with a facing or lining; revet. **18.** *Bookbinding.* to bind (a book) in a case. **19.** *Cards Slang.* **a.** to arrange (cards or a pack of cards) in a dishonest manner. **b.** to remember the quantity, suit, or denomination of (the cards played). [1250–1300; ME *cas* < AF *cas(s)e,* OF *chasse* < L *capsa* cylindrical case for holding books in scroll form, receptacle] **—cas′er,** *n.*

ca•se•ate (kā′sē āt′), *v.i.,* **-at•ed, -at•ing.** *Pathol.* to undergo caseation. [1870–75; < L *cāse(us)* CHEESE + -ATE[1]]

ca•se•a•tion (kā′sē ā′shən), *n.* **1.** *Pathol.* transformation of tissue into a soft cheeselike mass, as in tuberculosis. **2.** *Biochem.* the formation of cheese from casein during the coagulation of milk. [1865–70; CASEATE + -ION]

case′ bay′, *Carpentry.* (in a roof or floor) the section between two principals. [1875–80]

case•book (kās′bo͝ok′), *n.* a book in which detailed records of a case are kept and from which illustrative material can be taken in the presentation of a thesis, lecture, or the like. [1755–65; CASE[1] + BOOK]

case•bound (kās′bound′), *adj. Bookbinding.* **1.** bound in hard covers. **2.** bound by gluing sewn sheets into a separately made cover. [CASE[2] + BOUND[1]]

case•box (kās′boks′), *n. Faro.* a device, similar to an abacus, for recording the cards as they are drawn from the dealing box. Also called **case.** [CASE[2] + BOX[1]]

case′ card′, case (def. 10).

case′ end′ing, *Gram.* a suffix on an inflected noun, pronoun, or adjective that indicates its grammatical function. [1870–75]

ca•se•fy (kā′sə fī′), *v.t., v.i.,* **-fied, -fy•ing.** to make or become like cheese. [< L *cāse(us)* CHEESE + -FY]

case′ glass′, glass composed of two or more layers of glass in different colors, often having the top layer cut or ground away so that the lower layer can serve as background or contrast. Also, **cased′ glass′.** Also called **overlay glass.**

case′ goods′, furniture designed for storage, as cupboards, chests of drawers, or wardrobes. [1920–25]

case′ gram′mar, *Ling.* a form of generative grammar that views case roles, as agent, experiencer, instrument, and object, based on the semantic relationship of noun phrases to verbs, to be basic categories in deep structure and derives grammatical relations, as subject and direct object, from these case roles.

case•hard•en (kās′här′dn), *v.t.* **1.** *Metall.* to make the outside surface of (an alloy having an iron base) hard by carburizing and heat treatment, leaving the interior tough and ductile. **2.** to harden in spirit so as to render insensible or insensitive to external impressions or influences; make callous. [1670–80; CASE[2] + HARDEN]

case′ his′tory, all the relevant information or material gathered about an individual, family, group, etc., and arranged so as to serve as an organized record and have analytic value for a social worker, student, or the like: used esp. in social work, sociology, psychiatry, and medicine. [1910–15]

ca•sein (kā′sēn, -sē in, kā sēn′), *n.* **1.** *Biochem.* a protein precipitated from milk, as by rennet, and forming the basis of cheese and certain plastics. **2.** *Fine Arts.* **a.** an emulsion made from a solution of this precipitated protein, water, and ammonia carbonate. **b.** a paint in which this emulsion is used as a binder. **c.** a picture produced with this paint and emulsion. [1835–45; < L *cāse(us)* CHEESE + -IN[2]]

ca•sein•ate (kā′sē nāt′, -sē ə-, kā sē′nāt), *n. Chem.* a metallic salt of casein. [CASEIN + -ATE[2]]

CONCISE PRONUNCIATION KEY: *act, cāpe, dâre, pärt; set, ēqual; if, īce; ox, ōver, ôrder, oil, bo͝ok, bo͞ot, out; up, ûrge; child; sing; shoe; thin, that;* zh as in *treasure.* ə = *a* as in *alone, e* as in *system, i* as in *easily, o* as in *gallop, u* as in *circus;* ᵊ as in *fire* (fīᵊr), *hour* (ouᵊr). l and n can serve as syllabic consonants, as in *cradle* (krād′l), and *button* (but′n). See the full key inside the front cover.

ca′sein glue′, a glue made from casein, used for plywood, cabinetwork, etc. [1885–90]

case•keep•er (kās′kē′pər), *n. Faro.* the person who records in the casebox a tally of cards as they appear in the box. [1865–70; CASE[2] + KEEPER]

case′ knife′, **1.** a knife carried or kept in a case or sheath. **2.** a table knife. [1695–1705]

case′ law′, law established by judicial decisions in particular cases, instead of by legislative action. [1860–65]

case•load (kās′lōd′), *n.* the number of cases handled by a court, an agency, a social worker, etc., either at any given moment or over a stated period. Also, **case′ load′**. [1945–50; CASE[1] + LOAD]

case•mak•er (kās′mā′kər), *n.* **1.** a person or thing that makes cases, esp. for books. **2.** a worker on leather articles who pastes the pieces together for sewing. [1325–75; ME. See CASE[2], MAKER]

case′mak•ing clothes′ moth′ (kās′mā′king). See under **clothes moth.**

case•mate (kās′māt′), *n.* **1.** an armored enclosure for guns in a warship. **2.** a vault or chamber, esp. in a rampart, with embrasures for artillery. [1565–75; < MF < OIt *casamatta,* alter. (by folk etymology) of Gk *chásmata* embrasures, lit., openings, pl. of *chásma* CHASM] —**case′mat′ed,** *adj.*

case•ment (kās′mənt), *n.* **1.** a window sash opening on hinges that are generally attached to the upright side of its frame. **2.** Also called **case′ment win′dow.** a window with such a sash or sashes. **3.** a casing or covering. [1375–1425; late ME. See CASE[2], -MENT] —**case′ment•ed,** *adj.*

Case•ment (kās′mənt), *n.* **(Sir) Roger (David),** 1864–1916, Irish patriot: hanged by the British for treason.

case′ment cloth′, a sheer fabric made of a variety of fibers, used for window curtains and as backing for heavy drapery or decorative fabrics. [1900–05]

case′ment door′. See **French door.**

case′ meth′od, **1.** Also called **case′-stud′y meth′•od** (kās′stud′ē). the teaching or elucidation of a subject or issue through analysis and discussion of actual cases, as in business education. **2.** See **case system.**

ca•se•ous (kā′sē əs), *adj.* of or like cheese. [1655–65; < L *cāse(us)* CHEESE + -OUS]

ca•sern (kə sûrn′), *n.* a lodging for soldiers in a garrison town; barracks. Also, **ca•serne′.** [1690–1700; < F *caserne,* orig. small room for guardsmen < OPr *cazerna* foursome < L *quaterna,* neut. pl. of *quaterni* four at a time, equiv. to *quater-* (deriv. of *quattuor* FOUR) + *-nī* distributive suffix]

case′ shot′, a collection of small projectiles in a case, to be fired from a cannon. Also called **canister, canister shot.** [1665–75]

case′ stud′y, **1.** a study of an individual unit, as a person, family, or social group, usually emphasizing developmental issues and relationships with the environment, esp. in order to compare a larger group to the individual unit. **2.** See **case history.** [1930–35]

case′ sys′tem, a method of teaching or studying law that focuses on analysis and discussion of cases. [1885–90]

case•work[1] (kās′wûrk′), *n.* **1.** the work of investigation, advice, supervision, etc., by social workers or the like, in cases handled by them. **2.** *Sociol.* a close study of psychological and sociological factors in the history of an individual or family in unfavorable circumstances, with a view to improving personal and family conditions. Also, **case′ work′.** [CASE[1] + WORK]

case•work[2] (kās′wûrk′), *n.* cabinetwork (def. 1). [CASE[2] + WORK]

case•work•er (kās′wûr′kər), *n.* **1.** a person who does casework. **2.** an investigator, esp. of a social agency, who aids disadvantaged individuals or families chiefly by analysis of their problems and through personal counseling. Also, **case′-work′er, case′ work′er.** [1930–35; CASE[1] + WORKER]

case•worm (kās′wûrm′), *n.* a caddisworm or other insect larva that constructs a case around its body. [1600–10; CASE[2] + WORM]

Ca•sey (kā′sē), *n.* a male given name: from an Irish word meaning "brave."

cash[1] (kash), *n.* **1.** money in the form of coins or banknotes, esp. that issued by a government. **2.** money or an equivalent, as a check, paid at the time of making a purchase. —*v.t.* **3.** to give or obtain cash for (a check, money order, etc.). **4.** *Cards.* **a.** to win (a trick) by leading an assured winner. **b.** to lead (an assured winner) in order to win a trick: *He cashed his ace and led the queen.* **5. cash in, a.** to turn in and get cash for (one's chips), as in a gambling casino. **b.** to end or withdraw from a business agreement; convert one's assets into cash. **c.** *Slang.* to die: *After her parents cashed in, she lived with her grandmother.* **6. cash in on,** to profit from; use to one's advantage: *swindlers who cash in on the credulity of the public.* **7. cash in one's chips,** *Slang.* to die. [1590–1600; appar. back formation from CASHIER[1]] —**cash′a•ble,** *adj.* —**cash′a•bil′i•ty,** *n.* —**cash′a•ble•ness,** *n.*

cash[2] (kash), *n., pl.* **cash.** any of several low-denomination coins of China, India, and the East Indies, esp. a Chinese copper coin. [1590–1600; < Pg *caixa* < Tamil *kācu* copper coin < Skt *karṣa* a weight (of precious metal)]

Cash (kash), *n.* **John** (*Johnny*), born 1932, U.S. country-and-western singer, musician, and composer.

CONCISE ETYMOLOGY KEY: <, descended or borrowed from; >, whence; b., blend of, blended; c., cognate with; cf., compare; deriv., derivative; equiv., equivalent; imit., imitative; obl., oblique; r., replacing; s., stem; sp., spelling, spelled; resp., respelling, respelled; trans., translation; ?, origin unknown; *, unattested; ‡, probably earlier than. See the full key inside the front cover.

cash′ account′, **1.** an account in which all transactions are in money. **2.** *Finance.* an account in which purchases are paid for in full, as distinguished from purchasing on credit or margin.

cash-and-car•ry (kash′ən kar′ē), *adj.* **1.** sold for cash payment and no delivery service. **2.** operated on such a basis: *a cash-and-carry business.* [1915–20]

cash′ au′dit, an audit confined to cash transactions for a prescribed period, for the purpose of determining the amount of cash on hand or on deposit in a bank.

ca•shaw (kə shô′), *n.* cushaw.

cash′ bar′, a bar selling drinks to persons attending a special function. Cf. **open bar.**

cash′ ba′sis, a method of recording income and expenses in which each item is entered as received or paid. Cf. **accrual basis.**

cash•book (kash′bo͝ok′), *n.* a book in which to record money received and paid out. [1615–25; CASH[1] + BOOK]

cash•box (kash′boks′), *n.* a box or container for money, esp. with compartments for coins and bills of different denominations. [1825–35; CASH[1] + BOX[1]]

cash′ cow′, *Informal.* any business venture, operation, or product that is a dependable source of income or profit.

cash′ crop′, **1.** any crop that is considered easily marketable, as wheat or cotton. **2.** a crop for direct sale in a market, as distinguished from a crop for use as livestock feed or for other purposes. [1865–70, *Amer.*]

cash′ cus′tomer, a purchaser who pays cash rather than by check, credit card, or charge account.

cash′ dis′count, **1.** a term of sale by which the buyer deducts a percentage from the bill if it is paid immediately in cash or within a stipulated period by check or cash. **2.** the amount deducted. [1915–20]

cash•drawer (kash′drôr′), *n.* a drawer, as in a cash register, that has separate compartments for coins and bills of different denominations. [CASH[1] + DRAWER]

cash•ew (kash′o͞o, kə sho͞o′), *n.* **1.** a tree, *Anacardium occidentale,* native to tropical America, having milky juice, simple, leathery leaves, and yellowish-pink flowers in open clusters. **2.** Also called **cash′ew nut′.** the small, kidney-shaped, edible nut of this tree. [1695–1705; < Pg *cajú,* aph. var. of *acajú* < Tupi *aka'iu*]

cash′ew fam′ily, the plant family Anacardiaceae, typified by trees, shrubs, or vines having resinous and sometimes poisonous juice, alternate leaves, small flowers, and a nut or fleshy fruit, and including the cashew, mango, pistachio, poison ivy, and sumac.

cash′ flow′, the sum of the after-tax profit of a business plus depreciation and other noncash charges: used as an indication of internal funds available for stock dividends, purchase of buildings and equipment, etc. [1950–55]

cash•ier[1] (ka shēr′), *n.* **1.** an employee, as in a market or department store, who collects payments for customer purchases. **2.** an executive who has charge of money, esp. one who superintends monetary transactions, as in a bank. **3.** an employee of a business establishment who keeps a record of financial transactions. [1570–80; < MF *caissier* custodian of a money-box (perh. via D), equiv. to *caisse* money-box (< Pr *caissa* < L *capsa;* see CASE[2]) + *-ier* -IER[2]]

cash•ier[2] (ka shēr′), *v.t.* **1.** to dismiss (a military officer) from service, esp. with disgrace. **2.** to discard; reject. [1570–80; < MD *kasseren* < MF *casser* to break, discharge, annul < L *quassāre* to shatter; see QUASH]

cashier's′ check′, a check drawn by a bank on its own funds and signed by its cashier. [1865–70, *Amer.*]

cash-in (kash′in′), *n.* redemption, as of mutual-fund shares. [1935–40; n. use of v. phrase *cash in*]

cash′ jour′nal, cashbook.

cash•less (kash′lis), *adj.* having or using no cash. [1825–35; CASH[1] + -LESS] —**cash′less•ness,** *n.*

cash′less soci′ety, a society in which purchases of goods or services are made by credit card or electronic funds transferral rather than with cash or checks. Also called **checkless society.** [1970–75]

cash′ let′ter, *Banking.* a deposit list from one bank to another containing items to be credited to the account of the depositing bank.

cash′ machine′. See **automated-teller machine.**

cash•mere (kazh′mēr, kash′-), *n.* **1.** the fine, downy wool at the roots of the hair of the Kashmir goat. **2.** a garment made of this wool. **3.** a yarn made from this wool. **4.** a wool or cashmere fabric of plain or twill weave. Also, **kashmir.** [1815–25; named after CASHMERE]

Cash•mere (kash mēr′), *n.* Kashmir. —**Cash•mer′i•an,** *adj. n.*

Cash′mere goat′. See **Kashmir goat.**

cash′ mon′ey, *South Midland and Southern U.S.* cash, as distinguished from a check or money order. [1895–1900; *Amer.*]

cash′ on deliv′ery. See **C.O.D.** [1850–55]

ca•shoo (kə sho͞o′), *n.* catechu. [var. sp. of CACHOU]

cash-out (kash′out′), *n.* **1.** Also, **cash′out′.** a direct cash payment or a cash profit or remainder: *The store owner lived on a cash-out of fifty dollars a day.* **2.** a payment of winnings or a cashing in of chips, as in a casino. **3.** cash-in.

cash•point (kash′point′), *n.* See **automated-teller machine.**

cash′ reg′ister, a business machine that indicates to customers the amounts of individual sales, has a money drawer from which to make change, records and totals receipts, and may automatically calculate the change due. Also called **sales register.** [1875–80, *Amer.*]

cash′ val′ue, *Insurance.* the nonforfeiture value of a life-insurance policy payable to the insured in cash upon its surrender. Also called **cash′ surren′der val′ue, surrender value.** [1895–1900]

cas•i•mere (kas′ə mēr′), *n.* cassimere. Also, **cas′i•mire′.**

cas•ing (kā′sing), *n.* **1.** a case or covering; housing. **2.** material for a case or covering. **3.** the framework around a door or window. **4.** the outermost covering of an automobile tire. **5.** any frame or framework. **6.** a steel pipe or tubing, esp. as used in oil and gas wells. **7.** a layer of glass that has been fused to an underlying layer of glass of a different color or of different properties. **8.** the thin, tubular membrane of the intestines of sheep, cattle, or hogs, or a synthetic facsimile, for encasing processed meat in making sausages, salamis, etc. **9.** *Naut.* the walls surrounding a funnel. **10.** a channel created in a garment or other article to carry a drawstring or elastic, as by sewing a strip of cloth to the basic material with two parallel rows of stitches. [1565–75; CASE[2] + -ING[1]]

cas′ing•head gas′ (kā′sing hed′), natural gas obtained from an oil well. [1925–30, *Amer.;* CASING + HEAD]

cas′ing knife′, a knife for trimming wallpaper after it has been attached.

cas′ing nail′, a nail having a small, conical head, slenderer than a common nail of the same length, used for laying floors, fastening matchboarding, and other work in which the head may remain visible. Cf. **finishing nail.**

ca•si•no (kə sē′nō), *n., pl.* **-nos** for 1. **1.** a building or large room used for meetings, entertainment, dancing, etc., esp. such a place equipped with gambling devices, gambling tables, etc. **2.** (in Italy) a small country house or lodge. **3.** Also, **cassino.** *Cards.* a game in which cards that are face up on the table are taken with eligible cards in the hand. [1780–90; < It, equiv. to *cas(a)* house + *-ino* dim. suffix]

ca•si•ta (kə sē′tə; *Sp.* kä sē′tä), *n., pl.* **-tas** (-təz; *Sp.* -täs). **1.** a small crude dwelling forming part of a shantytown inhabited by Mexican laborers in the southwestern U.S. **2.** a luxurious bungalow serving as private guest accommodations at a resort hotel, esp. in the southwestern U.S. or Mexico. [1920–25; < AmerSp, Sp, equiv. to *cas(a)* house, home (< L) + *-ita* dim. suffix]

cask (kask, käsk), *n.* **1.** a container made and shaped like a barrel, esp. one larger and stronger, for holding liquids. **2.** the quantity such a container holds: *wine at 32 guineas a cask.* —*v.t.* **3.** to place or store in a cask. [1425–75; late ME; back formation from CASKET, the *-et* being taken as the dim. suffix] —**cask′like′,** *adj.*

cas•ket (kas′kit, kä′skit), *n.* **1.** a coffin. **2.** a small chest or box, as for jewels. —*v.t.* **3.** to put or enclose in a casket. [1425–75; late ME < ?] —**cas′ket•like′,** *adj.*

Cask′ of Amontilla′do, The, a short story (1846) by Edgar Allan Poe.

Cas•lon (kaz′lən), *n.* **1. William,** 1692–1766, English type founder and designer. **2.** *Print.* an old-style type modeled after the types designed by William Caslon.

Cas•o•ron (kas′ə ron′), *Hort. Trademark.* a brand of dichlobenil.

Cas•par (kas′pər), *n.* **1.** one of the three Magi. **2.** a male given name.

Cas′par Milque′toast, milquetoast.

Cas•per (kas′pər), *n.* **1.** a city in central Wyoming. 51,016. **2.** a male given name.

Cas•pi•an (kas′pē ən), *adj.* **1.** of or pertaining to the Caspian Sea. —*n.* **2.** See **Caspian Sea.** [1580–90]

Cas′pian Sea′, a salt lake between SE Europe and Asia: the largest inland body of water in the world. ab. 169,000 sq. mi. (438,000 sq. km); 85 ft. (26 m) below sea level.

casque (kask), *n.* **1.** an open, conical helmet with a nose guard, commonly used in the medieval period. **2.** any helmet-shaped head covering. **3.** *Zool.* a process or formation on the head, resembling a helmet. [1570–80; < MF < Sp *casco* helmet, head, earthen pot; akin to CASCARA] —**casqued** (kaskt), *adj.*

Cass (kas), *n.* **1. Lewis,** 1782–1866, U.S. statesman. **2.** a male or female given name.

cas•sa•ba (kə sä′bə), *n.* casaba.

Cas•san•der (kə san′dər), *n.* c354-297 B.C., king of Macedonia 301-297 (son of Antipater).

Cas•san•dra (kə san′drə), *n.* **1.** Also called **Alexandra.** *Class. Myth.* a daughter of Priam and Hecuba, a prophet cursed by Apollo so that her prophecies, though true, were fated never to be believed. **2.** a person who prophesies doom or disaster. **3.** a female given name: from a Greek word meaning "helper of men."

cas•sa•pan•ca (kas′ə pang′kə), *n.* a carved bench of the Italian Renaissance, the seat of which is used as a chest. [< It, equiv. to *cassa* box, chest (see CASE[2]) + *panca,* var. of *banca* bench; see BANK[2]]

cas•sa•reep (kas′ə rēp′), *n.* the juice of bitter cassava root, boiled down to a syrup and used as a flavoring for food, esp. in West Indian cookery. [1825–35; apocopated var. of earlier *cassarepo* < Carib]

cas•sa•tion (ka sā′shən, kə-), *n.* **1.** annulment; cancellation; reversal. **2.** *Music.* an 18th-century instrumental suite for outdoor performance, similar to the divertimento and the serenade. [1375–1425; late ME *cassacio(u)n* < ML *cassātiōn-* (s. of *cassātiō*), equiv. to LL *cassāt(us)* ptp. of *cassāre* to annul (*cass-* var. of L *quass-* (see QUASH) + *-ātus* -ATE[1]) + *-iōn-* -ION] —**cas•sa′tion•al,** *adj.*

Cas•satt (kə sat′), *n.* **Mary,** 1845–1926, U.S. painter.

cas•sa•va (kə sä′və), *n.* **1.** any of several tropical American plants belonging to the genus *Manihot,* of the spurge family, as *M. esculenta* **(bitter cassava)** and *M. dulcis* **(sweet cassava),** cultivated for their tuberous roots, which yield important food products. **2.** a nutritious starch from the roots, the source of tapioca. [1545–55; < Sp *cazabe* cassava bread or meal < Taino *caçábi*]

Cas′se•grain tel′escope (kas′ə grān′), *Astron.* a reflecting telescope in which the light, passing through a central opening in the primary mirror, is brought into focus a short distance behind it by a secondary mirror. Also called **Cas•se•grain′i•an tel′escope** (kas′ə grā′nē ən). [1805–15; named after N. *Cassegrain,* 17th-century French scientist, its inventor]

Cas•sel (kas′əl; *Ger.* kä′səl), *n.* Kassel.

Cas•sel•ber•ry (kas′əl ber′ē, -bə rē), *n.* a city in central Florida. 15,247.

Cas′sel brown′, (*sometimes l.c.*) See **Vandyke brown.** Also called **Cas′sel earth′.** [1855–60; named after CASSEL]

Cas′sel yel′low, a lemon-yellow color. [1880–85; see CASSEL BROWN]

cas•se•role (kas′ə rōl′), *n., v.,* **-roled, -rol•ing.** —*n.* **1.** a baking dish of glass, pottery, etc., usually with a cover. **2.** any food, usually a mixture, cooked in such a dish. **3.** a small dish with a handle, used in chemical laboratories. —*v.t.* **4.** to bake or cook (food) in a casserole. [1700–10; < F: ladlelike pan, equiv. to *casse* small saucepan (< OPr *cassa* large spoon, akin to ML *cattia* crucible; of disputed orig.) + *-role* dim. suffix]

cas•sette (kə set′, ka-), *n.* **1.** Also called **cassette′ tape′.** a compact case containing a length of magnetic tape that runs between two small reels: used for recording or playback in a tape recorder or cassette deck and by some small computer systems to store programs and data. Cf. **microcassette, minicassette. 2.** an audio cassette or videocassette. **3.** *Photog.* a lightproof metal or plastic container for a roll of film, having a single spool for supplying and rewinding the film. [1955–60; < F, equiv. to *casse* box (see CASE[2]) + *-ette* -ETTE]

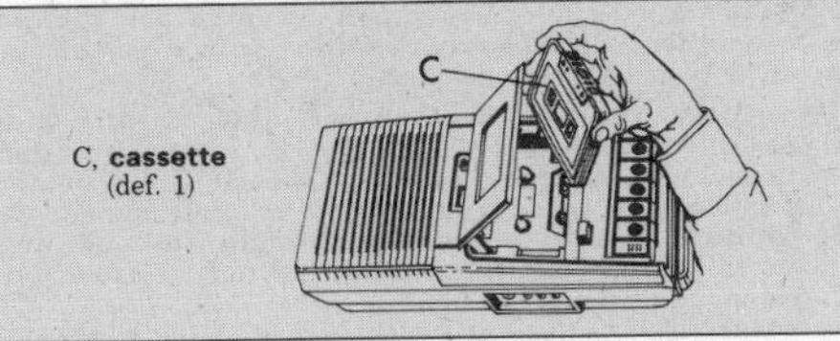

C, **cassette** (def. 1)

cassette′ deck′, a tape deck for playing and recording cassette tapes.

cas•sia (kash′ə, kas′ē ə), *n.* **1.** Also called **cas′sia bark′, Chinese cinnamon.** a variety of cinnamon derived from the cassia-bark tree. **2.** any of numerous plants, trees, and shrubs belonging to the genus *Cassia,* of the legume family, several species of which yield medicinal products. **3.** Also called **cas′sia pods′.** the pods of *Cassia fistulosa,* a tree widely cultivated as an ornamental. **4.** Also called **cas′sia pulp′.** the pulp of these pods, used medicinally and as a flavoring. [bef. 1000; ME *cas(s)ia,* OE < L < Gk *kas(s)ía* < Sem; cf. Heb *qəṣīʿāh*]

cas′sia-bark tree′ (kash′ə bärk′, kas′ē ə-), a lauraceous tree, *Cinnamomum cassia,* of eastern Asia.

cas•sie (kas′ē), *n.* huisache. [< F < Pr *cacio,* for *acacia* ACACIA]

Cas•sie (kas′ē), *n.* a male or female given name, form of **Cass.**

cas•si•mere (kas′ə mēr′), *n.* a twill-weave, worsted suiting fabric, often with a striped pattern. Also, **casimere, casimire.** [1695–1705; var. of CASHMERE]

Cas•sin (KA SAN′), *n.* **Re•né** (Rə nā′), 1887–1976, French diplomat and human-rights advocate: at the United Nations 1946–68; Nobel peace prize 1968.

Cas•si•ni (kə sē′nē, kä-), *n.* **1. O•leg** (ō′leg), (*Oleg Cassini-Loiewski*), born 1913, U.S. fashion designer and businessman, born in France. **2.** a walled plain in the first quadrant of the face of the moon: about 36 miles (56 km) in diameter. **3.** *Geom.* See **oval of Cassini.**

Cassi′ni divi′sion, *Astron.* a 3000-mi. (4800-km) wide dark region that separates the middle and outermost rings of the planet Saturn. [named after Italian astronomer Giovanni Domenico *Cassini* (1625–1712), who discovered it in 1675]

cas•si•no (kə sē′nō), *n.* casino (def. 3).

Cas•si•no (kə sē′nō; *It.* käs sē′nô), *n.* a town in SE Latium, in central Italy, NNW of Naples: site of Monte Cassino. 24,695.

Cas•si•o•do•rus (kas′ē ə dôr′əs, -dōr′-), *n.* **Flavius Magnus Aurelius,** died A.D. 575, Roman statesman and writer.

cas•si•o•pe (kə sī′ə pē′), *n.* **1.** (*sometimes cap.*) any evergreen shrub belonging to the genus *Cassiope,* of the heath family, having nodding white or pinkish solitary flowers and scalelike or needlelike leaves. **2.** (*cap.*) Cassiopeia. [< NL, L < Gk *Kassiópē* CASSIOPEIA]

Cas•si•o•pe•ia (kas′ē ə pē′ə), *n., gen.* **-pe•iae** (-pē′ē) for 1. **1.** *Astron.* a northern constellation between Cepheus and Perseus. **2.** *Class. Myth.* the wife of Cepheus and mother of Andromeda. —**Cas′si•o•pe′ian,** *adj.*

Cas•si•rer (kä sēr′ər, kə-), *n.* **Ernst** (ûrnst, ernst), 1874–1945, German philosopher.

cas•sis (ka sēs′; *Fr.* KA sēs′), *n.* **1.** See **crème de cassis. 2.** (*italics*) *French.* **a.** a black currant. **b.** a brandy distilled from black currants. [< F]

Cas•site (kas′īt), *n.* Kassite.

cas•sit•er•ite (kə sit′ə rīt′), *n.* a brown or black mineral, tin dioxide, SnO_2, that crystallizes in the tetragonal system; tinstone: the principal ore of tin. [1855–60; < Gk *kassíter(os)* tin + -ITE[1]]

Cas•sius (kash′əs), *n.* a male given name.

Cas′sius Lon•gi′nus (lon jī′nəs), **Ga•ius** (gā′əs), died 42 B.C., Roman general: leader of the conspiracy against Julius Caesar.

cas•sock (kas′ək), *n.* **1.** a long, close-fitting garment worn by members of the clergy or others participating in church services. **2.** a lightweight, double-breasted ecclesiastical coat or jacket, worn under the Geneva gown. **3.** a member of the clergy. [1540–50; < MF *casaque,* perh. < a Turkic word akin to the source of COSSACK]

cas•sol•ette (kas′ə let′), *n.* a container for cooking and serving an individual portion of food, usually made of pottery, silver, or paper, or sometimes of baked dough. [1650–60; < F, equiv. to *cassole* (*casse* small saucepan (see CASSEROLE) + *-ole* dim. suffix) + *-ette* -ETTE]

cas•so•ne (kə sō′nē; *It.* käs sô′ne), *n., pl.* **-ni** (-nē). a large Italian chest of the Middle Ages and Renaissance, usually highly ornamented. [1880–85; < It, equiv. to *cass(a)* box (see CASE[2]) + *-one* aug. suffix]

cas•sou•let (kas′ə lā′; *Fr.* KA soo le′), *n.* a white-bean stew of French origin, often containing pork, mutton, garlic sausage, and preserved goose or duck. [1925–30; < F < Pr (Languedoc) dim. of *cassolo* earthen pan, dish; see CASSOLETTE]

cassowary, *Casuarius casuarius,* height 5 ft. (1.5 m)

cas•so•war•y (kas′ə wer′ē), *n., pl.* **-war•ies.** any of several large flightless, ratite birds of the genus *Casuarius,* of Australia, New Guinea, and adjacent islands, characterized by a bony casque on the front of the head. [1605–15; by uncert. mediation < Central Moluccan *kasuwari, kasuwali*]

cast (kast, käst), *v.,* **cast, cast•ing,** *n., adj.* —*v.t.* **1.** to throw or hurl; fling: *The gambler cast the dice.* **2.** to throw off or away: *He cast the advertisement in the wastebasket.* **3.** to direct (the eye, a glance, etc.), esp. in a cursory manner: *She cast her eyes down the page.* **4.** to cause to fall upon something or in a certain direction; send forth: *to cast a soft light; to cast a spell; to cast doubts.* **5.** to draw (lots), as in telling fortunes. **6.** *Angling.* **a.** to throw out (a fishing line, net, bait, etc.): *The fisherman cast his line.* **b.** to fish in (a stream, an area, etc.): *He has often cast this brook.* **7.** to throw down or bring to the ground: *She cast herself on the sofa.* **8.** to part with; lose: *The horse cast a shoe.* **9.** to shed or drop (hair, fruit, etc.): *The snake cast its skin.* **10.** (of an animal) to bring forth (young), esp. abortively. **11.** to send off (a swarm), as bees do. **12.** to throw or set aside; discard or reject; dismiss: *He cast the problem from his mind.* **13.** to throw forth, as from within; emit or eject; vomit. **14.** to throw up (earth, sod, etc.), as with a shovel. **15.** to put or place, esp. hastily or forcibly: *to cast someone in prison.* **16.** to deposit or give (a ballot or vote). **17.** to bestow; confer: *to cast blessings upon someone.* **18.** to make suitable or accordant; tailor: *He cast his remarks to fit the occasion.* **19.** *Theat.* **a.** to select actors for (a play, motion picture, or the like). **b.** to allot a role to (an actor). **c.** to assign an actor to (a role). **20.** to form (an object) by pouring metal, plaster, etc., in a fluid state into a mold and letting it harden. **21.** to form (metal, plaster, etc.) into a particular shape by pouring it into a mold in a fluid state and letting it harden. **22.** to tap (a blast furnace). **23.** to compute or calculate; add, as a column of figures. **24.** to compute or calculate (a horoscope) astrologically; forecast. **25.** to turn or twist; warp. **26.** *Naut.* to turn the head of (a vessel), esp. away from the wind in getting under way. **27.** *Fox Hunting.* (of a hunter) to lead or direct (hounds) over ground believed to have been recently traveled by a fox. **28.** *Archaic.* to contrive, devise, or plan. **29.** *Obs.* to ponder.
—*v.i.* **30.** to throw. **31.** to receive form in a mold. **32.** to calculate or add. **33.** to conjecture; forecast. **34.** (of hounds) to search an area for scent: *The setter cast, but found no scent.* **35.** to warp, as timber. **36.** *Naut.* (of a vessel) to turn, esp. to get the head away from the wind; tack. **37.** to select the actors for a play, motion picture, or the like. **38.** *Obs.* **a.** to consider. **b.** to plan or scheme. **39. cast about, a.** to look, as to find something; search; seek: *We cast about for something to do during the approaching summer vacation.* **b.** to scheme; plan: *He cast about how he could avoid work.* **40. cast away, a.** Also, **cast aside.** to reject; discard. **b.** to shipwreck. **c.** to throw away; squander: *He will cast away this money just as he has done in the past.* **41. cast back,** to refer to something past; revert to: *The composer casts back to his earlier work.* **42. cast down,** to lower; humble. **43. cast off, a.** to discard; reject. **b.** to let go or let loose, as a vessel from a mooring. **c.** *Print.* to determine the quantity of type or space that a given amount of text will occupy when set. **d.** *Textiles.* to make (the final stitches) in completing a knitted fabric. **e.** to throw (a falcon) off from the fist to pursue game. **44. cast on,** *Textiles.* to set (yarn) on a needle in order to form the initial stitches in knitting. **45. cast out,** to force out; expel; eject. **46. cast up, a.** to add up; compute. **b.** to vomit; eject. **c.** *Chiefly Scot.* to turn up; appear.
—*n.* **47.** act of casting or throwing. **48.** that which is thrown. **49.** the distance to which a thing may be cast or thrown. **50.** *Games.* **a.** a throw of dice. **b.** the number rolled. **51.** *Angling.* **a.** act of throwing a line or net onto the water. **b.** a spot for casting; a fishing place. **52.** *Theat.* the group of performers to whom parts are assigned; players. **53.** *Hunting.* a searching of an area for a scent by hounds. **54.** a stroke of fortune; fortune or lot. **55.** a ride offered on one's way; lift. **56.** the form in which something is made or written; arrangement. **57.** *Metall.* **a.** act of casting or founding. **b.** the quantity of metal cast at one time. **58.** something formed from a material poured into a mold in a molten or liquid state; casting. **59.** an impression or mold made from something. **60.** *Med.* a rigid surgical dressing, usually made of bandage treated with plaster of Paris. **61.** outward form; appearance. **62.** sort; kind; style. **63.** tendency; inclination. **64.** a permanent twist or turn: *to have a cast in one's eye.* **65.** a warp. **66.** a slight tinge of some color; hue; shade: *A good diamond does not have a yellowish cast.* **67.** a dash or trace; a small amount. **68.** computation; calculation; addition. **69.** a conjecture; forecast. **70.** *Zool.* something that is shed, ejected, or cast off or out, as molted skin, a feather, food from a bird's crop, or the coil of sand and waste passed by certain earthworms. **71.** *Ornith.* pellet (def. 6). **72.** *Falconry.* a pair of hawks put in flight together. **73.** *Pathol.* effused plastic matter produced in the hollow parts of various diseased organs. **74.** low-grade, irregular wool. **75. at a single cast,** through a single action or event: *He bankrupted himself at a single cast.*
—*adj.* **76.** (of an animal, esp. a horse) lying in such a position that it is unable to return to its feet without assistance. [1175–1225; ME *casten* < ON *kasta* to throw] —**cast′a•ble,** *adj.* —**cast′a•bil′i•ty,** *n.*
—**Syn. 1.** See **throw. 63.** See **turn.**

Cas•ta•gno (kä stä′nyô), *n.* **An•dre•a del** (än dRe′ä del), (*Andrea di Bartolo di Bargilla*), c1423–57, Florentine painter.

cas•ta•net (kas′tə net′), *n.* either of a pair of concave pieces of wood held in the palm of the hand and clicked together, usually to accompany dancing. [1640–50; < Sp *castañeta,* equiv. to *castañ(a)* chestnut (< L *castanea*) + *-eta* dim. suffix; see -ET, -ETTE]

castanets

cast•a•way (kast′ə wā′, käst′-), *n.* **1.** a shipwrecked person. **2.** anything cast adrift or thrown away. **3.** an outcast. —*adj.* **4.** cast adrift. **5.** thrown away. [1520–30; n., adj. use of v. phrase *cast away*]
—**Syn. 3.** pariah, outlaw, leper.

caste (kast, käst), *n.* **1.** *Sociol.* **a.** an endogamous and hereditary social group limited to persons of the same rank, occupation, economic position, etc., and having mores distinguishing it from other such groups. **b.** any rigid system of social distinctions. **2.** *Hinduism.* any of the social divisions into which Hindu society is traditionally divided, each caste having its own privileges and limitations, transferred by inheritance from one generation to the next; jati. Cf. **class.** (def. 13). **3.** any class or group of society sharing common cultural features: *low caste; high caste.* **4.** social position conferred upon one by a caste system: *to lose caste.* **5.** *Entomol.* one of the distinct forms among polymorphous social insects, performing a specialized function in the colony, as a queen, worker or soldier. —*adj.* **6.** of, pertaining to, or characterized by caste: *a caste society; a caste system; a caste structure.* [1545–55; < Pg *casta* race, breed, n. use of *casta,* fem. of *casto* < L *castus* pure, CHASTE] —**caste′ism,** *n.* —**caste′less,** *adj.*

Cas•tel Gan•dol•fo (kä stel′ gän dôl′fô), a village in central Italy, 15 mi. (24 km) SE of Rome: papal palace serving as the summer residence of the pope.

cas•tel•lan (kas′tl n, ka stel′ən), *n.* the governor of a castle. [1350–1400; < ML *castellānus* (n.) governor, occupant of a castle, (adj.) of a castle (L: of a fortress), equiv. to *castell(um)* CASTELLUM, CASTLE + *-ānus* -AN; r. ME *castelain* < ONF < L, as above] —**cas′tel•lan•ship′,** *n.*

Cas•te•lla•nos (käs′te yä′nôs), *n.* **Ju•lio** (ho͞o′lyô), 1905–47, Mexican painter.

cas•tel•la•nus (kas′tl ā′nəs), *adj. Meteorol.* (of a cloud) having small turrets. [< NL, L *castellānus;* see CASTELLAN]

cas•tel•la•ny (kas′tl ā′nē), *n., pl.* **-nies. 1.** the rank, office, or jurisdiction of a castellan. **2.** the land belonging to a castle. [1325–75; ME; see CASTELLAN, -Y[3]]

cas•tel•lat•ed (kas′tl ā′tid), *adj.* **1.** *Archit.* built like a castle, esp. with turrets and battlements. **2.** having many castles. [< ML *castellāt(us)* (see CASTLE, -ATE[1]) + -ED[2]] **—cas′tel·la′tion,** *n.*

cas′tellated beam′, a rolled metal beam the web of which is first divided by a lengthwise zigzag cut, then welded together so as to join the peaks of both halves, thus increasing its depth and strength. [1670–80]

cas′tellated nut′, a tall lock nut, having on its outer face radial slits allowing for insertion of a cotter pin or wire in both the nut and a hole in its bolt, so as to prevent the nut from coming loose. See illus. under **nut.** Also called **castle nut.** [1900–05]

cas·tel·la·tus (kas′tl ā′təs), *adj. Meteorol.* (formerly) castellanus. [< NL, ML *castellātus* CASTELLATED]

Cas·te·llón de la Pla·na (käs′te lyôn′ de lä plä′nä, -yôn′), a seaport in E Spain. 93,968.

cas·tel·lum (ka stel′əm), *n., pl.* **cas·tel·li** (ka stel′ī). *Archaeol.* a small isolated fortress, or one of a series of such fortresses, of the ancient Romans. [< L: fortified settlement, fortress < **casterlom* < **castrlom* < **castrelom,* equiv. to *castr(a)* (neut. pl.) fortified camp + **-elom* dim. suffix; see -ULE, -ELLE]

Cas·tel·nuo·vo-Te·des·co (kä′stel nwô′vô te de′skô), *n.* **Ma·rio** (mä′ryô), 1895–1968, U.S. composer, born in Italy.

Cas·te·lo Bran·co (käs te′lŏŏ brän′kŏŏ), **Hum·ber·to de A·len·car** (ōōn ber′tŏŏ di ä len kär′), 1900–67, Brazilian general and statesman: president 1964–67.

Cas·tel·ve·tro (kas′tl ve′trō; *It.* kä′stel ve′trô), *n.* **Lo·do·vi·co** (lō′də vē′kō; *It.* lô′dô vē′kô), 1505–71, Italian philologist and literary critic.

caste′ mark′, **1.** (in India) a mark, usually on the forehead, symbolizing and identifying caste membership. **2.** a distinctive trait, associated with a group or class and marking a person as a member. [1900–05]

cast·er (kas′tər, kä′stər), *n.* **1.** a person or thing that casts. **2.** a small wheel on a swivel, set under a piece of furniture, a machine, etc., to facilitate moving it. **3.** a bottle or cruet for holding a condiment. **4.** a stand containing a set of such bottles. **5.** a metal container for sugar, pepper, etc., having a perforated top to permit sprinkling; dredger; muffineer. **6.** *Auto.* the angle that the kingpin makes with the vertical. Automobiles are usually designed with the upper end of the kingpin inclined rearward **(positive caster)** for improved directional stability. *—v.i.* **7.** (of a wheel) to swivel freely in a horizontal plane. Also, **castor** (for defs. 2–5). [1300–50; ME; see CAST[1], -ER[1]] **—cast′er·less,** *adj.*

cas·ti·gate (kas′ti gāt′), *v.t.,* **-gat·ed, -gat·ing.** **1.** to criticize or reprimand severely. **2.** to punish in order to correct. [1600–10; < L *castīgātus* lit., driven to be faultless (ptp. of *castīgāre* to chasten), equiv. to *cast(us)* pure, CHASTE + *-ig-,* comb. form of *agere* to drive, incite + *-ātus* -ATE[1]] **—cas′ti·ga′tion,** *n.* **—cas′ti·ga′tive, cas·ti·ga·to·ry** (kas′ti gə tôr′ē, -tōr′ē), *adj.* **—cas′ti·ga′tor,** *n.*
—Syn. 1. scold, reprove. **2.** discipline, chastise, chasten.

Cas·ti·glio·ne (kä′stē lyô′ne), *n.* **Bal·das·sa·re** (bäl′däs sä′re), 1478–1529, Italian diplomat and author.

Cas·tile (ka stēl′), *n.* **1.** Spanish, **Cas·ti·lla** (käs tē′lyä, -yä). a former kingdom comprising most of Spain. **2.** Also called **Castile′ soap′.** a variety of mild soap, made from olive oil and sodium hydroxide. **3.** any hard soap made from fats and oils, often partly from olive oil.

Cas·til·ian (ka stil′yən), *n.* **1.** the dialect of Spanish spoken in Castile. **2.** the official standard form of the Spanish language as spoken in Spain, based on this dialect. **3.** a native or inhabitant of Castile. *—adj.* **4.** of or pertaining to Castile. [1520–30; CASTILE + -IAN]

Cas·ti·lla (käs tē′yä), *n.* **Ra·món** (rä môn′), 1797–1867, Peruvian general and statesman: president of Peru 1845–51 and 1855–62.

Cas·ti·lla la Nue·va (käs tē′lyä lä nwe′vä, -yä), Spanish name of **New Castile.**

Cas·ti·lla la Vie·ja (käs tē′lyä lä vye′hä, -yä), Spanish name of **Old Castile.**

Cas·ti·llo (käs tē′lyô, -yô), *n.* **An·to·nio** (än tô′nyô), (*Antonio Cánovas del Castillo del Rey*), born 1908, Spanish fashion designer.

cast·ing (kas′ting, kä′sting), *n.* **1.** the act or process of a person or thing that casts. **2.** something cast; any article that has been cast in a mold. **3.** the act or process of choosing actors to play the various roles in a theatrical production, motion picture, etc. **4.** the act or skill of throwing a fishing line out over the water by means of a rod and reel: *I'll have to improve my casting if I'm ever going to learn to fish well.* **5.** *Zool.* cast (def. 70). [1250–1300; ME; see CAST[1], -ING[1]]

cast′ing couch′, *Facetious.* a couch in the office of a casting director, supposedly used with actors or actresses willing to trade sexual favors for roles. [1940–45]

cast′ing direc′tor, the person responsible for selecting the cast of a theatrical production, motion picture, etc. [1920–25]

cast′ing rod′, a fishing rod, generally 4–8 ft. (1.2–2.4 m) long, for casting bait or lures with a reel mounted near the handle that enables the thumb or finger to control the line during a cast, including rods used for bait casting and spinning.

cast′ing vote′, the deciding vote of the presiding officer of a deliberative body, made when the other votes are equally divided. Also called **cast′ing voice′.** [1685–95]

cast′ing wheel′, *Metall.* a wheel having on its circumference molds for receiving molten metal.

cast′ i′ron, an alloy of iron, carbon, and other elements, cast as a soft and strong, or as a hard and brittle, iron, depending on the mixture and methods of molding. [1655–65; *cast* (ptp. of CAST[1]) + IRON]

cast-i·ron (kast′ī′ərn, käst′-), *adj.* **1.** made of cast iron. **2.** not subject to change or exception: *a cast-iron rule.* **3.** hardy: *a cast-iron stomach.* [1655–65]

cast′-i′ron plant′, aspidistra.

cas·tle (kas′əl, kä′səl), *n., v.,* **-tled, -tling.** *—n.* **1.** a fortified, usually walled residence, as of a prince or noble in feudal times. **2.** the chief and strongest part of the fortifications of a medieval city. **3.** a strongly fortified, permanently garrisoned stronghold. **4.** a large and stately residence, esp. one, with high walls and towers, that imitates the form of a medieval castle. **5.** any place providing security and privacy: *It may be small, but my home is my castle.* **6.** *Chess.* the rook. *—v.t.* **7.** to place or enclose in or as in a castle. **8.** *Chess.* to move (the king) in castling. *—v.i. Chess.* **9.** to move the king two squares horizontally and bring the appropriate rook to the square the king has passed over. **10.** (of the king) to be moved in this manner. [bef. 1000; ME, OE *castel* < L *castellum* CASTELLUM] **—cas′tle·like′,** *adj.*
—Syn. 1. fortress, citadel. **4.** palace, château.

Cas·tle (kas′əl, kä′səl), *n.* **Irene (Foote),** 1893–1969, born in the U.S., and her husband and partner **Vernon** (*Vernon Castle Blythe*), 1887–1918, born in England, U.S. ballroom dancers.

Castle, The, (German, *Das Schloss*), a novel (1926) by Franz Kafka.

cas′tle in the air′, a fanciful or impractical notion or hope; daydream. Also called **air castle, cas′tle in Spain′.** [1570–80]

cas′tle nut′. See **castellated nut.** [1900–05]

Cas·tle·reagh (kas′əl rā′, kä′səl-), *n.* **Robert Stewart, Viscount** (*2nd Marquess of Londonderry*), 1769–1822, British statesman.

Cas′tle Shan′non, a city in SW Pennsylvania. 10,164.

Cas′tle walk′, a ballroom dance of the pre–World War I era, consisting of a sedate step to each beat. [named after Vernon and Irene CASTLE]

cast·off (kast′ôf′, -of′, käst′-), *adj.* **1.** thrown away; rejected; discarded: *castoff clothing.* *—n.* **2.** a person or thing that has been cast off. **3.** *Print.* the estimate by a compositor of how many pages copy will occupy when set in type. [1735–45; adj., n. use of v. phrase *cast off*]

cas·tor[1] (kas′tər, kä′stər), *n.* **1.** Also, **castoreum.** a brownish, unctuous substance with a strong, penetrating odor, secreted by certain glands in the groin of the beaver, used in medicine and perfumery. **2.** a hat made of beaver or rabbit fur. **3.** a heavy woolen cloth used mainly for coats. **4.** a beaver. [1350–1400; ME < L < Gk *kástōr* beaver]

cas·tor[2] (kas′tər, kä′stər), *n.* caster (defs. 2–5).

Cas·tor (kas′tər, kä′stər), *n. Astron.* a star of the second magnitude in the constellation Gemini, the more northerly of the two bright stars in this constellation. [named after *Castor;* see CASTOR AND POLLUX]

Cas′tor and Pol′lux, *Class. Myth.* twin sons of Leda and brothers of Helen, famous for their fraternal affection and regarded as the protectors of persons at sea. Also, **Kastor and Pollux.**

cas′tor bean′, **1.** the seed of the castor-oil plant. **2.** See **castor-oil plant.** [1810–20, *Amer.*; short for *castor-oil bean*] **—cas′tor-bean′,** *adj.*

cas·tor·e·um (ka stôr′ē əm, -stōr′-), *n.* castor[1] (def. 1). [< L < Gk *kastórion,* equiv. to *kastor-* (s. of *kástōr*) beaver + *-ion,* neut. of *-ios* adj. suffix]

cas′tor oil′, a colorless to pale yellow, viscid liquid, usually obtained from the castor bean by a pressing process: used as a lubricant, in the manufacture of certain soaps and creams, and in medicine chiefly as a cathartic. Also called **ricinus oil.** [1740–50; *castor* (perh. var. sp. of CASTER) + OIL; perh. so called because of its purgative effect]

cas′tor-oil′ plant′ (kas′tər oil′, kä′stər-), a tall plant, *Ricinus communis,* of the spurge family, cultivated for its ornamental foliage and having poisonous seeds that are the source of castor oil. Also called **castor bean.** [1835–45]

cas′tor sug′ar, *Chiefly Brit.* finely ground or powdered sugar. [1850–55]

cas·trate (kas′trāt), *v.,* **-trat·ed, -trat·ing,** *n.* *—v.t.* **1.** to remove the testes of; emasculate; geld. **2.** to remove the ovaries of. **3.** *Psychol.* to render impotent, literally or metaphorically, by psychological means, esp. by threatening a person's masculinity or femininity. **4.** to deprive of strength, power, or efficiency; weaken: *Without those ten new submarines, our navy will be castrated.* *—n.* **5.** a castrated person or animal. [1605–15; < L *castrātus* ptp. of *castrāre* to geld, equiv. to *castr-* geld + *-ātus* -ATE[1]] **—cas·tra′tion,** *n.* **—cas′tra·tor,** *n.*

castra′tion com′plex, *Psychoanal.* an unconscious fear of losing the genital organs, esp. as punishment for oedipal feelings. [1910–15]

cas·tra·to (ka strä′tō, kə-; *It.* kä strä′tô), *n., pl.* **-ti** (-tē). a male singer, esp. in the 18th century, castrated before puberty to prevent his soprano or contralto voice range from changing. [1755–65; < It < L *castrāt(us);* see CASTRATE]

Cas·tries (kas′trēz, -trēs, kä strē′), *n.* a port in and the capital of the state of St. Lucia, on the NW coast. 45,000.

Cas·tro (kas′trō; *Sp.* käs′trô), *n.* **1. Ci·pri·a·no** (sip′rē ä′nō; *Sp.* sē′prē ä′nô), 1858?–1924, Venezuelan military and political leader: president 1901–08; exiled 1908. **2. Fidel** (fi del′; *Sp.* fē thel′), (*Fidel Castro Ruz*) born 1927, Cuban revolutionary and political leader: prime minister 1959–76 and president since 1976.

Cas·tro·ism (kas′trō iz′əm, kä′strō-), *n.* the political, social, and revolutionary theories and policies advocated by Fidel Castro. [1955–60; Fidel CASTRO + -ISM] **—Cas′tro·ist, Cas′tro·ite′,** *n., adj.*

Ca·strop-Rau·xel (*Ger.* kä′strôp rouk′səl), *n.* a city in central North Rhine-Westphalia, in W Germany. 81,900. Also, **Kastrop-Rauxel.**

Cas′tro Val′ley (kas′trō), a town in W California, near San Francisco Bay. 44,011.

cast′ steel′, any of various steels cast in molds to form objects. [1770–80] **—cast′-steel′,** *adj.*

cast′ stone′, a concrete with a fine aggregate, used to imitate natural stone. [1920–25]

cas·u·al (kazh′ōō əl), *adj.* **1.** happening by chance; fortuitous: *a casual meeting.* **2.** without definite or serious intention; careless or offhand; passing: *a casual remark.* **3.** seeming or tending to be indifferent to what is happening; apathetic; unconcerned: *a casual, nonchalant air.* **4.** appropriate for wear or use on informal occasions; not dressy: *casual clothes; casual wear.* **5.** irregular; occasional: *a casual visitor.* **6.** accidental: *a casual mishap.* **7.** *Obs.* uncertain. *—n.* **8.** a worker employed only irregularly. **9.** a soldier temporarily at a station or other place of duty, and usually en route to another station. [1325–75; ME < L *cāsuālis,* equiv. to *cāsu(s)* CASE[1] + *-ālis* -AL[1]; r. ME *casuel* < MF < L as above] **—cas′u·al·ly,** *adv.* **—cas′u·al·ness,** *n.*
—Syn. 1. unexpected, fortuitous, unforeseen. See **accidental. 5.** random. **—Ant. 1.** planned.

cas′ual con′tact, the level of contact at which a person is not subject to contracting a communicable disease from another, esp. nonsexual contact with a person infected with a venereal disease.

cas·u·al·ty (kazh′ōō əl tē), *n., pl.* **-ties.** **1.** *Mil.* **a.** a member of the armed forces lost to service through death, wounds, sickness, capture, or because his or her whereabouts or condition cannot be determined. **b. casualties,** loss in numerical strength through any cause, as death, wounds, sickness, capture, or desertion. **2.** one who is injured or killed in an accident: *There were no casualties in the traffic accident.* **3.** any person, group, thing, etc., that is harmed or destroyed as a result of some act or event: *Their house was a casualty of the fire.* **4.** a serious accident, esp. one involving bodily injury or death. [1375–1425; CASUAL + -TY[2]; r. late ME *casuelte,* equiv. to *casuel* (see CASUAL) + *-te* -TY[2]]

cas′ualty insur′ance, insurance providing coverage against accident and property damages, as automobile, theft, liability, and explosion insurance, but not including life insurance, fire insurance, or marine insurance. [1900–05]

cas·u·ist (kazh′ōō ist), *n.* **1.** an oversubtle or disingenuous reasoner, esp. in questions of morality. **2.** a person who studies and resolves moral problems of judgment or conduct arising in specific situations. [1600–10; < Sp *casuista* < L *cāsu(s)* CASE[1] + *-ista* -IST]

cas·u·is·tic (kazh′ōō is′tik), *adj.* **1.** pertaining to casuists or casuistry. **2.** oversubtle; intellectually dishonest; sophistical: *casuistic distinctions.* Also, **cas′u·is′ti·cal.** [1650–60; CASUIST + -IC] **—cas′u·is′ti·cal·ly,** *adv.*

cas·u·ist·ry (kazh′ōō ə strē), *n., pl.* **-ries.** **1.** specious, deceptive, or oversubtle reasoning, esp. in questions of morality; fallacious or dishonest application of general principles; sophistry. **2.** the application of general ethical principles to particular cases of conscience or conduct. [1715–25; CASUIST + -RY]

ca·sus bel·li (kā′səs bel′ī, bel′ē; *Lat.* kä′sŏŏs bel′lē), *pl.* **ca·sus bel·li** (kā′səs bel′ī, bel′ē; *Lat.* kä′sōōs bel′lē). an event or political occurrence that brings about a declaration of war. [1840–50; < NL: lit., occurrence of war]

cat (kat), *n., v.,* **cat·ted, cat·ting.** *—n.* **1.** a small domesticated carnivore, *Felis domestica* or *F. catus,* bred in a number of varieties. **2.** any of several carnivores of the family Felidae, as the lion, tiger, leopard or jaguar, etc. **3.** *Slang.* **a.** a person, esp. a man. **b.** a devotee of jazz. **4.** a woman given to spiteful or malicious gossip. **5.** the fur of the domestic cat. **6.** a cat-o'-nine-tails. **7.** *Games.* **a.** *Chiefly Brit.* the tapering piece of wood used in the game of tipcat. **b.** *Chiefly Brit.* the game itself. **c.** See **four old cat, one old cat, three old cat, two old cat. 8.** a catboat. **9.** a catamaran. **10.** a catfish. **11.** *Naut.* a tackle used in hoisting an anchor to the cathead. **12.** a double tripod having six legs but resting on only three no matter how it is set down, usually used before or over a fire. **13.** *Navy Informal.* catapult (def. 2). **14.** (in medieval warfare) a movable shelter for providing protection when approaching a fortification. **15. bell the cat,** to attempt something formidable or dangerous. **16. let the cat out of the bag,** to divulge a secret, esp. inadvertently or carelessly: *He let the cat out of the bag, and the surprise party wasn't a surprise after all.* *—v.t.* **17.** to flog with a cat-o'-nine-tails. **18.** *Naut.* to hoist (an anchor) and secure to a cathead. *—v.i.* **19.** *Brit. Slang.* to vomit. **20. cat around,** *Slang.* **a.** to spend one's time aimlessly or idly. **b.** to seek sexual activity in-

CONCISE ETYMOLOGY KEY: <, descended or borrowed from; >, whence; b., blend of, blended; c., cognate with; cf., compare; deriv., derivative; equiv., equivalent; imit., imitative; obl., oblique; r., replacing; s., stem; sp., spelling, spelled; resp., respelling, respelled; trans., translation; ?, origin unknown; *, unattested; ‡, probably earlier than. See the full key inside the front cover.

discriminately; tomcat. [bef. 900; ME *cat, catte,* OE *catt* (masc.), *catte* (fem.); c. OFris, MD *katte,* OHG *kazza,* ON *kǫttr,* Ir *cat,* Welsh *cath* (Slavic **kotŭ,* Lith *katė̃* perh. < Gmc), LL *cattus, catta* (first attested in the 4th century, presumably with the introduction of domestic cats); ult. orig. obscure]

Cat (kat), *Trademark.* a Caterpillar tractor. [by shortening]

CAT, 1. clear-air turbulence. **2.** *Med.* computerized axial tomography. Cf. **CAT scanner.**

cat., 1. catalog; catalogue. **2.** catechism.

cata-, a prefix meaning "down," "against," "back," occurring originally in loanwords from Greek (*cataclysm; catalog; catalepsy*); on this model, used in the formation of other compound words (*catagenesis; cataphyll*). Also, **cat-, cath-, kata-.** [< Gk *kata-,* comb. form of *katá* down, through, against, according to, towards, during]

cat·a·bap·tist (kat′ə bap′tist), *n. Eccles.* a person who is opposed to baptism. [1555–65; < LGk *katabaptistḗs.* See CATA-, BAPTIST]

ca·tab·a·sis (kə tab′ə sis), *n., pl.* **-ses** (-sēz′). katabasis.

ca·tab·o·lism (kə tab′ə liz′əm), *n. Biol., Physiol.* destructive metabolism; the breaking down in living organisms of more complex substances into simpler ones, with the release of energy (opposed to *anabolism*). [1875–80; < Gk *katabol(ḗ)* a throwing down (*kata-* CATA- + *bolḗ* a throw; cf. *katabállein* to throw down) + -ISM] —**cat·a·bol·ic** (kat′ə bol′ik), *adj.* —**cat′a·bol′i·cal·ly,** *adv.*

ca·tab·o·lite (kə tab′ə līt′), *n. Biol., Physiol.* a product of catabolic action. [1905–10; CATABOL(ISM) + -ITE[1]]

ca·tab·o·lize (kə tab′ə līz′), *v.,* **-lized, -liz·ing.** —*v.t.* **1.** to cause (a nutrient or other substance) to undergo catabolism. —*v.i.* **2.** to be subjected to catabolism. Also, *esp. Brit.,* **ca·tab′o·lise′.** [1925–30; CATABOL(ISM) + -IZE]

cat·a·caus·tic (kat′ə kô′stik), *Math., Optics.* —*adj.* **1.** noting a caustic surface or curve formed by the reflection of light. —*n.* **2.** a catacaustic surface or curve. [1700–10; CATA- + CAUSTIC]

cat·a·chre·sis (kat′ə krē′sis), *n.* misuse or strained use of words, as in a mixed metaphor, occurring either in error or for rhetorical effect. [1580–90; < L < Gk: a misuse (akin to *katachrêsthai* to misuse), equiv. to *kata-* CATA- + *chrêsis* use (*chrê(sthai)* to use, need + *-sis* -SIS)] —**cat·a·chres·tic** (kat′ə kres′tik), **cat′a·chres′ti·cal,** *adj.* —**cat′a·chres′ti·cal·ly,** *adv.*

cat·a·cla·sis (kat′ə klā′sis, kə tak′lə sis), *n. Petrol.* a process of deformation or metamorphism in which the grains of a rock are fractured and rotated. [< Gk *katáklasis* refraction, equiv. to *katakla-,* s. of *kataklân* to break off, refract, break down (*kata-* CATA- + *klân* to break) + *-sis* -SIS; cf. Norw *kataklasstruktur* (1885)] —**cat·a·clas·tic** (kat′ə klas′tik), *adj.*

cat·a·clysm (kat′ə kliz′əm), *n.* **1.** any violent upheaval, esp. one of a social or political nature. **2.** *Physical Geog.* a sudden and violent physical action producing changes in the earth's surface. **3.** an extensive flood; deluge. [1625–35; < LL *cataclysmos* (Vulgate) < Gk *kataklysmós* flood (akin to *kataklýzein* to flood), equiv. to *kata-* CATA- + *klysmós* a washing]
—**Syn. 1.** See **disaster.**

cat·a·clys·mic (kat′ə kliz′mik), *adj.* **1.** of, pertaining to, or resulting from a cataclysm. **2.** of the nature of, or having the effect of, a cataclysm: *cataclysmic changes.* Also, **cat′a·clys′mal.** [1850–55; CATACLYSM + -IC] —**cat′a·clys′mi·cal·ly,** *adv.*

cat·a·comb (kat′ə kōm′), *n.* **1.** Usually, **catacombs.** an underground cemetery, esp. one consisting of tunnels and rooms with recesses dug out for coffins and tombs. **2. the Catacombs,** the subterranean burial chambers of the early Christians in and near Rome, Italy. **3.** an underground passageway, esp. one full of twists and turns. [bef. 900; ME *catacombe,* OE *catacumbe* < LL *catacumbās* (acc. pl.); of disputed orig.; perh. < Gk **katakýmbās,* equiv. to *kata-* CATA- + *kýmbās,* acc. pl. of *kýmbē* hollow, cup] —**cat·a·cum·bal** (kat′ə kum′bəl), *adj.*

cat·a·di·op·tric (kat′ə dī op′trik), *adj. Optics.* pertaining to or produced by both reflection and refraction. [1715–25; CATA- + DIOPTRIC]

ca·tad·ro·mous (kə tad′rə məs), *adj.* (of fish) migrating from fresh water to spawn in the sea, as eels of the genus *Anguilla* (distinguished from *anadromous*). [1880–85; CATA- + -DROMOUS]

cat·a·falque (kat′ə fôk′, -fôlk′, -falk′), *n.* **1.** a raised structure on which the body of a deceased person lies or is carried in state. **2.** a hearse. [1635–45; < F < It *catafalco* < LL **catafalicum* SCAFFOLD, equiv. to *cata-* CATA- + *fal(a)* wooden siege tower + *-icum,* neut. of *-icus* -IC]

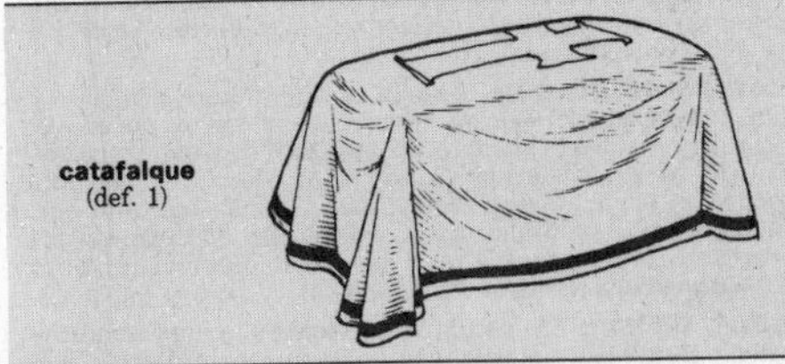
catafalque (def. 1)

cat·a·gen·e·sis (kat′ə jen′ə sis), *n. Biol.* the retrogressive evolution of a species. Cf. **anagenesis** (def. 1). [1880–85; CATA- + GENESIS] —**cat·a·ge·net·ic** (kat′ə jə net′ik), *adj.*

Cat·a·lan (kat′l an′, -ən, kat′l an′), *adj.* **1.** pertaining to Catalonia, its inhabitants, or their language. —*n.* **2.** a native or inhabitant of Catalonia. **3.** a Romance language closely related to Provençal, spoken in Catalonia, Valencia, the Balearic Islands, Andorra, southern France, and western Sardinia. [1375–1425; late ME < Sp]

cat·a·lase (kat′l ās′, -āz′), *n. Biochem.* an enzyme that decomposes hydrogen peroxide into oxygen and water. [1900–05; CATAL(YSIS) + -ASE] —**cat·a·lat·ic** (kat′l at′ik), *adj.*

cat·a·lec·tic (kat′l ek′tik), *Pros.* —*adj.* **1.** (of a line of verse) lacking part of the last foot; metrically incomplete, as the second line of *One more unfortunate,/Weary of breath.* —*n.* **2.** a catalectic line of verse. Cf. **acatalectic, hypercatalectic.** [1580–90; < LL *catalēcticus* < Gk *katalēktikós* incomplete, equiv. to *katalēk-,* var. s. of *katalḗgein* to leave off (*kata-* CATA- + *lḗgein* to end) + *-tikos* -TIC]

cat·a·lep·sy (kat′l ep′sē), *n. Pathol., Psychiatry.* a physical condition usually associated with catatonic schizophrenia, characterized by suspension of sensation, muscular rigidity, fixity of posture, and often by loss of contact with environment. Also, **cat′a·lep′sis.** [1350–1400; < ML *catalēpsia,* var. of LL *catalēpsis* < Gk *katálēpsis* seizure (akin to *katalambánein* to hold down), equiv. to *kata-* CATA- + *lêpsis* a grasping (*lēp-,* var. s. of *lambánein* to grasp + *-sis* -SIS); r. ME *cathalempsia* < ML] —**cat′a·lep′tic,** *adj., n.* —**cat′a·lep′ti·cal·ly,** *adv.*

cat·a·lex·is (kat′l ek′sis), *n., pl.* **cat·a·lex·es** (kat′l-ek′sēz). *Pros.* the absence of a syllable at the beginning or end of a line of metrical verse resulting in an incomplete foot, most often occurring in the last foot at the end of a verse; a catalectic line. [1820–30; < Gk *katálēxis* ending, final syllable; see CATALECTIC, -SIS]

Ça·tal·hü·yük (chät′l ho͞o yo͝ok′), a 32-acre Neolithic site in south-central Turkey, dated c6500–5500 B.C., one of the first true cities, characterized by a fully developed agriculture and extensive trading, particularly in obsidian, and having frescoed temples, mud-brick fortifications and houses, and mother-goddess figures. Also, **Ça′tal Hü·yük′.**

Cat·a·lin (kat′l in), *Trademark.* a synthetic resin used esp. for costume jewelry.

Cat′a·li′na Is′land (kat′l ē′nə, kat′-). See **Santa Catalina.** Also called **Cat′a·li′na.**

cat·a·log (kat′l ôg′, -og′), *n.* **1.** a list or record, as of items for sale or courses at a university, systematically arranged and often including descriptive material: *a stamp catalog.* **2.** something that contains such a list or record, as a book, leaflet, or file. **3.** a list of the contents of a library or a group of libraries, arranged according to any of various systems. Cf. **card catalog, on-line catalog, union catalog. 4.** any list or record: *a catalog of complaints.* —*v.t.* **5.** to enter (items) in a catalog; make a catalog of. —*v.i.* **6.** to produce a catalog. **7.** to have a specified price as listed in a catalog: *This model catalogs for $49.95.* **8.** to offer merchandise in a mail-order catalog. —*adj.* **9.** of, pertaining to, or carrying on business through a mail-order catalog: *catalog sales.* [1425–75; late ME *cataloge* < LL *catalogus* < Gk *katálogos* a register (akin to *katalégein* to count up), equiv. to *kata-* CATA- + *-logos* reckoning] —**cat′a·log′ist,** *n.* —**cat·a·log·ic** (kat′l oj′ik), **cat′a·log′i·cal, cat·a·lo·gis·tic** (kat′l ō jis′tik), *adj.*
—**Syn. 1, 3.** roster, register, record. See **list**[1].

cat′alog code′, *Library Science.* the principles, rules, and regulations for entering and describing books or other library material in a catalog.

cat·a·log·er (kat′l ô′gər, -og′ər), *n.* **1.** a person who catalogs. **2.** a person or firm that offers merchandise in a catalog from which buyers may order by mail. Also, **cat′a·logu′er.** [1835–45; CATALOG + -ER[1]]

cat·a·logue (kat′l ôg′, -og′), *n., v.t., v.i., adj.* **-logued, -logu·ing.** catalog. —**cat′a·logu′ist,** *n.*

ca·ta·logue rai·son·né (kat′l ôg′ rez′ə nā′, -og′; *Fr.* KA TA lôg RE zô nā′), *pl.* **ca·ta·logues rai·son·nés** (kat′l ôgz′ rez′ə nā′, -ogz′; *Fr.* KA TA lôg RE zô nā′). a catalog, as of paintings or books, with notes or commentary on the items listed; a classified, descriptive catalog. [1775–85; < F: lit., reasoned catalog]

cat′alog verse′, verse made by compiling long lists of everyday objects, names, or events, united by a common theme and often didactic in tone.

Cat·a·lo·ni·a (kat′l ō′nē ə, -ōn′yə), *n.* a region in NE Spain, bordering on France and the Mediterranean: formerly a province. Spanish, **Ca·ta·lu·ña** (kä′tä lo͞o′nyä).

Cat·a·lo·ni·an (kat′l ō′nē ən), *adj., n.* Catalan.

Catalo′nian jas′mine. See **Spanish jasmine.**

ca·tal·pa (kə tal′pə), *n.* any of several trees constituting the genus *Catalpa,* of the bignonia family, esp. *C. speciosa,* of the central U.S., or *C. bignonioides,* of the southern U.S., having opposite, sometimes whorled leaves, clusters of white flowers, and long, beanlike seed pods. Also called **Indian bean.** [1720–30, *Amer.*; (< NL) < Creek *katałpa,* equiv. to *ka-,* comb. form of *iká* head + *tałpa* wing (appar. so called from the shape of the flower)]

cat·a·lu·fa (kat′l o͞o′fə), *n., pl.* (*esp. collectively*) **-fa,** (*esp. referring to two or more kinds or species*) **-fas.** any of several bigeyes, as *Pristigenys serrula* **(popeye catalufa),** found in the Pacific Ocean. [< Cuban Sp *catalufa, cataluja,* var. of *catalineta,* deriv. of the personal name *Catalina*]

ca·tal·y·sis (kə tal′ə sis), *n., pl.* **-ses** (-sēz′). **1.** *Chem.* the causing or accelerating of a chemical change by the addition of a catalyst. **2.** an action between two or more persons or forces, initiated by an agent that itself remains unaffected by the action: *social catalyses occasioned by controversial writings.* [1645–55; < NL < Gk *katálysis* dissolution, equiv. to *kataly̆(ein)* to dissolve (*kata-* CATA- + *lýein* to loosen) + *-sis* -SIS] —**cat·a·lyt·ic** (kat′l it′ik), *adj., n.* —**cat′a·lyt′i·cal,** *adj.* —**cat′a·lyt′i·cal·ly,** *adv.*

cat·a·lyst (kat′l ist), *n.* **1.** *Chem.* a substance that causes or accelerates a chemical reaction without itself being affected. **2.** something that causes activity between two or more persons or forces without itself being affected. **3.** a person or thing that precipitates an event or change: *His imprisonment by the government served as the catalyst that helped transform social unrest into revolution.* **4.** a person whose talk, enthusiasm, or energy causes others to be more friendly, enthusiastic, or energetic. [1900–05; CATALY(SIS) + (-I)ST]

catalyt′ic convert′er, an antipollution device in an automotive exhaust system that contains a catalyst for chemically converting some pollutants in the exhaust gases, as carbon monoxide, unburned hydrocarbons, and oxides of nitrogen, into harmless compounds. [1960–65]

cat′alyt′ic crack′ing, the reduction of the molecular weight of hydrocarbons by a catalyst, accomplished in a petroleum refinery by a type of chemical reactor **(cat′alyt′ic crack′er).** Cf. **cracker** (def. 8), **cracking** (def. 1).

cat·a·lyze (kat′l īz′), *v.t.,* **-lyzed, -lyz·ing.** to act upon by catalysis. Also, *esp. Brit.,* **cat′a·lyse′.** [1885–90; CATALY(SIS) + (-I)ZE] —**cat′a·lyz′er,** *n.*

cat·a·ma·ran (kat′ə mə ran′), *n.* **1.** a vessel, usually propelled by sail, formed of two hulls or floats held side by side by a frame above them. Cf. **trimaran. 2.** a float or sailing raft formed of a number of logs lashed together, used in certain parts of India, South America, etc. **3.** a quarrelsome person, esp. a woman. **4.** *Canadian Dial.* a wooden sled. [1690–1700; < Tamil *kaṭṭamaram* tied wood]

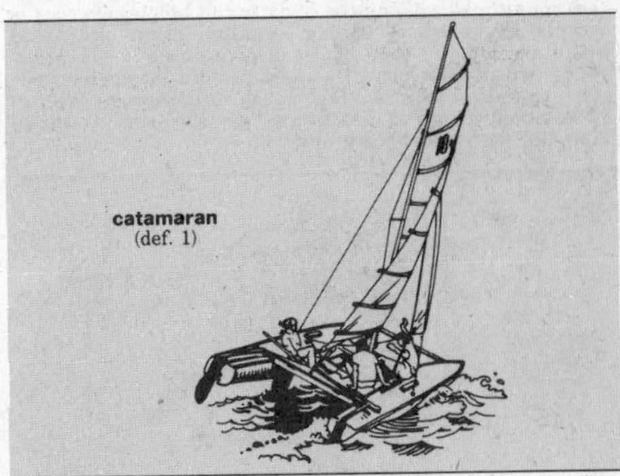
catamaran (def. 1)

Cat·a·mar·ca (kat′ə mär′kə; *Sp.* kä′tä mäʀ′kä), *n.* a city in N Argentina. 88,432.

cat·a·me·ni·a (kat′ə mē′nē ə), *n.* (*used with a singular or plural v.*) *Physiol.* menses. [1745–55; < NL < Gk *kataménia,* neut. pl. of Gk *kataménios* monthly, equiv. to *kata-* CATA- + *mḗn* MONTH + *-ios* -IOUS] —**cat′a·me′ni·al,** *adj.*

cat·a·mite (kat′ə mīt′), *n.* a boy or youth who is in a sexual relationship with a man. [1585–95; < L *Catamītus* < Etruscan *Catmite* < Gk *Ganymḗdēs* GANYMEDE]

cat·am·ne·sis (kat′am nē′sis), *n., pl.* **-ses** (-sēz). a medical history following the onset of an illness. [CATA- + (ANA)MNESIS] —**cat·am·nes·tic** (kat′am nes′tik), *adj.*

cat·a·mount (kat′ə mount′), *n.* **1.** a wild animal of the cat family, esp. the cougar or the lynx. **2.** catamountain. [1655–65; short for CATAMOUNTAIN]

cat·a·moun·tain (kat′ə moun′tn), *n.* a wild animal of the cat family, as the European wildcat, the leopard, or panther. Also, **cat-o′-mountain.** [1400–50; var. of *cat o′ mountain,* late ME *cat of the mountaine*]

cat-and-dog (kat′n dôg′, -dog′), *adj.* **1.** continuously or unceasingly vicious and destructive: *cat-and-dog competition.* **2.** *Slang.* (of a security) highly speculative and of questionable value. [1570–80]

cat′ and mouse′, 1. Also called **cat′ and rat′.** a children's game in which players in a circle keep a player from moving into or out of the circle and permit a second player to move into or out of the circle to escape the pursuing first player. **2.** *Western U.S.* tick-tack-toe (def. 1). **3. play cat and mouse,** to engage in a gamelike relationship in which evasion and pursuit are used: *They played cat and mouse for a while before she consented to go out with him.* **4. play cat and mouse with, a.** to toy or trifle with. **b.** to use strategy on one's opponent, esp. while waiting to strike: *The detective played cat and mouse with the suspect.* [1910–15]

CONCISE PRONUNCIATION KEY: act, cāpe, dâre, pärt; set, ēqual; if, ice; ox, ōver, ôrder, oil, bo͝ok, bo͞ot, out; up, ûrge; child; sing; shoe; thin, *th*at; zh as in *treasure.* ə = *a* as in *alone, e* as in *system, i* as in *easily, o* as in *gallop, u* as in *circus;* ə as in *fire* (fīər), *hour* (ouər). l and n can serve as syllabic consonants, as in *cradle* (krād′l), and *button* (but′n). See the full key inside the front cover.

Ca•ta•nia (kä tä′nyä), *n.* a seaport in E Sicily. 400,242.

Ca•ta•ño (kə tän′yō; *Sp.* kä tä′nyô), *n.* a city in NE Puerto Rico, SW of San Juan. 26,243.

Ca•tan•za•ro (kä′tän dzä′rô), *n.* a city in S Italy. 92,277.

cat•a•pha•sia (kat′ə fā′zhə, -zhē ə, -zē ə), *n. Pathol.* a speech disorder in which a person constantly repeats a word or phrase. [CATA- + -PHASIA]

ca•taph•o•ra (kə taf′ər ə), *n. Gram.* the use of a word or phrase to refer to a following word or group of words, as the use of the phrase *as follows.* Cf. **anaphora.** [CATA- + (ANA)PHORA] —**cat•a•phor•ic** (kat′ə fôr′ik, -for′-), *adj.* —**cat′a•phor′i•cal•ly,** *adv.*

cat•a•pho•re•sis (kat′ə fə rē′sis), *n.* **1.** *Med.* the causing of medicinal substances to pass through or into living tissues in the direction of flow of a positive electric current. **2.** *Physical Chem.* electrophoresis. [1885–90; < NL, equiv. to *cata-* CATA- + NGk *phórēsis* a being borne, equiv. to *phorē-* (var. s. of *phérein* to BEAR[1], carry) + *-sis* -SIS] —**cat•a•pho•ret•ic** (kat′ə fə ret′ik), *adj.* —**cat′a•pho•ret′i•cal•ly,** *adv.*

cat•a•phract (kat′ə frakt′), *n.* **1.** a heavily armed war galley of ancient Greece. **2.** a suit of ancient Roman scale armor for a man or horse. **3.** *Zool.* the bony plates or scales covering the body of certain fishes or reptiles. [1575–85; < L *cataphractus* fully armored < Gk *katáphraktos* (akin to *kataphrássein* to clothe fully in armor), equiv. to *kata-* CATA- + *phraktós* fenced, protectively clothed (*phrag-* fence + *-tos* verbal adj. suffix)] —**cat′•a•phrac′tic,** *adj.*

cat•a•phract•ed (kat′ə frak′tid), *adj. Zool.* covered with an armor of horny or bony plates or scales. [1880–85; CATAPHRACT + -ED[3]]

cat•a•phyll (kat′ə fil), *n. Bot.* a simplified leaf form, as a bud scale or a scale on a cotyledon or rhizome. [CATA- + -PHYLL] —**cat′a•phyl′la•ry,** *adj.*

cat•a•plane (kat′ə plān′), *n.* an aircraft designed to be launched by a catapult. [CATA(PULT) + (AIR)PLANE]

cat•a•pla•sia (kat′ə plā′zhə, -zhē ə, -zē ə), *n. Biol.* degeneration of a cell or tissue. [CATA- + -PLASIA] —**cat•a•plas•tic** (kat′ə plas′tik), *adj.*

cat•a•plasm (kat′ə plaz′əm), *n. Med.* poultice. [1555–65; < L *cataplasma* < Gk *katáplasma.* See CATA-, -PLASM]

cat•a•plex•y (kat′ə plek′sē), *n. Pathol.* a condition characterized by sudden, brief attacks of muscle weakness sometimes causing the body to fall helplessly, that is usually triggered by strong emotion: often associated with narcolepsy. [1880–85; < G *Kataplexie* < Gk *katáplēxis* (with suffix prob. by analogy with *Apoplexie* APOPLEXY) fixation (of the eyes), equiv. to *kataplēk-* (var. s. of *kataplḗssein* to strike down) + *-sis* -SIS] —**cat•a•plec•tic,** (kat′ə plek′tik), adj.

catapult (def. 1)

cat•a•pult (kat′ə pult′, -po͝olt′), *n.* **1.** an ancient military engine for hurling stones, arrows, etc. **2.** a device for launching an airplane from the deck of a ship. **3.** *Brit.* a slingshot. —*v.t.* **4.** to hurl from a catapult. **5.** to thrust or move quickly or suddenly: *His brilliant performance in the play catapulted him to stardom.* **6.** *Brit.* **a.** to hurl (a missile) from a slingshot. **b.** to hit (an object) with a missile from a slingshot. —*v.i.* **7.** to be catapulted. **8.** to move or spring up suddenly, quickly, or forcibly, as if by means of a catapult: *The car catapulted down the highway. When he heard the alarm he catapulted out of bed.* [1570–80; < L *catapulta* < Gk *katapéltēs,* equiv. to *kata-* CATA- + *péltēs* hurler, akin to *pállein* to hurl] —**cat′a•pul′tic,** *adj.*
—**Syn. 5.** throw, fling, propel, pitch, shoot.

cat•a•ract (kat′ə rakt′), *n.* **1.** a descent of water over a steep surface; a waterfall, esp. one of considerable size. **2.** any furious rush or downpour of water; deluge. **3.** *Ophthalm.* **a.** an abnormality of the eye, characterized by opacity of the lens. **b.** the opaque area. [1350–1400; ME *cataracte* < L *catar(r)acta* < Gk *katarráktēs* waterfall, floodgate, portcullis (n.), downrushing (adj.), akin to *katarássein* to dash down, equiv. to *kat-* CATA- + *arássein* to smite] —**cat′a•rac′tal, cat′a•rac′tous,** *adj.* —**cat′a•ract′ed,** *adj.*

ca•tarrh (kə tär′), *n. Pathol.* inflammation of a mucous membrane, esp. of the respiratory tract, accompanied by excessive secretions. [1350–1400; ME < LL *catarrhus* < Gk *katárrous* lit., down-flowing, equiv. to *katarr(eîn)* to flow down (*kata-* CATA- + *rhein* to flow) + *-ous,* var. of *-eos* (theme vowel + adj. suffix)] —**ca•tarrh′al, ca•tarrh′ous,** *adj.* —**ca•tarrh′al•ly,** *adv.*

catarrh′al fe′ver, *Vet. Pathol.* bluetongue. [1780–90]

cat•ar•rhine (kat′ə rīn′), *adj.* **1.** belonging or pertaining to the group Catarrhini, comprising humans, anthropoid apes, and Old World monkeys, having the nostrils close together and opening downward and a nonprehensile, often greatly reduced or vestigial tail. —*n.* **2.** a catarrhine animal. Also, **cat•ar•rhin•i•an** (kat′ə rin′ē ən). [1860–65; < NL *Catarrhini,* pl. of *catarrhinus* < Gk *katarrhin* hook-nosed, equiv. to *kata-* CATA- + *-rhīn* -nosed, adj. deriv. of *rhís* nose, snout]

CONCISE ETYMOLOGY KEY: <, descended or borrowed from; >, whence; b., blend of, blended; c., cognate with; cf., compare; deriv., derivative; equiv., equivalent; imit., imitative; obl., oblique; r., replacing; s., stem; sp., spelling, spelled; resp., respelling, respelled; trans., translation; ?, origin unknown; *, unattested; ‡, probably earlier than. See the full key inside the front cover.

ca•tas•ta•sis (kə tas′tə sis), *n., pl.* **-ses** (-sēz′). the part of a drama, preceding the catastrophe, in which the action is at its height; the climax of a play. Cf. **catastrophe** (def. 4), **epitasis, protasis.** [1650–60; < Gk *katástasis* stability, akin to *kathistánai* to make stand, settle. See CATA-, STASIS]

ca•tas•tro•phe (kə tas′trə fē), *n.* **1.** a sudden and widespread disaster: *the catastrophe of war.* **2.** any misfortune, mishap, or failure; fiasco: *The play was so poor our whole evening was a catastrophe.* **3.** a final event or conclusion, usually an unfortunate one; a disastrous end: *the great catastrophe of the Old South at Appomattox.* **4.** (in a drama) the point at which the circumstances overcome the central motive, introducing the close or conclusion; dénouement. Cf. **catastasis, epitasis, protasis.** **5.** *Geol.* a sudden, violent disturbance, esp. of a part of the surface of the earth; cataclysm. **6.** Also called **catas′trophe func′tion.** *Math.* any of the mathematical functions that describe the discontinuities that are treated in catastrophe theory. [1570–80; < Gk *katastrophḗ* an overturning, akin to *katastréphein* to overturn. See CATA-, STROPHE] —**cat•a•stroph•ic** (kat′ə strof′ik), **cat′a•stroph′i•cal, ca•tas′tro•phal,** *adj.* —**cat′a•stroph′i•cal•ly,** *adv.*
—**Syn. 1.** misfortune, calamity. **1, 3.** See **disaster.**
—**Ant. 1, 3.** triumph.

catas′trophe the′ory, *Math.* a theory, based on topology, for studying discontinuous processes and the mathematical models that describe them. [1970–75]

ca•tas•tro•phism (kə tas′trə fiz′əm), *n. Geol.* the doctrine that certain vast geological changes in the earth's history were caused by catastrophes rather than gradual evolutionary processes. [1865–70; CATASTROPHE + -ISM] —**ca•tas′tro•phist,** *n.*

cat•a•to•ni•a (kat′ə tō′nē ə, -tōn′yə), *n. Psychiatry.* a syndrome seen most frequently in schizophrenia, characterized by muscular rigidity and mental stupor, sometimes alternating with great excitement and confusion. [1915–20; CATA- + -TONIA] —**cat′a•to′ni•ac′,** *n.* —**cat•a•ton•ic** (kat′ə ton′ik), *adj., n.*

cat•a•wam•pus (kat′ə wom′pəs), *Chiefly Midland and Southern U.S.* —*adj.* **1.** askew; awry. **2.** positioned diagonally; cater-cornered. —*adv.* **3.** diagonally; obliquely: *We took a shortcut and walked catawampus across the field.* Also, **cattywampus.** [1830–40 for earlier sense "utterly"; *cata-* diagonally (see CATER-CORNERED) + *-wampus,* perh. akin to WAMPISH]

Ca•taw•ba (kə tô′bə), *n.* **1.** a Siouan language of North and South Carolina. **2.** a river flowing from W North Carolina into South Carolina, where it becomes the Wateree River. Cf. **Wateree.** **3.** *Hort.* **a.** a reddish variety of grape. **b.** the vine bearing this fruit, grown in the eastern U.S. **4.** a light, dry, white wine made from this grape. [1710–20, *Amer.*; appar. ult. < Catawba (yį) *kátapu* a village name, lit., (people of) the fork; perh. via Shawnee *kata·pa*]

cat•bird (kat′bûrd′), *n.* any of several American or Australian birds having catlike cries, esp. *Dumetella carolinensis* **(gray catbird),** of North America. [1700–10, *Amer.*; CAT[1] + BIRD]

cat′bird seat′, *Informal.* an advantageous situation or condition: *His appointment as acting dean put him in the catbird seat.* [1940–45, *Amer.*]

cat•boat (kat′bōt′), *n.* a boat having one mast set well forward with a single large sail. [1875–80; CAT[1] + BOAT]

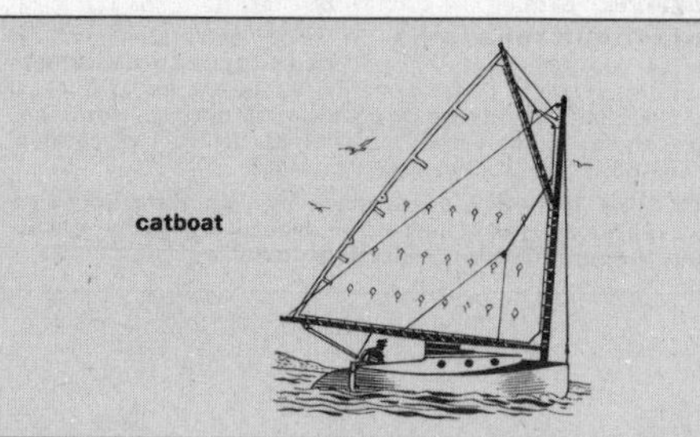

catboat

cat•bri•er (kat′brī′ər), *n.* any prickly vine of the genus *Smilax,* esp. *S. rotundifolia,* of eastern North America, growing in tangled masses. Also called **greenbrier, bullbrier, horsebrier.** [1830–40, *Amer.*; CAT[1] + BRIER[1]]

cat-built (kat′bilt′), *adj.* (of a sailing vessel) having a bluff bow and straight stern without a figurehead.

cat′ bur′glar, a burglar who breaks into buildings by climbing through upstairs windows, across roofs, etc., esp. with great stealth and agility. [1905–10]

cat•call (kat′kôl′), *n.* **1.** a shrill, whistlelike sound or loud raucous shout made to express disapproval at a theater, meeting, etc. **2.** an instrument for producing such a sound. —*v.i.* **3.** to sound catcalls. —*v.t.* **4.** to express disapproval of by catcalls. [1650–60; CAT[1] + CALL] —**cat′call′er,** *n.*
—**Syn. 1.** boo, hiss, jeer.

catch (kach), *v.,* **caught, catch•ing,** *n., adj.* —*v.t.* **1.** to seize or capture, esp. after pursuit: *to catch a criminal; to catch a runaway horse.* **2.** to trap or ensnare: *to catch a fish.* **3.** to intercept and seize; take and hold (something thrown, falling, etc.): *to catch a ball; a barrel to catch rain.* **4.** to come upon suddenly; surprise or detect, as in some action: *I caught him stealing the pumpkin.* **5.** to receive, incur, or contract: *to catch a cold.* **6.** to be in time to get aboard (a train, boat, etc.). **7.** to lay hold of; grasp; clasp: *He caught her arm.* **8.** to grip, hook, or entangle: *The closing door caught his arm.* **9.** to allow (something) to become gripped, hooked, snagged, or entangled: *He caught his coat on a nail.* **10.** to attract or arrest: *The painting caught his fancy. His speech caught our attention.* **11.** to check or restrain suddenly (often used reflexively): *She caught her breath in surprise. He caught himself before he said the wrong thing.* **12.** to see or attend: *to catch a show.* **13.** to strike; hit: *The blow caught him on the head.* **14.** to become inspired by or aware of: *I caught the spirit of the occasion.* **15.** to fasten with or as if with a catch: *to catch the clasp on a necklace.* **16.** to deceive: *No one was caught by his sugary words.* **17.** to attract the attention of; captivate; charm: *She was caught by his smile and good nature.* **18.** to grasp with the intellect; comprehend: *She failed to catch his meaning.* **19.** to hear clearly: *We caught snatches of their conversation.* **20.** to apprehend and record; capture: *The painting caught her expression perfectly.* **21.** *South Midland and Southern U.S.* to assist at the birth of: *The town doctor caught more than four hundred children before he retired.* —*v.i.* **22.** to become gripped, hooked, or entangled: *Her foot caught in the net.* **23.** to overtake someone or something moving (usually fol. by *up, up with,* or *up to*). **24.** to take hold: *The door lock doesn't catch.* **25.** *Baseball.* to play the position of catcher: *He catches for the Yankees.* **26.** to become lighted; take fire; ignite: *The kindling caught instantly.* **27.** to become established, as a crop or plant, after germination and sprouting. **28. catch a crab,** (in rowing) to bungle a stroke by failing to get the oar into the water at the beginning or by failing to withdraw it properly at the end. **29. catch at,** to grasp at eagerly; accept readily: *He caught at the chance to get free tickets.* **30. catch a turn,** *Naut.* to wind a rope around a bitt, capstan, etc., for one full turn. **31. catch it,** *Informal.* to receive a reprimand or punishment: *He'll catch it from his mother for tearing his good trousers again.* **32. catch on, a.** to become popular: *That new song is beginning to catch on.* **b.** to grasp mentally; understand: *You'd think he'd catch on that he's boring us.* **c.** *New England.* (in cooking) to scorch or burn slightly; sear: *A pot roast is better if allowed to catch on.* **33. catch out,** *Chiefly Brit.* to catch or discover (a person) in deceit or an error. **34. catch up, a.** to lift or snatch suddenly: *Leaves were caught up in the wind.* **b.** to bring or get up to date (often fol. by *on* or *with*): *to catch up on one's reading.* **c.** to come up to or overtake (something or someone) (usually fol. by *with*): *to catch up with the leader in a race.* **d.** to become involved or entangled with: *caught up in the excitement of the crowd.* **e.** to point out to (a person) minor errors, untruths, etc. (usually fol. by *on*): *We caught the teacher up on a number of factual details.* **f.** *Falconry.* to capture for further training (a hawk that has been flown at hack). **g.** *South Midland and Southern U.S.* to harness (a horse or mule).
—*n.* **35.** the act of catching. **36.** anything that catches, esp. a device for checking motion, as a latch on a door. **37.** any tricky or concealed drawback: *It seems so easy that there must be a catch somewhere.* **38.** a slight, momentary break or crack in the voice. **39.** that which is caught, as a quantity of fish: *The fisherman brought home a large catch.* **40.** a person or thing worth getting, esp. a person regarded as a desirable matrimonial prospect: *My mother thinks Pat would be quite a catch.* **41.** a game in which a ball is thrown from one person to another: *to play catch; to have a catch.* **42.** a fragment: *catches of a song.* **43.** *Music.* a round, esp. one in which the words are so arranged as to produce ludicrous effects. **44.** *Sports.* the catching and holding of a batted or thrown ball before it touches the ground. **45.** *Rowing.* the first part of the stroke, consisting of the placing of the oar into the water. **46.** *Agric.* the establishment of a crop from seed: *a catch of clover.*
—*adj.* **47.** catchy (def. 3). [1175–1225; ME *cacchen* to chase, capture < ONF *cachier* < VL **captiāre,* for L *captāre* to grasp at, seek out, try to catch, freq. of *capere* to take] —**catch′a•ble,** *adj.*
—**Syn. 1.** apprehend, arrest. **7.** CATCH, CLUTCH, GRASP, SEIZE imply taking hold suddenly of something. To CATCH may be to reach after and get: *He caught my hand.* To CLUTCH is to take firm hold of (often out of fear or nervousness), and retain: *The child clutched her mother's hand.* To GRASP also suggests both getting and keeping hold of, with a connotation of eagerness and alertness, rather than fear (literally or figuratively): *to grasp someone's hand in welcome; to grasp an idea.* To SEIZE implies the use of force or energy in taking hold of suddenly (literally or figuratively): *to seize a criminal; to seize an opportunity.* **17.** enchant, fascinate, win. **35.** capture, apprehension, arrest. **36.** ratchet, bolt.
—**Ant. 1, 7, 35.** release.

catch•all (kach′ôl′), *n.* **1.** a bag, basket, or other receptacle for odds and ends. **2.** something that covers a wide variety of items or situations: *The list is just a catchall of things I want to see or do on vacation.* —*adj.* **3.** covering a wide variety of items or situations: *The anthology is a catchall collection.* [1830–40, *Amer.*; n. use of v. phrase *catch all*]

catch-as-catch-can (kach′əz kach′kan′), *adj.* **1.** Also, **catch′-can′.** taking advantage of any opportunity; using any method that can be applied: *a catch-as-catch-can life, as an itinerant handyman.* —*adv.* **2.** without specific plan or order: *They lived catch-as-catch-can.* —*n.* **3.** a style of wrestling in which the contestants are permitted to trip, tackle, and use holds below the waist. Cf. **Greco-Roman** (def. 3). [1885–90]

catch′ ba′sin, a receptacle, located where a street gutter opens into a sewer, designed to retain matter that would not readily pass through the sewer. [1870–75]

catch-colt (kach′kōlt′), *n. Chiefly Inland North and Western U.S.* **1.** the offspring of a mare bred accidentally. **2.** a child born out of wedlock.

catch-cord (kach′kôrd′), *n. Textiles.* a cord or wire located near a selvage, used to form a loop or deflect the filling yarn not intended to be woven permanently in with the regular selvage.

catch′ crop′, a crop that reaches maturity in a relatively short time, often planted as a substitute for a crop that has failed or at a time when the ground would ordinarily lie fallow, as between the plantings of two staple crops. [1880–85] **—catch′ crop′ping.**

catch′ dog′, *Florida, Georgia.* a dog used to help round up livestock. [1855–60, *Amer.*]

catch•er (kach′ər), *n.* **1.** a person or thing that catches. **2.** *Baseball.* the player stationed behind home plate, whose chief duty is to catch pitches not hit by the batter. **3.** a member of an aerialist team, as in a circus, who hangs head down from a trapeze and catches another member who has completed a jump or somersault through the air. **4.** *Metalworking.* a person who feeds metal rods through a looping mill. **5.** *Electronics.* catcher resonator. See under **Klystron.** [1300–50; ME; see CATCH, -ER[1]]

Catch′er in the Rye′, The, a novel (1951) by J. D. Salinger.

catch′er res′onator, *Electronics.* See under **Klystron.**

catch′er's box′, *Baseball.* box (def. 15d).

catch•fly (kach′flī′), *n., pl.* **-flies.** any of various plants, esp. of the genera *Silene* and *Lychnis,* having a viscid secretion on the stem and calyx in which small insects are sometimes caught. [1590–1600; from phrase *catch (the) fly*]

catch•ing (kach′ing), *adj.* **1.** tending to be transmitted from one person to another; contagious or infectious: *a disease that is catching; His enthusiasm is catching.* **2.** attractive; fascinating; captivating; alluring: *a catching personality.* [1375–1425; late ME; see CATCH, -ING[2]] **—catch′ing•ly,** *adv.* **—catch′ing•ness,** *n.*

catch•line (kach′līn′), *n.* **1.** a word, phrase, or sentence used, esp. in advertising or journalism, to arouse or call attention. **2.** a line in which a catchword appears. **3.** a line of lesser importance, set shorter or sometimes in smaller type than the lines above and beneath it. **4.** *Theat.* a line of comic dialogue expected to elicit laughter. **5.** slug[1] (def. 10a). [1865–70; CATCH + LINE[1]]

catch•ment (kach′mənt), *n.* **1.** the act of catching water. **2.** something for catching water, as a reservoir or basin. **3.** the water that is caught in such a catchment. [1840–50; CATCH + -MENT]

catch′ment ar′ea, **1.** an area served by a hospital, social service agency, etc. **2.** See **drainage basin.**

catch•pen•ny (kach′pen′ē), *adj., n., pl.* **-nies.** *—adj.* **1.** made to sell readily at a low price, regardless of value or use. *—n.* **2.** something that is catchpenny. [1750–60; from phrase *catch (a) penny*]

catch′ phrase′, **1.** a phrase that attracts or is meant to attract attention. **2.** a phrase, as a slogan, that comes to be widely and repeatedly used, often with little of the original meaning remaining. Also, **catch′phrase′.** [1840–50; CATCH(WORD) + PHRASE]

catch•pole (kach′pōl′), *n.* (formerly) a petty officer of justice, esp. one arresting persons for debt. Also, **catch′•poll′.** [bef. 1050; ME *cacchepol,* late OE *cæcephol* < ML *cacepollus* tax-gatherer, lit., chase-fowl, equiv. to *cace-* (< ONF; see CATCH) + *pollus* < L *pullus* chick; see PULLET] **—catch′pol′er•y, catch′poll′er•y,** *n.*

catch′ stitch′, *Sewing.* a large cross-stitch used in finishing seams and in hemming. Also called **catstitch.** [1840–50]

Catch-22 (kach′twen′tē to͞o′), *n., pl.* **Catch-22's, Catch-22s.** **1.** a frustrating situation in which one is trapped by contradictory regulations or conditions. **2.** any illogical or paradoxical problem or situation; dilemma. **3.** a condition, regulation, etc., preventing the resolution of a problem or situation; catch. [from a military regulation in a novel of the same name (1961) by U.S. novelist Joseph Heller (born 1923)]

catch-up (kach′up′), *n.* **1.** an effort to reach or pass a norm, esp. after a period of delay: *After the slowdown there was a catch-up in production.* **2.** an effort to catch up with or surpass a competitor, as in a sports contest. **3.** an instance of catching up. **4. play catch-up,** *Informal.* to make a special effort to overcome a late start, a liability, or the advantage a competitor has: *After Russia launched the first space satellite, other countries had to play catch-up.* *—adj.* **5.** intended to keep up with or surpass a norm or competitor: *a catch-up pay raise to offset inflation.* [1835–45, *Amer.*; n., adj. use of v. phrase *catch up*]

catch•up (kach′əp, kech′-), *n.* ketchup.

catch•weed (kach′wēd′), *n.* cleavers. [1770–80]

catch•weight (kach′wāt′), *n. Sports.* the chance or optional weight of a contestant, as contrasted with a weight fixed by agreement or rule. [1810–20; CATCH + WEIGHT]

catch•word (kach′wûrd′), *n.* **1.** a memorable or effective word or phrase that is repeated so often that it becomes a slogan, as in a political campaign or in advertising a product. **2.** Also called **headword, guide word.** a word printed at the top of a page in a dictionary or other reference book to indicate the first or last entry or article on that page. Cf. **running head.** **3.** a device, used esp. in old books, to assist the binder in assembling signatures by inserting at the foot of each page the first word of the following page. **4.** keyword (def. 4). [1720–30; CATCH + WORD]

catch•y (kach′ē), *adj.,* **catch•i•er, catch•i•est.** **1.** pleasing and easily remembered: *a catchy tune.* **2.** likely to attract interest or attention: *a catchy title for a movie.* **3.** tricky; deceptive: *a catchy question.* **4.** occurring in snatches; fitful: *a catchy wind.* [1795–1805; CATCH + -Y[1]] **—catch′i•ness,** *n.*

cat•claw (kat′klô′), *n.* **1.** a prickly plant, *Schrankia nutallii,* of the legume family, native to the midwestern U.S. having pinnate leaves and tiny pink flowers forming a spherical cluster. **2.** cat's-claw. [CAT[1] + CLAW]

cat′ distem′per, *Vet. Pathol.* distemper[1] (def. 1c).

cate (kāt), *n.* Usually, **cates.** *Archaic.* a choice food; delicacy; dainty. [1425–75; back formation from late ME *cates,* aph. var. of ME *acates* things bought, pl. of *acat* buying < ONF, deriv. of *acater* to buy < VL **accaptāre,* equiv. to L *ac-* AC- + *captāre* to seek out; see CATCH]

cat•e•che•sis (kat′i kē′sis), *n., pl.* **-ses** (-sēz). oral religious instruction, formerly esp. before baptism or confirmation. [1745–55; < LL < Gk *katḗchēsis* oral teaching, equiv. to *katēchē-* (var. s. of *katēcheîn* to teach by word of mouth; see CATECHIST) + *-sis* -SIS]

cat•e•chet•i•cal (kat′i ket′i kəl), *adj.* **1.** of or pertaining to catechesis. **2.** pertaining to teaching by question and answer. Also, **cat′e•chet′ic.** [1610–20; < late ML *catēchēticus* (< Gk *katēchē-* (see CATECHESIS) + ML *-ticus* -TIC) + -AL[1]] **—cat′e•chet′i•cal•ly,** *adv.*

cat•e•chin (kat′i chin, -kin), *n.* a water-soluble, astringent yellow compound, $C_{15}H_{14}O_6$, found in gambier, used chiefly in tanning and dyeing. [1850–55; CATECH(U) + -IN[2]]

cat•e•chism (kat′i kiz′əm), *n.* **1.** *Eccles.* **a.** an elementary book containing a summary of the principles of the Christian religion, esp. as maintained by a particular church, in the form of questions and answers. **b.** the contents of such a book. **2.** a similar book of instruction in other subjects. **3.** a series of formal questions put, as to political candidates, to bring out their views. **4.** catechetical instruction. [1495–1505; < LL *catēchismus* appar. equiv. to *catēch(izāre)* to CATECHIZE + *-ismus* -ISM] **—cat′e•chis′mal,** *adj.*

cat•e•chist (kat′i kist), *n.* **1.** a person who catechizes. **2.** *Eccles.* a person appointed to instruct catechumens in the principles of religion as a preparation for baptism. [1555–65; < LL *catēchista* < Gk *katēchistḗs,* equiv. to *katēch(eîn)* to teach by word of mouth, orig. to din down, i.e. to get results by shouting (*kat-* CATA- + *ēcheîn* to sound) + *istēs* -IST] **—cat′e•chis′tic, cat′e•chis′ti•cal,** *adj.* **—cat′e•chis′ti•cal•ly,** *adv.*

cat•e•chize (kat′i kīz′), *v.t.,* **-chized, -chiz•ing.** **1.** to instruct orally by means of questions and answers, esp. in Christian doctrine. **2.** to question with reference to belief. **3.** to question closely. Also, *esp. Brit.,* **cat′e•chise′.** [1375–1425; late ME < LL *catēchizāre* < Gk *katēchízein* to make (someone) learn by teaching orally, equiv. to *katēch(eîn)* to teach orally (see CATECHIST) + *-izein* -IZE] **—cat′e•chiz′a•ble,** *adj.* **—cat′e•chi•za′•tion,** *n.* **—cat′e•chiz′er,** *n.*
—Syn. 3. interrogate, quiz, examine, probe.

cat•e•chol (kat′i kôl′, -kol′), *n.* a colorless, crystalline, dihydroxyl derivative of benzene, $C_6H_6O_2$, the ortho isomer, used chiefly in photography, for dyeing, and as a reagent; pyrocatechol. [1875–80; CATECH(U) + -OL[1]]

cat•e•chol•a•mine (kat′i kol′ə mēn′, -kō′lə-), *n. Biochem.* any of a group of chemically related neurotransmitters, as epinephrine and dopamine, that have similar effects on the sympathetic nervous system. [1950–55; CATECHOL + -AMINE]

cat•e•chu (kat′i cho͞o′, -kyo͞o′), *n.* any of several astringent substances obtained from various tropical plants, esp. from the wood of two East Indian acacias, *Acacia catechu* and *A. suma:* used in medicine, dyeing, tanning, etc. Also called **cashoo, cutch.** [1670–80; < NL < Pg; perh. a conflation of Marathi *kāt* catechu and *kāccu,* with same sense, alleged to be < Malayalam; *cashoo, cutch* perh. < Malay *kacu* < Malayalam, or a cognate Dravidian word]

cat•e•chu•men (kat′i kyo͞o′mən), *n.* **1.** *Eccles.* a person under instruction in the rudiments of Christianity, as in the early church; a neophyte. **2.** a person being taught the elementary facts, principles, etc., of any subject. [1325–75; < LL *catēchūmenus* < Gk *katēchoúmenos* (one who is) being taught orally, equiv. to *katēche-,* s. of *katēcheîn* to teach orally (see CATECHIST) + *-omenos* middle prp. suffix; r. ME *cathecumyn* < MF *cathecumine* < LL, as above] **—cat′e•chu′me•nal, cat•e•chu•men•i•cal** (kat′i kyo͞o men′i kəl), *adj.* **—cat′e•chu•men′i•cal•ly,** *adv.* **—cat•e•chu•me•nate** (kat′i-kyo͞o′mə nāt′, -nit), *n.* **—cat′e•chu′men•ism,** *n.*

cat•e•gor•e•mat•ic (kat′i gôr′ə mat′ik, -gor′-), *adj.* **1.** *Traditional Logic.* of or pertaining to a word having independent meaning so that it can be used as a term in a proposition. **2.** *Contemporary Logic.* of or pertaining to a word or symbol having an independent meaning apart from the context of other words or symbols. [1820–30; < Gk *katēgorēmat-,* s. of *katēgórēma* predicate (in logic), accusation, charge (equiv. to *katēgorē-,* var. s. of *katēgoreîn* to predicate, prove (see CATEGORY) + *-ma* n. suffix) + -IC]

cat•e•go•ri•al (kat′i gôr′ē əl, -gōr′-), *adj. Ling.* **1.** of or pertaining to a categorial grammar. **2.** (in generative grammar) of or pertaining to the part of the base component that contains rules for establishing syntactic categories and ordering the elements within them. [CATEGORY + -AL[1]; cf. G *categorial* (1880) pertaining to categories in logic]

catego′rial gram′mar, a grammar in which linguistic elements are categorized in terms of their ability to combine with one another to form larger constituents.

cat•e•gor•i•cal (kat′i gôr′i kəl, -gor′-), *adj.* **1.** without exceptions or conditions; absolute; unqualified and unconditional: *a categorical denial.* **2.** *Logic.* **a.** (of a proposition) analyzable into a subject and an attribute related by a copula, as in the proposition "All humans are mortal." **b.** (of a syllogism) having categorical propositions as premises. **3.** of, pertaining to, or in a category. Also, **cat′e•gor′ic.** [1590–1600; < LL *catēgoric(us)* (< Gk *katēgorikós;* see CATEGORY, -IC) + -AL[1]] **—cat′e•gor′i•cal•ly,** *adv.* **—cat′e•gor′i•cal•ness,** *n.*
—Syn. 1. positive, flat, downright.

categor′ical imper′ative, **1.** *Ethics.* the rule of Immanuel Kant that one must do only what one can will that all others should do under similar circumstances. **2.** the unconditional command of conscience. [1820–30]

cat′egor′ic con′tact, *Sociol.* behavior toward an individual on the basis of the type or group of people that person represents rather than on the basis of personal makeup. Cf. **sympathetic contact.**

cat•e•go•rize (kat′i gə rīz′), *v.t.,* **-rized, -riz•ing.** **1.** to arrange in categories or classes; classify. **2.** to describe by labeling or giving a name to; characterize. Also, *esp. Brit.,* **cat′e•go•rise′.** [1695–1705; CATEGOR(Y) + -IZE] **—cat•e•go•rist** (kat′i gôr′ist, -gōr′-), *n.* **—cat′e•go•ri•za′tion,** *n.*

cat•e•go•ry (kat′i gôr′ē, -gōr′ē), *n., pl.* **-ries.** **1.** any general or comprehensive division; a class. **2.** a classificatory division in any field of knowledge, as a phylum or any of its subdivisions in biology. **3.** *Metaphys.* **a.** (in Aristotelian philosophy) any of the fundamental modes of existence, such as substance, quality, and quantity, as determined by analysis of the different possible kinds of predication. **b.** (in Kantian philosophy) any of the fundamental principles of the understanding, as the principle of causation. **c.** any classification of terms that is ultimate and not susceptible to further analysis. **4. categories.** Also called **Guggenheim.** (*used with a singular v.*) a game in which a key word and a list of categories, as dogs, automobiles, or rivers, are selected, and in which each player writes down a word in each category that begins with each of the letters of the key word, the player writing down the most words within a time limit being declared the winner. **5.** *Math.* a type of mathematical object, as a set, group, or metric space, together with a set of mappings from such an object to other objects of the same type. **6.** *Gram.* See **part of speech.** [1580–90; < LL *catēgoria* < Gk *katēgoría* accusation (also, kind of predication), equiv. to *katēgor(os)* accuser, affirmer (*katēgor(eîn)* to accuse, affirm, lit., speak publicly against, equiv. to *kata-* CATA- + *-agorein* to speak before the AGORA + *-os* n. suffix) + *-ia* -Y[3]]
—Syn. 1. group, grouping, type.

ca•te•na (kə tē′nə), *n., pl.* **-nae** (-nē), a chain or connected series, esp. of extracts from the writings of the fathers of the Christian church. [1635–45; < L *catēna* a chain]

cat•e•nane (kat′n ān′), *n.* any of the class of chemical compounds containing two or more rings that are interlocked without being bonded chemically. [CATEN(A) + -ANE]

cat•e•nar•y (kat′n er′ē; *esp. Brit.* kə tē′nə rē), *n., pl.* **-nar•ies,** *adj.* *—n.* **1.** *Math.* the curve assumed approximately by a heavy uniform cord or chain hanging freely from two points not in the same vertical line. Equation: $y = k \cosh(x/k)$. **2.** (in electric railroads) the cable, running above the track, from which the trolley wire is suspended. *—adj.* **3.** of, pertaining to, or resembling a catenary. **4.** of or pertaining to a chain or linked series. [1780–90; < L *catēnārius* relating to a chain, equiv. to *catēn(a)* a chain + *-ārius* -ARY]

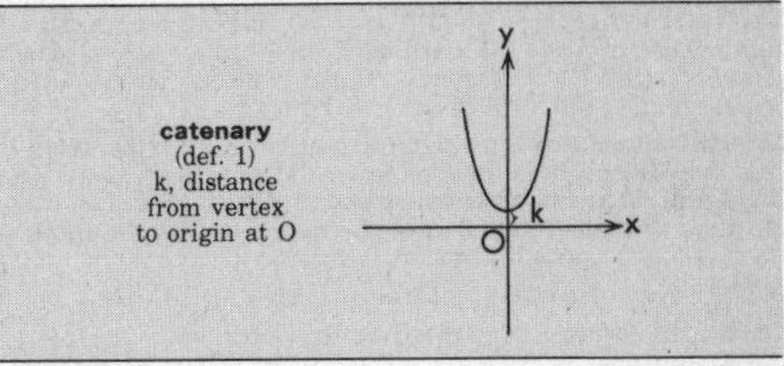

catenary (def. 1) k, distance from vertex to origin at O

cat•e•nate (kat′n āt′), *v.t.,* **-nat•ed, -nat•ing.** to link together; form into a connected series: *catenated cells.* [1615–25; < L *catēnātus* chained, equiv. to *catēn(a)* a chain + *-ātus* -ATE[1]]

cat•e•na•tion (kat′n ā′shən), *n.* **1.** the act or process of catenating. **2.** *Chem.* the linking of identical atoms to form chainlike molecules. [1635–45; < L *catēnātiōn-,* s. of *catēnātiō;* see CATENATE, -ION]

cat•e•noid (kat′n oid′), *n. Geom.* the surface generated by rotating a catenary about its axis of symmetry. [1875–80; < L *catēn(a)* a chain + -OID]

ca•ten•u•late (kə ten′yə lit, -lāt′), *adj.* characterized by a chainlike form, as certain bacterial colonies. [1875–80; < LL *catēnul(a),* dim. of L *catēna* chain + -ATE[1]]

ca•ter (kā′tər), *v.i.* **1.** to provide food, service, etc., as for a party or wedding: *to cater for a banquet.* **2.** to provide or supply what amuses, is desired, or gives pleasure, comfort, etc. (usually fol. by *to* or *for*): *to cater to popular demand; to cater to an invalid.* *—v.t.* **3.** to provide food and service for: *to cater a party.* [1350–1400; v. use of obs. *cater,* ME *catour,* aph. var. of *acatour* buyer < AF, equiv. to *acat(er)* to buy (see CATE) + *-our* -OR[2]] **—ca′ter•ing•ly,** *adv.*
—Syn. 2. humor, indulge, please.

cat•er•an (kat′ər ən), *n.* (formerly) a freebooter or marauder of the Scottish Highlands. [1325–75; < ML *caterānus,* Latinized form of ME (Scots) *catherein* < ScotGael *ceatharn;* see KERN[1]]

cat•er-cor•nered (kat′i kôr′nərd, kat′ē-, kat′ər-), *adj.* **1.** diagonal. *—adv.* **2.** diagonally. Also, **cat′er•cor′ner, cat′er-cor′ner, catty-corner, catty-cornered, kitty-corner, kitty-cornered.** [1830–40; dial. *cater* (adv.) diagonally (prob. to be identified with obs. *cater* four < MF *quatre* < L *quattuor*) + CORNERED]

ca•ter-cous•in (kā′tər kuz′ən), *n.* **1.** an intimate friend. **2.** *Obs.* a cousin. [1540–50; perh. CATER + COUSIN, though original literal sense is unclear]

ca•ter•er (kā′tər ər), *n.* **1.** one whose business is to provide food, supplies, and sometimes service at social gatherings. **2.** one who caters. [1585–95; CATER + -ER[1]]

Cat•e•ri•na (kat′ə rē′nə), *n.* a female given name, form of **Catherine.**

cat•er•pil•lar[1] (kat′ə pil′ər, kat′ər-), *n.* **1.** the worm-

CONCISE PRONUNCIATION KEY: act, cāpe, dâre, pärt; set, ēqual; if, īce; ox, ōver, ôrder, oil, bo͝ok, bo͞ot, out; up, ûrge; child; sing; shoe; thin, *th*at; zh as in *treasure.* ə = *a* as in *alone, e* as in *system, i* as in *easily, o* as in *gallop, u* as in *circus;* ᵊ as in *fire* (fīᵊr), *hour* (ouᵊr). l and n can serve as syllabic consonants, as in *cradle* (krād′l), and *button* (but′n). See the full key inside the front cover.

like larva of a butterfly or a moth. **2.** a person who preys on others; extortioner. [1400–50; late ME *catyrpel*, prob. alter. of an ONF var. of OF *chatepelose*, equiv. to *chate* CAT¹ + *pelose* hairy (<< L *pilōsus*; see PILOSE); *-yr* prob. by assoc. with *cater* tomcat (see CATERWAUL); final *-er* prob. by assoc. with *piller* despoiler (see PILLAGE, -ER¹); cf. CHENILLE]

Cat•er•pil•lar (kat′ə pil′ər, kat′ər-), *Trademark.* a tractor intended for rough terrain, propelled by two endless belts or tracks that pass over a number of wheels.

cat•er•waul (kat′ər wôl′), *v.i.* **1.** to utter long wailing cries, as cats in rutting time. **2.** to utter a similar sound; howl or screech. **3.** to quarrel like cats. —*n.* Also, **cat′•er•waul′ing. 4.** the cry of a cat in rutting time. **5.** any similar sound. [1350–1400; ME *cater(wawen)* (equiv. to *cater* tomcat (< MD) + *wawen* to howl, OE *wāwan* to blow, said of the wind) + *waul*, var. of WAIL] —**cat′er•waul′er,** *n.*
—**Syn. 2.** wail, shriek, squawk, yowl.

cat-eyed (kat′īd′), *adj.* **1.** having eyes resembling those of a cat. **2.** capable of seeing in dark places. [1605–15]

cat•fight (kat′fīt′), *n.* a dispute carried out with intense hostility and bitterness. [CAT¹ + FIGHT]

cat•fish (kat′fish′), *n. pl.* (*esp. collectively*) **-fish,** (*esp. referring to two or more kinds or species*) **-fish•es. 1.** any of the numerous fishes of the order or suborder Nematognathi (or Siluroidei), characterized by barbels around the mouth and the absence of scales. **2.** a wolffish of the genus *Anarhichas.* **3.** any of various other fishes having a fancied resemblance to a cat. [1605–15; CAT¹ + FISH]

channel catfish, *Ictalurus punctatus,* length to 4 ft. (1.2 m)

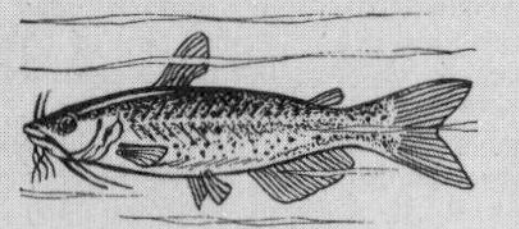

cat′ flea′. See under **flea.**

cat-foot (kat′fo͝ot′), *v.i.* to move in the soft, stealthy manner of a cat; pussyfoot. [1590–1600; CAT¹ + FOOT]

cat•foot•ed (kat′fo͝ot′id), *adj.* **1.** having feet resembling those of a cat. **2.** catlike in the manner of walking; characterized by noiseless, stealthy steps: *a catfooted jewel thief.* [1590–1600; CAT¹ + FOOTED]

cat•gut (kat′gut′), *n.* **1.** a strong cord made by twisting the dried intestines of animals, as sheep, used in stringing musical instruments and tennis rackets, for surgical sutures, etc. **2.** goat's-rue. [1590–1600; appar. CAT¹ + GUT, though allusion is obscure]

cath-, var. of **cata-** before an aspirate: *cathode.*

Cath., 1. (*often l.c.*) cathedral. **2.** Catholic.

Cath•ar (kath′är), *n., pl.* **-a•ri** (-ə rī′), **-ars.** (in medieval Europe) a member of any of several rigorously ascetic Christian sects maintaining a dualistic theology. Also called **Cath•a•rist** (kath′ər ist). [1630–40; < LL *Cathari* (pl.) < LGk *hoi Katharoí* Novatians, lit., the pure; applied in ML to various sects] —**Cath′a•rism,** *n.* —**Cath′a•ris′tic,** *adj.*

cath′ar•ine wheel′ (kath′rin, -ər in). See **Catherine wheel.**

cat-har•pin (kat′här′pin), *n. Naut.* any of a number of short ropes or rods for gathering in shrouds near their tops. [var. of *cat-harping;* etym. uncert.]

ca•thar•sis (kə thär′sis), *n., pl.* **-ses** (-sēz). **1.** the purging of the emotions or relieving of emotional tensions, esp. through certain kinds of art, as tragedy or music. **2.** *Med.* purgation. **3.** *Psychiatry.* **a.** psychotherapy that encourages or permits the discharge of pent-up, socially unacceptable affects. **b.** discharge of pent-up emotions so as to result in the alleviation of symptoms or the permanent relief of the condition. [1795–1805; < NL < Gk *kátharsis* a cleansing, equiv. to *kathar-* (var. s. of *kathaírein* to cleanse, deriv. of *katharós* pure) + *-sis* -SIS]

ca•thar•tic (kə thär′tik), *adj.* **1.** of or pertaining to catharsis. **2.** Also, **ca•thar′ti•cal.** evacuating the bowels; purgative. —*n.* **3.** a purgative. [1605–15; < LL *catharticus* < Gk *kathartikós* fit for cleansing. See CATHARSIS, -TIC] —**ca•thar′ti•cal•ly,** *adv.* —**ca•thar′ti•cal•ness,** *n.*
—**Syn. 3.** laxative, physic.

Ca•thay (ka thā′), *n. Literary or Archaic.* China. [< ML *Cat(h)aya* < Turkic; cf. Tatar *Kïtai*]

cat•head (kat′hed′), *n. Naut.* a projecting timber or metal beam to which an anchor is hoisted and secured. [1620–30; CAT¹ + HEAD]

ca•thect (kə thekt′, ka-), *v.t. Psychoanal.* to invest emotion or feeling in (an idea, object, or another person). [1930–35; back-formation from *cathectic* relating to CATHEXIS]

ca•the•dra (kə thē′drə, kath′i-), *n., pl.* **-drae** (-drē, -drē′). **1.** the seat or throne of a bishop in the principal church of a diocese. **2.** an official chair, as of a professor in a university. **3.** an ancient Roman chair used by women, having an inclined, curved back and curved legs flaring outward: the Roman copy of the Greek klismos. [1625–35; < L < Gk *kathédra*, deriv. of *kathézomai* to sit down; see CAT-, SIT; cf. CHAIR]

ca•the•dral (kə thē′drəl), *n.* **1.** the principal church of a diocese, containing the bishop's throne. **2.** (in nonepiscopal denominations) any of various important churches. —*adj.* **3.** pertaining to or containing a bishop's throne. **4.** pertaining to or emanating from a chair of office or authority. [1250–1300; ME < LL *cathedrālis* (*ecclesia*) a cathedral (church). See CATHEDRA, -AL¹] —**ca•the′dral•like′,** *adj.*

cathe′dral ceil′ing, 1. a high ceiling formed by or suggesting an open-timbered roof. **2.** a ceiling, as in a living room, higher than that of other rooms in a house.

cathe′dral glass′, a semitransparent sheet of rolled glass having a decorative pattern. [1840–50]

cathe′dral hull′, a motorboat hull having a bottom characterized by two or more, usually three, V-shaped hull profiles meeting below the waterline.

ca•thep•sin (kə thep′sin), *n. Biochem.* any of a class of intracellular proteolytic enzymes, occurring in animal tissue, esp. the liver, spleen, kidneys, and intestine, that catalyze autolysis in certain pathological conditions and after death. [1925–30; < Gk *kathéps(ein)* to digest (*cat-* CAT- + *hépsein* to boil) + -IN²] —**ca•thep•tic** (kə thep′tik), *adj.*

Cath•er (kath′ər *or, often,* kath′-), *n.* **Wil•la (Si•bert)** (wil′ə sē′bərt), 1876–1947, U.S. novelist.

Cath•er•ine (kath′ər in, kath′rin), *n.* a female given name. Also, **Cath′er•yn.**

Catherine I, (*Marfa Skavronskaya*) 1684?–1727, Lithuanian wife of Peter the Great: empress of Russia 1725–27.

Catherine II, (*Sophia Augusta of Anhalt-Zerbst*) ("*Catherine the Great*") 1729–96, empress of Russia 1762–96.

Ca•the•rine de Mé•di•cis (kaᵗ rēn də mā dē sēs′), (*Caterina de' Medici*) 1518–89, queen of Henry II of France (mother of Francis II, Charles IX, and Henry III). Also, **Cath•er•ine de' Med•i•ci** (kath′rin də med′i chē, mā′di-, dä, kath′ər in), **Cath′erine de Med′ici.**

Cath′erine How′ard, 1520?–42, fifth queen consort of Henry VIII of England.

Cath′erine of Alexan′dria, Saint, A.D. c310, Christian martyr.

Cath′erine of Ar′a•gon (ar′ə gən, -gon′), 1485–1536, first queen consort of Henry VIII of England (mother of Mary I of England).

Cath′erine of Sie′na, Saint, 1347–80, Italian ascetic and mystic.

Cath′erine Parr′ (pär), 1512–48, sixth queen consort of Henry VIII of England.

Cath′erine wheel′, 1. a firework that revolves on a pin, making a wheel of fire or sparks; pinwheel. **2.** See **wheel window.** Also, **catharine wheel.** [1175–1225; ME; named after St. CATHERINE of Alexandria, from wheel used to torture her]

cath•e•ter (kath′i tər), *n. Med.* a flexible or rigid hollow tube employed to drain fluids from body cavities or to distend body passages, esp. one for passing into the bladder through the urethra to draw off urine or into the heart through a leg vein or arm vein for diagnostic examination. [1595–1605; < LL < Gk *kathetḗr* kind of tube, lit., something sent or let down, equiv. to *kathe-* (var. s. of *kathiénai*, equiv. to *kat-* CATA- + *hiénai* to send, let go) + *-tēr* agent suffix]

cath•e•ter•ize (kath′i tə rīz′), *v.t.,* **-ized, -iz•ing.** to introduce a catheter into. Also, *esp. Brit.,* **cath′e•ter•ise′.** [1880–85; CATHETER + -IZE] —**cath′e•ter•i•za′•tion,** *n.*

cath•e•tus (kath′i təs, kə thē′təs), *n., pl.* **-ti** (-tī′, -tī). (in an Ionic capital) the vertical guideline through the eye of a volute, from which the form of the volute is determined. [1565–75; < L (n.) < Gk *káthetos* perpendicular, equiv. to *kathe-* (see CATHETER) + *-tos* adj. suffix]

ca•thex•is (kə thek′sis), *n., pl.* **-thex•es** (-thek′sēz). *Psychoanal.* **1.** the investment of emotional significance in an activity, object, or idea. **2.** the charge of psychic energy so invested. [1920–25; < NL < Gk *káthexis* a keeping, equiv. to *kathek-* (var. s. of *katéchein* to keep, hold on to, equiv. to *cat* CAT- + *échein* to have, hold) + *-sis* -SIS, as trans. of G *Besetzung* a taking possession of (Freud's term)] —**ca•thec•tic** (kə thek′tik), *adj.*

Cath•ie (kath′ē), *n.* a female given name, form of **Catherine.**

ca•this•ma (*Gk.* kä′thēz mä; *Eng.* ka thiz′mə), *n., pl.* **ca•this•ma•ta** (*Gk.* kä thēz′mä tä; *Eng.* ka thiz′mə tə). kathisma.

Cath•leen (kath lēn′), *n.* a female given name, Irish form of **Catherine.**

cath•ode (kath′ōd), *n.* **1.** the electrode or terminal by which current leaves an electrolytic cell, voltaic cell, battery, etc. **2.** the positive terminal of a voltaic cell or battery. **3.** the negative terminal, electrode, or element of an electron tube or electrolytic cell. [1825–35; < Gk *káthodos* a way down, equiv. to *kat-* CAT- + *hodós* way]

cath′ode dark′ space′. See **Crookes dark space.** [1910–15]

cath′ode glow′, a luminous region between the Aston dark space and the Crookes dark space in a vacuum tube, occurring when the pressure is low.

cath′ode ray′, a flow of electrons emanating from a cathode in a vacuum tube and focused into a narrow beam. [1875–80]

cath′ode-ray tube′ (kath′ōd rā′), a vacuum tube generating a focused beam of electrons that can be deflected by electric fields, magnetic fields, or both. The terminus of the beam is visible as a spot or line of luminescence caused by its impinging on a sensitized screen at one end of the tube. Cathode-ray tubes are used to study the shapes of electric waves, to reproduce images in television receivers, to display alphanumeric and graphical information on computer monitors, as an indicator in radar sets, etc. *Abbr.:* CRT [1900–05]

ca•thod•ic (ka thod′ik, -thō′dik, kə-), *adj.* pertaining to a cathode or phenomena in its vicinity. Also, **cath•o•dal** (kath′ə dl). [1830–40; CATHODE + -IC] —**ca•thod′i•cal•ly, cath′o•dal•ly,** *adv.*

cathod′ic protec′tion, protection of ferrous metals against electrolysis by the attachment of sacrificial anodes. Also called **electrolytic protection.** [1930–35]

cath•o•do•lu•mi•nes•cence (kath′ə dō lo͞o′mə nes′-əns), *n.* light emitted by a substance undergoing bombardment by cathode rays. [1905–10; CATHODE + -O- + LUMINESCENCE] —**cath′o•do•lu′mi•nes′cent,** *adj.*

cath•o•lic (kath′ə lik, kath′lik), *adj.* **1.** broad or wide-ranging in tastes, interests, or the like; having sympathies with all; broad-minded; liberal. **2.** universal in extent; involving all; of interest to all. **3.** pertaining to the whole Christian body or church. [1300–1350; ME < L *catholicus* < Gk *katholikós* general, equiv. to *kathól(ou)* universally (contr. of phrase *katà hólou* according to the whole; see CATA-, HOLO-) + *-ikos* -IC] —**ca•thol•i•cal•ly, ca•thol•ic•ly** (kə thol′ik lē), *adv.* —**ca•thol′i•cal•ness, cath′o•lic•ness,** *n.*

Cath•o•lic (kath′ə lik, kath′lik), *adj.* **1.** of or pertaining to a Catholic church, esp. the Roman Catholic Church. **2.** *Theol.* **a.** (among Roman Catholics) claiming to possess exclusively the notes or characteristics of the one, only, true, and universal church having unity, visibility, indefectibility, apostolic succession, universality, and sanctity: used in this sense, with these qualifications, only by the Church of Rome, as applicable only to itself and its adherents and to their faith and organization; often qualified, especially by those not acknowledging these claims, by prefixing the word *Roman.* **b.** (among Anglo-Catholics) noting or pertaining to the conception of the church as the body representing the ancient undivided Christian witness, comprising all the orthodox churches that have kept the apostolic succession of bishops, and including the Anglican Church, the Roman Catholic Church, the Eastern Orthodox Church, Church of Sweden, the Old Catholic Church (in the Netherlands and elsewhere), etc. **3.** pertaining to the Western Church. —*n.* **4.** a member of a Catholic church, esp. of the Roman Catholic Church. [1300–50; ME; special uses of CATHOLIC]

Cath′olic Apostol′ic Church′, a nearly extinct English Protestant church established between 1832 and 1835, stressing the imminent coming of the millennium and the reestablishment of the primitive church's ministries. Cf. **Irvingite.**

ca•thol•i•cate (kə thol′i kāt′, -kit), *n.* the see of a catholicos. [1875–80; < ML *catholicātus*, equiv. to *catholic(us)* CATHOLICOS + *-ātus* -ATE³]

Cath′olic Church′, *Rom. Cath. Ch.* a visible society of baptized Christians professing the same faith under the authority of the invisible head (Christ) and the authority of the visible head (the pope and the bishops in communion with him). [1400–50; late ME]

Cath′olic Emancipa′tion Act′, *Eng. Hist.* an act of Parliament (1829) permitting Roman Catholics to hold parliamentary office and repealing other laws that imposed civil disabilities on Catholics.

Cath′olic Epis′tles, the New Testament Epistles of James, I and II Peter, I John, and sometimes II and III John and Jude, addressed to the entire church.

Ca•thol•i•cism (kə thol′ə siz′əm), *n.* **1.** the faith, system, and practice of the Catholic Church, esp. the Roman Catholic Church. **2.** (*l.c.*) catholicity. [1600–10; CATHOLIC + -ISM]

cath•o•lic•i•ty (kath′ə lis′i tē), *n.* **1.** broad-mindedness or liberality, as of tastes, interests, or views. **2.** universality; general inclusiveness. **3.** (*cap.*) the Roman Catholic Church, or its doctrines and usages. [1820–30; CATHOLIC + -ITY]

ca•thol•i•con (kə thol′i kən), *n.* a universal remedy; panacea. [1375–1425; late ME < ML < Gk *katholikón* neut. of *katholikós* CATHOLIC]

ca•thol•i•cos (kə thol′i kəs, -kos′), *n., pl.* **-cos•es, -coi** (-koi′). **1.** (*often cap.*) *Eastern Ch.* **a.** any of the heads of certain autocephalous churches. **b.** (in some autocephalous churches) a primate subject to a patriarch and having authority over metropolitans. **2.** (in the early Christian church) the head of monasteries in the same city. Also, **catholicus, katholikos.** [1615–25; < LGk *katholikós*, n. use of Gk adj.; see CATHOLIC]

ca•thol•i•cus (kə thol′i kəs), *n., pl.* **-i•ci** (-ə sī′, -i kē′). catholicos. [< ML]

cat•house (kat′hous′), *n., pl.* **-hous•es** (-hou′ziz). *Slang.* brothel; whorehouse. [1595–1605, for earlier sense of siege tower; 1930–35 for current sense; CAT¹ (in obs. sense of harlot) + HOUSE]

Cath•y (kath′ē), *n.* a female given name, form of **Catherine.**

Cat•i•li•nar•i•an (kat′l ə nâr′ē ən), *adj.* **1.** pertaining to or resembling Catiline. —*n.* **2.** a person who participated in Catiline's conspiracy. **3.** a person who resembles or imitates Catiline; conspirator. [1815–25; < L *Catilin(a)* CATILINE + -ARIAN]

Cat•i•line (kat′l īn′), *n.* (*Lucius Sergius Catilina*) 108?–62 B.C., Roman politician and conspirator.

cat•i•on (kat′ī′ən, -on), *n. Physical Chem.* **1.** a positively charged ion that is attracted to the cathode in electrolysis. **2.** any positively charged atom or group of atoms (opposed to *anion*). Also, **kation.** [1825–35; < Gk *katión* going down (neut. of *katiṓn*, prp. of *kateînai*), equiv. to *kat-* CAT- + *-i-* go + *-on* neut. prp. suffix] —**cat•i•on•ic** (kat′ī on′ik), *adj.* —**cat′i•on′i•cal•ly,** *adv.*

cation′ic deter′gent, any of a class of synthetic compounds, as benzalkonium chloride, whose cations are colloidal in solution: used as antiseptics, wetting agents, and emulsifiers. Also called **invert soap.** [1960–65]

cat•kin (kat′kin), *n. Bot.* a spike of unisexual, apetalous flowers having scaly, usually deciduous bracts, as of a willow or birch. Also called **ament.** [1570–80; < D *katteken* little cat (now obs.). See CAT[1], -KIN] —**cat•kin•ate** (kat′kə nāt′), *adj.*

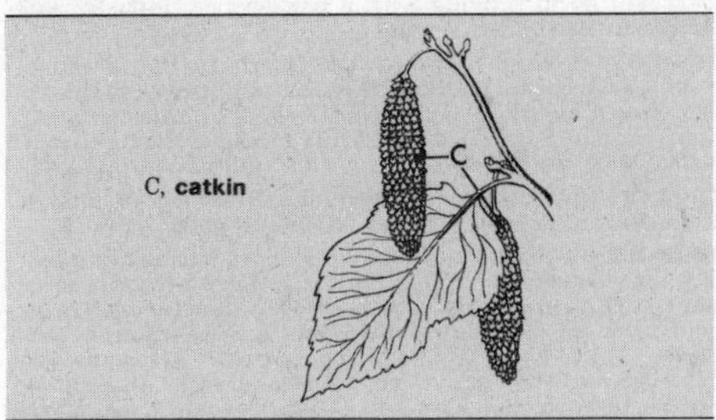

C, **catkin**

cat•like (kat′līk′), *adj.* **1.** resembling or typical of a cat: *catlike eyes.* **2.** swift and graceful. **3.** stealthy and noiseless: *The scouts crept up on their quarry with catlike tread.* [1590–1600; CAT[1] + -LIKE]

Cat•lin (kat′lin), *n.* **George,** 1796–1872, U.S. painter.

cat′ lit′ter, pulverized absorbent clay used for lining a box in which a cat can eliminate waste.

cat•mint (kat′mint′), *n. Chiefly Brit.* catnip. [1225–75; ME *cattesminte* equiv. to *cattes,* gen. of CAT[1] + *minte* MINT[1]]

cat•nap (kat′nap′), *n., v.,* **-napped, -nap•ping.** —*n.* **1.** a short, light nap or doze. —*v.i.* **2.** to doze or sleep lightly. [1815–25, *Amer.*; CAT + NAP]

cat•nap•per[1] (kat′nap′ər), *n.* a person who takes catnaps, esp. regularly or habitually. [CATNAP + -ER[1]]

cat•nap•per[2] (kat′nap′ər), *n.* a person who steals cats. Also, **cat′nap′er.** [1940–45; CAT[1] + -NAP + -ER[1]]

cat•nip (kat′nip), *n.* a plant, *Nepeta cataria,* of the mint family, having egg-shaped leaves containing aromatic oils that are a cat attractant. Also, *esp. Brit.,* **catmint.** [1705–15, *Amer.*; CAT[1] + *nip,* var. of ME *nep* catnip, apocopated var. of OE *nepte* < ML *nepta,* var. of L *nepeta*]

Ca•to (kā′tō), *n.* **1. Marcus Por•ci•us** (pôr′shē əs, -shəs), (*"the Elder"* or *"the Censor"*), 234–149 B.C., Roman statesman, soldier, and writer. **2.** his great-grandson, **Marcus Porcius** (*"the Younger"*), 95–46 B.C., Roman statesman, soldier, and Stoic philosopher.

Ca•toc′tin Moun′tain Park′ (kə tok′tin), a federal park in N central Maryland: site of Camp David. 9 sq. mi. (23 sq. km).

Catoc′tin Moun′tains, a mountain range extending NE from NE Virginia through central Maryland: part of the Appalachian Mountains.

cat-o′-moun•tain (kat′ə moun′tn), *n.* catamountain.

Cat′ on a Hot′ Tin′ Roof′, a play (1955) by Tennessee Williams.

cat-o′-nine-tails (kat′ə nīn′tālz′), *n., pl.* **-tails.** a whip, usually having nine knotted lines or cords fastened to a handle, used for flogging. [1685–95; so called in allusion to a cat's scratches]

Ca•tons•ville (kāt′nz vil′), *n.* a town in central Maryland, near Baltimore. 33,208.

ca•top•trics (kə top′triks), *n.* (*used with a singular v.*) the branch of optics dealing with the formation of images by mirrors. [1560–70; < Gk *katoptrikós,* equiv. to *kátoptr(on)* mirror (*kat-* CAT- + *op-* see + *-tron* suffix of instruments) + *-ikos* -IC; see -ICS] —**ca•top′tric, ca•top′tri•cal,** *adj.* —**ca•top′tri•cal•ly,** *adv.*

ca•touse (kə tous′), *n. New Eng.* a noisy disturbance; commotion. [1855–60; prob. CA- + TOUSE]

cat′ rig′, *Naut.* the typical rig of a catboat, consisting of a single mast with a long boom, set well forward and carrying a single gaff or jib-headed sail. [1865–70, *Amer.*]

CAT′ scan′ (kat), **1.** an examination performed with a CAT scanner. **2.** an x-ray image obtained by examination with a CAT scanner. Also, **CT scan.** [1970–75; C(OMPUTERIZED) A(XIAL) T(OMOGRAPHY)]

CAT′ scan′ner, (kat), a specialized x-ray instrument that displays computerized cross-sectional images of the body, providing a noninvasive means of visualizing the brain, lungs, liver, spleen, and other soft tissue. Also called **CT scanner.**

cat's-claw (kats′klô′), *n.* a spiny shrub or small tree, *Pithecellobium unguis-cati,* of Central America, having greenish-yellow flowers and reddish, spirally twisted pods. Also, **catclaw.** Also called **blackbead.** [1750–60]

cat's′ cra′dle, **1.** a children's game in which two players alternately stretch a looped string over their fingers in such a way as to produce different designs. **2.** the intricate design formed by the string in this game. **3.** intricacy; complexity. [1760–70]

cat′-scratch disease′ (kat′skrach′), *Pathol.* a disorder characterized by fever and swelling of the lymph glands, caused by a viral infection resulting from the scratch or bite of a cat. Also called **cat′-scratch fe′ver.**

cat's′ cry′ syn′drome, *Pathol.* a complex of congenital malformations in human infants caused by a chromosomal aberration and in which the infant emits a mewing cry. Also called **cri du chat.**

cat's-ear (kats′ēr′), *n.* **1.** Also called **gosmore.** any of several Old World composite plants of the genus *Hypochaeris,* having leaves in a rosette at the base and dandelionlike yellow or white flowers, esp. *H. radicata,* naturalized as a weed in the western U.S. **2.** any western American plant of the genus *Calochortus,* of the lily family, as *C. coeruleus* or *C. elegans,* having white or bluish bell-shaped flowers. [1840–50]

cat's-eye (kats′ī′), *n., pl.* **-eyes.** **1.** any of certain gems having a chatoyant luster, esp. chrysoberyl. **2.** a playing marble marked with eyelike concentric circles. [1545–55]

Cats′kill Moun′tains (kats′kil), a range of low mountains in E New York: resort area. Highest peak, Slide Mountain, 4204 ft. (1281 m). Also called **Cats′kills.**

cat•skin•ner (kat′skin′ər), *n. Informal.* an operator of a vehicle or machine with caterpillar treads. [CAT[2] + (MULE) SKINNER]

cat•slide (kat′slīd′), *n.* (in early American architecture) a steep roof ending close to the ground, as on a saltbox. [CAT[1] + SLIDE]

cat's′ paja′mas, *Older Slang.* someone or something wonderful or remarkable. Also called **cat's′ meow′.**

cat's-paw (kats′pô′), *n.* **1.** a person used to serve the purposes of another; tool. **2.** *Naut.* **a.** a hitch made in the bight of a rope so that two eyes are formed to hold the hook of one block of a tackle. **b.** a light breeze that ruffles the surface of the water over a comparatively small area. **c.** the small area ruffled by such a breeze. Also, **cats′paw′.** [1650–60]

cat′ squir′rel, *Chiefly South Atlantic States.* the gray squirrel, as distinguished from the fox squirrel.

cat's′-tail speed′well (kats′tāl′), a widely cultivated Eurasian plant, *Veronica spicata,* of the figwort family, having blue flowers in long, spikelike clusters.

cat•stick (kat′stik′), *n.* a broomstick or other stick used as a bat, esp. in playing tipcat. [1620–30; CAT[1] + STICK[1]]

cat•stitch (kat′stich′), *n.* See **catch stitch.** [by reanalysis of 1st syll. as CAT[1]]

cat′ suit′, *Chiefly Brit.* a jumpsuit. [1955–60]

cat•sup (kat′səp, kech′əp, kach′-), *n.* ketchup.

cat's′ whisk′er. See **cat whisker.** [1910–15]

Catt (kat), *n.* **Carrie Chapman Lane,** 1859–1947, U.S. leader in women's suffrage movements.

cat′ tack′le, *Naut.* a tackle for hoisting an anchor.

cat•tail (kat′tāl′), *n.* any tall, reedlike marsh plant of the genus *Typha,* esp. *T. latifolia,* having long, sword-shaped leaves and dense, cylindrical clusters of minute brown flowers. Also called **bulrush, reed mace.** [1425–75; late ME *cattestail.* See CAT[1], TAIL[1]]

cattails,
Typha latifolia

cat•ta•lo (kat′l ō′), *n., pl.* **-loes, -los.** beefalo. [1885–90; b. CATTLE and BUFFALO]

Cat•te•gat (kat′i gat′, kä′ti gät′), *n.* Kattegat.

Cat•tell (kə tel′), *n.* **James Mc•Keen** (mə kēn′), 1860–1944, U.S. psychologist, educator, and editor.

cat•te•ry (kat′ə rē), *n., pl.* **-ries.** a place where cats are kept and bred. [1785–95; CAT[1] + -ERY]

cat•tish (kat′ish), *adj.* **1.** catlike; feline. **2.** spiteful; malicious. [1590–1600; CAT[1] + -ISH[1]] —**cat′tish•ly,** *adv.* —**cat′tish•ness,** *n.*

cat•tle (kat′l), *n.* (*used with a plural v.*) **1.** bovine animals, esp. domesticated members of the genus *Bos.* **2.** *Bib.* such animals together with other domesticated quadrupeds, as horses, swine, etc. **3.** *Disparaging.* human beings. [1175–1225; ME *catel* < ONF: (personal) property < ML *capitāle* wealth; see CAPITAL[1]] —**cat′•tle•less,** *adj.*

cat′tle call′, *Slang.* a theatrical audition that is open to everyone, esp. to those who do not belong to a theatrical union. [1950–55]

cat′tle car′, **1.** *Railroads.* See **stock car** (def. 2). **2.** *Slang.* a railroad passenger car providing little comfort and few amenities. [1860–65, *Amer.*]

cat•tle•duff•er (kat′l duf′ər), *n. Australian.* a cattle thief. [1885–90; CATTLE + DUFFER]

cat′tle e′gret, an egret, *Bubulcus ibis,* cosmopolitan in warmer regions, often associating with grazing animals for the insects that hover around them. [1900–05]

cat′tle grub′, the larva or adult of a warble fly, esp. *Hypoderma lineatum,* a common pest of cattle in North America. Also called **heel fly.** [1925–30, *Amer.*]

cat′tle guard′, a structure consisting typically of parallel bars over a shallow ditch, used to prevent cattle from straying. [1835–45]

cat•tle•man (kat′l mən, -man′), *n., pl.* **-men** (-mən, -men′). **1.** a person who tends or breeds cattle. **2.** a rancher who raises cattle on a large scale; the owner of a cattle ranch. [1860–65, *Amer.*; CATTLE + MAN[1]]

cat′tle plague′, *Vet. Pathol.* rinderpest. [1865–70]

cat′tle prod′, a rod-shaped, usually electrified device designed for prodding or driving livestock, esp. cattle.

cat′tle run′, **1.** a barnyard or fenced area adjacent to a barn used as a limited grazing area or exercise lot for cattle. **2.** a passageway used for cattle. [1850–55]

cat•tle•ship (kat′l ship′), *n.* a large vessel for the transportation of livestock. [1620–30; CATTLE + SHIP]

cat′tle show′, **1.** an exhibition of prize cattle by cattle breeders, as at a livestock exposition. **2.** *Informal.* a public appearance by the contenders for a political office, a job, or the like, at which they may be judged by voters, prospective employers, etc. [1805–15]

cat′tle tick′, a dark brown tick, *Boophilus annulatus,* that infests cattle and is a vector for parasitic diseases of cattle, as babesiosis. [1865–70, *Amer.*]

catt•ley•a (kat′lē ə, kat lē′ə, -lā′ə), *n.* any of several tropical American orchids of the genus *Cattleya,* having showy flowers ranging from white to purple. [1820–30; after William *Cattley* (d. 1832), English botany enthusiast; see -A[2]]

Cat•ton (kat′n), *n.* **(Charles) Bruce,** 1899–1978, U.S. journalist and historian.

cat-train (kat′trān′), *n. Chiefly Canadian.* a train of sleds and other vehicles mounted on runners, the whole procession drawn by a tractor with caterpillar treads. [1945–50]

cat•ty[1] (kat′ē), *adj.,* **-ti•er, -ti•est.** **1.** catlike; feline. **2.** slyly malicious; spiteful: *a catty gossip.* [1885–90; CAT[1] + -Y[1]] —**cat′ti•ly,** *adv.* —**cat′ti•ness,** *n.*
—**Syn. 2.** mean, nasty, malevolent; bitchy.

cat•ty[2] (kat′ē), *n., pl.* **-ties.** (in China and southeast Asia) a weight equal to about $1^1/_2$ pounds (680 grams) avoirdupois. [1545–55; < Malay *kati*]

cat•ty-cor•nered (kat′ē kôr′nərd), *adj., adv. Chiefly South Midland and Southern U.S.* cater-cornered. Also, **cat′ty-cor′ner.** [1830–40, *Amer.*]

cat•ty•wam•pus (kat′ē wom′pəs, kat′ə-), *adj., adv. Chiefly Midland and Southern U.S.* catawampus.

Ca•tul•lus (kə tul′əs), *n.* **Ga•ius Va•le•ri•us** (gā′əs və lēr′ē əs), 84?–54? B.C., Roman poet. —**Ca•tul•li•an** (kə tul′ē ən), *adj.*

CATV, community antenna television: a cable television system that receives television broadcasts by antenna and relays them by cable to paying subscribers in areas where direct reception is either poor or not possible.

cat•walk (kat′wôk′), *n.* a narrow walkway, esp. one high above the surrounding area, used to provide access or allow workers to stand or move, as over the stage in a theater, outside the roadway of a bridge, along the top of a railroad car, etc. [1880–85; CAT[1] + WALK]

cat′ whisk′er, **1.** *Radio.* a stiff wire forming one contact in a crystal detector and used for probing the crystal. **2.** *Electronics.* any wire for making contact with a semiconductor. Also, **cat's whisker.** Also called **whisker.** [1910–15]

cat′ yawl′, a yawl having the mainmast close to the stem and the after mast on the counter.

Cau•ca (kou′kä), *n.* a river in W Colombia: tributary of the Magdalena. 600 mi. (965 km) long.

Cau•ca•sia (kô kā′zhə, -shə), *n.* Caucasus (def. 2).

Cau•ca•sian (kô kā′zhən, -shən, -kazh′ən, -kash′-), *adj.* Also, **Cau•cas•ic** (kô kas′ik, -kaz′-). **1.** *Anthropol.* of, pertaining to, or characteristic of one of the traditional racial divisions of humankind, marked by fair to dark skin, straight to tightly curled hair, and light to very dark eyes, and originally inhabiting Europe, parts of North Africa, western Asia, and India: no longer in technical use. **2.** of or pertaining to the Caucasus mountain range. **3.** of or related to the non-Indo-European, non-Turkic languages of the Caucasus region. —*n.* **4.** *Anthropol.* a member of the peoples traditionally classified as the Caucasian race, esp. those peoples having light to fair skin: no longer in technical use. **5.** a native of Caucasia. [1800–10; < L *Caucasi(us)* (< Gk *Kaukásios,* equiv. to *Kaúkas(os)* CAUCASUS + *-ios* adj. suffix) + -AN]

Cauca′sian lil′y, a tall lily plant, *Lilium monadelphum,* having large, fragrant, drooping golden-yellow flowers.

Cau•ca•soid (kô′kə soid′), *adj., n.* Caucasian (defs. 1, 4). [1900–05; CAUCAS(IAN) + -OID]

Cau•ca•sus (kô′kə səs), *n.* **the, 1.** Also called **Cau′•casus Moun′tains.** a mountain range in Caucasia, between the Black and Caspian seas, along the border between the Russian Federation, Georgia, and Azerbaijan. Highest peak, Mt. Elbrus, 18,481 ft. (5633 m). **2.** Also, **Caucasia.** a region between the Black and Caspian seas: divided by the Caucasus Mountains into Ciscaucasia in Europe and Transcaucasia in Asia.

cau•cho (kou′chō, -shōō), *n.* rubber obtained from the latex of any of several tropical American trees of the genus *Castilla,* esp. *C. elastica,* of Central America. Also called **ule.** [1895–1900; < AmerSp, var. of *cauchuc* CAOUTCHOUC]

Cau•chy (kō shē′), *n.* **Au•gus•tin Louis** (ō gʏ staɴ′ lwē′), 1789–1857, French mathematician.

Cau′chy in′tegral for′mula, *Math.* a theorem that gives an expression in terms of an integral for the value of an analytic function at any point inside a simple closed curve of finite length in a domain. [named after A. L. CAUCHY]

Cau′chy in′tegral the′orem, *Math.* the theorem that the integral of an analytic function about a closed curve of finite length in a finite, simply connected domain is zero. [named after A. L. CAUCHY]

Cau′chy-Rie′mann equa′tions (kō′shē rē′män, kō shē′-), *Math.* equations relating the partial derivatives of the real and imaginary parts of an analytic function of a complex variable, as $f(z) = u(x,y) + iv(x,y)$, by

CONCISE PRONUNCIATION KEY: act, cāpe, dâre, pärt; set, ēqual; *if,* ice; ox, ōver, ôrder, oil, bŏŏk, bōōt, out; up, ûrge; child; sing; shoe; thin, *th*at; zh as in *treasure.* ə = *a* as in *alone, e* as in *system, i* as in *easily, o* as in *gallop, u* as in *circus;* ᵊ as in *fire* (fīᵊr), *hour* (ouᵊr). l and n can serve as syllabic consonants, as in *cradle* (krād′l), and *button* (but′n). See the full key inside the front cover.

$\delta u/\delta x = \delta v/\delta y$ and $\delta u/\delta y = -\delta v/\delta x$. [named after A. L. CAUCHY and G. F. B. RIEMANN]

Cau′chy-Schwarz′ inequal′ity (kō′shē shwôrts′, kō shē′shvärts′), *Math.* See **Schwarz inequality** (def. 2).

Cau′chy se′quence, *Math.* See **fundamental sequence.** [named after A. L. CAUCHY]

Cau′chy's inequal′ity, *Math.* See **Schwarz inequality** (def. 1). [named after A. L. CAUCHY]

cau•cus (kô′kəs), *n., pl.* **-cus•es,** *v.* —*n.* **1.** *U.S. Politics.* **a.** a meeting of party leaders to select candidates, elect convention delegates, etc. **b.** a meeting of party members within a legislative body to select leaders and determine strategy. **c.** (*often cap.*) a faction within a legislative body that pursues its interests through the legislative process: *the Women's Caucus; the Black Caucus.* **2.** any group or meeting organized to further a special interest or cause. —*v.i.* **3.** to hold or meet in a caucus. —*v.t.* **4.** to bring up or hold for discussion in a caucus: *The subject was caucused. The group caucused the meeting.* [1755–65, *Amer.*; appar. first used in the name of the *Caucus Club* of colonial Boston; perh. < ML *caucus* drinking vessel, LL *caucum* < Gk *kaûkos;* alleged Virginia Algonquian orig. less probable]

cau•da (kou′də, kô′-), *n., pl.* **-dae** (-dē). *Anat., Zool.* a tail or taillike appendage. [1690–1700; < L: tail]

cau•da•ite (kô′də īt′), *n.* a small meteorite, generally less than one half millimeter in diameter, containing crystals of more or less pure magnetite. [< L *caud(a)* tail + -ITE[1]]

cau•dal (kôd′l), *adj.* **1.** *Anat., Zool.* of, at, or near the tail or the posterior end of the body. **2.** *Zool.* taillike: *caudal appendages.* —*n.* **3.** *Med.* a caudal anesthetic [1655–65; < NL *caudālis,* equiv. to L *caud(a)* tail + *-ālis* -AL[1]] —**cau′dal•ly,** *adv.*

cau′dal anesthe′sia, *Med.* anesthesia below the pelvis, induced by injecting an anesthetic into the sacral portion of the spinal canal.

cau′dal fin′, the terminal vertical fin of a fish. Also called **tail fin.** See diag. under **fish.**

cau•date (kô′dāt), *adj. Zool.* having a tail or taillike appendage. Also, **cau′dat•ed.** [1590–1600; < NL *caudātus,* equiv. to L *caud(a)* tail + *-ātus* -ATE[1]] —**cau•da′•tion,** *n.*

cau•dex (kô′deks), *n., pl.* **-di•ces** (-də sēz′), **-dex•es.** *Bot.* **1.** the main stem of a tree, esp. a palm or tree fern. **2.** the woody or thickened persistent base of an herbaceous perennial. [1820–30; < L: tree trunk; cf. CODEX]

cau•dil•lo (kô dēl′yō, -dē′ō; *Sp.* kou t͟hē′lyō, -t͟hē′yō), *n., pl.* **-dil•los** (-dēl′yōz, -dē′ōz; *Sp.* -t͟hē′lyôs, -t͟hē′yôs). (in Spanish-speaking countries) a head of state, esp. a military dictator. [1850–55; < Sp < LL *capitellum,* equiv. to L *capit-* (s. of *caput*) head + *-ellum* dim. suffix; see -ELLE]

Cau′dine Forks′ (kô′dīn), two mountain passes in S Italy, in the Apennines near Benevento.

cau•dle (kôd′l), *n.* a warm drink for the sick, as of wine or ale mixed with eggs, bread, sugar, spices, etc. [1250–1300; ME *caudel* < ONF < ML *caldellum,* equiv. to L *calid(um)* warmed watered wine (n. use of neut. of *calidus* warm) + *-ellum* dim. suffix; see -ELLE]

cau′dle cup′, a deep drinking cup having two handles and, usually, a cover. [1650–60]

caught (kôt), *v.* pt. and pp. of **catch.**

caul[1] (kôl), *n.* **1.** a part of the amnion sometimes covering the head of a child at birth. **2.** See **greater omentum. 3.** a net lining in the back of a woman's cap or hat. **4.** a cap or hat of net formerly worn by women. [1300–50; ME *calle* < MF *cale,* prob. back formation from *calotte* kind of cap; see CALOTTE]

caul[2] (kôl), *n.* a form or plate for pressing a veneer or veneers being glued to a backing or to each other. [< F *cale* shim < G *Keil* wedge]

cauld (kôld, käld, kôd), *adj., n. Scot.* cold.

caul•dron (kôl′drən), *n.* a large kettle or boiler. Also, **caldron.** [1250–1300; ME, alter. (by assoc. with L *caldus* warm) of ME *cauderon* < AF, equiv. to *caudere* (< LL *caldāria;* see CALDERA) + *-on* n. suffix]

cau•les•cent (kô les′ənt), *adj. Bot.* having an obvious stem rising above the ground. [1785–95; < L *caul(is)* a stalk, stem + -ESCENT]

cau•li•flow•er (kô′lə flou′ər, -lē-, kol′ə-, kol′ē-), *n.* **1.** a form of cultivated plant, *Brassica oleracea botrytis,* of the mustard family, whose inflorescence forms a compact, usually whitish head. Cf. **broccoli. 2.** this head, used as a vegetable. [1590–1600; < L *cauli(s)* COLE + FLOWER; r. *coleflorie* < It *ca(v)olfiore,* equiv. to *cavol* cole + *fiore* (< L *flōri-* (s. of *flōs*) flower]

cau′liflower ear′, an ear that has been deformed by repeated injury, resulting in an irregular thickening of scar tissue. [1905–10, *Amer.*]

cau•li•flow•er•ette (kô′lə flou ə ret′, kô′lē-, kol′ə-, kol′ē-), *n.* a single floret from the head of a cauliflower. Also, **cau′li•flow•er•et′.** [1945–50; CAULIFLOWER + -ETTE]

cau′liflower fun′gus, a large edible white to yellowish cauliflowerlike mushroom, *Sparassis radicata,* widely distributed in North America. Also called **sparassis.**

cau•line (kô′lin, -līn), *adj. Bot.* of or pertaining to a stem, esp. pertaining to or arising from the upper part of a stem. [1750–60; < L *caul(is)* a stalk, stem + -INE[1]]

CONCISE ETYMOLOGY KEY: <, descended or borrowed from; >, whence; b., blend of, blended; c., cognate with; cf., compare; deriv., derivative; equiv., equivalent; imit., imitative; obl., oblique; r., replacing; s., stem; sp., spelling, spelled; resp., respelling, respelled; trans., translation; ?, origin unknown; *, unattested; ‡, probably earlier than. See the full key inside the front cover.

caulk (kôk), *v.t.* **1.** to fill or close seams or crevices of (a tank, window, etc.) in order to make watertight, airtight, etc. **2.** to make (a vessel) watertight by filling the seams between the planks with oakum or other material driven snug. **3.** to fill or close (a seam, joint, etc.), as in a boat. **4.** to drive the edges of (plating) together to prevent leakage. —*n.* **5.** Also, **caulk•ing** (kô′king). a material or substance used for caulking. Also, **calk.** [1350–1400; < L *calcāre* to trample, tread on (v. deriv. of *calx* heel), conflated with ME *cauken* < OF *cauquer* to trample < L, as above]

caulk•er (kô′kər), *n.* **1.** a person who caulks the seams of boats or the like. **2.** a caulking tool or device. Also, **calker.** [1485–95; CAULK + -ER[1]]

Cau•lo•nia (kou lô′nyä), *n.* a town in S Calabria, in S Italy: ruins of ancient Achaean colony. 10,282.

Cau•que•nes (kou ke′nes), *n.* a city in central Chile. 20,300.

cau•ri (kou′rē), *n.* a monetary unit of Guinea, the 100th part of a syli.

caus., causative.

caus•al (kô′zəl), *adj.* **1.** of, constituting, or implying a cause. **2.** *Gram.* expressing a cause, as the conjunctions *because* and *since.* [1520–30; < L *causālis,* equiv. to *caus(a)* CAUSE + *-ālis* -AL[1]] —**caus′al•ly,** *adv.*

cau•sal•gi•a (kô zal′jē ə, -jə), *n.* a neuralgia distinguished by a burning pain along certain nerves, usually of the upper extremities. [1870–75; < NL, equiv. to Gk *kaûs(is)* a burning + NL *-algia* -ALGIA; see CAUSTIC] —**cau•sal′gic,** *adj.*

cau•sal•i•ty (kô zal′i tē), *n., pl.* **-ties. 1.** the relation of cause and effect: *The result is the same, however differently the causality is interpreted.* **2.** causal quality or agency. [1595–1605; CAUSAL + -ITY]

cau•sa si•ne qua non (kou′sä si′ne kwä nōn′; *Eng.* kô′zə sī′nē kwā non′, kô′zə sin′ā kwä nōn′), *Latin.* an indispensable condition; requisite. [lit., a cause without which not]

cau•sa•tion (kô zā′shən), *n.* **1.** the action of causing or producing. **2.** the relation of cause to effect; causality. **3.** anything that produces an effect; cause. [1640–50; < ML *causātiōn-* (s. of *causātiō*), equiv. to *causāt(us)* (ptp. of *causāre* to cause) (L *caus(a)* CAUSE + *-ātus* -ATE[1]) + *-iōn-* -ION] —**cau•sa′tion•al,** *adj.*

cau•sa•tion•ism (kô zā′shə niz′əm), *n.* the doctrine or theory that every event is the result of a prior and adequate cause. [1840–50; CAUSATION + -ISM] —**cau•sa′tion•ist,** *n.*

caus•a•tive (kô′zə tiv), *adj.* **1.** acting as a cause; producing (often fol. by *of*): *a causative agency; an event causative of war.* **2.** *Gram.* noting causation. The causative form of *to fall* is *to fell.* Gothic *-jan* is a causative suffix in *fulljan "to cause to be full; to fill."* —*n.* **3.** *Gram.* a word, esp. a verb, noting causation, as *made* in *He made me eat the apple.* [1375–1425; late ME < L *causātīvus,* equiv. to *causāt(us)* caused (see CAUSATION) + *-īvus* -IVE] —**caus′a•tive•ly,** *adv.* —**caus′a•tive•ness, caus′a•tiv′i•ty,** *n.*

cause (kôz), *n., v.,* **caused, caus•ing.** —*n.* **1.** a person or thing that acts, happens, or exists in such a way that some specific thing happens as a result; the producer of an effect: *You have been the cause of much anxiety. What was the cause of the accident?* **2.** the reason or motive for some human action: *The good news was a cause for rejoicing.* **3.** good or sufficient reason: *to complain without cause; to be dismissed for cause.* **4.** *Law.* **a.** a ground of legal action; the matter over which a person goes to law. **b.** a case for judicial decision. **5.** any subject of discussion or debate. **6.** a principle, ideal, goal, or movement to which a person or group is dedicated: *the Socialist cause; the human rights cause.* **7.** the welfare of a person or group, seen as a subject of concern: *support for the cause of the American Indian.* **8.** *Philos.* **a.** the end or purpose for which a thing is done or produced. **b.** *Aristotelianism.* any of the four things necessary for the movement or the coming into being of a thing, namely a material **(material cause),** something to act upon it **(efficient cause),** a form taken by the movement or development **(formal cause),** and a goal or purpose **(final cause). 9. make common cause,** to unite in a joint effort; work together for the same end: *They made common cause with neighboring countries and succeeded in reducing tariffs.* —*v.t.* **10.** to be the cause of; bring about. [1175–1225; ME < L *causa* reason, sake, case] —**caus′a•ble,** *adj.* —**caus′a•bil′i•ty,** *n.* —**cause′less,** *adj.* —**cause′less•ly,** *adv.* —**cause′less•ness,** *n.* —**caus′er,** *n.*

—**Syn. 1.** CAUSE, OCCASION refer to the starting of effects into motion. A CAUSE is an agency, perhaps acting through a long time, or a long-standing situation, that produces an effect: *The cause of the quarrel between the two men was jealousy.* An OCCASION is an event that provides an opportunity for the effect to become evident, or perhaps promotes its becoming evident: *The occasion was the fact that one man's wages were increased.* **3.** See **reason. 10.** effect, make, create, produce.

'cause (kôz, kuz, *unstressed* kəz), *conj. Informal.* because. [1400–50; late ME; aph. var.]

cause-and-ef•fect (kôz′ənd i fekt′, -ən-), *adj.* noting a relationship between actions or events such that one or more are the result of the other or others.

cause cé•lè•bre (kôz′ sə leb′rə, -leb′; *Fr.* kōz sā-leb′Rᵊ), *pl.* **causes cé•lè•bres** (kôz′ sə leb′rəz, sə lebz′, kô′ziz sə leb′rə, -leb′; *Fr.* kōz sā leb′Rᵊ). any controversy that attracts great public attention, as a celebrated legal case or trial. [1755–65; < F: lit., famous case]

cau•se•rie (kō′zə rē′; *Fr.* kōz° Rē′), *n., pl.* **-ries** (-rēz′; *Fr.* -Rē′). **1.** an informal talk or chat. **2.** a short, informal essay, article, etc. [1820–30; < F, equiv. to *caus(er)* to chat (< L *causārī* to plead at law, deriv. of *causa* case) + *-erie* -ERY]

cau•seuse (kō zœz′), *n., pl.* **-seuses** (-zœz′). *Fr. Furniture.* an upholstered settee for two persons. [1835–45; < F, equiv. to *caus(er)* to chat (see CAUSERIE) + *-euse* -EUSE]

cause•way (kôz′wā′), *n.* **1.** a raised road or path, as across low or wet ground. **2.** a highway or paved way. —*v.t.* **3.** to pave (a road or street) with cobblestones or pebbles. **4.** to provide with a causeway. [1400–50; late ME; see CAUSEY, WAY]

cau•sey (kô′zē), *n., pl.* **-seys. 1.** *Brit. Dial.* a causeway. **2.** *Archaic.* an ancient Roman highway. [1125–75; ME *cauce* < AF < ONF *caucie,* var. of *cauciee* < LL (*via*) *calciāta* (road) paved with limestone, equiv. to L *calci-* (s. of *calx*) limestone + *-āta,* fem. of *-ātus* -ATE[1]]

caus•ist (kô′zist), *n.* a person who supports or defends a cause, esp. a social cause. [CAUSE + -IST]

caus•tic (kô′stik), *adj.* **1.** capable of burning, corroding, or destroying living tissue. **2.** severely critical or sarcastic: *a caustic remark.* —*n.* **3.** a caustic substance. **4.** *Optics.* **a.** See **caustic curve. b.** See **caustic surface.** [1350–1400; ME < L *causticus* < Gk *kaustikós* burning, caustic, equiv. to *kaust(ós)* burnt (v. adj. of *kaíein* to burn) + *-ikos* -IC] —**caus′ti•cal•ly, caus′tic•ly,** *adv.* —**caus•tic•i•ty** (kô stis′i tē), **caus′tic•ness,** *n.*

—**Syn. 2.** biting, mordant, bitter, scathing, acid.

caus′tic al′cohol. See **sodium ethylate.** [1785–95]

caus′tic bary′ta, baryta (def. 2).

caus′tic curve′, *Optics.* a curve formed by a plane section of a caustic surface. Also called **caustic.** [1720–30]

caus′tic lime′, lime[1] (def. 1). [1805–15]

caus′tic pot′ash. See **potassium hydroxide.** [1865–70]

caus′tic so′da. See **sodium hydroxide.** [1875–80]

caus′tic sur′face, *Optics.* the surface to which all light rays emanating from a single point and reflected by a curved surface, as a concave mirror, are tangent. Also called **caustic.** [1865–70]

cau•ter•ant (kô′tər ənt), *Med.* —*n.* **1.** a caustic agent. —*adj.* **2.** caustic. [1535–45; CAUTER(IZE) + -ANT]

cau•ter•ize (kô′tə rīz′), *v.t.,* **-ized, -iz•ing.** to burn with a hot iron, electric current, fire, or a caustic, esp. for curative purposes; treat with a cautery. Also, *esp. Brit.,* **cau′ter•ise′.** [1350–1400; ME < LL *cautērizāre* to brand, equiv. to *cautēr-* (< Gk *kautḗr* branding iron, equiv. to *kau-,* var. s. of *kaíein* to burn (cf. CAUSTIC), + *-tēr* agent suffix) + *-izāre* -IZE] —**cau′ter•i•za′tion,** *n.*

cau•ter•y (kô′tə rē), *n., pl.* **-ter•ies. 1.** an escharotic substance, electric current, or hot iron used to destroy tissue. **2.** the process of destroying tissue with a cautery. [1350–1400; ME < L *cautērium* < Gk *kautḗrion,* equiv. to *kautḗr* branding iron (see CAUTERIZE) + *-ion* dim. suffix]

cau•tion (kô′shən), *n.* **1.** alertness and prudence in a hazardous situation; care; wariness: *Landslides ahead—proceed with caution.* **2.** a warning against danger or evil; anything serving as a warning: *By way of caution, he told me the difficulties I would face.* **3.** *Informal.* a person or thing that astonishes or causes mild apprehension: *She's a caution. The way he challenges your remarks is a caution.* —*v.t.* **4.** to give warning to; advise or urge to take heed. —*v.i.* **5.** to warn or advise: *The newspapers caution against overoptimism.* [1250–1300; ME *caucion* < L *cautiōn-* (s. of *cautiō*) a taking care, equiv. to *caut(us),* ptp. of *cavēre* to guard against (*cautake care, guard* + *-tus* ptp. suffix) + *-iōn-* -ION] —**cau′tion•er,** *n.*

—**Syn. 1.** circumspection, discretion, watchfulness, heed, vigilance. **2.** admonition, advice, counsel. **4.** admonish, forewarn. See **warn.** —**Ant. 1.** carelessness.

cau•tion•ar•y (kô′shə ner′ē), *adj.* of the nature of or containing a warning: *cautionary advice; a cautionary tale.* [1590–1600; CAUTION + -ARY]

cau•tious (kô′shəs), *adj.* showing, using, or characterized by caution: *a cautious man; To be cautious is often to show wisdom.* [1630–40; CAUTI(ON) + -OUS] —**cau′•tious•ly,** *adv.* —**cau′tious•ness,** *n.*

—**Syn.** prudent, guarded, wary, chary, circumspect, watchful, vigilant. See **careful.**

Cau•ver•y (kô′və rē), *n.* a river in S India, flowing SE from the Western Ghats in Mysore state through Madras state to the Bay of Bengal: sacred to the Hindus. 475 mi. (765 km) long. Also, **Kaveri.**

cav., 1. cavalier. **2.** cavalry. **3.** cavity.

ça va (SA VA′), *French.* all right; fine. [lit., that goes]

ca•vae•di•um (kə vē′dē əm, kä-, kā-), *n., pl.* **-di•a** (-dē ə). atrium (def. 1a). [< L, contr. of *cavum aedium,* lit., hollow of rooms (i.e. house); see CAVE, EDIFICE]

Ca•va•fy (kä vä′fē), *n.* **Constantine** (*Konstantinos Kavafis*), 1863–1933, Greek poet in Egypt.

cav•al•cade (kav′əl kād′, kav′əl kād′), *n.* **1.** a procession of persons riding on horses, in horsedrawn carriages, in cars, etc. **2.** any procession. **3.** any noteworthy series, as of events or activities. [1585–95; < MF < early It *cavalcata* horseback raid, equiv. to *cavalc(are)* to ride on horseback (< LL *caballicāre,* equiv. to *caball(us)* horse (see CAVALIER) + *-icā-* v. suffix + *-re* inf. ending) + *-ata* -ADE[1]]

—**Syn. 2.** parade, retinue.

cav•a•lier (kav′ə lēr′, kav′ə lēr′), *n.* **1.** a horseman, esp. a mounted soldier; knight. **2.** one having the spirit or bearing of a knight; a courtly gentleman; gallant. **3.** a man escorting a woman or acting as her partner in dancing. **4.** (*cap.*) an adherent of Charles I of England in his contest with Parliament. —*adj.* **5.** haughty, disdainful, or supercilious: *an arrogant and cavalier attitude toward others.* **6.** offhand or unceremonious: *The very dignified officials were confused by his cavalier manner.* **7.** (*cap.*) of or pertaining to the Cavaliers. **8.** (*cap.*) of, pertaining to, or characteristic of the Cavalier poets or their work. —*v.i.* **9.** to play the cavalier. **10.** to be haughty or domineering. [1590–1600; < MF: horseman, knight < OIt *cavaliere* < OPr < LL *caballārius* man on horseback, equiv. to L *caball(us)* horse (cf. CAPERCAILLIE) + *-ārius*

-ARY] —**cav′a·lier′ism, cav′a·lier′ness,** *n.* —**cav′a·lier′ly,** *adv.*
—**Syn. 5.** indifferent, offhand, uncaring, thoughtless, condescending.

Ca·va·lie·ri (kav′əl yâr′ē; *It.* kä′vä lye′rē), *n.* **Fran·ces·co Bo·na·ven·tu·ra** (frän ches′kô bô′nä ven to͞o′rä), 1598–1697, Italian mathematician.

cav′alier King′ Charles′ span′iel, one of a breed of small dogs developed from the English toy spaniel, having a long silky coat, usually white with chestnut markings, with fringes of longer hair on the ears, legs, tail, and feet.

Cav′alier po′ets, a group of English poets, including Herrick, Carew, Lovelace, and Suckling, mainly at the court of Charles I. [1875–80]

ca·va·lier ser·ven·te (kä′vä lyer′ ser ven′te), *pl.* ***ca·va·lie·ri ser·ven·ti*** (kä′vä lye′rē ser ven′tē). *Italian.* a lover; suitor. [lit., serving cavalier]

ca·val·la (kə val′ə, -vī′ə), *n., pl.* **-las,** (*esp. collectively*) **-la.** See **king mackerel.** [< Sp *caballa,* fem. deriv. of *caballo* horse < L *caballus* (see CAPERCAILLIE); for a parallel E use of "horse" for a fish, see REDHORSE]

Ca·val·le·ri·a Rus·ti·ca·na (kav′ə lə rē′ə rus′ti-kan′ə, ro͞os′-; *It.* käv′äl le rē′ä ro͞os′tē kä′nä), an opera (1890) by Pietro Mascagni.

cav·al·ry (kav′əl rē), *n., pl.* **-ries. 1.** *Mil.* **a.** the part of a military force composed of troops that serve on horseback. **b.** mounted soldiers collectively. **c.** the motorized, armored units of a military force organized for maximum mobility. **2.** horsemen, horses, etc., collectively. [1585–95; syncopated var. of *cavallery* < It *cavalleria,* deriv. of *cavaliere* CAVALIER]

cav·al·ry·man (kav′əl rē mən, -man′), *n., pl.* **-men** (-mən, -men′). a soldier in the cavalry. [1855–60; CAVALRY + MAN[1]]

cav′alry twill′, a strong cotton, wool, or worsted fabric constructed in double twill, used for apparel. Also called **tricotine.** [1940–45]

Cav·an (kav′ən), *n.* **1.** a county in Ulster, in the N Republic of Ireland. 53,763; 730 sq. mi. (1890 sq. km). **2.** the seat of this county. 3219.

ca·vate (kā′vāt), *adj.* hollowed out, as a space excavated from rock: *cavate cliff dwellings.* [1725–35; < L *cavātus* made hollow (ptp.), equiv. to *cav(āre)* to hollow + *-ātus* -ATE[1]]

ca·va·ti·na (kav′ə tē′nə; *It.* kä′vä tē′nä), *n., pl.* **-ne** (-nā; *It.* -ne). *Music.* a simple song or melody, properly one without a second part or a repeat; an air. [1830–40; < It, equiv. to *cavat(a)* song (lit., something drawn out, n. use of fem. of *cavata* < L *cavātus* hollowed out, hollow; see CAVE, -ATE[1]) + *-ina* -INE[1]]

cave (kāv), *n., v.,* **caved, cav·ing.** —*n.* **1.** a hollow in the earth, esp. one opening more or less horizontally into a hill, mountain, etc. **2.** a storage cellar, esp. for wine. **3.** *Eng. Hist.* a secession, or a group of seceders, from a political party on some special question. —*v.t.* **4.** to hollow out. **5.** *Mining.* **a.** to cause (overlying material) to fall into a stope, sublevel, or the like. **b.** to cause (supports, as stulls or sets) to collapse beneath overlying material. **c.** to fill (a stope or the like) with caved-in material: *sub-level caving.* —*v.i.* **6.** to cave in. **7. cave in, a.** to fall in; collapse. **b.** to cause to fall in or collapse. **c.** *Informal.* to yield; submit; surrender: *The opposition caved in before our superior arguments.* [1175–1225; ME < OF < LL *cava* (fem. sing.), L *cava,* neut. pl. of *cavum* hole, n. use of neut. of *cavus* hollow] —**cave′like′,** *adj.*

cave′ art′, paintings and engravings on the walls of caves and rock-shelters, esp. naturalistic depictions of animals, produced by Upper Paleolithic peoples of western Europe between about 28,000 and 10,000 years ago. [1920–25]

ca·ve·at (kav′ē ät′, -at′, kä′vē-, kā-), *n.* **1.** a warning or caution; admonition. **2.** *Law.* a legal notice to a court or public officer to suspend a certain proceeding until the notifier is given a hearing: *a caveat filed against the probate of a will.* [< L: let him beware, 3rd person sing. pres. subj. of *cavēre* to take care; see CAUTION]

ca·ve·at emp·tor (kav′ē ät′ emp′tôr, -at′, kä′vē-, kā-; *Lat.* kä′we ät′ emp′tōr). let the buyer beware: the principle that the seller of a product cannot be held responsible for its quality unless it is guaranteed in a warranty. [1515–25; < L]

ca·ve·a·tor (kav′ē ā′tər, -at′ər, kä′vē-, kä′vē ā′tər), *n. Law.* a person who files or enters a caveat. [1880–85; CAVEAT + -OR[2]]

cave′ bear′, an extinct bear, *Ursus spelaeus,* that lived in caves in Europe during the Pleistocene Epoch.

ca·ve ca·nem (kä′we kä′nem; *Eng.* kā′vē kā′nəm, kā′vä), *Latin.* beware of the dog.

cave′ crick′et, any of several nocturnal, wingless, cricketlike long-horned grasshoppers of the family Gryllacrididae, characterized by a humpbacked appearance and inhabiting dark moist habitats, as caves, cellars, hollow trees, and the ground under logs and stones. Also called **camel cricket.**

cave′ dwell′er, 1. a person whose home is a cave. **2.** a prehistoric person who lived in caves. **3.** *Facetious.* a person who lives in an apartment building or the like in a large city. [1860–65]

cave·fish (kāv′fish′), *n., pl.* (*esp. collectively*) **-fish,** (*esp. referring to two or more kinds or species*) **-fish·es.** any of several fishes that live in cave waters, as species of the genus *Amblyopsis,* having no body pigment and rudimentary, functionless eyes. [1870–75; CAVE + FISH]

cave-in (kāv′in′), *n.* **1.** a collapse, as of anything hollow: *the worst cave-in in the history of mining.* **2.** a place or site of such a collapse. **3.** submission to something or someone previously opposed or resisted: *His cave-in to such unreasonable demands shocked us.* [1700–10; n. use of v. phrase *cave in*]

Cav·ell (kav′əl), *n.* **Edith Louisa,** 1865–1915, English nurse: executed by the Germans in World War I.

cave′ man′, 1. a cave dweller, esp. of the Stone Age. **2.** a man who behaves in a rough, primitive manner, esp. toward women. [1860–65]

cav·en·dish (kav′ən dish), *n.* tobacco that has been softened, sweetened, and pressed into cakes. [1830–40; presumably named after maker or handler]

Cav·en·dish (kav′ən dish), *n.* **1. Henry,** 1731–1810, English chemist and physicist. **2. William, 4th Duke of Devonshire,** 1720–64, British statesman: prime minister 1756–57.

Cav′endish exper′iment, *Physics.* the experiment, conducted by Henry Cavendish, that determined the constant of gravitation by using a torsion balance and measuring the torsion produced by two masses placed at given distances from the masses on the balance.

cav·er (kā′vər), *n.* a person who studies or explores caves. [1645–55; CAVE + -ER[1]]

cav·ern (kav′ərn), *n.* **1.** a cave, esp. one that is large and mostly underground. **2.** *Pathol.* a cavity that is produced by disease, esp. one produced in the lungs by tuberculosis. —*v.t.* **3.** to enclose in or as if in a cavern. **4.** to hollow out to form a cavern. [1325–75; ME *caverne* < L *caverna,* equiv. to *cav(us)* hollow + *-erna,* as in *cisterna* CISTERN]

cav·er·nic·o·lous (kav′ər nik′ə ləs), *adj.* living in caverns or caves, as certain animals. [1885–90; CAVERN + -I- + -COLOUS]

cav·ern·ous (kav′ər nəs), *adj.* **1.** being, resembling, or suggestive of a cavern: *a vast, cavernous room.* **2.** deep-set: *cavernous eyes.* **3.** hollow and deep-sounding: *a cavernous voice.* **4.** containing caverns. **5.** full of small cavities; porous. [1350–1400; ME < L *cavernōsus.* See CAVERN, -OUS] —**cav′ern·ous·ly,** *adv.*

cav·es·son (kav′ə sən), *n.* the noseband of a bridle or a halter. [1590–1600; < It *cavezzone* noseband halter, equiv. to *cavezz(a)* halter (< Gmc; cf. OE *cælf* halter, muzzle) + *-one* aug. suffix]

ca·vet·to (kə vet′ō; *It.* kä vet′tô), *n., pl.* **-ti** (-tē), **-tos.** *Archit.* a concave molding the outline of which is a quarter circle. See illus. under **molding.** [1670–80; < It, equiv. to *cav(o)* (< L *cavus* or *cavum* hollow place; see CAVE) + *-etto* -ET]

cav·i·ar (kav′ē är′, kav′ē är′), *n.* the roe of sturgeon, esp. the beluga, or other fish, usually served as an hors d'oeuvre or appetizer. Also, **cav′i·are′.** [1585–95; appar. back formation from *caviarie* (taken, perh. rightly, as *caviar* + pl. ending, L or It *-i*), of uncert. orig.; cf. It *caviaro,* Turk *havyar*]

cav·i·corn (kav′i kôrn′), *adj. Zool.* hollow-horned, as the ruminants with true horns, as distinguished from bony antlers. [< NL *cavicornis* hollow-horned, equiv. to *cavi-* (comb. form of L *cavus* hollow) + *cornis* (L *corn(ū)* horn + *-is* adj. suffix)]

cav·il (kav′əl), *v.,* **-iled, -il·ing** or (*esp. Brit.*) **-illed, -il·ling,** *n.* —*v.i.* **1.** to raise irritating and trivial objections; find fault with unnecessarily (usually fol. by *at* or *about*): *He finds something to cavil at in everything I say.* —*v.t.* **2.** to oppose by inconsequential, frivolous, or sham objections: *to cavil each item of a proposed agenda.* —*n.* **3.** a trivial and annoying objection. **4.** the raising of such objections. [1540–50; < L *cavillāri* to jeer, scoff, quibble, v. deriv. of *cavilla* jesting, banter] —**cav′il·er;** *esp. Brit.,* **cav′il·ler,** *n.* —**cav′il·ing·ly;** *esp. Brit.,* **cav′il·ling·ly,** *adv.*
—**Syn. 1.** carp, complain, criticize.

Cav·ill (kav′əl), *n.* **1. Frederick,** 1839–1927, Australian swimmer and coach, born in England: developed the Australian crawl. **2.** his son **Sydney St. Leonards** (len′ərdz), died 1945, Australian-American swimmer and coach: developed the butterfly stroke.

cav·ing (kā′ving), *n.* spelunking. [1865–70; CAVE[1] + -ING[1]]

cav·i·tar·y (kav′i ter′ē), *adj. Anat., Pathol.* of, pertaining to, or characterized by a cavity or cavities. [1825–35; CAVIT(Y) + -ARY]

cav·i·ta·tion (kav′i tā′shən), *n.* **1.** the rapid formation and collapse of vapor pockets in a flowing liquid in regions of very low pressure, a frequent cause of structural damage to propellers, pumps, etc. **2.** such a pocket formed in a flowing liquid. [1890–95; CAVIT(Y) + -ATION]

Ca·vi·te (kä vē′te, kə-), *n.* a seaport on W central Luzon, in the N Philippines, on Manila Bay: naval base. 87,666.

cav·i·ty (kav′i tē), *n., pl.* **-ties. 1.** any hollow place; hollow. **2.** *Anat.* a hollow space within the body, an organ, a bone, etc. **3.** a hollow space or a pit in a tooth, most commonly produced by caries. A cavity may be artificially made to support dental restorations. [1535–45; < MF *cavite* < LL *cavitās* hollowness, equiv. to L *cav(us)* hollow + *-itās* -ITY] —**cav′i·tied,** *adj.*
—**Syn. 1.** See **hole.**

cav′ity res′onator, *Electronics.* See under **resonator** (def. 4a).

cav′ity wall′, *Masonry.* a wall built with an enclosed inner space to prevent penetration by water. [1905–10]

ca·vo-re·lie·vo (kä′vō ri lē′vō, kā′-), *n., pl.* **-vos.** *Fine Arts.* **1.** a form of relief sculpture in which the volumes are carved or incised so that the highest points are below or level with the original surface. Cf. **intaglio** (defs. 1–3). **2.** a piece of sculpture in this form. Also called **sunk relief.** [< It *cavo-rilievo* hollow relief. See CAVE, RELIEF]

ca·vort (kə vôrt′), *v.i.* **1.** to prance or caper about. **2.** to behave in a high-spirited, festive manner; make merry. [1785–95, *Amer.*; earlier *cavault,* perh. CUR(VET) + VAULT[2]] —**ca·vort′er,** *n.*

Ca·vour (kä vo͞or′), *n.* **Ca·mil·lo Ben·so di** (kä mēl′lô ben′sô dē), 1810–61, Italian statesman: leader in the unification of Italy.

ca·vy (kā′vē), *n., pl.* **-vies.** any of several short-tailed or tailless South American rodents of the family Caviidae, as the guinea pig, capybara, or agouti. [1790–1800; < NL *Cavia* name of the genus < Carib (Galibi) *cabiai*]

caw (kô), *n.* **1.** the harsh, grating cry of the crow, raven, etc. —*v.i.* **2.** to utter this cry or a similar sound. [1580–90; imit.]

Cawn·pore (kôn′pôr′, -pōr′), *n.* former name of **Kanpur.** Also, **Cawn·pur** (kôn′po͝or′).

Ca·xi·as (kä shē′əs), *n.* a city in NE Brazil. 124,403.

Caxi′as do Sul′ (do͝o so͞ol′), a city in S Brazil. 107,487.

C-ax·is (sē′ak′sis), *n., pl.* **C-ax·es** (sē′ak′sēz). *Crystall.* the vertical crystallographic axis. Cf. **A-axis, B-axis.**

Cax·ton (kak′stən), *n.* **1. William,** 1422?–91, English printer, translator, and author: established first printing press in England 1476. **2.** *Bibliog.* any one of the books printed by Caxton, all of which are in black letter. **3.** *Print.* a kind of type imitating Caxton's black letter. —**Cax·to·ni·an** (kak stō′nē ən), *adj.*

cay (kā, kē), *n.* a small low island; key. [1700–10; < Sp *cayo;* see KEY[2]]

Cay·ce (kā′sē), *n.* a town in central South Carolina. 11,701.

cay·enne (kī en′, kā-), *n.* **1.** a hot, biting condiment composed of the ground pods and seeds of the pepper *Capsicum annuum longum.* **2.** the long, wrinkled, twisted fruit of this plant. **3.** the plant itself. Also called **cayenne′ pep′per.** [1750–60; short for *cayenne pepper,* formerly *cayan* < Tupi *kyinha,* but long associated with CAYENNE] —**cay·enned′,** *adj.*

Cay·enne (kī en′, kā-), *n.* **1.** a seaport in and the capital of French Guiana. 19,668. **2.** (*l.c.*) Also called **cayenne′ whist′.** a variety of whist played with two full packs of 52 cards each.

Cayes (kā), *n.* **Les.** See **Les Cayes.**

Ca·ye·y (kä ye′ē), *n.* a city in central Puerto Rico. 23,305.

Cay·ley (kā′lē), *n.* **Arthur,** 1821–95, English mathematician.

cay·man (kā′mən), *n., pl.* **-mans.** caiman.

Cay′man Is′lands (kā′man′, -mən), three islands in the West Indies, NW of Jamaica: a British crown colony. 10,249; 104 sq. mi. (269 sq. km).

Ca·yu·ga (kā yo͞o′gə, kī-), *n., pl.* **-gas,** (*esp. collectively*) **-ga. 1.** a member of a tribe of North American Indians, the smallest tribe of the Iroquois Confederacy. **2.** the dialect of the Seneca language spoken by the Cayuga. **3.** Also called **Cayu′ga duck′.** one of an American breed of domestic ducks having black plumage. [1735–45, *Amer.*; < Cayuga **kayo·kwę,* name of a 17th-century village; cf. Cayuga *kayokwęhó·nǫʔ* Cayuga (people) (or < a related form in another N Iroquoian language)]

Cayu′ga Lake′, a lake in central New York: one of the Finger Lakes. 40 mi. (64 km) long.

cay·use (kī yo͞os′, kī′o͞os), *n.* **1.** *Western U.S.* a horse, esp. an Indian pony. **2.** Also called **cayuse′ wind′.** *Northwestern U.S.* a cold wind blowing from the east. [1830–40, *Amer.*; named after the CAYUSE]

Cay·use (kī yo͞os′, kī′o͞os), *n., pl.* **-us·es,** (*esp. collectively*) **-use.** a member of a tribe of North American Indians now living in Oregon.

CB, 1. See **Citizens Band. 2.** *Mil.* construction battalion. **3.** See **continental breakfast.** [1960–65]

Cb, *Symbol, Chem.* columbium.

C.B., 1. Bachelor of Surgery. [< L *Chirurgiae Baccalaureus*] **2.** *Brit.* Companion of the Bath.

CBAT, College Board Achievement Test.

C battery, *Electronics.* an electric battery for supplying a constant voltage bias to a control electrode of a vacuum tube. Cf. **A battery, B battery.**

CBC, 1. Also, **C.B.C.** Canadian Broadcasting Corporation. **2.** *Med.* complete blood count.

C.B.D., 1. cash before delivery. **2.** central business district.

C.B.E., Commander of the Order of the British Empire.

C.B.E.L., Cambridge Bibliography of English Literature. Also, **CBEL**

CBer (sē′bē′ər), *n. Informal.* **1.** a person who owns and operates a CB radio. **2.** an enthusiast or devotee of CB radio. Also, **CB′er.** [1960–65; CB + -ER[1]]

C-bi·as (sē′bī′əs), *n. Electronics.* See **grid bias.**

CBing (sē′bē′ing), *n. Informal.* the operating of a CB radio. [CB + -ING[1]]

CBO, Congressional Budget Office.

CB radio, 1. a device that transmits and receives radio signals only within a designated band of frequencies. Cf. **Citizens Band. 2.** a system of private radio communication built around such a device.

CBT, Chicago Board of Trade.

CBW, chemical and biological warfare.

CC, *Symbol.* a quality rating for a corporate or municipal bond, lower than CCC and higher than C.

Cc, cirrocumulus.

cc, 1. See **carbon copy** (def. 1). **2.** copies. **3.** cubic centimeter.

cc., 1. See **carbon copy** (def. 1). **2.** chapters. **3.** copies. **4.** cubic centimeter. Also, **c.c.**

C.C., 1. See **carbon copy** (def. 1). **2.** cashier's check. **3.** chief clerk. **4.** circuit court. **5.** city council. **6.** city councilor. **7.** civil court. **8.** company commander. **9.**

CONCISE PRONUNCIATION KEY: act, cāpe, dâre, pärt; set, ēqual; if, īce; ox, ōver, ôrder, oil, bo͝ok, bo͞ot, out; up, ûrge; child; sing; shoe; thin, *th*at; zh as in *treasure.* ə = *a* as in *alone, e* as in *system, i* as in *easily, o* as in *gallop, u* as in *circus;* ᵊ as in *fire* (fīᵊr), *hour* (ouᵊr). l and n can serve as syllabic consonants, as in *cradle* (krād′l), and *button* (but′n). See the full key inside the front cover.

county clerk. **10.** county commissioner. **11.** county council. **12.** county court. Also, **c.c.**

C.C.A., **1.** Chief Clerk of the Admiralty. **2.** Circuit Court of Appeals. **3.** County Court of Appeals.

CCC, **1.** Civilian Conservation Corps: the former U.S. federal agency (1933–1943), organized to utilize the nation's unemployed youth by building roads, improving parks, etc. **2.** Commodity Credit Corporation.

CCC, *Symbol.* a quality rating for a corporate or municipal bond, lower than B and higher than CC.

CCD, **1.** *Electronics.* See **charge-coupled device.** **2.** Confraternity of Christian Doctrine.

C.C.I.A., Consumer Credit Insurance Association.

CCK, cholecystokinin.

C-clamp (sē′klamp′), *n.* a C-shaped clamp having a screw that is threaded through one tip in the direction of the other tip. See illus. under **clamp.**

C clef, *Music.* a clef that, according to its position, locates middle C on the first, third, or fourth line of the staff.

C.Cls., Court of Claims.

CCP, Chinese Communist Party.

C.C.P., **1.** *Law.* Code of Civil Procedure. **2.** Court of Common Pleas.

CCR, Commission on Civil Rights.

CCTV, closed-circuit television.

CCU, See **coronary-care unit.**

ccw, counterclockwise.

CD, **1.** See **certificate of deposit.** **2.** Civil Defense. **3.** Community Development. **4.** See **compact disk.**

Cd, *Symbol, Chem.* cadmium.

cd, **1.** candela; candelas. **2.** Also, **cd.** cord; cords.

C/D, See **certificate of deposit.** Also, **c/d**

C.D., **1.** See **certificate of deposit.** **2.** Civil Defense. **3.** civil disobedience. **4.** Congressional District.

c.d., cash discount.

CDC, Centers for Disease Control.

CD-I, compact disk-interactive. Also, **CD/I, CD I**

cDNA, complementary DNA: a DNA molecule that is complementary to a specific messenger RNA. [1985–90]

CD player. See **compact disk player.**

Cdr., Commander. Also, **CDR**

CD-ROM (sē′dē′rom′), *n.* a compact disk on which a large amount of digitized read-only data can be stored. Cf. **ROM.** [*c*(*ompact*) *d*(*isk*) *r*(*ead-*)*o*(*nly*) *m*(*emory*)]

CD single, a compact disk, usually three inches in diameter, containing one or two popular songs.

CDT, Central daylight time. Also, **C.D.T.**

Ce, *Symbol, Chem.* cerium.

-ce, a multiplicative suffix occurring in *once, twice, thrice.* [ME, OE *-es* adv. suffix, orig. gen. sing. ending; see *-s*[1]]

C.E., **1.** Chemical Engineer. **2.** chief engineer. **3.** Church of England. **4.** Civil Engineer. **5.** common era. **6.** Corps of Engineers.

c.e., **1.** buyer's risk. [< L *cāveat emptor* may the buyer beware] **2.** compass error.

CEA, See **Council of Economic Advisers.**

ce·a·no·thus (sē′ə nō′thəs), *n., pl.* **-thus·es.** any North American shrub or small tree of the largely western genus *Ceanothus,* having clusters of small white or blue flowers. [< NL (Linnaeus) < Gk *keánōthos* a species of thistle]

Ce·a·rá (*Port.* se′ä Rä′), *n.* Fortaleza.

cease (sēs), *v.,* **ceased, ceas·ing,** *n.* —*v.i.* **1.** to stop; discontinue: *Not all medieval beliefs have ceased to exist.* **2.** to come to an end: *At last the war has ceased.* **3.** *Obs.* to pass away; die out. —*v.t.* **4.** to put a stop or end to; discontinue: *He begged them to cease their quarreling.* —*n.* **5.** cessation: *The noise of the drilling went on for hours without cease.* [1250–1300; ME *ces(s)en* < OF *cesser* < L *cessāre* to leave off, equiv. to *cess(us)* (ptp. of *cēdere* to withdraw, go; *ced-* go + *-tus* ptp. suffix) + *-ā-* thematic vowel + *-re* inf. ending; see CEDE]
—**Syn.** **2.** terminate, end, culminate.

cease′-and-de·sist′ or′der (sēs′ən di zist′, -sist′), an order by a government agency to a person or corporation to terminate a business practice found by the agency to be illegal or unfair. [1925–30]

cease-fire (sēs′fīr′), *n.* **1.** a cessation of hostilities; truce. **2.** *Mil.* an order issued for a cease-fire. [1840–50; n. use of v. phrase *cease fire*]

cease·less (sēs′lis), *adj.* without stop or pause; unending; incessant. [1580–90; CEASE + -LESS] —**cease′less·ly,** *adv.* —**cease′less·ness,** *n.*
—**Syn.** endless, continuous, constant, unceasing.

Ceau·şes·cu (chou shes′ko͞o), *n.* **Ni·co·lae** (nē′kô lī′), 1918–89, Rumanian political leader: president 1967–89.

Ce·bú (se bo͞o′), *n.* **1.** an island in the S central Philippines. 2,091,602; 1703 sq. mi. (4411 sq. km). **2.** a seaport on this island. 490,281.

CONCISE ETYMOLOGY KEY: <, descended or borrowed from; >, whence; b., blend of, blended; c., cognate with; cf., compare; deriv., derivative; equiv., equivalent; imit., imitative; obl., oblique; r., replacing; s., stem; sp., spelling, spelled; resp., respelling, respelled; trans., translation; ?, origin unknown; *, unattested; ‡, probably earlier than. See the full key inside the front cover.

CEC, Commodity Exchange Commission.

Čech·y (che′ḵē), *n.* Czech name of **Bohemia.**

ce·ci (chech′ē), *n.pl.* chickpeas. Also called **ce′ci beans′.** [< It, pl. of *cece* < L *cicer;* cf. CHICKPEA]

Cec·il (ses′əl, sis′- *or, for 5,* sē′səl), *n.* **1. (Edgar Algernon) Robert** (*1st Viscount Cecil of Chelwood*), 1864–1958, British statesman: Nobel peace prize 1937. **2. Robert** (*1st Earl of Salisbury* and *1st Viscount Cecil of Cranborne*), 1563–1612, British statesman (son of William Cecil). **3. Robert Arthur Talbot Gascoyne-.** See **Salisbury** (def. 1). **4. William** (*1st Baron Burghley* or *Burleigh*), 1520–98, British statesman: adviser to Elizabeth I. **5.** a male given name: from a Latin word meaning "blind."

Ce·cile (si sēl′), *n.* a female given name, form of **Cecilia.**

Ce·cil·ia (si sēl′yə), *n.* **1. Saint,** died A.D. 230?, Roman martyr: patron saint of music. **2.** Also, **Ce·cil′lia.** a female given name: from a Latin word meaning "blind."

Cec·i·ly (ses′ə lē), *n.* a female given name, form of **Cecilia.**

Ce·cro′pi·a moth′ (si krō′pē ə), (*sometimes l.c.*) a large North American silkworm moth, *Hyalophora cecropia,* the larvae of which feed on the foliage of forest and other trees. Also called **Ce·cro′pi·a.** [1865–70, *Amer.;* < NL *Cecropia* name of the genus, L: fem. of *Cecropius* pertaining to *Cecrops,* legendary ruler of Attica]

ce·cum (sē′kəm), *n., pl.* **-ca** (-kə). *Anat., Zool.* a cul-de-sac, esp. that in which the large intestine begins. Also, **caecum.** [1715–25; short for L *intestinum caecum* blind gut] —**ce′cal,** *adj.* —**ce′cal·ly,** *adv.*

CED, Committee for Economic Development.

ce·dant ar·ma to·gae (kā′dänt äʀ′mä tō′gī; *Eng.* sē′dant är′mə tō′jē). *Latin.* let military power be subject to civil authority: motto of Wyoming. [lit., let arms yield to the toga]

ce·dar (sē′dər), *n.* **1.** any of several Old World, coniferous trees of the genus *Cedrus,* having wide, spreading branches. Cf. **cedar of Lebanon.** **2.** any of various junipers, as the red cedar, *Juniperus virginiana,* of the cypress family, having reddish-brown bark and dark-blue, berrylike fruit. **3.** any of various other coniferous trees. Cf. **incense cedar, white cedar.** **4.** any of several trees belonging to the genus *Cedrela,* of the mahogany family. **5.** Also called **cedarwood.** the fragrant wood of any of these trees, used in furniture and as a moth repellent. [bef. 1000; ME *cedir,* OE *ceder* < L *cedrus* < Gk *kédros;* r. ME *cedre* < OF < L, as above]

ce′dar ap′ple, a brown gall on the branches of the juniper, produced by several rust fungi of the genus *Gymnosporangium.* [1840–50, *Amer.*]

ce′dar chest′, a chest made of or lined with cedar, used to store clothing, blankets, etc., esp. for protection against moths. [1765–75, *Amer.*]

Ce′dar Cit′y, a town in SW Utah. 10,972.

Ce′dar Falls′, a city in central Iowa. 36,322.

ce·darn (sē′dərn), *adj. Archaic.* resembling or made of cedar. [1625–35; CEDAR + -(E)N[2]]

ce′dar of Leb′anon, a cedar, *Cedrus libani,* of Asia Minor, having horizontally spreading branches. [bef. 1000; ME, OE]

Ce′dar Rap′ids, a city in E Iowa. 110,243.

ce′dar robe′, *Dial.* a cedar chest or cedar-lined wardrobe. [1965–70]

ce′dar wax′wing, a North American waxwing, *Bombycilla cedrorum,* having light yellowish-brown plumage. Also called **ce′dar bird′.** [1835–45, *Amer.*]

cedar waxwing,
Bombycilla cedrorum,
length 7 in. (18 cm)

ce·dar·wood (sē′dər wo͝od′), *n.* cedar (def. 5). [1605–15; CEDAR + WOOD[1]]

ce′darwood oil′, an aromatic oil obtained from the wood of the red cedar and used in the manufacture of soaps, perfumes, and insecticides.

cede (sēd), *v.t.,* **ced·ed, ced·ing.** to yield or formally surrender to another: *to cede territory.* [1625–35; < L *cēdere* to go, yield] —**ced′er,** *n.*
—**Syn.** relinquish, abandon; grant, transfer, convey.

ce·di (sā′dē), *n., pl.* **-di, -dis.** a paper money and monetary unit of Ghana, equal to 100 pesewas.

ce·dil·la (si dil′ə), *n.* **1.** a mark (̧) placed under a consonant letter, as under *c* in French, in Portuguese, and formerly in Spanish, to indicate that it is pronounced (s), under *c* and *s* in Turkish to indicate that they are pronounced, respectively, (ch) and (sh), or under *t* and *s* in Rumanian to indicate that they are pronounced, respectively, (ts) and (sh). **2.** this mark used as a diacritic of arbitrary value in transliteration of words from non-Roman into Roman alphabetic characters. [1590–1600; < Sp. var. sp. of *zedilla* little *z,* equiv. to *zed(a)* ZED + *-illa* dim. suffix; the mark was so called from its original form]

Ced·ric (sed′rik, sē′drik), *n.* a male given name.

cee (sē), *n.* **1.** the letter *C.* —*adj.* **2.** shaped or formed like the letter *C.* [1535–45; conventional spelling of the pronunciation of the letter *C*]

CEEB, College Entrance Examination Board.

C.E.F., Canadian Expeditionary Force.

cef·a·clor (sef′ə klôr′, -klōr′), *n. Pharm.* a cephalosporin antibiotic, $C_{15}H_{14}ClN_3O_4$, used in the treatment of infections. [resp. of CEPHA(LOSPORIN) + CHLOR(INE)]

ce·fox·i·tin (sə fok′si tin), *n. Pharm.* a broad-spectrum, crystalline, semisynthetic cephalosporin antibiotic, $C_{16}H_{17}N_3O_7$, used in the treatment of serious infections caused by susceptible Gram-positive and Gram-negative bacteria. [*cef-* (see CEFACLOR) + OX- + *-itin,* of unclear derivation]

cei·ba (sā′bə *or, for 2,* sī′-; *Sp.* thā′vä, sā′-), *n., pl.* **-bas** (-bəz; *Sp.* -väs). **1.** the silk-cotton tree, *Ceiba pentandra.* **2.** silk cotton; kapok. [1805–15; < Sp < Taino *ceyba* or its cognate in another Arawakan language]

ceil (sēl), *v.t.* **1.** to overlay (the ceiling of a building or room) with wood, plaster, etc. **2.** to provide with a ceiling. [1400–50; late ME *celen* to cover, to panel < ?]

cei·lidh (kā′lē), *n. Irish, Scot., and Canadian* (*chiefly Prince Edward Island*). a party, gathering, or the like, at which singing and storytelling are the usual forms of entertainment. [< Ir *céilidhe,* ScotGael *cèilidh,* MIr *céilide,* deriv. of OIr *céile* companion]

ceil·ing (sē′ling), *n.* **1.** the overhead interior surface of a room. **2.** the top limit imposed by law on the amount of money that can be charged or spent or the quantity of goods that can be produced or sold. **3.** *Aeron.* **a.** the maximum altitude from which the earth can be seen on a particular day, usually equal to the distance between the earth and the base of the lowest cloud bank. **b.** Also called **absolute ceiling.** the maximum altitude at which a particular aircraft can operate under specified conditions. **4.** *Meteorol.* the height above ground level of the lowest layer of clouds that cover more than half of the sky. **5.** a lining applied for structural reasons to a framework, esp. in the interior surfaces of a ship or boat. **6.** Also called **ceil′ing piece′.** *Theat.* the ceiling or top of an interior set, made of cloth, a flat, or two or more flats hinged together. **7.** the act or work of a person who makes or finishes a ceiling. **8.** vaulting, as in a medieval church. **9. hit the ceiling,** *Informal.* to become enraged: *When he saw the amount of the bill, he hit the ceiling.* [1350–1400, for def. 7; ME; see CEIL, -ING[1]] —**ceil′inged,** *adj.*

ceil·om·e·ter (sē lom′i tər, si-), *n.* an automatic device for measuring and recording the height of clouds by projecting a modulated beam of light onto a cloud base, receiving the reflection of light through a photoelectric apparatus, and computing the height by triangulation. [1940–45; CEIL(ING) + -O- + -METER]

cein·ture (san to͝or′, -tyo͝or′, san′chər; *Fr.* saɴ tʏʀ′), *n., pl.* **-tures** (-to͝orz′, -tyo͝orz′, -chərz; *Fr.* -tʏʀ′). cincture (defs. 1, 2). [< F; OF *ceingture* < L *cinctūra;* see CINCTURE]

cel (sel), *n.* a transparent celluloid sheet on which a character, scene, etc., is drawn or painted and which constitutes one frame in the filming of an animated cartoon: may be overlapped for change of background or foreground. Also, **cell.** [by shortening of CELLULOID]

Ce·la (the′lä), *n.* **Ca·mi·lo Jo·sé** (kä mē′lô hô se′), born 1916, Spanish writer.

cel·a·don (sel′ə don′, -dn), *n.* **1.** any of several Chinese porcelains having a translucent, pale green glaze. **2.** any porcelain imitating these. **3.** a pale gray-green. —*adj.* **4.** having the color celadon. [1760–70; named after *Céladon,* name of a character in *L'Astrée,* a tale by H. d'Urfé (1568–1625), French writer]

Ce·lae·no (sə lē′nō), *n.* **1.** *Class. Myth.* a Pleiad. **2.** *Astron.* one of the six visible stars of the Pleiades.

cel·an·dine (sel′ən dīn′, -dēn′), *n.* **1.** Also called **greater celandine, swallowwort.** an Old World plant, *Chelidonium majus,* of the poppy family, having yellow flowers. **2.** Also called **lesser celandine.** an Old World plant, *Ranunculus ficaria,* of the buttercup family, having fleshy, heart-shaped leaves and solitary yellow flowers. [1275–1325; ME *selandyne,* var. of *celydon* < L *chelīdonia* greater celandine, *chelīdonium* lesser celandine < Gk *chelidónion,* deriv. of *chelidṓn* swallow; said to be so called because it blooms when the swallows return in spring]

cel′andine pop′py, a poppy, *Stylophorum diphyllum,* of the east-central U.S., having one pair of deeply lobed leaves and yellow flowers. [1855–60, *Amer.*]

Cel·a·nese (sel′ə nēz′, sel′ə nēz′), *Trademark.* a brand name for an acetate rayon yarn or fabric.

cel·a·ture (sel′ə cho͝or′), *n.* the art of embossing metal. [1375–1425; late ME < L *caelātūra* art of engraving, equiv. to *caelāt(us)* (ptp. of *caelāre* to engrave) + *-ūra* -URE]

-cele[1], a combining form meaning "tumor," used in the formation of compound words: *variocele.* [comb. form repr. Gk *kḗlē* a tumor; akin to OE *hēala* hydrocele]

-cele[2], var. of **-coele:** *blastocele.*

ce·leb (sə leb′), *n. Slang.* a celebrity. [1910–15; by shortening]

Cel·e·bes (sel′ə bēz′, sə lē′bēz; *Du.* se lā′bes), *n.* former name of **Sulawesi.** —**Cel·e·be·sian** (sel′ə bē′zhən), *adj.*

Cel′ebes Sea′, an arm of the Pacific Ocean, N of Sulawesi and S of the Philippines.

cel·e·brant (sel′ə brənt), *n.* **1.** a participant in any celebration. **2.** the officiating priest in the celebration of the Eucharist. **3.** a participant in a public religious rite. [1830–40; < L *celebrant-* (s. of *celebrāns* prp. of *celebrāre* to solemnize, celebrate), equiv. to *celebr-* (see CELEBRATE) + *-ant-* -ANT]

cel·e·brate (sel′ə brāt′), *v.,* **-brat·ed, -brat·ing.** —*v.t.* **1.** to observe (a day) or commemorate (an event) with ceremonies or festivities: *to celebrate Christmas; to celebrate the success of a new play.* **2.** to make known publicly; proclaim: *The newspaper celebrated the end of the war in red headlines.* **3.** to praise widely or to present

to widespread and favorable public notice, as through newspapers or novels: *a novel celebrating the joys of marriage; the countryside celebrated in the novels of Hardy.* **4.** to perform with appropriate rites and ceremonies; solemnize: *to celebrate a marriage.* —*v.i.* **5.** to observe a day or commemorate an event with ceremonies or festivities. **6.** to perform a religious ceremony, esp. Mass or the Lord's Supper. **7.** to have or participate in a party, drinking spree, or uninhibited good time: *You look like you were up celebrating all night.* [1425–75; late ME < L *celebrātus* ptp. of *celebrāre* to solemnize, celebrate, honor, equiv. to *celebr-* (s. of *celeber*) often repeated, famous + *-ātus* -ATE¹] —**cel′e•bra′tive,** *adj.* —**cel′e•bra′tor, cel′e•brat′er,** *n.* —**cel•e•bra•to•ry** (sel′ə brə tôr′ē, -tōr′ē, sə leb′rə-), *adj.*
—**Syn. 1.** honor, solemnize. **3.** laud, glorify, honor.

cel•e•brat•ed (sel′ə brā′tid), *adj.* renowned; well-known: *the celebrated authors of best-selling books.* [CELEBRATE + -ED²] —**cel′e•brat′ed•ness,** *n.*
—**Syn.** illustrious. See **famous.**

Cel′ebrated Jump′ing Frog′ of Cal•a•ver′as Coun′ty, The (kal′ə ver′əs), a short story (1865) by Mark Twain.

cel•e•bra•tion (sel′ə brā′shən), *n.* **1.** an act of celebrating. **2.** the festivities engaged in to celebrate something. [1520–30; < L *celebrātiōn-* (s. of *celebrātiō*) big assembly. See CELEBRATE, -ION]

ce•leb•ri•ty (sə leb′ri tē), *n., pl.* **-ties** for 1. **1.** a famous or well-known person. **2.** fame; renown. [1350–1400; ME < L *celebritās* multitude, fame, festal celebration, equiv. to *celebr-* (s. of *celeber*) often repeated, famous + *-itās* -ITY]
—**Syn. 2.** distinction, note, eminence, stardom.

ce•leb•u•tante (sə leb′yŏŏ tänt′), *n.* a person seeking the limelight through association with celebrities. [1985–90; b. CELEBRITY and DEBUTANTE]

ce•ler•i•ac (sə ler′ē ak′, -lēr′-), *n.* a variety of celery, *Apium graveolens rapaceum,* of the parsley family, having a large, edible, turniplike root. Also called **knob celery, turnip-rooted celery.** [1735–45; CELERY + -AC]

ce•ler•i•ty (sə ler′i tē), *n.* swiftness; speed. [1480–90; earlier *celerite* < MF < L *celeritās,* equiv. to *celer* swift + *-itās* -ITY]
—**Syn.** alacrity, dispatch, briskness. See **speed.**

cel•er•y (sel′ə rē, sel′rē), *n.* a plant, *Apium graveolens,* of the parsley family, whose leafstalks are eaten raw or cooked. [1655–65; < F *céleri* < It *seleri,* pl. of *selero* << Gk *sélinon* parsley]

cel′ery cab′bage. See **Chinese cabbage.** [1925–30]

cel′ery salt′, a seasoning of finely ground celery seed and salt. [1895–1900]

ce•les•ta (sə les′tə), *n.* a musical instrument consisting principally of a set of graduated steel plates struck with hammers that are activated by a keyboard. [1895–1900; < F *célesta,* for *céleste,* lit., heavenly (see CELESTIAL); the *-a* for *-e* makes the name pseudo-It]

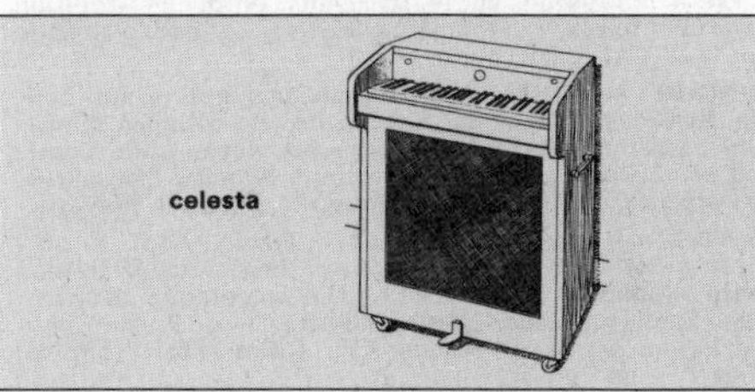
celesta

Ce•leste (sə lest′), *n.* a female given name: from a Latin word meaning "heavenly."

ce•les•tial (sə les′chəl), *adj.* **1.** pertaining to the sky or visible heaven. **2.** pertaining to the spiritual or invisible heaven; heavenly; divine: *celestial bliss.* **3.** of or pertaining to celestial navigation: *a celestial fix.* **4.** (*cap.*) of or pertaining to the former Chinese Empire or the Chinese people. —*n.* **5.** an inhabitant of heaven. **6.** (*cap.*) a citizen of the Celestial Empire. [1350–1400; ME < ML *cēlestiālis,* equiv. to L *caelesti(s)* heavenly (*cael(um)* heaven, sky + *-estis* adj. suffix) + *-ālis* -AL¹] —**ce•les′tial•ly,** *adv.* —**ce•les′tial•ness, ce•les•ti•al•i•ty** (sə les′chē al′i tē), *n.*

Celes′tial Cit′y, 1. the goal of Christian's journey in Bunyan's *Pilgrim's Progress;* the heavenly Jerusalem. **2.** See **New Jerusalem.**

Celes′tial Em′pire, the former Chinese Empire. [1815–25]

celes′tial equa′tor, *Astron., Navig.* the great circle of the celestial sphere, lying in the same plane as the earth's equator. Also called **equator, equinoctial, equinoctial circle, equinoctial line.** [1870–75]

celes′tial globe′. See under **globe** (def. 3). [1755–65]

celes′tial guid′ance, a guidance system for an aeronautical or space vehicle by which an automatic device in the vehicle takes periodic fixes on celestial bodies to determine the vehicle's position and to guide it along a particular flight path. Also called **astro-inertial guidance.** Cf. **celestial navigation, command guidance, inertial guidance.**

celes′tial hi′erarchy, hierarchy (def. 6). [1880–85]

celes′tial hori′zon, *Astron.* See under **horizon** (def. 2b). [1895–1900]

celes′tial lat′itude, *Astron.* the angular distance from the ecliptic of a point on the celestial sphere.

celes′tial lon′gitude, *Astron.* the angular distance of a point on the celestial sphere from the great circle that is perpendicular to the ecliptic at the point of the vernal equinox, measured through 360° eastward parallel to the ecliptic.

celes′tial mar′riage, the rite or state of marriage, performed in a Mormon temple by the Church of Jesus Christ of Latter-day Saints and believed to continue beyond death. [1920–25]

celes′tial mechan′ics, the branch of astronomy that deals with the application of the laws of dynamics and Newton's law of gravitation to the motions of heavenly bodies. [1815–25]

celes′tial naviga′tion, navigation by means of observations made of the apparent position of heavenly bodies. Also called **astronavigation, celo-navigation.** [1935–40]

celes′tial pole′, *Astron.* each of the two points in which the extended axis of the earth cuts the celestial sphere and about which the stars seem to revolve. Also called **pole.** [1900–05]

celes′tial sphere′, the imaginary spherical shell formed by the sky, usually represented as an infinite sphere, the center of which is a given observer's position. [1875–80]

Cel•es•tine I (sel′ə stīn′, si les′tin, -tīn), **Saint,** died A.D. 432, Italian ecclesiastic: pope 422–432.

Celestine II, (*Guido di Castello*), fl. 12th century, Italian ecclesiastic: pope 1143–44.

Celestine III, (*Giacinto Bobone*), died 1198, Italian ecclesiastic: pope 1191–98.

Celestine IV, (*Godfrey Castiglione*), died 1241, Italian ecclesiastic: pope 1241.

Celestine V, Saint (*Pietro di Murrone* or *Morone*), 1215–96, Italian ascetic: pope 1294.

cel•es•tite (sel′ə stīt′), *n.* a white to pale-blue mineral, strontium sulfate, $SrSO_4$, occurring in tabular crystals, the principal ore of strontium. Also, **cel•es•tine** (sel′i stin, -stīn′). [1850–55; *celest(ine)* celestite (< G *Zölestin* < L *coelest(is),* var. of *caelestis* CELESTIAL + G *-in* -IN²) + -ITE¹]

Cel•ia (sēl′yə), *n.* a female given name, form of **Cecilia.**

ce•li•ac (sē′lē ak′), *adj. Anat.* of, pertaining to, or located in the cavity of the abdomen. Also, **coeliac.** [1655–65; < L *coeliacus* < Gk *koiliakós* of the bowels, equiv. to *koilí(a)* bowels (deriv. of *koîlos* hollow; see COEL-) + *-akos* -AC]

ce′liac disease′, a hereditary digestive disorder involving intolerance to gluten, usually occurring in young children, characterized by marked abdominal distention, malnutrition, wasting, and the passage of large, fatty, malodorous stools. Also called **ce•li•ac-sprue** (sē′lē ak-sprōō′). [1935–40]

ce′liac plex′us, *Anat.* See **solar plexus** (def. 1). [1830–40]

cel•i•ba•cy (sel′ə bə sē), *n.* **1.** abstention from sexual relations. **2.** abstention by vow from marriage: *the celibacy of priests.* **3.** the state of being unmarried. [1655–65; < L *caelibā(tus)* celibacy (*caelib-,* s. of *caelebs* single + *-ātus* -ATE³) + -CY] —**cel•i•bat•ic** (sel′ə bat′ik), *adj.*

cel•i•bate (sel′ə bit, -bāt′), *n.* **1.** a person who abstains from sexual relations. **2.** a person who remains unmarried, esp. for religious reasons. —*adj.* **3.** observing or pertaining to sexual abstention or a religious vow not to marry. **4.** not married. [1605–15; < L *caelib-* (s. of *caelebs*) unmarried + -ATE¹]

Cé•line (sā lēn′), *n.* **Louis-Fer•di•nand** (lwē fer dē-näN′), (*Louis F. Destouches*), 1894–1961, French novelist and physician.

ce•li•o•scope (sē′lē ə skōp′), *n. Med.* celoscope. —**ce•li•os•co•py** (sē′lē os′kə pē), *n.*

ce•li•ot•o•my (sē′lē ot′ə mē), *n., pl.* **-mies.** *Surg.* laparotomy (def. 2). [< Gk *koilí(a)* bowels (see CELIAC + -O- + -TOMY]

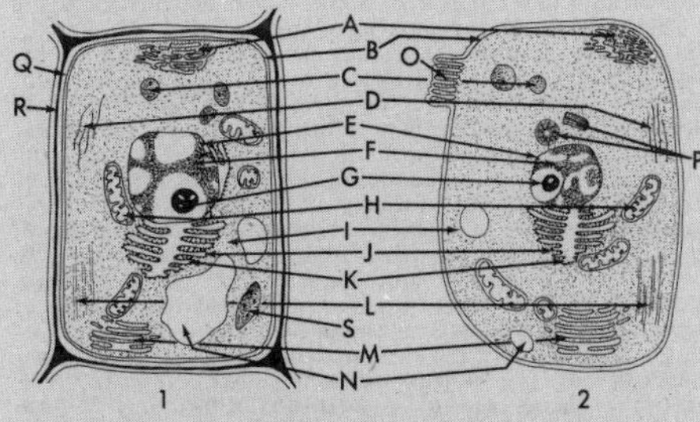

cells (def. 4)
1, plant cell; 2, animal cell:
A, smooth endoplasmic reticulum; B, cell membrane; C, lysosome; D, microfibril; E, nuclear envelope; F, chromatin; G, nucleolus; H, mitochondrion; I, cytoplasm; J, ribosome; K, rough endoplasmic reticulum; L, microtubule; M, Golgi body; N, vacuole; O, microvilli; P, centrioles; Q, cell wall; R, lamella; S, chloroplast

cell¹ (sel), *n.* **1.** a small room, as in a convent or prison. **2.** any of various small compartments or bounded areas forming part of a whole. **3.** a small group acting as a unit within a larger organization: *a local cell of the Communist party.* **4.** *Biol.* a usually microscopic structure containing nuclear and cytoplasmic material enclosed by a semipermeable membrane and, in plants, a cell wall; the basic structural unit of all organisms. **5.** *Entomol.* one of the areas into which the wing of an insect is divided by the veins. **6.** *Bot.* locule. **7.** *Elect.* **a.** Also called **battery, electric cell, galvanic cell, voltaic cell.** a device that generates electrical energy from chemical energy, usually consisting of two different conducting substances placed in an electrolyte. Cf. **dry cell. b.** See **solar cell. 8.** Also called **electrolytic cell.** *Physical Chem.* a device for producing electrolysis, consisting essentially of the electrolyte, its container, and the electrodes. **9.** *Aeron.* the gas container of a balloon. **10.** *Eccles.* a monastery or nunnery, usually small, dependent on a larger religious house. **11.** *Telecommunications.* See under **cellular phone.** —*v.i.* **12.** to live in a cell: *The two prisoners had celled together for three years.* [bef. 1150; 1665–75 for def. 4; ME *celle* < OF *celle* < ML *cella* monastic cell, L: room (see CELLA); OE *cell* < ML, as above; see CELLA] —**cell′-like′,** *adj.*

cell² (sel) *n.* cel.

cel•la (sel′ə), *n., pl.* **cel•lae** (sel′ē). *Archit.* **1.** the principal enclosed chamber of a classical temple. **2.** the entire central structure of a classical temple. Also called **naos.** [1670–80; < L: storeroom, shrine, akin to *cēlāre* to hide; see CONCEAL]

cel•lar (sel′ər), *n.* **1.** a room, or set of rooms, for the storage of food, fuel, etc., wholly or partly underground and usually beneath a building. **2.** an underground room or story. **3.** See **wine cellar. 4.** *Sports.* the lowest position in a group ranked in order of games won: *The team was in the cellar for most of the season.* —*v.t.* **5.** to place or store in a cellar. [1175–1225; ME *celer* < AF < L *cellārium* storeroom, equiv. to *cell(a)* CELL¹ + *-ārium* -ARY; later resp. to reflect L form; see -ER², -AR²]

cel•lar•age (sel′ər ij), *n.* **1.** cellar space. **2.** charges for storage in a cellar. [1505–15; CELLAR + -AGE]

cel•lar•et (sel′ə ret′), *n.* a compartment, cabinet, or stand fitted for wine bottles. Also, **cel′lar•ette′.** [1800–10; CELLAR + -ET]

cel′lar fun′gus, a fungus, *Coniophora puteana,* that causes dry rot in timber.

cel•lar•man (sel′ər mən), *n., pl.* **-men.** a person who is in charge of the alcoholic-beverage supply of a hotel or restaurant. [1650–60; CELLAR + -MAN]

cel•lar•mas•ter (sel′ər mas′tər, -mä′stər), *n.* a person in charge of a wine cellar. [CELLAR + MASTER]

cel′lar sash′, a window sash of relatively small size, having two or three panes horizontally arranged.

cell′ biol′ogy, the branch of biology dealing with the study of cells, esp. their formation, structure, components, and function.

cell•block (sel′blok′), *n.* a unit of a prison consisting of a number of cells. [CELL¹ + BLOCK]

cell′ bod′y, *Biol.* the compact area of a nerve cell that constitutes the nucleus and surrounding cytoplasm, excluding the axons and dendrites. Also called **perikaryon.** [1875–80]

cell′ cy′cle, the cycle of growth and asexual reproduction of a cell, consisting of interphase followed in actively dividing cells by prophase, metaphase, anaphase, and telophase. [1970–75]

cell′ divi′sion, *Biol.* the division of a cell in reproduction or growth. [1880–85]

celled (seld), *adj.* having a cell or cells (often used in combination): *The ameba is a single-celled animal.* [1640–50; CELL¹ + -ED³]

cell′ fu′sion, *Biol.* the merging of two or more cells into a single cell. [1970–75]

cell•house (sel′hous′), *n.* a prison building containing separate cells, each usually intended for one or two prisoners. [1930–35; CELL¹ + HOUSE]

Cel•li•ni (chə lē′nē; *It.* chel lē′nē), *n.* **Ben•ve•nu•to** (ben′və nōō′tō, -nyōō′-; *It.* ben′ve nōō′tō), 1500–71, Italian, metalsmith, sculptor, and autobiographer.

Celli′ni's ha′lo, heiligenschein. [named after Benvenuto CELLINI, who described the effect]

cel•list (chel′ist), *n.* a person who plays the cello. [1885–90; short for VIOLONCELLIST]

cell′ line′, *Cell Biol.* a perpetuating strain of cells in laboratory culture. [1950–55]

cell•mate (sel′māt′), *n.* a fellow inmate in a prison cell. [CELL¹ + MATE¹]

cell′-me•di•at•ed immu′nity (sel′mē′dē ā′tid), *Immunol.* immunity independent of antibody but dependent on the recognition of antigen by T cells and their subsequent destruction of cells bearing the antigen or on the secretion by T cells of lymphokines that enhance the ability of phagocytes to eliminate the antigen. Also called **cellular immunity.** Cf. **antibody-mediated immunity.** [1970–75]

cell′ mem′brane, *Biol.* the semipermeable membrane enclosing the cytoplasm of a cell. [1865–70]

cel•lo¹ (chel′ō), *n., pl.* **-los.** the second largest member of the violin family, rested vertically on the floor between the performer's knees when being played. Also called **violoncello.** [1875–80; short for VIOLONCELLO]

cello

CONCISE PRONUNCIATION KEY: act, cāpe, dâre, pärt; set, ēqual; *if,* īce; ox, ōver, ôrder, oil, bŏŏk, bōōt, out; up, ûrge; child; sing; shoe; thin, *th*at; zh as in *treasure.* ə = *a* as in *alone, e* as in *system, i* as in *easily, o* as in *gallop, u* as in *circus;* ᵊ as in *fire* (fīᵊr), *hour* (ouᵊr). l and n can serve as syllabic consonants, as in *cradle* (krād′l), and *button* (but′n). See the full key inside the front cover.

cel·lo[2] (sel′ō), *n., adj. Informal.* cellophane. [by shortening]

cel·lo·bi·ose (sel′ō bī′ōs), *n.* a white, crystalline, water-soluble disaccharide, $C_{12}H_{22}O_{11}$, that is obtained by the breakdown of cellulose or lichenin and yields glucose upon hydrolysis: used chiefly in bacteriology as a reagent. [1900–05; CELL(ULOSE) + -O- + BI-[2] + -OSE[2]]

cel·loi·din (sə loi′din), *n.* a concentrated form of pyroxylin used to embed tissues for cutting and microscopic examination. [1880–85; CELL(ULOSE) + -OID + -IN[2]]

cel·lo·phane (sel′ə fān′), *n.* **1.** a transparent, paperlike product of viscose, impervious to moisture, germs, etc., used to wrap and package food, tobacco, etc. —*adj.* **2.** of, made of, or resembling cellophane. [1910–15; formerly trademark]

Cel·lo·solve (sel′ə solv′), *Chem., Trademark.* a brand name for any of a group of industrial solvents consisting of ethers of ethylene glycol and their derivatives.

cell′ pack′, a container made of cellular plastic, as one used for holding flowers or plants.

cell′ plate′, (in plant cells) a plate that develops at the midpoint between the two groups of chromosomes in a dividing cell and that is involved in forming the wall between the two new daughter cells. [1880–85]

cell′ sap′, the watery fluid within the central vacuole of a plant cell. [1885–90]

cell′ the′ory, a basic tenet of modern biology, first stated by Matthias Schleiden and Theodor Schwann in 1838–39, that cells are the basic units of structure and function in living organisms.

cel·lu·lar (sel′yə lər), *adj.* **1.** pertaining to or characterized by cellules or cells, esp. minute compartments or cavities. **2.** of or pertaining to cellular phones. [1745–55; < NL *cellulāris,* equiv. to *cellul(a)* live cell (L: little room; see CELLULE) + *-āris* -AR[1]] —**cel′lu·lar′i·ty,** *n.* —**cel′lu·lar·ly,** *adv.*

cel′lular immu′nity. See **cell-mediated immunity.**

cel′lular phone′, a mobile telephone system using low-powered radio transmitters, with each transmitter covering a distinct geographical area **(cell),** and computer equipment to switch a call from one area to another, thus enabling large-scale car or portable phone service. Also called **cel′lular mo′bile ra′dio, cel′lular tel′ephone, mobile phone.**

cel′lular respira′tion, *Physiol.* the oxidation of organic compounds that occurs within cells, producing energy for cellular processes.

cel·lu·lase (sel′yə lās′, -lāz′), *n. Biochem.* any of several enzymes, produced primarily by fungi and bacteria, that catalyze the hydrolysis of cellulose. [1900–05; CELLUL(OSE) + -ASE]

cel·lu·late (*adj.* sel′yə lit, -lāt′; *v.* sel′yə lāt′), *adj., v.,* **-lat·ed, -lat·ing.** —*adj.* **1.** cellular. —*v.t.* **2.** to form into cells. [1685–95; < NL *cellul(a)* (see CELLULAR) + -ATE[1]] —**cel′lu·la′tion,** *n.*

cel·lule (sel′yo͞ol), *n.* a minute cell. [1645–55; < L *cellula* small room. See CELL[1], -ULE]

cel·lu·lite (sel′yə līt′, -lēt′), *n.* (not in technical use) lumpy fat deposits, esp. in the thighs and buttocks. [1970–75; < F: formation of fatty deposits under the skin, orig., cellulitis, equiv. to *cellule* cell (see CELLULE) + *-ite* -ITIS, taken in E as -ITE[1]]

cel·lu·li·tis (sel′yə lī′tis), *n. Pathol.* inflammation of cellular tissue. [1860–65; < NL, equiv. to *cellul(a)* (see CELLULAR) + *-itis* -ITIS]

cel·lu·loid (sel′yə loid′), *n.* **1.** a tough, highly flammable substance consisting essentially of cellulose nitrate and camphor, used in the manufacture of motion-picture and x-ray film and other products. **2.** motion-picture film. —*adj.* **3.** *Informal.* of or involving motion pictures. [former trademark; CELLUL(OSE) + -OID]

cel·lu·lo·lyt·ic (sel′yə lō lit′ik), *adj. Biochem.* (of bacteria or enzymes) capable of hydrolyzing cellulose. [1940–45; CELLUL(OSE) + -O- + -LYTIC]

cel·lu·lose (sel′yə lōs′), *n.* an inert carbohydrate, $(C_6H_{10}O_5)_n$, the chief constituent of the cell walls of plants and of wood, cotton, hemp, paper, etc. [1745–55; < NL *cellul(a)* live cell (see CELLULAR) + -OSE[2]] —**cel·lu·los·i·ty** (sel′yə los′i tē), *n.*

cel′lulose ac′etate, any of a group of acetic esters of cellulose, used to make yarns, textiles, nonflammable photographic films, rubber and celluloid substitutes, etc. [1890–95]

cel′lulose gum′, carboxymethylcellulose.

cel′lulose ni′trate, any of a group of nitric esters of cellulose, used in the manufacture of lacquers and explosives. Also called **nitrocellulose, nitrocotton.** [1890–95]

cel′lulose triac′etate, a triacetic ester of cellulose characterized by its resistance to most solvents, used chiefly in the manufacture of textile fibers.

cel·lu·lo·sic (sel′yə lō′sik), —*adj.* **1.** of, containing, or derived from cellulose. —*n.* **2.** any cellulosic compound or substance. [1880–85; CELLULOSE + -IC]

cell′ wall′, *Biol.* the definite boundary or wall that is part of the outer structure of certain cells, as a plant cell. See diag. under **cell.** [1840–50]

ce·lom (sē′ləm), *n., pl.* **ce·loms, ce·lo·ma·ta** (si lō′mə tə). coelom.

ce·lo·nav·i·ga·tion (sē′lō nav′i gā′shən, sel′ō-), *n.* See **celestial navigation.** [CEL(ESTIAL) + -O- + NAVIGATION]

ce·lo·scope (sē′lə skōp′), *n. Med.* an instrument for examining a body cavity. Also, **celioscope, coeloscope.** [< Gk *koîlo(s)* hollow or *koîlo(n)* a hollow + -SCOPE]

ce·lo·sia (si lō′zhə, -zhē ə), *n.* any plant of the genus *Celosia,* having small, usually red or yellowish flowers in dense, crested or plumelike spikes. Cf. **cockscomb** (def. 3). [< NL (Linnaeus), appar. an irreg. deriv. of Gk *kéleos* burning, from the burnt appearance of the flowers of some species; see -IA]

Cel·o·tex (sel′ə teks′), *Trademark.* a brand of board made of cane fiber, used for insulation or as a vapor barrier, siding, or layer under a roof.

Cels., Celsius.

Cel·si·us (sel′sē əs, -shē-), *adj.* **1.** Also, **Centigrade.** pertaining to or noting a temperature scale **(Cel′sius scale′)** in which 0° represents the ice point and 100° the steam point. *Symbol:* C See illus. under **thermometer. 2.** *Thermodynam.* of or pertaining to a temperature scale having the same units as the Celsius scale but in which the zero point has been shifted so that the triple point of water has the exact value 0.01°; Celsius temperatures are computed from Kelvin values by subtracting 273.15 from the latter. *Symbol:* C Cf. **Kelvin** (def. 3). [named after Anders *Celsius* (1701–44), Swedish astronomer who devised the scale]

celt (selt), *n. Archaeol.* an ax of stone or metal without perforations or grooves, for hafting. [1705–15; < LL **celtis* chisel, found only in the abl. case *celte* (Vulgate, Job XIX, 24)]

Celt (kelt, selt), *n.* a member of an Indo-European people now represented chiefly by the Irish, Gaels, Welsh, and Bretons. Also, **Kelt.** [1695–1705; < L *Celtae* (pl.); in Gk *Keltoí* (pl.)]

Celt, Celtic (def. 1).

Celt., Celtic.

Celt·ic (kel′tik, sel′-), *n.* **1.** a branch of the Indo-European family of languages, including esp. Irish, Scots Gaelic, Welsh, and Breton, which survive now in Ireland, the Scottish Highlands, Wales, and Brittany. *Abbr.:* Celt —*adj.* **2.** of the Celts or their languages. Also, **Keltic.** [1600–10; < L *Celticus,* equiv. to *Celt(ae)* the Celts (see CELT) + *-icus* -IC] —**Celt′i·cal·ly,** *adv.*

Celt′ic cross′, a cross shaped like a Latin cross and having a ring that intersects each segment of the shaft and crossbar at a point equidistant from their junction. See illus. under **cross.** [1870–75]

Celt·i·cism (kel′tə siz′əm, sel′-), *n.* a Celtic custom or usage. [1850–55; CELTIC + -ISM]

Celto-, a combining form of **Celt** or **Celtic:** *Celto-Iberian.*

Cel·to-Ger·man·ic (kel′tō jər man′ik, sel′-), *adj.* **1.** having the characteristics of both the Celtic and Germanic peoples. **2.** pertaining to or designating a style of art developed in northern and western Europe from about the 5th to 9th centuries A.D., chiefly characterized by the use of recognizable human or animal motifs elaborated into complex interlaced patterns. Also, **Celt′ic-German′ic.**

cel·tuce (sel′tis), *n.* a variety of lettuce, *Lactuca sativa asparagina,* having characteristics of both celery and lettuce, and eaten raw or cooked. [b. CELERY and LETTUCE]

cel·ure (sel′yər), *n.* an ornamented canopy, as for a bed or dais. [1300–50; ME, equiv. to *cel(en)* to drape (see CEIL) + -URE]

CEMA, Council for Economic Mutual Assistance.

cem·ba·lo (chem′bə lō′), *n., pl.* **-li** (-lē′), **-los.** *Music.* harpsichord. [1795–1805; < It *(clavi)cembalo* < L *cymbalum* CYMBAL]

ce·ment (si ment′), *n.* **1.** any of various calcined mixtures of clay and limestone, usually mixed with water and sand, gravel, etc., to form concrete, that are used as a building material. **2.** any of various soft, sticky substances that dry hard or stonelike, used esp. for mending broken objects or for making things adhere. **3.** *Petrog.* the compact groundmass surrounding and binding together the fragments of clastic rocks. **4.** anything that binds or unites: *Time is the cement of friendship.* **5.** *Dentistry.* **a.** a hardening, adhesive, plastic substance, used in the repair of teeth for anchoring fillings or inlays, for filling, or for fastening crowns. **b.** *Informal.* cementum. —*v.t.* **6.** to unite by or as if by cement: *to cement stones to form a wall; to cement a relationship.* **7.** to coat or cover with cement: *to cement a floor.* —*v.i.* **8.** to become cemented; join together or unite; cohere. [1250–1300; < L *cēmentum,* var. of *caementum* (sing. of *caementa* unprocessed cuttings from the quarry, i.e., rough stone and chips) < **caed-mentom,* equiv. to *caed(ere)* to cut + *-mentum* -MENT; r. ME *cyment* < OF *ciment* < L, as above] —**ce·ment′a·ble,** *adj.* —**ce·ment′er,** *n.* —**ce·ment′less,** *adj.*
—**Syn. 6.** merge, join, bind, fuse, secure.

ce·men·ta·tion (sē′mən tā′shən, -men-, sem′ən-), *n.* **1.** the act, process, or result of cementing. **2.** *Metall.* the heating of two substances in contact in order to effect some change in one of them, esp., the formation of steel by heating iron in powdered charcoal. [1585–95; CEMENT + -ATION]

ce·ment·ite (si men′tīt), *n. Metall.* an iron carbide, Fe_3C, a constituent of steel and cast iron, sometimes with part of its iron replaced by another metal, as manganese. [1885–90; CEMENT + -ITE[1]]

ce·men·ti·tious (sē′mən tish′əs, -men-, sem′ən-), *adj.* having the properties of a cement. [1820–30; CEMENT + -ITIOUS]

cement′ mix′er, a machine having a revolving drum, often motor-driven, for mixing cement, sand, gravel, and water to produce concrete. Also called **concrete mixer.**

cement′ steel′, steel produced by the cementation of wrought iron or mild steel. Also called **converted steel.** [1880–85]

ce·men·tum (si men′təm), *n. Dentistry.* the bonelike tissue that forms the outer surface of the root of the tooth. See diag. under **tooth.** [1605–15; < L, var. of *caementum* rough stone; see CEMENT]

cem·e·te·ri·al (sem′i tēr′ē əl, -târ′-), *adj.* of or pertaining to a cemetery or to burial. [1600–10; CEMETERY + -IAL]

cem·e·ter·y (sem′i ter′ē), *n., pl.* **-ter·ies.** an area set apart for or containing graves, tombs, or funeral urns, esp. one that is not a churchyard; burial ground; graveyard. [1375–1425; late ME < LL *coemētērium* < Gk *koimētḗrion* a sleeping place, equiv. to *koimē-* (var. s. of *koimân* to put to sleep) + *-tērion* suffix of locality]

cen., **1.** central. **2.** century.

cen·a·cle (sen′ə kəl), *n.* the room where the Last Supper took place. [1375–1425; late ME < F *cénacle* < L *cēnāculum* top story, attic (orig., presumably, dining room), equiv. to *cēnā(re)* to dine (deriv. of *cēna* dinner) + *-culum* -CLE[2]]

Ce·nae·um (si nē′əm), *n.* (in ancient geography) a NW promontory of Euboea.

Cen·ci (chen′chē), *n.* **Be·a·tri·ce** (be′ä trē′che), 1577–1599, Italian parricide whose life is the subject of various novels and poems.

Cen·ci, The (chen′chē), a verse tragedy (1819) by Shelley.

cen·dal (sen′dl), *n.* sendal.

-cene, var. of **ceno-**[1] as final element of a compound word: *Pleistocene.*

ce·nes·the·sia (sē′nəs thē′zhə, -zhē ə, -zē ə, sen′əs-), *n. Psychol.* coenesthesia. Also, **ce·nes·the·sis** (sē′nis thē′sis, sen′is-).

Ce·nis (sə nē′), *n.* **Mont,** a mountain pass between SE France and Italy, in the Alps. 6834 ft. (2083 m) high.

ce·ni·zo (sə nē′zō, -sō), *n., pl.* **-zos.** chamiso.

ceno-[1], a combining form meaning "new," "recent," used in the formation of compound words: *cenogenesis.* Also, **caeno-, caino-.** [comb. form repr. Gk *kainós*]

ceno-[2], a combining form meaning "common," used in the formation of compound words: *cenobite.* Also, **coeno-.** [< Gk *koino-,* comb. form of *koinós*]

ce·no·bite (sē′nə bīt′, sen′ə-), *n.* a member of a religious order living in a convent or community. Also, **coenobite.** [1630–40; < LL *coenobīta,* equiv. to *coenob-* (< Gk *koinóbios* (adj.) conventual, living together, equiv. to *koino-* CENO-[2] + *bi-* BI-[2] + *-os* adj. suffix) + *-īta* -ITE[1]] —**ce·no·bit·ic** (sē′nə bit′ik, sen′ə-), **ce′no·bit′i·cal, ce·no·bi·an** (si nō′bē ən), *adj.* —**ce′no·bit′i·cal·ly,** *adv.* —**ce·no·bit·ism** (sē′nə bī′tiz əm, sen′ə-), *n.*

ce·no·spe·cies (sē′nə spē′shēz, -sēz, sen′ə-), *n., pl.* **-cies.** *Genetics.* a group of different species the individuals of which produce partially fertile hybrids when crossbred. [1920–25; CENO-[2] + SPECIES]

cen·o·taph (sen′ə taf′, -täf′), *n.* a sepulchral monument erected in memory of a deceased person whose body is buried elsewhere. [1595–1605; < L *cenotaphium* < Gk *kenotáphion,* equiv. to *kenó(s)* empty + *-taphion* (*táph(os)* tomb + *-ion* dim. suffix)] —**cen·o·taph·ic** (sen′ə taf′ik), *adj.*

ce·no·te (sə nō′tē), *n.* a deep natural well or sinkhole, esp. in Central America, formed by the collapse of surface limestone that exposes ground water underneath, and sometimes used by the ancient Mayans for sacrificial offerings. [1835–45; < MexSp < Yucatec Mayan]

Ce·no·zo·ic (sē′nə zō′ik, sen′ə-), *Geol.* —*adj.* **1.** noting or pertaining to the present era, beginning 65 million years ago and characterized by the ascendancy of mammals. See table under **geologic time.** —*n.* **2.** the Cenozoic Era or group of systems. Also, **Cainozoic.** [1850–55; CENO-[1] + ZO- + -IC]

cense (sens), *v.t.,* **censed, cens·ing.** to burn incense near or in front of; perfume with incense. [1300–50; ME, aph. var. of INCENSE[1]]

cen·ser (sen′sər), *n.* a container, usually covered, in which incense is burned, esp. during religious services; thurible. [1200–50; ME < AF, aph. var. of *ensenser* < ML *incensārium.* See INCENSE[1], -ER[2]]

censer

cen·sor (sen′sər), *n.* **1.** an official who examines books, plays, news reports, motion pictures, radio and television programs, letters, cablegrams, etc., for the purpose of suppressing parts deemed objectionable on moral, political, military, or other grounds. **2.** any person who supervises the manners or morality of others. **3.** an adverse critic; faultfinder. **4.** (in the ancient Roman republic) either of two officials who kept the register or census of the citizens, awarded public contracts, and supervised manners and morals. **5.** (in early Freudian dream theory) the force that represses ideas, impulses, and feelings, and prevents them from entering consciousness in their original, undisguised forms. —*v.t.* **6.** to examine and act upon as a censor. **7.** to delete (a word or passage of text) in one's capacity as a censor. [1525–35; < L *cēnsor,* equiv. to *cēns(ēre)* to give as one's opinion, recommend, assess + *-tor* -TOR; *-sor* for **-stor* by analogy with derivatives from dentals, as *tōnsor* barber (see TONSORIAL)] —**cen′sor·a·ble,** *adj.* —**cen·so·ri·al** (sen sôr′ē əl, -sōr′-), **cen·so′ri·an,** *adj.*

cen·so·ri·ous (sen sôr′ē əs, -sōr′-), *adj.* severely crit-

CONCISE ETYMOLOGY KEY: <, descended or borrowed from; >, whence; b., blend of, blended; c., cognate with; cf., compare; deriv., derivative; equiv., equivalent; imit., imitative; obl., oblique; r., replacing; s., stem; sp., spelling, spelled; resp., respelling, respelled; trans., translation; ?, origin unknown; *, unattested; ‡, probably earlier than. See the full key inside the front cover.

ical; faultfinding; carping. [1530–40; < L *cēnsōrius* of a censor, hence, austere, moral; see CENSOR, -TORY[1]] —**cen·so′ri·ous·ly,** *adv.* —**cen·so′ri·ous·ness,** *n.*

cen·sor·ship (sen′sər ship′), *n.* **1.** the act or practice of censoring. **2.** the office or power of a censor. **3.** the time during which a censor holds office. **4.** the inhibiting and distorting activity of the Freudian censor. [1585–95; CENSOR + -SHIP]

cen·sur·a·ble (sen′shər ə bəl), *adj.* deserving censure or blame. [1625–35; CENSURE + -ABLE] —**cen′sur·a·ble·ness, cen′sur·a·bil′i·ty,** *n.* —**cen′sur·a·bly,** *adv.*

cen·sure (sen′shər), *n., v.,* **-sured, -sur·ing.** —*n.* **1.** strong or vehement expression of disapproval: *The newspapers were unanimous in their censure of the tax proposal.* **2.** an official reprimand, as by a legislative body of one of its members. —*v.t.* **3.** to criticize or reproach in a harsh or vehement manner: *She is more to be pitied than censured.* —*v.i.* **4.** to give censure, adverse criticism, disapproval, or blame. [1350–1400; ME < L *cēnsūra* censor's office, assessment, equiv. to *cēns(us)* ptp. of *cēnsēre* (see CENSOR) + *-ūra* -URE] —**cen′sur·er,** *n.* —**cen′sure·less,** *adj.*
—**Syn. 1.** condemnation, reproof, reproach, reprehension, rebuke, reprimand, stricture, animadversion. See **abuse. 3.** reprove, rebuke, chide. See **blame, reprimand.** —**Ant. 1–3.** praise.

cen·sus (sen′səs), *n., pl.* **-sus·es,** *v.* —*n.* **1.** an official enumeration of the population, with details as to age, sex, occupation, etc. **2.** (in ancient Rome) the registration of citizens and their property, for purposes of taxation. —*v.t.* **3.** to take a census of (a country, city, etc.): *The entire nation is censused every 10 years.* [1605–15; < L: a listing and property assessment of citizens, equiv. to *cēns(ēre)* to assess, register (citizens) in a census + *-tus* suffix of v. action; for *-s-* in place of *-st-* see CENSOR] —**cen·su·al** (sen′sho͞o əl), *adj.*

cen′sus tak′er, a person who gathers information for a census. [1830–40, *Amer.*]

cen′sus tract′, a standard area in certain large American cities used by the U.S. Bureau of the Census for purposes of population enumeration.

cent (sent), *n.* **1.** a bronze coin of the U.S., the 100th part of a U.S. dollar: made of steel during part of 1943. *Symbol:* ¢ **2.** the 100th part of the monetary units of various other nations, including Australia, the Bahamas, Barbados, Belize, Bermuda, Canada, Ethiopia, Fiji, Guyana, Hong Kong, Jamaica, Kenya, Liberia, Mauritius, the Netherlands, New Zealand, the Seychelles, Sierra Leone, the Solomon Islands, Somalia, South Africa, Sri Lanka, Swaziland, Tanzania, Trinidad and Tobago, and Uganda. **3.** sen[3]. [1325–75; ME < L *centēsimus* hundredth (by shortening), equiv. to *cent(um)* 100 (see HUNDRED) + *-ēsimus* ordinal suffix]

cent-, var. of **centi-** before a vowel: *centare.*

cent., **1.** centigrade. **2.** central. **3.** centum. **4.** century.

cen·tal (sen′tl), *n.* **1.** hundredweight (def. 1). **2.** *Chiefly Brit.* a hundredweight of 112 lb. (50.8 kg). [1865–70; < L *cent(um)* 100 + (QUINT)AL]

cen·tare (sen′târ; *Fr.* säN TAR′), *n., pl.* **-tares** (-târz; *Fr.* -TAR′). centiare.

cen·tas (sen′täs), *n., pl.* **-tai** (-tī). a former bronze coin of Lithuania, the 100th part of a litas. [< Lith *centas,* ult. < E CENT]

cen·taur (sen′tôr), *n.* **1.** *Class. Myth.* one of a race of monsters having the head, trunk, and arms of a man, and the body and legs of a horse. **2.** (*cap.*) *Astron.* the constellation Centaurus. **3.** a skillful horseman or horsewoman. **4.** (*cap.*) *Rocketry.* a U.S. upper stage, with a restartable liquid-propellant engine, used with an Atlas or Titan booster to launch satellites and probes. [1325–75; ME, OE < L *centaurus* < Gk *kéntauros*] —**cen·tau′ri·al, cen·tau′ri·an, cen·tau′ric,** *adj.*

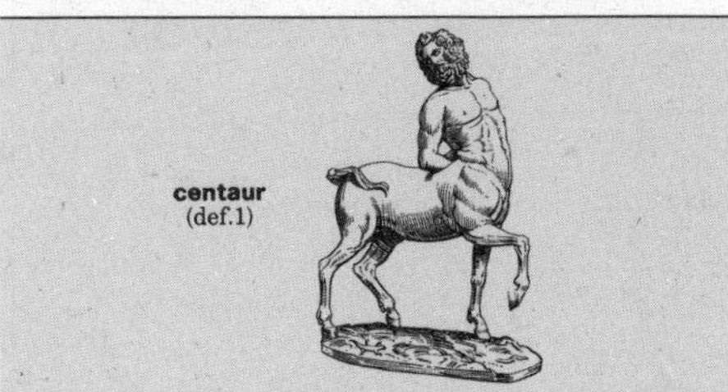
centaur (def.1)

cen·tau·re·a (sen tôr′ē ə), *n.* any of numerous composite plants of the genus *Centaurea,* having tubular flowers in a variety of colors. Cf. **cornflower** (def. 1), **knapweed.** [< NL (Linnaeus) by suffix change from ML *centauria;* see CENTAURY, -EA]

Cen·tau·rus (sen tôr′əs), *n., gen.* **-tau·ri** (-tôr′ī). *Astron.* the Centaur, a southern constellation between Lupus and Vela, containing the triple-star system Alpha Centauri. [< L; see CENTAUR]

cen·tau·ry (sen′tô rē), *n., pl.* **-ries. 1.** any of various plants belonging to the genus *Centaurium,* of the gentian family, having clusters of small pink or red flowers. **2.** any of several other plants of the genera *Centaurea* and *Sabatia.* [bef. 1000; ME, OE *centaurie* < ML *centauria,* appar. < Gk *kentaúria,* neut. pl. (taken in ML as fem. sing.) of *kentaúrion,* n. use of neut. of *kentaúrios* (adj.), equiv. to *kéntaur(os)* centaur + *-ios* adj. suffix; said to be in reference to the centaur Chiron, known for his knowledge of medicinal plants]

cen·ta·vo (sen tä′vō; *Sp.* sen tä′vô), *n., pl.* **-vos** (-vōz; *Sp.* -vôs). the 100th part of the monetary units of various nations, including Argentina, Bolivia, Brazil, Cape Verde, Chile, Colombia, Cuba, the Dominican Republic, Ecuador, El Salvador, Guatemala, Guinea-Bissau, Honduras, Mexico, Mozambique, Nicaragua, Peru, the Philippines, and Portugal. [1880–85; < Sp: the 100th part, equiv. to *cent-* 100 (see CENT) + *-avo* < L *-āvum* as in *octāvum* eighth; see OCTAVO]

cen·te·nar·i·an (sen′tn âr′ē ən), *adj.* **1.** pertaining to or having lived 100 years. —*n.* **2.** a person who has reached the age of 100. [1840–50; < L *centēnāri(us)* (see CENTENARY) + -AN]

cen·ten·ar·y (sen ten′ə rē, sen′tn er′ē; *esp. Brit.* sen tē′nə rē), *adj., n., pl.* **-ar·ies.** —*adj.* **1.** of or pertaining to a period of 100 years. **2.** recurring once in every 100 years: *a centenary celebration.* —*n.* **3.** a centennial. **4.** a period of 100 years; century. [1600–10; < L *centēnārius* (adj.), equiv. to *centēn(ī)* a hundred each (*cent(um)* 100 + *-ēnī* distributive suffix) + *-ārius* -ARY]

cen·ten·i·o·na·lis (sen ten′ē ō nā′lis), *n., pl.* **-les** (-lēz). a silver coin of ancient Rome, first issued by Diocletian as the 100th part of a solidus, later greatly debased. [< L *centēniōnālis (nummus)*]

cen·ten·ni·al (sen ten′ē əl), *adj.* **1.** pertaining to, or marking the completion of, a period of 100 years. **2.** pertaining to a 100th anniversary. **3.** lasting 100 years. **4.** 100 years old. —*n.* **5.** a 100th anniversary or its celebration; centenary. [1790–1800; < L *cent-* 100 (see CENT) + E *-ennial* pertaining to a period of years (extracted from BIENNIAL)] —**cen·ten′ni·al·ly,** *adv.*

Centen′nial State′, Colorado (used as a nickname).

cen·ter (sen′tər), *n.* **1.** *Geom.* the middle point, as the point within a circle or sphere equally distant from all points of the circumference or surface, or the point within a regular polygon equally distant from the vertices. **2.** a point, pivot, axis, etc., around which anything rotates or revolves: *The sun is the center of the solar system.* **3.** the source of an influence, action, force, etc.: *the center of a problem.* **4.** a point, place, person, etc., upon which interest, emotion, etc., focuses: *His family is the center of his life.* **5.** a principal point, place, or object: *a shipping center.* **6.** a building or part of a building used as a meeting place for a particular group or having facilities for certain activities: *a youth center; The company has a complete recreation center in the basement.* **7.** an office or other facility providing a specific service or dealing with a particular emergency: *a flood-relief center; a crisis center.* **8.** a person, thing, group, etc., occupying the middle position, esp. a body of troops. **9.** the core or middle of anything: *chocolate candies with fruit centers.* **10.** a store or establishment devoted to a particular subject or hobby, carrying supplies, materials, tools, and books as well as offering guidance and advice: *a garden center; a nutrition center.* **11.** See **shopping center. 12.** (*usually cap.*) *Govt.* **a.** the part of a legislative assembly, esp. in continental Europe, that sits in the center of the chamber, a position customarily assigned to members of the legislature who hold political views intermediate between those of the Right and Left. **b.** the members of such an assembly who sit in the Center. **c.** the political position of persons who hold moderate views. **d.** politically moderate persons, taken collectively; Centrists; middle-of-the-roaders: *Unfortunately, his homeland has always lacked a responsible Center.* **13.** *Football.* **a.** a lineman who occupies a position in the middle of the line and who puts the ball into play by tossing it between his legs to a back. **b.** the position played by this lineman. **14.** *Basketball.* **a.** a player who participates in a center jump. **b.** the position of the player in the center of the court, where the center jump takes place at the beginning of play. **15.** *Ice Hockey.* a player who participates in a face-off at the beginning of play. **16.** *Baseball.* See **center field. 17.** *Physiol.* a cluster of nerve cells governing a specific organic process: *the vasomotor center.* **18.** *Math.* **a.** the mean position of a figure or system. **b.** the set of elements of a group that commute with every element of the group. **19.** *Mach.* **a.** a tapered rod, mounted in the headstock spindle **(live center)** or the tailstock spindle **(dead center)** of a lathe, upon which the work to be turned is placed. **b.** one of two similar points on some other machine, as a planing machine, enabling an object to be turned on its axis. **c.** a tapered indentation, in a piece to be turned on a lathe, into which a center is fitted. **20. on center,** from the centerline or midpoint of a structural member, an area of a plan, etc., to that of a similar member, area, etc.: *The studs are set 30 inches on center. Abbr.:* o.c.
—*v.t.* **21.** to place in or on a center: *She centered the clock on the mantelpiece.* **22.** to collect to or around a center; focus: *He centered his novel on the Civil War.* **23.** to determine or mark the center of: *A small brass star centered the tabletop.* **24.** to adjust, shape, or modify (an object, part, etc.) so that its axis or the like is in a central or normal position: *to center the lens of a telescope; to center the work on a lathe.* **25.** to place (an object, part, etc.) so as to be equidistant from all bordering or adjacent areas. **26.** *Football.* snap (def. 20). **27.** to pass (a basketball, hockey puck, etc.) from any place along the periphery toward the middle of the playing area.
—*v.i.* **28.** to be at or come to a center. **29.** to come to a focus; converge; concentrate (fol. by *at, about, around, in,* or *on*): *The interest of the book centers specifically on the character of the eccentric hero. Political power in the town centers in the position of mayor.* **30.** to gather or accumulate in a cluster; collect (fol. by *at, about, around, in,* or *on*): *Shops and municipal buildings center around the city square.* Also, *esp. Brit.,* **centre.** [1325–75; var. of ME *centre* < L *centrum* < Gk *kéntron* needle, spur, pivoting point in drawing a circle, deriv. of *kenteîn* to sting] —**cen′ter·a·ble,** *adj.* —**cen′ter·less,** *adj.*
—**Syn. 1.** See **middle.** —**Ant. 1.** edge.
—**Usage. 29.** Although sometimes condemned for alleged illogicality, the phrases CENTER ABOUT and CENTER AROUND have appeared in edited writing for more than a century to express the sense of gathering or collecting as if around a center: *The objections center around the question of fiscal responsibility.*

cen′ter back′, *Volleyball, Water Polo.* the player in the middle of the back line.

cen′ter bit′, *Carpentry.* a bit having a sharp, projecting point for fixing it at the center of the hole to be drilled. [1785–95]

cen·ter·board (sen′tər bôrd′, -bōrd′), *n. Naut.* a pivoted fin keel that can be swung upward and aft within a watertight trunk when not in use. Also called **drop keel.** Cf. **daggerboard.** [1840–50, *Amer.;* CENTER + BOARD]

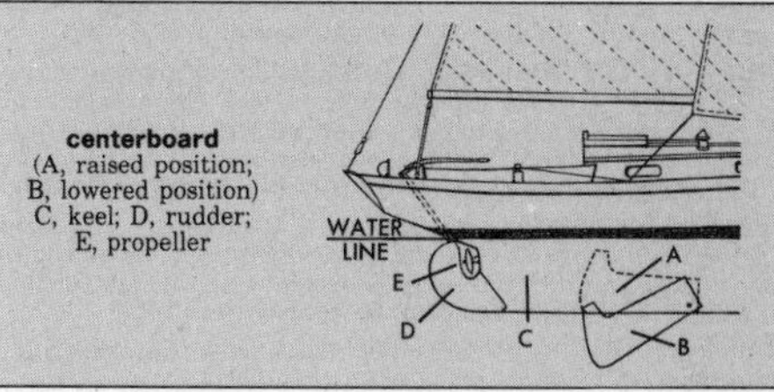

centerboard
(A, raised position; B, lowered position) C, keel; D, rudder; E, propeller

cen·tered (sen′tərd), *adj.* **1.** having a central axis: *a centered arc.* **2.** equidistant from all bordering or adjacent areas; situated in the center: *The illustration was centered on the page.* **3.** *Print.* set above the base line at approximately the level of the hyphen: *a centered dot between syllables.* [1580–90; CENTER + -ED[3]]

cen′ter field′, *Baseball.* **1.** the area of the outfield beyond second base and between right field and left field. **2.** the position of the player covering this area. [1855–60, *Amer.*]

cen′ter field′er, *Baseball.* the player whose position is center field. [1865–70, *Amer.*]

cen·ter-fire (sen′tər fīər′), *adj.* **1.** (of a cartridge) having the primer in the center of the base. Cf. **rimfire** (def. 1). **2.** (of firearms) designed for the use of such cartridges. Also, **central-fire.** [1870–75, *Amer.*]

cen·ter·fold (sen′tər fōld′), *n.* **1.** See **center spread. 2.** a gatefold bound into the center of a magazine or book signature. **3.** a photograph of a woman or man in a nude or seminude pose appearing on a magazine centerfold. **4.** the person in such a photograph. [1950–55, *Amer.;* CENTER + FOLD[1]]

cen′ter for′ward, *Soccer.* an offensive player who covers the center of the field and who usually starts the kickoff. [1890–95]

cen′ter half′back, **1.** *Field Hockey.* the player in the middle among the halfbacks. **2.** *Soccer.* the player in the middle of his or her own half of the field who carries out both offensive and defensive duties. [1875–80]

cen·ter·ing (sen′tər ing), *n.* a temporary framework for supporting a masonry arch during construction until it is able to stand by itself. [1760–70; CENTER + -ING[1]]

cen′ter jump′, *Basketball.* a jump ball between the centers of the opposing teams, held in the circle at the center of the court, as at the beginning of each period.

cen·ter·line (sen′tər līn′), *n.* **1.** any line that bisects a plane figure: *the centerline of a building plan.* **2.** a line along the center of a road or highway dividing it into separate sections for traffic moving in opposite directions. **3.** *Radio.* the perpendicular bisector of the line connecting two radio transmitters. Also, **cen′ter line′.** [1800–10; CENTER + LINE[1]]

cen′ter of cur′vature, *Math.* the center of the circle of curvature. [1865–70]

cen′ter of grav′ity, **1.** *Mech.* the point through which the resultant of gravitational forces on a body passes and from which the resultant force of attraction of the body on other bodies emanates: coincident with the center of mass in a uniform gravitational field. **2.** a person, thing, or idea that is the vital or pivotal focus of interest or activity within a larger entity. [1650–60]

cen′ter of mass′, *Mech.* the point at which the entire mass of a body may be considered concentrated for some purposes; formally, the point such that the first moment of a physical or geometric object about every line through the point is zero. Cf. **moment** (def. 8). [1875–80]

cen′ter of percus′sion, *Mech.* the point on a rigid body, suspended so as to be able to move freely about a fixed axis, at which the body may be struck without changing the position of the axis. [1720–30]

cen′ter of sym′metry, *Crystall.* a point within a crystal through which any straight line extends to points on opposite surfaces of the crystal at equal distances. Also called **inversion center.** Cf. **symmetry element.**

cen·ter·piece (sen′tər pēs′), *n.* **1.** an ornamental object used in a central position, esp. on the center of a dining-room table. **2.** the central or outstanding point or feature: *The centerpiece of the evening was a play put on by the employees.* [1830–40; CENTER + PIECE]

cen′ter pin′, *Railroads.* a cylindrical device passing through the center plates of both the body bolster and the truck bolster, permitting the truck to swivel beneath the car body while the stress is taken by the center plate. [1795–1805]

cen′ter-piv·ot irriga′tion (sen′tər piv′ət), a method of irrigation, used mainly in the western U.S., in which water is dispersed through a long, segmented arm that revolves about a deep well and covers a circular area from a quarter of a mile to a mile in diameter. [1970–75]

cen′ter plate′, *Railroads.* one of a pair of plates

that fit together and support the body of a car on a truck, while allowing the truck to rotate with respect to the body. One plate **(body center plate)** is attached to the underside of the car body and the other **(truck center plate)** is part of the car truck. [1880–85]

cen′ter punch′, a punch for making shallow indentations in metal work, as to center drill bits. [1875–80]

cen•ter•punch (sen′tər punch′), *v.t.* to mark with a center punch. [v. use of CENTER PUNCH]

Cen′ters for Disease′ Control′, the branch of the U.S. Public Health Service under the Department of Health and Human Services charged with the investigation and control of contagious disease in the nation. *Abbr.:* CDC Formerly, **Communicable Disease Center.**

cen′ter spread′, *Journalism.* **1.** the pair of pages facing each other at the center of a magazine or newspaper, printed and made up as a single unit. **2.** matter occupying this space. Cf. **double truck** (def. 2).

Cen•ter•ville (sen′tər vil′), *n.* a town in W Ohio. 18,886.

cen′ter-weight•ed light′ me′ter (sen′tər wā′tid), *Photog.* an exposure meter that gives priority to light measured near the center of the picture area, with sensitivity gradually decreasing toward the edges. Cf. **averaging light meter.**

cen′ter wheel′, *Horol.* the wheel driving the minute and hour hands of a timepiece. [1880–85]

cen•tes•i•mal (sen tes′ə məl), *adj.* hundredth; pertaining to division into hundredths. [1675–85; < L *centēsim(us)* hundredth (*cent(um)* 100 + *-ēsimus* ordinal suffix) + -AL[1] —**cen•tes′i•mal•ly,** *adv.*

cen•tes•i•mo (sen tes′ə mō′; *It.* chen te′zē mô; *Sp.* sen te′sē mô′), *n., pl. It.* **-mi** (-mē), **-mos** (-mōz′; *Sp.* -môs′). **1.** a money of account of Italy, the 100th part of a lira. **2.** a cupronickel coin of Uruguay, the 100th part of a peso. **3.** a copper coin of Panama, the 100th part of a balboa. [1850–55; < It, Sp < L *centēsimus;* see CENTESIMAL]

cen•te•sis (sen tē′sis), *n., pl.* **-ses** (-sēz). *Surg.* **1.** a puncture or perforation. **2.** a puncture into a body cavity, usually to remove fluid. [< NL < Gk, equiv. to *kentē-* (var. s. of *kenteîn* to prick) + *-sis* -SIS]

centi-, a combining form meaning "hundredth" or "hundred," used in the formation of compound words: *centiliter; centimeter; centipede.* Also, *esp. before a vowel,* **cent-.** [< L, comb. form of *centum*]

cen•ti•are (sen′tē âr′; *Fr.* säɴ tyAR′), *n., pl.* **-ti•ares** (-tē ârz′; *Fr.* -tyAR′). a square meter. *Abbr.:* ca Also, **centare.** [< F; see CENTI-, ARE[2]]

cen•ti•bar (sen′tə bär′), *n.* a centimeter-gram-second unit of pressure, equal to 1/100 bar or 10,000 dynes per square centimeter. [CENTI- + BAR[3]]

cen•ti•grade (sen′ti grād′), *adj.* **1.** divided into 100 degrees, as a scale. **2.** (*cap.*) Celsius (def. 1). *Abbr.:* cent. *Symbol:* C See illus. under **thermometer.** [1805–15; < F; see CENTI-, -GRADE]

cen•ti•gram (sen′ti gram′), *n.* one 100th of a gram, equivalent to 0.1543 grain. *Abbr.:* cg Also, *esp. Brit.,* **cen′ti•gramme′.** [1795–1805; < F *centigramme.* See CENTI-, -GRAM[2]]

cen•tile (sen′til, -tīl), *n.* (not in technical use) a percentile. [< L *cent(um)* HUNDRED + -ILE]

cen•ti•li•ter (sen′tl ē′tər), *n.* one 100th of a liter, equivalent to 0.6102 cubic inch, or 0.338 U.S. fluid ounce. *Abbr.:* cl Also, *esp. Brit.,* **cen′ti•li′tre.** [1795–1805; < F *centilitre.* See CENTI-, LITER]

cen•til•lion (sen til′yən), *n., pl.* **-lions,** (*as after a numeral*) **-lion,** *adj.* —*n.* **1.** a cardinal number represented in the U.S. by 1 followed by 303 zeros, and in Great Britain by 1 followed by 600 zeros. —*adj.* **2.** amounting to one centillion in number. [1850–55; < L *cent(um)* 100 + *-illion* (as in *million, billion,* etc.)] —**cen•til′lionth,** *adj., n.*

cen•time (sän′tēm; *Fr.* säɴ tēm′), *n., pl.* **-times** (-tēmz′; *Fr.* -tēm′). **1.** the 100th part of the franc of various nations and territories, as Belgium, France, Lichtenstein, Luxembourg, Martinique, Senegal, Switzerland, and Tahiti. **2.** a money of account of Haiti, the 100th part of a gourde. **3.** an aluminum coin and monetary unit of Algeria, the 100th part of a dinar. **4.** an aluminum coin and monetary unit of Morocco, the 100th part of a dirham. [1795–1805; < F; OF *centiesme* < L *centēsimum,* acc. of *centēsimus* hundredth; see CENT]

cen•ti•me•ter (sen′tə mē′tər), *n.* one 100th of a meter, equivalent to 0.3937 inch. *Abbr.:* cm Also, *esp. Brit.,* **cen′ti•me′tre.** [1795–1805; < F *centimètre.* See CENTI-, METER[1]]

cen•ti•me•ter-gram-sec•ond (sen′tə mē′tər gram′-sek′ənd), *adj.* of or pertaining to the system of units in which the centimeter, gram, and second are the principal units of length, mass, and time. *Abbr.:* cgs [1870–75]

cen•ti•mo (sen′tə mō′; *Sp.* then′tē mô′, sen′-), *n., pl.* **-mos** (-mōz′; *Sp.* -môs′). the 100th part of the monetary units of various countries, as Costa Rica, Equatorial Guinea, Paraguay, Spain, and Venezuela. [1895–1900; < Sp < F *centime.* See CENTIME]

cen•ti•pede (sen′tə pēd′), *n.* any of numerous predaceous, chiefly nocturnal arthropods constituting the class Chilopoda, having an elongated, flattened body composed of from 15 to 173 segments, each with a pair of legs, the first pair being modified into poison fangs. [1595–1605; < L *centipeda.* See CENTI-, -PEDE] —**cen•tip•e•dal** (sen tip′i dl, sen′tə pēd′l), *adj.*

CONCISE ETYMOLOGY KEY: <, descended or borrowed from; >, whence; b., blend of, blended; c., cognate with; cf., compare; deriv., derivative; equiv., equivalent; imit., imitative; obl., oblique; r., replacing; s., stem; sp., spelling, spelled; resp., respelling, respelled; trans., translation; ?, origin unknown; *, unattested; ‡, probably earlier than. See the full key inside the front cover.

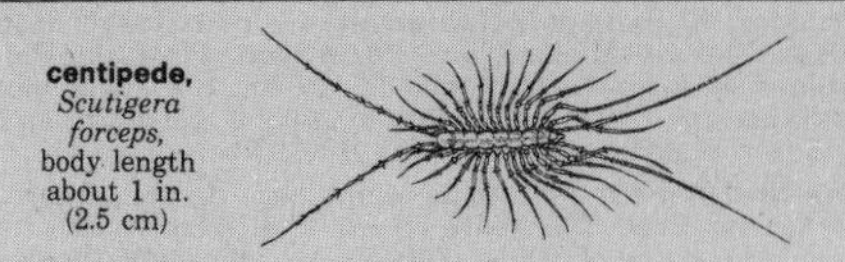
centipede, *Scutigera forceps,* body length about 1 in. (2.5 cm)

cen′tipede grass′, a slow-growing grass, *Eremochloa ophiuroides,* introduced into the U.S. from China and used for lawns in warm areas.

cen•ti•poise (sen′tə poiz′), *n.* a centimeter-gram-second unit of viscosity, equal to 1/100 poise. *Abbr.:* cP, cp [1915–20; CENTI- + POISE[2]]

cen•ti•stere (sen′tə stēr′), *n.* one 100th of a stere. [< F *centistère.* See CENTI-, STERE]

cen•ti•stoke (sen′tə stōk′), *n.* a centimeter-gram-second unit of kinematic viscosity, equal to 1/100 stoke. *Abbr.:* cS, cs [1930–35; CENTI- + STOKE[2]]

cent•ner (sent′nər), *n.* **1.** (in several European countries) a unit of weight of 50 kilograms, equivalent to 110.2 pounds avoirdupois. **2.** a unit of 100 kilograms. [1675–85 for sense "hundredweight"; < LG; cf. G *Zentner,* OHG *centenari* < L *centēnārius* of a hundred; see CENTENARY]

cen•to (sen′tō), *n., pl.* **-tos. 1.** a piece of writing, esp. a poem, composed wholly of quotations from the works of other authors. **2.** anything composed of incongruous parts; conglomeration. **3.** *Obs.* a patchwork. [1595–1605; < L *centō* patchwork quilt or curtain] —**cen•ton•i•cal** (sen ton′i kəl), *adj.* —**cen•to•nism** (sen′tn iz′əm), **cen•to•ni•za•tion** (sen′tn ə zā′shən), *n.*

CENTO (sen′tō), *n.* a former organization (1959–79) for economic and military cooperation, established as successor to the Baghdad Pact, and comprising Great Britain, Iran, Pakistan, and Turkey. The U.S. had affiliate status. [*Cen(tral) T(reaty) O(rganization)*]

centr-, var. of **centri-** before a vowel: *centroid.*

cen•tra (sen′trə), *n.* a pl. of **centrum.**

cen•tral[1] (sen′trəl), *adj.* **1.** of or forming the center: *the central hut in the village.* **2.** in, at, or near the center: *a central position.* **3.** constituting something from which other related things proceed or upon which they depend: *a central office.* **4.** principal; chief; dominant: *the play's central character.* **5.** *Anat., Zool.* **a.** of or pertaining to the central nervous system. **b.** of or pertaining to the centrum of a vertebra. **6.** *Phonet.* (of a speech sound) produced with the tongue articulating neither expressly forward nor in the back part of the mouth, as any of the sounds of *lull.* **7.** *Physics.* (of a force) directed to or from a fixed point. —*n.* **8.** (formerly) **a.** a main telephone exchange. **b.** a telephone operator at such an exchange. [1640–50; < L *centrālis,* equiv. to *centr(um)* CENTER + *-ālis* -AL[1]] —**cen′tral•ly,** *adv.* —**Syn. 4.** major, main, key, leading, primary.

cen•tral[2] (sen träl′; *Sp.* sen träl′), *n., pl.* **-trals,** *Sp.* **-tra•les** (-trä′les). (in Spanish America and the Philippines) a mill for crushing cane into raw sugar. [< AmerSp, special use of Sp *central* CENTRAL[1]]

Cen•tral (sen′trəl), *n.* a region in central Scotland. 269,281. 1016 sq. mi. (2631 sq. km).

Cen′tral Af′rican, 1. of or pertaining to the Central African Republic, its inhabitants, or their language. **2.** an inhabitant or native of the Central African Republic.

Cen′tral Af′rican Em′pire, a former name (1976–79) of **Central African Republic.**

Cen′tral Af′rican Federa′tion. See **Rhodesia and Nyasaland, Federation of.**

Cen′tral Af′rican Repub′lic, a republic in central Africa: a member of the French Community. 2,100,000; 238,000 sq. mi. (616,420 sq. km). *Cap.:* Bangui. Formerly, **Central African Empire, Ubangi-Shari.**

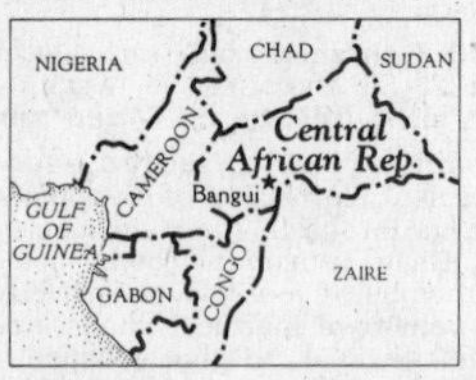

Cen′tral Amer′ica, continental North America, S of Mexico, usually considered as comprising Guatemala, Belize, El Salvador, Honduras, Nicaragua, Costa Rica, and Panama. 18,600,000; 227,933 sq. mi. (590,346 sq. km). See map below. —**Cen′tral Amer′ican.**

cen′tral an′gle, *Geom.* an angle formed at the center of a circle by two radii. [1900–05]

cen′tral bank′, a bank, as the Federal Reserve Bank, that holds basic banking reserves, issues currency, and acts as lender of last resort and controller of credit. [1920–25]

cen′tral cast′ing, *Motion Pictures.* an agency, studio department, etc., responsible for hiring actors, esp. bit players or extras. [1925–30, *Amer.*]

cen′tral cit′y, a city at the center of a metropolitan area. Also called **core city.** Cf. **inner city.** [1945–50]

cen′tral cyl′inder, *Bot.* stele (def. 4).

Cen′tral Falls′, a city in NE Rhode Island. 16,995.

cen•tral-fire (sen′trəl fīᵊr′), *adj.* center-fire. [1880–85]

cen′tral heat′ing, a system that supplies heat to an entire building from a single source through ducts or through pipes. [1905–10]

Cen•tra•lia (sen trāl′yə, -trā′lē ə), *n.* **1.** a city in central Illinois. 15,126. **2.** a town in SW Washington. 10,809.

Cen′tral In′dia, a former political agency in central India uniting various native states and subordinate agencies: now incorporated into Madhya Pradesh. Also called **Cen′tral In′dian A′gency.**

Cen′tral Intel′ligence A′gency. See **CIA.**

Cen′tral I′slip, a town on S Long Island, in SE New York. 19,734.

cen•tral•ism (sen′trə liz′əm), *n.* a centralizing system; centralization. [1825–35, *Amer.;* CENTRAL[1] + -ISM] —**cen′tral•ist,** *n., adj.* —**cen•tral•is•tic** (sen′trə lis′-tik), *adj.*

cen•tral•i•ty (sen tral′i tē), *n., pl.* **-ties. 1.** a central position or state: *the centrality of the sun.* **2.** a vital, critical, or important position: *the centrality of education to modern civilization.* [1640–50; CENTRAL[1] + -ITY]

cen•tral•i•za•tion (sen′trə lə zā′shən), *n.* **1.** the act or fact of centralizing; fact of being centralized. **2.** the concentration of administrative power in a central government, authority, etc. **3.** *Chiefly Sociol.* **a.** a process

whereby social groups and institutions become increasingly dependent on a central group or institution. **b.** concentration of control or power in a few individuals. [1795–1805; CENTRALIZE + -ATION]

cen·tral·ize (sen′trə līz′), *v.*, **-ized, -iz·ing.** —*v.t.* **1.** to draw to or gather about a center. **2.** to bring under one control, esp. in government: *to centralize budgeting in one agency.* —*v.i.* **3.** to come together at or to form a center. Also, *esp. Brit.,* **cen′tral·ise′.** [1790–1800; CENTRAL[1] + -IZE] —**cen′tral·iz′er,** *n.*

cen′tralized school′. See **consolidated school.**

cen′tral lim′it the′orem, *Statistics.* any of several theorems stating that the sum of a number of random variables obeying certain conditions will assume a normal distribution as the number of variables becomes large. [1950–55]

cen′tral mo′ment, *Statistics.* a moment about the center of a distribution, usually the mean.

cen′tral nerv′ous sys′tem, the part of the nervous system comprising the brain and spinal cord. Also called **cerebrospinal nervous system.** [1890–95]

Cen′tral Park′, a public park in central Manhattan, New York City. 840 acres (340 hectares).

Cen′tral Pow′ers, (in World War I) Germany and Austria-Hungary, often with their allies Turkey and Bulgaria, as opposed to the Allies.

cen′tral proc′essing u′nit, *Computers.* See **CPU.** Also called **cen′tral proc′essor.** [1965–70]

cen′tral projec′tion, *Geom.* a projection of one plane onto a second plane such that a point on the first plane and its image on the second plane lie on a straight line through a fixed point not on either plane.

Cen′tral Prov′inces, *Canadian.* the Canadian provinces of Ontario and Quebec.

Cen′tral Prov′inces and Be·rar′ (bā rär′), a former province in central India: became the state of Madhya Pradesh 1950.

Cen′tral Sudan′ic, a group of languages belonging to the Nilo-Saharan family, spoken in northeastern Zaire, northern Uganda, southern Sudan, Chad, and the Central African Republic, and including Mangbetu.

cen′tral sul′cus, *Anat.* the sulcus separating the frontal and parietal lobes of the cerebrum. Also called **fissure of Rolando.**

cen′tral tend′ency, *Statistics.* the tendency of samples of a given measurement to cluster around some central value. Cf. **measure of central tendency.** [1925–30]

Cen′tral time′. See under **standard time.** Also called **Cen′tral Stand′ard Time′.** [1880–85, *Amer.*]

Cen′tral Trea′ty Organiza′tion. See **CENTO.**

Cen′tral Val′ley, the chief wine-producing region of California, centered in San Joaquin County.

cen·tre (sen′tər), *n., v.,* **-tred, -tring.** *Chiefly Brit.* center.

centri-, a combining form of **center:** *centrifuge.* Also, **centr-, centro-.** [< NL, comb. form of *centrum* CENTER]

cen·tric (sen′trik), *adj.* **1.** pertaining to or situated at the center; central. **2.** *Anat., Physiol.* pertaining to or originating at a nerve center. Also, **cen′tri·cal.** [1580–90; < Gk *kentrikós* of, pertaining to a cardinal point, equiv. to *kéntr(on)* (see CENTER) + *-ikos* -IC] —**cen′tri·cal·ly,** *adv.* —**cen·tric·i·ty** (sen tris′i tē), *n.*

-centric, a combining form with the meanings "having a center or centers" of the specified number or kind (*polycentric*); "centered upon, focused around" that named by the first element (*ethnocentric; heliocentric*). [see CENTR-, -IC]

cen·trif·u·gal (sen trif′yə gəl, -ə gəl), *adj.* **1.** moving or directed outward from the center (opposed to *centripetal*). **2.** pertaining to or operated by centrifugal force: *a centrifugal pump.* **3.** *Physiol.* efferent. —*n.* **4.** *Mach.* **a.** a machine for separating different materials by centrifugal force; centrifuge. **b.** a rotating, perforated drum holding the materials to be separated in such a machine. [1715–25; < NL *centrifug(us)* center-fleeing (*centri-* CENTRI- + L *-fugus,* deriv. of *fugere* to flee) + -AL[1]] —**cen·trif′u·gal·ly,** *adv.*

centrif′ugal box′, *Textiles.* a revolving chamber, used in the spinning of manufactured filaments, in which the plastic fibers, subjected to centrifugal force, are slightly twisted and emerge in the form of yarn wound into the shape of a hollow cylinder. Also called **centrif′ugal pot′, spinning box, spinning pot.**

centrif′ugal cast′ing, *Metall.* casting that utilizes centrifugal force within a spinning mold to force the metal against the walls. [1920–25]

centrif′ugal force′, an outward force on a body rotating about an axis, assumed equal and opposite to the centripetal force and postulated to account for the phenomena seen by an observer in the rotating body. [1715–25]

cen·trif·u·gal·ize (sen trif′yə gə līz′, -ə gə-), *v.t.,* **-ized, -iz·ing.** centrifuge (def. 2). Also, *esp. Brit.,* **cen·trif′u·gal·ise′.** [1875–80; CENTRIFUGAL + -IZE] —**cen·trif′u·gal·i·za′tion,** *n.*

centrif′ugal spin′ning. See **pot spinning.**

cen·trif·u·gate (sen trif′yə git, -gāt′, -trif′ə-), *n.* the denser of the centrifuged materials. [1875–80; CENTRIFUG(AL) + -ATE[1]]

cen·tri·fuge (sen′trə fyo͞oj′), *n., v.,* **-fuged, -fug·ing.** —*n.* **1.** an apparatus that rotates at high speed and by centrifugal force separates substances of different densities, as milk and cream. —*v.t.* **2.** Also, **centrifugalize.** to subject to the action of a centrifuge. [1795–1805; < F, n. use of *centrifuge* (adj.) < NL *centrifugus* center-fleeing; see CENTRIFUGAL] —**cen·trif·u·ga·tion** (sen trif′yə gā′shən, -trif′ə-), *n.*

cen·tri·ole (sen′trē ōl′), *n. Cell Biol.* a small, cylindrical cell organelle, seen near the nucleus in the cytoplasm of most eukaryotic cells, that divides in perpendicular fashion during mitosis, the new pair of centrioles moving ahead of the spindle to opposite poles of the cell as the cell divides: identical in internal structure to a basal body. See diag. under **cell.** [1895–1900; CENTRI- + -OLE[1]]

cen·trip·e·tal (sen trip′i tl), *adj.* **1.** directed toward the center (opposed to *centrifugal*). **2.** operating by centripetal force. **3.** *Physiol.* afferent. [1700–10; < NL *centripet(us)* center-seeking (*centri-* CENTRI- + *-petus,* deriv. of L *petere* to seek) + -AL[1]] —**cen·trip′e·tal·ism,** *n.* —**cen·trip′e·tal·ly,** *adv.*

centrip′etal force′, the force, acting upon a body moving along a curved path, that is directed toward the center of curvature of the path and constrains the body to the path. [1700–10]

cen·trist (sen′trist), *n.* **1.** (esp. in continental Europe) a member of a political party of the Center; moderate. —*adj.* **2.** of or pertaining to centrists or to their political views; middle-of-the-road. Also, **Cen′trist.** [1870–75; < F *centriste.* See CENTER, -IST] —**cen′trism,** *n.*

centro-, var. of **centri-:** *centrosphere.*

cen·tro·bar·ic (sen′trə bar′ik), *adj.* pertaining to the center of gravity. [1695–1705; CENTRO- + BARIC[2]]

cen·troid (sen′troid), *n.* **1.** *Mech.* the point that may be considered as the center of a one- or two-dimensional figure, the sum of the displacements of all points in the figure from such a point being zero. Cf. **center of mass. 2.** Also called **median point.** *Geom.* that point where the medians of a triangle intersect. [1875–80; CENTR- + -OID] —**cen·troi′dal,** *adj.*

cen·tro·lec·i·thal (sen′trō les′ə thəl), *adj. Embryol.* having a centrally located yolk, as certain insect eggs or ova. [1875–80; CENTRO- + LECITHAL]

cen·tro·lin·e·ad (sen′trō lin′ē ad′, -əd), *n.* a drafting instrument for drawing lines converging on a vanishing point outside the drawing. [1805–15; CENTRO- + L *line(a)* LINE[1] + *ad* to]

cen·tro·mere (sen′trə mēr′), *n. Cell Biol.* a specialized structure on the chromosome, appearing during cell division as the constricted central region where the two chromatids are held together and form an X shape. [1920–25; CENTRO- + -MERE] —**cen·tro·mer·ic** (sen′trə-mer′ik, -mēr′-), *adj.*

cen·tro·some (sen′trə sōm′), *n. Cell Biol.* a small region near the nucleus in the cell cytoplasm, containing the centrioles. [1895–1900; CENTRO- + -SOME[3]] —**cen·tro·som·ic** (sen′trə som′ik), *adj.*

cen·tro·sphere (sen′trə sfēr′), *n.* **1.** *Cell Biol.* the protoplasm around a centrosome; the central portion of an aster, containing the centrosome. **2.** *Geol.* the central or interior portion of the earth. [1895–1900; CENTRO- + -SPHERE]

cen·tro·sym·met·ric (sen′trō si me′trik), *adj.* symmetric in relation to a center. Also, **cen′tro·sym·met′ri·cal.** [1875–80; CENTRO- + SYMMETRIC] —**cen·tro·sym·met·ry** (sen′trō sim′i trē), *n.*

cen·trum (sen′trəm), *n., pl.* **-trums, -tra** (-trə). **1.** a center. **2.** *Anat., Zool.* the body of a vertebra. **3.** *Mycol.* collectively, all the structures enclosed within the ascocarp of a fungus. [1850–55; < L; see CENTER]

cent′ sign′, the symbol ¢ placed after a number to indicate that the number represents cents.

cents-off (sents′ôf′, -of′), *adj.* of or pertaining to a marketing device, as a coupon, that entitles a buyer to a specified amount off the regular price. [1960–65]

cen·tum[1] (sen′təm), *n.* one hundred. [< L; see HUNDRED]

cen·tum[2] (ken′təm, -to͝om), *adj.* belonging to or consisting of those branches of the Indo-European family of languages that show distinctive preservation of the Proto-Indo-European labiovelars and that show a historical development of velar articulations, as the sounds (k) or (KH), from Proto-Indo-European palatal phonemes. The centum branches are Germanic, Celtic, Italic, Hellenic, Anatolian, and Tocharian. Cf. **satem.** [1900–05; < L, exemplifying in c- the outcome of IE palato-velar stops characteristic of the group]

cen·tu·ple (sen′tə pəl, -tyə-), *adj., v.,* **-pled, -pling.** —*adj.* **1.** a hundred times as great; hundredfold. —*v.t.* **2.** to increase 100 times. [1600–10; < MF < LL *centuplus,* equiv. to L *centu(m)* 100 + *-plus* -FOLD]

cen·tu·pli·cate (*v.* sen to͞o′pli kāt′, -tyo͞o′-; *adj., n.* sen to͞o′pli kit, -kāt′, -tyo͞o′-), *v.,* **-cat·ed, -cat·ing,** *adj., n.* —*v.t.* **1.** to increase 100 times; centuple. —*adj.* **2.** a hundredfold. —*n.* **3.** a number or quantity increased a hundredfold. [1825–35; < L *centuplic-* (s. of *centuplex*) hundredfold, equiv. to *centu(m)* 100 + *plic-* (s. of *plicāre* to fold) + -ATE[1]] —**cen·tu′pli·ca′tion,** *n.*

cen·tu·ri·al (sen to͝or′ē əl, -tyo͝or′-), *adj.* pertaining to a century. [1600–10; < L *centuriālis,* equiv. to *centuri(a)* CENTURY + *-ālis* -AL[1]]

cen·tu·ried (sen′chə rēd), *adj.* **1.** existing for an indefinite number of centuries. **2.** very old; ancient. [1810–20; CENTURY + -ED[3]]

cen·tu·ri·on (sen to͝or′ē ən, -tyo͝or′-), *n.* **1.** (in the ancient Roman army) the commander of a century. **2.** (*cap.*) *Mil.* any one of various British battle tanks in service from 1945 to 1967. [1225–75; ME < L *centuriōn-* (s. of *centuriō*), equiv. to *centur(ia)* CENTURY + *-iōn-* -ION]

cen·tu·ry (sen′chə rē), *n., pl.* **-ries. 1.** a period of 100 years. **2.** one of the successive periods of 100 years reckoned forward or backward from a recognized chronological epoch, esp. from the assumed date of the birth of Jesus. **3.** any group or collection of 100: *a century of limericks.* **4.** (in the ancient Roman army) a company, consisting of approximately 100 men. **5.** one of the voting divisions of the ancient Roman people, each division having one vote. **6.** (*cap.*) *Print.* a style of type. **7.** *Slang.* a hundred-dollar bill; 100 dollars. **8.** *Sports.* a race of 100 yards or meters, as in track or swimming, or of 100 miles, as in bicycle racing. **9.** *Cricket.* a score of at least 100 runs made by one batsman in a single inning. [1525–35; < L *centuria* unit made up of 100 parts, esp. company of soldiers, equiv. to *cent(um)* 100 + *-uria,* perh. extracted from *decuria* DECURY]

cen′tury plant′, any New World plant of the genus *Agave,* requiring many years to mature and blooming once before dying, esp. the widely cultivated species *A. americana,* having leaves in a basal rosette and a tall flower stalk. [1755–65, *Amer.*]

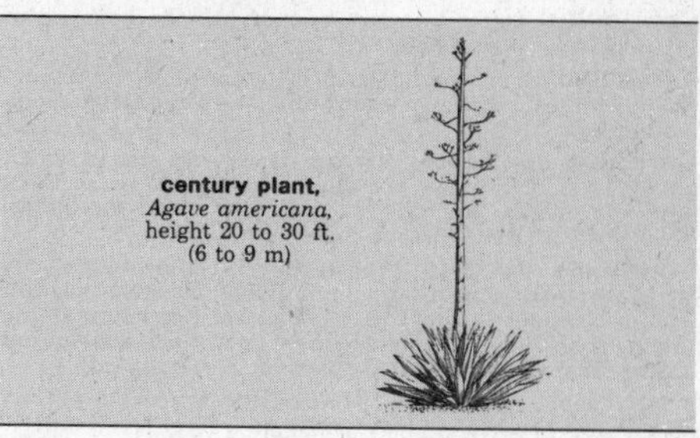
century plant, *Agave americana,* height 20 to 30 ft. (6 to 9 m)

CEO, chief executive officer. Also, **C.E.O.**

ceorl (chā′ôrl), *n. Obs.* churl (def. 4). [bef. 1000; this form borrowed (17th century) < OE] —**ceorl′ish,** *adj.*

cep (sep), *n.* an edible mushroom, *Boletus edulis,* that grows wild under pine or other evergreen trees: prized for its flavor. [1860–65; < F *cèpe* < Gascon *cep* mushroom, tree trunk < L *cip(p)us* boundary stone, pillar]

cèpe (sep), *n. French Cookery.* cep.

cephal-, var. of **cephalo-** before a vowel: *cephalate.*

ceph·a·lal·gia (sef′ə lal′jə, -jē ə), *n. Med.* headache (def. 1). [1540–50; CEPHAL- + -ALGIA] —**ceph′a·lal′gic,** *adj.*

ceph·a·late (sef′ə lit, -lāt′), *adj. Zool.* having a head or headlike part. [1860–65; CEPHAL- + -ATE[1]]

ceph·a·lex·in (sef′ə lek′sin), *n. Pharm.* an oral, antimicrobial drug, $C_{16}H_{7}N_{3}O_{4}S$, used in treating minor respiratory and urinary tract infections and as a backup or alternative to penicillin treatment. [1965–70; CEPHAL(OSPORIN) + *-ex-* of unclear derivation + -IN[2]]

ce·phal·ic (sə fal′ik), *adj.* **1.** of or pertaining to the head. **2.** situated or directed toward the head. [1590–1600; < L *cephalicus* < Gk *kephalikós* of the head. See CEPHAL-, -IC] —**ce·phal′i·cal·ly,** *adv.*

-cephalic, var. of **-cephalous:** *brachycephalic.* [< Gk *-kephal(os)* -CEPHALOUS + -IC]

cephal′ic in′dex, *Cephalom., Craniom.* the ratio of the greatest breadth of the head to its greatest length from front to back, multiplied by 100. [1865–70]

ceph·a·lin (sef′ə lin), *n. Biochem.* any of several phosphatides occurring in animal tissue, esp. of the brain, and having marked blood-clotting properties. [1895–1900; CEPHAL- + -IN[2]]

ceph·a·li·tis (sef′ə lī′tis), *n. Pathol.* encephalitis. [1805–15; CEPHAL- + -ITIS]

ceph·a·li·za·tion (sef′ə lə zā′shən), *n. Zool.* a tendency in the development of animals to localization of important organs or parts in or near the head. [1860–65; CEPHAL- + -IZATION]

cephalo-, a combining form meaning "head," used in the formation of compound words: *cephalometry.* Also, **cephal-, -cephalic, -cephalous, -cephaly.** [< Gk *kephalo-,* comb. form of *kephalḗ* head; akin to GABLE]

ceph·a·lo·chor·date (sef′ə lō kôr′dāt), *adj.* **1.** belonging or pertaining to the Cephalochordata. —*n.* **2.** any chordate animal of the subphylum Cephalochordata, having fishlike characters but lacking a spinal column, comprising the lancelets. [< NL *Cephalochordata;* see CEPHALO-, CHORDATE]

cephalom., cephalometry.

ceph·a·lom·e·ter (sef′ə lom′i tər), *n.* an instrument for measuring the human head. Cf. **craniometer.** [1875–80; CEPHALO- + -METER] —**ceph·a·lo·met·ric** (sef′ə lō me′trik), *adj.*

ceph·a·lom·e·try (sef′ə lom′i trē), *n.* the science of measuring the human head, used esp. in plastic surgery and orthodontics. [1895–1900; CEPHALO- + -METRY]

ceph·a·lon (sef′ə lon′, -lən), *n., pl.* **-la** (-lə). *Zool.* the head, esp. of an arthropod. [1870–75; < NL, for Gk *kephalḗ* head]

Ceph·a·lo·ni·a (sef′ə lō′nē ə, -lōn′yə), *n.* the largest of the Ionian Islands, off the W coast of Greece. 36,742; 287 sq. mi. (743 sq. km). Greek, **Kephallenia.**

ceph·a·lo·pod (sef′ə lə pod′), *n.* **1.** any mollusk of the class Cephalopoda, having tentacles attached to the head, including the cuttlefish, squid, and octopus. —*adj.* **2.** Also, **ceph′a·lo·pod′ic, ceph·a·lop·o·dous** (sef′ə-lop′ə dəs). belonging or pertaining to the Cephalopoda. [1820–30; < NL *Cephalopoda;* see CEPHALO-, -POD]

ceph·a·lo·spo·rin (sef′ə lō spôr′in, -spōr′-), *n. Pharm.* any of a group of widely used broad-spectrum antibiotics, originally isolated as a product of fermentation from the fungus *Cephalosporium acremonium.* [1950–55; < NL *Cephalospor(ium)* the genus (see CEPHALO-, -SPORE, -IUM) + -IN[2]]

ceph·a·lo·tho·rax (sef′ə lō thôr′aks, -thōr′-), *n., pl.* **-tho·rax·es, -tho·ra·ces** (-thôr′ə sēz′, -thōr′-). *Zool.* the anterior part of the body in certain arachnids and crustaceans, consisting of the coalesced head and thorax. [1825–35; CEPHALO- + THORAX] **—ceph•a•lo•tho•rac•ic** (sef′ə lō thə ras′ik), *adj.*

ceph•a•lous (sef′ə ləs), *adj.* having a head. [1870–75; CEPHAL- + -OUS]

-cephalous, a combining form meaning "having a head or heads" of the specified sort or number: *brachycephalous.* Also, **-cephalic.** [< Gk *-kephalos* -headed, deriv. of *kephalḗ* head; see -OUS]

Ceph•a•lus (sef′ə ləs), *n. Class. Myth.* the husband of Procris. Also, **Kephalos.**

-cephaly, a combining form of nouns that correspond to adjectives ending in **-cephalic** or **-cephalous:** *dolichocephaly.*

Ce′pheid var′iable, *Astron.* a variable star in which changes in brightness are due to alternate contractions and expansions in volume. Also, **ce′pheid var′iable.** [1900–05; CEPHE(US) + -ID[1]]

Ce•phe•us (sē′fē əs, -fyōōs), *n., gen.* **-phe•i** (-fē ī′) for 1. **1.** *Astron.* a northern circumpolar constellation between Cassiopeia and Draco. **2.** Also, **Kepheus.** *Class. Myth.* an Ethiopian king, the husband of Cassiopeia and father of Andromeda. **—Ce•phe•id** (sē′fē id), *adj.*

'cept (sept), *prep. Informal.* except[1].

cer-, var. of **cero-** before a vowel: *ceraceous.*

ce•ra (sēr′ə), *n.* (in prescriptions) wax. [< L *cēra*]

ce•ra•ceous (sə rā′shəs), *adj.* waxlike; waxy: *a ceraceous surface.* [1760–70; < L *cēr(a)* wax (cf. Gk *kērós* wax) + -ACEOUS]

Ce•ram (sē ram′; *Port.* se RÄN′; *Du.* sā′räm), *n.* an island of the Moluccas in Indonesia, W of New Guinea. 100,000; 7191 sq. mi. (18,625 sq. km). Also called **Serang.**

ce•ram•al (sə ram′əl), *n.* cermet. [CERAM(IC) + AL(LOY)]

ce•ram•ic (sə ram′ik), *adj.* **1.** of or pertaining to products made from clay and similar materials, as pottery and brick, or to their manufacture: *ceramic art.* —*n.* **2.** ceramic material. [1840–50; var. of *keramic* < Gk *keramikós,* equiv. to *kéram(os)* potters' clay + *-ikos* -IC]

ceram′ic engineer′ing, the branch of engineering concerned with the development and production of ceramics.

ce•ram•ics (sə ram′iks), *n.* **1.** (*used with a singular v.*) the art or technology of making objects of clay and similar materials treated by firing. **2.** (*used with a plural v.*) articles of earthenware, porcelain, etc. [1855–60; see CERAMIC, -ICS]

ce•ram•ist (sə ram′ist, ser′ə mist), *n.* **1.** a person who makes ceramics. **2.** a technician in a dental laboratory who makes dentures from porcelain. Also, **ce•ram•i•cist** (sə ram′ə sist). [1850–55; CERAM(IC) + -IST]

ce•rar•gy•rite (sə rär′jə rīt′), *n.* a very soft mineral, silver chloride, AgCl, used as an ore of silver; horn silver. [1865–70; < Gk *kér(as)* horn (see CERAT-) + *árgyr(os)* silver + -ITE[1]; cf. F *kérargyre*]

ce•ras•tes (sə ras′tēz), *n., pl.* **-tes.** any of several small vipers of the genus *Cerastes,* including the horned viper, that have a sideways looping motion like that of a sidewinder and inhabit deserts of northern Africa and southwestern Asia. [1768; < NL < Gk *kerástēs* lit., something horned, equiv. to *kerat-* s. of *kéras* horn + *-tēs* n. suffix; earlier in sense "asp," ME < ML, L, as above]

ce•ras•ti•um (sə ras′tē əm), *n., pl.* **-ums.** any of various low-growing plants of the genus *Cerastium,* having leaves covered with whitish or grayish down and small white flowers, and including mouse-ear chickweed and snow-in-summer. [< NL (Linnaeus) < Gk *kerást(ēs)* horned (see CERASTES) + NL *-ium* -IUM; so called from the horn-shaped seed capsules of some species]

cerat-, a combining form meaning "horn," "cornea," used in the formation of compound words: *ceratodus.* Also, **kerat-.** Also, *esp. before a consonant,* **cerato-, kerato-.** [< Gk *kerat-,* comb. form of *kéras;* akin to L *cornū* CORNU, HORN]

ce•rate (sēr′āt), *n.* **1.** *Pharm.* an unctuous, often medicated, preparation for external application, consisting of lard or oil mixed with wax, rosin, or the like, esp. one that has a firmer consistency than a typical ointment and does not melt when in contact with the skin. —*adj.* **2.** Also, **cerated.** *Ornith.* having a cere. [1375–1425; late ME < L *cērātum,* neut. of *cērātus* (ptp. of *cērāre* to cover or smear with wax), equiv. to *cēr(a)* wax + *-ātus* -ATE[1]; cf. Gk *kērōtḗn* in same sense]

ce•rat•ed (sēr′ā tid), *adj.* **1.** covered with wax. **2.** *Ornith.* cerate (def. 2). [1720–30; < L *cērāt(us)* waxed (see CERATE) + -ED[2]]

cerato- var. of **cerat-** before a consonant: *ceratosaur.*

ce•rat•o•dus (sə rat′ə dəs, ser′ə tō′dəs), *n., pl.* **-dus•es.** a lungfish of either of two genera, *Ceratodus* or *Neoceratodus,* having hornlike ridges on the teeth. Cf. **barramunda.** [1870–75; < NL, equiv. to *cerat-* CERAT- + *-odus* < Gk *odoús* TOOTH]

cer•a•toid (ser′ə toid′), *adj.* hornlike; horny. [< Gk *kerātoeidḗs* hornlike. See CERAT-, -OID]

cer•a•top•si•an (ser′ə top′sē ən), *n.* any of several four-footed, herbivorous dinosaurs of the suborder Ceratopsia, of the late Cretaceous Period, having an enlarged skull with a beak, a large perforated frill at the back, and, in some species, one or three horns. Also called **horned dinosaur.** [< NL *Ceratopsi(a)* (see CERAT-, -OPSIS, -IA) + -AN]

cer•a•to•saur (ser′ə tə sôr′), *n.* a carnivorous, swift-running North American theropod dinosaur of the genus *Ceratosaurus* and closely related genera, of the Jurassic Period, having a large skull with a short horn between the nostrils and a bony knob in front of each eye, and reaching a length of 20 ft. (6.1 m). [1884; < NL *Ceratosaurus;* see CERATO-, -SAUR]

Cer•ber•us (sûr′bər əs), *n., pl.* **-ber•us•es, -ber•i** (-bə rī′) for 2. **1.** Also, **Kerberos.** *Class. Myth.* a dog, usually represented as having three heads, that guarded the entrance of the infernal regions. **2.** a formidable and often surly keeper or guard. **—Cer•be•re•an** (sər bēr′ē ən), **Cer′ber•ic,** *adj.*

cer•car•i•a (sər kâr′ē ə), *n., pl.* **-car•i•ae** (-kâr′ē ē′). *Zool.* the disk-shaped larva of flukes of the class Trematoda, having a taillike appendage. [1830–40; < NL, equiv. to *cerc-* (< Gk *kérkos* tail) + *-āria* -ARIA] **—cer•car′i•al,** *adj.* **—cer•car′i•an,** *adj., n.*

cer•cis (sûr′sis), *n.* any shrub or small tree of the genus *Cercis,* as the redbud or Judas tree. [< NL (Linnaeus) < Gk *kerkís* redbud, lit., weaver's shuttle (perh. after the shape of the fruit), deriv. of *kérkos* tail]

cer•cus (sûr′kəs, ker′-), *n., pl.* **cer•ci** (sûr′sī, ker′kē). one of a pair of appendages at the rear of the abdomen of certain insects and other arthropods, serving as tactile organs. [1820–30; < NL < Gk *kérkos* tail] **—cer′cal,** *adj.*

cere[1] (sēr), *n. Ornith.* a fleshy, membranous covering of the base of the upper mandible of a bird, esp. a bird of prey or a parrot, through which the nostrils open. [1480–90; earlier *sere,* sp. var. of **cere* < ML *cēra* lit., wax < L] **—cered,** *adj.* **—cere′less,** *adj.*

cere[2] (sēr), *v.t.,* **cered, cer•ing. 1.** *Archaic.* to wrap in or as if in a cerecloth, esp. a corpse. **2.** *Obs.* to wax. [1375–1425; late ME *ceren* < L *cērāre* to wax, v. deriv. of *cēra* wax]

Cer.E., Ceramic Engineer.

ce•re•al (sēr′ē əl), *n.* **1.** any plant of the grass family yielding an edible grain, as wheat, rye, oats, rice, or corn. **2.** the grain itself. **3.** some edible preparation of it, esp. a breakfast food. —*adj.* **4.** of or pertaining to grain or the plants producing it. [1590–1600; < L *Cereālis* of, pertaining to CERES; see -AL[1]]

ce′real leaf′ bee′tle, an Old World leaf beetle, *Oulema melanopus,* introduced into North America in 1962: a serious pest of small grains, esp. oats and cereal grasses. [1960–65]

cer•e•bel•lum (ser′ə bel′əm), *n., pl.* **-bel•lums, -bel•la** (-bel′ə). *Anat., Zool.* a large portion of the brain, serving to coordinate voluntary movements, posture, and balance in humans, being in back of and below the cerebrum and consisting of two lateral lobes and a central lobe. See illus. under **brain.** [1555–65; < L: brain, dim. of *cerebrum;* see CEREBRUM; for formation, see CASTELLUM] **—cer′e•bel′lar,** *adj.*

cerebr-, var. of **cerebro-** before a vowel: *cerebritis.*

ce•re•bral (sə rē′brəl, ser′ə-), *adj.* **1.** *Anat., Zool.* of or pertaining to the cerebrum or the brain. **2.** betraying or characterized by the use of the intellect rather than intuition or instinct: *His is a cerebral music that leaves many people cold.* **3.** *Phonet.* retroflex (def. 2). —*n.* **4.** *Phonet.* a cerebral sound. [1795–1805; < NL *cerebrālis.* See CEREBRUM, -AL[1]] **—ce•re′bral•ly,** *adv.*

cere′bral cor′tex, the furrowed outer layer of gray matter in the cerebrum of the brain, associated with the higher brain functions, as voluntary movement, coordination of sensory information, learning and memory, and the expression of individuality. [1925–30]

cere′bral hem′isphere, either of the rounded halves of the cerebrum of the brain, divided laterally by a deep fissure and connected at the bottom by the corpus callosum. Cf. **left brain, right brain.** [1810–20]

cere′bral hem′orrhage, *Pathol.* hemorrhage from a blood vessel into the cerebrum, often followed by neurologic damage; a type of stroke. [1870–75]

cere′bral pal′sy, *Pathol.* a form of paralysis believed to be caused by a prenatal brain defect or by brain injury during birth, most marked in certain motor areas and characterized by difficulty in control of the voluntary muscles. [1920–25] **—cere′bral pal′sied.**

cere′bral thrombo′sis, *Pathol.* formation of a clot or other blockage in one of the blood vessels of the brain, often followed by neurologic damage; a type of stroke.

cer•e•brate (ser′ə brāt′), *v.i., v.t.,* **-brat•ed, -brat•ing.** to use the mind; think or think about. [1870–75; back formation from *cerebration.* See CEREBRUM, -ATION] **—cer′e•bra′tion,** *n.* **—cer′e•bra′tion•al,** *adj.*

ce•re•bric (sə rē′brik, -reb′rik, ser′ə brik), *adj.* pertaining to or derived from the brain. [1830–40; CEREBR(UM) + -IC]

cer•e•bri•tis (ser′ə brī′tis), *n.* inflammation of the brain, esp. of the cerebrum. [1865–70; CEREBR- + -ITIS]

cerebro-, a combining form of **cerebrum:** *cerebrospinal.* Also, *esp. before a vowel,* **cerebr-.**

ce•re•broid (sə rē′broid, ser′ə broid′), *adj. Anat.* resembling the cerebrum or the brain. [1850–55; CEREBR- + -OID]

ce•re•bro•side (sə rē′brə sīd′, ser′ə-), *n. Biochem.* any of a class of glycolipids, found in brain tissue and the medullary sheaths of nerves, that, upon hydrolysis, yield sphingosine, galactose or certain other sugars, and a fatty acid. [1880–85; CEREBR- + -OSE[2] + -IDE]

ce•re•bro•spi•nal (sə rē′brō spīn′l, ser′ə-), *adj. Anat., Physiol.* **1.** pertaining to or affecting the brain and the spinal cord. **2.** of or pertaining to the central nervous system. [1820–30; CEREBRO- + SPINAL]

cerebrospi′nal flu′id, *Physiol.* the fluid in the ventricles of the brain, between the arachnoid and pia mater, and surrounding the spinal cord. [1895–1900]

cerebrospi′nal meningi′tis, *Pathol.* an acute inflammation of the meninges of the brain and spinal cord, caused by a specific organism, accompanied by fever and occasionally red spots on the skin. Also called **brain fever, cer′ebrospi′nal fe′ver.** [1885–90]

cere′brospi′nal nerv′ous sys′tem. See **central nervous system.** [1865–70]

ce•re•bro•vas•cu•lar (se rē′brō vas′kyə lər, ser′ə-), *adj. Anat.* of, pertaining to, or affecting the cerebrum and its associated blood vessels. [1930–35; CEREBRO- + VASCULAR]

cere′brovas′cular ac′cident, *Pathol.* stroke (def. 6). *Abbr.:* CVA [1930–35]

ce•re•brum (sə rē′brəm, ser′ə-), *n., pl.* **-brums, -bra** (-brə). *Anat., Zool.* **1.** the anterior and largest part of the brain, consisting of two halves or hemispheres and serving to control voluntary movements and coordinate mental actions. **2.** the forebrain and the midbrain. See illus. under **brain.** [1605–15; < L: brain; akin to CRANIUM, HORN]

cere•cloth (sēr′klôth′, -kloth′), *n., pl.* **-cloths** (-klôthz′, -klothz′, -klôths′, -kloths′). **1.** cloth coated or impregnated with wax so as to be waterproof, formerly used for wrapping the dead, for bandages, etc. **2.** a piece of such cloth. [1400–50; late ME; earlier *cered cloth;* see CERE[2]]

cere•ment (sēr′mənt, ser′ə-), *n.* Usually, **cerements. 1.** a cerecloth used for wrapping the dead. **2.** any graveclothes. [1595–1605; CERE[2] + -MENT]

cer•e•mo•ni•al (ser′ə mō′nē əl), *adj.* **1.** of, pertaining to, or characterized by ceremony; formal; ritual: *a ceremonial occasion.* **2.** used in or in connection with ceremonies: *ceremonial robes.* —*n.* **3.** a system of ceremonies, rites, or formalities prescribed for or observed on any particular occasion; a rite. **4.** *Rom. Cath. Ch.* **a.** the order for rites and ceremonies. **b.** a book containing it. **5.** formal behavior found at, or appropriate to, a certain occasion: *the ceremonial of a state banquet.* [1350–1400; ME < ML *cērēmōniālis,* LL *caerimōniālis.* See CEREMONY, -AL[1]] **—cer′e•mo′ni•al•ism,** *n.* **—cer′e•mo′ni•al•ist,** *n.* **—cer′e•mo′ni•al•ly,** *adv.*
—Syn. 1. solemn, conventional, ceremonious. **3.** ritual, liturgy. **—Ant. 1.** informal.

cer′emo′nial tea′, a Japanese green tea made from choice shade-grown leaves that are cured by a steaming, drying, and powdering process: used in chanoyu.

cer•e•mo•ni•ous (ser′ə mō′nē əs), *adj.* **1.** carefully observant of ceremony; formally or elaborately polite: *He greeted his rival with a ceremonious display of friendship.* **2.** pertaining to, marked by, or consisting of ceremony; formal: *a ceremonious reception.* [1545–55; CEREMONY + -OUS; cf. MF *cerimonieux* < LL *caerimōniōsus*] **—cer′e•mo′ni•ous•ly,** *adv.* **—cer′e•mo′ni•ous•ness,** *n.*
—Syn. 1. ceremonial; conventional, punctilious.

cer•e•mo•ny (ser′ə mō′nē), *n., pl.* **-nies. 1.** the formal activities conducted on some solemn or important public or state occasion: *the coronation ceremony.* **2.** a formal religious or sacred observance; a solemn rite: *a marriage ceremony.* **3.** formal observances or gestures collectively; ceremonial observances: *The breathless messenger had no time for ceremony.* **4.** any formal act or observance, esp. a meaningless one: *His low bow was mere ceremony.* **5.** a gesture or act of politeness or civility: *the ceremony of a handshake.* **6.** strict adherence to conventional forms; formality: *to leave a room without ceremony.* **7. stand on ceremony,** to behave in a formal or ceremonious manner. [1350–1400; ME *ceremonie* < ML *cērēmōnia,* L *caerimōnia* sacred rite; r. ME *cerymonye* < MF *cerimonie* < L, as above]
—Syn. 1, 2. CEREMONY, RITE, RITUAL refer to set observances and acts traditional in religious services or on public occasions. CEREMONY applies to more or less formal dignified acts on religious or public occasions: *a marriage ceremony; an inaugural ceremony.* A RITE is an established, prescribed, or customary form of religious or other solemn practice: *the rite of baptism.* RITUAL refers to the form of conducting worship or to a code of ceremonies in general: *Masonic rituals.*

Ce•ren•kov (chə reng′kôf, -kof, -ren′-; *Russ.* chyi-RYIN kôf′), *n.* **Pa•vel A.** (pä′vəl; *Russ.* pä′vyil), born 1904, Russian physicist: Nobel prize 1958. Also, **Cherenkov.**

Ceren′kov radia′tion, *Physics.* radiation produced by a particle passing through a medium at a speed greater than that of light through the medium. [1935–40; named after P. A. CERENKOV]

cer•e•ous (sēr′ē əs), *adj. Obs.* waxlike. [1595–1605; < L *cēreus* waxen, equiv. to *cēr(a)* wax + *-eus* -EOUS]

Ce•res (sēr′ēz), *n.* **1.** a pre-Roman goddess of agriculture under whose name the Romans adopted the worship of the Greek goddess Demeter. **2.** *Astron.* the first asteroid to be discovered, being the largest and one of the brightest. **3.** a town in central California. 13,281.

ce•re•us (sēr′ē əs), *n., pl.* **-us•es. 1.** any of various plants of the genus *Cereus,* of the cactus family, having large, usually white, funnel-shaped flowers. **2.** any of several related, similar plants, esp. of the genera *Hylocereus, Nyctocereus,* and *Selenicereus.* [1720–30; < NL, L *cēreus* wax candle, n. use of *cēreus* CEREOUS]

Cerf (sûrf), *n.* **Bennett (Alfred),** 1898–1971, U.S. book publisher, editor, and writer.

ce•ri•a (sēr′ē ə), *n.* a white-to-yellow, heavy powder, cerium dioxide, CeO_2, usually derived from cerium nitrate by decomposition with heat: used chiefly in ceramics, glass polishing, and decolorizing. [CERI(UM) + -A[4]]

ce•ric (sēr′ik, ser′-), *adj.* containing cerium, esp. in the tetravalent state. [1860–65; CER(IUM) + -IC]

ce•rif•er•ous (si rif′ər əs), *adj.* producing or secreting wax, as a gland. [CER- + -I- + -FEROUS]

Ce•ri•go (cher′i gō′), *n.* a Greek island in the Mediterranean, S of Peloponnesus: site of former ancient temple of Aphrodite. 3961; 108 sq. mi. (280 sq. km). Also called **Cythera.** Greek, **Kythira.**

cer•i•man (ser′ə mən, ser′ə man′, -män′), *n., pl.* **-mans. 1.** a climbing, tropical American plant, *Monstera deliciosa,* of the arum family, characterized by cordlike, aerial roots and large, perforated leaves. **2.**

CONCISE ETYMOLOGY KEY: <, descended or borrowed from; >, whence; b., blend of, blended; c., cognate with; cf., compare; deriv., derivative; equiv., equivalent; imit., imitative; obl., oblique; r., replacing; s., stem; sp., spelling, spelled; resp., respelling, respelled; trans., translation; ?, origin unknown; *, unattested; ‡, probably earlier than. See the full key inside the front cover.

the greenish-yellow, edible, sweet fruit of this plant. Also called **false breadfruit.** [1870–75; < AmerSp]

ce·rin′ic ac′id (si rin′ik). See **cerotic acid.** [CER- + -IN[2] + -IC]

cer·iph (ser′if), *n. Chiefly Brit.* serif.

ce·rise (sə rēs′, -rēz′), *adj., n.* moderate to deep red. [1855–60; < F; see CHERRY]

ce·ri·um (sēr′ē əm), *n.* a steel-gray, ductile metallic element of the rare-earth group found only in combination. *Symbol:* Ce; *at. wt.:* 140.12; *at. no.:* 58. [1795–1805; CER(ES) + -IUM]

ce′rium met′al, *Chem.* any of a subgroup of rare-earth metals, of which the terbium and yttrium metals comprise the other two subgroups.

cer·met (sûr′met), *n.* a durable, heat-resistant alloy formed by compacting and sintering a metal and a ceramic substance, used under conditions of high temperature and stress. Also called **ceramal.** [1950–55; CER(AMIC) + MET(AL)]

CERN, European Laboratory for Particle Physics; formerly called European Organization for Nuclear Research: an international research organization based in Geneva, Switzerland. [< F, for C*(onseil)* e*(uropéen pour la)* r*(echerche)* n*(ucléaire)*]

Cer·nan (sûr′nən), *n.* **Eugene Andrew,** born 1934, U.S. astronaut.

Cer·nă·u·ţi (*Rum.* cheʀ′nə ōōts′), *n.* a city in SW Ukraine, on the Prut river: formerly in Rumania. 254,000. German, **Czernowitz.** Russian, **Chernovtsy.**

Cer·nu·da (sər nōō′də, -nyōō′-; *Sp.* theʀ nōō′thä, seʀ-), *n.* **Lu·is** (lōō ēs′), 1902–63, Spanish poet, in England after 1939.

cer·nu·ous (sûrn′yōō əs, sûr′nōō-), *adj. Bot.* drooping, as a flower; nodding. [1645–55; < L *cernuus* falling forwards, face down; see -OUS]

ce·ro (sēr′ō), *n., pl.* (*esp. collectively*) **-ro,** (*esp. referring to two or more kinds or species*) **-ros. 1.** a large Atlantic and Gulf Coast mackerel game fish, *Scomberomorus regalis.* **2.** any of various related fishes. [1880–85, *Amer.*; alter. of SIERRA]

cero-, a combining form meaning "wax," used in the formation of compound words: *cerotype.* Also, *esp. before a vowel,* **cer-.** [< Gk *kēro-,* comb. form of *kērós* wax]

ce·ro·graph (sēr′ə graf′, -gräf′), *n.* a drawing, design, or text incised into a wax surface. [1585–95; CERO- + -GRAPH] —**ce·ro·graph·ic** (sēr′ə graf′ik), **ce′ro·graph′i·cal,** *adj.* —**ce·rog·ra·phist** (si rog′rə fist), *n.*

ce·rog·ra·phy (si rog′rə fē), *n.* the process of writing or engraving on wax. [1585–95; < Gk *kērographía.* See CERO-, -GRAPHY]

ce·ro·pe·gi·a (sēr′ə pē′jē ə, -jə), *n.* any of various, usually climbing or trailing, plants of the genus *Ceropegia,* native to the Old World tropics and often cultivated as houseplants. [< NL (Linnaeus) < Gk *kēro-* CERO- + NL *-pegia,* perh. < Gk *-pēgia,* n. deriv. of *pēgnýnai* to stick in, fix in; perh. to be taken as "candle holder"; cf. Linnaeus' specific name *candelabrum*]

ce·ro·plas·tic (sēr′ə plas′tik), *adj.* **1.** pertaining to modeling in wax. **2.** modeled in wax. [1795–1805; < Gk *kēroplastikós.* See CERO-, PLASTIC] —**ce′ro·plas′tics,** *n.*

ce·rot·ic (si rot′ik, -rō′tik), *adj.* of or derived from cerotic acid. [1840–50; < L *cērōt(um)* wax salve (< Gk *kērōtón,* n. use of neut. of *kērōtós* waxed, v. adj. of *kēroûn* to wax, v. deriv. of *kērós* wax) + -IC]

cerot′ic ac′id, a white, crystalline, water-insoluble, odorless wax, $C_{26}H_{52}O_2$, usually obtained from beeswax or carnauba wax. Also called **cerinic acid, hexacosanoic acid.** [1860–65]

ce·ro·type (sēr′ə tīp′), *n.* a process of engraving in which the design or the like is cut on a wax-coated metal plate from which a printing surface is subsequently produced by stereotyping or by electrotyping. [CERO- + -TYPE]

ce·rous (sēr′əs), *adj. Chem.* containing trivalent cerium. [1860–65; CER(IUM) + -OUS]

cer·ra·do (sə rä′dō; *Port.* si Rä′dōō), *n., pl.* **-dos** (-dōz; *Port.* -dōōs). *Ecol.* a type of plains community characterized by vegetation ranging from tropical broadleaf woodlands to scrublands, occurring in extensive areas of Brazil. [< Brazilian Pg; Pg: n. use of *cerrado* thick, dense, lit., shut, ptp. of *cerrar* to close < VL **serrāre;* c in Pg, Sp perh. by assoc. with *cercar* to enclose, surround]

Cer·ri·tos (sə rē′təs), *n.* a city in SW California. 52,756.

cer·ro (ser′ō), *n., pl.* **-ros.** *Southwestern U.S.* a hill or peak. [1825–35, *Amer.*; < AmerSp; Sp: hill, backbone, neck of an animal < L *cirrus* curl, tuft (with shift: curly hair > hair on an animal's neck > neck or spine > hill)]

Cer·ro de Pas·co (seʀ′Rô the päs′kô), a town in central Peru: silver-mining district. 25,000; 14,280 ft. (4353 m) above sea level.

Cer·ro Gor·do (seʀ′Rô gôʀ′dô), a mountain pass in E Mexico between Veracruz and Jalapa: defeat of Mexican troops by U.S. troops 1847.

Cer′ro To·lo′lo Inter-Amer′ican Observ′atory (ser′ō tə lō′lō; *Sp.* seʀ′Rô tô lô′lô), an astronomical observatory in the Chilean Andes having a 156-in. (4-m) reflecting telescope.

cert., **1.** certificate. **2.** certification. **3.** certified. **4.** certify.

cer·tain (sûr′tn), *adj.* **1.** free from doubt or reservation; confident; sure: *I am certain he will come.* **2.** destined; sure to happen (usually fol. by an infinitive): *He is certain to be there.* **3.** inevitable; bound to come: *They realized then that war was certain.* **4.** established as true or sure; unquestionable; indisputable: *It is certain that he tried.* **5.** fixed; agreed upon; settled: *on a certain day; for a certain amount.* **6.** definite or particular, but not named or specified: *A certain person phoned. He had a certain charm.* **7.** that may be depended on; trustworthy; unfailing; reliable: *His aim was certain.* **8.** some though not much: *a certain reluctance.* **9.** *Obs.* steadfast. **10. for certain,** without a doubt; surely: *I know for certain that I have seen that face before.* —*pron.* **11.** certain ones: *Certain of the members declined the invitation.* [1250–1300; ME < OF < VL **certānus,* equiv. to L *cert(us)* sure, settled (*cer-* base of *cernere* to decide, + *-tus* ptp. suffix) + *-ānus* -AN]
—**Syn. 1.** convinced, satisfied. See **sure. 4.** indubitable, incontestable, irrefutable, incontrovertible, obvious, plain, clear. **5.** determined.

cer·tain·ly (sûr′tn lē), *adv.* **1.** with certainty; without doubt; assuredly: *I'll certainly be there.* **2.** yes, of course: *Certainly, take the keys.* **3.** surely; to be sure: *He certainly is successful.* [1250–1300; ME; see CERTAIN, -LY]

cer·tain·ty (sûr′tn tē), *n., pl.* **-ties. 1.** the state of being certain. **2.** something certain; an assured fact. **3. for** or **of a certainty,** certainly; without a doubt: *I suspect it, but I don't know it for a certainty.* [1250–1300; ME *certeinte* < AF, equiv. to *certein* CERTAIN + *-te* -TY[2]]
—**Syn. 1.** certitude, assurance, confidence. See **belief. 2.** truth.

cer·tes (sûr′tēz), *adv. Archaic.* certainly; in truth. [1200–50; ME < OF phrase *a certes* < L **ā certīs,* lit., from sure (things); see A-[4], CERTAIN]

certif., **1.** certificate. **2.** certificated.

cer·ti·fi·a·ble (sûr′tə fī′ə bəl, sûr′tə fī′-), *adj.* **1.** capable of being certified. **2.** legally committable to a mental institution. **3.** *Sometimes Facetious.* fit or ready for an insane asylum. **4.** uncontrollable; insane: *a certifiable desire.* [1840–50; CERTIFY + -ABLE] —**cer′ti·fi′a·ble·ness,** *n.* —**cer′ti·fi′a·bly,** *adv.*

cer·tif·i·cate (*n.* sər tif′i kit; *v.* sər tif′i kāt′), *n., v.,* **-cat·ed, -cat·ing.** —*n.* **1.** a document serving as evidence or as written testimony, as of status, qualifications, privileges, or the truth of something. **2.** a document attesting to the fact that a person has completed an educational course, issued either by an institution not authorized to grant diplomas, or to a student not qualifying for a diploma. **3.** *Law.* a statement, written and signed, which is by law made evidence of the truth of the facts stated, for all or for certain purposes. **4.** *Finance.* **a.** See **gold certificate. b.** See **silver certificate.** —*v.t.* **5.** to furnish with or authorize by a certificate. **6.** to issue an official certificate attesting to the training, aptitude, and qualification of: *to certificate a teacher.* [1375–1425; late ME *certificat* < ML *certificātum,* n. use of neut. of *certificātus* certified (ptp. of *certificāre*), equiv. to *certific-* (see CERTIFY) + *-ātus* -ATE[1]] —**cer·tif·i·ca·to·ry** (sər tif′ə ki tôr′ē, -tōr′ē), *adj.*

certif′icate of admeas′urement, *Naut.* a certificate issued by a government authority, showing the registered tonnages of a commercial vessel.

certif′icate of depos′it, a written acknowledgment of a bank that it has received from the person named a specified sum of money as a deposit, often for a fixed term at a specified interest rate. *Abbr.:* CD, C.D.

certif′icate of enroll′ment, a document issued to a U.S. vessel of 20 tons gross or more, engaged in fishing or in trade along the U.S. coast, on the Great Lakes, or on U.S. inland waters.

certif′icate of incorpora′tion, a statement filed with a state official in forming a corporation, stating its name, purposes, the distribution of its stock, etc.

certif′icate of indebt′edness, a short-term, negotiable, interest-bearing note representing indebtedness.

certif′icate of or′igin, a document certifying the country of manufacture of a commodity, often required by the customs office before importation.

certif′icate of reg′istry, *Naut.* a document issued to a U.S. vessel engaged in foreign trade, stating its name, nationality, ownership, etc., and claiming for it all privileges pertaining to U.S. nationality.

certif′icate of stock′. See **stock certificate.**

cer·ti·fi·ca·tion (sûr′tə fi kā′shən, sər tif′ə-), *n.* **1.** the act of certifying. **2.** the state of being certified. **3.** a certified statement. **4.** the writing on the face of a check by which it is certified. **5.** *Law.* a certificate attesting the truth of some statement or event. [1400–50; late ME *certificacio(u)n* < ML *certificātiōn-* (s. of *certificātiō*). See CERTIFICATE, -ION]

certifica′tion mark′, a mark that certifies the origin, material, quality, mode of manufacture, accuracy, or other characteristic of a product or service: *"UL" is a certification mark for appliances meeting the safety standards of Underwriters Laboratories, Inc.*

cer·ti·fied (sûr′tə fīd′), *adj.* **1.** having or proved by a certificate: *a certified representative.* **2.** guaranteed; reliably endorsed: *a certified check.* **3.** legally declared insane. **4.** committed to a mental institution. [1605–15; CERTIFY + -ED[2]]

cer′tified check′, a check bearing a guarantee of payment by the bank on which the check is drawn. [1875–80, *Amer.*]

cer′tified mail′, uninsured first-class mail requiring proof of delivery. [1950–55]

cer′tified milk′, milk, either pasteurized or unpasteurized, that is processed in dairies conforming to official medical standards of sanitation.

cer′tified profes′sional sec′retary, a person holding an official certificate, issued by the National Secretaries Association, attesting to the holder's having specific secretarial knowledge and skills. *Abbr.:* CPS

cer′tified pub′lic account′ant, an accountant certified by a state examining board as having fulfilled the requirements of state law to be a public accountant. *Abbr.:* C.P.A. [1910–15, *Amer.*]

cer·ti·fy (sûr′tə fī′), *v.,* **-fied, -fy·ing.** —*v.t.* **1.** to attest as certain; give reliable information of; confirm: *He certified the truth of his claim.* **2.** to testify to or vouch for in writing: *The medical examiner will certify his findings to the court.* **3.** to guarantee; endorse reliably: *to certify a document with an official seal.* **4.** to guarantee (a check) by writing on its face that the account against which it is drawn has sufficient funds to pay it. **5.** to award a certificate to (a person) attesting to the completion of a course of study or the passing of a qualifying examination. **6.** to declare legally insane and committable to a mental institution. **7.** *Archaic.* to assure or inform with certainty. —*v.i.* **8.** to give assurance; testify; vouch for the validity of something (usually fol. by *to*). [1300–50; ME *certifien* < MF *certifier* < LL *certificāre,* equiv. to L *certi-* (comb. form of *certus* decided; see CERTAIN) + *-ficāre* -FY] —**cer′ti·fi′er,** *n.*
—**Syn. 1.** corroborate, verify, validate, guarantee.

cer·ti·o·ra·ri (sûr′shē ə râr′ī, -rär′ē), *n. Law.* a writ issuing from a superior court calling up the record of a proceeding in an inferior court for review. Also called **writ of certiorari.** [1515–25; < L: to be informed, certified, lit., made surer, pass. inf. of *certiōrāre* to inform, v. deriv. of *certior,* comp. of *certus* sure (see CERTAIN); so called because v. form occurred in the L original]

cer·ti·tude (sûr′ti tōōd′, -tyōōd′), *n.* freedom from doubt, esp. in matters of faith or opinion; certainty. [1375–1425; late ME < LL *certitūdō,* equiv. to L *certi-* (comb. form of *certus* sure; see CERTAIN) + *-tūdō* -TUDE]
—**Syn.** assurance, conviction, belief.

cer·to·si·na (chûr′tə sē′nə; *It.* cheʀ′tô sē′nä), *n.* a technique of inlaying light-colored material, as bone, ivory, metal, or pale wood, in elaborate designs on a dark ground. [< It, fem. of *certosino* Carthusian]

ce·ru·le·an (sə rōō′lē ən), *adj., n.* **1.** deep blue; sky blue; azure. **2.** *Heraldry.* a sky-blue tincture, used esp. on the Continent. [1660–70; < L *caerule(us)* dark blue, azure (akin to *caelum* sky) + -AN]

ceru′lean blue′, **1.** a light-blue to strong greenish-blue color. **2.** a pigment used in painting consisting mainly of oxides of tin and cobalt, chiefly characterized by its greenish-blue color and permanence. [1885–90]

ceru′lean war′bler, a North American wood warbler, *Dendroica cerulea,* the male of which is blue above and white below. [1820–30, *Amer.*]

ce·ru·lo·plas·min (sə rōō′lə plaz′min), *n. Biochem.* a serum glycoprotein involved in the storage and transport of copper and iron. [1950–55; < NL *cerulo-,* comb. form repr. L *caeruleus* (see CERULEAN, -O-) + PLASM(A) + -IN[2]]

ce·ru·men (si rōō′mən), *n.* earwax. [1735–45; < NL, equiv. to L *cēr(a)* wax + *(alb)umen* ALBUMEN] —**ce·ru′mi·nous,** *adj.*

ce·ruse (sēr′ōōs, si rōōs′), *n.* a pigment composed of white lead. [1350–1400; ME < L *cērussa*]

ce·rus·site (sēr′ə sīt′, si rus′īt), *n.* a mineral, lead carbonate, $PbCO_3$, found in masses or in colorless, transparent crystals: an important ore of lead. [1840–50; < L *cēruss(a)* CERUSE + -ITE[1]]

Cer·van·tes (sər van′tēz; *Sp.* theʀ vän′tes, seʀ-), *n.* **Mi·guel de** (mi gel′ dā; *Sp.* mē gel′ de), (*Miguel de Cervantes Saavedra*), 1547–1616, Spanish novelist and short-story writer.

cer·ve·lat (sûr′və lat′, -lä′, ser′-), *n.* a type of smoked sausage made of beef or pork, fat, and seasonings: originally made of brains. Also, **cer·ve·las** (sur′və-lä′, ser′-). [1605–15; F (now obs.); see SAVELOY]

cer·vel·lière (sûr′vəl yâr′), *n. Armor.* a close-fitting cap of mail or plate; coif. Also, **cer′ve·lière′.** [< F, deriv. of *cervelle* brain. See CEREBELLUM; for formation, see BRASSIERE]

Cer·ve·ra y To·pe·te (theʀ ve′Rä ē tô pe′te, seʀ-), **Pas·cual** (päs kwäl′), 1839–1909, Spanish admiral.

cer·ve·za (seʀ ve′sä, theʀ ve′thä; *Eng.* sər vā′sə), *n., pl.* ***-zas*** (-säs, -thäs; *Eng.* -səz). *Spanish.* beer.

cer·vi·cal (sûr′vi kəl), *adj. Anat.* of or pertaining to the cervix or neck. [1675–85; < L *cervīc-* (s. of *cervīx*) neck + -AL[1]]

cer′vical cap′, a contraceptive device made of rubberlike plastic and fitted over the cervix, where it may be kept for long periods without removal. [1920–25]

cer′vical plex′us, a network of nerves branching from the spinal nerves of the neck region and innervating the neck, chest, diaphragm, and part of the face.

cer·vi·ces (sər vī′sēz, sûr′və sēz′), *n.* a pl. of **cervix.**

cer·vi·ci·tis (sûr′və sī′tis), *n. Pathol.* inflammation of the cervix. [1885–90; < L *cervīc-* (see CERVICAL) + -ITIS]

cer·vid (sûr′vid), *n. Zool.* any member of the deer family, Cervidae, comprising deer, caribou, elk, and moose, characterized by the bearing of antlers in the male or in both sexes. [1885–90; < NL *Cervidae,* equiv. to *Cerv(us)* a genus of the family (L: stag, deer) + *-idae* -ID[2]]

Cer·vin (seʀ vaɴ′), *n.* **Mont** (môɴ). French name of the **Matterhorn.**

cer·vine (sûr′vin, -vin), *adj.* **1.** deerlike. **2.** of deer or the deer family. **3.** of a deep tawny color. [1825–35; < L *cervīnus* of, pertaining to a deer, equiv. to *cerv(us)* deer + *-īnus* -INE[1]]

cer·vix (sûr′viks), *n., pl.* **cer·vix·es, cer·vi·ces** (sər-vī′sēz, sûr′və sēz′). *Anat.* **1.** the neck, esp. the back part. **2.** any necklike part, esp. the constricted lower end of the uterus. [1375–1425; late ME < L *cervix* neck, nape, uterine cervix] —**cer·vi·cal** (sûr′vi kəl), *adj.*

Cer′y·ne′an stag′ (ser′ə nē′ən, ser′-), *Class. Myth.* a stag living in Arcadia, captured by Hercules as one of his labors. Also called **Cer′yne′an hind′.**

CONCISE PRONUNCIATION KEY: *act, cāpe, dâre, pärt; set, ēqual; if, īce; ox, ōver, ôrder, oil, bo͝ok, bo͞ot, out; up, ûrge; child; sing; shoe; thin, that;* zh as in *treasure.* ə = *a* as in *alone, e* as in *system, i* as in *easily, o* as in *gallop, u* as in *circus;* ᵊ as in *fire* (fīᵊr), *hour* (ouᵊr). l and n can serve as syllabic consonants, as in *cradle* (krād′l), and *button* (but′n). See the full key inside the front cover.

Cé•saire (sā zer′), *n.* **Ai•mé Fer•nand** (e mā′ fer-nän′), born 1913, West Indian poet.

Ce•sar•e•an (si zâr′ē ən), *n.* (*sometimes l.c.*) **1.** Also called **Cesarean section, C-section.** an operation by which a fetus is taken from the uterus by cutting through the walls of the abdomen and uterus. —*adj.* **2.** of or pertaining to a Cesarean. **3.** Caesarean. Also, **Caesarean, Caesarian, Cesarian** (for defs. 1, 2).

ce•sar•e•vitch (si zâr′ə vich, -zär′-), *n.* the eldest son of a czar. Cf. **czarevitch.** [1830–40; see CZAREVITCH]

Ces′ca chair′ (ches′kə), a chair, with or without arms, designed by Marcel Breuer in 1928, having a cantilevered frame of chromium-plated or stainless tubular steel and a seat and back of bentwood-framed canework. Also called **Breuer chair.** [said to have been named after Breuer's daughter *Cesca* (Franciska)]

Ce•se•na (che ze′nä), *n.* a city in E central Italy. 86,070.

ce•si•um (sē′zē əm), *n.* a rare, highly reactive, soft, metallic element of the alkali metal group, used chiefly in photoelectric cells. *Symbol:* Cs; *at. wt.:* 132.905; *at. no.:* 55; *sp. gr.:* 1.9 at 20°C; melts at 28.5°C. Also, **caesium.** [1930–35; < NL, special use of L *caesium,* neut. of *caesius* bluish-grey; see -IUM]

cesium 137, *Chem.* the radioactive cesium isotope with mass number 137 and a half-life of 33 years: used for gamma irradiation of certain foods and for radiation therapy. Also called **radiocesium.**

Čes•ké Bu•dě•jo•vi•ce (ches′ke bo͝o′dye yô vi tse), a city in the S Czech Republic, on the Vltava River. 90,415. German, **Budweis.**

ces•pi•tose (ses′pi tōs′), *adj. Bot.* forming mats; growing in dense tufts. Also, **caespitose.** [1785–95; < NL *cespitōsus,* equiv. to L *cēspit-* (s. of *cēspes,* var. of *caespes* turf) + *-ōsus* -OSE[1]] —**ces′pi•tose′ly,** *adv.*

cess[1] (ses), *n.* **1.** *Brit.* a tax, assessment, or lien. **2.** (in Scotland) a land tax. **3.** (in Ireland) a military assessment. **4.** (in India) an import or sales tax on a commodity. —*v.t.* **5.** *Brit.* to tax; assess. [1400–50; late ME; aph. var. of obs. *assess* assessment, n. use of ASSESS (v.)]

cess[2] (ses), *n. Irish Eng. Informal.* luck (usually used in the expression *bad cess to*): *Bad cess to them!* [1855–60; perh. aph. var. of SUCCESS]

ces•sa•tion (se sā′shən), *n.* a temporary or complete stopping; discontinuance: *a cessation of hostilities.* [1350–1400; ME *cessacio(u)n* < L *cessātiōn-* (s. of *cessātiō*) delay, inactivity, stoppage, equiv. to *cessāt(us)* ptp. of *cessāre* to delay, stop (*cess(us)* yielded, ceded (*ced*-CEDE + *-tus* ptp. suffix) + *-ātus* -ATE[1]) + *-iōn-* -ION]

ces•sa•tive (ses′ə tiv, se sā′-), *adj.* (of a verbal form or aspect) expressing cessation. [< L *cessāt(us)* (ptp. of *cessāre* to delay) + -IVE]

ces•sion (sesh′ən), *n.* **1.** act of ceding, as by treaty. **2.** something that is ceded, as territory. [1350–1400; ME < L *cessiōn-* (s. of *cessiō*) a giving up, equiv. to *cess(us)* ptp. of *cēdere* to yield (*ced-* perfect s. + *-tus* ptp. suffix) + *-iōn-* -ION]

ces•sion•ar•y (sesh′ə ner′ē), *n., pl.* **-ar•ies.** *Law.* an assignee or grantee. [1605–15; < ML *cessiōnārius,* equiv. to *cessiōn-* CESSION + *-ārius* -ARY]

cess•pipe (ses′pīp′), *n.* a waste pipe, esp. one discharging from a cesspool. [CESS(POOL) + PIPE[1]]

cess•pit (ses′pit′), *n.* a pit for receiving wastes, as sewage, or other refuse. [1860–65; CESS(POOL) + PIT[1]]

cess•pool (ses′po͞ol′), *n.* **1.** a cistern, well, or pit for retaining the sediment of a drain or for receiving the sewage from a house. **2.** any filthy receptacle or place. **3.** any place of moral filth or immorality: *a cesspool of iniquity.* [1575–85; *cess* (< It *cesso* privy < L *rēcessus* RECESS, place of retirement) + POOL[1]]

ces•ta (ses′tə), *n. Jai Alai.* a narrow, curved basket fitted on one end to a wooden handle with a glovelike compartment at the base, for catching and throwing the ball. [1900–05; < Sp: lit., basket < L *cista* CHEST]

c'est-à-dire (se tA dēr′), *French.* that is to say.

Ces•ti (ches′tē), *n.* **Marc•an•to•nio** (mär′kän tô′nyô), 1623–69, Italian composer.

c'est la guerre (se lA ger′), *French.* such is war.

c'est la vie (se lA vē′), *French.* that's life; such is life.

ces•tode (ses′tōd), *n.* **1.** a parasitic platyhelminth or flatworm of the class Cestoda, which comprises the tapeworms. —*adj.* **2.** belonging or pertaining to the Cestoda. [1830–40; < NL *Cestoda.* See CESTUS[1], -ODE[1]]

ces•toid (ses′toid), *adj.* **1.** *Zool.* (of worms) ribbonlike. —*n.* **2.** cestode. [1830–40; < NL *cestoīdēs.* See CESTUS[1], -OID]

ces•tus[1] (ses′təs), *n., pl.* **-ti** (-tī). **1.** a girdle or belt, esp. as worn by women of ancient Greece. **2.** *Class. Myth.* the girdle of Venus, decorated with every object that could arouse amorous desire. Also, *esp. Brit.,* **ces′•tos.** [1570–80; < L < Gk *kestós* a girdle, lit., (something) stitched, equiv. to *kes-* (var. s. of *kentein* to stitch; see CENTER) + *-tos* v. adj. suffix]

ces•tus[2] (ses′təs), *n., pl.* **-tus•es.** *Rom. Antiq.* a hand covering made of leather strips and often covered with metal studs, worn by boxers. [1725–35; < L *cestus, caestus*]

ce•su•ra (sə zho͝or′ə, -zo͝or′ə, siz yo͝or′ə), *n., pl.* **ce•su•ras, ce•su•rae** (sə zho͝or′ē, -zo͝or′ē, siz yo͝or′ē). caesura. —**ce•su′ral,** *adj.*

cet-, a combining form meaning "whale," used in the formation of compound words: *cetane.* [comb. form repr. Gk *kêtos* whale]

CONCISE ETYMOLOGY KEY: <, descended or borrowed from; >, whence; b., blend of, blended; c., cognate with; cf., compare; deriv., derivative; equiv., equivalent; imit., imitative; obl., oblique; r., replacing; s., stem; sp., spelling, spelled; resp., respelling, respelled; trans., translation; ?, origin unknown; *, unattested; ‡, probably earlier than. See the full key inside the front cover.

CETA (sē′tə), *n.* Comprehensive Employment and Training Act.

ce•ta•cean (si tā′shən), *adj.* **1.** belonging to the Cetacea, an order of aquatic, chiefly marine mammals, including the whales and dolphins. —*n.* **2.** a cetacean mammal. [1830–40; < NL *Cetace(a)* name of the order (see CET-, -ACEA) + -AN] —**ce•ta′ceous,** *adj.*

ce•ta•ce•um (sē tā′shē əm, -sē əm), *n.* spermaceti. [< NL, neut. of *cētāceus;* see CETACEAN]

ce•tane (sē′tān), *n.* a colorless, liquid hydrocarbon of the alkane series, $C_{16}H_{34}$, used as a solvent and in cetane number determinations. [1930–35; CET(YL) + -ANE]

ce′tane num′ber, a measure of the ignition quality of a diesel engine fuel by comparison with various mixtures in which the alpha form of methylnaphthalene is given a standard value of 0 and cetane is given a standard value of 100. Also called **ce′tane rat′ing.** [1930–35]

Ce•ta•tea Al•bă (che tä′tyä äl′bə), Rumanian name of **Belgorod-Dnestrovsky.**

cete (sēt), *n.* a number of badgers together. [1400–50; late ME, of obscure orig.; perh. var. of ME *cite* CITY, a usage suggested by similarity of ME forms for BOROUGH and BURROW]

ce•te•ris pa•ri•bus (kā′te rēs′ pä′ri bo͝os′; *Eng.* set′ər is par′ə bəs), *Latin.* other things being equal.

ce•tin (sēt′n), *n. Biochem.* a white, crystalline, water-insoluble fat, $C_{32}H_{64}O_2$, obtained from spermaceti by extraction with ether: used chiefly as an emulsive agent in the manufacture of pharmaceuticals and cosmetics and as a base in the manufacture of candles and soaps. Also called **ce′tyl pal′mitate.** [CET- + -IN[2]]

Ce•tin•je (tse′ti nye), *n.* a city in S Yugoslavia: former capital of Montenegro. 22,032.

ceto-, var. of **cet-** before a consonant: *cetology.*

ce•tol•o•gy (sē tol′ə jē), *n.* the branch of zoology dealing with whales and dolphins. [1850–55; CET- + -O- + -LOGY] —**ce•to•log•i•cal** (sēt′l oj′i kəl), *adj.* —**ce•tol′o•gist,** *n.*

cet. par., See ***ceteris paribus.***

Ce•tur•a (si to͝or′ə), *n. Douay Bible.* Keturah.

Ce•tus (sē′təs, sā′-), *n., gen.* **Ce•ti** (sē′tī, sā′tē). *Astron.* the Whale, a constellation lying above the equator, containing the variable star Mira. [< L; see CET-]

ce′tyl al′cohol (sēt′l), a white, crystalline, water-insoluble solid, $C_{16}H_{34}O$, used chiefly as an emollient in cosmetics and pharmaceuticals. Also, **ce•tyl′ic al′cohol** (si til′ik). Also called **ethal.** [1870–75; CET- + -YL (so called because some of its compounds are found in spermaceti)]

cetyl′ic ac′id. See **palmitic acid.** [CETYL + -IC]

Ceu•ta (syo͞o′tə; *Sp.* the′o͞o tä, se′-), *n.* a seaport and enclave of Spain in N Morocco, on the Strait of Gibraltar. 67,187.

Cé•vennes (sā ven′), *n.* (*used with a plural v.*) a mountain range in S France. Highest peak, Mt. Mézenc, 5753 ft. (1754 m).

ce•vi•che (sə vē′chā, -chē), *n.* an appetizer of small pieces of raw fish marinated in lime or lemon juice, often with onions, peppers, and spices. Also, **seviche.** [1950–55; < AmerSp (Peru, Ecuador, etc.) *cebiche, ceviche, seviche,* said to be der. of Sp *cedo* fodder, fish pieces used for bait < L *cibus* food]

Ce•wa (chā′wä), *n., pl.* **-was,** (*esp. collectively*) **-wa.** Chewa.

Cey•lon (si lon′, sā-), *n.* former name of **Sri Lanka.**

Ceylon′ cin′namon. See under **cinnamon** (def. 1).

Cey•lon•ese (sē′lə nēz′, -nēs′, sā′-), *adj., n., pl.* **-ese.** —*adj.* **1.** of or pertaining to Ceylon (now Sri Lanka), its people, or their language. —*n.* **2.** a native or inhabitant of Ceylon. [1790–1800; CEYLON + -ESE]

Ceylon′ goose′berry, kitembilla.

Ceylon′ moss′, a seaweed, *Gracilaria lichenoides,* of Ceylon and the East Indies: one of the algae from which agar is obtained. [1860–65]

Cé•zanne (si zan′; *Fr.* sā zAn′), *n.* **Paul** (pôl), 1839–1906, French painter.

CF, 1. Also, **cf** cubic foot; cubic feet. **2.** cystic fibrosis.

Cf, *Symbol, Chem.* californium.

cf., 1. *Bookbinding.* calf. **2.** *Music.* cantus firmus. **3.** *Baseball.* center fielder. **4.** compare. [< L *confer*]

c/f, *Bookkeeping.* carried forward.

C.F., cost and freight. Also, **c.f.**

CFA, *Trademark.* Chartered Financial Analyst.

CFA franc, a monetary unit used by several countries in West Africa, including Benin, Ivory Coast, Niger, Senegal, Togo, and Burkina Faso. Also, **C.F.A. franc.** [abbrev. of *Communauté financière africaine* African Financial Community]

cfd, cubic feet per day.

CFG, Camp Fire Girls. See under **Camp Fire.**

cfh, cubic feet per hour.

C.F.I., cost, freight, and insurance. Also, **c.f.i.**

cfm, cubic feet per minute.

CFNP, Community Food and Nutrition Programs.

CFO, chief financial officer. Also, **C.F.O.**

CFP, certified financial planner.

CFR, Code of Federal Regulations.

CFS, chronic fatigue syndrome.

cfs, cubic feet per second.

CFT, *Med.* See **complement fixation test.**

CFTC, See **Commodity Futures Trading Commission.**

cg, centigram; centigrams.

C.G., 1. Captain of the Guard. **2.** center of gravity. **3.** Coast Guard. **4.** Commanding General. **5.** Consul General.

c.g., 1. Captain of the Guard. **2.** center of gravity. **3.** Commanding General. **4.** Consul General.

cgm., centigram; centigrams.

cGMP, cyclic GMP.

cgs, centimeter-gram-second. Also, **CGS, c.g.s.**

ch, *Survey., Civ. Engin.* chain; chains.

Ch., 1. Chaldean. **2.** Chaldee. **3.** *Television.* channel. **4.** chapter. **5.** Château. **6.** *Chess.* check. **7.** China. **8.** Chinese. **9.** church.

ch., 1. chaplain. **2.** chapter. **3.** *Chess.* check. **4.** chief. **5.** child; children. **6.** church.

c.h., 1. candle hours. **2.** clearinghouse. **3.** courthouse. **4.** custom house.

chab•a•zite (kab′ə zīt′), *n.* a zeolite mineral, essentially a hydrated sodium calcium aluminum silicate, occurring usually in red to colorless rhombohedral crystals. [1795–1805; earlier *chabaz(ie)* (< F *chabasie* < LGk *chabázios,* misspelling of *chalázios* hailstonelike (stone), equiv. to *cháláz(a)* hail, hailstone + *-ios* adj. suffix) + -ITE[1]; cf. G *Chabasit*]

Cha•blis (sha blē′, shə-, shä-, shab′lē; *Fr.* shA blē′), *n., pl.* **Cha•blis** (sha blēz′, shə-, shä-, shab′lēz; *Fr.* shA-blē′). **1.** a dry white wine from the Burgundy region in France. **2.** a similar wine produced elsewhere. [1660–70; named after *Chablis,* a town in the region]

cha•bouk (chä′bo͝ok), *n.* (in the Orient) a horsewhip, often used for inflicting corporal punishment. Also, **cha′buk.** [1805–15; < Urdu *chābuk* < Pers]

Cha•bri•er (shä′brē ā′; *Fr.* shA brē ā′), *n.* **A•lex•is Em•man•u•el** (ə lek′sis i man′yo͞o əl; *Fr.* A lek sē′ e mA ny el′), 1841–94, French composer.

cha-cha (chä′chä′), *n., pl.* **-chas,** *v.,* **-chaed, -cha•ing.** —*n.* **1.** a fast ballroom dance of Latin American origin, similar to the mambo, that follows a rhythmic pattern based upon a quick three-step movement. —*v.i.* **2.** to dance the cha-cha. Also, **cha′-cha′-cha′.** [1950–55; < AmerSp (Cuban) *cha-cha-cha,* prob. imit. of the musical accompaniment]

cha•cha•la•ca (chä′chə lä′kə; *Sp.* chä′chä lä′kä), *n., pl.* **-cas** (-kəz; *Sp.* -käs). any of several slender guans of the genus *Ortalis,* of Central America, Mexico, and southern Texas, having loud, harsh cries. [1850–55, *Amer.;* < MexSp < Nahuatl: to chatter, esp. of birds; cf. Nahuatl *chachalacametl* the chachalaca]

chach•ka (choch′kə), *n.* tchotchke.

chack•le (chak′əl), *v.i.,* **chack•led, chack•ling.** *Brit. Dial.* to chatter; jabber. [expressive form; cf. CHATTER, CACKLE]

chac•ma (chak′mə), *n.* a large, brownish-gray baboon, *Papio ursinus,* of southern Africa. [1825–35; (< D) < Khoikhoi, first recorded as *chöachamma* (1691)]

chacma, *Papio ursinus,* about 2 ft. (0.6 m) high at shoulder; head and body 2½ ft. (0.8 m); tail 1½ ft. (0.5 m)

Cha•co (chä′kô), *n.* **1.** a part of the Gran Chaco region in central South America, in Bolivia, Paraguay, and Argentina. ab. 100,000 sq. mi. (259,000 sq. km). **2.** See **Gran Chaco.**

cha•conne (sha kôn′, -kon′, shä-; *Fr.* shA kôn′), *n., pl.* **-connes** (-kônz′, -konz′; *Fr.* -kôn′). **1.** an ancient dance, probably of Spanish origin, in moderate triple meter. **2.** a musical form based on the continuous variation of a series of chords or of a ground bass. [1675–85; < F < Sp *chacona*]

cha•cun à son goût (shA kœ nA sôN go͞o′), *French.* each to one's own taste.

chad (chad), *n. Computers.* a small paper disk or square formed when a hole is punched in a punch card or paper tape. [1945–50; orig. uncert.]

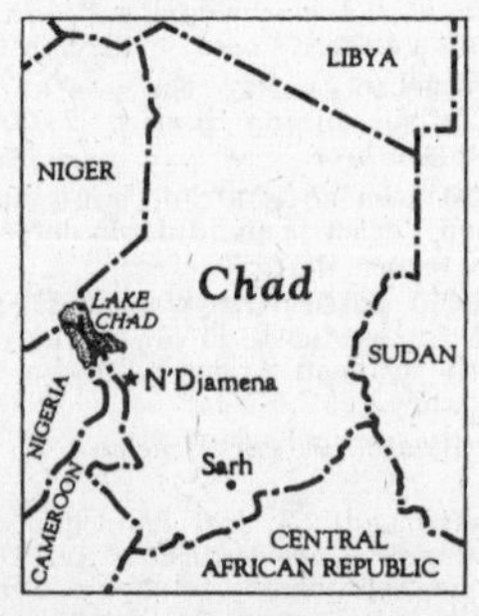

Chad (chad), *n.* **1. Lake,** a lake in Africa at the junction of four countries: Cameroon, Chad, Niger, and Nigeria. 5000 to 10,000 sq. mi. (13,000 to 26,000 sq. km) (seasonal variation). **2.** Official name, **Republic of Chad.** a republic in N central Africa, E of Lake Chad: a member of the French Community; formerly part of French Equatorial Africa. 4,100,000; 501,000 sq. mi. (1,297,590 sq. km). *Cap.:* N'Djamena. **3.** Chadic. **4.** a male given name. French, **Tchad** (for defs. 1, 2).

cha·da·rim (KHə dä′Rim), *n. Yiddish.* pl. of **cheder.**

Chad·i·an (chad′ē ən), *adj.* **1.** of or pertaining to the Republic of Chad, its inhabitants, or their language. —*n.* **2.** an inhabitant or native of the Republic of Chad. [CHAD + -IAN]

Chad·ic (chad′ik), *n.* a branch of the Afroasiatic family of languages, of which Hausa is the most widely spoken representative. [CHAD + -IC]

chad·or (chud′ər), *n.* the traditional garment of Muslim and Hindu women, consisting of a long, usually black or drab-colored cloth or veil that envelops the body from head to foot and covers all or part of the face. Also **chad′ar, chad′dar, chuddar.** [1605–15; < Hindi < Pers *chaddar, chādur* veil, sheet]

Chad·wick (chad′wik), *n.* **1. Florence (May),** born 1918, U.S. long-distance swimmer. **2. George Whitefield,** 1854–1931, U.S. composer. **3. James,** 1891–1974, English physicist: discoverer of the neutron; Nobel prize 1935.

Chaer·o·ne·a (ker′ə nē′ə), *n.* an ancient city in E Greece, in Boeotia: victory of Philip of Macedon over the Athenians, Thebans, and their allies, 338 B.C.

chae·ta (kē′tə), *n., pl.* **-tae** (-tē). *Zool.* a bristle or seta, esp. of a chaetopod. [< NL < Gk *chaítē* long hair]

chaeto-, a combining form meaning "hair," used in the formation of compound words: *chaetophorous.* [1865–70; comb. form repr. Gk *chaítē;* see CHAETA]

chae·tog·nath (kē′tog nath′, -təg-), *n.* **1.** any animal of the phylum Chaetognatha, comprising the arrowworms. —*adj.* **2.** Also, **chae·tog·na·than** (kē tog′nə thən), **chae·tog′na·thous.** belonging or pertaining to the Chaetognatha. [1885–90; < NL *Chaetognatha,* neut. pl. of *chaetognathus;* see CHAETO-, -GNATHOUS]

chae·toph·o·rous (ki tof′ər əs), *adj. Zool.* bearing bristles; setigerous. [1875–80; CHAETO- + -PHOROUS]

chae·to·pod (kē′tə pod′), *n.* any annelid of the class or group Chaetopoda, having the body composed of more or less similar segments with muscular processes bearing setae. [1860–65; < NL *Chaetopoda;* see CHAETO-, -POD]

chae·to·tax·y (kē′tə tak′sē), *n. Entomol.* the arrangement of bristles on the exoskeleton of an insect. [1890–95; CHAETO- + -TAXY] —**chae·to·tac·tic** (kē′tə-tak′tik), *adj.*

chafe (chāf), *v.,* **chafed, chaf·ing,** *n.* —*v.t.* **1.** to wear or abrade by rubbing: *He chafed his shoes on the rocks.* **2.** to make sore by rubbing: *Her collar chafed her neck.* **3.** to irritate; annoy: *The dripping of the faucet chafed her nerves.* **4.** to warm by rubbing: *to chafe cold hands.* **5.** *Obs.* to heat; make warm. —*v.i.* **6.** to become worn or sore from rubbing: *His neck began to chafe from the starched collar.* **7.** to rub; press with friction: *The horse chafed against his stall.* **8.** to be irritated or annoyed: *He chafed at their constant interruptions.* **9. chafe at the bit,** to become impatient at delay: *The work was going very slowly, and he began to chafe at the bit.* —*n.* **10.** irritation; annoyance. **11.** heat, wear, or soreness caused by rubbing. [1275–1325; ME *chaufen* to heat, rub, chafe < MF *chaufer* < VL **calfāre,* var. of L *cal(e)facere,* equiv. to *cale-* (s. of *calēre* to be hot) + *facere* to make]
—**Syn. 3.** exasperate, vex, trouble, provoke.

chaf·er (chā′fər), *n.* any scarabaeid beetle. [bef. 1000; ME *cheaffer, chaver,* OE *ceofor;* akin to G *Käfer*]

chafe·weed (chāf′wēd′), *n.* See **wood cudweed.** [1540–50; CHAFE + WEED[1]]

chaff[1] (chaf, chäf), *n.* **1.** the husks of grains and grasses that are separated during threshing. **2.** straw cut up for fodder. **3.** worthless matter; refuse. **4.** the membranous, usually dry, brittle bracts of the flowers of certain plants. **5.** Also called **window.** *Mil.* strips of metal foil dropped by an aircraft to confuse enemy radar by creating false blips. [bef. 1000; ME *chaf,* OE *ceaf;* c. MLG, D *kaf*] —**chaff′less,** *adj.* —**chaff′like′,** *adj.*

chaff[2] (chaf, chäf), *v.t., v.i.* **1.** to mock, tease, or jest in a good-natured way; banter: *She chaffed him for working late. They joked and chaffed with each other.* —*n.* **2.** good-natured ridicule or teasing; raillery. [1640–50; perh. from CHAFF[1]] —**chaff′ing·ly,** *adv.*

chaf·fer[1] (chaf′ər), *n.* **1.** bargaining; haggling. —*v.i.* **2.** to bargain; haggle: *to chaffer over a price.* **3.** to bandy words; chatter: *to chaffer about nothing in particular.* —*v.t.* **4.** to bandy (words). **5.** *Obs.* to trade or deal in; barter. [1175–1225; ME *chaffare,* deriv. of *chapfare* trading journey, equiv. to OE *cēap* trade (see CHEAP) + *faru* journey; see FARE] —**chaff′er·er,** *n.*

chaf·fer[2] (chaf′ər), *n.* a person who chaffs or banters. [1850–55; CHAFF[2] + -ER[1]]

chaf·finch (chaf′inch), *n.* a common finch, *Fringilla coelebs,* of the Old World, often kept as a pet. [1400–50; late ME *chaffynche,* OE *ceaffinc.* See CHAFF[1], FINCH]

chaff·y (chaf′ē, chä′fē), *adj.,* **chaff·i·er, chaff·i·est.** consisting of, covered with, or resembling chaff. [1545–55; CHAFF[1] + -Y[1]] —**chaff′i·ness,** *n.*

chaf′ing dish′ (chā′fing), **1.** an apparatus consisting of a metal dish with a lamp or heating appliance beneath it, for cooking food or keeping it hot at the table. **2.** a vessel that holds charcoal or the like, for heating anything set over it. [1400–50; late ME *chafing* warming (see CHAFE, -ING[1])]

Cha·ga (chä′gə), *n., pl.* **-gas,** (*esp. collectively*) **-ga** for 1. **1.** a member of a Bantu people of northern Tanzania. **2.** the Bantu language spoken by the Chaga. Also, **chag′ga.**

cha·gal (chä′gəl), *n.* chagul.

Cha·gall (shə gäl′), *n.* **Marc,** 1887–1985, Russian painter in France.

Cha′gas′ disease′ (shä′gəs), *Pathol.* an infectious disease caused by the protozoan *Trypanosoma cruzi,* occurring chiefly in tropical America and characterized by irregular fever, palpable lymph nodes, and often heart damage. Also called **American trypanosomiasis.** [1910–15; named after C. *Chagas* (1879–1934), Brazilian physician, its describer]

Cha·ga·tai (chä′gə tī′, chag′ə-, chä′gə tī′, chag′ə-), *n.* a Turkic literary language of medieval Central Asia. Also, **Jagatai, Jaghatai.**

Cha′gos Archipel′ago (chä′gōs, -gəs), a group of islands in the British Indian Ocean Territory. ab. 75 sq. mi. (195 sq. km).

Cha·gres (chä′gRes), *n.* a river in Panama, flowing through Gatun Lake into the Caribbean Sea.

cha·grin (shə grin′), *n., v.,* **-grined** or **-grinned, -grin·ing** or **-grin·ning.** —*n.* **1.** a feeling of vexation, marked by disappointment or humiliation. —*v.t.* **2.** to vex by disappointment or humiliation: *The rejection of his proposal chagrined him deeply.* **3.** *Obs.* shagreen (def. 1). [1650–60; < F < ?]
—**Syn. 1.** See **shame.**

cha·gul (chä′gəl), *n.* a bag made of goatskin: used in the Orient for carrying water. Also, **chagal.** [1905–10; < Hindi *chāgal* < Skt *chāgala* of a goat]

Cha·har (chä′häR′), *n. Older Spelling.* Qahar.

chai (she), *n., pl.* ***chais*** (she). *French.* a shed or other aboveground building where a winemaker stores wine in casks.

Chai·kov·ski (chī kôf′skē, -kof′-; *Russ.* chye kôf′skyē), *n.* **Pëtr Il·ich** (*Russ.* pyôtR ē lyēch′). See **Tchaikovsky, Pëtr Ilich.**

chain (chān), *n.* **1.** a series of objects connected one after the other, usually in the form of a series of metal rings passing through one another, used either for various purposes requiring a flexible tie with high tensile strength, as for hauling, supporting, or confining, or in various ornamental and decorative forms. **2.** Often, **chains.** something that binds or restrains; bond: *the chain of timidity; the chains of loyalty.* **3. chains, a.** shackles or fetters: *to place a prisoner in chains.* **b.** bondage; servitude: *to live one's life in chains.* **c.** *Naut.* (in a sailing vessel) the area outboard at the foot of the shrouds of a mast: the customary position of the leadsman in taking soundings. **d.** See **tire chain. 4.** a series of things connected or following in succession: *a chain of events.* **5.** a range of mountains. **6.** a number of similar establishments, as banks, theaters, or hotels, under one ownership or management. **7.** *Chem.* two or more atoms of the same element, usually carbon, attached as in a chain. Cf. **ring**[1] (def. 17). **8.** *Survey., Civ. Engin.* **a.** a distance-measuring device consisting of a chain of 100 links of equal length, having a total length either of 66 ft. (20 m) **(Gunter's chain** or **surveyor's chain)** or of 100 ft. (30 m) **(engineer's chain). b.** a unit of length equal to either of these. **c.** a graduated steel tape used for distance measurements. *Abbr.:* ch **9.** *Math.* See **totally ordered set. 10.** *Football.* a chain 10 yd. (9 m) in length for determining whether a first down has been earned. **11. drag the chain,** *Australian Slang.* to lag behind or shirk one's fair share of work. **12. in the chains,** *Naut.* standing outboard on the channels or in some similar place to heave the lead to take soundings. —*v.t.* **13.** to fasten or secure with a chain: *to chain a dog to a post.* **14.** to confine or restrain: *His work chained him to his desk.* **15.** *Survey.* to measure (a distance on the ground) with a chain or tape. **16.** *Computers.* to link (related items, as records in a file or portions of a program) together, esp. so that items can be run in sequence. **17.** to make (a chain stitch or series of chain stitches), as in crocheting. —*v.i.* **18.** to form or make a chain. [1250–1300; ME *chayne* < OF *chaeine* < L *catēna* fetter; see CATENA] —**chain′less,** *adj.* —**chain′like′,** *adj.*
—**Syn. 4.** sequence, succession, train, set.

Chain (chān), *n.* **Sir Ernst Boris** (ûrnst, ẹrnst), 1906–79, English biochemist, born in Germany: Nobel prize for medicine 1945.

chain·age (chā′nij), *n.* a length as measured by a surveyor's chain or tape. [1605–15; CHAIN + -AGE]

chain·belt (chān′belt′), *n.* a belt made up of metal links, used as a conveyor or with a chain gear. Also, **chain′ belt′.** [1965–70; CHAIN + BELT]

chain′ cor′al, coral of the extinct genus *Halysites,* from the Ordovician and Silurian periods, consisting of oval, laterally compressed corallites united to form a chainlike structure. [1800–10]

chain′ drive′, a driving mechanism transmitting power by means of an endless chain. [1900–05] —**chain-driv·en** (chān′driv′ən), *adj.*

chaî·né (she nā′), *n., pl.* **-nés** (-nāz′; *Fr.* -nā′). *Ballet.* a series of short, usually rapid, turns performed in a straight line across the stage. [1945–50; < F, n. use of ptp. of *chaîner* to CHAIN]

Chained′ La′dy, *Astron.* the constellation Andromeda.

chain′ fern′, any of several ferns of the genus *Woodwardia,* having a chainlike row of sori on either side of the midrib of each fertile leaflet. [1865–70, *Amer.*]

chain′ gang′, a group of convicts chained together, esp. when working outside. [1825–35]

chain′ gear′, a gear assembly in which motion is transmitted by means of a chain. [1875–80]

chain′ let′ter, a letter sent to a number of people, each of whom is asked to make and mail copies to other people who are to do likewise, often used as a means of spreading a message or raising money. [1905–10]

chain′ light′ning, 1. *Chiefly Northeastern and Western U.S.* lightning that seems to move very quickly in wavy or zigzag lines. **2.** See **bead lightning.** [1825–35, *Amer.*]

chain-link (chān′lingk′), *adj.* of, pertaining to, or resembling a chain-link fence, as in its diamond shapes or linked couplings: *a chain-link fabric.* [1895–1900]

chain′-link fence′, a mesh fence made of thick steel wire and having a diamond-shaped pattern.

chain′ lock′er, *Naut.* a compartment where the chain or cable of an anchor is stowed when the anchor is raised.

chain′ mail′, *Armor.* mail[2] (def. 1). [1815–25]

chain·man (chān′mən), *n., pl.* **-men.** *Survey.* a person who holds and positions a chain in taking measurements. [1705–15, *Amer.;* CHAIN + -MAN]

chain′ meas′ure, measurement of distance using a chain 66 ft. (20 m) long, of which one link equals 7.9 in. (20.1 cm).

chain′ of command′, a series of administrative or military ranks, positions, etc., in which each has direct authority over the one immediately below. [1910–15]

chain′ pick′erel. See under **pickerel** (def. 1). [1900–05, *Amer.*]

chain′ plate′, *Naut.* any of the metal plates secured to the hull of a sailing vessel or elsewhere to hold shrouds and backstays at their lower ends. [1685–95]

chain′ pump′, a pump consisting of buckets, plates, or the like, rising upon a chain within a cylinder for raising liquids entering the cylinder at the bottom. [1610–20]

chain-re·act (chān′rē akt′), *v.i.* to undergo or produce a chain reaction: *Riots chain-reacted from one area to another in the city.*

chain′-reacting pile′, *Physics.* reactor (def. 4). [1945–50]

chain′ reac′tion, 1. *Physics.* a self-sustaining reaction in which the fission of nuclei of one generation of nuclei produces particles that cause the fission of at least an equal number of nuclei of the succeeding generation. **2.** *Chem.* a reaction that results in a product necessary for the continuance of the reaction. **3.** a series of events in which each event is the result of the one preceding and the cause of the one following. [1925–30]

chain′ reac′tor, *Physics.* reactor (def. 4). [1940–45]

chain′ rule′, *Math.* the theorem that defines the method for taking the derivative of a composite function. [1860–65]

chain′ saw′, a power saw, usually portable, having teeth set on an endless chain. [1840–50, *Amer.*]

chain-saw (chān′sô′), *v.t.* **1.** to cut or cut down (lumber, a tree, etc.) with a chain saw. —*v.i.* **2.** to use a chain saw. Also, **chain′saw′.**

chain′ shot′, cannon shot consisting of two balls or half balls connected by a short chain, formerly used in naval artillery to destroy the masts and sails of enemy ships. [1575–85]

chains·man (chānz′mən), *n., pl.* **-men.** *Naut.* a person who stands in the chains to take soundings; leadsman. [CHAIN + 'S[1] + -MAN]

chain-smoke (chān′smōk′), *v.i., v.t.,* **-smoked, -smok·ing.** to smoke continually, as by lighting one cigarette, cigar, etc., from the preceding one. [1930–35] —**chain′ smok′er.** —**chain′-smok′er,** *n.*

chain′ stitch′, 1. a kind of ornamental hand stitching in which each stitch forms a loop through the forward end of the next. **2.** a basic crochet stitch in which yarn is pulled with the crochet hook through a loop on the hook to form a continuous strand of interlocking single loops. **3.** a machine stitch forming a chain on the underside of the fabric. [1590–1600]

chain·stitch (chān′stich′), *v.t., v.i.* to sew or crochet using a chain stitch. [1860–65; v. use of CHAIN STITCH]

chain′ store′, one of a group of retail stores under the same ownership and selling similar merchandise. [1905–10, *Amer.*]

chain′ wale′, *Naut.* channel[2]. Also, **chain-wale** (chān′wāl′, chan′l). [1605–15]

chain·wheel (chān′hwēl′, -wēl′), *n. Mach.* sprocket (def. 1). [1835–45; CHAIN + WHEEL]

chain·work (chān′wûrk′), *n.* any decorative product, handiwork, etc., in which parts are looped or woven together, like the links of a chain. [1545–55; CHAIN + WORK]

chair (châr), *n.* **1.** a seat, esp. for one person, usually having four legs for support and a rest for the back and often having rests for the arms. **2.** something that serves as a chair or supports like a chair: *The two men clasped hands to make a chair for their injured companion.* **3.** a seat of office or authority. **4.** a position of authority, as of a judge, professor, etc. **5.** the person occupying a seat of office, esp. the chairperson of a meeting: *The speaker addressed the chair.* **6.** (in an orchestra) the position of a player, assigned by rank; desk: *first clarinet chair.* **7. the chair,** *Informal.* See **electric chair. 8.** chairlift. **9.** See **sedan chair. 10.** (in reinforced-concrete construction) a device for maintaining the position of reinforcing rods or strands during the pouring operation. **11.** a glassmaker's bench having extended arms on which a blowpipe is rolled in shaping glass. **12.** *Railroads Brit.* a metal block for supporting a rail and securing it to a crosstie or the like. **13. get the chair,** to be sentenced to die in the electric chair. **14. take the chair, a.** to begin or open a meeting. **b.** to preside at a meeting; act as chairperson. —*v.t.* **15.** to place or seat in a chair. **16.** to install in office. **17.** to preside over; act as chairperson of: *to chair a committee.* **18.** *Brit.* to carry (a hero or victor) aloft in triumph. —*v.i.* **19.** to preside over a meeting, committee, etc. [1250–

CONCISE PRONUNCIATION KEY: act, cāpe, dâre, pärt; set, ēqual; *if,* īce; ox, ōver, ôrder, oil, bo͝ok, bo͞ot, out; up, ûrge; child; sing; shoe; thin, that; zh as in *treasure.* ə = *a* as in *alone, e* as in *system, i* as in *easily, o* as in *gallop, u* as in *circus;* ə as in *fire* (fīər), *hour* (ouər). l and n can serve as syllabic consonants, as in *cradle* (krād′l), and *button* (but′n). See the full key inside the front cover.

1300; ME *chaiere* < OF < L *cathedra;* see CATHEDRA] —**chair′less,** *adj.*
—**Usage. 5.** See **chairperson.**

chair′ bed′, 1. a chair that can be opened out to form a bed. **2.** See **bed chair.** [1795–1805]

chair•borne (châr′bôrn′, -bōrn′), *adj.* (of military, esp. Air Force, personnel) having a desk job rather than a field or combat assignment. [1940–45; b. CHAIR and AIRBORNE]

chair′ car′, *Railroads.* **1.** a day coach having two adjustable seats on each side of a central aisle. **2.** (not in technical use) See **parlor car.** [1865–70, *Amer.*]

chair•la•dy (châr′lā′dē), *n., pl.* **-dies.** chairwoman. [1920–25; CHAIR + LADY]

chair•lift (châr′lift′), *n.* a series of chairs suspended from an endless cable driven by motors, for conveying skiers up the side of a slope. Also, **chair′ lift′.** [1935–40, *Amer.;* CHAIR + LIFT]

chair•man (châr′mən), *n., pl.* **-men,** *v.* **-maned** or **-manned, -man•ing** or **-man•ning.** —*n.* **1.** the presiding officer of a meeting, committee, board, etc. **2.** the administrative head of a department in a high school, college, or university. **3.** someone employed to carry or wheel a person in a chair. —*v.t.* **4.** to act as or be chairman of (a meeting, committee, etc.). [1645–55; CHAIR + -MAN]
—**Usage.** See **chairperson.**

chair′man of the board′, the chief officer of a business corporation, elected by its board of directors and charged with the supervision and management of high-level affairs of the company, as making corporate policy or approving actions of the president and vice presidents. Also called **board chairman.**

chair•man•ship (châr′mən ship′), *n.* the office or rank of chairman. [1840–50; CHAIRMAN + -SHIP]

chair•per•son (châr′pûr′sən), *n.* **1.** a person who presides over a meeting, committee, board, etc. **2.** the administrative head of a department in a high school, college, or university. [1970–75; CHAIR(MAN) + -PERSON] —**chair′per′son•ship′,** *n.*
—**Usage.** CHAIRPERSON has, since the 1960's, come to be used widely as an alternative to either CHAIRMAN or CHAIRWOMAN. This change has sprung largely from a desire to avoid CHAIRMAN, which is felt by many to be inappropriate and even sexually discriminatory when applied to a woman. In some organizations, notably academic and, to a lesser extent, governmental, CHAIRPERSON has been adopted as the official term for anyone who fills the position in question. Some publishers and publications specify the use of CHAIRPERSON in their style guides.
Despite such widespread acceptance, some newspapers, press associations, and other news media do not use CHAIRPERSON at all, usually on the grounds that it is awkward and that CHAIRMAN is a well-established generic term covering both sexes. Some publications and organizations use the term CHAIR to designate the presiding officer, thus avoiding charges of both sexism and awkwardness: *Jim will be chair of the entertainment committee this year, and Jane will be chair next year.* CHAIRPERSON is standard in all varieties of speech and writing. See also **-man, -person, -woman.**

chair′ rail′, a molding on an interior wall for preventing the backs of chairs from rubbing against plaster. [1835–45]

chair′ ta′ble, an article of furniture, produced esp. in colonial America, that can serve as either a table or a chair, having, as a chair, a large, usually circular, hinged back that can be pulled down and rested on the arms to form a tabletop. [1550–60]

chair′ warm′er, *Informal.* **1.** an officeholder, employee, or the like, who accomplishes little, esp. a person who holds an interim position. **2.** a person who lounges for long periods sitting in a chair, as in a hotel lobby or clubroom. [1905–10]

chair•wom•an (châr′wo͝om′ən), *n., pl.* **-wom•en.** a woman who presides over a meeting, committee, department, etc. Also called **chairlady.** [1690–1700; CHAIR + WOMAN]
—**Usage.** See **chairperson.**

chaise (def. 1)

chaise (shāz), *n.* **1.** a light, open carriage, usually with a hood, esp. a one-horse, two-wheeled carriage for two persons; shay. **2.** See **post chaise. 3.** a chaise longue, esp. a light one used out of doors. **4.** Also called **chaise d'or** (shāz dôr′). *Numis.* **a.** a gold coin of France, first issued in the early 14th century, which bears a figure of the king seated on a large throne. **b.** an Anglo-Gallic copy of this coin, issued by Edward III. [1695–1705; < F, var. of *chaire* CHAIR]

chaise longue (shāz′ lông′, chāz′; *Fr.* shez lôɴ′), *pl.* **chaise longues,** *Fr.* **chaises longues** (shez lôɴ′). a chair, with or without arms, for reclining, having a seat lengthened to form a complete leg rest and sometimes an adjustable back. Also, **chaise lounge** (shāz′ lounj′, chāz′). [1790–1800; < F: long chair; *chaise lounge* by folk etym.]

chait•ya (chīt′yə), *n.* a Buddhist shrine in India; stupa. [1870–75; < Skt *caitya,* deriv. of *citā* funeral pyre, akin to *cinoti* (he) piles up]

chak•ra (chuk′rə), *n. Yoga.* cakra.

chak•ra•var•tin (chuk′rə vär′tin), *n.* cakravartin.

Chal., 1. Chaldaic. **2.** Chaldean. **3.** Chaldee.

cha•la•za (kə lā′zə), *n., pl.* **-zas, -zae** (-zē). **1.** *Zool.* one of the two albuminous twisted cords which fasten an egg yolk to the shell membrane. **2.** *Bot.* the point of an ovule or seed where the integuments are united to the nucellus. See diag. under **orthotropous.** [1695–1705; < NL < Gk: hail, lump] —**cha•la′zal, cha•la•zi•an** (kə lā′zē ən), *adj.*

cha•la•zi•on (kə lā′zē ən), *n., pl.* **-zi•a** (-zē ə). *Ophthalm.* sty. [1700–10; < Gk, dim. of *chálaza;* see CHALAZA]

chal•can•thite (kal kan′thīt), *n. Mineral.* See **blue vitriol.** [1855–60; < L *chalcanth(um)* (< Gk *chálkanthon* blue vitriol, lit., flower of copper, equiv. to *chalk(ós)* copper + *ánth(os)* flower + *-on* neut. suffix) + -ITE[1]]

Chal•ce•don (kal′si don′, kal sēd′n), *n.* **1.** an ancient city in NW Asia Minor, on the Bosporus, opposite Byzantium. **2. Council of,** the ecumenical council held there in A.D. 451. —**Chal•ce•do•ni•an** (kal′si dō′nē ən), *adj., n.*

chal•ced•o•ny (kal sed′n ē, kal′sə dō′nē), *n., pl.* **-nies.** a microcrystalline, translucent variety of quartz, often milky or grayish. [1275–1325; ME *calcedonie* < LL *chalcēdōnius* (Vulgate, Rev. XIX, 19), equiv. to *chalcēdōn-* (< Gk *chalkēdṓn* chalcedony, identified by Saint Jerome with *Chalcedon,* the city) + *-ius* -IOUS] —**chal•ce•don•ic** (kal′si don′ik), **chal•ced′o•nous,** *adj.*

chal•cid•fly (kal′sid flī′), *n., pl.* **-flies.** any of numerous small flies of the family Chalcididae, often having bright metallic coloration, the larvae of which are chiefly parasitic on various stages of other insects. Also called **chal•cid** (kal′sid), **chal′cid fly′, chal′cid wasp′.** [1890–95; < Gk *chalk(ós)* copper, brass (with allusion to the coloration) + -ID[2] + FLY[2]]

Chal•cid•i•ce (kal sid′ə sē), *n.* a peninsula in NE Greece. Greek, **Khalkidike.**

chal•cid•i•cum (kal sid′i kəm), *n., pl.* **-ca** (-kə). **1.** an annex of an ancient Roman basilica. **2.** an annex or appendage, esp. a narthex, of an early Christian basilica. [1720–30; < L, n. use of neut. of *Chalcidicus* < Gk *Chalkidikós,* equiv. to *Chalkid-* (s. of *Chalkís*) CHALCIS + *-ikos* -IC]

Chal•cis (kal′sis; *Gr.* KHäl kēs′), *n.* a city on Euboea, in SE Greece. 36,300.

chalco-, a learned borrowing from Greek meaning "copper," used in the formation of compound words: *chalcolithic.* [< Gk *chalko-,* comb. form of *chalkós* copper]

chal•co•cite (kal′kə sīt′), *n.* a common mineral, cuprous sulfide, Cu_2S: an important ore of copper. [1865–70; irreg. CHALCO- + (ANTHRA)CITE]

chal•co•gen (kal′kə jən, -jen′), *n. Chem.* any of the elements oxygen, sulfur, selenium, tellurium, and polonium, which form the VIa group in the periodic table. [1960–65; CHALCHO- + -GEN]

chal•co•gen•ide (kal′kə jə nīd′, kal koj′ə-), *n. Chem.* a binary compound consisting of a chalcogen and a more electropositive element or radical. [CHALCOGEN + -IDE]

chal•cog•ra•phy (kal kog′rə fē), *n.* the art of engraving on copper or brass. [1655–65; CHALCO- + -GRAPHY] —**chal•cog′ra•pher, chal•cog′ra•phist,** *n.* —**chal•co•graph•ic** (kal′kə graf′ik), **chal′co•graph′i•cal,** *adj.*

chal•co•lite (kal′kə līt′), *n. Mineral.* torbernite. [1795–1805; CHALCO- + -LITE]

Chal•co•lith•ic (kal′kə lith′ik), *adj.* of, pertaining to, or characteristic of the Copper Age; Aeneolithic. [1900–05; CHALCO- + -LITHIC]

chal•co•phile (kal′kə fīl′), *adj.* **1.** (of a chemical element in the earth) having an affinity for sulfur. —*n.* **2.** a chalcophile element. [CHALCO- + -PHILE]

chal•co•py•rite (kal′kə pī′rīt), *n.* a very common mineral, copper iron sulfide, $CuFeS_2$, occurring in brass-yellow crystals or masses: the most important ore of copper; copper pyrites. [1825–35; CHALCO- + PYRITE]

chal•co•stib•ite (kal′kə stib′īt), *n.* a mineral, antimony copper sulfide, $CuSbS_2$, occurring in lead-gray crystals. [1865–70; CHALCO- + STIB(IUM) + -ITE[1]]

chal•co•trich•ite (kal′kə trik′īt), *n. Mineral.* a fibrous variety of cuprite. [1865–70; < G *Chalkotrichit;* see CHALCO-, TRICH-, -ITE[1]]

Chald., 1. Chaldaic. **2.** Chaldean. **3.** Chaldee.

Chal•da•ic (kal dā′ik), *n., adj.* Chaldean. [< L *Chaldaicus* < Gk *Chaldaïkós.* See CHALDEAN, -IC]

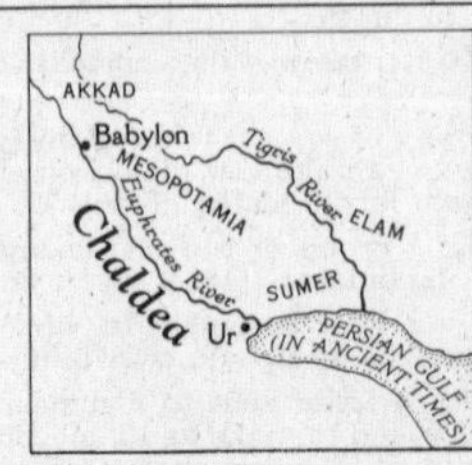

Chal•de•a (kal dē′ə), *n.* **1.** an ancient region in the lower Tigris and Euphrates valley, in S Babylonia. **2.** Babylonia. Also, **Chal•dae′a.**

Chal•de•an (kal dē′ən), *n.* **1.** one of an ancient Semitic people that formed the dominant element in Babylonia. **2.** the indigenous Semitic language of the Chaldeans, Aramaic being used as an auxiliary language. **3.** See **Biblical Aramaic. 4.** an astrologer, soothsayer, or enchanter. Dan. 1:4; 2:2. —*adj.* **5.** of or belonging to ancient Chaldea. **6.** pertaining to astrology, occult learning, etc. Also, **Chal•dee** (kal dē′, kal′dē). [1575–85; < L *Chaldae(us)* (< Gk *Chaldaîos* Chaldaea, an astrologer) + -AN]

chal•dron (chôl′drən), *n.* an English dry measure formerly used for coal, coke, lime, and the like, varying locally from 32 to 36 bushels or more. [1375–1425; late ME, earlier *chaudron* < MF *chauderon* CAULDRON]

cha•let (sha lā′, shal′ā; *Fr.* shä le′), *n., pl.* **cha•lets** (sha lāz′, shal′āz; *Fr.* shä le′). **1.** a herdsman's hut in the Swiss Alps. **2.** a kind of farmhouse, low and with wide eaves, common in Alpine regions. **3.** any cottage, house, ski lodge, etc., built in this style. [1810–20; < F, SwissF, equiv. to **chale* shelter (c. OPr *cala* COVE[1]) + *-et* -ET]

chalet (def. 3)

Cha•leur′ Bay′ (shə lo͝or′, -lûr′), an inlet of the Gulf of St. Lawrence between NE New Brunswick and SE Quebec, in SE Canada: rich fishing ground. ab. 85 mi. (135 km) long; 15–25 mi. (24–40 km) wide.

Cha•lia•pin (shäl yä′pin; *Russ.* shu lyä′pyin), *n.* **Fë•dor I•va•no•vich** (fyô′dər ē vä′nə vyich), 1873–1938, Russian operatic bass.

chal•ice (chal′is), *n.* **1.** *Eccles.* **a.** a cup for the wine of the Eucharist or Mass. **b.** the wine contained in it. **2.** a drinking cup or goblet. **3.** a cuplike blossom. [bef. 900; ME < MF < L *calici-* (s. of *calix*) cup; r. ME *caliz, calc,* OE *calic* < L *calici-,* as above] —**chal•iced** (chal′ist), *adj.*

chal•i•co•there (kal′i kō thēr′), *n.* a horselike fossil of the genus *Chalicotherium* and related genera, common in Europe, Asia, and Africa during the Tertiary Period, having a sloping back and three-toed, clawed feet. [< NL *Chalicotherium* (1833) < Gk *chalik-,* s. of *chálix* gravel + *-o-* -O- + *thḗrion* -THERE]

chalk (chôk), *n.* **1.** a soft, white, powdery limestone consisting chiefly of fossil shells of foraminifers. **2.** a prepared piece of chalk or chalklike substance for marking, as a blackboard crayon. **3.** a mark made with chalk. **4.** a score or tally. —*v.t.* **5.** to mark or write with chalk. **6.** to rub over or whiten with chalk. **7.** to treat or mix with chalk: *to chalk a billiard cue.* **8.** to make pale; blanch: *Terror chalked her face.* —*v.i.* **9.** (of paint) to powder from weathering. **10. chalk up, a.** to score or earn: *They chalked up two runs in the first inning.* **b.** to charge or ascribe to: *It was a poor performance, but may be chalked up to lack of practice.* —*adj.* **11.** of, made of, or drawn with chalk. [bef. 900; ME *chalke,* OE *cealc* < L *calc-* (s. of *calx*) lime] —**chalk′like′,** *adj.*

chalk•board (chôk′bôrd′, -bōrd′), *n.* a blackboard, esp. a green or other light-colored one. [1935–40, *Amer.;* CHALK + BOARD]

chalk′ line′, *Building Trades.* **1.** a chalked string for making a straight line on a large surface, as a wall, by holding the string taut against the surface and snapping it to transfer the chalk. **2.** the line so made. [1400–50; late ME]

chalk•rail (chôk′rāl′), *n.* a troughlike molding or strip holding chalk, erasers, etc., under a blackboard. [CHALK + RAIL[1]]

chalk•stone (chôk′stōn′), *n. Pathol.* a chalklike concretion in the tissues or small joints of a person with gout. [1350–1400; ME, for sense "limestone"; 1730–40 for current sense. See CHALK, STONE] —**chalk′ston′y,** *adj.*

chalk′ stripe′, (on a fabric) a pattern of thin white lines on a dark ground. [1940–45]

chalk′ talk′, a talk or lecture in which the speaker illustrates points by drawing on a blackboard: *The coach gave a chalk talk before the big game.* [1830–40, *Amer.*]

chalk•y (chô′kē), *adj.,* **chalk•i•er, chalk•i•est. 1.** of or like chalk. **2.** of a chalklike consistency: *chalky soil.* **3.** without resonance, color, warmth, etc.: *several high tones that were quite chalky.* **4.** *Photog.* lacking in detail, due to extreme contrast: *a chalky print.* [1425–75; late ME; see CHALK, -Y[1]] —**chalk′i•ness,** *n.*

chal•lah (KHä′lə, hä′), *n.* a loaf of rich white bread leavened with yeast and containing eggs, often braided before baking, prepared esp. for the Jewish Sabbath. Also, **chal′leh, hallah.** [< Heb *ḥallāh*]

chal•lenge (chal′inj), *n., v.,* **-lenged, -leng•ing,** *adj.* —*n.* **1.** a call or summons to engage in any contest, as of skill, strength, etc. **2.** something that by its nature or character serves as a call to battle, contest, special effort, etc.: *Space exploration offers a challenge to humankind.* **3.** a call to fight, as a battle, a duel, etc. **4.** a demand to explain, justify, etc.: *a challenge to the treasurer to itemize expenditures.* **5.** difficulty in a job or undertaking that is stimulating to one engaged in it. **6.** *Mil.* the demand of a sentry for identification or a countersign. **7.** *Law.* a formal objection to the qualifications of a partic-

ular juror, to his or her serving, or to the legality of an entire jury. Cf. **peremptory challenge.** **8.** the assertion that a vote is invalid or that a voter is not legally qualified. **9.** *Biol.* the process of inducing or assessing physiological or immunological activity by exposing an organism to a specific substance. **10.** *Hunting.* the crying of a hound on finding a scent. —*v.t.* **11.** to summon to a contest of skill, strength, etc. **12.** to take exception to; call in question: *to challenge the wisdom of a procedure.* **13.** to demand as something due or rightful. **14.** *Mil.* to halt and demand identification or countersign from. **15.** *Law.* to take formal exception to (a juror or jury). **16.** to have a claim to; invite; arouse; stimulate: *a matter which challenges attention.* **17.** to assert that (a vote) is invalid. **18.** to assert that (a voter) is not qualified to vote. **19.** to expose an organism to a specific substance in order to assess its physiological or immunological activity. **20.** *Archaic.* to lay claim to. —*v.i.* **21.** to make or issue a challenge. **22.** *Hunting.* (of hounds) to cry or give tongue on picking up the scent. —*adj.* **23.** donated or given by a private, corporate, or government benefactor on condition that the recipient raise an additional specified amount from the public: *a challenge grant.* [1175–1225; ME *chalenge* < OF, var. of *chalonge* < L *calumnia* CALUMNY] —**chal′lenge·a·ble,** *adj.*
—**Syn. 11.** dare, bid, invite. **12.** question, impute, doubt.

chal·leng·er (chal′in jər), *n.* **1.** a person or thing that challenges. **2.** *Boxing.* a boxer who fights a champion for his championship title. **3.** *Radio.* interrogator (def. 2). **4.** (*cap., italics*) *U.S. Aerospace.* the second space shuttle to orbit and return to earth: exploded 1½ min. after launch on Jan. 28, 1986, causing the death of all seven on board. [1250–1300; ME; see CHALLENGE, -ER[1]]

chal·leng·ing (chal′in jing), *adj.* **1.** offering a challenge; testing one's ability, endurance, etc: *a challenging course; a challenging game.* **2.** stimulating, interesting, and thought-provoking: *a challenging suggestion.* **3.** provocative; intriguing: *a challenging smile.* [1300–50; ME, as ger.; 1835–45 for def. 1; see CHALLENGE, -ING[2]] —**chal′leng·ing·ly,** *adv.*

chal·lis (shal′ē), *n.* a soft fabric of plain weave in wool, cotton, rayon, or other staple fiber, either in a solid color or, more often, a small print. Also, **chal′lie, chal′ly.** [1840–50; perh. after *Challis,* a surname]

Chal·mers (chä′mərz, chal′-), *n.* **Alexander,** 1759–1834, Scottish biographer, editor, and journalist.

chal·one (kal′ōn), *n. Physiol.* an endocrine secretion that depresses or inhibits physiological activity. [1910–15; < Gk *chalôn,* prp. of *chalân* to slacken, loosen; on the model of HORMONE]

Châ·lons (shä lôn′), *n.* **1.** Also called **Châ·lons-sur-Marne** (shä lôn syr marn′). a city in and the capital of Marne, in NE France: defeat of Attila A.D. 451. 55,709. **2.** Also called **Châ·lons-sur-Saône** (shä lôn syr sōn′). a city in E France, on the Saône River. 60,451.

Cha·lu·kya (chä′lə kyə), *n.* a dynasty of central India, ruling A.D. c500–753, and restored A.D. 973–1190. —**Cha′lu·kyan,** *adj.*

chal·u·meau (shal′yə mō′; *Fr.* shä ly mō′), *n., pl.* **-meaux** (-mōz′, *Fr.* -mō′). **1.** *Music.* the low register of the clarinet. **2.** a 17th- or 18th-century woodwind instrument. [1705–15; < F: orig., flute made from a reed, stem of a reed; OF *chalemel* < LL *calamellus* narrow reed; see CALAMUS, -ELLE]

cha·lu·pa (chə lo͞o′pə; *Sp.* chä lo͞o′pä), *n., pl.* **-pas** (-pəz; *Sp.* -päs). *Mexican Cookery.* a fried tortilla spread with bean paste or ground cooked meat and topped with shredded cheese, lettuce, chopped tomato, and often hot sauce. [1890–95, *Amer.*; < MexSp; Sp: boat, launch < F *chaloupe;* see SHALLOP, SLOOP]

cha·lutz (KHä lo͞ots′), *n., pl.* **-lutz·im** (-lo͞o tsēm′). *Hebrew.* halutz.

cha·lyb·e·ate (kə lib′ē it, -āt′), *adj.* **1.** containing or impregnated with salts of iron, as a mineral spring or medicine. —*n.* **2.** a chalybeate water, medicine, or the like. [1625–35; < NL *chalybeātus,* L *chalybē(ius)* of steel (< Gk *chalybēis,* equiv. to *chalybē-,* var. s. of *chálybs* iron + *-is* adj. suffix) + *-ātus* -ATE[1]; see CHALYBITE]

chal·y·bite (kal′ə bīt′), *n. Mineral.* siderite (def. 1). [1855–60; < Gk *chalyb-* (s. of *chálybs*) iron, also ironworker, member of the Chalybes, a tribe of Asia Minor noted for their blacksmiths + -ITE[1]]

cham (kam), *n. Archaic.* khan[1].

cha·made (shə mäd′), *n. Mil. Archaic.* a signal by drum or trumpet inviting an enemy to a parley. [1675–85; < F < Pg *chamada,* equiv. to *cham(ar)* to sound (< L *clamāre* to shout; see CLAIM) + *-ada* -ADE[1]]

cham·ae·do·re·a (kam′i dôr′ē ə, -dōr′-), *n.* any of various small, slender palms of the genus *Chamaedorea,* several species of which are cultivated as houseplants. [< NL (1806) < Gk *chamaí* on the ground, low-growing + *dór(u)* tree + NL *-ea* -EA]

Cha·mae·le·on (kə mē′lē ən, -mēl′yən), *n., gen.* **-mae·le·on·tis** (-mē′lē on′tis). *Astron.* a small southern constellation between Musca and Hydrus. Also, **Chameleon.** [< L]

cham·ae·phyte (kam′ə fīt′), *n. Bot.* a plant having dormant vegetative buds at, or slightly above, ground level. [1910–15; < Gk *chamaí* on the ground + -PHYTE]

cham·ber (chām′bər), *n.* **1.** a room, usually private, in a house or apartment, esp. a bedroom: *She retired to her chamber.* **2.** a room in a palace or official residence. **3.** the meeting hall of a legislative or other assembly. **4. chambers,** *Law.* **a.** a place where a judge hears matters not requiring action in open court. **b.** the private office of a judge. **c.** (in England) the quarters or rooms that lawyers use to consult with their clients, esp. in the Inns of Court. **5.** a legislative, judicial, or other like body: *the upper or the lower chamber of a legislature.* **6.** an organization of individuals or companies for a specified purpose. **7.** the place where the moneys due a government are received and kept; a treasury or chamberlain's office. **8.** (in early New England) any bedroom above the ground floor, generally named for the ground-floor room beneath it. **9.** a compartment or enclosed space; cavity: *a chamber of the heart.* **10.** (in a canal or the like) the space between any two gates of a lock. **11.** a receptacle for one or more cartridges in a firearm, or for a shell in a gun or other cannon. **12.** (in a gun) the part of the barrel that receives the charge. **13.** See **chamber pot.** —*adj.* **14.** of, pertaining to, or performing chamber music: *chamber players.* —*v.t.* **15.** to put or enclose in, or as in, a chamber. **16.** to provide with a chamber. [1175–1225; ME *chambre* < OF < L *camera,* var. of *camara* vaulted room, vault < Gk *kamára*]

cham′ber con′cert, a concert of chamber music. [1830–40]

cham·bered (chām′bərd), *adj.* having compartmental chambers: *a spiral chambered seashell.* [1350–1400; ME. See CHAMBER, -ED[3]]

cham′bered nau′tilus, nautilus (def. 1). [1855–60]

cham·ber·er[1] (chām′bər ər), *n. Archaic.* a man who frequents ladies' chambers; gallant. [1200–50; ME: chamberlain < AF; see CHAMBER, -ER[2]]

cham·ber·er[2] (chām′bər ər), *n. Obs.* chambermaid. [1350–1400; ME *chamberere* < AF, fem. of *chamberer* chamberlain; see CHAMBERER[1]]

cham·ber·lain (chām′bər lin), *n.* **1.** an official charged with the management of the living quarters of a sovereign or member of the nobility. **2.** an official who receives rents and revenues, as of a municipal corporation; treasurer. **3.** the high steward or factor of a member of the nobility. **4.** a high official of a royal court. [1175–1225; ME < OF, var. of *chamberlenc* < Frankish **kamerling,* equiv. to *kamer* (< L *camera* room; see CHAMBER) + *-ling* -LING[1]]

Cham·ber·lain (chām′bər lin), *n.* **1. (Arthur) Neville,** 1869–1940, British statesman: prime minister 1937–40. **2. Joseph,** 1836–1914, British statesman (father of Sir Austen and Neville Chamberlain). **3. Sir (Joseph) Austen,** 1863–1937, British statesman: Nobel peace prize 1925. **4. Owen,** born 1920, U.S. physicist: Nobel prize 1959. **5. Wilt(on Norman)** ("*Wilt the Stilt*"), born 1936, U.S. basketball player.

cham·ber·maid (chām′bər mād′), *n.* a maid who cleans bedrooms and bathrooms. [1580–90; CHAMBER + MAID]

cham′ber mug′, *Chiefly New England Older Use.* a chamber pot. [1945–50, *Amer.*]

cham′ber mu′sic, music suited for performance in a room or a small concert hall, esp. for two or more, but usually fewer than ten, solo instruments. [1780–90]

cham′ber of com′merce, an association, primarily of people in business, to promote the commercial interests of an area. *Abbr.:* C of C [1780–90]

cham′ber of dep′uties, the lower house of the legislature of certain countries, as Italy. Also, **Cham′ber of Dep′uties.**

cham′ber of hor′rors, **1.** a place for the exhibition of gruesome or horrible objects. **2.** a group of such objects, as instruments of torture or murder. **3.** any collection of things or ideas that inspire horror. [1840–50]

cham′ber op′era, an opera requiring few performers and a small orchestra.

cham′ber or′chestra, a small orchestra, commonly of about 25 players. [1925–30]

cham′ber pot′, a portable container, esp. for urine, used in bedrooms. [1560–70]

Cham·bers (chām′bərz), *n.* **1. Robert,** 1802–71, Scottish publisher and editor. **2. Robert William,** 1865–1933, U.S. novelist and illustrator. **3. Whittaker** (*Jay David Chambers*), 1901–61, U.S. journalist, Communist spy, and accuser of Alger Hiss.

Cham·bers·burg (chām′bərz bûrg′), *n.* a city in central Pennsylvania. 16,174.

Cham·ber·tin (shän ber tan′), *n.* a dry, red wine from the Gevrey-Chambertin commune of the Burgundy region in France.

cham′ber tomb′, *Archaeol.* a type of late Neolithic to Bronze Age tomb found in Britain and Europe, usually of megaliths covered by mounds, sometimes decorated, and used for successive family or clan burials spanning a number of generations. Cf. **dolmen, passage grave.** [1890–95]

Cham·bé·ry (shän bā rē′), *n.* **1.** a city in and the capital of Savoie, in SE France. 56,788. **2.** a dry vermouth from this city.

Cham·bly (sham′blē, shäm′-; *Fr.* shän blē′), *n.* a city in S Quebec, in E Canada. 12,190.

cham·bray (sham′brā), *n.* a fine cloth of cotton, silk, or linen, commonly of plain weave with a colored warp and white weft. [1805–15, *Amer.*; var. of CAMBRIC]

African chameleon, *Chamaeleo chamaeleon,* length 8 in. (20 cm)

cha·me·le·on (kə mē′lē ən, -mēl′yən), *n.* **1.** any of numerous Old World lizards of the family Chamaeleontidae, characterized by the ability to change the color of their skin, very slow locomotion, and a projectile tongue. **2.** any of several American lizards capable of changing the color of the skin, esp. *Anolis carolinensis* **(American chameleon),** of the southeastern U.S. **3.** a changeable, fickle, or inconstant person. **4.** (*cap.*) *Astron.* Chamaeleon. [1300–50; var. of *chamaeleon* < L < Gk *chamailéōn,* equiv. to *chamaí* on the ground, dwarf (akin to HUMUS) + *léōn* LION; r. ME *camelion* < MF < L, as above] —**cha·me·le·on·ic** (kə mē′lē on′ik), *adj.* —**cha·me′le·on·like′,** *adj.*

cha·metz (*Seph.* KHä mets′; *Ashk.* KHô′mits), *n. Hebrew.* hametz.

cham·fer (cham′fər), *n.* **1.** a cut that is made in wood or some other material, usually at a 45° angle to the adjacent principal faces. Cf. **bevel.** —*v.t.* **2.** to make a chamfer on or in. [1595–1605; back formation from *chamfering* (taken as *chamfer* + -ING[1]) < MF *chamfrein,* var. of *chanfreint* beveled edge, orig. ptp. of *chanfraindre* to bevel, equiv. to *chant* edge (< L *canthus;* see CANT[2]) + *fraindre* to break < L *frangere;* see FRANGIBLE] —**cham′fer·er,** *n.*

cham′fer bit′, a bit for beveling the edge of a hole. [1875–80]

cham·fron (cham′frən), *n. Armor.* chanfron.

Cha·mi·nade (shä mē nad′), *n.* **Cé·cile Louise Sté·pha·nie** (sā sēl′ lwēz stā fä nē′), 1857–1944, French pianist and composer.

cha·mi·so (shə mē′zō, chə-), *n., pl.* **-sos.** a saltbush, *Atriplex canescens,* of the western U.S. and Mexico, having grayish, scurfy foliage. Also, **cha·mi·za** (shə mē′zə, chə-). Also called **cenizo.** [1840–50; < MexSp]

cham·my (sham′ē), *n., pl.* **-mies,** *v.t.,* **-mied, -my·ing.** chamois (defs. 2–4, 6, 7).

cham·ois (sham′ē; *Fr.* shä mwä′), *n., pl.* **cham·ois, cham·oix** (sham′ēz; *Fr.* shä mwä′), *v.,* **cham·oised** (sham′ēd), **cham·ois·ing** (sham′ē ing). —*n.* **1.** an agile, goatlike antelope, *Rupicapra rupicapra,* of high mountains of Europe: now rare in some areas. **2.** a soft, pliable leather from any of various skins dressed with oil, esp. fish oil, originally prepared from the skin of the chamois. **3.** a piece of this leather. **4.** a cotton cloth finished to simulate this leather. **5.** a medium to grayish yellow color. —*v.t.* **6.** to dress (a pelt) with oil in order to produce a chamois. **7.** to rub or buff with a chamois. Also, **chammy, shammy, shamoy** (for defs. 2–4, 6, 7). [1525–35; < MF < LL *camox,* presumably of pre-L orig.; cf. GEMS]

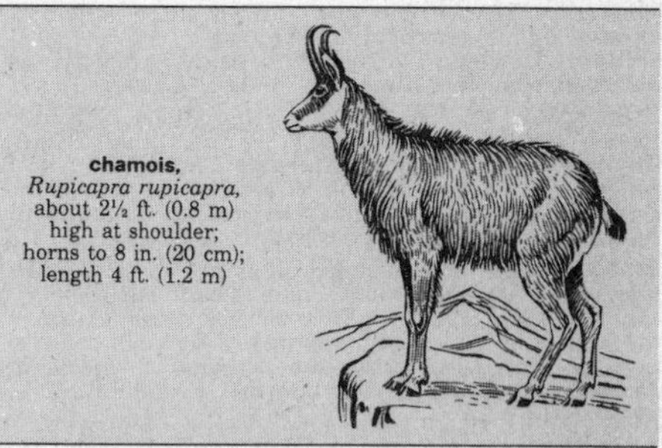
chamois, *Rupicapra rupicapra,* about 2½ ft. (0.8 m) high at shoulder; horns to 8 in. (20 cm); length 4 ft. (1.2 m)

cham·o·mile (kam′ə mīl′, -mēl′), *n.* **1.** a composite plant, *Chamaemelium nobile* (or *Anthemis nobilis*), native to the Old World, having strongly scented foliage and white ray flowers with yellow centers used medicinally and as a tea. **2.** any of several allied plants of the genera *Matricaria* and *Tripleurospermum.* Also, **camomile.** [1350–1400; ME *camamyll, camomille* < MF, OF *camomille* or ML *camomilla,* for L *chamaemēlon* < Gk *chamaímēlon,* equiv. to *chamaí* on the ground + *mêlon* apple; allegedly so called from the applelike odor of the flowers]

Cha·mo·nix (sham′ə nē′, sham′ə nē; *Fr.* shä mô nē′), *n.* a mountain valley in E France, N of Mont Blanc. Also, **Cha·mou·ni** (*Fr.* shä mo͞o nē′).

Cha·mor·ro (chə môr′ō; *Sp.* chä môr′rô), *n., pl.* **-mor·ros** (-môr′ōz; *Sp.* -môr′rôs), (*esp. collectively*) **-mor·ro** for 1. **1.** a people inhabiting the Mariana Islands. **2.** the Austronesian language of the Chamorro.

Cha·mos (kā′mos), *n. Douay Bible.* Chemosh.

cham·o·site (sham′ə zīt′), *n.* a mineral of the chlorite group, hydrous aluminum silicate of iron, occurring in gray or black crystals in oolitic iron ore. [1825–35; var. of *camoisite,* named after *Chamoison* in the Valais, Switzerland, where found; see -ITE[1]]

cha·motte (shə mot′), *n. Metall.* grog (def. 3). [1885–90; prob. < F < G *Schamotte*]

champ[1] (champ, chomp), *v.t.* **1.** to bite upon or grind, esp. impatiently: *The horses champed the oats.* **2.** to crush with the teeth and chew vigorously or noisily; munch. **3.** to mash; crush. —*v.i.* **4.** to make vigorous chewing or biting movements with the jaws and teeth. **5. champ at the bit,** to betray impatience, as to begin some action. —*n.* **6.** the act of champing. Also, **chomp.** [1520–30; perh. akin to CHAP[1]; see CHOP[1]] —**champ′er,** *n.* —**champ′y,** *adj.*

champ[2] (champ), *n. Informal.* a champion. [by shortening]

cham·pac (cham′pak, chum′puk), *n.* a southern Asian tree, *Michelia champaca,* of the magnolia family, having fragrant yellow or orange flowers and yielding an oil **(cham′paca oil′)** used in perfumes. Also, **cham·pa·ca** (cham′pə kə, chum′-), **cham′pak.** [1760–70; < Hind *campak* < Skt *campaka*]

cham·pagne (sham pān′), *n.* **1.** (*cap.*) the sparkling, dry, white table wine from the region of Champagne in France. **2.** a similar sparkling wine produced elsewhere. **3.** (formerly) the nonsparkling, dry, white table wine produced in the region of Champagne in France. **4.** a

CONCISE PRONUNCIATION KEY: act, cāpe, dâre, pärt; set, ēqual; *if,* ice; ox, ōver, ôrder, oil, bo͝ok, bo͞ot, out; up, ûrge; child; sing; shoe; thin, *th*at; zh as in *treasure.* ə = a as in *alone,* e as in *system,* i as in *easily,* o as in *gallop,* u as in *circus;* ᵊ as in *fire* (fīᵊr), *hour* (ouᵊr). l and n can serve as syllabic consonants, as in *cradle* (krād′l), and *button* (but′n). See the full key inside the front cover.

very pale yellow or greenish-yellow color. **5.** anything considered the best or luxurious. —*adj.* **6.** having the color of champagne. **7.** luxurious or expensive: *champagne tastes.* [1655–65; after CHAMPAGNE]

Cham•pagne (sham pān′; *Fr.* shäN pan′yə), *n.* a region and former province in NE France.

cham•paign (sham pān′), *n.* **1.** level, open country; plain. **2.** *Obs.* a battlefield. —*adj.* **3.** level and open: *champaign fields.* [1350–1400; ME *champai(g)ne* < MF *champa(i)gne* < L *campānia;* see CAMPAIGN]

Cham•paign (sham pān′), *n.* a city in E Illinois, adjoining Urbana. 58,133.

cham•pers (sham′pərz), *n. Brit. Slang.* champagne (def. 1). [1950–55; CHAMP(AGNE) + -ERS]

cham•per•ty (cham′pər tē), *n. Law.* a sharing in the proceeds of litigation by one who agrees with either the plaintiff or defendant to help promote it or carry it on. [1300–50; ME *champartie,* equiv. to *champart* (< MF: share of the produce, lit., of the field, equiv. to *champ* field (see CAMP[1]) + *part* share, see PART) + *-ie* -Y[3]] —**cham′per•tous,** *adj.*

cham•pi•gnon (sham pin′yən *or, esp. Brit.,* cham-; *Fr.* shäN pē nyôN′), *n., pl.* **-pi•gnons** (-pin′yənz; *Fr.* -pē nyôN′). mushroom (defs. 1, 2). [1570–80; < MF, appar. << VL **campīn(us)* of the field (see CAMP[1], -INE[1]) + L *-iōn-* -ION]

cham•pi•on (cham′pē ən), *n.* **1.** a person who has defeated all opponents in a competition or series of competitions, so as to hold first place: *the heavyweight boxing champion.* **2.** anything that takes first place in competition: *the champion of a cattle show.* **3.** an animal that has won a certain number of points in officially recognized shows: *This dog is a champion.* **4.** a person who fights for or defends any person or cause: *a champion of the oppressed.* **5.** a fighter or warrior. —*v.t.* **6.** to act as champion of; defend; support: *to champion a cause.* **7.** *Obs.* to defy. —*adj.* **8.** first among all contestants or competitors. **9.** *Informal.* first-rate. [1175–1225; ME < OF < LL *campiōn-* (s. of *campiō*) < WGmc **kampiōn-,* equiv. to *kamp-* battle (< L *campus* field, battlefield) + *-iōn-* n. suffix; cf. OE *cempa* warrior, etc.] —**cham′pi•on•less,** *adj.* —**cham′pi•on•like′,** *adj.*
—**Syn. 1.** winner, victor. **4.** defender, protector. **6.** maintain, fight for, advocate. —**Ant. 1.** loser.

Cham′pion of Eng′land, a hereditary official at British coronations, representing the king **(King's Champion)** or the queen **(Queen's Champion)** who is being crowned, and having originally the function of challenging to mortal combat any person disputing the right of the new sovereign to rule.

cham•pi•on•ship (cham′pē ən ship′), *n.* **1.** the distinction or condition of being a champion: *to win a championship.* **2.** advocacy or defense: *championship of the underdog.* **3. championships,** a series of competitions or contests to determine a champion: *the tennis championships.* [1815–25; CHAMPION + -SHIP]

Cham•plain (sham plān′; *for 1 also Fr.* shäN plaN′), *n.* **1. Sa•mu•el de** (sam′yo͞o əl də; *Fr.* sa my el′ də), 1567–1635, French explorer in the Americas: founder of Quebec; first colonial governor 1633–35. **2. Lake,** a lake between New York and Vermont. 125 mi. (200 km) long; ab. 600 sq. mi. (1550 sq. km).

champ•le•vé (shäN lə vā′), *adj., n., pl.* **-vés** (-vā′, -vāz′). —*adj.* **1.** of or pertaining to an enamel piece or enameling technique in which enamel is fused onto the incised or hollowed areas of a metal base. —*n.* **2.** an enamel piece made by the champlevé method. **3.** the technique used to produce champlevé enamels. [1855–60; < F, ptp. of *champlever* to lift (i.e., take out) a field (i.e., a flat part), make hollow places on the ground to be engraved; see CAMP[1], LEVER]

Cham•pol•lion (shäN pô lyôN′), *n.* **Jean Fran•çois** (zhäN fräN swa′), 1790–1832, French Egyptologist.

Champs É•ly•sées (shäN zā lē zā′), a boulevard in Paris, France, noted for its cafés, shops, and theaters.

Ch'an (chän), *n. Chinese.* Zen (def. 1).

Chan., **1.** Chancellor. **2.** Chancery. Also, **Chanc.**

Cha•naan (kā′nən, -nā ən), *n. Douay Bible.* Canaan (def. 4).

chanc., **1.** chancellor. **2.** chancery.

chance (chans, chäns), *n., v.,* **chanced, chanc•ing,** *adj.* —*n.* **1.** the absence of any cause of events that can be predicted, understood, or controlled: often personified or treated as a positive agency: *Chance governs all.* **2.** luck or fortune: *a game of chance.* **3.** a possibility or probability of anything happening: *a fifty-percent chance of success.* **4.** an opportune or favorable time; opportunity: *Now is your chance.* **5.** *Baseball.* an opportunity to field the ball and make a put-out or assist. **6.** a risk or hazard: *Take a chance.* **7.** a share or ticket in a lottery or prize drawing: *The charity is selling chances for a dollar each.* **8. chances,** probability: *The chances are that the train hasn't left yet.* **9.** *Midland and Southern U.S.* a quantity or number (usually fol. by *of*). **10.** *Archaic.* an unfortunate event; mishap. **11. by chance,** without plan or intent; accidentally: *I met her again by chance in a department store in Paris.* **12. on the chance,** in the mild hope or against the possibility: *I'll wait on the chance that she'll come.* **13. on the off chance,** in the very slight hope or against the very slight possibility. —*v.i.* **14.** to happen or occur by chance: *It chanced that our arrivals coincided.* —*v.t.* **15.** to take the chances or risks of; risk (often fol. by impersonal *it*): *I'll have to chance it, whatever the outcome.* **16. chance on** or **upon,** to come upon by chance; meet unexpectedly: *She chanced on a rare kind of mushroom during her walk through the woods.* —*adj.* **17.** not planned or expected; accidental: *a chance occurrence.* [1250–1300; ME < OF *chance, cheance* < VL **cadentia* a befalling, happening; see CADENZA] —**chance′less,** *adj.*
—**Syn. 2.** accident, fortuity. **3.** contingency. **4.** opening. **14.** befall. See **happen. 17.** casual, fortuitous. —**Ant. 1.** necessity.

chance•ful (chans′fəl, chäns′-), *adj.* **1.** full of chance or chances. **2.** *Archaic.* **a.** dependent on chance. **b.** risky. [1585–95; CHANCE + -FUL] —**chance′ful•ly,** *adv.*

chan•cel (chan′səl, chän′-), *n.* the space about the altar of a church, usually enclosed, for the clergy and other officials. [1275–1325; ME < MF < LL *cancellus* lattice, railing or screen before the altar of a church, L *cancell(ī)* (pl.) lattice, railing, grating; see CANCEL] —**chan′celed, chan′celled,** *adj.*

chan•cel•ler•y (chan′sə lə rē, -slə rē, -səl rē, chän′-), *n., pl.* **-ler•ies. 1.** the position of a chancellor. **2.** the office or department of a chancellor. **3.** the office attached to an embassy or consulate. **4.** a building or room occupied by a chancellor's department. [1250–1300; ME *chancellerie* < AF, equiv. to *chanceller* CHANCELLOR + *-ie* -Y[3]]

chan•cel•lor (chan′sə lər, -slər, chän′-), *n.* **1.** the chief minister of state in certain parliamentary governments, as in Germany; prime minister; premier. **2.** the chief administrative officer in certain American universities. **3.** a secretary, as to a king or noble or of an embassy. **4.** the priest in charge of a Roman Catholic chancery. **5.** the title of various important judges and other high officials. **6.** (in some states of the U.S.) the judge of a court of equity or chancery. **7.** *Brit.* the honorary, nonresident, titular head of a university. Cf. **vice-chancellor.** [bef. 1100; ME *chanceler* < AF < LL *cancellārius* doorkeeper, lit., man at the barrier (see CHANCEL, -ER[2]); r. ME *canceler,* OE << LL, as above]

Chan′cellor of the Exche′quer, the minister of finance in the British government. [1350–1400; ME]

chan•cel•lor•ship (chan′sə lər ship′, -slər-, chän′-), *n.* **1.** the office or rank of chancellor. **2.** a chancellor's term of office. [1425–75; late ME *chanceler-schepp.* See CHANCELLOR, -SHIP]

Chan•cel•lors•ville (chan′sə lərz vil′, -slərz-, chän′-), *n.* a village in NE Virginia: site of a Confederate victory 1863.

chance-med•ley (chans′med′lē, chäns′-), *n. Law.* **1.** a killing occurring during a sudden and unpredicted encounter. **2.** aimless and random action. [1485–95; < AF *chance medlee*]

chance′ mu′sic, aleatory music. [1960–65]

chanc•er (chan′sər, chän′-), *n. Chiefly Brit.* a person who takes many risks. [1880–85; CHANCE + -ER[1]]

chan•cer•y (chan′sə rē, chän′-), *n., pl.* **-cer•ies. 1.** the office or department of a chancellor; chancellery. **2.** an office of public records, esp. those of the Lord Chancellor in England. **3.** (in England) the Lord Chancellor's court, now a division of the High Court of Justice. **4.** *Law.* **a.** Also called **court of chancery.** a court having jurisdiction in equity; court of equity. **b.** equity (defs. 3a, b). **5.** the administrative office of a diocese. **6.** *Rom. Cath. Ch.* a department of the Curia Romana now having the responsibility for issuing bulls to establish new dioceses, benefices, etc. **7. in chancery, a.** *Law.* in litigation in a court of chancery. **b.** *Wrestling, Boxing.* (of a contestant's head) held under an opponent's arm. **c.** in a helpless or embarrassing position. [1325–75; ME *chancerie,* var. of *chancelrie,* syncopated var. of *chancellerie* CHANCELLERY]

Chan Chan (chän′ chän′), the site of the ancient capital city of the Chimu people, near the modern city of Trujillo, Peru, characterized by large walled enclosures and houses made of unfired mud brick covered with frescoes in brilliant colors.

chan•cre (shang′kər), *n. Pathol.* the initial lesion of syphilis and certain other infectious diseases, commonly a more or less distinct ulcer or sore with a hard base. [1595–1605; < MF << L *cancrum,* acc. of *cancer* CANCER] —**chan•crous,** *adj.*

chan•croid (shang′kroid), *n. Pathol.* an infectious venereal ulcer with a soft base. Also called **simple chancre, soft chancre.** [1860–65; CHANCRE + -OID] —**chan•croi′dal,** *adj.*

chanc•y (chan′sē, chän′-), *adj.,* **chanc•i•er, chanc•i•est. 1.** uncertain, hazardous, or risky. **2.** random; haphazard; subject to chance. **3.** *Chiefly Scot.* lucky. [1505–15; CHANCE + -Y[1]] —**chanc′i•ness,** *n.*
—**Syn. 1.** precarious, doubtful, dubious, venturesome. —**Ant. 1.** sure, certain, predictable.

chan•de•lier (shan′dl ēr′), *n.* a decorative, sometimes ornate, light fixture suspended from a ceiling, usually having branched supports for a number of lights. [1655–65; < F: lit., something that holds candles; see CHANDLER] —**chan′de•liered′,** *adj.*

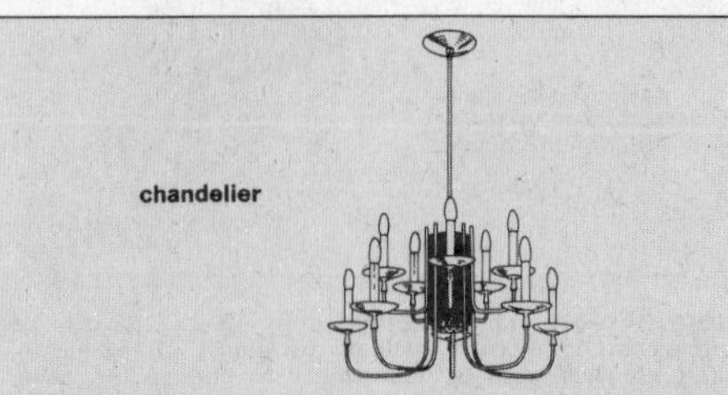

chan•delle (shan del′, shäN-), *n., v.* **-delled, -dell•ing.** *Aeron.* —*n.* **1.** an abrupt climbing turn in which an aircraft almost stalls while using its momentum to gain a higher rate of climb. —*v.i.* **2.** to perform a chandelle. [1915–20; < F: lit., CANDLE]

Chan•der•na•gor (chun′dər nə gôr′, -gōr′), *n.* a port in S West Bengal, in E India, on the Hooghly River: a former French dependency. 421,256. Also, **Chan•dar•na•gar** (chun′dər nug′ər).

Chan•di•garh (chun′di gur′), *n.* a city in and a union territory of India, in the N part: joint capital of Punjab and Haryana states. 450,061.

chan•dler (chand′lər, chänd′-), *n.* **1.** a person who makes or sells candles and sometimes other items of tallow or wax, as soap. **2.** a dealer or trader in supplies, provisions, etc., of a specialized type: *a ship chandler.* **3.** a retailer of provisions, groceries, etc. [1275–1325; ME *chandeler* candlestick, maker or seller of candles < AF, OF *chandelier,* lit., someone or something connected with candles, equiv. to *chandelle* CANDLE + *-ier* -IER[2]]

Chan•dler (chand′lər, chänd′-), *n.* **1. Charles Frederick,** 1836–1925, U.S. scientist, educator, and public-health expert. **2. Raymond (Thornton),** 1888–1959, U.S. writer of detective novels. **3.** a town in central Arizona. 29,673.

Chan′dler pe′riod, **(Chan′dler wob′ble)** of the period of the oscillation of the earth's axis, varying between 416 and 433 days. [named after Seth *Chandler* (1846–1913), U.S. astronomer]

chan•dler•y (chand′lə rē, chänd′-), *n., pl.* **-dler•ies. 1.** a storeroom for candles. **2.** the warehouse, wares, or business of a chandler. [1595–1605; CHANDLER + -Y[3]]

Chan•dra•gup•ta (chun′drə go͝op′tə), *n.* (*Chandragupta Maurya*) died 286? B.C., king of northern India 322?–298 B.C.: founder of the Maurya empire. Greek, **Sandrakottos** or **Sandrocottus.**

Chan•dra•se′khar lim′it (shän′drə sā′kär), *Astron.* the mass limit above which a star has too much mass to become a white dwarf after gravitational collapse, approximately 1.44 solar masses. [1975–80; after U.S. astrophysicist Subrahmanyan *Chandrasekhar* (born 1910), who formulated it]

Cha•nel (shə nel′; *Fr.* sha nel′), *n.* **Ga•bri•elle** (ga brē el′), ("*Coco*"), 1882–1971, French fashion designer.

Cha•ney (chā′nē), *n.* **Lon** (lon), 1883–1930, U.S. film actor.

chan•fron (chan′frən), *n.* a piece of plate armor for defending a horse's head. Also, **chamfron.** Also called **frontstall.** [late ME *shamfron* < AF, OF *champfrein,* perh. for **chafrein* (with *-m-* perh. from *chamfrein* CHAMFER, though the senses are unrelated), n. deriv. of *chafre(s)ner* lit., to put a bridle on < VL **cap(um)* head (for *caput;* see CHIEF) + **-frenāre,* v. deriv. of L *frēnum* bridle]

Chang•an (chäng′än′), *n. Pinyin, Wade-Giles.* former name of **Xian.**

Chang•chia•k'ou (*Chin.* chäng′jyä′kō′), *n. Wade-Giles.* Zhangjiakou.

Chang•chou (chang′chou′; *Chin.* chäng′jō′), *n. Wade-Giles.* Zhangzhou. Also, *Older Spelling,* **Chang′chow′.**

Ch'ang•chou (*Chin.* chäng′jō′), *n. Wade-Giles.* Changzhou.

Chang•chun (chäng′cho͝on′), *n. Pinyin, Wade-Giles.* a city in and the capital of Jilin province, in NE China: former capital of Manchuria. 1,200,000. Formerly, **Hsinking.**

Ch'ang Ch'un (chäng′ cho͝on′), monastic name of **Ch'iu Ch'u-chi.**

Chang•de (chäng′dœ′), *n. Pinyin.* a city in N Hunan province, in E China. 225,000. Also, **Changteh.**

change (chānj), *v.,* **changed, chang•ing,** *n.* —*v.t.* **1.** to make the form, nature, content, future course, etc., of (something) different from what it is or from what it would be if left alone: *to change one's name; to change one's opinion; to change the course of history.* **2.** to transform or convert (usually fol. by *into*): *The witch changed the prince into a toad.* **3.** to substitute another or others for; exchange for something else, usually of the same kind: *She changed her shoes when she got home from the office.* **4.** to give and take reciprocally; interchange: *to change places with someone.* **5.** to transfer from one (conveyance) to another: *You'll have to change planes in Chicago.* **6.** to give or get smaller money in exchange for: *to change a five-dollar bill.* **7.** to give or get foreign money in exchange for: *to change dollars into francs.* **8.** to remove and replace the covering or coverings of: *to change a bed; to change a baby.* —*v.i.* **9.** to become different: *Overnight the nation's mood changed.* **10.** to become altered or modified: *Colors change if they are exposed to the sun.* **11.** to become transformed or converted (usually fol. by *into*): *The toad changed into a prince again.* **12.** to pass gradually into (usually fol. by *to* or *into*): *Summer changed to autumn.* **13.** to make a change or an exchange: *If you want to sit next to the window, I'll change with you.* **14.** to transfer between trains or other conveyances: *We can take the local and change to an express at the next stop.* **15.** to change one's clothes: *She changed into jeans.* **16.** (of the moon) to pass from one phase to another. **17.** (of the voice) to become deeper in tone; come to have a lower register: *The boy's voice began to change when he was thirteen.* **18. change front,** *Mil.* to shift a military force in another direction. **19. change hands.** See **hand** (def. 34). **20. change off, a.** to take turns with another, as at doing a task. **b.** to alternate between two tasks or between a task and a rest break. **21. change one's mind,** to change one's opinions or intentions. —*n.* **22.** the act or fact of changing; fact of being changed. **23.** a transformation or modification; alteration: *They noticed the change in his facial expression.* **24.** a variation or deviation: *a change in the daily routine.* **25.** the substitution of one thing for another: *We finally made the change to an oil-burning furnace.* **26.** variety or novelty: *Let's try a new restaurant for a change.* **27.** the passing from one place, state, form, or phase to another: *a change of seasons; social change.* **28.** *Jazz.* harmonic progression from one tonality to another; modulation. **29.** the supplanting of one thing by another. **30.** anything that is or may be substituted for another. **31.** a fresh set of clothing. **32.** money given in exchange for an equivalent of higher denomination. **33.**

CONCISE ETYMOLOGY KEY: <, descended or borrowed from; >, whence; b., blend of, blended; c., cognate with; cf., compare; deriv., derivative; equiv., equivalent; imit., imitative; obl., oblique; r., replacing; s., stem; sp., spelling, spelled; resp., respelling, respelled; trans., translation; ?, origin unknown; *, unattested; ‡, probably earlier than. See the full key inside the front cover.

a balance of money that is returned when the sum tendered in payment is larger than the sum due. **34.** coins of low denomination. **35.** any of the various sequences in which a peal of bells may be rung. **36.** Also, **'change.** *Brit.* exchange (def. 10). **37.** *Obs.* changefulness; caprice. **38. ring the changes, a.** to perform all permutations possible in ringing a set of tuned bells, as in a bell tower of a church. **b.** to vary the manner of performing an action or of discussing a subject; repeat with variations. [1175–1225; (v.) ME *cha(u)ngen* < AF, OF *changer* < LL *cambiāre,* L *cambīre* to exchange; (n.) ME *cha(u)nge* < AF, OF, n. deriv. of the v.] **—chang·ed·ness** (chān′jid nis, chānjd′-), *n.*

—Syn. 1. transmute, transform; vary, mutate; amend, modify. CHANGE, ALTER both mean to make a difference in the state or condition of a thing or to substitute another state or condition. To CHANGE is to make a material difference so that the thing is distinctly different from what it was: *to change one's opinion.* To ALTER is to make some partial change, as in appearance, but usually to preserve the identity: *to alter a dress* (*to change a dress* would mean to put on a different one). **3.** replace, trade. **4.** trade. **7.** convert. **10.** vary, mutate, amend. **22.** transmutation, mutation, conversion, vicissitude. **25.** exchange. **29, 30.** replacement. **—Ant. 10.** remain. **22.** permanence.

change·a·ble (chān′jə bəl), *adj.* **1.** liable to change or to be changed; variable. **2.** of changing color or appearance: *changeable silk.* [1200–50; ME; see CHANGE, -ABLE] **—change′a·bil′i·ty, change′a·ble·ness,** *n.* **—change′a·bly,** *adv.*

—Syn. 1. erratic, inconstant, fickle, flighty, unstable.

change·ful (chānj′fəl), *adj.* full of changes; variable; inconstant. [1600–10; CHANGE + -FUL] **—change′ful·ly,** *adv.* **—change′ful·ness,** *n.*

change′ key′, a key opening only one lock.

change·less (chānj′lis), *adj.* unchanging; constant; steadfast. [1570–80; CHANGE + -LESS] **—change′less·ly,** *adv.* **—change′less·ness,** *n.*

change·ling (chānj′ling), *n.* **1.** a child surreptitiously or unintentionally substituted for another. **2.** (in folklore) an ugly, stupid, or strange child left by fairies in place of a pretty, charming child. **3.** *Philately.* a postage stamp that, by accident or intention, has been chemically changed in color. **4.** *Archaic.* **a.** a renegade or turncoat. **b.** an imbecile. [1545–55; CHANGE + -LING[1]]

change·mak·er (chānj′mā′kər), *n.* **1.** a person or thing that changes bills or coins for ones of smaller denominations. **2.** a device for supplying coins of specific denominations when a key is moved. [CHANGE + MAKER]

change·ment de pied (*Fr.* shänzh mänd[ə] pyā′), *pl.* **change·ments de pied** (*Fr.* shänzh mänd[ə] pyā′). *Ballet.* a jump in which the dancer's feet are reversed from the starting position. [1830–40; < F: lit., change of foot]

change′ of heart′, a reversal of one's feelings, intentions, opinions, etc.: *At first Mother said we couldn't go, but she had a change of heart and let us.* [1820–30]

change′ of life′, menopause. [1825–35]

change′ of pace′, 1. a temporary shift or variation in a normal routine or regular pattern of activity: *Reading a mystery novel has been a real change of pace for me.* **2.** Also called **change-up** (chānj′up′). *Baseball.* a ball that is thrown by a pitcher with the same motion as for a fastball but that travels with less speed, making the pitch more difficult for the batter to time. [1935–40]

change′ of ven′ue, *Law.* the removal of a trial to another jurisdiction.

change·o·ver (chānj′ō′vər), *n.* a conversion or complete change from one thing, condition, or system to another, as in equipment, personnel, methods of production, etc.: *a changeover to automated equipment.* [1905–10; n. use of v. phrase *change over*]

change·pock·et (chānj′pok′it), *n.* a small pocket or compartment for holding coins. [CHANGE + POCKET]

chang·er (chān′jər), *n.* **1.** a person or thing that changes something. **2.** See **record changer. 3.** *Obs.* a moneychanger. [1350–1400; ME. See CHANGE, -ER[1]]

change′ ring′ing, the art of ringing a series of tuned bells of different tones, as those hung in a church tower, according to any of various orderly sequences. [1870–75]

change·room (chānj′ro͞om′, -ro͝om′), *n.* a room for use in changing one's clothes. [CHANGE + ROOM]

chang′ing bag′, a lightproof bag with openings made to fit closely around the arms, used in place of a darkroom in some photographic procedures.

chang′ing room′, *Brit.* a locker room, usually with showers, for athletes. [1935–40]

chang′ing tone′, cambiata. Also called **chang′ing note′.**

Chang Jiang (chäng′ jyäng′), *Pinyin.* a river in E Asia, flowing from the Tibetan plateau through central China to the East China Sea. ab. 3200 mi. (5150 km) long. Also called **Yangtze, Yangtze Kiang.**

Chang·sha (chäng′shä′), *n. Pinyin, Wade-Giles.* a city in and the capital of Hunan province, in SE China. 825,000.

Chang·teh (chäng′du′), *n. Older Spelling.* Changde.

Chang Tso-lin (jäng′ tsō′lin′), 1873–1928, Chinese general: military ruler of Manchuria 1918–28.

Chang·zhou (chäng′jō′), *n. Pinyin.* a city in S Jiangsu province, in E China. 300,000. Also, **Ch'ang·chou.** Formerly, **Wujin.**

chank (changk), *v.i. Chiefly New Eng. and West Midland U.S.* to eat noisily or greedily. [1870–75; expressive v. akin to CHAMP[1], CHOMP]

chan·nel[1] (chan′l), *n., v.,* **-neled, -nel·ing** or (*esp. Brit.*) **-nelled, -nel·ling.** —*n.* **1.** the bed of a stream, river, or other waterway. **2.** *Naut.* a navigable route between two bodies of water. **3.** the deeper part of a waterway. **4.** a wide strait, as between a continent and an island. **5.** a course into which something may be directed: *He hoped to direct the conversation to a new channel.* **6.** a route through which anything passes or progresses: *channels of trade.* **7. channels,** the specific, prescribed, or official course or means of communication: *In an emergency he was able to reach the governor without going through channels.* **8.** a groove or furrow. **9.** a means of access: *He considers the Senate a channel to the White House.* **10.** *Archit.* **a.** a flute in a column, esp. one having no fillet between it and other flutes. **b.** any of the prominent vertical grooves in a triglyph. **11.** (in jazz or popular music) a bridge. **12.** a frequency band of sufficient width for one- or two-way communication from or to a transmitter used for television, radio, CB radio, telephone, or telegraph communication. **13.** *Computers.* a path for the transfer of signals or data within a computer or between a computer and its peripheral equipment. **14.** either of the two signals in stereophonic or any single signal in multichannel sound recording and reproduction. **15.** *Cell Biol.* a transient opening made by a protein embedded in a cell membrane, permitting passage of specific ions or molecules into or out of the cell: *calcium channel.* **16.** a tubular passage for liquids or fluids. **17.** *Building Trades.* **a.** any structural member, as one of reinforced concrete, having the form of three sides of a rectangle. **b.** a number of such members: *channel in 100-foot lengths.* **c.** See **channel iron.** —*v.t.* **18.** to convey through or as through a channel: *He channeled the information to us.* **19.** to direct toward or into some particular course: *to channel one's interests.* **20.** to excavate as a channel. **21.** to form a channel in; groove. —*v.i.* **22.** to become marked by a channel: *Soft earth has a tendency to channel during a heavy rain.* [1250–1300; ME *chanel* < OF < L *canālis* waterpipe; see CANAL] **—chan′nel·er;** *esp. Brit.,* **chan′nel·ler,** *n.*

chan·nel[2] (chan′l), *n.* a horizontal timber or ledge built outboard from the side of a sailing vessel to spread shrouds and backstays outward. Also, **chain wale, chain-wale.** [1760–70; var. of CHAIN WALE]

chan′nel back′, an upholstered chair or sofa back having deep vertical grooves.

chan′nel bass′ (bas). See **red drum.** [1885–90, *Amer.*]

chan·nel·bill (chan′l bil′), *n.* a large, gray Australian cuckoo, *Scythrops novaehollandiae,* with a grooved bill. Also called **chan′nel-billed cuck′oo** (chan′l bild′). [CHANNEL[1] + BILL[2]]

chan′nel black′. See **gas black.**

chan′nel cat′fish, a food fish, *Ictalurus punctatus,* common in fresh waters throughout central U.S. See illus. under **catfish.** Also called **chan′nel cat′.** [1830–40, *Amer.*]

chan·nel·ing (chan′l ing), *n.* **1.** *Archit., Furniture.* ornamentation with flutes or channels. **2.** the practice of professedly entering a meditative or trancelike state in order to convey messages from a spiritual guide. Also, *esp. Brit.,* **chan′nel·ling.** [1570–80; CHANNEL[1] + -ING[1]]

chan′nel i′ron, a rolled steel or iron shape having a U-shaped cross section, with two narrower sides at right angles to a broader one. See illus. under **shape.** Also called **chan′nel bar′.** [1885–90]

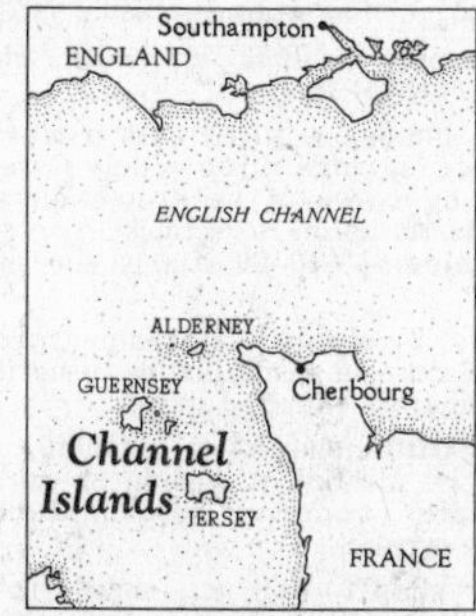

Chan′nel Is′lands, a British island group in the English Channel, near the coast of France, consisting of Alderney, Guernsey, Jersey, and smaller islands. 126,156; 75 sq. mi. (194 sq. km).

chan·nel·ize (chan′l īz′), *v.t., v.i.,* **-ized, -iz·ing.** to channel. Also, *esp. Brit.,* **chan′nel·ise′.** [1600–10; CHANNEL[1] + -IZE] **—chan′nel·i·za′tion,** *n.*

chan·ner·y (chan′ə rē), *n.* an accumulation of thin, flat fragments of sandstone, limestone, or schist with diameters up to 6 in. (15 cm): used in Scotland and Ireland for gravel. [Scots dial.: lit., gravelly, equiv. to *channer* gravel (alter. of *channel* gravel, CHANNEL[1]) + -Y[1]]

Chan·ning (chan′ing), *n.* **1. Edward,** 1856–1931, U.S. historian. **2. William El·ler·y** (el′ə rē), 1780–1842, U.S. Unitarian clergyman and writer.

cha·no·yu (chä′nô yo͞o′), *n.* a Japanese ceremony at which tea is prepared, served, and taken with an ancient and involved ritual. [< Japn, equiv. to *cha* TEA + *no* (particle) + *yu* hot water]

chan·son (shan′sən; *Fr.* shäN sôN′), *n., pl.* **-sons** (-sənz; *Fr.* -sôN′). any of several types of song with French lyrics, occurring from the Middle Ages to the present in a variety of musical styles. [1595–1605; < F < L *cantiōn-* (s. of *cantiō*) song; see CANZONE]

chan·son d'a·mour (shäN sôN dȧ mo͞or′), *pl.* ***chan·sons d'a·mour*** (shäN sôN dȧ mo͞or′). *French.* love song.

chan·son de geste (shäN sôN də zhest′), *pl.* **chan·sons de geste** (shäN sôN də zhest′). (in medieval French literature) an epic poem written in assonant verse or rhyme about historical or legendary events or figures. [1865–70; < F: lit., song of deeds; see CHANSON, GEST]

Chan·son de Ro·land (*Fr.* shäN sôN də rō läN′), (English, *The Song of Roland*), a chanson de geste (c1100) relating Roland's brave deeds and death at Roncesvalles and Charlemagne's revenge.

chan·son·ette (shäN sô net′; *Eng.* shan′sə net′), *n., pl.* ***-son·ettes*** (-sô net′; *Eng.* -sə nets′). *French.* a little song; ditty.

chan·son·nier (shan′sən yā′; *Fr.* shäN sô nyā′), *n., pl.* **-son·niers** (-sən yāz′; *Fr.* -sô nyā′). a singer or writer of chansons, esp. a cabaret performer who specializes in songs that are a combination of melody and rapid spoken patter. [1885–90; < F; see CHANSON, -IER[2]]

chant (chant, chänt), *n.* **1.** a short, simple melody, esp. one characterized by single notes to which an indefinite number of syllables are intoned, used in singing psalms, canticles, etc., in church services. **2.** a psalm, canticle, or the like, chanted or for chanting. **3.** the singing or intoning of all or portions of a liturgical service. **4.** any monotonous song. **5.** a song; singing: *the chant of a bird.* **6.** a monotonous intonation of the voice in speaking. **7.** a phrase, slogan, or the like, repeated rhythmically and insistently, as by a crowd. —*v.t.* **8.** to sing to a chant, or in the manner of a chant, esp. in a church service. **9.** to sing. **10.** to celebrate in song. **11.** to repeat (a phrase, slogan, etc.) rhythmically and insistently. —*v.i.* **12.** to sing. **13.** to utter a chant. [1350–1400; (v.) ME *chanten* < MF *chanter* < L *cantāre,* freq. of *canere* to sing; (n.) < F *chant* < L *cantus;* see CANTO] **—chant′a·ble,** *adj.* **—chant′ing·ly,** *adv.*

chan·tage (shäN tȧzh′), *n. French.* blackmail. [1870–75]

chan·tant (shäN täN′; *Fr.* shäN täN′), *adj. Music.* melodious; tuneful. [1780–90; < F: prp. of *chanter* to sing; see CHANT]

Chant de guerre pour l'ar·mée du Rhin (*Fr.* shäN də ger′ po͞or lȧr mā′ dʏ rȧN′), Marseillaise.

chante·fa·ble (*Fr.* shäNt fä′bl[ə]), *n., pl.* **-fa·bles** (-fä′bl[ə]). (in medieval French literature) a prose narrative interspersed with verse. [< F; see CHANT, FABLE]

chant·er (chan′tər, chän′-), *n.* **1.** a person who chants; singer. **2.** a chorister; precentor. **3.** the chief singer or priest of a chantry. **4.** the pipe of a bagpipe provided with finger holes for playing the melody. [1250–1300; CHANT + -ER[1]; r. ME *chantour* < AF, var. of OF *chanteor* < L *cantātōr-,* equiv. to *cantā(re)* to sing (see CHANT) + *-tor* -TOR] **—chant′er·ship′,** *n.*

chan·te·relle (shan′tə rel′, chan′-), *n.* a mushroom, *Cantharellus cibarius,* having a bright yellow-to-orange funnel-shaped cap, a favorite edible species in France. [1765–75; < F < NL *cantharella,* equiv. to L *canthar(us)* tankard (< Gk *kántharos*) + *-ella* dim. suffix]

chan·teur (shan tûr′; *Fr.* shäN tœr′), *n., pl.* **-teurs** (-tûrz′; *Fr.* -tœr′). a male singer, esp. one who sings in nightclubs and cabarets. [< F; OF *chanteor;* see CHANTER, -EUR]

chan·teuse (shan to͞os′; *Fr.* shäN tœz′), *n., pl.* **-teuses** (-to͞o′siz; *Fr.* -tœz′). a female singer, esp. one who sings in nightclubs and cabarets. [1885–90; < F, fem. of CHANTEUR; see -EUSE]

chant·ey (shan′tē, chan′-), *n., pl.* **-eys.** a sailors' song, esp. one sung in rhythm to work. Also, **chanty, shantey, shanty.** [1855–60; alter. of F *chanter* to sing; see CHANT]

chan·ti·cleer (chan′tə klēr′), *n. Now Literary.* a rooster: used as a proper name in medieval fables. Also, **chan·te·cler** (chan′tə klâr′). [1250–1300; ME *Chauntecler* < OF *Chantecler* n. use of v. phrase *chante cler* sing clear. See CHANT, CLEAR]

Chan·til·ly (shan til′ē; *Fr.* shäN tē yē′), *n.* **1.** a town in N France, N of Paris: lace manufacture. 10,684. **2.** (*sometimes l.c.*) Also called **Chantil′ly lace′.** a delicate silk, linen, or synthetic bobbin lace, in black or white, scalloped along one edge and often having an outlined design of scrolls or vases or baskets of flowers, widely used for bridal gowns and evening gowns. **3.** a dessert topping of whipped cream, sweetening, and flavoring, esp. vanilla. **4.** Also called **Chantil′ly sauce′.** mousseline (def. 1). —*adj.* **5.** (of cream) whipped and flavored, esp. with vanilla. **6.** (of food) prepared or served with whipped cream: *strawberries Chantilly.*

chant·ress (chan′tris, chän′-), *n.* a woman who chants or sings. [1400–50; late ME *chanteresse.* See CHANTER, -ESS]

—Usage. See **-ess.**

chan·try (chan′trē, chän′-), *n., pl.* **-tries.** *Eccles.* **1.** an endowment for the singing or saying of Mass for the souls of the founders or of persons named by them. **2.** a chapel or the like so endowed. **3.** the priests of a chantry endowment. **4.** a chapel attached to a church, used for minor services. [1300–50; ME *chanterie* < MF. See CHANT, -ERY]

chant·y (shan′tē, chan′-), *n., pl.* **chant·ies.** chantey.

Cha·nu·kah (KHä′nə kə, hä′-; *Ashk. Heb.* KHä′nə kə; *Seph. Heb.* KHä nōō kä′), *n. Judaism.* Hanukkah.

Cha·nute (shə nōōt′), *n.* a town in SE Kansas. 10,506.

Cha·ny (chä′nē, *Russ.* chyi ni′), *n.* **Lake,** a salt lake in SW Siberia, in the W Soviet Union in Asia. ab. 1300 sq. mi. (3365 sq. km).

Chao′·an (*Chin.* chou′än′), *n. Pinyin, Wade-Giles.* former name of **Chaozhou.** Also, **Chao′an′.**

Chao·chow (*Chin.* chou′jō′), *n. Older Spelling.* Chaozhou.

Chao K′uang-yin (jou′ kwäng′yin′), (*T′ai Tsu*) 927–976 A.D., Chinese emperor 960–976: founder of the Sung dynasty.

Chao Phra·ya (chou′ prä yä′), a river in N Thailand, flowing S to the Gulf of Thailand. 150 mi. (240 km) long. Formerly, **Menam, Nam.**

cha·os (kā′os), *n.* **1.** a state of utter confusion or disorder; a total lack of organization or order. **2.** any confused, disorderly mass: *a chaos of meaningless phrases.* **3.** the infinity of space or formless matter supposed to have preceded the existence of the ordered universe. **4.** (*cap.*) the personification of this in any of several ancient Greek myths. **5.** *Obs.* a chasm or abyss. [1400–50; late ME < L < Gk; akin to CHASM, YAWN, GAPE]
—Syn. 1. disarray, jumble, turmoil, tumult. **—Ant. 1.** order, peace, calm.

cha·ot·ic (kā ot′ik), *adj.* completely confused or disordered: *a chaotic mass of books and papers.* [1705–15; CHAO(S) + -TIC] **—cha·ot′i·cal·ly,** *adv.*
—Ant. orderly, systematic.

Chao·zhou (chou′zhō′), *n. Pinyin.* a city in E Guangdong province, in SE China. 101,000. Also, **Chaochow.** Formerly, **Chao′an.**

chap[1] (chap), *v.,* **chapped, chap·ping,** *n.* **—***v.t.* **1.** to crack, roughen, and redden (the skin): *The windy, cold weather chapped her lips.* **2.** to cause (the ground, wood, etc.) to split, crack, or open in clefts: *The summer heat and drought chapped the riverbank.* **—***v.i.* **3.** to become chapped. **—***n.* **4.** a fissure or crack, esp. in the skin. **5.** *Scot.* a knock; rap. [1275–1325; ME *chappen;* c. D *kappen* to cut; akin to CHIP[1]]

chap[2] (chap), *n.* **1.** *Informal.* a fellow; man or boy. **2.** *Chiefly Midland and Southern U.S.* a baby or young child. **3.** *Brit. Dial.* a customer. [1570–80; short for CHAPMAN]

chap[3] (chop, chap), *n.* chop[3]. [1325–75; ME; perh. special use of CHAP[1]]

chap., 1. Chaplain. **2.** chapter. Also, **Chap.**

Cha·pa·la (chə pä′lə; *Sp.* chä pä′lä), *n.* **Lake,** the largest lake in Mexico, located in Jalisco state. 651 sq. mi. (1686 sq. km).

cha·pa·ra·jos (shap′ə rā′ōs; *Sp.* chä′pä rä′hôs), *n.* (*used with a plural v.*) (in Mexico) chaps. Also, **cha·pa·re·jos** (shap′ə rā′ōs; *Sp.* chä′pä re′hôs). [1860–65, *Amer.;* < MexSp, var. of *chaparejos,* prob. b. *chaparral* CHAPARRAL and *aparejos,* pl. of *aparejo* gear; akin to APAREL]

chap·ar·ral (shap′ə ral′, chap′-), *n. Southwestern U.S.* a dense growth of shrubs or small trees. [1835–45, *Amer.;* < Sp, equiv. to *chaparr(o)* evergreen oak (< Basque *tshapar*) + *-al* collective suffix]

chaparral′ bird′, roadrunner. Also called **chaparral′ cock′.**

chaparral′ lil′y, a lily, *Lilium rubescens,* of the western coast of the U.S., having pale lilac-colored flowers that turn rose-purple. [1915–20, *Amer.*]

chaparral′ pea′, a spiny bush, *Pickeringia montana,* of the legume family, having large purple flowers and sometimes forming dense thickets in the Pacific coast regions of the U.S. [1905–10, *Amer.*]

cha·pa·ti (chə pä′tē, -pat′ē), *n., pl.* **-ti, -tis, -ties.** *Indian Cookery.* a flat pancakelike bread, usually of whole-wheat flour, baked on a griddle. Also, **chapat′ti.** [1855–60; < Hindi *capāti*]

chap·book (chap′bo͝ok′), *n.* **1.** a small book or pamphlet of popular tales, ballads, etc., formerly hawked about by chapmen. **2.** a small book or pamphlet, often of poetry. [1790–1800; *chap* (as in CHAPMAN) + BOOK]

chape (chāp), *n.* the lowermost terminal mount of a scabbard. [1350–1400; ME < MF: (metal) covering < LL *cappa;* see CAP[1], CAPE[1]] **—chape′less,** *adj.*

cha·peau (sha pō′; *Fr.* shA pō′), *n., pl.* **-peaux** (-pōz′; *Fr.* -pō′), **-peaus. 1.** a hat. **2.** *Heraldry.* **a.** a representation of a low-crowned hat with a turned-up brim, usually of a different tincture, used either as a charge or as part of a crest. **b.** a cap depicted within a representation of a crown or coronet. [1515–25; < F; OF *chapel* wreath, hat < LL *cappellus* hood, hat, equiv. to *capp(a)* (see CAP[1]) + *-ellus* dim. suffix]

chapeau′ bras′ (brä), a small three-cornered hat, worn by gentlemen in full dress in the 18th century, that could be folded flat and carried under the arm. [1755–65; < F: arm hat]

chap·el (chap′əl), *n., v.,* **-eled, -el·ing** or (*esp. Brit.*) **-elled, -el·ling,** *adj.* **—***n.* **1.** a private or subordinate place of prayer or worship; oratory. **2.** a separately dedicated part of a church, or a small independent churchlike edifice, devoted to special services. **3.** a room or building for worship in an institution, palace, etc. **4.** (in Great Britain) a place of worship for members of various dissenting Protestant churches, as Baptists or Methodists. **5.** a separate place of public worship dependent on the church of a parish. **6.** a religious service in a chapel: *Don't be late for chapel!* **7.** a funeral home or the room in which funeral services are held. **8.** a choir or orchestra of a chapel, court, etc. **9.** a print shop or printing house. **10.** an association of employees in a print shop for dealing with their interests, problems, etc. **—***v.t.* **11.** *Naut.* to maneuver (a sailing vessel taken aback) by the helm alone until the wind can be recovered on the original tack. **—***adj.* **12.** (in England) belonging to any of various dissenting Protestant sects. [1175–1225; ME *chapele* < OF < LL *cappella* hooded cloak, equiv. to *capp(a)* (see CAP[1]) + *-ella* dim. suffix; first applied to the sanctuary where the cloak of St. Martin (4th-century bishop of Tours) was kept as a relic]

cha·pel de fer (sha pel′ də fâr′), *pl.* **cha·pels de fer.** a medieval open helmet, often having a broad brim for deflecting blows from above. Also called **war hat, kettle hat.** [1895–1900; < OF: hat of iron; see CHAPEAU, FERROUS]

Chap′el Hill′, a city in central North Carolina. 32,421.

chap′el of ease′, *Rom. Cath. Ch.* a chapel in a remote part of a large parish, in which Mass is celebrated. [1530–40]

chap·er·on (shap′ə rōn′), *n.* **1.** a person, usually a married or older woman, who, for propriety, accompanies a young unmarried woman in public or who attends a party of young unmarried men and women. **2.** any adult present in order to maintain order or propriety at an activity of young people, as at a school dance. **3.** a round headdress of stuffed cloth with wide cloth streamers that fall from the crown or are draped around it, worn in the 15th century. **—***v.t.* **4.** to attend or accompany as chaperon. **—***v.i.* **5.** to act as chaperon. Also, **chaperone.** [1350–1400; ME < AF, MF: hood, cowl, equiv. to *chape* CAPE[1] + *-eron* n. suffix; figurative sense < F (18th century)] **—chap·er·on·age** (shap′ə rō′nij), *n.* **—chap′er·on′less,** *adj.*
—Syn. 1, 4. escort.

chap·er·one (shap′ə rōn′), *n., v.t., v.i.,* **-oned, -on·ing.** chaperon.

chap·fall·en (chop′fô′lən, chap′-), *adj.* dispirited; chagrined; dejected. Also, **chopfallen.** [1590–1600; CHAP[3] + FALLEN]

chap·lain (chap′lin), *n.* **1.** an ecclesiastic attached to the chapel of a royal court, college, etc., or to a military unit. **2.** a person who says the prayer, invocation, etc., for an organization or at an assembly. [bef. 1100; ME *chapelain* < MF < LL *cappellānus* custodian of St. Martin's cloak (see CHAPEL, -AN); r. OE *capellan* < LL, as above] **—chap′lain·cy, chap′lain·ship′, chap′lain·ry,** *n.*

chap·let (chap′lit), *n.* **1.** a wreath or garland for the head. **2.** a string of beads. **3.** *Rom. Cath. Ch.* **a.** a string of beads, one-third of the length of a rosary, for counting prayers. **b.** the prayers recited over this. **4.** *Archit.* a small molding carved to resemble a string of beads; astragal. **5.** *Metall.* an object for separating the core of a mold from a wall, composed of the same metal as the casting and forming an integral part of it. [1325–75; ME *chapelet* wreath < OF. See CHAPEAU, -ET] **—chap′let·ed,** *adj.*

Chap·lin (chap′lin), *n.* **Sir Charles Spencer** (*Charlie*), 1889–1977, English film actor, producer, and director; in U.S. 1910–52.

Chap·lin·esque (chap′lə nesk′), *adj.* characteristic of or resembling the comedy or filmmaking style of Charlie Chaplin. [1920–25; (Charles) CHAPLIN + -ESQUE]

chap·man (chap′mən), *n., pl.* **-men. 1.** *Brit.* a peddler. **2.** *Archaic.* a merchant. [bef. 900; ME; OE *cēapman* (*cēap* buying and selling + *man* MAN[1]); c. D *koopman,* G *Kaufmann;* see CHEAP] **—chap′man·ship′,** *n.*

Chap·man (chap′mən), *n.* **1. Frank Mich·ler** (mik′lər), 1864–1945, U.S. ornithologist, museum curator, and author. **2. George,** 1559–1634, English poet, dramatist, and translator. **3. John.** See **Appleseed, Johnny.**

chappe (shap), *n.* See **schappe silk.** [1815–25]

chap·pie (chap′ē), *n. Brit. Informal.* chap[2] (def. 1). Also, **chappy.** [1815–25; CHAP[2] + -IE]

chaps (chaps, shaps), *n.* (*used with a plural v.*) a pair of joined leather leggings, often widely flared, worn over trousers, esp. by cowboys, as protection against burs, rope burns, etc., while on horseback. Also called **chaparajos, chaparejos.** [1810–20, *Amer.;* short for CHAPARAJOS]

Chap′ Stick′, *Trademark.* a brand of medicated, often flavored petrolatum in a small tube, used as a salve for or protection against chapped lips.

chap·tal·i·za·tion (shap′tə lə zā′shən), *n.* a method of increasing the alcohol in a wine by adding sugar to the must before or during fermentation. [1890–95; CHAPTALIZE + -ATION]

chap·tal·ize (shap′tə līz′), *v.t.,* **-ized, -iz·ing.** to subject (wine) to chaptalization. Also, *esp. Brit.,* **chap′tal·ise′.** [< F *chaptaliser,* named after J. A. Chaptal (d. 1832), French chemist; see -IZE]

chap·ter (chap′tər), *n.* **1.** a main division of a book, treatise, or the like, usually bearing a number or title. **2.** a branch, usually restricted to a given locality, of a society, organization, fraternity, etc.: *the Connecticut chapter of the American Red Cross.* **3.** an important portion or division of anything: *The atomic bomb opened a new chapter in history.* **4.** *Eccles.* **a.** an assembly of the monks in a monastery, of those in a province, or of the entire order. **b.** a general assembly of the canons of a church. **c.** a meeting of the elected representatives of the provinces or houses of a religious community. **d.** the body of such canons or representatives collectively. **5.** any general assembly. **6.** *Liturgy.* a short scriptural quotation read at various parts of the office, as after the last psalm in the service of lauds, prime, tierce, etc. **7.** *Horol.* any of the marks or numerals designating the hours on a dial. **—***v.t.* **8.** to divide into or arrange in chapters. [1175–1225; ME *chapiter,* var. of *chapitre* < OF < L *capitulum* little head (*capit-,* s. of *caput* head + *-ulum* -ULE); in LL: section of a book; in ML: section read at a meeting, hence, the meeting, esp. one of canons, hence, a body of canons] **—chap′ter·al,** *adj.*
—Syn. 3. era, episode, period, phase.

Chapter 11, *U.S. Law.* a section of the Bankruptcy Code that provides for the reorganization of an insolvent corporation under court supervision and can establish a schedule for the payment of debts and, in some cases, a new corporation that can continue to do business. Also, **Chap′ter Elev′en, Chapter XI.**

chap′ter and verse′, 1. any specific chapter and verse of the Bible, as used when citing the text. **2.** full, cited authority, as for any quotation, opinion, action, etc.: *Give me chapter and verse for the information you've provided so far.* **3.** *Informal.* **a.** detailed information. **b.** a set of regulations or rules. [1620–30]

chap′ter head′, printed material appearing before and usually above the text of a chapter, as a title, number, quotation, etc.

chap′ter house′, 1. *Eccles.* a building attached to or a hall forming part of a cathedral or monastery, used as a meeting place for the chapter. **2.** a building used by a chapter of a society, fraternity, sorority, etc. [bef. 1150; ME *chapitelhus,* OE *captelhus*]

chap′ter ring′, a ringlike band on the dial of a clock that bears the numerals or other symbols of the hours.

chap·trel (chap′trəl), *n. Archit.* **1.** a capital, as on a pilaster or vaulting shaft, engaged in masonry on one or more sides. **2.** a small capital. [1670–80; CHAPTER + *-el* < L *-ellum* dim. suffix]

Cha·pul·te·pec (chə pul′tə pek′; *Sp.* chä pōōl′te-pek′), *n.* a fortress and military school at the outskirts of Mexico City: captured by U.S. forces (1847) in the Mexican War; now a park.

cha·que·ta (chə kā′tə), *n.* a heavy jacket, esp. a leather one worn by cowboys in the American Southwest. [1890–95; < AmerSp; Sp < F *jacquette,* MF *jacquete;* see JACKET, -ETTE]

char[1] (chär), *v.,* **charred, char·ring,** *n.* **—***v.t.* **1.** to burn or reduce to charcoal: *The fire charred the paper.* **2.** to burn slightly; scorch: *The flame charred the steak.* **—***v.i.* **3.** to become charred. **—***n.* **4.** a charred material or surface. **5.** charcoal. **6.** a superior carbon-rich fuel, a by-product of the conversion of coal into gaseous or liquid fuel. [1670–80; appar. extracted from CHARCOAL; see CHARK]
—Syn. 2. singe, sear.

char[2] (chär), *n., pl.* (*esp. collectively*) **char,** (*esp. referring to two or more kinds or species*) **chars.** any trout of the genus *Salvelinus* (or *Cristovomer*), esp. the Arctic char. [1655–65; perh. OE **ceorra* lit., turner, deriv. of *ceorran* to turn, it being thought of as swimming to and fro time and again; see CHAR[3]]

char[3] (chär), *n., v.,* **charred, char·ring.** *Chiefly Brit.* **—***n.* **1.** a charwoman. **2.** a task, esp. a household chore. **3. chars,** odd jobs, esp. of housework, for which one is paid by the hour or day. **—***v.i.* **4.** to work at housecleaning by the day or hour; hire oneself out to do odd jobs. **—***v.t.* **5.** to do (housework, odd jobs, or chores); clean or repair. Also, **chare.** [1375–1425; late ME, OE *cerr, cierr* turn, time, occasion, affair, deriv. of *cierran* to turn]

char[4] (chär), *n. Brit. Informal.* tea. [1915–20; < Hindi *cā* TEA; for sp. with *r* cf. ARVO, PARCHEESI]

Char (shAR), *n.* **Re·né** (rə nā′), born 1907, French poet.

char., 1. character. **2.** charter.

char-à-banc (shar′ə bang′, -bangk′; *Fr.* shA RA bäN′), *n., pl.* **-bancs** (-bangz′, -bangks′; *Fr.* -bäN′). *Brit.* a large bus used on sightseeing tours, esp. one with open sides and no center aisle. Also, **char′a·banc′.** [1810–20; back formation from F *char-à-bancs* lit., car with benches, the *-s* being taken as pl. ending of word as a whole]

char·a·cin (kar′ə sin), *n.* any freshwater fish of the family Characidae, of Africa and Central and South America. Also, **char′a·cid.** [1880–85; < NL *Characinidae* name of family, equiv. to *Characin(us)* the genus (*charac-* (< Gk *charak-,* s. of *chárax* pointed stake, a sea fish) + *-inus* -IN[1]) + *-idae* -IDAE]

char·ac·ter (kar′ik tər), *n.* **1.** the aggregate of features and traits that form the individual nature of some person or thing. **2.** one such feature or trait; characteristic. **3.** moral or ethical quality: *a man of fine, honorable character.* **4.** qualities of honesty, courage, or the like; integrity: *It takes character to face up to a bully.* **5.** reputation: *a stain on one's character.* **6.** good repute. **7.** an account of the qualities or peculiarities of a person or thing. **8.** a person, esp. with reference to behavior or personality: *a suspicious character.* **9.** *Informal.* an odd, eccentric, or unusual person. **10.** a person represented in a drama, story, etc. **11.** a part or role, as in a play or film. **12.** a symbol as used in a writing system, as a letter of the alphabet. **13.** the symbols of a writing system collectively. **14.** a significant visual mark or symbol. **15.** status or capacity: *the character of a justice of the peace.* **16.** a written statement from an employer concerning the qualities of a former employee. **17.** *Literature.* (esp. in 17th- and 18th-century England) a formal character sketch or descriptive analysis of a particular human virtue or vice as represented in a person or type. Cf. **character sketch. 18.** *Genetics.* any trait, function, structure, or substance of an organism resulting from the effect of one or more genes as modified by the environment. **19.** *Computers.* **a.** any symbol, as a number, letter, punctuation mark, etc., that represents data and that, when encoded, is usable by a machine. **b.** one of a set of basic symbols that singly or in a series of two or more represents data and, when encoded, is usable in a computer. **20.** a style of writing or printing. **21.** *Rom. Cath. Theol.* the ineffaceable imprint received on the soul through the sacraments of baptism, confirmation,

CONCISE ETYMOLOGY KEY: <, descended or borrowed from; >, whence; b., blend of, blended; c., cognate with; cf., compare; deriv., derivative; equiv., equivalent; imit., imitative; obl., oblique; r., replacing; s., stem; sp., spelling, spelled; resp., respelling, respelled; trans., translation; ?, origin unknown; *, unattested; ‡, probably earlier than. See the full key inside the front cover.

and ordination. **22.** (formerly) a cipher or cipher message. **23. in character, a.** in harmony with one's personal character or disposition: *Such behavior is not in character for him.* **b.** in accordance with the role or personality assumed in a performance: *an actor in character.* **24. out of character, a.** out of harmony with one's personal character or disposition: *Her remarks were out of character.* **b.** away from the role or personality assumed in a performance: *The actor stepped out of character.*
—*adj.* **25.** *Theat.* **a.** (of a part or role) representing a personality type, esp. by emphasizing distinctive traits, as language, mannerisms, physical makeup, etc. **b.** (of an actor or actress) acting or specializing in such roles.
—*v.t. Archaic.* **26.** to portray; describe. **27.** to engrave; inscribe. [1275–1325; < L < Gk *charaktḗr* graving tool, its mark, equiv. to *charak-* (base of *charáttein* to engrave) + *-tēr* agent suffix; r. ME *caractere* < MF < L, as above] —**char′ac·ter·less,** *adj.*
—**Syn. 1.** CHARACTER, INDIVIDUALITY, PERSONALITY refer to the sum of the characteristics possessed by a person. CHARACTER refers esp. to moral qualities, ethical standards, principles, and the like: *a man of sterling character.* INDIVIDUALITY refers to the distinctive qualities that make one recognizable as a person differentiated from others: *a woman of strong individuality.* PERSONALITY refers particularly to the combination of outer and inner characteristics that determine the impression that a person makes upon others: *a child of vivid or pleasing personality.* **5.** name, repute. See **reputation. 14.** sign.

char′acter assassina′tion, a slandering attack, esp. one intended to damage the reputation of a public or political figure. [1945–50]

char′acter defense′, a personality trait, as a habitual tendency to idealize or rationalize, that serves some unconscious defensive purpose.

char′acter disor′der, *Psychiatry.* a disorder characterized by socially undesirable behavior, as poor control of impulses or inability to maintain close emotional relationships, and by absence of anxiety or guilt.

char·ac·ter·ful (kar′ik tər fəl), *adj.* **1.** highly expressive of character: *a characterful face.* **2.** having remarkable character: *a characterful prose style.* [1900–05; CHARACTER + -FUL]

char′acter gen′erator, *Television.* a device used in television studios to incorporate text or other symbols into the television screen image.

char·ac·ter·is·tic (kar′ik tə ris′tik), *adj.* **1.** Also, **char′ac·ter·is′ti·cal.** pertaining to, constituting, or indicating the character or peculiar quality of a person or thing; typical; distinctive: *Red and gold are the characteristic colors of autumn.* —*n.* **2.** a distinguishing feature or quality: *Generosity is his chief characteristic.* **3.** *Math.* **a.** the integral part of a common logarithm. Cf. **mantissa. b.** the exponent of 10 in a number expressed in scientific notation. **c.** the smallest positive integer *n* such that each element of a given ring added to itself *n* times results in 0. [1655–65; < Gk *charaktēristikós.* See CHARACTER, -ISTIC] —**char′ac·ter·is′ti·cal·ly,** *adv.*
—**Syn. 1.** special, peculiar. **2.** attribute, property, trait. See **feature.**

char′acteris′tic curve′, *Photog.* a graph used in sensitometry to show the relationship between exposure time and image density under constant developing conditions. Also called **sensitometric curve.** [1900–05]

characteris′tic equa′tion, 1. *Math.* **a.** the characteristic polynomial of a given matrix, equated to zero. **b.** Also called **auxiliary equation.** an equation with one variable and equated to zero, which is derived from a given linear differential equation and in which the coefficient and power of the variable in each term correspond to the coefficient and order of a derivative in the original equation. **2.** *Physics.* See **equation of state.** [1920–25]

char′acteris′tic func′tion, *Math.* **1.** a function defined on a given set, having value 1 for every element of the set and value 0 for every element not contained in the set. **2.** See **characteristic polynomial.** [1875–80]

characteris′tic polyno′mial, *Math.* an expression obtained from a given matrix by taking the determinant of the difference between the matrix and an arbitrary variable times the identity matrix. [1955–60]

char′acteris′tic root′, *Math.* **1.** a scalar for which there exists a nonzero vector such that the scalar times the vector equals the value of the vector under a given linear transformation on a vector space. **2.** a root of the characteristic equation of a given matrix. Also called **char′acteris′tic val′ue, eigenvalue, latent root, proper value.** [1955–60]

char′acteris′tic vec′tor, *Math.* a vector for which there exists a scalar such that the value of the vector under a given transformation is equal to the scalar times the vector. Also called **eigenvector.** [1955–60]

characteris′tic veloc′ity, *Aerospace.* **1.** a measure of the effectiveness with which the combustion in a rocket engine produces high temperature and pressure, equal to the exhaust velocity divided by the thrust coefficient. **2.** the total of all velocities a space vehicle must develop to complete a given mission. **3.** an expression of the performance of a propellant or a propulsion system under given operating pressures.

char′acteris′tic x′-ray, *Physics.* an x-ray that is emitted from an atom when an electron is displaced from an inner shell.

char·ac·ter·i·za·tion (kar′ik tər ə zā′shən, -trə zā′-), *n.* **1.** portrayal; description: *the actor's characterization of a politician.* **2.** the act of characterizing. **3.** the creation and convincing representation of fictitious characters. [1560–70; < ML *charactērizāt(us)* marked (ptp. of *charactērizāre;* see CHARACTERIZE; see -ATE[1]) + L *-iōn-* -ION]
—**Syn. 1.** representation, depiction, delineation.

char·ac·ter·ize (kar′ik tə rīz′), *v.t.,* **-ized, -iz·ing. 1.** to mark or distinguish as a characteristic; be a characteristic of: *Rich metaphors characterize his poetry.* **2.** to describe the character or individual quality of: *He characterized her in a few well-chosen words.* **3.** to attribute character to: *to characterize him as a coward.* Also, *esp. Brit.,* **char′ac·ter·ise′.** [1585–95; < ML *charactērizāre* < Gk *charaktērízein.* See CHARACTER, -IZE] —**char′ac·ter·iz′a·ble,** *adj.* —**char′ac·ter·iz′er,** *n.*

char′acter piece′, *Music.* a short, simple piece, usually for piano, of a type developed chiefly during the 19th century, often of a descriptive or seemingly improvisatory character.

char′acter set′, *Computers.* the numbers, letters, punctuation marks, and special symbols that can be used by a particular device, as a printer, or in a coding method, as ASCII.

char′acter sketch′, *Literature.* a short essay describing a person; literary profile. Cf. **character** (def. 17). [1880–85]

char′acter stud′y, a work of fiction in which the delineation of the central character's personality is more important than the plot.

char′acter wit′ness, a person who testifies as to the moral character and reputation of a litigant in a court of law or other legal proceeding. [1950–55]

char·ac·ter·y (kar′ik tə rē, -trē), *n.* **1.** the use of characters or symbols for the expression of meaning. **2.** characters or symbols collectively. [1580–90; CHARACTER + -Y[3]]

char·ac·to·nym (kar′ik tə nim), *n.* a name given to a literary character that is descriptive of a quality or trait of the character. [CHARACT(ER) + -ONYM]

cha·rade (shə rād′; *esp. Brit.* shə räd′), *n.* **1. charades,** (*used with a singular v.*) a game in which the players are typically divided into two teams, members of which take turns at acting out in pantomime a word, phrase, title, etc., which the members of their own team must guess. **2.** a word or phrase acted out in this game. **3.** a blatant pretense or deception, esp. something so full of pretense as to be a travesty. [1770–80; < F < Pr *charrad(o)* entertainment, equiv. to *charr(á)* to chat, chatter (from imit. root) + *-ado* -ADE[1]]

cha·ran·go (chə rang′gō) *n., pl.* **-gos.** a small South American guitar made from the shell of an armadillo or similar animal and having two to five strings. [< Sp, alter. of *charanga* brass band, of imit. orig.]

cha·ras (chär′əs), *n.* **1.** hashish. **2.** marijuana. [1870–75; < Hindi: resin of the hemp plant]

Char·cas (kär′kəs), *n. Douay Bible.* Carcas.

Char·che·mish (kär′kə mish, kär kē′-), *n.* Carchemish.

char·co (chär′kō), *n., pl.* **-cos.** *Southwestern U.S.* a water hole, pool, or puddle. [1885–90, *Amer.;* < AmerSp, Sp; of obscure orig.]

char·coal (chär′kōl′), *n.* **1.** the carbonaceous material obtained by heating wood or other organic substances in the absence of air. **2.** a drawing pencil of charcoal. **3.** a drawing made with charcoal. —*v.t.* **4.** to blacken, write, or draw with charcoal. **5.** to cook (food) over charcoal, esp. on a grill. —*v.i.* **6.** to cook food over charcoal, esp. on a grill. [1300–50; ME *charcole,* perh. *cherre* CHAR[3] + *cole* COAL, though literal sense of the compound is unclear] —**char′coal′y,** *adj.*

char′coal burn′er, 1. a device that burns charcoal, as a stove or brazier. **2.** a person employed in the manufacture of charcoal. [1815–25]

char′coal rot′, a disease of plants, esp. sorghum, corn, etc., characterized by basal stem lesions and a black discoloration and dry rot of the internal tissues at the base of the stem and upper roots, caused by a fungus, *Macrophomina phaseoli.*

Char·cot (shar kō′), *n.* **1. Jean Bap·tiste É·tienne Au·guste** (zhän ba tēst′ ā tyen′ ō gyst′), 1867–1936, French explorer. **2.** his father, **Jean Mar·tin** (zhän mar tan′), 1825–93, French neuropathologist.

char·cu·te·rie (shär ko͞o′tə rē′, shär ko͞o′tə rē; *Fr.* shar kyt[ə] rē′), *n., pl.* **-ries** (-rēz′, -rēz; *Fr.* -rē′). (in France) **1.** a store where pork products, as hams, sausages, and pâtés are sold. **2.** the items sold in such a store. [1855–60; < F; MF *chaircuterie,* equiv. to *chaircut(ier)* CHARCUTIER + *-erie* -ERY]

char·cu·tier (shär ko͞o′tē ā′, shär ko͞o′tē ā′; *Fr.* shar ky tyā′), *n., pl.* **-tiers** (-tē āz′, -āz′; *Fr.* -tyā′). (in France) a pork butcher. [1890–95; < F; MF *chaircutier,* equiv. to *chair* flesh + *cuite* cooked, fem. of *cuit,* ptp. of *cuire* (< L *coquere;* see COOK) + *-ier* -IER[2]]

chard (chärd), *n.* a variety of beet, *Beta vulgaris cicla,* having leaves and leafstalks that are used as a vegetable. Also called **Swiss chard, leaf beet.** [1650–60; appar. < F *chardon* thistle; see CARDOON]

Char·din (shar dan′), *n.* **1. Jean Bap·tiste Si·mé·on** (zhän ba tēst′ sē mā ôn′), 1699–1779, French painter. **2. Pierre Teil·hard de** (pyer te yar′ də). See **Teilhard de Chardin, Pierre.**

Char·don·nay (shär′dn ā′; *Fr.* shar dô ne′), **1.** a white grape used in winemaking. **2.** a dry white wine made with this grape. Also called **Pinot Chardonnay.** [< F *chardon(n)ay*]

Char·don·net (shär′dn ā′; *Fr.* shar dô ne′), *n.* **Hi·laire Ber·ni·gaud** (ē ler′ ber nē gō′), **Comte de,** 1839–1924, French chemist and inventor.

Char·dzhou (chär jō′; *Russ.* chyir jō′), *n.* a city in E Turkmenistan, on the Amu Darya. 140,000.

chare (châr), *n., v.,* **chared, char·ing.** *Chiefly Brit.* char[3].

Cha·rente (sha ränt′), *n.* a department in W France. 337,064; 2306 sq. mi. (5975 sq. km). *Cap.:* Angoulême.

Cha·rente-Ma·ri·time (sha ränt ma rē tēm′), *n.* a department in W France. 497,859; 2792 sq. mi. (7230 sq. km). *Cap.:* La Rochelle.

cha·rette (shə ret′), *n.* charrette.

charge (chärj), *v.,* **charged, charg·ing,** *n.* —*v.t.* **1.** to impose or ask as a price or fee: *That store charges $25 for leather gloves.* **2.** to impose on or ask of (someone) a price or fee: *He didn't charge me for it.* **3.** to defer payment for (a purchase) until a bill is rendered by the creditor: *The store let me charge the coat.* **4.** to hold liable for payment; enter a debit against. **5.** to attack by rushing violently against: *The cavalry charged the enemy.* **6.** to accuse formally or explicitly (usually fol. by *with*): *They charged him with theft.* **7.** to impute; ascribe the responsibility for: *He charged the accident to his own carelessness.* **8.** to instruct authoritatively, as a judge does a jury. **9.** to lay a command or injunction upon: *He charged his secretary with the management of his correspondence.* **10.** to fill or furnish (a thing) with the quantity, as of powder or fuel, that it is fitted to receive: *to charge a musket.* **11.** to supply with a quantity of electric charge or electrical energy: *to charge a storage battery.* **12.** to change the net amount of positive or negative electric charge of (a particle, body, or system). **13.** to suffuse, as with emotion: *The air was charged with excitement.* **14.** to fill (air, water, etc.) with other matter in a state of diffusion or solution: *The air was charged with pollen.* **15.** *Metall.* to load (materials) into a furnace, converter, etc. **16.** to load or burden (the mind, heart, etc.): *His mind was charged with weighty matters.* **17.** to put a load or burden on or in. **18.** to record the loan of, as books or other materials from a library (often fol. by *out*): *The librarian will charge those books at the front desk.* **19.** to borrow, as books or other materials from a library (often fol. by *out*): *How many magazines may I charge at one time?* **20.** *Heraldry.* to place charges on (an escutcheon).
—*v.i.* **21.** to make an onset; rush, as to an attack. **22.** to place the price of a thing to one's debit. **23.** to require payment: *to charge for a service.* **24.** to make a debit, as in an account. **25.** (of dogs) to lie down at command. **26. charge off, a.** to write off as an expense or loss. **b.** to attribute to: *I charged off the blunder to inexperience.* **27. charge up,** *Informal.* **a.** to agitate, stimulate, or excite: *a fiery speaker who can charge up an audience.* **b.** to put or be under the influence of narcotic drugs.
—*n.* **28.** expense or cost: *improvements made at a tenant's own charge.* **29.** a fee or price charged: *a charge of three dollars for admission.* **30.** a pecuniary burden, encumbrance, tax, or lien; cost; expense; liability to pay: *After his death there were many charges on his estate.* **31.** an entry in an account of something due. **32.** an impetuous onset or attack, as of soldiers. **33.** a signal by bugle, drum, etc., for a military charge. **34.** a duty or responsibility laid upon or entrusted to one. **35.** care, custody, or superintendence: *The child was placed in her nurse's charge.* **36.** anything or anybody committed to one's care or management: *The nurse was careful to let no harm come to her charge.* **37.** *Eccles.* a parish or congregation committed to the spiritual care of a pastor. **38.** a command or injunction; exhortation. **39.** an accusation: *He was arrested on a charge of theft.* **40.** *Law.* an address by a judge to a jury at the close of a trial, instructing it as to the legal points, the weight of evidence, etc., affecting the verdict in the case. **41.** the quantity of anything that an apparatus is fitted to hold, or holds, at one time: *a charge of coal for a furnace.* **42.** a quantity of explosive to be set off at one time. **43.** *Elect.* **a.** See **electric charge. b.** the process of charging a storage battery. **44.** *Slang.* a thrill; kick. **45.** *Rocketry.* grains of a solid propellant, usually including an inhibitor. **46.** a load or burden. **47.** *Heraldry.* any distinctive mark upon an escutcheon, as an ordinary or device, not considered as belonging to the field; bearing. **48. in charge, a.** in command; having supervisory power. **b.** *Brit.* under arrest; in or into the custody of the police. **49. in charge of, a.** having the care or supervision of: *She is in charge of two libraries.* **b.** Also, **in the charge of.** under the care or supervision of: *The books are in the charge of the accounting office.* [1175–1225; 1950–55 for def. 41; (v.) ME *chargen* < AF, OF *charg(i)er* < LL *carricāre* to load a wagon, equiv. to *carr(us)* wagon (see CAR[1]) + *-icā-* v. suffix. + *-re* inf. ending; (n.) ME < AF, OF, n. deriv. of the v.] —**charge′less,** *adj.*
—**Syn. 5.** assault. **6.** indict, arraign, impeach. **9.** enjoin, exhort, urge, bid, require, order. **29.** See **price. 32.** onslaught, assault. **34.** commission, trust. **35.** management. **39.** indictment, imputation, allegation. **46.** cargo, freight. —**Ant. 6.** acquit, absolve, exculpate, exonerate.

char·gé (shär zhā′, shär′zhā; *Fr.* shar zhā′), *n., pl.* **-gés** (-zhāz′, -zhāz; *Fr.* -zhā′). a chargé d'affaires. [by shortening]

charge·a·ble (chär′jə bəl), *adj.* **1.** that may or should be charged: *chargeable duty.* **2.** liable to be accused or held responsible; indictable: *He was held chargeable for the theft.* **3.** liable to become a charge on the public. [1350–1400; ME; see CHARGE, -ABLE] —**charge′a·ble·ness, charge′a·bil′i·ty,** *n.* —**charge′a·bly,** *adv.*

charge′ account′, an account, esp. in retailing, that permits a customer to buy merchandise and be billed for it at a later date. [1900–05, *Amer.*]

charge-a-plate (chärj′ə plāt′), *n.* See **charge plate.** [1955–60; alteration of former trademark *Charga-plate*]

charge·back (chärj′bak′), *n.* *Banking.* a debit to a depositor's account for an item that has been previously credited, as for a returned bad check. [CHARGE + BACK[2]]

charge′ card′, an identification card used to make purchases on a charge account; a charge plate.

charge′ car′rier, *Physics.* carrier (def. 13).

charge′ conjuga′tion, *Physics.* the mathematical operation of replacing every elementary particle by its antiparticle. *Symbol:* C

charge′-cou·pled device′ (chärj′kup′əld), *Electronics.* a semiconductor chip with a grid of light-sensi-

CONCISE PRONUNCIATION KEY: act, cāpe, dâre, pärt; set, ēqual; *if,* ice; ox, ōver, ôrder, oil, bo͝ok, bo͞ot, out; up, ûrge; child; sing; shoe; thin, *th*at; zh as in *treasure.* ə = *a* as in *alone, e* as in *system, i* as in *easily, o* as in *gallop, u* as in *circus;* ᵊ as in *fire* (fīᵊr), *hour* (ouᵊr). l and n can serve as syllabic consonants, as in *cradle* (krād′l), and *button* (but′n). See the full key inside the front cover.

tive elements, used for converting light images, as in a television camera, into electrical signals. *Abbr.:* CCD [1970–75]

charged (chärjd), *adj.* **1.** intense; impassioned: *an emotionally charged speech.* **2.** fraught with emotion: *the charged atmosphere of the room.* **3.** capable of producing violent emotion, arousing controversy, etc.: *the highly charged issue of birth control.* **4.** *Elect.* pertaining to a particle, body, or system possessing a net amount of positive or negative electric charge. [1275–1325; ME, for sense "laden, filled"; 1785–95 for def. 1; see CHARGE, -ED[2]]

char·gé d'af·faires (shär zhā′ də fâr′, shär′zhā; *Fr.* shAR zhā dA feR′), *pl.* **char·gés d'af·faires** (shär zhāz′ də fâr′, shär′zhāz; *Fr.* shAR zhā dA feR′). *Govt.* **1.** Also called **chargé′ d'affaires′ ad in′terim.** an official placed in charge of diplomatic business during the temporary absence of the ambassador or minister. **2.** an envoy to a state to which a diplomat of higher grade is not sent. [1760–70; < F: lit., one in charge of things]

charge·ful (chärj′fəl), *adj. Obs.* costly; expensive. [1350–1400; ME. See CHARGE, -FUL]

charge-off (chärj′ôf′, -of′), *n.* a writeoff, esp. of a bad loan by a bank. Also, **charge′off′.** [CHARGE + (WRITE)-OFF]

charge′ of quar′ters, 1. an enlisted person, usually a noncommissioned officer, who remains on duty and handles administrative matters in a military or other unit during the night or on holidays. **2.** the duty of a charge of quarters. [1915–20]

Charge′ of the Light′ Brigade′, The, a poem (1854) by Tennyson, celebrating the British cavalry attack on the Russian position at Balaklava during the Crimean War.

charge′ plate′, an identification plate, esp. one from which an impression can be taken, issued to a customer and used to make purchases on a credit basis. Also, **charge-a-plate.**

charg·er[1] (chär′jər), *n.* **1.** a person or thing that charges. **2.** a horse of a kind suitable to be ridden in battle. **3.** *Elect.* an apparatus that charges storage batteries. [1475–85; CHARGE + -ER[1]]

charg·er[2] (chär′jər), *n.* **1.** a platter. **2.** a large, shallow dish for liquids. [1275–1325; ME *chargeour.* See CHARGE, -OR[2]]

Cha·ri (*Fr.* shA Rē′), *n.* Shari.

Chā·ri·kār (chä′Rē kär′), *n.* a city in E Afghanistan, in the Hindu Kush range. 100,443.

char·i·ly (châr′ə lē), *adv.* **1.** carefully; warily. **2.** sparingly; frugally. [1570–80; CHARY + -LY]
—Syn. 1. guardedly, cautiously. **—Ant. 1.** boldly. **2.** liberally.

char·i·ness (châr′ē nis), *n.* **1.** the state or quality of being chary. **2.** *Obs.* scrupulous integrity. [1565–75; CHARY + -NESS]

Char′ing Cross′ (char′ing), a square and district in central London, England: major railroad terminals.

char·i·ot (char′ē ət), *n.* **1.** a light, two-wheeled vehicle for one person, usually drawn by two horses and driven from a standing position, used in ancient Egypt, Greece, Rome, etc., in warfare, racing, hunting, etc. **2.** a light, four-wheeled pleasure carriage. **3.** any stately carriage. **4.** *Facetious.* an automobile. —*v.t.* **5.** to convey in a chariot. —*v.i.* **6.** to ride in or drive a chariot. [1275–1325; ME < MF, OF, equiv. to *char* CAR[1] + *-iot* dim. suffix] **—char′i·ot·like′,** *adj.*

chariot (def. 1)

char·i·ot·eer (char′ē ə tēr′), *n.* **1.** a chariot driver. **2.** (*cap.*) *Astron.* the constellation Auriga. [1300–50; CHARIOT + -EER; r. ME *charietere* < MF *charetier,* equiv. to OF *charete* cart (*char* CAR[1] + *-ete* -ETTE) + *-ier* -EER]

Cha·ris (kā′ris) *n. Class. Myth.* **1.** one of the Graces, married to Hephaestus. **2.** sing. of **Charites.**

cha·ris·ma (kə riz′mə), *n., pl.* **-ma·ta** (-mə tə). **1.** *Theol.* a divinely conferred gift or power. **2.** a spiritual power or personal quality that gives an individual influence or authority over large numbers of people. **3.** the special virtue of an office, function, position, etc., that confers or is thought to confer on the person holding it an unusual ability for leadership, worthiness of veneration, or the like. Also, **char·ism** (kar′iz əm). [1635–45; < LL < Gk, equiv. to *char-* (base of *cháris* favor, *charízesthai* to favor; akin to YEARN, EXHORT) + *-isma* -ISM]
—Syn. 2. charm, magnetism, presence.

char·is·mat·ic (kar′iz mat′ik), *adj.* **1.** of, having, or characteristic of charisma. **2.** characterizing Christians of various denominations who seek an ecstatic religious experience, sometimes including speaking in tongues and instantaneous healing. —*n.* **3.** a Christian who emphasizes such a religious experience. [1865–70; < Gk *charismat-,* s. of *chárisma* CHARISMA + -IC]

CONCISE ETYMOLOGY KEY: <, descended or borrowed from; >, whence; b., blend of, blended; c., cognate with; cf., compare; deriv., derivative; equiv., equivalent; imit., imitative; obl., oblique; r., replacing; s., stem; sp., spelling, spelled; resp., respelling, respelled; trans., translation; ?, origin unknown; *, unattested; ‡, probably earlier than. See the full key inside the front cover.

cha·ris·ma·tize (kə riz′mə tīz′), *v.,* **-tized, -tiz·ing.** —*v.t.* **1.** to impress or influence by charisma. —*v.i.* **2.** to impress or influence people by charisma. Also, *esp. Brit.,* **cha·ris′ma·tise′.** [CHARISMAT(IC) + -IZE]

char·i·ta·ble (char′i tə bəl), *adj.* **1.** generous in donations or gifts to relieve the needs of indigent, ill, or helpless persons, or of animals: *a charitable man giving much money to feed the poor.* **2.** kindly or lenient in judging people, acts, etc.: *charitable in his opinions of others.* **3.** pertaining to or concerned with charity: *a charitable institution.* [1300–50; ME < OF, equiv. to *charit(e)* CHARITY + *-able* -ABLE] **—char′i·ta·ble·ness,** *n.* **—char′i·ta·bly,** *adv.*
—Syn. 1. beneficent, liberal, bountiful, benevolent. See **generous. 2.** broad-minded, considerate, mild. **—Ant. 1.** selfish. **2.** severe, intolerant.

char′itable trust′, a trust designed for the benefit of the general public, as for educational or other charitable purposes (opposed to *private trust*). Also called **public trust.** [1855–60]

Char·i·tes (kar′i tēz′), *n.pl., sing.* **Cha·ris** (kā′ris). the ancient Greek name for the Graces.

char·i·ty (char′i tē), *n., pl.* **-ties. 1.** generous actions or donations to aid the poor, ill, or helpless: *to devote one's life to charity.* **2.** something given to a person or persons in need; alms: *She asked for work, not charity.* **3.** a charitable act or work. **4.** a charitable fund, foundation, or institution: *He left his estate to a charity.* **5.** benevolent feeling, esp. toward those in need or in disfavor: *She looked so poor that we fed her out of charity.* **6.** leniency in judging others; forbearance: *She was inclined to view our selfish behavior with charity.* **7.** Christian love; agape. [1125–75; ME *charite* < OF < L *cāritāt-* (s. of *cāritās*), equiv. to *cār(us)* dear (akin to CARESS, CHERISH, KAMA, WHORE) + *-itāt-* -ITY] **—char′i·ty·less,** *adj.*
—Syn. 5. kindliness, consideration, humanity, benignity, sympathy. **—Ant. 5.** malevolence.

Char·i·ty (char′i tē), *n.* a female given name.

char′ity school′, *U.S. Hist.* an elementary school, usually funded by charitable persons or organizations, for those unable to pay: a forerunner of the public-school system. [1675–85]

cha·ri·va·ri (shiv′ə rē′, shiv′ə rē′, shə riv′ə rē′ *or, esp. Brit.,* shär′ə vär′ē), *n., pl.* **-ris,** *v.t.,* **-ried, -ri·ing.** shivaree. Also, **chivaree, chivari.** [< F, MF, of obscure orig.; said to be < LL *caribaria* headache < Gk *karēbaría,* equiv. to *karē-,* comb. form of *kárā, kárē* head + *-baria* (*bar(ys)* heavy + *-ia* -IA), on the hypothesis that such a noisy procession would cause a headache]

chark (chärk), *n. Brit. Dial.* **1.** charcoal (def. 1). **2.** coke[1]. —*v.t.* **3.** to char; convert into coke. [1485–95; earlier *charke cole,* back formation from CHARCOAL]

char·kha (chär′kə), *n.* (in India and the East Indies) a cotton gin or spinning wheel. Also, **char′ka.** [1875–80; < Urdu < Pers]

char·la·dy (chär′lā′dē), *n., pl.* **-dies.** *Brit.* a charwoman. [1905–10; CHAR(WOMAN) + LADY]

char·la·tan (shär′lə tn), *n.* a person who pretends to more knowledge or skill than he or she possesses; quack. [1595–1605; < MF < It *ciarlatano,* equiv. to *ciarla(tore)* chatterer (deriv. of *ciarlare* to chatter; from imit. root) + *(cerre)tano* hawker, quack, lit., native of *Cerreto,* a village in Umbria, known for its quacks] **—char·la·tan·ic** (shär′lə tan′ik), **char′la·tan′i·cal, char′la·tan·ish, char′la·tan·is′tic,** *adj.* **—char′la·tan′i·cal·ly,** *adv.*
—Syn. impostor, mountebank, fraud, fake, phony.

char·la·tan·ism (shär′lə tn iz′əm), *n.* **1.** the practice or method of a charlatan. **2.** an instance of this. [1795–1805; CHARLATAN + -ISM]

char·la·tan·ry (shär′lə tn rē), *n., pl.* **-ries.** charlatanism. [1630–40; CHARLATAN + -RY]

Char·le·magne (shär′lə mān′; *Fr.* shAR lə mAN′yᵊ), *n.* ("*Charles the Great*") A.D. 742–814, king of the Franks 768–814; as Charles I, emperor of the Holy Roman Empire 800–814.

Char·lene (shär lēn′), *n.* a female given name, form of **Caroline.** Also, **Char·leen′.**

Char·le·roi (shAR lə RWA′), *n.* a city in S Belgium. 21,700. Also **Char·le·roy′.**

Charles (chärlz), *n.* **1.** (*Prince of Edinburgh and of Wales*) born 1948, heir apparent to the throne of Great Britain (son of Elizabeth II). **2. Cape,** a cape in E Virginia, N of the entrance to the Chesapeake Bay. **3.** a river in E Massachusetts, flowing between Boston and Cambridge into the Atlantic. 47 mi. (75 km) long. **4.** a male given name: from a Germanic word meaning "man."

Charles I (chärlz; *Fr.* shARl), **1.** Charlemagne. **2.** ("*the Bald*") A.D. 823–877, king of France 840–877; as Charles II, emperor of the Holy Roman Empire 875–877. **3.** 1500–58, king of Spain 1516–56; as Charles V, emperor of the Holy Roman Empire 1519–56. **4.** 1600–49, king of Great Britain 1625–49 (son of James I). **5.** 1887–1922, emperor of Austria 1916–18; as Charles IV, king of Hungary 1916–18.

Charles II, 1. See **Charles I** (def. 2). **2.** ("*Charles the Fat*") A.D. 839–888, king of France 884–887; as Charles III, emperor of the Holy Roman Empire 881–887. **3.** 1630–85, king of Great Britain 1660–85 (son of Charles I of England). **4.** 1661–1700, king of Spain 1665–1700.

Charles III, 1. See **Charles II** (def. 2). **2.** ("*Charles the Simple*") A.D. 879–929, king of France 898–923. **3.** See **Charles VI** (def. 2). **4.** 1716–1788, king of Spain 1759–88; as Charles IV, king of Naples 1734–59.

Charles IV, 1. ("*Charles the Fair*") 1294–1328, king of France 1322–28. **2.** (*Charles of Luxembourg*) 1316–78, king of Germany 1347–78 and Bohemia 1346–78; emperor of the Holy Roman Empire 1355–78. **3.** See **Charles I** (def. 5). **4.** See **Charles III** (def. 4).

Charles V, 1. ("*Charles the Wise*") 1337–81, king of France 1364–80. **2.** See **Charles I** (def. 3).

Charles VI, 1. ("*Charles the Mad*" or "*Charles the Well-beloved*") 1368–1422, king of France 1380–1422. **2.** 1685–1740, emperor of the Holy Roman Empire 1711–40; as Charles III, king of Hungary 1711–40.

Charles VII, 1. ("*Charles the Victorious*") 1403–61, king of France 1422–61 (son of Charles VI). **2.** (*Charles Albert*) 1697–1745, elector of Bavaria 1726–45; emperor of the Holy Roman Empire 1742–45.

Charles VIII, 1470–98, king of France 1483–98 (son of Louis XI).

Charles IX, 1. 1550–74, king of France 1560–74. **2.** 1550–1611, king of Sweden 1604–11 (son of Gustavus I).

Charles X, 1. (*Charles Gustavus*) 1622–60, king of Sweden 1654–60. **2.** 1757–1836, king of France 1824–30.

Charles XI, 1655–97, king of Sweden 1660–97 (son of Charles X).

Charles XII, 1682–1718, king of Sweden 1697–1718.

Charles XIV. See **Bernadotte, Jean Baptiste Jules.**

Charles·bourg (shärl′bŏŏrg; *Fr.* shARl bōōR′), *n.* a city in S Quebec, in E Canada, near Quebec. 68,326.

Charles′ Ed′ward Stu′art. See **Stuart, Charles Edward.**

Charles′' law′, *Thermodynam.* See **Gay-Lussac's law.** [named after J. A. C. *Charles* (1746–1823), French physicist, who stated it]

Charles′ Lou′is, (*Karl Ludwig Johann*) 1771–1847, archduke of Austria.

Charles′ Mar·tel′ (mär tel′; *Fr.* mAR tel′), A.D. 690?–741, ruler of the Franks 714–741 (grandfather of Charlemagne).

Charles's Wain (chärl′ziz wān′), *Brit.* See **Big Dipper.** [bef. 1000; OE *Carles wægn* Carl's wagon (*Carl* for Charlemagne); see WAIN]

Charles′ the Great′, Charlemagne.

Charles·ton (chärlz′tən, chärl′stən), *n.* **1.** a seaport in SE South Carolina. 69,510. **2.** a city in and the capital of West Virginia, in the W part. 63,968. **3.** a city in E central Illinois. 19,355.

Charles·ton (chärlz′tən, chärl′stən), *n.* **1.** a vigorous, rhythmic ballroom dance popular in the 1920's. —*v.i.* **2.** to dance the Charleston. [named after CHARLESTON, South Carolina]

Charles·town (chärlz′toun′), *n.* a former city in E Massachusetts: since 1874 a part of Boston; navy yard; battle of Bunker Hill June 17, 1775.

Charle·ton (chärl′tn), *n.* a male given name.

Char·ley (chär′lē), *n., pl.* **-leys.** *Mil. Slang.* See **Victor Charley.** Also, **Charlie.**

char′ley horse′ (chär′lē), a painful, involuntary cramp of an arm or leg muscle resulting from excessive muscular strain or a blow. [1885–90; orig. baseball slang]

Char·lie (chär′lē), *n.* **1.** a word used in communications to represent the letter *C.* **2.** *Mil. Slang.* Charley. **3.** a male given name, form of **Charles. 4.** a female given name.

Char·line (shär lēn′), *n.* a female given name, form of **Caroline.**

char·lock (chär′lək), *n.* a wild mustard, *Brassica kaber,* having lobed, ovate leaves and clusters of small, yellow flowers, often troublesome as a weed in grainfields. [bef. 1000; ME *cherlok,* OE *cerlic* < ?]

Char·lot (shär′lō; *Fr.* shAR lō′), *n.* **Jean** (jēn; *Fr.* zhäN), born 1898, U.S. painter, lithographer, and illustrator; born in France.

char·lotte (shär′lət), *n.* **1.** a dessert of many varieties, served hot or cold and commonly made by lining a mold with cake or bread and filling it with fruit, whipped cream, custard, or gelatin. **2.** the mold used in making this dessert. [1790–1800; < F, special use of woman's name]

Char·lotte (shär′lət), *n.* **1. Grand Duchess** (*Charlotte Aldegonde Elise Marie Wilhelmine*), 1896–1985, sovereign of Luxembourg 1919–64. **2.** a city in S North Carolina. 314,447. **3.** a female given name: derived from *Charles.*

Char·lotte A·ma·li·e (shär′lət ə mä′lē ə), a seaport in and the capital of the Virgin Islands, on St. Thomas. 12,372. Formerly, **St. Thomas.**

Char·lot·ten·burg (shär lot′n bûrg′; *Ger.* shäR lôt′n-bŏŏRk′), *n.* a residential neighborhood in Berlin, Germany: 17th century palace.

char′lotte russe′ (rōōs), **1.** a dessert made by lining a mold with sponge cake or ladyfingers and filling it with Bavarian cream. **2.** a simpler version of this, consisting of a small piece of sponge cake topped with whipped cream and a candied cherry. [1835–45; < F: lit., Russian charlotte]

Char•lottes•ville (shär′ləts vil′), *n.* a city in central Virginia. 45,010.

Char•lotte•town (shär′lət toun′), *n.* a seaport on and the capital of Prince Edward Island, in SE Canada. 17,063.

Charl•ton (chärl′tn), *n.* a male given name.

Char•lyne (shär′lin, shär lēn′), *n.* a female given name, form of **Caroline.** Also, **Char•lyn** (shär′lin).

charm[1] (chärm), *n.* **1.** a power of pleasing or attracting, as through personality or beauty: *charm of manner; the charm of a mountain lake.* **2.** a trait or feature imparting this power. **3. charms,** attractiveness. **4.** a trinket to be worn on a bracelet, necklace, etc. **5.** something worn or carried on one's person for its supposed magical effect; amulet. **6.** any action supposed to have magical power. **7.** the chanting or recitation of a magic verse or formula. **8.** a verse or formula credited with magical power. **9.** *Physics.* a quantum number assigned the value +1 for one kind of quark, −1 for its antiquark, and 0 for all other quarks. *Symbol:* C Cf. **charmed quark.** —*v.t.* **10.** to delight or please greatly by beauty, attractiveness, etc.; enchant: *She charmed us with her grace.* **11.** to act upon (someone or something) with or as with a compelling or magical force: *to charm a bird from a tree.* **12.** to endow with or protect by supernatural powers. **13.** to gain or influence through personal charm: *He charmed a raise out of his boss.* —*v.i.* **14.** to be fascinating or pleasing. **15.** to use charms. **16.** to act as a charm. [1250–1300; ME *charme* < OF < L *carminem,* acc. of *carmen* song, magical formula < **canmen* (by dissimilation), equiv. to *can(ere)* to sing + *-men* n. suffix] —**charm•ed•ly** (chär′mid lē), *adv.* —**charm′er,** *n.* —**charm′less,** *adj.* —**charm′•less•ly,** *adv.*
—**Syn. 1.** attractiveness, allurement. **4.** bauble. **5.** talisman. **6.** enchantment, spell. **8.** spell. **10.** fascinate, captivate, entrance, enrapture, ravish; allure, bewitch.

charm[2] (chärm), *n. Brit. Dial.* blended singing of birds, children, etc. [bef. 1000; ME *cherm(e),* OE *cerm, ceorm,* var. of *ci(e)rm* outcry]

charmed (chärmd), *adj.* **1.** marked by good fortune or privilege: *a charmed life.* **2.** *Physics.* (of a particle) having a nonzero value of charm. [1250–1300; ME. See CHARM[1], -ED[2]]

charmed′ cir′cle, an exclusive or privileged group: *the charmed circle of concert violinists.* [1895–1900]

charmed′ quark′, *Physics.* the quark having electric charge ⅔ times the elementary charge and charm C = +1. It is more massive than the up, down, and strange quarks. Also called **c quark.**

char•meuse (shär mo͞oz′, -mo͞os′; *Fr.* shar mœz′), *n.* a soft, lightweight, drapable fabric of silk or synthetic fibers, having a semilustrous satin face and a dull back. [1905–10; formerly trademark]

Char•mi•an (chär′mē ən, shär′-), *n.* a female given name: from a Greek word meaning "source of joy."

charm•ing (chär′ming), *adj.* **1.** pleasing; delightful: *a charming child.* **2.** using charm; exercising magic power. [1250–1300; ME; see CHARM[1], -ING[2]] —**charm′•ing•ly,** *adv.* —**charm′ing•ness,** *n.*
—**Syn. 1.** lovely, winning, winsome, engaging.

char•mo•ni•um (chär mō′nē əm), *n. Physics.* any meson composed of a charmed quark and a charmed antiquark. [1970–75; CHARM[1] + *-onium,* prob. extracted from POSITRONIUM]

charm′ school′, a school for teaching the social graces, grooming and dress, etc. [1945–50]

char•nel (chär′nl), *n.* **1.** a repository for dead bodies. —*adj.* **2.** of, like, or fit for a charnel; deathlike; sepulchral. [1350–1400; ME < MF < LL *carnāle,* n. and adj. use of neut. of *carnālis* CARNAL]

char′nel house′, a house or place in which the bodies or bones of the dead are deposited. [1550–60]

Cha•ro•lais (shar′ə lā′), *n.* one of a breed of large white or cream-colored beef cattle, originally of France, often used in crossbreeding. Also, **Cha•ro•laise** (shar′ə-lāz′). [1890–95; < F *charolais* (masc.), *charolaise* (fem.) lit., pertaining to the town of *Charolles* (Saône-et-Loire) and *le Charolais* its environs]

Char•on (kâr′ən, kar′-), *n.* **1.** *Class. Myth.* the ferryman who conveyed the souls of the dead across the Styx. **2.** (usually used ironically) any ferryman. **3.** *Astron.* the natural satellite of Pluto, discovered in 1978. —**Cha•ro•ni•an** (kə rō′nē ən), **Cha•ron•ic** (kə ron′ik), *adj.*

char•o•phyte (kar′ə fīt′), *n.* any green algae of the class Charophyceae (or group Charophyta), comprising the stoneworts. [< NL *Charophyta,* equiv. to *Char(a)* a genus of stoneworts (L: a plant of uncert. identity found in Epirus) + -o- -o- + Gk *phŷta,* pl. of *phŷton* -PHYTE]

cha•ro•seth (*Seph.* khä rō′set; *Ashk.* khä rō′sis), *n. Hebrew.* haroseth. Also, ***cha•ro′set.***

Char•pen•tier (shar pän tyā′), *n.* **1. Gus•tave** (gy-stav′), 1860–1956, French composer. **2. Marc An•toine** (mark än twan′), 1634–1704, French composer.

char•poy (chär′poi′), *n.* a light bedstead used in India. Also, **char•pai** (chär′pī′). [1835–45; < Urdu *chārpāi* < Pers, equiv. to *ch(ah)ār* FOUR + *pāy* FOOT]

char•qui (chär′kē), *n.* jerky[2]. [< AmerSp < Quechua *ch′arki*] —**char•quid** (chär′kid), *adj.*

char•rette (shə ret′), *n.* a final, intensive effort to finish a project, esp. an architectural design project, before a deadline. Also, **charette.** [1965–70; < F: cart, OF, equiv. to *char* chariot, wagon (see CAR[1]) + *-ette* -ETTE, from the idea of speed of wheels]

char•ro (chär′ō; *Sp.* chär′rô), *n., pl.* **char•ros** (chär′ōz; *Sp.* chär′rôs). a Mexican horseman or cowboy, typically one wearing an elaborate outfit, often with silver decorations, of tight trousers, ruffled shirt, short jacket, and sombrero. [1925–30; < MexSp; Sp: rustic, countrylike < Basque *txar* poor, weak]

char•ry (chär′ē), *adj.,* **-ri•er, -ri•est.** of, like, or covered with charcoal. [1780–90; CHAR[1] + -Y[1]]

chart (chärt), *n.* **1.** a sheet exhibiting information in tabular form. **2.** a graphic representation, as by curves, of a dependent variable, as temperature, price, etc.; graph. **3.** a map, esp. a hydrographic or marine map. **4.** an outline map showing special conditions or facts: *a weather chart.* **5.** *Astrol.* horoscope (def. 1). **6.** *Jazz.* a musical arrangement. **7. the charts,** ratings of the popularity of popular-music records, usually based on nationwide sales for a given week: *Their album is number three on the charts this week.* —*v.t.* **8.** to make a chart of. **9.** to plan: *to chart a course of action.* **10.** *Informal.* to rank in the charts: *The new song gets charted number four this week.* [1565–75; < MF *charte* < L *c(h)arta;* see CHARTA] —**chart′a•ble,** *adj.*
—**Syn. 3.** See **map. 9.** draft, outline, draw up.

chart., (in prescriptions) a paper. [< L *charta*]

char•ta (kär′tə), *n., pl.* **-tae** (-tē). *Pharm.* **1.** a strip of paper that is impregnated with a medicinal substance, for external application. **2.** Also called **chartula, powder paper.** a paper folded so as to form a packet for a powdered medicament. [bef. 1000; OE, for earlier sense of "letter, document" < ML; < NL, L: sheet of paper, document < Gk *chártēs* papyrus leaf, sheet of paper, lit., something to make marks on; see CHARACTER]

char•ta•ceous (kär tā′shəs), *adj.* of or like paper; papery. [1645–55; < L *chartāceus* made of papyrus. See CHARTA, -ACEOUS]

chart. cerat., (in prescriptions) waxed paper. [< L *charta cērāta*]

char•ter (chär′tər), *n.* **1.** a document, issued by a sovereign or state, outlining the conditions under which a corporation, colony, city, or other corporate body is organized, and defining its rights and privileges. **2.** (*often cap.*) a document defining the formal organization of a corporate body; constitution: *the Charter of the United Nations.* **3.** authorization from a central or parent organization to establish a new branch, chapter, etc. **4.** a grant by a sovereign power creating a corporation, as the royal charters granted to British colonies in America. **5.** Also called **charter party.** a contract by which part or all of a ship is leased for a voyage or a stated time. **6.** a tour, vacation, or trip by charter arrangement: *The travel agency is offering charters to Europe and the Caribbean.* **7.** special privilege or immunity. —*v.t.* **8.** to establish by charter: *to charter a bank.* **9.** to lease or hire for exclusive use: *The company will charter six buses for the picnic.* **10.** to give special favor or privilege to. —*adj.* **11.** of or pertaining to a method of travel in which the transportation is specially leased or hired for members of a group or association: *a charter flight to Europe.* **12.** that can be leased or hired for exclusive or private use: *a charter boat for deep-sea fishing.* **13.** done or held in accordance with a charter: *a charter school.* [1200–50; ME *chartre* < OF < L *chartul(a)* little paper (by assimilation), equiv. to *chart(a)* (see CHARTA) + *-ula* -ULE] —**char′ter•a•ble,** *adj.* —**char′ter•age,** *n.* —**char′ter•er,** *n.* —**char′ter•less,** *adj.*
—**Syn. 9.** See **hire.**

char′ter col′ony, *Amer. Hist.* a colony, as Virginia, Massachusetts, Connecticut, or Rhode Island, chartered to an individual, trading company, etc., by the British crown. Cf. **royal colony** (def. 2). [1760–70]

char′tered account′ant, *Brit.* a member of the Institute of Accountants. *Abbr.:* C.A. [1850–55]

char′tered bank′, *Canadian.* a private bank operating under authorization by the federal government of Canada.

Char•ter•house (chär′tər hous′), *n., pl.* **-hous•es** (-hou′ziz). **1.** a Carthusian monastery. **2.** the hospital and charitable institution founded in London, in 1611, on the site of a Carthusian monastery. **3.** the public school into which this hospital was converted. **4.** the modern heir of this school, now located in Surrey. [1400–50; late ME < AF *chartrouse* (taken as CHARTER + HOUSE), after *Chatrousse,* village in Dauphiné near which the order was founded; see CARTHUSIAN, whence the first *r* of the AF word]

Char′terhouse of Par′ma, The (pär′mə), (French, *La Chartreuse de Parme*), a novel (1839) by Stendhal.

char′ter mem′ber, one of the original members or founders of a club, organization, etc. [1905–10, *Amer.*] —**char′ter mem′bership.**

Char′ter of Rights′, *Canadian.* a section of the Canadian Constitution containing a statement of the basic rights of citizens of Canada.

char′ter par′ty, charter (def. 5). [1530–40]

chart′ house′, *Naut.* a room or deckhouse for storing and working with charts, navigational instruments, etc. Also called **chart room.** [1890–95]

Chart•ism (chär′tiz əm), *n.* the principles or movement of a party of political reformers, chiefly workingmen, in England from 1838 to 1848: so called from the document **(People's Charter** or **National Charter)** that contained a statement of their principles and demands. [1830–40; CHART charter (now obs.) + -ISM; r. *Charterism;* see CHARTER] —**Chart′ist,** *n., adj.*

chart•ist (chär′tist), *n.* **1.** a specialist in the stock market who studies and draws charts of trading actions. **2.** a cartographer. [1960–65; CHART + -IST]

chart•less (chärt′lis), *adj.* uncharted or unknown: *chartless regions of space.* [1800–10; CHART + -LESS]

chart•let (chärt′lit), *n. Navig.* a small chart indicating some special thing, as information relative to a radio navigational aid. [CHART + -LET]

char•to•phy•la•cium (kär′tō fi lā′shəm), *n., pl.* **-cia** (-shə). (in a medieval church) a place for the keeping of records and documents. [< LGk *chartophylákion,* equiv. to *charto-* (comb. form of *chártēs;* see CHARTA) + *phylákion* a guard, watch; see PHYLACTERY]

char•to•phy•lax (kär tof′ə laks′), *n. Gk. Orth. Ch.* an official who serves chiefly as the chancellor and archivist of a diocese. [1875–80; < LGk, Gk, equiv. to *charto-* (see CHARTOPHYLACIUM) + *phýlax* watcher, guard]

Char•tres (shär′trə, shärt; *Fr.* shar′trᵊ), *n.* a city in and the capital of Eure-et-Loir, in N France, SW of Paris: cathedral. 41,251.

Char•treuse (shär tro͞oz′, -tro͞os′; *Fr.* shar trœz′), *n.* **1.** an aromatic liqueur, usually yellow or green, made by the Carthusian monks at Grenoble, France, and, at one time, at Tarragona, Spain. **2.** (*l.c.*) a clear, light green with a yellowish tinge. —*adj.* **3.** (*l.c.*) of the color chartreuse. [1865–70; < F, after La Grande *Chartreuse,* Carthusian monastery near Grenoble, where the liqueur is made]

chart′ room′, *Naut.* See **chart house.** [1875–80]

char•tu•la (kär′chə lə), *n., pl.* **-lae** (-lē′). *Pharm.* charta (def. 2). [< NL, L, equiv. to *chart(a)* piece of paper (see CHARTA) + *-ula* -ULE]

char•tu•lar•y (kär′chə ler′ē), *n., pl.* **-lar•ies. 1.** a register of charters, title deeds, etc. **2.** an archivist. Also, **cartulary.** [1565–75; < ML *chartulārium,* equiv. to L *chartul(a)* CHARTER + *-ārium* -ARY]

Char•va•ka (chär′vä kə, -və-), *n.* Lokayatika.

char•vet (shär′vā, shär vā′), *n.* a soft, lusterless silk or rayon tie fabric, often made with a faint stripe effect. [named after the French firm]

char•wom•an (chär′wo͝om′ən), *n., pl.* **-wom•en.** a woman hired to do general cleaning, esp. in an office or large house. [1590–1600; CHAR[3] + WOMAN]

char•y (châr′ē), *adj.,* **char•i•er, char•i•est. 1.** cautious or careful; wary: *He was chary of investing in oil wells.* **2.** shy; timid. **3.** fastidious; choosy: *She is excessively chary about her friends.* **4.** sparing (often fol. by *of*): *chary of his praise.* [bef. 1000; ME; OE *cearig* sorrowful (c(e)ar(u) CARE + *-ig* -Y[1]); c. OS *karag,* OHG *karag* (G *karg* scanty, paltry)] —**char′i•ly,** *adv.*
—**Syn. 1.** circumspect. **4.** frugal. —**Ant. 1.** trustful. **2.** confident. **3.** uncritical. **4.** lavish.

Cha•ryb•dis (kə rib′dis), *n.* **1.** a whirlpool in the Strait of Messina off the NE coast of Sicily. Modern, **Galofalo, Garofalo. 2.** *Class. Myth.* a daughter of Gaea and Poseidon, a monster mentioned in Homer and later identified with the whirlpool Charybdis. Cf. **Scylla** (def. 2). —**Cha•ryb′di•an,** *adj.*

Chas., Charles.

chase[1] (chās), *v.,* **chased, chas•ing,** *n.* —*v.t.* **1.** to pursue in order to seize, overtake, etc.: *The police officer chased the thief.* **2.** to pursue with intent to capture or kill, as game; hunt: *to chase deer.* **3.** to follow or devote one's attention to with the hope of attracting, winning, gaining, etc.: *He chased her for three years before she consented to marry him.* **4.** to drive or expel by force, threat, or harassment: *She chased the cat out of the room.* —*v.i.* **5.** to follow in pursuit: *to chase after someone.* **6.** to rush or hasten: *We spent the weekend chasing around from one store to another.* —*n.* **7.** the act of chasing; pursuit: *The chase lasted a day.* **8.** an object of pursuit; something chased. **9.** *Chiefly Brit.* a private game preserve; a tract of privately owned land reserved for, and sometimes stocked with, animals and birds to be hunted. **10.** *Brit.* the right of keeping game or of hunting on the land of others. **11.** a steeplechase. **12. give chase,** to pursue: *The hunt began and the dogs gave chase.* **13. the chase,** the sport or occupation of hunting. [1250–1300; ME *chacen* < MF *chasser* to hunt, OF *chacier* < VL **captiāre;* see CATCH] —**chase′a•ble,** *adj.*
—**Syn. 4.** oust, rout, scatter. **7.** hunt, quest.

chase[2] (chās), *n.* **1.** a rectangular iron frame in which composed type is secured or locked for printing or platemaking. **2.** *Building Trades.* a space or groove in a masonry wall or through a floor for pipes or ducts. **3.** a groove, furrow, or trench; a lengthened hollow. **4.** *Ordn.* **a.** the part of a gun in front of the trunnions. **b.** the part containing the bore. [1570–80; < MF *chas, chasse* < LL *capsus* (masc.), *capsum* (neut.) fully or partly enclosed space, var. of *capsa* CASE[2]]

chase[3] (chās), *v.t.,* **chased, chas•ing. 1.** to ornament (metal) by engraving or embossing. **2.** to cut (a screw thread), as with a chaser or machine tool. [1400–50; late ME *chased* (ptp.); aph. var. of ENCHASE]

Chase (chās), *n.* **1. Mary Ellen,** 1887–1973, U.S. educator, novelist, and essayist. **2. Sal•mon Portland** (sal′-mən), 1808–73, U.S. jurist and statesman: secretary of the Treasury 1861–64; Chief Justice of the U.S. 1864–73. **3. Samuel,** 1741–1811, U.S. jurist and leader in the American Revolution: associate justice of the U.S. Supreme Court 1796–1811. **4. Stuart,** 1888–1985, U.S. economist and writer.

chase′ mor′tise, a mortise having one inclined narrow side. [1825–35] —**chase′ mor′tised.**

chas•er[1] (chā′sər), *n.* **1.** a person or thing that chases or pursues. **2.** a drink of a milder beverage taken after a drink of liquor. **3.** Also called **chase′ gun′.** (on a vessel) a gun esp. for use when in chase or when being chased. **4.** a hunter. **5.** *Theat.* **a.** *Chiefly Brit.* the final act or musical number of a vaudeville or variety show. **b.** the music played as the audience leaves a theater. [1250–1300; ME; see CHASE[1], -ER[1]]

chas•er[2] (chā′sər), *n.* a tool with multiple teeth for cutting screw threads. [1700–10; CHASE[2] + -ER[1]]

CONCISE PRONUNCIATION KEY: *act, cāpe, dâre, pärt; set, ēqual; if, īce; ox, ōver, ôrder, oil, bo͝ok, bo͞ot, out; up, ûrge; child; sing; shoe; thin, that;* zh as in *treasure.* ə = a as in *alone,* e as in *system,* i as in *easily,* o as in *gallop,* u as in *circus;* ᵊ as in *fire* (fīᵊr), *hour* (ouᵊr). l and n can serve as syllabic consonants, as in *cradle* (krād′l), and *button* (but′n). See the full key inside the front cover.

chas·er[3] (chā′sər), *n.* a person who engraves metal. [1700–10; CHASE[3] + -ER[1]]

Cha·sid (KHä′sid, hä′-; *Ashk. Heb.* KHô′sid; *Seph. Heb.* KHä sēd′), *n., pl.* **Cha·sid·im** (KHä sid′im, hä-; *Ashk. Heb.* KHô sē′dim; *Seph. Heb.* KHä sē dēm′). *Judaism.* Hasid. Also, **Chassid.** —**Cha·sid·ic** (KHä sid′ik, hä-), *adj.* —**Cha′sid·ism,** *n.*

chas·ing (chā′sing), *n.* **1.** a design chased on metal. **2.** an object decorated by chasing. [1825–35; CHASE[3] + -ING[1]]

Chasles (shäl), *n.* **Mi·chel** (mē shel′), 1793–1880, French mathematician.

chasm (kaz′əm), *n.* **1.** a yawning fissure or deep cleft in the earth's surface; gorge. **2.** a breach or wide fissure in a wall or other structure. **3.** a marked interruption of continuity; gap: *a chasm in time.* **4.** a sundering breach in relations, as a divergence of opinions, beliefs, etc., between persons or groups. [1590–1600; apocopated var. of *chasma* < L < Gk, equiv. to *cha-* (root of *chainein* to gape; see YAWN) + -*(a)sma* resultative suffix] —**chas′·mal, chas′mic,** *adj.* —**chasmed,** *adj.* —**chasm′y,** *adj.*

chas·mog·a·mous (kaz mog′ə məs), *adj. Bot.* pertaining to or having pollination occur in a fully opened flower. Cf. **cleistogamous.** [1955–60] —**chas·mog′a·my,** *n.*

chas·sé (sha sā′ *or, esp. in square dancing,* sa shā′), *n., v.,* **chas·séd, chas·sé·ing.** *Dancing.* —*n.* **1.** a gliding step in which one foot is kept in advance of the other. —*v.i.* **2.** to execute a chassé. [1795–1805; < F: lit., chased, followed, ptp. of *chasser* to CHASE[1]]

chasse gar·dée (shAs gAR dā′), *pl.* ***chasses gar·dées*** (shAs gAR dā′). *French.* **1.** a private hunting preserve. **2.** private grounds.

chasse·pot (shas′pō; *Fr.* shAs pō′), *n., pl.* **-pots** (-pōz; *Fr.* -pō′). a breechloading rifle, closed with a sliding bolt, introduced into the French army after 1866. [1865–70; named after A. A. *Chassepot* (1833–1905), French mechanic, who invented it]

chas·seur (sha sûr′; *Fr.* shA sœR′), *n., pl.* **-seurs** (-sûrz′; *Fr.* -sœR′). **1.** (in the French army) one of a body of cavalry or infantry troops equipped and trained for rapid movement. **2.** a uniformed footman or attendant; liveried servant. **3.** a hunter. **4.** Also called **hunter's sauce.** *French Cookery.* a brown sauce, usually containing mushrooms, tomatoes, shallots, white wine, etc. [1790–1800; < F: lit., chaser; see CHASE[1], -EUR]

Chas·sid (KHä′sid, hä′-; *Ashk. Heb.* KHô′sid; *Seph. Heb.* KHä sēd′), *n., pl.* **Chas·sid·im** (KHä sid′im, hä-; *Ashk. Heb.* KHô sē′dim; *Seph. Heb.* KHä sē dēm′). *Judaism.* Hasid. Also, **Chasid.** —**Chas·sid·ic** (hä sid′ik, hə-), *adj.* —**Chas′sid·ism,** *n.*

chas·sis (chas′ē, -is, shas′ē), *n., pl.* **chas·sis** (chas′ēz, shas′-). **1.** *Auto.* the frame, wheels, and machinery of a motor vehicle, on which the body is supported. **2.** *Ordn.* the frame or railway on which a gun carriage moves backward and forward. **3.** the main landing gear of an aircraft; that portion of the landing gear that supports an aircraft. **4.** *Radio and Television.* a frame for mounting the circuit components of a radio or television set. **5.** a construction forming the sides, top, and bottom of a cabinet, showcase, or the like. [1655–65; < F *châssis* frame; akin to CHASE[2]]

chaste (chāst), *adj.,* **chast·er, chast·est. 1.** refraining from sexual intercourse that is regarded as contrary to morality or religion; virtuous. **2.** virgin. **3.** not engaging in sexual relations; celibate. **4.** free from obscenity; decent: *chaste conversation.* **5.** undefiled or stainless: *chaste, white snow.* **6.** pure in style; not excessively or ornamented; simple. **7.** *Obs.* unmarried. [1175–1225; ME < OF < L *castus* clean, pure, chaste] —**chaste′ly,** *adv.* —**chaste′ness,** *n.*
—**Syn. 1.** continent. **4.** clean, elevated. **5.** unsullied. **6.** unaffected, unadorned, neat; classic; elegant. —**Ant. 1.** immoral. **4.** coarse. **5.** debased. **6.** ornate.

chas·ten (chā′sən), *v.t.* **1.** to inflict suffering upon for purposes of moral improvement; chastise. **2.** to restrain; subdue: *Age has chastened his violent temper.* **3.** to make chaste in style. [1520–30; CHASTE + -EN[1]; r. *chaste* (v.), ME *chastien* < OF *chastier* < L *castīgāre;* see CASTIGATE] —**chas′ten·er,** *n.* —**chas′ten·ing·ly,** *adv.* —**chas′ten·ment,** *n.*
—**Syn. 1.** discipline, punish. **2.** humble. **3.** purify, simplify. —**Ant. 1.** indulge.

chaste′ tree′, a shrub or small tree, *Vitex agnus-castus,* of southern Europe, having aromatic, hairy leaves and long clusters of fragrant, pale lilac-blue flowers. Also called **hemp tree, monk's pepper tree.** [1555–65; trans. of L *agnus castus,* var. of *agnos castus* (by influence of *agnus* lamb) < Gk *ágnos* kind of willow + L *castus* chaste, reinforcement of the idea thought to be in *ágnos* by confusion with Gk *hagnós* pure]

chas·tise (chas tīz′, chas′tīz), *v.t.,* **-tised, -tis·ing. 1.** to discipline, esp. by corporal punishment. **2.** to criticize severely. **3.** *Archaic.* to restrain; chasten. **4.** *Archaic.* to refine; purify. [1275–1325; ME *chastisen,* equiv. to *chasti(en)* to CHASTEN + *-s-* < ? + *-en* inf. suffix] —**chas·tis′a·ble,** *adj.* —**chas·tise·ment** (chas′tiz-mənt, chas tīz′-), *n.* —**chas·tis′er,** *n.*
—**Syn. 1.** punish, castigate; whip, beat, flog, spank.

chas·ti·ty (chas′ti tē), *n.* the state or quality of being chaste. [1175–1225; ME *chastite,* var. of *chastete* < OF < L *castitāt-* (s. of *castitās*), equiv. to *cast(us)* CHASTE + *-itāt-* -ITY]

chas′tity belt′, a beltlike device, worn by women esp. in the Middle Ages, designed to prevent sexual intercourse. [1930–35]

CONCISE ETYMOLOGY KEY: <, descended or borrowed from; >, whence; b., blend of, blended; c., cognate with; cf., compare; deriv., derivative; equiv., equivalent; imit., imitative; obl., oblique; r., replacing; s., stem; sp., spelling, spelled; resp., respelling, respelled; trans., translation; ?, origin unknown; *, unattested; ‡, probably earlier than. See the full key inside the front cover.

chas·u·ble (chaz′yə bəl, -ə bəl, chas′-), *n. Eccles.* a sleeveless outer vestment worn by the celebrant at Mass. [1250–1300; < F < LL *casubla,* unexplained var. of *casula* hooded cloak, L: little house (see CASA, -ULE); r. ME *chesible* < AF < LL] —**chas′u·bled,** *adj.*

A, **chasuble;**
B, maniple

chat (chat), *v.,* **chat·ted, chat·ting,** *n.* —*v.i.* **1.** to converse in a familiar or informal manner. —*v.t.* **2. chat up,** *Chiefly Brit.* **a.** to talk flirtatiously with. **b.** to talk to in a friendly, open way. —*n.* **3.** informal conversation: *We had a pleasant chat.* **4.** any of several small Old World thrushes, esp. of the genus *Saxicola,* having a chattering cry. **5.** See **yellow-breasted chat.** [1400–50; late ME; short for CHATTER] —**chat′ta·ble,** *adj.*
—**Syn. 1, 3.** talk, chitchat, gossip, visit.

Chât., (esp. in Bordeaux wines) Château.

châ·teau (sha tō′; *Fr.* shä tō′), *n., pl.* **-teaus, -teaux** (-tōz′; *Fr.* -tō′). **1.** (in France) a castle or fortress. **2.** a stately residence imitating a distinctively French castle. **3.** a country estate, esp. a fine one, in France or elsewhere on the Continent. **4.** (*often cap.*) a winegrower's estate, esp. in the Bordeaux region of France: often used as part of the name of a wine. Also, **cha·teau′.** [1730–40; < F << L *castellum* CASTELLUM]

Châ·teau·bri·and (shä tō brē äN′; *Eng.* sha tō′brē-äN′), *n.* **1. Fran·çois Re·né** (fRäN swA′ Rə nā′), **Vicomte de,** 1768–1848, French author and statesman. **2.** (*l.c.*) a thick slice of tenderloin, broiled and served with potatoes and a sauce, often a béarnaise sauce. [1875–80, def. 2]

châ·teau d'eau (shä tō dō′), *pl.* ***châ·teaux d'eau*** (shä tō dō′). *French.* an architecturally treated fountain or cistern. [lit: castle of water]

Châ·teau·guay (shat′ə gā′, -gē; *Fr.* shä tō gā′), *n.* a town in S Quebec, in E Canada, on the St. Lawrence. 36,928.

Châ·teau·neuf-du-Pape (shä tō nœf dY pAp′), *n.* a dry red or white wine from the Rhone valley near Avignon. [1850–55; named after a village, center of its production]

Châ·teau·roux (shä tō Ro͞o′), *n.* a city in and capital of Indre, in central France. 55,629.

Châ·teau-Thier·ry (sha tō′tē′ə rē; *Fr.* shä tō tye-Rē′), *n.* a town in N France, on the Marne River: scene of heavy fighting 1918. 13,856.

château′ wine′, wine made at a vineyard estate in the Bordeaux region of France. [1885–90]

chat·e·lain (shat′l ān′; *Fr.* shät[ə] laN′), *n., pl.* **chat·e·lains** (shat′l ānz′; *Fr.* shät[ə] laN′). a castellan. [< MF < L *castellānus* CASTELLAN]

chat·e·laine (shat′l ān′; *Fr.* shät[ə] len′), *n., pl.* **chat·e·laines** (shat′l ānz′; *Fr.* shät[ə] len′). **1.** the mistress of a castle. **2.** the mistress of an elegant or fashionable household. **3.** a hooklike clasp or a chain for suspending keys, trinkets, scissors, a watch, etc., worn at the waist by women. **4.** a woman's lapel ornament resembling this. [1835–45; < F *châtelaine.* See CHATELAIN]

Chat·ham (chat′əm), *n.* **1. 1st Earl of.** See **Pitt, William, 1st Earl of Chatham. 2.** a city in N Kent, in SE England. 56,921. **3.** a city in SW Ontario, in S Canada, near Lake St. Clair. 40,952.

Chat′ham Is′lands, a group of islands in the S Pacific, E of and belonging to New Zealand. 372 sq. mi. (963 sq. km).

cha·ton (shA tôN′), *n., pl.* **-tons** (-tôN′). **1.** Also called **chaton′ foil′.** an imitation gem of paste that has its pavilion backed with metal foil or silver to reflect light. **2.** a bezel in a ring. [1570–80; < F, OF *chastun* gem setting < Gmc; cf. OHG *kasto* container]

cha·toy·ant (shə toi′ənt), *adj.* **1.** changing in luster or color: *chatoyant silk.* **2.** *Jewelry.* reflecting a single streak of light when cut in a cabochon. —*n.* **3.** *Jewelry.* a cabochon-cut gemstone having this reflected streak, as a chrysoberyl cat's-eye. [1790–1800; < F, special use of prp. of *chatoyer* to change luster like a cat's eye, equiv. to *chat* CAT[1] + *-oy-* v. suffix + *-ant* -ANT] —**cha·toy′ance, cha·toy′an·cy,** *n.*

chat′ show′, *Brit.* a television talk show. [1970–75]

Chat·ta·hoo·chee (chat′ə ho͞o′chē), *n.* a river flowing S from N Georgia along part of the boundary between Alabama and Georgia into the Apalachicola River. ab. 418 mi. (675 km) long.

Chat·ta·noo·ga (chat′ə no͞o′gə), *n.* a city in SE Tennessee, on the Tennessee River: Civil War battle 1863. 169,565. —**Chat′ta·noo′gan, Chat·ta·noo·gi·an** (chat′-ə no͞o′jē ən), *adj., n.*

chat·tel (chat′l), *n.* **1.** *Law.* a movable article of personal property. **2.** any article of tangible property other than land, buildings, and other things annexed to land. **3.** a slave. [1175–1225; ME *chatel* < OF. See CATTLE]
—**Syn. 1.** See **property.**

chat′tel mort′gage, a mortgage on household, movable, or other personal property. [1855–60, *Amer.*]

chat·ter (chat′ər), *v.i.* **1.** to talk rapidly in a foolish or purposeless way; jabber. **2.** to utter a succession of quick, inarticulate, speechlike sounds, as monkeys or certain birds. **3.** to make a rapid clicking noise by striking together: *His teeth were chattering from the cold.* **4.** *Mach.* (of a cutting tool or piece of metal) to vibrate during cutting so as to produce surface flaws on the work. —*v.t.* **5.** to utter rapidly or purposelessly. **6.** to cause to chatter, as the teeth from cold. —*n.* **7.** purposeless or foolish talk. **8.** a series of waves or ridges on the surface of a piece of metal that has been imperfectly drawn or extruded. **9.** the act or sound of chattering. [1200–50; ME *chateren;* imit.] —**chat′ter·ing·ly,** *adv.* —**chat′·ter·y,** *adj.*
—**Syn. 2.** clatter, click.

chat·ter·box (chat′ər boks′), *n.* an excessively talkative person. [1765–75; i.e., person whose voice box chatters constantly]

chat·ter·er (chat′ər ər), *n.* **1.** a person who chatters; a chatterbox. **2.** any of several passerine birds having a chattering cry, as certain waxwings and cotingas. [1400–50; late ME *chaterer.* See CHATTER, -ER[1]]

Chat·ter·ji (chä′tər jē), *n.* **Ban·kim Chan·dra** (bung′-kim chun′drə), 1838–94, Indian novelist in the Bengali language. Also, **Chat′ter·jee.**

chat′ter mark′, 1. a mark left by a tool that has been chattering. **2.** *Geol.* any of a series of irregular gouges made on rock surfaces by the slipping of rock fragments held in the lower portion of a glacier. [1885–90]

Chat·ter·ton (chat′ər tən), *n.* **Thomas,** 1752–70, English poet.

chat·ty (chat′ē), *adj.,* **-ti·er, -ti·est. 1.** characterized by friendly and informal talk or writing, often about minor or personal matters: *a long, chatty letter from my sister.* **2.** given to such talk: *a lovable, chatty old man.* [1755–65; CHAT[1] + -Y[1]] —**chat′ti·ly,** *adv.* —**chat′ti·ness,** *n.*
—**Syn. 1.** talky, voluble, gossipy, talkative, newsy.

Chau·cer (chô′sər), *n.* **Geoffrey,** 1340?–1400, English poet.

Chau·ce·ri·an (chô sēr′ē ən), *adj.* **1.** of, pertaining to, or characteristic of Chaucer's writings: *Chaucerian wit.* —*n.* **2.** a scholar devoted to the study of Chaucer and his writings. [1650–60; CHAUCER + -IAN]

chaud·froid (*Fr.* shō fRwä′), *n.* **1.** a cooked dish of fowl or game, served cold with aspic, jelly, or a sauce. **2.** the aspic glaze covering the cold food. Also, **chaud-froid′.** [1890–95; < F: lit., hot-cold, equiv. to *chaud* (< L *cal(i)dus;* see CALDARIUM) + *froid* < L *frīgidus* FRIGID]

chauf·fer (chô′fər), *n.* a small, portable stove. [1815–25; var. of obs. *chafer,* ME *chafer* (see CHAFE, -ER[1]), prob. influenced by + F *chauffoir* heater]

chauf·feur (shō′fər, shō fûr′), *n.* **1.** a person employed to drive a private automobile or limousine for the owner. **2.** a person employed to drive a car or limousine that transports paying passengers. —*v.t.* **3.** to drive (a vehicle) as a chauffeur. **4.** to transport by car: *Saturday mornings I have to chauffeur the kids to their music lessons.* —*v.i.* **5.** to work as a chauffeur: *He chauffeured for a time right after the war.* [1895–1900; < F, equiv. to *chauff(er)* to heat (see CHAFE) + *-eur* -EUR]

chauf·feuse (shō fœz′), *n., pl.* **-feuses** (-fœz′). *Fr. Furniture.* a fireside chair having a low seat and a high back. [1900–05; < F, fem. of *chauffeur.* See CHAUFFEUR]

chaul·moo·gra (chôl mo͞o′grə), *n.* any of several trees of the genus *Hydnocarpus* (or *Taraktogenos*), of southeastern Asia, esp. *H. kurzii,* the seeds of which yield chaulmoogra oil. [1805–15; < Bengali *cālmugrā*]

chaulmoo′gra oil′, a brownish-yellow oil or soft fat expressed from the seeds of a chaulmoogra tree, used formerly in the treatment of leprosy and skin diseases. [1805–15]

Chau·mont (shō mônˊ), *n.* a city in and the capital of Haute-Marne, in NE France. 29,329. Also called **Chau·mont-en-Bas·si·gny** (shō môN′äN bA sē nyē′).

Chaun·cey (chôn′sē, chän′-), *n.* a male given name.

chaunt (chônt, chänt), *n., v.t., v.i. Obs.* chant.

chausses (shōs), *n.* (*used with a plural v.*) **1.** medieval armor of mail for the legs and feet. **2.** tights worn by men in medieval times over the legs and feet. [1350–1400; ME *chauces* < MF, pl. of *chauce* << L *calceus* shoe, equiv. to *calc-* (s. of *calx*) heel + *-eus* -EOUS]

Chaus·son (shō sôN′), *n.* **Er·nest** (eR nest′), 1855–99, French composer.

chaus·sure (shō sYR′), *n., pl.* **-sures** (-sYR′). *French.* any foot covering, as a shoe or boot; footwear.

Chau·tau·qua (shə tô′kwə, chə-), *n.* **1. Lake,** a lake in SW New York. 18 mi. (29 km) long. **2.** a village on this lake: summer educational center. **3.** an annual educational meeting, originating in this village in 1874, providing public lectures, concerts, and dramatic performances during the summer months, usually in an outdoor setting. **4.** (*usually l.c.*) any similar assembly, esp. one of a number meeting in a circuit of communities. —*adj.* **5.** of or pertaining to a system of education flourishing in the late 19th and early 20th centuries, originating at Lake Chautauqua, New York. **6.** (*usually l.c.*) pertaining to a chautauqua: *a chautauqua program.*

Chau·temps (shō täN′), *n.* **Ca·mille** (kA mē′y[ə]), 1885–1963, French politician: premier 1930, 1933–34, 1937–38.

chau·vin·ism (shō′və niz′əm), *n.* **1.** zealous and aggressive patriotism or blind enthusiasm for military glory. **2.** biased devotion to any group, attitude, or cause. Cf. **male chauvinism.** [1865–70; < F *chauvinisme,* equiv. to *chauvin* jingo (named after N. *Chauvin,* a soldier in Napoleon's army noted for loud-mouthed patriotism) + *-isme* -ISM] **—chau′vin·ist,** *n.* **—chau′vin·is′tic,** *adj.* **—chau′vin·is′ti·cal·ly,** *adv.*

Cha·vannes (shᴀ vᴀɴ′), *n.* **Pu·vis de** (ᴘʏ vē′ də). See **Puvis de Chavannes, Pierre.**

Chá·vez (chä′vez or, *for 2,* shä′-, shə vez′; *Sp.* chä′ves), *n.* **1. Car·los** (kär′lōs; *Sp.* kär′lôs), 1899–1978, Mexican composer and conductor. **2. Ce·sar (Es·tra·da)** (sē′zər e strä′də; *Sp.* se′säʀ es tʀä′thä), 1927–93, U.S. labor leader: organizer of migrant farmworkers.

Cha·vin (chə vēn′), *adj.* of, pertaining to, or characteristic of a Peruvian culture flourishing from the 1st to the 6th century A.D. [named after *Chavin,* town in Peru]

cha·vu·rah (*Seph., Ashk.* ᴋʜä′vo͞o rä′; *Eng.* ᴋʜä′vo͝o-rä′), *n., pl.* ***-roth, -rot*** (*Seph.* -ʀôt′; *Ashk.* -ʀōs′), *Eng.* **-rahs.** *Hebrew.* havurah.

chaw (chô), *v.t., v.i., n. Dial.* chew. **—chaw′er,** *n.*

chay (shā), *n.* chaise; shay.

Chay·ef·sky (chī ef′skē), *n.* **Pad·dy** (pad′ē), 1923–1981, U.S. playwright and director.

cha·yo·te (chī ō′tē), *n.* **1.** a tropical American vine, *Sechium edule,* of the gourd family, having triangular leaves and small, white flowers. **2.** the green or white, furrowed, usually pear-shaped, edible fruit of this plant. Also, **choyote.** Also called **christophene, mirliton, vegetable pear.** [1885–90, *Amer.;* < MexSp < Nahuatl *chayohtli*]

cha·zan (*Seph.* ᴋʜä zän′; *Ashk., Eng.* ᴋʜä′zən), *n., pl.* ***cha·zan·im*** (*Seph.* ᴋʜä′zä nēm′; *Ashk.* ᴋʜä zô′nim), *Eng.* **cha·zans** (ᴋʜä′zənz). *Hebrew.* hazan. Also, ***chaz·zan′.***

cha·ze·rei (ᴋʜä′zə ʀī′; *Eng.* hä′zə rī′), *n. Yiddish.* anything of little value; junk; garbage. Also, ***chaz′ze·rei′, chozerei.***

Ch.B., Bachelor of Surgery. [< L *Chirurgiae Baccalaureus*]

Ch.E., Chemical Engineer.

cheap (chēp), *adj.,* **-er, -est,** *adv., n.* **—*adj.* 1.** costing very little; relatively low in price; inexpensive: *a cheap dress.* **2.** costing little labor or trouble: *Words are cheap.* **3.** charging low prices: *a very cheap store.* **4.** of little account; of small value; mean; shoddy: *cheap conduct; cheap workmanship.* **5.** embarrassed; sheepish: *He felt cheap about his mistake.* **6.** obtainable at a low rate of interest: *when money is cheap.* **7.** of decreased value or purchasing power, as currency depreciated due to inflation. **8.** stingy; miserly: *He's too cheap to buy his own brother a cup of coffee.* **9. cheap at twice the price,** exceedingly inexpensive: *I found this old chair for eight dollars—it would be cheap at twice the price.* **—*adv.* 10.** at a low price; at small cost: *He is willing to sell cheap.* **—*n.* 11. on the cheap,** *Informal.* inexpensively; economically: *She enjoys traveling on the cheap.* [bef. 900; ME *cheep* (short for phrases, as *good cheep* cheap, lit., good bargain), OE *cēap* bargain, market, trade; c. G *Kauf,* ON *kaup;* all < L *caupō* innkeeper, tradesman; see CHAPMAN] **—cheap′ish,** *adj.* **—cheap′ish·ly,** *adv.* **—cheap′ly,** *adv.* **—cheap′ness,** *n.*
—Syn. 1, 4. CHEAP, INEXPENSIVE agree in their suggestion of low cost. CHEAP now usually suggests shoddiness, inferiority, showy imitation, complete unworthiness, and the like: *a cheap kind of fur.* INEXPENSIVE emphasizes lowness of price (although more expensive than CHEAP) and suggests that the value is fully equal to the cost: *an inexpensive dress.* It is often used as an evasion for the more specific CHEAP. **4.** paltry, low, poor, inferior, base. **—Ant. 1.** costly, dear, expensive. **8.** generous, charitable.

cheap·en (chē′pən), *v.t.* **1.** to make cheap or cheaper. **2.** to lower in esteem; bring into contempt: *Constant swearing cheapened him.* **3.** to decrease the quality or beauty of; make inferior or vulgar: *She cheapened the dress by adding a fringe to it.* **4.** *Archaic.* to bargain for. **—*v.i.* 5.** to become cheap or cheaper. [1555–65; CHEAP + -EN[1]; r. ME *chepen* (> obs. E *cheap* (v.)) to price, bargain, OE *cēapian* to bargain, trade, buy; c. ON *kaupa,* Goth *kaupōn,* G *kaufen*] **—cheap′en·er,** *n.*

cheap·ie (chē′pē), *Informal.* **—*n.* 1.** a cheaply made, often inferior, product: *The movie studio made a dozen cheapies last year.* **2.** any item that is inexpensive as compared with others of its kind: *All brands of margarine taste alike to me, so I buy a cheapie.* **3.** a stingy or miserly person: *That cheapie wouldn't buy anyone a gift!* **—*adj.* 4.** of, being, or pertaining to a cheap or inferior product: *cheapie shoes.* **5.** stingy; miserly. Also, **cheapy.** [1940–45; CHEAP + -IE]

cheap-jack (chēp′jak′), *n.* **1.** a peddler, esp. of inferior articles. **—*adj.* 2.** of or suitable for a cheap-jack; cheap or inferior. **3.** without scruples or principles; underhanded: *using cheap-jack methods to evict tenants.* Also, **cheap′jack′, cheap-john** (chēp′jon′). [1850–55]

cheap·o (chē′pō), *adj., n. Slang.* cheapie. Also, **el cheapo.** [1970–75; CHEAP + -O]

cheap′ shot′, 1. a covert, unsportsmanlike, and illegal act of deliberate roughness, esp. in football, often calculated to injure an opponent. **2.** any mean or unsportsmanlike remark or action, esp. one directed at a defenseless or vulnerable person.

Cheap·side (chēp′sīd′), *n.* a district and thoroughfare in London, England.

cheap·skate (chēp′skāt′), *n., v.,* **-skat·ed, -skat·ing.** *Informal.* **—*n.* 1.** a person who is stingy and miserly. **—*v.i.* 2.** to act in a stingy or miserly way. [1895–1900, *Amer.;* CHEAP + SKATE[3]]

cheap·y (chē′pē), *n., pl.* **cheap·ies,** *adj. Informal.* cheapie. [CHEAP + -Y[2]]

cheat (chēt), *v.t.* **1.** to defraud; swindle: *He cheated her out of her inheritance.* **2.** to deceive; influence by fraud: *He cheated us into believing him a hero.* **3.** to elude; deprive of something expected: *He cheated the law by suicide.* **—*v.i.* 4.** to practice fraud or deceit: *She cheats without regrets.* **5.** to violate rules or regulations: *He cheats at cards.* **6.** to take an examination or test in a dishonest way, as by improper access to answers. **7.** *Informal.* to be sexually unfaithful (often fol. by *on*): *Her husband knew she had been cheating all along. He cheated on his wife.* **—*n.* 8.** a person who acts dishonestly, deceives, or defrauds: *He is a cheat and a liar.* **9.** a fraud; swindle; deception: *The game was a cheat.* **10.** *Law.* the fraudulent obtaining of another's property by a pretense or trick. **11.** an impostor: *The man who passed as an earl was a cheat.* [1325–75; ME *chet* (n.) (aph. for *achet,* var. of *eschet* ESCHEAT); *cheten* to escheat, deriv. of *chet* (n.)] **—cheat′a·ble,** *adj.* **—cheat′ing·ly,** *adv.*
—Syn. 1. mislead, dupe, delude; gull, con; hoax, fool. CHEAT, DECEIVE, TRICK, VICTIMIZE refer to the use of fraud or artifice deliberately to hoodwink or obtain an unfair advantage over someone. CHEAT implies conducting matters fraudulently, esp. for profit to oneself: *to cheat at cards.* DECEIVE suggests deliberately misleading or deluding, to produce misunderstanding or to prevent someone from knowing the truth: *to deceive one's parents.* To TRICK is to deceive by a stratagem, often of a petty, crafty, or dishonorable kind: *to trick someone into signing a note.* To VICTIMIZE is to make a victim of; the emotional connotation makes the cheating, deception, or trickery seem particularly dastardly: *to victimize a blind man.* **8.** swindler, trickster, sharper, dodger, charlatan, fraud, fake, phony, mountebank. **9.** imposture, artifice, trick, hoax.

cheat·er (chē′tər), *n.* **1.** a person or thing that cheats. **2. cheaters,** *Slang.* **a.** eyeglasses; spectacles. **b.** falsies. [1300–50; ME; see CHEAT, -ER[1]]

che·bec (chi bek′), *n.* See **least flycatcher.** [imit.]

che·beck (shi bek′), *n. Naut.* xebec.

Che·bo·ksa·ry (cheb′ək sär′ē; *Russ.* chyi bu ksä′ʀi), *n.* a port in and the capital of the Chuvash Autonomous Republic, in the Russian Federation in Europe, on the Volga. 420,000.

Che·by·shev′ equa′tion (chə bə shôf′), *Math.* See **Tchebycheff equation.**

Chebyshev′ polyno′mial, *Math.* See **Tchebycheff polynomial.**

che·cha·ko (chē chä′kō), *n., pl.* **-kos.** (in the Pacific Northwest) cheechako.

Che·chen (chə chen′), *n., pl.* **-chens,** (*esp. collectively*) **-chen** for 1. **1.** a member of a Sunni Muslim people living in the Chechen-Ingush Autonomous Republic and adjacent areas, closely related to the Ingush. **2.** the Caucasian language spoken by the Chechen.

Che·chen′-In·gush′ Auton′omous Repub′lic (chə chen′in go͞osh′), an autonomous republic of the Russian Federation, in Caucasia. 1,277,000; 7,350 sq. mi. (19,300 sq. km). *Cap.:* Grozny. Also, **Che·chen′o-In·gush′ Auton′omous Repub′lic** (chə chen′ō in go͞osh′).

ché·chia (shāsh′yä), *n.* a close-fitting, cylindrical cap with a tuft or tassel. [1905–10; < F < North African dial. var. of Ar *shāshīyah,* after *Shāsh,* city in Persia where it was once made]

check[1] (chek), *v., n., pl.* **checks** or, for 45, **chex,** *adj., interj.* **—*v.t.* 1.** to stop or arrest the motion of suddenly or forcibly: *He checked the horse at the edge of the cliff.* **2.** to restrain; hold in restraint or control: *They built a high wall to check the tides.* **3.** to cause a reduction, as in rate or intensity; diminish: *The new measures checked the rapidity with which the epidemic was spreading.* **4.** to investigate or verify as to correctness: *She checked the copy against the original.* **5.** to make an inquiry into, search through, etc.: *We checked the files, but the letter was missing.* **6.** to inspect or test the performance, condition, safety, etc., of (something): *Check a used car thoroughly before buying it.* **7.** to mark (something) so as to indicate examination, correctness, preference, etc. (often fol. by *off*): *Please check the correct answer. They checked off the names of people they wanted to invite.* **8.** to leave in temporary custody: *Check your umbrellas at the door.* **9.** to accept for temporary custody: *We accept responsibility for any article we check here.* **10.** to send (baggage) on a passenger's ticket, usually on the same carrier used by the passenger, for pickup at the destination: *We checked two trunks through to Portland.* **11.** to accept (baggage) for conveyance, and to convey, under the privilege of a passenger's ticket: *Check this trunk to Portland.* **12.** to mark with or in a pattern of squares: *to check fabric.* **13.** *Agric.* to plant in checkrows. **14.** *Chess.* to place (an opponent's king) under direct attack. **15.** *Ice Hockey.* to obstruct or impede the movement or progress of (an opponent). Cf. **back-check, fore-check.** **—*v.i.* 16.** to prove to be right; correspond accurately: *The reprint checks with the original, item for item.* **17.** to make an inquiry, investigation, etc., as for verification (often fol. by *up, into,* etc.): *He checked to make sure his answer was correct. Check into the matter.* **18.** to make a sudden stop; pause: *The horse checked before he jumped.* **19.** *Chess.* to make a move that puts the opponent's king under direct attack. **20.** to crack or split, usually in small checks: *Painted surfaces may check with age.* **21.** *Poker.* to decline to initiate the betting in a betting round, usually to force another player to make the first bet rather than raise it. **22.** *Hunting.* (of hounds) to stop, esp. because the line of scent has been lost. **23.** *Falconry.* (of a hawk) to forsake the proper prey and follow baser game (fol. by *at*). **24. check in,** to register, as at a hotel; indicate one's arrival or presence at a place, function, etc., usually by signing an appropriate form: *We checked in at the reception desk.* **25. check on** or **up on,** to investigate, scrutinize, or inspect: *Don't forget to check on his work. We have to check up on him.* **26. check out, a.** to vacate and pay for one's quarters at a hotel. **b.** to verify or become verified; examine or investigate. **c.** to fulfill requirements, as by passing a test: *The engine checked out and we proceeded on our way.* **d.** to itemize, total the cost of, and collect payment for (a purchase): *The supermarket cashier was exhausted from checking out groceries all day long.* **e.** to have the cost added up and pay for merchandise. **f.** to borrow (an item) by having it listed as one's temporary responsibility: *The adding machine was checked out in your name.* **g.** *Informal.* to depart quickly or abruptly; leave in a hurry. **h.** *Slang.* to die. **27. check over,** to examine or investigate, esp. thoroughly. **28. check the helm,** *Naut.* to alter the helm of a turning vessel to keep the bow from swinging too far or too rapidly.
—*n.* 29. Also, *Brit.,* **cheque.** *Banking.* a written order, usually on a standard printed form, directing a bank to pay money. **30.** a slip or ticket showing the amount owed, esp. a bill for food or beverages consumed. **31.** a ticket or token that when matched with a counterpart identifies an article left in the temporary custody of another, the purchaser of a ticket, a person who is to be served next, etc. **32.** a criterion, standard, or means to insure against error, fraud, etc.: *This handmade sample is a check that the machine-made samples have to match.* **33.** an inquiry, search, or examination: *We made a quick check but found nothing missing.* **34.** Also called **check mark.** a mark, often indicated by (✓), as on a list, to indicate that something has been considered, acted upon, or approved. **35.** a person or thing that stops, limits, slows, or restrains: *The increase of duty was an effective check on imports. He was a check on her enthusiasm.* **36.** a sudden arrest or stoppage; repulse; rebuff: *Taxation caused a check in the accumulation of vast fortunes.* **37.** a control, test, or inspection that ascertains performance or prevents error: *They ran a check on the dependability of the automobile.* **38.** a pattern formed of squares, as on a checkerboard. **39.** one of the squares in such a pattern. **40.** a fabric having a check pattern. **41.** *Chess.* the exposure of the king to direct attack: *The king was in check.* **42.** *Ice Hockey.* any of several maneuvers designed to obstruct or impede the forward progress of an opponent. Cf. **board check, body check, cross-check** (def. 5), **hook check, poke check, sweep check.** **43.** a counter used in card games, as the chip in poker. **44.** a small crack: *There were several checks in the paint.* **45.** an egg, designated for market, having a slightly cracked shell and an intact inner membrane. **46.** *Masonry.* a rabbet-shaped cutting on the edge of a stone, by which it is fitted to another stone. **47.** *Hunting.* **a.** the losing of the scent by a dog or pack. **b.** (in fox hunting) a period in a hunt, following the losing of the scent by the hounds, during which the field rests quietly while the hounds cast to regain the scent. **48. in check,** under restraint: *He held his anger in check.*
—*adj.* 49. serving to check, control, verify, etc.: *a check system.* **50.** ornamented with a checkered pattern; checkered: *a check border.*
—*interj.* 51. *Chess.* (used as a call to warn one's opponent that his or her king is exposed to direct attack, having just one move in which to escape or parry.) **52.** *Informal.* all right! agreed! [1275–1325; ME *chek, chekke* (at chess) < OF *eschec* (by aphesis), var. of *eschac* < Ar *shāh* check (at chess) < Pers: lit., king (an exclamation: i.e., look out, your king is threatened); see SHAH] **—check′less,** *adj.*
—Syn. 1. See **stop. 2.** hinder, hamper, obstruct, curtail; chain, bridle, hobble. CHECK, CURB, REPRESS, RESTRAIN refer to putting a control on movement, progress, action, etc. CHECK implies arresting suddenly, halting or causing to halt: *to check a movement toward reform.* CURB implies the use of a means such as a chain, strap, frame, wall, etc., to guide or control or to force to stay within definite limits: *to curb a horse.* REPRESS, formerly meaning to suppress, now implies preventing the action or development that might naturally be expected: *to repress evidence of excitement.* RESTRAIN implies the use of force to put under control, or chiefly, to hold back: *to restrain a person from violent acts.* **6.** examine, scrutinize. **16.** agree. **30.** receipt, tab, counterfoil. **31.** coupon, tag, stub. **35.** obstacle, obstruction, hindrance, restriction, restraint, impediment, control, deterrent; bar, barrier; damper; curb, bridle, bit, rein. **—Ant. 1.** advance.

check[2] (chek), *n. South Midland and Southern U.S.* **1.** Often, **checks.** the game of checkers. **2.** any of the playing pieces used in this game. [by shortening]

check·a·ble (chek′ə bəl), *adj.* **1.** capable of being checked, as by inquiry or verification: *The fact is checkable from available records.* **2.** (of money deposited in a bank) capable of being withdrawn by bank check: *a checkable account.* [1875–80; CHECK[1] + -ABLE] **—check′a·bil′i·ty,** *n.*

check·back (chek′bak′), *n.* a check or verification of a process, tabulation, etc., already completed. [1925–30; n. use of v. phrase *check back*]

check′ bit′, *Computers.* a binary digit used as part of a unit of information that is intended to indicate whether or not an error has occurred in the transmission or storage of the information. Cf. **parity bit.**

check·book (chek′bo͝ok′), *n.* a book containing blank checks or orders on a bank. [1770–80, *Amer.;* CHECK[1] + BOOK]

checked (chekt), *adj.* **1.** having a pattern of squares; checkered: *a checked shirt.* **2.** *Phonet.* (of a vowel) situated in a closed syllable (opposed to *free*). [1375–1425; late ME. See CHECK[1], -ED[2]]

check·ed·y (chek′i dē), *adj.* checkered; having a checked pattern. [1915–20, *Amer.;* appar. CHECKED + -Y[1]]

check·er[1] (chek′ər), *n.* **1.** a small, usually red or black disk of plastic or wood, used in playing checkers. **2. checkers, a.** Also called, *Brit.,* **draughts.** (*used with a singular v.*) a game played by two persons, each with 12 playing pieces, on a checkerboard. **b.** (in a regenerative furnace) loosely stacked brickwork through which furnace gases and incoming air are passed in turn, so that the heat of the exhaust is absorbed and later transferred to the incoming air. See diag. under **open hearth.** **3.** a checkered pattern. **4.** one of the squares of a

CONCISE PRONUNCIATION KEY: *act, cāpe, dâre, pärt; set, ēqual; if, īce; ox, ōver, ôrder, oil, bo͝ok, bo͞ot, out; up, ûrge; child; sing; shoe; thin, that;* zh as in *treasure.* ə = *a* as in *alone, e* as in *system, i* as in *easily, o* as in *gallop, u* as in *circus;* ᵊ as in *fire* (fīᵊr), *hour* (ouᵊr). l and n can serve as syllabic consonants, as in *cradle* (krād′l), and *button* (but′n). See the full key inside the front cover.

checkered pattern. —*v.t.* **5.** to mark like a checkerboard. **6.** to diversify in color; variegate. **7.** to diversify in character; subject to alternations: *Sorrow and joy have checkered his life.* Also, *Brit.,* **chequer.** [1250–1300; ME *checker* chessboard < AF *escheker* (by aphesis), equiv. to *eschec* CHECK + *-er* -ER[2]]

check•er[2] (chek′ər), *n.* **1.** a person or thing that checks. **2.** a cashier, as in a supermarket or cafeteria. **3.** a person who checks coats, baggage, etc. [1525–35; CHECK[1] + -ER[1]]

check•er•ber•ry (chek′ər ber′ē), *n., pl.* **-ries. 1.** the red fruit of the American wintergreen, *Gaultheria procumbens.* **2.** the plant itself. **3.** any of several other plants bearing similar fruit, or the fruit itself. [1770–80, *Amer.*; perh. so named from its appearance]

check•er•bloom (chek′ər blo͞om′), *n.* a western North American plant, *Sidalcea malviflora,* of the mallow family, having long, loose clusters of rose-colored flowers. Also called **wild hollyhock.** [1920–25; CHECKER[1] + BLOOM[1]]

check•er•board (chek′ər bôrd′, -bōrd′), *n.* **1.** a board marked off into 64 squares of two alternating colors, arranged in eight vertical and eight horizontal rows, on which checkers or chess is played. **2.** a design resembling this: *The garden was laid out in a checkerboard.* —*v.t.* **3.** to arrange in or mark with a checkerboard pattern: *a wall checkerboarded with black and white tiles.* Also called, *Brit.,* **draughtboard** (for def. 1). [1765–75; CHECKER[1] + BOARD]

check•ered (chek′ərd), *adj.* **1.** marked by numerous and various shifts or changes; variegated: *a checkered career.* **2.** marked by dubious episodes; suspect in character or quality: *a checkered past.* **3.** marked with squares: *a checkered fabric.* **4.** diversified in color; alternately light and shadowed: *the checkered shade beneath trees.* [1350–1400; ME. See CHECKER[1], -ED[2]]
—**Syn. 1.** varied, uneven, irregular, seesaw.

check′ered flag′, (in automobile racing) **1.** a flag having a pattern of black and white squares, used to signal that a car has crossed the finish line and completed its race. **2.** this signal indicating the first car to cross the finish line or the winner.

check′ered lil′y, a lily, *Fritillaria meleagris,* native to Europe, having solitary, checkered, red-purple flowers mottled with greenish yellow. Also called **guinea-hen flower, snake's-head.**

check•er•spot (chek′ər spot′), *n.* any of several butterflies of the genus *Melitaea,* having black wings with yellowish-brown, checkerlike markings. [CHECKER[1] + SPOT]

check•er•work (chek′ər wûrk′), *n.* a pile of loosely stacked bricks in the regenerator of a regenerative furnace. [CHECKER[1] + WORK]

check•hook (chek′ho͝ok′), *n.* a hook on the saddle of a harness, for holding the end of the checkrein. [CHECK(REIN) + HOOK]

check-in (chek′in′), *n.* the act or fact of checking in. [1915–20; n. use of v. phrase *check in*]

check′ing account′, a bank deposit against which checks can be drawn by the depositor. Cf. **savings account.** [1920–25, *Amer.*]

check′less soci′ety. See **cashless society.**

check′ line′, 1. a checkrein. **2.** *Naut.* a line for controlling the progress of a vessel, as along a quay.

check•list (chek′list′), *n.* **1.** Also, **check′ list′.** a list of items, as names or tasks, for comparison, verification, or other checking purposes. —*v.t.* **2.** to enter (an item) on a checklist. —*v.i.* **3.** to enter items on a checklist. [1850–55, *Amer.*; CHECK[1] + LIST[1]]

check′ mark′. check[1] (def. 34). [1915–20]

check•mark (chek′märk′), *v.t.* to indicate by a check mark. [1955–60; CHECK[1] + MARK[1]]

check•mate (chek′māt′), *n., v.,* **-mat•ed, -mat•ing,** *interj.* —*n.* **1.** Also called **mate.** *Chess.* **a.** an act or instance of maneuvering the opponent's king into a check from which it cannot escape, thus bringing the game to a victorious conclusion. **b.** the position of the pieces when a king is checkmated. **2.** a complete check; defeat: *His efforts to escape met with a checkmate.* —*v.t.* **3.** *Chess.* to maneuver (an opponent's king) into a check from which it cannot escape; mate. **4.** to check completely; defeat: *Napoleon was checkmated at Waterloo.* —*interj.* **5.** *Chess.* (used by a player to announce that he or she has put the opponent's king into inextricable check.) [1300–50; ME *chek mat(e)* < MF *escec mat* < Ar *shāh māt* < Pers: lit., the king (is) checked, nonplussed]

check•off (chek′ôf′, -of′), *n.* **1.** the collection of union dues by employers through compulsory deduction from each worker's wages. **2.** a voluntary contribution from one's income tax for a specific purpose, as the public financing of election campaigns, made by checking off the appropriate box on a tax return. **3.** *Football.* audible (def. 2). [1910–15, *Amer.*; n. use of v. phrase *check off*]

check•out (chek′out′), *n.* **1.** the procedure of vacating and paying for one's quarters at a hotel. **2.** the time before which a hotel room must be vacated if another day's charge is not to be made. **3.** an examination of fitness for performance: *The checkout of the new plane was successful.* **4.** a series of sequential actions to familiarize oneself with new equipment. **5.** itemization and collection of amounts due for purchases. **6.** Also called **check′out count′er.** a counter where customers pay for purchases: *The supermarket has five checkouts.* Also, **check′-out′.** [1920–25, *Amer.*; n. use of v. phrase *check out*]

check•o•ver (chek′ō′vər), *n.* a thorough examination or investigation. [n. use of v. phrase *check over*]

check•point (chek′point′), *n.* **1.** a place along a road, border, etc., where travelers are stopped for inspection. **2.** a point or item, esp. in a procedure, for notation, inspection, or confirmation. [1935–40; CHECK[1] + POINT]

Check′point Char′lie, a checkpoint in Berlin at which passage was permitted between East and West Berlin.

check′ protec′tor, checkwriter.

check′ rail′, (in a window sash) a meeting rail, esp. one closing against the corresponding rail with a diagonal or rabbeted overlap. Also, **check′rail′.** Cf. **plain rail.** [1875–80]

check•rein (chek′rān′), *n.* **1.** a short rein passing from the bit to the saddle of a harness, to prevent the horse from lowering its head. Cf. **overcheck** (def. 2), **sidecheck.** See illus. under **harness. 2.** a short rein joining the bit of one of a span of horses to the driving rein of the other. [1800–10; CHECK[1] + REIN]

check•room (chek′ro͞om′, -ro͝om′), *n.* a room where hats, coats, parcels, etc., may be checked. [1895–1900, *Amer.*; CHECK[1] + ROOM]

check•row (chek′rō′), *Agric.* —*n.* **1.** one of a number of rows of trees or plants, esp. corn, in which the distance between adjacent trees or plants is equal to that between adjacent rows. —*v.t.* **2.** to plant in checkrows. [1855–60, *Amer.*; CHECK[1] + ROW[1]]

checks′ and bal′ances, limits imposed on all branches of a government by vesting in each branch the right to amend or void those acts of another that fall within its purview. [1780–90]

check•up (chek′up′), *n.* **1.** a comprehensive physical examination: *He went to the doctor for a checkup.* **2.** an examination or close scrutiny, as for verification, accuracy, or comparison: *They gave the motor a checkup.* [1885–90, *Amer.*; n. use of v. phrase *check up*]

check′ valve′, a valve permitting liquids or gases to flow in one direction only. [1875–80]

check•weigh•man (chek′wā′mən), *n., pl.* **-men.** a representative elected by coal miners to check the findings of the mine owner's weighman where miners are paid by the weight of coal mined. Also called **check•weigh•er** (chek′wā′ər). [1885–90; CHECK[1] + WEIGHMAN]

check•writ•er (chek′rī′tər), *n.* a machine for printing amounts on checks, as by perforations, so as to prevent alterations. [CHECK[1] + WRITER]

check•y (chek′ē), *adj. Heraldry.* divided into several rows of squares of two alternating tinctures: *a fess checky, or and azure.* Also, **chequy.** [1400–50; late ME *cheke(e)* < MF *escheque* checked, chequered in pattern, ptp. of *eschequer,* deriv. of *eschec* CHECK[1]]

ched•dar (ched′ər), *n.* (*often cap.*) a hard, smooth-textured cheese, made usually from the whole milk of cows and varying in color from white to deep yellow and in flavor from mild to sharp as it ages. Also called **ched′dar cheese′.** [1655–65; named after *Cheddar,* village in Somersetshire, England, where it was first made] —**ched′dar•y,** *adj.*

ched′dar pink′, a low, mat-forming European plant, *Dianthus gratianopolitanus,* of the pink family, having solitary, fragrant, rose-colored flowers with fringed petals. [1835–45; named after *Cheddar,* England; see PINK[1]]

chedd•ite (ched′īt, shed′-), *n. Chem.* an explosive for blasting, composed of a chlorate or perchlorate mixed with a fatty substance, as castor oil. [1905–10; named after *Chedde,* town in Savoy where it was first made; see -ITE[1]]

che•der (KHā′dər; *Eng.* KHā′dər, hā′-), *n., pl.* ***cha•da•rim*** (KHə dä′ʀim), *Eng.* **che•ders.** *Yiddish.* heder.

chee•cha•ko (chē chä′kō), *n., pl.* **-kos.** (*sometimes cap.*) *Informal.* (in Alaska and Northern Canada) a tenderfoot; greenhorn; newcomer. Also, **chechako, cheecha′co.** [1895–1900; < Chinook Jargon; *chee* just now, new < Lower Chinook *čxi* straightway + *chako* come < Nootka *čokʷa·* come! (impv. particle)]

cheek (chēk), *n.* **1.** either side of the face below the eye and above the jaw. **2.** the side wall of the mouth between the upper and lower jaws. **3.** something resembling the side of the human face in form or position, as either of two parts forming corresponding sides of various objects: *the cheeks of a vise.* **4.** impudence or effrontery: *He's got a lot of cheek to say that to me!* **5.** *Slang.* either of the buttocks. **6.** *Archit.* **a.** one side of an opening, as a reveal. **b.** either of two similar faces of a projection, as a buttress or dormer. **7.** *Carpentry.* **a.** a piece of wood removed from the end of a timber in making a tenon. **b.** a piece of wood on either side of a mortise. **8.** one side of a hammer head. **9.** *Horol.* one of two pieces placed on both sides of the suspension spring of a pendulum to control the amplitude of oscillation or to give the arc of the pendulum a cycloidal form. **10.** one of the two main vertical supports forming the frame of a hand printing press. **11.** *Mach.* either of the sides of a pulley or block. **12.** *Naut.* either of a pair of fore-and-aft members at the lower end of the head of a lower mast, used to support trestletrees which in turn support a top and often the heel of a topmast; one of the hounds of a lower mast. **13.** *Metall.* any part of a flask between the cope and the drag. **14. cheek by jowl,** in close intimacy; side by side: *a row of houses cheek by jowl.* **15. (with) tongue in cheek.** See **tongue** (def. 29). [bef. 900; ME *cheke,* OE *cē(a)ce;* akin to D *kaak,* MLG *kake*] —**cheek′less,** *adj.*
—**Syn. 4.** nerve, audacity, brass, gall.

cheek•bone (chēk′bōn′), *n.* **1.** the zygomatic bone. **2.** the part of that bone below the eye forming the prominence of the cheek. **3.** the area of the cheek overlying this bone. [bef. 1000; ME *chekbon,* OE *ceacban.* See CHEEK, BONE[1]]

cheeked (chēkt), *adj.* having cheeks of the kind indicated (used in combination): *rosy-cheeked youngsters.* [CHEEK + -ED[3]]

cheek•piece (chēk′pēs′), *n.* **1.** either of two vertical bars of a bit, one on each end of the mouthpiece. See illus. under **snaffle. 2.** See **cheek strap.** [1750–60; CHEEK + PIECE]

cheek′ pouch′, a sac in the cheek of certain animals, as squirrels, in which food may be carried. [1825–35]

cheek′ strap′, (of a bridle) one of two straps passing over the cheeks of the horse and connecting the crown piece with the bit or noseband. Also called **cheekpiece.** See illus. under **harness.**

cheek′ tooth′, any of the three posterior chewing teeth on each side of the upper and lower jaws in human adults; molar. [1350–1400; ME]

Cheek•to•wa•ga (chēk′tə wä′gə), *n.* a town in NW New York, near Buffalo. 109,442.

cheek•y (chē′kē), *adj.,* **cheek•i•er, cheek•i•est.** impudent; insolent: *a cheeky fellow; cheeky behavior.* [1855–60; CHEEK + -Y[1]] —**cheek′i•ly,** *adv.* —**cheek′i•ness,** *n.*
—**Syn.** saucy, audacious, bold.

cheep (chēp), *v.i.* **1.** to chirp; peep. **2.** *Chiefly South Midland U.S.* to reveal or tell a secret (usually used in the phrase *cheep it*). —*v.t.* **3.** to express by cheeps. —*n.* **4.** a chirp. [1505–15; imit.] —**cheep′er,** *n.*

cheer (chēr), *n.* **1.** a shout of encouragement, approval, congratulation, etc.: *The cheers of the fans filled the stadium.* **2.** a set or traditional form of shout used by spectators to encourage or show enthusiasm for an athletic team, contestant, etc., as *rah! rah! rah!* **3.** something that gives joy or gladness; encouragement; comfort: *words of cheer.* **4.** a state of feeling or spirits: *Their good cheer overcame his depression.* **5.** gladness, gaiety, or animation: *full of cheer and good spirits.* **6.** food and drink: *tables laden with cheer.* **7.** *Archaic.* facial expression. **8. be of good cheer,** (used as an exhortation to be cheerful): *Be of good cheer! Things could be much worse.* **9. with good cheer,** cheerfully; willingly: *She accepted her lot with good cheer.* —*interj.* **10. cheers,** (used as a salutation or toast.) —*v.t.* **11.** to salute with shouts of approval, congratulation, triumph, etc.: *The team members cheered their captain.* **12.** to gladden or cause joy to; inspire with cheer (often fol. by *up*): *The good news cheered her.* **13.** to encourage or incite: *She cheered him on when he was about to give up.* —*v.i.* **14.** to utter cheers of approval, encouragement, triumph, etc. **15.** to become happier or more cheerful (often fol. by *up*): *She cheered up as soon as the sun began to shine.* **16.** *Obs.* to be or feel in a particular state of mind or spirits. [1175–1225; ME *chere* face < AF; cf. OF *chiere* < LL *cara* face, head < Gk *kárā* head] —**cheer′er,** *n.* —**cheer′ing•ly,** *adv.*
—**Syn. 3.** solace. **5.** joy, mirth, glee, merriment. **11.** applaud. **12.** exhilarate, animate. CHEER, GLADDEN, ENLIVEN mean to make happy or lively. TO CHEER is to comfort, to restore hope and cheerfulness to (now often CHEER UP, when thoroughness, a definite time, or a particular point in the action is referred to): *to cheer a sick person; She soon cheered him up.* (Cf. **eat up.**) TO GLADDEN does not imply a state of sadness to begin with, but suggests bringing pleasure or happiness to someone: *to gladden someone's heart with good news.* ENLIVEN suggests bringing vivacity and liveliness: *to enliven a dull evening, a party.* **13.** inspirit. —**Ant. 12.** discourage, depress.

cheer•er-up•per (chēr′ər up′ər), *n. Informal.* a person or thing that cheers a person up: *A good joke is the best cheerer-upper.* [*cheer up* + -ER[1], joined pleonastically to both v. and particle]

cheer•ful (chēr′fəl), *adj.* **1.** full of cheer; in good spirits: *a cheerful person.* **2.** promoting or inducing cheer; pleasant; bright: *cheerful surroundings.* **3.** characterized by or expressive of good spirits or cheerfulness: *cheerful songs.* **4.** hearty or ungrudging: *cheerful giving.* [1400–50; late ME *cherfull.* See CHEER, -FUL] —**cheer′ful•ly,** *adv.* —**cheer′ful•ness,** *n.*
—**Syn. 1.** cheery, gay, blithe, happy, joyful, joyous, buoyant, sunny, jolly. **4.** generous. —**Ant. 1.** miserable. **4.** grudging.

cheer•i•o (chēr′ē ō′, chēr′ē ō′), *interj., n., pl.* **cheer•i•os.** *Chiefly Brit.* —*interj.* **1.** good-bye; good-bye and good luck. **2.** (used as a toast to one's drinking companions.) —*n.* **3.** a good-bye or farewell. **4.** a toast of "cheerio!" [1905–10; see CHEERO; source of *-i-* is unclear]

cheer•lead (chēr′lēd′), *v.,* **-led, -lead•ing.** —*v.t.* **1.** to act as cheerleader for. **2.** to encourage by or as if by cheerleading. —*v.i.* **3.** to act as cheerleader. [by back formation from CHEERLEADER OR CHEERLEADING]

cheer•lead•er (chēr′lē′dər), *n.* a person who leads spectators in traditional or formal cheering, esp. at a pep rally or athletic event. [1900–05, *Amer.*; CHEER + LEADER]

cheer•lead•ing (chēr′lē′ding), *n.* the action or skill of a cheerleader. [1950–55; CHEER + LEADING[1]]

cheer•less (chēr′lis), *adj.* without cheer; joyless; gloomy: *drab, cheerless surroundings.* [1570–80; CHEER + -LESS] —**cheer′less•ly,** *adv.* —**cheer′less•ness,** *n.*

cheer•ly (chēr′lē), *adv. Archaic.* cheerily; cheeringly. [CHEER + -LY]

cheer•o (chēr′ō), *interj., n., pl.* **cheer•os.** *Brit.* cheerio. [1905–10; see CHEER, -O]

cheer•y (chēr′ē), *adj.,* **cheer•i•er, cheer•i•est. 1.** in good spirits; gay. **2.** promoting cheer; enlivening. [1840–50; CHEER + -Y[1]] —**cheer′i•ly,** *adv.* —**cheer′i•ness,** *n.*

cheese[1] (chēz), *n., v.,* **cheesed, chees•ing.** —*n.* **1.** the curd of milk separated from the whey and prepared in many ways as a food. **2.** a definite mass of this substance, often in the shape of a wheel or cylinder. **3.** something of similar shape or consistency, as a mass of pomace in cider-making. **4.** *Informal.* partly digested milk curds sometimes spit up by infants. **5. cheeses,** any of several mallows, esp. *Malva neglecta,* a sprawling, weedy plant having small lavender or white flowers and round, flat, segmented fruits thought to resemble little wheels of cheese. **6.** *Slang (vulgar).* smegma. **7.** *Metalworking.* **a.** a transverse section cut from an ingot, as for making into a tire. **b.** an ingot or billet made into a convex, circular form by blows at the ends. **8.** a low curtsy. —*v.i.* **9.** *Informal.* (of infants) to spit up partly digested milk curds. —*v.t.* **10.** *Metalworking.* to forge (an ingot or billet) into a cheese. [bef. 1000; ME *chese,* OE *cēse* (c. OS *kāsi,* G *Käse*) < L *cāseus*]

cheese[2] (chēz), *v.t.,* **cheesed, chees•ing.** *Slang.* **1.** to stop; desist. —*interj.* **2. cheese it, a.** look out! **b.** run away! [1805–15; perh. alter. of CEASE]

cheese[3] (chēz), *n. Slang.* a person or thing that is important or splendid. [1905–10; perh. < Urdu *chiz* thing < Pers]

cheese•board (chēz′bôrd′, -bōrd′), *n.* **1.** a tray or platter for serving a variety of cheeses. **2.** a selection of cheeses provided, as before or after a meal. Also called **cheese tray.** [1935–40; CHEESE[1] + BOARD]

cheese′box seat′ (chēz′boks′), a chair seat, usually of rush, having a rounded form and surrounded with a thin strip of wood. [CHEESE[1] + BOX[1]]

cheese•burg•er (chēz′bûr′gər), *n.* a hamburger cooked with a slice of cheese on top of it. [1935–40, *Amer.;* CHEESE[1] + -BURGER]

cheese•cake (chēz′kāk′), *n.* **1.** Also, **cheese′ cake′.** a cake having a firm custardlike texture, made with cream cheese, cottage cheese, or both, and sometimes topped with a jamlike fruit mixture. **2.** *Informal.* Also called **leg art.** photographs featuring scantily clothed attractive women. [1400–50; 1930–35, for def. 2; late ME *chese kake;* see CHEESE[1], CAKE]

cheese•cloth (chēz′klôth′, -kloth′), *n.* a lightweight cotton fabric of open texture. Also called, *esp. Brit.,* **butter muslin.** [1650–60; so called because first used to wrap cheese]

cheesed (chēzd), *adj. Chiefly Brit. Slang.* disgusted; fed up (usually fol. by *off*). [1940–45; orig. obscure]

cheese′ eat′er, *Slang.* **1.** an informer; rat. **2.** a person who betrays, denies, or abandons his or her associates, social group, beliefs, etc.

cheese•mak•er (chēz′mā′kər), *n.* a person or thing that makes cheese. [1865–70; CHEESE[1] + MAKER] —**cheese′mak′ing,** *n., adj.*

cheese•par•ing (chēz′pâr′ing), *adj.* **1.** meanly economical; parsimonious. —*n.* **2.** something of little or no value. **3.** niggardly economy. [1590–1600; CHEESE[1] + PARING] —**cheese′par′er,** *n.*

cheese′ pie′, a pie, usually made with cream cheese, having a creamier consistency than cheesecake.

cheese′ prod′uct, a processed cheese consisting in the U.S. of at least 50 percent cheese to which cheese whey or whey albumin may be added.

cheese′ spread′, a processed cheese of smooth and spreadable consistency.

cheese′ steak′, a sandwich of sliced steak topped with melted cheese and fried onions, usually served on a long roll. Also, **cheese′steak′.**

cheese′ tray′, cheeseboard.

chees•y (chē′zē), *adj.,* **chees•i•er, chees•i•est. 1.** of or like cheese: *a cheesy aroma; a cheesy taste.* **2.** *Slang.* inferior or cheap; chintzy: *The movie's special effects are cheesy and unconvincing.* [1350–1400; ME. See CHEESE[1], -Y[1]] —**chees′i•ly,** *adv.* —**chees′i•ness,** *n.*

chee•tah (chē′tə), *n.* a cat, *Acinonyx jubatus,* of southwestern Asia and Africa, resembling a leopard but having certain doglike characteristics, often trained for hunting deer, antelope, etc.: an endangered species. [1695–1705; < Hindi *cītā* < Skt *citraka* leopard; cf. Pali *cittaka,* Prakrit *cittaya*]

cheetah, *Acinonyx jubatus,* 2½ ft. (0.8 m) high at shoulder; head and body 5 ft. (1.5 m); tail 2½ ft. (0.8 m)

Chee•ver (chē′vər), *n.* **John,** 1912–82, U.S. novelist and short-story writer.

chef (shef), *n.* **1.** the chief cook, esp. in a restaurant or hotel, usually responsible for planning menus, ordering foodstuffs, overseeing food preparation, and supervising the kitchen staff. **2.** any cook. [1835–45; < F; see CHIEF]

chef de cui•sine (shef də kwē zēn′), *pl.* ***chefs de cui•sine*** (shef də kwē zēn′). *French.* chef (def. 1). [lit., head of kitchen]

chef-d'oeu•vre (*Fr.* she dœ′vrᵊ), *n., pl.* **chefs-d'oeu•vre** (she dœ′vrᵊ). a masterpiece, esp. in art, literature, or music. [1610–20; < F]

Che•foo (*Chin.* ju′fo͞o′), *n. Older Spelling.* Zhifu.

chef's′ sal′ad, a salad typically consisting of thin strips of chicken, ham, and Swiss cheese on a bed of lettuce, sometimes with slices or quarters of hard-boiled eggs and tomatoes; usually served as a main course.

chei•li•tis (kī lī′tis), *n. Pathol.* inflammation of the lips. [1835–45; CHEIL(O)- + -ITIS]

cheilo-, var. of **chilo-**[1].

chei•lo•plas•ty (kī′lə plas′tē), *n., pl.* **-ties.** *Surg.* plastic surgery of the lip. Also, **chiloplasty.** [1835–45; CHEILO- + -PLASTY]

cheiro-, var. of **chiro-:** *cheiromancy.*

Chei•ron (kī′ron), *n. Class. Myth.* Chiron.

Che•ju (che′jo͞o′), *n.* **1.** formerly, **Quelpart.** an island S of and belonging to South Korea. 365,522; 718 sq. mi. (1860 sq. km). **2.** a city on and the capital of this island, on the N coast. 91,300.

Che•ka (che′kä), *n.* (in the Soviet Union) the state secret-police organization (1917–22), succeeded by the GPU. Cf. **KGB.** [1920–25; < Russ *Cheká, Vecheká,* names of the initial letters of *Vserossíĭskaya chrezvycháĭnaya Kommíssiya (po bor′bé s kontrarevolyútsieĭ, spekulyátsieĭ i sabotázhem)* All-Russian Extraordinary Commission (for the Struggle against Counterrevolution, Speculation and Sabotage)] —**Che′kist,** *n.*

Che•khov (chek′ôf, -of; *Russ.* chye′khəf), *n.* **An•ton Pa•vlo•vich** (an′ton pav lō′vich; *Russ.* un tôn′ pu vlô′vyich), 1860–1904, Russian short-story writer and dramatist. Also, **Tchekhov.**

Che•khov•i•an (che kō′vē ən, -kô′fē-, -kof′ē-; chek′ô fē ən, -of ē-), *adj.* of, pertaining to, or characteristic of Anton Chekhov or his writings, esp. as they are evocative of a mood of introspection and frustration. [1920–25; CHEKHOV + -IAN]

Che•kiang (che′kyang′; *Chin.* ju′gyäng′), *n. Older Spelling.* Zhejiang.

che•la[1] (kē′lə), *n., pl.* **-lae** (-lē). the pincerlike organ or claw terminating certain limbs of crustaceans and arachnids. [1640–50; < NL < Gk *chēlḗ* claw]

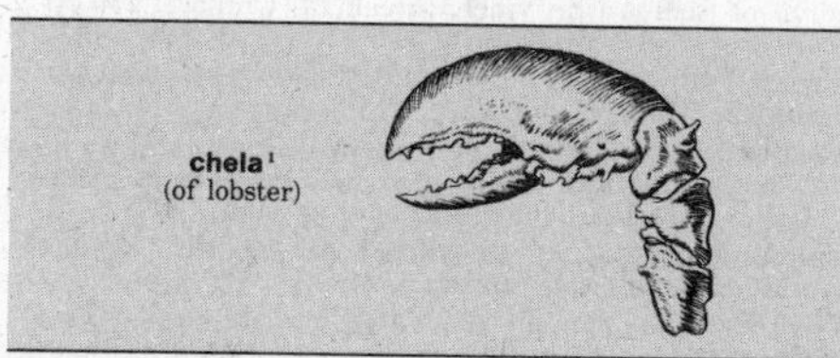

chela[1] (of lobster)

che•la[2] (chā′lä), *n.* (in India) a disciple of a religious teacher. [1825–35; < Hindi *celā;* cf. Pali *cellaka* monk, Prakrit *cilla* boy, student] —**che′la•ship′,** *n.*

che•late (kē′lāt), *adj., n., v.,* **-lat•ed, -lat•ing.** —*adj.* **1.** *Chem.* **a.** of or noting a heterocyclic compound having a central metallic ion attached by covalent bonds to two or more nonmetallic atoms in the same molecule. **b.** of or noting a compound having a cyclic structure resulting from the formation of one or more hydrogen bonds in the same molecule. **2.** *Zool.* having a chela or chelae. —*n.* **3.** *Chem.* a chelate compound. —*v.i. Chem.* **4.** (of a heterocyclic compound) to react to form a chelate. **5.** (of a compound) to form a ring by forming one or more hydrogen bonds. —*v.t.* **6.** *Chem.* to combine (an organic compound) with a metallic ion to form a chelate. [1820–30; CHEL(A)[1] + -ATE[1]] —**che′lat•a•ble,** *adj.*

che′lating a′gent, *Chem.* a ligand that forms chelates. Also called **che•la•tor** (kē′lā tər).

che•la•tion (kē lā′shən), *n.* **1.** *Chem.* the process of chelating. **2.** *Med.* **a.** a method of removing certain heavy metals from the bloodstream, used esp. in treating lead or mercury poisoning. **b.** a controversial treatment for arteriosclerosis that attempts to remove calcium deposits from the inner walls of the coronary arteries. [1930–35; CHELATE + -ION]

cheli-, a combining form meaning "claws," used in the formation of compound words: *cheliferous.* [comb. form repr. Gk *chēlḗ* CHELA[1]]

che•lic•er•a (kə lis′ər ə), *n., pl.* **-er•ae** (-ə rē′). one member of the first pair of usually pincerlike appendages of spiders and other arachnids. Cf. **pedipalp.** [1825–35; < NL, equiv. to *cheli-* CHELI- + Gk *kér(as)* horn + L *-a* fem. n. ending] —**che•lic′er•al,** *adj.* —**che•lic•er•ate** (kə lis′ə rāt′, -ər it), *adj.*

che•lif•er•ous (kə lif′ər əs), *adj.* bearing chelae. [1750–60; CHELI- + -FEROUS]

che•li•form (kē′lə fôrm′, kel′ə-), *adj.* shaped like a chela. [1790–1800; CHELI- + -FORM]

che•li•ped (kē′lə ped′, kel′ə-), *n.* (in decapod crustaceans) either of the pair of appendages bearing a chela. [1865–70; CHELI- + -PED]

Chel•le•an (shel′ē ən), *adj.* Abbevillian. [1890–95; < F *chelléen,* after *Chelles,* France, where Paleolithic tools were unearthed; see -AN]

Chełm•no (khewm′nô), *n.* a Nazi concentration camp in central Poland.

Chelms•ford (chelms′fərd, chelmz′-), *n.* a city in NE Massachusetts. 31,174.

che•loid (kē′loid), *n. Pathol.* keloid.

che•lo•ni•an (ki lō′nē ən), *adj.* **1.** belonging or pertaining to the order Chelonia, comprising the turtles. —*n.* **2.** a turtle. [1820–30; < NL *Cheloni(a)* (< Gk *chelṓn(ē)* turtle + NL *-ia,* neut. pl. n. suffix) + -AN]

Chel•sea (chel′sē), *n.* **1.** a former borough in Greater London, England: now part of Kensington and Chelsea; many residences of artists and writers. **2.** a city in E Massachusetts, near Boston. 25,431. **3.** a female given name.

Chel•ten•ham (chelt′nəm *for 1, 3;* chel′tn ham′ *for 2*), *n.* **1.** a city in N Gloucestershire, in W England: resort. 86,500. **2.** a town in SE Pennsylvania, near Philadelphia. 35,509. **3.** *Print.* a style of type.

Chel•ya•binsk (chel yä′binsk; *Russ.* chyi lyä′byinsk), *n.* a city in the S Russian Federation in Asia, E of the Ural Mountains. 1,143,000.

Chel•yus•kin (chel yo͝os′kin; *Russ.* chyi lyo͞os′kyin), *n.* **Cape,** a cape in the N Russian Federation in Asia: the northernmost point of the Asia mainland.

chem-, var. of **chemo-** before a vowel: *chemosmosis.*

chem., **1.** chemical. **2.** chemist. **3.** chemistry.

Chem.E., Chemical Engineer.

chemi-, var. of **chemo-,** esp. before elements of Latin origin: *chemisorption.*

chem•ic (kem′ik), *adj.* **1.** of or pertaining to alchemy; alchemic. **2.** of or pertaining to chemistry; chemical. [1570–80; < Gk *chēm(ía)* alchemy + -IC; r. *chimic* < ML *(al)chimicus*]

chem•i•cal (kem′i kəl), *n.* **1.** a substance produced by or used in a chemical process. **2. chemicals,** *Slang.* narcotic or mind-altering drugs or substances. —*adj.* **3.** of, used in, produced by, or concerned with chemistry or chemicals: *a chemical formula; chemical agents.* [1570–80; CHEMIC + -AL[1]; r. *chimical* chemic] —**chem′i•cal•ly,** *adv.*

chem′ical bond′, bond (def. 15).

chem′ical depend′ency, addiction to drugs or alcohol.

chem′ical engineer′ing, the science or profession of applying chemistry to industrial processes. [1900–05] —**chem′ical engineer′.**

Chem′ical Mace′, *Trademark.* Mace.

chem′ical poten′tial, *Thermodynam.* a quantity that determines the transport of matter from one phase to another: a component will flow from one phase to another when the chemical potential of the component is greater in the first phase than in the second.

chem′ical pulp′, wood pulp made from chemically treated and cooked wood fibers and used in the manufacture of better grades of paper. Cf. **groundwood pulp.**

chem′ical sympathec′tomy, *Med.* sympathectomy (def. 2).

chem′ical toi′let, a toilet that is not connected to sewage pipes but has a holding compartment where waste is chemically treated until disposal.

chem′ical ton′er, *Photog.* toner (def. 4).

chem′ical war′fare, warfare with asphyxiating, poisonous, or corrosive gases, oil flames, etc. [1915–20]

che•mig•ra•phy (kə mig′rə fē), *n.* any technique for making engravings or etchings using chemicals and without the aid of photography. [1890–95; CHEMI- + -GRAPHY] —**che•mig′ra•pher,** *n.* —**chem•i•graph•ic** (kem′i graf′ik), *adj.* —**chem′i•graph′i•cal•ly,** *adv.*

chem•i•lum•i•nes•cence (kem′ə lo͞o′mə nes′əns), *n.* (in chemical reactions) the emission of light by an atom or molecule that is in an excited state. [1900–05; CHEMI- + LUMINESCENCE] —**chem′i•lu′mi•nes′cent,** *adj.*

che•min de fer (shə man′ də fâr′; *Fr.* shə mand fer′), *Cards.* a variation of baccarat. [1890–95; < F: lit., railroad; so called from the speed of the game]

che•mise (shə mēz′), *n.* **1.** a woman's loose-fitting, shirtlike undergarment. **2.** (in women's fashions) a dress designed to hang straight from the shoulders and fit loosely at the waist, sometimes more tightly at the hip. **3.** a revetment for an earth embankment. [bef. 1050; ME < AF, OF: shirt < LL *camīsa* linen undergarment, shirt; r. ME *kemes,* OE *cemes* < LL *camisa*]

chem•i•sette (shem′ə zet′), *n.* a woman's garment of linen, lace, or the like, worn, toward the end of the Victorian era, over a low-cut or open bodice to cover the neck and breast. [1800–10; < F; see CHEMISE, -ETTE]

chem•ism (kem′iz əm), *n.* chemical action. [1850–55; CHEM- + -ISM, modeled on F *chimisme,* equiv. to *chim(ie)* chemistry + *-isme* -ISM]

chem•i•sorb (kem′ə sôrb′, -zôrb′), *v.t. Chem.* to take up by chemisorption. [1930–35; CHEMI- + (AD)SORB]

chem•i•sorp•tion (kem′ə sôrp′shən, -zôrp′-), *n. Chem.* adsorption involving a chemical linkage between the adsorbent and the adsorbate. [1930–35; CHEMI- + (AD)SORPTION]

chem•ist (kem′ist), *n.* **1.** a specialist in chemistry. **2.** *Brit.* a druggist. **3.** *Obs.* alchemist. [1555–65; < Gk *chēm(ía)* alchemy + -IST; r. *chymist* < ML *alchimista*]

chem•is•try (kem′ə strē), *n., pl.* **-tries. 1.** the science that deals with the composition and properties of substances and various elementary forms of matter. Cf. **element** (def. 2). **2.** chemical properties, reactions, phenomena, etc.: *the chemistry of carbon.* **3.** the interaction of one personality with another: *The chemistry between him and his boss was all wrong.* **4.** sympathetic understanding; rapport: *the astonishing chemistry between the actors.* **5.** any or all of the elements that make up something: *the chemistry of love.* [1590–1600; CHEMIST + -RY; r. *chymistry, chimistry*]

chem•my (shem′ē), *n. Informal.* chemin de fer. [1920–25; by shortening and alter.]

Chem•nitz (kem′nits), *n.* a city in E Germany. 314,437. Formerly (1953–90), **Karl-Marx Stadt.**

che•mo (kē′mō, kem′ō), *n., pl.* **-mos.** *Informal.* chemotherapy or a chemotherapy treatment. [by shortening; see -O]

chemo-, a combining form with the meanings "chemical," "chemically induced," "chemistry," used in the formation of compound words: *chemotherapy.* Also, *esp. before elements of Latin origin,* **chemi-.** Also, *esp. before a vowel,* **chem-.** [*chem-,* extracted from CHEMICAL or CHEMISTRY + -O- or -I-]

che•mo•ki•ne•sis (kē′mō ki nē′sis, -kī-, kem′ō-), *n.* increased activity of an organism due to a chemical substance. [1895–1900; CHEMO- + KINESIS] —**che•mo•ki•net•ic** (kē′mō ki net′ik, -kī-, kem′ō-), *adj.*

che•mo•nite (kē′mə nīt′, kem′ə-), *n. Chem.* a solution consisting of copper hydroxide, arsenic trioxide, am-

CONCISE PRONUNCIATION KEY: *act, cāpe, dâre, pärt; set, ēqual; if, īce; ox, ōver, ôrder, oil, bo͝ok, bo͞ot, out; up, ûrge; child; sing; shoe; thin, that;* zh as in *treasure.* ə = *a* as in *alone, e* as in *system, i* as in *easily, o* as in *gallop, u* as in *circus;* ᵊ as in *fire* (fīᵊr), *hour* (ouᵊr). l and n can serve as syllabic consonants, as in *cradle* (krād′l), and *button* (but′n). See the full key inside the front cover.

monia, acetic acid, and water: used as a wood preservative. [CHEMO- + -*n*- + -ITE[1]]

che•mo•nu•cle•ol•y•sis (kē′mō no͞o′klē ol′ə sis, -nyo͞o′-, kem′ō-), *n.* treatment for a herniated spinal disk in which chymopapain is injected into the disk to dissolve tissue. [CHEMO- + NUCLEO- + -LYSIS]

che•mo•pal•li•dec•to•my (kē′mō pal′i dek′tə mē, kem′ō-), *n., pl.* **-mies.** *Surg.* an operation for treating Parkinson's disease and certain other diseases characterized by muscular rigidity, consisting of destroying a specific part of the corpus striatum by injecting it with a chemical, usually alcohol. [CHEMO- + NL *pallid*(*um*) a muscle (n. use of neut. of L *pallidus* pale) + -ECTOMY]

che•mo•pro•phy•lax•is (kē′mō prō′fə lak′sis, -prof′ə-, kem′ō-), *n.* prevention of disease by means of chemical agents or drugs or by food nutrients. Also called **che•mo•pre•ven•tion** (kē′mō pri ven′shən). [1935–40; CHEMO- + PROPHYLAXIS] **—che•mo•pro•phy•lac•tic** (kē′mō prō′fə lak′tik, kem′ō-), *adj.*

che•mo•re•cep•tion (kē′mō ri sep′shən, kem′ō-), *n.* the physiological response to chemical stimuli. [1915–20; CHEMO- + RECEPTION] **—che•mo•re•cep•tive** (kē′mō-ri sep′tiv, kem′ō-), *adj.*

che•mo•re•cep•tor (kē′mō ri sep′tər, kem′ō-), *n. Physiol.* a receptor stimulated by chemical means. [1905–10; CHEMO- + RECEPTOR]

che•mo•re•flex (kē′mō rē′fleks, kem′ō-), *n. Physiol.* a reflex caused by a chemical stimulus. [1900–05; CHEMO- + REFLEX]

che•mo•sen•so•ry (kē′mō sen′sə rē, kem′ō-), *adj. Physiol.* sensitive to chemical stimuli, as the sensory nerve endings that mediate taste and smell. [1970–75; CHEMO- + SENSORY]

Che•mosh (kē′mosh), *n.* a Moabite god. Jer. 48.

che•mos•mo•sis (kē′moz mō′sis, -mos-, kem′oz-, -os-), *n.* chemical action between substances that occurs through an intervening, semipermeable membrane. [CHEM- + OSMOSIS] **—che•mos•mot•ic** (kē′moz mot′ik, -mos-, kem′oz-, -os-), *adj.*

che•mo•sphere (kē′mə sfēr′, kem′ə-), *n.* the region of the atmosphere most characterized by chemical, esp. photochemical, activity, starting in the stratosphere and including the mesosphere and perhaps part of the thermosphere. [1945–50; CHEMO- + -SPHERE]

che•mo•ster•i•lant (kē′mō ster′ə lənt, kem′ō-), *n.* a chemical that causes an animal to become irreversibly sterile without changing its mating behavior or longevity. [1960–65; CHEMO- + STERILANT]

che•mo•ster•i•lize (kē′mō ster′ə līz′, kem′ō-), *v.t.,* **-lized, -liz•ing.** to sterilize (insects or other animals) with a chemosterilant. Also, *esp. Brit.,* **che′mo•ster′i•lise′.** [CHEMO- + STERILIZE] **—che′mo•ster′i•li•za′tion,** *n.*

che•mo•sur•ger•y (kē′mō sûr′jə rē, kem′ō-), *n. Surg.* the use of chemical substances to destroy diseased or unwanted tissue. [1940–45; CHEMO- + SURGERY] **—che′mo•sur′gi•cal,** *adj.*

che•mo•syn•the•sis (kē′mō sin′thə sis, kem′ō-), *n. Biol., Biochem.* the synthesis of organic compounds within an organism, with chemical reactions providing the energy source. [1900–05; CHEMO- + SYNTHESIS] **—che•mo•syn•thet•ic** (kē′mō sin thet′ik, kem′ō-), *adj.* **—che′mo•syn•thet′i•cal•ly,** *adv.*

che′mosynthet′ic bacte′ria, bacteria that synthesize organic compounds, using energy derived from the oxidation of organic or inorganic materials without the aid of light. [1955–60; CHEMO- + SYNTHETIC]

che•mo•tax•is (kē′mō tak′sis, kem′ō-), *n. Biol.* oriented movement toward or away from a chemical stimulus. [1890–95; CHEMO- + -TAXIS] **—che•mo•tac•tic** (kē′mō tak′tik, kem′ō-), *adj.* **—che′mo•tac′ti•cal•ly,** *adv.*

che•mo•tax•on•o•my (kē′mō tak son′ə mē, kem′ō-), *n. Biochem., Biol.* the identification and classification of organisms by comparative analysis of their biochemical composition. [1960–65; CHEMO- + TAXONOMY] **—che•mo•tax•o•nom•ic** (kē′mō tak′sə nom′ik, kem′ō-), **che′mo•tax′o•nom′i•cal,** *adj.* **—che′mo•tax′o•nom′i•cal•ly,** *adv.* **—che′mo•tax•on′o•mist,** *n.*

che•mo•ther•a•peu•tics (kē′mō ther′ə pyo͞o′tiks, kem′ō-), *n.* (*used with a singular v.*) chemotherapy. [1910–15; CHEMO- + THERAPEUTICS] **—che′mo•ther′a•peu′tic, che′mo•ther′a•peu′ti•cal,** *adj.* **—che′mo•ther′a•peu′ti•cal•ly,** *adv.*

che•mo•ther•a•py (kē′mō ther′ə pē, kem′ō-), *n. Med.* the treatment of disease by means of chemicals that have a specific toxic effect upon the disease-producing microorganisms or that selectively destroy cancerous tissue. Cf. **pharmacotherapy.** [1905–10; CHEMO- + THERAPY] **—che′mo•ther′a•pist,** *n.*

che•mo•troph (kē′mə trof′, -trôf′, -trōf′, kem′ə-), *n. Bacteriol., Biol.* any organism that oxidizes inorganic or organic compounds as its principal energy source. [CHEMO- + *-troph* < Gk *trophḗ* food] **—che•mo•troph•ic** (kē′mə trof′ik, -trō′fik, kem′ə-), *adj.*

che•mot•ro•pism (ki mo′trə piz′əm), *n. Biol.* oriented growth or movement in response to a chemical stimulus. [1895–1900; CHEMO- + -TROPISM] **—che•mo•trop•ic** (kē′mə trop′ik, -trō′pik, kem′ə-), *adj.* **—che′mo•trop′i•cal•ly,** *adv.*

Che•mul•po (*Korean.* che′mo͞ol pô′), *n.* Inchon.

chem•ur•gy (kem′ûr jē, kə mûr′-), *n.* a division of applied chemistry concerned with the industrial use of organic substances, esp. substances obtained from farm produce, as soybeans or peanuts. [1930–35; CHEM- + -URGY] **—chem•ur′gic, chem•ur′gi•cal,** *adj.* **—chem•ur′gi•cal•ly,** *adv.*

Ch'en (chun), *n.* a dynasty that ruled in China A.D. 557–89. Also, **Chen.**

Che•nab (chi näb′), *n.* a river in S Asia, flowing SW from N India to the Sutlej River in E Pakistan. ab. 675 mi. (1085 km) long.

Chen•chiang (*Chin.* jun′jyäng′), *n. Wade-Giles.* Zhenjiang.

Chen Du•xiu (jun′ do͞o′shyo͞o′), 1879–1942, Chinese intellectual, journalist, and cofounder of the Chinese Communist party. Also, **Ch'en Tu-hsiu.**

che•neau (shä nō′), *n., pl.* **-neaus, -neaux** (-nōz′). *Archit.* **1.** an ornamented cresting on a cornice or coping. **2.** a gutter, esp. an ornamented one, at the eaves of a building. [< F *chéneau,* earlier *chenau;* OF *chenal* < L *canālis* CANAL]

Cheng•chow (*Chin.* jung′jō′), *n. Older Spelling.* Zhengzhou.

Ch'eng′-Chu′ school′ (cheng′jo͞o′), *Philos.* See **School of Law.** Also, **Cheng′-Zhu′ school′.**

Cheng•de (chœng′dœ′), *n. Pinyin.* a city in NE Hebei province, in NE China: former summer residence of the Manchu emperors. 200,000. Also, *Older Spelling,* **Cheng•teh** (chung′du′). Formerly, **Jehol.**

Cheng•du (chœng′dy′), *n. Pinyin.* a city in and the capital of Sichuan province, in central China. 1,250,000. Also, *Older Spelling,* **Cheng′tu′.**

Ch'eng Tsu (*Chin.* chung′ dzo͞o′). See **Yung Lo.** Also, **Cheng Zu** (chung′ zo͞o′).

che•nier (shin′ə rē), *n.* a hummock in a marshy region, with stands of evergreen oaks. Also, **chê′nière.** [< LaF, equiv. to F *chêne* oak + *-ier* -IER[2]]

Ché•nier (shā nyā′), *n.* **An•dré Ma•rie de** (äɴ drā′ mȧ rē′ də), 1762–94, French poet.

che•nille (shə nēl′), *n.* **1.** a velvety cord or yarn of silk or worsted, for embroidery, fringes, etc. **2.** fabric made with a fringed silken thread used as the weft in combination with wool or cotton. **3.** any fabric with a protruding pile, as in certain rayon bedspreads. **4.** a deep-pile, durable, woolen carpeting with chenille weft: the most expensive power-loomed floor covering. [1730–40; < F: velvety cord, lit., caterpillar < L *canicula,* with etymological sense "little dog," though attested only in senses "shrewish woman, dogfish, Sirius" (see CANICULAR); for parallel use of "cat" in same sense, see CATERPILLAR]

chenille′ plant′, an East Indian plant, *Acalypha hispida,* of the spurge family, having long, drooping, reddish-purple spikes of flowers.

Che•nin Blanc (shen′in blängk′; *Fr.* shə naɴ bläɴ′), a grape used in the making of white wine, esp. in the lower Loire valley of France and in California.

Chen•nault (shə nôlt′), *n.* **Claire Lee** (klâr), 1890–1958, U.S. Air Force general.

che•no•pod (kē′nə pod′, ken′ə-), *n.* any plant of the goosefoot family Chenopodiaceae. [1545–55; < Gk *chēno-* (comb. form of *chḗn* GOOSE) + -POD; cf. NL *Chenopodium* genus name]

che•no•po•di•a•ceous (kē′nə pō′dē ā′shəs, ken′ə-), *adj.* belonging to the Chenopodiaceae, the goosefoot family of plants. Cf. **goosefoot family.** [1865–70; < NL *Chenopodiace*(*ae*) family name (*Chenopodi*(*um*) (see CHENOPOD) + *-aceae* -ACEAE) + -OUS]

che•no•po′di•um oil′ (kē′nə pō′dē əm, ken′ə-), a colorless or yellowish oil obtained from the seeds and leaves of Mexican tea, used chiefly in medicine as an agent for killing or expelling intestinal worms. Also called **wormseed oil.** [1910–15; < NL *Chenopodium.* See CHENOPOD, -IUM]

Ch'en Tu-hsiu (chun′ do͞o′shyo͞o′), *Wade-Giles.* See **Chen Duxiu.**

cheong•sam (chông′säm′), *n.* a form-fitting, knee-length dress with a mandarin collar and slit skirt, worn chiefly by Oriental women. [1955–60; < Chin dial. (Guangdong) *chèuhngsāam,* equiv. to Chin *chángshān* long dress]

Che•ops (kē′ops), *n.* fl. early 26th century B.C., king of Egypt: builder of the great pyramid at Giza (father of Khafre). Also called **Khufu.**

Cheph•ren (kef′rən), *n.* Khafre.

cheque (chek), *n. Brit.* check (def. 29).

cheq•uer (chek′ər), *n. Brit.* checker[1].

chequ•y (chek′ē), *adj. Heraldry.* checky.

cher (sheʀ; *Eng.* shâr), *adj. French.* dear; beloved: used in referring to or addressing a man or boy.

Cher (shâr; *Fr.* sheʀ), *n.* **1.** a river in central France, flowing NW to the Loire River. 220 mi. (355 km) long. **2.** a department in central France. 316,350; 2820 sq. mi. (7305 sq. km). *Cap.:* Bourges. **3.** a female given name.

Cher•bourg (shâr′bo͝org; *Fr.* sheʀ bo͞oʀ′), *n.* a seaport in NW France. 34,637.

cher•chez la femme (sheʀ shā′ lȧ fȧm′), *French.* look for the woman: advice offered facetiously in any situation, esp. one of doubt or mystery.

chère (sheʀ), *adj. French.* dear; beloved: used in referring to or addressing a woman or girl.

che•rem (*Seph.* ᴋʜe′rem; *Ashk.* ᴋʜä′rəm), *n. Hebrew.* herem.

cher•eme (ker′ēm), *n. Ling.* any of a small set of elements, analogous to the phoneme in speech, proposed as the basic structural units by which the signs of a sign language are represented, and including the handshapes, hand movements, and locations of the hands in relation to the body employed in a particular sign language. Cf. **allocher.** [irreg. < Gk *cheír* hand (cf. CHIRO-) + -EME; coined by U.S. linguist William C. Stokoe (born 1919) in 1960] **—che•re•mic** (kə rē′mik, ke-), *adj.*

Cher•e•mis (cher′ə mis′, -mēs′, cher′ə mis′, -mēs′), *n., pl.* **-mis•es,** (*esp. collectively*) **-mis.** Mari. Also, **Cher′e•miss′.** [< Russ *cheremís,* earlier *cheremísin,* ORuss (pl.) *chermisy,* prob. < Chuvash *śarmís, śarmîś* Mari]

Che•rem•kho•vo (chə rem′kə vō′; *Russ.* chyi ʀyim-ᴋʜô′və), *n.* a city in the SE Russian Federation in Asia, on the Trans-Siberian Railroad, near Lake Baikal. 110,000.

Che•ren•kov (chə reng′kôf, -kof, -ren′-; *Russ.* chyi-ʀyin kôf′), *n.* **Pa•vel A.** (pä′vəl; *Russ.* pä′vyil). See **Cerenkov, Pavel A.**

Che•re•po•vets (cher′ə pə vets′; *Russ.* chyi ʀyi pu-vyets′), *n.* a city in the NW Russian Federation in Europe, N of Rybinsk Reservoir. 315,000.

ché•rie (shā ʀē′), *n., pl.* **-ries** (-ʀē′). *French.* dear; sweetheart: used in referring to or addressing a woman or girl.

Cher•ie (sher′ē), *n.* a female given name. Also, **Cher′i.**

cher•i•moy•a (cher′ə moi′ə), *n.* **1.** a tropical American tree, *Annona cherimola,* having leaves with velvety, hairy undersides and yellow-to-brown fragrant flowers. **2.** the large, edible fruit of this tree, having leathery, scalelike skin and soft pulp. Also, **cher•i•moy•er** (cher′ə-moi′ər), **cher•i•mol•la** (cher′ə moi′ə), **chirimoya.** [1730–40; < AmerSp *chirimoya* name of the fruit; of uncert. orig.; alleged analysis as Quechua *chiri* cold + *muyu* wheel, circle is prob. spurious]

cher•ish (cher′ish), *v.t.* **1.** to hold or treat as dear; feel love for: *to cherish one's native land.* **2.** to care for tenderly; nurture: *to cherish a child.* **3.** to cling fondly or inveterately to: *to cherish a memory.* [1275–1325; ME *cherisshen* < MF *cheriss-* (long s. of *cherir*), equiv. to *cher* dear (< L *cārus*) + *-iss* -ISH[2]; akin to CHARITY] **—cher′ish•a•ble,** *adj.* **—cher′ish•er,** *n.* **—cher′ish•ing•ly,** *adv.*

—Syn. 1, 2. CHERISH, FOSTER, HARBOR imply giving affection, care, or shelter to something. CHERISH suggests regarding or treating something as an object of affection or as valuable: *to cherish a friendship.* FOSTER implies sustaining and nourishing something with care, esp. in order to promote, increase, or strengthen it: *to foster a hope; to foster enmity.* HARBOR suggests giving shelter to or entertaining something undesirable, esp. evil thoughts or intentions: *to harbor malice or a grudge.* **2.** nurse, nourish, sustain. **—Ant. 2.** neglect, ignore, abandon. **3.** relinquish.

Cher•kas•sy (chûr kä′sē, -kas′ē; *Russ.* chyiʀ käs′si), *n.* a city in central Ukraine, on the Dnieper River, SE of Kiev. 287,000.

Cher•kessk′ Auton′omous Re′gion (chûr kesk′; *Russ.* chyiʀ kyesk′). See **Karachai-Cherkessk Autonomous Region.**

Cher•ni•gov (chûr nē′gôf, -gof; *Russ.* chyiʀ nyē′gəf), *n.* a city in N Ukraine, on the Desna River. 291,000.

Cher•no•byl (chûr nō′bəl; *Russ.* chyiʀ nô′bil), *n.* a city in N Ukraine, 80 mi. NW of Kiev: nuclear-plant accident 1986.

Cher•nov•tsy (chyiʀ nuf tsī′), *n.* Russian name of **Cernăuţi.**

cher•no•zem (chûr′nə zem′, châr′-; *Russ.* chyiʀ nu-zyôm′), *n.* a soil common in cool or temperate semiarid climates, very black and rich in humus and carbonates. [1835–45; < Russ *chernozëm,* equiv. to *chërn*(*yĭ*) black + *-o-* -O- + *-zëm,* var., in compounds, of *zemlyá* earth, land; see HUMUS]

Cher•o•kee (cher′ə kē′, cher′ə kē′), *n., pl.* **-kees,** (*esp. collectively*) **-kee** for 1. **1.** a member of an important tribe of North American Indians whose first known center was in the southern Alleghenies and who presently live in North Carolina and Oklahoma. **2.** the Iroquoian language of the Cherokee, written since 1822 in a syllabic script invented for the language by Sequoya.

Cher′okee rose′, the fragrant white rose of a prickly, climbing shrub, *Rosa laevigata,* originally from China and naturalized in the southern U.S.: the state flower of Georgia. [1815–25, *Amer.*]

che•root (shə ro͞ot′), *n.* a cigar having open, untapered ends. [1660–70; < Tamil *curuṭṭu* roll (of tobacco)]

cher′ries ju′bilee, a dessert of black cherries that have been flambéed with brandy or kirsch and spooned over vanilla ice cream.

cher•ry (cher′ē), *n., pl.* **-ries,** *adj.* **—***n.* **1.** the fruit of any of various trees belonging to the genus *Prunus,* of the rose family, consisting of a pulpy, globular drupe enclosing a one-seeded smooth stone. **2.** the tree bearing such a fruit. **3.** the wood of such a tree. **4.** any of various fruits or plants resembling the cherry. **5.** bright red; cerise. **6.** *Slang* (*often vulgar*). **a.** the hymen. **b.** the state of virginity. **7.** *Slang.* **a.** something new or unused. **b.** a novice. **8.** *Underworld Slang.* a first offender. **9.** *Bowling.* the striking down of only the forward pin or pins in attempting to make a spare. **—***adj.* **10.** bright-red; cerise. **11.** (of food and beverages) made with or containing cherries or cherrylike flavoring: *cherry pie; cherry soda.* **12.** (of furniture, woodwork, etc.) made of or covered or decorated with wood from the cherry tree. **13.** *Slang* (*often vulgar*). being a virgin. **14.** *Slang.* **a.** new or unused: *a three-year-old car in cherry condition.* **b.** inexperienced; being an innocent novice. [1300–50; ME *cheri* var. of *chirie,* back formation from OE *ciris-* (taken for pl.) << VL **ceresium* for **cerasium* (L *cerasum*) < Gk *kerásion* cherry] **—cher′ry•like′,** *adj.*

cher′ry birch′. See **sweet birch.** [1800–10, *Amer.*]

cher•ry-bob (cher′ē bob′), *n. Brit.* a pair of cherries joined at the end of their stems. [CHERRY + BOB[2]]

cher′ry bomb′, a red, globe-shaped firecracker with a long fuse and high explosive capability. [1950–55]

cher′ry coal′, a type of bituminous coal that burns readily and gives a hot fire.

CONCISE ETYMOLOGY KEY: <, descended or borrowed from; >, whence; b., blend of, blended; c., cognate with; cf., compare; deriv., derivative; equiv., equivalent; imit., imitative; obl., oblique; r., replacing; s., stem; sp., spelling, spelled; resp., respelling, respelled; trans., translation; ?, origin unknown; *, unattested; ‡, probably earlier than. See the full key inside the front cover.

cher′ry lau′rel, **1.** Also called **English laurel.** a rosaceous evergreen shrub or small tree, *Prunus laurocerasus,* of Eurasia, having clusters of white flowers and dark purple fruit. **2.** See **laurel cherry.** [1655–65]

Cher′ry Or′chard, The, a play (1904) by Chekhov.

cher′ry pep′per, a variety of pepper, *Capsicum annuum cerasiforme,* having rounded, usually pungent fruit. [1825–35]

cher•ry-pick (cher′ē pik′), *Informal.* —*v.t.* **1.** to select with great care: *You can cherry-pick your own stereo components.* —*v.i.* **2.** (in retail use) to buy only the sale items and ignore the other merchandise. [1970–75]

cher′ry pick′er, **1.** a moveable boom, having a bucketlike attachment at its top that is large enough to carry a worker: used for repairing telephone lines, pruning trees, etc. **2.** a vehicle equipped with such a boom. Also, **cher′ry-pick′er, cher′ry•pick′er.** [1860–65]

cher′ry pie′, any of several plants having flowers with an odor suggestive of cherries, as the heliotrope. [1825–35]

cher′ry plum′, **1.** a small tree, *Prunus cerasifera,* bearing edible yellow or reddish fruit. **2.** the fruit of this tree. Also called **myrobalan.**

cher′ry red′, a bright red; cherry. [1585–95]

cher•ry•stone (cher′ē stōn′), *n.* **1.** the one-seeded smooth stone of the cherry. **2.** the quahog, *Venus mercenaria,* when larger than a littleneck. [1300–50; ME *cheriston.* See CHERRY, STONE]

cher′ry toma′to, a variety of tomato, *Lycopersicon lycopersicum cerasiforme,* having cherry-sized, edible, red or yellow fruit. [1840–50, *Amer.*]

cher•so•nese (kûr′sə nēz′, -nēs′), *n.* a peninsula. [1595–1605; < L *chersonēsus* < Gk *chersónēsos,* equiv. to *chérso(s)* dry + *nēsos* island]

chert (chûrt), *n.* a compact rock consisting essentially of microcrystalline quartz. [1670–80; orig. uncert.] —**chert′y,** *adj.*

cher•ub (cher′əb), *n., pl.* **cher•ubs** for 3, 4; **cher•u•bim** (cher′ə bim, -yo͞o bim) for 1, 2. **1.** a celestial being. Gen. 3:24; Ezek. 1, 10. **2.** *Theol.* a member of the second order of angels, often represented as a beautiful rosy-cheeked child with wings. **3.** a beautiful or innocent person, esp. a child. **4.** a person, esp. a child, with a sweet, chubby, innocent face. [bef. 900; ME < L < Gk < Heb *kərūbh;* r. ME *cherubin,* OE *c(h)erubin, cerubim* (all sing.) < L *cherūbīm* < Gk < Heb *kərūbhīm* (pl.)] —**che•ru•bic** (chə ro͞o′bik), **che•ru′bi•cal,** *adj.* —**che•ru′bi•cal•ly,** *adv.* —**cher′ub•like′,** *adj.*

cher•ub•fish (cher′əb fish′), *n., pl.* **-fish•es,** (*esp. collectively*) **-fish.** a brilliantly colored butterflyfish, *Centropyge argi,* found in the West Indies: kept in home aquariums. [CHERUB + FISH]

Che•ru•bi•con (*Gk.* KHE′RO͞O vē kōn′; *Eng.* chi ro͞o′bikon′), *n. Eastern Ch.* the hymn sung during the Great Entrance by the choir, which represents the cherubim. Also, **Che′ru•bi•kon′.** Also called **Cheru′bic Hymn′.**

Che•ru•bi•ni (ker′o͞o bē′nē; *It.* ke′RO͞O bē′nē), *n.* **Ma•ri•a Lu•i•gi Car•lo Ze•no•bio Sal•va•to•re** (mä Rē′ä lo͞o ē′jē kär′lô dze nô′byô säl′vä tô′Re), 1760–1842, Italian composer, esp. of opera; in France after 1788.

cher•vil (chûr′vil), *n.* **1.** an herb, *Anthriscus cerefolium,* of the parsley family, having aromatic leaves used to flavor soups, salads, etc. **2.** any of several other plants of the same genus or allied genera. [bef. 900; ME *chervelle,* OE *cerfelle* < L *chaerephylla,* pl. of *chaerephyllum* < Gk *chairéphyllon,* equiv. to *chaíre* hail (greeting) + *phýllon* leaf]

cher•vo•nets (chər vô′nits, -nets; *Russ.* chyiR vô′nyits), *n., pl.* **-von•tsi** (-vônt′sē; *Russ.* -vôn′tsi). a former gold coin and monetary unit of the U.S.S.R., equal to ten rubles. Also, **tchervonetz.** [1920–25; < Russ *chervónets,* ORuss *chervon(n)yi* a similar gold coin < Pol *czerwony* a gold coin, lit., red (appar. because gold of a high purity was thought to have a reddish cast), c. Czech *červený,* Serbo-Croatian *crven, cr(v)ljen,* Bulg *chervén* < Slavic **črvljen,* orig. ptp. of **črviti* to dye red, deriv. of **črvĭ* worm, KERMES (Serbo-Croatian *crv,* Pol *czerw,* Russ *cherv′*), a by-form of **črmĭ;* cf. OCS *chrŭmĭnŭ* red; see CRIMSON, VERMILION]

Cher•yl (sher′əl), *n.* a female given name.

Cher•y•lene (sher′ə lēn′), *n.* a female given name.

Ches•a•peake (ches′ə pēk′), *n.* **1.** (*italics*) a U.S. frigate boarded in 1807 by the British, who removed part of its crew and impressed some members into British service: captured by the British in naval battle near Boston in 1813. **2.** a city in SE Virginia. 114,486.

Ches′apeake and Del′aware Canal′, a canal between N Delaware and NE Maryland, connecting the Chesapeake and Delaware bays. ab. 19 mi. (31 km) long.

Ches′apeake Bay′, an inlet of the Atlantic, in Maryland and Virginia. 200 mi. (320 km) long; 4–40 mi. (6–64 km) wide.

Ches′apeake Bay′ retriev′er, one of an American breed of retrievers having a short, thick, oily coat ranging in color from brown to a light tan. [1905–10]

che sa•rà sa•rà (ke′ sä Rä′ sä Rä′), *Italian.* what will be, will be.

Chesh•ire (chesh′ər, -ēr), *n.* **1.** formerly, **Chester.** a county in NW England. 910,900; 899 sq. mi. (2328 sq. km). **2.** a town in central Connecticut. 21,788. **3.** Also called **Chesh′ire cheese′, Chester.** a hard cheese, yellowish, orange, or white in color, made of cow's milk and similar to cheddar.

Chesh′ire cat′, **1.** a constantly grinning cat in Lewis Carroll's *Alice's Adventures in Wonderland.* **2. grin like a Cheshire cat,** to smile or grin inscrutably.

Chesh•van (*Seph. Heb.* KHesh vän′; *Ashk. Heb.* KHesh′vän; *Eng.* KHesh′vən, hesh′-), *n.* Heshvan.

ches•key (ches′kē), *n., pl.* **-keys.** *Slang (disparaging and offensive).* **1.** a person of Czech extraction. **2.** the Czech language. [1890–95; < Czech *český* Czech (adj.)]

Ches•nutt (ches′nət, -nut), *n.* **Charles Wad•dell** (wodel′), 1858–1932, U.S. short-story writer and novelist.

chess[1] (ches), *n.* a game played by two persons, each with 16 pieces, on a chessboard. [1150–1200; ME < OF *esches,* pl. of *eschec* CHECK[1]]

chess[2] (ches), *n., pl.* **chess, chess•es.** one of the planks forming the roadway of a floating bridge. [1425–75; late ME *ches* tier, layer < ?]

chess•board (ches′bôrd′, -bōrd′), *n.* the board, identical with a checkerboard, used for playing chess. [1400–50; late ME. See CHESS[1], BOARD]

chess′ clock′, a timer for chess players, having a dial for each player on which his or her accumulated time is recorded and a device for stopping one timer and starting the other at the end of each move. [1885–90]

chess•man (ches′man′, -mən), *n., pl.* **-men** (-men′, -mən). any piece used in the game of chess. [1275–1325; ME; earlier *chesse meyne,* equiv. to *chesse* CHESS[1] + *meyne* household (*man, men* by folk etymology) < MF *mesniée* < L *mansiōn-* (s. of *mansiō*); see MANSION]

chess′ pie′, *Southern Cookery.* a dessert of cornmeal, sugar, butter, egg yolks, milk, and flavorings baked in a pastry shell. [1930–35; appar. for *chest pie; chest* perh. alluding to its depth]

chess•tree (ches′trē′), *n. Naut.* (in the 17th and 18th centuries) a wooden fastening with one or more sheaves, attached to the topside of a sailing vessel, through which the windward tack of a course was rove. [1620–30; perh. by folk etymology < F *châssis* frame; see CHASSIS]

chest (chest), *n.* **1.** *Anat.* the trunk of the body from the neck to the abdomen; thorax. **2.** a box, usually with a lid, for storage, safekeeping of valuables, etc.: *a toy chest; a jewelry chest.* **3.** the place where the funds of a public institution or charitable organization are kept; treasury; coffer. **4.** the funds themselves. **5.** a box in which certain goods, as tea, are packed for transit. **6.** the quantity contained in such a box: *a chest of spices.* **7.** See **chest of drawers. 8.** a small cabinet, esp. one hung on a wall, for storage, as of toiletries and medicines: *a medicine chest.* **9. get (something) off one's chest,** *Informal.* to relieve oneself of (problems, troubling thoughts, etc.) by revealing them to someone. **10. play it close to the chest.** See **vest** (def. 8). [bef. 900; ME; OE *cest, cist* < L *cista* < Gk *kístē* box] —**chest•ful** (chest′fo͝ol), *n.*

chest•ed (ches′tid), *adj.* having a chest of a specified kind (often used in combination): *broad-chested; barrel-chested.* [1400–50; late ME. See CHEST, -ED[3]]

Ches•ter (ches′tər), *n.* **1.** a city in Cheshire, in NW England: only English city with the Roman walls still intact. 117,200. **2.** a city in SE Pennsylvania. 45,794. **3.** Cheshire (def. 3). **4.** former name of Cheshire (def. 1). **5.** a male given name: from a Latin word meaning "camp."

ches•ter•bed (ches′tər bed′), *n. Chiefly Canadian.* a sofa or chesterfield that opens into a bed. [CHESTER(FIELD) + BED]

ches•ter•field (ches′tər fēld′), *n.* **1.** (*sometimes cap.*) a single- or double-breasted topcoat or overcoat with a fly front and a narrow velvet collar. **2.** a large, overstuffed sofa or divan with a back and upholstered arms. **3.** *Chiefly Canadian.* any large sofa or couch. [1885–90; named after an Earl of *Chesterfield* in the 19th century]

Ches•ter•field (ches′tər fēld′), *n.* **Philip Dor•mer Stan•hope** (dôr′mər stan′əp), **4th Earl of,** 1694–1773, British statesman and author.

Ches•ter•field•i•an (ches′tər fēl′dē ən), *adj.* of, pertaining to, or like the 4th Earl of Chesterfield or his writings; elegant; urbane; suave. [1770–80; CHESTERFIELD + -IAN]

Ches•ter•ton (ches′tər tən), *n.* **G(ilbert) K(eith),** 1874–1936, English essayist, critic, and novelist.

Ches′ter White′, one of an American breed of white hogs, having drooping ears. [1855–60, *Amer.*; named after *Chester,* county in Pennsylvania where first bred]

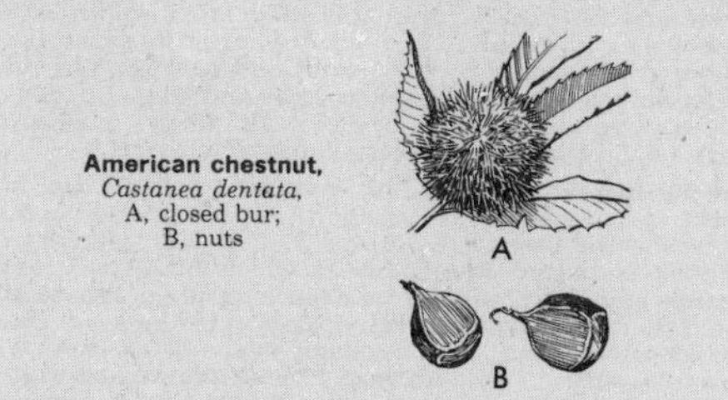

American chestnut, *Castanea dentata,* A, closed bur; B, nuts

chest•nut (ches′nut′, -nət), *n.* **1.** any of the several deciduous trees constituting the genus *Castanea,* of the beech family, having toothed, oblong leaves and bearing edible nuts enclosed in a prickly bur, and including *C. dentata* **(American chestnut),** which has been virtually destroyed by the chestnut blight, *C. sativa* **(European chestnut),** *C. mollissima* **(Chinese chestnut),** and *C. crenata* **(Japanese chestnut). 2.** the edible nut of such a tree. **3.** the wood of any of these trees. **4.** any fruit or tree resembling the chestnut, as the horse chestnut. **5.** reddish brown. **6.** an old or stale joke, anecdote, etc. **7.** the callosity on the inner side of the leg of a horse. See diag. under **horse. 8.** a reddish-brown horse having the mane and tail of the same color. Cf. **bay**[5] (def. 2). **9.** Also called **liver chestnut.** a horse of a solid, dark-brown color. **10. pull someone's chestnuts out of the fire,** to rescue someone from a difficulty. —*adj.* **11.** reddish-brown. **12.** (of food) containing or made with chestnuts: *turkey with chestnut stuffing.* [1350–1400; 1880–85 for def. 6; earlier *chesten nut,* ME *chesten,* OE *cysten* chestnut tree (< L *castanea* < Gk *kastanéa*) + NUT] —**chest′nut′ty,** *adj.*

chest′nut blight′, *Plant Pathol.* a disease of chestnuts, esp. the American chestnut, characterized by bark lesions that girdle and eventually kill the tree, caused by a fungus, *Endothia parasitica.* [1905–10, *Amer.*]

chest′nut bot′tle, an American glass bottle or flask of the 19th century, having slightly flattened sides.

chest′nut clam′, Astarte (def. 2). Also called **chest′nut shell′.**

chest′nut coal′, anthracite in sizes ranging from $1\frac{3}{16}$ to $1\frac{5}{8}$ in. (3 to 4 cm). Also called **nut coal.** [1805–15, *Amer.*]

chest′nut oak′, any of several North American oaks, as *Quercus prinus,* having serrate or dentate leaves resembling those of the chestnut. [1695–1705, *Amer.*]

chest′ of drawers′, *Furniture.* a piece of furniture consisting of a set of drawers in a frame set on short legs, or feet, for holding clothing, household linens, etc. [1670–80]

chest′ of vi′ols, *Music.* a set of several viols, usually played together as an ensemble.

chest-on-chest (chest′on chest′, -ôn-), *n.* a chest of drawers placed upon a slightly wider chest of drawers. [1810–20, *Amer.*]

chest′ protec′tor, *Baseball.* a protective pad worn over the chest by a catcher or umpire to shield the body from foul tips. [1885–90, *Amer.*]

chest′ reg′ister, *Music.* the low register of the human voice. [1840–50]

chest-thump•ing (chest′thum′ping), *n.* the act or practice of boasting.

chest•y (ches′tē), *adj.,* **chest•i•er, chest•i•est. 1.** having a well-developed chest or bosom. **2.** proud; conceited. [1895–1900, *Amer.*; CHEST + -Y[1]] —**chest′i•ly,** *adv.* —**chest′i•ness,** *n.*

Chet (chet), *n.* a male given name, form of **Chester.**

cheth (het, hes; *Seph. Heb.* KHet; *Ashk. Heb.* KHes), *n.* heth. [< Heb *ḥeth*]

Chet•nik (chet nēk′, chet′nik), *n.* a member of a Serbian nationalist group that fought against the Turks in the early part of the 20th century and carried on guerrilla warfare during World War I and II. [1905–10; < Serbo-Croatian *čètnik* guerrilla, equiv. to *čět(a)* troop (c. ORuss *cheta,* Czech *četa*) + *-nik* agent suffix (cf. -NIK)]

che•trum (chē′trəm, che′-), *n.* a coin and monetary unit of Bhutan, the hundredth part of a ngultrum.

Che•tu•mal (che′to͞o mäl′), *n.* a city in and the capital of Quintana Roo, in SE Mexico. 23,685.

che•val de ba•taille (shə vAl də bA tä′y[ə]), *pl.* ***che•vaux de ba•taille*** (shə vōd[ə] bA tä′y[ə]). *French.* **1.** a horse used in battle; charger. **2.** a favorite topic of discussion, argument, etc.

che•val-de-frise (shə val′də frēz′), *n., pl.* **che•vaux-de-frise** (shə vō′də frēz′). Usually, **chevaux-de-frise.** a portable obstacle, usually a sawhorse, covered with projecting spikes or barbed wire, for military use in closing a passage, breaking in a defensive wall, etc. [1680–90; < F; lit., horse of Friesland, so called because first used by Frisians]

che•va•let (shev′ə lā′, shə val′ā), *n.* the bridge on a stringed musical instrument, as a violin. [1800–10; < F: more generally, any wooden frame for holding or supporting something, equiv. to *cheval* horse (< L *caballus*) + *-et* -ET; cf. parallel sense of HORSE]

che•val′ glass′ (shə val′), a full-length mirror mounted so that it can be tilted in a frame. [1830–40; < F *cheval* horse, supporting framework (see CHEVALET)]

chev•a•lier (shev′ə lēr′ *or, esp. for 1, 2,* shə val′yā, -väl′-), *n.* **1.** a member of certain orders of honor or merit: *a chevalier of the Legion of Honor.* **2.** *Fr. Hist.* the lowest title of rank in the old nobility. **3.** a chivalrous man; cavalier. **4.** *Archaic.* a knight. [1250–1300; < MF; r. late ME *chivaler* < AF. See CAVALIER]

Che•va•lier (shə val′yā, -väl′-; *Fr.* shə vA lyā′), *n.* **Mau•rice (Au•guste)** (mô rēs′ ô′gəst; *Fr.* mō Rēs′ ō gYst′), 1888–1972, French actor and singer.

Che•va•lier-Mon•tra•chet (shə val′yā mōn′trə shā′, -mon′-, -väl′-; *Fr.* shə vA lyā′MÔN RA she′), *n.* a white wine from Burgundy.

cheval′ screen′, a fire screen, usually with a cloth panel, having supports at the ends and mounted on legs. [see CHEVAL GLASS]

che•vaux-de-frise (shə vō′də frēz′), *n.* pl. of **cheval-de-frise.**

che•vee (shə vā′), *n. Jewelry.* **1.** cuvette (def. 1). **2.** a smooth gem with a slightly depressed surface. [< F *chevée,* n. use of fem. of *chevé,* ptp. of *chever* to make a hollow in < L *cavāre,* deriv. of *cavus* hollow; see CAVE]

cheve•ret (shev′rit, shev ret′), *n.* a small English table of the 18th century, having an oblong top, one or two rows of drawers, and slender legs joined near the bottom by a shelf. Also, **sheveret.** [perh. alter. of F *chevalet* CHEVALET]

che•vet (shə vā′), *n.* an apse, as of a Gothic cathedral. [1800–10; < F, earlier *chevès,* OF *chevez* << L *capitium* opening or covering for the head. See CAPUT]

che•ville (shə vē′), *n. Pros.* a word or expression whose only function is to fill a metrical gap in a verse or to balance a sentence. Cf. **expletive** (def. 2). [1880–85; < F: plug, peg < L *clāvicula* tendril. See CLAVICLE]

Chev•i•ot (shiv′ē ət, shev′- *for 1;* chev′ē ət, chē′vē-for 2, 3; for 3 also shev′ē ət), n. **1.** a city in SW Ohio. 10,394. **2.** one of a British breed of sheep, noted for its heavy fleece of medium length. **3.** (l.c.) a woolen fabric in a coarse twill weave, for coats, suits, etc. [1805–15; named after the CHEVIOT HILLS]

Chev′i•ot Hills′ (chev′ē ət, chē′vē-), a range of hills on the boundary between England and Scotland: highest point, 2676 ft. (816 m).

chev•on (shev′ən), n. the flesh of goats, used as food. [chev- (< F chèvre goat < L capra she-goat, fem. of caper goat) + -on, extracted from MUTTON[1]]

chè•vre (shev′rə, shev; Fr. she′vrᵊ), n. any cheese made from goat's milk. Also, **chev•ret** (shə vrā′). [< F chèvre goat. See CHEVON]

chev•rette (shə vret′), n. a soft, thin kidskin. [1725–35; < F: she-kid, equiv. to chèvre goat (see CHEVON) + -ette -ETTE]

chev•ron (shev′rən), n. **1.** a badge consisting of stripes meeting at an angle, worn on the sleeve by noncommissioned officers, police officers, etc., as an indication of rank, service, or the like. **2.** an ornament in this form, as on a molding. **3.** Also called **chev′ron weave′.** herringbone (def. 2a). **4.** Heraldry. an ordinary in the form of an inverted V. [1300–50; ME cheveroun < OF: rafter, chevron < VL *capriōn- (s. of *capriō), deriv. of L caper goat] **—chev′roned,** adj.

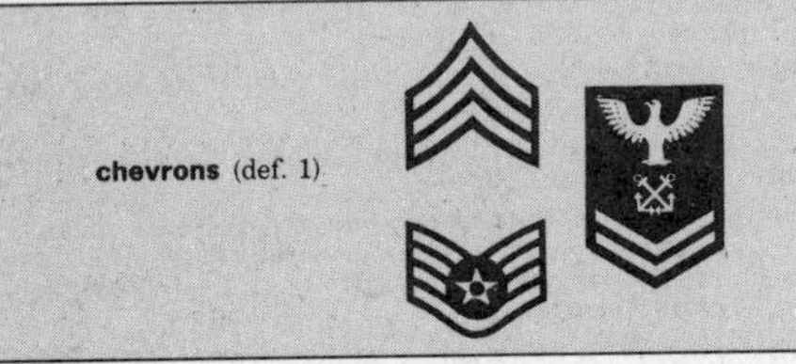
chevrons (def. 1)

chev•ron•el (shev′rə nel′), n. Heraldry. a narrow chevron, one-half the usual breadth or less. [1565–75; CHEVRON + -el dim. suffix]

chev•ro•tain (shev′rə tān′, -tin), n. any very small, deerlike ruminant of the family Tragulidae, of Africa, tropical Asia, the Malay Peninsula, etc. Also called **mouse deer.** [< F, appar. Buffon's alter. of chevrotin roe deer under the age of six months, equiv. to MF chevrot kid (chevre goat (see CHEVON) + -ot dim. suffix) + -in -INE[1]]

chev•y (chev′ē), v., **chev•ied, chev•y•ing,** n., pl. **chev•ies.** Brit. —v.t. **1.** to chase; run after. **2.** to harass; nag; torment. —v.i. **3.** to race; scamper. —n. **4.** a hunting cry. **5.** a hunt, chase, or pursuit. **6.** the game of prisoner's base. Also, **chivvy, chivy.** [1775–85; perh. short for CHEVY CHASE]

Chev′y Chase′, (The Ballad of Chevy Chase) a 15th-century English ballad describing the battle of Otterburn between the Percys and the Douglases.

chew (cho͞o), v.t. **1.** to crush or grind with the teeth; masticate. **2.** to crush, damage, injure, etc., as if by chewing (often fol. by up): The faulty paper feeder chewed the letters up. **3.** to make by or as if by chewing: The puppy chewed a hole in my slipper. **4.** to meditate on; consider deliberately (often fol. by over): He chewed the problem over in his mind. —v.i. **5.** to perform the act of crushing or grinding with the teeth. **6.** Informal. to chew tobacco. **7.** to meditate. **8. chew out,** Slang. to scold harshly: The sergeant chewed out the recruits. **9. chew the fat,** Informal. to converse at length in a relaxed manner; chat: They liked to sit around chewing the fat. Also, **chew the rag.** —n. **10.** an act or instance of chewing. **11.** something chewed or intended for chewing: a chew of tobacco; taffy chews. [bef. 1000; ME chewen, OE cēowan; c. OHG kiuwan (G kauen)] **—chew′er,** n.

Che•wa (chā′wä), n. **1.** a member of a Bantu-speaking people of Malawi. **2.** Also called **Chichewa.** the Bantu language of the Chewa people, widely spoken in Malawi. Also, **Cewa.**

chew•a•ble (cho͞o′ə bəl), adj. **1.** capable of being chewed: chewable aspirin. —n. **2.** something that can be chewed: Now that the baby is getting its teeth, add chewables to its diet. [1840–50; CHEW + -ABLE]

chew′ing gum′ (cho͞o′ing), a sweetened and flavored preparation for chewing, usually made of chicle. [1755–65, Amer.]

chew′ing louse′. See under **louse** (def. 2).

Chew′ings fes′cue (cho͞o′ingz), a hardy, fine-leaved variety of fescue, Festuca rubra commutata, grown in the U.S. and New Zealand as a lawn grass. [1915–20; named after Charles Chewings (d. 1937), Australian scientist]

chew′ing tobac′co, tobacco, in the form of a plug, usually flavored, for chewing rather than smoking. [1780–90, Amer.]

che•wink (chi wingk′), n. a towhee, Pipilo erythrophthalmus, of eastern North America. [1785–95, Amer.; imit.]

chew•y (cho͞o′ē), adj., **chew•i•er, chew•i•est.** (of food) not easily chewed, as because of toughness or stickiness; requiring much chewing. [1920–25; CHEW + -Y[1]] **—chew′i•ness,** n.

chex (cheks), n. a pl. of **check[1].**

CONCISE ETYMOLOGY KEY: <, descended or borrowed from; >, whence; b., blend of, blended; c., cognate with; cf., compare; deriv., derivative; equiv., equivalent; imit., imitative; obl., oblique; r., replacing; s., stem; sp., spelling, spelled; resp., respelling, respelled; trans., translation; ?, origin unknown; *, unattested; ‡, probably earlier than. See the full key inside the front cover.

Chey•enne (shī en′, -an′), n., pl. **-ennes,** (esp. collectively) **-enne** for 1. **1.** a member of a North American Indian people of the western plains, formerly in central Minnesota and North and South Dakota, and now divided between Montana and Oklahoma. **2.** an Algonquian language, the language of the Cheyenne Indians. **3.** a city in and the capital of Wyoming, in the S part. 47,283.

Chey′enne Riv′er, a river flowing NE from E Wyoming to the Missouri River in South Dakota. ab. 500 mi. (800 km) long.

Chey•ne (chā′nē, chān), n. **Thomas Kel•ly** (kel′ē), 1841–1915, English clergyman and Biblical scholar.

chez (shā), prep. French. at or in the home of; with.

chg., **1.** change. **2.** charge. Also, **chge.**

chi[1] (kī), n., pl. **chis.** **1.** the twenty-second letter of the Greek alphabet (X, χ). **2.** the consonant sound represented by this letter. [< Gk]

chi[2] (chē), n. the vital life force in the body supposedly regulated by acupuncture. [< Chin qì breath]

Chi (chī), n. Chicago. [by shortening]

Ch'i (chyē), n. one of two dynasties that ruled in China A.D. 479–502 and, as the Northern Ch'i, A.D. 550–77.

chi•a (chē′ə), n. **1.** a plant, Salvia columbariae, of the mint family, native to the southwestern U.S. and Mexico, having mostly basal, oblong leaves and small blue flowers: the seeds are used as food and as the source of a beverage. **2.** any of several similar related plants. **3.** a beverage brewed from the seeds of any of these plants. [1875–80; < MexSp chía < Nahuatl chiah, chian]

chi•ack (chī′ək), v.t. Australian. to jeer at; tease; deride. Also, **chyack.** [1870–75; prob. alter. of CHEEK]

Chia•i (jyä′ē′), n. Wade-Giles. a city on W Taiwan. 250,000. Also, **Chia′-i′, Chiayi, Jiayi.**

Chia•mu•ssu (Chin. jyä′mo͞o′so͞o′), n. Wade-Giles. Jiamusi.

Chi•an (kī′ən), adj. **1.** of or pertaining to Chios or its inhabitants. —n. **2.** a native or inhabitant of Chios. [1625–35; CHI(os) + -AN]

Chiang Ch'ing (Chin. jyäng′ ching′), Wade-Giles. See **Jiang Qing.**

Chiang Ching-kuo (jyäng′ jing′gwô′), 1910–88, Chinese political leader: president of the Republic of China 1978–88 (son of Chiang Kai-shek).

Chiang Kai-shek (chang′ kī shek′, jyäng′), (Chiang Chung-cheng) 1886?–1975, Chinese army officer and political leader: president of the Republic of China 1950–75. Also, **Chiang Chieh-shih** (jyäng′ jye′shœ′).

Chiang•ling (Chin. jyäng′ling′), n. Wade-Giles. Jiangling.

Chiang Mai (chyäng′ mī′), a city in NW Thailand. 100,000. Also **Chiang′mai′, Chiengmai.**

Chi•a•ni•na (kē′ə nē′nə), n., pl. **-ni.** one of a large breed of beef cattle, originally of Italy, used also as a draft animal. [< It, fem. of chianino lit., pertaining to Chiana, a river and valley in Tuscany]

Chi•an•ti (kē än′tē, -an′-; It. kyän′tē), n. a dry, red, Italian table wine, originally put up in straw-covered bottles. [1825–35; after the Chianti region of Tuscany, source of the wine]

Chi′an tur′pentine (kī′ən), turpentine (def. 2). [1885–90]

chiao (jyou), n., pl. **chiao.** Wade-Giles. jiao.

Chiao•chou (Chin. jyou′jō′), n. Wade-Giles. Jiaozhou.

Chiao′chou′ Bay′. See **Jiaozhou Bay.**

Chi•a•pas (chē ä′päs), n. a state in S Mexico. 1,933,000; 28,732 sq. mi. (74,415 sq. km). Cap.: Tuxtla Gutiérrez.

chi•a•ro•scu•ro (kē är′ə sky͝or′ō), n., pl. **-ros.** **1.** the distribution of light and shade in a picture. **2.** Painting. the use of deep variations in and subtle gradations of light and shade, esp. to enhance the delineation of character and for general dramatic effect: Rembrandt is a master of chiaroscuro. **3.** a woodcut print in which the colors are produced by the use of different blocks with different colors. **4.** a sketch in light and shade. [1680–90; < It, equiv. to chiaro bright (< L clārus) + oscuro dark (< L obscūrus). See CLEAR, OBSCURE]

chi•as•ma (kī az′mə), n., pl. **-mas, -ma•ta** (-mə tə). **1.** Anat. a crossing or decussation, as that of the optic nerves at the base of the brain. **2.** Cell Biol. a point of overlap of paired chromatids at which fusion and exchange of genetic material take place during prophase of meiosis. Also, **chi•asm** (kī′az əm). [1830–40; < Gk: crosspiece of wood, cross-bandage, equiv. to chi CHI[1] + -asma n. suffix] **—chi•as′mal, chi•as′mic, chi•as•mat•ic** (kī′az mat′ik), adj.

chi•as•ma•typ•y (kī az′mə tī′pē), n. Genetics. the process of chiasma formation, which is the basis for crossing over. Cf. **crossing over.** [CHIASMA + -TYPE + -Y[3]] **—chi•as′ma•type′,** adj., n.

chi•as•mus (kī az′məs), n., pl. **-mi** (-mī). Rhet. a reversal in the order of words in two otherwise parallel phrases, as in "He went to the country, to the town went she." [1870–75; < Gk chiasmós, equiv. to chi CHI[1] + -asmos masc. n. suffix, akin to -asma; see CHIASMA]

chi•as•tic (kī as′tik), adj. Rhet. characterized by chiasmus. [1865–70; < Gk chiast(ós) diagonally arranged (see CHIASMA) + -IC]

chi•as•to•lite (kī as′tl īt′), n. a variety of the mineral andalusite having cruciform carbonaceous inclusions. [1795–1805; alter. of chiastolith (see -LITE), equiv. to Gk chiastó(s) set crosswise (see CHIASMA) + -LITH]

chiaus (chous, choush), n., pl. **chiaus•es.** **1.** (in the Ottoman Empire) a court official who served as an ambassador, emissary, or member of a ceremonial escort. **2.** a Turkish military rank approximating that of sergeant. [1590–1600; < Turk çavuş < Pers chāwush]

Chia•yi (Chin. jyä′ē′), n. Wade-Giles. Chiai.

Chi•ba (chē′bä′), n. a city on SE Honshu, in central Japan, near Tokyo. 746,428.

Chib•cha (chib′chə), n., pl. **-chas,** (esp. collectively) **-cha** for 1. **1.** a member of a now extinct tribe of South American Indians, having an advanced culture, who lived on a high plateau of Bogotá, Colombia. **2.** the extinct language of the Chibcha.

Chib•chan (chib′chən), n. a family of languages indigenous to Central America, Colombia, and Ecuador. [1905–10; CHIBCH(A) + -AN]

Chi•bou•ga•mau (shi bo͞o′gə mo͞o′, -mō′; Fr. shē bo͞o-gа mo͞o′, -mō′), n. a town in S Quebec, in E Canada. 10,732.

chi•bouk (chi bo͝ok′, -bo͞ok′), n. a Turkish tobacco pipe with a stiff stem sometimes 4 or 5 ft. (1.2 or 1.5 m) long. Also, **chi•bouque′.** [1805–15; < Turk çibuk, var. of çubuk lit., shoot, sapling, staff]

chic (shēk), adj., **-er, -est.** **1.** attractive and fashionable; stylish: a chic hat. —n. **2.** style and elegance, esp. in dress: Paris clothes have such chic. **3.** stylishness; modishness: the chic of the firstnighters. [1855–60; < F < G Schick skill] **—chic′ly,** adv. **—chic′ness,** n.
—Syn. **1.** smart, elegant, modish.
—Pronunciation. The spelling pronunciation (chik) is considered nonstandard except when used facetiously.

Chi•ca•go (shi kä′gō, -kô′-), n. a city in NE Illinois, on Lake Michigan: second largest city in the U.S. 3,005,072. **—Chi•ca′go•an,** n.

Chica′go Board′ of Trade′, a major exchange in the United States that deals in futures, notably of grains and metals. Abbr.: CBT

Chica′go Fire′, U.S. Hist. a three-day fire in Chicago, Ill., in 1871 that largely destroyed the city and took several hundred lives.

Chica′go Heights′, a city in NE Illinois, S of Chicago. 37,026.

Chica′go Ridge′, a town in NE Illinois. 13,473.

Chica′go School′, a group of Chicago architects active between c1880 and c1910 and known for major developments in skyscraper design and for experiments in a modern architectural style appropriate esp. to business and industrial buildings: two of the best-known members were Louis Sullivan and John Wellborn Root.

Chica′go steak′, a strip steak or, sometimes, a shell steak. Also called **Chica′go cut′.**

Chica′go style′, a style of jazz flourishing in Chicago esp. in the early 1920's, constituting a direct offshoot of New Orleans style, and differing from its predecessor chiefly in the diminished influence of native folk sources, the greater tension of its group improvisation, the increased emphasis on solos, and the regular use of the tenor saxophone as part of the ensemble. [1940–45]

Chica′go win′dow, a composite window, horizontal in character, consisting of a large, fixed sheet of glass between two vertical windows with sash for ventilation, first popularized in commercial buildings in Chicago in the 1880's and 1890's.

Chi•ca•na (chi kä′nə, -kan′ə), n. **1.** a Mexican-American girl or woman. —adj. **2.** of or pertaining to female Mexican-Americans or their culture: a conference on Chicana issues. [1965–70; < MexSp, fem. of CHICANO]

chi•cane (shi kān′, chi-), n., v., **-caned, -can•ing.** —n. **1.** deception; chicanery. —v.t. **2.** to trick by chicanery. **3.** to quibble over; cavil at. [1665–75; < F chicane (n.), chicaner (v.), perh. < MLG schikken to arrange] **—chi•can′er,** n.

chi•can•er•y (shi kā′nə rē, chi-), n., pl. **-er•ies.** **1.** trickery or deception by quibbling or sophistry: He resorted to the worst flattery and chicanery to win the job. **2.** a quibble or subterfuge used to trick, deceive, or evade. [1605–15; < F chicanerie. See CHICANE, -ERY]
—Syn. **1.** fraud, deception, knavery. **2.** evasion.

chi•ca•nis•mo (chē′kä nēz′mô; Eng. chē′kä nēz′mō, -niz′mō), n. Spanish. **1.** pride in one's heritage as a Mexican-American. **2.** the heritage, background, culture, etc., of Mexican-Americans.

Chi•ca•no (chi kä′nō, -kan′ō), n., pl. **-nos.** **1.** a Mexican-American. —adj. **2.** of or pertaining to Mexican-Americans or their culture. Cf. **la raza.** [1960–65; < MexSp, by shortening and alter. of mexicano Mexican]

chic•co•ry (chik′ə rē), n., pl. **-ries.** chicory.

chi•cha (chē′chə), n. a beer made from fermented corn in South and Central America. [1750–60; < AmerSp]

Chi•chén It•zá (chē chen′ ēt sä′, ēt′sə), the ruins of an ancient Mayan city, in central Yucatán state, Mexico.

Chi•che•wa (chi chā′wä), n. Chewa (def. 2).

chi•chi (shē′shē′), adj. **1.** showily or affectedly elegant or trendy; pretentious. —n. **2.** a chichi person or thing. **3.** the quality of being chichi. [1905–10; < F]
—Syn. **1.** flashy, ostentatious, flamboyant.

Chi•chi•har (*Chin.* chē′chē′här′), *n. Wade-Giles.* Qiqihar. Also, **Chi′chi′haerh′.**

Chich•i•vache (chich′ə väsh′), *n.* (in early English literature) a mythical animal, usually depicted as a cow verging on starvation, that existed solely by devouring virtuous women. Cf. **Bicorn.** [1350–1400; ME < MF (north) *chichefache* thin face, ugly face, monster (hence *vache* cow, by folk etymology, r. *fache*)]

chick (chik), *n.* **1.** a young chicken or other bird. **2.** a child. **3.** *Slang* (*often offensive*). a girl or young woman. [1275–1325; ME *chike,* var. of *chiken* CHICKEN]

chick•a•dee (chik′ə dē′), *n.* any of several North American birds of the genus *Parus,* of the titmouse family, esp. *P. atricapillus* **(black-capped chickadee),** having the throat and top of the head black. [1820–30; imit.]

black-capped chickadee, *Parus atricapillus,* length 5¼ in. (13 cm)

Chick•a•hom•i•ny (chik′ə hom′ə nē), *n., pl.* **-nies,** (*esp. collectively*) **-ny.** a member of a North American Indian tribe of the Powhatan confederacy that inhabited eastern Virginia.

Chick•a•mau•ga (chik′ə mô′gə), *n.* a creek in NW Georgia: scene of a Confederate victory 1863.

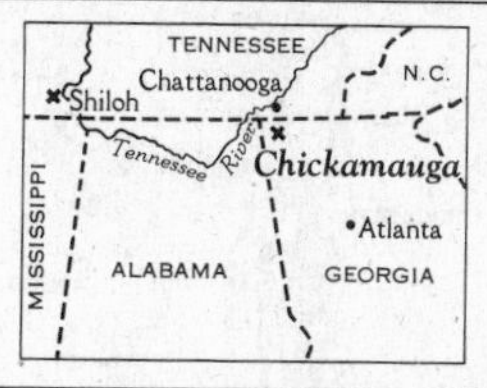

chick•a•ree (chik′ə rē′), *n.* See **red squirrel.** [1795–1805, *Amer.;* imit.]

Chick•a•saw (chik′ə sô′), *n., pl.* **-saws,** (*esp. collectively*) **-saw.** **1.** a member of a tribe of North American Indians, formerly in northern Mississippi, now in Oklahoma. **2.** the Muskogean language of the Chickasaw.

Chick•a•sha (chik′ə shā′), *n.* a city in central Oklahoma. 15,828.

chic•kee (chi kē′, chik′ē), *n.* **1.** Also, **chikee.** (among the Seminole Indians) an open-sided structure, usually thatched with palms and serving as a dwelling. **2.** a similar structure, used to provide shelter from the sun, as at a beach. [< Mikasuki *čikî·* dwelling]

chick•en (chik′ən), *n.* **1.** a domestic fowl, *Gallus domesticus,* descended from various jungle fowl of southeastern Asia and developed in a number of breeds for its flesh, eggs, and feathers. **2.** the young of this bird, esp. when less than a year old. **3.** the flesh of the chicken, esp. of the young bird, used as food. **4.** *Informal.* a young or inexperienced person, esp. a young girl. **5.** *Slang.* **a.** a cowardly or fearful person. **b.** petty details or tasks. **c.** unnecessary discipline or regulations. **d.** a young male homosexual, esp. one sought as a sexual partner by older men. **6.** a contest in which two cars approach each other at high speed down the center of a road, the object being to force one's opponent to veer away first. **7.** a policy or strategy of challenging an opponent to risk a clash or yield: *diplomats playing chicken at the conference table.* **8. count one's chickens before they are hatched,** to rely on a benefit that is still uncertain: *They were already spending in anticipation of their inheritance, counting their chickens before they were hatched.* —*adj.* **9.** (of food) containing, made from, or having the flavor of chicken: *chicken salad; chicken soup.* **10.** *Slang.* **a.** cowardly. **b.** petty or trivial: *a chicken regulation.* **c.** obsessed with petty details, regulations, etc.: *He's quitting this chicken outfit to become his own boss.* —*v.i.* **11. chicken out,** *Slang.* **a.** to refrain from doing something because of fear or cowardice: *I chickened out when I saw how deep the water was.* **b.** to renege or withdraw: *You can't chicken out of this business deal now.* [bef. 950; 1605–15 for def. 5a; 1940–45 for def. 7; ME *chiken,* OE *cicen;* akin to MD *kieken* (D *kuiken*), LG *küken*]

chick′en ad′der, *Chiefly New Eng.* See **milk snake.** [1965–70, *Amer.*]

chick•en-and-egg (chik′ən ən eg′, -ənd-), *adj.* of, pertaining to, or being a dilemma of which of two things came first or of which is the cause and which the effect: *a chicken-and-egg question of whether matter or energy is the basis of the universe.* Also, **chick•en-or-egg** (chik′ən ər eg′). [1955–60]

chick′en breast′, *Pathol.* a congenital or acquired malformation of the chest in which there is abnormal projection of the sternum and the sternal region, often associated with rickets. Also called **pigeon breast.** [1840–50] —**chick′en-breast′ed,** *adj.* —**chick′en-breast′ed•ness,** *n.*

chick′en chol′era, *Vet. Pathol.* See **fowl cholera.** [1880–85]

chick′en colo′nel, *Mil. Slang.* a full colonel, as distinguished from a lieutenant colonel. Also called **bird colonel.** [1945–50, *Amer.*]

chick′en coop′, **1.** a coop for chickens. **2.** *Fox Hunting.* a device for making it easier for a horse to jump wire fences, consisting of two wooden panels set on opposite sides of the fence with the tops of the panels joined at an angle so as to cover the wire. [1780–90]

chick′en feed′, *Slang.* **1.** an insignificant sum of money: *He's so rich that $1000 is chicken feed to him.* **2.** small change, as pennies and nickels. [1830–40, *Amer.*]

chick•en-fry (chik′ən frī′), *v.,* **-fried, -fry•ing,** *n.* —*v.t.* **1.** to dip (meat, vegetables, etc.) in batter and fry, usually in deep fat: *chicken-fried steak.* —*n.* **2.** food or a meal prepared in this way: *He claims to do the best chicken-fry in Texas.*

chick′en hawk′, **1.** Also called **hen hawk.** (not used scientifically) any of various hawks said to prey on poultry. **2.** *Slang.* an older man who seeks out young boys as sexual partners. [1820–30, *Amer.*]

chick•en-heart•ed (chik′ən här′tid), *adj. Informal.* timid; fearful; cowardly. [1675–85, *Amer.*] —**chick′•en-heart′ed•ly,** *adv.* —**chick′en-heart′ed•ness,** *n.*

chick′en Ki′ev, boned chicken breasts rolled around seasoned butter, breaded, and deep-fried.

chick′en lad′der, *Building Trades.* an inclined plank with transverse cleats.

Chick′en Lit′tle, a person who constantly warns that a calamity is imminent; a vociferous pessimist: *The Chicken Littles are warning that the stock market will collapse.* [from a character in nursery tales (also known as Henny Penny, Chicken-Diddle, or Chicken-Licken) who, when struck on the head by an object from above, panics and believes that the sky is falling]

chick•en-liv•ered (chik′ən liv′ərd), *adj. Informal.* timid; fearful; cowardly. [1870–75, *Amer.*]

chick′en lob′ster, a young lobster weighing 1 lb. (0.4 kg) or less. [1965–70, *Amer.*]

chick′en mush′room, an edible yellow-to-orange bracket fungus, *Laetiporus sulphureus,* common on tree trunks, in which it causes wood decay. Also called **sulfur polypore, sulfur shelf.**

chick•en•pox (chik′ən poks′), *n.* a disease, commonly of children, caused by the varicella zoster virus and characterized by mild headache and fever, malaise, and eruption of blisters on the skin and mucous membranes. Also, **chick′en pox′.** Also called **varicella.** [1720–30]

chick•en•shit (chik′ən shit′), *Slang* (*vulgar*). —*n.* **1.** boring or annoying details or unimportant tasks. —*adj.* **2.** obsessed with petty details. **3.** menial or petty. **4.** cowardly or fainthearted. [1945–50; *Amer.*]

chick′en snake′, a striped rat snake, *Elaphe obsoleta,* of the southeastern U.S., reaching a length of 4 to 7 ft. (1.2 to 2.1 m). [1700–10, *Amer.*]

chick′en switch′, *Rocketry Slang.* **1.** a device by which an astronaut may eject the capsule in which he or she rides in the event that a rocket malfunctions. **2.** See **egads button.**

chick′en tet•ra•zi′ni (te′trə zē′nē), diced chicken in a cream sauce, baked in a casserole with noodles and cheese, usually flavored with sherry. [named after Luisa TETRAZZINI]

chick′en tur′tle, an edible, freshwater turtle, *Deirochelys reticularia,* of the southeastern U.S., characterized by a long neck and by the network of fine, yellow lines marking the dark carapace.

chick′en wire′, a light, wire netting having a large, hexagonal mesh, used esp. as fencing. [1915–20, *Amer.*]

chick•pea (chik′pē′), *n.* **1.** Also called **garbanzo.** a widely cultivated plant, *Cicer arietinum,* of the legume family, bearing pods containing pealike seeds. **2.** the seeds of this plant, used extensively as a food. [1540–50; alter. of *chich-pea,* equiv. to late ME *chiche* (< MF << L *cicer* chickpea) + PEA]

chick•weed (chik′wēd′), *n.* **1.** any plant of the genus *Stellaria,* of the pink family, as *S. media,* a common Old World weed whose leaves and seeds are relished by birds. **2.** any of various allied plants. [1325–75; ME *chiken wede.* See CHICK, WEED[1]]

chick′weed win′tergreen, a starflower, *Trientalis borealis.*

Chi•cla•yo (chē klä′yō), *n.* a city in NW Peru. 187,809.

chic•le (chik′əl), *n.* a gumlike substance obtained from the latex of certain tropical American trees, as the sapodilla, used chiefly in the manufacture of chewing gum. Also called **chic′le gum′.** [1860–65, *Amer.;* < MexSp < Nahuatl *tzictli*]

Chic•lets (chik′lits), *Trademark.* a brand of chewing gum made in small, rectangular, sugarcoated lozenges.

chi•co (chē′kō), *n., pl.* **-cos.** greasewood (def. 1). [short for CHICALOTE]

Chi•co (chē′kō), *n.* **1.** a city in central California. 26,601. **2.** a male given name.

Chi•com (chī′kom′), *Disparaging.* —*n.* **1.** a Communist Chinese. —*adj.* **2.** of or pertaining to the People's Republic of China.

Chic•o•pee (chik′ə pē′), *n.* a city in S Massachusetts, on the Connecticut River. 55,112.

chic•o•ry (chik′ə rē), *n., pl.* **-ries.** **1.** a composite plant, *Cichorium intybus,* having bright-blue flower heads and toothed oblong leaves, cultivated as a salad plant and for its root, which is used roasted and ground as a substitute for or additive to coffee. Cf. **endive** (def. 2). **2.** the root of this plant. Also, **chiccory.** [1350–1400; < MF *chicorée,* alter. of earlier *cicoree* (by influence of It *cicoria*) < L *cichorēa* < Gk *kichória, kíchora* (neut. plurals); r. ME *cicoree* < MF]

Chi•cou•ti•mi (shi ko͞o′tə mē; *Fr.* shē ko͞o tē mē′), *n.* a city in S Quebec, in E Canada. 60,064.

Chic Sale (chik′ sāl′), *Facetious.* an outside privy. [from the pen name of Charles Partlow (1885–1936), American actor and author of *The Specialist* (1929), a humorous treatise on outhouse construction]

chide (chīd), *v.,* **chid•ed** or **chid** (chid), **chid•ed** or **chid** or **chid•den** (chid′n), **chid•ing.** —*v.t.* **1.** to express disapproval of; scold; reproach: *The principal chided the children for their thoughtless pranks.* **2.** to harass, nag, impel, or the like by chiding: *She chided him into apologizing.* —*v.i.* **3.** to scold or reproach; find fault. [bef. 1000; ME *chiden,* OE *cīdan*] —**chid′er,** *n.* —**chid′ing•ly,** *adv.*
—**Syn. 1, 3.** reprove, rebuke, censure, upbraid, blame.
—**Ant. 1, 3.** praise.

chief (chēf), *n.* **1.** the head or leader of an organized body of people; the person highest in authority: *the chief of police.* **2.** the head or ruler of a tribe or clan: *an Indian chief.* **3.** (*cap.*) *U.S. Army.* a title of some advisers to the Chief of Staff, who do not, in most instances, command the troop units of their arms or services: *Chief of Engineers; Chief Signal Officer.* **4.** *Informal.* boss or leader: *We'll have to talk to the chief about this.* **5.** *Heraldry.* **a.** the upper area of an escutcheon. **b.** an ordinary occupying this area. **6. in chief, a.** in the chief position; highest in rank (used in combination): *editor in chief; commander in chief.* **b.** *Heraldry.* in the upper part of an escutcheon. —*adj.* **7.** highest in rank or authority: *the chief priest; the chief administrator.* **8.** most important; principal: *his chief merit; the chief difficulty.* —*adv.* **9.** *Archaic.* chiefly; principally. [1250–1300; ME < AF *chief, chef,* OF *chef* < VL **capum,* re-formation of L *caput* HEAD] —**chief′less,** *adj.* —**chief′ship,** *n.*
—**Syn. 8.** foremost, leading, prime, paramount, cardinal. See **capital**[1]. —**Ant. 7.** subordinate.

chief′ con′stable, *Brit.* chief of police.

chief•dom (chēf′dəm), *n.* **1.** the rank or office of a chief. **2.** the territory or people over which a chief rules. [1570–80; CHIEF + -DOM]

Chief′ Exec′utive, **1.** the president of the United States. **2.** (*l.c.*) the governor of a U.S. state. **3.** (*l.c.*) the head of a government. [1825–35, *Amer.*]

chief′ jus′tice, **1.** *Law.* the presiding judge of a court having several members. **2.** (*caps.*) Official title, **Chief′ Jus′tice of the Unit′ed States′.** the presiding judge of the U.S. Supreme Court. See table under **Supreme Court.** [1685–95] —**chief′ jus′tice•ship′.**

chief•ly (chēf′lē), *adv.* **1.** primarily; essentially: *He phoned chiefly to let us know he was feeling better.* **2.** mainly; mostly: *This dish consists chiefly of noodles.* —*adj.* **3.** of, pertaining to, or like a chief: *his chiefly responsibilities.* [1300–50; ME; see CHIEF, -LY]
—**Syn. 1, 2.** See **especially.**

chief′ mas′ter ser′geant, the highest noncommissioned officer rank in the U.S. Air Force. [1955–60]

chief′ mate′, *Naut.* See **first mate.** Also called **chief′ of′ficer.**

Chief′ of Na′val Opera′tions, the highest officer in the U.S. Navy and a member of the Joint Chiefs of Staff. [1910–15]

Chief′ of Staff′, **1.** the senior officer of the U.S. Army or Air Force, a member of the Joint Chiefs of Staff, responsible to the secretary of a service branch. **2.** (*l.c.*) the senior or principal staff officer in a brigade or division or higher unit in the U.S. Army or Marine Corps, in a numbered unit in the U.S. Air Force, or in a unit in the U.S. Navy commanded by a rear admiral or one of higher rank. **3.** (*l.c.*) the senior officer in command of a general staff, esp. that of the military forces of a nation. **4.** (*l.c.*) the head of any staff: *the chief of staff for the First Lady.* [1880–85]

chief′ of state′, the titular head of a nation, as a president or king. [1945–50]

chief′ pet′ty of′ficer, *U.S. Navy and Coast Guard.* a noncommissioned rank above petty officer first class and below senior petty officer. *Abbr.:* CPO, C.P.O., c.p.o. [1885–90, *Amer.*]

chief•tain (chēf′tən, -tin), *n.* **1.** the chief of a clan or a tribe. **2.** a leader of a group, band, etc.: *the robbers' chieftain.* **3.** (*cap.*) *Mil.* Britain's main battle tank since 1969, fitted with a 120mm gun and two machine guns and weighing 55 tons (50 m tons). [1275–1325; ME *cheftayne,* var. of *chevetaine* < OF < LL *capitāneus* CAPTAIN] —**chief′tain•cy, chief′tain•ship′,** *n.*

chief′ war′rant of′ficer, *U.S. Mil.* a warrant officer ranking immediately below a second lieutenant or ensign in the armed forces.

chield (chēld), *n. Scot.* a young man; fellow. Also, **chiel** (chēl). [1525–35; var. of CHILD]

Chieng•mai (*Thai.* chyeng′mī′), *n.* See **Chiang Mai.**

Ch'ien Lung (chyen′ lo͝ong′), (*Kao Tsung*) 1711–99, Chinese emperor of the Ch'ing dynasty 1736–96. Also, **Kien Lung.**

chiff•chaff (chif′chaf′, -chäf′), *n.* a common, greenish Old World warbler, *Phylloscopus collybita.* [1770–80; gradational compound; imit.]

chif•fon (shi fon′, shif′on), *n.* **1.** a sheer fabric of silk, nylon, or rayon in plain weave. **2.** any women's dress ornament, as ribbon or lace. —*adj.* **3.** (of dresses, scarves, etc.) resembling or made of chiffon. **4.** (in cooking) having a light, frothy texture, as certain pies and cakes containing beaten egg whites. [1755–65; < F, equiv. to *chiffe* rag (< Ar *shiff* sheer fabric) + *-on* n. suffix]

chif•fo•nade (shif′ə näd′, -näd′), *adj.* a mixture of finely cut vegetables, herbs, or the like, for use in soups, salads, etc. [1875–80; < F; see CHIFFON, -ADE[1]]

chif•fo•nier (shif′ə nēr′), *n.* **1.** a high chest of drawers or bureau, often having a mirror on top. See illus. on next page. **2.** a low bookcase of the English Regency,

CONCISE PRONUNCIATION KEY: act, cāpe, dâre, pärt; set, ēqual; *if,* ice; ox, ōver, ôrder, oil, bo͝ok, bo͞ot, out; up, ûrge; child; sing; shoe; thin, *th*at; zh as in *treasure.* ə = *a* as in *alone, e* as in *system, i* as in *easily, o* as in *gallop, u* as in *circus;* ᵊ as in *fire* (fīᵊr), *hour* (ouᵊr). l and n can serve as syllabic consonants, as in *cradle* (krād′l), and *button* (but′n). See the full key inside the front cover.

with grille doors or doorless. **3.** a shallow, tall, open piece of furniture, of the 18th century, having shelves for the display of china. Also, **chif′fon·nier′.** [1800–10; < F *chiffonnier.* See CHIFFON, -IER[2]]

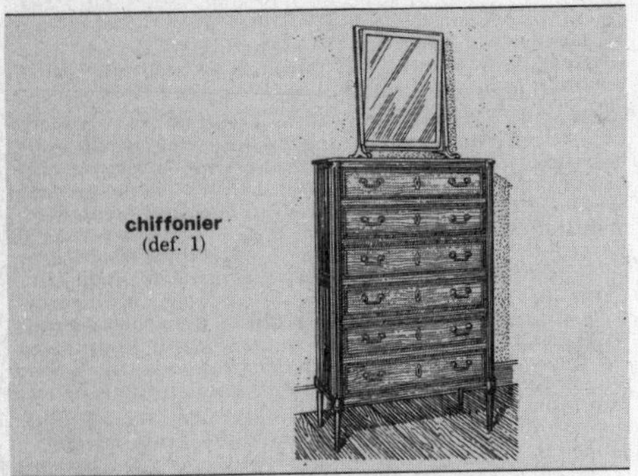
chiffonier (def. 1)

chif·fon·nière (shif′ə nēr′; *Fr.* shē fô nyeʀ′), *n., pl.* **-nières** (-nērz′; *Fr.* -nyeʀ′). *Fr. Furniture.* a worktable of the 18th century, having several tiers of shallow drawers. [1800–10; < F, fem. of *chiffonnier.* See CHIFFONIER]

chif·fo·robe (shif′ə rōb′, shif′rōb′), *n.* a piece of furniture having both drawers and space for hanging clothes. Also, **chif′fe·robe′, chiff·robe** (shif′rōb). [1905–10, *Amer.*; CHIFFO(NIER) + (WARD)ROBE]

Chif·ley (chif′lē), *n.* **Joseph Benedict,** 1885–1951, Australian statesman: prime minister 1945–49.

chig·e·tai (chig′i tī′), *n.* a Mongolian wild ass, *Equus hemionus hemionus,* related to the onager. Also called **dziggetai.** [< Mongolian *chikitei* lit., with ears, eared, deriv. of *chiki(n)* ear]

chig·ger (chig′ər), *n.* **1.** Also called **harvest mite, redbug.** the six-legged larva of a mite of the family Trombiculidae, parasitic on humans and other vertebrates, sucking blood and causing severe itching and acting as a vector of scrub typhus and other infectious diseases. **2.** chigoe. Also, **jigger.** [1735–45, *Amer.*; var. of CHIGOE]

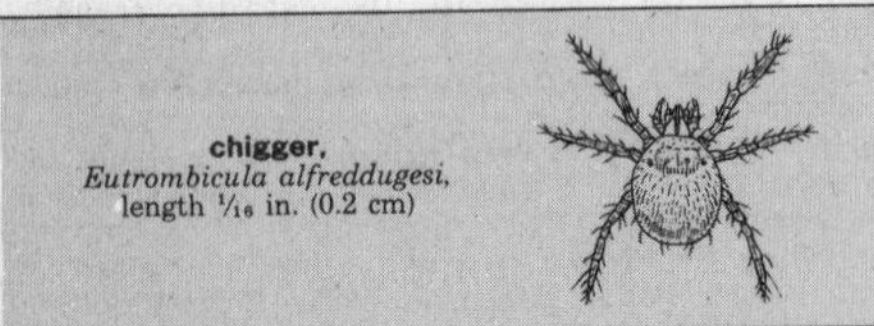
chigger, *Eutrombicula alfreddugesi,* length 1/16 in. (0.2 cm)

chi·gnon (shēn′yon, shēn yun′; *Fr.* shē nyôɴ′), *n., pl.* **chi·gnons** (shēn′yonz, shēn yunz′; *Fr.* shē nyôɴ′). a large, smooth twist, roll, or knot of hair, worn by women at the nape of the neck or the back of the head. [1775–85; < F: nape, roll of hair at nape, b. MF *chaignon* (var. of *chainon* link, equiv. to *chaine* CHAIN + *-on* n. suffix) and *tignon* twist of hair (*tigne* (< L *tinea* worm) + *-on* n. suffix)] **—chi′gnoned,** *adj.*

chig·oe (chig′ō), *n.* a flea, *Tunga penetrans,* of tropical America and Africa, the impregnated female of which embeds itself in the skin, esp. of the feet, of humans and animals and becomes greatly distended with eggs. Also called **chig′oe flea′, chigger, jigger, sand flea.** [1685–95; < Carib]

Chih·li (chē′lē; *Chin.* jœ′lē′), *n. Wade-Giles.* **1.** former name of **Hebei. 2. Gulf of,** former name of **Bohai.**

Chi·hua·hua (chi wä′wä, -wə), *n.* **1.** a state in N Mexico. 2,000,000; 94,831 sq. mi. (245,610 sq. km). **2.** the capital of this state. 386,000. **3.** one of a Mexican or Aztec breed of very small dogs having either short or long hair of any one of a variety of colors.

Chi·ka·ma·tsu (chē′kä mä′tso͞o), *n.* **Mon·za·e·mon** (môn′zä e môn′), 1653–1724, Japanese playwright.

chi·kee (chi kē′, chik′ē), *n.* chickee (def. 1).

chil·blain (chil′blān), *n.* Usually, **chilblains.** *Pathol.* an inflammation of the hands and feet caused by exposure to cold and moisture. Also called **pernio.** [1540–50; CHILL + BLAIN] **—chil′blained,** *adj.*

Chil·cat (chil′kat), *n., pl.* **-cats,** (*esp. collectively*) **-cat.** Chilkat. [1835–45, *Amer.*]

child (chīld), *n., pl.* **chil·dren. 1.** a person between birth and full growth; a boy or girl: *books for children.* **2.** a son or daughter: *All my children are married.* **3.** a baby or infant. **4.** a childish person: *He's such a child about money.* **5.** a descendant: *a child of an ancient breed.* **6.** any person or thing regarded as the product or result of particular agencies, influences, etc. **7.** a person regarded as conditioned or marked by a given circumstance, situation, etc.: *a child of poverty.* **8.** *Brit. Dial. Archaic.* a female infant. **9.** *Archaic.* childe. **10. with child,** pregnant: *She's with child.* [bef. 950; ME; OE *cild;* akin to Goth *kilthai* womb] **—child′less,** *adj.* **—child′less·ness,** *n.*

Child (chīld), *n.* **Lydia Maria (Francis),** 1802–80, U.S. author, abolitionist, and social reformer.

child′ abuse′, mistreatment of a child by a parent or guardian, including neglect, beating, and sexual molestation. [1970–75]

CONCISE ETYMOLOGY KEY: <, descended or borrowed from; >, whence; b., blend of, blended; c., cognate with; cf., compare; deriv., derivative; equiv., equivalent; imit., imitative; obl., oblique; r., replacing; s., stem; sp., spelling, spelled; resp., respelling, respelled; trans., translation; ?, origin unknown; *, unattested; ‡, probably earlier than. See the full key inside the front cover.

child·bat·ter·ing (chīld′bat′ər ing), *n.* the physical abuse of a child by a parent or guardian, as by beating. [1970–75] **—child′-bat′ter·er,** *n.*

child·bear·ing (chīld′bâr′ing), *n.* **1.** the act of producing or bringing forth children. *—adj.* **2.** capable of, suitable for, or relating to the bearing of a child or of children: *the childbearing years.* [1350–1400; ME; see CHILD, BEARING]

child·bed (chīld′bed′), *n.* the circumstance or situation of a woman giving birth to a child; parturition: *to lie in childbed.* [1150–1200; ME; see CHILD, BED]

child′bed fe′ver, *Pathol.* See **puerperal fever.** [1925–30]

child·birth (chīld′bûrth′), *n.* an act or instance of bringing forth a child; parturition: *a difficult childbirth.* [1400–50; late ME; see CHILD, BIRTH]

child′ bride′, a very young bride. [1835–45]

child·care (chīld′kâr′), *n.* **1.** the care or supervision of another's child, esp. at a day-care center. *—adj.* **2.** Also, **child′-care′.** of, pertaining to, or providing childcare. [1910–15; CHILD + CARE]

child′ cus′tody, *Law.* custody (def. 4).

childe (chīld), *n. Archaic.* a youth of noble birth. [sp. var. of CHILD]

Childe (chīld), *n.* **Vere Gordon** (vēr), 1892–1957, English anthropologist, archaeologist, and writer; born in Australia.

Childe′ Har′old's Pil′grimage, a narrative poem (1812, 1816, 1818) by Byron.

Chil·der·mas (chil′dər məs), *n. Chiefly Brit.* See **Holy Innocents' Day.** [bef. 1000; ME *chyldermasse,* equiv. to OE *cildra* (gen. pl. of *cild* CHILD) + *mæsse* MASS]

Childe′ Ro′land to the Dark′ Tow′er Came′, a poem (1855) by Robert Browning.

child·free (chīld′frē′), *adj.* having no children; childless, esp. by choice. [CHILD + -FREE]

child′ guid′ance, the reeducation, therapeutic treatment, or study of children with emotional and behavioral problems, conducted by psychologists, teachers, or other trained specialists. [1925–30]

child·hood (chīld′ho͝od), *n.* **1.** the state or period of being a child. **2.** the early stage in the existence of something: *the childhood of the human race.* [bef. 950; ME *childhode,* OE *cildhād.* See CHILD, -HOOD]

child·ing (chīl′ding), *adj. Archaic.* bearing children; pregnant. [1250–1300; ME; see CHILD, -ING[2]]

child·ish (chīl′dish), *adj.* **1.** of, like, or befitting a child: *childish games.* **2.** puerile; weak; silly: *childish fears.* [bef. 1000; ME *childisch,* OE *cildisc.* See CHILD, -ISH[1]] **—child′ish·ly,** *adv.* **—child′ish·ness,** *n.*
—Syn. CHILDISH, INFANTILE, CHILDLIKE refer to characteristics or qualities of childhood. The ending *-ish* often has unfavorable connotations; CHILDISH therefore refers to characteristics that are undesirable and unpleasant: *childish selfishness, outbursts of temper.* INFANTILE, originally a general word, now often carries an even stronger idea of disapproval or scorn than does CHILDISH: *infantile reasoning, behavior.* The ending *-like* has pleasing or neutral connotations; CHILDLIKE therefore refers to the characteristics that are desirable and admirable: *childlike innocence, trust.* **—Ant.** mature, adult.

child′ la′bor, the gainful employment of children below an age determined by law or custom. [1875–80]

child·like (chīld′līk′), *adj.* like a child, as in innocence, frankness, etc.; befitting a child: *childlike trust.* [1580–90; CHILD + -LIKE] **—child′like′ness,** *n.*
—Syn. young, ingenuous, simple, guileless, trusting, innocent. See **childish. —Ant.** sophisticated, adult.

child·ly (chīld′lē), *adj. Rare.* childlike; childish. [bef. 900; ME *childely,* OE *cildlīc.* See CHILD, -LY]

child·mind·er (chīld′mīn′dər), *n. Brit.* a baby-sitter. [1940–45; CHILD + MIND + -ER[1]]

child·ness (chīld′nis), *n. Archaic.* the quality of being a child. [1605–15; CHILD + -NESS]

child′ pornog′raphy, pornography using a child or children as the subject.

child·proof (chīld′pro͞of′), *adj.* **1.** resistant to being opened, tampered with, or operated by a child: *a childproof medicine bottle.* **2.** made free of hazard for a child: *a childproof home.* **3.** made safe from damage by children: *a childproof living room free of breakable objects.* *—v.t.* **4.** to make childproof: *to childproof a home.* Also, **child-proof.** [1955–60; CHILD + -PROOF]

child′ psychi′atry, 1. the branch of psychiatry specializing in the treatment of children. **2.** psychiatric techniques used in therapy for children.

child′ psychol′ogy, 1. the study of the mental states and processes of children. **2.** the application of psychological techniques to children. [1895–1900]

chil·dren (chil′drən), *n.* pl. of **child.**

Chil′dren of God′, a highly disciplined, fundamentalist Christian sect, active esp. in the early 1970's, whose mostly young converts live in communes.

Chil′dren of Her′cules, Heraclidae.

chil′dren of Is′rael, the Hebrews; Jews.

Chil′dren's Crusade′, a crusade to recover Jerusalem from the Saracens, undertaken in 1212 by thousands of French and German children who perished, were sold into slavery, or were turned back.

Chil′dren's Day′, the second Sunday in June, celebrated by Protestant churches with special programs for children: first started in the U.S. in 1868.

Chil′dren's Hour′, The, a play (1934) by Lillian Hellman.

child-re·sist·ant (chīld′ri zis′tənt), *adj.* that resists being opened, tampered with, or damaged by a child; childproof: *a child-resistant medicine cabinet.* [1970–75]

child's′ play′, something very easily done. [1350–1400; ME]

child′ support′, money paid for the care of one's minor child, esp. payments to a divorced spouse or a guardian under a decree of divorce.

child′ wel′fare, social work aimed at improving the lives of disadvantaged children. [1905–10]

child′ wife′, a very young wife. [1835–45]

chil·e (chil′ē), *n.* chili.

Chil·e (chil′ē; *Sp.* chē′le), *n.* a republic in SW South America, on the Pacific Coast. 10,800,000; 286,396 sq. mi. (741,765 sq. km). *Cap.:* Santiago. **—Chil′e·an,** *adj., n.*

Chil′ean gua′va, a tropical shrub or small tree, *Ugni molinae,* of the myrtle family, having leathery, oval leaves, rose-pink flowers, and blue-black, edible fruit. [1955–60]

Chil·e-bells (chil′ē belz′), *n., pl.* **-bells.** (*used with a singular or plural v.*) a vine, *Lapageria rosea,* native to Chile, having leathery evergreen leaves and showy red-dish flowers: the national flower of Chile. Also called **Chil′ean bell′flower, copihue.**

chil·e con car·ne (chil′ē kon kär′nē; *Sp.* chē′le kôn kär′ne). See **chili con carne.**

chil′e rel·le′no (rə yā′nō, rəl yā′-; *Sp.* ʀe ye′nô), *pl.* **chil·es rel·le·nos** (-nōz, -nōs). a green chili pepper stuffed with cheese or meat, dipped in batter, and fried. [1890–95, *Amer.*; < MexSp: stuffed chili pepper]

Chil′e salt′peter. *Mineral.* See **soda niter.** [1870–75]

chil·i (chil′ē), *n., pl.* **chil·ies. 1.** Also called **chili pepper.** the pungent pod of any of several species of *Capsicum,* esp. *C. annuum longum:* used in cooking for its pungent flavor. **2.** See **chili con carne. 3.** a meatless version of chili con carne. Also, **chile, chilli.** [1655–65; < MexSp *chile* < Nahuatl *chīlli* chili pepper]

chil·i·ad (kil′ē ad′), *n.* **1.** a group of 1000. **2.** a period of 1000 years. [1590–1600; < LL *chiliad-* (s. of *chīlias*) < Gk, equiv. to *chīli(oi)* 1000 + *-ad-* -AD[1]] **—chil′i·ad′·al, chil′i·ad′ic,** *adj.*

chil·i·arch (kil′ē ärk′), *n.* (in ancient Greece) the military commander of 1000 men. [1650–60; < L *chiliarchēs* (or *chiliarchus*) < Gk *chiliárchēs* (or *chiliárchos*), equiv. to *chīli(oi)* 1000 + *-archēs* (or *-archos*) -ARCH] **—chil′i·arch′y,** *n.*

chil·i·asm (kil′ē az′əm), *n. Theol.* the doctrine of Christ's expected return to reign on earth for 1000 years; millennialism. [1600–10; < Gk *chiliasmós,* equiv. to *chīli(oi)* 1000 + *-asmos,* var. of *-ismos* -ISM before stems ending in *-i-*] **—chil·i·ast** (kil′ē ast′), *n.* **—chil′i·as′·tic,** *adj.*

chil·i·burg·er (chil′ē bûr′gər), *n.* a hamburger served with a topping of chili con carne. [CHILI + -BURGER]

chil·i con car·ne (chil′ē kon kär′nē), a Mexican-style dish made with chilies or chili powder, ground or diced beef, and usually kidney beans and tomatoes. Also, **chile con carne.** Also called **chile, chili, chilli.** [< Sp *chile con carne* chili with meat]

chil′i dog′, a frankfurter garnished with chili con carne. Also, **chil′i·dog′.** [1970–75, *Amer.*]

Chi·lien Shan (*Chin.* chē′lyen′ shän′), *Wade-Giles.* See **Qilian Shan.**

Chi·lin (*Chin.* jē′lin′), *n. Wade-Giles.* Jilin.

chil′i oil′, an edible oil spiced with chili peppers, often used in Chinese cookery.

chil′i pep′per, chili (def. 1).

chil·i·pep·per (chil′ē pep′ər), *n.* an edible, crimson rockfish, *Sebastes goodei,* of coastal waters off California. [CHILI + PEPPER]

chil′i pow′der, a powdered mixture of dried chilies, cumin, oregano, garlic, etc., used as a seasoning.

chil′i sauce′, a sauce made of tomatoes simmered with chili peppers and spices. [1880–85, *Amer.*]

chil′is relle′nos, *Mexican Cookery.* green chili peppers, stuffed usually with white cheese, tomato sauce, and sometimes meat. [1890–95, *Amer.*; < MexSp *chiles rellenos* stuffed chili peppers]

chi·li ver·de (chil′ē vâr′dē, -dā, vûr′-; *Sp.* chē′lē beʀ′the), *Southwest Cookery.* a stew of beef or pork, or both, flavored with hot green peppers. [< AmerSp *chile verde* green chili pepper]

Chil·kat (chil′kat), *n., pl.* **-kats,** (*esp. collectively*) **-kat.** a member of an Indian people of the Pacific coastal area of southeastern Alaska belonging to the Tlingit group of Indians. Also, **Chilcat.**

Chil′koot Pass′ (chil′ko͞ot), a mountain pass on the boundary between SE Alaska and British Columbia, Canada, in the Coast Range. ab. 3500 ft. (1065 m) high.

chill (chil), *n.* **1.** coldness, esp. a moderate but uncomfortably penetrating coldness: *the chill of evening.* **2.** a sensation of cold, usually with shivering: *She felt a slight chill from the open window.* **3.** a feeling of sudden fear, anxiety, or alarm. **4.** sudden coldness of the body, as during the cold stage of an ague: *fevers and chills.* **5.** a depressing influence or sensation: *His presence cast a chill over everyone.* **6.** lack of warmth of feeling; unfriendliness; coolness. **7.** *Foundry.* an inserted object or a surface in a mold capable of absorbing large amounts of heat, used to harden the surface of a casting or to increase its rate of solidification at a specific point. **8.** bloom[1] (def. 10). —*adj.* **9.** moderately cold; tending to cause shivering; chilly: *a chill wind.* **10.** shivering with or affected by cold; chilly. **11.** depressing or discouraging: *chill prospects.* **12.** *Slang.* cool (def. 14). **13.** unduly formal; unfriendly; chilly: *a chill reception.* —*v.i.* **14.** to become cold: *The earth chills when the sun sets.* **15.** to be seized with a chill; shiver with cold or fear. **16.** *Foundry.* (of a casting) to become hard on the surface by contact with a chill or chills. —*v.t.* **17.** to affect with cold; make chilly: *The rain has chilled me to the bone.* **18.** to make cool: *Chill the wine before serving.* **19.** to depress; discourage; deter: *The news chilled his hopes.* **20.** *Foundry.* to harden the surface of (a casting) by casting it in a mold having a chill or chills. **21.** bloom[1] (def. 19). **22.** *Slang.* to kill; murder. **23. chill out,** *Slang.* to calm down; relax. [bef. 900; ME *chile,* OE *ci(e)le, cele* coolness; akin to GELID, COOL, COLD] —**chill′·ing·ly,** *adv.* —**chill′ness,** *n.*
—**Syn. 9.** See **cold. 13.** cold, aloof, hostile, stiff.

Chi·llán (chē yän′), *n.* a city in central Chile: earthquakes 1835, 1939. 102,210.

chill′ bumps′, *South Midland and Southern U.S.* goose flesh. [1955–60, *Amer.*]

chill·er (chil′ər), *n.* **1.** a person or thing that chills. **2.** *Informal.* a frightening or suspenseful story or film; melodrama. **3.** a device for cooling or refrigerating. [1790–1800; CHILL + -ER[1]]

chill·er-dill·er (chil′ər dil′ər), *n. Informal.* chiller (def. 2). [rhyming compound based on CHILLER; *d-* perh. from DILLY]

chill′ fac′tor, *Meteorol.* See **windchill factor.** [1960–65]

chil·li (chil′ē), *n., pl.* **-lies.** chili.

Chil·li·coth·e (chil′ə koth′ē), *n.* a city in S Ohio. 23,420.

chill·ing (chil′ing), *adj.* causing or likely to cause a chill: *the chilling effect of the high unemployment rate.* [CHILL + -ING[2]]

Chil·lon (shə lon′, shil′ən; *Fr.* shē yôN′), *n.* an ancient castle in W Switzerland, at the end of Lake Geneva.

chil·lum (chil′əm), *n.* **1.** the part of a hookah that contains the tobacco, marijuana, or other substance being smoked. **2.** the substance that is smoked. **3.** a hookah or other water pipe adapted for smoking marijuana, that can be passed in ritual fashion among a group of participants: used esp. by Rastafarians. [1775–85; < Hindi *cilam*]

Chil·lum (chil′əm), *n.* a city in central Maryland, near Washington, D.C. 32,775.

chill·y (chil′ē), *adj.,* **chill·i·er, chill·i·est,** *adv.* —*adj.* **1.** mildly cold or producing a sensation of cold; causing shivering; chill: *a chilly breeze.* **2.** feeling cold; sensitive to cold: *Her hands were chilly.* **3.** without warmth of feeling; cool: *a chilly reply.* **4.** producing or likely to produce a feeling of fear; frightening: *He told a chilly story of ghosts and murder.* —*adv.* **5.** Also, **chill′i·ly.** in a chill manner: *The wind blew chilly.* [1560–70; CHILL + -Y[1]] —**chill′i·ness,** *n.*
—**Syn. 1.** See **cold.**

chilo-[1], a combining form meaning "lip," used in the formation of compound words: *chiloplasty.* Also, **cheilo-.** [comb. form of Gk *cheîlos* lip]

chilo-[2], var. of **kilo-:** *chilopod.*

Chi·lo·e′ Is′land (chil′ō ā′; *Sp.* chē′lô e′), an island off the SW coast of Chile. 4700 sq. mi. (12,175 sq. km).

chi·log·nath (kī′ləg nath′), *n.* any member of the diplopod subclass Chilognatha, including millipedes having exoskeletons heavily sclerotized with calcium carbonate. [< NL *Chilognatha* subclass name, equiv. to Gk *cheilo-* CHILO-[1] + *-gnatha,* neut. pl. of *-gnathos* -GNATHOUS] —**chi·log·na·than** (kī log′nə thən), *n., adj.* —**chi·log′na·thous,** *adj.*

chi·lom·o·nad (kī lom′ə nad′), *n.* any of the colorless protozoalike algae of the genus *Chilomonas* (phylum Cryptophyta), chiefly saprozoic flagellates found in fresh waters that have become stagnant: popular in laboratory studies. [< NL *chilomonad-,* s. of CHILOMONAS]

Chi·lom·on·as (kī lom′ə nəs), *n.* a genus of flagellate algae comprising the chilomonads. [< NL, equiv. to *chilo-*[1] CHILO- + Gk *monás* (gen. *monádos*) unit; see MONAD]

Chi·lon (kī′lon), *n.* fl. 556 B.C., Greek sage and ephor at Sparta. Also, **Chi·lo** (kī′lō).

chi·lo·plas·ty (kī′lə plas′tē), *n., pl.* **-ties.** *Surg.* cheiloplasty.

chi·lo·pod (kī′lə pod′), *n.* any arthropod of the class Chilopoda, comprising the centipedes. [1820–30; < NL *Chilopoda;* see CHILO-, -POD] —**chi·lop·o·dous** (kī lop′ə dəs), *adj.*

Chil·pan·cin·go (chēl′pän sēng′gô), *n.* a city in and the capital of Guerrero, in SW Mexico. 56,904.

Chil′tern Hun′dreds (chil′tərn), *Brit.* **1.** certain crown lands, the stewardship of which is nominally bestowed on a member of the House of Commons to provide an excuse to resign, as members are not allowed to hold titular office from the crown. **2. to apply for the Chiltern Hundreds,** to resign or express a desire to resign from the House of Commons.

Chi·lu·ba (chi lo͞o′bə), *n.* Luba (def. 2).

Chi·lung (chē′lo͝ong′), *n. Wade-Giles.* a seaport on the N coast of Taiwan. 363,000. Also, **Jilong, Keelung.**

chi·mae·ra (ki mēr′ə, kī-), *n.* **1.** any fish of the family Chimaeridae, the male of which has a spiny clasping organ over the mouth. **2.** any similar fish of the group Holocephali, which includes this family. **3.** chimera. [1795–1805; see CHIMERA]

chim·ar (chim′ər, shim′-), *n.* chimere.

chimb (chīm), *n.* chime[2].

Chim·bo·ra·zo (chim′bə rä′zō, -rā′-; *Sp.* chēm′bô-rä′sô), *n.* a volcano in central Ecuador, in the Andes. 20,702 ft. (6310 m).

Chim·bo·te (chim bō′tē; *Sp.* chēm bô′te), *n.* a city in NW Peru, on the W coast at the mouth of the Santa River. 159,045.

chime[1] (chīm), *n., v.,* **chimed, chim·ing.** —*n.* **1.** an apparatus for striking a bell so as to produce a musical sound, as one at the front door of a house by which visitors announce their presence. **2.** Often, **chimes. a.** a set of bells or of slabs of metal, stone, wood, etc., producing musical tones when struck. **b.** a musical instrument consisting of such a set, esp. a glockenspiel. **c.** the musical tones thus produced. **d.** carillon. **3.** harmonious sound in general; music; melody. **4.** harmonious relation; accord: *the battling duo, in chime at last.* —*v.i.* **5.** to sound harmoniously or in chimes, as a set of bells: *The church bells chimed at noon.* **6.** to produce a musical sound by striking a bell, gong, etc.; ring chimes: *The doorbell chimed.* **7.** to speak in cadence or singsong. **8.** to harmonize; agree: *The scenery chimed perfectly with the play's eerie mood.* —*v.t.* **9.** to give forth (music, sound, etc.), as a bell or bells. **10.** to strike (a bell, set of bells, etc.) so as to produce musical sound. **11.** to put, bring, indicate, announce, etc., by chiming: *Bells chimed the hour.* **12.** to utter or repeat in cadence or singsong: *The class chimed a greeting to the new teacher.* **13. chime in, a.** to break suddenly and unwelcomely into a conversation, as to express agreement or voice an opinion. **b.** to harmonize with, as in singing. **c.** to be consistent or compatible; agree: *The new building will not chime in with the surrounding architecture.* [1250–1300; ME *chymbe belle,* by false analysis of **chimbel,* OE *cimbal* CYMBAL] —**chim′er,** *n.*

chime[2] (chīm), *n.* the edge or brim of a cask, barrel, or the like, formed by the ends of the staves projecting beyond the head or bottom. Also, **chimb, chine.** [1350–1400; ME *chimb(e);* cf. OE *cimbing* chime; c. MLG, MD *kimme* edge]

chime′ hoop′, a hoop used to secure the chimes of a barrel.

chi·me·ra (ki mēr′ə, kī-), *n., pl.* **-ras. 1.** (*often cap.*) a mythological, fire-breathing monster, commonly represented with a lion's head, a goat's body, and a serpent's tail. **2.** any similarly grotesque monster having disparate parts, esp. as depicted in decorative art. **3.** a horrible or unreal creature of the imagination; a vain or idle fancy: *He is far different from the chimera your fears have made of him.* **4.** *Genetics.* an organism composed of two or more genetically distinct tissues, as an organism that is partly male and partly female, or an artificially produced individual having tissues of several species. Also, **chimaera.** [1350–1400; ME *chimera* < L *chimaera* < Gk *chímaira* she-goat; akin to ON *gymbr,* E *gimmer* ewe-lamb one year (i.e., one winter) old, L *hiems* winter (see HIEMAL), Gk *cheimṓn* winter]
—**Syn. 3.** dream, fantasy, delusion.

chi·mere (chi mēr′, shi-), *n.* a loose upper robe, esp. of a bishop, to which the lawn sleeves are usually attached. Also, **chimar, chim·er** (chim′ər, shim′-). [1325–75; ME *chemer, chymere* < AL *chimēra,* special use of CHIMERA]

chi·mer·i·cal (ki mer′i kəl, -mēr′-, kī-), *adj.* **1.** unreal; imaginary; visionary: *a chimerical terrestrial paradise.* **2.** wildly fanciful; highly unrealistic: *a chimerical plan.* Also, **chi·mer′ic.** [1630–40; CHIMER(A) + -ICAL] —**chi·mer′i·cal·ly,** *adv.*
—**Syn. 1.** illusory, fantastic. —**Ant. 1.** real.

chi·mi·chan·ga (chim′ē chäng′gə; *Sp.* chē′mē-chäng′gä), *n., pl.* **-gas** (-gəz; *Sp.* -gäs). *Mexican Cookery.* a crisp, often deep-fried tortilla containing a spicy filling of pork, chicken, etc., usually served as an appetizer with sour cream, green chili sauce, melted cheese, etc. [< MexSp (Veracruz, Tabasco) *chimichanga, chivichanga* trinket, trifle; of unexplained orig.]

Chim·kent (chim kent′; *Russ.* chyim kyent′), *n.* a city in S Kazakhstan, N of Tashkent. 321,000.

chim·ney (chim′nē), *n., pl.* **-neys,** *v.,* **-neyed, -ney·ing.** —*n.* **1.** a structure, usually vertical, containing a passage or flue by which the smoke, gases, etc., of a fire or furnace are carried off and by means of which a draft is created. **2.** the part of such a structure that rises above a roof. **3.** *Now Rare.* the smokestack or funnel of a locomotive, steamship, etc. **4.** a tube, usually of glass, surrounding the flame of a lamp to promote combustion and keep the flame steady. **5.** *Geol.* **a.** the vent of a volcano. **b.** a narrow vertical fissure between two rock faces or in a rock formation. **6.** *Mining.* a nearly vertical cylindrical oreshoot. **7.** *Brit. Dial.* fireplace. —*v.t.* **8.** *Mountain Climbing.* to ascend or descend (a chimney) by repeated bracing of one's feet or back and feet against opposite walls. —*v.i.* **9.** *Mountain Climbing.* to ascend or descend a chimney. [1300–50; ME *chimenai* < MF *cheminee* < L (*camera*) *camīnāta* (room) having a fireplace, equiv. to *camīn(us)* (< Gk *káminos* furnace) + *-āta* -ATE[1]] —**chim′ney·less,** *adj.* —**chim′ney·like′,** *adj.*

chim′ney breast′, a part of a chimney or fireplace that projects out from the wall, usually inside the building. [1835–45]

chim′ney cap′, a raised cover for the top of a chimney, usually in the form of a slab or cornice. [1840–50; *Amer.*]

chim′ney cor′ner, 1. the corner or side of a fireplace. **2.** a place near the fire. **3.** fireside; hearth. [1570–80]

chim′ney piece′, 1. *Chiefly Brit.* mantelpiece. **2.** *Obs.* a decoration over a fireplace. [1605–15]

chim′ney place′, an open hearth.

chim′ney pot′, *Chiefly Brit.* an earthenware or metal pipe or deflector, often cylindrical, fitted on the top of a chimney to increase draft and reduce or disperse smoke. [1820–30]

chim′ney-pot hat′ (chim′nē pot′), *Brit.* a high silk hat; top hat. [1850–55]

chim′ney rock′, a column of rock rising above the level of the surrounding area or isolated on the face of a steep slope. [1840–50, *Amer.*]

chim′ney swal′low, 1. *Brit.* See **barn swallow. 2.** See **chimney swift.** [1765–75]

chim′ney sweep′, a person whose business it is to clean out chimneys. Also, **chim′ney sweep′er.** [1605–15]

chim′ney swift′, an American swift, *Chateura pelagica,* which often builds its nest in an unused chimney. [1840–50]

chim′ney wheel′, smokejack.

chimp (chimp), *n. Informal.* chimpanzee. [1875–80; by shortening]

chim·pan·zee (chim′pan zē′, chim pan′zē), *n.* a large, somewhat arboreal anthropoid ape, *Pan troglodytes,* of equatorial Africa, having a brown-to-black coat, a relatively hairless face with a rounded muzzle, prominent ears, and hands adapted for knuckle-walking, noted for its intelligence and humanlike behavior: now greatly reduced in number and threatened with extinction in the wild. Cf. **pygmy chimpanzee.** [1730–40; presumably < a Bantu language of the Atlantic coast]

chimpanzee,
Pan troglodytes,
height about 4 ft. (1.2 m)

Chi·mu (chē mo͞o′), *n., pl.* **-mus,** (*esp. collectively*) **-mu.** —*n.* **1.** a member of an Amerindian people inhabiting the northern coast of Peru and having a highly developed urban culture that lasted until its destruction by the Incas. **2.** the language of this people. —*adj.* **3.** of, pertaining to, or characteristic of the Chimu, their language, or their culture.

chin (chin), *n., v.,* **chinned, chin·ning.** —*n.* **1.** the lower extremity of the face, below the mouth. **2.** the prominence of the lower jaw. **3.** *Informal.* chin-up. **4. keep one's chin up,** to maintain a cheerful disposition in spite of difficulties, disappointments, etc. Also, **chin up. 5. take it on the chin,** *Informal.* **a.** to suffer defeat; fail completely. **b.** to endure suffering or punishment. —*v.t.* **6.** *Gymnastics.* **a.** to bring one's chin up to (a horizontal bar, from which one is hanging by the hands), by bending the elbows. **b.** to raise (oneself) to this position. **7.** to raise or hold to the chin, as a violin. **8.** *Archaic.* to talk to; chatter with. —*v.i.* **9.** *Gymnastics.* to chin oneself. **10.** *Slang.* to talk; chatter: *We sat up all night chinning about our college days.* [bef. 1000; ME; OE *cin(n);* c. D *kin,* G *Kinn* chin, ON *kinn,* Goth *kinnus* cheek, L *gena,* Gk *génus* chin, *gnáthos* jaw (see GENIAL[2], -GNATHOUS), Skt *hanus* jaw] —**chin′less,** *adj.*

Chin (jin), *n.* **1.** Also, **Tsin.** any of three dynasties that ruled in China, A.D. 265–316 (the Western Chin), A.D. 317–420 (the Eastern Chin), and A.D. 936–46 (the Later Chin). **2.** a dynasty that ruled in China 1115–1234. Also, **Jin.**

ch'in (chin; *Chin.* chēn), *n.* a Chinese zither consisting of an oblong, slightly curved wooden box over which are stretched strings that are stopped with one hand and plucked with the other. [< Chin (Wade-Giles) *ch'in*[2], (Pinyin) *qín*]

Ch'in (chin; *Chin.* chēn), *n.* a dynasty in ancient China, 221–206 B.C., marked by the emergence of a unified empire and the construction of much of the Great Wall of China. Also, **Qin.**

Chin., 1. China. **2.** Chinese. Also, **Chin**

chi•na (chī′nə), *n.* **1.** a translucent ceramic material, biscuit-fired at a high temperature, its glaze fired at a low temperature. **2.** any porcelain ware. **3.** plates, cups, saucers, etc., collectively. **4.** figurines made of porcelain or ceramic material, collectively: *a collection of china.* **5.** *Chiefly Midland and Southern U.S.* a playing marble of china, or sometimes of porcelain or glass. —*adj.* **6.** made of china. **7.** indicating the twentieth event of a series, as a wedding anniversary. See table under **wedding anniversary.** [1645–55; by ellipsis from CHINAWARE]

Chi•na (chī′nə), *n.* **1. People's Republic of,** a country in E Asia. 1,008,175,288; 3,691,502 sq. mi. (9,560,990 sq. km). *Cap.:* Beijing. **2. Republic of.** Also called **Nationalist China.** a republic consisting mainly of the island of Taiwan off the SE coast of mainland China: under Nationalist control since 1948 but claimed by the People's Republic of China. 16,100,000; 13,885 sq. mi. (35,960 sq. km). *Cap.:* Taipei. See map above.

Chi′na as′ter, an asterlike composite plant, *Callistephus chinensis,* cultivated in numerous varieties having white, yellow, blue, red, or purple flowers. [1810–20]

China aster, *Callistephus chinensis*

chi′na bark′ (kī′nə, kē′nə), cinchona (def. 1).

chi•na•ber•ry (chī′nə ber′ē), *n., pl.* **-ries.** a tree, *Melia azedarach,* of the mahogany family, native to Asia but widely planted elsewhere for its ornamental yellow fruits and long clusters of fragrant purplish flowers. Also called **chi′naberry tree′, China tree.** [1885–90, *Amer.;* CHINA + BERRY]

chi′na blue′, a bright greenish blue. Also, **Chi′na blue′.** [1865–70]

chi′na clay′, kaolin. [1830–40]

chi′na clos′et, a cabinet or cupboard for storing or exhibiting chinaware. Also, **chi′na cab′inet.** [1765–75]

Chi′na grass′ cloth′. See **grass cloth.** [1875–80]

Chi•na•man (chī′nə mən), *n., pl.* **-men. 1.** *Usually Offensive.* a Chinese or a person of Chinese descent. **2.** (*l.c.*) a person who imports or sells china. **3.** (*often l.c.*) *Political Slang.* a person regarded as one's benefactor, sponsor, or protector: *to see one's chinaman about a favor.* **4. a Chinaman's chance,** *Usually Offensive.* the slightest chance: *He hasn't a Chinaman's chance of getting that job.* [1765–75; CHINA + -MAN]

Chi•nan (*Chin.* jē′nän′), *n. Wade-Giles.* Jinan.

Chi•nan•de•ga (chē′nän de′gä), *n.* a city in W Nicaragua. 36,885.

Chi′na oil′. See **Peru balsam.**

Chi′na rose′, 1. Also called **Bengal rose.** a rose, *Rosa chinensis,* of China, having slightly fragrant crimson, pink, or white flowers. **2.** Also called **Chinese hibiscus, rose of China.** a tropical Asian shrub, *Hibiscus rosa-sinensis,* of the mallow family, having showy, usually rose-red flowers. [1725–35]

Chi′na Sea′, the East China Sea and the South China Sea, taken together.

Chi′na silk′, a lightweight silk fabric constructed in plain weave, often used for linings, blouses, slips, etc. [1605–15]

Chi′na syn′drome, a hypothetical nuclear-reactor accident in which the fuel would melt through the floor of the containment structure and burrow into the earth. [1970–75; from the jocular notion that the hot reactor core would pass through to the other side of the earth]

Chi•na•town (chī′nə toun′), *n.* the main Chinese district in any city outside China. [CHINA + TOWN]

Chi′na tree′, chinaberry.

chi•na•ware (chī′nə wâr′), *n.* dishes, ornaments, etc., made of china. [1625–35; CHINA + WARE[1]; r. *Cheney ware,* prob. < Hindi < Pers *chīnī* Chinese]

Chi′na White′, *Slang.* a very potent form of synthetic heroin.

chin•beak (chin′bēk′), *n. Archit.* a molding having a convex upper surface and a concave lower one, with a fillet between them; beak. [CHIN + BEAK]

chin•bone (chin′bōn′), *n.* the anterior portion of the mandible, forming the prominence of the chin. [bef. 1000; ME, OE. See CHIN, BONE]

chin′ cac′tus, any of various globular cacti of the genus *Gymnocalycium,* native to South America, having white or pinkish flowers and a chinlike protrusion below each cluster of spines.

chin•ca•pin (ching′kə pin), *n.* chinquapin.

chinch (chinch), *n.* **1.** See **chinch bug. 2.** (loosely) a bedbug. [1615–25; < Sp *chinche* < L *cimic-* (s. of *cimex*) bug]

chinch′ bug′, a small lygaeid bug, *Blissus leucopterus,* that feeds on corn, wheat, and other grains. [1775–85, *Amer.*]

chin•che•rin•chee (chin′chə rin chē′, -rin′chē, ching′kə-), *n.* a bulbous plant, *Ornithogalum thyrsoides,* of the lily family, native to southern Africa, having dense clusters of cream-colored or white flowers. [1925–30; < Afrik *tjienkerientjee,* perh. *tjienker-* (< ?) + *-uintjie* name for various edible bulbs (cf. *uietjie,* dim. of *ui* onion); often alleged to be imit. representation of the sound produced when the stalks are rubbed together]

chinchilla, *Chinchilla laniger,* head and body to 14 in. (35.6 cm); tail to 6 in. (15 cm)

chin•chil•la (chin chil′ə), *n.* **1.** a small, South American rodent, *Chinchilla laniger,* raised for its soft, silvery gray fur: now rare in the wild. **2.** the fur of this animal. **3.** something, as a coat or jacket, made of chinchilla fur: *a floor-length chinchilla.* **4.** a thick, napped, woolen fabric for coats. [1595–1605; < Sp, perh., equiv. to *chinche* CHINCH + *-illa* < L *-illa* dim. suffix]

chin-chin (chin′chin′), *n., v.,* **-chinned, -chin•ning,** *interj.* —*n.* **1.** polite and ceremonious speech. **2.** light conversation; chitchat. —*v.i.* **3.** to speak politely and ceremoniously. **4.** to talk casually and lightly; chat. —*interj.* **5.** (used as a greeting or farewell.) **6.** (used as a toast, as in drinking to someone's health.) [1785–95; < Chin *qǐng-qǐng* please-please]

Chin•chow (*Chin.* jin′jō′), *n. Older Spelling.* Jinzhou.

chinch•y (chin′chē), *adj.,* **chinch•i•er, chinch•i•est.** *Chiefly Midland and Southern U.S.* stingy; miserly; cheap. [1400–50; late ME, deriv. of *chinche* (n. and adj.) < OF *chinche, chiche* < VL **ciccus* for L *ciccum* a bagatelle; see -Y[1]]

Chin•co•teague (shing′kə tēg′, ching′-), *n.* a town on a small island in a lagoon (**Chin′coteague Bay′**) in E Virginia: annual wild pony roundup. 1607.

Chin′coteague po′ny, a wild pony found on certain islands off the Virginia coast, apparently descended from Moorish ponies shipwrecked in this vicinity in the 16th century. [after *Chincoteague* Island, off the Virginia coast]

Chin•dwin (chin′dwin′), *n.* a river in N Burma, flowing S to the Irrawaddy River. 550 mi. (885 km) long.

chine[1] (chīn), *n. Brit. Dial.* a ravine formed in rock by the action of running water. [bef. 900; ME; OE *cinu* crevice, fissure; c. MD *kene;* cf. OE *cīnan* to gape, crack open]

chine[2] (chīn), *n., v.,* **chined, chin•ing.** —*n.* **1.** the backbone or spine, esp. of an animal. **2.** the whole or a piece of the backbone of an animal with adjoining parts, cut for cooking. **3.** a ridge or crest, as of land. **4.** *Naut.* **a.** an angular intersection of the sides and bottom of a vessel. **b.** a longitudinal member running behind this. —*v.t.* **5.** (in butchering) to sever the backbone of. [1250–1300; ME *eschine* < OF *eschine* < Gmc. See SHIN]

chine[3] (chīn), *n.* chime[2].

chi•né (shē nā′), *adj.* noting or pertaining to a fabric having a variegated pattern produced by warp threads that have been dyed, printed, or painted before weaving. [1850–55; < F, ptp. of *chiner,* v. deriv. of *Chine* China]

Chi•nese (chī nēz′, -nēs′), *n., pl.* **-nese,** *adj.* —*n.* **1.** the standard language of China, based on the speech of Beijing; Mandarin. **2.** a group of languages of the Sino-Tibetan family, including standard Chinese and most of the other languages of China. *Abbr.:* Chin., Chin **3.** any of the Chinese languages, which vary among themselves to the point of mutual unintelligibility. **4.** a native or descendant of a native of China. —*adj.* **5.** of or pertaining to China, its inhabitants, or one of their languages. **6.** noting or pertaining to the partly logographic, partly phonetic script used for the writing of Chinese, Japanese, and other languages, consisting of thousands of brushstroke characters written in vertical columns from right to left. [1570–80; CHIN(A) + -ESE]

Chi′nese an′ise. See **star anise.**

Chi′nese ar′tichoke, a hairy plant, *Stachys affinis,* of China and Japan, having numerous small, white, edible tubers. Also called **chorogi, Japanese artichoke, knotroot.** [1900–05]

Chinese′ banan′a. See **dwarf banana.**

Chi′nese box′es, a matched set of boxes, usually elaborately decorated and decreasing in size so that each fits inside the next larger one. [1825–30]

Chi′nese cab′bage, a plant, *Brassica rapa pekinensis,* forming a long, dense head of broad, whitish leaves used in salads and Oriental cuisine. Also called **celery cabbage, Chi′nese cel′ery, napa, pe-tsai.** [1835–45, *Amer.*]

Chi′nese cal′endar, the former calendar of China, in which the year consisted of 12 lunar months with an intercalary month added seven times every 19 years to reconcile the lunar year of 354 days with the solar year of 365 days, time being reckoned in 60-year cycles with the first cycle dating from 2637 B.C.

Chi′nese cat′fish, puntat.

Chi′nese check′ers, a board game for two to six players each of whom has ten marbles resting in holes on a player's section of a six-pointed star: the winner is the first to move all of his or her marbles to the opposite side by jumping intervening pieces or moving to adjacent holes that are unoccupied. [1935–40]

Chi′nese chess′, a Chinese game, resembling chess, played on a board consisting of two halves, each eight squares by four, with a strip separating them: pieces representing the military of ancient China are placed on the intersections of the lines and the game is won when a general is checkmated.

Chi′nese chest′nut. See under **chestnut** (def. 1). [1905–10]

Chi′nese Chip′pendale, (esp. in furniture) an English rococo style using Chinese or quasi-Chinese motifs. [1920–25]

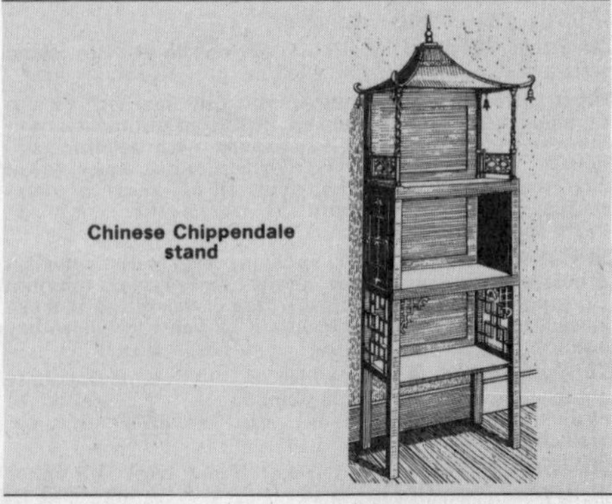
Chinese Chippendale stand

CONCISE ETYMOLOGY KEY: <, descended or borrowed from; >, whence; b., blend of, blended; c., cognate with; cf., compare; deriv., derivative; equiv., equivalent; imit., imitative; obl., oblique; r., replacing; s., stem; sp., spelling, spelled; resp., respelling, respelled; trans., translation; ?, origin unknown; *, unattested; ‡, probably earlier than. See the full key inside the front cover.

Chi′nese cin′namon, cassia (def. 1).

Chi′nese cop′y, *Facetious (sometimes offensive).* an exact copy, including all errors. [1915–20]

Chi′nese cres′cent, crescent (def. 6). [1875–80]

Chi′nese date′, **1.** an Old World tree, *Ziziphus jujuba,* thriving in hot, dry regions. **2.** the edible, plumlike fruit of this tree. Also called **Chinese jujube, jujube.** [1935–40, *Amer.*]

Chi′nese Em′pire, China under the rule of various imperial dynasties, including China proper and other domains, as Manchuria, Mongolia, Sinkiang, and Tibet: replaced by a republic in January, 1912. [1875–80]

Chi′nese ev′ergreen, a tropical Asian plant, *Aglaonema modestum,* of the arum family, often grown indoors, in water or soil, for its glossy green foliage.

Chi′nese fan′ palm′, a fan palm, *Livistona chinensis,* of southern Japan, having very large, deeply cleft leaves and bluish-green, ovalish fruit. Also called **fan palm.**

Chi′nese fin′ger trap′, a child's toy, consisting of a small cylinder of woven straw or paper into which the forefingers are placed, one in each end: the harder one pulls, the more securely the fingers are held. Also called **Chi′nese hand′cuff.**

Chi′nese fire′ drill′, *Informal (sometimes offensive).* a state of chaotic, often clamorous disorder. [‡1960–65]

Chi′nese fleece′-vine. See **silver-lace vine.**

Chinese′ forget′-me-not, an eastern Asian plant, *Cynoglossum amabile,* of the borage family, having lance-shaped leaves and clustered, showy, blue, pink, or white flowers.

Chi′nese gel′atin, agar (def. 1). Also called **Chi′nese i′singlass.**

Chi′nese goose′berry, **1.** a climbing shrub, *Actinidia chinensis,* native to China and cultivated commercially in New Zealand for its edible fruit. **2.** kiwi (def. 2). Also called **yang tao.** [1920–25]

Chinese′ hibis′cus. See **China rose** (def. 2).

Chi′nese hous′es, (*used with a singular or plural v.*) a plant, *Collinsia heterophylla,* of the figwort family, native to California, having clusters of double-lipped purple and white flowers.

Chi′nese ink′. See **India ink.**

Chi′nese ju′jube, See **Chinese date.**

Chi′nese ju′niper, a shrub or tree, *Juniperus chinensis,* of China, Mongolia, and Japan, having scalelike leaves and small, round, purplish-brown fruit.

Chi′nese lac′quer, lacquer (def. 2). [1895–1900]

Chi′nese lan′tern, a collapsible lantern of thin, colored paper, often used for decorative lighting. Also called **Japanese lantern.** [1815–25]

Chi′nese lan′tern plant′. See **winter cherry** (def. 1). [1900–05]

Chi′nese liv′er fluke′ (liv′ər), a parasitic Asian flatworm, *Clonorchis sinensis,* that infects the gastrointestinal tract and bile duct following ingestion of contaminated raw or insufficiently cooked freshwater fish. Cf. **trematode.**

Chi′nese lug′, a lugsail stiffened by battens and kept flat when hoisted: used in Chinese sailing vessels. [1875–80]

Chi′nese mon′ey, *Informal (sometimes offensive).* See **funny money** (def. 3).

Chi′nese pars′ley, coriander.

Chinese′ pavil′ion, crescent (def. 6).

Chi′nese prim′rose. See under **primrose** (def. 1). [1815–25]

Chi′nese puz′zle, **1.** a very complicated puzzle. **2.** anything very complicated or perplexing. [1805–15]

Chi′nese rad′ish, daikon.

Chi′nese red′, vermilion; orange red; red chrome. [1890–95]

Chi′nese-res′tau·rant syn′drome (chī′nēz res′tər ənt, -tə ränt′, -nēs-), a reaction, as headache, sweating, etc., to monosodium glutamate, sometimes added to food in Chinese restaurants. [1965–70]

Chinese′ Revolu′tion, **1.** the revolution in China in 1911, resulting in the overthrow of the Manchu dynasty and in the establishment of a republic in 1912. **2.** the events that culminated in the overthrow of the Nationalist regime and the establishment of the People's Republic of China by the Chinese Communist party in 1949.

Chi′nese sa′cred lil′y, a variety of narcissus, *Narcissus tazetta orientalis,* that has fragrant yellow flowers, and is often grown for indoor winter bloom.

Chi′nese schol′ar tree′. See **pagoda tree.**

Chinese′ Shar-Pei′, Shar-Pei.

Chi′nese snow′ball, a Chinese shrub, *Viburnum macrocephalum,* of the honeysuckle family, having scurfy, hairy twigs, hairy leaves, and white flowers in large, showy, globelike clusters.

Chi′nese tag′, a variety of the game of tag in which the tagged player must hold one hand on the part of the body where he or she was tagged.

Chi′nese tour′, *Informal (sometimes offensive).* a tour in which visitors are shown only what those in charge want them to see. [1975–80]

Chi′nese trum′pet creep′er, a showy, woody vine, *Campsis grandiflora,* of China, having aerial rootlets and large red flowers.

Chi′nese Turk′estan. See under **Turkestan.**

Chinese′ vermil′ion, **1.** pimento (def. 3). **2.** vermilion (def. 2). [1890–95]

Chi′nese Wall′, *Informal.* **1.** See **Great Wall of China.** **2.** an insuperable barrier or obstacle, as to understanding. [1905–10]

Chi′nese wa′termelon. See **wax gourd.**

Chi′nese wax′, a white to yellowish-white, gelatinous, water-insoluble substance obtained from the wax secreted by certain insects, esp. a Chinese scale (*Ericerus pela*): used chiefly in the manufacture of polishes, sizes, and candles. Also called **Chi′nese tree′ wax′, insect wax.**

Chi′nese white′, a white pigment made from zinc oxide, largely used in watercolors and for giving opacity to other colors.

Chi′nese wind′lass. See **differential windlass.** [1870–75]

Chinese′ wiste′ria, a high-climbing Chinese vine, *Wisteria sinensis,* of the legume family, having hanging clusters of fragrant, bluish-violet flowers and long, velvety pods.

Chi′nese wood′ oil′. See **tung oil.**

chin·fest (chin′fest), *n. Slang.* gabfest; bull session; rap session. [1935–40; CHIN + -FEST]

Ch'ing (ching), *n.* See under **Manchu** (def. 1). Also, **Qing.** Also called **Ta Ch'ing.**

Ch'ing Hai (ching′ hī′). See **Qing Hai.**

Ch'ing·hai (ching′hī′), *n. Wade-Giles.* Qinghai.

ching·ma (ching′mä′), *n.* the fiber of the Indian mallow. [< Chin *qīngmá* lit., blue hemp]

Chin·go·la (ching gō′lə), *n.* a town in N central Zambia. 214,000.

Ching·te·chen (*Chin.* jing′tu′jun′), *n. Wade-Giles.* Jingdezhen.

Ching-t'u (jing′tōō′), *n. Chinese.* See **Pure Land.**

Chin·huang·tao (*Chin.* chin′hwäng′dou′), *n. Wade-Giles.* Qinhuangdao.

chin′ic ac′id (kin′ik, kwin′-), *Chem.* See **quinic acid.**

Chin·ju (jin′jōō′), *n.* Jinju.

chink[1] (chingk), *n.* **1.** a crack, cleft, or fissure: *a chink in a wall.* **2.** a narrow opening: *a chink between two buildings.* —*v.t.* **3.** to fill up chinks in. [1350–1400; ME; perh. CHINE[1] + *-k* suffix (see -OCK)]
—Syn. 1. breach, rent, cut.

chink[2] (chingk), *v.t., v.i.* **1.** to make, or cause to make, a short, sharp, ringing sound, as of coins or glasses striking together. —*n.* **2.** a chinking sound: *the chink of ice in a glass.* **3.** *Slang.* coin or ready cash. [1565–75; imit.]

Chink (chingk), *n.* (*sometimes l.c.*) Slang (*disparaging and offensive*). a Chinese. [1900–05; earlier *Chinkie* appar. alter. of CHINA, CHINESE by assoc. with CHINK[1] (from the stereotypical Western image of Chinese as narrow-eyed); see -IE]

chin·ka·pin (ching′kə pin), *n.* chinquapin.

Chin·kiang (chin′kyang′), *n. Older Spelling.* Zhenjiang.

Chin·men (*Chin.* chin′mun′), *n. Wade-Giles.* Quemoy.

chin′ mu′sic, *Older Slang.* idle talk; gossip. [1825–35, *Amer.*]

chi·no[1] (chē′nō), *n., pl.* **-nos** for 2, *adj.* —*n.* **1.** a tough, twilled cotton cloth used for uniforms, sports clothes, etc. **2.** Usually, **chinos.** trousers made of this material. —*adj.* **3.** made of chino. [1940–45, *Amer.*; of uncert. orig.]

chi·no[2] (chē′nō), *n., pl.* **-nos.** *Sometimes Disparaging and Offensive.* Chicano. [< MexSp: person of mixed racial ancestry, usually Negro and Indian; further etym. disputed]

Chi·no (chē′nō), *n.* a city in SE California. 40,165.

Chino-, a combining form representing **Chinese** in compound words: *Chino-Tibetan.*

chi·noi·se·rie (shēn wä′zə rē′, -wä′zə rē; *Fr.* shē-nwaz[ə] rē′), *n., pl.* **-ries** (-rēz′, -rēz; *Fr.* -rē′) for 2. (*sometimes cap.*) **1.** a style of ornamentation current chiefly in the 18th century in Europe, characterized by intricate patterns and an extensive use of motifs identified as Chinese. **2.** an object decorated in this style or an example of this style: *The clock was an interesting chinoiserie.* [1880–85; < F, equiv. to *chinois* CHINESE + *-erie* -ERY]

chi·none (kin′ōn, kwin′-), *n. Chem.* quinone.

Chi·nook (shi nŏŏk′, -nŏŏk′, chi-), *n., pl.* **-nooks,** (*esp. collectively*) **-nook.** **1.** a member of a formerly numerous North American Indian people originally inhabiting the northern shore of the mouth of the Columbia River and the adjacent territory. **2.** either of the two languages of the Chinook Indians. Cf. **Lower Chinook, Upper Chinook.** **3.** (*l.c.*) a warm, dry wind that blows at intervals down the eastern slopes of the Rocky Mountains. **4.** (*l.c.*) See **chinook salmon.** **5.** a U.S. Army cargo helicopter in service since 1962 and capable of ferrying 12 tons of supplies and troops.

Chi·nook·an (shi nŏŏk′ən, -nōō′kən, chi-), *n.* **1.** a language family comprising only Lower Chinook and Upper Chinook. —*adj.* **2.** of or pertaining to the Chinooks or to Chinookan. [1885–90; CHINOOK + -AN]

Chinook′ Jar′gon, a pidgin based largely on Nootka, Lower Chinook, French, and English, once widely used as a lingua franca from Alaska to Oregon. [1830–40]

chinook′ salm′on, a large salmon, *Oncorhynchus tshawytscha,* found in the northern Pacific Ocean. Also called **king salmon, quinnat salmon.** See illus. under **salmon.** [1850–55, *Amer.*]

chin·qua·pin (ching′kə pin), *n.* **1.** a shrubby chestnut, *Castanea pumila,* of the beech family, native to the southeastern U.S., having toothed, oblong leaves and small edible nuts. **2.** a Pacific coast evergreen tree, *Castanopsis chrysophylla,* of the beech family, having deeply furrowed bark, dark green lance-shaped leaves, and inedible nuts. **3.** the nut of either of these trees. Also, **chincapin, chinkapin.** [1605–15, *Amer.*; < Virginia Algonquian (E sp.) *chechinquamins*]

chin′ rest′, a device fixed to the top of a violin or viola to provide a firm rest for the player's chin.

Ch'in Shih Huang Ti (*Chin.* chin′ shœ′ hwäng′ dē′). See **Shih Huang Ti.**

chin′ strap′, **1.** a strap attached to a hat for passing under the chin of the wearer. **2.** a strap to support the chin in cosmetic facial treatment. **3.** a strap on a bridle or halter that joins the throatlatch and noseband. [1865–70]

chintz (chints), *n.* **1.** a printed cotton fabric, glazed or unglazed, used esp. for draperies. **2.** a painted or stained calico from India. [1605–15; earlier *chints,* pl. of *chint* < Gujarati *chīṭ*]

chintz·y (chint′sē), *adj.,* **chintz·i·er, chintz·i·est.** **1.** of, like, or decorated with chintz. **2.** cheap, inferior, or gaudy. **3.** stingy; miserly: *a chintzy way to entertain guests.* [1850–55; CHINTZ + -Y[1]; cf. CHINCHY, which has reinforced figurative senses]
—Syn. 3. cheap, close, niggardly, stinting.

chin-up (chin′up′), *n.* an act or instance of chinning a horizontal bar, rod, or the like. [1880–85]

chin·wag (chin′wag′), *v.,* **-wagged, -wag·ging,** *n. Slang.* —*v.i.* **1.** to chat idly; gossip. —*n.* **2.** an idle chat; gossiping. [1875–80; CHIN + WAG]

Chin·wang·tao (*Chin.* chin′wäng′dou′), *n. Older Spelling.* Qinhuangdao.

chi·o·no·dox·a (kī′ə nō dok′sə, kī on′ə-), *n.* any of several plants belonging to the genus *Chionodoxa,* of the lily family, having blue, white, or pink clusters of flowers on short stalks, and including the glory-of-the-snow. [1844; < NL < Gk *chiono-,* comb. form of *chiṓn* snow + *dóxa* glory]

Chi·os (kī′os, -ōs, kē′-; *Gk.* KHē′ôs), *n.* **1.** a Greek island in the Aegean, near the W coast of Turkey. 53,942; 322 sq. mi. (834 sq. km). **2.** a seaport on and the capital of this island. 52,487. Greek, **Khios.**

chip[1] (chip), *n., v.,* **chipped, chip·ping.** —*n.* **1.** a small, slender piece, as of wood, separated by chopping, cutting, or breaking. **2.** a very thin slice or small piece of food, candy, etc.: *chocolate chips.* **3.** a mark or flaw made by the breaking off or gouging out of a small piece: *This glass has a chip.* **4.** any of the small round disks, usually of plastic or ivory, used as tokens for money in certain gambling games, as roulette or poker; counter. **5.** Also called **microchip.** *Electronics.* a tiny slice of semiconducting material, generally in the shape of a square a few millimeters long, cut from a larger wafer of the material, on which a transistor or an entire integrated circuit is formed. Cf. **microprocessor.** **6.** a small cut or uncut piece of a diamond or crystal. **7.** anything trivial or worthless. **8.** something dried up or without flavor. **9.** a piece of dried dung: *buffalo chips.* **10.** wood, straw, etc., in thin strips for weaving into hats, baskets, etc. **11.** *Golf.* See **chip shot.** **12.** *Tennis.* a softly sliced return shot with heavy backspin. **13.** the strip of material removed by a recording stylus as it cuts the grooves in a record. **14. chips,** *Chiefly Brit.* French fries. **15. chip off the old block,** a person who resembles one parent in appearance or behavior: *His son is just a chip off the old block.* **16. chip on one's shoulder,** a disposition to quarrel: *You will never make friends if you go around with a chip on your shoulder.* **17. in the chips,** *Slang.* wealthy; rich: *Don't look down on your old friends now that you're in the chips.* **18. when the chips are down,** in a discouraging or disadvantageous situation; in bad or pressing times: *When the chips are down he proves to be a loyal friend.*
—*v.t.* **19.** to hew or cut with an ax, chisel, etc. **20.** to cut, break off, or gouge out (bits or fragments): *He chipped a few pieces of ice from the large cube.* **21.** to disfigure by breaking off a fragment: *to chip the edge of a saucer.* **22.** to shape or produce by cutting or flaking away pieces: *to chip a figure out of wood.* **23.** *Games.* to bet by means of chips, as in poker. **24.** *Tennis.* to slice (a ball) on a return shot, causing it to have heavy backspin. **25.** *Slang.* to take (a narcotic drug) occasionally, esp. only in sufficient quantity to achieve a mild euphoria. **26.** *Chiefly Brit. Sports.* to hit or kick (a ball) a short distance forward. **27.** *Brit. Slang.* to jeer or criticize severely; deride; taunt. **28.** *Australian.* to hoe; harrow. —*v.i.* **29.** to break off in small pieces. **30.** *Golf.* to make a chip shot. **31. chip in, a.** to contribute money or assistance; participate. **b.** *Games.* to bet a chip or chips, as in poker. **c.** to interrupt a conversation to say something; butt in: *We all chipped in with our suggestions for the reunion.* [1300–50; (n.) ME *chip* (cf. OE *cipp* plowshare, beam, i.e., piece cut off); (v.) late ME *chippen* (cf. OE *-cippian* in *forcippian* to cut off); akin to MLG, MD *kippen* to chip eggs, hatch] **—chip′pa·ble,** *adj.*

chip[2] (chip), *v.,* **chipped, chip·ping,** *n.* —*v.i.* **1.** to utter a short chirping or squeaking sound; cheep. —*n.* **2.** a short chirping or squeaking cry. [1880–85; var. of CHEEP]

chip[3] (chip), *n. Wrestling.* a tricky or special method by which an opponent can be thrown. [1820–30; n. use of *chip* to trip up; c. G *kippen* to tip over, ON *kippa* to pull]

chip′ and dip′, a bowl or plate for holding potato chips or crackers with a smaller bowl, often placed in the center, for holding dip: usually sold as a set. Also, **chip 'n dip** (chip′n dip′), **chip & dip.**

CONCISE PRONUNCIATION KEY: act, *cāpe, dâre, pärt; set, ēqual; if, īce; ox, ōver, ôrder,* oil, *bŏŏk, bōōt,* out; *up, ûrge; child; sing; shoe; thin, that;* zh as in *treasure.* ə = *a* as in *alone, e* as in *system, i* as in *easily, o* as in *gallop, u* as in *circus;* ə as in *fire* (fīər), *hour* (ouər). l and n can serve as syllabic consonants, as in *cradle* (krād′l), and *button* (but′n). See the full key inside the front cover.

chip•board (chip′bôrd′, -bōrd′), *n.* **1.** a low grade of cardboard, used as a backing for pads of paper, a stiffener for photographs in mailing, etc. **2.** a thin, stiff sheet material made from wastepaper. **3.** a type of board made from compressed waste wood bound together with synthetic resin. [1915–20; CHIP[1] + BOARD]

chip′ carv′ing, wood carving, usually executed with a knife and characterized by small incisions and simple geometrical patterns. [1890–95]

Chip•e•wy•an (chip′ə wī′ən), *n., pl.* **-ans,** (*esp. collectively*) **-an** for 1. **1.** a member of a North American Indian tribe that inhabits northwestern Canada between Hudson Bay and the Rocky Mountains. **2.** the Athabaskan language spoken by the Chipewyan.

chip′ log′, *Naut.* a log for measuring the speed of a vessel. Also called **hand log.** [1825–35]

chip•mak•er (chip′mā′kər), *n.* a manufacturer of electronic chips. [CHIP[1] + MAKER] —**chip′mak′ing,** *n.*

chip•munk (chip′mungk), *n.* any of several small, striped, terrestrial squirrels of the genera *Tamias,* of North America, and *Eutamia,* of Asia and North America, esp. *T. striatus,* of eastern North America. [1825–35, *Amer.*; assimilated var. of earlier *chitmunk,* appar. < Ojibwa *ačitamo·nʔ* red squirrel, equiv, to *ačit-* headfirst, face-down + derivational elements; so called from the squirrel's manner of descending trees]

chipmunk, *Tamias striatus,* head and body 6 in. (15 cm); tail 4 in. (10 cm)

chi•pot•le (chi pōt′lā; *Sp.* chē pôt′le), *n., pl.* **-les** (-lāz; *Sp.* -les). *Mexican Cookery.* a pungent red pepper, often pickled and eaten as an appetizer or added to meat stews, sauces, etc. [< MexSp < Nahuatl *xipotli*]

chip•page (chip′ij), *n.* the fact or an instance of chipping: *The pottery could not be insured against chippage.* [CHIP[1] + -AGE]

chipped′ beef′, very thin slices or shavings of dried, smoked beef, often served in a cream sauce. [1855–60, *Amer.*]

Chip•pen•dale (chip′ən dāl′), *n.* **1. Thomas,** 1718?–79, English cabinetmaker and furniture designer. —*adj.* **2.** of or in the style of Thomas Chippendale.

chip•per[1] (chip′ər), *adj.* marked by or being in sprightly good humor and health. [1830–40; of uncert. orig.]
—**Syn.** jaunty, peppy, pert.

chip•per[2] (chip′ər), *v.i.* **1.** to chirp or twitter. **2.** to chatter or babble. [1705–15; CHIP[2] + -ER[6]]

chip•per[3] (chip′ər), *n.* **1.** a person or thing that chips or cuts. **2.** a machine that grinds up logs, tree trunks, discarded Christmas trees, etc., into wood chips. **3.** *Slang.* a person who uses narcotic drugs only occasionally or in small doses. [1505–15; CHIP[1] + -ER[1]]

Chip•pe•wa (chip′ə wä′, -wā′, -wə), *n., pl.* **-was,** (*esp. collectively*) **-wa.** Ojibwa. [1665–75, *Amer.*]

Chip′pewa Falls′, a city in W Wisconsin. 11,845.

Chip•pe•way (chip′ə wā′), *n., pl.* **-ways,** (*esp. collectively*) **-way.** Chippewa.

chip′ping spar′row, a small, North American sparrow, *Spizella passerina,* common in urban areas. [1785–95, *Amer.*; CHIP[2] + -ING[2]]

chip•proof (chip′pro͞of′), *adj.* resistant to chipping.

chip•py[1] (chip′ē), *n., pl.* **-pies. 1.** Also, **chip′pie.** *Slang.* **a.** a promiscuous woman. **b.** a prostitute. **2.** See **chipping sparrow.** [1860–65, *Amer.*; CHIPP(ING SPARROW) + -Y[2]; def. 1 appar. deriv. of this sense, or from CHIP[2]]

chip•py[2] (chip′ē), *n., pl.* **-pies.** a chipmunk. [CHIP(MUNK) + -Y[2]]

chip•py[3] (chip′ē), *adj.,* **-pi•er, -pi•est. 1.** *Ice Hockey.* using or characterized by aggressive, rough play or commission of fouls: *a chippy player; a chippy second period.* **2.** *Canadian.* irritable; ill-tempered. [1890–95, for def. 2; CHIP[1] (cf. *chip on one's shoulder*) + -Y[1]]

chippy[4] (chip′ē), *n., pl.* **-pies.** *Brit. Informal.* **1.** a carpenter. **2.** a store selling fish and chips. [CHIP[1] + -Y[2]]

chip′ shot′, *Golf.* a shot that is purposely hit fairly high into the air and is meant to roll upon landing, used in approaching the green. Also called **pitch-and-run shot, pitch-and-run.** Cf. **pitch shot.** [1905–10]

Chi•qui•ta (chi kē′tə; *Sp.* chē kē′tä), *n.* a female given name: from a Spanish word meaning "small."

Chi•rac (shē räk′), *n.* **Jacques (Re•né)** (zhäk Rə nā′), born 1932, French political leader: prime minister 1986–88.

chi•ral (kī′rəl), *adj. Chem.* (of a molecule) not superimposable on its mirror image. [1894; *chir-* < Gk *cheír* hand + -AL[1]; coined by Lord Kelvin] —**chi•ral•i•ty** (kī ral′i tē), *n.*

Chir•chik (chər chēk′; *Russ.* chyiʀ chyēk′), *n.* a city in E Uzbekistan, E of Tashkent. 132,000.

CONCISE ETYMOLOGY KEY: <, descended or borrowed from; >, whence; b., blend of, blended; c., cognate with; cf., compare; deriv., derivative; equiv., equivalent; imit., imitative; obl., oblique; r., replacing; s., stem; sp., spelling, spelled; resp., respelling, respelled; trans., translation; ?, origin unknown; *, unattested; ‡, probably earlier than. See the full key inside the front cover.

Chi-Rho (kē′rō′, kī′-), *n., pl.* **-Rhos.** the Christian monogram (☧) made from the first two letters of the Greek word for Christ. Also called **chrismon.** [first two letters of Gk *Christós* CHRIST. See CHI, RHO]

Chir•i•ca•hua (chir′i kä′wə), *n., pl.* **-huas,** (*esp. collectively*) **-hua** for 1. **1.** a member of an Apache Indian group, formerly located in the southwestern U.S. and northern Mexico, now living primarily in Oklahoma and New Mexico. **2.** the Athabaskan language of the Chiricahua, differing only dialectically from Navaho.

Chi•ri•co (kē′ʀē kô), *n.* **Gior•gio de** (jôʀ′jô de), 1888–1978, Italian painter.

chir•i•moy•a (chir′ə moi′ə), *n.* cherimoya.

chirk (chûrk), *v.i.* **1.** to make a shrill, chirping noise. —*v.t.* **2.** *Informal.* to cheer (usually fol. by *up*). [bef. 1000; ME *chirken* to creak, chirrup, OE *circian* to roar]

chi•ro (chēr′ō), *n., pl.* **-ros.** the ladyfish, *Elops saurus.* [orig. uncert.]

chiro-, a combining form meaning "hand," used in the formation of compound words: *chiromancy.* Also, **cheiro-.** [comb. form of Gk *cheír* hand]

chi•rog•ra•phy (kī rog′rə fē), *n.* handwriting; penmanship. [1645–55; CHIRO- + -GRAPHY] —**chi•rog′ra•pher,** *n.* —**chi•ro•graph•ic** (kī′rə graf′ik), **chi′ro•graph′i•cal,** *adj.*

chi•ro•man•cy (kī′rə man′sē), *n.* palmistry. [1520–30; CHIRO- + -MANCY] —**chi′ro•man′cer,** *n.* —**chi′ro•man′tic, chi′ro•man′ti•cal,** *adj.*

Chi•ron (kī′ron), *n.* **1.** *Class. Myth.* a wise and beneficent centaur, teacher of Achilles, Asclepius, and others. **2.** *Astron.* an asteroid located between Saturn and Uranus, about 100 mi. (160 km) in diameter: discovered in 1977. Also, **Cheiron.**

chi•rop•o•dist (ki rop′ə dist, kī- *or, often,* shə-), *n.* a podiatrist. [1775–85; CHIRO- + -POD + -IST]

chi•rop•o•dy (ki rop′ə dē, kī- *or, often,* shə-), *n.* podiatry. [1885–90; CHIRO- + *-pody;* see -POD, -Y[3]]

chi•ro•prac•tic (kī′rə prak′tik), *n.* **1.** a therapeutic system based primarily upon the interactions of the spine and nervous system, the method of treatment usually being to adjust the segments of the spinal column. **2.** a chiropractor. [1895–1900, *Amer.*; CHIRO- + *-practic* < Gk *praktikós;* see PRACTICAL]

chi•ro•prac•tor (kī′rə prak′tər), *n.* one whose occupation is the practice of chiropractic. [1900–05; CHIROPRACT(IC) + -OR[2], as if a L noun with -TOR]

chi•rop•ter (kī rop′tər), *n.* any mammal of the order Chiroptera, comprising the bats. [< NL *Chiroptera,* equiv. to *chiro-* CHIRO- + Gk *-ptera,* neut. pl. of *-pteros* -PTEROUS; so named because the wing membranes are supported by the extended digits of the forelimbs; cf. -PTER]

chi•rop•ter•an (kī rop′tər ən), *n.* **1.** chiropter. —*adj.* **2.** of or pertaining to a chiropter. [1825–35; < NL *Chiropter(a)* (see CHIROPTER) + -AN]

chirp (chûrp), *v.i.* **1.** to make a characteristic short, sharp sound, as small birds and certain insects. **2.** to make any similar sound: *The children chirped with amusement.* —*v.t.* **3.** to sound or utter in a chirping manner: *The little girl chirped her joy.* —*n.* **4.** a chirping sound. [1400–50; late ME *chyrpynge* (ger.); expressive word akin to CHEEP, CHIRK, etc.] —**chirp′er,** *n.* —**chirp′ing•ly,** *adv.*

chirp•y (chûr′pē), *adj.,* **chirp•i•er, chirp•i•est. 1.** chirping or tending to chirp: *chirpy birds.* **2.** cheerful; lively; gay. [1830–40; CHIRP + -Y[1]] —**chirp′i•ly,** *adv.* —**chirp′i•ness,** *n.*

chirr (chûr), *v.i.* **1.** to make a characteristic shrill, trilling sound, as a grasshopper. —*n.* **2.** the sound of chirring. Also, **chirre, churr.** [1590–1600; alter. of CHIRP]

chir•rup (chēr′əp, chûr′-), *v.,* **-ruped, -rup•ing,** *n.* —*v.i.* **1.** to chirp: *robins chirruping on the lawn.* **2.** to make a similar sound: *She chirruped softly to encourage the horse.* —*v.t.* **3.** to utter with chirps. **4.** to make a chirping sound to. —*n.* **5.** the act or sound of chirruping: *a chirrup of birds.* [1570–80; var. of CHIRP] —**chir′rup•per,** *n.*

chir•rup•y (chēr′ə pē, chûr′-), *adj.* chirpy; gay. [1800–10; CHIRRUP + -Y[1]]

chir•u (chir′o͞o), *n.* a goat antelope, *Pantholops hodgsoni,* of Tibet, the male of which has very long, straight horns. Also called **Tibetan antelope.** [perh. < Nepali *jarayo*]

chi•rur•geon (kī rûr′jən), *n. Archaic.* a surgeon. [1250–1300; < L *chīrūr(gus)* (< Gk *cheirourgós* handworker, surgeon; see CHIRO-, DEMIURGE) + (SUR)GEON; r. ME *cirurgian* < OF *cirurgien;* see SURGEON]

chi•rur•ger•y (kī rûr′jə rē), *n. Archaic.* surgery. [1350–1400; CHIRURG(EON) + -ERY; r. ME *sirurgerie* < MF *cirurgerie* < L *chīrūrg(ia)* (< Gk *cheirourgía;* see CHIRURGEON, -IA) + OF *-erie* -ERY] —**chi•rur′gic, chi•rur′gi•cal,** *adj.*

Chis•an•bop (chiz′ən bop′), *Math., Trademark.* a system for performing basic arithmetic calculations, esp. addition, by counting on one's fingers in a specified way. [< Korean *chi-* finger + *san(p)pŏp* calculation, < MChin, equiv. to Chin *zhǐ suànfǎ*]

chis•el (chiz′əl), *n., v.,* **-eled, -el•ing** or (*esp. Brit.*) **-elled, -el•ling.** —*n.* **1.** a wedgelike tool with a cutting edge at the end of the blade, often made of steel, used for cutting or shaping wood, stone, etc. **2.** See **chisel plow. 3.** (*cap.*) *Astron.* the constellation Caelum. —*v.t.* **4.** to cut, shape, or fashion by or as if by carving with a chisel. **5.** to cheat or swindle (someone): *He chiseled me out of fifty dollars.* **6.** to get (something) by cheating or trickery: *He chiseled fifty dollars out of me.* —*v.i.* **7.** to work with a chisel. **8.** to trick; cheat. [1325–75; ME < AF, var. of OF *cisel* < VL **cisellus,* dim. of **cisus,* for L *caesus,* ptp. of *caedere* to cut, with -i- generalized from prefixed derivatives; cf. EXCIDE] —**chis′el•like′,** *adj.*

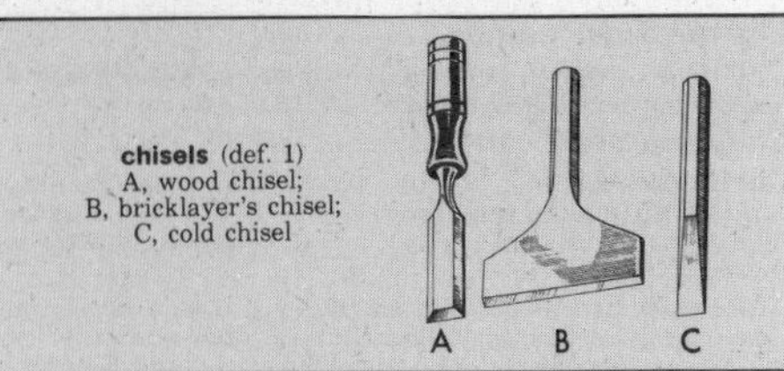

chisels (def. 1) A, wood chisel; B, bricklayer's chisel; C, cold chisel

chis•eled (chiz′əld), *adj.* **1.** cut, shaped, etc., with a chisel: *chiseled stone.* **2.** sharply or clearly shaped; clear-cut: *She has finely chiseled features.* Also, *esp. Brit.,* **chis′elled.** [1730–40; CHISEL + -ED[2]]

chis•el•er (chiz′ə lər, chiz′lər), *n.* **1.** a person who cheats or tricks; swindler. **2.** a person who uses a chisel, as a wood carver. Also, *esp. Brit.,* **chis′el•ler.** [1880–85; CHISEL + -ER[1]]

chis′el plow′, a soil tillage device pulled by a tractor or animal, used to break up and stir soil a foot or more beneath the surface without turning it. Also called **chisel.**

chis′el point′, a nail or spike with the point formed by two flat inclined sides meeting at a sharp angle.

Chi•shi•ma (chē′shē mä′), *n.* Japanese name of the **Kurile Islands.**

Chis•holm (chiz′əm), *n.* **Shirley (Anita St. Hill),** born 1924, U.S. politician: congresswoman 1969–83; first black woman elected to the House of Representatives.

Chis′holm Trail′, a cattle trail leading N from San Antonio, Tex., to Abilene, Kan.: used for about twenty years after the Civil War. [named after Jesse *Chisholm* (1806–68), American scout]

Chish•ti•ya (chish′tē yə), *n.* a Sufi order of the Indian subcontinent. [named after the founder, Mu'in al-Dīn Hasan *Chishtī* (1141–1236)]

Chi•și•nă•u (kē′shē nu′o͞o), *n.* Rumanian name of **Kishinev.**

chi-square (kī′skwâr′), *n. Statistics.* a quantity equal to the summation over all variables of the quotient of the square of the difference between the observed and expected values divided by the expected value of the variable. [1935–40]

chi′-square test′, *Statistics.* a test devised by Karl Pearson that uses the quantity chi-square for testing the mathematical fit of a frequency curve to an observed frequency distribution. Also, **chi′-squared test′** (kī′skwârd′). [1935–40]

chit[1] (chit), *n.* **1.** a signed note for money owed for food, drink, etc. **2.** any receipt, voucher, or similar document, esp. of an informal nature. **3.** *Chiefly Brit.* a note; short memorandum. [1775–85; short for *chitty* < Hindi *ciṭṭī*]

chit[2] (chit), *n.* a child or young person, esp. a pert girl. [1350–1400; for sense of "the young of an animal"; 1615–25 for current sense; ME; perh. akin to KITTEN or KID]

chit[3] (chit), *n. Hinduism.* cit.

Chi•ta (chi tä′; *Russ.* chyi tä′), *n.* a city in the SE Russian Federation in Asia. 349,000.

chi•tal (chēt′l), *n.* See **axis deer.** [< Hindi *cītal;* cf. Skt *citrala* variegated, CHEETAH]

chi•tar•ro•ne (kē′tə rō′nā; *It.* kē′tär rô′ne), *n., pl.* **-ni** (-nē). an early musical stringed instrument of the lute family with a long neck and two pegboxes, one above the other. [1730–40; < It, aug. of *chitarra* < Gk *kithára* lyre]

chit•chat (chit′chat′), *n., v.,* **-chat•ted, -chat•ting.** —*n.* **1.** light conversation; casual talk; gossip. —*v.i.* **2.** to indulge in chitchat; gossip. [1700–10; gradational compound based on CHAT] —**chit′chat′ty,** *adj.*

chi•tin (kī′tin), *n. Biochem.* a nitrogen-containing polysaccharide, related chemically to cellulose, that forms a semitransparent horny substance and is a principal constituent of the exoskeleton, or outer covering, of insects, crustaceans, and arachnids. [1830–40; < F *chitine* < Gk *chitṓn* tunic, CHITON + F *-ine* -IN[2]] —**chi′tin•ous,** *adj.* **chi′tin•oid′,** *adj.*

chit•lings (chit′linz, -lingz), *n.* chitterlings. Also, **chit•lins** (chit′linz).

chi•ton (kīt′n, kī′ton), *n.* **1.** Also called **sea cradle.** a mollusk of the class Amphineura, having a mantle covered with calcareous plates, found adhering to rocks. **2.** a gown or tunic, with or without sleeves, worn by both sexes in ancient Greece. [1810–20; < Gk *chitṓn* tunic < Sem (cf. Heb *kuttōneth* tunic); ult. < Sumerian]

chi•to•san (kī′tə san′), *n. Chem.* a derivative of chitin, used in waste-water treatment. [1890–95; CHIT(IN) + -OSE[2] + *-an,* special use of -AN]

Chi-tse (*Chin.* jē′dzu′), *n.* See **Ki Tse.** Also, **Chi′tzu′.**

Chit•ta•gong (chit′ə gong′), *n.* a port in SE Bangladesh, near the Bay of Bengal. 416,733.

chit•tam•wood (chit′əm wo͝od′), *n.* **1.** See **American smoke tree. 2.** cascara. [1835–45, *Amer.*; *chittam* (< ?; alleged AmerInd orig. unsubstantiated) + WOOD[1]]

chit•ter (chit′ər), *v.i.* to twitter. [1350–1400; ME *che(a)teren, chiteren,* var. of *chateren* to CHATTER]

chit•ter•lings (chit′linz, -lingz), *n.* (*used with a singular or plural v.*) the small intestine of swine, esp. when prepared as food. Also, **chitlings, chitlins.** [1250–1300; ME *cheterling;* akin to G *Kutteln* in same sense]

Ch'iu Ch'u-chi (chyo͞o′cho͞o′jē′), (*Ch'ang Ch'un*) 1148–1227, Chinese Taoist philosopher and author.

Chiung•chou (*Chin.* chyung′jō′), *n. Wade-Giles.* Qiongzhou.

Ch'iung•shan (*Chin.* chyung′shän′), *n. Wade-Giles.* Qiongshan.

Chiu·si (kyo͞o′sē), *n.* a town in central Italy, in Tuscany; Etruscan tombs. 8756. Ancient, **Clusium.**

chiv (shiv), *n.* shiv. [1855–60, *Amer.*]

chi·val·ric (shi val′rik, shiv′əl rik), *adj.* pertaining to chivalry; chivalrous. [1790–1800; CHIVALR(Y) + -IC]

chiv·al·rous (shiv′əl rəs), *adj.* **1.** having the qualities of chivalry, as courage, courtesy, and loyalty. **2.** considerate and courteous to women; gallant. **3.** gracious and honorable toward an enemy, esp. a defeated one, and toward the weak or poor. [1300–50; ME *chevalrous* < MF *chevalerous,* equiv. to *chevalier* CHEVALIER + *-ous* -OUS] —**chiv′al·rous·ly,** *adv.* —**chiv′al·rous·ness,** *n.*
—**Syn. 1.** fearless, dauntless, valiant; courtly; faithful, true, devoted. —**Ant. 1.** cowardly, rude, disloyal.

chiv·al·ry (shiv′əl rē), *n., pl.* **-ries** for 6. **1.** the sum of the ideal qualifications of a knight, including courtesy, generosity, valor, and dexterity in arms. **2.** the rules and customs of medieval knighthood. **3.** the medieval system or institution of knighthood. **4.** a group of knights. **5.** gallant warriors or gentlemen: *fair ladies and noble chivalry.* **6.** *Archaic.* a chivalrous act; gallant deed. [1250–1300; ME *chivalrie* < AF, OF *chevalerie,* equiv. to *chevalier* CHEVALIER + *-ie* -Y[3]]

chiv·a·ree (shiv′ə rē′, shiv′ə rē′), *n., v.t.,* **-reed, -ree·ing.** shivaree. Also, **chiv′a·ri′.**

chive (chīv), *n.* a small bulbous plant, *Allium schoenoprasum,* related to the leek and onion, having long, slender leaves that are used as a seasoning. [1350–1400; ME *cive* < AF *chive,* OF *cive* << L *caepa* onion]

chiv·vy (chiv′ē), *v.t., v.i.,* **-vied, -vy·ing,** *n., pl.* **-vies.** chevy. Also, **chiv′y.**

Ch. J., Chief Justice.

Chka·lov (*Russ.* chkä′ləf), *n.* former name of **Orenburg.**

chlam·y·date (klam′i dāt′), *adj. Zool.* having a mantle or pallium, as a mollusk. [< L *chlamydātus* dressed in a chlamys, equiv. to Gk *chlamyd-* (s. of *chlamys*) CHLAMYS + *-ātus* -ATE[1]]

chla·myd·e·ous (klə mid′ē əs), *adj. Bot.* pertaining to or having a floral envelope. [< Gk *chlamyd-* (s. of *chlamýs*) CHLAMYS + -EOUS]

chla·myd·i·a (klə mid′ē ə), *n., pl.* **-mid·i·ae** (-mid′ē ē′). **1.** *Microbiol.* any coccoid rickettsia of the genus *Chlamydia,* parasitic in birds and mammals, including humans, and causing various infections, esp. of the eyes, as trachoma, lungs, as psittacosis, and genitourinary tract, as urethritis or chlamydia. **2.** *Pathol.* Also called **lymphogranuloma venereum.** a widespread, often asymptomatic sexually transmitted disease caused by *Chlamydia trachomatis,* a major cause of nongonococcal urethritis in men and pelvic inflammatory disease and ectopic pregnancy in women. [1945; < NL < Gk *chlamyd-,* s. of *chlamýs* CHLAMYS + NL *-ia* -IA]

chla·myd·o·spore (klə mid′ə spôr′, -spōr′), *n.* a thick-walled, asexual, resting spore of certain fungi and algae. [1880–85; < Gk *chlamyd-* (s. of *chlamýs*) CHLAMYS + -O- + -SPORE]

chla·mys (klā′mis, klam′is), *n., pl.* **chla·mys·es** (klā′mi siz, klam′i-), **chlam·y·des** (klam′i dēz′). a short, fine woolen mantle worn by men in ancient Greece. [1740–50; < L < Gk *chlamýs*]

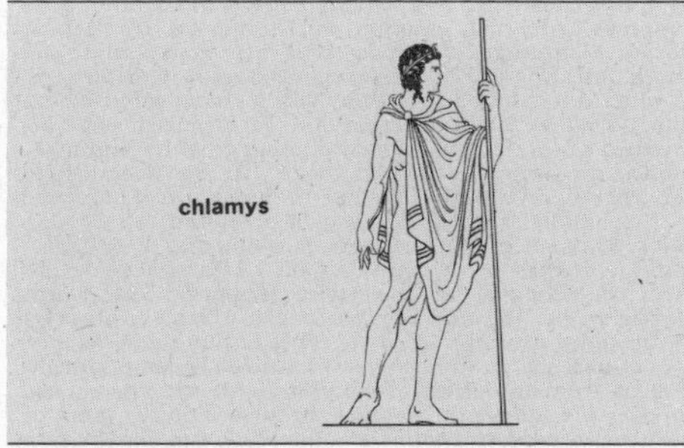
chlamys

chlo·an·thite (klō an′thīt), *n. Mineral.* a nickel-rich variety of skutterudite, used as an ore of nickel. [< Gk *chloanth(és)* (*chlo-* (s. of *chlóē;* see CHLOE) + *-anthēs* comb. form, akin to *ánthos* flower) + -ITE[1]]

chlo·as·ma (klō az′mə), *n. Pathol.* a condition in which light-brown spots occur on the skin, caused by exposure to sun, dyspepsia, or certain specific diseases. [1875–80; < NL < LGk: greenness, deriv. of Gk *chloázein* to be green, deriv. of *chlóos* green]

Chlod·wig (klōt′viKH), *n.* German name of **Clovis I.**

Chlo·e (klō′ē), *n.* **1.** the lover of Daphnis in a Greek pastoral romance. **2.** a female given name. [< Gk *chlóē* young green vegetation, akin to *chlōrós* CHLOR-[1]]

chlor-[1], a combining form meaning "green," used in the formation of compound words: *chlorine.* Also, *esp. before a consonant,* **chloro-**[1]. [comb. form of Gk *chlōrós* light green, greenish yellow; akin to YELLOW, GOLD, GLEAM]

chlor-[2], a combining form used in the names of chemical compounds in which chlorine is present: *chloramine.* Also, *esp. before a consonant,* **chloro-**[2].

chlo′ra·ce′tic ac′id (klôr′ə sē′tik, -set′ik, klōr′-, klôr′-, klōr′-). See **chloroacetic acid.** [1840–50]

chlor·ac·e·to·phe·none (klôr as′i tō fə nōn′, -ə sē′-tō-, klōr-), *n.* chloroacetophenone.

chlor·ac·ne (klôr ak′nē, klōr-), *n. Pathol.* a severe and sometimes persistent form of acne resulting from exposure to chlorine compounds, such as dioxin. [1925–30; CHLOR(INE) + ACNE]

chlo·ral (klôr′əl, klōr′-), *n.* **1.** Also called **trichloroacetaldehyde, trichloroacetic acid aldehyde.** a colorless, oily liquid, C_2Cl_3HO, having a pungent odor, usually derived by the chlorination of ethyl alcohol or of acetaldehyde and combining with water to form chloral hydrate. **2.** Also called **chlo′ral hy′drate.** *Pharm.* a white, crystalline solid, $C_2H_3Cl_3O_2$, formed by combining liquid chloral with water: used as a hypnotic. [1825–35; CHLOR-[2] + -AL[3]]

chlo·ral·ose (klôr′ə lōs′, klōr′-), *n.* a crystalline compound, $C_8H_{11}Cl_3O_6$, used as an animal anesthetic and bird repellent. Also called **glucochlorose.** [1890–95; CHLORAL + -OSE[2]]

chlo·ram·bu·cil (klô ram′byə sil, klō-), *n. Pharm.* a nitrogen mustard, $C_{14}H_{19}Cl_2NO_2$, used in the treatment of chronic lymphocytic leukemia, malignant lymphomas, and Hodgkin's disease. [1955–60; *chlor(oethyl)* + *a-m(inophen)* + BU(TYRIC ACID), components of the chemical name + *-cil* of uncert. derivation]

chlo·ra·mine (klôr′ə mēn′, klōr′-, klô ram′ēn, klō-), *n.* **1.** an unstable, colorless liquid, NH_2Cl, with a pungent odor, derived from ammonia. **2.** any of a class of compounds obtained by replacing a hydrogen atom of an $=NH$ or $-NH_2$ group with chlorine. [1890–95; CHLOR-[2] + AMINE]

chlo·ram·phen·i·col (klôr′am fen′i kôl′, -kol′, klōr′-), *n. Pharm.* a colorless, crystalline, slightly water-soluble antibiotic, $C_{11}H_{12}Cl_2N_2O_5$, obtained from cultures of *Streptomyces venezuelae* or synthesized: used chiefly in the treatment of infections caused by certain bacteria, by rickettsiae, and by certain viruses. [1945–50; CHLOR-[2] + AM(IDO)- + PHE(N)- + NI(TR)- + (GLY)COL]

chlo·ran·il (klô ran′l, klō-, klôr′ə nil, klōr′-), *n.* a yellow, crystalline, water-insoluble solid, $C_6Cl_4O_2$, used chiefly as a fungicide and as an intermediate in the manufacture of dyes. [CHLOR-[2] + ANIL(INE)]

chlo·rate (klôr′āt, -it, klōr′-), *n.* a salt of chloric acid. [1815–25; CHLOR-[2] + -ATE[2]]

chlor·cy·cli·zine (klôr sī′klə zēn′, klōr-), *n. Pharm.* a substance, $C_{18}H_{21}ClN_2$, used as an antihistamine in the symptomatic treatment of certain allergic disorders and in motion sickness. [CHLOR-[2] + CYCL- + *-i-* + (PIPERA)ZINE]

chlor·dane (klôr′dān, klōr′-), *n.* a colorless, viscous, water-insoluble, toxic liquid, $C_{10}H_6Cl_8$, used as an insecticide. Also, **chlor·dan** (klôr′dan, klōr′-). [1945–50; CHLOR-[2] + *(in)dane* an oily cyclic hydrocarbon, equiv. to IND- + -ANE]

chlor·de·cone (klôr′di kōn′, klōr′-), *n.* a toxic chlorinated hydrocarbon, formerly widely used as a pesticide and now a major contaminant of rivers and streams. [1970–75; CHLOR-[2] + DEC- + (KET)ONE]

chlor·di·az·e·pox·ide (klôr′dī az′ə pok′sīd, klōr′-), *n. Pharm.* a compound, $C_{16}H_{14}ClN_3O$, used as a tranquilizer. [CHLOR-[2] + DIAZ(O)- + EPOX(Y) + -IDE]

chlo·rel·la (klə rel′ə), *n.* any freshwater, unicellular green alga of the genus *Chlorella.* [1890; < NL; see CHLOR-[1], -ELLA] —**chlo·rel·la·ceous** (klôr′ə lā′shəs, klōr′-), *adj.*

chlo·ren·chy·ma (klə reng′kə mə), *n. Bot.* parenchymal tissue containing chlorophyll. [1890–95; CHLOR(OPHYLL) + (PAR)ENCHYMA]

chlo·ric (klôr′ik, klōr′-), *adj.* of or containing chlorine in the pentavalent state. [1800–10; CHLOR(INE) + -IC]

chlo′ric ac′id, a hypothetical acid, $HClO_3$, known only in solution or in the form of its salts. [1860–65]

chlo·ride (klôr′īd, -id, klōr′-), *n.* **1.** a salt of hydrochloric acid consisting of two elements, one of which is chlorine, as sodium chloride, NaCl. **2.** a compound containing chlorine, as methyl chloride, CH_3Cl. [1805–15; CHLOR-[2] + -IDE]

chlo′ride of lime′. See **bleaching powder.** [1820–30]

chlo′ride pa′per, *Photog.* a relatively slow printing paper coated with an emulsion of silver chloride: used mostly for contact prints.

chlo·ri·dize (klôr′i dīz′, klōr′-), *v.t.,* **-dized, -diz·ing.** to convert (the metal of an ore) into a chloride by treating with chlorine or hydrochloric acid. Also, *esp. Brit.,* **chlo′ri·dise′.** [1865–70; CHLORIDE + -IZE]

chlo·ri·nate (klôr′ə nāt′, klōr′-), *v.t.,* **-nat·ed, -nat·ing. 1.** *Chem.* **a.** to combine or treat with chlorine. **b.** to introduce chlorine atoms into an organic compound by an addition or substitution reaction. **2.** to disinfect (water) by means of chlorine. **3.** *Metall.* to treat (a gold ore) with chlorine gas in order that the gold may be removed as a soluble chloride. [1855–60; CHLORINE + -ATE[1]] —**chlo′ri·na′tion,** *n.* —**chlo′ri·na′tor,** *n.*

chlo′rinated lime′. See **bleaching powder.** [1875–80]

chlo·rine (klôr′ēn, -in, klōr′-), *n.* a halogen element, a heavy, greenish-yellow, incombustible, water-soluble, poisonous gas that is highly irritating to the respiratory organs, obtained chiefly by electrolysis of sodium chloride brine: used for water purification, in the making of bleaching powder, and in the manufacture both of chemicals that do not contain chlorine, as ethylene glycol, and of those that do. *Symbol:* Cl; *at. wt.:* 35.453; *at. no.:* 17. [1800–10; CHLOR-[1] + -INE[2]] —**chlo′rin·ous,** *adj.*

chlorine 36, the radioactive isotope of chlorine having a mass number 36 and a half-life of about 440,000 years, used chiefly as a tracer.

chlo′rine diox′ide, an orange, water-soluble, unstable, extremely explosive gas, ClO_2, used chiefly as a bleaching agent for wood pulp, fats, oils, and flour.

chlo·rin·i·ty (klô rin′i tē, klō-), *n.* the quality, state, or degree of being chlorinous. [1930–35; CHLORINE + -ITY]

chlo·rite[1] (klôr′īt, klōr′-), *n.* a group of minerals, hydrous silicates of aluminum, ferrous iron, and magnesium, occurring in green platelike crystals or scales. [1595–1605; CHLOR-[1] + -ITE[1]] —**chlo·rit·ic** (klô rit′ik, klō-), *adj.*

chlo·rite[2] (klôr′īt, klōr′-), *n.* a salt of chlorous acid, as potassium chlorite, $KClO_2$. [1850–55; CHLOR-[2] + -ITE[1]]

chlor·mer·o·drin (klôr mer′ə drin, klōr-), *n.* a white, bitter, odorless powder, $ClHgN_2H_{11}O_2$, soluble in methanol and ethanol and slightly soluble in water, used in medicine as a diuretic. [CHLOR-[2] + MER(CURY) + -O- + *-(hy)drin;* see CHLOROHYDRIN]

chloro-[1], var. of **chlor-**[1] before a consonant: *chlorophyll.*

chloro-[2], var. of **chlor-**[2] before a consonant: *chloroform.*

chlo·ro·a·ce·tic (klôr′ō ə sē′tik, -ə set′ik, klōr′-), *adj.* of or derived from chloroacetic acid. [CHLORO-[2] + ACETIC]

chlo′roace′tic ac′id, a colorless, crystalline, deliquescent, water-soluble powder, $C_2H_3ClO_2$, usually derived from acetic acid by chlorination: used chiefly in the manufacture of dyes and other organic compounds. Also, **chloracetic acid.** Also called **monochloroacetic acid.**

chlo·ro·ac·e·tone (klôr′ō as′i tōn′, klōr′-), *n.* a colorless, lachrymatory, poisonous liquid, C_3H_5ClO, used chiefly in organic synthesis and in the manufacture of insecticides and perfumes. [CHLORO-[2] + ACETONE]

chlo·ro·a·ce·to·phe·none (klôr′ō ə sē′tō fə nōn′, -as′i tō-, klōr′-), *n.* a white, crystalline, water-insoluble, poisonous solid, C_8H_7ClO, used in solution as a tear gas. *Abbr.:* CN Also, **chloracetophenone.** [CHLORO-[2] + ACETOPHENONE]

chlo·ro·ben·zene (klôr′ə ben′zēn, -ben zēn′, klōr′-), *n.* a colorless, volatile, water-insoluble, flammable liquid, C_6H_5Cl, having an almondlike odor, prepared from benzene by chlorination: used as a solvent for resins, paints, and lacquers, and in the synthesis of benzene derivatives, as DDT and certain drugs and perfumes. [CHLORO-[2] + BENZENE]

chlo·ro·bro′mide pa′per (klôr′ə brō′mīd, -mid, klōr′-), *Photog.* a relatively fast printing paper coated with an emulsion of silver chloride and silver bromide. Also, **chlo·ro·bro′mid pa′per** (klôr′ō brō′mid, klōr′-). [CHLORO-[2] + BROMIDE]

chlo·ro·bro·mo·meth·ane (klôr′ə brō′mə meth′ān, klōr′-), *n.* a clear, colorless, volatile, nonflammable liquid, CH_2ClBr, used chiefly as an extinguishing agent in fire extinguishers and as a solvent in organic synthesis. Also called **bromochloromethane.** [CHLORO-[2] + BROMO- + METHANE]

chlo·ro·car·bon (klôr′ə kär′bən, klōr′-), *n.* a chemical compound containing carbon and chlorine, as carbon tetrachloride, or containing carbon, chlorine, and hydrogen, as chloroform. [1810–20; CHLORO-[2] + CARBON]

chlo·ro·eth·ane (klôr′ō eth′ān, klōr′-), *n.* See **ethyl chloride.** [CHLORO-[2] + ETHANE]

chlo·ro·eth·ene (klôr′ō eth′ēn, klōr′-), *n.* See **vinyl chloride.** Also, **chlo·ro·eth·yl·ene** (klôr′ō eth′ə lēn′, klōr′-). [CHLORO-[2] + ETHENE]

chlo·ro·fluor·o·car·bon (klôr′ō flo͝or′ō kär′bən, -flôr′-; klōr′ō flo͝or′ō kär′bən, -flōr′-), *n.* any of several volatile, inert, saturated compounds of carbon, fluorine, chlorine, and hydrogen: used as refrigerants, foam-blowing agents, solvents, and, formerly, as aerosol propellants until scientists became concerned about depletion of the atmospheric ozone layer. Cf. **chlorofluoromethane.** [1945–50; CHLORO-[2] + FLUOROCARBON]

chlo·ro·fluor·o·meth·ane (klôr′ō flo͝or′ō meth′ān, -flôr′-; klōr′ō flo͝or′ō meth′ān, -flōr′-), *n.* any of a series of gaseous or volatile methanes substituted with chlorine and fluorine and containing little or no hydrogen: used as refrigerants and, formerly, as aerosol propellants until scientists became concerned about depletion of the atmospheric ozone layer. Cf. **chlorofluorocarbon.** [1960–65; CHLORO-[2] + FLUORO- + METHANE]

chlo·ro·form (klôr′ə fôrm′, klōr′-), *n.* **1.** Also called **trichloromethane.** *Chem., Pharm.* a colorless, volatile, nonflammable, slightly water-soluble, pungent, sweet-tasting liquid, $CHCl_3$, usually derived from acetone, acetaldehyde, or ethyl alcohol by the reaction of chloride of lime: used chiefly in medicine as a solvent and formerly as an anesthetic. —*v.t.* **2.** to administer chloroform to, esp. in order to anesthetize, make unconscious, or kill. **3.** to put chloroform on (a cloth, object, etc.). [1830–40; CHLORO-[2] + FORM(YL)] —**chlo′ro·for′mic,** *adj.*

chlo′ro·for·myl chlo′ride (klôr′ə fôr′məl, klōr′-), phosgene. [CHLORO-[2] + FORMYL]

chlo′ro·gen′ic ac′id (klôr′ə jen′ik, klōr′-, klôr′-, klōr′-), *Biochem.* a colorless crystalline acid, $C_{16}H_{18}O_9$, that is important in plant metabolism and is purportedly responsible for the browning or blackening of cut apples, potatoes, and other fruits and vegetables. [1885–90; CHLORO-[1] + -GENIC; so named because in an ammonia solution it turns green when exposed to air]

chlo·ro·hy·drin (klôr′ə hī′drin, klōr′-), *n.* any of a class of organic chemical compounds containing a chlorine atom and a hydroxyl group, usually on adjacent carbon atoms. [1885–90; CHLORO-[2] + HYDR-[2] + -IN[2]]

chlo·ro·hy·dro·qui·none (klôr′ə hī′drō kwi nōn′, klōr′-), *n.* a white to light-tan, crystalline, water-soluble solid, $C_6H_3Cl(OH)_2$, used chiefly in organic synthesis and as a developer in photography. [CHLORO-[2] + HYDROQUINONE]

chlo·ro·meth·ane (klôr′ə meth′ān, klōr′-), *n.* See **methyl chloride.** [1870–75; CHLORO-[2] + METHANE]

Chlo·ro·my·ce·tin (klôr′ō mī sēt′n, klōr′-), *Pharm., Trademark.* a brand of chloramphenicol.

chlo·ro·naph·tha·lene (klôr′ə naf′thə lēn′, -nap′-, klōr′-), *n.* **1.** either of two isomeric naphthalene compounds containing one chlorine atom. **2.** any of a group of compounds prepared from naphthalene and containing one or more chlorine atoms. [CHLORO-[2] + NAPHTHALENE]

chlo·ro·phe·nol (klôr′ə fē′nôl, -nol, klōr′-), *n. Chem.* **1.** any of three isomers having the formula C_6H_5ClO, derived from chlorine and phenol, used chiefly as intermediates in the manufacture of dyes. **2.** any derivative of phenol of which one or more hydrogen atoms have been replaced by chlorine atoms. Also, **chlorphenol.** [CHLORO-[2] + PHENOL]

chlo′rophe′nol red′, *Chem.* an acid-base indicator, $C_{19}H_{12}Cl_2O_5S$, that changes color from yellow to red as the acidity of a solution decreases.

chlo·ro·phe·no·thane (klôr′ə fē′nə thān′, klōr′-), *n.* See **DDT.** [*(di)chloro(di)phen(yltrichlōr)o(e)thane*]

chlo·ro·phyll (klôr′ə fil, klōr′-), *n. Bot., Biochem.* the green coloring matter of leaves and plants, essential to the production of carbohydrates by photosynthesis, and occurring in a bluish-black form, $C_{55}H_{72}MgN_4O_5$ **(chlorophyll a)**, and a dark-green form, $C_{55}H_{70}MgN_4O_6$ **(chlorophyll b).** Also, **chlo′ro·phyl.** [1810–20; CHLORO-[1] + -PHYLL] **—chlo′ro·phyl′loid,** *adj.*

chlo·ro·phyl·lase (klôr′ə fil′ās, -āz, klōr′-; klôr′ə fəlās′, -lāz′, klōr′-), *n. Biochem.* an enzyme found in plants that decomposes chlorophyll by removing the phytol chain. [CHLOROPHYLL + -ASE]

chlo·ro·phyl·lous (klôr′ə fil′əs, klōr′-), *adj.* of or containing chlorophyll. Also, **chlo·ro·phyl·lose** (klôr′əfil′ōs, klōr′-). [1870–75; CHLOROPHYLL + -OUS]

chlo·ro·pic·rin (klôr′ə pik′rin, -pī′krin, klōr′-), *n. Chem., Mil.* a colorless, somewhat oily, water-insoluble, poisonous liquid, CCl_3NO_2, that causes lachrymation and headache: used as an insecticide, a fungicide, in organic synthesis, and as a war gas. Also, **chlorpicrin.** Also called **nitrochloroform.** [1885–90; CHLORO-[2] + PICR(IC ACID) + -IN[2]]

chlo·ro·plast (klôr′ə plast′, klōr′-), *n. Bot.* a plastid containing chlorophyll. See diag. under **cell.** [1885–90; CHLORO(PHYLL) + -PLAST] **—chlo′ro·plas′tic,** *adj.*

chlo·ro·pla·tin·ic (klôr′ə plə tin′ik, klōr′-), *adj.* of or derived from chloroplatinic acid. [1835–45; CHLORO-[2] + PLATINIC]

chlo′roplatin′ic ac′id, a red-brown, crystalline, water-soluble solid, $H_2PtCl_6·6H_2O$, used chiefly in platinizing glass, metals, and ceramic ware. Also called **platinic chloride.**

chlo·ro·prene (klôr′ə prēn′, klōr′-), *n.* a colorless, slightly water-soluble liquid, C_4H_5Cl, usually produced by the reaction of vinylacetylene with hydrochloric acid, that polymerizes to neoprene. [1930–35; CHLORO-[2] + (ISO)PRENE]

chlo·ro·quine (klôr′ə kwin, -kwēn′, klōr′-), *n. Pharm.* a synthetic substance, $C_{18}H_{26}ClN_3$, used chiefly to control malaria attacks. [1945–50; CHLORO-[2] + QUIN(OLIN)E]

chlo·ro·sis (klô rō′sis, klō-), *n.* **1.** an abnormally yellow color of plant tissues, resulting from partial failure to develop chlorophyll, caused by a nutrient deficiency or the activities of a pathogen. **2.** Also called **greensickness.** *Pathol.* a benign type of iron-deficiency anemia in adolescent girls, marked by a pale yellow-green complexion. [1675–85; CHLOR-[1] + -OSIS] **—chlo·rot·ic** (klôrot′ik, klō-), *adj.* **—chlo·rot′i·cal·ly,** *adv.*

chlo·ro·spi·nel (klôr′ō spi nel′, -spin′l, klōr′-), *n. Mineral.* a variety of spinel used as a gem, colored grass-green by the presence of copper. [1840–50; CHLORO-[1] + SPINEL]

chlo′ro·sul·fon′ic ac′id (klôr′ō sul fon′ik, klōr′-, klôr′-, klōr′-), a colorless or yellowish, highly corrosive, pungent liquid, $HClO_3S$, usually produced by treating sulfur trioxide with hydrogen chloride: used in organic synthesis to introduce the sulfonyl chloride group, $=SO_2Cl$. [CHLORO-[2] + SULFONIC ACID]

chlo·ro·thi·a·zide (klôr′ə thī′ə zīd′, klōr′-), *n. Pharm.* a white, crystalline, slightly water-soluble powder, $C_7H_6ClN_3O_4S_2$, used as a diuretic and in the treatment of hypertension. [1955–60; CHLORO-[2] + THIAZ(OLE) + -IDE]

chlo·ro·tri·fluor·o·eth·yl·ene (klôr′ō trī flo͝or′ōeth′ə lēn′, -flôr′-; klōr′ō trī flo͝or′-, -flōr′-), *n.* a colorless, flammable gas, C_2H_2ClF, that polymerizes to form oils, greases, and waxes. [CHLORO-[2] + TRI- + FLUOR-[1] + -O- + ETHYLENE]

chlo·ro·tri·fluor·o·meth·ane (klôr′ō trī flo͝or′ōmeth′ān, -flôr′-; klōr′ō trī flo͝or′-, -flōr′-), *n.* a colorless gas, $CClF_3$, used chiefly as a refrigerant, in the hardening of metals, and in pharmaceutical processing. Also called **trifluorochloromethane.** [CHLORO-[2] + TRI- + FLUOR- + -O- + METHANE]

chlo·rous (klôr′əs, klōr′-), *adj.* **1.** containing trivalent chlorine. **2.** of or derived from chlorous acid. [1835–45; CHLOR-[2] + -OUS]

chlo′rous ac′id, a hypothetical acid, $HClO_2$, known only in solution or in the form of its salts. [1835–45]

chlor·phe·nir·a·mine (klôr′fə nir′ə mēn′, klōr′-), *n. Pharm.* an antihistaminic compound, $C_{20}H_{23}ClN_2O_4$, used in treating the symptoms of allergies. [CHLOR-[2] + PHEN- + (P)YR- + -AMINE]

chlor·phe·nol (klôr fē′nôl, -nol, klōr-), *n. Chem.* chlorophenol.

chlor·pic·rin (klôr pik′rin, klōr-), *n. Chem.* chloropicrin.

chlor·prom·a·zine (klôr prom′ə zēn′, klōr-), *n.* a grayish-white, crystalline powder, $C_{17}H_{19}ClN_2S$, derived from phenothiazine, used chiefly to inhibit nausea and vomiting and as a major tranquilizer in the management of schizophrenia and related psychoses. [1950–55; CHLOR-[2] + PRO(PYL) + (A)M(INE) + AZINE]

chlor·prop·a·mide (klôr prop′ə mīd′, -prō′pə-, klōr-), *n. Pharm.* an oral hypoglycemic substance, $C_{10}H_{13}ClN_2O_3S$, used to augment insulin secretion in the treatment of certain kinds of diabetes mellitus. [1955–60; CHLOR-[2] + PROP(ANE) + AMIDE]

chlor·pyr·i·fos (klôr pir′ə fos′, klōr-), *n.* a broad-spectrum insecticide, $C_9H_{11}Cl_3NO_3PS$, used on lawns and ornamental plants. [CHLOR-[2] + PYRI(DINE) + *-fos,* for PHOSPHORUS]

chlor·tet·ra·cy·cline (klôr te′trə sī′klin, -klēn, klōr-), *n. Pharm.* a yellow, crystalline, antibiotic powder, $C_{22}H_{23}N_2O_8Cl$, biosynthesized by *Streptomyces aureofaciens,* used in the treatment of infections. [1950–55; CHLOR-[2] + TETRACYCLINE]

chlor·thal·i·done (klôr thal′i dōn′, klōr-), *n. Pharm.* a sulfonamide diuretic, $C_{14}H_{11}ClN_2O_4S$, used in the management of hypertension. [CHLOR-[2] + *(ph)thali(mi)d(ine)* a chemical component of the drug + (KET)ONE]

Chlor-Tri·me·ton (klôr trī′mi ton′, klōr-), *Pharm., Trademark.* a brand of chlorpheniramine.

chm., **1.** chairman. **2.** checkmate.

chmn., chairman.

cho·a·no·cyte (kō′ə nə sīt′, kō an′ə-), *n. Zool.* one of the flagellated cells lining the inner cavity of a sponge, having a collar of protoplasm encircling the base of the flagellum. Also called **collar cell.** [1885–90; < Gk *choán(ē)* funnel + -O- + -CYTE] **—cho′a·no·cyt′al,** *adj.*

cho·a·no·flag·el·late (kō′ə nō flaj′ə lāt′), *n. Zool.* any flagellate of the genera *Monosiga* and *Proterospongia,* having a protoplasmic collar encircling the base of the flagellum. [1895–1900; < NL *Choanoflagellata* name of the order. See CHOANOCYTE, FLAGELLATA]

Choate (chōt), *n.* **1. Joseph Hodges,** 1832–1917, U.S. lawyer and diplomat. **2. Rufus,** 1799–1859, U.S. lawyer, orator, and statesman.

choc., chocolate.

chock (chok), *n.* **1.** a wedge or block of wood, metal, or the like, for filling in a space, holding an object steady, etc. **2.** *Naut.* **a.** any of various heavy metal fittings on a deck or wharf that serve as fairleads for cables or chains. **b.** a shaped support or cradle for a ship's boat, barrel, etc. **c.** a small wooden piece or timber for filling a gap, reinforcing an angle, etc., in a wooden vessel. **3.** *Metalworking.* a bearing supporting the end of a rolling mill. **4.** *Mining.* a roof support made of cribbing filled with stones. Cf. **cog**[3] (def. 2). *—v.t.* **5.** to furnish with or secure by a chock or chocks. **6.** *Naut.* to place (a boat) upon chocks. *—adv.* **7.** as close or tight as possible: *chock against the edge.* [ME < AF *choque* (cf. modern Picard *choke* big log, Normandy dial. *chouque*), OF *çoche* (F *soche*); of uncert. orig.]

chock
(def. 2a)

chock·a·block (chok′ə blok′), *adj.* **1.** extremely full; crowded; jammed: *a room chockablock with furniture and plants.* **2.** *Naut.* having the blocks drawn close together, as when the tackle is hauled to the utmost. *—adv.* **3.** in a crowded manner: *books piled chockablock on the narrow shelf.* Also, **chock′-a-block′.** [cf. *chock* close (up to), appar. as back formation from CHOCKFUL]

chock-full (chok′fo͝ol′, chuk′-), *adj.* full to the limit; crammed. Also, **chock′-ful′, chuck-full, choke-full.** [1350–1400; ME *chokke-fulle,* equiv. to *chokke* (< ?) + *fulle* FULL[1]]

choc·o·hol·ic (chô′kə hô′lik, -hol′ik, chok′ə-), *n.* a person who is excessively fond of chocolate. [CHOCO(LATE) + -HOLIC]

choc·o·late (chô′kə lit, chok′ə-, chôk′lit, chok′-), *n.* **1.** a preparation of the seeds of cacao, roasted, husked, and ground, often sweetened and flavored, as with vanilla. **2.** a beverage made by dissolving such a preparation in milk or water, served hot or cold: *a cup of hot chocolate.* **3.** candy made from such a preparation. **4.** an individual piece of this candy. **5.** any syrup or flavoring made from this preparation or artificially imitating its flavor. **6.** a dark brown color. *—adj.* **7.** made, flavored, or covered with chocolate: *chocolate cake; chocolate ice cream.* **8.** having the color of chocolate; dark-brown. [1595–1605; < Sp < Nahuatl *chocolātl*] **—choc′o·lat·y,** *adj.*

choc·o·late-box (chô′kə lit boks′, chok′ə-, chôk′lit-, chok′-), *adj.* excessively decorative and sentimental, as the pictures or designs on some boxes of chocolate candy; prettified: *decorous, chocolate-box paintings of Victorian garden parties.* [1900–05]

choc′olate milk′, milk flavored with chocolate syrup or powdered chocolate.

choc′olate sol′dier, a nonfighting soldier; a serviceman not assigned to combat duty. [1895–1900]

choc′olate tree′, cacao (def. 1). [1825–35]

cho·co·la·tier (chô′kə lə tēr′, chok′ə-, chôk′lə-, chok′-; *Fr.* shô kô lᴀ tyā′), *n., pl.* **-tiers** (-tērz′; *Fr.* -tyā′). a person or firm that makes and sells chocolate candy. [< F; see CHOCOLATE, -IER[2]]

Choc·taw (chok′tô), *n., pl.* **-taws,** (*esp. collectively*) **-taw** for 1. **1.** a member of a large Muskhogean tribe of North American Indians, formerly living chiefly in southern Mississippi, now in Oklahoma. **2.** the language of the Choctaw, closely related to Chickasaw. **3.** something unintelligible, as speech, illegible handwriting, or an ineffectual explanation; gibberish: *My best efforts at clarity were Choctaw to him.*

Cho·ëph·o·ri (kō ef′ə rī′), *n.* a tragedy (458 B.C.) by Aeschylus. Also called ***The Libation-bearers.*** Cf. ***Oresteia.***

choice (chois), *n., adj.,* **choic·er, choic·est.** *—n.* **1.** an act or instance of choosing; selection: *Her choice of a computer was made after months of research. His parents were not happy with his choice of friends.* **2.** the right, power, or opportunity to choose; option: *The child had no choice about going to school.* **3.** the person or thing chosen or eligible to be chosen: *This book is my choice. He is one of many choices for the award.* **4.** an alternative: *There is another choice.* **5.** an abundance or variety from which to choose: *a wide choice of candidates.* **6.** something that is preferred or preferable to others; the best part of something: *Mare's Nest is the choice in the sixth race.* **7.** a carefully selected supply: *This restaurant has a fine choice of wines.* **8.** a choice grade of beef. **9. of choice,** that is generally preferred: *A detached house is still the home of choice.* *—adj.* **10.** worthy of being chosen; excellent; superior. **11.** carefully selected: *choice words.* **12.** (in the grading of beef in the U.S.) rated between prime and good. [1250–1300; ME *chois* < OF, deriv. of *choisir* to perceive, choose < Gmc; see CHOOSE] **—choice′less,** *adj.* **—choice′ly,** *adv.* **—choice′ness,** *n.*

—Syn. 2. CHOICE, ALTERNATIVE, OPTION, PREFERENCE all suggest the power of choosing between things. CHOICE implies the opportunity to choose: *a choice of evils.* ALTERNATIVE suggests that one has a choice between only two possibilities. It is often used with a negative to mean that there is no second possibility: *to have no alternative.* OPTION emphasizes free right or privilege of choosing: *to exercise one's option.* PREFERENCE applies to a choice based on liking or partiality: *to state a preference.* **10.** select, rare, uncommon, valuable, precious. See **fine**[1].

choir (kwīᵊr), *n.* **1.** a company of singers, esp. an organized group employed in church service. **2.** any group of musicians or musical instruments; a musical company, or band, or a division of one: *string choir.* **3.** *Archit.* **a.** the part of a church occupied by the singers of the choir. **b.** the part of a cruciform church east of the crossing. **4.** (in medieval angelology) one of the orders of angels. *—adj.* **5.** professed to recite or chant the divine office: *a choir monk.* *—v.t., v.i.* **6.** to sing or sound in chorus. [1250–1300; ME *quer* < OF *cuer* < L *chorus* CHORUS; r. OE *chor* choir < L] **—choir′like′,** *adj.*

choir·boy (kwīᵊr′boi′), *n.* a boy who sings in a choir, esp. a church choir. [1830–40; CHOIR + BOY]

choir·girl (kwīᵊr′gûrl′), *n.* a girl who sings in a choir. [CHOIR + GIRL]

choir′ loft′, a gallery in a church in which the choir is placed. [1925–30]

choir·mas·ter (kwīᵊr′mas′tər, -mä′stər), *n.* the director of a choir. [1855–60; CHOIR + MASTER]

Choi·seul (*Fr.* shwᴀ zœl′), *n.* an island in the W central Pacific Ocean: part of the independent Solomon Islands. 8021; 1500 sq. mi. (3885 sq. km).

choke (chōk), *v.,* **choked, chok·ing,** *n.* *—v.t.* **1.** to stop the breath of by squeezing or obstructing the windpipe; strangle; stifle. **2.** to stop by or as if by strangling or stifling: *The sudden wind choked his words.* **3.** to stop by filling; obstruct; clog: *Grease choked the drain.* **4.** to suppress (a feeling, emotion, etc.) (often fol. by *back* or *down*): *I managed to choke back my tears.* **5.** to fill chock-full: *The storeroom was choked with furniture.* **6.** to seize (a log, felled tree, etc.) with a chain, cable, or the like, so as to facilitate removal. **7.** to enrich the fuel mixture of (an internal-combustion engine) by diminishing the air supply to the carburetor. **8.** *Sports.* to grip (a bat, racket, or the like) farther than usual from the end of the handle; shorten one's grip on (often fol. by *up*). *—v.i.* **9.** to suffer from or as from strangling or suffocating: *He choked on a piece of food.* **10.** to become obstructed, clogged, or otherwise stopped: *The words choked in her throat.* **11. choke off,** to stop or obstruct by or as by choking: *to choke off a nation's fuel supply.* **12. choke up, a.** to become or cause to become speechless, as from the effect of emotion or stress: *She choked up over the sadness of the tale.* **b.** to become too tense or nervous to perform well: *Our team began to choke up in the last inning.* *—n.* **13.** the act or sound of choking. **14.** a mechanism by which the air supply to the carburetor of an internal-combustion engine can be diminished or stopped. **15.** *Mach.* any mechanism that, by blocking a passage, regulates the flow of air, gas, etc. **16.** *Elect.* See **choke coil. 17.** a narrowed part, as in a chokebore. **18.** the bristly upper portion of the receptacle of the artichoke. [1150–1200; ME *choken, cheken,* var. of *achoken, acheken,* OE *āceocian* to suffocate; akin to ON *kōk* gullet] **—choke′a·ble,** *adj.*

—Syn. 3. block, dam, plug.

choke·ber·ry (chōk′ber′ē, -bə rē), *n., pl.* **-ries. 1.** the berrylike fruit of any North American shrub of the genus *Aronia,* of the rose family, esp. *A. arbutifolia* **(red chokeberry),** *A. melanocarpa* **(black chokeberry),** or *A. prunifolia* **(purple chokeberry). 2.** the plant that bears this fruit. [1770–80, *Amer.*; CHOKE + BERRY]

choke·bore (chōk′bôr′, -bōr′), *n.* **1.** a bore in a shotgun that narrows toward the muzzle to prevent shot from scattering too widely. **2.** a shotgun with such a bore. [1870–75; CHOKE + BORE[1]]

choke·cher·ry (chōk′cher′ē), *n., pl.* **-ries.** *Chiefly Northern U.S.* **1.** any of several cherries, esp. *Prunus virginiana,* of North America, that bear an astringent fruit. **2.** the fruit itself. [1775–85, *Amer.*; CHOKE + CHERRY]

choke′ coil′, *Elect.* a coil of large inductance that gives relatively large impedance to alternating current. Also called **choke.** [1905–10]

choke′ col′lar, a nooselike collar for controlling untrained or powerful dogs. Also called **choke′ chain′.**

choke·damp (chōk′damp′), *n. Mining.* mine atmosphere so low in oxygen and high in carbon dioxide as to

CONCISE ETYMOLOGY KEY: <, descended or borrowed from; >, whence; b., blend of, blended; c., cognate with; cf., compare; deriv., derivative; equiv., equivalent; imit., imitative; obl., oblique; r., replacing; s., stem; sp., spelling, spelled; resp., respelling, respelled; trans., translation; ?, origin unknown; *, unattested; ‡, probably earlier than. See the full key inside the front cover.

cause choking. Also called **blackdamp.** [1635–45; CHOKE + DAMP]

choke-full (chōk′fo͝ol′), *adj.* chock-full.

choke′ hold′, a restraining hold, as when one person encircles the neck of another from behind in a viselike grip with the arm. Also, **choke′hold′.**

choke•point (chōk′point′), *n.* a place of greatest congestion and often hazard; bottleneck. [1965–70]

chok•er (chō′kər), *n.* **1.** a person or thing that chokes. **2.** a necklace that fits snugly around the neck. **3.** a neckcloth or high collar. **4.** a chain or cable used to haul logs from the woods. [1545–55; CHOKE + -ER[1]]

chok•er-set•ter (chō′kər set′ər), *n.* (in logging) a worker whose job is to fasten a choker to logs.

chokes (chōks), *n. Informal.* a manifestation of caisson disease that is characterized by dyspnea, coughing, and choking. [see CHOKE, -S[3]]

chok•ing (chō′king), *adj.* **1.** (of the voice) husky and strained, esp. because of emotion. **2.** causing the feeling of being choked: *a choking cloud of smoke.* [CHOKE + -ING[2]] **—chok′ing•ly,** *adv.*

chok•y (chō′kē), *adj.,* **chok•i•er, chok•i•est.** tending to choke: *a choky collar.* [1570–80; CHOKE + -Y[1]]

chol-, var. of **chole-** before a vowel: *choline.*

cho•la (chō′lə), *n. Chiefly Southwestern U.S.* (esp. among Mexican-Americans) a teenage girl who associates closely with a gang of cholos or is the girlfriend of a cholo. [1850–55; < AmerSp, fem. of CHOLO]

cho•la•gogue (kō′lə gôg′, -gog′, kol′ə-), *Med.* —*adj.* **1.** Also, **cho•la•gog•ic** (kō′lə goj′ik, kol′ə-). promoting the flow of bile. —*n.* **2.** a cholagogue agent. [1605–15; < F < Gk *cholagōgós.* See CHOL-, -AGOGUE]

cho•lan•gi•og•ra•phy (kə lan′jē og′rə fē, kō-), *n.* x-ray examination of the bile ducts using a radiopaque contrast medium. [1935–40; CHOL- + ANGIO- + -GRAPHY]

cho•late (kō′lāt), *n. Biochem.* the salt form of cholic acid. [1835–45; CHOL(IC ACID) + -ATE[2]]

chole-, a combining form meaning "bile," "gall," used in the formation of compound words: *cholesterol.* Also, *esp. before a vowel,* **chol-.** [comb. form of Gk *cholḗ* bile; akin to CHLOR-[1]]

cho•le•cal•cif•er•ol (kō′lə kal sif′ə rōl′, -rol′, kol′ə-), *n.* See **vitamin D.** [1930–35; CHOLE- + CALCI- + -FER + -OL[1]]

cho•le•cyst (kō′lə sist′, kol′ə-), *n. Anat.* gallbladder. [1865–70; CHOLE- + -CYST] **—cho′le•cys′tic,** *adj.*

cho•le•cys•tec•to•my (kō′lə si stek′tə mē, kol′ə-), *n., pl.* **-mies.** *Surg.* removal of the gallbladder. [1880–85; CHOLECYST + -ECTOMY]

cho•le•cys•ti•tis (kō′lə si stī′tis, kol′ə-), *n. Pathol.* inflammation of the gallbladder. [1865–70; CHOLE- + CYSTITIS]

cho•le•cys•tog•ra•phy (kō′lə si stog′rə fē, kol′ə-), *n. Med.* the production of x-ray photographs of the gallbladder following administration of a radiopaque substance that is secreted by the liver into the gallbladder. [1920–25; CHOLECYST + -O- + -GRAPHY] **—cho•le•cys•to•gram** (kō′lə sis′tə gram′, kol′ə-), *n.*

cho•le•cys•to•ki•nin (kō′lə sis′tə kī′nin, kol′ə-), *n.* a hormone secreted by the upper portion of the intestine that stimulates contraction of the gallbladder and increases secretion of pancreatic juice. *Abbr.:* CCK [1925–30; CHOLECYST + -O- + -KININ]

cho•le•cys•tos•to•my (kō′lə si stos′tə mē, kol′ə-), *n., pl.* **-mies.** *Surg.* formation of an opening through the abdominal wall into the gallbladder, usually done for drainage and to remove gallstones. [CHOLECYST + -O- + -STOMY]

cho•le•cys•tot•o•my (kō′lə si stot′ə mē, kol′ə-), *n., pl.* **-mies.** *Surg.* incision of the gallbladder. [1875–80; CHOLE- + CYSTO- + -TOMY]

cho•led•o•chos•to•my (kə led′i kos′tə mē, kō′lə dō-kos′-, kol′i-), *n., pl.* **-mies.** *Surg.* formation of a temporary opening through the abdominal wall into the common bile duct, usually to remove stones. [< NL *choledoch(us)* (< Gk *cholēdóchos,* equiv. to *cholē-* CHOLE- + *dóchos* DUCT) + -O- + -STOMY]

cho•led•o•chot•o•my (kə led′i kot′ə mē, kō′lə dō-kot′-, kol′i-), *n., pl.* **-mies.** *Surg.* incision of the common bile duct. [1890–95; < NL *choledoch(us)* (see CHOLEDOCHOSTOMY) + -O- + -TOMY]

cho•lee (chō′lē), *n.* choli.

cho•le•lith (kō′lə lith, kol′ə-), *n. Pathol.* a gallstone. Also, **chololith.** [CHOLE- + -LITH]

cho•le•li•thi•a•sis (kō′lə li thī′ə sis, kol′ə-), *n. Pathol.* the presence of gallstones. [1855–60; CHOLELITH + -IASIS]

cho•lent (chô′lənt, chul′ənt; *Yiddish* chôlnt), *n. Jewish Cookery.* a stewed or baked dish, esp. of meat and beans, served on the Sabbath but cooked the day before or overnight over a slow fire. [< Yiddish *tsholnt, tshulnt,* perh. < OF < L *calentem,* acc. prp. of *calēre* to be hot (> F, OF *chaloir,* attested only in derived sense "to be of interest, matter"); cf. NONCHALANT); cf. Heb (post-Biblical) *ḥammin* cholent, deriv. of *ḥam* hot]

chol•er (kol′ər), *n.* **1.** irascibility; anger; wrath; irritability. **2.** *Old Physiol.* See **yellow bile. 3.** *Obs.* biliousness. [1350–1400; ME *colera* < ML, L *cholera* < Gk *choléra* CHOLERA]

chol•er•a (kol′ər ə), *n.* **1.** Also called **Asiatic cholera.** *Pathol.* an acute, infectious disease, endemic in India and China and occasionally epidemic elsewhere, characterized by profuse diarrhea, vomiting, cramps, etc. **2.** *Vet. Pathol.* any of several diseases of domesticated animals that are characterized by depression, sleepiness, lack of appetite, and diarrhea. Cf. **fowl cholera, hog cholera.** [1350–1400 for sense of CHOLER (def. 2); 1565–75 for current senses; ME < L < Gk *choléra* name of several intestinal diseases] **—chol•e•ra•ic** (kol′ə rā′-ik), *adj.*

chol′era in•fan′tum (in fan′təm), *Pathol.* an often fatal form of gastroenteritis occurring in infants, not of the same cause as cholera but having somewhat similar characteristics. [1820–30, *Amer.*; < NL: cholera of infants]

chol•er•ic (kol′ər ik, kə ler′ik), *adj.* **1.** extremely irritable or easily angered; irascible: *a choleric disposition.* **2.** *Obs.* **a.** bilious. **b.** causing biliousness. [1300–50; ME *colerik* < ML *colericus* bilious, L *cholericus* < Gk *cholerikós.* See CHOLERA, -IC] **—chol′er•i•cal•ly, chol′•er•ic•ly,** *adv.* **—chol′er•ic•ness,** *n.*
—Syn. 1. wrathful, testy, impatient, touchy. **—Ant. 1.** phlegmatic, tranquil.

cho•le•sta•sis (kō′lə stā′sis, -stas′is, kol′ə-), *n. Pathol.* total or partial suppression of the flow of bile. [1930–35; CHOLE- + STASIS] **—cho•le•stat•ic** (kō′lə-stat′ik, kol′ə-), *adj.*

cho•les•ter•e•mi•a (kə les′tə rē′mē ə), *n. Pathol.* cholesterolemia.

cho•les•ter•ic (kə les′tər ik, kō′lə ster′ik), *adj. Chem., Physics.* of or pertaining to a form of liquid crystal having molecules arranged in thick, regular layers, and displaying marked color effects, esp. in polarized light. [CHOLESTER(OL) + -IC]

cho•les•ter•ol (kə les′tə rōl′, -rôl′), *n. Biochem.* **1.** a sterol, $C_{27}H_{46}O$, that occurs in all animal tissues, esp. in the brain, spinal cord, and adipose tissue, functioning chiefly as a protective agent in the skin and myelin sheaths of nerve cells, a detoxifier in the bloodstream, and as a precursor of many steroids: deposits of cholesterol form in certain pathological conditions, as gallstones and atherosclerotic plaques. **2.** the commercial form of this compound, obtained from the spinal cord of cattle, used chiefly as an emulsifying agent in cosmetics and pharmaceuticals, and in the synthesis of vitamin D. Also, **cho•les•ter•in** (kə les′tər in). [1890–95; CHOLE- + Gk *ster(eós)* solid + -OL[1]]

cho•les•ter•ol•e•mi•a (kə les′tər ə lē′mē ə), *n. Pathol.* the presence of an abnormal amount of cholesterol in the blood. Also, **cholesteremia.** [CHOLESTEROL + -EMIA]

Chol Ha•mo•ed (*Seph.* KHôl′ hä mô ed′; *Ashk.* KHôl′ hä mō′äd, -moid′), *Hebrew.* See ***Hol Hamoed.***

cho•li (chō′lē), *n.* a short-sleeved blouse or bodice, often one exposing part of the midriff, worn by Hindu women in India. Also, **cholee.** [1905–10; < Hindi *colī*]

cho•li•am•bus (kō′lē am′bəs), *n., pl.* **-bi** (-bī). *Pros.* a line of iambic meter with a spondee or trochee replacing the last foot. [< Gk *chōlíambos,* equiv. to *chōl(ós)* lame, halting + *íambos* IAMB]

cho′lic ac′id (kō′lik, kol′ik), **1.** *Biochem.* a bile acid, $C_{24}H_{40}O_5$, related to the sex hormones and cholesterol. **2.** the commercial form of this compound, obtained from beef bile, used chiefly in the manufacture of drugs and in research. [1840–50; < Gk *cholikós* bilious (*chol(ḗ)* bile + *-ikos* -IC); see CHOLE-]

cho•line (kō′lēn, kol′ēn), *n.* **1.** *Biochem.* a quaternary ammonium cation, $C_5H_{14}N^{+}O$, one of the B-complex vitamins, found in the lecithin of many plants and animals. **2.** choline hydroxide, $C_5H_{15}NO_2$, the viscous, strongly alkaline commercial form of this compound, usually synthesized, used as a feed supplement, esp. for poultry, and in medicine in certain liver conditions. **3.** choline chloride, $C_5H_{14}ClNO$. [1855–60; CHOL- + -INE[2]]

cho′line chlo′ride car′bamate, *Chem.* carbachol.

cho•lin•er•gic (kō′lə nûr′jik, kol′ə-), *adj. Biochem.* **1.** resembling acetylcholine in pharmacological action. **2.** stimulated by or releasing acetylcholine or a related compound. [1930–35; (ACETYL)CHOLINE + -ERGIC]

cho•lin•es•ter•ase (kō′lə nes′tə rās′, -rāz′, kol′ə-), *n. Biochem.* an enzyme, found esp. in the heart, brain, and blood, that hydrolyzes acetylcholine to acetic acid and choline. [1930–35; CHOLINE + ESTERASE]

cho•li•no•lyt•ic (kō′lə nl it′ik), *adj. Biochem., Pharm.* **1.** capable of blocking the action of acetylcholine and related compounds. —*n.* **2.** a drug or other substance that has cholinolytic properties. [1955–60; CHOLINE + -O- + -LYTIC]

cho•li•no•mi•met•ic (kō′lə nō mi met′ik, -mī-), *adj. Biochem., Pharm.* **1.** mimicking the action of choline, esp. acetylcholine. **2.** a drug or other substance that has cholinometric properties. [1965–70; CHOLINE + -O- + MIMETIC]

chol•la (chōl′yä, -yə; *Sp.* chô′yä), *n., pl.* **chol•las** (chōl′yäz, -yəz; *Sp.* chô′yäs). any of several spiny treelike cacti belonging to the genus *Opuntia,* esp. *O. fulgida* of the southwestern U.S. and Mexico, having knobby outgrowths and yellow spines. [1855–60, *Amer.*; < MexSp *cholla* head (perh. < OF (dial.) *cholle* ball < Gmc); see KEEL[1]]

cho•lo (chō′lō), *n., pl.* **-los.** *Chiefly Southwestern U.S.* **1.** (esp. among Mexican-Americans) a teenage boy who is a member of a street gang. **2.** *Disparaging.* a Mexican or Mexican-American. **3.** a mestizo of Spanish America. [1850–55; < Mex Sp: mestizo, peasant, allegedly shortening of *Cholollán* (< Nahuatl *Chōlōllān,* modern Cholula), a city-state in pre-conquest Mexico]

cho•lo•lith (kō′lə lith′, kol′ə-), *n. Pathol.* cholelith.

Cho•lon (chə lun′; *Fr.* shô lôN′), *n.* a suburb of Ho Chi Minh City, in S Vietnam.

Cho•lu•la (chô lo͞o′lä), *n.* a town in S Mexico, SE of Mexico City: ancient Aztec ruins. 20,913.

Cho•lu•te•ca (chô′lo͞o te′kä), *n.* a city in S Honduras. 43,551.

chomp (chomp), *v.t., v.i., n.* champ[1].

Chom•sky (chom′skē), *n.* **(Avram) Noam** (nōm, nō′-əm), born 1928, U.S. linguist and political activist.

Chom•sky•an (chom′skē ən), *adj.* of or pertaining to Noam Chomsky or his linguistic theories, esp. to transformational-generative grammar. [CHOMSKY + -AN]

chon (chun), *n., pl.* **chon. 1.** Also, **jun.** a monetary unit of North Korea, the hundredth part of a won. **2.** Also, **jeon.** a monetary unit of South Korea, the hundredth part of a won. [< Korean *chŏn* < Chin; akin to Chin *qián*; cf. SEN[1]]

chondr-, var. of **chondrio-** before a vowel.

chon•dral (kon′drəl), *adj. Anat., Zool.* of or pertaining to cartilage or a cartilage. [CHONDR- + -AL[1]]

chon•dri•a (kon′drē ə), *n.* a profusely branched red alga, *Chondria tenuissima,* of the Atlantic and Pacific coasts of North America. [< NL, fem. deriv. of Gk *chondríon,* dim. of *chóndros* cartilage; see -A[2]]

chon•drich•thi•an (kon drik′thē ən), *n.* any member of the class Chondrichthyes, comprising the cartilaginous fishes. [< NL, equiv. to *chondr-* CHONDR- + Gk *ichthýes* (pl.) fish]

chon•dri•fy (kon′drə fī′), *v.,* **-fied, -fy•ing.** —*v.t.* **1.** to change (a precursor tissue) into cartilage. —*v.i.* **2.** to become cartilage. [1870–75; CHONDR- + -IFY]

chondrio-, a combining form meaning "cartilage," used in the formation of compound words: *chondriosome.* Also, **chondr-, chondro-.** [< Gk *chondríon,* dim. of *chóndros* cartilage]

chon•drite (kon′drīt), *n.* a stony meteorite containing chondrules. [1880–85; CHONDR- + -ITE[1]] **—chon•drit•ic** (kon drit′ik), *adj.*

chondro-, var. of **chondrio-:** *chondrosarcoma.*

chon•dro•cra•ni•um (kon′drō krā′nē əm) *n., pl.* **-ni•ums, -ni•a** (-nē ə). a braincase composed of cartilage rather than bone, as the skull of sharks and of the vertebrate embryo before ossification. [1870–75; CHONDRO- + CRANIUM]

chon•droid (kon′droid), *adj.* cartilaginous or resembling cartilage. [1840–50; CHONDR- + -OID]

chon•dro•ma (kon drō′mə), *n., pl.* **-mas, -ma•ta** (-mə tə). *Pathol.* a benign cartilaginous tumor or growth. [CHONDR- + -OMA] **—chon•dro′ma•tous,** *adj.*

chon•dro•ma•la•cia (kon′drō mə lā′shə, -shē ə, -sē ə), *n. Pathol.* degeneration of cartilage in the knee, usually caused by excessive wear between the patella and lower end of the femur. Also called **runner's knee.** [CHONDRO- + MALACIA]

chon•drule (kon′dro͞ol), *n.* a small round mass of olivine or pyroxene found in stony meteorites. [1885–90; CHONDR- + -ULE]

Chong•jin (chœng′jin′), *n.* a seaport in W North Korea. 200,000.

Chong•ju (chung′jo͞o′), *n.* a city in central South Korea. 192,707.

Chong•qing (chông′ching′), *n. Pinyin.* a city in SE Sichuan province, in S central China, on the Chang Jiang: provisional capital of China 1937–46. 2,400,000. Also, **Chungking.**

Chon•ju (chœn′jo͞o′), *n.* a city in SW South Korea. 262,816.

choo-choo (cho͞o′cho͞o′), *n., v.,* **-chooed, -choo•ing.** *Baby Talk.* —*n.* **1.** a train. **2.** the sound of a steam locomotive. —*v.i.* **3.** to make a sound like that made by a steam locomotive. **4.** to travel by train. [1900–05; imit.]

chook (cho͝ok, cho͞ok), *n.* **1.** *Australian.* a hen. **2.** *Slang.* a woman. —*interj.* **3.** (used as a call for poultry or pigs.) Also, **chook•ie** (cho͝ok′ē, cho͞o′kē). [1885–90; cf. Brit. dial. *chuck, chook* call to poultry, CHUCK[3], CHICKEN]

choom (cho͝om), *n. Australian.* an Englishman. [1915–20; facetious resp. of CHUM[1], with *-oo-* repr. English Midlands pron. of the vowel]

choo•ra (cho͝or′ə), *n.* an Indian dagger having a sharply pointed, single-edged blade. [< Hindi]

choose (cho͞oz), *v.,* **chose; cho•sen** or (*Obs.*) **chose; choos•ing.** —*v.t.* **1.** to select from a number of possibilities; pick by preference: *She chose Sunday for her departure.* **2.** to prefer or decide (to do something): *He chose to speak.* **3.** to want; desire. **4.** (esp. in children's games) to contend with (an opponent) to decide, as by odd or even, who will do something: *I'll choose you to see who gets to bat first.* —*v.i.* **5.** to make a choice: *He chose carefully.* **6.** to be inclined: *You may stay here, if you choose.* **7.** (esp. in children's games) to decide, as by means of odd or even, who will do something: *Let's choose to see who bats first.* **8. cannot choose but,** cannot do otherwise than: *He cannot choose but obey.* **9. choose up, a.** to select (players) for a contest or game: *The boys chose up sides for the game.* **b.** to select players for a contest or game: *We have to choose up before we can play.* [bef. 1000; ME *chosen, chēsen,* OE *cēosan*; c. Goth *kiusan,* OHG *kiosan* (G *kiesen*); akin to Gk *geúesthai* to enjoy, L *gustāre* to taste (see GUSTO)] **—choos′a•ble,** *adj.* **—choos′er,** *n.*
—Syn. 1. CHOOSE, SELECT, PICK, ELECT, PREFER indicate a decision that one or more possibilities are to be regarded more highly than others. CHOOSE suggests a decision on one of a number of possibilities because of its apparent superiority: *to choose a course of action.* SELECT suggests a choice made for fitness: *to select the proper golf club.* PICK, an informal word, suggests a selection on personal grounds: *to pick a winner.* The formal word ELECT suggests a kind of official action: *to elect a representative.* PREFER, also formal, emphasizes the desire or liking for one thing more than for another or others: *to prefer coffee to tea.* **—Ant. 1.** reject.

choos•y (cho͞o′zē), *adj.,* **choos•i•er, choos•i•est.** hard to please, particular; fastidious, esp. in making a selection: *She's too choosy about food.* [1860–65, *Amer.*; CHOOSE + -Y[1]] **—choos′i•ness,** *n.*

chop[1] (chop), *v.*, **chopped, chop•ping,** *n.* —*v.t.* **1.** to cut or sever with a quick, heavy blow or a series of blows, using an ax, hatchet, etc. (often fol. by *down, off,* etc.): *to chop down a tree.* **2.** to make or prepare for use by so cutting: *to chop logs.* **3.** to cut in pieces; mince (often fol. by *up*): *to chop up an onion; to chop meat.* **4.** (in tennis, cricket, etc.) to hit (a ball) with a chop stroke. **5.** to weed and thin out (growing cotton) with a hoe. **6.** *Fox Hunting.* (of a hound or pack) to attack and kill (a fox that has not begun to run). —*v.i.* **7.** to make a quick, heavy stroke or a series of strokes, as with an ax. **8.** *Boxing.* to throw or deliver a short blow, esp. a downward one while in a clinch. **9.** (in tennis, cricket, etc.) to employ or deliver a chop stroke. **10.** to go, come, or move suddenly or violently. **11. chop** or **cut down to size.** See **cut** (def. 49). —*n.* **12.** an act or instance of chopping. **13.** a cutting blow. **14.** *Boxing.* a short blow, esp. a downward one, executed while in a clinch. **15.** a piece chopped off. **16.** an individual cut or portion of meat, as mutton, lamb, veal, or pork, usually one containing a rib. **17.** crushed or ground grain used as animal feed. **18.** a short, irregular, broken motion of waves; choppiness: *There's too much chop for rowing today.* **19.** rough, turbulent water, as of a sea or lake. **20.** See **chop stroke.** [1350–1400; ME *choppen;* var. of CHAP[1]]
—**Syn. 1.** See **cut.**

chop[2] (chop), *v.i.*, **chopped, chop•ping. 1.** to turn, shift, or change suddenly: *The wind chopped to the west.* **2.** to vacillate; change one's mind. **3.** *Obs.* **a.** to barter. **b.** to bandy words; argue. **4. chop logic,** to reason or dispute argumentatively; draw unnecessary distinctions. [1425–75; var. of obs. *chap* barter, ME *chappen* (with vowel as in CHAPMAN), *chepen,* OE *cēapian* to trade (deriv. of *cēap* sale, trade; see CHEAP)]

chop[3] (chop), *n.* **1.** Usually, **chops.** the jaw. **2. chops, a.** the oral cavity; mouth. **b.** *Slang.* the embouchure or technique necessary to play a wind instrument. **c.** *Slang.* musical ability on any instrument, esp. in playing jazz or rock; technical virtuosity. **d.** *Slang.* the music or musical part played by an instrumentalist, esp. a solo passage. **3.** an entranceway, as into a body of water. **4.** *Horol.* either of two pieces clasping the end of the suspension spring of a pendulum. **5. bust one's chops,** *Slang.* to exert oneself. **6. bust someone's chops,** *Slang.* to annoy with nagging or criticism: *Stop busting my chops —I'll get the job done.* **7. lick one's chops,** to await with pleasure; anticipate; relish: *He was already licking his chops over the expected inheritance.* Also, **chap.** [1350–1400; ME; perh. special use of CHOP[1]]

chop[4] (chop), *n.* **1.** an official stamp or seal, or a permit or clearance, esp. as formerly used in India and China. **2.** a design, corresponding to a brand or trademark, stamped on goods to indicate their identity or quality. **3.** the signature stamp of an artist, printmaker, etc., testifying to the authenticity of a work. **4.** quality, class, or grade: *a musician of the first chop.* [1605–15; < Hindi *chāp* impression, stamp]

cho•pa (chō′pə, chop′ə), *n., pl.* (*esp. collectively*) **-pa,** (*esp. referring to two or more kinds or species*) **-pas.** any of several fishes, esp. of the sea chub family, Kyphosidae, and the nibbler family, Girellidae. [1880–85; < Sp < Pg *choupa* < L *clupea;* see CLUPEID]

chop•block (chop′blok′), *n.* **1.** butcher-block. **2.** See **chopping block.** [CHOP[1] + BLOCK]

chop-chop (chop′chop′), *adv.* with haste; quickly. [1825–35; repetitive compound based on Chin Pidgin English *chop* quick, of uncert. orig.]

chop•fall•en (chop′fô′lən), *adj.* chapfallen. [1595–1605]

chop•house (chop′hous′), *n., pl.* **-hous•es** (-hou′ziz). a restaurant specializing in chops, steaks, and the like. [1680–90; CHOP[1] + HOUSE]

chop•in[1] (chop′in), *n.* **1.** an old Scottish unit of liquid measure equivalent to about a quart. **2.** a container holding this amount. [1225–75; ME < MF *chopine* < MLG *schōpe* SCOOP < MD *schoepe*]

chop•in[2] (chop′in), *n.* chopine.

Cho•pin (shō′pan; *for 1 also Fr.* shô paN′), *n.* **1. Fré•dé•ric Fran•çois** (fred′ə rik fran swä′, fred′rik; *Fr.* frā dā rēk′ frän swa′), 1810–49, Polish composer and pianist, in France after 1831. **2. Kate O'Flaherty,** 1851–1904, U.S. short-story writer and novelist.

cho•pine (chō pēn′, chop′in), *n.* a shoe having a thick sole, usually of cork, suggesting a short stilt, worn esp. by women in 18th-century Europe after its introduction from Turkey. Also, **chopin.** [1570–80; < Sp *chapín,* equiv. to *chap(a)* (< MF *chape* CHAPE) + *-in* -IN[1]]

chop•log•ic (chop′loj′ik), *n.* **1.** sophistic or overly complicated argumentation. —*adj.* **2.** Also, **chop′log′i•cal.** exhibiting or indulging in choplogic. [1520–30; CHOP[2] + LOGIC]

chop′ mark′, a notch or other mark made in a coin to indicate verification of its authenticity, esp. by a banker or merchant in the Far East during the 18th or 19th centuries. [1945–50]

chopped (chopt), *adj.* **1.** diced, minced, or cut into small bits. **2.** (of an automobile) streamlined; lowered. [1540–50]

chopped′ liv′er, cooked liver chopped with onions and hard-boiled eggs and seasoned.

chopped′ steak′, ground, cooked beef, usually served as a main course. Also, **chopsteak.**

chop•per (chop′ər), *n.* **1.** a person or thing that chops. **2.** a short ax with a large blade, used for cutting up meat, fish, etc.; butcher's cleaver. **3.** a prehistoric implement made by striking flakes off one or both sides of a stone, considered the oldest known worked stone tool. **4. choppers,** *Slang.* the teeth. **5.** *Informal.* a helicopter. **6.** *Slang.* a motorcycle. **7.** a device for interrupting an electric current or a beam of light at regular intervals. —*v.i.* **8.** *Informal.* **a.** to travel by helicopter: *We choppered into midtown from the airport.* **b.** to travel by motorcycle. [1545–55; 1950–55 for def. 5; CHOP[1] + -ER[1]]

chop′ping block′, a thick, often large block of wood on which meat, vegetables, etc., are placed for cutting, trimming, chopping, and the like. [1695–1705]

chop•py (chop′ē), *adj.*, **-pi•er, -pi•est. 1.** (of the sea, a lake, etc.) forming short, irregular, broken waves. **2.** (of the wind) shifting or changing suddenly or irregularly; variable. **3.** uneven in style or quality or characterized by poorly related parts: *The book was a choppy first novel.* [1595–1605; CHOP[2] + -Y[1]] —**chop′pi•ly,** *adv.* —**chop′pi•ness,** *n.*

chop′ shop′, *Informal.* a garage where stolen cars are dismantled so that their parts can be sold separately.

chop•steak (chop′stāk′), *n.* See **chopped steak.** [CHOP[1] + STEAK]

chop•stick (chop′stik′), *n.* one of a pair of thin, tapered sticks, often of wood or ivory, held in one hand between the thumb and fingers and used chiefly in China, Japan, and other Asian countries for lifting food to the mouth. [1690–1700; Chin Pidgin English *chop* quick (see CHOP-CHOP) + STICK[1]]

chopsticks

chop•sticks (chop′stiks′), *n.* (*used with a singular v.*) a harmonically and melodically simple waltz for piano played typically with the forefinger of each hand and sometimes having an accompanying part for a second player. [1890–95; perh. after CHOPSTICK from the way the fingers are held]

chop′ stroke′, (in tennis, cricket, etc.) a stroke made with a sharp downward movement of the racket, bat, etc., imparting a backspin to the ball. Also called **chop.**

chop′ su′ey (chop′so͞o′ē), a Chinese-style American dish consisting of small pieces of meat, chicken, etc., cooked together with bean sprouts, onions, mushrooms, or other vegetables and seasoning, in a gravy, often served with rice and soy sauce. Also, **chop′ soo′y.** [1885–90, *Amer.*; < dial. Chin (Guangdong) *jaahp seui* mixed bits, akin to Chin *zá suì*]

cho•ra•gus (kə rā′gəs, kō-, kô-), *n., pl.* **-gi** (-jī), **-gus•es. 1.** (in ancient Greece) **a.** the leader of a dramatic chorus. **b.** a person who undertook the expense of providing for such a chorus. **2.** any conductor of an entertainment or festival. Also, **choregus.** [1620–30; < L < Gk *chorāgós,* dial. var. of *chorēgós,* equiv. to *chor(ós)* CHORUS + *-ēgos,* comb. form of *ágein* to lead] —**cho•rag•ic** (kə raj′ik, -rā′jik), *adj.*

cho•ral (*adj.* kôr′əl, kōr′-; *n.* kə ral′, kô-, kō-, kôr′əl, kōr′-), *adj.* **1.** of a chorus or a choir: *She heads our new choral society.* **2.** sung by, adapted for, or containing a chorus or a choir. —*n.* **3.** chorale. [1580–90; < ML *chorālis,* equiv. to *chor(us)* CHORUS + *-ālis* -AL[1]] —**cho′ral•ly,** *adv.*

cho•rale (kə ral′, -räl′, kô-, kō-; kôr′əl, kōr′-), *n.* **1.** a hymn, esp. one with strong harmonization: *a Bach chorale.* **2.** a group of singers specializing in singing church music; choir. [1835–45; < G *Choral,* short for *Choralgesang,* trans. of L *cantus chorālis* choral singing; see CHORAL]

cho′rale pre′lude, *Music.* a composition usually for organ that is based on a chorale or other hymn tune and is typically contrapuntal in style. [1920–25]

cho′ral speak′ing, the recitation of poetry or prose by an ensemble or chorus.

chord[1] (kôrd), *n.* **1.** a feeling or emotion: *His story struck a chord of pity in the listeners.* **2.** *Geom.* the line segment between two points on a given curve. **3.** *Engin., Building Trades.* a principal member of a truss extending from end to end, usually one of a pair of such members, more or less parallel and connected by a web composed of various compression and tension members. **4.** *Aeron.* a straight line joining the trailing and leading edges of an airfoil section. **5.** *Anat.* cord (def. 6). [1350–1400; ME < L *chorda* < Gk *chordḗ* gut, string; r. CORD in senses given] —**chord′ed,** *adj.*

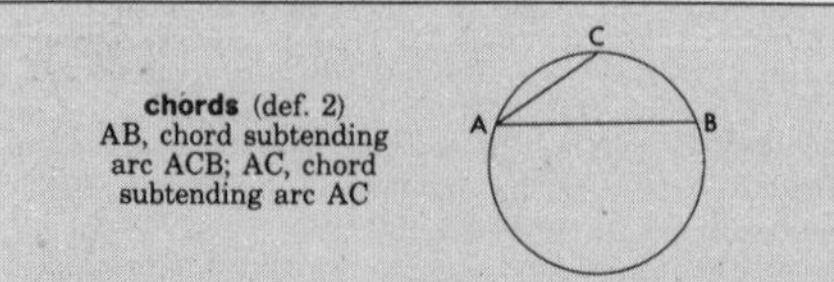

chords (def. 2)
AB, chord subtending arc ACB; AC, chord subtending arc AC

chord[2] (kôrd), *n.* **1.** a combination of usually three or more musical tones sounded simultaneously. —*v.t.* **2.** to establish or play a chord or chords for (a particular harmony or song); harmonize or voice: *How would you chord that in B flat?* [1350–1400; earlier *cord,* ME, short for ACCORD; *ch-* from CHORD[1]]

chord•al (kôr′dl), *adj.* **1.** of, pertaining to, or resembling a chord. **2.** of or pertaining to music that is marked principally by vertical harmonic movement rather than by linear polyphony. [1610–20; CHORD[2] + -AL[1]]

chor•da•mes•o•derm (kôr′də mez′ə dûrm′, -mes′-, -mē′zə-, -sə-), *n. Embryol.* the part of the blastoderm of a young embryo that forms the notochord and related structures. [1935–40; < NL *chorda* (see CHORD[1]) + MESODERM] —**chor′da•mes′o•der′mal, chor′da•mes′o•der′mic,** *adj.*

Chor•da•ta (kôr dā′tə, -dä′-), *n. Zool.* the phylum comprising the chordates. [1875–80; < NL, equiv. to *chord(a)* (see CHORD[1]) + L *-āta,* neut. pl. of *-ātus* -ATE[1]]

chor•date (kôr′dāt), *Zool.* —*adj.* **1.** belonging or pertaining to the phylum Chordata, comprising the true vertebrates and those animals having a notochord, as the lancelets and tunicates. —*n.* **2.** a chordate animal. [1885–90; see CHORDATA]

chor•da ten•din•e•a (kôr′də ten din′ē ə), *pl.* **chor•dae ten•din•e•ae** (kôr′dē ten din′ē ē′). *Anat.* any of the tendons extending from the papillary muscles to the atrioventricular valves and preventing the valves from moving into the atria during ventricular contraction. [1800–10; < NL: tendinous cord]

chord′ chart′, a chart indicating by means of symbols the identity, sequence, and duration of the musical chords occurring in the accompaniment to a melody.

chor•dee (kôr′dē, -dā, kōr′-), *n. Pathol.* a downward bowing of the penis, of a congenital nature or caused by gonorrhea. [1700–10; < F *cordée* (fem. ptp.) corded, in the phrase *chaude-pisse cordée* corded gonorrhea]

chord′ of the sixth′, *Music.* See **sixth chord.**

chor•do•phone (kôr′də fōn′), *n.* a stringed instrument of a group including the harps, lutes, lyres, and zithers. [1935–40; CHORD[1] + -O- + -PHONE]

chord′ or′gan, an electronic organ having a small keyboard for the right hand and for the left hand a set of buttons each of which produces a full chord when pushed. [1950–55]

chor•dot•o•my (kôr dot′ə mē), *n., pl.* **-mies.** cordotomy. [CHORD[1] + -O- + -TOMY]

chor•do•to•nal (kôr′də tōn′l), *adj.* (of an insect) responsive to sound vibrations, as certain organs or parts. [1885–90; CHORD[1] + -O- + TONAL]

chore (chôr, chōr), *n.* **1.** a small or odd job; routine task. **2. chores,** the everyday work around a house or farm. **3.** a hard or unpleasant task: *Solving the problem was quite a chore.* [1375–1425; late ME *char,* OE *cyrr,* var. of *cierr, cerr* CHAR[3]]
—**Syn. 1.** duty, work, errand, stint. **1, 2.** See **task.**

cho•re•a (kə rē′ə, kô-, kō-), *n. Pathol.* **1.** any of several diseases of the nervous system characterized by jerky, involuntary movements, chiefly of the face and extremities. **2.** Also called **St. Vitus's dance.** such a disease occurring chiefly in children and associated with rheumatic fever. **3.** *Vet. Pathol.* a disease of the central nervous system caused by bacterial or organic degeneration, most common in dogs following canine distemper, characterized by irregular, jerky, involuntary muscular movements. [1680–90; < Gk *choreía* a dance, equiv. to *chor(ós)* CHORUS + *-eia* -Y[3]] —**cho•re′al, cho•re′ic, cho•re•at•ic** (kôr′ē at′ik, kōr′-), *adj.* —**cho•re•oid** (kôr′ē oid′, kōr′-), *adj.*

cho•re•gus (kə rē′gəs, kô-, kō-), *n., pl.* **-gi** (-jī), **-gus•es.** choragus.

cho•re•i•form (kə rē′ə fôrm′), *adj. Pathol.* of, pertaining to, or resembling chorea. [1905–10; CHORE(A) + -I- + -FORM]

chore•man (chôr′mən, -man′, chōr′-), *n., pl.* **-men** (-mən -men′). a menial worker, as in a logging camp. [1870–75; CHORE + MAN[1]]

cho•re•o•graph (kôr′ē ə graf′, -gräf′, kōr′-), *v.t.* **1.** to provide the choreography for: *to choreograph a musical comedy.* **2.** to manage, maneuver, or direct: *The author is a genius at choreographing a large cast of characters.* —*v.i.* **3.** to work as a choreographer. [1875–80; back formation from CHOREOGRAPHY]

cho•re•og•ra•pher (kôr′ē og′rə fər, kōr′-), *n.* a person who creates dance compositions and plans and arranges dance movements and patterns for dances and esp. for ballets. [1885–90; CHOREOGRAPH(Y) + -ER[1]]

cho•re•og•ra•phy (kôr′ē og′rə fē, kōr′-), *n.* **1.** the art of composing ballets and other dances and planning and arranging the movements, steps, and patterns of dancers. **2.** the technique of representing the various movements in dancing by a system of notation. **3.** the arrangement or manipulation of actions leading up to an event: *the choreography of a surprise birthday party.* [1780–90; < Gk *chore-* (s. of *choreía* CHOREA) + -O- + -GRAPHY] —**cho•re•o•graph•ic** (kôr′ē ə graf′ik, kōr′-), *adj.* —**cho′re•o•graph′i•cal•ly,** *adv.*

cho•re•ol•o•gy (kôr′ē ol′ə jē, kōr′-), *n.* **1.** the study of dance notation. **2.** the recording of dance movement by notation. [1965–70; *choreo-* (see CHOREOGRAPHY) + -LOGY] —**cho′re•ol′o•gist,** *n.*

cho•reu•tic (kə ro͞o′tik), *adj.* of or belonging to a chorus. [< Gk *choreutikós* pertaining to choral song and dance, equiv. to *choreut(ḗs)* choral dancer (*choreú(ein)* to dance a choral dance, deriv. of *chorós* CHORUS + *-tēs* agent suffix) + *-ikos* -IC]

cho•reu•tics (kə ro͞o′tiks), *n.* (*used with a singular v.*) *Dance.* a system that analyzes form in movement, developed by Rudolf von Laban (1879–1958), Hungarian choreographer and dance theorist. [see CHOREUTIC, -ICS]

chori-, var. of **chorio-.**

cho•ri•amb (kôr′ē amb′, -am′, kōr′-), *n. Pros.* a foot of four syllables, two short between two long or two unstressed between two stressed. [1835–45; short for CHORIAMBUS] —**cho′ri•am′bic,** *adj.*

cho•ri•am•bus (kôr′ē am′bəs, kōr′-), *n., pl.* **-bi** (-bī), **-bus•es.** choriamb. [1840–50; < LL < Gk *choríambos,* equiv. to *chor(eîos)* choric + *íambos* IAMB]

cho•ric (kôr′ik, kōr′-), *adj.* of, pertaining to, or written for a chorus. [1810–20; < LL *choricus* < Gk *chorikós,* equiv. to *chor(ós)* CHORUS + *-ikos* -IC]

cho·rine (kôr′in, kōr′ēn), *n.* a chorus girl. [1920–25, *Amer.;* CHOR(US) + -INE[2]]

chorio-, a combining form meaning "chorion," "choroid," used in the formation of compound words: *chorioallantois.* Also, **chori-.** [comb. form repr. Gk *chórion*]

cho·ri·o·al·lan·to·is (kôr′ē ō ə lan′tō is, -tois, kōr′-), *n. Embryol., Zool.* a vascular, extraembryonic membrane of birds, reptiles, and certain mammals, formed by the fusion of the wall of the chorion with the wall of the allantois. Also called **cho′rioallanto′ic mem′brane.** [1930–35; CHORIO- + ALLANTOIS] —**cho·ri·o·al·lan·to·ic** (kôr′ē ō al′ən tō′ik, kōr′-) *adj.*

cho·ri·o·car·ci·no·ma (kôr′ē ō kär′sə nō′mə, kōr′-), *n., pl.* **-mas, -ma·ta** (-mə tə). *Pathol.* chorioma. [1900–05; CHORIO- + CARCINOMA]

cho·ri·oid (kôr′ē oid′, kōr′-), *adj., n. Anat.* choroid. Also, **cho′ri·oi′dal.** [< Gk *chorioeidḗs.* See CHORI-, -OID]

cho·ri·o·ma (kôr′ē ō′mə, kōr′-), *n., pl.* **-mas, -ma·ta** (-mə tə). *Pathol.* any benign or malignant tumor of chorionic tissue; choriocarcinoma. [by shortening]

cho·ri·on (kôr′ē on′, kōr′-), *n.* **1.** *Embryol.* the outermost of the extraembryonic membranes of land vertebrates, contributing to the formation of the placenta in the placental mammals. **2.** *Zool.* the membrane around the eggs of certain insects, secreted by cells of the ovary. [1535–45; < NL < Gk *chórion* membrane enclosing the fetus] —**cho′ri·on′ic, cho′ri·al,** *adj.*

chorion′ic gonadotro′pin, 1. Also called **human chorionic gonadotropin.** *Biochem.* a hormone, produced in the incipient placenta of pregnant women, that stimulates the production of estrogen and progesterone: its presence in blood or urine is an indication of pregnancy. **2.** *Pharm.* a commercial form of this substance, obtained from the urine of pregnant mares, used in medicine in the treatment of testicular disorders and functional uterine bleeding, and in veterinary medicine in the treatment of cystic ovaries, esp. in cows and mares. Also, **chorion′ic gonadotro′phin.** [GONADOTROP(IC) + -IN[2]]

cho′rion′ic vil′lus, *Embryol.* one of the branching outgrowths of the chorion that, together with maternal tissue, form the placenta.

chorion′ic vil′lus sam′pling, a prenatal test for detecting birth defects at an early stage of pregnancy, involving removal by needle of fluid from the chorionic villus, and examination of the cells obtained.

cho·ri·pet·al·ous (kôr′ə pet′l əs, kōr′-), *adj. Bot.* having unconnected petals. [1875–80; < Gk *chōri,* var. of *chōris* apart + PETALOUS]

cho·ri·so (chə rē′sō), *n., pl.* **-sos.** chorizo.

chor·is·ter (kôr′ə stər, kor′-), *n.* **1.** a singer in a choir. **2.** a choirboy. **3.** a choir leader. [1325–75; < ML *chorist(a)* singer in a choir + -ER[1]; r. ME *queristre* < AF, equiv. to *quer* CHOIR + *-istre* -IST]

cho·ri·zo (chə rē′zō; *Sp.* chô rē′sô, -thô), *n., pl.* **-zos** (-zōz; *Sp.* -sôs, -thôs). *Spanish Cookery.* a pork sausage spiced with garlic, peppers, and juniper berries and smoked and dried. Also, **choriso.** [< Sp, of uncert. orig.]

C horizon, the layer in a soil profile below the B horizon and immediately above the bedrock, consisting chiefly of weathered, partially decomposed rock. [1930–35]

cho·ro·gi (chôr′ō gē′, chōr′-), *n.* See **Chinese artichoke.** [< Japn, of uncert. orig.; *-gi* perh. comb. form of *ki* onion, plant]

cho·rog·ra·phy (kə rog′rə fē, kô-, kō-), *n., pl.* **-phies.** *Geog.* a systematic, detailed description and analysis of a region or regions. [1550–60; < L *chōrographia* < Gk *chōrographía,* equiv. to *chōro-,* comb. form of *chṓra* region + *-graphia* -GRAPHY] —**cho·rog′ra·pher,** *n.* —**cho·ro·graph·ic** (kôr′ə graf′ik, kōr′-), **cho′ro·graph′i·cal,** *adj.* —**cho′ro·graph′i·cal·ly,** *adv.*

cho·roid (kôr′oid, kōr′-), *Anat.* —*adj.* **1.** like the chorion; membranous. —*n.* **2.** See **choroid coat.** Also, **cho·roi′dal, chorioid, chorioidal.** [1625–35; < Gk *choroeidḗs* false reading for *chorioeidḗs* CHORIOID]

cho′roid coat′, *Ophthalm.* a pigmented, highly vascular membrane of the eye that is continuous with the iris and lies between the sclera and the retina, functioning to nourish the retina and absorb scattered light. See diag. under **eye.** Also called **choroid, cho′roid mem′·brane.** [1735–45]

cho·roid·i·tis (kôr′oi dī′tis, kōr′-), *n. Ophthalm.* inflammation of the choroid coat. [1875–80; < NL; see CHOROID, -ITIS]

chor·ten (chôr′ten), *n.* (in Tibet) a monument to a distinguished Buddhist, esp. a lama. [1890–95; < Tibetan *chörten* (sp. *mchod rten*)]

chor·tle (chôr′tl), *v.,* **-tled, -tling,** *n.* —*v.i.* **1.** to chuckle gleefully. —*v.t.* **2.** to express with a gleeful chuckle: *to chortle one's joy.* —*n.* **3.** a gleeful chuckle. [b. CHUCKLE and SNORT; coined by Lewis Carroll in *Through the Looking-Glass* (1871)] —**chor′tler,** *n.*

cho·rus (kôr′əs, kōr′-), *n., pl.* **-rus·es,** *v.,* **-rused, -rus·ing.** —*n.* **1.** *Music.* **a.** a group of persons singing in unison. **b.** (in an opera, oratorio, etc.) such a group singing choral parts in connection with soloists or individual singers. **c.** a piece of music for singing in unison. **d.** a part of a song that recurs at intervals, usually following each verse; refrain. **2.** simultaneous utterance in singing, speaking, shouting, etc. **3.** the sounds so uttered: *a chorus of jeers.* **4.** (in a musical show) **a.** a company of dancers and singers. **b.** the singing, dancing, or songs performed by such a company. **5.** (in ancient Greece) **a.** a lyric poem, believed to have been in dithyrambic form, that was sung and danced to, originally as a religious rite, by a company of persons. **b.** an ode or series of odes sung by a group of actors in ancient Greek drama. **c.** the group of actors that performed the chorus and served as major participants in, commentators on, or as a supplement to the main action of the drama. **6.** *Theat.* **a.** a group of actors or a single actor having a function similar to that of the Greek chorus, as in Elizabethan drama. **b.** the part of a play performed by such a group or individual. **7. in chorus,** in unison; with all speaking or singing simultaneously: *They responded in chorus to the minister's questions.* —*v.t., v.i.* **8.** to sing or speak in chorus. [1555–65; < L < Gk *chorós* a dance, band of dancers and singers]

cho′rus boy′, a male singer or dancer of the chorus of a musical comedy, vaudeville show, etc. [1940–45]

cho′rus frog′, any of several small North American frogs of the genus *Pseudacris,* having a loud call commonly heard in the early spring.

cho′rus girl′, a female singer or dancer of the chorus of a musical comedy, vaudeville show, etc. [1890–95]

Cho·rzów (hô′zho͞of), *n.* a city in S Poland. 156,000. German, **Königshütte.** Formerly, **Królewska Huta.**

chose[1] (chōz), *v.* **1.** pt. of **choose. 2.** *Obs.* pp. of **choose.**

chose[2] (shōz), *n. Law.* a thing; an article of personal property. [1350–1400 for earlier senses; 1660–70 for current sense; ME < F < L *causa* case, thing. See CAUSE]

cho·sen (chō′zən), *v.* **1.** a pp. of **choose.** —*adj.* **2.** selected from several; preferred: *my chosen profession.* **3.** *Theol.* elect (def. 9). —*n.* **4.** elect. —**cho′sen·ness,** *n.*

Cho·sen (chō′sen′), *n.* Japanese name of **Korea.**

cho′sen peo′ple, (*often caps.*) the Israelites. Ex. 19. [1525–35]

cho·sis·me (shō zēz′mə), *n.* a writing style in which plot and characterization are de-emphasized and people, events, and setting are recorded as though seen by the author through the lens of a camera. [< F, equiv. to *chose* thing (see CHOSE[2]) + *-isme* -ISM]

chotch·ke (chäch′kə), *n. Slang.* tchotchke.

chott (shot), *n.* a shallow brackish or saline marsh or lake in N Africa, usually dry during the summer. Also, **shott.** [1970–75; < F < Ar *shaṭṭ*]

chou (sho͞o), *n., pl.* **choux** (sho͞oz *for 1;* sho͞o *for 2*). **1.** a cabbage-shaped decoration, as a rosette or knot on a woman's dress, hat, etc. **2.** See **cream puff.** [1700–10; < F: cabbage < L *caulis* stem; see CAULIS]

Chou (jō), *n.* a dynasty in China, 1122?–256 B.C., marked by the division of China into separate feudal states and the emergence of important philosophical schools, esp. Confucianism and Taoism. Also, **Chow, Zhou.**

chou·croute (sho͞o kro͞ot′), *n. French.* sauerkraut.

Chou En-lai (jō′ en′lī′), *Wade-Giles.* See **Zhou Enlai.**

chou·ette (sho͞o et′), *n.* a variation of a two-handed game, as backgammon, allowing the participation of three or more persons, in which one player accepts the bets of all the others on the outcome of a game between that player and one other active player, who is permitted to receive advice from the nonplayers. [1885–90; < F, from the phrase *faire la chouette* to play alone against a group of opponents (in billiards, etc.), lit., to play the barn owl, perh. alluding to the owl's watchful look]

chough (chuf), *n.* any of several crowlike Old World birds, esp. *Pyrrhocorax pyrrhocorax,* of Europe. [1275–1325; ME *choghe;* akin to OE *cēo,* D *kauw,* Dan *kaa*]

Chou·kou·tien (jō′kō′tyen′), *n. Wade-Giles.* Zhoukoudian.

chou′ pas′try. See **cream puff paste.** [1950–55]

chouse (chous), *v.,* **choused, chous·ing,** *n.* —*v.t.* **1.** to swindle; cheat (often fol. by *of* or *out of*). —*n.* **2.** a swindle. **3.** *Archaic.* a swindler. **4.** *Archaic.* a dupe. [1600–10; perh. to be identified with CHIAUS] —**chous′·er,** *n.*

chow[1] (chou), *Informal.* —*n.* **1.** food, esp. hearty dishes or a meal. —*v.i.* **2. chow down,** to eat; eat a meal, esp. the main meal of the day: *In the army we usually chow down at 6* P.M. [1855–60, *Amer.;* short for CHOW-CHOW]

chow[2] (chou), (*often cap.*) *n.* See **chow chow.** [short form]

Chow (chou; *Chin.* jō), *n.* Chou.

Chow (chou), *n. Australian Disparaging.* a Chinese. [1870–75; special use of CHOW[1]]

chow chow (chou′ chou′), (*often caps.*) one of a Chinese breed of medium-sized dogs having a thick black, blue, red, or cream coat and a blue-black tongue. Also, **chow.** [1785–95; said to be < dial. Chin; cf. Guangdong dial. *gáu* dog]

chow chow
20 in. (51 cm)
high at shoulder

chow-chow (chou′chou′), *n.* **1.** a Chinese mixed fruit preserve. **2.** a relish of chopped mixed pickles in mustard sauce. [1785–95; < Chin Pidgin English]

chow·der (chou′dər), *n.* a thick soup or stew made of clams, fish, or vegetables, with potatoes, onions, and other ingredients and seasonings. [1735–45, *Amer.;* < F *chaudière* pot, kettle < LL *caldāria* CAULDRON]

chow·der·head (chou′dər hed′), *n. Slang.* a stupid person; blockhead. [1825–35; cf. Brit. dial. (Lancashire) *chowterhead,* phon. var. of *cholterhead,* dial. var. of *jolterhead,* earlier *joltheed,* equiv. to *jolt-, jolter-* (prob. akin to JOLT, but sense uncert.) + HEAD] —**chow′der·head′ed,** *adj.*

chow·hound (chou′hound′), *n. Slang.* a person who eats food in large quantities or with great gusto; glutton. [1940–45; CHOW[1] + HOUND[1]]

chow mein (chou′ mān′), a Chinese-style dish of steamed or stir-fried vegetables, topped with shredded chicken, shrimp, etc., and served with fried noodles. [1900–05, *Amer.;* < Chin *chǎo* fry + *miàn* noodles, or < cognate dial. forms]

chow·time (chou′tīm′), *n. Slang.* mealtime. [1910–15; CHOW[1] + TIME]

cho·yo·te (choi ō′tē), *n.* chayote.

choz·e·rei (KHä′zə RĪ′; *Eng.* hä′zə rī′), *n. Yiddish.* chazerei.

CHQ, Corps Headquarters.

Chr., 1. Christ. **2.** Christian.

chrem·zel (krem′zəl; *Yiddish* KHREM′zəl), *n., pl.* **chremz·lach** (kremz′lək, -läk; *Yiddish* KHREMZ′ləKH, -läKH). *Jewish Cookery.* a flat cake made from matzo meal, topped or stuffed with a filling, as of ground meat or fruit and nuts. Also, **chrem′sel.** [< Yiddish *khremzl*]

Chres·tien de Troyes (krā tyaN′ də trwä′), c1140–c90, French poet. Also, **Chré·tien′ de Troyes′.**

chres·tom·a·thy (kres tom′ə thē), *n., pl.* **-thies.** a collection of selected literary passages, often by one author and esp. from a foreign language. [1825–35; < NL *chrestomathia* < Gk *chrēstomátheia,* equiv. to *chrēstó(s)* useful (*chrēs-,* s. of *chrēsthai* to use + *-tos* v. adj. suffix) + *math-* (var. s. of *manthánein* to learn) + *-eia* -Y[3]] —**chres·to·math·ic** (kres′tə math′ik), *adj.*

Chris (kris), *n.* **1.** a male given name, form of **Christopher. 2.** a female given name, form of **Christine.**

chrism (kriz′əm), *n.* a consecrated oil, usually mixed with balsam or balsam and spices, used by certain churches in various rites, as in baptism, confirmation, and the like. Also, **chrisom.** [bef. 900; learned respelling of ME *crisme,* OE *crisma* < L *chrisma* < Gk *chrîsma* unguent, unction] —**chris′mal,** *adj.*

chris·ma·to·ry (kriz′mə tôr′ē, -tōr′ē), *n., pl.* **-ries,** a receptacle for chrism. [1375–1425; late ME *crismatorie* < ML *chrismatōrium,* equiv. to *chrismat-* (s. of *chrisma*) CHRISM + *-ōrium* for L *-tōrium* -TORY[2]]

chris·mon (kriz′mon), *n.* Chi-Rho. [< L *Chris(tus)* CHRIST + LL *mon(ogramma)* MONOGRAM]

chris·om (kriz′əm), *n.* **1.** chrism. **2.** a white cloth or robe put on a person at baptism to signify innocence. [1400–50; late ME *krysom, crysum,* var. of CHRISM]

chris′om child′, a baptized child that dies in its first month. [1535–45]

Christ (krīst), *n.* **1.** Jesus of Nazareth, held by Christians to be the fulfillment of prophecies in the Old Testament regarding the eventual coming of a Messiah. **2.** the Messiah prophesied in the Old Testament (used chiefly in versions of the New Testament). **3.** someone regarded as similar to Jesus of Nazareth. [learned respelling of ME, OE *Crist* < L *Christus* < Gk *christos* anointed, trans. of Heb *māshīaḥ* anointed, Messiah]

Christ·church (krīst′chûrch′), *n.* a city on E South Island, in New Zealand. 325,710.

christ·cross (kris′krôs′, -kros′), *n.* the figure or mark of a cross. [1350–1400; ME *Crist cross*]

christ·cross-row (kris′krôs′rō′, -kros′-), *n.* the alphabet. [1555–65]

chris·ten (kris′ən), *v.t.* **1.** to receive into the Christian church by baptism; baptize. **2.** to give a name to at baptism: *They christened her Mary.* **3.** to name and dedicate: *to christen a ship.* **4.** to make use of for the first time. [bef. 900; ME *cristenen,* OE *cristnian,* deriv. of *cristen* CHRISTIAN] —**chris′ten·er,** *n.*

Chris·ten·dom (kris′ən dəm), *n.* **1.** Christians collectively. **2.** the Christian world. **3.** Christianity. [bef. 900; ME; OE *cristendōm.* See CHRISTIAN, -DOM]

chris·ten·ing (kris′ə ning, kris′ning), *n.* **1.** the ceremony of baptism, esp. as accompanied by the giving of a name to a child. **2.** a public ceremony in which a new ship is formally named and launched. **3.** an act or instance of naming or dedicating something new. [1250–1300; ME; see CHRISTEN, -ING[1]]

Christ·hood (krīst′ho͝od), *n.* the condition of being a Christ. [1375–1425; late ME; see CHRIST, -HOOD]

Chris·tian (kris′chən), *adj.* **1.** of, pertaining to, or derived from Jesus Christ or His teachings: *a Christian faith.* **2.** of, pertaining to, believing in, or belonging to the religion based on the teachings of Jesus Christ: *Spain is a Christian country.* **3.** of or pertaining to Christians: *many Christian deaths in the Crusades.* **4.** exhibiting a spirit proper to a follower of Jesus Christ; Christlike: *She displayed true Christian charity.* **5.** decent; respectable: *They gave him a good Christian burial.* **6.** human; not brutal; humane: *Such behavior isn't Christian.* —*n.* **7.** a person who believes in Jesus Christ; adherent of Christianity. **8.** a person who exemplifies in his or her life the teachings of Christ: *He died like a true Christian.* **9.** a member of any of certain Protestant churches, as the Disciples of Christ and the Plymouth Brethren. **10.** the hero of Bunyan's *Pilgrim's Progress.* **11.** a male given name. [1250–1300; < L *Christiānus* < Gk *Christiānós,* equiv. to *Christ(ós)* CHRIST + *-iānos* < L *-iānus* -IAN; r. ME, OE *cristen* < L, as above]

Christian IX, 1818–1906, king of Denmark 1863–1906.

Christian X, 1870–1947, king of Denmark 1912–47.

Chris′tian Breth′ren. See **Plymouth Brethren.** [1880–85]

CONCISE PRONUNCIATION KEY: *act, cāpe, dâre, pärt; set, ēqual; if, īce; ox, ōver, ôrder, oil, bo͝ok, bo͞ot, out; up, ûrge; child; sing; shoe; thin, that;* zh as in *treasure.* ə = *a* as in *alone, e* as in *system, i* as in *easily, o* as in *gallop, u* as in *circus;* ᵊ as in *fire* (fīᵊr), *hour* (ouᵊr). l and n can serve as syllabic consonants, as in *cradle* (krād′l), and *button* (but′n). See the full key inside the front cover.

Chris′tian Broth′er. See **Brother of the Christian Schools.** [1810–20]

Chris′tian Endeav′or, an organization of young people of various evangelical Protestant churches, formed in 1881 to promote Christian principles and service. [1890–95, *Amer.*]

Chris′tian E′ra, the period since the assumed year of Jesus' birth. [1650–60]

Chris•ti•an•i•a (kris′chē an′ē ə, -ä′nē ə, kris′tē-), *n.* **1.** former name of **Oslo. 2.** (*sometimes l.c.*) Also called **Christie, Christy.** any of several skiing turns executed in order to change direction on a downhill run or for decreasing speed or stopping, esp. a turn in which the body is swung around with the skis kept parallel. [1900–05]

Chris•tian•ism (kris′chə niz′əm), *n.* the beliefs and practices of Christians. [1570–80; < LL *Chrīstiānismus* < Gk *Christianismós* Christianity, equiv. to *christiān(ós)* CHRISTIAN + *-ismos* -ISM]

Chris•ti•an•i•ty (kris′chē an′i tē), *n., pl.* **-ties. 1.** the Christian religion, including the Catholic, Protestant, and Eastern Orthodox churches. **2.** Christian beliefs or practices; Christian quality or character: *Christianity mixed with pagan elements; the Christianity of Augustine's thought.* **3.** a particular Christian religious system: *She followed fundamentalist Christianity.* **4.** the state of being a Christian. **5.** Christendom. **6.** conformity to the Christian religion or to its beliefs or practices. [1250–1300; ME *cristianite* < L *christiānitāt-* (s. of *christiānitās*), equiv. to *christiān-* CHRISTIAN + *-itāt-* -ITY; r. ME *cristiente* < MF < L, as above]

Chris•tian•ize (kris′chə nīz′), *v.t.,* **-ized, -iz•ing. 1.** to make Christian. **2.** to imbue with Christian principles. Also, *esp. Brit.,* **Chris′tian•ise′.** [1585–95; CHRISTIAN + -IZE] **—Chris′tian•i•za′tion,** *n.* **—Chris′tian•iz′er,** *n.*

Chris•tian•like (kris′chən līk′), *adj.* like or befitting a Christian. [1565–75; CHRISTIAN + -LIKE]

Chris•tian•ly (kris′chən lē), *adj.* **1.** like a Christian; Christianlike. **—***adv.* **2.** in a Christian manner. [1375–1425; late ME *cristenli.* See CHRISTIAN, -LY]

Chris′tian name′, 1. Also called **baptismal name.** the name given one at baptism, as distinguished from the family name. **2.** a person's first or given name. [1540–50]

Chris′tian Reformed′, of or pertaining to a Protestant denomination **(Chris′tian Reformed′ Church′)** organized in the U.S. in 1857 by groups that had seceded from the Dutch Reformed Church.

Chris•tian•sand (kris′chən sand′; *Norw.* kʀɪs′tyän sän′), *n.* former name of **Kristiansand.**

Chris•tians•burg (kris′chənz bûrg′), *n.* a town in SW Virginia. 10,345.

Chris′tian Sci′ence, a system of religious teaching, founded in 1866 by Mary Baker Eddy and based on the Scriptures, the most notable application of which is the practice of spiritual healing. [1860–65, *Amer.*]

Chris′tian Sci′entist, a believer in Christian Science; a member of the Church of Christ, Scientist.

Chris′tian So′cialist, a member of any of certain European political parties advocating a form of social organization based on Christian and socialistic principles. [1855–60] **—Chris′tian So′cialism.**

Chris′tian year′, a year in the ecclesiastical calendar, used esp. in reference to the various feast days and special seasons. Also called **church year.**

Chris•tie (kris′tē), *n.* (*sometimes l.c.*) *Skiing.* Christiania (def. 2). [1915–20; by shortening; see -IE]

Chris•tie (kris′tē), *n.* **1. Agatha,** 1891–1976, English novelist of detective fiction. **2.** a male given name, form of **Christopher. 3.** a female given name, form of **Christine.**

Chris•ti•na (kri stē′nə), *n.* **1.** 1626–89, queen of Sweden 1632–54 (daughter of Gustavus Adolphus). **2.** a female given name.

Chris•tine (kri stēn′), *n.* a female given name: derived from *Christian.*

Christ′ Je′sus, Jesus (def. 1).

Christ•less (krīst′lis), *adj.* being without the teachings or spirit of Christ; unchristian. [1645–55; CHRIST + -LESS]

Christ•like (krīst′līk′), *adj.* like Christ; showing the spirit of Christ. [1670–80; CHRIST + -LIKE]

Christ•ly (krīst′lē), *adj.* Christlike. [bef. 1000; OE *cristlic* (unrecorded in ME; mod. E *Christly* appar. a reformation on the model of GODLY, MANLY, etc.); see CHRIST, -LY] **—Christ′li•ness,** *n.*

Christ•mas (kris′məs), *n.* **1.** the annual festival of the Christian church commemorating the birth of Jesus: celebrated on December 25 and now generally observed as a legal holiday and an occasion for exchanging gifts. **2.** Christmastime. **3.** Christmastide. [bef. 1150; ME *cristmasse;* OE *Cristes mæsse* MASS of CHRIST] **—Christ′•mas•sy, Christ′mas•y,** *adj.*

Christ•mas•ber•ry (kris′məs ber′ē), *n., pl.* **-ries.** toyon. [1895–1900, *Amer.;* CHRISTMAS + BERRY]

Christ′masberry tree′. See **Brazilian pepper tree.**

Christ′mas cac′tus, a cactus, *Schlumbergera bridgesii* (or *Zygocactus bridgesii*), native to Brazil, having stems with leaflike segments and showy, purplish-red flowers, and often cultivated as a houseplant. [1895–1900]

Christ′mas card′, a printed and often decorated card for mailing at Christmas to express good wishes. [1880–85]

CONCISE ETYMOLOGY KEY: <, descended or borrowed from; >, whence; b., blend of, blended; c., cognate with; cf., compare; deriv., derivative; equiv., equivalent; imit., imitative; obl., oblique; r., replacing; s., stem; sp., spelling, spelled; resp., respelling, respelled; trans., translation; ?, origin unknown; *, unattested; ‡, probably earlier than. See the full key inside the front cover.

Christ′mas Car′ol, A, a story (1843) by Dickens.

Christ′mas club′, a savings account in a bank in which regular deposits are made, usually throughout one year, as to provide funds for Christmas shopping. [1905–10]

Christ′mas disease′, *Pathol.* a hereditary disease characterized by an inability of the blood to clot because of a deficiency of a coagulation factor. [1952; after S. *Christmas,* the first sufferer from the disease to be examined in detail]

Christ′mas Eve′, the evening or the day preceding Christmas. [1350–1400; ME]

Christ′mas fac′tor, *Biochem.* a blood constituent necessary for clotting, the absence of which is characterized by a hemophilialike condition. Also called **factor IX, plasma thromboplastic component.** [see CHRISTMAS DISEASE]

Christ′mas fern′, an evergreen fern, *Polystichum acrostichoides,* having dense clusters of stiff fronds growing from a central rootstock. Also called **dagger fern.** [1875–80]

Christ′mas Is′land, 1. an Australian island in the Indian Ocean, ab. 190 mi. (300 km) S of Java. 3300; 52 sq. mi. (135 sq. km). **2.** one of the Line Islands, in Kiribati (Gilbert Islands), in the central Pacific; sovereignty disputed by U.S.: largest atoll in the Pacific; former U.S. test center for nuclear warheads. ab. 220 sq. mi. (575 sq. km).

Christ′mas pan′tomime, pantomime (def. 5).

Christ′mas pud′ding. See **plum pudding.** [1855–60]

Christ′mas rose′, a European hellebore, *Helleborus niger,* having evergreen leaves and white-to-purplish flowers that bloom in the winter. Also called **winter rose.** [1680–90]

Christ′mas seal′, a decorative stamp sold by some charitable organizations during the Christmas season to raise money.

Christ′mas stock′ing, a stocking or stocking-shaped bag traditionally hung on a mantelpiece or Christmas tree by children on Christmas Eve to hold small gifts that Santa Claus is credited with bringing. [1850–55, *Amer.*]

Christ•mas•tide (kris′məs tīd′), *n.* **1.** the festival season from Christmas to after New Year's Day. **2.** the period from Christmas Eve to Epiphany, esp. in England. [1620–30; CHRISTMAS + TIDE[1]]

Christ•mas•time (kris′məs tīm′), *n.* the Christmas season. [1830–40; CHRISTMAS + TIME]

Christ′mas tree′, 1. an evergreen tree decorated at Christmas with ornaments and lights. **2.** a control board or panel containing a variety of colored lights for indicating the status of various functions, elements, components, etc. **3.** an elaborate arrangement of pipes, valves, etc., as for controlling the flow of oil or gas. [1780–90, *Amer.*]

Christo-, a combining form representing **Christ** in compound words: *Christophany.* [see CHRIST, -O-]

Chris•to•cen•tric (kris′tə sen′trik), *adj.* having as the theological focal point the teachings and practices of Jesus Christ. [1870–75; CHRISTO- + -CENTRIC] **—Chris′to•cen′trism,** *n.*

Chris•to•gram (kris′tə gram′), *n.* a symbol of Christ, esp. the Chi-Rho. [1895–1900; CHRISTO- + -GRAM[1]]

Chris•tol•o•gy (kri stol′ə jē), *n., pl.* **-gies** for 2. **1.** the branch of theology dealing with the nature, person, and deeds of Jesus Christ. **2.** an interpretation of the nature, person, and deeds of Christ. [1665–75; CHRISTO- + -LOGY] **—Chris•to•log•i•cal** (kris′tl oj′i kəl), *adj.* **—Chris•tol′o•gist,** *n.*

Chris•toph•a•ny (kri stof′ə nē), *n., pl.* **-nies.** an appearance of Christ after His Resurrection, esp. as recorded in the New Testament. [1840–50; CHRISTO- + -PHANY]

Chris•tophe (krē stôf′), *n.* **Hen•ri** (äɴ ʀē′), (*"Henri I"*), 1767–1820, Haitian revolutionary general, born in Grenada: king 1811–20. Also, **Cristophe.**

chris•to•phene (kris′tə fēn′), *n.* chayote.

Chris•to•pher (kris′tə fər), *n.* **1. Saint,** died A.D. c250, Christian martyr. **2.** a male given name: from a Greek word meaning "Christ-bearer."

Christ's-thorn (krīsts′thôrn′), *n.* any of certain Old World thorny shrubs or small trees supposed to have been used for Christ's crown of thorns, as the Jerusalem thorn, *Paliurus spina-christi,* or the jujube, *Ziziphus jujuba.* [1555–65; trans. of L *spina Christī*]

Christ′ Within′. See **Inner Light.**

Chris•ty (kris′tē), *n., pl.* **-ties.** (*sometimes l.c.*) *Skiing.* Christiania (def. 2). [by shortening]

Chris•ty (kris′tē), *n.* **1. Edwin P.,** 1815–62, U.S. minstrel-show performer and producer. **2. Howard Chan•dler** (chand′lər, chänd′-), 1873–1952, U.S. illustrator and painter. **3.** a male given name, form of **Christopher. 4.** a female given name, form of **Christine.**

-chroic, var. of **-chroous.**

chrom-, 1. a combining form meaning "color," used in the formation of compound words: *chromhydrosis.* **2.** *Chem.* **a.** a combining form used in the names of chemical compounds in which chromium is present. **b.** a combining form that, when prefixed to the name of a chemical compound, denotes its colored form. Also, **-chrome;** *esp. before a consonant,* **chromo-.** [def. 1, for Gk *chrôma* color (see CHROMA); def. 2, for CHROMIUM]

chro•ma (krō′mə), *n.* **1.** the purity of a color, or its freedom from white or gray. **2.** intensity of distinctive hue; saturation of a color. [1885–90; < Gk *chrôma* color]

chro•maf•fin (krō′mə fin), *adj. Histol.* having an affinity for stains containing chromium salts, indicating the presence of epinephrine or norepinephrine. [< G *Chromaffine* (1898), equiv. to *chrom-* CHROM- + L *affinis* next to, inclined to; see AFFINITY]

chro′ma key′, *Television.* an electronic special-effects system for combining a desired background with live foreground action. [1970–75]

chromat-, var. of **chromato-** before a vowel: *chromatid.*

chro•mate (krō′māt), *n.* a salt of chromic acid, as potassium chromate, K_2CrO_4. [1810–20; CHROM(IC ACID) + -ATE[2]]

chro•mat•ic (krō mat′ik, krə-), *adj.* **1.** pertaining to color or colors. **2.** *Music.* **a.** involving a modification of the normal scale by the use of accidentals. **b.** progressing by semitones, esp. to a tone having the same letter name, as in C to C sharp. [1590–1600; < Gk *chrōmatikós,* equiv. to *chrōmat-* (see CHROMATO-) + *-ikos* -IC] **—chro•mat′i•cal•ly,** *adv.*

chromat′ic aberra′tion, *Optics.* the variation of either the focal length or the magnification of a lens system with different wavelengths of light, characterized by prismatic coloring at the edges of the optical image and color distortion within it. Also called **chromatism.** [1825–35]

chro•mat•i•cism (krō mat′ə siz′əm, krə-), *n. Music.* **1.** the use of chromatic tones. **2.** a style in which chromatic tones predominate. [1875–80; CHROMATIC + -ISM]

chro•ma•tic•i•ty (krō′mə tis′i tē), *n. Optics.* the quality of a color as determined by its dominant wavelength and its purity. [1900–05; CHROMATIC + -ITY]

chro•mat•ics (krō mat′iks, krə-), *n.* (*used with a singular v.*) the science of colors. Also called **chromatology.** [1700–10; see CHROMATIC, -ICS] **—chro•ma•tist** (krō′mə tist), *n.*

chromat′ic scale′, *Music.* a scale progressing entirely by semitones. [1780–90]

chromat′ic sign′, *Music.* accidental (def. 5).

chro•ma•tid (krō′mə tid), *n. Genetics.* one of two identical chromosomal strands into which a chromosome splits longitudinally preparatory to cell division. [1895–1900; CHROMAT- + -ID[3]]

chro•ma•tin (krō′mə tin), *n. Cell Biol.* the readily stainable substance of a cell nucleus, consisting of DNA, RNA, and various proteins, that forms chromosomes during cell division. See diag. under **cell.** [1880–85; CHROMAT- + -IN[2]] **—chro′ma•tin′ic,** *adj.* **—chro′ma•toid′,** *adj.*

chro•ma•tism (krō′mə tiz′əm), *n.* **1.** See **chromatic aberration. 2.** the abnormal coloration of leaves or other normally green parts of a plant. [1715–25; CHROMAT- + -ISM]

chromato-, a combining form meaning "color," used in the formation of compound words in this sense and in the specialized sense of "chromatin": *chromatophore; chromatolysis.* Also, *esp. before a vowel,* **chromat-.** [< Gk *chromat-,* s. of *chrôma* color + -o-]

chro•mat•o•gram (krə mat′ə gram′, krō′mə tə-), *n. Chem.* the column, gel layer, or paper strip on which some or all of the constituents of a mixture have been separated by being adsorbed at different locations. [1920–25; CHROMATO- + -GRAM[1]]

chro•mat•o•graph (krə mat′ə graf′, -gräf′, krō′mə-tə-), *Chem.* **—***v.t.* **1.** to separate mixtures by chromatography. **—***n.* **2.** a piece of equipment used to produce a chromatogram. [1855–60; CHROMATO- + -GRAPH]

chro•ma•tog•ra•phy (krō′mə tog′rə fē), *n. Chem.* the separation of mixtures into their constituents by preferential adsorption by a solid, as a column of silica **(column chromatography)** or a strip of filter paper **(paper chromatography)** or by a gel. [1725–35; CHROMATO- + -GRAPHY] **—chro′ma•tog′ra•pher,** *n.* **—chro•mat•o•graph•ic** (krə mat′ə graf′ik, krō′mə tə-), *adj.* **—chro′ma•to•graph′i•cal•ly,** *adv.*

chro•ma•tol•o•gy (krō′mə tol′ə jē), *n.* **1.** chromatics. **2.** a treatise on colors. [1840–50; CHROMATO- + -LOGY]

chro•ma•tol•y•sis (krō′mə tol′ə sis), *n. Cell Biol., Pathol.* the dissolution and disintegration of chromatin. [1900–05; CHROMATO- + -LYSIS] **—chro•mat•o•lyt•ic** (krə mat′l it′ik, krō′mə tl it′-), *adj.*

chro•mat•o•phil (krə mat′ə fil, krō′mə tə-), *Histol.* **—***adj.* **1.** Also, **chro•mat′o•phil′ic, chro•ma•toph•i•lous** (krō′mə tof′ə ləs). chromophil (def. 1). **—***n.* **2.** chromophil (def. 2). Also, **chro•ma•to•phile** (krō′mə tə fil′, -fil, krō mat′ə-, krə-). [CHROMATO- + -PHIL]

chro•mat•o•phil•i•a (krə mat′ə fil′ē ə, -fēl′yə, krō′-mə tə-), *n. Histol.* chromophilia. [CHROMATO- + -PHILIA]

chro•mat•o•phore (krə mat′ə fôr′, -fōr′, krō′mə-tə-), *n.* **1.** *Zool.* a cell containing pigment, esp. one that through contraction and expansion produces a temporary color, as in cuttlefishes. **2.** *Bot.* one of the colored plastids in plant cells. [1860–65; CHROMATO- + -PHORE] **—chro•mat•o•phor•ic** (krə mat′ə fôr′ik, -for′ik, krō′-mə tə-), **chro•ma•toph•or•ous** (krō′mə tof′ər əs), *adj.*

chrome (krōm), *n., v.,* **chromed, chrom•ing. —***n.* **1.** chromium. **2.** chromium-plated or other bright metallic trim, as on an automobile. **3.** (of dyeing) the dichromate of potassium or sodium. **4.** *Photog.* a positive color transparency; kodachrome. **—***v.t.* **5.** (of dyeing) to subject to a bath of dichromate of potassium or sodium. **6.** to plate (metal) with a compound of chromium. **7.** to treat or tan (a hide or leather) with a chromium compound. [1790–1800; < F < Gk *chrôma* color; (in defs. 1, 2, 6, 7) shortened form of CHROMIUM]

-chrome, var. of **chrom-** as the final element of a compound word: *polychrome.*

chrome′ al′um, 1. Also called **ammonium chrome alum, ammonium chromic sulfate.** a green, crystalline, water-soluble powder, chromium ammonium sulfate, $CrNH_4(SO_4)_2 \cdot 12H_2O$, used chiefly as a mordant in dyeing. **2.** a violet, crystalline, water-soluble powder, potassium chromium sulfate, $CrK(SO_4)_2 \cdot 12H_2O$, used chiefly as a mordant in dyeing.

chrome′ dome′, *Slang.* **1.** a baldheaded person. **2.** an intellectual; egghead.

chrome′ green′, the permanent green color made from chromic oxide, or any similar pigment made largely from chromic oxide, used chiefly in printing textiles. [1875–80]

Chro•mel (krō′məl), *Trademark.* a brand name for a group of nickel-chromium alloys, some with an iron content, having high electrical resistance: used in heating devices and thermocouples.

chrome′ leath′er, leather tanned with chrome. [1880–85]

chrome•plate (krōm′plāt′), *v.t.,* **-plat•ed, -plat•ing.** to plate with chromium. [CHROME + PLATE[1]]

chrome′ red′, a bright-red pigment consisting of the basic chromate of lead. [1860–65]

chrome′ steel′, any of various steels containing chromium. Also called **chromium steel.** [1875–80]

chrome′ yel′low, any of several yellow pigments in shades from lemon to deep orange, composed chiefly of chromates of lead, barium, or zinc. [1810–20]

chrom•hi•dro•sis (krō′mi drō′sis, krōm′hi-, -hī-), *n. Pathol.* the secretion of pigmented sweat. Also, **chro•mi•dro•sis** (krō′mi drō′sis). [CHROM- + HIDROSIS]

chro•mic (krō′mik), *adj.* **1.** of or containing chromium in the trivalent state, as chromic hydroxide, $Cr(OH)_3$. **2.** of or derived from chromic acid. [1790–1800; CHROM(IUM) + -IC]

chro′mic ac′etate, a grayish-green, water-soluble powder, $Cr(C_2H_3O_2)_3 \cdot H_2O$, used chiefly as a mordant in dyeing and printing textiles. Also called **chromium acetate.**

chro′mic ac′id, a hypothetical acid, H_2CrO_4, known only in solution or in the form of its salts. [1790–1800]

chro′mic chlo′ride, a violet, crystalline compound, $CrCl_3$, occurring in both water-soluble and water-insoluble forms, or a green or violet, water-soluble deliquescent compound, $CrCl_3 \cdot 6H_2O$: used chiefly as a mordant, in chrome-steel plating, and in the synthesis of chromium salts. Also called **chromium chloride.**

chro′mic fluor′ide, a green, crystalline, water-insoluble powder, $CrF_3 \cdot 4H_2O$ or $CrF_3 \cdot 9H_2O$: used chiefly in printing and dyeing woolens.

chro′mic ox′ide, a bright-green crystalline powder, Cr_2O_3, insoluble in water: used in metallurgy and as the pigment chrome green. Also called **chromium oxide, green cinnabar.**

chro•mi•nance (krō′mə nəns), *n. Optics.* the difference in color quality between a color and a reference color that has an equal brightness and a specified chromaticity. [1950–55; CHROM- + (LUM)INANCE]

chro•mite (krō′mīt), *n.* **1.** *Chem.* a salt of chromium in the bivalent state. **2.** *Mineral.* a cubic mineral, ferrous chromate, $Fe_3Cr_2O_3$, usually with much of the ferrous iron and aluminum replaced by magnesium, and some of the chromium by ferric iron: the principal ore of chromium. [1830–40; CHROM(IUM) or CHROM(ATE) + -ITE[1]]

chro•mi•um (krō′mē əm), *n.* **1.** a lustrous, hard, brittle, metallic element used in alloy steels for hardness and corrosion resistance, as in stainless steel, and for plating other metals: chromium salts are used as pigments and mordants. *Symbol:* Cr; *at. wt.:* 51.996; *at. no.:* 24; *sp. gr.:* 7.1. **2.** chrome (def. 2). [1800–10; CHROME + -IUM]

chromium 51, the radioactive isotope of chromium having a mass number 51 and a half-life of 27.8 days: used as a tracer.

chro′mium ac′etate. See **chromic acetate.**

chro′mium chlo′ride. See **chromic chloride.**

chro′mium diox′ide, a strongly magnetic, black, semiconducting substance, CrO_2, used as the active material in a type of recording tape.

chro′mium ox′ide. See **chromic oxide.**

chro′mium steel′. See **chrome steel.**

chro•mo (krō′mō), *n., pl.* **-mos.** chromolithograph. [by shortening; cf. -O]

chromo-, var. of **chrom-** before a consonant: *chromophore.*

chro•mo•cen•ter (krō′mə sen′tər), *n. Biol.* karyosome (def. 1). [1925–30; CHROMO- + CENTER]

chro•mo•dy•nam•ics (krō′mō dī nam′iks), *n.* (*used with a singular v.*) *Physics.* See **quantum chromodynamics.** [1975–80; CHROMO- + DYNAMICS] —**chro′mo•dy•nam′ic,** *adj.*

chro•mo•gen (krō′mə jən, -jen′), *n.* **1.** *Chem.* **a.** any substance found in organic fluids that forms colored compounds when oxidized. **b.** a colored compound that, though not a dye itself, can be converted into a dye. **2.** a chromogenic bacterium. [1855–60; CHROMO- + -GEN]

chro•mo•gen•ic (krō′mə jen′ik), *adj.* **1.** producing color. **2.** *Chem.* pertaining to chromogen or a chromogen. **3.** (of bacteria) producing some characteristic color or pigment that is useful as a means of identification. [1880–85; CHROMO- + -GENIC]

chro•mo•lith•o•graph (krō′mə lith′ə graf′, -gräf′), *n.* a picture produced by chromolithography. Also called **chromo.** [1855–60; CHROMO- + LITHOGRAPH]

chro•mo•li•thog•ra•phy (krō′mō li thog′rə fē), *n.* the process of lithographing in colors from a series of plates or stones. [1830–40; CHROMO- + LITHOGRAPHY] —**chro′mo•li•thog′ra•pher,** *n.* —**chro•mo•lith•o•graph•ic** (krō′mə lith′ə graf′ik), *adj.*

chro•mo•mere (krō′mə mēr′), *n.* **1.** *Genetics.* one of the beadlike granules arranged in a linear series in a chromonema. **2.** *Anat.* the central, granular part of a blood platelet. Cf. **hyalomere.** [1895–1900; CHROMO- + -MERE] —**chro•mo•mer•ic** (krō′mə mer′ik, -mēr′-), *adj.*

chro•mo•ne•ma (krō′mə nē′mə), *n., pl.* **-ma•ta** (-mə tə). *Genetics.* a chromosome thread that is relatively uncoiled at early prophase but assumes a spiral form at metaphase. [1920–25; CHROMO- + Gk *nêma* thread] —**chro•mo•ne•mat•ic** (krō′mə nə mat′ik, -nē-), *adj.*

chro•mo•phil (krō′mə fil), *Histol.* —*adj.* **1.** Also, **chro′mo•phil′ic, chro•moph•i•lous** (krō mof′ə ləs), **chromatophilic, chromatophilous.** staining readily. —*n.* **2.** a chromophil cell, tissue, or substance. Also, **chro•mo•phile** (krō′mə fīl′, -fil), **chromatophil, chromatophile.** [1895–1900; CHROMO- + -PHIL]

chro•mo•phil•i•a (krō′mə fil′ē ə, -fēl′yə), *n. Histol.* the property of staining readily. Also, **chromatophilia.** [CHROMO- + -PHILIA]

chro•mo•phobe (krō′mə fōb′), *adj.* **1.** Also, **chro′•mo•pho′bic.** *Histol.* not staining readily. —*n.* **2.** *Cell Biol.* a chromophobe cell in the pituitary gland. [1895–1900; CHROMO- + -PHOBE]

chro•mo•phore (krō′mə fôr′, -fōr′), *n.* any chemical group that produces color in a compound, as the azo group —N=N—. [1875–80; CHROMO- + -PHORE] —**chro•mo•phor•ic** (krō′mə fôr′ik, -for′ik), *adj.*

chro•mo•plasm (krō′mə plaz′əm), *n. Cell Biol.* chromatin. [CHROMO- + -PLASM] —**chro′mo•plas′mic,** *adj.*

chro•mo•plast (krō′mə plast′), *n. Bot.* a plastid containing coloring matter other than chlorophyll. [1880–85; CHROMO- + -PLAST]

chro•mo•pro•tein (krō′mə prō′tēn, -tē in), *n. Biochem.* a protein, as hemoglobin or rhodopsin, containing a pigmented nonprotein group, such as heme, riboflavin, or retinal. [1920–25; CHROMO- + PROTEIN]

chromoso′mal aberra′tion, *Genetics.* any irregularity or abnormality of chromosome distribution, number, structure, or arrangement. Cf. **deletion, duplication, inversion, translocation.**

chro•mo•some (krō′mə sōm′), *n. Genetics.* any of several threadlike bodies, consisting of chromatin, that carry the genes in a linear order: the human species has 23 pairs, designated 1 to 22 in order of decreasing size and X and Y for the female and male sex chromosomes respectively. [1885–90; CHROMO- + -SOME[3]] —**chro′•mo•so′mal,** *adj.* —**chro′mo•so′mal•ly,** *adv.*

chro′mosome num′ber, *Genetics.* the characteristic number of chromosomes contained in the cell nucleus of a given species. [1905–10]

chro•mo•sphere (krō′mə sfēr′), *n. Astron.* **1.** a scarlet, gaseous envelope surrounding the sun outside the photosphere, from which enormous quantities of hydrogen and other gases are erupted. **2.** a gaseous envelope surrounding a star. [1865–70; CHROMO- + -SPHERE] —**chro•mo•spher•ic** (krō′mə sfer′ik, -sfēr′-), *adj.*

chro•mous (krō′məs), *adj.* containing chromium in the divalent state, as chromous carbonate, $CrCO_3$. [1830–40; CHROM(IUM) + -OUS]

chrom•y (krō′mē), *adj.,* **chrom•i•er, chrom•i•est.** decorated with or abounding in chrome: *a chromy car.* [1880–85; CHROME + -Y[1]] —**chrom′i•ness,** *n.*

chro•myl (krō′məl), *adj.* containing chromium in the hexavalent state, as chromyl chloride, CrO_2Cl_2. [CHROM(IUM) + -YL]

chron-, var. of **chrono-** before a vowel: *chronaxie.*

Chron., *Bible.* Chronicles.

chron., **1.** chronicle. **2.** chronograph. **3.** chronological. **4.** chronology.

chro•nax•ie (krō′nak sē, kron′ak-), *n. Physiol.* the minimum time that an electric current of twice the threshold strength must flow in order to excite a tissue. Also, **chro′nax•y.** [1915–20; < F, equiv. to *chron-* CHRON- + *-axie* < Gk *axía* worth, value]

chron•ic (kron′ik), *adj.* **1.** constant; habitual; inveterate: *a chronic liar.* **2.** continuing a long time or recurring frequently: *a chronic state of civil war.* **3.** having long had a disease, habit, weakness, or the like: *a chronic invalid.* **4.** (of a disease) having long duration (opposed to *acute*). Also, **chron′i•cal.** [1595–1605; < L *chronicus* < Gk *chronikós,* equiv. to *chrón(os)* time + *-ikos* -IC] —**chron′i•cal•ly,** *adv.* —**chro•nic•i•ty** (kro-nis′i tē), *n.*

chron′ic fatigue′ syn′drome, a viral disease of the immune system, usu. characterized by debilitating fatigue and flu-like symptoms. [1988]

chron′ic glauco′ma, *Ophthalm.* See under **glaucoma.**

chron•i•cle (kron′i kəl), *n., v.,* **-cled, -cling.** —*n.* **1.** a chronological record of events; a history. —*v.t.* **2.** to record in or as in a chronicle. [1275–1325; ME *cronicle* < AF, var., with *-le* -ULE, of OF *cronique* < ML *cronica* (fem. sing.), L *chronica* (neut. pl.) < Gk *chroniká* annals, chronology; see CHRONIC] —**chron′i•cler,** *n.*

chron′icle play′, a drama based on historical material, usually consisting of a series of short episodes or scenes arranged chronologically. Also called **chron′icle his′tory.** [1900–05]

Chron•i•cles (kron′i kəlz), *n.* (*used with a singular v.*) either of two books of the Old Testament, I Chronicles or II Chronicles. *Abbr.:* I Chron., II Chron.

chron′ic obstruc′tive pul′monary disease′, *Pathol.* any of various lung diseases leading to poor pulmonary aeration, including emphysema and chronic bronchitis. *Abbr.:* COPD

chron•o (kron′ō), *n., pl.* **chron•os.** chronometer. [by shortening; see -O]

chrono-, a combining form meaning "time," used in the formation of compound words: *chronometer.* Also, *esp. before a vowel,* **chron-.** [< Gk, comb. form of *chrónos*]

chron•o•bi•ol•o•gy (kron′ō bī ol′ə jē), *n.* the science or study of the effect of time, esp. rhythms, on living systems. [1975–80; CHRONO- + BIOLOGY] —**chron•o•bi•o•log•i•cal** (kron′ō bī′ə loj′i kəl), *adj.* —**chron′o•bi•ol′o•gist,** *n.*

chron•o•gram (kron′ə gram′), *n.* **1.** an inscription in which certain Roman numeral letters express a date or epoch on being added together by their values. **2.** a record made by a chronograph. [1615–25; CHRONO- + -GRAM[1]] —**chron•o•gram•mat•ic** (kron′ō grə mat′ik), **chron′o•gram•mat′i•cal,** *adj.* —**chron′o•gram•mat′i•cal•ly,** *adv.* —**chron′o•gram′ma•tist,** *n.*

chron•o•graph (kron′ə graf′, -gräf′), *n.* **1.** a timepiece fitted with a recording device, as a stylus and rotating drum, used to mark the exact instant of an occurrence, esp. in astronomy. **2.** a timepiece capable of measuring extremely brief intervals of time accurately, as a stopwatch able to record fractions of a second as well as elapsed time. [1655–65; CHRONO- + -GRAPH] —**chro•nog•ra•pher** (krə nog′rə fər), *n.* —**chron•o•graph•ic** (kron′ə graf′ik), *adj.* —**chron′o•graph′i•cal•ly,** *adv.* —**chro•nog′ra•phy,** *n.*

chronol., **1.** chronological. **2.** chronology.

chron•o•log•i•cal (kron′l oj′i kəl), *adj.* **1.** arranged in the order of time: *a chronological list of events.* **2.** pertaining to or in accordance with chronology: *a chronological process.* Also, **chron′o•log′ic.** [1605–15; CHRONOLOG(Y) + -ICAL] —**chron′o•log′i•cal•ly,** *adv.*

chronolog′ical age′, *Psychol.* the number of years a person has lived, esp. when used as a standard against which to measure behavior, intelligence, etc.

chro•nol•o•gist (krə nol′ə jist), *n.* a person versed in chronology. Also, **chro•nol′o•ger.** [1605–15; CHRONOLOG(Y) + -IST]

chro•nol•o•gize (krə nol′ə jīz′), *v.t.,* **-gized, -giz•ing.** to arrange in chronological order. Also, *esp. Brit.,* **chro•nol′o•gise′.** [1610–20; CHRONOLOG(Y) + -IZE]

chro•nol•o•gy (krə nol′ə jē), *n., pl.* **-gies.** **1.** the sequential order in which past events occur. **2.** a statement of this order. **3.** the science of arranging time in periods and ascertaining the dates and historical order of past events. **4.** a reference work organized according to the dates of events. [1585–95; CHRONO- + -LOGY]

chro•nom•e•ter (krə nom′i tər), *n.* **1.** a timepiece or timing device with a special mechanism for ensuring and adjusting its accuracy, for use in determining longitude at sea or for any purpose where very exact measurement of time is required. **2.** any timepiece, esp. a wristwatch, designed for the highest accuracy. [1705–15; CHRONO- + -METER] —**chron•o•met•ric** (kron′ə me′trik), **chron′o•met′ri•cal,** *adj.* —**chron′o•met′ri•cal•ly,** *adv.*

chro•nom•e•try (krə nom′i trē), *n.* **1.** the art of measuring time accurately. **2.** measurement of time by periods or divisions. [1825–35; CHRONO- + -METRY]

chro•non (krō′non), *n.* a hypothetical unit of time, taken as a ratio between the diameter of the electron and the velocity of light, equivalent to approximately 10^{-24} second. [1975–80; < Gk *chrón(os)* time + -ON[1]]

chron•o•pher (kron′ə fər, krō′nə-), *n.* an instrument for transmitting time signals electronically. [1865–70; CHRONO- + *-pher,* for -FER, with *ph* from -PHORE]

chron•o•scope (kron′ə skōp′, krō′nə-), *n.* an electronic instrument for measuring accurately very brief intervals of time, as in determining the velocity of projectiles. [1695–1705; CHRONO- + -SCOPE] —**chron•o•scop•ic** (kron′ə skop′ik), *adj.* —**chron′o•scop′i•cal•ly,** *adv.* —**chro•nos•co•py** (krə nos′kə pē), *n.*

chron•o•ther•a•py (kron′ə ther′ə pē, krō′nə-), *n. Med.* a treatment for insomnia in which a person's normal cycle of waking and sleeping is altered. [1975–80; CHRONO- + THERAPY]

Chron•o•tron (kron′ə tron′, krō′nə-), *Trademark.* a brand name for a device for measuring extremely brief time intervals by comparing electric pulses.

chron•o•trop•ic (kron′ə trop′ik, -trō′pik), *adj.* affecting the rate or timing of a physiologic process, as the heart rate. [CHRONO- + -TROPIC]

-chroous, a combining form meaning "having a color" of the kind specified by the initial element: *isochroous.* Also, **-chroic.** [comb. form repr. Gk *chrṓs* skin, skin color; see -OUS]

chrys-, var. of **chryso-** before a vowel: *chryselephantine.*

chrys•a•lid (kris′ə lid), *Entomol.* —*n.* **1.** a chrysalis. —*adj.* **2.** of a chrysalis. [1770–80; repr. s. of Gk *chrȳsallís* CHRYSALIS]

chrys•a•lis (kris′ə lis), *n., pl.* **chrys•a•lis•es, chry•sal•i•des** (kri sal′i dēz′). the hard-shelled pupa of a moth or butterfly; an obtect pupa. [1650–60; < L *chrȳsalis* < Gk *chrȳsallís,* equiv. to *chrȳs-* CHRYS- + *-allis* suffix, prob. with dim. value]

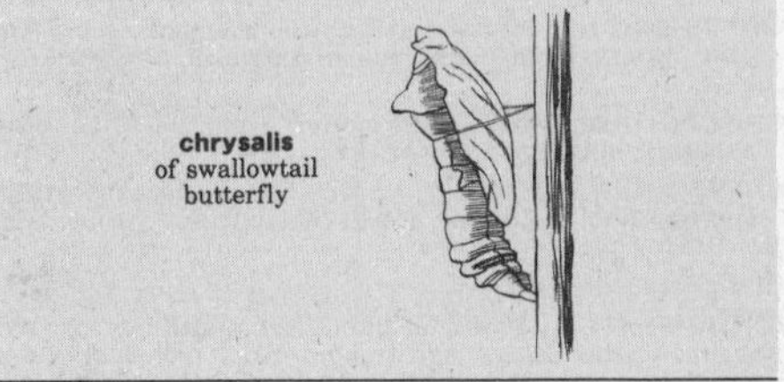

chrysalis of swallowtail butterfly

chry•san•the•mum (kri san′thə məm), *n.* **1.** any of several composite plants of the genus *Chrysanthemum,* as *C. leucanthemum,* the oxeye daisy, having white ray flowers with a yellow center. **2.** any cultivated variety of the plant *C. morifolium,* native to China, and of other species of *Chrysanthemum,* notable for the diversity of

CONCISE PRONUNCIATION KEY: act, cāpe, dâre, pärt; set, ēqual; *if,* ice; ox, ōver, ôrder, oil, bo͝ok, bo͞ot, out; up, ûrge; child; sing; shoe; thin, *th*at; zh as in *treasure.* ə = *a* as in *alone, e* as in *system, i* as in *easily, o* as in *gallop, u* as in *circus;* ° as in *fire* (fī°r), *hour* (ou°r). l and n can serve as syllabic consonants, as in *cradle* (krād′l), and *button* (but′n). See the full key inside the front cover.

color and size of their autumnal flowers. **3.** the flower of any such plant. [1570–80; < L < Gk *chrȳsánthemon,* equiv. to *chrȳs-* CHRYS- + *ánthemon* flower, akin to *ánthos;* see ANTHO-]

chrys•a•ro•bin (kris′ə rō′bin), *n. Pharm.* a mixture of compounds obtained from Goa powder, used in the treatment of psoriasis and other skin conditions. [1885–90; CHRYS- + (AR)AROB(A) + -IN[2]]

chrys•el•e•phan•tine (kris′el ə fan′tin, -tīn), *adj.* made of or overlaid with gold and ivory, as certain objects made in ancient Greece. [1820–30; < Gk *chryselephántinos,* equiv. to *chrȳs-* CHRYS- + *elephántinos* (*elephant-,* s. of *eléphās* ELEPHANT, ivory + *-inos* -INE[1]]

Chry•se Pla•ni•tia (krī′sē plə nish′ə), *Astron.* a plain on Mars, the landing site of the Viking I spacecraft.

Chry•sip•pus (krī sip′əs, kri-), *n.* 280–209? B.C., Greek Stoic philosopher.

Chrys•ler (krīs′lər), *n.* **Walter Percy,** 1875–1940, U.S. automobile manufacturer.

chryso-, a combining form meaning "gold," used in the formation of compound words: *chrysolite.* Also, *esp. before a vowel,* **chrys-.** [comb. form of Gk *chrȳsós*]

chrys•o•ber•yl (kris′ə ber′əl), *n.* a mineral, beryllium aluminate, $BeAl_2O_4$, occurring in green or yellow crystals, sometimes used as a gem. Also called **cymophane.** [1350–1400; ME < L *chrȳsoberyllus* < Gk *chrȳsobéryllos,* equiv. to *chrȳso-* CHRYSO- + *béryllos* BERYL]

chrys•o•cale (kris′ə kāl′), *n.* a copper alloy containing zinc and lead. [appar. alter. of L *chrȳsocolla* CHRYSOCOLLA]

chrys•o•car•pous (kris′ə kär′pəs), *adj. Bot.* bearing golden-yellow fruit. [CHRYSO- + -CARPOUS]

chrys•o•col•la (kris′ə kol′ə), *n.* a mineral, hydrous copper silicate, $CuSiO_3 \cdot 2H_2O$, occurring in compact, green or blue masses, sometimes used in ornaments. [1590–1600; < L *chrȳsocolla* < Gk *chrȳsókolla* gold solder, equiv. to *chrȳso-* CHRYSO- + *kólla* glue (cf. COLLAGE)]

chrys•o•graph (kris′ə graf′, -gräf′), *n.* **1.** a manuscript, esp. of the Middle Ages, written in gold or gold and silver ink. —*v.t.* **2.** to write with gold ink. [1830–40; see CHRYSOGRAPHY, -GRAPH] —**chry•sog•ra•pher** (kri sog′rə fər), *n.*

chry•sog•ra•phy (kri sog′rə fē), *n.* **1.** the art of writing in ink made of powdered gold suspended in a small amount of glair or gum. **2.** the gold writing produced by this art. [1850–55; < Gk *chrȳsographía.* See CHRYSO-, -GRAPHY]

chry•so•i•dine (kri sō′i din, -dēn′), *n. Chem.* a red-brown or greenish-black, crystalline solid, $C_{12}H_{13}N_4Cl$, that yields orange colors in aqueous or alcohol solution: used chiefly in dyeing cotton and silk. [1875–80; < Gk *chrȳsoeid(és)* like gold (*chrȳs-* CHRYS- + *-oeidēs* -OID) + -INE[2]]

chrys•o•lite (kris′ə līt′), *n. Mineral.* olivine. [1250–1300; ME < L *chrȳsolithus* < Gk *chrȳsólithos,* equiv. to *chrȳso-* CHRYSO- + *líthos* stone; see -LITE] —**chrys•o•lit•ic** (kris′ə lit′ik), *adj.*

chrys•o•mel•id (kris′ə mel′id, -mē′lid), *n.* **1.** any beetle of the family Chrysomelidae, comprising the leaf beetles. —*adj.* **2.** belonging or pertaining to the family Chrysomelidae. [1920–25; < NL *Chrysomelidae* name of the family, equiv. to *Chrysomel(a)* a genus (fem. deriv. of Gk *chrȳsomélon* quince, equiv. to *chrȳso-* CHRYSO- + *mêlon* apple; see -A[4]) + *-idae* -ID[2]]

chry•som•o•nad (kri som′ə nad′), *n. Biol.* any golden-yellow to brown freshwater algae of the class Chrysomonadales (phylum Chrysophyta), living singly or in colonies; blooms may color the water brown. [< NL *Chrysomonad-,* s. of *Chrysomonas* a genus name, equiv. to L *chrȳso-* CHRYSO- + Gk *monás* unit; see MONAD]

chry•soph•e•nine (kri sof′ə nēn′, -nin), *n. Chem.* a bright yellow dye derived from stilbene, used chiefly for dyeing leather and textiles. [CHRYSO- + PHEN- + -INE[2]]

chrys•o•phyte (kris′ə fīt′), *n. Biol.* any algae of the phylum Chrysophyta, comprising the yellow-green algae, golden-brown algae, and diatoms, distinguished by having in various proportions the three pigment groups chlorophyll (green), carotene (yellow), and xanthophyll (brown), and storing food reserves as oil rather than starch. [1955–60; < NL *Chrysophyta;* see CHRYSO-, -PHYTE]

chrys•o•prase (kris′ə prāz′), *n. Mineral.* a green variety of chalcedony, sometimes used as a gem. [1250–1300; ME < L *chrȳsoprasus* < Gk *chrȳsóprasos,* equiv. to *chrȳso-* CHRYSO- + *prás(on)* leek + *-os* n. suffix]

Chrys•os•tom (kris′ə stəm, kri sos′təm), *n.* **Saint John,** A.D. 347?–407, ecumenical patriarch of Constantinople.

chrys•o•ther•a•py (kris′ə ther′ə pē), *n.* See **gold therapy.** [CHRYSO- + THERAPY]

chrys•o•tile (kris′ə til), *n. Mineral.* a fibrous variety of serpentine; asbestos. [1840–50; CHRYSO- + Gk *tílos* something plucked]

chs., chapters.

chtho•ni•an (thō′nē ən), *adj. Class. Myth.* of or pertaining to the deities, spirits, and other beings dwelling under the earth. Also, **chthon•ic** (thon′ik). [1840–50; < Gk *chthóni(os)* (*chthon-,* s. of *chthṓn* earth + *-ios* adj. suffix) + -AN; akin to L *humus* earth (see HUMUS)]

Chuan•chow (*Chin.* chwän′jō′), *n. Older Spelling.* Quanzhou.

Chuang-tzu (jwäng′dzu′), *n.* **1.** Also, **Chwang-tse** (*Chuang Chow*). fl. 4th century B.C., Chinese mystic and philosopher. **2.** (*italics*) a fundamental work on Taoism by Chuang-tzu, dating from the 4th century B.C.

chub (chub), *n., pl.* (*esp. collectively*) **chub,** (*esp. referring to two or more kinds or species*) **chubs. 1.** a common freshwater fish, *Leuciscus cephalus,* of European waters, having a thick, fusiform body. **2.** any of various related fishes. **3.** any of several unrelated American fishes, esp. the tautog and whitefishes of the genus *Coregonus,* of the Great Lakes. [1400–50; late ME *chubbe,* of obscure orig.]

chub•by (chub′ē), *adj.,* **-bi•er, -bi•est.** round and plump: *a chubby child; a chubby face.* [1605–15; CHUB + -Y[1]] —**chub′bi•ly,** *adv.* —**chub′bi•ness,** *n.*
—**Syn.** pudgy, heavy, fleshy, roly-poly. —**Ant.** lean, svelte, thin, skinny.

chub′ mack′erel, a small mackerel, *Scomber japonicus,* of Atlantic and Pacific seas and parts of the Indian Ocean. Also called **tinker.** [1805–15, *Amer.*]

chub•suck•er (chub′suk′ər), *n.* any of several stout suckers of the genus *Erimyzon,* inhabiting sluggish streams, backwaters, and lakes of the central and eastern U.S. [1810–20, *Amer.;* CHUB + SUCKER]

Chuch•chi (cho͝ok′chē), *n., pl.* **-chis,** (*esp. collectively*) **-chi.** Chukchi.

Chu•chow (*Chin.* jo͞o′jō′), *n. Older Spelling.* Zhuzhou.

chuck[1] (chuk), *v.t.* **1.** to toss; throw with a quick motion, usually a short distance. **2.** *Informal.* to resign from; relinquish; give up: *He's chucked his job.* **3.** to pat or tap lightly, as under the chin. **4.** *Informal.* to eject (a person) from a public place (often fol. by *out*): *They chucked him from the bar.* **5.** *Slang.* to vomit; upchuck. **6. chuck it,** *Brit. Slang.* stop it; shut up. —*n.* **7.** a light pat or tap, as under the chin. **8.** a toss or pitch; a short throw. **9.** a sudden jerk or change in direction. [1575–85; orig. uncert.]
—**Syn. 1.** fling, pitch, heave, hurl.

chuck[2] (chuk), *n.* **1.** the cut of beef between the neck and the shoulder blade. See diag. under **beef. 2.** a block or log used as a chock. **3.** *Mach.* **a.** a device for centering and clamping work in a lathe or other machine tool. **b.** a device for holding a drill bit. —*v.t.* **4.** *Mach.* to hold or secure with a chuck. [1665–75; var. of CHOCK. See CHUNK[1]]

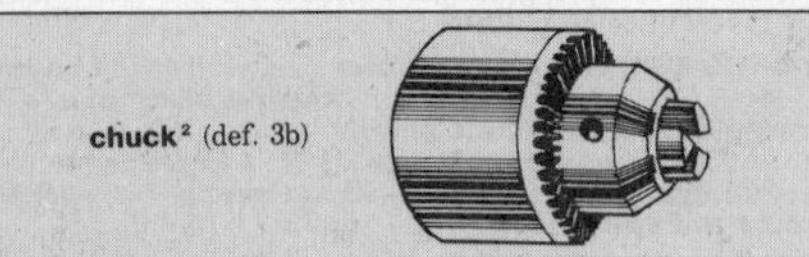

chuck[2] (def. 3b)

chuck[3] (chuk), *v.t., v.i.* **1.** to cluck. —*n.* **2.** a clucking sound. **3.** *Archaic.* (used as a term of endearment): *my love, my chuck.* [1350–1400; ME *chuk,* expressive word, appar. imit.]

chuck[4] (chuk), *n. Western U.S. Slang.* food; provisions. [1840–50; special use of CHUCK[2]]

chuck[5] (chuk), *n. Informal.* woodchuck. [by shortening]

chuck[6] (chuk), *n. Canadian Slang.* **1.** water. **2.** any body of water. [1855–60; < Chinook Jargon, prob. < Nootka *č'a'ak* water, reinforced by Lower Chinook *ł-čuq* water]

Chuck (chuk), *n.* **1.** a male given name, form of **Charles. 2.** *Usually Disparaging.* **a.** a white man. **b.** white society, culture, and values.

chuck-a-luck (chuk′ə luk′), *n.* a game played with three dice at which the players bet that a certain number will come up on one die, that the three dice will total a certain number, or that the total will be an odd number, even number, a high number, or a low number. Also, **chuck-luck** (chuk′luk′). [1830–40, *Amer.*]

Chuck•chi (cho͝ok′chē), *n., pl.* **-chis,** (*esp. collectively*) **-chi.** Chukchi.

chuck•er[1] (chuk′ər), *n. Baseball.* a pitcher. [1750–60, for literal sense; CHUCK[1] + -ER[1]]

chuck•er[2] (chuk′ər), *n. Informal.* woodchuck. [(WOOD)-CHUCK + -ER[1]]

chuck•er-out (chuk′ər out′), *n., pl.* **chuck•ers-out.** *Brit. Slang.* bouncer (def. 2). [1875–80; *chuck out* + -ER[1]]

chuck-full (chuk′fo͝ol′), *adj.* chock-full.

chuck•hole (chuk′hōl′), *n. Chiefly Midland U.S.* a hole or pit in a road or street; pothole. [1830–40; CHUCK[1] + HOLE]

chuck•le (chuk′əl), *v.,* **chuck•led, chuck•ling,** *n.* —*v.i.* **1.** to laugh softly or amusedly, usually with satisfaction: *They chuckled at the child's efforts to walk.* **2.** to laugh to oneself: *to chuckle while reading.* **3.** *Obs.* to cluck, as a fowl. —*n.* **4.** a soft laugh, usually of satisfaction. **5.** *Obs.* the cluck of a hen. [1590–1600; CHUCK[3] + -LE] —**chuck′ler,** *n.* —**chuck′ling•ly,** *adv.*
—**Syn. 4.** See **laugh.**

chuck•le•head (chuk′əl hed′), *n. Slang.* a stupid person; blockhead. [1725–35; *chuckle* clumsy (CHUCK[2] + -LE) + HEAD] —**chuck′le•head′ed,** *adj.*

chuck′ wag′on, *Western U.S.* a wagon carrying cooking facilities and food for serving people working outdoors, as at a ranch or lumber camp. [1860–65]

chuck•wal•la (chuk′wä′lə), *n.* an iguanid lizard, *Sauromalis obesus,* of arid parts of the southwestern U.S. and Mexico, that feeds on desert plants. [1865–70, *Amer.;* < California Sp *chacahuala* < Cahuilla *čáxwal*]

chuck-will's-wid•ow (chuk′wilz wid′ō), *n.* a goatsucker, *Caprimulgus carolinensis,* of the southern U.S., resembling the whippoorwill but larger. [1785–95; fanciful representation of its incessant call]

chuck•y (chuk′ē), *n., pl.* **chuck•ies.** *Brit. Dial.* a chicken; fowl. [1720–30; CHUCK[3] + -Y[2]]

chud•dar (chud′ər), *n.* chador. Also, **chud′der.**

Chud•sko•ye O•ze•ro (chyo͞ot skô′yə ô′zyi rə), Russian name of **Peipus.**

chu•fa (cho͞o′fə), *n.* an African plant, *Cyperus esculentus sativus,* of the sedge family, having a tuberous, edible root. Also called **earth almond.** [1850–55, *Amer.;* < Sp]

chuff[1] (chuf), *n.* **1.** a rustic. **2.** a boor; churl. **3.** a miserly fellow. [1400–50; late ME *chuffe,* of obscure orig.]

chuff[2] (chuf, cho͝of), *adj. Brit. Dial.* **1.** chubby; fat. **2.** swollen with pride; proud; elated. [1600–10; cf. earlier *chuff* puffed cheek, perh. repr. ME *cholle* JOWL[2] conflated with uncert. elements]

chuff[3] (chuf), *n.* **1.** a sound of or like the exhaust of a steam engine. —*v.i.* **2.** to emit or proceed with chuffs: *The train chuffed along.* [1910–15; imit.]

chuffed[1] (chuft), *adj. Brit. Informal.* delighted; pleased; satisfied. [1855–60; see CHUFF[2], -ED[2]]

chuffed[2] (chuft), *adj. Brit. Informal.* annoyed; displeased; disgruntled. [1825–35; cf. dial. (mainly S England) *chuff, choff* ill-tempered, surly, prob. to be identified with CHUFF[1]]

chuf•fle (chuf′əl), *v.,* **-fled, -fling,** *n.* —*v.i.* **1.** (of the larger species of cats) to make a low snuffling sound analogous to the purring of smaller cat species, often as a greeting. —*n.* **2.** such a sound. [imit.; cf. CHUFF[3], -LE]

chuff•y (chuf′ē), *adj.,* **chuff•i•er, chuff•i•est.** churlish; surly. [1690–1700; CHUFF[1] + -Y[1]] —**chuff′i•ly,** *adv.* —**chuff′i•ness,** *n.*

chug[1] (chug), *n., v.,* **chugged, chug•ging.** —*n.* **1.** a short, dull, explosive sound: *the steady chug of an engine.* —*v.i.* **2.** to make this sound: *The motor chugged.* **3.** to move while making this sound: *The train chugged along.* [1865–70, *Amer.;* imit.] —**chug′ger,** *n.*

chug[2] (chug), *v.,* **chugged, chug•ging,** *n. Slang.* —*v.t.* **1.** chug-a-lug. —*v.i.* **2.** to drink something in large gulps: *to chug on a bottle of beer.* —*n.* **3.** a large gulp or swallow: *He finished his beer in two chugs.* [imit.]

chug-a-lug (chug′ə lug′), *v.,* **-lugged, -lug•ging,** *adv. Slang.* —*v.t.* **1.** to drink (a container of beverage) in one continuous draught. —*v.i.* **2.** to drink a beverage in one continuous draught. —*adv.* **3.** in one continuous draught: *drinking their soft drinks chug-a-lug.* [1955–60, *Amer.;* imit. rhyming compound]

chug•ger (chug′ər), *n. Angling.* a type of plug that rests on the surface of the water and makes a popping sound when retrieved. Also called **popper.** [Scot *chug* to tug + -ER[1]]

chug•hole (chug′hōl′), *n. Chiefly South Midland U.S.* chuckhole.

Chu Hsi (jo͞o′ shē′), 1130–1200, Chinese philosopher.

chu•kar (chu kär′), *n.* a partridge, *Alectoris chukar,* of Asia and the Near East, introduced into North America as a game bird. Also called **chukar′ par′tridge.** [< Hindi *cakor* < Skt *cakora*]

Chuk•chee (cho͝ok′chē), *n., pl.* **-chees,** (*esp. collectively*) **-chee.** Chukchi.

Chuk•chi (cho͝ok′chē), *n., pl.* **-chis,** (*esp. collectively*) **-chi** for 1. **1.** a member of a Paleo-Asiatic people of northeastern Siberia. **2.** the Chukotian language of the Chukchi people, noted for having different pronunciations for men and women. Also, **Chuchchi, Chuckchi, Chukchee.**

Chuk•chi-Kam•chat•kan (cho͝ok′chē kam chät′kən, -chat′-), *n.* Chukotian.

Chuk′chi Penin′sula, a peninsula in the NE Russian Federation, across the Bering Strait from Alaska.

Chuk′chi Sea′, a part of the Arctic Ocean, N of the Bering Strait. Russian, **Chukotskoye More.**

Chu Kiang (*Chin.* jo͞o′ gyäng′). *Older Spelling.* See **Zhu Jiang.**

chuk′ka boot′ (chuk′ə), an ankle-high shoe, laced through two pairs of eyelets, often made of suede. Also called **chuk′ka.** Cf. **jodhpur** (def. 2). [1945–50; so called from its resemblance to a polo boot. See CHUKKER]

chuk•ker (chuk′ər), *n. Polo.* one of the periods of play. Also, **chuk′kar.** [1895–1900; < Hindi *chakkar* < Skt *cakra* WHEEL]

Chu•ko•tian (chə kō′shən), *n.* a group of genetically related languages spoken on the Chukchi and Kamchatka peninsulas in eastern Siberia, including Chukchi, Kamchadal, and Koryak. Also called **Chukchi-Kamchatkan, Chu•kot•ko-Kam•chat•kan** (chə kot′kō kamchät′kən, -chat′-), **Luoravetlan.** [< Russ *chukót(skiĭ)* Chukchi (adj.) + -IAN]

Chu•kot•sko•ye Mo•re (chyo͞o kôt′skə yə mô′ryə), Russian name of the **Chukchi Sea.**

Chu•la Vis•ta (cho͞o′lə vis′tə), a city in SW California, near San Diego. 83,927.

chu•le•ta (cho͞o le′tä), *n., pl.* **-tas** (-täs). *Spanish.* a cutlet or chop.

chu•lo (cho͞o′lô; *Eng.* cho͞o′lō), *n., pl.* **-los** (-lôs; *Eng.* -lōz). *Spanish.* **1.** a dandified or effeminate man. **2.** pimp.

chul•pa (cho͞ol′pə), *n. Archaeol.* a type of prehistoric stone tower, found in Brazil and Peru, having living quarters over a burial chamber. Also, **chull′pa.** [< AmerSp < Aymara *chullpa*]

chum[1] (chum), *n., v.,* **chummed, chum•ming.** —*n.* **1.** a close or intimate companion: *boyhood chums.* **2.** a roommate, as at college. —*v.i.* **3.** to associate closely. **4.** to share a room or rooms with another, esp. in a dormitory at a college or prep school. [1675–85; of uncert. orig.]

chum[2] (chum), *n., v.,* **chummed, chum•ming.** —*n.* **1.** cut or ground bait dumped into the water to attract fish to the area where one is fishing. **2.** fish refuse or scraps discarded by a cannery. —*v.i.* **3.** to fish by attracting fish by dumping cut or ground bait into the water. —*v.t.*

CONCISE ETYMOLOGY KEY: <, descended or borrowed from; >, whence; b., blend of, blended; c., cognate with; cf., compare; deriv., derivative; equiv., equivalent; imit., imitative; obl., oblique; r., replacing; s., stem; sp., spelling, spelled; resp., respelling, respelled; trans., translation; ?, origin unknown; *, unattested; ‡, probably earlier than. See the full key inside the front cover.

4. to dump chum into (a body of water) so as to attract fish. 5. to lure (fish) with chum: *They chummed the fish with hamburger.* [1855–60, *Amer.*; of uncert. orig.]

chum[3] (chum), *n.* See **chum salmon.**

Chu•mash (cho͞o′mash), *n., pl.* **-mash•es,** (*esp. collectively*) **-mash** for 1. **1.** a member of an American Indian people who formerly inhabited the southern California coast from San Luis Obispo to Santa Monica Bay, as well as the Santa Barbara Islands and the interior westward to the San Joaquin Valley: noted for their sophisticated seacraft and rock paintings. **2.** any of the Hokan languages of the Chumash, at least six in number, all now extinct.

Chu•mash (*Seph.* KHo͞o mäsh′; *Ashk.* KHo͝om′əsh), *n., pl.* ***Chu•ma•shim*** (*Seph.* KHo͞o′mä shēm′; *Ashk.* KHo͞o-mô′shim). *Hebrew.* Humash.

chum•my (chum′ē), *adj.,* **-mi•er, -mi•est.** *Informal.* friendly; intimate; sociable. [1825–35; CHUM[1] + -Y[1]] —**chum′mi•ly,** *adv.* —**chum′mi•ness,** *n.*
—**Syn.** close, devoted, familiar, congenial.

chump[1] (chump), *n.* **1.** *Informal.* a stupid person; dolt: *Don't be a chump—she's kidding you along.* **2.** a short, thick piece of wood. **3.** the thick, blunt end of anything. **4.** *Slang.* the head. **5. off one's chump,** *Brit. Slang.* crazy. [1695–1705; perh. b. CHUNK[1] and LUMP] —**chump′ish,** *adj.* —**chump′ish•ness,** *n.*

chump[2] (chump), *v.t., v.i.* to bite or chew; munch. Also, **chomp.** [1850–55; var. of CHAMP[1]]

chum′ salm′on, a Pacific salmon, *Oncorhynchus keta,* occurring from southern California to Alaska and off the coasts of Japan and Korea, fished commercially and for sport. Also called **chum, dog salmon, keta.** [1905–10; *chum* < Chinook Jargon *cam* mixed colors, spotted, striped < Lower Chinook *c'ə́m(·)* variegated]

Chun•chon (cho͞on′chun′), *n.* a city in N South Korea. 120,517.

chun•der (chun′dər), *Australian Informal.* —*v.i., v.t.* **1.** to vomit. —*n.* **2.** vomit. [1920–25; orig. variously explained; perh. ult. an expressive formation akin to dial. (mainly N England) *chunder* grumble, complain; cf. CHUNTER]

chun•der•ous (chun′dər əs), *adj. Australian Informal* (*vulgar*). thoroughly unpleasant or nauseating; revolting. [CHUNDER + -OUS]

Chun Doo Hwan (jœn′ dō′ hwän′), born 1931, South Korean political leader: president since 1980.

chung (jo͝ong), *n. Chinese.* (in Confucianism) conscientiousness in one's dealings with others.

Chung•ju (chung′jo͞o′) *n.* a city in central South Korea. 105,274.

Chung•king (cho͝ong′king′; *Chin.* jo͝ong′ging′), *n. Older Spelling.* Chongqing.

chunk[1] (chungk), *n.* **1.** a thick mass or lump of anything: *a chunk of bread; a chunk of firewood.* **2.** *Informal.* a thick-set and strong person. **3.** a strong and stoutly built horse or other animal. **4.** a substantial amount of something: *Rent is a real chunk out of my pay.* —*v.t.* **5.** to cut, break, or form into chunks: *Chunk that wedge of cheese and put the pieces on a plate.* **6.** to remove a chunk or chunks from (often fol. by *out*): *Storms have chunked out the road.* —*v.i.* **7.** to form, give off, or disintegrate into chunks: *My tires have started to chunk.* [1685–95; nasalized var. of CHUCK[2]]
—**Syn. 1.** hunk, piece, wad, gob.

chunk[2] (chungk), *v.t. South Midland and Southern U.S.* **1.** to toss or throw; chuck: *chunking pebbles at the barn door.* **2.** to make or rekindle (a fire) by adding wood, coal, etc., or by stoking (sometimes followed by *up*). [1825–35, *Amer.*; perh. nasalized var. of CHUCK[1]]

chunk•y (chung′kē), *adj.,* **chunk•i•er, chunk•i•est. 1.** thick or stout; stocky. **2.** in chunks. **3.** full of chunks; coarse: *chunky peanut butter; The soup was so chunky it was almost a stew.* [1745–55, *Amer.*; CHUNK[1] + -Y[1]] —**chunk′i•ly,** *adv.* —**chunk′i•ness,** *n.*

Chun•nel (chun′l), *n.* a railroad tunnel under the English Channel between Great Britain and France, approved for construction in 1986. Also, **chun′nel.** [1925–30; b. CHANNEL[1] and TUNNEL]

chun•ter (chun′tər), *v.i. Brit. Informal.* to grumble or grouse mildly or tediously. [1590–1600; orig. dial. (Midlands, N England) *chunter, chunder, chunner;* cf. Scots *channer* in same sense; expressive word of obscure orig.]

chup•pah (*Seph.* KHo͞o pä′; *Ashk., Eng.* KHo͝op′ə), *n., pl.* ***chup•poth, chup•pot*** (*Seph.* KHo͞o pôt′; *Ashk.* KHo͞o-pōs′), *Eng.* **chup•pahs.** *Hebrew.* huppah.

Chur (ko͞or), *n.* a town in and the capital of Grisons, in E Switzerland. 32,600.

church (chûrch), *n.* **1.** a building for public Christian worship. **2.** public worship of God or a religious service in such a building: *to attend church regularly.* **3.** (*sometimes cap.*) the whole body of Christian believers; Christendom. **4.** (*sometimes cap.*) any division of this body professing the same creed and acknowledging the same ecclesiastical authority; a Christian denomination: *the Methodist Church.* **5.** that part of the whole Christian body, or of a particular denomination, belonging to the same city, country, nation, etc. **6.** a body of Christians worshipping in a particular building or constituting one congregation: *She is a member of this church.* **7.** ecclesiastical organization, power, and affairs, as distinguished from the state: *separation of church and state; The missionary went wherever the church sent him.* **8.** the clergy and religious officials of a Christian denomination. **9.** the Christian faith: *a return of intellectuals to the church.* **10.** (*cap.*) the Christian Church before the Reformation. **11.** (*cap.*) the Roman Catholic Church. **12.** the clerical profession or calling: *After much study and contemplation, he was prepared to enter the church.* **13.** a place of public worship of a non-Christian religion. **14.** any non-Christian religious society, organization, or congregation: *the Jewish church.* —*v.t.* **15.** to conduct or bring to church, esp. for special services. **16.** *South Midland and Southern U.S.* to subject to church discipline. **17.** to perform a church service of thanksgiving for (a woman after childbirth). [bef. 900; ME *chir(i)che,* OE *cir(i)ce* << Gk *kȳri(a)kón* (*dôma*) the Lord's (house), neut. of *kȳriakós* of the master, equiv. to *kȳri(os)* master (*kȳr(os)* power + *-ios* n. suffix) + *-akos,* var. of *-ikos* -IC; akin to D *kerk,* G *Kirche,* ON *kirkja.* See KIRK]

church′ book′, any of various books commonly used by a church, as a service book or a parish register. [bef. 1050; ME, OE]

church′ cal′endar. See **ecclesiastical calendar** (def. 2).

church′ coun′cil, (in certain Lutheran churches) a body of lay delegates chosen from the congregation and charged with supporting the pastor in religious instruction, contributions to the church, etc.

church′ expect′ant, *Theol.* the church living in its earthly struggles and in anticipation of God's ultimate victory at the Final Judgment. Cf. **church triumphant.**

church′ fa′ther, father (def. 13). [1855–60]

church•go•er (chûrch′gō′ər), *n.* **1.** a person who goes to church, esp. habitually. **2.** *Chiefly Brit.* a member of the Established Church, in contrast to a Nonconformist. [1600–90; CHURCH + GO[1] + -ER[1]] —**church′go′ing,** *n.*

Church•ill (chûr′chil, -chəl), *n.* **1. John, 1st Duke of Marlborough,** ("*Corporal John*"), 1650–1722, British military commander. **2. Lord Randolph (Henry Spencer),** 1849–95, British statesman (father of Winston L. S. Churchill). **3. Winston,** 1871–1947, U.S. novelist. **4. Sir Winston (Leonard Spencer),** 1874–1965, British statesman and author: prime minister 1940–45, 1951–55; Nobel prize for literature 1953. **5.** a river in Canada, flowing NE from E Saskatchewan through Manitoba to Hudson Bay. ab. 1000 mi. (1600 km) long. **6.** Also called **Church′ill Riv′er.** Formerly, **Hamilton River.** a river in SW Labrador, Newfoundland, in E Canada, flowing SE and N through Lake Melville to the Atlantic Ocean. ab. 600 mi. (965 km) long. **7.** a seaport and railway terminus in NE Manitoba, on Hudson Bay at the mouth of this river. 1700.

Church′ill Falls′, waterfalls near the head of the Churchill River in SW Labrador, Newfoundland, in E Canada: site of hydroelectric power plant. ab. 200 ft. (60 m) wide; 316 ft. (96 m) high. Formerly, **Grand Falls.** [named after Sir Winston CHURCHILL in 1965]

Church•ill•i•an (chûr chil′ē ən), *adj.* **1.** of, pertaining to, or characteristic of Winston Churchill, his life, works, etc. —*n.* **2.** a specialist in the life and works of Winston Churchill. [CHURCHILL + -IAN]

Church′ill Res′ervoir, a series of irregularly shaped lakes in W Labrador, Newfoundland, in E Canada: the source of the Churchill River.

church′ invis′ible, *Theol.* the entire body of Christian believers on earth and in heaven. Cf. **church visible.** [1840–50]

church′ key′, *Slang.* a small metal can opener having a sharp triangular pointed end for punching holes in the top of a beverage can, as of beer. [1950–55]

church•less (chûrch′lis), *adj.* **1.** without a church. **2.** not belonging to or attending any church. **3.** without church approval or ceremony. [1635–45; CHURCH + -LESS]

church•like (chûrch′līk′), *adj.* resembling or appropriate to a church: *churchlike silence.* [1585–95; CHURCH + -LIKE]

church•ly (chûrch′lē), *adj.* of or appropriate for the church or a church; ecclesiastical: *churchly vestments.* [bef. 900; OE *ciriclic,* equiv. to *cirice* CHURCH + *-līc* -LY] —**church′li•ness,** *n.*

church•man (chûrch′mən), *n., pl.* **-men. 1.** an ecclesiastic; clergyman. **2.** an adherent or active supporter of a church. **3.** *Brit.* a member of the Established Church. [1350–1400; ME. See CHURCH, -MAN] —**church′man•ly,** *adj.* —**church′man•ship′,** *n.*

church′ mil′itant, *Theol.* those Christians on earth who are engaged in a continuous war against evil and the enemies of Christ. Cf. **church triumphant.** [1530–40]

church′ mode′, *Music.* a mode belonging to a codified system of modes in use in Gregorian chant and in other music to c1600. Also called **Gregorian mode.** [1860–65]

Church′ of Christ′, Sci′entist, the official name of the Christian Science Church.

Church′ of Eng′land, the established church in England, Catholic in faith and order, but incorporating many principles of the Protestant Reformation and independent of the papacy.

Church′ of God′, any of numerous Protestant denominations that stress personal conversion, sanctification, the imminent return of Jesus Christ, baptism by immersion, and, among some, speaking in tongues.

Church′ of Je′sus Christ′ of Lat′ter-day Saints′, the name of the largest denomination of the Mormon Church.

Church′ of Rome′. See **Roman Catholic Church.**

Church′ of the Breth′ren, the official name of the church of the Dunkers.

Church′ of the New′ Jeru′salem. See **New Jerusalem Church.**

church′ rate′, *Eccles.* (formerly in England and Ireland) a compulsory assessment imposed on the parishioners' holdings of houses or land in order to repair the parish church and maintain its services. [1705–15]

church′ reg′ister. See **parish register.** [1840–50]

church′ school′, a primary or secondary private school affiliated with a Christian denomination. [1860–65]

Church′ Slav′ic, a liturgical language used in Eastern Orthodox churches in Slavic countries since the 11th or 12th century, representing a development of Old Church Slavonic through contact with the national Slavic languages. [1840–50]

church′ suf′fering, *Rom. Cath. Ch.* the souls in purgatory.

church′ text′, *Print.* See **Old English** (def. 2). [1675–85]

church′ trium′phant, *Theol.* those Christians in heaven who have triumphed over evil and the enemies of Christ. Cf. **church militant.** [1545–55]

church′ vis′ible, *Theol.* the entire body of Christian believers on earth. Cf. **church invisible.** [1555–65]

church•ward (chûrch′wərd), *adv.* **1.** Also, **church′•wards.** toward the church. —*adj.* **2.** directed toward the church: *a churchward summons.* [1325–75; ME *chircheward.* See CHURCH, -WARD]

church•ward•en (chûrch′wôr′dn), *n.* **1.** *Anglican Ch.* a lay officer who looks after the secular affairs of the church, and who, in England, is the legal representative of the parish. **2.** *Episc. Ch.* a lay church officer who, with other members of the vestry, is in charge of the temporal management of the parish. **3.** a long-stemmed clay pipe for smoking. [1400–50; late ME *chirche wardeyn*]

church•wom•an (chûrch′wo͝om′ən), *n., pl.* **-wom•en.** a female member, adherent, or active supporter of a church. [1715–25; CHURCH + WOMAN]

church•y (chûr′chē), *adj.,* **church•i•er, church•i•est. 1.** adhering strictly to the prescribed form in ecclesiastical matters. **2.** intolerant of dissent in one's religion. **3.** of, characteristic of, or suggestive of a church: *The stained-glass windows gave the room a churchy look.* [1835–45; CHURCH + -Y[1]] —**church′i•ness,** *n.*

church•yard (chûrch′yärd′), *n.* the yard or ground adjoining a church, often used as a graveyard. [1125–75; ME *chirche yeard;* see CHURCH, YARD[2]]

church′ year′. See **Christian year.**

chu•rin•ga (cho͝o ring′gə), *n., pl.* **-ga, -gas.** an object carved from wood or stone by Aboriginal tribes in central Australia and held by them to be sacred. [1895–1900; < Aranda *jwerreŋe*]

churl (chûrl), *n.* **1.** a rude, boorish, or surly person. **2.** a peasant; rustic. **3.** a niggard; miser: *He was a churl in his affections.* **4.** *Eng. Hist.* a freeman of the lowest rank. [bef. 900; ME *cherl,* OE *ceorl* man, freeman; c. D *kerel,* G *Kerl;* akin to CARL]

churl•ish (chûr′lish), *adj.* **1.** like a churl; boorish; rude: *churlish behavior.* **2.** of a churl; peasantlike. **3.** niggardly; mean. **4.** difficult to work or deal with, as soil. [bef. 1000; ME *cherlish,* OE *ceorlisc.* See CHURL, -ISH[1]] —**churl′ish•ly,** *adv.* —**churl′ish•ness,** *n.*
—**Syn. 1.** coarse, uncouth, vulgar, loutish; ill-natured, uncivil. —**Ant. 1.** courteous.

churn (chûrn), *n.* **1.** a container or machine in which cream or milk is agitated to make butter. **2.** any of various containers or machines similar in shape or action to a butter churn, as a device for mixing beverages. **3.** *Brit.* a large milk can. **4.** an act of churning stocks by a stockbroker. —*v.t.* **5.** to agitate in order to make into butter: *to churn cream.* **6.** to make (butter) by the agitation of cream. **7.** to shake or agitate with violence or continued motion: *The storm churned the sea.* **8.** (of a stockbroker) to trade (a customer's securities) excessively in order to earn more in commissions. —*v.i.* **9.** to operate a churn. **10.** to move or shake in agitation, as a liquid or any loose matter: *The leaves churned along the ground.* **11.** (of a stockbroker) to engage in the practice of churning. **12. churn out,** to produce mechanically, hurriedly, or routinely: *He was hired to churn out verses for greeting cards.* [bef. 1000; ME *chirne* (n.), OE *cyrne cyr(i)n;* c. MLG *kerne,* ON *kjarni, kirna*] —**churn′a•ble,** *adj.* —**churn′a•bil′i•ty,** *n.* —**churn′er,** *n.*

churn′ drill′, a portable drill rig using a bit fashioned on a massive steel cylinder that is alternately lifted and dropped to drill a hole in earth and rock.

churn•ing (chûr′ning), *n.* **1.** the act of a person or thing that churns. **2.** the butter made at any one time. [1400–50; late ME *chyrnynge.* See CHURN, -ING[1]]

churn′ mold′ing, a molding decorated with chevrons.

churr (chûr), *v.i., n.* chirr.

chur•ras•co (chə ras′kō; *Sp.* cho͞oR räs′kô), *n., pl.* **-cos** (-kōz; *Sp.* -kôs) for 2. *Latin American Cookery.* **1.** meat cooked over an open fire. **2.** a large piece of meat suitable for barbecuing. [< AmerSp (Argentina, Uruguay); cf. dial. Sp (Salamanca region) *churrusco* piece of burnt toast, *churruscar* to begin to burn, Sp *socarrar* to scorch, singe, all from a pre-L etymon]

chur•ri•gue•resque (cho͝or′ē gə resk′), *adj.* noting or pertaining to the baroque architecture of Spain and its colonies in the late 17th and early 18th centuries, characterized by fantastic and lavish detailing. Also, **chur•ri•gue•res•co** (*Sp.* cho͞oR Rē′ge Res′kô). [1835–45; < F < Sp *churrigueresco,* after José Churriguera (1650–1725), baroque architect and sculptor + *-esco* -ESQUE]

chur•ro (cho͝or′ō; *Sp.* cho͞oR′Rô), *n., pl.* **chur•ros** (cho͝or′ōz; *Sp.* cho͞oR′Rôs). *Mexican Cookery.* a long, slender, deep-fried pastry resembling a cruller. [1885–90, *Amer.*; < Sp, perh. after dial. *churro* name for the inhabitants of the mountainous parts of Valencia (lit., a kind of coarse-wooled sheep), the approximate area where the pastry originated]

chuse (cho͞oz), *v.t., v.i.,* **chused, chus•ing.** *Archaic.* choose.

chute[1] (sho͞ot), *n., v.,* **chut•ed, chut•ing.** —*n.* **1.** an inclined channel, as a trough, tube, or shaft, for conveying water, grain, coal, etc., to a lower level. **2.** a waterfall or steep descent, as in a river. **3.** a water slide, as at an amusement park. **4.** a steep slope, as for tobogganing. **5. out of the chute,** at the start; at the very beginning: *The new business made mistakes right out of the chute and failed within a year.* —*v.t.* **6.** to move or deposit, by or as if by means of a chute: *The dock had facilities for chuting grain directly into the hold of a vessel.* —*v.i.* **7.** to descend by or as if by means of a chute. [1715–25; < F, MF, repr. OF *cheoite* a fall, nominalized fem. ptp. of *cheoir* to fall (< VL **cadēre,* for L *cadere;* cf. CADENCE, CASE[1]), with vowel of MF *chue,* OF *cheue,* a variant ptp.; some senses influenced by SHOOT]

chute[2] (sho͞ot), *n., v.,* **chut•ed, chut•ing.** —*n.* **1.** a parachute. —*v.i.* **2.** to descend from the air by or as if by a parachute. —*v.t.* **3.** to drop from an aircraft by means of a parachute: *Supplies were chuted to the snowbound mountain climbers.* [1915–20, *Amer.;* by shortening]

Chu Teh (*Chin.* jo͞o′ du′), *Wade-Giles.* See **Zhu De.**

chute′ the chute′, to ride or slide on, or as if on, a chute-the-chute. [1905–10, *Amer.*] Also, **chute′ the chutes′, shoot the chutes.**

chute-the-chute (sho͞ot′thə sho͞ot′, sho͞ot′ə sho͞ot′), *n.* **1.** a ride or coaster, as at an amusement park or carnival, that provides thrills or excitement by moving passengers down steep dips and around sharp curves, esp. one having a track that ends in water. Cf. **roller coaster. 2.** a steep or curving slide used for purposes of amusement. **3.** any ride, motion, or experience that produces a sensation of rapid or curving descent: *an emotional chute-the-chute.* Also, **chute′-the-chutes′.** [1890–95, *Amer.;* see CHUTE[1]]

chut•ist (sho͞o′tist), *n.* a parachutist. [1915–20; CHUTE[2] + -IST]

chut•ney (chut′nē), *n.* a sauce or relish of East Indian origin, often compounded of both sweet and sour ingredients, as fruits and herbs, with spices and other seasoning. Also, **chut′nee.** [1805–15; < Hindi *chaṭnī*]

chutz•pa (ᴋʜo͝ot′spə, ho͝ot′-), *n. Slang.* unmitigated effrontery or impudence; gall. Also, **chutz′pah, hutzpa, hutzpah.** [1890–95; < Yiddish *khutspe* < Aram *ḥūṣpā*]

Chu•vash (cho͞o vash′; *Russ.* chyo͞o väsh′), *n., pl.* **Chu•vash•es, Chu•va•shi** (cho͞o vä′shē; *Russ.* chyo͞o vä′shi, -vu shi′), (*esp. collectively*) **Chu•vash** for 1. **1.** a member of a people of mixed Uralic and Altaic ancestry who live in the middle Volga basin, mainly in the Chuvash Autonomous Republic. **2.** the language of the Chuvash, generally considered Turkic though markedly divergent from all other modern Turkic languages.

Chuvash′ Auton′omous Repub′lic, an autonomous republic in the Russian Federation in Europe. 1,336,000; 7064 sq. mi. (18,300 sq. km). *Cap.:* Cheboksary.

Ch'ü Yüan (chʏ′ yʏän′), 343–289 B.C., Chinese poet: author of the *Li-sao.*

Chwang-tse (*Chin.* jwäng′dzu′), *n.* Chuang-tzu (def. 1).

chy•ack (chī′ək), *v.t. Australian.* chiack.

chy•la•ceous (kī lā′shəs), *adj.* of or resembling chyle. [1690–1700; CHYLE + -ACEOUS]

chyle (kīl), *n.* a milky fluid containing emulsified fat and other products of digestion, formed from the chyme in the small intestine and conveyed by the lacteals and the thoracic duct to the veins. [1535–45; < LL *chȳlus* < Gk *chȳlós* juice, akin to *cheîn* to pour, L *fundere* to pour (see FUSE[2]), E GUT] —**chy′lous,** *adj.*

chylo- a combining form meaning "juice," used in the formation of compound words: *chylophyllous.* [comb. for repr. Gk *chȳlós;* see CHYLE]

chy•lo•cau•lous (kī′lə kô′ləs), *adj. Bot.* having fleshy stems. [< G *Chylocaul* (see CHYLO-, CAULO-, -OUS)] —**chy′lo•cau′lous•ly,** *adv.*

chy•lo•mi•cron (kī′lə mī′kron), *n. Biochem.* a large plasma lipoprotein particle, occurring as a droplet consisting primarily of triglycerides and functioning in the transport of neutral lipids from the intestine to the tissues by way of the lymph. [1920–25; CHYLO- + MICRON]

chy•lo•phyl•lous (kī′lə fil′əs), *adj. Bot.* having fleshy leaves, as certain desert plants. [CHYLO- + -PHYLLOUS] —**chy′lo•phyl′lous•ly,** *adv.*

chyme (kīm), *n.* the semifluid mass into which food is converted by gastric secretion and which passes from the stomach into the small intestine. [1600–10; < L *chȳmus* < Gk *chȳmós* juice, akin to *chȳlós* CHYLE] —**chy′mous,** *adj.*

chym•is•try (kim′ə strē), *n. Archaic.* chemistry. —**chym′ic,** *adj.* —**chym′ist,** *n.*

chy•mo•pa•pa•in (kī′mō pə pā′in, -pī′in), *n. Pharm.* an enzyme derived from the tropical papaya fruit that is used in some circumstances to treat herniated disks. [1970–75; CHYME + -O- + PAPAIN]

chy•mo•tryp•sin (kī′mō trip′sin), *n. Biochem.* a proteolytic enzyme, found in pancreatic juice, that catalyzes the hydrolysis of proteins into polypeptides and amino acids. [1930–35; CHYME + -O- + TRYPSIN] —**chy•mo•tryp•tic** (kī′mō trip′tik), *adj.*

chy•mo•tryp•sin•o•gen (kī′mō trip sin′ə jən, -jen′), *n. Biochem.* a zymogen that is converted by trypsin to chymotrypsin. [1930–35; CHYMOTRYPSIN + -O- + -GEN]

chy•trid (kī′trid, ki′-), *n.* any of the simple, algaelike fungi constituting the class Chytridiomycetes, order Chytridiales, of aquatic and soil environments, having flagellated zoospores and little or no mycelium. [< NL *Chytridiales,* equiv. to *Chytridi(um)* the type genus (< Gk *chytrídion,* dim. of *chýtra* pipkin) + *-ales* -ALES]

CI, counterintelligence.

Ci, curie; curies.

C.I., Channel Islands.

CIA, Central Intelligence Agency: the U.S. federal agency that coordinates governmental intelligence activities outside the United States. Also, **C.I.A.**

Cia., Company. [< Sp *Compañía*]

Cia•no (chä′nō; *It.* chä′nô), *n.* **Count Ga•le•az•zo** (gä′le ät′tsô), (*Ciano di Cortellazzo*), 1903–44, Italian Fascist statesman: minister of foreign affairs 1936–43.

cia•o (chä′ô; *Eng.* chou), *interj. Italian.* (used as a word of greeting or parting): hello; goodbye; so long; see you later.

Ciar•di (chär′dē), *n.* **John,** 1916–86, U.S. poet.

cib., (in prescriptions) food. [< L *cibus*]

ci•bar•i•um (si bâr′ē əm), *n., pl.* **-bar•i•a** (-bâr′ē ə). *Entomol.* a food pouch in front of the mouth in certain insects. [< NL, equiv. to L *cib(us)* food + *-ārium* -ARY] —**ci•bar′i•al,** *adj.*

Cib•ber (sib′ər), *n.* **Col•ley** (kol′ē), 1671–1757, English actor and dramatist: poet laureate 1730–57.

Ci•bo•la (sē′bə lə), *n.* **the Seven Cities of,** legendary cities of great wealth believed by earlier Spanish explorers to exist in the SW United States.

ci•bo•ri•um (si bôr′ē əm, -bōr′-), *n., pl.* **-bo•ri•a** (-bôr′ē ə, -bōr′-). **1.** a permanent canopy placed over an altar; baldachin. **2.** any container designed to hold the consecrated bread or sacred wafers for the Eucharist. **3.** *Archaic.* a severy. [1645–55; < L: drinking-cup < Gk *kibṓrion* lit., the seed vessel of the Egyptian lotus, which the cup appar. resembled]

ciborium (def. 2)

C.I.C., 1. Combat Information Center. **2.** Commander in Chief. **3.** Counterintelligence Corps.

ci•ca•da (si kā′də, -kä′-), *n., pl.* **-das, -dae** (-dē). any large homopterous insect of the family Cicadidae, the male of which produces a shrill sound by means of vibrating membranes on the underside of the abdomen. [1350–1400; ME < L *cicāda*]

cicada, *Magicicada septendecim,* length about 1 in. (2.5 cm)

cica′da kill′er, a black or rust-colored digger wasp, *Sphecius speciosis,* with a yellow-banded abdomen, that preys on cicadas. [1890–95]

ci•ca•la (si kä′lə; *It.* chē kä′lä), *n., pl.* **-las,** *It.* **-le** (-le). cicada. [< It < L *cicāda* CICADA]

cicatri′cial tis′sue. See **scar tissue.** [1880–85]

cic•a•trix (sik′ə triks, si kā′triks), *n., pl.* **cic•a•tri•ces** (sik′ə trī′sēz). **1.** *Physiol.* new tissue that forms over a wound and later contracts into a scar. **2.** *Bot.* a scar left on a tree or plant by a fallen leaf, seed, etc. Also, **cic•a•trice** (sik′ə tris). [1350–1400; ME < L: scar] —**cic•a•tri•cial** (sik′ə trish′əl), *adj.* —**ci•cat•ri•cose** (si ka′trikōs′, sik′ə-), *adj.*

cic•a•trize (sik′ə trīz′), *v.,* **-trized, -triz•ing.** —*v.t.* **1.** *Physiol.* to heal by inducing the formation of a cicatrix. —*v.i.* **2.** to become healed by the formation of a cicatrix. Also, *esp. Brit.,* **cic′a•trise′.** [1350–1400; ME < ML *cicātrizāre.* See CICATRIX, -IZE] —**cic′a•tri′zant,** *adj.* —**cic′a•tri•za′tion,** *n.* —**cic′a•triz′er,** *n.*

cic•e•ly (sis′ə lē), *n., pl.* **-lies.** a plant, *Myrrhis odorata,* of the parsley family, having a fragrant aroma and sometimes used as a potherb. [1590–1600; < L *seseli* < Gk *séselis, séseli* hartwort, resp. through influence of proper name *Cicely*]

Cic•e•ly (sis′ə lē), *n.* a female given name, form of **Cecilia.**

cic•e•ro (sis′ə rō′), *n., pl.* **-ros.** *Print.* a Continental unit of measurement for type, equal to 12 Didot points, or 0.178 in. (4.5 mm), roughly comparable to a pica. [named after the type cast for a 15th-century edition of Cicero's *De Oratore*]

Cic•e•ro (sis′ə rō′), *n.* **1. Marcus Tul•li•us** (tul′ē əs), (*"Tully"*), 106–43 B.C., Roman statesman, orator, and writer. **2.** a city in NE Illinois, near Chicago. 61,232.

cic•e•ro•ne (sis′ə rō′nē, chich′ə-; *It.* chē′che rô′ne), *n., pl.* **-nes,** *It.* **-ni** (-nē). a person who conducts sightseers; guide. [1720–30; It < L *Cicerōnem,* acc. of *Cicerō* CICERO, the guide being thought of as having the knowledge and eloquence of Cicero]

Cic•e•ro•ni•an (sis′ə rō′nē ən), *adj.* **1.** of or pertaining to Cicero or his writings: *the Ciceronian orations.* **2.** in the style of Cicero: characterized by melodious language, clarity, and forcefulness of presentation: *Ciceronian invective.* —*n.* **3.** a person who is an expert on or specializes in the study of the works of Cicero. **4.** a person who admires or imitates the style of Cicero. [1575–85; < L *Cicerōniānus,* equiv. to *Cicerōn-* (s. of *Cicerō*) CICERO + *-iānus* -IAN]

Cic•e•ro•ni•an•ism (sis′ə rō′nē ə niz′əm), *n.* imitation of the style of Cicero, esp. as practiced by some writers and orators during the Renaissance. [1580–90; CICERONIAN + -ISM]

cich•lid (sik′lid), *n.* **1.** any of the spiny-rayed, freshwater fishes constituting the family Cichlidae, of South America, Africa, and southern Asia, superficially resembling the American sunfishes and popular in home aquariums. —*adj.* **2.** belonging or pertaining to the family Cichlidae. Also, **cich•loid** (sik′loid). [1880–85; < NL *Cichlidae,* equiv. to *Cichl(a)* a genus (< Gk *kíchlē* thrush, wrasse) + *-idae* -ID[2]]

ci•cis•be•ism (chē′chiz bā′iz əm *or, older,* si sis′bē-), *n.* the social custom of having a *cicisbeo,* as practiced esp. in Italy in the 17th and 18th centuries. [1735–45; < It *cicisbeismo.* See CICISBEO, -ISM]

ci•cis•be•o (chē′chiz bā′ō *or, older,* si sis′bē ō′; *It.* chē′chēz be′ô), *n., pl.* **-be•i** (-bā′ē *or, older,* -bē ī′; *It.* -be′ē). (esp. in Italy during the 17th and 18th centuries) an escort or lover of a married woman. [< It]

Cid (sid; *Sp.* thēd), *n.* **1. The,** (*"El Cid Campeador"*) (*Rodrigo Díaz de Bivar*), c1040–99, Spanish soldier: hero of the wars against the Moors. **2.** (*italics*) **Le.** See ***Le Cid.***

C.I.D., Criminal Investigation Department of Scotland Yard.

c.i.d., *Auto.* cubic-inch displacement: the displacement of an engine measured in cubic inches: *My old car had a 302 c.i.d. engine.* Also, **cid, CID**

-cidal, a combination of **-cide** and **-al**[1] found on adjectives that correspond to nouns ending in **-cide:** *homicidal.* [-CIDE + -AL[1]]

-cide, a learned borrowing from Latin meaning "killer," "act of killing," used in the formation of compound words: *pesticide, homicide.* [late ME < L *-cīda* killer, *-cīdium* act of killing, derivatives of *caedere* to cut down, kill (in compounds *-cīdere*)]

ci•der (sī′dər), *n.* the juice pressed from apples (or formerly from some other fruit) used for drinking, either before fermentation **(sweet cider)** or after fermentation **(hard cider),** or for making applejack, vinegar, etc. Also, *Brit.,* **cyder.** [1250–1300; ME *sidre* < MF < OF *si(s)dre* < LL *sīcera* strong drink < Septuagint Gk *síkera* < Heb *shēkhār* (Levit. 10:9); r. ME *sithere* < OF *sidre*] —**ci′der•ish, ci′der•like′,** *adj.*

ci′der press′, a press for crushing apples for cider. [1665–75]

ci′der vin′egar, vinegar produced by fermentation of cider. [1850–55]

ci-de•vant (sēdᵊ väɴ′), *adj. French.* former: used esp. in reference to a retired officeholder. [lit., heretofore]

Cie., company. Also, **cie.** [< F *Compagnie*]

cié•na•ga (syā′nə gə, syen′ə-, sin′-), *n. Southwestern U.S.* a swamp or marsh, esp. one formed and fed by springs. Also, **cie′ne•ga.** [1840–50, *Amer.;* < Sp, deriv. of *cieno* mud, slime < L *caenum* filth]

Cié•na•ga (sye′nä gä′), *n.* a city in N Colombia, on the SE coast of the Caribbean Sea. 69,100.

Cien•fue•gos (syen fwe′gôs), *n.* a seaport in S Cuba. 225,615.

C.I.F., cost, insurance, and freight: used by a seller to indicate that the price quoted includes the cost of the merchandise, packing, and freight to a specified destination plus insurance charges. Also, **CIF, c.i.f.**

cig (sig), *n. Slang.* a cigarette. [1885–90; by shortening]

ci•gar (si gär′), *n.* **1.** a more or less cylindrical roll of tobacco cured for smoking, of any of various lengths, thicknesses, degrees of straightness, etc., usually wrapped in a tobacco leaf. **2. no cigar,** *Informal.* not being a winning or successful effort, as if not good enough to earn a cigar as a prize: *He made a good try at fielding the ball, but no cigar.* [1625–35; < Sp *cigarro*] —**ci•gar′less,** *adj.* —**ci•gar′like′,** *adj.*

cig•a•rette (sig′ə ret′, sig′ə ret′), *n.* a cylindrical roll of finely cut tobacco cured for smoking, considerably smaller than most cigars and usually wrapped in thin white paper. Also, **cig′a•ret′.** [1820–30; < F, equiv. to *cigare* CIGAR + *-ette* -ETTE]

cigarette′ bee′tle, a small cylindrical beetle, *Lasioderma serricorne,* that is a pest, esp. of dried tobacco. Also called **tobacco beetle, tow bug.** [1890–95]

cigarette′ girl′, a woman who sells cigars and cigarettes, usually from a tray displaying various brands, to customers in a restaurant or nightclub. [1865–70]

cigarette′ hold′er, a mouthpiece of plastic, ivory, etc., for holding a cigarette while it is being smoked. [1920–25]

cig•a•ril•lo (sig′ə ril′ō), *n., pl.* **-los. 1.** a small, thin cigar, longer than a cigarette. **2.** a cigarette with a wrapping of tobacco instead of paper. [1825–35; < Sp, dim. of *cigarro* CIGAR]

cigar′ store′, a retail store specializing in tobacco products, as cigars and cigarettes. [1840–50, *Amer.*]

ci•gar′-store In′dian (si gär′stôr′, -stōr′), a wooden statue of an American Indian, traditionally displayed at the entrance of cigar stores. [1925–30]

Cig•fa (kig′vä), *n. Welsh Legend.* wife of Pryderi.

cig•gy (sig′ē), *n., pl.* **-gies.** *Slang.* a cigarette. Also, **cig′gie.** [1960–65; CIG(ARETTE) + -Y[2]]

ci•lan•tro (si län′trō, -lan′-), *n.* coriander. [1900–05; < Sp, var. of *culantro* < VL, dissimilated form of L *coriandrum* CORIANDER]

cil•i•a (sil′ē ə), *n.pl., sing.* **cil•i•um** (sil′ē əm). **1.** *Biol.* minute hairlike organelles, identical in structure to flagella, that line the surfaces of certain cells and beat in rhythmic waves, providing locomotion to ciliate protozoans and moving liquids along internal epithelial tissue in animals. See diag. under **paramecium.** **2.** *Anat.* the eyelashes. [1705–15; NL, pl. of *cilium* eyelash, L: upper eyelid, perh. a back formation from *supercilium* eyebrow; see SUPERCILIUM]

cil•i•ar•y (sil′ē er′ē), *adj.* **1.** *Anat.* noting or pertaining to various anatomical structures in or about the eye. **2.** pertaining to cilia. [1685–95; CILI(A) + -ARY]

cil′iary bod′y, *Anat.* the part of the tunic of the eye, between the choroid coat and the iris, consisting chiefly of the ciliary muscle and the ciliary processes.

cil′iary mus′cle, *Anat.* the smooth muscle in the ciliary body, the action of which affects the accommodation of the eye. See diag. under **eye.** [1875–80]

cil′iary proc′ess, *Anat.* one of the folds on the ciliary body, connected with the suspensory ligament of the crystalline lens. See diag. under **eye.** [1825–35]

Cil•i•a•ta (sil′ē ā′tə), *n.* the class comprising the ciliate protozoans, considered as belonging in the kingdom Animalia. [< NL; see CILIATE]

cil•i•ate (sil′ē it, -āt′), *Biol.* —*n.* **1.** Also called **cil•i•oph•o•ran** (sil′ē of′ər ən). any protozoan of the phylum Ciliophora (or in some classification schemes, class Ciliata), as those of the genera *Paramecium, Tetrahymena, Stentor,* and *Vorticella,* having cilia on part or all of the surface. —*adj.* **2.** Also, **cil•i•at•ed** (sil′ē ā′tid). having cilia. **3.** belonging or pertaining to the phylum Ciliophora. [1785–95; < NL *ciliātus,* equiv. to *cili(a)* CILIA + *-ātus* -ATE[1]] —**cil′i•ate•ly,** *adv.* —**cil′i•a′tion,** *n.*

cil•ice (sil′is), *n.* **1.** a garment of haircloth formerly worn by monks; a hair shirt. **2.** haircloth. [bef. 950; < MF; r. OE *cilic* < L *cilicium* < Gk *kilíkion,* neut. of *kilíkios* Cilician, so called because first made of Cilician goathair]

Ci•li•cia (si lish′ə), *n.* an ancient country in SE Asia Minor: later a Roman province. —**Ci•li′cian,** *adj., n.*

Cili′cian Gates′, a mountain pass in SE Asia Minor, connecting Cappadocia and Cilicia. Turkish, **Gülek Boğaz.**

cil•i•o•late (sil′ē ə lit, -lāt′), *adj.* having cilia. [1865–70; < NL *ciliol(um)* (equiv. to *cili(um)* (see CILIA) + *-olum* -OLE[1]) + -ATE[1]]

Cil•i•oph•o•ra (sil′ē of′ər ə), *n. Biol.* a phylum of protozoa in the kingdom Protista, comprising the ciliates. [< NL, equiv. to *cili(um)* CILIUM + *-o-* -O- + Gk *-phora,* neut. pl. of *-phoros* -PHOROUS]

cil•i•um (sil′ē əm), *n.* sing. of **cilia.** [< L]

Cil•la (sil′ə), *n. Class. Myth.* a sister of Priam who, with her infant son, was slain by Priam because it had been prophesied that a mother and child of the royal house would cause the destruction of Troy.

Ci•lu•ba (chi lo͞o′bə), *n.* Luba (def. 2).

CIM, **1.** computer input from microfilm. **2.** computer-integrated manufacturing.

Ci•ma•bu•e (chē′mä bo͞o′e), *n.* **Gio•van•ni** (jô vän′nē), (*Cenni di Pepo*), c1240–1302?, Italian painter and mosaicist.

ci•maise (sē mez′), *n.* cymaise.

Ci•ma•ro•sa (chē′mə rō′zə; *It.* chē′mä rô′sä), *n.* **Do•me•ni•co** (dô me′nē kô), 1749–1801, Italian conductor and composer.

cim•ar•ron (sim′ə ron′, -rōn′, -ər ən; sim′ə rōn′), *n.* bighorn. [1840–50; < AmerSp (*carnero*) *cimarrón* wild (sheep); Sp: wild, prob. equiv. to *cim(a)* peak, summit (< L *cȳma* spring shoots of a vegetable < Gk; see CYME) + *-arrón* adj. suffix; cf. MAROON[2]]

Cim•ar•ron (sim′ə ron′, -rōn′, -ər ən; sim′ə rōn′), *n.* a river flowing E from NE New Mexico to the Arkansas River in Oklahoma. 600 mi. (965 km) long.

cim•ba•lom (sim′bə ləm), *n.* cymbalom.

Cim•bri (sim′brī, -brē, kim′-), *n.* (*used with a plural v.*) a Germanic or Celtic people, supposed to have originated in Jutland, who invaded Gaul and northern Italy, and were destroyed by the Romans in 101 B.C. —**Cim′bri•an,** *adj., n.* —**Cim′bric,** *adj.*

ci•me•li•a (si mē′lē ə, -mēl′yə), *n.pl., sing.* **-me•li•um** (-mē′lē əm, -mēl′yəm). treasures, esp. church treasures, as art objects or jeweled vestments. [1655–65; < ML < Gk *keimḗlion* heirloom, treasure, akin to *keîsthai* to lie, be stored away; see CEMETERY]

ci•me•li•arch (si mē′lē ärk′), *n.* a room for keeping the valuables of a church. [1650–60; < LL *cīmēliarcha* < LGk *keimēliárchē* treasury guard. See CIMELIA, -ARCH]

ci•met•i•dine (sə met′i dēn′), *n. Pharm.* a substance, $C_{10}H_{16}N_6S$, that is used alone or in combination with antacids to inhibit gastric secretion in the treatment of duodenal ulcers. [1975–80; prob. *ci-,* resp. of CY(ANO)-[3] + MET(HYL) + (GUAN)IDINE]

ci•mex (sī′meks), *n., pl.* **cim•i•ces** (sim′ə sēz′). a bedbug of the genus *Cimex.* [1575–85; < NL, L *cīmex* bedbug]

Cim•me•ri•an (si mēr′ē ən), *adj.* **1.** *Class. Myth.* of, pertaining to, or suggestive of a western people believed to dwell in perpetual darkness. **2.** very dark; gloomy: *deep, Cimmerian caverns.* —**Cim•me′ri•an•ism,** *n.*

Ci•mon (sī′mən), *n.* 507–449 B.C., Athenian military leader, naval commander, and statesman (son of Miltiades).

C. in C., Commander in Chief. Also, **C-in-C**

cinch[1] (sinch), *n.* **1.** a strong girth used on stock saddles, having a ring at each end to which a strap running from the saddle is secured. **2.** a firm hold or tight grip. **3.** *Informal.* **a.** something sure or easy: *This problem is a cinch.* **b.** a person or thing certain to fulfill an expectation, esp. a team or contestant certain to win a sporting event: *The Giants are a cinch to win Sunday's game.* —*v.t.* **4.** to gird with a cinch; gird or bind firmly. **5.** *Informal.* to seize on or make sure of; guarantee: *Ability and hard work cinched her success.* [1855–60, *Amer.*; < Sp *cincha* < L *cingula* girth, equiv. to *cing(ere)* to gird + *-ula* -ULE]

cinch[2] (sinch), *n. Cards.* a variety of the game all fours. [1885–90; perh. < Sp *cinco* five, a card game]

cinch′ belt′, a wide belt of elastic, leather, or fabric with a clasp or lacing in front, worn tightly to make the waist look smaller. Also called **cinch.**

cin•cho•na (sing kō′nə, sin-), *n.* **1.** any of several trees or shrubs of the genus *Cinchona,* of the madder family, esp. *C. calisaya,* native to the Andes, cultivated there and in Java and India for its bark, which yields quinine and other alkaloids. **2.** Also called **Jesuit's bark, Peruvian bark.** the medicinal bark of such trees or shrubs. [< NL, the Linnaean genus name, after Francisca Enriques de Ribera, Countess of *Chinchón* (d. 1641), who was associated with the introduction of quinine into Europe, in several accounts now considered spurious] —**cin•chon•ic** (sin kon′ik), *adj.*

cin•chon•i•dine (sing kon′i dēn′, -din, sin-), *n. Pharm.* a white, crystalline, slightly water-soluble, levorotatory alkaloid, $C_{19}H_{22}N_2O$, stereoisomeric with cinchonine and similarly derived, used chiefly as a quinine substitute. [1850–55; CINCHON(A) + -ID[3] + -INE[2]]

cin•cho•nine (sing′kə nēn′, -nin, sin′-), *n. Pharm.* a colorless, crystalline, slightly water-soluble alkaloid, $C_{19}H_{22}N_2O$, a stereoisomer of cinchonidine, obtained from the bark of various species of cinchona and used chiefly as a quinine substitute. [1815–25; CINCHON(A) + -INE[2]]

cin•chon•ism (sing′kə niz′əm, sin′-), *n. Pathol.* poisoning by any of the cinchona alkaloids, characterized by headache, deafness, and ringing in the ears. [1855–60; CINCHON(A) + -ISM]

Cin•cin•nat•i (sin′sə nat′ē), *n.* **1.** a city in SW Ohio, on the Ohio River. 385,457. **2.** *Bowling Slang.* a split in which the eight and ten pins remain standing.

Cin•cin•na•tus (sin′sə nā′təs, -nat′əs), *n.* **Lucius Quinc•ti•us** (kwingk′tē əs), 519?–439? B.C., Roman general and statesman: dictator 458, 439.

Cin•co de Ma•yo (*Sp.* sēng′kô the mä′yô), a Mexican holiday marking the victory of Mexican troops over French forces in Puebla, Mexico, on May 5, 1862. [< Sp: May 5]

cinc•ture (singk′chər), *n., v.,* **-tured, -tur•ing.** —*n.* **1.** a belt or girdle. **2.** something that surrounds or encompasses as a girdle does; a surrounding border: *The midnight sky had a cincture of stars.* **3.** (on a classical column) a fillet at either end of a shaft, esp. one at the lower end. Cf. **orle** (def. 3b). **4.** the act of girding or encompassing. —*v.t.* **5.** to gird with or as if with a cincture; encircle; encompass. [< L *cinctūra,* equiv. to *cinct(us)* (*cinc-,* var. s. of *cingere* to gird, CINCH + *-tus* ptp. suffix) + *-ūra* -URE]

cin•der (sin′dər), *n.* **1.** a partially or mostly burned piece of coal, wood, etc. **2. cinders, a.** any residue of combustion; ashes. **b.** *Geol.* coarse scoriae erupted by volcanoes. **3.** a live, flameless coal; ember. **4.** *Metall.* **a.** slag (def. 1). **b.** a mixture of ashes and slag. —*v.t.* **5.** to spread cinders on: *The highway department salted and cindered the icy roads.* **6.** *Archaic.* to reduce to cinders. —*v.i.* **7.** to spread cinders on a surface, as a road or sidewalk: *My neighbor began cindering as soon as the first snowflake fell.* [bef. 900; ME *synder,* OE *sinder* slag; c. G *Sinter,* ON *sindr*; c- (for s-) < F *cendre* ashes] —**cin′der•y, cin′der•ous,** *adj.* —**cin′der•like′,** *adj.*

cin′der block′, a concrete building block made with a cinder aggregate. [1925–30]

cin′der con′crete, concrete having small coal clinkers as an aggregate.

cin′der cone′, *Geol.* a small, conical volcano built of ash and cinders. [1840–50]

Cin•der•el•la (sin′də rel′ə), *n.* **1.** a heroine of a fairy tale or folk tale who is maltreated by a malevolent stepmother but achieves happiness and marries a prince through the benevolent intervention of a fairy godmother. **2.** (*italics*) the tale itself, the earliest version of which is in Chinese and dates from the 9th century A.D. **3.** (*italics*) a ballet (1945) with musical score by Sergei Prokofiev. **4.** a person or thing of merit, undeservedly neglected or forced into a wretched or obscure existence. **5.** a person who achieves unexpected or sudden success or recognition, esp. after obscurity, neglect, or misery.

cin′der patch′, *Metall.* a defect on steel caused by the accidental picking up of matter, as from the bottom of a soaking pit.

cin′der track′, a track covered with small cinders, for use in running races. [1885–90]

Cin•dy (sin′dē), *n.* a female given name, form of **Cynthia.**

cin•e (sin′ē, sin′ā), *n.* **1.** a film; motion picture. **2.** a motion-picture theater. Also, **cin′é.** [1895–1900; short for CINEMA]

cine-, a combining form meaning "motion picture," used in the formation of compound words: *cineradiograph.* [extracted from CINEMA]

cin•e•an•gi•og•ra•phy (sin′ē an′jē og′rə fē), the recording by motion pictures of blood vessels following injection of a radiopaque contrast medium. [CINE- + ANGIO- + -GRAPHY] —**cin•e•an•gi•o•graph•ic** (sin′ē-an′jē ə graf′ik), *adj.*

cin•e•aste (sin′ē ast′, sin′ā-), *n.* **1.** any person, esp. a director or producer, associated professionally with filmmaking. **2.** an aficionado of filmmaking. Also, **cin′e•ast′, cin′é•aste′.** [1925–30; < F *cinéaste,* equiv. to *ciné-* CINE- + *-aste,* as in *ecclésiaste, gymnaste,* etc.]

cin•e•ma (sin′ə mə), *n.* **1.** *Chiefly Brit.* See **motion picture. 2. the cinema,** motion pictures collectively, as an art. **3.** *Chiefly Brit.* a motion-picture theater. [1895–1900; short for CINEMATOGRAPH] —**cin•e•mat•ic** (sin′ə mat′ik), *adj.* —**cin′e•mat′i•cal•ly,** *adv.*

Cin•e•ma•Scope (sin′ə mə skōp′), *Motion Pictures, Trademark.* a wide-screen process using anamorphic lenses in photographing and projecting the film. —**Cin•e•ma•Scop•ic** (sin′ə mə skop′ik), *adj.*

cin•e•ma•theque (sin′ə mə tek′), *n.* a motion-picture theater, often part of a university or private archive, showing experimental or historically important films. Also, **cin•é•ma•thèque** (*Fr.* sē nä mȧ tek′). [1965–70; < F *cinémathèque* film archive, equiv. to *cinéma-* prefixal use of *cinéma* CINEMA + *-thèque,* as in *bibliothèque* library, *discothèque* collection of phonograph records; see THECA]

cin•e•mat•ics (sin′ə mat′iks), *n.* (*used with a singular or plural v.*) the art of making motion pictures; cinematography. [1925–30; CINEMAT(OGRAPH) + -ICS]

cin•e•ma•tize (sin′ə mə tīz′), *v.t., v.i.,* **-tized, -tiz•ing.** **1.** to adapt (a novel, play, etc.) for motion pictures. **2.** *Chiefly Brit.* cinematograph (def. 3). Also, *esp. Brit.,* **cin′e•ma•tise′.** [CINEMA + (DRAMA)TIZE]

cinematog., cinematography.

cin•e•mat•o•graph (sin′ə mat′ə graf′, -gräf′), *Chiefly Brit.* —*n.* **1.** a motion-picture projector. **2.** a motion-picture camera. —*v.t., v.i.* **3.** to photograph with a motion-picture camera. Also, **kinematograph.** [1895–1900; < F *cinématographe,* equiv. to *cinémat-* (< Gk *kīnēmat-,* s. of *kī́nēma* motion) + *-o-* -O- + *-graphe* -GRAPH] —**cin•e•mat•o•graph•ic** (sin′ə mat′ə graf′ik), *adj.* —**cin′e•mat′o•graph′i•cal•ly,** *adv.*

cin•e•ma•tog•ra•pher (sin′ə mə tog′rə fər), *n.* **1.** a person whose profession is motion-picture photography. **2.** See **director of photography.** Also, *esp. Brit.,* **cin′e•ma•tog′ra•phist.** [1895–1900; CINEMATOGRAPH + -ER[1]]

cin•e•ma•tog•ra•phy (sin′ə mə tog′rə fē), *n.* the art or technique of motion-picture photography. [1895–1900; see CINEMATOGRAPH, -GRAPHY]

ci•né•ma vé•ri•té (sin′ə mə ver′i tā′; *Fr.* sē nä mä vā rē tā′), **1.** a technique of documentary filmmaking in which the camera records actual persons and events without directorial control: introduced in France in the 1950's. **2.** a film using this technique or a simulation of it. [1960–65; < F *cinéma-vérité* lit., cinema-truth, coined as a trans. of Russ *kinoprávda,* a documentary technique developed by the Soviet filmmaker Dziga Vertov (1896–1954)]

cin•e•mi•cro•graph (sin′ə mī′krə graf′, -gräf′), *n.* a motion picture filmed through a microscope. Also, **cin•e•pho•to•mi•cro•graph** (sin′ə fō′tō mī′krə graf′, -gräf′). Cf. **photomicrograph.** [CINE- + MICROGRAPH] —**cin•e•mi•crog•ra•pher** (sin′ə mī krog′rə fər), *n.* —**cin•e•mi•cro•graph•ic** (sin′ə mī′krə graf′ik), **cin′e•mi′cro•graph′i•cal,** *adj.* —**cin′e•mi′cro•graph′i•cal•ly,** *adv.*

cin•e•mi•crog•ra•phy (sin′ə mī krog′rə fē), *n. Micros.* the cinematographic recording of microscopic pictures, e.g., for the study of bacterial motion. [1940–45; CINE- + MICROGRAPHY]

cin•e•ole (sin′ē ōl′), *n. Chem., Pharm.* a colorless, oily, slightly water-soluble liquid terpene ether, $C_{10}H_{18}O$, having a camphorlike odor and a pungent, spicy, cooling taste, found in eucalyptus, cajeput, and other essential oils: used in flavoring, perfumery, and medicine chiefly as an expectorant. Also, **cin•e•ol** (sin′ē ōl′, -ol′). Also called **cajeputol, cajuputol, eucalyptol.** [alter. of NL *oleum cinae,* equiv. to *oleum* oil + gen. sing. of *cina* wormseed]

cin•e•phile (sin′ə fīl′), *n.* a devoted moviegoer, esp. one knowledgeable about the cinema. [1965–70; < F, equiv. to *ciné-* CINE- + *-phile* -PHILE]

cin•e•ra•di•og•ra•phy (sin′ə rā′dē og′rə fē), *n.* the filming of motion pictures through a fluoroscope or x-ray machine. [1930–35; CINE- + RADIOGRAPHY]

Cin•e•ram•a (sin′ə ram′ə, -rä′mə), *Motion Pictures, Trademark.* a wide-screen process using three adjacent, synchronized cameras for photographing and three corresponding projectors for showing the film.

cin•e•rar•i•a (sin′ə râr′ē ə), *n.* any of several horticultural varieties of a composite plant, *Senecio hybridus,* of the Canary Islands, having clusters of flowers with white, blue, purple, red, or variegated rays. [1590–1600; < NL, fem. of *cinerārius* ashen, equiv. to L *ciner-* (s. of *cinis* ashes) + *-ārius* -ARY; so named from ash-colored down on leaves]

cin•e•rar•i•um (sin′ə râr′ē əm), *n., pl.* **-rar•i•a** (-râr′ē ə). a place for depositing the ashes of the dead after cremation. [1875–80; < L; see CINERARIA, -ARIUM]

cin•e•rar•y (sin′ə rer′ē), *adj.* holding or intended for ashes, esp. the ashes of cremated bodies: *a cinerary urn.* [1740–50; < NL *cinerārius*; see CINERARIA]

cin•er•a•tor (sin′ə rā′tər), *n.* an incinerator. [< L *ciner-,* s. of *cinis* ash + -ATOR] —**cin′e•ra′tion,** *n.*

ci•ne•re•ous (si nēr′ē əs), *adj.* **1.** in the state of or reduced to ashes: *cinereous bodies.* **2.** resembling ashes. **3.** ashen; ash-colored; grayish: *a cinereous bird.* Also, **cin•er•i•tious** (sin′ə rish′əs). [1655–65; < L *cinereus,* equiv. to *ciner-* (s. of *cinis*) ashes + *-eus* -EOUS]

Cin•ga•lese (sing′gə lēz′, -lēs′), *adj., n., pl.* **-lese.** Singhalese.

cin•gu•lum (sing′gyə ləm), *n., pl.* **-la** (-lə). **1.** *Anat., Zool.* a belt, zone, or girdlelike part. **2.** *Dentistry.* See **basal ridge.** [1835–45; < L: girdle, zone, equiv. to *cing-* (s. of *cingere* to gird; see CINCTURE) + *-ulum* -ULE] —**cin•gu•late** (sing′gyə lit, -lāt′), **cin′gu•lat′ed, cin′gu•lar,** *adj.*

cin•na•bar (sin′ə bär′), *n.* **1.** a mineral, mercuric sulfide, HgS, occurring in red crystals or masses: the

CONCISE PRONUNCIATION KEY: act, cāpe, dâre, pärt; set, ēqual; *if,* īce; ox, ōver, ôrder, oil, bo͝ok, bo͞ot, out; up, ûrge; child; sing; shoe; thin, *th*at; zh as in *treasure.* ə = *a* as in *alone, e* as in *system, i* as in *easily, o* as in *gallop, u* as in *circus;* ᵊ as in *fire* (fīᵊr), *hour* (ouᵊr). l and n can serve as syllabic consonants, as in *cradle* (krād′l), and *button* (but′n). See the full key inside the front cover.

principal ore of mercury. **2.** red mercuric sulfide, used as a pigment. **3.** bright red; vermillion. [1350–1400; < L *cinnabaris* < Gk *kinnábari* < ?; r. ME *cynoper* < ML, L as above] —**cin•na•bar•ine** (sin′ə bə rēn′, -bər in, -bär′in, -ēn), **cin•na•bar•ic** (sin′ə bar′ik), *adj.*

cin•na•mene (sin′ə mēn′), *n. Chem.* styrene. [1870–75; *cinnam-* (comb. form of L *cinnamōmum* CINNAMON) + -ENE]

cin•nam•ic (si nam′ik, sin′ə mik), *adj.* of or obtained from cinnamon. [1880–85; CINNAM(ON) + -IC]

cinnam′ic ac′id, *Chem.* a white, crystalline, water-insoluble powder, $C_9H_8O_2$, usually obtained from cinnamon or synthesized: used chiefly in the manufacture of perfumes and medicines. [1880–85]

cinnam′ic al′cohol, *Chem.* a white, water-insoluble, crystalline solid, $C_9H_{10}O$, having a hyacinthine odor, used chiefly as a scent in the manufacture of perfumes.

cinnam′ic al′dehyde, *Chem.* a yellowish oil, C_9H_8O, having a cinnamonlike odor, used chiefly as a scent in the manufacture of flavorings and perfumes.

cin•na•mon (sin′ə mən), *n.* **1.** the aromatic inner bark of any of several East Indian trees belonging to the genus *Cinnamonum*, of the laurel family, esp. the bark of *C. zeylanicum* **(Ceylon cinnamon)**, used as a spice, or that of *C. loureirii* **(Saigon cinnamon)**, used in medicine as a cordial and carminative. **2.** a tree yielding such bark. **3.** any allied or similar tree. **4.** a common culinary spice of dried rolled strips of this bark, often made into a powder. **5.** cassia (def. 1). **6.** a yellowish or reddish brown. —*adj.* **7.** (of food) containing or flavored with cinnamon. **8.** reddish-brown or yellowish-brown. [1400–50; < L < LGk *kínnamon* < Sem (cf. Heb *qinnā-mōn*); r. late ME *cinamome* < MF < L *cinnamōmum* < Gk *kinnámōmon* < Sem as above] —**cin′na•moned,** *adj.* —**cin•na•mon•ic** (sin′ə mon′ik), *adj.*

cin′namon bear′, a cinnamon-colored variety of the black bear of North America. [1815–25]

cin′namon bun′, a honey bun flavored with cinnamon and often containing raisins.

cin′namon fern′, a common coarse fern, *Osmunda cinnamomea*, having rusty-woolly stalks, growing in wet, low woods or thickets. [1810–20]

cin′namon stone′, *Mineral.* essonite. [1795–1805]

cin′namon teal′, a small, freshwater, wild duck, *Anas cyanoptera*, of North and South America, having chiefly cinnamon-red plumage. [1890–95, *Amer.*]

cin′namon vine′. See **Chinese yam.**

cin•nam′yl ac′etate (si nam′əl), *Chem.* a colorless liquid, $C_{11}H_{12}O_2$, having a piquant, flowerlike odor: used as a fixative in the manufacture of perfumes. [CINNAM(IC ACID) + -YL]

cin•quain (sing kān′, sing′kān), *n.* **1.** a group of five. **2.** *Pros.* **a.** a short poem consisting of five, usually unrhymed lines containing, respectively, two, four, six, eight, and two syllables. **b.** any stanza of five lines. [1705–15; < F < LL *cinque* (see CINQUE) + F *-ain* collective suffix. See QUATRAIN]

cinque (singk), *n.* the five at dice, cards, etc. [1350–1400; ME *cink* < OF *cinq* < VL **cinque*, for L *quinque* FIVE]

cin•que•cen•tist (ching′kwi chen′tist), *n.* an Italian writer or artist of the 16th century. [1870–75; < It *cinquecentista*, equiv. to *cinquecent(o)* (see CINQUECENTO) + *-ista* -IST]

cin•que•cen•to (ching′kwi chen′tō), *n.* (*often cap.*) the 16th century, with reference to Italy, esp. to the Italian art or literature of that period. [1750–60; < It, short for *mil cinque cento* 1500, used for period A.D. 1500–99] —**cin′que•cen′tism,** *n.*

cin•que•de•a (ching′kwi dē′ə, -dā′ə), *n.* an Italian short sword of the late 15th and early 16th centuries having a broad, tapering blade, often richly ornamented. [1895–1900; < It, equiv. to *cinque* five (<< L *quinque*) + *dea* (dial.) fingers, akin to *dito* finger (< L *digitus;* see DIGIT)]

cinquefoil (def. 2)

cinque•foil (singk′foil′), *n.* **1.** any of several plants belonging to the genus *Potentilla*, of the rose family, having yellow, red, or white five-petaled flowers, as *P. reptans* **(creeping cinquefoil)**, of the Old World, or *P. argentea* **(silvery cinquefoil)**, of North America. **2.** Also called **quinquefoil, quintefoil.** *Archit.* a panellike ornament consisting of five lobes, divided by cusps, radiating from a common center. **3.** *Heraldry.* a charge in the form of a five-leaved clover. [1375–1425; late ME *sink foil* < MF *cincfoille* < L *quinque folia* five leaves, trans. of Gk *pentáphyllon*]

Cinque′ Ports′ (singk), a former association of maritime towns in SE England: originally (1278) numbering five (Hastings, Romney, Hythe, Dover, and Sandwich) and receiving special privileges in return for aiding in the naval defense of England. [1275–1325; ME *cink pors* < OF *cink porz*. See CINQUE, PORT[1]]

C.I.O., **1.** chief investment officer. **2.** See **Congress of Industrial Organizations.** Also, **CIO**

ci•on (sī′ən), *n.* scion (def. 2).

-cion, var. of **-tion:** *suspicion.* [< L, equiv. to *-c-* final in v. stem + *-iōn-* -ION]

ciop•pi•no (chə pē′nō; *It.* chôp pē′nô), *n. Italian Cookery.* a stew of fish, shellfish, tomatoes, and seasonings. [1935–40; appar. < dial. It]

CIP, Cataloging in Publication: a program sponsored by the Library of Congress and cooperating publishers in which a partial bibliographic description of a work appears on the verso of its title page.

Ci•pan•go (si pang′gō), *n. Archaic.* Japan.

ci•pher (sī′fər), *n.* **1.** zero. **2.** any of the Arabic numerals or figures. **3.** Arabic numerical notation collectively. **4.** something of no value or importance. **5.** a person of no influence; nonentity. **6.** a secret method of writing, as by transposition or substitution of letters, specially formed symbols, or the like. Cf. **cryptography.** **7.** writing done by such a method; a coded message. **8.** the key to a secret method of writing. **9.** a combination of letters, as the initials of a name, in one design; monogram. —*v.i.* **10.** to use figures or numerals arithmetically. **11.** to write in or as in cipher. —*v.t.* **12.** to calculate numerically; figure. **13.** to convert into cipher. Also, *esp. Brit.,* **cypher.** [1350–1400; ME *siphre* < ML *ciphra* < Ar *ṣifr* empty, zero; trans. of Skt *śūnyā* empty] —**ci′pher•a•ble,** *adj.* —**ci′pher•er,** *n.*

ci•pher•text (sī′fər tekst′), *n.* the encoded version of a message or other text; cryptogram. Cf. **plain-text.** [1935–40; CIPHER + TEXT]

ci•pho•ny (sī′fə nē), *n.* the process of encrypting telecommunication signals, as to prevent information from being intercepted by an enemy or competitor. [1955–60; b. CIPHER and TELEPHONY]

cip•o•lin (sip′ə lin), *n.* an impure variety of marble with alternate white and greenish zones and a layered structure. [1790–1800; < F < It *cipollino*, equiv. to *cipoll(a)* onion (< LL *cēpulla*, equiv. to L *cēp(a)* onion + *-ulla* dim. suffix) + *-ino* -INE[1]]

cip•pus (sip′əs), *n., pl.* **cip•pi** (sip′ī, sip′ē). (in classical architecture) a stele. [1615–25; < L: pillar, gravestone]

cir., **1.** about: *cir. 1800.* [< L *circā, circiter, circum*] **2.** circular.

circ (sûrk), *n.* circular (def. 9).

circ., **1.** about: *circ. 1800.*[< L *circā, circiter, circum*] **2.** circuit. **3.** circular. **4.** circulation. **5.** circumference.

cir•ca (sûr′kə), *prep., adv.* about: (used esp. in) approximate dates: *The Venerable Bede was born circa 673. Abbr.:* ca, ca., c., c, cir., circ. [1860–65; < L: around, about, akin to *circus* CIRCUS]

cir•ca•di•an (sûr kā′dē ən, -kad′ē-, sûr′kə dē′ən), *adj.* noting or pertaining to rhythmic biological cycles recurring at approximately 24-hour intervals. [1955–60; < L *circā* about + *di(ēs)* day + -AN]

circ•an•nu•al (sûr kan′yo͞o əl), *adj. Biol.* noting or pertaining to a biological activity or cycle that recurs yearly. [1970–75; CIRC(A) + ANNUAL]

Cir•cas•sia (sər kash′ə, -ē ə), *n.* a region in the S Russian Federation in Europe, bordering on the Black Sea.

Cir•cas•sian (sər kash′ən, -ē ən), *n.* **1.** a native or inhabitant of Circassia. **2.** a group of North Caucasian languages, including Kabardian. **3.** a literary language based on the western dialects of the Circassian group. —*adj.* **4.** of or pertaining to Circassia, its inhabitants, often with respect to their legendary beauty, or their language. [1545–55; < ML or NL *Circassi(a)* + -AN]

Circas′sian wal′nut, the hard, intricately grained wood of the English walnut. [1910–15]

Cir•ce (sûr′sē), *n.* **1.** Also, **Kirke.** Also called **Aeaea.** *Class. Myth.* the enchantress represented by Homer as turning the companions of Odysseus into swine by means of a magic drink. **2.** a dangerously or irresistibly fascinating woman. —**Cir•ce•an, Cir•cae•an** (sər sē′ən), *adj.*

cir•ci•nate (sûr′sə nāt′), *adj.* **1.** made round; ring-shaped. **2.** *Bot., Mycol.* rolled up on the axis at the apex, as a leaf or fruiting body. [1820–30; < L *circinātus* (ptp. of *circināre* to make round), equiv. to *circin(us)* pair of compasses (akin to CIRCUS) + *-ātus* -ATE[1]] —**cir′ci•nate•ly,** *adv.*

circinate fronds of a young fern

Cir•ci•nus (sûr′sə nəs), *n., gen.* **-ni** (-nī′). *Astron.* the Compasses, a small southern constellation between Triangulum and Centaurus. [1830–40; < L]

cir•cle (sûr′kəl), *n., v.,* **-cled, -cling.** —*n.* **1.** a closed plane curve consisting of all points at a given distance from a point within it called the center. Equation: $x^2 + y^2 = r^2$. **2.** the portion of a plane bounded by such a curve. **3.** any circular or ringlike object, formation, or arrangement: *a circle of dancers.* **4.** a ring, circlet, or crown. **5.** the ring of a circus. **6.** a section of seats in a theater: *dress circle.* **7.** the area within which something acts, exerts influence, etc.; realm; sphere: *A politician has a wide circle of influence.* **8.** a series ending where it began, esp. when perpetually repeated; cycle: *the circle of the year.* **9.** *Logic.* an argument ostensibly proving a conclusion but actually assuming the conclusion or its equivalent as a premise; vicious circle. **10.** a complete series forming a connected whole; cycle: *the circle of the sciences.* **11.** a number of persons bound by a common tie; coterie: *a literary circle; a family circle.* **12.** *Govt.* an administrative division, esp. of a province. **13.** *Geog.* a parallel of latitude. **14.** *Astron.* **a.** (formerly) the orbit of a heavenly body. **b.** See **meridian circle.** **15.** *Survey.* a glass or metal disk mounted concentrically with the spindle of a theodolite or level and graduated so that the angle at which the alidade is set may be read. **16.** a sphere or orb: *the circle of the earth.* **17.** a ring of light in the sky; halo. —*v.t.* **18.** to enclose in a circle; surround; encircle: *Circle the correct answer on the exam paper. The enemy circled the hill.* **19.** to move in a circle or circuit around; rotate or revolve around: *He circled the house cautiously.* **20.** to change course so as to pass by or avoid collision with; bypass; evade: *The ship carefully circled the iceberg.* **21. circle the wagons, a.** (in the early U.S. West) to form the wagons of a covered-wagon train into a circle for defensive purposes, as against Indian attack. **b.** *Slang.* to prepare for an all-out, unaided defensive fight: *The company has circled the wagons since its market share began to decline.* —*v.i.* **22.** to move in a circle or circuit: *The plane circled for half an hour before landing.* **23.** *Motion Pictures, Television.* to iris (usually fol. by *in* or *out*). [bef. 1000; < L *circulus*, equiv. to *circ(us)* (see CIRCUS) + *-ulus* -ULE; r. ME *cercle* < OF < L, as above; r. OE *circul* < L, as above] —**cir′cler,** *n.*

—**Syn.** **3.** ring, halo, corona. **11.** CIRCLE, CLUB, COTERIE, SET, SOCIETY are terms applied to restricted social groups. A CIRCLE may be a little group; in the plural it often suggests a whole section of society interested in one mode of life, occupation, etc.: *a sewing circle; a language circle; in theatrical circles.* CLUB implies an association with definite requirements for membership and fixed dues: *an athletic club.* COTERIE suggests a little group closely and intimately associated because of congeniality: *a literary coterie.* SET refers to a number of persons of similar background, interests, etc., somewhat like a CLIQUE (see RING[1]) but without disapproving connotations; however, it often implies wealth or interest in social activities: *the country club set.* A SOCIETY is a group associated to further common interests of a cultural or practical kind: *a Humane Society.*

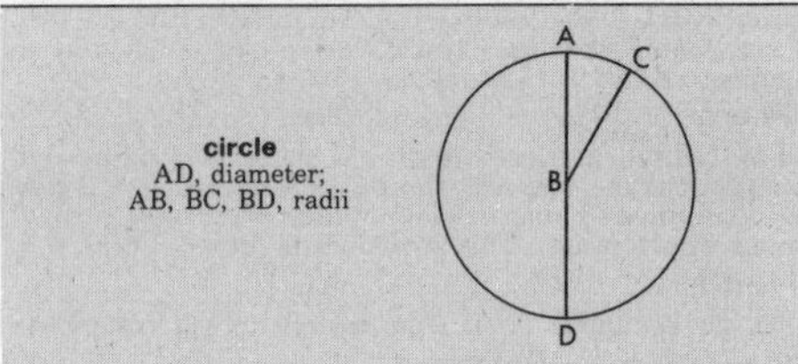

circle AD, diameter; AB, BC, BD, radii

cir′cle graph′, *Statistics, Math.* See **pie chart.** [1925–30]

cir•cle-in (sûr′kəl in′), *n. Motion Pictures, Television.* iris-in.

cir′cle jerk′, *Slang* (*vulgar*). mutual masturbation among three or more persons.

cir′cle of confu′sion, *Photog.* a circular spot on a film, resulting from the degree to which a pencil of light reflected from the field of view is focused in front of or behind the film, or from aberration of the lens, or from both. [1905–10]

cir′cle of conver′gence, *Math.* a circle associated with a given power series such that the series converges for all values of the variable inside the circle and diverges for all values outside it. Cf. **interval of convergence.**

cir′cle of cur′vature, *Math.* the circle with its center on the normal to the concave side of a curve at a given point on the curve and with its radius equal to the radius of curvature at the point. Also called **osculating circle.**

cir′cle of declina′tion, *Astron.* See **hour circle.** [1585–95]

cir′cle of least′ confu′sion, *Optics.* the smallest cross section in a beam of paraxial rays, lying in the plane of least spherical aberration. [1865–70]

cir•cle-out (sûr′kəl out′), *n. Motion Pictures, Television.* iris-out.

cir•clet (sûr′klit), *n.* **1.** a small circle. **2.** a ring. **3.** a ring-shaped ornament, esp. for the head. [1475–85; CIRCLE + -ET; r. late ME *serclett* < MF]

Cir•cle•ville (sûr′kəl vil′), *n.* a city in S central Ohio. 11,700.

cir′cling disease′, *Vet. Pathol.* listeriosis.

cir•cuit (sûr′kit), *n.* **1.** an act or instance of going or moving around. **2.** a circular journey or one beginning and ending at the same place; a round. **3.** a roundabout journey or course. **4.** a periodical journey from place to place, to perform certain duties, as by judges to hold court, ministers to preach, or salespeople covering a route. **5.** the persons making such a journey. **6.** the route followed, places visited, or district covered by such a journey. **7.** the line going around or bounding any area or object; the distance about an area or object. **8.** the space within a bounding line; district: *the circuit of the valley.* **9.** *Elect.* **a.** Also called **electric circuit.** the complete path of an electric current, including the generating apparatus, intervening resistors, or capacitors. **b.** any well-defined segment of a complete circuit. **10.** *Telecommunications.* a means of transmitting communication signals or messages, usually comprising two channels for interactive communication. Cf. **channel**[1] (def. 12). **11.** a number of theaters, nightclubs, etc., controlled by the same owner or manager or visited in turn by the same entertainers or acting companies. **12.** a

league or association: *He used to play baseball for the Texas circuit.* **13. ride circuit,** *Law.* (of a judge) to travel a judicial county or district in order to conduct judicial proceedings. —*v.t.* **14.** to go or move around; make the circuit of. —*v.i.* **15.** to go or move in a circuit. [1350–1400; ME < L *circuitus,* var. of *circumitus* circular motion, cycle, equiv. to *circu(m)i-,* var. s. of *circu(m)ire* to go round, circle (*circum-* CIRCUM- + *ire* to go) + *-tus* suffix of v. action; cf. AMBIT, EXIT] —**cir′cuit·al,** *adj.*
—**Syn. 2.** tour, revolution, orbit. **7.** circumference, perimeter, periphery, boundary, compass. **8.** region, compass, area, range, field. **11.** chain.

cir′cuit an′alyzer, *Elect.* multimeter. [1960–65]

cir′cuit bind′ing, a bookbinding having soft edges that project beyond and fold over the edges of the pages to protect them. Also called **divinity circuit, yapp, yapp binding.** [1905–10, *Amer.*]

cir′cuit board′, 1. *Electronics.* a sheet of insulating material used for the mounting and interconnection (often by a printed circuit) of components in electronic equipment. **2.** *Computers.* **a.** board (def. 13a). **b.** a piece of material on which printed or integrated circuits are installed. Also called **board** (for defs. 1, 2b).

cir′cuit break′er, 1. *Elect.* Also called **breaker.** a device for interrupting an electric circuit to prevent excessive current, as that caused by a short circuit, from damaging the apparatus in the circuit or from causing a fire. **2.** any property-tax relief measure that reduces or limits property taxes for certain eligible taxpayers, as those with low income or the elderly. [1870–75, *Amer.*]

cir′cuit court′, 1. a court holding sessions at various intervals in different sections of a judicial district. **2.** (*caps.*) the court of general jurisdiction in a number of U.S. states. [1700–10, *Amer.*]

cir′cuit court′ of appeals′, any of the courts of appeals in the U.S. federal judicial system before 1948. [1940–45, *Amer.*]

cir′cuit edg′es, the soft edges of a circuit binding. [1905–10]

cir·cuit·er (sûr′ki tər), *n.* a person who travels a circuit. [1645–55; CIRCUIT + -ER[1]]

cir′cuit judge′, a judge of a circuit court. [1795–1805, *Amer.*]

cir·cu·i·tous (sər kyo͞o′i təs), *adj.* roundabout; not direct: *a circuitous route; a circuitous argument.* [1655–65; < ML *circuitōsus,* equiv. to *circuit(us)* CIRCUIT + *-ōsus* -OUS] —**cir·cu′i·tous·ly,** *adv.* —**cir·cu′i·tous·ness,** *n.*
—**Syn.** circular, winding, indirect, meandering. —**Ant.** straight, direct.

cir′cuit rid′er, 1. (formerly) a minister who rode horseback from place to place to preach and perform religious ceremonies. **2.** someone, as a public official or a nurse, who travels throughout a given territory to provide services. [1830–40, *Amer.*]

cir·cuit·ry (sûr′ki trē), *n.* **1.** the science of designing electric or electronic circuits. **2.** the circuits themselves. **3.** the components of such circuits. [1945–50; CIRCUIT + -RY]

cir·cu·i·ty (sər kyo͞o′i tē), *n., pl.* **-ties.** circuitous quality or roundabout character. [1535–45; CIRCUIT + -Y[3]]

cir·cu·lar (sûr′kyə lər), *adj.* **1.** having the form of a circle; round: *a circular tower.* **2.** of or pertaining to a circle: *a circular plane.* **3.** moving in or forming a circle or a circuit: *the circular rotation of the earth.* **4.** moving or occurring in a cycle or round: *the circular succession of the seasons.* **5.** roundabout; indirect; circuitous: *a circular route.* **6.** *Logic.* of or pertaining to reasoning in which the conclusion is ostensibly proved, but in actuality it or its equivalent has been assumed as a premise. **7.** pertaining to a circle or set of persons. **8.** (of a letter, memorandum, etc.) addressed to a number of persons or intended for general circulation. —*n.* **9.** a letter, advertisement, notice, or statement for circulation among the general public. [1375–1425; late ME < L *circulāris,* equiv. to *circul(us)* CIRCLE + *-āris* -AR[1]] —**cir′cu·lar′i·ty, cir′cu·lar·ness,** *n.* —**cir′cu·lar·ly,** *adv.*
—**Syn. 9.** handbill, flier, leaflet.

cir′cular defini′tion, *Logic.* a definition in which the definiendum (the expression being defined) or a variant of it appears in the definiens (the expression that defines it).

cir′cular di′chroism, *Optics.* selective absorption of one of the two possible circular polarizations of light. [1960–65]

cir′cular er′ror, 1. *Horol.* loss of isochronism in a pendulum moving through circular arcs of different sizes: sometimes avoided by causing the pendulum to move through cycloidal arcs. **2.** *Mil.* error measured as the distance from the center of a target to the point of impact of a bomb or shell, or to the ground zero of an aerial burst. [1880–85]

cir′cular file′, *Facetious.* a wastebasket. [1960–65]

cir′cular func′tion, *Math.* See **trigonometric function** (def. 1). [1880–85]

cir·cu·lar·ize (sûr′kyə lə rīz′), *v.t.,* **-ized, -iz·ing. 1.** to circulate (a letter, memorandum, etc.). **2.** to send circulars to. **3.** to publicize, esp. by mailing or handing out circulars. **4.** to make circular. Also, *esp. Brit.,* **cir′cu·lar·ise′.** [1790–1800; CIRCULAR + -IZE] —**cir′cu·lar·i·za′tion,** *n.* —**cir′cu·lar·iz′er,** *n.*

cir·cu·lar-knit (sûr′kyə lər nit′), *adj.* noting, pertaining to, or made of a fabric made by circular knitting. Cf. **flat-knit.**

cir′cular knit′ting, 1. a technique of knitting in circular or tubular form with curved or straight needles. **2.** (in machine knitting) a process of knitting tubular and seamless fabrics by using special needles and shaping the fabric by varying the tension or length of the stitches. Cf. **flat knitting.**

cir′cular light′, *Optics.* light that is circularly polarized.

cir′cular meas′ure, a measurement system for circles: 1 circle = 360 degrees (4 quadrants); 1 quadrant = 90 degrees; 1 degree = 60 minutes; 1 minute = 60 seconds. [1870–75]

cir′cular mil′, a unit used principally for measuring the cross-sectional area of wires, being the area of a circle having a diameter of one mil.

cir′cular pitch′, *Mach.* See under **pitch**[1] (def. 49a).

cir′cular polariza′tion, *Optics.* polarization in which the vector representing the instantaneous intensity of the electromagnetic field describes a circular helix in the direction of propagation. Cf. **elliptical polarization.** [1965–70]

cir′cular sail′ing. See **spherical sailing.**

cir′cular saw′, 1. a power saw having a disk-shaped blade, usually with a toothed edge. **2.** the blade of such a saw. See illus. under **saw.** [1810–20]

cir′cular tri′angle, a triangle whose sides are arcs of circles.

cir′cular veloc′ity, the velocity at which a body must move in order to maintain an orbit at the outer edge of the earth's atmosphere. Cf. **orbital velocity.**

cir·cu·late (sûr′kyə lāt′), *v.,* **-lat·ed, -lat·ing.** —*v.i.* **1.** to move in a circle or circuit; move or pass through a circuit back to the starting point: *Blood circulates throughout the body.* **2.** to pass from place to place, from person to person, etc.: *She circulated among her guests.* **3.** to be distributed or sold, esp. over a wide area. **4.** *Library Science.* (of books and other materials) to be available for borrowing by patrons of a library for a specified period of time. —*v.t.* **5.** to cause to pass from place to place, person to person, etc.; disseminate; distribute: *to circulate a rumor.* **6.** *Library Science.* to lend (books and other materials) to patrons of a library for a specified period of time. [1425–75 for earlier senses; 1665–75 for current senses; late ME < L *circulātus* (ptp. of *circulārī* to gather round one, ML *circulāre* to encircle), equiv. to *circul(us)* CIRCLE + *-ātus* -ATE[1]] —**cir′cu·lat′a·ble,** *adj.* —**cir·cu·la·tive** (sûr′kyə lā′tiv, -lə tiv), *adj.* —**cir·cu·la·to·ry** (sûr′kyə lə tôr′ē, -tōr′ē), *adj.*
—**Syn. 3.** disperse, spread, promulgate.

cir′culating cap′ital, the portion of capital goods that consists of goods in process, inventories of finished goods, and raw materials. Also called **cir′culating cap′ital goods′.** Cf. **fixed capital.** [1770–80]

cir′culating dec′imal, *Math.* See **repeating decimal.** [1760–70]

cir′culating li′brary, 1. a library whose books can be borrowed by its members or subscribers. **2.** See **lending library.** [1735–45]

cir′culating me′dium, 1. any coin or note passing, without endorsement, as a medium of exchange. **2.** such coins or notes collectively. [1790–1800]

cir·cu·la·tion (sûr′kyə lā′shən), *n.* **1.** an act or instance of circulating, moving in a circle or circuit, or flowing. **2.** the continuous movement of blood through the heart and blood vessels, which is maintained chiefly by the action of the heart, and by which nutrients, oxygen, and internal secretions are carried to and wastes are carried from the body tissues. **3.** any similar circuit, passage, or flow, as of the sap in plants or air currents in a room. **4.** the transmission or passage of anything from place to place or person to person: *the circulation of a rumor; the circulation of money.* **5.** the distribution of copies of a periodical among readers. **6.** the number of copies of each issue of a newspaper, magazine, etc., distributed. **7.** coins, notes, bills, etc., in use as money; currency. **8.** *Library Science.* **a.** the lending of library books and other materials. **b.** the number of books and materials that a library has lent. **c.** the processes connected with providing for the use of library materials, including reserve operations, recall, and record-keeping. **9.** *Hydraul.* a quantity analogous to work and equal to the line integral of the component of fluid velocity about a closed contour. **10. in circulation,** participating actively in social or business life: *After a month in the hospital, he's back in circulation.* [1400–50 for an earlier alchemical sense; 1645–55 for def. 1; late ME *circulacioun* < L *circulātiōn-* (s. of *circulātiō*), equiv. to *circulāt(us)* (see CIRCULATE) + *-iōn-* -ION] —**cir·cu·la·ble** (sûr′kyə lə bəl), *adj.*

cir·cu·la·tor (sûr′kyə lā′tər), *n.* **1.** a person who moves from place to place. **2.** a person who circulates money, information, etc. **3.** a talebearer or scandalmonger. **4.** any of various devices for circulating gases or liquids. **5.** *Obs.* a mountebank. [1600–10; < L *circulātor* itinerant vendor who gathers a circle of people round himself (see CIRCULATE, -TOR); later as CIRCULATE + -OR[2]]

cir′culatory sys′tem, *Anat., Zool.* the system of organs and tissues, including the heart, blood, blood vessels, lymph, lymphatic vessels, and lymph glands, involved in circulating blood and lymph through the body. [1860–65]

cir·cu·lus (sûr′kyə ləs), *n., pl.* **-li** (-lī′). any of the concentric circles on each scale of a fish, each of which indicates the annual growth of that scale. [< L: CIRCLE]

circum-, a prefix with the meaning "round about, around," found in Latin loanwords, esp. derivatives of verbs that had the general senses "to encompass or surround" (*circumference; circumjacent; circumstance*) or "to go around" by the means or in the manner specified by the verb (*circumnavigate; circumscribe*); on this basis forming adjectives in English with the meaning "surrounding" that named by the stem (*circumocular; circumpolar*). [< L *circum* around (acc. of *circus;* see CIRCUS, CIRCLE), orig. as an adv. fixed in relation to the v., later construed as a prefix]

circum., circumference.

cir·cum·am·bi·ent (sûr′kəm am′bē ənt), *adj.* surrounding; encompassing: *circumambient gloom.* [1625–35; < LL *circumambient-* (s. of *circumambiēns*). See CIRCUM-, AMBIENT] —**cir′cum·am′bi·ence, cir′cum·am′bi·en·cy,** *n.* —**cir′cum·am′bi·ent·ly,** *adv.*

cir·cum·am·bu·late (sûr′kəm am′byə lāt′), *v.t., v.i.,* **-lat·ed, -lat·ing.** to walk or go about or around, esp. ceremoniously. [1650–60; < LL *circumambulātus* (ptp. of *circumambulāre*). See CIRCUM-, AMBULATE] —**cir′cum·am′bu·la′tion,** *n.* —**cir′cum·am′bu·la′tor,** *n.* —**cir′cum·am′bu·la·to′ry,** *adj.*

cir·cum·ba·sal (sûr′kəm bā′səl), *adj.* surrounding the base. [1875–80; CIRCUM- + BASAL]

cir·cum·bend·i·bus (sûr′kəm ben′də bəs), *n., pl.* **-bus·es.** *Informal.* a roundabout way; circumlocution. [1675–85; CIRCUM- + BEND[1] + L *-ibus* abl. pl. ending]

cir·cum·cen·ter (sûr′kəm sen′tər), *n. Geom.* the center of a circumscribed circle; that point where any two perpendicular bisectors of the sides of a polygon inscribed in the circle intersect. [1885–90; CIRCUM- + CENTER]

cir·cum·cir·cle (sûr′kəm sûr′kəl), *n. Geom.* a circle circumscribed about a figure. [1880–85; CIRCUM- + CIRCLE]

cir·cum·cise (sûr′kəm sīz′), *v.t.,* **-cised, -cis·ing. 1.** to remove the prepuce of (a male), esp. as a religious rite. **2.** to remove the clitoris, prepuce, or labia of (a female). **3.** to purify spiritually. [1200–50; ME *circumcisen* < L *circumcīsus* (ptp. of *circumcīdere* to cut around), equiv. to *circum-* CIRCUM- + *-cīsus* (*-cīd-* cut + *-tus* ptp. suffix; see -CIDE)] —**cir′cum·cis′er,** *n.*

cir·cum·ci·sion (sûr′kəm sizh′ən), *n.* **1.** an act, instance, or the rite of circumcising. **2.** clitoridectomy. **3.** spiritual purification. **4.** (*cap.*) a church festival in honor of the circumcision of Jesus, observed on January 1. [1125–75; ME < LL *circumcīsiōn-* (s. of *circumcīsiō*), equiv. to L *circumcīs(us)* (see CIRCUMCISE) + *-iōn-* -ION]

cir·cum·col·um·nar (sûr′kəm kə lum′nər), *adj. Archit.* surrounding a column. [1875–80; CIRCUM- + COLUMNAR]

cir·cum·fer·ence (sər kum′fər əns), *n.* **1.** the outer boundary, esp. of a circular area; perimeter: *the circumference of a circle.* **2.** the length of such a boundary: *a one-mile circumference.* **3.** the area within a bounding line: *the vast circumference of his mind.* [1350–1400; ME < LL *circumferentia,* equiv. to *circum-* CIRCUM- + *fer-* (s. of *ferre* to carry) + *-entia* -ENCE]
—**Syn. 1.** periphery, circuit.

cir·cum·fer·en·tial (sər kum′fə ren′shəl), *adj.* **1.** of, at, or near the circumference; surrounding; lying along the outskirts. **2.** lying within the circumference. **3.** circuitous; indirect: *a circumferential manner of speech.* [1600–10; < L *circumferenti(a)* CIRCUMFERENCE + -AL[1]]

cir·cum·fer·en·tor (sər kum′fə ren′tər), *n. Survey.* an alidade equipped with a compass and two diametrically opposed vertical arms with slits for sighting through. [1600–10; < L *circumferent(ia)* CIRCUMFERENCE + -OR[2]]

cir·cum·flex (sûr′kəm fleks′), *adj.* **1.** consisting of, indicated by, or bearing the mark ˆ, ˜, or ¯, placed over a vowel symbol in some languages to show that the vowel or the syllable containing it is pronounced in a certain way, as, in French, that the vowel so marked is of a certain quality and long, in Albanian, that the vowel is nasalized and stressed, or, in Classical Greek, that the syllable bears the word accent and is pronounced, according to the ancient grammarians, with a rise and fall in pitch. **2.** pronounced with or characterized by the quality, quantity, stress, or pitch indicated by such a mark. **3.** bending or winding around. —*n.* **4.** a circumflex mark or accent. —*v.t.* **5.** to bend around. [1555–65; < L *circumflexus,* equiv. to *circum-* CIRCUM- + *flexus,* ptp. of *flectere* to bend; see FLEX]

cir·cum·flu·ent (sər kum′flo͞o ənt), *adj.* flowing around; encompassing. [1570–80; < L *circumfluent-* (s. of *circumfluēns,* prp. of *circumfluere* to flow around). See CIRCUM-, FLUENT] —**cir·cum′flu·ence,** *n.*

cir·cum·flu·ous (sər kum′flo͞o əs), *adj.* **1.** circumfluent. **2.** surrounded by water. [1605–15; < L *circumfluus,* equiv. to *circum-* CIRCUM- + *-fluus,* deriv. of *fluere* to flow; see -OUS]

cir·cum·fuse (sûr′kəm fyo͞oz′), *v.t.,* **-fused, -fus·ing. 1.** to pour around; diffuse. **2.** to surround as with a fluid; suffuse: *An atmosphere of joy circumfused the celebration.* [1590–1600; < L *circumfūsus* (ptp. of *circumfundere* to pour around). See CIRCUM-, FUSE[2]] —**cir·cum·fu·sion** (sûr′kəm fyo͞o′zhən), *n.*

cir·cum·gy·ra·tion (sûr′kəm jī rā′shən), *n.* a revolution or circular movement. [1595–1605; < LL *circumgȳrātiōn-* (s. of *circumgȳrātiō*). See CIRCUM-, GYRATION] —**cir·cum·gy·ra·to·ry** (sûr′kəm jī′rə tôr′ē, -tōr′ē), *adj.*

cir·cum·in·ces·sion (sûr′kəm in sesh′ən), *n. Theol.* the reciprocal existence in one another of the three persons of the Trinity. Also, **cir′cum·in·ses′sion.** [1635–45; < ML *circumincessiōn-* (s. of *circumcessiō*), equiv. to L *circum-* CIRCUM + ML *incessiōn-* < L *incess(us)* (ptp. of *incedere* to give in, to go along with, equiv. to *in-* IN-[2] + *cēd(ere)* to go + *-tus* ptp. suffix) + *-iōn-* -ION; see CEDE, CESSION]

cir·cum·ja·cent (sûr′kəm jā′sənt), *adj.* lying around; surrounding. [1480–90; < L *circumjacent-* (s. of *circumjacēns,* prp. of *circumjacēre* to lie around), equiv. to *circum-* CIRCUM- + *jac-* lie + *-ent-* -ENT] —**cir′cum·ja′cence, cir′cum·ja′cen·cy,** *n.*

cir·cum·lo·cu·tion (sûr′kəm lō kyo͞o′shən), *n.* **1.** a roundabout or indirect way of speaking; the use of more words than necessary to express an idea. **2.** a roundabout expression. [1375–1425; late ME < L *circumlocūtiōn-* (s. of *circumlocūtiō*). See CIRCUM-, LOCUTION] —**cir·cum·loc·u·to·ry** (sûr′kəm lok′yə tôr′ē, -tōr′ē), **cir′cum·lo·cu′tion·al, cir′cum·lo·cu′tion·ar′y,** *adj.*
—**Syn. 1.** rambling, meandering, verbosity, prolixity.

cir·cum·lu·nar (sûr′kəm lo͞o′nər), *adj.* rotating about or surrounding the moon. [1905–10; CIRCUM- + LUNAR]

cir·cum·nav·i·gate (sûr′kəm nav′i gāt′), *v.t.,* **-gat·ed, -gat·ing. 1.** to sail or fly around; make the circuit of by navigation: *to circumnavigate the earth.* **2.** to go or maneuver around: *to circumnavigate the heavy downtown traffic.* [1625–35; < L *circumnāvigātus* (ptp. of *circumnāvigāre*), equiv. to *circum-* CIRCUM- + *nāvigātus;* see NAVIGATE] **—cir·cum·nav·i·ga·ble** (sûr′kəm nav′i gə bəl), *adj.* **—cir′cum·nav′i·ga′tion,** *n.* **—cir′cum·nav′i·ga′tor,** *n.* **—cir·cum·nav·i·ga·to·ry** (sûr′kəm nav′i gə tôr′ē, -tōr′ē), *adj.*

cir·cum·nu·tate (sûr′kəm no͞o′tāt, -nyo͞o′-), *v.i.,* **-tat·ed, -tat·ing.** (of the apex of a stem or other growing part of a plant) to bend or move around in an irregular circular or elliptical path. [1875–80; CIRCUM- + *nutate* < L *nūtātus,* ptp. of *nūtāre* to nod in assent, sway, totter] **—cir′cum·nu·ta′tion,** *n.* **—cir·cum·nu·ta·to·ry** (sûr′kəm no͞o′tə tôr′ē, -tōr′ē, -nyo͞o′-), *adj.*

cir·cum·oc·u·lar (sûr′kəm ok′yə lər), *adj. Ophthalm.* surrounding the eye. [CIRCUM- + OCULAR]

cir·cum·po·lar (sûr′kəm pō′lər), *adj.* around or near a pole, as of the earth. [1680–90; CIRCUM- + POLAR]

cir·cum·ra·di·us (sûr′kəm rā′dē əs), *n., pl.* **-di·i** (-dē′ ī′), **-di·us·es.** *Geom.* the radius of the circle circumscribed around a triangle. [CIRCUM- + RADIUS]

cir·cum·ro·tate (sûr′kəm rō′tāt), *v.i.,* **-tat·ed, -tat·ing.** to rotate like a wheel. [< L *circumrotātus* (ptp. of *circumrotāre*), equiv. to *circum-* CIRCUM- + *rotātus;* see ROTATE] **—cir′cum·ro·ta′tion,** *n.* **—cir·cum·ro·ta·to·ry** (sûr′kəm rō′tə tôr′ē, -tōr′ē), *adj.*

cir·cum·scis·sile (sûr′kəm sis′il), *adj. Bot.* opening along a transverse circular line, as a seed vessel. [1825–35; CIRCUM- + SCISSILE]

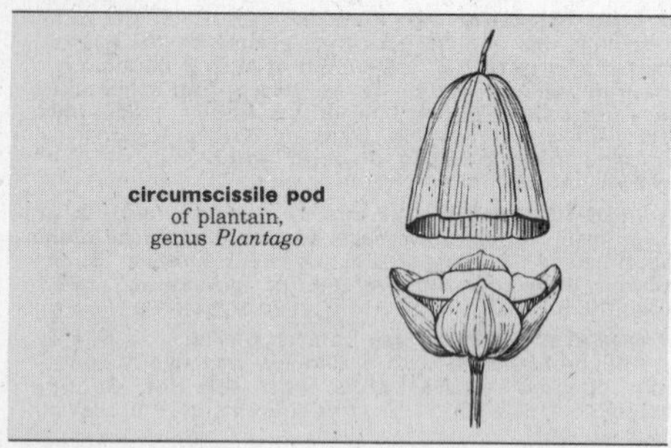
circumscissile pod of plantain, genus *Plantago*

cir·cum·scribe (sûr′kəm skrīb′, sûr′kəm skrīb′), *v.t.,* **-scribed, -scrib·ing. 1.** to draw a line around; encircle: *to circumscribe a city on a map.* **2.** to enclose within bounds; limit or confine, esp. narrowly: *Her social activities are circumscribed by school regulations.* **3.** to mark off; define; delimit: *to circumscribe the area of a science.* **4.** *Geom.* **a.** to draw (a figure) around another figure so as to touch as many points as possible. **b.** (of a figure) to enclose (another figure) in this manner. [1350–1400; ME < L *circumscrībere,* equiv. to *circum-* CIRCUM- + *scrībere* to write] **—cir′cum·scrib′a·ble,** *adj.* **—cir′·cum·scrib′er,** *n.*
—Syn. 2. restrict, restrain, check, hamper, hinder.

cir·cum·script (sûr′kəm skript′), *adj.* **1.** *Rare.* limited or confined. **2.** *Obs.* enclosed or encompassed. [1640–50; < L *circumscrīptus,* ptp. of *circumscrībere* to CIRCUMSCRIBE; see CIRCUM-, SCRIPT]

cir·cum·scrip·tion (sûr′kəm skrip′shən), *n.* **1.** an act or instance of circumscribing. **2.** circumscribed state; limitation. **3.** anything that circumscribes, surrounds, or encloses; boundary. **4.** periphery; outline. **5.** a circumscribed area. **6.** a circular inscription on a coin, seal, etc. **7.** limitation of a meaning; definition. [1375–1425; late ME < L *circumscrīptiōn-* (s. of *circumscrīptiō*), equiv. to *circumscrīpt(us)* (ptp. of *circumscrībere* to CIRCUMSCRIBE; see CIRCUM-, SCRIPT) + *-iōn-* -ION] **—cir′cum·scrip′·tive,** *adj.* **—cir′cum·scrip′tive·ly,** *adv.*

cir·cum·so·lar (sûr′kəm sō′lər), *adj.* directed, traveling, etc., around the sun: *the earth's circumsolar course.* [1840–50; CIRCUM- + SOLAR]

cir·cum·spect (sûr′kəm spekt′), *adj.* **1.** watchful and discreet; cautious; prudent: *circumspect behavior.* **2.** well-considered: *circumspect ambition.* [1375–1425; late ME < L *circumspectus* (ptp. of *circumspicere* to look around), equiv. to *circum-* CIRCUM- + *spec(ere)* to look + *-tus* ptp. suffix] **—cir′cum·spect′ly,** *adv.* **—cir′·cum·spect′ness,** *n.*
—Syn. 1. careful, vigilant, guarded. **—Ant. 1.** careless, indiscreet.

cir·cum·spec·tion (sûr′kəm spek′shən), *n.* circumspect observation or action; caution; prudence: *He approached with circumspection.* [1350–1400; ME < L *circumspectiōn-* (s. of *circumspectiō*), equiv. to *circumspect(us)* CIRCUMSPECT + *-iōn-* -ION]

cir·cum·spec·tive (sûr′kəm spek′tiv), *adj.* given to or marked by circumspection; watchful; cautious: *His behavior was circumspective.* [1625–35; CIRCUMSPECT + -IVE] **—cir′cum·spec′tive·ly,** *adv.*

cir·cum·stance (sûr′kəm stans′ *or, esp. Brit.,* -stəns), *n., v.,* **-stanced, -stanc·ing. —***n.* **1.** a condition, detail, part, or attribute, with respect to time, place, manner, agent, etc., that accompanies, determines, or modifies a fact or event; a modifying or influencing factor: *Do not judge his behavior without considering every circumstance.* **2.** Usually, **circumstances.** the existing conditions or state of affairs surrounding and affecting an agent: *Circumstances permitting, we sail on Monday.* **3.** an unessential or secondary accompaniment of any fact or event; minor detail: *The author dwells on circumstances rather than essentials.* **4. circumstances,** the condition or state of a person with respect to income and material welfare: *a family in reduced circumstances.* **5.** an incident or occurrence: *His arrival was a fortunate circumstance.* **6.** detailed or circuitous narration; specification of particulars: *The speaker expatiated with great circumstance upon his theme.* **7.** *Archaic.* ceremonious accompaniment or display: *pomp and circumstance.* **8. under no circumstances,** regardless of events or conditions; never: *Under no circumstances should you see them again.* **9. under the circumstances,** because of the conditions; as the case stands: *Under the circumstances, there is little hope for an early settlement.* Also, **in the circumstances. —***v.t.* **10.** to place in particular circumstances or relations. **11.** *Obs.* **a.** to furnish with details. **b.** to control or guide by circumstances. [1175–1225; ME < L *circumstantia* (*circumstant-,* s. of *circumstāns,* prp. of *circumstāre* to stand round), equiv. to *circum-* CIRCUM- + *stā-* STAND + *-nt* prp. suffix + *-ia* n. suffix; see -ANCE]
—Syn. 7. ritual, formality, splendor.

cir·cum·stanced (sûr′kəm stanst′ *or, esp. Brit.,* -stənst), *v.* **1.** pt. and pp. of **circumstance.** **—***adj.* **2.** being in a condition, or state, esp. with respect to income and material welfare, as specified: *They were well circumstanced.* [1595–1605; CIRCUMSTANCE + -ED[2]]

cir·cum·stan·tial (sûr′kəm stan′shəl), *adj.* **1.** of pertaining to, or derived from circumstances: *a circumstantial result.* **2.** of the nature of a circumstance; secondary; incidental: *of circumstantial importance.* **3.** dealing with or giving circumstances; detailed; particular: *a circumstantial report of a business conference.* **4.** pertaining to conditions of material welfare. [1590–1600; < L *circumstanti(a)* CIRCUMSTANCE + -AL[1]] **—cir′cum·stan′tial·ly,** *adv.*
—Syn. 3. minute, thorough, exact, precise.

cir′cumstan′tial ev′idence, proof of facts offered as evidence from which other facts are to be inferred (contrasted with *direct evidence*). Also called **indirect evidence.** [1730–40]

cir·cum·stan·ti·al·i·ty (sûr′kəm stan′shē al′i tē), *n., pl.* **-ties** for 2, 3. **1.** the quality of being circumstantial; minuteness; fullness of detail. **2.** a circumstance; a detail. **3.** *Psychiatry.* a pattern of speech that seems to wander because of excessive detail but eventually reaches its goal idea. [1725–35; CIRCUMSTANTIAL + -ITY]

cir·cum·stan·ti·ate (sûr′kəm stan′shē āt′), *v.t.,* **-at·ed, -at·ing. 1.** to set forth or support with circumstances or particulars: *Documents circumstantiated her evidence.* **2.** to describe fully or minutely: *He circumstantiated the accident.* [1640–50; < L *circumstanti(a)* CIRCUMSTANCE + -ATE[1]] **—cir′cum·stan′ti·a′tion,** *n.*

cir·cum·stel·lar (sûr′kəm stel′ər), *adj.* surrounding a star. [1950–55; CIRCUM- + STELLAR]

cir·cum·ter·res·tri·al (sûr′kəm tə res′trē əl), *adj.* surrounding or revolving about the earth. [1820–30; CIRCUM- + TERRESTRIAL]

cir·cum·val·late (sûr′kəm val′āt), *adj., v.,* **-lat·ed, -lat·ing. —***adj.* **1.** surrounded by or as if by a rampart. **2.** *Anat.* surrounded by a depression or wall-like ridge. **—***v.t.* **3.** to surround with or as if with a rampart. [1655–65; < L *circumvallātus* (ptp. of *circumvallāre* to surround with a wall), equiv. to *circum-* CIRCUM- + *vall(um)* rampart, wall + *-ātus* -ATE[1]] **—cir′cum·val·la′tion,** *n.*

cir·cum·vent (sûr′kəm vent′, sûr′kəm vent′), *v.t.* **1.** to go around or bypass: *to circumvent the lake; to circumvent the real issues.* **2.** to avoid (defeat, failure, unpleasantness, etc.) by artfulness or deception; avoid by anticipating or outwitting: *He circumvented capture by anticipating their movements.* **3.** to surround or encompass, as by stratagem; entrap: *to circumvent a body of enemy troops.* [1545–55; < L *circumventus* (ptp. of *circumvenīre* to come around, surround, oppress, defraud), equiv. to *circum-* CIRCUM- + *ven(īre)* to come + *-tus* ptp. suffix] **—cir′cum·vent′er, cir′cum·ven′tor,** *n.* **—cir′cum·ven′tion,** *n.* **—cir′cum·ven′tive,** *adj.*
—Syn. 2. escape, elude, evade, outwit.

cir·cum·vo·lu·tion (sûr′kəm və lo͞o′shən), *n.* **1.** the act of rolling or turning around: *planetary circumvolution.* **2.** a single complete turn or cycle. **3.** a winding or folding about something: *the circumvolutions of a boa.* **4.** a fold so wound: *the circumvolution of a snail shell.* **5.** a winding in a sinuous course; a sinuosity: *the circumvolutions of the river.* **6.** a roundabout course or procedure, or an instance of such: *The speaker's circumvolutions bored the audience to tears.* [1400–50; late ME < ML *circumvolūtiōn-* (s. of *circumvolūtiō*), equiv. to L *circumvolūt(us)* (ptp. of *circumvolvere* to CIRCUMVOLVE) (*circum-* CIRCUM- + *volū-* ptp. s. of *volvere* to roll + *-tus* ptp. suffix) + *-iōn-* -ION] **—cir·cum·vo·lu·to·ry** (sur′kəm və lo͞o′tə rē), *adj.*

cir·cum·volve (sûr′kəm volv′), *v.t., v.i.,* **-volved, -volv·ing.** to revolve or wind about. [1590–1600; < L *circumvolv(ere),* equiv. to *circum-* CIRCUM- + *volvere* to roll (see EVOLVE)]

cir·cus (sûr′kəs), *n., pl.* **-cus·es. 1.** a large public entertainment, typically presented in one or more very large tents or in an outdoor or indoor arena, featuring exhibitions of pageantry, feats of skill and daring, performing animals, etc., interspersed throughout with the slapstick antics of clowns. Cf. **big top. 2.** a troupe of performers, esp. a traveling troupe, that presents such entertainments, together with officials, other employees, and the company's performing animals, traveling wagons, tents, cages, and equipment. **3.** a circular arena surrounded by tiers of seats, in which public entertainments are held; arena. **4.** (in ancient Rome) **a.** a large, usually oblong or oval, roofless enclosure, surrounded by tiers of seats rising one above another, for chariot races, public games, etc. **b.** an entertainment given in this Roman arena, as a chariot race or public game: *The Caesars appeased the public with bread and circuses.* **5.** anything resembling the Roman circus, or arena, as a natural amphitheater or a circular range of houses. **6.** See **flying circus. 7.** *Brit.* an open circle, square, or plaza where several streets converge: *Piccadilly Circus.* **8.** fun, excitement, or uproar; a display of rowdy sport. **9.** *Obs.* a circlet or ring. [1350–1400; ME < L: circular region of the sky, oval space for games, akin to (or borrowed from) Gk *kírkos* ring, circle] **—cir′cus·y,** *adj.*

Cir′cus Max′i·mus (mak′sə məs), the great ancient Roman circus between the Palatine and Aventine hills.

ci·ré (si rā′), *n.* **1.** a brilliant, highly glazed surface produced on fabrics by subjecting them to a wax, heat, and calendering treatment. **2.** a double fabric having such a finish. [1920–25; < F < L *cērātus* waxed, equiv. to *cēr(a)* wax (see CERE) + *-ātus* -ATE[1]]

Ci·re·bon (chir′ə bôn′), *n.* a seaport on N Java, in S central Indonesia. 178,529. Also, **Tjirebon.**

Cir·e·na·i·ca (sir′ə nā′i kə, sī′rə-; *It.* chē ʀe nä′ē kä), *n.* Cyrenaica.

cire per·due (sēr′ per do͞o′, -dyo͞o′; *Fr.* sēʀ peʀ dʏ′), *Metall.* See **lost-wax process.** [1875–80; short for F *moulage à cire perdue* mold on lost wax]

cir·i·o (sir′ē ō′), *n., pl.* **cir·i·os.** See **boojum tree.** [< MexSp; Sp: wax candle < L *cēreus,* n. use of *cēreus* made of wax, equiv. to *cēr(a)* wax + *-eus* -EOUS]

cirque (sûrk), *n.* **1.** circle; ring. **2.** a bowl-shaped, steep-walled mountain basin carved by glaciation, often containing a small, round lake. [1595–1605; < F < L *circus;* see CIRCUS]

cir·rate (sir′āt), *adj. Bot., Zool.* having cirri. [1820–30; < L *cirrātus,* equiv. to *cirr(us)* a curl + *-ātus* -ATE[1]]

cir·rho·sis (si rō′sis), *n. Pathol.* a disease of the liver characterized by increase of connective tissue and alteration in gross and microscopic makeup. [1830–40; < Gk *kirrh(ós)* orange-tawny + -OSIS] **—cir·rhot·ic** (si rot′ik), *adj.* **—cir·rhosed′,** *adj.*

cir·rhus (sir′əs), *n., pl.* **cir·rhi** (sir′ī). *Mycol.* a mucus-bound ribbonlike mass of spores that is exuded from a fungus. [< NL, a pseudo-Gk form of L *cirrus* CIRRUS]

cir·ri (sir′ī), *n. Bot., Zool.* a pl. of **cirrus.**

cirri-, var. of **cirro-.**

cir·ri·form (sir′ə fôrm′), *adj.* of or pertaining to clouds composed of ice crystals, as cirrus, cirrostratus, and cirrocumulus clouds. [1805–15; CIRRI- + -FORM]

cir·ri·ped (sir′ə ped′), *n.* **1.** any crustacean of the subclass Cirripedia, chiefly comprising the barnacles, typically free-swimming in the larval stage and attached or parasitic in the adult stage, with slender, bristly appendages for gathering food. **—***adj.* **2.** having legs like cirri. **3.** belonging or pertaining to the Cirripedia. [1820–30; < NL *Cirripedia;* see CIRRI-, PED]

cirro-, a combining form representing **cirrus** in compound words: *cirrostratus.* Also, **cirri-.**

cir·ro·cu·mu·lus (sir′ō kyo͞o′myə ləs), *n., pl.* **-lus.** a cirriform cloud of a class characterized by thin, white patches, each of which is composed of very small granules or ripples: of high altitude, ab. 20,000–40,000 ft. (6000–12,000 m). [1795–1805; CIRRO- + CUMULUS] **—cir′ro·cu′mu·lar, cir·ro·cu·mu·la·tive** (sir′ō kyo͞o′myə lā′tiv, -lə tiv), **cir′ro·cu′mu·lous,** *adj.*

cir·rose (sēr′ōs, si rōs′), *adj. Bot. Zool.* **1.** having a cirrus or cirri. **2.** resembling cirri. Also, **cir·rous** (sir′əs). [1650–60; < NL *cirrōsus.* See CIRRO-, -OSE[1]] **—cir′·rose·ly,** *adv.*

cir·ro·stra·tus (sir′ō strā′təs, -strat′əs), *n., pl.* **-tus.** a cloud of a class characterized by a composition of ice crystals and often by the production of halo phenomena and appearing as a whitish and usually somewhat fibrous veil, often covering the whole sky and sometimes so thin as to be hardly discernible: of high altitude, ab. 20,000–40,000 ft. (6000–12,000 m). [1795–1805; CIRRO- + STRATUS] **—cir′ro·stra′tive,** *adj.*

cir·rus (sir′əs), *n., pl.* **cir·rus** for 1, **cir·ri** (sir′ī) for 2, 3. **1.** *Meteorol.* **a.** a cloud of a class characterized by thin white filaments or narrow bands and a composition of ice crystals: of high altitude, ab. 20,000–40,000 ft. (6000–12,000 m). **b.** a cirriform cloud. **2.** *Bot.* a tendril. **3.** *Zool.* **a.** a filament or slender appendage serving as a foot, tentacle, barbel, etc. **b.** the male copulatory organ of flatworms and various other invertebrates. [1700–10; < L: a curl, tuft, plant filament like a tuft of hair]

cis-, 1. a prefix occurring in loanwords from Latin meaning "on the near side of" (*cisalpine*); on this model, used in the formation of compound words (*cisatlantic*). **2.** *Chem.* a specialization of this denoting a geometric isomer having a pair of identical atoms or groups attached on the same side of two atoms linked by a double bond. Cf. **trans-** (def. 2). [< L; akin to HERE]

C.I.S., Commonwealth of Independent States.

cis·ac′o·nit′ic ac′id (sis ak′ə nit′ik, -ak′-), *Biochem.* a stereoisomer of 1-propene-1,2,3 tricarboxylic acid, $C_6H_6O_6$, an important intermediate in the Krebs cycle. [CIS- + ACONITE + -IC]

cis·al·pine (sis al′pīn, -pin), *adj.* on this (the Roman or south) side of the Alps. [1535–45; < L *Cisalpinus,* equiv. to *cis-* CIS- + *Alpinus* ALPINE]

Cisal′pine Gaul′. See under **Gaul** (def. 1).

cis·at·lan·tic (sis′ət lan′tik), *adj.* on this (the speaker's or writer's) side of the Atlantic. [1775–85, *Amer.;* CIS- + ATLANTIC]

CISC (sisk), *n.* complex instruction set computer: a computer whose central processing unit recognizes a relatively large number of instructions. Compare **RISC**

Cis·cau·ca·sia (sis′kô kā′zhə, -shə), *n.* the part of Caucasia north of the Caucasus Mountains. [CIS- + CAUCASIA]

cis·co (sis′kō), *n., pl.* (*esp. collectively*) **-co,** (*esp. referring to two or more kinds or species*) **-coes, -cos.** any of several whitefishes of the genus *Coregonus,* of the Great

CONCISE ETYMOLOGY KEY: <, descended or borrowed from; >, whence; b., blend of, blended; c., cognate with; cf., compare; deriv., derivative; equiv., equivalent; imit., imitative; obl., oblique; r., replacing; s., stem; sp., spelling, spelled; resp., respelling, respelled; trans., translation; ?, origin unknown; *, unattested; ‡, probably earlier than. See the full key inside the front cover.

Lakes and smaller lakes of eastern North America. [1840–50, *Amer.*; < CanF, back formation from *ciscoette, ciscaouette* < Ojibwa; see SISCOWET]

ci•seaux (sē zō′), *n., pl.* **-seaux** (-zōz′, -zō′). *Ballet.* a jump in which the dancer's legs are opened wide in the air and closed on landing. [1890–95; < F: lit., scissors]

ci•se•lé (sē′zə lā′; *Fr.* sēzᵊ lā′), *adj.* noting or pertaining to velvet having a chiseled or embossed pattern produced by contrasting cut and uncut pile. [< F: chiseled (ptp. of *ciseler;* see CHISEL)]

Cis•kei (sis′kī), *n.* a self-governing Bantu territory of South Africa on the Indian Ocean: granted independence in 1981 by South Africa, but not recognized by any other country as an independent state. 2,100,000; 3200 sq. mi. (8300 sq. km). *Cap.:* Bisho. **—Cis•kei′an,** *adj., n.*

cis•lu•nar (sis lo͞o′nər), *adj. Astron.* of or pertaining to the space between the earth and the orbit of the moon. [1865–70; CIS- + LUNAR]

cis•mon•tane (sis mon′tān), *adj.* on this (the speaker's or writer's) side of the mountains, esp. the Alps. [1820–30; < L *cismontānus,* equiv. to *cis-* CIS- + *montānus* MONTANE]

cis•plat•in (sis plat′n), *n. Pharm.* a platinum-containing white powder, $PtCl_2H_6N_2$, used to treat ovarian carcinoma and other cancers. Also, **cis•plat•i•num** (sis-plat′n əm, -plat′nəm). [1975–80; CIS- + PLATIN(UM)]

cis•soid (sis′oid), *n. Geom.* a curve having a cusp at the origin and a point of inflection at infinity. Equation: $r = 2a\sin\theta\tan\theta$. [1650–60; < Gk *kissoeidḗs,* equiv. to *kiss(ós)* ivy + *-oeidēs* -OID] **—cis•soi′dal,** *adj.*

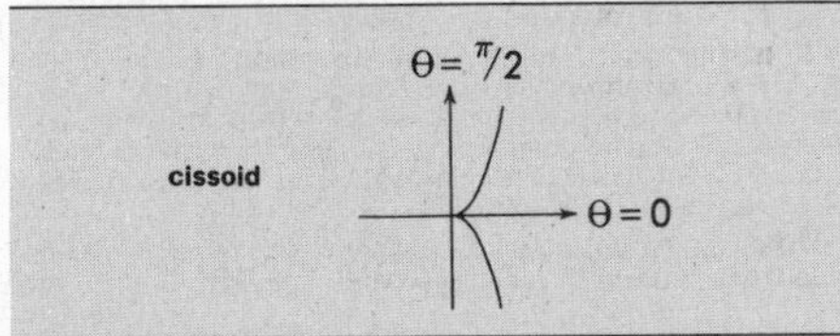

cissoid

cis•sus (sis′əs), *n.* any of numerous tropical and subtropical vines of the genus *Cissus,* including the grape ivy and the kangaroo vine. [< NL < Gk *kissós* ivy]

Cis•sy (sis′ē), *n.* a female given name, form of **Cecilia.**

cist[1] (sist), *n. Class. Antiq.* a box or chest, esp. for sacred utensils. [1795–1805; < L *cista* < Gk *kístē* CHEST]

cist[2] (sist, kist), *n.* a prehistoric sepulchral tomb or casket. Also, **kist.** [1795–1805; < Welsh < L *cista.* See CIST[1]] **—cist′ed,** *adj.* **—cis′tic,** *adj.*

cis•ta•ceous (si stā′shəs), *adj.* belonging to the Cistaceae, the rockrose family of plants. Cf. **rockrose family.** [< Gk *kíst(os),* var. of *kísthos* rockrose + -ACEOUS]

Cis•ter•cian (si stûr′shən), *n.* **1.** a member of an order of monks and nuns founded in 1098 at Citeaux, near Dijon, France, under the rule of St. Benedict. —*adj.* **2.** of or pertaining to the Cistercians. [1595–1605; < ML *Cisterciānus* < L *Cisterci(um)* placename (now *Cîteaux*) + *-ānus* -AN] **—Cis•ter′cian•ism,** *n.*

cis•tern (sis′tərn), *n.* **1.** a reservoir, tank, or container for storing or holding water or other liquid. **2.** *Anat.* a reservoir or receptacle of some natural fluid of the body. [1250–1300; ME *cistern(e)* < L *cisterna,* equiv. to *cist(a)* (see CIST[1]) + *-erna* n. suffix]

cis•ter•na (si stûr′nə), *n., pl.* **cis•ter•nae** (si stûr′nē) *Anat.* cistern (def. 2). [< NL, L] **—cis•ter′nal,** *adj.*

cis′tern barom′eter, a mercury barometer in which the lower mercury surface has a greater area than the upper. Also called **cup barometer.**

cis•tron (sis′tron), *n. Genetics.* a segment of DNA that encodes for the formation of a specific polypeptide chain; a structural gene. [1955–60; CIS- + TR(ANS)- + -ON[1]] **—cis•tron′ic,** *adj.*

cist•vaen (kist′vīn, -vān), *n.* cist[2]. [< Welsh *cist faen* lit., stone box]

cit (chit), *n. Hinduism.* pure consciousness. Also, **chit.** Cf. **Sat-cit-ananda.** [< Skt]

cit., **1.** citation. **2.** cited. **3.** citizen. **4.** citrate.

C.I.T., counselor in training.

cit•a•del (sit′ə dl, -ə del′), *n.* **1.** a fortress that commands a city and is used in the control of the inhabitants and in defense during attack or siege. **2.** any strongly fortified place; stronghold. **3.** (formerly) a heavily armored structure on a warship, for protecting the engines, magazines, etc. [1580–90; < MF *citadelle* < OIt *cittadella,* equiv. to *cittad(e)* CITY + *-ella* -ELLE]

ci•ta•tion (si tā′shən), *n.* **1.** *Mil.* mention of a soldier or a unit in orders, usually for gallantry: *Presidential citation.* **2.** any award or commendation, as for outstanding service, hard work, or devotion to duty, esp. a formal letter or statement recounting a person's achievements. **3.** a summons, esp. to appear in court. **4.** a document containing such a summons. **5.** the act of citing or quoting a reference to an authority or a precedent. **6.** a passage cited; quotation. **7.** a quotation showing a particular word or phrase in context. **8.** mention or enumeration. [1250–1300; ME *citacio(u)n* < LL *citātiōn-* (s. of *citātiō*), equiv. to L *citāt(us)* ptp. of *citāre* (see CITE[1]) + *-iōn-* -ION] **—ci•ta′tion•al,** *adj.*
—Syn. 7. excerpt, passage, extract, cite, quote.

cita′tion form′, *Ling.* **1.** the spoken form a word has when produced in isolation, such as when cited for purposes of illustration, as distinguished from the form it would have when produced in the normal stream of speech. **2.** the form of a lexical set that represents its entire inflectional paradigm in linguistic discussions and dictionary entries: *"Be" is the citation form for "be," "am," "is," "are," "was," "were," "been."*

cite[1] (sīt), *v.t.,* **cit•ed, cit•ing. 1.** to quote (a passage, book, author, etc.), esp. as an authority: *He cited the Constitution in his defense.* **2.** to mention in support, proof, or confirmation; refer to as an example: *He cited many instances of abuse of power.* **3.** to summon officially or authoritatively to appear in court. **4.** to call to mind; recall: *citing my gratitude to him.* **5.** *Mil.* to mention (a soldier, unit, etc.) in orders, as for gallantry. **6.** to commend, as for outstanding service, hard work, or devotion to duty. **7.** to summon or call; rouse to action. [1400–50; late ME < LL *citāre* to summon before a church court; in L, to hurry, set in motion, summon before a court, freq. of *ciēre* to move, set in motion] **—cit′a•ble, cite′a•ble,** *adj.* **—cit′er,** *n.*

cite[2] (sīt), *n.* citation (defs. 7, 8). [by shortening]

cith•a•ra (sith′ər ə), *n.* kithara. **—cith′a•rist,** *n.*

cit•ied (sit′ēd), *adj.* **1.** occupied by a city or cities. **2.** formed into or like a city. [1605–15; CITY + -ED[3]]

cit•i•fied (sit′i fīd′), *adj.* **1.** made into a city. **2.** having city habits, fashions, etc. Also, **cityfied.** [1820–30, *Amer.;* CITY + -FY + -ED[2]]

cit•i•fy (sit′i fī′), *v.t.,* **-fied, -fy•ing. 1.** to make into a city; urbanize. **2.** to cause to conform to city habits, fashions, etc. [1860–65; CITY + -FY] **—cit′i•fi•ca′tion,** *n.*

cit•i•zen (sit′ə zən, -sən), *n.* **1.** a native or naturalized member of a state or nation who owes allegiance to its government and is entitled to its protection (distinguished from *alien*). **2.** an inhabitant of a city or town, esp. one entitled to its privileges or franchises. **3.** an inhabitant, or denizen: *The deer is a citizen of our woods.* **4.** a civilian, as distinguished from a soldier, police officer, etc. [1275–1325; ME *citisein* < AF *citesein,* OF *citeain,* equiv. to *cite* CITY + *-ain* -AN; AF *s* perh. by assoc. with *deinzain* DENIZEN] **—cit′i•zen•ly,** *adj.*

cit•i•zen•ess (sit′ə zə nis, -sə-), *n.* a woman who is a citizen. [1790–1800; CITIZEN + -ESS]
—Usage. See **-ess.**

Cit′izen Kane′, an American film (1941), directed by and starring Orson Welles.

cit•i•zen•ry (sit′ə zən rē, -sən-), *n., pl.* **-ries.** citizens collectively. [1810–20; CITIZEN + -RY]

cit′izen's arrest′, *Law.* an arrest made by a private citizen whose authority derives from the fact of citizenship. [1950–55]

Cit′izens Band′, a two-way radio service (**Cit′izens Ra′dio Serv′ice**) licensed by the FCC to a U.S. citizen for short-distance personal or business communications between fixed or mobile stations. *Abbr.:* CB [1960–65]

cit•i•zen•ship (sit′ə zən ship′, -sən-), *n.* **1.** the state of being vested with the rights, privileges, and duties of a citizen. **2.** the character of an individual viewed as a member of society; behavior in terms of the duties, obligations, and functions of a citizen: *an award for good citizenship.* [1605–15; CITIZEN + -SHIP]

cit′izenship pa′pers, 1. a certificate of citizenship, as one issued to a U.S. citizen born abroad. **2.** (loosely) a certificate of naturalization conferring citizenship on a resident alien.

Ci•tlal•te•petl (sē′tläl tā′pet l), *n.* Orizaba (def. 1).

cit•ole (sit′ōl, si tōl′), *n.* cittern. [1350–1400; ME < MF < L *cit(hara)* KITHARA + MF *-ole* dim. suffix]

cit•ral (si′trəl), *n. Chem.* a pale yellow, water-insoluble, liquid aldehyde, $C_{10}H_{16}O$, having a strong lemonlike odor, consisting in natural form of two isomers (**citral a** or **geranial** and **citral b** or **neral**), usually obtained from the oils of lemon and orange or synthetically: used chiefly in perfumery, flavoring, and the synthesis of vitamin A. [1890–95; CITR(US) + -AL[1]]

cit•rate (si′trāt, si′-), *n. Chem.* a salt or ester of citric acid. [1785–95; CITR(IC ACID) + -ATE[2]]

cit•re•ous (si′trē əs), *adj.* lemon-yellow; greenish-yellow. [1865–70; < L *citreus* of the citrus tree; see -OUS]

cit•ric (si′trik), *adj. Chem.* of or derived from citric acid. [1790–1800; CITR(US) + -IC]

cit′ric ac′id, a white, crystalline, water-soluble powder, $C_6H_8O_7 \cdot H_2O$, a tribasic acid having a strong acidic taste, an intermediate in the metabolism of carbohydrates occurring in many fruits, esp. limes and lemons, obtained chiefly by fermentation of crude sugar or corn sugar: used chiefly in the flavoring of beverages, confections, and pharmaceuticals. [1805–15]

cit′ric ac′id cy′cle, *Biochem.* See **Krebs cycle.** [1940–45]

cit•ri•cul•ture (si′tri kul′chər), *n.* the cultivation of citrus fruits. [1915–20; CITR(US) + -I- + CULTURE] **—cit′ri•cul′tur•ist,** *n.*

cit•rin (si′trin), *n. Biochem.* bioflavonoid. [1935–40; < G *Citrin;* see CITRUS, -IN[2]]

cit•rine (si′trēn, -trin, -trin, si trēn′), *adj.* **1.** pale-yellow; lemon-colored. —*n.* **2.** a translucent, yellow variety of quartz, often sold as topaz; false topaz; topaz quartz. [1350–1400; ME < AF; see CITRUS, -INE[1]]

cit•ron (si′trən), *n.* **1.** a pale-yellow fruit resembling the lemon but larger and with thicker rind, borne by a small tree or large bush, *Citrus medica,* allied to the lemon and lime. **2.** the tree itself. **3.** the rind of the fruit, candied and preserved. **4.** a grayish-green yellow color. **5.** See **citron melon.** —*adj.* **6.** having the color citron. [1375–1425; late ME < MF < It *citrone* < L *citr(us)* CITRUS + It *-one* aug. suffix]

cit•ro•na•lis (si′trə nā′lis), *n.* See **lemon verbena.** [< NL; see CITRON, -AL[1]]

cit•ron•el•la (si′trə nel′ə), *n.* **1.** a fragrant grass, *Cymbopogon nardus,* of southern Asia, cultivated as the source of citronella oil. **2.** See **citronella oil.** [1855–60; < NL < F *citronelle,* equiv. to *citron* CITRON + *-elle* dim. suffix]

cit•ron•el•lal (si′trə nel′al, -əl), *n.* a colorless, slightly water-soluble liquid mixture of isomeric aldehydes having the formula $C_{10}H_{18}O$, with a strong lemonlike odor, occurring in many essential oils, usually derived from lemon, citronella oil, and other oils: used chiefly as a flavoring agent and in the manufacture of perfume. [1890–95; CITRONELL(A) + -AL[3]]

citronel′la oil′, a light-yellowish pungent oil, distilled from citronella, used in the manufacture of liniment, perfume, and soap, and as an insect repellent. Also called **citronella.** [1880–85]

cit•ro•nel•lol (si′trə nel′ôl, -ol), *n.* a clear, colorless liquid mixture of isomeric alcohols having the formula $C_{10}H_{20}O$, usually obtained from an essential oil, as citronella oil, and having a roselike odor: used chiefly as a scent in the manufacture of perfume. [1870–75; CITRONELL(A) + -OL[1]]

cit′ron mel′on, a round, hard-fleshed watermelon, *Citrullus lanatus citroides,* used candied or pickled. Also called **citron.** [1800–10, *Amer.*]

cit′ron wood′, 1. the wood of the citron. **2.** the wood of the sandarac. [1705–15]

cit•rul•line (si′trə lēn′), *n. Biochem.* an amino acid, $NH_2CONH(CH_2)_3CHNH_2COOH$, abundant in watermelons and an intermediate compound in the urea cycle. [1930; < NL *citrull(us)* the watermelon genus (ML *citrul(l)us, citrolus,* Latinization of South It *citrulo,* Tuscan *citri(u)olo* < LL *citrium* watermelon (deriv. of L *citrus* (see CITRUS); appar. in reference to the citron-colored fruit of some types of watermelon), with *-uolo* < L *-eolus*) + -INE[2]]

cit•rus (si′trəs), *n., pl.* **-rus•es. 1.** any small tree or spiny shrub of the genus *Citrus,* of the rue family, including the lemon, lime, orange, tangerine, grapefruit, citron, kumquat, and shaddock, widely cultivated for fruit or grown as an ornamental. **2.** the tart-to-sweet, pulpy fruit of any of these trees or shrubs, having a characteristically smooth, shiny, stippled skin. —*adj.* **3.** Also, **cit′rous.** of or pertaining to such trees or shrubs, or their fruit. [1815–25; < NL, L: citron tree]

cit′rus can′ker, *Plant Pathol.* a disease of citrus trees caused by the bacterium *Xanthomonas citri,* characterized by spongy eruptions on leaves and fruit.

Cit′rus Heights′, a city in central California, near Sacramento. 85,911.

cit′rus red′ mite′, a large mite, *Panonychus citri,* that is an important pest of citrus. Also called **cit′rus red′ spi′der, purple mite.** [1930–35]

cit′rus white′fly. See under **whitefly.**

cit•ta (chit′ə), *n. Hinduism.* the intellect or cognitive facility. Cf. **Skt.** [< Skt]

Cit•tà del Va•ti•ca•no (chēt tä′ del vä′tē kä′nô), Italian name of **Vatican City.**

cit•tern (sit′ərn), *n.* an old musical instrument related to the guitar, having a flat, pear-shaped soundbox and wire strings. [1550–60; b. CITHER and GITTERN]

cittern

cit•y (sit′ē), *n., pl.* **cit•ies. 1.** a large or important town. **2.** (in the U.S.) an incorporated municipality, usually governed by a mayor and a board of aldermen or councilmen. **3.** the inhabitants of a city collectively: *The entire city is mourning his death.* **4.** (in Canada) a municipality of high rank, usually based on population. **5.** (in Great Britain) a borough, usually the seat of a bishop, upon which the dignity of the title has been conferred by the crown. **6. the City, a.** the major metropolitan center of a region; downtown: *I'm going to the City to buy clothes and see a show.* **b.** the commercial and financial area of London, England. **7.** a city-state. [1175–1225; ME *cite* < AF, OF *cite(t)* < L *cīvitāt-* (s. of *cīvitās*) citizenry, town, equiv. to *cīvi(s)* citizen + *-tāt-* -TY[2]] **—cit′y•less,** *adj.* **—cit′y•like′,** *adj.*
—Syn. 1. See **community.**

cit•y-born (sit′ē bôrn′), *adj.* born in a city. [1590–1600; CITY + BORN]

cit•y-bred (sit′ē bred′), *adj.* reared in a city. [1880–85; CITY + BRED]

cit′y chick′en. See **mock chicken.**

cit′y clerk′, a city official who maintains public records and vital statistics, issues licenses, etc. [1915–20]

cit′y coun′cil, a municipal body having legislative and administrative powers, such as passing ordinances and appropriating funds. [1780–90]

cit′y desk′, 1. a newspaper department responsible for editing local news. **2.** Also, **Cit′y desk′.** *Brit.* the department of a newspaper handling financial news. [1900–05, *Amer.*]

Cit′y Diony′sia. See **Greater Dionysia.**

cit′y edi′tion, an early edition of a daily newspaper on sale locally, usually a later edition than the one sent for out-of-town distribution.

cit′y ed′itor, 1. a newspaper editor in charge of local news and assignments to reporters. **2.** Also, **Cit′y ed′-**

itor. *Brit.* a newspaper or magazine editor in charge of the financial and commercial news. [1825–35, *Amer.*]

cit′y fa′ther, any of the officials or prominent citizens of a city. [1835–45, *Amer.*]

cit•y•fied (sit′i fīd′), *adj.* citified.

cit′y hall′, (*often caps.*) **1.** the administration building of a city government. **2.** a city administration or government. **3.** *Informal.* a bureaucracy or bureaucratic rules and regulations, esp. that of a city government: *You can't fight city hall.* [1665–75, *Amer.*]

cit′y man′ager, a person not publicly elected but appointed by a city council to manage a city. [1910–15, *Amer.*]

Cit′y of Broth′erly Love′, Philadelphia, Pa. (used as a nickname).

Cit′y of Da′vid, 1. Jerusalem. II Sam. 5:6–7. **2.** Bethlehem. Luke 2:4.

Cit′y of God′, the New Jerusalem; heaven.

Cit′y of God′, The, (Latin, *De Civitate Dei*) a work in 22 books (A.D. 413–26) by St. Augustine of Hippo, expounding an early Christian view of society and history.

Cit′y of Light′, Paris, France (used as a nickname).

Cit′y of Sev′en Hills′, Rome, Italy (used as a nickname).

Cit′y of the Dalles′. See **Dalles, The.**

cit′y plan′, the developmental plan for a city or town arrived at through the process of city planning.

cit′y plan′ning, the activity or profession of determining the future physical arrangement and condition of a community, involving an appraisal of the present condition, a forecast of future requirements, a plan for the fulfillment of these requirements, and proposals for constructional, legal, and financial programs to implement the plan. Also called **town planning, urbanism, urban planning.** [1910–15] —**cit′y plan′ner.**

cit′y room′, 1. the room in which local news is handled for a newspaper, a radio or television station, or for another journalistic agency. **2.** the editorial staff of this room. [1915–20]

cit•y•scape (sit′ē skāp′), *n.* **1.** a view of a city, esp. a large urban center: *The cityscape is impressive as one approaches New York from the sea.* **2.** a picture representing such a view. **3.** the characteristic appearance of a city: *She has been documenting changes in the cityscape for 20 years.* [1855–60, *Amer.*; CITY + -SCAPE]

cit′y slick′er, *Often Disparaging.* a worldly, nattily dressed city dweller. [1920–25, *Amer.*]

cit•y-state (sit′ē stāt′), *n.* a sovereign state consisting of an autonomous city with its dependencies. [1890–95]

cit•y•ward (sit′ē wərd), *adv.* to, toward, or in the direction of the city. Also, **cit′y•wards.** [1350–1400; ME; see CITY, -WARD]

cit•y•wide (sit′ē wīd′), *adj.* **1.** occurring throughout a city; including an entire city: *citywide school board elections.* **2.** open to including, or affecting all the inhabitants of or groups in a city: *a citywide track meet.* [1960–65; CITY + -WIDE]

Ciu•dad Bo•lí•var (syo͞o thäth′ bô lē′vär), a port in E Venezuela, on the Orinoco River. 103,728.

Ciu•dad del Car•men (syo͞o thäth′ thel kär′men), a city in SE Mexico, on the Gulf of Campeche. 36,511. Also called **Carmen.**

Ciu•dad Gua•ya•na (syo͞o thäth′ gwä yä′nä). See **Santo Tomé de Guayana.**

Ciu•dad Juá•rez (syo͞o thäth′ hwä′res), a city in N Mexico, across the Rio Grande from El Paso, Texas. 570,000.

Ciu•dad Ma•de•ro (syo͞o thäth′ mä the′rô), a city in Tamaulipas, in E Mexico, on the W coast of the Gulf of Mexico, N of Tampico. 121,782.

Ciu•dad O•bre•gón (syo͞o thäth′ ô vre gôn′), a city in W Mexico. 152,834.

Ciu•dad Tru•jil•lo (syo͞o thäth′ tro͞o hē′yô), former name (1936–61) of **Santo Domingo.**

Ciu•dad Vic•to•ria (syo͞o thäth′ bēk tô′ryä), a city in and the capital of Tamaulipas state, in NE Mexico. 94,304.

Civ., 1. civil. **2.** civilian.

African civet, *Civettictis civetta,* head and body 2½ ft. (0.76 m); tail 1½ ft. (0.5 m)

civ•et (siv′it), *n.* **1.** a yellowish, unctuous substance with a strong musklike odor, obtained from a pouch in the genital region of civets and used in perfumery. **2.** any catlike, carnivorous mammal of the subfamily Viverrinae, chiefly of southern Asia and Africa, having a coarse-haired, spotted coat, rounded ears, and a narrow muzzle. **3.** any of various related or similar animals, as the palm civet. **4.** cacomistle. [1525–35; < MF *civette* < Catalan *civetta* << Ar *zabād* civet perfume; see ZIBET] —**civ′et•like′,** *adj.*

civ′et cat′, 1. cacomistle. **2.** the fur of the cacomistle. **3.** *Western U.S.* skunk. Also called **California mink** (for defs. 1, 2). [1600–10, *Amer.*]

civ•ic (siv′ik), *adj.* **1.** of or pertaining to a city; municipal: *civic problems.* **2.** of or pertaining to citizenship; civil: *civic duties.* **3.** of citizens: *civic pride.* [1535–45; < L *cīvicus,* equiv. to *cīv(is)* citizen + *-icus* -IC] —**civ′i•cal•ly,** *adv.*

civ′ic cen′ter, 1. a building complex housing a theater or theaters for the performing arts and sometimes exhibition halls, a museum, etc., and usually constructed or maintained by municipal funds. **2.** a building or building complex containing a municipality's administrative offices, various departmental headquarters, courts, etc., and sometimes an auditorium, libraries, or other community or cultural facilities. **3.** a theater, meeting hall, or the like for community or public use. [1905–10]

civ•ic-mind•ed (siv′ik mīn′did), *adj.* concerned with the well-being of the community. [1940–45] —**civ′•ic-mind′ed•ly,** *adv.* —**civ′ic-mind′ed•ness,** *n.*

civ•ics (siv′iks), *n.* (*used with a singular v.*) the study or science of the privileges and obligations of citizens. [1880–85, *Amer.*; see CIVIC, -ICS]

civ•ies (siv′ēz), *n.pl.* civvy (def. 1).

civ•il (siv′əl), *adj.* **1.** of, pertaining to, or consisting of citizens: *civil life; civil society.* **2.** of the commonwealth or state: *civil affairs.* **3.** of citizens in their ordinary capacity, or of the ordinary life and affairs of citizens, as distinguished from military and ecclesiastical life and affairs. **4.** of the citizen as an individual: *civil liberty.* **5.** befitting a citizen: *a civil duty.* **6.** of, or in a condition of, social order or organized government; civilized: *civil peoples.* **7.** adhering to the norms of polite social intercourse; not deficient in common courtesy: *After their disagreement, their relations were civil though not cordial.* **8.** marked by benevolence: *He was a very civil sort, and we liked him immediately.* **9.** (of divisions of time) legally recognized in the ordinary affairs of life: *the civil year.* **10.** of or pertaining to civil law. [1350–1400; ME < L *cīvīlis,* equiv. to *cīv(is)* citizen + *-īlis* -IL] —**civ′il•ness,** *n.*

—**Syn. 7, 8.** respectful, deferential, gracious, complaisant, suave, affable, urbane, courtly. CIVIL, AFFABLE, COURTEOUS, POLITE all imply avoidance of rudeness toward others. CIVIL suggests a minimum of observance of social requirements. AFFABLE suggests ease of approach and friendliness. COURTEOUS implies positive, dignified, sincere, and thoughtful consideration for others. POLITE implies habitual courtesy, arising from a consciousness of one's training and the demands of good manners. —**Ant. 7, 8.** boorish, churlish.

Civ′il Aeronaut′ics Board′, *U.S. Govt.* the former federal agency (1938–85) that regulated airline fares and assigned routes. *Abbr.:* CAB, C.A.B.

Civ′il Air′ Patrol′, a voluntary organization performing emergency services, as assisting the U.S. Air Force on search missions, and offering aerospace-education and youth programs: founded 1941. *Abbr.:* CAP

civ′il day′, *Astron.* day (def. 3c). [1595–1605]

civ′il defense′, plans or activities organized by civilians and civilian authorities for the protection of civilian population and property in times of such disasters or emergencies as war or floods. [1935–40]

civ′il disobe′dience, 1. the refusal to obey certain laws or governmental demands for the purpose of influencing legislation or government policy, characterized by the employment of such nonviolent techniques as boycotting, picketing, and nonpayment of taxes. Cf. **noncooperation** (def. 2), **passive resistance. 2.** (*caps., italics*) an essay (1848) by Thoreau. [1865–70]

civ′il engineer′, a person who designs public works, as roads, bridges, canals, dams, and harbors, or supervises their construction or maintenance. [1785–95]

civ′il engineer′ing, the work or profession of a civil engineer.

ci•vil•ian (si vil′yən), *n.* **1.** a person who is not on active duty with a military, naval, police, or fire fighting organization. **2.** *Informal.* anyone regarded by members of a profession, interest group, society, etc., as not belonging; nonprofessional; outsider: *We need a producer to run the movie studio, not some civilian from the business world.* **3.** a person versed in or studying Roman or civil law. —*adj.* **4.** of, pertaining to, formed by, or administered by civilians. [1350–1400; ME: student of civil law < OF *civilien* (adj.); see CIVIL, -IAN]

civil′ian clothes′, 1. everyday or ordinary clothing, as distinguished from a military uniform. **2.** *Informal.* ordinary clothing as distinguished from a uniform, clerical garb, or work clothes. [1885–90]

Civil′ian Conserva′tion Corps′. See **CCC.**

ci•vil•ian•ize (si vil′yə nīz′), *v.t.,* **-ized, -iz•ing. 1.** to assign to civilians or place under civilian direction or control: *a decision to civilianize the teaching of history at the naval academy.* **2.** to make less military in form or character: *He charged that the union movement is civilianizing the army.* Also, *esp. Brit.,* **ci•vil′ian•ise′.** [1865–70; CIVILIAN + -IZE] —**ci•vil′ian•i•za′tion,** *n.*

civil′ian review′ board′, a quasi-judicial board of appointed or elected citizens that investigates complaints against the police. [1965–70]

ci•vil•i•ty (si vil′i tē), *n., pl.* **-ties. 1.** courtesy; politeness. **2.** a polite action or expression: *an exchange of civilities.* **3.** *Archaic.* civilization; culture; good breeding. [1350–1400; ME *civilite* < MF < L *cīvīlitāt-* (s. of *cīvīlitās*) courtesy. See CIVIL, -ITY]

—**Syn. 1.** affability, amiability, manners, tact.

civ•i•li•za•tion (siv′ə lə zā′shən), *n.* **1.** an advanced state of human society, in which a high level of culture, science, industry, and government has been reached. **2.** those people or nations that have reached such a state. **3.** any type of culture, society, etc., of a specific place, time, or group: *Greek civilization.* **4.** the act or process of civilizing or being civilized: *Rome's civilization of barbaric tribes was admirable.* **5.** cultural refinement; refinement of thought and cultural appreciation: *The letters of Madame de Sévigné reveal her wit and civilization.* **6.** cities or populated areas in general, as opposed to unpopulated or wilderness areas: *The plane crashed in the jungle, hundreds of miles from civilization.* **7.** modern comforts and conveniences, as made possible by science and technology: *After a week in the woods, without television or even running water, the campers looked forward to civilization again.* [1765–75; < F *civilisation;* see CIVILIZE, -ATION] —**civ′i•li•za′tion•al,** *adj.*

civ•i•lize (siv′ə līz′), *v.t.,* **-lized, -liz•ing.** to bring out of a savage, uneducated, or rude state; make civil; elevate in social and private life; enlighten; refine: *Rome civilized the barbarians.* Also, *esp. Brit.,* **civ′i•lise′.** [1595–1605; < F *civiliser;* see CIVIL, -IZE] —**civ′i•liz′a•ble,** *adj.* —**civ•i•liz•a•to•ry** (siv′ə lī′zə tôr′ē, -tōr′ē), *adj.* —**civ′i•liz′er,** *n.*

—**Syn.** educate, teach, instruct, polish, sophisticate.

civ•i•lized (siv′ə līzd′), *adj.* **1.** having an advanced or humane culture, society, etc. **2.** polite; well-bred; refined. **3.** of or pertaining to civilized people: *The civilized world must fight ignorance.* **4.** easy to manage or control; well organized or ordered: *The car is quiet and civilized, even in sharp turns.* [1605–15; CIVILIZE + -ED[2]] —**civ•i•liz•ed•ness** (siv′ə lī′zid nis, -līzd′), *n.*

civ′il law′, 1. the body of laws of a state or nation regulating ordinary private matters, as distinct from laws regulating criminal, political, or military matters. **2.** *Rom. Hist.* the body of law proper to the city or state of Rome, as distinct from that common to all nations. Cf. **jus civile. 3.** systems of law influenced significantly and in various ways by Roman law, esp. as contained in the Corpus Juris Civilis, as distinct from the common law and canon or ecclesiastical law. [1375–1425; late ME] —**civ′il-law′,** *adj.*

civ′il libertar′ian, a person who actively supports or works for the protection or expansion of civil liberties.

civ′il lib′erty, Usually, **civil liberties. 1.** the freedom of a citizen to exercise customary rights, as of speech or assembly, without unwarranted or arbitrary interference by the government. **2.** such a right as guaranteed by the laws of a country, as in the U.S. by the Bill of Rights. [1635–45]

civ•il•ly (siv′ə lē), *adv.* **1.** politely; courteously. **2.** in accordance with civil law. [1400–50; late ME. See CIVIL, -LY]

civ′il mar′riage, a marriage performed by a government official, as distinguished from a member of the clergy. [1890–95]

civ′il right′er, a civil rightist. Also, **civ′il-right′er.** [CIVIL RIGHT(S) + -ER[1]]

civ′il right′ist, a person who actively supports or works for safeguarding or obtaining civil rights. [CIVIL RIGHT(S) + -IST]

civ′il rights′, (*often caps.*) **1.** rights to personal liberty established by the 13th and 14th Amendments to the U.S. Constitution and certain Congressional acts, esp. as applied to an individual or a minority group. **2.** the rights to full legal, social, and economic equality extended to blacks. [1715–25] —**civ′il-rights′,** *adj.*

civ′il serv′ant, a civil-service employee. [1790–1800]

civ′il serv′ice, 1. those branches of public service concerned with all governmental administrative functions outside the armed services. **2.** the body of persons employed in these branches. **3.** a system or method of appointing government employees on the basis of competitive examinations, rather than by political patronage. [1775–85]

civ′il war′, a war between political factions or regions within the same country. Cf. **American Civil War, English Civil War, Spanish Civil War.** [1540–50]

civ′il year′. See under **year** (def. 1).

civ•ism (siv′iz əm), *n.* good citizenship. [1785–95; < F *civisme* < L *cīv(is)* citizen + F *-isme* -ISM]

Civ•i•tan (siv′i tan′), *n.* a member of Civitan International, a service club founded 1918. [appar. < L *cīvit(ās)* CIVITAS + -AN]

civ•i•tas (siv′i tas′; *Lat.* kē′wi täs′), *n., pl.* **civ•i•ta•tes** (siv′i tā′tēz; *Lat.* kē′wi tä′tās). **1.** the body of citizens who constitute a state, esp. a city-state, commonwealth, or the like. **2.** citizenship, esp. as imparting shared responsibility, a common purpose, and sense of community. [< L *cīvitās.* See CITY]

civ•vy (siv′ē), *n., pl.* **-vies. 1.** civvies. Also, **civies.** See **civilian clothes. 2.** a civilian. [1885–90; CIV(ILIAN) + -Y[2]]

CJ, Chief Justice.

ck., 1. cask. **2.** check. **3.** cook.

ckw., clockwise.

CL, common law.

Cl, *Symbol, Chem.* chlorine.

cl, centiliter; centiliters.

cl., 1. carload. **2.** claim. **3.** class. **4.** classification. **5.** clause. **6.** clearance. **7.** clerk. **8.** close. **9.** closet. **10.** cloth.

C/L, 1. carload. **2.** carload lot. **3.** cash letter.

c.l., 1. carload. **2.** carload lot. **3.** center line. **4.** civil law. **5.** common law.

CLA, College Language Association.

clab•ber (klab′ər), *South Midland and Southern U.S.* —*n.* **1.** milk that has soured and thickened; curdled milk. —*v.i.* **2.** (of milk) to curdle; to become thick in souring. Also, **clobber.** [1625–35; < Ir *clabar* short for *bainne clabair* BONNYCLABBER]

—**Regional Variation.** CLABBER has many regional variations, including BONNYCLABBER and its variant BONNYCLAPPER in the Northern and Midland U.S., THICK MILK in the Hudson River Valley and North Midland U.S., LOBBER and its variant LOBBERED MILK in the Inland North, CLOBBER in the South Midland and Southern U.S., and CRUD in some widely scattered areas.

clab′ber cheese′, *Chiefly South Midland U.S. and South Atlantic States.* cottage cheese.

cla•chan (klä′khən, kla′-), *n. Scot., Irish.* a small vil-

CONCISE ETYMOLOGY KEY: <, descended or borrowed from; >, whence; b., blend of, blended; c., cognate with; cf., compare; deriv., derivative; equiv., equivalent; imit., imitative; obl., oblique; r., replacing; s., stem; sp., spelling, spelled; resp., respelling, respelled; trans., translation; ?, origin unknown; *, unattested; ‡, probably earlier than. See the full key inside the front cover.

lage or hamlet. [1375–1425; late ME (Scots) < ScotGael, equiv. to *clach* stone + *-an* dim. suffix]

clack (klak), *v.i.* **1.** to make a quick, sharp sound, or a succession of such sounds, as by striking or cracking: *The loom clacked busily under her expert hands.* **2.** to talk rapidly and continually or with sharpness and abruptness; chatter. **3.** to cluck or cackle. —*v.t.* **4.** to utter by clacking. **5.** to cause to clack: *He clacked the cup against the saucer.* —*n.* **6.** a clacking sound. **7.** something that clacks, as a rattle. **8.** rapid, continual talk; chatter. [1200–50; ME *clacken;* imit.]

clack•ers (klak′ərz), *n.* (*used with a singular or plural v.*) any of various percussion toys consisting of balls or blocks joined by a cord. [1630–40, for an earlier sense; CLACK + -ER[1] + -S[3]]

Clack•man•nan (klak man′ən), *n.* a historic county in central Scotland. Also called **Clack•man•nan•shire** (klak man′ən shēr′, -shər).

clack′ valve′, a valve having a hinged flap permitting flow only in the direction in which the flap opens. Also called **flap valve.** [1855–60]

Clac•to•ni•an (klak tō′nē ən), *adj.* of, pertaining to, or characteristic of a Lower Paleolithic culture in England marked by the production of tools made from stone flakes. [1930–35; < F *clactonien,* after *Clacton(-on-Sea),* English town where the tools were first unearthed; see -IAN]

clad[1] (klad), *v.* **1.** a pt. and pp. of **clothe.** —*adj.* (usually used in combination) **2.** dressed: *ill-clad vagrants.* **3.** covered: *vine-clad cottages.* [bef. 950; ME *cladd(e),* OE *clāthod(e)* clothed. See CLOTHE, -ED[2]]

clad[2] (klad), *v.t.,* **clad, clad•ding.** to bond a metal to (another metal), esp. to provide with a protective coat. [1935–40; special use of CLAD[1]]

clad-, var. of **clado-** before a vowel.

cla•dan•thous (klə dan′thəs), *adj. Bot.* pleurocarpous. [CLAD- + -ANTHOUS]

clad•ding (klad′ing), *n.* **1.** the act or process of bonding one metal to another, usually to protect the inner metal from corrosion. **2.** metal bonded to an inner core of another metal. [1880–85; CLAD[2] + -ING[1]]

clade (klād), *n. Biol.* a taxonomic group of organisms classified together on the basis of homologous features traced to a common ancestor. [1957; < Gk *kládos* branch]

clad•ism (klad′iz əm, klā′diz-), *n. Biol.* the cladistic method of classification. [1965; CLAD- + -ISM]

cla•dis•tics (klə dis′tiks), *n. Biol.* (*used with a plural v.*) classification of organisms based on the branchings of descendant lineages from a common ancestor. [1965–70; *cladist(ic)* (see CLAD-, -ISTIC) + -ICS] —**cla•dis′tic,** *adj.* —**cla•dis′ti•cal•ly,** *adv.*

clado-, a combining form meaning "branch," used in the formation of compound words: *cladophyll.* Also, *esp. before a vowel,* **clad-.** [comb. form of Gk *klados*]

clad•o•car•pous (klad′ə kär′pəs, klā′də-), *adj. Bot.* pleurocarpous. [1855–60; CLADO- + -CARPOUS]

cla•doc•er•an (klə dos′ər ən), *n.* **1.** any or several small, transparent crustaceans of the order Cladocera, having the body covered by a bivalve shell from which the head and antennae extend. —*adj.* **2.** Also, **cla•doc•er•ous** (klə dos′ər əs). belonging or pertaining to the Cladocera. [1905–10; < NL *Cladocer(a)* (*clado-* CLADO- + *-cera,* neut. pl. of *-cerus* horned; see CERO-) + -AN]

clad•ode (klad′ōd), *n. Bot.* cladophyll. [1865–70; < NL *cladodium;* see CLAD-, -ODE[1], -IUM] —**cla•do′di•al,** *adj.*

clad•o•gen•e•sis (klad′ə jen′ə sis, klā′də-), *n. Biol.* evolutionary change by the branching off of new species from common ancestral types. [1950–55; < G *Kladogenese;* see CLADO-, -GENESIS] —**clad•o•ge•net•ic** (klad′ō jə net′ik, klā′dō-), *adj.* —**clad′o•ge•net′i•cal•ly,** *adv.*

clad•o•gram (klad′ə gram′, klā′də-), *n. Biol.* a branching diagram depicting the successive points of species divergence from common ancestral lines without regard to the degree of deviation. Cf. **dendrogram, phenogram.** [1965–70; CLADO- + -GRAM[1]]

clad•o•phyll (klad′ə fil, klā′də-), *n. Bot.* a leaflike flattened branch that resembles and functions as a leaf. Also called **cladode.** [1875–80; CLADO- + -PHYLL]

cladophyll

clad•op•to•sis (klad′op tō′sis, klā′dop-), *n. Bot.* the annual shedding of twigs or branches instead of leaves, as in certain cypresses. [1880–85; CLADO- + PTOSIS]

Clai•borne (klā′bôrn, -bōrn), *n.* a male given name.

claim (klām), *v.t.* **1.** to demand by or as by virtue of a right; demand as a right or as due: *to claim an estate by inheritance.* **2.** to assert and demand the recognition of (a right, title, possession, etc.); assert one's right to: *to claim payment for services.* **3.** to assert or maintain as a fact: *She claimed that he was telling the truth.* **4.** to require as due or fitting: *to claim respect.* —*v.i.* **5.** to make or file a claim: *to claim for additional compensation.* —*n.* **6.** a demand for something as due; an assertion of a right or an alleged right: *He made unreasonable claims on the doctor's time.* **7.** an assertion of something as a fact: *He made no claims to originality.* **8.** a right to claim or demand; a just title to something: *His claim to the heavyweight title is disputed.* **9.** something that is claimed, esp. a piece of public land for which formal request is made for mining or other purposes. **10.** a request or demand for payment in accordance with an insurance policy, a workers' compensation law, etc.: *We filed a claim for compensation from the company.* **11. lay claim to,** to declare oneself entitled to: *I have never laid claim to being an expert in tax laws.* [1250–1300; (*v.*) ME *claimen* < AF, OF *claimer* < L *clāmāre* to cry out; (*n.*) ME < AF, OF *cla(i)me,* n. deriv. of the v.] —**claim′a•ble,** *adj.* —**claim′less,** *adj.*
—**Syn. 1.** See **demand. 6.** request, requisition, call.

claim•ant (klā′mənt), *n.* a person who makes a claim. [1740–50; CLAIM + -ANT]

claim•er (klā′mər), *n.* **1.** a person who makes a claim; claimant. **2.** *Horse Racing.* **a.** a horse participating in a claiming race. **b.** See **claiming race.** [1400–50; late ME; see CLAIM, -ER[1]]

claim′ing race′, *Horse Racing.* a race in which any horse entered can be purchased at a fixed price by anyone who has made a bid or claim before the start of the race. Cf. **selling race.** [1930–35]

claim-jump•er (klām′jum′pər), *n.* a person who seizes another's claim of land, esp. for mineral rights. [1825–35] —**claim′-jump′ing,** *n.*

claims•man (klāmz′mən), *n., pl.* **-men.** an insurance adjuster, esp. one dealing with casualty-insurance claims; claims adjuster. [*claims* (pl. of CLAIM) + -MAN]

Clair (klâr; *Fr.* klεR), *n.* **1. Re•né** (Rə nā′), 1898–1981, French motion-picture director and writer. **2.** a male or female given name.

clair•au•di•ence (klâr ô′dē əns), *n.* the power to hear sounds said to exist beyond the reach of ordinary experience or capacity, as the voices of the dead. [1860–65; CLAIR(VOYANCE) + AUDIENCE (in sense "hearing")] —**clair•au′di•ent,** *n., adj.* —**clair•au′di•ent•ly,** *adv.*

Clai•raut (klâ rō′; *Fr.* kle Rō′), *n.* **A•le•xis Claude** (A lek sē′ klōd), 1713–65, French mathematician.

Clairaut′ equa′tion, *Math.* a differential equation of the form $y = xy' + f(y')$. [named after A. C. CLAIRAUT]

clair de lune (klâr′ dl o͞on′, də lo͞on′), **1.** a pale-green color. **2.** a very pale blue color, tinged with lavender, used as a glaze on Chinese porcelain. **3.** porcelain glazed with this color. [1875–80; < F: lit., moonlight]

Clair de Lune (klâr′ dl o͞on′, də lo͞on′; *Fr.* klεR də lYN′), a work for the piano by Claude Debussy, third movement of the *Suite bergamasque.*

Claire (klâr), *n.* **1. Ina,** 1892–1985, U.S. actress. **2.** a female given name, form of **Clara.**

clair-ob•scure (klâr′əb skyo͝or′), *n.* chiaroscuro. Also, **clare-obscure.** [1710–20; < F, trans. of It *chiaroscuro* CHIAROSCURO; see CLEAR, OBSCURE]

clair•seach (*Scot.* klâr′saKH, -səKH, klär′-), *n.* clarsach.

Clair•ton (klâr′tn), *n.* a city in SW Pennsylvania. 12,188.

clair•voy•ance (klâr voi′əns), *n.* **1.** the supernatural power of seeing objects or actions removed in space or time from natural viewing. **2.** quick, intuitive knowledge of things and people; sagacity. [1840–50; < F, equiv. to *clairvoy(ant)* CLAIRVOYANT + *-ance* -ANCE]
—**Syn. 2.** intuition, penetration, discernment, vision.

clair•voy•ant (klâr voi′ənt), *adj.* **1.** having or claiming to have the power of seeing objects or actions beyond the range of natural vision. **2.** of, by, or pertaining to clairvoyance. —*n.* **3.** a clairvoyant person. [1665–75; < F, equiv. to *clair* CLEAR + *voyant* seeing (prp. of *voir* to see < L *vidēre;* see -ANT)] —**clair•voy′ant•ly,** *adv.*

clam[1]
genus
Anodonta

clam[1] (klam), *n., v.,* **clammed, clam•ming.** —*n.* **1.** any of various bivalve mollusks, esp. certain edible species. Cf. **quahog, soft-shell clam. 2.** *Informal.* a secretive or silent person. **3.** clamminess. **4.** *Slang.* a dollar or the sum of a dollar: *I only made 60 clams a week.* —*v.i.* **5.** to gather or dig clams. **6. clam up,** *Slang.* to refuse to talk or reply; refrain from talking or divulging information: *The teacher asked who had thrown the eraser, but the class clammed up.* [1585–95; short for *clam-shell,* i.e., bivalve with a shell that clamps. See CLAM[2], SHELL] —**clam′like′,** *adj.* —**clam′mer,** *n.*

clam[2] (klam), *n.* **1.** *Brit. Dial.* clamp[1] (defs. 1–3). **2.** *Mach.* (formerly) pincers. [bef. 1000; ME; OE, deriv. of *clamm* fetter, grasp; c. G *Klamm* fetter; akin to CLAMP]

cla•mant (klā′mənt, klam′ənt), *adj.* **1.** clamorous; noisy. **2.** compelling or pressing; urgent: *a clamant need for reform.* [1630–40; < L *clāmant-* (s. of *clāmāns,* prp. of *clāmāre* to shout), equiv. to *clām-* (see CLAIM) + *-ant-* -ANT] —**cla′mant•ly,** *adv.*

clam•a•to•ri•al (klam′ə tôr′ē əl, -tōr′-), *adj.* of or pertaining to the Clamatores, a large group of passerine birds with relatively simple vocal organs and little power of song, as the flycatchers. [1870–75; < NL *Clamator(es)* (pl. of L *clāmātor* shouter, equiv. to *clāmā(re)* to shout) + *-tor* -TOR) + -IAL]

clam•bake (klam′bāk′), *n.* **1.** a picnic or social gathering at the seashore at which clams and other seafood are baked, sometimes with corn and other items, traditionally on hot stones under a covering of seaweed. **2.** *Informal.* any social gathering, esp. a very noisy one. [1825–35, *Amer.;* CLAM[1] + BAKE]

clam•ber (klam′bər, klam′ər), *v.t., v.i.* **1.** to climb, using both feet and hands; climb with effort or difficulty. —*n.* **2.** an act or instance of clambering. [1325–75; ME *clambren,* equiv. to *clamb-* (akin to CLIMB) + *-r-* -ER[6] + *-en* inf. suffix] —**clam′ber•er,** *n.*

clam•ber•ing (klam′bər ing, klam′ər-), *adj. Bot.* of or pertaining to plants that creep or climb like vines, but without benefit of tendrils. [CLAMBER + -ING[1]]

clam′ dig′gers, casual pants that end slightly below the knee. Also, **clam′dig′gers.** [1850–55, for literal sense]

clam•my (klam′ē), *adj.* **-mi•er, -mi•est. 1.** covered with a cold, sticky moisture; cold and damp: *clammy hands.* **2.** sickly; morbid: *She had a clammy feeling that something was wrong at home.* [1350–1400; ME, equiv. to ME *clam* sticky, cold and damp + -y -Y[1]] —**clam′mi•ly,** *adv.* —**clam′mi•ness,** *n.*

clam•or[1] (klam′ər), *n.* **1.** a loud uproar, as from a crowd of people: *the clamor of the crowd at the gates.* **2.** a vehement expression of desire or dissatisfaction: *the clamor of the proponents of the law.* **3.** popular outcry: *The senators could not ignore the clamor against higher taxation.* **4.** any loud and continued noise: *the clamor of traffic; the clamor of birds and animals in the zoo.* —*v.i.* **5.** to make a clamor; raise an outcry. —*v.t.* **6.** to drive, force, influence, etc., by clamoring: *The newspapers clamored him out of office.* **7.** to utter noisily: *They clamored their demands at the meeting.* Also, *esp. Brit.,* **clam′our.** [1350–1400; ME *clamor* (< AF) < L, equiv. to *clām-* (see CLAIM) + *-or* -OR[1]; ME *clamour* < MF < L *clāmōr-* (s. of *clāmor*)] —**clam′or•er, clam′or•ist,** *n.*
—**Syn. 1.** shouting. **2.** vociferation. **4.** See **noise.**
—**Usage.** See **-our.**

clam•or[2] (klam′ər), *v.t. Obs.* to silence. [1605–15; perh. sp. var. of *clammer,* obs. var. of CLAMBER in sense "to clutch," hence "reduce to silence"]

clam•or•ous (klam′ər əs), *adj.* **1.** full of, marked by, or of the nature of clamor. **2.** vigorous in demands or complaints. [1375–1425; late ME. See CLAMOR[1], -OUS] —**clam′or•ous•ly,** *adv.* —**clam′or•ous•ness,** *n.*

clamp (klamp), *n.* **1.** a device, usually of some rigid material, for strengthening or supporting objects or fastening them together. **2.** an appliance with opposite sides or parts that may be adjusted or brought closer together to hold or compress something. **3.** one of a pair of movable pieces, made of lead or other soft material, for covering the jaws of a vise and enabling it to grasp without bruising. **4.** Also called **clamp′ rail′.** *Carpentry.* a rail having a groove or a number of mortises for receiving the ends of a number of boards to bind them into a flat piece, as a drawing board or door. **5.** *Naut.* **a.** a horizontal timber in a wooden hull, secured to ribs to support deck beams and to provide longitudinal strength. **b.** See **mast clamp.** —*v.t.* **6.** to fasten with or fix in a clamp. **7. clamp down,** to become more strict: *There were too many tax loopholes, so the government clamped down.* **8. clamp down on,** to impose or increase controls on. [1350–1400; ME (n.) < MD *clampe* clamp, cleat; c. MLG *klampe*]
—**Syn. 6.** clinch, clench, secure.

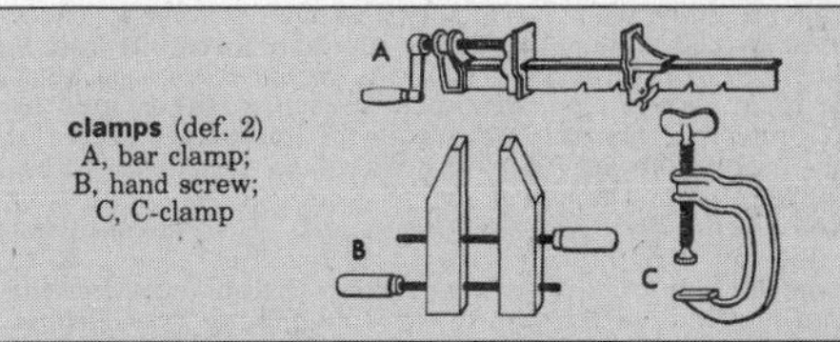

clamps (def. 2)
A, bar clamp;
B, hand screw;
C, C-clamp

clamp•down (klamp′doun′), *n.* crackdown. [1935–40; n. use of v. phrase *clamp down*]

clamp•er (klam′pər), *n.* **1.** a clamp; pincer. **2.** a spiked metal plate worn on the sole of a shoe to prevent slipping on ice. [1815–25; CLAMP + -ER[1]]

clam•shell (klam′shel′), *n.* **1.** the shell of a clam. **2.** *Mach.* **a.** Also called **clam′shell buck′et.** a dredging bucket opening at the bottom, consisting of two similar pieces hinged together at the top. **b.** a machine equipped with such a bucket. **3.** *Print.* a platen press. [1490–1500; earlier *clam-shell;* see CLAM[1], SHELL]

clam′shell door′, Often, **clamshell doors.** a door consisting of two panels that spread open vertically, as those located on the underside of some cargo planes.

clam•worm (klam′wûrm′), *n.* any of several burrowing polychaete worms of the genus *Nereis,* used as bait for fishing. [1795–1805; CLAM[1] + WORM]

clan (klan), *n.* **1.** a group of families or households, as among the Scottish Highlanders, the heads of which claim descent from a common ancestor: *the Mackenzie clan.* **2.** a group of people of common descent; family: *Our whole clan got together for Thanksgiving.* **3.** a group of people, as a clique, set, society, or party, esp. as united by some common trait, characteristic, or interest: *a clan of actors and directors.* **4.** *Anthropol.* **a.** the principal social unit of tribal organization, in which descent is reckoned exclusively in either the paternal or the maternal line. **b.** a group of people regarded as being descended from a common ancestor. [1375–1425; late ME (Scots) < ScotGael *clann* < OIr *cland* offspring < L *planta* scion, PLANT, perh. directly < Brit. Celtic; cf. Welsh *plant* children] —**clan′less,** *adj.*

clan•des•tine (klan des′tin), *adj.* characterized by, done in, or executed with secrecy or concealment, esp. for purposes of subversion or deception; private or surreptitious: *Their clandestine meetings went undiscovered for two years.* [1560–70; < L *clandestinus,* equiv. to **clande, *clamde,* var. of *clam* secretly (with *-de* adv. particle) + *-stinus,* prob. after *intestinus* internal; see INTESTINE] —**clan•des′tine•ly,** *adv.* —**clan•des′tine•ness, clan′des•tin′i•ty,** *n.*
—**Syn.** hidden, underhand, confidential, illicit.

clang (klang), *v.i.* **1.** to give out a loud, resonant sound, as that produced by a large bell or two heavy pieces of metal striking together: *The bells clanged from the steeples.* **2.** to move with such sounds: *The old truck clanged down the street.* —*v.t.* **3.** to cause to resound or ring loudly. —*n.* **4.** a clanging sound. [1570–80; < L *clangere* to resound, clang]
—**Syn. 1.** clash, din, clank, jangle.

clang•er (klang′ər), *n.* **1.** a person or thing that clangs. **2.** *Brit. Slang.* **a.** a blunder; faux pas. **b. drop a clanger,** to blunder. [1945–50; CLANG + -ER]

clang•ing (klang′ing), *n.* a pattern of speech observed in some types of mental illness, as manic disorder, in which associations are based on punning or rhyming. [*clang-* prob. < G *Klang* sound, taken as CLANG + -ING[1]]

clang•or (klang′ər, klang′gər), *n.* **1.** a loud, resonant sound; clang. **2.** clamorous noise. —*v.i.* **3.** to make a clangor; clang. Also, *esp. Brit.,* **clang′our.** [1585–95; < L: loud sound, noise, equiv. to *clang(ere)* to CLANG + *-or* -OR[1]] —**clang′or•ous,** *adj.* —**clang′or•ous•ly,** *adv.*
—**Usage.** See **-our.**

clank (klangk), *n.* **1.** a sharp, hard, nonresonant sound, like that produced by two pieces of metal striking, one against the other: *the clank of chains; the clank of an iron gate slamming shut.* —*v.i.* **2.** to make such a sound. **3.** to move with such sounds: *The old jalopy clanked up the hill.* —*v.t.* **4.** to cause to make a sharp sound, as metal in collision: *He clanked the shovel against the pail.* **5.** to place, put, set, etc., with a clank: *to clank the cell door shut.* [1605–15; < D *klank* sound] —**clank′ing•ly,** *adv.* —**clank′ing•ness,** *n.* —**clank′•less,** *adj.*

clan•nish (klan′ish), *adj.* **1.** of, pertaining to, or characteristic of a clan. **2.** inclined to associate exclusively with the members of one's own group; cliquish: *the clannish behavior of the original members of the country club.* **3.** imbued with or influenced by the sentiments, prejudices, or the like, of a clan. [1770–80; CLAN + -ISH[1]] —**clan′nish•ly,** *adv.* —**clan′nish•ness,** *n.*
—**Syn. 2.** exclusive, snobbish, distant, aloof, narrow.

clans•man (klanz′mən), *n., pl.* **-men.** a member of a clan. [1800–10; CLAN + 's[1] + -MAN]

clans•wom•an (klanz′wo͝om′ən), *n., pl.* **-wom•en.** a woman who belongs to a clan. [1895–1900; CLAN + 's + WOMAN]

clap[1] (klap), *v.* **clapped, clap•ping,** *n.* —*v.t.* **1.** to strike the palms of (one's hands) against one another resoundingly, and usually repeatedly, esp. to express approval: *She clapped her hands in appreciation.* **2.** to strike (someone) amicably with a light, open-handed slap, as in greeting, encouragement, or the like: *He clapped his friend on the back.* **3.** to strike (an object) against something quickly and forcefully, producing an abrupt, sharp sound, or a series of such sounds: *to clap a book on the table.* **4.** to bring together forcefully (facing surfaces of the same object): *She clapped the book shut.* **5.** to applaud (a performance, speech, speaker, etc.) by clapping the hands: *The audience clapped the actors at the end of the act.* **6.** to put or place quickly or forcefully: *to clap a lid on a jar; She clapped her hand over his mouth. They clapped him in jail.* **7.** to make or arrange hastily (often fol. by *up* or *together*). —*v.i.* **8.** to clap the hands, as to express approval; applaud: *After the audience stopped clapping, the tenor sang two encores.* **9.** to make an abrupt, sharp sound, as of flat surfaces striking against one another: *The shutters clapped in the wind.* **10.** to move or strike with such a sound: *She clapped across the room in her slippers.* **11. clap eyes on.** See **eye** (def. 38). **12. clap hold of,** *Naut.* to take hold of. —*n.* **13.** an act or instance of clapping. **14.** the abrupt, sharp sound produced by clapping. **15.** a resounding blow; slap. **16.** a loud and abrupt or explosive noise, as of thunder. **17.** a sudden stroke, blow, or act. **18.** *Print.* clapper (def. 5). **19.** *Obs.* a sudden mishap. [1175–1225; ME *clappen,* OE *clæppan;* c. MLG *kleppen*]

clap[2] (klap), *n. Slang (vulgar).* gonorrhea (often prec. by *the*). [1580–90; akin to MF *clapoir* bubo, *clapier* brothel, OPr *clapier* warren]

clap•board[1] (klab′ərd, klap′bôrd′, -bōrd′), *n.* **1.** *Chiefly Northeastern U.S.* a long, thin board, thicker along one edge than along the other, used in covering the outer walls of buildings, being laid horizontally, the thick edge of each board overlapping the thin edge of the board below it. See illus. under **siding. 2.** *Brit.* a size of oak board used for making barrel staves and for wainscoting. —*adj.* **3.** of or made of clapboard: *a clapboard house.* [1510–20; earlier *clap bord,* alter. of obs. *clapholt* < LG *klappholt* (c. D *klaphout*) split wood used for barrel staves; see CLAP[1], HOLT]

clap•board[2] (klap′bôrd′, -bōrd′), *n. Motion Pictures.* a small board with a hinged stick attached that is clapped down at the beginning of the filming of a shot for use later in synchronizing sound and image in the editing of the film. Also called **clap′per board′, clap•stick** (klap′stik′). [CLAP[1] + BOARD]

clapped-out (klapt′out′), *adj. Brit. Informal.* **1.** (of machinery or appliances) worn-out; dilapidated. **2.** (of a person) exhausted; fatigued. [1945–50]

clap•per (klap′ər), *n.* **1.** a person who applauds. **2.** the tongue of a bell. **3.** *Slang.* the tongue. **4.** Usually, **clappers.** two flat sticks held between the fingers and struck rhythmically against each other to produce abrupt, sharp sounds. **5.** *Print.* a platen press. [1250–1300; ME *claper.* See CLAP[1], -ER[1]]

clap′per rail′, a long-billed rail, *Rallus longirostris,* of coastal marshes of the Americas, having a harsh, cackling cry. [1805–15, *Amer.*]

CONCISE ETYMOLOGY KEY: <, descended or borrowed from; >, whence; b., blend of, blended; c., cognate with; cf., compare; deriv., derivative; equiv., equivalent; imit., imitative; obl., oblique; r., replacing; s., stem; sp., spelling, spelled; resp., respelling, respelled; trans., translation; ?, origin unknown; *, unattested; ‡, probably earlier than. See the full key inside the front cover.

clapt (klapt), *v. Archaic.* pt. or pp. of **clap**[1].

clap•trap (klap′trap′), *n.* **1.** pretentious but insincere or empty language: *His speeches seem erudite but analysis reveals them to be mere claptrap.* **2.** any artifice or expedient for winning applause or impressing the public. [1720–30; CLAP[1] + TRAP[1]]
—**Syn. 1.** sham, humbug, hokum, nonsense, bunk.

claque (klak), *n.* **1.** a group of persons hired to applaud an act or performer. **2.** a group of sycophants. [1860–65; < F, deriv. of *claquer* to clap]

cla•queur (kla kûr′), *n.* a member of a claque. Also, **claqu•er** (klak′ər). [1830–40; < F, equiv. to *claque* CLAQUE + *-eur* -EUR]

clar., clarinet.

Clar•a (klâr′ə, klar′ə), *n.* a female given name: from a Latin word meaning "clear, bright."

Clar•a•belle (klâr′ə bel′, klar′-), *n.* a female given name.

clar•ain (klâr′ān), *n.* the coal forming the bright layers in banded bituminous coal. Cf. **durain, vitrain.** [1915–20; < L *clār(us)* CLEAR, bright + F *-ain,* as in DURAIN]

Clare (klâr), *n.* **1.** a county in W Republic of Ireland. 87,489; 1231 sq. mi. (3190 sq. km). *Co. seat:* Ennis. **2.** a male or female given name.

Clare•mont (klâr′mont), *n.* **1.** a town in SW California. 30,950. **2.** a city in W New Hampshire. 14,557.

Clare•more (klâr′môr, -mōr), *n.* a town in NE Oklahoma. 12,085.

clar•ence (klar′əns), *n.* a closed, four-wheeled carriage, usually with a glass front, with seats inside for four persons. [1830–40; named after Duke of *Clarence* (1765–1837), later William IV]

Clar•ence (klar′əns), *n.* a male given name: from a Latin word meaning "clear one."

Clar•en•don (klar′ən dən), *n.* **1. Edward Hyde, 1st Earl of,** 1609–74, British statesman and historian. **2. Council of,** the ecumenical council (1164) occasioned by the opposition of Thomas à Becket to Henry II. **3.** (*l.c.*) *Print.* a condensed form of printing type, like roman in outline but with thicker serifs.

clare-ob•scure (klâr′əb skyo͝or′), *n.* chiaroscuro.

Clare′ of Assi′si, Saint, 1194–1253, Italian nun: founder of the Franciscan order of nuns. Also, **Clar′a of Assi′si.**

clar•et (klar′it), *n.* **1.** the red table wine produced in the Bordeaux region of France: originally it was light red or yellowish. **2.** a similar wine made elsewhere. **3.** Also called **clar′et red′.** a deep purplish red. **4.** *Slang.* blood. —*adj.* **5.** deep purplish-red. [1350–1400; ME < AF, MF *claret, cleret,* alter., by suffix substitution, of OF *claré* wine mixed with honey and herbs or spices < ML *clarātum,* equiv. to L *clār(us)* CLEAR + *-ātus* -ATE[1]]

clar′et cup′, an iced beverage made of claret and carbonated water with lemon juice, brandy or other spirits, fruits, and sugar. [1875–80]

Cla•re•tian (kla rē′shən, klə-), *Rom. Cath. Ch.* —*n.* **1.** a member of the "Congregation of the Missionary Sons of the Immaculate Heart of Mary," founded in Spain in 1849, and devoted chiefly to missionary work. —*adj.* **2.** of or pertaining to the Claretians. [after St. Anthony *Claret* (1807–70), founder of the order; see -IAN]

Clar•i•bel (klâr′ə bel′, klar′-), *n.* a female given name.

Clar•ice (klar′is, klə rēs′; *Fr.* klA RĒS′), *n.* a female given name, form of **Clara.**

cla•rif•i•cant (kla rif′i kənt), *n. Chem.* any substance for clarifying a liquid. [< LL *clārificant-* (s. of *clārificāns*), prp. of *clārificāre* to CLARIFY; see -ANT]

clar•i•fy (klar′ə fī′), *v.,* **-fied, -fy•ing.** —*v.t.* **1.** to make (an idea, statement, etc.) clear or intelligible; to free from ambiguity. **2.** to remove solid matter from (a liquid); to make into a clear or pellucid liquid. **3.** to free (the mind, intelligence, etc.) from confusion; revive: *The short nap clarified his thoughts.* —*v.i.* **4.** to become clear, pure, or intelligible: *The political situation clarified.* [1350–1400; ME < MF *clarifier* < LL *clārificāre,* equiv. to L *clār(us)* clear + *-ificāre* -IFY] —**clar′i•fi•ca′tion,** *n.* —**clar′i•fi′er,** *n.*
—**Syn. 1.** explain, illuminate, elucidate, resolve.

Cla•rin•da (klə rin′də), *n.* a female given name, form of **Clara.**

clar•i•net (klar′ə net′), *n.* a woodwind instrument in the form of a cylindrical tube with a single reed attached to its mouthpiece. [1790–1800; < F *clarinette,* equiv. to OF *clarin* CLARION + *-ette* -ETTE] —**clar′i•net′ist, clar′i•net′tist,** *n.*

cla•ri•no (klə rē′nō), *n., pl.* **-ni** (-nē), **-nos.** a valveless trumpet used in the 17th and 18th centuries for playing rapid passages in the high register. Also called **cla•rin′ trum′pet** (klə rēn′). Cf. **Bach trumpet.** [< It: trumpet, prob. < Sp *clarin* < F; see CLARINET]

clar•i•on (klar′ē ən), *adj.* **1.** clear and shrill: *the clarion call of a battle trumpet.* —*n.* **2.** an ancient trumpet with a curved shape. **3.** the sound of this instrument. **4.** any similar sound. [1275–1325; ME < ML *clāriōn-* (s. of *clāriō*) trumpet, equiv. to L *clār-* CLEAR + *-iōn-* -ION]

Cla•ris•sa (klə ris′ə), *n.* a female given name, form of **Clara.**

clar•i•ty (klar′i tē), *n.* **1.** clearness or lucidity as to perception or understanding; freedom from indistinctness or ambiguity. **2.** the state or quality of being clear or transparent to the eye; pellucidity: *the clarity of pure water.* [1300–50; ME *clarite* < L *clāritās* (see CLEAR, -ITY); r. ME *clarte* < MF < L as above]
—**Syn. 1.** intelligibility, exactness, simplicity.

Clark (klärk), *n.* **1. Alvan,** 1804–87, and his son **Alvan Graham,** 1832–97, U.S. astronomers and telescope-lens manufacturers. **2. Champ** (champ), (*James Beauchamp*), 1850–1921, U.S. political leader: Speaker of the House 1911–19. **3. (Charles) Joseph** (*Joe*), born 1939, Canadian political leader: prime minister 1979–80. **4. George Rogers,** 1752–1818, U.S. soldier. **5. John Bates** (bāts), 1847–1938, U.S. economist and educator. **6. Kenneth B(ancroft),** born 1914, U.S. psychologist and educator, born in the Panama Canal Zone. **7. Mark Wayne,** 1896–1984, U.S. general. **8. Thomas Campbell** (*Tom*), 1899–1977, associate justice of the U.S. Supreme Court 1949–67. **9. Walter Van Til•burg** (van til′bərg), 1909–71, U.S. author. **10. William,** 1770–1838, U.S. soldier and explorer (brother of George R. Clark): on expedition with Meriwether Lewis 1804–06. **11.** a male given name: a surname, ultimately derived from *clerk.*

Clarke (klärk), *n.* **Arthur C(harles),** born 1917, English science-fiction writer.

Clarke's′ gazelle′, dibatag. [perh. after George S. *Clarke,* Baron Sydenham (1848–1933), English soldier and colonial administrator]

clark•i•a (klär′kē ə), *n.* any of various western U.S. plants belonging to the genus *Clarkia,* of the evening primrose family, having narrow leaves and ornamental red or purple flowers. [< NL (1814); named after William CLARK; see -IA]

Clarks•burg (klärks′bûrg), *n.* a city in N West Virginia, on the Monongahela River. 22,371.

Clarks•dale (klärks′dāl′), *n.* a city in NW Mississippi. 21,137.

Clark's′ nut′crack•er, a nutcracker, *Nucifraga columbiana,* of western North America, having pale gray plumage and black and white wings and tail. Also, **Clark′ nut′crack•er.** Also called **Clark's′ crow′.** [1910–15, *Amer.;* named after William CLARK; see NUTCRACKER]

Clarks•ville (klärks′vil), *n.* **1.** a city in N Tennessee. 54,777. **2.** a town in SE Indiana. 15,164.

clar•o (klär′ō), *adj., n., pl.* **clar•os.** —*adj.* **1.** (of cigars) light-colored and, usually, mild. —*n.* **2.** such a cigar. [1890–95; < Sp < L *clārus* CLEAR]

clar•sach (klär′sax, -səx, klär′-), *n.* an ancient Irish and Scottish harp. Also, **clairseach, clar•seach** (klär′sax, -səx, klär′-), **clar•sech, clar•seth** (klâr′səx, klär′-). [< ScotGael *clàrsach* (cf. Scots *clareschaw*) or Ir *cláirseach,* MIr *cláirsech*]

clar•y (klâr′ē), *n., pl.* **clar•ies.** any of several aromatic herbs of the genus *Salvia,* esp. *S. sclarea,* having hairy, heart-shaped leaves and open clusters of lilac or blue flowers, used as a seasoning, a wine flavoring, and an ingredient in perfumes. [bef. 1000; ME *clare, sclari,* OE *slarege* < ML *sclareia*]

-clase, a combining form used in the formation of compound words that denote minerals with a particular cleavage, as specified by the initial element: *oligoclase; plagioclase.* [< F < Gk *klásis;* see -CLASIS]

clash (klash), *v.i.* **1.** to make a loud, harsh noise: *The gears of the old car clashed and grated.* **2.** to come together or collide, esp. noisily: *The cymbals clashed.* **3.** to conflict; disagree: *Their stories of the accident clashed completely.* **4.** (of juxtaposed colors) to be offensive to the eye. **5.** to engage in a physical conflict or contest, as in a game or a battle (often fol. by *with*): *The Yankees clash with the White Sox for the final game of the season.* —*v.t.* **6.** to strike with a resounding or violent collision: *He clashed his fist against the heavy door.* **7.** to produce (sound) by or as by collision: *The tower bell clashed its mournful note.* —*n.* **8.** a loud, harsh noise, as of a collision: *The automobiles collided with a terrible clash.* **9.** a collision, esp. a noisy one. **10.** a conflict; opposition, esp. of views or interests: *a clash between nations.* **11.** a battle, fight, or skirmish: *The clash between the border patrols left three men dead.* [1490–1500; b. CLAP[1] and DASH[1]] —**clash′er,** *n.* —**clash′ing•ly,** *adv.*
—**Syn. 1.** clang, crash. **10.** disagreement, altercation, dispute. See **struggle.** —**Ant. 10.** agreement, cooperation.

Clash′ing Rocks′, Symplegades.

-clasis, a combining form meaning "a breaking," used in the formation of compound words: *thromboclasis.* [< NL < Gk *klásis*]

clasp (klasp, kläsp), *n., v.,* **clasped** or (*Archaic*) **claspt** (klaspt, kläspt); **clasping.**—*n.* **1.** a device, usually of metal, for fastening together two or more things or parts of the same thing: *a clasp for paper money; a clasp on a necklace.* **2.** a firm grasp or grip: *a clasp of hands.* **3.** a tight embrace: *She held the child in a loving clasp.* **4.** a small bar or metal design, as a star, for affixing to the ribbon of a military decoration to indicate that the bearer has been awarded the decoration an additional time. —*v.t.* **5.** to fasten with or as with a clasp. **6.** to furnish with a clasp. **7.** to seize, grasp, or grip with the hand: *She clasped the club in her hand.* **8.** to hold in a tight embrace; hug: *He clasped the child to him.* —*v.i.* **9.** to embrace or hug: *The lovers clasped.* [1275–1325; ME *clasp* (n.), *claspen* (v.), perh. b. *clippen* CLIP[2] and *haspe* HASP]
—**Syn. 1.** brooch, pin, clip, hook, catch. **3.** hug.

clasp•er (klas′pər, klä′spər), *n.* **1.** a person or thing that clasps. **2.** (in insects, fishes, crustaceans, etc.) one of the modified, usually paired organs or parts by which the male clasps the female during copulation. [1545–55; CLASP + -ER[1]]

clasp•ing (klas′ping, klä′sping), *adj.* (of a leaf) partly or wholly surrounding the stem. [1870–75; CLASP + -ING[2]]

clasp′ knife′, a large pocket knife having a blade or blades that may be folded into the handle. [1745–55]

class (klas, kläs), *n.* **1.** a number of persons or things regarded as forming a group by reason of common attributes, characteristics, qualities, or traits; kind; sort: *a class of objects used in daily living.* **2.** a group of students meeting regularly to study a subject under the guidance of a teacher: *The class had arrived on time for the lecture.* **3.** the period during which a group of students meets for instruction. **4.** a meeting of a group of students for instruction. **5.** a classroom. **6.** a number of pupils in a school, or of students in a college, pursuing the same studies, ranked together, or graduated in the same year: *She graduated from Ohio State, class of '72.* **7.** a social stratum sharing basic economic, political, or cultural characteristics, and having the same social position: *Artisans form a distinct class in some societies.* **8.** the system of dividing society; caste. **9.** social rank, esp. high rank. **10.** the members of a given group in society, regarded as a single entity. **11.** any division of persons or things according to rank or grade: *Hotels were listed by class, with the most luxurious ones listed first.* **12.** excellence; exceptional merit: *She's a good performer, but she lacks class.* **13.** *Hinduism.* any of the four social divisions, the Brahman, Kshatriya, Vaisya, and Shudra, of Hindu society; varna. Cf. **caste** (def. 2). **14.** *Informal.* elegance, grace, or dignity, as in dress and behavior: *He may be a slob, but his brother has real class.* **15.** any of several grades of accommodations available on ships, airplanes, and the like: *We bought tickets for first class.* **16.** *Informal.* the best or among the best of its kind: *This new plane is the class of the wide-bodied airliners.* **17.** *Biol.* the usual major subdivision of a phylum or division in the classification of organisms, usually consisting of several orders. **18.** *Brit. Univ.* any of three groups into which candidates for honors degrees are divided according to merit on the basis of final examinations. **19.** drafted or conscripted soldiers, or persons available for draft or conscription, all of whom were born in the same year. **20.** *Gram.* See **form class.** **21.** *Eccles.* classis. **22.** (in early Methodism) one of several small companies, each composed of about 12 members under a leader, into which each society or congregation was divided. **23.** *Statistics.* a group of measurements that fall within a specified interval. **24.** *Math.* a set; a collection. **25. the classes,** the higher ranks of society, as distinguished from the masses.
—*adj.* **26.** *Informal.* of high quality, integrity, status, or style: *class players on a mediocre team.*
—*v.t.* **27.** to place or arrange in a class; classify: *to class justice with wisdom.*
—*v.i.* **28.** to take or have a place in a particular class: *those who class as believers.* **29. class up,** *Informal.* to improve the quality, tone, or status of; add elegance, dignity, style, etc., to: *The new carpet and curtains really class up this room.* [1590–1600; earlier *classis,* pl. *classes* < L: class, division, fleet, army; sing. *class* back formation from pl.] —**class′a·ble,** *adj.* —**class′er,** *n.*
—**Syn. 27.** group, categorize, type, rank, rate.
—**Usage.** See **collective noun.**

class., **1.** classic. **2.** classical. **3.** classification. **4.** classified.

class′ act′, *Informal.* something or someone regarded as outstanding or elegant in quality or performance. [1975–80]

class′ ac′tion, a legal proceeding in which persons representing interests common to a large group participate as representatives of the group or class. [1950–55] —**class-ac·tion** (klas′ak′shən, kläs′-), *adj.*

class·book (klas′bŏŏk′, kläs′-), *n.* **1.** a book kept by a teacher recording student attendance, grades, etc. **2.** a souvenir book of a graduating class, containing photographs, articles, etc. [1825–35, *Amer.*; CLASS + BOOK]

class′ con′flict. See **class struggle** (def. 1). [1895–1900]

class′ con′sciousness, **1.** awareness of one's own social or economic rank in society. **2.** a feeling of identification and solidarity with those belonging to the same social or economic class as oneself. [1885–90] —**class-con·scious** (klas′kon′shəs, kläs′-), *adj.*

class′ day′, (*sometimes cap.*) a day during the commencement season on which the members of the graduating class in U.S. colleges and schools celebrate the completion of their course with special ceremonies. [1825–35, *Amer.*]

clas·sic (klas′ik), *adj.* **1.** of the first or highest quality, class, or rank: *a classic piece of work.* **2.** serving as a standard, model, or guide: *the classic method of teaching arithmetic.* **3.** of or pertaining to Greek and Roman antiquity, esp. with reference to literature and art. **4.** modeled upon or imitating the style or thought of ancient Greece and Rome: *The 17th and 18th centuries were obsessed with classic ideals.* **5.** of or adhering to an established set of artistic or scientific standards or methods: *a classic example of mid-Victorian architecture.* **6.** basic; fundamental: *the classic rules of warfare.* **7.** of enduring interest, quality, or style: *a classic design; classic clothes.* **8.** of literary or historical renown: *the classic haunts of famous writers.* **9.** traditional or typical: *a classic comedy routine.* **10.** definitive: *the classic reference work on ornithology.* **11.** of or pertaining to automobiles distinguished by elegant styling, outstanding engineering, and fine workmanship that were built between about 1925 and 1948. —*n.* **12.** an author or a literary work of the first rank, esp. one of demonstrably enduring quality. **13.** an author or literary work of ancient Greece or Rome. **14. classics,** the literature and languages of ancient Greece and Rome (often prec. by *the*). **15.** an artist or artistic production considered a standard. **16.** a work that is honored as definitive in its field: *His handbook on mushrooms is a classic.* **17.** something noteworthy of its kind and worth remembering: *His reply was a classic.* **18.** an article, as of clothing, unchanging in style: *Her suit was a simple classic.* **19.** a typical or traditional event, esp. one that is considered to be highly prestigious or the most important of its kind: *The World Series is the fall classic of baseball.* **20.** *Archaic.* a classicist. Also, **classical** (for defs. 1–5, 8, 10). [1605–15; (< F *classique*) < L *classicus* belonging to a class, belonging to the first or highest class, equiv. to *class(is)* CLASS + *-icus* -IC]

clas·si·cal (klas′i kəl), *adj.* **1.** of, pertaining to, or characteristic of Greek and Roman antiquity: *classical literature; classical languages.* **2.** conforming to ancient Greek and Roman models in literature or art, or to later systems modeled upon them. **3.** marked by classicism: *classical simplicity.* **4.** *Music.* **a.** of, pertaining to, or constituting the formally and artistically more sophisticated and enduring types of music, as distinguished from popular and folk music and jazz. Classical music includes symphonies, operas, sonatas, song cycles, and lieder. **b.** of, pertaining to, characterized by, or adhering to the well-ordered, chiefly homophonic musical style of the latter half of the 18th and the early 19th centuries: *Haydn and Mozart are classical composers.* **5.** *Archit.* **a.** noting or pertaining to the architecture of ancient Greece and Rome, esp. the religious and public architecture, characterized by the employment of orders. Cf. **order** (def. 27b). **b.** noting or pertaining to any of several styles of architecture closely imitating the architecture of ancient Greece or Rome; neoclassic. **c.** noting or pertaining to architectural details or motifs adapted from ancient Greek or Roman models. **d.** (of an architectural design) simple, reposeful, well-proportioned, or symmetrical in a manner suggesting the architecture of ancient Greece and Rome. **6.** (*often cap.*) pertaining to or designating the style of fine arts, esp. painting and sculpture, developed in Greece during the 5th and 4th centuries B.C., chiefly characterized by balanced composition, the separation of figures from an architectural background, and the naturalistic rendering of anatomical details, spatial movement, and distribution of weight in a figure. Cf. **archaic** (def. 4), **Hellenistic** (def. 5). **7.** of or pertaining to a style of literature and art characterized by conformity to established treatments, taste, or critical standards, and by attention to form with the general effect of regularity, simplicity, balance, proportion, and controlled emotion (contrasted with *romantic*). **8.** pertaining to or versed in the ancient classics: *a classical scholar.* **9.** relating to or teaching academic branches of knowledge, as the humanities, general sciences, etc., as distinguished from technical subjects. **10.** (of a given field of knowledge) accepted as standard and authoritative, as distinguished from novel or experimental: *classical physics.* **11.** classic (defs. 1–5, 8, 10). **12.** *Eccles.* pertaining to a classis. —*n.* **13.** classical music: *a jazz pianist who studied classical for years.* [1580–90; CLASSIC + -AL[1]] —**clas′si·cal′i·ty, clas′si·cal·ness,** *n.* —**clas′si·cal·ly,** *adv.*

clas′sical condi′tioning, conditioning (def. 2). [1945–50]

clas′sical econom′ics, a system or school of economic thought developed by Adam Smith, Jeremy Bentham, Thomas Malthus, and David Ricardo, advocating minimum governmental intervention, free enterprise, and free trade, considering labor the source of wealth and dealing with problems concerning overpopulation. —**clas′sical econ′omist.**

Clas′sical Greek′, **1.** the form of Greek used in classical literature, esp. the literary Attic Greek of the 5th and 4th centuries B.C. **2.** (loosely) ancient Greek.

Clas′sical Lat′in, the form of Latin used in classical literature, esp. the literary Latin of the 1st century B.C. and the 1st and 2nd centuries A.D.

clas′sical mechan′ics, *Physics.* the branch of mechanics that is based on Newton's laws of motion and that is applicable to systems that are so large that Planck's constant can be regarded as negligibly small (distinguished from *quantum mechanics*). Also called **Newtonian mechanics.** [1930–35]

clas′sical Na′huatl, Aztec (def. 2).

clas′sical San′skrit, Sanskrit of an ancient period earlier than that of the Prakrits and later than Vedic.

clas·si·cism (klas′ə siz′əm), *n.* **1.** the principles or styles characteristic of the literature and art of ancient Greece and Rome. **2.** adherence to such principles. **3.** the classical style in literature and art, or adherence to its principles (contrasted with *romanticism*). Cf. **classical** (def. 7). **4.** a Greek or Latin idiom or form, esp. one used in some other language. **5.** classical scholarship or learning. Also, **clas·si·cal·ism** (klas′i kə liz′əm). [1820–30; CLASSIC + -ISM] —**clas·si·cis·tic** (klas′ə sis′tik), *adj.*

clas·si·cist (klas′ə sist), *n.* **1.** an adherent of classicism in literature or art (contrasted with *romanticist*). **2.** an authority on the classics; a classical scholar. **3.** a person who advocates study of the ancient Greek and Roman classics. Also, **clas·si·cal·ist** (klas′i kə list). [1820–30; CLASSIC + -IST]

clas·si·cize (klas′ə sīz′), *v.,* **-cized, -ciz·ing.** —*v.t.* **1.** to make classic. —*v.i.* **2.** to conform to the classic style. Also, *esp. Brit.,* **clas′si·cise′.** [1850–55; CLASSIC + -IZE]

clas·si·fi·ca·tion (klas′ə fi kā′shən), *n.* **1.** the act of classifying. **2.** the result of classifying or being classified. **3.** one of the groups or classes into which things may be or have been classified. **4.** *Biol.* the assignment of organisms to groups within a system of categories distinguished by structure, origin, etc. The usual series of categories is *phylum* (or, esp. in botany, *division*), *class, order, family, genus, species,* and *variety.* See table under **taxonomy.** **5.** the category, as *restricted, confidential, secret,* or *top secret,* to which information, a document, etc., is assigned, as by a government or military agency, based on the degree of protection considered necessary to safeguard it from unauthorized use. **6.** *Library Science.* any of various systems for arranging books and other materials, esp. according to subject or format. [1780–90; < L *classi(s)* CLASS + -FICATION] —**clas·si·fi·ca·to·ry** (klə sif′i kə tôr′ē, -tōr′ē, klas′ə fi- *or, esp. Brit.,* klas′ə fi kā′tə rē), *adj.* —**cla·si′fi·ca·to′ri·ly,** *adv.* —**clas′si·fi·ca′tion·al,** *adj.*

clas·si·fied (klas′ə fīd′), *adj.* **1.** arranged or distributed in classes or according to class: *We plan to review all the classified specimens in the laboratory.* **2.** of or designating the part or parts of a publication that contain advertisements or lists arranged by category: *Look under "plumbers" in the classified pages of the telephone book. He found a job for a "typist" in the classified section of the newspaper.* **3.** (of information, a document, etc.) **a.** bearing the designation *classified.* **b.** available only to authorized persons. Cf. **classification** (def. 5). **4.** confidential or secret: *The firm's promotional budget for next year is classified information.* **5.** identified as belonging to a specific group or category, as one to which benefits or restrictions apply: *Classified buildings are eligible for state-funded restoration. The bank has a list of classified customers to whom it will not make large loans.* —*n.* **6.** See **classified ad.** [1885–90; 1940–45 for def. 3; CLASSIFY + -ED[2]]

clas′sified ad′, an advertisement in a newspaper, magazine, or the like generally dealing with offers of or requests for jobs, houses, apartments, used cars, and the like. Also called **classified, clas′sified advertise′·ment, want ad.** [1905–10]

clas′sified ad′vertising, **1.** classified ads collectively. **2.** the business or practice of selling space for classified ads. **3.** the department of a newspaper or other publication that handles classified advertising. [1930–35, *Amer.*]

clas·si·fi·er (klas′ə fī′ər), *n.* **1.** a person or thing that classifies. **2.** a device for separating solids of different characteristics by controlled rates of settling. **3.** *Gram.* (in Chinese, Japanese, and other languages) a word or morpheme that corresponds to a semantic class of nouns and regularly accompanies any noun of that class in certain syntactic constructions, such as those of numeration. [1810–20; CLASSIFY + -ER[1]]

clas·si·fy (klas′ə fī′), *v.t.,* **-fied, -fy·ing.** **1.** to arrange or organize by classes; order according to class. **2.** to assign a classification to (information, a document, etc.). Cf. **classification** (def. 5). **3.** to limit the availability of (information, a document, etc.) to authorized persons. [1790–1800; < L *classi(s)* CLASS + -FY] —**clas′si·fi′a·ble,** *adj.*
—**Syn. 1.** class, rank, rate, categorize, group.

class′ inclu′sion, *Logic.* the relation between two classes in which all members of one class are included in the other, as in the proposition "All humans are animals."

class′ in′terval, *Statistics.* one of a set of intervals of arbitrary width into which the range of a sample of measurement is partitioned. [1925–30]

clas·sis (klas′is), *n., pl.* **clas·ses** (klas′ēz). (in certain Reformed churches) **1.** the organization of pastors and elders that governs a group of local churches; a presbytery. **2.** the group of churches governed by such an organization. [1585–95; < L: class]

class·ism (klas′iz əm), *n.* **1.** a biased or discriminatory attitude based on distinctions made between social or economic classes. **2.** the viewing of society as being composed of distinct classes. [1835–45; CLASS + -ISM]

class·less (klas′lis, kläs′-), *adj.* **1.** of or pertaining to a society in which there are no economic or social distinctions. **2.** (of an individual) not having membership in a social or economic class or group. [1875–80; CLASS + -LESS] —**class′less·ness,** *n.*

class′ mark′, *Statistics.* the midpoint of a class interval. [1885–90, for an earlier sense]

class·mate (klas′māt′, kläs′-), *n.* a member of the same class at a school or college. [1705–15, *Amer.*; CLASS + MATE[1]]

class′ mean′ing, *Gram.* **1.** the meaning of a grammatical category or a form class, common to all forms showing the category or to all members of the form class, as in the meaning of number common to all Latin nouns or the meaning of singular common to all Latin singular noun and verb forms. **2.** the part of the meaning of a linguistic form that it has by virtue of membership in a particular form class, as the past tense meaning of *ate.* [1925–30]

class·room (klas′rōōm′, -rŏŏm′, kläs′-), *n.* **1.** a room, as in a school or college, in which classes are held. **2.** any place where one learns or gains experience: *The sea is the sailor's classroom.* [1865–70, *Amer.*; CLASS + ROOM]

class′ strug′gle, **1.** Also called **class conflict.** conflict between different classes in a community resulting from different social or economic positions and reflecting opposed interests. **2.** Also called **class′ war′, class′ war′fare.** (in Marxist thought) the struggle for political and economic power carried on between capitalists and workers. [1840–50]

class·work (klas′wûrk′, kläs′-), *n.* **1.** the written or oral work done in a classroom by a student (distinguished from *homework*). **2.** the work done in a classroom by the students and teacher jointly. [CLASS + WORK]

class·y (klas′ē, klä′sē), *adj.,* **class·i·er, class·i·est.** *Informal.* of high class, rank, or grade; stylish; admirably smart; elegant. [1890–95; CLASS + -Y[1]] —**class′i·ly,** *adv.* —**class′i·ness,** *n.*

clast (klast), *n.* a grain of sediment, silt, sand, gravel, etc., esp. as a constituent fragment of a clastic rock formation, as distinguished from a chemical or biogenic component of such a formation. [1950–55; prob. back formation from CLASTIC]

clas·tic (klas′tik), *adj.* **1.** *Biol.* breaking up into fragments or separate portions; dividing into parts. **2.** pertaining to an anatomical model made up of detachable pieces. **3.** *Geol.* noting or pertaining to rock or rocks

CONCISE PRONUNCIATION KEY: act, cāpe, dâre, pärt; set, ēqual; *if,* īce; ox, ōver, ôrder, oil, bŏŏk, bōōt, out; up, ûrge; child; sing; shoe; thin, *that;* zh as in *treasure.* ə = *a* as in *alone, e* as in *system, i* as in *easily, o* as in *gallop, u* as in *circus;* ə as in *fire* (fīər), *hour* (ouər). l and n can serve as syllabic consonants, as in *cradle* (krād′l), and *button* (but′n). See the full key inside the front cover.

composed of fragments or particles of older rocks or previously existing solid matter; fragmental. [1870–75; < Gk *klastós* broken in pieces (*klas-* var. s. of *klân* to break + *-tos* verbal adj. suffix) + -IC]

clath·rate (klath′rāt), *adj.* **1.** *Biol.* resembling a lattice; divided or marked like latticework. —*n.* **2.** *Chem.* a substance in which a molecule of one compound fills a cavity within the crystal lattice of another compound. Cf. **adduct.** [1615–25; < L *clāt(h)rātus,* ptp. of *clāt(h)rāre* to fit with bars, v. deriv. of *clāt(h)ra* bars, lattice < Gk, Doric equiv. of Attic *klâithra,* pl. of *klêithron* bar; see CLITHRAL]

clath·rin (klath′rin), *n. Cell Biol.* a basketlike network of protein molecules that forms on the cell membrane in response to the attachment of ligands to receptors and becomes the inside surface of the coated vesicle during endocytosis. [prob. CLATHR(ATE) + -IN[2]]

clat·ter (klat′ər), *v.i.* **1.** to make a loud, rattling sound, as that produced by hard objects striking rapidly one against the other: *The shutters clattered in the wind.* **2.** to move rapidly with such a sound: *The iron-wheeled cart clattered down the street.* **3.** to talk fast and noisily; chatter: *They clattered on and on about their children.* —*v.t.* **4.** to cause to clatter: *clattering the pots and pans in the sink.* —*n.* **5.** a rattling noise or series of rattling noises: *The stagecoach made a terrible clatter going over the wooden bridge.* **6.** noisy disturbance; din; racket. **7.** noisy talk; din of voices: *They had to shout over the clatter at the cocktail party.* **8.** idle talk; gossip. [bef. 1050; ME *clateren,* OE *clatr-* (in *clatrunge*); c. D *klateren* to rattle; see -ER[6]] —**clat′ter·er,** *n.* —**clat′ter·ing·ly,** *adv.* —**clat′ter·y,** *adj.*

claucht (klôKHt, kläKHt), *v.* a pt. of **cleek.**

Claude (klôd; *Fr.* klōd), *n.* **1. Albert,** 1899–1983, U.S. biologist, born in Belgium: Nobel prize for medicine 1974. **2.** Also, **Claud.** a male given name: from a Roman family name meaning "lame."

Clau·del (klō del′), *n.* **Paul (Louis Charles)** (pôl lwē sharl), 1868–1955, French diplomat, poet, and dramatist.

Clau·dette (klō det′; *Fr.* klō det′), *n.* a female given name, form of **Claudia.**

Clau·di·a (klô′dē ə), *n.* a female given name: from a Roman family name meaning "lame."

clau·di·ca·tion (klô′di kā′shən), *n.* **1.** a limp or a lameness. **2.** leg weakness associated with circulation difficulties, relieved by rest. [1375–1425; late ME < L *claudicātiōn-* (s. of *claudicātiō*), equiv. to *claudic(āre)* to limp (deriv. of *claudus* lame) + *-ātiōn-* -ATION]

Clau·dine (klô dēn′; *Fr.* klō dēn′), *n.* a female given name, form of **Claudia.**

Clau·di·us I (klô′dē əs), 10 B.C.–A.D. 54, Roman emperor A.D. 41–54.

Claudius II, (*"Gothicus"*) A.D. 214–270, Roman emperor 268–270.

claught (klôKHt, kläKHt), *v.* a pt. of **cleek.**

clause (klôz), *n.* **1.** *Gram.* a syntactic construction containing a subject and predicate and forming part of a sentence or constituting a whole simple sentence. **2.** a distinct article or provision in a contract, treaty, will, or other formal or legal written document. [1175–1225; ME *claus(e)* (< AF) < ML *clausa,* back formation from L *clausula* CLAUSULA] —**claus′al,** *adj.*

Clau·se·witz (klou′zə vits), *n.* **Karl von** (kärl fən), 1780–1831, German military officer and author of books on military science.

Clau·si·us (klou′zē əs), *n.* **Ru·dolf Jul·ius E·man·u·el** (ro͞o′dolf jo͞ol′yəs i man′yo͞o əl; *Ger.* Ro͞o′dôlf yo͞o′lē-o͞os′ ā mä′no͞o el′), 1822–88, German mathematical physicist: pioneer in the field of thermodynamics.

Clau′si·us cy′cle (klô′zē əs, klou′-), *Thermodynam.* See **Rankine cycle.**

claus·thal·ite (klou′stə līt′), *n.* a rare mineral, lead selenide, PbSe, occurring in grayish, granular crystals that have a metallic luster. [named after *Clausthal*-Zellerfeld, mining city in Germany; see -ITE[1]]

claus·tral (klô′strəl), *adj.* cloistral; cloisterlike. [1400–50; late ME < LL *claustrālis,* equiv. to *claustr(um)* bolt, barrier (see CLAUSTRUM) + *-ālis* -AL[1]]

claus·tro·phobe (klô′strə fōb′), *n.* a person who suffers from claustrophobia. [see CLAUSTROPHOBIA, -PHOBE]

claus·tro·pho·bi·a (klô′strə fō′bē ə), *n.* an abnormal fear of being in enclosed or narrow places. [1875–80; < L *claustr(um)* bolt (see CLAUSTRUM) + -O- + -PHOBIA]

claus·tro·pho·bic (klô′strə fō′bik), *adj.* **1.** pertaining to or suffering from claustrophobia. **2.** tending to induce claustrophobia: *a small, airless, claustrophobic room.* [see CLAUSTROPHOBIA, -PHOBIC] —**claus′tro·pho′bi·cal·ly,** *adv.*

claus·trum (klô′strəm, klou′-), *n., pl.* **claus·tra** (klô′-strə, klou′-). *Anat.* barrier. [1840–50; < NL; L: bolt, barrier, equiv. to *claud(ere)* to CLOSE, shut + *-trum* instrumental suffix; cf. CLOISTER]

clau·su·la (klô′zhə lə), *n., pl.* **-lae** (-lē′). *Music.* an ornamented cadence esp. in early Renaissance music. [< L: a closing, conclusion, equiv. to *claus(us)* (ptp. of *claudere* to close) + *-ula* -ULE] —**clau′su·lar,** *adj.*

cla·va (klā′və, klä′-), *n., pl.* **cla·vae** (klā′vē, klä′vī). *Entomol.* the two or more enlarged distal segments that form the bulbous end of a clavate antenna. [< LL *clāva* staff, club] —**cla′val,** *adj.*

CONCISE ETYMOLOGY KEY: <, descended or borrowed from; >, whence; b., blend of, blended; c., cognate with; cf., compare; deriv., derivative; equiv., equivalent; imit., imitative; obl., oblique; r., replacing; s., stem; sp., spelling, spelled; resp., respelling, respelled; trans., translation; ?, origin unknown; *, unattested; ‡, probably earlier than. See the full key inside the front cover.

clav·a·cin (klav′ə sin), *n. Pharm.* patulin. [1942; < NL *clava(tus)* short for *Aspergillus clavatus,* species of fungus found to produce the substance (see CLAVATE) + *-cin,* as in ACTINOMYCIN]

cla·vate (klā′vāt), *adj.* club-shaped; claviform. [1655–65; < NL *clāvātus,* equiv. to LL *clāv(a)* club + *-ātus* -ATE[1]] —**cla′vate·ly,** *adv.*

clave[1] (klāv), *v. Archaic.* pt. of **cleave.**

cla·ve[2] (klä′vā), *n.* one of a pair of wooden sticks or blocks that are held one in each hand and are struck together to accompany music and dancing. [1925–30; AmerSp, Sp: keystone < L *clāvis* key]

cla·ver (klā′vər, klä′-), *n. Scot. and North Eng.* idle talk; gossip. [1680–90; orig. uncert.]

clav·i·cem·ba·lo (klav′i chem′bə lō′), *n., pl.* **-li** (-lē′). a harpsichord. [1730–40; < It < ML *clāvicymbalum,* equiv. to L *clāvi(s)* key + *cymbalum* CYMBAL] —**clav′i·cem′bal·ist,** *n.*

clav·i·chord (klav′i kôrd′), *n.* an early keyboard instrument producing a soft sound by means of metal blades attached to the inner ends of the keys gently striking the strings. [1425–75; late ME < ML *clāvichordium,* equiv. to L *clāvi(s)* key + *chord(a)* CHORD[2] + *-ium* -IUM] —**clav′i·chord′ist,** *n.*

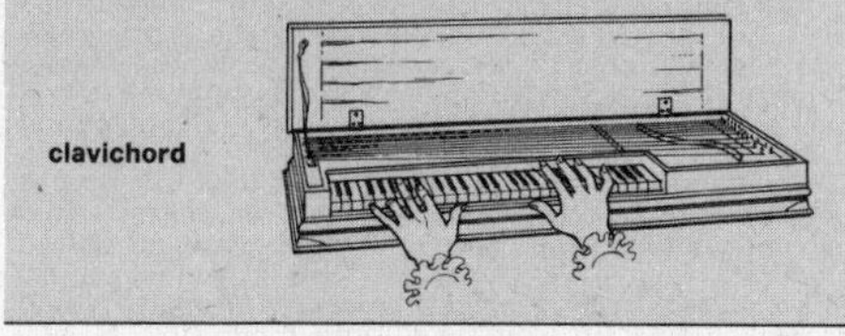

clav·i·cle (klav′i kəl), *n. Anat., Zool.* **1.** a bone of the pectoral arch. **2.** (in humans) either of two slender bones, each articulating with the sternum and a scapula and forming the anterior part of a shoulder; collarbone. See diag. under **shoulder.** [1605–15; < ML *clāvicula* collarbone, L: tendril, door-bolt, little key, equiv. to *clāvi(s)* key + *-cula* -CULE[1]] —**cla·vic·u·lar** (klə vik′yə-lər), *adj.* —**cla·vic·u·late** (klə vik′yə lāt′), *adj.*

clav·i·corn (klav′i kôrn′), *adj.* **1.** having club-shaped antennae, as many beetles of the group Clavicornia. **2.** belonging or pertaining to the group Clavicornia. —*n.* **3.** a clavicorn beetle. [1830–40; < NL *clavicornis,* equiv. to LL *clāv(a)* club + *-i-* -I- + *-cornis,* comb. form of *cornū* HORN]

clav·i·cy·the·ri·um (klav′ə sī thēr′ē əm), *n., pl.* **-the·ri·a** (-thēr′ē ə). an upright harpsichord. [1505–15; *clavi-* < ML *clāvis* key + *cytherium,* for L *citara* KITHARA]

cla·vier[1] (klə vēr′, klav′ē ər, klā′vē-), *n.* the keyboard of a musical instrument. [1700–10; < F: keyboard, in OF, keyholder, equiv. to L *clāvi(s)* key + *-ier* -IER[2]]

cla·vier[2] (klə vēr′, klav′ē ər, klā′vē-), *n.* any musical instrument having a keyboard, esp. a stringed keyboard instrument, as a harpsichord, clavichord, or piano. Also, **klavier.** [1835–45; < G *Klavier* < F *clavier* keyboard; see CLAVIER[1]] —**cla·vier′ist,** *n.*

clav·i·form (klav′ə fôrm′), *adj.* club-shaped; clavate. [1810–20; < LL *clāv(a)* club + -I- + -FORM]

clav·o·la (klav′ə lə), *n., pl.* **-lae** (-lē′). *Entomol.* **1.** the terminal, enlarged, usually club-shaped portion of a capitate, lamellate, or clavate antenna. **2.** flagellum (def. 3). [< NL, equiv. to LL *clāv(a)* club + *-ola,* var. of *-ula* -ULE]

cla·vus (klā′vəs, klä′-), *n., pl.* **-vi** (-vī, -vē). **1.** *Psychiatry.* an intense headache in which the pain is likened to one that would be produced by a sharp object driven into the skull. **2.** (in ancient Rome) a vertical stripe or band of purple worn on the tunic by senators and equites. **3.** *Entomol.* clavola. [1800–10; < L: lit., nail; akin to *claudere* to close]

claw (klô), *n.* **1.** a sharp, usually curved, nail on the foot of an animal, as on a cat, dog, or bird. **2.** a similar curved process at the end of the leg of an insect. **3.** the pincerlike extremity of specific limbs of certain arthropods: *lobster claws.* **4.** any part or thing resembling a claw, as the cleft end of the head of a hammer. **5.** *Typography.* the hooklike projection from the right side of an *r* or from the bowl of a *g.* **6.** (in a motion-picture mechanism) a device having one or two teeth that hook into the perforations of a length of film and move it one frame at a time at any given speed. **7.** *Jewelry.* one of a group of slender, tapering metal projections rising from the base of a jewelry setting, used to hold a transparent or faceted gemstone in position. Cf. **prong** (def. 4). —*v.t.* **8.** to tear, scratch, seize, pull, etc., with or as if with claws: *The kitten clawed my sweater to shreds.* **9.** to make by or as if by scratching, digging, etc., with hands or claws: *to claw a hole in the earth.* **10.** to proceed by or as if by using the hands: *He clawed his way through the crowd.* —*v.i.* **11.** to scratch, tear, or dig with or as if with claws: *The cat clawed and hissed in fear.* **12.** to make fumbling motions: *He clawed at the door. She clawed for the light switch.* **13.** *Scot.* to scratch gently, as to relieve itching. [bef. 900; (n.) ME; OE *clawu;* c. OHG *chlō(a),* akin to D *klauw,* G *Klaue;* (v.) ME *clawen,* OE *claw(i)an,* deriv. of *clawu* (n.); akin to D *klauwen,* G *klauen*] —**claw′er,** *n.* —**claw′less,** *adj.*

claw′-and-ball′ foot′ (klô′ən bôl′), *Furniture.* See **ball-and-claw foot.** [1900–05]

claw′ bar′, a crowbar or lever having a bend at one end with a claw for pulling spikes. [1870–75, *Amer.*]

clawed (klôd), *adj.* having claws (sometimes used in combination): *sharp-clawed.* [1250–1300; ME *claued.* See CLAW, -ED[3]]

claw′ foot′, **1.** a foot with claws. **2.** a representation of the claws of an animal or bird, esp. on the foot of a piece of furniture. **3.** a pathological distortion of the human foot, consisting chiefly of an abnormally high longitudinal arch. [1815–25]

claw′ ham′mer, **1.** a hammer having a head with one end curved and cleft for pulling out nails. See illus. under **hammer.** **2.** *Informal.* a dress coat. [1760–70] —**claw′ham′mer,** *adj.*

Claw·son (klô′sən), *n.* a city in SE Michigan. 15,103.

clax·on (klak′sən), *n.* klaxon. [naturalized English spelling]

clay[1] (klā), *n.* **1.** a natural earthy material that is plastic when wet, consisting essentially of hydrated silicates of aluminum: used for making bricks, pottery, etc. **2.** earth; mud. **3.** earth, esp. regarded as the material from which the human body was formed. **4.** the human body, esp. as distinguished from the spirit or soul; the flesh. **5.** human character as estimated according to fineness of constitution, endowments, etc.: *The saints and heroes seem of a different clay from most of us.* —*v.t.* **6.** to treat or mix with clay; cover, daub, or fill with clay. **7.** to filter through clay. [bef. 1000; ME; OE *clǣg,* c. D, G *Klei,* akin to GLUE] —**clay′like′,** *adj.*

clay[2] (klā), *n.* a lusterless serge having a rough texture. Also called **clay′ wor′sted.** [perh. short for *clay drab* clay-colored cloth]

Clay (klā), *n.* **1. Bertha M.** (*Charlotte Monica Braeme*), 1836–84, English author: originator of a long series of romantic novels. **2. Cassius Marcellus,** 1810–1903, U.S. antislavery leader and diplomat. **3. Cassius Marcellus, Jr.,** original name of **Muhammad Ali.** **4. Henry,** 1777–1852, U.S. statesman and orator. **5. Lucius (Du·Bi·gnon)** (do͞o′bin yon′), 1897–1978, U.S. general. **6.** a male given name.

clay·bank (klā′bangk′), *n.* **1.** a dull yellow color; dun; brownish-yellow. **2.** a horse of this color [1745–55; CLAY[1] + BANK[1]]

Clay·born (klā′bôrn, -bərn), *n.* a male given name.

clay′-col·ored rob′in (klā′kul′ərd). See under **robin**[1] (def. 3).

clay′-colored spar′row, a sparrow, *Spizella pallida,* of the interior of North America, having buff, brown, and white plumage with a pale-gray breast. [1865–70, *Amer.*]

clay′ court′, an outdoor tennis court having a clay surface. Cf. **grass court, hard court.** [1915–20]

clay′ eat′er, *Usually Disparaging.* (in the South Atlantic States) a poor, uneducated person from a rural area. [1835–45, *Amer.*]

clay·ey (klā′ē), *adj.,* **clay·i·er, clay·i·est.** **1.** covered or smeared with clay. **2.** like or resembling clay. **3.** full of or abounding in clay. Also, **clay′ish.** [bef. 1050; ME *cleii,* OE *clǣig;* see CLAY[1], -EY[1]]

clay′ flour′, *Ceram.* dried and pulverized clay.

clay′ min′eral, any of a group of hydrous aluminum silicate minerals, as kaolinite, illite, and montmorillonite, that constitute the major portion of most clays. [1945–50]

clay·more (klā′môr′, -mōr′), *n.* **1.** a two-handed sword with a double-edged blade, used by Scottish Highlanders in the 16th century. **2.** a Scottish broadsword with a basket hilt. [1765–75; < ScotGael *claidheamh mòr* great sword]

clay′more mine′, *Mil.* an antipersonnel mine designed to produce a direction-guided, fan-shaped pattern of fragments. [1965–70; perh. after CLAYMORE]

clay·pan (klā′pan′), *n.* **1.** hardpan (def. 1). **2.** *Australian.* a shallow, normally dry depression in the ground that holds water after a heavy rain. [1830–40, *Amer.;* CLAY[1] + PAN[1]]

clay′ pig′eon, **1.** *Trapshooting, Skeet.* a disk of baked clay or other material hurled into the air from a trap as a target. **2.** *Slang.* a person in a situation likely to be taken advantage of by others. [1885–90, *Amer.*]

clay′ stone′, *Geol.* argillite. Also, **clay′stone′.** [1770–80]

Clay·ton (klāt′n), *n.* **1. John Middleton,** 1796–1856, U.S. jurist and politician: senator 1829–36, 1845–49, 1853–56; Secretary of State 1849–50. **2.** a city in E Missouri, near St. Louis. 14,219. **3.** a male given name.

Clay′ton Antitrust′ Act′, an act of Congress in 1914 supplementing the Sherman Antitrust Act and establishing the FTC.

Clay′ton-Bul′wer Trea′ty (klāt′n bo͝ol′wər), an agreement between the U.S. and Great Britain in 1850 guaranteeing that any canal built to connect the Atlantic and Pacific across Central America would be jointly controlled, open to all nations, and unfortified. Cf. **Hay-Pauncefote Treaty.**

Clay′ton fern′. See **interrupted fern.**

clay·to·ni·a (klā tō′nē ə), *n.* any of the low, succulent plants constituting the genus *Claytonia* of the purslane family, having basal leaves and long clusters of white or rose-colored flowers. [< NL (Linnaeus), named after Dr. John *Clayton* (1693–1773), Virginia botanist; see -IA]

cld., **1.** *Stock Exchange.* (of bonds) called. **2.** cleared.

-cle[1], a suffix found in French loanwords of Latin origin, originally diminutive nouns, and later in adaptations of words borrowed directly from Latin or in Neo-Latin coinages: *article; conventicle; corpuscle; particle.* [< F, OF < L *-culus, -cula, -culum,* var. of *-ulus* -ULE with nouns of the 3d, 4th and 5th declensions, usually with the same gender as the base noun]

-cle[2], a suffix found in French loanwords of Latin origin, later in adaptations of words borrowed directly from Latin; in Latin, this suffix formed from verbs nouns that denoted a place appropriate to the action of the verb (*cubicle, receptacle*) or a means by which the action is performed (*vehicle*). [< F, OF < L *-culum, -cula* < **-tlom, *-tlā*]

Cle·a (klē′ə), *n.* a female given name, form of **Cleopatra.**

clean (klēn), *adj.,* **-er, -est,** *adv.,* **-er, -est,** *v.* —*adj.* **1.** free from dirt; unsoiled; unstained: *She bathed and put on a clean dress.* **2.** free from foreign or extraneous matter: *clean sand.* **3.** free from pollution; unadulterated; pure: *clean air; clean water.* **4.** habitually free of dirt: *Cats are considered clean animals.* **5.** characterized by a fresh, wholesome quality: *the clean smell of pine.* **6.** free from all writing or marking: *a clean sheet of paper.* **7.** having few or no corrections; easily readable: *The publisher demanded clean proofs from the printer.* **8.** free from roughness or irregularity: *He made a clean cut with a razor.* **9.** not ornate; gracefully spare; forceful and simple; trim; streamlined: *a clean literary style; the clean lines of a ship.* **10.** complete; unqualified: *a clean break with tradition.* **11.** morally pure; innocent; upright; honorable: *to lead a clean life.* **12.** showing good sportsmanship; fair: *a clean fighter.* **13.** inoffensive in language or content; without obscenity. **14.** (of a document, record, etc.) bearing no marks of discreditable or unlawful conduct; listing no offenses: *a clean driver's license.* **15.** *Slang.* **a.** innocent of any crime. **b.** not having a criminal record. **c.** carrying or containing no evidence of unlawful activity or intent, as controlled substances, unlicensed weapons, or contraband: *The agents searched the car for drugs, but it was clean.* **d.** not using narcotics. **16.** (of a nuclear weapon) producing little or no radioactive fallout. **17.** not radioactive. **18.** (of a document or financial instrument) free from qualifications or restrictions: *a clean bill of lading.* **19.** free from defects or flaws: *a clean diamond.* **20.** free from encumbrances or obstructions. **21.** neatly or evenly made or proportioned; shapely; trim: *a clean profile.* **22.** made without any unanticipated difficulty or interference: *The bank robbers made a clean getaway.* **23.** *Chiefly Biblical.* having no physical or moral blemish or carrying no taboo so as to make impure according to the laws, esp. the dietary or ceremonial laws: *a clean animal; clean persons.* **24.** dexterously performed; adroit: *a clean serve in tennis.* **25.** (of a jump over an obstacle) made without touching the obstacle. **26.** *Slang.* having no direct associations, business interests, etc., that could prejudice one's official acts or decisions: *The new governor is clean because he's sold his construction business and doesn't owe political favors to anyone.* **27.** *Slang.* without money or funds. **28.** (of wine) having a taste that is unusually refreshing and smooth. **29.** *Naut.* (of an anchorage, harbor, etc.) free of obstructions or hazards (opposed to *foul*). **30.** (of the legs of a horse) free from injury or blemish, as capped hocks, splints, or scars. **31.** *Foreign Exchange.* (of currency floats) not influenced by exchange-rate manipulation (opposed to *dirty*).
—*adv.* **32.** in a clean manner; cleanly: *Nobody wants to box with him because he doesn't fight clean.* **33.** so as to be clean: *This shirt will never wash clean.* **34.** *Informal.* wholly; completely; quite: *The sharp carving knife sliced clean through the roast. In a year, he had gone clean through his inheritance.* **35. clean full,** *Naut.* **a.** (of a sail or sails) filled with wind; rap full. **b.** (of a sailing vessel) with all sails full of wind; rap full. **36. come clean,** *Slang.* to tell the truth, esp. to admit one's guilt.
—*v.t.* **37.** to make clean: *Clean those dirty shoes.* **38.** to remove or consume the contents of; empty; clear: *She sat down to dinner ravenous and within five minutes had cleaned her plate.* **39.** to dry-clean. **40.** to remove the entrails and other inedible parts from (poultry, fish, etc.); dress. **41.** *Slang.* to take away or win all or almost all the money or possessions of (often fol. by *out*): *The cards were marked and I got cleaned.* **42.** *Metall.* to remove the seams from (a casting) by filing or grinding. **43.** *Philately.* to delete intentionally the cancellation from (a postage or revenue stamp).
—*v.i.* **44.** to perform or undergo a process of cleaning: *This kind of fabric cleans easily. Detergents clean better than most soaps.* **45.** to get rid of dirt, soil, etc. (often fol. by *up*): *to spend the morning cleaning.* **46. clean house,** to wipe out corruption, inefficiency, etc., as in an organization: *It's time for the city government to clean house.* **47. clean out, a.** to empty in order to straighten or clean. **b.** to use up; exhaust: *He had cleaned out his savings.* **c.** *Informal.* to drive out by force. **d.** to empty or rid (a place) of occupants, contents, etc.: *Eager customers cleaned out the store on the first day of the sale. The thief cleaned out the safe.* **e.** *Slang.* to cause to lose all or almost all one's money or possessions. **48. clean up, a.** to wash or tidy up. **b.** to rid of undesirable persons or features: *They cleaned up the local bars.* **c.** to put an end to; finish: *to clean up yesterday's chores.* **d.** *Informal.* to make a large profit: *They cleaned up in the stock market.* **49. clean up one's act.** See **act** (def. 10). [bef. 900; ME *clene,* OE *clǣne* pure, clear, c. OHG *kleini* (G *klein* small)] —**clean′ness,** *n.*
—**Syn. 1.** neat, immaculate. CLEAN, CLEAR, PURE refer to freedom from soiling, flaw, stain, or mixture. CLEAN refers esp. to freedom from soiling: *a clean shirt.* CLEAR refers particularly to freedom from flaw or blemish: *a clear pane of glass.* PURE refers esp. to freedom from mixture or stain: *a pure metal; not diluted but pure and full strength.* **7.** legible. **11.** unsullied, chaste, virtuous. **19.** unblemished, flawless. **34.** entirely, thoroughly. **37.** scour, scrub, sweep, brush, wipe, mop, dust, wash, rinse, lave, deterge, purify, clear; decontaminate. CLEAN, CLEANSE refer to removing dirt or impurities. To CLEAN is the general word with no implication of method or means: *to clean windows, a kitchen, streets.* CLEANSE is esp. used of thorough cleaning by chemical or other technical process; figuratively it applies to moral or spiritual purification: *to cleanse parts of machinery; to cleanse one's soul of guilt.* —**Ant. 1.** dirty. **17.** contaminated, radioactive. **37.** soil.

clean·a·bil·i·ty (klē′nə bil′i tē), *n.* the ability to be cleaned, esp. easily or without damage: *fabrics rated for their cleanability.* [CLEAN + -ABILITY] —**clean′a·ble,** *adj.*

clean′ and jerk′, *Weight Lifting.* a lift in which a barbell is raised from the floor to shoulder height where it is brought to rest and then, with a lunging movement by the lifter, is thrust overhead so the arms extend straight in the air, being held in this position for a short, specified length of time. [1935–40]

clean′ bill′ of health′, **1.** a certificate of health attesting the lack of a contagious disease, as on a ship. **2.** an assurance, as by a doctor, that one is in good health. **3.** Also, **clean′ bill′.** an assurance, esp. an official verdict by a committee, that a group or an individual has proved, under investigation, to be morally sound, fit for office, etc. [1850–55]

clean-cut (klēn′kut′), *adj.* **1.** having distinct, regular shape: *a face with clean-cut features.* **2.** clearly outlined. **3.** neat and wholesome: *a polite, clean-cut young man.* **4.** unambiguously clear; unmistakable; clear-cut: *The case against him is a clean-cut one.* [1835–45]

clean′ en′ergy, energy, as electricity or nuclear power, that does not pollute the atmosphere when used, as opposed to coal and oil, that do.

clean·er (klē′nər), *n.* **1.** a person who cleans, esp. one whose regular occupation is cleaning offices, buildings, equipment, etc. **2.** an apparatus or machine for cleaning, as a vacuum cleaner. **3.** a preparation for use in cleaning, as a detergent or chemical bleach. **4.** the owner or operator of a dry-cleaning establishment: *The cleaner said he couldn't get the spot off my coat.* **5.** Usually, **cleaners.** a dry-cleaning establishment: *My suit is at the cleaners.* **6. take to the cleaners.** *Slang.* to cause to lose all or a great deal of one's money or personal property, as through gambling or a bad investment: *He got taken to the cleaners in the poker game last night.* [1425–75; late ME *clener.* See CLEAN, -ER[1]]

clean′er tooth′, *Carpentry.* See **raker tooth.**

clean-hand·ed (klēn′han′did), *adj.* free from wrongdoing; guiltless. [1720–30] —**clean′hand′ed·ness,** *n.*

clean′ hands′, freedom from guilt, wrongdoing, or dishonesty; innocence; guiltlessness: *He came out of the bribery investigation triumphantly when it was proved that he had clean hands.* [1590–1600]

clean·ing (klē′ning), *n.* **1.** an act or instance of making clean: *Give the house a good cleaning.* **2.** *Slang.* an overwhelming or complete defeat, financial loss, or failure: *Our team took a cleaning in yesterday's game.* **3.** *Informal.* killing (def. 3). [1655–75; CLEAN + -ING[1]]

clean′ing wom′an, a woman employed to sweep, mop, dust, or do general cleaning in a house, office, hotel, or the like. Also called **clean′ing la′dy.**

clean-limbed (klēn′limd′), *adj.* having slender, well-proportioned arms and legs: *a clean-limbed athlete.* [1425–75; late ME]

clean-liv·ing (klēn′liv′ing), *adj.* conducting one's life so as to be beyond moral reproach. [1915–20]

clean·ly (*adj.* klen′lē; *adv.* klēn′lē), *adj.,* **-li·er, -li·est,** *adv.* —*adj.* **1.** personally neat; careful to keep or make clean: *The cat is by nature a cleanly animal.* **2.** habitually kept clean. **3.** *Obs.* cleansing; making clean. —*adv.* **4.** in a clean manner. [bef. 900; ME *clenlich(e),* OE *clǣnlic,* equiv. to *clǣne* CLEAN + *-lic* -LY] —**clean·li·ness** (klen′lē nis), *n.*

clean·out (klēn′out′), *n.* **1.** an act of cleaning out. **2.** an opening or passage giving access to a place that requires occasional cleaning, as a soil pipe. [1885–90, *Amer.*; n. use of v. phrase *clean out*]

clean′ room′, a room in which contaminants such as dust are reduced to a very low level by special procedures so that operations such as the manufacture and assembly of delicate equipment or the manipulation of biological materials can be performed effectively. [1960–65, *Amer.*]

cleanse (klenz), *v.,* **cleansed, cleans·ing.** —*v.t.* **1.** to make clean. **2.** to remove by or as if by cleaning: *to cleanse sin from the soul.* —*v.i.* **3.** to become clean. [bef. 900; ME *clensen,* OE *clǣnsian,* equiv. to *clǣne* CLEAN + *-si-* v. suffix + *-an* inf. suffix] —**cleans′a·ble,** *adj.*
—**Syn. 1.** See **clean.**

cleans·er (klen′zər), *n.* **1.** a preparation for cleansing, as a liquid or powder for scouring sinks, bathtubs, etc., or a cream for cleaning the face. **2.** a person or thing that cleanses. **3.** *Chiefly Eastern New Eng.* a dry-cleaning establishment. [bef. 1000; ME; OE *clǣnsere;* see CLEANSE, -ER[1]]

clean-shav·en (klēn′shā′vən), *adj.* (of a man) having the beard and mustache shaved off. [1860–65]

cleans′ing tis′sue, a small piece of absorbent paper, used esp. for removing cleansing cream and cosmetics and also serving as a disposable handkerchief.

clean′ sweep′, **1.** an overwhelming or decisive victory, as by a political candidate who wins in all or almost all election districts. **2.** the winning of all the prizes, rounds, contests, etc., in a competition or of all the games in a series. **3.** a thorough or sweeping change, esp. one effected by the large-scale removal or elimination of unwanted persons or things: *The new president made a clean sweep when he joined the company, replacing all the department heads.*

Cle·an·thes (klē an′thēz), *n.* c300–232? B.C., Greek Stoic philosopher.

clean·up (klēn′up′), *n.* **1.** the act or process of cleaning up. **2.** *Slang.* a very large profit: *The company made a real cleanup on their new invention.* **3.** *Baseball.* **a.** the fourth position in the batting order: *Our best home-run hitter is batting cleanup.* **b.** the player who bats in this position. [1865–70, *Amer.*; n. use of v. phrase *clean up*]

clear (klēr), *adj.,* **-er, -est,** *adv.,* **-er, -est,** *v., n.* —*adj.* **1.** free from darkness, obscurity, or cloudiness; light: *a clear day.* **2.** transparent; pellucid: *clear water.* **3.** without discoloration, defect, or blemish: *a clear complexion; a clear pane of glass.* **4.** of a pure, even color: *a clear yellow.* **5.** easily seen; sharply defined: *a clear outline.* **6.** distinctly perceptible to the ear; easily heard: *a clear sound.* **7.** free from hoarse, harsh, or rasping qualities: *a clear voice; clear as a bell.* **8.** easily understood; without ambiguity: *clear, concise answers.* **9.** entirely comprehensible; completely understood: *The ultimate causes of inflation may never be clear.* **10.** distinct; evident; plain: *a clear case of misbehavior.* **11.** free from confusion, uncertainty, or doubt: *clear thinking.* **12.** perceiving or discerning distinctly: *a clear mind.* **13.** convinced; certain: *He was not clear on the first point that she made but agreed with the others.* **14.** free from anything that would disturb or blame: *a clear conscience.* **15.** free from suspicion of guilt or complicity: *She was entirely clear of the crime until one of her accomplices turned informer.* **16.** serene; calm; untroubled: *a clear brow.* **17.** free from obstructions or obstacles; open: *a clear view; a clear path.* **18.** free from entanglement or contact: *He kept clear of her after the argument. She managed to keep her dress clear of the mud.* **19.** without limitation or qualification; absolute: *a clear victory.* **20.** free from obligation, liability, or debt: *After twenty years, our house is clear of the mortgage. Municipal bonds were returning as much as 9 percent, clear of taxes.* **21.** without deduction or diminution: *a clear $1000 after taxes.* **22.** freed or emptied of contents, cargo, etc. **23.** (of tree trunks or timber) free from branches, knots, or other protruding or rough parts: *The trunk was clear for 20 feet above the ground.* **24.** *Phonet.* **a.** (of an *l*-sound) having front-vowel resonance; situated before a vowel in the same syllable. Cf. **dark** (def. 16a). **b.** (of a speech sound) produced without frication or aspiration. **25.** (in cryptography) not coded or enciphered. Cf. **plaintext. 26.** bright; shining: *a clear flame.* **27.** *Obs.* illustrious.
—*adv.* **28.** in a clear or distinct manner; clearly. **29.** so as not to be in contact with or near; away (often fol. by *of*): *Stand clear of the closing doors.* **30.** entirely; completely; clean: *to cut a piece clear off; to climb clear to the top; to run clear off the road.*
—*v.t.* **31.** to remove people or objects from (usually fol. by *of*): *to clear a courtroom of photographers; to clear the table of dishes.* **32.** to remove (people or objects) (usually fol. by *from*): *to clear the photographers from the courtroom; to clear the dishes from the table.* **33.** to make clear, transparent, or pellucid; free from cloudiness or impurities: *to clear a liquid by means of a filter.* **34.** to make free of confusion, doubt, or uncertainty: *He spoke to his supervisor to clear his mind about their working relationship.* **35.** to make understandable or lucid; free from ambiguity or obscurity: *She rephrased the report in order to clear the essential points.* **36.** to make (a path, road, etc.) by removing any obstruction: *He had to cut away the underbrush to clear a path.* **37.** to eat all the food on: *to clear one's plate.* **38.** to relieve (the throat) of some obstruction, as phlegm, by forcing air through the larynx, usually producing a rasping sound. **39.** to make a similar rasping noise in (the throat), as to express disapproval or to attract attention. **40.** to remove from (the brow) any traces of tension or anxiety, as folds or wrinkles. **41.** to free of anything defamatory or discrediting: *to clear one's name.* **42.** to free from suspicion, accusation, or imputation of guilt; prove or declare innocent: *The jury cleared the defendant of the charge.* **43.** to remove instructions or data from (a computer, calculator, etc.). **44.** to pass by or over without contact or entanglement: *The ship cleared the reef. The fisherman cleared his line.* **45.** to pass through or away from: *The ship cleared the harbor. The bill cleared the Senate.* **46.** to pass (checks or other commercial paper) through a clearinghouse. **47.** (of mail, telephone calls, etc.) to process, handle, reroute, etc.: *The dispatcher clears hundreds of items each day.* **48.** to free from debt: *Just a few dollars more would clear him. The widow had to borrow money to clear her husband's estate.* **49.** to gain as clear profit: *to clear $1000 in a transaction.* **50.** to pay (a debt) in full. **51.** to receive authorization before taking action on: *You'll have to clear your plan with headquarters.* **52.** to give clearance to; authorize: *The chairperson has to clear our speeches before the meeting.* **53.** to authorize (a person, agency, etc.) to use classified information, documents, etc.: *He has finally been cleared for highly classified information.* **54.** to remove trees, buildings, or other obstructions from (land), as for farming or construction. **55.** to free (a ship, cargo, etc.) from legal detention at a port by satisfying customs and other requirements. **56.** to try or otherwise dispose of (the cases awaiting court action): *to clear the docket.* **57.** (of a commodity) to buy up or sell out the existing supply of. **58.** *Skin Diving.* to drain or expel unwanted water in: *to clear a snorkel by sharp exhalations; to clear a regulator and face mask while underwater.* **59.** *Bridge.* to establish one or more winning cards in (a given suit) by leading the suit until all the outstanding cards have been drawn: *He cleared the heart suit before attacking spades.*
—*v.i.* **60.** to become clear. **61.** to exchange checks and bills, and settle balances, as in a clearinghouse. **62.** to become free from doubt, anxiety, misunderstanding, etc.: *His mind cleared when he heard the truth.* **63.** to pass an authority for review, approval, etc.: *The bill must clear through the assembly before it becomes legal.* **64.** to remove dishes, food, etc., from a table following a meal: *Is it my turn to clear?* **65.** to remove previously inserted instructions or data from a computer, calculator, typewriter, or the like. **66.** *Naut.* **a.** to comply with customs and other requirements legally imposed on entering or leaving a port (often fol. by *in* or *out*). **b.** to leave port after having complied with such requirements. **67.** (of a commodity for sale) to sell out; become bought out: *Wheat cleared rapidly.* **68. clear away** or **off, a.** to remove in order to make room. **b.** to leave; escape: *We were warned to clear off before the floods came.* **c.** to disappear; vanish: *When the smoke cleared*

away, we saw that the house was in ruins. **69. clear out, a.** to remove the contents of: *Clear out the closet.* **b.** to remove; take away: *Clear out your clothes from the closet.* **c.** to go away, esp. quickly or abruptly. **d.** to drive or force out: *The police cleared out the pickets by force.* **70. clear up, a.** to make clear; explain; solve. **b.** to put in order; tidy up. **c.** to become better or brighter, as the weather.
—*n.* **71.** a clear or unobstructed space. **72.** plaintext. **73.** a piece of clear lumber. **74. in the clear, a.** absolved of blame or guilt; free: *He was suspected of the theft, but evidence put him in the clear.* **b.** See **en clair.** [1250–1300; ME *clere* < AF, OF *cler* < L *clārus*] —**clear′a•ble,** *adj.* —**clear′ness,** *n.*
—**Syn. 1.** fair, cloudless, sunny. **2.** translucent, limpid, crystalline, diaphanous. **3.** See **clean. 8.** intelligible, comprehensible, lucid, plain, perspicuous. **10.** obvious, manifest, apparent, unmistakable. **17.** unimpeded, unobstructed. **18.** unhampered, unencumbered. **33.** clarify, purify, refine. **42.** exonerate, absolve, vindicate, excuse. —**Ant. 1.** cloudy, dark. **8, 10.** obscure. **13.** uncertain.

clear′-air′ tur′bulence (klēr′âr′), atmospheric turbulence, sometimes severe, occurring in air devoid of clouds or other visible indicators that turbulence might be present. *Abbr.:* CAT [1950–55]

clear•ance (klēr′əns), *n.* **1.** the act of clearing. **2.** the distance between two objects; an amount of clear space: *The bridge allowed a clearance of 37 feet at mean high water.* **3.** a formal authorization permitting access to classified information, documents, etc. **4.** Also called **clear′ance sale′.** the disposal of merchandise at reduced prices to make room for new goods: *He bought the coat for half price at a clearance.* **5.** a clear space; a clearing: *The house stood in a clearance among the trees.* **6.** *Banking.* an exchange of checks and other commercial paper drawn on members of a clearinghouse, usually effected at a daily meeting of the members. **7.** *Mach.* a space between two moving parts, left to avoid clashing or to permit relatively free motion. **8.** the angle between a face of a cutting tool, as a lathe tool, and the work. **9.** *Naut.* **a.** the clearing of a ship at a port. **b.** Also called **clear′ance pa′pers.** the official papers certifying this. **10.** *Med.* a test of the excretory function of the kidneys based on the volume of blood that is cleared of a specific substance per minute by renal excretion. [1555–65; CLEAR + -ANCE] —**clear′er,** *n.*

clear′ chan′nel, *Radio.* **1.** a radio broadcast channel cleared for long-distance broadcasting during nighttime hours. **2.** a broadcast channel free of undesirable interference. —**clear′-chan′nel,** *adj.*

Cle•ar•chus (klē är′kəs), *n.* died 401 B.C., Spartan general.

clear-coat•ing (klēr′kō′ting), *n.* an automotive painting technique in which a coating of clear lacquer or other synthetic liquid is applied over the base color to enhance the shine and durability of the paint.

clear•cole (klēr′kōl′), *n.* size mixed with white lead, used esp. as a priming in house painting. [1815–25; < F *claire colle,* equiv. to *claire* fem. of *clair* CLEAR + *colle* < Gk *kólla* glue]

clear-cut (klēr′kut′ *for 1, 2;* klēr′kut′ *for 3–5*), *adj., n., v.,* **-cut, -cut•ting.** —*adj.* **1.** formed with or having clearly defined outlines: *a face with clear-cut features.* **2.** unambiguously clear; completely evident; definite: *His sale of secrets was a clear-cut example of treachery.* **3.** of or pertaining to a section of forest where all trees have been cut down for harvesting. —*n.* **4.** a section of forest where all trees have been cut down for harvesting. —*v.t.* **5.** to fell all the trees in (a section of forest) for harvesting. Also, **clear′ cut′, clear′cut′** (for defs. 3–5). [1850–55] —**clear′-cut′ness,** *n.*
—**Syn. 1.** chiseled, crisp, precise, positive, definite.

clear-eye (klēr′ī′), *n., pl.* **-eyes.** the clary, *Salvia sclarea.* [1575–85; alter. by folk etym. of CLARY]

clear-eyed (klēr′īd′), *adj.* **1.** having clear eyes. **2.** mentally acute or perceptive; realistic; clear-sighted: *a clear-eyed appraisal.* [1520–30]

Clear•field (klēr′fēld′), *n.* a town in N Utah. 17,982.

clear•head•ed (klēr′hed′id), *adj.* having or showing an alert mind. [1700–10; CLEAR + -HEADED] —**clear′•head′ed•ly,** *adv.* —**clear′head′ed•ness,** *n.*

clear′ ice′, glaze ice, esp. on aircraft.

clear•ing (klēr′ing), *n.* **1.** the act of a person or thing that clears; the process of becoming clear. **2.** a tract of land, as in a forest, that contains no trees or bushes. **3.** the reciprocal exchange between banks of checks and drafts, and the settlement of the differences. **4. clearings,** the total of claims settled at a clearinghouse. [1350–1400; ME *clering.* See CLEAR, -ING[1]]

clear′ing bath′, *Photog.* any solution for removing material from the surface of a photographic image, as silver halide, metallic silver, or a dye or stain.

clear•ing•house (klēr′ing hous′), *n., pl.* **-hous•es** (-hou′ziz). **1.** a place or institution where mutual claims and accounts are settled, as between banks. **2.** a central institution or agency for the collection, maintenance, and distribution of materials, information, etc. Also, **clear′•ing house′.** [1825–35]

clear′ing loan′. See **day loan.**

clear′ing mark′, *Navig.* either of a pair of landmarks or marks on a mariner's chart lying upon a line (**clear′ing line′**) along which a vessel can sail to avoid navigational hazards.

clear•ly (klēr′lē), *adv.* **1.** in a clear manner: *It is difficult to explain complex matters clearly.* **2.** without equivocation; decidedly: *It is clearly out of the question to drop the case.* [1250–1300; ME *clerli.* See CLEAR, -LY]
—**Syn. 1.** plainly, understandably. CLEARLY, DEFINITELY, DISTINCTLY, EVIDENTLY imply the way in which something is plainly understood or understandable. CLEARLY suggests without doubt or obscurity: *expressed clearly.* DEFINITELY means explicitly; with precision: *definitely phrased.* DISTINCTLY means without blurring or confusion: *distinctly enunciated.* EVIDENTLY means patently, unquestionably: *evidently an error.*

clear-sight•ed (klēr′sī′tid), *adj.* **1.** having clear or sharp eyesight. **2.** having or marked by keen perception or sound judgment: *a clear-sighted, analytical approach.* [1580–90] —**clear′-sight′ed•ly,** *adv.* —**clear′-sight′•ed•ness,** *n.*

clear•sto•ry (klēr′stôr′ē, -stōr′ē), *n., pl.* **-ries.** clerestory. —**clear′sto′ried,** *adj.*

clear′ text′, plaintext.

Clear•wa•ter (klēr′wô′tər, -wot′ər), *n.* a city in W Florida. 85,450.

Clear′water Moun′tains, a group of mountains in N Idaho.

clear•way (klēr′wā′), *n. Brit.* a road on which only emergency stops are permitted. [1880–85, for an earlier sense; CLEAR + WAY[1]]

clear•weed (klēr′wēd′), *n.* a plant, *Pilea pumila,* of the nettle family, having drooping, green flower clusters and smooth stems. Also called **richweed.** [1815–25, *Amer.;* CLEAR + WEED[1]; so called from its translucent leaves and stems]

clear•wing (klēr′wing′), *n.* a moth having wings mostly devoid of scales and transparent, esp. any of the family Aegeriidae, many species of which are injurious to plants. [1865–70; CLEAR + WING]

cleat (klēt), *n.* **1.** a wedge-shaped block fastened to a surface to serve as a check or support: *He nailed cleats into the sides of the bookcase to keep the supports from slipping.* **2.** a strip of metal, wood, or the like, fastened across a surface, as a ramp or gangway, to provide sure footing or to maintain an object in place. **3.** a strip of wood, metal, etc., fastened across a surface, as of a plank or series of adjacent planks, for strength or support. **4.** a conical or rectangular projection, usually of hard rubber, or a metal strip with sharp projections, built into or attached to the sole of a shoe to provide greater traction. **5.** a shoe fitted with such projections. **6.** a metal plate fastened to the sole or heel of a shoe, to protect against wear. **7.** *Shipbuilding.* a hook-shaped piece of metal supporting a small structural member. **8.** Also called **belaying cleat.** *Naut.* an object of wood or metal having one or two projecting horns to which ropes may be belayed, esp. as fixed to the deck, bulkhead, or stanchion of a vessel. **9.** the cleavage plane of coal as found in a mine. —*v.t.* **10.** to supply or strengthen with cleats; fasten to or with a cleat. [1350–1400; ME *clete* wedge, c. OHG *klōz* lump, ball, D *kloot;* akin to CLOT]

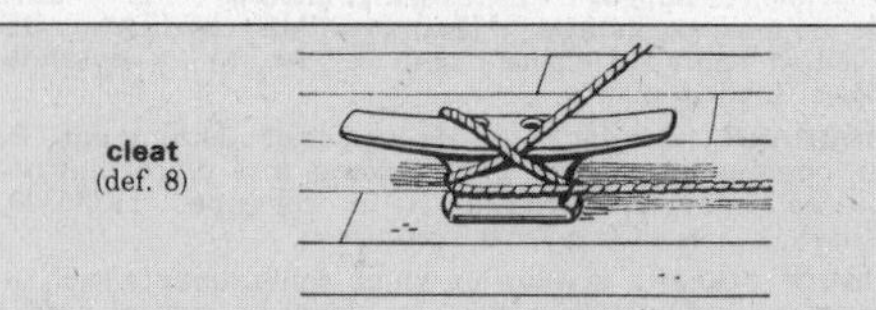
cleat (def. 8)

cleav•a•ble (klē′və bəl), *adj.* capable of being cleft or split. [1840–50; CLEAVE[2] + -ABLE] —**cleav′a•bil′i•ty,** *n.*

cleav•age (klē′vij), *n.* **1.** the act of cleaving or splitting. **2.** the state of being cleft. **3.** the area between a woman's breasts, esp. when revealed by a low-cut neckline. **4.** a critical division in opinion, beliefs, interests, etc., as leading to opposition between two groups: *a growing cleavage between the Conservative and Liberal wings of the party.* **5.** the tendency of crystals, certain minerals, rocks, etc., to break in preferred directions so as to yield more or less smooth surfaces (**cleav′age planes′**). **6.** *Embryol.* the total or partial division of the egg into smaller cells or blastomeres. **7.** Also called **scission.** *Chem.* the breaking down of a molecule or compound into simpler structures. [1810–20; CLEAVE[2] + -AGE]

cleave[1] (klēv), *v.i.,* **cleaved** or (*Archaic*) **clave; cleaved; cleav•ing. 1.** to adhere closely; stick; cling (usually fol. by *to*). **2.** to remain faithful (usually fol. by *to*): *to cleave to one's principles in spite of persecution.* [bef. 900; ME *cleven,* OE *cleofian,* c. OHG *klebēn* (G *kleben*)] —**cleav′ing•ly,** *adv.*

cleave[2] (klēv), *v.,* **cleft** or **cleaved** or **clove, cleft** or **cleaved** or **clo•ven, cleav•ing.** —*v.t.* **1.** to split or divide by or as if by a cutting blow, esp. along a natural line of division, as the grain of wood. **2.** to make by or as if by cutting: *to cleave a path through the wilderness.* **3.** to penetrate or pass through (air, water, etc.): *The bow of the boat cleaved the water cleanly.* **4.** to cut off; sever: *to cleave a branch from a tree.* —*v.i.* **5.** to part or split, esp. along a natural line of division. **6.** to penetrate or advance by or as if by cutting (usually fol. by *through*). [bef. 950; ME *cleven,* OE *clēofan,* c. OHG *klioban* (G *klieben*), ON *kljūfa;* akin to Gk *glyphein* to carve, L *glūbere* to peel]
—**Syn. 1.** halve, rend, rive.

cleav•er (klē′vər), *n.* **1.** a heavy, broad-bladed knife or long-bladed hatchet, esp. one used by butchers for cutting meat into joints or pieces. **2.** a person or thing that cleaves. [1325–75; ME *clevere.* See CLEAVE[2], -ER[1]]

cleav•ers (klē′vərz), *n., pl.* **-ers. 1.** a North American plant, *Galium aparine,* of the madder family, having short, hooked bristles on the stems and leaves and bearing very small white flowers. **2.** any of certain related species. Also, **clivers.** Also called **catchweed, goose grass.** [bef. 1000; ME *clivre,* OE *clife* burdock (*-re* prob. by assoc. with ME *clivres* (pl.) claws, or with the agent n. from *cleven* to CLEAVE[1], whence the modern sp.)]

Cle•burne (klē′bərn), *n.* a city in N Texas, near Fort Worth. 19,218.

cleek (klēk), *n., v.,* **claught** or **cleeked** or **claucht, cleeked, cleek•ing.** —*n.* **1.** *Chiefly Scot.* a large hook, esp. one fixed to the inside walls of a house to hold clothing, pots, or food. **2.** *Golf Older Use.* a club with an iron head, a narrow face, and little slope, used for shots from a poor lie on the fairway and sometimes for putting. —*v.t.* **3.** *Chiefly Scot.* to grasp or seize (something) suddenly and eagerly; snatch. [1350–1400; ME (Scots) *cleke* hook, deriv. of *cleke* to take hold of, var. of *cleche,* akin to CLUTCH[1]]

clef (klef), *n. Music.* a symbol placed upon a staff to indicate the name and pitch of the notes corresponding to its lines and spaces. Cf. **bass clef, treble clef, C clef.** [1570–80; < MF < L *clāvis* key]

clefs
A, treble clef (G clef); B, bass clef (F clef); C, alto clef

cleft[1] (kleft), *n.* **1.** a space or opening made by cleavage; a split. **2.** a division formed by cleaving. **3.** a hollow area or indentation: *a chin with a cleft.* **4.** *Vet. Pathol.* a crack on the bend of the pastern of a horse. [1300–50; ME *clift,* OE (*ge*)*clyft* split, cracked; c. OHG, ON *kluft;* akin to CLEAVE[2]]
—**Syn. 1.** fissure, crevice, crack, rift, cranny, chasm, crevasse.

cleft[2] (kleft), *v.* **1.** a pt. and pp. of **cleave**[2]. —*adj.* **2.** cloven; split; divided. **3.** (of a leaf, corolla, lobe, or other expanded plant part) having divisions formed by incisions or narrow sinuses that extend more than halfway to the midrib or the base. [see CLEFT[1]]

cleft′ lip′, harelip.

cleft′ pal′ate, a congenital defect of the palate in which a longitudinal fissure exists in the roof of the mouth. [1840–50]

cleft′ sen′tence, *Gram.* **1.** a sentence in which a simpler sentence is paraphrased by being divided into two parts, each with its own verb, in order to emphasize certain information, esp. a sentence beginning with expletive *it* and a form of *be* followed by the information being emphasized, as *It was a mushroom that Alice ate* instead of *Alice ate a mushroom.* **2.** Also called **pseudo-cleft sentence.** a two-part sentence in which a subject or subject complement expresses information being emphasized and an indefinite relative clause corresponds to the rest of a simpler sentence that has been paraphrased, as *A mushroom was what Alice ate* or *What Alice ate was a mushroom.*

clei•do•ic (klī dō′ik), *adj. Embryol.* isolated from the environment, as certain eggs enclosed within a shell or membrane. [1930–35; < Gk *kleido*(*ûn*) to lock up (v. deriv. of *kleís* (gen. *kleidós*) bolt, key) + -IC]

Cleis•the•nes (klīs′thə nēz′), *n.* active c515–c495 B.C., Athenian statesman. Also, **Clisthenes.**

cleisto-, a combining form meaning "closed," "capable of being closed," used in the formation of compound words: *cleistogamy; cleistothecium.* [comb. form repr. Gk *kleistós*]

cleis•to•carp (klī′stə kärp′), *n. Mycol.* cleistothecium. Also, **clistocarp.** [1880–85; CLEISTO- + -CARP]

cleis•to•car•pous (klī′stə kär′pəs), *adj.* **1.** *Mycol.* having cleistothecia. **2.** *Bot.* having a closed capsule, as certain mosses. Also, **clistocarpous.** [1885–90; CLEISTO- + -CARPOUS]

cleis•tog•a•mous (klī stog′ə məs), *adj. Bot.* pertaining to or having pollination occurring in unopened flowers. Also, **cleis•to•gam•ic** (klī′stə gam′ik). Cf. **chasmogamous.** [1880–85; CLEISTO- + -GAMOUS] —**cleis•tog′a•mous•ly, cleis′to•gam′i•cal•ly,** *adv.* —**cleis•tog′a•my,** *n.*

cleis•to•the•ci•um (klī′stə thē′shē əm, -sē əm), *n., pl.* **-ci•a** (-shē ə, -sē ə). (in certain ascomycetous fungi) a closed, globose ascocarp from which the ascospores are released only by its rupture or decay. Also, **clistothecium.** [CLEISTO- + THECIUM]

clem (klem), *v.t., v.i.,* **clemmed, clem•ming.** *Brit. Dial.* to starve. [1530–40; akin to ME *forclemmed* (ptp.) pinched with hunger, OE *beclemman* to fetter]

Clem (klem), *n.* a male given name, form of **Clement.**

clem•a•stine fu•ma•rate (klem′ə stēn′ fyo͞o′mə-rāt′), *Pharm.* an antihistamine, $C_{25}H_{30}ClNO_5$, that has drying and some sedative effects, used for symptomatic relief of allergy. [perh. a rearrangement of *meclastine* an alternate name, perh. ME(THYL) + C(H)L(ORO)- + *-astine,* alter. and shortening of ANTIHISTAMINE]

clem•a•tis (klem′ə tis, kli mat′is), *n.* any of numerous plants or woody vines of the genus *Clematis,* including many species cultivated for their showy, variously colored flowers. Cf. **traveler's-joy, virgin's-bower.** [1545–55; < L < Gk *klēmatís* name of several climbing plants]

Cle•men•ceau (klem′ən sō′; *Fr.* kle mäɴ sō′), *n.* **Georges Eu•gène Ben•ja•min** (jôrj yo͞o jēn′ ben′jə-min, yo͞o′jēn; *Fr.* zhôrzh œ zhen′ baɴ zhA maɴ′), ("*the Tiger*"), 1841–1929, French statesman, journalist, and editor: premier 1906–09, 1917–20.

clem•en•cy (klem′ən sē), *n., pl.* **-cies. 1.** the quality of being clement; disposition to show forbearance, compassion, or forgiveness in judging or punishing; leniency; mercy. **2.** an act or deed showing mercy or leniency. **3.** (of the weather) mildness or temperateness. [1375–1425; late ME (< AF) < L *clēmentia.* See CLEMENT, -CY]
—**Syn. 1.** forgivingness, gentleness, mercifulness. —**Ant. 1.** harshness. **3.** severity.

CONCISE ETYMOLOGY KEY: <, descended or borrowed from; >, whence; b., blend of, blended; c., cognate with; cf., compare; deriv., derivative; equiv., equivalent; imit., imitative; obl., oblique; r., replacing; s., stem; sp., spelling, spelled; resp., respelling, respelled; trans., translation; ?, origin unknown; *, unattested; ‡, probably earlier than. See the full key inside the front cover.

Clem•ens (klem′ənz), *n.* **Samuel Lang•horne** (lang′hôrn, -ərn), (*"Mark Twain"*), 1835–1910, U.S. author and humorist.

clem•ent (klem′ənt), *adj.* **1.** mild or merciful in disposition or character; lenient; compassionate: *A clement judge reduced his sentence.* **2.** (of the weather) mild or temperate; pleasant. [1425–75; late ME (< OF) < L *clēment-*, s. of *clēmēns* gentle, merciful] **—clem′ent•ly,** *adv.*

Clem•ent (klem′ənt), *n.* a male given name.

Clement I, Saint (*Clement of Rome*), A.D. c30–c100, first of the Apostolic Fathers: pope 88?–97?

Clement II, (*Suidger*) died 1047, pope 1046–47.

Clement III, (*Paolo Scolari*) died 1191, Italian ecclesiastic: pope 1187–91.

Clement IV, (*Guy Foulques*) died 1268, French ecclesiastic: pope 1265–68.

Clement V, (*Bertrand de Got*) 1264–1314, French ecclesiastic: pope 1305–14.

Clement VI, (*Pierre Roger*) 1291–1352, French ecclesiastic: pope 1342–52.

Clement VII, (*Giulio de' Medici*) 1478–1534, Italian ecclesiastic: pope 1523–34 (nephew of Lorenzo de' Medici).

Clement VIII, (*Ippolito Aldobrandini*) 1536–1605, Italian ecclesiastic: pope 1592–1605.

Clement IX, (*Giulio Rospigliosi*) 1600–69, Italian ecclesiastic: pope 1667–69.

Clement X, (*Emilio Altieri*) 1590–1676, Italian ecclesiastic: pope 1670–76.

Clement XI, (*Giovanni Francesco Albani*) 1649–1721, Italian ecclesiastic: pope 1700–21.

Clement XII, (*Lorenzo Corsini*) 1652–1740, Italian ecclesiastic: pope 1730–40.

Clement XIII, (*Carlo della Torre Rezzonico*) 1693–1769, Italian ecclesiastic: pope 1758–69.

Clement XIV, (*Giovanni Vincenzo Antonio Ganganelli* or *Lorenzo Ganganelli*) 1705–74, Italian ecclesiastic: pope 1769–74.

Cle•men•ti (klə men′tē; *It.* kle men′te), *n.* **Mu•zio** (mo͞o′tsyô), 1752–1832, Italian pianist and composer in England.

clem•en•tine (klem′ən tīn′, -tēn′), *n.* a small, sweet variety of tangerine with orange-red skin. [< F *clémentine* (1902), said to be named after a Father *Clément,* who developed the fruit near Oran; see -INE[1]]

Clem•en•tine (klem′ən tīn′, -tēn′; *Fr.* kle mäɴ tēn′), *n.* a female given name: derived from *Clement.* Also, **Clem•en•ti•na** (klem′ən tē′nə).

Clem′ent of Alexan′dria, A.D. c150–c215, Greek Christian theologian and writer.

clench (klench), *v.t.* **1.** to close (the hands, teeth, etc.) tightly. **2.** to grasp firmly; grip. **3.** clinch (def. 1). **4.** clinch (defs. 2–4). —*v.i.* **5.** to close or knot up tightly: *His hands clenched as he faced his enemy.* —*n.* **6.** the act of clenching. **7.** a tight hold; grip. **8.** something that clenches or holds fast. **9.** clinch (defs. 9, 11, 12). [1200–50; ME *clenchen*; cf. OE *beclencan* hold fast] **—Syn. 2.** clasp, clutch.

Cle•o (klē′ō), *n.* a female given name.

Cle•o•bu•lus (klē′ō byo͞o′ləs, klē′ə-, klē ob′yə ləs), *n.* fl. 560 B.C., Greek sage and lyric poet, a native and tyrant of Lindus, Rhodes.

cle•oid (klē′oid), *n. Dentistry.* a claw-shaped dental instrument used to remove carious material from a cavity. [< Gk *kle(ís)* catch, hook + -OID]

cle•o•me (klē ō′mē), *n.* any of numerous strong-smelling plants or shrubs belonging to the genus *Cleome,* of the caper family, mostly natives of tropical regions, and often bearing showy flowers. Also called **spider plant.** [< NL (Linnaeus), of uncert. orig.]

Cle•om•e•nes III (klē om′ə nēz′), died c220 B.C., king of Sparta c235–c220.

Cle•on (klē′on), *n.* died 422 B.C., Athenian general and political opponent of Pericles.

Cle•o•pa•tra (klē′ə pa′trə, -pä′-, -pā′-), *n.* **1.** 69–30 B.C., queen of Egypt 51–49, 48–30. **2.** a female given name: from Greek words meaning "fame" and "father."

Cle′opa′tra's Nee′dle, 1. an ancient Egyptian obelisk, now in Central Park, New York City. **2.** an ancient Egyptian obelisk, now on the Thames River embankment, in London.

clepe (klēp), *v.t.,* **cleped** or **clept** (also **y•cleped** or **y•clept**), **clep•ing.** *Archaic.* to call; name (now chiefly in the pp. as *ycleped* or *yclept*). [bef. 900; ME *clepen,* OE *cleopian,* var. of *clipian;* akin to MLG *kleperen* to rattle]

clep•sy•dra (klep′si drə), *n., pl.* **-dras, -drae** (-drē′). an ancient device for measuring time by the regulated flow of water or mercury through a small aperture. [1640–50; < L < Gk *klepsýdra,* equiv. to *kleps-* (*klep-,* s. of *kléptein* to steal, conceal + *-s-* formative in derivation) + *hydra,* deriv. of *hýdōr* water]

clept (klept), *v.* a pt. and pp. of **clepe.**

clep•to•bi•o•sis (klep′tō bī ō′sis), *n., pl.* **-ses** (-sēz). an ecological relationship in which members of one species, as of ants, steal food from another. [< Gk *klépt(ein)* to steal + *-o-* + -BIOSIS] **—clep•to•bi•ot•ic** (klep′tō bī ot′ik), *adj.*

clep•to•ma•ni•a (klep′tə mā′nē ə, -mān′yə), *n. Psychol.* kleptomania. [< Gk *klépt(ein)* to steal + *-o-* + -MANIA] **—clep′to•ma′ni•ac′,** *n.*

Clerc (kleʀ), *n.* **Lau•rent** (lō ʀäɴ′), 1785–1869, French educator of the deaf, in the U.S. after 1816.

clere•sto•ry (klēr′stôr′ē, -stōr′ē), *n., pl.* **-ries. 1.** *Archit.* a portion of an interior rising above adjacent rooftops and having windows admitting daylight to the interior. **2.** a raised construction, as on the roof of a railroad car, having windows or slits for admitting light or air. Also, **clearstory.** [1375–1425; late ME, equiv. to *clere* CLEAR + *story* STORY[2]] **—clere′sto′ried,** *adj.*

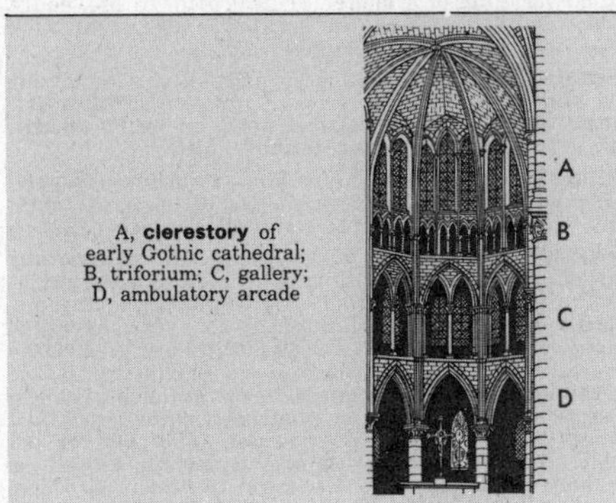

A, **clerestory** of early Gothic cathedral; B, triforium; C, gallery; D, ambulatory arcade

cler•gy (klûr′jē), *n., pl.* **-gies.** the group or body of ordained persons in a religion, as distinguished from the laity. [1175–1225; ME *clerge, clergie* < OF *clergé* (< LL *clericātus* office of a priest; see CLERIC, -ATE[3]), *clergie,* equiv. to *clerc* CLERIC + *-ie* -Y[3], with *-g-* after *clergé*] **—cler′gy•like′,** *adj.*
—Usage. See **collective noun.**

cler•gy•man (klûr′jē mən), *n., pl.* **-men. 1.** a member of the clergy. **2.** an ordained Christian minister. [1570–80; CLERGY + -MAN]

cler•gy•per•son (klûr′jē pûr′sən), *n.* **1.** a member of the clergy. **2.** an ordained Christian minister. [CLERGY(MAN) + -PERSON]
—Usage. See **-person.**

cler•gy•wom•an (klûr′jē wo͝om′ən), *n., pl.* **-wom•en. 1.** a female member of the clergy. **2.** a woman who is an ordained Christian minister. [CLERGY(MAN) + -WOMAN]

cler•ic (kler′ik), *n.* **1.** a member of the clergy. **2.** a member of a clerical party. **3. clerics,** (*used with a plural v.*) half-sized or small-sized reading glasses worn on the nose, usually rimless or with a thin metal frame. —*adj.* **4.** pertaining to the clergy; clerical. [1615–25; < LL *clēricus* priest < Gk *klērikós,* equiv. to *klêr(os)* lot, allotment + *-ikos* -IC]

cler•i•cal (kler′i kəl), *adj.* **1.** of, pertaining to, appropriate for, or assigned to an office clerk or clerks: *a clerical job.* **2.** doing the work of a clerk or clerks: *a clerical assistant; a clerical staff.* **3.** of, pertaining to, or characteristic of the clergy or a member of the clergy: *clerical garb.* **4.** advocating the power or influence of the clergy in politics, government, etc.: *a clerical party.* —*n.* **5.** a cleric. **6. clericals,** *Informal.* clerical garments. **7.** a person or a party advocating the power or influence of the church in politics, government, etc. **8.** a person who does clerical work; office worker; clerk. **9.** Also called **cler′ical er′ror.** a minor error, as in the keeping of records, the transcribing of documents, or the handling of correspondence. [1425–75 for sense "learned"; 1585–95 for def. 3; late ME < LL *clēricālis,* equiv. to *clēric(us)* CLERIC + *-ālis* -AL[1]] **—cler′i•cal′i•ty,** *n.* **—cler′i•cal•ly,** *adv.*

cler′ical col′lar, a stiff, narrow, bandlike white collar fastened at the back of the neck, worn by certain clerics. Also called **reversed collar, Roman collar.** [1945–50]

cler•i•cal•ism (kler′i kə liz′əm), *n.* **1.** clerical principles. **2.** clerical power or influence in government, politics, etc. (distinguished from *laicism*). **3.** support of such power or influence. [1860–65; CLERICAL + -ISM] **—cler′i•cal•ist,** *n.*

cler•i•hew (kler′ə hyo͞o′), *n. Pros.* a light verse form, usually consisting of two couplets, with lines of uneven length and irregular meter, the first line usually containing the name of a well-known person. [1925–30; named after E. *Clerihew* Bentley (1875–1956), English writer, its inventor]

cler•i•sy (kler′ə sē), *n.* learned persons as a class; literati; intelligentsia. [1818; < G *Klerisei* clergy < ML *clēricia,* equiv. to *clēric(us)* CLERIC + *-ia* -IA; introduced by S.T. Coleridge]

clerk (klûrk; *Brit.* klärk), *n.* **1.** a person employed, as in an office, to keep records, file, type, or perform other general office tasks. **2.** a salesclerk. **3.** a person who keeps the records and performs the routine business of a court, legislature, board, etc. **4.** a member of the clergy; ecclesiastic. **5.** a lay person charged with various minor ecclesiastical duties. **6.** *Archaic.* **a.** a person who is able to read, or to read and write. **b.** a scholar. —*v.i.* **7.** to act or serve as a clerk. [bef. 1000; ME, OE *clerc,* var. of *cleric* < LL *clēricus* CLERIC] **—clerk′ish,** *adj.* **—clerk′like′,** *adj.* **—clerk′ship,** *n.*

clerk•ly (klûrk′lē; *Brit.* klärk′lē), *adj.,* **-li•er, -li•est,** *adv.* —*adj.* **1.** of, pertaining to, or characteristic of a clerk. **2.** *Archaic.* scholarly. —*adv.* **3.** in the manner of a clerk. [1400–50; late ME *clerkli.* See CLERK, -LY] **—clerk′li•ness,** *n.*

clerk′ vic′ar. See **lay vicar.**

Cler•mont-Fer•rand (kleʀ môɴ fe ʀäɴ′), *n.* a city in and the capital of Puy-de-Dôme, in central France. 161,203.

cle•ro•den•drum (klēr′ə den′drəm, kler′-), *n.* any of numerous tropical trees or shrubs of the genus *Clerodendrum,* having clusters of variously colored flowers. Also, **cle•ro•den•dron** (klēr′ə den′drən, kler′-). [< NL (Linnaeus), equiv. to Gk *klēro-* (comb. form of *klêros* lot, chance) + *déndron* tree; allegedly so named in reference to the varying uses of its species, some being medicinal, some poisonous]

cle•ro•man•cy (klēr′ə man′sē, kler′-), *n.* the casting of lots as a means of divination. [1600–10; < ML *clēromantia,* equiv. to Gk *klêro(s)* lot + *manteía* -MANCY]

Cle•tus (klē′təs), *n.* **1.** Anacletus. **2.** a male given name.

Cle•ve (klā′və *for 1;* klēv *for 2*), *n.* **1. Per Te•o•dor** (paʀ tā′ô dôʀ′), 1840–1905, Swedish chemist. **2.** a male given name.

Cleve•land (klēv′lənd), *n.* **1. (Stephen) Gro•ver** (grō′vər), 1837–1908, 22nd and 24th president of the U.S. 1885–89, 1893–97. **2.** a port in NE Ohio, on Lake Erie. 573,822. **3.** a county in N England. 565,400; 225 sq. mi. (583 sq. km). **4.** a city in SE Tennessee. 26,415. **5.** a city in NW Mississippi. 14,524. **6.** a male given name.

Cleve′land Heights′, a city in NE Ohio, near Cleveland. 56,438.

clev•er (klev′ər), *adj.,* **-er, -est. 1.** mentally bright; having sharp or quick intelligence; able. **2.** superficially skillful, witty, or original in character or construction; facile: *It was an amusing, clever play, but of no lasting value.* **3.** showing inventiveness or originality; ingenious: *His clever device was the first to solve the problem.* **4.** adroit with the hands or body; dexterous or nimble. **5.** *Older Use.* **a.** suitable; convenient; satisfactory. **b.** good-natured. **c.** handsome. **d.** in good health. [1175–1225; ME *cliver,* akin to OE *clifer* claw, *clife* burdock. See CLEAVERS] **—clev′er•ish,** *adj.* **—clev′er•ish•ly,** *adv.* **—clev′er•ly,** *adv.* **—clev′er•ness,** *n.*
—Syn. 1. ingenious, talented, quick-witted; smart, gifted; apt, expert. **4.** skillful, agile, handy. **—Ant. 1.** stupid. **4.** clumsy.

Cleves (klēvz), *n.* a city in W North Rhine-Westphalia, in W West Germany. 43,447. German, **Kleve.**

clev•is (klev′is), *n.* a U-shaped yoke at the end of a chain or rod, between the ends of which a lever, hook, etc., can be pinned or bolted. [1585–95; akin to CLEAVE[2]]

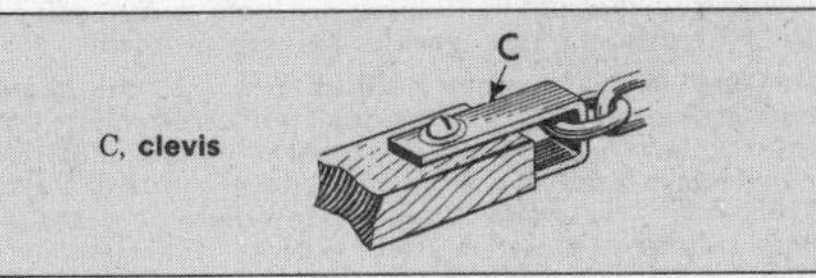

C, **clevis**

clew (klo͞o), *n.* **1.** clue (def. 1). **2.** *Naut.* either lower corner of a square sail or the after lower corner of a fore-and-aft sail. See diag. under **sail. 3.** a ball or skein of thread, yarn, etc. **4.** Usually, **clews.** the rigging for a hammock. **5.** *Theat.* a metal device holding scenery lines controlled by one weighted line. **6.** *Class. Myth.* the thread by which Theseus found his way out of the labyrinth. **7. spread a large clew,** *Naut.* **a.** to carry a large amount of sail. **b.** to present an impressive appearance. —*v.t.* **8.** to coil into a ball. **9.** clue (def. 3). **10.** *Theat.* **a.** to draw up the bottom edge of (a curtain, drop, etc.) and fold out of view; bag. **b.** to secure (lines) with a clew. **11. clew down,** *Naut.* to secure (a sail) in an unfurled position. **12. clew up,** *Naut.* to haul (the lower corners of a square-rig sail) up to the yard by means of the clew lines. [bef. 900; ME *clewe,* OE *cleowen, cliewen,* equiv. to *cliew-* (c. OHG *kliu* ball) + *-en* -EN[5]; akin to D *kluwen*]

Cli•burn (klī′bərn), *n.* **Van** (van), (*Harvey Lavan Cliburn, Jr.*), born 1934, U.S. pianist.

cli•ché (klē shā′, kli-), *n.* **1.** a trite, stereotyped expression; a sentence or phrase, usually expressing a popular or common thought or idea, that has lost originality, ingenuity, and impact by long overuse, as *sadder but wiser,* or *strong as an ox.* **2.** (in art, literature, drama, etc.) a trite or hackneyed plot, character development, use of color, musical expression, etc. **3.** anything that has become trite or commonplace through overuse. **4.** *Print. Brit.* **a.** a stereotype or electrotype plate. **b.** a reproduction made in a like manner. —*adj.* **5.** trite; hackneyed; stereotyped; clichéd. Also, **cli•che′.** [1825–35; < F: stereotype plate, stencil, cliché, n. use of ptp. of *clicher* to make such a plate, said to be imit. of the sound of the metal pressed against the matrix]
—Syn. 1. platitude, bromide, stereotype, commonplace.

cli•chéd (klē shād′, kli-), *adj.* **1.** full of or characterized by clichés: *a clichéd, boring speech.* **2.** representing or expressing a cliché or stereotype; trite; hackneyed; commonplace: *the old clichéd argument that girls are more affectionate than boys.* [1925–30; CLICHÉ + -ED[3]]

Cli•chy (klē shē′), *n.* an industrial suburb of Paris, France, on the Seine. 47,956.

click[1] (klik), *n.* **1.** a slight, sharp sound: *At the click of the latch, the dog barked.* **2.** a small device for preventing backward movement of a mechanism, as a detent or pawl. **3.** *Phonet.* any one of a variety of ingressive, usually implosive, speech sounds, phonemic in some languages, produced by suction occlusion and plosive or affricative release. **4.** any one of a variety of familiar sounds used in calling or urging on horses or other animals, in expressing reprimand or sympathy, or produced in audible kissing. —*v.i.* **5.** to emit or make a slight, sharp sound, or series of such sounds, as by the cocking of a pistol: *The door clicked shut.* **6.** *Informal.* **a.** to succeed; make a hit: *If the play clicks, the producer will be rich.* **b.** to fit together; function well together: *They get along in public, but their personalities don't really click.* **c.** to become intelligible. **7.** *Computers.* to depress

CONCISE PRONUNCIATION KEY: act, cāpe, dâre, pärt; set, ēqual; if, īce; ox, ōver, ôrder, oil, bo͝ok, bo͞ot, out; up, ûrge; child; sing; shoe; thin, *th*at; zh as in *treasure.* ə = *a* as in *alone, e* as in *system, i* as in *easily, o* as in *gallop, u* as in *circus;* ᵊ as in *fire* (fīᵊr), *hour* (ouᵊr). l and n can serve as syllabic consonants, as in *cradle* (krād′l), and *button* (but′n). See the full key inside the front cover.

and release a mouse button rapidly, as to select an icon. —*v.t.* **8.** to cause to click. **9.** to strike together with a click: *He clicked his heels and saluted.* [1575–85; perh. imit., but perh. < D *klick* (n.), *klikken* (v.)] —**click′er,** *n.* —**click′less,** *adj.*

click[2] (klik), *n. Slang.* a kilometer. Also, **klick, klik.** [‡1970–75; prob. special use of CLICK[1], but sense development unclear]

click′ bee′tle, any of numerous beetles of the family Elateridae, having the ability to spring up with a clicking sound when placed on their backs. Also called **skipjack, snapping beetle.** [1860–65]

click•e•ty-clack (klik′i tē klak′), *n.* a rhythmic, swiftly paced succession of alternating clicks and clacks, as the sound produced by the wheels of a train moving over tracks. Also called **click•e•ty-click** (klik′i tē klik′). [1875–80; metrical compound from CLICK[1], CLACK]

click′ stop′, a control device, as in a camera, that can be turned or rotated so that when it reaches a specific setting it engages with an audible click. [1945–50]

cli•ent (klī′ənt), *n.* **1.** a person or group that uses the professional advice or services of a lawyer, accountant, advertising agency, architect, etc. **2.** a person who is receiving the benefits, services, etc., of a social welfare agency, a government bureau, etc. **3.** a customer. **4.** anyone under the patronage of another; a dependent. **5.** See **client state. 6.** (in ancient Rome) a plebeian who lived under the patronage of a patrician. —*adj.* **7.** being a regular customer: *a client company.* **8.** economically, and often militarily, dependent upon a more prosperous, more powerful nation. [1350–1400; ME < L *client-*, s. of *cliēns* person seeking the protection or influence of someone powerful; perh. akin to *clīnāre* to bend (see INCLINE)] —**cli•en•tal** (klī en′tl, klī′ən tl), *adj.*

cli•ent•age (klī′ən tij), *n.* **1.** a body of clients; clientele. **2.** Also, **cli′ent•hood′.** the relationship of a client to a patron; dependency. [1625–35; CLIENT + -AGE]

cli′ent-cen•tered ther′apy (klī′ənt sen′tərd), *Psychol.* a nondirective method of psychotherapy in which treatment consists of helping patients to use effectively their own latent resources in solving problems.

cli•en•tele (klī′ən tel′, klē′än-), *n.* **1.** the clients or customers, as of a professional person or shop, considered collectively; a group or body of clients: *This jewelry store has a wealthy clientele.* **2.** dependents or followers. [1555–65; < L *clientēla*, equiv. to *client-* (see CLIENT) + *-ēla* collective n. suffix; (def. 1) prob. < F *clientèle* < L]

cli′ent state′, a country that is dependent on a larger and more powerful country for its political, economic, or military welfare. [1915–20]

cliff (klif), *n.* a high steep face of a rock. [bef. 900; ME *clif*, OE, c. D, LG, ON *klif*] —**cliff′like′,** *adj.*
—**Syn.** bluff, promontory, ledge, crag.

Cliff (klif), *n.* a male given name, form of **Clifford.**

cliff′ brake′, any of several common ferns of the genus *Pellaea*, usually growing in pockets of thin soil on rocks. [1865–70, *Amer.*]

cliff′ dwell′er, 1. (*usually cap.*) a member of a prehistoric people of the southwestern U.S., who were ancestors of the Pueblo Indians and built shelters in caves or on the ledges of cliffs. **2.** a person who lives in an apartment house, esp. in a large city. [1880–85, *Amer.*] —**cliff′ dwell′ing.**

cliff-hang (klif′hang′), *v.i.*, **-hung, -hang•ing.** *Informal.* to wait eagerly for the outcome of a suspenseful situation or contest. Also, **cliff′hang′.** [1935–40]

cliff-hang•er (klif′hang′ər), *n.* **1.** a melodramatic adventure serial in which each installment ends in suspense in order to interest the reader or viewer in the next installment. **2.** a situation or contest of which the outcome is suspensefully uncertain up to the very last moment: *The game was a cliff-hanger, but our team finally won.* Also, **cliff′hang′er.** [1935–40, *Amer.*]

cliff-hang•ing (klif′hang′ing), *adj.* of, pertaining to, or characteristic of a cliff-hanger: *a cliff-hanging vote of 20–19.* Also, **cliff′hang′ing.** [1935–40, *Amer.*]

Clif•ford (klif′ərd), *n.* **1. William King•don** (king′dən), 1845–79, English mathematician and philosopher. **2.** a male given name.

Clif′ford trust′, *Law.* a type of living trust set up for at least a 10-year period, during which the income goes to a beneficiary and after which the principal reverts to the grantor. [after George B. *Clifford*, plaintiff in a suit against the Internal Revenue Service in 1940; regulations resulting from the suit defined the trust]

Cliff′side Park′ (klif′sīd′), a city in NE New Jersey. 21,464.

cliff′ swal′low, any of several North American birds of the genus *Hirundo*, esp. *H. pyrrhonota*, that live colonially and build bottle-shaped mud nests on cliffs and walls. [1815–25, *Amer.*]

cliff•y (klif′ē), *adj.*, **cliff•i•er, cliff•i•est.** abounding in or formed by cliffs: *a cliffy shoreline.* [1530–40; CLIFF + -Y[1]]

clift (klift), *n. South Midland U.S.* cliff. [1350–1400; ME, alter. of CLIFF (perh. by influence of CLEFT[1])]

Clif•ton (klif′tən), *n.* **1.** a city in NE New Jersey. 74,388. **2.** a male given name.

cli•mac•ter•ic (klī mak′tər ik, klī′mak ter′ik), *n.* **1.** *Physiol.* a period of decrease of reproductive capacity in men and women, culminating, in women, in the menopause. **2.** any critical period. **3.** a year in which important changes in health, fortune, etc., are held by some theories to occur, as one's sixty-third year **(grand climacteric). 4.** the period of maximum respiration in a fruit, during which it becomes fully ripened. —*adj.* **5.** Also, **cli•mac•ter•i•cal** (klī′mak ter′i kəl). critical; crucial. [1595–1605; < L *clīmactēricus* < Gk *klimaktērikós* (*klīmaktḗr* rung of a ladder, critical point in life, equiv. to *klīmak-*, s. of *klîmax* (see CLIMAX) + *-tēr* n. suffix) + *-ikos* -IC] —**cli′mac•ter′i•cal•ly,** *adv.*

CONCISE ETYMOLOGY KEY: <, descended or borrowed from; >, whence; b., blend of, blended; c., cognate with; cf., compare; deriv., derivative; equiv., equivalent; imit., imitative; obl., oblique; r., replacing; s., stem; sp., spelling, spelled; resp., respelling, respelled; trans., translation; ?, origin unknown; *, unattested; ‡, probably earlier than. See the full key inside the front cover.

cli•mac•tic (klī mak′tik), *adj.* pertaining to or coming to a climax: *the climactic scene of a play.* Also, **cli•mac′ti•cal.** [1870–75; from CLIMAX, perh. on model of SYNTAX, SYNTACTIC] —**cli•mac′ti•cal•ly,** *adv.*

cli•mant (klī′mənt), *adj. Heraldry.* rampant, as a goat: *a goat climant.* [modeled on, or partial trans. of, *rampant* (< F, prp. of *ramper* to climb). See CLIMB, -ANT]

cli•mate (klī′mit), *n.* **1.** the composite or generally prevailing weather conditions of a region, as temperature, air pressure, humidity, precipitation, sunshine, cloudiness, and winds, throughout the year, averaged over a series of years. **2.** a region or area characterized by a given climate: *to move to a warm climate.* **3.** the prevailing attitudes, standards, or environmental conditions of a group, period, or place: *a climate of political unrest.* [1350–1400 for earlier senses; 1595–1605 for def. 2; ME *climat* < L *clīmat-* (s. of *clīma*) < Gk *klímat-*, s. of *klíma* slope, equiv. to *kli-* (akin to *klī́nein* to slope, lean) + *-ma* n. suffix]
—**Syn. 3.** mood, atmosphere, spirit, tone, temper.

cli′mate control′, a thermostat for controlling a heating or air-conditioning system. —**cli′mate-controlled′,** *adj.*

cli•mat•ic (klī mat′ik), *adj.* **1.** of or pertaining to climate. **2.** (of ecological phenomena) due to climate rather than to soil or topography. Also, **cli•mat′i•cal, cli•mat•al** (klī′mi tl). [1820–30; CLIMATE + -IC] —**cli•mat′i•cal•ly,** *adv.*

cli•ma•tize (klī′mə tīz′), *v.t.* **-tized, -tiz•ing. 1.** to acclimate to a new environment. **2.** to prepare or modify (a building, vehicle, etc.) for use or comfort in a specific climate, esp. one that includes extreme cold or extreme heat: *to climatize a house by adding insulation and storm windows.* Also, *esp. Brit.*, **cli′ma•tise′.** [1820–30; CLIMATE + -IZE] —**cli′ma•ti•za′tion,** *n.*

cli•ma•tol•o•gy (klī′mə tol′ə jē), *n.* the science that deals with the phenomena of climates or climatic conditions. [1835–45; CLIMATE + -O- + -LOGY] —**cli•ma•to•log•ic** (klī′mə tl oj′ik), **cli′ma•to•log′i•cal,** *adj.* —**cli′ma•to•log′i•cal•ly,** *adv.* —**cli′ma•tol′o•gist,** *n.*

cli•max (klī′maks), *n.* **1.** the highest or most intense point in the development or resolution of something; culmination: *His career reached its climax when he was elected president.* **2.** (in a dramatic or literary work) a decisive moment that is of maximum intensity or is a major turning point in a plot. **3.** *Rhet.* **a.** a figure consisting of a series of related ideas so arranged that each surpasses the preceding in force or intensity. **b.** the last term or member of this figure. **4.** an orgasm. **5.** *Ecol.* the stable and self-perpetuating end stage in the ecological succession or evolution of a plant and animal community. —*v.t., v.i.* **6.** to bring to or reach a climax. [1580–90; < LL < Gk *klîmax* ladder, akin to *klī́nein* to lean]
—**Syn. 1.** summit, zenith, acme, apex.

climb (klīm), *v.i.* **1.** to go up or ascend, esp. by using the hands and feet or feet only: *to climb up a ladder.* **2.** to rise slowly by or as if by continued effort: *The car laboriously climbed to the top of the mountain.* **3.** to ascend or rise: *The plane climbed rapidly and we were soon at 35,000 feet. Temperatures climbed into the 80's yesterday.* **4.** to slope upward: *The road climbs steeply up to the house.* **5.** to ascend by twining or by means of tendrils, adhesive tissues, etc., as a plant: *The ivy climbed to the roof.* **6.** to proceed or move by using the hands and feet, esp. on an elevated place; crawl: *to climb along a branch; to climb around on the roof.* **7.** to ascend in prominence, fortune, etc.: *From lowly beginnings he climbed to the highest office in the land.* —*v.t.* **8.** to ascend, go up, or get to the top of, esp. by the use of the hands and feet or feet alone or by continuous or strenuous effort: *to climb a rope; to climb the stairs; to climb a mountain.* **9.** to go to the top of and over: *The prisoners climbed the wall and escaped.* **10. climb down, a.** to descend, esp. by using both hands and feet. **b.** to retreat, as from an indefensible opinion or position: *He was forced to climb down from his untenable position.* **11. climb the walls.** See **wall** (def. 7). —*n.* **12.** a climbing; an ascent by climbing: *It was a long climb to the top of the hill.* **13.** a place to be climbed: *That peak is quite a climb.* [bef. 1000; ME *climben*, OE *climban;* c. D, G *klimmen;* akin to CLAMBER] —**climb′a•ble,** *adj.*
—**Syn. 8.** CLIMB, ASCEND, MOUNT, SCALE imply a moving upward. To CLIMB is to make one's way upward, often with effort: *to climb a mountain.* ASCEND, in its literal meaning ("to go up"), is general, but it now usually suggests a gradual or stately movement, with or without effort, often to a considerable degree of altitude: *to ascend the heights; to ascend the Himalayas.* MOUNT may be interchangeable with ASCEND, but also suggests climbing on top of or astride of: *to mount a platform, a horse.* SCALE, a more literary word, implies difficult or hazardous climbing up or over something: *to scale a summit.* —**Ant. 1, 8.** descend. **12.** descent.

climb-down (klīm′doun′), *n.* a retreat, as from an indefensible opinion or position. [1885–90; n. use of v. phrase *climb down*]

climb•er (klī′mər), *n.* **1.** a person or thing that climbs. **2.** a climbing plant. **3.** See **social climber. 4.** a device to assist in climbing, as a climbing iron. [1375–1425; late ME; see CLIMB, -ER[1]]

climb′ in′dicator, *Aeron.* an instrument that shows the rate of ascent or descent of an aircraft, operating on a differential pressure principle. [1935–40]

climb′ing bit′tersweet, bittersweet (def. 4).

climb′ing fern′, any of several chiefly tropical, vinelike ferns of the genus *Lygodium*, having climbing or trailing stems. [1810–20, *Amer.*]

climb•ing•fish (klī′ming fish′), *n., pl.* **-fish•es,** (*esp. collectively*) **-fish.** See **climbing perch.** [CLIMBING + FISH]

climb′ing hydran′gea, a woody vine, *Hydrangea anomala*, of eastern Asia, having shiny, egg-shaped leaves and flat-topped white flower clusters, and climbing by aerial rootlets.

climb′ing i′ron, one of a pair of spiked iron frames, strapped to the shoe, leg, or knee, to help in climbing trees, telephone poles, etc. Also called **climb′ing spur′, spur.** [1855–60]

climb′ing lil′y. See **gloriosa lily.**

climb′ing perch′, a brown labyrinth fish, *Anabas testudineus*, of southeastern Asia and the Malay Archipelago, having a specialized breathing apparatus that enables it to leave the water and move about on land. [1870–75]

climb′ing rose′, any of various roses that ascend and cover a trellis, arbor, etc., chiefly by twining about the supports. [1830–40]

clime (klīm), *n.* climate. [1535–45; < L *clima;* see CLIMATE]

clin., clinical.

cli•nan•dri•um (kli nan′drē əm), *n., pl.* **-dri•a** (-drē ə). a cavity in the apex of the column in orchids, in which the anthers rest; the androclinium. [1860–65; < NL; see ANDROCLINIUM]

clinch (klinch), *v.t.* **1.** to settle (a matter) decisively: *After they clinched the deal they went out to celebrate.* **2.** to secure (a nail, screw, etc.) in position by beating down the protruding point: *He drove the nails through the board and clinched the points flat with a hammer.* **3.** to fasten (objects) together by nails, screws, etc., secured in this manner. **4.** *Naut.* to fasten by a clinch. —*v.i.* **5.** *Boxing.* to engage in a clinch: *The boxers clinched and were separated by the referee.* **6.** *Slang.* to embrace, esp. passionately. **7.** (of a clinched nail, screw, etc.) to hold fast; be secure. —*n.* **8.** the act of clinching. **9.** *Boxing.* an act or instance of one or both boxers holding the other about the arms or body in order to prevent or hinder the opponent's punches. **10.** *Slang.* a passionate embrace. **11.** a clinched nail or fastening. **12.** the bent part of a clinched nail, screw, etc. **13.** a knot or bend in which a bight or eye is made by making a loop or turn in the rope and seizing the end to the standing part. **14.** *Archaic.* a pun. Also, **clench** (for defs. 1–4, 9, 11, 12). [1560–70; later var. of ME CLENCH] —**clinch′ing•ly,** *adv.*
—**Syn. 1.** cinch, secure, close, conclude, confirm.

clinch•er (klin′chər), *n.* **1.** a person or thing that clinches. **2.** a statement, argument, fact, situation, or the like, that is decisive or conclusive: *The heat was the clincher that made us decide to leave the city.* **3.** a nail, screw, etc., for clinching. **4.** *Auto.* a clincher tire. [1485–95; var. of ME *clencher* (CLENCH + -ER[1])]

clinch•er-built (klin′chər bilt′), *adj. Shipbuilding.* clinker-built (def. 2). [1760–70]

clinch′er tire′, *Auto.* an automobile tire having on each side of its inner circumference a rubber flange that fits under the turned-over edge of the wheel rim.

clin•da•my•cin (klin′də mī′sin), *n. Pharm.* a toxic semisynthetic antibiotic, $C_{18}H_{33}ClN_2O_5S$, used to treat serious infections chiefly due to various anaerobic bacteria, esp. *Bacteroides.* [1965–70; by contr. and rearrangement of *chloro-deoxylincomycin* an alternate name, equiv. to CHLORO-[2] + DEOXY- + *lincomycin* an antibiotic produced by *Streptomyces lincolnensis;* see -MYCIN]

cline (klīn), *n.* **1.** *Biol.* the gradual change in certain characteristics exhibited by members of a series of adjacent populations of organisms of the same species. **2.** *Ling.* (in systemic linguistics) a scale of continuous gradation; continuum. [1935–40; < Gk *klī́nein* to LEAN[1]] —**clin′al,** *adj.* —**clin′al•ly,** *adv.*

cling[1] (kling), *v.,* **clung, cling•ing,** *n.* —*v.i.* **1.** to adhere closely; stick to: *The wet paper clings to the glass.* **2.** to hold tight, as by grasping or embracing; cleave: *The children clung to each other in the dark.* **3.** to be or remain close: *The child clung to her mother's side.* **4.** to remain attached, as to an idea, hope, memory, etc.: *Despite the predictions, the candidate clung to the belief that he would be elected.* **5.** to cohere. —*n.* **6.** the act of clinging; adherence; attachment. [bef. 900; ME *clingen*, OE *clingan* to stick together, shrink, wither; akin to CLENCH] —**cling′er,** *n.* —**cling′ing•ly,** *adv.* —**cling′ing•ness,** *n.*
—**Syn. 2.** clutch, grab, hug.

cling[2] (kling), *n.* a clingstone. [1835–45; by shortening from *clingstone*, or special use of CLING[1] (n.)]

cling•fish (kling′fish′), *n., pl.* (*esp. collectively*) **-fish,** (*esp. referring to two or more kinds or species*) **-fish•es.** any fish of the family Gobiesocidae, having a sucking disk on the abdomen for clinging to stones, debris, etc. [1890–95; CLING[1] + FISH]

cling′ing vine′, *Informal.* a person who behaves in a helpless and dependent manner in relationships with others. [1960–65, *Amer.*]

Cling′mans Dome′ (kling′mənz), a mountain on the border between North Carolina and Tennessee: the highest peak in the Great Smoky Mountains. 6642 ft. (2024 m).

cling′ peach′, a clingstone peach. [1870–75, *Amer.*]

cling•stone (kling′stōn′), *adj.* **1.** having a pit to which the pulp adheres closely, as certain peaches and plums. —*n.* **2.** a clingstone peach. [1695–1705, *Amer;* CLING[1] + STONE]

cling•y (kling′ē), *adj.*, **cling•i•er, cling•i•est.** apt to cling; adhesive or tenacious: *a clingy fabric.* [1700–10; CLING[1] + -Y[1]] —**cling′i•ness,** *n.*

clin•ic (klin′ik), *n.* **1.** a place, as in connection with a medical school or a hospital, for the treatment of nonresident patients, sometimes at low cost or without charge.

2. a group of physicians, dentists, or the like, working in cooperation and sharing the same facilities. **3.** a class or group convening for instruction or remedial work or for the diagnosis and treatment of specific problems: *a reading clinic; a speech clinic; a summer baseball clinic for promising young players.* **4.** the instruction of medical students by examining or treating patients in their presence or by their examining or treating patients under supervision. **5.** a class of students assembled for such instruction. **6.** *Sports Slang.* a performance so thoroughly superior by a team or player as to be a virtual model or demonstration of excellence; rout or mismatch. **—adj. 7.** of a clinic; clinical. [1620–30; 1885–90 for def. 1; < L *clinicus* < Gk *klinikós* pertaining to a (sick) bed, equiv. to *klín(ē)* bed + *-ikos* -IC]

clin·i·cal (klin′i kəl), *adj.* **1.** pertaining to a clinic. **2.** concerned with or based on actual observation and treatment of disease in patients rather than experimentation or theory. **3.** extremely objective and realistic; dispassionately analytic; unemotionally critical: *She regarded him with clinical detachment.* **4.** pertaining to or used in a sickroom: *a clinical bandage.* **5.** *Eccles.* **a.** (of a sacrament) administered on a deathbed or sickbed. **b.** (of a convert or conversion) made on a deathbed or sickbed. [1770–80; CLINIC + -AL[1]] **—clin′i·cal·ly,** *adv.*

clin′ical depres′sion, *Psychiatry.* a depression so severe as to be considered abnormal, either because of no obvious environmental causes, or because the reaction to unfortunate life circumstances is more intense or prolonged than would generally be expected.

clin′ical pathol′ogy, the branch of pathology dealing with the study of disease and disease processes by means of chemical, microscopic, and serologic examinations.

clin′ical psychol′ogy, the branch of psychology dealing with the diagnosis and treatment of personality and behavioral disorders. **—clin′ical psychol′ogist.**

clin′ical thermom′eter, a small thermometer used to measure body temperature. [1875–80]

cli·ni·cian (kli nish′ən), *n.* **1.** a physician or other qualified person who is involved in the treatment and observation of living patients, as distinguished from one engaged in research. **2.** a person who teaches or conducts sessions at a clinic. [1870–75; CLINIC + -IAN]

clin·i·co·path·o·log·ic (klin′i kō path′ə loj′ik), *adj. Med.* of or relating to the combined study of disease symptoms and pathology. Also, **clin′i·co·path′o·log′i·cal.** [1895–1900; CLINIC + -O- + PATHOLOGIC] **—clin′i·co·path′o·log′i·cal·ly,** *adv.* **—clin·i·co·pa·thol·o·gy** (klin′i kō pə thol′ə jē), *n.*

clin·id (klin′id), *n.* **1.** any of the blennioid fishes of the family Clinidae, of tropical and subtropical seas. **—adj. 2.** belonging or pertaining to the family Clinidae. [< NL *Clinidae,* equiv. to *Clin(us)* genus name (of uncert. orig.) + *-idae* -ID[2]]

clink[1] (klingk), *v.t., v.i.* **1.** to make or cause to make a light, sharp, ringing sound: *The coins clinked together. He clinked the fork against a glass.* **—n. 2.** a clinking sound. **3.** *Metall.* a small crack in a steel ingot resulting from uneven expanding or contracting. **4.** a pointed steel bar for breaking up road surfaces. **5.** *Archaic.* a rhyme; jingle. [1275–1325; ME *clinken,* perh. < MD *clinken* to sound, ring, resound]

clink[2] (klingk), *n. Slang.* a prison; jail; lockup. [1505–15; after *Clink,* name of prison in Southwark, London, perh. < D *klink* door-latch]

clink·er[1] (kling′kər), *n.* **1.** a mass of incombustible matter fused together, as in the burning of coal. **2.** a hard Dutch brick, used esp. for paving. **3.** a partially vitrified mass of brick. **4.** the scale of oxide formed on iron during forging. **5.** *Geol.* a mass of vitrified material ejected from a volcano. **—v.i. 6.** to form clinkers in burning. [1635–45; < D *klinker* kind of brick, slag]

clink·er[2] (kling′kər), *n.* a person or thing that clinks. [1680–90; CLINK[1] + -ER[1]]

clink·er[3] (kling′kər), *n. Slang.* **1.** a wrong note in a musical performance. **2.** any mistake or error. **3.** something that is a failure; a product of inferior quality. **4.** *Brit.* someone or something wonderful or exceedingly well-liked. [1830–40; special use of CLINKER[2]]

clink·er-built (kling′kər bilt′), *adj.* **1.** faced or surfaced with boards, plates, etc., each course of which overlaps the one below, lapstrake. **2.** Also, **clincher-built.** *Shipbuilding.* noting a hull whose shell is formed of planking **(clink′er plank′ing)** or plating **(clink′er plat′ing)** in which each strake overlaps the next one below and is overlapped by the next one above. Cf. **carvel-built.** [1760–70; *clinker* (var. of CLINCHER) + BUILT]

clink·e·ty-clank (kling′ki tē klangk′), *n.* a succession of alternating clinks and clanks: *the clinkety-clank of armored vehicles on the rough road.* [1900–05; alter. of CLINK[1] + CLANK]

clino-, a combining form meaning "slope, incline," and, in mineralogy, "monoclinic," used in the formation of compound words: *clinometer.* [< L *-clin(āre)* (c. Gk *klínein* to cause to lean, Skt *śrayati* he causes to lean) + -O-]

cli·no·graph (klī′nə graf′, -gräf′), *n.* **1.** (in mining, construction, etc.) an instrument that records the deviation of boreholes or the like from the vertical. **2.** *Drafting.* a pair of straightedges hinged together so as to be adjustable to any angle. [1880–85; CLINO- + -GRAPH] **—cli·no·graph·ic** (klī′nə graf′ik), *adj.*

cli·nom·e·ter (klī nom′i tər, kli-), *n.* an instrument for determining angles of inclination or slope. [1805–15; CLINO- + -METER] **—cli·nom′e·try,** *n.*

cli·no·met·ric (klī′nə me′trik), *adj.* **1.** (of crystals) having oblique angles between one or all axes. **2.** pertaining to or determined by a clinometer. Also, **cli′no·met′ri·cal.** [CLINO- + -METRIC]

Clin·o·ril (klin′ə ril), *Pharm., Trademark.* a brand of sulindac.

cli·no·zo·i·site (klī′nə zō′ə sīt′), *n.* a monoclinic mineral, hydrous calcium aluminum silicate, a variety of epidote, dimorphous with zoisite. [CLINO- + ZOISITE]

clin·quant (kling′kənt), *adj.* **1.** glittering, esp. with tinsel; decked with garish finery. **—n. 2.** imitation gold leaf; tinsel; false glitter. [1585–95; < MF: clinking, prp. of *clinquer* (< D *klinken* to sound); see -ANT]

Clint (klint), *n.* a male given name, form of **Clinton.**

Clin·ton (klin′tn), *n.* **1. De Witt** (də wit′), 1769–1828, U.S. political leader and statesman: governor of New York 1817–21, 1825–28 (son of James Clinton). **2. George,** 1739–1812, governor of New York 1777–95, 1801–04: vice president of the U.S. 1805–12. **3. Sir Henry,** 1738?–95, commander in chief of the British forces in the American Revolutionary War. **4. Hillary Rodham,** born 1947, U.S. attorney and social reformer (wife of William J. Clinton). **5. James,** 1733–1812, American general in the Revolutionary War (brother of George Clinton). **6. William Jefferson** (*Bill*), born 1946, 42nd president of the U.S. since 1993. **7.** a city in E Iowa, on the Mississippi River. 32,828. **8.** a city in central Maryland. 16,438. **9.** a town in W Mississippi. 14,660. **10.** a city in central Massachusetts. 12,771. **11.** a town in S Connecticut. 11,195. **12.** a male given name.

clin·to·ni·a (klin tō′nē ə), *n.* any plant of the genus *Clintonia,* of the lily family, comprising stemless plants with a few broad, ribbed, basal leaves, and white, greenish-yellow, or rose-colored flowers on a short stalk. [1818; named after De Witt CLINTON; see -IA]

Clin·ton·om·ics (klin′tə nom′iks), *n.* (*used with a singular v.*) the economic policies set forth by President Bill Clinton. [1993; b. CLINTON and ECONOMICS]

Cli·o (klē′ō: *for 1 also* klī′ō), *n., pl.* **Cli·os** for 2. **1.** *Class. Myth.* the Muse of history. **2.** an award presented annually by the advertising industry for achievement in television commercials. **3.** a female given name. [< L < Gk *Kleió,* equiv. to *klei-* (s. of *klein* to make famous) + *-ō* suffix used for women's names]

cli·o·met·rics (klē′ō me′triks, klī′ō-), *n.* (*used with a singular v.*) the study of historical data by the use of statistical, often computerized, techniques. [1965–70; CLIO + -METRICS] **—cli′o·met′ric,** *adj.* **—cli′o·met′ri·cal·ly,** *adv.* **—cli·o·me·tri·cian** (klē′ō mi trish′ən, klī′ō-), *n.*

clip[1] (klip), *v.,* **clipped, clipped** or **clipt, clip·ping,** *n.* **—v.t. 1.** to cut, or cut off or out, as with shears: *to clip a rose from a bush.* **2.** to trim by cutting: *to clip a hedge.* **3.** to cut or trim the hair or fleece of; shear: *to clip a poodle.* **4.** to pare the edge of (a coin). Cf. **sweat** (def. 22). **5.** to cut short; curtail: *We clipped our visit by a week to return home earlier.* **6.** to pronounce rapidly, with precise articulation and with omission of certain sounds, as of unstressed vowels: *an annoying habit of clipping his words.* **7.** to shorten (a word or phrase) by dropping one or more syllables. **8.** *Informal.* to hit with a quick, sharp blow: *He clipped him on the jaw with a sudden punch.* **9.** *Slang.* to take or get money from by dishonest means; swindle; rook. **—v.i. 10.** to clip or cut something. **11.** to cut articles or pictures from a newspaper, magazine, etc. **12.** to move swiftly: *He clipped along the highway on his motorcycle.* **13.** *Archaic.* to fly rapidly. **—n. 14.** the act of clipping. **15.** anything clipped off, esp. the wool shorn at a single shearing of sheep. **16.** the amount of wool shorn in one season. **17. clips,** (*used with a plural v.*) an instrument for clipping; shears. **18.** See **film clip. 19.** *Informal.* clipping (def. 2). **20.** *Informal.* a quick, sharp blow: *a clip on the jaw.* **21.** rate; pace: *at a rapid clip.* [1150–1200; ME *clippen* < ON *klippa* to clip, cut] **—clip′pa·ble,** *adj.*

clip[2] (klip), *n., v.,* **clipped, clip·ping.** **—n. 1.** a device that grips and holds tightly. **2.** a metal or plastic clasp for holding together papers, letters, etc. **3.** See **cartridge clip. 4.** an article of jewelry or other decoration clipped onto clothing, shoes, hats, etc. **5.** a flange on the upper surface of a horseshoe. **6.** Also called **lug.** *Shipbuilding.* a short length of angle iron connecting and maintaining the angle between two members or surfaces. **7.** *Archaic.* an embrace. **—v.t., v.i. 8.** to grip tightly; fasten with or as if with a clip. **9.** to encircle; encompass. **10.** *Football.* to block by illegally throwing the body across a player's legs from behind. **11.** *Archaic.* to embrace or hug. [bef. 900; ME *clippen,* OE *clyppan* to embrace, surround; c. OFris *kleppa*]

clip·board (klip′bôrd′, -bōrd′), *n.* a small board having at the top a clip for holding papers and serving as a portable writing surface. [1905–10; CLIP[2] + BOARD]

clip′ bond′, a form of brickwork raking bond for a facing of all stretchers, in which the stretchers are tied in to the backing every few courses by diagonally set bricks that project from the backing into angles made by cutting off the concealed corners of the face brick.

clip-clop (klip′klop′), *n.* clippety-clop. [1880–85]

clip-fed (klip′fed′), *adj.* (of a rifle) loading from a cartridge clip into the magazine. [CLIP[2] + FED]

clip′ joint′, 1. *Slang.* a business, esp. a place of entertainment, that makes a practice of overcharging or cheating customers. **2.** *Masonry.* a mortar joint made higher than usual in order to level the course above. [1930–35, *Amer.*]

clip-on (klip′on′, -ôn′), *adj.* **1.** designed to be clipped on easily, esp. by a self-attached clip: *a clip-on bow tie.* **—n. 2.** a clip-on device, ornament, or the like. [1905–10; adj., n. use of v. phrase *clip on*]

clip-out (klip′out′), *adj.* intended to be clipped out, as from a newspaper: *a clip-out coupon.* [adj. use of v. phrase *clip out*]

clipped (klipt), *adj.* characterized by quick, terse, and clear enunciation. [CLIP[1] + -ED[2]]

clipped′ form′, a word formed by dropping one or more syllables from a longer word or phrase with no change in meaning, as *deli* from *delicatessen* or *flu* from *influenza.* Also called **clipped′ word′, clipping, shortening.** Cf. **back clipping, fore clipping.**

clip·per (klip′ər), *n.* **1.** a person or thing that clips or cuts. **2.** Often, **clippers.** (*often used with a plural v.*) a cutting tool, esp. shears: *hedge clippers.* **3.** Usually, **clippers.** (*usually used with a plural v.*) a mechanical or electric tool for cutting hair, fingernails, or the like: *He told the barber, "No clippers on the sides, please."* **4.** *Naut.* Also called **clipper ship.** a sailing ship built and rigged for speed, esp. a type of three-masted ship with a fast hull form and a lofty rig, built in the U.S. from c1845, and in Great Britain from a later date, until c1870, and used in trades in which speed was more important than cargo capacity. **5.** *Electronics.* a device that gives output only for an input above or below a certain critical value. **6.** a person or thing that moves along swiftly. [1350–1400; ME; see CLIP[1], -ER[1]]

clipper (def. 4)

clip′per bow′ (bou), *Naut.* a bow having a concave stem and a hollow entrance. Also called **fiddle bow.**

clip·per-built (klip′ər bilt′), *adj. Naut.* (of a hull) having fast lines, with a high ratio of length to beam and a fine entrance. [1825–35]

clip′per ship′, clipper (def. 4).

clip·pe·ty-clop (klip′i tē klop′), *n.* the sound struck by the hoofs of a horse trotting on pavement, or any staccato, rhythmic sound resembling it. Also, **clip-clop.** [1925–30; imit.]

clip·ping (klip′ing), *n.* **1.** the act of a person or thing that clips. **2.** a piece clipped off or out, esp. an article, advertisement, etc., clipped from a newspaper or magazine. **3.** See **clipped form. —adj. 4.** serving or tending to clip. **5.** *Informal.* swift: *a clipping pace.* [1300–50; ME. See CLIP[1], -ING[2], -ING[1]] **—clip′ping·ly,** *adv.*

clip·sheet (klip′shēt′), *n. Journalism.* a sheet of paper printed on one side for convenience in cutting and reprinting, containing news items, features, cartoons, etc., and distributed by public relations firms, publishers, and similar organizations. [CLIP[1] + SHEET[1]]

clipt (klipt), *v.* a pp. of **clip[1].**

clique (klēk, klik), *n., v.,* **cliqued, cli·quing. —n. 1.** a small, exclusive group of people; coterie; set. **—v.i. 2.** *Informal.* to form, or associate in, a clique. [1705–15; < F, appar. metaphorical use of MF *clique* latch, or n. deriv. of *cliquer* to make noise, resound, imit. word parallel to CLICK[1]] **—clique′less,** *adj.* **—cli′quey, cli′quy,** *adj.* **—cli′quism,** *n.*
—Syn. 1. See **circle, ring[1].**

cli·quish (klē′kish, klik′ish), *adj.* **1.** associating exclusively with the members of one's own clique; clannish. **2.** tending to divide into cliques: *a cliquish neighborhood.* **3.** of, pertaining to, or characteristic of a clique: *narrow, cliquish notions about art.* [1850–55; CLIQUE + -ISH[1]] **—cli′quish·ly,** *adv.* **—cli′quish·ness,** *n.*

clish·ma·cla·ver (klish′mə klā′vər, klēsh′-), *n. Scot.* gossip; idle or foolish talk. [1720–30; *clish(-clash)* gossip (gradational compound based on CLASH) + *-ma-* (< ?) + CLAVER]

Clis·the·nes (klīs′thə nēz′), *n.* Cleisthenes.

clis·to·carp (klī′stə kärp′), *n. Mycol.* cleistocarp.

clis·to·car·pous (klī′stə kär′pəs), *adj. Bot., Mycol.* cleistocarpous.

clis·to·the·ci·um (klī′stə thē′shē əm, -sē əm), *n., pl.* **-ci·a** (-shē ə, -sē ə). *Mycol.* cleistothecium.

clit (klit), *n. Slang* (*vulgar*). clitoris. [by shortening]

Cli·te (klī′tē), *n. Class. Myth.* the wife of Cyzicus, who hanged herself when her husband was mistakenly killed by the Argonauts.

cli·tel·lum (klī tel′əm), *n., pl.* **-tel·la** (-tel′ə). a ring or saddle-shaped region of glandular tissue in the body wall of certain annelids, as earthworms and some leeches, that after copulation secretes a cocoon in which the eggs and sperm are deposited for fertilization and development. [1830–40; < NL, neut. n. based on L *clitellae* packsaddle]

clith·ral (klīth′rəl), *adj.* (of a classical temple) roofed over. Cf. **hypethral.** [< Gk *kleîthr(on)* bar for closing a door (deriv. of *kleíein* to close, shut) + -AL[1]; cf. CLATHRATE]

clit·ic (klit′ik), *Gram.* **—adj. 1.** (of a word) functioning as a bound form; closely connected in pronunciation with a preceding or following word and not having an independent accent or phonological status. **—n. 2.** a clitic word; enclitic or proclitic. [1945–50; extracted from ENCLITIC and PROCLITIC]

clit·i·cize (klit′ə sīz′), *v.i.,* **-cized, -ciz·ing.** *Ling.* to become attached to a word or phrase as a clitic. Also, *esp. Brit.,* **clit′i•cise′.** [CLITIC + -IZE] —**clit′i•ci•za′tion,** *n.*

clit•o•ri•dec•to•my (klit′ər i dek′tə mē), *n., pl.* **-mies.** the excision of the clitoris, usually performed as part of female initiation rites, mainly among certain African peoples, but also sometimes used in various societies to curb sexual desire; female circumcision. Cf. **infibulation.** [1865–70; *clitorid-* (comb. form repr. Gk *kleitorís* (gen. *kleitorídos*) CLITORIS) + -ECTOMY]

clit•o•ris (klit′ər is, klī′tər-, kli tôr′is, -tōr′-), *n. Anat.* the erectile organ of the vulva, homologous to the penis of the male. [1605–15; < Gk *kleitorís,* akin to *kleíein* to shut] —**clit′o•ral, cli•tor•ic** (kli tôr′ik, -tor′-, klī-), **clit•o•rid•e•an** (klit′ə rid′ē ən, klī′tə-), *adj.*

Clive (klīv), *n.* **1. Robert** (*Baron Clive of Plassey*), 1725–74, British general and statesman in India. **2.** a male given name, form of **Cleve.**

cliv•ers (kliv′ərz), *n., pl.* **-ers.** cleavers.

cli•vi•a (klī′vē ə, kliv′ē ə), *n.* See **Kaffir lily.** [< NL (1828), named in honor of Lady Charlotte Florentia (née *Clive*), Duchess of Northumberland (1787–1866); see -IA]

clk., **1.** clerk. **2.** clock.

clo., clothing.

clo•a•ca (klō ā′kə), *n., pl.* **-cae** (-sē). **1.** *Zool.* **a.** the common cavity into which the intestinal, urinary, and generative canals open in birds, reptiles, amphibians, many fishes, and certain mammals. **b.** a similar cavity in invertebrates. **2.** a sewer, esp. an ancient sewer. [1650–60; < L *clo(u)āca, cluāca* sewer, drain; prob. akin to Gk *klýzein* to wash, wash away] —**clo•a′cal,** *adj.*

cloak (klōk), *n.* **1.** a loose outer garment, as a cape or coat. **2.** something that covers or conceals; disguise; pretense: *He conducts his affairs under a cloak of secrecy.* —*v.t.* **3.** to cover with or as if with a cloak: *She arrived at the opera cloaked in green velvet.* **4.** to hide; conceal: *The mission was cloaked in mystery.* [1175–1225; ME *cloke* (< OF) < ML *cloca,* var. of *clocca* bell-shaped cape, bell; see CLOCK¹] —**cloak′less,** *adj.*
—**Syn. 2.** cover, mask, veil.

cloak-and-dag•ger (klōk′ən dag′ər), *adj.* pertaining to, characteristic of, or dealing in espionage or intrigue, esp. of a romantic or dramatic kind. [1835–45]

cloak-and-suit•er (klōk′ən sōō′tər), *n. Informal.* a manufacturer or seller of clothing.

cloak-and-sword (klōk′ən sôrd′), *adj.* (of a drama or work of fiction) dealing with characters who wear cloaks and swords; concerned with the customs and romance of the nobility in bygone times. [1800–10]

cloak•room (klōk′rōōm′, -rŏŏm′), *n.* **1.** a room in which outer garments, hats, umbrellas, etc., may be left temporarily, as in a club, restaurant, etc.; checkroom. **2.** a room adjacent to a legislative chamber or legislative room, where legislators may leave their coats, relax, or engage in informal conversation. **3.** *Brit.* **a.** a bathroom; a public rest room. **b.** a baggage room, as at a railway station, where packages and luggage may be left temporarily or checked through to one's destination. [1850–55; CLOAK + ROOM]

clob•ber¹ (klob′ər), *v.t. Slang.* **1.** to batter severely; strike heavily: *He tried to clobber me with his club.* **2.** to defeat decisively; drub; trounce. **3.** to denounce or criticize vigorously. [1940–45, *Amer.*; orig. uncert.]
—**Syn. 2.** whip, thrash, lick.

clob•ber² (klob′ər), *n. Brit., Australian Slang.* (*used with a plural v.*) clothes. [1875–80; of obscure orig.; cf. CLOBBER³]

clob•ber³ (klob′ər), *v.t.,* to paint over existing decoration on (a ceramic piece). [1850–55; earlier, to mend, patch up (clothes or shoes); of obscure orig.]

clob•ber⁴ (klob′ər), *n., v.i. South Midland and Southern U.S.* clabber.
—**Regional Variation.** See **clabber.**

cloche (klōsh, klôsh), *n.* **1.** a woman's close-fitting hat with a deep, bell-shaped crown and often a narrow, turned-down brim. **2.** a bell-shaped glass cover placed over a plant to protect it from frost and to force its growth. **3.** a bell-shaped metal or glass cover placed over a plate to keep food warm or fresh. [1905–10; < F: bell, bell-jar < ML *clocca.* See CLOAK]

clock¹ (klok), *n.* **1.** an instrument for measuring and recording time, esp. by mechanical means, usually with hands or changing numbers to indicate the hour and minute: not designed to be worn or carried about. **2.** See **time clock. 3.** a meter or other device, as a speedometer or taximeter, for measuring and recording speed, distance covered, or other quantitative functioning. **4.** See **biological clock. 5.** (*cap.*) *Astron.* the constellation Horologium. **6.** *Computers.* the circuit in a digital computer that provides a common reference train of electronic pulses for all other circuits. **7. around the clock, a.** during all 24 hours; ceaselessly. **b.** without stopping for rest; tirelessly: *working around the clock to stem the epidemic.* **8. kill the clock,** *Sports.* to use up as much game time as possible when one is winning, as to protect a lead in basketball, ice hockey, or football. Also, **run out the clock. 9. stop the clock,** to postpone an official or legal deadline by ceasing to count the hours that elapse, as when a new union contract must be agreed upon before an old contract runs out. —*v.t.* **10.** to time, test, or determine by means of a clock or watch: *The racehorse was clocked at two minutes thirty seconds.* —*v.i.* **11. clock in,** to begin work, esp. by punching a time clock: *She clocked in at 9 on the dot.* **12. clock out,** to end work, esp. by punching a time clock: *He clocked out early yesterday.* [1350–1400; ME *clok(ke)* < MD *clocke* bell, clock; akin to OE *clucge,* OHG *glocka* (G *Glocke*), OIr *clocc* bell; cf. CLOAK]

clock² (klok), *n.* **1.** a short embroidered or woven ornament on each side or on the outer side of a sock or stocking, extending from the ankle upward. —*v.t.* **2.** to embroider with such an ornament. [1520–30; orig. uncert.]

clock•er (klok′ər), *n.* **1.** a person who times racehorses during tryouts to determine their speed. **2.** an official who times a race. **3.** a person who maintains a record of the flow of traffic, as of visitors to a museum. [CLOCK¹ + -ER¹]

clock-hour (klok′ouᵊr′, -ou′ər), *n.* a full 60-minute period, as of class instruction or therapeutic consultation. Cf. **hour** (def. 11). [1870–75]

clock′ jack′, *Horol.* jack¹ (def. 18). [1925–30; earlier *jack of the clock-(house), jackaclock;* see JACK¹]

clock•like (klok′līk′), *adj.* highly systematic, precise, and dependable: *The mail carrier arrives at noon with clocklike regularity.* [1735–45; CLOCK¹ + -LIKE]

clock•mak•er (klok′mā′kər), *n.* a person who makes or repairs clocks. [1400–50; late ME. See CLOCK¹, MAKER] —**clock′mak′ing,** *n.*

clock′ punch′er, a worker with a routine job in a factory or office, as one who punches a time clock at the beginning and end of a work shift.

clock′ ra′dio, a radio combined with an alarm clock in a compact cabinet, the clock serving as a timer to turn the radio on or off at a preset time. [1960–65, *Amer.*]

clock-tim•er (klok′tī′mər), *n.* timer (def. 4).

clock′ watch′, a watch that strikes the hours. Cf. **repeater** (def. 3). [1675–85]

clock′ watch′er, 1. an employee who demonstrates lack of interest in a job by watching the time closely to be sure to stop work as soon as the workday or shift is over. **2.** any person who watches the time closely, as in expectation of some news or event. —**clock′ watch′ing.** [1885–90]

clock•wise (klok′wīz′), *adv.* **1.** in the direction of the rotation of the hands of a clock as viewed from the front or above; circularly to the right from a point taken as the top. —*adj.* **2.** directed clockwise: *a clockwise movement.* [1885–90; CLOCK¹ + -WISE]

clock•work (klok′wûrk′), *n.* **1.** the mechanism of a clock. **2.** any mechanism similar to that of a clock. **3. like clockwork,** with perfect regularity or precision: *The launching of the spacecraft went off like clockwork.* [1620–30; CLOCK¹ + WORK]

clod (klod), *n.* **1.** a lump or mass, esp. of earth or clay. **2.** a stupid person; blockhead; dolt. **3.** earth; soil. **4.** something of lesser dignity or value, as the body as contrasted with the soul: *this corporeal clod.* **5.** a part of a shoulder of beef. [1400–50; late ME *clodde,* OE *clod-* (in *clodhamer* fieldfare); see CLOUD] —**clod′di•ly,** *adv.* —**clod′di•ness,** *n.* —**clod′like′,** *adj.* —**clod′dy,** *adj.*
—**Syn. 2.** boor, yokel, lout, oaf, dunce.

clod•dish (klod′ish), *adj.* of, pertaining to, or resembling a clod or boor; doltish; stolid. [1835–45; CLOD + -ISH¹] —**clod′dish•ly,** *adv.* —**clod′dish•ness,** *n.*

clod•hop•per (klod′hop′ər), *n.* **1.** a clumsy boor; rustic; bumpkin. **2. clodhoppers,** strong, heavy shoes. [1680–90; CLOD + HOPPER, modeled on GRASSHOPPER]
—**Syn. 1.** hick, yokel, lout, hayseed, lummox.

clod•hop•ping (klod′hop′ing), *adj.* loutish; boorish. [1835–45; CLODHOPP(ER) + -ING²]

clod•poll (klod′pōl′), *n. Archaic.* a stupid person; blockhead. [1595–1605; CLOD + POLL¹]

Clo•ë (klō′ē), *n.* a female given name, form of **Chloe.**

Cloe•te (klōō′tē), *n.* **Stuart,** 1897–1976, South African novelist, born in France.

clo•fi•brate (klō fī′brāt, -fib′rāt), *n. Pharm.* a substance, $C_{12}H_{15}ClO_3$, used principally to reduce elevated plasma triglyceride and cholesterol levels. [1960–65; *clofibr(ic acid)* (perh. C(H)LO(RO)-² + FIBR- + -IC) + -ATE²]

clog (klog, klôg), *v.,* **clogged, clog•ging,** *n.* —*v.t.* **1.** to hinder or obstruct with thick or sticky matter; choke up: *to clog a drain.* **2.** to crowd excessively, esp. so that movement is impeded; overfill: *Cars clogged the highway.* **3.** to encumber; hamper; hinder. —*v.i.* **4.** to become clogged, encumbered, or choked up. **5.** to stick; stick together. **6.** to do a clog dance. —*n.* **7.** anything that impedes motion or action; an encumbrance; a hindrance. **8.** a shoe or sandal with a thick sole of wood, cork, rubber, or the like. **9.** a similar but lighter shoe worn in the clog dance. **10.** a heavy block, as of wood, fastened to a person or beast to impede movement. **11.** See **clog dance. 12.** *Brit. Dial.* a thick piece of wood. [1350–1400; ME, of uncert. orig.] —**clog′gi•ly,** *adv.* —**clog′gi•ness,** *n.* —**clog′gy,** *adj.*
—**Syn. 3.** impede, trammel, fetter.

clog′ dance′, a dance in which clogs, or heavy shoes, are worn for hammering out the lively rhythm. [1880–85] —**clog′ danc′er.** —**clog′ danc′ing.**

cloi•son•né (kloi′zə nā′; *Fr.* klwa zô nā′), *n.* **1.** enamelwork in which colored areas are separated by thin metal bands fixed edgewise to the ground. —*adj.* **2.** pertaining to, forming, or resembling cloisonné or the pattern of cloisonné. [1860–65; < F, equiv. to *cloison* partition (OF < VL **clausiōn-,* s. of **clausiō;* L *claus(us)* closed (see CLAUSE, CLOSE) + *-iō* -ION) + *-é* < L *-ātus* -ATE¹]

clois•ter (kloi′stər), *n.* **1.** a covered walk, esp. in a religious institution, having an open arcade or colonnade usually opening onto a courtyard. **2.** a courtyard, esp. in a religious institution, bordered with such walks. **3.** a place of religious seclusion, as a monastery or convent. **4.** any quiet, secluded place. **5.** life in a monastery or convent. —*v.t.* **6.** to confine in a monastery or convent. **7.** to confine in retirement; seclude. **8.** to furnish with a cloister or covered walk. **9.** to convert into a monastery or convent. [1250–1300; ME *cloistre* < AF, OF, b. *cloison* partition (see CLOISONNÉ) and *clostre* (< L *claustrum* barrier (LL: enclosed place); see CLAUSTRUM)] —**clois′ter•less,** *adj.* —**clois′ter•like′,** *adj.*
—**Syn. 3.** abbey, priory.

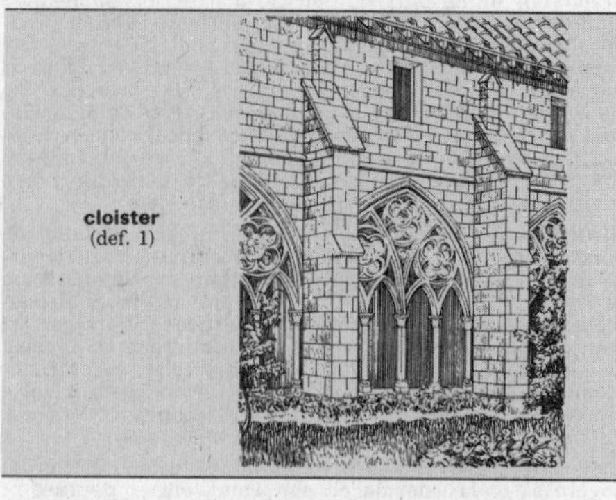
cloister (def. 1)

clois•tered (kloi′stərd), *adj.* **1.** secluded from the world; sheltered: *a cloistered life.* **2.** having a cloister or cloisters. [1575–85; CLOISTER + -ED²]
—**Syn. 1.** withdrawn, isolated, aloof, sequestered.

clois′tered vault′, a vault having the form of a number of intersecting coves. Also, **clois′ter vault′.** Also called **coved vault.**

clois′ter garth′, garth (def. 1). [1840–50]

clois•tral (kloi′strəl), *adj.* **1.** of, pertaining to, or living in a cloister. **2.** cloisterlike. [1595–1605; CLOIST(E)R + -AL¹]

clois•tress (kloi′stris), *n. Obs.* a nun. [1595–1605; *cloist(e)r(er)* monk + -ESS]

clo•ky (klō′kē), *n., pl.* **-kies,** *adj.* cloque.

clomb (klōm), *v. Chiefly Eastern Virginia.* pt. and pp. of **climb.**

Clom•id (klom′id, klō′mid), *Pharm., Trademark.* a brand of clomiphene.

clom•i•phene (klom′ə fēn′, klō′mə-), *n. Pharm.* a substance, $C_{26}H_{28}ClNO$, used for inducing ovulation in certain infertile women. [1960–65; C(H)LO(RO)-² + (A)MI(NE) + PHEN(YL), extracted from the chemical name]

clomp (klomp), *v.i.* clump (def. 6).

clo•naz•e•pam (klō nā′zə pam′), *n. Pharm.* a benzodiazepine, $C_{15}H_{10}ClN_3O_3$, used in the control of certain epilepsies. [*c(h)lo(rophe)n(yl)* + *(di)azep(in),* extracted from the chemical name + *-am,* of uncert. derivation]

clone (klōn), *n., v.,* **cloned, clon•ing.** —*n.* **1.** *Biol.* **a.** a cell, cell product, or organism that is genetically identical to the unit or individual from which it was derived. **b.** a population of identical units, cells, or individuals that derive from the same ancestral line. **2.** a person or thing that duplicates, imitates, or closely resembles another in appearance, function, performance, or style: *All the fashion models seemed to be clones of one another.* —*v.t.* **3.** to produce a copy or imitation of. **4.** *Biol.* **a.** to cause to grow as a clone. **b.** to separate (a batch of cells or cell products) so that each portion produces only its own kind. —*v.i.* **5.** *Biol.* to grow as a clone. [1900–05; < Gk *klṓn* a slip, twig] —**clon′al,** *adj.* —**clon′al•ly,** *adv.* —**clon′er,** *n.*

clon•ic (klon′ik, klō′nik), *adj. Pathol.* of or relating to clonus. [1840–50; CLON(US) + -IC] —**clo•nic•i•ty** (klō nis′i tē, klo-), *n.* —**clon′ism** (klō′niz əm), *n.*

clon′ic spasm′, *Med.* See under **spasm** (def. 1). [1840–50]

clon•i•dine (klon′i dēn′, klō′ni-), *n. Pharm.* a synthetic white crystalline substance, $C_9H_9Cl_2N_3$, used in the treatment of high blood pressure. [1965–70; C(H)LO(RO)-² + (A)NI(LINE) + (IMI)D(E), extracted from the chemical name + -INE²]

clon•ing (klō′ning), *n. Biol.* the process of producing a clone. [1955–60; CLONE + -ING¹]

clonk (klongk, klôngk), *n.* **1.** a low, dull sound of impact, as of a heavy object striking against another. —*v.i., v.t.* **2.** to make or cause to make such a sound. Also, **clunk.** [1925–30; imit.]

clo•nus (klō′nəs), *n., pl.* **-nus•es.** *Pathol.* a rapid succession of flexions and extensions of a group of muscles, usually signifying an affection of the brain or spinal cord. [1810–20; < NL < Gk *klónos* turmoil]

cloot (klōōt; *Scot.* klʏt), *n. Scot. and North Eng.* **1.** a cloven hoof; one of the divisions of the cloven hoof of the swine, sheep, etc. **2.** (*usually cap.*) Often, **Cloots.** Satan; the devil. [1715–25; perh. akin to D *klauwtje,* equiv. to *klauw* CLAW + *-tje* dim. suffix]

cloot•ie (klōō′tē; *Scot.* klʏ′tē), *n. Scot. and North Eng.* (*usually cap.*) cloot (def. 2). [CLOOT + -IE]

Cloots (klōts), *n.* **Jean Bap•tiste du Val-de-Grâce** (zhäɴ ba tēst′ dʏ val də gräs′), **Baron de** (*"Anacharsis Clootz"*), 1755–94, Prussian leader in the French Revolution.

clop (klop), *n., v.,* **clopped, clop•ping.** —*n.* **1.** a sound made by or as if by a horse's hoof striking the ground. —*v.i.* **2.** to make or move with such a sound. [1895–1900; imit.]

clop-clop (*n.* klop′klop′; *v.* klop′klop′), *n., v.,* **-clopped, -clop•ping.** —*n.* **1.** a clattering sound of repeated clops. —*v.i.* **2.** to make or move with such a sound. [1900–05]

clo•que (klō kā′), *n.* **1.** an embossed or quilted fabric.

CONCISE ETYMOLOGY KEY: <, descended or borrowed from; >, whence; b., blend of, blended; c., cognate with; cf., compare; deriv., derivative; equiv., equivalent; imit., imitative; obl., oblique; r., replacing; s., stem; sp., spelling, spelled; resp., respelling, respelled; trans., translation; ?, origin unknown; *, unattested; ‡, probably earlier than. See the full key inside the front cover.

—*adj.* **2.** having a small, irregular pattern or figured motif woven into a fabric to give a puckered or quilted effect. Cf. **matelassé.** Also, **clo·qué′, cloky.** [1945–50; < F: *cloqué* embossed, blistered, equiv. to dial. F (Picard) *cloque* bell, blister (see CLOAK) + -*é* < L -*ātus* -ATE[1]]

Clo·quet (klō kā′), *n.* a town in NE Minnesota. 11,142.

clo·raz·e·pate (klô raz′ə pāt′, klō-), *n. Pharm.* a benzodiazepine, $C_{16}H_{13}ClN_2O_4$, used in the treatment of chronic anxiety states and as an adjunct in the treatment of alcohol withdrawal. [C(H)LOR-[2] + *azep(ine)* + -ATE[2]]

Clo·rin·da (klô rin′də, klō-), *n.* a female given name.

Clo·ris (klôr′is, klōr′-), *n.* a male or female given name.

clos, *Real Estate.* closet.

clos (klō), *n., pl.* ***clos.*** *French.* a walled vineyard. [lit., closed]

close (*v.* klōz; *adj., adv.* klōs *or, for 56,* klōz; *n.* klōz *for 66, 67, 70–72, 74, 75,* klōs *for 68, 69, 73*), *v.,* **closed, clos·ing,** *adj.,* **clos·er, clos·est,** *adv., n.* —*v.t.* **1.** to put (something) in a position to obstruct an entrance, opening, etc.; shut. **2.** to stop or obstruct (a gap, entrance, aperture, etc.): *to close a hole in a wall with plaster.* **3.** to block or hinder passage across or access to: *to close a border to tourists; to close the woods to picnickers.* **4.** to stop or obstruct the entrances, apertures, or gaps in: *He closed the crate and tied it up.* **5.** (of the mind) to make imperceptive or inaccessible: *to close one's mind to the opposite opinion.* **6.** to bring together the parts of; join; unite (often fol. by *up*): *Close up those ranks! The surgeon closed the incision.* **7.** *Elect.* to complete (an electrical circuit) by joining the circuit elements: *The circuit was closed so the current could be measured.* **8.** to bring to an end: *to close a debate.* **9.** to arrange the final details of; to conclude negotiations about: *to close a deal to everyone's satisfaction.* **10.** to complete or settle (a contract or transaction); consummate: *We close the sale of the house next week.* **11.** to stop rendering the customary services of: *to close a store for the night.* **12.** to terminate or suspend the operation of; to halt the activities of: *The epidemic forced authorities to close the schools. The police closed the bar for selling liquor to minors.* **13.** *Naut.* to come close to: *We closed the cruiser to put our injured captain on board.* **14.** *Metalworking.* to reduce the internal diameter of (a tube or the like). **15.** *Archaic.* to shut in or surround on all sides; enclose; cover in: *to close a bird in a cage.*

—*v.i.* **16.** to become closed; shut: *The door closed with a bang. This window is stuck and will not close tight.* **17.** to come together; unite: *Her lips closed firmly.* **18.** to come close: *His pursuers closed rapidly.* **19.** to grapple; engage in close encounter (often fol. by *with*): *We closed with the invaders shortly before sundown.* **20.** to come to an end; terminate: *The service closed with a hymn.* **21.** to cease to offer the customary activities or services: *The school closed for the summer.* **22.** to enter into or reach an agreement, usually as a contract: *The builder closed with the contractor after negotiations.* **23.** (of a theatrical production) to cease to be performed: *The play closed in New York yesterday and will open in Dallas next week.* **24.** (of a stock, group of stocks, etc.) to be priced or show a change in price as specified at the end of a trading period: *The market closed low for the fourth straight day.* **25. close down, a.** to terminate the operation of; discontinue: *to close down an air base because of budget cuts.* **b.** to attempt to control or eliminate: *The city must close down drug traffic.* **26. close in on** or **upon, a.** to approach so as to capture, attack, arrest, etc.: *The hoodlums closed in on their victim.* **b.** to surround or envelop so as to entrap: *a feeling that the room was closing in upon her.* **27. close out, a.** to reduce the price of (merchandise) for quick sale: *That store is closing out its stock of men's clothing.* **b.** to liquidate or dispose of finally and completely: *They closed out their interests after many years in this city.* **28. close ranks,** to unite forces, esp. by overlooking petty differences, in order to deal with an adverse or challenging situation; to join together in a show of unity, esp. to the public: *When the newspaper story broke suggesting possible corruption in the government, the politicians all closed ranks.* **29. close up, a.** to come together in close array; converge: *The enemy was closing up on us from both flanks.* **b.** to bring to an end; cease: *The company is closing up its overseas operations.* **c.** to become silent or uncommunicative. **d.** to reduce or eliminate spacing material between (units of set type).

—*adj.* **30.** having the parts or elements near to one another: *a close formation of battleships.* **31.** compact; dense: *a close texture; a close weave.* **32.** being in or having proximity in space or time: *The barn is so close to the house that you can hear the animals. His birthday is in May, close to mine.* **33.** marked by similarity in degree, action, feeling, etc.: *This dark pink is close to red. He left her close to tears.* **34.** near, or near together, in kind or relationship: *a flower close to a rose; a close relative.* **35.** intimate or confidential; dear. **36.** based on a strong uniting feeling of respect, honor, or love: *a close circle of friends.* **37.** fitting tightly: *a close, clinging negligee.* **38.** (of a haircut or shave, the mowing of a lawn, etc.) so executed that the hair, grass, or the like is left flush with the surface or very short. **39.** not deviating from the subject under consideration. **40.** strict; searching; minute: *The matter requires close investigation.* **41.** not deviating from a model or original: *a close, literal translation.* **42.** nearly even or equal: *a close contest.* **43.** strictly logical: *close reasoning.* **44.** shut; shut tight; not open: *a close hatch.* **45.** shut in; enclosed. **46.** completely enclosing or surrounding: *a close siege preventing all escape.* **47.** without opening; with all openings covered or closed. **48.** confined; narrow: *close quarters.* **49.** lacking fresh or freely circulating air: *a hot, close room.* **50.** heavy; oppressive: *a spell of close, sultry weather.* **51.** narrowly confined, as a prisoner. **52.** practicing or keeping secrecy; secretive; reticent: *She is so close that you can tell her all your secrets.* **53.** parsimonious; stingy: *He is very close with his money.* **54.** scarce, as money. **55.** not open to public or general admission, competition, etc.: *The entire parish participated in the close communication.* **56.** (of a delimiting punctuation mark) occurring at the end of a group of words or characters that is set off, as from surrounding text: *close parentheses; close quotes; close brackets.* Cf. **open** (def. 32). **57.** *Hunting, Angling.* closed (def. 8). **58.** *Phonet.* (of a vowel) articulated with a relatively small opening between the tongue and the roof of the mouth. Cf. **high** (def. 23), **open** (def. 34a). **59.** *Heraldry.* (of a bird) represented as having folded wings: *an eagle close.* **60.** *Archaic.* viscous; not volatile.

—*adv.* **61.** in a close manner; closely. **62.** near; close by. **63.** *Heraldry.* immediately behind the ears, so as to show no neck: *a bear's head couped close.* **64. close to the wind,** *Naut.* in a direction nearly opposite to that from which the wind is coming: *to sail close to the wind.* **65. close up, a.** from close range; in a detailed manner; intimately. **b.** *Naut.* fully raised; at the top of the halyard: *an answering pennant flown close up.* Cf. **dip** (def. 37).

—*n.* **66.** the act of closing. **67.** the end or conclusion: *at the close of day; the close of the speech.* **68.** an enclosed place or enclosure, esp. one about or beside a cathedral or other building. **69.** any piece of land held as private property. **70.** See **complimentary close. 71.** *Music.* cadence (def. 7). **72.** *Stock Exchange.* **a.** the closing price on a stock. **b.** the closing prices on an exchange market. **73.** *Scot.* **a.** a narrow entry or alley terminating in a dead end. **b.** a courtyard enclosed except for one narrow entrance. **74.** *Archaic.* a junction; union. **75.** *Obs.* a close encounter; a grapple: *The fighters met in a fierce close.* [bef. 1050; (n., adj.) ME *clos* < AF, OF < L *clausus,* ptp. of *claudere* to close (cf. CLAUSE); (v.) ME *closen,* v. deriv. of the adj. (cf. OE *clȳsan, beclȳsan* to shut in, enclose, v. deriv. of *clūse* bar, enclosure < ML *clūsa,* for L *clausa,* fem. of *clausus*); n. and adj. senses with voiced pron. of *s* are presumably modern deverbal derivatives] —**clos·a·ble, close·a·ble** (klō′zə bəl), *adj.* —**close·ly** (klōs′lē), *adv.* —**close·ness** (klōs′nis), *n.*

—**Syn. 2.** bar; clog; choke. CLOSE, SHUT mean to cause something not to be open. CLOSE suggests blocking an opening or vacant place: *to close a breach in a wall.* The word SHUT refers esp. to blocking or barring openings intended for entering and leaving: *to shut a door, gate, etc.,* and CLOSE can be used in this sense, too: *to close a door, gate, etc.* **8.** complete, end, conclude, terminate, finish. **21.** stop; suspend. **31.** firm, solid. **32.** immediate, proximate, nearby. **40.** intent, concentrated. **41.** scrupulous, exacting, accurate, faithful. **50.** muggy, thick. **52.** taciturn, uncommunicative, reserved. **53.** penurious, miserly, tight, mean. See **stingy. 66.** See **end**[1].

close-at-hand (klōs′ət hand′), *adj.* lying in the near future or vicinity; nearby or imminent.

close-by (klōs′bī′), *adj.* nearby; adjacent; neighboring. [1620–30]

close′ call′ (klōs), a narrow escape from danger or trouble. [1880–85, *Amer.*]

close′ commun′ion (klōs), *Eccles.* a communion service in which only members of the same denomination or the same church can participate. Cf. **intercommunion, open communion.** [1815–25, *Amer.*] —**close′ commun′ion·ist.**

close′ corpora′tion (klōs). See **closed corporation.** [1915–20]

close-cropped (klōs′kropt′), *adj.* **1.** clipped or trimmed short: *close-cropped hair.* **2.** having one's hair clipped or trimmed short: *a close-cropped wrestler.* [1890–95]

closed (klōzd), *adj.* **1.** having or forming a boundary or barrier: *He was blocked by a closed door. The house had a closed porch.* **2.** brought to a close; concluded: *It was a closed incident with no repercussions.* **3.** not public; restricted; exclusive: *a closed meeting; a closed bid at a private auction.* **4.** not open to new ideas or arguments. **5.** self-contained; independent or self-sufficient: *a closed, symbiotic relationship.* **6.** *Phonet.* (of a syllable) ending with a consonant or a consonant cluster, as *has, hasp.* Cf. **open** (def. 35b). **7.** *Ling.* (of a class of items) limited in membership and not readily expanded to include new items, as the class of inflectional affixes, articles, pronouns, or auxiliaries (opposed to *open*). **8.** *Hunting, Angling.* restricted as to the kind of game that may be legally taken and as to where or when it may be taken: *woods closed to deer hunters.* **9.** *Math.* **a.** (of a set in which a combining operation between members of the set is defined) such that performing the operation between members of the set produces a member of the set, as multiplication in the set of integers. **b.** (of an interval) containing both of its endpoints. **c.** (of a map from one topological space to another) having the property that the image of a closed set is a closed set. **d.** (of a curve) not having endpoints; enclosing an area. **e.** (of a surface) enclosing a volume. **f.** (of a function or operator) having as its graph a closed set. [1175–1225; ME; see CLOSE, -ED[2]]

closed′-an·gle glauco′ma (klōzd′ang′gəl), *Pathol.* angle-closure glaucoma. See under **glaucoma.**

closed′ book′, something that is not known or cannot be understood; a mystery or puzzle: *Abstract art is a closed book as far as I'm concerned.* [1910–15]

closed-cap·tioned (klōzd′kap′shənd), *adj.* (of a television program) broadcast with captions, as for the hearing-impaired, that are visible only with the use of a decoder attached to the television set. [1975–80]

closed′ chain′, *Chem.* three or more atoms linked together to form a ring or cycle and represented accordingly by its structural formula. Cf. **open chain.** [1900–05]

closed′ cir′cuit, *Elect.* a circuit without interruption, providing a continuous path through which a current can flow. Cf. **open circuit.** [1820–30] —**closed′-cir′cuit,** *adj.*

closed′-circuit tel′evision, a system of televising by cable to designated viewing sets, as within a factory for monitoring production operations, in a theater for viewing a special event taking place elsewhere, or in an office building as an aid to maintaining security. [1945–50]

closed′ cor′nice, 1. a slightly projecting wooden cornice composed of a frieze board and a crown molding without a soffit. **2.** See **box cornice.**

closed′ corpora′tion, an incorporated business the stock of which is owned by a small group. Also, **close corporation.**

closed′ cou′plet, a couplet that concludes with an end-stopped line. Cf. **open couplet.** [1905–10]

closed-door (klōzd′dôr′, -dōr′), *adj.* held in strict privacy; not open to the press or the public: *a closed-door strategy meeting of banking executives.* [1930–35]

closed′ ec′osystem, *Ecol.* a self-replenishing ecosystem in which life can be maintained without external factors or outside aid.

closed-end (klōzd′end′), *adj.* of, pertaining to, or like a closed-end investment company. [1935–40; *Amer.*]

closed′-end invest′ment com′pany, an investment company that issues its shares in large blocks at infrequent intervals and is not obligated to redeem or repurchase them. Cf. **open-end investment company.**

closed′ frac′ture. See **simple fracture.** [1960–65]

closed′ gen′tian, a gentian, *Gentiana andrewsii,* of the eastern and central U.S., having tight clusters of dark blue, closed flowers. Also called **bottle gentian.** [1855–60, *Amer.*]

closed′ loop′, *Computers, Electronics.* the complete path followed by a signal as it is fed back from the output of a circuit, device, or system to the input and then back to the output. Cf. **feedback loop.**

closed-loop (klōzd′lo͞op′), *adj. Engin.* **1.** of or pertaining to a processing system in which effluents are recycled, that is, treated and returned for reuse. **2.** of or pertaining to an automatic control system operating on a feedback principle. Cf. **feedback** (def. 2). [1950–55]

closed-mind·ed (klōzd′mīn′did), *adj.* having a mind firmly unreceptive to new ideas or arguments: *It's hard to argue with, much less convince, a closed-minded person.* [modeled after OPEN-MINDED]

close·down (klōz′doun′), *n.* a termination or suspension of operations; shutdown: *a temporary closedown of a factory.* [1885–90, *Amer.;* n. use of v. phrase *close down*]

closed′ plan′, an office floor plan consisting of fully enclosed office spaces. Cf. **open plan.**

closed′ posi′tion, (in ballet, modern dance, and jazz dance) any position in which the feet touch each other.

closed′ pri′mary, a direct primary in which only persons meeting tests of party membership may vote. [1940–45, *Amer.*]

closed′ rule′, *Parl. Proc.* a rule that prohibits amendments to a bill from the floor.

closed′ sea′son, a period, usually for a specific part of the year, during which angling or hunting for a given species is legally prohibited: *closed season on ducks.*

closed′ set′, *Math.* a set that contains all of its accumulation points, as the set of points on and within a circle; a set having an open set as its complement.

closed′ shelf′, *Library Science.* a library stack with access restricted to the staff of the library or to a limited group of library users.

closed′ shell′, *Physics.* **1.** (in atomic structure) a shell that contains the maximum number of electrons permitted by the exclusion principle. **2.** (in nuclear structure) a shell that contains the maximum number of nucleons permitted by the exclusion principle.

closed′ shop′, a factory, office, or other business establishment in which union membership is a condition of being hired as well as of continued employment. Cf. **open shop.** [1900–05, *Amer.*]

closed-stack (klōzd′stak′), *adj. Library Science.* having access to the stacks limited to the staff of the library or to a limited group of library users. Also, **closed-shelf** (klōzd′shelf′). Cf. **open-stack.**

closed′ stance′, *Baseball.* a batting stance in which the front foot is positioned closer to the inside of the batter's box than the back foot. [1930–35]

closed′ sys′tem, *Thermodynam.* a region that is isolated from its surroundings by a boundary that admits no transfer of matter or energy across it. Cf. **open system.** [1895–1900]

closed′ trav′erse, *Survey.* a traverse ending at its point of origin.

closed′ un′ion, a labor union in which admission of new members is restricted by rigid requirements. Cf. **open union.**

closed′ u′niverse, (in cosmology) a hypothetical expanding universe that contains sufficient matter to reverse the observed expansion through its gravitational contraction. Cf. **open universe.**

close·fist·ed (klōs′fis′tid), *adj.* stingy; miserly; tight. [1565–75; CLOSE + FIST[1] + -ED[3]] —**close′fist′ed·ly,** *adv.* —**close′fist′ed·ness,** *n.*

—**Syn.** niggardly, penurious, tight-fisted.

close-fit·ting (klōs′fit′ing), *adj.* (of a garment) fitting tightly or snugly to the body: *A close-fitting jacket showed off her small waist.* Cf. **loose-fitting.** [1865–70]

close-grained (klōs′grānd′), *adj.* (of wood) fine in texture or having inconspicuous annual rings. [1745–55]

CONCISE PRONUNCIATION KEY: act, cāpe, dâre, pärt; set, ēqual; *if,* ice; ox, ōver, ôrder, oil, bo͝ok, bo͞ot, out; up, ûrge; child; sing; shoe; thin, that; zh as in *treasure.* ə = *a* as in *alone, e* as in *system, i* as in *easily, o* as in *gallop, u* as in *circus;* ᵊ as in *fire* (fīᵊr), *hour* (ouᵊr). l and n can serve as syllabic consonants, as in *cradle* (krād′l), and *button* (but′n). See the full key inside the front cover.

close′ har′mony (klōs), *Music.* harmony in which the voices, excluding the bass, occur within an octave or, sometimes, within the interval of a tenth. [1875–80]

close-hauled (klōs′hôld′), *adj., adv. Naut.* as close to the wind as a vessel will sail, with sails as flat as possible; full and by. [1760–70]

close′ hel′met (klōz), *Armor.* a completely closed helmet of the late 15th century and after, having a facial defense composed of a visor and beaver or of a visor, ventail, and beaver attached to a pivot on each side.

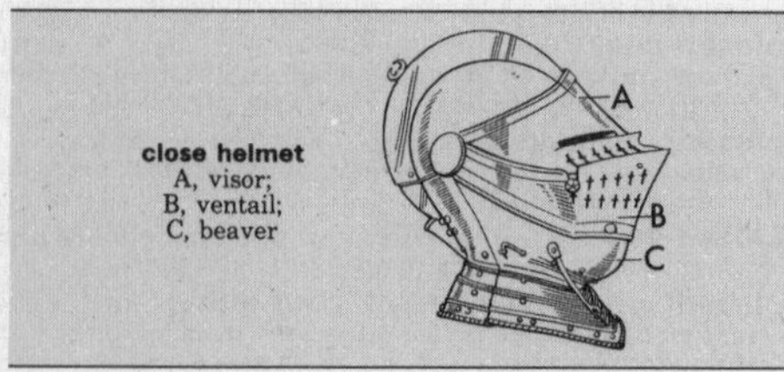

close helmet
A, visor;
B, ventail;
C, beaver

close-in (klōs′in′), *adj.* **1.** near, as to a common center; adjacent, esp. to a city: *The city is enveloping its close-in suburbs.* **2.** occurring or provided at close quarters: *Fighter planes provided daring close-in air support.*

close′ junc′ture (klōs), *Phonet.* continuity in the articulation of two successive sounds, as in the normal transition between sounds within a word; absence of juncture (opposed to *open juncture*). Cf. **juncture** (def. 7), **open juncture, terminal juncture.**

close-knit (klōs′nit′), *adj.* tightly united, connected, or organized. [1925–30]

close-lipped (klōs′lipt′), *adj.* not talking or telling much.

close•mouthed (klōs′mouthd′, -moutht′), *adj.* reticent; uncommunicative. [1880–85; CLOSE + MOUTH + -ED[3]]
—Syn. tight-lipped, diffident, taciturn, secretive.

close′-or•der drill′ (klōs′ôr′dər), *Mil.* practice in formation marching and other movements, in the carrying of arms during formal marching, and in the formal handling of arms for ceremonies and guard.

close•out (klōz′out′), *n.* **1.** a sale on all goods in liquidating a business. **2.** a sale on goods of a type that will no longer be carried by the store. **3.** an article of merchandise offered for sale at a closeout. [1920–25; n. use of v. phrase *close out*]

close′ posi′tion (klōs), *Music.* arrangement of a chord so that the voices, excluding the bass, occur within an octave.

close′ quar′ters (klōs), **1.** a small, cramped place or position. **2.** direct and close contact in a fight: *They met at close quarters, exchanging many quick jabs.* [1745–55]

close′ quote′ (klōz), **1.** the quotation mark used to end a quotation, usually ” or ’. **2.** (used by a speaker to indicate the end of a quotation.) Also, **close′ quotes′.**

clos•er[1] (klō′zər), *n.* **1.** a person or thing that closes. **2.** Also, **closure.** *Masonry.* any of various specially formed or cut bricks for spacing or filling gaps between regular bricks or courses of regular brickwork. [1350–1400; ME. See CLOSE, -ER[1]]

clos•er[2] (klō′sər), *adj.* comparative of **close.**

close′ reach′ (klōs), *Naut.* See under **reach** (def. 26). [1895–1900]

close-reefed (klōs′rēfd′, klōz′-), *adj. Naut.* having most or all of the sail reefs taken in. [1750–60]

close′ shave′ (klōs), *Informal.* a narrow escape from serious danger or trouble: *We weren't hit when the truck swerved at us, but it was a close shave.* [1825–35, *Amer.*]

close′ shot′ (klōs), *Motion Pictures, Television.* closeup (def. 2).

close′ stitch′ (klōs). See **buttonhole stitch.**

close-stool (klōz′sto͞ol′, klōs′-), *n.* a stool having a seat with a hole, beneath which a chamber pot is placed. Also called **necessary stool.** [1375–1425; late ME]

clos•et (kloz′it), *n.* **1.** a small room, enclosed recess, or cabinet for storing clothing, food, utensils, etc. **2.** a small private room, esp. one used for prayer, meditation, etc. **3.** a state or condition of secrecy or carefully guarded privacy: *Some conservatives remain in the closet except on election day. Gay liberation has encouraged many gay people to come out of the closet.* **4.** See **water closet.** *—adj.* **5.** private; secluded. **6.** suited for use or enjoyment in privacy: *closet reflections; closet prayer.* **7.** engaged in private study or speculation; speculative; unpractical: *a closet thinker with no practical experience.* **8.** being or functioning as such in private; secret: *a closet anarchist.* *—v.t.* **9.** to shut up in a private room for a conference, interview, etc. (usually used in the passive voice): *The Secretary of State was closeted with the senator for three hours in a tense session.* [1300–50; ME < AF, MF, equiv. to *clos* CLOSE (n.) + *-et* -ET]

clos′et dra′ma, 1. drama appropriate for reading rather than for acting. **2.** a play in this form.

clos•et•ed (kloz′i tid), *adj.* functioning in private; secret; closet. [1675–85; CLOSET + -ED[2]]

clos•et•ful (kloz′it fo͝ol′), *n., pl.* **-fuls.** an amount sufficient to fill a closet: *a closetful of new clothes.* [CLOSET + -FUL]
—Usage. See **-ful.**

CONCISE ETYMOLOGY KEY: <, descended or borrowed from; >, whence; b., blend of, blended; c., cognate with; cf., compare; deriv., derivative; equiv., equivalent; imit., imitative; obl., oblique; r., replacing; s., stem; sp., spelling, spelled; resp., respelling, respelled; trans., translation; ?, origin unknown; *, unattested; ‡, probably earlier than. See the full key inside the front cover.

clos′et queen′, *Slang (disparaging).* a homosexual male who denies his homosexuality to himself or keeps it hidden from others. [1965–70]

close•up (klōs′up′), *n.* **1.** a photograph taken at close range or with a long focal-length lens, on a relatively large scale. **2.** Also called **close shot.** *Motion Pictures, Television.* a camera shot taken at a very short distance from the subject, to permit a close and detailed view of an object or action. Cf. **long shot** (def. 3), **medium shot.** **3.** an intimate view or presentation of anything. *—adj.* **4.** of or resembling a closeup. **5.** intimate or detailed; close-in. [1910–15, *Amer.*; n. use of adverbial phrase *close up*]

clos•ing (klō′zing), *n.* **1.** the end or conclusion, as of a speech. **2.** something that closes; a fastening, as of a purse. **3.** the final phase of a transaction, esp. the meeting at which procedures are carried out in the execution of a contract for the sale of real estate. **4.** an act or instance of failing or going bankrupt: *an increase in bank closings.* **5.** See **complimentary close.** [1350–1400; ME; see CLOSE, -ING[1]]

clos′ing costs′, *Real Estate.* **1.** fees charged to a purchaser by a bank, lawyer, etc. for services related to a sale, as title search, appraisal, etc. **2.** any expenses over the purchase price of a house, land, etc., that is paid by the purchaser or seller at the completion of the sale.

clos′ing er′ror, *Survey.* See **error of closure.**

clos′ing price′, *Stock Exchange.* the final price of a stock or bond at the end of a trading day.

clos•trid•i•um (klo strid′ē əm), *n., pl.* **clos•trid•i•a** (klo strid′ē ə). *Bacteriol.* any of several rod-shaped, spore-forming, anaerobic bacteria of the genus *Clostridium,* found in soil and in the intestinal tract of humans and animals. [1880–85; < NL < Gk *klōstr-,* var. s. of *klōstḗr* spindle (*klōs-,* var. s. of *klṓthein* (see CLOTHO) + *-tēr* agent suffix) + NL *-idium* -IDIUM] **—clos•trid′i•al, clos•trid′i•an,** *adj.*

clo•sure (klō′zhər), *n., v.,* **-sured, -sur•ing.** *—n.* **1.** the act of closing; the state of being closed. **2.** a bringing to an end; conclusion. **3.** something that closes or shuts. **4.** closer (def. 2). **5.** an architectural screen or parapet, esp. one standing free between columns or piers. **6.** *Phonet.* an occlusion of the vocal tract as an articulatory feature of a particular speech sound. Cf. **constriction** (def. 5). **7.** *Parl. Proc.* a cloture. **8.** *Survey.* completion of a closed traverse in such a way that the point of origin and the endpoint coincide within an acceptably small margin of error. Cf. **error of closure.** **9.** *Math.* **a.** the property of being closed with respect to a particular operation. **b.** the intersection of all closed sets that contain a given set. **10.** *Psychol.* **a.** the tendency to see an entire figure even though the picture of it is incomplete, based primarily on the viewer's past experience. **b.** a sense of psychological certainty or completeness: *a need for closure.* **11.** *Obs.* something that encloses or shuts in; enclosure. *—v.t., v.i.* **12.** *Parl. Proc.* to cloture. [1350–1400; ME < MF < L *clausūra.* See CLOSE, -URE]

clot (klot), *n., v.,* **clot•ted, clot•ting.** *—n.* **1.** a mass or lump. **2.** a semisolid mass, as of coagulated blood. **3.** a small compact group of individuals: *a clot of sightseers massed at the entrance.* **4.** *Brit. Informal.* blockhead, dolt, clod. *—v.i.* **5.** to form into clots; coagulate. *—v.t.* **6.** to cause to clot. **7.** to cover with clots: *Carefully aimed snowballs clotted the house.* **8.** to cause to become blocked or obscured: *to clot the book's narrative with too many characters.* [bef. 1000; ME; OE *clott* lump; c. MD *klotte,* G *Klotz* block, log (cf. KLUTZ)]

cloth (klôth, kloth), *n., pl.* **cloths** (klôthz, klothz, klôths, kloths), *adj.* *—n.* **1.** a fabric formed by weaving, felting, etc., from wool, hair, silk, flax, cotton, or other fiber, used for garments, upholstery, and many other items. **2.** a piece of such a fabric for a particular purpose: *an altar cloth.* **3.** the particular attire of any profession, esp. that of the clergy. Cf. **man of the cloth.** **4. the cloth,** the clergy: *men of the cloth.* **5.** *Naut.* **a.** one of the lengths of canvas or duck of standard width sewn side by side to form a sail, awning, or tarpaulin. **b.** any of various pieces of canvas or duck for reinforcing certain areas of a sail. **c.** a number of sails taken as a whole. **6.** *Obs.* a garment; clothing. *—adj.* **7.** of or made of cloth: *She wore a cloth coat trimmed with fur.* **8.** clothbound. [bef. 900; ME *cloth, clath* cloth, garment, OE *clāth;* c. D *kleed,* G *Kleid*] **—cloth′like′,** *adj.*

cloth′ beam′. See **cloth roll.**

cloth•bound (klôth′bound′, kloth′-), *adj.* (of a book) bound with cloth rather than paper, leather, etc. [1855–60; CLOTH + BOUND[1]]

cloth-cap (klôth′kap′, kloth′-), *adj. Brit.* pertaining to or characteristic of the working class. [1850–55]

clothe (klōth), *v.t.,* **clothed** or **clad, cloth•ing. 1.** to dress; attire. **2.** to provide with clothing. **3.** to cover with or as with clothing. [bef. 950; ME *clothen,* OE *clāthian,* deriv. of *clāth* CLOTH]
—Syn. 1. robe, garb, array, accouter, bedeck.

clothes (klōz, klōthz), *n.pl.* **1.** garments for the body; articles of dress; wearing apparel. **2.** bedclothes. [bef. 900; ME; OE *clāthas,* pl. of *clāth* CLOTH]
—Syn. 1. clothing, attire, raiment, costume, garb; vestments, habiliments.

clothes•bas•ket (klōz′bas′kit, -bä′skit, klōthz′-), *n.* a basket for holding and carrying laundry. [1800–10; CLOTHES + BASKET]

clothes•horse (klōz′hôrs′, klōthz′-), *n.* **1.** *Informal.* a person whose chief interest and pleasure is dressing fashionably. **2.** a frame on which to hang wet laundry for drying. [1765–75; CLOTHES + HORSE]

clothes•line (klōz′līn′, klōthz′-), *n.* a strong, narrow rope, cord, wire, etc., usually stretched between two poles, posts, or buildings, on which clean laundry is hung to dry. [1820–30; CLOTHES + LINE[1]]

clothes′ moth′, any of several small moths of the family Tineidae, the larvae of which feed on wool, fur, etc., esp. *Tinea pellionella* **(casemaking clothes moth).** [1745–55]

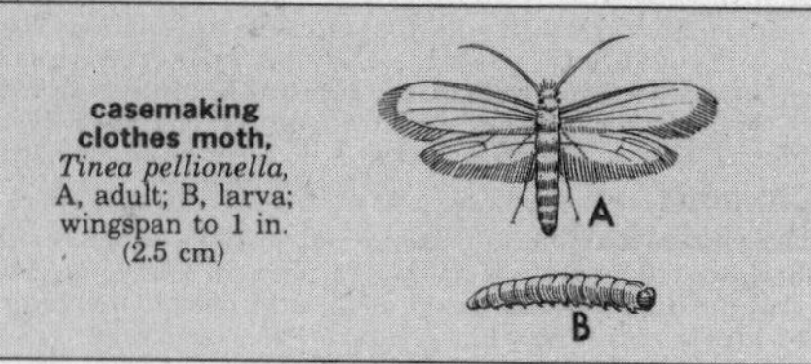

casemaking clothes moth,
Tinea pellionella,
A, adult; B, larva;
wingspan to 1 in.
(2.5 cm)

clothes-peg (klōz′peg′, klōthz′-), *n. Brit.* a clothespin. [1815–25]

clothes•pin (klōz′pin′, klōthz′-, klōs′-), *n.* a device, such as a forked piece of wood or plastic, for fastening articles to a clothesline. [1840–50, *Amer.*; CLOTHES + PIN]

clothes′ pole′, a pole used for supporting a clothesline. [1860–65, *Amer.*]

clothes•press (klōz′pres′, klōthz′-), *n.* a receptacle for clothes, as a chest, wardrobe, or closet. [1705–15; CLOTHES + PRESS[1]]

clothes′ tree′, an upright pole with hooks near the top for hanging coats, hats, etc.

cloth•ier (klōth′yər, -ē ər), *n.* **1.** a retailer of clothing. **2.** a person who makes or sells cloth. [1325–75; CLOTH + -IER[1]; r. ME *clother*]

cloth•ing (klō′thing), *n.* **1.** garments collectively; clothes; raiment; apparel. **2.** a covering. [1150–1200; ME; see CLOTHE, -ING[1]]

Clo•tho (klō′thō), *n. Class. Myth.* the Fate who spins the thread of life. [< L < Gk *Klōthṓ* lit., Spinner, equiv. to *klṓth(ein)* to spin + *-ō* suffix used in fem. names]

cloth-of-gold (klôth′əv gōld′, kloth′-), *n.* a garden plant, *Crocus augustifolius,* of the iris family, native to the Crimean mountains, having orange-red flowers.

cloth′ roll′, a roller, located at the front of a loom, on which woven material is wound after it leaves the breast beam. Also called **cloth beam.**

cloth′ yard′, a unit of measure for cloth, formerly 37 inches (0.93 meter), now the equivalent of the standard yard (0.91 meter); 36 inches; 3 feet. [1425–75; late ME]

clot′ted cream′, cream that has been clotted by cooking. Also called, *Brit.,* **Devon cream, Devonshire cream.** [1875–80]

clot•ty (klot′ē), *adj.,* **-ti•er, -ti•est. 1.** full of clots. **2.** tending to clot. [1375–1425; late ME. See CLOT, -Y[1]]

clo•ture (klō′chər), *n., v.,* **-tured, -tur•ing.** *U.S. Parl. Proc.* *—n.* **1.** a method of closing a debate and causing an immediate vote to be taken on the question. *—v.t., v.i.* **2.** to close (a debate) by cloture. [1870–75; < F *clôture,* MF *closture* < VL **clōstūra,* alter. of L *clōstra, claustra,* pl. of *claustrum* barrier. See CLAUSTRAL, -URE]

clou (klo͞o), *n.* a major point of interest or attention. [1880–85; < F: lit., a nail < L *clāvus*]

cloud (kloud), *n.* **1.** a visible collection of particles of water or ice suspended in the air, usually at an elevation above the earth's surface. **2.** any similar mass, esp. of smoke or dust. **3.** a dim or obscure area in something otherwise clear or transparent. **4.** a patch or spot differing in color from the surrounding surface. **5.** anything that obscures or darkens something, or causes gloom, trouble, suspicion, disgrace, etc. **6.** a great number of insects, birds, etc., flying together: *a cloud of locusts obscuring the sun.* **7. in the clouds, a.** in a condition of absent-mindedness; lost in reverie. **b.** impractical: *Their schemes are usually up in the clouds.* **8. on a cloud,** *Informal.* exceedingly happy; in high spirits: *On the night of the prom the seniors were on a cloud.* **9. under a cloud,** in disgrace; under suspicion: *After going bankrupt he left town under a cloud.* *—v.t.* **10.** to overspread or cover with, or as with, a cloud or clouds: *The smoke from the fire clouded the sun from view.* **11.** to overshadow; obscure; darken: *The hardships of war cloud his childhood memories.* **12.** to make gloomy. **13.** (of distress, anxiety, etc.) to reveal itself in (a part of one's face): *Worry clouded his brow.* **14.** to make obscure or indistinct; confuse: *Don't cloud the issue with unnecessary details.* **15.** to place under suspicion, disgrace, etc. **16.** to variegate with patches of another color. *—v.i.* **17.** to grow cloudy; become clouded. **18.** (of a part of one's face) to reveal one's distress, anxiety, etc.: *His brow clouded with anger.* [bef. 900; ME; OE *clūd* rock, hill; prob. akin to CLOD] **—cloud′like′,** *adj.*
—Syn. 1. vapor. **6.** swarm, horde, multitude, throng, host, crowd, army. **7.** CLOUD, FOG, HAZE, MIST differ somewhat in their figurative uses. CLOUD connotes esp. daydreaming: *His mind is in the clouds.* FOG and HAZE connote esp. bewilderment or confusion: *to go around in a fog (haze).* MIST has an emotional connotation and suggests tears: *a mist in one's eyes.* **14.** muddle, distort.

cloud•age (klou′dij), *n. Meteorol.* See **cloud cover.** [1810–20; CLOUD + -AGE]

cloud′ ban′ner, *Meteorol.* See **banner cloud.** [1905–10]

cloud′ base′, the apparent lower surface of a cloud or cloud layer. [1950–55]

cloud•ber•ry (kloud′ber′ē, -bə rē), *n., pl.* **-ries. 1.** the orange-yellow edible fruit of a creeping plant, *Rubus chamaemorus,* of the rose family, related to the raspberries and blackberries and restricted to northern regions. **2.** the plant itself. Also called **bake apple.** [1590–1600; CLOUD + BERRY]

cloud•burst (kloud′bûrst′), *n.* a sudden and very heavy rainfall. [1810–20, *Amer.*; CLOUD + BURST]

cloud′ cap′, *Meteorol.* See **cap cloud.**

cloud-capped (kloud′kapt′), *adj.* surrounded at the top by clouds: *cloud-capped mountains.* [1600–10]

cloud′ cham′ber, *Physics.* an apparatus for determining the movements of charged particles, consisting of a chamber containing a supersaturated mixture of gas and vapor, the vapor condensing around ions created by the particle in its passing, thereby revealing the path of the particle. Also called **expansion chamber, Wilson cloud chamber.** Cf. **bubble chamber.** [1895–1900]

cloud′ cov′er, **1.** a covering of clouds over all or part of the sky. **2.** the fraction of sky covered by clouds. Also called **cloudage.** Cf. **sky cover.** [1940–45]

cloud-cuck·oo-land (kloud′ko͞o′ko͞o land′, -ko͝ok′-o͞o-), *n.* an idealized, illusory domain of imagination; cloudland: *the cloud-cuckoo-land of technicolor cartoon whimsy.* [1815–25; trans. of Gk *Nephelokokkygía,* the realm which separates the gods from mankind in Aristophanes' *The Birds*]

cloud′ ear′, a thin, blackish edible mushroom, *Auricularia polytricha,* used esp. in Chinese cookery. Also called **mu ehr.** [appar. an erroneous trans. of Chin *mùêr,* equiv. to *mù* tree + *êr* ear(s)]

cloud·ed (klou′did), *adj.* **1.** confused; muddled; disordered: *a mind clouded by sorrow.* **2.** covered with or as if with clouds. [1590–1600; CLOUD + -ED²]

cloud′ed leop′ard, a medium-sized wild cat, *Felis nebulosa,* with brownish-gray fur spotted or striped with black, native to southeastern Asia and Indonesia: an endangered species. Also called **cloud′ed ti′ger.** [1905–10]

cloud′ed sul′fur. See **common sulfur.**

cloud′ grass′, a grass, *Agrostis nebulosa,* of Spain, having clusters of tiny spikelets on slender stalks, used in bouquets.

cloud·land (kloud′land′), *n.* **1.** the sky. **2.** a region of unreality, imagination, etc.; dreamland. [1810–20; CLOUD + -LAND]

cloud′ lay′er, a continuous or fragmented distribution of clouds all sharing the same cloud base. Also called **cloud′ deck′.**

cloud·less (kloud′lis), *adj.* having no clouds; clear: *a cloudless sky.* [1350–1400; ME. See CLOUD, -LESS] **—cloud′less·ly,** *adv.* **—cloud′less·ness,** *n.*

cloud·let (kloud′lit), *n.* a small cloud. [1780–90; CLOUD + -LET]

cloud′ nine′, *Informal.* a state of perfect happiness (usually in the phrase *on cloud nine*). [1955–60]

cloud′ phys′ics, the science of the physical properties and processes of clouds.

cloud′ rack′, rack⁴ (def. 1). [1840–50]

Clouds, The, a comedy (423 B.C.) by Aristophanes.

cloud′ seed′ing, any technique of adding material to a cloud to alter its natural development, usually to increase or obtain precipitation. [1945–50]

cloud·y (klou′dē), *adj.,* **cloud·i·er, cloud·i·est.** **1.** full of or overcast by clouds: *a cloudy sky.* **2.** having little or no sunshine: *a cloudy but rainless day.* **3.** of or like a cloud or clouds; pertaining to clouds. **4.** having cloudlike markings: *cloudy marble.* **5.** not clear or transparent: *He could not see through the cloudy liquid.* **6.** obscure; indistinct. **7.** darkened by gloom, trouble, etc. **8.** under suspicion, disgrace, etc.: *a gambler with a cloudy reputation.* [bef. 900; ME *cloudi,* OE *clūdig* rocky, hilly. See CLOUD, -Y¹] **—cloud′i·ly,** *adv.* **—cloud′i·ness,** *n.*
—Syn. 1, 2. murky, lowering, shadowy, gloomy, depressing. **5.** murky, turbid, muddy, opaque, shadowy. **6.** dim, blurred, shadowy, unclear, befogged, muddled, confused. **7.** gloomy, lowering. **8.** shadowy.

Clough (kluf), *n.* **Arthur Hugh,** 1819–61, English poet.

clout (klout), *n.* **1.** a blow, esp. with the hand; cuff: *The bully gave him a painful clout on the head.* **2.** *Informal.* pull; strong influence; muscle, esp. political power: *a wealthy campaign contributor with clout at city hall.* **3.** *Baseball.* a long hit, esp. an extra-base hit: *A hard clout to deep center field drove in the winning run.* **4.** *Archery.* **a.** the mark or target shot at, esp. in long-distance shooting. **b.** a shot that hits the mark. **5.** Also called **clout′ nail′.** a nail for attaching sheet metal to wood, having a short shank with a broad head. **6.** *Archaic.* **a.** a patch or piece of cloth or other material used to mend something. **b.** any worthless piece of cloth; rag. **c.** an article of clothing (usually used contemptuously). —*v.t.* **7.** to strike, esp. with the hand; cuff. **8.** *Archaic.* **a.** to bandage. **b.** to patch; mend. [bef. 900; ME; OE *clūt* piece of cloth or metal; c. MLG *klūte,* ON *klūtr*] **—clout′er,** *n.*

clove¹ (klōv), *n.* **1.** the dried flower bud of a tropical tree, *Syzygium aromaticum,* of the myrtle family, used whole or ground as a spice. **2.** the tree itself. [1175–1225; ME *clow(e),* short for *clow-gilofre* < OF *clou de gilofre.* See CLOU, GILLYFLOWER]

clove² (klōv), *n. Bot.* one of the small bulbs formed in the axils of the scales of a mother bulb, as in garlic. [bef. 1000; ME; OE *clufu* bulb (c. MD *clōve,* D *kloof*); akin to CLEAVE²]

clove³ (klōv), *v.* a pt. of **cleave².**

clove⁴ (klōv), *n.* a British unit of weight for wool, cheese, etc., usually equivalent to 8 pounds (3.6 kilograms). [1300–50; ME *claue* < AF *clove,* earlier *clou,* equiv. to AL *clāvus,* L: nail; see CLOVE¹]

clove′ hitch′, a knot or hitch for fastening a rope to a spar or larger rope, consisting of two half hitches made in opposite directions, the two parts of the rope emerging also in opposite directions. Also called **builder's knot.** See illus. under **knot.** [1760–70; see CLOVE³]

clo·ven (klō′vən), *v.* **1.** a pp. of **cleave²** —*adj.* **2.** cleft; split; divided: *Goats have cloven hoofs.*

clo′ven hoof′, the figurative indication of Satan or evil temptation. Also called **clo′ven foot′.**

clo·ven-hoofed (klō′vən ho͞oft′, -ho͝oft′), *adj.* **1.** having split hoofs, once assumed to represent the halves of a single undivided hoof, as in cattle. **2.** devilish; Satanic. Also, **clo·ven-foot·ed** (klō′vən fo͝ot′id). [1640–50]

clove′ pink′, a pink, *Dianthus caryophyllus,* having a spicy scent resembling that of cloves. Cf. **carnation** (def. 1). [1865–70]

clo·ver (klō′vər), *n., pl.* **-vers,** (*esp. collectively*) **-ver.** **1.** any of various plants of the genus *Trifolium,* of the legume family, having trifoliolate leaves and dense flower heads, many species of which, as *T. pratense,* are cultivated as forage plants. **2.** any of various plants of allied genera, as melilot. **3. in clover,** enjoying luxury or comfort; wealthy or well-off: *They struggled to make their fortune, and now they're in clover.* [bef. 900; ME *clovere,* OE *clāfre;* akin to G *Klee*] **—clo′vered,** *adj.* **—clo′ver·y,** *adj.*

white clover, *Trifolium repens*

clo·ver·leaf (klō′vər lēf′), *n., pl.* **-leafs, -leaves,** *adj.* —*n.* **1.** a road arrangement, resembling a four-leaf clover in form, for permitting easy traffic movement between two intersecting high-speed highways. One highway passes over the other, and both are joined by a system of curved feeder roads permitting vehicles to enter and leave the highways. —*adj.* **2.** shaped like or resembling a leaf or leaves of clover. [1930–35; CLOVER + LEAF] **—clo′ver·leafed′,** *adj.*

cloverleaf (def. 1)

Clo·vis (klō′vis), *n.* **1.** a town in central California. 33,021. **2.** a city in E New Mexico. 31,194. **3.** a male given name.

Clo·vis (klō′vis), *adj.* of or pertaining to a Paleo-Indian cultural tradition of North America, esp. the American Southwest, dated 10,000–9000 B.C. and characterized by a usually bifacial, fluted stone projectile point **(Clo′vis point′)** used in big-game hunting. [1955–60; after CLOVIS, New Mexico, near where such projectile points were found]

Clo·vis I (klō′vis; *Fr.* klô vēs′), A.D. c465–511, king of the Franks 481–511. German, **Chlodwig.**

clowd·er (klou′dər), *n.* a group or cluster of cats. [1795–1805; var. of dial. *clodder* clotted mass, n. use of *clodder* to clot, coagulate, ME *clothered, clothred* (ptp.), var. of *clotered;* cf. obs. *clotter* to huddle together; see CLUTTER]

clown (kloun), *n.* **1.** a comic performer, as in a circus, theatrical production, or the like, who wears an outlandish costume and makeup and entertains by pantomiming common situations or actions in exaggerated or ridiculous fashion, by juggling or tumbling, etc. **2.** a person who acts like a clown; comedian; joker; buffoon; jester. **3.** a prankster; a practical joker. **4.** *Slang.* a coarse, ill-bred person; a boor. **5.** a peasant; rustic. —*v.i.* **6.** to act like a clown. [1555–65; earlier *cloyne, clowne,* perh. akin to ON *klunni* boor, Dan dial. *klunds,* Sw dial. *klunn* log] **—clown′ish,** *adj.* **—clown′ish·ly,** *adv.* **—clown′ish·ness,** *n.*
—Syn. 3. lout, churl. **4.** bumpkin.

clown′ anem′one, a widely distributed anemone fish, *Amphiprion ocellaris,* having broad bands of orange and white: popular in home aquariums. Also called **clown′ fish′.**

clown·er·y (klou′nə rē), *n., pl.* **-er·ies** for 2. **1.** clownish behavior. **2.** an instance of this. [1580–90; CLOWN + -ERY]

clown′ white′, *Theat.* white facial makeup used by performers, as clowns.

clox·a·cil·lin (klok′sə sil′in), *n. Pharm.* a semisynthetic penicillin, $C_{19}H_{17}ClN_3NaO_5S$, used chiefly against penicillin-resistant staphylococcal infections. [1965–70; b. CHLOR-² and OXACILLIN]

cloy (kloi), *v.t.* **1.** to weary by an excess of food, sweetness, pleasure, etc.; surfeit; satiate. —*v.i.* **2.** to become uninteresting or distasteful through overabundance: *A diet of cake and candy soon cloys.* [1350–1400; aph. var. of ME *acloyen* < MF *enclo(y)er* < LL *inclāvāre* to nail in, equiv. to *in-* IN-² + *-clāvāre,* v. deriv. of *clāvus* nail]
—Syn. 1. glut, sate, bore.

cloy·ing (kloi′ing), *adj.* **1.** causing or tending to cause disgust or aversion through excess: *a perfume of cloying sweetness.* **2.** overly ingratiating or sentimental. [1540–50; CLOY + -ING²] **—cloy′ing·ly,** *adv.*

cloze (klōz), *adj.* **1.** pertaining to or being a procedure used to measure comprehension or text difficulty, in which a person is called upon to supply elements that have been systematically deleted from a text. —*n.* **2.** a cloze procedure or test. [1953; back formation from CLOSURE (def. 10), resp. to make it distinct from CLOSE]

clpbd, *Real Estate.* clapboard.

clr., clear.

CLU, Civil Liberties Union.

C.L.U., Chartered Life Underwriter.

club (klub), *n., v.,* **clubbed, club·bing,** *adj.* —*n.* **1.** a heavy stick, usually thicker at one end than at the other, suitable for use as a weapon; a cudgel. **2.** a group of persons organized for a social, literary, athletic, political, or other purpose: *They organized a computer club.* **3.** the building or rooms occupied by such a group. **4.** an organization that offers its subscribers certain benefits, as discounts, bonuses, or interest, in return for regular purchases or payments: *a book club; a record club; a Christmas club.* **5.** *Sports.* **a.** a stick or bat used to drive a ball in various games, as golf. **b.** See **Indian club. 6.** a nightclub or cabaret: *Last night we went to all the clubs in town.* **7.** a black trefoil-shaped figure on a playing card. **8.** a card bearing such figures. **9. clubs,** (*used with a singular or plural v.*) the suit so marked: *Clubs is trump. Clubs are trump.* **10.** See **club sandwich. 11.** *Naut.* **a.** a short spar attached to the end of a gaff to allow the clew of a gaff topsail to extend beyond the peak of the gaff. **b.** a short spar attached to the truck of a mast to support the upper part of a club topsail. **c.** clubfoot (def. 3). —*v.t.* **12.** to beat with or as with a club. **13.** to gather or form into a clublike mass. **14.** to unite; combine; join together. **15.** to contribute as one's share toward a joint expense; make up by joint contribution (often fol. by *up* or *together*): *They clubbed their dollars together to buy the expensive present.* **16.** to defray by proportional shares. **17.** to hold (a rifle, shotgun, etc.) by the barrel, so as to use the stock as a club. —*v.i.* **18.** to combine or join together, as for a common purpose. **19.** to attend a club or a club's activities. **20.** to gather into a mass. **21.** to contribute to a common fund. **22.** *Naut.* to drift in a current with an anchor, usually rigged with a spring, dragging or dangling to reduce speed. —*adj.* **23.** of or pertaining to a club. **24.** consisting of a combination of foods offered at the price set on the menu: *They allow no substitutions on the club luncheon.* [1175–1225; ME *clubbe* < ON *klubba* club; akin to CLUMP]
—Syn. 1. bludgeon, billy. **2, 4.** association, society. See **circle. 12.** bludgeon, batter, maul, cudgel.

club·ba·ble (klub′ə bəl), *adj.* fit to be a member of a social club; sociable. Also, **club′a·ble.** [1775–85; CLUB + -ABLE] **—club′ba·bil′i·ty, club′a·bil′i·ty,** *n.*

club′ bag′, a soft, usually leather, two-handled bag suitable for use in traveling or for general utility. [1925–30]

club·ber (klub′ər), *n.* **1.** a person or thing that clubs. **2.** a member of a club. [1625–35; CLUB + -ER¹]

club·by (klub′ē), *adj.,* **-bi·er, -bi·est.** **1.** characteristic of a club: *The room had a warm, clubby atmosphere.* **2.** very friendly; intimate; chummy: *He became clubby with the bartender, who slipped him many free drinks.* **3.** socially exclusive; cliquish: *Their group is very clubby and unfriendly.* **4.** inclined to join clubs. [1855–60; CLUB + -Y¹] **—club′bi·ly,** *adv.* **—club′bi·ness,** *n.*

club′ car′, a railroad passenger car equipped with easy chairs, card tables, a buffet, etc. [1890–95, *Amer.*]

club′ chair′, a heavily upholstered chair having solid sides and a low back. [1915–20]

club′ fight′er, *Boxing.* a prizefighter who fights regularly at local boxing clubs, but who is not nationally known or regarded as having the ability or skill to win a division championship.

club′ foot′, *Furniture.* a knoblike foot formed from the end of a cabriole leg as a continuation of its lines: less flat than a pad foot but otherwise similar.

club·foot (klub′fo͝ot′), *n., pl.* **-feet** for 1. **1.** a congenitally deformed or distorted foot. **2.** the condition of having such a foot; talipes. **3.** Also called **club.** *Naut.* a short boom for fastening to the foot of a jib. [1530–40; CLUB + FOOT] **—club′foot′ed,** *adj.*

club′ fun′gus, any basidiomycete fungus belonging to the family Clavariaceae. [1905–10]

club′ grass′, cattail. [1780–90]

club·hand (klub′hand′), *n.* **1.** a deformed or distorted hand, similar in nature to a clubfoot. **2.** the condition of having such a hand. [1865–70; CLUB + HAND]

club·house (klub′hous′), *n., pl.* **-hous·es** (-hou′ziz). **1.** a building or room occupied by a club. **2.** a building or area used for social or recreational activities by occupants of an apartment complex, institution, etc. **3.** an athletic team's dressing room. [1810–20; CLUB + HOUSE]

club·man (klub′mən, -man′), *n., pl.* **-men** (-mən, -men′). a man who belongs to a club, esp. a fashionable club, and is active in club life. [1590–1600; CLUB + MAN¹] **—club′man·ship′,** *n.*

club′ moss′, any plant of the genus *Lycopodium.* [1590–1600]

club·room (klub′ro͞om′, -ro͝om′), *n.* a room used by a club. [CLUB + ROOM]

club·root (klub′ro͞ot′, -ro͝ot′), *n. Plant Pathol.* a disease of cabbage and other cruciferous plants, characterized by enlarged, malformed roots, caused by a slime mold, *Plasmodiophora brassicae.* [1840–50; CLUB + ROOT¹]

club′ sand′wich, a sandwich, typically on three slices of toast, interlaid with pieces of cold chicken or turkey and bacon or ham and containing lettuce, tomato, mayonnaise, etc. Also called **three-decker, triple-decker.** [1900–05, *Amer.*]

club′ so′da. See **soda water** (def. 1). [1940–45]

club′ so′fa, a heavily upholstered sofa having solid sides and a low back.

club′ steak′, a beefsteak cut from the rib end of the short loin, or sometimes a porterhouse or T-bone steak from which the tenderloin has been trimmed. Also called **Delmonico, rib steak.** [1910–15, *Amer.*]

club′ wheat′, a wheat, *Triticum compactum,* characterized by compact, club-shaped spikes, used for making pastry flour and the like. [1840–50, *Amer.*]

club•wom•an (klub′wo͝om′ən), *n., pl.* **-wom•en.** a woman who engages in club activities, esp. one prominent in social or civic organizations. [1890–95, *Amer.*; CLUB + -WOMAN]

cluck[1] (kluk), *v.i.* **1.** to utter the cry of a hen brooding or calling her chicks. **2.** to make a similar sound; express concern, approval, etc., by such a sound. —*v.t.* **3.** to call or utter by clucking. —*n.* **4.** the sound uttered by a hen when brooding, or in calling her chicks. **5.** any clucking sound. [1475–85; var. of *clock* (now dial. and Scot), ME *clokken,* OE *cloccian* to cluck; c. D *klokken*]

cluck[2] (kluk), *n. Slang.* a dull-witted, stupid person; blockhead; dolt. [1900–05, *Amer.*; special use of CLUCK[1]]

clue (klo͞o), *n., v.,* **clued, clu•ing.** —*n.* **1.** anything that serves to guide or direct in the solution of a problem, mystery, etc. **2.** clew (defs. 1–4, 6, 7). —*v.t.* **3.** to direct or point out by a clue. **4.** clew (def. 8). **5. clue in, a.** to provide with useful or reliable information: *Clue us in on how these forms are to be filled out.* **b.** to make familiar or aware: *Has she been clued in about the rules of this office?* [var. sp. of CLEW]
—**Syn. 1.** sign, hint, trace, evidence, mark, key.

Cluj-Na•po•ca (klo͞ozh′nä pô′kä), *n.* a city in NW Rumania. 274,095. German, **Klausenberg.** Hungarian, **Kolozsvár.** Formerly, **Cluj** (klo͞ozh).

clum′ber span′iel (klum′bər), one of an English breed of short-legged, stocky spaniels having a chiefly white coat, used esp. for retrieving game. [1880–85; after *Clumber,* estate in Nottinghamshire, England, where dogs were bred]

clumber spaniel 1½ ft. (0.5 m) high at shoulder

clump (klump), *n.* **1.** a small, close group or cluster, esp. of trees or other plants. **2.** a lump or mass. **3.** a heavy, thumping step, sound, etc. **4.** *Immunol.* a cluster of agglutinated bacteria, red blood cells, etc. **5.** a thick extra sole on a shoe. —*v.i.* **6.** Also, **clomp.** to walk heavily and clumsily. **7.** *Immunol.* to gather or be gathered into clumps; agglutinate. —*v.t.* **8.** to gather or form into a clump; mass. [1580–90; akin to D *klompe* lump, mass, OE *clympre* lump of metal] —**clump′y, clump′ish, clump′like′,** *adj.*

clum•sy (klum′zē), *adj.,* **-si•er, -si•est. 1.** awkward in movement or action; without skill or grace: *He is very clumsy and is always breaking things.* **2.** awkwardly done or made; unwieldy; ill-contrived: *He made a clumsy, embarrassed apology.* [1590–1600; *clums* benumbed with cold (now obs.) + -Y[1]; akin to ME *clumsen* to be stiff with cold, dial. Sw *klumsig* benumbed, awkward, *klums* numbskull, ON *klumsa* lockjaw. See CLAM[2]] —**clum′si•ly,** *adv.* —**clum′si•ness,** *n.*
—**Syn. 1.** ungraceful, ungainly, lumbering, lubberly. **2.** unhandy, unskillful, maladroit, inexpert, bungling, bumbling, heavy-handed, inept. —**Ant. 2.** adroit, skillful.

clung (klung), *v.* pt. and pp. of **cling.**

clunk (klungk), *v.i., v.t.* **1.** to hit hard, esp. on the head. **2.** clonk (def. 2). —*n.* **3.** a hard hit, esp. on the head. **4.** *Informal.* a stupid person; clunkhead. **5.** clonk (def. 1). **6.** *Informal.* clunker (def. 2) [1790–1800; imit.; cf. CLINK[1], CLANK]

clunk•er (klung′kər), *n. Informal.* **1.** something worthless or inferior. **2.** Also, **klunker.** an old, worn-out vehicle or machine, esp. a car. **3.** clunk (def. 4). [1940–45, *Amer.*; CLUNK + -ER[1]; cf. CLINKER[3]]

clunk•head (klungk′hed′), *n. Slang.* a stupid or foolish person. [1950–55, *Amer.*; CLUNK + HEAD]

clunk•y (klung′kē), *adj.,* **clunk•i•er, clunk•i•est.** *Informal.* awkwardly heavy or clumsy: *clunky metal jewelry; clunky shoes.* [1965–70; CLUNK + -Y[1]]

Clu•ny (klo͞o′nē; *Fr.* kly nē′), *n.* a town in E France, N of Lyons: ruins of a Benedictine abbey. 4000.

Clu′ny lace′, 1. ivory-white bobbin lace made of strong linen or cotton thread. **2.** a machine lace, usually of cotton, copied from it. [1870–75; named after CLUNY, France]

clu•pe•id (klo͞o′pē id), *n.* **1.** any of the Clupeidae, a family of chiefly marine, teleostean fishes, including the herrings, sardines, menhaden, and shad. —*adj.* **2.** belonging or pertaining to the family Clupeidae. [1875–80; < NL *Clupeidae,* equiv. to *Clupe(a)* the type genus (L: a small river fish) + *-idae* -ID[2]]

clu•pe•oid (klo͞o′pē oid′), *adj.* **1.** resembling a fish of the family Clupeidae; clupeid. —*n.* **2.** a clupeoid fish. [1875–80; < NL *Clupeid(ae)* (see CLUPEID) + -OID]

CONCISE ETYMOLOGY KEY: <, descended or borrowed from; >, whence; b., blend of, blended; c., cognate with; cf., compare; deriv., derivative; equiv., equivalent; imit., imitative; obl., oblique; r., replacing; s., stem; sp., spelling, spelled; resp., respelling, respelled; trans., translation; ?, origin unknown; *, unattested; ‡, probably earlier than. See the full key inside the front cover.

Clur•man (klûr′mən), *n.* **Harold (Edgar),** 1901–80, U.S. theatrical director, author, and critic.

Clu•si•um (klo͞o′sē əm), *n.* ancient name of **Chiusi.**

clus•ter (klus′tər), *n.* **1.** a number of things of the same kind, growing or held together; a bunch: *a cluster of grapes.* **2.** a group of things or persons close together: *There was a cluster of tourists at the gate.* **3.** *U.S. Army.* a small metal design placed on a ribbon representing an awarded medal to indicate that the same medal has been awarded again: *oak-leaf cluster.* **4.** *Phonet.* a succession of two or more contiguous consonants in an utterance, as the *str-* cluster of *strap.* **5.** *Astron.* a group of neighboring stars, held together by mutual gravitation, that have essentially the same age and composition and thus supposedly a common origin. Cf. **globular cluster, open cluster, stellar association.** —*v.t.* **6.** to gather into a cluster or clusters. **7.** to furnish or cover with clusters. —*v.i.* **8.** to form a cluster or clusters: *The people clustered around to watch.* [bef. 900; ME; OE *cluster, clyster* bunch; c. LG *kluster*] —**clus′ter•ing•ly,** *adv.* —**clus′•ter•y,** *adj.*
—**Syn. 8.** group, gather, throng, crowd, bunch.

clus′ter bomb′, a canister that can be dropped from an aircraft and that opens to release a number of small fragmentation explosives over a wide area. [1960–65]

clus′ter col′lege, a small residential college affiliated with a university but semi-independent and specializing in one field of study.

clus′ter cup′, aecium. [1880–85]

clus′ter fly′, a black fly, *Pollenia rudis,* slightly larger than the housefly, commonly found hibernating in large numbers in homes in the fall.

clus′ter head′ache, *Pathol.* a type of severe recurrent headache associated with dilated carotid arteries and the release of histamine, characterized by sudden attacks of intense pain behind the nostril and eye on one side and accompanied by runny nose, tearing, and flushed skin. [1950–55]

clus′ter leg′, *Furniture.* a leg having the form of a cluster of columns or shafts.

clus′ter point′, *Math.* **1.** a point of a net having the property that the net is frequently in each neighborhood of the point. **2.** See **accumulation point. 3.** a point of a filter having the property that every neighborhood of the point has points in common with every set in the filter.

clus′ter var′iable, *Astron.* See **RR Lyrae star.** [1900–05]

clutch[1] (kluch), *v.t.* **1.** to seize with or as with the hands or claws; snatch: *The bird swooped down and clutched its prey with its claws.* **2.** to grip or hold tightly or firmly: *She clutched the child's hand as they crossed the street.* **3.** *Slang.* to spellbind; grip a person's emotions, attention, or interest: *Garbo movies really clutch me.* —*v.i.* **4.** to try to seize or grasp (usually fol. by *at*): *He clutched at the fleeing child. She clutched at the opportunity.* **5.** *Slang.* to become tense with fright; panic (sometimes fol. by *up*): *I clutched up on the math exam.* **6.** to operate the clutch in a vehicle. —*n.* **7.** the hand, claw, etc., when grasping. **8.** Usually, **clutches.** power of disposal or control; mastery: *She fell into the clutches of the enemy.* **9.** the act of clutching; a snatch or grasp. **10.** a tight grip or hold. **11.** a device for gripping something. **12.** *Auto., Mach.* **a.** a mechanism for readily engaging or disengaging a shaft with or from another shaft or rotating part. Cf. **coupling** (def. 2a). **b.** a control, as a pedal, for operating this mechanism. **13.** *Sports.* an extremely important or crucial moment of a game: *He was famous for his coolness in pitching in the clutch.* **14.** any critical position or situation; emergency: *She kept complete control in the clutch.* **15.** Also called **clutch bag, clutch purse.** a woman's small purse that can be carried in the hand and usually has no handle or strap. —*adj.* **16.** done or accomplished in a critical situation: *a clutch shot that won the basketball game.* **17.** dependable in crucial situations: *a clutch player.* **18.** (of a coat) without fasteners; held closed in front by one's hand or arm. [1175–1225; ME *clucchen,* var. of *clicchen,* OE *clyccan* to clench] —**clutch′ing•ly,** *adv.* —**clutch′y,** *adj.*
—**Syn. 1.** See **catch. 2.** clench, squeeze, hug.

clutch[2] (kluch), *n.* **1.** a hatch of eggs; the number of eggs produced or incubated at one time. **2.** a brood of chickens. **3.** a number of similar individuals: *a clutch of books; a whole clutch of dancers.* —*v.t.* **4.** to hatch (chickens). [1715–25; var. of *cletch* (now dial.); akin to Scots *cleck* to hatch < ON *klekja* to hatch]

clutch′ bag′, clutch (def. 15). Also called **clutch′ purse′.** [1945–50]

Clu•tha (klo͞o′thə), *n.* a river in S New Zealand, on S South Island, flowing NE to the Pacific Ocean. ab. 200 mi. (320 km) long.

clut•ter (klut′ər), *v.t.* **1.** to fill or litter with things in a disorderly manner: *All kinds of papers cluttered the top of his desk.* —*v.i.* **2.** *Brit. Dial.* to run in disorder; move with bustle and confusion. **3.** *Brit. Dial.* to make a clatter. **4.** to speak so rapidly and inexactly that distortions of sound and phrasing result. —*n.* **5.** a disorderly heap or assemblage; litter: *It's impossible to find anything in all this clutter.* **6.** a state or condition of confusion. **7.** confused noise; clatter. **8.** an echo or echoes on a radar screen that do not come from the target and can be caused by such factors as atmospheric conditions, objects other than the target, chaff, and jamming of the radar signal. [1550–60; var. of *clotter* (now obs.), equiv. to CLOT + -ER[6]]
—**Syn. 5.** mess, disorder, jumble.

Clw•yd (klo͞o′id), *n.* a county in N Wales. 374,800; 937 sq. mi. (2426 sq. km).

clyde (klīd), *n. Slang.* **1.** (*sometimes cap.*) a stupid, inept, or boorish person. **2.** the brain or mind. [prob. generic use of the personal name]

Clyde (klīd), *n.* **1.** a river in S Scotland, flowing NW into the Firth of Clyde. 106 mi. (170 km) long. **2. Firth of,** an inlet of the Atlantic, in SW Scotland. 64 mi. (103 km) long. **3.** a male given name: a Scottish family name, after the Clyde River.

Clyde•bank (klīd′bangk′), *n.* a city in SW Scotland, on the Clyde River. 56,529.

Clydes•dale (klīdz′dāl′), *n.* one of a Scottish breed of strong, hardy draft horses, having a feathering of long hairs along the backs of the legs. [1780–90; after *Clydesdale,* Scotland]

clyp•e•ate (klip′ē it, -āt′), *adj. Biol.* shaped like a round shield or buckler. Also, **clyp•e•i•form** (klip′ē ə fôrm′). [1705–15; < L *clypeātus.* See CLYPEUS, -ATE[1]]

clyp•e•us (klip′ē əs), *n., pl.* **clyp•e•i** (klip′ē ī′, -ē ē′). the area of the facial wall of an insect's head between the labrum and the frons, usually separated from the latter by a groove. [1825–35; < NL, special use of L *clypeus, clipeus* round shield] —**clyp′e•al,** *adj.*

cly•sis (klī′sis), *n., pl.* **-ses** (-sēz). *Med.* **1.** the administration of an enema. **2.** intravenous administration of any of a number of solutions to provide nutriment, replace lost body fluid or control blood pressure. [< NL < Gk *klýsis* flushing by an enema; see CLYSTER, -SIS]

clys•ter (klis′tər), *n. Med.* an enema. [1350–1400; ME < L < Gk *klystér,* equiv. to **klyd-* (base of *klýzein* to rinse out; cf. CATACLYSM) + *-tēr* agent n. suffix]

Cly•tem•nes•tra (klī′təm nes′trə), *n. Class. Myth.* the daughter of Tyndareus and Leda, the wife of Agamemnon, and the mother of Orestes, Electra, and Iphigenia. She killed Agamemnon and was herself killed, along with her lover, Aegisthus, by Orestes. Also, **Cly′taem•nes′ra.**

Cly•ti•us (klish′ē əs), *n. Class. Myth.* **1.** (in the *Iliad*) a brother of Priam killed by Hercules. **2.** a companion of Jason. **3.** one of the Gigantes.

CM, Common Market.

Cm, *Symbol, Chem.* curium.

cm, centimeter; centimeters. Also, **cm.**

c/m, (of capital stocks) call of more.

C.M., *Rom. Cath. Ch.* Congregation of the Mission.

c.m., 1. church missionary. **2.** common meter. **3.** corresponding member. **4.** court-martial.

CMA, Canadian Medical Association.

C.M.A., certificate of management accounting.

CMC, 1. certified management consultant. **2.** Commandant of the Marine Corps.

cmd., command.

cmdg., commanding.

Cmdr., Commander.

CME, Chicago Mercantile Exchange.

CMEA, Council for Mutual Economic Assistance. See **COMECON.**

C.M.G., Companion of the Order of St. Michael and St. George.

cml., commercial.

c'mon (kmon, kə mon′), *Informal.* contraction of *come on.* See **come** (defs. 45e, f). [1930–35]

CMOS (sē′môs′, -mos′), *n. Electronics.* complementary metal oxide semiconductor.

CMP, cytidine monophosphate.

CMV, cytomegalovirus.

CN, chloroacetophenone.

C/N, 1. circular note. **2.** credit note.

cne•mis (nē′mis), *n., pl.* **cnem•i•des** (nem′i dēz′). *Anat., Zool.* the tibia or shin. [< Gk *knēmis* greave, akin to *knḗmē* tibia] —**cne′mic, cne′mi•al,** *adj.*

cni•da (nī′də), *n., pl.* **-dae** (-dē). *Zool.* a nematocyst. [1875–80; < L *cnidē* nettle < Gk *knídē*]

Cni•dar•i•a (nī dâr′ē ə), *n. Zool.* an alternative name for the invertebrate phylum Coelenterata, giving emphasis to the stinging structures as characteristic of the phylum. [< NL; see CNIDA, -ARIA]

cni•dar•i•an (nī dâr′ē ən), *n.* **1.** any invertebrate animal, as a hydra, jellyfish, sea anemone, or coral, considered as belonging to the phylum Cnidaria, characterized by the specialized stinging structures in the tentacles surrounding the mouth; a coelenterate. —*adj.* **2.** belonging or pertaining to the Cnidaria. [CNIDARI(A) + -AN]

cnido-, a combining form representing **cnida** in compound words: *cnidophore.*

cni•do•blast (nī′də blast′), *n. Zool.* the cell within which a nematocyst is developed. [1880–85; CNIDO- + -BLAST]

cni•do•cil (nī′də sil), *n. Zool.* a hairlike sensory process projecting from the surface of a cnidoblast, believed to trigger the discharge of the nematocyst. [1880–85; CNIDO- + *-cil* < NL *cilium;* see CILIA]

cni•do•cyst (nī′də sist′), *n. Zool.* a nematocyst. [1885–90; CNIDO- + -CYST]

cni•dog•e•nous (nī doj′ə nəs), *adj. Zool.* producing or containing nematocysts. [1900–05; CNIDO- + -GENOUS]

cni•do•phore (nī′də fôr′, -fōr′), *n. Zool.* a part or organ bearing cnidoblasts. [1885–90; CNIDO- + -PHORE] —**cni•doph•o•rous** (nī dof′ər əs), *adj.*

Cni•dus (nī′dəs), *n.* an ancient city in SW Asia Minor, in Caria: the Athenians defeated the Spartans in a naval battle near here 394 B.C. —**Cni′de•an,** *adj.*

CNM, Certified Nurse Midwife.

CNO, Chief of Naval Operations.

Cnos•sus (nos′əs, kə nos′-), *n.* Knossos. —**Cnos′si•an,** *adj.*

C-note (sē′nōt′), *n.* C (def. 11).

CNS, central nervous system. Also, **cns**

Cnut (kə no͞ot′, -nyo͞ot′), *n.* Canute.

CO, 1. Colorado (approved esp. for use with zip code). 2. Commanding Officer. 3. conscientious objector.

Co, *Symbol, Chem.* cobalt.

co-, var. of **com-** before a vowel, *h,* and *gn: coadjutor; cohabit; cognate.* The prefix **co-** now productively forms new words from bases beginning with any sound (*co-conspirator; co-manage; coseismic*), sometimes with the derived sense "auxiliary, subsidiary" (*coenzyme; copilot*), and, in mathematics and astronomy, with the sense "complement" (*codeclination*).

Co., 1. Company. 2. County. Also, **co.**

C/O, 1. cash order. 2. certificate of origin.

C/o, 1. care of. 2. *Bookkeeping.* carried over.

c/o, 1. care of. 2. *Bookkeeping.* carried over. 3. cash order.

C.O., 1. cash order. 2. Commanding Officer. 3. conscientious objector. 4. correction officer.

c.o., 1. care of. 2. carried over.

COA, change of address.

CoA, coenzyme A.

co·ac·er·vate (*n.* kō as′ər vit, -vāt′, kō′ə sûr′vit; *v.* kō as′ər vāt′, kō′ə sûr′vāt), *n., v.,* **-vat·ed, -vat·ing.** —*n.* 1. *Physical Chem.* a reversible aggregation of liquid particles in an emulsion. —*v.t., v.i.* 2. to make or become a coacervate. [1620–30; < L *coacervātus* (ptp. of *coacervāre* to heap up), equiv. to *co-* CO- + *acerv(us)* heap, multitude + *-ātus* -ATE[1]]

co·ac·er·va·tion (kō as′ər vā′shən), *n. Physical Chem.* the process of becoming a coacervate. [1350–1400; ME *coacervacioun* < L *coacervātiōn-* (s. of *coacervātiō*), equiv. to *coacervāt(us)* (see COACERVATE) + *-iōn-* -ION]

coach (kōch), *n.* 1. a large, horse-drawn, four-wheeled carriage, usually enclosed. 2. a public motorbus. 3. *Railroads.* See **day coach.** 4. Also called **air coach.** a class of airline travel providing less luxurious accommodations than first class at a lower fare. 5. a person who trains an athlete or a team of athletes: *a football coach.* 6. a private tutor who prepares a student for an examination. 7. a person who instructs an actor or singer. 8. *Baseball.* a playing or nonplaying member of the team at bat who is stationed in the box outside first or third base to signal instructions to and advise base runners and batters. 9. *Naut.* an after cabin in a sailing ship, located beneath the poop deck, for use esp. by the commander of the ship. 10. a type of inexpensive automobile with a boxlike, usually two-door, body manufactured in the 1920's. 11. See **mobile home.** —*v.t.* 12. to give instruction or advice to in the capacity of a coach; instruct: *She has coached the present tennis champion.* —*v.i.* 13. to act as a coach. 14. to go by or in a coach. —*adv.* 15. by coach or in coach-class accommodations: *We flew coach from Denver to New York.* [1550–60; 1840–50 for sense "tutor"; earlier *coche(e)* < MF *coche* < G *Kotsche, Kutsche* < Hungarian *kocsi,* short for *kocsi szekér* cart of Kocs, town on the main road between Vienna and Budapest; senses referring to tutoring, from the conception of the tutor as one who carries the student through examinations] —**coach′a·ble,** *adj.* —**coach′a·bil′i·ty,** *n.*
—**Syn.** 6. mentor, preceptor.

coach (def. 1)

coach-and-four (kōch′ən fôr′, -fōr′), *n.* a coach together with the four horses by which it is drawn. [1880–85]

coach′ box′, the seat for the driver of a coach or carriage. [1645–55]

coach′ dog′, Dalmatian (def. 3). [1830–40]

coach·er (kō′chər), *n.* 1. a person who coaches; coach. 2. See **coach horse.** [1580–90; COACH + -ER[1]]

coach′ horse′, a horse, usually strong and heavily built, for drawing a coach. [1580–90]

coach′ house′, a small building, usually part of an estate or adjacent to a main house, used for housing coaches, carriages, and other vehicles. Also called **carriage house.** [1670–80]

coach′ing glass′, a small drinking glass of the early 19th century having no foot. Also called **fuddling glass.**

coach·man (kōch′mən), *n., pl.* **-men.** 1. a man employed to drive a coach or carriage. 2. *Angling.* See **royal coachman.** [1570–80; COACH + MAN]

coach′ screw′. See **lag screw.** [1870–75]

coach·whip (kōch′hwip′, -wip′), *n.* 1. a whip, usually having a long lash, used in driving a coach horse. 2. Also called **coach′whip snake′.** a long, slender snake, *Masticophis flagellum,* of the southern U.S. and Mexico, having a thin tail resembling a braided whip. [1730–40; COACH + WHIP]

co·act (kō akt′), *v.t., v.i.* to do or act together. [1375–1425 for earlier adj. senses "compelled or forced (to do something)"; 1600–10 for current (intrans.) sense; late ME; see CO-, ACT] —**co·ac′tor,** *n.*

co·ac·tion[1] (kō ak′shən), *n.* force or compulsion, either in restraining or in impelling. [1350–1400; ME < L *coāctiōn-* (s. of *coāctiō*), equiv. to *coāct(us)* (ptp. of *cōgere;* see COGENT, CO-, ACT) + *-iōn-* -ION]

co·ac·tion[2] (kō ak′shən), *n.* 1. joint action. 2. *Ecol.* any interaction among organisms within a community. [1615–25; CO- + ACTION]

co·ac·tive[1] (kō ak′tiv), *adj.* compulsory; coercive. [1590–1600; COACT(ION)[1] + -IVE] —**co·ac′tive·ly,** *adv.* —**co′ac·tiv′i·ty,** *n.*

co·ac·tive[2] (kō ak′tiv), *adj.* acting together. [1590–1600; CO- + ACTIVE] —**co·ac′tive·ly,** *adv.* —**co′ac·tiv′i·ty,** *n.*

co·ad·ap·ta·tion (kō′ad əp tā′shən), *n.* 1. *Biol.* the correlation of structural or behavioral characteristics in two or more interacting organisms in a community or organs in an organism resulting from progressive accommodation by natural selection. 2. Also called **integration.** *Genetics.* the accumulation in a population's gene pool of genes that interact by harmonious epistasis in the development of an organism. [1830–40; CO- + ADAPTATION] —**co′ad·ap·ta′tion·al,** *adj.* —**co′ad·ap·ta′tion·al·ly,** *adv.*

co·a·dapt·ed (kō′ə dap′tid), *adj.* having undergone coadaptation; mutually accommodating. [CO- + ADAPT + -ED[2]]

Coade′ stone′ (kōd), a ceramic imitation of carved stonework popular in England around 1800. [named after Eleanor *Coade,* late 18th-century English manufacturer]

co·ad·ju·tant (kō aj′ə tənt), *adj.* 1. helping reciprocally; cooperating. —*n.* 2. an assistant; aide. [1700–10; CO- + ADJUTANT]

co·ad·ju·tor (kō aj′ə tər, kō′ə jo͞o′tər), *n.* 1. an assistant. 2. an assistant to a bishop or other ecclesiastic. 3. a bishop who assists another bishop, with the right of succession. [1400–50; late ME < L, equiv. to *co-* CO- + *adjūtor* helper (*adjū-* base of *adjuvāre* to help (cf. ADJUTANT) + *-tor* -TOR)]

co·ad·u·nate (kō aj′ə nit, -nāt′), *adj. Zool., Bot.* united by growth. [1600–10; < LL *coadūnātus* (ptp. of *coadūnāre* to unite), equiv. to *co-* CO- + *ad-* AD- + *ūn(us)* one + *-ātus* -ATE[1]] —**co·ad′u·na′tion,** *n.*

co·ad·ven·ture (kō′əd ven′chər), *n., v.,* **-tured, -turing.** —*n.* 1. adventure in which two or more share. —*v.i.* 2. to share in an adventure. [1635–45; CO- + ADVENTURE] —**co′ad·ven′tur·er,** *n.*

co·a·gen·cy (kō ā′jən sē), *n., pl.* **-cies.** joint agency. [1605–15; CO- + AGENCY]

co·a·gent (kō ā′jənt), *n.* a joint agent. [1590–1600; CO- + AGENT]

co·ag·u·la·ble (kō ag′yə lə bəl), *adj.* capable of being coagulated. [1645–55; COAGUL(ATE) + -ABLE] —**co·ag′u·la·bil′i·ty,** *n.*

co·ag·u·lant (kō ag′yə lənt), *n.* a substance that produces or aids coagulation. Also, **co·ag·u·la·tor** (kō ag′yə lā′tər). [1760–70; < L *coāgulant-* (s. of *coāgulāns,* prp. of *coāgulāre* to COAGULATE), equiv. to *coāgul(um)* COAGULUM + *-ant-* -ANT]

co·ag·u·late (*v.* kō ag′yə lāt′; *adj.* kō ag′yə lit, -lāt′), *v.,* **-lat·ed, -lat·ing,** *adj.* —*v.t., v.i.* 1. to change from a fluid into a thickened mass; curdle; congeal: *Let the pudding stand two hours until it coagulates.* 2. *Biol.* (of blood) to form a clot. 3. *Physical Chem.* (of colloidal particles) to flocculate or cause to flocculate by adding an electrolyte to an electrostatic colloid. —*adj.* 4. *Obs.* coagulated. [1350–1400 for earlier ptp. senses "solidified, clotted," 1605–15 for def. 1; ME < L *coāgulāt(us)* (ptp. of *coāgulāre*), equiv. to *coāgul(um)* COAGULUM + *-ātus* -ATE[1]] —**co·ag′u·la′tion,** *n.* —**co·ag·u·la·to·ry** (kō ag′yə lə tôr′ē, -tōr′ē), **co·ag·u·la·tive** (kō ag′yə lā′tiv, -lə tiv), *adj.*
—**Syn.** 1. clot, set, solidify, thicken.

co·ag·u·lum (kō ag′yə ləm), *n., pl.* **-la** (-lə). any coagulated mass; precipitate; clump; clot. [1650–60; < L: that which binds together or coagulates, rennet, equiv. to *co-* CO- + *āg-,* comb. form, in n. derivation, of *agere* to drive, do (see AMBAGES, INDAGATE) + *-ulum* -ULE; cf. *cōgere* to make congeal, lit., to drive together; see COGENT]

Co·a·hui·la (kô′ä wē′lä), *n.* a state in N Mexico. 1,334,000; 58,067 sq. mi. (150,395 sq. km). *Cap.:* Saltillo.

coak (kōk), *n. Carpentry.* 1. (in a scarf joint) a tenon in one member fitting into a corresponding recess of the other. 2. a dowel through overlapping timbers to prevent one from sliding across the other. [1785–95; of uncert. orig.]

coal (kōl), *n.* 1. a black or dark-brown combustible mineral substance consisting of carbonized vegetable matter, used as a fuel. Cf. **anthracite, bituminous coal, lignite.** 2. a piece of glowing, charred, or burned wood or other combustible substance. 3. charcoal (def. 1). 4. **heap coals of fire on someone's head,** to repay evil with good in order to make one's enemy repent. 5. **rake, haul, drag, call,** or **take over the coals,** to reprimand; scold: *They were raked over the coals for turning out slipshod work.* —*v.t.* 6. to burn to coal or charcoal. 7. to provide with coal. —*v.i.* 8. to take in coal for fuel. [bef. 900; ME *cole,* OE *col;* c. D *kool,* G *Kohle,* ON *kol*] —**coal′less,** *adj.*

co·a·la (kō ä′lə), *n.* koala.

coal′ ball′, a spherical mass of mineral and plant material embedded in coal beds, ranging in size from that of a pea to that of a boulder. [1735–45]

coal·bin (kōl′bin′), *n.* a bin used for holding coal. [1860–65, *Amer.;* COAL + BIN]

coal′ car′, 1. a railroad car designed to carry coal. 2. a car for hauling coal in or from a mine. [1855–60, *Amer.*]

coal′ cut′ter, a machine for cutting a kerf, esp. in longwall mining. [1870–75]

coal·er (kō′lər), *n.* a railroad, ship, etc., used mainly to haul or supply coal. [1865–70; COAL + -ER[1]]

co·a·lesce (kō′ə les′), *v.,* **-lesced, -lesc·ing.** —*v.i.* 1. to grow together or into one body: *The two lakes coalesced into one.* 2. to unite so as to form one mass, community, etc.: *The various groups coalesced into a crowd.* 3. to blend or come together: *Their ideas coalesced into one theory.* —*v.t.* 4. to cause to unite in one body or mass. [1535–45; < L *coalēscere,* equiv. to *co-* CO- + *al-* (s. of *alere* to nourish, make grow) + *-ēscere* -ESCE] —**co′a·les′cence,** *n.* —**co′a·les′cent,** *adj.*
—**Syn.** 1, 2. unite, combine, join. 2. amalgamate, fuse, blend, merge.

coal′ field′, an area containing significant coal deposits. [1805–15]

coal·fish (kōl′fish′), *n., pl.* **-fish·es,** (*esp. collectively*) **-fish.** 1. a sablefish. 2. a pollack. [1595–1605; COAL + FISH]

coal′ gas′, 1. a gas used for illuminating and heating, produced by distilling bituminous coal and consisting chiefly of hydrogen, methane, and carbon monoxide. 2. the gas formed by burning coal. [1800–10]

coal′ heav′er, a person who carries or shovels coal. [1755–65]

coal′ hod′, a small pail for carrying coal; a coal scuttle. [1815–25]

coal·i·fi·ca·tion (kō′lə fi kā′shən), *n. Geol.* the conversion of plant material into coal by natural processes, as by diagenesis and, in some instances, metamorphism. [1910–15; COAL + -I- + -FICATION]

coal′ing sta′tion, a place at which coal is supplied to ships, locomotives, etc. [1865–70]

co·a·li·tion (kō′ə lish′ən), *n.* 1. a combination or alliance, esp. a temporary one between persons, factions, states, etc. 2. a union into one body or mass; fusion. [1605–15; < L *coalitiōn-* (s. of *coalitiō*), equiv. to *coalit(us),* ptp. of *coalēscere* (*co-* CO- + *ali-,* ptp. s. of *alere* to nourish + *-tus* ptp. suffix) + *-iōn-* -ION; see COALESCE] —**co′a·li′tion·al,** *adj.* —**co′a·li′tion·er,** *n.*
—**Syn.** 1. partnership; league.

co·a·li·tion·ism (kō′ə lish′ə niz′əm), *n.* the idea, principle, or policy of favoring or supporting the concept of coalition or a specific coalition, esp. in politics. [1920–25; COALITION + -ISM] —**co′a·li′tion·ist,** *n.*

coal′ meas′ures, *Geol.* 1. coal-bearing strata. 2. (*caps.*) in Europe, a portion of the Carboniferous System, characterized by widespread coal deposits. [1655–65]

coal′ mine′, a mine or pit from which coal is obtained. [1605–15] —**coal′ min′er.** —**coal′ min′ing.**

coal′ oil′, *Older U.S. Use and Canadian.* 1. petroleum obtained by the destructive distillation of bituminous coal. 2. kerosene. [1855–60, *Amer.*]

coal′ pit′, 1. a pit where coal is dug. 2. a place where charcoal is made. [bef. 1050; ME *colpytte,* OE *collpytt*]

Coal·sack (kōl′sak′), *n. Astron.* a dark nebula in the southern constellation Crux, whose dust particles obscure light from Milky Way stars behind it. Also, **Coal′ Sack′.** Also called **Southern Coalsack.** [1625–35; COAL + SACK[1]]

coal′ scut′tle, a metal bucket, usually with a lip, for holding and carrying coal. [1765–75]

coal′ seam′, a bed of coal. [1840–50]

coal′ tar′, a thick, black, viscid liquid formed during the distillation of coal, that upon further distillation yields compounds, as benzene, anthracene, and phenol, from which are derived a large number of dyes, drugs, and other synthetic compounds, and that yields a final residuum (**coal′-tar pitch′**), which is used chiefly in making pavements. [1775–85] —**coal-tar** (kōl′tär′), *adj.*

coal′-tar cre′osote, impure phenol or carbolic acid, distinct from the creosote of wood tar.

coal·y (kō′lē), *adj.,* **coal·i·er, coal·i·est.** of, resembling, or containing coal. [1555–65; COAL + -Y[1]]

coam·ing (kō′ming), *n.* a raised border around an opening in a deck, roof, or floor, designed to prevent water from running below. [1605–15; earlier *coming,* appar. equiv. to COMB (in sense "crest") + -ING[1]]

C, coaming

Co·a·mo (kô ä′mô), *n.* a city in S central Puerto Rico. 12,851.

co·an·chor (kō ang′kər), *v.t.* 1. to anchor (a news broadcast or other program) jointly with another. —*v.i.* 2. to anchor a news broadcast or other program jointly with another. —*n.* 3. a person who coanchors. [1965–70; CO- + ANCHOR] —**co·an′chor·ship′,** *n.*

Co·an·da (kô än dä′), *n.* **Hen·ri Ma·rie** (äN rē′ ma-rē′), 1885–1972, French engineer and inventor.

co·apt (kō apt′), *v.t.* to bring close together: *The surgeons coapted the edges of the wound.* [1560–70; < L *coapt(āre),* equiv. to *co-* CO- + *aptāre* to put into position, v. deriv. of *aptus* APT]

CONCISE PRONUNCIATION KEY: act, cāpe, dâre, pärt; set, ēqual; *if,* īce; ox, ōver, ôrder, oil, bo͝ok, bo͞ot, out; up, ûrge; child; sing; shoe; thin, *th*at; zh as in *treasure.* ə = *a* as in *alone, e* as in *system, i* as in *easily, o* as in *gallop, u* as in *circus;* [ə] as in *fire* (fī[ə]r), *hour* (ou[ə]r). l and n can serve as syllabic consonants, as in *cradle* (krād′l), and *button* (but′n). See the full key inside the front cover.

co·ap·ta·tion (kō′ap tā′shən), *n.* a joining or adjustment of parts to one another: *the coaptation of a broken bone.* [1555–65; < LL *coaptātiōn-,* s. of *coaptātiō;* see COAPT, -ATION]

co·arc·tate (kō ärk′tāt, -tit), *adj.* (of a pupa) having the body enclosed in a hardened shell or puparium. [1375–1425 for sense "confined, restricted," 1810–20 for current sense; late ME < L *coarctātus,* var. of *coartātus* (ptp. of *coartāre* to press together), equiv. to *co-* CO- + *art(us)* tight (see ARTICLE) + *-ātus* -ATE[1]]

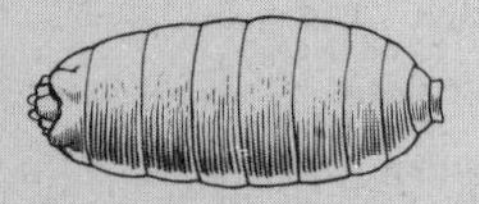
coarctate pupa of a fly

co·arc·ta·tion (kō′ärk tā′shən), *n.* **1.** *Pathol.* **a.** a narrowing of the lumen of a blood vessel. **b.** a congenital anomaly of the heart in which there is a narrowing of the aorta, resulting in abnormal blood flow. **2.** *Entomol.* the condition of having the body enclosed in a hardened shell or puparium. [1400–50; late ME *coartacioun* pressure, constriction < L *coar(c)tātiōn-,* s. of *coar(c)tātiō;* see COARCTATE, -ION]

coarse (kôrs, kōrs), *adj.,* **coars·er, coars·est.** **1.** composed of relatively large parts or particles: *The beach had rough, coarse sand.* **2.** lacking in fineness or delicacy of texture, structure, etc.: *The stiff, coarse fabric irritated her skin.* **3.** harsh; grating. **4.** lacking delicacy, taste, or refinement; unpolished: *He had coarse manners but an absolutely first-rate mind.* **5.** of inferior or faulty quality; common; base. **6.** vulgar; obscene; crude: *His coarse language angered us.* **7.** (of metals) unrefined. **8.** (of a metal file) having the maximum commercial grade of coarseness. [1550–60; earlier *cors(e), course, cowarce;* of obscure orig.] **—coarse′ly,** *adv.* **—coarse′ness,** *n.*
—Syn. 2, 4. crude, rude, rough. **4.** vulgar, gross, crass. **6.** indelicate. **—Ant. 4.** refined, sensitive.

coarse-grained (kôrs′grānd′, kōrs′-), *adj.* **1.** having a coarse texture or grain. **2.** indelicate; crude; vulgar; gross: *a coarse-grained person with vulgar manners.* [1760–70] **—coarse′-grained′ness,** *n.*

coars·en (kôr′sən, kōr′-), *v.t., v.i.* to make or become coarse. [1795–1805; COARSE + -EN[1]]

coars·er (kôr′sər, kōr′-), *adj. Math.* of or pertaining to a topology on a topological space whose open sets are included among the open sets of a second specified topology on the space. Cf. **finer.** [COARSE + -ER[4]]

co·ar·tic·u·la·tion (kō′är tik′yə lā′shən), *n. Phonet.* **1.** concomitance of articulation, as in *fro,* ostensibly a succession of three discrete sounds but physically a single articulation (f-) blending into a coarticulation (-fr-), which blends into an articulation (-r-), which blends into a coarticulation (-ro-), which blends into an articulation (-o). **2.** Also called **secondary articulation.** the movement during the articulation of a given sound of one or more articulators not directly involved in producing the sound. [1605–15; CO- + ARTICULATION]

coast (kōst), *n.* **1.** the land next to the sea; seashore: *the rocky coast of Maine.* **2.** the region adjoining it: *They live on the coast, a few miles from the sea.* **3.** a hill or slope down which one may slide on a sled. **4.** a slide or ride down a hill or slope, as on a sled. **5.** *Obs.* the boundary or border of a country. **6. the Coast,** *Informal.* (in the U.S. and Canada) the region bordering on the Pacific Ocean; the West Coast: *I'm flying out to the Coast next week.* **7. the coast is clear,** no danger or impediment exists; no persons are in the path or vicinity: *The boys waited until the coast was clear before climbing over the wall.* —*v.i.* **8.** to slide on a sled down a snowy or icy hillside or incline. **9.** to descend a hill or the like, as on a bicycle, without using pedals. **10.** to continue to move or advance after effort has ceased; keep going on acquired momentum: *We cut off the car engine and coasted for a while.* **11.** to advance or proceed with little or no effort, esp. owing to one's actual or former assets, as wealth, position, or name, or those of another: *The actor coasted to stardom on his father's name.* **12.** to sail along, or call at the various ports of, a coast. **13.** *Obs.* to proceed in a roundabout way. —*v.t.* **14.** to cause to move along under acquired momentum: *to coast a rocket around the sun.* **15.** to proceed along or near the coast of. **16.** *Obs.* to keep alongside of (a person moving). **17.** *Obs.* to go by the side or border of. [1325–75; (n.) ME *cost(e)* < AF, MF < L *costa* rib, side, wall; (v.) ME *cost(e)yen, costen* < AF *costeier,* OF *costoier,* deriv. of the n.]
—Syn. 1. strand, seaside, littoral. See **shore[1].**

coast·al (kōs′tl), *adj.* of, relating to, bordering on, or located near a coast: *The coastal regions are inundated at high tide.* [1880–85; COAST + -AL[1]] **—coast′al·ly,** *adv.*

coast′al plain′, a plain extending along a coast. [1895–1900, *Amer.*]

coast′ artil′lery, **1.** artillery used for defending coastal areas. **2.** a military unit manning such artillery.

coast·er (kō′stər), *n.* **1.** a person or thing that coasts. **2.** a small dish, tray, or mat, esp. for placing under a glass to protect a table from moisture. **3.** a ship engaged in coastwise trade. **4.** a sled for coasting. **5.** a tray for holding a decanter to be passed around a dining table. **6.** See **roller coaster.** [1565–75; COAST + -ER[1]]

coast′er brake′, a brake on the hub of the rear wheel of freewheel bicycles, operated by back pressure on the pedals. [1885–90]

Coast′ Guard′, **1.** *U.S. Mil.* a military service under the Department of Transportation, which in peacetime enforces maritime laws, saves lives and property at sea, and maintains aids to navigation, and which in wartime may be placed under the Navy Department to augment the navy. **2.** (*l.c.*) any similar organization for aiding navigation, preventing smuggling, etc. **3.** (*l.c.*) Also called **coastguardsman.** a member of any such organization. [1825–35]

coast′-guard cut′ter (kōst′gärd′), a cutter used by the U.S. Coast Guard.

coast·guards·man (kōst′gärdz′mən), *n., pl.* **-men.** See **Coast Guard** (def. 3). [1840–50; COAST GUARD + -'S[1] + MAN[1]]

coast′ing lead′ (led), *Naut.* a lead used in sounding depths of from 20 to 60 fathoms.

coast′ing trade′, trade between ports along the same coast. [1735–45]

coast′ing wag′on, a toy wagon for children, often used for coasting down hills.

coast·land (kōst′land′), *n.* land along a coast; seacoast. [1850–55; COAST + LAND]

coast·line (kōst′līn′), *n.* **1.** the outline or contour of a coast; shoreline. **2.** the land and water lying adjacent to a shoreline. [1855–60; COAST + LINE[1]]

coast′ live′ oak′. See **California live oak.** [1880–85, *Amer.*]

coast′ pi′lot, **1.** Also called **pilot.** a manual published by a government for mariners, containing descriptions of coastal waters, harbor facilities, etc., for a specific area. **2.** a pilot of coasting vessels.

Coast′ Range′, a series of mountain ranges along the Pacific coast of North America, extending from Lower California to SE Alaska. Also, **Coast′ Moun′tains.**

coast′ red′wood, the redwood, *Sequoia sempervirens.*

coast′ rhododen′dron, a rhododendron, *Rhododendron macrophyllum,* of western North America, having large clusters of rose-purple flowers spotted with brown: the state flower of Washington. Also called **California rosebay, pink rhododendron.**

coast-to-coast (kōst′tə kōst′), *adj.* extending, going, or operating from one coast of the U.S. to the other: *a coast-to-coast television network.* [1910–15]

coast·ward (kōst′wərd), *adv.* **1.** Also, **coast′wards.** toward the coast: *We left the sinking ship in lifeboats and rowed coastward.* —*adj.* **2.** directed toward the coast: *a coastward migration.* [1850–55; COAST + -WARD]

coast·ways (kōst′wāz′), *adv., adj. Archaic.* coastwise. [1695–1705]

coast·wise (kōst′wīz′), *adv.* **1.** along the coast: *We sailed coastwise for days before finding a harbor.* —*adj.* **2.** following the coast. [1685–95; COAST + -WISE]

coat (kōt), *n.* **1.** an outer garment with sleeves, covering at least the upper part of the body: *a new fur coat; a coat for formal wear.* **2.** a natural integument or covering, as the hair, fur, or wool of an animal, the bark of a tree, or the skin of a fruit. **3.** a layer of anything that covers a surface: *That wall needs another coat of paint.* **4.** a mucous layer covering or lining an organ or connected parts, as on the tongue. **5.** See **coat of arms. 6.** *Archaic.* a petticoat or skirt. **7.** *Obs.* **a.** a garment indicating profession, class, etc. **b.** the profession, class, etc., so indicated. —*v.t.* **8.** to cover with a layer or coating: *He coated the wall with paint. The furniture was coated with dust.* **9.** to cover thickly, esp. with a viscous fluid or substance: *Heat the mixture until it coats a spoon. The boy was coated with mud from head to foot.* **10.** to cover or provide with a coat. [1250–1300; ME *cote* < AF, OF < Gmc; cf. G *Kotze,* OS *cott* woolen coat] **—coat′er,** *n.* **—coat′less,** *adj.*
—Syn. 8. spread, smear, encrust.

Coat·bridge (kōt′brij′), *n.* a city in the Strathclyde region, in central Scotland, near Glasgow. 51,985.

coat′ card′. See **face card.** [1555–65]

coat·dress (kōt′dres′), *n.* a tailored dress of medium or heavy fabric, styled like a coat and worn in place of a suit or similar outfit. [1910–15; COAT + DRESS]

coat·ed (kō′tid), *adj.* **1.** having a coat. **2.** (of paper) having a highly polished coating applied to provide a smooth surface for printing. **3.** (of a fabric) having a coating, as of plastic, paint, or pyroxylin, to make it impervious to moisture. [1555–65; COAT + -ED[3]]

coat′ed pit′, *Cell Biol.* a clathrin-lined depression in the outer surface of a cell membrane, formed of receptors and their specific ligands, that becomes a coated vesicle upon endocytosis.

coat′ed ves′icle, *Cell Biol.* a clathrin-covered vesicle that forms from the closure of a coated pit, engulfing the ligand-receptor complex in endocytosis.

coat·ee (kō tē′), *n.* a close-fitting short coat, esp. one with tails or skirts. [1750–60, *Amer.;* formation modeled on GOATEE]

Coates (kōts), *n.* **1. Eric,** 1886–1957, English violist and composer. **2. Joseph Gordon,** 1878–1943, New Zealand statesman: prime minister 1925–28.

Coates·ville (kōts′vil), *n.* a city in SE Pennsylvania. 10,698.

coat′ flow′er, a plant, *Petrorhagia saxifraga,* of the pink family, native to Eurasia, having pink or white flowers in terminal branching clusters. Also called **tunic flower.**

coat′ hang′er, hanger (def. 1). [1890–95]

co·a·ti (kō ä′tē), *n., pl.* **-tis.** any tropical American carnivore of the genus *Nasua,* related to the raccoon, having an elongated body, long, ringed tail, and a slender, flexible snout. Also, **co·a·ti·mon·di, co·a·ti·mun·di** (kō ä′tē mun′dē). [1670–80; < Pg < Tupi]

coati, *Nasua nasua,* 1 ft. (0.3 m) high at shoulder; head and body 1½ ft. (0.46 m); tail to 2½ ft. (0.8 m)

coat·ing (kō′ting), *n.* **1.** a layer of any substance spread over a surface. **2.** fabric for making coats. [1760–70; COAT + -ING[1]]
—Syn. 1. coat, covering, film, sheet, veneer.

coat′ of arms′, **1.** a surcoat or tabard embroidered with heraldic devices, worn by medieval knights over their armor. **2.** a heraldic achievement of arms. [1325–75; ME; parallel to F *cotte d'armes*]

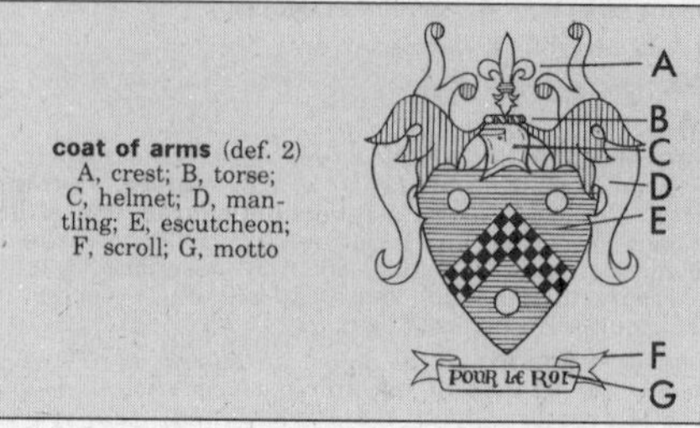

coat of arms (def. 2) A, crest; B, torse; C, helmet; D, mantling; E, escutcheon; F, scroll; G, motto

coat′ of mail′, a long defensive garment made of interlinked metal rings; hauberk; byrnie. [1480–90; parallel to F *cotte de mailles*]

coat′ pro′tein, any protein that is a constituent of the capsid of a virus. [1975–80]

coat·rack (kōt′rak′), *n.* a rack or stand for the temporary hanging or storing of coats, hats, etc. [1910–15; COAT + RACK[1]]

coat·room (kōt′ro͞om′, -ro͝om′), *n.* cloakroom (def. 1). [1865–70; COAT + ROOM]

Coats·worth (kōts′wûrth′), *n.* **Elizabeth,** 1893–1986, U.S. writer, esp. of children's books.

coat·tail (kōt′tāl′), *n.* **1.** the back of the skirt on a man's coat or jacket. **2.** one of the two back parts of the skirt of a coat, esp. one of the tails on a tail coat. **3. on someone's coattails,** aided by association with another person: *The senator rode into office on the President's coattails.* **4. on the coattails of,** immediately after or as a result of: *His decline in popularity followed on the coattails of the scandal.* —*adj.* **5.** gained by association with another, esp. with a successful or celebrated person: *coattail benefits.* [1590–1600; COAT + TAIL[1]]

coat-trail·ing (kōt′trā′ling), *n. Brit.* behavior that is deliberately provocative. [1925–30; from the phrase *trail one's coat,* provoking someone to step on it]

coat′ tree′. See **clothes tree.** [1940–45]

co·au·thor (kō ô′thər, kō′ô′-), *n.* **1.** one of two or more joint authors. —*v.t.* **2.** to write in joint authorship. [1860–65; CO- + AUTHOR]

coax[1] (kōks), *v.t.* **1.** to attempt to influence by gentle persuasion, flattery, etc.; cajole: *He coaxed her to sing, but she refused.* **2.** to obtain by coaxing: *We coaxed the secret from him.* **3.** to manipulate to a desired end by adroit handling or persistent effort: *He coaxed the large chair through the door.* **4.** *Obs.* **a.** to fondle. **b.** to fool; deceive. —*v.i.* **5.** to use gentle persuasion. [1580–90; v. use of *cokes* fool (now obs.), perh. var. of COXCOMB] **—coax′er,** *n.* **—coax′ing·ly,** *adv.*

co·ax[2] (kō aks′, kō′aks), *n. Elect.* See **coaxial cable.** [1945–50; by shortening]

co·ax·i·al (kō ak′sē əl), *adj.* **1.** Also, **co·ax·al** (kō-ak′səl). having a common axis or coincident axes. **2.** *Geom.* **a.** (of a set of circles) having the property that each pair of circles has the same radical axis. **b.** (of planes) intersecting in a straight line. **3.** (of a loudspeaker) having two or more cones with their centers mounted on the same axis. [1880–85; CO- + AXIAL] **—co·ax′i·al·ly,** *adv.*

coax′ial ca′ble, *Elect.* a cable that consists of an insulated conducting tube through which a central, insulated conductor runs, used for transmitting high-frequency telephone, telegraph, digital, or television signals. Also called **coax.** [1935–40]

cob (kob), *n.* **1.** a corncob. **2.** a male swan. **3.** a short-legged, thick-set horse, often having a high gait and frequently used for driving. **4.** *Brit.* a mixture of clay and straw, used as a building material. **5.** *Brit. Dial.* a rounded mass or lump. **6.** a crude silver or gold Spanish-American coin of the 16th to 18th centuries, characteristically irregular in shape and bearing only a partial impression of the dies from which it was struck. [1375–1425; late ME *cobbe* male swan, leader of a gang; these and various subsequent senses are obscurely related and prob. in part of distinct orig.]

co·bal·a·min (kō bal′ə min), *n.* See **vitamin B_{12}.** Also, **co·bal·a·mine** (kō bal′ə mēn′). [1945–50; CO-BAL(T) + (VIT)AMIN]

co·balt (kō′bôlt), *n.* a silver-white metallic element with a faint pinkish tinge, occurring in compounds whose silicates afford important blue coloring substances for ceramics. *Symbol:* Co; *at. wt.:* 58.933; *at. no.:* 27; *sp. gr.:* 8.9 at 20°C. [1675–85; < G *Kobalt,* var. of *Kobold* KOBOLD]

cobalt 60, *Chem.* a radioactive isotope of cobalt having a mass number of 60 and a half-life of 5.2 years, used chiefly in radiotherapy. [1945–50]

co·balt·am·mine (kō′bôlt am′ēn, -ə mēn′), *n.* any of

CONCISE ETYMOLOGY KEY: <, descended or borrowed from; >, whence; b., blend of, blended; c., cognate with; cf., compare; deriv., derivative; equiv., equivalent; imit., imitative; obl., oblique; r., replacing; s., stem; sp., spelling, spelled; resp., respelling, respelled; trans., translation; ?, origin unknown; *, unattested; ‡, probably earlier than. See the full key inside the front cover.

the various complex derivatives of cobalt containing one or more molecules of ammonia bonded to the cobalt. [1880–85; < F *cobaltamine;* see COBALT, AMMINE]

co′balt bloom′, *Mineral.* erythrite (def. 1) [1770–80]

co′balt blue′, **1.** a deep blue to a strong greenish-blue color. **2.** any of a number of pigments containing an oxide of cobalt. Also called **king's blue, Thenard's blue.** [1825–35]

co′balt green′, **1.** a medium, yellowish-green color. **2.** Also called **zinc green.** a pigment used in painting consisting mainly of oxides of cobalt and zinc, characterized chiefly by its green color, fast drying rate, permanence, and lack of tinting strength. [1870–75]

co•bal•tic (kō bôl′tik), *adj.* of or containing cobalt, esp. in the trivalent state. [1775–85; COBALT + -IC]

co•bal•tite (kō bôl′tīt, kō′bôl tīt′), *n.* a mineral, cobalt arsenic sulfide, CoAsS, silver-white with a reddish tinge: an end member of a series of solid solutions that includes gersdorffite; used as an ore of cobalt. [1865–70; COBALT + -ITE[1]]

co•bal•tous (kō bôl′təs), *adj.* containing bivalent cobalt. [1860–65; COBALT + -OUS]

cobal′tous hydrox′ide, a rose-red, amorphous, water-insoluble powder, $Co_2O_3·3H_2O$, used chiefly in the preparation of cobalt salts and in the manufacture of paint and varnish driers. Also, **co′balt hydrox′ide, cobal′tic hydrox′ide.**

co′balt vi′olet deep′, **1.** a medium to strong purple color. **2.** a pigment consisting mainly of phosphate of cobalt, characterized by its violet color, fast drying rate, permanence, and lack of tinting strength.

co′balt vi′olet light′, a pigment used in painting consisting mainly of arsenate of cobalt, characterized chiefly by its violet color, permanence, and poisonous properties.

co′balt yel′low, **1.** aureolin. **2.** Also called **co′balt potas′sium ni′trite.** See **potassium cobaltinitrite.** [1870–75]

Cobb (kob), *n.* **1. How•ell** (hou′əl), 1815–68, U.S. politician: Speaker of the House 1849–51. **2. Irvin S(hrewsbury),** 1876–1944, U.S. humorist and writer. **3. Ty(rus Raymond)** (tī′rəs), (*"the Georgia Peach"*), 1886–1961, U.S. baseball player.

cob•ber (kob′ər), *n. Australian.* a close fellow male friend; chum; pal. [1890–95; of uncert. orig.]

Cob•bett (kob′it), *n.* **William** (*"Peter Porcupine"*), 1763–1835, English political essayist and journalist in the U.S. and England.

cob•bing (kob′ing), *n. Metall.* old refractory material removed from furnaces. [1760–70; *cob* (v.) to break up, special use of COB + -ING[1]]

cob•ble[1] (kob′əl), *v.t.* **-bled, -bling.** **1.** to mend (shoes, boots, etc.); patch. **2.** to put together roughly or clumsily. [1490–1500; appar. back formation from COBBLER]

cob•ble[2] (kob′əl), *n., v.,* **-bled, -bling.** —*n.* **1.** a cobblestone. **2. cobbles,** coal in lumps larger than a pebble and smaller than a boulder. **3.** *Metalworking.* **a.** a defect in a rolled piece resulting from loss of control over its movement. **b.** *Slang.* a piece showing bad workmanship. —*v.t.* **4.** to pave with cobblestones. [1595–1605; perh. COB + -LE; see COBBLESTONE]

cob•bler (kob′lər), *n.* **1.** a person who mends shoes. **2.** a deep-dish fruit pie with a rich biscuit crust, usually only on top. **3.** an iced drink made of wine or liquor, fruits, sugar, etc. **4.** a fabric rejected because of defective dyeing or finishing. **5.** a mummichog. **6.** *Archaic.* a clumsy workman. [1250–1300; ME *cobelere,* equiv. to *cobel* (< ?) + *-ere* -ER[1]]

cob•ble•stone (kob′əl stōn′), *n.* a naturally rounded stone, larger than a pebble and smaller than a boulder, formerly used in paving. [1400–50; late ME *cobylstone.* See COBBLE[1], STONE] —**cob′ble•stoned′,** *adj.*

cob′ coal′, coal in large round lumps. [1795–1805]

Cob•den (kob′dən), *n.* **Richard,** 1804–65, English manufacturer, merchant, economist, and statesman.

co•bel•lig•er•ent (kō′bə lij′ər ənt), *n.* a state or individual that cooperates with, but is not bound by a formal alliance to another in waging war. [1805–15; CO- + BELLIGERENT]

Cóbh (kōv), *n.* a seaport in S Republic of Ireland: port for Cork. 6586. Formerly, **Queenstown.**

Cob•ham (kob′əm), *n.* **Sir John.** See **Oldcastle, Sir John.**

co•bi•a (kō′bē ə), *n.* a large, fusiform fish, *Rachycentron canadum,* found off the eastern coast of temperate and tropical America, in the East Indies, and in Japan. [1870–75; *Amer.*; of obscure orig.]

Co•blenz (kō′blents), *n.* a city in W West Germany, at the junction of the Rhine and Moselle rivers. 118,394. Also, **Koblenz.**

cob•nut (kob′nut′), *n.* **1.** the nut of certain cultivated varieties of hazel, *Corylus avellana grandis.* **2.** a tree bearing such nuts. [1400–50; late ME *cobylle nutt.* See COBBLE[1], NUT]

COBOL (kō′bôl), *n. Computers.* a programming language particularly suited for writing programs to process large files of data, using a vocabulary of common English words, phrases, and sentences. [1955–60; *co(mmon) b(usiness)-o(riented) l(anguage)*]

co•boss (kə bôs′, -bos′, kō-), *interj. Chiefly Northern U.S.* (used to summon cows from the pasture.) [1890–95; co reduced form of COME + BOSS[3]]

Co•bourg (kō′bûrg), *n.* a town in SE Ontario, in S Canada, on Lake Ontario: summer resort. 11,385.

cob′ pie′, *Rhode Island.* a deep-dish pie, esp. an apple cobbler.

co•bra[1] (kō′brə), *n.* **1.** any of several highly venomous, Old World elapid snakes of the genera *Naja* and *Ophiophagus,* characterized by the ability to flatten the neck into a hoodlike form when disturbed. **2.** any of several similar, related African snakes, as the ringhals. **3.** leather made from the skin of a cobra. **4.** (*cap.*) *Mil.* a single-engine, two-seat U.S. Army attack helicopter armed with missiles, rockets, and a 20mm cannon and in service since 1977. [1810–20; short for COBRA DE CAPELLO]

Indian cobra, *Naja naja,* length to 6 ft. (1.8 m)

co•bra[2] (kō′brə, kob′rə), *n. Australian.* head; skull. [1825–35; < Dharuk *gabarā*]

co•bra de ca•pel•lo (kō′brə dē kə pel′ō), *pl.* **co•bras de ca•pel•lo.** See **Indian cobra.** [1660–70; < Pg: hooded snake (*cobra* < L *colubra* snake; *capello* < LL *cappellus* hood, equiv. to *capp(a)* CAP[1] + *-ellus* ELLE)]

co•burg (kō′bûrg), *n.* a piece-dyed or printed twill dress fabric or lining cloth. Also, **co•bourg** (kō′bŏŏrg). [1880–85; named after Prince Albert of Saxe-*Coburg*]

Co•burg (kō′bûrg; *Ger.* kō′bŏŏʀk), *n.* a city in N Bavaria, in E West Germany. 45,900.

cob•web (kob′web′), *n., v.,* **-webbed, -web•bing.** —*n.* **1.** a web spun by a spider to entrap its prey. **2.** a single thread spun by a spider. **3.** something resembling a cobweb; anything finespun, flimsy, or insubstantial. **4.** a network of plot or intrigue; an insidious snare. **5. cobwebs,** confusion, indistinctness, or lack of order: *I'm so tired my head is full of cobwebs.* —*v.t.* **6.** to cover with or as with cobwebs: *Spiders cobwebbed the cellar.* **7.** to confuse or muddle: *Drunkenness cobwebbed his mind.* [1275–1325; ME *coppeweb,* deriv. of OE *-coppe* spider (in *ātorcoppe* poison spider); c. MD *koppe;* see WEB]

cob•web•by (kob′web′ē), *adj.* **1.** bearing an accumulation of cobwebs. **2.** having the form, texture, or quality of cobwebs. [1735–45; COBWEB + -Y[1]]

cob′web house′leek, a small southern European plant, *Sempervivum arachnoideum,* of the stonecrop family, having a dense, globular cluster of cobwebby leaves and red flowers on hairy stalks.

co•ca (kō′kə), *n.* **1.** a shrub, *Erythroxylon coca,* native to the Andes, having simple, alternate leaves and small yellowish flowers. **2.** the dried leaves of this shrub, which are chewed for their stimulant properties and which yield cocaine and other alkaloids. [1610–20; < Sp < Quechua *kuka*]

Co•ca-col•o•nize (kō′kə kol′ə nīz′, -kō′lə-), *v.t.,* **-nized, -niz•ing.** to bring (a foreign country) under the influence of U.S. trade, popular culture, and attitudes. Also, *esp. Brit.,* **Co′ca-col′o•nise′.** [b. *Coca-cola* (a brand name of a cola drink, considered a typical American product) and COLONIZE] —**Co′ca-col′o•ni•za′tion,** *n.*

co•caine (kō kān′, kō′kān), *n. Pharm.* a bitter, crystalline alkaloid, $C_{17}H_{21}NO_4$, obtained from coca leaves, used as a local anesthetic and also widely used as an illicit drug for its stimulant and euphorigenic properties. [1870–75; COCA + -INE[1]]

co•cain•ism (kō kā′niz əm, kō′kə niz′əm), *n. Pathol.* an abnormal condition due to excessive or habitual use of cocaine. [COCAINE + -ISM]

co•cain•ize (kō kā′nīz, kō′kə nīz′), *v.t.,* **-ized, -iz•ing.** to treat with or affect by cocaine. Also, *esp. Brit.,* **co•cain′ise.** [1885–90; COCAINE + -IZE] —**co•cain′i•za′•tion,** *n.*

-coccal, a combining form of adjectives corresponding to nouns formed with **-coccus:** *streptococcal.*

coc•ci (kok′sī, -sē), *n.* **1.** pl. of **coccus. 2.** coccidioidomycosis.

coc•cid (kok′sid), *n.* any of various related bugs of the superfamily Coccoidea, comprising the scale insects. [COCC(US) + -ID[2]]

coc•cid•i•oi•do•my•co•sis (kok sid′ē oi′dō mī kō′sis), *n. Pathol.* a disease caused by inhaling spores of *Coccidioides* fungi, characterized by fever, respiratory infection, and reddish bumps on the skin, common in hot, semiarid regions, esp. in southwestern U. S. and Mexico. Also called **cocci, desert fever, San Joaquin Valley fever, valley fever.** [1935–40; < NL *Coccidioid(es)* name of the genus (see COCCIDIUM, -OID) + -O- + MYCOSIS]

coc•cid•i•o•sis (kok sid′ē ō′sis), *n. Vet. Pathol.* any of a series of specific infectious diseases caused by epithelial protozoan parasites, which may affect the intestines of birds, domestic animals, or dogs. [1890–95; < NL *Coccidi(a)* (see COCCIDIUM) + -OSIS]

coc•cid•i•um (kok sid′ē əm), *n., pl.* **-cid•i•a** (-sid′ē ə). *Microbiol.* any sporozoan of the order Coccidia, often parasitic in the digestive tracts of certain animals and a cause of coccidiosis. [< NL *Coccidium,* orig. a genus name; see COCCUS, -IDIUM]

coc•co•ba•cil•lus (kok′ō bə sil′əs), *n., pl.* **-cil•li** (-sil′ī, -sil′ē). *Bacteriol.* a spherelike bacillus. [COCC(US) + -O- + BACILLUS]

coc•coid (kok′oid), *adj.* **1.** Also, **coc•coi′dal.** resembling a coccus; globular. —*n.* **2.** a coccoid cell or organism. [1910–15; COCC(US) + -OID]

coc•co•lith (kok′ə lith′), *n.* a microscopic calcareous disk or ring making up part of the covering of certain marine plankton and forming much of the content of chalk rocks. [1865–70; < NL *Coccolithus* orig. a genus name; see COCCUS, -O-, -LITH] —**coc′co•lith′ic,** *adj.*

coc•cus (kok′əs), *n., pl.* **-ci** (-sī, -sē). **1.** *Bacteriol.* a spherical bacterium. See diag. under **bacteria. 2.** *Bot.* one of the carpels of a schizocarp. [1755–65; < NL < Gk *kókkos* grain, seed, berry] —**coc′cal, coc•cic** (kok′sik), *adj.* —**coc′cous,** *adj.*

-coccus, a combining form representing **coccus** in compound words: *streptococcus.*

coc•cyx (kok′siks), *n., pl.* **coc•cy•ges** (kok sī′jēz, kok′si jēz′). **1.** a small triangular bone forming the lower extremity of the spinal column in humans, consisting of four ankylosed rudimentary vertebrae. See diag. under **spinal column. 2.** a corresponding part in certain animals. [1605–15; < NL < Gk *kókkyx* cuckoo, from its resemblance to a cuckoo's beak] —**coc•cyg•e•al** (kok sij′ē əl), *adj.*

coch., (in prescriptions) a spoonful. [< L *cochlear*]

Co•cha•bam•ba (kô′chä bäm′bä), *n.* a city in central Bolivia. 245,230; 8394 ft. (2558 m) above sea level.

co•chair (kō châr′), *v.t., v.i.* **1.** to chair along with another person or persons. —*n.* **2.** a cochairperson. [CO- + CHAIR (v.)]
—**Usage.** See **chairperson.**

co•chair•man (kō châr′mən), *n., pl.* **-men.** one of two or more joint chairmen. [1930–35; CO- + CHAIRMAN]
—**Usage.** See **chairperson, -man.**

co•chair•per•son (kō châr′pûr′sən), *n.* one of two or more joint chairpersons. [CO- + CHAIRPERSON]
—**Usage.** See **chairperson.**

coch. amp., (in prescriptions) a tablespoonful. [< L *cochlear amplum* large spoon(ful)]

co•chin (kō′chin, koch′in), *n.* one of an Asian breed of chickens, resembling the Brahma but slightly smaller. [1850–55; short for *Cochin-China fowl*]

Co•chin (kō′chin), *n.* **1.** a seaport in W Kerala, in SW India: first European fort in India, built by Portuguese 1503. 438,420. **2.** a former state in SW India; merged with Travancore 1949; a part of Kerala state since 1956.

Co•chin-Chi•na (kō′chin chī′nə, koch′in-), *n.* a former state in S French Indochina: now part of Vietnam. French, **Co•chin•chine** (kô shaɴ shēn′).

coch•i•neal (koch′ə nēl′, kō′chə-, koch′ə nēl′, kō′chə-), *n.* a red dye prepared from the dried bodies of the females of the cochineal insect, *Dactylopius coccus,* which lives on cactuses of Mexico, Central America, and other warm regions. [1575–85; < MF *cochenille* < Sp *cochinilla* the insect; of obscure orig.; perh. to be identified with Sp *cochinilla* sow bug (assuming a likeness between it and the female cochineal insect), dim. of *cochina* sow, but chronology is doubtful]

coch′ineal cac′tus, a treelike cactus, *Nopalea cochenillifera,* of Mexico and Central America, that is a principal source of food of the cochineal insect. Also called **coch′ineal plant′.**

coch′ineal in′sect, any of various small red scale insects of the family Dactylopiidae, related to the mealybugs and characterized by an oval segmented body with white waxy plates and short legs and antennae: the source of cochineal. [1795–1805]

Co•chise (kō chēs′), *adj.* of, pertaining to, or characteristic of a prehistoric American Indian culture of southeastern Arizona, dating from around 9000 B.C. [named after *Cochise* County, Arizona]

Co•chise (kō chēs′), *n.* c1815–74, a chief of the Chiricahua Apaches.

coch•le•a (kok′lē ə, kō′klē ə), *n., pl.* **-le•ae** (-lē ē′, -lē-ī′), **-le•as.** *Anat.* a spiral-shaped cavity forming a division of the internal ear in humans and in most other mammals. See diag. under **ear.** [1530–40; < L < Gk *kochlías* snail (with spiral shell), screw, prob. akin to *kónchē* CONCH] —**coch′le•ar,** *adj.*

coch′lear duct′, *Anat.* a spiral tube enclosed in the bony canal of the cochlea.

coch′lear im′plant, a device consisting of microelectrodes that deliver electrical stimuli directly to the auditory nerve when surgically implanted into the cochlea, enabling a person with sensorineural deafness to hear. Also called **artificial ear.**

coch•le•ate (kok′lē it, -āt′), *adj.* shaped like a snail shell; spiral. Also, **coch′le•at′ed.** [1825–35; < L *cochleātus* spiral, equiv. to *cochle(a)* COCHLEA + *-ātus* -ATE[1]]

coch. mag., (in prescriptions) a tablespoonful. [< L *cochlear magnum* large spoon(ful)]

coch. med., (in prescriptions) a dessertspoonful. [< L *cochlear medium* medium-sized spoon(ful)]

coch. parv., (in prescriptions) a teaspoonful. [< L *cochlear parvum* little spoon(ful)]

Coch•ran (kok′rən), *n.* **Jacqueline,** 1910?–80, U.S. aviator.

co•ci•ne•ro (kō′sə nâr′ō), *n., pl.* **-ros.** *Southwestern U.S.* a cook, esp. one working on a ranch or a trail drive. [1835–45, *Amer.*; < AmerSp, Sp: cook, equiv. to *cocin(a)* cooking, kitchen (see CUISINE, KITCHEN) + *-ero* < L *-ārius* -ARY]

cock[1] (kok), *n.* **1.** a male chicken; rooster. **2.** the male of any bird, esp. of the gallinaceous kind. **3.** Also called **stopcock.** a hand-operated valve or faucet, esp. one opened or closed by rotating a cylindrical or tapered plug having part of the passage pierced through it from side to side. **4.** (in a firearm) **a.** the part of the lock that, by its fall or action, causes the discharge; hammer. See diag. under **flintlock. b.** the position into which the cock, or hammer, is brought by being drawn partly or completely back, preparatory to firing. **5.** *Slang* (*vulgar*). **a.** penis. **b.** sexual relations with a man. **6.** a weathercock. **7.** a

CONCISE PRONUNCIATION KEY: *act, cāpe, dâre, pärt; set, ēqual; if, īce; ox, ōver, ôrder, oil, bŏŏk, bŏŏt, out; up, ûrge; child; sing; shoe; thin, that;* zh as in *treasure.* ə = *a* as in *alone, e* as in *system, i* as in *easily, o* as in *gallop, u* as in *circus;* ᵊ as in *fire* (fīᵊr), *hour* (ouᵊr). l and n can serve as syllabic consonants, as in *cradle* (krād′l), and *button* (but′n). See the full key inside the front cover.

leader; chief person. **8.** *Chiefly Brit. Informal.* pal; chum. **9.** *Brit. Slang.* nonsense. **10.** *Horol.* a bracket-like plate holding bearings, supported at one end only. Cf. **bridge**[1] (def. 17). **11.** *Archaic.* the time of the crowing of the cock; early in the morning; cockcrow. —*v.t.* **12.** to pull back and set the cock, or hammer, of (a firearm) preparatory to firing. **13.** to draw back in preparation for throwing or hitting: *He cocked his bat and waited for the pitch.* **14.** to set (a camera shutter or other mechanism) for tripping. Cf. **trip**[1] (def. 29). —*v.i.* **15.** to cock the firing mechanism of a firearm. [bef. 900; ME *cock,* OE *cocc;* c. ON *kokkr;* orig. imit.] —**cock′like′,** *adj.*

cock[2] (kok), *v.t.* **1.** to set or turn up or to one side, often in an assertive, jaunty, or significant manner: *He cocked his eyebrow questioningly.* —*v.i.* **2.** to stand or stick up conspicuously. **3.** *Scot. and New England.* to strut; swagger; put on airs of importance. **4. cock a snook.** See **snook**[2] (def. 2). —*n.* **5.** the act of turning the head, a hat, etc., up or to one side in a jaunty or significant way. **6.** the position of anything thus placed. [1705–15; prob. special use of COCK[1]]

cock[3] (kok), *n. Chiefly Northern and North Midland U.S.* **1.** a conical pile of hay, dung, etc. —*v.t.* **2.** to pile (hay, dung, etc.) in cocks. [1350–1400; ME; c. dial. G *Kocke* heap of hay or dung, Norw *kok* heap, lump; akin to ON *kǫkkr* lump]

cock•ade (ko kād′), *n.* a rosette, knot of ribbon, etc., usually worn on the hat as part of a uniform, as a badge of office, or the like. [1650–60; alter. of *cocarde* < F, equiv. to *coq* COCK[2] + *-arde* -ARD] —**cock•ad′ed,** *adj.*

cock-a-doo•dle-doo (kok′ə do͞od′l do͞o′), *interj., n., pl.* **-doos,** *v.,* **-dooed, -doo•ing.** —*interj.* **1.** (used as a conventionalized expression to suggest the crowing of a rooster, as in stories for children.) —*n.* **2.** the loud crow of a cock. **3.** *Baby Talk.* a rooster. —*v.i.* **4.** to crow. [1565–75; fanciful imit.]

cock-a-hoop (kok′ə ho͞op′, -ho͝op′, kok′ə ho͞op′, -ho͝op′), *adj.* **1.** in a state of unrestrained joy or exultation; boastfully elated: *He was cock-a-hoop over his victory.* **2.** askew; out of kilter: *He knocked his hat cock-a-hoop.* [1520–30; orig. uncert.]

Cock•aigne (ko kān′), *n.* a fabled land of luxury and idleness. Also, **Cockayne.** [1250–1300; ME *cokaygn(e)* < MF *(paide) cocaigne* (land of) Cockaigne, idler's paradise < MLG *kōkenje,* equiv. to *kōken* (see COOKIE) + *-je* dim. suffix]

cock-a-leek•ie (kok′ə lē′kē), *n. Scottish Cookery.* a soup made with chicken broth, chopped leeks, and sometimes a little oatmeal. [1765–75; var. of *cockie-leekie,* equiv. to COCK[1] + -IE + LEEK + -IE]

cock•a•lo•rum (kok′ə lôr′əm, -lōr′-), *n.* a self-important little man. [1705–15; mock Latin, equiv. to COCK[1] + fanciful *-al-* + L gen. pl. ending *-ōrum*]

cock•a•ma•mie (kok′ə mā′mē), *adj. Slang.* ridiculous, pointless, or nonsensical: *full of wild schemes and cockamamie ideas.* Also, **cock′a•ma′my.** [‡1940–45, *Amer.*; in orig. sense, paper strip with an image which could be transferred to the skin when moistened, appar. alter. of DECALCOMANIA; sense "ridiculous" prob. by assoc. with COCK-AND-BULL STORY, POPPYCOCK, etc.]

cock′-and-bull′ sto′ry (kok′ən bo͝ol′), an absurd, improbable story presented as the truth: *Don't ask him about his ancestry unless you want to hear a cock-and-bull story.* [1600–10; prob. with orig. reference to some fable in which a cock and bull figure]

cock•a•poo (kok′ə po͞o′), *n., pl.* **-poos.** one of a variety of dogs crossbred from a cocker spaniel and a miniature poodle. Also, **cock′-a-poo′.** [1965–70; COCK(ER)[1] + POO(DLE), with *-a-* from COCKATOO]

cock•a•tiel (kok′ə tēl′), *n.* a small, crested, long-tailed Australian parrot, *Nymphicus hollandicus,* often kept as a pet. Also, **cock′a•teel′.** [1875–80; < D *kaketielje,* < Pg *cacatilha,* equiv. to *cacat(ua)* COCKATOO + *-ilha* < L *-illa* dim. suffix]

cockatoo, *Cacatua galerita,* length 1½ ft. (0.5 m)

cock•a•too (kok′ə to͞o′, kok′ə to͞o′), *n., pl.* **-toos. 1.** any of numerous large, noisy, crested parrots of the genera *Cacatua, Callocephalon, Calyptorhynchus,* etc., of the Australasian region, having chiefly white plumage tinged with yellow, pink, or red: popular as a pet. **2.** *Australian.* **a.** a person who owns and works a small farm or ranch. **b.** *Slang.* a lookout posted by criminals or the operators of illegal gambling games. [1610–20; < D *kaketoe* < Malay *kakatua,* perh. etymologizing alter. of Central Moluccan *jaka* any psittacine bird, by assoc. with Malay *kakak* sibling, *kakak tua* older sibling); sp. copies COCK[1]]

cock•a•trice (kok′ə tris), *n.* **1.** a legendary monster with a deadly glance, supposedly hatched by a serpent from the egg of a cock, and commonly represented with the head, legs, and wings of a cock and the body and tail of a serpent. Cf. **basilisk** (def. 1). **2.** a venomous serpent. Isa. 11:8. [1350–1400; ME *cocatrice* < MF *cocatris* < ML *caucātrices* (pl.), L **calcātrix* (see -TRIX), fem. of **calcātor* tracker, equiv. to *calcā(re)* to tread, v. deriv. of *calx* heel + *-tor* -TOR; rendering Gk *ichneúmon* ICHNEUMON]

Cock•ayne (ko kān′), *n.* Cockaigne.

cock•boat (kok′bōt′), *n.* a small boat, esp. one used as a tender. Also, **cockleboat.** [1400–50; late ME *cokboot,* var. of *cogboot,* equiv. to *cog* boat, ship (akin to ON *kuggi* small ship) + *boot* BOAT]

cock•chaf•er (kok′chā′fər), *n.* any of certain scarab beetles, esp. the European species, *Melolontha melolontha,* which is very destructive to forest trees. [1685–95; COCK[1] (with reference to its size) + CHAFER]

Cock•croft (kok′krôft, -kroft), *n.* **Sir John Douglas,** 1897–1967, English physicist: Nobel prize 1951.

cock•crow (kok′krō′), *n.* the time at which a cock characteristically crows; daybreak; dawn. Also, **cock′crow′ing.** [1350–1400; ME. See COCK[1], CROW[2]]

cocked hat (def. 1)

cocked′ hat′, 1. a man's hat, worn esp. in the 18th century, having a wide, stiff brim turned up on two or three sides toward a peaked crown. Cf. **bicorne, tricorne. 2. knock into a cocked hat,** *Informal.* to destroy completely; render unachievable. [1665–75; COCK[2] + -ED[2]]

cock•er[1] (kok′ər), *n.* See **cocker spaniel.** [1805–15; (WOOD)COCK + -ER[1], i.e., woodcock starter]

cock•er[2] (kok′ər), *n.* a person who promotes or patronizes cockfights. [1680–90; (GAME)COCK + -ER[1], i.e., gamecock fancier]

cock•er[3] (kok′ər), *v.t.* to pamper: *to cocker a child.* [1495–1505; orig. uncert.]

cock•er•el (kok′ər əl, kok′rəl), *n.* a young domestic cock. [1400–50; late ME *cokerelle.* See COCK[1], -REL]

cock′er span′iel, one of a breed of small spaniels having a flat or slightly waved, soft, dense coat of any of several colors. [1880–85]

cocker spaniel 15 in. (38 cm) high at shoulder

cock•eye (kok′ī′), *n., pl.* **-eyes.** an eye that squints or is affected with strabismus. [1815–25; COCK[2] (v.) + EYE]

cock•eyed (kok′īd′), *adj.* **1.** cross-eyed. **2.** having a squinting eye. **3.** twisted, tilted, or slanted to one side. **4.** *Slang.* **a.** foolish; absurd. **b.** intoxicated; drunk. **c.** completely wrong. [1715–25; COCK[2] (v.) + EYED] —**cock•eyed•ly** (kok′īd′lē, -ī′id-), *adv.* —**cock′eyed′•ness,** *n.*
—**Syn. 4a.** ridiculous, preposterous, insane, nutty, cockamamie, weird.

cock′eyed bob′, *Australian.* a short, violent storm. [1890–95; of uncert. orig.]

Cock•eys•ville (kok′ēz vil′), *n.* a town in N Maryland. 17,013.

cock•fight (kok′fīt′), *n.* a fight between specially bred gamecocks usually fitted with spurs. [1485–95; COCK[1] + FIGHT] —**cock′fight′ing,** *n., adj.*

cock′fight chair′, a chair designed to be sat on backward, having a bell seat and a crest rail that serves as an armrest.

cock•horse (kok′hôrs′), *n.* a child's rocking horse or hobbyhorse. [1530–40; orig. father's leg, astride which child rides, from COCK[1] in sense "projection" + HORSE]

cock•ish (kok′ish), *adj.* cocky[1]. [1540–50; COCK[1] + -ISH[1]]

cock•le[1] (kok′əl), *n., v.,* **-led, -ling.** —*n.* **1.** any bivalve mollusk of the genus *Cardium,* having somewhat heart-shaped, radially ribbed valves, esp. *C. edule,* the common edible species of Europe. **2.** any of various allied or similar mollusks. **3.** cockleshell (defs. 1, 2). **4.** a wrinkle; pucker: *a cockle in fabric.* **5.** a small, crisp candy of sugar and flour, bearing a motto. **6. cockles of one's heart,** the depths of one's emotions or feelings: *The happy family scene warmed the cockles of his heart.* —*v.i.* **7.** to contract into wrinkles; pucker: *This paper cockles easily.* **8.** to rise in short, irregular waves; ripple: *The waves cockled along the shore.* —*v.t.* **9.** to cause to wrinkle, pucker, or ripple: *The wind cockled the water.* [1350–1400; ME *cokille* < MF *coqille* < VL **cocchilia,* L *conchylia,* pl. of *conchylium* < Gk *konchýlion,* equiv. to *konchýl(ē)* mussel + *-ion* dim. suffix; cf. OE *-cocc,* in *sǣcocc* lit., sea-cockle < VL **coccus* for L *concha* CONCH]

cock•le[2] (kok′əl), *n.* a weed, as the darnel *Lolium temulentum,* or rye grass, *L. perenne.* [bef. 1000; ME; OE *coccel*]

cock•le•boat (kok′əl bōt′), *n.* cockboat. [1615–25; COCKLE[1] + BOAT]

cock•le•bur (kok′əl bûr′), *n.* **1.** any composite plant of the genus *Xanthium,* comprising coarse weeds with spiny burs. **2.** the burdock, *Arctium lappa.* [1795–1805; COCKLE[2] + BUR[1]]

cock•le•shell (kok′əl shel′), *n.* **1.** a shell of the cockle. **2.** a shell of some other mollusk, as the scallop. **3.** *Naut.* any light or frail vessel. [1375–1425; late ME *cokille shell.* See COCKLE[1], SHELL]

cock•loft (kok′lôft′, -loft′), *n. Older Use.* **1.** a small loft or attic above the highest finished ceiling of a building. **2.** a completely enclosed space between rafters and a suspended ceiling. [1580–90; COCK[1] + LOFT]

cock•ney (kok′nē), *n., pl.* **-neys,** *adj.* —*n.* **1.** (*sometimes cap.*) a native or inhabitant of the East End district of London, England, traditionally, one born and reared within the sound of Bow bells. **2.** (*sometimes cap.*) the pronunciation or dialect of cockneys. **3.** *Obs.* **a.** a pampered child. **b.** a squeamish, affected, or effeminate person. —*adj.* **4.** (*sometimes cap.*) of or pertaining to cockneys or their dialect. [1325–75; ME *cokeney* foolish person, lit., cock's egg (i.e., malformed egg), equiv. to *coken,* gen. pl. of *cok* COCK[1] + *ey,* OE *æg;* c. G *Ei,* ON *egg* EGG] —**cock′ney•ish,** *adj.* —**cock′ney•ish•ly,** *adv.*

cock•ney•fy (kok′ni fī′), *v.t.,* **-fied, -fy•ing.** to give a cockney character to: *to cockneyfy the word "horse" by pronouncing it "'orse."* [1815–25; COCKNEY + -FY] —**cock′ney•fi•ca′tion,** *n.*

cock•ney•ism (kok′nē iz′əm), *n.* **1.** cockney quality or character. **2.** a cockney peculiarity, as of speech. [COCKNEY + -ISM]

cock-of-the-rock (kok′əv *th*ə rok′), *n., pl.* **cocks-of-the-rock.** a brilliant orange-red bird of the genus *Rupicola,* of northern South America, having an erect crest that conceals the bill. [1815–25]

cock-of-the-rock, *Rupicola rupicola,* length 1 ft. (0.3 m)

cock′ of the walk′, the leader in a group, esp. one with a conceited, domineering manner. [1850–55]

cock′ of the woods′. See **pileated woodpecker.**

cock•pit (kok′pit′), *n.* **1.** a space, usually enclosed, in the forward fuselage of an airplane containing the flying controls, instrument panel, and seats for the pilot and copilot or flight crew. **2.** a sunken, open area, generally in the after part of a small vessel, as a yacht, providing space for the pilot, part or all of the crew, or guests. **3.** the space, including the seat and instrumentation, surrounding the driver of an automobile. **4.** a pit or enclosed place for cockfights. **5.** a place where a contest is fought or which has been the scene of many contests or battles. **6.** (formerly) a space below the water line in a warship, occupied by the quarters of the junior officers and used as a dressing station for those wounded in action. [1580–90; COCK[1] + PIT[1]]

cock•roach (kok′rōch′), *n.* any of numerous orthopterous insects of the family Blattidae, characterized by a flattened body, rapid movements, and nocturnal habits and including several common household pests. Also called **roach.** Cf. **American cockroach, German cockroach, oriental cockroach.** [1615–25; < Sp *cucaracha,* of uncert. orig., assimilated by folk etym. to COCK[1], ROACH[2]]

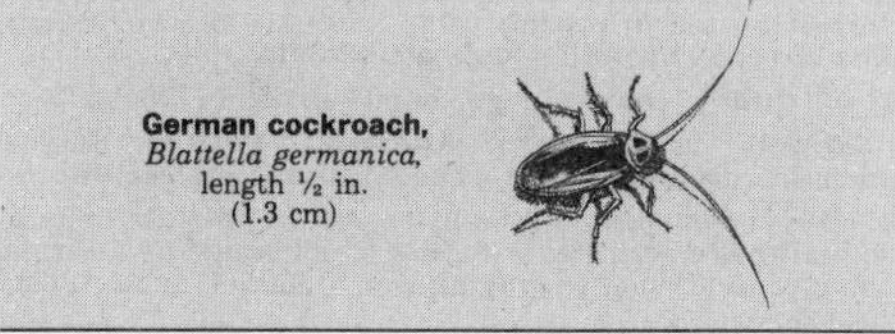
German cockroach, *Blattella germanica,* length ½ in. (1.3 cm)

cocks•comb (koks′kōm′), *n.* **1.** the comb or caruncle of a cock. **2.** the cap, resembling a cock's comb, formerly worn by professional fools. **3.** a garden plant, *Celosia cristata,* of the amaranth family, with flowers, commonly crimson or purple, in a broad spike somewhat resembling the comb of a cock. **4.** any of several other species of the genus *Celosia.* **5.** an elongate prickleback, *Anoplarchus purpurescens,* living among submerged rocks along the Pacific coast of North America. **6.** a gaslight burner having four or more jets. **7.** coxcomb (def. 1). [1350–1400; ME; see COCK, 'S[1], COMB[1]]

cock's-foot (koks′fo͝ot′), *n.* See **orchard grass.** Also, **cocks′foot′.** [1690–1700; so called from the appearance of the panicles]

cock•shut (kok′shut′), *n. Brit. Dial.* the close of the day; evening; twilight. [1585–95; COCK[1] + SHUT]

cock•shy (kok′shī′), *n., pl.* **-shies.** *Brit.* **1.** the act or sport of throwing missiles at a target. **2.** the target itself. [1785–95; COCK[1] + SHY[2]]

cock•spur (kok′spûr′), *n.* **1.** a North American hawthorn, *Crataegus crus-galli,* having leathery, toothed leaves and red fruit, cultivated as a small ornamental tree. **2.** a gaslight burner having three jets. [1585–95; for *cock's spur*]

cock•suck•er (kok′suk′ər), *n. Slang (vulgar).* **1.** a person who performs fellatio. **2.** a mean or contemptible person. [1890–95; COCK[1] + SUCKER]

cock•sure (kok′sho͝or′, -shûr′), *adj.* **1.** perfectly sure or certain; completely confident in one's own mind: *She was cocksure that she was able to do the job better than* *anyone else.* **2.** too certain; overconfident: *He was so cocksure he would win the election that he didn't even bother to campaign.* **3.** *Obs.* perfectly secure or safe. [1510–20; COCK[1] + SURE] **—cock′sure′ly,** *adv.* **—cock′sure′ness,** *n.*

cock•swain (kok′sən; *spelling pron.* kok′swān′), *n.* coxswain.

cock•tail[1] (kok′tāl′), *n.* **1.** any of various short mixed drinks, consisting typically of gin, whiskey, rum, vodka, or brandy, with different admixtures, as vermouth, fruit juices, or flavorings, usually chilled and frequently sweetened. **2.** a portion of food, as seafood served with a sauce, a mixture of fruits, or juice, served as the appetizer course of a meal. **3.** *Pharm.* a beverage or solution concocted of various drugs. **4.** any eclectic mixture or miscellaneous collection. *—v.i.* **5.** to drink cocktails, esp. at a cocktail party. *—adj.* **6.** (of women's clothing) styled for semiformal wear: *a cocktail dress.* **7.** of, pertaining to, used in, or suitable to the serving of cocktails: *cocktail onions; cocktail napkins.* [1800–10, *Amer.*; orig. obscure; none of numerous attempts to explain the orig. of this word or its relationship to COCKTAIL[2] have won general acceptance]

cock•tail[2] (kok′tāl′), *n.* **1.** a horse with a docked tail. **2.** a horse that is not a thoroughbred. **3.** a man of little breeding who passes for a gentleman. [1590–1600; COCK[2] + TAIL[1]]

cock′tail glass′, a glass for serving cocktails, typically bell-shaped and having a foot and a stem.

cock′tail hour′, the interval before the evening meal during which cocktails and other alcoholic beverages are often served. [1925–30]

cock′tail lounge′, **1.** a public room, as in a hotel or airline terminal, where cocktails and other drinks are served. **2.** a bar. [1935–40]

cock′tail par′ty, a social gathering, often held during the cocktail hour, at which cocktails and other alcoholic beverages, hors d'oeuvres, and canapés are served. [1925–30]

Cock′tail Par′ty, The, a play in verse (1950) by T. S. Eliot.

cock′tail sauce′, any of various sauces served with a seafood cocktail, typically one consisting of ketchup, Worcestershire sauce, Tabasco sauce, horseradish, and seasonings.

cock′tail ta′ble. See **coffee table.** [1960–65]

cock•teas•er (kok′tē′zər), *n. Slang (vulgar).* a girl or woman who purposely excites or arouses a male sexually but then refuses to have intercourse. [1890–95; COCK[1] + TEASER]

cock•up (kok′up′), *n.* **1.** an upward turn or curl at the top of something. **2.** a cap or hat with the front turned up. **3.** *Brit. Slang.* mess; botch. [1685–95; COCK[2] + UP]

cock•y[1] (kok′ē), *adj.,* **cock•i•er, cock•i•est.** arrogant; pertly self-assertive; conceited: *He walked in with a cocky air.* [1540–50; COCK[1] + -Y[1]] **—cock′i•ly,** *adv.* **—cock′i•ness,** *n.*

cock•y[2] (kok′ē), *n., pl.* **cock•ies. 1.** *Australian.* **a.** cockatoo (def. 1). **b.** cockatoo (def. 2a). **2.** cockatiel. [1885–90; COCK(ATOO), COCK(ATIEL) + -Y[2]]

cock•y[3] (kok′ē), *v.i.,* **cock•ied, cock•y•ing.** *Newfoundland.* copy (def. 16). [appar. a playful alter., by assoc. with COCKY[1]]

co•co (kō′kō), *n., pl.* **-cos. 1.** See **coconut palm. 2.** coconut (def. 1). [1545–55; < Pg: grimace; the three holes at the nut's base give it this appearance]

Co•co (kō′kō; *Sp.* kô′kô), *n.* a river rising in N Nicaragua and flowing NE along the Nicaragua-Honduras border to the Caribbean Sea. ab. 300 mi. (485 km) long. Also called **Segovia.**

co•coa[1] (kō′kō), *n.* **1.** a powder made from roasted, husked, and ground seeds of the cacao, *Theobroma cacao,* from which much of the fat has been removed. **2.** cacao (def. 2). **3.** a beverage made by mixing cocoa powder with hot milk or water. **4.** yellowish or reddish brown. *—adj.* **5.** of or pertaining to cocoa. **6.** of the color of cocoa. [1700–10; earlier *cocao, cacoa,* var. of CACAO]

co•coa[2] (kō′kō), *n.* coco. [1545–55; misspelling of coco, by confusion with COCOA[1]]

Co•coa (kō′kō), *n.* a city in E central Florida. 16,096.

Co′coa Beach′, a town in E central Florida. 10,926.

co′coa bean′. See **cacao bean.**

co′coa but′ter. a fatty substance obtained from the seeds of the cacao, used in making soaps, cosmetics, and other products. Also, **cacao butter.** [1895–1900]

co•coa•nut (kō′kə nut′, -nət), *n.* coconut.

co•co•bo•lo (kō′kə bō′lō), *n.* the hard, durable wood of any of several tropical trees of the genus *Dalbergia,* of the legume family, used for making furniture. Also, **co•co•bo•la** (kō′kə bō′lə). [1840–50; < Sp < Arawak *kakaboli*]

co•co-de-mer (kō′kō də mâr′), *n.* See **double coconut.** [< F: lit., sea coconut]

COCOM (kō′kom′), *n.* a nontreaty organization of the NATO nations except Iceland, and with the addition of Japan, that sets rules on exports of strategic goods to Communist countries: formed in 1949. Also, **Co′com′.** [*Co(ordinating) Com(mittee)*]

co•co•mat (kō′kō mat′), *n.* **1.** matting made of the fiber from the outer husk of the coconut. **2.** a mat, esp. a doormat, made from this. [COCO(NUT) + MAT[1]]

co-con•spir•a•tor (kō′kən spir′ə tər), *n.* a fellow conspirator; associate or collaborator in a conspiracy. Also, **co′con•spir′a•tor.** [1860–65]

co•co•nut (kō′kə nut′, -nət), *n.* **1.** the large, hard-shelled seed of the coconut palm, lined with a white edible meat, and containing a milky liquid. **2.** the meat of the coconut, often shredded and used in cooking, as a flavoring, and as a dessert topping. **3.** See **coconut palm.** Also, **cocoanut.** [1605–15; COCO + NUT]

coconut, *Cocos nucifera,* A, coconut husk; B, half-opened husk; C, fruit

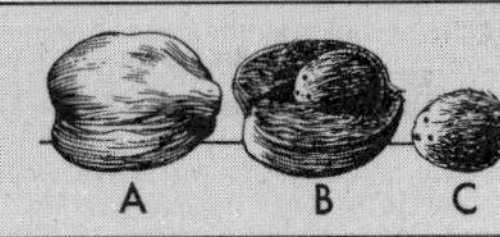

co′conut but′ter, a vegetable butter made by churning coconut cream.

co′conut crab′, a large, terrestrial crab, *Birgus latro,* of islands in the South Pacific, that feeds on coconuts. Also called **palm crab, purse crab, tree crab.**

co′conut cream′, 1. Also called **cream of coconut.** a creamy white liquid skimmed from the top of coconut milk that has been made by soaking grated coconut meat in water, used in East Indian cookery, mixed drinks, etc. **2.** a custard pie with shredded or ground coconut.

co′conut milk′. 1. the clear, potable liquid contained within the young hollow seed of the coconut palm. **2.** the milky, potable but highly perishable liquid contained within the mature hollow coconut. **3.** the milky, potable liquid extracted from grated coconut meat by infusion with boiling water.

co′conut oil′, a white, semisolid fat or nearly colorless fatty oil extracted from coconuts, used chiefly in foods and in the manufacture of soaps, cosmetics, and candles. [1830–40]

co′conut palm′, a tall, tropical palm, *Cocos nucifera,* bearing large, hard-shelled seeds enclosed in a thick, fibrous husk. Cf. **coconut** (def. 3). [1830–40]

co•coon (kə ko͞on′), *n.* **1.** the silky envelope spun by the larvae of many insects, as silkworms, serving as a covering while they are in the pupal stage. **2.** any of various similar protective coverings in nature, as the silky case in which certain spiders enclose their eggs. **3.** a protective covering, usually consisting of polyvinyl chloride, sprayed over machinery, large guns on board ships, etc., to provide an airtight seal and prevent rust during long periods of storage. **4.** any encompassingly protective or hermetic wrapping or enclosure resembling a cocoon: *a cocoon of gauze.* *—v.i.* **5.** to produce a cocoon. *—v.t.* **6.** to wrap or enclose tightly, as if in a cocoon. **7.** to provide (machinery, guns, etc.) with a protective, airtight covering by spraying with polyvinyl chloride or the like. **8.** to envelop or surround protectively; insulate. [1690–1700; < F *cocon* < Pr *coucoun* egg-shell, equiv. to *coco* shell (< L *coccum;* see COCHINEAL) + F *-on* dim. suffix] **—co•coon′like′,** *adj.*

co•coon•ing (kə ko͞o′ning), *n.* the practice of spending leisure time at home, esp. watching television or using a VCR. [1985–90, *Amer.*]

Co′cos Is′lands (kō′kōs), an Australian group of 27 coral islands in the Indian Ocean, SW of Java. 569; 5.5 sq. mi. (14 sq. km). Also called **Keeling Islands.**

Co′cos Plate′, *Geol.* a tectonic division of the earth's crust, coincident with the oceanic Guatemala Basin, and bounded on the north and east by the Central American Trench, on the west by the East Pacific Rise, and on the south by the Nazca Plate.

co•cotte[1] (kō kot′, kə-; *Fr.* kô kôt′), *n., pl.* **-cottes** (-kots′; *Fr.* -kôt′). prostitute. [1865–70; < F: orig. a child's word for a hen, equiv. to *coq* COCK[1] + *-otte* fem. suffix]

co•cotte[2] (kō kot′, kə-; *Fr.* kô kôt′), *n., pl.* **-cottes** (-kots′; *Fr.* -kôt′). a round or oval casserole, usually of earthenware or fireproof porcelain, used especially for cooking an individual portion of meat, fowl, or game. [1865–70; < F: small cast-iron pot for stewing meat; alter., by suffix substitution, of MF *cocasse, coquasse* applied to various receptacles, obscurely akin to *coquemar* kettle, by uncert. mediation < MGk *koukoumárion* (or its presumed VL source), ult. deriv. of L *cucuma* kettle]

coc•o•zel•le (kok′ə zel′ē), *n.* **1.** a variety of summer squash having a dark-green skin that is usually striped with light green or yellow. **2.** the plant itself. [of unclear orig., perh. < dial. form of It *cocuzza* gourd, pumpkin < LL *cucutia,* perh. a re-formation of L *cucurbita* GOURD; see -ELLE]

Coc•teau (kok tō′; *Fr.* kôk tō′), *n.* **Jean** (zhäɴ), 1889–1963, French author and painter.

co•cur•ric•u•lar (kō′kə rik′yə lər), *adj. Education.* related but only complementary to the official curriculum, as a civic or service activity outside the classroom. [1945–50; CO- + CURRICULAR]

cod[1] (kod), *n., pl. (esp. collectively)* **-cod,** *(esp. referring to two or more kinds or species)* **-cods. 1.** any of several soft-rayed food fishes of the family Gadidae, esp. *Gadus morhua,* of cool, North Atlantic waters. **2.** a closely related fish, *Gadus macrocephalus,* of the North Pacific. **3.** any of several unrelated fishes, as rockfishes of the genus *Sebastes.* [1325–75; ME orig. uncert.]

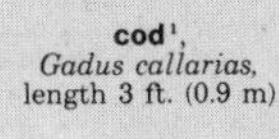
cod[1], *Gadus callarias,* length 3 ft. (0.9 m)

cod[2] (kod), *n. Slang (vulgar).* testicle. [bef. 1000; ME; OE *codd;* akin to ON *koddi* pillow]

Cod (kod), *n.* **Cape.** See **Cape Cod.**

COD., codex. Also, **cod.**

C.O.D., *Com.* cash, or collect, on delivery (payment to be made when delivered to the purchaser). Also, **c.o.d.** [1855–60, *Amer.*]

co•da (kō′də), *n.* **1.** *Music.* a more or less independent passage, at the end of a composition, introduced to bring it to a satisfactory close. **2.** *Ballet.* the concluding section of a ballet, esp. the final part of a pas de deux. **3.** a concluding section or part, esp. one of a conventional form and serving as a summation of preceding themes, motifs, etc., as in a work of literature or drama. **4.** anything that serves as a concluding part. **5.** *Phonet.* the segment of a syllable following the nucleus, as the *d*-sound in *good.* Cf. **core** (def. 14), **onset** (def. 3). [1745–55; < It < L *cauda* tail; cf. QUEUE]

co-day (kə dā′, -di′), *interj. Northern U.S.* (used to summon sheep and, sometimes, cows). Also **co-dack** (kə dak′). [see CO-BOSS; *day* appar. reduced from *Dick* as an animal's name]

cod•dle (kod′l), *v.t.,* **-dled, -dling. 1.** to treat tenderly; nurse or tend indulgently; pamper: *to coddle children when they're sick.* **2.** to cook (eggs, fruit, etc.) in water that is just below the boiling point; cook gently. [1590–1600; var. of *caudle,* v. use of CAUDLE] **—cod′dler,** *n.*

code (kōd), *n., v.,* **cod•ed, cod•ing.** *—n.* **1.** a system for communication by telegraph, heliograph, etc., in which long and short sounds, light flashes, etc., are used to symbolize the content of a message: *Morse code.* **2.** a system used for brevity or secrecy of communication, in which arbitrarily chosen words, letters, or symbols are assigned definite meanings. **3.** any set of standards set forth and enforced by a local government agency for the protection of public safety, health, etc., as in the structural safety of buildings **(building code),** health requirements for plumbing, ventilation, etc. **(sanitary** or **health code),** and the specifications for fire escapes or exits **(fire code). 4.** a systematically arranged collection or compendium of laws, rules, or regulations. **5.** any authoritative, general, systematic, and written statement of the legal rules and principles applicable in a given legal order to one or more broad areas of life. **6.** a word, letter, number, or other symbol used in a code system to mark, represent, or identify something: *The code on the label shows the date of manufacture.* **7.** *Computers.* the symbolic arrangement of statements or instructions in a computer program in which letters, digits, etc. are represented as binary numbers; the set of instructions in such a program: *That program took 3000 lines of code.* Cf. **ASCII, object code, source code. 8.** any system or collection of rules and regulations: *a gentleman's code of behavior.* **9.** *Med.* a directive or alert to a hospital team assigned to emergency resuscitation of patients. **10.** *Genetics.* See **genetic code. 11.** *Ling.* **a.** the system of rules shared by the participants in an act of communication, making possible the transmission and interpretation of messages. **b.** (in sociolinguistic theory) one of two distinct styles of language use that differ in degree of explicitness and are sometimes thought to be correlated with differences in social class. Cf. **elaborated code, restricted code.** *—v.t.* **12.** to translate (a message) into a code; encode. **13.** to arrange or enter (laws or statutes) in a code. **14.** *Computers.* to translate (a program) into language that can be communicated to the computer. *—v.i.* **15.** *Genetics.* to specify the amino acid sequence of a protein by the sequence of nucleotides comprising the gene for that protein: *a gene that codes for the production of insulin.* [1275–1325; ME < AF, OF < L *cōdex* CODEX] **—cod′er,** *n.* **—code′less,** *adj.*

code′ blue′, *(often caps.)* a medical emergency in which paramedics are dispatched to aid a person undergoing cardiac arrest. [1980–85]

code′ book′, a book containing a list of code signals with their meanings, usually arranged alphabetically.

co•dec•li•na•tion (kō′dek lə nā′shən), *n. Astron.* the complement of declination; the angular distance along a great circle from the celestial pole. [1805–15; CO- + DECLINATION]

code′ dat′ing, the practice of placing a code indicating the date and site of packaging on certain products, as canned goods. [1970–75]

co•de•fend•ant (kō′di fen′dənt), *n.* a joint defendant. [1630–40; CO- + DEFENDANT]

code′ flag′, *Naut.* **1.** a flag forming part of a signal code. **2.** a flag indicating that a certain signal code is being used. **3.** See **answering pennant.**

co•deine (kō′dēn), *n. Pharm.* a white, crystalline, slightly bitter alkaloid, $C_{18}H_{21}NO_3$, obtained from opium, used chiefly as an analgesic or sedative and to inhibit coughing. Also, **co•de•ia** (kō dē′ə), **co•de•i•na** (kō′dē ē′nə). [1830–40; < Gk *kṓde(ia)* head, poppy-head + -INE[2]]

code′ name′, 1. a name assigned to conceal the real identity of a person, as a spy, or to conceal the existence or purpose of a plan, military operation, etc. **2.** Also called **code′ phrase′.** a word or phrase assigned a meaning understood only by those who are secretly informed of it. [1915–20]

code-name (kōd′nām′), *v.t.,* **-named, -nam•ing.** to assign a code name to. [1955–60]

Code Na•po•lé•on (kôd nᴀ pô lā ôɴ′), the civil code of France, enacted in 1804 and officially designated in 1807. Also called **Napoleonic Code.**

Code′ of Hammura′bi, a Babylonian legal code of the 18th century B.C. or earlier, instituted by Hammurabi and dealing with criminal and civil matters.

co•de•pend•ent (kō′di pen′dənt), *adj.* **1.** of or pertaining to a relationship in which one person is physically or psychologically addicted, as to alcohol or gambling, and the other person is psychologically dependent on the first in an unhealthy way. *—n.* **2.** one who is codependent or in a codependent relationship. [1985–90] **—co′de•pend′en•cy, co′de•pend′ence,** *n.*

code-switch•ing (kōd′swich′ing), *n. Ling.* the alternate use of two or more languages or varieties of language, esp. within the same discourse. [1955–60]

co•de•ter•mi•na•tion (kō′di tûr′mə nā′shən), *n.* the determination of policy through cooperation, as between management and labor. [CO- + DETERMINATION]

code′ word′, 1. See **code name. 2.** a euphemistic or politically acceptable catchword or phrase used instead of a blunter or less acceptable term: *The official report said the diplomats had a "frank and serious discussion"—code words for "angry argument."* [1880–85]

co•dex (kō′deks), *n., pl.* **co•di•ces** (kō′də sēz′, kod′ə-). **1.** a quire of manuscript pages held together by stitching: the earliest form of book, replacing the scrolls and wax tablets of earlier times. **2.** a manuscript volume, usually of an ancient classic or the Scriptures. **3.** *Archaic.* a code; book of statutes. [1575–85; < L *cōdex, caudex* tree-trunk, book (formed orig. from wooden tablets); cf. CODE]

Co′dex Ju′ris Ca•no′ni•ci (jŏŏr′is kə non′ə sī′), *Rom. Cath. Ch.* an official collection of general church law made effective in 1918.

cod•fish (kod′fish′), *n., pl.* (*esp. collectively*) **-fish,** (*esp. referring to two or more kinds or species*) **-fish•es.** cod[1]. [1880–85; COD[1] + FISH]

codg•er (koj′ər), *n.* an eccentric man, esp. one who is old. [1750–60; perh. var. of obs. *cadger;* see CADGE]

co•di•ces (kō′də sēz′, kod′ə-), *n.* pl. of **codex.**

cod•i•cil (kod′ə səl), *n.* **1.** a supplement to a will, containing an addition, explanation, modification, etc., of something in the will. **2.** any supplement; appendix. [1375–1425; late ME < LL *cōdicillus* (in L, commonly in pl. only), equiv. to L *cōdic-* (s. of *cōdex*) CODEX + *-illus* dim. suffix]

cod•i•cil•la•ry (kod′ə sil′ə rē), *adj.* of, pertaining to, or of the nature of a codicil. [1720–30; CODICIL + -ARY]

cod•i•fi•ca•tion (kod′ə fi kā′shən, kō′də-), *n.* **1.** the act, process, or result of arranging in a systematic form or code. **2.** *Law.* **a.** the act, process, or result of stating the rules and principles applicable in a given legal order to one or more broad areas of life in this form of a code. **b.** the reducing of unwritten customs or case law to statutory form. [1810–20; CODE + -I- + -FICATION]

cod•i•fy (kod′ə fī′, kō′də-), *v.t.,* **-fied, -fy•ing. 1.** to reduce (laws, rules, etc.) to a code. **2.** to make a digest of; arrange in a systematic collection. [1795–1805; CODE + -IFY] **—cod•i•fi•a•bil•i•ty**(kod′ə fī′ə bil′i tē, kō′də-), *n.* **—cod′i•fi′er,** *n.*
—Syn. 2. classify, catalog, order, organize, group.

cod•ing (kō′ding), *n. Statistics.* the transforming of a variate into a more convenient variate. [CODE + -ING[1]]

cod′ing trip′let, *Genetics.* codon.

co•dis•cov•er•er (kō′di skuv′ər ər), *n.* one of two or more joint discoverers. [1870–75; CO- + DISCOVERER]

cod•line (kod′lin′), *n. Naut.* an untarred cord of hemp or cotton, used for fishing and for various purposes aboard a ship. Also called **whiteline.** [1625–35; COD[1] + LINE[1]]

cod•ling[1] (kod′ling), *n.* **1.** *Brit.* any of several varieties of elongated apples, used for cooking purposes. **2.** an unripe, half-grown apple. Also, **cod•lin** (kod′lin). [1400–50; late ME *querdling,* equiv. to *querd* (of obscure orig.) + *-ling* -LING[1]]

cod•ling[2] (kod′ling), *n.* the young of the cod. [1250–1300; ME; see COD[1], -LING[1]]

cod′ling moth′, a small, olethreutid moth, *Carpocapsa pomonella,* the larvae of which feed on the pulp of apples and other fruits. [1740–50]

cod′-liv•er oil′ (kod′liv′ər), a pale-yellow, fixed oil, extracted from the liver of the common cod or of allied species, used in medicine chiefly as a source of vitamins A and D. [1605–15]

Co•dó (kŏŏ dô′), *n.* a city in NE Brazil. 100,933.

co•dom•i•nant (kō dom′ə nənt), *adj.* **1.** *Ecol.* being one of two or more species that are equally dominant in a biotic community: *a forest in which oak and hickory are codominant.* **2.** *Genetics.* of or pertaining to two different alleles that are fully expressed in a heterozygous individual. [1895–1900; CO- + DOMINANT] **—co•dom′i•nance,** *n.*

co•don (kō′don), *n. Genetics.* a triplet of adjacent nucleotides in the messenger RNA chain that codes for a specific amino acid in the synthesis of a protein molecule. Also called **coding triplet.** Cf. **anticodon.** [1960–65, *Amer.;* CODE + -ON[1]]

cod•piece (kod′pēs′), *n.* **1.** (in the 15th and 16th centuries) a flap or cover for the crotch in men's hose or tight-fitting breeches, usually matching the costume and often decorated. **2.** *Obs.* penis. [1400–50; late ME. See COD[2], PIECE]

cods•wal•lop (kodz′wol′əp), *n. Brit. Slang.* nonsense; rubbish. [1960–65; orig. obscure]

Co•dy (kō′dē), *n.* **1. William Frederick** (*"Buffalo Bill"*), 1846–1917, U.S. Army scout and showman. **2.** a male given name.

co•ed (kō′ed′, -ed′), *n.* **1.** a female student in a coeducational institution, esp. in a college or university. *—adj.* **2.** coeducational (def. 1). **3.** of, pertaining to, or being a coed or coeds: *coed fads.* **4.** for or serving both men and women alike. Also, **co′-ed′.** [1885–90, *Amer.;* short for *coeducational student*]

co•ed•it (kō ed′it), *v.t.* to edit jointly with another. [CO- + EDIT]

co•e•di•tion (kō′i dish′ən), *n.* one of two or more simultaneously released editions of the same book, sometimes published by different publishers in different countries. [1960–65]

co•ed•i•tor (kō ed′i tər), *n.* a person who cooperates or collaborates as editor with another. [1860–65; CO- + EDITOR] **—co•ed′i•tor•ship′,** *n.*

co•ed•u•ca•tion (kō′ej ŏŏ kā′shən), *n.* the joint education of both sexes at the same institution and in the same classes. [1850–55, *Amer.;* CO- + EDUCATION]

co•ed•u•ca•tion•al (kō′ej ŏŏ kā′shə nl), *adj.* **1.** educating both sexes jointly at the same institution or classes: *a coeducational state college.* **2.** of or pertaining to coeducation: *coeducational programs.* [1880–85, *Amer.;* CO- + EDUCATIONAL] **—co′ed•u•ca′tion•al•ism,** *n.* **—co′ed•u•ca′tion•al•ly,** *adv.*

co•ef•fi•cient (kō′ə fish′ənt), *n.* **1.** *Math.* a number or quantity placed (generally) before and multiplying another quantity, as *3* in the expression *3x.* **2.** *Physics.* a number that is constant for a given substance, body, or process under certain specified conditions, serving as a measure of one of its properties: *coefficient of friction.* *—adj.* **3.** acting in consort; cooperating. [1655–65; < NL *coefficient-* (s. of *coefficiēns*). See CO-, EFFICIENT] **—co′•ef•fi′cient•ly,** *adv.*

coeffi′cient of accelera′tion, *Econ.* See **acceleration coefficient.**

coeffi′cient of correla′tion, *Statistics.* See **correlation coefficient.** [1905–10]

coeffi′cient of drag′. See **drag coefficient.**

coeffi′cient of elastic′ity, *Physics.* See **modulus of elasticity.** [1875–80]

coeffi′cient of expan′sion, *Physics.* the fractional change in length, area, or volume per unit change in temperature of a solid, liquid, or gas at a given constant pressure. Also called **expansivity.** [1870–75]

coeffi′cient of fine′ness, *Naval Archit.* See **block coefficient.**

coeffi′cient of perform′ance, *Thermodynam.* a constant that denotes the efficiency of a refrigerator, expressed as the amount of heat removed from a substance being refrigerated divided by the amount of work necessary to remove the heat. *Abbr.:* COP

coeffi′cient of restitu′tion, *Physics.* the ratio of the relative velocity after impact to the relative velocity before the impact of two colliding bodies, equal to 1 for an elastic collision and 0 for an inelastic collision. [1875–80]

coeffi′cient of viscos′ity, *Physics.* the measure of the viscosity of a fluid, equal to the force per unit area required to maintain a difference of velocity of one unit distance per unit time between two parallel planes in the fluid that lie in the direction of flow and are separated by one unit distance: usually expressed in poise or centipoise. Also called **absolute viscosity, dynamic viscosity.** [1920–25]

coel-, a combining form meaning "cavity," used in the formation of compound words: *coelenteron.* Also, **-cele, -coele.** [comb. form repr. Gk *koîlos* hollow; akin to CAVE]

coe•la•canth (sē′lə kanth′), *n.* a crossopterygian fish, *Latimeria chalumnae,* thought to have been extinct since the Cretaceous Period but found in 1938 off the coast of southern Africa. [1605–15; < NL *Coelacanthus* orig. a genus name, equiv. to *coel-* COEL- + Gk *-akanthos* -spined, -thorned, adj. deriv of *ákantha* spine, thorn] **—coe•la•can•thine** (sē′lə kan′thin, -thin), *adj.*

coelacanth,
Latimeria chalumnae,
length 5 to 6 ft.
(1.5 to 1.8 m)

coe•lan•a•glyph•ic (si lan′ə glif′ik), *adj.* (of a carving) executed in cavo-relievo. [COEL- + ANAGLYPHIC]

-coele, var. of **coel-** as final element of a compound word: *enterocoele.* Also, **-cele, -coel.**

Coe•len•ter•a•ta (si len′tə rā′tə), *n.* the phylum comprising the coelenterates. Cf. **Cnidaria.** [1870–75; < NL; see COELENTERON, -ATA[1]]

coe•len•ter•ate (si len′tə rāt′, -tər it), *n.* **1.** any invertebrate animal of the phylum Coelenterata, including the hydras, jellyfishes, sea anemones, and corals, characterized by a single internal cavity serving for digestion, excretion, and other functions and having tentacles on the oral end. Cf. **cnidarian.** *—adj.* **2.** belonging or pertaining to the Coelenterata. [1870–75; see COELENTERATA]

coe•len•ter•on (si len′tə ron′), *n., pl.* **-ter•a** (-tər ə). *Zool.* the body cavity of a coelenterate. [1890–95; COEL- + ENTERON]

coe•li•ac (sē′lē ak′), *adj.* celiac.

coe•lom (sē′ləm), *n., pl.* **coe•loms, coe•lo•ma•ta** (si lō′mə tə). *Zool.* the body cavity of higher metazoans, between the body wall and intestine, lined with a mesodermal epithelium. Also, **coe•lome** (sē′lōm), **celom.** [1875–80; < Gk *koílōma* cavity, equiv. to *koilō-,* var. s. of *koiloûn* to hollow out (v. deriv. of *koîlos* hollow) + *-ma* n. suffix denoting result] **—coe•lom•ic** (si lom′ik, -lō′mik), *adj.*

coe•lo•mate (sē′lə māt′, si lō′mit), *adj.* **1.** having a coelom. *—n.* **2.** a coelomate animal. [1880–85; COELOM + -ATE[1]]

coe•lo•scope (sē′lə skōp′), *n. Med.* celoscope. [COEL- + -O- + -SCOPE]

coe•lo•stat (sē′lə stat′), *n. Astron.* an apparatus consisting of a mirror driven by clockwork, used to enable a fixed telescope to keep the same area of sky in its field of view by compensating for the apparent rotation of the celestial sphere. Cf. **siderostat.** [1895–1900; *coelo-* (for L *caeli-,* comb. form of *caelum* sky) + -STAT]

coe•nes•the•sia (sē′nəs thē′zhə, -zhē ə, -zē ə, sen′əs-), *n. Psychol.* the aggregate of impressions arising from organic sensations that forms the basis of one's awareness of body or bodily state, as the feeling of health, vigor, or lethargy. Also, **coe•nes•the•sis** (sē′nəs thē′sis, sen′əs-), **cenesthesia, cenesthesis.** [1880–85; COEN(O)- + ESTHESIA]

coeno-, var. of **ceno-**[2]: *coenocyte.*

coe•no•bite (sē′nə bīt′, sen′ə-), *n.* cenobite. **—coe•no•bit•ic** (sē′nə bit′ik, sen′ə-), **coe′no•bit′i•cal,** *adj.* **—coe•no•bit•ism** (sē′nə bī tiz əm, sen′ə-), *n.*

coe•no•cyte (sē′nə sīt′, sen′ə-), *n. Biol.* an organism made up of a multinucleate, continuous mass of protoplasm enclosed by one cell wall, as in some algae and fungi. [1895–1900; COENO- + -CYTE] **—coe•no•cyt•ic** (sē′nə sit′ik, sen′ə-), *adj.*

coe•no•sarc (sē′nə särk′, sen′ə-), *n. Zool.* the tubular tissue connecting the polyps of a hydroid colony. [1840–50; COENO- + Gk *sark-,* s. of *sárx* flesh] **—coe′no•sar′•cal, coe′no•sar′cous,** *adj.*

co•en•zyme (kō en′zīm), *n. Biochem.* a molecule that provides the transfer site for biochemical reactions catalyzed by an enzyme. [1905–10; < G *Ko-enzym;* see CO-, ENZYME] **—co•en•zy•mat•ic** (kō en′zi mat′ik, -zī-), *adj.,* **—co•en′zy•mat′i•cal•ly,** *adv.*

coenzyme A, *Biochem.* a coenzyme, composed of a phosphorylated derivative of pantothenic acid linked to adenylic acid, that participates in the transfer of acyl groups in fatty acid metabolism and amino acid metabolism. *Abbr.:* CoA [1935–40]

co•e•qual (kō ē′kwəl), *adj.* **1.** equal with another or each other in rank, ability, extent, etc.: *The two top students were coequal.* *—n.* **2.** a coequal person or thing. [1350–1400; ME. See CO-, EQUAL] **—co•e•qual•i•ty** (kō′i kwol′i tē), **co•e′qual•ness,** *n.* **—co•e′qual•ly,** *adv.*

co•erce (kō ûrs′), *v.t.,* **-erced, -erc•ing. 1.** to compel by force, intimidation, or authority, esp. without regard for individual desire or volition: *They coerced him into signing the document.* **2.** to bring about through the use of force or other forms of compulsion; exact: *to coerce obedience.* **3.** to dominate or control, esp. by exploiting fear, anxiety, etc.: *The state is based on successfully coercing the individual.* [1425–75; late ME < L *coercēre* to hold in, restrain, equiv. to *co-* CO- + *-ercēre,* comb. form of *arcēre* to keep in, keep away, akin to *arca* ARK] **—co•erc′er,** *n.* **—co•er′ci•ble,** *adj.*

co•er•cion (kō ûr′shən), *n.* **1.** the act of coercing; use of force or intimidation to obtain compliance. **2.** force or the power to use force in gaining compliance, as by a government or police force. [1515–25; < ML *coerciōn-* (s. of *coerciō*), L *coerctiōn-,* syncopated var. of *coercitiōn-,* equiv. to *coercit(us)* (ptp. of *coercēre* to COERCE) + *-iōn-* -ION; r. late ME *cohercion* < MF < L as above] **—co•er′cion•ar•y,** *adj.* **—co•er′cion•ist,** *n.*

co•er•cive (kō ûr′siv), *adj.* serving or tending to coerce. [1590–1600; COERCE + -IVE] **—co•er′cive•ly,** *adv.* **—co•er′cive•ness,** *n.*

co•er•civ•i•ty (kō′ər siv′i tē), *n. Elect.* the magnetic intensity needed to reduce to zero the magnetic flux density of a fully magnetized magnetic specimen or to demagnetize a magnet. Also called **coer′cive force′.** [1895–1900; COERCIVE + -ITY]

coes•ite (kō′sīt), *n. Mineral.* a rare form of silicon dioxide, a denser polymorph of quartz, originally synthesized from quartz at high temperatures and pressures: later discovered in nature. Cf. **stishovite.** [1950–55; named after Loring *Coes,* Jr., 20th-century American who synthesized it; see -ITE[1]]

co•es•sen•tial (kō′i sen′shəl), *adj.* united in essence; having the same essence or nature. [1425–75; late ME. See CO-, ESSENTIAL] **—co′es•sen′ti•al′i•ty, co′es•sen′•tial•ness,** *n.* **—co′es•sen′tial•ly,** *adv.*

co•e•ta•ne•ous (kō′i tā′nē əs), *adj.* of the same age or duration. [1600–10; < L *coaetāneus,* equiv. to *co-* CO- + *aet(ās)* age + *-āneus* compound adj. suffix; see -AN, -EOUS] **—co′e•ta′ne•ous•ly,** *adv.* **—co•e•ta•ne•i•ty** (kō′i tə nē′i tē), **co′e•ta′ne•ous•ness,** *n.*

co•e•ter•nal (kō′i tûr′nl), *adj.* existing with another eternally. [1400–50; late ME. See CO-, ETERNAL] **—co′e•ter′nal•ly,** *adv.* **—co′e•ter′ni•ty,** *n.*

Coeur d'A•lene (kûr′ dl ān′), **1.** a member of an Indian people in N Idaho around Coeur d'Alene Lake. **2.** a Salishan language. **3.** a city in N Idaho. 20,054.

Coeur de Li•on (kûr′ də lē′ən; *Fr.* kœʀ də lyôɴ′). See **Richard I,** meaning "lionhearted."

co•e•val (kō ē′vəl), *adj.* **1.** of the same age, date, or duration; equally old: *Analysis has proved that this manuscript is coeval with that one.* **2.** coincident: *Leonardo da Vinci and Michelangelo were only approximately coeval.* *—n.* **3.** a contemporary: *He is more serious than his coevals.* [1595–1605; < LL *coaev(us)* (*co-* CO- + *-aevus,* adj. deriv. of *aevum* age) + -AL[1]] **—co•e•val•i•ty** (kō′i val′i tē), *n.* **—co•e′val•ly,** *adv.*
—Syn. 1, 2. See **contemporary.**

co•ev•o•lu•tion (kō′ev ə lōō′shən *or, esp. Brit.,* -ē və-), *n.* evolution involving a series of reciprocal changes in two or more noninterbreeding populations that have a close ecological relationship and act as agents of natural selection for each other, as the succession of adaptations of a predator for pursuing and of its prey for fleeing or evading. [1960–65; CO- + EVOLUTION] **—co′ev•o•lu′•tion•ar•y,** *adj.*

co•e•volve (kō′i volv′), *v.i.,* **-volved, -volv•ing.** to undergo coevolution. [CO- + EVOLVE]

co•ex•ec•u•tor (kō′ig zek′yə tər), *n.* a joint executor. [1400–50; late ME. See CO-, EXECUTOR]

co•ex•ec•u•trix (kō′ig zek′yə triks), *n., pl.* **-ex•ec•u•tri•ces** (-ig zek′yə trī′sēz). a joint executrix. [1840–50; CO- + EXECUTRIX]
—Usage. See **-trix.**

co•ex•ist (kō′ig zist′), *v.i.* **1.** to exist together or at the same time. **2.** to exist separately or independently but peaceably, often while remaining rivals or adversaries: *Although their ideologies differ greatly, the two great powers must coexist.* [1670–80; CO- + EXIST]

CONCISE ETYMOLOGY KEY: <, descended or borrowed from; >, whence; b., blend of, blended; c., cognate with; cf., compare; deriv., derivative; equiv., equivalent; imit., imitative; obl., oblique; r., replacing; s., stem; sp., spelling, spelled; resp., respelling, respelled; trans., translation; ?, origin unknown; *, unattested; ‡, probably earlier than. See the full key inside the front cover.

co•ex•ist•ence (kō′ig zis′təns), *n.* **1.** the act or state of coexisting. **2.** a policy of living peacefully with other nations, religions, etc., despite fundamental disagreements. [1640–50; CO- + EXISTENCE] —**co′ex•ist′ent,** *adj.*

co•ex•tend (kō′ik stend′), *v.t., v.i.* to extend equally through the same space or duration. [1610–20; CO- + EXTEND] —**co•ex•ten•sion** (kō′ik sten′shən), *n.*

co•ex•ten•sive (kō′ik sten′siv), *adj.* equal or coincident in space, time, or scope. [1670–80; CO- + EXTENSIVE] —**co′ex•ten′sive•ly,** *adv.*

co•ex•tru•sion (kō′ik strōō′zhən), *n. Engin.* simultaneous extrusion of two or more different yet compatible metals or plastics through the same die. [CO- + EXTRUSION]

co•fac•tor (kō′fak′tər), *n.* **1.** *Biochem.* any of various organic or inorganic substances necessary to the function of an enzyme. **2.** *Math.* **a.** a prefactor or postfactor. **b.** the product of the minor of a given element of a matrix times −1 raised to the power of the sum of the indices of the row and column crossed out in forming the minor. [1935–40; CO- + FACTOR]

COFC, container-on-flatcar.

C of C, Chamber of Commerce.

co•fea•ture (kō′fē′chər), *n.* a movie that shares a bill with another movie. [CO- + FEATURE]

cof•fee (kô′fē, kof′ē), *n.* **1.** a beverage consisting of a decoction or infusion of the roasted ground or crushed seeds **(cof′fee beans′)** of the two-seeded fruit **(cof′fee ber′ry)** of certain coffee trees. **2.** the seeds or fruit themselves. **3.** any tropical tree or shrub of the genus *Coffea,* of the madder family, esp. *C. arabica* and *C. canephora,* cultivated commercially. Cf. **Arabian coffee, robusta coffee. 4.** a cup of coffee: *We ordered four coffees and three doughnuts.* **5.** a social gathering at which coffee and other refreshments are served. **6.** medium to dark brown. —*adj.* **7.** coffee-colored. [1590–1600; < It *caffè* < Turk *kahve* < Ar *qahwah*]

cof•fee-and (kô′fē and′, kof′ē-), *n. Informal.* coffee and a snack. [1900–05, *Amer.*]

cof•fee•ber•ry (kô′fē ber′ē, kof′ē-), *n., pl.* **-ries.** an evergreen shrub, *Rhamnus californica,* of the buckthorn family, common in the western U.S., having small, greenish flowers and red fruit that turns black, grown as a bee plant. [1655–65, *Amer.*; COFFEE + BERRY]

cof′fee break′, a break from work for coffee, a snack, etc. [1940–45]

cof•fee•cake (kô′fē kāk′, kof′ē-), *n.* a cake or sweetened bread, often flavored with cinnamon and made or topped with nuts, raisins, candied fruit, etc., and glazed with melted sugar, usually served with coffee. [1875–80, *Amer.*; COFFEE + CAKE]

cof•fee-col•ored (kô′fē kul′ərd, kof′ē-), *adj.* having the medium-brown color of coffee mixed with cream or milk; moderately brown. [1685–95]

cof′fee cream′, cream for use in coffee; light cream. [1905–10]

cof′fee hour′, 1. an informal gathering of people at which coffee and refreshments are served. **2.** See **coffee break.** [1950–55]

cof•fee•house (kô′fē hous′, kof′ē-), *n., pl.* **-hous•es** (-hou′ziz), *v.,* **-housed, -hous•ing.** —*n.* **1.** a public place that specializes in serving coffee and other refreshments and that sometimes provides informal entertainment. **2.** (in 17th- and 18th-century England) a similar establishment where groups met for a particular purpose, as for informal discussions or card playing. —*v.i.* **3.** *Informal.* to engage in aimless talk or chitchat. **4.** *Cards.* to make remarks and gestures during play with the purpose of misleading opponents as to the cards one holds. [1605–15; COFFEE + HOUSE] —**cof′fee•hous′er,** *n.*

cof′fee klatsch′ (klach, kläch), a social gathering for informal conversation at which coffee is served. Also, **cof′fee klatch′, kaffee klatsch.** [1880–85; < G *Kaffeeklatsch,* equiv. to *Kaffee* COFFEE + *Klatsch* noise (e.g., of conversation)]

cof•fee-klatsch (kô′fē klach′, -kläch′, kof′ē-), *v.i.* to gather for a coffee klatsch. Also, **cof′fee-klatch′.** [1890–95]

cof′fee mak′er, 1. Also, **cof′fee•mak′er.** an apparatus for brewing coffee; coffeepot. **2.** a person or company that blends, roasts, or brews coffee. [1925–30]

cof′fee mill′, a small mill for grinding roasted coffee beans. [1685–95]

cof•fee•pot (kô′fē pot′, kof′ē-), *n.* a container, usually with a handle and a spout or lip, in which coffee is made or served, or both. [1695–1705; COFFEE + POT[1]]

cof′fee ring′, a coffeecake shaped like a ring, plain or fruited, often with a topping of raisins, ground nuts, and icing. [1920–25]

cof′fee roy′al. See **café royale.** [1920–25]

cof′fee shop′, a small, usually inexpensive, restaurant where refreshments and light meals are served. [1830–40, *Amer.*]

cof′fee spoon′, a small spoon used with demitasse cups. [1695–1705]

cof′fee ta′ble, a low table, usually placed in front of a sofa, for holding ashtrays, snack bowls, glasses, magazines, etc. Also called **cocktail table.** [1875–80]

cof′fee-ta•ble book′ (kô′fē tā′bəl, kof′ē-), an oversize, expensive, and usually illustrated book suitable for displaying, as on a coffee table. [1960–65]

cof′fee tree′, 1. any tree, as *Coffea arabica,* yielding coffee beans. **2.** See **Kentucky coffee tree.** [1735–45]

cof•fer (kô′fər, kof′ər), *n.* **1.** a box or chest, esp. one for valuables. **2. coffers,** a treasury; funds: *The coffers of the organization were rapidly filled by the contributions.* **3.** any of various boxlike enclosures, as a cofferdam. **4.** Also called **caisson, lacunar.** *Archit.* one of a number of sunken panels, usually square or octagonal, in a vault, ceiling, or soffit. —*v.t.* **5.** to deposit or lay up in or as in a coffer or chest. **6.** to ornament with coffers or sunken panels. [1250–1300; ME *cofre* < OF << L *cophinus* basket; see COFFIN] —**cof′fer•like′,** *adj.*

coffers (def. 4) of a ceiling

cof•fer•dam (kô′fər dam′, kof′ər-), *n.* **1.** a watertight enclosure placed or constructed in waterlogged soil or under water and pumped dry so that construction or repairs can proceed under normal conditions. **2.** *Naut.* a sealed void between two bulkheads, as for insulation or as an extra barrier to the escape of liquids or vapors. [1730–40; COFFER + DAM[1]]

cof•fered (kô′fərd, kof′ərd), *adj.* (of a vault, ceiling, or soffit) having coffers. [1580–90; COFFER + -ED[3]]

Cof•fey•ville (kô′fē vil′, kof′ē-), *n.* a city in SE Kansas. 15,185.

cof•fin (kô′fin, kof′in), *n.* **1.** the box or case in which the body of a dead person is placed for burial; casket. **2.** the part of a horse's foot containing the coffin bone. **3.** *Print.* **a.** the bed of a platen press. **b.** the wooden frame around the bed of an early wooden press. —*v.t.* **4.** to put or enclose in or as in a coffin. [1300–50; ME *cofin* < ONF < L *cophinus* < Gk *kóphinos* a kind of basket] —**cof′fin•less,** *adj.*

Cof•fin (kô′fin, kof′in), *n.* **1. Levi,** 1798–1877, U.S. abolitionist leader. **2. Robert P(eter) Tristram,** 1892–1955, U.S. poet, essayist, and biographer.

cof′fin bone′, the terminal phalanx in the foot of the horse and allied animals, enclosed in the hoof. [1710–20]

cof′fin cor′ner, *Football.* a corner of the field inside the ten-yard line, esp. as the target of a punt intended to go out of bounds in this area and so put the receiving team in a position near its goal line. [1940–45]

cof•fin•ite (kô′fi nīt, kof′i-), *n.* a mineral, black uranous silicate, $USiO_4$, an important ore of uranium. [1950–55; COFFIN + -ITE[1]]

cof′fin nail′, *Slang.* a cigarette. [1885–90]

Coff's′ Har′bour (kôfs, kofs), a seaport in E Australia. 16,020.

co•fi•nal (kō fīn′l), *adj. Math.* of or pertaining to a subset of a set with a partial order relation, as "greater than" or "equal to," in which corresponding to each element in the set is an element in the subset that is in relation to the given element. [CO- + FINAL]

co•found•er (kō foun′dər), *n.* a person who founds or establishes something with another. Also, **co-found′er.** [1595–1605; CO- + FOUNDER[1]]

C. of S., Chief of Staff.

co•func•tion (kō′fungk′shən), *n. Trigonom.* the function of the complement of a given angle or arc: *cosθ is the cofunction of sinθ.* [1905–10; CO- + FUNCTION]

cog[1] (kog, kôg), *n., v.,* **cogged, cog•ging.** —*n.* **1.** (not in technical use) a gear tooth, formerly esp. one of hardwood or metal, fitted into a slot in a gearwheel of less durable material. **2.** a cogwheel. **3.** a person who plays a minor part in a large organization, activity, etc.: *He's just a small cog in the financial department.* —*v.i.* **4.** (of an electric motor) to move jerkily. —*v.t.* **5.** to roll or hammer (an ingot) into a bloom or slab. **6. slip a cog,** to make a blunder; err: *One of the clerks must have slipped a cog.* [1200–50; ME *cogge,* prob. < Scand; cf. Sw, Norw *kugg* cog]

cog[2] (kog, kôg), *v.,* **cogged, cog•ging.** —*v.t.* **1.** to manipulate or load (dice) unfairly. —*v.i.* **2.** to cheat, esp. at dice. [1525–35; orig. uncert.]

cog[3] (kog, kôg), *n., v.,* **cogged, cog•ging.** —*n.* **1.** *Carpentry.* (in a cogged joint) the tongue in one timber, fitting into a corresponding slot in another. **2.** *Mining.* a cluster of timber supports for a roof. Cf. **chock** (def. 4). —*v.t., v.i.* **3.** *Carpentry.* to join with a cog. [1855–60; special use of COG[1]; r. *cock* in same sense, special use of COCK[1] (in sense of projection); see COAK]

cog., cognate.

co•gen•cy (kō′jən sē), *n.* the quality or state of being convincing or persuasive: *The cogency of the argument was irrefutable.* [1680–90; COG(ENT) + -ENCY]

co•gen•e•ra•tion (kō′jen ə rā′shən), *n. Energy.* utilization of the normally wasted heat energy produced by a power plant or industrial process, esp. to generate electricity. [1975–80; CO- + GENERATION]

co•gent (kō′jənt), *adj.* **1.** convincing or believable by virtue of forcible, clear, or incisive presentation; telling. **2.** to the point; relevant; pertinent. [1650–60; < L *cōgent-* (s. of *cōgēns,* prp. of *cōgere* to drive together, collect, compel), equiv. to *cōg-* (*co-* CO- + *ag-,* s. of *agere* to drive) + *-ent-* -ENT] —**co′gent•ly,** *adv.*

Cog•gan (kog′ən), *n.* **(Frederick) Donald,** born 1909, English clergyman: archbishop of Canterbury 1974–80.

cogged (kogd), *adj.* having cogs. [1815–25; COG[1] + -ED[3]]

cog•i•ta•ble (koj′i tə bəl), *adj.* able to be considered; conceivable; thinkable: *The thought of space flights to other galaxies has become more cogitable.* [1425–75; late ME < L *cōgitābilis,* equiv. to *cōgitā(re)* (see COGITATE) + *-bilis* -BLE] —**cog′i•ta•bil′i•ty,** *n.*

cog•i•tate (koj′i tāt′), *v.,* **-tat•ed, -tat•ing.** —*v.i.* **1.** to think hard; ponder; meditate: *to cogitate about a problem.* —*v.t.* **2.** to think about; devise: *to cogitate a scheme.* [1555–65; < L *cōgitātus* (ptp. of *cōgitāre*), equiv. to *co-* CO- + *agitātus*; see AGITATE] —**cog′i•tat′ing•ly,** *adv.* —**cog′i•ta′tor,** *n.*
—**Syn. 1.** deliberate, reflect. **2.** weigh.

cog•i•ta•tion (koj′i tā′shən), *n.* **1.** concerted thought or reflection; meditation; contemplation: *After hours of cogitation he came up with a new proposal.* **2.** the faculty of thinking: *She was a serious student and had a great power of cogitation.* **3.** a thought; design or plan: *to jot down one's cogitations.* [1175–1225; ME *cogitaciun* < AF, OF < L *cōgitātiōn-* (s. of *cōgitātiō*), equiv. to *cōgitāt(us)* (see COGITATE) + *-iōn-* -ION]

cog•i•ta•tive (koj′i tā′tiv), *adj.* **1.** meditating; contemplating: *The cogitative faculty distinguishes humans from animals.* **2.** given to meditation; thoughtful: *The leaders sat in cogitative silence.* [1375–1425; late ME < ML *cōgitātīvus,* equiv. to *cōgitāt(us)* (see COGITATE) + *-īvus* -IVE] —**cog′i•ta′tive•ly,** *adv.* —**cog′i•ta′tive•ness,** *n.*

co•gi•to, er•go sum (kō′gi tō′ er′gō sŏŏm′; *Eng.* koj′i tō′ ûr′gō sum′, er′gō), *Latin.* I think, therefore I am (stated by Descartes as the first principle in resolving universal doubt).

cog′ locomo′tive. See **rack locomotive.**

co•gnac (kōn′yak, kon′-; *Fr.* kô nyak′), *n.* **1.** (*often cap.*) the brandy distilled in and shipped from the legally delimited area surrounding the town of Cognac, in W central France. **2.** any French brandy. **3.** any good brandy. [1585–95; < F]

cog•nate (kog′nāt), *adj.* **1.** related by birth; of the same parentage, descent, etc. **2.** *Ling.* descended from the same language or form: *such cognate languages as French and Spanish.* **3.** allied or similar in nature or quality. —*n.* **4.** a person or thing cognate with another. **5.** a cognate word: *The English word* cold *is a cognate of German* kalt. [1635–45; < L *cognātus,* equiv. to *co-* CO- + *-gnātus* (ptp. of *gnāscī, nāscī* to be born)] —**cog′•nate•ness,** *n.* —**cog•nat•ic** (kog nat′ik), *adj.*

cog′nate ob′ject, *Gram.* a substantive functioning as the object of a verb, esp. of a verb that is usually intransitive, when both object and verb are derived from the same root. *Speech* in *Speak the speech* is a cognate object. [1875–80]

cog•na•tion (kog nā′shən), *n.* cognate relationship. [1350–1400; ME *cognacioun* (< AF, OF) < L *cognātiōn-* (s. of *cognātiō*) kinship, equiv. to *cognāt(us)* COGNATE + *-iōn-* -ION]

cog•ni•tion (kog nish′ən), *n.* **1.** the act or process of knowing; perception. **2.** the product of such a process; something thus known, perceived, etc. **3.** knowledge. [1375–1425; late ME *cognicioun* < L *cognitiōn-* (s. of *cognitiō*), equiv. to *cognit(us),* ptp. of *cognōscere* (*co-* CO- + *gni-,* var. s. of *gnōscere, nōscere,* to learn (see KNOW[1]) + *-tus* ptp. suffix) + *-iōn-* -ION] —**cog•ni′tion•al,** *adj.*

cog•ni•tive (kog′ni tiv), *adj.* **1.** of or pertaining to cognition. **2.** of or pertaining to the mental processes of perception, memory, judgment, and reasoning, as contrasted with emotional and volitional processes. [1580–90; < ML *cognitīvus,* equiv. to L *cognit(us)* known (see COGNITION) + *-īvus* -IVE] —**cog′ni•tive•ly,** *adv.* —**cog′ni•tiv′i•ty,** *n.*

cog′nitive devel′opment, the process of acquiring intelligence and increasingly advanced thought and problem-solving ability from infancy to adulthood.

cog′nitive dis′sonance, *Psychol.* anxiety that results from simultaneously holding contradictory or otherwise incompatible attitudes, beliefs, or the like, as when one likes a person but disapproves strongly of one of his or her habits. [1960–65]

cog′nitive psychol′ogy, the branch of psychology studying the mental processes involved in perception, learning, memory, and reasoning. [1945–50]

cog′nitive sci′ence, the study of the precise nature of different mental tasks and the operations of the brain that enable them to be performed, engaging branches of psychology, computer science, philosophy, and linguistics.

cog′nitive ther′apy, a form of therapy for depression in which the goal is to diminish symptoms by correcting distorted thinking based on negative self-perceptions and expectations. Also called **cog′nitive behav′ior ther′apy.**

cog•ni•za•ble (kog′nə zə bəl, kon′ə-, kog nī′-), *adj.* **1.** capable of being perceived or known. **2.** being within the jurisdiction of a court. [1670–80; COGNIZ(ANCE) + -ABLE] —**cog′ni•za•bly,** *adv.*

cog•ni•zance (kog′nə zəns, kon′ə-), *n.* **1.** awareness, realization, or knowledge; notice; perception: *The guests took cognizance of the snide remark.* **2.** *Law.* **a.** judicial notice as taken by a court in dealing with a cause. **b.** the right of taking jurisdiction, as possessed by a court. **c.** acknowledgment; admission, as a plea admitting the fact alleged in the declaration. **3.** the range or scope of knowledge, observation, etc.: *Such understanding is beyond his cognizance.* **4.** *Heraldry.* a device by which a person or a person's servants or property can be recognized; badge. [1250–1300; ME *conisa(u)nce* < MF *con(o)is(s)ance,* equiv. to *conois(tre)* to know (< L *cognōscere*; see COGNITION) + *-ance* -ANCE; forms with *-g-* (< L) from the 16th century]
—**Syn. 1.** note, heed, attention, regard, scrutiny.

cog•ni•zant (kog′nə zənt, kon′ə-), *adj.* **1.** having cognizance; aware (usually fol. by *of*): *He was cognizant of*

CONCISE PRONUNCIATION KEY: *act, cāpe, dâre, pärt; set, ēqual; if, ice; ox, ōver, ôrder, oil, bŏŏk, bōōt, out; up, ûrge; child; sing; shoe; thin, that;* zh as in *treasure.* ə = *a* as in *alone, e* as in *system, i* as in *easily, o* as in *gallop, u* as in *circus;* ə as in *fire* (fīər), *hour* (ouər). l and n can serve as syllabic consonants, as in *cradle* (krād′l), and *button* (but′n). See the full key inside the front cover.

the difficulty. **2.** having legal cognizance. [1810–20; COGNIZ(ANCE) + -ANT]
—Syn. 1. See **conscious.**

cog•nize (kog′nīz), *v.t.*, **-nized, -niz•ing.** to perceive; become conscious of; know. Also, *esp. Brit.*, **cog′nise.** [1650–60; back formation from COGNIZANCE] **—cog′niz•er,** *n.*

cog•no•men (kog nō′mən), *n., pl.* **-no•mens, -nom•i•na** (-nom′ə nə). **1.** a surname. **2.** any name, esp. a nickname. **3.** the third and commonly the last name of a citizen of ancient Rome, indicating the person's house or family, as "Caesar" in "Gaius Julius Caesar." Cf. **agnomen** (def. 1). [1800–10; < L, equiv. to *co-* CO- + *nōmen* name, with *-g-* on model of *nōsci: cognōsci;* see COGNITION] **—cog•nom•i•nal** (kog nom′ə nəl, -nō′mə-), *adj.* **—cog•nom′i•nal•ly,** *adv.*

cog•no•scen•ti (kon′yə shen′tē, kog′nə-), *n.pl., sing.* **-te** (-tē). persons who have superior knowledge and understanding of a particular field, esp. in the fine arts, literature, and world of fashion. Also, **conoscenti.** [1770–80; < It, Latinized var. of *conoscente* (prp. of *conoscere* to know) < L. See COGNITION, -ENT]

cog•nos•ci•ble (kog nos′ə bəl), *adj.* capable of being known. [1635–45; < LL *cognōscibilis,* equiv. to *cognōscere* (see COGNIZANCE) + *-ibilis* -IBLE] **—cog•nos′ci•bil′i•ty,** *n.*

cog•nos•ci•tive (kog nos′i tiv), *adj.* having the ability to know or discover: *cognoscitive powers.* [1630–40; < L *cognōsc(ere)* to know, come to know + -ITIVE] **—cog•nos′ci•tive•ly,** *adv.*

cog•no•vit (kog nō′vit), *n. Law.* an acknowledgment or confession by a defendant that the plaintiff's cause, or part of it, is just, wherefore the defendant, to save expense, permits judgment to be entered without trial. [1755–65; < L: 3rd pers. sing. perfect of *cognōscere* to recognize; see COGNIZANCE]

co•gon (kō gōn′), *n.* a tall, coarse grass, *Imperata cylindrica,* of the tropics and subtropics, used widely for thatching. [1895–1900; < Sp < Tagalog *kugon*]

cog′ rail′way, a railroad having locomotives with a cogged center driving wheel engaging with a cogged rail, to provide sufficient traction for climbing steeper grades than is possible with ordinary wheels. Also called **rack railway.** [1895–1900, *Amer.*]

Cogs′well chair′ (kogz′wel, -wəl), an armchair having a fixed, sloping back, open sides, and cabriole legs. Also, **Coxwell chair.**

cog•wheel (kog′hwēl′, -wēl′), *n.* (not in technical use) a gearwheel, esp. one having teeth of hardwood or metal inserted into slots. [1375–1425; late ME; see COG[1], WHEEL]

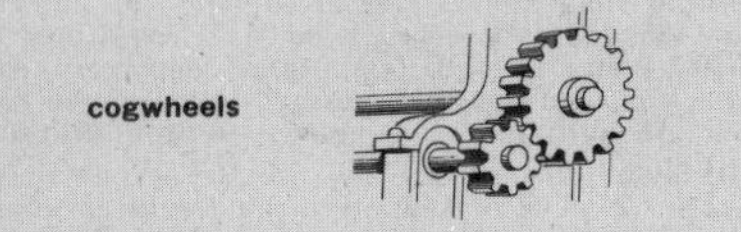
cogwheels

cog′wheel ore′, *Mineral.* bournonite.

co•hab (kō′hab′, kō hab′), *n. Informal.* a person who cohabits. [by shortening]

co•hab•it (kō hab′it), *v.i.* **1.** to live together as husband and wife, usually without legal or religious sanction. **2.** to live together in an intimate relationship. **3.** to dwell with another or share the same place, as different species of animals. [1520–30; < LL *cohabitāre,* equiv. to *co-* CO- + *habitāre* to have possession, abide (freq. of *habēre* to have, own)] **—co•hab′it•ant, co•hab′it•er,** *n.* **—co•hab′i•ta′tion,** *n.*

co•hab•i•tate (kō hab′i tāt′), *v.i.*, **-tat•ed, -tat•ing.** cohabit. [1625–35; < LL *cohabitātus,* ptp. of *cohabitāre* COHABIT; see -ATE[1]]

Co•han (kō han′, kō′han), *n.* **George M(ichael),** 1878–1942, U.S. actor, playwright, and producer.

co•heir (kō âr′), *n.* a joint heir. [1350–1400; ME. See CO-, HEIR] **—co•heir′ship,** *n.*

co•heir•ess (kō âr′is), *n.* a joint heiress. [CO- + HEIRESS]
—Usage. See **-ess.**

Co•hen (kō′ən), *n.* **1. Morris Raphael,** 1880–1947, U.S. philosopher and educator, born in Russia. **2. Octav•us Roy** (ok tav′əs), 1891–1959, U.S. short-story writer and novelist.

Co•hen (kō′ən; *Seph. Heb.* kô hen′ *Ashk. Heb.* kō-hān′, kō′hän, koin), *n., pl.* **Co•ha•nim** (*Seph. Heb.* kô-hä nēm′; *Ashk. Heb.* kō hä nim′, -hä′nim), *Eng.* **Co•hens.** a member of the Jewish priestly class, descended from Aaron, having sacrificial, ministerial, and other sacred functions from Aaronic times to about the 1st century A.D. and now having essentially honorific religious duties and prerogatives. Also, **Kohen.** [< Heb *kōhēn* priest]

co•hen•ite (kō′ə nīt′), *n.* a rare microscopic mineral, carbide of iron, nickel, or cobalt, $(Fe, Ni, Co)_3C$, found in lunar rocks and some meteorites. [named after E. W. Cohen, 19th-century German mineralogist; see -ITE[1]]

co•here (kō hēr′), *v.i.*, **-hered, -her•ing. 1.** to stick together; be united; hold fast, as parts of the same mass: *The particles of wet flour cohered to form a paste.* **2.** *Physics.* (of two or more similar substances) to be united within a body by the action of molecular forces. **3.** to be naturally or logically connected: *Without sound reasoning no argument will cohere.* **4.** to agree; be congruous: *Her account of the incident cohered with his.* [1590–1600; < L *cohaerēre,* equiv. to *co-* CO- + *haerēre* to stick, cling]
—Syn. 1. See **stick**[2]. **3.** follow.

co•her•ence (kō hēr′əns, -her′-), *n.* **1.** the act or state of cohering; cohesion. **2.** logical interconnection; overall sense or understandability. **3.** congruity; consistency. **4.** *Physics, Optics.* (of waves) the state of being coherent. **5.** *Ling.* the property of unity in a written text or a segment of spoken discourse that stems from the links among its underlying ideas and from the logical organization and development of its thematic content. Cf. **cohesion** (def. 4). Also, **co•her′en•cy.** [1570–80; COHER(ENT) + -ENCE]
—Syn. 3. correspondence, harmony, agreement, rationality.

coher′ence the′ory, *Philos.* the theory of truth that every true statement, insofar as it is true, describes its subject in the totality of its relationship with all other things. Cf. **correspondence theory, pragmatic theory.** [1905–10]

co•her•ent (kō hēr′ənt, -her′-), *adj.* **1.** logically connected; consistent: *a coherent argument.* **2.** cohering; sticking together: *a coherent mass of sticky candies.* **3.** having a natural or due agreement of parts; harmonious: *a coherent design.* **4.** *Physics, Optics.* of or pertaining to waves that maintain a fixed phase relationship, as in coherent light. Cf. **laser.** [1570–80; < ML *cohērent-,* var. of L *cohaerent-* (s. of *cohaerēns*), prp. of *cohaerēre.* See COHERE, -ENT] **—co•her′ent•ly,** *adv.*

coher′ent light′, light in which the electromagnetic waves maintain a fixed and predictable phase relationship with each other over a period of time.

co•her•er (kō hēr′ər, -her′-), *n.* **1.** a person or thing that coheres. **2.** *Radio.* a device usually used in detecting radio waves, as a tube filled with a conducting substance in granular form, whose electrical resistance increases when struck by radio waves. [1890–95; COHERE + -ER[1]]

co•he•sion (kō hē′zhən), *n.* **1.** the act or state of cohering, uniting, or sticking together. **2.** *Physics.* the molecular force between particles within a body or substance that acts to unite them. Cf. **adhesion** (def. 4). **3.** *Bot.* the congenital union of one part with another. **4.** *Ling.* the property of unity in a written text or a segment of spoken discourse that stems from links among its surface elements, as when words in one sentence are repeated in another, and esp. from the fact that some words or phrases depend for their interpretation upon material in preceding or following text, as in the sequence *Be assured of this. Most people do not want to fight. However, they will do so when provoked,* where *this* refers to the two sentences that follow, *they* refers back to *most people, do so* substitutes for the preceding verb *fight,* and *however* relates the clause that follows to the preceding sentence. Cf. **coherence** (def. 5). [1670–80; var. of *cohaesion* < L *cohaes-* (var. s. of *cohaerēre* to COHERE) + *-iōn-* -ION] **—co•he′sion•less,** *adj.*

co•he•sive (kō hē′siv), *adj.* **1.** characterized by or causing cohesion: *a cohesive agent.* **2.** cohering or tending to cohere; well-integrated; unified: *a cohesive organization.* **3.** *Physics.* of or pertaining to the molecular force within a body or substance acting to unite its parts. [1720–30; COHES(ION) + -IVE] **—co•he′sive•ly,** *adv.* **—co•he′sive•ness,** *n.*

Cohn (kōn), *n.* **1. Edwin Joseph,** 1892–1953, U.S. chemist and researcher on blood proteins. **2. Fer•di•nand Ju•li•us** (fûr′dn and′ jo͞ol′yəs; *Ger.* feʀ′di nänt′ yo͞o′lē o͞os′), 1828–98, German botanist and bacteriologist.

co•ho (kō′hō), *n., pl.* **-hos,** (*esp. collectively*) **-ho.** See **coho salmon.** Also, **co′hoe.**

co•ho•ba (kō hō′bə), *n.* parica. [< AmerSp, said to be < Arawak]

co•ho•bate (kō′hō bāt′), *v.t.*, **-bat•ed, -bat•ing.** *Pharm.* to distill again from the same or a similar substance, as by pouring a distilled liquid back upon the matter remaining in the vessel, or upon another mass of similar matter. [1635–45; < NL *cohobātus* (ptp. of *cohobāre*), equiv. to *kohob* repetition (Paracelsian term, perh. < dial. Ar *ka'ab* second) + *-ātus* -ATE[1]] **—co′ho•ba′tion,** *n.* **—co′ho•ba′tor,** *n.*

Co•hoes (kō hōz′), *n.* a city in E New York, on the Hudson River. 18,144.

co•hort (kō′hôrt), *n.* **1.** a group or company: *She has a cohort of admirers.* **2.** a companion or associate. **3.** one of the ten divisions in an ancient Roman legion, numbering from 300 to 600 soldiers. **4.** any group of soldiers or warriors. **5.** an accomplice; abettor: *He got off with probation, but his cohorts got ten years apiece.* **6.** a group of persons sharing a particular statistical or demographic characteristic: *the cohort of all children born in 1980.* **7.** *Biol.* an individual in a population of the same species. [1475–85; < MF *cohorte* < L *cohort-* (s. of *cohors*) farmyard, armed force (orig. from a particular place or camp), cohort, retinue, equiv. to *co-* CO- + *hort-* (akin to *hortus* garden); r. late ME *cohors* < L nom. sing.]
—Syn. 2. friend, comrade, fellow, chum, pal, buddy.
—Usage. A COHORT was originally one of the ten divisions of a legion in the Roman army, containing from 300 to 600 men. The most common use of COHORT today is in the sense "group" or "company": *A cohort of hangers-on followed the singer down the corridor.* In a development emphasizing the idea of companionship, COHORT has also come to mean a single companion, associate, or the like: *The senator strode into the room followed by his faithful cohort, his son-in-law.*

co•hor•ta•tive (kō hôr′tə tiv), *adj. Gram.* (of a verbal mood or form) expressing encouragement or exhortation. [1850–55; < L *cohortāt(us)* (ptp. of *cohortāre* to urge; see COHORT) + -IVE]

co′ho salm′on, a small salmon, *Oncorhynchus kisutch,* of the North Pacific coasts and also in the Great Lakes, where it was introduced: important as a game and food fish. Also, **co′hoe salm′on.** Also called **blue jack, coho, cohoe, silver salmon.** [1865–70; earlier *cohose* (construed as pl.) < Halkomelem (mainland dial.) *kʷóxʷəθ*]

co•hosh (kō′hosh, kō hosh′), *n.* either of two unrelated plants of the eastern U.S., *Cimicifuga racemosa* **(black cohosh),** of the buttercup family, or *Caulophyllum thalictroides* **(blue cohosh),** of the barberry family, both used medicinally. [1790–1800, *Amer.*; < Eastern Abenaki *kkʷə̀has*]

co-host (*v.* kō hōst′, kō′hōst′; *n.* kō′hōst′), *Radio and Television.* **—***v.t., v.i.* **1.** to host (a program) jointly with another. **—***n.* **2.** a person who co-hosts.

co•hune (kō ho͞on′), *n.* a pinnate-leaved palm, *Orbignya cohune,* native to Central America, bearing large nuts whose meat yields an oil resembling that of the coconut. Also, **cohune′ palm′.** [1795–1805; < NL < AmerSp, of uncert. orig.]

Coi•ba (koi′bə; *Sp.* koi′vä), *n.* an island in the Pacific Ocean, S of SW Panama. 20 mi. (32 km) long; 10 mi. (16 km) wide.

coif[1] (koif), *n.* **1.** a hood-shaped cap, usually of white cloth and with extended sides, worn beneath a veil, as by nuns. **2.** any of various hoodlike caps, varying through the centuries in shape and purpose, worn by men and women. **3.** a cap similar to a skullcap, formerly worn by sergeants at law. **4.** *Armor.* a covering for the head and neck, made of leather, padded cloth, or mail. **5.** *Brit.* the rank or position of a sergeant at law. **—***v.t.* **6.** to cover or dress with or as with a coif. [1250–1300; ME *coyf(e)* < AF *coife,* OF *coiffe* < LL *cofia, cofea* headdress, sort of cap < WGmc **kuf(f)ja*]

coif[2] (kwäf, koif), *n., v.t.* coiffure (defs. 1, 3). Also **coiffe.** [prob. back formation from COIFFURE, or < F *coiffer,* its base]

coiffe (kwäf), *n., v.t.,* **coiffed, coiff•ing.** coiffure (defs. 1, 3).

coif•feur (kwᴀ fœʀ′), *n., pl.* ***-feurs*** (-fœʀ′). *French.* a man who is a hairdresser.

coif•feuse (kwᴀ fœz′), *n., pl.* ***-feuses*** (-fœz′). *French.* a woman who is a hairdresser.

coif•fure (kwä fyo͝or′; *Fr.* kwᴀ fʏʀ′), *n., pl.* **-fures** (-fyo͝orz′; *Fr.* -fʏʀ′), *v.,* **-fured** (-fyo͝ord′), **-fur•ing** (-fyo͝or′ing). **—***n.* **1.** a style of arranging or combing the hair. **2.** a head covering; headdress. **—***v.t.* **3.** to provide with a coiffure. [1625–35; < F, equiv. to *coiff(er)* to dress the hair (see COIF[1]) + *-ure* -URE]

coif•fur•ist (kwä fyo͝or′ist), *n.* a person who styles hair, esp. for women. [COIFFURE + -IST]

coign (koin), *n., v.t.* quoin.

coigne (koin), *n., v.t.,* **coigned, coign•ing.** quoin.

coign′ of van′tage, a good position for observation, judgment, criticism, action, etc. [1595–1605]

coil[1] (koil), *v.t.* **1.** to wind into continuous, regularly spaced rings one above the other: *to coil a wire around a pencil.* **2.** to wind on a flat surface into rings one around the other: *He coiled the rope on the deck.* **3.** to gather (rope, wire, etc.) into loops: *She coiled the garden hose and hung it on the hook.* **—***v.i.* **4.** to form rings, spirals, etc.; gather or retract in a circular way: *The snake coiled, ready to strike.* **5.** to move in or follow a winding course: *The river coiled through the valley.* **—***n.* **6.** a connected series of spirals or rings into which a rope or the like is wound. **7.** a single such ring. **8.** an arrangement of pipes, coiled or in a series, as in a radiator. **9.** a continuous pipe having inlet and outlet, or flow and return ends. **10.** *Med.* an intrauterine device. **11.** *Elect.* **a.** a conductor, as a copper wire, wound up in a spiral or other form. **b.** a device composed essentially of such a conductor. **c.** See **ignition coil. 12.** *Philately.* **a.** a stamp issued in a roll, usually of 500 stamps, and usually perforated vertically or horizontally only. **b.** a roll of such stamps. [1605–15; perh. var. of CULL] **—coil′a•ble,** *adj.* **—coil′a•bil′i•ty,** *n.*

coil[2] (koil), *n.* **1.** a noisy disturbance; commotion; tumult. **2.** trouble; bustle; ado. [1560–70; orig. uncert.]

coil′ spring′, any spring of wire coiled helically, having a cylindrical or conical outline. See illus. under **spring.** [1875–80]

Co•im•ba•tore (kō im′bä tôr′, -tōr′), *n.* a city in W Tamil Nadu, in SW India. 405,592.

Coim•bra (kwēɴ′bʀə), *n.* a city in central Portugal: noted university founded at Lisbon 1290, transferred here 1537. 55,985.

coin (koin), *n.* **1.** a piece of metal stamped and issued by the authority of a government for use as money. **2.** a number of such pieces. **3.** *Informal.* money; cash: *He's got plenty of coin in the bank.* **4.** *Archit.* quoin (defs. 1, 2). **5.** *Archaic.* a corner cupboard of the 18th century. **6. pay someone back in his** or **her own coin,** to reciprocate or behave toward in a like way, esp. inamicably; retaliate: *If they persist in teasing you, pay them back in their own coin.* **7. the other side of the coin,** the other side, aspect, or point of view; alternative consideration. **—***adj.* **8.** operated by, or containing machines operated by, inserting a coin or coins into a slot: *a coin laundry.* **—***v.t.* **9.** to make (coinage) by stamping metal: *The mint is coining pennies.* **10.** to convert (metal) into coinage: *The mint used to coin gold into dollars.* **11.** to make; invent; fabricate: *to coin an expression.* **12.** *Metalworking.* to shape the surface of (metal) by squeezing between two dies. Cf. **emboss** (def. 3). **—***v.i.* **13.** *Brit. Informal.* to counterfeit, esp. to make counterfeit money. **14. coin money,** *Informal.* to make or gain money rapidly: *Those who own stock in that restaurant chain are coining money.* [1300–50; ME *coyn(e), coygne* < AF; MF *coin, cuigne* wedge, corner, die < L *cuneus* wedge] **—coin′a•ble,** *adj.* **—coin′er,** *n.*

COIN (koin), *n., adj.* counterinsurgency. [*co(unter) in(surgency)*]

coin•age (koi′nij), *n.* **1.** the act, process, or right of making coins. **2.** the categories, types, or quantity of coins issued by a nation. **3.** coins collectively; currency. **4.** the act or process of inventing words; neologizing. **5.**

CONCISE ETYMOLOGY KEY: <, descended or borrowed from; >, whence; b., blend of, blended; c., cognate with; cf., compare; deriv., derivative; equiv., equivalent; imit., imitative; obl., oblique; r., replacing; s., stem; sp., spelling, spelled; resp., respelling, respelled; trans., translation; ?, origin unknown; *, unattested; ‡, probably earlier than. See the full key inside the front cover.

an invented or newly created word or phrase: *"Ecdysiast" is a coinage of H. L. Mencken.* **6.** anything made, invented, or fabricated. [1350–1400; ME < MF *coignaige.* See COIN, -AGE]

coin′age bronze′, an alloy of 95 percent copper, 4 percent tin, and 1 percent zinc.

coin′ box′, a locked container or receptacle for holding coins deposited in a pay telephone, pinball machine, turnstile, or other coin-operated machine. [1905–10]

coin′ chang′er, **1.** a machine that gives change rapidly, as to a customer, typically operated by a manual keyboard and often used in association with a cash register. **2.** a machine that supplies change, as small coins for large or large coins for small, esp. for the use of other coin-operated machines.

co•in•cide (kō′in sīd′), *v.i.,* **-cid•ed, -cid•ing.** **1.** to occupy the same place in space, the same point or period in time, or the same relative position: *The centers of concentric circles coincide. Our vacations coincided this year.* **2.** to correspond exactly, as in nature, character, etc.: *His vocation coincides with his avocation.* **3.** to agree or concur, as in thought or opinion: *Their opinions always coincide.* [1635–45; < ML *coincidere,* equiv. to L co- CO- + *incidere* to befall; see INCIDENT]
—Syn. 3. accord, correspond, match, tally, jibe, square.
—Ant. 3. differ, contradict.

co•in•ci•dence (kō in′si dəns), *n.* **1.** a striking occurrence of two or more events at one time apparently by mere chance: *Our meeting in Venice was pure coincidence.* **2.** the condition or fact of coinciding. **3.** an instance of this. [1595–1605; COINCID(ENT) + -ENCE]
—Syn. 1. accident, luck, fate.

co•in•ci•dent (kō in′si dənt), *adj.* **1.** happening at the same time. **2.** coinciding; occupying the same place or position. **3.** exactly corresponding. **4.** in exact agreement (usually fol. by *with*). [1555–65; < ML *coincident-* (s. of *coincidēns*) prp. of *coincidere* to COINCIDE; see -ENT]
—Syn. 1. simultaneous, synchronous. See **contemporary.**

co•in•ci•den•tal (kō in′si den′tl), *adj.* **1.** happening by or resulting from coincidence; by chance: *a coincidental meeting.* **2.** existing or occurring at the same time. [1790–1800; COINCIDENT + -AL[1]] **—co•in′ci•den′tal•ly, co•in•ci•dent•ly** (kō in′si dənt lē), *adv.*

coin′cident in′dicator, an economic indicator, as gross national product, that typically fluctuates in correlation with the total economy.

co•in•fec′tious immu′nity (kō′in fek′shəs), premunition.

co•in•her•it•ance (kō′in her′i təns), *n.* joint inheritance. [1590–1600; CO- + INHERITANCE]

coin′ lock′, a lock that is opened by the insertion of a coin. [1925–30]

coin′ machine′, **1.** See **slot machine** (def. 2). **2.** a coin-operated machine, esp. one for dispensing soft drinks, cigarettes, candy, etc. [1915–20]

coin′ of the realm′. See **legal tender.**

coin-op•er•at•ed (koin′op′ə rā′tid), *adj. Informal.* **1.** Also, **coin-op** (koin′op′). activated by inserting a coin or coins into a slot: *a coin-operated washing machine.* **—n.** **2.** a coin-operated machine. **3.** a place with such machines, esp. a self-service laundry. [1955–60]

coin′ sil′ver, silver having the standard fineness for coinage purposes.

co•in•stan•ta•ne•ous (kō′in stən tā′nē əs), *adj.* occurring or existing at the same instant; simultaneous. [1760–70; CO- + INSTANTANEOUS] **—co′in•stan•ta′ne•ous•ly,** *adv.*

co•in•sur•ance (kō′in shŏŏr′əns, -shûr′-), *n.* **1.** insurance underwritten jointly with another or others. **2.** a form of property insurance in which an insurer assumes liability only for that proportion of a loss which the amount of insurance bears to a specified percentage of the value of the property. [1885–90; CO- + INSURANCE]

co•in•sure (kō′in shŏŏr′, -shûr′-), *v.t., v.i.,* **-sured, -sur•ing.** **1.** to insure jointly with another or others. **2.** to insure on the basis of coinsurance. [1895–1900; CO- + INSURE] **—co′in•sur′a•ble,** *adj.*

co•in•sur•er (kō′in shŏŏr′ər, -shûr′-), *n.* **1.** a person or firm that contracts as an insurer jointly with another or others. **2.** an insured who is liable to bear part of the loss under a coinsurance provision. [CO- + INSURER]

Coin•treau (kwän′trō; *Fr.* kwaɴ trō′), *Trademark.* a colorless, orange-flavored liqueur.

co•in•ven•tor (kō′in ven′tər), *n.* one of two or more joint inventors. [1885–90; CO- + INVENTOR]

coir (koir), *n.* the prepared fiber of the husk of the coconut fruit, used in making rope, matting, etc. [1575–85; < Malayalam *kayaru* cord; r. *cairo* < Pg < Tamil *kayiṟu* rope]

cois•trel (koi′strəl), *n. Archaic.* a scoundrel; knave. [1570–80; ME *custrell,* appar. < MF *coustillier, coustelier,* one armed with a *cou(s)telle* dagger (fem. deriv. of *coutel* knife < L *cultellus;* see -IER[2]), with *-r-* perh. from *quystroun* knave, page, scullion < AF (OF *coistron* < VL **coquistrō*)]

co′ital exanthe′ma, *Vet. Pathol.* a common venereal disease affecting horses and cattle, caused by a virus and characterized by the appearance of pustules on the mucous membranes of the genital organs and neighboring skin. [< L *coit(us)* (see COITUS) + -AL[1]]

co•i•tion (kō ish′ən), *n.* coitus. [1535–45; < L *coitiōn-* (s. of *coitiō*) a coming together, equiv. to *coi-* var. s. of *coīre* to come together (*co-* CO- + *īre* to go) + *-tiōn* -TION] **—co•i′tion•al,** *adj.*

co•i•tus (kō′i təs), *n.* sexual intercourse, esp. between a man and a woman. [1705–15; < L: a coming together, uniting, sexual intercourse, equiv. to *coi-* (see COITION) + *-tus* suffix of v. action] **—co′i•tal,** *adj.* **—co′i•tal•ly,** *adv.*

co′itus in•ter•rup′tus (in′tə rup′təs), *pl.* **coitus in•ter•rup•ti** (in′tə rup′tī). **1.** coitus that is intentionally interrupted by withdrawal before ejaculation of semen into the vagina. **2.** an act or instance of this. [1895–1900; < NL: interrupted coitus]

co•jo•nes (kō hô′nes; *Eng.* kə hō′nās, -nēz), *n. Spanish (sometimes vulgar).* **1.** (*used with a plural v.*) testicles. **2.** courage.

coke[1] (kōk), *n., v.,* **coked, cok•ing.** *Chem.* **—n.** **1.** the solid product resulting from the destructive distillation of coal in an oven or closed chamber or by imperfect combustion, consisting principally of carbon: used chiefly as a fuel in metallurgy to reduce metallic oxides to metals. **—v.t., v.i.** **2.** to convert into or become coke. [1375–1425; late ME *colke, coke,* equiv. to OE *col* COAL + *-(o)ca* -OCK] **—coke′like′, cok′y,** *adj.*

coke[2] (kōk), *Slang.* **—n.** **1.** cocaine. **—v.t.** **2.** to affect with a narcotic drug, esp. with cocaine (usually fol. by *up* or *out*). [1905–10, *Amer.*; short for COCAINE]

Coke (kŏŏk), *n.* **Sir Edward,** 1552–1634, English jurist and writer on law. Also, **Cooke.**

coke•head (kōk′hed′), *n. Slang.* a cocaine addict or habitual user. Also called **coke′ fiend′, coker, snowbird.** [COKE[2] + HEAD]

coke′ ov′en, an oven for the conversion of coal into coke by heating the coal in the absence of air so as to distill the volatile ingredients. [1830–40]

cok•er[1] (kō′kər), *n.* Often, **cokers.** an inhabitant of the mountains of the coal-mining regions of West Virginia and Pennsylvania. [1785–95; COKE[1] + -ER[1]]

cok•er[2] (kō′kər), *n. Slang.* cokehead. [COKE[2] + -ER[1]]

co•ker•nut (kō′kər nut′), *n. Chiefly Brit.* coconut.

col (kol; *Fr.* kôl), *n., pl.* **cols** (kolz; *Fr.* kôl). **1.** *Physical Geog.* a pass or depression in a mountain range or ridge. **2.** *Meteorol.* the region of relatively low pressure between two anticyclones. [1850–55; < F < L *collum* neck]

COL, cost of living.

col-[1], var. of **com-** before *l: collateral.*

col-[2], var. of **colo-** before a vowel: *colectomy.*

Col., **1.** Colombia. **2.** Colonel. **3.** Colorado. **4.** Colossians.

col., **1.** (in prescriptions) strain. [< L *colā*] **2.** collected. **3.** collector. **4.** college. **5.** collegiate. **6.** colonial. **7.** colony. **8.** color. **9.** colored. **10.** column.

co•la[1] (kō′lə), *n.* a carbonated soft drink containing an extract made from kola nuts, together with sweeteners and other flavorings. Also, **kola.** [1920–25; sp. var. of KOLA, extracted from the trademark names of such drinks, as *Coca-Cola, Pepsi-Cola,* etc.]

co•la[2] (kō′lə), *n.* a pl. of **colon.**

COLA (kō′lə), *n.* an escalator clause, esp. in union contracts, that grants automatic wage increases to cover the rising cost of living due to inflation. [*c(ost) o(f) l(iving) a(djustment)*]

col•a•co•bi•o•sis (kol′ə kō bī ō′sis), *n., pl.* **-ses** (-sēz). (among social insects) life in which one species lives as a parasite in the community of another species. [< Gk *kolak-* (s. of *kólax*) parasite + -o- + -BIOSIS] **—col•a•co•bi•ot•ic** (kol′ə kō bī ot′ik), *adj.*

co•la•da (kō lä′də), *n.* **1.** See **piña colada.** **2.** a tall mixed drink of rum, cream of coconut, ice, and fruit or fruit juice, usually mixed in a blender and served with a fruit garnish: *banana colada; strawberry colada.* [see PIÑA COLADA]

co•la•mine (kō′lə mēn′, kō lam′in), *n. Chem.* ethanolamine. [said to be (AL)CO(HO)L + AMINE]

col•an•der (kul′ən dər, kol′-), *n.* a metal or plastic container with a perforated bottom, for draining and straining foods. Also, **cullender.** [1400–50; late ME *colyndore,* perh. (with nasalization) < OPr *colador* < ML *cōlātōrium,* equiv. to L *cōlā(re)* to strain (v. deriv. of *cōlum* strainer) + *-tōrium* -TORY[2]]

co′la nut′. See **kola nut.**

colat., (in prescriptions) strained. [< L *colātus*]

Co•la•ti•na (kô′lä tē′nä), *n.* a city in SE Brazil. 140,729.

co•lat•i•tude (kō lat′i tōōd′, -tyōōd′), *n. Astron., Navig.* the complement of the latitude; the difference between a given latitude and 90°. [1780–90; CO- + LATITUDE]

Col•bath (kōl′bath, -bäth), *n.* **Jeremiah Jones.** See **Wilson, Henry.** Also, **Col′baith.**

Col•bert (kôl beʀ′), *n.* **Jean Bap•tiste** (zhäɴ ba tēst′), 1619–83, French statesman and finance minister under Louis XIV.

col•by (kōl′bē), *n.* (*often cap.*) a mild, cheddar-type cheese that is softer and more open in texture than standard cheddar. Also called **col′by cheese′.** [1940–45; appar. after a proper name]

col•can•non (kəl kan′ən, kôl′kan-), *n.* an Irish dish made of cabbage, kale, or other greens, and potatoes boiled and mashed together. [1765–75; < Ir *cál ceannann,* equiv. to *cál* (< L *caulis* cabbage) + *ceann* head + *-ann,* weak var. of *fionn* white]

Col•ches•ter (kōl′ches′tər, -chə stər), *n.* **1.** a city in NE Essex, in E England. 140,000. **2.** a town in W Vermont. 12,629.

col•chi•cine (kol′chə sēn′, -sin, kol′kə-), *n. Pharm.* a pale yellow, crystalline alkaloid, $C_{22}H_{25}NO_6$, the active principle of colchicum. [1850–55; COLCHIC(UM) + -INE[2]]

col•chi•cum (kol′chi kəm, kol′ki-), *n.* **1.** any Old World plant of the genus *Colchicum,* of the lily family, esp. the autumn crocus, *C. autumnale.* **2.** the dried seeds or corms of this plant. **3.** *Pharm.* a medicine or drug prepared from them, used in medicine chiefly in the treatment of gout. [1590–1600; < NL, L < Gk *kolchikón* meadow saffron, n. use of neut. of *Kolchikós* of COLCHIS, appar. by assoc. with Medea, the plant being considered poisonous]

Col•chis (kol′kis), *n.* an ancient country in Asia, S of the Caucasus and bordering on the Black Sea: the land of the Golden Fleece and of Medea in Greek mythology.

col•co•thar (kol′kə thər), *n. Chem.* the brownish-red oxide of iron produced by heating ferrous sulfate: used chiefly as a pigment in paints and theatrical rouge, and as a polishing agent. Also called **jewelers' rouge.** [1595–1605; < ML < OSp *colcotar,* SpAr *qulquṭār,* perh. < Gk *chálkanthos* copper sulfate solution]

cold (kōld), *adj.,* **-er, -est,** *n., adv.* **—adj.** **1.** having a relatively low temperature; having little or no warmth: *cold water; a cold day.* **2.** feeling an uncomfortable lack of warmth; chilled: *The skaters were cold.* **3.** having a temperature lower than the normal temperature of the human body: *cold hands.* **4.** lacking in passion, emotion, enthusiasm, ardor, etc.; dispassionate: *cold reason.* **5.** not affectionate, cordial, or friendly; unresponsive: *a cold reply; a cold reception.* **6.** lacking sensual desire: *She remained cold to his advances.* **7.** failing to excite feeling or interest: *the cold precision of his prose.* **8.** unexcitable; imperturbable: *cold impassivity.* **9.** depressing; dispiriting: *the cold atmosphere of a hospital waiting room.* **10.** unconscious because of a severe blow, shock, etc.: *I knocked him cold with an uppercut.* **11.** lacking the warmth of life; lifeless: *When the doctor arrived, the body was already cold.* **12.** faint; weak: *The dogs lost the cold scent.* **13.** (in games) distant from the object of search or the correct answer. **14.** *Slang.* (in sports and games) not scoring or winning; ineffective: *Cold shooting and poor rebounding were their undoing.* **15.** *Art.* **a.** having cool colors, esp. muted tones tending toward grayish blue. **b.** being a cool color. **16.** slow to absorb heat, as a soil containing a large amount of clay and hence retentive of moisture. **17.** *Metalworking.* noting or pertaining to any process involving plastic deformation of a metal at a temperature below that at which recrystallization can occur because of the strain: *cold working.* **18.** **go cold,** *Slang.* (in sports and games) to become unproductive or ineffective; be unable to score. **19.** **in cold blood.** See **blood** (def. 18). **20.** **throw cold water on,** to disparage; disapprove of; dampen the enthusiasm of. **—n.** **21.** the relative absence of heat: *Everyone suffered from the intense cold.* **22.** the sensation produced by loss of heat from the body, as by contact with anything having a lower temperature than that of the body: *He felt the cold of the steel door against his cheek.* **23.** cold weather: *He can't take the cold.* **24.** Also called **common cold.** a respiratory disorder characterized by sneezing, sore throat, coughing, etc., caused by an allergic reaction or by a viral, bacterial, or mixed infection. **25.** **catch** or **take cold,** to get or suffer from a cold: *We all caught cold during that dreadful winter.* **26.** **in from the cold,** out of a position or condition of exile, concealment, isolation, or alienation: *Since the new government promised amnesty, fugitive rebels are coming in from the cold.* **27.** **left out in the cold,** neglected; ignored; forgotten: *After the baby came, the young husband felt left out in the cold.* Also, **out in the cold.** **—adv.** **28.** with complete competence, thoroughness, or certainty; absolutely: *He learned his speech cold.* **29.** without preparation or prior notice: *She had to play the lead role cold.* **30.** in an abrupt, unceremonious manner: *He quit the job cold.* **31.** *Metalworking.* at a temperature below that at which recrystallization can occur (sometimes used in combination): *to cold-hammer an iron bar; The wire was drawn cold.* [bef. 950; ME; OE *cald, ceald;* c. Goth *kalds,* ON *kaldr,* G *kalt,* D *koud;* akin to L *gel-* in *gelidus* GELID] **—cold′ish,** *adj.* **—cold′ly,** *adv.* **—cold′ness,** *n.*
—Syn. 1. frigid, gelid, frozen, freezing. COLD, CHILL, CHILLY, COOL refer to various degrees of absence of heat. COLD refers to temperature possibly so low as to cause suffering: *cold water.* CHILL suggests a penetrating cold which causes shivering and numbness: *There was a chill wind blowing.* CHILLY is a weaker word, though it also connotes shivering and discomfort: *a chilly room.* COOL means merely somewhat cold, not warm: *cool and comfortable.* All have figurative uses. **4.** indifferent, uninvolved, cool, unconcerned, imperturbable. **5.** apathetic, unsympathetic, unfeeling, heartless, polite, formal, reserved, unfriendly, inimical, hostile. **7.** uninspiring, dull. **8.** calm, deliberate. **—Ant. 1.** hot. **4.** warm, emotional. **13.** warm.

cold-blood•ed (kōld′blud′id), *adj.* **1.** designating or pertaining to animals, as fishes and reptiles, whose blood temperature ranges from the freezing point upward, in accordance with the temperature of the surrounding medium; poikilothermal. **2.** without emotion or feeling; dispassionate; cruel: *a cold-blooded murder.* **3.** sensitive to cold. [1585–95] **—cold′-blood′ed•ly,** *adv.* **—cold′-blood′ed•ness,** *n.*

cold′ call′, a visit or telephone call to a prospective customer without an appointment or a previous introduction. [1980–85]

cold′ cash′, money immediately available: *They will accept payment in cold cash only.* [1920–25]

cold′ cath′ode, *Electronics.* a cathode, in an electron tube (**cold′-cath′ode tube′**) or lamp, that emits electrons without having to be heated. [1925–30]

cold′ cel′lar, *Chiefly Northeastern U.S.* root cellar. [1960–65, *Amer.*]

cold′ chis′el, a steel chisel used on cold metal. See illus. under **chisel.**

cold-chis•el (kōld′chiz′əl), *v.t.,* **-eled, -el•ing** or (*esp. Brit.*) **-elled, -el•ling.** to work upon (metal) with a cold chisel. [1690–1700]

cold-cock (kōld′kok′), *v.t. Slang.* to knock (someone) unconscious, as with the fist. [1925–30]

CONCISE PRONUNCIATION KEY: act, cāpe, dâre, pärt; set, ēqual; if, īce; ox, ōver, ôrder, oil, bŏŏk, bōōt, out; up, ûrge; child; sing; shoe; thin, *th*at; zh as in *treasure.* ə = *a* as in *alone, e* as in *system, i* as in *easily, o* as in *gallop, u* as in *circus;* ᵊ as in *fire* (fīᵊr), *hour* (ouᵊr). l and n can serve as syllabic consonants, as in *cradle* (krād′l), and *button* (but′n). See the full key inside the front cover.

cold′ col′or, a paint fixed to glass or to a ceramic object without firing.

cold′ com′fort, slight or negligible comfort; scarce consolation. [1565–75]

cold′ cream′, a creamy cosmetic, typically of oily consistency, used to cleanse or soothe the skin, esp. of the face and neck, or to remove makeup. [1700–10]

cold′ cuts′, slices of unheated salami, bologna, ham, liverwurst, turkey, or other meats and sometimes cheeses. [1940–45, *Amer.*]

cold′ deck′, *Cards Slang.* a pack with the cards in prearranged order, secretly exchanged for the one in use; stacked deck. [1855–60, *Amer.*]

cold-draw (kōld′drô′), *v.t.*, **-drew, -drawn, -draw•ing.** *Metalworking.* to draw (wire, tubing, etc.) without preheating the metal. [1710–20]

cold′ duck′, **1.** a pink sparkling wine originally from Germany. **2.** a drink made typically by mixing dry white wine, champagne, lemon juice, and sugar. [1965–70; trans. of G *Kalte Ente* with sense of def. 2; literal application unclear]

Col•den (kōl′dən), *n.* **Cadwallader,** 1688–1776, Scottish physician, botanist, and public official in America, born in Ireland.

cold′ feet′, *Informal.* a loss or lack of courage or confidence; an onset of uncertainty or fear: *She got cold feet when asked to sing a solo.* [1890–95]

cold′ fish′, *Informal.* a person who is very reserved or aloof in manner or who lacks normal cordiality, sympathy, or other feeling. [1940–45]

cold′ frame′, a bottomless, boxlike structure, usually covered with glass or transparent plastic, and the bed of earth that it covers, used to protect plants. [1850–55]

cold′ front′, the zone separating two air masses, of which the cooler, denser mass is advancing and replacing the warmer. [1920–25]

cold′ fu′sion, a hypothetical form of nuclear fusion postulated to occur at relatively low temperatures and pressures, as at room temperature and at one atmosphere. [1985–90]

Cold′ Har′bor, a locality in Virginia, NE of Richmond: Civil War battle in 1864.

cold-heart•ed (kōld′här′tid), *adj.* lacking sympathy or feeling; indifferent; unkind. [1600–10] **—cold′-heart′ed•ly,** *adv.* **—cold′-heart′ed•ness,** *n.*

cold′ light′, light emitted by a source that is not incandescent, as from a firefly. [1890–95]

cold′ one′, *Informal.* a glass, can, or bottle of cold beer.

cold′ pack′, **1.** a cold towel, ice bag, etc., applied to the body to reduce swelling, relieve pain, etc. **2.** Also called **cold′-pack meth′od, raw-pack method.** a method of canning uncooked food by placing it in hot jars or cans and sterilizing in a bath of boiling water or steam. Cf. **hot pack.** [1905–10]

cold-pack (kōld′pak′), *v.t.* **1.** to place a cold pack on: *to cold-pack a feverish patient.* **2.** to can (food) by the cold-pack method. [1920–25]

cold′ patch′, a patch that may be applied by cement to the tube of an automobile tire or the like without vulcanization.

cold-patch (kōld′pach′), *v.t.* to apply a cold patch to.

cold′ pole′, the location in the northern or southern hemisphere having the coldest annual mean temperature in that hemisphere. Also called **pole of cold.** [1905–10]

cold-roll (kōld′rōl′), *v.t. Metalworking.* to roll (metal) at a temperature below that at which recrystallization occurs.

cold′ rub′ber, a synthetic rubber made at a relatively low temperature (about 40°F or 4°C) and having greater strength and durability than that made at the usual temperature (about 120°F or 49°C): used chiefly for retreading tires. [1945–50]

cold′ shoul′der, a show of deliberate indifference or disregard. [1810–20]

cold-shoul•der (kōld′shōl′dər), *v.t.* to snub; show indifference to. [1810–20]

cold•slaw (kōld′slô′, kōl′-), *n.* coleslaw. [by folk etym.]

cold′ snap′, a sudden onset of a relatively brief period of cold weather. Also called **cold′ spell′.** [1770–80]

cold′ sore′, a vesicular eruption on the face, usually on or near the mouth, often accompanying a cold or a febrile condition; herpes simplex. Also called **fever blister.** [1905–10]

cold′ spot′, *Physiol.* a sensory area in the skin that responds to a decrease in temperature. [1890–95]

cold′ steel′, a weapon made of steel, as a sword.

cold′ stor′age, **1.** the storage of food, furs, etc., in an artificially cooled place. **2.** a condition of suspension of action or activity; abeyance. [1890–95]

cold′ store′, a refrigerated compartment or building for keeping foods, furs, etc., in cold storage. [1890–95; by back formation from COLD STORAGE]

cold-store (kōld′stôr′, -stōr′, -stôr′, -stōr′), *v.t.*, **-stored, -stor•ing.** to store in cold storage.

Cold•stream (kōld′strēm′), *n.* a town in SE Berwick, in SE Scotland, on the Tweed River. 1649.

Cold′stream Guards′, a guard regiment of the English royal household: formed in Coldstream, Scotland, 1659–60, and instrumental in restoring the English monarchy under Charles II. Also called **Cold•stream•ers** (kōld′strē′mərz).

CONCISE ETYMOLOGY KEY: <, descended or borrowed from; >, whence; b., blend of, blended; c., cognate with; cf., compare; deriv., derivative; equiv., equivalent; imit., imitative; obl., oblique; r., replacing; s., stem; sp., spelling, spelled; resp., respelling, respelled; trans., translation; ?, origin unknown; *, unattested; ‡, probably earlier than. See the full key inside the front cover.

cold′ sweat′, a chill accompanied by perspiration, caused by fear, nervousness, or the like. [1700–10]

cold′ tone′, *Photog.* a bluish or greenish tinge in a black-and-white print. Cf. **warm tone.**

cold′ tur′key, *Informal.* **1.** abrupt and complete withdrawal from the use of an addictive substance, as a narcotic drug, alcohol, or tobacco. **2. go cold turkey, a.** to stop using an addictive substance abruptly and completely. **b.** to undergo sudden and complete withdrawal from a habitual activity or behavior pattern. **c.** to begin or do something without planning, preparation, or practice. [1915–20, *Amer.*; prob. from the phrase *to talk cold turkey* to speak bluntly about something unpleasant, var. of *to talk turkey;* see TURKEY]

cold-tur•key (kōld′tûr′kē), *Slang.* —*v.t.* **1.** to withdraw from (an addictive substance or a habit) abruptly and completely. —*v.i.* **2.** to withdraw from an addictive substance or a habit abruptly and completely. —*adj.* **3.** abrupt and complete: *cold-turkey withdrawal from drugs.*

cold′ type′, *Print.* type set by a method other than the casting of molten metal, as text composed on a typewriter and photographed. Cf. **hot metal.** [1945–50]

cold′ war′, **1.** intense economic, political, military, and ideological rivalry between nations, short of military conflict; sustained hostile political policies and an atmosphere of strain between opposed countries. **2.** a continuing state of resentful antagonism between two parties short of open hostility or violence. **3.** (*caps.*) rivalry after World War II between the Soviet Union and its satellites and the democratic countries of the Western world, under the leadership of the United States.

cold′ war′rior, a person who advocates or participates in a cold war.

cold′-wa•ter flat′ (kōld′wô′tər, -wot′ər), *Chiefly Northeastern U.S.* (formerly) an apartment provided with only cold running water, often in a building with no central heating. [1940–45]

cold′ wave′, **1.** *Meteorol.* a rapid and considerable drop in temperature, usually affecting a large area. **2.** a permanent wave in the hair set by special chemical solutions without the aid of any heating device. [1875–80]

cold-weld (kōld′weld′), *v.t.* **1.** to weld (metal objects) by extreme high pressure with no application of heat. **2.** to weld (metal objects) by contact in a high vacuum, as in space.

cold-work (kōld′wûrk′), *v.t.* to work (metal) at a temperature below that at which recrystallization occurs. [1930–35]

cole (kōl), *n.* any of various plants of the genus *Brassica*, of the mustard family, esp. kale and rape. Also called **colewort.** [bef. 1000; ME *col(e)*, OE *cāl, cāw(e)l* < L *caulis* stalk, cabbage; c. Gk *kaulós* stalk. See KOHLRABI]

Cole (kōl), *n.* **1. Thomas,** 1801–48, U.S. painter, born in England: a founder of the Hudson River School of landscape painting. **2. Timothy,** 1852–1931, U.S. wood engraver, born in England. **3.** a male given name.

co•lec•ti•vo (kō′lek tē′vō; *Sp.* kô′lek tē′vô), *n., pl.* **-vos** (-vōz; *Sp.* -vôs). (in Latin America) a small public bus. [< AmerSp: lit., collective, i.e., a vehicle used collectively; Sp < L *collēctīvus* COLLECTIVE]

co•lec•to•my (kə lek′tə mē), *n., pl.* **-mies.** *Surg.* the removal of all or part of the colon or large intestine. [COL-[2] + -ECTOMY]

Cole•man (kōl′mən), *n.* **1. Or•nette** (ôr net′), born 1930, U.S. jazz saxophonist and composer. **2.** a male given name.

cole•man•ite (kōl′mə nīt′), *n.* a mineral, hydrous calcium borate, $Ca_2B_6O_{11}·5H_2O$, occurring in colorless or milky-white crystals. [named in 1884 after W. T. *Coleman* of San Francisco, in whose mine it was found; see -ITE[1]]

colent., (in prescriptions) let them be strained. Also, **colen.** [< L *colentur*]

Co•le•op•ter•a (kō′lē op′tər ə, kol′ē-), *n.* the order comprising the beetles. [1755–65; < NL < Gk *koleóptera*, neut. pl. of *koleópteros* sheath-winged, equiv. to *koleo-* (comb. form repr. *koleón* sheath, scabbard; see -O-) + *-pteros* -PTEROUS; term used by Aristotle in describing beetles]

co•le•op•ter•an (kō′lē op′tər ən, kol′ē-), *adj.* **1.** belonging or pertaining to the order Coleoptera. —*n.* **2.** a beetle. [1840–50; COLEOPTER(A) + -AN]

co•le•op•ter•on (kō′lē op′tər ən, kol′ē-), *n., pl.* **-ter•a** (-tər ə). a coleopterous insect; beetle. See illus. under **beetle.** [1755–65; < NL < Gk: sing. of COLEOPTERA]

co•le•op•ter•ous (kō′lē op′tər əs, kol′ē-), *adj.* belonging or pertaining to the order Coleoptera, comprising the beetles. [1785–95; see COLEOPTERA, -OUS]

co•le•op•tile (kō′lē op′til, kol′ē-), *n. Bot.* (in grasses) the first leaf above the ground, forming a sheath around the stem tip. [1865–70; < NL *coleoptilum* < Gk *koleó(n)* sheath, scabbard + *ptílon* soft feathers, down]

co•le•o•rhi•za (kō′lē ə rī′zə, kol′ē-), *n., pl.* **-zae** (-zē). *Bot.* the sheath that envelops the radicle in certain plants and that is penetrated by the root in germination. [1865–70; < NL < Gk *koleó(n)* sheath, scabbard + *rhiza* ROOT[1]]

Cole•ridge (kōl′rij), *n.* **Samuel Taylor,** 1772–1834, English poet, critic, and philosopher. **—Cole•ridg′i•an,** *adj.*

Cole•ridge-Tay•lor (kōl′rij tā′lər), *n.* **Samuel,** 1875–1912, English composer.

cole•seed (kōl′sēd′), *n.* **1.** the seed of the rape. **2.** rape[2]. [bef. 1000; ME; OE *cawel sǣd.* See COLE, SEED]

cole•slaw (kōl′slô′), *n.* a salad of finely sliced or chopped raw cabbage, usually moistened with a mayonnaise dressing. [1785–95; < D *koolsla*, equiv. to *kool* cabbage, COLE + *sla*, contr. of *salade* SALAD]

Col•et (kol′it), *n.* **John,** 1467?–1519, English educator and clergyman.

colet., (in prescriptions) let it be strained. [< L *colētur*]

Co•lette (kō let′, kə-, ko-; *Fr.* kô let′), *n.* **1.** (*Sidonie Gabrielle Claudine Colette*) 1873–1954, French author. **2.** a female given name.

co•le•us (kō′lē əs), *n., pl.* **-us•es.** any of several tropical Asian or African plants belonging to the genus *Coleus*, of the mint family, certain species of which are cultivated for their showy, colored foliage and blue flowers. [1865–70; < NL < Gk *koleós*, var. of *koleón* sheath, scabbard; akin to CONCEAL, HULL[1]]

cole•wort (kōl′wûrt′, -wôrt′), *n.* cole. [1350–1400; ME; see COLE, WORT[2]]

Col•fax (kōl′faks), *n.* **Schuyler,** 1823–85, U.S. political leader: vice president of the U.S. 1869–73.

col•ic (kol′ik), *Pathol., Vet. Pathol.* —*n.* **1.** paroxysmal pain in the abdomen or bowels. —*adj.* **2.** pertaining to or affecting the colon or the bowels. [1400–50; late ME *colike* (< MF *colique*) < L *colica* (*passiō*) (suffering) of the colon < Gk *kolikós*, equiv. to *kól(on)* COLON[2] + *-ikos* -IC] **—col′ick•y,** *adj.*

col•i•cin (kol′ə sin), *n. Pharm.* any bacteriocin produced by certain strains of *Escherichia coli* and having a lethal effect on strains other than the producing strain. [1945–50; < F *colicine*, equiv. to *coli-* (see COLIFORM) + *-cine*, prob. extracted from names of antibiotics ending in *-mycine* -MYCIN]

col•i•cin•o•gen (kol′ə sin′ə jən, -jen′), *n.* any bacterium that produces a colicin. [COLICIN + -O- + -GEN] **—col•i•ci•no•gen•ic** (kol′ə sə nə jen′ik), *adj.*

col•ic•root (kol′ik ro͞ot′, -ro͝ot′), *n.* **1.** either of two North American plants, *Aletris farinosa* or *A. aurea*, of the lily family, having small yellow or white flowers in a spikelike cluster and a root reputed to relieve colic. **2.** any of certain other plants having roots reputed to cure colic. **3.** the blazing star, *Liatris squarrosa.* [1830–40, *Amer.*; COLIC + ROOT[1]]

col•i•form (kol′ə fôrm′, kō′lə-), *adj.* **1.** of, pertaining to, or resembling a coliform bacillus. —*n.* **2.** See **coliform bacillus.** [1850–55; < NL *coli*, gen. of L *colum*, *colon* COLON[2] (the specific epithet of various species of bacteria inhabiting the colon, as *Escherichia coli;* construed as *col-* + -I-) + -FORM]

col′iform bacil′lus, *Bacteriol.* any of several bacilli, esp. *Escherichia coli* and members of the genus *Aerobacter*, found as commensals in the large intestine of humans and certain other animals, the presence of which in water indicates fecal pollution. Also called **col′iform bacte′rium, colon bacillus.**

Co•li•gny (kô lē nyē′), *n.* **Gas•pard de** (ga spar′ də), 1519–72, French admiral and Huguenot leader. Also, **Co•li•gni′.**

Co•li•ma (kô lē′mä), *n.* **1.** a state in SW Mexico, on the Pacific Coast. 317,000; 2010 sq. mi. (5205 sq. km). **2.** a city in and the capital of this state, in the E part. 72,074. **3.** a volcano NW of this city, in Jalisco state. 12,631 ft. (3850 m).

col•in (kol′in), *n.* any of several American quails, esp. the bobwhite. [1620–30; < MexSp *colín*, perh. < Nahuatl *zōlin*, through misreading of the older sp. *çolin*]

Col•in (kol′in, kō′lin; *Fr.* kô lan′; *Ger.* kō′lin, -lēn), *n.* a male given name.

co•lin•e•ar (kə lin′ē ər), *adj.* collinear. **—co•lin′e•ar′i•ty,** *n.*

col•i•phage (kol′ə fāj′), *n.* any bacteriophage that specifically infects the *Escherichia coli* bacterium. [1940–45; < NL *coli-* (see COLIFORM) + -PHAGE]

col•i•se•um (kol′i sē′əm), *n.* **1.** Also, **colosseum.** an amphitheater, stadium, large theater, or other special building for public meetings, sporting events, exhibitions, etc. **2.** (*cap.*) Colosseum. [1700–10; < ML *Colisseum;* see COLOSSEUM]

col′ise′um i′vy. See **kenilworth ivy.**

co•lis•tin (kə lis′tin), *n. Pharm.* a toxic antibiotic polypeptide, $C_{45}H_{85}O_{10}N_{13}$, produced by the bacterium *Bacillus colistinus*, used in sulfate form against a broad spectrum of microorganisms and in the treatment of gastroenteritis. [1950–55; < NL *colistinus* epithet for a variety of *Bacillus polymyxa*, equiv. to *coli-* (see COLIFORM) + *-stinus*, appar. an arbitrarily chosen suffix; cf. -IN[2]]

co•li•tis (kə lī′tis, kō-), *n. Pathol.* inflammation of the colon. [COL-[2] + -ITIS] **—co•lit•ic** (kə lit′ik, kō-), *adj.*

coll., **1.** collateral. **2.** collect. **3.** collection. **4.** collective. **5.** collector. **6.** college. **7.** collegiate. **8.** colloquial. **9.** (in prescriptions) an eyewash. [L *collyrium*]

collab., **1.** collaboration. **2.** collaborator.

col•lab•o•rate (kə lab′ə rāt′), *v.i.*, **-rat•ed, -rat•ing.** **1.** to work, one with another; cooperate, as on a literary work: *They collaborated on a novel.* **2.** to cooperate, usually willingly, with an enemy nation, esp. with an enemy occupying one's country: *He collaborated with the Nazis during World War II.* [1870–75; < LL *collabōrātus* (ptp. of *collabōrāre*), equiv. to *col-* COL-[1] + *labor* work + *-ātus* -ATE[1]] **—col•lab′o•ra′tor,** *n.*

col•lab•o•ra•tion (kə lab′ə rā′shən), *n.* **1.** the act or process of collaborating. **2.** a product resulting from collaboration: *This dictionary is a collaboration of many minds.* [1855–60; < F < LL *collabōrāt(us)* (see COLLABORATE) + F *-ion* -ION]

col•lab•o•ra•tion•ist (kə lab′ə rā′shə nist), *n.* a person who collaborates with an enemy; collaborator. [1920–25; COLLABORATION + -IST] **—col•lab′o•ra′tion•ism,** *n.*

col•lab•o•ra•tive (kə lab′ə rā′tiv, -ər ə tiv), *adj.* characterized or accomplished by collaboration: *collaborative methods; a collaborative report.* [COLLABORATE + -IVE] **—col•lab′o•ra′tive•ly,** *adv.*

col•lage (kə läzh′, kō-), *n., v.*, **-laged, -lag•ing.** —*n.*

1. a technique of composing a work of art by pasting on a single surface various materials not normally associated with one another, as newspaper clippings, parts of photographs, theater tickets, and fragments of an envelope. **2.** a work of art produced by this technique. Cf. **assemblage** (def. 3). **3.** an assemblage or occurrence of diverse elements or fragments in unlikely or unexpected juxtaposition: *The experimental play is a collage of sudden scene shifts, long monologues, musical interludes, and slapstick.* **4.** a film that presents a series of seemingly unrelated scenes or images or shifts from one scene or image to another suddenly and without transition. —*v.t.* **5.** to make a collage of: *The artist has collaged old photos, cartoon figures, and telephone numbers into a unique work of art.* [1915–20; < F, equiv. to *colle* paste, glue (< Gk *kólla*) + *-age* -AGE] **—col•lag′ist,** *n.*

col•la•gen (kol′ə jən), *n. Biochem.* any of a class of extracellular proteins abundant in higher animals, esp. in the skin, bone, cartilage, tendon, and teeth, forming strong insoluble fibers and serving as connective tissue between cells, yielding gelatin when denatured by boiling. [1860–65; < Gk *kólla* glue + -GEN] **—col•lag•e•nous** (kə laj′ə nəs), *adj.*

col′lagen disease′, *Pathol.* any of a group of diseases, as systemic lupus erythematosus, polyarteritis, scleroderma, and rheumatoid arthritis, involving inflammation or degeneration of connective tissue and accompanied by deposition of fibrinous material. Also called **connective tissue disease.** [1940–45]

col•lap•sar (kə lap′sär), *n. Astron.* (formerly) a gravitationally collapsed star. Cf. **black hole.** [1970–75; COLLAPSE + *-ar*, extracted from PULSAR, QUASAR, etc.]

col•lapse (kə laps′), *v.*, **-lapsed, -laps•ing,** *n.* —*v.i.* **1.** to fall or cave in; crumble suddenly: *The roof collapsed and buried the crowd.* **2.** to be made so that sections or parts can be folded up, as for convenient storage: *This bridge table collapses.* **3.** to break down; come to nothing; fail: *Despite all their efforts the peace talks collapsed.* **4.** to fall unconscious or as if unconscious or physically depleted, as from a stroke, heart attack, disease, or exhaustion. **5.** *Pathol.* **a.** to sink into extreme weakness. **b.** (of lungs) to come into an airless state. —*v.t.* **6.** to cause to collapse: *He collapsed the table easily.* —*n.* **7.** a falling in or together: *Three miners were trapped by the collapse of the tunnel roof.* **8.** a sudden, complete failure; breakdown: *The bribery scandal brought about the complete collapse of his industrial empire.* [1725–35; < L *collāpsus* (ptp. of *collābī* to fall, fall in ruins), equiv. to *col-* COL-[1] + *lāp-*, var. s. of *lābī* to fall + *-sus*, var. of *-tus* ptp. ending]

col•laps•i•ble (kə lap′sə bəl), *adj.* **1.** capable of collapsing or of being collapsed, as for carrying or storing. —*n.* **2.** something that is collapsible: *The auditorium chairs are collapsibles that store easily.* Also, **col•laps′a•ble.** [1835–45; COLLAPSE + -IBLE] **—col•laps′i•bil′i•ty, col•laps′a•bil′i•ty,** *n.*

col•lar (kol′ər), *n.* **1.** the part of a shirt, coat, dress, blouse, etc., that encompasses the neckline of the garment and is sewn permanently to it, often so as to fold or roll over. **2.** a similar but separate, detachable article of clothing worn around the neck or at the neckline of a garment. Cf. **clerical collar.** **3.** anything worn or placed around the neck. **4.** a leather or metal band or a chain, fastened around the neck of an animal, used esp. as a means of restraint or identification. **5.** the part of the harness that fits across the withers and over the shoulders of a draft animal, designed to distribute the pressure of the load drawn. See diag. under **harness.** **6.** an ornamental necklace worn as insignia of an order of knighthood. **7.** a narrow strip of leather or other material stitched around the top of a shoe as reinforcement or trimming. **8.** *Zool.* any of various collarlike markings or structures around the neck; torque. **9.** *Metall.* **a.** a raised area of metal for reinforcing a weld. **b.** a raised rim at the end of a roll in a rolling mill to check lateral expansion of the metal being rolled. **10.** *Mach.* a short ring formed on or fastened over a rod or shaft as a locating or holding part. **11.** (in iron or steel construction) a rigid frame for maintaining the form of an opening. **12.** the upper rim of a borehole, shot hole, or mine shaft. **13.** Also called **bracelet.** a narrow horizontal molding encircling the top or bottom of a furniture leg. **14.** *Glassmaking.* merese. **15.** *Informal.* **a.** an arrest; capture. **b.** a person placed under arrest. **16. hot under the collar,** *Informal.* angry; excited; upset. —*v.t.* **17.** to put a collar on; furnish with a collar: *They finally succeeded in collaring the unwilling dog.* **18.** to seize by the collar or neck: *We collared the little fellow and brought him, struggling all the while, into the house.* **19.** to detain (someone anxious to leave) in conversation: *The reporters collared the witness for an hour.* **20.** to lay hold of, seize, or take. **21.** *Informal.* to place under arrest. **22.** to roll up and bind (meat, fish, etc.) for cooking. —*v.i.* **23.** *Metalworking.* (of a piece being rolled) to wrap itself around a roller. [1250–1300; ME *coler* < AF; OF *colier* < L *collāre* neckband, collar, equiv. to *coll(um)* neck + *-āre*, neut. (as n.) of *-āris* -AR[1]; sp. later conformed to L (cf. -AR[2])] **—col′lar•less,** *adj.*

col•lar•bone (kol′ər bōn′), *n.* the clavicle. [1605–15; COLLAR + BONE]

col′lar but′ton, a button or stud for fastening a detachable collar to the neckband of a shirt or for fastening together the ends of a collar or neckband. [1885–90]

col′lar cell′, choanocyte. [1885–90]

coll′ ar•co (kō lär′kō; *It.* kôl är′kō), *Music.* (of performance with a stringed instrument) with the bow. [< It]

col•lard (kol′ərd), *n.* **1.** a variety of kale, *Brassica oleracea acephala*, grown in the southern U.S., having a rosette of green leaves. **2. collards.** Also called **col′lard greens′.** the leaves of this plant, eaten as a vegetable. [1745–55; var. of COLEWORT, with assimilation of *-wort* to -ARD]

col′lared liz′ard, any of several species of long-tailed iguanid lizards of the genus *Crotaphytus*, of central and western U.S. and northern Mexico, usually having a collar of two black bands.

col′lared pec′cary. See under **peccary.** Also called **javelina.**

col•lar•et (kol′ə ret′), *n.* a small ornamental collar of fur, lace, or other material, worn by women. Also, **col′lar•ette′.** [1680–90; COLLAR + -ET, modeled on F *collerette*]

col′lar point′, *Heraldry.* See **honor point.**

col′lar rot′, *Plant Pathol.* a disease of plants, characterized by cankers that girdle the stem, caused by any of several fungi, as *Alternaria solani.* [1950–55]

collat., collateral.

col•late (kə lāt′, kō-, ko-, kō′lāt, kol′āt), *v.t.*, **-lat•ed, -lat•ing.** **1.** to gather or arrange in their proper sequence (the pages of a report, the sheets of a book, the pages of several sets of copies, etc.). **2.** *Bookbinding.* to verify the arrangement of (the gathered sheets of a book), usually by inspecting the signature at the foot of the first page of each sheet or the mark printed on the back of each sheet or on the spine of each signature. **3.** to compare (texts, statements, etc.) in order to note points of agreement or disagreement. **4.** *Bibliog.* to verify the number and order of the sheets of (a volume) as a means of determining its completeness. **5.** *Computers.* to merge (sequenced data from two or more data sets or files) to produce a new sequenced data set or file. **6.** *Eccles.* to present by collation, as to a benefice. [1550–60; < L *collātus* (ptp. of *conferre* to bring together), equiv. to *col-* COL-[1] + *lā-* (suppletive s. of *ferre*) + *-tus* ptp. ending] **—col•lat′a•ble,** *adj.* **—col•la′tor,** *n.*

col•lat•er•al (kə lat′ər əl), *n.* **1.** security pledged for the payment of a loan: *He gave the bank some stocks and bonds as collateral for the money he borrowed.* **2.** *Anat.* **a.** a subordinate or accessory part. **b.** a side branch, as of a blood vessel or nerve. **c.** See **collateral circulation.** **3.** a relative descended from the same stock, but in a different line. —*adj.* **4.** accompanying; auxiliary: *He received a scholarship and collateral aid.* **5.** additional; confirming: *collateral evidence; collateral security.* **6.** secured by collateral: *a collateral loan.* **7.** aside from the main subject, course, etc.; secondary: *These accomplishments are merely collateral to his primary goal.* **8.** descended from the same stock, but in a different line; not lineal: *A cousin is a collateral relative.* **9.** pertaining to those so descended. **10.** situated at the side: *a collateral wing of a house.* **11.** situated or running side by side; parallel: *collateral ridges of mountains.* **12.** *Bot.* standing side by side. [1350–1400; ME (< AF) < ML *collaterālis*, equiv. to *col-* COL-[1] + *laterālis* LATERAL] **—col•lat•er•al•i•ty** (kō lat′ə ral′i tē), **col•lat′er•al•ness,** *n.* **—col•lat′er•al•ly,** *adv.*

collat′eral circula′tion, circulation of blood through a network of minor vessels that become enlarged and joined with adjacent vessels when a major vein or artery is impaired, as by obstruction. [1875–80]

collat′eral dam′age, **1.** the killing of civilians in a military attack. **2.** any damage incidental to an activity. [1985–90]

col•lat•er•al•ize (kə lat′ər ə līz′), *v.t.*, **-ized, -iz•ing.** **1.** to secure (a loan) with collateral. **2.** to pledge (property, securities, etc.) as collateral. Also, *esp. Brit.*, **col•lat′er•al•ise′.** [1940–45; COLLATERAL + -IZE] **—col•lat′er•al•i•za′tion,** *n.*

col•la•tion (kə lā′shən, kō-, ko-), *n.* **1.** the act of collating. **2.** *Bibliog.* the verification of the number and order of the leaves and signatures of a volume. **3.** a light meal that may be permitted on days of general fast. **4.** any light meal. **5.** (in a monastery) the practice of reading and conversing on the lives of the saints or the Scriptures at the close of the day. **6.** the presentation of a member of the clergy to a benefice, esp. by a bishop who is the patron or has acquired the patron's rights. [1175–1225; ME *collacion* (< AF) < ML *collāciōn-*, *collātiōn-* (s. of *collātiō*), equiv. to L *collāt(us)* (see COLLATE) + *-iōn-* -ION]

col•la•tive (kə lā′tiv, kō-, ko-, kō′lā-, kol′ā-), *adj.* **1.** marked by collation. **2.** *Eccles.* presented by collation: *collative benefices.* [1610–20; < L *collātīvus.* See COLLATE, -IVE]

col•league (kol′ēg), *n.* an associate. [1515–25; < MF *collegue* < L *collēga*, equiv. to *col-* COL-[1] + *-lēga*, deriv. of *legere* to choose, gather] **—col′league•ship′,** *n.*

col•lect[1] (kə lekt′), *v.t.* **1.** to gather together; assemble: *The professor collected the students' exams.* **2.** to accumulate; make a collection of: *to collect stamps.* **3.** to receive or compel payment of: *to collect a bill.* **4.** to regain control of (oneself or one's thoughts, faculties, composure, or the like): *At the news of her promotion, she took a few minutes to collect herself.* **5.** to call for and take with one: *He drove off to collect his guests. They collected their mail.* **6.** *Manège.* to bring (a horse) into a collected attitude. **7.** *Archaic.* to infer. —*v.i.* **8.** to gather together; assemble: *The students collected in the assembly hall.* **9.** to accumulate: *Rain water collected in the barrel.* **10.** to receive payment (often fol. by *on*): *He collected on the damage to his house.* **11.** to gather or bring together books, stamps, coins, etc., usually as a hobby: *He's been collecting for years.* **12.** *Manège.* (of a horse) to come into a collected attitude. —*adj., adv.* **13.** requiring payment by the recipient: *a collect telephone call; a telegram sent collect.* [1375–1425; late ME < L *collēctus* (ptp. of *colligere* to collect), equiv. to *col-* COL-[1] + *leg-* (s. of *legere* to gather) + *-tus* ptp. suffix]
—**Syn. 1.** See **gather.** **1, 2.** amass, aggregate.

col•lect[2] (kol′ekt), *n.* any of certain brief prayers used in Western churches esp. before the epistle in the communion service. [1150–1200; ME *collecte* < ML, short for *ōrātiō ad collēctam* prayer at collection (see COLLECT[1])]

col•lec•ta•ne•a (kol′ek tā′nē ə), *n.pl.* collected passages, esp. as arranged in a miscellany or anthology. [1785–95; < L, neut. pl. of *collēctāneus* gathered together, equiv. to *collēct(us)* (ptp. of *colligere*; see COLLECT[1]) + *-āneus* adj. suffix]

collect′ call′, a long-distance telephone call that is to be paid for by the person or station receiving it. [1965–70]

col•lect•ed (kə lek′tid), *adj.* **1.** having control of one's faculties; self-possessed: *Despite all the turmoil around him, Bob remained calm and collected.* **2.** brought or placed together; forming an aggregation from various sources: *the money collected to build an orphanage; the collected essays of Thoreau.* **3.** *Manège.* **a.** (of a moving horse) noting a compact pose in which the legs are well under the body, the head is arched at the poll, the jaw is relaxed, etc. Cf. **extended** (def. 8a). **b.** (of a gait of such a horse) characterized by short, elevated strides. Cf. **extended** (def. 8b). [1600–10; COLLECT[1] + -ED[2]] **—col•lect′ed•ly,** *adv.* **—col•lect′ed•ness,** *n.*
—**Syn. 1.** See **calm.**

collect′ed edi′tion, a comprehensive edition of the writings of a particular author.

col•lect•i•ble (kə lek′tə bəl), *adj.* **1.** capable of being collected. —*n.* **2.** an object suitable for a collection, originally a work of fine art or an antique, now including also any of a wide variety of items collected as a hobby, for display, or as an investment whose value may appreciate. Also, **col•lect′a•ble.** [1640–50; COLLECT[1] + -IBLE]

collect′ing tu′bule, *Anat.* the part of a nephron that collects the urine from the distal convoluted tubule and discharges it into the pelvis of the kidney.

col•lec•tion (kə lek′shən), *n.* **1.** the act of collecting. **2.** something that is collected; a group of objects or an amount of material accumulated in one location, esp. for some purpose or as a result of some process: *a stamp collection; a collection of unclaimed hats in the checkroom; a collection of books on Churchill.* **3.** the works of art constituting the holdings of an art museum: *a history of the museum and of the collection.* **4.** the gathered or exhibited works of a single painter, sculptor, etc.: *an excellent Picasso collection.* **5. collections,** the various holdings of an art museum organized by category, as painting, sculpture, works on paper, photography, or film: *the director of the collections.* **6.** the clothes or other items produced by a designer, esp. for a seasonal line: *the spring collection.* **7.** a sum of money collected, esp. for charity or church use. **8.** *Manège.* act of bringing or coming into a collected attitude. [1350–1400; ME *colleccioun* (< AF) < L *collēctiōn-* (s. of *collēctiō*), equiv. to *collēct(us)* (ptp. of *colligere*; see COLLECT[1]) + *-iōn-* -ION] **—col•lec′tion•al,** *adj.*
—**Syn. 2.** accumulation, aggregation, mass, heap, pile, hoard, store. **7.** contribution(s), alms.

collec′tion a′gency, a firm that collects unpaid bills for other firms and is usually compensated by receiving a percentage of the amount collected.

collec′tion box′, **1.** a box or other container used to collect offerings of money, esp. in a church. **2.** mailbox (def. 1).

collec′tion plate′, plate (def. 7). [1875–80]

col•lec•tive (kə lek′tiv), *adj.* **1.** formed by collection. **2.** forming a whole; combined: *the collective assets of a corporation and its subsidiaries.* **3.** of or characteristic of a group of individuals taken together: *the collective wishes of the membership.* **4.** organized according to the principles of collectivism: *a collective farm.* —*n.* **5.** See **collective noun.** **6.** a collective body; aggregate. **7.** a business, farm, etc., jointly owned and operated by the members of a group. **8.** a unit of organization or the organization in a collectivist system. [1400–50; late ME *collectif* (< MF) < L *collēctīvus*, equiv. to *collēct(us)* (ptp. of *colligere*; see COLLECT[1]) + *-īvus* -IVE] **—col•lec′tive•ly,** *adv.*

collec′tive agree′ment, **1.** the contract, written or oral, made between an employer or employers and a union on behalf of all the employees represented by the union. **2.** the schedule of wages, rules, and working conditions agreed upon. [1935–40]

collec′tive bar′gaining, the process by which wages, hours, rules, and working conditions are negotiated and agreed upon by a union with an employer for all the employees collectively whom it represents. [1890–95]

collec′tive behav′ior, *Sociol.* the spontaneous, unstructured, and temporary behavior of a group of people in response to the same event, situation, etc.

collec′tive farm′, (esp. in the Soviet Union) a farm, or a number of farms organized as a unit, worked by a community under the supervision of the state. [1915–20]

collec′tive mark′, a trademark or service mark used by the members of a cooperative, a union, or other collective association to identify themselves as members. [1965–70]

collec′tive noun′, *Gram.* a noun, as *herd, jury,* or *clergy,* that appears singular in formal shape but denotes a group of persons or objects. [1510–20]
—**Usage.** Whether a COLLECTIVE NOUN, which is singular in form, is used with a singular or plural verb depends on whether the word is referring to the group as a unit or to its members as individuals. In American English, a COLLECTIVE NOUN naming an organization regarded as a unit is usually treated as singular: *The corporation is holding its annual meeting. The team is having a winning season. The government has taken action.* In British English, such nouns are commonly treated as plurals: *The corporation are holding their annual meeting. The team are playing well. The government are in agreement.* When a COLLECTIVE NOUN naming a group of persons is treated as singular, it is referred to by the relative pronoun *that* or *which*: *His crew is one that* (or *which*) *works hard.* When such a noun is treated as plural, the pronoun is *who*: *His crew are specialists who volunteered for the project.* In formal

speech and writing, COLLECTIVE NOUNS are usually not treated as both singular and plural in the same sentence: *The enemy is fortifying its* (not *their*) *position. The enemy are bringing up their heavy artillery.*

When the COLLECTIVE NOUNS *couple* and *pair* refer to people, they are usually treated as plurals: *The newly married couple have found a house near good transportation. The pair are busy furnishing their new home.* The COLLECTIVE NOUN *number,* when preceded by *a,* is treated as a plural: *A number of solutions were suggested.* When preceded by *the,* it is treated as a singular: *The number of solutions offered was astounding.*

Other common COLLECTIVE NOUNS are *class, crowd, flock, panel, committee, group, audience, staff,* and *family.*

collec′tive uncon′scious, (in Jungian psychology) inborn unconscious psychic material common to humankind, accumulated by the experience of all preceding generations. Cf. **archetype** (def. 2). [1915–20]

col·lec·tiv·ism (kə lek′tə viz′əm), *n.* the political principle of centralized social and economic control, esp. of all means of production. [1875–80; < F *collectivisme*; see COLLECTIVE, -ISM] —**col·lec′tiv·ist,** *n., adj.* —**col·lec′tiv·is′tic,** *adj.* —**col·lec′tiv·is′ti·cal·ly,** *adv.*

col·lec·tiv·i·ty (kol′ek tiv′i tē), *n., pl.* **-ties. 1.** collective character. **2.** a collective whole. **3.** the people collectively. [1860–65; COLLECTIVE + -ITY]

col·lec·ti·vize (kə lek′tə vīz′), *v.t.,* **-vized, -viz·ing.** to organize (a people, industry, economy, etc.) according to the principles of collectivism. Also, *esp. Brit.,* **col·lec′·ti·vise′.** [1890–95; COLLECTIVE + -IZE] —**col·lec′ti·vi·za′tion,** *n.*

collect′ on deliv′ery. See **C.O.D.**

col·lec·tor (kə lek′tər), *n.* **1.** a person or thing that collects. **2.** a person employed to collect debts, duties, taxes, etc. **3.** a person who collects books, paintings, stamps, shells, etc., esp. as a hobby. **4.** *Elect.* a device for accumulating current from contact conductors. **5.** *Electronics.* an electrode in a transistor or vacuum tube for collecting electrons, ions, or holes. **6.** *Metall.* promoter (def. 5). **7.** *Energy.* See **solar collector.** [1375–1425; late ME (< AF) < ML, equiv. to L *colleg-* (var. s. of *colligere*; see COLLECT[1]) + *-tor* -TOR] —**col·lec′tor·ship′, col·lec′tor·ate,** *n.*

collec′tor elec′trode, *Electronics.* See under **Klystron.**

collec′tor's i′tem, an article or object of particular interest or value because of its uniqueness or scarcity. [1930–35]

col·leen (kol′ēn, ko lēn′), *n.* an Irish girl. [1820–30; < Ir *cailín,* equiv. to *caile* girl, wench + *-ín* dim. suffix]

Col·leen (kol′ēn, ko lēn′), *n.* a female given name: from an Irish word meaning "girl."

col·lege (kol′ij), *n.* **1.** an institution of higher learning, esp. one providing a general or liberal arts education rather than technical or professional training. Cf. **university. 2.** a constituent unit of a university, furnishing courses of instruction in the liberal arts and sciences, usually leading to a bachelor's degree. **3.** an institution for vocational, technical, or professional instruction, as in medicine, pharmacy, agriculture, or music, often a part of a university. **4.** an endowed, self-governing association of scholars incorporated within a university, as at the universities of Oxford and Cambridge in England. **5.** a similar corporation outside a university. **6.** the building or buildings occupied by an institution of higher education. **7.** the administrators, faculty, and students of a college. **8.** (in Britain and Canada) a private secondary school. **9.** an organized association of persons having certain powers and rights, and performing certain duties or engaged in a particular pursuit: *The electoral college formally selects the president.* **10.** a company; assemblage. **11.** Also called **collegium.** a body of clergy living together on a foundation for religious service or similar activity. **12.** *Brit. Slang.* a prison. [1350–1400; ME < AF, MF < L *collēgium,* equiv. to *col-* COL-[1] + *lēg-,* var. s. of *legere* to gather + *-ium* -IUM; cf. COLLEAGUE]

Col′lege Boards′, *Trademark.* a standard set of examinations administered by a college entrance examination board to evaluate aptitude and achievement in several fields of study for students seeking college admission. Cf. **Scholastic Aptitude Test.**

Col′lege of Arms′. See **Heralds' College.**

Col′lege of Car′dinals, the chief ecclesiastical body of the Roman Catholic Church, electing and advising the pope and comprising all of the cardinals of the church. Official name, **Sacred College of Cardinals.**

Col′lege of Propagan′da. See under **propaganda** (def. 4b).

Col′lege Park′, 1. a city in N Georgia. 24,632. **2.** a city in central Maryland. 23,614.

col·lege-pre·par·a·to·ry (kol′ij pri pâr′ə tôr′ē, -tōr′ē), *adj.* preparing a student for academic work at the college level.

col′lege ra′dio, 1. radio broadcasting from stations affiliated with a college or university, often at a frequency below 92 MHz FM. **2.** the usually eclectic or unconventional programming featured by such stations.

Col′lege Sta′tion, a city in E central Texas. 37,272.

col′lege try′, *Informal.* maximum effort for success on behalf of one's group, team, alma mater, etc. (usually prec. by the phrase *the old*): *We may not make the deadline, but we'll give it the old college try.* [1950–55]

col·le·gial (kə lē′jəl, -jē əl; *for 2 also* kə lē′gē əl), *adj.* **1.** collegiate. **2.** of or characterized by the collective responsibility shared by each of a group of colleagues, with minimal supervision from above. [1300–50; ME < L *collēgiālis.* See COLLEGE, -AL[1]] —**col·le′gi·al·ly,** *adv.*

col·le·gi·al·i·ty (kə lē′jē al′i tē, -gē-), *n.* cooperative interaction among colleagues. [1885–90; COLLEGIAL + -ITY]

col·le·gian (kə lē′jən, -jē ən), *n.* **1.** a student in, or a graduate of, a college. **2.** a member of a college. [1350–1400; ME < ML *collēgiānus,* equiv. to *collēgi(um)* COLLEGE + *-ānus* -AN]

col·le·giate (kə lē′jit, -jē it), *adj.* **1.** of or pertaining to a college: *collegiate life.* **2.** of, characteristic of, or intended for college students: *collegiate clothes; a collegiate dictionary.* **3.** of the nature of or constituted as a college. —*n.* **4.** (in Canada) See **collegiate institute.** [1400–50; late ME < LL *collēgiātus.* See COLLEGE, -ATE[1]] —**col·le′giate·ly,** *adv.* —**col·le′giate·ness,** *n.*

colle′giate church′, 1. a church that is endowed for a chapter of canons, usually with a dean, and that has no bishop's see. **2.** (in the U.S.) a church or group of churches under the general management of one consistory or session. **3.** a consolidation of formerly distinct churches under one or more pastors. **4.** (in Scotland) a church or congregation the active pastor of which is the colleague and successor of the emeritus pastor. [1400–50; late ME]

colle′giate in′stitute, (in Canada) a fully accredited high school teaching academic subjects under the supervision of a provincial government.

col·le·gi·um (kə lē′jē əm), *n., pl.* **-gi·a** (-jē ə), **-gi·ums. 1.** *Eccles.* college (def. 11). **2.** a group of ruling officials each with equal rank and power, esp. one that formerly administered a Soviet commissariat. [1915–20; < L; see COLLEGE]

col·le·gi·um mu·si·cum (kə lē′jē əm myōō′zi kəm; *Lat.* kō leg′ē ŏŏm′ mōō′si kŏŏm′), a group of usually amateur musicians, often connected with a university, who meet to study and perform chiefly old or little-known music. [< NL: musical society]

col le·gno (kō lān′yō; *It.* kôl le′nyô), *Music.* (of performance with the bow on the strings of a stringed instrument) with the wood. [< It]

col·lem·bo·lan (kə lem′bə lən), *adj.* **1.** Also, **col·lem′bo·lous.** belonging or pertaining to the insect order Collembola, comprising the springtails. —*n.* **2.** a collembolan insect; springtail. [1870; < NL *Collembol(a)* order name (equiv. to Gk *kóll(a)* glue + *émbola,* pl. of *émbolon* wedge, stopper (see EMBOLUS); so named from the collophore) + -AN]

col·len·chy·ma (kə leng′kə mə), *n. Bot.* a layer of modified tissue consisting of cells that are thickened at the angles and usually elongated. [1825–35; < NL < Gk *kóll(a)* glue + *énchyma* contents (*en-* EN-[2] + *chy-,* s. of *cheîn* to pour + *-ma* n. suffix denoting result of action)] —**col·len·chym·a·tous** (kol′ən kim′ə təs), **col·len·chy·mat·ic** (kə leng′kə mat′ik), *adj.*

col·let (kol′it), *n., v.,* **-let·ed, -let·ing.** —*n.* **1.** a collar or enclosing band. **2.** the enclosing rim within which a jewel is set. **3.** a slotted cylindrical clamp inserted tightly into the tapered interior of a sleeve or chuck on a lathe to hold a cylindrical piece of work. **4.** *Horol.* the tiny collar that supports the inner terminal of a hairspring. —*v.t.* **5.** to set (a gem or other stone) in a collet. [1520–30; < F, equiv. to *col* neck (< L *collum*) + *-et* -ET]

col·lide (kə līd′), *v.,* **-lid·ed, -lid·ing.** —*v.i.* **1.** to strike one another or one against the other with a forceful impact; come into violent contact; crash. **2.** to clash; conflict. —*v.t.* **3.** to cause to collide. [1615–25; < L *collīdere* to strike together, equiv. to *col-* COL-[1] + *-līdere,* comb. form of *laedere* to strike]

—**Syn. 1.** hit, smash, clash.

col·lid′ing-beam′ machine′ (kə lī′ding bēm′), *Physics.* a particle accelerator in which positively and negatively charged particles circulate in opposite directions and collide head-on. Also called **col·lid·er** (kə lī′dər).

col·lie (kol′ē), *n.* one of a breed of dogs having a usually long, black, tan, and white or sable and white coat, raised originally in Scotland for herding sheep. [1645–55; perh. Scots *colle* COAL (in reference to the original coloration of the breed) + -IE; cf. ME *Colle* dog's name] —**col′lie·like′,** *adj.*

collie
2 ft. (0.6 m)
high at shoulder

col·lier (kol′yər), *n.* **1.** a ship for carrying coal. **2.** a coal miner. **3.** *Obs.* a person who carries or sells coal. [1300–50; ME *coliere*; see COAL, -IER[1]]

Col·lier (kol′yər), *n.* **Jeremy,** 1650–1726, English clergyman and author.

col·lier·y (kol′yə rē), *n., pl.* **-lier·ies.** a coal mine, including all buildings and equipment. [1625–35; COLLIER + -Y[3]]

col·lie·shang·ie (kol′ē shang′ē), *n. Scot.* a noisy row; brawl. [1735–45; of obscure orig.]

col·li·gate (kol′i gāt′), *v.t.,* **-gat·ed, -gat·ing. 1.** to bind or fasten together. **2.** *Logic.* to link (facts) together by a general description or by a hypothesis that applies to them all. [1425–75 for obs. adj. sense "bound together"; 1535–45 for def. 1; < L *colligātus* (ptp. of *colligāre*), equiv. to *col-* COL-[1] + *ligā-* (s. of *ligāre* to bind) + *-tus* ptp. ending] —**col′li·ga′tion,** *n.*

col·li·ga·tive (kol′i gā′tiv), *adj. Physical Chem.* (of the properties of a substance) depending on the number of molecules or atoms rather than on their nature. [1900–05; COLLIGATE + -IVE]

col·li·mate (kol′ə māt′), *v.t.,* **-mat·ed, -mat·ing. 1.** to bring into line; make parallel. **2.** to adjust accurately the line of sight of (a telescope). [1615–25; < L *collimātus,* misreading of *collineātus,* ptp. of *collineāre* to direct in a straight line, equiv. to *col-* COL-[1] + *-lineā-,* v. deriv. of *linea* LINE[1] + *-tus* ptp. suffix] —**col′li·ma′tion,** *n.*

col·li·ma·tor (kol′ə mā′tər), *n.* **1.** *Optics.* **a.** a fixed telescope for use in collimating other instruments. **b.** an optical system that transmits parallel rays of light, as the receiving lens or telescope of a spectroscope. **2.** *Physics.* a device for producing a beam of particles in which the paths of all the particles are parallel. [1815–25; COLLIMATE + -OR[2]]

col·lin·e·ar (kə lin′ē ər, kō-), *adj.* lying in the same straight line. [1720–30; COL-[1] + LINEAR] —**col·lin′e·ar′i·ty,** *n.* —**col·lin′e·ar·ly,** *adv.*

Col·lings·wood (kol′ingz wŏŏd′), *n.* a city in SW New Jersey. 15,838.

Col·ling·wood (kol′ing wŏŏd′), *n.* **1.** a city in SE Australia, near Melbourne. 20,906. **2.** a town in S Ontario, in S Canada, on Georgian Bay of Lake Huron. 12,064.

col·lins (kol′inz), *n.* (*often cap.*) a tall drink made with gin, whiskey, rum, or vodka, and lemon or lime juice, soda water, and sugar. [1940–45; after the proper name *Collins*]

Col·lins (kol′inz), *n.* **1. Edward Trowbridge** (*Eddie*), 1887–1951, U.S. baseball player. **2. Michael,** 1890–1922, Irish revolutionist and patriot. **3. Michael,** born 1930, U.S. astronaut. **4. William,** 1721–59, English poet. **5. (William) Wil·kie** (wil′kē), 1824–89, English novelist.

col·lin·si·a (kə lin′sē ə, -zē ə), *n.* any plant belonging to the genus *Collinsia,* of the figwort family, having whorled leaves and usually clusters of variously colored flowers. [1817; after Zaccheus *Collins* (1764–1831), U.S. botanist; see -IA]

Col·lins·ville (kol′inz vil′), *n.* a city in SW Illinois. 19,613.

col·li·sion (kə lizh′ən), *n.* **1.** the act of colliding; a coming violently into contact; crash: *the collision of two airplanes.* **2.** a clash; conflict: *a collision of purposes.* **3.** *Physics.* the meeting of particles or of bodies in which each exerts a force upon the other, causing the exchange of energy or momentum. [1400–50; late ME < LL *collīsiōn-* (s. of *collīsiō*), equiv. to *collīs(us)* (ptp. of *collīdere* to COLLIDE) + *-iōn-* -ION] —**col·li′sion·al,** *adj.*

colli′sion course′, 1. a course or path of a vehicle, projectile, etc., that, if unchanged, will lead to a collision with another object. **2.** any plan, attitude, or course of action that leads to a confrontation or conflict with another. [1940–45]

colli′sion den′sity, *Physics.* the rate at which collisions are occurring per unit volume per unit time, usually pertaining to the collisions of neutrons in a nuclear reactor.

colli′sion diam′eter, *Physics.* the distance between the centers of two colliding molecules when at their closest point of approach.

colli′sion insur′ance, insurance protecting an automobile owner against loss or damage to the automobile resulting from a collision or other accident.

col·lo·blast (kol′ə blast′), *n. Zool.* one of the cells covered with sticky granules on the tentacles of a ctenophore, which aid in capturing prey. Also called **glue cell.** [< Gk *kóll(a)* glue + -O- + -BLAST]

col·lo·cate (kol′ə kāt′), *v.,* **-cat·ed, -cat·ing,** *n.* —*v.t.* **1.** to set or place together, esp. side by side. **2.** to arrange in proper order: *to collocate events.* —*v.i.* **3.** *Ling.* to enter into a collocation. —*n.* **4.** *Ling.* a lexical item that collocates with another. [1505–15; < L *collocātus* (ptp. of *collocāre*), equiv. to *col-* COL-[1] + *loc(us)* place + *-ātus* -ATE[1]]

col·lo·ca·tion (kol′ə kā′shən), *n.* **1.** the act of collocating. **2.** the state or manner of being collocated. **3.** the arrangement, esp. of words in a sentence. **4.** *Ling.* a co-occurrence of lexical items, as *perform* with *operation* or *commit* with *crime.* [1595–1605; < L *collocātiōn-* (s. of *collocātiō*), equiv. to *collocāt(us)* (see COLLOCATE) + *-iōn-* -ION] —**col′lo·ca′tion·al, col′lo·ca′tive,** *adj.*

Col·lo·di (kə lō′dē; *It.* kôl lô′dē), *n.* **Car·lo** (kär′lō; *It.* kär′lô), (*Carlo Lorenzini*), 1826–90, Italian writer: creator of the story of Pinocchio.

col·lo·di·on (kə lō′dē ən), *n.* a yellowish, viscous, highly flammable solution of pyroxylin in ether and alcohol: used in the manufacture of photographic film, in engraving and lithography, and in medicine chiefly for cementing dressings and sealing wounds. [1850–55; alter. of NL *collodium* < Gk *kollṓd(ēs)* glutinous (*kóll(a)* glue + *-ōdēs* -ODE[1]) + *-ium* -IUM]

collo′dion proc′ess, *Photog.* See **wet plate process.** [1865–60]

col·logue (kə lōg′), *v.i.,* **-logued, -lo·guing.** *Dial.* **1.** to confer secretly. **2.** to plot mischief; conspire. [1595–1605; perh. b. COLLUDE and DIALOGUE]

col·loid (kol′oid), *n.* **1.** *Physical Chem.* a substance made up of a system of particles with linear dimensions in the range of about 10^{-7} to 5×10^{-5} cm dispersed in a continuous gaseous, liquid, or solid medium whose properties depend on the large specific surface area. The particles can be large molecules like proteins, or solid, liquid, or gaseous aggregates and they remain dispersed indefinitely. Cf. **aerosol, emulsion, gel, sol[4], suspension. 2.** *Med.* a colloidal substance in the body, as a stored secretion or a cyst. —*adj.* **3.** *Physical Chem.* colloidal. [1840–50; < Gk *kóll(a)* glue + -OID]

col·loi·dal (kə loid′l), *adj. Physical Chem.* pertaining to or of the nature of a colloid: *colloidal gold and silver.* [1860–65; COLLOID + -AL[1]] —**col·loi·dal·i·ty** (kol′oi dal′i tē), *n.* —**col·loi′dal·ly,** *adv.*

CONCISE ETYMOLOGY KEY: <, descended or borrowed from; >, whence; b., blend of, blended; c., cognate with; cf., compare; deriv., derivative; equiv., equivalent; imit., imitative; obl., oblique; r., replacing; s., stem; sp., spelling, spelled; resp., respelling, respelled; trans., translation; ?, origin unknown; *, unattested; ‡, probably earlier than. See the full key inside the front cover.

colloi′dal suspen′sion. See under **suspension** (def. 6).

col′loid chem′istry, the study of colloids.

col·lop (kol′əp), *n.* **1.** a small slice of meat, esp. a small rasher of bacon. **2.** a small slice, portion, or piece of anything. **3.** a fold or roll of flesh on the body. [1350–1400; ME *collop(pe), colhoppe,* perh. < Scand; cf. OSw *kolhuppadher* roasted on coals, Sw *kalops,* dial. *kollops* dish of stewed meat]

col·lo·phane (kol′ə fān′), *n. Mineral.* a massive, cryptocrystalline variety of apatite that is the principal component of phosphate rock and fossil bone. Also, **col·loph·a·nite** (kə lof′ə nīt′, kol′ə fə-). [1915–20; < G *Kollophan,* equiv. to Gk *koll(a)* glue + -o- -o- + *-phan* -PHANE]

col·lo·phore (kol′ə fôr′, -fōr′), *n. Entomol.* a ventral tubelike structure on the abdomen of a springtail. [1875–80; < Gk *koll(a)* glue + -o- + -PHORE]

colloq., **1.** colloquial. **2.** colloquialism. **3.** colloquially.

col·lo·qui·al (kə lō′kwē əl), *adj.* **1.** characteristic of or appropriate to ordinary or familiar conversation rather than formal speech or writing; informal. **2.** involving or using conversation. [1745–55; COLLOQUY + -AL[1]] **—col·lo′qui·al·ly,** *adv.* **—col·lo′qui·al·ness, col·lo′qui·al′i·ty,** *n.*
—Syn. 1, 2. COLLOQUIAL, CONVERSATIONAL, INFORMAL refer to types of speech or to usages not on a formal level. COLLOQUIAL is often mistakenly used with a connotation of disapproval, as if it meant "vulgar" or "bad" or "incorrect" usage, whereas it is merely a familiar style used in speaking and writing. CONVERSATIONAL refers to a style used in the oral exchange of ideas, opinions, etc.: *an easy conversational style.* INFORMAL means without formality, without strict attention to set forms, unceremonious: *an informal manner of speaking;* it describes the ordinary, everyday language of cultivated speakers. **—Ant. 1.** formal.

col·lo·qui·al·ism (kə lō′kwē ə liz′əm), *n.* **1.** a colloquial expression. **2.** colloquial style or usage. [1800–10; COLLOQUIAL + -ISM] **—col·lo′qui·al·ist,** *n.*

col·lo·qui·um (kə lō′kwē əm), *n., pl.* **-qui·ums, -qui·a** (-kwē ə). a conference at which scholars or other experts present papers on, analyze, and discuss a specific topic. [1600–10; < L, equiv. to *colloqu(i)* (*col-* COL-[1] + *loquī* to speak) + *-ium* -IUM]

col·lo·quy (kol′ə kwē), *n., pl.* **-quies. 1.** a conversational exchange; dialogue. **2.** a conference. [1555–65; < L *colloquium* COLLOQUIUM] **—col′lo·quist,** *n.*

col·lo·type (kol′ə tīp′), *n., v.,* **-typed, -typ·ing.** **—n.** Also called **albertype, artotype, heliotype. 1.** any photomechanical process of printing from a plate coated with gelatin. **2.** the plate used for this. **3.** a print made from such a plate. **—v.t. 4.** to produce (a print) by collotype; albertype; artotype; heliotype. [1880–85; < Gk *kóll(a)* glue + -o- + -TYPE] **—col·lo·typ·ic** (kol′ə tip′ik), *adj.* **—col·lo·typ·y** (kol′ə tī′pē), *n.*

col·lude (kə lo͞od′), *v.i.,* **-lud·ed, -lud·ing. 1.** to act together through a secret understanding, esp. with evil or harmful intent. **2.** to conspire in a fraud. [1515–25; (< MF) < L *collūdere* to play together, equiv. to *col-* COL-[1] + *lūdere* to play] **—col·lud′er,** *n.*

collun., (in prescriptions) a nose wash. [see COLLUNARIUM]

col·lu·nar·i·um (kol′yə nâr′ē əm), *n., pl.* **-nar·i·a** (-nâr′ē ə). *Med.* a solution for application in the nose; nose drops. [< NL, equiv. to L *collu(ere)* to rinse (see COLLUTORY) + *nār(ēs)* nostrils (akin to NOSE) + *-ium* -IUM]

col·lu·sion (kə lo͞o′zhən), *n.* **1.** a secret agreement, esp. for fraudulent or treacherous purposes; conspiracy: *Some of his employees were acting in collusion to rob him.* **2.** *Law.* a secret understanding between two or more persons to gain something illegally, to defraud another of his or her rights, or to appear as adversaries though in agreement: *collusion of husband and wife to obtain a divorce.* [1350–1400; ME (< MF) < L *collūsiōn-* (s. of *collūsiō*), equiv. to *collūs(us)* (ptp. of *collūdere* to COLLUDE) + *-iōn-* -ION]
—Syn. 1. intrigue, connivance, complicity.

col·lu·sive (kə lo͞o′siv), *adj.* involving collusion; fraudulently contrived by agreement: *a collusive agreement to increase prices.* [1665–75; COLLUS(ION) + -IVE] **—col·lu′sive·ly,** *adv.* **—col·lu′sive·ness,** *n.*

collut., (in prescriptions) collutory.

col·lu·to·ri·um (kol′ə tôr′ē əm, -tōr′-), *n., pl.* **-to·ri·a** (-tôr′ē ə, -tōr′-). *Med.* collutory.

col·lu·to·ry (kol′ə tôr′ē, -tōr′ē), *n., pl.* **-ries.** *Med.* mouthwash. Also, **collutorium.** [< NL *collūtōrium,* equiv. to *collū-* (s. of L *colluere* to rinse, wash out; *col-* COL-[1] + *-luere,* comb. form of *lavere* to wash) + *-tōrium* -TORY[1]]

col·lu·vi·um (kə lo͞o′vē əm), *n., pl.* **-vi·a** (-vē ə), **-vi·ums.** *Geol.* loose earth material that has accumulated at the base of a hill, through the action of gravity, as piles of talus, avalanche debris, and sheets of detritus moved by soil creep or frost action. [1935–40; < NL, equiv. to L *colluv-,* base of *colluere* to wash out (see COLLUTORY) + *-ium* -IUM, on the model of L *alluvium* ALLUVIUM, *dīluvium* DELUGE] **—col·lu′vi·al,** *adj.*

col·ly (kol′ē), *v.,* **-lied, -ly·ing,** *n. Brit. Dial.* **—v.t. 1.** to blacken as with coal dust; begrime. **—n. 2.** grime; soot. [1555–65; var. of *collow* (v.), ME *colwen,* deriv. of OE *col* COAL; see -Y[1]]

collyr., (in prescriptions) an eyewash. [< L *collyrium*]

col·lyr·i·um (kə lēr′ē əm), *n., pl.* **-lyr·i·a** (-lēr′ē ə), **-lyr·i·ums.** eyewash (def. 1). [1350–1400; ME < L < Gk *kollýrion* eye salve]

col·ly·wob·bles (kol′ē wob′əlz), *n.* (*used with a singular or plural v.*) *Informal.* **1.** intestinal cramps or other intestinal disturbances. **2.** a feeling of fear, apprehension, or nervousness. [1815–25; coinage presumably based on COLIC, WOBBLE; see -S[3]]

Col·mar (*Fr.* kôl MAR′; *Ger.* kôl′mär), *n.* a city in and the capital of Haut-Rhin, in NE France. 67,410.

Cöln (kœln), *n.* former German name of **Cologne.**

colo-, a combining form representing **colon**[2] in compound words: *colostomy.* Also, *esp. before a vowel,* **col-.**

Colo., Colorado.

col·o·bus (kol′ə bəs, kə lō′-), *n., pl.* **-bus·es, -bi** (-bī′, -bī). any of several large, slender African monkeys of the genus *Colobus,* lacking thumbs and having long silky fur of black and white (*C. polykomos*), black and reddish-brown (*C. badius*), or olive (*C. verus*): now dwindling. [1811; < NL, the genus name < Gk *kolobós* docked, maimed; so named from the mutilated appearance of the thumbless hands]

co·lo·cate (kō lō′kāt), *v.t., v.i.,* **-cat·ed, -cat·ing.** to locate or be located in jointly or together, as two or more groups, military units, or the like; share or designate to share the same place. Also, **co-lo′cate.** [1965–70; CO- + LOCATE] **—co′lo·ca′tion, co′-lo·ca′tion,** *n.*

col·o·cynth (kol′ə sinth), *n.* **1.** a plant, *Citrullus colocynthis,* belonging to the gourd family, of the warmer parts of Asia, the Mediterranean region, etc., bearing a round, yellow or green fruit with a bitter pulp. **2.** the fruit of this plant. **3.** *Pharm.* the drug derived from the pulp of the unripe but full-grown fruit of this plant, used in medicine chiefly as a purgative. Also called **bitter apple** (for defs. 1, 2). [1555–65; < L *colocynthis* < Gk *kolokynthís,* var. of *kolókyntha* bitter gourd, bitter cucumber]

co·log (kō′lôg, -log), *n. Symbol, Math.* cologarithm.

co·log·a·rithm (kō lô′gə rith′əm, -rith′əm, -log′ə-), *n. Math.* the logarithm of the reciprocal of a number, often used in expressing the logarithm of a fraction: log $\frac{7}{25}$ = log 7 + colog 25. *Symbol:* colog [1880–85; CO- + LOGARITHM]

co·logne (kə lōn′), *n.* a mildly perfumed toilet water; eau de Cologne. Also called **Cologne′ wa′ter.** [short for *Cologne water,* made in COLOGNE since 1709] **—co·logned′,** *adj.*

Co·logne (kə lōn′), *n.* a city in W Germany. 914,300. German, **Köln.** Formerly, **Cöln.**

Cologne′ brown′. See **Vandyke brown.**

col·om·bard (kol′əm bärd′), *n.* **1.** a dry white wine, made esp. in California. **2.** the white grape used to make this wine. Also called **French colombard.** [< F *colombar(d),* equiv. to *colombe* dove (< L *columba*) + *-ard* -ARD; presumably alluding to the color of the grapes]

Co·lomb-Bé·char (*Fr.* kô lôN bā SHAR′), *n.* former name of **Béchar.**

Co·lombes (kô lôNb′), *n.* a city in N France, NW of Paris. 83,518.

Co·lom·bi·a (kə lum′bē ə; *Sp.* kô lôm′byä), *n.* a republic in NW South America. 24,500,000; 439,828 sq. mi. (1,139,155 sq. km). *Cap.:* Bogotá. **—Co·lom′bi·an,** *adj., n.*

Colom′bian gold′, *Slang.* a potent marijuana grown in South America. [1975–80]

Co·lom·bo (kə lum′bō), *n.* a seaport in and the capital of Sri Lanka, on the W coast. 562,160.

co·lon[1] (kō′lən), *n., pl.* **-lons** for 1, **-la** (-lə) for 2. **1.** the sign (:) used to mark a major division in a sentence, to indicate that what follows is an elaboration, summation, implication, etc., of what precedes; or to separate groups of numbers referring to different things, as hours from minutes in *5:30;* or the members of a ratio or proportion, as in *1 : 2 : : 3 : 6.* **2.** *Class. Pros.* one of the members or sections of a rhythmical period, consisting of a sequence of from two to six feet united under a principal ictus or beat. [1580–90; < L < Gk *kôlon* limb, member, clause]

co·lon[2] (kō′lən), *n., pl.* **-lons, -la** (-lə). **1.** *Anat.* the part of the large intestine extending from the cecum to the rectum. See diag. under **intestine. 2.** *Zool.* the portion of the digestive tract that is posterior to the stomach or gizzard and extends to the rectum. [1350–1400; ME < L < Gk *kólon* large intestine]

co·lon[3] (kō lōn′; *Sp.* kô lôn′), *n., pl.* **-lons,** *Sp.* **-lo·nes** (-lô′nes). **1.** the paper monetary unit of El Salvador, equal to 100 centavos. *Abbr.:* C. **2.** a cupronickel or steel coin and monetary unit of Costa Rica, equal to 100 centimos. [1890–95; < AmerSp, after (*Cristobal*) *Colón* (Christopher) Columbus]

co·lon[4] (kō′lon, kə lon′), *n.* a colonial farmer or plantation owner, esp. in Algeria. [1600–10, in sense "husbandmen"; 1955–60 in present sense; < F < L *colōnus* colonist]

Co·lón (kō lon′; *Sp.* kô lôn′), *n.* a seaport in Panama at the Atlantic end of the Panama Canal. 85,600.

Colón′ Archipel′ago. See **Galápagos Islands.**

co′lon bacil′lus (kō′lən), *Bacteriol.* See **coliform bacillus.** [1905–10]

colo·nel (kûr′nl), *n.* **1.** an officer in the U.S. Army, Air Force, or Marine Corps ranking between lieutenant colonel and brigadier general: corresponding to a captain in the U.S. Navy. **2.** a commissioned officer of similar rank in the armed forces of some other nations. **3.** an honorary title bestowed by some Southern states, as to those who have brought honor to the state, prominent businesspersons, visiting celebrities, or the like: *When the vice president visited the state he was made a Kentucky colonel.* **4.** *Older Use.* (in the South) a title of respect prefixed to the name of distinguished elderly men. [1540–50; < MF < It *colon(n)ello,* equiv. to *colonn(a)* COLUMN + *-ello* < L *-ellus* dim. suffix; r. (in writing) *coronel* < MF, dissimilated var. of *colonel;* so named because such an officer orig. headed the first column or company of a regiment]
—Pronunciation. COLONEL (kûr′nl), with its medial *l* pronounced as (r), illustrates one source for the apparent vagaries of English spelling: divergence between a word's orthographic development and its established pronunciation. In this case, English borrowed from French two variant forms of the same word, one with medial and final (l), and a second reflecting dissimilation of the first (l) to (r). After a period of competition, the dissimilated form triumphed in pronunciation, while the spelling *colonel* became the orthographic standard.

Colo′nel Blimp′, an elderly, pompous British reactionary, esp. an army officer or government official. [after a character appearing in cartoons by David Low]

colo·nel·cy (kûr′nl sē), *n.* the rank, position, or status of a colonel. Also, **colo′nel·ship′.** [1790–1800; COLONEL + -CY]

co·lo·ni·a (kə lō′nē ə, -lōn′yə; *Sp.* kô lô′nyä), *n., pl.* **-lo·ni·as** (-lō′nē əz, -lōn′yəz; *Sp.* -lô′nyäs). (in the southwestern U.S.) a city neighborhood or a rural settlement inhabited predominantly by Mexicans or Mexican Americans. [< MexSp: newly built or settled district of a city; Sp: plantation, COLONY]

co·lo·ni·al (kə lō′nē əl), *adj.* **1.** of, concerning, or pertaining to a colony or colonies: *the colonial policies of France.* **2.** of, concerning, or pertaining to colonialism; colonialistic. **3.** (*often cap.*) pertaining to the 13 British colonies that became the United States of America, or to their period. **4.** *Ecol.* forming a colony. **5.** (*cap.*) *Archit., Furniture.* **a.** noting or pertaining to the styles of architecture, ornament, and furnishings of the British colonies in America in the 17th and 18th centuries, mainly adapted to local materials and demands from prevailing English styles. **b.** noting or pertaining to various imitations of the work of American colonial artisans. **—n. 6.** an inhabitant of a colony. **7.** a house in or imitative of the Colonial style. [1770–80, *Amer.;* COLONY + -AL[1]] **—co·lo′ni·al·ly,** *adv.*

colo′nial an′imal, *Biol.* **1.** a collective life form comprising associations of individual organisms that are incompletely separated, as corals and moss animals. **2.** any of the individual organisms in such a life form. [1880–85]

Colo′nial Heights′, a town in central Virginia. 16,509.

co·lo·ni·al·ism (kə lō′nē ə liz′əm), *n.* **1.** the control or governing influence of a nation over a dependent country, territory, or people. **2.** the system or policy by which a nation maintains or advocates such control or influence. **3.** the state or condition of being colonial. **4.** an idea, custom, or practice peculiar to a colony. [1850–55; COLONIAL + -ISM] **—co·lo′ni·al·ist,** *n., adj.* **—co·lo′ni·al·is′tic,** *adj.*

co·lo·ni·al·i·ty (kə lō′nē al′i tē), *n. Animal Behav.* the state or condition of associating in colonies. [COLONIAL + -ITY]

co·lo·ni·al·i·za·tion (kə lō′nē ə lə zā′shən), *n.* **1.** the act of bringing into subjection or subjugation by colonializing. **2.** the state or fact of being colonialized. [1760–70; COLONIAL + -IZATION]

co·lo·ni·al·ize (kə lō′nē ə līz′), *v.t.,* **-ized, -iz·ing.** to make colonial. Also, *esp. Brit.,* **co·lo′ni·al·ise′.** [1860–65; COLONIAL + -IZE]

colo′nial sid′ing, *Carpentry.* siding composed of boards with parallel faces laid horizontally so that the upper overlaps the one below.

co·lon·ic (kō lon′ik, kə-), *adj. Anat.* **1.** of or pertaining to the colon. **—n. 2.** an enema. [1905–10; COLON[2] + -IC]

col·o·nist (kol′ə nist), *n.* **1.** an inhabitant of a colony. **2.** a member of a colonizing expedition. **3.** (*often cap.*) an inhabitant of the 13 British colonies that became the United States of America. [1695–1705, *Amer.;* COLON(Y) + -IST]

col·o·nize (kol′ə nīz′), *v.,* **-nized, -niz·ing.** **—v.t. 1.** to establish a colony in; settle: *England colonized Australia.* **2.** to form a colony of: *to colonize laborers in a mining region.* **—v.i. 3.** to form a colony: *They went out to Australia to colonize.* **4.** to settle in a colony.

CONCISE PRONUNCIATION KEY: act, cāpe, dâre, pärt; set, ēqual; *if,* ice; ox, ōver, ôrder, oil, bo͝ok, bo͞ot, out; up, ûrge; child; sing; shoe; thin, *th*at; zh as in *treasure.* ə = *a* as in *alone, e* as in *system, i* as in *easily, o* as in *gallop, u* as in *circus;* ᵊ as in *fire* (fīᵊr), *hour* (ouᵊr). l and n can serve as syllabic consonants, as in *cradle* (krād′l), and *button* (but′n). See the full key inside the front cover.

Also, *esp. Brit.*, **col′o·nise′.** [1615–25; COLON(Y) + -IZE] **—col′o·niz′a·ble,** *adj.* **—col′o·niz′a·bil′i·ty,** *n.* **—col′o·ni·za′tion,** *n.* **—col′o·ni·za′tion·ist,** *n.* **—col′o·niz′er,** *n.*

Co·lon·na (kə lō′nə), *n.* **Cape.** See **Sounion, Cape.**

col·on·nade (kol′ə nād′), *n.* **1.** *Archit.* a series of regularly spaced columns supporting an entablature and usually one side of a roof. Cf. **arcade. 2.** a series of trees planted in a long row, as on each side of a driveway or road. [1710–20; < F, equiv. to *colonne* COLUMN + *-ade* -ADE[1], on the model of It *colonnato*] **—col′on·nad′ed,** *adj.*

co·lon·o·scope (kō lon′ə skōp′, kə-), *n. Med.* a flexible, lighted, tubular instrument using fiber optics to permit visualization of the colon. [COLON[2] + -O- + -SCOPE] **—co·lon·os·co·py** (kō′lə nos′kə pē), *n.*

co·lo·nus (kə lō′nəs), *n., pl.* **-ni** (-nī, -nē). a serf in the latter period of the Roman Empire or in the early feudal period. [1885–90; < L *colōnus* inhabitant of a colony, tenant-farmer, farmer, deriv. of *colere* to inhabit, till, cultivate; cf. CULT, CULTIVATE]

col·o·ny (kol′ə nē), *n., pl.* **-nies. 1.** a group of people who leave their native country to form in a new land a settlement subject to, or connected with, the parent nation. **2.** the country or district settled or colonized: *Many Western nations are former European colonies.* **3.** any people or territory separated from but subject to a ruling power. **4. the Colonies,** those British colonies that formed the original 13 states of the United States: New Hampshire, Massachusetts, Rhode Island, Connecticut, New York, New Jersey, Pennsylvania, Delaware, Maryland, Virginia, North Carolina, South Carolina, and Georgia. **5.** a number of people coming from the same country, or speaking the same language, residing in a foreign country or city, or a particular section of it; enclave: *the Polish colony in Israel; the American colony in Paris.* **6.** any group of individuals having similar interests, occupations, etc., usually living in a particular locality; community: *a colony of artists.* **7.** the district, quarter, or dwellings inhabited by any such number or group: *The Greek island is now an artists' colony.* **8.** an aggregation of bacteria growing together as the descendants of a single cell. **9.** *Ecol.* a group of organisms of the same kind living or growing in close association. [1350–1400; ME *colonie* (< MF) < L *colōnia,* equiv. to *colōn(us)* COLONUS + *-ia* -Y[3]]
—Syn. 6. body, band.

Col·o·ny (kol′ə nē), *n.* **The,** a city in NE Texas. 11,586.

col·o·phon (kol′ə fon′, -fən), *n.* **1.** a publisher's or printer's distinctive emblem, used as an identifying device on its books and other works. **2.** an inscription at the end of a book or manuscript, used esp. in the 15th and 16th centuries, giving the title or subject of the work, its author, the name of the printer or publisher, and the date and place of publication. [1615–25; < L < Gk *kolophṓn* summit, finishing touch] **—col′o·phon′ic,** *adj.*

Col·o·phon (kol′ə fon′), *n.* an ancient city in Asia Minor: one of the 12 Ionian cities banded together in the 8th century B.C.: largely depopulated in 286 B.C.

Col·o·pho·ni·an (kol′ə fō′nē ən), *n.* **1.** a native of Colophon. **2. the,** Antimachus (def. 1). **—***adj.* **3.** of or pertaining to Colophon. [< L *colophōni(us)* (< Gk; see COLOPHONY) + -AN]

col·o·pho·ny (kol′ə fō′nē, kə lof′ə nē), *n.* rosin. [1300–50; ME *colofonie* (< AF) < L *Colophōnia* (*rēsina*) (resin) of Colophon < Gk *Kolophōnía,* fem. of *Kolophṓnios,* equiv. to *Kolophṓn* Colophon + *-ios* adj. suffix; see -Y[3]]

col·o·quin·ti·da (kol′ə kwin′ti də), *n.* colocynth (defs. 1, 2). [1350–1400; ME < ML < Gk *kolokýnthida,* acc. of *kolokynthís* COLOCYNTH]

col·or (kul′ər), *n.* **1.** the quality of an object or substance with respect to light reflected by the object, usually determined visually by measurement of hue, saturation, and brightness of the reflected light; saturation or chroma; hue. **2.** the natural appearance of the skin, esp. of the face; complexion: *She has a lovely color.* **3.** a ruddy complexion: *The wind and sun had given color to the sailor's face.* **4.** a blush: *His remarks brought the color to her face.* **5.** vivid or distinctive quality, as of a literary work: *Melville's description of a whaling voyage is full of color.* **6.** details in description, customs, speech, habits, etc., of a place or period: *The novel takes place in New Orleans and contains much local color.* **7.** something that is used for coloring; pigment; paint; tint; dye. **8.** background information, as anecdotes about players or competitors or analyses of plays, strategy, or performance, given by a sportscaster to heighten interest in a sportscast. **9. colors, a.** any distinctive color or combination or pattern of colors, esp. of a badge, ribbon, uniform, or the like, worn or displayed as a symbol of or to identify allegiance to, membership in, or sponsorship by a school, group, or organization. **b.** nature, viewpoint, or attitude; character; personality: *His behavior in a crisis revealed his true colors.* **c.** a flag, ensign, etc., particularly the national flag. **d.** *U.S. Navy.* the ceremony of hoisting the national flag at 8 A.M. and of lowering it at sunset. **10.** skin complexion of a particular people or race, esp. when other than white: *a man of color.* **11.** outward appearance or aspect; guise or show: *It was a lie, but it had the color of the truth.* **12.** a pretext: *She did it under the color of doing a good deed.* **13.** *Painting.* the general use or effect of the pigments in a picture. **14.** *Phonet.* timbre. **15.** *Chiefly Law.* an apparent or prima facie right or ground: *to hold possession under color of title.* **16.** *Music.* See **tone color. 17.** a trace or particle of valuable mineral, esp. gold, as shown by washing auriferous gravel. **18.** *Physics.* any of the labels red, green, or blue that designate the three states in which quarks are expected to exist, or any of the corresponding labels for antiquark states. Cf. **quantum chromodynamics, quark model. 19.** *Print.* the amount of ink used. **20.** *Heraldry.* a tincture other than a fur or metal, usually including gules, azure, vert, sable, and purpure. **21. call to the colors,** to summon for service in the armed forces: *Thousands are being called to the colors.* **22. change color, a.** to blush as from embarrassment. **b.** to turn pale, as from fear: *When he saw the size of his opponent, he changed color.* **23. with flying colors.** See **flying colors.**
—*adj.* **24.** involving, utilizing, yielding, or possessing color: *a color TV.*
—*v.t.* **25.** to give or apply color to; tinge; paint; dye: *She colored her hair dark red.* **26.** to cause to appear different from the reality: *In order to influence the jury, he colored his account of what had happened.* **27.** to give a special character or distinguishing quality to: *His personal feelings color his writing.*
—*v.i.* **28.** to take on or change color: *The ocean colored at dawn.* **29.** to flush; blush: *He colored when confronted with the incriminating evidence.* Also, *esp. Brit.,* **colour.** [1250–1300; ME *col(o)ur* < AF (F *couleur*) < L *color-* (s. of *color*) hue] **—col′or·er,** *n.*
—Syn. 26. bias, twist.
—Usage. See **-or**[1].

color., (in prescriptions) let it be colored. [< L *colōrētur*]

col·or·a·ble (kul′ər ə bəl), *adj.* **1.** capable of being colored. **2.** seemingly valid, true, or genuine; plausible. **3.** pretended; deceptive. [1400–50; late ME; see COLOR, -ABLE] **—col′or·a·bil′i·ty, col′or·a·ble·ness,** *n.* **—col′or·a·bly,** *adv.*

col·o·rad·o (kol′ə rad′ō, -rä′dō), *adj.* (of cigars) of medium color and strength. [< Sp < L *colōrātus* colored. See COLOR, -ATE[1]]

Col·o·rad·o (kol′ə rad′ō, -rä′dō), *n.* **1.** a state in the W United States. 2,888,834; 104,247 sq. mi. (270,000 sq. km). *Cap.:* Denver. *Abbr.:* CO (for use with zip code), Col., Colo. **2.** a river flowing SW from N Colorado through Utah and Arizona into the Gulf of California: Grand Canyon; Boulder Dam. 1450 mi. (2335 km) long. **3.** a river flowing SE from W Texas to the Gulf of Mexico. 840 mi. (1350 km) long. **—Col′o·rad′an, Col′o·rad′o·an,** *adj., n.*

Col′orad′o blue′ spruce′. See **blue spruce.** [1895–1900, *Amer.*]

Col′orad′o Des′ert, an arid region in SE California, W of the Colorado River. ab. 2500 sq. mi. (6475 sq. km).

col·o·rad·o·ite (kol′ə rad′ō it′, -rä′dō-), *n.* a mineral, mercury telluride, HgTe, occurring in the form of grayish-black masses. [1875–80; named after COLORADO; see -ITE[1]]

Colorad′o Plateau′, a plateau in the SW United States, in N Arizona, NW New Mexico, S Utah, and SW Colorado: location of the Grand Canyon.

Colorad′o pota′to bee′tle, a black and yellow leaf beetle, *Leptinotarsa decemlineata,* originally of Colorado and neighboring states but now a common pest in all potato-growing regions of the U.S. Also called **Col′orad′o bee′tle, potato beetle, potatobug.** [1865–70, *Amer.*]

Col′orad′o red′ ce′dar. See **Rocky Mountain juniper.**

Col′orad′o Springs′, a city in central Colorado: resort; U.S. Air Force Academy. 215,150.

Col′orad′o spruce′. See **blue spruce.**

Col′orad′o tick′ fe′ver, *Pathol.* a usually mild viral disease occurring in the Rocky Mountain regions of the United States, carried by a tick, *Dermacentor andersoni,* and characterized by fever, sensitivity to light, headache, and leg and back pain. [1955–60]

col·or·ant (kul′ər ənt), *n.* something used as a coloring matter; pigment; dye. [1880–85; < F, prp. of *colorer* < L *colōrāre* to color. See COLOR, -ANT]

col·or·a·tion (kul′ə rā′shən), *n.* appearance with regard to color arrangement or use of colors; coloring: *the bold coloration of some birds.* [1605–15; COLOR + -ATION] **—col′o·ra′tion·al,** *adj.* **—col′o·ra′tion·al·ly,** *adv.*

col·o·ra·tu·ra (kul′ər ə to͝or′ə, -tyo͝or′ə, kol′-, kōl′-), *n.* **1.** runs, trills, and other florid decorations in vocal music. **2.** a lyric soprano of high range who specializes in such music. Also, **col·or·a·ture** (kul′ər ə cho͝or′). [1730–40; < It < LL: lit., coloring. See COLOR, -ATE[1], -URE]

col′or bar′. See **color line** (def. 1). [1910–15]

col·or·bear·er (kul′ər bâr′ər), *n.* a person who carries the colors or standard, esp. of a military body. Cf. **guidon** (def. 2). [1890–95; COLOR + BEARER]

col·or-blind (kul′ər blīnd′), *adj.* **1.** *Ophthalm.* pertaining to or affected with color blindness. **2.** *Photog.* (of an emulsion) sensitive only to blue, violet, and ultraviolet rays. **3.** showing or characterized by freedom from racial bias. [1850–55]

col′or blind′ness, 1. inability to distinguish one or several chromatic colors, independent of the capacity for distinguishing light and shade. **2.** complete inability to distinguish colors of the spectrum, with all objects appearing as shades of gray, black, and white, varying only as to lightness and darkness; achromatopsia. [1835–45]

col·or·breed (kul′ər brēd′), *v.i.,* **-bred, -breed·ing.** *Genetics.* to breed plants or animals selectively for the production of new varieties having a specific color or shade. [COLOR + BREED]

col·or·cast (kul′ər kast′, -käst′), *n., v.,* **-cast, -cast·ing.** **—***n.* **1.** a television program broadcast in color. **—***v.t., v.i.* **2.** to broadcast or televise in color. [1945–50; COLOR + (BROAD)CAST]

col·or·cast·er (kul′ər kas′tər, -kä′stər), *n. Radio and Television.* an announcer, esp. in sports, who provides supplementary information or comment. Also called **col′or com′mentator.** [COLOR + (BROAD)CASTER]

col′or cir′cle, a circular diagram displaying the colors of the spectrum as a sequence of segments of the circle and showing complementary colors opposite each other. [1875–80]

col′or code′, any system of marking or visual designation that uses specific colors for indicating or simplifying, as on a chart or map or in an industrial plant.

col·or-code (kul′ər kōd′), *v.t.,* **-cod·ed, -cod·ing.** to distinguish or classify with a color code. [1955–60]

col·or-co·or·di·nat·ed (kul′ər kō ôr′dn ā′tid), *adj.* with all parts or elements related, blended, or matched to a particular color scheme.

co·lo·rec·tal (kō′lə rek′tl), *adj. Anat.* pertaining to or involving the colon and rectum: *colorectal cancer.* [COLO- + RECTAL]

col·ored (kul′ərd), *adj.* **1.** having color. **2.** *Often Offensive.* belonging wholly or in part to a race other than the white, esp. to the black race. **3.** *Often Offensive.* pertaining to the black race. **4.** influenced or biased: *colored opinions.* **5.** specious; deceptive: *The authorities detected a colored quality in her statement.* **6.** *Bot.* of some hue other than green. **—***n.* **7.** *Often Offensive.* **a.** a black person. **b. the colored,** black persons as a group. **8.** See **Cape Colored.** [1275–1325; ME; see COLOR, -ED[3]]
—Usage. 2, 3, 7. See **black.**

col′ored stone′, *Jewelry.* any gemstone, colored or colorless, other than a diamond.

col·or·fast (kul′ər fast′, -fäst′), *adj.* maintaining color without fading or running: *colorfast textile.* [1925–30; COLOR + FAST[1]] **—col′or·fast′ness,** *n.*

col·or·field (kul′ər fēld′), *adj.* of, pertaining to, or characteristic of abstract painting in which large, flat areas of color are spread to cover the entire canvas and dominate over form and texture. Also, **col′or-field′.** [1960–65; COLOR + FIELD]

col′or fil′ter, *Photog.* a screen of dyed gelatin or glass for controlling or modifying the reproduction of the colors of the subject as photographed. Cf. **filter** (def. 5). [1895–1900]

col′or force′, *Physics.* See **strong force** (def. 2). [1975–80]

col·or·ful (kul′ər fəl), *adj.* **1.** abounding in color: *In their tartans, the Scots guard made a colorful array.* **2.** richly eventful or picturesque: *a colorful historical period.* **3.** presenting or suggesting vivid or striking scenes: *a colorful narrative.* [1885–90; COLOR + -FUL] **—col′or·ful·ly,** *adv.* **—col′or·ful·ness,** *n.*
—Syn. 3. vigorous, spirited, dynamic.

col′or guard′, the group of persons, as in the armed forces or at military institutions, who carry or escort the flag or colors during parades, reviews, etc. [1815–25]

col·or·if·ic (kul′ə rif′ik), *adj.* **1.** producing or imparting color. **2.** pertaining to color. [1670–80; COLOR + -I- + -FIC]

col·or·im·e·ter (kul′ə rim′i tər), *n.* a device that analyzes color by measuring a given color in terms of a standard color, a scale of colors, or certain primary colors. [1860–65; COLOR + -I- + -METER] **—col·or·i·met·ric** (kul′er ə me′trik), **col′or·i·met′ri·cal,** *adj.* **—col′·or·i·met′ri·cal·ly,** *adv.* **—col′or·im′e·trist,** *n.* **—col′·or·im′e·try,** *n.*

col′or in′dex, *Astron.* **1.** the difference between the apparent photographic magnitude and the apparent visual magnitude of a star. **2.** the difference between the magnitudes of a star in any two spectral regions. [1920–25]

col·or·ing (kul′ər ing), *n.* **1.** the act or method of applying color. **2.** appearance as to color: *healthy coloring.* **3.** a substance used to color something: *food coloring made from vegetable dyes.* **4.** aspect or tone: *The ethical coloring of the story balanced the rawness of its language.* **5.** specious appearance; show. [1375–1425; late ME; see COLOR, -ING[1]]

col′oring book′, a children's book of outline drawings for coloring in crayons, watercolors, etc.

col·or·ist (kul′ər ist), *n.* **1.** a person who uses color skillfully. **2.** a painter who emphasizes color relationships in a work of art. **3.** a person who colors photographs. **4.** a hairdresser who is skilled in coloring or tinting hair. **5.** a musical performer or composer who is skilled in bringing musical color. [1680–90; COLOR + -IST; cf. F *coloriste*] **—col′or·is′tic,** *adj.* **—col′or·is′ti·cal·ly,** *adv.*

col·or·ize (kul′ə rīz′), *v.t.,* **-ized, -iz·ing.** to cause to appear in color; enhance with color, esp. by computer: *to colorize old black-and-white movies for television.* Also, *esp. Brit.,* **col′or·ise′.** [COLOR + -IZE] **—col′or·i·za′·tion,** *n.*

col·or-key (kul′ər kē′), *v.t.,* **-keyed, -key·ing.** color-code.

col·or·less (kul′ər lis), *adj.* **1.** without color: *Pure water is colorless.* **2.** pallid; dull in color: *a colorless complexion.* **3.** lacking vividness or distinctive character; dull; insipid: *a colorless description of the parade.* **4.** unbiased; neutral. [1350–1400; ME; see COLOR, -LESS] **—col′or·less·ly,** *adv.* **—col′or·less·ness,** *n.*
—Syn. 3. unexciting, dreary, drab, lackluster.

CONCISE ETYMOLOGY KEY: <, descended or borrowed from; >, whence; b., blend of, blended; c., cognate with; cf., compare; deriv., derivative; equiv., equivalent; imit., imitative; obl., oblique; r., replacing; s., stem; sp., spelling, spelled; resp., respelling, respelled; trans., translation; ?, origin unknown; *, unattested; ‡, probably earlier than. See the full key inside the front cover.

col′or line′, 1. Also called **color bar.** social or political restriction or distinction based on differences of skin pigmentation, as between white and black people. 2. **draw the color line,** to observe a color line. [1860–65, *Amer.*]

col′or phase′, 1. a genetically controlled variation in the colors of the skin, pelt, or plumage of an animal. 2. one of two or more colorings assumed by an animal, varying with age or season. [1925–30]

col′or point′, *Heraldry.* See **honor point.**

col′or scheme′, an arrangement or pattern of colors or colored objects conceived of as forming an integrated whole: *the color scheme of a living room.* [1885–90]

col′or ser′geant, a sergeant who has charge of battalion or regimental colors. [1805–15]

col•or•slide (kul′ər slīd′), *n.* a color transparency, mounted usually between cardboard or plastic masks or glass plates, for projection onto a screen. [1950–55; COLOR + SLIDE]

col′or tem′perature, *Optics, Photog.* a temperature defined in terms of the temperature of a black body at which it emits light of a specified spectral distribution: used to specify the color of a light source. [1915–20]

col′or transpar′ency, a positive color image photographically produced on transparent film or glass and viewed by transmitted light, usually by projection. [1910–15]

col′or wheel′. See under **complementary color** (def. 1a). [1890–95]

Co•los•sae (kə los′ē), *n.* an ancient city in SW Phrygia: seat of an early Christian church to which Paul wrote the Epistle to the Colossians.

co•los•sal (kə los′əl), *adj.* 1. extraordinarily great in size, extent, or degree; gigantic; huge. 2. of or resembling a colossus. [1705–15; COLOSS(US) + -AL[1]] —**co•los•sal•i•ty** (kol′ə sal′i tē), *n.* —**co•los′sal•ly,** *adv.* —**Syn.** 1. See **gigantic.**

Col•os•se•um (kol′ə sē′əm), *n.* 1. an ancient amphitheater in Rome, begun A.D. c70 by Vespasian, having the form of an oval 617 by 512 ft. (188 by 156 m). 2. (*l.c.*) coliseum. [< L, n. use of neut. of *colossēus* gigantic < Gk *kolossiaîos,* equiv. to *koloss(ós)* COLOSSUS + *-iaios* adj. suffix]

Co•los•sian (kə losh′ən), *n.* 1. a native or inhabitant of Colossae. 2. one of the Christians of Colossae, to whom Paul addressed one of his Epistles. —*adj.* 3. of or pertaining to Colossae or its inhabitants. [< L *Coloss(ae)* (< Gk *Kolossaî*) + -IAN]

Co•los•sians (kə losh′ənz), *n.* (*used with a singular v.*) a book of the New Testament, written by Paul. *Abbr.:* Col.

co•los•sus (kə los′əs), *n., pl.* **-los•si** (-los′ī), **-los•sus•es.** 1. (*cap.*) the legendary bronze statue of Helios at Rhodes. Cf. **Seven Wonders of the World.** 2. any statue of gigantic size. 3. anything colossal, gigantic, or very powerful. [1350–1400; ME < L < Gk *kolossós* statue, image, presumably < a pre-Hellenic Mediterranean language]

Colos′sus of Mem′non, an ancient Egyptian stone monument near Thebes, erected by Amenhotep III, that consists of two seated figures 38 ft. (12 m) high. Cf. **Vocal Memnon.**

co•los•to•my (kə los′tə mē), *n., pl.* **-mies.** *Surg.* 1. the construction of an artificial opening from the colon through the abdominal wall, thus bypassing a diseased portion of the lower intestine and permitting the passage of intestinal contents. 2. the opening so constructed. [1885–90; COLO- + -STOMY]

co•los•trum (kə los′trəm), *n.* a yellowish liquid, esp. rich in immune factors, secreted by the mammary gland of female mammals a few days before and after the birth of their young. Also called **foremilk.** [1570–80; < L *colostrum, colustrum* beestings] —**co•los′tral,** *adj.*

co•lot•o•my (kə lot′ə mē), *n., pl.* **-mies.** *Surg.* incision or opening of the colon. [1865–70; COLO- + -TOMY]

col•our (kul′ər), *n., adj. v.t., v.i. Chiefly Brit.* color. —**Usage.** See **-or**[1].

-colous, a combining form meaning "inhabiting" the thing or place specified by the initial element, used in the formation of compound words: *nidicolous.* [< L *-col(a),* comb. form repr. *colere* to inhabit (cf. COLONUS) + -OUS]

col•pi•tis (kol pī′tis), *n. Pathol.* vaginitis. [1875–80; < Gk *kólp(os)* bosom, womb + -ITIS]

col•po•da (kol pō′də), *n.* any ciliated protozoan of the genus *Colpoda,* common in fresh water. [1790; < NL, equiv. to Gk *kolpōd(ēs)* embosomed, embayed (*kólp(os)* bosom + *-ōdēs* -ODE[1]) + L *-a* -A[2]]

col•por•tage (kol′pôr′tij, -pōr′-; *Fr.* kôl pôr tazh′), *n.* the work of a colporteur. [1840–50; < F, equiv. to *colport(er)* to hawk (lit., carry on the neck; see COL, PORT[5]) + *-age* -AGE]

col•por•teur (kol′pôr′tər, -pōr′-; *Fr.* kôl pôr tœr′), *n., pl.* **-teurs** (-tərz; *Fr.* -tœr′). 1. a person who travels to sell or publicize Bibles, religious tracts, etc. 2. a peddler of books. [1790–1800; < F, equiv. to *colport(er)* (see COLPORTAGE) + *-eur* -EUR]

col•po•scope (kol′pə skōp′), *n.* an instrument that magnifies the cells of the cervix and vagina to permit direct observation and study of the living tissue. [1935–40; < Gk *kólp(os)* womb, vagina + -O- + -SCOPE] —**col•po•scop•ic** (kol′pə skop′ik), *adj.* —**col•pos•co•pist** (kol-pos′kə pist), *n.*

col•pos•co•py (kol pos′kə pē), *n., pl.* **-pies.** an examination by means of a colposcope. [1935–40; < Gk *kólp(os)* womb, vagina + -O- + -SCOPY]

col•pot•o•my (kol pot′ə mē), *n., pl.* **-mies.** *Surg.* incision of the vagina. Also called **vaginotomy.** [*colpo-* (see COLPOSCOPE) + -TOMY]

colt (kōlt), *n.* 1. a young male animal of the horse family. 2. a male horse of not more than four years of age. 3. a young or inexperienced person. [bef. 1000; ME, OE; cf. dial. Sw *kult* little pig]

Colt (kōlt), *Trademark.* a brand of revolver.

Colt (kōlt), *n.* **Samuel,** 1814–62, U.S. inventor of the Colt revolver.

colt′ distem′per, *Vet. Pathol.* distemper[1] (def. 1b).

col•ter (kōl′tər), *n.* a sharp blade or wheel attached to the beam of a plow, used to cut the ground in advance of the plowshare. Also, **coulter.** [1300–50; ME, OE *culter* < L: knife, plowshare]

colt•ish (kōl′tish), *adj.* 1. playful; frolicsome. 2. of, pertaining to, or resembling a colt. 3. not trained or disciplined; unruly; wild. [1350–1400; ME. See COLT, -ISH[1]] —**colt′ish•ly,** *adv.* —**colt′ish•ness,** *n.*

Col•ton (kōl′tn), *n.* a city in SW California, near Los Angeles. 27,419.

Col•trane (kōl′trān), *n.* **John (William),** 1926–67, U.S. jazz saxophonist and composer.

colts•foot (kōlts′fo͝ot′), *n., pl.* **-foots.** a composite plant, *Tussilago farfara,* having yellow, daisylike flowers, native to the Old World but widespread as a weed, formerly used as a cough remedy. [1545–55; COLT + 's[1] + FOOT, so called from the shape of the leaves]

col•u•brid (kol′ə brid, -yə-), *n.* 1. any of numerous, typically harmless snakes constituting the family Colubridae, having no vestigial limbs, a scale-covered head and body with a mostly bare face, and belly scales usually as wide as the body, including garter snakes, bull snakes, water snakes, racers, vine and tree snakes, and other temperate-to-tropical species, comprising about two-thirds of all living snakes. —*adj.* 2. belonging or pertaining to the Colubridae. [1885–90; < NL *Colubridae* name of the family, equiv. to *Colubr-* (s. of *Coluber* a genus, L *coluber* snake) + *-idae* -ID[2]]

col•u•brine (kol′ə brīn′, -brin, -yə-), *adj.* 1. of or resembling a snake; snakelike. 2. belonging or pertaining to the subfamily Colubrinae, comprising the typical colubrid snakes. [1520–30; < L *colubrīnus,* equiv. to *colubr-* (s. of *coluber*) snake + *-īnus* -INE[1]]

co•lu•go (kə lo͞o′gō), *n., pl.* **-gos.** See **flying lemur.** [1885–90; < NL, first recorded as *colago* (1702) and alleged to be < Bisayan]

Col•um (kol′əm), *n.* **Pa•draic** (pô′drik), 1881–1972, Irish poet and dramatist, in the U.S. from 1914.

Co•lum•ba (kə lum′bə), *n., gen.* **-bae** (-bē) for 2. 1. **Saint,** A.D. 521–597, Irish missionary in Scotland. 2. Also called **Colum′ba No′ae** (nō′ē). *Astron.* the Dove, or Noah's Dove, a southern constellation between Caelum and Canis Major. —**Co•lum′ban,** *adj.*

col•um•bar•i•um (kol′əm bâr′ē əm), *n., pl.* **-bar•i•a** (-bâr′ē ə). 1. a sepulchral vault or other structure with recesses in the walls to receive the ashes of the dead. 2. any one of these recesses. 3. columbary. [1840–50; < L: lit., a nesting box for pigeons, equiv. to *columb(a)* pigeon, dove + *-ārium* -ARY]

col•um•bar•y (kol′əm ber′ē), *n., pl.* **-bar•ies.** a dovecote or pigeon house. Also, **columbarium.** [1540–50; see COLUMBARIUM]

co•lum•bate (kə lum′bāt, -bit), *n. Chem.* niobate. [1810–20; COLUMB(IUM) + -ATE[2]]

Co•lum•bi•a (kə lum′bē ə), *n.* 1. a river in SW Canada and the NW United States, flowing S and W from SE British Columbia through Washington along the boundary between Washington and Oregon and into the Pacific. 1214 mi. (1955 km) long. 2. a city in and the capital of South Carolina, in the central part. 99,296. 3. a city in central Missouri. 62,061. 4. a city in central Maryland. 52,518. 5. a city in central Tennessee. 25,767. 6. a city in SE Pennsylvania. 10,466. 7. *Literary.* the United States of America. 8. one of an American breed of large sheep, developed by crossbreeding the Lincoln and Rambouillet, noted for its good market lambs and heavy fleece of medium length. 9. (*italics*) *U.S. Aerospace.* the first space shuttle to orbit and return to earth.

Colum′bia Heights′, a city in SE Minnesota, near Minneapolis. 20,029.

Co•lum•bi•an (kə lum′bē ən), *adj.* 1. *Literary.* pertaining to America or the United States. 2. pertaining to Christopher Columbus. —*n.* 3. *Print.* a 16-point type of a size between English and great primer. [1750–60; COLUMBI(A) + -AN or COLUMB(US) + -IAN]

co•lum•bic (kə lum′bik), *adj. Chem.* niobic. [1800–10; COLUMB(IUM) + -IC]

col•um•bine[1] (kol′əm bīn′), *n.* 1. a plant, *Aquilegia caerula,* of the buttercup family, having showy flowers with white petals and white to blue sepals that form long, backward spurs: the state flower of Colorado. 2. any of various other plants of the genus *Aquilegia,* characterized by divided leaves and showy flowers of various colors. [1275–1325; ME < ML *columbīna* (*herba*) dove-like (plant), fem. of L *columbīnus* (see COLUMBINE[2]); the inverted flower looks like a group of doves]

col•um•bine[2] (kol′əm bīn′, -bin), *adj.* 1. of a dove. 2. dovelike; dove-colored. [1350–1400; ME < L *columbīnus,* equiv. to *columb(a)* dove + *-īnus* -INE[1]]

Col•um•bine (kol′əm bīn′), *n.* 1. a female character in commedia dell'arte and pantomime: sweetheart of Harlequin. 2. a female given name. [1720–30; < It *Columbina* lit., dovelike girl; see COLUMBINE[2]]

co•lum•bite (kə lum′bīt), *n.* a black, crystalline mineral, iron niobate, $(Fe, Mn)Nb_2O_6$, the principal ore of niobium, an end member of a series of solid solutions in which manganese and tantalum combine to form tantalite. [1795–1805; COLUMB(IUM) + -ITE[1]]

co•lum•bi•um (kə lum′bē əm), *n. Chem.* (formerly) niobium. *Symbol:* Cb [1801; COLUMB(IA) (def. 7) + -IUM]

co•lum•bous (kə lum′bəs), *adj. Chem.* niobous. [COLUMB(IUM) + -OUS]

Co•lum•bus (kə lum′bəs), *n.* 1. **Christopher** (Sp. *Cristóbal Colón;* It. *Cristoforo Colombo*), 1446?–1506, Italian navigator in Spanish service: traditionally considered the discoverer of America 1492. 2. a city in and the capital of Ohio, in the central part. 564,871. 3. a city in W Georgia. 169,441. 4. a city in central Indiana. 30,292. 5. a city in E Mississippi. 27,383. 6. a city in E Nebraska. 17,328.

Colum′bus Air′ Force′ Base′, U.S. Air Force installation in NE Mississippi, NW of Columbus.

Colum′bus Day′, a day, October 12, observed as a holiday in various states of the U.S. in honor of the discovery of the New World by Columbus and his landing in the West Indies on October 12, 1492: observed in some states as the second Monday in October. [1890–95, *Amer.*]

col•u•mel•la (kol′yə mel′ə), *n., pl.* **-mel•lae** (-mel′ē). *Biol.* 1. a. any of various small, columnlike structures of animals or plants; rod or axis. b. *Mycol.* a small central column of sterile tissue within the sporangium of certain fungi, liverworts, and mosses. 2. a small bone in the ear of amphibians, reptiles, and birds. [1575–85; < L: small column, equiv. to *colum-* (var. of *column-,* s. of *columna* COLUMN) + *-ella* -ELLE] —**col′u•mel′lar,** *adj.* —**col•u•mel•late** (kol′yə mel′it, -āt), *adj.*

col•u•mel•li•form (kol′yə mel′ə fôrm′), *adj.* like a columella. [1830–40; COLUMELL(A) + -I- + -FORM]

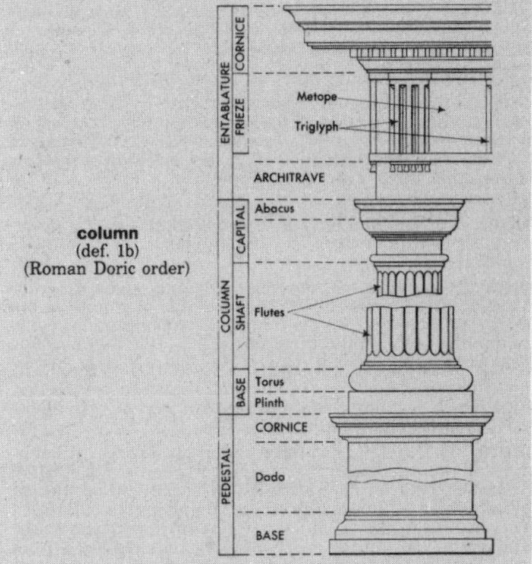

column
(def. 1b)
(Roman Doric order)

col•umn (kol′əm), *n.* 1. *Archit.* a. a rigid, relatively slender, upright support, composed of relatively few pieces. b. a decorative pillar, most often composed of stone and typically having a cylindrical or polygonal shaft with a capital and usually a base. 2. any column-like object, mass, or formation: *a column of smoke.* 3. a vertical row or list: *Add this column of figures.* 4. a vertical arrangement on a page of horizontal lines of type, usually typographically justified: *There are three columns on this page.* 5. a regular feature or series of articles in a newspaper, magazine, or the like, usually having a readily identifiable heading and the byline of the writer or editor, that reports or comments upon a particular field of interest, as politics, theater, or etiquette, or which may contain letters from readers, answers to readers' queries, etc. 6. a long, narrow formation of troops in which there are more members in line in the direction of movement than at right angles to the direction (distinguished from *line*). 7. a formation of ships in single file. 8. *Bot.* a columnlike structure in an orchid flower, composed of the united stamens and style. [1400–50; late ME *columne* < L *columna,* equiv. to *colum(e)n* peak + *-a* fem. ending; akin to EXCEL; r. late ME *colompne* < AF < L, as above] —**col′umned** (kol′-əmd), **col•um•nat•ed** (kol′əm nā′tid), *adj.*
—**Syn.** 1. COLUMN, PILLAR refer to upright supports in architectural structures. PILLAR is the general word: *the pillars supporting the roof.* A COLUMN is a particular kind of pillar, esp. one with an identifiable shaft, base, and capital: *columns of the Corinthian order.*

co•lum•nar (kə lum′nər), *adj.* 1. shaped like a column. 2. characterized by columns: *columnar architecture.* 3. Also, **co•lum′nal.** printed, arranged, etc., in columns: *data in columnar form.* [1720–30; < LL *columnāris,* equiv. to *column(a)* COLUMN + *-āris* -AR[1]] —**co•lum•nar•i•ty** (kol′əm nar′i tē), *n.*

colum′nar epithe′lium, *Biol.* epithelium consisting of one or more layers of elongated cells of cylindrical or prismatic shape.

CONCISE PRONUNCIATION KEY: act, cāpe, dâre, pärt; set, ēqual; if, īce; ox, ōver, ôrder, oil, bo͝ok, bo͞ot, out; up, ûrge; child; sing; shoe; thin, *th*at; zh as in *treasure.* ə = *a* as in *alone, e* as in *system, i* as in *easily, o* as in *gallop, u* as in *circus;* ə as in *fire* (fīər), *hour* (ouər). l and n can serve as syllabic consonants, as in *cradle* (krād′l), and *button* (but′n). See the full key inside the front cover.

co·lum·nar·ized (kə lum′nə rīzd′), *adj.* columnar (def. 3). [COLUMNAR + -IZE + -ED[2]]

colum′nar joint′ing, (in basaltic igneous rocks) a series of generally hexagonal columns formed by vertical joints as a result of contraction during cooling.

col′umn chromatog′raphy, *Chem.* See under **chromatography.**

co·lum·ne·a (kə lum′nē ə), *n.* any of various vines or shrubs of the genus *Columnea,* native to tropical America, that have tubular, showy, two-lipped flowers and are often cultivated as houseplants. [< NL (Linnaeus), equiv. to *column(a),* Latinized form of Fabio *Colonna* (1567–ca. 1640), Italian writer on plants + *-ea* -EA]

co·lum·ni·a·tion (kə lum′nē ā′shən), *n. Archit.* **1.** the employment of columns. **2.** the system of columns in a structure. [1585–95; extracted from INTERCOLUMNIATION]

col′umn inch′, *Print.* type one column wide and 1 in. (2.54 cm) deep. [1935–40]

col·um·nist (kol′əm nist, -ə mist), *n.* the writer or editor of a newspaper or magazine column. [1915–20; *Amer.*; COLUMN + -IST]

col′umn kra′ter, kelebe.

col′umn vec′tor, *Math.* a collection of numbers, as the components of a vector, written vertically. Cf. **row vector.**

co·lure (kə lo͝or′, kō-, kō′lo͝or), *n. Astron.* either of two great circles of the celestial sphere intersecting each other at the poles, one passing through both equinoxes and the other through both solstices. [1540–50; < LL *colūrus* < Gk *kólouros* dock-tailed, equiv. to *kól(os)* docked + *-ouros* -tailed, adj. deriv. of *ourá* tail; so called because the lower part is permanently hidden beneath the horizon]

co·ly (kō′lē), *n., pl.* **-lies.** any of several slender, fruit-eating, African birds constituting the family Coliidae, having grayish-brown plumage and a long, pointed tail. Also called **mousebird.** [< NL *colius* < Gk *koliós* green woodpecker]

col·za (kol′zə, kōl′-), *n.* rape[2]. [1705–15; < F < D *koolzaad,* equiv. to *kool* COLE + *zaad* SEED]

col′za oil′. *Chem.* See **rape oil.**

COM (kom), *n.* computer output on microfilm.

com-, a prefix meaning "with," "together," "in association," and (with intensive force) "completely," occurring in loanwords from Latin (*commit*): used in the formation of compound words before *b, p, m: combine; compare; commingle.* Also, **co-, col-, con-, cor-.** [< L, var. of prep. *cum* with]

Com., 1. Commander. **2.** Commission. **3.** Commissioner. **4.** Committee. **5.** Commodore. **6.** Commonwealth.

com., 1. comedy. **2.** comma. **3.** command. **4.** commander. **5.** commerce. **6.** commercial. **7.** commission. **8.** commissioner. **9.** committee. **10.** common. **11.** commonly. **12.** communications.

co·ma[1] (kō′mə), *n., pl.* **-mas.** a state of prolonged unconsciousness, including a lack of response to stimuli, from which it is impossible to rouse a person. [1640–50; < Gk *kôma* deep sleep]

co·ma[2] (kō′mə), *n., pl.* **-mae** (-mē). **1.** *Astron.* the nebulous envelope around the nucleus of a comet. **2.** *Optics.* a monochromatic aberration of a lens or other optical system in which the image from a point source cannot be brought into focus, the image of a point having the shape of a comet. **3.** *Bot.* **a.** a tuft of silky hairs at the end of a seed. **b.** the leafy crown of a tree; cluster of leaves at the end of a stem. **c.** a terminal cluster of bracts, as in the pineapple. [1660–70; < L: hair < Gk *kómē*]

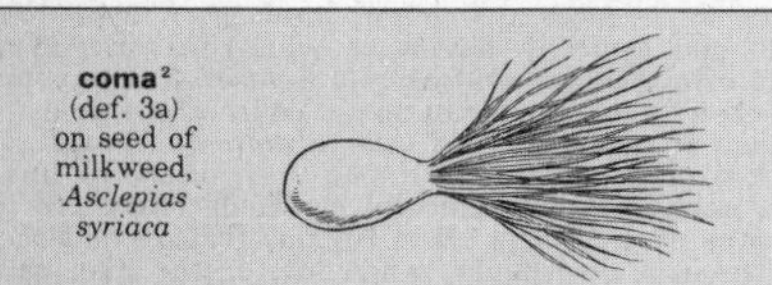
coma[2] (def. 3a) on seed of milkweed, *Asclepias syriaca*

Co·ma Ber·e·ni·ces (kō′mə ber′ə nī′sēz), *gen.* **Co·mae Ber·e·ni·ces** (kō′mē ber′ə nī′sēz). *Astron.* Berenice's Hair, a northern constellation situated north of Virgo and between Boötes and Leo. [< L]

co·mak·er (kō mā′kər, kō′mā′kər), *n. Finance.* a person who formally undertakes to discharge the duties of the maker of an instrument, esp. a promissory note, in the event of the maker's default. [1930–35; CO- + MAKER]

co·mal (kō mäl′; *Sp.* kô mäl′), *n., pl.* **co·mals,** *Sp.* ***co·ma·les*** (kô mä′les). a griddle made from sandstone or earthenware. [1835–45, *Amer.*; < MexSp < Nahuatl *comālli*]

co·man·age (kō man′ij), *v.t., v.i.,* **-aged, -ag·ing.** to manage jointly. —**co·man′a·ger,** *n.* —**co·man′age·ment,** *n.*

Co·man·che (kə man′chē, kō-), *n., pl.* **-ches,** (*esp. collectively*) **-che** for 1. **1.** a member of a Shoshonean tribe, the only tribe of the group living entirely on the Plains, formerly ranging from Wyoming to Texas, now in Oklahoma. **2.** the dialect of Shoshone spoken by the Comanche. [1800–10, *Amer.*; < AmerSp < Southern Paiute *kimmanci-,* as in *kimmanciŋʷt* strangers, Shoshones; or < a related word in another Numic language]

co·man·che·ro (kō′man châr′ō; *Sp.* kô′män che′rô), *n., pl.* **-che·ros** (-châr′ōz; *Sp.* -che′rôs). an Indian trader in the U.S. Southwest, esp. in the 19th century. [< AmerSp (Texas, New Mexico), equiv. to *comanch(e)* COMANCHE + *-ero* < L *-ārius* -ARY]

co·man·dan·te (kom′ən dan′tē; *Sp., It.* kô′män dän′te), *n., pl.* **-tes** (-tēz; *Sp.* -tes), *It.* **-ti** (-tē). commandant. [< Sp, It]

Co·ma·neci (kō′mə nēch′, -näch′; *Rum.* kô′mä-nech′), *n.* **Na·di·a** (nä′dē ə, näd′yə), born 1961, Rumanian gymnast.

co·mate[1] (kō māt′), *n.* a mate or companion. [1570–80; CO- + MATE[1]]

co·mate[2] (kō′māt), *adj.* **1.** *Bot.* having a coma. **2.** hairy; tufted. [1590–1600; < L *comātus.* See COMA[2], -ATE[1]]

co·mat·ic (kō mat′ik), *adj. Optics.* of, pertaining to, or blurred as a result of a coma. [COMA[2] + -IC; *-t-* irreg. by influence of COMATOSE]

com·a·tose (kom′ə tōs′, kō′mə-), *adj.* **1.** affected with or characterized by coma. **2.** lacking alertness or energy; torpid: *comatose from lack of sleep.* [1745–55; < Gk *komat-* (s. of *kôma* COMA[1]) + -OSE[1]] —**com′a·tose′·ly,** *adv.* —**com′a·tose′ness, com·a·tos·i·ty** (kom′ə-tos′i tē), *n.*

co·mat·u·lid (kə mach′ə lid), *n.* a free-swimming, stalkless crinoid; feather star. [1880–85; < NL *Comatulidae,* equiv. to *Comatul(a)* genus name (see COMATE[2], -ULE) + *-idae* -ID[2]]

Co·ma·ya·gua (kô′mä yä′gwä), *n.* a city in W central Honduras. 27,261.

comb[1] (kōm), *n.* **1.** a toothed strip of plastic, hard rubber, bone, wood, or metal, used for arranging the hair, untangling it, or holding it in place. **2.** a currycomb. **3.** any comblike instrument, object, or formation. **4.** the fleshy, more or less serrated outgrowth on the head of certain gallinaceous birds, esp. the domestic fowl. **5.** something resembling or suggesting this, as the crest of a wave. **6.** a honeycomb, or any similar group of cells. **7.** a machine for separating choice cotton or wool fibers from noil. **8.** a comblike instrument for imparting a grainlike finish to a painted surface. **9.** *Chiefly Midland and Southern U.S.* a ridge of a roof. **10.** a series of springlike prongs projecting from a spine, usually of plastic, for making a loose-leaf binding. **11.** a trowel having a notched edge for applying adhesives in setting tiles or the like. **12.** *Armor.* a ridge along the top of a helmet, esp. of the morion. **13.** *Masonry.* drag (def. 31). **14.** the upper edge of the buttstock of a rifle or shotgun. —*v.t.* **15.** to arrange or adorn (the hair) with a comb. **16.** to use (something) in the manner of a comb: *She was slowly combing her fingers through her hair.* **17.** to remove (anything undesirable) with or as if with a comb: *She combed the snarls out of her hair. They combed the cowards from the group.* **18.** to search everywhere in: *He combed the files for the missing letter.* **19.** to separate (textile fibers) with a comb. **20.** to scrape with or as with a comb. **21.** to sweep across; rake: *High winds combed the seacoast.* —*v.i.* **22.** to roll over or break at the crest, as a wave. [bef. 900; ME; OE *comb, camb;* c. OHG *kamb* (G *Kamm*), ON *kambr,* Gk *gómphos* pin, peg, *gomphíos* molar tooth; see CAM] —**comb′less,** *adj.* —**comb′less·ness,** *n.*

comb[2] (ko͞om, kōm), *n.* combe.

comb., 1. combination. **2.** combined. **3.** combining. **4.** combustion.

com·bat (*v.* kəm bat′, kom′bat, kum′-; *n.* kom′bat, kum′-), *v.,* **-bat·ed, -bat·ing** or (*esp. Brit.*) **-bat·ted, -bat·ting,** *n.* —*v.t.* **1.** to fight or contend against; oppose vigorously: *to combat crime.* —*v.i.* **2.** to battle; contend: *to combat with disease.* —*n.* **3.** *Mil.* active, armed fighting with enemy forces. **4.** a fight, struggle, or controversy, as between two persons, teams, or ideas. [1535–45; < MF *combat* (n.), *combattre* (v.) < LL *combattere,* equiv. to L *com-* COM- + LL *battere,* for L *battuere* to strike, beat] —**com·bat′a·ble,** *adj.*
—**Syn. 1, 2.** struggle, contest.

com·bat·ant (kəm bat′nt, kom′bə tənt, kum′-), *n.* **1.** a nation engaged in active fighting with enemy forces. **2.** a person or group that fights. —*adj.* **3.** combating; fighting: *the combatant armies.* **4.** disposed to combat; combative. [1425–75; late ME *combataunt* < MF *combatant.* See COMBAT, -ANT]

com′bat boot′, a heavy, usually laced and close-fitting boot of hard leather extending above the ankle and having a sole and heel of hard rubber.

com′bat fatigue′. See **battle fatigue.** [1940–45]

Com′bat In′fantryman Badge′, *Mil.* a badge awarded to an infantryman in recognition of satisfactory performance of duty in ground combat against the enemy.

com·bat·ive (kəm bat′iv, kom′bə tiv, kum′-), *adj.* ready or inclined to fight; pugnacious: *He displayed a most unpleasant, combative attitude.* [1825–35; COMBAT + -IVE] —**com·bat′ive·ly,** *adv.* —**com·bat′ive·ness, com·ba·tiv·i·ty** (kom′bə tiv′i tē), *n.*

com′bat jack′et. See **battle jacket.**

com′bat neuro′sis. See **battle fatigue.** [1955–60]

com·bat-read·y (kom′bat red′ē, kum′-), *adj.* sufficiently equipped, trained, and numerically strong to engage an enemy.

com′bat team′, *Mil.* a combination of military units, usually of different types, as infantry and artillery, temporarily under one command while on special combat mission.

com′bat zone′, 1. *Mil.* an area in a theater of operations where combat forces operate, extending typically from the front line to the communications zone. **2.** *Slang.* an area in some cities, usually in an older mid-town section, where pornography stores, striptease bars, etc., flourish, or are tolerated because of being concentrated in one district. [1935–40]

comb′ back′, a Windsor chair back in which the vertical spindles are surmounted by a broad, carved crest rail resembling a comb. [1900–05]

combe (ko͞om, kōm), *n. Brit.* a narrow valley or deep hollow, esp. one enclosed on all but one side. Also, **comb, coomb, coombe.** [OE *cumb* valley < British Celtic; cf. CWM]

Combe′-Ca·pelle′ man′ (kōm′ka pel′), a skeleton of the early Upper Paleolithic Perigordian culture in France. [1910–15; named after *Combe-Capelle* (near Périgueux, France) where the remains were found]

combed′ yarn′, cotton or worsted yarn of fibers laid parallel, superior in smoothness to carded yarn.

comb·er (kō′mər), *n.* **1.** a person or thing that combs. **2.** a long, curling wave. [1640–50; COMB[1] + -ER[1]]

comb′er board′, (in weaving) a wooden frame pierced with a series of small holes through which the harness cords are threaded, used to regulate the cords and determine the texture and width of a repeat in a fabric. [1825–35]

comb′-foot·ed spi′der (kōm′fo͝ot′id), any of numerous spiders constituting the family Theridiidae, having a comblike row of bristles on the tarsi of the hind legs.

com·bin·a·ble (kəm bī′nə bəl), *adj.* capable of combining or being combined. [1740–50; COMBINE + -ABLE] —**com·bin′a·bil′i·ty, com·bin′a·ble·ness,** *n.* —**com·bin′a·bly,** *adv.*

com·bi·na·tion (kom′bə nā′shən), *n.* **1.** the act of combining or the state of being combined. **2.** a number of things combined: *a combination of ideas.* **3.** something formed by combining: *A chord is a combination of notes.* **4.** an alliance of persons or parties: *a combination in restraint of trade.* **5.** the set or series of numbers or letters used in setting the mechanism of a combination lock. **6.** the parts of the mechanism operated by this. **7.** Often, **combinations.** a suit of underwear in one piece. **8.** *Math.* **a.** the arrangement of elements into various groups without regard to their order in the group. **b.** a group thus formed. Cf. **permutation** (def. 1). [1350–1400; ME *combinacyoun* (< MF) < LL *combinātiōn-* (s. of *combinātiō*), equiv. to *combināt(us)* combined (see COMBINE, -ATE[1]) + *-iōn-* -ION] —**com′bi·na′tion·al,** *adj.*
—**Syn. 1.** association, conjunction, union, coalescence, blending. **2.** mixture, amalgamation, amalgam. **4.** association, federation, league, coalition, cartel, combine, monopoly, bloc, cabal, conspiracy.

combina′tion door′, an outside door having a frame into which different types of panels can be inserted, as a screen for summer or storm sash for winter.

combina′tion last′, a shoe last that has a narrower heel or instep than the standard last.

combina′tion lock′, a lock opened by rotating one or more specially marked dials a given number of times through a particular set of positions in a prescribed order and direction. [1850–55]

combina′tion prin′ciple, *Physics.* See **Ritz combination principle.** [1835–45]

combina′tion shot′, a shot in pool in which the cue ball strikes at least one object ball before contact is made with the ball to be pocketed. [1905–10]

combina′tion square′, an adjustable device for carpenters, used as a try square, miter square, level, etc.

com·bi·na·tive (kom′bə nā′tiv, kəm bī′nə-), *adj.* **1.** tending or serving to combine. **2.** of, pertaining to, or resulting from combination. [1850–55; COMBINAT(ION) + -IVE]

com·bi·na·to·ri·al (kəm bī′nə tôr′ē əl, -tōr′-, kom′-bə-), *adj.* **1.** of, pertaining to, or involving the combination of elements, as in phonetics or music. **2.** of or pertaining to the enumeration of the number of ways of doing some specific task or of arranging items in a specific configuration. **3.** *Math.* of or pertaining to combination, or the modes, properties, etc., of combinations. [1810–20; COMBINATORY + -AL[1]] —**com·bi′na·to′ri·al·ly,** *adv.*

combinato′rial anal′ysis, *Math.* the branch of mathematics that deals with permutations and combinations, esp. used in statistics and probability. [1810–20]

combinato′rial topol′ogy, *Math.* the branch of topology that deals with the properties of geometric figures by considering the figures as being composed of elementary geometric figures, as points or lines. [‡1950–55]

com·bi·na·tor·ics (kəm bī′nə tôr′iks, -tor′-, kom′-bə-), *n.* (*used with singular v.*) See **combinatorial analysis.**

com·bin·a·to·ry (kəm bī′nə tôr′ē, -tōr′ē), *adj.* **1.** combinative. **2.** combinatorial. [1640–50; COMBINAT(ION) + -ORY[1]]

com·bine (*v.* kəm bīn′ *for 1, 2, 6,* kom′bīn *for 3, 7; n.* kom′bīn, kəm bīn′ *for 8, 9,* kom′bīn *for 10*), *v.,* **-bined, -bin·ing,** *n.* —*v.t.* **1.** to bring into or join in a close union or whole; unite: *She combined the ingredients to make the cake. They combined the two companies.* **2.** to possess or exhibit in union: *a plan that combines the best features of several other plans.* **3.** to harvest (grain) with a combine. —*v.i.* **4.** to unite; coalesce: *The clay combined with the water to form a thick paste.* **5.** to unite for a common purpose; join forces: *After the two factions combined, they proved invincible.* **6.** to enter into chemical union. **7.** to use a combine in harvesting. —*n.* **8.** a combination. **9.** a combination of persons or groups for the furtherance of their political, commercial, or other interests, as a syndicate, cartel, or trust. **10.** a harvesting machine for cutting and threshing grain in the field. [1375–1425; late ME *combinen* (< MF *combiner*) < LL *combināre,* equiv. to *com-* COM- + *-bināre,* v. deriv. of *bīnī* by twos (cf. BINARY)] —**com·bin′er,** *n.*
—**Syn. 1.** compound, amalgamate. See **mix. 9.** merger, monopoly, alignment, bloc. —**Ant. 1, 4.** separate.

com•bined (kəm bīnd′), *adj.* **1.** made by combining; joined; united, as in a chemical compound. **2.** taken as a whole or considered together; in the aggregate: *outselling all other brands combined.* [1375–1425; late ME; see COMBINE, -ED[2]] —**com•bined•ly** (kəm bīnd′lē, -bī′nid-), *adv.* —**com•bined′ness,** *n.*

combined′ opera′tions, war operations carried out cooperatively by two or more allied nations or by coordination of the land, sea, and air forces of one or more nations. [1835–45]

comb•ings (kō′mingz), *n.pl.* hairs removed with a comb or a brush. [1565–75; COMB[1] + -ING[1] + -S[3]]

combin′ing form′, *Gram.* a linguistic form that occurs only in combination with other forms. In word formation, a combining form may conjoin with an independent word (*mini-* + *skirt*), another combining form (*photo-* + *-graphy*), or an affix (*cephal-* + *-ic*); it is thus distinct from an affix, which can be added to either a free word or a combining form but not solely to another affix (*Iceland* + *-ic* or *cephal-* + *-ic* but not *pro-* + *-ic*). There are three types of combining forms: (1) forms borrowed from Greek or Latin that are derivatives of independent nouns, adjectives, or verbs in those languages; these combining forms, used in the formation of learned coinages, often semantically parallel independent words in English (cf., for example, *cardio-* in relation to *heart*, *-phile* in relation to *lover*) and usually appear only in combination with other combining forms of Greek or Latin origin (*bibliophile,* not *bookphile*); (2) the compounding form of a free-standing English word; such a combining form usually has only a single, restricted sense of the free word, and may differ from the word phonetically. Cf. **-proof, -wide, -worthy, -land, -man;** (3) a form extracted from an existing free word and used as a bound form, typically maintaining the meaning of the free word, or some facet of it. Cf. **heli-**[2]**, mini-, para-**[3]**, -aholic, -gate, -orama.** Note that the term "combining form" does not specify placement before or after the element to which the form is attached. Cf. **affix.** [1880–85]

combin′ing weight′, *Chem.* the atomic weight of an atom or radical divided by its valence.

comb′ jel′ly (kōm), any marine invertebrate of the phylum Ctenophora, comprising various nearly transparent creatures having rounded, oval, or band-shaped bodies propelled by eight iridescent appendages composed of cilia arranged like teeth on a comb. Also called **ctenophore.** [1885–90]

com•bo (kom′bō), *n., pl.* **-bos. 1.** *Informal.* **a.** a small jazz or dance band. Cf. **big band. b.** combination (defs. 2–4). **2.** *Australian Slang.* a white man living with Aborigines or having an Aborigine wife, usually in a common-law marriage. [1920–25; COMB(INATION) + -O]

com′bo store′, *Informal.* a combined drugstore and supermarket.

comb-out (kōm′out′), *n.* a thorough combing or brushing of the hair. [1915–20; n. use of v. phrase *comb out*]

com•bust (kəm bust′), *v.i., v.t.* burn. [1325–75; ME < L *combūstus* (ptp. of *combūrere* to burn up, equiv. to *com-* COM- + *-ūs-* var. s. of *ūrere* to burn + *-tus* ptp. suffix; *-b-* by misanalysis of *ambūrere,* another deriv., as *am-* + *-būrere*)]

com•bus•ti•ble (kəm bus′tə bəl), *adj.* **1.** capable of catching fire and burning; inflammable; flammable: *Gasoline vapor is highly combustible.* **2.** easily excited: *a high-strung, combustible nature.* —*n.* **3.** a combustible substance: *Trucks carrying combustibles will not be allowed to use this tunnel.* [1520–30; < LL *combūstibilis.* See COMBUST, -IBLE] —**com•bus′ti•bil′i•ty, com•bus′ti•ble•ness,** *n.* —**com•bus′ti•bly,** *adv.*

com•bus•tion (kəm bus′chən), *n.* **1.** the act or process of burning. **2.** *Chem.* **a.** rapid oxidation accompanied by heat and, usually, light. **b.** chemical combination attended by production of heat and light. **c.** slow oxidation not accompanied by high temperature and light. **3.** violent excitement; tumult. [1400–50; late ME (< MF) < LL *combūstiōn-* (s. of *combūstiō*). See COMBUST, -ION] —**com•bus′tive,** *adj.*

combus′tion cham′ber, *Mach.* a chamber, as in an engine or boiler, where combustion occurs. [1850–55]

combus′tion en′gine, any of various types of engines driven by energy produced by combustion.

combus′tion tube′, a tube of hard glass used esp. in a furnace for burning a substance in a current of air or oxygen. [1860–65]

com•bus•tor (kəm bus′tər), *n. Aeron.* the apparatus in a ramjet or other jet engine for initiating and sustaining combustion, consisting of the igniter, fuel-injection system, combustion chamber, and flameholder. [1940–45; COMBUST(ION) + -OR[2]]

comd. command.

comdg., commanding.

Comdr., commander. Also, **comdr.**

Comdt., commandant. Also, **comdt.**

come (kum), *v.,* **came, come, com•ing,** *n.* —*v.i.* **1.** to approach or move toward a particular person or place: *Come here. Don't come any closer!* **2.** to arrive by movement or in the course of progress: *The train from Boston is coming.* **3.** to approach or arrive in time, in succession, etc.: *Christmas comes once a year. I'll come to your question next.* **4.** to move into view; appear. **5.** to extend; reach: *The dress comes to her knees.* **6.** to take place; occur; happen: *Success comes to those who strive.* **7.** to occur at a certain point, position, etc.: *Tuesday comes after Monday. Her aria comes in the third act.* **8.** to be available, produced, offered, etc.: *Toothpaste comes in a tube.* **9.** to occur to the mind: *The idea just came to me.* **10.** to befall: *They promised no harm would come to us.* **11.** to issue; emanate; be derived: *Peaches come from trees. Good results do not come from careless work.* **12.** to arrive or appear as a result: *This comes of carelessness.* **13.** to enter or be brought into a specified state or condition: *to come into popular use.* **14.** to do or manage; fare: *She's coming along well with her work.* **15.** to enter into being or existence; be born: *The baby came at dawn.* **16.** to have been a resident or to be a native of (usually fol. by *from*): *She comes from Florida.* **17.** to become: *His shoes came untied.* **18.** to seem to become: *His fears made the menacing statues come alive. The work will come easy with a little practice.* **19.** (used in the imperative to call attention or to express impatience, anger, remonstrance, etc.): *Come, that will do!* **20.** to germinate, as grain. **21.** *Informal.* to have an orgasm.
—*v.t.* **22.** *Chiefly Brit.* to do; perform; accomplish. **23.** *Informal.* to play the part of: *to come the grande dame.* **24. come about, a.** to come to pass; happen. **b.** *Naut.* to tack. **25. come across, a.** Also, **come upon.** to find or encounter, esp. by chance: *I came across this picture when I was cleaning out the attic. We suddenly came upon a deer while walking in the woods.* **b.** *Informal.* to make good one's promise, as to pay a debt, do what is expected, etc.: *to come across with the rent.* **c.** to be understandable or convincing: *The moral of this story doesn't come across.* **d.** *Informal.* to make a particular impression; comport oneself: *She comes across as a very cold person.* **26. come again,** (used as a request to repeat a statement). **27. come along, a.** to accompany someone, attend as part of a group: *He didn't come along on the last trip.* **b.** to proceed, develop, or advance sufficiently or successfully: *The new project was coming along quite smoothly.* **c.** to appear; emerge as a factor or possibility: *Even if another job comes along this summer, I won't take it.* **28. come and go,** to occur briefly or suddenly but never for long; appear and disappear. **29. come around** or **round, a.** to recover consciousness; revive. **b.** to change one's opinion, decision, etc., esp. to agree with another's. **c.** to visit: *Come around more often.* **d.** to cease being angry, hurt, etc. **30. come at, a.** to arrive at; attain. **b.** to rush at; attack: *The watchdog came at the intruder.* **31. come back, a.** to return, esp. to one's memory: *It all comes back to me now.* **b.** to return to a former position or state. **c.** to talk back; retort: *to come back with a witty remark.* **32. come between,** to cause to be estranged or antagonized: *Love of money came between the brothers.* **33. come by,** to obtain; acquire: *How did he ever come by so much money?* **34. come down, a.** to lose wealth, rank, etc.; be reduced in circumstances or status. **b.** to be handed down by tradition or inheritance. **c.** to be relayed or passed along from a source of higher rank or authority: *The general's orders will come down tomorrow.* **d.** *Slang.* to take place; happen. **e.** *Slang.* to lose one's euphoria, enthusiasm, or esp. the effects of a drug high. **35. come down on** or **upon, a.** to voice one's opposition to: *She came down on increased spending and promised to cut the budget.* **b.** to reprimand; scold: *He came down on me for getting to work late.* **36. come down on the side of,** to support or favor: *I want to come down on the side of truth and justice.* **37. come down with,** to become afflicted with (an illness): *Many people came down with the flu this year.* **38. come forward,** to offer one's services; present oneself; volunteer: *When the president called for volunteers, several members of our group came forward.* **39. come home,** *Naut.* **a.** (of an anchor) to begin to drag. **b.** (of an object) to move when hauled upon. **40. come in, a.** to enter. **b.** to arrive. **c.** to come into use or fashion. **d.** to begin to produce or yield: *The oil well finally came in.* **e.** to be among the winners: *His horse came in and paid 5 to 1.* **f.** to finish in a race or any competition, as specified: *Our bobsled team came in fifth.* **41. come in for,** to receive; get; be subjected to: *This plan will no doubt come in for a great deal of criticism.* **42. come into, a.** to acquire; get. **b.** to inherit: *He came into a large fortune at the age of 21.* **43. come off,** *Informal.* **a.** to happen; occur. **b.** to reach the end; acquit oneself: *to come off with honors.* **c.** to be given or completed; occur; result: *Her speech came off very well.* **d.** to succeed; be successful: *The end of the novel just doesn't come off.* **44. come off it,** *Informal.* to stop being wrong, foolish, or pretentious; be truthful or honest: *Come off it—we know you're as poor as the rest of us.* **45. come on, a.** Also, **come upon.** to meet or find unexpectedly. **b.** to make progress; develop; flourish. **c.** to appear on stage; make one's entrance. **d.** to begin; appear: *The last showing will be coming on in a few minutes.* **e.** *Informal.* (used chiefly in the imperative) to hurry; begin: *Come on, before it rains!* **f.** *Informal.* (as an entreaty or attempt at persuasion) please: *Come on, go with us to the movies.* **g.** *Slang.* to try to make an impression or have an effect; present oneself: *She comes on a bit too strong for my taste.* **h.** *Slang.* to make sexual advances: *a Lothario who was always coming on with the women at the office.* **46. come on to,** *Slang.* to make sexual advances to. **47. come out, a.** to be published; appear. **b.** to become known; be revealed. **c.** to make a debut in society, the theater, etc. **d.** to end; terminate; emerge: *The fight came out badly, as both combatants were injured.* **e.** to make more or less public acknowledgment of being homosexual. **48. come out for,** to endorse or support publicly: *The newspaper came out for the reelection of the mayor.* **49. come out with, a.** to speak, esp. to confess or reveal something. **b.** to make available to the public; bring out: *The publisher is coming out with a revised edition of the textbook.* **50. come over, a.** to happen to; affect: *What's come over him?* **b.** to change sides or positions; change one's mind: *He was initially against the plan, but he's come over now.* **c.** to visit informally: *Our neighbors came over last night and we had a good chat.* **51. come round, a.** See **come** (def. 29). **b.** *Naut.* (of a sailing vessel) to head toward the wind; come to. **52. come through, a.** to endure or finish successfully. **b.** *Informal.* to do as expected or hoped; perform; succeed: *We knew you'd come through for us.* **c.** *Informal.* to experience religious conversion. **53. come to, a.** to recover consciousness. **b.** to amount to; total. **c.** *Naut.* to take the way off a vessel, as by bringing her head into the wind or anchoring. **54. come to pass,** to happen; occur. **55. come under, a.** to fit into a category or classification: *This play comes under the heading of social criticism.* **b.** to be the province or responsibility of: *This matter comes under the State Department.* **56. come up, a.** to be referred to; arise: *The subject kept coming up in conversation.* **b.** to be presented for action or discussion: *The farm bill comes up for consideration next Monday.* **57. come upon.** See **come** (defs. 25a, 45a). **58. come up to, a.** to approach; near: *A panhandler came up to us in the street.* **b.** to compare with as to quantity, excellence, etc.; match; equal: *This piece of work does not come up to your usual standard.* **59. come up with,** to produce; supply: *Can you come up with the right answer?* **60. come what may,** no matter what may happen; regardless of any opposition, argument, or consequences: *Come what may, he will not change his mind.* **61. where one is coming from,** *Slang.* where the source of one's beliefs, attitudes, or feelings lies: *It's hard to understand where your friend is coming from when he says such crazy things.*
—*n.* **62.** *Slang (vulgar).* semen. [bef. 900; ME *comen,* OE *cuman;* c. D *komen,* G *kommen,* Goth *qiman,* ON *koma,* L *venire* (see AVENUE), Gk *baínein* (see BASIS), Skt *gácchati* (he) goes]
—**Ant. 2.** leave, depart.

come-all-ye (kum′ôl′yē′), *n.* a street ballad, esp. in England. Also, **come-all-you** (kum′ôl′yōō′). [1885–90; after the invitation that often forms the opening line of such ballads]

come•back (kum′bak′), *n.* **1.** a return to a former higher rank, popularity, position, prosperity, etc.: *The ex-champion kept trying to make a comeback.* **2.** a clever or effective retort; rejoinder; riposte: *That was a great comeback the comedian made to the hecklers.* **3.** *Informal.* a basis or cause of complaint: *If you insist on buying these pointed shoes, you'll have no comeback when your toes start to hurt.* [1815–25; n. use of v. phrase *come back*]

COMECON (kom′i kon′), *n.* an economic association of Communist countries, established in 1949, to facilitate trade and development. Also, **Com′e•con.** Cf. **Common Market.** [*Co*(*uncil for*) *M*(*utual*) *Econ*(*omic Assistance*)]

co•me•di•an (kə mē′dē ən), *n.* **1.** a professional entertainer who amuses by relating anecdotes, acting out comical situations, engaging in humorous repartee, etc. **2.** an actor in comedy. **3.** a writer of comedy. **4.** any comical or amusing person. [1575–85; < MF *comediain;* see COMEDY, -IAN]

co•me•dic (kə mē′dik, -med′ik), *adj.* of, pertaining to, or of the nature of comedy. Also, **co•me′di•cal.** [1630–40; < L *cōmoedicus* < Gk *kōmōidikós,* equiv. to *kōmōid*(*ía*) COMEDY + *-ikos* -IC] —**co•me′di•cal•ly,** *adv.*

Co•mé•die Fran•çaise (kô mā dē fräɴ sez′), the French national theater, founded in Paris in 1680, famous for its repertoire of classical French drama. Also called **La Maison de Molière, Théâtre-Français.**

co•me•di•enne (kə mē′dē en′, -mā′-), *n.* a woman who is a comic entertainer or actress. [1855–60; < F *comédienne;* see COMEDIAN, -ENNE]
—**Usage.** See **-enne.**

com•e•dist (kom′i dist), *n.* a writer of comedies. [1810–20; COMED(Y) + -IST]

com•e•do (kom′i dō′), *n., pl.* **com•e•dos, com•e•do•nes** (kom′i dō′nēz). *Med.* a thickened secretion plugging a duct of the skin, esp. of a sebaceous gland; blackhead. [1865–70; < NL; L: glutton, equiv. to *comed*(*ere*) to consume, eat up (*com-* COM- + *edere* to EAT) + *-ō* agent suffix]

come•down (kum′doun′), *n.* an unexpected or humiliating descent from dignity, importance, or wealth. [1555–65; n. use of v. phrase *come down*]

com•e•dy (kom′i dē), *n., pl.* **-dies. 1.** a play, movie, etc., of light and humorous character with a happy or cheerful ending; a dramatic work in which the central motif is the triumph over adverse circumstance, resulting in a successful or happy conclusion. **2.** that branch of the drama which concerns itself with this form of composition. **3.** the comic element of drama, of literature generally, or of life. **4.** any literary composition dealing with a theme suitable for comedy, or employing the methods of comedy. **5.** any comic or humorous incident or series of incidents. [1350–1400; ME *comedye* < ML *cōmēdia,* L *cōmoedia* < Gk *kōmōidía,* equiv. to *kōmōid*(*ós*) comedian (*kômo*(*s*) merry-making + *aoidós* singer) + *-ia* -Y[3]] —**co•me•di•al** (kə mē′dē əl), *adj.*
—**Syn. 5.** jesting, humor, pleasantry, banter.

Com′edy of Er′rors, The, an early comedy (1594) by Shakespeare.

com′edy of man′ners, a comedy satirizing the manners and customs of a social class, esp. one dealing with the amorous intrigues of fashionable society. [1815–25]

come-hith•er (kum′hith′ər, kə mith′-), *adj.* inviting or enticing, esp. in a sexually provocative manner; beckoning: *a come-hither look.* [1895–1900; adj., n. use of impv. phrase *come hither*] —**come′-hith′er•ness,** *n.*

come•ly (kum′lē), *adj.,* **-li•er, -li•est. 1.** pleasing in appearance; attractive; fair: *a comely face.* **2.** proper; seemly; becoming: *comely behavior.* [bef. 1000; ME *cumli,* OE *cȳmlic* lovely, equiv. to *cȳme* exquisite (c. MHG *kūme* weak, tender, G *kaum* (adv.) with difficulty, OHG *kūmo*) + *-lic* -LY] —**come′li•ly,** *adv.* —**come′li•ness,** *n.*
—**Syn. 1.** pretty, handsome, beautiful, good-looking, personable. —**Ant. 1.** unattractive.

Co•me•ni•us (kə mē′nē əs), *n.* **John Amos** (*Jan Amos Komenský*), 1592–1670, Moravian educational reformer and bishop.

come-on (kum′on′, -ôn′), *n. Slang.* inducement; lure. [1895–1900, *Amer.*; n. use of v. phrase *come on*]

come-out•er (kum′ou′tər), *n. Informal.* an outspoken or very active supporter of a cause, esp. a reformer or a social activist. [1830–40, *Amer.*; *come out* + -ER[1]]

com•er (kum′ər), *n.* **1.** *Informal.* a person or thing

CONCISE PRONUNCIATION KEY: act, cāpe, dâre, pärt; set, ēqual; *if,* ice; ox, ōver, ôrder, oil, bŏŏk, bōōt, out; up, ûrge; child; sing; shoe; thin, that; zh as in *treasure.* ə = *a* as in *alone, e* as in *system, i* as in *easily, o* as in *gallop, u* as in *circus;* ə as in *fire* (fīər), *hour* (ouər). l and n can serve as syllabic consonants, as in *cradle* (krād′l), and *button* (but′n). See the full key inside the front cover.

that is progressing well or is very promising: *He looks like a comer in state politics.* **2.** a person or thing that arrives. [1325–75; ME; see COME, -ER[1]]

co•mes (kō′mēz), *n., pl.* **com•i•tes** (kom′i tēz′). **1.** *Astron.* companion[1] (def. 6). **2.** *Anat.* a blood vessel accompanying another vessel or a nerve. [1675–85; < L: traveling companion, prob. < **com-it-s,* equiv. to *com-* COM- + *-it-* n. deriv. of *īre* to go + *-s* nom. sing. ending]

co•mes•ti•ble (kə mes′tə bəl), *adj.* **1.** edible; eatable. —*n.* **2.** Usually, **comestibles.** articles of food; edibles: *The table was spread with all kinds of comestibles.* [1475–85; < LL *comēstibilis,* equiv. to L *comēst(us),* ptp. of *comedere* to eat up (see COMEDO; *-ēstus* for *-ēs(s)us* by analogy with *gestus, ūstus,* etc.; see GEST[1], COMBUST) + *-ibilis* -IBLE; see EAT]

com•et (kom′it), *n. Astron.* a celestial body moving about the sun, usually in a highly eccentric orbit, consisting of a central mass surrounded by an envelope of dust and gas that may form a tail that streams away from the sun. [1150–1200; ME *comete* < AF, OF < L *comētēs, comēta* < Gk *komḗtēs* wearing long hair, equiv. to *komē-,* var. s. of *komân* to let one's hair grow (deriv. of *kómē* hair) + *-tēs* agent suffix] —**com•et•ar•y** (kom′i ter′ē), **co•met•ic** (kə met′ik), **co•met′i•cal,** *adj.* —**com′et•like′,** *adj.*

com•eth (kum′ith), *v. Archaic.* 3rd pers. sing. pres. indic. of **come.**

come•up•pance (kum′up′əns), *n. Informal.* deserved reward or just deserts, usually unpleasant: *He finally got his comeuppance for his misbehavior.* [1855–60, *Amer.*; from phrase *come up* + -ANCE]

COMEX (kō′meks), *n.* Commodity Exchange, New York.

com•fit (kum′fit, kom′-), *n.* a candy containing a nut or piece of fruit. [1300–50; ME *confit* < MF < L *confectum* something prepared. See CONFECT]

com•fort (kum′fərt), *v.t.* **1.** to soothe, console, or reassure; bring cheer to: *They tried to comfort her after her loss.* **2.** to make physically comfortable. **3.** *Obs.* to aid; support or encourage. —*n.* **4.** relief in affliction; consolation; solace: *Her presence was a comfort to him.* **5.** a feeling of relief or consolation: *Her forgiveness afforded him great comfort.* **6.** a person or thing that gives consolation: *She was a great comfort to him.* **7.** a cause or matter of relief or satisfaction: *The patient's recovery was a comfort to the doctor.* **8.** a state of ease and satisfaction of bodily wants, with freedom from pain and anxiety: *He is a man who enjoys his comfort.* **9.** something that promotes such a state: *His wealth allows him to enjoy a high degree of comfort.* **10.** *Chiefly Midland and Southern U.S.* a comforter or quilt. **11.** *Obs.* strengthening aid; assistance. [1175–1225; (v.) ME *comfortien,* var. of *confortien, conforten* < AF, OF *conforter* < LL *confortāre* to strengthen, equiv. to *con-* CON- + *-fortāre* v. deriv. of L *fortis* strong; (n.) ME < AF, OF, n. deriv. of the v.] —**com′fort•less,** *adj.*
—**Syn. 1.** pacify, calm, solace, gladden. COMFORT, CONSOLE, RELIEVE, SOOTHE imply assuaging sorrow, worry, discomfort, or pain. To COMFORT is to lessen the sadness or sorrow of someone and to strengthen by inspiring with hope and restoring a cheerful outlook: *to comfort a despairing person.* CONSOLE, a more formal word, means to make grief or distress seem lighter, by means of kindness and thoughtful attentions: *to console a bereaved parent.* RELIEVE means to lighten, lessen, or remove pain, trouble, discomfort, or hardship: *to relieve a needy person.* SOOTHE means to pacify or calm: *to soothe a child.* **1, 2.** ease. **8.** See **ease.**

com•fort•a•ble (kumf′tə bəl, kum′fər tə bəl), *adj.* **1.** (of clothing, furniture, etc.) producing or affording physical comfort, support, or ease: *a comfortable chair; comfortable shoes.* **2.** being in a state of physical or mental comfort; contented and undisturbed; at ease: *to be comfortable in new shoes; I don't feel comfortable in the same room with her.* **3.** (of a person, situation, etc.) producing mental comfort or ease; easy to accommodate oneself to or associate with: *She's a comfortable person to be with.* **4.** more than adequate or sufficient: *a comfortable salary.* **5.** *Obs.* cheerful. —*n.* **6.** *Chiefly Northern U.S.* a quilted bedcover; comforter. [1350–1400; ME < AF *confortable.* See COMFORT, -ABLE] —**com′fort•a•ble•ness, com′fort•a•bil′i•ty,** *n.* —**com′fort•a•bly,** *adv.*

com•fort•er (kum′fər tər), *n.* **1.** a person or thing that comforts. **2.** a quilt. **3.** a long, woolen scarf, usually knitted. **4. the Comforter.** See **Holy Ghost.** [1300–50; ME *comfortour* < AF, OF *conforteor,* equiv. to *confort(er)* (see COMFORT) + *-eor* < L *-ōr-* -OR[1] or *-ātōr-* -ATOR]

com•fort•ing kum′fər ting), *adj.* affording comfort or solace. [1250–1300; ME; see COMFORT, -ING[2]] —**com′•fort•ing•ly,** *adv.*

com′fort let′ter, an informal statement assuring the financial soundness or backing of a company.

com′fort sta′tion, a room or building with toilet and lavatory facilities for public use. [1905–10, *Amer.*]

com′fort zone′, the range of atmospheric temperature and humidity considered comfortable for most people.

com•frey (kum′frē), *n., pl.* **-freys.** any coarse Eurasian plant belonging to the genus *Symphytum,* of the borage family, as the widely cultivated *S. officinale,* having hairy, lance-shaped leaves and drooping clusters of small, white, rose-colored, or purplish flowers. [1275–1325; ME *cumfirie, cumfere* < AF *cumfirie,* OF *confire* < ML **confervia* for L *conferva* CONFERVA]

com•fy (kum′fē), *adj.,* **-fi•er, -fi•est.** *Informal.* comfortable. [1820–30; COMF(ORTABLE) + -Y[2], anomalously forming an adj.] —**com′fi•ly,** *adv.* —**com′fi•ness,** *n.*

com•ic (kom′ik), *adj.* **1.** of, pertaining to, or characterized by comedy: *comic opera.* **2.** of or pertaining to a person who acts in or writes comedy: *a comic actor; a comic dramatist.* **3.** of, pertaining to, or characteristic of comedy: *comic situations; a comic sense.* **4.** provoking laughter; humorous; funny; laughable. —*n.* **5.** a comedian. **6.** See **comic book. 7. comics,** comic strips. **8. the comic,** the element or quality of comedy in literature, art, drama, etc.: *An appreciation of the comic came naturally to her.* [1350–1400; ME < L *cōmicus* < Gk *kōmikós,* equiv. to *kôm(os)* a revel + *-ikos* -IC]

com•i•cal (kom′i kəl), *adj.* **1.** producing laughter; amusing; funny: *a comical fellow.* **2.** *Obs.* pertaining to or of the nature of comedy. [1400–50; late ME; see COMIC, -AL[1]] —**com′i•cal′i•ty, com′i•cal•ness,** *n.* —**com′i•cal•ly,** *adv.*
—**Syn. 1.** See **amusing.**

com′ic book′, a magazine with one or more comic strips. Also called **comic, funny book.** [1940–45]

Co•mice (kə mēs′), *n.* a large, juicy variety of pear.

com′ic op′era, 1. a diverting opera with spoken dialogue and a happy ending. **2.** the tradition or genre of such operas. [1905–10]

com•ic-op•er•a (kom′ik op′ər ə, -op′rə), *adj.* comically vainglorious; having farcically self-important aspects: *a comic-opera army, proud in its ceremonial splendor but inept on the battlefield.*

com′ic relief′, 1. an amusing scene, incident, or speech introduced into serious or tragic elements, as in a play, in order to provide temporary relief from tension, or to intensify the dramatic action. **2.** relief from tension caused by the introduction or occurrence of a comic element, as by an amusing human foible. [1815–25]

com′ic strip′, a sequence of drawings, either in color or black and white, relating a comic incident, an adventure or mystery story, etc., often serialized, typically having dialogue printed in balloons, and usually printed as a horizontal strip in daily newspapers and in an uninterrupted block or longer sequence of such strips in Sunday newspapers and in comic books. [1915–20, *Amer.*]

Com. in Chf., Commander in Chief.

Co•mines (kō mēn′), *n.* **Phi•lippe de** (fē lēp′ də), 1445?–1511?, French historian and diplomat. Also, **Commines.**

Com•in•form (kom′in fôrm′), *n.* an organization (1947–56) established by the Communist parties of nine European countries for mutual advice and coordinated activity. [*Com(munist) Inform(ation Bureau)*] —**Com′in•form′ist,** *n.*

com•ing (kum′ing), *n.* **1.** approach; arrival; advent: *His coming here was a mistake.* —*adj.* **2.** following or impending; next; approaching: *the coming year.* **3.** promising future fame or success: *a coming actor.* [1250–1300; ME; see COME, -ING[1] -ING[2]]

co•min•gle (kə ming′gəl), *v.t., v.i.,* **-gled, -gling.** commingle. Also, **co-min′gle.**

com•ing-out (kum′ing out′), *n.* **1.** a debut into society, esp. a formal debut by a debutante. **2.** an acknowledgment of one's homosexuality, either to oneself or publicly. [1805–15; n. use of v. phrase *come out;* see -ING[1]]

com•int (kom′int′), *n.* the gathering of political or military intelligence by interception of wire or radio communications. Cf. **elint, humint, sigint.** [1965–70; *com(munications) int(elligence)*]

Com•in•tern (kom′in tûrn′, kom′in tûrn′), *n.* See **Third International.** Also, **Komintern.** [< Russ *Komintérn,* for *Kommunistícheskiĭ Internatsionál* COMMUNIST INTERNATIONAL]

com•i•ta•tive (kom′i tā′tiv, -tə tiv), *Gram.* —*adj.* **1.** noting a case whose distinctive function is to indicate accompaniment. —*n.* **2.** the comitative case. [1855–60; < L *comitāt(us)* retinue, escort (*comit-,* s. of *comes* companion (see COMES) + *-ātus* -ATE[3]) + -IVE]

co•mi•ti•a (kə mish′ē ə), *n. Rom. Hist.* an assembly of the people convened to pass on laws, nominate magistrates, etc. [1615–25; < L, pl. of *comitium* assembly, equiv. to *com-* COM- + *-it-,* n. deriv. of *īre* to go (cf. COMES) + *-ium* -IUM] —**co•mi•tial** (kə mish′əl), *adj.*

com•i•ty (kom′i tē), *n., pl.* **-ties. 1.** mutual courtesy; civility. **2.** Also called **com′ity of na′tions.** courtesy between nations, as in respect shown by one country for the laws, judicial decisions, and institutions of another. [1535–45; < L *cōmitās,* equiv. to *cōm(is)* affable + *-itās* -ITY]

com•ix (kom′iks), *n.* (*used with a plural v.*) comic strips or comic art, often luridly sexual or political in character. [1970–75; resp. of COMICS]

coml., commercial.

comm., 1. commander. **2.** commerce. **3.** commission. **4.** committee. **5.** commonwealth.

com•ma (kom′ə), *n.* **1.** the sign (,), a mark of punctuation used for indicating a division in a sentence, as in setting off a word, phrase, or clause, esp. when such a division is accompanied by a slight pause or is to be noted in order to give order to the sequential elements of the sentence. It is also used to separate items in a list, to mark off thousands in numerals, to separate types or levels of information in bibliographic and other data, and, in Europe, as a decimal point. **2.** *Class. Pros.* **a.** a fragment or smaller section of a colon. **b.** the part of dactylic hexameter beginning or ending with the caesura. **c.** the caesura itself. **3.** *Music.* the minute, virtually unheard difference in pitch between two enharmonic tones, as G♯ and A♭. **4.** any of several nymphalid butterflies, as *Polygonia comma,* having a comma-shaped silver mark on the underside of each hind wing. [1520–30; < LL: mark of punctuation, L: division of a phrase < Gk *kómma* piece cut off (referring to the phrase so marked), equiv. to *kop-* (base of *kóptein* to strike, chop) + *-ma* n. suffix denoting result of action (with assimilation of *p*)]

com′ma bacil′lus, a curved, rod-shaped bacterium, *Vibrio cholerae,* causing Asiatic cholera. [1885–90]

Com•mack (kō′mak, kom′ak), *n.* a town on central Long Island, in SE New York. 34,719.

com′ma fault′, *Gram.* the use of a comma, rather than a semicolon, colon, or period, to separate related main clauses in the absence of a coordinating conjunction: often considered to be incorrect or undesirable, esp. in formal writing. Also called **comma splice.** [1930–35]

Com•ma•ger (kom′ə jər), *n.* **Henry Steele,** born 1902, U.S. historian, author, and teacher.

com•mand (kə mand′, -mänd′), *v.t.* **1.** to direct with specific authority or prerogative; order: *The captain commanded his men to attack.* **2.** to require authoritatively; demand: *She commanded silence.* **3.** to have or exercise authority or control over; be master of; have at one's bidding or disposal: *The Pharaoh commanded 10,000 slaves.* **4.** to deserve and receive (respect, sympathy, attention, etc.): *He commands much respect for his attitude.* **5.** to dominate by reason of location; overlook: *The hill commands the sea.* **6.** to have authority over and responsibility for (a military or naval unit or installation); be in charge of. —*v.i.* **7.** to issue an order or orders. **8.** to be in charge; have authority. **9.** to occupy a dominating position; look down upon or over a body of water, region, etc. —*n.* **10.** the act of commanding or ordering. **11.** an order given by one in authority: *The colonel gave the command to attack.* **12.** *Mil.* **a.** an order in prescribed words, usually given in a loud voice to troops at close-order drill: *The command was "Right shoulder arms!"* **b.** the order of execution or the second part of any two-part close-order drill command, as *face* in *Right face!* **c.** (*cap.*) a principal component of the U.S. Air Force: *Strategic Air Command.* **d.** a body of troops or a station, ship, etc., under a commander. **13.** the possession or exercise of controlling authority: *a lieutenant in command of a platoon.* **14.** expertise; mastery: *He has a command of French, Russian, and German.* **15.** *Brit.* a royal order. **16.** power of dominating a region by reason of location; extent of view or outlook: *the command of the valley from the hill.* **17.** *Computers.* **a.** an electric impulse, signal, or set of signals for initiating an operation in a computer. **b.** a character, symbol, or item of information for instructing a computer to perform a specific task. **c.** a single instruction. —*adj.* **18.** of, pertaining to, or for use in the exercise of command: *a command car; command post.* **19.** of or pertaining to a commander: *a command decision.* **20.** ordered by a sovereign, as if by a sovereign, or by the exigencies of a situation: *a command performance.* [1250–1300; (v.) ME *coma(u)nden* < AF *com(m)a(u)nder,* OF *comander* < ML *commandāre,* equiv. to L *com-* COM- + *mandāre* to entrust, order (cf. COMMEND); (n.) late ME *comma(u)nde* < AF, OF, n. deriv. of the v.] —**command′a•ble,** *adj.*
—**Syn. 1.** bid, demand, charge, instruct, enjoin. See **direct. 3.** govern, control, oversee, manage, lead. See **rule. 4.** exact, compel, require, claim, secure. **10.** direction, bidding, injunction, charge, mandate, instruction. **13.** ascendancy, sway, domination. —**Ant. 1, 7.** obey.

com•man•dant (kom′ən dant′, -dänt′, kom′ən dant′, -dänt′), *n.* **1.** the commanding officer of a place, group, etc.: *the commandant of a naval base.* **2.** the title of the senior officer and head of the U.S. Marine Corps. **3.** *U.S. Army.* a title generally given to the heads of military schools. **4.** a commander. [1680–90; < F, n. use of prp. of *commander* to COMMAND; see -ANT]

command′ car′, *Mil.* a vehicle for use by a commander and staff. [1955–60, *Amer.*]

com•man•deer (kom′ən dēr′), *v.t.* **1.** to order or force into active military service. **2.** to seize (private property) for military or other public use: *The police officer commandeered a taxi and took off after the getaway car.* **3.** to seize arbitrarily. [1880–85; < Afrik *kommandeer* < F *commander* to COMMAND]

com•mand•er (kə man′dər, -män′-), *n.* **1.** a person who commands. **2.** a person who exercises authority; chief officer; leader. **3.** the commissioned officer in command of a military unit. **4.** *U.S. Navy.* an officer ranking below a captain and above a lieutenant commander. **5.** a police officer in charge of a precinct or other unit. **6.** the chief officer of a commandery in the medieval orders of Knights Hospitalers, Knights Templars, and others. **7.** a member of one of the higher classes or ranks in certain modern fraternal orders, as in the Knights Templars. [1250–1300; ME < OF *comandere,* equiv. to *comand(er)* to COMMAND + *-ere* < L *-ātōr-* -ATOR] —**com•mand′er•ship′,** *n.*

command′er in chief′, *pl.* **commanders in chief. 1.** Also, **Command′er in Chief′.** the supreme commander of the armed forces of a nation or, sometimes, of several allied nations: *The president is the Commander in Chief of the U.S. Army, Navy, and Air Force.* **2.** an officer in command of a particular portion of an armed force who has been given this title by specific authorization. [1635–45]

com•mand•er•y (kə man′də rē, -män′-), *n., pl.* **-er•ies. 1.** the office or rank of a commander. **2.** the district of a commander. **3.** a district controlled by a commander of certain medieval orders of knights. **4.** a local branch or lodge of certain secret or fraternal orders. [1400–50; late ME. See COMMANDER, -Y[3]]

command′ guid′ance, *Electronics.* a missile guidance system in which commands for controlling the flight of the vehicle originate from a source on the ground or in another vehicle. Cf. **inertial guidance.** [1945–50]

com•mand•ing (kə man′ding, -män′-), *adj.* **1.** being in command: *a commanding officer.* **2.** appreciably superior or imposing; winning; sizable: *a commanding position; a commanding lead in the final period.* **3.** having the air, tone, etc., of command; imposing; authoritative: *a man of commanding appearance; a commanding voice.* **4.** dominating by position, usually elevation; overlooking: *a commanding bluff at the mouth of the river.* **5.** (of a view, or prospect) provided by a commanding location and so permitting dominance: *a commanding view of the mouth of the river.* [1475–85; COMMAND + -ING[2]] —**com·mand′ing·ly,** *adv.* —**com·mand′ing·ness,** *n.*

command′ing of′ficer, *Army.* a commander of any rank from second lieutenant to colonel. [1790–1800]

com·mand·ment (kə mand′mənt, -mänd′-), *n.* **1.** a command or mandate. **2.** (*sometimes cap.*) any of the Ten Commandments. **3.** the act or power of commanding. [1200–50; ME *com(m)and(e)ment* < AF, OF *com(m)andement.* See COMMAND, -MENT]

command′ mod′ule, (*often caps.*) *U.S. Aerospace.* the portion of the Apollo spacecraft that contained the crew's living compartment and the on-board controls. [1960–65]

com·man·do (kə man′dō, -män′-), *n., pl.* **-dos, -does. 1.** (in World War II) **a.** any of the specially trained Allied military units used for surprise, hit-and-run raids against Axis forces. **b.** a member of any of these units. Cf. **ranger** (def. 3). **2.** any military unit organized for operations similar to those of the commandos of World War II. **3.** a member of a military assault unit or team trained to operate quickly and aggressively in especially urgent, threatening situations, as against terrorists holding hostages. [1785–95; < Afrik *kommando* raid, raiding party, a unit of militia < Pg *commando* unit commanded, n. deriv. of *commandar* to COMMAND]

command′ perfor′mance, a performance of a play, opera, ballet, or the like, given at the request of a sovereign or head of state. [1895–1900]

command′ post′, 1. *Army.* the headquarters of the commander of a military unit. **2.** a headquarters of a civilian group or organization dealing with an emergency situation, special event, or the like. [1915–20, *Amer.*]

com′ma posi′tion, *Skiing.* angulation (def. 3).

com′ma splice′, *Gram.* See **comma fault.** [1920–25]

com·meas·ur·a·ble (kə mezh′ər ə bəl), *adj.* having the same measure or extent; commensurate. [1660–70; COM- + MEASURABLE]

com·meas·ure (kə mezh′ər), *v.t.,* **-ured, -ur·ing.** to equal in measure or extent; be coextensive with. [1605–15; COM- + MEASURE]

comme ci, comme ça (kôm sē′ kôm SA′), *French.* so-so; neither good nor bad. [lit., like this, like that]

com·me·dia dell'ar·te (kə mā′dē ə del är′tē; *It.* kôm me′dyä del lär′te), *pl.* **com·me·di·a dell'ar·tes, com·me·di·as dell'ar·te,** *It.* ***com·me·die dell'ar·te*** (kôm me′dye del lär′te). Italian popular comedy, developed chiefly during the 16th–18th centuries, in which masked entertainers improvised from a plot outline based on themes associated with stock characters and situations. [1875–80; < It: lit., comedy of art]

comme il faut (kô mēl fō′; *Eng.* kum′ ēl fō′), *French.* as it should be; proper; fitting; fittingly.

com·mem·o·rate (kə mem′ə rāt′), *v.t.,* **-rat·ed, -rat·ing. 1.** to serve as a memorial or reminder of: *The monument commemorates the signing of the Declaration of Independence.* **2.** to honor the memory of by some observance: *to commemorate the dead by a moment of silence; to commemorate Bastille Day.* **3.** to make honorable mention of. [1590–1600; < L *commemorātus* (ptp. of *commemorāre*) to recall, put on record, equiv. to *com-* COM- + *memor* mindful + *-ātus* -ATE[1]] —**com·mem′o·ra·ble,** *adj.* —**com·mem′o·ra′tor,** *n.*

com·mem·o·ra·tion (kə mem′ə rā′shən), *n.* **1.** the act of commemorating. **2.** a service, celebration, etc., in memory of some person or event. **3.** a memorial. **4.** (in many Christian churches) a special service or prayer for commemorating the lesser feast on days on which two feasts of unequal rank are celebrated. [1350–1400; ME (< MF) < L *commemorātiōn-* (s. of *commemorātiō*), equiv. to *commemorāt(us)* (see COMMEMORATE) + *-iōn* -ION] —**com·mem′o·ra′tion·al,** *adj.*

com·mem·o·ra·tive (kə mem′ə rā′tiv, -ər ə tiv), *adj.* **1.** serving to commemorate: *a commemorative monument; a commemorative dinner.* **2.** (of a coin, medal, or postage stamp) issued to commemorate a historical event, to honor the memory of a personage, etc. —*n.* **3.** anything that commemorates. [1605–15; COMMEMORAT(ION) + -IVE] —**com·mem′o·ra′tive·ly,** *adv.* —**com·mem′o·ra′tive·ness,** *n.*

com·mem·o·ra·to·ry (kə mem′ər ə tôr′ē, -tōr′ē), *adj.* commemorative (def. 1). [1685–95; COMMEMORATE + -ORY[1]]

com·mence (kə mens′), *v.i., v.t.,* **-menced, -menc·ing.** to begin; start. [1250–1300; ME *commencen* < AF, MF *comencer* < VL **cominitiāre,* equiv. to L *com-* COM- + *initiāre* to begin; see INITIATE] —**com·mence′a·ble,** *adj.* —**com·menc′er,** *n.*
—**Syn.** originate, inaugurate. See **begin.**

com·mence·ment (kə mens′mənt), *n.* **1.** an act or instance of commencing; beginning: *the commencement of hostilities.* **2.** the ceremony of conferring degrees or granting diplomas at the end of the academic year. **3.** the day on which this ceremony takes place. [1225–75; ME < AF, OF. See COMMENCE, -MENT]

com·mend (kə mend′), *v.t.* **1.** to present, mention, or praise as worthy of confidence, notice, kindness, etc.; recommend: *to commend a friend to another; to commend an applicant for employment.* **2.** to entrust; give in charge; deliver with confidence: *I commend my child to your care.* **3.** to cite or name with approval or special praise: *to commend a soldier for bravery.* **4.** *Feudal Law.* to place (oneself or one's land) under another's protection so as to become his vassal. **5.** *Archaic.* to recommend (a person) to the kind remembrance of another. [1350–1400; ME *commenden* < L *commendāre,* equiv. to *com-* COM- + *-mendāre,* comb. form of *mandāre;* see MANDATE] —**com·mend′a·ble,** *adj.* —**com·mend′a·ble·ness,** *n.* —**com·mend′a·bly,** *adv.* —**com·mend′er,** *n.* —**com·mend′ing·ly,** *adv.*
—**Syn. 1.** acclaim, laud, extol. See **approve. 2.** commit, consign, relegate, convey. —**Ant. 1.** censure.

com·men·dam (kə men′dam), *n. Eccles.* **1.** the tenure of a benefice to be held until the appointment of a regular incumbent, the benefice being said to be held *in commendam.* **2.** a benefice so held. [1555–65; < ML, short for *(dare) in commendam* (to give) in trust; *commendam,* acc. sing. of *commenda,* n. deriv. of L *commendāre* to COMMEND]

com·men·da·tion (kom′ən dā′shən), *n.* **1.** the act of commending; recommendation; praise: *commendation for a job well done.* **2.** something that commends, as a formal recommendation or an official citation or award: *a commendation for bravery.* **3.** *Feudal Law.* the placing of oneself or one's land under the protection of a lord so as to become his vassal. **4. commendations,** *Archaic.* a complimentary greeting or message. [1175–1225; ME *commendacioun* (< AF) < L *commendātiōn-* (s. of *commendātiō*) a commending to God. See COMMEND, -ATION]
—**Syn. 1.** approval, approbation, applause. **2.** eulogy, encomium, panegyric, laudation. —**Ant. 1, 2.** condemnation.

com·mend·a·to·ry (kə men′də tôr′ē, -tōr′ē), *adj.* **1.** serving to commend; approving; praising. **2.** holding a benefice in commendam. **3.** held in commendam. [1545–55; < LL *commendātōrius,* equiv. to *commendā(re)* to COMMEND + *-tōrius* -TORY[1]]

com·men·sal (kə men′səl), *adj.* **1.** eating together at the same table. **2.** (of an animal, plant, fungus, etc.) living with, on, or in another, without injury to either. **3.** *Sociol.* (of a person or group) not competing while residing in or occupying the same area as another individual or group having independent or different values or customs. —*n.* **4.** a companion at table. **5.** a commensal organism. [1350–1400; ME < ML *commēnsālis.* See COM-, MENSAL[2]] —**com·men′sal·ism,** *n.* —**com·men·sal·i·ty** (kom′en sal′i tē), *n.* —**com·men′sal·ly,** *adv.*

com·men·su·ra·ble (kə men′sər ə bəl, -shər ə-), *adj.* **1.** having the same measure or divisor: *The numbers 6 and 9 are commensurable since they are divisible by 3.* **2.** suitable in measure; proportionate. [1550–60; < LL *commēnsūrābilis,* equiv. to L *com-* COM- + *mēnsūrābilis* (equiv. to *mēnsūrā(re)* (see COMMENSURATE) + *-bilis* -BLE)] —**com·men′su·ra·bil′i·ty, com·men′su·ra·ble·ness,** *n.* —**com·men′su·ra·bly,** *adv.*

com·men·su·rate (kə men′sər it, -shər-), *adj.* **1.** having the same measure; of equal extent or duration. **2.** corresponding in amount, magnitude, or degree: *Your paycheck should be commensurate with the amount of time worked.* **3.** proportionate; adequate. **4.** having a common measure; commensurable. [1635–45; < LL *commēnsūrātus,* equiv. to L *com-* COM- + *mēnsūrātus* (ptp. of *mēnsūrāre* to MEASURE); see -ATE[1]] —**com·men′su·rate·ly,** *adv.* —**com·men′su·rate·ness,** *n.* —**com·men·su·ra·tion** (kə men′sə rā′shən, -shə-), *n.*

com·ment (kom′ent), *n.* **1.** a remark, observation, or criticism: *a comment about the weather.* **2.** gossip; talk: *His frequent absences gave rise to comment.* **3.** a criticism or interpretation, often by implication or suggestion: *The play is a comment on modern society.* **4.** a note in explanation, expansion, or criticism of a passage in a book, article, or the like; annotation. **5.** explanatory or critical matter added to a text. **6.** Also called **rheme.** *Ling.* the part of a sentence that communicates new information about the topic. Cf. **topic** (def. 4). —*v.i.* **7.** to make remarks, observations, or criticisms: *He refused to comment on the decision of the court.* **8.** to write explanatory or critical notes upon a text. —*v.t.* **9.** to make comments or remarks on; furnish with comments; annotate. [1350–1400; ME *coment* < L *commentum* device, fabrication (LL: interpretation, commentary), n. use of neut. of *commentus* (ptp. of *comminīscī* to devise), equiv. to *com-* COM- + *men-* (base of *mēns, mentis* MIND) + *-tus* ptp. ending] —**com′ment·a·ble,** *adj.* —**com′ment·er,** *n.*
—**Syn. 1.** See **remark. 4.** addendum, commentary. **8.** annotate, elucidate.

com·men·tar·y (kom′ən ter′ē), *n., pl.* **-tar·ies. 1.** a series of comments, explanations, or annotations: *a commentary on the Bible; news followed by a commentary.* **2.** an explanatory essay or treatise: *a commentary on a play; Blackstone's commentaries on law.* **3.** anything serving to illustrate a point, prompt a realization, or exemplify, esp. in the case of something unfortunate: *The dropout rate is a sad commentary on our school system.* **4.** Usually, **commentaries.** records of facts or events: *Commentaries written by Roman lawyers give us information on how their courts functioned.* [1375–1425; late ME *commentaries* (pl.) < L *commentārium* notebook, n. use of neut. of *commentārius,* equiv. to *comment(um)* COMMENT + *-ārius* -ARY] —**com·men·tar·i·al** (kom′ən târ′ē əl), *adj.*

com·men·tate (kom′ən tāt′), *v.,* **-tat·ed, -tat·ing.** —*v.t.* **1.** to deliver a commentary on: *to commentate a fashion show.* **2.** to write a commentary on; annotate: *to commentate the Book of Job.* —*v.i.* **3.** to serve as a commentator: *The senior staff member will commentate, as usual.* **4.** to make explanatory or critical comments, as upon a text: *the manuscript on which I am commentating.* [1785–95; back formation from COMMENTATOR]
—**Usage.** Since the late 18th century, COMMENTATE has been used transitively with the meaning "to annotate" and, since the mid 19th, intransitively with the meaning "to make explanatory or critical comments." These uses are now rare. Recently, COMMENTATE has developed the additional transitive sense "to deliver a commentary on" and the intransitive sense "to serve as a commentator." These uses are occasionally criticized as journalistic jargon.

com·men·ta·tive (kom′ən tā′tiv), *adj.* of or pertaining to comment or commentary. [1710–20; COMMENTAT(OR) + -IVE]

com·men·ta·tor (kom′ən tā′tər), *n.* **1.** a person who discusses news, sports events, weather, or the like, as on television or radio. **2.** a person who makes commentaries. [1350–1400; ME < LL *commentātor* interpreter, equiv. to *commentā(rī)* to interpret (L: to think about, prepare, discuss, write, perh. freq. of *comminīscī* to devise; see COMMENT) + L *-tor* -TOR] —**com·men·ta·to·ri·al** (kə men′tə tôr′ē əl, -tōr′-), *adj.* —**com·men′ta·to′ri·al·ly,** *adv.*

com·merce (kom′ərs), *n.* **1.** an interchange of goods or commodities, esp. on a large scale between different countries (**foreign commerce**) or between different parts of the same country (**domestic commerce**); trade; business. **2.** social relations, esp. the exchange of views, attitudes, etc. **3.** sexual intercourse. **4.** intellectual or spiritual interchange; communion. **5.** (*cap.*) Also called **Com′merce Depart′ment.** *Informal.* the Department of Commerce. [1530–40; < MF < L *commercium,* equiv. to *commerc(ārī)* to trade together (*com-* COM- + *mercārī* to buy, deal, deriv. of *merc-,* s. of *merx* goods) + *-ium* -IUM]
—**Syn. 1.** See **trade.**

Com·merce (kom′ərs), *n.* a town in SW California. 10,509.

Com′merce Cit′y, a city in central Colorado. 16,234.

com·mer·cial (kə mûr′shəl), *adj.* **1.** of, pertaining to, or characteristic of commerce. **2.** engaged in commerce. **3.** prepared, done, or acting with sole or chief emphasis on salability, profit, or success: *a commercial product; His attitude toward the theater is very commercial.* **4.** able to yield or make a profit: *We decided that the small oil well was not commercial.* **5.** suitable or fit for a wide, popular market: *Communications satellites are gradually finding a commercial use.* **6.** suitable for or catering to business rather than private use: *commercial kitchen design; commercial refrigeration.* **7.** (of a vehicle or its use) **a.** engaged in transporting passengers or goods for profit. **b.** civilian and public, as distinguished from military or private. **8.** not entirely or chemically pure: *commercial soda.* **9.** catering esp. to traveling salespeople by offering reduced rates, space for exhibiting products, etc.: *a commercial hotel.* **10.** (in U.S. government grading of beef) graded between standard and utility. **11.** paid for by advertisers: *commercial television.* —*n.* **12.** *Radio and Television.* a paid advertisement or promotional announcement. **13.** (in U.S. government grading of beef) **a.** a low-quality grade of beef between standard and utility. **b.** a cut of beef of this grade. **14.** *Brit. Informal.* a traveling salesperson. [1680–90; COMMERCE + -IAL] —**com·mer′cial·ly,** *adv.*
—**Syn. 1.** COMMERCIAL, MERCANTILE refer to the activities of business, industry, and trade. COMMERCIAL is the broader term, covering all the activities and relationships of industry and trade. In a derogatory sense it may mean such a preoccupation with the affairs of commerce as results in indifference to considerations other than wealth: *commercial treaties; a merely commercial viewpoint.* MERCANTILE applies to the purchase and sale of goods, or to the transactions of business: *a mercantile house or class.*

commer′cial a′gency, a concern that investigates for the benefit of its subscribers the financial standing, reputation, and credit rating of individuals, firms, corporations, or others. [1895–1900, *Amer.*]

commer′cial art′, graphic art created specifically for commercial uses, esp. for advertising, illustrations in magazines or books, or the like. Cf. **fine art.** [1920–25] —**com·mer′cial art′ist.**

commer′cial attaché′, an attaché in an embassy or legation representing the commercial interests of his or her country.

commer′cial bank′, a bank specializing in checking accounts and short-term loans. [1905–10]

commer′cial break′, a short interruption during radio or television programming for the broadcasting of a commercial or commercials.

commer′cial code′, a telegraphic code designed to convey a message with a minimum number of words and thereby reduce toll costs.

commer′cial col′lege, a school that trains people for careers in business. [1795–1805]

commer′cial cred′it, credit issued by a bank to a business to finance trading or manufacturing operations.

commer′cial fer′tilizer, fertilizer manufactured chemically, as distinguished from natural fertilizer, as manure. [1885–90, *Amer.*]

com·mer·cial·ism (kə mûr′shə liz′əm), *n.* **1.** the principles, practices, and spirit of commerce. **2.** a commercial attitude in noncommercial affairs; inappropriate or excessive emphasis on profit, success, or immediate results. **3.** a commercial custom or expression. [COMMERCIAL + -ISM] —**com·mer′cial·ist,** *n.* —**com·mer′cial·is′tic,** *adj.*

com·mer·ci·al·i·ty (kə mûr′shē al′i tē), *n.* commercial quality or character; ability to produce a profit: *Distributors were concerned about the film's commerciality compared with last year's successful pictures.* [1860–65; COMMERCIAL + -ITY]

com·mer·cial·ize (kə mûr′shə līz′), *v.t.,* **-ized, -iz·ing. 1.** to make commercial in character, methods, or spirit. **2.** to emphasize the profitable aspects of, esp. at the expense of quality: *to commercialize one's artistic talent.* **3.** to offer for sale; make available as a commodity. Also, *esp. Brit.,* **com·mer′cial·ise′.** [COMMERCIAL + -IZE] —**com·mer′cial·i·za′tion,** *n.* —**com·mer′cial·iz′er,** *n.*

com·mer′cial law′, the legal regulations governing transactions and related matters in business and trade. [1755–65]

com·mer′cial pa′per, 1. negotiable paper, as drafts, bills of exchange, etc., given in the course of business. **2.** corporate promissory notes, usually short-term and unsecured, sold in the open market. [1830–40, *Amer.*]

com·mer′cial pi′lot, an airplane pilot licensed to transport passengers, goods, etc.

com·mer′cial trav′eler, a traveling sales representative. [1800–10]

com·mie[1] (kom′ē), *n., adj.* (*often cap.*) *Informal* (*disparaging and offensive*). communist. Also, **commy.** [1935–40; COMM(UNIST) + -IE]

com·mie[2] (kom′ē), *n.* a playing marble, esp. one not used as a shooter. [1920–25; *comm(on marble)* + -IE]

com·mi·nate (kom′ə nāt′), *v.t., v.i.,* **-nat·ed, -nat·ing. 1.** to threaten with divine punishment or vengeance. **2.** to curse; anathematize. [1605–15; back formation from COMMINATION]

com·mi·na·tion (kom′ə nā′shən), *n.* **1.** a threat of punishment or vengeance. **2.** a denunciation. **3.** (in the Church of England) a penitential office read on Ash Wednesday in which God's anger and judgments are proclaimed against sinners. [1400–50; late ME (< AF) < L *commīnātiōn-* (s. of *commīnātiō*), equiv. to *commīnāt(us)*, ptp. of *commīnārī* to threaten (*com-* COM- + *minārī* to threaten) + *-iōn-* -ION] **—com′mi·na′tor,** *n.* **—com·min·a·to·ry** (kə min′ə tôr′ē, -tōr′ē, kom′ə nə-), **com′mi·na′tive,** *adj.*

Com·mines (kô mēn′), *n.* **Phi·lippe de** (fē lēp′ də). See **Comines, Philippe de.**

com·min·gle (kə ming′gəl), *v.t., v.i.,* **-gled, -gling.** to mix or mingle together; combine. [1620–30; COM- + MINGLE] **—com·min′gler,** *n.*

com·mi·nute (kom′ə no͞ot′, -nyo͞ot′), *v.,* **-nut·ed, -nut·ing,** *adj.* —*v.t.* **1.** to pulverize; triturate. —*adj.* **2.** comminuted; divided into small parts. **3.** powdered; pulverized. [1620–30; < L *comminūtus*, ptp. of *comminuere*, equiv. to *com-* COM- + *minuere* to lessen, akin to *minor* MINOR] **—com′mi·nu′tion,** *n.*

com′minuted frac′ture, a fracture of a bone in which the separated parts are splintered or fragmented. See illus. under **fracture.** [1825–35]

com·mi·nu·tor (kom′ə no͞o′tər, -nyo͞o′-), *n.* a machine that pulverizes solids, as in waste treatment. [COMMINUTE + -OR[2]]

com·mis (kô mē′; *Eng.* kə mē′), *n., pl.* **-mis** (-mē′; *Eng.* -mēz′). *French.* an assistant, esp. to a chef.

com·mis·er·ate (kə miz′ə rāt′), *v.,* **-at·ed, -at·ing.** —*v.t.* **1.** to feel or express sorrow or sympathy for; empathize with; pity. —*v.i.* **2.** to sympathize (usually fol. by *with*): *They commiserated with him over the loss of his job.* [1585–95; < L *commiserātus* (ptp. of *commiserārī*), equiv. to *com-* COM- + *miser* pitiable (see MISERY) + *-ātus* -ATE[1]] **—com·mis′er·a·ble,** *adj.* **—com·mis′·er·a′tion,** *n.* **—com·mis′er·a′tive,** *adj.* **—com·mis′·er·a′tive·ly,** *adv.* **—com·mis′er·a′tor,** *n.*

com·mis·sar (kom′ə sär′, kom′ə sär′), *n.* **1.** the head of any of the major governmental divisions of the U.S.S.R.: called *minister* since 1946. **2.** an official in any communist government whose duties include political indoctrination, detection of political deviation, etc. [1915–20; < Russ *komissár* < G *Kommissar* < ML *commissārius* COMMISSARY]

com·mis·sar·i·at (kom′ə sâr′ē ət), *n.* **1.** any of the major governmental divisions of the U.S.S.R.: called *ministry* since 1946. **2.** the organized method or manner by which food, equipment, transport, etc., is delivered to armies. **3.** the department of an army charged with supplying provisions. [1600–10; < NL *commissāriātus*, equiv. to ML *commissāri(us)* COMMISSARY + *-ātus* -ATE[3]; (def. 1) < Russ *komissariát* << NL, as above]

com·mis·sar·y (kom′ə ser′ē), *n., pl.* **-sar·ies. 1.** a store that sells food and supplies to the personnel or workers in a military post, mining camp, lumber camp, or the like. **2.** a dining room or cafeteria, esp. one in a motion-picture studio. **3.** a person to whom some responsibility or role is delegated by a superior power; a deputy. **4.** (in France) a police official, usually just below the police chief in rank. **5.** commissar. [1350–1400; ME *commissarie* (< AF) < ML *commissārius*, equiv. to L *commiss(us)* (ptp. of *committere* to COMMIT) + *-ārius* -ARY] **—com·mis·sar·i·al** (kom′i sâr′ē əl), *adj.*

com·mis·sion (kə mish′ən), *n.* **1.** the act of committing or giving in charge. **2.** an authoritative order, charge, or direction. **3.** authority granted for a particular action or function. **4.** a document granting such authority. **5.** a document conferring authority issued by the president of the U.S. to officers in the Army, Navy, and other military services, and by state governments to justices of the peace and others. **6.** the power thus granted. **7.** the position or rank of an officer in any of the armed forces. **8.** a group of persons authoritatively charged with particular functions: *a parks commission.* **9.** the condition of being placed under special authoritative responsibility or charge. **10.** a task or matter committed to one's charge; official assignment: *The architect received a commission to design an office building.* **11.** the act of committing or perpetrating a crime, error, etc.: *The commission of a misdemeanor is punishable by law.* **12.** something that is committed. **13.** authority to act as agent for another or others in commercial transactions. **14.** a sum or percentage allowed to agents, sales representatives, etc., for their services: *to work on a 20 percent commission.* **15. in commission, a.** in service. **b.** in operating order: *A great deal of work will be necessary to put this car in commission again.* **c.** Also, **into commission.** *Navy.* (of a ship) manned and in condition for or ordered to active service. **16. on commission,** paid entirely or partially with commissions from sales one has made or for work one has done: *The salespeople who are on commission earn 6 percent of the total amount they sell.* **17. out of commission, a.** not in service. **b.** not in operating order: *The stove is out of commission.* —*v.t.* **18.** to give a commission to: *to commission a graduate of a military academy.* **19.** to authorize; send on a mission. **20.** to give the order that places a warship, military command, etc., in a state of complete readiness for active duty. **21.** to give a commission or order for: *The owners commissioned a painting for the building's lobby.* [1300–50; ME (< AF) < L *commissiōn-* (s. of *commissiō*) a committing. See COM-, MISSION, COMMIT] **—com·mis′sion·a·ble,** *adj.* **—com·mis′sion·al,** *adj.* **—com·mis′sive,** *adj.* **—com·mis′·sive·ly,** *adv.*

com·mis·sion·aire (kə mish′ə nâr′), *n. Brit.* a uniformed attendant, as a doorkeeper or usher. [1755–65; < F *commissionnaire;* see COMMISSION, -AIRE]

commis′sioned of′ficer, a military or naval officer holding rank by commission. [1675–85]

com·mis·sion·er (kə mish′ə nər), *n.* **1.** a person commissioned to act officially; member of a commission. **2.** a government official or representative in charge of a department or district: *the police commissioner; the commissioner of a colony.* **3.** an official chosen by an athletic association to exercise broad administrative or judicial authority: *the baseball commissioner.* [1400–50; late ME < AF. See COMMISSION, -ER[2]] **—com·mis′sion·er·ship′,** *n.*

commis′sion house′, a brokerage firm that buys and sells securities on commission. [1825–35, *Amer.*]

commis′sion plan′, a system of municipal government in which all the legislative and executive powers of the city are concentrated in the hands of a commission. [1915–20]

commissure (def. 2) AB, line of the commissural faces of the two carpels

com·mis·sure (kom′ə sho͝or′, -shûr′), *n.* **1.** a joint; seam; suture. **2.** *Bot.* the joint or face by which one carpel coheres with another. **3.** *Anat., Zool.* a connecting band of nerve fiber, esp. one joining the right and left sides of the brain or spinal cord. [1375–1425; late ME (< MF) < L *commissūra*, equiv. to *commiss(us)* (see COMMISSARY) + *-ūra* -URE] **—com·mis·su·ral** (kə mish′ər əl, kom′ə sho͝or′əl, -shûr′-), *adj.*

com·mis·sur·ot·o·my (kom′ə shə rot′ə mē), *n., pl.* **-mies.** *Surg.* the incision of a band of commissures, esp. of mitral fibers, to correct mitral stenosis. Cf. **valvulotomy.** [COMMISSURE + -O- + -TOMY]

com·mit (kə mit′), *v.,* **-mit·ted, -mit·ting.** —*v.t.* **1.** to give in trust or charge; consign. **2.** to consign for preservation: *to commit ideas to writing; to commit a poem to memory.* **3.** to pledge (oneself) to a position on an issue or question; express (one's intention, feeling, etc.): *Asked if he was a candidate, he refused to commit himself.* **4.** to bind or obligate, as by pledge or assurance; pledge: *to commit oneself to a promise; to be committed to a course of action.* **5.** to entrust, esp. for safekeeping; commend: *to commit one's soul to God.* **6.** to do; perform; perpetrate: *to commit murder; to commit an error.* **7.** to consign to custody: *to commit a delinquent to a reformatory.* **8.** to place in a mental institution or hospital by or as if by legal authority: *He was committed on the certificate of two psychiatrists.* **9.** to deliver for treatment, disposal, etc.; relegate: *to commit a manuscript to the flames.* **10.** to send into a battle: *The commander has committed all his troops to the front lines.* **11.** *Parl. Proc.* to refer (a bill or the like) to a committee for consideration. —*v.i.* **12.** to pledge or engage oneself: *an athlete who commits to the highest standards.* [1350–1400; ME *committen* (< AF *committer*) < L *committere*, equiv. to *com-* COM- + *mittere* to send, give over] **—com·mit′ta·ble,** *adj.* **—com·mit′ter,** *n.*
—Syn. 6. carry out, effect, execute.

com·mit·ment (kə mit′mənt), *n.* **1.** the act of committing. **2.** the state of being committed. **3.** the act of committing, pledging, or engaging oneself. **4.** a pledge or promise; obligation: *We have made a commitment to pay our bills on time.* **5.** engagement; involvement: *They have a sincere commitment to religion.* **6.** perpetration or commission, as of a crime. **7.** consignment, as to prison. **8.** confinement to a mental institution or hospital: *The psychiatrist recommended commitment.* **9.** an order, as by a court or judge, confining a person to a mental institution or hospital. **10.** *Law.* a written order of a court directing that someone be confined in prison; mittimus. **11.** *Parl. Proc.* the act of referring or entrusting to a committee for consideration. **12.** *Stock Exchange.* **a.** an agreement to buy or sell securities. **b.** a sale or purchase of securities. Also, **committal** (for defs. 1, 3–11). [1605–15; COMMIT + -MENT]

com·mit·tal (kə mit′l), *n.* an act or instance of committing; commitment. [1615–25; COMMIT + -AL[2]]

com·mit·tee (kə mit′ē), *n.* **1.** a person or group of persons elected or appointed to perform some service or function, as to investigate, report on, or act upon a particular matter. **2.** See **standing committee. 3.** *Law.* an individual to whom the care of a person or a person's estate is committed. [1425–75; late ME < AF; see COMMIT, -EE] **—com·mit′tee·ism, com·mit′tee·ship′,** *n.*
—Usage. See **collective noun.**

com·mit·tee·man (kə mit′ē mən, -man′), *n., pl.* **-men** (-mən, -men′). **1.** a member of a committee. **2.** the leader of a political ward or precinct. **3.** See **shop steward.** [1645–55; COMMITTEE + MAN[1]]
—Usage. See **-man.**

Commit′tee of Correspond′ence, *Amer. Hist.* **1.** an intercolonial committee organized 1772 by Samuel Adams in Massachusetts to keep colonists informed of British anticolonial actions and to plan colonial resistance or countermeasures. **2.** (*sometimes l.c.*) any of various similar organizations formed for the same purpose during the late colonial period. Also called **Correspondence Committee.** [1760–70, *Amer.*]

commit′tee of one′, an individual person designated to function alone as a committee. [1840–50, *Amer.*]

commit′tee of the whole′, the entire membership of a legislative body, sitting in a deliberative rather than a legislative capacity, for informal debate and preliminary consideration of matters awaiting legislative action. [1745–55]

com·mit·tee·per·son (kə mit′ē pûr′sən), *n.* **1.** a member of a committee. **2.** the leader of a political ward or precinct. [COMMITTEE(MAN) + -PERSON]
—Usage. See **-person.**

com·mit·tee·wom·an (kə mit′ē wo͝om′ən), *n., pl.* **-wom·en. 1.** a woman serving as a member of a committee. **2.** a woman who is the leader of a political ward or precinct. [1850–55; COMMITTEE + WOMAN]
—Usage. See **-woman.**

com·mix (kə miks′), *v.t., v.i.* to mix together; blend. [1375–1425; back formation from *commixt* (ptp.), ME < L *commixtus* (ptp. of *commiscēre*), equiv. to *com-* COM- + *mix-* (var. s. of *miscēre* to mix) + *-tus* ptp. ending]

com·mix·ture (kə miks′chər), *n.* **1.** the act or process of commixing. **2.** the condition of being commixed; mixture. **3.** (in a Eucharistic service) the placing of a part of the Host in the chalice. [1580–90; < L *commixtūra*, equiv. to *commixt(us)* (see COMMIX) + *-ūra* -URE]

com·mo (kom′ō), *n., pl.* **-mos.** *Australian Informal.* communist. [1915–20; COMM(UNIST) + -O]

com·mode (kə mōd′), *n.* **1.** a low cabinet or similar piece of furniture, often highly ornamental, containing drawers or shelves. **2.** a stand or cupboard containing a chamber pot or washbasin. **3.** toilet (def. 1). **4.** a portable toilet, esp. one on a chairlike frame with wheels, as for an invalid. **5.** an elaborate headdress consisting chiefly of a high framework decorated with lace, ribbons, etc., worn perched on top of the hair by women in the late 17th and early 18th centuries. [1680–90; < F < L *commodus* convenient, equiv. to *com-* COM- + *modus* MODE[1]]

commode (def. 1)

com·mo·di·ous (kə mō′dē əs), *adj.* **1.** spacious and convenient; roomy: *a commodious apartment.* **2.** ample or adequate for a particular purpose: *a commodious harbor.* [1375–1425; late ME < ML *commodiōsus*, equiv. to L *commodi(tās)* convenience (see COMMODITY) + *-ōsus* -OUS] **—com·mo′di·ous·ly,** *adv.* **—com·mo′di·ous·ness,** *n.*

com·mod·i·ty (kə mod′i tē), *n., pl.* **-ties. 1.** an article of trade or commerce, esp. a product as distinguished from a service. **2.** something of use, advantage, or value. **3.** *Stock Exchange.* any unprocessed or partially processed good, as grain, fruits, and vegetables, or precious metals. **4.** *Obs.* a quantity of goods. [1375–1425; late ME *commodite* < AF < L *commoditās* timeliness, convenience, equiv. to *commod(us)* (see COMMODE) + *-itās* -ITY]

commod′ity exchange′, an exchange for the buying and selling of futures contracts on commodities, as butter, coffee, sugar, and grains. [1930–35]

Commod′ity Fu′tures Trad′ing Commis′sion, *U.S. Govt.* an independent regulatory agency, created in 1975, that supervises the trading of futures on commodity exchanges. *Abbr.:* CFTC

com·mo·dore (kom′ə dôr′, -dōr′), *n.* **1.** *Navy.* a grade of flag officer next in rank below a rear admiral. **2.** *Brit. Navy.* an officer in temporary command of a squadron, sometimes over a captain on the same ship. **3.** *Navy.* the senior captain when two or more ships of war are cruising in company. **4.** (in the U.S. Navy and Merchant Marine) the officer in command of a convoy. **5.** the senior captain of a line of merchant vessels. **6.** the president or head of a yacht club or boat club. [1685–95; earlier *commandore*, perh. < D *komandeur* < F *commandeur* COMMANDER]

Com·mo·dus (kom′ə dəs), *n.* **Lucius Ae·li·us Aurelius** (ē′lē əs), A.D. 161–192, Roman emperor 180–192; son and successor of Marcus Aurelius.

com·mon (kom′ən), *adj.,* **-er, -est,** *n.* —*adj.* **1.** belonging equally to, or shared alike by, two or more or all

CONCISE ETYMOLOGY KEY: <, descended or borrowed from; >, whence; b., blend of, blended; c., cognate with; cf., compare; deriv., derivative; equiv., equivalent; imit., imitative; obl., oblique; r., replacing; s., stem; sp., spelling, spelled; resp., respelling, respelled; trans., translation; ?, origin unknown; *, unattested; ‡, probably earlier than. See the full key inside the front cover.

in question: *common property; common interests.* **2.** pertaining or belonging equally to an entire community, nation, or culture; public: *a common language or history; a common water-supply system.* **3.** joint; united: *a common defense.* **4.** widespread; general; ordinary: *common knowledge.* **5.** of frequent occurrence; usual; familiar: *a common event; a common mistake.* **6.** hackneyed; trite. **7.** of mediocre or inferior quality; mean; low: *a rough-textured suit of the most common fabric.* **8.** coarse; vulgar: *common manners.* **9.** lacking rank, station, distinction, etc.; unexceptional; ordinary: *a common soldier; common people; the common man; a common thief.* **10.** *Dial.* friendly; sociable; unaffected. **11.** *Anat.* forming or formed by two or more parts or branches: *the common carotid arteries.* **12.** *Pros.* (of a syllable) able to be considered as either long or short. **13.** *Gram.* **a.** not belonging to an inflectional paradigm; fulfilling different functions that in some languages require different inflected forms: *English nouns are in the common case whether used as subject or object.* **b.** constituting one of two genders of a language, esp. a gender comprising nouns that were formerly masculine or feminine: *Swedish nouns are either common or neuter.* **c.** noting a word that may refer to either a male or a female: *French* élève *has common gender. English lacks a common gender pronoun in the third person singular.* **d.** (of a noun) belonging to the common gender. **14.** *Math.* bearing a similar relation to two or more entities. **15.** of, pertaining to, or being common stock: *common shares.*
—*n.* **16.** Often, **commons.** *Chiefly New England.* a tract of land owned or used jointly by the residents of a community, usually a central square or park in a city or town. **17.** *Law.* the right or liberty, in common with other persons, to take profit from the land or waters of another, as by pasturing animals on another's land **(com′mon of pas′turage)** or fishing in another's waters **(com′mon of pis′cary).** **18. commons,** (*used with a singular or plural v.*) **a.** the commonalty; the nonruling class. **b.** the body of people not of noble birth or not ennobled, as represented in England by the House of Commons. **c.** (*cap.*) the representatives of this body. **d.** (*cap.*) the House of Commons. **19. commons, a.** (*used with a singular v.*) a large dining room, esp. at a university or college. **b.** (*usually used with a plural v.*) *Brit.* food provided in such a dining room. **c.** (*usually used with a plural v.*) food or provisions for any group. **20.** (*sometimes cap.*) *Eccles.* **a.** an office or form of service used on a festival of a particular kind. **b.** the ordinary of the Mass, esp. those parts sung by the choir. **c.** the part of the missal and breviary containing Masses and offices of those saints assigned to them. **21.** *Obs.* **a.** the community or public. **b.** the common people. **22. in common,** in joint possession or use; shared equally: *They have a love of adventure in common.* [1250–1300; ME *comun* < AF, OF < L *commūnis* common, presumably orig. "sharing common duties," akin to *mūnia* duties of an office, *mūnus* task, duty, gift < a base **moin-,* c. MEAN[2]; cf. COM-, IMMUNE] —**com′mon·ness,** *n.*
—**Syn. 4.** universal, prevalent, popular. See **general. 5.** customary, everyday. **7, 8, 9.** COMMON, VULGAR, ORDINARY refer, often with derogatory connotations of cheapness or inferiority, to what is usual or most often experienced. COMMON applies to what is accustomed, usually experienced, or inferior, to the opposite of what is exclusive or aristocratic: *The park is used by the common people.* VULGAR properly means belonging to the people, or characteristic of common people; it connotes low taste, coarseness, or ill breeding: *the vulgar view of things; vulgar in manners and speech.* ORDINARY refers to what is to be expected in the usual order of things; it means average or below average: *That is a high price for something of such ordinary quality.*

com·mon·a·ble (kom′ə nə bəl), *adj.* **1.** held jointly; for general use; public: *commonable lands.* **2.** allowed to be pastured on common land: *commonable cattle.* [1610–20; COMMON + -ABLE]

com·mon·age (kom′ə nij), *n.* **1.** the joint use of anything, esp. a pasture. **2.** the state of being held in common. **3.** something that is so held, as land. **4.** commonalty. [1600–10; COMMON + -AGE]

com·mon·al·i·ty (kom′ə nal′i tē), *n., pl.* **-ties. 1.** a sharing of features or characteristics in common; possession or manifestation of common attributes. **2.** a feature or characteristic held in common: *Historians perceive commonalities of behavior in many eras.* **3.** commonalty (def. 1). [1350–1400; ME; partial Latinization of COMMONALTY, on basis of presumed L **commūnālitās* (see -ITY)]

com·mon·al·ty (kom′ə nl tē), *n., pl.* **-ties. 1.** Also, **commonality.** the ordinary people, as distinguished from those with authority, rank, station, etc.; the common people. **2.** an incorporated body or its members. [1250–1300; ME < MF *comunalte,* equiv. to *comunal-* COMMUNAL + *-te* -TY[2]; r. ME *communaute* < OF]

com′mon bond′, *Masonry.* See **American bond.**

com′mon busi′ness or′iented lan′guage, *Computers.* See **COBOL.**

com′mon canar′y. See under **canary** (def. 1).

com′mon carot′id ar′tery, *Anat.* the part of a carotid artery between its origin and its point of division into branches.

com′mon car′rier, 1. *Transp.* (in federal regulatory and other legal usage) a carrier offering its services at published rates to all persons for interstate transportation. **2.** a public service or public utility company, as a telephone or telegraph company, engaged in the transmitting of messages for the public. Also called **carrier.** —**com′mon-car′ri·er,** *adj.* —**com′mon car′riage.**

com′mon cold′, cold (def. 24). [1780–90]

com′mon cost′, *Accounting.* costs assignable to two or more products, operations, departments, etc., of a company.

com′mon coun′cil, the local legislative body of a municipal government. [1680–90]

com′mon denom′inator, 1. *Math.* a number that is a multiple of all the denominators of a set of fractions. **2.** a trait, characteristic, belief, or the like common to or shared by all members of a group: *Dedication to the cause of freedom was the common denominator of the American revolutionaries.* [1585–95]

com′mon dif′ference, *Math.* the difference between any two consecutive terms in an arithmetic progression. [1890–95]

com′mon disas′ter, *Insurance.* the death of an insured party and a beneficiary occurring at the same time in the same accident.

com′mon divi′sor, *Math.* a number that is a submultiple of all the numbers of a given set. Also called **com′mon fac′tor.** [1840–50]

com·mon·er (kom′ə nər), *n.* **1.** a common person, as distinguished from one with rank, status, etc. **2.** *Brit.* **a.** any person ranking below a peer; a person without a title of nobility. **b.** a member of the House of Commons. **c.** (at Oxford and some other universities) a student who pays for his or her commons and other expenses and is not supported by any scholarship or foundation. **3.** a person who has a joint right in common land. [1275–1325; ME *cominer.* See COMMON, -ER[1]]

Com′mon E′ra. See **Christian Era.**

com′mon frac′tion, *Arith.* a fraction represented as a numerator above and a denominator below a horizontal or diagonal line. Also called **vulgar fraction.** Cf. **decimal fraction, mixed number.** [1890–95]

com′mon grack′le, a large songbird, *Quiscalus quiscula,* of the family Icteridae, of central and eastern North America, having iridescent black plumage varying in color. Cf. **purple grackle, bronzed grackle.**

com′mon ground′, a foundation of common interest or comprehension, as in a social relationship or a discussion. [1925–30]

com′mon il′iac ar′tery, *Anat.* See **iliac artery** (def. 1).

com′mon law′, 1. the system of law originating in England, as distinct from the civil or Roman law and the canon or ecclesiastical law. **2.** the unwritten law, esp. of England, based on custom or court decision, as distinct from statute law. **3.** the law administered through the system of courts established for the purpose, as distinct from equity or admiralty. [1300–50; ME]

com·mon-law (kom′ən lô′), *adj.* of, pertaining to, or established by common law: *a common-law spouse.* [1905–10]

com′mon-law mar′riage, a marriage without a civil or ecclesiastical ceremony, generally resulting from an agreement to marry followed by the couple's living together as husband and wife. [1905–10]

com′mon log′arithm, *Math.* a logarithm having 10 as the base. Also called **Briggsian logarithm.** Cf. **natural logarithm.** [1890–95]

com·mon·ly (kom′ən lē), *adv.* **1.** usually; generally; ordinarily. **2.** in a common manner. [1250–1300; ME *communeli(che).* See COMMON, -LY]

com′mon mal′low, cheese (def. 5).

Com′mon Mar′ket, 1. Official name, **European Economic Community.** an economic association established in 1958 and originally composed of Belgium, France, Italy, Luxembourg, the Netherlands, and West Germany, created chiefly to abolish barriers to free trade among member nations and to adopt common import duties on goods from other countries: the United Kingdom, the Republic of Ireland, and Denmark joined in 1973, Greece joined in 1981, and Spain and Portugal joined in 1986. *Abbr.:* CM **2.** (*sometimes l.c.*) any economic association of nations created for a similar purpose. [1950–55]

com′mon meas′ure, 1. See **common time. 2.** Also called **com′mon me′ter, hymnal stanza.** *Pros.* a ballad stanza of four iambic lines and strict rhymes, often used in hymns, rhyming *abcb* or *abab.* [1710–20]

com′mon mul′tiple, *Math.* a number that is a multiple of all the numbers of a given set. [1885–90]

com′mon nail′, a cut or wire nail having a slender shaft and a broad, flat head. See illus. under **nail.**

com′mon noun′, *Gram.* a noun that may be preceded by an article or other limiting modifier and that denotes any or all of a class of entities and not an individual, as *man, city, horse, music.* Also called **com′mon name′.** Cf. **proper noun.** [1860–65]

com·mon·place (kom′ən plās′), *adj.* **1.** ordinary; undistinguished or uninteresting; without individuality: *a commonplace person.* **2.** trite; hackneyed; platitudinous: *a commonplace remark.* —*n.* **3.** a well-known, customary, or obvious remark; a trite or uninteresting saying. **4.** anything common, ordinary, or uninteresting. **5.** *Archaic.* a place or passage in a book or writing noted as important for reference or quotation. [1525–35; trans. of L *locus commūnis,* itself trans. of Gk *koinòs tópos*] —**com′mon·place′ly,** *adv.* —**com′mon·place′ness,** *n.*
—**Syn. 2.** COMMONPLACE, BANAL, HACKNEYED, STEREOTYPED, TRITE describe words, remarks, and styles of expression that are lifeless and uninteresting. COMMONPLACE characterizes thought that is dull, ordinary, and platitudinous: *commonplace and boring.* Something is BANAL that seems inane, insipid, and pointless: *a heavy-handed and banal affirmation of the obvious.* HACKNEYED characterizes something that seems stale and worn out through overuse: *a hackneyed comparison.* STEREOTYPED emphasizes the fact that situations felt to be similar invariably call for the same thought in exactly the same form and the same words: *so stereotyped as to seem automatic.* TRITE describes something that was originally striking and apt, but which has become so well-known and been so commonly used that all interest has been worn out of it: *true but trite.*

com′monplace book′, a book in which noteworthy quotations, comments, etc., are written. [1570–80]

com′mon pleas′, *Law.* **1.** civil actions or proceedings between private citizens. **2.** Also, **Com′mon Pleas′.** See **court of common pleas.** [1175–1225; ME]

com′mon pray′er, 1. prayer for reciting by a group of worshipers, esp. the liturgy for public worship prescribed by the Church of England. **2.** (*caps.*) See **Book of Common Prayer.** [1520–30]

com′mon prop′erty, 1. property belonging to all members of a community. **2.** someone or something regarded as belonging to the public in general: *The personal lives of celebrities often become common property.* **3.** information that is commonly known; common knowledge: *His secret was soon common property.*

com′mon raft′er, a rafter having no function other than to bear roofing. Cf. **principal rafter.** See diag. under **king post.** [1815–25]

com′mon ra′tio, *Math.* See **geometric ratio.**

com′mon rhythm′, *Pros.* See **running rhythm.**

com′mon room′, a room or lounge for informal use by all. [1660–70]

com′mon salt′, salt[1] (def. 1). [1670–80]

com′mon school′, a public school usually including both primary and secondary grades but sometimes primary grades alone. [1650–60, *Amer.*]

com′mon scold′, (in early common law) a habitually rude and brawling woman whose conduct was subject to punishment as a public nuisance. [1760–70]

com′mon sen′nit. See **flat sennit.** [‡1960–65]

com′mon sense′, sound practical judgment that is independent of specialized knowledge, training, or the like; normal native intelligence. [1525–35; trans. of L *sēnsus commūnis,* itself trans. of Gk *koinḕ aísthēsis*] —**com′mon-sense′, com′mon·sense′,** *adj.* —**com′·mon·sen′si·cal, com′mon·sen′si·ble,** *adj.* —**com′·mon·sen′si·cal·ly, com′mon·sen′si·bly,** *adv.*

com′mon-sense re′alism, *Philos.* See **naive realism.** —**com′mon-sense re′alist.**

com′mon si′tus pick′eting, the picketing of an entire construction project by a union having a dispute with only one subcontractor working at the site. Also called **com′mon site′ pick′eting, situs picketing.**

com′mon snipe′. See under **snipe** (def. 1).

com′mon stock′, 1. stock that ordinarily has no preference in the matter of dividends or assets and represents the residual ownership of a corporate business. **2.** *Animal Husb.* stock that is not purebred. [1840–50]

com′mon sul′fur, a sulfur butterfly, *Colias philodice,* having yellow wings with black edges and larvae that feed on clover and other legumes. Also called **clouded sulfur.**

com′mon tan′nin, *Chem.* See under **tannin.**

com′mon teal′, *Brit.* See **green-winged teal.**

com′mon tern′. See under **tern**[1].

com′mon time′, *Music.* a meter or tempo of four beats per measure, with each of four quarter notes receiving a single beat. *Symbol:* C Also called **common measure.** [1665–75]

com′mon to′paz, topaz (def. 2).

com′mon touch′, the ability to communicate with, appeal to, or inspire ordinary people. [1940–45]

com·mon·weal (kom′ən wēl′), *n.* **1.** the common welfare; the public good. **2.** *Archaic.* the body politic; a commonwealth. Also, **com′mon weal′.** [1350–1400; ME *comen wele.* See COMMON, WEAL[1]]

com·mon·wealth (kom′ən welth′), *n.* **1.** (*cap.*) a group of sovereign states and their dependencies associated by their own choice and linked with common objectives and interests: *the British Commonwealth.* **2. the Commonwealth.** See **Commonwealth of Nations. 3.** (*cap.*) a federation of states: *the Commonwealth of Australia.* **4.** (*cap.*) a self-governing territory associated with the U.S.: official designation of Puerto Rico. **5.** (*cap.*) *Eng. Hist.* the English government from the abolition of the monarchy in 1649 until the establishment of the Protectorate in 1653, sometimes extended to include the restoration of Charles II in 1660. **6.** (*cap.*) the official designation (rather than "State") of four states of the U.S.: Kentucky, Massachusetts, Pennsylvania, and Virginia. **7.** any group of persons united by some common interest. **8.** the whole body of people of a nation or state; the body politic. **9.** a state in which the supreme power is held by the people; a republican or democratic state. **10.** *Obs.* the public welfare. [1375–1425; late ME *commun welthe*]

Com′monwealth Day′, a holiday observed in some countries of the Commonwealth of Nations, originally on May 24, the anniversary of Queen Victoria's birth, but now on varying dates. Formerly, **Empire Day.** [1955–60]

Com′monwealth of Eng′land, commonwealth (def. 5).

Com′monwealth of In′dependent States′, an alliance of former Soviet republics formed in December 1991, including: Armenia, Azerbaijan, Belarus, Kazakhstan, Kyrgyzstan, Moldova, Russian Federation, Tajikistan, Ukraine, and Uzbekistan. *Abbr.:* C.I.S.

Com′monwealth of Na′tions, a voluntary association of independent nations and dependent territories linked by historical ties (as parts of the former British

Empire) and cooperating on matters of mutual concern, esp. regarding economics and trade. See table. Also called **the Commonwealth.** Formerly, **British Commonwealth, British Commonwealth of Nations.**

INDEPENDENT MEMBER COUNTRIES OF THE COMMONWEALTH OF NATIONS

Antigua and Barbuda	New Zealand
Australia	Nigeria
The Bahamas	Pakistan
Bangladesh	Papua New Guinea
Barbados	St. Christopher and Nevis
Belize	St. Lucia
Botswana	St. Vincent and the Grenadines
Brunei	Seychelles
Canada	Sierra Leone
Cyprus	Singapore
Dominica	Solomon Islands
The Gambia	Sri Lanka
Ghana	Swaziland
Grenada	Tanzania
Guyana	Tonga
India	Trinidad and Tobago
Jamaica	Tuvalu
Kenya	Uganda
Kiribati	United Kingdom of Great Britain and Northern Ireland
Lesotho	Vanuatu
Malawi	Western Samoa
Malaysia	Zambia
Maldives	Zimbabwe
Malta	
Mauritius	
Namibia	
Nauru	

com′mon year′, an ordinary year of 365 days; a year having no intercalary period. Cf. **leap year.** [1905–10]

com′mon yel′low throat′, a widely distributed wood warbler, *Geothlypis trichas,* of North America and Mexico, in the male having a black facial mask and yellow underparts.

com•mo•ran•cy (kom′ər ən sē), *n., pl.* **-cies.** *Law.* a dwelling in a place; usual or temporary residence in a place. [1580–90; commor(ant) residing (< L *commorant-,* s. of *commorāns,* prp. of *commorārī* to remain, delay, equiv. to *com-* COM- + *morārī* to delay, deriv. of *mora* delay) + -ANCY] —**com′mo•rant,** *adj.*

com•mo•tion (kə mō′shən), *n.* **1.** violent or tumultuous motion; agitation; noisy disturbance: *What's all the commotion in the hallway?* **2.** political or social disturbance or upheaval; sedition; insurrection. [1520–30; < L *commōtiōn-* (s. of *commōtiō*), equiv. to *commōt(us)* ptp. of *commovēre* to COMMOVE + *-iōn-* -ION] —**com•mo′•tion•al,** *adj.* —**com•mo′tive,** *adj.*
—**Syn. 1.** disorder, turmoil, tumult, riot, turbulence, bustle. See **ado.**

com•move (kə mōōv′), *v.t.,* **-moved, -mov•ing.** to move violently; agitate; excite. [1350–1400; ME *commeven* < AF *commoveir,* MF *com(m)ovoir* < L *commovēre,* equiv. to *com-* COM- + *movēre* to MOVE]

com•mu•nal (kə myōōn′l, kom′yə nl), *adj.* **1.** used or shared in common by everyone in a group: *a communal jug of wine.* **2.** of, by, or belonging to the people of a community; shared or participated in by the public: *communal land; Building the playground was a communal project.* **3.** pertaining to a commune or a community: *communal life.* **4.** engaged in by or involving two or more communities: *communal conflict.* [1805–15; < F < L *commūnālis,* equiv. to *commūn(e)* COMMUNE[3] + *-ālis* -AL[1]] —**com•mu′nal•ly,** *adv.*
—**Syn. 2.** public, common, collective.

com•mu•nal•ism (kə myōōn′l iz′əm, kom′yə nl-), *n.* **1.** a theory or system of government according to which each commune is virtually an independent state and the nation is merely a federation of such states. **2.** the principles or practices of communal ownership. **3.** strong allegiance to one's own ethnic group rather than to society as a whole. [1870–75; COMMUNAL + -ISM] —**com•mu′•nal•ist,** *n.* —**com•mu′nal•is′tic,** *adj.*

com•mu•nal•i•ty (kom′yə nal′i tē), *n.* **1.** the state or condition of being communal. **2.** a feeling or spirit of cooperation and belonging arising from common interests and goals. [1900–05; COMMUNAL + -ITY]

com•mu•nal•ize (kə myōōn′l iz′, kom′yə nl-), *v.t.,* **-ized, -iz•ing.** to make communal; to make (land, a business, etc.) the property of the community: *The town communalized the estate for a public park.* Also, *esp. Brit.,* **com•mu′nal•ise′.** [1880–85; COMMUNAL + -IZE] —**com•mu′nal•i•za′tion,** *n.*

commu′nal mar′riage. See **group marriage.** [1865–70]

Com•mu•nard (kom′yə närd′), *n.* **1.** (*often l.c.*) *Fr. Hist.* a member or supporter of the Commune of 1871. Cf. **commune**[3] (def. 8b). **2.** (*l.c.*) a person who lives in a commune. [1870–75; < F; see COMMUNE[3], -ARD]

com•mune[1] (*v.* kə myōōn′; *n.* kom′yōōn), *v.,* **-muned, -mun•ing,** *n.* —*v.i.* **1.** to converse or talk together, usually with profound intensity, intimacy, etc.; interchange thoughts or feelings. **2.** to be in intimate communication or rapport: *to commune with nature.* —*n.* **3.** interchange of ideas or sentiments. [1250–1300; ME *com(m)unen* < MF *comuner* to share, deriv. of *comun* COMMON] —**com•mun′er,** *n.*

CONCISE ETYMOLOGY KEY: <, descended or borrowed from; >, whence; b., blend of, blended; c., cognate with; cf., compare; deriv., derivative; equiv., equivalent; imit., imitative; obl., oblique; r., replacing; s., stem; sp., spelling, spelled; resp., respelling, respelled; trans., translation; ?, origin unknown; *, unattested; ‡, probably earlier than. See the full key inside the front cover.

com•mune[2] (kə myōōn′), *v.i.,* **-muned, -mun•ing.** to partake of the Eucharist. [1275–1325; ME; back formation from COMMUNION]

com•mune[3] (kom′yōōn), *n.* **1.** a small group of persons living together, sharing possessions, work, income, etc., and often pursuing unconventional lifestyles. **2.** a close-knit community of people who share common interests. **3.** the smallest administrative division in France, Italy, Switzerland, etc., governed by a mayor assisted by a municipal council. **4.** a similar division in some other country. **5.** any community organized for the protection and promotion of local interests, and subordinate to the state. **6.** the government or citizens of a commune. **7.** See **people's commune. 8. the Commune.** Also called **Com′mune of Par′is, Paris Commune. a.** a revolutionary committee that took the place of the municipality of Paris in the revolution of 1789, usurped the authority of the state, and was suppressed by the National Convention in 1794. **b.** a socialistic government of Paris from March 18 to May 27, 1871. [1785–95; < F < ML *commūna* (fem.), alter. of L *commūne* community, state, orig. neut. of *commūnis* COMMON]

com•mu•ni•ca•ble (kə myōō′ni kə bəl), *adj.* **1.** capable of being easily communicated or transmitted: *communicable information; a communicable disease.* **2.** talkative; communicative. [1350–1400; ME < LL *commūnicābilis,* equiv. to *commūnicā(re)* (see COMMUNICATE) + *-bilis* -BLE] —**com•mu′ni•ca•bil′i•ty, com•mu′ni•ca•ble•ness,** *n.* —**com•mu′ni•ca•bly,** *adv.*

Commu′nicable Disease′ Cen′ter, former name of **Centers for Disease Control.**

com•mu•ni•cant (kə myōō′ni kənt), *n.* **1.** a person who partakes or is entitled to partake of the Eucharist; a member of a church. **2.** a person who communicates. —*adj.* **3.** communicating; imparting. [1545–55; < L *commūnicant-* (s. of *commūnicāns*), equiv. to *commūnic(āre)* to share with (see COMMUNICATE) + *-ant-* -ANT]

com•mu•ni•cate (kə myōō′ni kāt′), *v.,* **-cat•ed, -cat•ing.** —*v.t.* **1.** to impart knowledge of; make known: *to communicate information; to communicate one's happiness.* **2.** to give to another; impart; transmit: *to communicate a disease.* **3.** to administer the Eucharist to. **4.** *Archaic.* to share in or partake of. —*v.i.* **5.** to give or interchange thoughts, feelings, information, or the like, by writing, speaking, etc.: *They communicate with each other every day.* **6.** to express thoughts, feelings, or information easily or effectively. **7.** to be joined or connected: *The rooms communicated by means of a hallway.* **8.** to partake of the Eucharist. **9.** *Obs.* to take part or participate. [1520–30; < L *commūnicātus,* ptp. of *commūnicāre* to impart, make common, equiv. to *commūn(is)* COMMON + *-icāre* v. suffix]
—**Syn. 1.** divulge, announce, disclose, reveal. COMMUNICATE, IMPART denote giving to a person or thing a part or share of something, now usually something immaterial, as knowledge, thoughts, hopes, qualities, or properties. COMMUNICATE, the more common word, implies often an indirect or gradual transmission: *to communicate information by means of letters, telegrams, etc.; to communicate one's wishes to someone else.* IMPART usually implies directness of action: *to impart information.*
—**Ant. 1.** withhold, conceal.

com•mu•ni•ca•tion (kə myōō′ni kā′shən), *n.* **1.** the act or process of communicating; fact of being communicated. **2.** the imparting or interchange of thoughts, opinions, or information by speech, writing, or signs. **3.** something imparted, interchanged, or transmitted. **4.** a document or message imparting news, views, information, etc. **5.** passage, or an opportunity or means of passage, between places. **6. communications, a.** means of sending messages, orders, etc., including telephone, telegraph, radio, and television. **b.** routes and transportation for moving troops and supplies from a base to an area of operations. **7.** *Biol.* **a.** activity by one organism that changes or has the potential to change the behavior of other organisms. **b.** transfer of information from one cell or molecule to another, as by chemical or electrical signals. [1375–1425; ME *communicacioun* < MF < L *commūnicātiōn-* (s. of *commūnicātiō*), equiv. to *commūnicāt(us)* (see COMMUNICATE) + *-iōn-* -ION] —**com•mu′ni•ca′tion•al,** *adj.*

communica′tions sat′ellite, an artificial earth satellite that facilitates communications, as radio, television, and telephone transmissions, by means of the reflection or the amplification and retransmission of signals between stations on earth or in space. [1960–65]

communica′tion the′ory. See **information theory.** [1945–50]

com•mu•ni•ca•tive (kə myōō′ni kā′tiv, -kə tiv), *adj.* **1.** inclined to communicate or impart; talkative: *He isn't feeling very communicative today.* **2.** of or pertaining to communication. Also, **com•mu•ni•ca•to•ry** (kə myōō′ni-kə tôr′ē, -tōr′ē). [1350–1400; ME < ML *commūnicātīvus,* equiv. to *commūnicāt(us)* (see COMMUNICATE) + *-īvus* -IVE] —**com•mu′ni•ca′tive•ly,** *adv.* —**com•mu′•ni•ca′tive•ness,** *n.*
—**Syn. 1.** free-spoken, loquacious, voluble, expansive.

commu′nicative com′petence, *Ling.* a speaker's internalized knowledge both of the grammatical rules of a language and of the rules for appropriate use in social contexts.

com•mu•ni•ca•tor (kə myōō′ni kā′tər), *n.* **1.** a person who communicates, esp. one skilled at conveying information, ideas, or policy to the public. **2.** a person in the business of communications, as television or magazine publishing. [1655–65; < LL *commūnicātor;* see COMMUNICATE, -TOR]

com•mun•ion (kə myōōn′yən), *n.* **1.** (*often cap.*) Also called **Holy Communion.** *Eccles.* **a.** the act of receiving the Eucharistic elements. **b.** the elements of the Eucharist. **c.** the celebration of the Eucharist. **d.** the antiphon sung at a Eucharistic service. **2.** a group of persons having a common religious faith; a religious denomination: *Anglican communion.* **3.** association; fellowship. **4.** interchange or sharing of thoughts or emotions; intimate communication: *communion with nature.* **5.** the act of sharing, or holding in common; participation. **6.** the state of things so held. [1350–1400; ME (< AF) < L *commūniōn-* (s. of *commūniō*) a sharing, equiv. to *commūn(is)* COMMON + *-iōn-* -ION] —**com•mun′ion•a•ble,** *adj.* —**com•mun′ion•al,** *adj.*

commun′ion cloth′, corporal[3]. [1625–35]

commun′ion cup′, *Eccles.* a chalice from which a communicant drinks. [1635–45]

com•mun•ion•ist (kə myōōn′yə nist), *n. Eccles.* **1.** a person with a particular view or interpretation of communion, as specified. **2.** a communicant. [1635–45; COMMUNION + -IST]

commun′ion of saints′, the spiritual fellowship existing among all faithful Christians, both living and dead.

commun′ion plate′, *Rom. Cath. Ch.* the plate held under the chin of a communicant to catch the Host if it should fall.

commun′ion rail′, *Eccles.* the altar rail where communion is received by the congregation. [1840–50]

Commun′ion Sun′day, *Eccles.* any Sunday on which communion is administered. [1875–80]

commun′ion ta′ble, *Eccles.* the table used in the celebration of communion, or the Lord's Supper; the Lord's table. [1560–70]

com•mu•ni•qué (kə myōō′ni kā′, kə myōō′ni kā′), *n.* an official bulletin or communication, usually to the press or public. [1850–55; < F: lit., communicated, ptp. of *communiquer* < L *commūnicāre* to COMMUNICATE]

com•mu•nism (kom′yə niz′əm), *n.* **1.** a theory or system of social organization based on the holding of all property in common, actual ownership being ascribed to the community as a whole or to the state. **2.** (*often cap.*) a system of social organization in which all economic and social activity is controlled by a totalitarian state dominated by a single and self-perpetuating political party. **3.** (*cap.*) the principles and practices of the Communist party. **4.** communalism. [1835–45; < F *communisme.* See COMMON, -ISM]

Com′munism Peak′, a peak of the Pamir mountains, in NE Tajikistan. 24,590 ft. (7495 m). Formerly, **Stalin Peak.**

com•mu•nist (kom′yə nist), *n.* **1.** (*cap.*) a member of the Communist party or movement. **2.** an advocate of communism. **3.** a person who is regarded as supporting politically leftist or subversive causes. **4.** (*usually cap.*) a Communard. —*adj.* **5.** (*cap.*) of or pertaining to the Communist party or to Communism. **6.** pertaining to communists or communism. [1835–45; < F *communiste.* See COMMON, -IST] —**com′mu•nis′tic, com′mu•nis′ti•cal,** *adj.* —**com′mu•nis′ti•cal•ly,** *adv.*

Com′munist Chi′na. *Informal.* See **China, People's Republic of.**

Com′munist Interna′tional. See **Third International.**

Com′munist Manifes′to, a pamphlet (1848) by Karl Marx and Friedrich Engels: first statement of the principles of modern communism.

Com′munist par′ty, a political party advocating the principles of communism, esp. as developed by Marx and Lenin. [1840–50]

com•mu•ni•tar•i•an (kə myōō′ni târ′ē ən), *n.* **1.** a member of a communistic community. **2.** an advocate of such a community. [1835–45; COMMUNIT(Y) + -ARIAN]

com•mu•ni•tas (kə myōō′ni täs′), *n. Anthropol.* the sense of sharing and intimacy that develops among persons who experience liminality as a group. [< L; see COMMUNITY]

com•mu•ni•ty (kə myōō′ni tē), *n., pl.* **-ties. 1.** a social group of any size whose members reside in a specific locality, share government, and often have a common cultural and historical heritage. **2.** a locality inhabited by such a group. **3.** a social, religious, occupational, or other group sharing common characteristics or interests and perceived or perceiving itself as distinct in some respect from the larger society within which it exists (usually prec. by *the*): *the business community; the community of scholars.* **4.** a group of associated nations sharing common interests or a common heritage: *the community of Western Europe.* **5.** *Eccles.* a group of men or women leading a common life according to a rule. **6.** *Ecol.* an assemblage of interacting populations occupying a given area. **7.** joint possession, enjoyment, liability, etc.: *community of property.* **8.** similar character; agreement; identity: *community of interests.* **9. the community,** the public; society: *the needs of the community.* [1325–75; < L *commūnitās,* equiv. to *commūni(s)* COMMON + *-tās* -TY[2]; r. ME *comunete* < MF < L as above] —**com•mu′ni•tal,** *adj.*
—**Syn. 1.** COMMUNITY, HAMLET, VILLAGE, TOWN, CITY are terms for groups of people living in somewhat close association, and usually under common rules. COMMUNITY is a general term, and TOWN is often loosely applied. A commonly accepted set of connotations envisages HAMLET as a small group, VILLAGE as a somewhat larger one, TOWN still larger, and CITY as very large. Size is, however, not the true basis of differentiation, but properly sets off only HAMLET. Incorporation, or the absence of it, and the type of government determine the classification of the others. **8.** similarity, likeness.

commu′nity anten′na tel′evision. See **CATV.** [1950–55]

commu′nity cen′ter, a building or other place in which members of a community may gather for social, educational, or cultural activities. [1910–15, *Amer.*]

commu′nity chest′, a fund for local welfare activities, built up by voluntary contributions. [1920–25, *Amer.*]

Commu′nity Chests′ and Coun′cils of Amer′•ica, a former name (1918–65) of the United Way of America. See under **United Way.**

commu′nity church′, an independent or denominational church in a particular community. [1930–35, *Amer.*]

commu′nity col′lege, a nonresidential junior college established to serve a specific community and typically supported in part by local government funds. [1945–50, *Amer.*]

commu′nity med′icine, public-health services targeted to a given community, often a low-income population.

commu′nity men′tal health′ cen′ter, a health-care facility or network of agencies that is part of a system originally authorized by the U.S. government to provide a coordinated program of continuing mental health care to a specific population.

commu′nity prop′erty, *U.S. Law.* (in some states) property acquired by a husband, wife, or both together, that is considered by law to be jointly owned and equally shared. [1920–25]

commu′nity serv′ice, *Law.* a punitive sentence that requires a convicted person to perform unpaid work for the community in lieu of imprisonment.

Commu′nity Serv′ices Administra′tion, *U.S. Govt.* a former independent agency (abolished 1981) that helped low-income persons attain economic self-sufficiency. *Abbr.:* CSA Formerly, **Office of Economic Opportunity.**

com•mu•nize (kom′yə nīz′), *v.t.,* **-nized, -niz•ing.** **1.** (*often cap.*) to impose Communist principles or systems of government on (a country or people). **2.** to make communistic. **3.** to make (something, as land or a house) the property of the community; to transfer from individual to community ownership. Also, *esp. Brit.,* **com′mu•nise′.** [1885–90; back formation from *communization,* equiv. to L *commūn(is)* COMMON + -IZATION] **—com′•mu•ni•za′tion,** *n.*

com•mut•a•ble (kə myo͞o′tə bəl), *adj.* that may be commuted; exchangeable or interchangeable. [1640–50; < L *commūtābilis,* equiv. to *commūtā(re)* to COMMUTE + *-bilis* -BLE] **—com•mut′a•bil′i•ty, com•mut′a•ble•ness,** *n.*

com•mu•tate (kom′yə tāt′), *v.t.,* **-tat•ed, -tat•ing.** *Elect.* **1.** to reverse the direction of (a current or currents), as by a commutator. **2.** to convert (alternating current) into direct current by use of a commutator. [1645–55; back formation from COMMUTATION]

com•mu•ta•tion (kom′yə tā′shən), *n.* **1.** the act of substituting one thing for another; substitution; exchange. **2.** the changing of a prison sentence or other penalty to another less severe. **3.** the act of commuting, as to and from a place of work. **4.** the substitution of one kind of payment for another. **5.** *Elect.* the act or process of commutating. **6.** Also called **commuta′tion test′.** *Ling.* the technique, esp. in phonological analysis, of substituting one linguistic item for another while keeping the surrounding elements constant, used as a means of determining the constituent units in a sequence and their contrasts with other units. [1400–50; late ME *commutacioun* < L *commūtātiōn-* (s. of *commūtātiō*) change. See COMMUTE, -ATION]

commuta′tion tick′et, a ticket issued at a reduced rate, as by a railroad or bus company, entitling the holder to travel over a given route a fixed number of times or during a specified period. [1835–45]

com•mu•ta•tive (kə myo͞o′tə tiv, kom′yə tā′tiv), *adj.* **1.** of or pertaining to commutation, exchange, substitution, or interchange. **2.** *Math.* **a.** (of a binary operation) having the property that one term operating on a second is equal to the second operating on the first, as $a \times b = b \times a$. **b.** having reference to this property: *commutative law for multiplication.* [1525–35; < ML *commūtātivus,* equiv. to L *commūtāt(us)* (ptp. of *commūtāre;* see COMMUTE, -ATE[1]) + *-ivus* -IVE] **—com•mu′ta•tive•ly,** *adv.* **—com•mu′ta•tiv′i•ty,** *n.*

commu′tative law′, *Logic.* a law asserting that the order in which certain logical operations are performed is indifferent. [1835–45]

com•mu•ta•tor (kom′yə tā′tər), *n.* **1.** *Elect.* **a.** a device for reversing the direction of a current. **b.** (in a DC motor or generator) a cylindrical ring or disk assembly of conducting members, individually insulated in a supporting structure with an exposed surface for contact with current-collecting brushes and mounted on the armature shaft, for changing the frequency or direction of the current in the armature windings. **2.** *Math.* the element equal to the product of two given elements in a group multiplied on the right by the product of the inverses of the elements. [1830–40; COMMUTATE + -OR[2]]

com′mutator group′, *Math.* the subgroup of a given group, which consists of all the commutators in the group. [1960–65]

com•mute (kə myo͞ot′), *v.,* **-mut•ed, -mut•ing,** *n.* —*v.t.* **1.** to change (a prison sentence or other penalty) to a less severe one: *The death sentence was commuted to life imprisonment.* **2.** to exchange for another or for something else; give and take reciprocally; interchange. **3.** to change: *to commute base metal into gold.* **4.** to change (one kind of payment) into or for another, as by substitution. —*v.i.* **5.** to travel regularly over some distance, as from a suburb into a city and back: *He commutes to work by train.* **6.** to make substitution. **7.** to serve as a substitute. **8.** to make a collective payment, esp. of a reduced amount, as an equivalent for a number of payments. **9.** *Math.* to give the same result whether operating on the left or on the right. —*n.* **10.** a trip made by commuting: *It's a long commute from his home to his office.* **11.** an act or instance of commuting. [1400–50; 1885–90 for def. 5; late ME < L *commūtāre* to change, replace, exchange, equiv. to *com-* COM- + *mūtāre* to change]

com•mut•er (kə myo͞o′tər), *n.* **1.** a person who commutes, esp. between home and work. —*adj.* **2.** of or for commuting; serving commuters: *a commuter railroad.* **3.** of or pertaining to a flight, plane, or airline that carries passengers over relatively short distances and usually serves small communities. [1860–65, *Amer.;* COMMUTE + -ER[1]]

commut′er air′plane. See **air taxi.**

commut′er belt′, a suburban region housing many people who commute to a nearby city in which they work. [1960–65]

commut′er mar′riage, a marriage between spouses who live apart, usually because of the locations of their jobs, and who regularly travel to be together, as on weekends.

commut′er tax′, an income tax imposed by a locality on those who work within its boundaries but reside elsewhere. [1965–70]

com•mu•tu•al (kə myo͞o′cho͞o əl), *adj. Archaic.* mutual; reciprocal. [1595–1605; COM- + MUTUAL] **—com•mu•tu•al•i•ty** (kə myo͞o′cho͞o al′i tē), *n.*

com•my (kom′ē), *n., pl.* **-mies,** *adj.* (*often cap.*) *Informal (disparaging and offensive).* communist. Also, **commie.** [COMM(UNIST) + -Y[2]]

Com•ne•nus (kom nē′nəs), *n.* a dynasty of Byzantine emperors that ruled at Constantinople, 1057?–1185, and at Trebizond in Asia Minor, 1204–1461?. **—Com•ne•ni•an** (kom nē′nē ən), *adj.*

Co•mo (kō′mō; *It.* kô′mô), *n.* **1. Lake,** a lake in N Italy, in Lombardy. 35 mi. (56 km) long; 56 sq. mi. (145 sq. km). **2.** a city at the SW end of this lake. 97,169.

Co•mo•do•ro Ri•va•da•via (kô′mô ᵺô′rô rē′vä-ᵺä′vyä), a city in E Argentina. 96,865.

Com•o•ran (kom′ər ən), *adj.* **1.** Also, **Co•mo•ri•an** (kə môr′ē ən). of or pertaining to the Comoros or its inhabitants. —*n.* **2.** a native or inhabitant of the Comoros. [COMOR(O) + -AN]

Com•o•rin (kom′ər in), *n.* **Cape,** a cape on the S tip of India, extending into the Indian Ocean.

Com′o•ro Is′lands (kom′ə rō′), a group of islands in the Indian Ocean between N Madagascar and E Africa: formerly an overseas territory of France; now divided between the Comoros and France. 290,000; ab. 800 sq. mi. (2070 sq. km). French, **Îles Comores.**

Com•o•ros (kom′ə rōz′), *n.* **Federal and Islamic Republic of the,** a republic comprising three of the Comoro Islands (Grand Comoro, Mohéli, and Anjouan): a former overseas territory of France; declared independence 1975. 344,000; 719 sq. mi. (1862 sq. km). *Cap.:* Moroni.

co•mose (kō′mōs), *adj.* hairy; comate. [1785–95; < L *comōsus,* equiv. to *com(a)* (< Gk *kómē* hair, foliage of trees or plants) + *-ōsus* -OSE[1]]

comp[1] (komp), *Informal.* —*n.* **1.** a compositor. **2.** composition. —*v.t.* **3.** to compose (type). [1865–70; shortened form]

comp[2] (komp), *Informal.* —*n.* **1.** a ticket, book, service, etc., provided free of charge to specially chosen recipients. —*adj.* **2.** complimentary; free of charge: *I received a comp copy of her book.* —*v.t.* **3.** to provide with a comp: *Some casinos comped the biggest spenders, providing rooms and meals on the house.* **4.** to provide free of charge: *His meals and drinks at the hotel were often comped.* [1885–90; by shortening of COMPLIMENTARY]

comp[3] (komp), *v.i. Jazz.* to accompany a soloist with a succession of irregularly spaced chords that punctuate the rhythm. [1945–50, *Amer.;* shortening of ACCOMPANY]

comp[4] (komp), *n.* Often, **comps.** *Informal.* comprehensive (def. 4). [by shortening]

comp[5] (komp), *n. Informal.* compensation: *workers' comp; unemployment comp.* [by shortening]

comp., **1.** comparative. **2.** compare. **3.** compensation. **4.** compilation. **5.** compiled. **6.** compiler. **7.** complement. **8.** complete. **9.** composition. **10.** compositor. **11.** compound. **12.** comprehensive.

com•pact[1] (*adj.* kəm pakt′, kom-, kom′pakt; *v.* kəm-pakt′; *n.* kom′pakt), *adj.* **1.** joined or packed together; closely and firmly united; dense; solid: *compact soil.* **2.** arranged within a relatively small space: *a compact shopping center; a compact kitchen.* **3.** designed to be small in size and economical in operation. **4.** solidly or firmly built: *the compact body of a lightweight wrestler.* **5.** expressed concisely; pithy; terse; not diffuse: *a compact review of the week's news.* **6.** composed or made (usually fol. by *of*): *a book compact of form and content.* **7.** Also, **bicompact.** *Math.* (of a set) having the property that in any collection of open sets whose union contains the given set there exists a finite number of open sets whose union contains the given set; having the property that every open cover has a finite subcover. —*v.t.* **8.** to join or pack closely together; consolidate; condense. **9.** to make firm or stable. **10.** to form or make by close union or conjunction; make up or compose. **11.** *Metall.* to compress (metallic or metallic and nonmetallic powders) in a die to be sintered. **12.** to crush into compact form for convenient disposal or for storage until disposal: *to compact rubbish.* —*n.* **13.** a small case containing a mirror, face powder, a puff, and sometimes rouge. **14.** Also called **com′pact car′.** an automobile that is smaller than an intermediate but larger than a subcompact and generally has a combined passenger and luggage volume of 100–110 cu. ft. (2.8–3.1 m^3). **15.** *Metall.* (in powder metallurgy) an object to be sintered formed of metallic or of metallic and nonmetallic powders compressed in a die. [1375–1425; late ME < L *compāctus* (ptp. of *compingere* to shut away, bind together), equiv. to *com-* COM- + *pag-,* var. s. of *pangere* to fix, arrange (akin to *pāx* PEACE; cf. PACT, COMPACT[2]) + *-tus* ptp. suffix] **—com•pact′ed•ly,** *adv.* **—com•pact′ed•ness,** *n.* **—com•pact′ly,** *adv.* **—com•pact′ness,** *n.*
—Syn. 2. small, snug. **5.** concise, succinct, brief. **8.** compress. **9.** stabilize, solidify.

com•pact[2] (kom′pakt), *n.* a formal agreement between two or more parties, states, etc.; contract: *the proposed economic compact between Germany and France.* [1580–90; < L *compactum, compectum,* n. use of neut. of *compactus* (ptp. of *compacisci* to make an agreement), equiv. to *com-* COM- + *pac-* (s. of *pacisci* to secure by negotiation, akin to *pāx* settlement ending hostilities, PEACE) + *-tus* ptp. ending]
—Syn. treaty, pact, entente, convention, concordat. See **agreement.**

Com′pact Disc′, *Trademark.* a brand of compact disk.

com′pact disk′, an optical disk approximately 4¾ in. (12 cm) in diameter, on which a program, data, music, etc., is digitally encoded for a laser beam to scan, decode, and transmit to a playback system, computer monitor, or television set. *Abbr.:* CD Cf. **optical disk** (def. 1).

com′pact disk′ play′er, a device for playing compact disks. Also called **CD player.**

com•pact•i•ble (kəm pak′tə bəl), *adj.* capable of being compacted: *compactible rubbish.* [1615–25; COMPACT[1] + -IBLE] **—com•pact′i•bil′i•ty,** *n.*

com•pac•tion (kəm pak′shən, kom-), *n.* **1.** the act of compacting or the state of being compacted. **2.** *Geol.* the consolidation of sediments resulting from the weight of overlying deposits. [1350–1400; ME *compaccioun* < L *compāctiōn-* (s. of *compāctiō*) a joining, frame, equiv. to *compāct(us)* COMPACT[1] + *-iōn-* -ION]

com•pac•tor (kəm pak′tər, kom′pak-), *n.* an appliance that crushes and compresses trash into small convenient bundles. [1945–50; COMPACT[1] + -OR[2]]

com•pa•dre (kəm pä′drā), *n. Chiefly Southwestern U.S.* a friend, companion, or close associate. [1825–35, *Amer.;* < AmerSp; Sp: godfather < early ML *compater;* see COMPÈRE]

com•pa•gnie (kôɴ pa nyē′), *n., pl.* **-gnies** (-nyē′). *French.* company.

com•pand•er (kəm pan′dər), *n. Electronics.* (in a communications path) a combination of a compressor at one point and an expander at another, the compressor reducing the volume of a signal and the expander restoring it. Also, **com•pan′dor.** [1965–70; COM(PRESS) + (EX)PAND + -ER[1]]

com•pand•ing (kəm pan′ding), *n.* a process in which the dynamic range of a signal is reduced for recording purposes and then expanded to its original value for reproduction or playback. [1965–70; COMPAND(ER) + -ING[1]]

com•pa•ñe•ra (kom′pən yâr′ə; *Sp.* kôm′pä nye′rä), *n., pl.* **-pa•ñe•ras** (-pən yâr′əz; *Sp.* -pä nye′räs). **1.** (in the southwestern U.S.) a female companion; friend. **2.** (in Latin America) a female worker, coworker, or comrade. [1835–45; *Amer.;* < Sp, fem. of COMPAÑERO]

com•pa•ñe•ro (kom′pən yâr′ō; *Sp.* kôm′pä nye′rô), *n., pl.* **-pa•ñe•ros** (-pən yâr′ōz; *Sp.* -pä nye′rôs). **1.** (in the southwestern U.S.) a male companion or partner. **2.** (in Latin America) a male worker, coworker, or comrade. [1835–45, *Amer.;* < Sp, equiv. to *compañ(a)* COMPANY + *-ero* < L *-ārius* -ARY]

com•pa•ñi•a (kôm′pä nyē′ä), *n., pl.* **-ñi•as** (-nyē′äs). *Spanish.* company.

com•pan•ion[1] (kəm pan′yən), *n.* **1.** a person who is frequently in the company of, associates with, or accompanies another: *my son and his two companions.* **2.** a person employed to accompany, assist, or live with another in the capacity of a helpful friend. **3.** a mate or match for something: *White wine is the usual companion of fish.* **4.** a handbook or guide: *a bird watcher's companion.* **5.** a member of the lowest rank in an order of knighthood or of a grade in an order. **6.** Also called **companion star, comes.** *Astron.* the fainter of the two stars that constitute a double star. Cf. **primary** (def. 19b). **7.** *Obs.* a fellow. —*v.t.* **8.** to be a companion to; accompany. [1250–1300; ME *compainoun* < AF; OF *compaignon* < LL *compāniōn-* (s. of *compāniō*) messmate, equiv. to *com-* COM- + *pān(is)* bread + *-iōn-* -ION; presumably as trans. of a Gmc word; cf. Goth *gahlaiba,* OHG *galeipo*] **—com•pan′ion•less,** *adj.*
—Syn. 1. comrade, partner, mate. See **acquaintance.**

com•pan•ion[2] (kəm pan′yən), *n. Naut.* **1.** a covering over the top of a companionway. **2.** a companionway. [1755–65; alter. of D *kampanje* quarterdeck < F (*chambre de la*) *compagne* pantry of a medieval galley]

com•pan•ion•a•ble (kəm pan′yə nə bəl), *adj.* possessing the qualities of a good companion; pleasant to be with; congenial. [1350–1400; ME. See COMPANION[1], -ABLE] **—com•pan′ion•a•bil′i•ty, com•pan′ion•a•ble•ness,** *n.* **—com•pan′ion•a•bly,** *adv.*

com•pan•ion•ate (kəm pan′yə nit), *adj.* **1.** of, by, or like companions. **2.** tastefully harmonious. [1650–60; COMPANION[1] + -ATE[1]]

compan′ionate mar′riage, a form of marriage in which the partners agree not to have children and can be divorced by mutual consent, leaving neither spouse legally responsible for the financial welfare of the other. Cf. **trial marriage.** [1925–30]

compan′ion cell′, *Bot.* any of a number of specialized parenchymal cells adjacent to a sieve tube in the phloem of flowering plants, believed to regulate the flow of nutrients through the tube. [1885–90]

compan′ion lad′der, *Naut.* an inboard ladder or stair, as in a companionway. [1820–30]

compan′ion piece′, a literary or musical work that has a close relationship to another work by the same author or composer. [1835–45]

com•pan•ion•ship (kəm pan′yən ship′), *n.* **1.** association as companions; fellowship. **2.** *Print.* a group of compositors working under a foreman. [1540–50; COMPANION[1] + -SHIP]

CONCISE PRONUNCIATION KEY: *act, cāpe, dâre, pärt; set, ēqual; if, īce; ox, ōver, ôrder, oil, bo͝ok, bo͞ot, out; up, ûrge; child; sing; shoe; thin, that;* zh as in *treasure.* ə = *a* as in *alone, e* as in *system, i* as in *easily, o* as in *gallop, u* as in *circus;* ᵊ as in *fire* (fīᵊr), *hour* (ouᵊr). l and n can serve as syllabic consonants, as in *cradle* (krād′l), and *button* (but′n). See the full key inside the front cover.

compan′ion star′, *Astron.* companion[1] (def. 6). [1775–85]

com•pan•ion•way (kəm pan′yən wā′), *n. Naut.* **1.** a stair or ladder within the hull of a vessel. **2.** the space occupied by this stair or ladder. [1830–40; COMPANION[2] + WAY]

com•pa•ny (kum′pə nē), *n., pl.* **-nies,** *v.,* **-nied, -ny•ing.** —*n.* **1.** a number of individuals assembled or associated together; group of people. **2.** a guest or guests: *We're having company for dinner.* **3.** an assemblage of persons for social purposes. **4.** companionship; fellowship; association: *I always enjoy her company.* **5.** one's usual companions: *I don't like the company he keeps.* **6.** society collectively. **7.** a number of persons united or incorporated for joint action, esp. for business: *a publishing company; a dance company.* **8.** (*cap.*) the members of a firm not specifically named in the firm's title: *George Higgins and Company.* **9.** *Mil.* **a.** the smallest body of troops, consisting of a headquarters and two or three platoons. **b.** any relatively small group of soldiers. **c.** *Army.* a basic unit with both tactical and administrative functions. **10.** a unit of firefighters, including their special apparatus: *a hook-and-ladder company.* **11.** Also called **ship's company.** a ship's crew, including the officers. **12.** a medieval trade guild. **13. the Company,** *Informal.* a nation's major intelligence-gathering and espionage organization, as the U.S. Central Intelligence Agency. **14. keep company, a.** to associate with; be a friend of. **b.** *Informal.* to go together, as in courtship: *My sister has been keeping company with a young lawyer.* **15. part company, a.** to cease association or friendship with: *We parted company 20 years ago after the argument.* **b.** to take a different or opposite view; differ: *He parted company with his father on politics.* **c.** to separate: *We parted company at the airport.* —*v.i.* **16.** *Archaic.* to associate. —*v.t.* **17.** *Archaic.* to accompany. [1200–50; ME < AF; OF *compaignie* companionship, equiv. to *compain* (< LL *compānio*; see COMPANION[1]) + *-ie* -Y[3]] —**com′pa•ny•less,** *adj.*
—**Syn. 1.** group, assemblage, body. COMPANY, BAND, PARTY, TROOP refer to a group of people formally or informally associated. COMPANY is the general word and means any group of people: *a company of motorists.* BAND, used esp. of a band of musicians, suggests a relatively small group pursuing the same purpose or sharing a common fate: *a concert by a band; a band of survivors.* PARTY, except when used of a political group, usually implies an indefinite and temporary assemblage, as for some common pursuit: *a spelunking party.* TROOP, used specifically of a body of cavalry, usually implies a number of individuals organized as a unit: *a troop of cavalry.* **3.** gathering, crowd. **6.** firm, house, corporation.

com′pany grade′, military rank applying to army officers below major, as second and first lieutenants and captains. Cf. **field grade.**

com′pany man′, an employee whose allegiance to his employer comes before personal beliefs or loyalty to fellow workers. [1920–25]

com′pany of′ficer, *Army and Marine Corps.* a captain or lieutenant serving in a company. [1835–45]

Com′pany of Je′sus, former name of the Society of Jesus.

com′pany store′, a retail store operated by a company for the convenience of the employees, who are required to buy from the store. Also called **industrial store.** [1870–75, *Amer.*]

com′pany town′, a town whose inhabitants are mainly dependent on one company for employment, housing, supplies, etc. [1930–35, *Amer.*]

com′pany un′ion, 1. a labor union dominated by management rather than controlled by the membership. **2.** a union confined to employees of one business or corporation. [1910–15]

compar., comparative.

com•pa•ra•ble (kom′pər ə bəl *or, sometimes,* kəm pâr′-), *adj.* **1.** capable of being compared; having features in common with something else to permit or suggest comparison: *He considered the Roman and British empires to be comparable.* **2.** worthy of comparison: *shops comparable to those on Fifth Avenue.* **3.** usable for comparison; similar: *We have no comparable data on Russian farming.* [1375–1425; late ME < L *comparābilis,* equiv. to *comparā(re)* to COMPARE + *-bilis* -BLE] —**com′pa•ra•bil′i•ty, com′pa•ra•ble•ness,** *n.* —**com′•pa•ra•bly,** *adv.*
—**Syn. 1.** like, equal, equivalent, similar.

com′parable worth′, the doctrine that a woman's and man's pay should be equal when their work requires equal training, skills, and responsibilities.

com•par•a•tist (kəm par′ə tist), *n.* a specialist in comparative linguistics or comparative literature. [1930–35; < F *comparatiste* < L *comparāt(us)* (ptp. of *comparāre* to COMPARE) + F *-iste* -IST]

com•par•a•tive (kəm par′ə tiv), *adj.* **1.** of or pertaining to comparison. **2.** proceeding by, founded on, or using comparison as a method of study: *comparative anatomy.* **3.** estimated by comparison; not positive or absolute; relative: *a comparative newcomer in politics; to live in comparative luxury.* **4.** *Gram.* being, noting, or pertaining to the intermediate degree of the comparison of adjectives, as *better* and *more beautiful,* the comparative forms of *good* and *beautiful,* and of adverbs, as *nearer* and *more carefully,* the comparative forms of *near* and *carefully.* Cf. **positive** (def. 20), **superlative** (def. 2). —*n. Gram.* **5.** the comparative degree. **6.** a form in the comparative. [1400–50; late ME < L *comparātīvus,* equiv. to *comparāt(us)* (ptp. of *comparāre* to COMPARE; see -ATE[1]) + *-īvus* -IVE] —**com•par′a•tive•ly,** *adv.* —**com•par′a•tive•ness,** *n.*

CONCISE ETYMOLOGY KEY: <, descended or borrowed from; >, whence; b., blend of, blended; c., cognate with; cf., compare; deriv., derivative; equiv., equivalent; imit., imitative; obl., oblique; r., replacing; s., stem; sp., spelling, spelled; resp., respelling, respelled; trans., translation; ?, origin unknown; *, unattested; ‡, probably earlier than. See the full key inside the front cover.

compar′ative ad′vertising, advertising in which a competing product is identified and compared unfavorably with the advertiser's product. [1970–75]

compar′ative gov′ernment, the study and comparison of different forms of government.

compar′ative linguis′tics, the study of the correspondences between languages that have a common origin. —**compar′ative lin′guist.**

compar′ative lit′erature, the study of the literatures of two or more groups differing in cultural background and, usually, in language, concentrating on their relationships to and influences upon each other.

compar′ative meth′od, *Historical Ling.* a body of procedures and criteria used by linguists to determine whether and how two or more languages are related and to reconstruct forms of their hypothetical parent language.

compar′ative musicol′ogy, ethnomusicology.

compar′ative philol′ogy. See **comparative linguistics.** [1880–85]

compar′ative psychol′ogy, a branch of psychology involving the study and comparison of the behaviors of diverse animal species, often under controlled laboratory experiments, in order to discover general principles of behavior. [1940–45]

compar′ative reli′gion, a field of study seeking to derive general principles from a comparison and classification of the growth and influence of various religions.

compar′ative state′ment, a financial statement with figures arranged in two or more parallel columns, each column representing a fiscal year or other period, used to compare performance between periods.

com•par•a•tor (kəm par′ə tər, kom′pə rā′-), *n.* **1.** any of various instruments for making comparisons, as of lengths or distances, tints of colors, etc. **2.** *Electronics.* a circuit for comparing two signals, as readings of duplicate information stored in a digital computer, and for giving an indication of agreement or disagreement between them. [1880–85; < LL *comparātor* a comparer. See COMPARE, -TOR]

com•pare (kəm pâr′), *v.,* **-pared, -par•ing,** *n.* —*v.t.* **1.** to examine (two or more objects, ideas, people, etc.) in order to note similarities and differences: *to compare two pieces of cloth; to compare the governments of two nations.* **2.** to consider or describe as similar; liken: *Shall I compare thee to a summer's day?* **3.** *Gram.* to form or display the degrees of comparison of (an adjective or adverb). —*v.i.* **4.** to be worthy of comparison; be held equal: *Dekker's plays cannot compare with Shakespeare's.* **5.** to appear in a similar standing: *His recital certainly compares with the one he gave last year.* **6.** to differ in quality or accomplishment as specified: *Their development compares poorly with that of neighbor nations.* **7.** to vie; rival. **8.** to make a comparison: *The only way we can say which product is better is to compare.* **9. compare notes.** See **note** (def. 25). —*n.* **10.** comparison: *Her beauty is beyond compare.* [1375–1425; late ME *comparen* < L *comparāre* to place together, match, v. deriv. of *compar* alike, matching (see COM-, PAR); r. ME *comperen* < OF *comperer* < L] —**com•par′•er,** *n.*
—**Usage.** The traditional rule about which preposition to use after COMPARE states that COMPARE should be followed by TO when it points out likenesses or similarities between two apparently dissimilar persons or things: *She compared his handwriting to knotted string.* COMPARE should be followed by WITH, the rule says, when it points out similarities or differences between two entities of the same general class: *The critic compared the paintings in the exhibit with magazine photographs.* This rule is by no means always observed, however, even in formal speech and writing. The usual practice is to employ TO for likenesses between members of different classes: *A language may be compared to a living organism.* But when the comparison is between members of the same category, both TO and WITH are used: *The article compares the Chicago of today with* (or *to*) *the Chicago of the 1890's.* Following the past participle COMPARED, either TO or WITH is used regardless of whether differences or similarities are stressed or whether the things compared belong to the same or different classes: *Compared with* (or *to*) *the streets of 18th-century London, New York's streets are models of cleanliness and order.*

com•par•i•son (kəm par′ə sən), *n.* **1.** the act of comparing. **2.** the state of being compared. **3.** a likening; illustration by similitude; comparative estimate or statement. **4.** *Rhet.* the considering of two things with regard to some characteristic that is common to both, as the likening of a hero to a lion in courage. **5.** capability of being compared or likened. **6.** *Gram.* **a.** the function of an adverb or adjective that is used to indicate degrees of superiority or inferiority in quality, quantity, or intensity. **b.** the patterns of formation involved therein. **c.** the degrees of a particular word, displayed in a fixed order, as *mild, milder, mildest, less mild, least mild.* [1300–50; ME *comparesoun* < OF *comparaison* < L *comparātiōn-* (s. of *comparātiō*). See COMPARE, -ATION]
—**Syn. 5.** likeness, resemblance, similarity.

compar′ison mi′croscope, *Optics.* a microscope having two objective lenses and using a system of prisms to form in one eyepiece adjacent images of two different objects. [1935–40]

com•par•i•son-shop (kəm par′ə sən shop′), *v.,* **-shopped, -shop•ping.** —*v.i.* **1.** to compare prices and quality of competing merchandise. —*v.t.* **2.** to compare prices and quality of merchandise in (competing stores) to determine the best value. **3.** to compare prices and quality of (competing merchandise). [1965–70]

compar′ison shop′per, an employee of a retail store hired to visit competing stores in order to gather information regarding styles, quality, prices, etc., of merchandise offered by competitors.

compar′ison test′, *Math.* the theorem that a given infinite series converges if the absolute value of each term of the given series is less than or equal to the corresponding term in a known convergent series.

com•par•sa (kəm pär′sə), *n.* a song and folk dance of Cuba. [< AmerSp, Sp: masquerade, group of theatrical supernumeraries < It: supernumerary (fem.), appearance, n. use of fem. of *comparso,* ptp. of *comparire* < L *compārēre* become visible. See COM-, APPEAR]

com•part (kəm pärt′), *v.t.* **1.** to separate or mark out in parts; subdivide. **2.** to distribute and give proportional relationships to the parts of (an architectural design). [1565–75; < LL *compartīre* to divide up. See COM-, PART]

com•par•ti•men•to (kôm pär′tē men′tô), *n., pl.* **-ti** (-tē). *Italian.* any of the 18 administrative districts into which Italy is divided.

com•part•ment (kəm pärt′mənt), *n.* **1.** a part or space marked or partitioned off. **2.** a separate room, section, etc.: *a baggage compartment.* **3.** *U.S. Railroads.* a private bedroom with toilet facilities. **4.** a separate aspect, function, or the like: *the compartments of the human mind.* **5.** *Archit.* a distinct major division of a design. **6.** *Heraldry.* a decorative base, as a grassy mound, on which the supporters of an escutcheon stand or rest. —*v.t.* **7.** to divide into compartments. [1555–65; < MF *compartiment* < It *compartimento.* See COMPART, -MENT]
—**Syn. 1.** division, section. **1, 2.** See **apartment.**

com•part•men•tal (kəm pärt men′tl, kom′pärt-), *adj.* divided into compartments: *a compartmental office; a compartmental agency.* [1855–60; COMPARTMENT + -AL[1]] —**com•part•men′tal•ly,** *adv.*

com•part•men•tal•ize (kəm pärt men′tl īz′, kom′pärt-), *v.t.,* **-ized, -iz•ing.** to divide into categories or compartments. Also, *esp. Brit.,* **com•part•men′tal•ise′.** [1920–25; COMPARTMENTAL + -IZE] —**com•part•men′•tal•i•za′tion,** *n.*

com•part•men•ta•tion (kəm pärt′mən tā′shən), *n. Naut.* subdivision of a hull into spaces enclosed by watertight bulkheads and sometimes by watertight decks. [1955–60; COMPARTMENT + -ATION]

com•pass (kum′pəs), *n.* **1.** an instrument for determining directions, as by means of a freely rotating magnetized needle that indicates magnetic north. **2.** the enclosing line or limits of any area; perimeter: *You can find anything you want downtown within the compass of ten square blocks.* **3.** space within limits; area; extent; range; scope: *the narrow compass of the strait; the broad compass of the novel.* **4.** Also called **range.** the total range of tones of a voice or of a musical instrument. **5.** due or proper limits; moderate bounds: *Their behavior stayed within the compass of propriety.* **6.** a passing round; circuit: *the compass of a year.* **7.** Often, **compasses.** an instrument for drawing or describing circles, measuring distances, etc., consisting generally of two movable, rigid legs hinged to each other at one end (usually used with *pair of*): *to spread the legs of a compass and draw a larger circle.* **8.** (*cap.*) *Astron.* **a.** Also called **Mariner's Compass.** the constellation Pyxis. **b. Compasses,** the constellation Circinus. —*adj.* **9.** curved; forming a curve or arc: *a compass timber; compass roof.* —*v.t.* **10.** to go or move round; make the circuit of: *It would take a week to compass his property on foot.* **11.** to extend or stretch around; hem in; surround; encircle: *An old stone wall compasses their property.* **12.** to attain or achieve; accomplish; obtain. **13.** to contrive; plot; scheme: *to compass a treacherous plan.* **14.** to make curved or circular. **15.** to comprehend; to grasp, as with the mind: *His mind could not compass the extent of the disaster.* [1250–1300; (v.) ME *compassen* < OF *compasser* to measure < VL **compāssāre,* equiv. to *compāss(us)* equal step (L *com-* COM- + *pāssus* PACE[1]) + *-āre* v. suffix; (n.) ME *compas* < OF, deriv. of *compasser*] —**com′pass•a•ble,** *adj.* —**com′pass•less,** *adj.*
—**Syn. 3.** See **range.**

com′pass card′, *Navig.* a circular card with magnets attached to its underside, the face divided on its rim into points of the compass, degrees clockwise from north, or both, and floating or suspended from a pivot so as to rotate freely. [1870–75]

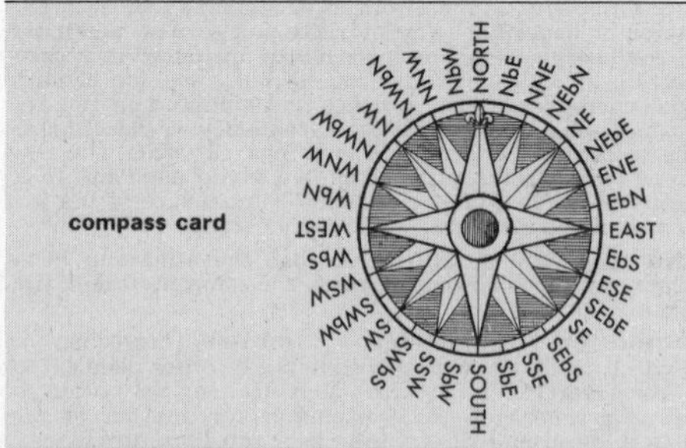

compass card

com′pass course′, *Naut.* a course whose bearing is relative to the meridian as given by the navigator's compass, no compensation being made for variation or deviation. Cf. **true course, magnetic course.** [1850–55]

com′pass devia′tion, deviation (def. 4).

com′pass devia′tion card′, a card, sheet, or the like, with two compass roses printed on it concentrically, for recording, on a given voyage, the amount of deviation for which the navigator must compensate in using the ship's compass to steer a magnetic course.

com•pas•sion (kəm pash′ən), *n.* **1.** a feeling of deep sympathy and sorrow for another who is stricken by misfortune, accompanied by a strong desire to alleviate the suffering. —*v.t.* **2.** *Archaic.* to compassionate. [1300–50; ME (< AF) < LL *compassiōn-* (s. of *compassiō*). See COM-, PASSION] —**com•pas′sion•less,** *adj.*
—**Syn. 1.** commiseration, mercy, tenderness, heart,

clemency. See **sympathy.** —**Ant.** **1.** mercilessness, indifference.

com•pas•sion•ate (*adj.* kəm pash′ə nit; *v.* kəm pash′ə nāt′), *adj., v.,* **-at•ed, -at•ing.** —*adj.* **1.** having or showing compassion: *a compassionate person; a compassionate letter.* **2.** granted in an emergency: *compassionate military leave granted to attend a funeral.* **3.** *Obs.* pitiable. —*v.t.* **4.** to have compassion for; pity. [1580–90; COMPASSION + -ATE[1]] —**com•pas′sion•ate•ly,** *adv.* —**com•pas′sion•ate•ness,** *n.*
—**Syn. 1.** pitying, sympathizing, sympathetic, tender.

com′pass north′, *Navig.* magnetic north, as indicated on a particular compass at a given moment.

com′pass plane′, *Carpentry.* a plane for smoothing curved surfaces. [1840–50]

com′pass plant′, any of various plants having leaves that tend to lie in a plane at right angles to the strongest light, hence usually north and south, esp. *Silphium laciniatum.* [1840–50]

com′pass raft′er, a rafter cut to a curve on one or both edges.

com′pass rose′, **1.** *Navig.* a circle divided into 32 points or 360° numbered clockwise from true or magnetic north, printed on a chart or the like as a means of determining the course of a vessel or aircraft. **2.** a similar design, often ornamented, used on maps to indicate the points of the compass.

com′pass saw′, *Carpentry.* a small handsaw with a narrow, tapering blade for cutting curves of small radii; whipsaw. Cf. **keyhole saw.** [1670–80]

com•pa•ter•ni•ty (kom′pə tûr′ni tē), *n.* the relationship between the godparents of a child or between the godparents and the child's parents. [1400–50; late ME *compaternite* < ML *compaternitās,* equiv. to *compater* godfather (see COM-, PATER) + (*pater*)*nitās* PATERNITY]

com•pa•thy (kom′pə thē), *n.* feelings, as happiness or grief, shared with another or others. [COM- + -PATHY]

com•pat•i•ble (kəm pat′ə bəl), *adj.* **1.** capable of existing or living together in harmony: *the most compatible married couple I know.* **2.** able to exist together with something else: *Prejudice is not compatible with true religion.* **3.** consistent; congruous (often fol. by *with*): *His claims are not compatible with the facts.* **4.** *Computers.* **a.** (of software) capable of being run on another computer without change. **b.** (of hardware) capable of being connected to another device without the use of special equipment or software. **5.** *Electronics.* (of a device, signal, etc.) capable of being used with equipment in a system without the need for special modification or conversion. **6.** noting a system of television in which color broadcasts can be received on ordinary sets in black and white. —*n.* **7.** something, as a machine or piece of electronic equipment, that is designed to perform the same tasks as another, often in the same way and using virtually identical parts, programmed instructions, etc.: *Software written for one computer will probably run on its close compatibles.* [1425–75; late ME < ML *compatibilis,* deriv. of LL *compati* (L *com-* COM- + *pati* to suffer, undergo). See -IBLE] —**com•pat′i•bil′i•ty, com•pat′i•ble•ness,** *n.* —**com•pat′i•bly,** *adv.*

com•pa•tri•ot (kəm pā′trē ət *or, esp. Brit.,* -pa′-), *n.* **1.** a native or inhabitant of one's own country; fellow countryman or countrywoman. —*adj.* **2.** of the same country. [1605–15; < LL *compatriōta.* See COM-, PATRIOT] —**com•pa•tri•ot•ic** (kəm pā′trē ot′ik *or, esp. Brit.,* -pa′-), *adj.* —**com•pa′tri•ot•ism,** *n.*

Comp•a•zine (kom′pə zēn′), *Pharm., Trademark.* a brand of prochlorperazine.

compd., compound.

com•peer (kəm pēr′, kom′pēr), *n.* **1.** an equal in rank, ability, accomplishment, etc.; peer; colleague. **2.** close friend; comrade. —*v.t.* **3.** *Archaic.* to be the equal of; match. [1325–75; ME *comper* < MF. See COM-, PEER[1]]

com•pel (kəm pel′), *v.,* **-pelled, -pel•ling.** —*v.t.* **1.** to force or drive, esp. to a course of action: *His disregard of the rules compels us to dismiss him.* **2.** to secure or bring about by force. **3.** to force to submit; subdue. **4.** to overpower. **5.** *Archaic.* to drive together; unite by force; herd. —*v.i.* **6.** to use force. **7.** to have a powerful and irresistible effect, influence, etc. [1350–1400; ME *compellen* (< AF) < L *compellere* to crowd, force, equiv. to *com-* COM- + *pellere* to push, drive] —**com•pel′la•ble,** *adj.* —**com•pel′la•bly,** *adv.* —**com•pel′lent,** *adj.* —**com•pel′ler,** *n.* —**com•pel′ling•ly,** *adv.*
—**Syn. 1.** constrain, oblige, coerce. COMPEL, IMPEL agree in the idea of using physical or other force to cause something to be done. COMPEL means to constrain someone, in some way, to yield or to do what one wishes: *to compel a recalcitrant debtor to pay; Fate compels us to face danger and trouble.* IMPEL may mean literally to push forward, but is usually applied figuratively, meaning to provide a strong motive or incentive toward a certain end: *Wind impels a ship. Curiosity impels me to ask.* **3.** overpower, bend.

com•pel•la•tion (kom′pə lā′shən), *n.* **1.** the act of addressing a person. **2.** manner or form of address; appellation. [1595–1605; < L *compellātiōn-* (s. of *compellātiō*) an accosting, a rebuke. See COM-, APPELLATION]

com•pel•ling (kəm pel′ing), *adj.* **1.** tending to compel; overpowering: *compelling reasons.* **2.** having a powerful and irresistible effect; requiring acute admiration, attention, or respect: *a man of compelling integrity; a compelling drama.* [1490–1500; COMPEL + -ING[2]]

com•pen•di•ous (kəm pen′dē əs), *adj.* of or like a compendium; containing the substance of a subject, often an exclusive subject, in a brief form; concise: *a compendious history of the world.* [1350–1400; ME < L *compendiōsus.* See COMPENDIUM, -OUS] —**com•pen′di•ous•ly,** *adv.* —**com•pen′di•ous•ness,** *n.*
—**Syn.** summary, comprehensive, succinct, packed.

com•pen•di•um (kəm pen′dē əm), *n., pl.* **-di•ums, -di•a** (-dē ə). **1.** a brief treatment or account of a subject, esp. an extensive subject; concise treatise: *a compendium of medicine.* **2.** a summary, epitome, or abridgment. **3.** a full list or inventory: *a compendium of their complaints.* Also, **com•pend** (kom′pend). [1575–85; < L: gain, saving, shortcut, abridgment, equiv. to *com-* COM- + *pend-* (s. of *pendere* to cause to hang down, weigh) + *-ium* -IUM]
—**Syn. 1.** survey, digest, conspectus.

com•pen•sa•ble (kəm pen′sə bəl), *adj.* eligible for or subject to compensation, esp. for a bodily injury. [1655–65; COMPENS(ATE) + -ABLE] —**com•pen′sa•bil′i•ty,** *n.*

com•pen•sate (kom′pən sāt′), *v.,* **-sat•ed, -sat•ing.** —*v.t.* **1.** to recompense for something: *They gave him ten dollars to compensate him for his trouble.* **2.** to counterbalance; offset; be equivalent to: *He compensated his homely appearance with great personal charm.* **3.** *Mech.* to counterbalance (a force or the like); adjust or construct so as to offset or counterbalance variations or produce equilibrium. **4.** to change the gold content of (a monetary unit) to counterbalance price fluctuations and thereby stabilize its purchasing power. —*v.i.* **5.** to provide or be an equivalent; make up; make amends (usually fol. by *for*): *His occasional courtesies did not compensate for his general rudeness.* **6.** *Psychol.* to develop or employ mechanisms of compensation. [1640–50; < L *compēnsātus* (ptp. of *compēnsāre* to counterbalance, orig., to weigh together). See COM-, PENSIVE, -ATE[1]] —**com′pen•sat′ing•ly,** *adv.* —**com′pen•sa′tor,** *n.*
—**Syn. 1.** remunerate, reward, pay. **2.** counterpoise, countervail. **5.** atone.

com′pensated grade′, *Railroads.* a grade that has been reduced along a curve to offset the additional resistance due to the curve.

com′pensating bal′ance, 1. Also, **com′pensated bal′ance, compensa′tion bal′ance.** a balance wheel in a timepiece, designed to compensate for variations in tension in the hair spring caused by changes in temperature. **2.** *Banking.* a deposit balance that is required to be left on deposit by a company to maintain or guarantee credit. [1795–1805]

com•pen•sa•tion (kom′pən sā′shən), *n.* **1.** the act or state of compensating. **2.** the state of being compensated. **3.** something given or received as an equivalent for services, debt, loss, injury, suffering, lack, etc.; indemnity: *The insurance company paid him $2000 as compensation for the loss of his car.* **4.** *Biol.* the improvement of any defect by the excessive development or action of another structure or organ of the same structure. **5.** *Psychol.* a mechanism by which an individual attempts to make up for some real or imagined deficiency of personality or behavior by developing or stressing another aspect of the personality or by substituting a different form of behavior. [1350–1400; ME *compensacioun* < L *compēnsātiōn-* (s. of *compēnsātiō*), equiv. to *compēnsāt(us)* (see COMPENSATE) + *-iōn-* -ION] —**com′pen•sa′tion•al,** *adj.*
—**Syn. 3.** recompense, payment, amends, reparation; requital, satisfaction, indemnification.

compensa′tion neuro′sis, *Psychiatry.* an unconscious attempt to retain physical or psychological symptoms of illness when some advantage may be obtained (distinguished from *malingering*). [1920–25]

com•pen•sa•to•ry (kəm pen′sə tôr′ē, -tōr′ē), *adj.* **1.** serving to compensate, as for loss, lack, or injury. **2.** countercyclical. Also, **com•pen•sa•tive** (kom′pən sā′tiv, kəm pen′sə-). [1595–1605; COMPENSATE + -ORY[1]]

compen′satory dam′ages, *Law.* damages, measured by the harm suffered, awarded to the injured person as due compensation. Cf. **punitive damages.**

compen′satory length′ening, *Historical Ling.* the lengthening of a vowel when a following consonant is weakened or lost, as the change from Old English *niht* (nɪKHt) to *night* (nīt), with loss of (KH) and lengthening of (i) to a vowel that eventually became (ī).

com•père (kom′pâr), *n., v.,* **-pèred, -pèr•ing.** *Brit.* —*n.* **1.** a host, master of ceremonies, or the like, esp. of a stage revue or television program. —*v.t.* **2.** to act as compère for: *to compère the new game show.* Also, **com′•pere.** [1730–40; < F: lit., godfather; OF < early ML *compater,* equiv. to L *com-* COM- + *pater* FATHER]

com•pete (kəm pēt′), *v.i.,* **-pet•ed, -pet•ing.** to strive to outdo another for acknowledgment, a prize, supremacy, profit, etc.; engage in a contest; vie: *to compete in a race; to compete in business.* [1610–20; < L *competere* to meet, coincide, be fitting, suffice (LL: seek, ask for), equiv. to *com-* COM- + *petere* to seek; LL and E sense influenced by COMPETITOR] —**com•pet′er,** *n.* —**com•pet′ing•ly,** *adv.*
—**Syn.** struggle. COMPETE, CONTEND, CONTEST mean to strive to outdo or excel. COMPETE implies having a sense of rivalry and of striving to do one's best as well as to outdo another: *to compete for a prize.* CONTEND suggests opposition or disputing as well as rivalry: *to contend with an opponent, against obstacles.* CONTEST suggests struggling to gain or hold something, as well as contending or disputing: *to contest a position or ground (in battle); to contest a decision.*

com•pe•tence (kom′pi təns), *n.* **1.** the quality of being competent; adequacy; possession of required skill, knowledge, qualification, or capacity: *He hired her because of her competence as an accountant.* **2.** sufficiency; a sufficient quantity. **3.** an income sufficient to furnish the necessities and modest comforts of life. **4.** *Law.* (of a witness, a party to a contract, etc.) legal capacity or qualification based on the meeting of certain minimum requirements of age, soundness of mind, citizenship, or the like. **5.** *Embryol.* the sum total of possible developmental responses of any group of blastemic cells under varied external conditions. **6.** *Ling.* the implicit, internalized knowledge of a language that a speaker possesses and that enables the speaker to produce and understand the language. Cf. **performance** (def. 8). **7.** *Immunol.* immunocompetence. **8.** *Geol.* the ability of a fluid medium, as a stream or the wind, to move and carry particulate matter, measured by the size or weight of the largest particle that can be transported. [1585–95; COMPET(ENT) + -ENCE]

com•pe•ten•cy (kom′pi tən sē), *n., pl.* **-cies.** competence (defs. 1–4). [1585–95; (< MF) < ML *competentia* suitability, competence (L: proportion). See COMPETENT, -CY]

com•pe•tent (kom′pi tənt), *adj.* **1.** having suitable or sufficient skill, knowledge, experience, etc., for some purpose; properly qualified: *He is perfectly competent to manage the bank branch.* **2.** adequate but not exceptional. **3.** *Law.* (of a witness, a party to a contract, etc.) having legal competence. **4.** *Geol.* (of a bed or stratum) able to undergo folding without flowage or change in thickness. [1350–1400; ME (< AF) < L *competent-* (s. of *competēns,* prp. of *competere* to meet, agree). See COMPETE, -ENT] —**com′pe•tent•ly,** *adv.*
—**Syn. 1.** fit, capable, proficient. See **able.**

com•pe•ti•tion (kom′pi tish′ən), *n.* **1.** the act of competing; rivalry for supremacy, a prize, etc.: *The competition between the two teams was bitter.* **2.** a contest for some prize, honor, or advantage: *Both girls entered the competition.* **3.** the rivalry offered by a competitor: *The small merchant gets powerful competition from the chain stores.* **4.** a competitor or competitors: *What is your competition offering?* **5.** *Sociol.* rivalry between two or more persons or groups for an object desired in common, usually resulting in a victor and a loser but not necessarily involving the destruction of the latter. **6.** *Ecol.* the struggle among organisms, both of the same and of different species, for food, space, and other vital requirements. [1595–1605; < LL *competītiōn-* (s. of *competītiō*), equiv. to *competīt(us)* (ptp. of *competere* to meet, come together) + *-iōn-* -ION; sense influenced by COMPETITOR]
—**Syn. 1.** emulation. **2.** struggle.

com•pet•i•tive (kəm pet′i tiv), *adj.* **1.** of, pertaining to, involving, or decided by competition: *competitive sports; a competitive examination.* **2.** well suited for competition; having a feature that makes for successful competition: *a competitive price.* **3.** having a strong desire to compete or to succeed. **4.** useful to a competitor; giving a competitor an advantage: *He was careful not to divulge competitive information about his invention.* [1820–30; < L *competīt(us)* (ptp. of *competere;* see COMPETITION) + -IVE] —**com•pet′i•tive•ly,** *adv.* —**com•pet′i•tive•ness,** *n.*

com•pet•i•tor (kəm pet′i tər), *n.* a person, team, company, etc., that competes; rival. [1525–35; < L *competītor* rival for an office, equiv. to *com-* COM- + *petītor* seeker, claimant (see PETITOR)] —**com•pet′i•tor•ship′,** *n.*
—**Syn.** See **opponent.**

com•pet•i•to•ry (kəm pet′i tôr′ē, -tōr′ē), *adj.* competitive. [1725–35; COMPETI(TOR) + -TORY[1]]

Comp. Gen., Comptroller General.

Com•piègne (kôN pyen′yᵊ), *n.* a city in N France, on the Oise River: nearby were signed the armistices between the Allies and Germany 1918, and between Germany and France 1940. 40,720.

com•pi•la•tion (kom′pə lā′shən), *n.* **1.** the act of compiling: *the compilation of documents.* **2.** something compiled, as a reference book. [1400–50; late ME < L *compīlātiōn-* (s. of *compīlātiō*). See COMPILE, -ATION] —**com•pil•a•to•ry** (kəm pī′lə tôr′ē, -tōr′ē), *adj.*
—**Syn. 2.** collection, assemblage, assortment.

com•pile (kəm pīl′), *v.t.,* **-piled, -pil•ing.** **1.** to put together (documents, selections, or other materials) in one book or work. **2.** to make (a book, writing, or the like) of materials from various sources: *to compile an anthology of plays; to compile a graph showing changes in profit.* **3.** to gather together: *to compile data.* **4.** *Computers.* to translate (a computer program) from a high-level language into another language, usually machine language, using a compiler. [1275–1325; ME < L *compīlāre* to rob, pillage, steal from another writer, equiv. to *com-* COM- + *-pīlāre,* perh. akin to *pīla* column, pier, PILE[1], *pīlāre* to fix firmly, plant (hence, pile up, accumulate)]

com•pil•er (kəm pī′lər), *n.* **1.** a person who compiles. **2.** Also called **compil′ing routine′.** *Computers.* a computer program that translates a program written in a high-level language into another language, usually machine language. Cf. **interpreter** (def. 3a). [1300–50; ME *compilour* < AF; OF *compileor* < LL *compīlātōr-.* See COMPILE, -ER[2]]

com•pla•cen•cy (kəm plā′sən sē), *n., pl.* **-cies.** **1.** a feeling of quiet pleasure or security, often while unaware of some potential danger, defect, or the like; self-satisfaction or smug satisfaction with an existing situation, condition, etc. **2.** *Archaic.* **a.** friendly civility; inclination to please; complaisance. **b.** a civil act. Also, **com•pla•cence** (kəm plā′səns). [1635–45; < ML *complacentia.* See COMPLACENT, -CY]

com•pla•cent (kəm plā′sənt), *adj.* **1.** pleased, esp. with oneself or one's merits, advantages, situation, etc., often without awareness of some potential danger or de-

fect; self-satisfied: *The voters are too complacent to change the government.* **2.** pleasant; complaisant. [1650–60; < L *complacent-* (s. of *complacēns,* prp. of *complacēre* to take the fancy of, please, equiv. to *com-* COM- + *placēre* to PLEASE] —**com•pla′cent•ly,** *adv.*
—**Syn. 1.** smug, unbothered, untroubled.

com•plain (kəm plān′), *v.i.* **1.** to express dissatisfaction, pain, uneasiness, censure, resentment, or grief; find fault: *He complained constantly about the noise in the corridor.* **2.** to tell of one's pains, ailments, etc.: *to complain of a backache.* **3.** to make a formal accusation: *If you think you've been swindled, complain to the police.* [1350–1400; ME *compleinen* < AF *compleign-,* s. of *compleindre,* OF *complaindre* < VL **complangere,* equiv. to L *com-* COM- + *plangere* to lament; see PLAINT] —**com•plain′a•ble,** *adj.* —**com•plain′er,** *n.* —**com•plain′ing•ly,** *adv.*
—**Syn. 1.** COMPLAIN, GRUMBLE, GROWL, WHINE are terms for expressing dissatisfaction or discomfort. To COMPLAIN is to protest against or lament a wrong: *to complain about high prices.* To GRUMBLE is to utter ill-natured complaints half to oneself: *to grumble about the service.* GROWL may express more anger than GRUMBLE: *to growl in reply to a question.* To WHINE is to complain in a meanspirited way, using a nasal tone: *to whine like a coward, like a spoiled child.* —**Ant. 1.** rejoice.

com•plain•ant (kəm plā′nənt), *n.* a person, group, or company that makes a complaint, as in a legal action. [1375–1425; late ME < AF *compleignant* (prp. of *compleindre*). See COMPLAIN, -ANT]

com•plaint (kəm plānt′), *n.* **1.** an expression of discontent, regret, pain, censure, resentment, or grief; lament; faultfinding: *his complaint about poor schools.* **2.** a cause of discontent, pain, grief, lamentation, etc. **3.** a cause of bodily pain or ailment; malady: *The doctor says I suffer from a rare complaint.* **4.** *Law.* the first pleading of the plaintiff in a civil action, stating the cause of action. [1350–1400; ME *compleynte* < MF *complainte* < L *com-* COM- + *plancta* PLAINT]
—**Syn. 3.** sickness, illness, ailment.

com•plai•sance (kəm plā′səns, -zəns, kom′plə zans′), *n.* **1.** the quality of being complaisant. **2.** a complaisant act. [1645–55; < F; see COMPLAISANT, -ANCE]

com•plai•sant (kəm plā′sənt, -zənt, kom′plə zant′), *adj.* inclined or disposed to please; obliging; agreeable or gracious; compliant: *the most complaisant child I've ever met.* [1640–50; < F (prp. of *complaire*) < L *complacent-* (s. of *complacēns,* prp. of *complacēre;* see COMPLACENT)] —**com•plai′sant•ly,** *adv.*

com•pla•nate (kom′plə nāt′), *adj.* made level; put into or on one plane. [1635–45; < L *complānātus* (ptp. of *complānāre* to make level), equiv. to *com-* COM- + *plān(us)* PLAIN, PLANE[1] + *-ātus* -ATE[1]] —**com′pla•na′tion,** *n.*

com•pleat (kəm plēt′), *adj.* highly skilled and accomplished in all aspects; complete; total: *the compleat actor, at home in comedy and tragedy.* [1875–80; earlier sp. of COMPLETE, used phrasally in allusion to THE COMPLEAT ANGLER]

Compleat′ An′gler, The, a book on fishing (1653) by Izaak Walton.

com•plect (kəm plekt′), *v.t. Obs.* to interweave; intertwine. [1515–25; < L *complecti* to embrace, enfold, equiv. to *com-* COM- + *plect(ere)* to PLAIT, braid + *-ī* pass. inf. ending; cf. COMPLEX]

com•plect•ed (kəm plek′tid), *adj. Informal.* complexioned: *a light-complected boy.* [1800–10, *Amer.*; *complect-* (back formation from COMPLEXION, presumably taken as **complection*) + -ED[3]]
—**Usage.** COMPLECTED, a back formation from COMPLEXION, is an Americanism dating from the early 19th century. Although it has been criticized by some as a dialectal or nonstandard substitution for COMPLEXIONED, it occurs in the speech of educated persons and occasionally in edited writing.

com•plec•tion (kəm plek′shən), *n.* complexion. [by misanalysis; see COMPLECTED]

com•ple•ment (*n.* kom′plə mənt; *v.* kom′plə ment′), *n.* **1.** something that completes or makes perfect: *A good wine is a complement to a good meal.* **2.** the quantity or amount that completes anything: *We now have a full complement of packers.* **3.** either of two parts or things needed to complete the whole; counterpart. **4.** full quantity or amount; complete allowance. **5.** the full number of officers and crew required on a ship. **6.** *Gram.* **a.** a word or group of words that completes a grammatical construction in the predicate and that describes or is identified with the subject or object, as *small* in *The house is small* or *president* in *They elected her president.* Cf. **object complement, subject complement. b.** any word or group of words used to complete a grammatical construction, esp. in the predicate, including adverbials, as *on the table* in *He put it on the table,* infinitives, as *to go* in *They are ready to go,* and sometimes objects, as *ball* in *He caught the ball.* **7.** *Geom.* the quantity by which an angle or an arc falls short of 90° or a quarter of a circle. Cf. **supplement** (def. 4). **8.** Also called **absolute complement.** *Math.* the set of all the elements of a universal set not included in a given set. **9.** *Music.* the interval that completes an octave when added to a given interval. **10.** *Immunol.* **a.** a system in vertebrate blood of 12 or more proteins that react in a cascade to a cell displaying immune complexes or foreign surfaces, acting in various combinations to coat the cell and promote phagocytosis, make holes in the cell wall, or enhance the inflammatory response. **b.** any of the proteins in the complement system, designated C1, C2, etc. **11.** See **complementary color.** —*v.t.* **12.** to complete; form a complement to: *This belt complements the dress better than that one.* **13.** *Obs.* to compliment. —*v.i.* **14.** *Obs.* to compliment. [1350–1400; ME < L *complēmentum* something that completes, equiv. to *complē(re)* to fill up (see COMPLETE) + *-mentum* -MENT] —**com′ple•ment′er,** *n.*
—**Syn. 12.** COMPLEMENT, SUPPLEMENT both mean to make additions to something. To COMPLEMENT is to provide something felt to be lacking or needed; it is often applied to putting together two things, each of which supplies what is lacking in the other, to make a complete whole: *Two statements from different points of view may complement each other.* To SUPPLEMENT is merely to add to: *Some additional remarks may supplement his address.*
—**Usage.** COMPLEMENT and COMPLIMENT, which are pronounced alike and originally shared some meanings, have become separate words with entirely different meanings. As a noun, COMPLEMENT means "something that completes or makes perfect": *The rare old brandy was a perfect complement to the delicious meal.* As a verb, COMPLEMENT means "to complete": *A bright scarf complements a dark suit.* The noun COMPLIMENT means "an expression of praise, commendation, or admiration": *The members paid her the compliment of a standing ovation.* The verb COMPLIMENT means "to pay a compliment to": *Everyone complimented him after the recital.*

complement (def. 8)
A, given set;
U, universal set

com•ple•men•tal (kom′plə men′tl), *adj.* **1.** complementary; completing. **2.** *Obs.* **a.** accomplished. **b.** ceremonious. **c.** complimentary. [1595–1605; COMPLEMENT + -AL[1]] —**com′ple•men′tal•ly,** *adv.*

com•ple•men•tar•i•ty (kom′plə men tar′i tē), *n.* the quality or state of being complementary. [1910–15; COMPLEMENTAR(Y) + -ITY]

complementar′ity prin′ciple, *Physics.* the principle that experiments on physical systems of atomic size or smaller, as electrons or photons, can exhibit either particle or wave behavior but not both simultaneously.

com•ple•men•ta•ry (kom′plə men′tə rē, -trē), *adj., n., pl.* **-ries.** —*adj.* **1.** forming a complement; completing. **2.** complementing each other. —*n.* **3.** See **complementary color** (def. 1). [1590–1600; COMPLEMENT + -ARY] —**com′ple•men′ta•ri•ness,** *n.*

com′plemen′tary an′gle, *Math.* either of two angles that added together produce an angle of 90°. Cf. **supplementary angle.**

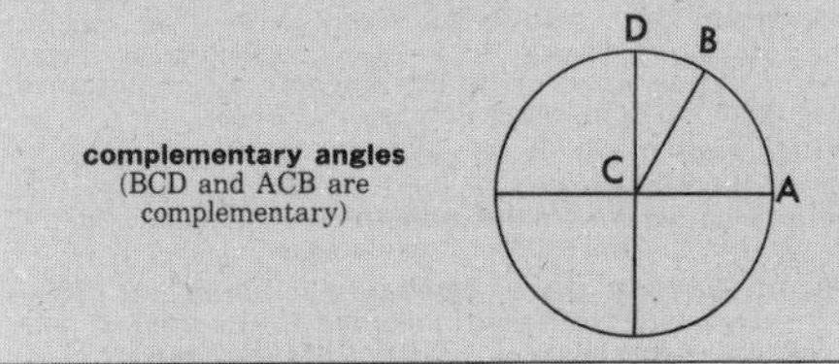

complementary angles
(BCD and ACB are complementary)

com′plemen′tary base′, *Genetics.* either of the nucleotide bases linked by a hydrogen bond on opposite strands of DNA or double-stranded RNA: guanine is the complementary base of cytosine, and adenine is the complementary base of thymine in DNA and of uracil in RNA. Cf. **base pair.**

complemen′tary cells′, *Bot.* cells fitting closely together in the lenticel. [1880–85]

com′plemen′tary col′or, 1. *Art.* **a.** one of a pair of primary or secondary colors opposed to the other member of the pair on a schematic chart or scale (**color wheel**), as green opposed to red, orange opposed to blue, or violet opposed to yellow. **b.** the relationship of these pairs of colors perceived as completing or enhancing each other. **2.** See **secondary color.** [1820–30]

complemen′tary distribu′tion, *Ling.* a relation such that the members of a pair or set of phones, morphs, or other linguistic units have no environment in common, as aspirated "p" and unaspirated "p" in English, the first occurring only in positions where the second does not. Also called **complementation.** Cf. **free variation.** [1930–35]

com′plemen′tary strand′, *Biochem.* **1.** either of the two chains that make up a double helix of DNA, with corresponding positions on the two chains being composed of a pair of complementary bases. **2.** a section of one nucleic acid chain that is bonded to another by a sequence of base pairs.

com•ple•men•ta•tion (kom′plə mən tā′shən), *n.* **1.** See **complementary distribution. 2.** *Genetics.* the occurrence of a wild-type phenotype when two closely related, interacting mutant genes are expressed in the same cell. **3.** *Gram.* **a.** complement (def. 6). **b.** the use of grammatical complements. **4.** cooperation in lowering tariffs to permit the movement of components among different countries when it is more profitable for each country to produce parts of a product than the whole. [1935–40; COMPLEMENT + -ATION]

com′plement clause′, *Ling.* a subordinate clause that functions as the subject, direct object, or prepositional object of a verb, as *that you like it* in *I'm surprised that you like it.* Also called **com′plement sen′tence.**

com•ple•ment•ed (kom′plə men′tid), *adj.* **1.** having a complement or complements. **2.** *Math.* (of a lattice containing a smallest element and a greatest element) having the property that corresponding to each element of the lattice is a second element such that the greatest lower bound of the two elements is the smallest element of the lattice and the least upper bound of the two elements is the greatest element of the lattice. [COMPLEMENT + -ED[3]]

com′plement fixa′tion, *Immunol.* the binding of complement to immune complexes or to certain foreign surfaces, as those of invading microorganisms. [1905–10]

com′ple•ment-fix•a′tion test′ (kom′plə mənt fik sā′shən), *Med.* a test for diagnosing an infectious disease by detecting the presence of antibody in the blood, based on the fixing of a known quantity of complement to the antigen being tested and the specific antibody that combines with it. *Abbr.:* CFT [1910–15]

com•ple•men•tiz•er (kom′plə mən tī′zər), *n. Ling.* an element or elements marking a complement clause, as *that* in *We thought that you forgot, for . . . to* in *For you to go all the way there would be silly,* or possessive *. . . -ing* in *Barbara's leaving so early worried them.* [COMPLEMENT + -IZE + -ER[1]]

com•plete (kəm plēt′), *adj., v.,* **-plet•ed, -plet•ing.** —*adj.* **1.** having all parts or elements; lacking nothing; whole; entire; full: *a complete set of Mark Twain's writings.* **2.** finished; ended; concluded: *a complete orbit.* **3.** having all the required or customary characteristics, skills, or the like; consummate; perfect in kind or quality: *a complete scholar.* **4.** thorough; entire; total; undivided, uncompromised, or unmodified: *a complete victory; a complete mess.* **5.** *Gram.* having all modifying or complementary elements included: *The complete subject of "The dappled pony gazed over the fence" is "The dappled pony."* Cf. **simple** (def. 20). **6.** Also, **completed.** *Football.* (of a forward pass) caught by a receiver. **7.** *Logic.* (of a set of axioms) such that every true proposition able to be formulated in terms of the basic ideas of a given system is deducible from the set. Cf. **incomplete** (def. 4b). **8.** *Engin.* noting a determinate truss having the least number of members required to connect the panel points so as to form a system of triangles. Cf. **incomplete** (def. 3), **redundant** (def. 5c). **9.** (of persons) accomplished; skilled; expert. **10.** *Math.* **a.** of or pertaining to an algebraic system, as a field with an order relation defined on it, in which every set of elements of the system has a least upper bound. **b.** of or pertaining to a set in which every fundamental sequence converges to an element of the set. Cf. **fundamental sequence. c.** (of a lattice) having the property that every subset has a least upper bound and a greatest lower bound. —*v.t.* **11.** to make whole or entire: *I need three more words to complete the puzzle.* **12.** to make perfect: *His parting look of impotent rage completed my revenge.* **13.** to bring to an end; finish: *Has he completed his new novel yet?* **14.** to consummate. **15.** *Football.* to execute (a forward pass) successfully: *He completed 17 passes in 33 attempts.* [1325–75; ME (< MF) < L *complētus* (ptp. of *complēre* to fill up, fulfill, equiv. to *com-* COM- + *plē-* FILL + *-tus* ptp. suffix] —**com•plet′a•ble,** *adj.* —**com•plet′ed•ness,** *n.* —**com•plete′ly,** *adv.* —**com•plete′ness,** *n.* —**com•plet′er,** *n.* —**com•ple′tive,** *adj.* —**com•ple′tive•ly,** *adv.*
—**Syn. 1.** unbroken, unimpaired, undivided. **1–3.** COMPLETE, ENTIRE, INTACT, PERFECT imply that there is no lack or defect, nor has any part been removed. COMPLETE implies that a certain unit has all its parts, fully developed or perfected, and may apply to a process or purpose carried to fulfillment: *a complete explanation.* ENTIRE means whole, having unbroken unity: *an entire book.* INTACT implies retaining completeness and original condition: *a package delivered intact.* PERFECT emphasizes not only completeness but also high quality and absence of defects or blemishes: *a perfect diamond.* **3.** developed. **11.** conclude, consummate, perfect, accomplish, achieve. —**Ant. 1.** partial. **3.** defective.
—**Usage.** Occasionally there are objections to modifying COMPLETE with qualifiers like *almost, more, most, nearly,* and *quite,* because they suggest that COMPLETE is relative rather than absolute: *an almost complete record; a more complete proposal; the most complete list available.* However, such uses are fully standard and occur regularly in all varieties of spoken and written English. See also **perfect, unique.**

complete′ blood′ count′, a diagnostic test that determines the exact numbers of each type of blood cell in a fixed quantity of blood. *Abbr.:* CBC

complete′ fer′tilizer, a fertilizer containing nitrogen, phosphorus, and potassium, the three principal elements required for plant nutrition. [1895–1900]

complete′ frac′ture, a bone fracture in which the bone is split completely across.

complete′ly nor′mal space′, *Math.* a normal topological space in which every subspace is normal.

complete′ly reg′ular space′, *Math.* a topological space in which, for every point and a closed set not containing the point, there is a continuous function that has value 0 at the given point and value 1 at each point in the closed set.

complete′ metamor′phosis, insect development in which egg, larval, pupal, and adult stages occur, each differing greatly in morphology. [1840–50]

complete′ quadrilat′eral, *Geom.* a plane figure composed of four straight lines and their points of intersection.

complet′er set′, a set of supplementary pieces that completes a set of dishes, as creamer, sugar bowl, platter, gravy boat, and vegetable dish.

complet′ing the square′, *Math.* a method, usually of solving quadratic equations, by which a quadratic expression, as $x^2 - 4x + 3$, is written as the sum or difference of a perfect square and a constant, $x^2 - 4x + 4 + 3 - 4 = (x - 2)^2 - 1$, by addition and subtraction of appropriate constant terms.

com•ple•tion (kəm plē′shən), *n.* **1.** the act of completing. **2.** the state of being completed. **3.** conclusion; fulfillment: *Her last novel represented the completion of her literary achievement.* **4.** *Football.* a forward pass

CONCISE ETYMOLOGY KEY: <, descended or borrowed from; >, whence; b., blend of, blended; c., cognate with; cf., compare; deriv., derivative; equiv., equivalent; imit., imitative; obl., oblique; r., replacing; s., stem; sp., spelling, spelled; resp., respelling, respelled; trans., translation; ?, origin unknown; *, unattested; ‡, probably earlier than. See the full key inside the front cover.

that has been completed. [1650–60; < LL *complētiōn-* (s. of *complētiō*). See COMPLETE, -ION]
—Syn. 1. termination, ending, closing.

com•plex (*adj., v.* kəm pleks′, kom′pleks; *n.* kom′pleks), *adj.* **1.** composed of many interconnected parts; compound; composite: *a complex highway system.* **2.** characterized by a very complicated or involved arrangement of parts, units, etc.: *complex machinery.* **3.** so complicated or intricate as to be hard to understand or deal with: *a complex problem.* **4.** *Gram.* **a.** (of a word) consisting of two parts, at least one of which is a bound form, as *childish,* which consists of the word *child* and the bound form *-ish.* **b.** See **complex sentence. 5.** *Math.* pertaining to or using complex numbers: *complex methods; complex vector space.* —*n.* **6.** an intricate or complicated association or assemblage of related things, parts, units, etc.: *the entire complex of our educational system; an apartment complex.* **7.** *Psychol.* a system of interrelated, emotion-charged ideas, feelings, memories, and impulses that is usually repressed and that gives rise to abnormal or pathological behavior. **8.** a fixed idea; an obsessive notion. **9.** *Math.* **a.** an arbitrary set of elements of a group. **b.** a collection of simplexes having specified properties. **10.** Also called **coordination compound.** *Chem.* a compound in which independently existing molecules or ions of a nonmetal **(complexing agent)** form coordinate bonds with a metal atom or ion. Cf. **ligand** (def. 2). **11.** *Biochem.* an entity composed of molecules in which the constituents maintain much of their chemical identity: *receptor-hormone complex, enzyme-substrate complex.* —*v.t.* **12.** *Chem.* to form a complex with. —*v.i.* **13.** *Chem.* to form a complex. [1645–55; 1905–10 for def. 7; (adj.) < L *complexus,* ptp. of *complecti, complectere* to embrace, encompass, include, equiv. to *complect-* (see COMPLECT) + *-tus* ptp. suffix; (n.) < LL *complexus* totality, complex (L: inclusion, grasping, embrace), equiv. to *complect(ere)* + *-tus* suffix of v. action; reanalysis of the L v. as "to intertwine (completely)" has influenced sense of the adj.] **—com•plex′ly,** *adv.* **—com•plex′ness,** *n.*
—Syn. 3. knotty, tangled, labyrinthine. **6.** network, web, tangle, labyrinth. **—Ant. 2, 3.** simple.

com′plex anal′ysis, *Math.* the branch of mathematics dealing with analytic functions of a complex variable.

com′plex carbohy′drate, a carbohydrate, as sucrose or starch, that consists of two or more monosaccharide units.

com′plex frac′tion, *Math.* a fraction in which the numerator or the denominator or both contain one or more fractions. Also called **compound fraction.** [1820–30]

com•plex′ing a′gent (kəm plek′sing), *Chem.* See under **complex** (def. 10).

com′plex i′on, *Chem.* a charged complex. Cf. **complex** (def. 10).

com•plex•ion (kəm plek′shən), *n.* **1.** the natural color, texture, and appearance of the skin, esp. of the face: *a clear, smooth, rosy complexion.* **2.** appearance; aspect; character: *His confession put a different complexion on things.* **3.** viewpoint, attitude, or conviction: *one's political complexion.* **4.** (in old physiology) constitution or nature of body and mind, regarded as the result of certain combined qualities. **5.** *Obs.* nature; disposition; temperament. Also, **complection.** [1300–50; ME < ML *complexiōn-* (s. of *complexiō*) constitution, temperament, L: combination, group, lit., the act of embracing. See COMPLEX, -ION] **—com•plex′ion•al,** *adj.* **—com•plex′ion•al•ly,** *adv.*

com•plex•ioned (kəm plek′shənd), *adj.* having a specified complexion (usually used in combination): *a light-complexioned person.* [1375–1425; late ME; see COMPLEXION, -ED[3]]
—Usage. See **complected.**

com•plex•ion•less (kəm plek′shən lis), *adj.* lacking in usual color; wan. [1855–60; COMPLEXION + -LESS]

com•plex•i•ty (kəm plek′si tē), *n., pl.* **-ties** for 2. **1.** the state or quality of being complex; intricacy: *the complexity of urban life.* **2.** something complex: *the complexities of foreign policy.* [1715–25; COMPLEX + -ITY]

com′plex machine′, *Mech.* machine (def. 4c).

com′plex num′ber, a mathematical expression ($a + bi$) in which a and b are real numbers and $i^2 = -1$. [1825–35]

com•plex•om•e•try (kom′plek som′i trē), *n.* a chemical technique using the formation of a colored complex to indicate the end of a titration. Also called **com•plex•o•met′ric titra′tion** (kəm plek′ sə me′trik). [COMPLEX + -O- + -METRY]

com′plex plane′, *Math.* a plane the points of which are complex numbers. Cf. **Argand diagram.** [1905–10]

com′plex sen′tence, a sentence containing one or more dependent clauses in addition to the main clause, as *When the bell rings* (dependent clause), *walk out* (main clause). [1880–85]

com′plex var′iable, *Math.* a variable to which complex numbers may be assigned as value. [1875–80]

com•pli•a•ble (kəm plī′ə bəl), *adj. Archaic.* compliant. [1625–35; COMPLY + -ABLE] **—com•pli′a•ble•ness,** *n.* **—com•pli′a•bly,** *adv.*

com•pli•ance (kəm plī′əns), *n.* **1.** the act of conforming, acquiescing, or yielding. **2.** a tendency to yield readily to others, esp. in a weak and subservient way. **3.** conformity; accordance: *in compliance with orders.* **4.** cooperation or obedience: *Compliance with the law is expected of all.* **5.** *Physics.* **a.** the strain of an elastic body expressed as a function of the force producing the strain. **b.** a coefficient expressing the responsiveness of a mechanical system to a periodic force. [1635–45; COMPLY + -ANCE]

com•pli•an•cy (kəm plī′ən sē), *n., pl.* **-cies.** compliance (defs. 1, 2, 4). [COMPLY + -ANCY]

com•pli•ant (kəm plī′ənt), *adj.* complying; obeying, obliging, or yielding, esp. in a submissive way: *a man with a compliant nature.* [1635–45; COMPLY + -ANT] **—com•pli′ant•ly,** *adv.*

com•pli•ca•cy (kom′pli kə sē), *n., pl.* **-cies** for 2. **1.** the state of being complicated; complicatedness. **2.** a complication: *the numerous complicacies of travel in such a remote country.* [1820–30; COMPLIC(ATE) + -ACY, modeled on such pairs as CONFEDERACY, CONFEDERATE]

com•pli•cate (*v.* kom′pli kāt′; *adj.* kom′pli kit), *v.,* **-cat•ed, -cat•ing,** *adj.* —*v.t.* **1.** to make complex, intricate, involved, or difficult: *His recovery from the operation was complicated by an allergic reaction.* —*adj.* **2.** complex; involved. **3.** *Entomol.* folded longitudinally one or more times, as the wings of certain insects. [1615–25; < L *complicātus* (ptp. of *complicāre* to fold together), equiv. to *com-* COM- + *-plic-* (comb. form of *plecāre* to fold, akin to *plecti* to PLAIT; see COMPLEX) + *-ātus* -ATE[1]]

com•pli•cat•ed (kom′pli kā′tid), *adj.* **1.** composed of elaborately interconnected parts; complex: *complicated apparatus for measuring brain functions.* **2.** difficult to analyze, understand, explain, etc.: *a complicated problem.* [1640–50; COMPLICATE + -ED[2]] **—com′pli•cat′ed•ly,** *adv.* **—com′pli•cat′ed•ness,** *n.*
—Syn. 2. involved, tangled, knotty.

com•pli•ca•tion (kom′pli kā′shən), *n.* **1.** the act of complicating. **2.** a complicated or involved state or condition. **3.** a complex combination of elements or things. **4.** something that introduces, usually unexpectedly, some difficulty, problem, change, etc.: *Because of the complications involved in traveling during the strike, we decided to postpone our trip.* **5.** *Pathol.* a concurrent disease, accident, or adverse reaction that aggravates the original disease. **6.** the act of forming a unified idea or impression from a number of sense data, memories, etc. [1605–15; < LL *complicātiōn-* (s. of *complicātiō*), equiv. to *complicāt(us)* (see COMPLICATE) + *-iōn-* -ION] **—com′pli•ca′tive,** *adj.*
—Syn. 4. drawback, handicap, obstacle.

com•plice (kom′plis), *n. Archaic.* an accomplice or associate. [1425–75; late ME < MF < LL *complice-,* obl. s. of *complex* confederate (formation modeled on *simplex* SIMPLEX), equiv. to *com-* COM- + *-plex* -FOLD]

com•plic•i•ty (kəm plis′i tē), *n., pl.* **-ties.** the state of being an accomplice; partnership or involvement in wrongdoing: *complicity in a crime.* [1650–60; < LL *complic-,* s. of *complex* COMPLICE + -ITY] **—com•plic′i•tous,** *adj.*
—Syn. collusion, intrigue, implication, connivance.

com•pli•er (kəm plī′ər), *n.* a person, group, etc., that complies. [1605–15; COMPLY + -ER[1]]

com•pli•ment (*n.* kom′plə mənt; *v.* kom′plə ment′), *n.* **1.** an expression of praise, commendation, or admiration: *A sincere compliment boosts one's morale.* **2.** a formal act or expression of civility, respect, or regard: *The mayor paid him the compliment of escorting him.* **3. compliments,** a courteous greeting; good wishes; regards: *He sends you his compliments.* **4.** *Archaic.* a gift; present. —*v.t.* **5.** to pay a compliment to: *She complimented the child on his good behavior.* **6.** to show kindness or regard for by a gift or other favor: *He complimented us by giving a party in our honor.* **7.** to congratulate; felicitate: *to compliment a prince on the birth of a son.* —*v.i.* **8.** to pay compliments. [1570–80; < F < It *complimento* < Sp *cumplimiento,* equiv. to *cumpli-* (see COMPLY) + *-miento* -MENT; earlier identical in sp. with COMPLEMENT] **—com′pli•ment′a•ble,** *adj.* **—com′pli•ment′er,** *n.* **—com′pli•ment′ing•ly,** *adv.*
—Syn. 1. kudos, tribute, eulogy, panegyric. **5.** commend, praise, honor. **—Ant. 1.** disparagement.
—Usage. See **complement.**

com•pli•men•ta•ry (kom′plə men′tə rē, -trē), *adj., n., pl.* **-ries.** —*adj.* **1.** of the nature of, conveying, or expressing a compliment, often one that is politely flattering: *a complimentary remark.* **2.** given free as a gift or courtesy: *a complimentary ticket.* —*n.* **3.** something given or supplied without charge, as lodging, transportation, or meals, esp. as an inducement to prospective customers. [1620–30; COMPLIMENT + -ARY] **—com′pli•men′ta•ri•ly,** *adv.* **—com′pli•men′ta•ri•ness,** *n.*
—Syn. 1. commendatory, praising, laudatory. **—Ant. 1.** abusive, unflattering.

com′plimen′tary close′ (klōz), the part of a letter that by convention immediately precedes the signature, as "Very truly yours," "Cordially," or "Sincerely yours." Also, **com′plimen′tary clos′ing.** Also called **closing, close.** [1915–20]

com•pline (kom′plin, -plīn), *n. Eccles.* the last of the seven canonical hours, or the service for it, originally occurring after the evening meal but now usually following immediately upon vespers. Also, **com•plin** (kom′plin). [1175–1225; ME *comp(e)lin,* equiv. to *compli, cump(e)lie* (< OF *complie, cumplie* < L *complēta* (*hōra*) COMPLETE (hour) + *-in* (of MATIN)]

com•plot (*n.* kom′plot′; *v.* kəm plot′), *n., v.,* **-plot•ted, -plot•ting.** —*n.* **1.** a plot involving several participants; conspiracy. —*v.t., v.i.* **2.** to plot together; conspire. [1570–80; < MF; cf. OF *complot* dense crowd, accord, understanding, conspiracy, *complote* assembly (of troops); of obscure orig.] **—com•plot′ment,** *n.* **—com•plot′ter,** *n.*

com•ply (kəm plī′), *v.i.,* **-plied, -ply•ing. 1.** to act or be in accordance with wishes, requests, demands, requirements, conditions, etc.; agree (sometimes fol. by *with*): *They asked him to leave and he complied. She has complied with the requirements.* **2.** *Obs.* to be courteous or conciliatory. [1595–1605; < It *complire* < Sp *cumplir* (see COMPLIMENT) to fulfill, accomplish < L *complēre,* equiv. to *com-* COM- + *plē-* FILL + *-re* inf. suffix]
—Syn. 1. acquiesce, yield, conform, obey, consent, assent. **—Ant. 1.** refuse, resist.

com•po (kom′pō), *n., pl.* **-pos.** composition material. [by shortening; cf. -O]

com•po•nent (kəm pō′nənt, kom-), *n.* **1.** a constituent part; element; ingredient. **2.** a part of a mechanical or electrical system: *hi-fi components.* **3.** *Physics.* the projection of a vector quantity, as force or velocity, along an axis. **4.** *Physical Chem.* one of the set of the minimum number of chemical constituents by which every phase of a given system can be described. **5.** *Math.* **a.** a connected subset of a set, not contained in any other connected subset of the set. **b.** a coordinate of a vector. **6.** *Ling.* **a.** one of the major subdivisions of a generative grammar: *base component; transformational component; semantic component; phonological component.* Cf. **level** (def. 17). **b.** a feature determined by componential analysis. —*adj.* **7.** being or serving as an element (in something larger); composing; constituent: *the component parts of a computer system.* [1555–65; < L *compōnent-* (s. of *compōnēns,* prp. of *compōnere* to put together), equiv. to *com-* COM- + *pōn(ere)* to put + *-ent-* -ENT] **—com•po•nen•tial** (kom′pə nen′shəl), **com′po•nen′tal,** *adj.* **—com•po′nent•ed,** *adj.*
—Syn. 1. See **element.**

componen′tial anal′ysis, *Ling.* the analysis of a set of related linguistic items, esp. word meanings, into combinations of features in terms of which each item may be compared with every other, as in the analysis of *man* into the semantic features 'male,' 'mature,' and 'human,' *woman* into 'female,' 'mature,' and 'human,' *girl* into 'female,' 'immature,' and 'human,' and *bull* into 'male,' 'mature,' and 'bovine.' [1945–50]

com•po•nen•try (kəm pō′nən trē), *n.* the components of a machine, vehicle, stereo system, etc. [COMPONENT + -RY]

com•po•ny (kəm pō′nē), *adj. Heraldry.* composed of a single row of squares, metal and color alternating; gobony. Also, **com•po•né** (kəm pō′nē; *Fr.* kôɴ pô nā′). [1565–75; < MF *compone,* nasalized var. of *copone,* equiv. to *copon* COUPON + *-e* -EE]

com•port[1] (kəm pôrt′, -pōrt′), *v.t.* **1.** to bear or conduct (oneself); behave: *He comported himself with dignity.* —*v.i.* **2.** to be in agreement, harmony, or conformity (usually followed by *with*): *His statement does not comport with the facts.* —*n.* **3.** *Obs.* comportment. [1350–1400; ME < MF *comporter* < L *comportāre* to transport, equiv. to *com-* COM- + *portāre* to PORT[5]]
—Syn. 1. deport.

com•port[2] (kom′pôrt, -pōrt), *n.* a large English glass dish of the 18th century used for holding fruit or candy and having a wide, shallow top supported by heavy stem and foot; compote. [1765–75; alter. of F *compotier* a dish for COMPOTE; see -IER[2]]

com•port•ance (kəm pôr′tns, -pōr′-), *n. Obs.* comportment. [1580–90; COMPORT[1] + -ANCE]

com•port•ment (kəm pôrt′mənt, -pōrt′-), *n.* personal bearing or conduct; demeanor; behavior. [1590–1600; < MF *comportement.* See COMPORT[1], -MENT]
—Syn. See **behavior.**

com•pose (kəm pōz′), *v.,* **-posed, -pos•ing.** —*v.t.* **1.** to make or form by combining things, parts, or elements: *He composed his speech from many research notes.* **2.** to be or constitute a part or element of: *a rich sauce composed of many ingredients.* **3.** to make up or form the basis of: *Style composes the essence of good writing.* **4.** to put or dispose in proper form or order: *to compose laws into a coherent system.* **5.** *Art.* to organize the parts or elements of (a picture or the like). **6.** to create (a musical, literary, or choreographic work). **7.** to end or settle (a quarrel, dispute, etc.): *The union and management composed their differences.* **8.** to bring (oneself, one's mind, etc.) to a condition of calmness, repose, etc.; calm; quiet. **9.** *Print.* **a.** to set (type). **b.** to set type for (an article, book, etc.). —*v.i.* **10.** to engage in composition, esp. musical composition. **11.** to enter into composition; fall into an arrangement: *a scene that composes well.* [1375–1425; late ME < MF *composer.* See COM-, POSE[1]] **—com•pos′a•ble,** *adj.*
—Syn. 8. settle, collect.

com•posed (kəm pōzd′), *adj.* calm; tranquil; serene: *His composed face reassured the nervous passengers.* [1475–85; COMPOSE + -ED[2]] **—com•pos•ed•ly** (kəm pō′zid lē), *adv.* **—com•pos′ed•ness,** *n.*
—Syn. See **calm. —Ant.** agitated, perturbed.

com•pos•er (kəm pō′zər), *n.* **1.** a person or thing that composes. **2.** a person who writes music. **3.** an author. [1555–65; COMPOSE + -ER[1]]

compos′ing room′, a room in which compositors work in a printing establishment. [1730–40]

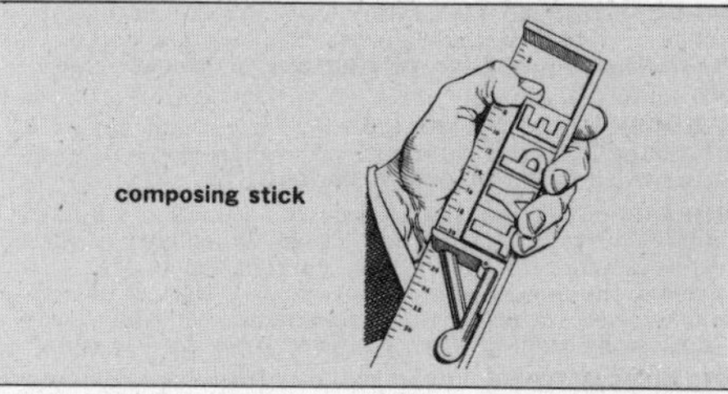

composing stick

compos′ing stick′, *Print.* a portable, adjustable, usually metal tray that the compositor holds in one hand while placing in it type gathered with the other hand. Also called **job stick.** [1670–80]

com•pos•ite (kəm poz′it), *adj., n., v.,* **-it•ed, -it•ing.** —*adj.* **1.** made up of disparate or separate parts or elements; compound: *a composite drawing; a composite philosophy.* **2.** *Bot.* belonging to the Compositae. Cf. **composite family. 3.** (*cap.*) *Archit.* noting or pertaining to

CONCISE PRONUNCIATION KEY: act, cāpe, dâre, pärt; set, ēqual; if, īce; ox, ōver, ôrder, oil, bo͝ok, bo͞ot, out; up, ûrge; child; sing; shoe; thin, *th*at; zh as in *treasure.* ə = *a* as in *alone, e* as in *system, i* as in *easily, o* as in *gallop, u* as in *circus;* ᵊ as in *fire* (fīᵊr), *hour* (ouᵊr). l and n can serve as syllabic consonants, as in *cradle* (krād′l), and *button* (but′n). See the full key inside the front cover.

one of the five classical orders, popular esp. since the beginning of the Renaissance but invented by the ancient Romans, in which the Roman Ionic and Corinthian orders are combined, so that four diagonally set Ionic volutes, variously ornamented, rest upon a bell of Corinthian acanthus leaves. Cf. **Corinthian** (def. 2), **Doric** (def. 3), **Ionic** (def. 1), **Tuscan** (def. 2). See illus. under **order. 4.** *Rocketry.* **a.** (of a rocket or missile) having more than one stage. **b.** (of a solid propellant) composed of a mixture of fuel and oxidizer. **5.** *Naut.* noting a vessel having frames of one material and shells and decking of another, esp. one having iron or steel frames with shells and decks planked. **6.** *Math.* of or pertaining to a composite function or a composite number. *—n.* **7.** something composite; a compound. **8.** *Bot.* a composite plant. **9.** a picture, photograph, or the like, that combines several separate pictures. *—v.t.* **10.** to make a composite of. [1350–1400; ME (< MF) < L *compositus* (ptp. of *compōnere* to put together), equiv. to *com-* COM- + *positus* placed; see POSIT] **—com•pos′ite•ly,** *adv.* **—com•pos′ite•ness,** *n.*

compos′ite fam′ily, the large and varied plant family Compositae (or Asteraceae), typified by herbaceous plants having alternate, opposite, or whorled leaves and a whorl of bracts surrounding the flower heads, which are usually composed of a disk containing tiny petalless flowers and a ray of petals extending from the flowers at the rim of the disk, some flower heads being composed only of a disk or a ray and some plants having clusters of flower heads, and including the aster, daisy, dandelion, goldenrod, marigold, ragweed, sunflower, thistle, and zinnia.

compos′ite func′tion, *Math.* a function obtained from two given functions, where the range of one function is contained in the domain of the second function, by assigning to an element in the domain of the first function that element in the range of the second function whose inverse image is the image of the element. Also called **compound function.** [1960–65]

compos′ite num′ber, *Math.* a number that is a multiple of at least two numbers other than itself and 1. [1720–30]

compos′ite pho′tograph, a photograph characterized by overlapping or juxtaposed images resulting from a multiple exposure or the combining of negatives (**composite print**).

compos′ite print′, 1. *Motion Pictures.* a positive print having the picture and soundtrack placed side by side on the same strand of film after all postproduction work on picture and sound has been completed. **2.** *Photog.* See under **composite photograph.**

compos′ite school′, (in Canada) a secondary school offering academic, commercial, and industrial subjects. Also called **comprehensive school.** [1940–45]

compos′ite shot′. *Motion Pictures, Television.* See **split screen.**

com•po•si•tion (kom′pə zish′ən), *n.* **1.** the act of combining parts or elements to form a whole. **2.** the resulting state or product. **3.** manner of being composed; structure: *This painting has an orderly composition.* **4.** makeup; constitution: *His moral composition was impeccable.* **5.** an aggregate material formed from two or more substances: *a composition of silver and tin.* **6.** a short essay written as a school exercise. **7.** the act or process of producing a literary work. **8.** an academic course for teaching the techniques of clear, expository writing. **9.** the art of putting words and sentences together in accordance with the rules of grammar and rhetoric. **10.** a piece of music. **11.** the art of composing music. **12.** *Fine Arts.* the organization or grouping of the different parts of a work of art so as to achieve a unified whole. **13.** *Gram.* the formation of compounds or derivatives: *the composition of "aircraft" from "air" and "craft."* **14.** a settlement by mutual agreement. **15.** an agreement or compromise, esp. one by which a creditor or group of creditors accepts partial payment from a debtor. **16.** a sum of money so paid. **17.** *Print.* **a.** the setting up of type for printing. **b.** Also called **pagination.** the makeup of pages for printing. **18.** *Math.* the process of making a composite function of two given functions. [1350–1400; ME *composicioun* < AF < L *compositiōn-* (s. of *compositiō*), equiv. to *composit(us)* (see COMPOSITE) + *-iōn-* -ION] **—com′po•si′tion•al,** *adj.* **—com′po•si′tion•al•ly,** *adv.* **—com•pos•i•tive** (kəm poz′i tiv), *adj.* **—com•pos′i•tive•ly,** *adv.*

composi′tion of forc′es, *Mech.* the union or combination of two or more forces into a single force. Cf. **parallelogram law, parallelogram of forces.** [1800–10]

composi′tion se′ries, *Math.* a normal series of subgroups in which no additional subgroups can be inserted. Also called **principal series.**

com•pos•i•tor (kəm poz′i tər), *n.* a person who sets the type or text for printing. [1325–75 for earlier sense "referee, arbiter"; 1560–70 for current sense; ME < L: one who composes, equiv. to *composi-*, var. s. of *compōnere* (see COMPONENT, COMPOSITE) + *-tor* -TOR] **—com•pos•i•to•ri•al** (kəm poz′i tôr′ē əl, -tōr′-), *adj.*

com•pos men•tis (kōm′pōs men′tis; *Eng.* kom′pəs men′tis), *Latin.* sane; mentally sound. [lit., being in full possession of one's mind]

com•pos•si•ble (kom pos′ə bəl, kəm-), *adj.* **1.** compatible; potentially consistent, as with another statement, theory, etc. **2.** able to exist or happen together. [1630–40; < ML *compossibilis.* See COM-, POSSIBLE] **—com•pos′si•bil′i•ty,** *n.*

com•post (kom′pōst), *n.* **1.** a mixture of various decaying organic substances, as dead leaves or manure, used for fertilizing soil. **2.** a composition; compound. *—v.t.* **3.** to use in compost; make compost of: *to compost manure and kitchen scraps.* **4.** to apply compost to (soil). *—v.i.* **5.** to make compost: *Shredded leaves will compost easily.* [1350–1400; ME < AF, MF < L *compositum,* n. use of neut. of *compositus* COMPOSITE; cf. COMPOTE] **—com′post•a•ble,** *adj.* **—com′post•er,** *n.*

com•po•sure (kəm pō′zhər), *n.* serene, self-controlled state of mind; calmness; tranquillity: *Despite the hysteria and panic around him, he retained his composure.* [1590–1600; COMPOSE + -URE]
—Syn. equability, serenity, quiet, coolness, equanimity, self-possession. **—Ant.** agitation.

com•po•ta•tion (kom′pə tā′shən), *n.* an act or instance of drinking or tippling together. [1585–95; < L *compōtātiōn-* (s. of *compōtātiō,* trans. of Gk *sympósion* SYMPOSIUM). See COM-, POTATION]

com•po•ta•tor (kom′pə tā′tər), *n.* a person who drinks or tipples with another. [1725–35; < LL; see COMPOTATION, -TOR] **—com•po•ta•to•ry** (kəm pō′tə tôr′ē, -tōr′ē), *adj.*

com•pote (kom′pōt; *Fr.* kôɴ pôt′), *n., pl.* **-potes** (-pōts; *Fr.* -pôt′). **1.** fruit stewed or cooked in a syrup, usually served as a dessert. **2.** Also, **compotier.** a dish, usually of glass, china, or silver, having a base, stem, and often a lid, and used for serving fruit, nuts, candy, etc. [1685–95; < F; OF *composte* < L *composita,* fem. of *compositus* COMPOSITE; cf. COMPOST]

com•po•tier (kom′pə tēr′; *Fr.* kôɴ pô tyā′), *n., pl.* **-tiers** (-tērz′; *Fr.* -tyā′). compote (def. 2). [1745–55; < F; see COMPOTE, -IER[2]]

com•pound[1] (*adj.* kom′pound, kom pound′; *n.* kom′pound; *v.* kəm pound′, kom′pound), *adj.* **1.** composed of two or more parts, elements, or ingredients: *Soap is a compound substance.* **2.** having or involving two or more actions or functions: *The mouth is a compound organ.* **3.** *Gram.* of or pertaining to a compound sentence or compound-complex sentence. **4.** (of a word) **a.** consisting of two or more parts that are also bases, as *housetop, many-sided, playact,* or *upon.* **b.** consisting of any two or more parts that have identifiable meaning, as a base and a noninflectional affix (*return, follower*), a base and a combining form (*biochemistry*), two combining forms (*ethnography*), or a combining form and a noninflectional affix (*aviary, dentoid*). **5.** (of a verb tense) consisting of an auxiliary verb and a main verb, as *are swimming, have spoken,* or *will write* (opposed to *simple*). **6.** *Bot.* composed of several similar parts that combine to form a whole: *a compound fruit.* **7.** *Zool.* composed of a number of distinct individuals that are connected to form a united whole or colony, as coral. **8.** *Music.* of or pertaining to compound time. **9.** *Mach.* noting an engine or turbine expanding the same steam or the like in two successive chambers to do work at two ranges of pressure.
—n. **10.** something formed by compounding or combining parts, elements, etc. **11.** *Chem.* a pure substance composed of two or more elements whose composition is constant. **12.** a compound word, esp. one composed of two or more words that are otherwise unaltered, as *moonflower* or *rainstorm.*
—v.t. **13.** to put together into a whole; combine: *to compound drugs to form a new medicine.* **14.** to make or form by combining parts, elements, etc.; construct: *to compound a new plan from parts of several former plans.* **15.** to make up or constitute: *all the organs and members that compound a human body.* **16.** to settle or adjust by agreement, esp. for a reduced amount, as a debt. **17.** *Law.* to agree, for a consideration, not to prosecute or punish a wrongdoer for: *to compound a crime or felony.* **18.** to pay (interest) on the accrued interest as well as the principal: *My bank compounds interest quarterly.* **19.** to increase or add to: *The misery of his loneliness was now compounded by his poverty.* **20.** *Elect.* to connect a portion of the field turns of (a direct-current dynamo) in series with the armature circuit.
—v.i. **21.** to make a bargain; come to terms; compromise. **22.** to settle a debt, claim, etc., by compromise. **23.** to form a compound. [1350–1400; (v.) ME *compounen* < MF *compon-* (s. of *compondre*) < L *compōnere,* equiv. to *com-* COM- + *pōnere* to put; (adj.) ME *compouned,* ptp. of *compounen,* as above] **—com•pound′a•ble,** *adj.* **—com•pound′ed•ness,** *n.* **—com•pound′er,** *n.*

com•pound[2] (kom′pound), *n.* **1.** (in the Far East) an enclosure containing residences, business offices, or other establishments of Europeans. **2.** (in Africa) a similar enclosure for native laborers. **3.** any enclosure, esp. for prisoners of war. **4.** any separate cluster of homes, often owned by members of the same family. [1670–80; alter., by assoc. with COMPOUND[1], of Malay *kampung* village, collection, gathering; cf. KAMPONG]

com′pound-com′plex sen′tence (kom′pound-kom′pleks), a sentence having two or more coordinate independent clauses and one or more dependent clauses, as *The lightning flashed* (independent clause) *and the rain fell* (independent clause) *as he entered the house* (dependent clause). [1920–25]

com′pound eye′, an arthropod eye subdivided into many individual, light-receptive elements, each including a lens, a transmitting apparatus, and retinal cells. [1830–40]

com′pound flow′er, the flower head of a composite plant. [1770–80]

com′pound frac′tion, *Math.* See **complex fraction.** [1800–10]

com′pound frac′ture, a fracture in which the broken bone is exposed through a wound in the skin. [1535–45]

com′pound func′tion, *Math.* See **composite function.**

com′pound in′terest, interest paid on both the principal and on accrued interest. [1650–60]

com′pound in′terval, *Music.* an interval that is greater than an octave, as a ninth or a thirteenth.

com′pound leaf′, a leaf composed of a number of leaflets on a common stalk, arranged either palmately, as the fingers of a hand, or pinnately, as the leaflets of a fern; the leaflets themselves may be compound.

com′pound lens′, an optical system consisting of two or more lenses having the same axis.

com′pound mag′net, a magnet consisting of two or more separate magnets placed together with like poles pointing in the same direction.

com′pound mi′croscope, an optical instrument for forming magnified images of small objects, consisting of an objective lens with a very short focal length and an eyepiece with a longer focal length, both lenses mounted in the same tube. See illus. under **microscope.** [1865–70]

com′pound num′ber, a quantity expressed in more than one denomination or unit, as one foot six inches or one minute twenty seconds. [1550–60]

com′pound o′vary, *Bot.* an ovary composed of more than one carpel.

com′pound pen′dulum, *Physics.* See **physical pendulum.** [1820–30]

compound Q, trichosanthin: an antiviral drug derived from the root of a Chinese cucumber plant, used in the treatment of AIDS. [1985–90; *Q* for *cu(cumber)*]

com′pound sen′tence, a sentence containing two or more coordinate independent clauses, usually joined by one or more conjunctions, but no dependent clause, as *The lightning flashed* (independent clause) *and* (conjunction) *the rain fell* (independent clause). [1765–75]

com′pound time′, *Music.* metrical time beaten so that three beats are counted as one; time in which each beat is divisible by three. [1840–50]

com•pound-wound (kom′pound wound′), *adj. Elect.* noting an electric device in which part of the field circuit is in parallel with the armature circuit and part is in series with it. **—com′pound wind′ing** (wīn′ding).

com•pra•dor (kom′prə dôr′), *n.* (formerly in China) a native agent or factotum, as of a foreign business house. Also, **com′pra•dore′.** [1605–15; < Pg: buyer < L *comparātor,* equiv. to *comparā(re)* to furnish, provide, prepare (see COM-, PREPARE) + *-tor* -TOR]

com•pre•hend (kom′pri hend′), *v.t.* **1.** to understand the nature or meaning of; grasp with the mind; perceive: *He did not comprehend the significance of the ambassador's remark.* **2.** to take in or embrace; include; comprise: *The course will comprehend all facets of Japanese culture.* [1350–1400; ME *comprehenden* < L *comprehendere,* equiv. to *com-* COM- + *prehendere* to grasp; see PREHENSILE] **—com′pre•hend′er,** *n.* **—com′pre•hend′ing•ly,** *adv.*
—Syn. 1. See **know[1]. 2.** See **include.**

com•pre•hen•si•ble (kom′pri hen′sə bəl), *adj.* capable of being comprehended or understood; intelligible. Also, **com•pre•hend•i•ble** (kom′pri hen′də bəl). [1520–30; < L *comprehēnsibilis.* See COMPREHENSION, -IBLE] **—com′pre•hen′si•bil′i•ty, com′pre•hen′si•ble•ness,** *n.* **—com′pre•hen′si•bly,** *adv.*

com•pre•hen•sion (kom′pri hen′shən), *n.* **1.** the act or process of comprehending. **2.** the state of being comprehended. **3.** perception or understanding: *His comprehension of physics is amazing for a young student.* **4.** capacity of the mind to perceive and understand; power to grasp ideas; ability to know. **5.** *Logic.* the connotation of a term. **6.** inclusion. **7.** comprehensiveness. [1400–50; late ME < L *comprehēnsiōn-* (s. of *comprehēnsiō*), equiv. to *comprehēns(us)* (ptp. of *comprehendere* to COMPREHEND) + *-iōn-* -ION]

com•pre•hen•sive (kom′pri hen′siv), *adj.* **1.** of large scope; covering or involving much; inclusive: *a comprehensive study of world affairs.* **2.** comprehending mentally; having an extensive mental range or grasp. **3.** *Insurance.* covering or providing broad protection against loss. *—n.* **4.** Often, **comprehensives.** Also called **comprehen′sive examina′tion.** an examination of extensive coverage given to measure a student's general progress, proficiency in his or her major field of study, or the like. **5.** the detailed layout of an advertisement, showing placement of photographs, illustrations, copy, etc., as for presentation to a client. Cf. **visual** (def. 7). [1605–15; < LL *comprehēnsīvus.* See COMPREHENSION, -IVE] **—com′pre•hen′sive•ly,** *adv.* **—com′pre•hen′sive•ness,** *n.*

comprehen′sive school′. See **composite school.** [1945–50]

com•press (*v.* kəm pres′; *n.* kom′pres), *v.t.* **1.** to press together; force into less space. **2.** to cause to become a solid mass: *to compress cotton into bales.* **3.** to condense, shorten, or abbreviate: *The book was compressed by 50 pages.* *—n.* **4.** *Med.* a soft, cloth pad held in place by a bandage and used to provide pressure or to supply moisture, cold, heat, or medication. **5.** an apparatus for compressing cotton bales. **6.** a warehouse for storing cotton bales before shipment. [1350–1400; (v.) ME (< MF *compresser*) < LL *compressāre,* freq. of L *comprimere* to squeeze together (see COM-, PRESS[1]); (n.) < MF *compresse,* n. deriv. of the v.] **—com•press′i•ble,** *adj.* **—com•press′i•bly,** *adv.* **—com•press′ing•ly,** *adv.*
—Syn. 1. condense, squeeze, constrict. See **contract.**

com•pressed (kəm prest′), *adj.* **1.** pressed into less space; condensed: *compressed gases.* **2.** pressed together: *compressed lips.* **3.** flattened by or as if by pressure: *compressed wallboard.* **4.** *Zool., Bot.* flattened laterally. [1325–75; ME; see COMPRESS, -ED[2]] **—com•press′ed•ly,** *adv.*
—Ant. 1. expanded.

compressed′ air′, air compressed, esp. by mechanical means, to a pressure higher than the surrounding atmospheric pressure. [1660–70]

compressed′ petro′leum gas′. See **liquefied petroleum gas.**

compressed′ speech′, speech reproduced on tape

CONCISE ETYMOLOGY KEY: <, descended or borrowed from; >, whence; b., blend of, blended; c., cognate with; cf., compare; deriv., derivative; equiv., equivalent; imit., imitative; obl., oblique; r., replacing; s., stem; sp., spelling, spelled; resp., respelling, respelled; trans., translation; ?, origin unknown; *, unattested; ‡, probably earlier than. See the full key inside the front cover.

at a faster rate than originally spoken, but without loss of intelligibility, by being filtered through a mechanism that deletes very small segments of the original signal at random intervals. [1965–70]

com•press•i•bil•i•ty (kəm pres′ə bil′i tē), *n., pl.* **-ties** for 2. **1.** the quality or state of being compressible. **2.** *Physics.* the reciprocal of the bulk modulus, equal to the ratio of the fractional change in volume to the stress applied to a body. [1685–95; COMPRESSIBLE + -ITY]

com•pres•sion (kəm presh′ən), *n.* **1.** the act of compressing. **2.** the state of being compressed. **3.** the effect, result, or consequence of being compressed. **4.** (in internal-combustion engines) the reduction in volume and increase of pressure of the air or combustible mixture in the cylinder prior to ignition, produced by the motion of the piston toward the cylinder head after intake. Also, **com•pres•sure** (kəm presh′ər) (for defs. 1, 2). [1350–1400; ME (< AF) < L *compressiōn-* (s. of *compressiō*), equiv. to *compress(us)* ptp. of *comprimere* to press together (see COM-, PRESS[1]) + *-iōn-* -ION] **—com•pres′sion•al,** *adj.*

compres′sion igni′tion, ignition of engine fuel by the heat of air compressed in the cylinders into which the fuel is introduced. [1925–30] **—com•pres′sion-ig•ni′tion,** *adj.*

compres′sion mold′ing, a method of molding thermosetting plastic by closing a mold on it, forming the material by heat and pressure. [1935–40]

compres′sion ra′tio, *Auto.* the ratio of the cylinder volume enclosed by the piston at its outermost position to the volume enclosed by it at its innermost position. [1905–10]

compres′sion wave′, a shock wave that compresses the medium through which it is transmitted. Also, **compres′sional wave′.** Cf. **expansion wave.** [1885–90]

com•pres•sive (kəm pres′iv), *adj.* compressing; tending to compress. [1375–1425; late ME. See COMPRESS, -IVE] **—com•pres′sive•ly,** *adv.*

com•pres•sor (kəm pres′ər), *n.* **1.** a person or thing that compresses. **2.** *Anat.* a muscle that compresses some part of the body. **3.** *Surg.* an instrument for compressing a part of the body. **4.** a pump or other machine for reducing volume and increasing pressure of gases in order to condense the gases, drive pneumatically powered machinery, etc. **5.** *Electronics.* a transducer that produces an output with a range of voltages whose ratio is smaller than that of the range of the input signal. Cf. **expander** (def. 2). [1745–55; COMPRESS + -OR[2]]

com•pri•mar•i•o (kom′prə mâr′ē ō′, -mär′-), *n., pl.* **-mar•i•os.** a singer in an opera company who ranks below the lead singers and who usually sings secondary roles. [< It, equiv. to *com-* COM- + *primario* PRIMARY]

com•prise (kəm prīz′), *v.t.,* **-prised, -pris•ing. 1.** to include or contain: *The Soviet Union comprises several socialist republics.* **2.** to consist of; be composed of: *The advisory board comprises six members.* **3.** to form or constitute: *Seminars and lectures comprised the day's activities.* **4. be comprised of,** to consist of; be composed of: *The sales network is comprised of independent outlets and chain stores.* [1400–50; late ME *comprisen* < MF *compris* (ptp. of *comprendre*) < L *comprehēnsus;* see COMPREHENSION] **—com•pris′a•ble,** *adj.* **—com•pris′•al,** *n.*

—Syn. 1. See **include.**

—Usage. COMPRISE has had an interesting history of sense development. In addition to its original senses, dating from the 15th century, "to include" and "to consist of" (*The United States of America comprises 50 states*), COMPRISE has had since the late 18th century the meaning "to form or constitute" (*Fifty states comprise the United States of America*). Since the late 19th century it has also been used in passive constructions with a sense synonymous with that of one of its original meanings "to consist of, be composed of": *The United States of America is comprised of 50 states.* These later uses are often criticized, but they occur with increasing frequency even in formal speech and writing.

com•prize (kəm prīz′), *v.t.,* **-prized, -priz•ing.** comprise. **—com•priz′a•ble,** *adj.* **—com•priz′al,** *n.*

com•pro•mis (kom′prə mē′), *n., pl.* **-mises** (-mēz′). *Internat. Law.* a formal document, executed in common by nations submitting a dispute to arbitration, that defines the matter at issue, the rules of procedure and the powers of the arbitral tribunal, and the principles for determining the award. [1590–1600; < F: lit., compromise]

com•pro•mise (kom′prə mīz′), *n., v.,* **-mised, -mis•ing.** —*n.* **1.** a settlement of differences by mutual concessions; an agreement reached by adjustment of conflicting or opposing claims, principles, etc., by reciprocal modification of demands. **2.** the result of such a settlement. **3.** something intermediate between different things: *The split-level is a compromise between a ranch house and a multistoried house.* **4.** an endangering, esp. of reputation; exposure to danger, suspicion, etc.: *a compromise of one's integrity.* —*v.t.* **5.** to settle by a compromise. **6.** to expose or make vulnerable to danger, suspicion, scandal, etc.; jeopardize: *a military oversight that compromised the nation's defenses.* **7.** *Obs.* **a.** to bind by bargain or agreement. **b.** to bring to terms. —*v.i.* **8.** to make a compromise or compromises: *The conflicting parties agreed to compromise.* **9.** to make a dishonorable or shameful concession: *He is too honorable to compromise with his principles.* [1400–50; late ME < AF *compromisse,* MF *compromis* < L *comprōmissum.* See COM-, PROMISE] **—com′pro•mis′er,** *n.* **—com′pro•mis′ing•ly,** *adv.* **—com•prom•is•sa•ry** (kom prom′ə ser′ē), *adj.*

com•pro•mised (kom′prə mīzd′), *adj. Pathol.* unable to function optimally, esp. with regard to immune response, owing to underlying disease, harmful environmental exposure, or the side effects of a course of treatment. [COMPROMISE + -ED[2]]

com′promise joint′, *Railroads.* a joint for linking together rails having different sections.

com′promise rail′, *Railroads.* a rail for linking rails having different sections.

comp•sog•na•thus (komp sog′nə thəs), *n.* any bipedal carnivorous dinosaur of the genus *Compsognathus,* of late Jurassic age, having a slender body that reached a length of 30 in. (76 cm). [< NL (1859) < Gk *kompsó(s)* elegant + *-gnathos* -GNATHOUS]

compt (kount), *v.t., v.i., n. Archaic.* count′.

compt., comptroller.

compte ren•du (kôɴт räɴ dy′), *pl.* ***comptes ren•dus*** (kôɴт räɴ dy′). *French.* a report of a transaction or proceedings. [lit., account rendered]

Comp•ton (komp′tən), *n.* **1. Arthur Hol•ly** (hol′ē), 1892–1962, U.S. physicist: Nobel prize 1927. **2.** his brother, **Karl Taylor** (kärl), 1887–1954, U.S. physicist. **3. Spencer, Earl of Wilmington,** 1673?–1743, British statesman: prime minister 1742–43. **4.** a city in SW California. 81,286.

Comp′ton effect′, *Physics.* the increase in wavelength of monochromatic, electromagnetic radiation, as a beam of photons or x-rays, when it is scattered by particles whose size is small compared to the wavelength of the radiation. Also called **Comp′ton-De•bye′ effect′** (komp′tən de bī′). [1920–25; named after A. H. COMPTON]

comp•trol•ler (kən trō′lər; *spelling pron.* komp trō′lər), *n.* controller (def. 1). [by confusion with COMPT] **—comp•trol′ler•ship′,** *n.*

Comptrol′ler Gen′eral of the Unit′ed States′, the director of the General Accounting Office. [1920–25]

Comptrol′ler of the Cur′rency, an official of the U.S. Department of the Treasury who regulates the national banks and administers the issuance and redemption of Federal Reserve notes. [1870–75]

com•pul•sion (kəm pul′shən), *n.* **1.** the act of compelling; constraint; coercion. **2.** the state or condition of being compelled. **3.** *Psychol.* a strong, usually irresistible impulse to perform an act, esp. one that is irrational or contrary to one's will. [1375–1425; late ME (< AF) < LL *compulsiōn-* (s. of *compulsiō*), equiv. to L *compulsus*) ptp. of *compellere* to COMPEL (*com-* COM- + *pul-* var. s. + *-sus* ptp. suffix) + *-iōn-* -ION]

com•pul•sive (kəm pul′siv), *adj.* **1.** compelling; compulsory. **2.** *Psychol.* **a.** pertaining to, characterized by, or involving compulsion: *a compulsive desire to cry.* **b.** governed by an obsessive need to conform, be scrupulous, etc., coupled with an inability to express positive emotions. —*n.* **3.** *Psychol.* a person whose behavior is governed by a compulsion. [1595–1605; obs. *compulse* v. (< L *compuls(us),* ptp. of *compellere;* see COMPULSION) + -IVE] **—com•pul′sive•ly,** *adv.* **—com•pul′sive•ness, com•pul•siv•i•ty** (kəm pul siv′i tē, kom′pul-), *n.*

com•pul•so•ry (kəm pul′sə rē), *adj., n., pl.* **-ries.** —*adj.* **1.** required; mandatory; obligatory: *compulsory education.* **2.** using compulsion; compelling; constraining: *compulsory measures to control rioting.* —*n.* **3.** something, as an athletic feat, that must be performed or completed as part of a contest or competition: *The ice skater received a higher score on the compulsories than on her freestyle performance.* [1510–20; < ML *compulsōrius,* equiv. to L *compul-,* var. s. of *compellere* (see COMPEL) + *-sōrius,* for *-tōrius* -TORY[1]; cf. COMPULSIVE] **—com•pul′so•ri•ly,** *adv.* **—com•pul′so•ri•ness,** *n.*

com•punc•tion (kəm pungk′shən), *n.* **1.** a feeling of uneasiness or anxiety of the conscience caused by regret for doing wrong or causing pain; contrition; remorse. **2.** any uneasiness or hesitation about the rightness of an action. [1350–1400; ME *compunccion* (< AF) < LL *compūnctiōn-* (s. of *compūnctiō*), equiv. to L *compūnct(us),* ptp. of *compungere* to prick severely (*com-* COM- + *pungere* to prick; cf. POINT) + *-iōn-* -ION] **—com•punc′•tion•less,** *adj.*

com•punc•tious (kəm pungk′shəs), *adj.* causing or feeling compunction; regretful. [1595–1605; COMPUNCT(ION) + -IOUS] **—com•punc′tious•ly,** *adv.*

com•pur•ga•tion (kom′pər gā′shən), *n.* an early common-law method of trial in which the defendant is acquitted on the sworn endorsement of a specified number of friends or neighbors. [1650–60; < ML *compurgātiōn-* (s. of *compurgātiō*), equiv. to *com-* COM- + *purgāt(us)* (ptp. of *purgāre* to PURGE) + *-iōn-* -ION]

com•pur•ga•tor (kom′pər gā′tər), *n.* a person who vouches for the innocence and truthful testimony of another. [1525–35; < ML, equiv. to *compurgā(re)* (see COMPURGATION) + *-tor* -TOR]

com•pu•ta•tion (kom′pyo͝o tā′shən), *n.* **1.** an act, process, or method of computing; calculation. **2.** a result of computing. **3.** the amount computed. [1375–1425; late ME < L *computātiōn-* (s. of *computātiō*), equiv. to *computāt(us)* (ptp. of *computāre;* see COMPUTE) + *-iōn-* -ION] **—com′pu•ta′tion•al,** *adj.* **—com′pu•ta′tive,** *adj.* **—com′pu•ta′tive•ly,** *adv.*

computa′tional linguis′tics, the study of the applications of computers in processing and analyzing language, as in automatic machine translation and text analysis. [1960–65]

com•pute (kəm pyo͞ot′), *v.,* **-put•ed, -put•ing,** *n.* —*v.t.* **1.** to determine by calculation; reckon; calculate: *to compute the period of Jupiter's revolution.* **2.** to determine by using a computer or calculator. —*v.i.* **3.** to reckon; calculate. **4.** to use a computer or calculator. **5.** *Informal.* to make sense; add up: *His reasons for doing that just don't compute.* —*n.* **6.** computation: *outer space that is vast beyond compute.* [1375–1425 for earlier sense; 1580–90 for def. 6; (v.) < L *computāre,* equiv. to *com-* COM- + *putāre* to think; (n.) late ME < MF < LL *computus* calculation, number, n. deriv. of *computāre;* cf. PUTATIVE, COUNT[1]] **—com•put′a•ble,** *adj.* **—com•put′•a•bil′i•ty,** *n.* **—com•put′a•bly,** *adv.* **—com•put•ist** (kəm pyo͞o′tist, kom′pyo͝o-), *n.*

—Syn. 1. estimate, count, figure.

comput′ed tomog′raphy. See **computerized axial tomography.** *Abbr.:* CT

com•put•er (kəm pyo͞o′tər), *n.* **1.** Also called **processor.** an electronic device designed to accept data, perform prescribed mathematical and logical operations at high speed, and display the results of these operations. Cf. **analog computer, digital computer. 2.** a person who computes; computist. [1640–50; COMPUTE + -ER[1]; cf. MF *computeur*] **—com•put′er•like′,** *adj.*

com•put′er-aid•ed pub′lishing (kəm pyo͞o′tər ā′did). See **desktop publishing.** *Abbr.:* CAP

com•put′er-as•sist•ed make′up (kəm pyo͞o′tər ə sis′tid), *Print.* pagination (def. 4a).

comput′er-assisted tomog′raphy. See **computerized axial tomography.**

comput′er crime′, unauthorized use of a computer for personal gain, as in the illegal transfer of funds or to alter the data or property of others. [1970–75] **—comput′er crim′inal.**

com•put•er•ese (kəm pyo͞o′tə rēz′, -rēs′), *n.* the jargon and technical terms associated with computers and their operation. [1955–60; COMPUTER + -ESE]

comput′er graph′ics, 1. pictorial computer output produced on a display screen, plotter, or printer. **2.** the study of the techniques used to produce such output. [1970–75]

com•put•er•ist (kəm pyo͞o′tə rist), *n.* a person who works with computers, esp. a computer hobbyist or amateur programmer. [COMPUTER + -IST]

com•put•er•ize (kəm pyo͞o′tə rīz′), *v.,* **-ized, -iz•ing.** —*v.t.* **1.** to control, perform, process, or store (a system, operation, or information) by means of or in an electronic computer or computers. **2.** to equip with or automate by computers: *to computerize a business.* —*v.i.* **3.** to make use of computers: *The entire industry is expected to computerize by the end of the year.* Also, *esp. Brit.,* **com•put′er•ise′.** [1955–60; COMPUTER + -IZE] **—com•put′er•iz′a•ble,** *adj.* **—com•put′er•i•za′tion,** *n.*

comput′erized ax′ial tomog′raphy, the process of producing a CAT scan. Also called **computed tomography, computer-assisted tomography, comput′•erized tomog′raphy.** Cf. **CAT scanner.** [1970–75]

comput′er lan′guage, a programming language, as BASIC, COBOL, or FORTRAN, devised for communicating instructions to a computer. [1965–70]

comput′er law′, a body of law arising out of the special conditions relating to the use of computers, as in computer crime or software copyright.

comput′er lit′eracy, familiarity with computers and how they work, esp. a nontechnical understanding of microcomputers and of the role computers play in modern society. [1975–80] **—com•put•er•lit•er•ate** (kəm pyo͞o′tər lit′ər it), *adj.*

comput′er mem′ory, memory (def. 11).

comput′er sci′ence, the science that deals with the theory and methods of processing information in digital computers, the design of computer hardware and software, and the applications of computers. [1970–75] **—comput′er sci′entist.**

comput′er vi′rus, virus (def. 4). [1985–90]

comput′er vi′sion, 1. a robot analogue of human vision in which information about the environment is received by one or more video cameras and processed by computer: used in navigation by robots, in the control of automated production lines, etc. **2.** a similar system for the blind that converts optical information into tactile signals. Also called **machine vision, vision.**

com•put•ing (kəm pyo͞o′ting), *n.* **1.** the use of a computer to process data or perform calculations. **2.** the act of calculating or reckoning. [1640–50; COMPUTE + -ING[1]]

Comr., Commissioner.

com•rade (kom′rad, -rid), *n.* **1.** a person who shares in one's activities, occupation, etc.; companion, associate, or friend. **2.** a fellow member of a fraternal group, political party, etc. **3.** a member of the Communist party or someone with strongly leftist views. [1585–95; < MF *camarade* < Sp *camarada* group of soldiers billeted together, equiv. to *cámar(a)* room (< L; see CAMERA) + *-ada* < L *-āta,* fem. of *-ātus* -ATE[1]] **—com′•rade•ship′,** *n.*

—Syn. 1. crony, fellow, mate.

com′rade in arms′, a fellow soldier. [1840–50]

com•rade•ly (com′rad lē, -rid-), *adj.* of, like, or befitting a comrade: *a comradely pat on the shoulder.* [1875–80; COMRADE + -LY] **—com′rade•li•ness,** *n.*

com•rade•ry (kom′rad rē, -rid-), *n.* camaraderie.

Com•sat (kom′sat′), **1.** *Trademark.* a privately owned corporation servicing the global communications satellite system and acting as the U.S. representative to and participant in Intelsat. —*n.* **2.** (*often l.c.*) a communications satellite. [*Com(munications) Sat(ellite Corporation)*]

Com•so•mol (kom′sə môl′, kom′sə môl′), *n.* Komsomol.

Com•stock (kum′stok, kom′-), *n.* **Anthony,** 1844–1915, U.S. author and reformer.

Com•stock•er•y (kum′stok ə rē, kom′-), *n.* overzealous moral censorship of the fine arts and literature, often mistaking outspokenly honest works for salacious ones. [1900–05; after A. COMSTOCK; see -ERY] **—Com′•stock′er,** *n.* **—Com•stock′i•an,** *adj.*

Com′stock Lode′, the most valuable deposit of silver ore ever recorded, discovered in 1859 by Henry T. P. Comstock near Virginia City, Nev. Also called **Com′•stock Sil′ver Lode′.**

com•symp (kom′simp′), *n.* (*sometimes cap.*) *Disparaging.* a person who sympathizes with communists. [1960–65; *com(munist) symp(athizer)*]

comte (kôNt), *n., pl.* ***comtes*** (kôNt). *French.* count².

Comte (kôNt; *Fr.* kôNt), *n.* **(I·si·dore) Au·guste (Ma·rie Fran·çois)** (ē zē dôr′ ō gyst′ MA RĒ′ fRäN swa′), 1798–1857, French founder of the philosophical system of positivism.

com·tesse (kôN tes′), *n., pl.* **-tesses** (-tes′). *French.* countess.

Com·ti·an (kom′tē ən, kôN′-), *adj.* **1.** Also, **Com′te·an.** of or pertaining to the philosophy of Auguste Comte. —*n.* **2.** a follower of the philosophy of Auguste Comte. [1850–55; A. COMTE + -IAN]

Comt·ism (kom′tiz əm, kôN′-), *n.* the philosophy of Auguste Comte; positivism. [1870–75; A. COMTE + -ISM] —**Com′tist,** *n., adj.*

Co·mus (kō′məs), *n.* an ancient Greek and Roman god of drinking and revelry. Also, **Komos.** [< L < Gk *kômos* revel; akin to COMEDY]

Com. Ver., Common Version (of the Bible).

con¹ (kon), *adv.* **1.** against a proposition, opinion, etc.: *arguments pro and con.* —*n.* **2.** the argument, position, arguer, or voter against something. Cf. **pro¹.** [1575–85; short for L *contrā* in opposition, against]

con² (kon), *v.t.,* **conned, con·ning. 1.** to learn; study; peruse or examine carefully. **2.** to commit to memory. [bef. 1000; ME *cunnen,* OE *cunnan* var. of CAN¹ in sense "become acquainted with, learn to know"]

con³ (kon), *v.,* **conned, con·ning,** *n. Naut.* —*v.t.* **1.** to direct the steering of (a ship). —*n.* **2.** the station of the person who cons. **3.** the act of conning. Also, **conn.** [1350–1400; earlier *cond,* apocopated var. of ME *condie, condue* < MF *cond(u)ire* < L *condūcere* to CONDUCT]

con⁴ (kon), *adj., v.,* **conned, con·ning,** *n. Informal.* —*adj.* **1.** involving abuse of confidence: *a con trick.* —*v.t.* **2.** to swindle; trick: *That crook conned me out of all my savings.* **3.** to persuade by deception, cajolery, etc. —*n.* **4.** a confidence game or swindle. **5.** a lie, exaggeration, or glib self-serving talk: *He had a dozen different cons for getting out of paying traffic tickets.* [1895–1900, *Amer.*; by shortening of CONFIDENCE]

con⁵ (kon), *n. Slang.* a convict. [1715–25; by shortening]

con⁶ (kon), *v.t.,* **conned, con·ning.** *Brit. Dial.* **1.** to strike, hit, or rap (something or someone). **2.** to hammer (a nail or peg). **3.** to beat or thrash a person with the hands or a weapon. [1890–95; perh. akin to F *cognée* hatchet, *cogner* to knock in, drive (a nail) home]

con-, var. of **com-** before a consonant (except *b, h, l, p, r*) and, by assimilation, before *n: convene; condone; connection.* [< L]

Con., 1. Conformist. **2.** Consul.

con., 1. concerto. **2.** conclusion. **3.** connection. **4.** consolidated. **5.** consul. **6.** continued. **7.** against. [< L *contrā*]

CONAD (kon′ad), *n.* Continental Air Defense Command.

Co·na·kry (*Fr.* kô nA kRē′), *n.* a seaport in and the capital of Guinea, in NW Africa. 525,671 with suburbs. Also, **Konakri.**

con a·mo·re (kon ə môr′ē, -môr′ā, -mōr′ē, -mōr′ā, kōn; *It.* kôn ä mô′Re). **1.** (*italics*) *Italian.* with love, tender enthusiasm, or zeal. **2.** tenderly and lovingly (used as a musical direction). [1730–40]

Co·nan (kō′nən), *n.* a male given name.

con a·ni·ma (kon an′ə mä′, kōn ä′nē mä′; *It.* kôn ä′nē mä), with spirit; animatedly (used as a musical direction). [1905–10; < It: lit., with spirit]

Co·nant (kō′nənt), *n.* **James Bryant,** 1893–1978, U.S. chemist and educator: president of Harvard University 1933–53.

con′ ar′tist, *Informal.* **1.** a person adept at lying, cajolery, or glib self-serving talk. **2.** a person adept at swindling by means of confidence games; swindler.

co·na·tion (kō nā′shən), *n. Psychol.* the part of mental life having to do with striving, including desire and volition. [1605–15; < L *cōnātiōn-* (s. of *cōnātiō*) an effort, equiv. to *cōnāt(us)* (ptp. of *cōnārī* to try) + *-iōn-* -ION]

con·a·tive (kon′ə tiv, kō′nə-), *adj.* **1.** *Psychol.* pertaining to or of the nature of conation. **2.** *Gram.* expressing endeavor or effort: *a conative verb.* —*n.* **3.** *Gram.* a conative word, affix, or verbal aspect. [1680–90; CONAT(ION) + -IVE]

co·na·tus (kō nā′təs), *n., pl.* **-tus. 1.** an effort or striving. **2.** a force or tendency simulating a human effort. **3.** (in the philosophy of Spinoza) the force in every animate creature toward the preservation of its existence. [1655–65; < L: exertion, equiv. to *cōnā(rī)* to attempt + *-tus* suffix of v. action]

con bri·o (kon brē′ō, kōn; *It.* kôn bRē′ô), with vigor; vivaciously (used as a musical direction). [1890–95; < It]

conc., 1. concentrate. **2.** concentrated. **3.** concentration. **4.** concerning. **5.** concrete.

con·cat·e·nate (kon kat′n āt′), *v.,* **-nat·ed, -nat·ing,** *adj.* —*v.t.* **1.** to link together; unite in a series or chain. —*adj.* **2.** linked together, as in a chain. [1425–75; late ME (ptp.) < LL *concatēnātus* (ptp. of *concatēnāre*), equiv. to *con-* CON- + L *catēn(a)* CHAIN + *-ātus* -ATE¹] —**con·cat′e·na′tor,** *n.*

con·cat·e·na·tion (kon kat′n ā′shən), *n.* **1.** the act of concatenating. **2.** the state of being concatenated; connection, as in a chain. **3.** a series of interconnected or interdependent things or events. [1595–1605; < LL *concatēnātiōn-* (s. of *concatēnātiō*), equiv. to *concatēnāt(us)* CONCATENATE + *-iōn-* -ION]

con·cave (*adj., v.* kon kāv′, kon′kāv; *n.* kon′kāv), *adj., n., v.,* **-caved, -cav·ing.** —*adj.* **1.** curved like a segment of the interior of a circle or hollow sphere; hollow and curved. Cf. **convex** (def. 1). **2.** *Geom.* (of a polygon) having at least one interior angle greater than 180°. **3.** *Obs.* hollow. —*n.* **4.** a concave surface, part, line, or thing. **5.** *Mach.* a concave piece, as one against which a drum rotates. —*v.t.* **6.** to make concave. [1375–1425; late ME (< MF) < L *concavus,* hollow. See CON-, CAVE] —**con·cave′ly,** *adv.* —**con·cave′·ness,** *n.*

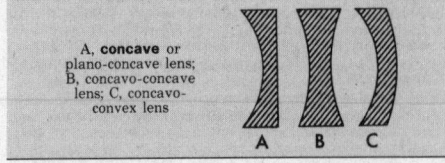

A, **concave** or plano-concave lens; B, concavo-concave lens; C, concavo-convex lens

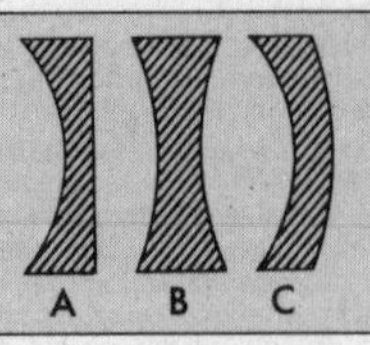

A B C

con·cav·i·ty (kon kav′i tē), *n., pl.* **-ties** for 2. **1.** the state or quality of being concave. **2.** a concave surface or thing; cavity. [1350–1400; ME *concavite* < LL *concavitāt-* (s. of *concavitās*). See CON-, CAVE, -ITY]

con·ca·vo-con·cave (kon kā′vō kon kāv′), *adj.* concave on both sides. [< L *concav(us)* + -o- + CONCAVE]

con·ca·vo-con·vex (kon kā′vō kon veks′), *adj.* **1.** Also, **convexo-concave.** concave on one side and convex on the other. **2.** *Optics.* pertaining to or noting a lens in which the concave face has a greater degree of curvature than the convex face. [1670–80; < L *concav(us)* + -o- + CONVEX]

con·ceal (kən sēl′), *v.t.* **1.** to hide; withdraw or remove from observation; cover or keep from sight: *He concealed the gun under his coat.* **2.** to keep secret; to prevent or avoid disclosing or divulging: *to conceal one's identity by using a false name.* [1275–1325; ME *conselen, concelen* < AF *conceler* < L *concēlāre,* equiv. to *con-* CON- + *cēlāre* to hide (akin to HULL¹, Gk *koleón* scabbard (see COLEOPTERA); cf. OCCULT)] —**con·ceal′a·ble,** *adj.* —**con·ceal′a·bil′i·ty,** *n.* —**con·ceal′ed·ly,** *adv.* —**con·ceal′ed·ness,** *n.* —**con·ceal′er,** *n.*
—**Syn. 1.** See **hide¹.**

con·ceal·ment (kən sēl′mənt), *n.* **1.** the act of concealing. **2.** the state of being concealed. **3.** a means or place of hiding. [1275–1325; ME *concelement* < AF. See CONCEAL, -MENT]

con·cede (kən sēd′), *v.,* **-ced·ed, -ced·ing.** —*v.t.* **1.** to acknowledge as true, just, or proper; admit: *He finally conceded that she was right.* **2.** to acknowledge (an opponent's victory, score, etc.) before it is officially established: *to concede an election before all the votes are counted.* **3.** to grant as a right or privilege; yield: *to concede a longer vacation for all employees.* —*v.i.* **4.** to make concession; yield; admit: *She was so persistent that I conceded at last.* [1625–35; < L *concēdere,* equiv. to *con-* CON- + *cēdere* to withdraw, yield, CEDE] —**con·ced′ed·ly,** *adv.* —**con·ced′er,** *n.* —**con·ces′si·ble,** *adj.*
—**Syn. 1.** grant. —**Ant. 1.** deny. **3.** refuse.

con·ceit (kən sēt′), *n.* **1.** an excessively favorable opinion of one's own ability, importance, wit, etc. **2.** something that is conceived in the mind; a thought; idea: *He jotted down the conceits of his idle hours.* **3.** imagination; fancy. **4.** a fancy; whim; fanciful notion. **5.** an elaborate, fanciful metaphor, esp. of a strained or far-fetched nature. **6.** the use of such metaphors as a literary characteristic, esp. in poetry. **7.** a fancy, purely decorative article. **8.** *Brit. Dial.* **a.** favorable opinion; esteem. **b.** personal opinion or estimation. **9.** *Obs.* the faculty of conceiving; apprehension. **10. out of conceit with,** displeased or dissatisfied with. —*v.t.* **11.** to flatter (esp. oneself). **12.** *Brit. Dial.* to take a fancy to; have a good opinion of. **13.** *Obs.* **a.** to imagine. **b.** to conceive; apprehend. [1350–1400; ME *conceyte, conceipt,* deriv. of CONCEIVE by analogy with DECEIVE, DECEIT and RECEIVE, RECEIPT; cf. AF *conceite;* see CONCEPT]
—**Syn. 1.** self-esteem, vanity, egotism, complacency. See **pride.** —**Ant. 1.** humility.

con·ceit·ed (kən sē′tid), *adj.* **1.** having an excessively favorable opinion of one's abilities, appearance, etc. **2.** *Archaic.* **a.** having an opinion. **b.** fanciful; whimsical. **3.** *Obs.* intelligent; clever. [1535–45; CONCEIT + -ED²] —**con·ceit′ed·ly,** *adv.* —**con·ceit′ed·ness,** *n.*
—**Syn. 1.** vain, proud, egotistical, self-important, self-satisfied.

con·ceiv·a·ble (kən sē′və bəl), *adj.* capable of being conceived; imaginable. [1425–75; late ME. See CONCEIVE, -ABLE] —**con·ceiv′a·bil′i·ty, con·ceiv′a·ble·ness,** *n.* —**con·ceiv′a·bly,** *adv.*

con·ceive (kən sēv′), *v.,* **-ceived, -ceiv·ing.** —*v.t.* **1.** to form (a notion, opinion, purpose, etc.): *He conceived the project while he was on vacation.* **2.** to form a notion or idea of; imagine. **3.** to hold as an opinion; think; believe: *I can't conceive that it would be of any use.* **4.** to experience or form (a feeling): *to conceive a great love for music.* **5.** to express, as in words. **6.** to become pregnant with. **7.** to beget. **8.** to begin, originate, or found (something) in a particular way (usually used in the passive): *a new nation conceived in liberty.* **9.** *Archaic.* to understand; comprehend. —*v.i.* **10.** to form an idea; think (usually fol. by *of*). **11.** to become pregnant. [1250–1300; ME < AF, OF *conceivre* < L *concipere* to take fully, take in, equiv. to *con-* CON- + *-cipere,* comb. form of *capere* to take] —**con·ceiv′er,** *n.*
—**Syn. 2, 8.** See **imagine.**

con·cel·e·brant (kən sel′ə brənt, kon-), *n.* a member of the clergy who participates in a concelebration. [1930–35; CONCELEBR(ATE) + -ANT]

con·cel·e·brate (kən sel′ə brāt′, kon-), *v.,* **-brat·ed, -brat·ing.** —*v.i.* **1.** to participate in a concelebration. —*v.t.* **2.** to celebrate (a Eucharist or Mass) with other members of the clergy. [1565–75; < L *concelebrātus,* ptp. of *concelebrāre;* see COM-, CELEBRATE]

con·cel·e·bra·tion (kən sel′ə brā′shən, kon-), *n.* the celebration of a Eucharist or Mass by two or more members of the clergy. [1840–50; CONCELEBRATE + -ION]

con·cent (kən sent′), *n. Archaic.* concord of sound, voices, etc.; harmony. [1575–85; < L *concentus* harmony, chorus, lit., singing or playing together, equiv. to *concen-,* var. s. of *concinere* to sing together (*con-* CON- + *-cinere,* comb. form of *canere* to sing; cf. CHANT) + *-tus* suffix of v. action]

con·cen·ter (kon sen′tər, kən-), *v.t., v.i.* to bring or converge to a common center; concentrate. Also, *esp. Brit.,* **concentre.** [1585–95; < MF *concentrer,* equiv. to *con-* CON- + *centrer* to CENTER]

con·cen·trate (kon′sən trāt′), *v.,* **-trat·ed, -trat·ing,** *n.* —*v.t.* **1.** to bring or draw to a common center or point of union; converge; direct toward one point; focus: *to concentrate one's attention on a problem; to concentrate the rays of the sun with a lens.* **2.** to put or bring into a single place, group, etc.: *The nation's wealth had been concentrated in a few families.* **3.** to intensify; make denser, stronger, or purer, esp. by the removal or reduction of liquid: *to concentrate fruit juice; to concentrate a sauce by boiling it down.* **4.** *Mining.* to separate (metal or ore) from rock, sand, etc., so as to improve the quality of the valuable portion. —*v.i.* **5.** to bring all efforts, faculties, activities, etc., to bear on one thing or activity (often fol. by *on* or *upon*): *to concentrate on solving a problem.* **6.** to come to or toward a common center; converge; collect: *The population concentrated in one part of the city.* **7.** to become more intense, stronger, or purer. —*n.* **8.** a concentrated form of something; a product of concentration: *a juice concentrate.* [1630–40; CONCENTR(IC) + -ATE²; cf. F *concentrer,* It *concentrare*] —**con·cen·tra·tive** (kon′sən trā′tiv, kən sen′trə-), *adj.* —**con′cen·tra′tive·ness,** *n.* —**con′cen·tra′tor,** *n.*
—**Syn. 1.** See **contract.** —**Ant. 1.** dissipate, disperse. **5.** diverge.

con·cen·trat·ed (kon′sən trā′tid), *adj.* **1.** applied with all one's attention, energy, etc.: *their concentrated efforts to win the election.* **2.** clustered or gathered together closely. **3.** treated to remove or reduce an inessential ingredient, esp. liquid: *concentrated orange juice.* [1680–90; CONCENTRATE + -ED²]

con·cen·tra·tion (kon′sən trā′shən), *n.* **1.** the act of concentrating; the state of being concentrated. **2.** exclusive attention to one object; close mental application. **3.** something concentrated: *a concentration of stars.* **4.** *Mil.* **a.** the assembling of military or naval forces in a particular area in preparation for further operations. **b.** a specified intensity and duration of artillery fire placed on a small area. **5.** the focusing of a student's academic program on advanced study in a specific subject or field. **6.** *Chem.* (in a solution) a measure of the amount of dissolved substance contained per unit of volume. **7.** Also called **memory.** *Cards.* a game in which all 52 cards are spread out face down on the table and each player in turn exposes two cards at a time and replaces them face down if they do not constitute a pair, the object being to take the most pairs by remembering the location of the cards previously exposed. [1625–35; CONCENTR(IC) + -ATION]

concentra′tion camp′, a guarded compound for the detention or imprisonment of aliens, members of ethnic minorities, political opponents, etc., esp. any of the camps established by the Nazis prior to and during World War II for the confinement and persecution of prisoners. [1900–05, applied orig. to camps where noncombatants were placed during the Boer War]

concentra′tion cell′, *Physical Chem.* a galvanic cell consisting of two electrodes of the same metal each in different concentrations of a solution of the same salt of that metal. [1895–1900]

con·cen·tre (kon sen′tər, kən-), *v.t., v.i.,* **-tred, -tring.** *Chiefly Brit.* concenter.

con·cen·tric (kən sen′trik), *adj.* having a common center, as circles or spheres. Also, **con·cen′tri·cal.** [1350–1400; ME *consentrik* < ML *concentricus.* See CON-, CENTER, -IC] —**con·cen′tri·cal·ly,** *adv.* —**con·cen·tric·i·ty** (kon′sən tris′i tē, -sen-), *n.*

Con·cep·ción (kôn′sep syôn′; *Eng.* kən sep′sē ōn′, -sep′shən), *n.* **1.** a city in central Chile, near the mouth of the Bío-Bío River. 196,000. **2.** a city in central Paraguay, on the Paraguay River. 19,200.

con·cept (kon′sept), *n.* **1.** a general notion or idea; conception. **2.** an idea of something formed by mentally combining all its characteristics or particulars; a construct. **3.** a directly conceived or intuited object of thought. —*v.t.* **4.** *Informal.* to develop a concept of; conceive: *Experts pooled their talents to concept the new car.* [1550–60; < L *conceptum* something conceived, orig. neut. of *conceptus* (ptp. of *concipere*), equiv. to *con-* CON- + *cep-* (var. s. of *-cipere,* comb. form of *capere* to seize) + *-tus* ptp. ending]

con·cep·ta·cle (kən sep′tə kəl), *n. Biol.* an organ or cavity enclosing reproductive bodies. [1605–15; < L *conceptāculum,* equiv. to *concept(us)* conceived (see CONCEPT) + *-āculum* (see RECEPTACLE)] —**con·cep·tac·u·lar** (kon′sep tak′yə lər), *adj.*

con′cept art′. See **conceptual art.**

con·cep·tion (kən sep′shən), *n.* **1.** the act of conceiving; the state of being conceived. **2.** fertilization; inception of pregnancy. **3.** a notion; idea; concept: *She has some odd conceptions about life.* **4.** something that is conceived: *That machine is the conception of a genius.* **5.** origination; beginning: *The organization has been beset by problems from its conception.* **6.** a design; plan. **7.** a sketch of something not actually existing: *an artist's conception of ancient Athens.* **8.** the act or power of forming notions, ideas, or concepts. [1300–50; ME *concepcion* < L *conceptiōn-* (s. of *conceptiō*), equiv. to L *concept-* (see CONCEPT) + *-iōn-* -ION] —**con·cep′tion·al,** *adj.* —**con·cep′tive,** *adj.*
—**Syn. 3.** See **idea.**

CONCISE ETYMOLOGY KEY: <, descended or borrowed from; >, whence; b., blend of, blended; c., cognate with; cf., compare; deriv., derivative; equiv., equivalent; imit., imitative; obl., oblique; r., replacing; s., stem; sp., spelling, spelled; resp., respelling, respelled; trans., translation; ?, origin unknown; *, unattested; ‡, probably earlier than. See the full key inside the front cover.

con•cep•tor (kən sep′tər), *n.* a person who generates or conceives ideas or plans. [CONCEPT + -OR²]

con•cep•tu•al (kən sep′cho͞o əl), *adj.* pertaining to concepts or to the forming of concepts. [1655–65; < ML *conceptuālis.* See CONCEPTUS, -AL¹] **—con•cep•tu•al•i•ty** (kən sep′cho͞o al′i tē), *n.* **—con•cep′tu•al•ly,** *adv.*

concep′tual art′, art in which emphasis is placed on the means and processes of producing art objects rather than on the objects themselves and in which the various tools and techniques, as photographs, photocopies, video records, and the construction of environments and earthworks, are used to convey the message to the spectator. Also called **concept art.** **—concep′tual art′ist.**

con•cep•tu•al•ism (kən sep′cho͞o ə liz′əm), *n. Philos.* any of several doctrines existing as a compromise between realism and nominalism and regarding universals as concepts. Cf. **nominalism, realism** (def. 5). [1830–40; CONCEPTUAL + -ISM] **—con•cep′tu•al•ist,** *n.* **—con•cep′tu•al•is′tic,** *adj.* **—con•cep′tu•al•is′ti•cal•ly,** *adv.*

con•cep•tu•al•ize (kən sep′cho͞o ə līz′), *v.,* **-ized, -iz•ing.** —*v.t.* **1.** to form into a concept; make a concept of. —*v.i.* **2.** to form a concept; think in concepts. Also, *esp. Brit.,* **con•cep′tu•al•ise′.** [1875–80; CONCEPTUAL + -IZE] **—con•cep′tu•al•i•za′tion,** *n.* **—con•cep′tu•al•iz′er,** *n.*

concep′tual re′alism, *Philos.* the doctrine that universals have real and independent existence. **—concep′tual re′alist.**

con•cep•tus (kən sep′təs), *n., pl.* **-tus•es.** the embryo and associated membranes of humans and other highly developed animals. [1935–40; < NL; L: the action of conceiving, hence, something that is conceived, fetus, embryo, equiv. to *concep-* (var. s. of *concipere* to CONCEIVE; see CONCEPT) + *-tus* suffix of v. action]

con•cern (kən sûrn′), *v.t.* **1.** to relate to; be connected with; be of interest or importance to; affect: *The water shortage concerns us all.* **2.** to interest or engage (used reflexively or in the passive, often fol. by *with* or *in*): *She concerns herself with every aspect of the business.* **3.** to trouble, worry, or disquiet: *I am concerned about his health.* —*n.* **4.** something that relates or pertains to a person; business; affair: *Law is the concern of lawyers.* **5.** a matter that engages a person's attention, interest, or care, or that affects a person's welfare or happiness: *The party was no concern of his.* **6.** worry, solicitude, or anxiety: *to show concern for someone in trouble.* **7.** important relation or bearing: *This news is of concern to all of us.* **8.** a commercial or manufacturing company or establishment: *the headquarters of an insurance concern.* **9.** *Informal.* any material object or contrivance. [1375–1425; late ME *concernen* (< MF *concerner*) < ML *concernere* to relate to, distinguish (LL: to mix for sifting), equiv. to L *con-* CON- + *cernere* to sift]
—Syn. 1. touch, involve. **3.** disturb. **5.** burden, responsibility. CONCERN, CARE, WORRY connote an uneasy and burdened state of mind. CONCERN implies an anxious sense of interest in something: *concern over a friend's misfortune.* CARE suggests a heaviness of spirit caused by dread, or by the constant pressure of burdensome demands: *Poverty weighs a person down with care.* WORRY is an active state of agitated uneasiness and restless apprehension: *He was distracted by worry over the stock market.* **8.** firm, house. **—Ant. 6.** indifference.

con•cerned (kən sûrnd′), *adj.* **1.** interested or affected: *concerned citizens.* **2.** troubled or anxious: *a concerned look.* **3.** having a connection or involvement; participating: *They arrested all those concerned in the kidnapping.* [1650–60; CONCERN + -ED²] **—con•cern•ed•ly** (kən sûr′nid lē), *adv.* **—con•cern′ed•ness,** *n.*

con•cern•ing (kən sûr′ning), *prep.* relating to; regarding; about: *a discussion concerning foreign aid.* [1375–1425; late ME; see CONCERN, -ING²]

con•cern•ment (kən sûrn′mənt), *n.* **1.** importance or moment: *a matter of concernment to all voters.* **2.** relation or bearing. **3.** anxiety or solicitude. **4.** a thing in which one is involved or interested. **5.** interest; participation; involvement. [1600–10; CONCERN + -MENT]

con•cert (*n., adj.* kon′sûrt, -sərt; *v.* kən sûrt′), *n.* **1.** a public musical performance in which a number of singers or instrumentalists, or both, participate. **2.** a public performance, usually by an individual singer, instrumentalist, or the like; recital: *The violinist has given concerts all over the world.* **3.** agreement of two or more individuals in a design or plan; combined action; accord or harmony: *His plan was greeted with a concert of abuse.* **4. in concert,** together; jointly: *to act in concert.* —*adj.* **5.** designed or intended for concerts: *concert hall.* **6.** performed at concerts: *concert music.* **7.** performing or capable of performing at concerts: *a concert pianist.* —*v.t.* **8.** to contrive or arrange by agreement: *They were able to concert a settlement of their differences.* **9.** to plan; devise: *A program of action was concerted at the meeting.* —*v.i.* **10.** to plan or act together. [1595–1605; (n.) < F < It *concerto;* see CONCERTO; (v.) < F *concerter* < It *concertare* to organize, arrange by mutual agreement, perh. parasynthetically from *con* with + *certo* CERTAIN; L *concertāre* (see CONCERTATION) is remote in sense]

con•cer•tan•te (kon′sər tän′tē; *It.* kôn′cheʀ tän′te), *adj., n., pl.* **-ti** (-tē). *Music.* —*adj.* **1.** brilliantly virtuosic: *a concertante part for solo violin.* **2.** solo rather than accompanying: *a sonata for recorder and harpsichord concertante.* —*n.* **3.** an 18th-century symphonic work with sections for solo instruments. Also, **concertato.** [1720–30; < It, prp. of *concertare* to give a CONCERT; see -ANT]

con•cer•ta•tion (kon′sər tā′shən; *Fr.* kôɴ seʀ tA-syôɴ′), *n.* (esp. in European politics) cooperation, as among opposing factions, aimed at effecting a unified proposal or concerted action. [1500–10; < F < L *concertātiōn-* (s. of *concertātiō* strife, controversy), equiv. to *concertāt(us)* ptp. of *concertāre* to contend, fight (*con-* CON- + *certāre* to contend, freq. of *cernere* to decide, determine, lit., to sift; cf. CERTAIN) + *-iōn-* -ION; though influenced by F *concerter* (see CONCERT) and perh. a new formation]

con•cer•ta•to (kon′sər tä′tō; *It.* kôn′cheʀ tä′tô), *adj., n., pl.* **-tos** (-tōz), **-ti** (*It.* -tē). concertante. [‡1960–65; < It, ptp. of *concertare* to give a concert; see -ATE¹]

con•cert•ed (kən sûr′tid), *adj.* **1.** contrived or arranged by agreement; planned or devised together: *a concerted effort.* **2.** done or performed together or in cooperation: *a concerted attack.* **3.** *Music.* arranged in parts for several voices or instruments. [1710–20; CONCERT (v.) + -ED²] **—con•cert′ed•ly,** *adv.* **—con•cert′•ed•ness,** *n.*
—Syn. 1. 2. united, joint, cooperative.

con•cert•go•er (kon′sərt gō′ər), *n.* a person who attends concerts esp. frequently. [1850–55; CONCERT + GOER] **—con′cert•go′ing,** *n., adj.*

con′cert grand′, a grand piano of the largest size, being typically 9 ft. (2.7 m) in length. Also called **con′•cert grand′ pian′o.** [1890–95]

con•cer•ti•na (kon′sər tē′nə), *n., v.,* **-naed** (-nəd), **-na•ing** (-nə ing), *adj.* —*n.* **1.** a musical instrument resembling an accordion but having buttonlike keys, hexagonal bellows and ends, and a more limited range. **2.** See **concertina wire.** —*v.i.* **3.** to fold, crush together, or collapse in the manner of a concertina: *The car concertinaed when it hit the truck.* —*v.t.* **4.** to cause to fold or collapse in the manner of a concertina. —*adj.* **5.** of, pertaining to, or resembling a concertina: *concertina pleats.* [appar. coined by the original instrument's inventor, English instrument-maker Charles Wheatstone (1802–75), who patented it in 1829; cf. CONCERTINO, *seraphina* a similar instrument] **—con′cer•ti′nist,** *n.*

concertina

concerti′na move′ment, a principle of table construction in which hinged sections of the frame, ordinarily folded inward out of sight, can be pulled into line with the parts of the frame ordinarily seen to permit the addition of leaves. Also called **concerti′na ac′tion.**

concerti′na ta′ble, an extensible table having a hinged double top falling onto a hinged frame that unfolds like an accordion when pulled out.

concerti′na wire′, wire with razor-sharp edges or projections, placed in coils as a barrier along the tops of fences or walls, as at a prison. Also called **concertina, barbed tape, razor wire.** [1925–30]

con•cer•ti•no (kon′chər tē′nō; *It.* kôn′cheʀ tē′nô), *n., pl.* **-ni** (-nē). *Music.* **1.** a short concerto. **2.** the group of solo instruments in a concerto grosso. **3.** a section in a concerto grosso played by these instruments. [1720–30; < It, equiv. to *concert(o)* (see CONCERTO) + *-ino* dim. suffix]

con•cert•ize (kon′sər tīz′), *v.i.,* **-ized, -iz•ing.** to give concerts or recitals professionally, esp. on tour. Also, *esp. Brit.,* **con′cert•ise′.** [1880–85; CONCERT + -IZE] **—con′cert•iz′er,** *n.*

con•cert•mas•ter (kon′sərt mas′tər, -mä′stər), *n.* the leader of the first violins in a symphony orchestra, who is usually also the assistant to the conductor. [1875–80; trans. of G *Konzertmeister.* See CONCERT (n.), MASTER]

con•cer•to (kən cher′tō; *It.* kôn cheʀ′tô), *n., pl.* **-tos, -ti** (-tē). *Music.* a composition for one or more principal instruments, with orchestral accompaniment, now usually in symphonic form. [1720–30; < It, deriv. of *concertare;* see CONCERT (v.)]

con•cer•to gros•so (kən cher′tō grō′sō; *It.* kôn-cheʀ′tô gʀôs′sô), *pl.* **con•cer•ti gros•si** (kən cher′tē grō′sē; *It.* kôn cheʀ′tē gʀôs′sē), **con•cer•to gros•sos.** a musical form, common in the Baroque period, in which contrasting sections are played by full orchestra and by a small group of soloists. [1715–25; < It: lit., big concert; see GROSS]

con′cert par′ty, *Brit.* a form of theatrical entertainment popular at seaside resorts, in which specialty acts, songs, dances, etc., are presented. [1880–85]

con′cert pitch′, **1.** *Music.* a standard of pitch used for tuning orchestral instruments, usually established at 440 vibrations per second for A above middle C. **2.** a state of heightened eagerness, readiness, or tension: *Spring training had brought the athletes up to concert pitch for the beginning of the season.* [1760–70]

con•ces•sion (kən sesh′ən), *n.* **1.** the act of conceding or yielding, as a right, a privilege, or a point or fact in an argument: *He made no concession to caution.* **2.** the thing or point yielded: *Management offered a shorter workweek as a concession.* **3.** something conceded by a government or a controlling authority, as a grant of land, a privilege, or a franchise. **4.** a space or privilege within certain premises for a subsidiary business or service: *the refreshment concession at a movie theater.* **5.** *Canadian.* any of the usually sixteen divisions of a township, each division being 10 sq. mi. (26 sq. km) in area and containing thirty-two 200-acre lots. [1605–15; 1910–15 for def. 4; < L *concessiōn-* (s. of *concessiō*), equiv. to *concess(us)* (ptp. of *concēdere* to CONCEDE) + *-iōn-* -ION] **—con•ces′sion•al,** *adj.*

con•ces•sion•aire (kən sesh′ə nâr′), *n.* a person, group, or company to whom a concession has been granted, esp. to operate a subsidiary business or service: *a popcorn concessionaire at a baseball park.* Also, **con•ces•sion•er** (kən sesh′ə nər). [1860–65; < F *concessionnaire.* See CONCESSION, -AIRE]

con•ces•sion•ar•y (kən sesh′ə ner′ē), *adj., n., pl.* **-ar•ies.** —*adj.* **1.** pertaining to concession; of the nature of a concession: *concessionary agreements.* —*n.* **2.** a concessionaire. [1720–30; CONCESSION + -ARY]

conces′sion road′, *Canadian.* a road built between two concessions of a township.

con•ces•sive (kən ses′iv), *adj.* **1.** tending or serving to concede. **2.** *Gram.* expressing concession, as the English conjunction *though.* [1705–15; < LL *concessīvus.* See CONCESSION, -IVE] **—con•ces′sive•ly,** *adv.*

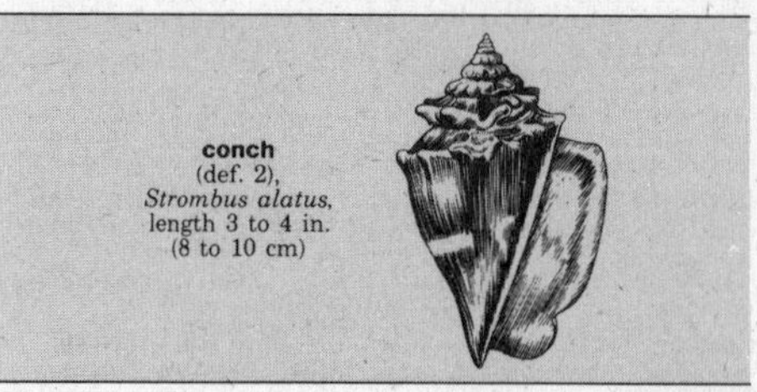
conch (def. 2), *Strombus alatus,* length 3 to 4 in. (8 to 10 cm)

conch (kongk, konch), *n., pl.* **conchs** (kongks), **con•ches** (kon′chiz). **1.** the spiral shell of a gastropod, often used as a horn. **2.** any of various marine gastropods. **3.** the fabled shell trumpet of the Tritons. **4.** (*often cap.*) *Slang* (*sometimes disparaging*). **a.** a native or inhabitant of the Florida Keys. **b.** a Bahamian. **5.** Also, **concha.** *Archit.* a smooth concave surface consisting of or resembling the interior of a semidome, as the surface of a vault, a trompe, or the head of a niche. [1350–1400; ME < L *concha* < Gk *kónchē* mussel, shell] **—conch•ate** (kong′kāt, kon′chāt), **conched,** *adj.*

con•cha¹ (kong′kə), *n., pl.* **-chae** (-kē). **1.** *Anat.* **a.** a shell-like structure, esp. the external ear. See diag. under **ear. b.** any turbinate bone, esp. in the nose. **2.** *Archit.* conch (def. 5). [1605–15; < NL, L: CONCH] **—con′chal,** *adj.*

con•cha² (kong′kə), *n., pl.* **-chae** (-kē). a disk, traditionally of hammered silver and resembling a shell or flower, used as decoration on belts, harness, etc. [< AmerSp, Sp < LL *conchula,* dim. of L *concha* CONCHA¹, CONCH]

conch•fish (kongk′fish′, konch′-), *n., pl.* **fish•es,** (*esp. collectively*) **-fish.** a cardinalfish, *Astropogon stellatus,* of the Atlantic Ocean. [CONCH + FISH]

con•chif•er•ous (kong kif′ər əs), *adj.* having a shell. [1820–30; CONCH + -I- + -FEROUS]

con•chi•o•lin (kong kī′ə lin), *n. Biochem.* a fibrous protein that forms the iridescent inner layer, as mother-of-pearl, in the shells of mollusks. [1865–70; CONCH + -I- + *-ol-* (< L *-olus* -OLE¹) + -IN²]

Con•chi•ta (kən chē′tə; *Sp.* kôn chē′tä), *n.* a female given name.

Con•cho•bar (kong′kō wər, kon′ə ho͝or′, kon′o͝or), *n. Irish Legend.* a king of Ulster, the uncle of Cuchulainn and the abductor of Deirdre.

con•choid (kong′koid), *n. Geom.* a plane curve such that if a straight line is drawn from a certain fixed point, called the pole of the curve, to the curve, the part of the line intersected between the curve and its asymptote is always equal to a fixed distance. Equation: $r = b \pm a \sec \theta$. [1790–1800; < Gk *konchoeidḗs.* See CONCH, -OID]

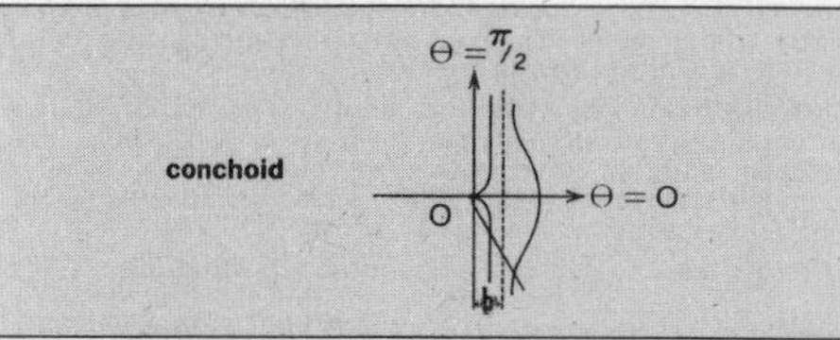

conchoid

con•choi•dal (kong koid′l), *adj. Mineral.* noting a shell-like fracture form produced on certain minerals by a blow. [1660–70; CONCHOID + -AL¹] **—con•choi′dal•ly,** *adv.*

con•chol•o•gy (kong kol′ə jē), *n.* the branch of zoology dealing with the shells of mollusks. [1770–80; CONCH + -O- + -LOGY] **—con•cho•log•i•cal** (kong′kə loj′i-kəl), *adj.* **—con′cho•log′i•cal•ly,** *adv.* **—con•chol′o•gist,** *n.*

Con•chos (kôn′chôs; *Eng.* kon′chōs), *n.* a river in NE Mexico, flowing E and N to the Rio Grande. ab. 350 mi. (565 km) long.

con•chy (kon′chē), *n., pl.* **-chies.** *Slang* (*often disparaging*). conscientious objector. Also, **con′chie.** [1915–20; *conch-* (shortening and resp. of CONSCIENTIOUS) + -Y²]

con•cierge (kon′sē ârzh′; *Fr.* kôɴ syeʀzh′), *n., pl.* **-cierges** (-sē âr′zhiz; *Fr.* -syeʀzh′). **1.** (esp. in France) a person who has charge of the entrance of a building and is often the owner's representative; doorkeeper. **2.** a member of a hotel staff in charge of special services for guests, as arranging for theater tickets or tours. **3.** an employee stationed in an apartment house lobby who screens visitors, controls operation of elevators, accepts deliveries to the tenants, etc. **4.** a janitor. **5.** *Obs.* a custodian or warden. [1640–50; < F; OF *cumserges* < L *con-* CON- + *serviēns* prp. of *servīre* to SERVE]

con•cil•i•ar (kən sil′ē ər), *adj.* of, pertaining to, or issued by a council. [1650–60; < L *concili(um)* COUNCIL + -AR[1]] —**con•cil′i•ar•ly,** *adv.*

con•cil•i•ate (kən sil′ē āt′), *v.,* **-at•ed, -at•ing.** —*v.t.* **1.** to overcome the distrust or hostility of; placate; win over: *to conciliate an angry competitor.* **2.** to win or gain (goodwill, regard, or favor). **3.** to make compatible; reconcile. —*v.i.* **4.** to become agreeable or reconciled: *Efforts to conciliate in the dispute proved fruitless.* [1540–50; < L *conciliātus* (ptp. of *conciliāre* to bring together, unite, equiv. to *concili(um)* COUNCIL + *-ātus* -ATE[1]] —**con•cil•i•a•ble** (kən sil′ē ə bəl), *adj.* —**con•cil′i•at′ing•ly,** *adv.* —**con•cil′i•a′tion,** *n.*
—**Syn. 1.** See **appease.**

con•cil•i•a•tor (kən sil′ē ā′tər), *n.* **1.** a person who conciliates. **2.** arbitrator. [1565–75; < L *conciliātor,* equiv. to *conciliā(re)* (see CONCILIATE) + *-tor* -TOR]

con•cil•i•a•to•ry (kən sil′ē ə tôr′ē, -tōr′ē), *adj.* tending to conciliate: *a conciliatory manner; conciliatory comments.* Also, **con•cil•i•a•tive** (kən sil′ē ā′tiv, -ə tiv, -sil′yə-). [1570–80; CONCILIATE + -ORY[1]] —**con•cil′i•a•to′ri•ly,** *adv.* —**con•cil′i•a•to′ri•ness,** *n.*

con•cin•nate (kon′sə nāt′), *v.t.,* **-nat•ed, -nat•ing.** to arrange or blend together skillfully, as parts or elements; put together in a harmonious, precisely appropriate, or elegant manner. [1595–1605; < L *concinnātus,* ptp. of *concinnāre* to prepare, set in order; cf. CONCINNOUS]

con•cin•ni•ty (kən sin′i tē), *n., pl.* **-ties. 1.** *Rhet.* **a.** a close harmony of tone as well as logic among the elements of a discourse. **b.** an instance of this. **2.** any harmonious adaptation of parts. [1525–35; < L *concinnitās,* equiv. to *concinn(us)* CONCINNOUS + *-itās* -ITY]

con•cin•nous (kən sin′əs), *adj.* characterized by concinnity; elegant; harmonious; stylistically congruous. [1645–55; < L *concinnus* neatly arranged, elegant; see -OUS] —**con•cin′nous•ly,** *adv.*

con•cise (kən sīs′), *adj.* expressing or covering much in few words; brief in form but comprehensive in scope; succinct; terse: *a concise explanation of the company's retirement plan.* [1580–90; < L *concīsus* cut short (ptp. of *concīdere*), equiv. to *con-* CON- + *-cīd-* (comb. form of *caedere* to cut) + *-tus* ptp. ending] —**con•cise′ly,** *adv.*
—**Syn.** pithy, compendious, laconic. CONCISE, SUCCINCT, TERSE all refer to speech or writing that uses few words to say much. CONCISE usually implies that unnecessary details or verbiage have been eliminated from a more wordy statement: *a concise summary of the speech.* SUCCINCT, on the other hand, implies that the message is as originally composed and is expressed in as few words as possible: *a succinct statement of the problem.* TERSE sometimes suggests brevity combined with wit or polish to produce particularly effective expression: *a terse, almost aphoristic, style.* It may also suggest brusqueness or curtness: *a terse reply that was almost rude.*

con•cise•ness (kən sīs′nis), *n.* the quality of being concise. [1650–60; CONCISE + -NESS]
—**Syn.** terseness, pithiness. See **brevity.**

con•ci•sion (kən sizh′ən), *n.* **1.** concise quality; brevity; terseness. **2.** *Archaic.* a cutting up or off; mutilation. [1350–1400; ME (< MF) < L *concīsiōn-* (s. of *concīsiō*), equiv. to *concīs(us)* CONCISE + *-iōn-* -ION]

con•clave (kon′klāv, kong′-), *n.* **1.** a private or secret meeting. **2.** an assembly or gathering, esp. one that has special authority, power, or influence: *a conclave of political leaders.* **3.** the assembly or meeting of the cardinals for the election of a pope. **4.** the body of cardinals; the College of Cardinals. **5.** the place in which the cardinals of the Roman Catholic Church meet in private for the election of a pope. [1350–1400; ME < ML, L *conclāve* room, enclosed space, repr. *(camera) cum clāve* (room) with key. See CON-, CLEF]

con•clav•ist (kon′klā vist, kong′-), *n.* either of two persons who attend upon a cardinal at a conclave, one usually being an ecclesiastical secretary and the other a personal servant. [1590–1600; < It *conclavista* < ML *conclāv(e)* CONCLAVE + *-ista* -IST]

con•clude (kən klōōd′), *v.,* **-clud•ed, -clud•ing.** —*v.t.* **1.** to bring to an end; finish; terminate: *to conclude a speech with a quotation from the Bible.* **2.** to say in conclusion: *At the end of the speech he concluded that we had been a fine audience.* **3.** to bring to a decision or settlement; settle or arrange finally: *to conclude a treaty.* **4.** to determine by reasoning; deduce; infer: *They studied the document and concluded that the author must have been an eyewitness.* **5.** to decide, determine, or resolve: *He concluded that he would go no matter what the weather.* **6.** *Obs.* **a.** to shut up or enclose. **b.** to restrict or confine. —*v.i.* **7.** to come to an end; finish: *The meeting concluded at ten o'clock.* **8.** to arrive at an opinion or judgment; come to a decision; decide: *The jury concluded to set the accused free.* [1250–1300; ME < L *conclūdere* to close, end an argument, equiv. to *con-* CON- + *-clūdere,* comb. form of *claudere* to CLOSE] —**con•clud′a•ble, con•clud′i•ble,** *adj.* —**con•clud′er,** *n.*

con•clu•sion (kən klōō′zhən), *n.* **1.** the end or close; final part. **2.** the last main division of a discourse, usually containing a summing up of the points and a statement of opinion or decisions reached. **3.** a result, issue, or outcome; settlement or arrangement: *The restitution payment was one of the conclusions of the negotiations.* **4.** final decision: *The judge has reached his conclusion.* **5.** a reasoned deduction or inference. **6.** *Logic.* a proposition concluded or inferred from the premises of an argument. **7.** *Law.* **a.** the effect of an act by which the person performing the act is bound not to do anything inconsistent therewith; an estoppel. **b.** the end of a pleading or conveyance. **8.** *Gram.* apodosis. **9. in conclusion,** finally: *In conclusion, I would like to thank you for your attention.* **10. try conclusions with,** to engage oneself in a struggle for victory or mastery over, as a person or an impediment. [1300–50; ME < L *conclūsiōn-* (s. of *conclūsiō*), equiv. to *conclūs(us)* closed, ptp. of *conclūdere* (*conclūd-* to CONCLUDE + *-tus* ptp. suffix) + *-iōn-* -ION] —**con•clu′sion•al,** *adj.* —**con•clu′sion•al•ly,** *adv.*
—**Syn. 1.** ending, termination, completion, finale. See **end**[1]. **2.** summation. —**Ant. 1.** beginning.

con•clu•sive (kən klōō′siv), *adj.* **1.** serving to settle or decide a question; decisive; convincing: *conclusive evidence.* **2.** tending to terminate; closing. [1580–90; < LL *conclūsīvus,* equiv. to L *conclūs(us)* (ptp. of *conclūdere* to CONCLUDE; see CONCLUSION) + *-īvus* -IVE] —**con•clu′sive•ly,** *adv.* —**con•clu′sive•ness,** *n.*
—**Syn. 1.** definitive, determining.

con•clu•so•ry (kən klōō′sə rē), *adj.* conclusive. [1840–50; see CONCLUSIVE, -ORY[1]]

con•coct (kon kokt′, kən-), *v.t.* **1.** to prepare or make by combining ingredients, esp. in cookery: *to concoct a meal from leftovers.* **2.** to devise; make up; contrive: *to concoct an excuse.* [1525–35; < L *concoctus* (ptp. of *concoquere* to cook together), equiv. to *con-* CON- + *coc-,* var. s. of *coquere* to boil, COOK[1] (akin to Gk *péptein;* see PEPSIN, PEPTIC) + *-tus* ptp. ending] —**con•coct′er, con•coc′tor,** *n.* —**con•coc′tive,** *adj.*
—**Syn. 2.** invent, fabricate, hatch.

con•coc•tion (kon kok′shən, kən-), *n.* **1.** the act or process of concocting. **2.** something concocted: *a delicious concoction of beans, rice, and meat.* [1525–35; < L *concoctiōn-* (s. of *concoctiō*) digestion, equiv. to *concoct(us)* (see CONCOCT) + *-iōn-* -ION]
—**Syn. 2.** mixture, medley, blend.

con•com•i•tance (kon kom′i təns, kən-), *n.* **1.** the quality or relation of being concomitant. **2.** concomitant (def. 2). **3.** *Rom. Cath. Ch.* the coexistence of the body and blood of Christ in the Eucharistic bread. [1525–35; < ML *concomitantia.* See CONCOMITANT, -ANCE]

con•com•i•tan•cy (kon kom′i tən sē, kən-), *n., pl.* **-cies.** concomitance. [1555–65; < ML *concomitantia.* See CONCOMITANT, -ANCY]

con•com•i•tant (kon kom′i tənt, kən-), *adj.* **1.** existing or occurring with something else, often in a lesser way; accompanying; concurrent: *an event and its concomitant circumstances.* —*n.* **2.** a concomitant quality, circumstance, or thing. [1595–1605; < L *concomitant-* (s. of *concomitāns,* prp. of *concomitārī*), equiv. to *con-* CON- + *comit-* (s. of *comes*) COMES + *-ant-* -ANT] —**con•com′i•tant•ly,** *adv.*
—**Syn. 1.** associated.

con•cord (kon′kôrd, kong′-), *n.* **1.** agreement between persons, groups, nations, etc.; concurrence in attitudes, feelings, etc.; unanimity; accord: *There was complete concord among the delegates.* **2.** agreement between things; mutual fitness; harmony. **3.** *Gram.* agreement (def. 6). **4.** peace; amity. **5.** a treaty; compact; covenant. **6.** *Music.* a stable, harmonious combination of tones; a chord requiring no resolution. [1250–1300; ME *concorde* < OF < L *concordia,* equiv. to *concord-* (s. of *concors*) harmonious (*con-* CON- + *cord-,* s. of *cors* HEART) + *-ia* -IA] —**con•cord′al,** *adj.*
—**Syn. 4.** harmony, goodwill, friendship. —**Ant. 4.** ill will, animosity.

Con•cord (kong′kərd *for 1, 2, 5, 6;* kon′kôrd, kong′- *for 3, 4; for 5, 6 also* kon′kôrd, kong′-), *n.* **1.** a town in E Massachusetts, NW of Boston: second battle of the Revolution fought here April 19, 1775. 16,293. **2.** a city in W California, near San Francisco. 103,251. **3.** a city in and the capital of New Hampshire, in the S part. 30,400. **4.** a city in central North Carolina. 16,942. **5.** See **Concord grape. 6.** a sweet red wine with a strong grapelike taste, made from the Concord grape.

con•cord•ance (kon kôr′dns, kən-), *n.* **1.** agreement; concord; harmony: *the concordance of the membership.* **2.** an alphabetical index of the principal words of a book, as of the Bible, with a reference to the passage in which each occurs. **3.** an alphabetical index of subjects or topics. **4.** (in genetic studies) the degree of similarity in a pair of twins with respect to the presence or absence of a particular disease or trait. [1350–1400; ME *concordaunce* < AF, equiv. to MF *concordance* < ML *concordantia.* See CONCORD, -ANCE]

con•cord•ant (kon kôr′dnt, kən-), *adj.* agreeing; harmonious. [1475–85; < AF, MF *concordant.* See CONCORD, -ANT] —**con•cord′ant•ly,** *adv.*

con•cor•dat (kon kôr′dat), *n.* **1.** an agreement or compact, esp. an official one. **2.** an agreement between the pope and a secular government regarding the regulation of church matters. [1610–20; < F; r. *concordate* < ML *concordātum,* L: neut. of *concordātus,* ptp. of *concordāre* to be in agreement. See CONCORD, -ATE[1]] —**con•cor•da•to•ry** (kon kôr′də tôr′ē, -tōr′ē), *adj.*

Con′cord coach′, a type of sturdy 19th-century U.S. stagecoach. [1820–30]

Con•corde (kon′kôrd, kong′-, kon kôrd′, kong-), *Trademark.* a supersonic passenger aircraft manufactured and operated jointly by England and France.

Con′cord grape′ (kong′kərd, kon′kôrd, kong′-), a cultivated variety of the fox grape, *Vitis labrusca,* used in making jelly, juice, and wine. [1855–60, *Amer.*]

Con•cor•di•a (kon kôr′dē ə), *n.* the ancient Roman goddess of harmony or peace. [< L; see CONCORD]

con•cor•po•rate (*v.* kon kôr′pə rāt′; *adj.* kon kôr′pər it, -prit), *v.,* **-rat•ed, -rat•ing,** *adj. Archaic.* —*v.t., v.i.* **1.** to unite in one body, unit, or mass. —*adj.* **2.** united in one body, unit, or mass. [1375–1425; late ME < L *concorporātus* (ptp. of *concorporāre* to unite in one body). See CON-, CORPORATE] —**con•cor′po•ra′tion,** *n.*

con•cours (*Fr.* kôN kōōr′; *Eng.* kong kōōr′), *n., pl.* **-cours** (*Fr.* -kōōr′; *Eng.* -kōōrz′). **1.** a public contest or competition. **2.** See **concours d'élégance.** [1935–40; < F, OF; see CONCOURSE]

con•cours d'é•lé•gance (*Fr.* kôN kōōr dā lā gäNs′; *Eng.* kong kōōr′ del′i gäns′, -gans′), *pl.* **con•cours d'é•lé•gance** (*Fr.* kôN kōōr dā lā gäNs′; *Eng.* kong kōōrz′ del′i gäns′, -gans′). a public exhibition and competition in which automobiles or other vehicles are judged, chiefly on the basis of elegance and beauty. [1935–40; < F: lit., elegance competition]

con•course (kon′kôrs, -kōrs, kong′-), *n.* **1.** an assemblage; gathering: *a concourse of people.* **2.** a driveway or promenade, esp. in a park. **3.** a boulevard or other broad thoroughfare. **4.** a large open space for accommodating crowds, as in a railroad station. **5.** an area or grounds for racing, athletic sports, etc. **6.** an act or instance of running or coming together; confluence: *a concourse of events.* [1350–1400; ME *concours* < MF; r. ME *concurs* < L *concursus* assembly, verbal n. corresponding to *concurrere* to assemble, collide. See CONCUR, COURSE]

con•cres•cence (kon kres′əns), *n. Biol.* a growing together, as of tissue or embryonic parts; coalescence. [1600–10; < L *concrēscentia,* equiv. to *concrēscent-* (s. of *concrēscēns,* prp. of *concrēscere* to harden, set; see CON-, CRESCENT) + *-ia* -IA; see -ENCE] —**con•cres′cent,** *adj.*

con•crete (kon′krēt, kong′-, kon krēt′, kong- *for 1–10, 11, 14, 15;* kon krēt′, kong- *for 12, 13*), *adj., n., v.,* **-cret•ed, -cret•ing.** —*adj.* **1.** constituting an actual thing or instance; real: *a concrete proof of his sincerity.* **2.** pertaining to or concerned with realities or actual instances rather than abstractions; particular (opposed to *general*): *concrete ideas.* **3.** representing or applied to an actual substance or thing, as opposed to an abstract quality: *The words "cat," "water," and "teacher" are concrete, whereas the words "truth," "excellence," and "adulthood" are abstract.* **4.** made of concrete: *a concrete pavement.* **5.** formed by coalescence of separate particles into a mass; united in a coagulated, condensed, or solid mass or state. —*n.* **6.** an artificial, stonelike material used for various structural purposes, made by mixing cement and various aggregates, as sand, pebbles, gravel, or shale, with water and allowing the mixture to harden. Cf. **reinforced concrete. 7.** any of various other artificial building or paving materials, as those containing tar. **8.** a concrete idea or term; a word or notion having an actual or existent thing or instance as its referent. **9.** a mass formed by coalescence or concretion of particles of matter. **10. set** or **cast in concrete,** to put (something) in final form; finalize so as to prevent change or reversal: *The basic agreement sets in concrete certain policies.* —*v.t.* **11.** to treat or lay with concrete: *to concrete a sidewalk.* **12.** to form into a mass by coalescence of particles; render solid. **13.** to make real, tangible, or particular. —*v.i.* **14.** to coalesce into a mass; become solid; harden. **15.** to use or apply concrete. [1375–1425; late ME *concret* < L *concrētus* (ptp. of *concrēscere* to grow together), equiv. to *con-* CON- + *crē-* (s. of *crēscere* to grow, increase; see -ESCE) + *-tus* ptp. ending] —**con•crete′ly,** *adv.* —**con•crete′ness,** *n.* —**con•cre′tive,** *adj.* —**con•cre′tive•ly,** *adv.*
—**Syn. 1.** solid, factual, substantial. —**Ant. 1, 2.** abstract.

con′crete mix′er. See **cement mixer.** [1905–10]

con′crete mu′sic. See ***musique concrète.*** [1950–55]

con′crete noun′, *Gram.* a noun denoting something material and nonabstract, as *chair, house,* or *automobile.* Cf. **abstract noun.**

con′crete num′ber, *Arith.* a number that relates to a particular object or thing. [1585–95]

con′crete po′et, a writer of concrete poetry. [1965–70]

con′crete po′etry, poetry in which effects are created by the physical arrangement of words in patterns or forms rather than by the use of traditional language structure. [1955–60, *Amer.*; prob. as trans. of Pg *poesia concreta* or G *konkrete Dichtung*]

con′crete univer′sal, *Hegelianism.* a principle that necessarily has universal import but is also concrete by virtue of its arising in historical situations. [1860–65]

con•cre•tion (kon krē′shən, kong-), *n.* **1.** the act or process of concreting or becoming substantial; coalescence; solidification. **2.** the state of being concreted. **3.** a solid mass formed by or as if by coalescence or cohesion: *a concretion of melted candies.* **4.** anything that is made real, tangible, or particular. **5.** *Pathol.* a solid or calcified mass in the body formed by a disease process. **6.** *Geol.* a rounded mass of mineral matter occurring in sandstone, clay, etc., often in concentric layers about a nucleus. [1535–45; < L *concrētiōn-* (s. of *concrētiō*). See CONCRETE, -ION]

con•cre•tion•ar•y (kon krē′shə ner′ē, kong-), *adj.* formed by concretion; consisting of concreted matter or masses. [1820–30; CONCRETION + -ARY]

con•cret•ism (kon krē′tiz əm, kong-, kon′krē tiz′əm, kong′-), *n.* the theory or practice of concrete poetry. [CONCRETE + -ISM] —**con•cret′ist,** *n.*

con•cre•tize (kon′krə tīz′, kong′-; kon krē′tīz, kong-, kən-, kəng-), *v.t.,* **-tized, -tiz•ing.** to make concrete, real, or particular; give tangible or definite form to: *to concretize abstractions.* Also, *esp. Brit.,* **con′cre•tise′.** [1880–85; CONCRETE + -IZE] —**con•cret′i•za′tion,** *n.*

con•cu•bi•nage (kon kyōō′bə nij, kong-), *n.* **1.** cohabitation of a man and woman without legal or formal marriage. **2.** the state or practice of being a concubine. [1350–1400; ME; see CONCUBINE, -AGE]

con•cu•bi•nar•y (kon kyōō′bə ner′ē, kong-), *adj., n., pl.* **-nar•ies.** —*adj.* **1.** of, pertaining to, or living in concubinage. —*n.* **2.** a person who lives in concubinage. [1555–65; < ML *concubīnārius.* See CONCUBINE, -ARY]

con•cu•bine (kong′kyə bīn′, kon′-), *n.* **1.** a woman who cohabits with a man to whom she is not legally married. **2.** (among polygamous peoples) a secondary wife, usually of inferior rank. **3.** (esp. formerly in Muslim societies) a woman residing in a harem and kept, as by a sultan, for sexual purposes. [1250–1300; ME (< AF) < L *concubīna,* equiv. to *concub-* (var. s. of *concumbere* to lie together; see CON-, INCUMBENT) + *-īna* fem. suffix]

CONCISE ETYMOLOGY KEY: <, descended or borrowed from; >, whence; b., blend of, blended; c., cognate with; cf., compare; deriv., derivative; equiv., equivalent; imit., imitative; obl., oblique; r., replacing; s., stem; sp., spelling, spelled; resp., respelling, respelled; trans., translation; ?, origin unknown; *, unattested; ‡, probably earlier than. See the full key inside the front cover.

con•cu•pis•cence (kon kyōō′pi səns, kong-), *n.* **1.** sexual desire; lust. **2.** ardent, usually sensuous, longing. [1300–50; ME < LL *concupiscentia.* See CONCUPISCENT, -ENCE]

con•cu•pis•cent (kon kyōō′pi sənt, kong-), *adj.* **1.** lustful or sensual. **2.** eagerly desirous. [1400–50; < L *concupiscent-* (s. of *concupiscēns,* prp. of *concupiscere* to conceive ardent desire for), equiv. to *con-* CON- + *cup-* (s. of *cupere* to desire) + *-iscent-,* var. of *-ēscent-* -ESCENT]

con•cu•pis•ci•ble (kon kyōō′pi sə bəl, kong-), *adj. Archaic.* worthy of being desired. [1490–1500; < MF *concupiscible* < LL *concupiscibil(is),* equiv. to L *concupisc(ere)* (see CONCUPISCENT) + *-ibilis* -IBLE]

con•cur (kən kûr′), *v.i.,* **-curred, -cur•ring. 1.** to accord in opinion; agree: *Do you concur with his statement?* **2.** to cooperate; work together; combine; be associated: *Members of both parties concurred.* **3.** to coincide; occur at the same time: *His graduation concurred with his birthday.* **4.** *Obs.* to run or come together; converge. [1375–1425; late ME < L *concurrere* to run together, meet, be in agreement, equiv. to *con-* CON- + *currere* to run; cf. CONCOURSE, CURRENT] **—con•cur′ring•ly,** *adv.*
—Syn. 1. See **agree.**

con•cur•rence (kən kûr′əns, -kur′-), *n.* **1.** the act of concurring. **2.** accordance in opinion; agreement: *With the concurrence of several specialists, our doctor recommended surgery.* **3.** cooperation, as of agents or causes; combined action or effort. **4.** simultaneous occurrence; coincidence: *the concurrence of several unusual events.* **5.** *Geom.* a point that is in three or more lines simultaneously. **6.** *Law.* a power equally held or a claim shared equally. **7.** *Archaic.* competition; rivalry. Also, **con•cur′ren•cy** (for defs. 1–4). [1515–25; < ML *concurrentia.* See CONCURRENT, -ENCE]

con•cur•rent (kən kûr′ənt, -kur′-), *adj.* **1.** occurring or existing simultaneously or side by side: *concurrent attacks by land, sea, and air.* **2.** acting in conjunction; cooperating: *the concurrent efforts of several legislators to pass the new law.* **3.** having equal authority or jurisdiction: *two concurrent courts of law.* **4.** accordant or agreeing: *concurrent testimony by three witnesses.* **5.** tending to or intersecting at the same point: *four concurrent lines.* —*n.* **6.** something joint or contributory. **7.** *Archaic.* a rival or competitor. [1375–1425; late ME (< MF) < L *concurrent-* (s. of *concurrēns,* prp. of *concurrere* to run together; see CONCUR); see CON-, CURRENT] **—con•cur′rent•ly,** *adv.*

concur′rent resolu′tion, a resolution adopted by both branches of a legislative assembly that, unlike a joint resolution, does not require the signature of the chief executive. [1795–1805]

concur′ring opin′ion, *Law.* (in appellate courts) an opinion filed by a judge that agrees with the majority or plurality opinion on the case but that bases this conclusion on different reasons or on a different view of the case.

con•cuss (kən kus′), *v.t.* to injure by concussion: *He was mildly concussed by the falling books.* [1590–1600; < L *concussus,* ptp. of *concutere,* equiv. to *con-* CON- + *-cut-,* comb. form of *quat-,* s. of *quatere* to shake + *-tus* ptp. ending]

con•cus•sion (kən kush′ən), *n.* **1.** *Pathol.* injury to the brain or spinal cord due to jarring from a blow, fall, or the like. **2.** shock caused by the impact of a collision, blow, etc. **3.** the act of violently shaking or jarring. [1350–1400; ME < L *concussiōn-* (s. of *concussiō*) a shaking. See CONCUSS, -ION] **—con•cus′sion•al, con•cus•sant** (kən kus′ənt), *adj.* **—con•cus′sive,** *adj.*

concus′sion grenade′, a grenade designed to inflict damage by the force of its detonation rather than by the fragmentation of its casing.

con•cyc•lic (kən sī′klik, -sik′lik), *adj. Geom.* (of a system of points) lying on the circumference of a circle. [1870–75; CON- + CYCLIC]

cond., 1. condenser. **2.** condition; conditional. **3.** conductivity. **4.** conductor.

Con•dé (kôN dā′), *n.* **Louis II de Bour•bon** (lwē, də bo͝or bôN′), **Prince de,** (*Duc d'Enghien*) (*"the Great Condé"*) 1621–86, French general.

con•demn (kən dem′), *v.t.* **1.** to express an unfavorable or adverse judgment on; indicate strong disapproval of; censure. **2.** to pronounce to be guilty; sentence to punishment: *to condemn a murderer to life imprisonment.* **3.** to give grounds or reason for convicting or censuring: *His acts condemn him.* **4.** to judge or pronounce to be unfit for use or service: *to condemn an old building.* **5.** *U.S. Law.* to acquire ownership of for a public purpose, under the right of eminent domain: *The city condemned the property.* **6.** to force into a specific state or activity: *His lack of education condemned him to a life of menial jobs.* **7.** to declare incurable. [1350–1400; ME *condempnen* < AF, OF *condem(p)ner* < L *condemnāre.* See CON-, DAMN] **—con•dem•na•ble** (kən dem′nə bəl), *adj.* **—con•dem′na•bly,** *adv.* **—con•demn•er** (kən dem′ər), **con•dem•nor** (kən dem′ər, kən dem nôr′), *n.* **—con•demn′ing•ly,** *adv.*
—Syn. 1. See **blame. —Ant. 2.** exonerate, liberate.

con•dem•na•tion (kon′dem nā′shən, -dəm-), *n.* **1.** the act of condemning. **2.** the state of being condemned. **3.** strong censure; disapprobation; reproof. **4.** a cause or reason for condemning. **5.** *U.S. Law.* the seizure, as of property, for public use. [1350–1400; ME *condempnacioun* (< MF) < LL *condemnātiōn-* (s. of *condemnātiō*). See CONDEMN, -ATION]

con•dem•na•to•ry (kən dem′nə tôr′ē, -tōr′ē), *adj.* serving to condemn. [1555–65; CONDEMNAT(ION) + -ORY[1]]

con•den•sa•ble (kən den′sə bəl), *adj.* capable of being condensed. Also, **condensible.** [1635–45; CONDENSE + -ABLE] **—con•den′sa•bil′i•ty,** *n.*

con•den•sate (kən den′sāt, kon′dən sāt′), *n.* a product of condensation, as a liquid reduced from a gas or vapor. [1545–55; < L *condēnsātus* (ptp. of *condēnsāre* to CONDENSE), equiv. to *condēns(us)* very dense (see CON-, DENSE) + *-ātus* -ATE[1]]

con•den•sa•tion (kon′den sā′shən, -dən-), *n.* **1.** the act of condensing; the state of being condensed. **2.** the result of being made more compact or dense. **3.** reduction of a book, speech, statement, or the like, to a shorter or terser form; abridgment. **4.** a condensed form: *Did you read the whole book or just a condensation?* **5.** a condensed mass. **6.** (in nontechnical usage) condensate. **7.** the act or process of reducing a gas or vapor to a liquid or solid form. **8.** *Chem.* a reaction between two or more organic molecules leading to the formation of a larger molecule and the elimination of a simple molecule such as water or alcohol. **9.** *Meteorol.* the process by which atmospheric water vapor liquefies to form fog, clouds, or the like, or solidifies to form snow or hail. **10.** *Psychoanal.* the representation of two or more ideas, memories, feelings, or impulses by one word or image, as in a person's humor, accidental slips, or dreams. **11.** *Physics.* the relative amount by which the density of an elastic medium varies from its average value as a sound wave passes through it. [1595–1605; < LL *condēnsātiōn-* (s. of *condēnsātiō*), equiv. to *condēnsāt(us)* CONDENSATE + *-iōn-* -ION] **—con′den•sa′tion•al,** *adj.* **—con′•den•sa′tive,** *adj.*

condensa′tion nu′cleus, *Meteorol.* nucleus (def. 5). [1910–15]

condensa′tion point′, *Math.* a point of which every neighborhood contains an uncountable number of points of a given set.

condensa′tion polymeriza′tion, *Chem.* See under **polymerization** (def. 2).

condensa′tion trail′, contrail. [1940–45]

con•dense (kən dens′), *v.,* **-densed, -dens•ing.** —*v.t.* **1.** to make more dense or compact; reduce the volume or extent of; concentrate. **2.** to reduce to a shorter form; abridge: *Condense your answer into a few words.* **3.** to reduce to another and denser form, as a gas or vapor to a liquid or solid state. —*v.i.* **4.** to become denser or more compact or concentrated. **5.** to reduce a book, speech, statement, or the like, to a shorter form. **6.** to become liquid or solid, as a gas or vapor: *The steam condensed into droplets.* [1475–85; < MF *condenser* < L *condēnsāre,* equiv. to *con-* CON- + *dēnsāre* to thicken, v. deriv. of *dēnsus* DENSE]
—Syn. 1. compress, consolidate. **2.** digest, epitomize, abstract, abbreviate. See **contract. —Ant. 1.** expand.

con•densed (kən denst′), *adj.* **1.** reduced in volume, area, length, or scope; shortened: *a condensed version of the book.* **2.** made denser, esp. reduced from a gaseous to a liquid state. **3.** thickened by distillation or evaporation; concentrated: *condensed lemon juice.* **4.** *Print.* (of type) narrow in proportion to its height. Cf. **expanded** (def. 3). [1375–1425; late ME; see CONDENSE, -ED[2]] **—con•densed′ly,** *adv.* **—con•densed′ness,** *n.*

condensed′ milk′, whole milk reduced by evaporation to a thick consistency, with sugar added. [1855–60]

con•dens•er (kən den′sər), *n.* **1.** a person or thing that condenses. **2.** an apparatus for condensing. **3.** any device for reducing gases or vapors to liquid or solid form. **4.** *Optics.* a lens or combination of lenses that gathers and concentrates light in a specified direction, often used to direct light onto the projection lens in a projection system. **5.** *Elect.* capacitor. [1680–90; CONDENSE + -ER[1]]

con•den•si•ble (kən den′sə bəl), *adj.* condensable. **—con•den′si•bil′i•ty,** *n.*

con•de•scend (kon′də send′), *v.i.* **1.** to behave as if one is conscious of descending from a superior position, rank, or dignity. **2.** to stoop or deign to do something: *He would not condescend to misrepresent the facts.* **3.** to put aside one's dignity or superiority voluntarily and assume equality with one regarded as inferior: *He condescended to their intellectual level in order to be understood.* **4.** *Obs.* **a.** to yield. **b.** to assent. [1300–50; ME *condescenden* < LL *condēscendere* (see CON-, DESCEND); r. ME *condescendre* < MF] **—con′des•cend′er, con′•des•cend′ent,** *n.*

con•de•scend•ence (kon′də sen′dəns), *n.* **1.** condescension. **2.** *Scot.* a list or specification of particulars. [1630–40; CONDESCEND + -ENCE]

con•de•scend•ing (kon′də sen′ding), *adj.* showing or implying a usually patronizing descent from dignity or superiority: *They resented the older neighbors' condescending cordiality.* [1630–40; CONDESCEND + -ING[2]] **—con′de•scend′ing•ly,** *adv.*
—Syn. patronizing, disdainful, supercilious.

con•de•scen•sion (kon′də sen′shən), *n.* **1.** an act or instance of condescending. **2.** behavior that is patronizing or condescending. **3.** voluntary assumption of equality with a person regarded as inferior. [1635–45; < LL *condēscēnsiōn-* (s. of *condēscēnsiō*). See CON-, DESCENSION] **—con•de•scen•sive** (kon′də sen′siv), *adj.* **—con′de•scen′sive•ly,** *adv.*

con•dign (kən dīn′), *adj.* well-deserved; fitting; adequate: *condign punishment.* [1375–1425; late ME *condigne* < AF, MF < L *condignus,* equiv. to *con-* CON- + *dignus* worthy; see DIGNITY] **—con•dign′ly,** *adv.*
—Syn. appropriate, suitable.

con•dig•ni•ty (kən dig′ni tē), *n. Scholasticism.* merit earned through good works while in a state of grace, and having a just claim on such rewards as heavenly glory. Cf. **congruity** (def. 4). [1545–55; < ML *condignitās;* see CONDIGN, -ITY]

Con•dil•lac (kôN dē yak′), *n.* **É•tienne Bon•not de** (ā tyen′ bô nō′ də), 1715–80, French philosopher.

con•di•ment (kon′də mənt), *n.* something used to give a special flavor to food, as mustard, ketchup, salt, or spices. [1400–50; late ME < MF < L *condimentum* spice, equiv. to *condi(re)* to season + *-mentum* -MENT] **—con′di•men′tal, con′di•men′ta•ry,** *adj.*

con•dis•ci•ple (kon′də sī′pəl), *n.* a fellow student or disciple. [1375–1425; late ME < L *condiscipulus* schoolmate. See CON-, DISCIPLE]

con•di•tion (kən dish′ən), *n.* **1.** a particular mode of being of a person or thing; existing state; situation with respect to circumstances. **2.** state of health: *He was reported to be in critical condition.* **3.** fit or requisite state: *to be out of condition; to be in no condition to run.* **4.** social position: *in a lowly condition.* **5.** a restricting, limiting, or modifying circumstance: *It can happen only under certain conditions.* **6.** a circumstance indispensable to some result; prerequisite; that on which something else is contingent: *conditions of acceptance.* **7.** Usually, **conditions.** existing circumstances: *poor living conditions.* **8.** something demanded as an essential part of an agreement; provision; stipulation: *He accepted on one condition.* **9.** *Law.* **a.** a stipulation in an agreement or instrument transferring property that provides for a change consequent on the occurrence or nonoccurrence of a stated event. **b.** the event upon which this stipulation depends. **10.** *Informal.* an abnormal or diseased state of part of the body: *heart condition; skin condition.* **11.** *U.S. Educ.* **a.** a requirement imposed on a college student who fails to reach the prescribed standard in a course at the end of the regular period of instruction, permitting credit to be established by later performance. **b.** the course or subject to which the requirement is attached. **12.** *Gram.* protasis. **13.** *Logic.* the antecedent of a conditional proposition. **14. on** or **upon condition that,** with the promise or provision that; provided that; if: *She accepted the position on condition that there would be opportunity for advancement.* —*v.t.* **15.** to put in a fit or proper state. **16.** to accustom or inure: *to condition oneself to the cold.* **17.** to air-condition. **18.** to form or be a condition of; determine, limit, or restrict as a condition. **19.** to subject to particular conditions or circumstances: *Her studies conditioned her for her job.* **20.** *U.S. Educ.* to impose a condition on (a student). **21.** to test (a commodity) to ascertain its condition. **22.** to make (something) a condition; stipulate. **23.** *Psychol.* to establish a conditioned response in (a subject). **24.** *Textiles.* **a.** to test (fibers or fabrics) for the presence of moisture or other foreign matter. **b.** to replace moisture lost from (fibers or fabrics) in manipulation or manufacture. —*v.i.* **25.** to make conditions. [1275–1325; ME *condicioun* < AF; OF < L *condiciōn-* (s. of *condiciō*) agreement, equiv. to *con-* CON- + *dic-* say (see DICTATE) + *-iōn-* -ION; sp. with *t* by influence of LL or ML forms; cf. F *condition*] **—con•di′tion•a•ble,** *adj.*
—Syn. 1. See **state. 8.** requirement, proviso.

con•di•tion•al (kən dish′ə nl), *adj.* **1.** imposing, containing, subject to, or depending on a condition or conditions; not absolute; made or allowed on certain terms: *conditional acceptance.* **2.** *Gram.* (of a sentence, clause, mood, or word) involving or expressing a condition, as the first clause in the sentence *If it rains, he won't go.* **3.** *Logic.* **a.** (of a proposition) asserting that the existence or occurrence of one thing or event depends on the existence or occurrence of another thing or event; hypothetical. **b.** (of a syllogism) containing at least one conditional proposition as a premise. **4.** *Math.* (of an inequality) true for only certain values of the variable, as $x + 3 > 0$ is only true for real numbers greater than −3. Cf. **absolute** (def. 12). —*n.* **5.** *Gram.* **a.** (in some languages) a mood, tense, or other category used in expressing conditions, often corresponding to an English verb phrase beginning with *would,* as Spanish *comería* "he would eat." **b.** a sentence, clause, or word expressing a condition. [1350–1400; ME *condicionel* < AF, MF < LL *condiciōnālis,* equiv. to *condiciōn-* (s. of *condiciō*) CONDITION + *-ālis* -AL[1]] **—con•di′tion•al′i•ty,** *n.* **—con•di′•tion•al•ly,** *adv.*
—Syn. 1. dependent, contingent, relative.

condi′tional conver′gence, *Math.* the property of an infinite series that converges while the series formed by replacing each term in the given series with its absolute value diverges; the property of an infinite series that converges when the order of the terms is altered. Cf. **absolute convergence** (def. 1).

condi′tional opera′tion, *Computers.* a step in a computer program that determines which of two or more instructions or instruction sequences to execute next, depending on whether or not one or more specified conditions have been met.

condi′tional probabil′ity, *Statistics, Math.* the probability that an event will occur under the condition that another event occurs first: equal to the probability that both will occur divided by the probability that the first will occur. [1960–65]

condi′tional sale′, a sale in which the title of a property remains with the seller until some condition is met, as the payment of the full purchase price.

con•di•tioned (kən dish′ənd), *adj.* **1.** existing under or subject to conditions. **2.** characterized by a predictable or consistent pattern of behavior or thought as a result of having been subjected to certain circumstances or conditions. **3.** *Psychol.* proceeding from or dependent on a conditioning of the individual; learned; acquired: *conditioned behavior patterns.* Cf. **unconditioned** (def. 2). **4.** made suitable for a given purpose. **5.** air-conditioned. **6.** accustomed; inured. [1400–50; late ME; see CONDITION, -ED[2]]
—Ant. 1. free, absolute.

condi′tioned response′, *Psychol.* a response that becomes associated with a previously unrelated stimulus as a result of pairing the stimulus with another stimulus normally yielding the response. Also called **condi′tioned re′flex.** [1930–35]

con•di•tion•er (kən dish′ə nər), *n.* **1.** a person or

CONCISE PRONUNCIATION KEY: act, cāpe, dâre, pärt; set, ēqual; if, ice; ox, ōver, ôrder, oil, bo͝ok, bo͞ot, out; up, ûrge; child; sing; shoe; thin, *th*at; zh as in *treasure.* ə = *a* as in *alone, e* as in *system, i* as in *easily, o* as in *gallop, u* as in *circus;* ′ as in *fire* (fī′ər), *hour* (ou′ər). l and n can serve as syllabic consonants, as in *cradle* (krād′l), and *button* (but′n). See the full key inside the front cover.

thing that conditions. **2.** something added to a substance to increase its usability, as a water softener. **3.** a cream or liquid preparation applied to the hair or skin, esp. for its emollient qualities. **4.** a trainer of athletes. **5.** an air conditioner. **6.** *Textiles.* a person who conditions fibers or fabrics. [1590–1600; CONDITION + -ER[1]]

con•di•tion•ing (kən dish′ə ning), *n. Psychol.* **1.** Also called **operant conditioning, instrumental conditioning.** a process of changing behavior by rewarding or punishing a subject each time an action is performed until the subject associates the action with pleasure or distress. **2.** Also called **classical conditioning, Pavlovian conditioning, respondent conditioning.** a process in which a stimulus that was previously neutral, as the sound of a bell, comes to evoke a particular response, as salivation, by being repeatedly paired with another stimulus that normally evokes the response, as the taste of food. [1915–20; CONDITION + -ING[1]]

con•do (kon′dō), *n., pl.* **-dos.** *Informal.* condominium (defs. 1, 2). [1970–75, *Amer.*; by shortening; cf. -O]

con•dole (kən dōl′), *v.,* **-doled, -dol•ing.** —*v.i.* **1.** to express sympathy with a person who is suffering sorrow, misfortune, or grief (usually fol. by *with*): *to condole with a friend whose father has died.* —*v.t.* **2.** *Obs.* to grieve with. [1580–90; < LL *condolēre,* equiv. to *con-* CON- + *dolēre* to feel pain; akin to DOLOR] —**con•do•la•to•ry** (kən dō′lə tôr′ē, -tōr′ē), *adj.* —**con•dol′er,** *n.* —**con•dol′ing•ly,** *adv.*

con•do•lence (kən dō′ləns), *n.* Often, **condolences.** expression of sympathy with a person who is suffering sorrow, misfortune, or grief. Also, **con•dole′ment.** [1595–1605; CONDOLE + -ENCE]

con•do•lent (kən dō′lənt), *adj.* feeling or expressing sorrow, sympathy, compassion, or the like. [1480–90; < LL *condolent-* (s. of *condolēns,* prp. of *condolēre*). See CONDOLE, -ENT]

con do•lo•re (kon′ də lôr′ā, -lōr′ā, kōn′; *It.* kôn dô-lô′re), sorrowfully (used as a direction in music). [< It: lit., with sadness; see DOLOR]

con•dom (kon′dəm, kun′-), *n.* a thin sheath, usually of very thin rubber, worn over the penis during sexual intercourse to prevent conception or sexually transmitted disease. [1700–10; of obscure orig., but popularly supposed to have been named after an 18th-century English physician, who allegedly devised it]

con•do•min•i•um (kon′də min′ē əm), *n.* **1.** an apartment house, office building, or other multiple-unit complex, the units of which are individually owned, each owner receiving a recordable deed to the individual unit purchased, including the right to sell, mortgage, etc., that unit and sharing in joint ownership of any common grounds, passageways, etc. **2.** a unit in such a building. **3.** *Internat. Law.* **a.** joint sovereignty over a territory by several states. **b.** the territory itself. **4.** joint or concurrent dominion. [1705–15; < NL. See CON-, DOMINIUM]

Con•don (kon′dən), *n.* **Edward Uh•ler** (yōō′lər), 1902–74, U.S. physicist.

con•do•na•tion (kon′dō nā′shən), *n.* the act of condoning; the overlooking or implied forgiving of an offense. Also, **con•don•ance** (kən dō′nəns). [1615–25; < NL *condōnātiōn-* (s. of *condōnātiō*), L: a giving away, equiv. to *condōnāt(us)* (ptp. of *condōnāre*; see CONDONE) + *-iōn-* -ION. See CON-, DONATION]

con•done (kən dōn′), *v.t.,* **-doned, -don•ing.** **1.** to disregard or overlook (something illegal, objectionable, or the like). **2.** to give tacit approval to: *By his silence, he seemed to condone their behavior.* **3.** to pardon or forgive (an offense); excuse. **4.** to cause the condonation of. **5.** *Law.* to forgive or act so as to imply forgiveness of (a violation of the marriage vow). [1615–25, but in general currency from its use in the British Divorce Act of 1857 (see def. 5); < L *condōnāre* to absolve, grant pardon, equiv. to *con-* CON- + *dōnāre* to give; see DONATE] —**con•don′a•ble,** *adj.* —**con•don′er,** *n.*

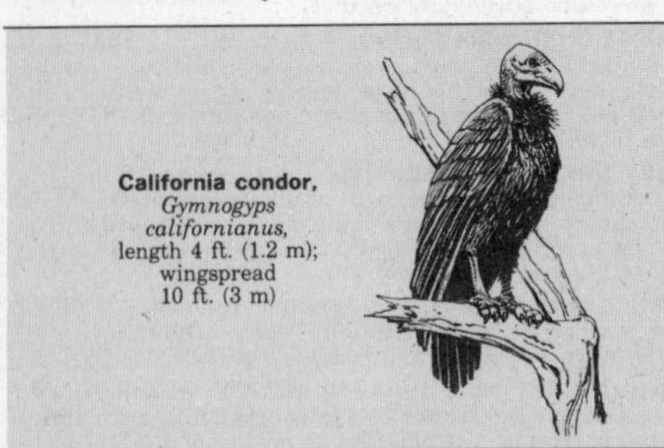

California condor, *Gymnogyps californianus,* length 4 ft. (1.2 m); wingspread 10 ft. (3 m)

con•dor (kon′dər, -dôr), *n.* **1.** either of two large, New World vultures of the family Cathartidae, *Gymnogyps californianus* **(California condor)** or *Vultur gryphus* **(Andean condor),** the largest flying birds in the Western Hemisphere: the California condor is almost extinct; the Andean condor is greatly reduced in number and rare in many areas. **2.** a former coin of Chile equal to 10 pesos. **3.** a former coin of Ecuador equal to 10 sucres. [1595–1605; < Sp < AmerSp < Quechua *kuntur*]

Con•dor•cet (kôn dôr se′), *n.* **Ma•rie Jean An•toine Ni•co•las Ca•ri•tat** (MA RĒ′ ZHÄN ÄN TWAN′ NĒ KÔ LÄ′ KA RĒ TA′), **Marquis de,** 1743–94, French mathematician and philosopher.

CONCISE ETYMOLOGY KEY: <, descended or borrowed from; >, whence; b., blend of, blended; c., cognate with; cf., compare; deriv., derivative; equiv., equivalent; imit., imitative; obl., oblique; r., replacing; s., stem; sp., spelling, spelled; resp., respelling, respelled; trans., translation; ?, origin unknown; *, unattested; ‡, probably earlier than. See the full key inside the front cover.

con•dot•tie•re (kôn′də tyâr′ā, -tyâr′ē; *It.* kôn′dôt-tye′re), *n., pl.* **-tie•ri** (-tyâr′ē; *It.* -tye′rē). **1.** a leader of a private band of mercenary soldiers in Italy, esp. in the 14th and 15th centuries. **2.** any mercenary; soldier of fortune. [1785–95; < It, equiv. to *condott(o)* (< L *conductus* hired man, ptp. of *condūcere* to CONDUCE; see CONDUCT) + *-iere* < L *-ārius* -ARY]

con•duce (kən dōōs′, -dyōōs′), *v.i.,* **-duced, -duc•ing.** to lead or contribute to a result (usually fol. by *to* or *toward*): *qualities that conduce to success.* [1350–1400; ME < L *condūcere* to lead, bring together, equiv. to *con-* CON- + *dūcere* to lead, akin to *dux* (see DUKE) and to TOW[1], TUG] —**con•duc′er,** *n.* —**con•duc′i•ble,** *adj.* —**Ant.** hinder.

con•du•cive (kən dōō′siv, -dyōō′-), *adj.* tending to produce; conducing; contributive; helpful; favorable (usually fol. by *to*): *Good eating habits are conducive to good health.* [1640–50; CONDUCE + -IVE] —**con•du′cive•ness,** *n.*

con•duct (*n.* kon′dukt; *v.* kən dukt′), *n.* **1.** personal behavior; way of acting; bearing or deportment. **2.** direction or management; execution: *the conduct of a business.* **3.** the act of conducting; guidance; escort: *The curator's conduct through the museum was informative.* **4.** *Obs.* a guide; an escort. —*v.t.* **5.** to behave or manage (oneself): *He conducted himself well.* **6.** to direct in action or course; manage; carry on: *to conduct a meeting; to conduct a test.* **7.** to direct (an orchestra, chorus, etc.) as leader. **8.** to lead or guide; escort: *to conduct a tour.* **9.** to serve as a channel or medium for (heat, electricity, sound, etc.): *Copper conducts electricity.* —*v.i.* **10.** to lead. **11.** to act as conductor, esp. of a musical group. [1250–1300; late ME < ML *conductus* escort, n. use of L *conductus* (ptp. of *condūcere* to CONDUCE), equiv. to *con-* CON- + *duc-* lead + *-tus* ptp. suffix; r. ME *conduyt(e)* < AF < L as above; see CONDUIT] —**con•duct′i•ble,** *adj.* —**con•duct′i•bil′i•ty,** *n.*
—**Syn. 1.** demeanor, comportment, actions, manners. See **behavior. 2.** guidance, administration. **5.** deport, bear. **6.** supervise, administer. **8.** See **guide.**

con•duct•ance (kən duk′təns), *n. Elect.* the conducting power, esp. the power to conduct alternating current, of a conductor, equal to the real part of the admittance, and in a circuit with no reactance equal to the reciprocal of the resistance. *Symbol:* G [1880–85; CONDUCT + -ANCE]

con•duc•tion (kən duk′shən), *n.* **1.** the act of conducting, as of water through a pipe. **2.** *Physics.* **a.** the transfer of heat between two parts of a stationary system, caused by a temperature difference between the parts. **b.** transmission through a conductor. **c.** conductivity. **3.** *Physiol.* the carrying of sound waves, electrons, heat, or nerve impulses by a nerve or other tissue. [1530–40; < L *conductiōn-* (s. of *conductiō*) a bringing together, a hiring, equiv. to *conduct(us)* (see CONDUCT) + *-iōn-* -ION] —**con•duc′tion•al,** *adj.*

con•duc•tive (kən duk′tiv), *adj.* having the property or capability of conducting. [1520–30; < L *conduct(us)* (see CONDUCT) + -IVE] —**con•duc′tive•ly,** *adv.*

con•duc•tiv•i•ty (kon′duk tiv′i tē), *n., pl.* **-ties. 1.** *Physics.* the property or power of conducting heat, electricity, or sound. **2.** Also called **specific conductance.** *Elect.* a measure of the ability of a given substance to conduct electric current, equal to the reciprocal of the resistance of the substance. *Symbol:* σ [1830–40; CONDUCTIVE + -ITY]

con•duc•to•met′ric titra′tion (kən duk′tə me′-trik), *Chem.* titration in which the end point is determined by measuring the resistance of the solution to an electric current that is passed through it. [CONDUCT + -O- + -METRIC]

con•duc•tor (kən duk′tər), *n.* **1.** a person who conducts; a leader, guide, director, or manager. **2.** an employee on a bus, train, or other public conveyance, who is in charge of the conveyance and its passengers, collects fares or tickets, etc. **3.** a person who directs an orchestra or chorus, communicating to the performers by motions of a baton or the hands his or her interpretation of the music. **4.** a substance, body, or device that readily conducts heat, electricity, sound, etc.: *Copper is a good conductor of electricity.* **5.** See **lightning rod.** [1400–50; < L (see CONDUCE, -TOR); r. late ME *cond(u)itour* < AF, equiv. to MF *conduiteur* < L as above; see CONDUIT] —**con•duc•to•ri•al** (kon′duk tôr′ē əl, -tōr′-), *adj.* —**con•duc′tor•ship′,** *n.*

con•duc•tress (kən duk′tris), *n.* **1.** a woman who conducts; a female leader, guide, director, or manager. **2.** a woman who is employed as a conductor on a bus, train, or other public conveyance. [1615–25; CONDUCT(O)R + -ESS]
—**Usage.** See **-ess.**

con•duc•tus (kən duk′təs), *n., pl.* **-tus.** any of various forms of medieval song with a Latin text. [1795–1805; < ML, equiv. to L *conduc-,* var. s. of *condūcere* (see CONDUCE) + *-tus* suffix of v. action; cf. CONDUCT]

con•duit (kon′dwit, -dōō it, -dyōō it, -dit), *n.* **1.** a pipe, tube, or the like, for conveying water or other fluid. **2.** a similar natural passage. **3.** *Elect.* a structure containing one or more ducts. **4.** *Archaic.* a fountain. [1300–50; ME < AF, OF < ML *conductus* pipe channel; see CONDUCE, DUCT]
—**Syn. 1.** duct, main, channel.

con•du•pli•cate (kon dōō′pli kit, -dyōō′-), *adj. Bot.* (of a leaf in the bud) folded lengthwise with the upper face of the blade within. [1770–80; < L *conduplicātus* (ptp. of *conduplicāre* to double), equiv. to *con-* CON- + *duplicātus* DUPLICATE] —**con•du•pli•ca′tion,** *n.*

con•dy•larth (kon′dl ärth′), *n.* any of the primitive ungulate mammals of the extinct order Condylarthra, from the Paleocene and Eocene epochs, having a slender body, low-crowned teeth, and five-toed feet, each toe ending in a small hoof. [1880–85; < NL *Condylarthra* (neut. pl.) < Gk *kóndyl(os)* CONDYLE + *-arthra,* neut. pl. of *arthrus* -jointed, deriv. of *árthron* joint]

condylarth, genus *Ectoconus,* 1½ ft. (0.5 m) high at shoulder; length 3 ft. (0.9 m)

con•dyle (kon′dil, -dl), *n.* **1.** *Anat.* the smooth surface area at the end of a bone, forming part of a joint. **2.** (in arthropods) a similar process formed from the hard integument. [1625–35; var. of *condyl* < NL *condylus* knuckle < Gk *kóndylos*] —**con′dy•lar,** *adj.*

con•dy•loid (kon′dl oid′), *adj.* of or like a condyle. [1735–45; CONDYLE + -OID]

con•dy•lo•ma (kon′dl ō′mə), *n., pl.* **-mas, -ma•ta** (-mə tə). *Pathol.* a wartlike growth on the skin, usually in the region of the anus or genitals. [1650–60; < NL, L < Gk *kondylōma.* See CONDYLE, -OMA] —**con•dy•lom•a•tous** (kon′dl om′ə təs, -dl ō′mə-), *adj.*

condylo′ma a•cu•mi•na′tum (ə kyōō′mə nā′təm). See **venereal warts.** [< NL; see CONDYLOMA, ACUMINATE]

cone (kōn), *n., v.,* **coned, con•ing.** —*n.* **1.** *Geom.* **a.** a solid whose surface is generated by a line passing through a fixed point and a fixed plane curve not containing the point, consisting of two equal sections joined at a vertex. **b.** a plane surface resembling the cross section of a solid cone. **2.** anything shaped like a cone: *sawdust piled up in a great cone; the cone of a volcano.* **3.** See **ice-cream cone. 4.** *Bot.* **a.** the more or less conical multiple fruit of the pine, fir, etc., consisting of overlapping or valvate scales bearing naked ovules or seeds; a strobile. **b.** a similar fruit, as in cycads or club mosses. **5.** *Anat.* one of the cone-shaped cells in the retina of the eye, sensitive to color and intensity of light. Cf. **rod** (def. 17). **6.** one of a series of cone-shaped markers placed along a road, as around an area of highway construction, esp. to exclude or divert motor vehicles. **7.** (in a taper thread screw or bevel gear) an imaginary cone or frustum of a cone concentric to the axis and defining the pitch surface or one of the extremities of the threads or teeth. **8.** *Ceram.* See **pyrometric cone.** —*v.t.* **9.** to shape like a cone or a segment of a cone. [1480–90; < L *cōnus* < Gk *kônos* pine-cone, cone-shaped figure; akin to HONE[1]]

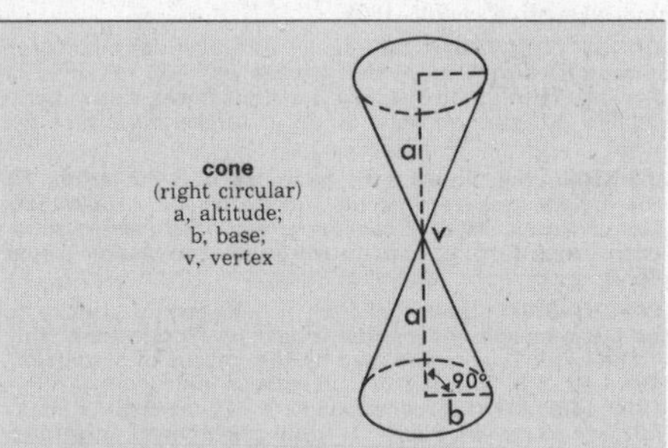

cone (right circular) a, altitude; b, base; v, vertex

cone•flow•er (kōn′flou′ər), *n.* **1.** any of several composite plants of the genus *Rudbeckia,* having flowers usually with yellow rays and a brown or black disk. **2.** any of various allied plants, as the prairie coneflower. [1810–20, *Amer.*; CONE + FLOWER]

cone•head (kōn′hed′), *n. Slang.* **1.** a stupid person; domehead. **2.** *Usually Disparaging.* an intellectual, esp. one with little or no interest in mundane affairs. [CONE + HEAD]

Con•el•rad (kon′l rad′), *n.* a system formerly used by the U.S. civil defense system to prevent enemy planes or missiles from homing on radio and television frequencies. [1955–60; *con(trol of) el(ectromagnetic) rad(iation)*]

cone•nose (kōr′nōz′), *n.* any of several bloodsucking assassin bugs of the genus *Triatoma,* some of which inflict a painful bite and serve as vectors of Chagas' disease. [1890–95; CONE + NOSE]

cone′ of si′lence, a space, in the shape of an inverted cone, above a radio beacon, in which there is a sharp reduction in the intensity of transmitted signals.

co•ne•pa•ti (kō′nə pä′tē), *n.* See **hog-nosed skunk** (def. 2). [1765–75; < MexSp *conepate* < Nahuatl *conēpatl,* equiv. to *conē(tl)* child, offspring + *(e)patl* skunk]

cone′ pep′per, 1. a tropical, woody pepper plant, *Capsicum annuum conoides,* having upright, cone-shaped, very pungent fruit of red, yellow, or purple. **2.** the fruit itself.

cone′ plant′, any dwarf succulent of the genus *Conophytum,* native to southern Africa.

cone′ pul′ley, (on a lathe) a pulley consisting of a conelike arrangement of graduated, concentric pulleys for driving the headstock at different speeds.

cone′ shell′, any of numerous, chiefly tropical, marine gastropods of the genus *Conus,* having a smooth, brightly colored, conical shell with a short, flattened spire. Also called **cone′ snail′.**

con es•pres•si•o•ne (kon′ i spres′ē ō′nē, -nā, kōn′; *It.* kôn es′pres syô′ne), with expression; expressively (used as a direction in music). [1890–95; < It: lit., with expression]

Con′es•to′ga wag′on (kon′ə stō′gə, kon′-), a large, heavy, broad-wheeled covered wagon, used esp.

for transporting pioneers and freight across North America during the early westward migration. Also called **Con′es·to′ga.** [1690–1700; named after *Conestoga*, Pa., where it was first made]

co·ney (kō′nē, kun′ē), *n., pl.* **-neys. 1.** a serranid fish, *Epinephelus fulvus*, of tropical American waters. **2.** cony. [sp. var. of CONY]

Co′ney Is′land (kō′nē), an area in S Brooklyn in New York City: amusement park and beach.

conf., 1. (in prescriptions) a confection. [< L *confectiō*] **2.** compare. [< L *confer*] **3.** conference. **4.** confessor. **5.** confidential.

con·fab (*n.* kon′fab; *v.* kən fab′, kon′fab), *n., v.,* **-fabbed, -fab·bing.** *Informal.* **—*n.* 1.** a confabulation. **—*v.i.* 2.** to confabulate: *They spent the morning confabbing over coffee in my office.* [1695–1705; by shortening]

con·fab·u·late (kən fab′yə lāt′), *v.i.,* **-lat·ed, -lat·ing. 1.** to converse informally; chat. **2.** *Psychiatry.* to engage in confabulation. [1605–15; < L *confābulātus* (ptp. of *confābulārī* to talk together), equiv. to *con-* CON- + *fābul(a)* conversation (see FABLE) + *-ātus* -ATE[1]] **—con·fab′u·la′tor,** *n.*

con·fab·u·la·tion (kən fab′yə lā′shən), *n.* **1.** the act of confabulating; conversation; discussion. **2.** *Psychiatry.* the replacement of a gap in a person's memory by a falsification that he or she believes to be true. [1490–1500; < LL *confabulātiōn-* (s. of *confābulātiō*) conversation, equiv. to *confābulāt(us)* (see CONFABULATE) + *-iōn-* -ION] **—con·fab·u·la·to·ry** (kən fab′yŏŏ lə tôr′ē, -tōr′ē), *adj.*

con·far·re·a·tion (kon far′ē ā′shən), *n.* (among the ancient Romans) a form of marriage ceremony, limited to patricians and obligatory for holders of certain ritual offices, marked by the offering of a cake. [1590–1600; < L *confarreātiōn-* (s. of *confarreātiō*) equiv. to *confarreā(re)* to contract such a marriage (*con-* CON- + *-farreāre*, v. deriv. of *farreum* cake made of emmer, deriv. of *far* emmer; see BARLEY[1]) + *-tiōn-* -TION] **—con·far·re·ate** (kən far′ē it, -āt′), **con·far′re·at′ed,** *adj.*

con·fect (*v.* kən fekt′; *n.* kon′fekt), *v.t.* **1.** to make up, compound, or prepare from ingredients or materials: *to confect a herbal remedy for colds.* **2.** to make into a preserve or confection. **3.** to construct, form, or make: *to confect a dress from odds and ends of fabric.* **—*n.* 4.** a preserved, candied, or other sweet confection. [1350–1400; ME *confecten* < L *confectus* (ptp. of *conficere* to produce, effect), equiv. to *con-* CON- + *-fec-* (var. s. of *-ficere*, comb. form of *facere* to make; see FACT) + *-tus* ptp. suffix]

con·fec·tion (kən fek′shən), *n.* **1.** a sweet preparation of fruit or the like, as a preserve or candy. **2.** the process of compounding, preparing, or making something. **3.** a frivolous, amusing, or contrived play, book, or other artistic or literary work. **4.** something made up or confected; a concoction: *He said the charges were a confection of the local police.* **5.** something, as a garment or decorative object, that is very delicate, elaborate, or luxurious and usually nonutilitarian. **6.** *Pharm.* a medicated preparation made with the aid of sugar, honey, syrup, or the like. **—*v.t.* 7.** *Archaic.* to prepare as a confection. [1300–50; ME < L *confectiōn-* (s. of *confectiō*) completion, equiv. to *confect-* (see CONFECT) + *-iōn-* -ION]

con·fec·tion·ar·y (kən fek′shə ner′ē), *n., pl.* **-ar·ies,** *adj.* **—*n.* 1.** a candy; sweetmeat. **2.** a place where confections are kept or made. **3.** confectionery (def. 3). **—*adj.* 4.** pertaining to or of the nature of confections or their production. [1590–1600; < ML *confectiōnārius*, equiv. to *confectiōn-* CONFECTION + *-ārius* -ARY]

con·fec·tion·er (kən fek′shə nər), *n.* a person who makes or sells candies and, sometimes, ice cream, cakes, etc. [1585–95; CONFECTION + -ER[1]]

confec′tioners' sug′ar, an extra-fine variety of powdered sugar, with cornstarch added to preserve dryness, used in icings, confections, etc. *Symbol:* XXXX [1890–95]

con·fec·tion·er·y (kən fek′shə ner′ē), *n., pl.* **-er·ies. 1.** confections or sweetmeats collectively. **2.** the work or business of a confectioner. **3.** a confectioner's shop. [1535–45; CONFECTION + -ERY]

confed., 1. confederacy. **2.** confederate. **3.** confederation.

con·fed·er·a·cy (kən fed′ər ə sē, -fed′rə sē), *n., pl.* **-cies. 1.** an alliance between persons, parties, states, etc., for some purpose. **2.** a group of persons, parties, states, etc., united by such a confederacy. **3.** a combination of persons for unlawful purposes; conspiracy. **4. the Confederacy.** See **Confederate States of America.** [1350–1400; ME *confederacie* < AF; see CONFEDERATE, -ACY]

con·fed·er·al (kən fed′ər əl, -fed′rəl), *adj.* of, pertaining to, or involving two or more nations: *confederal agreements.* [1775–85; CONFEDER(ATION) + -AL[1], on model of FEDERATION and FEDERAL] **—con·fed′er·al·ist,** *n.*

con·fed·er·ate (*adj., n.* kən fed′ər it, -fed′rit; *v.* kən-fed′ə rāt′), *adj., n., v.,* **-at·ed, -at·ing. —*adj.* 1.** united in a league, alliance, or conspiracy. **2.** (*cap.*) of or pertaining to the Confederate States of America: *the Confederate army.* **—*n.* 3.** a person, group, nation, etc., united with others in a confederacy; an ally. **4.** an accomplice, esp. in a mischievous or criminal act. **5.** (*cap.*) *U.S. Hist.* a supporter of the Confederate States of America. **—*v.t., v.i.* 6.** to unite in a league, alliance, or conspiracy. [1350–1400; ME *confederat* < LL *confoederātus* (ptp. of *confoederāre* to unite in a league), equiv. to *con-* CON- + *foeder-* (s. of *foedus*) treaty (see FIDELITY) + *-ātus* -ATE[1]]
—Syn. 3. associate, partner, cohort.

Confed′erate jas′mine, (*sometimes l.c.*) See **star jasmine.** [1895–1900, *Amer.*]

Confed′erate Memo′rial Day′, a day set aside in the South to pay tribute to those who served with the Confederate forces during the American Civil War. It is observed on April 26 in Alabama, Florida, Georgia, and Mississippi; on May 10 in North Carolina and South Carolina; on May 30 in Virginia; and on June 3 in Kentucky, Louisiana, and Tennessee. [1895–1900]

Confed′erate States′ of Amer′ica, the group of 11 Southern states that seceded from the United States in 1860–61. Also called **the Confederacy.**

Confed′erate War′, *Chiefly South Atlantic States.* the American Civil War.

con·fed·er·a·tion (kən fed′ə rā′shən), *n.* **1.** the act of confederating. **2.** the state of being confederated. **3.** a league or alliance. **4.** a group of confederates, esp. of states more or less permanently united for common purposes. **5. the Confederation,** the union of the 13 original U.S. states under the Articles of Confederation 1781–89. **6.** (*cap.*) the federation of Ontario, Quebec, New Brunswick, and Nova Scotia, formed in 1867 and constituting the Dominion of Canada. [1375–1425; late ME < LL *confoederātiōn-* (s. of *confoederātiō*) an agreement, equiv. to *confoederāt(us)* CONFEDERATE + *-iōn-* -ION] **—con·fed′er·a′tion·ism,** *n.* **—con·fed′er·a′tion·ist,** *n.*
—Syn. 3. coalition, federation. See **alliance.**

con·fed·er·a·tive (kən fed′ə rā′tiv, -ər ə tiv, -fed′rə-), *adj.* pertaining to or characteristic of a confederation. [1810–20; CONFEDERATE + -IVE]

con·fer (kən fûr′), *v.,* **-ferred, -fer·ring. —*v.i.* 1.** to consult together; compare opinions; carry on a discussion or deliberation. **—*v.t.* 2.** to bestow upon as a gift, favor, honor, etc.: *to confer a degree on a graduate.* **3.** *Obs.* to compare. [1400–50 for earlier sense "to summon"; 1520–30 for current senses; late ME *conferen* < L *conferre* to bring together, compare, consult with, equiv. to *con-* CON- + *ferre* to carry, BEAR[1]] **—con·fer′ment,** *n.* **—con·fer′ra·ble,** *adj.* **—con·fer′rer,** *n.*
—Syn. 1. See **consult. 2.** See **give.**

con·fer·ee (kon′fə rē′), *n.* **1.** a person on whom something is conferred, esp. the recipient of an academic degree. **2.** a person, group, etc., that confers or takes part in a conference. Also, **conferree.** [1765–75, *Amer.*; CONFER + -EE]

con·fer·ence (kon′fər əns, -frəns), *n., v.,* **-enced, -enc·ing. —*n.* 1.** a meeting for consultation or discussion: *a conference between a student and his adviser.* **2.** the act of conferring or consulting together; consultation, esp. on an important or serious matter. **3.** *Govt.* a meeting, as of various committees, to settle disagreements between the two branches of the legislature. **4.** an association of athletic teams; league: *an intercollegiate conference.* **5.** *Eccles.* **a.** an official assembly of clergy or of clergy and laity, customary in many Christian denominations. **b.** a group of churches whose representatives regularly meet in such an assembly. **—*v.i.* 6.** to hold or participate in a conference or series of conferences. [1530–40; < ML *conferentia.* See CONFER, -ENCE] **—con·fer·en·tial** (kon′fə ren′shəl), *adj.*
—Syn. 1. parley, colloquium. See **convention.**

con′ference call′, a telephone call that interconnects three or more phones simultaneously. [1940–45]

Con′ference on Secu′rity and Coopera′tion in Eu′rope, an agreement signed in Helsinki, Finland, in 1975, by 35 countries including the U.S. and the Soviet Union, that promotes human rights as well as cooperation in economic, social, and cultural progress. *Abbr.:* CSCE

con·fer·enc·ing (kon′fər ən sing, -frən-), *n.* **1.** the holding of a series of meetings or conferences. **2.** participation in a conference that involves use of a particular electronic technology: *audio conferencing; computer conferencing.* Cf. **teleconferencing** (def. 1), **videoconferencing.** [1860–65; CONFERENCE + -ING[1]]

con·fer·ral (kən fûr′əl), *n.* the act of conferring or bestowing; conferment: *the conferral of an honorary doctorate on the president.* [1875–80; CONFER + -AL[2]]

con·fer·ree (kon′fə rē′), *n.* conferee.

con·fer·va (kon fûr′və), *n., pl.* **-vae** (-vē), **-vas.** any simple filamentous green algae, many of which were formerly classified in the genus *Conferva.* [1630–40; < L: a certain water plant supposed to heal wounds, akin to *confervēre* to grow together, heal (see CON-, FERVENT)] **—con·fer′val, con·fer·vous** (kən fûr′vəs), *adj.* **—con·fer·void** (kon fûr′void), *adj., n.*

con·fess (kən fes′), *v.t.* **1.** to acknowledge or avow (a fault, crime, misdeed, weakness, etc.) by way of revelation. **2.** to own or admit as true: *I must confess that I haven't read the book.* **3.** to declare or acknowledge (one's sins), esp. to God or a priest in order to obtain absolution. **4.** (of a priest) to hear the confession of (a person). **5.** to acknowledge one's belief or faith in; declare adherence to. **6.** to reveal by circumstances. **—*v.i.* 7.** to make confession; plead guilty; own: *to confess to a crime.* **8.** to make confession of sins, esp. to a priest. **9.** (of a priest) to hear confession. [1300–50; ME *confessen* < AF, OF *confesser* < ML *confessāre*, v. deriv. of L *confessus*, ptp. of *confitērī* to admit, confess, equiv. to *con-* CON- + *-fitērī*, comb. form of *fatērī* to admit] **—con·fess′a·ble,** *adj.* **—con·fess′ingly,** *adv.*
—Syn. 1. See **acknowledge. 2.** grant, concede. **—Ant. 1.** conceal. **2.** deny.

con·fess·ed·ly (kən fes′id lē), *adv.* by confession or acknowledgment; admittedly. [1630–40; CONFESS + -ED[2] + -LY]

con·fes·sion (kən fesh′ən), *n.* **1.** acknowledgment; avowal; admission: *a confession of incompetence.* **2.** acknowledgment or disclosure of sin or sinfulness, esp. to a priest to obtain absolution. **3.** something that is confessed. **4.** a formal, usually written, acknowledgment of guilt by a person accused of a crime. **5.** Also called **confession of faith.** a formal profession of belief and acceptance of doctrines, as before being admitted to church membership. **6.** the tomb of a martyr or confessor or the altar or shrine connected with it. [1350–1400; < L *confessiōn-* (s. of *confessiō*), equiv. to *confess-* (see CONFESS) + *-iōn-* -ION; r. ME *confessioun* < AF]

con·fes·sion·al (kən fesh′ə nl), *adj.* **1.** of, pertaining to, characteristic of, or based on confession: *confessional release.* **—*n.* 2.** the place set apart for the hearing of confessions by a priest. **3.** *Fr. Furniture.* a high, upholstered wing chair of the 18th century. [1590–1600; < ML *confessiōnāle*, neut. of *confessiōnālis* (adj.); see CONFESSION, -AL[1]; in def. 2, 3 < F < ML]

con·fes·sion·al·ism (kən fesh′ə nl iz′əm), *n.* advocacy of the maintenance of a confession of faith. [1875–80; CONFESSIONAL + -ISM] **—con·fes·sion·a·li·an** (kən-fesh′ə nā′lē ən), *adj., n.*

con·fes·sion·al·ist (kən fesh′ə nl ist), *n.* a person who confesses in or as if in a confessional. [1820–30; CONFESSIONAL + -IST]

con·fes·sion·ar·y (kən fesh′ə ner′ē), *adj., n., pl.* **-ar·ies. —*adj.* 1.** of or pertaining to confession, esp. auricular confession of sins. **—*n.* 2.** *Archaic.* a confessional. [1600–10; < ML *confessiōnārius*, equiv. to *confessiōn-* CONFESSION + *-ārius* -ARY]

confes′sion of faith′, confession (def. 5). [1530–40]

Confes′sions of an Eng′lish O′pium Eat′er, an autobiographical work (1822) by Thomas De Quincey.

con·fes·sor (kən fes′ər), *n.* **1.** a person who confesses. **2.** a priest authorized to hear confessions. **3.** a person who confesses faith in and adheres to the Christian religion, esp. in spite of persecution and torture but without suffering martyrdom. **4. the Confessor.** See **Edward the Confessor.** Also, **con·fess′er.** [bef. 1000; ME, OE (in pl: *confessores*) < LL; see CONFESS, -TOR]

con·fet·ti (kən fet′ē *for 1; It.* kôn fet′tē *for 2*), *n.pl., sing.* **-fet·to** (*It.* -fet′tô) for 2. **1.** (*used with a singular v.*) small bits of paper, usually colored, thrown or dropped from a height to enhance the gaiety of a festive event, as a parade, wedding, or New Year's Eve party. **2.** confections; bonbons. [1805–15; < It, pl. of *confetto* COMFIT]

con·fi·dant (kon′fi dant′, -dänt′, -dənt, kon′fi dant′, -dänt′), *n.* a close friend or associate to whom secrets are confided or with whom private matters and problems are discussed. [1705–15; < F *confident* < It *confidente*, n. use of adj.; see CONFIDENT]

con·fi·dante (kon′fi dant′, -dänt′, kon′fi dant′, -dänt′), *n.* **1.** a woman to whom secrets are confided or with whom private matters and problems are discussed. **2.** *Furniture.* confidente. [1700–10; < F *confidente*]

con·fide (kən fīd′), *v.,* **-fid·ed, -fid·ing. —*v.i.* 1.** to impart secrets trustfully; discuss private matters or problems (usually fol. by *in*): *She confides in no one but her husband.* **2.** to have full trust; have faith: *They confided in their own ability.* **—*v.t.* 3.** to tell in assurance of secrecy: *He confided all his plans to her.* **4.** to entrust; commit to the charge or knowledge of another: *She confided her jewelry to her sister.* [1625–35; < L *confīdere*, equiv. to *con-* CON- + *fīdere* to trust, akin to *foedus*; see CONFEDERATE, FIDELITY] **—con·fid′er,** *n.*
—Syn. 3. disclose, reveal, divulge, impart.

con·fi·dence (kon′fi dəns), *n.* **1.** full trust; belief in the powers, trustworthiness, or reliability of a person or thing: *We have every confidence in their ability to succeed.* **2.** belief in oneself and one's powers or abilities; self-confidence; self-reliance; assurance: *His lack of confidence defeated him.* **3.** certitude; assurance: *He described the situation with such confidence that the audience believed him completely.* **4.** a confidential communication: *to exchange confidences.* **5.** (esp. in European politics) the wish to retain an incumbent government in office, as shown by a vote in a particular issue: *a vote of confidence.* **6.** presumption; impudence: *Her disdainful look crushed the confidence of the brash young man.* **7.** *Archaic.* something that gives confidence; ground of trust. **8. in confidence,** as a secret or private matter, not to be divulged or communicated to others; with belief in a person's sense of discretion: *I told him in confidence.* [1350–1400; ME (< MF) < L *confīdentia.* See CONFIDE, -ENCE]
—Syn. 1. faith, reliance, dependence. See **trust. 2.** CONFIDENCE, ASSURANCE both imply a faith in oneself. CONFIDENCE may imply trust in oneself or arrogant self-conceit. ASSURANCE implies even more sureness of oneself; this may be shown as undisturbed calm or as offensive boastfulness. **—Ant. 1.** mistrust.

con′fidence game′, any swindle in which the swindler, after gaining the confidence of the victim, robs the victim by cheating at a gambling game, appropriating funds entrusted for investment, or the like. Also called, *Brit.,* **con′fidence trick′.** [1855–60, *Amer.*]

con′fidence in′terval, *Statistics.* the interval bounded by confidence limits. Cf. **interval estimation.** [1930–35]

con′fidence lim′its, *Statistics.* a pair of numbers used to estimate a characteristic of a population, such that the numbers can be stated with a specified probability that the population characteristic is included between them. [1935–40]

con′fidence man′, a person who swindles others by means of a confidence game; swindler. [1840–50, *Amer.*]

con·fi·dent (kon′fi dənt), *adj.* **1.** having strong belief or full assurance; sure: *confident of fulfillment.* **2.** sure of oneself; having no uncertainty about one's own abilities, correctness, successfulness, etc.; self-confident; bold: *a confident speaker.* **3.** excessively bold; presumptuous. **4.** *Obs.* trustful or confiding. **—*n.* 5.** a confidant. [1570–80; < L *confident-* (s. of *confīdēns*), prp. of *confīdere.* See CONFIDE, -ENT] **—con′fi·dent·ly,** *adv.*
—Syn. 1. certain, positive. See **sure. 2.** self-reliant, assured, intrepid. **—Ant. 2.** modest, diffident.

con·fi·dente (kon′fi dant′, -dänt′, kon′fi dant′, -dänt′), *n.* a sofa or settee, esp. of the 18th century, having a triangular seat at each end divided from the

CONCISE PRONUNCIATION KEY: act, cāpe, dâre, pärt; set, ēqual; *if,* īce; ox, ōver, ôrder, oil, bŏŏk, bōōt, out; up, ûrge; child; sing; shoe; thin, that; zh as in *treasure.* ə = *a* as in *alone, e* as in *system, i* as in *easily, o* as in *gallop, u* as in *circus;* ᵊ as in *fire* (fīᵊr), *hour* (ouᵊr). l and n can serve as syllabic consonants, as in *cradle* (krād′l), and *button* (but′n). See the full key inside the front cover.

greater part of the seat by an armrest. Also, **confidante.** [< F, special use of *confidente* female confidant]

con·fi·den·tial (kon′fi den′shəl), *adj.* **1.** spoken, written, acted on, etc., in strict privacy or secrecy; secret: *a confidential remark.* **2.** indicating confidence or intimacy; imparting private matters: *a confidential tone of voice.* **3.** having another's trust or confidence; entrusted with secrets or private affairs: *a confidential secretary.* **4.** (of information, a document, etc.) **a.** bearing the classification *confidential,* usually being above *restricted* and below *secret.* **b.** limited to persons authorized to use information, documents, etc., so classified. Cf. **classification** (def. 5). [1645–55; < L *confidenti(a)* CONFIDENCE + -AL[1]] **—con′fi·den′ti·al′i·ty, con′fi·den′tial·ness,** *n.* **—con′fi·den′tial·ly,** *adv.*
—Syn. 1. restricted, private. **2.** intimate, familiar. **3.** trusted, trustworthy, private. See **familiar.**

confiden′tial communica′tion, *Law.* a confidential statement made to a lawyer, doctor, or pastor, or to one's husband or wife, privileged against disclosure in court if the privilege is claimed by the client, patient, penitent, or spouse. Also called **privileged communication.** [1790–1800]

con·fid·ing (kən fī′ding), *adj.* trustful; credulous or unsuspicious: *a confiding nature.* [1635–45; CONFIDE + -ING[2]] **—con·fid′ing·ly,** *adv.* **—con·fid′ing·ness,** *n.*

con·fig·u·rate (kən fig′yə rāt′), *v.t.,* **-rat·ed, -rat·ing.** to give a configuration, form, or design to. [by back formation from CONFIGURATION]

con·fig·u·ra·tion (kən fig′yə rā′shən), *n.* **1.** the relative disposition or arrangement of the parts or elements of a thing. **2.** external form, as resulting from this; conformation. **3.** *Astron.* **a.** the relative position or aspect of heavenly bodies. **b.** a group of stars. **4.** *Chem.* an atomic spatial arrangement that is fixed by the chemical bonding in a molecule and that cannot be altered without breaking bonds (contrasted with *conformation*). **5.** *Computers.* the totality of a computer and the devices connected to it: *A common microcomputer configuration consists of a computer, two disk drives, a monitor, and a printer.* [1550–60; < LL *configūrātiōn-* (s. of *configūrātiō*), equiv. to L *configūrāt(us)* shaped like its model, ptp. of *configūrāre* to mold, shape (*con-* CON- + *figūr(a)* FIGURE + *-ātus* -ATE[1]) + *-iōn-* -ION] **—con·fig′u·ra′tion·al, con·fig·u·ra·tive** (kən fig′yər ə tiv, -yə rā′tiv), *adj.* **—con·fig′u·ra′tion·al·ly,** *adv.*

con·fig·u·ra·tion·ism (kən fig′yə rā′shə niz′əm), *n.* See **Gestalt psychology.** [1920–25; CONFIGURATION + -ISM] **—con·fig′u·ra′tion·ist,** *n.*

con·fig·ure (kən fig′yər), *v.t.,* **-ured, -ur·ing. 1.** to design or adapt to form a specific configuration or for some specific purpose: *The planes are being configured to hold more passengers in each row.* **2.** *Computers.* **a.** to put (a computer system) together by supplying a specific computer with appropriate peripheral devices, as a monitor and disk drive, and connecting them. **b.** to insert batch files into (a program) to enable it to run with a particular computer. [back formation from CONFIGURATION]

con·fine (kən fīn′ *for 1, 2, 5, 6;* kon′fīn *for 3, 4*), *v.,* **-fined, -fin·ing,** *n.* —*v.t.* **1.** to enclose within bounds; limit or restrict: *She confined her remarks to errors in the report. Confine your efforts to finishing the book.* **2.** to shut or keep in; prevent from leaving a place because of imprisonment, illness, discipline, etc.: *For that offense he was confined to quarters for 30 days.* —*n.* **3.** Usually, **confines.** a boundary or bound; limit; border; frontier. **4.** Often, **confines.** region; territory. **5.** *Archaic.* confinement. **6.** *Obs.* a place of confinement; prison. [1350–1400 for n.; 1515–25 for v.; (n.) ME < MF *confins, confines* < ML *confinia,* pl. of L *confinis* boundary, border (see CON-, FINE[2]); (v.) < MF *confiner,* v. deriv. of *confins* < L, as above] **—con·fin′a·ble, con·fine′a·ble,** *adj.* **—con·fine′less,** *adj.* **—con·fin′er,** *n.*
—Syn. 1. circumscribe. **—Ant. 1, 2.** free.

con·fined (kən fīnd′), *adj.* **1.** limited or restricted. **2.** unable to leave a place because of illness, imprisonment, etc. **3.** being in childbirth; being in parturition. [CONFINE + -ED[2]] **—con·fin·ed·ly** (kən fī′nid lē, -fīnd′lē), *adv.* **—con·fin′ed·ness,** *n.*

con·fin·ee (kən fī nē′, -fī′nē), *n.* a person held in confinement. [CONFINE + -EE]

con·fine·ment (kən fīn′mənt), *n.* **1.** the act of confining. **2.** the state of being confined. **3.** the lying-in of a woman in childbed; accouchement; childbirth. **4.** *Mil.* incarceration in a guardhouse or prison while awaiting trial or as a punishment (distinguished from *arrest*). [1640–50; CONFINE + -MENT; cf. F *confinement*]

con·firm (kən fûrm′), *v.t.* **1.** to establish the truth, accuracy, validity, or genuineness of; corroborate; verify: *This report confirms my suspicions.* **2.** to acknowledge with definite assurance: *Did the hotel confirm our room reservation?* **3.** to make valid or binding by some formal or legal act; sanction; ratify: *to confirm a treaty; to confirm her appointment to the Supreme Court.* **4.** to make firm or more firm; add strength to; settle or establish firmly: *Their support confirmed my determination to run for mayor.* **5.** to strengthen (a person) in habit, resolution, opinion, etc.: *The accident confirmed him in his fear of driving.* **6.** to administer the religious rite of confirmation to. [1250–1300; < L *confirmāre* to strengthen, confirm (see CON-, FIRM[1]); r. ME *confermen* < OF < L, as above] **—con·firm′a·ble,** *adj.* **—con·firm′a·bil′i·ty,** *n.* **—con·firm′er;** *Law,* **con·fir·mor** (kon′fər môr′, kən fûr′mər), *n.* **—con·firm′ing·ly,** *adv.*
—Syn. 1. prove, substantiate, authenticate, validate. **4.** fix. **—Ant. 1.** disprove. **3.** invalidate. **4.** shake.

con·fir·mand (kon′fər mand′, kon′fər mand′), *n.* a candidate for or recipient of religious confirmation. [1880–85; < L *confirmandus* to be confirmed, ger. of *confirmāre* to CONFIRM]

con·fir·ma·tion (kon′fər mā′shən), *n.* **1.** the act of confirming. **2.** the state of being confirmed. **3.** something that confirms, as a corroborative statement or piece of evidence: *His birth certificate served as confirmation of his citizenship.* **4.** a rite administered to baptized persons, in some churches as a sacrament for confirming and strengthening the recipient in the Christian faith, in others as a rite without sacramental character by which the recipient is admitted to full communion with the church. **5.** a solemn ceremony among Reform and certain Conservative Jews that is held in the synagogue, usually on Shavuoth, to admit formally as adult members of the Jewish community Jewish boys and girls 14 to 16 years of age who have successfully completed a prescribed course of study in Judaism. [1275–1325; ME < L *confirmātiōn-* s. of *confirmātiō.* See CONFIRM, -ATION] **—con′fir·ma′tion·al,** *adj.*

con·firm·a·to·ry (kən fûr′mə tôr′ē, -tōr′ē), *adj.* serving to confirm; corroborative. Also, **con·firm′a·tive.** [1630–40; < ML *confirmātōrius,* equiv. to L *confirmā(re)* (see CONFIRM) + *-tōrius* -TORY[1]]

con·firmed (kən fûrmd′), *adj.* **1.** made certain as to truth, accuracy, validity, availability, etc.: *confirmed reports of new fighting at the front; confirmed reservations on the three o'clock flight to Denver.* **2.** settled; ratified. **3.** firmly established in a habit or condition; inveterate: *a confirmed bachelor.* **4.** given additional determination; made resolute. **5.** having received the religious rite of confirmation. [1350–1400; ME *confermyd.* See CONFIRM, -ED[2]] **—con·firm·ed·ly** (kən fur′mid lē), *adv.* **—con·firm·ed·ness** (kən fûr′mid nis, -fûrmd′-), *n.*

con·fis·ca·ble (kən fis′kə bəl, kon′fə skə bəl), *adj.* liable to be confiscated. [1720–30; CONFISC(ATE) + -ABLE]

con·fis·cate (kon′fə skāt′, kən fis′kāt), *v.,* **-cat·ed, -cat·ing,** *adj.* —*v.t.* **1.** to seize as forfeited to the public domain; appropriate, by way of penalty, for public use. **2.** to seize by or as if by authority; appropriate summarily: *The border guards confiscated our movie cameras.* —*adj.* **3.** seized. [1525–35; < L *confiscātus* (ptp. of *confiscāre* to seize for the public treasury), equiv. to *con-* CON- + *fisc(us)* basket, moneybag, public treasury (see FISCAL) + *-ātus* -ATE[1]] **—con′fis·cat′a·ble,** *adj.* **—con′fis·ca′tion,** *n.* **—con′fis·ca′tor,** *n.*

con·fis·ca·to·ry (kən fis′kə tôr′ē, -tōr′ē), *adj.* characterized by, effecting, or resulting in confiscation. [1790–1800; CONFISCATE + -ORY[1]]

con·fit (kôN fē′), *n. French Cookery.* duck or goose cooked in its own fat and preserved. [< F; see COMFIT]

Con·fit·e·or (kən fit′ē ôr′), *n. Rom. Cath. Ch.* a prayer in the form of a general confession said at the beginning of the Mass and on certain other occasions. [1150–1200; ME; after first word of Latin prayer: I confess]

con·fi·ture (kon′fi cho͝or′), *n.* a confection; a preserve, as of fruit. [1350–1400; ME < MF. See COMFIT, -URE]

con·fla·grant (kən flā′grənt), *adj.* blazing; burning; on fire. [1650–60; < L *conflagrant-* (s. of *conflagrāns*), prp. of *conflagrāre.* See CONFLAGRATION, -ANT]

con·fla·gra·tion (kon′flə grā′shən), *n.* a destructive fire, usually an extensive one. [1545–55; < L *conflagrātiōn-* (s. of *conflagrātiō*), equiv. to *conflagrāt(us)* ptp. of *conflagrāre* to burn up (*con-* CON- + *flagr-* (akin to *fulgur* lightning, *flamma* FLAME, Gk *phlóx;* see PHLOX) + *-ātus* -ATE[1]) + *-iōn-* -ION] **—con′fla·gra′tive,** *adj.*
—Syn. See **flame.**

con·flate (kən flāt′), *v.t.,* **-flat·ed, -flat·ing.** to fuse into one entity; merge: *to conflate dissenting voices into one protest.* [1600–10; < L *conflātus,* ptp. of *conflāre* to fuse together, equiv. to *con-* CON- + *flāre* to BLOW[2]]

con·fla·tion (kən flā′shən), *n.* **1.** the process or result of fusing items into one entity; fusion; amalgamation. **2.** *Bibliog.* **a.** the combination of two variant texts into a new one. **b.** the text resulting from such a combination. [1400–50; late ME < LL *conflātiō.* See CONFLATE, -ION]

con·flict (*v.* kən flikt′; *n.* kon′flikt), *v.i.* **1.** to come into collision or disagreement; be contradictory, at variance, or in opposition; clash: *The account of one eyewitness conflicted with that of the other. My class conflicts with my going to the concert.* **2.** to fight or contend; do battle. —*n.* **3.** a fight, battle, or struggle, esp. a prolonged struggle; strife. **4.** controversy; quarrel: *conflicts between parties.* **5.** discord of action, feeling, or effect; antagonism or opposition, as of interests or principles: *a conflict of ideas.* **6.** a striking together; collision. **7.** incompatibility or interference, as of one idea, desire, event, or activity with another: *a conflict in the schedule.* **8.** *Psychiatry.* a mental struggle arising from opposing demands or impulses. [1375–1425; late ME (n.) < L *conflictus* a striking together, equiv. to *conflig(ere)* to strike together, contend (*con-* CON- + *fligere* to strike) + *-tus* suffix of v. action; (v.) < L *conflictus,* ptp. of *confligere,* or by v. use of the n.] **—con·flic′tion,** *n.* **—con·flic′tive, con·flic·to·ry** (kən flik′tə rē), *adj.*
—Syn. 1. collide, oppose. **3.** encounter, siege. See **fight. 5.** contention, opposition. **—Ant. 4.** accord.

con·flict·ed (kən flik′tid), *adj.* full of conflicting emotions or impulses: *a situation that makes one feel very conflicted.* [CONFLICT + -ED[2]]

con·flict·ing (kən flik′ting), *adj.* being in conflict or disagreement; not compatible: *conflicting viewpoints.* [1600–10; CONFLICT + -ING[2]] **—con·flict′ing·ly,** *adv.*

con′flict of in′terest, 1. the circumstance of a public officeholder, business executive, or the like, whose personal interests might benefit from his or her official actions or influence: *The senator placed his stocks in trust to avoid possible conflict of interest.* **2.** the circumstance of a person who finds that one of his or her activities, interests, etc., can be advanced only at the expense of another of them. [1950–55]

con′flict of laws′, 1. dissimilarity or discrepancy between the laws of different legal orders, such as states or nations, with regard to the applicable legal rules and principles in a matter that each legal order wishes to regulate. **2.** Also called **private international law.** the branch of law dealing with the determination of the law applicable to a private-law matter, of the legal order having jurisdiction to adjudicate such a matter, and of the extent to which an adjudication in such a matter by another legal order is to be recognized and enforced locally.

con·flu·ence (kon′flo͞o əns), *n.* **1.** a flowing together of two or more streams, rivers, or the like: *the confluence of the Missouri and Mississippi rivers.* **2.** their place of junction: *St. Louis is at the confluence of the Missouri and Mississippi rivers.* **3.** a body of water formed by the flowing together of two or more streams, rivers, or the like. **4.** a coming together of people or things; concourse. **5.** a crowd or throng; assemblage. Also, **con·flux** (kon′fluks). [1375–1425; late ME (< MF) < LL *confluentia;* see CONFLUENT, -ENCE]
—Syn. 4. union, joining, meeting.

con·flu·ent (kon′flo͞o ənt), *adj.* **1.** flowing or running together; blending into one: *confluent rivers; confluent ideas.* **2.** *Pathol.* **a.** running together: *confluent efflorescences.* **b.** characterized by confluent efflorescences: *confluent smallpox.* —*n.* **3.** one of two or more confluent streams. **4.** a tributary stream. [1425–75; late ME (< MF) < L *confluent-* (s. of *confluēns,* prp. of *confluere* to flow together), equiv. to *con-* CON- + *flu-* (s. of *fluere* to flow) + *-ent-* -ENT; see FLUENT, FLUID]

con·fo·cal (kon fō′kəl), *adj. Math.* having the same focus or foci. [1865–70; CON- + FOCAL]

con·form (kən fôrm′), *v.i.* **1.** to act in accordance or harmony; comply (usually fol. by *to*): *to conform to rules.* **2.** to act in accord with the prevailing standards, attitudes, practices, etc., of society or a group: *One has to conform in order to succeed in this company.* **3.** to be or become similar in form, nature, or character. **4.** to be in harmony or accord. **5.** to comply with the usages of an established church, esp. the Church of England. —*v.t.* **6.** to make similar in form, nature, or character. **7.** to bring into agreement, correspondence, or harmony. —*adj.* **8.** *Archaic.* conformable. [1275–1325; ME *confo(u)rmen* < AF, MF *conformer* < L *confōrmāre* to shape. See CON-, FORM] **—con·form′er,** *n.* **—con·form′ing·ly,** *adv.*
—Syn. 1. yield, agree, consent. **3.** correspond, agree, tally. **7.** adapt, adjust, accommodate. **—Ant. 1, 5.** dissent. **3.** differ.

con·form·a·ble (kən fôr′mə bəl), *adj.* **1.** corresponding in form, nature, or character; similar. **2.** compliant; obedient; submissive: *a conformable disposition.* **3.** *Geol.* of or pertaining to an unbroken sequence of strata or beds, characteristic of uninterrupted deposition. See illus. under **unconformable.** [1425–75; late ME. See CONFORM, -ABLE]

con·for·mal (kən fôr′məl), *adj.* of, pertaining to, or noting a map or transformation in which angles and scale are preserved. [1640–50; < LL *confōrmālis* of the same shape. See CON-, FORMAL[1]]

confor′mal projec′tion, *Cartog.* a map projection in which angles formed by lines are preserved: a map made using this projection preserves the shape of any small area. Also called **orthomorphic projection.**

con·form·ance (kən fôr′məns), *n.* the act of conforming; conformity. [1600–10; CONFORM + -ANCE]

con·for·ma·tion (kon′fôr mā′shən), *n.* **1.** manner of formation; structure; form, as of a physical entity. **2.** symmetrical disposition or arrangement of parts. **3.** the act or process of conforming; adaptation; adjustment. **4.** the state of being conformed. **5.** *Chem.* an atomic spatial arrangement that results from rotation of carbon atoms about single bonds within an organic molecule. (contrasted with *configuration*). [1505–15; < L *confōrmātiōn-* (s. of *confōrmātiō*), equiv. to *confōrmāt(us)* ptp. of *confōrmāre* to shape (*con-* CON- + *fōrm(a)* FORM + *-āt(us)* -ATE[1]) + *-iōn-* -ION] **—con′for·ma′tion·al,** *adj.*
—Syn. 1. configuration, shape.

con·form·ist (kən fôr′mist), *n.* **1.** a person who conforms, esp. unquestioningly, to the usual practices or standards of a group, society, etc. **2.** (*often cap.*) a person who conforms to the usages of an established church, esp. the Church of England. —*adj.* **3.** of or characterized by conforming, esp. in action or appearance. [1625–35; CONFORM + -IST] **—con·form′ism,** *n.*

con·form·i·ty (kən fôr′mi tē), *n., pl.* **-ties. 1.** action in accord with prevailing social standards, attitudes, practices, etc. **2.** correspondence in form, nature, or character; agreement, congruity, or accordance. **3.** compliance or acquiescence; obedience. **4.** (*often cap.*) compliance with the usages of an established church, esp. the Church of England. **5.** *Geol.* the relationship between adjacent conformable strata. Cf. **unconformity** (def. 2a). [1375–1425; late ME *conformite* < MF < LL *confōrmitās.* See CONFORM, -ITY]

con·found (kon found′, kən-; *for 6 usually* kon′found′), *v.t.* **1.** to perplex or amaze, esp. by a sudden disturbance or surprise; bewilder; confuse: *The complicated directions confounded him.* **2.** to throw into confusion or disorder: *The revolution confounded the people.* **3.** to throw into increased confusion or disorder. **4.** to treat or regard erroneously as identical; mix or associate by mistake: *truth confounded with error.* **5.** to mingle so that the elements cannot be distinguished or separated. **6.** to damn (used in mild imprecations): *Confound it!* **7.** to contradict or refute: *to confound their arguments.* **8.** to put to shame; abash. **9.** *Archaic.* **a.** to defeat or overthrow. **b.** to bring to ruin or naught. **10.** *Obs.* to spend uselessly; waste. [1250–1300; ME *conf(o)unden* < AF *confoundre* < L *confundere* to mix, equiv. to *con-* CON- + *fundere* to pour] **—con·found′a·ble,** *adj.* **—con·found′er,** *n.* **—con·found′ing·ly,** *adv.*
—Syn. 1. dumbfound, daze, nonplus, astound.

con·found·ed (kon foun′did, kən-), *adj.* **1.** bewildered; confused; perplexed. **2.** damned (used euphemistically): *That is a confounded lie.* [1325–75; ME; see CONFOUND, -ED[2]] **—con·found′ed·ly,** *adv.* **—con·found′ed·ness,** *n.*

con·fra·ter·ni·ty (kon′frə tûr′ni tē), *n., pl.* **-ties. 1.** a

---

CONCISE ETYMOLOGY KEY: <, descended or borrowed from; >, whence; b., blend of, blended; c., cognate with; cf., compare; deriv., derivative; equiv., equivalent; imit., imitative; obl., oblique; r., replacing; s., stem; sp., spelling, spelled; resp., respelling, respelled; trans., translation; ?, origin unknown; *, unattested; ‡, probably earlier than. See the full key inside the front cover.

lay brotherhood devoted to some purpose, esp. to religious or charitable service. **2.** a society or organization, esp. of men, united for some purpose or in some profession. [1425–75; late ME *confraternite* < ML *confrāternitās*, deriv. of *confrāter* (see CONFRERE), on the model of L *frāternitās* FRATERNITY] **—con′fra•ter′nal,** *adj.*

con•frere (kon′frâr), *n.* a fellow member of a fraternity, profession, etc.; colleague: *my confreres in the medical profession.* [1425–75; late ME < MF < ML *confrāter* colleague, equiv. to L *con-* CON- + *frāter* BROTHER]

con•front (kən frunt′), *v.t.* **1.** to face in hostility or defiance; oppose: *The feuding factions confronted one another.* **2.** to present for acknowledgment, contradiction, etc.; set face to face: *They confronted him with evidence of his crime.* **3.** to stand or come in front of; stand or meet facing: *The two long-separated brothers confronted each other speechlessly.* **4.** to be in one's way: *the numerous obstacles that still confronted him.* **5.** to bring together for examination or comparison. [1595–1605; < ML *confrontārī*, equiv. to L *con-* CON- + *-frontārī*, deriv. of L *frōns* forehead, FRONT] **—con•front′al, con•front′ment,** *n.* **—con•front′er,** *n.*

con•fron•ta•tion (kon′frən tā′shən, -frun-), *n.* **1.** an act of confronting. **2.** the state of being confronted. **3.** a meeting of persons face to face. **4.** an open conflict of opposing ideas, forces, etc. **5.** a bringing together of ideas, themes, etc., for comparison. **6.** *Psychol.* a technique used in group therapy, as in encounter groups, in which one is forced to recognize one's shortcomings and their possible consequences. [1625–35; CONFRONT + -ATION; cf. ML *confrontātiō*, F, MF *confrontation*]

con•fron•ta•tion•al (kon′frən tā′shə nl, -frun-), *adj.* tending toward or ready for confrontation: *They came to the meeting with a confrontational attitude.* Also, **con•fron•ta•tive** (kon′frən tā′tiv, kən frun′tə-). [CONFRONTATION + -AL[1]]

con•fron•ta•tion•ist (kon′frən tā′shə nist, -frun-), *n.* **1.** a person who confronts opposition, esp. aggressively. *—adj.* **2.** characteristic of confrontation or confrontationists: *confrontationist language.* [1965–70; CONFRONTATION + -IST] **—con′fron•ta′tion•ism,** *n.*

Con•fu•cian (kən fyoo′shən), *n.* **1.** an adherent of the teachings of Confucius. **2.** Also called **Ju.** a member of the school of philosophers, founded by Confucius, who codified in their teachings the traditional Chinese principles of ethics, morals, and politics. *—adj.* **3.** of, pertaining to, or resembling the teachings of Confucius. [1830–40; CONFUCI(US) + -AN]

Con•fu•cian•ism (kən fyoo′shə niz′əm), *n.* the system of ethics, education, and statesmanship taught by Confucius and his disciples, stressing love for humanity, ancestor worship, reverence for parents, and harmony in thought and conduct. [1860–65; CONFUCIAN + -ISM] **—Con•fu′cian•ist,** *n., adj.*

Con•fu•cius (kən fyoo′shəs), *n.* (*K'ung Ch'iu*) 551? B.C.–478? B.C., Chinese philosopher and teacher. Chinese, **K'ung Fu-tzŭ.**

con fuo•co (kon fwô′kō, fōō ô′-, kōn; *It.* kôn fōō ô′-kô), with great vigor and speed (used as a musical direction). [< It: lit., with fire]

con•fuse (kən fyooz′), *v.t.*, **-fused, -fus•ing. 1.** to perplex or bewilder: *The flood of questions confused me.* **2.** to make unclear or indistinct: *The rumors and angry charges tended to confuse the issue.* **3.** to fail to distinguish between; associate by mistake; confound: *to confuse dates; He always confuses the twins.* **4.** to disconcert or abash: *His candor confused her.* **5.** to combine without order; jumble; disorder: *Try not to confuse the papers on the desk.* **6.** *Archaic.* to bring to ruin or naught. [back formation from *confused* (since early 19th century), ME *confused* < AF *confus* (with *-ed* -ED[2] maintaining participial sense) < L *confūsus*, ptp. of *confundere*; see CONFOUND] **—con•fus′a•ble,** *adj.* **—con•fus′a•bil′i•ty,** *n.* **—con•fus′a•bly,** *adv.* **—con•fus•ed•ly** (kən fyoo′zid lē, -fyoozd′-), *adv.* **—con•fus′•ed•ness,** *n.*

—Syn. 1. mystify, nonplus. CONFUSE, DISCONCERT, EMBARRASS imply temporary interference with the clear working of one's mind. To CONFUSE is to produce a general bewilderment: *to confuse someone by giving complicated directions.* To DISCONCERT is to disturb one's mind by irritation, perplexities, etc.: *to disconcert someone by asking irrelevant questions.* To EMBARRASS is to cause one to be ill at ease or uncomfortable, so that one's usual judgment and presence of mind desert one: *to embarrass someone by unexpected rudeness.* **4.** mortify, shame. **5.** disarray, disarrange, disturb.

confused′ flour′ bee′tle, a brown flour beetle, *Tribolium confusum*, that feeds on stored grain and grain products. [appar. so called because it is confused with similar beetles]

con•fus•ing (kən fyoo′zing), *adj.* causing or tending to cause confusion: *a confusing attempt at explanation.* [1840–50; CONFUSE + -ING[2]] **—con•fus′ing•ly,** *adv.* **—con•fus′ing•ness,** *n.*

con•fu•sion (kən fyoo′zhən), *n.* **1.** the act of confusing. **2.** the state of being confused. **3.** disorder; upheaval; tumult; chaos: *The army retreated in confusion.* **4.** lack of clearness or distinctness: *a confusion in his mind between right and wrong.* **5.** perplexity; bewilderment: *The more difficult questions left us in complete confusion.* **6.** embarrassment or abashment: *He blushed in confusion.* **7.** *Psychiatry.* a disturbed mental state; disorientation. **8.** *Archaic.* defeat, overthrow, or ruin. [1300–50; ME (< AF) < L *confūsiōn-* (s. of *confūsiō*). See CONFUSE, -ION] **—con•fu′sion•al,** *adj.*

—Syn. 2. distraction. **3.** turmoil, jumble, mess, disarray. **6.** shame, mortification.

con•fu•ta•tion (kon′fyoo tā′shən), *n.* **1.** the act of confuting. **2.** something that confutes. **3.** *Class. Oratory.* the fourth section of a speech, given over to direct refutation. [1425–75; late ME *confutacioun* (< MF) < L *confūtātiōn-* (s. of *confūtātiō*), equiv. to *confūtāt(us)* silenced (ptp. of *confūtāre*; see CONFUTE, -ATE[1]) + *-iōn-* -ION] **—con•fut•a•tive** (kən fyoo′tə tiv), *adj.*

con•fute (kən fyoot′), *v.t.*, **-fut•ed, -fut•ing. 1.** to prove to be false, invalid, or defective; disprove: *to confute an argument.* **2.** to prove (a person) to be wrong by argument or proof: *to confute one's opponent.* **3.** *Obs.* to bring to naught; confound. [1520–30; < L *confūtāre* to abash, silence, refute, equiv. to *con-* CON- + *-fūtāre*; cf. REFUTE] **—con•fut′a•ble,** *adj.* **—con•fut′er,** *n.*

Cong (kong), *n. Informal.* Vietcong. [by shortening]

Cong., 1. Congregational. **2.** Congregationalist. **3.** Congress. **4.** Congressional.

cong., gallon. [< L *congius*]

con•ga (kong′gə), *n., pl.* **-gas,** *v.,* **-gaed, -ga•ing.** *—n.* **1.** a Cuban ballroom dance that consists of three steps forward followed by a kick, characteristically performed by a group following a leader in a single line. **2.** the music for this dance. **3.** Also called **con′ga drum′.** a tall, conical, Afro-Cuban drum played with the hands. *—v.i.* **4.** to dance a conga. [1930–35; < Cuban Sp]

con′ game′, *Slang.* See **confidence game.** [1950–55]

Con•ga•ree (kong′gə rē′), *n.* a river flowing E in central South Carolina, joining with the Wateree River to form the Santee River. ab. 60 mi. (97 km) long.

con•gé (kon′zhā, -jā; *Fr.* kôN zhā′), *n., pl.* **-gés** (-zhāz, -jāz; *Fr.* -zhā′). **1.** leave-taking; farewell. **2.** permission to depart. **3.** sudden dismissal. **4.** a bow or obeisance. **5.** *Archit.* a concave molding, as an apophyge, formed by a quadrant curving away from a given surface and terminating perpendicular to a fillet parallel to that surface. Also, **congee.** [1695–1705; < F; see CONGEE]

con•geal (kən jēl′), *v.t., v.i.* **1.** to change from a soft or fluid state to a rigid or solid state, as by cooling or freezing: *The fat congealed on the top of the soup.* **2.** to curdle; coagulate, as a fluid. **3.** to make or become fixed, as ideas, sentiments, or principles: *Some philosophic systems lost their vitality and congealed.* [1350–1400; ME *congelen* (< MF *congeler*) < L *congelāre*, equiv. to *con-* CON- + *gelāre* to freeze; see GELID] **—con•geal′a•ble,** *adj.* **—con•geal′a•bil′i•ty, con•geal′a•ble•ness,** *n.* **—con•geal′ed•ness,** *n.* **—con•geal′er,** *n.* **—con•geal′ment,** *n.*

—Syn. 1. harden, set, jell, solidify.

con•gee (kon′jē), *n., v.,* **-geed, -gee•ing.** *—n.* **1.** congé. *—v.i. Obs.* **2.** to take one's leave. **3.** to bow ceremoniously. [1350–1400; (n.) late ME *conge, c(o)unge* < AF *cung(i)é*, OF *congié* < L *commeātus* furlough, lit., passage, coming and going, equiv. to *commeā(re)* to go, travel (*com-* COM- + *meāre* to proceed, pass, travel) + *-tus* suffix of v. action; (v.) ME *congeien* < AF, v. deriv. of n.]

con•ge•la•tion (kon′jə lā′shən), *n.* **1.** the act or process of congealing; the state of being congealed. **2.** the product of congealing; a concretion; coagulation. [1375–1425; late ME (< MF) < L *congelātiōn-* (s. of *congelātiō*). See CONGEAL, -ATION]

con•gel•i•frac•tion (kən jel′ə frak′shən), *n. Geol.* the shattering or splitting of rock or frozen soil due to the action of frost. [*congelifract* (< L *congel(āre)* (see CONGEAL) + -I- + L *fract(us)* broken; see FRACTURE) + -ION]

con•gel•i•tur•ba•tion (kən jel′i tûr bā′shən), *n. Geol.* the churning, heaving, and thrusting of soil material due to the action of frost. [< L *congel(āre)* to cause to freeze up (see CONGEAL) + -I- + L *turb(āre)* to agitate (see DISTURB, TURBID) + -ATION]

con•ge•ner (kon′jə nər), *n.* **1.** a person or thing of the same kind or class as another. **2.** a plant, animal, fungus, etc., belonging to the same genus as another. **3.** Also, **congeneric.** a secondary product formed in alcohol during fermentation that determines largely the character of the final liquor. [1720–30; < L, equiv. to *con-* CON- + *gener-* (s. of *genus*); see GENUS, GENERAL]

con•ge•ner•ic (kon′jə ner′ik), *adj.* **1.** Also, **con•gen•er•ous** (kən jen′ər əs). of the same kind or genus. **2.** offering a group of closely related services: *a congeneric investment company.* *—n.* **3.** congener (def. 3). **4.** a congeneric company, service, or the like. [1825–35; CONGENER + -IC; see GENERIC]

con•ge•net•ic (kon′jə net′ik), *adj.* alike in origin. [1825–35; CON- + GENETIC]

con•gen•ial (kən jēn′yəl), *adj.* **1.** agreeable, suitable, or pleasing in nature or character: *congenial surroundings.* **2.** suited or adapted in spirit, feeling, temper, etc.; compatible: *a congenial couple.* [1615–25; < L *con-* CON- + *geni(us)* GENIUS + -AL[1]] **—con•ge•ni•al•i•ty** (kən jē′nē al′i tē), **con•gen′ial•ness,** *n.* **—con•gen′ial•ly,** *adv.*

—Syn. 1. favorable, pleasant, complaisant, sympathetic. **—Ant. 1, 2.** disagreeable.

con•gen•i•tal (kən jen′i tl), *adj.* **1.** of or pertaining to a condition present at birth, whether inherited or caused by the environment, esp. the uterine environment. **2.** having by nature a specified character: *a congenital fool.* [1790–1800; < L *congenit(us)* connate (*con-* CON- + *geni-*, var. s. of *gignere* to give birth + *-tus* ptp. suffix) + -AL[1]] **—con•gen′i•tal•ly,** *adv.* **—con•gen′i•tal•ness,** *n.*

—Syn. 1. See **innate.**

congen′ital de′fect. See **birth defect.**

con•ger (kong′gər), *n.* **1.** a large marine eel, *Conger conger*, sometimes reaching a length of 10 ft. (3 m), used for food. **2.** any other eel of the family Congridae. Also called **con′ger eel′.** [1250–1300; ME *kunger, congre* < OF *congre* < L *conger* < Gk *góngros* sea-eel, gnarl, protuberance]

con•ge•ries (kon jēr′ēz, kon′jə rēz), *n.* (*used with a singular or plural v.*) a collection of items or parts in one mass; assemblage; aggregation; heap: *From the airplane the town resembled a congeries of tiny boxes.* [1610–20; < L: a heap, equiv. to *conger-* (s. of *congerere* to collect, heap up, equiv. to *con-* CON- + *gerere* to bear, carry) + *-iēs* n. suffix; cf. RABIES, SERIES]

con•gest (kən jest′), *v.t.* **1.** to fill to excess; overcrowd or overburden; clog: *The subway entrance was so congested that no one could move.* **2.** *Pathol.* to cause an unnatural accumulation of blood or other fluid in (a body part or blood vessel): *The cold congested her sinuses.* **3.** *Obs.* to heap together. *—v.i.* **4.** to become congested: *His throat congested with phlegm.* [1530–40; < L *congestus* (ptp. of *congerere*; see CONGERIES), equiv. to *con-* CON- + *ges-* (var. s. of *gerere*) + *-tus* ptp. suffix] **—con•gest′i•ble,** *adj.* **—con•ges′tive,** *adj.*

con•ges•tion (kən jes′chən), *n.* **1.** overcrowding; clogging: *severe traffic congestion.* **2.** an excessive or abnormal accumulation of blood or other fluid in a body part or blood vessel: *pulmonary congestion.* [1585–95; < L *congestiō.* See CONGEST, -ION]

conges′tive heart′ fail′ure. See **heart failure** (def. 2). [1930–35]

con•gi•us (kon′jē əs), *n., pl.* **-gi•i** (-jē ī′). **1.** (in prescriptions) a gallon (3.7853 liters). **2.** an ancient Roman unit of liquid measure equal to about 0.8 U.S. gallon (3.2 liters). [1350–1400; ME < L, alter. of Gk *konchíon*, equiv. to *kónch(ē)* CONCH + *-ion* dim. suffix]

con•glo•bate (kon glō′bāt, kong-, kong′glō bāt′), *adj.*, *v.,* **-bat•ed, -bat•ing.** *—adj.* **1.** formed into a ball. *—v.t., v.i.* **2.** to collect or form into a ball or rounded mass. [1625–35; < L *conglobātus*, ptp. of *conglobāre.* See CONGLOBE, -ATE[1]] **—con•glo′bate•ly,** *adv.* **—con′glo•ba′tion,** *n.*

con•globe (kon glōb′, kong-), *v.t., v.i.*, **-globed, -glob•ing.** to conglobate. [1525–35; < L *conglobāre*, equiv. to *con-* CON- + *glob(us)* ball, sphere + *-āre* inf. ending]

con•glom•er•ate (*n., adj.* kən glom′ər it, kəng-; *v.* kən glom′ə rāt′, kəng-), *n., adj., v.,* **-at•ed, -at•ing.** *—n.* **1.** anything composed of heterogeneous materials or elements. **2.** a corporation consisting of a number of subsidiary companies or divisions in a variety of unrelated industries, usually as a result of merger or acquisition. **3.** *Geol.* a rock consisting of pebbles or the like embedded in a finer cementing material; consolidated gravel. *—adj.* **4.** gathered into a rounded mass; consisting of parts so gathered; clustered. **5.** consisting of heterogeneous parts or elements. **6.** of or pertaining to a corporate conglomerate. **7.** *Geol.* of the nature of a conglomerate. *—v.t.* **8.** to bring together into a cohering mass. **9.** to gather into a ball or rounded mass. *—v.i.* **10.** to collect or cluster together. **11.** (of a company) to become part of or merge with a conglomerate. [1565–75; < L *conglomerātus* (ptp. of *conglomerāre*), equiv. to *con-* CON- + *glomer-* (s. of *glomus*) ball of yarn + *-ātus* -ATE[1]] **—con•glom•er•at•ic** (kən glom′ə rat′ik, kəng-), **con•glom•er•it•ic** (kən glom′ə rit′ik, kəng-), *adj.*

con•glom•er•a•teur (kən glom′ər ə tûr′, kəng-), *n.* a person who forms a corporate conglomerate by acquiring a group of companies, services, etc. Also, **con•glom•er•a•tor** (kən glom′ə rā′tər, kəng-). [1965–70; CONGLOMERATE + *-eur*, prob. extracted from ENTREPRENEUR]

con•glom•er•a•tion (kən glom′ə rā′shən, kəng-), *n.* **1.** the act of conglomerating; the state of being conglomerated. **2.** a cohering mass; cluster. **3.** a heterogeneous combination: *a conglomeration of ideas.* [1620–30; < LL *conglomerātiōn-* (s. of *conglomerātiō*), equiv. to *conglomerāt(us)* CONGLOMERATE + *-iōn-* -ION] **—con•glom•er•a•tive** (kən glom′ər ə tiv, -ə rā′tiv, kəng-), *adj.*

—Syn. 2, 3. agglomeration, aggregate, aggregation, conglomerate.

con•glom•er•a•tize (kən glom′ər ə tiz′, kəng-), *v.t., v.i.*, **-tized, -tiz•ing.** to form into or become a conglomerate. Also, *esp. Brit.*, **con•glom′er•a•tise′.** [CONGLOMERATE + -IZE] **—con•glom′er•a•ti•za′tion,** *n.*

con•glu•ti•nant (kən gloot′n ənt, kəng-), *adj. Med.* promoting the union of a wound's edges. [1820–30; < L *conglūtinant-*, s. of *conglūtināns*, prp. of *conglūtināre* to make cohere; see CONGLUTINATE]

con•glu•ti•nate (kən gloot′n āt′, kəng-), *v.,* **-nat•ed, -nat•ing,** *adj.* *—v.t., v.i.* **1.** to join or become joined with or as if with glue. *—adj.* **2.** glued together; adhering. [1375–1425; late ME < L *conglūtinātus* (ptp. of *conglūtināre*), equiv. to *con-* CON- + *glūtin-* (var. s. of *glūten*) GLUE (see GLUTEN, CLAY) + *-ātus* -ATE[1]] **—con•glu′ti•na′tion,** *n.* **—con•glu′ti•na′tive,** *adj.*

con•go (kong′gō), *n.* congou.

Con•go (kong′gō), *n.* **1. People's Republic of the,** a republic in central Africa, W of Zaire: formerly an overseas territory in French Equatorial Africa; now an independent member of the French Community. 1,300,020; 132,046 sq. mi. (341,999 sq. km). *Cap.:* Brazzaville. Formerly, **French Congo, Middle Congo. 2. Democratic Republic of the,** a former name of **Zaire** (def. 1). **3.** Also called **Zaire.** a river in central Africa, flowing in a great loop from SE Zaire to the Atlantic. ab. 3000 mi. (4800 km) long. Cf. **Zaire** (def. 2). **4.** Kongo.

Con′go col′or, *Chem.* any of a group of azo dyes derived from benzidine that will dye cotton and other vegetable fibers without the aid of a mordant. Also called **Con′go dye′.**

Con′go Free′ State′, a former name of **Zaire** (def. 1).

Con•go•lese (kong′gə lēz′, -lēs′), *adj., n., pl.* **-lese.** —*adj.* **1.** of or pertaining to the People's Republic of the Congo or the Congo region, its inhabitants, or their languages. —*n.* **2.** an inhabitant or native of the People's Republic of the Congo or of the Congo region. [1895–1900; < F *congolais,* irreg. formation; see -ESE]

Con′go red′, *Chem.* a water-soluble powder, $C_{32}H_{22}O_6N_6S_2Na_2$, one of the Congo colors that is not acid-fast or lightfast: used chiefly as a dye, biological stain, and chemical indicator. [1880–85]

con′go snake′, any of several eel-shaped salamanders, as the amphiuma or siren. Also called **con′go eel′.** [1825–35, *Amer.*]

con•gou (kong′gōō), *n.* a black tea from China. Also, **congo.** [1715–25; < dial. Chin (Xiamen), equiv. to Chin *gōngfū(-chá)* lit., effort (tea)]

con•grats (kən grats′, kəng-), *n., interj. Informal.* congratulations. [1880–85; by shortening]

con•grat•u•lant (kən grach′ə lənt *or, often,* -graj′-, kəng-), *adj.* **1.** expressing or conveying congratulation. —*n.* **2.** a person who congratulates. [1660–70; < L *congrātulant-* (s. of *congrātulāns,* prp. of *congrātulārī*), equiv. to *con-* CON- + *grātul-* (*grāt-,* s. of *grātus* pleasing + *-ul-* adj. suffix) + *-ant-* -ANT]

con•grat•u•late (kən grach′ə lāt′ *or, often,* -graj′-, kəng-), *v.t.,* **-lat•ed, -lat•ing. 1.** to express pleasure to (a person), as on a happy occasion: *They congratulated him on his marriage.* **2.** *Archaic.* to express sympathetic joy or satisfaction at (an event). **3.** *Obs.* to salute. [1540–50; < L *congrātulātus,* ptp. of *congrātulārī.* See CONGRATULANT, -ATE[1]] —**con•grat′u•la′tor,** *n.*

con•grat•u•la•tion (kən grach′ə lā′shən *or, often,* -graj′-, kəng-), *n.* **1.** the act of congratulating. **2. congratulations,** an expression of joy in the success or good fortune of another. —*interj.* **3. congratulations,** (used to express joy in the success or good fortune of another): *Congratulations! You have just won the lottery!* [1400–50; late ME < LL *congrātulātiōn-* (s. of *congrātulātiō*), equiv. to *congrātulāt(us)* (see CONGRATULATE) + *-iōn-* -ION] —**con•grat′u•la′tion•al,** *adj.*

con•grat•u•la•to•ry (kən grach′ə lə tôr′ē, -tōr′ē *or, often,* -graj′-, kəng-), *adj.* expressing or conveying congratulations: *a congratulatory telegram.* [1515–25; < ML *congrātulātōrius,* equiv. to L *congrātulā(rī)* (see CONGRATULATE) + *-tōrius* -TORY[1]]

con•gre•gant (kong′gri gənt), *n.* a person who is part of a congregation: *The voices of the congregants were raised in prayer.* [1885–90; CONGREG(ATE) + -ANT]

con•gre•gate (*v.* kong′gri gāt′; *adj.* kong′gri git, -gāt′), *v.,* **-gat•ed, -gat•ing,** *adj.* —*v.i.* **1.** to come together; assemble, esp. in large numbers: *People waiting for rooms congregated in the hotel lobby.* —*v.t.* **2.** to bring together in a crowd, body, or mass; assemble; collect. —*adj.* **3.** congregated; assembled. **4.** formed by collecting; collective. [1350–1400; ME (adj.) < L *congregātus* (ptp. of *congregāre* to flock together), equiv. to *con-* CON- + *greg-* (s. of *grex*) flock + *-ātus* -ATE[1]] —**con′gre•ga′tive,** *adj.* —**con′gre•ga′tive•ness,** *n.* —**con′gre•ga′tor,** *n.*
—**Syn. 1.** gather, collect, throng, cluster.

con′gregate hous′ing, a type of housing in which each individual or family has a private bedroom or living quarters but shares with other residents a common dining room, recreational room, or other facilities.

con•gre•ga•tion (kong′gri gā′shən), *n.* **1.** an assembly of persons brought together for common religious worship. **2.** the act of congregating or the state of being congregated. **3.** a gathered or assembled body; assemblage. **4.** an organization formed for the purpose of providing for worship of God, for religious education, and for other church activities; a local church society. **5.** the people of Israel. Ex. 12:3,6; Lev. 4:13. **6.** *New Testament.* the Christian church in general. **7.** *Rom. Cath. Ch.* **a.** a committee of cardinals or other ecclesiastics. **b.** a community of men or women, either with or without vows, observing a common rule. **8.** (at English universities) the general assembly of the doctors, fellows, etc. **9.** (in colonial North America) a parish, town, plantation, or other settlement. [1300–50; ME *congregacio(u)n* (< AF) < L *congregātiōn-* (s. of *congregātiō*); see CONGREGATE, -ION]

con•gre•ga•tion•al (kong′gri gā′shə nl), *adj.* **1.** of or pertaining to a congregation: *congregational singing.* **2.** (*cap.*) pertaining or adhering to a form of Protestant church government in which each local church acts as an independent, self-governing body, while maintaining fellowship with like congregations. [1570–80; CONGREGATION + -AL[1]] —**con′gre•ga′tion•al•ly,** *adv.*

con•gre•ga•tion•al•ism (kong′gri gā′shə nl iz′əm), *n.* **1.** a form of Protestant church government in which each local religious society is independent and self-governing. **2.** (*cap.*) the system of government and doctrine of Congregational churches. [1640–50; CONGREGATIONAL + -ISM] —**con′gre•ga′tion•al•ist,** *n., adj.*

con•gress (*n.* kong′gris; *v.* kən gres′, kəng-), *n.* **1.** (*cap.*) **a.** the national legislative body of the U.S., consisting of the Senate, or upper house, and the House of Representatives, or lower house, as a continuous institution. **b.** this body as it exists for a period of two years during which it has the same membership: *the 96th Congress.* **c.** a session of this body: *to speak in Congress.* **2.** the national legislative body of a nation, esp. of a republic. **3.** a formal meeting or assembly of representatives for the discussion, arrangement, or promotion of some matter of common interest. **4.** the act of coming together; an encounter; meeting. **5.** an association, esp. one composed of representatives of various organizations. **6.** familiar relations; dealings; intercourse. **7.** coitus; sexual intercourse. —*v.i.* **8.** to assemble together; meet in congress. [1350–1400 for earlier sense "body of attendants, following"; 1520–30 for current senses; ME < L *congressus* assembly, intercourse, meeting, equiv. to *congred(ī)* to approach, meet (*con-* CON- + *-gredī,* comb. form of *gradī* to step; cf. GRADE) + *-tus* suffix of v. action]
—**Syn. 3.** conference, council, convention.

CONCISE ETYMOLOGY KEY: <, descended or borrowed from; >, whence; b., blend of, blended; c., cognate with; cf., compare; deriv., derivative; equiv., equivalent; imit., imitative; obl., oblique; r., replacing; s., stem; sp., spelling, spelled; resp., respelling, respelled; trans., translation; ?, origin unknown; *, unattested; ‡, probably earlier than. See the full key inside the front cover.

con′gress boot′, a high shoe with elastic sides, worn by men in the U.S. in the late 19th and early 20th centuries. [1840–50, *Amer.*]

con•gres•sion•al (kən gresh′ə nl, kəng-), *adj.* **1.** of or pertaining to a congress. **2.** (*usually cap.*) of or pertaining to the Congress of the U.S.: *a Congressional committee.* [1685–95; < L *congressiōn-* (s. of *congressiō*) a coming together, equiv. to *congress(us)* (see CONGRESS) + *-iōn-* -ION + -AL[1]] —**con•gres′sion•al•ist,** *n.* —**con•gres′sion•al•ly,** *adv.*

Congres′sional dis′trict, *U.S. Govt.* one of a fixed number of districts into which a state is divided, each district electing one member to the national House of Representatives. Cf. **assembly district, Senatorial district.** [1805–15, *Amer.*]

Congres′sional Med′al of Hon′or. See **Medal of Honor.**

Congres′sional Rec′ord, the record of the proceedings of the U.S. Congress, with a transcript of the discussion, published daily by the government while Congress is in session. [1825–35, *Amer.*]

con•gress•man (kong′gris mən), *n., pl.* **-men.** (*often cap.*) a member of a congress, esp. of the U.S. House of Representatives. [1770–80, *Amer.*; CONGRESS + -MAN]
—**Usage.** See **-man.**

con•gress•man-at-large (kong′gris mən ət lärj′), *n., pl.* **con•gress•men-at-large** (kong′gris mən ət lärj′). a U.S. congressman who is elected from a state as a whole and not from a district. [1880–85, *Amer.*]

con•gress•mem•ber (kong′gris mem′bər), *n.* (*often cap.*) a member of a congress, esp. of the U.S. House of Representatives. [CONGRESS + MEMBER]

Con′gress of Indus′trial Organiza′tions, a federation of affiliated industrial labor unions, founded 1935 within the American Federation of Labor but independent of it 1938–55. *Abbr.:* C.I.O., CIO

Con′gress of Vien′na, an international conference (1814–15) held at Vienna after Napoleon's banishment to Elba, with Metternich as the dominant figure, aimed at territorial resettlement and restoration to power of the crowned heads of Europe.

con•gress•per•son (kong′gris pûr′sən), *n.* (*often cap.*) congressmember. [1970–75; CONGRESS(MAN) + -PERSON]
—**Usage.** See **-person.**

con•gress•wom•an (kong′gris wŏŏm′ən), *n., pl.* **-wom•en.** (*often cap.*) a female member of a congress, esp. of the U.S. House of Representatives. [1915–20; CONGRESS + -WOMAN]
—**Usage.** See **-woman.**

Con•greve (kon′grēv, kong′-), *n.* **1. William,** 1670–1729, English dramatist. **2. Sir William,** 1772–1828, English engineer and inventor.

con•gru•ence (kong′grōō əns, kən grōō′-, kəng-), *n.* **1.** the quality or state of agreeing or corresponding. **2.** *Math.* a relation between two numbers indicating that the numbers give the same remainder when divided by some given number. Cf. **residue** (def. 4b). [1400–50; late ME < L *congruentia,* deriv. of *congruent-* CONGRUENT; see -ENCE]

con•gru•en•cy (kong′grōō ən sē, kən grōō′-, kəng-), *n., pl.* **-cies.** congruence. [1485–95; < L *congruentia.* See CONGRUENCE, -CY]

con•gru•ent (kong′grōō ənt, kən grōō′-, kəng-), *adj.* **1.** agreeing; accordant; congruous. **2.** *Math.* of or pertaining to two numbers related by a congruence. **3.** *Geom.* coinciding at all points when superimposed: *congruent triangles.* [1375–1425; late ME < L *congruent-* (s. of *congruēns,* prp. of *congruere* to come together, fit in, agree), equiv. to *con-* CON- + *-gru-* base of uncert. meaning (attested only in this v. and *ingruere* to fall upon) + *-ent-* -ENT] —**con′gru•ent•ly,** *adv.*

con•gru•i•ty (kən grōō′i tē, kon-, kəng-, kong-), *n., pl.* **-ties. 1.** the state or quality of being congruous; harmony; appropriateness: *a congruity of ideas.* **2.** the state or quality of being geometrically congruent. **3.** a point of agreement. **4.** *Scholasticism.* merit bestowed as a divine gift rather than earned. Cf. **condignity.** [1350–1400; ME *congruite* < MF < LL *congruitāt-* (s. of *congruitās*), equiv. to L *congru(us)* CONGRUOUS + *-itāt-* -ITY]

con•gru•ous (kong′grōō əs), *adj.* **1.** exhibiting harmony of parts. **2.** appropriate or fitting. [1590–1600; < L *congruus,* equiv. to *con-* CON- + *gru-* (see CONGRUENT) + *-us* -OUS] —**con′gru•ous•ly,** *adv.* —**con′gru•ous•ness,** *n.*

con•ic (kon′ik), *adj.* **1.** Also, **con′i•cal.** having the form of, resembling, or pertaining to a cone. —*n.* **2.** *Geom.* See **conic section.** [1560–70; < Gk *kōnikós,* equiv. to *kôn(os)* CONE + *-ikos* -IC] —**con′i•cal•ly,** *adv.* —**co•nic•i•ty** (kō nis′i tē), **con′i•cal•ness,** *n.*

con′ical pen′dulum, *Horol.* a clock pendulum oscillating in a circle rather than in a straight line.

con•i•coid (kon′i koid′, kō′ni-), *n. Geom.* a quadric, esp. a hyperboloid, paraboloid, or ellipsoid. [1860–65; CONIC + -OID]

con′ic projec′tion, *Cartog.* a map projection based on the concept of projecting the earth's surface on a conical surface, which is then unrolled to a plane surface.

con•ics (kon′iks), *n.* (*used with a singular v.*) the branch of geometry that deals with conic sections. [see CONIC, -ICS]

con′ic sec′tion, *Geom.* a curve formed by the intersection of a plane with a right circular cone; an ellipse, a circle, a parabola, or a hyperbola. Also called **conic.** [1655–65]

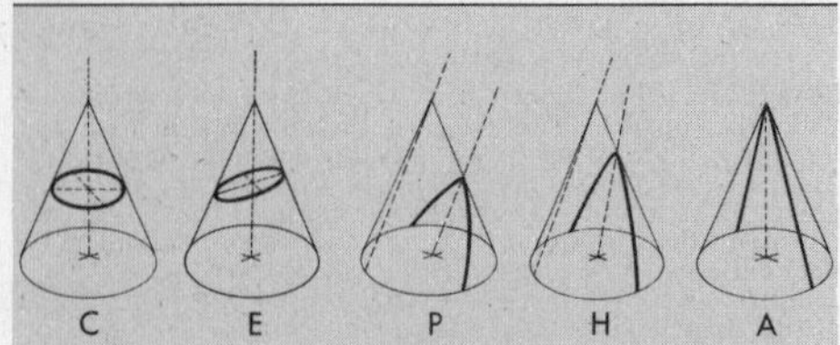

conic sections
the two principal forms are E, ellipse, and H, hyperbola; P, parabola, is an intermediate case; C, circle, is an ellipse perpendicular to the axis of the cone; A, angle, is a hyperbola whose axis coincides with that of the cone

co•nid•i•o•phore (kō nid′ē ə fôr′, -fōr′, kə-), *n. Bot.* (in fungi) a special stalk or branch of the mycelium, bearing conidia. [1880–85; *conidio-* (comb. form of CONIDIUM) + -PHORE] —**co•nid•i•oph•o•rous** (kə nid′ē of′ər əs), *adj.*

co•nid•i•um (kō nid′ē əm, kə-), *n., pl.* **-nid•i•a** (-nid′ē ə). *Bot.* (in fungi) an asexual spore formed by abstriction at the top of a hyphal branch. [1865–70; < Gk *kó-n(is)* dust (akin to INCINERATE) + -IDIUM] —**co•nid′i•al, co•nid′i•an,** *adj.*

co•ni•fer (kō′nə fər, kon′ə-), *n.* **1.** any of numerous, chiefly evergreen trees or shrubs of the class Coniferinae (or group Coniferales), including the pine, fir, spruce, and other cone-bearing trees and shrubs, and also the yews and their allies that bear drupelike seeds. **2.** a plant producing naked seeds in cones, or single naked seeds as in yews, but with pollen always borne in cones. [1350–1400; ME *conefere* < L *cōnifer* coniferous, equiv. to *cōn(us)* CONE + *-i-* + *-fer* -FER]

co•nif•er•in (kō nif′ər in, kə-), *n. Chem.* a grayish-white, water-soluble powder, $C_{16}H_{22}O_8{\cdot}2H_2O$, obtained from the cambium of coniferous trees and from asparagus: used chiefly in the manufacture of vanillin. [1865–70; CONIFER + -IN[2]]

co•nif•er•ous (kō nif′ər əs, kə-), *adj. Bot.* belonging or pertaining to the conifers. Cf. **conifer** (def. 1). [1655–65; see CONIFER, -OUS]

co•ni•ine (kō′nē ēn′, -in, -nēn), *n.* a volatile, highly poisonous alkaloid, $C_8H_{17}N$, constituting the active principle of the poison hemlock. Also, **co•nin** (kō′nin), **co•nine** (kō′nēn, -nin). [1825–35; CONI(UM) + -INE[2]]

co•ni•ros•tral (kō′ni ros′trəl, kon′i-), *adj. Ornith.* having a conical bill, as a finch. [1830–40; *coni-* (comb. form of L *cōnus* CONE) + ROSTRAL] —**co•ni•ros•ter** (kō′ni ros′tər, kon′i-), *n.*

co•ni•um (kō′nē əm), *n.* the poison hemlock, *Conium maculatum.* [1860–65; < NL; LL < Gk *kṓneion*]

conj., 1. conjugation. **2.** conjunction. **3.** conjunctive.

con•jec•tur•al (kən jek′chər əl), *adj.* **1.** of, of the nature of, or involving conjecture; problematical: *Theories about the extinction of dinosaurs are highly conjectural.* **2.** given to making conjectures: *a conjectural thinker.* [1545–55; < L *conjectūrālis,* equiv. to *conjectūr(a)* CONJECTURE + *-ālis* -AL[1]] —**con•jec′tur•al•ly,** *adv.*
—**Syn. 1.** speculative, theoretical, doubtful.

con•jec•ture (kən jek′chər), *n., v.,* **-tured, -tur•ing.** —*n.* **1.** the formation or expression of an opinion or theory without sufficient evidence for proof. **2.** an opinion or theory so formed or expressed; guess; speculation. **3.** *Obs.* the interpretation of signs or omens. —*v.t.* **4.** to conclude or suppose from grounds or evidence insufficient to ensure reliability. —*v.i.* **5.** to form conjectures. [1350–1400; (n.) ME < L *conjectūra* (< MF) inferring, reasoning, equiv. to *conject(us)* ptp. of *conjicere* to throw together, form a conclusion (*con-* CON- + *-jicere,* comb. form of *jacere* to throw) + *-ūra* -URE; (v.) late ME *conjecturen* (< MF) < LL *conjectūrāre,* deriv. of the n.] —**con•jec′tur•a•ble,** *adj.* —**con•jec′tur•a•bly,** *adv.* —**con•jec′tur•er,** *n.*
—**Syn. 2.** surmise, inference, supposition, theory, hypothesis. **4.** surmise, suppose, presume. See **guess.**

con′ job′, *Informal.* **1.** an act or instance of duping or swindling. **2.** an act or instance of lying or talking glibly to convince others or get one's way. [1950–55]

con•join (kən join′), *v.t., v.i.* **1.** to join together; unite; combine; associate. **2.** *Gram.* to join as coordinate elements, esp. as coordinate clauses. [1325–75; ME *conjoignen* < AF, MF *conjoign-* (s. of *conjoindre*) < L *conjungere.* See CON-, JOIN] —**con•join′er,** *n.*

con•joined (kən joind′), *adj.* **1.** joined together, united, or linked. **2.** *Numis.* accolated. [1560–70; CONJOIN + -ED[2]] —**con•join•ed•ly** (kən joi′nid lē, -joind′lē), *adv.*

con•joint (kən joint′), *adj.* **1.** joined together; united; combined; associated. **2.** pertaining to or formed by two or more in combination; joint. —*n.* **3. conjoints,** husband and wife, esp. as joint owners of property. [1350–1400; ME < MF < L *conjunctus* (ptp. of *conjungere*). See CON-, JOINT] —**con•joint′ly,** *adv.* —**con•joint′ness,** *n.*

con•ju•gal (kon′jə gəl), *adj.* **1.** of, pertaining to, or characteristic of marriage: *conjugal vows.* **2.** pertaining to the relation of husband and wife. [1535–45; < L *conjugālis,* equiv. to *con-* CON- + *jug(um)* YOKE + *-ālis* -AL[1]] —**con′ju•gal′i•ty,** *n.* —**con′ju•gal•ly,** *adv.*
—**Syn. 1.** matrimonial, nuptial, connubial. **2.** marital.

con′jugal rights′, the sexual rights and privileges conferred on husband and wife by the marriage bond. [1890–95]

con·ju·gant (kon′jə gənt), *n. Biol.* either of two organisms participating in the process of conjugation. [1905–10; CONJUG(ATE) + -ANT]

con·ju·gate (*v.* kon′jə gāt′; *adj., n.* kon′jə git, -gāt′), *v.,* **-gat·ed, -gat·ing,** *adj., n.* —*v.t.* **1.** *Gram.* **a.** to inflect (a verb). **b.** to recite or display all or some subsets of the inflected forms of (a verb), in a fixed order: *One conjugates the present tense of the verb "be" as "I am, you are, he is, we are, you are, they are."* **2.** to join together, esp. in marriage. —*v.i.* **3.** *Biol.* to unite; to undergo conjugation. **4.** *Gram.* to be characterized by conjugation: *The Latin verb* esse *does not conjugate in the passive voice.* —*adj.* **5.** joined together, esp. in a pair or pairs; coupled. **6.** *Bot.* (of a pinnate leaf) having only one pair of leaflets. **7.** *Gram.* (of words) having a common derivation. **8.** *Bibliog.* (of two leaves in a book) forming one sheet. **9.** *Math.* **a.** (of two points, lines, etc.) so related as to be interchangeable in the enunciation of certain properties. **b.** (of an element) so related to a second element of a group that there exists a third element of the group that, multiplying one element on the right and the other element on the left, results in equal elements. **c.** (of two complex numbers) differing only in the sign of the imaginary part. **10.** *Chem.* **a.** of or noting two or more liquids in equilibrium with one another. **b.** (of an acid and a base) related by the loss or gain of a proton: *NH_3 is a base conjugate to NH_4^+. NH_4^+ is an acid conjugate to NH_3.* **c.** Also, **con′ju·gat′ed.** (of an organic compound) containing two or more double bonds each separated from the other by a single bond. —*n.* **11.** one of a group of conjugate words. **12.** *Math.* **a.** either of two conjugate points, lines, etc. **b.** Also called **con′jugate com′plex num′ber.** either of a pair of complex numbers of the type $a + bi$ and $a - bi$, where a and b are real numbers and i is imaginary. [1425–75; late ME (adj.) < L *conjugātus* (ptp. of *conjugāre* to yoke together), equiv. to *con-* CON- + *jug(um)* YOKE + *-ātus* -ATE[1]] —**con·ju·ga·ble** (kon′jə gə bəl), *adj.* —**con′ju·ga·bly,** *adv.* —**con′ju·ga′tive,** *adj.* —**con′ju·ga′tor,** *n.*

con′jugate ax′is, *Geom.* **1.** the axis of a hyperbola perpendicular to the transverse axis at a point equidistant from the foci. **2.** the segment of this axis equal to one side of a rectangle that has its other side equal to the transverse axis and diagonals that are along the asymptotes of the hyperbola. [1875–80]

con′jugated pro′tein, *Biochem.* a complex protein, as a lipoprotein or metalloprotein, combining amino acids with other substances (contrasted with *simple protein*). [1920–25]

con′jugate num′bers, *Math.* the set of roots of an algebraic equation that cannot be factored. [1905–10]

con′jugate solu′tion, *Chem.* a system of liquids, each partially miscible in the other, existing with a common interface, consisting of a saturated solution of one in the other. [1905–10]

con·ju·ga·tion (kon′jə gā′shən), *n.* **1.** *Gram.* **a.** the inflection of verbs. **b.** the whole set of inflected forms of a verb or the recital or display thereof in a fixed order: *The conjugation of the Latin verb* amo *begins* amō, amas, amat. **c.** a class of verbs having similar sets of inflected forms: *the Latin second conjugation.* **2.** an act of joining: *a conjugation of related ideas.* **3.** the state of being joined together; union; conjunction. **4.** *Biol.* **a.** the reproductive process in ciliate protozoans in which two organisms of different mating types exchange nuclear material through a temporary area of fusion. **b.** temporary union or permanent fusion as a form of sexual reproduction in certain algae and fungi, the male gametes of one organism uniting with female gametes of the other. **c.** a temporary union of two bacteria, in *Escherichia* and related groups, in which genetic material is transferred by migration of a plasmid, either solitary or as part of a chromosome, from one bacterium, the donor, to the other, the recipient; sometimes also including the transfer of resistance to antibiotics. [1400–50; late ME *conjugacion* (< AF) < LL *conjugātiōn-* (s. of *conjugātiō*), equiv. to *conjugāt(us)* (see CONJUGATE) + *-iōn-* -ION] —**con′ju·ga′tion·al,** *adj.* —**con′ju·ga′tion·al·ly,** *adv.*

con·junct (*adj.* kən jungkt′, kon′jungkt; *n.* kon′jungkt), *adj.* **1.** bound in close association; conjoined; combined; united: *conjunct ideas; conjunct influences.* **2.** formed by conjunction. **3.** *Gram.* **a.** occurring only in combination with an immediately preceding or following form of a particular class, and constituting with this form a single phonetic unit, as *'ll* in English *he'll,* and *n't* in *isn't.* **b.** (of a pronoun) having enclitic or proclitic form and occurring with a verb, as French *me, le, se.* **c.** pertaining to a word so characterized. **4.** *Music.* progressing melodically by intervals of a second: *conjunct motion of an ascending scale.* —*n.* **5.** *Logic.* either of the propositions in a conjunction. **6.** *Gram.* a conjunctive adverb. [1425–75; late ME (ptp.) < L *conjunctus* joined, connected (ptp. of *conjungere* to join together), equiv. to *con-* CON- + *junc-* (var. s. of *jungere* to join) + *-tus* ptp. suffix] —**con·junct′ly,** *adv.*

con·junc·tion (kən jungk′shən), *n.* **1.** *Gram.* **a.** any member of a small class of words distinguished in many languages by their function as connectors between words, phrases, clauses, or sentences, as *and, because, but, however.* **b.** any other word or expression of similar function, as *in any case.* **2.** the act of conjoining; combination. **3.** the state of being conjoined; union; association: *The police, in conjunction with the army, established order.* **4.** a combination of events or circumstances. **5.** *Logic.* **a.** a compound proposition that is true if and only if all of its component propositions are true. **b.** the relation among the components of such a proposition, usually expressed by AND or & or •. **6.** *Astron.* **a.** the coincidence of two or more heavenly bodies at the same celestial longitude. **b.** the state of two or more such coinciding heavenly bodies. **7.** *Astrol.* the coincidence of two or more heavenly bodies at the same celestial longitude, characterized by a unification of the planetary energies; an astrological aspect. [1350–1400; ME *conjunccio(u)n* (< AF) < L *conjunctiōn-* (s. of *conjunctiō*). See CONJUNCT, -ION] —**con·junc′tion·al,** *adj.* —**con·junc′tion·al·ly,** *adv.*
—**Syn. 2.** joining, meeting, associating.

con·junc·ti·va (kon′jungk tī′və), *n., pl.* **-vas, -vae** (-vē). *Anat.* the mucous membrane that lines the exposed portion of the eyeball and inner surface of the eyelids. See diag. under **eye.** [1350–1400; ME; short for ML *membrāna conjunctiva* conjunctive membrane; see CONJUNCTIVE] —**con′junc·ti′val,** *adj.*

con·junc·tive (kən jungk′tiv), *adj.* **1.** serving to connect; connective: *conjunctive tissue.* **2.** conjoined; joint: *a conjunctive action.* **3.** *Gram.* **a.** (of a mode) subjunctive. **b.** (of a pronoun) conjunct. **c.** of the nature of a conjunction. **d.** (of an adverb) serving to connect two clauses or sentences, as *however* or *furthermore.* **4.** *Logic.* characterizing propositions that are conjunctions. —*n.* **5.** *Gram.* a conjunctive word; a conjunction. [1400–50; late ME *conjunctif* < LL *conjunctīvus.* See CONJUNCT, -IVE] —**con·junc′tive·ly,** *adv.*

con·junc·ti·vi·tis (kən jungk′tə vī′tis), *n. Ophthalm.* inflammation of the conjunctiva. [1825–35; CONJUNCTIV(A) + -ITIS]

con·junc·ture (kən jungk′chər), *n.* **1.** a combination of circumstances; a particular state of affairs. **2.** a critical state of affairs; crisis. **3.** conjunction; joining. [1595–1605; CONJUNCT + -URE] —**con·junc′tur·al,** *adj.*

con·ju·ra·tion (kon′jə rā′shən), *n.* **1.** the act of calling on or invoking a sacred name. **2.** an incantation; magical charm. **3.** supernatural accomplishment by invocation or spell. **4.** the practice of legerdemain. **5.** supplication; solemn entreaty. [1350–1400; ME *conjuracio(u)n* (< AF) < L *conjūrātiōn-* (s. of *conjūrātiō*), equiv. to *conjūrāt(us),* ptp. of *conjūrāre* to swear together (*con-* CON- + *jūr-* (s. of *jūs*) right, justice, duty + *-ātus* -ATE[1]) + *-iōn-* -ION]

con·jur·a·tor (kon′jə rā′tər), *n.* **1.** a person who practices conjuration. **2.** *Law.* a conspirator. [1400–50; late ME (< AF) < ML, equiv. to L *conjūrā(re)* to CONJURE + *-tor* -TOR]

con·jure (kon′jər, kun′- *for 1–5, 8–10, 12;* kən jŏŏr′ *for 6, 7, 11*), *v.,* **-jured, -jur·ing,** *n.* —*v.t.* **1.** to affect or influence by or as if by invocation or spell. **2.** to effect, produce, bring, etc., by or as by magic: *to conjure a miracle.* **3.** to call upon or command (a devil or spirit) by invocation or spell. **4.** to call or bring into existence by or as if by magic (usually fol. by *up*): *She seemed to have conjured up the person she was talking about.* **5.** to bring to mind; recall (usually fol. by *up*): *to conjure up the past.* **6.** to appeal to solemnly or earnestly: *I conjure you to hear my plea.* **7.** *Obs.* to charge solemnly. —*v.i.* **8.** to call upon or command a devil or spirit by invocation or spell. **9.** to practice magic. **10.** to practice legerdemain. **11.** *Obs.* to conspire. —*n.* **12.** *Chiefly Southern U.S.* an act or instance of witchcraft or voodoo, esp. a spell. [1250–1300; ME *conjuren* < AF, OF *conjurer* < L *conjūrāre,* equiv. to *con-* CON- + *jūrāre* to swear, deriv. of *jūs* law; cf. JURY[1], JUSTICE]
—**Syn. 3.** summon, raise, invoke.

con′jure man′ (kon′jər, kun′-), (in the southern U.S. and the West Indies) a conjurer; witch doctor. [1905–10, *Amer.*]

con·jur·er (kon′jər ər, kun′- *for 1, 2;* kən jŏŏr′ər *for 3*), *n.* **1.** a person who conjures spirits or practices magic; magician. **2.** a person who practices legerdemain; juggler. **3.** a person who solemnly charges or entreats. Also, **con′ju·ror.** [1300–1350; ME; see CONJURE, -ER[1]]

conk[1] (kongk, kôngk), *Slang.* —*n.* **1.** the head. **2.** a blow on the head. **3.** *Brit.* the nose. —*v.t.* **4.** to hit or strike on the head. [1805–15; of obscure orig.]

conk[2] (kongk, kôngk), *v.i. Slang.* **1.** to break or fail, as a machine or engine (often fol. by *out*): *The engine conked out halfway there.* **2.** to slow down or stop; lose energy (often fol. by *out*). **3.** to go to sleep (usually fol. by *off* or *out*). **4.** to lose consciousness; faint (usually fol. by *out*). **5.** to die (usually fol. by *out*). [1915–20; perh. of imit. orig.]

conk[3] (kongk, kôngk), *n. Mycol.* the shelflike fruiting body of certain wood-decaying fungi; bracket. [1850–55, *Amer.*; of obscure orig.] —**conk′y,** *adj.*

conk[4] (kongk, kôngk), *Slang.* —*n.* **1.** a method of chemically straightening the hair. **2.** a hairstyle in which the hair has been chemically straightened and sometimes set into waves. —*v.t.* **3.** to straighten (kinky hair) by the use of chemicals: *to have one's hair conked.* Also, **process.** [prob. shortening and alter. of *congolene,* alleged to be the name of a hair straightener made from Congo copal]

conk·er (kong′kər, kông′-), *n. Brit. Informal.* **1.** a horse chestnut. **2.** the hollowed-out shell of a horse chestnut. **3. conkers,** a game in which a child swings a horse chestnut on a string in an attempt to break that of another player. [1840–50; prob. orig. CONQUER; cf. *conquering* a game played with snail shells (the name of the game presumably later transferred to the playing pieces)]

Conk·ling (kong′kling), *n.* **Roscoe,** 1829–88, U.S. lawyer and politician: senator 1867–81.

con mae·stà (kon mī stä′, kōn; *It.* kôn mä es tä′), majestically (used as a musical direction). [< It: lit., with majesty]

con′ man′, *Slang.* See **confidence man.**

con mo·to (kon mō′tō, kōn; *It.* kôn mô′tô), with spirited drive; animatedly (used as a musical direction). [1890–95; < It: with animation]

conn (kon), *v.t.* **1.** con[3] (def. 1). —*n.* **2.** responsibility for the steering of a ship. **3.** con[3] (defs. 2, 3). [1800–10]

Conn., Connecticut (def. 1).

Con·nacht (*Irish.* kon′əKHt, -ət), *n.* Irish name of **Connaught.**

con·nate (kon′āt), *adj.* **1.** existing in a person or thing from birth or origin; inborn: *a connate sense of right and wrong.* **2.** associated in birth or origin. **3.** allied or agreeing in nature; cognate. **4.** *Anat.* firmly united; fused. **5.** *Bot.* congenitally joined, as leaves. **6.** *Geol.* trapped in sediment at the time the sediment was deposited: *connate water.* [1635–45; < LL *connātus* (ptp. of *connāscī* to be born at the same time with), equiv. to L *con-* CON- + *nā-* (short s. of *nāscī*) + *-tus* ptp. suffix (see NASCENT)] —**con′nate·ly,** *adv.* —**con′nate·ness,** *n.* —**con·na·tion** (kə nā′shən), *n.*

con·nat·u·ral (kə nach′ər əl, -nach′rəl), *adj.* **1.** belonging to a person or thing by nature or from birth or origin; inborn. **2.** of the same or a similar nature. [1585–95; < ML *connātūrālis,* equiv. to L *con-* CON- + *nātūrālis* NATURAL] —**con·nat′u·ral·ly,** *adv.* —**con·nat′u·ral′i·ty, con·nat′u·ral·ness,** *n.*

Con·naught (kon′ôt), *n.* a province in the NW Republic of Ireland. 423,915; 6610 sq. mi. (17,120 sq. km). Irish, **Connacht.**

Con·ne·aut (kon′ē ot′), *n.* a city in NE Ohio. 13,835.

con·nect (kə nekt′), *v.t.* **1.** to join, link, or fasten together; unite or bind: *to connect the two cities by a bridge; Communication satellites connect the local stations into a network.* **2.** to establish communication between; put in communication: *Operator, will you please connect me with Mr. Jones?* **3.** to have as an accompanying or associated feature: *pleasures connected with music.* **4.** to cause to be associated, as in a personal or business relationship: *to connect oneself with a group of like-minded persons; Our bank is connected with major foreign banks.* **5.** to associate mentally or emotionally: *She connects all telegrams with bad news.* **6.** to link to an electrical or communications system; hook up: *to connect a telephone.* —*v.i.* **7.** to become connected; join or unite: *These two parts connect at the sides.* **8.** (of trains, buses, etc.) to run so as to make connections (often fol. by *with*): *This bus connects with a northbound bus.* **9.** *Informal.* to have or establish successful communication; make contact: *I connected with two new clients today.* **10.** *Informal.* to relate to or be in harmony with another person, one's work, etc.: *We knew each other well but never connected.* **11.** *Slang.* (of an addict or drug dealer) to make direct contact for the illegal sale or purchase of narcotics. **12.** *Sports.* to hit successfully or solidly: *The batter connected for a home run. The boxer connected with a right.* —*adj.* **13.** of or pertaining to a connection or connections: *connect charges for a new cable television channel.* [1400–50; late ME < L *connectere,* equiv. to *con-* CON- + *nectere* to tie; see NEXUS] —**con·nect′i·ble, con·nect′a·ble,** *adj.* —**con·nect′i·bil′i·ty, con·nect′a·bil′i·ty,** *n.*
—**Syn. 1.** See **join.** —**Ant. 1.** divide. **4.** dissociate.

con·nect·ed (kə nek′tid), *adj.* **1.** united, joined, or linked. **2.** having a connection. **3.** joined together in sequence; linked coherently: *connected ideas.* **4.** related by family ties. **5.** having social or professional relationships, esp. with influential or powerful persons. **6.** *Math.* pertaining to a set for which no cover exists, consisting of two open sets whose intersections with the given set are disjoint and nonempty. [1705–15; CONNECT + -ED[2]] —**con·nect′ed·ly,** *adv.* —**con·nect′ed·ness,** *n.*

con·nect·er (kə nek′tər), *n.* connector. [CONNECT + -ER[1]]

Con·nect·i·cut (kə net′i kət), *n.* **1.** a state in the NE United States. 3,107,576; 5009 sq. mi. (12,975 sq. km). *Cap.:* Hartford. *Abbr.:* Conn., Ct., CT (for use with zip code). **2.** a river flowing S from N New Hampshire along the boundary between New Hampshire and Vermont and then through Massachusetts and Connecticut into Long Island Sound. 407 mi. (655 km) long.

Connect′icut chest′, *Furniture.* a chest made in Connecticut in the late 17th and early 18th centuries, having three front panels of which the center panel has a conventional sunflower design in low relief and the end panels have tulip designs. Also called **sunflower chest.**

Connect′icut Com′promise, *Amer. Hist.* a compromise adopted at the Constitutional Convention, providing the states with equal representation in the Senate and proportional representation in the House of Representatives. Cf. **New Jersey plan, Virginia plan.**

Connect′icut war′bler, a North American wood warbler, *Oporornis agilis,* olive-green above with a gray head and throat and yellow below. [1805–15, *Amer.*]

Connect′icut Yan′kee in King′ Ar′thur's Court′, A, a novel (1889) by Mark Twain.

connec′ting rod′, *Mach.* a rod or link for transmitting motion and force between a rotating and a reciprocating part, as between a piston and a crankshaft. See diag. under **piston.** [1830–40]

con·nec·tion (kə nek′shən), *n.* **1.** the act or state of connecting. **2.** the state of being connected: *the connec-*

CONCISE PRONUNCIATION KEY: act, cāpe, dâre, pärt; set, ēqual; *if,* īce; ox, ōver, ôrder, oil, bŏŏk, bōōt, out; up, ûrge; child; sing; shoe; thin, *th*at; zh as in *treasure.* ə = *a* as in *alone, e* as in *system, i* as in *easily, o* as in *gallop, u* as in *circus;* ′ as in *fire* (fī′r), *hour* (ou′r). l and n can serve as syllabic consonants, as in *cradle* (krād′l), and *button* (but′n). See the full key inside the front cover.

tion between cause and effect. **3.** anything that connects; connecting part; link; bond: *an electrical connection.* **4.** association; relationship: *the connection between crime and poverty; no connection with any other firm of the same name.* **5.** a circle of friends or associates or a member of such a circle. **6.** association with or development of something observed, imagined, discussed, etc.: *to make a connection between the smell of smoke and the presence of fire; I have a few thoughts in connection with your last remarks.* **7.** contextual relation; context, as of a word. **8.** the meeting of trains, planes, etc., for transfer of passengers: *There are good connections between buses in Chicago.* **9.** Often, **connections.** a transfer by a passenger from one conveyance to another: *to miss connections.* **10.** a specific vehicle, airplane, ship, etc., boarded in making connections: *My connection for Hartford is the 10:58.* **11.** a relative, esp. by marriage or distant blood relationship. **12.** *Slang.* a person who sells drugs directly to addicts. **13.** a source of supply for goods, material, etc., that is scarce, difficult, or illegal to obtain: *a connection to obtain guns and ammunition for the rebels.* **14.** a group of persons connected as by political or religious ties. **15.** Usually, **connections.** associates, relations, acquaintances, or friends, esp. representing or having some influence or power: *European connections; good connections in Congress.* **16.** a religious denomination: *the Methodist connection.* **17.** a channel of communication: *a bad telephone connection.* **18.** sexual intercourse. Also, *Brit.,* **connexion.** [1350–1400; var. sp. of *connexion;* ME *conneccioun, connexioun* (< MF) < L *connexiōn-* (s. of *connexiō*), equiv. to *connex(us)* (ptp. of *connectere* to CONNECT) + *-iōn-* -ION] —**con·nec′tion·al,** *adj.*
—**Syn. 1.** junction, conjunction, union. **3.** tie, coupling, yoke. **5.** affiliation, alliance. **11.** relation.

con·nec·tion·ism (kə nek′shə niz′əm), *n. Psychol.* the theory that all mental processes can be described as the operation of inherited or acquired bonds between stimulus and response. [CONNECTION + -ISM]

con·nec·tive (kə nek′tiv), *adj.* **1.** serving or tending to connect: *connective remarks between chapters.* —*n.* **2.** something that connects. **3.** *Gram.* a word used to connect words, phrases, clauses, and sentences, as a conjunction. **4.** *Bot.* the tissue joining the two cells of the anther. [1645–55; CONNECT + -IVE] —**con·nec′tive·ly,** *adv.* —**con·nec·tiv·i·ty** (kon′ek tiv′i tē), *n.*

connec′tive tis′sue, *Anat.* a tissue, usually of mesoblastic origin, that connects, supports, or surrounds other tissues, organs, etc. [1880–85]

connec′tive tis′sue disease′. See **collagen disease.**

con·nec·tor (kə nek′tər), *n.* **1.** a person or thing that connects. **2.** any of various devices for connecting one object to another. **3.** (formerly) a person who couples railroad cars. Also, **connecter.** [1785–95; CONNECT + -OR^2]

Con·nells·ville (kon′lz vil′), *n.* a town in SW Pennsylvania. 10,319.

Con·nel·ly (kon′l ē), *n.* **Marc**(**us Cook**), 1890–1980, U.S. dramatist.

Con·ners·ville (kon′ərz vil′), *n.* a city in E Indiana. 17,023.

con·nex (kon′eks), *n.* a large metal cargo container used by the U.S. Army for shipping supplies, as to overseas bases. Also called **con′nex box′.** [appar. resp. of *conex,* from *con(tainer for) ex(port)*]

con′nex′ion (kə nek′shən), *n. Brit.* connection. —**con·nex′ion·al,** *adj.*

Con·nie (kon′ē), *n.* **1.** a female given name, form of **Constance. 2.** a male given name, form of **Conrad** or **Cornelius.**

conn′ing tow′er (kon′ing), **1.** the low observation tower of a submarine, constituting the main entrance to the interior. **2.** the low, dome-shaped, armored pilothouse of a warship. [1865–70; CON^3 + -ING^2]

con·nip·tion (kə nip′shən), *n.* Often, **conniptions.** *Informal.* a fit of hysterical excitement or anger. Also called **connip′tion fit′.** [1825–35, *Amer.;* orig. uncert.]

con·niv·ance (kə nī′vəns), *n.* **1.** the act of conniving. **2.** *Law.* **a.** tacit encouragement or assent (without participation) to wrongdoing by another. **b.** the consent by a person to a spouse's conduct, esp. adultery, that is later made the basis of a divorce proceeding or other complaint. Also, **con·niv′ence.** [1590–1600; earlier *connivence* (< F) < L *connīventia.* See CONNIVE, -ENCE, -ANCE]

con·nive (kə nīv′), *v.i.,* **-nived, -niv·ing. 1.** to cooperate secretly; conspire (often fol. by *with*): *They connived to take over the business.* **2.** to avoid noticing something that one is expected to oppose or condemn; give aid to wrongdoing by forbearing to act or speak (usually fol. by *at*): *The policeman connived at traffic violations.* **3.** to be indulgent toward something others oppose or criticize (usually fol. by *at*): *to connive at childlike exaggerations.* [1595–1605; (< F *conniver*) < L *co(n)nīvēre* to close the eyes in sleep, turn a blind eye, equiv. to *con-* CON- + *-nīvēre,* akin to *nictāre* to blink (cf. NICTITATE)] —**con·niv′er,** *n.* —**con·niv′ing·ly,** *adv.*
—**Syn. 1.** plan, plot, collude.

con·niv·ent (kə nī′vənt), *adj. Bot., Zool.* converging, as petals. [1635–45; < L *connīvent-* (s. of *connīvēns,* prp. of *connīvēre*). See CONNIVE, -ENT]

con·niv·er·y (kə nī′və rē), *n.* the practice of conniving. [CONNIVE + -ERY]

con·nois·seur (kon′ə sûr′, -sŏŏr′), *n.* **1.** a person who is especially competent to pass critical judgments in an art, particularly one of the fine arts, or in matters of taste: *a connoisseur of modern art.* **2.** a discerning judge of the best in any field: *a connoisseur of horses.* [1705–15; < F; OF *conoiseor* < L *cognōscitōr-* (s. of *cognōscitor*) knower. See COGNOSCIBLE, -TOR] —**con′nois·seur′ship,** *n.*
—**Syn.** critic, aesthete.

Con·nol·ly (kon′l ē), *n.* **Maureen** (*Maureen Catherine Connolly Brinker*) ("*Little Mo*"), 1934–69, U.S. tennis player.

Con·nor (kon′ər), *n.* **Ralph** (*Charles William Gordon*), 1860–1937, Canadian novelist and clergyman.

con·no·ta·tion (kon′ə tā′shən), *n.* **1.** an act or instance of connoting. **2.** the associated or secondary meaning of a word or expression in addition to its explicit or primary meaning: *A possible connotation of "home" is "a place of warmth, comfort, and affection."* Cf. **denotation** (def. 1). **3.** *Logic.* the set of attributes constituting the meaning of a term and thus determining the range of objects to which that term may be applied; comprehension; intension. [1375–1425 for earlier sense; 1525–35 for current senses; late ME *connotacion* < ML *connotātiōn-* (s. of *connotātiō*), equiv. to *connotāt(us)* (ptp. of *connotāre* to CONNOTE; see -ATE^1) + *-iōn-* -ION] —**con·no·ta·tive** (kon′ə tā′tiv, kə nō′tə-), **con·no′tive,** *adj.* —**con′no·ta′tive·ly, con·no′tive·ly,** *adv.*
—**Syn. 2.** undertone, implication, import.

con·note (kə nōt′), *v.,* **-not·ed, -not·ing.** —*v.t.* **1.** to signify or suggest (certain meanings, ideas, etc.) in addition to the explicit or primary meaning: *The word "fireplace" often connotes hospitality, warm comfort, etc.* **2.** to involve as a condition or accompaniment: *Injury connotes pain.* —*v.i.* **3.** to have significance only by association, as with another word: *Adjectives can only connote, nouns can denote.* [1645–55; < ML *connotāre,* equiv. to L *con-* CON- + *notāre* to NOTE]
—**Syn. 1.** intimate, imply.

con·nu·bi·al (kə nōō′bē əl, -nyōō′-), *adj.* of marriage or wedlock; matrimonial; conjugal: *connubial love.* [1650–60; < ML *connūbiālis,* L *cōnūbiālis,* equiv. to *cōnūbi(um)* (*cō-* CO- + *nūb(ere)* to marry + *-ium* -IUM) + *-ālis* -AL^1] —**con·nu′bi·al′i·ty,** *n.* —**con·nu′bi·al·ly,** *adv.*
—**Syn.** nuptial, marital.

co·no·dont (kō′nə dont′, kon′ə-), *n.* a Paleozoic microfossil occurring in various jagged or toothlike shapes and constituting the hard remains of an extinct marine animal of the order Conodonta (or Conodontophorida), found abundantly worldwide in sedimentary rock. [1855–60; < G *Conodonten* (pl.) < Gk *kôn(os)* CONE + *-odont* -ODONT]

co·noid (kō′noid), *adj.* **1.** Also, **co·noi′dal.** resembling a cone in shape; cone-shaped. —*n.* **2.** a geometrical solid formed by the revolution of a conic section about one of its axes. [1650–60; < Gk *kōnoeidēs.* See CONE, -OID] —**co·noi′dal·ly,** *adv.*

Co·non (kō′non), *n.* died A.D. 687, pope 686–687.

co·no·scen·ti (kō′nə shen′tē, kon′ə-; *It.* kô′nô shen′tē), *n.pl., sing.* **-te** (-tē; *It.* -te). cognoscenti. [1760–70]

co·no·scope (kō′nə skōp′, kon′ə-), *n. Optics.* a polarizing microscope for giving interference figures and for determining the principal axis of a crystal. [< Gk *kôno(s)* CONE + -SCOPE] —**co·no·scop·ic** (kō′nə skop′ik, kon′ə-), *adj.*

con·quer (kong′kər), *v.t.* **1.** to acquire by force of arms; win in war: *to conquer a foreign land.* **2.** to overcome by force; subdue: *to conquer an enemy.* **3.** to gain, win, or obtain by effort, personal appeal, etc.: *conquer the hearts of his audience.* **4.** to gain a victory over; surmount; master; overcome: *to conquer disease and poverty; to conquer one's fear.* —*v.i.* **5.** to be victorious; make conquests; gain the victory: *Despite their differences, their love will conquer.* [1200–50; ME *conqueren* < AF *conquerir,* OF *conquerre* < VL **conquērere* to acquire (for L *conquīrere* to seek out). See CON-, QUERY] —**con′quer·a·ble,** *adj.* —**con′quer·a·ble·ness,** *n.* —**con′quer·ing·ly,** *adv.*
—**Syn. 2.** vanquish, overpower, overthrow, subjugate. See **defeat.**

con·quer·or (kong′kər ər), *n.* a person who conquers or vanquishes; victor. [1250–1300; ME *conquerour* < AF; OF *conquereor,* equiv. to *conquer-* CONQUER + *-eor* < L *-ōr-* -OR^1 or *-ātōr-* -ATOR]
—**Syn.** vanquisher, winner.

con·quest (kon′kwest, kong′-), *n.* **1.** the act or state of conquering or the state of being conquered; vanquishment. **2.** the winning of favor, affection, love, etc.: *the conquest of Antony by Cleopatra.* **3.** a person whose favor, affection, etc., has been won: *He's another one of her conquests.* **4.** anything acquired by conquering, as a nation, a territory, or spoils. **5. the Conquest.** See **Norman Conquest.** [1275–1325; ME *conqueste* < AF, OF < VL **conquēsta* (for L *conquīsita,* fem. ptp. of *conquīrere*). See CON-, QUEST]
—**Syn. 1.** subjugation, defeat, mastery. See **victory. 2.** seduction, enchantment. —**Ant. 1.** surrender.

con·qui·an (kong′kē ən), *n. Cards.* a variety of rummy for two players. [1885–90; < Sp *¿con quién?* with whom?]

con·quis·ta·dor (kon kwis′tə dôr′, kong-; *Sp.* kông-kēs′tä ᵺôʀ′), *n., pl.* **-dors,** *Sp.* **-do·res** (-ᵺô′ʀes). one of the Spanish conquerors of Mexico and Peru in the 16th century. [1540–50; < Sp. equiv. to *conquist(ar)* to conquer (see CONQUEST) + *-ador* -ATOR]

Con·rad (kon′rad), *n.* **1. Charles, Jr.,** born 1930, U.S. astronaut. **2. Joseph** (*Teodor Jozef Konrad Korzeniowski*), 1857–1924, English novelist and short-story writer, born in Poland. **3.** a male given name: from Germanic words meaning "bold" and "counsel."

Conrad I, died A.D. 918, king of Germany 911–918.

Conrad II, c990–1039, king of Germany 1024–39 and emperor of the Holy Roman Empire 1027–39.

Conrad III, 1093–1152, king of Germany 1138–52; uncrowned emperor of the Holy Roman Empire: founder of the Hohenstaufen dynasty.

Conrad IV, 1228–54, king of Germany 1237–54 and Sicily 1251–54; uncrowned emperor of the Holy Roman Empire (son of Frederick II).

Con·rail (kon′rāl′), *n.* a government-supported corporation that combined six bankrupt railroads to provide freight and commuter service in 17 states from Boston to St. Louis. [*Con(solidated) Rail (Corporation)*]

Con·roe (kon′rō), *n.* a town in E Texas. 18,034.

Cons., 1. Conservative. **2.** Constable. **3.** Constitution. **4.** Consul. **5.** Consulting.

cons., 1. consecrated. **2.** conservative. **3.** (in prescriptions) conserve; keep. [< L *conservā*] **4.** consolidated. **5.** consonant. **6.** constable. **7.** constitution. **8.** constitutional. **9.** construction. **10.** consul. **11.** consulting.

con·san·guin·e·ous (kon′sang gwin′ē əs), *adj.* having the same ancestry or descent; related by blood. Also, **con·san·guine** (kon sang′gwin), **con′san·guin′e·al.** [1595–1605; < L *consanguineus,* equiv. to *con-* CON- + *sanguin-* (s. of *sanguis*) blood + *-eus* -EOUS] —**con′san·guin′e·ous·ly,** *adv.*

con·san·guin·i·ty (kon′sang gwin′i tē), *n.* **1.** relationship by descent from a common ancestor; kinship (distinguished from *affinity*). **2.** close relationship or connection. [1350–1400; ME *consanguinite* (< AF) < L *consanguinitās.* See CONSANGUINEOUS, -ITY]

con·sarned (kon′särnd′, kən-), *adj. Older Use.* confounded; damned. [1835–45, *Amer.;* alter. of CONCERNED, used as a euphemism for CONFOUNDED]

con·science (kon′shəns), *n.* **1.** the inner sense of what is right or wrong in one's conduct or motives, impelling one toward right action: *to follow the dictates of conscience.* **2.** the complex of ethical and moral principles that controls or inhibits the actions or thoughts of an individual. **3.** an inhibiting sense of what is prudent: *I'd eat another piece of pie but my conscience would bother me.* **4.** conscientiousness. **5.** *Obs.* consciousness; self-knowledge. **6.** *Obs.* strict and reverential observance. **7. have something on one's conscience,** to feel guilty about something, as an act that one considers wrong: *She behaves as if she had something on her conscience.* **8. in all conscience, a.** in all reason and fairness. **b.** certainly; assuredly. Also, **in conscience.** [1175–1225; ME < AF < L *conscientia* knowledge, awareness, conscience. See CON-, SCIENCE] —**con′science·less,** *adj.* —**con′science·less·ly,** *adv.* —**con′science·less·ness,** *n.*

con′science clause′, a clause or article in an act or law that exempts persons whose conscientious or religious scruples forbid their compliance. [1865–70]

con′science mon′ey, money paid, often anonymously, to relieve one's conscience, as for an obligation previously evaded or a wrong done. [1840–50]

con·science-strick·en (kon′shəns strik′ən), *adj.* greatly troubled or disturbed by the knowledge of having acted wrongfully. [1810–20]

con·sci·en·tious (kon′shē en′shəs, kon′sē-), *adj.* **1.** controlled by or done according to conscience; scrupulous: *a conscientious judge.* **2.** meticulous; careful; painstaking; particular: *conscientious application to the work at hand.* [1605–15; < ML *conscientiōsus,* equiv. to L *conscienti(a)* CONSCIENCE + *-ōsus* -OUS] —**con′sci·en′tious·ly,** *adv.* —**con′sci·en′tious·ness,** *n.*
—**Syn. 1.** just, upright, honest, faithful, devoted, dedicated. **2.** See **painstaking.**

conscien′tious objec′tion, refusal on moral or religious grounds to bear arms in a military conflict or to serve in the armed forces. [1895–1900] —**conscien′tious objec′tor.**

con·scion·a·ble (kon′shə nə bəl), *adj.* being in conformity with one's conscience; just. [1540–50; *conscion-* (back formation from *conscions,* var. of CONSCIENCE, the final *-s* taken for pl. sign) + -ABLE] —**con′scion·a·ble·ness,** *n.* —**con′scion·a·bly,** *adv.*

con·scious (kon′shəs), *adj.* **1.** aware of one's own existence, sensations, thoughts, surroundings, etc. **2.** fully aware of or sensitive to something (often fol. by *of*): *conscious of one's own faults; He wasn't conscious of the gossip about his past.* **3.** having the mental faculties fully active: *He was conscious during the operation.* **4.** known to oneself; felt: *conscious guilt.* **5.** aware of what one is doing: *a conscious liar.* **6.** aware of oneself; self-conscious. **7.** deliberate; intentional: *a conscious insult; a conscious effort.* **8.** acutely aware of or concerned about: *money-conscious; a diet-conscious society.* **9.** *Obs.* inwardly sensible of wrongdoing. —*n.* **10. the conscious,** *Psychoanal.* the part of the mind comprising psychic material of which the individual is aware. [1625–35; < L *conscius* sharing knowledge with, equiv. to *con-* CON- + *sci-* (s. of *scīre* to know; see SCIENCE) + *-us* -OUS; cf. NICE] —**con′scious·ly,** *adv.*
—**Syn. 2.** knowing, percipient. CONSCIOUS, AWARE, COGNIZANT refer to an individual sense of recognition of something within or without oneself. CONSCIOUS implies to be awake or awakened to an inner realization of a fact, a truth, a condition, etc.: *to be conscious of an extreme weariness.* AWARE lays the emphasis on sense perceptions insofar as they are the object of conscious recognition: *He was aware of the odor of tobacco.* COGNIZANT lays the emphasis on an outer recognition more on the level of reason and knowledge than on the sensory level alone: *He was cognizant of their drawbacks.*

con·scious·ness (kon′shəs nis), *n.* **1.** the state of being conscious; awareness of one's own existence, sensations, thoughts, surroundings, etc. **2.** the thoughts and feelings, collectively, of an individual or of an aggregate of people: *the moral consciousness of a nation.* **3.** full activity of the mind and senses, as in waking life: *to regain consciousness after fainting.* **4.** awareness of something for what it is; internal knowledge: *consciousness of wrongdoing.* **5.** concern, interest, or acute awareness: *class consciousness.* **6.** the mental activity of which a person is aware as contrasted with unconscious mental processes. **7.** *Philos.* the mind or the mental faculties as characterized by thought, feelings, and volition. **8. raise one's consciousness,** to increase one's awareness and understanding of one's own needs, behavior, attitudes, etc., esp. as a member of a particular social or political group. [1625–35; CONSCIOUS + -NESS]

con•scious•ness-ex•pand•ing (kon′shəs nis ik-span′ding), *adj.* mind-expanding. [1965–70]

con•scious•ness-rais•ing (kon′shəs nis rā′zing), *n.* **1.** *Psychol.* a group-therapy technique in which the aim is to enhance the participants' awareness of their particular needs and goals as individuals or as a group. **2.** any method for increasing interpersonal awareness or sensitivity by teaching people to experience a situation or point of view radically different from their own: *The women's group has tried to change macho attitudes through consciousness-raising.* **3.** an act or instance of increasing the awareness of one's own or another's needs, behavior, attitudes, or problems. [1970–75, *Amer.*]

con•scribe (kən skrīb′), *v.t.*, **-scribed, -scrib•ing.** **1.** to constrict or limit; circumscribe. **2.** to force into military service; conscript. [1540–50; < L *conscrībere* to enroll, enlist, equiv. to *con-* CON- + *scribere* to write]

con•script (*v.* kən skript′; *n., adj.* kon′skript), *v.t.* **1.** to draft for military or naval service. **2.** to compel into service. —*n.* **3.** a recruit obtained by conscription. —*adj.* **4.** enrolled or formed by conscription; drafted: *a conscript soldier.* [1525–35; < L *conscrīptus,* ptp. of *conscrībere* to CONSCRIBE; see CON-, SCRIPT] —**con•script′a•ble,** *adj.*
—**Syn. 1.** induct, impress, recruit, mobilize.

con•script•ee (kən skrip tē′, kon′skrip-), *n.* a person who has been drafted for military service; conscript. [CONSCRIPT + -EE]

con′script fa′thers, **1.** the senators of ancient Rome. **2.** any legislators. [1525–35]

con•scrip•tion (kən skrip′shən), *n.* **1.** compulsory enrollment of persons for military or naval service; draft. **2.** a compulsory contribution of money to a government during a time of war. [1350–1400 for earlier sense "piece of writing"; 1795–1805 for current senses; ME *conscripcioun* < L *conscrīptiōn-* (s. of *conscrīptiō*) a drawing up in writing, levying of troops, equiv. to *conscript(us)* (see CONSCRIPT) + *-iōn-* -ION] —**con•scrip′tion•al,** *adj.*

con•scrip•tion•ist (kən skrip′shə nist), *n.* an advocate or supporter of conscription. [1900–05; CONSCRIPTION + -IST]

con•se•crate (kon′si krāt′), *v.,* **-crat•ed, -crat•ing,** *adj.* —*v.t.* **1.** to make or declare sacred; set apart or dedicate to the service of a deity: *to consecrate a new church building.* **2.** to make (something) an object of honor or veneration; hallow: *a custom consecrated by time.* **3.** to devote or dedicate to some purpose: *a life consecrated to science.* **4.** to admit or ordain to a sacred office, esp. to the episcopate. **5.** to change (bread and wine) into the Eucharist. —*adj.* **6.** consecrated; sacred. [1325–75; ME *consecraten* < L *consecrātus* (ptp. of *consecrāre*), equiv. to *con-* CON- + *-secr-* (var., in non-initial syllables, of *sacer*) SACRED, holy + *-ātus* -ATE[1]] —**con′se•crat′ed•ness,** *n.* —**con′se•cra′tor, con′se•crat′er,** *n.* —**con•se•cra•to•ry** (kon′si krə tôr′ē, -tōr′ē), **con′se•cra′tive,** *adj.*
—**Syn. 2.** sanctify, venerate. **3.** See **devote.** —**Ant. 1.** desecrate.

con•se•cra•tion (kon′si krā′shən), *n.* **1.** the act of consecrating; dedication to the service and worship of a deity. **2.** the act of giving the sacramental character to the Eucharistic elements of bread and wine, esp. in the Roman Catholic Church. **3.** ordination to a sacred office, esp. to the episcopate. [1350–1400; ME *consecracio(u)n* (< AF) < L *consecrātiōn-* (s. of *consecrātiō*). See CONSECRATE, -ION]

con•se•cu•tion (kon′si kyōō′shən), *n.* **1.** succession; sequence. **2.** logical sequence; chain of reasoning. [1525–35; < L *consecūtiōn-* (s. of *consecūtiō*), equiv. to *con-* CON- + *secūt(us),* ptp. of *sequī* to follow + *-iōn-* -ION]

con•sec•u•tive (kən sek′yə tiv), *adj.* **1.** following one another in uninterrupted succession or order; successive: *six consecutive numbers, such as 5, 6, 7, 8, 9, 10.* **2.** marked by logical sequence. **3.** *Gram.* expressing consequence or result: *a consecutive clause.* [1605–15; CONSECUT(ION) + -IVE] —**con•sec′u•tive•ly,** *adv.* —**con•sec′u•tive•ness,** *n.*
—**Syn. 1.** continuous.

con•sen•su•al (kən sen′shōō əl), *adj.* **1.** formed or existing merely by consent: *a consensual transaction.* **2.** *Physiol.* (of an action) involuntarily correlative with a voluntary action, as the contraction of the iris when the eye is opened. [1745–55; < L *consēnsu-,* s. of *consēnsus* CONSENSUS + -AL[1]] —**con•sen′su•al•ly,** *adv.*

con•sen•sus (kən sen′səs), *n., pl.* **-sus•es.** **1.** majority of opinion: *The consensus of the group was that they should meet twice a month.* **2.** general agreement or concord; harmony. [1850–55; < L, equiv. to *consent(ire)* to be in agreement, harmony (*con-* CON- + *sentire* to feel; cf. SENSE) + *-tus* suffix of v. action]
—**Usage.** Many say that the phrase CONSENSUS OF OPINION is redundant and hence should be avoided: *The committee's statement represented a consensus of opinion.* The expression is redundant, however, only if CONSENSUS is taken in the sense "majority of opinion" rather than in its equally valid and earlier sense "general agreement or concord." Criticism of CONSENSUS OF OPINION has been so persistent and widespread that the phrase, even though in common use, occurs only infrequently in edited formal writing. The phrase *general consensus* is objected to for similar reasons. CONSENSUS is now widely used attributively, esp. in the phrase *consensus politics.*

con•sen•sus gen•ti•um (kōn sen′sōōs gen′tē ōōm′; *Eng.* kən sen′səs jen′shē əm), *Latin.* agreement of the people.

con•sent (kən sent′), *v.i.* **1.** to permit, approve, or agree; comply or yield (often fol. by *to* or an infinitive): *He consented to the proposal. We asked her permission, and she consented.* **2.** *Archaic.* to agree in sentiment, opinion, etc.; be in harmony. —*n.* **3.** permission, approval, or agreement; compliance; acquiescence: *He gave his consent to the marriage.* **4.** agreement in sentiment, opinion, a course of action, etc.: *By common consent he was appointed official delegate.* **5.** *Archaic.* accord; concord; harmony. [1175–1225; (v.) ME *consenten* < AF, OF *consentir* < L *consentīre* (see CONSENSUS); (n.) ME < AF, OF, n. deriv. of the v.] —**con•sent′er,** *n.* —**con•sent′•ing•ly,** *adv.*
—**Syn. 1.** See **agree.**

con•sen•ta•ne•ous (kon′sen tā′nē əs), *adj.* **1.** agreeing; accordant. **2.** done by common consent; unanimous. [1615–25; < L *consentāneus,* equiv. to *consent-* (s. of *consentīre* to CONSENT) + *-āneus* (*-ān(us)* -AN + *-eus* -EOUS)] —**con′sen•ta′ne•ous•ly,** *adv.* —**con•sen•ta•ne•i•ty** (kən sen′tə nē′i tē), **con′sen•ta′ne•ous•ness,** *n.*

consent′ decree′, *Law.* **1.** an agreement, approved by the court, pursuant to which the defendant ceases activities alleged by the government to be illegal and the government's action is dropped, esp. in antitrust and other regulatory matters. **2.** an agreement made in court by the parties to settle a suit in equity. [1920–25]

con•sen•tience (kən sen′shəns), *n.* **1.** agreement or unity of opinion; concurrence. **2.** the faculty of synthesizing sensations, without the use of the intellect or without consciousness, in reflex or involuntary actions. [1875–80; CONSENTI(ENT) + -ENCE]

con•sen•tient (kən sen′shənt), *adj.* **1.** agreeing; accordant. **2.** acting in harmonious agreement. **3.** unanimous, as an opinion. **4.** characterized by or having consentience. [1615–25; < L *consentient-* (s. of *consentiēns,* prp. of *consentīre* to CONSENT; see -ENT)] —**con•sen′•tient•ly,** *adv.*

consent′ judg′ment, *Law.* a judgment settled and agreed to by the parties to the action. Cf. **consent decree** (def. 2).

con•sen•tu•al (kən sen′chōō əl), *adj. Law.* involving or carried out by mutual consent: *a consentual divorce.* [CONSENT + -AL[1], with *-u-* after CONSENSUAL, or by assoc. with phonetically similar ACCENTUAL, EVENTUAL, etc.]

con•se•quence (kon′si kwens′, -kwəns), *n.* **1.** the effect, result, or outcome of something occurring earlier: *The accident was the consequence of reckless driving.* **2.** an act or instance of following something as an effect, result, or outcome. **3.** the conclusion reached by a line of reasoning; inference. **4.** importance or significance: *a matter of no consequence.* **5.** importance in rank or position; distinction: *a man of great consequence in art.* **6.** **in consequence,** consequently; as a result; hence: *He withdrew from the world, and in consequence was forgotten.* **7.** **in consequence of,** as a result of; on account of: *A trial was held in consequence of the investigation.* [1350–1400; ME (< AF) < L *consequentia.* See CONSEQUENT, -ENCE]
—**Syn. 1.** outcome, issue, upshot, sequel. See **effect. 4.** moment, weight. See **importance.** —**Ant. 1.** cause.

con•se•quent (kon′si kwent′, -kwənt), *adj.* **1.** following as an effect or result; resulting (often fol. by *on, upon,* or *to*): *a fall in price consequent to a rise in production.* **2.** following as a logical conclusion: *a consequent law.* **3.** following or progressing logically: *consequent reasoning.* —*n.* **4.** anything that follows upon something else, with or without a causal relationship. **5.** *Logic.* the second member of a conditional proposition, as *"Caesar was a great general"* in *"If Caesar conquered Gaul, he was a great general."* **6.** *Math.* **a.** the second term of a ratio. **b.** the second of two vectors in a dyad. [1350–1400; ME (n.) < L *consequent-* (s. of *consequēns,* prp. of *consequī* to follow closely). See CON-, SEQUENT]

con•se•quen•tial (kon′si kwen′shəl), *adj.* **1.** following as an effect, result, or outcome; resultant; consequent. **2.** following as a logical conclusion or inference; logically consistent. **3.** of consequence or importance: *a consequential man in his field.* **4.** self-important; pompous. [1620–30; < L *consequenti(a)* CONSEQUENCE + -AL[1]] —**con′se•quen′ti•al′i•ty, con′se•quen′tial•ness,** *n.* —**con′se•quen′tial•ly,** *adv.*

con•se•quent•ly (kon′si kwent′lē, -kwənt-), *adv.* as a result, effect, or outcome; therefore: *There has been a great deal of rain and consequently the reservoirs are full.* [1375–1425; late ME; see CONSEQUENT, -LY]
—**Syn.** See **therefore.**

con′sequent stream′, *Geol.* a stream the course of which was determined by the original slope of the land. Cf. **obsequent stream.** [1955–60]

con•serv•a•ble (kən sûr′və bəl), *adj.* capable of being conserved: *conservable fruits.* [1615–25; < LL *conservābilis.* See CONSERVE, -ABLE]

con•serv•an•cy (kən sûr′vən sē), *n., pl.* **-cies.** **1.** conservation of natural resources. **2.** an association dedicated to the protection of the environment and its resources. **3.** *Brit.* a commission regulating navigation, fisheries, etc. [1550–60; < ML *conservantia* (see CONSERVE, -ANCY); r. *conservacy* < ML *conservātia;* see -ACY] —**con•serv′ant,** *adj.*

con•ser•va•tion (kon′sər vā′shən), *n.* **1.** the act of conserving; prevention of injury, decay, waste, or loss; preservation: *conservation of wildlife; conservation of human rights.* **2.** official supervision of rivers, forests, and other natural resources in order to preserve and protect them through prudent management. **3.** a district, river, forest, etc., under such supervision. **4.** the careful utilization of a natural resource in order to prevent depletion. **5.** the restoration and preservation of works of art. [1350–1400; ME *conservacioun* < L *conservātiōn-* (s. of *conservātiō*), equiv. to *conservāt(us)* (ptp. of *conservāre* to CONSERVE; see -ATE[1]) + *-iōn-* -ION] —**con′ser•va′tion•al,** *adj.*
—**Syn. 1.** care, husbandry, protection.

con•ser•va•tion•ist (kon′sər vā′shə nist), *n.* a person who advocates or promotes conservation, esp. of natural resources. [1865–70; CONSERVATION + -IST]

conserva′tion law′, *Physics, Chem.* any law stating that some quantity or property remains constant during and after an interaction or process, as conservation of charge or conservation of linear momentum. [1945–50]

conserva′tion of an′gular momen′tum, *Physics.* the principle that the total angular momentum of a system has constant magnitude and direction if the system is subjected to no external force. Also called **law of conservation of angular momentum.**

conserva′tion of bar′yon num′ber, *Physics.* the principle that the total baryon number remains constant in all processes involving the interaction of elementary particles.

conserva′tion of charge′, *Physics.* the principle that the total electric charge of a system is constant. Also called **law of conservation of charge.** [1945–50]

conserva′tion of en′ergy, *Physics.* the principle that in a system that does not undergo any force from outside the system, the amount of energy is constant, irrespective of its changes in form. Also called **law of conservation of energy.** [1850–55]

conserva′tion of lep′ton num′ber, *Physics.* the principle that the total lepton number remains constant in any process involving elementary particles.

conserva′tion of lin′ear momen′tum, *Physics.* the principle that the linear momentum of a system has constant magnitude and direction if the system is subjected to no external force. Also called **law of conservation of linear momentum.**

conserva′tion of mass′, *Physics.* the principle that in any closed system subjected to no external forces, the mass is constant irrespective of its changes in form; the principle that matter cannot be created or destroyed. Also called **law of conservation of mass, conserva′•tion of mat′ter.** [1880–85]

con•serv•a•tism (kən sûr′və tiz′əm), *n.* **1.** the disposition to preserve or restore what is established and traditional and to limit change. **2.** the principles and practices of political conservatives. [1825–35; CONSERVAT(IVE) + -ISM]

con•serv•a•tive (kən sûr′və tiv), *adj.* **1.** disposed to preserve existing conditions, institutions, etc., or to restore traditional ones, and to limit change. **2.** cautiously moderate or purposefully low: *a conservative estimate.* **3.** traditional in style or manner; avoiding novelty or showiness: *conservative suit.* **4.** (*often cap.*) of or pertaining to the Conservative party. **5.** (*cap.*) of, pertaining to, or characteristic of Conservative Jews or Conservative Judaism. **6.** having the power or tendency to conserve; preservative. **7.** *Math.* (of a vector or vector function) having curl equal to zero; irrotational; lamellar. —*n.* **8.** a person who is conservative in principles, actions, habits, etc. **9.** a supporter of conservative political policies. **10.** (*cap.*) a member of a conservative political party, esp. the Conservative party in Great Britain. **11.** a preservative. [1350–1400; < LL *conservātīvus,* equiv. to L *conservāt(us)* (see CONSERVATION) + *-īvus* -IVE; r. ME *conservatif* < MF < L, as above] —**con•serv′a•tive•ly,** *adv.* —**con•serv′a•tive•ness,** *n.*

Conserv′ative Bap′tist, a member of a Protestant denomination **(Conserv′ative Bap′tist Associa′tion of Amer′ica)** organized in Milwaukee, Wisconsin, in 1948.

Conserv′ative Jew′, a Jew who adheres for the most part to the principles and practices of traditional Judaism with the reservation that, taking into account contemporary conditions, certain modifications or rejections are permissible. Cf. **Orthodox Jew, Reform Jew.**

Conserv′ative Ju′daism, Judaism as observed by Conservative Jews. [1945–50]

Conserv′ative par′ty, a political party in Great Britain founded about 1832 as successor to the Tory party and characterized by moderate progressivism.

con•serv•a•tize (kən sûr′və tīz′), *v.t., v.i.,* **-tized, -tiz•ing.** to make or become conservative. Also, *esp. Brit.,* **con•serv′a•tise′.** [1840–50; CONSERVAT(IVE) + -IZE] —**con•serv′a•ti•za′tion,** *n.*

con•ser•va•toire (kən sûr′və twär′, -sûr′və twär′; *Fr.* kôn ser va twar′), *n., pl.* **-toires** (-twärz′, -twärz′; *Fr.* -twar′). a conservatory, as of music or theatrical arts. [1765–75; < F < It *conservatorio* CONSERVATORY, orig., orphanage; early schools of music originated in orphanages where a musical education was given]

con•ser•va•tor (kon′sər vā′tər, kən sûr′və-), *n.* **1.** a person who conserves or preserves; preserver; protector. **2.** a person who repairs, restores, or maintains the condition of objects, as paintings or sculptures in an art museum, or books in a library. **3.** *Law.* a guardian; a custodian. **4.** *Brit.* a person employed by the conservancy commission; a conservation worker. [1400–50; late ME < L, equiv. to *conservā(re)* (see CONSERVE) + *-tor* -TOR] —**con•serv•a•to•ri•al** (kən sûr′və tôr′ē əl, -tōr′-), *adj.* —**con′ser•va′tor•ship′,** *n.*

con•serv•a•to•ry (kən sûr′və tôr′ē, -tōr′ē), *n., pl.* **-ries,** *adj.* —*n.* **1.** a school giving instruction in one or more of the fine or dramatic arts; specifically, a school of music. **2.** a greenhouse, usually attached to a dwelling, for growing and displaying plants. **3.** *Archaic.* a place where things are preserved. —*adj.* **4.** serving or adapted to conserve; preservative. [1555–65; < L *conservā(re)* (see CONSERVE) + -TORY[2]; in the sense "music school" < F or It; see CONSERVATOIRE]

con•serve (*v.* kən sûrv′; *n.* kon′sûrv, kən sûrv′), *v.,* **-served, -serv•ing,** *n.* —*v.t.* **1.** to prevent injury, decay, waste, or loss of: *Conserve your strength for the race.* **2.** to use or manage (natural resources) wisely; preserve;

save: *Conserve the woodlands.* **3.** *Physics, Chem.* to hold (a property) constant during an interaction or process: *the interaction conserved linear momentum.* **4.** to preserve (fruit) by cooking with sugar or syrup. *—n.* **5.** Often, **conserves.** a mixture of several fruits cooked to jamlike consistency with sugar and often garnished with nuts and raisins. [1325–75; (v.) ME < L *conservāre* to save, preserve, equiv. to *con-* CON- + *servāre* to watch over, guard (akin to *servus* slave, *servīre* to SERVE); (n.) ME < MF *conserve,* n. deriv. of *conserver* < L, as above] **—con·serv′er,** *n.*
—Syn. 2. husband, safeguard.

con·sid·er (kən sid′ər), *v.t.* **1.** to think carefully about, esp. in order to make a decision; contemplate; reflect on: *He considered the cost before buying the new car.* **2.** to regard as or deem to be: *I consider the story improbable.* **3.** to think, believe, or suppose: *We consider his reply unsatisfactory.* **4.** to bear in mind; make allowance for: *The arrest was justified if you consider his disorderly behavior.* **5.** to pay attention to; regard: *He considered the man for some time before speaking to him.* **6.** to regard with respect, thoughtfulness, honor, etc.; esteem. **7.** to think about (something that one might do, accept, buy, etc.): *to consider a job in Guatemala.* **8.** *Obs.* to view attentively; scrutinize. **9.** *Obs.* to recompense or remunerate. *—v.i.* **10.** to think deliberately or carefully; reflect. **11.** to view carefully or thoughtfully. [1350–1400; ME *consideren* (< AF) < L *considerāre* to examine, equiv. to *con-* CON- + *sīder-* (s. of *sīdus*) star-group, sky (see SIDEREAL) + *-āre* inf. suffix] **—con·sid′er·er,** *n.*
—Syn. 1. ponder, deliberate, weigh. See **study**[1].

con·sid·er·a·ble (kən sid′ər ə bəl), *adj.* **1.** rather large or great in size, distance, extent, etc.: *It cost a considerable amount. We took a considerable length of time to decide.* **2.** worthy of respect, attention, etc.; important; distinguished: *a considerable person.* *—n.* **3.** *Informal.* much; not a little: *He has done considerable for the community.* *—adv.* **4.** *Nonstandard (older use).* considerably; noticeably; much: *I'm feeling considerable better now.* [1400–50; late ME < ML *considerābilis,* equiv. to *considerā-* (see CONSIDER) + *-bilis* -BLE]

con·sid·er·a·bly (kən sid′ər ə blē), *adv.* to a noteworthy or marked extent; much; noticeably; substantially; amply. [CONSIDER(ABLE) + -ABLY]

con·sid·er·ance (kən sid′ər əns), *n. Obs.* consideration. [1400–50; late ME < L *considerantia.* See CONSIDER, -ANCE]

con·sid·er·ate (kən sid′ər it), *adj.* **1.** showing kindly awareness or regard for another's feelings, circumstances, etc.: *a very considerate critic.* **2.** carefully considered; deliberate. **3.** marked by consideration or reflection; deliberate; prudent. [1375–1425 for earlier sense; 1565–75 for current senses; late ME < L *considerātus* (ptp. of *considerāre* to CONSIDER), equiv. to *considerā-* (s. of *considerāre*) + *-tus* ptp. suffix] **—con·sid′er·ate·ly,** *adv.* **—con·sid′er·ate·ness,** *n.*
—Syn. 1. kind, patient, concerned. See **thoughtful.**

con·sid·er·a·tion (kən sid′ə rā′shən), *n.* **1.** the act of considering; careful thought; meditation; deliberation: *I will give your project full consideration.* **2.** something that is or is to be kept in mind in making a decision, evaluating facts, etc.: *Age was an important consideration in the decision.* **3.** thoughtful or sympathetic regard or respect; thoughtfulness for others: *They showed no consideration for his feelings.* **4.** a thought or reflection; an opinion based upon reflection. **5.** a recompense or payment, as for work done; compensation. **6.** importance or consequence. **7.** estimation; esteem: *He is held in great consideration by the community.* **8.** *Law.* **a.** something that suffices to make an informal promise legally binding, usually some value given in exchange for the promise. **b.** the hearing of a case by a tribunal. **9. in consideration of, a.** in view of. **b.** in return or recompense for: *She was offered money in consideration of her efforts.* **10. take into consideration,** to take into account; consider: *We failed to take into consideration the large number of tourists attending the exhibition.* [1350–1400; ME (< AF) < L *consīderātiōn-* (s. of *consīderātiō*), equiv. to *consīderāt(us)* (see CONSIDERATE) + *-iōn-* -ION]
—Syn. 1. reflection, contemplation, rumination, attention. **3.** kindness, kindliness, concern. **5.** remuneration, fee. **6.** weight, significance, moment. **7.** See **honor.**

con·sid·ered (kən sid′ərd), *adj.* **1.** thought about or decided upon with care: *a considered opinion.* **2.** regarded with respect or esteem: *a highly considered person.* [1595–1605; CONSIDER + -ED[2]]

con·sid·er·ing (kən sid′ər ing), *prep.* **1.** taking into account; in view of: *The campaign was a great success, considering the strong opposition.* *—adv.* **2.** *Informal.* with all things considered (used only after the statement it modifies): *He paints very well, considering.* *—conj.* **3.** taking into consideration that: *Considering they are newcomers, they've adjusted very well.* [CONSIDER + -ING[2]]

con·si·glie·re (kôn′sē lye′Re), *n., pl.* **-ri** (-Rē). *Italian.* a member of a criminal organization or syndicate who serves as an adviser to the leader.

con·sign (kən sīn′), *v.t.* **1.** to hand over or deliver formally or officially; commit (often fol. by *to*). **2.** to transfer to another's custody or charge; entrust. **3.** to set apart for or devote to (a special purpose or use): *to consign two afternoons a week to the club.* **4.** to banish or set apart in one's mind; relegate: *to consign unpleasant thoughts to oblivion.* **5.** *Com.* **a.** to ship, as by common carrier, esp. for sale or custody. **b.** to address for such shipment. **6.** *Obs.* to confirm or ratify, as with a seal or other token. *—v.i.* **7.** to agree or assent. **8.** *Obs.* to yield or submit. [1400–50; late ME; appar. (< MF *consigner*) < ML *consignāre* to mark with sign of cross, L: to mark with a seal. See CON-, SIGN] **—con·sign′a·ble,** *adj.* **—con·sig·na·tion** (kon′sig nā′shən), *n.*
—Syn. 1. relegate, assign. **2.** confide.

con·sign·ee (kon′sī nē′, -si-, kən sī-), *n.* a person or party to whom something, usually merchandise, is consigned. [1780–90; CONSIGN + -EE]

con·sign·ment (kən sīn′mənt), *n.* **1.** the act of consigning. **2.** something that is consigned. **3.** *Com.* property sent to an agent for sale, storage, or shipment. **4. on consignment,** (of goods) sent to an agent for sale, with title being held by the consignor until a sale is made. *—adj.* **5.** of, pertaining to, or shipped as goods on consignment: *consignment selling of gift items.* [1555–65; CONSIGN + -MENT]

consign′ment note′, *Chiefly Brit.* See **air waybill.**

con·sign·or (kən sī′nər, kon′sī nôr′), *n.* a person or company that consigns goods, merchandise, etc. Also, **con·sign·er** (kən sī′nər). [1780–90; CONSIGN + -OR[2]]

con·sist (*v.* kən sist′; *n.* kon′sist), *v.i.* **1.** to be made up or composed (usually fol. by *of*): *This cake consists mainly of sugar, flour, and butter.* **2.** to be comprised or contained (usually fol. by *in*): *Her charm does not consist only in her beauty.* **3.** *Archaic.* to exist together or be capable of existing together. **4.** *Obs.* to insist; urge. *—n.* **5.** *Railroads.* **a.** the rolling stock, exclusive of the locomotive, making up a train. **b.** a record made of this rolling stock. [1520–30; < L *consistere* to stand together, stand firm, equiv. to *con-* CON- + *sistere* to cause to stand, reduplicative v. akin to *stāre* to STAND]

con·sist·en·cy (kən sis′tən sē), *n., pl.* **-cies.** **1.** a degree of density, firmness, viscosity, etc.: *The liquid has the consistency of cream.* **2.** steadfast adherence to the same principles, course, form, etc.: *There is consistency in his pattern of behavior.* **3.** agreement, harmony, or compatibility, esp. correspondence or uniformity among the parts of a complex thing: *consistency of colors throughout the house.* **4.** the condition of cohering or holding together and retaining form; solidity or firmness. Also, **con·sist′ence.** [1585–95; CONSIST(ENT) + -ENCY]

con·sist·ent (kən sis′tənt), *adj.* **1.** agreeing or accordant; compatible; not self-contradictory: *His views and actions are consistent.* **2.** constantly adhering to the same principles, course, form, etc.: *a consistent opponent.* **3.** holding firmly together; cohering. **4.** *Archaic.* fixed; firm. [1565–75; < L *consistent-* (s. of *consistēns,* prp. of *consistere*). See CONSIST, -ENT] **—con·sist′ent·ly,** *adv.*
—Syn. 1. congruous, consonant, harmonious, conformable.

consist′ent equa′tions, *Math.* two or more equations that have at least one common solution.

con·sis·to·ry (kən sis′tə rē), *n., pl.* **-ries.** **1.** any of various ecclesiastical councils or tribunals. **2.** the place where such a council or tribunal meets. **3.** the meeting of any such body. **4.** *Rom. Cath. Ch.* a solemn assembly of the whole body of cardinals, summoned and presided over by the pope. **5.** *Anglican Ch.* a diocesan court for dealing with ecclesiastical and spiritual questions, held in the cathedral church and presided over by the bishop, the bishop's chancellor, or the commissary. **6.** (in certain Reformed churches) the governing board of a local church or congregation. **7.** any assembly or council. **8.** *Obs.* a council chamber. [1275–1325; ME *consistorie* < AF < LL *consistōrium* meeting place, equiv. to L *consist(ere)* (see CONSIST) + *-(t)ōrium* -TORY[2]] **—con·sis·to·ri·al** (kon′si stôr′ē əl, -stōr′-), **con′sis·to′ri·an,** *adj.*

con·so·ci·ate (*adj., n.* kən sō′shē it, -āt′, -sē-; *v.* kən sō′shē āt′, -sē-), *adj., n., v.i.,* **-at·ed, -at·ing.** associate. [1425–75; late ME (adj.) < L *consociātus* (ptp. of *consociāre* to bring into partnership), equiv. to *con-* CON- + *soci(us)* fellow, partner + *-ātus* -ATE[1]]

con·so·ci·a·tion (kən sō′sē ā′shən, -shē-), *n.* **1.** the act of uniting in association. **2.** an association of churches or religious orders. **3.** *Ecol.* a climax community in which a single species is dominant. [1585–95; < L *consociātiōn-,* s. of *consociātiō* an associating; see CONSOCIATE, -ION]

con·sol (kon′sol, kən sol′), *n.* sing. of **consols.**

consol., consolidated.

con·so·la·tion (kon′sə lā′shən), *n.* **1.** the act of consoling; comfort; solace. **2.** the state of being consoled. **3.** someone or something that consoles: *His faith was a consolation during his troubles. Her daughters are a consolation to her.* **4.** *Sports.* a game, match, or race for tournament entrants eliminated before the final round, as a basketball game between the losing semifinalists. [1325–75; ME *consolacioun* (< AF) < L *consōlātiōn-* (s. of *consōlātiō*), equiv. to *consōlāt(us),* ptp. of *consōlārī* (*con-* CON- + *sōlā-,* s. of *sōlārī* to comfort, + *-tus* ptp. suffix) + *-iōn-* -ION; see SOLACE]
—Syn. 1. relief, succor, help, support, cheer.

Consola′tion of Philos′ophy, The, (Latin, *De Consolatione Philosophiae*), a philosophical work (A.D. 523?) by Boethius.

consola′tion prize′, a prize, usually of minor value, given to the loser or runner-up in a contest, competition, etc., or to all losers who have performed well or met certain standards. [1885–90]

Con·so·la·to del Ma·re (kôn sô lä′tô del mä′Re), a code of maritime law compiled in the Middle Ages: it drew upon ancient law and has influenced modern law.

con·sol·a·to·ry (kən sol′ə tôr′ē, -tōr′ē), *adj.* giving comfort; consoling. [1400–50; late ME < L *consōlātōrius,* equiv. to *consōlā(re)* (see CONSOLE) + *-tōrius* -TORY[1]] **—con·sol′a·to′ri·ly,** *adv.* **—con·sol′a·to′ri·ness,** *n.*

con·sole[1] (kən sōl′), *v.t.,* **-soled, -sol·ing.** to alleviate or lessen the grief, sorrow, or disappointment of; give solace or comfort: *Only his children could console him when his wife died.* [1685–95; (< F *consoler*) < L *consōlārī,* equiv. to *con-* CON- + *sōlārī* to soothe (see SOLACE); perh. akin to OE *sǣl* happiness (see SEELY)] **—con·sol′a·ble,** *adj.* **—con·sol′er,** *n.* **—con·sol′ing·ly,** *adv.*
—Syn. See **comfort**[1].

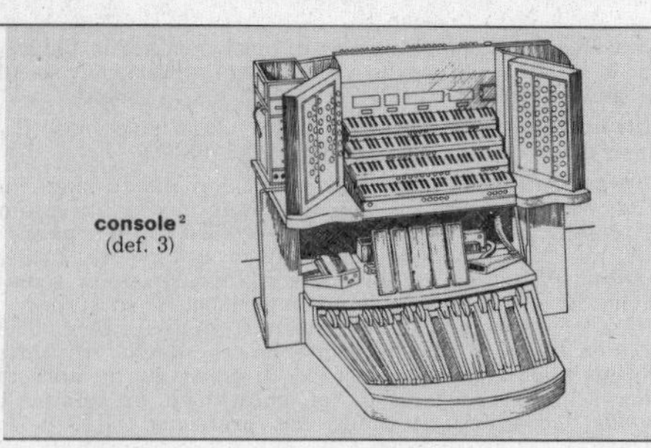
console[2] (def. 3)

con·sole[2] (kon′sōl), *n.* **1.** a television, phonograph, or radio cabinet designed to stand on the floor rather than on a table or shelf. **2.** the control or monitoring unit of a computer, containing the keyboard or keys, switches, etc. **3.** a desklike structure containing the keyboards, pedals, etc., by means of which an organ is played. **4.** a small cabinet standing on the floor and having doors. **5.** See **console table.** **6.** the control unit of a mechanical, electrical, or electronic system: *the console that controls a theater's lighting system.* **7.** *Archit.* an ornamental corbel or bracket, esp. one high in relation to its projection. **8.** *Auto.* a tray or container typically divided into compartments, mounted between bucket seats, and used for storing small items. **9.** *Naut.* a unit on a vessel containing steering apparatus, systems monitoring equipment, etc.: *a bridge console, an engine-room console.* [1700–10; < F; MF *consolle* bracket or support, appar. shortening of *consolateur* (attested in MF with same sense) lit., one who consoles (< LL *consōlātor;* see CONSOLE[1], -ATOR), perh. because such supports served as rests in choir stalls, etc.; cf. MISERICORD]

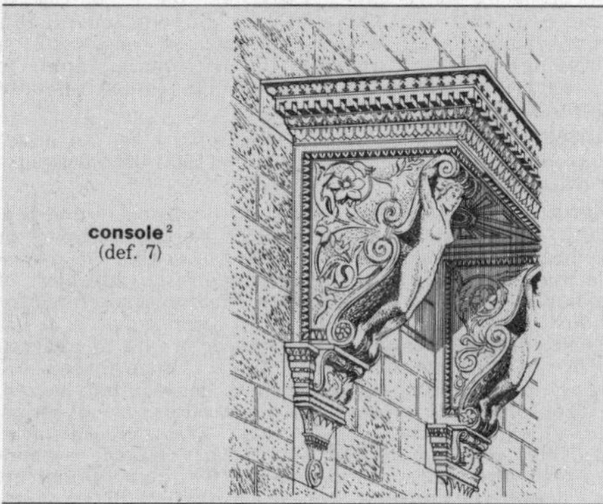
console[2] (def. 7)

con′sole ta′ble (kon′sōl), **1.** a table supported by consoles or brackets fixed to a wall. **2.** a table, often with bracketlike legs, designed to fit against a wall. [1805–15]

con·so·lette (kon′sə let′), *n.* **1.** a small shelf or recess in a handy location, as in the armrest, dashboard, or door panel of a car, in a shower stall, etc., for holding small, frequently used items. **2.** a small console television, phonograph, or radio. [1940–45; CONSOLE[2] + -ETTE]

con·sol·i·date (kən sol′i dāt′), *v.,* **-dat·ed, -dat·ing,** *adj.* *—v.t.* **1.** to bring together (separate parts) into a single or unified whole; unite; combine: *They consolidated their three companies.* **2.** to discard the unused or unwanted items of and organize the remaining: *She consolidated her home library.* **3.** to make solid or firm; solidify; strengthen: *to consolidate gains.* **4.** *Mil.* to strengthen by rearranging the position of ground combat troops after a successful attack. *—v.i.* **5.** to unite or combine. **6.** to become solid or firm. *—adj.* **7.** consolidated (def. 2). [1505–15; < L *consolidātus* (ptp. of *consolidāre*), equiv. to *con-* CON- + *solid(us)* SOLID + *-ātus* -ATE[1]] **—con·sol′i·da′tor,** *n.*

con·sol·i·dat·ed (kən sol′i dā′tid), *adj.* **1.** brought together into a single whole. **2.** having become solid, firm, or coherent. **3.** *Accounting.* taking into account the combined information gathered from the financial conditions of a parent corporation and its subsidiaries: *a consolidated balance sheet.* [1745–55; CONSOLIDATE + -ED[2]]

Consol′idated Fund′, a British national fund created to pay grants to the royal family, interest on public debt, etc., by consolidating various public securities. Cf. **consols.**

consol′idated school′, a public school formed from the pupils and teachers of a number of discontinued smaller schools, esp. in a rural district. Also called **centralized school.** [1910–15, *Amer.*]

con·sol·i·da·tion (kən sol′i dā′shən), *n.* **1.** an act or instance of consolidating; the state of being consolidated; unification: *consolidation of companies.* **2.** solidification; strengthening: *consolidation of principles and beliefs.* **3.** something that is or has been consolidated; a consolidated whole. **4.** *Law.* **a.** a statutory combination of two or more corporations. **b.** the union of two or more claims or actions at law for trial or appeal. **5.** (*cap.*) a steam locomotive having a two-wheeled front truck, eight driving wheels, and no rear truck. See table under **Whyte classification.** **6.** *Pathol.* the process of becoming solid, as changing of lung tissue from aerated and elastic to firm in certain diseases. **7.** *Geol.* lithification. [1350–1400; ME (< AF) < LL *consolidātiōn-* (s. of *consolidātiō*), equiv. to L *consolidāt(us)* (see CONSOLIDATE) + *-iōn-* -ION] **—con·sol′i·da′tive,** *adj.*

CONCISE ETYMOLOGY KEY: <, descended or borrowed from; >, whence; b., blend of, blended; c., cognate with; cf., compare; deriv., derivative; equiv., equivalent; imit., imitative; obl., oblique; r., replacing; s., stem; sp., spelling, spelled; resp., respelling, respelled; trans., translation; ?, origin unknown; *, unattested; ‡, probably earlier than. See the full key inside the front cover.

consolida′tion loan′, a loan made in order to consolidate several debts into one loan, usually for the purpose of reducing the monthly payments by extending them over a longer time period.

con·sols (kon′solz, kən solz′), *n.pl.* Sometimes, **consol.** the funded government securities of Great Britain that originated in the consolidation in 1751 of various public securities, chiefly in the form of annuities, into a single debt issue without maturity. Also called **bank annuities.** [short for *consolidated annuities*]

con·sol·ute (kon′sə lo͞ot′), *adj. Chem.* **1.** (of two liquids) mutually soluble in all proportions. **2.** soluble in each of two or more conjugate liquids. **3.** of or pertaining to two partially miscible liquids capable of becoming totally miscible under certain conditions. [< LL *consolūtus* dissolved together, equiv. to L *con-* CON- + *solūtus,* ptp. of *solvere* to SOLVE]

con·som·mé (kon′sə mā′, kon′sə mā′), *n.* a clear soup made by boiling meat or chicken, bones, vegetables, etc., to extract their nutritive properties: served hot or jellied. [1805–15; < F, n. use of *consommé,* ptp. of *consommer* to finish < L *consummāre* to add up, finish; see CONSUMMATE]
—Syn. broth.

con·so·nance (kon′sə nəns), *n.* **1.** accord or agreement. **2.** correspondence of sounds; harmony of sounds. **3.** *Music.* a simultaneous combination of tones conventionally accepted as being in a state of repose. Cf. **dissonance** (def. 2). See illus. under **resolution. 4.** *Pros.* **a.** the correspondence of consonants, esp. those at the end of a word, in a passage of prose or verse. Cf. **alliteration** (def. 1). **b.** the use of the repetition of consonants or consonant patterns as a rhyming device. **5.** *Physics.* the property of two sounds the frequencies of which have a ratio equal to a small whole number. Also, **con′so·nan·cy.** [1350–1400; ME (< AF) < L *consonantia* concord. See CONSONANT, -ANCE]
—Syn. 1. concord, harmony, correspondence. **—Ant. 1.** dissonance.

con·so·nant (kon′sə nənt), *n.* **1.** *Phonet.* **a.** (in English articulation) a speech sound produced by occluding with or without releasing (p, b; t, d; k, g), diverting (m, n, ng), or obstructing (f, v; s, z, etc.) the flow of air from the lungs (opposed to *vowel*). **b.** (in a syllable) any sound other than the sound of greatest sonority in the syllable, as *b, r,* and *g* in *brig* (opposed to *sonant*). Cf. **vowel** (def. 1b). **c.** (in linguistic function) a concept empirically determined as a phonological element in structural contrast with vowel, as the *b* of *be,* the *w* of *we,* the *y, s,* and *t* of *yeast,* etc. **2.** a letter that usually represents a consonant sound. *—adj.* **3.** in agreement; agreeable; in accord; consistent (usually fol. by *to* or *with*): *behavior consonant with his character.* **4.** corresponding in sound, as words. **5.** harmonious, as sounds. **6.** *Music.* constituting a consonance. **7.** *Physics.* noting or pertaining to sounds exhibiting consonance. **8.** consonantal. [1350–1400; ME *consona(u)nt* (< AF) < L *consonant-* (s. of *consonāns,* prp. of *consonāre* to sound with or together). See CON-, SONANT] **—con′so·nant·like′,** *adj.* **—con′·so·nant·ly,** *adv.*
—Syn. 3. concordant, congruous, conformant. **—Ant. 6.** dissonant.

con·so·nan·tal (kon′sə nan′tl), *adj.* **1.** of, or of the nature of, a consonant. **2.** marked by consonant sounds. Also, **con′so·nan′tic.** [1785–95; CONSONANT + -AL[1]] **—con′so·nan′tal·ly,** *adv.*

consonan′tal allitera′tion. See under **alliteration** (def. 1).

con·so·nan·tal·ize (kon′sə nan′tl īz′), *v.t., v.i.,* **-ized, -iz·ing.** *Phonet.* to change into or become changed into a consonant (contrasted with *vocalize*). Also, *esp. Brit.,* **con′so·nan′tal·ise′.** [CONSONANTAL + -IZE] **—con′so·nan′tal·i·za′tion,** *n.*

con·so·nant·ism (kon′sə nən tiz′əm), *n.* **1.** the system of consonants of a particular language. **2.** the nature, distribution, or phonology of the consonants of a word, group of words, or language. [1870–75; CONSONANT + -ISM]

con·so·nan·tize (kon′sə nən tīz′), *v.t., v.i.,* **-tized, -tiz·ing.** consonantalize. Also, *esp. Brit.,* **con′so·nan·tise′.** [1875–80]

con′sonant shift′, *Ling.* a set of changes that take place in the articulation of one or more consonant phonemes between an earlier and a later stage of a language. Cf. **first consonant shift, second consonant shift.** [1885–90]

con′sonant sys′tem, *Ling.* the consonant phonemes of a language, esp. when considered as forming an interrelated and interacting group. Cf. **vowel system.**

con sor·di·no (kon sôr dē′nō, kōn; *It.* kôn sôr dē′nô), with the mute (used as a direction in music to a string player). [1815–25; < It; see SORDINO]

con·sort (*n.* kon′sôrt, *v.* kən sôrt′), *n.* **1.** a husband or wife; spouse, esp. of a reigning monarch. Cf. **prince consort, queen consort. 2.** one vessel or ship accompanying another. **3.** *Music.* **a.** a group of instrumentalists and singers who perform music, esp. old music. **b.** a group of instruments of the same family, as viols, played in concert. **4.** a companion, associate, or partner: *a confidant and consort of heads of state.* **5.** accord or agreement. **6.** *Obs.* **a.** company or association. **b.** harmony of sounds. *—v.i.* **7.** to associate; keep company: *to consort with known criminals.* **8.** to agree or harmonize. *—v.t.* **9.** to associate, join, or unite. **10.** *Obs.* **a.** to accompany; espouse. **b.** to sound in harmony. [1375–1425; late ME < MF < L *consort-* (s. of *consors*) sharer, orig. sharing (adj.). See CON-, SORT] **—con·sort′a·ble,** *adj.* **—con·sort′er,** *n.* **—con·sor′tion,** *n.*

con·sor·ti·um (kən sôr′shē əm, -tē-), *n., pl.* **-ti·a** (-shē ə, -tē ə). **1.** a combination of financial institutions, capitalists, etc., for carrying into effect some financial operation requiring large resources of capital. **2.** any association, partnership, or union. **3.** *Law.* the legal right of husband and wife to companionship and conjugal intercourse with each other: *In a wrongful death action the surviving spouse commonly seeks damages for loss of consortium.* [1820–30; < L: partnership, equiv. to *consort-* CONSORT + *-ium* -IUM] **—con·sor′ti·al,** *adj.*

con·spe·cif·ic (kon′spi sif′ik), *adj. Biol.* **1.** belonging to the same species. *—n.* **2.** an organism belonging to the same species as another. [1855–60; *conspeci(es)* (see CON-, SPECIES) + -FIC]

con·spec·tus (kən spek′təs), *n., pl.* **-tus·es. 1.** a general or comprehensive view; survey. **2.** a digest; summary; résumé. [1830–40; < L: survey, view, act of seeing, equiv. to *conspec-,* var. s. of *conspicere* to see, catch sight of (*con-* CON- + *-spicere,* comb. form of *specere* to look) + *-tus* suffix of v. action]
—Syn. 2. compendium, brief, abstract, epitome.

consperg., (in prescriptions) dust; sprinkle. [< L *consperge*]

con·spic·u·ous (kən spik′yo͞o əs), *adj.* **1.** easily seen or noticed; readily visible or observable: *a conspicuous error.* **2.** attracting special attention, as by outstanding qualities or eccentricities: *He was conspicuous by his booming laughter.* [1535–45; < L *conspicuus* visible, conspicuous, equiv. to *conspic(ere)* (see CONSPECTUS) + *-uus* deverbal adj. suffix; cf. CONTIGUOUS, CONTINUOUS, -OUS] **—con·spic′u·ous·ly,** *adv.* **—con·spic′u·ous·ness, con·spi·cu·i·ty** (kon′spi kyo͞o′i tē), *n.*
—Syn. 1. manifest, noticeable, clear, marked, salient. **2.** prominent, striking, noteworthy.

conspic′uous consump′tion, public enjoyment of possessions that are known to be costly so that one's ability to pay for such things is flaunted. [used by Thorstein Veblen in *The Theory of the Leisure Class* (1899)]

con·spir·a·cy (kən spir′ə sē), *n., pl.* **-cies. 1.** the act of conspiring. **2.** an evil, unlawful, treacherous, or surreptitious plan formulated in secret by two or more persons; plot. **3.** a combination of persons for a secret, unlawful, or evil purpose: *He joined the conspiracy to overthrow the government.* **4.** *Law.* an agreement by two or more persons to commit a crime, fraud, or other wrongful act. **5.** any concurrence in action; combination in bringing about a given result. [1325–75; ME *conspiracie,* prob. < AF; see CONSPIRE, -ACY; r. ME *conspiracioun;* see CONSPIRATION] **—con·spir′a·tive,** *adj.* **—con·spir·a·to·ri·al** (kən spir′ə tôr′ē əl, -tōr′-), **con·spir′a·to′ry,** *adj.* **—con·spir′a·to′ri·al·ly,** *adv.*
—Syn. 1. collusion, sedition. **2.** CONSPIRACY, PLOT, INTRIGUE, CABAL all refer to surreptitious or covert schemes to accomplish some end, most often an evil one. A CONSPIRACY usually involves a group entering into a secret agreement to achieve some illicit or harmful objective: *a vicious conspiracy to control prices.* A PLOT is a carefully planned secret scheme, usually by a small number of persons, to secure sinister ends: *a plot to seize control of a company.* An INTRIGUE usually involves duplicity and deceit aimed at achieving either personal advantage or criminal or treasonous objectives: *the petty intrigues of civil servants.* CABAL refers either to a plan by a small group of highly-placed persons to overthrow or control a government, or to the group of persons themselves: *a cabal of powerful lawmakers.*

conspir′acy of si′lence, a usually secret or unstated agreement to remain silent among those who know something whose disclosure might be damaging, harmful, or against their own best interest or that of their associates. [1860–65]

con·spi·ra·tion (kon′spə rā′shən), *n.* **1.** joint effort. **2.** *Obs.* conspiracy. [1275–1325; ME *conspiracioun* < AF; MF *conspiration* < L *conspīrātiōn-* (s. of *conspīrātiō*), equiv. to *conspīrāt(us)* (ptp. of *conspīrāre* to CONSPIRE) + *-iōn-* -ION] **—con′spi·ra′tion·al,** *adj.*

con·spir·a·tor (kən spir′ə tər), *n.* a person who takes part in a conspiracy; plotter. [1375–1425; late ME *conspiratour* < AF < ML; see CONSPIRE, -TOR]
—Syn. traitor, schemer, conniver.

con·spire (kən spīər′), *v.,* **-spired, -spir·ing.** *—v.i.* **1.** to agree together, esp. secretly, to do something wrong, evil, or illegal: *They conspired to kill the king.* **2.** to act or work together toward the same result or goal. *—v.t.* **3.** to plot (something wrong, evil, or illegal). [1325–75; ME < L *conspīrāre* to act in harmony, conspire, equiv. to *con-* CON- + *spīrāre* to breathe; see SPIRANT, SPIRIT] **—con·spir′er,** *n.* **—con·spir′ing·ly,** *adv.*
—Syn. 1. complot, intrigue. See **plot. 2.** combine, concur, cooperate.

con spir·i·to (kon spir′i tō′, kōn; *It.* kôn spē′rē tô), with lively spirit; vigorously (used as a direction in music). [1890–95; < It: lit., with spirit]

Const., Constitution.

const., **1.** constable. **2.** constant. **3.** constitution. **4.** constitutional. **5.** construction.

con·sta·ble (kon′stə bəl *or, esp. Brit.,* kun′-), *n.* **1.** an officer of the peace, having police and minor judicial functions, usually in a small town, rural district, etc. **2.** *Chiefly Brit.* a police officer. **3.** an officer of high rank in medieval monarchies, usually the commander of all armed forces, esp. in the absence of the ruler. **4.** the keeper or governor of a royal fortress or castle. [1200–50; ME *conestable* < AF, OF < LL *comes stabuli* COUNT[2] of the STABLE[1]] **—con′sta·ble·ship′,** *n.*

Con·sta·ble (kun′stə bəl, kon′-), *n.* **John,** 1776–1837, English painter.

con′stable glass′, a drinking glass of the 18th century, having a heavy foot, a tall body, and a capacity of 1 qt. (0.946 l).

con·stab·u·lar·y[1] (kən stab′yə ler′ē), *n., pl.* **-lar·ies. 1.** the body of constables of a district. **2.** a body of officers of the peace organized on a military basis. [1350–1400; < ML *constabulāria,* fem. of *constabulārius* CONSTABULARY[2]; r. ME *constablerie* < OF < ML as above]

con·stab·u·lar·y[2] (kən stab′yə ler′ē), *adj.* pertaining to constables or their duties. Also, **con·stab·u·lar** (kən stab′yə lər). [1815–25; < ML *constabulārius;* see CONSTABLE, -ARY]

Con·stance (kon′stəns), *n.* **1. Lake.** German, **Bodensee.** a lake in W Europe, bounded by Germany, Austria, and Switzerland. 46 mi. (74 km) long; 207 sq. mi. (536 sq. km). **2.** German, **Konstanz.** a city in S Germany, on this lake: important church council 1414–18. 61,160. **3.** a female given name.

con·stan·cy (kon′stən sē), *n.* **1.** the quality of being unchanging or unwavering, as in purpose, love, or loyalty; firmness of mind; faithfulness. **2.** uniformity or regularity, as in qualities or conditions; invariableness. [1520–30; < L *constantia.* See CONSTANT, -ANCY]
—Syn. 1. resolution, steadfastness, fidelity, fealty, loyalty, devotion. **2.** permanence, regularity, dependability.
—Ant. 1. irresolution, infidelity. **2.** fickleness.

Con·stans I (kon′stanz), (*Flavius Julius Constans*) A.D. c323–350, emperor of Rome 337–350 (son of Constantine I).

con·stant (kon′stənt), *adj.* **1.** not changing or varying; uniform; regular; invariable: *All conditions during the three experiments were constant.* **2.** continuing without pause or letup; unceasing: *constant noise.* **3.** regularly recurrent; continual; persistent: *He found it impossible to work with constant interruption.* **4.** faithful; unswerving in love, devotion, etc.: *a constant lover.* **5.** steadfast; firm in mind or purpose; resolute. **6.** *Obs.* certain; confident. *—n.* **7.** something that does not or cannot change or vary. **8.** *Physics.* a number expressing a property, quantity, or relation that remains unchanged under specified conditions. **9.** *Math.* a quantity assumed to be unchanged throughout a given discussion. [1350–1400; ME < L *constant-* (s. of *constāns,* prp. of *constāre* to stand firm), equiv. to *con-* CON- + *stā-* STAND + *-nt-* prp. suffix] **—con′stant·ly,** *adv.*
—Syn. 1. unchanging, immutable, permanent. **2.** perpetual, unremitting, uninterrupted. **3.** incessant, ceaseless. **4.** loyal, staunch, true. See **faithful. 5.** steady, unwavering, unswerving. **—Ant. 1.** changeable. **2.** fitful. **3.** sporadic. **4.** unreliable. **5.** wavering.

Con·stant (kôn stän′), *n.* **1. Paul Hen·ri Ben·ja·min Bal·luat** (pôl äN RĒ′ baN zhA maN′ bA lwA′). See **Estournelles de Constant, Paul. 2. Jean Jo·seph Ben·ja·min** (zhäN zhô zef′ baN zhA maN′), 1845–1902, French painter.

Con·stan·ța (kôn stän′tsä), *n.* a seaport in SE Rumania, on the Black Sea. 279,308.

con·stant·an (kon′stən tan′), *n.* an alloy containing approximately 55 percent copper and approximately 45 percent nickel, used for electrical resistance heating and thermocouples. [1900–05; CONSTANT + -AN]

Con·stant de Re·becque (kôn stän′ də Rə bek′), **Hen·ri Ben·ja·min** (äN RĒ′ baN zhA maN′), (*Benjamin Constant*), 1767–1830, French statesman and author, born in Switzerland.

con′stant dol′lar, a dollar valued according to its purchasing power in an arbitrarily set year and then adjusted for price changes in other years so that real purchasing power can be compared by giving prices as they would presumably be in the base year.

Con·stan·tia (kon stan′shə, -shē ə), *n.* a female given name, form of **Constance.**

Con·stan·tine (kon′stən tēn′ *or, for 1, 3,* -tīn′; *for 2, 3, also Fr.* kôn staN tēn′), *n.* **1.** died A.D. 715, pope 708–715. **2.** a city in NE Algeria. 1,682,000. **3.** a male given name.

Con·stan·tine I (kon′stən tēn′, -tīn′), **1.** (*Flavius Valerius Aurelius Constantinus*) ("*the Great*") A.D. 288?–337, Roman emperor 324–337: named Constantinople as the new capital; legally sanctioned Christian worship. **2.** 1868–1923, king of Greece 1913–17, 1920–22. **—Con·stan·tin·i·an** (kon′stən tin′ē ən), *adj.*

Constantine II, **1.** (*Flavius Claudius Constantinus*) A.D. 317–340, emperor of Rome 337–340 (son of Constantine I). **2.** born 1940, king of Greece 1964–74, in exile since 1967.

Constantine XI Pa·lae·ol·o·gus (pā′lē ol′ə gəs, pal′ē-), (*Dragases*) 1404–53, last Byzantine emperor 1449–53.

Con·stan·ti·no·ple (kon′stan tn ō′pəl), *n.* former name of **Istanbul.**

Con′stan′ti·no·pol′i·tan Creed′ (kon stan′tn ō-pol′i tn, -stan′-). See under **Nicene Creed** (def. 2). [1670–80; < LL *Constantinopolitānus,* equiv. to *Constantinopol(is)* CONSTANTINOPLE (with Gk *polítēs* citizen r. *pólis* city) + *-ānus* -AN]

Constan′tinopol′itan rite′. See **Greek rite.**

con′stant of gravita′tion, *Physics.* See under **law of gravitation.** *Symbol:* G Also called **gravitational constant.**

con′stant of integra′tion, *Math.* a constant that is added to the function obtained by evaluating the indefinite integral of a given function, indicating that all indefinite integrals of the given function differ by, at most, a constant.

con′stant-ve·loc′i·ty joint′ (kon′stənt və los′i tē), *Auto.* a universal joint that is used in the drive train of front-wheel-drive cars and operates effectively even when the shafts being connected meet at a sharp angle. Also, **con′stant veloc′ity joint′.**

con·sta·tive (kən stā′tiv), *Philos., Ling.* *—adj.* **1.** (of an utterance) describing a state of affairs; making a statement that can be said to be true or false. *—n.* **2.** a constative utterance. Cf. **performative.** [1900–05; prob. < F *constat(er)* to affirm, verify (appar. v. deriv. of L *constat* (it) is apparent, 3d sing. pres. of *constāre;* cf. CONSTANT) + -IVE]

con·stel·late (kon′stə lāt′), *v.i., v.t.,* **-lat·ed, -lat·ing.** to cluster together, as stars in a constellation. [1615–25;

< LL *constellātus* star-studded, equiv. to L *con-* CON- + *stell(a)* star + *-ātus* -ATE[1]]

con•stel•la•tion (kon′stə lā′shən), *n.* **1.** *Astron.* **a.** any of various groups of stars to which definite names have been given, as Ursa Major, Ursa Minor, Boötes, Cancer, Orion. **b.** the section of the heavens occupied by such a group. **2.** *Astrol.* **a.** the grouping or relative position of the stars as supposed to influence events, esp. at a person's birth. **b.** *Obs.* character as presumed to be determined by the stars. **3.** a group or configuration of ideas, feelings, characteristics, objects, etc., that are related in some way: *a constellation of qualities that made her particularly suited to the job.* **4.** any brilliant, outstanding group or assemblage: *a constellation of great scientists.* [1275–1325; ME *constellacioun* (< AF) < LL *constellātiōn-* (s. of *constellātiō*). See CONSTELLATE, -ION] —**con•stel•la•to•ry** (kən stel′ə tôr′ē, -tōr′ē), *adj.*
—**Syn. 4.** gathering, company, circle.

con•ster (kon′stər), *v.t., v.i. Obs.* construe.

con•ster•nate (kon′stər nāt′), *v.t.,* **-nat•ed, -nat•ing.** to dismay, confuse, or terrify. [1645–55; < L *consternātus,* ptp. of *consternāre* to unsettle, throw into confusion, perh. intensive deriv. of *consternere* to cover, spread (with) (*con-* CON- + *sternere* to STREW; cf. STRATUM), though sense development uncert.]

con•ster•na•tion (kon′stər nā′shən), *n.* a sudden, alarming amazement or dread that results in utter confusion; dismay. [1605–15; < L *consternātiōn-* (s. of *consternātiō*). See CONSTERNATE, -ION]
—**Syn.** bewilderment, alarm, terror, fear, panic, fright, horror. —**Ant.** composure, equanimity.

con•sti•pate (kon′stə pāt′), *v.t.,* **-pat•ed, -pat•ing. 1.** to cause constipation in; make costive. **2.** *Informal.* to cause to become slow-moving or immobilized; restrict the action or effectiveness of: *Bureaucratic red tape can constipate the operations of any government agency.* **3.** *Obs.* to crowd or pack closely together. [1375–1425; late ME (ptp.) < L *constipātus* (ptp. of *constipāre*), equiv. to *con-* CON- + *stipā-* (s. of *stipāre* to crowd, press) + *-tus* ptp. suffix]

con•sti•pa•tion (kon′stə pā′shən), *n.* **1.** a condition of the bowels in which the feces are dry and hardened and evacuation is difficult and infrequent. **2.** *Informal.* a state of slowing down, sluggishness, or inactivity. **3.** *Obs.* the act of crowding anything into a smaller compass; condensation. [1375–1425; late ME *constipacioun* (< MF) < LL *constipātiōn-* (s. of *constipātiō*). See CONSTIPATE, -ION]

con•stit•u•en•cy (kən stich′o͞o ən sē), *n., pl.* **-cies. 1.** a body of constituents; the voters or residents in a district represented by an elective officer. **2.** the district itself. **3.** any body of supporters, customers, etc.; clientele. [1825–35; CONSTITU(ENT) + -ENCY]

con•stit•u•ent (kən stich′o͞o ənt), *adj.* **1.** serving to compose or make up a thing; component: *the constituent parts of a motor.* **2.** having power to frame or alter a political constitution or fundamental law, as distinguished from lawmaking power: *a constituent assembly.* —*n.* **3.** a constituent element, material, etc.; component. **4.** a person who authorizes another to act in his or her behalf, as a voter in a district represented by an elected official. **5.** *Gram.* an element considered as part of a construction. Cf. **immediate constituent, ultimate constituent.** [1615–25; < L *constituent-* (s. of *constituēns,* prp. of *constituere* to set up, found, constitute), equiv. to *con-* CON- + *-stitu-* (comb. form of *statuere* to set up) + *-ent-* -ENT] —**con•stit′u•ent•ly,** *adv.*
—**Syn. 3.** See **element.**

Constit′uent Assem′bly, *Fr. Hist.* the legislature of France 1789–91.

constit′uent struc′ture, *Ling.* See **phrase structure.** [1960–65]

con•sti•tute (kon′sti to͞ot′, -tyo͞ot′), *v.t.,* **-tut•ed, -tut•ing. 1.** to compose; form: *mortar constituted of lime and sand.* **2.** to appoint to an office or function; make or create: *He was constituted treasurer.* **3.** to establish (laws, an institution, etc.). **4.** to give legal form to (an assembly, court, etc.). **5.** to create or be tantamount to: *Imports constitute a challenge to local goods.* **6.** *Archaic.* to set or place. [1400–50; late ME < L *constitūtus* (ptp. of *constituere;* see CONSTITUENT), equiv. to *con-* CON- + *-stitūtus,* comb. form of *statūtum,* ptp. of *statuere* to set up. See STATUTE] —**con′sti•tut′er, con′sti•tu′tor,** *n.*
—**Syn. 3.** institute, commission.

con•sti•tu•tion (kon′sti to͞o′shən, -tyo͞o′-), *n.* **1.** the way in which a thing is composed or made up; makeup; composition: *the chemical constitution of the cleanser.* **2.** the physical character of the body as to strength, health, etc.: *He has a strong constitution.* **3.** *Med., Psychol.* the aggregate of a person's physical and psychological characteristics. **4.** the act or process of constituting; establishment. **5.** the state of being constituted; formation. **6.** any established arrangement or custom. **7.** (*cap.*) See **Constitution of the United States. 8.** the system of fundamental principles according to which a nation, state, corporation, or the like, is governed. **9.** the document embodying these principles. **10.** *Archaic.* character or condition of mind; disposition; temperament. [1350–1400; ME *constitucion* edict, ordinance < AF < L *constitūtiōn-* (s. of *constitūtiō*). See CONSTITUTE, -ION]

Constitution, The, an American 44-gun frigate, famous for its exploits in the War of 1812 and popularly called "Old Ironsides."

con•sti•tu•tion•al (kon′sti to͞o′shə nl, -tyo͞o′-), *adj.* **1.** of or pertaining to the constitution of a state, organization, etc. **2.** subject to the provisions of such a constitution: *a constitutional monarchy.* **3.** provided by, in accordance with, or not prohibited by, such a constitution: *the constitutional powers of the president; a constitutional law.* **4.** belonging to or inherent in the character or makeup of a person's body or mind: *a constitutional weakness for sweets.* **5.** pertaining to the constitution or composition of a thing; essential. **6.** beneficial to one's constitution; healthful: *constitutional exercise.* —*n.* **7.** a walk or other mild exercise taken for the benefit of one's health. [1675–85; CONSTITUTION + -AL[1]]

Constitu′tional Conven′tion, the convention in Philadelphia (1787) of representatives from each of the former Colonies, except Rhode Island, at which the Constitution of the United States was framed.

Constitu′tional Democrat′ic par′ty, a former Russian political party that advocated a right-wing policy in foreign and domestic affairs.

con•sti•tu•tion•al•ism (kon′sti to͞o′shə nl iz′əm, -tyo͞o′-), *n.* **1.** the principles of constitutional government or adherence to them. **2.** constitutional rule or authority. [1825–35; CONSTITUTIONAL + -ISM]

con•sti•tu•tion•al•ist (kon′sti to͞o′shə nl ist, -tyo͞o′-), *n.* **1.** an adherent or advocate of constitutionalism or of an existing constitution. **2.** an expert on a political constitution. [1760–70; CONSTITUTIONAL + -IST]

con•sti•tu•tion•al•i•ty (kon′sti to͞o′shə nal′i tē, -tyo͞o′-), *n.* **1.** the quality of being constitutional. **2.** accordance with the constitution of a country, state, etc. [1780–90, *Amer.;* CONSTITUTIONAL + -ITY]

con•sti•tu•tion•al•ize (kon′sti to͞o′shə nl īz′, -tyo͞o′-), *v.t.,* **-ized, -iz•ing. 1.** to incorporate in a constitution; make constitutional. **2.** to provide a constitution for. Also, *esp. Brit.,* **con′sti•tu′tion•al•ise′.** [1825–35; CONSTITUTIONAL + -IZE] —**con′sti•tu′tion•al•i•za′tion,** *n.*

con•sti•tu•tion•al•ly (kon′sti to͞o′shə nl ē, -tyo͞o′-), *adv.* **1.** in respect to physical makeup: *He is constitutionally fitted for heavy labor.* **2.** in respect to mental or emotional makeup: *constitutionally unable to speak before an audience.* **3.** with respect to a constitution: *constitutionally invalid law.* [1735–45; CONSTITUTIONAL + -LY]

constitu′tional mon′archy. See **limited monarchy.** [1795–1805] —**constitu′tional mon′arch.**

Constitu′tional Un′ion par′ty, *U.S. Hist.* the political party formed in 1859 chiefly by former Whigs to rally moderates desirous of preserving the Union. In 1860 it nominated John Bell for president and Edward Everett for vice president.

Constitu′tion clock′, an American banjo clock having depicted on its lower part the battle in the War of 1812 between the U.S. frigate *Constitution* and the British frigate *Guerrière.*

Constitu′tion mir′ror, *U.S. Furniture.* an oblong Chippendale mirror, usually of mahogany or walnut with gilt detail, having a frame with a fanciful outline emphasized by a raised molding that is topped with a scrolled broken pediment with a central finial, often in the form of a bird. Also called **Martha Washington mirror.**

Constitu′tion of the Unit′ed States′, the fundamental or organic law of the U.S., framed in 1787 by the Constitutional Convention. It went into effect March 4, 1789.

Constitu′tion State′, Connecticut (used as a nickname).

con•sti•tu•tive (kon′sti to͞o′tiv, -tyo͞o′-), *adj.* **1.** constituent; making a thing what it is; essential. **2.** having power to establish or enact. **3.** *Physics, Chem.* pertaining to a molecular property determined primarily by the arrangement of atoms in the molecule rather than by their nature or number. [1585–95; CONSTITUTE + -IVE] —**con′sti•tu′tive•ly,** *adv.*

constr., 1. construction. **2.** construed.

con•strain (kən strān′), *v.t.* **1.** to force, compel, or oblige: *He was constrained to admit the offense.* **2.** to confine forcibly, as by bonds. **3.** to repress or restrain: *Cold weather constrained the plant's growth.* [1275–1325; ME *constrei(g)nen* < AF, MF *constrei(g)n-* (s. of *constreindre*) < L *constringere.* See CON-, STRAIN[1]] —**con•strain′a•ble,** *adj.* —**con•strain′er,** *n.* —**con•strain′ing•ly,** *adv.*
—**Syn. 1.** coerce. **2.** check, bind. —**Ant. 2.** free.

con•strained (kən strānd′), *adj.* **1.** forced, compelled, or obliged: *a constrained confession.* **2.** stiff or unnatural; uneasy or embarrassed: *a constrained manner.* [1565–75; CONSTRAIN + -ED[2]] —**con•strain•ed•ly** (kən strā′nid lē), *adv.*

con•straint (kən strānt′), *n.* **1.** limitation or restriction. **2.** repression of natural feelings and impulses: *to practice constraint.* **3.** unnatural restraint in manner, conversation, etc.; embarrassment. **4.** something that constrains. **5.** the act of constraining. **6.** the condition of being constrained. **7.** *Ling.* a restriction on the operation of a linguistic rule or the occurrence of a linguistic construction. [1350–1400; ME *constreinte* < MF, n. use of fem. ptp. of *constreindre;* see CONSTRAIN]
—**Syn. 1.** force, obligation, pressure.

con•strict (kən strikt′), *v.t.* **1.** to draw or press in; cause to contract or shrink; compress. **2.** to slow or stop the natural course or development of: *Greed and aggressiveness constricted the nation's cultural life.* [1375–1425 for earlier ptp. sense; 1725–35 for current senses; late ME < L *constrictus* (ptp. of *constringere* to draw together, tie up), equiv. to *con-* CON- + *stric-* (var. s. of *stringere* to tie; see STRICT) + *-tus* ptp. suffix]
—**Syn. 1.** cramp, squeeze, bind, tighten. —**Ant. 1.** expand.

con•stric•tion (kən strik′shən), *n.* **1.** the act of constricting. **2.** the state of being constricted; tightness or inward pressure. **3.** a constricted part. **4.** something that constricts. **5.** *Phonet.* an articulated narrowing of the vocal tract that in consonants audibly obstructs the flow of air and in vowels defines an interconnection between or among resonance cavities. Cf. **closure** (def. 6). [1350–1400; ME < LL *constrictiōn-* (s. of *constrictiō*), equiv. to L *constrict(us)* (see CONSTRICT) + *-iōn-* -ION]
—**Syn. 2.** compression, contraction, stricture.

con•stric•tive (kən strik′tiv), *adj.* **1.** constricting; tending to constrict. **2.** pertaining to constriction. [1375–1425; late ME < LL *constrictīvus,* equiv. to *constrict(us)* (see CONSTRICT) + *-īvus* -IVE]

con•stric•tor (kən strik′tər), *n.* **1.** a snake that kills its prey by coiling tightly around it, causing suffocation. **2.** *Anat.* a muscle that constricts a hollow part of the body, as the pharynx. **3.** a person or thing that constricts. [1700–10; < NL; see CONSTRICT, -TOR]

con•stringe (kən strinj′), *v.t.,* **-stringed, -string•ing.** to constrict; compress; cause to contract. [1595–1605; < L *constringere* to draw tight, tie up, equiv. to *con-* CON- + *stringere* to draw; see CONSTRICT]

con•strin•gent (kən strin′jənt), *adj.* **1.** constricting. **2.** causing constriction. [1595–1605; < L *constringent-* (s. of *constringēns,* prp. of *constringere*). See CONSTRINGE, -ENT] —**con•strin′gen•cy,** *n.*

con•stru•a•ble (kən stro͞o′ə bəl), *adj.* capable of being construed. [1650–60; CONSTRUE + -ABLE] —**con•stru′a•bil′i•ty,** *n.*

con•struct (*v.* kən strukt′; *n.* kon′strukt), *v.t.* **1.** to build or form by putting together parts; frame; devise. **2.** *Geom.* to draw (a figure) fulfilling certain given conditions. —*n.* **3.** something constructed. **4.** an image, idea, or theory, esp. a complex one formed from a number of simpler elements. [1400–50 for earlier ptp. sense; 1655–65 for current senses; late ME < L *constrūctus* (ptp. of *construere* to CONSTRUE), equiv. to *con-* CON- + *strūc-* (var. s. of *struere* to build) + *-tus* ptp. suffix] —**con•struct′i•ble,** *adj.*
—**Syn. 1.** erect, form. See **make[1].**

con•struct•er (kən struk′tər), *n.* constructor (def. 1).

con•struc•tion (kən struk′shən), *n.* **1.** the act or art of constructing. **2.** the way in which a thing is constructed: *a building of solid construction.* **3.** something that is constructed; a structure. **4.** the occupation or industry of building: *He works in construction.* **5.** *Gram.* **a.** the arrangement of two or more forms in a grammatical unit. Constructions involving bound forms are often called morphological, as the bound forms *fif-* and *-teen.* Those involving only free forms are often called syntactic, as *the good man, in the house.* Cf. **bound form, free form. b.** a word or phrase consisting of two or more forms arranged in a particular way. **c.** a group of words or morphemes for which there is a rule in some part of the grammar. **6.** explanation or interpretation, as of a law, a text, or an action. [1350–1400; ME (< MF) < L *constrūctiōn-* (s. of *constrūctiō*) a putting together, building, equiv. to *constrūct(us)* (see CONSTRUCT) + *-iōn-* -ION] —**con•struc′tion•al,** *adj.* —**con•struc′tion•al•ly,** *adv.*
—**Syn. 6.** version, rendition, story.

constr :c′tional homonym′ity, *Gram.* the property of a string of morphemes that is susceptible of two or more syntactic analyses, as in *Flying planes can be dangerous, planes* may be either the object of *flying* or the subject of *can.*

con•struc•tion•ist (kən struk′shə nist), *n.* a person who construes or interprets, esp. laws or the like, in a specific manner: *a strict constructionist.* [1835–45; CONSTRUCTION + -IST] —**con•struc′tion•ism,** *n.*

construc′tion loan′, *Finance.* a short-term loan to finance the building phase of a real-estate project.

construc′tion pa′per, a heavy groundwood paper in sheets of various sizes and colors for use esp. in making posters and cutouts. [1920–25]

con•struc•tive (kən struk′tiv), *adj.* **1.** constructing or tending to construct; helping to improve; promoting further development or advancement (opposed to *destructive*): *constructive criticism.* **2.** of, pertaining to, or of the nature of construction; structural. **3.** deduced by inference or interpretation; inferential: *constructive permission.* **4.** *Law.* denoting an act or condition not directly expressed but inferred from other acts or conditions. [1670–80; < ML *constrūctīvus,* equiv. to L *constrūct(us)* (see CONSTRUCT) + *-īvus* -IVE] —**con•struc′tive•ly,** *adv.* —**con•struc′tive•ness,** *n.*
—**Syn. 1.** productive, helpful, handy, useful.

construc′tive interfer′ence, *Physics.* the interference of two or more waves of equal frequency and phase, resulting in their mutual reinforcement and producing a single amplitude equal to the sum of the amplitudes of the individual waves. Cf. **destructive interference.**

con•struc•tiv•ism (kən struk′tə viz′əm), *n.* (*sometimes cap.*) **1.** *Fine Arts.* a nonrepresentational style of art developed by a group of Russian artists principally in the early 20th century, characterized chiefly by a severely formal organization of mass, volume, and space, and by the employment of modern industrial materials. Cf. **suprematism. 2.** *Theat.* a style of scenic design characterized by abstraction, simplification, and stylization rather than realistic imitation. [1920–25; CONSTRUCTIVE + -ISM] —**con•struc′tiv•ist,** *n., adj.*

con•struc•tor (kən struk′tər), *n.* **1.** a person or thing that builds. **2.** a person or company engaged in the construction business. **3.** a person who devises crossword puzzles. Also, **constructer.** [1610–20; CONSTRUCT + -OR[2]]

con′struct state′ (kon′strukt), *Gram.* (in Semitic languages) the inflected form of a noun dependent on a following noun, with the combination expressing a genitive relationship, as Hebrew *beth David* "house of David," where *beth* "house of" is the construct form of *bayit* "house." [1815–25]

con•strue (*v.* kən stro͞o′ *or, esp. Brit.,* kon′stro͞o; *n.* kon′stro͞o), *v.,* **-strued, -stru•ing,** *n.* —*v.t.* **1.** to give the meaning or intention of; explain; interpret. **2.** to deduce by inference or interpretation; infer: *He construed her intentions from her gestures.* **3.** to translate, esp. orally. **4.** to analyze the syntax of; to rehearse the applicable grammatical rules of: *to construe a sentence.* **5.** to arrange or combine (words, phrases, etc.) syntactically. —*v.i.* **6.** to admit of grammatical analysis or interpretation. —*n.* **7.** the act of construing. **8.** something that is construed. [1325–75; ME *construen* < L *construere* to put together, build, equiv. to *con-* CON- + *struere* to pile up, arrange, perh. akin to *sternere* to spread, STREW; see STRATUM] —**con•stru′er,** *n.*

con•sub•stan•tial (kon′səb stan′shəl), *adj.* of one and the same substance, essence, or nature. [1350–1400; ME < LL *consubstantiālis,* equiv. to *con-* CON- + *substanti(a)* SUBSTANCE + *-ālis* -AL[1]] —**con′sub•stan′tial•ism,** *n.* —**con′sub•stan′tial•ist,** *n.* —**con′sub•stan′ti•al′i•ty,** *n.* —**con′sub•stan′tial•ly,** *adv.*

con•sub•stan•ti•ate (kon′səb stan′shē āt′), *v.,* **-at•ed, -at•ing.** —*v.i.* **1.** to profess the doctrine of consubstantiation. **2.** to become united in one common substance or nature. —*v.t.* **3.** to unite in one common substance or nature. **4.** to regard as so united. [1590–1600; < NL *consubstantiātus* (ptp. of *consubstantiāre*), equiv. to *con-* CON- + *substanti(a)* SUBSTANCE + *-ātus* -ATE[1]]

con•sub•stan•ti•a•tion (kon′səb stan′shē ā′shən), *n. Theol.* the doctrine that the substance of the body and blood of Christ coexist in and with the substance of the bread and wine of the Eucharist. [1590–1600; < NL *consubstantiātiōn-* (s. of *consubstantiātiō*), equiv. to *con-* CON- + *(trans)substantiātiōn-* TRANSUBSTANTIATION]

Con•sue•la (kon swā′lə; *It., Sp.* kôn swe′lä), *n.* a female given name: from a Latin word meaning "consolation."

con•sue•tude (kon′swi to͞od′, -tyo͞od′), *n.* custom, esp. as having legal force. [1350–1400; ME < L *consuētūdō,* equiv. to *con-* CON- + *suē-* (short s. of *suēscere* to become accustomed, akin to *suus* one's own) + *-tūdō* -TUDE]

con•sue•tu•di•nar•y (kon′swi to͞od′n er′ē, -tyo͞od′-), *adj.* customary or traditional. [1375–1425; late ME < LL *consuētūdinārius,* equiv. to *consuētūdin-* (s. of *consuētūdō*) CONSUETUDE + *-ārius* -ARY]

con•sul (kon′səl), *n.* **1.** an official appointed by the government of one country to look after its commercial interests and the welfare of its citizens in another country. **2.** either of the two chief magistrates of the ancient Roman republic. **3.** *Fr. Hist.* one of the three supreme magistrates of the First Republic during the period 1799–1804. [1350–1400; ME < L; traditionally taken to be a deriv. of *consulere* to CONSULT, but orig. and interrelationship of both words is unclear] —**con′su•lar,** *adj.* —**con′sul•ship′,** *n.*
—**Usage.** See **council.**

con′sular a′gent, a consular officer of the lowest rank, often a designated foreign national, stationed at a place where no full consular service is established.

con•su•late (kon′sə lit), *n.* **1.** the premises officially occupied by a consul. **2.** the position, work, authority, or term of service of a consul. **3.** (*often cap.*) a government by consuls, as in France from 1799 to 1804. [1350–1400; ME < L *consulātus,* equiv. to *consul* CONSUL + *-ātus* -ATE[3]]

con′sulate gen′eral, *pl.* **consulates general.** the office or establishment of a consul general. [1880–85]

con′sul gen′eral, *pl.* **consuls general.** a consular officer of the highest rank, as a person who is stationed at a place of considerable commercial importance or supervises other consuls. [1745–55]

con•sult (*v.* kən sult′; *n.* kon′sult, kən sult′), *v.t.* **1.** to seek advice or information from; ask guidance from: *Consult your lawyer before signing the contract.* **2.** to refer to for information: *Consult your dictionary for the spelling of the word.* **3.** to have regard for (a person's interest, convenience, etc.) in making plans. **4.** *Obs.* to meditate, plan, or contrive. —*v.i.* **5.** to consider or deliberate; take counsel; confer (usually fol. by *with*): *He consulted with his doctor.* **6.** to give professional or expert advice; serve as consultant. —*n.* **7.** a consultation. **8.** *Archaic.* a secret meeting, esp. one for seditious purposes. [1525–35; (< MF *consulter*) < L *consultāre* to deliberate, consult, freq. of *consulere* to consult, take counsel; cf. CONSUL]
—**Syn. 1.** CONSULT, CONFER imply talking over a situation or a subject with someone to decide points in doubt. To CONSULT is to seek from a presumably qualified person or source advice, opinion, etc.: *to consult an authority.* To CONFER is to exchange views: *The partners conferred concerning their business.*

con•sult•an•cy (kən sul′tn sē), *n., pl.* **-cies. 1.** the state of being a consultant; the position of a consultant: *a consultancy with a government agency.* **2.** a person or firm that provides consulting advice or services. **3.** consultation (defs. 1, 2). [CONSULT + -ANCY]

con•sult•ant (kən sul′tnt), *n.* **1.** a person who gives professional or expert advice: *a consultant on business methods.* **2.** a person who consults someone or something. [1690–1700; (< F) < L *consultant-* (s. of *consultāns,* prp. of *consultāre*). See CONSULT, -ANT]

con•sult•ant•ship (kən sul′tnt ship′), *n.* the state or office of being a consultant; consultancy. [CONSULTANT + -SHIP]

con•sul•ta•tion (kon′səl tā′shən), *n.* **1.** the act of consulting; conference. **2.** a meeting for deliberation, discussion, or decision. **3.** a meeting of physicians to evaluate a patient's case and treatment. **4.** *Eng. Law.* a writ returning a case to an ecclesiastical court from a temporal one. **5.** *Australian.* lottery. [1540–50; < L *consultātiōn-* (s. of *consultātiō*), equiv. to *consultāt(us)* (ptp. of *consultāre;* see CONSULT, -ATE[1]) + *-iōn-* -ION]

con•sul•ta•tive (kən sul′tə tiv, kon′səl tā′tiv), *adj.* of or pertaining to consultation; advisory. Also, **con•sul•ta•to•ry** (kən sul′tə tôr′ē, -tōr′ē), **con•sul′tive.** [1575–85; CONSULTAT(ION) + -IVE] —**con•sul′ta•tive•ly,** *adv.*

con•sult•ing (kən sul′ting), *adj.* **1.** employed or involved in giving professional advice to the public or to those practicing the profession: *a consulting physician.* **2.** of, pertaining to, or used for consultation: *a physician's consulting room.* [1790–1800; CONSULT + -ING[2]]

con•sul•tor (kən sul′tər), *n.* **1.** a member of a secular clergy who advises a bishop. **2.** a specialist who advises the Roman Curia. [1620–30; < L, equiv. to *consul(ere)* to CONSULT + *-tor* -TOR]

con•sum•a•ble (kən so͞o′mə bəl), *adj.* **1.** able or meant to be consumed, as by eating, drinking, or using: *consumable goods.* **2.** liable to be used up or depleted: *consumable resources.* —*n.* **3.** Usually, **consumables.** something that is produced to be consumed, as processed food or fuel. [1635–45; CONSUME + -ABLE] —**con•sum′•a•bil′i•ty,** *n.*

con•sume (kən so͞om′), *v.,* **-sumed, -sum•ing.** —*v.t.* **1.** to destroy or expend by use; use up. **2.** to eat or drink up; devour. **3.** to destroy, as by decomposition or burning: *Fire consumed the forest.* **4.** to spend (money, time, etc.) wastefully. **5.** to absorb; engross: *consumed with curiosity.* —*v.i.* **6.** to undergo destruction; waste away. **7.** to use or use up consumer goods. [1350–1400; ME (< MF *consumer*) < L *consūmere,* equiv. to *con-* CON- + *sūmere* to take up (perh. < **suzm-* < **subzm-* < **subs-(e)m-,* equiv. to *subs-,* var. of *sub-* SUB- + *emere* to take, buy)]
—**Syn. 1.** exhaust, deplete. **4.** squander, dissipate.

con•sum•ed•ly (kən so͞o′mid lē), *adv.* excessively; extremely: *a consumedly profound wish.* [1700–10; CONSUMED + -LY]

con•sum•er (kən so͞o′mər), *n.* **1.** a person or thing that consumes. **2.** *Econ.* a person or organization that uses a commodity or service. **3.** *Ecol.* an organism, usually an animal, that feeds on plants or other animals. [1375–1425 for earlier sense "squanderer," 1525–35 for current senses; ME; see CONSUME, -ER[1]] —**con•sum′er•ship′,** *n.*

consum′er ad′vocate, consumerist (def. 1).

consum′er cred′it, credit extended by a retail store, bank, finance company, or other lender, chiefly for the purchase of consumer goods. [1925–30]

consum′er goods′, *Econ.* goods that are ready for consumption in satisfaction of human wants, as clothing or food, and are not utilized in any further production (contrasted with *capital goods*). Also called **consumption goods.** [1885–90]

con•sum•er•ism (kən so͞o′mə riz′əm), *n.* **1.** a modern movement for the protection of the consumer against useless, inferior, or dangerous products, misleading advertising, unfair pricing, etc. **2.** the concept that an ever-expanding consumption of goods is advantageous to the economy. **3.** the fact or practice of an increasing consumption of goods: *a critic of American consumerism.* [1940–45, *Amer.;* CONSUMER + -ISM]

con•sum•er•ist (kən so͞o′mər ist), *n.* **1.** Also called **consumer advocate.** a person who is dedicated to protecting and promoting the welfare and rights of consumers. —*adj.* **2.** of or pertaining to consumer interests or consumerism. [1965–70; CONSUMER + -IST]

con•sum•er•ize (kən so͞o′mə rīz′), *v.t.,* **-ized, -iz•ing. 1.** to make (goods or a product) suitable or available for mass consumption: *to consumerize computers by making them cheaper.* **2.** to encourage or foster the widespread consumption of (goods or a product). Also, *esp. Brit.,* **con•sum′er•ise′.** [CONSUMER + -IZE] —**con•sum′er•i•za′tion,** *n.*

consum′er price′ in′dex, an index of the changes in the cost of goods and services to a typical consumer, based on the costs of the same goods and services at a base period. *Abbr.:* CPI Also called **cost-of-living index.** [1945–50]

Consum′er Prod′uct Safe′ty Commis′sion, *U.S. Govt.* an independent regulatory agency, created in 1972, that protects the public against risk of injury from consumer products. *Abbr.:* CPSC

consum′er strike′, a boycott of a product by consumers, often in protest over a raise in its price.

con•sum•ing (kən so͞o′ming), *adj.* strongly and urgently felt: *a consuming need to be successful.* [CONSUME + -ING[2]] —**con•sum′ing•ly,** *adv.* —**con•sum′ing•ness,** *n.*

con•sum•mate (*v.* kon′sə māt′; *adj.* kən sum′it, kon′sə mit), *v.,* **-mat•ed, -mat•ing,** *adj.* —*v.t.* **1.** to bring to a state of perfection; fulfill. **2.** to complete (an arrangement, agreement, or the like) by a pledge or the signing of a contract: *The company consummated its deal to buy a smaller firm.* **3.** to complete (the union of a marriage) by the first marital sexual intercourse. —*adj.* **4.** complete or perfect; supremely skilled; superb: *a consummate master of the violin.* **5.** being of the highest or most extreme degree: *a work of consummate skill; an act of consummate savagery.* [1400–50; late ME (adj.) < L *consummātus* (ptp. of *consummāre* to complete, bring to perfection), equiv. to *con-* CON- + *summ(a)* SUM + *-ātus* -ATE[1]] —**con•sum′mate•ly,** *adv.* —**con′sum•ma′tive, con•sum•ma•to•ry** (kən sum′ə tôr′ē, -tōr′ē), *adj.* —**con′sum•ma′tor,** *n.*
—**Syn. 1.** complete, perfect, finish, accomplish, achieve. —**Ant. 4.** imperfect, unfinished.

con•sum•ma•tion (kon′sə mā′shən), *n.* **1.** the act of consummating; completion. **2.** the state of being consummated; perfection; fulfillment. [1350–1400; ME *consummacioun* (< MF) < L *consummātiōn-* (s. of *consummātiō*). See CONSUMMATE, -ION]

consum′matory behav′ior, *Ethology.* a behavior pattern that occurs in response to a stimulus and that achieves the satisfaction of a specific drive, as the eating of captured prey by a hungry predator (distinguished from *appetitive behavior*). [1905–10]

con•sump•tion (kən sump′shən), *n.* **1.** the act of consuming, as by use, decay, or destruction. **2.** the amount consumed: *the high consumption of gasoline.* **3.** *Econ.* the using up of goods and services having an exchangeable value. **4.** *Pathol.* **a.** *Older Use.* tuberculosis of the lungs. **b.** progressive wasting of the body. [1350–1400; ME *consumpcyon* (< MF) < L *consūmptiōn-* (s. of *consūmptiō*) a consuming, wasting, equiv. to *consūmpt(us),* ptp. of *consūmere* to CONSUME (*con-* CON- + *sūmp-* (var. s. of *sūmere* to take up, spend) + *-tus* ptp. suffix) + *-iōn-* -ION]
—**Syn. 1.** depletion, exploitation, utilization.

consump′tion goods′. See **consumer goods.** [1890–95]

consump′tion tax′, a tax, as a sales tax, levied on consumer goods or services at the time of sale. [1900–05]

consump′tion weed′. See **groundsel tree.** [1820–30, *Amer.*]

con•sump•tive (kən sump′tiv), *adj.* **1.** tending to consume; destructive; wasteful. **2.** pertaining to consumption by use. **3.** *Pathol.* **a.** pertaining to or of the nature of consumption. **b.** disposed to or affected with consumption. —*n.* **4.** *Older Use.* a person who suffers from tuberculosis. [1375–1425; ME: eliminating morbid humors < ML *consūmptīvus* wasteful, destructive; see CONSUMPTION, -IVE] —**con•sump′tive•ly,** *adv.* —**con•sump′tive•ness,** *n.*

Cont., Continental.

cont., 1. containing. **2.** contents. **3.** continent. **4.** continental. **5.** continue. **6.** continued. **7.** contra. **8.** contract. **9.** contraction. **10.** control. **11.** (in prescriptions) bruised. [def. 11 < L *contūsus*]

con•tact (kon′takt), *n.* **1.** the act or state of touching; a touching or meeting, as of two things or people. **2.** immediate proximity or association. **3.** an acquaintance, colleague, or relative through whom a person can gain access to information, favors, influential people, and the like. **4.** *Elect.* a junction of electric conductors, usually metal, that controls current flow, often completing or interrupting a circuit. **5.** *Geol.* the interface, generally a planar surface, between strata that differ in lithology or age. **6.** *Med.* a person who has lately been exposed to an infected person. **7.** *Sociol.* a condition in which two or more individuals or groups are placed in communication with each other. Cf. **categoric contact, primary contact, secondary contact, sympathetic contact. 8.** See **contact lens.** —*v.t.* **9.** to put or bring into contact. **10.** to communicate with: *We'll contact you by mail or telephone.* —*v.i.* **11.** to enter into or be in contact. —*adj.* **12.** involving or produced by touching or proximity: *contact allergy.* [1620–30; < L *contāctus* a touching, equiv. to *contac-* < **contag-,* var. s. of *contingere* to touch (*con-* CON- + *-tingere,* comb. form of *tangere* to touch) + *-tus* suffix of v. action; cf. TANGO, ATTAIN] —**con•tac•tu•al** (kon tak′cho͞o əl), *adj.* —**con•tac′tu•al•ly,** *adv.*
—**Usage.** Many verbs in English have derived from nouns. One can *head* an organization or *toe* the mark; *butter* the bread or *bread* the cutlet. Hence, grammatically at least, there is no historical justification for the once frequently heard criticism of CONTACT used as a verb meaning "to communicate with": *The managing editor contacted each reporter personally.* Despite the earlier objections to it and probably largely because there is no other one-word verb in the language to express the same idea, this use of CONTACT has become standard in all types of speech and writing. CONTACT as a noun meaning "a person through whom one can gain access to information and the like" is also standard: *My contact at the embassy says that the coup has been successful.*

con•tac•tant (kən tak′tənt), *n. Med.* any substance that might induce an allergy by coming in contact with the skin or a mucous membrane. [CONTACT + -ANT]

con′tact bi′nary, *Astron.* a binary system in which the envelopes of gas surrounding each star are in contact.

con′tact cement′, synthetic adhesive that is applied separately to the surfaces to be joined and is allowed to dry, with the surfaces then being brought into contact: often used to join veneers.

con′tact dermati′tis, *Pathol.* inflammation of the skin caused by an allergic reaction to contact with an animal, vegetable, or chemical substance.

con•tact•ee (kon′tak tē′), *n.* **1.** a person or thing that is contacted. **2.** a person who claims to have communicated with or been contacted by visitors arriving from outer space. [CONTACT + -EE]

con′tact fly′ing, aircraft piloting in which visual reference is made to the horizon and its landmarks. [1935–40, *Amer.*]

con′tact inhibi′tion, *Biol.* the cessation of movement, growth, and division in cells that touch each other. [1960–65]

con′tact lens′, one of a pair of small plastic disks that are held in place over the cornea by surface tension and correct vision defects inconspicuously. Cf. **hard lens, intraocular lens, soft lens.** [1885–90]

con′tact metamor′phism, *Geol.* localized metamorphism resulting from the heat of an igneous intrusion. [1875–80]

con′tact mine′, a naval mine designed to explode on contact with the hull of a ship. Cf. **acoustic mine, magnetic mine.** [1880–85]

con•tac•tor (kon′tak tər, kən tak′tər), *n. Elect.* a mechanically operated switch for continuously establishing and interrupting an electric power circuit. [1905–10; CONTACT + -OR[2]]

con′tact pa′per, 1. *Photog.* sensitized paper on which a contact print is made. **2.** an adhesive-backed paper or paperlike product, used to line shelves, decorate surfaces, etc.

con′tact patch′, the area of contact between a tire on an automotive vehicle and the road surface.

con′tact poten′tial, *Elect.* the potential generated by the contact of two dissimilar materials in air or in a vacuum. Also called **Volta effect.** [1880–85]

con′tact print′, *Photog.* a photographic print made by placing a negative directly in contact with sensitized paper, with their emulsion surfaces facing, and exposing them to light. Cf. **projection print.** [1930–35]

con′tact print′er, an apparatus used for making contact prints, having a frame for holding printing paper and negatives together and a light source for making an exposure. Cf. **enlarger.**

con′tact print′ing, the process of making contact prints. Cf. **projection printing.** [1875–80]

con′tact proc′ess, *Chem.* a catalytic method for producing sulfuric acid from sulfur dioxide and oxygen. [1900–05]

con′tact sheet′, *Photog.* a contact print, usually of all frames of a developed roll of negative print film, used as a proof print.

con′tact sport′, any sport in which physical contact between players is an accepted part of play, as football, boxing, or hockey.

Con·ta·do·ra (kon′tə dôr′ə), *n.* **1.** See **Contadora Group.** —*adj.* **2.** Also, **Contadoran.** of, pertaining to, or characteristic of the Contadora Group.

Contado′ra Group′, a group of four Latin American nations, Colombia, Mexico, Panama, and Venezuela, formed in January, 1983, to help solve the problems of the region. [after *Contadora* Island, off the coast of Panama, where ministers of the four nations first met]

Con·ta·do·ran (kon′tə dôr′ən), *n.* **1.** a member nation of the Contadora Group: *action taken by the Contadorans.* —*adj.* **2.** Contadora. [CONTADOR(A) + -AN]

con·ta·gion (kən tā′jən), *n.* **1.** the communication of disease by direct or indirect contact. **2.** a disease so communicated. **3.** the medium by which a contagious disease is transmitted. **4.** harmful or undesirable contact or influence. **5.** the ready transmission or spread as of an idea or emotion from person to person: *a contagion of fear.* [1350–1400; ME (< MF) < L *contāgiōn-* (s. of *contāgiō*) contact, infection, equiv. to *con-* CON- + *tāg-* (var. s. of *tangere* to touch) + *-iōn-* -ION; cf. CONTACT] —**con·ta′gioned,** *adj.*

con·ta·gious (kən tā′jəs), *adj.* **1.** capable of being transmitted by bodily contact with an infected person or object: *contagious diseases.* **2.** carrying or spreading a contagious disease. **3.** tending to spread from person to person: *contagious laughter.* [1350–1400; ME < LL *contāgiōsus,* equiv. to *contāgi(ō)* CONTAGION + *-ōsus* -OUS] —**con·ta′gious·ly,** *adv.* —**con·ta′gious·ness, con·ta·gi·os·i·ty** (kən tā′jē os′i tē), *n.*

—**Syn. 1.** CONTAGIOUS, INFECTIOUS are usually distinguished in technical medical use. CONTAGIOUS, literally "communicable by contact," describes a very easily transmitted disease as influenza or the common cold. INFECTIOUS refers to a disease involving a microorganism that can be transmitted from one person to another only by a specific kind of contact; venereal diseases are usually infectious. In nontechnical senses, CONTAGIOUS emphasizes the rapidity with which something spreads: *Contagious laughter ran through the hall.* INFECTIOUS suggests the pleasantly irresistible quality of something: *Her infectious good humor made her a popular guest.*

conta′gious abor′tion, *Vet. Pathol.* **1.** brucellosis of domestic cattle, an infectious disease characterized by spontaneous abortion and caused by the bacterium *Brucella abortus;* Bang's disease. **2.** any of several diseases causing spontaneous abortion of domestic animals, as vibriosis or salmonellosis. [1905–10]

conta′gious ec′thyma, *Vet. Pathol.* ecthyma.

conta′gious mag′ic, magic that attempts to affect a person through something once connected with him or her, as a shirt once worn by the person or a footprint left in the sand; a branch of sympathetic magic based on the belief that things once in contact are in some way permanently so, however separated physically they may subsequently become. Cf. **imitative magic.**

con·ta·gium (kən tā′jəm, -jē əm), *n., pl.* **-gia** (-jə, -jē ə). *Pathol.* the causative agent of a contagious or infectious disease, as a virus. [1645–55; < L, equiv. to *contāg-* (see CONTAGION) + *-ium* -IUM]

con·tain (kən tān′), *v.t.* **1.** to hold or include within its volume or area: *This glass contains water. This paddock contains our best horses.* **2.** to be capable of holding; have capacity for: *The room will contain 75 persons safely.* **3.** to have as contents or constituent parts; comprise; include. **4.** to keep under proper control; restrain: *He could not contain his amusement.* **5.** to prevent or limit the expansion, influence, success, or advance of (a hostile nation, competitor, opposing force, natural disaster, etc.): *to contain an epidemic.* **6.** to succeed in preventing the spread of: *efforts to contain water pollution.* **7.** *Math.* (of a number) to be a multiple of; be divisible by, without a remainder: *Ten contains five.* **8.** to be equal to: *A quart contains two pints.* [1250–1300; ME *conte(y)nen* < AF *contener,* OF *contenir* < L *continēre,* equiv. to *con-* CON- + *tenēre* to hold (see TENET)] —**con·tain′a·ble,** *adj.*

—**Syn. 1.** CONTAIN, ACCOMMODATE, HOLD, express the idea that something is so designed that something else can exist or be placed within it. CONTAIN refers to what is actually within a given container. HOLD emphasizes the idea of keeping within bounds; it refers also to the greatest amount or number that can be kept within a given container. ACCOMMODATE means to contain comfortably or conveniently, or to meet the needs of a certain number. A passenger plane that ACCOMMODATES 50 passengers may be able to HOLD 60, but at a given time may CONTAIN only 30. **3.** embody, embrace.

con·tained (kən tānd′), *adj.* showing restraint or calmness; controlled; poised: *She was contained throughout the ordeal.* [1400–50; late ME *conteynyd.* See CONTAIN, -ED[2]] —**con·tain·ed·ly** (kən tā′nid lē), *adv.*

con·tain·er (kən tā′nər), *n.* **1.** anything that contains or can contain something, as a carton, box, crate, or can. **2.** a large, vanlike, reuseable box for consolidating smaller crates or cartons into a single shipment, designed for easy and fast loading and unloading of freight. [1400–50 for an earlier sense; 1495–1505 for def. 1; late ME *conteiner;* see CONTAIN, -ER[1]]

con·tain·er·board (kən tā′nər bôrd′, -bōrd′), *n.* any paperboard used in making containers, as corrugated paper or cardboard. Also, **contain′er board′.** [1920–25; CONTAINER + BOARD]

contain′er car′, a flatcar or gondola car for carrying a number of standard, separate, removable containers. [1925–30]

con·tain·er·i·za·tion (kən tā′nər ə zā′shən), *n.* *Transp.* a method of shipping freight in relatively uniform, sealed, movable containers whose contents do not have to be unloaded at each point of transfer. Cf. **break-bulk** (def. 1). [1955–60; CONTAINERIZE + -ATION]

con·tain·er·ize (kən tā′nə rīz′), *v.t.,* **-ized, -iz·ing. 1.** to package (freight) in uniform, sealed containers for shipment. **2.** to perform (a materials-handling operation) with the help of containerization. **3.** to make suitable for a containerization system. —*v.i.* **4.** to adopt containerization. Also, *esp. Brit.,* **con·tain′er·ise′.** [CONTAINER + -IZE]

con·tain·er·port (kən tā′nər pôrt′, -pōrt′), *n.* a seaport equipped with special facilities for loading and unloading containerships. [1965–70; CONTAINER + PORT[1]]

con·tain·er·ship (kən tā′nər ship′), *n.* a usually large ship built to transport containerized cargo. Also, **contain′er ship′.** Cf. **break-bulk** (def. 2). [CONTAINER + SHIP]

con·tain·ment (kən tān′mənt), *n.* **1.** the act or condition of containing. **2.** an act or policy of restricting the territorial growth or ideological influence of another, esp. a hostile nation. **3.** (in a nuclear power plant) an enclosure completely surrounding a nuclear reactor, designed to prevent the release of radioactive material in the event of an accident. [1645–55; CONTAIN + -MENT]

con·ta·ki·on (kôn tä′kē ôn; *Eng.* kən tä′kē on′), *n., pl.* **-ki·a** (-kē ä; *Eng.* -kē ə). *Gk. Orth. Ch.* kontakion.

con·tam·i·nant (kən tam′ə nənt), *n.* something that contaminates. [1920–25; < L *contāminant-* (s. of *contāminans*), prp. of *contāmināre.* See CONTAMINATE, -ANT]

con·tam·i·nate (*v.* kən tam′ə nāt′; *n., adj.* kən tam′ə nit, -nāt′), *v.,* **-nat·ed, -nat·ing,** *n., adj.* —*v.t.* **1.** to make impure or unsuitable by contact or mixture with something unclean, bad, etc.: *to contaminate a lake with sewage.* **2.** to render harmful or unusable by adding radioactive material to: *to contaminate a laboratory.* —*n.* **3.** something that contaminates or carries contamination; contaminant. —*adj.* **4.** *Obs.* contaminated. [1375–1425; late ME *contaminaten* < L *contāminātus,* ptp. of *contāmināre* to defile, spoil, equiv. to *con-* CON- + *-tāmināre,* v. deriv. of **tāmen* something touched < **tag-s-men,* equiv. to *tag-,* var. s. of *tangere* to touch + *-s-men* resultative n. suffix; cf. EXAMEN] —**con·tam′i·na·ble,** *adj.* —**con·tam′i·na′tive,** *adj.* —**con·tam′i·na′tor,** *n.* —**con·tam′i·nous,** *adj.*

—**Syn. 1.** defile, pollute, taint, infect, poison, corrupt.

con·tam·i·na·tion (kən tam′ə nā′shən), *n.* **1.** the act of contaminating. **2.** the state of being contaminated. **3.** something that contaminates. **4.** *Ling.* **a.** an alternation in a linguistic form due to the influence of a related form, as the replacement in English of earlier *femelle* with *female* through the influence of *male.* **b.** the process of forming blends. Cf. **blend** (def. 9). [1375–1425; late ME *contaminacioun* < LL *contāminātiōn-* (s. of *contāminātiō*), equiv. to *contāmināt(us)* (see CONTAMINATE) + *-iōn-* -ION]

con·tang·o (kən tang′gō), *n., pl.* **-gos, -goes.** (on the London stock exchange) a fee paid by a buyer of securities to the seller for the privilege of deferring payment. Also called **continuation.** Cf. **backwardation.** [1850–55; said to be alter. of CONTINUE OR CONTINGENT]

contd., continued.

con·te (kôn′te), *n., pl.* **-ti** (-tē). *Italian.* count.

Con·té (kôn tā′, kon′tē; *Fr.* kôn tā′), *pl.* **-tés** (-tāz′, -tēz; *Fr.* -tā′). *Trademark.* a brand of crayon made of graphite and clay, usually in black, red, or brown. Also called **Conté′ cray′on.** [1850–55; named after N. J. *Conté,* 18th-century French chemist, who invented it]

con·temn (kən tem′), *v.t.* to treat or regard with disdain, scorn, or contempt. [1375–1425; late ME *contempnen* (< MF) < L *contemnere* to despise, scorn, equiv. to *con-* CON- + *temnere* to slight; see CONTEMPT] —**con·temn·er** (kən tem′ər, -tem′nər), **con·tem·nor** (kən tem′nər), *n.* —**con·tem·ni·ble** (kən tem′nə bəl), *adj.* —**con·tem′ni·bly,** *adv.* —**con·temn′ing·ly,** *adv.*

—**Syn.** scorn, disdain, despise.

contemp., contemporary.

con·tem·pla·ble (kən tem′plə bəl), *adj.* fit to be or capable of being contemplated. [1400–50; late ME < LL *contemplābilis,* equiv. to L *contemplā(re), contemplā(rī)* (see CONTEMPLATE) + *-bilis* -BLE]

con·tem·plate (kon′təm plāt′, -tem-), *v.,* **-plat·ed, -plat·ing.** —*v.t.* **1.** to look at or view with continued attention; observe or study thoughtfully: *to contemplate the stars.* **2.** to consider thoroughly; think fully or deeply about: *to contemplate a difficult problem.* **3.** to have as a purpose; intend. **4.** to have in view as a future event: *to contemplate buying a new car.* —*v.i.* **5.** to think studiously; meditate; consider deliberately. [1585–95; < L *contemplātus* ptp. of *contemplāre, contemplārī* to survey, observe, equiv. to *con-* CON- + *templ(um)* space marked off for augural observation, TEMPLE + *-ātus* -ATE[1]] —**con′tem·plat′ing·ly,** *adv.* —**con′tem·pla′·tor,** *n.*

—**Syn. 1.** gaze at, behold, regard, survey. **2.** study, ponder. **3.** design, plan.

con·tem·pla·tion (kon′təm plā′shən, -tem-), *n.* **1.** the act of contemplating; thoughtful observation. **2.** full or deep consideration; reflection: *religious contemplation.* **3.** purpose or intention. **4.** prospect or expectation. [1175–1225; < L *contemplātiōn-* (s. of *contemplātiō*); see CONTEMPLATE, -ION; r. ME *contemplaci(o)un* < AF < L, as above]

con·tem·pla·tive (kən tem′plə tiv, kon′təm plā′-, -tem-), *adj.* **1.** given to or characterized by contemplation: *a contemplative mind.* —*n.* **2.** a person devoted to contemplation, as a monk. [1300–50; < L *contemplātīvus,* equiv. to *contemplāt(us)* (see CONTEMPLATE) + *-īvus* -IVE; r. ME *contemplatif* < AF < L, as above] —**con·tem′pla·tive·ly,** *adv.* —**con·tem′pla·tive·ness,** *n.*

—**Syn. 1.** thoughtful, reflective, meditative.

contem′plative or′der, a religious order whose members are devoted to prayer rather than works. [1880–85]

con·tem·po (kən tem′pō), *adj. Informal.* following or showing the latest style or fad: *contempo furniture.* [by shortening; see -O]

con·tem·po·ra·ne·ous (kən tem′pə rā′nē əs), *adj.* living or occurring during the same period of time; contemporary. [1650–60; < L *contemporāneus,* equiv. to *con-* CON- + *tempor-* (s. of *tempus* time) + *-āneus* (*-ān(us)* -AN + *-eus* -EOUS)] —**con·tem·po·ra·ne·i·ty** (kən tem′pər ə nē′i tē), **con·tem′po·ra′ne·ous·ness,** *n.* —**con·tem′po·ra′ne·ous·ly,** *adv.*

—**Syn.** simultaneous, concurrent. See **contemporary.**

con·tem·po·rar·y (kən tem′pə rer′ē), *adj., n., pl.* **-rar·ies.** —*adj.* **1.** existing, occurring, or living at the same time; belonging to the same time: *Newton's discovery of the calculus was contemporary with that of Leibniz.* **2.** of about the same age or date: *a Georgian table with a contemporary wig stand.* **3.** of the present time; modern: *a lecture on the contemporary novel.* —*n.* **4.** a person belonging to the same time or period with another or others. **5.** a person of the same age as another. [1625–35; < LL *contempor-* (see CONTEMPORIZE) + -ARY] —**con·tem′po·rar′i·ly,** *adv.* —**con·tem′po·rar′·i·ness,** *n.*

—**Syn. 1.** coexistent, concurrent, simultaneous. CONTEMPORARY, CONTEMPORANEOUS, COEVAL, COINCIDENT all mean happening or existing at the same time. CONTEMPORARY often refers to persons or their acts or achievements: *Hemingway and Fitzgerald, though contemporary, shared few values.* CONTEMPORANEOUS is applied chiefly to events: *the rise of industrialism, contemporaneous with the spread of steam power.* COEVAL refers either to very long periods of time—an era or an eon—or to remote or long ago times: *coeval stars, shining for millenia with equal brilliance; coeval with the dawning of civilization.* COINCIDENT means occurring at the same time but without causal or other relationships: *prohibition, coincident with the beginning of the 1920's.*

con·tem·po·rize (kən tem′pə rīz′), *v.,* **-rized, -riz·ing.** —*v.t.* **1.** to place in or regard as belonging to the same age or time. **2.** to give a modern or contemporary character or setting to; update: *The new production of* Romeo and Juliet *contemporizes it as the love of two modern teenagers in a Chicago high school.* —*v.i.* **3.** to be contemporary. Also, *esp. Brit.,* **con·tem′po·rise′.** [1640–50; < LL *contempor-* (s. of *contemporāre* to be at the same time), equiv. to *con-* CON- + *tempor-* (s. of *tempus* time) + -IZE]

con·tempt (kən tempt′), *n.* **1.** the feeling with which a person regards anything considered mean, vile, or worthless; disdain; scorn. **2.** the state of being despised; dishonor; disgrace. **3.** *Law.* **a.** willful disobedience to or open disrespect for the rules or orders of a court **(contempt′ of court′)** or legislative body. **b.** an act showing such disrespect. [1350–1400; ME (< AF) < L *contemptus* a slighting, equiv. to *contemn(ere)* to despise, scorn (see CONTEMN) + *-tus* suffix of v. action, with loss of *n* and intrusive *p*]

—**Syn. 1.** contumely. CONTEMPT, DISDAIN, SCORN imply strong feelings of disapproval combined with disgust or derision. CONTEMPT is disapproval tinged with disgust for what seems mean, base, or worthless: *to feel contempt for a weakling.* DISDAIN is a feeling that something is unworthy of one's notice or acceptance: *disdain for crooked dealing.* SCORN denotes derisive, open, or undisguised contempt, as for a thing thought unworthy of considerate treatment: *He showed only scorn for those who had not been as ambitious as himself.* —**Ant. 1.** respect.

con·tempt·i·ble (kən temp′tə bəl), *adj.* **1.** deserving of or held in contempt; despicable. **2.** *Obs.* contemptuous. [1350–1400; ME (< MF) < LL *contemptibilis,* equiv. to *contempt(us)* (see CONTEMPT) + *-ibilis* -IBLE] —**con·tempt′i·bil′i·ty, con·tempt′i·ble·ness,** *n.* —**con·tempt′i·bly,** *adv.*

—**Syn. 1.** mean, abject, low, base. —**Ant. 1.** admirable.

contempt′ of Con′gress, contempt of a U.S. Congressional body, as of an investigating committee, shown by a witness summoned or appearing before it.

con·temp·tu·ous (kən temp′cho͞o əs), *adj.* showing or expressing contempt or disdain; scornful. [1520–30; < L *contemptu-,* s. of *contemptus* CONTEMPT + -OUS] —**con·temp′tu·ous·ly,** *adv.* —**con·temp′tu·ous·ness,** *n.*

—**Syn.** disdainful, sneering, insolent, arrogant, supercilious, haughty. —**Ant.** respectful.

con·tend (kən tend′), *v.i.* **1.** to struggle in opposition: *to contend with the enemy for control of the port.* **2.** to strive in rivalry; compete; vie: *to contend for first prize.* **3.** to strive in debate; dispute earnestly: *to contend against falsehood.* —*v.t.* **4.** to assert or maintain earnestly: *He contended that taxes were too high.* [1400–50; late ME *contenden* < AF *contendre* < L *contendere* to

CONCISE ETYMOLOGY KEY: <, descended or borrowed from; >, whence; b., blend of, blended; c., cognate with; cf., compare; deriv., derivative; equiv., equivalent; imit., imitative; obl., oblique; r., replacing; s., stem; sp., spelling, spelled; resp., respelling, respelled; trans., translation; ?, origin unknown; *, unattested; ‡, probably earlier than. See the full key inside the front cover.

compete, strive, draw tight, equiv. to *con-* CON- + *tendere* to stretch; see TEND[1]] **—con·tend′er,** *n.* **—con·tend′ing·ly,** *adv.*
—Syn. 1. wrestle, grapple, battle, fight. **2.** See **compete. 3.** argue, wrangle. **4.** hold, claim. **—Ant. 3.** agree.

con·tent[1] (kon′tent), *n.* **1.** Usually, **contents. a.** something that is contained: *the contents of a box.* **b.** the subjects or topics covered in a book or document. **c.** the chapters or other formal divisions of a book or document: *a table of contents.* **2.** something that is to be expressed through some medium, as speech, writing, or any of various arts: *a poetic form adequate to a poetic content.* **3.** significance or profundity; meaning: *a clever play that lacks content.* **4.** that which may be perceived in something: *the latent versus the manifest content of a dream.* **5.** *Philos., Logic.* the sum of the attributes or notions comprised in a given conception; the substance or matter of cognition. **6.** power of containing; holding capacity: *The bowl's content is three quarts.* **7.** volume, area, or extent; size. **8.** the amount contained. **9.** *Ling.* the system of meanings or semantic values specific to a language (opposed to *expression*). **10. a.** *Math.* the greatest common divisor of all the coefficients of a given polynomial. Cf. **primitive polynomial. b.** any abstraction of the concept of length, area, or volume. [1375–1425; late ME (< AF) < ML *contentum,* n. use of neut. of L *contentus* (ptp. of *continēre* to contain), equiv. to *con-* CON- + *ten-* hold + *-tus* ptp. suffix]

con·tent[2] (kən tent′), *adj.* **1.** satisfied with what one is or has; not wanting more or anything else. **2.** *Brit.* agreeing; assenting. **3.** *Archaic.* willing. —*v.t.* **4.** to make content: *These things content me.* —*n.* **5.** the state or feeling of being contented; contentment: *His content was threatened.* **6.** (in the British House of Lords) an affirmative vote or voter. [1400–50; late ME < MF < L *contentus* satisfied, special use of ptp. of *continēre;* see CONTENT[1]] **—con·tent′a·ble,** *adj.* **—con·tent′ly,** *adv.* **—con·tent′ness,** *n.*
—Syn. 4. appease, gratify. See **satisfy. —Ant. 4.** dissatisfy.

con′tent anal′ysis, analysis to determine the meaning, purpose, or effect of any type of communication, as literature, newspapers, or broadcasts, by studying and evaluating the details, innuendoes, and implications of the content, recurrent themes, etc. [1950–55]

con·tent·ed (kən ten′tid), *adj.* content. [1515–25; CONTENT[2] + -ED[2]] **—con·tent′ed·ly,** *adv.* **—con·tent′ed·ness,** *n.*
—Syn. gratified, pleased, happy.

con·ten·tion (kən ten′shən), *n.* **1.** a struggling together in opposition; strife. **2.** a striving in rivalry; competition; contest. **3.** strife in debate; dispute; controversy. **4.** a point contended for or affirmed in controversy. [1350–1400; ME (< AF) < L *contentiōn-* (s. of *contentiō*), equiv. to *content(us),* ptp. of *contendere* to CONTEND (*con-* CON- + *tentus,* var. of *tēnsus;* see TENSE[1]) + *-iōn-* -ION] **—con·ten′tion·al,** *adj.*
—Syn. 1. conflict, combat. **3.** disagreement, dissension, debate, altercation. **—Ant. 3.** agreement.

con·ten·tious (kən ten′shəs), *adj.* **1.** tending to argument or strife; quarrelsome: *a contentious crew.* **2.** causing, involving, or characterized by argument or controversy: *contentious issues.* **3.** *Law.* pertaining to causes between contending parties. [1400–50; late ME *contencio*se < L *contentiōsus,* equiv. to *contenti(ō)* CONTENTION + *-ōsus* -OUS] **—con·ten′tious·ly,** *adv.* **—con·ten′tious·ness,** *n.*
—Syn. 1. disputatious, argumentative.

con·ten·tive (kən ten′tiv), *n. Ling.* a content word or a morpheme that is the root of a content word. Cf. **functor** (def. 2). [CONTENT[1] + -IVE]

con·tent·ment (kən tent′mənt), *n.* **1.** the state of being contented; satisfaction; ease of mind. **2.** *Archaic.* the act of making contentedly satisfied. [1400–50; late ME *contentement* < MF. See CONTENT[2], -MENT]
—Syn. 1. See **happiness.**

con′tent word′, a word, typically a noun, verb, adjective, or adverb, that carries semantic content, bearing reference to the world independently of its use within a particular sentence (distinguished from *function word*). [1935–40]

con·ter·mi·nous (kən tûr′mə nəs), *adj.* **1.** having a common boundary; bordering; contiguous. **2.** meeting at the ends; without an intervening gap: *In our calendar system, the close of one year is conterminous with the beginning of the next.* **3.** coterminous. Also, **con·ter′mi·nal, coterminal.** [1625–35; < L *conterminus* having a common border with, equiv. to *con-* CON- + *terminus* TERMINUS; see -OUS] **—con·ter′mi·nal·ly, con·ter′mi·nous·ly,** *adv.* **—con·ter′mi·nal′i·ty, con·ter′mi·nous·ness,** *n.*

con·tes·sa (kôn tes′sä; *Eng.* kən tes′ə), *n., pl.* ***-tes·se*** (-tes′e), *Eng.* **-tes·sas.** *n. Italian.* countess.

con·test (*n.* kon′test; *v.* kən test′), *n.* **1.** a race, conflict, or other competition between rivals, as for a prize. **2.** struggle for victory or superiority. **3.** strife in argument; dispute; controversy: *Their marriage was marred by perpetual contest.* —*v.t.* **4.** to struggle or fight for, as in battle. **5.** to argue against; dispute: *to contest a controversial question; to contest a will.* **6.** to call in question: *They contested his right to speak.* **7.** to contend for in rivalry. —*v.i.* **8.** to dispute; contend; compete. [1595–1605; (v.) < L *contestārī* to call to witness (in a lawsuit), equiv. to *con-* CON- + *testārī* to TESTIFY, deriv. of *testis* witness; (n.) deriv. of the v., or < F *conteste*] **—con·test′a·ble,** *adj.* **—con·test′a·ble·ness,** *n.* **—con·test′a·bly,** *adv.* **—con·test′er,** *n.* **—con·test′ing·ly,** *adv.*
—Syn. 1. contention, rivalry, match, tournament, tourney, game. **2.** battle, encounter. See **fight. 3.** debate, polemic, altercation. **4.** See **compete. 5.** controvert, oppose. **6.** challenge. **7.** strive, compete, vie.

con·test·ant (kən tes′tənt), *n.* **1.** a person who takes part in a contest or competition. **2.** a person who contests the results of an election. **3.** *Law.* the party who, in proceedings in the probate court, contests the validity of a will. [1655–65; < F; see CONTEST, -ANT]

con·tes·ta·tion (kon′te stā′shən), *n.* **1.** the act of contesting; controversy; dispute. **2.** an assertion contended for. [1540–50; (< MF) < L *contestātiōn-* (s. of *contestātiō*). See CONTEST, -ATION]

con·text (kon′tekst), *n.* **1.** the parts of a written or spoken statement that precede or follow a specific word or passage, usually influencing its meaning or effect: *You have misinterpreted my remark because you took it out of context.* **2.** the set of circumstances or facts that surround a particular event, situation, etc. **3.** *Mycol.* the fleshy fibrous body of the pileus in mushrooms. [1375–1425; late ME < L *contextus* a joining together, scheme, structure, equiv. to *contex(ere)* to join by weaving (*con-* CON- + *texere* to plait, weave) + *-tus* suffix of v. action; cf. TEXT] **—con′text·less,** *adj.*
—Syn. 2. background, milieu, climate.

con′text of situa′tion, *Ling.* the totality of extralinguistic features having relevance to a communicative act.

con·tex·tu·al (kən teks′cho͞o əl), *adj.* of, pertaining to, or depending on the context. [1805–15; < L *contextu-,* s. of *contextus* CONTEXT + -AL[1]] **—con·tex′tu·al·ly,** *adv.*

contex′tual defini′tion, *Logic, Philos.* definition of a word or symbol by explaining the meaning of the phrase or statement in which it occurs. [1930–35]

con·tex·tu·al·ism (kən teks′cho͞o ə liz′əm), *n.* **1.** (in motion-picture criticism) the theory that all incidents in a film must be viewed in the social, political, and cultural context with which the film concerns itself and in which it was made. **2.** *Archit.* the aesthetic position that a building or the like should be designed for harmony or a meaningful relationship with other such elements already existing in its vicinity. [1925–30; CONTEXTUAL + -ISM] **—con·tex′tu·al·ist,** *n., adj.*

con·tex·tu·al·ize (kən teks′cho͞o ə līz′), *v.t.,* **-ized, -iz·ing.** to put (a linguistic element, an action, etc.) in a context, esp. one that is characteristic or appropriate, as for purposes of study. Also, *esp. Brit.,* **con·tex′tu·al·ise′.** [1930–35; CONTEXTUAL + -IZE] **—con·tex′tu·al·i·za′tion,** *n.*

con·tex·ture (kən teks′chər), *n.* **1.** the arrangement and union of the constituent parts of anything; constitution; structure. **2.** an interwoven structure; fabric. **3.** the act of weaving together. **4.** the process or manner of being woven together. [1595–1605; < F; see CONTEXT, -URE] **—con·tex′tur·al,** *adj.* **—con·tex′tured,** *adj.*

contg., containing.

con·ti·gu·i·ty (kon′ti gyo͞o′i tē), *n., pl.* **-ties. 1.** the state of being contiguous; contact or proximity. **2.** a series of things in continuous connection; a continuous mass or extent. [1635–45; < LL *contiguitās.* See CONTIGUOUS, -ITY]

con·tig·u·ous (kən tig′yo͞o əs), *adj.* **1.** touching; in contact. **2.** in close proximity without actually touching; near. **3.** adjacent in time: *contiguous events.* [1605–15; < L *contiguus* bordering upon, equiv. to *con-* CON- + *tig-* (var. s. of *-tingere,* comb. form of *tangere* to touch; see TANGENT, CONTINGENT, CONTACT) + *-uus* deverbal adj. suffix; cf. -OUS, CONTINUOUS] **—con·tig′u·ous·ly,** *adv.* **—con·tig′u·ous·ness,** *n.*
—Syn. 1. bordering, adjoining, abutting. **2.** adjacent.

contin., continued.

con·ti·nence (kon′tn əns), *n.* **1.** self-restraint or abstinence, esp. in regard to sexual activity; temperance; moderation. **2.** *Physiol.* the ability to voluntarily control urinary and fecal discharge. Also, **con′ti·nen·cy.** [1350–1400; ME < L *continentia.* See CONTINENT, -ENCE]

con·ti·nent (kon′tn ənt), *n.* **1.** one of the main landmasses of the globe, usually reckoned as seven in number (Europe, Asia, Africa, North America, South America, Australia, and Antarctica). See table. **2.** a comparable landmass on another planet. **3.** the mainland, as distinguished from islands or peninsulas. **4. the Continent,** the mainland of Europe, as distinguished from the British Isles. **5.** a continuous tract or extent, as of land. **6.** *Archaic.* something that serves as a container or boundary. —*adj.* **7.** exercising or characterized by restraint in relation to the desires or passions and esp. to sexual desires; temperate. **8.** able to control urinary and fecal discharge. **9.** *Obs.* containing; being a container; capacious. **10.** *Obs.* restraining or restrictive. **11.** *Obs.* continuous; forming an uninterrupted tract, as land. [1350–1400; ME < L *continent-* (s. of *continēns,* prp. of *continēre* to CONTAIN), equiv. to *con-* CON- + *-tin-,* comb. form of *ten-* hold + *-ent-* -ENT]

CONTINENTS

Name	Approximate Land Area sq. mi.	Approximate Land Area sq. km	Estimated Population
Africa	11,700,000	30,303,000	551,000,000
Antarctica	5,000,000	12,950,000	(uninhabited)
Asia	16,000,000	41,440,000	2,896,700,000
Australia	2,948,366	7,636,270	14,576,330
Europe	4,017,000	10,404,000	702,300,000
North America	9,360,000	24,242,400	400,000,000
South America	6,900,000	17,871,000	271,000,000

con·ti·nen·tal (kon′tn en′tl), *adj.* **1.** of or of the nature of a continent. **2.** (*usually cap.*) of or pertaining to the mainland of Europe, to Europeans, or to European customs and attitudes. **3.** (*cap.*) of or pertaining to the 13 original American colonies during and immediately after the American Revolution. **4.** of or pertaining to the continent of North America. —*n.* **5.** (*cap.*) a soldier of the Continental Army in the American Revolution. **6.** a piece of paper currency issued by the Continental Congress during the American Revolution. **7.** a small amount: *advice that's not worth a continental.* **8.** an inhabitant of a continent. **9.** (*usually cap.*) an inhabitant of the mainland of Europe. [1750–60; CONTINENT + -AL[1]] **—con′ti·nen′tal·ly,** *adv.*

Con′tinen′tal Ar′my, *Amer. Hist.* the Revolutionary War Army, authorized by the Continental Congress in 1775 and led by George Washington.

con′tinen′tal break′fast, a light breakfast consisting typically of coffee and rolls. *Abbr.:* CB [1910–15]

Con′tinen′tal Cel′tic, Celtic as spoken and written in ancient times on the mainland of Europe. Cf. **Insular Celtic.**

con′tinen′tal code′. See **international Morse code.** [1920–25]

Con′tinen′tal Con′gress, *Amer. Hist.* either of two legislative congresses during and after the Revolutionary War. The first was in session from September 5 to October 26, 1774, to petition the British government for a redress of grievances. The second existed from May 10, 1775, to 1789, and issued the Declaration of Independence and established the Articles of Confederation.

continen′tal cuisine′, a style of cooking that includes the better-known dishes of various western European countries.

continen′tal divide′, 1. a divide separating river systems that flow to opposite sides of a continent. **2.** (*caps.*) (in North America) the line of summits of the Rocky Mountains, separating streams flowing toward the Gulf of California and the Pacific from those flowing toward the Gulf of Mexico, Hudson Bay, and the Arctic Ocean. [1865–70, *Amer.*]

con′tinen′tal drift′, *Geol.* the lateral movement of continents resulting from the motion of crustal plates. Cf. **plate tectonics.** [1925–30]

con·ti·nen·tal·ism (kon′tn en′tl iz′əm), *n.* **1.** an attitude, expression, etc., characteristic of a continent, esp. of Europe. **2.** an attitude or policy of favoritism or partiality to a continent: *American continentalism.* **3.** the belief or doctrine that the U.S. and Canada should merge into a North American nation, esp. for mutual economic benefit. [1850–55; CONTINENTAL + -ISM] **—con′ti·nen′·tal·ist,** *n.*

con·ti·nen·tal·i·ty (kon′tn ən tal′i tē), *n.* the degree to which the climate of a region typifies that of the interior of a large landmass. Cf. **oceanicity.** [1895–1900; CONTINENTAL + -ITY]

con·ti·nen·tal·ize (kon′tn en′tl īz′), *v.t.,* **-ized, -iz·ing. 1.** to make continental, as in scope or character. **2.** (*sometimes cap.*) to influence with European ideas or culture. Also, *esp. Brit.,* **con′ti·nen′tal·ise′.** [1850–55; CONTINENTAL + -IZE] **—con′ti·nen′tal·i·za′tion,** *n.*

con′tinen′tal mar′gin, *Physical Geog.* the offshore zone, consisting of the continental shelf, slope, and rise, that separates the dry-land portion of a continent from the deep ocean floor.

con′tinen′tal quilt′, *Brit.* duvet.

con′tinen′tal rise′, *Physical Geog.* the gently sloping transition between the continental slope and the deep ocean floor, usually characterized by coalescence of submarine alluvial fans.

con′tinen′tal seat′ing, a theater seating plan in which there is no center aisle, but with wide spacing between each row of seats to allow for ease of passage.

con′tinen′tal shelf′, *Physical Geog.* the part of a continent that is submerged in relatively shallow sea. [1940–45]

con′tinen′tal slope′, *Physical Geog.* a steep slope separating a continental shelf and a deep ocean basin. [1905–10]

continen′tal sys′tem. See **French system.** [1830–40]

con·ti·nent·ly (kon′tn ənt lē), *adv.* in a continent manner; temperately. [1520–30; CONTINENT + -LY]

con·tin·gence (kən tin′jəns), *n.* contact or tangency. [1520–30; CONTING(ENT) + -ENCE]

con·tin·gen·cy (kən tin′jən sē), *n., pl.* **-cies. 1.** dependence on chance or on the fulfillment of a condition; uncertainty; fortuitousness: *Nothing was left to contingency.* **2.** a contingent event; a chance, accident, or possibility conditional on something uncertain: *He was prepared for every contingency.* **3.** something incidental to a thing. [1555–65; CONTING(ENT) + -ENCY]
—Syn. 2. emergency, likelihood, predicament.

contin′gency fee′. See **contingent fee.**

contin′gency fund′, *Accounting.* money or securities set aside to cover unexpected conditions or losses in business, usually supplementing a contingency reserve. Also, **contingent fund.** [1880–85]

contin′gency plan′, 1. a course of action to be followed if a preferred plan fails or an existing situation changes. **2.** a plan or procedure that will take effect if an emergency occurs; emergency plan.

contin′gency reserve′, *Accounting.* an amount of money established from retained earnings to allow for unforeseen losses in business. Also, **contin′gent reserve′.** [1930–35]

contin′gency ta′ble, *Statistics.* the frequency distribution for a two-way statistical classification. [1945–50]

contin′gency tax′, any new tax that would be necessary in case of a shortfall in revenues.

CONCISE PRONUNCIATION KEY: *act, cāpe, dâre, pärt; set, ēqual; if, īce; ox, ōver, ôrder, oil, bo͝ok, bo͞ot, out; up, ûrge; child; sing; shoe; thin, that;* zh as in *treasure.* ə = *a* as in *alone, e* as in *system, i* as in *easily, o* as in *gallop, u* as in *circus;* ᵊ as in *fire* (fīᵊr), *hour* (ouᵊr). l and n can serve as syllabic consonants, as in *cradle* (krād′l), and *button* (but′n). See the full key inside the front cover.

con•tin•gent (kən tin′jənt), *adj.* **1.** dependent for existence, occurrence, character, etc., on something not yet certain; conditional (often fol. by *on* or *upon*): *Our plans are contingent on the weather.* **2.** liable to happen or not; uncertain; possible: *They had to plan for contingent expenses.* **3.** happening by chance or without known cause; fortuitous; accidental: *contingent occurrences.* **4.** *Logic.* (of a proposition) neither logically necessary nor logically impossible, so that its truth or falsity can be established only by sensory observation. —*n.* **5.** a quota of troops furnished. **6.** any one of the representative groups composing an assemblage: *the New York contingent at a national convention.* **7.** the proportion that falls to one as a share to be contributed or furnished. **8.** something contingent; contingency. [1350–1400; late ME (prp.) (< MF) < L *contingent-* (s. of *contingēns,* prp. of *contingere*), equiv. to *con-* CON- + *ting-,* var. s. of *tangere* to touch + *-ent-* -ENT] —**con•tin′gent•ly,** *adv.*

contin′gent benefi′ciary, *Insurance.* a person who becomes the beneficiary if the primary beneficiary dies or is otherwise disqualified.

contin′gent fee′, a fee paid to a lawyer conducting a suit, esp. a suit for damages, in the event that the suit is successful and generally based on a percentage of the sum recovered. Also called **contingency fee.**

contin′gent fund′. See **contingency fund.**

contin′gent liabil′ity, a liability dependent upon the occurrence of a particular event, as default by the maker of a guaranteed loan.

con•tin•u•al (kən tin′yo͞o əl), *adj.* **1.** of regular or frequent recurrence; often repeated; very frequent: *continual bus departures.* **2.** happening without interruption or cessation; continuous in time. [1300–50; < ML *continuālis,* equiv. to L *continu(us)* CONTINUOUS + *-ālis* -AL[1]; r. ME *continuel* < MF < L, as above] —**con•tin′u•al′i•ty, con•tin′u•al•ness,** *n.*
—**Syn. 1.** successive, recurrent, repetitive, repetitious. **2.** unceasing, ceaseless, incessant, uninterrupted, unremitting, unbroken, permanent, unending.
—**Usage.** Although usage guides generally advise that CONTINUAL may be used only to mean "intermittent" and CONTINUOUS only to mean "uninterrupted," the words are used interchangeably in all kinds of speech and writing with no distinction in meaning: *The President's life is under continual* (or *continuous*) *scrutiny. Continuous* (or *continual*) *bursts of laughter punctuated her testimony.* The adverbs CONTINUALLY and CONTINUOUSLY are also used interchangeably. To make a clear distinction between what occurs at short intervals and what proceeds without interruption, writers sometimes use the contrasting terms *intermittent* (*intermittent losses of power during the storm*) and *uninterrupted* (*uninterrupted reception during the storm*) or similar expressions. CONTINUOUS is not interchangeable with CONTINUAL in the sense of spatial relationship: *a continuous* (not *continual*) *series of passages.*

con•tin•u•al•ly (kən tin′yo͞o ə lē), *adv.* **1.** very often; at regular or frequent intervals; habitually. **2.** without cessation or intermission; unceasingly; always. [1175–1225; ME *continuelli, continueliche.* See CONTINUAL, -LY]
—**Usage.** See **continual.**

con•tin•u•ance (kən tin′yo͞o əns), *n.* **1.** an act or instance of continuing; continuation: *a continuance of war.* **2.** a remaining in the same place, condition, etc. **3.** continuation (def. 3). **4.** *Law.* adjournment of a step in a proceeding to a future day. [1325–75; ME < AF; see CONTINUE, -ANCE]
—**Syn. 1.** persistence, extension, prolongation.

con•tin•u•ant (kən tin′yo͞o ənt), *Phonet.* —*n.* **1.** a consonant, as *f* or *s,* that may be prolonged without change of quality. Cf. **stop** (def. 39). —*adj.* **2.** pertaining to or noting a continuant. [1600–10; < L *continuant-,* s. of *continuāns,* prp. of *continuāre* to CONTINUE; see -ANT]

con•tin•u•ate (kən tin′yo͞o āt′), *adj. Obs.* continuing; uninterrupted. [1375–1425; late ME < L *continuātus,* ptp. of *continuāre* to CONTINUE; see -ATE[1]] —**con•tin′u•ate′ly,** *adv.* —**con•tin′u•ate′ness,** *n.*

con•tin•u•a•tion (kən tin′yo͞o ā′shən), *n.* **1.** the act or state of continuing; the state of being continued. **2.** extension or carrying on to a further point: *to request the continuation of a loan.* **3.** something that continues some preceding thing by being of the same kind or having a similar content: *Today's weather will be a continuation of yesterday's.* **4.** *Library Science.* **a.** a supplement to a publication previously issued. **b.** a work published in continuance of a monograph, serial, or series. **5.** *Brit. Stock Exchange.* contango. [1350–1400; ME *continuacio(u)n* (< AF) < L *continuātiōn-* (s. of *continuātiō*). See CONTINUATE, -ION]

continua′tion school′, a school providing extension courses for people who have left school in the elementary grades to go to work. [1885–90]

con•tin•u•a•tive (kən tin′yo͞o ā′tiv, -ə tiv), *adj.* **1.** tending or serving to continue; causing continuation or prolongation. **2.** expressing continuance of thought. **3.** *Gram.* expressing a following event. In *They arrested a suspect, who gave his name as John Doe,* the second clause is continuative. **4.** *Gram.* (of a verbal form or aspect) expressing continuation. —*n.* **5.** something continuative. **6.** *Gram.* a continuative word or expression. [1520–30; < LL *continuātīvus* connecting, copulative. See CONTINUATE, -IVE] —**con•tin′u•a′tive•ly,** *adv.* —**con•tin′u•a′tive•ness,** *n.*

con•tin•u•a•tor (kən tin′yo͞o ā′tər), *n.* a person or thing that continues. [1640–50; CONTINUATE + -OR[2]]

con•tin•ue (kən tin′yo͞o), *v.,* **-ued, -u•ing.** —*v.i.* **1.** to go on after suspension or interruption: *The program continued after an intermission.* **2.** to go on or keep on, as in some course or action; extend: *The road continues for three miles.* **3.** to last or endure: *The strike continued for two months.* **4.** to remain in a particular state or capacity: *The general agreed to continue in command of the army.* **5.** to remain in a place; abide; stay: *Let us continue in this house forever.* —*v.t.* **6.** to go on with or persist in: *to continue an action.* **7.** to carry on from the point of suspension or interruption: *He continued the concert after the latecomers were seated.* **8.** to extend from one point to another in space; prolong. **9.** to say in continuation. **10.** to cause to last or endure; maintain or retain, as in a position. **11.** to carry over, postpone, or adjourn; keep pending, as a legal proceeding. [1300–50; ME (< AF) < L *continuāre* to make all one, v. deriv. of *continuus* CONTINUOUS] —**con•tin′u•a•ble,** *adj.* —**con•tin′u•er,** *n.* —**con•tin′u•ing•ly,** *adv.*
—**Syn. 3.** CONTINUE, ENDURE, PERSIST, PERSEVERE, LAST, REMAIN imply existing uninterruptedly for an appreciable length of time. CONTINUE implies duration or existence without break or interruption. ENDURE, used of people or things, implies persistent continuance against influences that tend to weaken, undermine, or destroy. PERSIST and PERSEVERE, used principally of people, both imply firm and steadfast continuance in the face of opposition. PERSIST suggests human opposition: *He persisted after he had been warned;* and PERSEVERE suggests opposition from any source, often an impersonal one: *He persevered despite fatigue.* LAST often applies to something that holds out to a desired end, fresh, unimpaired, or unexhausted, sometimes under conditions that tend to produce the opposite effect: *They had provisions enough to last all winter.* REMAIN is esp. applied to what continues without change in its essential state: *He remained a bachelor.* —**Ant. 2.** cease.

con•tin•ued (kən tin′yo͞od), *adj.* **1.** lasting or enduring without interruption: *continued good health.* **2.** going on after an interruption; resuming: *a continued TV series.* [CONTINUE + -ED[2]] —**con•tin′ued•ly,** *adv.* —**con•tin′ued•ness,** *n.*

contin′ued educa′tion. See **adult education.** Also called **contin′uing educa′tion.**

contin′ued frac′tion, *Math.* a fraction whose denominator contains a fraction whose denominator contains a fraction, and so on. [1860–65]

contin′ued propor′tion, *Math.* an ordered set of numbers such that the ratio between any two successive terms is the same, as 1:3:9:27:81. [1790–1800]

contin′uing resolu′tion, *U.S. Politics.* legislation enacted by Congress to allow government operations to continue until the regular appropriations are enacted: used when action on appropriations is not completed by the beginning of a fiscal year.

con•ti•nu•i•ty (kon′tn o͞o′i tē, -tn yo͞o′), *n., pl.* **-ties. 1.** the state or quality of being continuous. **2.** a continuous or connected whole. **3.** a motion-picture scenario giving the complete action, scenes, etc., in detail and in the order in which they are to be shown on the screen. **4.** the spoken part of a radio or television script that serves as introductory or transitional material on a nondramatic program. **5.** *Math.* the property of a continuous function. **6.** Usually, **continuities.** sets of merchandise, as dinnerware or encyclopedias, given free or sold cheaply by a store to shoppers as a sales promotion. [1375–1425; late ME *continuite* < AF < L *continuitās,* equiv. to *continu(us)* CONTINUOUS + *-itās* -ITY]
—**Syn. 2.** flow, progression.

continu′ity equa′tion, *Mech.* the mathematical statement in fluid mechanics that, for a fluid passing through a tube in a steady flow, the mass flowing through any section of the tube in a unit of time is constant. [1830–40]

con•tin•u•o (kən tin′yo͞o ō′), *n., pl.* **-tin•u•os.** *Music.* a keyboard accompanying part consisting originally of a figured bass, which in modern scores is usually realized, and serving to provide or fill out the harmonic texture. [1715–25; < It: lit., continuous]

con•tin•u•ous (kən tin′yo͞o əs), *adj.* **1.** uninterrupted in time; without cessation: *continuous coughing during the concert.* **2.** being in immediate connection or spatial relationship: *a continuous series of blasts; a continuous row of warehouses.* **3.** *Gram.* progressive (def. 7). [1635–45; < L *continuus* uninterrupted, equiv. to *contin(ēre)* to hold together, retain (*con-* CON- + *-tinēre,* comb. form of *tenēre* to hold; cf. CONTAIN) + *-uus* deverbal adj. suffix; cf. -OUS, CONTIGUOUS] —**con•tin′u•ous•ly,** *adv.* —**con•tin′u•ous•ness,** *n.*
—**Usage.** See **continual.**

contin′uous cast′ing, *Metall.* a technique of casting ingots, bars, etc., in which the metal is poured into an open-ended mold, being withdrawn as it solidifies so that the solid portion of the piece retains the fluid portion within the mold. —**contin′uous cast′er.**

contin′uous cut′ter, *Mining.* any of various machines that can remove coal from the mine face and load it into cars or conveyors. Also called **contin′uous min′er.** [1955–60]

con•tin′u•ous-ex•pan′sion en′gine (kən tin′yo͞o-əs ik span′shən), a steam engine in which a high-pressure cylinder is partly exhausted into a low-pressure cylinder during each stroke.

con•tin•u•ous-form (kən tin′yo͞o əs fôrm′), *adj.* of or pertaining to paper, blank forms, checks, etc., supplied in a folded stack or roll to a device, as a computer printer, generally with perforations between sheets for later separation and often with detachable punched edges used to advance the sheets through the device.

contin′uous func′tion, *Math.* **1.** (loosely) a mathematical function such that a small change in the independent variable, or point of the domain, produces only a small change in the value of the function. **2.** (at a point in its domain) a function that has a limit equal to the value of the function at the point; a function that has the property that for any small number, a second number can be found such that when the distance between any other point in the domain and the given point is less than the second number, the difference in the functional values at the two points is less than the first number in absolute value. **3.** (at a point in a topological space) a function having the property that for any open set containing the image of the point, an open set about the given point can be found such that the image of the set is contained in the first open set. **4.** (on a set in the domain of the function or in a topological space) a function that is continuous at every point of the set.

contin′uous hinge′. See **piano hinge.**

contin′uously var′iable transmis′sion, *Auto., Mach.* a transmission, typically using rubber belts and pulleys, in which the ratio of the rotational speeds of two shafts, as the drive shaft and driven shaft of a vehicle, can be varied continuously within a given range, providing an infinite number of possible ratios. *Abbr.:* CVT

contin′uous min′er. See **continuous cutter.** [1955–60]

contin′uous spec′trum, *Physics.* a spectrum apparently having all wavelengths over a comparatively wide range, usually characteristic of solids and other substances at high temperatures. Cf. **band spectrum, line spectrum, spectral line.** [1900–05]

contin′uous wave′, *Telecommunications.* an electromagnetic wave of constant amplitude and frequency: used to carry information by being modulated, as in radio or television, or by being interrupted as in radiotelegraphy. *Abbr.:* CW [1910–15]

contin′uous weld′ed rail′, *Railroads.* a long, continuous rail formed by welding many short rails.

con•tin•u•um (kən tin′yo͞o əm), *n., pl.* **-tin•u•a** (-tin′yo͞o ə). **1.** a continuous extent, series, or whole. **2.** *Math.* **a.** a set of elements such that between any two of them there is a third element. **b.** the set of all real numbers. **c.** any compact, connected set containing at least two elements. [1640–50; < L, n. use of neut. of *continuus* CONTINUOUS]

contin′uum hypoth′esis, *Math.* a conjecture of set theory that the first infinite cardinal number greater than the cardinal number of the set of all positive integers is the cardinal number of the set of all real numbers. [1935–40]

con•to (kon′tō; *Port.* kôn′to͞o), *n., pl.* **-tos** (-tōz; *in Portugal* -to͞osh; *in Brazil* -to͞os). **1.** a money of account of Portugal and Cape Verde, equal to 1000 escudos. **2.** a former money of account in Portugal and Brazil equal to 1000 milreis. [1595–1605; < Pg < LL *computus* reckoning, n. deriv. of L *computāre* to COMPUTE; see COUNT[1]]

con•toid (kon′toid), *Phonet.* —*adj.* **1.** of or pertaining to a sound characterized by stoppage or obstruction of the flow of air in the vocal tract; consonantlike. **2.** a contoid sound. Cf. **vocoid.** [1940–45; CON(SONAN)T + -OID]

con•tort (kən tôrt′), *v.t.* **1.** to twist, bend, or draw out of shape; distort. —*v.i.* **2.** to become twisted, distorted, or strained: *His face contorted into a grotesque sneer.* [1555–65; < L *contortus* twisted together, ptp. of *contorquēre.* See CON-, TORT]

con•tort•ed (kən tôr′tid), *adj.* **1.** twisted in a violent manner; distorted. **2.** twisted back on itself; convoluted. [1615–25; CONTORT + -ED[2]] —**con•tort′ed•ly,** *adv.* —**con•tort′ed•ness,** *n.*

con•tor•tion (kən tôr′shən), *n.* **1.** the act or process of contorting. **2.** the state of being contorted. **3.** a contorted position. **4.** something contorted or twisted, as in position or meaning: *His account of the incident was a complete contortion of fact.* [1605–15; < L *contortiōn-* (s. of *contortiō*) a whirling around. See CONTORT, -ION] —**con•tor′tion•al,** *adj.* —**con•tor′tioned,** *adj.*

con•tor•tion•ist (kən tôr′shə nist), *n.* **1.** a person who performs gymnastic feats involving contorted postures. **2.** a person who practices contortion: *a verbal contortionist.* [1855–60; CONTORTION + -IST] —**con•tor′tion•is′tic,** *adj.*

con•tor•tive (kən tôr′tiv), *adj.* characterized by, tending toward, or causing contortions or twisting: *contortive movements; contortive pain; contortive alleyways.* [1855–60; CONTORT + -IVE] —**con•tor′tive•ly,** *adv.*

con•tour (kon′to͝or), *n.* **1.** the outline of a figure or body; the edge or line that defines or bounds a shape or object. **2.** See **contour line. 3.** *Phonet.* a distinctive pattern of changes in pitch, stress, or tone extending across all or part of an utterance, esp. across a sentence, and contributing to meaning. —*v.t.* **4.** to mark with contour lines. **5.** to make or form the contour or outline of. **6.** to build (a road, railroad track, etc.) in conformity with the contour of the land. **7.** to mold or shape so as to fit a certain configuration: *cars with seats that are contoured for comfort.* —*adj.* **8.** molded or shaped to fit a particular contour or form: *contour seats.* **9.** *Agric.* of or used in a system of plowing, cultivating, sowing, etc., along the contour lines of the land in order to trap water runoff and prevent erosion. [1655–65; < F, equiv. to *con-* CON- + *tour* a turn (see TOUR), modeled on It *contorno,* deriv. of *contornare* to outline; see TURN]
—**Syn. 1.** configuration, form, boundary.

con′tour cur′tain, *Theat.* a curtain having lines attached to several points for drawing up into folds of various shapes.

con′tour feath′er, *Ornith.* one of the feathers that form the surface plumage of a bird, including those of the wings and tail but excluding such specialized types as downs and filoplumes. [1865–70]

con′tour integra′tion, *Math.* integration in the complex plane about a closed curve of finite length.

con′tour in′terval, the difference in elevation represented by each contour line on a topographic map.

con′tour line′, 1. a line joining points of equal elevation on a surface. **2.** the representation of such a line on a map. **3.** *Math.* a line parallel to a trace. Cf. **trace**[1] (def. 11). Also called **contour, level curve, level line.** [1835–45]

CONCISE ETYMOLOGY KEY: <, descended or borrowed from; >, whence; b., blend of, blended; c., cognate with; cf., compare; deriv., derivative; equiv., equivalent; imit., imitative; obl., oblique; r., replacing; s., stem; sp., spelling, spelled; resp., respelling, respelled; trans., translation; ?, origin unknown; *, unattested; ‡, probably earlier than. See the full key inside the front cover.

con′tour map′, a topographic map on which the shape of the land surface is shown by contour lines, the relative spacing of the lines indicating the relative slope of the surface. [1860–65]

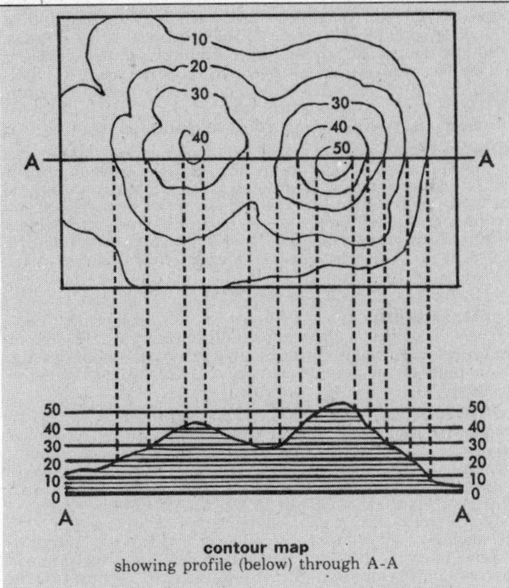

contour map
showing profile (below) through A-A

con′tour sheet′, a bed sheet designed to fit snugly over a mattress or the like, often having elastic material to hold down the corners.

contr., 1. contract. 2. contracted. 3. contraction. 4. contralto. 5. contrary. 6. contrasted. 7. control. 8. controller.

con•tra[1] (kon′trə), *prep.* 1. against; in opposition or contrast to: *Consider the problems of the teenager contra those of the adult.* —*adv.* 2. contrariwise; on or to the contrary. [1350–1400; ME < L *contrā*]

con•tra[2] (kōn′trə; *Sp.* kôn′trä), *n., pl.* **-tras** (-trəz; *Sp.* -träs). (*often cap.*) a member of a counterrevolutionary guerrilla group in Nicaragua. [< AmerSp, shortening of *contrarrevolucionario* COUNTERREVOLUTIONARY]

contra-[1], a prefix meaning "against," "opposite," "opposing," used in the formation of compound words: *contradistinction.* [< L, prefixal use of adv. and prep. *contrā*]

contra-[2], *Music.* a prefix meaning "pitched lower than normal": *contrabassoon.* [< It < L (see CONTRA-[1]); prob. generalized in E on the basis of It borrowings, e.g., CONTRABASS, CONTRALTO, CONTRAPUNTAL, etc.]

con•tra•band (kon′trə band′), *n.* 1. anything prohibited by law from being imported or exported. 2. goods imported or exported illegally. 3. illegal or prohibited trade; smuggling. 4. *Internat. Law.* See **contraband of war.** 5. (during the American Civil War) a black slave who escaped to or was brought within the Union lines. —*adj.* 6. prohibited from export or import. [1520–30; earlier *contrabanda* < Sp < It *contrabando* (now *contrabbando*), equiv. to *contra-* CONTRA-[1] + ML *bandum,* var. of *bannum* BAN[2]]

con•tra•band•ist (kon′trə ban′dist), *n.* a person engaged in contraband trade; smuggler. [1810–20; < Sp *contrabandista.* See CONTRABAND, -IST] —**con′tra•band′ism,** *n.*

con′traband of war′, *Internat. Law.* goods that a neutral nation cannot supply to a belligerent nation except at the risk of seizure and confiscation. [1795–1805]

con•tra•bass (kon′trə bās′), *Music.* —*n.* 1. (in any family of instruments) the member below the bass. 2. (in the violin family) the double bass. —*adj.* 3. of, pertaining to, or characteristic of such instruments: *a contrabass trombone.* [1590–1600; < It; see CONTRABASSO] —**con•tra•bass•ist** (kon′trə bā′sist, -bas′ist), *n.*

con•tra•bas•so (kon′trə bas′ō, -bä′sō; *It.* kôn′trä bäs′sô), *n., pl.* **-bas•sos, -bas•si** (-bas′ē, -bä′sē; *It.* -bäs′sē), *adj. Music.* contrabass. [< It *contrabbasso,* equiv. to *contra-* CONTRA-[2] + *basso* BASS[1]]

con•tra•bas•soon (kon′trə ba sōōn′, -bə-), *n.* a bassoon larger in size and an octave lower in pitch than the ordinary bassoon; a double bassoon. [1890–95; CONTRA-[2] + BASSOON] —**con′tra•bas•soon′ist,** *n.*

con•tra•cept (kon′trə sept′), *v.t.* 1. to prevent the conception of (offspring). 2. to prevent pregnancy or impregnation in; provide with the means for birth control. [1965–70; back formation from CONTRACEPTION]

con•tra•cep•tion (kon′trə sep′shən), *n.* the deliberate prevention of conception or impregnation by any of various drugs, techniques, or devices; birth control. [1885–90; CONTRA-[1] + (CON)CEPTION]

con•tra•cep•tive (kon′trə sep′tiv), *adj.* 1. tending or serving to prevent conception or impregnation. 2. pertaining to contraception. —*n.* 3. a contraceptive device, drug, foam, etc. [1890–95; CONTRA-[1] + (CON)CEPTIVE]

con•tra•clock•wise (kon′trə klok′wīz′), *adj., adv.* counterclockwise. [CONTRA-[1] + CLOCKWISE]

con•tract (*n., adj., and usually for v. 16–18, 22, 23* kon′trakt; *otherwise v.* kən trakt′), *n.* 1. an agreement between two or more parties for the doing or not doing of something specified. 2. an agreement enforceable by law. 3. the written form of such an agreement. 4. the division of law dealing with contracts. 5. Also called **con′tract bridge′.** a variety of bridge in which the side that wins the bid can earn toward game only that number of tricks named in the contract, additional points being credited above the line. Cf. **auction bridge.** 6. (in auction or contract bridge) **a.** a commitment by the declarer and his or her partner to take six tricks plus the number specified by the final bid made. **b.** the final bid itself. **c.** the number of tricks so specified, plus six. 7. the formal agreement of marriage; betrothal. 8. *Slang.* an arrangement for a hired assassin to kill a specific person. 9. **put out a contract on,** *Slang.* to hire or attempt to hire an assassin to kill (someone): *The mob put out a contract on the informer.* —*adj.* 10. under contract; governed or arranged by special contract: *a contract carrier.* —*v.t.* 11. to draw together or into smaller compass; draw the parts of together: *to contract a muscle.* 12. to wrinkle: *to contract the brows.* 13. to shorten (a word, phrase, etc.) by combining or omitting some of its elements: *Contracting "do not" yields "don't."* 14. to get or acquire, as by exposure to something contagious: *to contract a disease.* 15. to incur, as a liability or obligation: *to contract a debt.* 16. to settle or establish by agreement: *to contract an alliance.* 17. to assign (a job, work, project, etc.) by contract: *The publisher contracted the artwork.* 18. to enter into an agreement with: *to contract a free-lancer to do the work.* 19. to enter into (friendship, acquaintance, etc.). 20. to betroth. —*v.i.* 21. to become drawn together or reduced in compass; become smaller; shrink: *The pupils of his eyes contracted in the light.* 22. to enter into an agreement: *to contract for snow removal.* 23. **contract out,** to hire an outside contractor to produce or do. [1275–1325; (n.) ME (< AF) < L *contractus* undertaking a transaction, agreement, equiv. to *contrac-,* var. s. of *contrahere* to draw in, bring together, enter into an agreement (*con-* CON- + *trahere* to drag, pull; cf. TRACTION) + *-tus* suffix of v. action; (v.) < L *contractus,* ptp. of *contrahere*] —**con′tract•ee′,** *n.* —**con•tract′i•ble,** *adj.* —**con•tract′i•bil′i•ty, con•tract′i•ble•ness,** *n.* —**con•tract′i•bly,** *adv.*
—**Syn.** 1. See **agreement.** 11. reduce, shorten, lessen, narrow, shrivel, shrink. CONTRACT, COMPRESS, CONCENTRATE, CONDENSE imply retaining original content but reducing the amount of space occupied. CONTRACT means to cause to draw more closely together: *to contract a muscle.* COMPRESS suggests fusing to become smaller by means of fairly uniform external pressure: *to compress gases into liquid form.* CONCENTRATE implies causing to gather around a point: *to concentrate troops near an objective; to concentrate one's strength.* CONDENSE implies increasing the compactness, or thickening the consistency of a homogeneous mass: *to condense milk.* It is also used to refer to the reducing in length of a book or the like. —**Ant.** 11. expand.

con′tract bond′, an indemnity agreement to protect against loss due to breach of contract. Cf. **performance bond.**

con•tract•ed (kən trak′tid), *adj.* 1. drawn together; reduced in compass or size; made smaller; shrunken. 2. condensed; abridged. 3. (of the mind, outlook, etc.) narrow or illiberal; restricted: *a contracted view of human rights.* [1540–50; CONTRACT + -ED[2]] —**con•tract′ed•ly,** *adv.* —**con•tract′ed•ness,** *n.*

con′tract fur′niture, furniture designed and manufactured for commercial installation, as in offices, waiting rooms, or lobbies.

con•trac•tile (kən trak′tl, -til), *adj.* capable of contracting or causing contraction. [1700–10; CONTRACT + -ILE] —**con•trac•til•i•ty** (kon′trak til′i tē), *n.*

contrac′tile vac′uole, *Cell Biol.* a membrane-enveloped cellular organelle, found in many microorganisms, that periodically expands, filling with water, and then contracts, expelling its contents to the cell exterior: thought to be important in maintaining hydrostatic equilibrium. See diags. under **ameba, paramecium.** [1875–80]

con•trac•tion (kən trak′shən), *n.* 1. an act or instance of contracting. 2. the quality or state of being contracted. 3. a shortened form of a word or group of words, with the omitted letters often replaced in written English by an apostrophe, as *e'er* for *ever, isn't* for *is not, dep't* for *department.* 4. *Physiol.* the change in a muscle by which it becomes thickened and shortened. 5. a restriction or withdrawal, as of currency or of funds available as call money. 6. a decrease in economic and industrial activity (opposed to *expansion*). [1375–1425; late ME (< MF) < L *contractiōn-* (s. of *contractiō*), equiv. to *contract(us)* drawn together, ptp. of *contrahere* (see CONTRACT) + *-iōn-* -ION] —**con•trac′tion•al,** *adj.*
—**Usage.** Contractions such as *isn't, couldn't, can't, weren't, he'll, they're* occur chiefly, although not exclusively, in informal speech and writing. They are common in personal letters, business letters, journalism, and fiction; they are rare in scientific and scholarly writing. Contractions occur in formal writing mainly as representations of speech.

contrac′tion joint′, *Archit., Civ. Engin.* a joint between two parts of a structure, designed to compensate for the contraction to which either part may be subject. [1905–10]

con•trac•tive (kən trak′tiv), *adj.* 1. serving or tending to contract. 2. capable of contracting. [1615–25; CONTRACT + -IVE] —**con•trac′tive•ly,** *adv.* —**con•trac′tive•ness,** *n.*

con′tract la′bor, 1. labor coercible by the enforceable provisions of a contract. 2. foreign labor supplied under contract for a particular job.

con•trac•tor (kon′trak tər, kən trak′tər), *n.* 1. a person who contracts to furnish supplies or perform work at a certain price or rate. 2. something that contracts, esp. a muscle. 3. *Bridge.* the player or team who makes the final bid. [1540–50; < LL; see CONTRACT, -TOR]

con′tract prac′tice, the medical treatment of a group of persons by a physician or physicians with fees and services mutually agreed upon in advance.

con•trac•tu•al (kən trak′chōō əl), *adj.* of, pertaining to, or secured by a contract. [1860–65; < L *contractu-,* s. of *contractus* CONTRACT + -AL[1]] —**con•trac′tu•al•ly,** *adv.*

con•trac•ture (kən trak′chər), *n. Pathol.* a shortening or distortion of muscular or connective tissue due to spasm, scar, or paralysis of the antagonist of the contracting muscle. [1650–60; < L *contractūra,* equiv. to *contract(us)* drawn together (ptp. of *contrahere;* see CONTRACT) + *-ūra* -URE] —**con•trac′tured,** *adj.*

con•tra•cy•cli•cal (kon′trə sī′kli kəl, -sik′li-), *adj.* countercyclical. [CONTRA-[1] + CYCLICAL] —**con′tra•cy′•cli•cal′i•ty,** *n.*

con•tra•dance (kon′trə dans′, -däns′), *n.* contredanse.

con•tra•dict (kon′trə dikt′), *v.t.* 1. to assert the contrary or opposite of; deny directly and categorically. 2. to speak contrary to the assertions of: *to contradict oneself.* 3. (of an action or event) to imply a denial of: *His way of life contradicts his stated principles.* 4. *Obs.* to speak or declare against; oppose. —*v.i.* 5. to utter a contrary statement. [1560–70; < L *contrādictus* (ptp. of *contrādīcere* to gainsay), equiv. to *contrā-* CONTRA-[1] + *dic-* (var. s. of *dīcere* to speak) + *-tus* ptp. suffix] —**con′tra•dict′a•ble,** *adj.* —**con′tra•dict′er, con′tra•dic′tor,** *n.*
—**Syn.** 1, 2. gainsay, impugn, controvert, dispute. See **deny.** —**Ant.** 1. support.

con•tra•dic•tion (kon′trə dik′shən), *n.* 1. the act of contradicting; gainsaying or opposition. 2. assertion of the contrary or opposite; denial. 3. a statement or proposition that contradicts or denies another or itself and is logically incongruous. 4. direct opposition between things compared; inconsistency. 5. a contradictory act, fact, etc. [1350–1400; ME *contradiccioun* (< AF) < L *contrādictiōn-* (s. of *contrādictiō*). See CONTRADICT, -ION]

con•tra•dic•tious (kon′trə dik′shəs), *adj.* 1. inclined to contradict; disputatious. 2. *Archaic.* self-contradictory. [1595–1605; CONTRADICT + -IOUS] —**con′tra•dic′•tious•ly,** *adv.* —**con′tra•dic′tious•ness,** *n.*

con•tra•dic•tive (kon′trə dik′tiv), *adj.* tending or inclined to contradict; involving contradiction; contradictory. [1620–30; CONTRADICT + -IVE] —**con′tra•dic′•tive•ly,** *adv.* —**con′tra•dic′tive•ness,** *n.*

con•tra•dic•to•ry (kon′trə dik′tə rē), *adj., n., pl.* **-ries.** —*adj.* 1. asserting the contrary or opposite; contradicting; inconsistent; logically opposite: *contradictory statements.* 2. tending or inclined to contradict. —*n.* 3. *Logic.* a proposition so related to a second that it is impossible for both to be true or both to be false. [1350–1400; ME < LL *contrādictōrius,* equiv. to *contrādīc(ere)* (see CONTRADICT) + *-tōrius* -TORY[1]] —**con′tra•dic′to•ri•ly,** *adv.* —**con′tra•dic′to•ri•ness,** *n.*
—**Syn.** 1. irreconcilable, paradoxical.

con•tra•dis•tinc•tion (kon′trə di stingk′shən), *n.* distinction by opposition or contrast: *plants and animals in contradistinction to humans.* [1640–50; CONTRA-[1] + DISTINCTION] —**con′tra•dis•tinc′tive,** *adj.* —**con′tra•dis•tinc′tive•ly,** *adv.*

con•tra•dis•tin•guish (kon′trə di sting′gwish), *v.t.* to distinguish by contrasting opposite qualities. [1615–25; CONTRA-[1] + DISTINGUISH]

con′tra-guide rud′der (kon′trə gīd′), *Naut.* a rudder having a horizontal offset of its upper and lower halves to improve the flow characteristics of the propeller race.

con•trail (kon′trāl), *n.* a visible condensation of water droplets or ice crystals from the atmosphere, occurring in the wake of an aircraft, rocket, or missile under certain conditions. Also called **condensation trail, vapor trail.** [1940–45; CON(DENSATION) TRAIL]

con•tra•in•di•cate (kon′trə in′di kāt′), *v.t.,* **-cat•ed, -cat•ing.** *Med.* (of a symptom or condition) to give indication against the advisability of (a particular or usual remedy or treatment). [1660–70; prob. back formation from *contraindication.* See CONTRA-[1], INDICATION] —**con′tra•in′di•cant** (kon′trə in′di kənt), *n.* —**con′•tra•in′di•ca′tion,** *n.*

con•tra•lat•er•al (kon′trə lat′ər əl), *adj.* (of the body) pertaining to, situated on, or coordinated with the opposite side. [1880–85; CONTRA-[1] + LATERAL]

con•tral•to (kən tral′tō), *n., pl.* **-tos,** *adj. Music.* —*n.* 1. the lowest female voice or voice part, intermediate between soprano and tenor. 2. the alto, or highest male voice or voice part. 3. a singer with a contralto voice. —*adj.* 4. pertaining to the contralto voice or its compass. [1720–30; < It, equiv. to *contr(a)* CONTRA-[2] + *alto* ALTO]

con•tra•oc•tave (kon′trə ok′tiv, -tāv), *n. Music.* the octave between the second and third C's below middle C. [1890–95; CONTRA-[2] + OCTAVE]

con•tra•or•bi•tal (kon′trə ôr′bi tl), *adj.* of or pertaining to flight in the orbit of, but in a direction contrary to, a given rocket, ballistic missile, satellite, etc. [CONTRA-[1] + ORBITAL] —**con′tra•or′bi•tal•ly,** *adv.*

con•tra•plete (kon′trə plēt′), *n. Philos.* either of two opposed and complementary elements in a relationship. [CONTRA-[1] + (COM)PLETE] —**con′tra•ple′tal,** *adj.*

con•tra•pose (kon′trə pōz′), *v.t.,* **-posed, -pos•ing.** to place in contraposition. [1610–20; back formation from *contraposed* < L *contrāpositus,* ptp. of *contrāpōnere* to place against, with -ED[2] for L *-itus* ptp. suffix]

con•tra•po•si•tion (kon′trə pə zish′ən), *n.* 1. placement opposite or against. 2. opposition, contrast, or antithesis. 3. *Logic.* the inference drawn from a proposition by negating its terms and changing their order, as by inferring "Not B implies not A" from "A implies B." [1545–55; < LL *contrāposition-* (s. of *contrāpositiō*). See CONTRA-[1], POSITION]

con•tra•pos•i•tive (kon′trə poz′i tiv), *Logic.* —*adj.* 1. of or pertaining to contraposition. —*n.* 2. a contrapositive statement of a proposition. [1855–60; CONTRAPOSIT(ION) + -IVE]

con•trap•pos•to (kŏn′trə pos′tō), *n., pl.* **-tos.** *Fine Arts.* a representation of the human body in which the forms are organized on a varying or curving axis to provide an asymmetrical balance to the figure. [1900–05; < It < L *contrāpositus,* ptp. of *contrāpōnere* to place against. See CONTRA-[1], POSIT]

con•trap•tion (kən trap′shən), *n. Informal.* a mechanical contrivance; gadget; device. [1815–25; perh. CONTR(IVANCE) + (*ad*)*aption,* var. of ADAPTATION] —**con•trap′tious,** *adj.*

con•tra•pun•tal (kon′trə pun′tl), *adj. Music.* **1.** of or pertaining to counterpoint. **2.** composed of two or more relatively independent melodies sounded together. [1835–45; < It *contrappunt(o)* + -AL[1]. See COUNTERPOINT] —**con′tra•pun′tal•ly,** *adv.*

con•tra•pun•tist (kon′trə pun′tist), *n.* a person skilled in the practice of counterpoint. [1770–80; < It *contrappuntista.* See COUNTERPOINT, -IST]

con•trar•i•an (kən trâr′ē ən), *n.* a person who takes an opposing view, esp. one who rejects the majority opinion, as in economic matters. [CONTR(ARY) + -ARIAN]

con•tra•ri•e•ty (kon′trə rī′i tē), *n., pl.* **-ties** for 2. **1.** the quality or state of being contrary. **2.** something contrary or of opposite character; a contrary fact or statement. **3.** *Logic.* the relation between contraries. [1350–1400; ME *contrariete* (< AF) < LL *contrārietās.* See CONTRARY, -ITY]

con•trar•i•ous (kən trâr′ē əs), *adj.* **1.** *Chiefly Appalachian.* perverse; refractory. **2.** *Archaic.* adverse; unfavorable. [1250–1300; ME (< AF) < L *contrārius* CONTRARY; see -OUS] —**con•trar′i•ous•ly,** *adv.* —**con•trar′i•ous•ness,** *n.*

con•trar•i•wise (kon′trer ē wīz′ *or, for 3,* kən trâr′-), *adv.* **1.** in the opposite direction or way. **2.** on the contrary; in direct opposition to a statement, attitude, etc. **3.** perversely. [1300–50; ME *contrary-wyse.* See CONTRARY, -WISE]

con•trar•y (kon′trer ē; *for 5 also* kən trâr′ē), *adj., n., pl.* **-trar•ies,** *adv.,* —*adj.* **1.** opposite in nature or character; diametrically or mutually opposed: *contrary to fact; contrary propositions.* **2.** opposite in direction or position: *departures in contrary directions.* **3.** being the opposite one of two: *I will make the contrary choice.* **4.** unfavorable or adverse. **5.** perverse; stubbornly opposed or willful. —*n.* **6.** something that is contrary or opposite: *to prove the contrary of a statement.* **7.** either of two contrary things. **8.** *Logic.* a proposition so related to another proposition that both may not be true though both may be false, as with the propositions "All judges are male" and "No judges are male." **9. by contraries,** contrary to expectation. **10. on the contrary, a.** in opposition to what has been stated. **b.** from another point of view: *On the contrary, there may be some who would agree with you.* **11. to the contrary, a.** to the opposite effect: *I believe he is innocent, whatever they may say to the contrary.* **b.** to a different effect. —*adv.* **12.** in opposition; oppositely; counter: *to act contrary to one's own principles.* [1200–50; ME *contrarie* < AF < L *contrārius.* See CONTRA-[1], -ARY] —**con′trar•i•ly** (kon′trer ə lē, kən trâr′-), *adv.* —**con′trar•i•ness,** *n.*

—**Syn. 1.** contradictory, conflicting, counter. See **opposite. 4.** unfriendly, hostile. CONTRARY, ADVERSE both describe something that opposes. CONTRARY conveys an idea of something impersonal and objective whose opposition happens to be unfavorable: *contrary winds.* ADVERSE suggests something more personally unfriendly or even hostile; it emphasizes the idea of the resulting misfortune to that which is opposed: *The judge rendered a decision adverse to the defendant.* **5.** intractable, obstinate, headstrong, stubborn, pig-headed. —**Ant. 4.** favorable. **5.** obliging, complaisant.

con′trary mo′tion, *Music.* melodic motion in which one part rises in pitch while the other descends.

con•trast (*v.* kən trast′, kon′trast; *n.* kon′trast), *v.t.* **1.** to compare in order to show unlikeness or differences; note the opposite natures, purposes, etc., of: *Contrast the political rights of Romans and Greeks.* —*v.i.* **2.** to exhibit unlikeness on comparison with something else; form a contrast. **3.** *Ling.* to differ in a way that can serve to distinguish meanings: *The sounds (p) and (b) contrast in the words "pin" and "bin."* —*n.* **4.** the act of contrasting; the state of being contrasted. **5.** a striking exhibition of unlikeness. **6.** a person or thing that is strikingly unlike in comparison: *The weather down here is a welcome contrast to what we're having back home.* **7.** opposition or juxtaposition of different forms, lines, or colors in a work of art to intensify each element's properties and produce a more dynamic expressiveness. **8.** *Photog.* the relative difference between light and dark areas of a print or negative. **9.** *Television.* the brightness ratio of the lightest to the darkest part of the television screen image. **10.** *Ling.* a difference between linguistic elements, esp. sounds, that can serve to distinguish meanings. [1480–90; (v.) < MF *contraster* < It *contrastare* to contest < L *contrā-* CONTRA-[1] + *stāre* to STAND; (n.) earlier *contraste* < F < It *contrasto* conflict, deriv. of *contrastare*] —**con•trast′a•ble,** *adj.* —**con•trast′a•bly,** *adv.* —**con•trast′ing•ly,** *adv.*

—**Syn. 1.** differentiate, discriminate, distinguish, oppose.

con•tras•tive (kən tras′tiv), *adj.* **1.** tending to contrast; contrasting. *contrastive colors.* **2.** studying or exhibiting the congruences and differences between two languages or dialects without reference to their origins: *contrastive linguistics.* [1810–20; CONTRAST + -IVE] —**con•tras′tive•ly,** *adv.*

contras′tive stress′, *Phonet.* a stress imposed on a word or syllable contrary to its normal accentuation in order to contrast it with an alternative word or syllable or to focus attention on it, as the stress given to the normally unstressed word *of* in *government of the people, by the people, for the people* in order to point up the parallel between *of, by,* and *for* and to distinguish *of* from words such as *over* or *against.*

CONCISE ETYMOLOGY KEY: <, descended or borrowed from; >, whence; b., blend of, blended; c., cognate with; cf., compare; deriv., derivative; equiv., equivalent; imit., imitative; obl., oblique; r., replacing; s., stem; sp., spelling, spelled; resp., respelling, respelled; trans., translation; ?, origin unknown; *, unattested; ‡, probably earlier than. See the full key inside the front cover.

con′trast me′dium, *Med.* a radiopaque substance injected into a part of the body, as the stomach or duodenum, to provide a contrasting background for the tissues in an x-ray or fluoroscopic examination. [1950–55]

con•trast•y (kən tras′tē, kon′tras-), *adj. Photog.* (of a subject, photograph, or film stock) having or producing a preponderance of dark and light tones with few intermediate shades. [1890–95; CONTRAST + -Y[1]]

con•trate (kon′trāt), *adj. Horol.* (of a gear) having teeth at right angles to the plane of rotation. [1680–90; CONTRA-[1] + -ATE[1]]

con•tra•val•la•tion (kon′trə və lā′shən), *n. Fort.* a more or less continuous chain of redoubts and breastworks raised by besiegers outside the line of circumvallation of a besieged place to protect the besiegers from attacks from the outside, as by a relieving force. [1670–80; CONTRA-[1] + VALLATION; cf. F *contrevallation,* It *contravvallazione*]

con•tra•vene (kon′trə vēn′), *v.t.,* **-vened, -ven•ing. 1.** to come or be in conflict with; go or act against; deny or oppose: *to contravene a statement.* **2.** to violate, infringe, or transgress: *to contravene the law.* [1560–70; < LL *contrāvenīre,* equiv. to L *contrā* against + *venīre* to COME] —**con′tra•ven′er,** *n.*

con•tra•ven•tion (kon′trə ven′shən), *n.* an act of contravening; action counter to something; violation or opposition. [1570–80; CONTRAVENE + -TION; cf. MF *contrevention*]

con•tra•yer•va (kon′trə yûr′və), *n.* the root of certain tropical American plants of the genus *Dorstenia,* of the mulberry family, esp. *D. contrajerva,* used as a stimulant, diaphoretic, etc. [1650–60; < Sp *contrayerba, contrahierba* < L *contrā* CONTRA-[1] + *herba* HERB; so called from its being thought an antidote to poison]

con•tre•coup (kon′trə ko͞o′; *Fr.* kôNtʀə ko͞o′), *n. Med.* an injury of one point of an organ or part resulting from a blow on the opposite point. Also called **counterstroke.** [1820–30; < F *contre-coup.* See COUNTER-, COUP[1]]

con•tre•danse (kon′trə dans′, -däns′; *Fr.* kôN tʀə däNs′), *n., pl.* **-dans•es** (-dan′siz, -dän′-; *Fr.* -däNs′). **1.** a variation of the quadrille in which the dancers face each other. **2.** a piece of music suitable for such a dance. Also, **contradance.** [1795–1805; < F, equiv. to *contre-* COUNTER- + *danse* DANCE, misrendering of E COUNTRY-DANCE, by assoc. with the characteristic arrangement of dancers in rows facing each other]

con•tre-jour (kon′trə zho͞or′; *Fr.* kôNtʀə zho͞oʀ′), *adj.* (of a photograph) taken with the camera pointed more or less in the direction of the principal light source or with the strongest light behind the subject. [1920–25; < F, equiv. to *contre* COUNTER- + *jour* daylight, day; see JOURNEY]

cont. rem., (in prescriptions) let the medicines be continued. [< L *continuāntur remedia*]

con•tre-par•tie (*Fr.* kôNtʀə PAR tē′), *n. Furniture.* (in buhlwork) an inlay composed of a design in tortoise shell on a background of brass. Also called **counter-boulle.** Cf. **première partie.** [< F: counterpart]

con•tre•temps (kon′trə täN′; *Fr.* kôNtʀə täN′), *n., pl.* **-temps** (-täNz′; *Fr.* -täN′). an inopportune occurrence; an embarrassing mischance: *He caused a minor contretemps by knocking over his drink.* [1675–85; < F, equiv. to *contre-* COUNTER- + *temps* time (< L *tempus*); perh. alter. (by folk etym.) of MF *contrestant,* prp. of *contrester* to oppose; see CONTRAST]

contrib., 1. contribution. **2.** contributor.

con•trib•ute (kən trib′yo͞ot), *v.,* **-ut•ed, -ut•ing.** —*v.t.* **1.** to give (money, time, knowledge, assistance, etc.) to a common supply, fund, etc., as for charitable purposes. **2.** to furnish (an original written work, drawing, etc.) for publication: *to contribute stories to a magazine.* —*v.i.* **3.** to give (money, food, etc.) to a common supply, fund, etc.: *He contributes to many charities.* **4.** to furnish works for publication: *He contributed to many magazines.* **5. contribute to,** to be an important factor in; help to cause: *A sudden downpour contributed to the traffic jam.* [1520–30; < L *contribūtus* ptp. of *contribuere* to bring together. See CON-, TRIBUTE] —**con•trib′ut•a•ble,** *adj.* —**con•trib′u•tive,** *adj.* —**con•trib′u•tive•ly,** *adv.* —**con•trib′u•tive•ness,** *n.*

—**Syn. 1.** provide, furnish, donate.

con•tri•bu•tion (kon′trə byo͞o′shən), *n.* **1.** the act of contributing. **2.** something contributed. **3.** an article, story, drawing, etc., furnished to a magazine or other publication. **4.** an impost or levy. **5.** *Insurance.* the method of distributing liability, in case of loss, among several insurers whose policies attach to the same risk. [1350–1400; ME *contribucio(u)n* (< AF) < LL *contribūtiōn-* (s. of *contribūtiō*). See CONTRIBUTE, -ION] —**con′•tri•bu′tion•al,** *adj.*

—**Syn. 2.** gift, donation, benefaction.

con•trib•u•tor (kən trib′yə tər), *n.* **1.** a person who contributes money, assistance, etc. **2.** a person who contributes an article, story, etc., to a newspaper, magazine, or the like. [1400–50; late ME *contributour* < AF. See CONTRIBUTE, -TOR] —**con•trib•u•to•ri•al** (kən trib′yə tôr′ē əl, -tōr′-), *adj.*

con•trib•u•to•ry (kən trib′yə tôr′ē, -tōr′ē), *adj., n., pl.* **-ries.** —*adj.* **1.** pertaining to or of the nature of contribution; contributing. **2.** furnishing something toward a result: *a contributory factor.* **3.** of, pertaining to, or constituting an insurance or pension plan the premiums of which are paid partly by an employer and partly by employees. **4.** subject to contribution or levy. —*n.* **5.** a person or thing that contributes. [1375–1425; late ME *contributorie* < ML *contribūtōrius.* See CONTRIBUTE, -TORY[1]]

—**Syn. 2.** accessory, ancillary.

contrib′utory neg′ligence, *Law.* negligence on the part of an injured party that combines with the negligence of another in causing the injury, sometimes so as to diminish or bar the recovery of damages for the injury. [1870–75]

con•trite (kən trīt′, kon′trīt), *adj.* **1.** caused by or showing sincere remorse. **2.** filled with a sense of guilt and the desire for atonement; penitent: *a contrite sinner.* [1300–50; ME *contrit* (< AF) < L *contrītus* worn down, crushed, ptp. of *conterere.* See CON-, TRITE] —**con•trite′ly,** *adv.* —**con•trite′ness,** *n.*

—**Syn. 2.** rueful, remorseful, repentant.

con•tri•tion (kən trish′ən), *n.* **1.** sincere penitence or remorse. **2.** *Theol.* sorrow for and detestation of sin with a true purpose of amendment, arising from a love of God for His own perfections **(perfect contrition),** or from some inferior motive, as fear of divine punishment **(imperfect contrition).** [1250–1300; ME *contricio(u)n* (< AF) < LL *contrītiōn-* (s. of *contrītiō*). See CONTRITE, -ION]

—**Syn. 1.** compunction, regret.

con•triv•ance (kən trī′vəns), *n.* **1.** something contrived; a device, esp. a mechanical one. **2.** the act or manner of contriving; the faculty or power of contriving. **3.** a plan or scheme; expedient. [1620–30; CONTRIVE + -ANCE]

con•trive (kən trīv′), *v.,* **-trived, -triv•ing.** —*v.t.* **1.** to plan with ingenuity; devise; invent: *The author contrived a clever plot.* **2.** to bring about or effect by a plan, scheme, or the like; manage: *He contrived to gain their votes.* **3.** to plot (evil, treachery, etc.). —*v.i.* **4.** to form designs; plan. **5.** to plot. [1275–1325; ME *contreven* < MF *contreuv-,* tonic s. of *controver* to devise, invent, OF: to decide, agree upon < LL *contropāre* to compare, equiv. to *con-* CON- + **tropāre* (> F *trouver* to find; see TROVER); development of vowel unclear] —**con•triv′a•ble,** *adj.* —**con•triv′er,** *n.*

—**Syn. 1.** design, concoct. See **prepare. 3.** conspire, scheme. **5.** connive.

con•trived (kən trīvd′), *adj.* obviously planned or forced; artificial; strained: *a contrived story.* [1505–15; CONTRIVE + -ED[2]] —**con•triv•ed•ly** (kən trī′vid lē), *adv.*

con•trol (kən trōl′), *v.,* **-trolled, -trol•ling,** *n.* —*v.t.* **1.** to exercise restraint or direction over; dominate; command. **2.** to hold in check; curb: *to control a horse; to control one's emotions.* **3.** to test or verify (a scientific experiment) by a parallel experiment or other standard of comparison. **4.** to eliminate or prevent the flourishing or spread of: *to control a forest fire.* **5.** *Obs.* to check or regulate (transactions), originally by means of a duplicate register. —*n.* **6.** the act or power of controlling; regulation; domination or command: *Who's in control here?* **7.** the situation of being under the regulation, domination, or command of another: *The car is out of control.* **8.** check or restraint: *Her anger is under control.* **9.** a legal or official means of regulation or restraint: *to institute wage and price controls.* **10.** a standard of comparison in scientific experimentation. **11.** a person who acts as a check; controller. **12.** a device for regulating and guiding a machine, as a motor or airplane. **13. controls,** a coordinated arrangement of such devices. **14.** prevention of the flourishing or spread of something undesirable: *rodent control.* **15.** *Baseball.* the ability of a pitcher to throw the ball into the strike zone consistently: *The rookie pitcher has great power but no control.* **16.** *Philately.* any device printed on a postage or revenue stamp to authenticate it as a government issue or to identify it for bookkeeping purposes. **17.** a spiritual agency believed to assist a medium at a séance. **18.** the supervisor to whom an espionage agent reports when in the field. [1425–75; late ME *co(u)ntrollen* (v.) < AF *contreroller* to keep a duplicate account or roll, deriv. of *contrerolle* (n.). See COUNTER-, ROLL] —**con•trol′la•ble,** *adj., n.* —**con•trol′la•bil′i•ty, con•trol′la•ble•ness,** *n.* —**con•trol′la•bly,** *adv.* —**con•trol′less,** *adj.* —**con•trol′ling•ly,** *adv.*

—**Syn. 1.** manage, govern, rule. **2.** restrain, bridle, constrain. **6.** management, government, reign, rule, mastery. See **authority.**

control′ account′, a general account showing totals of transactions with detailed figures appearing in subsidiary ledgers. Also called **controlling account.**

control′ board′, a panel containing switches, dials, and other equipment for regulating electrical devices, lights, etc. Also called **control panel.** [1905–10]

control′ cen′ter, an administrative or operational center for a group of related activities: *the control center for the new military offensive.*

control′ char′acter, *Computers.* a character in a data stream that signals the device receiving the data to perform a particular control function, as changing the line spacing on a printer from single to double-spaced.

control′ chart′, *Statistics.* a chart on which observations are plotted as ordinates in the order in which they are obtained and on which control lines are constructed to indicate whether the population from which the observations are being drawn is remaining the same: used esp. in industrial quality control.

control′ elec′trode, *Electronics.* an electrode to which a varying signal is applied to vary the output of a transistor or vacuum tube. [1915–20]

control′ exper′iment, an experiment in which the variables are controlled so that the effects of varying one factor at a time may be observed. [1870–75]

control′ group′, (in an experiment or clinical trial) a group of subjects closely resembling the treatment group in many demographic variables but not receiving the active medication or factor under study and thereby serving as a comparison group when treatment results are evaluated. [1950–55]

con•trol•la•ble-pitch (kən trō′lə bəl pich′), *adj.* (of a marine or aircraft propeller) having blades whose pitch can be changed during navigation or flight; variable-pitch. Cf. **adjustable-pitch.** [1935–40]

con•trolled-re•lease (kən trōld′ri lēs′), *adj.* (of a

substance, as a medicine or insecticide) released or activated at predetermined intervals or gradually over a period of time.

controlled′ sub′stance, any of a category of behavior-altering or addictive drugs, as heroin or cocaine, whose possession and use are restricted by law. [1970–75]

con·trol·ler (kən trō′lər), *n.* **1.** an employee, often an officer, of a business firm who checks expenditures, finances, etc.; comptroller. **2.** a person who regulates, directs, or restrains. **3.** *Brit. Aeron.* a dispatcher. **4.** a regulating mechanism; governor. **5.** Also called **control unit, processor.** *Computers.* the key component of a peripheral device, as a terminal, printer, or external storage unit, that contains the circuitry necessary to interpret and execute instructions fed into the device. [1350–1400; ME *countrollour* < AF *countrero(u)llour,* MF *contrerolleur,* equiv. to *contrerolle* duplicate roll (see CONTROL) + *-eur, -our* < L *-ōr-* -OR[2] or *-ātōr-* -ATOR] —**con·trol′ler·ship′,** *n.*

control′ling account′. See **control account.**

control′ling im′age, a literary device employing repetition so as to stress the theme of a work or a particular symbol.

control′ling in′terest, ownership of enough stock in a company to exert control over policy and management. [1920–25]

control′ pan′el, **1.** See **control board.** **2.** *Computers.* **a.** the portion of a computer console that contains manual controls for regulating computer operations. **b.** plugboard (def. 2). [1920–1925]

control′ point′, *Aerial Photogrammetry.* a point located on the ground by precise surveying that when identified on aerial photographs provides the control necessary for producing a photomap. [1925–30]

control′ rock′et, a small rocket engine used to make corrections in the flight path of spacecraft or missiles.

control′ rod′, a neutron-absorbing material, as boron or cadmium, in the shape of a rod or other configuration, that can be moved into or out of the core of a nuclear reactor to regulate the rate of fission. [1940–45]

control′ room′, a room housing control equipment, as in a recording studio. [1925–30]

control′ stick′, *Aeron.* a lever by which a pilot controls the ailerons and elevator of an aircraft. [1930–35]

control′ sur′face, any movable airfoil, as a rudder, flap, or aileron, for guiding or controlling an aircraft or missile in flight. [1915–20]

control′ sur′vey, an accurate survey of a region forming a basis for more detailed surveys.

control′ tow′er, a glass-enclosed, elevated structure for the visual observation and control of the air and ground traffic at an airport. Also called **tower.** [1915–20]

control′ u′nit, *Computers.* **1.** the part of a CPU that interprets the instructions in programs and directs the operation of the entire system. **2.** controller (def. 5). [1960–65]

con·tro·ver·sial (kon′trə vûr′shəl), *adj.* **1.** of, pertaining to, or characteristic of controversy; polemical: *a controversial book.* **2.** subject to controversy; debatable: *a controversial decision.* **3.** given to controversy; disputatious. [1575–85; < LL *contrōversiālis,* equiv. to L *contrōversi(a)* CONTROVERSY + *-ālis* -AL[1]] —**con′tro·ver′sial·ism,** *n.* —**con′tro·ver′sial·ist,** *n.* —**con′tro·ver′sial·ly,** *adv.*
—**Syn. 2.** arguable, questionable.

con·tro·ver·sy (kon′trə vûr′sē; *Brit. also* kən trov′ər sē), *n., pl.* **-sies. 1.** a prolonged public dispute, debate, or contention; disputation concerning a matter of opinion. **2.** contention, strife, or argument. [1350–1400; ME *controversie* (< AF) < L *contrōversia,* equiv. to *contrōvers(us)* turned against, disputed (*contrō-,* var. of *contrā* against, + *versus,* ptp. of *vertere* to turn) + *-ia* -Y[3]]
—**Syn. 1.** disagreement, altercation. **2.** quarrel, wrangle. See **argument.**

con·tro·vert (kon′trə vûrt′, kon′trə vûrt′), *v.t.* **1.** to argue against; dispute; deny; oppose. **2.** to argue about; debate; discuss. [1600–10; alter. of earlier *controverse* (< L *contrōversus;* see CONTROVERSY) with *-vert* from ADVERT[1], CONVERT, etc.] —**con′tro·vert′er, con′tro·vert′ist,** *n.* —**con′tro·vert′i·ble,** *adj.* —**con′tro·vert′i·bly,** *adv.*
—**Syn. 1.** refute, rebut.

con·tu·ma·cious (kon′to͝o mā′shəs, -tyo͝o-), *adj.* stubbornly perverse or rebellious; willfully and obstinately disobedient. [1590–1600; CONTUMACY + -OUS] —**con′tu·ma′cious·ly,** *adv.* —**con′tu·ma′cious·ness, con·tu·mac·i·ty** (kon′to͝o mas′i tē, -tyo͝o-), *n.*
—**Syn.** contrary, pigheaded, factious, refractory, headstrong, intractable.

con·tu·ma·cy (kon′to͝o mə sē, -tyo͝o-), *n., pl.* **-cies.** stubborn perverseness or rebelliousness; willful and obstinate resistance or disobedience to authority. [1150–1200; ME *contumacie* < L *contumācia,* equiv. to *contumāc-,* s. of *contumāx* unyielding, stubborn (*con-* CON- + *-tum-* of uncert. sense, though connected by classical authors with both *contemnere* to regard with CONTEMPT and *tumēre* to swell) + *-āx* adj. suffix) + *-ia* -IA]

con·tu·me·ly (kon′to͝o mə lē, -tyo͝o-; kən to͞o′mə lē, -tyo͞o′-; kon′təm lē, -tyo͝om-, -chəm), *n., pl.* **-lies. 1.** insulting display of contempt in words or actions; contemptuous or humiliating treatment. **2.** a humiliating insult. [1350–1400; ME *contumelie* (< AF) < L *contumēlia,* perh. akin to *contumāx* (see CONTUMACY), though formation and sense development are unclear] —**con·tu·me·li·ous** (kon′to͝o mē′lē əs, -tyo͝o-), *adj.* —**con′tu·me′li·ous·ly,** *adv.* —**con′tu·me′li·ous·ness,** *n.*
—**Syn. 1.** abuse, scorn, disdain, rudeness.

con·tuse (kən to͞oz′, -tyo͞oz′), *v.t.,* **-tused, -tus·ing.** to injure (tissue), esp. without breaking the skin; bruise. [1375–1425; late ME < L *contūsus* ptp. of *contundere* to bruise, crush, equiv. to *con-* CON- + *tud-* (var. s. of *tundere* to beat) + *-tus* ptp. suffix] —**con·tu·sive** (kən to͞o′siv, -tyo͞o′-), *adj.*

con·tu·sion (kən to͞o′zhən, -tyo͞o′-), *n.* an injury, as from a blow with a blunt instrument, in which the subsurface tissue is injured but the skin is not broken; bruise. [1350–1400; ME (< MF) < L *contūsiōn-* (s. of *contūsiō*). See CONTUSE, -ION] —**con·tu′sioned,** *adj.*

co·nun·drum (kə nun′drəm), *n.* **1.** a riddle, the answer to which involves a pun or play on words, as *What is black and white and read all over? A newspaper.* **2.** anything that puzzles. [1590–1600; pseudo-L word of obscure orig.]

con·ur·ba·tion (kon′ər bā′shən), *n.* an extensive urban area resulting from the expansion of several cities or towns so that they coalesce but usually retain their separate identities. [1910–15; CON- + L *urb-* (s. of *urbs*) city + -ATION]

con·ure (kon′yər), *n.* any of several long-tailed New World parrots, esp. of the genus *Aratinga,* certain species of which are kept as pets. [1855–60; < NL *Conurus* earlier genus name < Gk *kôn(os)* cone + *-ouros* -tailed, adj. deriv. of *ourá* tail]

CONUS, continental United States.

co·nus ar·te·ri·o·sus (kō′nəs är tēr′ē ō′səs), *pl.* **co·ni ar·te·ri·o·si** (kō′nī är tēr′ē ō′sī, kō′nē är tēr′ē ō′sē). *Anat., Zool.* the most anterior part of the simple tubular heart of lower vertebrates and embryos of higher vertebrates, leading into the artery that leaves the heart; in mammals it forms a part of the upper wall of the right ventricle, in which the pulmonary artery originates. Also called **co′nus.** [1855–60; < NL: lit., arterial cone. See ARTERIO-, CONE]

conv., 1. convention; conventional. **2.** convertible. **3.** convocation.

con·va·lesce (kon′və les′), *v.i.,* **-lesced, -lesc·ing.** to recover health and strength after illness; make progress toward recovery of health. [1475–85; < L *convalēscere* to grow fully strong, equiv. to *con-* CON- + *valēscere* to grow strong (*val(ēre)* to be well + *-escere* -ESCE)]

con·va·les·cence (kon′və les′əns), *n.* **1.** the gradual recovery of health and strength after illness. **2.** the period during which one is convalescing. [1480–90; < LL *convalēscentia.* See CONVALESCE, -ENCE]

con·va·les·cent (kon′və les′ənt), *adj.* **1.** convalescing. **2.** of or pertaining to convalescence or convalescing persons. —*n.* **3.** a person who is convalescing. [1650–60; < L *convalēscent-* (s. of *convalēscēns*), prp. of *convalēscere* to CONVALESCE; see -ENT] —**con′va·les′cent·ly,** *adv.*

con·vect (kən vekt′), *v.t.* **1.** to transfer (heat or a fluid) by convection. —*v.i.* **2.** (of a fluid) to transfer heat by convection. [1880–85; back formation from *convected* < L *convect(us)* ptp. of *convehere* to carry together (see CON-, VECTOR) + -ED[2]] —**con·vec′tive,** *adj.* —**con·vec′tive·ly,** *adv.*

con·vec·tion (kən vek′shən), *n.* **1.** *Physics.* the transfer of heat by the circulation or movement of the heated parts of a liquid or gas. **2.** *Meteorol.* the vertical transport of atmospheric properties, esp. upward (distinguished from *advection*). **3.** the act of conveying or transmitting. [1615–25; < LL *convectiōn-* (s. of *convectiō*) a bringing together. See CONVECT, -ION] —**con·vec′tion·al,** *adj.*

convec′tion cell′, *Physics.* a distinct volume of circulating fluid, in a fluid medium under gravity, that is heated from below and cooled from above: usually found in large groupings.

convec′tion ov′en, a gas, electric, or microwave oven equipped with a fan that circulates and intensifies the heat, thereby decreasing the normal cooking time. [1970–75]

convec′tive activ′ity, *Meteorol.* any manifestation of convection in the atmosphere, as hail or thunderstorms.

convec′tive dis′charge, *Physics.* the repulsion of ions of a gas by a highly charged body, creating a discernible wind.

con·vec·tor (kən vek′tər), *n.* any fluid or device transferring heat by convection. [1905–10; CONVECT + -OR[2]]

con·ve·nance (kon′və näns′; *Fr.* kôNvə näNs′), *n., pl.* **-nanc·es** (-nän′siz; *Fr.* -näNs′). **1.** suitability; expediency; propriety. **2. convenances,** the social proprieties or conventionalities. [1475–85; < AF, equiv. to *convenir* to be proper + *-ance* -ANCE]

con·vene (kən vēn′), *v.,* **-vened, -ven·ing.** —*v.i.* **1.** to come together or assemble, usually for some public purpose. —*v.t.* **2.** to cause to assemble; convoke. **3.** to summon to appear, as before a judicial officer. [1400–50; late ME < AF *convenire* to come together, equiv. to *con-* CON- + *venire* to COME] —**con·ven′a·ble,** *adj.* —**con·ven′a·bly,** *adv.* —**con·ven′er, con·ve′nor,** *n.*
—**Syn. 1.** congregate, meet, collect, gather.

con·ven·ience (kən vēn′yəns), *n.* **1.** the quality of being convenient; suitability. **2.** anything that saves or simplifies work, adds to one's ease or comfort, etc., as an appliance, utensil, or the like. **3.** a convenient situation or time: *at your convenience.* **4.** advantage or accommodation: *a shelter for the convenience of travelers.* **5.** *Chiefly Brit.* See **water closet** (def. 1). —*adj.* **6.** easy to obtain, use, or reach; made for convenience: *convenience utensils that can be discarded after use.* [1350–1400; ME < L *convenientia* harmony, agreement. See CONVENIENT, -ENCE]
—**Syn. 1.** utility, handiness, availability.

conven′ience food′, any packaged food, dish, or meal that can be prepared quickly and easily, as by thawing or heating. [1960–65]

conven′ience store′, a retail store that carries a limited selection of basic items, as packaged foods and drugstore items, and is open long hours for the convenience of shoppers. [1960–65]

con·ven·ien·cy (kən vēn′yən sē), *n., pl.* **-cies.** *Archaic.* convenience. [1485–95; < L *convenientia.* See CONVENIENCE, -CY]

con·ven·ient (kən vēn′yənt), *adj.* **1.** suitable or agreeable to the needs or purpose; well-suited with respect to facility or ease in use; favorable, easy, or comfortable for use. **2.** at hand; easily accessible: *Their house is convenient to all transportation.* **3.** *Obs.* fitting; suitable. [1350–1400; ME < L *convenient-* (s. of *conveniēns*), prp. of *convenīre* to be suitable, COME together. See CONVENE, -ENT] —**con·ven′ient·ly,** *adv.*
—**Syn. 1.** adapted, serviceable, useful, helpful, advantageous. **2.** handy.

con·vent (kon′vent, -vənt), *n.* **1.** a community of persons devoted to religious life under a superior. **2.** a society or association of monks, friars, or nuns: now usually used of a society of nuns. **3.** the building or buildings occupied by such a society; a monastery or nunnery. **4.** *Obs.* assembly; meeting. [1175–1225; < ML *conventus;* L: assembly, coming together, equiv. to *conven(īre)* (see CONVENE) + *-tus* suffix of v. action; r. ME *covent* < AF < ML, as above]
—**Syn. 1.** abbey, priory. **3.** cloister.

con·ven·ti·cle (kən ven′ti kəl), *n.* **1.** a secret or unauthorized meeting, esp. for religious worship, as those held by Protestant dissenters in England in the 16th and 17th centuries. **2.** a place of meeting or assembly, esp. a Nonconformist meeting house. **3.** *Obs.* a meeting or assembly. [1350–1400; ME < L *conventiculum* a small assembly. See CONVENT, -I-, -CLE[1]] —**con·ven′ti·cler,** *n.* —**con·ven·tic·u·lar** (kon′ven tik′yə lər), *adj.*

con·ven·tion (kən ven′shən), *n.* **1.** a meeting or formal assembly, as of representatives or delegates, for discussion of and action on particular matters of common concern. **2.** *U.S. Politics.* a representative party assembly to nominate candidates and adopt platforms and party rules. **3.** an agreement, compact, or contract. **4.** an international agreement, esp. one dealing with a specific matter, as postal service or copyright. **5.** a rule, method, or practice established by usage; custom: *the convention of showing north at the top of a map.* **6.** general agreement or consent; accepted usage, esp. as a standard of procedure. **7.** conventionalism. **8.** *Bridge.* any of a variety of established systems or methods of bidding or playing that allows partners to convey certain information about their hands. [1375–1425; late ME *convencio(u)n* (< MF) < L *conventiōn-* (s. of *conventiō*) agreement, lit., a coming together. See CONVENE, -TION]
—**Syn. 1.** CONVENTION, ASSEMBLY, CONFERENCE, CONVOCATION name meetings for particular purposes. CONVENTION usually suggests a meeting of delegates representing political, church, social, or fraternal organizations. ASSEMBLY usually implies a meeting for a settled or customary purpose, as for discussion, legislation, or participation in a social function. CONFERENCE suggests a meeting for consultation and discussion about business or professional problems. CONVOCATION denotes a (church) assembly, the members of which have been summoned for a special purpose; chapel services at some colleges are called CONVOCATIONS. **3.** pact, treaty.

con·ven·tion·al (kən ven′shə nl), *adj.* **1.** conforming or adhering to accepted standards, as of conduct or taste: *conventional behavior.* **2.** pertaining to convention or general agreement; established by general consent or accepted usage; arbitrarily determined: *conventional symbols.* **3.** ordinary rather than different or original: *conventional phraseology.* **4.** not using, making, or involving nuclear weapons or energy; nonnuclear: *conventional warfare.* **5.** *Art.* **a.** in accordance with an accepted manner, model, or tradition. **b.** (of figurative art) represented in a generalized or simplified manner. **6.** of or pertaining to a convention, agreement, or compact. **7.** *Law.* resting on consent, express or implied. **8.** of or pertaining to a convention or assembly. [1575–85; < LL *conventiōnālis.* See CONVENTION, -AL[1]] —**con·ven′tion·al·ist,** *n.* —**con·ven′tion·al·ly,** *adv.*
—**Syn. 1.** See **formal**[1]. **2.** usual, habitual, customary.

con·ven·tion·al·ism (kən ven′shə nl iz′əm), *n.* **1.** adherence to or advocacy of conventional attitudes or practices. **2.** something conventional, as an expression or attitude. **3.** *Philos.* the view that fundamental principles are validated by definition, agreement, or convention. [1825–35; CONVENTIONAL + -ISM]

con·ven·tion·al·i·ty (kən ven′shə nal′i tē), *n., pl.* **-ties** for 3, 4. **1.** conventional quality or character. **2.** adherence to convention. **3.** a conventional practice, principle, form, etc. **4. conventionalities,** conventional rules of behavior. [1825–35; CONVENTIONAL + -ITY]

con·ven·tion·al·ize (kən ven′shə nl īz′), *v.t.,* **-ized, -iz·ing. 1.** to make conventional. **2.** *Art.* to represent in a conventional manner. Also, *esp. Brit.,* **con·ven′tion·al·ise′.** [1850–55; CONVENTIONAL + -IZE] —**con·ven′tion·al·i·za′tion,** *n.*

conven′tional weap′on, a nonnuclear weapon. [1950–55]

conven′tional wis′dom, something that is generally believed; prudence. [‡1965–70]

conven′tion cen′ter, a large civic building or group of buildings designed for conventions, industrial shows, and the like, having large unobstructed exhibit areas and often including conference rooms, hotel accommodations, restaurants, and other facilities.

con·ven·tion·eer (kən ven′shə nēr′), *n.* **1.** a person, as a political delegate, who participates in a convention. —*v.i.* **2.** to participate in a convention. [1930–35; CONVENTION + -EER]

con·ven·tion·er (kən ven′shə nər), *n.* **1.** a conven-

CONCISE PRONUNCIATION KEY: *act, cāpe, dâre, pärt; set, ēqual; if, īce; ox, ōver, ôrder, oil, bo͝ok, bo͞ot, out; up, ûrge; child; sing; shoe; thin, that;* zh *as in treasure.* ə = *a* as in *alone, e* as in *system, i* as in *easily, o* as in *gallop, u* as in *circus;* [ə] as in *fire* (fī[ə]r), *hour* (ou[ə]r). l and n can serve as syllabic consonants, as in *cradle* (krād′l), and *button* (but′n). See the full key inside the front cover.

tioneer. **2.** a member of a convention. [1685–95; CONVENTION + -ER[1]]

con•ven•tu•al (kən ven′cho͞o əl), *adj.* **1.** of, belonging to, or characteristic of a convent. —*n.* **2.** See **Friar Minor Conventual. 3.** a member of a convent or monastery. [1375–1425; late ME < ML *conventuālis*, equiv. to L *conventu-*, s. of *conventus* CONVENT + *-ālis* -AL[1]] —**con•ven′tu•al•ly,** *adj.*

Conven′tual Mass′, 1. the Mass celebrated daily in a convent church for all members of the conventual community. **2.** *Rom. Cath. Ch., Anglican Ch.* the Mass said daily in a cathedral or collegiate chapter.

con•verge (kən vûrj′), *v.*, **-verged, -verg•ing.** —*v.i.* **1.** to tend to meet in a point or line; incline toward each other, as lines that are not parallel. **2.** to tend to a common result, conclusion, etc. **3.** *Math.* **a.** (of a sequence) to have values eventually arbitrarily close to some number; to have a finite limit. **b.** (of an infinite series) to have a finite sum; to have a sequence of partial sums that converges. **c.** (of an improper integral) to have a finite value. **d.** (of a net) to be residually in every neighborhood of some point. —*v.t.* **4.** to cause to converge. [1685–95; < LL *convergere* to incline together. See CON-, VERGE[2]]
—**Syn. 1.** approach, focus, come together.

con•ver•gence (kən vûr′jəns), *n.* **1.** an act or instance of converging. **2.** a convergent state or quality. **3.** the degree or point at which lines, objects, etc., converge. **4.** *Ophthalm.* a coordinated turning of the eyes to bear upon a near point. **5.** *Physics.* **a.** the contraction of a vector field. **b.** a measure of this. **6.** *Meteorol.* a net flow of air into a given region. Cf. **divergence** (def. 2). **7.** *Biol.* similarity of form or structure caused by environment rather than heredity. Also, **con•ver′gen•cy** (for defs. 1–3). [1705–15; CONVERG(ENT) + -ENCE]

con•ver•gent (kən vûr′jənt), *adj.* characterized by convergence; tending to come together; merging. [1720–30; < LL *convergent-* (s. of *convergēns*, prp. of *convergere*). See CONVERGE, -ENT] —**con•ver′gent•ly,** *adv.*

conver′gent bound′ary, *Geol.* a major geologic discontinuity or suture marking the juncture of lithospheric plates that have been joined by plate tectonics.

conver′gent evolu′tion, the appearance of apparently similar structures in organisms of different lines of descent. [1965–70]

conver′gent se′quence, *Math.* See **fundamental sequence.**

converg′ing lens′, *Optics.* a lens that converts parallel rays of light to convergent rays and produces a real image. Also called **positive lens.** Cf. **diverging lens.** See diag. under **lens.**

con•vers•a•ble (kən vûr′sə bəl), *adj.* **1.** easy and pleasant to talk with; agreeable. **2.** able or disposed to converse. **3.** pertaining to or proper for conversation. [1590–1600; < ML *conversābilis.* See CONVERSE[1], -ABLE] —**con•vers′a•ble•ness,** *n.* —**con•vers′a•bly,** *adv.*

con•ver•sant (kən vûr′sənt, kon′vər-), *adj.* **1.** familiar by use or study (usually fol. by *with*): *conversant with Spanish history.* **2.** *Archaic.* having regular or frequent conversation; intimately associating; acquainted. [1250–1300; ME *conversa(u)nt* < L *conversant-* (s. of *conversāns*), prp. of *conversārī* to associate with. See CONVERSE[1], -ANT] —**con•ver′sance, con•ver′san•cy,** *n.* —**con•ver′sant•ly,** *adv.*
—**Syn. 1.** versed, learned, skilled, practiced, well-informed, proficient.

con•ver•sa•tion (kon′vər sā′shən), *n.* **1.** informal interchange of thoughts, information, etc., by spoken words; oral communication between persons; talk; colloquy. **2.** an instance of this. **3.** association or social intercourse; intimate acquaintance. **4.** See **criminal conversation. 5.** the ability to talk socially with others: *She writes well but has no conversation.* **6.** *Obs.* **a.** behavior or manner of living. **b.** close familiarity; intimate acquaintance, as from constant use or study. [1300–50; ME *conversacio(u)n* < L *conversātiōn-* (s. of *conversātiō*) society, intercourse, equiv. to *conversāt(us)* ptp. of *conversārī* to associate with (see CONVERSE[1]) + *-iōn-* -ION]
—**Syn. 1.** dialogue, chat.

con•ver•sa•tion•al (kon′vər sā′shə nl), *adj.* **1.** of, pertaining to, or characteristic of conversation: *a conversational tone of voice.* **2.** able or ready to converse; given to conversation. [1770–80; CONVERSATION + -AL[1]] —**con′ver•sa′tion•al•ly,** *adv.*
—**Syn. 1.** See **colloquial.**

conversa′tional im′plicature, *Philos., Ling.* an inference that can be drawn from an utterance, as from one that is seemingly illogical or irrelevant, by examining the degree to which it conforms to the canons of normal conversation and the way it functions pragmatically within the situation, as when "The phone is ringing," said in a situation where both speaker and listener can clearly hear the phone, can be taken as a suggestion to answer the phone. [1970–75]

con•ver•sa•tion•al•ist (kon′vər sā′shə nl ist), *n.* a person who enjoys and contributes to good conversation; an interesting person in conversation. [1830–40; CONVERSATIONAL + -IST]

conversa′tional qual′ity, (in public speaking) a manner of utterance that resembles the spontaneity and informality of relaxed personal conversation.

conversa′tion chair′, an English chair of the 18th century designed to be straddled facing the back of the chair with the elbows resting on the crest rail: an English imitation of the voyeuse. [1785–95]

conversa′tion piece′, 1. any object that arouses comment because of some striking or unusual quality. **2.** group portraiture representing more or less fashionable people either in an interior or landscape setting. **3.** a play that relies for its effect mainly on the cleverness of its dialogue rather than on plot or action. [1775–85]

conversa′tion pit′, a usually sunken portion of a room or living area with chairs, sofas, etc., often grouped around a fireplace, where people can gather to talk.

con•verse[1] (*v.* kən vûrs′; *n.* kon′vûrs), *v.*, **-versed, -vers•ing,** *n.* —*v.i.* **1.** to talk informally with another or others; exchange views, opinions, etc., by talking. **2.** *Archaic.* to maintain a familiar association (usually fol. by *with*). **3.** *Obs.* to have sexual intercourse (usually fol. by *with*). —*n.* **4.** familiar discourse or talk; conversation. [1300–50; ME *conversen* < MF *converser* < L *conversārī* to associate with. See CON-, VERSE] —**con•vers′er,** *n.*
—**Syn. 1.** chat, discuss. See **speak.**

con•verse[2] (*adj.* kən vûrs′, kon′vûrs; *n.* kon′vûrs), *adj.* **1.** opposite or contrary in direction, action, sequence, etc.; turned around. —*n.* **2.** something opposite or contrary. **3.** *Logic.* **a.** a proposition obtained from another proposition by conversion. **b.** the relation between two terms, one of which is related to the other in a given manner, as "younger than" to "older than." **4.** a group of words correlative with a preceding group but having a significant pair of terms interchanged, as "hot in winter but cold in summer" and "cold in winter but hot in summer." [1350–1400; ME *convers* (< AF) < L *conversus* ptp. of *convertere* to turn around, equiv. to *con-* CON- + *vert-* turn + *-tus* ptp. suffix; see CONVERT] —**con•verse•ly** (kən vûrs′lē, kon′vûrs-), *adv.*

Con•verse (kon′vûrs), *n.* **Frederick Shep•herd** (shep′ərd), 1871–1940, U.S. composer.

con•ver•sion (kən vûr′zhən, -shən), *n.* **1.** the act or process of converting; state of being converted. **2.** change in character, form, or function. **3.** spiritual change from sinfulness to righteousness. **4.** change from one religion, political belief, viewpoint, etc., to another. **5.** a change of attitude, emotion, or viewpoint from one of indifference, disbelief, or antagonism to one of acceptance, faith, or enthusiastic support, esp. such a change in a person's religion. **6.** a physical transformation from one material or state to another: *conversion of coal, water, and air into nylon.* **7.** the act of obtaining equivalent value, as of money or units of measurement, in an exchange or calculation: *conversion of francs into dollars.* **8.** a physical, structural, or design change or transformation from one state or condition to another, esp. to effect a change in function: *conversion of a freighter into a passenger liner.* **9.** a substitution of one component for another so as to effect a change: *conversion from oil heat to gas heat.* **10.** *Math.* a change in the form or units of an expression. **11.** *Logic.* the transposition of the subject and predicate of a proposition, as "No good man is unhappy" becomes by conversion "No unhappy man is good." **12.** *Law.* **a.** unauthorized assumption and exercise of rights of ownership over personal property belonging to another. **b.** change from realty into personalty, or vice versa, as in the sale or purchase of land or mining coal. **13.** *Football.* a score made on a try for a point after touchdown by place-kicking or drop-kicking the ball over the bar between the goalposts or by completing a pass in or running the ball into the end zone. **14.** *Psychoanal.* the process by which a repressed psychic event, idea, feeling, memory, or impulse is represented by a bodily change or symptom. **15.** *Physics.* the production of radioactive material in a process in which one nuclear fuel is converted into another by the capture of neutrons. Cf. **breeding** (def. 6). **16.** *Computers.* **a.** the process of changing software designed to run on one computer system to run on another. **b.** the change from an existing computer system to a new computer system. **c.** the act of transferring or copying data stored on one storage medium to another storage medium. **d.** the process of changing the base that a number or numbers are written in. **17.** the transformation of material from a form suitable for printing by one process to a form suitable for another process: *a halftone gravure conversion.* [1300–50; ME *conversio(u)n* (< AF) < L *conversiōn-* (s. of *conversiō*) a complete change. See CONVERSE[2], -ION] —**con•ver′sion•al, con•ver•sion•ar•y** (kən vûr′zhə ner′ē, -shə-), *adj.*

conver′sion disor′der, *Psychiatry.* a mental disorder in which physical symptoms, as paralysis or blindness, occur without apparent physical cause and instead appear to result from psychological conflict or need. Also called **conver′sion hyste′ria.**

conver′sion ra′tio, *Physics.* (in a reactor) the number of fissionable atoms produced by each fissionable atom that is destroyed. [1950–55]

conver′sion ta′ble, a tabular arrangement of the equivalent values of the weight or measure units of different systems.

con•ver•sus (kən vûr′səs), *n., pl.* **-si** (-sī, -sē). *Eccles.* a lay brother. [< L, ptp. of *convertere* to CONVERT[1]; see CONVERSE[2]]

con•vert[1] (*v.* kən vûrt′; *n.* kon′vûrt), *v.t.* **1.** to change (something) into a different form or properties; transmute; transform. **2.** to cause to adopt a different religion, political doctrine, opinion, etc.: *to convert the heathen.* **3.** to turn to another or a particular use or purpose; divert from the original or intended use: *They converted the study into a nursery for the baby.* **4.** to modify (something) so as to serve a different function: *to convert an automobile factory to the manufacture of tanks.* **5.** to obtain an equivalent value for in an exchange or calculation, as money or units of measurement: *to convert bank notes into gold; to convert yards into meters.* **6.** *Finance.* to exchange voluntarily (a bond or preferred stock) into another security, usually common stock, because of the greater value of the latter. **7.** to change in character; cause to turn from an evil life to a righteous one: *to convert a criminal.* **8.** *Chem.* to cause (a substance) to undergo a chemical change: *to convert sugar into alcohol.* **9.** to invert or transpose. **10.** *Law.* **a.** to assume unlawful rights of ownership of (personal property). **b.** to change the form of (property), as from realty to personalty or vice versa. **11.** to appropriate wrongfully to one's own use. **12.** *Logic.* to transpose the subject and predicate of (a proposition) by conversion. **13.** *Computers.* to subject to conversion. —*v.i.* **14.** to become converted. **15.** *Football.* to make a conversion. —*n.* **16.** one who has been converted, as to a religion or opinion. [1250–1300; ME *converten* < L *convertere* to change completely, equiv. to *con-* CON- + *vertere* to turn round (see VERSE); *convert* (n.) r. *converse*, ME *convers* (< AF) < L; see CONVERSE[2]] —**con•ver′•tive,** *adj.*
—**Syn. 1.** See **transform. 2.** proselytize. **16.** proselyte, neophyte, disciple.

con•vert[2] (kon′vûrt), *n. Informal.* **1.** a convertible automobile. **2.** a convertible bond. [by shortening of CONVERTIBLE]

con•vert•a•plane (kən vûr′tə plān′), *n.* convertiplane.

con•vert•ed (kən vûr′tid), *adj.* **1.** noting a specified type of person who has been converted from the religion, beliefs, or attitudes characteristic of that type: *a converted Christian; a converted thief.* **2.** noting anything, formerly of the type specified, that has been converted to something else: *His yacht is a converted destroyer escort.* [1585–95; CONVERT + -ED[2]]

convert′ed steel′. See **cement steel.** [1870–75]

con•vert•er (kən vûr′tər), *n.* **1.** a person or thing that converts. **2.** *Elect.* a device that converts alternating current to direct current or vice versa. Cf. **inverter, synchronous converter. 3.** *Metall.* a chamber or vessel through which an oxidizing blast of air is forced, as in making steel by the Bessemer process. **4.** *Television.* decoder (def. 5). **5.** *Radio and Television.* an auxiliary device that permits a receiver to pick up frequencies or channels for which it was not originally designed. **6.** *Physics.* a reactor for converting one kind of fuel into another kind. **7.** a person who is engaged in converting textile fabrics, esp. cotton cloths, from the raw state into the finished product ready for the market by bleaching, dyeing, etc. **8.** Also called **convert′er lens′.** *Photog.* an additional lens attached to a lens in use on a camera to alter focal length, mounted in front of a lens to produce a wide-angle effect **(wide-angle converter)** or between the lens and the camera body to produce a telephoto effect **(teleconverter** or **extender).** Also, **con•ver′tor.** [1525–35; CONVERT + -ER[1]]

con•vert•i•ble (kən vûr′tə bəl), *adj.* **1.** capable of being converted. **2.** having a folding top, as an automobile or pleasure boat. **3.** exchangeable for something of equal value: *debts payable only in convertible currencies.* —*n.* **4.** an automobile or a boat with a folding top. **5.** a sofa, couch, or chair whose seating section can be folded out into a bed. **6.** *Finance.* a convertible bond or security. [1350–1400; ME < ML *convertibilis.* See CONVERT, -IBLE] —**con•vert′i•bil′i•ty, con•vert′i•ble•ness,** *n.* —**con•vert′i•bly,** *adv.*

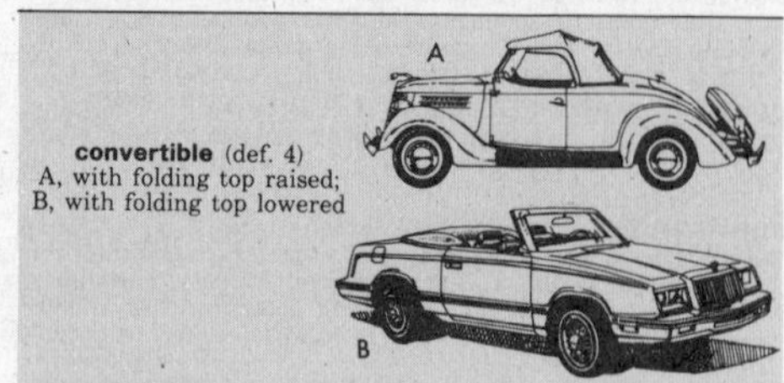

convertible (def. 4)
A, with folding top raised;
B, with folding top lowered

convert′ible bond′, a bond that can be exchanged for a fixed number of shares of the common stock of the issuing company at the holder's option.

convert′ible deben′ture, a convertible bond that is not secured with collateral.

convert′ible insur′ance, any form of life or health insurance, either individual or group, that enables the insured to change or convert the insurance to another form, as term to whole life insurance or group to individual health insurance.

convert′ible lens′, *Photog.* a lens containing two or more elements that can be used individually or in combination to provide a variety of focal lengths.

convert′ible preferred′ stock′, preferred stock that can be exchanged for a fixed number of shares of the common stock of the issuing company at the holder's option.

con•vert•i•plane (kən vûr′tə plān′), *n.* a plane capable of both vertical flight like a helicopter and fast, forward speed like a conventional airplane. Also, **converta-plane, con•vert′o•plane′.** [1945–50; CONVERT + -I- + PLANE[1]]

con•vert•ite (kon′vər tīt′), *n. Archaic.* **1.** a convert. **2.** a reformed prostitute. [1555–65; CONVERT + -ITE[1]]

con•vex (*adj.* kon veks′, kən-; *n.* kon′veks), *adj.* **1.** having a surface that is curved or rounded outward. Cf. **concave** (def. 1). **2.** *Math.* **a.** (of a polygon) having all interior angles less than or equal to 180°. **b.** (of a set) having the property that for each pair of points in the set the line joining the points is wholly contained in the set. —*n.* **3.** a convex surface, part, or thing. [1565–75; < L *convexus* equiv. to *con-* CON- + *-vexus*, perh. < **wek-sos*, deriv. of base of *vehere* to convey, if original sense was "brought together (to a single point)"] —**con•vex′ly, con•vex•ed•ly** (kən vek′sid lē), *adv.* —**con•vex′ed•ness,** *n.*

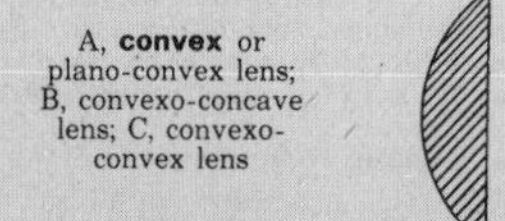
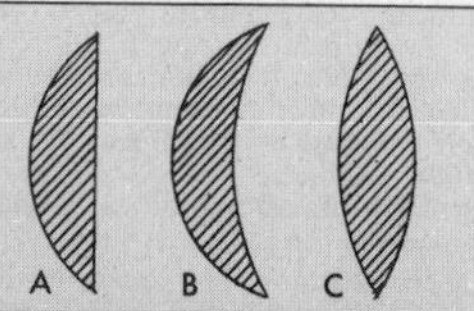

A, **convex** or plano-convex lens; B, convexo-concave lens; C, convexo-convex lens

CONCISE ETYMOLOGY KEY: <, descended or borrowed from; >, whence; b., blend of, blended; c., cognate with; cf., compare; deriv., derivative; equiv., equivalent; imit., imitative; obl., oblique; r., replacing; s., stem; sp., spelling, spelled; resp., respelling, respelled; trans., translation; ?, origin unknown; *, unattested; ‡, probably earlier than. See the full key inside the front cover.

con′vex hull′, *Math.* the smallest convex set containing a given set; the intersection of all convex sets that contain a given set. Also called **con′vex cov′er, con′vex span′.**

con·vex·i·ty (kən vek′si tē), *n., pl.* **-ties** for 2. **1.** the state of being convex. **2.** a convex surface or thing. [1590–1600; < L *convexitās.* See CONVEX, -ITY]

convexo-, a combining form representing **convex** in compound words: *convexo-concave.*

con·vex·o-con·cave (kən vek′sō kon kāv′), *adj.* **1.** concavo-convex. **2.** *Optics.* pertaining to or noting a lens in which the convex face has a greater degree of curvature than the concave face. [1685–95; CONVEXO- + CONCAVE]

con·vex·o-con·vex (kən vek′sō kon veks′), *adj.* convex on both sides; biconvex. [CONVEXO- + CONVEX]

con·vex·o-plane (kən vek′sō plān′), *adj.* plano-convex. [CONVEXO- + PLANE[1]]

con·vey (kən vā′), *v.t.* **1.** to carry, bring, or take from one place to another; transport; bear. **2.** to communicate; impart; make known: *to convey a wish.* **3.** to lead or conduct, as a channel or medium; transmit. **4.** *Law.* to transfer; pass the title to. **5.** *Archaic.* steal; purloin. **6.** *Obs.* to take away secretly. [1250–1300; ME *conveyen* < AF *conveier* < VL **conviāre,* equiv. to *con-* CON- + *-viāre,* deriv. of *via* way; see VIA] —**con·vey′a·ble,** *adj.*
—**Syn. 1.** move. See **carry.**

con·vey·ance (kən vā′əns), *n.* **1.** the act of conveying; transmission; communication. **2.** a means of transporting, esp. a vehicle, as a bus, airplane, or automobile. **3.** *Law.* **a.** the transfer of property from one person to another. **b.** the instrument or document by which this is effected. [1495–1505; CONVEY + -ANCE]

con·vey·anc·er (kən vā′ən sər), *n.* a person engaged in conveyancing. [1615–25; CONVEYANCE + -ER[1]]

con·vey·anc·ing (kən vā′ən sing), *n.* the branch of law practice consisting of examining titles, giving opinions as to their validity, and drawing of deeds, etc., for the conveyance of property from one person to another. [1670–80; CONVEYANCE + -ING[1]]

con·vey·or (kən vā′ər), *n.* **1.** a person or thing that conveys. **2.** See **conveyor belt.** Also, **con·vey′er.** [1505–15; CONVEY + -OR[2]]

convey′or belt′, *Mach.* an endless belt or chain, set of rollers, etc., for carrying materials or objects short distances, as from one part of a building to another. [1905–10]

con·vey·or·ize (kən vā′ə rīz′), *v.t.,* **-ized, -iz·ing.** to equip (a factory or the like) with conveyor belts. Also, *esp. Brit.,* **con·vey′or·ise′.** [1940–45, *Amer.;* CONVEYOR + -IZE] —**con·vey′or·i·za′tion,** *n.* —**con·vey′or·iz′er,** *n.*

con·vict (*v., adj.* kən vikt′; *n.* kon′vikt), *v.t.* **1.** to prove or declare guilty of an offense, esp. after a legal trial: *to convict a prisoner of a felony.* **2.** to impress with a sense of guilt. —*n.* **3.** a person proved or declared guilty of an offense. **4.** a person serving a prison sentence. —*adj.* **5.** *Archaic.* convicted. [1350–1400; (v.) ME *convicten* < L *convictus* ptp. of *convincere,* equiv. to *con-* CON- + *vic-* var. s. of *vincere* to overcome + *-tus* ptp. suffix (see CONVINCE); (n., adj.) ME *convict,* ptp. of *convicten* (or directly < L)] —**con·vict′a·ble, con·vict′i·ble,** *adj.* —**con·vic′tive,** *adj.* —**con·vic′tive·ly,** *adv.*

con·vict·fish (kon′vikt fish′), *n., pl.* **-fish·es,** (*esp. collectively*) **-fish.** See **painted greenling.** [CONVICT + FISH, so called from the fancied resemblance of its stripes to a convict's uniform]

con·vic·tion (kən vik′shən), *n.* **1.** a fixed or firm belief. **2.** the act of convicting. **3.** the state of being convicted. **4.** the act of convincing. **5.** the state of being convinced. [1400–50; late ME < LL *convictiōn-* (s. of *convictiō*) proof (of guilt). See CONVICT, -ION] —**con·vic′tion·al,** *adj.*
—**Syn. 1.** See **belief.** —**Ant. 5.** doubt, uncertainty.

con·vince (kən vins′), *v.t.,* **-vinced, -vinc·ing. 1.** to move by argument or evidence to belief, agreement, consent, or a course of action: *to convince a jury of his guilt; A test drive will convince you that this car handles well.* **2.** to persuade; cajole: *We finally convinced them to have dinner with us.* **3.** *Obs.* to prove or find guilty. **4.** *Obs.* to overcome; vanquish. [1520–30; < L *convincere* to prove (something) false or true, (somebody) right or wrong, equiv. to *con-* CON- + *vincere* to overcome; see VICTOR] —**con·vinc′ed·ly,** *adv.* —**con·vinc′ed·ness,** *n.* —**con·vinc′er,** *n.* —**con·vin′ci·ble,** *adj.* —**con·vinc′i·bil′i·ty,** *n.*
—**Syn. 1.** satisfy.
—**Usage.** CONVINCE, an often stated rule says, may be followed only by *that* or *of,* never by *to: We convinced him that he should enter* (not *convinced him to enter*) *the contest. He was convinced of the wisdom of entering.* In examples to support the rule, CONVINCE is often contrasted with PERSUADE, which may take *to, of,* or *that* followed by the appropriate construction: *We persuaded him to seek counseling* (or *of his need for counseling* or *that he should seek counseling*). The history of usage does not support the rule. CONVINCE (someone) TO has been in use since the 16th century and, despite objections by some, occurs freely today in all varieties of speech and writing and is fully standard: *Members of the cabinet are trying to convince the prime minister not to resign.*

con·vinc·ing (kən vin′sing), *adj.* **1.** persuading or assuring by argument or evidence: *They gave a convincing demonstration of the car's safety features.* **2.** appearing worthy of belief; plausible: *The excuse was not convincing.* [1605–15; CONVINCE + -ING[2]] —**con·vinc′ing·ly,** *adv.* —**con·vinc′ing·ness,** *n.*

con·vive (kon′vīv; *Fr.* kôN vēv′), *n., pl.* **-vives** (-vīvz; *Fr.* -vēv′). an eating or drinking companion; fellow diner or drinker. [1640–50; < F < L *conviva* table-companion, guest, equiv. to *con-* CON- + *-vīva,* deriv. of *vīvere* to live. See VITAL]

con·viv·i·al (kən viv′ē əl), *adj.* **1.** friendly; agreeable: *a convivial atmosphere.* **2.** fond of feasting, drinking, and merry company; jovial. **3.** of or befitting a feast; festive. [1660–70; < LL *convīviālis* festal, equiv. to L *convīvi(um)* feast (*convīv(ere)* to live together, dine together (*con-* CON- + *vīvere* to live) + *-ium* -IUM) + *-ālis* -AL[1]] —**con·viv′i·al·ist,** *n.* —**con·viv′i·al′i·ty,** *n.* —**con·viv′i·al·ly,** *adv.*
—**Syn. 1.** sociable, companionable, genial.

con·vo·ca·tion (kon′və kā′shən), *n.* **1.** the act of convoking. **2.** the state of being convoked. **3.** a group of people gathered in answer to a summons; assembly. **4.** *Anglican Ch.* either of the two provincial synods or assemblies of the clergy. **5.** *Prot. Episc. Ch.* **a.** an assembly of the clergy of part of a diocese. **b.** the area represented at such an assembly. **6.** a formal assembly at a college or university, esp. for a graduation ceremony. [1350–1400; ME *convocacio(u)n* (< MF) < L *convocātiōn-* (s. of *convocātiō*). See CONVOKE, -ATION] —**con′vo·ca′tion·al,** *adj.* —**con′vo·ca′tion·al·ly,** *adv.*
—**Syn. 3.** See **convention.**

con·vo·ca·tor (kon′və kā′tər), *n.* **1.** a person who convokes a meeting. **2.** a person who takes part in a convocation. [1595–1605; < ML, equiv. to *convocā(re)* to CONVOKE + *-tor* -TOR]

con·voke (kən vōk′), *v.t.,* **-voked, -vok·ing.** to call together; summon to meet or assemble. [1590–1600; (< MF *convoquer*) < L *convocāre,* equiv. to *con-* CON- + *vocāre* to call] —**con·voc·a·tive** (kən vok′ə tiv), *adj.* —**con·vok·er** (kən vō′kər), **con·vo·cant** (kon′və kənt), *n.*
—**Syn.** convene.

con·vo·lute (kon′və lo͞ot′), *v.,* **-lut·ed, -lut·ing,** *adj.* —*v.t., v.i.* **1.** to coil up; form into a twisted shape. —*adj.* **2.** rolled up together or with one part over another. **3.** *Bot.* coiled up longitudinally so that one margin is within the coil and the other without, as the petals of cotton. [1690–1700; < L *convolūtus* rolled up, equiv. to *convolū-* (s. of *convolvere* to CONVOLVE) + *-tus* ptp. suffix] —**con′vo·lute′ly,** *adv.*

con·vo·lut·ed (kon′və lo͞o′tid), *adj.* **1.** twisted; coiled. **2.** complicated; intricately involved: *a convoluted way of describing a simple device.* [1805–15; CONVOLUTE + -ED[2]] —**con′vo·lut′ed·ly,** *adj.* —**con′vo·lut′ed·ness,** *n.*

con′voluted tu′bule, *n. Anat.* a portion of the nephron in the kidney that functions in concentrating urine and in maintaining salt, water, and sugar balance. [1945–50]

con·vo·lu·tion (kon′və lo͞o′shən), *n.* **1.** a rolled up or coiled condition. **2.** a rolling or coiling together. **3.** a turn of anything coiled; whorl. **4.** *Anat.* one of the sinuous folds or ridges of the surface of the brain. [1535–45; < L *convolūt-* (see CONVOLUTE) + -ION] —**con′vo·lu′tion·al, con·vo·lu·tion·ar·y** (kon′və lo͞o′shə ner′ē), *adj.*
—**Syn. 3.** twist, winding, sinuosity.

con·volve (kən volv′), *v.i., v.t.,* **-volved, -volv·ing.** to roll or wind together; coil; twist. [1590–1600; < L *convolvere,* equiv. to *con-* CON- + *volvere* to roll, turn, twist] —**con·volve′ment,** *n.*

con·vol·vu·la·ceous (kən vol′vyə lā′shəs), *adj.* belonging to the Convolvulaceae, the morning glory family. Cf. **morning glory family.** [1840–50; < NL *Convolvulace(ae)* (see CONVOLVOLUS, -ACEAE) + -OUS]

con·vol·vu·lus (kən vol′vyə ləs), *n., pl.* **-lus·es, -li** (-lī′). any plant belonging to the genus *Convolvulus,* of the morning glory family, comprising twining or prostrate plants having trumpet-shaped flowers. [1545–55; < NL, L: bindweed, equiv. to *convolv(ere)* to CONVOLVE + *-ulus* -ULE]

con·voy (*v.* kon′voi, kən voi′; *n.* kon′voi), *v.t.* **1.** to accompany or escort, usually for protection: *A destroyer convoyed the merchant ship.* —*n.* **2.** the act of convoying. **3.** the protection provided by an escort. **4.** a ship, fleet, group of vehicles, etc., accompanied by a protecting escort. **5.** an armed force, warship, etc., that escorts, esp. for protection. **6.** any group of military vehicles traveling together under the same orders. **7.** *CB Radio Slang.* two or more CB-equipped vehicles traveling together. [1325–75; ME *convoyen* < MF *convoier,* AF *conveier* to CONVEY]
—**Syn. 1.** See **accompany.**

con·vul·sant (kən vul′sənt), *adj.* **1.** causing convulsions; convulsive. —*n.* **2.** a convulsant agent. [1870–75; CONVULSE + -ANT]

con·vulse (kən vuls′), *v.t.,* **-vulsed, -vuls·ing. 1.** to shake violently; agitate. **2.** to cause to shake violently with laughter, anger, pain, etc. **3.** to cause to suffer violent, spasmodic contractions of the muscles. [1635–45; < L *convulsus* ptp. of *convellere* to shatter, tear loose, equiv. to *con-* CON- + *vul-* (var. s. of *vellere* to pull, tear) + *-sus,* var. of *-tus* ptp. suffix] —**con·vuls′ed·ly,** *adv.* —**con·vuls′i·ble,** *adj.* —**con·vuls′i·bil′i·ty,** *n.*

con·vul·sion (kən vul′shən), *n.* **1.** contortion of the body caused by violent, involuntary muscular contractions of the extremities, trunk, and head. **2.** violent agitation or disturbance; commotion. **3.** an outburst of great, uncontrollable laughter. [1575–85; < L *convulsiōn-* (s. of *convulsiō*). See CONVULSE, -ION]

con·vul·sion·ar·y (kən vul′shə ner′ē), *adj., n., pl.* **-ar·ies.** —*adj.* **1.** of or affected with convulsion. —*n.* **2.** a person who has convulsions, esp. as a result of religious experience. [1735–45; CONVULSION + -ARY]

con·vul·sive (kən vul′siv), *adj.* **1.** of the nature of or characterized by convulsions or spasms. **2.** producing or accompanied by convulsion: *convulsive rage.* [1605–15; < L *convulsīvus.* See CONVULSE, -IVE] —**con·vul′sive·ly,** *adv.* —**con·vul′sive·ness,** *n.*
—**Syn. 1.** spasmodic.

convul′sive disor′der, any of various types of epilepsy.

Con·way (kon′wā), *n.* **1. Thomas,** 1735–1800?, Irish soldier of fortune in America and India. **2.** a city in central Arkansas. 20,375. **3.** a town in E South Carolina. 10,240. **4.** a male given name.

co·ny (kō′nē, kun′ē), *n., pl.* **-nies. 1.** the fur of a rabbit, esp. when dyed to simulate Hudson seal. **2.** the daman or other hyrax of the same genus. **3.** the pika. **4.** a rabbit. **5.** *Obs.* a person who is easily tricked; gull; dupe. Also, **coney.** [1150–1200; ME, back formation from *conyes* < OF *conis,* pl. of *conil* < L *cuniculus* rabbit, burrow, a word said to be of Iberian orig., according with evidence that the rabbit spread through Europe from NW Africa and the Iberian Peninsula]

coo[1] (ko͞o), *v.,* **cooed, coo·ing,** *n.* —*v.i.* **1.** to utter or imitate the soft, murmuring sound characteristic of doves. **2.** to murmur or talk fondly or amorously. —*v.t.* **3.** to utter by cooing. —*n.* **4.** a cooing sound. [1660–70; imit.] —**coo′er,** *n.* —**coo′ing·ly,** *adv.*

coo[2] (ko͞o), *interj. Brit. Slang.* (used to express surprise or amazement.) [1910–15; orig. uncert.]

Co·o (kô′ô), *n.* Italian name of **Kos.**

COO, chief operating officer.

coo·boo (ko͞o′bo͞o), *n., pl.* **-boos.** *Australian Informal.* an Aborigine child. [perh. < an Australian Aboriginal language]

co-oc·cur (kō′ə kûr′), *v.i.,* **-curred, -cur·ring.** to appear together in sequence or simultaneously. Also, **co′·oc·cur′.** [1950–55] —**co′-oc·cur′rence, co′oc·cur′·rence,** *n.*

cooch (ko͞och), *n.* a sinuous, quasi-Oriental dance performed by a woman and characterized chiefly by suggestive gyrating and shaking of the body. Also, **cootch.** Also called **cooch′ dance′, hootchy-kootchy, cooch·ie-cooch·ie** (ko͞o′chē ko͞o′chē). [1940–45; appar. short for HOOTCHY-KOOTCHY]

Cooch Be·har (ko͞och′ bə här′), **1.** a former state in NE India; now part of West Bengal. **2.** a city in West Bengal, in NE India. 53,734.

coo·ee (ko͞o′ē), *n., v.,* **coo·eed, coo·ee·ing.** —*n.* **1.** a prolonged, shrill, clear call or cry used as a signal by Australian Aborigines and adopted by the settlers in the country. —*v.i.* **2.** to utter the call "cooee." [1780–90; < Dharuk *gu-wi*]

coo·ey (ko͞o′ē), *n., pl.* **-eys,** *v.i.,* **-eyed, -ey·ing.** cooee.

coof (ko͝of), *n. Chiefly Scot.* a silly or stupid person. [1715–25; orig. uncert.]

cook[1] (ko͝ok), *v.t.* **1.** to prepare (food) by the use of heat, as by boiling, baking, or roasting. **2.** to subject (anything) to the application of heat. **3.** *Slang.* to ruin; spoil. **4.** *Informal.* to falsify, as accounts: *to cook the expense figures.* —*v.i.* **5.** to prepare food by the use of heat. **6.** (of food) to undergo cooking. **7.** *Slang.* **a.** to be full of activity and excitement: *Las Vegas cooks around the clock.* **b.** to perform, work, or do in just the right way and with energy and enthusiasm: *That new drummer is really cooking tonight. Now you're cooking!* **c.** to be in preparation; develop: *Plans for the new factory have been cooking for several years.* **d.** to take place; occur; happen: *What's cooking at the club?* **8. cook off,** (of a shell or cartridge) to explode or fire without being triggered as a result of overheating in the chamber of the weapon. **9. cook one's goose.** See **goose** (def. 9). **10. cook the books,** *Slang.* to manipulate the financial records of a company, organization, etc., so as to conceal profits, avoid taxes, or present a false financial report to stockholders. **11. cook up,** *Informal.* **a.** to concoct or contrive, often dishonestly: *She hastily cooked up an excuse.* **b.** to falsify: *Someone had obviously cooked up the alibi.* —*n.* **12.** a person who cooks: *The restaurant hired a new cook.* [bef. 1000; (n.) ME *cok(e),* OE *cōc* (cf. ON *kokkr,* G *Koch,* D *kok*) < L *cocus, coquus,* deriv. of *coquere* to cook; akin to Gk *péptein* (see PEPTIC); (v.) late ME *coken,* deriv. of the n.] —**cook′a·ble,** *adj.* —**cook′less,** *adj.*

cook[2] (ko͞ok, ko͝ok), *v.i. Scot.* to hide, esp. outdoors, as by crouching down behind a hedge. [1780–90; perh. b. ME *couche* bend, stoop (see COUCH) and ME *croke* bend, stoop (see CROOKED)]

Cook (ko͝ok), *n.* **1. Frederick Albert,** 1865–1940, U.S. physician and polar explorer. **2. George Cram** (kram), 1873–1924, U.S. novelist, dramatist, and poet. **3. Captain James,** 1728–79, English navigator and explorer in the S Pacific, Antarctic Ocean, and along the coasts of Australia and New Zealand. **4. Sir Joseph,** 1860–1947, Australian statesman, born in England: prime minister 1913–14. **5. Mount.** Also called **Aorangi.** a mountain in New Zealand, on South Island. 12,349 ft. (3764 m).

cook·book (ko͝ok′bo͝ok′), *n.* a book containing recipes and instructions for cooking. Also, *Brit.,* **cook′ery book′.** [1800–10, *Amer.;* COOK[1] + BOOK]

Cooke (ko͝ok), *n.* **1.** See **Coke, Sir Edward. 2. Jay,** 1821–1905, U.S. financier. **3. Terence (James), Cardinal,** 1921–83, U.S. Roman Catholic clergyman: archbishop of New York 1968–83.

cook·er (ko͝ok′ər), *n.* **1.** an appliance or utensil for cooking: *pressure cooker.* **2.** a person employed in certain industrial processes, as in brewing or distilling, to operate cooking apparatus. [1880–85; COOK[1] + -ER[1]]

cook·er·y (ko͝ok′ə rē), *n., pl.* **-er·ies. 1.** the art or practice of cooking. **2.** a place equipped for cooking. [1350–1400; ME *cokerie.* See COOK[1], -ERY]

cook′ery stove′, *Brit.* cookstove.

Cooke·ville (ko͝ok′vil), *n.* a town in central Tennessee. 20,350.

cook·house (ko͝ok′hous′), *n., pl.* **-hous·es** (-hou′ziz). a building or place for cooking, esp. a camp kitchen. [1785–95; COOK[1] + HOUSE]

cook·ie (ko͝ok′ē), *n.* **1.** a small cake made from stiff, sweet dough rolled and sliced or dropped by spoonfuls on a large, flat pan **(cookie sheet)** and baked. **2.** *Informal-*

CONCISE PRONUNCIATION KEY: act, cāpe, dâre, pärt; set, ēqual; *if,* ice; ox, ōver, ôrder, oil, bo͝ok, bo͞ot, out; up, ûrge; child; sing; shoe; thin, *th*at; zh as in *treasure.* ə = *a* as in *alone, e* as in *system, i* as in *easily, o* as in *gallop, u* as in *circus;* ᵊ as in *fire* (fīᵊr), *hour* (ouᵊr). l and n can serve as syllabic consonants, as in *cradle* (krād′l), and *button* (but′n). See the full key inside the front cover.

mal. dear; sweetheart (a term of address, usually connoting affection). **3.** *Slang.* **a.** a person: *a smart cookie; a tough cookie.* **b.** an alluring young woman. **4.** *South Atlantic U.S.* (*chiefly North Carolina*). a doughnut. **5.** *Scot.* a bun. **6. toss** or **spill one's cookies,** *Slang.* to vomit. Also, **cooky.** [1695–1705, < D *koekie,* dial. var. of *koekje,* equiv. to *koek* CAKE + *-je* dim. suffix]

cook′ie cut′ter, a device, usually of metal, for cutting shaped forms, as circles or stars, for cookies from dough that has been rolled flat. [1900–05, *Amer.*]

cook•ie-cut•ter (ko͝ok′ē kut′ər), *adj.* **1.** having the same configuration or look as many others of a given kind; identical: *rows of cookie-cutter houses.* **2.** lacking individuality; stereotyped or formulaic: *a novel filled with cookie-cutter characters.*

cook′ie jar′, **1.** a jar or other container for storing cookies. **2.** such a container used for storing money. **3. have one's hand in the cookie jar,** *Informal.* to take or attempt to take advantage of one's position by demanding or accepting favors or bribes: *They suspected the mayor's assistant had his hand in the cookie jar.* [1940–45, *Amer.*]

cook′ie press′, a device, operating in a manner similar to that of a syringe, in which dough is inserted in a chamber and extruded, by means of a plunger, through one of a number of interchangeable dies to form a shaped cylinder that is sliced into individual cookies.

cook′ie sheet′. See under **cookie** (def. 1). [1925–30]

cook•ing (ko͝ok′ing), *n.* **1.** the act of a person or thing that cooks. **2.** the art or practice of preparing food; cookery. —*adj.* **3.** used in preparing foods: *a cooking utensil.* **4.** fit to eat when cooked (distinguished from *eating*): *cooking apples.* [1635–45; COOK[1] + -ING[1], -ING[2]]

Cook′ In′let, an inlet of the Gulf of Alaska. 150 mi. (240 km) long.

Cook′ Is′lands, a group of islands in the S Pacific belonging to New Zealand. 21,317; 99 sq. mi. (256 sq. km).

cook•off (ko͝ok′ôf′, -of′), *n.* a cooking contest in which competitors gather to prepare their specialties. Also, **cook′-off′.** Cf. **Bake-Off.** [1955–60; COOK[1] + -OFF]

cook•out (ko͝ok′out′), *n.* **1.** a party or entertainment featuring the cooking and eating of a meal out of doors. **2.** the process of cooking and eating a meal outdoors. **3.** a meal cooked and eaten in the open. —*adj.* **4.** of, pertaining to, or intended for use or consumption at a cookout. Also, **cook′-out′.** [1945–50, *Amer.*; n. use of v. phrase *cook out*]

cook•shack (ko͝ok′shak′), *n.* a simple structure, as on a ranch or at a camp, where food is cooked. [1905–10; COOK[1] + SHACK[1]]

cook•shop (ko͝ok′shop′), *n.* a place where prepared food is sold or served; restaurant. [1545–55; COOK[1] + SHOP]

Cook's′ tour′ (ko͝oks), a guided but cursory tour of the major features of a place or area. [1905–10; after Thomas *Cook* (1808–92), English travel agent]

cook•stove (ko͝ok′stōv′), *n.* a wood- or coal-burning stove for use in cooking. [1805–15; COOK[1] + STOVE[1]]

Cook′ Strait′, a strait in New Zealand between North and South Islands.

cook•top (ko͝ok′top′), *n.* a cooking surface consisting of a flat sheet of heat-transmitting glass and ceramic material over heating elements, usually electric. [COOK[1] + TOP[1]]

cook•ware (ko͝ok′wâr′), *n.* pots, pans, and other cooking utensils. [1950–55; COOK[1] + WARE[1]]

cook•y (ko͝ok′ē), *n., pl.* **cook•ies.** cookie.

cool (ko͞ol), *adj.,* **-er, -est,** *adv., n., v.* —*adj.* **1.** moderately cold; neither warm nor cold: *a rather cool evening.* **2.** feeling comfortably or moderately cold: *I'm perfectly cool, but open the window if you feel hot.* **3.** imparting a sensation of moderate coldness or comfortable freedom from heat: *a cool breeze.* **4.** permitting such a sensation: *a cool dress.* **5.** not excited; calm; composed; under control: *to remain cool in the face of disaster.* **6.** not hasty; deliberate: *a cool and calculated action.* **7.** lacking in interest or enthusiasm: *a cool reply to an invitation.* **8.** lacking in warmth or cordiality: *a cool reception.* **9.** calmly audacious or impudent: *a cool lie.* **10.** aloof or unresponsive; indifferent: *He was cool to her passionate advances.* **11.** unaffected by emotions; disinterested; dispassionate: *She made a cool appraisal of all the issues in the dispute.* **12.** *Informal.* (of a number or sum) without exaggeration or qualification: *a cool million dollars.* **13.** (of colors) with green, blue, or violet predominating. **14.** *Slang.* **a.** great; fine; excellent: *a real cool comic.* **b.** characterized by great facility; highly skilled or clever: *cool maneuvers on the parallel bars.* **c.** socially adept: *It's not cool to arrive at a party too early.* —*adv.* **15.** *Informal.* coolly. —*n.* **16.** something that is cool; a cool part, place, time, etc.: *in the cool of the evening.* **17.** coolness. **18.** calmness; composure; poise: *an executive noted for maintaining her cool under pressure.* **19. blow one's cool.** See **blow**[2] (def. 34). —*v.i.* **20.** to become cool (sometimes fol. by *down* or *off*): *The soup cooled in five minutes. We cooled off in the mountain stream.* **21.** to become less ardent, cordial, etc.; become moderate. —*v.t.* **22.** to make cool; impart a sensation of coolness to. **23.** to lessen the ardor or intensity of; allay; calm; moderate: *Disappointment cooled his early zealousness.* **24. cool down,** to bring the body back to its normal physiological level after fast, vigorous exercise or activity by gradually slowing the pace of activity or by doing gentle exercises or stretches. **25. cool it,** *Slang.* calm down; take it easy. **26. cool off,** *Informal.* to become calmer or more reasonable: *Wait until he cools off before you talk to him again.* **27. cool one's heels.** See **heel**[1] (def. 18). **28. cool out,** *Slang.* to calm or settle down; relax: *cooling out at the beach.* [bef. 1000; ME *cole,* OE *cōl;* c. MLG *kōl,* OHG *kuoli* (G *kuhl*). See COLD, CHILL] —**cool′ing•ly,** *adv.* —**cool′ish,** *adj.* —**cool′ly,** *adv.* —**cool′ness,** *n.*
—**Syn. 1.** See **cold. 5.** collected, self-possessed, unruffled, placid, quiet. See **calm. 7, 8.** distant, apathetic, reserved, remote, lukewarm. **23.** temper, abate. —**Ant. 1, 3, 4, 7, 8.** warm.

coo•la•bah (ko͞o′lə bä′), *n.* any of several Australian gum trees of the genus *Eucalyptus,* esp. *E. microtheca,* abundant along riverbanks and having sickle-shaped leaves and wrinkled, cracked bark. Also, **coo′li•bah′.** [1885–90; < Kamilaroi *gulabā*]

coo•la•mon (ko͞o′lə mon′, -mən), *n.* a basinlike dish made from wood or bark by Australian Aborigines. [1840–50; < Kamilaroi *gulaman*]

cool•ant (ko͞o′lənt), *n.* **1.** a substance, usually a liquid or a gas, used to reduce the temperature of a system below a specified value by conducting away the heat produced in the operation of the system, as the liquid in an automobile cooling system or the fluid that removes heat from the core of a nuclear reactor. **2.** a lubricant that dissipates the heat caused by friction. [1925–30; COOL + -ANT]

cool•er (ko͞o′lər), *n.* **1.** a container or apparatus, as an insulated chest, in which something may be cooled or kept cool. **2.** anything that cools or makes cool; refrigerant. **3.** an air conditioner. **4.** a tall drink, consisting of liquor, soda, and a fruit garnish. **5.** See **water cooler. 6. the cooler,** *Slang.* jail: *He was in the cooler for three months for petty theft.* **7.** *Ice Hockey Slang.* See **penalty box.** [1565–75; COOL + -ER[1]]

Coo•ley (ko͞o′lē), *n.* **Charles Hor•ton** (hôr′tn), 1864–1929, U.S. author and pioneer in the field of sociology.

Coo′ley's ane′mia, thalassemia. [1930–35; named after Thomas Benton *Cooley* (1871–1945), U.S. pediatrician, who reported incidences of the disease]

cool-head•ed (ko͞ol′hed′id), *adj.* not easily excited; calm. [1770–80] —**cool′-head′ed•ly,** *adv.* —**cool′-head′ed•ness,** *n.*

Cool•idge (ko͞o′lij), *n.* **Calvin,** 1872–1933, 30th president of the U.S. 1923–29.

Cool′idge tube′, *Physics.* a cathode ray tube, used for x-ray production, in which a beam of thermoelectrons is produced by heating a wire cathode. [1910–15, *Amer.*; named after William D. *Coolidge* (1873–1975), U.S. physicist and chemist who devised it]

coo•lie (ko͞o′lē), *n. Offensive.* **1.** an unskilled laborer, esp. formerly in China and India. **2.** an unskilled laborer employed cheaply, esp. one brought from Asia. —*adj.* **3.** *Informal.* characteristic of or suitable for a coolie: *working for coolie wages.* Also, **cooly.** [1545–55; < Urdu *kūlī* < Tamil *kūli* hire, hireling]

coo′lie hat′, a wide, conical straw hat worn esp. as a shield against the sun. [1935–40]

cool′ing board′, *South Midland and Southern U.S. Older Use.* a plank for laying out a corpse. [1850–55]

cool′ing degree′-day, a degree-day above the standard temperature of 75°F (24°C), used in estimating the energy requirements for air conditioning and refrigeration. Cf. **growing degree-day, heating degree-day.**

cool′ing-off′ pe′riod, a period arranged by agreement to allow for negotiation and an abatement of tension between disputing parties: *The law calls for a cooling-off period before a strike can begin.* [1945–50]

cool′ing tow′er, *Energy.* a usually cylindrical structure, sometimes of very great size, in which heat is extracted from water that has been used for cooling, as in a nuclear reactor. [1900–05]

cool′ jazz′, a restrained, fluid modern-jazz style of the 1950's, marked by intricate harmonic structures, deemphasized dynamics, and carefully controlled phrasing and ensemble playing, often with a slight lagging behind the beat. Also called **West Coast jazz.** Cf. **bop**[1], **hard bop, modern jazz, progressive jazz.** [1945–50]

coolth (ko͞olth), *n. Usually Facetious.* coolness. [1540–50; COOL + -TH[1]]

coo•ly (ko͞o′lē), *n., pl.* **-lies,** *adj.* coolie.

coom (ko͞om), *n. Chiefly Scot. and North Eng.* **1.** soot; coal dust; smut. **2.** dust, esp. sawdust or dust from a gristmill. **3.** grease from bearings, axles, etc. Also, **coomb.** [1580–90; var. of CULM[1]]

coomb[1] (ko͞om, kōm), *n.* combe. Also, **coombe.**

coomb[2] (ko͞om), *n.* coom.

coon (ko͞on), *n.* **1.** raccoon. **2.** *Slang* (*disparaging and offensive*). a black person. **3.** a rustic or undignified person. [1735–45, *Amer.*; aph. form]

coon•ass (ko͞on′as′), *n. Vulgar, Disparaging, and Offensive.* (chiefly in Louisiana and Southeast Texas) a Cajun. [‡1960–65; prob. alter., by folk etym., of LaF, F *conasse* a contemptuous term for a woman, lit., vulva, equiv. to *con* vulva (< L *cunnus*) + *-asse* pejorative n. suffix]

coon•can (ko͞on′kan′), *n. Cards.* a variety of rummy for two players. [1885–90, *Amer.*; popular alter. of CONQUIAN]

coon′ cat′, cacomistle. [1900–05]

coon′ cheese′, a sharp crumbly cheddar cheese that has dark outer surfaces, usually enclosed in black wax. [1950–55]

coon′ dog′, any dog trained to hunt raccoons. [1825–35, *Amer.*]

coon•er (ko͞o′nər), *n.* See **coon dog.** [COON + -ER[1]]

coon•hound (ko͞on′hound′), *n.* **1.** See **coon dog. 2.** a hound of any of several breeds developed esp. for hunting raccoons. Cf. **black and tan coonhound, bluetick, Plott hound, redbone, Walker hound.** [1915–20, *Amer.*; COON + HOUND[1]]

Coon′ Rap′ids, a city in E Minnesota. 35,826.

coon's′ age′, *Informal.* a long time: *I haven't seen you in a coon's age!* [1835–45, *Amer.*]

coon•skin (ko͞on′skin′), *n.* **1.** the pelt of a raccoon. **2.** an article of clothing made of coonskin, esp. a cap with a tail. —*adj.* **3.** made of coonskin: *a coonskin cap.* [1615–25, *Amer.*; COON + SKIN]

coonskin (def. 2)

coon•tie (ko͞on′tē), *n.* **1.** either of two arrowroots, *Zamia integrifolia* or *Z. floridana,* of Florida, having a short trunk, pinnate leaves, and cones: *Z. floridana* is an endangered species. **2.** the flour produced from its starch. [1785–95, *Amer.*; < Florida Creek *kuntí·* applied to arrowroot and the starch derived therefrom, earlier (in Georgia) applied to the smilax]

coon•y (ko͞o′nē), *adj.,* **coon•i•er, coon•i•est.** sharp-witted and shrewd; wily; canny. [1900–05, *Amer.*; COON + -Y[1]]

co-op (*n., adv.* kō′op; *v.* kō′op, kō op′), *n., v.,* **-oped, -op•ing,** *adv.* —*n.* **1.** a cooperative store, dwelling, program, etc. —*v.t.* **2.** to place in a cooperative arrangement, esp. to convert (an apartment or building) to a cooperative. —*adv.* **3. go co-op,** to convert to a cooperative: *Our apartment building is going co-op.* [1860–65; shortened form] —**co′-op•er,** *n.*

coop (ko͞op, ko͝op), *n.* **1.** an enclosure, cage, or pen, usually with bars or wires, in which fowls or other small animals are confined for fattening, transportation, etc. **2.** any small or narrow place. **3.** *Slang.* a prison. **4.** *Sometimes Facetious.* a cooperative, esp. the cooperative bookstore of a college or university. **5. fly the coop,** *Informal.* to run off; depart abruptly; escape: *We stopped to see my sister, but she'd flown the coop.* —*v.t.* **6.** to place in or as if in a coop; confine narrowly (often fol. by *up* or *in*). —*v.i.* **7.** *Slang.* (of a police officer) to park and sleep inside one's patrol car while on duty. [1250–1300; ME *coupe* basket, perh. < Scand; cf. Norw *kaup* wooden can; akin to OE *cȳpa* basket]

coop., cooperative. Also, **co-op.**

coop•er (ko͞o′pər, ko͝op′ər), *n.* **1.** a person who makes or repairs casks, barrels, etc. —*v.t.* **2.** to make or repair (casks, barrels, etc.). **3.** to furnish or fix (usually fol. by *up*). —*v.i.* **4.** to work as a cooper. [1350–1400; ME *couper* < MLG *kūper* or MD *cūper* < ML *cūpārius* (L *cūp(a)* cask, vat + *-ārius* -ARY)]

Coo•per (ko͞o′pər, ko͝op′ər), *n.* **1. Anthony Ashley.** See **Shaftesbury, Anthony Ashley Cooper. 2. Hugh Lincoln,** 1865–1937, U.S. hydraulic engineer. **3. James Fen•i•more** (fen′ə môr′, -mōr′), 1789–1851, U.S. novelist. **4. Leon N.,** born 1930, U.S. physicist: Nobel prize 1972. **5. Peter,** 1791–1883, U.S. inventor, manufacturer, reformer, and philanthropist.

coop•er•age (ko͞o′pər ij, ko͝op′ər-), *n.* **1.** the work or business of a cooper. **2.** the place where such work is carried on. **3.** articles made by a cooper, as barrels or casks. **4.** the price paid or charged for coopers' work. [1425–75; late ME. See COOPER, -AGE]

co•op•er•ate (kō op′ə rāt′), *v.i.,* **-at•ed, -at•ing. 1.** to work or act together or jointly for a common purpose or benefit. **2.** to work or act with another or other persons willingly and agreeably. **3.** to practice economic cooperation. Also, **co-op′er•ate′.** [1595–1605; < LL *cooperātus* ptp. of *cooperārī* to work with. See CO-, OPERATE] —**co•op′er•a′tor, co-op′er•a′tor,** *n.*
—**Syn. 2.** collaborate, join, participate.

co•op•er•a•tion (kō op′ə rā′shən), *n.* **1.** an act or instance of working or acting together for a common purpose or benefit; joint action. **2.** more or less active assistance from a person, organization, etc.: *We sought the cooperation of various civic leaders.* **3.** willingness to cooperate: *to indicate cooperation.* **4.** *Econ.* the combination of persons for purposes of production, purchase, or distribution for their joint benefit: *producers' cooperation; consumers' cooperation.* **5.** *Sociol.* activity shared for mutual benefit. **6.** *Ecol.* mutually beneficial interaction among organisms living in a limited area. Also, **co-op′er•a′tion.** [1620–30; (< MF) < LL *cooperātiōn-* (s. of *cooperātiō*). See COOPERATE, -ION] —**co•op′er•a′tion•ist, co-op′er•a′tion•ist,** *n.*

co•op•er•a•tive (kō op′ər ə tiv, -op′rə tiv, -op′ə rā′tiv), *adj.* **1.** working or acting together willingly for a common purpose or benefit. **2.** demonstrating a willingness to cooperate: *The librarian was cooperative in helping us find the book.* **3.** pertaining to economic cooperation: *a cooperative business.* **4.** involving or denoting an educational program comprising both classroom study and on-the-job or technical training, esp. in colleges and universities. —*n.* **5.** a jointly owned enterprise engaging in the production or distribution of goods or the supplying of services, operated by its members for their mutual benefit, typically organized by consumers or farmers. **6.** Also called **co-op, coop′erative apart′ment. a.** a building owned and managed by a corporation in which shares are sold, entitling the shareholders to occupy individual units in the building. **b.** an apartment in such a building. Cf. **condominium** (defs. 1, 2). Also, **co-op′er•a′tive.** [1595–1605; < LL *cooperātīvus.* See COOPERATE, -IVE] —**co•op•er•a•tive•ly, co•op•er•a•tive•ly** (kō op′ər ə tiv lē, -op′rə tiv-, -op′ə rā′tiv-), *adv.* —**co•op′er•a′tive•ness, co-op′er•a′tive•ness,** *n.*

CONCISE ETYMOLOGY KEY: <, descended or borrowed from; >, whence; b., blend of, blended; c., cognate with; cf., compare; deriv., derivative; equiv., equivalent; imit., imitative; obl., oblique; r., replacing; s., stem; sp., spelling, spelled; resp., respelling, respelled; trans., translation; ?, origin unknown; *, unattested; ‡, probably earlier than. See the full key inside the front cover.

coop′erative bank′. See **savings and loan association.**

coop′erative cred′it un′ion. See **credit union.**

coop′erative store′, 1. a retail store owned and managed by consumer-customers who supply the capital and share in the profits by patronage dividends. 2. a store operated by a farmers' cooperative organization or by a cooperative chain. [1850–55]

co•op•er•a•tiv•i•ty (kō op′ər ə tiv′i tē), *n. Biochem.* the increase or decrease in the rate of interaction between a reactant and a protein as the reactant concentration increases. Also, **co-op′er•a•tiv′i•ty.** [COOPERATIVE + -ITY]

Coo′per Cit′y, a town in SE Florida. 10,140.

coop′ered joint′, *Joinery.* a joint made between pieces in a polygonal or curved construction, using either splines or dowels.

coop•er•ite (ko͞o′pə rit′), *n.* a mineral, sulfide and arsenide of platinum, occurring in igneous rocks in the form of steel-gray crystals. [after R. A. *Cooper,* who described it in 1920; see -ITE[1]]

Coo′per's hawk′, a North American hawk, *Accipiter cooperii,* having a bluish-gray back and a rusty breast. [1820–30, *Amer.*; named after William *Cooper* (d. 1864), American ornithologist]

Coo•pers•town (ko͞o′pərz toun′, ko͝op′ərz-), *n.* a town in central New York: location of the National Baseball Hall of Fame and Museum. 2342.

coop•e•ry (ko͞o′pə rē, ko͝op′ə-), *n., pl.* **-ries.** 1. the work of a cooper. 2. a cooper's shop. 3. articles made by a cooper. [1325–75; ME *couperie.* See COOPER, -Y[3]]

co•opt (kō opt′), *v.t.* 1. to elect into a body by the votes of the existing members. 2. to assimilate, take, or win over into a larger or established group: *The fledgling Labor party was coopted by the Socialist party.* 3. to appropriate as one's own; preempt: *The dissidents have coopted the title of her novel for their slogan.* Also, **co-opt′.** [1645–55; < L *cooptāre.* See CO-, OPT] —**co′•op•ta′tion, co′-op•ta′tion, co•op•tion, co-op′tion** (kō op′shən), *n.* —**co•op•ta•tive, co-op•ta•tive** (kō op′tə-tiv), **co•op′tive, co-op′tive,** *adj.*

co•or•di•nal (kō ôr′dn l), *adj. Biol.* belonging to the same order. [1870–75; CO- + ORDINAL[1]]

co•or•di•nate (*adj., n.* kō ôr′dn it, -dn āt′; *v.* kō ôr′-dn āt′), *adj., n., v.,* **-nat•ed, -nat•ing.** —*adj.* 1. of the same order or degree; equal in rank or importance. 2. involving coordination. 3. *Math.* using or pertaining to systems of coordinates. 4. *Gram.* of the same rank in grammatical construction, as *Jack* and *Jill* in the phrase *Jack and Jill,* or *got up* and *shook hands* in the sentence *He got up and shook hands.* —*n.* 5. a person or thing of equal rank or importance; an equal. 6. *Math.* any of the magnitudes that serve to define the position of a point, line, or the like, by reference to a fixed figure, system of lines, etc. 7. **coordinates,** articles of clothing, furniture, or the like, harmonizing in color, material, or style, designed to be worn or used together. —*v.t.* 8. to place or class in the same order, rank, division, etc. 9. to place or arrange in proper order or position. 10. to combine in harmonious relation or action. —*v.i.* 11. to become coordinate. 12. to assume proper order or relation. 13. to act in harmonious combination. Also, **co-or′di•nate.** [1635–45; CO- + (SUB)ORDINATE] —**co•or′di•nate•ly, co-or′di•nate•ly,** *adv.* —**co•or′di•nate•ness, co-or′di•nate•ness,** *n.* —**co•or•di•na•tive, co-or•di•na•tive,** (kō-ôr′dn ā′tiv, -ôr′dn ə-), *adj.*
—**Syn.** 9. order, correlate.

coor′dinate bond′, *Chem.* a type of covalent bond between two atoms in which the bonding electrons are supplied by one of the two atoms. Also called **dative bond.** [1935–40]

coor′dinate clause′, *Gram.* one of two or more clauses of equal status in a sentence, esp. when joined by a coordinating conjunction, as either *The sun came out* or *the ice started to melt* in *The sun came out and the ice started to melt.* [1870–75]

coor′dinate geom′etry. See **analytic geometry.** [1815–25]

coor′dinate pa′per. See **graph paper.**

coor′dinate sys′tem, *Math.* any method that uses numbers to represent a point, line, or the like.

coor′dinating conjunc′tion, *Gram.* a conjunction that connects two grammatical elements of identical construction, as *and* in *Sue and Andrea* or *or* in *He can't decide if he should stay or go.* Also, **coor′dinate conjunc′tion.** Cf. **subordinating conjunction.** [1875–80]

co•or•di•na•tion (kō ôr′dn ā′shən), *n.* 1. the act or state of coordinating or of being coordinated. 2. proper order or relationship. 3. harmonious combination or interaction, as of functions or parts. Also, **co-or′di•na′tion.** [1595–1605; < LL *coordinātiōn-* (s. of *coordinātiō*). See CO-, ORDINATION]

coordina′tion com′pound, *Chem.* complex (def. 10). Also called **coordina′tion com′plex.**

coordina′tion num′ber, *Crystall.* the number of anions surrounding a single cation in a stable crystal structure. [1905–10]

co•or•di•na•tor (kō ôr′dn ā′tər), *n.* 1. a person or thing that coordinates. 2. *Gram.* a coordinating conjunction. Also, **co-or′di•na′tor.** [1860–65; COORDINATE + -OR[2]]

Coorg (ko͝org), *n.* a former province in SW India; now part of Karnataka state. 1593 sq. mi. (4126 sq. km). Also, **Kurg.**

Coos (ko͞os), *n.* a language of a group of American Indians indigenous to the coast of Oregon.

Coos′ Bay′, a town in SW Oregon. 14,424.

coot (ko͞ot), *n.* 1. any aquatic bird of the genus *Fulica,* as *F. americana,* of North America, and *F. atra,* of the Old World, characterized by lobate toes and short wings and tail. 2. any of various other swimming or diving birds, esp. the scoters. 3. *Informal.* a foolish or crotchety person, esp. one who is old. [1250–1300; ME *cote;* c. D *koet*]

American coot, *Fulica americana,* length 16 in. (41 cm)

cootch (ko͞och), *n.* cooch.

coot•er (ko͞o′tər), *n. Chiefly Southern U.S.* any of several large aquatic turtles of the southern U.S. and northern Mexico. [1820–30; said to be < Bambara, Malinke *kuta* turtle (with related forms in other Niger-Congo languages); cf. *coot* to copulate (of sea turtles), first attested in the Caribbean in 1667]

coot•ie[1] (ko͞o′tē), *n. Informal.* a louse, esp. one affecting humans, as the body louse, head louse, or pubic louse. Also, **cooty.** [1910–15; perh. < Malay *kutu* biting body louse, with final syll. conformed to -IE]

coot•ie[2] (ko͞o′tē), *n. Scot.* a wooden container, esp. a wooden bowl, for storing or serving food or drink. Also, **cooty.** [1775–85; var. of Scots *cood,* of uncert. orig.]

coot•y[1] (ko͞o′tē), *n., pl.* **coot•ies.** cootie[1].

coot•y[2] (ko͞o′tē), *n., pl.* **coot•ies.** *Scot.* cootie[2].

co-own (kō ōn′, kō′ōn′), *v.t.* to own jointly with another: *a building I co-owned with my brother.*

cooze (ko͞oz), *n. Slang (vulgar).* vagina. Also, **coo•zie** (ko͞o′zē). [of obscure orig.]

cop[1] (kop), *v.t.,* **copped, cop•ping.** *Informal.* 1. to catch; nab. 2. to steal; filch. 3. to buy (narcotics). 4. **cop a plea, a.** to plead guilty or confess in return for receiving a lighter sentence. **b.** to plead guilty to a lesser charge as a means of bargaining one's way out of standing trial for a more serious charge; plea-bargain. 5. **cop out, a.** to avoid one's responsibility, the fulfillment of a promise, etc.; renege; back out (often fol. by *on* or *of*): *He never copped out on a friend in need. You agreed to go, and you can't cop out now.* **b.** cop a plea. [1695–1705; cf. *cap* (obs.) to arrest, Scots *cap* to seize << dial. OF *caper* to take, ult. < L *capere*]

cop[2] (kop), *n. Informal.* a police officer. [1855–60; cf. COPPER[2]]

cop[3] (kop), *n.* 1. a conical mass of thread, yarn, etc., wound on a spindle. 2. *Brit. Dial.* crest; tip. [bef. 1000; ME, OE *cop* tip, top (in ME also head), prob. c. D *kop,* G *Kopf* head; see CUP]

COP, *Thermodynam.* See **coefficient of performance.**

Cop., 1. Copernican. 2. Coptic.

cop., 1. copper. 2. copyright; copyrighted.

co•pa•cet•ic (kō′pə set′ik, -sē′tik), *adj. Slang.* fine; completely satisfactory; OK. Also, **copasetic, copesetic.** [1915–20, *Amer.*; of obscure orig; popular attributions of the word to LaF, It, Heb, etc., lack supporting evidence]

co•pai•ba (kō pā′bə, -pī′bə), *n.* an oleoresin obtained from several tropical, chiefly South American trees belonging to the genus *Copaifera,* of the legume family, used chiefly in varnishes and lacquers, for removing old oil varnish from or for brightening oil paintings, and formerly in medicine in the treatment of certain mucous-membrane conditions. Also called **balsam capivi, Jesuits' resin.** [1705–15; < Sp < Pg < Tupi *cupaiba*]

copai′ba oil′, a colorless, yellowish, or bluish liquid having a pepperlike odor and bitter taste, obtained from copaiba by distillation: used chiefly in the manufacture of perfumes and soaps. [1825–35]

co•pal (kō′pəl, -pal), *n.* a hard, lustrous resin obtained from various tropical trees and used chiefly in making varnishes. [1570–80; < MexSp < Nahuatl *copalli*]

Co•pán (*Sp.* kō pän′), *n.* See **Santa Rosa de Copán.**

co•par•ce•nar•y (kō pär′sə ner′ē), *n. Law.* a special kind of joint ownership arising esp. under common law upon the descent of real property to several female heirs. Also, **co•par•ce•ny** (kō pär′sə nē). [1495–1505; CO- + PARCENARY]

co•par•ce•ner (kō pär′sə nər), *n.* a member of a coparcenary. [1400–50; late ME. See CO-, PARCENER]

co•par•ent (*n.* kō′pâr′ənt, -par′-, kō pâr′-, -par′-; *v.* kō pâr′ənt, -par′-), *n.* 1. a divorced or separated parent who shares equally with the other parent in the custody and care of a child. —*v.t.* 2. to share equally with another parent in the care of (a child). —*v.i.* 3. to act as a co-parent. Also, **co′par′ent.**

co•part•ner (kō pärt′nər, kō′pärt′-), *n.* a partner or associate, as in a business. [1495–1505; CO- + PARTNER] —**co•part′ner•ship′,** *n.*

co•pa•set•ic (kō′pə set′ik, -sē′tik), *adj.* copacetic.

co•pay•ment (kō pā′mənt), *n.* a contributory payment by an employer, usually matching that of an employee, toward the payment of health-care or life-insurance premiums, a pension fund, etc. [CO- + PAYMENT]

COPD, See **chronic obstructive pulmonary disease.**

cope[1] (kōp), *v.,* **coped, cop•ing.** —*v.i.* 1. to struggle or deal, esp. on fairly even terms or with some degree of success (usually fol. by *with*): *I will try to cope with his rudeness.* 2. to face and deal with responsibilities, problems, or difficulties, esp. successfully or in a calm or adequate manner: *After his breakdown he couldn't cope any longer.* 3. *Archaic.* to come into contact; meet (usually fol. by *with*). —*v.t.* 4. *Brit. Informal.* to cope with. 5. *Obs.* to come into contact with; encounter. [1300–50; ME *coupen* < AF, OF *couper* to strike, deriv. of *coup* COUP[1]] —**cope′less,** *adj.* —**cope′less•ness,** *n.*
—**Syn.** 1. wrestle, strive, persevere.

cope[2] (kōp), *n., v.,* **coped, cop•ing.** —*n.* 1. a long mantle, esp. of silk, worn by ecclesiastics over the alb or surplice in processions and on other occasions. 2. any cloaklike or canopylike covering. 3. the sky. 4. a coping. 5. *Metall.* the upper half of a flask. Cf. **drag** (def. 32). —*v.t.* 6. to furnish with or as if with a cope or coping. [1175–1225; ME < ML *cāpa,* var. of *cappa* CAP[1]]

A, cope[2] (def. 1); B, crosier

cope[3] (kōp), *v.t.,* **coped, cop•ing.** 1. *Building Trades.* **a.** to join (two molded wooden members) by undercutting the end of one of them to the profile of the other so that the joint produced resembles a miter joint (usually fol. by *in* or *together*). **b.** to form (a joint between such members) in this way. **c.** to undercut the end of (a molded wooden member) in order to form a coped joint. **d.** to cut away (a flange of a metal member) so that it may be joined to another member at an angle. 2. *Falconry.* to clip or dull (the beak or talons of a hawk). [1565–75; < F *couper* to cut; see COPE[1]]

cope[4] (kōp), *v.t.,* **coped, cop•ing.** *Brit.* to barter; trade; exchange. [1400–50; late ME *copen* < LG; cf. MD *côpen* to buy]

co•peck (kō′pek), *n.* kopeck.

Co•pe•han (kō pā′ən, -hən), *n.* Wintun. [1891; < Patwin *Cop-éh* a village name (properly *ko·pe* lit., root) + -AN]

cope•mate (kōp′māt′), *n. Obs.* 1. an antagonist; opponent. 2. a comrade; partner. Also, **copes′mate′.** [1555–65; COPE[1] + MATE[1]]

co•pen (kō′pən), *n.* 1. Also called **co′pen blue′.** a medium blue color. —*adj.* 2. Also, **co′pen-blue′.** of the color copen. [1915–20; shortening of COPENHAGEN]

Co•pen•ha•gen (kō′pən hā′gən, -hä′-, kō′pən hā′-, -hä′-), *n.* a seaport in and the capital of Denmark, on the E coast of Zealand. 802,391; with suburbs, 1,380,204. Danish, **København.**

co′penha′gen blue′, gray-blue.

co•pe•pod (kō′pə pod′), *n.* any of numerous tiny marine or freshwater crustaceans of the order (or subclass) Copepoda, lacking compound eyes or a carapace and usually having six pairs of limbs on the thorax, some abundant in plankton and others parasitic on fish. [1830–40; < NL *Copepoda* name of the order < Gk *kṓpē* a handle, oar + *-poda* -PODA]

cop•er (kō′pər), *n. Brit.* a horse dealer. Also called **horse-coper.** [1600–10; COPE[4] + -ER[1]]

Co•per•ni•can (kō pûr′ni kən, kə-), *adj.* 1. of or pertaining to Copernicus or his theories. 2. important and radically different; thoroughgoing: *a Copernican revolution in modern art.* [1660–70; COPERNIC(US) + -AN]

Co•per•ni•cus (kō pûr′ni kəs, kə-), *n.* 1. **Nic•o•la•us** (nik′ə lā′əs), (*Mikolaj Kopernik*), 1473–1543, Polish astronomer who promulgated the now accepted theory that the earth and the other planets move around the sun (the **Coper′nican Sys′tem**). 2. a crater in the second quadrant of the face of the moon, having an extensive ray system: about 56 mi. (90 km) in diameter from crest to crest with walls rising about 12,000 ft. (3650 m) from its floor; having several central mountains the highest being about 2400 ft. (730 m).

co•pe•set•ic (kō′pə set′ik, -sē′tik), *adj.* copacetic.

cope•stone (kōp′stōn′), *n.* 1. the top stone of a building or other structure. 2. a stone used for or in coping. 3. the crown or completion; finishing touch. [1560–70; COPE[2] + STONE]

Copht (kopt), *n.* Copt.

Co•piague (kō′pāg, -peg), *n.* a town on SW Long Island, in SE New York. 20,132.

Co•pia•pó (kō′pyä pō′), *n.* a city in N Chile. 51,809.

cop•i•er (kop′ē ər), *n.* 1. a person or thing that copies; copyist. 2. photocopier. 3. See **copying machine.** [1590–1600; COPY + -ER[1]]

co•pi•hue (kō pē′wā), *n.* Chile-bells.

co•pi•lot (kō′pī′lət), *n.* a pilot who is second in command of an aircraft. Also called **first officer.** [1925–30; CO- + PILOT]

CONCISE PRONUNCIATION KEY: act, cāpe, dâre, pärt; set, ēqual; if, īce; ox, ōver, ôrder, oil, bo͝ok, bo͞ot, out; up, ûrge; child; sing; shoe; thin, *th*at; zh as in *treasure.* ə = *a* as in *alone, e* as in *system, i* as in *easily, o* as in *gallop, u* as in *circus;* ᵊ as in *fire* (fīᵊr), *hour* (ouᵊr). l and n can serve as syllabic consonants, as in *cradle* (krād′l), and *button* (but′n). See the full key inside the front cover.

cop•ing (kō′ping), *n.* **1.** a finishing or protective course or cap to an exterior masonry wall or the like. **2.** a piece of woodwork having its end shaped to fit together with a molding. [1595–1605; COPE[2] + -ING[1]]

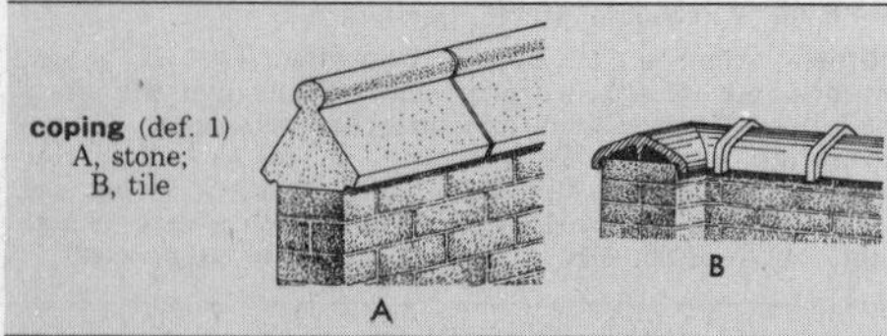

coping (def. 1) A, stone; B, tile

cop′ing mech′anism, *Psychol.* an adaptation to environmental stress that is based on conscious or unconscious choice and that enhances control over behavior or gives psychological comfort. Cf. **defense mechanism** (def. 2).

cop′ing saw′, a saw consisting of a thin, light blade held, under tension, in a U-shaped frame that has a handle: used for cutting small curves in wood. [1930–35]

coping saw

co•pi•ous (kō′pē əs), *adj.* **1.** large in quantity or number; abundant; plentiful: *copious amounts of food.* **2.** having or yielding an abundant supply: *a copious larder; a copious harvest.* **3.** exhibiting abundance or fullness, as of thoughts or words. [1350–1400; ME < L *cōpiōsus* plentiful, rich, equiv. to *cōpi(a)* wealth (*co-* CO- + *op(s)* OPS + *-ia* -IA) + *-ōsus* -OUS] **—co′pi•ous•ly,** *adv.* **—co′pi•ous•ness, co•pi•os•i•ty** (kō′pē os′i tē), *n.*
—Syn. 1. bountiful. **2.** See **ample. —Ant. 1.** scanty, scarce. **3.** meager.

co•pla•nar (kō plā′nər), *adj. Math.* being or operating in the same plane. [1860–65; CO- + *planar* < LL *plānāris*; see PLANE[1], -AR[1]] **—co′pla•nar′i•ty,** *n.*

Cop•land (kōp′lənd), *n.* **Aaron,** 1900–90, U.S. composer.

Cop•ley (kop′lē), *n.* **John Sin•gle•ton** (sing′gəl tən), 1738–1815, U.S. painter.

co•pol•y•mer (kō pol′ə mər), *n.* a chemical compound of high molecular weight produced by polymerizing two or more different monomers together. [1935–40; CO- + POLYMER]

co•po•lym•er•ize (kō′pə lim′ə rīz′, kō pol′ə mə-), *v.t., v.i.,* **-ized, -iz•ing.** *Chem.* to subject to or undergo a change analogous to polymerization but with a union of two or more different monomers. Also, *esp. Brit.,* **co′po•lym′er•ise′.** [1935–40; COPOLYMER + -IZE] **—co′po•lym′er•i•za′tion,** *n.*

cop-out (kop′out′), *n. Informal.* **1.** an act or instance of copping out; reneging; evasion: *The governor's platform was a cop-out.* **2.** a person who cops out: *Everyone helped as they had promised, except for one cop-out.* [1940–45; n. use of v. phrase *cop out*]

Cop•pel•ia (kō pāl′yə), *n.* a ballet (1870) by Délibes.

cop•per[1] (kop′ər), *n.* **1.** a malleable, ductile, metallic element having a characteristic reddish-brown color: used in large quantities as an electrical conductor and in the manufacture of alloys, as brass and bronze. *Symbol:* Cu; *at. wt.:* 63.54; *at. no.:* 29; *sp. gr.:* 8.92 at 20°C. **2.** a metallic reddish brown. **3.** a coin composed of copper, bronze, or the like, as the U.S. cent or the British penny. **4.** any of several butterflies of the family Lycaenidae, as *Lycaena hypophleas* **(American copper),** having copper-colored wings spotted and edged with black. **5.** a container made of copper. **6.** a tool partly or wholly made of copper: *a soldering copper.* **7.** *Brit.* a large kettle, now usually made of iron, used for cooking or to boil laundry. **—*adj.* 8.** made of copper: *copper kettles.* **9.** reddish-brown; coppery: *The copper sun sank into the sea.* **—*v.t.* 10.** to cover, coat, or sheathe with copper. **11.** *Informal.* hedge (def. 6). [bef. 1000; ME *coper,* OE *coper, copor* (c. ON *koparr,* G *Kupfer*) < LL *cuprum,* for L *(aes) Cyprium* CYPRIAN (metal)]

cop•per[2] (kop′ər), *n. Slang.* a police officer. [1840–50, *Amer.*; perh. COP[1] + -ER[1]]

Cop′per Age′, a cultural period intermediate between the Neolithic and the Bronze ages, marked by the development and use of copper tools. [1860–65]

cop•per•ah (kop′ər ə, kop′rə), *n.* copra.

cop′per ar′senite, a yellowish-green, water-insoluble, poisonous powder, $CuHAsO_3$, used chiefly as a pigment and as an insecticide.

cop•per•as (kop′ər əs), *n. Chem.* See **ferrous sulfate.** [1400–50; late ME *coperas,* var. of ME *coperose* < ML *(aqua) cuprōsa* copperish (water). See COPPER[1], -OSE[1]]

Cop′per•as Cove′ (kop′ər əs), a town in central Texas. 19,469.

cop′per beech′, a variety of the European beech, *Fagus sylvatica atropunicea,* having purplish or copper-red leaves. Also called **purple beech.**

cop′per cy′anide, *Chem.* See **cuprous cyanide.**

CONCISE ETYMOLOGY KEY: <, descended or borrowed from; >, whence; b., blend of, blended; c., cognate with; cf., compare; deriv., derivative; equiv., equivalent; imit., imitative; obl., oblique; r., replacing; s., stem; sp., spelling, spelled; resp., respelling, respelled; trans., translation; ?, origin unknown; *, unattested; ‡, probably earlier than. See the full key inside the front cover.

cop•per•head (kop′ər hed′), *n.* **1.** a venomous snake, *Agkistrodon (Ancistrodon) contortrix,* of the eastern and southern U.S., having a light-brown to copper-red body marked with darker bands. **2.** an extremely venomous but sluggish snake, *Denisonia superba,* of Australia and Tasmania, having a reddish to black body, depending on the region. **3.** *(cap.) U.S. Hist.* a Northern Democrat who opposed the Civil War, advocating peace and restoration of the Union even if slavery continued. **4.** *(cap.) Mil.* a finned, 155mm cannon-launched U.S. Army artillery shell that homes on the target, using the reflection of a laser beam projected by a forward observer. [1765–75, *Amer.*; COPPER[1] + HEAD]

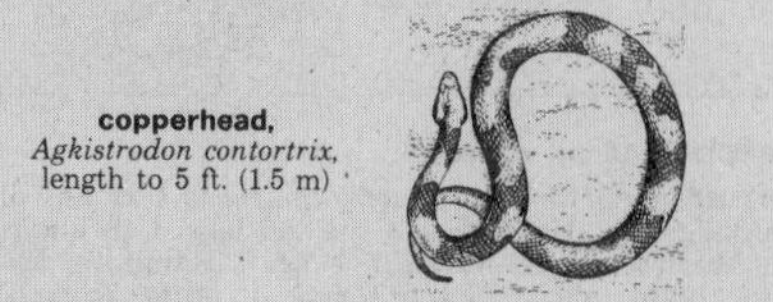
copperhead, *Agkistrodon contortrix,* length to 5 ft. (1.5 m)

Cop•per•head•ism (kop′ər hed iz′əm), *n. U.S. Hist.* (during the Civil War) the advocacy of peace negotiations to restore the Union to its prewar condition, with continued slavery in the South. [1860–65, *Amer.*; COPPERHEAD + -ISM]

cop′per hydrox′ide, a blue, water-insoluble, poisonous powder, $Cu(OH)_2$, used in the manufacture of rayon, as a source for copper salts, and as a mordant. Also called **cupric hydroxide.**

cop′per i′ris, an iris, *Iris fulva,* found from the Gulf Coast to southern Illinois, having copper-colored or reddish-brown flowers.

cop•per-leaf (kop′ər lēf′), *n., pl.* **-leaves.** a Pacific Islands plant, *Acalypha wilkesiana,* of the spurge family, having showy, bronzy-green, usually red-mottled foliage and grown as an ornamental or houseplant.

Cop•per•mine (kop′ər mīn′), *n.* a river in N Canada, in the central Northwest Territories, flowing N to the Arctic Ocean. 525 mi. (845 km) long.

cop′per naph′the•nate (naf′thə nāt′, nap′-), *Chem.* a green salt, soluble in benzene, used as an insecticide and a wood preservative, but harmless to plants. [NAPHTHENE + -ATE[2]]

cop•per•on (kop′ə ron′), *n. Chem.* cupferron.

cop•per•plate (kop′ər plāt′), *n.* **1.** a plate of polished copper on which a writing, picture, or design is made by engraving or etching. **2.** a print or impression from such a plate. **3.** engraving or printing of this kind. **4.** a fine, elegant style of handwriting. [1655–65; COPPER[1] + PLATE[1]]

cop′per pyri′tes, *Mineral.* chalcopyrite. [1770–80]

Cop′per Riv′er, a stream in S Alaska, flowing through the SE part. 300 mi. (483 km) long.

cop•per•smith (kop′ər smith′), *n.* **1.** a person who makes utensils, jewelry, etc., out of copper. **2.** a crimson-breasted barbet, *Megalaima haemacephala,* of India, southeast Asia, and adjacent islands, characterized by the ringing, metallic sound of its note. [1300–50; ME *copresmythe.* See COPPER[1], SMITH]

cop′per spot′, *Plant Pathol.* a disease of grasses characterized by coppery or orange spore masses covering the blades, caused by a fungus, *Gloeocercospora sorghi.*

cop′per sul′fate, *Chem.* See **blue vitriol.** [1890–95]

cop•per•tone (kop′ər tōn′), *n.* **1.** a reddish-brown color. **—*adj.* 2.** Also, **cop′per-toned′.** of or having such color: *coppertone appliances.* [COPPER[1] + TONE]

cop′per•y (kop′ə rē), *adj.* **1.** of, resembling, or containing copper. **2.** reddish-brown. [1785–95; COPPER[1] + -Y[1]]

cop•pice (kop′is), *n.* copse. [1375–1425; late ME *copies* < MF *copeis,* OF *copeiz* < VL **colpāticium* cutover area, equiv. to **colpāt(us)* ptp. of **colpāre* to cut (see COUP[1]) + *-icium* -ICE] **—cop′piced,** *adj.*

cop•ping (kop′ing), *n.* the winding of yarn into a cap from a cone, bobbin, etc. Also called **quilling.** [1785–95; COP[2] + -ING[1]]

Cop•po•la (kop′ə lə), *n.* **Francis Ford,** born 1939, U.S. film director and screenwriter.

copr-, var. of **copro-** before a vowel: *copremia.*

cop•ra (kop′rə, kō′prə), *n.* the dried kernel or meat of the coconut from which coconut oil is expressed. Also, **copperah.** [1575–85; < Pg < Malayalam *koppara* < Hindi *khoprā* coconut]

co•pre•cip•i•tate (kō′pri sip′i tāt′), *v.,* **-tat•ed, -tat•ing.** *Chem.* **—*v.t.* 1.** to cause to precipitate together. **—*v.i.* 2.** to precipitate together in the same reaction. [1930–35; CO- + PRECIPITATE] **—co′pre•cip′i•ta′tion,** *n.*

cop•re•mi•a (ko prē′mē ə), *n. Pathol.* poisoning due to the presence of fecal matter in the blood. Also, **cop•rae′mi•a.** [COPR- + -EMIA] **—cop•re•mic,** *adj.*

copro-, a combining form meaning "dung," used in the formation of compound words: *coprophagous.* Also, *esp. before a vowel,* **copr-.** [< Gk *kopro-,* comb. form of *kópros;* c. Skt *śakṛt*]

co•pro•duce (kō′prə dōōs′, -dyōōs′), *v.t.,* **-duced, -duc•ing. 1.** to produce (a motion picture, play, etc.) in collaboration with others. **2.** to manufacture (goods) in partnership with others. Also, **co′-pro•duce′.** [1705–15; CO- + PRODUCE] **—co•pro•duc•tion** (kō′prə duk′shən), *n.* **—co′pro•duc′er,** *n.*

co•prod•uct (kō′prod′əkt, -ukt), *n.* something produced jointly with another product. [1940–45; CO- + PRODUCT]

cop•ro•lag•ni•a (kop′rə lag′nē ə), *n. Psychiatry.* sexual arousal that is produced by the thought or sight of feces. [COPRO- + -LAGNIA] **—cop•ro•lag•nist** (kop′rə-lag′nist), *n.*

cop•ro•la•li•a (kop′rə lā′lē ə), *n. Psychiatry.* the obsessive use of scatological language. [COPRO- + -LALIA] **—cop•ro•la•li•ac** (kop′rə lā′lē ak′), *adj.*

cop•ro•lite (kop′rə līt′), *n.* a stony mass consisting of fossilized fecal matter of animals. [1820–30; COPRO- + -LITE] **—cop•ro•lit•ic** (kop′rə lit′ik), *adj.*

cop•rol•o•gy (kə prol′ə jē), *n.* scatology. [1855–60; COPRO- + -LOGY]

cop•roph•a•gous (kə prof′ə gəs), *adj.* feeding on dung, as certain beetles. [1820–30; COPRO- + -PHAGOUS] **—cop•ro•pha•gi•a** (kop′rə fā′jē ə, -jə), *n.* **—co•proph•a•gist** (kə prof′ə jist), *n.* **—cop•roph′a•gy,** *n.*

cop•ro•phil•i•a (kop′rə fil′ē ə), *n. Psychiatry.* an obsessive interest in feces. [1930–35; COPRO- + -PHILIA] **—cop′ro•phil′i•ac′,** *n.* **—cop′ro•phil′ic,** *adj.* **—co•proph•i•lism** (kə prof′ə liz′əm), *n.*

co•proph•i•lous (kə prof′ə ləs), *adj.* living or growing on dung, as certain fungi. [1900–05; COPRO- + -PHILOUS]

cop•ro•pho•bi•a (kop′rə fō′bē ə), *n. Psychiatry.* an abnormal fear of feces. [1930–35; COPRO- + -PHOBIA] **—cop′ro•pho′bic,** *adj.*

co•pros•e•cu•tor (kō pros′i kyōō′tər, kō′-), *n.* one of two or more joint prosecutors. [CO- + PROSECUTOR]

cops′ and rob′bers, a children's game in which a group of players imitate the behavior of police and of thieves, as in pursuing and capturing. [1900–05]

copse (kops), *n.* a thicket of small trees or bushes; a small wood. Also, **coppice.** [1570–80; alter. of COPPICE]

Copt (kopt), *n.* **1.** a member of the Coptic Church. **2.** a native Egyptian claiming descent from the ancient Egyptians. Also, **Copht.** [1605–15; < Ar *qubṭ,* back formation from *qubṭī* < Coptic *kyptios,* var. of *gyptios* < Gk *Aigýptios* EGYPTIAN]

cop•ter (kop′tər), *n. Informal.* helicopter. Also, **'cop′•ter.** [1945–50; by shortening]

Cop•tic (kop′tik), *n.* **1.** an Afroasiatic language of Egypt descended from ancient Egyptian, largely extinct as a spoken language since the 16th century but surviving as the liturgical language of the Coptic Church. **—*adj.* 2.** of or pertaining to Coptic or the Copts. [1670–80; COPT + -IC]

Cop′tic Church′, the native Christian church in Egypt, governed by a patriarch and characterized by an adherence to Monophysitism and the use of the Coptic language in its liturgy. [1840–50]

co-publish (kō pub′lish), *v.t.* to publish jointly with another publisher. Also, **co•pub′lish. —co-pub′lish•er, co•pub′lish•er,** *n.*

cop•u•la (kop′yə lə), *n., pl.* **-las, -lae** (-lē′). **1.** something that connects or links together. **2.** Also called **linking verb.** *Gram.* a verb, as *be, seem,* or *look,* that serves as a connecting link or establishes an identity between subject and complement. **3.** *Logic.* a word or set of words that acts as a connecting link between the subject and predicate of a proposition. [1640–50; < L *cōpula,* equiv. to *co-* CO- + *ap-* fasten (see APT) + *-ula* -ULE] **—cop′u•lar,** *adj.*

cop•u•late (*v.* kop′yə lāt′; *adj.* kop′yə lit), *v.,* **-lat•ed, -lat•ing,** *adj.* **—*v.i.* 1.** to engage in sexual intercourse. **—*adj.* 2.** connected; joined. [1375–1425; late ME < L *cōpulātus* bound together. See COPULA, -ATE[1]] **—cop•u•la•to•ry** (kop′yə lə tôr′ē, -tōr′ē), *adj.*

cop•u•la•tion (kop′yə lā′shən), *n.* **1.** sexual intercourse. **2.** a joining together or coupling. [1350–1400; ME *copulacion* < L *cōpulātiōn-* (s. of *cōpulātio*) a binding together. See COPULATE, -ION]

cop•u•la•tive (kop′yə lā′tiv, -lə tiv), *adj.* **1.** serving to unite or couple. **2.** *Gram.* **a.** involving or consisting of connected words or clauses: *a copulative sentence.* **b.** pertaining to or serving as a copula; serving to connect subject and complement: *a copulative verb.* **c.** serving to connect nouns, noun phrases, verbs, clauses, etc.: *a copulative conjunction.* **d.** of the dvandva type: Bittersweet *is a copulative compound.* **3.** of or pertaining to sexual intercourse. **—*n.* 4.** *Gram.* a copulative word. [1350–1400; ME *copulatif* < L *cōpulātīvus.* See COPULATE, -IVE] **—cop′u•la′tive•ly,** *adv.*

cop′ulative asyn′deton, *Rhet.* a staccato effect produced by omitting copulative connectives between two or more items in a group, as in "Friends, Romans, countrymen." Cf. **adversative asyndeton.**

cop•y (kop′ē), *n., pl.* **cop•ies,** *for 1, 2, 7, 9, v.,* **cop•ied, cop•y•ing. —*n.* 1.** an imitation, reproduction, or transcript of an original: *a copy of a famous painting.* **2.** one of the various examples or specimens of the same book, engraving, or the like. **3.** written matter intended to be reproduced in printed form: *The editor sent the copy for the next issue to the printer.* **4.** the text of a news story, advertisement, television commercial, etc., as distinguished from related visual material. **5.** the newsworthiness of a person, thing, or event (often prec. by *good* or *bad*): *The president is always good copy.* Cf. **news** (def. 4). **6.** *Genetics.* replication (def. 7). **7.** *Print.* pictures and artwork prepared for reproduction. **8.** *Brit. Informal.* (in schools) a composition; a written assignment. **9.** *Brit.* a size of drawing or writing paper, 16 × 20 in. (40 × 50 cm). **10.** *Archaic.* something that is to be reproduced; an example or pattern, as of penmanship to be copied by a pupil. **—*v.t.* 11.** to make a copy of; transcribe; reproduce: *to copy a set of figures from a book.* **12.** to receive and understand (a radio message or its sender). **13.** to follow as a pattern or model; imitate. **—*v.i.* 14.** to make a copy or copies. **15.** to undergo copying: *It copied poorly.* **16.** to hear or receive a radio message, as over a CB radio: *Do you copy?* **17.** Also, **cocky.** *Newfoundland.* to leap from one ice pan to another across open water. **18. copy the mail,** *CB Radio Slang.* See **mail**[1] (def. 5). [1300–50; ME *copie* (< AF) <

ML *cōpia* abundance, something copied, L: wealth, abundance; see COPIOUS; (def. 16) orig. a children's game, from the phrase *copy the leader*]
—**Syn. 1.** duplicate, carbon, facsimile. **13.** See **imitate.** —**Ant. 13.** originate.

cop•y•book (kop′ē bŏŏk′), *n.* **1.** a book containing models, usually of penmanship, for learners to imitate. **2.** a book for or containing copies, as of documents. —*adj.* **3.** commonplace; stereotyped: *a copybook sort of phrase.* [1550–60; COPY + BOOK]

cop•y•boy (kop′ē boi′), *n.* an employee who runs errands and carries copy from desk to desk in a newspaper office. [1885–90; COPY + BOY]

cop•y•cat (kop′ē kat′), *n., v.,* **-cat•ted, -cat•ting.** —*n.* Also, **cop′y cat′. 1.** a person or thing that copies, imitates, mimics, or follows the lead of another, as a child who says or does exactly the same as another child. —*adj.* **2.** imitating or repeating a recent, well-known occurrence: *a copycat murder.* —*v.t.* **3.** to imitate or mimic: *new domestic wines that copycat the expensive imports.* **4.** to copy slavishly; reproduce: *The clothes were copycatted straight from designer originals.* [1895–1900, *Amer.*; COPY + CAT[1]] —**cop′y•cat•ism,** *n.*

cop•y•cut•ter (kop′ē kut′ər), *n. Journalism.* an employee of a newspaper who separates copy into takes to facilitate printing. [COPY + CUTTER]

cop′y desk′, *Journalism.* the desk in a newspaper office at which copy is edited and prepared for printing. Cf. **slot**[1] (def. 5). [1925–30, *Amer.*]

cop•y•ed•it (kop′ē ed′it), *v.t.* **1.** to edit (a manuscript, document, text, etc.) for publication, esp. for punctuation, spelling, grammatical structure, style, etc. **2.** to copyread. Also, **cop′y-ed′it.** [1950–55; back formation from COPY EDITOR]

cop•y•ed•i•tor (kop′ē ed′i tər), *n.* **1.** a person who edits a manuscript, text, etc., for publication, esp. to find and correct errors in style, punctuation, and grammar. **2.** a copyreader. **3.** Also called **slot man.** the head copyreader on a newspaper. Also, **cop′y ed′itor.** [1895–1900, *Amer.*]

cop•y•fit•ting (kop′ē fit′ing), *n. Print.* the determining of the area to be occupied by given copy when set in type. [1945–50; COPY + FITTING] —**cop′y•fit′ter,** *n.*

cop•y•girl (kop′ē gûrl′), *n.* a female employee who runs errands and sometimes delivers copy in a newspaper office. [COPY + GIRL]

cop•y•hold (kop′ē hōld′), *n.* **1.** (formerly) a type of ownership of land in England, evidenced by a copy of the manor roll establishing the title. **2.** an estate held under such ownership. [1400–50; late ME; see COPY, HOLD[1]]

cop•y•hold•er (kop′ē hōl′dər), *n.* **1.** a person or thing that holds copy. **2.** a device for holding copy in its place, as on a printer's frame or on a typewriter. **3.** a proofreader's assistant who reads copy aloud or follows it while proof is read for the detection of deviations from it in proof. **4.** a person who holds an estate in copyhold. [1425–75; late ME. See COPYHOLD, -ER[1]]

cop′ying machine′, a machine that makes copies of original documents, esp. by xerography. Also called **copier, cop′y machine′.** Cf. **photocopier.** [1795–1805]

cop•y•ist (kop′ē ist), *n.* **1.** a person who transcribes copies, esp. of documents. **2.** an imitator. [1690–1700; COPY + -IST]

cop′y neg′ative, *Photog.* master (def. 22).

cop′y pa′per, paper specially prepared for the writing of advertising copy, newspaper copy, etc., usually having guidelines to indicate margins and the number of spaces per line. [1900–05]

cop′y protec′tion, *Computers.* a routine that is included in a program by its publisher to prevent the software from being duplicated except for a single backup copy. —**cop•y-pro•tect•ed** (kop′ē prə tek′tid), *adj.*

cop•y•read (kop′ē rēd′), *v.t.,* **-read** (-red), **-read•ing.** to work on (copy) as a copyreader. [1940–45; back formation from COPYREADER]

cop•y•read•er (kop′ē rē′dər), *n.* **1.** an editor concerned with the preparation of copy for the typesetter and printer. **2.** Also called **rim man.** a person who edits copy and writes headlines for a newspaper. Cf. **copy editor** (def. 3). [1890–95, *Amer.*; COPY + READER]

cop•y•right (kop′ē rīt′), *n.* **1.** the exclusive right to make copies, license, and otherwise exploit a literary, musical, or artistic work, whether printed, audio, video, etc.: works granted such right by law on or after January 1, 1978, are protected for the lifetime of the author or creator and for a period of 50 years after his or her death. —*adj.* **2.** of or pertaining to copyrights. **3.** Also, **cop′y•right′ed.** protected by copyright. —*v.t.* **4.** to secure a copyright on. [1725–35; COPY + RIGHT] —**cop′y•right′a•ble,** *adj.* —**cop′y•right′er,** *n.*

cop′yright block′, *Philately.* a block of four or more U.S. stamps that includes, in the selvage of the sheet, the copyright mark of the U.S. Postal Service.

cop•y•writ•er (kop′ē rī′tər), *n.* a writer of copy, esp. for advertisements or publicity releases. [1910–15; COPY + WRITER] —**cop′y•writ′ing,** *n.*

coq au vin (*Fr.* kôk ō vaN′), *French Cookery.* chicken stewed in a sauce of wine, diced pork, onions, garlic, and mushrooms. [1935–40; < F: lit., cock with wine]

Co•que•lin (kôk laN′), *n.* **Be•noît Con•stant** (bə nwa′ kôN stäN′), 1841–1909, French actor.

co•quet (kō ket′), *v.,* **-quet•ted, -quet•ting,** *adj., n.* —*v.i.* **1.** to try to attract the attention and admiration of men for mere self-gratification; flirt. **2.** to act without seriousness; trifle; dally. —*adj.* **3.** coquettish. —*n.* **4.** *Obs.* a male flirt. [1685–95; < F; lit., cockerel, equiv. to *coq* cock + *-et* -ET]
—**Syn. 1.** dally, tease.

co•quet•ry (kō′ki trē, kō ke′trē), *n., pl.* **-ries. 1.** the behavior or arts of a coquette; flirtation. **2.** dalliance; trifling. [1650–60; < F *coquetterie.* See COQUETTE, -ERY]

co•quette (kō ket′), *n.* **1.** a woman who flirts lightheartedly with men to win their admiration and affection; flirt. —*v.i.* **2.** to coquet. [1605–15; < F, fem. of COQUET] —**co•quet′tish,** *adj.* —**co•quet′tish•ly,** *adv.* —**co•quet′tish•ness,** *n.*
—**Syn. 1.** tease, vamp.
—**Usage.** See **-ette.**

Co•quil•hat•ville (kô kē ya vēl′), *n.* former name of **Mbandaka.**

co•quil•lage (kō′ki läzh′; *Fr.* kô kē yäzh′), *n.* an ornamental shell motif. [1850–55; < F: a shellfish. See COQUILLE, -AGE]

co•quil′la nut′ (ko kēl′yə, -kē′yə), the elongated oval fruit or nut of a South American palm, *Attalea funifera,* having a very hard brown shell used in turnery. [1850–55; < Pg *coquilho,* dim. of *côco* COCO]

co•quille (kō kēl′; *Fr.* kô kē′yᵊ), *n., pl.* **-quilles** (-kēlz′; *Fr.* -kē′yᵊ). **1.** any of various seafood or chicken dishes baked with a sauce and usually served in a scallop shell or a shell-shaped serving dish. **2.** the cooking utensil for baking such dishes, usually a scallop shell or small casserole resembling a shell. **3.** a cooking utensil, filled with charcoal, for roasting meat on a spit. **4.** the shell of an escargot. [< F: shell (of a mollusk, nut, etc.). See COCKLE[1]]

co•quilles St. Jacques (kō kēl′ saN zhak′, zhäk′; *Fr.* kô kē yᵊ saN zhak′), *French Cookery.* an appetizer of minced scallops in a wine and cream sauce topped with grated cheese and browned under a broiler: usually served in scallop shells. [< F: scallops, lit., St. James shells, after the scallop shells worn as badges by pilgrims to shrines of St. James; see COQUILLE]

co•qui•na (kō kē′nə), *n.* **1.** Also called **pompano, butterfly-shell clam.** a small clam, *Donax variabilis,* abundant in the intertidal zone of eastern and southern U.S. coastal beaches, having fanlike bands of various hues, the paired empty shells often spread in a butterfly shape. **2.** any similar clam, esp. of the genus *Donax.* **3.** a soft, whitish rock made up of fragments of marine shells and coral, used as a building material. [1830–40, *Amer.*; < Sp: lit., shellfish, equiv. to OSp *coc(a)* shellfish (< L *concha;* see CONCH) + *-ina* -INE[1]]

co•qui•to (kō kē′tō), *n., pl.* **-tos.** a palm, *Jubaea chilensis,* of Chile, from whose sap a honey is prepared and whose small, hard, edible nuts yield a useful oil. Also called **honey palm, wine palm.** [1855–60; < Sp, dim. of *coco* coco palm < Pg *côco* COCO]

cor[1] (kor), *interj. Brit. Dial.* gor. [1930–35]

cor[2] (kôr), *n. Chiefly Brit.* **1.** the tenor oboe. **2.** the English horn. [1865–70; prob. < F *cor (anglais)* (English) HORN]

cor[3] (kôr, kōr), *n., pl.* **cor•di•a** (kôr′dē ə, kōr′-). (in prescriptions) the heart. [< L]

cor-, var. of **com-** before *r: correlate.*

Cor., **1.** Corinthians. **2.** Coroner.

cor., **1.** corner. **2.** cornet. **3.** coroner. **4.** corpus. **5.** correct. **6.** corrected. **7.** correction. **8.** correlative. **9.** correspondence. **10.** correspondent. **11.** corresponding.

Co•ra (kôr′ə, kōr′ə), *n.* **1.** *Class. Myth.* Kore. **2.** a female given name: from a Greek word meaning "girl."

cor•a•cle (kôr′ə kəl, kor′-), *n.* a small, round, or very broad boat made of wickerwork or interwoven laths covered with a waterproof layer of animal skin, canvas, tarred or oiled cloth, or the like: used in Wales, Ireland, and parts of western England. [1540–50; < Welsh *corwgl, corwg;* akin to Ir *curach* boat; see CURRACH]

cor•a•coid (kôr′ə koid′, kor′-), *Anat., Zool.* —*adj.* **1.** pertaining to the bone that in reptiles, birds, and monotremes articulates with the scapula and the sternum and that in humans and other higher mammals is a reduced bony process of the scapula having no connection with the sternum. —*n.* **2.** a coracoid bone or process. [1700–10; < NL *coracoīdēs* < Gk *korakoeidēs* ravenlike, hooked like a raven's beak, equiv. to *korak-* (s. of *kórax*) raven + *-oeidēs* -OID]

co•ra•ji (kə rä′jē), *n. Australian.* boyla. [see KORADJI]

cor•al (kôr′əl, kor′-), *n.* **1.** the hard, variously colored, calcareous skeleton secreted by certain marine polyps. **2.** such skeletons collectively, forming reefs, islands, etc. **3.** the solitary or colonial polyp that secretes this calcareous skeleton. **4.** a reddish yellow; light yellowish red; pinkish yellow. **5.** the unimpregnated roe or eggs of the lobster that when boiled take on the color of red coral. **6.** something made of coral, as an ornament, piece of jewelry, or a child's toy. —*adj.* **7.** made of coral: *a coral reef; coral ornamentation.* **8.** making coral: *a coral polyp.* **9.** resembling coral, esp. in color; yellowish-red. [1275–1325; ME *corall(l)* < L *corāll(i)um* < Gk *korállion* red coral, equiv. to *korall-* (< Sem; cf. Heb *gōrāl* pebble) + *-ion* dim. suffix] —**cor′al•like′,** *adj.*

reef-building coral

Cor•al (kôr′əl, kor′-), *n.* a female given name.

cor′al bells′, an alumroot, *Heuchera sanguinea,* of southwestern North America, having red, bell-shaped flowers, cultivated in many varieties. [1895–1900]

cor•al•ber•ry (kôr′əl ber′ē, kor′-), *n., pl.* **-ries.** See **Indian currant.** [1855–60, *Amer.*; CORAL + BERRY]

cor′al fun′gi, any of a group of brightly colored fungi having erect, branching fruiting bodies that resemble coral.

Cor•al Ga•bles (kôr′əl gā′bəlz, kor′-), a city in SE Florida, near Miami. 43,241.

cor′al hon′eysuckle. See **trumpet honeysuckle.** [1860–65, *Amer.*]

cor•al•lif•er•ous (kôr′ə lif′ər əs, kor′-), *adj.* containing or bearing coral; producing coral. [1870–75; < L *corāll(ium)* CORAL + -I- + -FEROUS]

cor′al lil′y, a bulbous herb, *Lilium pumilum,* of eastern Asia, having scarlet flowers with recurved petals.

cor•al•line (kôr′ə lin, -līn′, kor′-), *adj.* **1.** composed of coral or having the structure of coral: *coralline limestone.* **2.** corallike. **3.** coral-colored; reddish-yellow; light yellowish-red; pinkish-yellow. —*n.* **4.** any red algae impregnated with lime. **5.** any of various corallike animals or calcareous algae. [1535–45; < LL *corallinus* coral red. See CORAL, -INE[1]]

cor•al•lite (kôr′ə līt′, kor′-), *n.* the skeleton of a single coral polyp. [1805–15; < L *corāll(ium)* CORAL + -ITE[1]]

cor•al•loid (kôr′ə loid′, kor′-), *adj.* having the form or appearance of coral. Also, **cor′al•loi′dal.** [1595–1605; < L *corāll(ium)* CORAL + -OID]

cor′al pink′, a light to medium yellowish-pink color. —**cor′al-pink′,** *adj.*

cor′al plant′, a South American tree, *Jatropha multifida,* of the spurge family, having showy, scarlet flowers. [1765–75]

cor′al reef′, a reef composed mainly of coral and other organic matter of which parts have solidified into limestone. [1735–45]

cor•al•root (kôr′əl rōōt′, -rŏŏt′, kor′-), *n.* a saprophytic orchid of the genus *Corallorhiza,* of the Northern Hemisphere, having elongated clusters of small flowers on a leafless stem. [1850–55; CORAL + ROOT[1]]

Cor′al Sea′, a part of the S Pacific, bounded by NE Australia, New Guinea, the Solomon Islands, and the New Hebrides: U.S. naval victory over the Japanese, May 1942.

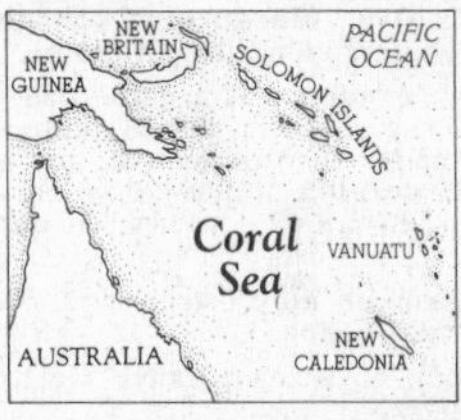

cor′al snake′, **1.** any of numerous venomous elapid snakes, found chiefly in the New World tropics, as *Micrurus fulvius* **(eastern coral snake),** of the southeastern U.S., often brilliantly marked with bands of red, yellow, and black. **2.** any of several other snakes, as of the genus *Calliophis,* of Asia, having red markings. [1750–50]

Cor′al Springs′, a town in SE Florida. 37,349.

cor′al tree′, any of various tropical shrubs or trees of the genus *Erythrina,* of the legume family, having large clusters of pealike flowers. [1625–35]

cor′al vine′, a Mexican climbing vine, *Antigonon leptopus,* of the buckwheat family, having arrow- or heart-shaped leaves and pink or white flowers. [1930–35]

co•ram ju•di•ce (kôr′am jōō′di sē′, kōr′am), *Law.* before a court having the authority to hear and decide (the case in question). [1600–10; < L: in the presence of a judge]

co•ram no•bis (kôr′am nō′bis, kōr′am), *Law.* a writ to correct an injury caused by a mistake of the court. [< L: before us]

co•ram non ju•di•ce (kôr′am non jōō′di sē′, kōr′am), *Law.* before a court lacking the authority to hear and decide the case in question. [1600–10; < L: in the presence of one not a judge]

cor an•glais (kôr′ äng glā′). See **English horn.** [1865–70; < F, equiv. to *cor* HORN + *anglais* ENGLISH]

co•ran•to (kə ran′tō, -rän′-, kō-), *n., pl.* **-tos, -toes.** courante. [1615–25; earlier *carranta* < It *cor(r)anta* < F *courante* COURANTE]

co•ra•zón (kô′rä sôn′, -thôn′), *n., pl.* **-zo•nes** (-sô′nes, -thô′-). *Spanish.* **1.** the heart. **2.** courage; spirit. **3.** love; affection; compassion or sympathy. **4.** (often used in direct address as a term of endearment) lover; beloved.

cor•ban (kôr′bən; *Seph. Heb.* kôr bän′; *Ashk. Heb.* kôr′bən), *n.* a sacrifice or offering made to God, esp. among the ancient Hebrews in fulfillment of a vow. Also, **korban.** [1350–1400; ME < Heb *qorbān* lit., a drawing near]

cor•beil (kôr′bəl; *Fr.* kôr bā′), *n.* a sculptured ornament, esp. on a capital, having the form of a basket. [1700–10; < F *corbeille* < LL *corbicula,* equiv. to L *corbi(s)* basket + *-cula* -CULE[1]]

cor•beille (kôr′bəl; *Fr.* kôr be′yᵊ), *n., pl.* **-beilles** (bəlz; *Fr.* -be′yᵊ). corbeil.

cor•bel (kôr′bəl), *n., v.,* **-beled, -bel•ing** or (*esp. Brit.*) **-belled, -bel•ling.** *Archit.* —*n.* **1.** any bracket, esp. one of brick or stone, usually of slight extent. **2.** a short horizontal timber supporting a girder. —*v.t.* **3.** to set (bricks, stones, etc.) so as to form a corbel or corbels (usually fol. by *out*). **4.** to support by means of a corbel or corbels. [1375–1425; late ME < MF < ML *corvellus*, equiv. to L *corv(us)* RAVEN[1] + *-ellus* dim. suffix]

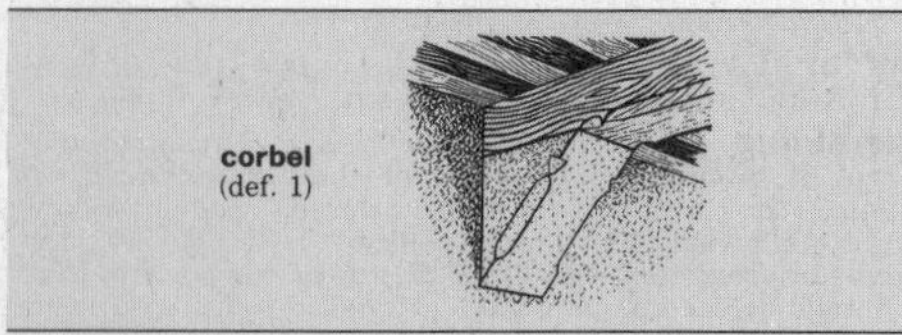
corbel (def. 1)

cor′bel arch′, a construction like an arch but composed of masonry courses corbeled until they meet.

cor•bel•ing (kôr′bə ling), *n. Archit.* **1.** the construction of corbels. **2.** a system of corbels. Also, *esp. Brit.,* **cor′bel•ling.** [1540–50; CORBEL + -ING[1]]

cor′bel ta′ble, a horizontal masonry construction, as a cornice or part of a wall, supported on corbels or on arches supported on corbels. [1400–50; ME]

cor′bel vault′, a structure having the form of a vault but constructed on the principle of a corbel arch.

Cor•bett (kôr′bit), *n.* **James John** (*"Gentleman Jim"*), 1866–1933, U.S. boxer: world heavyweight champion 1892–97.

cor•bic•u•la (kôr bik′yə lə), *n., pl.* **-lae** (-lē′). See **pollen basket.** [1810–20; < NL, little basket; see CORBEIL] —**cor•bic•u•late** (kôr bik′yə lit, -lāt′), *adj.*

cor•bie (kôr′bē), *n. Scot.* a raven or crow. [1150–1200; ME *corbin* < OF < L *corvinus* CORVINE]

cor′bie ga′ble, a gable with corbiesteps. [1850–55]

cor•bie•step (kôr′bē step′), *n.* any of a series of steplike portions of a masonry gable that terminate the gable above the surface of the roof. Also called **cor′bel step′, crowstep.** [1800–10; CORBIE + STEP]

Cor•bin (kôr′bin), *n.* **Margaret (Cochran),** 1751–1800, American Revolutionary military heroine.

cor•bi•na (kôr bē′nə), *n.* **1.** a game fish, *Menticirrhus undulatus,* of the croaker family, inhabiting Pacific coastal waters of North America. **2.** any of various related fish. Also, **corvina.** [1900–05; < Sp *corvina,* fem. of *corvino* < L *corvinus* CORVINE; so named from its color]

cor•bli•mey (kôr bli′mē), *interj. Brit. Slang.* blimey. Also, **cor•bli′my.** Cf. **gor.**

Cor•by (kôr′bē), *n.* a town in NE Northamptonshire, in S England. 55,300.

Cor•co•va•do (kôʀ′kô vä′do͞o *for 1;* kôʀ′kô vä′thô *for 2*), *n.* **1.** a mountain in SE Brazil, S of Rio de Janeiro: statue of Christ on peak. 2310 ft. (704 m). **2.** a volcano in S Chile. 7550 ft. (2301 m).

Cor•cy•ra (kôr sī′rə), *n.* ancient name of **Corfu.** —**Cor•cy•rae•an** (kôr′si rē′ən), *adj., n.*

cord (kôrd), *n.* **1.** a string or thin rope made of several strands braided, twisted, or woven together. **2.** *Elect.* a small, flexible, insulated cable. **3.** a ribbed fabric, esp. corduroy. **4.** a cordlike rib on the surface of cloth. **5.** any influence that binds or restrains: *cord of marriage.* **6.** *Anat.* a cordlike structure: *the spinal cord; umbilical cord.* **7.** a unit of volume used chiefly for fuel wood, now generally equal to 128 cu. ft. (3.6 cu. m), usually specified as 8 ft. long, 4 ft. wide, and 4 ft. high (2.4 m × 1.2 m × 1.2 m). *Abbr.:* cd, cd. **8.** a hangman's rope. —*v.t.* **9.** to bind or fasten with a cord or cords. **10.** to pile or stack up (wood) in cords. **11.** to furnish with a cord. [1250–1300; ME *coord(e)* < AF, OF *corde* < L *chorda* < Gk *chordḗ* gut; confused in part of its history with CHORD[1]] —**cord′er,** *n.* —**cord′like′,** *adj.*

cord•age (kôr′dij), *n.* **1.** fiber and wire ropes, lines, hawsers, etc., taken as a whole, esp. with reference to the rigging and other equipment of a vessel. **2.** a quantity of wood measured in cords. [1480–90; CORD + -AGE]

cor•date (kôr′dāt), *adj.* **1.** heart-shaped: *a cordate shell.* **2.** (of leaves) heart-shaped, with the attachment at the notched end. [1645–55; < NL *cordātus* heart-shaped, equiv. to L *cord-* (s. of *cor*) HEART + *-ātus* -ATE[1]] —**cor′date•ly,** *adv.*

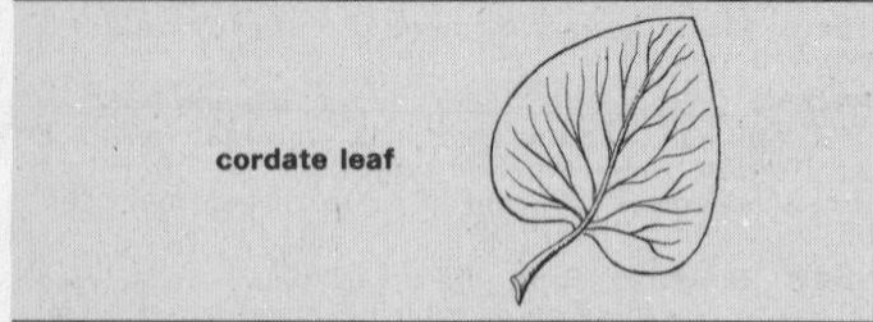
cordate leaf

Cor•day d'Ar•mont (kôr dā′ där môɴ′; *Fr.* kôʀ de dᴀʀ môɴ′), **(Ma•rie Anne) Char•lotte** (mə rē′ an shär′lət; *Fr.* mᴀ ʀē′ ᴀɴ shᴀʀ lôt′), 1768–93, French Revolutionary heroine who assassinated Marat.

cord•ed (kôr′did), *adj.* **1.** furnished with, made of, or in the form of cords. **2.** ribbed, as a fabric. **3.** bound with cords. **4.** (of wood) stacked up in cords. **5.** stringy, or ribbed, in appearance, esp. from the prominence of the muscles, veins, etc.: *a corded throat.* **6.** (of pottery) decorated with the imprint of twisted cords. [1350–1400; ME; see CORD, -ED[3]]

CONCISE ETYMOLOGY KEY: <, descended or borrowed from; >, whence; b., blend of, blended; c., cognate with; cf., compare; deriv., derivative; equiv., equivalent; imit., imitative; obl., oblique; r., replacing; s., stem; sp., spelling, spelled; resp., respelling, respelled; trans., translation; ?, origin unknown; *, unattested; ‡, probably earlier than. See the full key inside the front cover.

Cord′ed cul′ture. See **Battle-Ax culture.**

Cor•dele (kôr dēl′, kôr′dēl), *n.* a city in SW Georgia. 10,914.

Cor•del•ia (kôr dēl′yə), *n.* **1.** (in Shakespeare's *King Lear*) the youngest of Lear's three daughters and the only one who remains loyal to her father. Cf. **Goneril, Regan. 2.** a female given name.

Cor•de•lier (kôr′dl ēr′), *n.* **1.** a Franciscan friar: so called from the knotted cord worn as a girdle. **2. Cordeliers,** a political club in Paris that met at an old Cordelier convent at the time of the French Revolution. [1350–1400; < MF; r. ME *cordeler.* See CORDELLE, -ER[2]]

cor•delle (kôr del′), *n., v.,* **-delled, -dell•ing.** —*n.* **1.** a heavy rope formerly used for towing boats on rivers in Canada and the U.S. —*v.t.* **2.** to tow (a boat) by means of a cordelle. [1785–95; < F, dim. of *corde* CORD]

cord′ foot′, a quantity of wood 4 ft. high, 4 ft. wide, and 1 ft. long (1.2 m × 1.2 m × 0.3 m), or 16 cu. ft. (0.5 cu. m).

cord•grass (kôrd′gras′, -gräs′), *n.* any of several grasses of the genus *Spartina,* of coastal regions. Also called **marsh grass.** [CORD + GRASS]

cor•dial (kôr′jəl *or, esp. Brit.,* -dē əl), *adj.* **1.** courteous and gracious; friendly; warm: *a cordial reception.* **2.** invigorating the heart; stimulating. **3.** sincere; heartfelt: *a cordial dislike.* **4.** *Archaic.* of or pertaining to the heart. —*n.* **5.** a strong, sweetened, aromatic alcoholic liquor; liqueur. **6.** a stimulating medicine. **7.** anything that invigorates or exhilarates. [1350–1400; ME < ML *cordiālis,* equiv. to L *cordi-* (s. of *cor*) HEART + *-ālis* -AL[1]] —**cor′dial•ly,** *adv.* —**cor′dial•ness,** *n.*
—**Syn. 1.** affectionate, genial. **2.** cheering.

cor•dial•i•ty (kôr jal′i tē, kôr′jē al′- *or, esp. Brit.,* -dē-al′-), *n., pl.* **-ties** for 2. **1.** cordial quality or feeling. **2.** an expression of cordial feeling. [1590–1600; CORDIAL + -ITY]
—**Syn. 1.** warmth, friendliness, geniality, heartiness.

cor•di•er•ite (kôr′dē ə rīt′), *n.* a strongly dichroic blue mineral consisting of a silicate of magnesium, aluminum, and iron: common in metamorphic rocks. Also called **dichroite, iolite.** [1805–15; named after Pierre L. A. *Cordier* (1777–1861), French geologist; see -ITE[1]]

cor•di•form (kôr′də fôrm′), *adj.* heart-shaped. [1820–30; < L *cordi-* (s. of *cor*) HEART + -FORM]

cor•dil•le•ra (kôr′dl yâr′ə, -âr′ə, kôr dil′ər ə), *n.* a chain of mountains, usually the principal mountain system or mountain axis of a large landmass. [1695–1705; < Sp, deriv. of *cordilla,* dim. of *cuerda* string, mountain range (< L *chorda*); see CORD] —**cor′dil•le′ran,** *adj.*

Cor•di•lle•ra Cen•tral (kôʀ′thē ye′ʀä sen tʀäl′), **1.** a mountain range in Colombia: part of the Andes. Highest peak, Huila, 18,700 ft. (5700 m). **2.** a mountain range in the Dominican Republic. Highest peak, Pico Duarte, 10,414 ft. (3174 m). **3.** a mountain range in Peru: part of the Andes. **4.** a mountain range in Luzon, Philippines. Highest peak, Mt. Pulog, 9606 ft. (2928 m). **5.** a mountain range in central Puerto Rico. Highest peak, Cerro de Punta, 4389 ft. (1338 m).

Cor•di•lle•ra de Ta•la•man•ca (kôʀ′thē ye′ʀä the tä′lä mäng′kä), a mountain range running SE from central Costa Rica to W Panama.

Cor•di•lle•ra Oc•ci•den•tal (kôʀ′thē ye′ʀä ôk′sethen täl′), the western coastal ranges of the Andes, in Peru and Colombia.

Cor•di•lle•ra O•rien•tal (kôʀ′thē ye′ʀä ô′ʀyen täl′), the eastern ranges of the Andes, in Bolivia, Colombia, and Peru.

Cor•di•lle•ra Re•al (kôʀ′thē ye′ʀä ʀe äl′), **1.** a range of the Andes, in Bolivia. Highest peak, Illimani, 21,201 ft. (6462 m). **2.** a range of the Andes, in Ecuador. Highest peak, Chimborazo, 20,561 ft. (6267 m).

Cor•dil•le•ras (kôr′dl yâr′əz, -âr′-, kôr dil′ər əz; *Sp.* kôʀ′thē ye′ʀäs *for 1*), *n.* **1.** a mountain system in W South America: the Andes and its component ranges. **2.** a mountain system in W North America, including the Sierra Nevada, Coast Range, Cascade Range, and Rocky Mountains. **3.** the entire chain of mountain ranges parallel to the Pacific coast, extending from Cape Horn to Alaska. —**Cor′dil•le′ran,** *adj.*

cord•ing (kôr′ding), *n.* cord covered with yarns or fabric, used decoratively. [1565–75; CORD + -ING[1]]

cor•dis (kôr′dis, kōr′-), *adj.* (in prescriptions) of the heart. [< L]

cord•ite (kôr′dīt), *n.* a smokeless, slow-burning powder composed of 30 to 58 percent nitroglycerin, 37 to 65 percent cellulose nitrate, and 5 to 6 percent mineral jelly. Also called **pyrocellulose.** [1885–90; CORD + -ITE[1], so called from its cordlike form]

cord•less (kôrd′lis), *adj.* **1.** lacking a cord. **2.** (of an electrical appliance) requiring no wire leading to an external source of electricity because of a self-contained, often rechargeable, power supply; battery-powered. [1905–10; CORD + -LESS]

cor•do•ba (kôr′də bə, -və; *Sp.* kôʀ′thô vä), *n., pl.* **-bas** (-bəz, -vəz; *Sp.* -väs), a silver coin and monetary unit of Nicaragua, equal to 100 centavos.

Cór•do•ba (kôr′də bə, -və; *Sp.* kôr′thô vä), *n.* **1.** Also, **Cor′do•ba, Cordova.** a city in S Spain on the Guadalquivir River: the capital of Spain under Moorish rule. 253,632. **2.** a city in central Argentina. 982,018.

cor•don (kôr′dn), *n.* **1.** a line of police, sentinels, military posts, warships, etc., enclosing or guarding an area. **2.** a cord or braid worn for ornament or as a fastening. **3.** a ribbon worn usually diagonally across the breast as a badge of a knightly or honorary order. **4.** *Fort.* **a.** a projecting course of stones at the base of a parapet. **b.** the coping of a scarp. **5.** *Archit.* **a.** a stringcourse, esp. one having little or no projection. **b.** a cut-stone riser on a stepped ramp or the like. **6.** a fruit tree or shrub trained to grow along a support or a series of such supports. —*v.t.* **7.** to surround or blockade with or as with a cordon (usually fol. by *off*): *The police cordoned off the street.* [1400–50; ME < MF, dim. of *corde*]

cor•don bleu (*Fr.* kôʀ dôɴ blœ′), *pl.* **cor•dons bleus** (*Fr.* kôʀ dôɴ blœ′). **1.** the sky-blue ribbon worn as a badge by knights of the highest order of French knighthood under the Bourbons. **2.** some similar high distinction. **3.** one entitled to wear the cordon bleu. **4.** any person of great distinction in a specific field, esp. a distinguished chef. **5.** (of a dish made with thin slices of veal, chicken, etc.) interlaid or stuffed with ham and cheese and then sautéed: *chicken cordon bleu.* [1720–30; < F: lit., blue ribbon]

cor•don•bleu (kôr′dn blo͞o′, -don-), *n.* any of several small African finches of the genus *Uraeginthus,* having pale blue and buff plumage and commonly kept as cage birds. [< F *cordon bleu;* see CORDON BLEU]

cor•don•net (kôr′dn et′, -dn ā′), *n.* a thread, cord, or yarn used to outline a lace motif, form fringes, edge decorative braid, etc. [1855–60; < F; see CORDON, -ET]

cor•don sa•ni•taire (*Fr.* kôʀ dôɴ sa nē teʀ′), *pl.* **cor•dons sa•ni•taires** (*Fr.* kôʀ dôɴ sa nē teʀ′). **1.** a line around a quarantined area guarded to prevent the spread of a disease by restricting passage into or out of the area. **2.** a group of neighboring, generally neutral states forming a geographical barrier between two states having aggressive military or ideological aims against each other. [1840–50; < F; see CORDON, SANITARY]

cor•dot•o•my (kôr dot′ə mē), *n., pl.* **-mies.** the surgical severance of certain nerve fibers of the spinal cord to alleviate intractable pain. Also, **chordotomy.** [CORD + -O- + -TOMY]

Cor•do•va (kôr′də və), *n.* a coarse wool from Argentina used chiefly for carpet stock.

Cor•do•va (kôr′də və), *n.* Córdoba (def. 1).

Cor•do•van (kôr′də vən) *n.* **1.** a native or inhabitant of Córdoba, Spain. **2.** (*l.c.*) a soft, smooth leather originally made at Córdoba of goatskin but later made also of split horsehide, pigskin, etc. —*adj.* **3.** of Córdoba, Spain. **4.** (*l.c.*) designating or made of cordovan. [1585–95; CORDOV(A) + -AN]

cords (kôrdz), *n.* (*used with a plural v.*) clothing, esp. trousers, of corded fabric; corduroys. [1770–80; pl. of CORD]

cor•du•roy (kôr′də roi′, kôr′də roi′), *n.* **1.** a cotton-filling pile fabric with lengthwise cords or ridges. **2. corduroys,** trousers made of this fabric. —*adj.* **3.** of, pertaining to, or resembling corduroy. **4.** constructed of logs laid together transversely, as a road across swampy ground. —*v.t.* **5.** to form (a road or the like) by laying logs transversely. **6.** to make a corduroy road across or along. [1780–90; perh. CORD (cf. CORDS) + *duroy, deroy* (now obs.) a woolen fabric originating in W England; later taken as F *cord du roy* the king's cords, though the fabric had no connection with France]

cord•wain (kôrd′wān), *n. Archaic.* cordovan leather. [1350–1400; ME *cordewan* < MF < Sp *cordován* CORDOVAN]

cord•wain•er (kôrd′wā nər), *n. Archaic.* **1.** a person who makes shoes from cordovan leather. **2.** shoemaker; cobbler. [1150–1200; ME *cordewaner* < OF *cordewan(i)er.* See CORDWAIN, -ER[2]] —**cord′wain•er•y,** *n.*

cord•wood (kôrd′wo͝od′), *n.* **1.** wood stacked in cords for use as fuel. **2.** logs cut to a length of 4 feet (1.2 meters) to facilitate stacking in cords. **3.** trees intended for timber but of a quality suitable only for fuel. [1630–40; CORD + WOOD[1]]

core[1] (kôr, kōr), *n., v.,* **cored, cor•ing.** —*n.* **1.** the central part of a fleshy fruit, containing the seeds. **2.** the central, innermost, or most essential part of anything. **3.** Also called **magnetic core.** *Elect.* the piece of iron, bundle of iron wires, or other ferrous material forming the central or inner portion in an electromagnet, induction coil, transformer, or the like. See diag. under **electromagnet. 4.** (in mining, geology, etc.) a cylindrical sample of earth, mineral, or rock extracted from the ground by means of a corer so that the strata are undisturbed in the sample. **5.** the inside wood of a tree. **6.** *Anthropol.* a lump of stone, as flint, from which prehistoric humans struck flakes in order to make tools. Cf. **flake tool. 7.** *Carpentry.* **a.** a thickness of wood forming a base for a veneer. **b.** a wooden construction, as in a door, forming a backing for veneers. **8.** *Engin.* kern[2]. **9.** *Metall.* **a.** a thickness of base metal beneath a cladding. **b.** the softer interior of a piece of casehardened metal. **c.** a specially formed refractory object inserted into a mold to produce cavities or depressions in the casting that cannot be readily formed on the pattern. **10.** *Geol.* the central portion of the earth, having a radius of about 2100 mi. (3379 km) and believed to be composed mainly of iron and nickel in a molten state. Cf. **crust** (def. 6), **mantle** (def. 3). **11.** *Physics.* the region in a reactor that contains its fissionable material. **12.** Also called **magnetic core.** *Computers.* a small ring or loop of ferromagnetic material with two states of polarization that can be changed by changing the direction of the current applied in wires wound around the ring, used to store one bit of information or to perform switching or logical functions. **13.** *Ropemaking.* heart (def. 16). **14.** *Phonet.* the final segment of a syllable beginning with the vowel and including any following consonants; the nucleus plus the coda. Cf. **onset** (def. 3). —*v.t.* **15.** to remove the core of (fruit). **16.** to cut from the central part. **17.** to remove (a cylindrical sample) from the interior, as of the earth or a tree trunk: *to core the ocean bottom.* **18.** to form a cavity in (a molded object) by placing a core, as of sand, in the mold before pouring. [1275–1325; 1945–50 for def. 11; ME; orig. uncert.; perh. < OF *cors* body < L *corpus*] —**core′less,** *adj.*
—**Syn. 2.** essence, heart, gist, center.

core[2] (kôr, kōr), *n. Chiefly Scot.* a small company or group of people, esp. a gang of miners or a small corps of workers. [1150–1200; ME *chor(e)* dance, company of dancers or singers. See CHORUS]

Co•re (kôr′ē, kōr′ē), *n.* **1.** Korah. **2.** *Class. Myth.* Kore.

CORE (kôr, kōr), *n.* Congress of Racial Equality. Also, **C.O.R.E.**

core′ bar′rel, (in a core drill) a length of pipe for holding rock cores while they are being extracted from the drill hole.

co•re•cip•i•ent (kō′ri sip′ē ənt), *n.* one of two or more recipients, as of an award. [CO- + RECIPIENT]

core′ cit′y. See **central city.** [1960–65]

core′ curric′ulum, *Educ.* a curriculum in which all or some of the subjects or courses are based on a central theme in order to correlate the subjects and the theme.

core′ draw′ing, *Metalworking.* drawing of fine tubing using wire as a mandrel.

co•ref•er•ence (kō ref′ər əns, -ref′rəns), *n. Ling.* a relationship between two words or phrases in which both refer to the same person or thing and one stands as a linguistic antecedent of the other, as the two pronouns in *She taught herself* but not in *She taught her.* Also, **co-ref′er•ence.** [CO- + REFERENCE]

co•ref•er•en•tial (kō′ref ər en′shəl), *adj. Ling.* (of two words or phrases) having reference to the same person or thing. Also, **co′-ref•er•en′tial.** [CO- + REFERENTIAL] **—co′ref•er•en′ti•al′i•ty,** *n.*

core′ gen′der iden′tity. See **gender identity.**

cor′e•id bug′ (kôr′ē id). See **leaf-footed bug.** [< NL *Coreidae* the family which includes such bugs, equiv. to *Core(us)* a genus (based on Gk *kóris* bug) + *-idae* -ID[2]]

co•re•late (kôr′ə lāt′, kor′-), *v.t.,* **-lat•ed, -lat•ing.** *Chiefly Brit.* to correlate. [CO- + RELATE]

co•re•la•tion (kôr′ə lā′shən, kor′-), *n. Chiefly Brit.* correlation. [CO- + RELATION]

co•rel•a•tive (kə rel′ə tiv), *adj., n. Chiefly Brit.* correlative. [CO- + RELATIVE] **—co•rel′a•tive•ly,** *adv.*

co•re•li•gion•ist (kō′ri lij′ə nist), *n.* an adherent of the same religion as another. [1835–45; CO- + RELIGIONIST]

Co•rel•li (kô rel′ē, kō-; *for 1 also It.* kô REL′lē), *n.* **1. Ar•can•ge•lo** (äR kän′je lô′), 1653–1713, Italian violinist and composer. **2. Marie** (*Mary Mackay*), 1854?–1924, English novelist.

core•mak•er (kôr′mā′kər, kōr′-), *n. Metall.* a person who makes cores for foundry molds. [1880–85; CORE[1] + MAKER]

core′ mem′ory, *Computers.* the main memory of a computer that uses the magnetization of small ferrite rings to store data. [1960–65]

co•re•mi•um (kō rē′mē əm, kō-, kə-), *n., pl.* **-mi•a** (-mē ə). *Mycol.* the fruiting bodies of certain fungi, consisting of a loosely bound bundle of conidiophores. [1925–30; < NL < Gk *kórēm(a)* besom, broom + *-ium* -IUM]

co•re•op•sis (kôr′ē op′sis, kōr′-), *n.* any composite plant of the genus *Coreopsis,* including familiar garden species having yellow, brownish, or yellow-and-red ray flowers. [1745–55; < NL < Gk *kore-* (s. of *kóris*) bedbug + *-opsis* -OPSIS; so named from the shape of seed]

co•re•pres•sor (kō′ri pres′ər), *n. Genetics.* a molecule that is capable of combining with a specific repressor molecule and activating it, thereby blocking gene transcription. [1960–65; CO- + REPRESSOR]

co•req•ui•site (kō rek′wə zit), *n. Educ.* an academic course required to be taken in conjunction with another course. [1945–50; CO- + REQUISITE]

cor•er (kôr′ər, kōr′-), *n.* **1.** a person or thing that cores. **2.** a knife or other instrument for coring apples, pears, etc. **3.** a device having a hollow cylindrical drill or tube, used for taking samples of earth, rock, etc., from below the surface of the ground or ocean bottom. [1790–1800; CORE[1] + -ER[1]]

co•re•spond•ent (kō′ri spon′dənt), *n. Law.* a joint defendant, charged along with the respondent, esp. a person charged with adultery in a divorce proceeding. [1855–60; CO- + RESPONDENT]

core′ vocab′ulary. See **basic vocabulary.**

Cor•ey (kôr′ē, kōr′ē), *n.* a male given name.

corf (kôrf), *n., pl.* **corves** (kôrvz). *Brit.* **1.** *Mining.* **a.** a small wagon for carrying coal, ore, etc. **b.** a wicker basket formerly used for this purpose. **2.** a basket, cage, or boxlike structure with perforations for keeping lobsters or fish alive in water. [1350–1400; ME < MD (c. G *Korb*) < L *corbis* basket; cf. CORBEIL]

Cor•fam (kôr′fam), *Trademark.* a brand of synthetic flexible, microporous material, used as a leather substitute for shoes, handbags, belts, luggage, etc.

Cor•fu (kôr′fo͞o, -fyo͞o; *It.* kôR fo͞o′), *n.* **1.** Ancient, **Corcyra.** one of the Ionian Islands, off the NW coast of Greece. 89,664; 229 sq. mi. (593 sq. km). **2.** a seaport on this island. 29,374. Greek, **Kerkyra.**

cor•gi (kôr′gē), *n.* See **Welsh corgi.** [1925–30; < Welsh, equiv. to *cor* dwarf + *-gi,* combining form of *ci* dog, c. OIr *cú;* see HOUND[1]]

Co•ri (kôr′ē, kōr′ē), *n.* **Carl Ferdinand,** 1896–1984, and his wife, **Gerty Theresa,** 1896–1957, U.S. biochemists, born in Czechoslovakia: Nobel prize for medicine 1947.

co•ri•a (kôr′ē ə, kōr′-), *n.* pl. of **corium.**

co•ri•a•ceous (kôr′ē ā′shəs, kōr′-, kor′-), *adj.* of or like leather. [1665–75; < LL *coriāceus* leathern. See CORIUM, -ACEOUS]

co•ri•an•der (kôr′ē an′dər, kōr′-), *n.* an herb, *Coriandrum sativum,* of the parsley family, native to Europe, having strong-scented leaves used in cooking and aromatic seeds used as a seasoning and in medicine. Also called **Chinese parsley, cilantro.** [1350–1400; ME *coriandre* < L *coriandrum* < Gk *koríandron,* var. of *koríannon*]

cor•ing (kôr′ing, kōr′-), *n.* **1.** the act of removing a core or of cutting from a central part. **2.** *Geol., Mining.* core (def. 4). [1865–70; CORE[1] + -ING[1]]

Cor•inth (kôr′inth, kor′-), *n.* **1.** an ancient city in Greece, on the Isthmus of Corinth: one of the wealthiest and most powerful of the ancient Greek cities. **2.** a port in the NE Peloponnesus, in S Greece: NE of the site of ancient Corinth. **3. Gulf of.** Also called **Gulf of Lepanto.** an arm of the Ionian Sea, N of the Peloponnesus. **4. Isthmus of,** an isthmus at the head of the Gulf of Corinth, connecting the Peloponnesus with central Greece: traversed by a ship canal. **5.** a city in NE Mississippi. 13,839.

Co•rin•thi•an (kə rin′thē ən), *adj.* **1.** of, pertaining to, or characteristic of Corinth. **2.** *Archit.* noting or pertaining to one of the five classical orders invented in ancient Greece and similar in most respects to the Ionic but usually of slenderer proportions, and characterized by a deep capital with a round bell decorated with acanthus leaves and a square abacus with concave sides. The Corinthian capital has typically two distinct rows of acanthus leaves above which appear eight fluted sheaths, from each of which spring two scrolls **(helices),** of which one curls beneath a corner of the abacus as half of a volute and the other curls beneath the center of the abacus. Cf. **composite** (def. 3), **Doric** (def. 3), **Ionic** (def. 1), **Tuscan** (def. 2). See illus. under **order. 3.** ornate, as literary style. **4.** luxurious or licentious. **5.** pertaining to or designating a style of vase painting developed in Corinth, in the 7th and early 6th centuries B.C., characterized chiefly by human, animal, and ornamental motifs, painted boldly in a black figure style on a terra-cotta ground, often arranged in tiers around the vase. *—n.* **6.** a native or inhabitant of Corinth. **7.** a man about town, esp. one who lives luxuriously or, sometimes, dissolutely. **8.** an amateur yachtsman. **9.** *Manège.* a horse-show class in which each contestant must be a member of a recognized hunt and wear regulation hunt livery. Cf. **appointment** (def. 7). [1350–1400; ME *Corinthi(es)* men of Corinth (< L *Corinthii* < Gk *Korínthioi;* see CORINTH) + -AN]

Co•rin•thi•ans (kə rin′thē ənz), *n.* (*used with a singular v.*) either of two books of the New Testament, I Corinthians or II Corinthians, written by Paul. *Abbr.:* I Cor., II Cor.

Cor•i•o•la•nus (kôr′ē ə lā′nəs, kor′-), *n.* **1. Ga•ius** (or **Gnae•us**) **Mar•ci•us** (gā′əs *or* nē′əs, mär′shē əs), fl. late 5th century B.C., legendary Roman military hero. **2.** (*italics*) a tragedy (1608?) by Shakespeare.

Co•ri•o′lis effect′ (kôr′ē ō′lis), the apparent deflection **(Corio′lis accelera′tion)** of a body in motion with respect to the earth, as seen by an observer on the earth, attributed to a fictitious force **(Corio′lis force′)** but actually caused by the rotation of the earth and appearing as a deflection to the right in the Northern Hemisphere and a deflection to the left in the Southern Hemisphere. Also called **deflecting force.** [1965–70; named after Gaspard G. *Coriolis* (d. 1843), French civil engineer]

co•ri•ta (kə rē′tə), *n.* a boat resembling a large, woven basket, used by Indians of the southwestern U.S. [< AmerSp]

co•ri•um (kôr′ē əm, kōr′-), *n., pl.* **co•ri•a** (kôr′ē ə, kōr′-). **1.** *Anat., Zool.* dermis. **2.** *Entomol.* the thickened, leathery, basal portion of a hemelytron. [1645–55; < L: skin, hide, leather]

Co•riz•za (kô Rēt′tsä), *n.* Italian name of **Korçë.**

cork (kôrk), *n.* **1.** the outer bark of an oak, *Quercus suber,* of Mediterranean countries, used for making stoppers for bottles, floats, etc. **2.** Also called **cork oak.** the tree itself. **3.** something made of cork. **4.** a piece of cork, rubber, or the like used as a stopper, as for a bottle. **5.** *Angling.* a small float to buoy up a fishing line or to indicate that a fish is biting. **6.** Also called **phellem, suber.** *Bot.* an outer tissue of bark produced by and exterior to the phellogen. **7. blow** or **pop one's cork,** *Informal.* to lose one's temper; release one's emotional or physical tension. *—v.t.* **8.** to provide or fit with cork or a cork. **9.** to stop with or as if with a cork (often fol. by *up*). **10.** to blacken with burnt cork. [1275–1325; ME *cork(e)* < Ar *qurq* < L *quercus* oak]

Cork (kôrk), *n.* **1.** a county in Munster province, in S Republic of Ireland. 266,019; 2881 sq. mi. (7460 sq. km). **2.** a seaport in and the county seat of Cork, in the S part. 136,344.

cork•age (kôr′kij), *n.* a fee charged, as in a restaurant, for serving wine or liquor brought in by the patron. [1830–40; CORK + -AGE]

cork•board (kôrk′bôrd′, -bōrd′), *n.* **1.** an insulating material made of compressed cork, used in building, for industrial purposes, etc. **2.** a bulletin board made of this material. [1890–95; CORK + BOARD]

cork′ cam′bium, *Bot.* phellogen. [1875–80]

corked (kôrkt), *adj.* **1.** stopped or closed with a cork. **2.** corky (def. 2). **3.** blackened with burnt cork. [1510–20; CORK + -ED[3]]

cork•er (kôr′kər), *n.* **1.** a person or thing that corks. **2.** *Informal.* something that closes a discussion or settles a question. **3.** *Informal.* someone or something that is astonishing or excellent. [1715–25; CORK + -ER[1]; defs. 2–3 of unclear relation to def. 1 and perh. of distinct orig.]

cork•ing (kôr′king), *Informal.* *—adj.* **1.** excellent; fine. *—adv.* **2.** very: *a corking good time.* [1890–95; CORK + -ING[2]]

cork′ oak′, cork (def. 2). [1870–75]

cork•screw (kôrk′skro͞o′), *n.* **1.** an instrument typically consisting of a metal spiral with a sharp point at one end and a transverse handle at the other, used for drawing corks from bottles. *—adj.* **2.** resembling a corkscrew; helical; spiral. *—v.t., v.i.* **3.** to move in a spiral or zigzag course. [1805–15; CORK + SCREW]

cork′screw flow′er, snailflower. [1710–20]

cork′ tree′, **1.** the cork oak, *Quercus suber,* of the beech family. **2.** any of several Asian citrus trees of the genus *Phellodendron,* having a corky bark. [1400–50; late ME]

cork•wood (kôrk′wo͝od′), *n.* **1.** a stout shrub or small tree, *Leitneria floridana,* having light green deciduous leaves, woolly catkins, and a drupaceous fruit. **2.** any of certain trees and shrubs yielding a light and porous wood, as the balsa. [1750–60; CORK + WOOD[1]]

cork•y (kôr′kē), *adj.,* **cork•i•er, cork•i•est. 1.** of the nature of cork; corklike. **2.** Also, **corked.** (of wine, brandy, etc.) spoiled, esp. by a tainted cork. [1595–1605; CORK + -Y[1]] **—cork′i•ness,** *n.*

Cor•liss (kôr′lis), *n.* **George Henry,** 1817–88, U.S. engineer and inventor.

corm (kôrm), *n. Bot.* an enlarged, fleshy, bulblike base of a stem, as in the crocus. [1820–30; < NL *cormus* < Gk *kormós* a tree trunk with boughs lopped off, akin to *keírein* to cut off, hew] **—corm′like′,** *adj.* **—cor′moid,** *adj.* **—cor′mous,** *adj.*

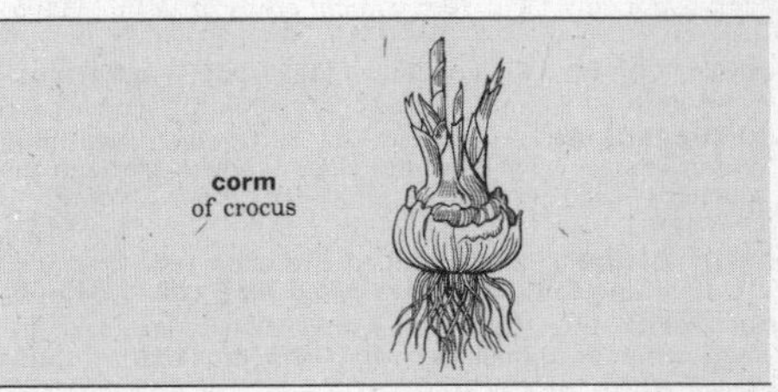
corm of crocus

cor•mel (kôr′məl, kôr mel′), *n.* a small new corm that is vegetatively propagated by a fully mature corm. [1895–1900; CORM + *-el* dim. suffix, as in CARPEL, PEDICEL, etc. (< L *-ellus;* see -ELLE)]

cor•mo•rant (kôr′mər ənt), *n.* **1.** any of several voracious, totipalmate seabirds of the family Phalacrocoracidae, as *Phalacrocorax carbo,* of America, Europe, and Asia, having a long neck and a distensible pouch under the bill for holding captured fish, used in China for catching fish. **2.** a greedy person. [1300–50; ME *cormera(u)nt* < MF *cormorant,* OF *cormareng* < LL *corvus marinus* sea-raven. See CORBEL, MARINE]

cormorant, *Phalacrocorax carbo,* length 3 ft. (0.9 m)

corn[1] (kôrn), *n.* **1.** Also called **Indian corn;** *esp. technical and Brit.,* **maize.** a tall cereal plant, *Zea mays,* cultivated in many varieties, having a jointed, solid stem and bearing the grain, seeds, or kernels on large ears. **2.** the grain, seeds, or kernels of this plant, used for human food or for fodder. **3.** the ears of this plant. **4.** the edible seed of certain other cereal plants, esp. wheat in England and oats in Scotland. **5.** the plants themselves. **6.** sweet corn. **7.** See **corn whiskey. 8.** *Skiing.* See **corn snow. 9.** *Informal.* old-fashioned, trite, or mawkishly sentimental material, as a joke, a story, or music. *—v.t.* **10.** to preserve and season with salt in grains. **11.** to preserve and season with brine. **12.** to granulate, as gunpowder. **13.** to plant (land) with corn. **14.** to feed with corn. [bef. 900; ME, OE; c. D *koren,* ON *korn,* G *Korn,* Goth *kaúrn;* akin to L *grānum* GRAIN, Russ *zernó*]

corn[2] (kôrn), *n. Pathol.* a horny induration or callosity of the epidermis, usually with a central core, formed esp. on the toes or feet and caused by undue pressure or friction. [1375–1425; late ME *corne* < AF, MF < L *cornū* HORN, hence a horny hardening of the cuticle. See CORNU]

-corn, a combining form meaning "having a horn," of the kind specified by the initial element: *longicorn.* [repr. L *-cornis* horned]

Corn., **1.** Cornish. **2.** Cornwall.

cor•na•ceous (kôr nā′shəs), *adj.* belonging to the Cornaceae, the dogwood family of plants. Cf. **dogwood family.** [< NL *Cornace(ae)* (*Corn(us)* the type genus (see CORNEL) + *-aceae* -ACEAE) + -OUS]

corn•ball (kôrn′bôl′), *n.* **1.** popcorn rolled into a ball and flavored with molasses or caramel. **2.** *Informal.* **a.** a person who indulges in clichés or sentimentality. **b.** a country bumpkin; hick. *—adj.* **3.** *Informal.* corny.

[1835–45, *Amer.*; CORN[1] + BALL[1]; defs. 2, 3, influenced by slang sense of *corn.* Cf. SCREWBALL, ODDBALL]

corn′ beef′, corned beef.

Corn′ Belt′, a region in the midwestern U.S., esp. Iowa, Illinois, and Indiana, excellent for raising corn and cornfed livestock. [1880–85]

corn′ bor′er, any of several pyralid moths, as *Pyrausta (ostrinia)* nubilalis **(European corn borer),** the larvae of which bore into the stem and crown of corn and other plants. [1915–20]

corn′ bread′, **1.** Also called **Indian bread.** a bread made of cornmeal. **2.** (esp. in northeastern U.S.) a sourdough rye bread, moist and heavy in texture. [1740–50, *Amer.*]

corn′ broom′, *Northeastern U.S. Older Use.* a broom made from the panicles of broomcorn. [1810–20]

corn′ cake′, *Midland and Southern U.S.* a flat corn bread baked on a griddle. [1785–95, *Amer.*]
—Regional Variation. See **pancake.**

corn′ chip′, a thin, crisp piece of snack food made from cornmeal. [1945–50]

corn·cob (kôrn′kob′), *n.* **1.** the elongated woody core in which the grains of an ear of corn are embedded. **2.** Also called **corn′cob pipe′.** a tobacco pipe with a bowl made from a corncob. [1780–90, *Amer.*; CORN[1] + COB[1]]

corn′ cock′le, a plant, *Agrostemma githago,* of the pink family, having magenta-purple flowers and occurring commonly as a weed among crops of grain. [1705–15]

corn′ col′or, light yellow. [1850–55] **—corn′-col′·ored,** *adj.*

corn-crack·er (kôrn′krak′ər), *n. Slang (disparaging and offensive).* one of a poor class of white people in the southern U.S.; cracker. [1825–35, *Amer.*; CORN[1] + CRACKER]

corn′ crake′, a short-billed Eurasian rail, *Crex crex,* frequenting grainfields. Also called **land rail.** [1545–55]

corn·crib (kôrn′krib′), *n.* a ventilated structure for the storage of unhusked corn. [1675–85; CORN[1] + CRIB]

corn′ dodg′er, **1.** *South Midland and Southern U.S.* a small, usually oval cake made of corn bread and baked or fried hard in a skillet. **2.** *Chiefly South Atlantic States and Eastern Virginia.* a boiled dumpling made of cornmeal.

corn′ dog′, a sandwich consisting of a frankfurter baked or fried in corn bread and usually spread with mustard before eating: often served on a stick. [1965–70, *Amer.*]

cor·ne·a (kôr′nē ə), *n. Anat.* the transparent anterior part of the external coat of the eye covering the iris and the pupil and continuous with the sclera. See diag. under **eye.** [1350–1400; ME < ML *cornea* (*tēla,* later *tunica*) horny (web or tunic), fem. of *corneus* CORNEOUS] **—cor′·ne·al,** *adj.*

cor′neal re′flex, **1.** *Physiol.* the closing of the eyelids induced by touching the cornea lightly. **2.** *Ophthalm.* the reflection of a keratoscope, as Placido's disk, on the surface of the cornea.

corn′ ear′worm (ēr′wûrm′), the larva of a cosmopolitan noctuid moth, *Heliothis zea,* that is highly destructive to crops, esp. corn, cotton, and tomato. Also called **bollworm, cotton bollworm, tomato fruitworm.** [1795–1805, *Amer.*]

corned (kôrnd), *adj.* marinated in brine, often containing garlic, peppercorns, cloves, etc.; preserved or cured with salt: *corned beef.* [1570–80; CORN[1] + -ED[2]]

Cor·neille (kôr nā′; *Fr.* kôʀ ne′yᵊ), *n.* **Pierre** (pē âr′; *Fr.* pyeʀ), 1606–84, French dramatist and poet.

cor·nel (kôr′nl), *n.* any tree or shrub of the genus *Cornus;* dogwood. [1400–50; late ME *corneille* < MF < VL **cornicul(a),* equiv. to L *corn(us)* cornel + *-i-* -I- + *-cula* -CULE[1]]

Cor·nel·ia (kôr nēl′yə), *n.* **1.** fl. 2nd century B.C., Roman matron: mother of Gaius and Tiberius Gracchus. **2.** fl. 1st century B.C., first wife of Julius Caesar 83–67?. Cf. **Calpurnia, Pompeia. 3.** a female given name.

cor·nel·ian (kôr nēl′yən), *n.* carnelian.

cornel′ian cher′ry, **1.** a Eurasian shrub or small tree, *Cornus mas,* of the dogwood family, having shiny, ovate leaves and yellow flowers. **2.** its tart, edible, scarlet berry. [1755–65; CORNEL + -IAN]

Cor·ne·li·us (kôr nēl′yəs, -nē′lē əs; *for 2, 3, also Ger.* kôʀ nā′lē o͝os′), *n.* **1. Saint,** died A.D. 253, Italian ecclesiastic: pope 251–253. **2. Pe·ter von** (pā′tər fən), 1783–1867, German painter. **3.** a male given name: from a Roman family name.

Cor·nell (kôr nel′), *n.* **1. Ezra,** 1809–74, U.S. capitalist and philanthropist. **2. Katharine,** 1898–1974, U.S. actress. **3.** a male given name.

cor·ne·ous (kôr′nē əs), *adj.* consisting of a horny substance; horny. [1640–50; < L *corneus* horny, equiv. to *corn(ū)* HORN + *-eus* -EOUS]

cor·ner (kôr′nər), *n.* **1.** the place at which two converging lines or surfaces meet. **2.** the space between two converging lines or surfaces near their intersection; angle: *a chair in the corner of the room.* **3.** a projecting angle, esp. of a rectangular figure or object: *He bumped into the corner of the table.* **4.** the point where two streets meet: *the corner of Market and Main Streets.* **5.** an end; margin; edge. **6.** any narrow, secluded, or secret place. **7.** an awkward or embarrassing position, esp. one from which escape is impossible. **8.** *Finance.* a monopolizing or a monopoly of the available supply of a stock or commodity to a point permitting control of price (applied only when monopoly price is exacted). **9.** region; part; quarter: *from every corner of the empire.* **10.** *Survey.* **a.** the point of intersection of the section lines of a land survey, often marked by a monument or some object, as a pipe that is set or driven into the ground. Cf. **section** (def. 5). **b.** a stake, tree, or rock marking the intersection of property lines. **11.** a piece to protect the corner of anything. **12.** *Baseball.* **a.** any point on the line forming the left or right boundary of home plate: *a pitch on the corner.* **b.** the area formed by the intersection of the foul line and the outfield fence. **13.** *Boxing.* **a.** the immediate area formed by any of the four angles in the ring. **b.** one of the two assigned corners where a boxer rests between rounds and behind which the handlers sit during a fight. **14.** *Soccer.* See **corner kick. 15. cut corners, a.** to use a shorter route. **b.** to reduce costs or care in execution: *cutting corners to meet the foreign competition.* **16. rough corners,** rude, boorish, or unsophisticated characteristics, manners, or the like: *Despite his rough corners, he was very likable.* **17. the four corners of the earth,** the most distant or remote regions: *They traveled to the four corners of the earth.* **18. turn the corner,** to pass through a crisis safely: *When the fever passed, we knew he had turned the corner.* —*adj.* **19.** situated on or at a corner where two streets meet: *a corner drugstore.* **20.** made to fit or be used in a corner: *a corner cabinet.* —*v.t.* **21.** to furnish with corners. **22.** to place in or drive into a corner. **23.** to force into an awkward or difficult position or one from which escape is impossible: *He finally cornered the thief.* **24.** to gain control of (a stock, commodity, etc.). —*v.i.* **25.** to meet in or be situated on or at a corner. **26.** to form a corner in a stock or commodity. **27.** (of an automobile) to turn, esp. at a speed relatively high for the angle of the turn involved. [1250–1300; ME < AF, equiv. to OF *corne* corner, HORN (< L *cornū* horn; cf. CORNU) + *-er* -ER[2]]
—Syn. 7. predicament, impasse, dead end.

CONCISE ETYMOLOGY KEY: <, descended or borrowed from; >, whence; b., blend of, blended; c., cognate with; cf., compare; deriv., derivative; equiv., equivalent; imit., imitative; obl., oblique; r., replacing; s., stem; sp., spelling, spelled; resp., respelling, respelled; trans., translation; ?, origin unknown; *, unattested; ‡, probably earlier than. See the full key inside the front cover.

cor·ner·back (kôr′nər bak′), *n. Football.* one of two defensive backs positioned in the secondary between the linebackers and safeties, responsible for covering the outside areas near the sidelines against end runs and pass plays. [1965–70; CORNER + BACK[1]]

Cor′ner Brook′, a city in Newfoundland, in E Canada, on the W part of the island. 24,339.

cor′ner cab′inet, a cabinet, usually triangular in design so as to fit into a corner of a room.

cor′ner chair′, a chair having an approximately square seat with a leg at each corner and a back extending around two adjacent sides. Also called **roundabout chair.**

cor·nered (kôr′nərd), *adj.* **1.** having corners (usually used in combination): *a six-cornered room.* **2.** having a given number of positions; sided (usually used in combination): *a four-cornered debate.* **3.** forced into an awkward, embarrassing, or inescapable position: *a cornered debater; a cornered fox.* [1300–50; ME; see CORNER, -ED[3]]

cor′ner kick′, *Soccer.* a direct free kick awarded to the attacking team when a defender last touched a ball that crossed entirely over the goal line, taken from the corner area on the side of the field where the ball went out of play. Also called **corner.** [1880–85]

cor·ner·man (kôr′nər man′, -mən), *n., pl.* **-men** (-men′, -mən). **1.** *Basketball.* a forward. **2.** *Ice Hockey.* a player who is adept at gaining control of the puck in the corner areas of the rink. [CORNER + MAN[1]]

cor·ner·stone (kôr′nər stōn′), *n.* **1.** a stone uniting two masonry walls at an intersection. **2.** a stone representing the nominal starting place in the construction of a monumental building, usually carved with the date and laid with appropriate ceremonies. **3.** something that is essential, indispensable, or basic: *The cornerstone of democratic government is a free press.* **4.** the chief foundation on which something is constructed or developed: *The cornerstone of his argument was that all people are created equal.* [1250–1300; ME; see CORNER, STONE]

cor′ner ta′ble, a table of the 18th century having a triangular top with a triangular drop leaf of the same size. Also called **handkerchief table.** [1920–25]

cor·ner·wise (kôr′nər wīz′), *adv.* **1.** with the corner in front. **2.** so as to form a corner. **3.** from corner to corner; diagonally. Also, **cor·ner·ways** (kôr′nər wāz′). [1425–75; late ME; see CORNER, -WISE]

cor·net (kôr net′ *for 1;* kôr′nit, kôr net′ *for 2–8*), *n.* **1.** *Music.* a valved wind instrument of the trumpet family. **2.** a small cone of paper twisted at the end and used for holding candy, nuts, etc. **3.** a pastry cone, usually filled with whipped cream. **4.** *Brit.* a conical wafer, as for ice cream; cone. **5.** a large, white, winged headdress formerly worn by the members of the Sisters of Charity. **6.** a woman's headdress, often cone-shaped, usually of delicate fabrics and having lappets of lace or other material, worn by women from the 14th to the 18th century. **7.** a pennant or flag used for signaling in a navy. **8.** (formerly) the officer who carried the colors in a troop of cavalry: *the cornet of horse.* [1325–75; ME < MF, OF, equiv. to *corn* HORN (< L *cornū;* see CORNU) + *-et* -ET]

cornet
(def. 1)

cor·net-à-pis·tons (kôr net′ə pis′tənz; *Fr.* kôʀ ne A-pē stôN′), *n., pl.* **cor·nets-à-pis·tons** (kôr nets′ə pis′-tənz; *Fr.* kôʀ ne zA pē stôN′). cornet (def. 1). [1830–40; < F: lit., cornet with valves]

cor·net·fish (kôr net′fish′), *n., pl.* (*esp. collectively*) **-fish,** (*esp. referring to two or more kinds or species*) **-fish·es.** any of several slender fishes of the family Fistulariidae, of tropical seas, having an elongated snout and bony plates instead of scales. [CORNET + FISH]

cor·net·ist (kôr net′ist), *n.* a musician who plays the cornet. Also, **cor·net′tist.** [1880–85, *Amer.*; CORNET + -IST]

corn·fed (kôrn′fed′), *adj.* **1.** fed on corn: *cornfed cattle.* **2.** having a well-fed, healthy, and guileless appearance: *the open enthusiasm of these handsome, cornfed youngsters.* [1350–1400; ME; see CORN[1], FED]

corn·field (kôrn′fēld′), *n.* a field in which corn is grown. [1275–1325; ME *cornfield.* See CORN[1], FIELD]

corn′field ant′, a small, brown ant, *Lasius alienus,* that lives in cornfields and feeds on honeydew of the corn-root aphid.

corn·flag (kôrn′flag′), *n.* a Mediterranean plant, *Gladiolus segetum,* of the iris family, having loose, one-sided spikes of pinkish-purple flowers. [1570–80; CORN[1] + FLAG[2]]

corn·flakes (kôrn′flāks′), *n.* (*used with a plural v.*) a packaged breakfast cereal in the form of small toasted flakes made from corn, for serving cold with milk, sugar, etc. Also, **corn′ flakes′.** [1905–10, *Amer.*; CORN[1] + *flakes,* pl. of FLAKE[1]]

corn′ flour′, **1.** flour made from corn. **2.** *Brit.* cornstarch. [1665–75, *Amer.*]

corn·flow·er (kôrn′flou′ər), *n.* **1.** Also called **bachelor's-button, bluebottle.** a European composite plant, *Centaurea cyanus,* growing in grainfields, having blue to white flower heads, often cultivated as an ornamental. **2.** Also called **corn′flower blue′.** a deep, vivid blue. **3.** See **corn cockle. 4.** strawflower (def. 2). [1570–80; CORN[1] + FLOWER]

Corn·forth (kôrn′fərth, -fōrth′, -fôrth′), *n.* **Sir John War·cup** (wôr′kup), born 1917, British chemist, born in Australia: Nobel prize 1975.

corn′ glu′ten, gluten separated from corn during milling, used primarily as a livestock feed.

corn′ grits′, (*used with a singular or plural v.*) hominy grits. [1830–40, *Amer.*]

corn·hole (kôrn′hōl′), *v.t.,* **-holed, -hol·ing.** *Slang (vulgar).* to have anal intercourse with. [CORN[1] + HOLE]

corn·house (kôrn′hous′), *n., pl.* **-hous·es** (-hou′ziz). *New Eng. and South Atlantic States.* a corncrib. [CORN[1] + HOUSE]

corn·husk (kôrn′husk′), *n.* the husk of an ear of corn. [1705–15, *Amer.*; CORN[1] + HUSK]

corn·husk·er (kôrn′hus′kər), *n.* **1.** a person or thing that husks corn. **2.** (*cap.*) a Nebraskan (used as a nickname). [1840–50, *Amer.*; CORN[1] +HUSK + -ER[1]]

Corn′husker State′, Nebraska (used as a nickname).

corn·husk·ing (kôrn′hus′king), *n.* **1.** the removing of the husks from corn. **2.** See **husking bee.** [1780–90, *Amer.*; CORN[1] + HUSK + -ING[1]]

cor·nice (kôr′nis), *n., v.,* **-niced, -nic·ing.** —*n.* **1.** *Archit.* **a.** any prominent, continuous, horizontally projecting feature surmounting a wall or other construction, or dividing it horizontally for compositional purposes. **b.** the uppermost member of a classical entablature, consisting of a bed molding, a corona, and a cymatium, with rows of dentils, modillions, etc., often placed between the bed molding and the corona. **2.** any of various other ornamental horizontal moldings or bands, as for concealing hooks or rods from which curtains are hung or for supporting picture hooks. **3.** a mass of snow, ice, etc., projecting over a mountain ridge. —*v.t.* **4.** to furnish or finish with a cornice. [1555–65; < It: lit., crow (< L *cornix*); for the meaning, cf. Gk *korōnē* crow, CROWN]

cor·niche (kôr′nish, kôr nēsh′), *n.* a winding road cut into the side of a steep hill or along the face of a coastal cliff. [1830–40; < F, by ellipsis from *route de corniche, route en corniche* (*corniche* rock ledge < It; see CORNICE)]

Cor·ni·chon (kôr′ni shon′), *n.* **1.** a black vinifera grape grown for table use. **2.** the vine itself. **3.** (*l.c.*) a cucumber pickle; gherkin. [1965–70; < F: lit., little horn, equiv. to *corne* HORN + *-ichon* dim. suffix]

cor·ni·cle (kôr′ni kəl), *n.* any of various small, horn-shaped processes, esp. one of a pair of tubes at the posterior end of the abdomen of aphids, from which a waxy fluid is emitted. [1640–50; < L *corniculum* little horn, equiv. to *corn-* (s. of *cornū*) HORN + *-i-* -I- + *-culum* -CLE[1]]

cor·nic·u·late (kôr nik′yə lit, -lāt′), *adj.* **1.** resembling a small horn in appearance. **2.** having horns or hornlike parts; horned. [1640–50; < L *corniculātus* horned, equiv. to *cornicul(um)* little horn (see CORNICLE) + *-ātus* -ATE[1]]

cor·ni·fi·ca·tion (kôr′nə fi kā′shən), *n. Biol.* the formation of a horny layer of skin, or horny skin structures, as hair, nails, or scales, from squamous epithelial cells. [1835–45; CORN[2] + -I- + -FICATION]

Cor·ning (kôr′ning), *n.* a city in S New York. 12,953.

Cor·nish (kôr′nish), *adj.* **1.** of, pertaining to, or characteristic of Cornwall, England, its inhabitants, or the Cornish language. —*n.* **2.** the Celtic language of Cornwall, extinct since c1800. **3.** one of an English breed of chickens raised chiefly for crossing with other breeds to produce roasters. [1350–1400; late ME, appar. syncopated var. of ME *Cornwelisse.* See CORNWALL, -ISH[1]]

Cor·nish·man (kôr′nish mən), *n., pl.* **-men.** a native or inhabitant of Cornwall. [1375–1425; late ME. See CORNISH, MAN[1]]

Corn′ Law′, *Eng. Hist.* any of the laws regulating domestic and foreign trading of grain, the last of which was repealed in 1846.

corn′-leaf a′phid (kôrn′lēf′), a green aphid,

Rhopalosiphum maidis, widely distributed in the U.S.: a pest of corn and other grasses. [1935–40]

corn′ lil′y, 1. any of several plants of the genus *Ixia,* of the iris family, native to southern Africa, having spikes of flowers and grown as an ornamental. **2.** a woodland plant, *Clintonia borealis,* of the lily family, native to eastern and midwestern North America, having broad leaves, nodding yellowish-green flowers, and dark-blue berries. Also called **bluebead.** [1945–50, *Amer.*]

corn′ liq′uor. See **corn whiskey.** [1920–25, *Amer.*]

corn′ mar′igold, a composite plant, *Chrysanthemum segetum,* of Eurasia, having daisylike, solitary yellow flowers. [1590–1600]

corn•meal (kôrn′mēl′), *n.* **1.** Also called, *esp. Brit.,* **Indian meal.** meal made of corn. **2.** *Scot.* oatmeal. [1740–50; CORN[1] + MEAL[2]]

corn′ muf′fin, a muffin, often shaped like a cupcake, made from cornmeal. [1835–45, *Amer.*]

corn′ oil′, a pale-yellow, water-insoluble liquid oil obtained by expressing the germs of corn kernels, used in the preparation of foodstuffs, lubricants, soaps, and hair dressings. Also called **maize oil.**

corn′ pick′er, a machine for picking the ears of corn from standing stalks and removing the husks. **—corn′ pick′ing.** [1940–45, *Amer.*]

corn′ plant′, any of several treelike tropical plants of the genus *Draecena,* esp. *D. fragrans massangeana,* widely cultivated as a houseplant.

corn′ pone′, *Southern U.S.* corn bread, esp. of a plain or simple kind. [1855–60, *Amer.*]

corn-pone (kôrn′pōn′), *adj. Usually Disparaging.* of or characteristic of an unsophisticated rural person, esp. from the South; hick: *a corn-pone accent.* [1965–70]

corn′ pop′py, a common Old World poppy, *Papaver rhoeas,* having bright-red flowers. Also called **field poppy, Flanders poppy.** [1875–80; so called from its growing in grainfields]

corn′-root a′phid (kôrn′ro͞ot′, -ro͝ot′), an aphid, *Anuraphis maidiradicis,* that lives as a symbiont in colonies of cornfield ants and feeds on the roots of corn: an agricultural pest.

corn′ root′worm, the larva of any of several leaf beetles of the genus *Diabrotica* that feeds on roots and underground stems: an agricultural pest, esp. of corn. [1890–95, *Amer.*]

corn•row (kôrn′rō′), *n.* **1.** a type of braid, originating in Africa, in which a narrow strip of hair is plaited tightly against the scalp from front to back or from side to side. **2.** Usually, **cornrows.** a hair style consisting of such braids in close parallel rows. —*v.t.* **3.** to arrange (hair) in cornrows. [1970–75, *Amer.*; CORN[1] + ROW[1]]

corn′ sal′ad, any of several plants of the genus *Valerianella,* of the valerian family, esp. *V. locusta* (or *V. olitoria*), having small light blue flowers and tender, narrow leaves eaten in salads. Also called **lamb's lettuce, mache.** [1590–1600]

corn′ silk′, the long, threadlike, silky styles on an ear of corn. [1850–55]

corn′ smut′, a disease of corn caused by a fungus, *Ustilago maydis,* and characterized by blackish, powdery masses of spores on the affected parts of the plant. [1880–85]

corn′ snake′, a large, harmless rat snake, *Elaphe guttata guttata,* of the southeastern U.S., having yellow, tan, or gray scales with dark-red blotches: once common in cornfields but now an endangered species. Also called **red rat snake.** [1670–80, *Amer.*]

corn′ snow′, *Skiing.* snow in the form of small pellets or grains produced by the alternate melting and freezing of a snow layer. Also called **corn, spring snow.** [1930–35]

corn′ stack′, *Delmarva Peninsula.* corncrib.

corn•stalk (kôrn′stôk′), *n.* the stalk or stem of corn, esp. Indian corn. [1635–45, *Amer.*; CORN[1] + STALK[1]]

corn•starch (kôrn′stärch′), *n.* a starch or a starchy flour made from corn and used for thickening gravies and sauces, making puddings, etc. Also called, *esp. Brit.,* **corn flour.** [1850–55, *Amer.*; CORN[1] + STARCH]

corn•stick (kôrn′stik′), *n. Southern Cookery.* a corn muffin baked in the form of a small ear of corn. [1940–45, *Amer.*; CORN[1] + STICK[1]]

corn′ sug′ar, dextrose. [1840–50, *Amer.*]

corn′ syr′up, syrup prepared from corn. [1900–05, *Amer.*]

cor•nu (kôr′no͞o, -nyo͞o), *n., pl.* **-nu•a** (-no͞o ə, -nyo͞o ə). a horn, esp. a bony part that resembles a horn. [1685–95; < L: HORN; akin to Gk *kéras* (see CERAT-), *krānīon* CRANIUM] **—cor′nu•al,** *adj.*

cor•nu•co•pi•a (kôr′nə kō′pē ə, -nyə-), *n.* **1.** *Class. Myth.* a horn containing food, drink, etc., in endless supply, said to have been a horn of the goat Amalthaea. **2.** a representation of this horn, used as a symbol of abundance. **3.** an abundant, overflowing supply. **4.** a horn-shaped or conical receptacle or ornament. [1585–95; < LL, equiv. to L *cornū* HORN (see CORNU) + *cōpiae* of plenty (gen. s. of *cōpia*); see COPIOUS] **—cor′nu•co′pi•an,** *adj.* **—cor•nu•co•pi•ate** (kôr′nə kō′pē it), *adj.*

cornucopia (def. 2)

cornuco′pia leg′, *Furniture.* a leg used on pieces in the Directoire and Empire styles, curving downward from the piece and curving upward again to a point and having a foot or caster at the lowest part of the curve.

cor•nute (kôr no͞ot′, -nyo͞ot′), *v.,* **-nut•ed, -nut•ing,** *adj.* —*v.t.* **1.** *Archaic.* to cuckold. —*adj.* **2.** cornuted. [1590–1600; < L *cornūtus* horned, equiv. to *cornū* HORN + *-tus* adj. suffix]

cor•nut•ed (kôr no͞o′tid, -nyo͞o′-), *adj.* **1.** having horns. **2.** shaped like a horn. **3.** *Archaic.* cuckolded. Also, **cornute.** [1605–15; CORNUTE + -ED[2]]

cor•nu•to (kôr no͞o′tō, -nyo͞o′-), *n., pl.* **-tos.** a cuckold. [1400–50; late ME < It: lit., one who is horned < L *cornūtus* HORNED. See CORNUTE]

Corn•wall (kôrn′wôl *or, esp. Brit.,* -wəl), *n.* **1.** a county in SW England. 397,200; 1369 sq. mi. (3545 sq. km). **2.** a city in SE Ontario, in S Canada, SW of Ottawa, on the St. Lawrence. 46,144.

Corn•wal•lis (kôrn wô′lis, -wol′is), *n.* **Charles, 1st Marquis,** 1738–1805, British general and statesman: surrendered to Washington at Yorktown, Virginia, October 19, 1781.

corn′ whis′key, whiskey made from a mash having at least 80 percent corn. Also called **corn, corn liquor.** [1835–45, *Amer.*]

corn•y[1] (kôr′nē), *adj.,* **corn•i•er, corn•i•est.** **1.** of or abounding in corn. **2.** *Informal.* **a.** old-fashioned, trite, or lacking in subtlety: *corny jokes.* **b.** mawkishly sentimental: *a corny soap opera.* [1350–1400; 1930–35 for def. 2; ME; see CORN[1], -Y[1]] **—corn′i•ly,** *adv.* **—corn′i•ness,** *n.*
—Syn. 2. hackneyed, banal, stale.

corn•y[2] (kôr′nē), *adj.,* **corn•i•er, corn•i•est.** pertaining to or affected with corns of the feet. [1700–10; CORN[2] + -Y[1]]

Co•ro (kô′rô), *n.* a city in NW Venezuela. 68,701.

cor•o•dy (kôr′ə dē, kor′-), *n., pl.* **-dies.** *Old Eng. Law.* **1.** a right to receive maintenance in the form of housing, food, or clothing, esp. the right enjoyed by the sovereign or a private benefactor to receive such maintenance from a religious house. **2.** the housing, food, or clothing so received. Also, **corrody.** [1375–1425; late ME *corrodie* < AF < ML *corrōdium* outfit, provision, var. of *conrēdium* < VL **conrēd(āre)* to outfit, provide with (equiv. to *con-* CON- + **-rēdāre* < Gmc; cf. OE *rǣdan* to equip, provide for, READY) + L *-ium* -IUM]

coroll., corollary. Also, **corol.**

co•rol•la (kə rol′ə), *n. Bot.* the inner envelope of floral leaves of a flower, usually of delicate texture and of some color other than green; the petals considered collectively. [1665–75; < L: little garland, equiv. to *corōn(a)* garland, CORONA + *-la* dim. suffix; see -ULE]

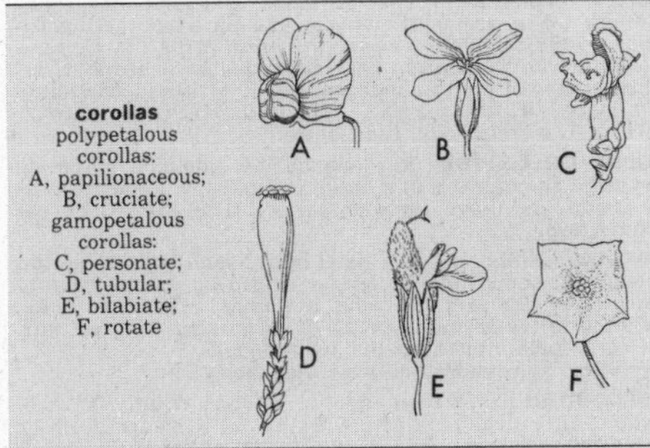

corollas
polypetalous corollas:
A, papilionaceous;
B, cruciate;
gamopetalous corollas:
C, personate;
D, tubular;
E, bilabiate;
F, rotate

cor•ol•la•ceous (kôr′ə lā′shəs, kor′-), *adj.* of, pertaining to, or resembling a corolla. [1765–75; COROLL(A) + -ACEOUS]

cor•ol•lar•y (kôr′ə ler′ē, kor′-; *esp. Brit.,* kə rol′ə rē), *n., pl.* **-lar•ies.** **1.** *Math.* a proposition that is incidentally proved in proving another proposition. **2.** an immediate consequence or easily drawn conclusion. **3.** a natural consequence or result. [1325–75; ME < LL *corollārium* corollary, in L: money paid for a garland, a gift, gratuity. See COROLLA, -ARY]

co•rol•late (kə rol′āt, -it, kôr′ə lāt′, -lit, kor′-), *adj. Bot.* having a corolla. Also, **co•rol•lat•ed** (kə rol′ā tid, kôr′ə lā′-, kor′-). [1860–65; COROLL(A) + -ATE[1]]

cor•o•man•del (kôr′ə man′dl, kor′-), *n.* **1.** the hard, brownish wood of a tropical Asian tree, *Diospyros melanoxylon.* **2.** the tree itself. Also called **cor′oman′del eb′ony.** [1835–45; after the COROMANDEL COAST; cf. CALIMANDER]

Cor′o•man′del Coast′ (kôr′ə man′dl, kor′-, kôr′-, kor′-), a coastal region in SE India, S of the Kistna River.

Coroman′del work′, lacquer work popular in England c1700 and marked by an incised design filled in with gold and color. Also called **Bantam work, Cor′oman′del lac′quer.** [after the COROMANDEL COAST, where objects decorated with such work were transshipped to Europe]

co•ro•na (kə rō′nə), *n., pl.* **-nas, -nae** (-nē). **1.** a white or colored circle or set of concentric circles of light seen around a luminous body, esp. around the sun or moon. **2.** *Meteorol.* such a circle or set of circles having a small radius and ranging in color from blue inside to red outside, attributable to the diffraction caused by thin clouds, mist, or sometimes dust (distinguished from *halo*). **3.** Also called **aureola, aureole.** *Astron.* a faintly luminous envelope outside of the sun's chromosphere, the inner part consisting of highly ionized elements. **4.** a long, straight, untapered cigar, rounded at the closed end. **5.** *Bot.* a crownlike appendage, esp. one on the inner side of a corolla, as in the narcissus. **6.** *Anat.* the upper portion or crown of a part, as of the head. **7.** *Elect.* See **corona discharge.** **8.** *Archit.* the projecting, slablike member of a classical cornice supported by the bed molding or by modillions, dentils, etc., and supporting the cymatium. **9.** the tonsure of a cleric. **10.** *Eccles.* a gold-colored stripe around the lower edge of a clerical headdress, as of a miter. **11.** a chandelier of wrought metal, having the form of one or more concentric hoops. [1555–65; < L *corōna* garland, CROWN < Gk *korṓnē* crown, curved object; akin to *korōnís* curved, beaked, *kórax* CROW, raven]

Co•ro•na (kə rō′nə), *n.* a city in SE California. 37,791.

Co•ro•na Aus•tra•lis (kə rō′nə ô strā′lis), *gen.* **Co•ro•nae Aus•tra•lis** (kə rō′nē ô strā′lis). *Astron.* the Southern Crown, a southern constellation touching the southern part of Sagittarius. [< L: lit., southern crown]

Co•ro•na Bo•re•al•is (kə rō′nə bôr′ē al′is, -ā′lis, -bōr′-), *gen.* **Co•ro•nae Bo•re•al•is** (kə rō′nē bôr′ē al′is, -ā′lis, -bōr′-). *Astron.* the Northern Crown, a northern constellation between Hercules and Boötes. [< L: lit., northern crown]

cor•o•nach (kôr′ə nəKH, kor′-), *n.* (in Scotland and Ireland) a song or lamentation for the dead; dirge. [1490–1500; < ScotGael *corranach,* Ir *coránach* dirge]

coro′na dis′charge, *Elect.* a discharge, frequently luminous, at the surface of a conductor or between two conductors of the same transmission line, accompanied by ionization of the surrounding atmosphere and often by a power loss. Also called **corona, electric glow, St. Elmo's fire.** Cf. **brush discharge.** [1915–20]

Co•ro•na•do (kôr′ə nä′dō, kor′-; *for 1 also Sp.* kô′rô-nä′thō), *n.* **1. Fran•cis•co Vás•quez de** (frän thēs′kô bäs′keth the, frän sēs′kô bäs′kes), 1510–54?, Spanish explorer in North America. **2.** a city in SW California, near San Diego. 16,859.

co•ro•na•graph (kə rō′nə graf′, -gräf′), *n. Astron.* an instrument for observing and photographing the sun's corona, consisting of a telescope fitted with lenses, filters, and diaphragms that simulate an eclipse. Also, **coronograph.** [1885–90; earlier *coronograph.* See CORONA, -GRAPH] **—co•ro•na•graph•ic** (kə rō′nə graf′ik), *adj.*

cor•o•nal (*n.* kôr′ə nl, kor′-; *adj.* kə rōn′l, kôr′ə nl, kor′-), *n.* **1.** a crown; coronet. **2.** a garland. —*adj.* **3.** of or pertaining to a coronal. **4.** *Anat.* **a.** of or pertaining to a corona. **b.** (of a plane along the long axis of the body) lying in the direction of the coronal suture. **c.** Also, **frontal.** lying in the direction of the frontal plane. **5.** *Phonet.* (of a speech sound) articulated with the tip of the tongue, esp. in a retroflex position. **6.** *Ling.* (in distinctive feature analysis) articulated with the blade of the tongue raised; dental, alveolar, or palato-alveolar. **7.** of or pertaining to the tip of the tongue. [1300–50; ME < L *corōnālis,* equiv. to L *corōn(a)* CROWN + *-ālis* -AL[1]] **—cor′o•naled;** *esp. Brit.,* **cor′o•nalled,** *adj.* **—co•ro′nal•ly,** *adv.*

coro′nal hole′, *Astron.* a part of the solar corona that appears dark on optical and x-ray images and is characterized by low temperature and low density. [1970–75]

coro′nal su′ture, *Anat.* a seam extending across the skull where the frontal bone and the parietal bones meet. [1605–15]

co•ro•na ra•di•a•ta (kə rō′nə rā′dē ā′tə), *pl.* **co•ro•nae ra•di•a•tae** (kə rō′nē rā′dē ā′tē). *Anat.* the layer of follicle cells surrounding an ovum and remaining attached to it following ovulation. [1840–50; < NL; see CORONA, RADIATE]

cor•o•nar•y (kôr′ə ner′ē, kor′-), *adj., n., pl.* **-nar•ies.** —*adj.* **1.** of or pertaining to the human heart, with respect to health. **2.** *Med.* **a.** pertaining to the arteries that supply the heart tissues and originate in the root of the aorta. **b.** encircling like a crown, as certain blood vessels. **3.** of or like a crown. —*n.* **4.** *Pathol.* a heart attack, esp. a coronary thrombosis. **5.** a coronary artery. [1600–10; < L *corōnārius,* equiv. to *corōn(a)* CROWN + *-ārius* -ARY; in reference to the heart, extended from CORONARY ARTERY, CORONARY VEIN, etc.]

cor′onary ar′tery, *Anat.* either of two arteries that originate in the aorta and supply the heart muscle with blood. See illus. under **heart.** [1735–45; so called from its crownlike envelopment of the heart]

cor′onary by′pass, the surgical revascularization of the heart, using healthy blood vessels of the patient, performed to circumvent obstructed coronary vessels and improve blood flow.

cor′o•nar•y-care′ u′nit (kôr′ə ner′ē kâr′, kor′-), a specialized hospital unit for the early care and treatment of heart-attack patients. *Abbr.:* CCU

cor′onary cush′ion, a thick band of vascular tissue in the coronet of horses and other hoofed animals that secretes the horny wall of the hoof. Also called **cor′onary ring′, cor′onary band′.**

cor′onary insuffi′ciency, *Pathol.* inadequate blood flow to the heart muscle.

cor′onary occlu′sion, *Pathol.* partial or total obstruction of a coronary artery, as by a thrombus, usually resulting in infarction of the myocardium. [1945–50]

cor′onary si′nus, *Anat.* a large venous channel in the heart wall that receives blood via the coronary veins and empties into the right atrium. [1825–35]

cor′onary thrombo′sis, *Pathol.* a coronary occlusion in which there is blockage of a coronary arterial branch by a blood clot within the vessel, usually at a site narrowed by arteriosclerosis. [1925–30]

cor′onary vein′, *Anat.* any of several veins that receive blood from the heart wall and empty into the coronary sinus. [1825–35; see CORONARY ARTERY]

cor•o•nate (kôr′ə nāt′, kor′-), *adj.*, *v.*, **-nat•ed, -nat•ing.** —*adj.* **1.** having or wearing a crown, coronet, or the like. —*v.t.* **2.** to crown (a sovereign). [1840–50; < L *corōnātus* ptp. of *corōnāre* to CROWN, equiv. to *corōn(a)* crown + *-ātus* -ATE[1]]

cor•o•na•tion (kôr′ə nā′shən, kor′-), *n.* the act or ceremony of crowning a king, queen, or other sovereign. [1350–1400; ME *coronacio(u)n* < AF *coronation* < L *corōnāt(us)* CROWNED (see CORONATE) + MF *-ion* -ION]

co•ro•na•vi•rus (kə rō′nə vī′rəs), *n., pl.* **-rus•es.** any of various RNA-containing spherical viruses of the family Coronaviridae, including several that cause acute respiratory illnesses. [1965–70; so called from the corona-like array of spikes projecting from the capsid]

cor•o•ner (kôr′ə nər, kor′-), *n.* an officer, as of a county or municipality, whose chief function is to investigate by inquest, as before a jury, any death not clearly resulting from natural causes. [1225–75; ME < AF *corouner* supervisor of the Crown's pleas, equiv. to *coroune* CROWN + *-er* -ER[2]] —**cor′o•ner•ship′,** *n.*

cor•o•net (kôr′ə nit, -net′, kor′-, kôr′ə net′, kor′-), *n.* **1.** a small crown. **2.** a crown worn by nobles or peers. **3.** a crownlike ornament for the head, as of gold or jewels. **4.** an ornament, more or less pedimental in form, situated over a door or window. **5.** the lowest part of the pastern of a horse or other hoofed animal, just above the hoof. **6.** Also called **crest coronet.** *Heraldry.* a crownlike support for a crest, used in place of a torse. [1350–1400; ME *corounet.* See CROWN, -ET] —**cor′o•net•like′,** *adj.*

cor•o•net•ed (kôr′ə ni tid, -net′id, kor′-, kôr′ə net′id, kor′-), *adj.* **1.** wearing or entitled to wear a coronet. **2.** of noble birth. Also, **cor′o•net′ted.** [1740–50; CORONET + -ED[3]]

cor•o•ni•tis (kôr′ə nī′tis, kor′-), *n. Vet. Pathol.* inflammation of the coronary cushion of hoofed animals. [1885–90; CORON(A) + -ITIS]

co•ro•ni•um (kə rō′nē əm), *n. Astron.* a hypothetical element once thought to exist because certain spectral lines in the emission spectrum of the solar corona could not be identified by known elements. These lines were subsequently found to be emitted by certain highly ionized metals. [1885–90; CORON(A) + -IUM]

co•ro•no•graph (kə rō′nə graf′, -gräf′), *n. Astron.* coronagraph. [1880–85] —**co•ro•no•graph•ic** (kə rō′nə-graf′ik), *adj.*

Co•rot (kō rō′, kə-; *Fr.* kô rō′), *n.* **Jean Bap•tiste Ca•mille** (zhäN ba tēst′ ka mē′yə), 1796–1875, French painter.

co•ro•tate (kō rō′tāt), *v.i.*, **-tat•ed, -tat•ing.** to rotate jointly, as with another rotating object or field. [1960–65; CO- + ROTATE[1]] —**co′ro•ta′tion,** *n.* —**co′ro•ta′tion•al,** *adj.*

corp., **1.** corporal. **2.** corporation. Also, **Corp.**

corpl., corporal. Also, **Corpl.**

corpn., corporation.

cor•po•ra (kôr′pər ə), *n.* a pl. of **corpus.**

cor•po•ral[1] (kôr′pər əl, -prəl), *adj.* **1.** of the human body; bodily; physical: *corporal suffering.* **2.** *Zool.* of the body proper, as distinguished from the head and limbs. **3.** personal: *corporal possession.* **4.** *Obs.* corporeal; belonging to the material world. [1350–1400; ME *corporall* (< AF) < L *corporālis* bodily, equiv. to *corpor-* (s. of *corpus* CORPUS) + *-ālis* -AL[1]] —**cor′po•ral′i•ty,** *n.* —**cor′po•ral•ly,** *adv.*
—**Syn. 1.** material. See **physical.**

cor•po•ral[2] (kôr′pər əl, -prəl), *n.* **1.** *Mil.* **a.** a noncommissioned officer ranking above a private first class in the U.S. Army or lance corporal in the Marines and below a sergeant. **b.** a similar rank in the armed services of other countries. **2.** (*cap.*) a U.S. surface-to-surface, single-stage ballistic missile. [1570–80; < MF, var. of *caporal* (influenced by *corporal* CORPORAL[1]) < It *caporale,* appar. contr. of phrase *capo corporale* corporal head, i.e., head of a body (of soldiers). See CAPUT] —**cor′po•ral•cy, cor′po•ral•ship′,** *n.*

cor•po•ral[3] (kôr′pər əl, -prəl), *n. Eccles.* a fine cloth, usually of linen, on which the consecrated elements are placed or with which they are covered. Also called **communion cloth.** [1350–1400; ME *corporalle* < ML *corporale* (*pallium*) eucharistic (altar cloth); r. earlier *corporas* < OF < L, as above]

cor′poral pun′ishment, **1.** *Law.* physical punishment, as flogging, inflicted on the body of one convicted of a crime: formerly included the death penalty, sentencing to a term of years, etc. **2.** physical punishment, as spanking, inflicted on a child by an adult in authority.

cor′poral's guard′, **1.** *Mil.* any small detachment. **2.** any small group, as of followers. [1835–45, *Amer.*]

cor•po•rate (kôr′pər it, -prit), *adj.* **1.** of, for, or belonging to a corporation or corporations: *a corporate executive; She considers the new federal subsidy just corporate welfare.* **2.** forming a corporation. **3.** pertaining to a united group, as of persons: *the corporate good.* **4.** united or combined into one. **5.** corporative. —*n.* **6.** a bond issued by a corporation. [1350–1400 for v. senses; 1505–15 for adj. senses; ME *corporaten* < L *corporātus* ptp. of *corporāre* to INCORPORATE; see CORPUS] —**cor′po•rate•ly,** *adv.* —**cor′po•rate•ness,** *n.*

cor′porate cul′ture, the philosophy, values, behavior, dress codes, etc., that together constitute the unique style and policies of a company.

cor′porate im′age, the impression of the policies, personnel, and operations of a corporation that is imparted to its employees and the public.

CONCISE ETYMOLOGY KEY: <, descended or borrowed from; >, whence; b., blend of, blended; c., cognate with; cf., compare; deriv., derivative; equiv., equivalent; imit., imitative; obl., oblique; r., replacing; s., stem; sp., spelling, spelled; resp., respelling, respelled; trans., translation; ?, origin unknown; *, unattested; ‡, probably earlier than. See the full key inside the front cover.

cor′porate lad′der, the hierarchical order of position, title, or rank, as in a large corporation: *to work one's way up the corporate ladder.*

cor′porate park′. See **office park.**

cor′porate raid′er, a person who seizes control of a company, as by secretly buying stock and gathering proxies. [1985–90]

cor•po•ra•tion (kôr′pə rā′shən), *n.* **1.** an association of individuals, created by law or under authority of law, having a continuous existence independent of the existences of its members, and powers and liabilities distinct from those of its members. **2.** (*cap.*) the group of principal officials of a borough or other municipal division in England. **3.** any group of persons united or regarded as united in one body. **4.** *Informal.* a paunch; potbelly. [1400–50; late ME < LL *corporātiōn-* (s. of *corporātiō*) guild, L: physical makeup, build. See CORPORATE, -ION] —**cor′po•ra′tion•al,** *adj.*
—**Usage.** See **collective noun.**

corpora′tion stop′, a cock controlling the flow of water or gas from mains to individual consumers. Also called **corpora′tion cock′.**

cor•po•rat•ism (kôr′pə rə tiz′əm, -prə tiz′-), *n.* the principles, doctrine, or system of corporative organization of a political unit, as a city or state. Also, **cor•po•rat•iv•ism** (kôr′pə rā′tə viz′əm, -pər ə tə-, -prə-). [1885–90; CORPORATE + -ISM] —**cor′po•rat•ist,** *adj.*

cor•po•ra•tive (kôr′pə rā′tiv, -pər ə tiv, -prə-), *adj.* **1.** of or pertaining to a corporation. **2.** of or pertaining to a political system under which the principal economic functions, as banking or industry, are organized as corporate unities. Also, **corporate.** [1825–35; < LL *corporātīvus,* equiv. to L *corporāt(us)* CORPORATE + *-īvus* -IVE]

cor•po•ra•tize (kôr′pər ə tīz′, -prə tīz′), *v.t.*, **-tized, -tiz•ing.** to develop into big business; bring under the control of a corporation. Also, *esp. Brit.,* **cor′po•ra•tise′.** [CORPORATE + -IZE] —**cor′po•ra•ti•za′tion,** *n.*

cor•po•ra•tor (kôr′pə rā′tər), *n.* a member of a corporation, esp. one of the original members. [1775–85; CORPORATE + -OR[2]]

cor•po•re•al (kôr pôr′ē əl, -pōr′-), *adj.* **1.** of the nature of the physical body; bodily. **2.** material; tangible: *corporeal property.* [1375–1425; late ME < L *corpore(us)* bodily (*corpor-* (s. of *corpus*) body + *-eus* adj. suffix) + -AL[1]] —**cor•po′re•al′i•ty, cor•po′re•al•ness,** *n.* —**cor•po′re•al•ly,** *adv.*
—**Syn. 1.** See **physical.** —**Ant. 1.** spiritual.

cor•po•re•i•ty (kôr′pə rē′i tē), *n.* material or physical nature or quality; materiality. [1615–25; < ML *corporeitās,* equiv. to L *corpore(us)* CORPOREAL + *-itās* -ITY]

corps (kôr, kōr), *n., pl.* **corps** (kôrz, kōrz). **1.** *Mil.* **a.** a military organization consisting of officers and enlisted personnel or of officers alone: *the U.S. Marine Corps; corps of cadets.* **b.** a military unit of ground combat forces consisting of two or more divisions and other troops. **2.** a group of persons associated or acting together: *the diplomatic corps; the press corps.* **3.** *Print.* a Continental designation that, preceded by a number, indicates size of type in Didot points of 0.0148 in. (3.8 mm): *14 corps.* **4.** *Obs.* corpse. [1225–75; ME *corps, cors* < MF < L *corpus* body; see CORPSE]

corps de bal•let (kôr′ də ba lā′, bal′ā; *Fr.* kôr də ba le′), the dancers in a ballet company who perform as a group and have no solo parts. [1820–30; < F; see CORPS, BALLET]

corpse (kôrps), *n.* **1.** a dead body, usually of a human being. **2.** something no longer useful or viable: *rusting corpses of old cars.* **3.** *Obs.* a human or animal body, whether alive or dead. [1225–75; ME *corps,* orig. sp. var. of *cors* CORSE but the *p* is now sounded]
—**Syn. 1.** remains, cadaver. See **body.**

corps•man (kôr′mən, kōr′-), *n., pl.* **-men. 1.** *U.S. Navy.* an enlisted person working as a pharmacist or hospital assistant. **2.** *U.S. Army.* an enlisted person in the Medical Corps who accompanies combat troops into battle to give first aid, carry off the wounded, etc. **3.** a member of any corps, as of the Peace Corps. [1940–45, *Amer.*; CORPS + -MAN]

Corps′ of Engineers′, a branch of the U.S. Army responsible for military and many civil engineering projects.

cor•pu•lence (kôr′pyə ləns), *n.* bulkiness or largeness of body; fatness; portliness. Also, **cor′pu•len•cy.** [1350–1400; ME < L *corpulentia.* See CORPULENT, -ENCE]

cor•pu•lent (kôr′pyə lənt), *adj.* large or bulky of body; portly; stout; fat. [1350–1400; ME < L *corpulentus,* equiv. to *corp(us)* body + *-ulentus* -ULENT] —**cor′pu•lent•ly,** *adv.*

cor pul•mo•na•le (kôr′ pŏŏl′mə nal′ē, -nä′lē, -nä′-, pul′-), *pl.* **cor•di•a pul•mo•na•li•a** (kôr′dē ə pŏŏl′mə-nal′ē ə, -nä′lē ə, -nä′-, pul′-). *Pathol.* a heart condition resulting from disease of the lungs or of their blood vessels. [1855–60; < NL: pulmonary heart]

cor•pus (kôr′pəs), *n., pl.* **-po•ra** (-pər ə) for 1–3, 5, **-pus•es** for 4. **1.** a large or complete collection of writings: *the entire corpus of Old English poetry.* **2.** the body of a person or animal, esp. when dead. **3.** *Anat.* a body, mass, or part having a special character or function. **4.** *Ling.* a body of utterances, as words or sentences, assumed to be representative of and used for lexical, grammatical, or other linguistic analysis. **5.** a principal or capital sum, as opposed to interest or income. [1225–75; ME < L]

cor•pus cal•lo•sum (kôr′pəs kə lō′səm), *pl.* **cor•po•ra cal•lo•sa** (kôr′pər ə kə lō′sə). *Anat., Zool.* a great band of deeply situated transverse white fibers uniting the two halves of the cerebrum in humans and other mammals. See illus. under **brain.** [1700–10; < NL: lit., firm body]

Cor•pus Chris•ti (kôr′pəs kris′tē, -tī), *Rom. Cath. Ch.* a festival in honor of the Eucharist, celebrated on the Thursday after Trinity Sunday. [1325–75; ME < ML: lit., body of Christ]

Cor•pus Chris•ti (kôr′pəs kris′tē), a seaport in S Texas. 231,999.

Cor′pus Chris′ti Bay′, a bay in S Texas, at the mouth of the Nueces River.

cor•pus•cle (kôr′pə səl, -pus əl), *n.* **1.** *Biol.* an unattached cell, esp. of a kind that floats freely, as a blood or lymph cell. **2.** *Anat.* a small mass or body forming a more or less distinct part, as the sensory receptors at nerve terminals. **3.** *Physical Chem.* a minute or elementary particle of matter, as an electron, proton, or atom. **4.** any minute particle. Also, **cor•pus•cule** (kôr pus′kyōōl). [1650–60; < L *corpusculum,* equiv. to *corpus* body + *-culum* -CLE[1]] —**cor•pus•cu•lar** (kôr-pus′kyə lər), **cor•pus•cu•lat•ed** (kôr pus′kyə lā′tid), **cor•pus′cu•lous,** *adj.* —**cor•pus•cu•lar•i•ty** (kôr pus′-kyə lar′i tē), *n.*

corpus′cular radia′tion, *Physics, Astron.* radiation consisting of atomic and subatomic particles, as alpha particles, beta particles, and neutrons.

corpus′cular the′ory, *Physics.* the theory that light is transmitted as a stream of particles. Cf. **wave theory.** [1825–35]

cor•pus de•lic•ti (kôr′pəs di lik′tī), *pl.* **cor•po•ra de•lic•ti** (kôr′pər ə di lik′tī). *Law.* **1.** the basic element or fact of a crime, as, in murder, the death of the murdered person. **2.** the object, as the body of a murdered person, upon which a crime has been committed and that serves as evidence proving that the crime was committed. [1825–35; < NL: lit., body of the offense]

cor•pus ju•ris (kôr′pəs jŏŏr′is), a compilation of law, or the collected law of a nation, state, etc. [1825–35; < LL: lit., body of law]

Cor•pus Ju•ris Ci•vi•lis (kôr′pəs jŏŏr′is si vī′lis, si-vil′is), the collective title of the body of ancient Roman law as compiled and codified under the emperor Justinian in the 6th century A.D.: comprises the Digest, the Institutes, the Justinian Code, and the Novels. [1890–95; < NL: lit., body of civil law]

cor•pus lu•te•um (kôr′pəs lōō′tē əm), *pl.* **cor•po•ra lu•te•a** (kôr′pər ə lōō′tē ə). **1.** *Anat., Zool.* a ductless gland developed within the ovary by the reorganization of a Graafian follicle following ovulation. **2.** *Pharm.* an extract of this gland, usually of the hog or cow, the chief product of which is progesterone. [1780–90; < NL: yellow body]

cor•pus stri•a•tum (kôr′pəs strī ā′təm), *pl.* **cor•po•ra stri•a•ta** (kôr′pər ə strī ā′tə). *Anat.* a mass of gray matter beneath the cortex and in front of the thalamus in each cerebral hemisphere. [1850–55; < NL: striated body]

corr., **1.** correct. **2.** corrected. **3.** correction. **4.** correspond. **5.** correspondence. **6.** correspondent. **7.** corresponding. **8.** corrupt. **9.** corrupted. **10.** corruption.

cor•rade (kə rād′, kô-), *v.*, **-rad•ed, -rad•ing.** —*v.i.* **1.** (of a moving agent, as running water, wind, or a glacier) to erode by the abrasion of materials carried along. **2.** to disintegrate as a result of corrasion, as the rock underlying the brink of a waterfall. —*v.t.* **3.** to wear down by corrasion; abrade. [1610–20; < L *corrādere* to scrape together, equiv. to *cor-* COR- + *rādere* to scrape. See ERASE, RAZE]

cor•ral (kə ral′), *n.*, *v.*, **-ralled, -ral•ling.** —*n.* **1.** an enclosure or pen for horses, cattle, etc. **2.** a circular enclosure formed by wagons during an encampment, as by covered wagons crossing the North American plains in the 19th century, for defense against attack. —*v.t.* **3.** to confine in or as if in a corral. **4.** *Informal.* **a.** to seize; capture. **b.** to collect, gather, or garner: *to corral votes.* **5.** to form (wagons) into a corral. [1575–85; < Sp < LL **currāle* enclosure for carts, equiv. to L *curr(us)* wagon, cart (deriv. of *currere* to run) + *-āle,* neut. of *-ālis* -AL[1]]

cor•ra•sion (kə rā′zhən), *n.* the mechanical erosion of soil and rock by the abrasive action of particles set in motion by running water, wind, glacial ice, and gravity. [1605–15; < L *corrās(us)* scraped together (ptp. of *corrādere*) + -ION. See CORRADE] —**cor•ra•sive** (kə rā′siv), *adj.*

cor•rect (kə rekt′), *v.t.* **1.** to set or make true, accurate, or right; remove the errors or faults from: *The native guide corrected our pronunciation. The new glasses corrected his eyesight.* **2.** to point out or mark the errors in: *The teacher corrected the examination papers.* **3.** to scold, rebuke, or punish in order to improve: *Should parents correct their children in public?* **4.** to counteract the operation or effect of (something hurtful or undesirable): *The medication will correct stomach acidity.* **5.** *Math., Physics.* to alter or adjust so as to bring into accordance with a standard or with a required condition. —*v.i.* **6.** to make a correction or corrections. **7.** (of stock prices) to reverse a trend, esp. temporarily, as after a sharp advance or decline in previous trading sessions. —*adj.* **8.** conforming to fact or truth; free from error; accurate: *a correct answer.* **9.** in accordance with an acknowledged or accepted standard; proper: *correct behavior.* [1300–50; (v.) ME *correcten* (< AF *correcter*) < L *corrēctus* ptp. of *corrigere* to make straight, equiv. to *cor-* COR- + *reg-* (s. of *regere* to DIRECT) + *-tus* ptp. suffix; (adj.) (< F *correct*) < L, as above] —**cor•rect′a•ble, cor•rect′i•ble,** *adj.* —**cor•rect′a•bil′i•ty, cor•rect′i•bil′i•ty,** *n.* —**cor•rect′ing•ly,** *adv.* —**cor•rect′ly,** *adv.* —**cor•rect′ness,** *n.* —**cor•rec′tor,** *n.*
—**Syn. 3.** warn, chasten, castigate. See **punish. 8.** faultless, perfect, exact. CORRECT, ACCURATE, PRECISE imply conformity to fact, standard, or truth. A CORRECT statement is one free from error, mistakes, or faults. An ACCURATE statement is one that shows careful conformity to fact, truth, or spirit. A PRECISE statement shows scrupulously strict and detailed conformity to fact.

correct′ing plate′, *Optics.* a thin lens used to correct incoming light rays in special forms of reflecting telescopes. Also, **corrector plate.**

cor•rec•tion (kə rek′shən), *n.* **1.** something that is substituted or proposed for what is wrong or inaccurate; emendation. **2.** the act of correcting. **3.** punishment intended to reform, improve, or rehabilitate; chastisement; reproof. **4.** Usually, **corrections.** the various methods, as incarceration, parole, and probation, by which society deals with convicted offenders. **5.** a quantity applied or other adjustment made in order to increase accuracy, as in the use of an instrument or the solution of a problem: *A five degree correction will put the ship on course.* **6.** a reversal of the trend of stock prices, esp. temporarily, as after a sharp advance or decline in the previous trading sessions. [1300–50; ME *correccio(u)n* (< AF) < L *corrēctiōn-* (s. of *corrēctiō*) a setting straight. See CORRECT, -ION]

cor•rec•tion•al (kə rek′shə nl), *adj.* of or pertaining to correction, esp. to penal correction. [1830–40; CORRECTION + -AL[1]]

correc′tional facil′ity, a prison, esp. for long-term confinement. Also, **correc′tion facil′ity.** [1970–75]

correc′tional of′ficer, an officer of a jail or prison, esp. a guard. Also, **correc′tion of′ficer, correc′tions of′ficer.** [1970–75]

correc′tion flu′id, an opaque, quick-drying fluid for obliterating handwritten or typewritten matter.

cor•rect•i•tude (kə rek′ti to͞od′, -tyo͞od′), *n.* correctness, esp. of manners and conduct. [1890–95; b. CORRECT and RECTITUDE]

cor•rec•tive (kə rek′tiv), *adj.* **1.** tending to correct or rectify; remedial: *corrective exercises.* —*n.* **2.** a means of correcting; corrective agent. [1525–35; (< AF) < ML *corrēctīvus.* See CORRECT, -IVE] —**cor•rec′tive•ly,** *adv.*

correc′tor plate′, *Optics.* See **correcting plate.**

Cor•reg•gio (kə rej′ō, -rej′ē ō′; *It.* kôr red′jô), *n.* **Antonio Al•le•gri da** (än tô′nyô äl le′grē dä), 1494–1534, Italian painter.

cor•reg•i•dor (kə reg′i dôr′, -dōr′; *Sp.* kôr re′hē-t͟hôr′), *n., pl.* **-dors, -do•res** (-dôr′ēz, -dōr′-; *Sp.* -t͟hô′res). **1.** the chief magistrate of a town in Spain. **2.** *Hist.* (in Spanish America) **a.** a minor administrative unit. **b.** the chief officer of such a district. [1585–95; < Sp, deriv. of *corregir* to CORRECT]

Cor•reg•i•dor (kə reg′i dôr′, -dōr′; *Sp.* kôr re′hē-t͟hôr′), *n.* an island in Manila Bay, in the Philippines: U.S. forces defeated by the Japanese in May, 1942. 2 sq. mi. (5 sq. km).

correl., correlative.

cor•re•late (*v., adj.* kôr′ə lāt′, kor′-; *n.* kôr′ə lit, -lāt′, kor′-), *v.,* **-lat•ed, -lat•ing,** *adj., n.* —*v.t.* **1.** to place in or bring into mutual or reciprocal relation; establish in orderly connection: *to correlate expenses and income.* —*v.i.* **2.** to have a mutual or reciprocal relation; stand in correlation: *The results of the two tests correlate to a high degree.* —*adj.* **3.** mutually or reciprocally related. —*n.* **4.** either of two related things, esp. when one implies the other. [1635–45; prob. back formation from CORRELATION and CORRELATIVE] —**cor′re•lat′a•ble,** *adj.*

cor•re•la•tion (kôr′ə lā′shən, kor′-), *n.* **1.** mutual relation of two or more things, parts, etc. **2.** the act of correlating or state of being correlated. **3.** *Statistics.* the degree to which two or more attributes or measurements on the same group of elements show a tendency to vary together. **4.** *Physiol.* the interdependence or reciprocal relations of organs or functions. **5.** *Geol.* the demonstrable equivalence, in age or lithology, of two or more stratigraphic units, as formations or members of such. Also, *esp. Brit.,* **corelation.** [1555–65; < ML *correlātiōn-* (s. of *correlātiō*). See COR-, RELATION] —**cor′re•la′tion•al,** *adj.*

correla′tion coeffi′cient, *Statistics.* one of a number of measures of correlation, usually assuming values from +1 to −1. Also called **coefficient of correlation.** [1905–10]

correla′tion ra′tio, *Statistics.* the ratio of the variance between arrays of data within a sample to the variance of the whole sample.

cor•rel•a•tive (kə rel′ə tiv), *adj.* **1.** so related that each implies or complements the other. **2.** being in correlation; mutually related. **3.** *Gram.* answering to or complementing one another and regularly used in association, as *either* and *or, not only* and *but.* **4.** *Biol.* (of a typical structure of an organism) found in correlation with another. —*n.* **5.** either of two things, as two terms, that are correlative. **6.** *Gram.* a correlative expression. Also, *esp. Brit.,* **corelative.** [1520–30; < ML *correlātīvus.* See COR-, RELATIVE] —**cor•rel′a•tive•ly,** *adv.* —**cor•rel′a•tive•ness, cor•rel′a•tiv′i•ty,** *n.*

correl′ative conjunc′tion, *Gram.* either member of a matched pair of words, of which the second is a coordinating conjunction, as *either . . . or, neither . . . nor, both . . . and,* or *not only . . . but.*

corresp., correspondence.

cor•re•spond (kôr′ə spond′, kor′-), *v.i.* **1.** to be in agreement or conformity (often fol. by *with* or *to*): *His actions do not correspond with his words.* **2.** to be similar or analogous; be equivalent in function, position, amount, etc. (usually fol. by *to*): *The U.S. Congress corresponds to the British Parliament.* **3.** to communicate by exchange of letters. [1520–30; < (< MF) ML *correspondēre.* See COR-, RESPOND] —**cor′re•spond′ing•ly,** *adv.*
—**Syn. 1.** harmonize, match, tally. CORRESPOND, AGREE, ACCORD imply comparing persons or things and finding that they harmonize. CORRESPOND suggests having an obvious similarity, though not agreeing in every detail: *Part of this report corresponds with the facts.* AGREE implies having or arriving at a condition in which no essential difference of opinion or detail is evident: *All the reports agree.* ACCORD emphasizes agreeing exactly, both in fact and in point of view: *This report accords with the other.*

cor•re•spond•ence (kôr′ə spon′dəns, kor′-), *n.* **1.** communication by exchange of letters. **2.** a letter or letters that pass between correspondents: *It will take me all day to answer this business correspondence.* **3.** Also, **correspondency.** an instance of corresponding. **4.** similarity or analogy. **5.** agreement; conformity. **6.** news, commentary, letters, etc., received from a newspaper or magazine correspondent. **7.** *Math.* function (def. 4a). [1375–1425; late ME (< MF) < ML *correspondentia.* See CORRESPONDENT, -ENCE]
—**Syn. 5.** accord, concord, consonance.

Correspond′ence Commit′tee. See **Committee of Correspondence.**

correspond′ence course′, a course of instruction provided by a correspondence school. [1900–05]

correspond′ence prin′ciple, *Physics.* the principle that the laws of quantum mechanics and of any new theory that may be developed reduce to the laws of Newtonian mechanics and electromagnetic theory when applied to systems in which Planck's constant can be regarded as negligible, wavelengths are comparatively small, dimensions are relatively large, etc. Also called **principle of correspondence.** [1920–25]

correspond′ence school′, a school operating on a system in which study materials and tests are mailed to the students, who in turn mail their work back to the school for grading. [1885–90]

correspond′ence the′ory, *Philos.* the theory of truth that a statement is rendered true by the existence of a fact with corresponding elements and a similar structure. Cf. **coherence theory, pragmatic theory.** [1900–05]

cor•re•spond•en•cy (kôr′ə spon′dən sē, kor′-), *n., pl.* **-cies.** correspondence (def. 3). [1580–90]

cor•re•spond•ent (kôr′ə spon′dənt, kor′-), *n.* **1.** a person who communicates by letters. **2.** a person employed by a news agency, periodical, television network, etc., to gather, report, or contribute news, articles, and the like regularly from a distant place. **3.** a person who contributes a letter or letters to a newspaper, magazine, etc. **4.** a person or firm that has regular business relations with another, esp. at a distance. **5.** a thing that corresponds to something else. —*adj.* **6.** consistent, similar, or analogous; corresponding. [1375–1425; late ME < ML *correspondent-* (s. of *correspondēns*), prp. of *correspondēre* to CORRESPOND; see -ENT] —**cor′re•spond′ent•ly,** *adv.*

correspond′ent bank′, a bank that performs services for one or more other banks. [1960–65] —**correspond′ent bank′ing.**

cor•re•spond•ing (kôr′ə spon′ding, kor′-), *adj.* **1.** identical in all essentials or respects: *corresponding fingerprints.* **2.** similar in position, purpose, form, etc.: *corresponding officials in two states.* **3.** associated in a working or other relationship: *a bolt and its corresponding nut.* **4.** dealing with correspondence: *a corresponding secretary.* **5.** employing the mails as a means of association: *a corresponding member of a club.* [1570–80; CORRESPOND + -ING[2]] —**cor′re•spond′ing•ly,** *adv.*

cor′respond′ing an′gles, *Geom.* two nonadjacent angles made by the crossing of two lines by a third line, one angle being interior, the other exterior, and both being on the same side of the third line. Cf. **alternate angles.** [1790–1800]

cor•re•spon•sive (kôr′ə spon′siv, kor′-), *adj.* responsive to effort or impulse; answering. [1600–10; < ML *correspons(us)* (ptp. of *correspondēre* to CORRESPOND, equiv. to *correspond-* v.s. + *-tus* ptp. suffix) + -IVE] —**cor′re•spon′sive•ly,** *adv.*

Cor•rèze (kô rez′), *n.* a department in central France. 240,363; 2273 sq. mi. (5885 sq. km). *Cap.:* Tulle.

cor•ri•da (kô rē′də; *Sp.* kôr rē′t͟hä), *n., pl.* **-das** (-dəz; *Sp.* -t͟häs). a bullfight. [1895–1900; < Sp, short for *corrida de toros* lit., course, running of bulls; *corrida,* fem. of *corrido,* ptp. of *correr* < L *currere* to run]

cor•ri•do (kô rē′dō; *Sp.* kôr rē′t͟hô), *n., pl.* **-dos** (-dōz; *Sp.* -t͟hôs). a Mexican ballad or folksong about struggle against oppression and injustice. [< MexSp, Sp; see CORRIDA]

cor•ri•dor (kôr′i dər, -dôr′, kor′-), *n.* **1.** a gallery or passage connecting parts of a building; hallway. **2.** a passage into which several rooms or apartments open. **3.** a passageway in a passenger ship or railroad car permitting access to separate cabins or compartments. **4.** a narrow tract of land forming a passageway, as one connecting two major cities or one belonging to an inland country and affording an outlet to the sea: *the Polish Corridor.* **5.** a usually densely populated region characterized by one or more well-traveled routes used by railroad, airline, or other carriers: *The Northeast corridor extends from Washington, D.C., to Boston.* **6.** *Aeron.* a restricted path along which an aircraft must travel to avoid hostile action, other air traffic, etc. **7.** *Aerospace.* a carefully calculated path through the atmosphere along which a space vehicle must travel after launch or during reentry in order to attain a desired orbit, to avoid severe acceleration and deceleration, or to minimize aerodynamic heating. [1585–95; < MF < Upper It *corridore* (Tuscan *corridoio*), equiv. to *corr(ere)* to run (< L *currere*) + *-idore* < L *-i-tōrium;* see -I-, -TORY[2]] —**cor′ri•dored,** *adj.*

cor•rie (kôr′ē, kor′ē), *n. Scot.* a circular hollow in the side of a hill or mountain. [1785–95; < ScotGael *coire* cauldron, whirlpool, hollow]

Cor•rie•dale (kôr′ē dāl′, kor′-), *n.* one of a breed of sheep raised originally in New Zealand and noted for their high-quality wool and good market lambs. [1900–05; after an estate near Otago Harbor, New Zealand, where the breed was developed]

Cor•ri•en•tes (kôr′rē en′tes), *n.* a port in NE Argentina, on the Paraná River. 179,590.

Cor•ri•gan (kôr′i gən, kor′-), *n.* **Mai•read** (mə rād′), born 1944, Northern Irish peace activist: Nobel peace prize 1976.

cor•ri•gen•dum (kôr′i jen′dəm, kor′-), *n., pl.* **-da** (-də). **1.** an error to be corrected, esp. an error in print. **2. corrigenda,** a list of corrections of errors in a book or other publication. [1840–50; < L: lit., (something) to be corrected (neut. ger. of *corrigere*); see CORRECT]

cor•ri•gi•ble (kôr′i jə bəl, kor′-), *adj.* **1.** capable of being corrected or reformed: *a corrigible criminal.* **2.** submissive to correction. **3.** subject to being revised, improved, or made more accurate: *a corrigible theory.* [1425–75; late ME (< MF) < ML *corrigibilis,* equiv. to L *corrig(ere)* to CORRECT + *-ibilis* -IBLE] —**cor′ri•gi•bil′i•ty, cor′ri•gi•ble•ness,** *n.* —**cor′ri•gi•bly,** *adv.*

cor•ri•val (kə rī′vəl), —*n.* **1.** a rival; competitor. —*adj.* **2.** rival; competitive. [1570–80; < L *corrīvālis* joint rival. See COR-, RIVAL] —**cor•ri′val•ry,** *n.*

cor•rob•o•rant (kə rob′ər ənt), *adj.* **1.** corroborating; confirming. **2.** *Archaic.* strengthening; invigorating, as a medicine. —*n.* **3.** something that corroborates or strengthens. **4.** *Archaic.* a strengthening medicine. [1620–30; < L *corrōborant-* (s. of *corrōborāns*) strengthening, prp. of *corrōborāre.* See CORROBORATE, -ANT]

cor•rob•o•rate (*v.* kə rob′ə rāt′; *adj.* kə rob′ər it), *v.,* **-rat•ed, -rat•ing,** *adj.* —*v.t.* **1.** to make more certain; confirm: *He corroborated my account of the accident.* —*adj.* **2.** *Archaic.* confirmed. [1520–30; < L *corrōborātus* ptp. of *corrōborāre* to strengthen, equiv. to *cor-* COR- + *rōbor(āre)* to make strong (deriv. of *rōbor, rōbur* oak (hence, strength); see ROBUST) + *-ātus* -ATE[1]] —**cor•rob•o•ra•tive** (kə rob′ə rā′tiv, -ər ə tiv), **cor•rob•o•ra•to•ry,** *adj.* —**cor•rob′o•ra′tive•ly, cor•rob′o•ra•to′ri•ly,** *adv.* —**cor•rob′o•ra′tor,** *n.*
—**Syn. 1.** verify, authenticate, support, validate.

cor•rob•o•ra•tion (kə rob′ə rā′shən), *n.* **1.** the act of corroborating. **2.** a corroboratory fact, statement, etc. [1425–75; late ME (< MF) < LL *corrōborātiōn-* (s. of *corrōborātiō*). See CORROBORATE, -ION]

cor•rob•o•ree (kə rob′ə rē), *n. Australian.* **1.** an assembly of Aborigines typified by singing and dancing, sometimes associated with traditional sacred rites. **2.** a social gathering, esp. of a boisterous nature. Also, **cor•rob′bo•ree.** [1793; < Dharuk *ga-ra-ba-ra* dance]

cor•rode (kə rōd′), *v.,* **-rod•ed, -rod•ing.** —*v.t.* **1.** to eat or wear away gradually as if by gnawing, esp. by chemical action. **2.** to impair; deteriorate: *Jealousy corroded his character.* —*v.i.* **3.** to become corroded. [1350–1400; ME (< MF) < L *corrōdere* to gnaw to pieces, equiv. to *cor-* COR- + *rōdere* to gnaw; akin to RODENT] —**cor•rod′ent,** *n.* —**cor•rod′er,** *n.* —**cor•rod′i•ble,** *adj.* —**cor•rod′i•bil′i•ty,** *n.*

cor•ro•dy (kôr′ə dē, kor′-), *n., pl.* **-dies.** *Old Eng. Law.* corody.

cor•ro•sion (kə rō′zhən), *n.* **1.** the act or process of corroding; condition of being corroded. **2.** a product of corroding, as rust. [1350–1400; ME (< MF) < LL *corrōsiōn-* (s. of *corrōsiō*) a gnawing away, equiv. to L *corrōs(us),* ptp. of *corrōdere* to CORRODE + *-iōn-* -ION] —**cor•ro′sion•al,** *adj.*

cor•ro•sive (kə rō′siv), *adj.* **1.** having the quality of corroding or eating away; erosive. **2.** harmful or destructive; deleterious: *the corrosive effect of poverty on their marriage.* **3.** sharply sarcastic; caustic: *corrosive comments on the speaker's integrity.* —*n.* **4.** something corrosive, as an acid or drug. [1350–1400; late ME (< MF) < ML *corrōsīvus,* equiv. to L *corrōs(us)* (see CORROSION) + *-īvus* -IVE; r. ME *corosif* < MF (< L as above)] —**cor•ro′sive•ly,** *adv.* —**cor•ro′sive•ness, cor•ro•siv•i•ty** (kôr′ō siv′i tē, kor′-), *n.*

corro′sive sub′limate. *Chem. Now Rare.* mercuric chloride. [1700–10]

cor•ru•gate (*v.* kôr′ə gāt′, kor′-; *adj.* kôr′ə git, -gāt′, kor′-), *v.,* **-gat•ed, -gat•ing,** *adj.* —*v.t.* **1.** to draw or bend into folds or alternate furrows and ridges. **2.** to wrinkle, as the skin or face. **3.** *Western U.S.* to make irrigation ditches in (a field). —*v.i.* **4.** to become corrugated; undergo corrugation. —*adj.* **5.** corrugated; wrinkled; furrowed. [1375–1425; late ME < L *corrūgātus* ptp. of *corrūgāre,* equiv. to *cor-* COR- + *rūg(āre)* to wrinkle + *-ātus* -ATE[1]] —**cor′ru•gat′ed,** *adj.* —**cor′ru•ga′tor,** *n.*

cor′rugated i′ron, a type of sheet iron or steel strengthened for use in construction by having a series of alternating grooves and ridges forced into it, and usually galvanized for weather resistance. [1885–90]

cor′rugated pa′per, heavy paper with ridges and grooves, used in packing fragile articles. [1895–1900]

cor•ru•ga•tion (kôr′ə gā′shən, kor′-), *n.* **1.** the act or state of corrugating or of being corrugated. **2.** a wrinkle; fold; furrow; ridge. [1520–30; < ML *corrūgātiōn-* (s. of *corrūgātiō*) a wrinkling. See CORRUGATE, -ION]

cor•rupt (kə rupt′), *adj.* **1.** guilty of dishonest practices, as bribery; lacking integrity; crooked: *a corrupt judge.* **2.** debased in character; depraved; perverted; wicked; evil: *a corrupt society.* **3.** made inferior by errors or alterations, as a text. **4.** infected; tainted. **5.** decayed; putrid. —*v.t.* **6.** to destroy the integrity of; cause to be dishonest, disloyal, etc., esp. by bribery. **7.** to lower morally; pervert: *to corrupt youth.* **8.** to alter (a language, text, etc.) for the worse; debase. **9.** to mar; spoil. **10.** to infect; taint. **11.** to make putrid or putrescent. **12.** *Eng. Law.* to subject (an attainted person) to corruption of blood. —*v.i.* **13.** to become corrupt. [1250–1300; ME (< AF) < L *corruptus* broken in pieces, corrupted (ptp. of *corrumpere*), equiv. to *cor-* COR- + *rup-* (var. s. of *rumpere* to break) + *-tus* ptp. suffix] —**cor•rupt′ed•ly,** *adv.* —**cor•rupt′ed•ness,** *n.* —**cor•rupt′er, cor•rup′tor,** *n.* —**cor•rup′tive,** *adj.* —**cor•rup′tive•ly,** *adv.* —**cor•rupt′ly,** *adv.* —**cor•rupt′ness,** *n.*
—**Syn. 1.** false, untrustworthy. CORRUPT, DISHONEST, VENAL apply to one, esp. in public office, who acts on mercenary motives, without regard to honor, right, or justice. A CORRUPT politician is one originally honest who has succumbed to temptation and begun questionable practices. A DISHONEST politician is one lacking native integrity. A VENAL politician is one so totally debased as to sell patronage. **3, 4.** contaminated. **4, 5.** putrescent, rotten, spoiled. **6.** demoralize, bribe. **7.** debase, vitiate. **10.** contaminate, pollute, spoil, defile. **11.** putrefy.

cor·rupt·i·ble (kə rup′tə bəl), *adj.* that can or might be corrupted. [1300–50; ME (< AF) < LL *corruptibilis* < L *corrupt(us)* (see CORRUPT) + *-ibilis* -IBLE] **—cor·rupt′i·bil′i·ty, cor·rupt′i·ble·ness,** *n.* **—cor·rupt′i·bly,** *adv.*

cor·rup·tion (kə rup′shən), *n.* **1.** the act of corrupting or state of being corrupt. **2.** moral perversion; depravity. **3.** perversion of integrity. **4.** corrupt or dishonest proceedings. **5.** bribery. **6.** debasement or alteration, as of language or a text. **7.** a debased form of a word. **8.** putrefactive decay; rottenness. **9.** any corrupting influence or agency. [1300–50; ME *corrupcio(u)n* (< AF) < L *corruptiōn-,* s. of *corruptiō.* See CORRUPT, -ION]
—Syn. 2. dissolution, immorality. **8.** rot, putrefaction, putrescence, foulness, pollution, contamination. **—Ant. 1–3.** purity. **3, 4.** honesty.

cor·rup·tion·ist (kə rup′shə nist), *n.* a person who practices or endorses corruption, esp. in politics. [1800–10; CORRUPTION + -IST]

corrup′tion of blood′, *Eng. Law.* the impurity before law that results from attainder and disqualifies the attainted person from inheriting, retaining, or bequeathing lands or interests in lands: abolished in 1870. [1555–65]

corrupt′ prac′tices act′, any of several U.S. statutes for ensuring the purity of elections by forbidding the purchase of votes, restricting the amount and source of political contributions, limiting campaign expenditures, and requiring the submission of an itemized statement of such expenditures. [1880–85]

cor·sage (kôr säzh′), *n.* **1.** a small bouquet worn at the waist, on the shoulder, on the wrist, etc., by a woman. **2.** the body or waist of a dress; bodice. [1475–85; < MF: bodily shape (later: bust, bodice, corsage), equiv. to *cors* body (< L *corpus*) + *-age* -AGE]

cor·sair (kôr′sâr), *n.* **1.** a fast ship used for piracy. **2.** a pirate, esp. formerly of the Barbary Coast. **3.** *(cap.) Mil.* a gull-winged, propeller-driven fighter plane built for the U.S. Navy in World War II and kept in service into the early 1950's. [1540–50; < MF *corsaire* < Pr *corsar(i)* < Upper It *corsaro* < ML *cursārius,* equiv. to L *curs(us)* COURSE + *-ārius* -ARY]

corse (kôrs), *n. Archaic.* corpse. [1225–75; ME *cors* < OF < L *corpus* body; see CORPSE]

Corse (kôrs), *n.* French name of **Corsica.**

cor·se·let (kôr′sə let′ *for 1;* kôrs′lit *for 2*), *n.* **1.** Also, **cor′se·lette′.** a woman's lightweight foundation garment combining a brassiere and girdle in one piece. **2.** Also, **corslet.** *Armor.* **a.** a suit of light half armor or three-quarter armor of the 16th century or later. **b.** cuirass (def. 1). [1490–1500; < MF, equiv. to *cors* bodice, body + *-elet* -LET]

C, **corselet** (def. 2a) of English pikeman (17th century); M, morion

cor·set (kôr′sit), *n.* **1.** Sometimes, **corsets.** a close-fitting undergarment, stiffened with whalebone or similar material and often capable of being tightened by lacing, enclosing the trunk: worn, esp. by women, to shape and support the body; stays. *—v.t.* **2.** to dress or furnish with or as if with a corset. **3.** to regulate strictly; constrict. [1225–75; ME < AF, OF, equiv. to *cors* bodice, body + *-et* -ET] **—cor′set·less,** *adj.*

cor′set cov′er, an undergarment, as a camisole, worn over the upper part of a corset.

cor·se·tiere (kôr′si tēr′), *n.* a person who specializes in making, fitting, or selling corsets, brassieres, or other foundation garments. [1840–50; < F *corsetière,* fem. of *corsetier;* see CORSET, -IER²]

Cor·si·ca (kôr′si kə), *n.* an island in the Mediterranean, SE of and forming a department of France. 220,000; 3367 sq. mi. (8720 sq. km). *Cap.:* Ajaccio. French, **Corse.** **—Cor′si·can,** *adj., n.*

Cor·si·can·a (kôr′si kan′ə), *n.* a city in E Texas. 21,712.

CONCISE ETYMOLOGY KEY: <, descended or borrowed from; >, whence; b., blend of, blended; c., cognate with; cf., compare; deriv., derivative; equiv., equivalent; imit., imitative; obl., oblique; r., replacing; s., stem; sp., spelling, spelled; resp., respelling, respelled; trans., translation; ?, origin unknown; *, unattested; ‡, probably earlier than. See the full key inside the front cover.

cors·let (kôrs′lit), *n.* corselet (def. 2).

cort., (in prescriptions) the bark. [< L *cortex*]

Cor·tá·zar (kôr tä′sär), *n.* **Ju·lio** (ho͞o′lyô), 1914–84, Argentine novelist and short-story writer; French citizen after 1981.

cor·tege (kôr tezh′, -tāzh′), *n.* **1.** a procession, esp. a ceremonial one: *a funeral cortege.* **2.** a line or train of attendants; retinue. Also, **cor·tège′.** [1670–80; < F < It *corteggio* courtly retinue, deriv. of *corteggiare* to court, itself deriv. of *corte* COURT]

Cor·tel·you (kôr′tl yo͞o′), *n.* **George Bruce,** 1862–1940, U.S. cabinet officer and public utility director.

Cor·tes (kôr′tiz; *Sp.* kôʀ′tes), *n.* (in Spain or Portugal) the two houses constituting the national legislative body. [1660–70; < Sp, pl. of *corte* COURT]

Cor·tés (kôr tez′; *Sp.* kôʀ tes′), *n.* **Her·nan·do** (eʀ nän′dô) or **Her·nán** (eʀ nän′), 1485–1547, Spanish conqueror of Mexico. Also, **Cor·tez′.**

cor·tex (kôr′teks), *n., pl.* **-ti·ces** (-tə sēz′). **1.** *Anat., Zool.* **a.** the outer region of an organ or structure, as the outer portion of the kidney. **b.** the cerebral cortex. **2.** *Bot.* **a.** the portion of a stem between the epidermis and the vascular tissue; bark. **b.** any outer layer, as rind. **3.** *Mycol.* the surface tissue layer of a fungus or lichen, composed of massed hyphal cells. [1650–60; < L: bark, rind, shell, husk]

Cor·ti (kôr′tē), *n.* **Al·fon·so** (al fon′sō; *It.* äl fôn′sô), 1822–76, Italian anatomist.

cor·ti·cal (kôr′ti kəl), *adj.* **1.** *Anat.* of, pertaining to, resembling, or consisting of cortex. **2.** *Physiol.* resulting from the function or condition of the cerebral cortex. **3.** *Bot.* of or pertaining to the cortex. [1665–75; < NL *corticālis,* equiv. to L *cortic-* (s. of *cortex*) CORTEX + *-ālis* -AL¹] **—cor′ti·cal·ly,** *adv.*

cor·ti·cate (kôr′ti kit, -kāt′), *adj.* having a cortex. Also, **cor′ti·cat′ed.** [1840–50; < L *corticātus,* equiv. to *cortic-* (s. of *cortex*) CORTEX + *-ātus* -ATE¹] **—cor′ti·ca′tion,** *n.*

cortico-, a combining form representing **cortex** in compound words: *corticosteroid.* [< L *cortic-* (s. of *cortex*) CORTEX) + -O-]

cor·tic·o·lous (kôr tik′ə ləs), *adj. Bot., Zool.* living or growing on or in bark. [1855–60; < L *corti(c)-* (s. of *cortex*) CORTEX + -COLOUS]

cor·ti·co·ster·oid (kôr′tə kō ster′oid, -stēr′-), *n. Biochem.* any of a class of steroids, as aldosterone, hydrocortisone, or cortisone, occurring in nature, esp. as a product of the adrenal cortex, or synthesized. Also called **cor·ti·coid** (kôr′tə koid′). [1940–45; CORTICO- + STEROID]

cor·ti·cos·ter·one (kôr′ti kos′tə rōn′, -kō stə rōn′), *n. Biochem.* a steroid hormone, secreted by the adrenal cortex, that is involved in regulation of the water and electrolyte balance of the body. [1935–40; CORTICO- + STER(OL) + -ONE]

cor·ti·co·tro·pin (kôr′ti kō trō′pin), *n. Biochem.* See **ACTH.** [1940–45; (ADRENO)CORTICOTROP(IC) + -IN²]

corticotro′pin releas′ing fac′tor, *Biochem.* a hormonelike factor, produced by the hypothalamus, that stimulates the increased release of corticotropin by the pituitary gland in response to stress. *Abbr.:* CRF

cor·ti·na (kôr tī′nə, -tē′nə), *n., pl.* **-ti·nae** (-tī′nē, -tē′nī). *Mycol.* a weblike, often evanescent veil covering the gills or hanging from the cap edge of certain mushrooms, particularly those of genus *Cortinarius,* and sometimes persisting as a ring or remnant of fibrils around the mushroom stalk. [1825–35; < NL; LL *cortina* CURTAIN]

cor·ti·sol (kôr′tə sôl′, -sol′), *n.* **1.** *Biochem.* one of several steroid hormones produced by the adrenal cortex and resembling cortisone in its action.. **2.** *Pharm.* hydrocortisone. [1950–55; CORTIS(ONE) + -OL¹]

cor·ti·sone (kôr′tə zōn′, -sōn′), *n.* **1.** *Biochem.* a steroid hormone of the adrenal cortex, $C_{21}H_{28}O_5$, active in carbohydrate and protein metabolism. **2.** *Pharm.* a commercial form of this compound, obtained by extraction from the adrenal glands of certain domesticated animals or produced synthetically, used chiefly in the treatment of arthritis, rheumatic fever, certain allergies, and other systemic conditions. [1949; shortening of *corticosterone;* see STEROL, -ONE]

Cort·land (kôrt′lənd), *n.* a city in central New York. 20,138.

Cort·land (kôrt′lənd), *n.* **1.** a crisp, red variety of apple. **2.** a tree bearing this fruit. [1940–45; *Amer.*]

Cor·to·na (kôʀ tô′nä), *n.* **Pie·tro da** (pye′tʀô dä), *(Pietro Berrettini),* 1596–1669, Italian painter and architect.

Co·rum·bá (kô′ʀo͞on bä′), *n.* a city in W Brazil. 89,199.

Co·ru·ña (kə ro͞on′yə; *Sp* kô ʀo͞o′nyä), *n.* See **La Coruña.** Also, **Co·run·na** (kə run′ə).

co·run·dum (kə run′dəm), *n.* a common mineral, aluminum oxide, Al_2O_3, notable for its hardness: transparent varieties, as sapphire and ruby, are used as gems, other varieties as abrasives: often made synthetically. [1720–30; < Tamil *kuruntam;* akin to Skt *kuruvinda* ruby]

co·rus·cant (kə rus′kənt, kôr′əs-, kor′-), *adj.* sparkling or gleaming; scintillating; coruscating. [1475–85; < L *coruscant-* s. of *coruscāns* prp. of *coruscāre* to quiver, flash, deriv. of *coruscus* quivering, flashing; see -ANT]

cor·us·cate (kôr′ə skāt′, kor′-), *v.i.,* **-cat·ed, -cat·ing.** to emit vivid flashes of light; sparkle; scintillate; gleam. [1695–1705; < L *coruscātus* ptp. of *coruscāre* to quiver, flash; see CORUSCANT, -ATE¹]

cor·us·ca·tion (kôr′ə skā′shən, kor′-), *n.* **1.** the act of coruscating. **2.** a sudden gleam or flash of light. **3.** a striking display of brilliance or wit. [1480–90; < LL *coruscātiōn-* (s. of *coruscātiō*). See CORUSCATE, -ION]

Cor·val·lis (kôr val′is), *n.* a city in W Oregon. 40,960.

cor·vée (kôr vā′), *n.* **1.** unpaid labor for one day, as on the repair of roads, exacted by a feudal lord. **2.** an obligation imposed on inhabitants of a district to perform services, as repair of roads, bridges, etc., for little or no remuneration. [1300–50; ME < MF < LL *corrogāta* contribution, collection, n. use of fem. of L *corrogātus* (ptp. of *corrogāre* to collect by asking), equiv. to *cor-* COR- + *rogā(re)* to ask + *-tus* ptp. suffix]

corves (kôrvz), *n.* pl. of **corf.**

cor·vette (kôr vet′), *n.* **1.** a warship of the old sailing class, having a flush deck and usually one tier of guns. **2.** a lightly armed, fast ship used mostly for convoy escort and ranging in size between a destroyer and a gunboat. Also, **cor·vet** (kôr vet′, kôr′vet). [1630–40; < F, MF < MD *corver* pursuit boat (deriv. of *corf* fishing boat, lit., basket), with suffix altered to *-ette* -ETTE]

cor·vi·na (kôr vē′nə), *n.* corbina. [1780–90; < MexSp, Sp: kind of fish, fem. deriv. of *corvino* CORVINE; so called from its color]

cor·vine (kôr′vīn, -vin), *adj.* **1.** pertaining to or resembling a crow. **2.** belonging or pertaining to the Corvidae, a family of birds including the crows, ravens, and jays. [1650–60; < L *corvinus,* equiv. to *corv(us)* raven + *-inus* -INE¹]

cor·vo (kôr′vō), *n.* a dry red or white wine of Sicily.

Cor·vus (kôr′vəs), *n., gen.* **-vi** (-vī). *Astron.* the Crow, a southern constellation between Virgo and Hydra.

Cor·win (kôr′win), *n.* **Norman (Lewis),** born 1910, U.S. dramatist and novelist.

Cor·y (kôr′ē), *n.* a male or female given name.

Cor·y·ate (kôr′ē it), *n.* **Thomas,** 1577–1617, English traveler and author. Also, **Cor·y·at** (kôr′ē it, kôr′yit).

Cor·y·bant (kôr′ə bant′, kor′-), *n., pl.* **Cor·y·ban·tes** (kôr′ə ban′tēz, kor′-), **Cor·y·bants. 1.** *Class. Myth.* any of the spirits or secondary divinities attending Cybele with wild music and dancing. **2.** an ancient Phrygian priest of Cybele. [1350–1400; ME < L *Corybant-* (s. of *Corybās*) < Gk *Korybant-* (s. of *Korýbās*)]

cor·y·ban·tic (kôr′ə ban′tik, kor′-), *adj.* **1.** frenzied; agitated; unrestrained. **2.** *(cap.)* Also, **Cor·y·ban·tian** (kôr′ə ban′shən, kor′-), **Cor·y·ban·tine** (kôr′ə ban′tin, -tīn, kor′-). of or pertaining to a Corybant. [1635–45; CORYBANT + -IC]

co·ryd·a·lis (kə rid′l is), *n.* any of the erect or climbing plants constituting the genus *Corydalis,* of the poppy family, having divided leaves, tuberous or fibrous roots, and clusters of irregular spurred flowers. [1810–20; < NL < Gk *korydallís,* extended var. of *korydós* crested lark, deriv. of *koryd-,* var. of *koryth-* (s. of *kórys*) helmet, head, crest; akin to *kára* head]

Cor·yell (kôr yel′), *n.* **John Russell,** 1848–1924, U.S. author of detective and adventure stories.

cor·ymb (kôr′imb, -im, kor′-), *n. Bot.* a form of inflorescence in which the flowers form a flat-topped or convex cluster, the outermost flowers being the first to open. See illus. under **inflorescence.** [1700–10; < L *corymbus* < Gk *kórymbos* head, top, cluster of fruit or flowers] **—cor′ymbed,** *adj.* **—cor′ymb′like′,** *adj.*

co·rym·bose (kə rim′bōs), *adj.* characterized by or growing in corymbs; corymblike. [1765–75; < NL *corymbōsus,* equiv. to *corymb(us)* CORYMB + *-ōsus* -OSE¹] **—co·rym′bose·ly,** *adv.*

cor·y·ne·bac·te·ri·um (kôr′ə nē bak tēr′ē əm, kə rin′ə-), *n., pl.* **-te·ri·a** (-tēr′ē ə). any of various rod-shaped bacteria of the genus *Corynebacterium,* many of which are pathogenic. [< NL (1896) < Gk *korýnē* club + *bacterium* BACTERIUM] **—cor′y·ne·bac·te′ri·al,** *adj.*

co·ryn·e·form (kə rin′ə fôrm′), *adj.* **1.** having a rodlike or clublike shape. *—n.* **2.** *Bacteriol.* any coryneform bacterium, esp. a corynebacterium or propionibacterium. [1950–55; CORYNE(BACTERIUM) + -FORM]

cor·y·phae·us (kôr′ə fē′əs, kor′-), *n., pl.* **-phae·i** (-fē′ī). **1.** the leader of the chorus in the ancient Greek drama. **2.** the leader of an operatic chorus or any group of singers. [1625–35; < L < Gk *koryphaîos* leading, equiv. to *koryph(ḗ)* head, top + *-aîos* n. suffix]

cor·y·phée (kôr′ə fā′, kor′-; *Fr.* kô ʀē fā′), *n., pl.* **-phées** (-fāz′; *Fr.* -fā′). a member of a ballet company who dances usually as part of a small group and who ranks below the soloists. [1820–30; < F < L *coryphaeus* CORYPHAEUS]

co·ryph·o·don (kə rif′ə don′), *n. Paleontol.* a primitive hoofed mammal of the extinct genus *Coryphodon,* of the early Eocene Epoch, having a long, thickset body, short legs, and five-toed feet, each toe ending in a small hoof. [1845; < NL < Gk *koryph(ḗ)* peak, top + *odṓn* tooth]

co·ry·za (kə rī′zə), *n.* **1.** *Pathol.* acute inflammation of the mucous membrane of the nasal cavities; cold in the head. **2.** *Vet. Pathol.* a contagious disease of birds, esp. poultry, characterized by the secretion of a thick mucus in the mouth and throat. [1625–35; < LL < Gk *kóryza* catarrh] **—co·ry′zal,** *adj.*

cos¹ (kos, kôs), *n.* romaine. [1690–1700; after Kos, where it originated]

cos² *Trigonom., Math.* cosine.

Cos (kos, kôs), *n.* Kos.

cos., 1. companies. **2.** consul. **3.** consulship. **4.** counties.

C.O.S., cash on shipment. Also, **c.o.s.**

Co·sa Nos·tra (kō′zə nōs′trə), a secret association engaged in organized crime in the U.S., modeled after and affiliated with the Mafia. [1960–65; < It: lit., our affair]

co·sce·nar·ist (kō′si nâr′ist, -när′-), *n.* one of two or more joint scenarists. [CO- + SCENARIST]

cose (kōs), *v.i.,* **cosed, cos·ing,** *n.* coze.

co·sec (kō′sēk′), *n.* cosecant.

co•se•cant (kō sē′kənt, -kant), *n. Trigonom.* **1.** (in a right triangle) the ratio of the hypotenuse to the side opposite a given angle. **2.** the secant of the complement, or the reciprocal of the sine, of a given angle or arc. *Abbr.:* csc Also, **cosec.** [1700–10; < NL *cosecant-* (s. of *cosecāns*). See CO-, SECANT]

cosecant
ACB being the angle, the ratio of BC to BA, or that of CL to CD, is the cosecant; or, CD being taken as unity, the cosecant is LC

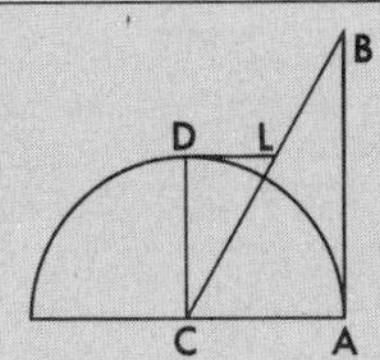

co•seis•mal (kō sīz′məl, -sīs′-), *adj.* of, pertaining to, or being in a line, curve, etc., connecting or comprising points on the earth's surface at which an earthquake wave arrives simultaneously. Also, **co•seis′mic.** [1850–55; CO- + SEISMAL]

Co•sen•za (kô zen′tsä), *n.* a city in S Italy. 102,475.

co•set (kō′set), *n. Math.* a subset of a group, formed by the consistent operation of a given element of the group on the left or right of all the elements of a subgroup of the group. [1925–30; CO- + SET]

Cos•grave (koz′grāv′), *n.* **William Thomas,** 1880–1965, Irish political leader: president of the executive council of the Irish Free State 1922–32.

cosh[1] (kosh), *Chiefly Brit. Slang.* —*n.* **1.** a blackjack; bludgeon. —*v.t.* **2.** to hit on the head with a cosh. [1865–70; perh. < Romany *kosh, koshter* stick]

cosh[2] (kosh), *n. Math.* hyperbolic cosine. [1870–75; COS(INE) + H(YPERBOLIC)]

cosh•er (kosh′ər), *v.t.* to treat with special fondness; pamper. [1860–65; perh. conflation of COCKER[3] with uncert. elements; Hiberno-E *cosher* to feast, live at the expense of kinsmen (< Ir *cóisir* feast, retinue) is remote in sense]

Co•shoc•ton (kə shok′tən), *n.* a city in E central Ohio. 13,405.

Co•sì fan tut•te (*It.* kô zē′ fän to͞ot′te), a comic opera (1790) by Wolfgang Amadeus Mozart.

co•sign (kō′sīn′, kō sīn′), *v.i., v.t.* to sign as a cosigner. [CO- + SIGN]

co•sig•na•to•ry (kō sig′nə tôr′ē, -tōr′ē), *adj., n., pl.* **-ries.** —*adj.* **1.** signing jointly with another or others. —*n.* **2.** a person who signs a document jointly with another or others; cosigner. [1860–65; CO- + SIGNATORY]

co•sign•er (kō′sī′nər, kō sī′-), *n.* **1.** a cosignatory. **2.** a joint signer of a negotiable instrument, esp. a promissory note. [1900–05; CO- + SIGNER]

Co•si•mo (kō′zə mō′; *It.* kô′zē mô), *n.* **Pie•ro di** (pē-âr′ō di; *It.* pye′RÔ dē). See **Piero di Cosimo.**

co•sine (kō′sīn), *n.* **1.** *Trigonom.* **a.** (in a right triangle) the ratio of the side adjacent to a given angle to the hypotenuse. **b.** the sine of the complement of a given angle or arc. *Abbr.:* cos **2.** *Math.* (of a real or complex number *x*) the function cos *x* defined by the infinite series $1 - (x^2/2!) + (x^4/4!) - + \ldots$, where ! denotes factorial. *Abbr.:* cos Cf. **sine** (def. 3), **factorial** (def. 1). [1625–35; < NL *cosinus.* See CO-, SINE[1]]

cosine
ACB being the angle, the ratio of AC to BC is the cosine; or, BC being taken as unity, the cosine is AC

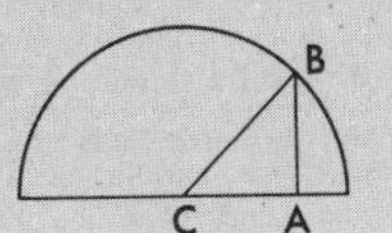

co′sine law′, *Optics.* See **Lambert's law.**

cos′ let′tuce, romaine. [1690–1700]

cosm-, var. of **cosmo-** before a vowel: *cosmism.*

-cosm, var. of **cosmo-** as final element of a compound word: *microcosm.*

cos•met•ic (koz met′ik), *n.* **1.** a powder, lotion, lipstick, rouge, or other preparation for beautifying the face, skin, hair, nails, etc. **2. cosmetics,** superficial measures to make something appear better, more attractive, or more impressive: *The budget committee opted for cosmetics instead of a serious urban renewal plan.* —*adj.* **3.** serving to beautify; imparting or improving beauty, esp. of the face. **4.** used or done superficially to make something look better, more attractive, or more impressive: *Alterations in the concert hall were only cosmetic and did nothing to improve the acoustics.* [1595–1605; < Gk *kosmētikós* relating to adornment, equiv. to *kosmē(ós)* adorned, arranged (verbid of *kosmeîn,* deriv. of *kósmos* order, arrangement) + *-ikos* -IC] —**cos•met′i•cal•ly,** *adv.*

cos•me•ti•cian (koz′mi tish′ən), *n.* **1.** a person who manufactures or sells cosmetics. **2.** a person professionally engaged in the application of cosmetics. [1925–30; COSMET(IC) + -ICIAN]

cos•met•i•cize (koz met′ə sīz′), *v.t.,* **-cized, -ciz•ing.** to improve superficially; cause to seem better or more attractive. Also, *esp. Brit.,* **cos•met′i•cise′.** [1815–25; COSMETIC + -IZE]

cosmet′ic sur′gery, plastic surgery for improving a person's appearance by restoration of damaged areas of skin, removal of wrinkles or blemishes, etc. [1925–30]

cos•me•tize (koz′mi tīz′), *v.t.,* **-tized, -tiz•ing.** to cosmeticize. Also, *esp. Brit.,* **cos′me•tise′.** [COSMET(IC) + -IZE]

cos•me•tol•o•gy (koz′mi tol′ə jē), *n.* the art or profession of applying cosmetics. [1850–55; < Gk *kosmētó(s)* adorned, arranged (see COSMETIC) + -LOGY, appar. modeled on F *cosmétologie*] —**cos•me•to•log•i•cal** (koz′mi-tl oj′i kəl), *adj.* —**cos′me•tol′o•gist,** *n.*

cos•mic (koz′mik), *adj.* **1.** of or pertaining to the cosmos: *cosmic laws.* **2.** characteristic of the cosmos or its phenomena: *cosmic events.* **3.** immeasurably extended in time and space; vast. **4.** forming a part of the material universe, esp. outside of the earth. Also, **cos′mi•cal.** [1640–50; < Gk *kosmikós* worldly, universal, equiv. to *kósm(os)* world, arrangement + *-ikos* -IC] —**cos•mi•cal•i•ty** (koz′mi kal′i tē), *n.* —**cos′mi•cal•ly,** *adv.*
—**Syn. 3.** immense, enormous, stupendous.

cos′mic back′ground radia′tion, *Astron.* electromagnetic radiation coming from every direction in the universe, considered the remnant of the big bang and corresponding to the black-body radiation of 3 K, the temperature to which the universe has cooled. Also called **cos′mic mi′crowave back′ground.**

cos′mic dust′, *Astron.* fine particles of matter in space. [1880–85]

cos′mic noise′, *Physics.* radio-frequency noise that originates outside the earth's atmosphere. [1945–50]

cos′mic ray′, *Physics.* a radiation of high penetrating power that originates in outer space and consists partly of high-energy atomic nuclei. [1920–25, *Amer.*]

cos•mism (koz′miz əm), *n.* the philosophy of cosmic evolution. [1860–65; COSM- + -ISM] —**cos′mist,** *n.*

cosmo-, a combining form meaning "world," "universe," used in the formation of compound words: *cosmography;* in contemporary usage, sometimes representing Russian *kosmo-,* it may mean "outer space," "space travel," or "cosmic ray": *cosmonaut.* Also, *esp. before a vowel,* **cosm-.** Cf. **astro-.** [< Gk *kosmo-,* comb. form of *kósmos* COSMOS]

cos•mo•chem•is•try (koz′mə kem′ə strē), *n.* the science dealing with the occurrence and distribution of chemical elements in the universe. [1935–40; COSMO- + CHEMISTRY] —**cos′mo•chem′ist,** *n.* —**cos•mo•chem•i•cal** (koz′mə kem′i kəl), *adj.*

cos•mo•drome (koz′mə drōm′), *n.* an aerospace center or launching site for spacecraft in the Soviet Union. [1950–55; < Russ *kosmodróm;* see COSMO-, -DROME]

cos•mog•o•ny (koz mog′ə nē), *n., pl.* **-nies.** a theory or story of the origin and development of the universe, the solar system, or the earth-moon system. [1860–65; < Gk *kosmogonía* creation of the world. See COSMO-, -GONY] —**cos•mog′o•nal, cos•mo•gon•ic** (koz′mə-gon′ik), **cos′mo•gon′i•cal,** *adj.* —**cos•mog′o•nist,** *n.*

cos•mog•ra•phy (koz mog′rə fē), *n., pl.* **-phies. 1.** a science that describes and maps the main features of the heavens and the earth, including astronomy, geography, and geology. **2.** a description or representation of the main features of the universe. [1350–1400; ME < Gk *kosmographía* description of the world. See COSMO-, -GRAPHY] —**cos•mog′ra•pher, cos•mog′ra•phist,** *n.* —**cos•mo•graph•ic** (koz′mə graf′ik), **cos′mo•graph′i•cal,** *adj.* —**cos′mo•graph′i•cal•ly,** *adv.*

cosmolog′ical ar′gument, *Philos.* an argument for the existence of God, asserting that the contingency of each entity, and of the universe composed wholly of such entities, demands the admission of an adequate external cause, which is God. Also called **cosmolog′ical proof′.** Cf. **first-cause argument.**

cosmolog′ical con′stant, *Astron.* a term introduced by Einstein into his field equations of general relativity to permit a stationary, nonexpanding universe: it has since been abandoned in most models of the universe. Cf. **Einstein model.** [1925–30]

cosmolog′ical prin′ciple, *Astron.* the hypothesis that the universe is isotropic and homogeneous on a large scale: used to simplify the equations of general relativity for models of the universe.

cosmolog′ical red′shift, *Astron.* the part of the redshift of celestial objects resulting from the expansion of the universe.

cos•mol•o•gy (koz mol′ə jē), *n.* **1.** the branch of philosophy dealing with the origin and general structure of the universe, with its parts, elements, and laws, and esp. with such of its characteristics as space, time, causality, and freedom. **2.** the branch of astronomy that deals with the general structure and evolution of the universe. [1650–60; < NL *cosmologia.* See COSMO-, -LOGY] —**cos•mol′o•ger, cos•mol′o•gist,** *n.* —**cos•mo•log•i•cal** (koz′mə loj′i kəl), **cos′mo•log′ic,** *adj.* —**cos′mo•log′i•cal•ly,** *adv.*

cos•mo•naut (koz′mə nôt′, -not′), *n.* a Russian or Soviet astronaut. [1955–60; COSMO- + (AERO)NAUT, repr. Russ *kosmonávt*] —**cos′mo•nau′tic,** *adj.* —**cos′mo•nau′ti•cal•ly,** *adv.*

cos•mo•nau•tics (koz′mə nô′tiks, -not′iks), *n.* (*used with a singular v.*) astronautics, esp. as applied to space flight. [1945–50; see COSMONAUTIC, -ICS]

cos•mop•o•lis (koz mop′ə lis), *n.* an internationally important city inhabited by many different peoples reflecting a great variety of cultures, attitudes, etc. [1890–95; COSMO- + -POLIS, modeled on METROPOLIS]

cos•mo•pol•i•tan (koz′mə pol′i tn), *adj.* **1.** free from local, provincial, or national ideas, prejudices, or attachments; at home all over the world. **2.** of or characteristic of a cosmopolite. **3.** belonging to all the world; not limited to just one part of the world. **4.** *Bot., Zool.* widely distributed over the globe. —*n.* **5.** a person who is free from local, provincial, or national bias or attachment; citizen of the world; cosmopolite. [1835–45; COSMOPOLITE + -AN] —**cos′mo•pol′i•tan•ism,** *n.* —**cos′•mo•pol′i•tan•ly,** *adv.*
—**Syn. 1.** sophisticated, urbane, worldly. —**Ant. 1.** provincial, parochial.

cos•mo•pol•i•tan•ize (koz′mə pol′i tn īz′), *v.t.,* **-ized, -iz•ing.** to make cosmopolitan. Also, *esp. Brit.,* **cos′mo•pol′i•tan•ise′.** [1875–80; COSMOPOLITAN + -IZE] —**cos′mo•pol′i•tan•i•za′tion,** *n.*

cos•mop•o•lite (koz mop′ə līt′), *n.* **1.** a person who is cosmopolitan in his or her ideas, life, etc.; citizen of the world. **2.** an animal or plant of worldwide distribution. [1590–1600; < Gk *kosmopolítēs* citizen of the world, equiv. to *kosmo-* COSMO- + *polítēs* citizen (*pól(is)* a city, state + *-ītēs* -ITE[1])] —**cos•mop′o•lit•ism,** *n.*

cos•mos (koz′məs, -mōs), *n., pl.* **-mos, -mos•es** for 2, 4. **1.** the world or universe regarded as an orderly, harmonious system. **2.** a complete, orderly, harmonious system. **3.** order; harmony. **4.** any composite plant of the genus *Cosmos,* of tropical America, some species of which, as *C. bipinnatus* and *C. sulphureus,* are cultivated for their showy ray flowers. **5.** Also, **Kosmos.** (*cap.*) *Aerospace.* one of a long series of Soviet satellites that have been launched into orbit around the earth. [1150–1200; ME < Gk *kósmos* order, form, arrangement, the world or universe]

cos•mo•tron (koz′mə tron′), *n. Physics.* a proton accelerator. [1945–50; COSMO- + -TRON]

co•spon•sor (kō spon′sər), *n.* **1.** a joint sponsor, as of a legislative bill. —*v.t.* **2.** to act as cosponsor for. [CO- + SPONSOR] —**co•spon′sor•ship′,** *n.*

coss (kōs), *n.* kos.

Cos•sack (kos′ak, -ək), *n.* (esp. in czarist Russia) a person belonging to any of certain groups of Slavs living chiefly in the southern part of Russia in Europe and forming an elite corps of horsemen. [1590–1600; < Polish *kozak* or Ukrainian *kozák,* ult. < a Turkic word taken to mean "adventurer, freebooter," adopted as an ethnic name by Turkic tribal groups of the Eurasian steppes]

cos•set (kos′it), *v.t.* **1.** to treat as a pet; pamper; coddle. —*n.* **2.** a lamb brought up without its dam; pet lamb. **3.** any pet. [1570–80; akin to OE *cossetung* kissing, verbal n. based on **cossettan* to kiss, deriv. of *coss* KISS]

cos•sie (koz′ē), *n. Australian Informal.* a bathing suit; bathers. [1915–20; (*swimming*) *cos*(*tume*) + -IE]

cost (kôst, kost), *n., v.,* **cost** or, for 11–13, **cost•ed, cost•ing.** —*n.* **1.** the price paid to acquire, produce, accomplish, or maintain anything: *the high cost of a good meal.* **2.** an outlay or expenditure of money, time, labor, trouble, etc.: *What will the cost be to me?* **3.** a sacrifice, loss, or penalty: *to work at the cost of one's health.* **4. costs,** *Law.* **a.** money allowed to a successful party in a lawsuit in compensation for legal expenses incurred, chargeable to the unsuccessful party. **b.** money due to a court or one of its officers for services in a cause. **5. at all costs,** regardless of the effort involved; by any means necessary: *The stolen painting must be recovered at all costs.* Also, **at any cost.** —*v.t.* **6.** to require the payment of (money or something else of value) in an exchange: *That camera cost $200.* **7.** to result in or entail the loss of: *Carelessness costs lives.* **8.** to cause to lose or suffer: *The accident cost her a broken leg.* **9.** to entail (effort or inconvenience): *Courtesy costs little.* **10.** to cause to pay or sacrifice: *That request will cost us two weeks' extra work.* **11.** to estimate or determine the cost of (manufactured articles, new processes, etc.). —*v.i.* **12.** to estimate or determine costs, as of manufacturing something. **13. cost out,** to calculate the cost of (a project, product, etc.) in advance: *to cost out a major construction project.* [1200–50; (v.) ME *costen* < AF, OF *co(u)ster* < L *constāre* to stand together, be settled, cost; cf. CONSTANT; (n.) ME < AF, OF n. deriv. of the v.] —**cost′less,** *adj.* —**cost′less•ness,** *n.*
—**Syn. 1.** charge, expense, expenditure, outlay. See **price. 3.** detriment.

cost-, var. of **costo-** before a vowel: *costate.*

cos•ta (kos′tə, kô′stə), *n., pl.* **cos•tae** (kos′tē, kô′stē). **1.** a rib or riblike part. **2.** the midrib of a leaf in mosses. **3.** a ridge. **4.** *Entomol.* **a.** Also called **cos′tal vein′.** a vein, usually marginal, in the anterior portion of the wing of certain insects. **b.** Also called **cos′tal mar′gin.** the anterior edge or border of the wing of certain insects. [1865–70; < L: rib, side. See COAST]

Cos•ta Bra•va (kos′tə brä′və, kô′stə, kō′-; *Sp.* kôs′tä bRä′vä), a coastal region in NE Spain, extending NE along the Mediterranean from Barcelona to France.

cost-ac•count (kôst′ə kount′, kost′-), *v.t.* to subject to cost accounting. [1895–1900]

cost′ account′ing, an accounting system indicating the cost of items involved in production. Also called, *esp. Brit.,* **costing.** [1910–15] —**cost′ account′ant.**

Cos•ta del Sol (kos′tə del sōl′, kô′stə, kō′-; *Sp.* kôs′tä thel sôl′), the S coast of Spain from Estepona to Motril: resort and retirement area.

Cos•tain (kos′tān), *n.* **Thomas Bertram,** 1885–1965, U.S. novelist, historian, and editor, born in Canada.

cos•tal (kos′tl, kôs′tl), *adj.* **1.** *Anat.* pertaining to the ribs or the upper sides of the body: *costal nerves.* **2.** *Bot., Zool.* pertaining to, involving, or situated near a costa. [1625–35; < ML *costālis* of the ribs, equiv. to L *cost(a)* rib, side + *-ālis* -AL[1]] —**cos′tal•ly,** *adv.*

Cos•ta Me•sa (kos′tə mā′sə, kô′stə, kō′-), a city in SW California, near Los Angeles. 82,291.

Cos•ta•no•an (kos′tə nō′ən, kô′stə-), *n.* **1.** a family of eight languages, now extinct, spoken by American Indian peoples of coastal California: part of the Penutian stock. **2.** any of the speakers of these languages, who formerly inhabited the coast and adjacent river valleys from San Francisco Bay south to Monterey Bay and Point Sur. —*adj.* **3.** of or pertaining to Costanoan or the Costanoans. [< Sp *costano* coast dweller (*cost(a)* COAST, shore + *-ano* -AN) + -AN]

co•star (*n.* kō′stär′; *v.* kō′stär′), *n., v.,* **-starred, -star•ring.** —*n.* **1.** a performer, esp. an actor or actress, who shares star billing with another. **2.** a performer whose status is slightly below that of a star. —*v.i.* **3.** to share star billing with another performer. **4.** to receive billing of slightly less status than that of a star. —*v.t.* **5.** to present (two or more actors) as having equal billing or prominence. **6.** to present as having slightly less status than that of a star. Also, **co′-star′.** [1915–20, *Amer.*; CO- + STAR]

cos•tard (kos′tərd, kô′stərd), *n.* **1.** a large English variety of apple. **2.** *Archaic.* the head. [1250–1300; ME, perh. < AF, equiv. to *coste* rib (see COAST) + *-ard* -ARD, alluding to the ridges or ribs of the variety]

Cos•ta Ri•ca (kos′tə rē′kə, kô′stə, kō′-; *Sp.* kôs′tä rē′kä), a republic in Central America, between Panama and Nicaragua. 2,012,000; 19,238 sq. mi. (49,825 sq. km). *Cap.:* San José. —**Cos′ta Ri′can.**

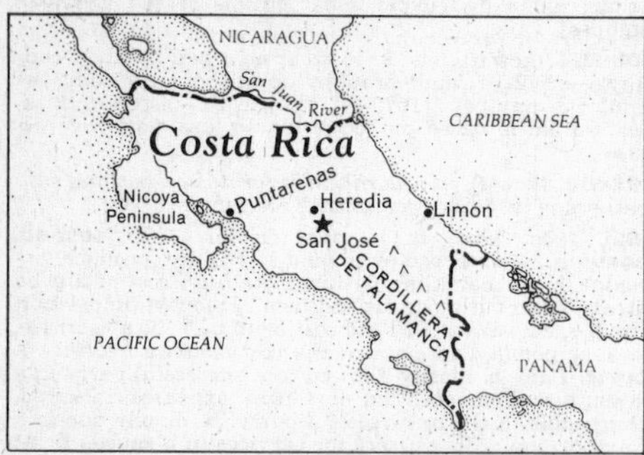

cos•tate (kos′tāt, kô′stāt), *adj.* **1.** *Anat.* having ribs. **2.** (of mosses) having a midrib or costa. [1810–20; < L *costātus* having ribs, ribbed, equiv. to *cost(a)* rib + *-ātus* -ATE[1]]

cost-ben•e•fit (kôst′ben′ə fit, kost′-), *adj.* of, pertaining to, or based on a cost-effective analysis. [1925–30]

cost′ card′. See **cost sheet.**

cost′ cen′ter, any unit of activity, group of employees or machines, line of products, etc., isolated or arranged in order to allocate and assign costs more easily.

cost-cut (kôst′kut′, kost′-), *v.t.,* **-cut, -cut•ting.** to reduce the cost of: *to cost-cut expenditures.* [1970–75]

cos•tec•to•my (ko stek′tə mē, kô-), *n., pl.* **-mies.** *Surg.* excision of part or all of a rib. Also called **thoracectomy.** [COST- + -ECTOMY]

cost-ef•fec•tive (kôst′i fek′tiv, kost′-), *adj.* producing optimum results for the expenditure. Also, **cost-efficient.** —**cost′-ef•fec′tive•ly,** *adv.* —**cost′-ef•fec′tive•ness,** *n.*

cost-ef•fi•cient (kôst′i fish′ənt, kost′-), *adj.* cost-effective. —**cost′-ef•fi′cien•cy,** *n.* —**cost′-ef•fi′cient•ly,** *adv.*

Cos•tel•lo (kos′tl ō′, ko stel′ō), *n.* **John Al•o•y•sius** (al′ō ish′əs, -ē əs), 1891–1976, Irish political leader: prime minister of the Republic of Ireland 1948–51, 1954–57.

cos•ter (kos′tər, kô′stər), *n.* costermonger.

Cos•ter•mans•ville (kos′tər mənz vil′, kô′stər-), *n.* former name of **Bukavu.**

cos•ter•mon•ger (kos′tər mung′gər, -mong′-, kô′stər-), *Chiefly Brit.* —*n.* **1.** Also called **coster.** a hawker of fruit, vegetables, fish, etc. —*v.i.* **2.** to sell fruit, vegetables, fish, etc., from a cart, barrow, or stall in the streets; coster. [1505–15; earlier *costerdmonger.* See COSTARD, MONGER]

cost•ing (kôs′ting, kos′-), *n. Chiefly Brit.* See **cost accounting.**

cost′, insur′ance, and freight′. See **C.I.F.**

cos•tive (kos′tiv, kô′stiv), *adj.* **1.** suffering from constipation; constipated. **2.** slow in action or in expressing ideas, opinions, etc. **3.** *Obs.* stingy; tight-fisted. [1350–1400; ME < AF **costif,* for MF *costivé,* ptp. of *costiver* to constipate < L *constipāre* (see CONSTIPATE)] —**cos′tive•ly,** *adv.* —**cos′tive•ness,** *n.*

cost-jus•ti•fy (kôst′jus′tə fī′, kost′-), *v.t.,* **-fied, -fy•ing.** to justify the allotment or spending of a specific sum of money for (an investment, procurement, etc.). —**cost′-jus′ti•fi′a•ble,** *adj.*

cost′ keep′er, a cost accountant. [1895–1900] —**cost′ keep′ing.**

cost′ ledg′er, a subsidiary ledger in which are recorded the costs of goods produced or services supplied.

cost•ly (kôst′lē, kost′-), *adj.,* **-li•er, -li•est. 1.** costing much; expensive; high in price: *a costly emerald bracelet; costly medical care.* **2.** resulting in great expense: *The upkeep of such a large house is costly.* **3.** resulting in great detriment: *It was a costly mistake because no one ever trusted him again.* **4.** of great value; very valuable; sumptuous. **5.** lavish; extravagant. [1350–1400; ME *costli.* See COST[1], -LY] —**cost′li•ness,** *n.*
—**Syn. 1.** dear, high-priced. See **expensive.**

CONCISE ETYMOLOGY KEY: <, descended or borrowed from; >, whence; b., blend of, blended; c., cognate with; cf., compare; deriv., derivative; equiv., equivalent; imit., imitative; obl., oblique; r., replacing; s., stem; sp., spelling, spelled; resp., respelling, respelled; trans., translation; ?, origin unknown; *, unattested; ‡, probably earlier than. See the full key inside the front cover.

cost•mar•y (kost′mâr′ē, kôst′-), *n., pl.* **-mar•ies.** a composite plant, *Chrysanthemum balsamita,* that has silvery, fragrant leaves and is used in salads and as a flavoring. Also called **mint geranium.** [1325–75; ME *costmarie,* equiv. to *cost* (OE *cost* costmary < L *costum, costus* a composite herb, *Saussurea lappa* < Gk *kóstos*) + *Marie* (the Virgin) Mary]

costo-, a combining form meaning "rib," used in the formation of compound words: *costoclavicular.* Also, *esp. before a vowel,* **cost-.** [< L *cost(a)* rib (see COSTA) + -O-]

cost′ of liv′ing, the average cost of food, clothing, and other necessary or usual goods and services paid by a person, family, etc., or considered as a standard by the members of a group. [1895–1900] —**cost′-of-liv′ing,** *adj.*

cost′-of-liv′ing in′dex, a former term for **consumer price index.** [1910–15]

cos•to•tome (kos′tə tōm′), *n. Surg.* an instrument, as shears or a knife, for incising or dividing a rib, as in costotomy. [COSTO- + -TOME]

cos•tot•o•my (ko stot′ə mē), *n., pl.* **-mies.** *Surg.* incision of a rib. [COSTO- + -TOMY]

cost′ o′verrun, cost in excess of that originally estimated or budgeted, esp. in a government contract: *Additional funds had to be allocated to cover the cost overrun on the new fighter plane.*

cost-plus (kôst′plus′, kost′-), *adj.* **1.** paid or providing for payment based on the cost of production plus an agreed-upon fee or rate of profit, as certain government contracts. **2.** of or pertaining to a cost-plus arrangement or contract. [1915–20]

cost-push (kôst′po͝osh′, kost′-), *adj.* **1.** of or pertaining to cost-push inflation: *a proponent of the cost-push theory.* —*n.* **2.** See **cost-push inflation.** [1955–60]

cost′-push infla′tion, inflation in which prices increase as a result of increased production costs, as labor and parts, even when demand remains the same. Cf. **demand-pull inflation.** [1965–70]

cos•trel (kos′trəl, kô′strəl), *n.* a flask made of leather, earthenware, or wood, usually with an ear or ears by which to suspend it, as from the waist. [1350–1400; ME < MF *costerel,* equiv. to *costier* worn at the side (< VL **costārius;* see COSTA, -ARY) + *-el* dim. suffix]

cost-share (kôst′shâr′, kost′-), *v.t.,* **-shared, -shar•ing.** to share the cost of: *to cost-share a joint venture.* [1975–80]

cost′ sheet′, a summary of costs involved in the production of a product. Also called **cost card.**

cos•tume (*n.* kos′to͞om, -tyo͞om; *v.* ko sto͞om′, -styo͞om′), *n., v.,* **-tumed, -tum•ing,** *adj.* —*n.* **1.** a style of dress, including accessories and hairdos, esp. that peculiar to a nation, region, group, or historical period. **2.** dress or garb characteristic of another period, place, person, etc., as worn on the stage or at balls. **3.** fashion of dress appropriate to a particular occasion or season: *dancing costume; winter costume.* **4.** a set of garments, esp. women's garments, selected for wear at a single time; outfit; ensemble. —*v.t.* **5.** to dress; furnish with a costume; provide appropriate dress for: *to costume a play.* —*adj.* **6.** of or characterized by the wearing of costumes: *a costume party.* **7.** meant for use with or appropriate to a specific costume: *costume accessories.* [1705–15; < F < It: usage, habit, dress; doublet of CUSTOM]
—**Syn. 1.** See **dress.**

cos′tume jew′elry, jewelry made of nonprecious metals, sometimes gold-plated or silver-plated, often set with imitation or semiprecious stones. [1930–35, *Amer.*]

cos•tum•er (kos′to͞o mər, -tyo͞o-; ko sto͞o′mər, -styo͞o′-), *n.* **1.** a person who makes, sells, or rents costumes, as for theatrical productions. **2.** a clothes tree. [1860–65, *Amer.*; COSTUME + -ER[1]]

cos•tum•er•y (ko sto͞o′mə rē, -styo͞o′-), *n.* **1.** items of costume. **2.** the art of designing, making, or providing costumes. [1830–40; COSTUME + -ERY]

cos•tum•i•er (ko sto͞o′mē ər, -styo͞o′-; *Fr.* kôs ty myā′), *n., pl.* **cos•tum•i•ers** (ko sto͞o′mē ərz, -styo͞o′-; *Fr.* kôs ty myā′). costumer (def. 1). [< F; see COSTUME, -IER[2]]

cos•tum•ing (kos′to͞o ming, -tyo͞o-), *n.* **1.** material for costumes. **2.** costumes collectively. **3.** the act of furnishing or designing costumes. [1855–60; COSTUME + -ING[1]]

cost′ u′nit, a quantity or unit of a product or service whose cost is computed, used as a standard for comparison with other costs.

co•sy (kō′zē), *adj.,* **-si•er, -si•est,** *n., pl.* **-sies,** *v.,* **-sied, -sy•ing.** cozy. [1700–10] —**co′si•ly,** *adv.* —**co′si•ness,** *n.*

Co•sy•ra (kō sī′rə), *n.* ancient name of **Pantelleria.**

cot[1] (kot), *n.* **1.** a light portable bed, esp. one of canvas on a folding frame. **2.** *Brit.* a child's crib. **3.** a light bedstead. **4.** *Naut.* a hammocklike bed stiffened by a suspended frame. [1625–35; < Hindi *khāṭ* < Prakrit *khaṭṭā* < Skt *khaṭvā;* akin to Tamil *kattil* bedstead]

cot[2] (kot), *n.* **1.** a small house; cottage; hut. **2.** a small place of shelter. **3.** a sheath or protective covering, as for an injured finger or toe. [bef. 900; ME, OE *cot* (neut.; cf. COTE[1]); c. ON *kot* hut; akin to CUBBY, COVE[1]]

cot, *Trig.* cotangent.

Co•ta•ba•to (kô′tä bä′tô), *n.* a city on W central Mindanao, in the S Philippines. 83,871.

co•tan•gent (kō tan′jənt, kō′tan′-), *n. Trig.* **1.** (in a right triangle) the ratio of the side adjacent to a given angle to the side opposite. **2.** the tangent of the complement, or the reciprocal of the tangent, of a given angle or arc. *Abbr.:* cot, ctn Also, **co•tan** (kō′tan′). [1625–35; < NL *cotangent-* (s. of *cotangēns*). See CO-, TANGENT] —**co•tan•gen•tial** (kō′tan jen′shəl), *adj.*

cotangent
ACB being the angle, the ratio of AC to AB, or that of DL to CD, is the cotangent; or, CD being taken as unity, the cotangent is DL

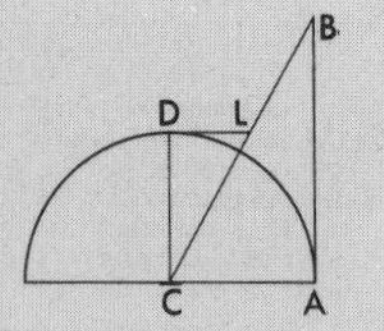

cot′ death′, *Brit.* See **sudden infant death syndrome.** [1965–70]

cote[1] (kōt), *n.* **1.** a shelter, coop, or small shed for sheep, pigs, pigeons, etc. **2.** *Brit. Dial.* a cottage; small house. [bef. 1050; ME, OE *cote* (fem.; cf. COT[2])]

cote[2] (kōt), *v.t.,* **cot•ed, cot•ing.** *Obs.* to pass by; outstrip; surpass. [1565–75; orig. uncert.]

côte (kōt), *n., pl.* **côtes** (kōt). *French.* a slope or hillside with vineyards.

co•teach (kō tēch′), *v.t., v.i.,* **-taught, -teach•ing.** to teach jointly. Also, **co-teach′.**

Côte d'A•zur (kōt dᴀ zyʀ′), French name of the **Riviera.**

Côte d'I•voire (kōt dē vwᴀʀ′), French name of **Ivory Coast.**

Côte-d'Or (kōt dôʀ′), *n.* a department in E France. 456,070; 3393 sq. mi. (8790 sq. km). *Cap.:* Dijon.

cote•har•die (kōt′är′dē, -här′-), *n.* (in the Middle Ages) a close-fitting outer garment with long sleeves, hip-length for men and full-length for women, often laced or buttoned down the front or back. [1300–50; ME < OF: lit., bold coat]

co•ten•ant (kō ten′ənt), *n.* a joint tenant. [1815–25; CO- + TENANT] —**co•ten′an•cy, co•ten•ure** (kō ten′yər), *n.*

co•te•rie (kō′tə rē), *n.* **1.** a group of people who associate closely. **2.** an exclusive group; clique. **3.** a group of prairie dogs occupying a communal burrow. [1730–40; < F, MF: an association of tenant farmers < ML *coterius* COTTER[2] + *-ie* -Y[3]]
—**Syn. 1.** See **circle.**

co•ter•mi•nous (kō tûr′mə nəs), *adj.* **1.** having the same border or covering the same area. **2.** being the same in extent; coextensive in range or scope. Also, **co•ter•mi•nal** (kō tûr′mə nl). [1790–1800; re-formation of CONTERMINUS; see CO-] —**co•ter′mi•nous•ly,** *adv.*

Côtes-du-Nord (kōt dʏ nôʀ′), *n.* a department in NW France. 525,556; 2787 sq. mi. (7220 sq. km). *Cap.:* Saint-Brieuc.

Côte-St.-Luc (kōt′sānt′lo͝ok′; *Fr.* kōt sᴀɴ lʏk′), *n.* a city in S Quebec, in E Canada: suburb of Montreal. 27,531.

coth•a•more (kō′thə môr′, -mōr′), *n.* a frieze fabric, often used in the manufacture of overcoats. [< Ir *cóta mór* lit., greatcoat]

co•thur•nus (kō thûr′nəs), *n., pl.* **-ni** (-nī). **1.** a grave and elevated style of acting; tragic acting; tragedy. **2.** buskin (def. 2). Also, **co•thurn** (kō′thûrn, kō thûrn′). [1720–30; < L < Gk *kóthornos* buskin, type of boot worn by tragic actors in heroic roles] —**co•thur′nal,** *adj.*

co•tid•al (kō tīd′l), *adj.* **1.** pertaining to a coincidence of tides. **2.** (on a chart or map) indicating a line connecting points at which high tide occurs at the same time. [1825–35; CO- + TIDAL]

co•til•lion (kə til′yən, kō-), *n.* **1.** a formal ball given esp. for debutantes. **2.** a lively French social dance originating in the 18th century, consisting of a variety of steps and figures and performed by couples. **3.** any of various dances resembling the quadrille. **4.** music arranged or played for these dances. **5.** a formalized dance for a large number of people, in which a head couple leads the other dancers through elaborate and stately figures. [1760–70; < F *cotillon* kind of dance, in OF: petticoat, equiv. to *cote* COAT + *-illon* dim. suffix]

co•til•lon (kə til′yən, kō-; *Fr.* kô tē yôɴ′), *n., pl.* **-til•lons** (-til′yənz; *Fr.* -tē yôɴ′). cotillion.

co•tin•ga (kō ting′gə, kə-), *n.* any of several songbirds constituting the family Cotingidae of chiefly tropical New World regions. Also called **bellbird.** [1775–85; < NL < F < Tupi]

co•to•ne•as•ter (kə tō′nē as′tər, kot′n ē′stər), *n.* any of various shrubs or small trees belonging to the genus *Cotoneaster,* of the rose family, having white or pink flowers and bearing a red or black, berrylike fruit, grown as an ornamental. [1789; < NL, equiv. to L *cotōne(a)* QUINCE + *-aster* -ASTER[2]]

Co•to•nou (kō′tə no͞o′), *n.* a seaport in SE Benin. 180,000.

Co•to•pax•i (kō′tə pak′sē; *Sp.* kô′tô pä′hē), *n.* a volcano in central Ecuador, in the Andes: the highest active volcano in the world. 19,498 ft. (5943 m).

cot•quean (kot′kwēn′), *n.* **1.** *Archaic.* a man who busies himself with traditionally women's household duties. **2.** *Archaic.* a coarse woman. [1540–50; COT[2] + QUEAN]

co•trans•duc•tion (kō′trans duk′shən, -tranz-), *n. Genetics.* the process by which two genetic markers are simultaneously packaged within a bacteriophage for transfer to a new host bacterium. Cf. **transduction.** [CO- + TRANSDUCTION]

Cots•wold (kots′wōld, -wəld), *n.* one of an English breed of large sheep having coarse, long wool. [named after the COTSWOLDS, where the breed originated]

Cots•wolds (kots′wōldz, -wəldz), *n.* (*used with a plural v.*) a range of hills in SW England, in Gloucestershire. Also called **Cots′wold Hills′.**

cot•ta (kot′ə, kô′tə), *n. Eccles.* **1.** a surplice. **2.** a short surplice, sleeveless or with short sleeves, worn esp. by choristers. [1840–50; < ML, var. of *cota* kind of tunic. See COAT]

cot•tage (kot′ij), *n.* **1.** a small house, usually of only one story. **2.** a small, modest house at a lake, mountain resort, etc., owned or rented as a vacation home. **3.** one of a group of small, separate houses, as for patients at a hospital, guests at a hotel, or students at a boarding school. [1350–1400; ME *cotage.* See COT[2], -AGE; cf. ML *cotagium,* appar. < AF] **—cot′taged,** *adj.*

cot′tage cheese′, an extremely soft, or loose, white, mild-flavored cheese made from skim-milk curds, usually without rennet. [1840–50, *Amer.*]
—Regional Variation. FARMER CHEESE and FARMER'S CHEESE are widely used throughout the U.S. as terms for a kind of COTTAGE CHEESE. This same kind of cheese, with varying curd size and sourness, is also called SOUR-MILK CHEESE in Eastern New England; CURD or CURD CHEESE, chiefly in the Northeastern and Southern U.S.; POT CHEESE, chiefly in the Hudson Valley; SMEARCASE, chiefly in the North Midland U.S., and sometimes CREAM CHEESE in the Gulf States.

cot′tage fries′, *Chiefly Northern and North Midland U.S.* See **home fries.** Also called **cot′tage-fried pota′toes** (kot′ij frīd′). [1965–70]

Cot′tage Grove′, a town in E Minnesota. 18,994.

cot′tage in′dustry, 1. the production, for sale, of goods at home, as the making of handicrafts by rural families. **2.** any small-scale, loosely organized industry. [1920–25]

cot′tage pud′ding, a pudding made by covering plain cake with a sweet sauce, often of fruit. [1905–10]

cot•tag•er (kot′i jər), *n.* **1.** a person who lives in a cottage. **2.** Also, **cotter, cot•ti•er** (kot′ē ər). *Brit.* a rural worker; a laborer on a farm or in a small village. **3.** a person having a private house at a vacation resort. [1540–50; COTTAGE + -ER[1]]

cot′tage tu′lip, a late-flowering type of tulip, usually having pointed or elongated flowers. [1925–30]

cot′tage win′dow, a double-hung window with an upper sash smaller than the lower. Also called **front window.**

Cott•bus (kot′bəs; *Ger.* kôt′bo͝os), *n.* a city in E Germany, on the Spree River. 107,623.

cot•ter[1] (kot′ər), *Mach.* **—n. 1.** a pin, wedge, key, or the like, fitted or driven into an opening to secure something or hold parts together. **2.** See **cotter pin.** **—v.t. 3.** to secure with a cotter. [1300–50; ME *coter;* akin to late ME *coterell* iron bracket; of uncert. orig.]

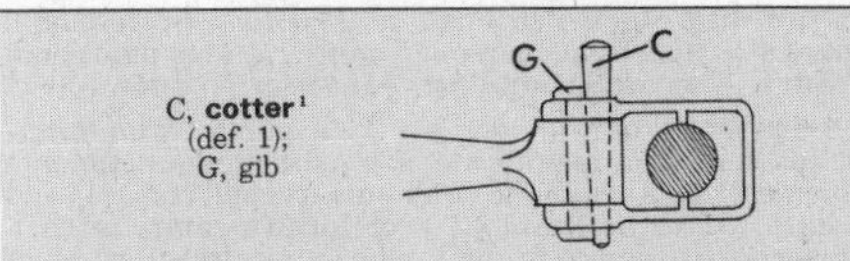

C, cotter[1] (def. 1); G, gib

cot•ter[2] (kot′ər), *n.* **1.** *Scot.* a person occupying a plot of land and cottage, paid for in services. **2.** cottager (def. 2). [1175–1225; ME *cotere* < AF *cot(i)er;* see COT[2], -ER[2]]

cot′ter pin′, *Mach.* a cotter having a split end that is spread after being pushed through a hole to prevent it from working loose. [1890–95]

cot′ter slot′, *Mach.* a slot cut into the end of a rod for the reception of another rod or part to be attached by a cotter.

Cot′ti•an Alps′ (kot′ē ən), a mountain range in SW Europe, in France and Italy: a part of the Alps. Highest peak, Monte Viso, 12,602 ft. (3841 m).

cot•ton (kot′n), *n.* **1.** a soft, white, downy substance consisting of the hairs or fibers attached to the seeds of plants belonging to the genus *Gossypium,* of the mallow family, used in making fabrics, thread, wadding, etc. **2.** the plant itself, having spreading branches and broad, lobed leaves. **3.** such plants collectively as a cultivated crop. **4.** cloth, thread, a garment, etc., of cotton. **5.** any soft, downy substance resembling cotton, but growing on other plants. **—v.i. 6.** *Informal.* to get on well together; agree. **7.** *Obs.* to prosper or succeed. **8. cotton to** or **on to,** *Informal.* **a.** to become fond of; begin to like. **b.** to approve of; agree with: *to cotton to a suggestion.* **c.** to come to a full understanding of; grasp: *More and more firms are cottoning on to the advantages of using computers.* [1250–1300; ME *coton* < OF < OIt *cotone* < Ar *qutun,* var. of *qutn*]

cotton boll

Cot•ton (kot′n), *n.* **John,** 1584–1652, U.S. clergyman, colonist, and author (grandfather of Cotton Mather).

cot•ton•ade (kot′n ād′), *n.* a heavy, coarse fabric made of cotton or mixed fibers and often resembling wool, used in the manufacture of work clothes. [1795–1805; < F *cotonnade.* See COTTON, -ADE[1]]

cot′ton bat′ting, absorbent cotton pressed into pads or layers for use in dressing wounds, filling quilts, etc. [1820–30, *Amer.*]

Cot′ton Belt′, (*sometimes l.c.*) the part of the southern U.S. where cotton is grown, originally Alabama, Georgia, and Mississippi, but now often extended to include parts of Texas and California. [1870–75, *Amer.*]

cot′ton boll′worm. See **corn earworm.** [1865–70, *Amer.*]

cot′ton cake′, a mass of compressed cottonseed after the oil has been extracted: used chiefly to feed cattle. Also called **cottonseed cake.** [1890–95]

cot′ton can′dy, a fluffy, sweet confection whipped from spun sugar and gathered or wound around a stick or cone-shaped paper core. [1925–30, *Amer.*]

cot′ton flan′nel. See **Canton flannel.** [1835–45]

cot′ton gin′, a machine for separating the fibers of cotton from the seeds. [1790–1800, *Amer.*]

cot′ton grass′, any rushlike plant constituting the genus *Eriophorum,* of the sedge family, common in swampy places and bearing spikes resembling tufts of cotton. [1590–1600; so called from its cottonlike heads]

cot′ton gum′. any of several tupelo trees, esp. *Nyssa aquatica.* [1855–60, *Amer.*; so called from the cottonlike hairs of its seeds]

cot′ton mill′, a factory for producing cotton fabrics, thread, etc. [1785–95]

cot•ton•mouth (kot′n mouth′), *n., pl.* **-mouths** (-mouths′, -mouthz′). a venomous snake, *Agkistrodon* (*Ancistrodon*) *piscivorus,* of swamps in southeastern U.S., that grows to about 4 ft. (1.2 m). Also called **water moccasin.** [1825–35, *Amer.*; COTTON + MOUTH, so called from the whiteness of its lips and mouth]

cot′ton pick′er, a machine for removing the ripe cotton fiber from the standing plant. [1825–35, *Amer.*]

cot•ton•pick•in′ (kot′n pik′ən), *adj. Slang.* damned; confounded: *That's a cottonpickin' lie.* Also, **cot•ton•pick•ing** (kot′n pik′ən, -pik′ing). [1950–55, *Amer.*; COTTON + PICK[1] + -ING[2]]

cot′ton press′, a press for baling cotton. [1800–10, *Amer.*]

cot•ton•seed (kot′n sēd′), *n., pl.* **-seeds,** (*esp. collectively*) **-seed.** the seed of the cotton plant, yielding an oil. [1785–95; COTTON + SEED]

cot′tonseed cake′. See **cotton cake.** [1865–70, *Amer.*]

cot′tonseed meal′, cotton cake when pulverized. [1855–60, *Amer.*]

cot′tonseed oil′, a brown-yellow, viscid oil with a nutlike odor, obtained from the seed of the cotton plant: used in the manufacture of soaps, hydrogenated fats, lubricants, and cosmetics, as a cooking and salad oil, and in medicine chiefly as a laxative. [1825–35, *Amer.*]

cot′ton stain′er, any of several large red-and-black bugs of the genus *Dysdercus* that puncture oranges and cotton bolls and discolor cotton fibers: a serious pest in America and India. [1855–60, *Amer.*]

Cot′ton State′, Alabama (used as a nickname). [1930–35]

cot•ton•tail (kot′n tāl′), *n.* any small North American rabbit of the genus *Sylvilagus,* having a brownish coat and fluffy white tail. [1865–70, *Amer.*; COTTON + TAIL[1]]

cottontail, *Sylvilagus floridanus,* head and body 13 in. (33 cm); tail 2 in. (5 cm)

cot′ton this′tle. See **Scotch thistle.** [1540–50]

cot′ton tie′, a light, narrow strip of metal for binding together bales of cotton, hemp, jute, etc. [1885–90]

cot′ton top′, a person with extremely light-colored hair. Also, **cot′ton•top′.** [1920–25]

cot•ton•weed (kot′n wēd′), *n.* any of various plants having stems and leaves covered with a soft, hoary pubescence. [1555–65; COTTON + WEED[1]]

cot•ton•wick (kot′n wik′), *n.* a grunt, *Haemulon melanurum,* of warm Atlantic seas. [1670–80; COTTON + WICK[1]]

cot•ton•wood (kot′n wo͝od′), *n.* any of several American poplars, as *Populus deltoides,* having toothed, triangular leaves and cottonlike tufts on the seeds. [1795–1805, *Amer.*; COTTON + WOOD[1]]

cot′ton wool′, 1. cotton in its raw state, as on the boll or gathered but unprocessed. **2.** *Brit.* See **absorbent cotton.** [1590–1600]

cot•ton•y (kot′n ē), *adj.* **1.** of or like cotton; soft. **2.** covered with a down or nap resembling cotton. [1570–80; COTTON + -Y[1]]

cot′ton•y-cush′ion scale′ (kot′n ē ko͝osh′ən), a scale insect, *Icerya purchasi,* native to Australia, now a common pest in the citrus-growing regions of California. [1885–90]

cot′tony ju′jube. See **Indian jujube.**

co•tul•a (kō tul′ə, kə-), *n., pl.* **-tul•ae** (-tul′ē). (in prescriptions) a measure. [1570–80; < L < Gk *kotýlē* cup; see COTYLOID]

co•tun•nite (kə tun′īt), *n.* a soft, white to yellowish mineral, lead chloride, $PbCl_2$, that forms as an alteration product of galena. [1825–35; < G *Cotunnit,* after Domenico Cotugno, in Latinized form *Cotunnius* (1736–1822), Italian anatomist; see -ITE[1]]

co•tur•nix (kə tûr′niks), *n.* any of several small Old World quails of the genus *Coturnix,* esp. *C. japonica* (**Japanese quail**), widely used as a laboratory animal. [1758; < NL; L *cōturnix, coturnix* quail]

cot•wal (kōt′wäl), *n.* kotwal.

Co•ty (kō tē′; *Fr.* kô tē′), *n.* **Re•né Jules Gus•tave** (rə nā′ zhyl gys tav′), 1882–1962, president of France 1954–59.

cot•y•le•don (kot′l ēd′n), *n. Bot.* **1.** the primary or rudimentary leaf of the embryo of seed plants. **2.** *Anat.* any of several lobules of the placenta. [1535–45; < L: navelwort < Gk *kotylēdṓn* a plant (prob. navelwort), lit., a cuplike hollow, deriv. of *kotýlē* cup] **—cot′y•le′don•al, cot•y•le•don•ar•y** (kot′l ēd′n er′ē), **cot′y•le′don•ous,** *adj.*

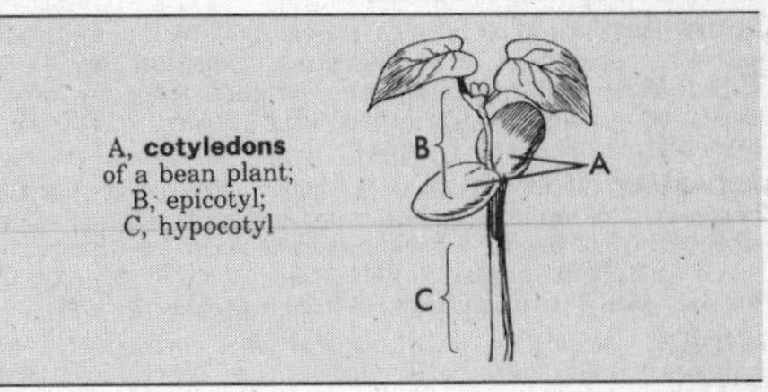

A, **cotyledons** of a bean plant; B, epicotyl; C, hypocotyl

cot•y•loid (kot′l oid′), *adj. Anat.* cup-shaped. [1750–60; < Gk *kotyloeidḗs,* equiv. to *kotýl(ē)* cup + *-oeidēs* -OID]

cot•y•lo•saur (kot′l ə sôr′), *n.* any member of the extinct order Cotylosauria, comprising heavy-bodied, splay-limbed, plant-eating reptiles that arose during the Carboniferous Period and that are considered to include the ancestors of all other reptiles. [1900–05; < NL *Cotylosauria,* equiv. to *cotyl(us)* a hollow space in the bones forming the distinctive articulation of skull and vertebrae, which orig. defined the order (masc. n. < Gk *kotýlē* socket, cup, anything hollow) + *-o-* -O- + *-sauria;* see -SAUR, -IA] **—cot′y•lo•sau′ri•an,** *adj.*

co•type (kō′tīp), *n.* a syntype. [1890–95; CO- + TYPE]

cou•cal (ko͞o′kəl), *n.* any of several Old World cuckoos of the genus *Centropus,* having harsh-textured plumage and a long, daggerlike hind claw. [1805–15; < F, said to be equiv. to *couc(ou)* CUCKOO + *al(ouette)* lark]

couch (kouch *or, for 6, 15,* ko͞och), *n.* **1.** a piece of furniture for seating from two to four people, typically in the form of a bench with a back, sometimes having an armrest at one or each end, and partly or wholly upholstered and often fitted with springs, tailored cushions, skirts, etc.; sofa. **2.** a similar article of furniture, with a headrest at one end, on which some patients of psychiatrists or psychoanalysts lie while undergoing treatment. **3.** a bed or other place of rest; a lounge; any place used for repose. **4.** the lair of a wild beast. **5.** *Brewing.* the frame on which barley is spread to be malted. **6.** *Papermaking.* the board or felt blanket on which wet pulp is laid for drying into paper sheets. **7.** *Fine Arts.* a primer coat or layer, as of paint. **8. on the couch,** *Informal.* undergoing psychiatric or psychoanalytic treatment. **—v.t. 9.** to arrange or frame (words, a sentence, etc.); put into words; express: *a simple request couched in respectful language.* **10.** to express indirectly or obscurely: *the threat couched under his polite speech.* **11.** to lower or bend down, as the head. **12.** to lower (a spear, lance, etc.) to a horizontal position, as for attack. **13.** to put or lay down, as for rest or sleep; cause to lie down. **14.** to lay or spread flat. **15.** *Papermaking.* to transfer (a sheet of pulp) from the wire to the couch. **16.** to embroider by couching. **17.** *Archaic.* to hide; conceal. **—v.i. 18.** to lie at rest or asleep; repose; recline. **19.** to crouch; bend; stoop. **20.** to lie in ambush or in hiding; lurk. **21.** to lie in a heap for decomposition or fermentation, as leaves. [1300–50; (n.) ME *couche* < AF, OF, deriv. of *coucher;* (v.) ME *couchen* < AF, OF *coucher,* OF *colcher* < L *collocāre* to put into place, equiv. to *col-* COL- + *locāre* to put, place; see LOCATE]

couch•ant (kou′chənt), *adj.* **1.** lying down; crouching. **2.** *Heraldry.* (of an animal) represented as lying on its stomach with its hind legs and forelegs pointed forward. [1400–50; late ME < MF, prp. of *coucher* to lay or lie. See COUCH, -ANT]

cou•ché (ko͞o shā′), *adj. Heraldry.* (of an escutcheon) depicted in a diagonal position, the sinister chief uppermost. [1720–30; < F, ptp. of *coucher* to lay down. See COUCH]

couch•er (ko͞o′chər, kou′-), *n. Papermaking.* the worker who transfers sheets of wet pulp to the couch. [1745–55; COUCH + -ER[1]]

cou•chette (ko͞o shet′), *n. Railroads.* **1.** a sleeping berth in a passenger compartment that can be collapsed to form a benchlike seat for daytime use. **2.** a compartment containing such berths. [< F; see COUCH, -ETTE]

couch′ grass′ (kouch, ko͞och), any of various grasses, esp. *Agropyron repens,* known chiefly as troublesome weeds and characterized by creeping rootstocks that spread rapidly. Also called **quitch.** [1570–80; *couch,* var. of QUITCH]

couch•ing (kou′ching), *n.* **1.** the act of a person or thing that couches. **2.** a method of embroidering in which a thread, often heavy, laid upon the surface of the material, is caught down at intervals by stitches taken with another thread through the material. **3.** work so made. [1325–75; ME; see COUCH, -ING[1]]

couch′ pota′to, *Informal.* a person whose leisure time is spent watching television. [1980–85]

couch′ roll′ (ko͞och, kouch), *Papermaking.* the roll on which a wet web is transferred from the paper machine to the couch. [1850–55]

cou·dé′ tel′escope (ko͞o dā′), a telescope in which light from the primary mirror is reflected along the polar axis to additional mirrors, and in which the focus **(coudé′ fo′cus)** is independent of the telescope's motion, permitting the use of heavy instruments without disturbing the delicate balance of the telescope. [1920–25; < F *coudé* bent, elbowed, ptp. of *couder* to bend, v. deriv. of *coude* elbow << L *cubitus* CUBIT]

Cou·é (ko͞o ā′), *n.* **É·mile** (ā mēl′), 1857–1926, French psychotherapist. Cf. **Couéism.**

Cou·é·ism (ko͞o ā′iz əm, ko͞o′ā iz′-), *n.* a method of self-help stressing autosuggestion, popular esp. in the U.S. c1920 and featuring the slogan "Day by day in every way I am getting better and better." [1920–25; < F *couéisme.* See COUÉ, -ISM]

Cou·ette′ flow′ (ko͞o et′), *Mech.* the flow of a fluid between two surfaces that have tangential relative motion, as of a liquid between two coaxial cylinders that have different angular velocities. [< F *couette,* lit., feather bed (in machinery, a bearing). See QUILT]

cou·gar (ko͞o′gər), *n., pl.* **-gars,** (*esp. collectively*) **-gar.** a large, tawny cat, *Felis concolor,* of North and South America: now greatly reduced in number and endangered in some areas. Also called **mountain lion, panther, puma.** [1765–75; < F *couguar* (Buffon) < NL *cuguacu ara,* appar. a misrepresentation of Guarani *guaçu ara*]

cougar, *Felis concolor,* head and body 5 ft. (1.5 m); tail to 3 ft. (0.9 m)

cough (kôf, kof), *v.i.* **1.** to expel air from the lungs suddenly with a harsh noise, often involuntarily. **2.** (of an internal-combustion engine) to make a similar noise as a result of the failure of one or more cylinders to fire in sequence. **3.** to make a similar sound, as a machine gun firing in spurts. —*v.t.* **4.** to expel by coughing (usually fol. by *up* or *out*): *to cough up phlegm.* **5. cough up,** *Slang.* **a.** to relinquish, esp. reluctantly; contribute; give. **b.** to blurt out; state, as by way of making a confession: *After several hours of vigorous questioning by the police, he finally coughed up the information.* —*n.* **6.** the act or sound of coughing. **7.** an illness characterized by frequent coughing. **8.** a sound similar to a cough, a machine gun, or an engine firing improperly. [1275–1325; ME *coghen,* appar. < OE **cohhian* (cf. its deriv. *cohhettan* to cough); akin to D *kuchen* to cough, G *keuchen* to wheeze] —**cough′er,** *n.*

cough′ drop′, a small, medicinal lozenge for relieving a cough, sore throat, hoarseness, etc. [1850–55]

Cough·lin (kôg′lin, kog′-), *n.* **Charles Edward** (*"Father Coughlin"*), 1891–1979, U.S. Roman Catholic priest, activist, radio broadcaster, and editor, born in Canada.

cough′ syr′up, a medicated, syruplike fluid, usually flavored and nonnarcotic or mildly narcotic, for relieving coughs or soothing irritated throats. Also called **cough′ med′icine.** [1875–80]

could (ko͝od; *unstressed* kəd), *v.* **1.** a pt. of **can**[1]. —*auxiliary verb.* **2.** (used to express possibility): *I wonder who that could be at the door. That couldn't be true.* **3.** (used to express conditional possibility or ability): *You could do it if you tried.* **4.** (used in making polite requests): *Could you open the door for me, please?* **5.** (used in asking for permission): *Could I borrow your pen?* **6.** (used in offering suggestions or advice): *You could write and ask for more information. You could at least have called me.* [ME *coude,* OE *cūthe;* modern *-l-* (from WOULD, SHOULD) first attested 1520–30]
—Usage. See **care.**

could·n't (ko͝od′nt), contraction of *could not.*
—Usage. See **care, contraction.**

couldst (ko͝odst, ko͝otst), *auxiliary v.* and *v. Archaic.* 2nd pers. sing. pt. of **can.**[1] Also, **could·est** (ko͝od′ist).

cou·lee (ko͞o′lē), *n.* **1.** *Chiefly Western U.S. and Western Canada.* a deep ravine or gulch, usually dry, that has been formed by running water. **2.** a small valley. **3.** a low-lying area. **4.** a small intermittent stream. **5.** *Geol.* a stream of lava. [1800–10, *Amer.;* < CanF, F: a flowing, n. use of fem of *coulé,* ptp. of *couler* to flow < L *cōlāre* to filter, strain, deriv. of *cōlum* strainer, sieve; cf. COLANDER, PORTCULLIS]

cou·li·biac (ko͞o lēb yäk′), *n. French-Russian Cookery.* a fish pie usually made with salmon or sturgeon combined with buckwheat, hard-boiled eggs, mushrooms, scallions, wine, herbs, and spices, and served in a brioche or puff pastry. [1895–1900; < F < Russ *kulebyáka* an oblong loaf of fish, meat, or vegetables, baked in a pastry shell; of uncert. orig.]

cou·lisse (ko͞o lēs′), *n.* **1.** a timber or the like having a groove for guiding a sliding panel. **2.** *Theat.* **a.** the space between two wing flats, leg drops, or the like. **b.** any space or area backstage. **c.** See **wing flat.** [1810–20; < F: groove, something that slides in a groove; see PORTCULLIS]

CONCISE ETYMOLOGY KEY: <, descended or borrowed from; >, whence; b., blend of, blended; c., cognate with; cf., compare; deriv., derivative; equiv., equivalent; imit., imitative; obl., oblique; r., replacing; s., stem; sp., spelling, spelled; resp., respelling, respelled; trans., translation; ?, origin unknown; *, unattested; ‡, probably earlier than. See the full key inside the front cover.

cou·loir (ko͞ol wär′; *Fr.* ko͞o lwAR′), *n., pl.* **cou·loirs** (ko͞ol wärz′, *Fr.* ko͞o lwAR′). a steep gorge or gully on the side of a mountain, esp. in the Alps. [1850–55; < F: lit., colander < LL *cōlātōrium* strainer, equiv. to L *cōlā(re)* to strain, filter + *-tōrium* -TORY[2]; see COULEE]

cou·lomb (ko͞o′lom, -lōm, ko͞o lom′, -lōm′), *n.* the SI unit of quantity of electricity, equal to the quantity of charge transferred in one second across a conductor in which there is a constant current of one ampere. *Abbr.:* C [1880–85; after COULOMB]

Cou·lomb (ko͞o′lom, -lōm, ko͞o lom′, -lōm′; *Fr.* ko͞o-lôN′), *n.* **Charles Au·gus·tin de** (sHARl ō gy stan′ də), 1736–1806, French physicist and inventor.

Cou′lomb's law′, *Elect.* the principle that the force between two point charges acts in the direction of the line between them and is directly proportional to the product of their electric charges divided by the square of the distance between them. [1850–55; after COULOMB]

cou·lom·e·ter (ko͞o lom′i tər, kə-), *n. Elect.* voltameter. Also, **cou·lomb·me·ter** (ko͞o′lom mē′tər, -lōm-). [1900–05; COULO(MB) + -METER]

cou·lom·e·try (ko͞o lom′i trē, kə-), *n. Chem.* a method used in quantitative analysis, whereby the amount of a substance set free or deposited during electrolysis is determined by measuring the number of coulombs that passed through the electrolyte. [1940–45; COULO(MB) + -METRY] —**cou·lo·met·ric** (ko͞o′lə me′-trik), *adj.* —**cou′lo·met′ri·cal·ly,** *adv.*

coul·ter (kōl′tər), *n.* colter.

Coul·ter (kōl′tər), *n.* **John Merle** (mûrl), 1851–1928, U.S. botanist.

Coul′ter pine′, a California pine, *Pinus coulteri,* having stout, bluish-green needles and heavy cones 9 to 14 in. (23 to 36 cm) long. Also called **big-cone pine.** [1885–90, *Amer.;* named after Thomas *Coulter* (d. 1843), Irish botanist]

Cou·ma·din (ko͞o′mə din), *Pharm., Trademark.* a brand name for warfarin (def. 2).

cou·ma·rin (ko͞o′mə rin), *n.* a fragrant crystalline substance, $C_9H_6O_2$, obtained from the tonka bean, sweet clover, and certain other plants or prepared synthetically, used chiefly in soaps and perfumery. Also, **cumarin.** [1820–30; < F *coumarine,* equiv. to *coumar(ou)* tonka-bean tree (< Sp *cumarú* < Pg < Tupi *cumaru*) + *-ine* -IN[2]]

cou·ma·rone (ko͞o′mə rōn′), *n. Chem.* a colorless liquid, C_8H_6O, derived from a naphtha distilled from coal tar: used chiefly in the synthesis of coumarone resins. Also, **cumarone.** Also called **benzofuran.** [1880–85; < G *Cumaron;* see COUMARIN, -ONE]

cou′marone res′in, any of the group of thermosetting resins derived by the polymerization of mixtures of coumarone and indene: used chiefly in the manufacture of paints, varnishes, and printing inks. Also called **cou′·ma·rone-in′dene res′in** (ko͞o′mə rōn′in′dēn).

coun·cil (koun′səl), *n.* **1.** an assembly of persons summoned or convened for consultation, deliberation, or advice. **2.** a body of persons specially designated or selected to act in an advisory, administrative, or legislative capacity: *the governor's council on housing.* **3.** (in certain British colonies or dependencies) an executive or legislative body assisting the governor. **4.** an ecclesiastical assembly for deciding matters of doctrine or discipline. **5.** *New Testament.* the Sanhedrin or other authoritative body. [1125–75; ME *co(u)nsile* < AF *cuncil(e),* OF *concile* < LL *concilium* synod, church council (L: assembly), prob. equiv. to L *con-* CON- + *-cil(āre),* comb. form of *calāre* to summon, convoke + *-ium* -IUM; ME *-s-* by assoc. with AF *cunseil* COUNSEL]
—Usage. COUNCIL, COUNSEL, and CONSUL are not interchangeable. COUNCIL is a noun. Its most common sense is "an assembly of persons convened for deliberation or the like." It is generally used with a singular verb. A member of such a group is a *councilor.* COUNSEL is both noun and verb. Its most common meaning as a noun is "advice given to another": *His counsel on domestic relations is sound.* A person giving such advice is a *counselor.* In law, COUNSEL means "legal adviser or advisers" and can be either singular or plural. As a verb, COUNSEL means "to advise." The noun CONSUL refers to the representative of a government who guards the welfare of its citizens in a foreign country.

Coun′cil Bluffs′, a city in SW Iowa, across the Missouri River from Omaha, Neb. 56,449.

coun′cil fire′, a fire kept burning continually during a council of American Indians. [1745–55, *Amer.*]

Coun′cil for Mu′tual Econom′ic Assis′tance. See **COMECON.**

coun·cil·lor (koun′sə lər, -slər), *n.* councilor. —**coun′·cil·lor·ship′,** *n.*

coun·cil·man (koun′səl mən), *n., pl.* **-men.** a member of a council, esp. the local legislative body of a city. [1650–60; COUNCIL + MAN[1]] —**coun·cil·man·ic** (koun′-səl man′ik), *adj.*
—Usage. See **-man.**

coun′cil-man′ag·er plan′ (koun′səl man′ə jər), a system of municipal government in which the administrative powers of the city are entrusted to a manager selected by the city council.

coun·cil·mem·ber (koun′səl mem′bər), *n.* a member of a council, esp. a legislative council. [COUNCIL + MEMBER]

Coun′cil of Econom′ic Advis′ers, *U.S. Govt.* a board, consisting of three members, established in 1946 to advise the president on economic matters. *Abbr.:* CEA

Coun′cil of Min′isters, 1. the policy-making body of the European Economic Community, representing all the member nations. **2.** (*sometimes l.c.*) the highest administrative body of various countries, usually serving in an advisory capacity to the chief executive; cabinet.

Coun′cil of National′ities. See under **Supreme Soviet.**

coun′cil of state′, a council that deliberates on high-level policies of a government. [1605–15]

Coun′cil of Ten′, the governing council of Venice from 1310 until its overthrow in 1797, composed originally of 10 and later 17 members.

Coun′cil of the Reich′, *German Hist.* the Reichsrat.

Coun′cil of the Un′ion. See under **Supreme Soviet.**

coun′cil of war′, 1. a conference of high-ranking military or naval officers, usually for discussing a major emergency or war problem. **2.** any conference for discussing or deciding upon a course of action. [1580–90]

coun·ci·lor (koun′sə lər, -slər), *n.* **1.** a member of a council. **2.** counselor. Also, **councillor.** [1300–50; COUNCIL + -OR[2]; r. ME *conseiler* < AF: adviser; see COUNSELOR] —**coun′ci·lor·ship′,** *n.*

coun·cil·per·son (koun′səl pûr′sən), *n.* a member of a city or local legislative council. [COUNCIL + -PERSON]
—Usage. See **-person.**

coun·cil·wom·an (koun′səl wo͝om′ən), *n., pl.* **-wom·en.** a female member of a council, esp. the local legislative body of a city. [1925–30; COUNCIL + -WOMAN]
—Usage. See **-woman.**

coun·sel (koun′səl), *n., pl.* **-sel** for 3, *v.,* **-seled, -sel·ing** or (*esp. Brit.*) **-selled, -sel·ling.** —*n.* **1.** advice; opinion or instruction given in directing the judgment or conduct of another. **2.** interchange of opinions as to future procedure; consultation; deliberation. **3.** *Law.* (*used with a singular or plural v.*) the advocate or advocates engaged in the direction of a cause in court; a legal adviser or counselor: *Is counsel for the defense present?* **4.** deliberate purpose; plan; design. **5.** *Theol.* one of the advisory declarations of Christ, considered by some Christians as not universally binding but as given for aid in attaining moral perfection. **6.** *Archaic.* a private or secret opinion or purpose. **7.** *Obs.* wisdom; prudence. **8. keep one's own counsel,** to conceal one's ideas or opinions; keep silent. **9. take counsel,** to ask for or exchange advice, ideas, or opinions; deliberate; consult. —*v.t.* **10.** to give advice to; advise. **11.** to urge the adoption of, as a course of action; recommend (a plan, policy, etc.): *He counseled patience during the crisis.* —*v.i.* **12.** to give counsel or advice. **13.** to get or take counsel or advice. [1175–1225; (n.) ME *counseil* < AF *cunseil,* OF *conseil* < L *consilium* debate, advice, advisory body, plan, equiv. to *consil-,* var. s. of *consulere* to apply for advice (see CONSULT) + *-ium* -IUM; (v.) < AF *cunseiler* (OF *conseillier*) < LL *consiliāre,* deriv. of *consilium*] —**coun′sel·a·ble;** *esp. Brit.,* **coun′sel·la·ble,** *adj.*
—Syn. 1. recommendation, suggestion. See **advice. 3.** lawyer, attorney; solicitor, barrister.
—Usage. See **council.**

coun·sel·ee (koun′sə lē′), *n.* a person who is being counseled. [1920–25; COUNSEL + -EE]

coun·sel·ing (koun′sə ling), *n. Psychol.* professional guidance in resolving personal conflicts and emotional problems. Also, **coun′sel·ling.** [COUNSEL + -ING[1]]

coun·se·lor (koun′sə lər), *n.* **1.** a person who counsels; adviser. **2.** a faculty member who advises students on personal and academic problems, career choices, and the like. **3.** an assistant at a children's camp, often a high-school or college student, who supervises a group of children or directs a particular activity, as nature study or a sport. **4.** a lawyer, esp. a trial lawyer; counselor-at-law. **5.** an official of an embassy or legation who ranks below an ambassador or minister. Also, *esp. Brit.,* **coun′·sel·lor.** [1175–1225; ME *counseiler* < AF *cunseiler, cunseiliour,* OF *conseilleor.* See COUNSEL, -EUR, -ER[2], -OR[2]] —**coun′se·lor·ship′;** *esp. Brit.,* **coun′sel·lor·ship′,** *n.*
—Syn. 4. counsel, attorney; solicitor, barrister.

coun·se·lor-at-law (koun′sə lər ət lô′), *n., pl.* **coun·se·lors-at-law.** counselor (def. 4). [1875–80]

count[1] (kount), *v.t.* **1.** to check over (the separate units or groups of a collection) one by one to determine the total number; add up; enumerate: *He counted his tickets and found he had ten.* **2.** to reckon up; calculate; compute. **3.** to list or name the numerals up to: *Close your eyes and count ten.* **4.** to include in a reckoning; take into account: *There are five of us here, counting me.* **5.** to reckon to the credit of another; ascribe; impute. **6.** to consider or regard: *He counted himself lucky to have survived the crash.* —*v.i.* **7.** to count the items of a collection one by one in order to determine the total: *She counted three times before she was satisfied that none was missing.* **8.** to list or name numerals in order: *to count to 100 by fives.* **9.** to reckon numerically. **10.** to have a specified numerical value. **11.** to be accounted or worth something: *That first try didn't count—I was just practicing.* **12.** to have merit, importance, value, etc.; deserve consideration: *Every bit of help counts.* **13.** to have worth; amount (usually fol. by *for*): *Intelligence counts for something.* **14. count coup.** See **coup**[1] (def. 4). **15. count down,** to count backward, usually by ones, from a given integer to zero. **16. count in,** to include: *If you're going to the beach, count me in.* **17. count off,** (often used imperatively, as in the army) to count aloud by turns, as to arrange positions within a group of persons; divide or become divided into groups: *Close up ranks and count off from the left by threes.* **18. count on** or **upon,** to depend or rely on: *You can always count on him to lend you money.* **19. count out, a.** *Boxing.* to declare (a boxer) a loser because of inability to stand up before the referee has counted 10 seconds. **b.** to exclude: *When it comes to mountain climbing, count me out.* **c.** to count and apportion or give out: *She counted out four cookies to each child.* **d.** to disqualify (ballots) illegally in counting, in order to control the election. —*n.* **20.** the act of counting; enumeration; reckoning; calculation: *A count of hands showed 23 in favor and 16 opposed.* **21.** the number representing the result of a process of counting; the total number. **22.** an accounting. **23.** *Baseball.* the number of balls and strikes, usually designated in that order, that have been called on a batter during a turn at bat: *a count of two* *balls and one strike.* **24.** *Law.* a distinct charge or theory of action in a declaration or indictment: *He was found guilty on two counts of theft.* **25.** *Textiles.* **a.** a number representing the size or quality of yarn, esp. the number based on the relation of weight to length of the yarn and indicating its degree of coarseness. **b.** the number of warp and filling threads per square inch in woven material, representing the texture of the fabric. **26.** *Bowling.* the number of pins struck down by the first ball rolled by a bowler in the frame following a spare and included in the score for the frame in which the spare was made. **27.** *Physics.* **a.** a single ionizing reaction registered by an ionization chamber, as in a Geiger counter. **b.** the indication of the total number of ionizing reactions registered by an ionization chamber in a given period of time. **28.** *Archaic.* regard; notice. **29.** **the count,** *Boxing.* the calling aloud by the referee of the seconds from 1 to 10 while a downed boxer remains off his feet. Completion of the count signifies a knockout, which the referee then declares: *A hard right sent the challenger down for the count.* Also called **the full count.** —*adj.* **30.** noting a number of items determined by an actual count: *The box is labeled 50 count.* [1275–1325; (v.) ME *counten* < AF *c(o)unter,* OF *conter* < L *computāre* to COMPUTE; (n.) ME *counte* < AF *c(o)unte,* OF *conte* < LL *computus* calculation, reckoning, n. deriv. of *computāre*]

count[2] (kount), *n.* (in some European countries) a nobleman equivalent in rank to an English earl. [1375–1425; late ME *counte* < AF *c(o)unte,* OF *conte, comte* < LL *comitem,* acc. of *comes* honorary title of various imperial functionaries, L: retainer, staff member, lit., companion; see COMES]

count·a·ble (koun′tə bəl), *adj.* **1.** able to be counted. **2.** *Math.* **a.** (of a set) having a finite number of elements. **b.** (of a set) having elements that form a one-to-one correspondence with the natural numbers; denumerable; enumerable. [1400–50; late ME. See COUNT[1], -ABLE] —**count′a·bil′i·ty, count′a·ble·ness,** *n.* —**count′a·bly,** *adv.*

count′ably ad′ditive func′tion, *Math.* a set function that upon operating on the union of a countable number of disjoint sets gives the same result as the sum of the functional values of each set. Cf. **finitely additive function.**

count′ably com′pact set′, *Math.* a set for which every cover consisting of a countable number of sets has a subcover consisting of a finite number of sets.

count·down (kount′doun′), *n.* **1.** the backward counting in fixed time units from the initiation of a project, as a rocket launching, with the moment of firing designated as zero. **2.** the final preparations made during this period. **3.** a period of increasing activity, tension, or anxiety, as before a deadline. [1950–55, *Amer.*; n. use of v. phrase *count down*]

coun·te·nance (koun′tn əns), *n., v.,* **-nanced, -nanc·ing.** —*n.* **1.** appearance, esp. the look or expression of the face: *a sad countenance.* **2.** the face; visage. **3.** calm facial expression; composure. **4.** approval or favor; encouragement; moral support. **5.** *Obs.* bearing; behavior. **6.** **out of countenance,** visibly disconcerted; abashed: *He was somewhat out of countenance at the prospect of an apology.* —*v.t.* **7.** to permit or tolerate: *You should not have countenanced his rudeness.* **8.** to approve, support, or encourage. [1250–1300; ME *cuntenaunce* behavior, bearing, self-control < AF *cuntena(u)nce,* OF *contenance* < L *continentia;* see CONTINENCE] —**coun′te·nanc′er,** *n.*
—**Syn. 2.** See **face.**

count·er[1] (koun′tər), *n.* **1.** a table or display case on which goods can be shown, business transacted, etc. **2.** (in restaurants, luncheonettes, etc.) a long, narrow table with stools or chairs along one side for the patrons, behind which refreshments or meals are prepared and served. **3.** a surface for the preparation of food in a kitchen, esp. on a low cabinet. **4.** anything used in keeping account, as a disk of metal or wood, used in some games, as checkers, for marking a player's position or for keeping score. **5.** an imitation coin or token. **6.** a coin; money. **7.** **over the counter, a.** (of the sale of stock) through a broker's office rather than through the stock exchange. **b.** (of the sale of merchandise) through a retail store rather than through a wholesaler. **8.** **under the counter,** in a clandestine manner, esp. illegally: *books sold under the counter.* [1300–50; ME *countour* < AF (OF *comptoir*) < ML *computātorium* place for computing, equiv. to L *computā(re)* to COMPUTE + *-tōrium* -TORY[2]; cf. COUNT[1]]

count·er[2] (koun′tər), *n.* **1.** a person who counts. **2.** a device for counting revolutions of a wheel, items produced, etc. **3.** *Cards.* See **card counter. 4.** *Computers.* a storage register or program variable used to tally how often something of interest occurs. **5.** *Electronics.* scaler (def. 2). **6.** *Physics.* any of various instruments for detecting ionizing radiation and for registering counts. Cf. **Geiger counter.** [1325–75; ME *countour* < AF (OF *conteor*) << L *computātor,* equiv. to *computā(re)* to COMPUTE + *-tor* -TOR]

coun·ter[3] (koun′tər), *adv.* **1.** in the wrong way; contrary to the right course; in the reverse or opposite direction. **2.** contrary; in opposition (usually prec. by *run* or *go*): *to run counter to the rules.* —*adj.* **3.** opposite; opposed; contrary. —*n.* **4.** something that is opposite or contrary to something else. **5.** a blow delivered in receiving or parrying another blow, as in boxing. **6.** a statement or action made to refute, oppose, or nullify another statement or action. **7.** *Fencing.* a circular parry. **8.** a piece of leather or other material inserted between the lining and outside leather of a shoe or boot quarter to keep it stiff. **9.** *Naut.* the part of a stern that overhangs and projects aft of the sternpost of a vessel. **10.** Also called **void.** *Typesetting.* any part of the face of a type that is less than type-high and is therefore not inked. **11.** *Engin., Building Trades.* a truss member subject to stress only under certain partial loadings of the truss. **12.** the part of a horse's breast that lies between the shoulders and under the neck. —*v.t.* **13.** to go counter to; oppose; controvert. **14.** to meet or answer (a move, blow, etc.) by another in return. —*v.i.* **15.** to make a counter or opposing move. **16.** to give a blow while receiving or parrying one, as in boxing. [1400–50; late ME *countre* < AF *co(u)ntre, cuntre,* OF *contre* < L *contrā* against. See COUNTER-]

coun·ter[4] (koun′tər), *v.t.* to encounter in opposition or combat. [1250–1300; ME *countren,* aph. var. of *acountren* < MF *acontrer.* See A-[5], ENCOUNTER]

counter-, a combining form of **counter**[3], used with the meanings "against," "contrary," "opposite," "in opposition or response to" (*countermand*); "complementary," "in reciprocation," "corresponding," "parallel" (*counterfoil; counterbalance*); "substitute," "duplicate" (*counterfeit*). [ME *countre-;* see COUNTER[3]]
—**Note.** The lists at the bottom of this and following pages provide the spelling, syllabification, and stress for words whose meanings may easily be inferred by combining the meaning of COUNTER- and an attached base word, or base word plus a suffix. Appropriate parts of speech are also shown. Words prefixed by COUNTER- that have special meanings or uses are entered in their proper alphabetical places in the main vocabulary or as derived forms run on at the end of a main vocabulary entry.

coun·ter·act (koun′tər akt′), *v.t.* to act in opposition to; frustrate by contrary action. [1670–80; COUNTER- + ACT] —**coun′ter·ac′tant,** *adj.* —**coun′ter·act′er, coun′ter·ac′tor,** *n.* —**coun′ter·act′ing·ly,** *adv.* —**coun′ter·ac′tion,** *n.* —**coun′ter·ac′tive,** *adj.* —**coun′ter·ac′tive·ly,** *adv.*
—**Syn.** neutralize, counterbalance, contravene, thwart.

coun·ter·ar·gu·ment (koun′tər är′gyə mənt), *n.* a contrasting, opposing, or refuting argument. [1860–65; COUNTER- + ARGUMENT]

coun·ter·at·tack (*n.* koun′tər ə tak′; *v.* koun′tər ə tak′, koun′tər ə tak′), *n.* **1.** an attack made as an offset or reply to another attack. **2.** *Mil.* an attack by a ground combat unit to drive back an enemy attack. —*v.t.* **3.** to make a counterattack against. —*v.i.* **4.** to deliver a counterattack. [1915–20; COUNTER- + ATTACK]

coun·ter·at·trac·tion (koun′tər ə trak′shən), *n.* a rival or opposite attraction. [1755–65; COUNTER- + ATTRACTION] —**coun′ter·at·trac′tive,** *adj.* —**coun′ter·at·trac′tive·ly,** *adv.*

coun·ter·bal·ance (*n.* koun′tər bal′əns; *v.* koun′tər bal′əns), *n., v.,* **-anced, -anc·ing.** —*n.* **1.** a weight balancing another weight; an equal weight, power, or influence acting in opposition; counterpoise. —*v.t., v.i.* **2.** to act against or oppose with an equal weight, force, or influence; offset. [1570–80; COUNTER- + BALANCE]
—**Syn. 2.** correct, countervail, rectify, balance.

coun·ter·blast (koun′tər blast′, -bläst′), *n.* an unrestrained and vigorously powerful response to an attacking statement. [1560–70; COUNTER- + BLAST]

coun·ter·blow (koun′tər blō′), *n.* a blow given in return or retaliation, as in boxing. Also called **counterpunch.** [1625–35; COUNTER- + BLOW[1]]

coun·ter·bore (koun′tər bôr′, -bōr′; koun′tər bôr′, -bōr′), *n., v.,* **-bored, -bor·ing.** —*n.* **1.** a tool for enlarging a drilled hole for a portion of its length, as to permit sinking a screw head. **2.** the portion of the hole so enlarged. —*v.t.* **3.** to enlarge (a drilled hole) along part of the length of the hole by drilling with a bit having a greater diameter. [1605–15; COUNTER- + BORE[1]] —**coun′ter·bor′er,** *n.*

coun·ter-boulle (koun′tər bo͞ol′), *n.* contre-partie. [COUNTER- + BOULLE]

coun·ter·brace (koun′tər brās′), *n.* *Engin., Building Trades.* a web member of a truss subject to tension or compression under varying conditions. [1815–25; COUNTER- + BRACE]

coun·ter·change (koun′tər chānj′), *v.t.,* **-changed, -chang·ing. 1.** to cause to change places, qualities, etc.; interchange. **2.** to diversify; checker. [1885–90; COUNTER- + CHANGE]

coun·ter·charge (*n.* koun′tər chärj′; *v.* koun′tər chärj′, koun′tər chärj′), *n., v.,* **-charged, -charg·ing.** —*n.* **1.** a charge by an accused person against the accuser. **2.** *Mil.* a retaliatory charge. —*v.t.* **3.** to make an accusation against (one's accuser). **4.** *Mil.* to charge in retaliation. [1605–15; COUNTER- + CHARGE]

count′er check′, a blank check available in a bank for the use of a depositor in making a withdrawal from that bank. [1855–60, *Amer.*]

coun·ter·check (*n.* koun′tər chek′; *v.* koun′tər chek′), *n.* **1.** a check that opposes or restrains. **2.** a check controlling or confirming another check. —*v.t.* **3.** to oppose or restrain (a tendency, force, trend, etc.) by contrary action. **4.** to control or confirm by a second check. [1550–60; COUNTER- + CHECK]

coun·ter·claim (*n.* koun′tər klām′; *v.* koun′tər klām′), *n.* **1.** a claim to offset another claim, esp. one made by the defendant in a legal action. —*v.t., v.i.* **2.** to claim so as to offset a previous claim. [1775–85; COUNTER- + CLAIM] —**coun′ter·claim′ant,** *n.*

coun·ter·clock·wise (koun′tər klok′wīz′), *adj., adv.* in a direction opposite to that of the normal rotation of the hands of a clock; not clockwise. Also, **contraclockwise;** *esp. Brit.,* **anticlockwise.** [1885–90; COUNTER- + CLOCKWISE]

coun·ter·con·di·tion·ing (koun′tər kən dish′ə ning), *n.* *Psychol.* the extinction of an undesirable response to a stimulus through the introduction of a more desirable, often incompatible, response. [1960–65; COUNTER- + CONDITIONING]

coun·ter·coup (koun′tər ko͞o′), *pl.* **-coups** (-ko͞oz′). *n.* a coup aimed at the replacement of a government that itself achieved power through an earlier coup. [1960–65; COUNTER- + COUP[1]]

coun·ter·cul·ture (koun′tər kul′chər), *n.* the culture and lifestyle of those people, esp. among the young, who reject or oppose the dominant values and behavior of society. [1965–70; COUNTER- + CULTURE] —**coun′ter·cul′tur·al,** *adj.* —**coun′ter·cul′tur·ist, coun′ter·cul′·tur·al·ist,** *n.*

coun·ter·cur·rent (koun′tər kûr′ənt), *n.* **1.** a current running in an opposite direction to another current. **2.** a movement, opinion, mood, etc., contrary to the prevailing one. [1675–85; COUNTER- + CURRENT] —**coun′·ter·cur′rent·ly,** *adv.*

coun·ter·cy·cli·cal (koun′tər sī′kli kəl, -sik′li-), *adj.,* opposing the trend of a business or economic cycle; countervailing: *a countercyclical monetary policy.* [COUNTER- + CYCLICAL]

coun·ter·earth (koun′tər ûrth′), *n.* (in Pythagorean astronomy) a planet, out of sight from our part of the earth, whose shadow upon the sun and moon, cast by a central fire that is also out of sight, causes the eclipses. Also called **antichthon.** [1855–60; COUNTER- + EARTH, as trans. of Gk *antíchthōn*]

coun·ter·e·con·o·my (koun′tər i kon′ə mē), *n., pl.* **-mies.** an economy operating simultaneously with or in opposition to the established economic system. [COUNTER- + ECONOMY]

coun′ter electromo′tive force′, *Elect.* an electromotive force that is created by a chemical or magnetic effect upon a circuit and that acts in opposition to the applied electromotive force of the circuit. Also called **back electromotive force.**

coun·ter·es·pi·o·nage (koun′tər es′pē ə näzh′, -nij), *n.* the detection and frustration of enemy espionage. [1895–1900; COUNTER- + ESPIONAGE]

coun·ter·ex·am·ple (koun′tər ig zam′pəl, -zäm′-), *n.* an example that refutes an assertion or claim. [1955–60; COUNTER- + EXAMPLE]

coun·ter·fac·tu·al (koun′tər fak′cho͞o əl), *n.* *Logic.* a conditional statement the first clause of which expresses something contrary to fact, as "If I had known." [1945–50; COUNTER- + FACTUAL] —**coun′ter·fact′,** *n.* —**coun′ter·fac′tu·al·ly,** *adv.*

coun·ter·feit (koun′tər fit′), *adj.* **1.** made in imitation so as to be passed off fraudulently or deceptively as genuine; not genuine; forged: *counterfeit dollar bills.* **2.** pretended; unreal: *counterfeit grief.* —*n.* **3.** an imitation intended to be passed off fraudulently or deceptively as genuine; forgery. **4.** *Archaic.* a copy. **5.** *Archaic.* a close likeness; portrait. **6.** *Obs.* impostor; pretender. —*v.t.* **7.** to make a counterfeit of; imitate fraudulently; forge. **8.** to resemble. **9.** to simulate. —*v.i.* **10.** to make counterfeits, as of money. **11.** to feign; dissemble. [1250–1300; (adj.) ME *countrefet* false, forged < AF *cuntrefet,* OF *contrefait,* ptp. of *contrefere* to copy, imitate, equiv. to *conter-* COUNTER- + *fere* to make, do << L *facere* (see FACT); (v.) ME *countrefeten,* v. deriv. of *countrefet*] —**coun′ter·feit′er,** *n.* —**coun′ter·feit′ly,** *adv.* —**coun′ter·feit′ness,** *n.*
—**Syn. 1.** spurious, bogus. See **false. 2.** sham, feigned, simulated, fraudulent; mock, fake, ersatz. **3.** falsification, sham. **7.** copy; falsify.

coun·ter·foil (koun′tər foil′), *n.* *Chiefly Brit.* a part of a bank check, money order, etc., that is kept by the issuer and on which a record of the transaction is made; stub. [1700–10; COUNTER- + FOIL[2]]

coun·ter·force (koun′tər fôrs′, -fōrs′), *n.* a contrary or opposing force, tendency, etc. [1600–10; COUNTER- + FORCE]

coun·ter·fort (koun′tər fôrt′, -fōrt′), *n.* **1.** a buttress, esp. one for strengthening a basement wall against the pressure of earth. **2.** a cantilevered weight, as in a retaining wall, having the form of a pier built on the side of the material to be retained. [1580–90; partial trans. of MF *contrefort,* equiv. to *contre* COUNTER- + *fort* strength (deriv. of *fort* (adj.) strong)]

coun·ter·glow (koun′tər glō′), *n.* *Astron.* gegenschein. [1850–55; trans. of G *Gegenschein.* See COUNTER-, GLOW]

coun′ter im′age, *Math.* See **inverse image.**

CONCISE PRONUNCIATION KEY: *act, cāpe, dâre, pärt; set, ēqual; if, ice; ox, ōver, ôrder, oil, bo͝ok, bo͞ot, out; up, ûrge; child; sing; shoe; thin, that;* zh as in *treasure.* ə = *a* as in *alone, e* as in *system, i* as in *easily, o* as in *gallop, u* as in *circus;* ᵊ as in *fire* (fīᵊr), *hour* (ouᵊr). l and n can serve as syllabic consonants, as in *cradle* (krād′l), and *button* (but′n). See the full key inside the front cover.

coun′ter·ac′cu·sa′tion, *n.*
coun′ter·ad′, *n.*
coun′ter·ad′ap·ta′tion, *n.*
coun′ter·ad′ver·tis′ing, *n.*
coun′ter·a′gent, *n.*
coun′ter·ag·gres′sion, *n.*
coun′ter·ar′gue, *v.,* **-gued, -gu·ing.**
coun′ter·as·sas′si·na′tion, *n.*
coun′ter·as·sault′, *v.t., n.*
coun′ter·bid′, *n., v.,* **-bade, -bad** or **-bid, -bid·den** or **-bid, -bid·ding.**
coun′ter·block·ade′, *n., v.,* **-ad·ed, -ad·ing.**
coun′ter·cam·paign′, *n.*
coun′ter·com·mer′cial, *adj.*
coun′ter·com·plaint′, *n.*
coun′ter·con·ven′tion, *n.*
coun′ter·crit′i·cism, *n.*
coun′ter·cry′, *n., pl.* **-cries.**
coun′ter·dec′la·ra′tion, *n.*
coun′ter·de·mand′, *n.*
coun′ter·dem′on·strate′, *v.i.,* **-strat·ed, -strat·ing.**
coun′ter·dem′on·stra′tion, *n.*
coun′ter·dem′on·stra′tor, *n.*
coun′ter·de·ploy′ment, *n.*
coun′ter·ed′u·ca′tion·al, *n.;* **-ly,** *adv.*
coun′ter·ef′fort, *n.*
coun′ter·ev′i·dence, *n.*
coun′ter·fire′, *n., v.i.,* **-fired, -fir·ing.**
coun′ter·gov′ern·ment, *n.*
coun′ter·guer·ril′la, *adj.*
coun′ter·hy·poth′e·sis, *n., pl.* **-ses.**
coun′ter·in·cen′tive, *n.*
coun′ter·in·fla′tion·ar′y, *adj.*
coun′ter·in′flu·ence, *n., v.t.,* **-enced, -enc·ing.**
coun′ter·in′stance, *n.*
coun′ter·in′sti·tu′tion, *n.*
coun′ter·mag′net, *n.*
coun′ter·man′i·fes′to, *n., pl.* **-toes.**
coun′ter·mem′o, *n., pl.* **-mem·os.**
coun′ter·mo′bi·li·za′tion, *n.*

coun•ter•in•sur•gen•cy (koun′tər in sûr′jən sē), *n., pl.* **-cies,** *adj.* —*n.* **1.** a program or an act of combating guerrilla warfare and subversion. —*adj.* **2.** of, pertaining to, or designed for combating guerrilla warfare and subversion: *counterinsurgency funds.* [1960–65; COUNTER- + INSURGENCY] —**coun′ter•in•sur′gent,** *n., adj.*

coun•ter•in•tel•li•gence (koun′tər in tel′i jəns), *n.* **1.** the activity of an intelligence service employed in thwarting the efforts of an enemy's intelligence agents to gather information or commit sabotage. **2.** an organization engaged in counterintelligence. [1935–40; COUNTER- + INTELLIGENCE]

coun•ter•in•tu•i•tive (koun′tər in to͞o′i tiv, -tyo͞o′-), *adj.* counter to what intuition would lead one to expect: *The direction we had to follow was counterintuitive—we had to go north first before we went south.* [1960–65; COUNTER- + INTUITIVE]

coun•ter•i•on (koun′tər ī′ən, -ī′on), *n. Physical Chem.* an ion in solution that associates itself with an ion of opposite charge on the surface of a member of a solute. [COUNTER- + ION]

coun•ter•ir•ri•tant (koun′tər ir′i tənt), *n.* **1.** *Med.* an agent for producing inflammation in superficial tissues to relieve pain or inflammation in deeper structures. **2.** any irritation or annoyance that draws attention away from another. —*adj.* **3.** *Med.* of or acting as a counterirritant. [1850–55; COUNTER- + IRRITANT]

count•er•jump•er (koun′tər jum′pər), *n. Slang (older use).* a clerk in a retail store. [1820–30; COUNTER[1] + JUMPER[1]]

coun•ter•light (*v.* koun′tər līt′; *n.* koun′tər līt′), *v.,* **-light•ed** or **-lit, -light•ing,** *n.* —*v.t.* **1.** to light (an interior) with windows or lights on opposite sides. **2.** to light (an object) with a window or light directly opposite. —*n.* **3.** a light or window that counterlights an interior or object. Cf. **crosslight.** [1720–30; COUNTER- + LIGHT[1]]

count•er•man (koun′tər man′), *n., pl.* **-men.** a person who waits on customers from behind a counter, as in a cafeteria. [1850–55; COUNTER[1] + MAN[1]]

coun•ter•mand (*v.* koun′tər mand′, -mänd′, koun′tər mand′, -mänd′; *n.* koun′tər mand′, -mänd′), *v.t.* **1.** to revoke or cancel (a command, order, etc.). **2.** to recall or stop by a contrary order. —*n.* **3.** a command, order, etc., revoking a previous one. [1375–1425; late ME *countermaunden* < AF *countermander* < MF *contremander,* equiv. to *contre-* COUNTER- + *mander* to command < L *mandāre;* see MANDATE] —**coun′ter•mand′a•ble,** *adj.*
—**Syn. 1.** rescind, abrogate, overrule, recall.

coun•ter•march (*n.* koun′tər märch′; *v.* koun′tər-märch′, koun′tər märch′), *n.* **1.** a march back over the same ground. **2.** a complete reversal of conduct or measures. —*v.i.* **3.** to execute a countermarch. —*v.t.* **4.** to cause to countermarch. [1590–1600; COUNTER- + MARCH[1]]

coun•ter•mark (*n.* koun′tər märk′; *v.* koun′tər-märk′), *Numis.* —*n.* **1.** Also called **counterstamp.** a sign or device stamped on a coin after its minting. —*v.t.* **2.** to stamp (a coin) with a countermark; counterstamp. [1495–1505; (n.) < MF *contremarque,* equiv. to *contre* COUNTER- + *marque* MARK[1]; (v.) < MF *contremarquer,* deriv. of *contremarque*]

coun•ter•meas•ure (koun′tər mezh′ər), *n.* an opposing, offsetting, or retaliatory measure. [1920–25; COUNTER- + MEASURE]

coun•ter•mel•o•dy (koun′tər mel′ə dē), *n., pl.* **-dies.** a melody heard, played, or sung simultaneously with another melody as an integral part of the composition. [1930–35; COUNTER- + MELODY]

coun•ter•mi•gra•tion (koun′tər mī grā′shən), *n.* a migration in the opposite direction. [COUNTER- + MIGRATION]

coun•ter•mine (*n.* koun′tər mīn′; *v.* koun′tər mīn′, koun′tər mīn′), *n., v.,* **-mined, -min•ing.** —*n.* **1.** *Mil.* a mine intended to intercept or destroy an enemy mine. **2.** a counterplot. —*v.t.* **3.** to oppose by a countermine. —*v.i.* **4.** to make a countermine. **5.** *Mil.* to intercept or destroy enemy mines. [1425–75; late ME; see COUNTER-, MINE[2]]

coun•ter•of•fen•sive (koun′tər ə fen′siv, koun′tər ə-fen′-), *n. Mil.* an attack by an army against an attacking enemy force. [1915–20; COUNTER- + OFFENSIVE]

coun•ter•of•fer (koun′tər ô′fər, -of′ər, koun′tər ô′-fər, -of′ər), *n.* an offer or proposal made to offset or substitute for an earlier offer made by another. [1780–90; COUNTER- + OFFER]

coun•ter•pane (koun′tər pān′), *n. Older Use.* a quilt or coverlet for a bed; bedspread. [1425–75; COUNTER- + PANE (in obs. sense bedspread); r. late ME *counterpoynte* < MF *contre-pointe* quilt, alter. (by assoc. with *contre-* COUNTER-) of *cou(s)tepointe, coitepointe* < L *culcita puncta* pricked pillow. See QUILT, POINT] —**coun′ter•paned′,** *adj.*

coun•ter•part (koun′tər pärt′), *n.* **1.** a person or thing closely resembling another, esp. in function: *Our president is the counterpart of your prime minister.* **2.** a copy; duplicate. **3.** *Law.* a duplicate or copy of an indenture. **4.** one of two parts that fit, complete, or complement one another. [1425–75; late ME; see COUNTER-, PART]

count•er•per•son (koun′tər pûr′sən), *n.* a person who waits on customers from behind a counter, as in a cafeteria. [COUNTER(MAN) + -PERSON]
—**Usage.** See **-person.**

coun•ter•pho•bic (koun′tər fō′bik), *adj. Psychiatry.* seeking out a situation that one fears in an attempt to overcome the fear. [COUNTER- + -PHOBIC]

coun•ter•pin (koun′tər pin′), *n. South Midland and Southern U.S.* bedspread. Also called **county pin.** [alter., by folk etym., of COUNTERPANE]

coun•ter•plan (koun′tər plan′), *n.* **1.** an opposing plan. **2.** an alternative or substitute plan. [1780–90; COUNTER- + PLAN]

coun•ter•plea (koun′tər plē′), *n. Law.* an answering plea, as a plaintiff's response to a defendant's plea. [1555–65; COUNTER- + PLEA]

coun•ter•plot (*n., v.* koun′tər plot′; *v. also* koun′tər-plot′), *n., v.,* **-plot•ted, -plot•ting.** —*n.* **1.** a plot directed against another plot. **2.** *Literature.* a secondary theme in a play or other literary work, used as a contrast to or variation of the main theme. Cf. **subplot.** —*v.i.* **3.** to devise a counterplot. —*v.t.* **4.** to plot against (a plot or plotter). [1590–1600; COUNTER- + PLOT]

coun•ter•point (koun′tər point′), *n.* **1.** *Music.* the art of combining melodies. **2.** *Music.* the texture resulting from the combining of individual melodic lines. **3.** a melody composed to be combined with another melody. **4.** Also called **coun′terpoint rhythm′.** *Pros.* syncopation (def. 2). **5.** any element that is juxtaposed and contrasted with another. —*v.t.* **6.** to emphasize or clarify by contrast or juxtaposition. [1400–50; late ME < MF *contrepoint,* trans. of ML *(cantus) contrāpūnctus* lit., (song) pointed or pricked against, referring to notes of an accompaniment written over or under the notes of a plainsong. See COUNTER-, POINT]

coun•ter•poise (koun′tər poiz′), *n., v.,* **-poised, -pois•ing.** —*n.* **1.** a counterbalancing weight. **2.** any equal and opposing power or force. **3.** the state of being in equilibrium; balance. **4.** *Radio.* a network of wires or other conductors connected to the base of an antenna, used as a substitute for the ground connection. —*v.t.* **5.** to balance by an opposing weight; counteract by an opposing force. **6.** to bring into equilibrium. **7.** *Archaic.* to weigh (one thing) against something else; consider carefully. [1375–1425; COUNTER- + POISE[1]; r. late ME *countrepeis* < AF, equiv. to OF *contrepois*]

coun•ter•pose (koun′tər pōz′), *v.t.,* **-posed, -pos•ing.** to offer or place in opposition, response, or contrast. [1585–95; COUNTER- + (PRO)POSE]

coun•ter•pres•sure (koun′tər presh′ər), *n.* pressure in the opposite direction or with opposing effect. [1645–55; COUNTER- + PRESSURE]

coun•ter•pro•duc•tive (koun′tər prə duk′tiv), *adj.* thwarting the achievement of an intended goal; tending to defeat one's purpose: *Living on credit while trying to save money is counterproductive.* [1960–65; COUNTER- + PRODUCTIVE] —**coun′ter•pro•duc′tive•ly,** *adv.*

coun•ter•prop•a•gan•da (koun′tər prop′ə gan′də), *n.* propaganda to offset or nullify unfriendly or enemy propaganda. [COUNTER- + PROPAGANDA]

coun•ter•pro•pos•al (koun′tər prə pō′zəl), *n.* a proposal offered to offset or substitute for a preceding one. [1880–85; COUNTER- + PROPOSAL]

coun•ter•prop•o•si•tion (koun′tər prop′ə zish′ən), *n.* a proposition made in place of or in opposition to a preceding one. [1860–65; COUNTER- + PROPOSITION]

coun•ter•punch (koun′tər punch′), *n.* counterblow. [1675–85; COUNTER- + PUNCH[1]]

coun•ter•pur•chase (koun′tər pûr′chəs), *n.* barter, esp. of products or materials between international companies or importers and exporters.

Coun′ter Reforma′tion, the movement within the Roman Catholic Church that followed the Protestant Reformation of the 16th century.

coun•ter•ref•or•ma•tion (koun′tər ref′ər mā′shən), *n.* a reformation opposed to or counteracting a previous reformation. [1830–40; COUNTER- + REFORMATION, as trans. of G *Gegenreformation*]

coun•ter•re•ply (*n.* koun′tər ri plī′; *v.* koun′tər ri-plī′, koun′tər ri plī′), *n., pl.* **-plies,** *v.,* **-plied, -ply•ing.** —*n.* **1.** a reply made in response to a reply; rejoinder. —*v.i.* **2.** to make a reply in response to a reply. —*v.t.* **3.** to reply with (a statement) in response to a reply. [COUNTER- + REPLY]

coun•ter•rev•o•lu•tion (koun′tər rev′ə lo͞o′shən), *n.* **1.** a revolution against a government recently established by a revolution. **2.** a political movement that resists revolutionary tendencies. [1785–95; COUNTER- + REVOLUTION, as trans. of F *contre-révolution*]

coun•ter•rev•o•lu•tion•ar•y (koun′tər rev′ə lo͞o′-shə ner′ē), *adj., n., pl.* **-ar•ies.** —*adj.* **1.** characteristic of or resulting from a counterrevolution. **2.** opposing a revolution or revolutionary government. —*n.* **3.** Also, **coun•ter•rev•o•lu•tion•ist** (koun′tər rev′ə lo͞o′shə nist). a person who advocates or engages in a counterrevolution. [1790–1800; COUNTERREVOLUTION + -ARY]

coun•ter•ro•tat•ing (koun′tər rō′tā ting, koun′-), *adj. Mach.* (of two corresponding or similar moving parts) rotating in opposite directions: *counterrotating propellers.* [COUNTER- + ROTATING]

coun•ter•scarp (koun′tər skärp′), *n. Fort.* the exterior slope or wall of the ditch of a fort, supporting the covered way. See diag. under **bastion.** [1565–75; COUNTER- + SCARP[1] (modeled on It *contrascarpa*); r. *counterscarfe,* with *scarfe* obs. var. of SCARP[1]]

coun•ter•shad•ing (koun′tər shā′ding), *n. Zool.* the development of dark colors on parts usually exposed to the sun and of light colors on parts usually shaded, esp. as serving for protection or concealment. [1895–1900; COUNTER- + SHADING]

coun•ter•shaft (koun′tər shaft′, -shäft′), *n. Mach.* jackshaft (def. 1). [1860–65; COUNTER- + SHAFT] —**coun′ter•shaft′ing,** *n.*

coun•ter•sign (*n., v.* koun′tər sīn′; *v. also* koun′tər-sīn′), *n.* **1.** a sign used in reply to another sign. **2.** *Mil.* a secret sign that must be given by authorized persons seeking admission through a guarded area. **3.** a signature added to another signature, esp. for authentication. —*v.t.* **4.** to sign (a document that has been signed by someone else), esp. in confirmation or authentication. [1585–95; COUNTER- + SIGN, modeled on MF *contresigne,* or its source, OIt *contrasegno*]

coun•ter•sig•na•ture (koun′tər sig′nə chər), *n.* a signature added by way of countersigning. [1835–45; COUNTER(SIGN) + SIGNATURE]

coun•ter•sink (*v., n.* koun′tər singk′; *v. also* koun′tər-singk′), *v.,* **-sank, -sunk, -sink•ing,** *n.* —*v.t.* **1.** to enlarge the upper part of (a cavity), esp. by chamfering, to receive the cone-shaped head of a screw, bolt, etc. **2.** to cause (the head of a screw, bolt, etc.) to sink into a prepared depression so as to be flush with or below the surface. —*n.* **3.** a tool for countersinking a hole. **4.** a countersunk hole. [1810–20; COUNTER- + SINK]

coun•ter•spy (koun′tər spī′), *n., pl.* **-spies.** a spy active in counterespionage. [1935–40; COUNTER- + SPY]

coun•ter•stain (*n.* koun′tər stān′; *v.* koun′tər stān′), *Histol.* *n.* **1.** a second stain of a different color applied to a microscopic specimen and used to color and contrast those parts not retaining the first stain. —*v.t.* **2.** to treat (a microscopic specimen) with a counterstain. —*v.i.* **3.** to become counterstained; take a counterstain. [1890–95; COUNTER- + STAIN]

coun•ter•stamp (*n.* koun′tər stamp′; *v.* koun′tər-stamp′), *n.* **1.** a stamp added to a stamped paper or document as a qualifying mark. **2.** *Numis.* countermark (def. 1). —*v.t.* **3.** to stamp (a paper or document) already stamped. **4.** *Numis.* countermark (def. 2). [COUNTER- + STAMP]

coun•ter•state•ment (koun′tər stāt′mənt), *n.* a statement made to deny or refute another statement. [1850–55; COUNTER- + STATEMENT]

coun•ter•stroke (koun′tər strōk′), *n.* **1.** a stroke or blow given in return. **2.** *Med.* contrecoup. [1590–1600; COUNTER- + STROKE[1]]

coun•ter•sub•ject (koun′tər sub′jikt), *n. Music.* a theme in a fugue that occurs simultaneously with the second and often the subsequent themes of the main subject. [1850–55; COUNTER- + SUBJECT]

coun•ter•sue (koun′tər so͞o′), *v.,* **-sued, -su•ing.** —*v.t.* **1.** to bring a civil action against (one's complainant). —*v.i.* **2.** to bring a civil action against one's complainant. [COUNTER- + SUE]

count′er ta′ble, a medieval English table having a top divided into appropriately marked spaces for various denominations of money.

coun•ter•ten•or (koun′tər ten′ər), *n. Music.* **1.** an adult male voice or voice part higher than the tenor. **2.** a singer with such a voice; a high tenor. Also called **male alto.** [1350–1400; ME *cowntyrtenur,* appar. < AF; cf. MF *contreteneur,* OIt *contratenore,* equiv. to *contra-* CONTRA-[2] + *tenore* TENOR]

coun•ter•ter•ror•ism (koun′tər ter′ə riz′əm), *n.* terrorism in reaction to or retaliation for some previous act of terrorism. [1965–70; COUNTER- + TERRORISM] —**coun′ter•ter′ror•ist,** *n., adj.*

count•er•top (koun′tər top′), *n.* **1.** a counter, as in a kitchen, esp. when covered with a heat- and stain-resistant material. —*adj.* **2.** designed to fit or be used on a countertop: *a countertop microwave oven.* [1895–1900; COUNTER[1] + TOP[1]]

coun•ter•trade (koun′tər trād′), *n.* trade, esp. international trade, carried on for payment wholly or partially in goods instead of cash or credit. [1915–20; COUNTER- + TRADE] —**coun′ter•trad′er,** *n.*

coun•ter•trans•fer•ence (koun′tər trans fûr′əns, -trans′fər əns), *n. Psychoanal.* transference on the part of the analyst of repressed feelings aroused by the patient. [COUNTER- + TRANSFERENCE]

coun•ter•turn (koun′tər tûrn′), *n.* **1.** a turn in an opposing or contrary direction. **2.** an unexpected twist or turn of events in the plot of a story, play, or the like. [1580–90; COUNTER- + TURN]

coun•ter•type (koun′tər tīp′), *n.* **1.** a corresponding type. **2.** an opposite type. [1615–25; COUNTER- + TYPE]

coun•ter•vail (koun′tər vāl′), *v.t.* **1.** to act or avail against with equal power, force, or effect; counteract. **2.** to furnish an equivalent of or a compensation for; offset. **3.** *Archaic.* to equal. —*v.i.* **4.** to be of equal force in opposition; avail. [1350–1400; ME *contrevailen* < AF *countrevail-,* tonic s. (subj.) of *countrevaloir* to equal, be

CONCISE ETYMOLOGY KEY: <, descended or borrowed from; >, whence; b., blend of, blended; c., cognate with; cf., compare; deriv., derivative; equiv., equivalent; imit., imitative; obl., oblique; r., replacing; s., stem; sp., spelling, spelled; resp., respelling, respelled; trans., translation; ?, origin unknown; *, unattested; ‡, probably earlier than. See the full key inside the front cover.

coun′ter•move′, *n.*
coun′ter•move′, *v.,* **-moved, -mov•ing.**
coun′ter•move′ment, *n.*
coun′ter•myth′, *n.*
coun′ter•or′der, *n., v.*
coun′ter•pe•ti′tion, *n., v.*
coun′ter•pick′et, *n., v.*
coun′ter•play′, *n.*
coun′ter•play′er, *n.*
coun′ter•ploy′, *n.*
coun′ter•pow′er, *n.*
coun′ter•proj′ect, *n.*
coun′ter•ques′tion, *n., v.*
coun′ter•raid′, *n., v.*
coun′ter•ral′ly, *n., pl.* **-lies,** *v.,* **-lied, -ly•ing.**
coun′ter•re•ac′tion, *n.*
coun′ter•re•form′er, *n.*
coun′ter•re•sponse′, *n.*
coun′ter•re•tal′i•a′tion, *n.*
coun′ter•ri′ot•er, *n.*
coun′ter•sci′en•tif′ic, *adj.*
coun′ter•shot′, *n.*
coun′ter•snip′er, *n.*
coun′ter•spell′, *n.*
coun′ter•state′, *v.,* **-stat•ed, -stat•ing.**
coun′ter•step′, *n., v.,* **-stepped, -step•ping.**
coun′ter•strat′e•gy, *n., pl.* **-gies.**
coun′ter•style′, *n.*
coun′ter•sub•ver′sive, *n.*
coun′ter•sug•ges′tion, *n.*
coun′ter•suit′, *n.*
coun′ter•sur•veil′lance, *n.*
coun′ter•tac′tics, *n.*
coun′ter•tend′en•cy, *n., pl.* **-cies.**
coun′ter•ter′ror, *n.*
coun′ter•threat′, *n.*
coun′ter•thrust′, *n.*
coun′ter•tra•di′tion, *n.*
coun′ter•trans′port, *n.*
coun′ter•trend′, *n.*
coun′ter•u′ni•ver′si•ty, *n., pl.* **-ties.**
coun′ter•vi′o•lence, *n.*
coun′ter•world′, *n.*

comparable to < L phrase *contrā valēre* to be of worth against (someone or something). See COUNTER-, -VALENT]
—Syn. 1. counterbalance, counterpoise, neutralize.

coun•ter•view (koun′tər vyo͞o′), *n.* an opposing or contrasting opinion. [1580–90; COUNTER- + VIEW]

coun•ter•weigh (koun′tər wā′), *v.t., v.i.* to counterbalance; counterpoise. [1400–50; late ME *countreweyen;* see COUNTER-, WEIGH]

coun•ter•weight (koun′tər wāt′), *n.* **1.** a weight used as a counterbalance. *—v.t.* **2.** to balance or equip with a counterweight. [1685–95; COUNTER- + WEIGHT]

count•er•word (koun′tər wûrd′), *n.* **1.** a word, often of short-lived popularity, widely used as an almost meaningless, automatic response. **2.** a word that has come to be used with a meaning much less specific than that which it had originally, as *swell, awful,* or *terrific.* [1670–80; COUNTER[1] + WORD]

coun•ter•work (*n.* koun′tər wûrk′; *v.* koun′tər-wûrk′, koun′tər wûrk′), *n.* **1.** work or action to oppose some other work or action. *—v.i.* **2.** to work in opposition. *—v.t.* **3.** to work in opposition to; hinder or frustrate. [1590–1600; COUNTER- + WORK] **—coun′ter-work′er,** *n.*

count•ess (koun′tis), *n.* **1.** the wife or widow of a count in the nobility of Continental Europe or of an earl in the British peerage. **2.** a woman having the rank of a count or earl in her own right. [1125–75; ME *c(o)untesse* < AF. See COUNT[2], -ESS]
—Usage. See **-ess.**

count′ing house′, a building or office used by the accounting and bookkeeping department of a business. [1400–50; late ME]

count′ing num′ber, *Math.* See **whole number** (def. 1). [1960–65]

count′ing room′, counting house. [1705–15]

count•less (kount′lis), *adj.* too numerous to count; innumerable: *the countless stars.* [1580–90; COUNT[1] + -LESS] **—count′less•ly,** *adv.*
—Syn. numberless, endless, myriad, unlimited.

count′ noun′, *Gram.* a noun, as *apple, table,* or *birthday,* that typically refers to a countable thing and that in English can be used in both the singular and the plural and can be preceded by the indefinite article *a* or *an* and by numerals. Cf. **mass noun.** [1950–55]

Count′ of Mon′te Cris′to, The (mon′tē kris′tō), (French, *Le Comte de Monte-Cristo),* a novel (1844–45) by Alexandre Dumas *père.*

count′ pal′atine, *pl.* **counts palatine. 1.** (formerly, in Germany) a count having jurisdiction in his fief or province. **2.** Also called **earl palatine.** *Eng. Hist.* an earl or other county proprietor who exercised royal prerogatives within his county. [1590–1600]

coun•tri•fied (kun′trə fīd′), *adj.* **1.** rustic or rural in appearance, conduct, etc.: *a countrified person; a countrified area amid the suburbs.* **2.** not sophisticated or cosmopolitan; provincial. Also, **countryfied.** [1645–55; COUNTRIFY + -ED[2]] **—coun′tri•fied′ness,** *n.*

coun•tri•fy (kun′trə fī′), *v.t.,* **-fied, -fy•ing.** to make countrified. [COUNTRY + -FY]

coun•try (kun′trē), *n., pl.* **-tries,** *adj.* *—n.* **1.** a state or nation: *What European countries have you visited?* **2.** the territory of a nation. **3.** the people of a district, state, or nation: *The whole country backed the president in his decision.* **4.** the land of one's birth or citizenship. **5.** rural districts, including farmland, parkland, and other sparsely populated areas, as opposed to cities or towns: *Many city dwellers like to spend their vacations in the country.* **6.** any considerable territory demarcated by topographical conditions, by a distinctive population, etc.: *mountainous country; the Amish country of Pennsylvania.* **7.** a tract of land considered apart from any geographical or political limits; region; district. **8.** the public. **9.** *Law.* the public at large, as represented by a jury. **10.** See **country music. 11. go to the country,** *Brit.* to dissolve a Parliament that has cast a majority vote disagreeing with the prime minister and cabinet and to call for the election of a new House of Commons. Also, **appeal to the country. 12. put oneself upon the** or **one's country,** *Law.* to present one's cause formally before a jury. *—adj.* **13.** of, from, or characteristic of the country; rural: *a winding country road.* **14.** of, pertaining to, or associated with country music: *That Nashville station plays country records all day long.* **15.** rude; unpolished; rustic: *country manners.* **16.** of, from, or pertaining to a particular country. **17.** *Obs.* of one's own country. [1200–50; ME *cuntree* < AF, OF < VL **(regiō) contrāta* terrain opposite the viewer, equiv. to L *contr(ā)* COUNTER[3] + *-āta,* fem. of *-ātus* -ATE[1]; cf. G *Gegend* region, deriv. of *gegen* AGAINST]

coun•try-and-west•ern (kun′trē ən wes′tərn), *n.* See **country music.** [1955–60]

coun•try-bred (kun′trē bred′), *adj.* raised or bred in the country. [1660–70]

coun′try club′, a club, usually in a suburban district, with a clubhouse and grounds, offering various social activities and generally having facilities for tennis, golf, swimming, etc. [1865–70, *Amer.*]

Coun′try Club′ Hills′, a city in NE Illinois, near Chicago. 14,676.

coun′try cous′in, a person from the country or from a small town, to whom the sights and activities of a large city are novel and bewildering. [1760–70]

coun•try-dance (kun′trē dans′, -däns′), *n.* a dance of rural English origin in which the dancers form circles or squares or in which they face each other in two rows. [1570–80]

coun′try fe′ver, *Older Use.* malaria. [1815–25; *Amer.*]

coun•try•fied (kun′tri fīd′), *adj.* countrified. **—coun′try•fied′ness,** *n.*

coun•try•folk (kun′trē fōk′), *n.* (*used with a plural v.*) **1.** people living or raised in the country; rustics. **2.** people from the same country; compatriots. Also called **countrypeople.** [1540–50; COUNTRY + FOLK]

coun′try fries′, *Dial.* See **home fries.** Also called **coun′try-fried pota′toes** (kun′trē frīd′).

coun′try gen′tleman, a wealthy man living in his country home or estate. [1625–35]

coun′try house′, a house in the country, esp. a large and impressive house on an estate. [1585–95]

coun′try kitch′en, a large kitchen with ample areas for food preparation and eating.

coun•try•man (kun′trē mən), *n., pl.* **-men. 1.** a native or inhabitant of one's own country. **2.** a native or inhabitant of a particular region. **3.** a person who lives in the country. **4.** an unsophisticated person, as one who lives in or comes from a rural area; rustic. [1275–1325; ME *contre man.* See COUNTRY, MAN[1]]
—Syn. 1. compatriot, fellow citizen, landsman. **3.** rustic, farmer, peasant. **—Ant. 1.** foreigner.
—Usage. See **-man.**

coun′try mile′, *Informal.* a long distance: *He can hit a baseball a country mile.* [1945–50]

coun′try mu′sic, a style and genre of largely string-accompanied American popular music having roots in the folk music of the Southeast and cowboy music of the West, usually vocalized, generally simple in form and harmony, and typified by romantic or melancholy ballads accompanied by acoustic or electric guitar, banjo, violin, and harmonica. Also called **country-and-western, coun•try-west•ern** (kun′trē wes′tərn). [1965–70]

coun•try•peo•ple (kun′trē pē′pəl), *n.* (*used with a plural v.*) countryfolk. [1570–80; COUNTRY + PEOPLE]

coun′try rock′, 1. a style of popular music combining the features of rock-'n'-roll and country music. Cf. **rockabilly. 2.** *Geol.* the rock surrounding and penetrated by mineral veins or igneous intrusions. Cf. **wall rock.** [1870–75]

coun•try•seat (kun′trē sēt′), *n. Brit.* a country mansion or estate, esp. one belonging to a distinguished family and large enough to accommodate house parties, hunt meetings, etc. [1575–85; COUNTRY + SEAT]

coun•try•side (kun′trē sīd′), *n.* **1.** a particular section of a country, esp. a rural section. **2.** its inhabitants. [1615–25; COUNTRY + SIDE[1]]

coun′try sing′er, a singer of country music songs. [1950–55]

coun′try store′, a general store, esp. in a rural or resort area. [1735–45, *Amer.*]

coun•try•wide (kun′trē wīd′), *adj.* extending across or throughout the whole country; nationwide: *a countrywide reaction; a countrywide highway system.* Also, **coun′try-wide′.** [1920–25; COUNTRY + WIDE]

coun•try•wom•an (kun′trē wo͝om′ən), *n., pl.* **-wom•en. 1.** a woman who is a native or inhabitant of one's own country. **2.** a woman who lives in the country. [1400–50; late ME; see COUNTRY, WOMAN]
—Usage. See **-woman.**

count•ship (kount′ship), *n.* **1.** the rank or position of a count. **2.** the territory or jurisdiction of a count. [1695–1705; COUNT[2] + -SHIP]

coun•ty[1] (koun′tē), *n., pl.* **-ties. 1.** the largest administrative division of a U.S. state: *Miami, Florida, is in Dade County.* **2.** one of the chief administrative divisions of a country or state, as in Great Britain and Ireland. **3.** one of the larger divisions for purposes of local administration, as in Canada and New Zealand. **4.** the territory of a county, esp. its rural areas: *We farmed out in the county before moving to town.* **5.** the inhabitants of a county: *It was supposed to be a secret, but you told the whole county.* **6.** the domain of a count or earl. [1250–1300; ME *counte* < AF *counté,* OF *cunté, conte* < LL *comitātus* imperial seat, office of a *comes* (see COUNT[2]), equiv. to L *comit-,* s. of *comes* + *-ātus* -ATE[3] (or by reanalysis of L *comitātus* escort, retinue, orig. v. noun of *comitārī* to accompany, deriv. of *comes*)]

coun•ty[2] (koun′tē), *n. Obs.* count[2]. [1540–50; < AF *counte* COUNT[2]; *-y* by confusion with COUNTY[1]]

coun′ty a′gent, a U.S. governmental official employed chiefly to advise farmers on farming and marketing techniques and to promote educational programs fitted to the needs of rural people. Also called **agricultural agent.** Cf. **extension agent.** [1695–1705, *Amer.*]

coun′ty board′, the governing body of a U.S. county consisting usually of three or more elected members. [1830–40, *Amer.*]

coun′ty clerk′, an elective county official in most U.S. states who generally keeps records of property titles, distributes ballots, issues licenses, etc. [1685–95]

coun′ty commis′sioner, a member of a U.S. county board overseeing the collection and disbursement of funds and other affairs of the county. [1680–90]

coun′ty court′, 1. (in the U.S.) **a.** an administrative board in counties in some states. **b.** a judicial tribunal in some states with jurisdiction extending over one or more counties. **2.** (in England) **a.** the lowest civil tribunal, having limited jurisdiction, mostly for the recovery of small debts. **b.** (formerly) the assembly of local residents who met periodically in each county under the presidency of the sheriff to transact the judicial and administrative business of the county. [1525–35]

coun′ty fair′, a competitive exhibition of farm products, livestock, etc., often held annually in the same place in the county. [1835–45]

coun′ty farm′, a farm maintained for the poor by a county. [1870–75, *Amer.*]

coun′ty home′, a county poorhouse. Also called **coun′ty house′.** [1910–15, *Amer.*]

coun′ty pal′atine, *pl.* **counties palatine.** the territory under the jurisdiction of a count palatine. [1400–50; late ME]

coun′ty pin′, *South Midland and Southern U.S.* counterpin.

coun′ty seat′, the seat of government of a county. [1795–1805, *Amer.*]

coup[1] (ko͞o), *n., pl.* **coups** (ko͞oz; *Fr.* ko͞o). **1.** a highly successful, unexpected stroke, act, or move; a clever action or accomplishment. **2.** (among the Plains Indians of North America) a brave or reckless deed performed in battle by a single warrior, as touching or striking an enemy warrior without sustaining injury oneself. **3.** See **coup d'état. 4. count coup,** (among Plains Indians of North America) **a.** to perform a coup. **b.** to recount or relate the coups one has performed. [1640–50; < F: lit., blow, stroke, OF *colp* < LL *colpus,* L *colaphus* < Gk *kólaphos*]

coup[2] (kop, ko͞op), *v.t., v.i. Scot.* overturn; upset. [1350–1400; ME *coupe* to pay for < ON *kaupa* to buy, barter; c. OE *cēapian,* G *kaufen.* See CHEAP]

coup de fou•dre (ko͞odᵊ fo͞o′drᵊ), *pl.* ***coups de foudre*** (ko͞odᵊ fo͞o′drᵊ). *French.* **1.** a thunderbolt. **2.** love at first sight.

coup de grâce (ko͞odᵊ gräs′), *pl.* ***coups de grâce*** (ko͞odᵊ gräs′). *French.* **1.** a death blow, esp. one delivered mercifully to end suffering. **2.** any finishing or decisive stroke. [lit., blow of mercy]

coup de main (ko͞odᵊ maN′), *pl.* ***coups de main*** (ko͞odᵊ maN′). *French.* a surprise attack; a sudden development. [lit., blow from the hand]

coup de maî•tre (ko͞odᵊ me′trᵊ), *pl.* ***coups de maître*** (ko͞odᵊ me′trᵊ). *French.* a master stroke.

coup de poing (*Fr.* ko͞odᵊ pwaN′), *pl.* **coups de poing** (*Fr.* ko͞odᵊ pwaN′). *Archaeol.* (no longer in technical use) a Lower Paleolithic stone hand ax, pointed or ovate in shape and having sharp cutting edges. [1910–15; < F: lit., blow of the fist]

coup d'es•sai (ko͞o de se′), *pl.* ***coups d'es•sai*** (ko͞o de se′). *French.* a first attempt. [lit., trial stroke]

coup d'é•tat (ko͞o′ dā tä′; *Fr.* ko͞o dā tA′), *pl.* **coups d'é•tat** (ko͞o′ dā täz′; *Fr.* ko͞o dā tA′). a sudden and decisive action in politics, esp. one resulting in a change of government illegally or by force. [1640–50; < F: lit., stroke concerning the state]
—Syn. overthrow, rebellion, revolution, uprising.

coup de thé•â•tre (ko͞odᵊ tā ä′trᵊ), *pl.* ***coups de thé•â•tre*** (ko͞odᵊ tā ä′trᵊ). *French.* **1.** a surprising or unexpected turn of events in a play. **2.** a sensational and unexpected turn in the plot of a drama. **3.** any theatrical trick intended to have a sensational effect.

coupe[1] (ko͞op), *n.* **1.** Also, **coupé.** a closed, two-door car shorter than a sedan of the same model. **2.** coupé (defs. 1–3). [1880–85; see COUPÉ]

coupe[2] (ko͞op), *n.* **1.** ice cream or sherbet mixed or topped with fruit, liqueur, whipped cream, etc. **2.** a glass container for serving such a dessert, usually having a stem and a wide, deep bowl. **3.** any rimless plate. [1375–1425 for earlier senses "wicker basket, tub, cask"; 1890–95 for current senses; ME < AF *co(u)pe,* OF *coupe* < LL *cuppa,* L *cūpa* cask, tub, barrel; cf. CUP]

cou•pé (ko͞o pā′ *or, for 1, 5,* ko͞op), *n.* **1.** a short, four-wheeled, closed carriage, usually with a single seat for two passengers and an outside seat for the driver. **2.** the end compartment in a European diligence or railroad car. **3.** *Ballet.* an intermediary step to transfer the weight from one foot to the other. **4.** (in Continental heraldry) party per fess. **5.** coupe[1] (def. 1). Also, **coupe** (for defs. 1–3). [1825–35; < F *coupé* (in defs. 1 and 2 short for *carrosse coupé* cut (i.e., shortened) coach), ptp. of *couper* to cut off, v. deriv. of *coup* COUP; cf. COPE[1]]

Cou•pe•rin (ko͞opᵊ RaN′), *n.* **Fran•çois** (fRäN swA′), 1668–1733, French composer.

Cou•pe•rus (ko͞o pä′rəs), *n.* **Lou•is** (lo͞o ē′), 1863–1923, Dutch novelist.

coup•ette (ko͞o pet′), *n.* a small coupe for serving dessert. [COUPE[2] + -ETTE]

cou•ple (kup′əl), *n., v.,* **-pled, -pling.** *—n.* **1.** two of the same sort considered together; pair. **2.** two persons considered as joined together, as a married or engaged pair, lovers, or dance partners: *They make a handsome couple.* **3.** any two persons considered together. **4.** *Mech.* a pair of equal, parallel forces acting in opposite directions and tending to produce rotation. **5.** Also called **couple-close.** *Carpentry.* a pair of rafters connected by a tie beam or collar beam. **6.** a leash for holding two hounds together. **7.** *Fox Hunting.* two hounds: *25 hounds or 12½ couple.* **8. a couple of,** more than two, but not many, of; a small number of; a few: *It will take a couple of days for the package to get there.* Also, **a couple.** *—v.t.* **9.** to fasten, link, or associate together in a pair or pairs. **10.** to join; connect. **11.** to unite in marriage or in sexual union. **12.** *Elect.* **a.** to join or associate by means of a coupler. **b.** to bring (two electric circuits or circuit components) close enough to permit an exchange of electromagnetic energy. *—v.i.* **13.** to join in a pair; unite. **14.** to copulate. [1175–1225; (n.) ME < AF *c(o)uple,* OF *cople, cuple* < L *cōpula* a tie, bond (see COPULA); (v.) ME *couplen* < AF *co(u)pler,* OF *copler, cupler* < L *copulāre* (see COPULATE)] **—cou′ple•a•ble,** *adj.*
—Usage. The phrase A COUPLE OF has been in standard use for centuries, especially with measurements of time and distance and in referring to amounts of money: *They walked a couple of miles in silence. Repairs will probably cost a couple of hundred dollars.* The phrase is used in all but the most formal speech and writing. The shortened phrase A COUPLE, without OF (*The gas station is a couple miles from here*), is an Americanism of recent development that occurs chiefly in informal speech or representations of speech. Without a following noun, the

CONCISE PRONUNCIATION KEY: act, cāpe, dâre, pärt; set, ēqual; if, ice; ox, ōver, ôrder, oil, bo͝ok, bo͞ot, out; up, ûrge; child; sing; shoe; thin, *th*at; zh as in *treasure.* ə = *a* as in *alone, e* as in *system, i* as in *easily, o* as in *gallop, u* as in *circus;* ᵊ as in *fire* (fīᵊr), *hour* (ouᵊr). l and n can serve as syllabic consonants, as in *cradle* (krād′l), and *button* (but′n). See the full key inside the front cover.

phrase is highly informal: *Jack shouldn't drive. I think he's had a couple.* (Here the noun *drinks* is omitted.)
In referring to two people, COUPLE, like many collective nouns, may take either a singular or a plural verb. Most commonly, it is construed as a plural: *The couple were traveling to Texas.* See also **collective noun.**

cou·ple-close (kup′əl klōs′), *n.* **1.** *Heraldry.* a narrow chevron, one-quarter the usual breadth. **2.** *Carpentry.* couple (def. 6). [1565–75]

cou·pler (kup′lər), *n.* **1.** a person or thing that couples or links together. **2.** *Mach.* a rod or link transmitting force and motion between a rotating part and a rotating or oscillating part. **3.** Also called **coupling.** *Railroads.* a device for joining pieces of rolling stock. **4.** a device in an organ or harpsichord for connecting keys, manuals, or a manual and pedals, so that they are played together when one is played. **5.** *Elect.* a device for transferring electrical energy from one circuit to another, as a transformer that joins parts of a radio apparatus together by induction. **6.** (in color photography) a chemical that reacts with the developer to produce one of the colors in a print or transparency. [1545–55; COUPLE + -ER[1]]

cou′ples ther′apy, a counseling procedure that attempts to improve the adaptation and adjustment of two people who form a conjugal unit.

cou·plet (kup′lit), *n.* **1.** a pair of successive lines of verse, esp. a pair that rhyme and are of the same length. **2.** a pair; couple. **3.** *Music.* any of the contrasting sections of a rondo occurring between statements of the refrain. [1570–80; < MF; see COUPLE, -ET]

cou·pling (kup′ling), *n.* **1.** the act of a person or thing that couples. **2.** *Mach.* **a.** a device for joining two rotating shafts semipermanently at their ends so as to transmit torque from one to the other. Cf. **clutch**[1] (def. 12a). **b.** a part with an inside thread for connecting two pipes of the same diameter. **c.** a fitting at the end of a length of hose into which the end of another such length can be screwed or fitted. **3.** *Railroads.* coupler (def. 3). **4.** *Elect.* **a.** the association of two circuits or systems in such a way that power may be transferred from one to the other. **b.** a device or expedient to ensure this. **5.** a short length of plumbing pipe having each end threaded on the inside. **6.** the part of the body between the tops of the shoulder blades and the tops of the hip joints in a dog, horse, etc. **7.** linkage (def. 5). [1300–50; ME; see COUPLE, -ING[1]]

coup′ling capac′itor, *Electronics.* See **blocking capacitor.**

cou·pon (ko͞o′pon, kyo͞o′-), *n.* **1.** a portion of a certificate, ticket, label, advertisement, or the like, set off from the main body by dotted lines or the like to emphasize its separability, entitling the holder to something, as a gift or discount, or for use as an order blank, a contest entry form, etc. **2.** a separate certificate, ticket, etc., for the same purpose. **3.** one of a number of small detachable certificates calling for periodic interest payments on a bearer bond. Cf. **coupon bond. 4.** *Metall.* a sample of metal or metalwork submitted to a chemical or testing agency for approval. [1815–25; < F; OF *colpon* piece cut off, equiv. to *colp(er)* to cut (see COPE[1]) + *-on* n. suffix] —**cou′pon·less,** *adj.*
—**Pronunciation.** COUPON, related to *cope* and *coup,* is of French origin. It has developed an American pronunciation variant (kyo͞o′pon) with an unhistorical *y*-sound not justified by the spelling. This pronunciation is used by educated speakers and is well-established as perfectly standard, although it is sometimes criticized. Its development may have been encouraged by analogy with words like *curious, cupid,* and *cute,* where *c* is followed by a "long *u*" and the (y) is mandatory.

cou′pon bond′, a bond, usually a bearer bond, that pays interest by means of coupons with specific cash values. [1860–65, *Amer.*]

cou′pon clip′per, a well-to-do person much of whose income is derived from clipping and cashing coupons from coupon bonds. [1880–85]

cou·pon·er (ko͞o′pon ər, kyo͞o′-), *n.* a person who seeks out or saves discount coupons, as for buying grocery items. [COUPON + -ER[1]]

cou·pon·ing (ko͞o′pon ing, kyo͞o′-), *n.* **1.** the practice of distributing discount coupons to consumers as a form of product promotion. **2.** the activity of seeking out or saving discount coupons to save money on food or household purchases. [1950–55; COUPON + -ING[1]]

cou′pon rate′, the interest rate fixed on a coupon bond or other debt instrument.

coup′ stick′ (ko͞o), a stick with which some North American Indian warriors sought to touch their enemies in battle as a sign of courage. [1875–80]

cour·age (kûr′ij, kur′-), *n.* **1.** the quality of mind or spirit that enables a person to face difficulty, danger, pain, etc., without fear; bravery. **2.** *Obs.* the heart as the source of emotion. **3. have the courage of one's convictions,** to act in accordance with one's beliefs, esp. in spite of criticism. [1250–1300; ME *corage* < OF, equiv. to *cuer* heart (< L *cor;* see HEART) + *-age* -AGE]
—**Syn. 1.** fearlessness, dauntlessness, intrepidity, pluck, spirit. COURAGE, BRAVERY, VALOR, BRAVADO refer to qualities of spirit and conduct. COURAGE permits one to face extreme dangers and difficulties without fear: *to take* (or *lose*) *courage.* BRAVERY implies true courage with daring and an intrepid boldness: *bravery in a battle.* VALOR implies heroic courage: *valor in fighting for the right.* BRAVADO is now usually a boastful and ostentatious pretense of courage or bravery: *empty bravado.* —**Ant. 1.** cowardice.

cou·ra·geous (kə rā′jəs), *adj.* possessing or characterized by courage; brave: *a courageous speech against the dictator.* [1250–1300; ME *corageous* < AF *curajous,* OF *corageus,* equiv. to *corage* COURAGE + *-eus* -EOUS] —**cou·ra′geous·ly,** *adv.* —**cou·ra′geous·ness,** *n.*
—**Syn.** See **brave.**

cou·rant (ko͝or′ənt *for 1;* ko͞o ränt′, *Fr.* ko͞o RÄN′ *for 2*), *adj.* **1.** *Heraldry.* (of an animal) represented in the act of running: *a greyhound courant.* —*n.* **2.** courante. [1595–1605; < F: lit., running, masc. prp. of *courir* to run; cf. CURRENT]

cou·rante (ko͞o ränt′; *Fr.* ko͞o RÄNT′), *n., pl.* **-rantes** (-ränts′; *Fr.* -RÄNT′). **1.** a dance dating back to the 17th century and characterized by a running or gliding step. **2.** a piece of music for or suited to this dance. **3.** *Music.* a movement following the allemande in the classical suite. Also, **courant.** [1580–90; < MF; lit., running, fem. prp. of *courir* to run; cf. CURRENT]

Cour·an·tyne (kôr′ən tīn′, kōr′-), *n.* a river in N South America, flowing N along the Guyana-Suriname border to the Atlantic Ocean. ab. 450 mi. (725 km) long.

Cour·bet (ko͞oR be′), *n.* **Gus·tave** (gys TAV′), 1819–77, French painter.

Cour·be·voie (ko͞oR bə VWA′), *n.* a city in N France, WNW of Paris. 54,578.

cou·reur de bois (ko͞o RŒR də bwä′), *pl.* ***cou·reurs de bois*** (ko͞o RŒR də bwä′). *French.* a French or French-Indian trapper of North America, esp. of Canada. [lit., runner, hunter of (the) woods]

cour·gette (ko͝or zhet′), *n. Chiefly Brit.* zucchini. [1930–35; < F, orig. dim. of *courge* gourd < VL **cucurbica,* for L *cucurbita;* cf. CUCURBIT, GOURD, -ETTE]

cour·i·er (kûr′ē ər, ko͝or′-), *n.* **1.** a messenger, usually traveling in haste, bearing urgent news, important reports or packages, diplomatic messages, etc. **2.** any means of carrying news, messages, etc., regularly. **3.** the conveyance used by a courier, as an airplane or ship. **4.** *Chiefly Brit.* a tour guide for a travel agency. [1350–1400; < MF *cour(r)ier* < It *corriere,* equiv. to *corr(ere)* to run (< L *currere*) + *-iere* < L *-ārius* -ARY; r. ME *corour* < AF *cor(i)our,* OF *coreor* < LL *curritor* runner; see CURRENT, -TOR]

cour·lan (ko͝or′lən), *n.* the limpkin. [< F *courlan* < Carib; akin to Galibi *kurliri*]

Cour·land (ko͝or′lənd), *n.* a former duchy on the Baltic: later, a province of Russia and, in 1918, incorporated into Latvia. Also, **Kurland.**

Cour·nand (ko͝or′nand, -nənd; *Fr.* ko͞oR nän′), *n.* **André Fré·dé·ric** (äN DRĀ′ fRā dā RēK′), born 1895, U.S. physiologist, born in France: Nobel prize for medicine 1956.

course (kôrs, kōrs), *n., v.,* **coursed, cours·ing.** —*n.* **1.** a direction or route taken or to be taken. **2.** the path, route, or channel along which anything moves: *the course of a stream.* **3.** advance or progression in a particular direction; forward or onward movement. **4.** the continuous passage or progress through time or a succession of stages: *in the course of a year; in the course of the battle.* **5.** the track, ground, water, etc., on which a race is run, sailed, etc.: *One runner fell halfway around the course.* **6.** a particular manner of proceeding: *a course of action.* **7.** a customary manner of procedure; regular or natural order of events: *as a matter of course; the course of a disease.* **8.** a mode of conduct; behavior. **9.** a systematized or prescribed series: *a course of lectures; a course of medical treatments.* **10.** a program of instruction, as in a college or university: *a course in economics.* **11.** a prescribed number of instruction periods or classes in a particular field of study. **12.** a part of a meal served at one time: *The main course was roast chicken with mashed potatoes and peas.* **13.** *Navig.* **a.** the line along the earth's surface upon or over which a vessel, an aircraft, etc., proceeds: described by its bearing with relation to true or magnetic north. **b.** a point of the compass. **14.** *Naut.* the lowermost sail on a fully square-rigged mast: designated by a special name, as foresail or mainsail, or by the designation of the mast itself, as fore course or main course. See diag. under **ship. 15.** *Building Trades.* a continuous and usually horizontal range of bricks, shingles, etc., as in a wall or roof. **16.** one of the pairs of strings on an instrument of the lute family, tuned in unison or in octaves to increase the volume. **17.** the row of stitches going across from side to side in knitting and other needlework (opposed to *wale*). **18.** Often, **courses.** the menses. **19.** a charge by knights in a tournament. **20.** a pursuit of game with dogs by sight rather than by scent. **21.** See **golf course. 22.** a race. **23. in due course,** in the proper or natural order of events; eventually: *They will get their comeuppance in due course.* **24. of course, a.** certainly; definitely: *Of course I'll come to the party.* **b.** in the usual or natural order of things: *Extra services are charged for, of course.* —*v.t.* **25.** to run through or over. **26.** to chase; pursue. **27.** to hunt (game) with dogs by sight rather than by scent. **28.** to cause (dogs) to pursue game by sight rather than by scent. **29.** *Masonry.* to lay (bricks, stones, etc.) in courses. —*v.i.* **30.** to follow a course; direct one's course. **31.** to run, race, or move swiftly: *The blood of ancient emperors courses through his veins.* **32.** to take part in a hunt with hounds, a tilting match, etc. [1250–1300; ME *co(u)rs* (n.) < AF *co(u)rs(e),* OF *cours* < L *cursus* a running, course, equiv. to *cur(rere)* to run + *-sus,* var. of *-tus* suffix of v. action]
—**Syn. 1.** way, road, track, passage. **2, 13a.** bearing. **6.** method, mode. **7.** process, career. **15.** row, layer.

course′ protrac′tor, a navigational instrument for measuring the bearing of a course as given on a chart, having a disk calibrated in degrees and an arm pivoted about the center of the disk.

cours·er[1] (kôr′sər, kōr′-), *n.* **1.** a person or thing that courses. **2.** a dog for coursing. [1585–95; COURSE + -ER[1]]

cours·er[2] (kôr′sər, kōr′-), *n. Literary.* a swift horse. [1250–1300; ME < AF, OF *coursier* < VL **cursārius,* equiv. to L *curs(us)* COURSE + *-ārius* -ARY; see -ER[2]]

cours·er[3] (kôr′sər, kōr′-), *n.* any of several swift-footed, ploverlike birds of the genera *Cursorius* and *Pluvianus,* chiefly of the desert regions of Asia and Africa. [1760–70; irreg. < NL *cursōrius* fitted for running, equiv. to L *cur(rere)* to run + *-sōrius,* for *-tōrius* -TORY[1]; cf. COURSE]

course·ware (kôrs′wâr′, kōrs′-), *n. Computers.* educational software designed esp. for use with classroom computers. [COURSE + (SOFT)WARE]

course·work (kôrs′wûrk′, kōrs′-), *n.* **1.** the work required of a student in a particular course of study; classroom work. **2.** curricular studies or academic work. [COURSE + WORK]

cours·ing (kôr′sing, kōr′-), *n.* **1.** the act of a person or thing that courses. **2.** the sport of pursuing game with dogs that follow by sight rather than by scent. [1530–40; COURSE + -ING[1]]

court (kôrt, kōrt), *n.* **1.** *Law.* **a.** a place where justice is administered. **b.** a judicial tribunal duly constituted for the hearing and determination of cases. **c.** a session of a judicial assembly. **2.** an area open to the sky and mostly or entirely surrounded by buildings, walls, etc. **3.** a high interior usually having a glass roof and surrounded by several stories of galleries or the like. **4.** *Chiefly Irish.* a stately dwelling. **5.** a short street. **6.** a smooth, level quadrangle on which to play tennis, basketball, etc. **7.** one of the divisions of such an area. **8.** the residence of a sovereign or other high dignitary; palace. **9.** a sovereign's or dignitary's retinue. **10.** a sovereign and councilors as the political rulers of a state. **11.** a formal assembly held by a sovereign. **12.** homage paid, as to a king. **13.** special or devoted attention in order to win favor, affection, etc.: *to pay court to the king.* **14.** the body of qualified members of a corporation, council, board, etc. **15.** a branch or lodge of a fraternal society. **16.** *Animal Behav.* **a.** an area where animals of a particular species gather to display. **b.** the group of insects, as honeybees, surrounding the queen; retinue. **17. hold court, a.** to have a formal assembly of a judicial tribunal or one held by a sovereign. **b.** to be surrounded by one's disciples or admirers, giving advice, exchanging gossip, receiving compliments, etc. **18. out of court, a.** without a legal hearing; privately: *The case will be settled out of court.* **b.** out of the question; undeserving of discussion: *This wild scheme is entirely out of court.* —*v.t.* **19.** to try to win the favor, preference, or goodwill of: *to court the rich.* **20.** to seek the affections of; woo. **21.** (of animals) to attempt to attract (a mate) by engaging in certain species-specific behaviors. **22.** to attempt to gain (applause, favor, a decision, etc.). **23.** to hold out inducements to; invite. **24.** to act in such a manner as to cause, lead to, or provoke: *to court disaster by reckless driving.* —*v.i.* **25.** to seek another's love; woo. **26.** (of animals) to engage in certain species-specific behaviors in order to attract individuals of the opposite sex for mating. [1125–75; ME *co(u)rt* < AF, OF < L *cohort-* (s. of *cohors*) farmyard; see COHORT]

Court (kôrt, kōrt), *n.* **Margaret Smith,** born 1942, Australian tennis player.

court-bouil·lon (ko͝or′bo͝ol yon′, -yôn′, kôr′-, kōr′-; *Fr.* ko͞oR bo͞o yôN′), *n., pl.* **courts-bouil·lons** (ko͝or′bo͝ol-yonz′, -yônz′, kôr′-, kōr′-; *Fr.* ko͞oR bo͞o yôN′). *French Cookery.* **1.** a vegetable broth or fish stock with herbs, used for poaching fish. **2.** a rich soup containing wine. [1715–25; < F: a preparation of salted water, white wine, herbs, and various other ingredients, in which fish, shellfish, or vegetables are cooked; lit., short broth]

court′ Chris′tian, *pl.* **courts Christian.** See **ecclesiastical court.** [1250–1300; ME]

court′ cup′board, *Eng. Furniture.* a sideboard of the 16th and 17th centuries, having three open tiers, the middle of which sometimes has a small closed cabinet with oblique sides. Cf. **press cupboard.** [1585–95]

court′ dance′, a dignified dance for performance at a court. Cf. **folk dance** (def. 1).

court′ dress′, the formal costume required to be worn at a royal court on ceremonial and other occasions. [1690–1700]

cour·te·ous (kûr′tē əs), *adj.* having or showing good manners; polite. [1225–75; COURT + -EOUS; r. ME *co(u)rteis* < AF; see COURT, -ESE] —**cour′te·ous·ly,** *adv.* —**cour′te·ous·ness,** *n.*
—**Syn.** mannerly, gracious, courtly. See **civil.**

cour·te·san (kôr′tə zən, kōr′-, kûr′-), *n.* a prostitute or paramour, esp. one associating with noblemen or men of wealth. Also, **cour′te·zan.** [1540–50; < MF *courtisane* < It *cortigiana,* lit., woman of the court, deriv. of *corte* COURT]

cour·te·sy (kûr′tə sē *or, for 5,* kûrt′sē), *n., pl.* **-sies,** *adj.* —*n.* **1.** excellence of manners or social conduct; polite behavior. **2.** a courteous, respectful, or considerate act or expression. **3.** indulgence, consent, or acquiescence: *a "colonel" by courtesy rather than by right.* **4.** favor, help, or generosity: *The costumes for the play were by courtesy of the local department store.* **5.** a curtsy. —*adj.* **6.** done or performed as a matter of courtesy or protocol: *a courtesy call on the mayor.* **7.** offered or provided free by courtesy of the management: *While waiting to board the airplane, we were provided with courtesy coffee.* [1175–1225; ME *curteisie* < AF, OF; see COURTEOUS, -Y[3]]
—**Syn. 1.** courteousness, civility, urbanity.

cour′tesy car′, **1.** a limousine or van provided by a hotel, airline, etc., for free transportation over a fixed route, as between an airport and a hotel. **2.** an automobile provided by a garage or repair shop for use while one's own car is being repaired.

cour′tesy card′, a card making the bearer eligible for special prices, privileges, or consideration, as at a club, hotel, store, or bank. [1930–35, *Amer.*]

cour′tesy light′, a light on the inside of an automobile that is turned on automatically when a door is opened. [1955–60]

cour′tesy ti′tle, **1.** a title applied or assumed through custom, courtesy, or association and without regard for its being officially merited. **2.** a title allowed by custom, as to the children of dukes. [1860–65]

CONCISE ETYMOLOGY KEY: <, descended or borrowed from; >, whence; b., blend of, blended; c., cognate with; cf., compare; deriv., derivative; equiv., equivalent; imit., imitative; obl., oblique; r., replacing; s., stem; sp., spelling, spelled; resp., respelling, respelled; trans., translation; ?, origin unknown; *, unattested; ‡, probably earlier than. See the full key inside the front cover.

court′ hand′, a style of handwriting formerly used in the English law courts. [1585–95]

court·house (kôrt′hous′, kōrt′-), *n., pl.* **-hous·es** (-hou′ziz). **1.** a building in which courts of law are held. **2.** a county seat. [1425–75; late ME; see COURT, HOUSE]

cour·ti·er (kôr′tē ər, kōr′-), *n.* **1.** a person who is often in attendance at the court of a king or other royal personage. **2.** a person who seeks favor by flattery, charm, etc. [1250–1300; ME *courteour* < AF *courte(i)our,* equiv. to OF *cortoy(er)* to attend at court (deriv. of *court* COURT) + AF *-our* < L *-ōr-* -OR[2]; suffix later conformed to -IER[1]]

court′ing chair′. See **love seat.**

court′ing mir′ror, *U.S. Furniture.* a small mirror of c1800 having a border and cresting of glass painted with leaves and flowers in imitation of a Chinese style.

court·ly (kôrt′lē, kōrt′-), *adj.,* **-li·er, -li·est,** *adv.* —*adj.* **1.** polite, refined, or elegant: *courtly manners.* **2.** flattering; obsequious. **3.** noting, pertaining to, or suitable for the court of a sovereign. —*adv.* **4.** in a courtly manner; politely or flatteringly. [1400–50; late ME; see COURT, -LY] —**court′li·ness,** *n.*

court′ly love′, a highly stylized code of behavior popular chiefly from the 12th to the 14th century that prescribed the rules of conduct between lovers, advocating idealized but illicit love, and which fostered an extensive medieval literature based on this tradition. [1895–1900]

court-mar·tial (kôrt′mär′shəl, -mär′-, kōrt′-), *n., pl.* **courts-mar·tial, court-mar·tials,** *v.,* **-tialed, -tial·ing** or (*esp. Brit.*) **-tialled, -tial·ling.** —*n.* **1.** a court consisting of military or naval personnel appointed by a commander to try charges of offenses by soldiers, sailors, etc., against military or naval law. **2.** a trial by such a court. **3.** a conviction by such a court: *He lost his privileges because of his court-martial.* **4.** a session of such a court: *He attended the court-martial this morning.* —*v.t.* **5.** to arraign and try by court-martial. [1565–75; earlier *martial court*]

Court′ of Appeal′. See under **Supreme Court of Judicature.**

court′ of appeals′, *Law.* **1.** (in the U.S. federal court system and some state court systems) an appellate court intermediate between the trial courts and the court of last resort. **2.** the highest appellate court of New York State. **3. Court of Appeal,** *Brit.* See under **Supreme Court of Judicature.** Also, **Court′ of Appeals′** (for defs. 1, 2). [1885–90]

court′ of chan′cery, *Law.* chancery (def. 4a).

court′ of claims′, *U.S. Law.* **1.** a court specialized in adjudicating claims against the federal government and its agencies. **2.** a special state court specialized in adjudicating claims against the state, its subdivisions, and its agencies. [1685–95]

court′ of com′mon pleas′, *Law.* **1.** (formerly in England) a court to hear civil cases between common citizens. **2.** (in some U.S. states) a court with general civil jurisdiction. Also, **Court′ of Com′mon Pleas′.** [1680–90]

court′ of domes′tic rela′tions, *Law.* a court, usually with a limited jurisdiction, that handles legal cases involving a family, esp. controversies between parent and child or husband and wife. Also called **domestic-relations court, family court.** Cf. **juvenile court.** [1925–30]

court′ of eq′uity, *Law.* a court having jurisdiction in equity or administering justice in accordance with the principles of equity.

Court′ of Excheq′uer, exchequer (def. 2c).

court′ of gen′eral ses′sions, a local court with general jurisdiction, both civil and criminal. [1695–1705, *Amer.*]

court′ of hon′or, 1. a body, esp. a military one, convened to hear complaints relating to personal honor. **2.** *Philately.* a noncompetitive exhibit of outstanding stamps forming part of a large exhibition. [1680–90]

Court′ of Hon′or, 1. the planning body of a girl-scout troop, composed of patrol leaders, the troop scribe, the troop treasurer, and the adult troop leader. **2.** a body of officials of a boy-scout organization that awards honor medals and certificates of promotion to members.

court′ of in′quiry, a military board or agency created to investigate and report on certain military matters, as an accusation against an officer. [1750–60]

court′ of law′, 1. a duly instituted organ of the government that administers justice, whether on the basis of legislation, previous court decisions, or other authoritative services. **2.** a court administering the rules developed by such organs as distinguished from the rules and principles developed and administered in courts of equity. Also called **law court.**

court′ of rec′ord, a court whose judgments and proceedings are kept on permanent record and that has the power to impose penalties for contempt. [1755–65]

Court′ of Ses′sion, (in Scotland) the highest civil court.

court′ of ses′sions, any of state courts of criminal jurisdiction in California, New York, and a few other states. [1695–1705]

Court′ of St. James′s, the British royal court: so called from St. James's Palace, London, the former scene of royal receptions. Also, **Court′ of Saint James′.**

court′ or′der, any rule or regulation of a court with which one must comply or risk a contempt action. [1640–50]

court′ pack′ing, *U.S. Hist.* an unsuccessful attempt by President Franklin D. Roosevelt in 1937 to appoint up to six additional justices to the Supreme Court, which had invalidated a number of his New Deal laws.

court′ plas′ter, cotton or other fabric coated on one side with an adhesive preparation, as of isinglass and glycerin, used on the skin for medical and cosmetic purposes. [1765–75; so called because of former use in courtly circles for making beauty spots]

Cour·trai (*Fr.* ko͞or trε′), *n.* a city in W Belgium, on the Lys River: important medieval city. 43,364. Flemish, **Kortrijk.**

court′ report′er, a stenographer employed to record and transcribe an official verbatim record of the legal proceedings of a court. [1890–95, *Amer.*]

court·room (kôrt′ro͞om′, -ro͝om′, kōrt′-), *n.* a room in which the sessions of a law court are held. [1670–80; COURT + ROOM]

court·ship (kôrt′ship, kōrt′-), *n.* **1.** the wooing of one person by another. **2.** the period during which such wooing takes place. **3.** solicitation of favors, applause, etc. **4.** *Ethology.* behavior in animals that occurs before and during mating, often including elaborate displays. **5.** *Obs.* courtly behavior; courtesy; gallantry. [1580–90; COURT + -SHIP]

court′ship display′, a stereotyped pattern of behavior in animals that functions to attract and arouse a prospective mate. [1920–25]

court′ shoe′, *Brit.* pump[2]. [1880–85; so called from the fact that high-heeled shoes were first worn in royal courts]

court·side (kôrt′sīd′, kōrt′-), *n.* (in sports) the area adjoining the official playing area of a court, as in basketball, tennis, or volleyball. [1965–70; COURT + SIDE[1]]

court′ ten′nis, a variety of tennis played indoors on a specially constructed court having high cement walls off which the ball may be played, points being made chiefly by stroking the ball into any of three openings in the walls of the court. Cf. **penthouse** (def. 7), **tambour** (def. 7), **winning opening.** See illus. under **racket.** [1910–15]

court·yard (kôrt′yärd′, kōrt′-), *n.* a court open to the sky, esp. one enclosed on all four sides. [1545–55; COURT + YARD[2]]

cou·ru (ko͝o ro͞o′; *Fr.* ko͞o RY′), *adj. Ballet.* done or executed with a running step. [< F, ptp. of *courir* to run << L *currere;* see CURRENT]

cous·cous (ko͞os′ko͞os), *n.* a North African dish consisting of steamed semolina, served with vegetables and meat. [1590–1600; < F < Ar *kuskus, kuskusū* < Berber *seksu*]

cous·in (kuz′ən), *n.* **1.** Also called **first cousin, full cousin, cousin-german.** the son or daughter of an uncle or aunt. **2.** one related by descent in a diverging line from a known common ancestor, as from one's grandparent or from one's father's or mother's sister or brother. **3.** a kinsman or kinswoman; relative. **4.** a person or thing related to another by similar natures, languages, geographical proximity, etc.: *Our Canadian cousins are a friendly people.* **5.** *Slang.* a gullible, innocent person who is easily duped or taken advantage of. **6.** a term of address used by a sovereign in speaking, writing, or referring to another sovereign or a high-ranking noble. [1250–1300; ME *cosin* < AF *co(u)sin,* OF *cosin* < L *consōbrīnus* cousin (properly, son of one's mother's sister), equiv. to *con-* CON- + *sōbrīnus* second cousin (presumably orig. "pertaining to the sister") < **swesrīnos,* equiv. to **swesr-,* gradational var. of **swesōr* (> *soror* SISTER) + **-īnos* -INE[1]; for *-sr-* > *-br-* cf. DECEMBER] —**cous′in·age, cous′in·hood′, cous′in·ship′,** *n.*

Cou·sin (ko͞o zaN′), *n.* **Vic·tor** (vēk tôr′), 1792–1867, French philosopher and educational reformer: founder of the method of eclecticism in French philosophy.

cous·in-ger·man (kuz′ən jûr′mən), *n., pl.* **cous·ins-ger·man** (kuz′ənz jûr′mən). cousin (def. 1). [1250–1300; ME *cosin germain.* See COUSIN, GERMAN]

Cous′in Jack′, *pl.* **Cousin Jacks.** a Cornishman, esp. a Cornish miner. [1875–80]

cous·in·ly (kuz′ən lē), *adj.* like or befitting a cousin. [1805–15; COUSIN + -LY]

cous·in·ry (kuz′ən rē), *n., pl.* **-ries.** cousins or relatives collectively. [1835–45; COUSIN + -RY]

Cous·teau (ko͞o stō′), *n.* **Jacques Yves** (zhäk ēv), born 1910, French naval officer, author, and underseas explorer: developed the Aqua-Lung.

Cou·sy (ko͞o′zē), *n.* **Robert Joseph** (*Bob*), born 1928, U.S. basketball player.

cou·teau (ko͞o tō′), *n., pl.* **-teaux** (-tōz′; *Fr.* -tō′). a knife, esp. a large double-edged one formerly carried as a weapon. [1670–80; < F; OF *coutel* < L *cultellus;* see CULTELLUS]

cou·ter (ko͞o′tər), *n. Armor.* a piece of plate armor for the elbow. See diag. under **armor.** [1325–75; ME < AF, equiv. to OF *coute* elbow (< L *cubitum;* see CUBIT) + AF *-er* -ER[2]]

couth[1] (ko͞oth), *Facetious.* —*adj.* **1.** showing or having good manners or sophistication; smooth: *Sending her flowers would be a very couth thing to do.* —*n.* **2.** good manners; refinement: *to be lacking in couth.* [1895–1900; back formation from UNCOUTH]

couth[2] (ko͞oth), *adj. Archaic.* known or acquainted with. [bef. 1000; ME, OE *cūth* ptp. of *cunnan* to KNOW (see CAN[1], COULD)]

couth·ie (ko͞o′thē), *adj. Scot.* agreeable; genial; kindly. [1715–25; COUTH[2] + *-ie,* sp. var. of -Y[1]] —**couth′i·ly,** *adv.* —**couth′i·ness,** *n.*

cou·til (ko͞o tēl′, -til′), *n.* a sturdy fabric constructed of a compactly woven herringbone twill. [1850–55; < F, OF, equiv. to *coute* QUILT + *-il* n. suffix]

cou·ture (ko͞o to͝or′; *Fr.* ko͞o TYR′), *n.* **1.** the occupation of a couturier; dressmaking and designing. **2.** fashion designers or couturiers collectively. **3.** the clothes and related articles designed by such designers. **4.** the business establishments of such designers, esp. where clothes are made to order. —*adj.* **5.** created or produced by a fashion designer: *couture clothes.* **6.** being, having, or suggesting the style, quality, etc., of a fashion designer; very fashionable: *the couture look.* [1905–10; < F: lit., sewing, seam < VL **cō(n)sūtūra,* equiv. to L *consūt(us)* ptp. of *consuere* to sew together (*con-* CON- + *suere* to SEW[1]) + *-ūra* -URE; cf. SUTURE, ACCOUTER]

cou·tu·ri·er (ko͞o to͝or′ē ā′, -ē ər, -to͝or′yā; *Fr.* ko͞o TY RYĀ′), *n., pl.* **-tu·riers** (-to͝or′ē āz′, -ē ərz, -to͝or′yāz; *Fr.* -TY RYĀ′). a person who designs, makes, and sells fashionable clothes for women. [1895–1900; < F, OF; see COUTURE, -IER[2]]

cou·tu·ri·ère (ko͞o to͝or′ē ər, -ē er′; *Fr.* ko͞o TY RYER′), *n., pl.* **-tu·ri·ères** (-to͝or′ē ərz, -erz′; *Fr.* -TY RYER′). a woman who is a couturier. Also called **cou·tu·ri·ere** (ko͞o to͝or′ē ər, -ē er′). [1810–20; < F]

cou·vade (ko͞o väd′; *Fr.* ko͞o VAD′), *n.* a practice among some peoples, as the Basques of Spain, in which a man, immediately preceding the birth of his child, takes to his bed in an enactment of the birth experience and subjects himself to various taboos usually associated with pregnancy. [1860–65; < F (now obs.), lit., a hatching, sitting on eggs, equiv. to *couv(er)* to hatch (< L *cubāre* to lie down) + *-ade* -ADE[1]; cf. COVEY]

co·va·lence (kō vā′ləns), *n. Chem.* the number of electron pairs that an atom can share with other atoms. [1915–20; CO- + VALENCE] —**co·va′lent,** *adj.* —**co·va′lent·ly,** *adv.*

cova′lent bond′, *Chem.* the bond formed by the sharing of a pair of electrons by two atoms. [1960–65]

co·var·i·ance (kō vâr′ē əns), *n. Statistics.* the expectation or mean value of the variable formed by multiplying the differences obtained by subtracting two given variates from their respective means; the product of the standard deviations of two given variates and the coefficient of correlation between them. [1875–80; CO- + VARIANCE]

co·var·i·ant (kō vâr′ē ənt), *adj. Math.* (of one magnitude with respect to another) varying in accordance with a fixed mathematical relationship: *The area of a square is covariant with the length of a side.* [1850–55; CO- + VARIANT]

Co·var·ru·bias (kō′və ro͞o′bē əs; *Sp.* kô′vär Ro͞o′byäs), *n.* **Mi·guel** (mē gel′), 1904–57, Mexican caricaturist, illustrator, and painter.

cove[1] (kōv), *n., v.,* **coved, cov·ing.** —*n.* **1.** a small indentation or recess in the shoreline of a sea, lake, or river. **2.** a sheltered nook. **3.** a hollow or recess in a mountain; cave; cavern. **4.** a narrow pass between woods or hills. **5.** a sheltered area between woods or hills. **6.** *Archit.* **a.** a concave surface or molding. **b.** a concave surface forming part of a ceiling at its edge so as to eliminate the usual interior angle between the wall and ceiling. —*v.t., v.i.* **7.** to make or become a cove. [bef. 900; ME; OE *cofa* cave, den, closet; c. ON *kofi* hut, Gk *gýpē* cave]

cove[2] (kōv), *n.* **1.** *Brit. Slang.* a person; fellow. **2.** *Australian Slang.* a manager, esp. of a sheep station. [1560–70; said to be < Romany *kova* creature]

coved′ vault′. See **cloistered vault.**

cove′ light′ing, indirect lighting directed upward from an interior cornice or the like toward a cove at the edge of the ceiling.

co·vel·lite (kō vel′īt, kō′və līt′), *n.* a mineral, copper sulfide, CuS, indigo in color and usually occurring as a massive coating on other copper minerals. [1840–50; named after Nicolò *Covelli* (1790–1829), Italian mineralogist who found it; see -ITE[1]]

cov·en (kuv′ən, kō′vən), *n.* an assembly of witches, esp. a group of thirteen. [1500–10 for sense "assembly"; 1655–65 for current sense; var. of obs. *covent* assembly, religious group, CONVENT]

cov·e·nant (kuv′ə nənt), *n.* **1.** an agreement, usually formal, between two or more persons to do or not do something specified. **2.** *Law.* an incidental clause in such an agreement. **3.** *Eccles.* a solemn agreement between the members of a church to act together in harmony with the precepts of the gospel. **4.** (*cap.*) *Hist.* **a.** See **National Covenant. b.** See **Solemn League and Covenant. 5.** *Bible.* **a.** the conditional promises made to humanity by God, as revealed in Scripture. **b.** the agreement between God and the ancient Israelites, in which God promised to protect them if they kept His law and were faithful to Him. **6.** *Law.* **a.** a formal agreement of legal validity, esp. one under seal. **b.** an early English form of action in suits involving sealed contracts. **7.** See **Covenant of the League of Nations.** —*v.i.* **8.** to enter into a covenant. —*v.t.* **9.** to promise by covenant; pledge. **10.** to stipulate. [1250–1300; ME < AF, OF, n. use of prp. of *covenir* < L *convenīre* to come together, agree; see -ANT] —**cov·e·nan·tal** (kuv′ə nan′tl), *adj.*

—**Syn. 1.** treaty, pact, convention.

cov·e·nan·tee (kuv′ə nən tē′, -nan-), *n.* a person to whom something is promised in a covenant. [1640–50; COVENANT + -EE]

cov·e·nant·er (kuv′ə nən tər; *for 2 also Scot.* kuv′ənan′tər), *n.* **1.** a person who makes a covenant. **2.** (*cap.*) *Scot. Hist.* a person who, by solemn agreement, pledged to uphold Presbyterianism, esp. an adherent of the National Covenant or the Solemn League and Covenant. [1630–40; COVENANT + -ER[1]]

Cov′enant of the League′ of Na′tions, the constitution of the League of Nations, included as the first 26 articles in the Treaty of Versailles, in which the organization and purpose of the League were set forth.

cov′enant of war′ranty, *Law.* warranty (def. 2b).

cov·e·nan·tor (kuv′ə nən tər), *n. Law.* the party who

is to perform the obligation expressed in a covenant. [1640–50; COVENANT + -OR[2]]

Cov′ent Gar′den (kuv′ənt, kov′-), **1.** a district in central London, England, formerly a vegetable and flower market. **2.** a theater in this district, first built 1731–32, important in English theatrical history: home of the Royal Opera and Royal Ballet.

Cov•en•try (kuv′ən trē, kov′-), *n.* **1.** a city in West Midlands, in central England: heavily bombed 1940; cathedral. 337,000. **2.** a town in central Rhode Island. 27,065. **3. send to Coventry,** to refuse to associate with; openly and pointedly ignore: *His friends sent him to Coventry after he was court-martialed.*

Cov′entry bell′, a perennial garden plant, *Campanula trachelium,* of Eurasia, having coarsely toothed leaves and bluish-purple flowers. [1570–80]

co•ven•ture (kō ven′chər), *n.* a business project or enterprise undertaken jointly by two or more companies, each sharing in the capitalization and in any profits or losses.

cov•er (kuv′ər), *v.t.* **1.** to be or serve as a covering for; extend over; rest on the surface of: *Snow covered the fields.* **2.** to place something over or upon, as for protection, concealment, or warmth. **3.** to provide with a covering or top: *Cover the pot with a lid.* **4.** to protect or conceal (the body, head, etc.) with clothes, a hat, etc; wrap. **5.** to bring upon (oneself): *He covered himself with glory by his exploits.* **6.** to hide from view; screen. **7.** to spread on or over; apply to: *to cover bread with honey.* **8.** to put all over the surface of: *to cover a wall with paint.* **9.** to include, deal with, or provide for; address: *The rules cover working conditions.* **10.** to suffice to defray or meet (a charge, expense, etc.): *Ten dollars should cover my expenses.* **11.** to offset (an outlay, loss, liability, etc.). **12.** to achieve in distance traversed; pass or travel over: *We covered 600 miles a day on our trip.* **13.** *Journalism.* **a.** to act as a reporter or reviewer of (an event, a field of interest, a performance, etc.); have as an assignment: *She covers sports for the paper.* **b.** to publish or broadcast a report or reports of (a news item, a series of related events, etc.): *The press covered the trial in great detail.* **14.** to pass or rise over and surmount or envelop: *The river covered the town during the flood.* **15.** *Insurance.* to insure against risk or loss. **16.** to shelter; protect; serve as a defense for. **17.** *Mil.* **a.** to be in line with by occupying a position directly before or behind. **b.** to protect (a soldier, force, or military position) during an expected period of ground combat by taking a position from which any hostile troops can be fired upon. **18.** to take temporary charge of or responsibility for in place of another: *Please cover my phone while I'm out to lunch.* **19.** to extend over; comprise: *The book covers 18th-century England.* **20.** to be assigned to or responsible for, as a territory or field of endeavor: *We have two sales representatives covering the Southwest.* **21.** to aim at, as with a pistol. **22.** to have within range, as a fortress does adjacent territory. **23.** to play a card higher than (the one led or previously played in the round). **24.** to deposit the equivalent of (money deposited), as in wagering. **25.** to accept the conditions of (a bet, wager, etc.). **26.** (in short selling) to purchase securities or commodities in order to deliver them to the broker from whom they were borrowed. **27.** *Baseball.* to take a position close to or at (a base) so as to catch a ball thrown to the base: *The shortstop covered second on the attempted steal.* **28.** *Sports.* to guard (an opponent on offense) so as to prevent him or her from scoring or carrying out his or her assignment: *to cover a potential pass receiver.* **29.** (esp. of a male animal) to copulate with. **30.** (of a hen) to brood or sit on (eggs or chicks).
—*v.i.* **31.** *Informal.* to serve as a substitute for someone who is absent: *We cover for the receptionist during lunch hour.* **32.** to hide the wrongful or embarrassing action of another by providing an alibi or acting in the other's place: *They covered for him when he missed roll call.* **33.** to play a card higher than the one led or previously played in the round: *She led the eight and I covered with the jack.* **34.** to spread over an area or surface, esp. for the purpose of obscuring an existing covering or of achieving a desired thickness and evenness: *This paint is much too thin to cover.* **35. cover one's ass,** *Slang (vulgar).* to take measures that will prevent one from suffering blame, loss, harm, etc. **36. cover up, a.** to cover completely; enfold. **b.** to keep secret; conceal: *She tried to cover up her part in the plot.*
—*n.* **37.** something that covers, as the lid of a container or the binding of a book. **38.** a blanket, quilt, or the like: *Put another cover on the bed.* **39.** protection; shelter; concealment. **40.** anything that veils, screens, or shuts from sight: *under cover of darkness.* **41.** woods, underbrush, etc., serving to shelter and conceal wild animals or game; a covert. **42.** *Ecol.* vegetation that serves to protect or conceal animals, such as birds, from excessive sunlight, from drying, or from predators. **43.** a set of eating utensils and the like, as plate, knife, fork, and napkin, placed for each person at a table. **44.** an assumed identity, occupation, or business that masks the true or real one: *His job at the embassy was a cover for his work as a spy.* **45.** a covering of snow, esp. when suitable for skiing. **46.** a pretense; feigning. **47.** a person who substitutes for another or stands ready to substitute if needed: *She was hired as a cover for six roles at the opera house.* **48.** See **cover charge. 49.** *Philately.* **a.** an envelope or outer wrapping for mail. **b.** a letter folded so that the address may be placed on the outside and the missive mailed. **50.** *Finance.* funds to cover liability or secure against risk of loss. **51.** *Music.* See **cover version. 52.** Also called **covering.** *Math.* a collection of sets having the property that a given set is contained in the union of the sets in the collection. **53. blow one's cover,** to divulge one's secret identity, esp. inadvertently: *The TV news story blew his carefully fabricated cover.* **54. break cover,** to emerge, esp. suddenly, from a place of concealment: *The fox broke cover and the chase was on.* **55. take cover,** to seek shelter or safety: *The hikers took cover in a deserted cabin to escape the sudden storm.* **56. under cover, a.** clandestinely; secretly: *Arrangements for the escape were made under cover.* **b.** within an envelope: *The report will be mailed to you under separate cover.* [1200–50; ME *coveren* < OF *covrir* < L *cooperire* to cover completely, equiv. to *co-* CO- + *operire* to shut, close, cover (*op-*, appar. for *ob-* OB- + *-erire;* see APERIENT)] **—cov′er•a•ble,** *adj.* **—cov′er•er,** *n.* **—cov′er•less,** *adj.*
—Syn. 2. overlay, overspread, envelop, enwrap. **6.** cloak, conceal. **11.** counterbalance, compensate for. **39, 40.** COVER, PROTECTION, SCREEN, SHELTER mean a defense against harm or danger and a provision for safety. The main idea in COVER is that of concealment, as in darkness, in a wood, or behind something: *The ground troops were left without cover when the air force was withdrawn.* SCREEN refers especially to something behind which one can hide: *A heavy fire formed a screen for ground operations.* PROTECTION and SHELTER emphasize the idea of a guard or defense, a shield against injury or death. A PROTECTION is any such shield: *In World War II, an air cover of airplanes served as a protection for troops.* A SHELTER is something that covers over and acts as a place of refuge: *An abandoned monastery acted as a shelter.*

cov•er•age (kuv′ər ij, kuv′rij), *n.* **1.** *Insurance.* protection provided against risks or a risk, often as specified: *Does the coverage include flood damage?* **2.** *Journalism.* the reporting and subsequent publishing or broadcasting of news: *The World Series receives international coverage.* **3.** the extent to which something is covered. **4.** the area, groups, or number of persons served or reached by a newspaper, radio or television station, advertising campaign, business, etc.; market. **5.** *Radio and Television.* the area within the broadcasting range of a station or network, usually calculated by the number of owners of radio or television receivers. **6.** *Finance.* the value of funds held to back up or meet liabilities. **7.** *Photog.* See **covering power.** [1910–15, *Amer.*; COVER + -AGE]

cov•er•all (kuv′ər ôl′), *n.* **1.** a loose-fitting, one-piece work garment, consisting of a trouserlike portion and a top with or without sleeves, worn over other clothing. **2.** overalls for women. [1820–30; COVER + ALL]

cov′er charge′, a fee, in addition to the cost of food and drink, charged by a restaurant, nightclub, etc., for entertainment. Also called **cover.** Cf. **minimum** (def. 4). [1920–25, *Amer.*]

cov′er crop′, a crop, usually a legume, planted to keep nutrients from leaching, soil from eroding, and land from weeding over, as during the winter. [1905–10]

Cov•er•dale (kuv′ər dāl′), *n.* **Miles,** 1488–1569, English divine: translator of the Bible into English 1535.

cov′ered-dish sup′per (kuv′ərd dish′), a meal to which guests contribute food, as casseroles.

cov′ered wag′on, 1. a large wagon with a high, bonnetlike canvas top, esp. such a wagon used by pioneers to transport themselves and their possessions across the North American plains during the westward migrations in the 19th century. **2.** *Brit. Railroads.* a boxcar. [1735–45, *Amer.*]

covered wagon (def. 1)

cov′er girl′, an attractive young woman whose picture is featured on a magazine cover. [1910–15, *Amer.*]

cov′er glass′, a thin, round or square piece of glass used to cover an object mounted on a slide for microscopic observation. Also called **cover slip.** [1880–85]

cov•er•ing (kuv′ər ing), *n.* **1.** something laid over or wrapped around a thing, esp. for concealment, protection, or warmth. **2.** *Math.* cover (def. 52). **3.** the buying of securities or commodities that one has sold short, in order to return them to the person from whom they were borrowed. [1350–1400; ME; see COVER, -ING[1]]

cov′ering let′ter, a letter that accompanies another letter, a package, or the like, to explain, commend, etc. Also, **cov′er let′ter.** [1885–90]

cov′ering pow′er, *Photog.* the maximum area of a scene that can be recorded with good definition by a particular lens. Also called **coverage.** [1890–95]

cov•er•let (kuv′ər lit), *n.* **1.** Also, **cov•er•lid** (kuv′ər-lid). a bed quilt that does not cover the pillow, used chiefly for warmth; bedspread. **2.** *Archaic.* any covering or cover. [1250–1300; ME *coverlite* < AF *cuver-lit* bedspread, equiv. to *cuver* to COVER + *lit* bed < L *lectus;* akin to LIE[2], LAY[1]]

Cov•er•ley (kuv′ər lē), *n.* **Sir Roger de,** a literary figure representing the ideal of the early 18th-century squire in *The Spectator,* by Addison and Steele.

cov′er point′, 1. *Cricket.* the position and the player stationed near the point. **2.** *Lacrosse.* the position and the player stationed before the point. [1840–50]

co′versed sine′ (kō′vûrst), *Math.* the versed sine of the complement of an angle or arc. Also called **versed cosine.** [1700–10]

cov′er slip′, *Micros.* See **cover glass.** [1850–55]

cov′er sto′ry, 1. a magazine article highlighted by an illustration on the cover. **2.** a fabricated story used to conceal a true purpose; alibi: *No one believed the cover story released to the press.* [1945–50]

co•vert (*adj.* kō′vərt, kuv′ərt; *n.* kuv′ərt, kō′vərt), *adj.* **1.** concealed; secret; disguised. **2.** covered; sheltered. **3.** *Law.* (of a wife) under the protection of one's husband. **—*n.* 4.** a covering; cover. **5.** a shelter or hiding place. **6.** concealment or disguise. **7.** *Hunting.* a thicket giving shelter to wild animals or game. **8.** Also called **tectrix.** *Ornith.* one of the small feathers that cover the bases of the large feathers of the wings and tail. See diag. under **bird. 9.** See **covert cloth.** [1275–1325; ME < AF, OF < L *coopertus,* ptp. of *cooperire* to cover completely; see COVER] **—co′vert•ly,** *adv.* **—co′vert•ness,** *n.*
—Syn. 1. clandestine, surreptitious, furtive.
—Pronunciation. COVERT, related to *cover,* has historically been pronounced (kuv′ərt), with (u), the same stressed vowel found in *cover.* This (u) is the traditional and unchallenged vowel in many other English words spelled with stressed *o* followed by *v,* voiced *th,* or a nasal in the same syllable, words of high frequency like *love* and *above, mother* and *other, some* and *honey.* The adjective COVERT, however, by analogy with *overt* (. . ., ō′vərt), its semantic opposite, has developed the pronunciation (kō′vərt), perhaps because of the frequent coupling of the two terms in the news media. This is now the more common pronunciation for the adjective in American English, though not in British English, which retains the historical pronunciation. For the noun senses, less likely to appear in the news or to be contrasted with *overt* and its (ō) sound, the historical (kuv′ərt) remains the more frequent pronunciation.

co′vert ac′tion, a secret action undertaken to influence the course of political events, as a government intelligence operation. Also called **co′vert opera′tion.** [1975–80]

cov′ert cloth′, a cotton, woolen, or worsted cloth of twill weave, the warp being of ply yarns one of which may be white. Also called **covert.** [1890–95]

cov′er text′, a text that conceals an encoded message.

cov•er•ture (kuv′ər chər), *n.* **1.** a cover or covering; shelter; concealment. **2.** *Law.* the status of a married woman considered as under the protection and authority of her husband. [1175–1225; ME < AF, OF. See COVERT, -URE]

cov•er-up (kuv′ər up′), *n.* **1.** any action, stratagem, or other means of concealing or preventing investigation or exposure. **2.** Also, **cov′er•up′.** any of various women's garments, as loose blouses, jump suits, caftans, or sarongs, worn over a swimsuit, exercise clothing, or the like. [1925–30; n. use of v. phrase *cover up*]

cov′er ver′sion, a recording of a song by a singer, instrumentalist, or group other than the original performer or composer. Also called **cover.** [1965–70]

cov•et (kuv′it), *v.t.* **1.** to desire wrongfully, inordinately, or without due regard for the rights of others: *to covet another's property.* **2.** to wish for, esp. eagerly: *He won the prize they all coveted.* **—*v.i.* 3.** to have an inordinate or wrongful desire. [1175–1225; ME *coveiten* < AF *coveiter,* OF *coveit(i)er* < VL **cupiditāre,* v. deriv. of **cupiditās,* for L *cupititās* CUPIDITY] **—cov′et•a•ble,** *adj.* **—cov′et•er,** *n.* **—cov′et•ing•ly,** *adv.*
—Syn. 1. See **envy. —Ant. 1.** renounce.

cov•et•ous (kuv′i təs), *adj.* **1.** inordinately or wrongly desirous of wealth or possessions; greedy. **2.** eagerly desirous. [1250–1300; ME *coveitous* < AF, OF; see COVET, -OUS] **—cov′et•ous•ly,** *adv.* **—cov′et•ous•ness,** *n.*
—Syn. 1. grasping, rapacious. See **avaricious.**

cov•ey (kuv′ē), *n., pl.* **-eys. 1.** a brood or small flock of partridges or similar birds. **2.** a group, set, or company. [1400–50; ME, var. of *covee* < AF, OF, n. use of fem. of ptp. of *cover* to hatch < L *cubāre* to lie down; cf. COUVADE, CONCUBINE]

Co•vi•na (kə vē′nə), *n.* a city in SW California, near Los Angeles. 33,751.

Cov•ing•ton (kuv′ing tən), *n.* **1.** a city in N Kentucky, on the Ohio River. 49,013. **2.** a town in central Georgia. 10,586.

cow[1] (kou), *n., pl.* **cows,** (*Archaic*) **kine. 1.** the mature female of a bovine animal, esp. of the genus *Bos.* **2.** the female of various other large animals, as the elephant or whale. **3.** *Informal.* a domestic bovine of either sex and any age. **4.** *Slang (disparaging and offensive).* a large, obese, and slovenly woman. **5.** *Offensive.* a woman who has a large number of children or is frequently pregnant. **6. till** or **until the cows come home,** for a long time; forever: *You can keep arguing till the cows come home, but I won't change my mind.* [bef. 900; ME *cou,* OE *cū;* c. G *Kuh,* D *koe,* ON *kȳr,* L *bōs,* Gk *boûs* ox; cf. BOVINE, GAUR] **—cow′like′,** *adj.*

cow[2] (kou), *v.t.* to frighten with threats, violence, etc.; intimidate; overawe. [1595–1605; < ON *kūga* to oppress, cow; cf. Dan *kue* to cow]
—Syn. terrorize, scare, bully.

cow•a•bun•ga (kou′ə bung′gə), *Interj.* (a yell of exhilaration, mainly used by surfers.) [of uncert. orig.]

cow•age (kou′ij), *n.* **1.** a tropical vine, *Mucuna pruriens,* of the legume family, bearing reddish or blackish pods. **2.** the pod itself, covered with bristlelike hairs that are irritating to the skin and cause intense itching. **3.** the hairs of the cowage mixed with a liquid vehicle and used to expel intestinal worms. Also, **cowhage, cowitch.** [1630–40; < Hindi *kāūch, kēvāc* (cf. *kavac* any husk or pod), reshaped in E by folk etym.]

Cow•ans•ville (kou′ənz vil′), *n.* a town in S Quebec, in E Canada. 12,240.

cow•ard (kou′ərd), *n.* **1.** a person who lacks courage in facing danger, difficulty, opposition, pain, etc.; a timid or easily intimidated person. **—*adj.* 2.** lacking courage; very fearful or timid. **3.** proceeding from or expressive of fear or timidity: *a coward cry.* [1175–1225; ME < OF *couard-, couart* cowardly, equiv. to *coue* tail (< L *cauda*) + *-art* -ARD]
—Syn. 1. craven, poltroon, dastard, recreant, milksop.

CONCISE ETYMOLOGY KEY: <, descended or borrowed from; >, whence; b., blend of, blended; c., cognate with; cf., compare; deriv., derivative; equiv., equivalent; imit., imitative; obl., oblique; r., replacing; s., stem; sp., spelling, spelled; resp., respelling, respelled; trans., translation; ?, origin unknown; *, unattested; ‡, probably earlier than. See the full key inside the front cover.

Cow•ard (kou′ərd), *n.* **Noel,** 1899–1973, English playwright, author, actor, and composer.

cow•ard•ice (kou′ər dis), *n.* lack of courage to face danger, difficulty, opposition, pain, etc. [1250–1300; ME *cowardise* < OF *co(u)ardise,* equiv. to *co(u)art* cowardly (see COWARD) + *-ise* -ICE]
—**Syn.** pusillanimity, timidity. —**Ant.** bravery.

cow•ard•ly (kou′ərd lē), *adj.* **1.** lacking courage; contemptibly timid. **2.** characteristic of or befitting a coward; despicably mean, covert, or unprincipled: *a cowardly attack on a weak, defenseless man.* —*adv.* **3.** like a coward. [1275–1325; ME (adv.); see COWARD, -LY] —**cow′•ard•li•ness,** *n.*
—**Syn. 1.** craven, poltroon, dastardly, pusillanimous, fainthearted, white-livered, lily-livered, chicken-hearted, fearful, afraid, scared. COWARDLY, TIMID, TIMOROUS refer to a lack of courage or self-confidence. COWARDLY means weakly or basely fearful in the presence of danger: *The cowardly wretch deserted his comrades in battle.* TIMID means lacking in boldness or self-confidence even when there is no danger present: *a timid person who stood in the way of his own advancement.* TIMOROUS suggests a timidity based on an exaggeration of dangers or on an imaginary creation of dangers: *timorous as a mouse.* —**Ant. 1.** brave.

cow•bane (kou′bān′), *n.* any of several poisonous plants of the parsley family, as *Oxypolis rigidior,* of swampy areas of North America, or the water hemlock, *Cicuta maculata.* [1770–80; cow[1] + BANE]

cow•bell (kou′bel′), *n.* **1.** a bell hung around a cow's neck to indicate its whereabouts. **2.** the bladder campion. [1805–15; cow[1] + BELL[1]]

cow•ber•ry (kou′ber′ē, -bə rē), *n., pl.* **-ries. 1.** the berry or fruit of any of various shrubs, esp. *Vaccinium vitis-idaea,* of the heath family, growing in pastures. **2.** any of these shrubs. [1790–1800; cow[1] + BERRY, for L *vaccinium* plant name (in NL: genus name), deriv. of *vaccinus* of cows; see VACCINE]

cow•bird (kou′bûrd′), *n.* any of several New World blackbirds of the genus *Molothrus,* esp. *M. ater,* of North America, that accompany herds of cattle. [1795–1805, *Amer.*; cow[1] + BIRD]

cow•boy (kou′boi′), *n.* **1.** a man who herds and tends cattle on a ranch, esp. in the western U.S., and who traditionally goes about most of his work on horseback. **2.** a man who exhibits the skills attributed to such cowboys, esp. in rodeos. **3.** *Chiefly Northeastern U.S.* a reckless or speedy automobile driver. **4.** *Informal.* a reckless or irresponsible person, esp. a show-off or one who undertakes a dangerous or sensitive task heedlessly: *They put foreign policy in the hands of cowboys.* **5.** (during the American Revolution) a member of a pro-British guerrilla band that operated between the American and British lines near New York City. —*v.i.* **6.** to work as a cowboy. [1715–25; cow[1] + BOY]

cow′boy boot′, a boot with a chunky, moderately high slanted heel, usually pointed toe, and decorative stitching or tooling, extending to mid-calf. [1890–95]

cow′boy hat′, a broad-brimmed hat with a high crown, usually of soft felt, as worn by cowboys and ranchers. [1890–95]

cow′boys and In′dians, a children's game in which players imitate the supposed behavior of cowboys and Indians in conflict, as in shooting, chasing, and capturing. [1885–90, *Amer.*]

cow′ cake′, *Slang.* cow dung. [1965–70]

cow•catch•er (kou′kach′ər), *n.* a triangular frame at the front of a locomotive, esp. a steam locomotive, designed for clearing the track of obstructions. Also called **pilot.** [1830–40, *Amer.*; cow[1] + CATCHER]

cow′ chips′, dried cow dung used esp. for fuel by early settlers, explorers, etc., in the American West. [1865–70, *Amer.*]

cow′ col′lege, *Informal.* **1.** an agricultural college. **2.** a small, relatively unknown rural college. [1910–15]

cow′ coun′try, a region of cattle ranches, as rural areas of the southwestern U.S., esp. Texas. [1880–85]

Cow•ell (kou′əl), *n.* **Henry (Dixon),** 1897–1965, U.S. composer.

cow•er (kou′ər), *v.i.* to crouch, as in fear or shame. [1250–1300; ME *couren;* c. Norw, Sw *kūra,* MLG *kūren,* G *kauern*] —**cow′er•ing•ly,** *adv.*
—**Syn.** cringe, recoil, flinch, quail.

Cowes (kouz), *n.* a seaport on the Isle of Wight, in S England: resort. 18,895.

cow•fish (kou′fish′), *n., pl.* (*esp. collectively*) **-fish,** (*esp. referring to two or more kinds or species*) **-fish•es. 1.** any of several marine fishes having hornlike projections over the eyes, esp. a trunkfish, *Lactophrys guadricornus,* found in the warm waters of the Atlantic Ocean. **2.** a sirenian, as the manatee. **3.** any of various small cetaceans, as a porpoise or dolphin or the grampus, *Grampus griseus.* [1625–35; cow[1] + FISH]

cow′ flop′, *Slang.* cow dung. [1900–05]

cow•girl (kou′gûrl′), *n.* **1.** a woman who herds and tends cattle on a ranch, esp. in the western U.S., and who traditionally goes about most of her work on horseback. **2.** a woman who exhibits the skills attributed to such cowgirls, esp. in rodeos. [1880–85, *Amer.*; cow[1] + GIRL]

cow•hage (kou′ij), *n.* cowage.

cow•hand (kou′hand′), *n.* a person employed on a cattle ranch; cowboy or cowgirl. [1885–90, *Amer.*; cow[1] + HAND]

cow•herb (kou′ûrb′, -hûrb′), *n.* a plant, *Vaccaria pyramidata,* of the pink family, native to Europe, having clusters of pink flowers. [1855–60; cow[1] + HERB]

cow•herd (kou′hûrd′), *n.* a person whose occupation is tending and herding cows. [bef. 1000; ME *couherde,* OE *cūherde;* see cow[1], HERD[2]]

cow•hide (kou′hīd′), *n., v.,* **-hid•ed, -hid•ing.** —*n.* **1.** the hide of a cow. **2.** the leather made from it. **3.** a strong, flexible whip made of rawhide or of braided leather. **4. cowhides,** *Informal.* a pair of boots or shoes, esp. those made of cowhide. —*v.t.* **5.** to whip with a cowhide. [1630–40; cow[1] + HIDE[2]]

cow′ horse′. See **cow pony.** [1850–55, *Amer.*]

co•win•ner (kō win′ər, kō′win′-), *n.* one of two or more joint winners. Also, **co-win′ner.** [CO- + WINNER]

cow•itch (kou′ich), *n.* cowage. [1795–1805]

cow′ kil′ler, the wingless female of any of several velvet ants, esp. *Dasymutilla occidentalis,* of the southern U.S., which inflicts a painful sting. [1885–90, *Amer.*]

cowl (def. 1)

cowl (koul), *n.* **1.** a hooded garment worn by monks. **2.** the hood of this garment. **3.** part of a garment that is draped to resemble a cowl or hood. **4.** the forward part of the body of a motor vehicle supporting the rear of the hood and the windshield and housing the pedals and instrument panel. **5.** a cowling. **6.** a hoodlike covering for increasing the draft of a chimney or ventilator. **7.** a wire netting fastened to the top of the smokestack of a locomotive to prevent large sparks from being discharged; a spark arrester. —*v.t.* **8.** to cover with or as if with a cowl. **9.** to put a monk's cowl on. **10.** to make a monk of. [bef. 1000; ME *cou(e)le,* OE *cugele, cūle* < LL *cuculla* monk's hood, var. of L *cucullus* hood]

Cowl (koul), *n.* **Jane,** 1884–1950, U.S. actress and playwright.

cowled (kould), *adj.* **1.** wearing a cowl. **2.** shaped like a cowl; cucullate. [1555–65; COWL + -ED[3]]

Cow•ley (kou′lē, ko͞o′-), *n.* **1. Abraham,** 1618–67, English poet. **2. Malcolm,** born 1898, U.S. writer, critic, and editor.

cow•lick (kou′lik′), *n.* a tuft of hair that grows in a direction different from that of the rest of the hair. [1590–1600; cow[1] + LICK]

cow′ lil′y, spatterdock. [1860–65, *Amer.*]

cowl•ing (kou′ling), *n.* a streamlined metal housing or removable covering for an engine, esp. an aircraft engine, often part of or forming a continuous line with the fuselage or wing. [1915–20; COWL + -ING[1]]

cowl•neck (koul′nek′), *n.* **1.** a style of neckline for a woman's garment having material draped in rounded folds. **2.** a garment with this type of neckline, esp. a sweater or dress. [COWL + NECK]

cow•man (kou′mən), *n., pl.* **-men. 1.** *Western U.S.* **a.** a person who owns cattle; rancher. **b.** a cowboy or cowherd. **2.** *Brit.* a farmworker who tends cows. [1670–80; cow[1] + MAN[1]]

co•work•er (kō′wûr′kər, kō wûr′-), *n.* a fellow worker; colleague. [1635–45; CO- + WORKER]

cow′ pars′nip, any of several tall, coarse plants of the genus *Heracleum,* of the parsley family, as *H. sphondylium* or *H. lanatum,* having large, flat clusters of white flowers. [1540–50]

cow•pea (kou′pē′), *n.* **1.** a plant, *Vigna unguiculata,* extensively cultivated in the southern U.S. for forage, soil improvement, etc. **2.** the seed of this plant, used for food. Also called **black-eyed pea.** [1810–20, *Amer.*; cow[1] + PEA]

Cow•per (ko͞o′pər, kou′-), *n.* **William,** 1731–1800, English poet and hymnologist.

Cow′per's gland′ (kou′pərz, ko͞o′-), *Anat., Zool.* either of two small glands that secrete a mucous substance into the male urethra. Also called **bulbourethral gland.** [1730–40; named after William *Cowper* (1666–1709), English anatomist, who discovered them]

cow′ pie′, *Slang.* a piece of cow dung.

cow′ pi′lot. See **sergeant major** (def. 3). [1880–85]

cow•poke (kou′pōk′), *n. Southwestern U.S.* a cowboy or cowgirl. [1880–85; cow[1] + POKE[1] (prob. formed after COWPUNCHER)]

cow′ po′ny, a small, fast, agile horse trained for use by cowhands in herding cattle. [1870–75, *Amer.*]

cow•pox (kou′poks′), *n. Vet. Pathol.* an eruptive disease appearing on the teats and udders of cows, in which small pustules form that contain a virus used in the vaccination of humans against smallpox. [1790–1800; cow[1] + POX]

COWPS, Council on Wage and Price Stability.

cow•punch•er (kou′pun′chər), *n.* a cowboy or cowgirl. [1875–80; cow[1] + *puncher* (see PUNCH[1], -ER[1])]

cow•rie (kou′rē), *n.* **1.** the highly polished, usually brightly colored shell of a marine gastropod of the genus *Cypraea,* as that of *C. moneta* **(money cowrie),** used as money in certain parts of Asia and Africa, or that of *C. tigris,* used for ornament. **2.** the gastropod itself. [1655–65; < Hindi *kaurī*]

co•write (kō rīt′), *v.t.,* **-wrote, -writ•ten, -writ•ing.** to coauthor. [CO- + WRITE] —**co•writ′er,** *n.*

cow•ry (kou′rē), *n., pl.* **-ries.** cowrie.

cow′ shark′, any of several sharks constituting the family Hexanchidae, having six or seven gill openings on each side of the head.

cow•shed (kou′shed′), *n.* a shed serving as a shelter for cows. [1825–35; cow[1] + SHED[1]]

cow•skin (kou′skin′), *n.* **1.** the skin of a cow. **2.** the leather made from it. [1730–40, *Amer.*; cow[1] + SKIN]

cow•slip (kou′slip), *n.* **1.** an English primrose, *Primula veris,* having fragrant yellow flowers. **2.** the marsh marigold. **3.** See **shooting star** (def. 2). **4.** See **Virginia cowslip.** [bef. 1000; ME *cowslyppe,* OE *cūslyppe,* equiv. to *cū* cow[1] + *slyppe, slypa* slime; see SLIP[3]]

cow•tail (kou′tāl′), *n.* a coarse wool of poor quality. [1665–75; cow[1] + TAIL[1]]

cow′ town′, 1. a small town, esp. one in a cattle-raising district in the western U.S. or Canada. **2.** a town or city, esp. in the western U.S. or Canada, from which cattle are shipped to market. [1880–85]

cow′ vetch′, a climbing plant, *Vicia cracca,* of the legume family, of Eurasia and North America, having elongated clusters of violet-purple flowers.

cox (koks), *Informal.* —*n.* **1.** coxswain. —*v.t.* **2.** to act as coxswain to (a boat). [1865–70; short form]

Cox (koks), *n.* **James Middleton,** 1870–1957, U.S. journalist and politician.

cox•a (kok′sə), *n., pl.* **cox•ae** (kok′sē). **1.** *Anat.* **a.** See **innominate bone. b.** the joint of the hip. **2.** *Zool.* the first or proximal segment of the leg of insects and other arthropods. [1700–10; < L: hip] —**cox′al,** *adj.*

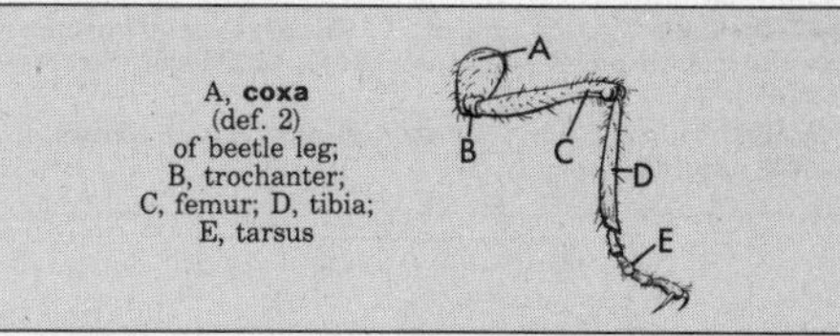

A, **coxa** (def. 2) of beetle leg; B, trochanter; C, femur; D, tibia; E, tarsus

cox•al•gi•a (kok sal′jē ə, -jə), *n.* pain in the hip. Also, **cox•al•gy** (kok′sal jē). [1855–60; COX(A) + -ALGIA] —**cox•al′gic,** *adj.*

cox•comb (koks′kōm′), *n.* **1.** a conceited, foolish dandy; pretentious fop. **2.** *Archaic.* head; pate. **3.** *Obs.* cockscomb (def. 2). [1565–75; sp. var. of COCKSCOMB] —**cox•comb•i•cal** (koks kom′i kəl, -kō′mi-), **cox•comb′ic,** *adj.* —**cox•comb′i•cal•ly,** *adv.*
—**Syn. 1.** dude, popinjay, jackanapes.

cox•comb•ry (koks′kōm′rē), *n., pl.* **-ries. 1.** the manners or behavior of a coxcomb. **2.** a foppish trait. [1600–10; COXCOMB + -RY]

Cox•ey (kok′sē), *n.* **Jacob Sech•ler** (sech′lər), 1854–1951, U.S. political reformer: led a group of unemployed marchers **(Cox′ey's ar′my)** in 1894 from Ohio to Washington, D.C., to petition Congress for legislation to create jobs and relieve poverty.

cox•sack•ie•vi•rus (kok sak′ē vī′rəs, ko͝ok sä′kē-), *n., pl.* **-rus•es.** any of a group of viruses closely related to the virus of poliomyelitis, causing certain diseases of humans, as herpangia and epidemic pleurodynia. Also, **Coxsack′ie vi′rus.** [1945–50; after *Coxsackie,* N.Y., where the first known case appeared]

cox•swain (kok′sən, -swān′), *n.* **1.** the steersman of a racing shell. **2.** a person who is in charge of a ship's boat and its crew, under an officer, and who steers it. Also, **cockswain.** [1425–75; late ME *cokeswayne.* See COCKBOAT, SWAIN]

Cox′well chair′ (kok′swəl, -swel). See **Cogswell chair.**

coy (koi), *adj.,* **-er, -est,** *v.* —*adj.* **1.** artfully or affectedly shy or reserved; slyly hesitant; coquettish. **2.** shy; modest. **3.** showing reluctance, esp. when insincere or affected, to reveal one's plans or opinions, make a commitment, or take a stand: *The mayor was coy about his future political aspirations.* **4.** *Archaic.* disdainful; aloof. **5.** *Obs.* quiet; reserved. —*v.i.* **6.** *Archaic.* to act in a coy manner. —*v.t. Obs.* **7.** to quiet; soothe. **8.** to pat; caress. [1300–50; ME < AF *coi, quoy* calm, OF *quei* < VL **quētus,* for L *quiētus* QUIET] —**coy′ish,** *adj.* —**coy′ish•ness,** *n.* —**coy′ly,** *adv.* —**coy′ness,** *n.*
—**Syn. 2.** retiring, diffident, bashful, demure.

coy•dog (kī′dôg′, -dog′), *n.* the offspring of a coyote and a dog. Also, **coy′-dog′.** [1945–50; COY(OTE) + DOG]

coy•o•te (kī ō′tē, kī′ōt), *n., pl.* **-tes,** (*esp. collectively*) **-te. 1.** Also called **prairie wolf.** a buffy-gray, wolflike canid, *Canis latrans,* of North America, distinguished from the wolf by its relatively small size and its slender build, large ears, and narrow muzzle. **2.** *Slang.* a contemptible person, esp. an avaricious or dishonest one. **3.** *Amer. Ind. Legend.* the coyote regarded as a culture hero and trickster by American Indian tribes of the West. **4.** *Slang.* a person who smuggles Mexican nationals across the border into the U.S. for a fee. [1825–35; earlier *cuiota, cayota* < MexSp *coyote* < Nahuatl *coyōtl*]

coyote, *Canis latrans,* 1½ ft. (0.5 m) high at shoulder; head and body 2½ ft. (0.76 m); tail 1 ft. (0.3 m)

CONCISE PRONUNCIATION KEY: act, cāpe, dâre, pärt; set, ēqual; *if,* īce; ox, ōver, ôrder, oil, bo͝ok, bo͞ot, out; up, ûrge; child; sing; shoe; thin, *that;* zh as in *treasure.* ə = *a* as in *alone, e* as in *system, i* as in *easily, o* as in *gallop, u* as in *circus;* ᵊ as in *fire* (fīᵊr), *hour* (ouᵊr). l and n can serve as syllabic consonants, as in *cradle* (krād′l), and *button* (but′n). See the full key inside the front cover.

Coyo′te State′, South Dakota (used as a nickname).

coy•pu (koi′po͞o), *n., pl.* **-pus,** (*esp. collectively*) **-pu.** a large, South American, aquatic rodent, *Myocastor* (or *Myopotamus*) *coypus,* yielding the fur nutria. [1785–95; < AmerSp *coipú* < Araucanian *coipu*]

coypu, *Myocastor coypus,* head and body 2 ft. (0.6 m); tail to 16 in. (41 cm)

coz (kuz), *n. Informal.* cousin. [short form]

coze (kōz), *v.,* **cozed, coz•ing,** *n.* —*v.i.* **1.** to converse in a friendly way; chat. —*n.* **2.** a friendly talk; a chat. Also, **cose.** [1820–30; < F *causer* to chat, OF: to reason, expound < L *causārī* to plead a cause, plead as an excuse, deriv. of *causa* CAUSE]

coz•en (kuz′ən), *v.t., v.i.* to cheat, deceive, or trick. [1565–75; perh. < ONF *coçonner* to resell, v. deriv. of *coçon* retailer (< L *coctiōnem,* acc. of *coctiō, cōciō* dealer), influenced by MF *cousin* dupe, lit., COUSIN] **—coz′en•er,** *n.* **—coz′en•ing•ly,** *adv.*

coz•en•age (kuz′ə nij), *n.* **1.** the practice of cozening. **2.** the condition of being cozened. [1555–65; COZEN + -AGE]

co•zey (kō′zē), *adj.,* **-zi•er, -zi•est,** *n., pl.* **-zeys,** *v.,* **-zied, -zy•ing.** cozy.

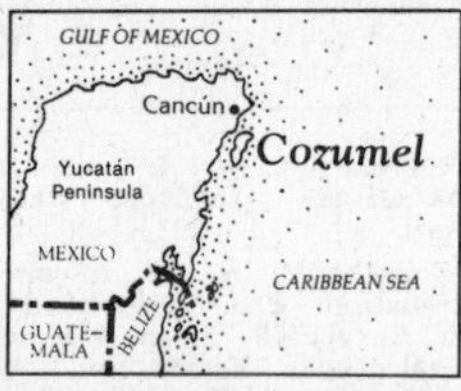

Co•zu•mel (kō′zə mel′; *Sp.* kō′so͞o mel′), *n.* an island off NE Quintana Roo state, on the Yucatán Peninsula, in SE Mexico: tourist resort.

co•zy (kō′zē), *adj.,* **-zi•er, -zi•est,** *n., pl.* **-zies,** *v.,* **-zied, -zy•ing.** —*adj.* **1.** snugly warm and comfortable: *a cozy little house.* **2.** convenient or beneficial, usually as a result of dishonesty or connivance: *a very cozy agreement between competing firms.* **3.** suggesting opportunistic or conspiratorial intimacy: *a cozy relationship between lobbyists and some politicians.* **4.** discreetly reticent or noncommittal: *The administrators are remaining cozy about which policy they plan to adopt.* —*n.* **5.** a padded covering for a teapot, chocolate pot, etc., to retain the heat. —*v.t.* **6.** to make more cozy (often fol. by *up*): *New curtains would cozy the room up a bit.* —*v.i.* **7. cozy up** or **up to,** *Informal.* **a.** to move closer for comfort or affection: *Come over to the fire and cozy up a bit.* **b.** to try to become friendly or intimate in order to further one's own ends; attempt to ingratiate oneself: *He's always cozying up to the boss.* Also, **cosy, cozey, co′zie.** [1700–10; orig. Scots; perh. < Scand; cf. Norw *koselig* cozy, *kose seg* to enjoy oneself] **—co′zi•ly,** *adv.* **—co′zi•ness,** *n.*
—**Syn. 1.** snug, comfy, homey, sheltered.

Coz•zens (kuz′ənz), *n.* **James Gould,** 1903–78, U.S. novelist.

CP, candlepower.

cP, centipoise. Also, **cp**

cp., compare.

C.P., 1. Chief Patriarch. **2.** command post. **3.** Common Prayer. **4.** Communist Party.

c.p., 1. chemically pure. **2.** circular pitch. **3.** command post. **4.** common pleas.

C.P.A., 1. See **certified public accountant. 2.** chartered public accountant.

CPB, Corporation for Public Broadcasting. Also, **C.P.B.**

CPCU, *Insurance.* Chartered Property and Casualty Underwriter. Also, **C.P.C.U.**

cpd., compound.

CPI, See **consumer price index.**

cpi, characters per inch.

cpl., corporal.

CPM, 1. *Com.* cost per thousand. **2.** Critical Path Method.

cpm, *Com.* cost per thousand.

CP/M, *Trademark.* Control Program/Microprocessors: a microcomputer operating system.

c.p.m., 1. *Music.* common particular meter. **2.** cycles per minute.

CPO, See **chief petty officer.** Also, **C.P.O., c.p.o.**

C power supply, *Electronics.* See **C supply.**

CPR, See **cardiopulmonary resuscitation.**

CPS, See **certified professional secretary.**

CONCISE ETYMOLOGY KEY: <, descended or borrowed from; >, whence; b., blend of, blended; c., cognate with; cf., compare; deriv., derivative; equiv., equivalent; imit., imitative; obl., oblique; r., replacing; s., stem; sp., spelling, spelled; resp., respelling, respelled; trans., translation; ?, origin unknown; *, unattested; ‡, probably earlier than. See the full key inside the front cover.

cps, 1. *Computers.* characters per second. **2.** cycles per second.

CPSC, See **Consumer Product Safety Commission.** Also, **C.P.S.C.**

cpt., counterpoint.

CPT theorem, the proposition that all the laws of physics are unchanged by the combined operations of charge conjugation (C), space inversion (P), and time reversal (T). Also called **PCT theorem, TCP theorem.**

CPU, *Computers.* central processing unit: the key component of a computer system, which contains the circuitry necessary to interpret and execute program instructions. Also called **central processor, microprocessor.** [1965–70]

CQ, 1. *Radio.* a signal sent at the beginning of radiograms conveying general information or sent by an amateur as an invitation for any other amateur to reply. **2.** *Mil.* charge of quarters.

c quark, *Physics.* See **charmed quark.**

CR, 1. conditioned reflex; conditioned response. **2.** consciousness-raising. **3.** critical ratio.

Cr, *Symbol, Chem.* chromium.

cr., 1. credit. **2.** creditor. **3.** crown.

C.R., 1. Costa Rica. **2.** *Banking.* credit report.

craal (kräl), *n.* kraal.

crab[1] (krab), *n., v.,* **crabbed, crab•bing.** —*n.* **1.** any decapod crustacean of the suborder Brachyura, having the eyes on short stalks and a short, broad, more or less flattened body, the abdomen being small and folded under the thorax. **2.** any of various other crustaceans, as the hermit crab, or other animals, as the horseshoe crab, resembling the true crabs. **3.** (*cap.*) *Astron., Astrol.* the zodiacal constellation or sign Cancer. **4.** (*cap.*) *Astron.* the Crab Nebula. **5.** any of various mechanical contrivances for hoisting or pulling. **6.** *Aeron.* the maneuver of crabbing. **7.** *Informal.* the crab louse. See under **louse** (def. 1). **8. crabs, a.** (*used with a singular v.*) a losing throw, as two aces, in the game of hazard. **b.** pediculosis. **9. catch a crab,** to make a faulty stroke in rowing, so that the oar strikes the water forcibly on the backstroke. —*v.i.* **10.** to catch or attempt to catch crabs. **11.** to move sideways, diagonally, or obliquely, esp. with short, abrupt bursts of speed; scuttle. **12.** *Aeron.* (of an aircraft) to head partly into the wind to compensate for drift. **13.** *Naut.* to drift or advance with some movement sideways, esp. when under tow. —*v.t.* **14.** to move (a vehicle or object) sideways, diagonally, or obliquely, esp. with short, abrupt movements. **15.** *Aeron.* to head (an aircraft) partly into the wind to compensate for drift. [bef. 1000; ME *crabbe,* OE *crabba;* c. D *krab,* ON *krabbi;* akin to G *Krebs*] **—crab′like′,** *adj.*

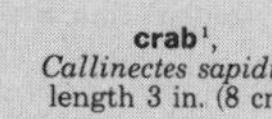

crab[1], *Callinectes sapidus,* length 3 in. (8 cm)

crab[2] (krab), *n.* a crab apple fruit or tree. [1300–50; ME *crabbe;* perh. special use of CRAB[1]]

crab[3] (krab), *n., v.,* **crabbed, crab•bing.** —*n.* **1.** *Informal.* an ill-tempered or grouchy person. —*v.i.* **2.** *Informal.* to find fault; complain. **3.** (of hawks) to claw each other. —*v.t.* **4.** *Informal.* to find fault with. **5.** to make ill-tempered or grouchy; embitter. **6.** (of a hawk) to claw (another hawk). **7.** *Slang.* to spoil. [1350–1400; ME; back formation from CRABBED] **—crab′ber,** *n.*

crab′ ap′ple, 1. a small, sour, wild apple. **2.** any of various small, tart, cultivated varieties of apple, used for making jelly and preserves. **3.** any tree bearing such fruit. [1705–15]

Crabb (krab), *n.* **George,** 1778–1851, English author and philologist.

Crabbe (krab), *n.* **George,** 1754–1832, English poet.

crab•bed (krab′id), *adj.* **1.** grouchy; ill-natured; irritable; churlish. **2.** perverse; contrary; obstinate. **3.** hard to understand; intricate and obscure. **4.** difficult to read or decipher, as handwriting. [1250–1300; ME; see CRAB[1], -ED[3]] **—crab′bed•ly,** *adv.* **—crab′bed•ness,** *n.*
—**Syn. 1.** cross, peevish, cantankerous.

crab•ber (krab′ər), *n.* **1.** a person who catches crabs. **2.** a boat used in catching crabs. [1840–50; CRAB[1] + ER[1]]

crab•bing (krab′ing), *n.* **1.** the activity or occupation of fishing for crabs. **2.** a finishing process for reducing shrinkage and creasing of woolens and worsteds by stretching the fabric on a rotating cylinder and immersing in hot or, sometimes, cold water. **3.** *Aeron.* the maneuver of heading partly into the wind to compensate for drift. [1870–75; CRAB[1] + -ING[1]]

crab•by (krab′ē), *adj.,* **-bi•er, -bi•est.** *Informal.* grouchy; ill-natured; irritable; peevish. [1540–50; CRAB[3] + -Y[1]] **—crab′bi•ly,** *adv.* **—crab′bi•ness,** *n.*

crab′ cac′tus, a cactus, *Schlumbergera truncata* (or *Zygocactus truncatus*), native to Brazil, having stems with leaflike segments and showy red flowers and often cultivated as a houseplant. Also called **Thanksgiving cactus.** [1895–1900, *Amer.*]

crab′ can′on, *Music.* a canon in which the imitating voice is the theme in retrograde motion.

crab•eat•er (krab′ē′tər), *n.* any of various animals that feed on crabs, as the cobia. [1805–15, *Amer.;* CRAB[1] + EATER] **—crab′eat′ing,** *n., adj.*

crab′ grass′, an annual grass, *Digitaria sanguinalis,* common in cultivated and waste grounds and often occurring as a pest weed in lawns. [1590–1600]

crab′ louse′. See under **louse** (def. 1). [1540–50]

crab•meat (krab′mēt′), *n.* the parts of a crab used for food. [CRAB[1] + MEAT]

Crab′ Neb′ula, *Astron.* the remnant of a supernova explosion, observed in 1054 A.D., in the constellation Taurus. [1885–90]

crab-plov•er (krab′pluv′ər, -plō′vər), *n.* a black and white wading bird, *Dromas ardeola,* of the northern and western shores of the Indian Ocean. [so called from its diet]

crab's′ eye′. See **Indian licorice.** [1875–80, *Amer.*]

crab′ spi′der, any crab-shaped spider of the family Thomisidae, characterized by its sideways manner of moving. [1860–65]

crab•stick (krab′stik′), *n.* **1.** a stick, cane, or club made of wood, esp. of the crab tree. **2.** an ill-tempered, grouchy person; crosspatch. [1695–1705; CRAB[2] + STICK[1]]

crab′ tree′, a tree bearing crab apples. [1300–50; ME]

crab•wise (krab′wīz′), *adv.* sideways: *patrons edging crabwise along the crowded row of theater seats.* [1900–05; CRAB + -WISE]

crab•wood (krab′wo͝od′), *n.* carapa. [1840–50; CRAB[2] + WOOD[1]]

crack (krak), *v.i.* **1.** to break without complete separation of parts; become fissured: *The plate cracked when I dropped it, but it was still usable.* **2.** to break with a sudden, sharp sound: *The branch cracked under the weight of the snow.* **3.** to make a sudden, sharp sound in or as if in breaking; snap: *The whip cracked.* **4.** (of the voice) to break abruptly and discordantly, esp. into an upper register, as because of weariness or emotion. **5.** to fail; give way: *His confidence cracked under the strain.* **6.** to succumb or break down, esp. under severe psychological pressure, torture, or the like: *They questioned him steadily for 24 hours before he finally cracked.* **7.** *Chem.* to decompose as a result of being subjected to heat. **8.** *Chiefly South Midland and Southern U.S.* to brag; boast. **9.** *Chiefly Scot.* to chat; gossip. —*v.t.* **10.** to cause to make a sudden sharp sound: *The driver cracked the whip.* **11.** to break without complete separation of parts; break into fissures. **12.** to break with a sudden, sharp sound: *to crack walnuts.* **13.** to strike and thereby make a sharp noise: *The boxer cracked his opponent on the jaw.* **14.** to induce or cause to be stricken with sorrow or emotion; affect deeply. **15.** to utter or tell: *to crack jokes.* **16.** to cause to make a cracking sound: *to crack one's knuckles.* **17.** to damage, weaken, etc.: *The new evidence against him cracked his composure.* **18.** to make mentally unsound. **19.** to make (the voice) harsh or unmanageable. **20.** to solve; decipher: *to crack a murder case.* **21.** *Informal.* to break into (a safe, vault, etc.). **22.** *Chem.* to subject to the process of cracking, as in the distillation of petroleum. **23.** *Informal.* to open and drink (a bottle of wine, liquor, beer, etc.). **24. crack a book,** *Informal.* to open a book in order to study or read: *He hardly ever cracked a book.* **25. crack a smile,** *Informal.* to smile. **26. crack down,** to take severe or stern measures, esp. in enforcing obedience to laws or regulations: *The police are starting to crack down on local drug dealers.* **27. crack off,** to cause (a piece of hot glass) to fall from a blowpipe or punty. **28. crack on,** *Naut.* **a.** (of a sailing vessel) to sail in high winds under sails that would normally be furled. **b.** (of a power vessel) to advance at full speed in heavy weather. **29. crack up,** *Informal.* **a.** to suffer a mental or emotional breakdown. **b.** to crash, as in an automobile or airplane: *He skidded into the telephone pole and cracked up.* **c.** to wreck an automobile, airplane, or other vehicle. **d.** to laugh or to cause to laugh unrestrainedly: *That story about the revolving door really cracked me up. Ed cracked up, too, when he heard it.* **30. crack wise,** *Slang.* to wisecrack: *We tried to be serious, but he was always cracking wise.* **31. get cracking,** *Informal.* **a.** to begin moving or working; start: *Let's get cracking on these dirty dishes!* **b.** to work or move more quickly.
—*n.* **32.** a break without complete separation of parts; fissure. **33.** a slight opening, as between boards in a floor or wall, or between a door and its doorpost. **34.** a sudden, sharp noise, as of something breaking. **35.** the snap of or as of a whip. **36.** a resounding blow: *He received a terrific crack on the head when the branch fell.* **37.** *Informal.* a witty or cutting remark; wisecrack. **38.** a break or change in the flow or tone of the voice. **39.** *Informal.* opportunity; chance; try: *Give him first crack at the new job.* **40.** a flaw or defect. **41.** Also called **rock.** *Slang.* pellet-size pieces of highly purified cocaine, prepared with other ingredients for smoking, and known to be especially potent and addicting. **42.** *Masonry.* check[1] (def. 46). **43.** a mental defect or deficiency. **44.** a shot, as with a rifle: *At the first crack, the deer fell.* **45.** a moment; instant: *He was on his feet again in a crack.* **46.** *Slang.* a burglary, esp. an instance of housebreaking. **47.** *Chiefly Brit.* a person or thing that excels in some respect. **48.** *Slang* (*vulgar*). the vulva. **49.** *Chiefly Scot.* conversation; chat. **50.** *Brit. Dial.* boasting; braggadocio. **51.** *Archaic.* a burglar. **52. fall through the cracks,** to be overlooked, missed, or neglected: *In any inspection process some defective materials will fall through the cracks.* Also, **slip between the cracks.**
—*adj.* **53.** first-rate; excellent: *a crack shot.*
—*adv.* **54.** with a cracking sound. [bef. 1000; ME *crak(k)en* (v.), *crak* (n.), OE *cracian* to resound; akin to G *krachen,* D *kraken* (v.), and G *Krach,* D *krak* (n.)] **—crack′a•ble,** *adj.* **—crack′less,** *adj.*

crack•a•jack (krak′ə jak′), *n., adj.* crackerjack.

crack•brain (krak′brān′), *n.* a foolish, senseless, or insane person. [1560–70; CRACK(ED) + BRAIN]

crack•brained (krak′brānd′), *adj.* foolish, senseless, or insane. [1625–35; CRACKBRAIN + -ED[3]]

crack•down (krak′doun′), *n.* the severe or stern enforcement of regulations, laws, etc., as to root out abuses or correct a problem. [1930–35, *Amer.;* n. use of v. phrase *crack down*]

cracked (krakt), *adj.* **1.** broken: *a container full of* *cracked ice.* **2.** broken without separation of parts; fissured. **3.** damaged; injured. **4.** *Informal.* eccentric; mad; daffy: *a charming person, but a bit cracked.* **5.** broken in tone, as the voice. **6. cracked up to be,** *Informal.* reported or reputed to be (usually used in the negative): *I hear the play is not what it's cracked up to be.* [1400–50; late ME *crachyd.* See CRACK, -ED[2]]

crack•er (krak′ər), *n.* **1.** a thin, crisp biscuit. **2.** a firecracker. **3.** Also called **crack′er bon′bon.** a small paper roll used as a party favor, that usually contains candy, trinkets, etc., and that pops when pulled sharply at one or both ends. **4.** (*cap.*) *Sometimes Disparaging and Offensive.* a native or inhabitant of Georgia (used as a nickname). **5.** *Slang* (*disparaging and offensive*). a poor white person living in some rural parts of the southeastern U.S. **6.** snapper (def. 5). **7.** braggart; boaster. **8.** a person or thing that cracks. **9.** a chemical reactor used for cracking. Cf. **catalytic cracking, fractionator.** —*adj.* **10. crackers,** *Informal.* wild; crazy: *They went crackers over the new styles.* [1400–50; late ME *craker.* See CRACK, -ER[1]; (defs. 4–5) perh. orig. in sense "braggart," applied to frontiersmen of the southern American colonies in the 1760's, though subsequently given other interpretations (cf. CORN-CRACKER); for *crackers* crazy, cf. CRACKED, -ERS]

crack•er-bar•rel (krak′ər bar′əl), *adj.* of or suggesting the simple rustic informality and directness thought to be characteristic of life in and around a country store: *homespun, cracker-barrel philosophy.* [1875–80, *Amer.*; adj. use of *cracker barrel,* around which rural people supposedly converse in old-style country stores]

crack•er•ber•ry (krak′ər ber′ē), *n., pl.* **-ries.** bunchberry. [1865–70, *Amer.*; so called from the sound made when it is crunched. See CRACKER, BERRY]

Crack′er Jack′, *Trademark.* a confection of caramel-coated popcorn and peanuts.

crack•er•jack (krak′ər jak′), *Informal.* —*n.* **1.** a person or thing that shows marked ability or excellence. —*adj.* **2.** of marked ability; exceptionally fine. Also, **crackajack.** [1890–95, *Amer.*; earlier *crackajack,* rhyming compound based on CRACK (adj.); *-a-* as in BLACKAMOOR; JACK[1] in sense "chap, fellow"]

Crack′er State′, *Sometimes Disparaging and Offensive.* Georgia (used as a nickname). [1870–75, *Amer.*]

crack•head (krak′hed′), *n. Slang.* a habitual user of cocaine in the form of crack. [1985–90]

crack•house (krak′hous′), *n., pl.* **-hous•es** (hou′ziz). a place where cocaine in the form of crack is bought, sold, and smoked. [1985–90]

crack•ie (krak′ē), *n. Canadian* (*chiefly Atlantic Provinces*). a small noisy dog. [1890–95; appar. CRACK + -IE; cf. dial. (Devonshire) *cracky* wren, any small creature]

crack•ing (krak′ing), *n.* **1.** (in the distillation of petroleum or the like) the process of breaking down certain hydrocarbons into simpler ones of lower boiling points by means of excess heat, distillation under pressure, etc., in order to give a greater yield of low-boiling products than could be obtained by simple distillation. Cf. **catalytic cracking.** —*adv.* **2.** extremely; unusually: *We saw a cracking good match at the stadium.* —*adj. Informal.* **3.** done with precision; smart: *A cracking salute from the honor guard.* **4. get cracking.** See **crack** (def. 31). [1250–1300; ME; see CRACK, -ING[1], -ING[2]]

crack•le (krak′əl), *v.,* **-led, -ling,** *n.* —*v.i.* **1.** to make slight, sudden, sharp noises, rapidly repeated. **2.** to form a network of fine cracks on the surface. **3.** (of ceramic glaze) to craze. **4.** to exhibit liveliness, vibrancy, anticipation, etc.: *The play crackled with wit.* —*v.t.* **5.** to cause to crackle. **6.** to break with a crackling noise. **7.** to craze (ceramic glaze). —*n.* **8.** the act of crackling. **9.** a crackling noise. **10.** a network of fine cracks, as in the glaze of some kinds of porcelain. **11.** crackleware. [1490–1500; CRACK + -LE]

crack•le•ware (krak′əl wâr′), *n.* ceramic ware having a crackled glaze. Also called **crackle.** [1880–85; CRACKLE + WARE[1]]

crack•ling (krak′ling *or, for 2, 3,* -lən), *n.* **1.** the making of slight cracking sounds rapidly repeated. **2.** the crisp browned skin or rind of roast pork. **3.** Usually, **cracklings.** *Southern U.S.* the crisp residue left when fat, esp. hog or chicken fat, is rendered. [1540–50; CRACKLE + -ING[1]]

crack•ly (krak′lē), *adj.,* **-li•er, -li•est.** apt to crackle. [1600–10; CRACKLE + -Y[1]]

crack•nel (krak′nl), *n.* **1.** a hard, brittle cake or biscuit. **2. cracknels,** small bits of fat pork fried crisp. Cf. **scrapple.** [1350–1400; ME *crak(e)nele* < MF **craquenelle,* metathetic alter. of *craquelin* < MD *crākelinc,* equiv. to *crāke(n)* to CRACK + *-linc* -LING[1]]

crack′ of dawn′, the part of morning when light first appears in the sky.

crack′ of doom′, **1.** the signal that announces the Day of Judgment. **2.** the end of the world; doomsday.

crack•pot (krak′pot′), *Informal.* —*n.* **1.** a person who is eccentric, unrealistic, or fanatical. —*adj.* **2.** eccentric; impractical; fanatical: *crackpot ideas.* [1860–65; from the phrase *cracked pot*]

cracks•man (kraks′mən), *n., pl.* **-men.** *Slang.* burglar; housebreaker. [1805–15; CRACK + -S[3] + MAN[1]]

crack′ the whip′, **1.** to demand obedience, hard work, or efficiency from others in a harsh or stern manner. **2.** Also called **snap the whip.** a game in which players in a line, each holding the next, run, roller-skate, or ice-skate for a distance until the leader veers suddenly in a new direction, causing the rest of the line to swing around rapidly and the players at the end of the line to lose their balance or to let go of the other players.

crack•up (krak′up′), *n.* **1.** a crash; collision. **2.** a breakdown in health, esp. a mental breakdown. **3.** collapse or disintegration: *the crackup of an alliance.* [1850–55; n. use of v. phrase *crack up*]

crack•y (krak′ē), *n.* See **by cracky.**

cra•co•vi•enne (krə kō′vē en′, krə kō′vē en′), *n.* krakowiak.

Crac•ow (krak′ou, krä′kou, krä′kō), *n.* a city in S Poland, on the Vistula: the capital of Poland 1320–1609. 685,000. German, **Krakau.** Polish, **Kraków.**

-cracy, a combining form occurring in loanwords from Greek (*aristocracy; democracy*); on this model used, with the meaning "rule," "government," "governing body," to form abstract nouns from stems of other origin: *mobocracy; bureaucracy.* Cf. **-crat.** [< MF *-cracie* (now *-cratie*) < LL *-cratia* < Gk *-kratia,* equiv. to *krát(os)* rule, strength, might (akin to HARD) + *-ia* -Y[3]]

cra•dle (krād′l), *n., v.,* **-dled, -dling.** —*n.* **1.** a small bed for an infant, usually on rockers. **2.** any of various supports for objects set horizontally, as the support for the handset of a telephone. **3.** the place where anything is nurtured during its early existence: *Boston was the cradle of the American Revolution.* **4.** *Agric.* **a.** a frame of wood with a row of long curved teeth projecting above and parallel to a scythe, for laying grain in bunches as it is cut. **b.** a scythe together with the cradle in which it is set. **5.** a wire or wicker basket used to hold a wine bottle in a more or less horizontal position while the wine is being served. **6.** *Artillery.* the part of a gun carriage on which a recoiling gun slides. **7.** a landing platform for ferryboats, rolling on inclined tracks to facilitate loading and unloading at different water levels. **8.** *Aeron.* a docklike structure in which a rigid or semirigid airship is built or is supported during inflation. **9.** *Auto.* creeper (def. 5). **10.** *Naut.* **a.** a shaped support for a boat, cast, etc.; chock. **b.** truss (def. 9). **11.** *Shipbuilding.* **a.** a moving framework on which a hull slides down the ways when launched. **b.** a built-up form on which plates of irregular form are shaped. **12.** *Med.* a frame that prevents the bedclothes from touching an injured part of a bedridden patient. **13.** *Mining.* a box on rockers for washing sand or gravel to separate gold or other heavy metal. **14.** an engraver's tool for laying mezzotint grounds. **15.** *Painting.* a structure of wooden strips attached to the back of a panel, used as a support and to prevent warping. **16. rob the cradle,** *Informal.* to marry, court, or date a person much younger than oneself. —*v.t.* **17.** to hold gently or protectively. **18.** to place or rock in or as in an infant's cradle. **19.** to nurture during infancy. **20.** to receive or hold as a cradle. **21.** to cut (grain) with a cradle. **22.** to place (a vessel) on a cradle. **23.** *Mining.* to wash (sand or gravel) in a cradle; rock. **24.** *Painting.* to support (a panel) with a cradle. —*v.i.* **25.** to lie in or as if in a cradle. **26.** to cut grain with a cradle scythe. [bef. 1000; ME *cradel,* OE *cradol;* akin to OHG *cratto* basket] —**cra′dler,** *n.*

cra•dle•board (krād′l bôrd′, -bōrd′), *n.* a wooden frame worn on the back, used by North American Indian women for carrying an infant. Also, **cra′dle board′.** [1875–80; CRADLE + BOARD]

cra′dle cap′, an inflammation of the scalp, occurring in infants and characterized by greasy, yellowish scales; seborrheic dermatitis of infants.

cra′dle roof′, **1.** a roof having trusses the undersides of which form an arch. **2.** a roof ceiled in the form of a barrel vault. [1835–45]

cra′dle scythe′, cradle (def. 4b). [1660–70]

cra•dle•song (krād′l sông′, -song′), *n.* a lullaby. [1350–1400; ME *cradel song.* See CRADLE, SONG]

cradle-to-grave (krād′l tə grāv′), *adj.* extending throughout one's life, from birth to death: *a cradle-to-grave system of health care.* Also, *Brit.,* **womb-to-tomb.** [1940–45]

cra′dle vault′, *Archit.* See **barrel vault.** [1870–75]

cra•dling (krād′l ing), *n.* framework for supporting a coved or vaulted ceiling. [1810–20; CRADLE + -ING[1]]

craft (kraft, kräft), *n., pl.* **crafts** or, for 5, 8, **craft,** *v.* —*n.* **1.** an art, trade, or occupation requiring special skill, esp. manual skill: *the craft of a mason.* **2.** skill; dexterity: *The silversmith worked with great craft.* **3.** skill or ability used for bad purposes; cunning; deceit; guile. **4.** the members of a trade or profession collectively; a guild. **5.** a ship or other vessel. **6.** a number of ships or other vessels taken as a whole: *The craft were warned of possible heavy squalls.* **7.** aircraft collectively. **8.** a single aircraft. —*v.t.* **9.** to make or manufacture (an object, objects, product, etc.) with skill and careful attention to detail. [bef. 900; ME; OE *cræft* strength, skill; c. G *Kraft,* D *kracht,* ON *kraptr*] —**craft′less,** *adj.*
—**Syn.** See **cunning.**

Craf•tint (kraf′tint′, kräf′-), *Print., Trademark.* a brand of prepared patterns, printed on clear plastic sheets, for pasting on artwork to produce effects of shading, crosshatching, etc.

crafts•man (krafts′mən, kräfts′-), *n., pl.* **-men.** **1.** a person who practices or is highly skilled in a craft; artisan. **2.** an artist. [1325–75; ME *craftes man* man of skill, earlier *craftman;* cf. OE *cræftiga* craftsman, workman (deriv. of *cræftig* CRAFTY)] —**crafts′man•like′,** *adj.* —**crafts′man•ly,** *adj.* —**crafts′man•ship′,** *n.*
—**Usage.** See **-man.**

crafts•peo•ple (krafts′pē′pəl, kräfts′-), *n.pl.* craftsmen and craftswomen collectively. [CRAFTS(MEN) + PEOPLE]

crafts•per•son (krafts′pûr′sən, kräfts′-), *n.* a person who practices or is highly skilled in a craft; artisan. [1970–75; CRAFTS(MAN) + -PERSON]
—**Usage.** See **-person.**

crafts•wom•an (krafts′wŏŏm′ən, kräfts′-), *n., pl.* **-wom•en.** a woman who practices or is highly skilled in a craft; artisan. [1885–90; CRAFTS(MAN) + -WOMAN]
—**Usage.** See **-woman.**

craft′ un′ion, a labor union composed only of people in the same craft. [1920–25] —**craft′ un′ionist.**

craft•work (kraft′wûrk′, kräft′-), *n.* **1.** work that requires special skill or artistry, esp. a handicraft. **2.** a piece of such work. [1350–1400; ME. See CRAFT, WORK] —**craft′work′er,** *n.*

craft•y (kraf′tē, kräf′-), *adj.,* **craft•i•er, craft•i•est.** **1.** skillful in underhand or evil schemes; cunning; deceitful; sly. **2.** *Obs.* skillful; ingenious; dexterous. [bef. 900; ME; OE *cræftig* skilled. See CRAFT, -Y[1]] —**craft′i•ly,** *adv.* —**craft′i•ness,** *n.*

crag[1] (krag), *n.* a steep, rugged rock; rough, broken, projecting part of a rock. [1275–1325; ME < British Celtic; akin to Welsh *craig* rock] —**crag′like′,** *adj.*

crag[2] (kRag), *n. Scot. and North Eng.* the neck, throat, or craw. [1425–75; late ME *cragge* < MD *crage* neck, throat; c. G *Kragen* collar; cf. CRAW]

crag•gy (krag′ē), *adj.,* **-gi•er, -gi•est.** **1.** full of crags. **2.** rugged; harsh; rough. Also, **crag•ged** (krag′id). [1350–1400; ME; see CRAG[1], -Y[1]] —**crag′gi•ly, crag′ged•ly,** *adv.* —**crag′gi•ness, crag′ged•ness,** *n.*

crags•man (kragz′mən), *n., pl.* **-men.** a person accustomed to or skilled in climbing crags. [1810–20; CRAG[1] + -S[3] + MAN[1]]

Craig (krāg), *n.* **1. Edward Gordon,** 1872–1966, English stage designer, producer, and author. **2.** a male given name: from a Welsh family name meaning "rock."

Craig•a•von (krāg ā′vən, -av′ən), *n.* **James Craig, 1st Viscount,** 1871–1940, first prime minister of Northern Ireland 1921–40.

Crai•gie (krā′gē), *n.* **Sir William (Alexander),** 1867–1957, Scottish lexicographer and philologist.

Cra•io•va (krä yô′vä), *n.* a city in SW Rumania. 220,893.

crake (krāk), *n.* any of several short-billed rails, esp. the corn crake. [1275–1325; ME < ON *krākr, krāki* CROW]

cra•kow (krä′kou), *n.* poulaine. [1325–75; ME *crakowe,* after CRACOW, the place of origin]

cram (kram), *v.,* **crammed, cram•ming,** *n.* —*v.t.* **1.** to fill (something) by force with more than it can easily hold. **2.** to force or stuff (usually fol. by *into, down,* etc.). **3.** to fill with or as with an excessive amount of food; overfeed. **4.** *Informal.* **a.** to prepare (a person), as for an examination, by having him or her memorize information within a short period of time. **b.** to acquire knowledge of (a subject) by so preparing oneself. **5.** *Archaic.* to tell lies to. —*v.i.* **6.** to eat greedily or to excess. **7.** to study for an examination by memorizing facts at the last minute. **8.** to press or force accommodation in a room, vehicle, etc., beyond normal or comfortable capacity; crowd; jam: *The whole team crammed into the bus.* —*n.* **9.** *Informal.* the act of cramming for an examination. **10.** a crammed state. **11.** a dense crowd; throng. [bef. 1000; ME *crammen,* OE *crammian* to stuff, akin to *crimman* to put in] —**cram′ming•ly,** *adv.*
—**Syn. 1.** crowd, pack, squeeze, compress, overcrowd. **3.** glut. **6.** gorge.

Cram (kram), *n.* **Ralph Adams,** 1863–1942, U.S. architect and writer.

cram•bo (kram′bō), *n., pl.* **-boes.** **1.** a game in which one person or side must find a rhyme to a word or a line of verse given by another. **2.** inferior rhyme. [1600–10; earlier *crambe* < L *crambē repetīta* phrase used by Juvenal in reference to unimaginative writing, lit., repeated (i.e., re-served) cabbage (< Gk *krámbē* kind of cabbage)]

cram′ course′, **1.** an intensive course of study designed to review or teach material needed for a specific purpose or, often, material previously taught but not mastered. **2.** See **crash course.**

Cra′mer's rule′ (krā′mərz), *Math.* a method involving the determinant of the coefficients, for calculating a unique solution for a given system of linear equations. [named after Gabriel Cramer (1704–72), Swiss mathematician]

cram-full (kram′fŏŏl′), *adj.* as full as possible; chockfull: *a box cram-full with toys.* [1830–40]

cram•oi•sy (kram′oi zē, -ə zē), *Archaic.* —*adj.* **1.** crimson. —*n.* **2.** crimson cloth. Also, **cram′oi•sie.** [1375–1425; < F *cramoisi,* earlier *crameisi* < Sp *carmesí* < Ar *qirmizī,* equiv. to *qirmiz* KERMES + *-ī* suffix of appurtenance; r. late ME *cremesye* < It *cremisi* < Ar, as above]

cramp[1] (kramp), *n.* **1.** Often, **cramps. a.** a sudden, involuntary, spasmodic contraction of a muscle or group of muscles, esp. of the extremities, sometimes with severe pain. **b.** a piercing pain in the abdomen. **c.** an intermittent, painful contraction of structures of a wall containing involuntary muscle, as in biliary colic or in the uterine contractions of menstruation or of labor. **2.** See **writer's cramp.** —*v.t.* **3.** to affect with or as if with a cramp. [1325–75; ME *crampe* < OF < Gmc; c. MD *crampe,* OS *krampo,* OHG *krampfo;* deriv. of adj. meaning narrow, constrained, bent; cf. OHG *krampf,* ON *krappr;* akin to CRIMP]

cramp[2] (kramp), *n.* **1.** See **cramp iron. 2.** a portable frame or tool with a movable part that can be screwed up to hold things together; clamp. **3.** anything that confines or restrains. **4.** a cramped state or part. —*v.t.* **5.** to fasten or hold with a cramp. **6.** to confine narrowly; restrict; restrain; hamper. **7.** to turn (the front wheels of a motor vehicle) by means of the steering gear; steer. **8. cramp one's style,** *Informal.* to prevent one from showing one's best abilities. —*adj.* **9.** cramped[2]. [1375–1425; late ME *crampe* < MD: hook. See CRAMP[1]] —**cramp′ing•ly,** *adv.*

cramped[1] (krampt), *adj.* affected with a cramp in a muscle or muscles. [1670–80; CRAMP[1] + -ED[3]]

cramped[2] (krampt), *adj.* **1.** confined or severely limited in space: *cramped closets.* **2. a.** (of handwriting) with characters written small and crowded together. **b.**

CONCISE PRONUNCIATION KEY: *act, cāpe, dâre, pärt; set, ēqual; if, īce; ox, ōver, ôrder, oil, bŏŏk, bōōt, out; up, ûrge; child; sing; shoe; thin, that;* zh as in *treasure.* ə = *a* as in *alone, e* as in *system, i* as in *easily, o* as in *gallop, u* as in *circus;* ª as in *fire* (fīªr), *hour* (ouªr). l and n can serve as syllabic consonants, as in *cradle* (krād′l), and *button* (but′n). See the full key inside the front cover.

(of a style of writing) hard to understand; crabbed. [1670–80; CRAMP² + -ED²] —**cramped′ness,** *n.*

cramp•fish (kramp′fish′), *n., pl.* **-fish•es,** (*esp. collectively*) **-fish.** See **electric ray.** [1585–95; CRAMP¹ + FISH]

cramp′ i′ron, a piece of iron with bent ends for holding together building stones or the like. [1555–65]

cram•pon (kram′pon), *n.* **1.** a spiked iron plate worn on boots or shoes for aid in climbing or to prevent slipping on ice, snow, etc. **2.** a device for grasping and lifting heavy loads, usually consisting of a pair of hooks suspended from a chain or cable, the upward pull on which provides tension for the hooks to grip the load on opposite sides. Also, **cram•poon** (kram po͞on′). [1275–1325; ME *cra(u)mpon* < OF *crampon* < Old Low Franconian **krampo,* c. OHG *krampfo,* MD *crampe;* see CRAMP²]

Cra•nach (krä′näkʜ), *n.* **1. Lucas** (*"the Elder"*), 1472–1553, German painter and graphic artist. **2.** his son, **Lucas the Younger,** 1515–86, German painter and graphic artist. Also, **Kranach, Kronach.**

cran•ber•ry (kran′ber′ē, -bə rē), *n., pl.* **-ries. 1.** the red, acid fruit or berry of certain plants of the genus *Vaccinium,* of the heath family, as *V. macrocarpon* **(large cranberry** or **American cranberry)** or *V. oxycoccus* **(small cranberry** or **European cranberry),** used in making sauce, relish, jelly, or juice. **2.** the plant itself, growing wild in bogs or cultivated in acid soils, esp. in the northeastern U.S. [1640–50, *Amer.;* < LG *kraanbere.* See CRANE, BERRY]

cran′berry bog′, a bog in which cranberry plants are cultivated. [1800–10, *Amer.*]

cran′berry bush′, 1. See **highbush cranberry. 2.** See **guelder rose.** [1770–80, *Amer.*]

cran′berry glass′, reddish-pink transparent glassware first made in England and the U.S. in the mid-19th century.

cran′berry gourd′, 1. a South American vine, *Abobra tenuifolia,* of the gourd family, having deeply lobed, ovate leaves and bearing a berrylike scarlet fruit. **2.** the fruit itself.

cran′berry tree′. See **highbush cranberry.** [1805–15, *Amer.*]

Cran•brook (kran′bro͝ok′), *n.* a city in SE British Columbia, in SW Canada. 15,915.

crance′ i′ron (krans), *Naut.* **1.** a metal ring or cap to which bobstays and shrouds are secured, at the forward end of a bowsprit. **2.** an iron mast fitting holding a yard that is not raised or lowered, as that of the foresail or mainsail on a large ship. [1840–50; cf. D *krans* wreath]

cranch (kränch), *v.t., v.i., n.* crunch. [1740–50; perh. b. CRASH¹ and CRUNCH]

cran•dall (kran′dl), *n.* a tool for dressing stone, having adjustable, pointed, steel rods held in a slot at the end of the handle. [prob. after the proper name]

Cran•dall (kran′dl), *n.* **Prudence,** 1803–90, U.S. educator and civil-rights activist.

crane (krān), *n., v.,* **craned, cran•ing.** —*n.* **1.** any large wading bird of the family Gruidae, characterized by long legs, bill, and neck and an elevated hind toe. **2.** (not used scientifically) any of various similar birds of other families, as the great blue heron. **3.** *Mach.* a device for lifting and moving heavy weights in suspension. **4.** any of various similar devices, as a horizontally swinging arm by a fireplace, used for suspending pots over the fire. **5.** *Motion Pictures, Television.* a vehicle having a long boom on which a camera can be mounted for taking shots from high angles. **6.** *Naut.* any of a number of supports for a boat or spare spar on the deck or at the side of a vessel. **7.** (*cap.*) *Astron.* the constellation Grus. —*v.t.* **8.** to hoist, lower, or move by or as by a crane. **9.** to stretch (the neck) as a crane does. —*v.i.* **10.** to stretch out one's neck, esp. to see better. **11.** to hesitate at danger, difficulty, etc. [bef. 1000; ME; OE *cran;* c. G *Kran,* Gk *géranos*]

whooping crane, *Grus americana,* height about 5 ft. (1.5 m); wingspread 7½ ft. (2.3 m)

Crane (krān), *n.* **1. (Harold) Hart,** 1899–1932, U.S. poet. **2. Stephen,** 1871–1900, U.S. novelist, poet, and short-story writer.

crane′ fly′, any of numerous nonbiting insects constituting the family Tipulidae, inhabiting damp areas and resembling a large mosquito with extremely long legs. [1650–60] —**crane′-fly′,** *adj.*

Cran•ford (kran′fərd), *n.* a township in NE New Jersey. 24,573.

cra•ni•al (krā′nē əl), *adj.* of or pertaining to the cranium or skull. [1790–1800; CRANI(UM) + -AL¹] —**cra′ni•al•ly,** *adv.*

cra′nial in′dex, *Cranium.* cephalic index. [1865–70]

CONCISE ETYMOLOGY KEY: <, descended or borrowed from; >, whence; b., blend of, blended; c., cognate with; cf., compare; deriv., derivative; equiv., equivalent; imit., imitative; obl., oblique; r., replacing; s., stem; sp., spelling, spelled; resp., respelling, respelled; trans., translation; ?, origin unknown; *, unattested; ‡, probably earlier than. See the full key inside the front cover.

cra′nial nerve′, *Anat.* any of the nerves arising from the brainstem and exiting to the periphery of the head through skull openings, including 10 pairs in fish and amphibians and 12 pairs in reptiles, birds, and mammals: in humans, these are the abducens nerve, accessory nerve, auditory nerve, facial nerve, glossopharyngeal nerve, hypoglossal nerve, oculomotor nerve, olfactory nerve, optic nerve, trigeminal nerve, trochlear nerve, and vagus nerve. [1830–40]

cra•ni•ate (krā′nē it, -āt′), *adj.* **1.** having a cranium or skull. —*n.* **2.** a craniate animal. [1875–80; CRANI(UM) + -ATE¹]

cranio-, a combining form representing **cranium** in compound words: *craniotomy.*

cra•ni•o•ce•re•bral (krā′nē ō sə rē′brəl, -ser′ə-), *adj.* pertaining to or involving both cerebrum and cranium. [1900–05; CRANIO- + CEREBRAL]

cra•ni•o•fa•cial (krā′nē ō fā′shəl), *adj.* of, pertaining to, or affecting the cranium and face. [1850–55; CRANIO- + FACIAL]

cra•ni•o•graph (krā′nē ə graf′, -gräf′), *n.* an instrument that outlines the skull. [1875–80; CRANIO- + -GRAPH]

cra•ni•og•ra•phy (krā′nē og′rə fē), *n.* examination of the skull as depicted by craniographs, photographs, and charts. [1860–65; CRANIO- + -GRAPHY]

craniol., craniology.

cra•ni•ol•o•gy (krā′nē ol′ə jē), *n.* the science that deals with the size, shape, and other characteristics of human skulls. [1800–10; CRANIO- + -LOGY] —**cra•ni•o•log•i•cal** (krā′nē ə loj′i kəl), *adj.* —**cra′ni•o•log′i•cal•ly,** *adv.* —**cra′ni•ol′o•gist,** *n.*

craniom., craniometry.

cra•ni•om•e•ter (krā′nē om′i tər), *n.* an instrument for measuring the external dimensions of skulls. [1875–80; CRANIO- + -METER]

cra•ni•om•e•try (krā′nē om′i trē), *n.* the science of measuring skulls, chiefly to determine their characteristic relationship to sex, body type, or genetic population. [1860–65; CRANIO- + -METRY] —**cra•ni•o•met•ric** (krā′nē ə me′trik), **cra′ni•o•met′ri•cal,** *adj.* —**cra′ni•o•met′ri•cal•ly,** *adv.* —**cra′ni•om′e•trist,** *n.*

cra•ni•o•phore (krā′nē ə fôr′, -fōr′), *n.* a device that holds a skull in place for measuring. [1875–80; CRANIO- + -PHORE]

cra•ni•o•sa•cral (krā′nē ō sā′krəl, -sak′rəl), *adj. Anat.* parasympathetic. [1920–25; CRANIO- + SACRAL²]

cra•ni•os•co•py (krā′nē os′kə pē), *n.* observation, examination, and description of the human skull. [1795–1805; CRANIO- + -SCOPY] —**cra•ni•o•scop•i•cal** (krā′nē ə skop′i kəl), *adj.* —**cra′ni•os′co•pist,** *n.*

cra•ni•ot•o•my (krā′nē ot′ə mē), *n., pl.* **-mies.** *Surg.* the operation of opening the skull, usually for operations on the brain. [1850–55; CRANIO- + -TOMY]

cra•ni•um (krā′nē əm), *n., pl.* **-ni•ums, -ni•a** (-nē ə). **1.** the skull of a vertebrate. **2.** the part of the skull that encloses the brain. Also called **braincase.** [1375–1425; late ME *craneum* < ML *crānium* < Gk *krānion* skull; akin to CERATO-, CEREBRUM, CORNU, HORN]

crank¹ (krangk), *n.* **1.** *Mach.* any of several types of arms or levers for imparting rotary or oscillatory motion to a rotating shaft, one end of the crank being fixed to the shaft and the other end receiving reciprocating motion from a hand, connecting rod, etc. **2.** *Informal.* an ill-tempered, grouchy person. **3.** an unbalanced person who is overzealous in the advocacy of a private cause. **4.** an eccentric or whimsical notion. **5.** a strikingly clever turn of speech or play on words. **6.** *Archaic.* a bend; turn. **7.** *Slang.* the nasal decongestant propylhexedrine, used illicitly for its euphoric effects. **8.** *Auto. Slang.* a crankshaft. —*v.t.* **9.** to bend into or make in the shape of a crank. **10.** to furnish with a crank. **11.** *Mach.* to rotate (a shaft) by means of a crank. **12.** to start (an internal-combustion engine) by turning the crankshaft manually or by means of a small motor. **13.** to start the engine of (a motor vehicle) by turning the crankshaft manually. —*v.i.* **14.** to turn a crank, as in starting an automobile engine. **15.** *Obs.* to turn and twist; zigzag. **16. crank down,** to cause to diminish or terminate: *the president's efforts to crank down inflation.* **17. crank in** or **into,** to incorporate as an integral part: *Overhead is cranked into the retail cost.* **18. crank out,** to make or produce in a mass-production, effortless, or mechanical way: *She's able to crank out one best-selling novel after another.* **19. crank up,** *Informal.* **a.** to get started or ready: *The theater season is cranking up with four benefit performances.* **b.** to stimulate, activate, or produce: *to crank up enthusiasm for a new product.* **c.** to increase one's efforts, output, etc.: *Industry began to crank up after the new tax incentives became law.* —*adj.* **20.** unstable; shaky; unsteady. **21.** of, pertaining to, or by an unbalanced or overzealous person: *a crank phone call; crank mail.* **22.** *Brit. Dial.* cranky¹ (def. 5). [bef. 1000; ME *cranke,* OE *cranc-,* in *crancstæf* crank (see STAFF¹)] —**crank′less,** *adj.*

crank² (krangk), *adj. Naut.* **1.** Also, **cranky.** having a tendency to roll easily, as a boat or ship; tender (opposed to *stiff*). —*n.* **2.** a crank vessel. [1690–1700; prob. to be identified with CRANK¹, but sense development unclear; cf. CRANK-SIDED]

crank³ (krangk), *adj. Brit. Dial.* lively; high-spirited. [1350–1400; ME *cranke,* of obscure orig.] —**crank′ly,** *adv.* —**crank′ness,** *n.*

crank•case (krangk′kās′), *n.* (in an internal-combustion engine) the housing that encloses the crankshaft, connecting rods, and allied parts. [1875–80; CRANK¹ + CASE²]

cran•kle (krang′kəl), *n., v.t., v.i.,* **-kled, -kling.** bend; turn; crinkle. [1585–95; CRANK¹ + -LE]

crank′ let′ter, a hostile or fanatical letter, often sent anonymously.

crank•pin (krangk′pin′), *n. Mach.* a short cylindrical pin at the outer end of a crank, held by and moving with a connecting rod or link. Also, **crank′ pin′.** Cf. **web** (def. 11). [1830–40; CRANK¹ + PIN]

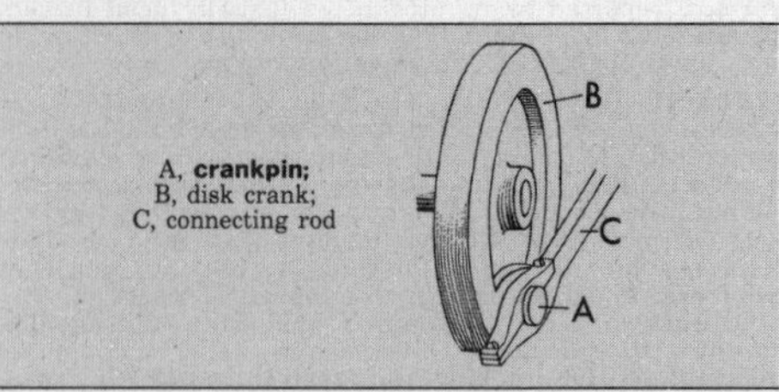

A, **crankpin;** B, disk crank; C, connecting rod

crank•shaft (krangk′shaft′, -shäft′), *n. Mach.* a shaft having one or more cranks, usually formed as integral parts. [1850–55; CRANK¹ + SHAFT]

crankshaft W, web; C, crankpin

crank-sid•ed (krangk′sī′did), *adj. Southern U.S.* lopsided; askew. [1880–85; see CRANK²]

crank-up (krangk′up′), *n.* an act or instance of cranking up. [1905–10; n. use of v. phrase *crank up*]

crank•y¹ (krang′kē), *adj.,* **crank•i•er, crank•i•est. 1.** ill-tempered; grouchy; cross: *I'm always cranky when I don't get enough sleep.* **2.** eccentric; queer. **3.** shaky; unsteady; out of order. **4.** full of bends or windings; crooked. **5.** *Brit. Dial.* sickly; in unsound or feeble condition; infirm. [1780–90; CRANK¹ + -Y¹] —**crank′i•ly,** *adv.* —**crank′i•ness,** *n.*
—**Syn. 1.** crotchety, cantankerous, perverse.

crank•y² (krang′kē), *adj. Naut.* crank² (def. 1). [1835–45; CRANK² + -Y¹]

Cran•mer (kran′mər), *n.* **Thomas,** 1489–1556, first Protestant archbishop of Canterbury: leader in the English Protestant Reformation in England.

cran•ne•quin (kran′i kin), *n.* a portable device for bending a crossbow. [< F, MF < MD *cranekijn;* see CRANE, -KIN]

cran•nied (kran′ēd), *adj.* having or full of crannies. [1400–50; late ME *cranyyd.* See CRANNY, -ED³]

cran•nog (kran′əg), *n.* **1.** (in ancient Ireland and Scotland) a lake dwelling, usually built on an artificial island. **2.** a small, artificial, fortified island constructed in bogs in ancient Scotland and Ireland. Also, **cran•noge** (kran′əj). [1850–55; < Ir *crannóg* wooden frame or vessel, pole, crannog, equiv. to *crann* beam, tree + *-óg* n. suffix]

cran•ny (kran′ē), *n., pl.* **-nies. 1.** a small, narrow opening in a wall, rock, etc.; chink; crevice; fissure: *They searched every nook and cranny for the missing ring.* **2.** a small out-of-the-way place or obscure corner; nook. [1400–50; late ME *crany,* perh. < MF *crené,* ptp. of *crener* to notch, groove; see CRENEL]

cran•reuch (krän′rəkʜ), *n. Scot.* hoarfrost. [1675–85; appar. < ScotGael phrase *crann reodhach* frosty tree, equiv. to *crann* tree + *reodh* frost, hoarfrost + *-ach* adj. suffix]

Cran•ston (kran′stən), *n.* a city in E Rhode Island, near Providence. 71,992.

crap¹ (krap), *n., v.,* **crapped, crap•ping.** —*n.* **1.** *Vulgar.* **a.** excrement. **b.** an act of defecation. **2.** *Slang (sometimes vulgar).* **a.** nonsense; drivel. **b.** falsehood, exaggeration, propaganda, or the like. **3.** refuse; rubbish; junk; litter: *Will you clean up that crap!* —*v.i.* **4.** *Vulgar.* to defecate. —*v.t.* **5.** *Slang (sometimes vulgar).* to talk nonsense to; attempt to deceive. **6. crap around,** *Slang (sometimes vulgar).* **a.** to behave in a foolish or silly manner. **b.** to avoid work. **7. crap on,** *Slang (sometimes vulgar).* **a.** to treat badly, esp. by humiliating, insulting, or slighting. **b.** to cause misery, misfortune, or discomfort. **8. crap up,** *Slang (sometimes vulgar).* to botch, ruin, or cheapen; make a mess of. [1375–1425; late ME *crap* chaff < MD (not recorded until 16th century) *krappe* anything cut off or separated]

crap² (krap), *n. v.,* **crapped, crap•ping.** —*n.* **1.** (in craps) a losing throw, in which the total on the two dice is 2, 3, or 12. **2.** craps. —*v.* **3. crap out, a.** Also called **seven out.** (in the game of craps) to throw a 7 rather than make one's point. **b.** *Slang.* to abandon a project, activity, etc., because of fear, cowardice, exhaustion, loss of enthusiasm, etc. **c.** *Slang.* to break a promise or fail to fulfill a duty or obligation; renege. [1835–45, *Amer.;* back formation from CRAPS]

cra•paud (kra pō′, krap′ō), *n.* a species of large frog, *Leptodactylus pentadactylus,* resembling a bullfrog, inhabiting South and Central America, and having deep orange or red coloring on the legs and sides during the breeding season, the rest of the body being dark-green or brown with black markings. Also called **South American bullfrog.** [< F: toad, OF *crapot,* perh. < Gmc **krappa* hook (see GRAPE, GRAPNEL), in reference to its hooklike feet; for *-aud,* see RIBALD]

crape (krāp), *n., v.t.,* **craped, crap•ing.** crepe. [Anglicized sp.] —**crape′like′,** *adj.*

crape•hang•er (krāp′hang′ər), *n.* a person who sees the gloomy side of things; pessimist. Also, **crepehanger.** [1915–20, *Amer.;* CRAPE + HANGER]

crape′ jas′mine, a shrub, *Tabernaemontana divaricata,* native to India, having white flowers that are fragrant at night.

crape′ myr′tle, a tall Chinese shrub, *Lagerstroemia indica,* of the loosestrife family, having clusters of crinkled red, pink, purple, or white flowers, grown as an ornamental in the southern and western U.S. Also, **crepe myrtle.** [1840–50, *Amer.*]

crap•o•la (kra pō′lə), *n. Slang.* crap[1] (def. 2). [CRAP[1] + -OLA]

crap•per (krap′ər), *n. Slang (vulgar).* **1.** a toilet. **2.** a bathroom. [1930–35; CRAP[1] + -ER[1]]

crap•pie (krap′ē), *n., pl.* **-pies,** (*esp. collectively*) **-pie.** either of two small sunfishes of central U.S. rivers, *Pomoxis nigromaculatus* **(black crappie)** or *P. annularis* **(white crappie).** Also, **croppie.** [1855–60, *Amer.*; < CanF *crapet*]

crap•py (krap′ē), *adj.*, **-pi•er, -pi•est.** *Slang (sometimes vulgar).* **1.** extremely bad, unpleasant, or inferior; lousy: *crappy weather.* **2.** nasty, humiliating, insulting, or unfair: *What a crappy thing to say about anyone!* **3.** cheaply made or done; shoddy: *a crappy job.* [1840–50, *Amer.*; CRAP[1] + -Y[1]] **—crap′pi•ness,** *n.*

craps (kraps), *n.* (*usually used with a singular v.*) a game in which two dice are thrown and in which a first throw of 7 or 11 wins, a first throw of 2, 3, or 12 loses, and a first throw of 4, 5, 6, 8, 9, or 10 can be won only by throwing the same number again before throwing a 7. [1835–45, *Amer.*; appar. < F *craps,* var. of *crabs* double-ace (lowest throw at hazard) < 18th-century E slang: pl. of CRAB[1]]

crap•shoot (krap′sho͞ot′), *n., v.,* **-shot, -shoot•ing.** *—n.* **1.** *Informal.* anything unpredictable, risky, or problematical; gamble. *—v.i.* **2.** to play craps. **3.** *Informal.* to take risks; gamble. [1970–75; CRAP[2] + SHOOT]

crap•shoot•er (krap′sho͞o′tər), *n.* **1.** a person who plays craps. **2.** *Informal.* a person inclined to take gambles or risks. [1890–95, *Amer.*; CRAP + SHOOTER]

crap•u•lent (krap′yə lənt), *adj.* sick from gross excess in drinking or eating. [1650–60; < LL *crāpulentus* drunk, deriv. of L *crāpula* drunkenness < Gk *kraipálē* drunkenness, a hangover; see -ENT] **—crap′u•lence, crap′u•len•cy,** *n.*

crap•u•lous (krap′yə ləs), *adj.* **1.** given to or characterized by gross excess in drinking or eating. **2.** suffering from or due to such excess. [1530–40; < LL *crāpulōsus.* See CRAPULENT, -OUS] **—crap′u•lous•ly,** *adv.* **—crap′u•lous•ness,** *n.*

cra•que•lure (krak lo͝or′, krak′lo͝or; *Fr.* KRAKᵊ LYR′), *n., pl.* **-lures** (-lo͝orz′, -lo͝orz; *Fr.* -LYR′). a network of fine cracks or crackles on the surface of a painting, caused chiefly by shrinkage of paint film or varnish. [1910–15; < F, equiv. to *craquel(er)* to crackle, crack (imit.) + *-ure* -URE]

crash[1] (krash), *v.i.* **1.** to make a loud, clattering noise, as of something dashed to pieces. **2.** to break or fall to pieces with noise. **3.** (of moving vehicles, objects, etc.) to collide, esp. violently and noisily. **4.** to move or go with a crash; strike with a crash. **5.** *Aeron.* to land in an abnormal manner, usually causing severe damage: *The airliner crashed.* **6.** to collapse or fail suddenly, as a financial enterprise: *The stock market crashed.* **7.** *Informal.* to gain admittance to a party, performance, etc., without an invitation, ticket, or permission. **8.** *Slang.* **a.** to sleep. **b.** to have a temporary place to sleep or live without payment: *He let me crash at his house.* **c.** to fall asleep: *I get home in the evening and I just crash till it's time for dinner.* **9.** *Slang.* to experience unpleasant sensations, as sudden exhaustion or depression, when a drug, esp. an amphetamine, wears off. **10.** *Med. Slang.* to suffer cardiac arrest. **11.** *Ecol.* (of a population) to decline rapidly. **12.** *Computers.* to shut down because of a malfunction of hardware or software. *—v.t.* **13.** to break into pieces violently and noisily; shatter. **14.** to force or drive with violence and noise (usually fol. by *in, through, out,* etc.). **15.** *Aeron.* to cause (an aircraft) to make a landing in an abnormal manner, usually damaging or wrecking the aircraft. **16.** *Informal.* **a.** to gain admittance to, even though uninvited: *to crash a party.* **b.** to enter without a ticket, permission, etc.: *to crash the gate at a football game.* *—n.* **17.** a sudden loud noise, as of something being violently smashed or struck: *the crash of thunder.* **18.** a breaking or falling to pieces with loud noise: *the sudden crash of dishes.* **19.** a collision or crashing, as of automobiles, trains, etc. **20.** the shock of collision and breaking. **21.** a sudden and violent falling to ruin. **22.** a sudden general collapse of a business enterprise, prosperity, the stock market, etc.: *the crash of 1929.* **23.** *Aeron.* an act or instance of crashing. **24.** *Ecol.* a sudden, rapid decline in the size of a population. *—adj.* **25.** characterized by an intensive effort, esp. to deal with an emergency, meet a deadline, etc.: *a crash plan to house flood victims; a crash diet.* [1350–1400; 1920–25 def. 16; 1870–75 for def. 22; ME *crasche,* b. *crase* to break (see CRAZE) and *masche* MASH] **—crash′er,** *n.*
—Syn. 13. smash. **21.** failure, ruin.

crash[2] (krash), *n.* **1.** a plain-weave fabric of rough, irregular, or lumpy yarns, for toweling, dresses, etc. **2.** *Bookbinding.* starched cotton fabric used to reinforce the spine of a bound book. [1805–15; prob. < Russ *krashenína* painted or dyed coarse linen, equiv. to *kráshen(yĭ)* painted (ptp. of *krásit'* to paint) + *-ina* n. suffix]

Crash•aw (krash′ô), *n.* **Richard,** 1613–49, English poet.

crash′ boat′, a small, fast boat used in rescue operations, esp. for airplane crashes. [1935–40, *Amer.*]

crash′ cart′, a movable cart or similar conveyance carrying supplies and equipment for the management of medical emergencies.

crash′ course′, a brief, intensive course of instruction, as to prepare one quickly for a test. Also called **cram course.**

crash′ dive′, a rapid dive by a submarine made at a steep angle, esp. to avoid attack from a surface vessel or airplane. [1915–20]

crash-dive (krash′dīv′, -dīv′), *v.i., v.t.,* **-dived** or **-dove, -dived, -div•ing.** to dive rapidly at a steep angle. [1925–30]

crash′ hel′met, a helmet for protecting the head in the event of an accident, worn by motorcyclists, automobile racers, etc. [1915–20]

crash•ing (krash′ing), *adj.* **1.** absolute; complete; utter: *a crashing bore.* **2.** unusual or superlative; exceptional: *a crashing celebration.* [1925–30; CRASH[1] + -ING[2]] **—crash′ing•ly,** *adv.*

crash-land (krash′land′), *v.t.* **1.** to land (an aircraft), under circumstances in which a normal landing is impossible, in such a way that damage to the aircraft is unavoidable. *—v.i.* **2.** to crash-land an aircraft. [1940–45; CRASH[1] + LAND] **—crash′-land′ing,** *n.*

crash′ pad′, 1. *Slang.* a place to sleep or live temporarily and at no cost. **2.** padding inside cars, tanks, or the like, for protecting passengers in the event of an accident, sudden stop, etc. [1935–40]

crash′ pro′gram, a plan of action entailing rapid and intensive production, growth, or the like, undertaken to meet a deadline or solve a pressing problem: *a crash program to develop a new fighter plane.* [1945–50]

crash•proof (krash′pro͞of′), *adj.* **1.** (of a vehicle) resistant to damage and as safe as possible for the occupants in the event of a crash. **2.** that cannot be smashed or broken. [CRASH[1] + -PROOF]

crash′ truck′, an emergency vehicle based at an airport. [1940–45, *Amer.*]

crash•wor•thi•ness (krash′wûr′thē nis), *n.* the ability of a car or other vehicle to withstand a collision or crash with minimal bodily injury to its occupants. [1945–50; CRASH[1] + -WORTHY + -NESS] **—crash′wor′•thy,** *adj.*

cra•sis (krā′sis), *n., pl.* **-ses** (-sēz). *Archaic.* composition; constitution; makeup. [1595–1605; < Gk *krâsis* mixture, blend, equiv. to *krā-* (base of *kerannýnai* to mix) + *-sis* -SIS]

crass (kras), *adj.,* **-er, -est. 1.** without refinement, delicacy, or sensitivity; gross; obtuse; stupid: *crass commercialism; a crass misrepresentation of the facts.* **2.** *Archaic.* thick; coarse. [1535–45; (< MF) < L *crassus* thick, dense, fat, heavy] **—crass′ly,** *adv.* **—crass′•ness,** *n.*
—Syn. 1. dull, boorish, oafish, indelicate.

cras•si•tude (kras′i to͞od′, -tyo͞od′), *n.* **1.** gross ignorance or stupidity. **2.** thickness; grossness. [1400–50; late ME (< MF) < L *crassitūdō* thickness. See CRASS, -I-, -TUDE]

cras•su•la•ceous (kras′yo͝o lā′shəs), *adj.* belonging to the Crassulaceae, the stonecrop family of plants. Cf. **stonecrop family.** [1650–60; < NL *Crassulace(ae)* (equiv. to *Crassul(a)* genus name (ML *crassula;* see CRASS, -ULE) + *-aceae* -ACEAE) + -OUS]

Cras•sus (kras′əs), *n.* **Marcus Li•cin•i•us** (li sin′ē əs), c115–53 B.C., Roman general: member of the first triumvirate.

-crat, a combining form meaning "ruler," "member of a ruling body," "advocate of a particular form of rule," used in the formation of compound words: *autocrat; technocrat.* Cf. **-cracy.** [< Gk *-kratēs* as in *autokratēs* AUTOCRAT; r. *-crate* < F < Gk, as above]

cratch (krach), *n. Archaic.* a crib for fodder; manger. [1175–1225; ME *cracche* < dial. OF *crache,* var. of *creche* CRÈCHE]

crate (krāt), *n., v.,* **crat•ed, crat•ing.** *—n.* **1.** a slatted wooden box or framework for packing, shopping, or storing fruit, furniture, glassware, crockery, etc. **2.** any completely enclosed boxlike packing or shipping case. **3.** *Informal.* something rickety and dilapidated, esp. an automobile: *They're still driving around in the old crate they bought 20 years ago.* **4.** a quantity, esp. of fruit, that is often packed in a crate approximately 2 × 1 × 1 ft. (0.6 × 0.3 × 0.3 m): *a crate of oranges.* *—v.t.* **5.** to pack in a crate. [1350–1400; 1915–20 for def. 3; ME, obscurely akin to L *crātis* wickerwork, hurdle]

cra•ter (krā′tər), *n., gen.* **Cra•te•ris** (krā tēr′is) for 9, *v.* *—n.* **1.** the cup-shaped depression or cavity on the surface of the earth or other heavenly body marking the orifice of a volcano. **2.** Also called **impact crater, meteorite crater.** (on the surface of the earth, moon, etc.) a bowl-shaped depression with a raised rim, formed by the impact of a meteoroid. Cf. **astrobleme. 3.** *Astron.* (on the surface of the moon) a circular or almost circular area having a depressed floor, almost always containing a central mountain and usually completely enclosed by walls that are often higher than those of a walled plain; ring formation; ring. Cf. **walled plain. 4.** the bowllike orifice of a geyser. **5.** the hole or pit in the ground where a bomb, shell, or military mine has exploded. **6.** *Elect.* the cavity formed in a positive carbon electrode by an electric arc. **7.** *Gk. and Rom. Antiq.* krater. **8.** *Metalworking.* a depression at the end of a bead produced by welding. **9.** (*cap.*) *Astron.* the Cup, a small southern constellation west of Corvus and north of Hydra. *—v.t.* **10.** to make craters in: *Bombs had cratered the landscape.* **11.** *Slang.* **a.** to cancel, abandon, or cast aside: *to crater the new project.* **b.** to destroy or ruin: *One more disappointment won't crater me.* *—v.i.* **12.** to form a crater or craters: *The surface of the concrete cratered and cracked under the repeated impacts.* [1605–15; < L < Gk *krātḗr* mixing bowl, lit., mixer, equiv. to *krā-* (base of *kerannýnai* to mix) + *-tēr* agentive suffix; cf. CRASIS] **—cra′ter•al, cra′ter•ous,** *adj.* **—cra′ter•like′,** *adj.*

Cra•ter (krā′tər), *n.* **Joseph Force** (fôrs, fōrs), 1889–?, a judge of the New York State Supreme Court: his mysterious disappearance on August 6, 1930, has never been solved.

cra′ter lake′, a body of water occupying a roughly circular, steep-sided volcanic crater or caldera. [1875–80]

Cra′ter Lake′, a lake in the crater of an extinct volcano in SW Oregon, in Crater Lake National Park. 20 sq. mi. (52 sq. km); 1996 ft. (608 m) deep.

Cra′ter Lake′ Na′tional Park′, a national park in SW Oregon, in the Cascade Range: Crater Lake. 250 sq. mi. (648 sq. km).

cra•ter•let (krā′tər lit), *n.* a small crater. [1880–85; CRATER + -LET]

Cra′ter Mound′, a bowl-shaped depression in the earth in central Arizona: believed to have been made by the impact of a meteoroid. 4000 ft. (1220 m) wide; 600 ft. (183 m) deep. Also called **Meteor Crater.**

Cra′ters of the Moon′, a national monument in S Idaho: site of scenic lava-flow formations.

C ration, any of various canned or prepackaged foods used as field rations in the U.S. armed forces.

cra•ton (krā′ton), *n. Geol.* a relatively rigid and immobile region of continental portions of the earth's crust. [1940–45; < G *Kraton,* based on Gk *krátos* power; cf. -CRACY, -ON[2]]

craunch (krônch, kränch), *v.t., v.i., n.* crunch. [1625–35; var. of CRANCH] **—craunch′ing•ly,** *adv.*

cra•vat (krə vat′), *n.* **1.** necktie (defs. 1, 2). **2.** a cloth, often made of or trimmed with lace, worn about the neck by men esp. in the 17th century. **3.** *Med.* a bandage made by folding a triangular piece of material into a band, used temporarily for a fracture or wound. [1650–60; < F *cravate* neckcloth, lit., Croat (< G *Krabate* < Serbo-Croatian *hr̀vāt*); so called because worn by Croatian mercenaries in the French army]

crave (krāv), *v.,* **craved, crav•ing.** *—v.t.* **1.** to long for; want greatly; desire eagerly: *to crave sweets; to crave affection.* **2.** to require; need: *a problem craving prompt attention.* **3.** to ask earnestly for (something); beg for. **4.** to ask (a person) earnestly for something or to do something. *—v.i.* **5.** to beg or plead (usually fol. by *for*). [bef. 1000; ME *craven,* OE *crafian;* akin to ON *krefja* to demand, lay claim to] **—crav′er,** *n.*
—Syn. 1. yearn for, hunger for.

cra•ven (krā′vən), *adj.* **1.** cowardly; contemptibly timid; pusillanimous. *—n.* **2.** a coward. **3. cry craven,** to yield; capitulate; give up. *—v.t.* **4.** to make cowardly. [1175–1225; ME *cravant, cravaunde* defeated < OF *cravente,* ptp. of *cravanter* to crush, overwhelm (< VL **crepantāre*), influenced by ME *creaunt* defeated (see RECREANT)] **—cra′ven•ly,** *adv.* **—cra′ven•ness,** *n.*
—Syn. 1. dastardly, fearful, timorous.

crav•ing (krā′ving), *n.* great or eager desire; yearning. [1250–1300; ME; see CRAVE, -ING[1]] **—crav′ing•ly,** *adv.* **—crav′ing•ness,** *n.*
—Syn. See **desire.**

craw (krô), *n.* **1.** the crop of a bird or insect. **2.** the stomach of an animal. **3. stick in one's craw,** to cause considerable or abiding resentment; rankle: *She said I was pompous, and that really stuck in my craw.* [1350–1400; ME *crawe,* prob. akin to CRAG[2]]

craw•dad (krô′dad′), *n.* crayfish (def. 1). Also, **craw•daddy.** [1900–05, *Amer.*; CRAW(FISH) + *dad* (perh. DAD[1]); cf. DOODAD]

craw•dad•dy (krô′dad′ē), *n., pl.* **-dies.** crawdad.

craw•fish (krô′fish′), *n., pl.* (*esp. collectively*) **-fish,** (*esp. referring to two or more kinds or species*) **-fish•es,** *v.* *—n.* **1.** crayfish. *—v.i.* **2.** *Informal.* to back out or retreat from a position or undertaking. [1615–25; earlier *crafish, cravish, cravis,* var. outcomes of MF *crevice* CRAYFISH]

Craw•ford (krô′fərd), *n.* **1. Cheryl,** 1902–86, U.S. stage director and producer. **2. Francis Marion,** 1854–1909, U.S. novelist, in Italy after 1885. **3. Thomas,** 1813?–57, U.S. sculptor. **4. William Harris,** 1772–1834, U.S. political leader: senator 1807–13, secretary of the Treasury 1816–25.

Craw•fords•ville (krô′fərdz vil′), *n.* a city in W central Indiana. 13,325.

crawl[1] (krôl), *v.i.* **1.** to move in a prone position with the body resting on or close to the ground, as a worm or caterpillar, or on the hands and knees, as a young child. **2.** (of plants or vines) to extend tendrils; creep. **3.** to move or progress slowly or laboriously: *The line of cars crawled behind the slow-moving truck. The work just crawled until we got the new machines.* **4.** to behave in a remorseful, abject, or cringing manner: *Don't come crawling back to me asking for favors.* **5.** to be, or feel as if, overrun with crawling things: *The hut crawled with lizards and insects.* **6.** *Ceram.* (of a glaze) to spread unevenly over the surface of a piece. **7.** (of paint) to raise or contract because of an imperfect bond with the underlying surface. *—v.t.* **8.** to visit or frequent a series of (esp. bars): *to crawl the neighborhood pubs.* *—n.* **9.** act of crawling; a slow, crawling motion. **10.** a slow pace or rate of progress: *Traffic slowed to a crawl.* **11.** *Swimming.* a stroke in a prone position, characterized by alternate overarm movements combined with the flutter kick. **12.** *Television, Motion Pictures.* titles that slowly move across a screen, providing information. [1150–1200; ME *crawlen* < ON *krafla;* cf. Dan *kravle* to crawl, creep] **—crawl′ing•ly,** *adv.*
—Syn. 1. CRAWL, CREEP refer to methods of moving like reptiles or worms, or on all fours. They are frequently interchangeable, but CRAWL is used of a more prostrate movement than CREEP: *A dog afraid of punishment crawls toward his master.* CREEP expresses slow progress: *A child creeps before walking or running.*

crawl[2] (krôl), *n. Chiefly South Atlantic States.* an enclosure in shallow water on the seacoast, as for confining fish, turtles, etc.: *a crab crawl.* [1650–60; < D *kraal* < Sp *corral* CORRAL; cf. KRAAL]

crawl•er (krô′lər), *n.* **1.** a person or thing that crawls. **2.** Also called **crawl′er trac′tor.** any of various large, heavy vehicles or machines that travel on endless belts or tracks, esp. as used in construction. **3.** hellgrammite. **4.** Often, **crawlers,** a garment with long pants, short sleeves or suspender straps, and sometimes feet for a baby who does not yet walk. **5.** *Australian Slang.* syco-phant. [1640–50; 1925–30 for def. 2; CRAWL[1] + -ER[1]]

crawl•space (krôl′spās′), *n.* (in a building) an area accessible by crawling, having a clearance less than human height, for access to plumbing or wiring, storage, etc. Also, **crawl′ space′.** [1950–55; CRAWL[1] + SPACE]

crawl•y (krô′lē), *adj.,* **crawl•i•er, crawl•i•est,** *n., pl.* **crawl•ies.** *Informal.* —*adj.* **1.** that crawls; noting or describing things, as worms or insects, that crawl, esp. imparting a queasy feeling; creepy. —*n.* **2.** a crawling insect, small reptile, etc. [1855–60; CRAWL[1] + -Y[1]]

crayer (krâr), *n.* a small sailing vessel formerly used in trade along the coasts of western Europe. [1275–1325; ME < AF *craier,* OF *croier* < MD *kraajer* three-masted boat]

cray•fish (krā′fish′), *n., pl.* (*esp. collectively*) **-fish,** (*esp. referring to two or more kinds or species*) **-fish•es.** **1.** Also called **crawdad, crawdaddy.** any freshwater decapod crustacean of the genera *Astacus* and *Cambarus,* closely related to but smaller than the lobsters. **2.** any of several similar marine crustaceans, esp. the spiny lobster. Also, **crawfish.** [1350–1400; alter. (by folk etym.) of ME *crevis* < MF *crevice* < OHG *krebiz* CRAB[1]]

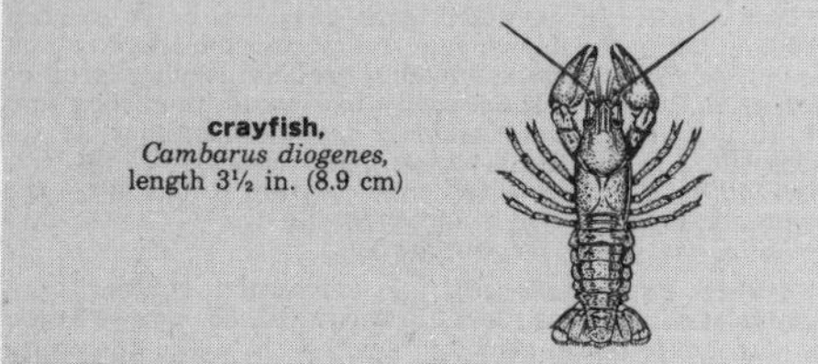

crayfish, *Cambarus diogenes,* length 3½ in. (8.9 cm)

Cray•o•la (krā ō′lə), *Trademark.* a brand of wax crayon, usually sold in assortments of bright colors.

cray•on (krā′on, -ən), *n.* **1.** a pointed stick or pencil of colored clay, chalk, wax, etc., used for drawing or coloring. **2.** a drawing in crayons. —*v.t.* **3.** to draw or color with a crayon or crayons. —*v.i.* **4.** to make a drawing with crayons. [1635–45; < F, equiv. to *craie* chalk (< L *crēta* clay, chalk) + *-on* n. suffix] —**cray′on•ist,** *n.*

craze (krāz), *v.,* **crazed, craz•ing,** *n.* —*v.t.* **1.** to derange or impair the mind of; make insane: *He was crazed by jealousy.* **2.** to make small cracks on the surface of (a ceramic glaze, paint, or the like); crackle. **3.** *Brit. Dial.* to crack. **4.** *Archaic.* to weaken; impair: *to craze one's health.* **5.** *Obs.* to break; shatter. —*v.i.* **6.** to become insane; go mad. **7.** to become minutely cracked, as a ceramic glaze; crackle. **8.** *Metall.* **a.** (of a case-hardened object) to develop reticulated surface markings; worm. **b.** (of an ingot) to develop an alligator skin as a result of being teemed into an old and worn mold. **9.** *Archaic.* to fall to pieces; break. —*n.* **10.** a popular or widespread fad, fashion, etc.; mania: *the newest dance craze.* **11.** insanity; an insane condition. **12.** a minute crack or pattern of cracks in the glaze of a ceramic object. **13.** *Obs.* flaw; defect. [1325–75; ME *crasen* to crush < Scand; cf. Sw, Norw *krasa* to shatter, crush]
—**Syn. 10.** vogue, mode.

crazed (krāzd), *adj.* **1.** insane; demented. **2.** suffering loss of emotional control: *crazed with fear.* **3.** (of a ceramic object) having small cracks in the glaze. [1425–75; late ME. See CRAZE, -ED[2]] —**craz•ed•ly** (krā′zid lē), *adv.*

cra•zy (krā′zē), *adj.,* **-zi•er, -zi•est,** *n., pl.* **-zies.** —*adj.* **1.** mentally deranged; demented; insane. **2.** senseless; impractical; totally unsound: *a crazy scheme.* **3.** *Informal.* intensely enthusiastic; passionately excited: *crazy about baseball.* **4.** *Informal.* very enamored or infatuated (usually fol. by *about*): *He was crazy about her.* **5.** *Informal.* intensely anxious or eager; impatient: *I'm crazy to try those new skis.* **6.** *Informal.* unusual; bizarre; singular: *She always wears a crazy hat..* **7.** *Slang.* wonderful; excellent; perfect: *That's crazy, man, crazy.* **8.** likely to break or fall to pieces. **9.** weak, infirm, or sickly. **10.** having an unusual, unexpected, or random quality, behavior, result, pattern, etc.: *a crazy reel that spins in either direction.* **11. like crazy, a.** *Slang.* with great enthusiasm or energy; to an extreme: *We shopped like crazy and bought all our Christmas gifts in one afternoon.* **b.** with great speed or recklessness: *He drives like crazy once he's out on the highway.* —*n.* **12.** *Slang.* an unpredictable, nonconforming person; oddball: *a house full of crazies who wear weird clothes and come in at all hours.* **13. the crazies,** *Slang.* a sense of extreme unease, nervousness, or panic; extreme jitters: *The crew was starting to get the crazies from being cooped up belowdecks for so long.* [1570–80; CRAZE + -Y[1]] —**cra′zi•ly,** *adv.* —**cra′zi•ness,** *n.*
—**Syn. 1.** crazed, lunatic. See **mad. 2.** foolish, imprudent, foolhardy. **8.** rickety, shaky, tottering. —**Ant. 1.** sane. **3.** calm, dispassionate. **8.** stable. **9.** strong; healthy.

cra′zy bone′, *Chiefly Northern, Midland, and Western U.S.* See **funny bone.** [1850–55, *Amer.*]

cra′zy eights′, (*used with a singular v.*) a card game played by two or more persons with a 52-card deck, the object of which is to be the first to get rid of one's hand by successively playing a card of the same suit or denomination as that played by the preceding player, with an eight counting for any desired suit. Also called **eights.** [1955–60]

CONCISE ETYMOLOGY KEY: <, descended or borrowed from; >, whence; b., blend of, blended; c., cognate with; cf., compare; deriv., derivative; equiv., equivalent; imit., imitative; obl., oblique; r., replacing; s., stem; sp., spelling, spelled; resp., respelling, respelled; trans., translation; ?, origin unknown; *, unattested; ‡, probably earlier than. See the full key inside the front cover.

Cra′zy Horse′, (*Tashunca-Uitco*), c1849–77, leader of the Oglala Sioux tribe: defeated General George Custer at battle of Little Bighorn.

cra′zy house′, **1.** *Slang.* an insane asylum. **2.** See **fun house.** [1885–90]

cra′zy quilt′, **1.** a patchwork quilt made of irregular patches combined with little or no regard to pattern. **2.** something that is irregular in pattern or shape, and suggestive of a crazy quilt; patchwork. [1885–90, *Amer.*] —**cra′zy-quilt′,** *adj.*

cra′zy top′, *Plant Pathol.* a disease of cotton, corn, etc., characterized by abnormal branching and small, misshapen leaves in the upper part of the plant, caused by water shortage, organic deficiencies in the soil, or unknown causes.

cra•zy•weed (krā′zē wēd′), *n.* locoweed. [1870–75; CRAZY + WEED[1]]

CRC, Civil Rights Commission.

C-re•ac•tive protein (sē′rē ak′tiv), *Biochem.* a globulin that increases in concentration in the bloodstream during infectious states and other abnormal conditions. *Abbr.:* CRP [1955–60; for *C-polysaccharide,* which is precipitated by this protein]

creak (krēk), *v.i.* **1.** to make a sharp, harsh, grating, or squeaking sound. **2.** to move with creaking. —*v.t.* **3.** to cause to creak. —*n.* **4.** a creaking sound. [1275–1325; ME *creken* to croak, appar. back formation from OE *crǣcettan,* var. of *crācettan* to CROAK] —**creak′ing•ly,** *adv.*

creak•y (krē′kē), *adj.,* **creak•i•er, creak•i•est.** **1.** creaking or apt to creak: *a creaky stairway.* **2.** rundown; dilapidated: *a creaky shack.* **3.** *Phonet.* (of the voice) produced by vibration of a small portion of the vocal cords while the arytenoid cartilages are held together, with little breath being released; laryngealized. [1825–35; CREAK + -Y[1]] —**creak′i•ly,** *adv.* —**creak′i•ness,** *n.*

cream (krēm), *n.* **1.** the fatty part of milk, which rises to the surface when the liquid is allowed to stand unless homogenized. **2.** a soft solid or thick liquid containing medicaments or other specific ingredients, applied externally for a prophylactic, therapeutic, or cosmetic purpose. **3.** Usually, **creams.** a soft-centered confection of fondant or fudge coated with chocolate. **4.** a purée or soup containing cream or milk: *cream of tomato soup.* **5.** the best part of anything: *the cream of society.* **6.** a yellowish white; light tint of yellow or buff. **7. cream of the crop,** the best or choicest: *a college that accepts only students who are the cream of the crop.* —*v.i.* **8.** to form cream. **9.** to froth; foam. **10.** *Informal.* to advance or favor only the wealthiest, most skilled or talented, etc., esp. so as to reap the benefits oneself: *Management is creaming by advancing only the most productive workers.* **11.** Also, **cream one's jeans.** *Slang* (*vulgar*). **a.** to have an orgasm, esp. to ejaculate or experience glandular lubrication of the vagina. **b.** to be overcome, as in rapturous admiration or delight. —*v.t.* **12.** to work (butter and sugar, or the like) to a smooth, creamy mass. **13.** to prepare (chicken, oysters, vegetables, etc.) with cream, milk, or a cream sauce. **14.** to allow (milk) to form cream. **15.** to skim (milk). **16.** to separate as cream. **17.** to take the cream or best part of. **18.** to use a cosmetic cream on. **19.** to add cream to (tea, coffee, etc.). **20.** *Slang.* **a.** to beat or damage severely; lambaste. **b.** to defeat decisively. **c.** to accomplish, esp. to pass (a test or course), with great ease and success: *She creamed the math test, getting the highest grade in the class.* —*adj.* **21.** of the color cream; cream-colored. [1300–50; ME *creme* < AF, OF *cresme* < LL *chrisma* CHRISM]

cream′ cheese′, **1.** a soft, white, smooth-textured, unripened, spreadable cheese made of sweet milk and sometimes cream. **2.** *Gulf States.* cottage cheese. [1575–85]
—**Regional Variation. 2.** See **cottage cheese.**

cream•cups (krēm′kups′), *n., pl.* **-cups.** (*used with a singular or plural v.*) a Californian plant, *Platystemon californicus,* of the poppy family, having narrow leaves and small, pale-yellow or cream-colored flowers. [1885–90, *Amer.*; CREAM + CUP + -S[3]]

cream•er (krē′mər), *n.* **1.** a person or thing that creams. **2.** a small jug, pitcher, etc., for holding cream. **3.** a container or apparatus for separating cream from milk. **4.** a refrigerator in which milk is placed to facilitate the formation of cream. **5.** a nondairy product in powder or liquid form, made chiefly from corn syrup solids and used as a substitute for cream, esp. for coffee cream. [1855–60; CREAM + -ER[1]]

cream•er•y (krē′mə rē), *n., pl.* **-er•ies.** **1.** a place where milk and cream are processed and where butter and cheese are produced. **2.** a place for the sale of milk and its products. **3.** a place where milk is set to form cream. [1870–75, *Amer.*; CREAM + -ERY]

cream′ ice′, *Brit.* See **ice cream.** [1840–50]

cream′ of co′conut. See **coconut cream** (def. 1).

cream′ of tar′tar, a white, crystalline, water-soluble powder, $C_4H_5KO_6$, used chiefly as an ingredient in baking powders and in galvanic tinning of metals. Also called **potassium bitartrate, potassium acid tartrate.** Cf. **tartar** (def. 3). [1655–65]

cream′ pail′, an open bowl of silver having a ladle or spoon for serving cream. Also called **piggin.**

cream′ puff′, **1.** a hollow pastry made with cream puff paste and filled with custard sauce or whipped cream. **2.** *Informal.* **a.** a weak or timid person; sissy. **b.** a vehicle or machine that has been kept in unusually good condition or is very easy to operate. [1885–90]

cream′ puff′ paste′, paste made with eggs, water or milk, butter, and flour, used in making éclairs, profiteroles, and other kinds of puffs. Also called **chou pastry, pâte à chou.**

cream′ sauce′, a white sauce made of cream or milk, flour, and butter.

cream′ so′da, a soft drink made with vanilla-flavored carbonated water colored brown with caramel. [1850–55, *Amer.*]

cream•y (krē′mē), *adj.,* **cream•i•er, cream•i•est.** **1.** containing cream. **2.** resembling cream in consistency or taste; soft and smooth. **3.** cream-colored. **4.** *Informal.* **a.** beneficial or profitable: *a creamy arrangement for profit sharing.* **b.** slick, facile, or superficial: *His later movies are too creamy.* [1425–75; late ME. See CREAM, -Y[1]] —**cream′i•ly,** *adv.* —**cream′i•ness,** *n.*

cre•ance (krē′əns), *n. Falconry.* a light cord attached to the leg of a hawk to prevent escape during training. [1300–50; ME < MF < VL **crēdentia* CREDENCE]

crease[1] (krēs), *n., v.,* **creased, creas•ing.** —*n.* **1.** a ridge or groove produced in anything by folding, heat, pressure, etc.; fold; furrow. **2.** a wrinkle, esp. one on the face. **3.** the straight, vertical edge or line produced in the front and back of trousers, esp. men's trousers, by pressing, as with a steam presser or iron. **4.** *Ice Hockey.* the marked rectangular area in front of each goal cage, into which an offensive player can skate only if that player has the puck, if the puck is already within the area, or if the goalie is absent. **5.** *Cricket.* **a.** See **bowling crease. b.** See **popping crease.** —*v.t.* **6.** to make a crease or creases in or on; wrinkle. **7.** to wound or stun by a furrowing or superficial shot: *The bullet merely creased his shoulder.* —*v.i.* **8.** to become creased. [1400–50; late ME *creeste, crest,* appar. special use of CREST] —**crease′less,** *adj.* —**creas′er,** *n.*
—**Syn. 6.** crimp, pucker, furrow, fold.

crease[2] (krēs), *n.* creese.

crease-re•sis•tant (krēs′ri zis′tənt), *adj.* (of a fabric) resistant to normal wrinkling. [1935–40]

creas•y (krē′sē), *adj.,* **creas•i•er, creas•i•est.** full of creases. [1855–60; CREASE[1] + -Y[1]]

cre•ate (krē āt′), *v.,* **-at•ed, -at•ing,** *adj.* —*v.t.* **1.** to cause to come into being, as something unique that would not naturally evolve or that is not made by ordinary processes. **2.** to evolve from one's own thought or imagination, as a work of art or an invention. **3.** *Theat.* to perform (a role) for the first time or in the first production of a play. **4.** to make by investing with new rank or by designating; constitute; appoint: *to create a peer.* **5.** to be the cause or occasion of; give rise to: *The announcement created confusion.* **6.** to cause to happen; bring about; arrange, as by intention or design: *to create a revolution; to create an opportunity to ask for a raise.* —*v.i.* **7.** to do something creative or constructive. **8.** *Brit.* to make a fuss. —*adj.* **9.** *Archaic.* created. [1350–1400; ME *creat* (ptp.) < L *creātus,* equiv. to *creā-* (s. of *creāre* to make) + *-tus* ptp. suffix] —**cre•at′a•ble,** *adj.*
—**Syn. 2.** originate, invent.

cre•a•tine (krē′ə tēn′, -tin), *n. Biochem.* an amino acid, $C_4H_9N_3O_2$, that is a constituent of the muscles of vertebrates and is phosphorylated to store energy used for muscular contraction. [1830–40; *creat-* (< Gk *kreat-,* s. of *kréas*) flesh + -INE[2]]

cre′atine ki′nase, *Biochem.* an enzyme that, during muscular activity, catalyzes the transfer of a phosphoryl group from phosphocreatine in muscle to produce ATP.

cre′atine phos′phate, *Biochem.* phosphocreatine. [1945–50]

cre•at•i•nine (krē at′n ēn′, -in), *n. Biochem.* a crystalline end product of creatine metabolism, $C_4H_7N_3O$, occurring in urine, muscle, and blood. [1850–55; < G *Kreatinin,* equiv. to *kreatin* CREATINE + *-in* -INE[2]]

cre•a•tion (krē ā′shən), *n.* **1.** the act of producing or causing to exist; the act of creating; engendering. **2.** the fact of being created. **3.** something that is or has been created. **4. the Creation,** the original bringing into existence of the universe by God. **5.** the world; universe. **6.** creatures collectively. **7.** an original product of the mind, esp. an imaginative artistic work: *the creations of a poetic genius.* **8.** a specially designed dress, hat, or other article of women's clothing, usually distinguished by imaginative or unique styling: *the newest Paris creations.* [1350–1400; ME *creacioun* < L *creātiōn-* (s. of *creātiō*). See CREATE, -ION] —**cre•a′tion•al, cre•a•tion•ar•y** (krē ā′shə ner′ē), *adj.*
—**Syn. 1.** production, development, formation.

cre•a•tion•ism (krē ā′shə niz′əm), *n.* **1.** the doctrine that matter and all things were created, substantially as they now exist, by an omnipotent Creator, and not gradually evolved or developed. **2.** (*sometimes cap.*) the doctrine that the true story of the creation of the universe is as it is recounted in the Bible, esp. in the first chapter of Genesis. **3.** the doctrine that God immediately creates out of nothing a new human soul for each individual born. Cf. **traducianism.** [1840–50; CREATION + -ISM] —**cre•a′tion•ist,** *n., adj.* —**cre•a′tion•is′tic,** *adj.*

crea′tion sci′ence, a form of creationism advocated as an alternative to the scientific theory of evolution, and holding that the creation of the universe and everything in it was supernatural and relatively recent. Cf. **scientific creationism.** —**crea′tion sci′entist.**

cre•a•tive (krē ā′tiv), *adj.* **1.** having the quality or power of creating. **2.** resulting from originality of thought, expression, etc.; imaginative: *creative writing.* **3.** originative; productive (usually fol. by *of*). **4.** *Facetious.* using or creating exaggerated or skewed data, information, etc.: *creative bookkeeping.* [1670–80; CREATE + -IVE] —**cre•a′tive•ly,** *adv.* —**cre•a′tive•ness,** *n.*

crea′tive imagina′tion. See under **imagination** (def. 6).

cre•a•tiv•i•ty (krē′ā tiv′i tē, krē′ə-), *n.* **1.** the state or quality of being creative. **2.** the ability to transcend traditional ideas, rules, patterns, relationships, or the like, and to create meaningful new ideas, forms, methods, interpretations, etc.; originality, progressiveness, or imagination: *the need for creativity in modern industry; creativity in the performing arts.* **3.** the process by which one utilizes creative ability: *Extensive reading stimulated his creativity.* [1870–75; CREATIVE + -ITY]

cre·a·tor (krē āʹtər), *n.* **1.** a person or thing that creates. **2. the Creator,** God. [1250–1300; ME *creato(u)r* < L *creātor,* equiv. to *creā(re)* to CREATE, be the home of, bear + *-tor* -TOR] —**cre·aʹtor·ship**ʹ, *n.*

crea·tur·al (krēʹchər əl), *adj.* of, pertaining to, or of the nature of a creature. [1635–45; CREATURE + -AL[1]]

crea·ture (krēʹchər), *n.* **1.** an animal, esp. a nonhuman: *the creatures of the woods and fields; a creature from outer space.* **2.** anything created, whether animate or inanimate. **3.** person; human being: *She is a charming creature. The driver of a bus is sometimes an irritable creature.* **4.** an animate being. **5.** a person whose position or fortune is owed to someone or something and who continues under the control or influence of that person or thing: *The cardinal was a creature of Louis XI.* **6.** *Scot. and Older U.S. Use.* intoxicating liquor, esp. whiskey (usually prec. by *the*): *He drinks a bit of the creature before bedtime.* [1250–1300; ME *creature* < LL *creātūra* act of creating. See CREATE, -URE]

creaʹture comʹforts, things that contribute to bodily comfort and ease, as food, warmth, a comfortable bed, hot water for bathing, etc. [1650–60]

crea·ture·ly (krēʹchər lē), *adj.* creatural. [1655–65; CREATURE + -LY] —**creaʹture·li·ness,** *n.*

crèche (kresh, krāsh; *Fr.* kresh), *n., pl.* **crèch·es** (kreshʹiz, krāʹshiz; *Fr.* kresh). **1.** a small or large modeled representation or tableau of Mary, Joseph, and others around the crib of Jesus in the stable at Bethlehem, as is displayed in homes or erected for exhibition in a community at Christmas season. **2.** a home for foundlings. **3.** *Brit.* a day-care center; day nursery. **4.** *Animal Behav.* an assemblage of dependent young that are cared for communally. [1785–95; < F, OF < Frankish **kripja* CRIB]

Cré·cy (kresʹē; *Fr.* krā sēʹ), *n.* **1.** Also, **Cressy.** a village in N France, NNW of Reims: English victory over the French 1346. 1390. —*adj.* **2.** (*sometimes l.c.*) (of food) prepared or garnished with carrots.

cre·dence (krēdʹns), *n.* **1.** belief as to the truth of something: *to give credence to a claim.* **2.** something giving a claim to belief or confidence: *letter of credence.* **3.** Also called **creʹdence taʹble, credenza.** *Eccles.* a small side table, shelf, or niche for holding articles used in the Eucharist service. **4.** *Furniture.* credenza (def. 1). [1300–50; ME < MF *credence* < ML *crēdentia.* See CREDENT, -ENCE]
—**Syn. 1.** credit, faith, confidence.

cre·den·dum (kri denʹdəm), *n., pl.* **-da** (-də). a doctrine that requires belief; article of faith. [< L, neut. of *crēdendus,* ger. of *crēdere* to believe]

cre·dent (krēdʹnt), *adj.* **1.** *Archaic.* believing. **2.** *Obs.* credible. [1595–1605; < L *crēdent-* (s. of *crēdēns*), prp. of *crēdere* to believe] —**creʹdent·ly,** *adv.*

cre·den·tial (kri denʹshəl), *n.* Usually, **credentials. 1.** evidence of authority, status, rights, entitlement to privileges, or the like, usually in written form: *Only those with the proper credentials are admitted.* **2.** anything that provides the basis for confidence, belief, credit, etc. —*v.t.* **3.** to grant credentials to, esp. educational and professional ones: *She has been credentialed to teach math.* —*adj.* **4.** providing the basis for confidence, belief, credit, etc. [1425–75; late ME *credencial* < ML *crēdenti(a)* CREDENCE + -AL[1]]

cre·den·tial·ism (kri denʹshə lizʹəm), *n.* excessive reliance on credentials, esp. academic degrees, in determining hiring or promotion policies. [1965–70; CREDENTIAL + -ISM]

cre·den·za (kri denʹzə), *n.* **1.** Also, **credence.** a sideboard or buffet, esp. one without legs. **2.** a closed cabinet for papers, office supplies, etc., often of desk height and matching the other furniture in an executive's office. **3.** *Eccles.* credence (def. 3). [1875–80; < It < ML *crēdentia* (in ecclesiastical usage) a sideboard for holding sacramental vessels; see CREDENCE]

credibilʹity gapʹ, **1.** a lack of popular confidence in the truth of the claims or public statements made by the federal government, large corporations, politicians, etc.: *a credibility gap between the public and the power company.* **2.** a perceived discrepancy between statements and actual performance or behavior. [1965–70, *Amer.*]

cred·i·ble (kredʹə bəl), *adj.* **1.** capable of being believed; believable: *a credible statement.* **2.** worthy of belief or confidence; trustworthy: *a credible witness.* [1350–1400; ME (< MF) < L *crēdibilis,* equiv. to *crēd(ere)* to believe + *-ibilis* -IBLE] —**credʹi·bilʹi·ty, credʹi·ble·ness,** *n.* —**credʹi·bly,** *adv.*
—**Syn. 1.** plausible, likely, reasonable, tenable.

cred·it (kredʹit), *n.* **1.** commendation or honor given for some action, quality, etc.: *Give credit where it is due.* **2.** a source of pride or honor: *You are a credit to your school.* **3.** the ascription or acknowledgment of something as due or properly attributable to a person, institution, etc.: *She got a screen credit for photography.* **4.** trustworthiness; credibility: *a witness of credit.* **5.** confidence in a purchaser's ability and intention to pay, displayed by entrusting the buyer with goods or services without immediate payment. **6.** reputation of solvency and probity, entitling a person to be trusted in buying or borrowing: *Your credit is good.* **7.** influence or authority resulting from the confidence of others or from one's reputation. **8.** time allowed for payment for goods or services obtained on trust: *90 days' credit.* **9.** repute; reputation; esteem. **10.** a sum of money due to a person; anything valuable standing on the credit side of an account: *He has an outstanding credit of $50.* **11.** *Educ.* **a.** official acceptance and recording of the work completed by a student in a particular course of study. **b.** a credit hour. **12.** *Bookkeeping.* **a.** an entry of payment or value received on an account. **b.** the right-hand side of an account on which such entries are made (opposed to *debit*). **c.** an entry, or the total shown, on the credit side. **13.** any deposit or sum of money against which a person may draw. **14. do someone credit,** to be a source of honor or distinction for someone. Also, **do credit to someone. 15. on credit,** by deferred payment: *Everything they have was bought on credit.* **16. to one's credit,** deserving of praise or recognition; admirable: *It is to his credit that he freely admitted his guilt.* —*v.t.* **17.** to believe; put confidence in; trust; have faith in. **18.** to bring honor, esteem, etc., to; reflect well upon. **19.** *Bookkeeping.* to enter upon the credit side of an account; give credit for or to. **20.** *Educ.* to award educational credits to (often fol. by *with*): *They credited me with three hours in history.* **21. credit to** or **with,** to ascribe to a (thing, person, etc.): *In former times many herbs were credited with healing powers.* [1535–45; < MF < OIt *credito* < L *crēditum* loan, n. use of neut. of *crēditus,* ptp. of *crēdere* to believe, confide, entrust, give credit] —**credʹit·less,** *adj.*
—**Syn. 4–7, 9.** CREDIT, REPUTE, REPUTATION, STANDING refer to one's status in the estimation of a community. CREDIT refers to business and financial status and the amount of money for which a person will be trusted. REPUTE is particularly what is reported about someone, the favor in which the person is held, etc.: *a man of fine repute among his acquaintances.* REPUTATION is the moral and other character commonly ascribed to someone: *of unblemished reputation.* STANDING is one's position in a community, or rank and condition in life: *a man of good standing and education.*

cred·it·a·ble (kredʹi tə bəl), *adj.* bringing or deserving credit, honor, reputation, or esteem. [1520–30; CREDIT + -ABLE] —**credʹit·a·ble·ness, credʹit·a·bilʹi·ty,** *n.* —**credʹit·a·bly,** *adv.*
—**Syn.** praiseworthy, meritorious, estimable, honorable.

credʹit buʹreau, a firm that investigates the creditworthiness of and assigns a credit rating to a client's customers or potential customers. Also called **credʹit aʹgency.**

credʹit cardʹ, a card that identifies a person as entitled to have food, merchandise, services, etc., billed on a charge account. [1885–90, *Amer.*]

credʹit hourʹ, hour (def. 12). [1925–30]

credʹit lifeʹ insurʹance, insurance guaranteeing payment of the unpaid portion of a loan if the debtor should die.

credʹit lineʹ, **1.** a line of text acknowledging the source or origin of published or exhibited material. **2.** Also called **credʹit limʹit, line of credit.** the maximum amount of credit that a customer of a store, bank, etc., is authorized to use. Cf. **revolving credit.** [1910–15]

credʹit manʹager, **1.** a person employed in a business firm to administer credit service to its customers, esp. to evaluate the extension and amount of credit to be granted. **2.** an employee who supervises the credit department in a bank or other business organization.

credʹit memoranʹdum, a memorandum issued to an account allowing a credit or reducing a debit, esp. one posted to a customer's account. Also called **credʹit memʹo, credit slip.**

Créd·it Mo·bil·ier (kredʹit mō bēlʹyər, mō bēl yāʹ; *Fr.* krā dē mō bē lyāʹ), *U.S. Hist.* a joint-stock company organized in 1863 and reorganized in 1867 to build the Union Pacific Railroad. It was involved in a scandal in 1872 in which high government officials were accused of accepting bribes.

cred·i·tor (kredʹi tər), *n.* **1.** a person or firm to whom money is due (opposed to *debtor*). **2.** a person or firm that gives credit in business transactions. **3.** *Bookkeeping.* credit (def. 12b, c). [1400–50; late ME *creditour* < L *crēditor,* equiv. to *crēdi-* var. s. of *crēdere* to believe, entrust (see CREDIT) + *-tor* -TOR] —**credʹi·tor·shipʹ,** *n.*

credʹit ratʹing, a classification of credit risk based on investigation of a customer's or potential customer's financial resources, prior payment pattern, and personal history or degree of personal responsibility for debts incurred. [1955–60]

credʹit riskʹ, **1.** the possibility of loss if a borrower defaults on a loan. **2.** a borrower regarded as likely to default on a loan.

credʹit slipʹ, **1.** See **deposit slip. 2.** See **credit memorandum.**

credʹit squeezeʹ, a restraint or limitation of credit. [1950–55]

credʹit standʹing, reputation for meeting financial obligations.

credʹit unʹion, a cooperative group that makes loans to its members at low rates of interest. Also called **cooperative credit union.** [1910–15, *Amer.*]

cred·it·wor·thy (kredʹit wûrʹthē), *adj.* having a satisfactory credit rating. [1555–65, for an earlier sense; CREDIT + -WORTHY] —**credʹit·worʹthi·ness,** *n.*

cre·do (krēʹdō, krāʹ-), *n., pl.* **-dos. 1.** (*often cap.*) the Apostles' Creed or the Nicene Creed. **2.** (*often cap.*) a musical setting of the creed, usually of the Nicene Creed. **3.** any creed or formula of belief. [1150–1200; ME < L: lit., I believe; first word of the Apostles' and Nicene Creeds in Latin]
—**Syn. 3.** doctrine, tenet, philosophy.

cre·du·li·ty (krə dōōʹli tē, -dyōōʹ-), *n.* willingness to believe or trust too readily, esp. without proper or adequate evidence; gullibility. [1375–1425; late ME *credulite* < L *crēdulitās.* See CREDULOUS, -ITY]

cred·u·lous (krejʹə ləs), *adj.* **1.** willing to believe or trust too readily, esp. without proper or adequate evidence; gullible. **2.** marked by or arising from credulity: *a credulous rumor.* [1570–80; < L *crēdulus,* equiv. to *crēd(ere)* to believe + *-ulus* adj. suffix denoting a quality or tendency; see -OUS] —**credʹu·lous·ly,** *adv.* —**credʹu·lous·ness,** *n.*
—**Syn. 1.** believing, trustful, unsuspecting.

Cree (krē), *n., pl.* **Crees,** (*esp. collectively*) **Cree. 1.** a member of a North American Indian people of Ontario, Manitoba, Saskatchewan, and Montana. **2.** an Algonquian language, the language of the Cree Indians.

creed (krēd), *n.* **1.** any system, doctrine, or formula of religious belief, as of a denomination. **2.** any system or codification of belief or of opinion. **3.** an authoritative, formulated statement of the chief articles of Christian belief, as the Apostles' Creed, the Nicene Creed, or the Athanasian Creed. **4. the creed.** See **Apostles' Creed.** [bef. 1000; ME *crede,* OE *crēda* < L *crēdō* I believe; see CREDO] —**creedʹal, credʹal,** *adj.* —**creedʹed,** *adj.* —**creedʹless,** *adj.* —**creedʹless·ness,** *n.*
—**Syn. 1, 2.** faith, conviction, credo, dogma.

creek (krēk, krik), *n.* **1.** *U.S., Canada, and Australia.* a stream smaller than a river. **2.** a stream or channel in a coastal marsh. **3.** *Chiefly Atlantic States and Brit.* a recess or inlet in the shore of the sea. **4.** an estuary. **5.** *Brit. Dial.* a narrow, winding passage or hidden recess. **6. up the creek,** *Slang.* in a predicament; in a difficult or seemingly hopeless situation. [1200–50; ME *creke,* var. of *crike* < ON *kriki* bend, crook]

Creek (krēk), *n., pl.* **Creeks,** (*esp. collectively*) **Creek. 1.** a member of a confederacy of North American Indians that in historic times occupied the greater part of Alabama and Georgia. **2.** Also called **Muskogee.** a Muskogean language that is the language of the Creek Indians.

Creekʹ Warʹ, *U.S. Hist.* an uprising in 1813–14 of the Creek Indians against settlers in Alabama: frontier militia from Tennessee, Georgia, and Mississippi under Andrew Jackson helped defeat the Creek, who ceded two-thirds of their land to the U.S.

creel (krēl), *n.* **1.** a wickerwork basket worn on the back or suspended from the shoulder, used esp. by anglers for carrying fish. **2.** a basket made of wicker or other material, for holding fish, lobsters, etc. **3.** a trap for fish, lobsters, etc., esp. one made of wicker. **4.** a framework, esp. one for holding bobbins in a spinning machine. [1275–1325; ME *crele,* of uncert. orig.]

creep (krēp), *v.,* **crept, creep·ing,** *n.* —*v.i.* **1.** to move slowly with the body close to the ground, as a reptile or an insect, or a person on hands and knees. **2.** to approach slowly, imperceptibly, or stealthily (often fol. by *up*): *We crept up and peeked over the wall.* **3.** to move or advance slowly or gradually: *The automobile crept up the hill. Time just seems to creep along on these hot summer days.* **4.** to sneak up behind someone or without someone's knowledge (usually fol. by *up on*): *The prisoners crept up on the guard and knocked him out.* **5.** to enter or become evident inconspicuously, gradually, or insidiously (often fol. by *in* or *into:*) *The writer's personal bias occasionally creeps into the account.* **6.** to move or behave timidly or servilely. **7.** to grow along the ground, a wall, etc., as a plant. **8.** to advance or develop gradually so as to infringe on or supplant something else: *creeping inflation; creeping socialism.* **9.** to slip, slide, or shift gradually; become displaced. **10.** (of a metal object) to become deformed, as under continuous loads or at high temperatures. **11.** *Naut.* to grapple (usually fol. by *for*): *The ships crept for their anchor chains.* —*v.t.* **12.** *Archaic.* to creep along or over. **13. make one's flesh creep,** to be frightening or repellent; cause one to experience uneasiness: *The eerie stories made our flesh creep.* —*n.* **14.** an act or instance of creeping. **15.** *Slang.* a boring, disturbingly eccentric, painfully introverted, or obnoxious person. **16.** *Slang.* an intelligence or counterintelligence agent; spy. **17.** *Geol.* **a.** the gradual movement downhill of loose soil, rock, gravel, etc.; solifluction. **b.** the slow deformation of solid rock resulting from constant stress applied over long periods. **18.** *Mech.* the gradual, permanent deformation of a body produced by a continued application of heat or stress. **19.** a grappling iron; grapnel. **20.** *Firearms.* the slack in a trigger mechanism before it releases the firing pin. **21.** See **creep feeder. 22. the creeps,** *Informal.* a sensation of horror, fear, disgust, etc., suggestive of the feeling induced by something crawling over the skin: *That horror movie gave me the creeps.* [bef. 900; ME *crepen,* OE *crēopan;* c. D *kruipen,* ON *krjūpa*] —**creepʹing·ly,** *adv.*
—**Syn. 1.** See **crawl. 3.** inch, crawl, dawdle, poke.

creep·age (krēʹpij), *n.* **1.** the act or process of creeping. **2.** slow, imperceptible movement. [1900–05; CREEP + -AGE]

creep·er (krēʹpər), *n.* **1.** a person or thing that creeps. **2.** *Bot.* a plant that grows upon or just beneath the surface of the ground, or upon any other surface, sending out rootlets from the stem, as ivy and couch grass. **3.** Often, **creepers.** a one-piece garment for an infant, the lower portion resembling briefs and having snaps or buttons across the crotch for convenience in diapering. **4.** *Chiefly Northeastern U.S.* a spiked iron plate worn on the shoe to prevent slipping on ice, rock, etc. **5.** Also called **cradle.** *Auto.* a flat framework on casters, on which a mechanic lies while working under an automobile or the like. **6.** *Ornith.* any of various birds that creep or climb about on trees, esp. of the family Certhiidae, as *Certhia americana* **(brown creeper** or **tree creeper),** of the Northern Hemisphere. **7.** a domestic fowl having malformed, short legs, due to a genetic defect. **8.** a grappling device for dragging a river, lake, etc. [bef. 1000; ME *crepere,* OE *crēopere.* See CREEP, -ER[1]]

creep-feed (krēpʹfēdʹ), *v.t.,* **-fed, -feed·ing.** to feed (animals) in a creep feeder. [1955–60]

creepʹ feedʹer, a pen so constructed as to exclude larger animals while permitting young animals to enter and obtain feed.

creepʹing Charʹlie, moneywort.

creepʹing cinqueʹfoil. See under **cinquefoil** (def. 1).

creepʹing erupʹtion, *Pathol.* a skin disorder caused by the burrowing of dog or cat hookworm larvae under the dermal tissue and manifested as a progressing red streak. [1925–30]

CONCISE PRONUNCIATION KEY: act, cāpe, dâre, pärt; set, ēqual; *if,* īce; ox, ōver, ôrder, oil, bŏŏk, bōōt, out; up, ûrge; child; sing; shoe; thin, *th*at; zh as in *treasure.* ə = a as in *alone,* e as in *system,* i as in *easily,* o as in *gallop,* u as in *circus;* ᵊ as in *fire* (fīᵊr), *hour* (ouᵊr). l and n can serve as syllabic consonants, as in *cradle* (krādʹl), and *button* (butʹn). See the full key inside the front cover.

creep′ing fes′cue. See **red fescue.**

creep′ing Jen′nie, moneywort. [1880–85]

creep′ing ju′niper, a prostrate central North American shrub, *Juniperus horizontalis,* of the cypress family, of central North America, having bluish-green or gray-blue leaves and blue fruit, growing well in sandy, rocky soil.

creeps (krēps), *n.* (*used with a singular v.*) *Vet. Pathol.* a disease of the bones in sheep and cattle that causes pain in walking, resulting from a deficiency of phosphorus in the diet. [so called from the effect on the animal's gait; see CREEP, -S[3]]

creep•y (krē′pē), *adj.,* **creep•i•er, creep•i•est. 1.** having or causing a creeping sensation of the skin, as from horror or fear: *a creepy ghost story.* **2.** that creeps: *a creepy insect.* **3.** *Slang.* of, pertaining to, or characteristic of a person who is a creep; obnoxious; weird. [1825–35; CREEP + -Y[1]] **—creep′i•ly,** *adv.* **—creep′i•ness,** *n.*

creep•y-crawl•y (krē′pē krô′lē), *n., pl.* **-crawl•ies,** *adj.,* **-crawl•i•er, -crawl•i•est.** *Informal.* **—***n.* **1.** a creeping or crawling animal, esp. an insect. **—***adj.* **2.** creepy (def. 1). [1855–60; see CREEP, CRAWL[1], -Y[1]]

creese (krēs), *n.* a short sword or heavy dagger with a wavy blade, used by the Malays. Also, **crease, kris.** [1570–80; < Malay *kəris* (sp. *keris*)]

Cre•feld (krā′feld; *Ger.* KRĀ′felt′), *n.* Krefeld.

cre•mains (kri mānz′), *n.pl.* the ashes of a cremated corpse. [1945–50; b. CREMATE and REMAINS]

cre•mas•ter (kri mas′tər), *n.* **1.** *Entomol.* a usually hooklike process on the posterior tip of a chrysalis, for attaching the pupa to a stem, twig, etc. **2.** *Anat.* the suspensory muscle of the testis. [1670–80; < L < Gk *kremastḗr* lit., suspender, akin to *kremannýnai* to hang] **—crem•as•te•ri•al** (krem′ə stēr′ē əl), **crem•as•ter•ic** (krem′ə ster′ik), *adj.*

cre•mate (krē′māt), *v.t.,* **-mat•ed, -mat•ing. 1.** to reduce (a dead body) to ashes by fire, esp. as a funeral rite. **2.** to consume by fire; burn. [1870–75; < L *cremātus* ptp. of *cremāre* to burn to ashes; see -ATE[1]] **—cre•ma•tion** (kri mā′shən), *n.*

cre•ma•tion•ist (kri mā′shə nist), *n.* a person who advocates cremation instead of burial of the dead. [1870–75; CREMATION + -IST] **—cre•ma′tion•ism,** *n.*

cre•ma•tor (krē′mā tər), *n.* **1.** a person who cremates. **2.** a furnace for cremating dead bodies. **3.** an incinerator, as for garbage. [1875–80; < LL, equiv. to L *cremā(re)* to CREMATE + *-tor* -TOR]

cre•ma•to•ri•um (krē′mə tôr′ē əm, -tōr′-, krem′ə-), *n., pl.* **-to•ri•ums, -to•ri•a** (-tôr′ē ə, -tōr′-). a crematory. [1875–80; Latinization of CREMATORY; see -TORY[2]]

cre•ma•to•ry (krē′mə tôr′ē, -tōr′ē, krem′ə-), *n., pl.* **-ries,** *adj.* **—***n.* **1.** a place, as a funeral establishment, at which cremation is done. **2.** a furnace for cremating. **—***adj.* **3.** of or pertaining to cremation. [1875–80; CREMATE + -ORY[2]]

crème (krem, krēm; *Fr.* KREM), *n., pl.* **crèmes** (kremz, krēmz; *Fr.* KREM). **1.** cream. **2.** one of a class of liqueurs of a rather thick consistency. Also, **creme.** [1815–25; < F; see CREAM]

crème an•glaise (krem′ ang glāz′, -glez′, krēm′; *Fr.* KREM ÄN glez′), *French Cookery.* a custard sauce flavored with vanilla or sometimes with rum, orange liqueur, kirsch, etc. [< F: lit., English cream]

crème brû•lée (krem′ brōō lā′, krēm′; *Fr.* KREM BRY lā′), *pl.* **crèmes brû•lées** (krem′ brōō lāz′, krēm′; *Fr.* KREM BRY lā′). *French Cookery.* a custard that has been sprinkled with sugar and placed under a broiler until a brown crust forms on top. [1885–90; < F: lit., burnt cream]

crème d'a•na•nas (krem′ dä nä nä′, krēm′; *Fr.* KREM DA NA nä′), a liqueur flavored with pineapple. [< F: lit., cream of pineapples]

crème de ba•nanes (krem′ də bä nän′, krēm′; *Fr.* KREM də BA NAN′), a liqueur flavored with bananas. Also, **crème′ de ba•nane′.** [< F: lit., cream of bananas]

crème de ca•ca•o (krem′ də kō′kō, kä kä′ō, krēm′; *Fr.* KREM də KA KA′ō), a liqueur flavored with cacao and vanilla beans. [1925–30; < F: lit., cream of cacao]

crème de cas•sis (krem′ də ka sēs′, krēm′; *Fr.* KREM də KA sēs′), a liqueur flavored with black currants. [< F: lit., cream of black currant]

crème de fraise (krem′ də frez′, krēm′; *Fr.* KREM də FREZ′), a liqueur flavored principally with strawberries. [< F: lit., cream of strawberry]

crème de fram•boise (krem′ də främ bwäz′, krēm′; *Fr.* KREM də FRÄN BWAZ′), a liqueur flavored with raspberries. [< F: lit., cream of raspberry]

crème de la crème (krem′ də lä krem′; *Fr.* KREM də LA KREM′), the very best; choicest parts or members. [1840–50; lit., cream of the cream]

crème de menthe (krem′ də menth′, mint′, krēm′; *Fr.* KREM də mänt′), a white or green liqueur flavored with mint. [1900–05; < F: lit., cream of mint]

crème de vi•o•lette (krem′ də vī′ə lit, krēm′; *Fr.* KREM də vyô let′), a liqueur flavored with vanilla extract and the essential oils of violets. [< F: lit., cream of violet]

crème fraîche (krem′ fresh′, krēm′; *Fr.* KREM fresh′), *French Cookery.* slightly fermented cream that has been thickened by lactic acids and natural fermentation. [< F: lit., fresh cream]

Cre•mer (krē′mər), *n.* **Sir William Randal,** 1838–1908, English union organizer: Nobel peace prize 1903.

CONCISE ETYMOLOGY KEY: <, descended or borrowed from; >, whence; b., blend of, blended; c., cognate with; cf., compare; deriv., derivative; equiv., equivalent; imit., imitative; obl., oblique; r., replacing; s., stem; sp., spelling, spelled; resp., respelling, respelled; trans., translation; ?, origin unknown; *, unattested; ‡, probably earlier than. See the full key inside the front cover.

Crem′nitz white′ (krem′nits). See **lead white.** [1870–75; after G *Kremnitz,* Slovak *Kremnica,* town in central Slovakia]

Cre•mo•na (kri mō′nə; *It.* KRE mô′nä), *n.* **1.** a city in N Italy, on the Po River. 82,411. **2.** one of a class of violins of superior quality made there during the 16th, 17th, and 18th centuries.

cre•morne′ bolt′ (kri môrn′), (on a French window or the like) a pair of rods, moved by a knob mechanism, sliding into sockets in the head and sill of the opening to provide a secure fastening. Also, **cre•mone′ bolt′** (kri-mōn′). [< F *crémone,* prob. after CREMONA]

cre•nate (krē′nāt), *adj.* having the margin notched or scalloped so as to form rounded teeth, as a leaf. Also, **cre′nat•ed.** [1785–95; < NL *crēnātus,* equiv. to L *crēn(a)* a notch, serration (a word occurring in some manuscripts of Pliny, identified with a semantically related set of Rom words; see CRENEL) + *-ātus* -ATE[1]]

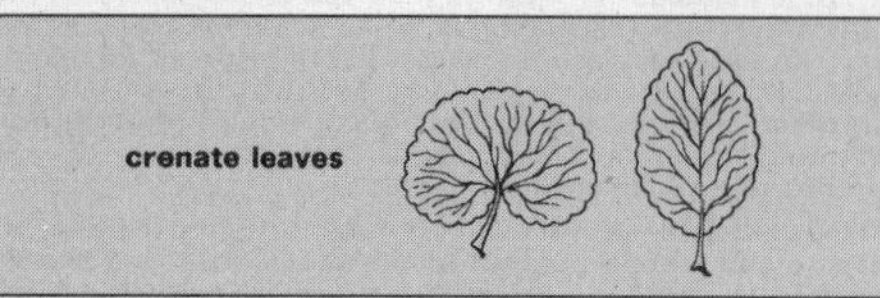

cre•na•tion (kri nā′shən), *n.* **1.** a rounded projection or tooth, as on the margin of a leaf. **2.** *Anat.* (in erythrocytes) the state of being or becoming shrunken with a notched or indented edge. **3.** a notch between teeth. [1840–50; CRENATE + -ION]

cren•a•ture (kren′ə chər, krē′nə-), *n.* **1.** a crenation. **2.** a notch or indentation between crenations. [1810–20; CRENATE + -URE]

cren•el (kren′l), *n., v.,* **-eled, -el•ing** or (*esp. Brit.*) **-elled, -el•ling. —***n.* **1.** any of the open spaces between the merlons of a battlement. See illus. under **battlement. 2.** a crenature. **—***v.t.* **3.** to crenelate. Also, **cre•nelle** (kri nel′). [1475–85; earlier *creneul, crennel* < MF, OF, appar. dim. of *cren* notch (attested since the 15th century), OF *cran,* of uncert. orig.; cf. CRENATE, CRANNY]

cren•el•ate (kren′l āt′), *v.,* **-at•ed, -at•ing,** *adj.* **—***v.t.* **1.** to furnish with crenels or battlements. **—***adj.* **2.** crenelated. Also, *esp. Brit.,* **cren′el•late′.** [1815–25; < F *crénel(er)* to crenelate (see CRENEL) + -ATE[1]] **—cren′el•a′tion;** *esp. Brit.,* **cren′el•la′tion,** *n.*

cren•el•at•ed (kren′l ā′tid), *adj.* furnished with crenelations, as a parapet or molding, in the manner of a battlement. Also, *esp. Brit.,* **cren′el•lat′ed.** [1815–25; CRENELATE + -ED[2]]

Cren′shaw mel′on (kren′shô), a variety of melon resembling the casaba, having pinkish flesh.

cren•u•late (kren′yə lāt′, -lit), *adj.* minutely crenate, as the margin of certain leaves. Also, **cren′u•lat′ed.** [1785–95; < NL *crēnulātus,* equiv. to *crēnul(a)* (dim. of *crēna* notch; see CRENATE) + *-ātus* -ATE[1]]

cren•u•la•tion (kren′yə lā′shən), *n.* **1.** a minute crenation. **2.** the state of being crenulate. [1840–50; CRENULATE + -ION]

cre•o•dont (krē′ə dont′), *n.* any of a diverse group of extinct predatory mammals, from the Paleocene to Pleistocene epochs, that constituted the suborder Creodonta, of the order Carnivora, developing along evolutionary lines somewhat parallel to those of the ancestors of modern carnivores and typically having a stocky, doglike body and a long, low skull. [< NL *Creodonta* (1875) name of the group, equiv. to *cre-* (< Gk *kréas* flesh) + *-odont-* -ODONT + *-a* neut. pl. ending]

Cre•ole (krē′ōl), *n.* **1.** a person born in the West Indies or Spanish America but of European, usually Spanish, ancestry. **2.** a person born in Louisiana but of usually French ancestry. **3.** (*sometimes l.c.*) a person of mixed black and European, esp. French or Spanish, ancestry who speaks a creolized form of French or Spanish. **4.** (*usually l.c.*) a creolized language; a pidgin that has become the native language of a speech community. Cf. **pidgin. 5.** the creolized French language of the descendants of the original settlers of Louisiana. Cf. **Cajun. 6.** See **Haitian Creole. 7.** (*usually l.c.*) *Archaic.* a black person born in the New World, as distinguished from one brought there from Africa. **—***adj.* **8.** (*sometimes l.c.*) of, pertaining to, or characteristic of a Creole or Creoles. **9.** (*usually l.c.*) *Cookery.* indicating a spicy sauce or dish made esp. with tomatoes, peppers, onions, celery, and seasonings, and often served with rice. **10.** (*sometimes l.c.*) bred or growing in a country, but of foreign origin, as an animal or plant. [1595–1605; < F < Sp *criollo* < Pg *crioulo* native, deriv. of *criar* to bring up < L *creāre;* see CREATE]

cre′ole contin′uum, *Ling.* a range of language varieties in an area undergoing decreolization showing a continuous gradation from forms more like the underlying creole to those approaching the standard language.

cre•ole-fish (krē′ōl fish′), *n., pl.* **-fish•es,** (*esp. collectively*) **-fish.** a deep-sea fish, *Paranthias furcifer,* of the sea bass family, inhabiting tropical Atlantic waters. [CREOLE + FISH]

cre′ole toma′to, *New Orleans.* See **cherry tomato.**

cre•o•lize (krē′ə līz′), *v.,* **-lized, -liz•ing. —***v.t.* **1.** to render (a language) creolized. **—***v.i.* **2.** to become creolized. Also, *esp. Brit.,* **cre′o•lise′.** [1810–20; CREOLE + -IZE] **—cre′o•li•za′tion,** *n.*

cre•o•lized (krē′ə līzd′), *adj.* (of a language) formerly a pidgin but now the native language of a group of speakers, with consequent enrichment of the vocabulary by borrowing and creation. [1875–80; CREOLIZE + -ED[2]]

Cre•on (krē′on), *n. Class. Myth.* a king of Thebes, the brother of Jocasta and the uncle of Eteocles, Polynices, and Antigone.

cre•o•sol (krē′ə sôl′, -sol′), *n. Chem.* a colorless oily liquid, $C_8H_{10}O_2$, having an agreeable odor and a burning taste, obtained from wood tar and guaiacum resin: used as a disinfectant, in the manufacture of resins, and in ore flotation. [1860–65; CREOS(OTE) + -OL[2]]

cre•o•sote (krē′ə sōt′), *n., v.,* **-sot•ed, -sot•ing. —***n.* **1.** an oily liquid having a burning taste and a penetrating odor, obtained by the distillation of coal and wood tar, used mainly as a preservative for wood and as an antiseptic. **2.** See **coal-tar creosote. —***v.t.* **3.** to treat with creosote. [< G *Kreosote* (1832) < Gk *kreo-,* comb. form of *kréas* flesh + *sōtḗr* savior, preserver (in reference to its antiseptic properties)] **—cre•o•sot•ic** (krē′ə-sot′ik), *adj.*

cre′osote bush′, any of several shrubs belonging to the genus *Larrea,* of the caltrop family, esp. *L. tridentata,* of arid regions of the southwestern U.S. and Mexico, having yellow flowers and resinous foliage with a strong odor of creosote. [1840–50, *Amer.*]

crepe (krāp), *n., v.,* **creped, crep•ing. —***n.* **1.** a lightweight fabric of silk, cotton, or other fiber, with a finely crinkled or ridged surface. **2.** a usually black band or piece of this material, worn as a token of mourning. **3.** a thin, light, delicate pancake. **4.** See **crepe paper. 5.** See **crepe rubber. —***v.t.* **6.** to cover, clothe, or drape with crepe. Also, **crape.,** [1790–1800; < F < L *crispus* curled, wrinkled]

crêpe (krāp; *for 2 also* krep *or, Fr.,* KREP), *n., pl.* **crêpes** (krāps; *for 2 also* kreps *or, Fr.,* KREP). **1.** crepe (defs. 1, 2). **2.** crepe (def. 3). [< F; see CREPE]

crepe de Chine (krāp′ də shēn′), a light, soft, silk or synthetic fabric with minute irregularities of surface. [1885–90; < F: lit., crepe from China]

crepe′ hair′, false hair, usually of plaited wool or vegetable fibers, used in theatrical makeup for making artificial beards, sideburns, etc. Also called **crepe′ wool′.** [1810–20]

crepe•hang•er (krāp′hang′ər), *n.* crapehanger. [1925–30, *Amer.*; CREPE + HANGER]

crepe′ mar′ocain, marocain.

crepe′ myr′tle. See **crape myrtle.** [1840–50]

crepe′ pa′per, thin paper densely wrinkled to resemble crepe, used for decorating, wrapping, etc. Also called **crepe.** [1890–95] **—crepe′-pa′per,** *adj.*

crêp•er•ie (krā′pə rē, krep′ə-; *Fr.* KREP[ə] RĒ′), *n., pl.* **crêp•er•ies** (krā′pə rēz, krep′ə-; *Fr.* KREP[ə] RĒ′). a restaurant specializing in crepes. [< F; see CRÊPE, -ERY]

crepe′ rub′ber, a type of crude or sometimes synthetic rubber pressed into crinkled sheets, used esp. in making shoe soles. Also called **crepe.** [1905–10]

crêpe su•zette (krāp′ sōō zet′, krep′; *Fr.* KREP SY-zet′), *pl.* **crêpe su•zettes** (krāp′ sōō zets′, krep′), *Fr.* **crêpes su•zette** (KREP SY zet′). a thin dessert pancake, usually rolled or folded in quarters, heated in a sauce of orange-flavored liqueur, and served flambé. Also, **crepe′ suzette′.** [1920–25; < F, allegedly after Suzanne (*Suzette*) Reichenberg (1853–1924), French actress, in whose honor they were first prepared]

crep•i•tate (krep′i tāt′), *v.i.,* **-tat•ed, -tat•ing.** to make a crackling sound; crackle. [1615–25; < L *crepitātus,* ptp. of *crepitāre* to rattle, rustle, chatter, freq. of *crepāre;* see -ATE[1]] **—crep′i•tant,** *adj.* **—crep′i•ta′•tion,** *n.*

cre•pon (krā′pon), *n.* a heavyweight crepe fabric. [1885–90; < F, equiv. to *crêpe* CREPE + *-on* n. suffix]

crept (krept), *v.* pt. and pp. of **creep.**

cre•pus•cu•lar (kri pus′kyə lər), *adj.* **1.** of, pertaining to, or resembling twilight; dim; indistinct. **2.** *Zool.* appearing or active in the twilight, as certain bats and insects. [1660–70; CREPUSCULE + -AR[1]]

crepus′cular ray′, a twilight ray of sunlight shining through breaks in high clouds and illuminating dust particles in the air.

cre•pus•cule (kri pus′kyōōl, krep′ə skyōōl′), *n.* twilight; dusk. Also, **cre•pus•cle** (kri pus′əl). [1350–1400; < L *crepuscul(um),* equiv. to *crepus-* (akin to *creper* obscure) + *-culum* -CULE[1]]

cres., *Music.* crescendo. Also, **cresc.**

Cres•cas (kres′kəs), *n.* **Has•dai** (KHÄS′dī), 1340–1412?, Jewish philosopher and theologian, born in Spain.

cre•scen•do (kri shen′dō, -sen′dō; *It.* KRE shen′dô), *n., pl.* **-dos, -di** (-dē), *adj., adv., v.* **—***n.* **1.** *Music.* **a.** a gradual, steady increase in loudness or force. **b.** a musical passage characterized by such an increase. **c.** the performance of a crescendo passage: *The crescendo by the violins is too abrupt.* **2.** a steady increase in force or intensity: *The rain fell in a crescendo on the rooftops.* **3.** the climactic point or moment in such an increase; peak: *The authorities finally took action when public outrage reached a crescendo.* **—***adj., adv.* **4.** gradually increasing in force, volume, or loudness (opposed to *decrescendo* or *diminuendo*). **—***v.i.* **5.** to grow in force or loudness. [1770–80; < It: lit., growing < L *crēscendum,* ger. of *crēscere* to grow; see CRESCENT]
—Ant. 1. diminuendo.

cres•cent (kres′ənt), *n.* **1.** a shape resembling a segment of a ring tapering to points at the ends. **2.** something, as a roll or cookie, having this shape. **3.** *Astron.* **a.** the figure of the moon in its first or last quarter, resembling a segment of a ring tapering to points at the ends. See diag. under **moon. b.** the similar figure of Mercury and Venus on either side of inferior conjunction, when seen through a telescope. **4.** the emblem of Turkey or of Islam. **5.** the power, religion, or civilization of Turkey or of Islam. **6.** Also called **Chinese crescent, Chinese pavilion, jingling Johnny, pavillon Chinois, Turkish crescent.** a musical percussion instrument of Turkish origin, consisting of a pole bearing a crescent-shaped metal plate, topped with a pavillon, and hung with small bells. **7.** *Chiefly Brit.* **a.** a curved street, often having solid façades of unified architectural design. **b.** the curve or curved portion of a street. **8.** *Heraldry.* a representation of a crescent moon, horns upward unless otherwise specified, used as the cadency mark of a second son. —*adj.* **9.** shaped like a crescent. **10.** increasing; growing. [1350–1400; < L *crēscent-* (s. of *crēscēns*) prp. of *crēscere* to grow (see CREATE, -ESCE); r. ME *cressaunt* < AF < L as above] —**cres·cen·tic** (kri-sen′tik), *adj.*

cres′cent truss′, a roof truss having upper and lower chords curving upward from a common point at each side. Also called **camelback truss.**

cre·scit e·un·do (kres′kit e ŏŏn′dō; *Eng.* kres′it ē un′dō), *Latin.* it grows as it goes: motto of the state of New Mexico.

cres·cive (kres′iv), *adj.* increasing; growing. [1560–70; < L *crēsc(ere)* to increase + -IVE]

Cres·lan (krez′lan), *Trademark.* a brand of acrylic textile fiber that is lightweight, strong, and wrinkle-resistant.

cre·sol (krē′sôl, -sol), *n.* any of three isomeric compounds having the formula C_7H_8O, usually derived from coal tar and wood tar, and used chiefly as a disinfectant. Also called **methyl phenol.** Cf. **tricresol.** [1860–65; *cres-* (irreg. from CREOSOTE) + -OL[2]]

cress (kres), *n.* **1.** any of various plants of the mustard family, esp. the watercress, having pungent-tasting leaves often used for salad and as a garnish. **2.** any of various similar plants. [bef. 900; ME *cresse,* OE *cress(a), cresse;* c. D *kers,* G *Kresse*] —**cress′y,** *adj.*

cres·set (kres′it), *n.* a metal cup or basket often mounted on a pole or suspended from above, containing oil, pitch, a rope steeped in rosin, etc., burned as a light or beacon. [1325–75; ME < AF, OF *craisset,* equiv. to *cras* GREASE + *-et* -ET]

cresset

Cres·si·da (kres′i də), *n.* (in medieval adaptations of the story of the Trojan wars) a Trojan woman portrayed as the lover of Troilus, whom she deserts for Diomedes.

Cres·sy (kres′ē), *n.* Crécy (def. 1).

crest (krest), *n.* **1.** the highest part of a hill or mountain range; summit. **2.** the head or top of anything. **3.** a ridge or ridgelike formation. **4.** the foamy top of a wave. **5.** the point of highest flood, as of a river. **6.** the highest point or level; climax; culmination. **7.** a tuft or other natural growth on the top of the head of an animal, as the comb of a rooster. **8.** anything resembling or suggesting such a tuft. **9.** the ridge of the neck of a horse, dog, etc. **10.** the mane growing from this ridge. **11.** an ornament or heraldic device surmounting a helmet. **12.** a helmet. **13.** a ridge running from front to back along the top of a helmet; comb. **14.** *Heraldry.* a figure borne above the escutcheon in an achievement of arms, either on a helmet or by itself as a distinguishing device. See illus. under **coat of arms. 15.** *Anat.* a ridge, esp. on a bone. **16.** a ridge or other prominence on any part of the body of an animal. **17.** *Archit.* a cresting. **18.** *Mach.* (in a screw or other threaded object) the ridge or surface farthest from the body of the object and defined by the flanks of the thread. Cf. **root** (def. 14a). —*v.t.* **19.** to furnish with a crest. **20.** to serve as a crest for; crown or top. **21.** to reach the crest or summit of (a hill, mountain, etc.). —*v.i.* **22.** to form or rise to a crest, as a wave or river. **23.** to reach the crest or highest level: *Interest in the project has crested.* [1275–1325; ME *creste* < OF < L *crista*] —**crest′ed,** *adj.* —**crest′less,** *adj.*

crest′ cloud′, a stationary cloud parallel to and near the top of a mountain ridge. Cf. **cap cloud** (def. 1).

crest′ cor′onet, *Heraldry.* coronet (def. 6).

crest′ed auk′let. See under **auklet.**

crest′ed i′ris. See **dwarf crested iris.**

crest′ed liz′ard. See **desert iguana.**

crest′ed swift′. See **tree swift.**

crest′ed wheat′grass, a forage grass, *Agropyron cristatum,* native to Eurasia and grown in the Great Plains as pasturage, hay, and for erosion control.

crest·fall·en (krest′fô′lən), *adj.* **1.** dejected; dispirited; discouraged. **2.** having a drooping crest or head. [1580–90; CREST + FALLEN] —**crest′fall′en·ly,** *adv.* —**crest′fall′en·ness,** *n.*

crest·ing (kres′ting), *n.* **1.** *Archit.* a decorative coping, balustrade, etc., usually designed to give an interesting skyline. **2.** *Furniture.* ornamentation either carved or sawed in the top rail of a piece or else added to it. **3.** a system of ornamental ridges or flutes on a piece of plate armor. [1865–70; CREST + -ING[1]]

crest′ rail′, the carved or profiled top rail of a chair, settee, or sofa.

Crest·wood (krest′wŏŏd′), *n.* **1.** a city in E Missouri. 12,815. **2.** a town in NE Illinois. 10,712.

cres·yl (kres′il, krē′sil), *adj. Chem.* tolyl. Also, **cre·syl·ic** (kri sil′ik). [1860–65; CRES(OL) + -YL]

cre·ta·ceous (kri tā′shəs), *adj.* **1.** resembling or containing chalk. **2.** (*cap.*) *Geol.* noting or pertaining to a period of the Mesozoic Era, from 140 million to 65 million years ago, characterized by the greatest development and subsequent extinction of dinosaurs and the advent of flowering plants and modern insects. See table under **geologic time.** —*n.* **3.** (*cap.*) *Geol.* the Cretaceous Period or System. [1665–70; < L *crētāceus,* equiv. to *crēt(a)* chalk, clay (cf. CRAYON) + *-āceus* -ACEOUS; the geological period was defined from the chalk beds of SE England and associated formations] —**cre·ta′ceous·ly,** *adv.*

Cre·tan (krēt′n), *adj.* **1.** of or pertaining to the island of Crete or its inhabitants. —*n.* **2.** a native or inhabitant of Crete. [< L *Crētānus.* See CRETE, -AN]

Cre′tan bull′, *Gk. Legend.* a savage bull, captured on Crete by Hercules and allowed to roam near Marathon in Greece until captured by Theseus. Also called **Marathonian bull.** [1930–35]

Crete (krēt), *n.* Also called **Candia.** a Greek island in the Mediterranean, SE of mainland Greece. 456,642; 3235 sq. mi. (8380 sq. km). *Cap.:* Canea.

cre·tin (krēt′n *or, esp. Brit.,* kret′n), *n.* **1.** a person suffering from cretinism. **2.** a stupid, obtuse, or mentally defective person. [1770–80; < F; Franco-Provençal *creitin, crestin* human being, lit., CHRISTIAN (hence one who is human despite deformities)] —**cre′ti·noid′,** *adj.* —**cre′tin·ous,** *adj.*

cre·tin·ism (krēt′n iz′əm *or, esp. Brit.,* kret′-), *n. Pathol.* a congenital disease due to absence or deficiency of normal thyroid secretion, characterized by physical deformity, dwarfism, and mental retardation, and often by goiter. [1795–1805; < F *crétinisme.* See CRETIN, -ISM]

cre·tin·ize (krēt′n īz′ *or, esp. Brit.,* kret′-), *v.t., v.i.,* **-ized, -iz·ing.** to make or become cretinous; cause (a person) to be incapable of normal intelligence or sound judgment. Also, *esp. Brit.,* **cre′tin·ise′.** [1855–60; CRETIN + -IZE]

cre·tonne (kri ton′, krē′ton), *n.* a heavy cotton material in colorfully printed designs, used esp. for drapery and slipcovers. [1865–70; < F, after *Creton,* Norman village where it was produced]

Cre·ü·sa (krē ōō′sə), *n. Class. Myth.* **1.** the bride to be of Jason, slain by Medea. **2.** a daughter of Priam and the wife of Aeneas who disappeared in the flight from Troy.

Creuse (krœz), *n.* a department in central France. 146,214; 2165 sq. mi. (5605 sq. km). *Cap.:* Guéret.

Creutz′feldt-Ja′kob disease′ (kroits′felt yä′kôp), *Pathol.* a rare, usually fatal brain disorder caused by an unidentified pathogen and characterized by progressive dementia, blindness, and involuntary movements. Also, **Creutz′feldt-Ja′cob disease′.** Also called **Jakob-Creutzfeldt disease.** [1965–70; after German physicians Hans G. *Creutzfeldt* (1885–1964) and Alfons *Jakob* (1884–1931)]

cre·val·le (krə val′ē, -val′ə), *n., pl.* (*esp. collectively*) **-le,** (*esp. referring to two or more kinds or species*) **-les.** any of several marine fishes of the jack family, Carangidae. [1895–1900, *Amer.;* obscurely akin to CAVALLA]

creval′le jack′. See under **jack**[1] (def. 6). Also called **jack crevalle.**

cre·vasse (krə vas′), *n., v.,* **-vassed, -vas·sing.** —*n.* **1.** a fissure, or deep cleft, in glacial ice, the earth's surface, etc. **2.** a breach in an embankment or levee. —*v.t.* **3.** to fissure with crevasses. [1805–15, *Amer.;* < F; see CREVICE]

Creve Coeur (krēv′ kŏŏr′), a town in E Missouri. 12,694.

Crève·coeur (krev kœr′), *n.* **Mi·chel Guil·laume Jean de** (mē shel′ gē yōm′ zhäN də), ("*J. Hector St. John*"), 1735–1813, French writer, statesman, and agriculturalist, in the U.S. after 1754.

crev·ice (krev′is), *n.* a crack forming an opening; cleft; rift; fissure. [1300–50; ME *crevace* < AF, OF, equiv. to *crev(er)* to crack (< L *crepāre*) + *-ace* n. suffix] —**crev′iced,** *adj.*

crew[1] (krōō), *n.* **1.** a group of persons involved in a particular kind of work or working together: *the crew of a train; a wrecking crew.* **2.** *Naut.* **a.** the people who sail or operate a ship or boat. **b.** the common sailors of a ship's company. **c.** a particular gang of a ship's company. **3.** the people who fly or operate an aircraft or spacecraft. **4.** the team that rows a racing shell: *varsity crew.* **5.** the sport of racing with racing shells: *He went out for crew in his freshman year.* **6.** a company; crowd: *He and his crew of friends filled the room.* **7.** any force or band of armed men. —*v.t.* **8.** to serve as a member of a crew on (a ship, aircraft, etc.). **9.** to obtain or employ a crew for (a ship, aircraft, etc.). —*v.i.* **10.** to serve as a member of a crew. [1425–75; late ME *crewe* augmentation, hence reinforcements, body of soldiers < MF *creue,* lit., increase, n. use of fem. of OF *creu,* ptp. of *creistre* to grow < L *crēscere;* see CRESCENT] —**crew′less,** *adj.* —**Usage.** See **collective noun.**

crew[2] (krōō), *v.* a pt. of **crow**[2].

crew′ cut′, a haircut in which the hair is very closely cropped. [1940–45, *Amer.*] —**crew′-cut′, crew′cut′,** *adj.*

crew·el (krōō′əl), *n.* **1.** Also called **crew′el yarn′.** a worsted yarn for embroidery and edging. **2.** crewelwork. [1485–95; earlier *crule;* orig. uncert.] —**crew′el·ist, crew′el·er,** *n.*

crew·el·work (krōō′əl wûrk′), *n.* decorative embroidery done with crewel yarn on cotton or linen, using simple stitches traditionally worked in floral or pastoral designs. [1860–65; CREWEL + WORK]

crew·man (krōō′mən), *n., pl.* **-men.** a member of a crew. [1935–40; CREW[1] + -MAN] —**crew′man·ship′,** *n.*

crew′ neck′, **1.** a collarless neckline, as on a sweater or jersey, that fits snugly at the base of the neck. **2.** a sweater, jersey, or other garment having such a neckline. [1935–40, *Amer.*] —**crew′-neck′, crew′-necked′,** *adj.*

crew′ socks′, short, thick casual socks usually ribbed above the ankles. [1945–50]

CRF, corticotropin releasing factor.

crib (krib), *n., v.,* **cribbed, crib·bing.** —*n.* **1.** a child's bed with enclosed sides. **2.** a stall or pen for cattle. **3.** a rack or manger for fodder, as in a stable or barn. **4.** a bin for storing grain, salt, etc. **5.** *Informal.* **a.** a translation, list of correct answers, or other illicit aid used by students while reciting, taking exams, or the like; pony. **b.** plagiarism. **c.** a petty theft. **6.** a room, closet, etc., in a factory or the like, in which tools are kept and issued to workers. **7.** a shallow, separate section of a bathing area, reserved for small children. **8.** any confined space. **9.** *Slang.* a house, shop, etc., frequented by thieves or regarded by thieves as a likely place for burglarizing. **10.** *Building Trades, Civil Engin.* any of various cellular frameworks of logs, squared timbers, or steel or concrete objects of similar form assembled in layers at right angles, often filled with earth and stones and used in the construction of foundations, dams, retaining walls, etc. **11.** a barrier projecting part of the way into a river and then upward, acting to reduce the flow of water and as a storage place for logs being floated downstream. **12.** a lining for a well or other shaft. **13.** *Slang.* one's home; pad. **14.** *Cribbage.* a set of cards made up by equal contributions from each player's hand, and belonging to the dealer. **15.** a cheap, ill-kept brothel. **16.** a wicker basket. **17.** *Brit., Australian.* lunch, esp. a cold lunch carried from home to work and eaten by a laborer on the job; snack. —*v.t.* **18.** *Informal.* to pilfer or steal, esp. to plagiarize (another's writings or ideas). **19.** to confine in or as if in a crib. **20.** to provide with a crib or cribs. **21.** to line with timber or planking. —*v.i.* **22.** *Informal.* **a.** to use a crib in examinations, homework, translating, etc. **b.** to steal; plagiarize. **23.** (of a horse) to practice cribbing. [bef. 1000; ME *cribbe,* OE *crib(b);* c. D *krib,* G *Krippe;* cf. CRÈCHE]

crib·bage (krib′ij), *n.* a card game for two or sometimes three or four players, a characteristic feature of which is the crib, and in which the object is to make counting combinations for points that are scored on a cribbage board. [1620–30; CRIB + -AGE]

crib′bage board′, a board for keeping score in cribbage, having holes into which pegs are placed to mark the score and progress of the players. [1775–85]

cribbage board

crib·ber (krib′ər), *n.* **1.** a person who cribs. **2.** a horse that practices cribbing. [1695–1705; CRIB + -ER[1]]

crib·bing (krib′ing), *n.* **1.** *Vet. Med.* Also called **crib-biting, wind-sucking.** an injurious habit in which a horse bites its manger and as a result swallows air. **2.** *Mining.* **a.** a timber lining, closely spaced, as in a shaft or raise. **b.** pieces of timber for lining a shaft, raise, etc. **3.** *Building Trades, Civil Engin.* a system of cribs, as for retaining earth or for a building or the like being moved or having its foundations rebuilt. [1635–45; CRIB + -ING[1]]

crib-bite (krib′bit′), *v.i.,* **-bit, -bit·ten** or **-bit, -bit·ing.** *Vet. Med.* to practice cribbing. [1835–45; back formation from *crib-biting, crib-biter;* see CRIBBING] —**crib′-bit′er,** *n.*

crib′ death′. See **sudden infant death syndrome.** [1965–70]

crib·note (krib′nōt′), *n.* crib (def. 5a). [CRIB + NOTE]

crib·ri·form (krib′rə fôrm′), *adj.* sievelike. Also, **crib·rous** (krib′rəs). [1735–45; < L *cribr(um)* a sieve + -I- + -FORM]

crib·work (krib′wûrk′), *n. Building Trades, Civil Engin.* a system of cribs; cribbing. [CRIB + WORK]

cri·ce·tid (krī sē′tid, -set′id, kri-), *n. Zool.* any of a diverse group of scampering, digging, or jumping rodents of the family Cricetidae, including the gerbils, hamsters, field mice, deer mice, voles, lemmings, muskrats, and several wood and field rats. [1955–60; < NL *Cricetidae,* equiv. to *Cricet(us)* a genus, including the common hamster (ML: hamster, perh. < Czech *křeček*) + *-idae* -ID[2]]

Crich·ton (krīt′n), *n.* **James** ("*the Admirable Crichton*"), 1560?–82, Scottish scholar and linguist.

crick[1] (krik), *n.* **1.** a sharp, painful spasm of the muscles, as of the neck or back. —*v.t.* **2.** to give a crick or wrench to (the neck, back, etc.). [1400–50; late ME *crikke,* perh. akin to CRICK[2]]

crick[2] (krik), *n. Northern, North Midland, and Western U.S.* creek (def. 1).

Crick (krik), *n.* **Francis Harry Compton,** born 1916, English biophysicist: Nobel prize for medicine 1962.

crick·et[1] (krik′it), *n.* **1.** any of several jumping, orthopterous insects of the family Gryllidae, characterized by long antennae and stridulating organs on the forewings of the male, as one of the species commonly found in pastures and meadows **(field cricket)** or on trees and shrubs **(tree cricket)**. **2.** a small metal toy with a flat metal spring that snaps back and forth with a clicking, cricketlike noise when pressed. [1275–1325; ME *criket* insect < OF *criquet,* equiv. to *criqu(er)* to creak (imit.) + *-et* -ET] **—crick′et·like′,** *adj.*

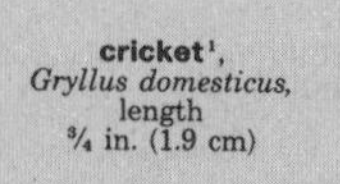
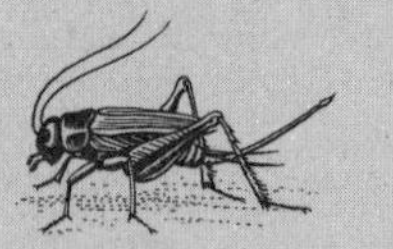
cricket[1], *Gryllus domesticus,* length ¾ in. (1.9 cm)

crick·et[2] (krik′it), *n.* **1.** a game, popular esp. in England, for two teams of 11 members each that is played on a field having two wickets 22 yards (20 m) apart, the object being to score runs by batting the ball far enough so that one is enabled to exchange wickets with the batsman defending the opposite wicket before the ball is recovered. **2.** fair play; honorable conduct: *It wouldn't be cricket to look at his cards.* **—***v.i.* **3.** to play cricket. [1590–1600; < MF *criquet* goal post, perh. < early D *krick(e)* arm, crosspiece, gallows] **—crick′et·er,** *n.*

crick·et[3] (krik′it), *n.* a small, low stool. [1635–45; of. obscure orig.; cf. *cracket,* with same sense]

crick·et[4] (krik′it), *n.* (on a sloping roof) a small roof for diverting rain water around an obstruction, as a chimney. [of uncert. orig.]

crick′et frog′, either of two tree frogs, *Acris gryllus* or *A. crepitans,* of eastern and central U.S., having a clicking call. [1790–1800]

crick′et ta′ble, a three-legged table of the Jacobean period.

cri·coid (krī′koid), *Anat.* **—***adj.* **1.** pertaining to a ring-shaped cartilage at the lower part of the larynx. **—***n.* **2.** the cricoid cartilage. See diag. under **larynx.** [1700–10; < NL *cricoīdes* < Gk *krikoeidēs* ring-shaped. See CIRCLE, -OID]

cri·co·pha·ryn·ge·al (krī′kō fə rin′jē əl, -jəl, -far′in jē′əl), *adj. Anat.* of, pertaining to, or involving the cricoid cartilage and the pharynx. [*crico-* (see CRICOID) + PHARYNGEAL]

cri de coeur (krēdᵊ kœr′; *Eng.* krē′ də kûr′), *pl.* ***cris de coeur*** (krēdᵊ kœr′; *Eng.* krēz′ də kûr′). *French.* an anguished cry of distress or indignation; outcry. [1900–05; lit., cry of (the) heart]

cri′ du chat′ (krē′ do͞o shä′, dyo͞o). See **cat's cry syndrome.** [< F: lit., cry of the cat]

cried (krīd), *v.* pt. and pp. of **cry.**

cri·er (krī′ər), *n.* **1.** a person who cries. **2.** a court or town official who makes public announcements. **3.** a hawker. [1250–1300; ME *criere* < OF. See CRY, -ER[1]]

cri·key (krī′kē), *interj.* (used as an exclamation of surprise, amazement, dismay, etc.) [1830–40; prob. euphemistic alter. of CHRIST]

Crile (krīl), *n.* **George Washington,** 1864–1943, U.S. surgeon.

crim., criminal.

crim. con., *Civil Law.* See **criminal conversation.**

crime (krīm), *n.* **1.** an action or an instance of negligence that is deemed injurious to the public welfare or morals or to the interests of the state and that is legally prohibited. **2.** criminal activity and those engaged in it: *to fight crime.* **3.** the habitual or frequent commission of crimes: *a life of crime.* **4.** any offense, serious wrongdoing, or sin. **5.** a foolish, senseless, or shameful act: *It's a crime to let that beautiful garden go to ruin.* [1200–50; ME < AF, OF < L *crīmin-* (s. of *crīmen*) charge, crime] **—crime′less,** *adj.* **—crime′less·ness,** *n.*
—Syn. 1. wrong; misdemeanor, tort, felony. **1, 4.** CRIME, OFFENSE, SIN agree in meaning a breaking of law. CRIME usually means any serious violation of human laws: *the crime of treason or robbery.* OFFENSE is used of an infraction of either human or divine law, and does not necessarily mean a serious one: *an offense leading to a jail sentence; an offense against morals.* SIN means a breaking of moral or divine law: *the sins of greed and lust.*

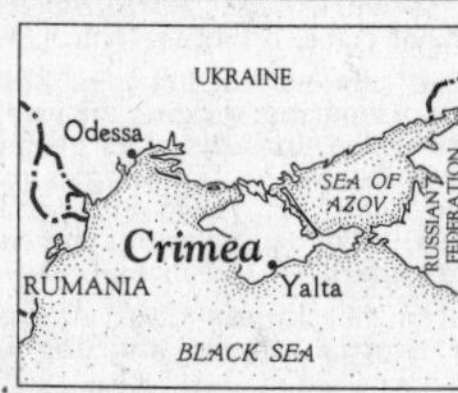

Cri·me·a (krī mē′ə, kri-), *n.* **the, 1.** a peninsula in SE Ukraine between the Black Sea and the Sea of Azov. **2.** a former autonomous republic of the Soviet Union, now a region of Ukraine. ab. 10,000 sq. mi. (25,900 sq. km). Russian, **Krim, Krym. —Cri·me′an,** *adj.*

crime′ against′ human′ity, a crime or series of crimes, such as genocide, directed against a large group because of race, religion, country of origin, or other reason unconnected with any individual's responsibility for having committed a criminal act. [1940–45]

crime′ against′ na′ture, 1. *Law.* sodomy. **2.** any act considered to be against the laws or designs of nature or one's religious teachings. [1920–25]

Crime′an Astrophys′ical Observ′atory, an astronomical observatory near Simferopol, in S Ukraine, having a 102.4-in. (2.6-m) reflecting telescope.

Crime′ and Pun′ishment, a novel (1866) by Feodor Dostoevsky.

Crime′an Goth′ic, a form of the Gothic language that survived in the Crimea after the extinction of Gothic elsewhere in Europe, known only from a list of words and phrases recorded in the 16th century.

Crime′an Ta′tar, 1. a member of a Turkic people who lived in the Crimea before emigration to Anatolia in the 18th and 19th centuries and deportations to Soviet central Asia after World War II. **2.** the Turkic language of the Crimean Tatars. Also, **Crime′an Tar′tar.**

Crime′an War′, a war between Great Britain, France, Turkey, and Sardinia on one side, and Russia on the other, fought chiefly in the Crimea 1853–56.

crime-fight·er (krīm′fī′tər), *n.* any person, as a law-enforcement officer or government official, who works to prevent crime or to enforce criminal laws.

crim·i·nal (krim′ə nl), *adj.* **1.** of the nature of or involving crime. **2.** guilty of crime. **3.** *Law.* of or pertaining to crime or its punishment: *a criminal proceeding.* **4.** senseless; foolish: *It's criminal to waste so much good food.* **5.** exorbitant; grossly overpriced: *They charge absolutely criminal prices.* **—***n.* **6.** a person guilty or convicted of a crime. [1350–1400; ME < AF < LL *crīminālis,* equiv. to L *crīmin-* (s. of *crīmen;* see CRIME) + *-ālis* -AL[1]] **—crim′i·nal·ly,** *adv.*
—Syn. 1. felonious, unlawful. See **illegal. 6.** malefactor, evildoer, transgressor, culprit, felon, crook, hoodlum, gangster. **—Ant. 1.** lawful. **2.** innocent.

crim′inal assault′, *Law.* **1.** an attack by physical force on a person for which the attacker is liable to criminal prosecution. **2.** a similar act with intent to commit rape.

crim′inal code′, *Law.* **1.** the aggregate of statutory enactments pertaining to criminal offenses. **2.** a systematic and integrated statement of the laws and principles pertaining to criminal offenses. [1780–90]

crim′inal contempt′, *Law.* any seriously disrespectful act committed against the dignity or authority of a court.

crim′inal conversa′tion, *Civil Law.* adultery. *Abbr.:* crim. con. [1760–70]

crim′inal court′, a court of law in which criminal cases are tried and determined. [1590–1600]

crim·i·nal·ist (krim′ə nl ist), *n.* **1.** an expert in criminalistics. **2.** a person who studies or practices criminology; criminologist. **3.** an expert in criminal law. [1625–35; CRIMINAL + -IST]

crim·i·nal·is·tics (krim′ə nl is′tiks), *n.* (*used with a singular v.*) **1.** the scientific study and evaluation of physical evidence in the commission of crimes. **2.** the science dealing with the detection of crime and the apprehension of criminals. [1945–50; CRIMINALIST + -ICS]

crim·i·nal·i·ty (krim′ə nal′i tē), *n., pl.* **-ties** for 2. **1.** the state of being criminal. **2.** a criminal act or practice. [1605–15; < ML *crīminālitās.* See CRIMINAL, -ITY]

crim·i·nal·ize (krim′ə nl īz′), *v.t.,* **-ized, -iz·ing. 1.** to make punishable as a crime: *To reduce the graffiti on subway cars, he wants to criminalize the selling of spray paint to minors.* **2.** to make a criminal of: *Drug use has criminalized him.* Also, *esp. Brit.,* **crim′i·nal·ise′.** [1955–60; CRIMINAL + -IZE] **—crim′i·nal·i·za′tion,** *n.*

crim′inal law′, the laws of a state or country dealing with criminal offenses and their punishments. [1580–90]

crim′inal law′yer, a person who specializes in the practice of criminal law. [1885–90]

crim′inal syn′dicalism, *Law.* the doctrine of recourse to acts of violence or terrorism, or the advocacy of such acts, as a means of effecting economic or political change: proscribed by statute in many U.S. states.

crim·i·nate (krim′ə nāt′), *v.t.,* **-nat·ed, -nat·ing. 1.** to charge with a crime. **2.** to incriminate. **3.** to censure (something) as criminal; condemn. [1635–45; < L *crīminātus* ptp. of *crīmināri* to accuse. See CRIME, -ATE[1]] **—crim′i·na′tion,** *n.* **—crim′i·na′tor,** *n.*

crim·i·na·tive (krim′ə nā′tiv, -nə tiv), *adj.* involving crimination; accusatory. Also, **crim·i·na·to·ry** (krim′ə nə tôr′ē, -tōr′ē). [1725–35; CRIMINATE + -IVE]

crim·i·no·gen·ic (krim′ə nə jen′ik), *adj.* producing or tending to produce crime or criminals: *a criminogenic environment.* Also, **crim·o·gen·ic** (krī′mə jen′ik). [CRIMIN(AL) + -O- + -GENIC]

criminol., 1. criminologist. **2.** criminology.

crim·i·nol·o·gy (krim′ə nol′ə jē), *n.* the study of crime and criminals: a branch of sociology. [1855–60; < L *crīmin-* (s. of *crīmen;* see CRIME) + -O- + -LOGY] **—crim·i·no·log·i·cal** (krim′ə nl oj′i kəl), **crim′i·no·log′ic,** *adj.* **—crim′i·no·log′i·cal·ly,** *adv.* **—crim′i·nol′o·gist,** *n.*

crim·i·nous (krim′ə nəs), *adj. Archaic.* criminal. [1425–75; late ME < OF *crimineux* < ML, L *crīminōsus,* equiv. to *crīmin-* (s. of *crīmen;* see CRIME) + *-ōsus* -OUS]

crim·mer (krim′ər), *n.* krimmer.

crimp[1] (krimp), *v.t.* **1.** to press into small regular folds; make wavy. **2.** to curl (hair), esp. with the use of a curling iron. **3.** to press or draw together, as the ends of something. **4.** to check, restrain, or inhibit; hinder: *Production was crimped by a shortage of workers.* **5.** *Cookery.* **a.** to pinch and press down the edges of (a pie crust), esp. to seal together the top and bottom layers of pastry. **b.** to gash (the flesh of a live fish or of one just killed) with a knife to make more crisp when cooked. **6.** to produce a corrugated surface in; corrugate, as sheet metal, cardboard, etc. **7.** to bend (leather) into shape. **8.** *Metalworking.* **a.** to bend the edges of (skelp) before forming into a tube. **b.** to fold the edges of (sheet metal) to make a lock seam. **—***n.* **9.** the act of crimping. **10.** a crimped condition or form. **11.** Usually, **crimps.** waves or curls, esp. in hair that has been crimped or that displays a crimped pattern. **12.** the waviness of wool fibers as naturally grown on sheep. **13.** the waviness imparted to natural or synthetic fibers by weaving, knitting, plaiting, or other processes. **14.** a crease formed in sheet metal or plate metal to make the material less flexible or for fastening purposes. **15. put a crimp in,** to interfere with; hinder: *His broken leg put a crimp in their vacation plans.* [1350–1400; ME *crympen,* OE *gecrympan* to curl, deriv. of *crump* crooked] **—crimp′er,** *n.*

crimp[2] (krimp), *n.* **1.** a person engaged in enlisting sailors, soldiers, etc., by persuasion, swindling, or coercion. **—***v.t.* **2.** to enlist (sailors, soldiers, etc.) by such means. [1630–40; special use of CRIMP[1]]

crim·ple (krim′pəl), *v.t., v.i.,* **-pled, -pling.** to wrinkle. [1400–50; late ME. See CRIMP[1], -LE]

crimp·y (krim′pē), *adj.,* **crimp·i·er, crimp·i·est. 1.** having a crimped form or appearance. **2.** *South Midland U.S.* (of weather) cold and disagreeable. [1885–90; CRIMP[1] + -Y[1]]

crim·son (krim′zən, -sən), *adj.* **1.** deep purplish-red. **2.** sanguinary. **—***n.* **3.** a crimson color, pigment, or dye. **—***v.t., v.i.* **4.** to make or become crimson. [1375–1425; late ME < ML *cremesinus* << Ar *qirmizī* (*qirmiz* KERMES + *-ī* suffix of appurtenance) + L *-inus* -INE[1]; see CRAMOISY] **—crim′son·ly,** *adv.* **—crim′son·ness,** *n.*

crim′son clo′ver, a European clover, *Trifolium incarnatum,* of the legume family, having heads of crimson flowers, cultivated as a forage plant in the U.S. Also called **Italian clover.**

crim′son flag′, a southern African plant, *Schizostylis coccinea,* of the iris family, having tubular red flowers. Also called **Kaffir lily.**

crine (krīn), *n.* hair; head of hair. [1605–15; < L *crīnis* hair] **—cri′nal,** *adj.*

cringe (krinj), *v.,* **cringed, cring·ing,** *n.* **—***v.i.* **1.** to shrink, bend, or crouch, esp. in fear or servility; cower. **2.** to fawn. **—***n.* **3.** servile or fawning deference. [1175–1225; ME *crengen, crenchen* (transit.); OE **crencean, crencgean,* causative of *cringan, crincan* to yield, fall (in battle)] **—cring′er,** *n.* **—cring′ing·ly,** *adv.* **—cring′ing·ness,** *n.*

crin·gle (kring′gəl), *n. Naut.* **1.** an eye or grommet formed on the boltrope of a sail to permit the attachment of lines. [1620–30; < LG *kringel,* equiv. to *kring* circle + *-el* dim. suffix; c. ME *Cringle* (in place-names), ON *kringla* circle]

cri·nite[1] (krī′nīt), *adj.* **1.** hairy. **2.** *Bot., Entomol.* having long hairs, or tufts of long, fine or limp hairs. [1590–1600; < L *crinītus,* equiv. to *crīn(is)* hair + *-ītus* -ITE[2]]

cri·nite[2] (krī′nīt, krin′īt), *n.* a fossil crinoid. [< Gk *krín(on)* lily + -ITE[1]]

crin·kle (kring′kəl), *v.,* **-kled, -kling,** *n.* **—***v.t., v.i.* **1.** to wrinkle; crimple; ripple. **2.** to make slight, sharp sounds; rustle. **3.** to turn or wind in many little bends and twists. **—***n.* **4.** a wrinkle or ripple. **5.** a crinkling sound. **6.** a turn or twist. [1350–1400; ME *crinklen;* akin to OE *crincan* to bend, yield, D *krinkelen* to crinkle; see CRINGLE, CRINGE, CRANK, -LE]

crin′kle leaf′, *Plant Pathol.* a disease of plants, characterized by puckering, mottling, and distortion of the leaves, caused by any of several viruses.

crin·kly (kring′klē), *adj.,* **-kli·er, -kli·est. 1.** having crinkles. **2.** making a rustling noise. [1820–30; CRINKLE + -Y[1]]

cri·no·gen·ic (krī′nə jen′ik, krin′ə-), *adj.* stimulating secretion. [< Gk *krín(ein)* to separate + -O- + -GENIC]

cri·noid (krī′noid, krin′oid), *n.* **1.** any echinoderm of the class Crinoidea, having a cup-shaped body to which are attached branched, radiating arms, comprising the sea lilies, feather stars, and various fossil forms. **—***adj.* **2.** belonging or pertaining to the Crinoidea. **3.** lilylike. [1825–35; < Gk *krinoeidḗs, equiv. to krín(on)* lily + *-oeidēs* -OID] **—cri·noi′dal,** *adj.*

crinoid (def. 1) (sea lily)

crin·o·line (krin′l in), *n.* **1.** a petticoat of haircloth or other stiff material, worn under a full skirt to keep it belled out. **2.** a stiff, coarse cotton material for interlining. **3.** a hoop skirt. **4.** a reinforcement of iron straps for holding together brickwork, as of a furnace or chimney. [1820–30; < F < It *crinolino,* equiv. to *crino* horsehair (<< L *crīnis* hair) + *lino* flax < L *līnum;* cf. LINEN]

crin′oline stretch′er, (on a Windsor chair) a stretcher having an inwardly curved piece connecting the front legs, and connected to the back legs by short, straight pieces.

cri·nose (krī′nōs, krin′ōs), *adj.* hairy. [< L *crīn(is)* hair + -OSE[1]] **—cri·nos·i·ty** (krī nos′i tē, kri-), *n.*

cri·num (krī′nəm), *n.* any of the tropical and subtropical bulbous plants constituting the genus *Crinum,* of the amaryllis family, usually having umbels of large, showy flowers. [< NL < Gk *krínon* lily]

CONCISE ETYMOLOGY KEY: <, descended or borrowed from; >, whence; b., blend of, blended; c., cognate with; cf., compare; deriv., derivative; equiv., equivalent; imit., imitative; obl., oblique; r., replacing; s., stem; sp., spelling, spelled; resp., respelling, respelled; trans., translation; ?, origin unknown; *, unattested; ‡, probably earlier than. See the full key inside the front cover.

cri•ol•la (krē ō′lə; *Sp.* krē ô′yä), *n., pl.* **-ol•las** (-ō′ləz; *Sp.* -ô′yäs). a woman or girl born in Spanish America but of European, usually Spanish, ancestry. [< Sp; fem. of CRIOLLO]

cri•ol•lo (krē ō′lō; *Sp.* krē ô′yô), *n., pl.* **-ol•los** (-ō′lōz; *Sp.* -ô′yôs), *adj.* —*n.* **1.** a person born in Spanish America but of European, usually Spanish, ancestry. Cf. **Creole** (def. 1). **2.** a domestic animal of any of several strains or breeds developed in Latin America. —*adj.* **3.** of, pertaining to, or characteristic of a criollo or criollos. [1905–10; < Sp; see CREOLE]

crip (krip), *n. Slang* (*offensive*). a cripple. [1915–20, *Amer.*; by shortening]

cripes (krīps), *interj.* (used as a mild oath or an exclamation of astonishment.) [1905–10; appar. euphemistic alter. of CHRIST]

crip•ple (krip′əl), *n., v.,* **-pled, -pling,** *adj.* —*n.* **1.** *Sometimes Offensive.* **a.** a person or animal that is partially or totally unable to use one or more limbs; a lame or disabled person or animal. **b.** a person who is disabled or impaired in any way: *a mental cripple.* **2.** anything that is impaired or flawed. **3.** a wounded animal, esp. one shot by a hunter. **4.** *Carpentry.* any structural member shorter than usual, as a stud beneath a window sill. **5.** *Delaware Valley.* a swampy, densely overgrown tract of land. —*v.t.* **6.** to make a cripple of; lame. **7.** to disable; impair; weaken. —*adj.* **8.** *Carpentry.* jack[1] (def. 29). [bef. 950; ME *cripel,* OE *crypel;* akin to CREEP] —**crip′pler,** *n.* —**crip′pling•ly,** *adv.*
—**Syn. 7.** maim. CRIPPLE, DISABLE mean to injure to a degree that interferes with normal activities. To CRIPPLE is to injure in such a way as to deprive of the use of a member, particularly a leg. DISABLE, a more general word, implies any such illness, injury, or impairment: *disabled by an attack of malaria; disabled by a wound.*

Crip′ple Creek′, a town in central Colorado: gold rush 1891. 655; 9600 ft. (2925 m) above sea level.

Cripps (krips), *n.* **Sir Stafford,** 1889–1952, British statesman and socialist leader.

crise (krēz), *n., pl.* ***crises*** (krēz). *French.* crisis.

cri•sis (krī′sis), *n., pl.* **-ses** (-sēz), *adj.* —*n.* **1.** a stage in a sequence of events at which the trend of all future events, esp. for better or for worse, is determined; turning point. **2.** a condition of instability or danger, as in social, economic, political, or international affairs, leading to a decisive change. **3.** a dramatic emotional or circumstantial upheaval in a person's life. **4.** *Med.* **a.** the point in the course of a serious disease at which a decisive change occurs, leading either to recovery or to death. **b.** the change itself. **5.** the point in a play or story at which hostile elements are most tensely opposed to each other. —*adj.* **6.** of, referring to, or for use in dealing with a crisis. [1375–1425; late ME < L < Gk *krísis* decision, equiv. to *kri-* var. s. of *krínein* to decide, separate, judge + *-sis* -SIS] —**cri′sic,** *adj.*
—**Syn. 1.** See **emergency.**

cri′sis cen′ter, 1. a central facility, telephone answering service, etc., where people may obtain informed help or advice in a personal crisis. **2.** an office, building, agency, etc., serving as a central point for receiving information and coordinating action during a disaster or emergency. [1970–75]

cri′sis man′agement, the techniques used, as by an employer or government, to avert or deal with strikes, riots, violence, or other crisis situations. [1960–65] —**cri′sis man′ager.**

cri′sis theol′ogy, a neoorthodox theology, advocated by Karl Barth and others, emphasizing the absolute necessity of faith and divine revelation in transcending the personal crisis, common to all humankind, that arises from the contradictions inherent in human nature and in the social order. Also called **theology of crisis.** —**cri′sis theolo′gian.**

crisp (krisp), *adj.,* **-er, -est,** *v., n.* —*adj.* **1.** (esp. of food) hard but easily breakable; brittle: *crisp toast.* **2.** (esp. of food) firm and fresh; not soft or wilted: *a crisp leaf of lettuce.* **3.** brisk; sharp; clear; decided: *a crisp reply.* **4.** lively; pithy; sparkling: *crisp repartee.* **5.** clean-cut, neat, and well-pressed; well-groomed. **6.** bracing; invigorating: *crisp air.* **7.** crinkled, wrinkled, or rippled, as skin or water. **8.** in small, stiff, or firm curls; curly. —*v.t., v.i.* **9.** to make or become crisp. **10.** to curl. —*n.* **11.** *Chiefly Brit.* See **potato chip. 12.** a dessert of fruit, as apples or apricots, baked with a crunchy mixture, usually of bread crumbs, chopped nutmeats, butter, and brown sugar. [bef. 900; ME, OE < L *crispus* curled] —**crisp′ly,** *adv.* —**crisp′ness,** *n.*
—**Syn. 6.** brisk, fresh, nippy.

crisp•en (kris′pən), *v.t., v.i.* to make or become crisp. [1940–45; CRISP + -EN[1]]

crisp•er (kris′pər), *n.* **1.** a person or thing that crisps, corrugates, or curls. **2.** a drawer or compartment in a refrigerator for keeping lettuce, celery, and other vegetables crisp. **3.** an ovenlike appliance for restoring the crispness of crackers, cookies, etc., by dry heating. [1825–35; CRISP + -ER[1]]

Cri•spi (krē′spē), *n.* **Fran•ce•sco** (frän che′skô), 1819–1910, prime minister of Italy 1887–91, 1893–96.

Cris•pin (kris′pin), *n.* **1. Saint,** with his brother **(Saint Crispinian)** martyred A.D. c285, Roman Christian missionaries in Gaul: patron saints of shoemakers. **2.** (*l.c.*) a shoemaker.

Cris•pin•i•an (kri spin′ē ən), *n.* **Saint.** See under **Crispin, Saint.**

crisp•y (kris′pē), *adj.,* **crisp•i•er, crisp•i•est. 1.** (esp. of food) brittle; crisp. **2.** curly or wavy. **3.** brisk. [1350–1400; ME *crispi.* See CRISP, -Y[1]] —**crisp′i•ly,** *adv.* —**crisp′i•ness,** *n.*

cris•sal (kris′əl), *adj.* of or pertaining to the crissum. [1870–75; < NL *crissālis.* See CRISSUM, -AL[1]]

criss•cross (kris′krôs′, -kros′), *v.t.* **1.** to move back and forth over: *students crisscrossing the field on their way to school.* **2.** to mark with crossing lines. —*v.i.* **3.** to proceed or pass back and forth; be arranged in a crisscross pattern: *The streets in that part of town crisscross confusingly.* —*adj.* **4.** Also, **criss′crossed′.** having many crossing lines, paths, etc. —*n.* **5.** a crisscross mark, pattern, etc. **6.** tick-tack-toe. —*adv.* **7.** in a crisscross manner; crosswise. **8.** awry; askew. [1810–20; var. of CHRISTCROSS]

cris•sum (kris′əm), *n., pl.* **cris•sa** (kris′ə). *Ornith.* **1.** the region surrounding the cloacal opening beneath the tail of a bird. **2.** the feathers of this region collectively. [1870–75; < NL, equiv. to L *criss(āre)* to move the haunches + *-um* n. suffix]

cris•ta (kris′tə), *n., pl.* **-tae** (-tē). *Anat., Zool.* a crest or ridge. [1840–50; < L: a CREST, tuft, comb]

cris•tate (kris′tāt), *adj.* **1.** having a crest; crested. **2.** forming a crest. Also, **cris′tat•ed.** [1655–65; < L *cristātus,* equiv. to *crist(a)* CRISTA + *-ātus* -ATE[1]]

Cris•to•bal (kri stō′bəl), *n.* a seaport in Panama at the Atlantic end of the Panama Canal, adjacent to Colón. 11,600. Spanish, **Cris•tó•bal** (krēs tô′bäl).

cris•to•bal•ite (kri stō′bə līt′), *n. Mineral.* a polymorph of quartz occurring in volcanic rock in the form of colorless, translucent crystals. [1885–90; named after San *Cristóbal,* a hill near Pachuca de Soto, Mexico; see -ITE[1]]

Cris•tophe (krē stôf′), *n.* **Henri.** See **Christophe, Henri.**

crit (krit), *n. Informal.* **1.** a critic. **2.** criticism. **3.** a critique. [1735–45; by shortening]

crit., 1. critic. **2.** critical. **3.** criticism. **4.** criticized.

cri•te•ri•on (krī tēr′ē ən), *n., pl.* **-te•ri•a** (-tēr′ē ə), **-te•ri•ons.** a standard of judgment or criticism; a rule or principle for evaluating or testing something. [1605–15; < Gk *kritḗrion* a standard, equiv. to *kri-* var. s. of *krínein* to separate, decide + *-tērion* neut. suffix of means (akin to L *-tōrium* -TORY[2])] —**cri•te′ri•al,** *adj.*
—**Syn.** measure, touchstone, yardstick. See **standard.**
—**Usage.** Like some other nouns borrowed from the Greek, CRITERION has both a Greek plural, CRITERIA, and a plural formed on the English pattern, CRITERIONS. The plural in *-a* occurs with far greater frequency than does the *-s* plural: *These are the criteria for the selection of candidates.* Although CRITERIA is sometimes used as a singular, most often in speech and rather infrequently in edited prose, it continues strongly in use as a plural in standard English, with CRITERION as the singular.

crit•ic (krit′ik), *n.* **1.** a person who judges, evaluates, or criticizes: *a poor critic of men.* **2.** a person who judges, evaluates, or analyzes literary or artistic works, dramatic or musical performances, or the like, esp. for a newspaper or magazine. **3.** a person who tends too readily to make captious, trivial, or harsh judgments; faultfinder. **4.** *Archaic.* **a.** criticism. **b.** critique. [1575–85; < L *criticus* < Gk *kritikós* skilled in judging (adj.), critic (n.), equiv. to *krī́t(ēs)* judge, umpire (*krī́(nein)* to separate, decide + *-tēs* agent suffix) + *-ikos* -IC]
—**Syn. 2.** reviewer, judge. **3.** censurer, carper.

crit•i•cal (krit′i kəl), *adj.* **1.** inclined to find fault or to judge with severity, often too readily. **2.** occupied with or skilled in criticism. **3.** involving skillful judgment as to truth, merit, etc.; judicial: *a critical analysis.* **4.** of or pertaining to critics or criticism: *critical essays.* **5.** providing textual variants, proposed emendations, etc.: *a critical edition of Chaucer.* **6.** pertaining to or of the nature of a crisis: *a critical shortage of food.* **7.** of decisive importance with respect to the outcome; crucial: *a critical moment.* **8.** of essential importance; indispensable: *a critical ingredient.* **9.** *Med.* (of a patient's condition) having unstable and abnormal vital signs and other unfavorable indicators, as loss of appetite, poor mobility, or unconsciousness. **10.** *Physics.* **a.** pertaining to a state, value, or quantity at which one or more properties of a substance or system undergo a change. **b.** (of fissionable material) having enough mass to sustain a chain reaction. [1580–90; CRITIC + -AL[1]] —**crit′i•cal•ly,** *adv.* —**crit′i•cal′i•ty, crit′i•cal•ness,** *n.*
—**Syn. 1.** captious, censorious, carping, faultfinding, caviling. **3.** discriminating, exact, precise.

crit′ical an′gle, 1. *Optics.* the minimum angle of incidence beyond which total internal reflection occurs for light traveling from a medium of higher to one of lower index of refraction; the angle of incidence for which refracted rays emerge tangent to the surface separating two media, the light traveling from the medium of higher to the medium of lower index of refraction. **2.** Also called **angle of stall, crit′ical an′gle of attack′, stalling angle.** *Aeron.* the angle of attack, greater than or equal to the angle of attack for maximum lift, at which there is a sudden change in the airflow around an airfoil with a subsequent decrease in lift and increase in drag. [1870–75]

crit′ical con′stant, *Physics.* any of three constants associated with the critical point of a pure element or compound. Cf. **critical density, critical pressure, critical temperature.**

crit′ical den′sity, *Physics.* the density of a pure element or compound at a critical point. Cf. **critical constant.**

crit′ical mass′, 1. *Physics.* the amount of a given fissionable material necessary to sustain a chain reaction at a constant rate. **2.** an amount necessary or sufficient to have a significant effect or to achieve a result: *a critical mass of popular support.* [1940–45]

crit′ical point′, 1. *Physics.* the point at which a substance in one phase, as the liquid, has the same density, pressure, and temperature as in another phase, as the gaseous. **2.** *Math.* **a.** (of a function of a single variable) a point at which the derivative of the function is zero. **b.** (of a function of several variables) a point at which all partial derivatives of the function are zero. [1875–80]

crit′ical pres′sure, *Physics.* the pressure of a pure element or compound at a critical point. Cf. **critical constant.** [1875–80]

crit′ical ra′tio, *Statistics.* a ratio associated with the probability of a sample, usually the ratio of the deviation from the mean to the standard deviation.

crit′ical re′gion, *Statistics.* the rejection region for the null hypothesis in the testing of a hypothesis. [1950–55]

crit′ical state′, *Physics.* the state of a pure element or compound when it is at a critical point. [1895–1900]

crit′ical tem′perature, *Physics.* the temperature of a pure element or compound at a critical point. Cf. **critical constant.** [1865–70]

crit′ical val′ue, *Statistics.* the value of the random variable at the boundary between the acceptance region and the rejection region in the testing of a hypothesis. [1905–10]

crit′ical vol′ume, *Physics.* the volume occupied by a certain mass, usually one gram molecule of a liquid or gaseous substance at its critical point. [1875–80]

crit•ic•as•ter (krit′i kas′tər), *n.* an incompetent critic. [1675–85; CRITIC + -ASTER[1]]

crit•i•cism (krit′ə siz′əm), *n.* **1.** the act of passing judgment as to the merits of anything. **2.** the act of passing severe judgment; censure; faultfinding. **3.** the act or art of analyzing and evaluating or judging the quality of a literary or artistic work, musical performance, art exhibit, dramatic production, etc. **4.** a critical comment, article, or essay; critique. **5.** any of various methods of studying texts or documents for the purpose of dating or reconstructing them, evaluating their authenticity, analyzing their content or style, etc.: *historical criticism; literary criticism.* **6.** investigation of the text, origin, etc., of literary documents, esp. Biblical ones: *textual criticism.* [1600–10; CRITIC + -ISM]
—**Syn. 2.** stricture, animadversion. **4.** See **review.**

crit•i•cize (krit′ə sīz′), *v.,* **-cized, -ciz•ing.** —*v.t.* **1.** to censure or find fault with. **2.** to judge or discuss the merits and faults of: *to criticize three novels in one review.* —*v.i.* **3.** to find fault; judge unfavorably or harshly. **4.** to make judgments as to merits and faults. Also, *esp. Brit.,* **crit′i•cise′.** [1640–50; CRITIC + -IZE] —**crit′i•ciz′a•ble,** *adj.* —**crit′i•ciz′er,** *n.* —**crit′i•ciz′•ing•ly,** *adv.*
—**Syn. 1.** condemn, blame. **2.** appraise, evaluate.

cri•tique (kri tēk′), *n., v.,* **-tiqued, -ti•quing.** —*n.* **1.** an article or essay criticizing a literary or other work; detailed evaluation; review. **2.** a criticism or critical comment on some problem, subject, etc. **3.** the art or practice of criticism. —*v.t.* **4.** to review or analyze critically. [1695–1705; < F < Gk *kritikḗ* the art of criticism, n. use of fem. of *kritikós* critical, skilled in judging; r. CRITIC]

Critique′ of Pure′ Rea′son, a philosophical work (1781) by Immanuel Kant.

Crit′ten•den Com′promise (krit′n dən), *U.S. Hist.* a series of constitutional amendments proposed in Congress in 1860 to serve as a compromise between proslavery and antislavery factions, one of which would have permitted slavery in the territories south but not north of latitude 36°30′N. Also called **Crit′tenden Plan′.** [named after its proponent, John J. *Crittenden* (1787–1863), U.S. Senator from Kentucky]

crit•ter (krit′ər), *n. Dial.* **1.** a domesticated animal. **2.** any creature. Also, **crit′tur.** [var. of CREATURE]

Cri•us (krī′əs), *n. Class. Myth.* a Titan, the son of Uranus and Gaea.

croak (krōk), *v.i.* **1.** to utter a low-pitched, harsh cry, as the sound of a frog or a raven. **2.** to speak with a low, rasping voice. **3.** *Slang.* to die. **4.** to talk despondingly; prophesy trouble or evil; grumble. —*v.t.* **5.** to utter or announce by croaking. **6.** *Slang.* to kill. —*n.* **7.** the act or sound of croaking. [1550–60; earlier *croke,* prob. imit.; cf. OE *crǣcetian* (of a raven) to croak]

croak•er (krō′kər), *n.* **1.** a person or thing that croaks. **2.** any of several sciaenoid fishes that make a croaking noise, esp. *Micropogonias undulatus* **(Atlantic croaker),** found off the Atlantic coast of the southern U.S. **3.** a person who grumbles or forebodes evil. **4.** *Slang.* doctor. [1630–40; CROAK + -ER[1]]

croak•y (krō′kē), *adj.,* **croak•i•er, croak•i•est.** low-pitched and hoarse; croaking. [1840–50; CROAK + -Y[1]] —**croak′i•ly,** *adv.* —**croak′i•ness,** *n.*

Cro•at (krō′at, -ät), *n.* a native or inhabitant of Croatia; Croatian.

Cro•a•tia (krō ā′shə, -shē ə), *n.* a republic in SE Europe: includes the historical regions of Dalmatia, Istria, and Slavonia; formerly a part of Yugoslavia. 4,660,000; 21,835 sq. mi. (56,555 sq. km). *Cap.:* Zagreb. Serbo-Croatian, **Hrvatska.**

Cro•a•tian (krō ā′shən, -shē ən), *adj.* **1.** of or pertaining to Croatia, its people, or their language. —*n.* **2.** a Croat. **3.** Serbo-Croatian as spoken and written in Croatia, differing from Serbian chiefly in its use of the Latin alphabet. [1545–55; CROATI(A) + -AN]

croc (krok), *n. Informal.* crocodile. [1880–85; by shortening]

Cro•ce (krô′che), *n.* **Be•ne•det•to** (be′ne det′tô), 1866–1952, Italian statesman, philosopher, and historian.

cro•ce•in (krō′sē in), *n. Chem.* any of several acid azo dyes producing orange or scarlet colors. Also, **cro•ce•ine** (krō′sē in, -ēn′). [< L *croce(us)* saffron-colored (see CROCUS, -EOUS) + -IN²]

cro•chet (krō shā′; *Brit.* krō′shā, -shē), *n., v.,* **-cheted** (-shād′; *Brit.* -shād, -shēd), **-chet•ing** (-shā′ing; *Brit.* -shā ing, -shē ing). —*n.* **1.** needlework done with a needle having a small hook at one end for drawing the thread or yarn through intertwined loops. —*v.t., v.i.* **2.** to form by crochet. [1840–50; < F: knitting needle, lit., small hook, dim. of *croche, croc* < ME or Scand. See CROOK¹, -ET] —**cro•chet•er** (krō shā′ər; *Brit.* krō′shā ər, -shē-), *n.*

crochet′ hook′, a needle with a hook at one end, used in crochet. Also called **crochet′ nee′dle.** [1840–50]

cro•chet•work (krō shā′wûrk′; *Brit.* krō′shā wûrk′, -shē-), *n.* needlework done by crocheting. [1855–60; CROCHET + WORK]

cro•cid•o•lite (krō sid′l īt′), *n. Mineral.* a bluish, asbestine variety of riebeckite. Also called **blue asbestos.** [1825–35; < Gk *krokid-* (s. of *krokís*) nap, wool + -O- + -LITE]

crock¹ (krok), *n.* **1.** an earthenware pot, jar, or other container. **2.** a fragment of earthenware; potsherd. [bef. 1000; ME *crokke,* OE *croc(c), crocca* pot; c. ON *krukka* jug]

crock² (krok), *n.* **1.** a person or thing that is old, decrepit, or broken-down. **2.** *Slang.* a person who complains about or insists on being treated for an imagined illness. **3.** an old ewe. **4.** an old worn-out horse. —*v.t.* **5.** *Brit. Slang.* to disable or injure. [1300–50; ME *crok* old ewe, perh. akin to CRACK (v.) and obs. *crack* whore; cf. LG *krakke* broken-down horse]

crock³ (krok), *n.* **1.** *Brit. Dial.* soot; smut. **2.** excess surface dye from imperfectly dyed cloth. —*v.t.* **3.** *Brit. Dial.* to soil with soot. —*v.i.* **4.** (of cloth) to give off excess surface dye when rubbed. [1650–60; orig. uncert.]

crock⁴ (krok), *n. Slang.* a lie; exaggeration; nonsense: *The entire story is just a crock.* [orig. unclear, though often taken as a euphemism for *a crock of shit*]

crocked (krokt), *adj. Slang.* drunk. [1925–30, *Amer.*; CROCK² + -ED²]

crock•er•y (krok′ə rē), *n.* crocks collectively; earthenware. [1710–20; CROCK¹ + -ERY]

crock•et (krok′it), *n. Archit.* a medieval ornament, usually in the form of a leaf that curves up and away from the supporting surface and returns partially upon itself. [1300–50; ME *croket* hook < AF, equiv. to *croc* hook (< Gmc; see CROOK¹) + *-et* -ET. See CROCHET, CROTCHET]

crockets on coping of a gable

Crock•ett (krok′it), *n.* **David** (*Davy*), 1786–1836, U.S. frontiersman, politician, and folklore hero.

Crock•pot (krok′pot′), *Trademark.* a brand of electric slow cooker.

croc•o•dile (krok′ə dīl′), *n.* **1.** any of several crocodilians of the genus *Crocodylus,* found in sluggish waters and swamps of the tropics. **2.** any reptile of the order Crocodylia; crocodilian. **3.** the tanned skin or hide of these animals, used in the manufacture of luggage and accessories, as belts, shoes, and wallets. **4.** *Chiefly Brit.* a file of people, esp. schoolchildren, out for a walk. **5.** *Archaic.* a person who makes a hypocritical show of sorrow. [1250–1300; < L *crocodilus* < Gk *krokódeilos* crocodile, orig. a kind of lizard, said to be equiv. to *krók(ē)* pebble + *-o-* -O- + *drîlos, dreîlos* worm (though attested only in sense "penis"), with *r* lost by dissimilation r. ME *cocodrille* < ML *cocodrillus*] —**croc•o•dil•oid** (krok′ə dil′oid, krok′ə di′loid), *adj.*

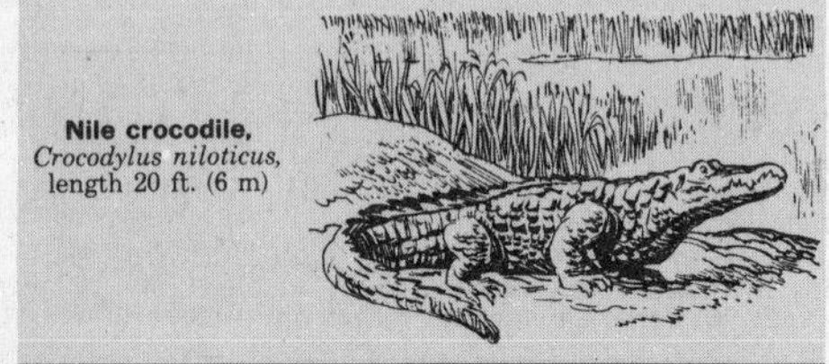
Nile crocodile, *Crocodylus niloticus,* length 20 ft. (6 m)

CONCISE ETYMOLOGY KEY: <, descended or borrowed from; >, whence; b., blend of, blended; c., cognate with; cf., compare; deriv., derivative; equiv., equivalent; imit., imitative; obl., oblique; r., replacing; s., stem; sp., spelling, spelled; resp., respelling, respelled; trans., translation; ?, origin unknown; *, unattested; ‡, probably earlier than. See the full key inside the front cover.

croc′odile bird′, an African courser, *Pluvianus aegyptius,* that often sits upon basking crocodiles and feeds on their insect parasites. [1865–70]

Croc′odile Riv′er, Limpopo.

croc′odile tears′, **1.** a hypocritical show of sorrow; insincere tears. **2.** *Pathol.* spontaneous tearing initiated by tasting or chewing food, occurring as a result of facial paralysis. [1555–65; so called from the the ancient belief that crocodiles shed tears while eating their victims]

croc•o•dil•i•an (krok′ə dil′ē ən), *n.* **1.** any reptile of the order Crocodylia, comprising the true crocodiles and the alligators, caimans, and gavials. —*adj.* **2.** of, like, or pertaining to a crocodile. **3.** hypocritical; insincere. [1625–35; CROCODILE + -IAN]

cro•co•ite (krō′kō īt′, krok′ō-), *n.* a yellow, orange, or red mineral, lead chromate, $PbCrO_4$, formed by replacement. Also called **cro•co•i•site** (krō′kō ə zīt′, krok′ō-). [1835–45; < Gk *krokó(eis)* saffron-colored + -ITE¹; see CROCUS]

cro•cus (krō′kəs), *n., pl.* **-cus•es. 1.** any of the small, bulbous plants of the genus *Crocus,* of the iris family, cultivated for their showy, solitary flowers, which are among the first to bloom in the spring. **2.** the flower or bulb of the crocus. **3.** a deep yellow; orangish yellow; saffron. **4.** Also called **cro′cus mar′tis** (mär′tis). a polishing powder consisting of iron oxide. [1350–1400; ME < L < Gk *krókos* saffron, crocus < Sem; cf. Ar *kurkum* saffron] —**cro′cused,** *adj.*

cro′cus sack′, *Southern U.S.* (*chiefly South Atlantic States*). a burlap bag. Also called **cro′cus bag′, croker sack.** [1780–90; orig. uncert.]
—**Regional Variation.** See **gunnysack.**

Croe•sus (krē′səs), *n., pl.* **-sus•es, -si** (-sī) for 2. **1.** died 546 B.C., king of Lydia 560–546: noted for his great wealth. **2.** a very rich man.

croft¹ (krôft, kroft), *n. Brit.* **1.** a small farm, esp. one worked by a tenant. **2.** a small plot of ground adjacent to a house and used as a kitchen garden, to pasture one or two cows, etc.; a garden large enough to feed a family or have commercial value. [bef. 1000; ME, OE: small field]

croft² (krôft, kroft), *n.* a small, portable filing cabinet of table height, having drop leaves for use as a table. [named after the Rev. Sir Herbert *Croft* (1757–1816), lexicologist, its inventor]

croft•er (krôf′tər, krof′-), *n. Brit.* a person who rents and works a small farm, esp. in Scotland or northern England. [1250–1300; ME; see CROFT¹, -ER¹]

Crohn's′ disease′ (krōnz), *Pathol.* a chronic inflammatory bowel disease that causes scarring and thickening of the intestinal walls and frequently leads to obstruction. Also called **regional ileitis, regional enteritis.** [named after Burrill Bernard *Crohn* (1884–1983), U.S. physician, one of the authors of a description of the disease published in 1932]

croi•sette (krô set′, kro-), *n.* crossette.

crois•sant (*Fr.* krwä sän′; *Eng.* krə sänt′), *n., pl.* **-sants** (*Fr.* -sän′; *Eng.* -sänts′). a rich, buttery, crescent-shaped roll of leavened dough or puff paste. [1895–1900; < F: lit., CRESCENT]

Croix de Guerre (krwädᵊ ger′), a French military award for heroism in battle. [1910–15; < F: lit., cross of war]

cro′ker sack′ (krō′kər). *Southern U.S.* (*chiefly Gulf States*). a crocus sack. Also called **cro′ker bag′.** [1875–80; *croker,* alter. of CROCUS]
—**Regional Variation.** See **gunnysack.**

Cro-Mag•non (krō mag′nən, -non, -man′yən), *n.* **1.** an Upper Paleolithic population of humans, regarded as the prototype of modern *Homo sapiens* in Europe. Skeletal remains found in an Aurignacian cave in southern France indicate that the Cro-Magnon had long heads, broad faces, and sunken eyes, and reached a height of approximately 5 ft. 9 in. (175 cm). See illus. under **hominid. 2.** a member of the Cro-Magnon population. [1865–70; named after the cave (near Périgueux, France) where the first remains were found]

Cro•mer (krō′mər), *n.* **1st Earl of.** See **Baring, Evelyn.**

crom•lech (krom′lek), *n. Archaeol.* (no longer in technical use) a megalithic chamber tomb. Cf. **chamber tomb, dolmen, passage grave.** [1595–1605; < Welsh, equiv. to *crom* bent, curved, crooked (fem. of *crwm*) + *lech,* comb. form of *llech* flat stone]

cro′mo•lyn so′dium (krō′mə lin), *Pharm.* a substance, $C_{23}H_{14}Na_2O_{11}$, used as a preventive inhalant for bronchial asthma and hay fever. [1970–75; contr. and rearrangement of the chemical name]

cro•morne (krō môrn′, krə-), *n.* crumhorn. [1685–95; < F, alter. of G *Krumhorn;* see CRUMHORN]

Cromp•ton (kromp′tən), *n.* **Samuel,** 1753–1827, English inventor of the spinning mule.

Crom•well (krom′wəl, -wel; *for 1–3 also* krum′-), *n.* **1. Oliver,** 1599–1658, English general, Puritan statesman, and Lord Protector of England, Scotland, and Ireland 1653–58. **2.** his son, **Richard,** 1626–1712, English soldier, politician, Lord Protector of England 1658–59. **3. Thomas, Earl of Essex,** 1485?–1540, English statesman. **4.** a town in central Connecticut. 10,265.

Crom′well Cur′rent. See **Equatorial Countercurrent.** [after Townsend *Cromwell* (1922–58), U.S. oceanographer]

Crom•wel•li•an (krom wel′ē ən, krum-), *adj.* **1.** of, pertaining to, or characteristic of the politics, practices, etc., of Oliver Cromwell or of the Commonwealth and Protectorate. **2.** noting or pertaining to a style of English furnishings of the middle 17th century, characterized by austerity, the use of oak and leather, and simple, decorative moldings. [1715–25; CROMWELL + -IAN]

Cromwel′lian chair′, *Eng. Furniture.* an upright oaken chair, often with arms, having all pieces turned and a seat and back panel of leather or cloth attached with brass-headed nails. [1900–05]

crone (krōn), *n.* a withered, witchlike old woman. [1350–1400; ME < MD *croonie* old ewe < ONF *caronie* CARRION] —**cron′ish,** *adj.*

Cro•nin (krō′nin), *n.* **A(rchibald) J(oseph),** 1896–1981, Scottish novelist and physician in the U.S.

Cron•jé (*Du.* krôn′yā), *n.* **Piet Ar•nol•dus** (*Du.* pēt är-nôl′do͝os), 1835?–1911, Boer general.

cronk (krongk, krôngk), *adj. Australian Slang.* sick or feeble. [1875–80; < Yiddish or G *krank,* MHG *kranc* weak]

Cro•nus (krō′nəs), *n. Class. Myth.* a Titan, son of Uranus and Gaea, who was dethroned by his son Zeus. Cf. **Saturn.**

cro•ny (krō′nē), *n., pl.* **-nies.** a close friend or companion; chum. [1655–65; alleged to be university slang; perh. < Gk *chrónios* for a long time, long-continued, deriv. of *chrónos* time; cf. CHRONO-]
—**Syn.** pal, buddy.

cro•ny•ism (krō′nē iz′əm), *n.* the practice of favoring one's close friends, esp. in political appointments. [1830–40; CRONY + -ISM]

Cro•nyn (krō′nin), *n.* **Hume,** born 1911, Canadian actor in the U.S.

crook¹ (kro͝ok), *n.* **1.** a bent or curved implement, piece, appendage, etc.; hook. **2.** the hooked part of anything. **3.** an instrument or implement having a bent or curved part, as a shepherd's staff hooked at one end or the crosier of a bishop or abbot. **4.** a dishonest person, esp. a sharper, swindler, or thief. **5.** a bend, turn, or curve: *a crook in the road.* **6.** the act of crooking or bending. **7.** a pothook. **8.** Also called **shank.** a device on some musical wind instruments for changing the pitch, consisting of a piece of tubing inserted into the main tube. —*v.t.* **9.** to bend; curve; make a crook in. **10.** *Slang.* to steal, cheat, or swindle: *She crooked a ring from that shop.* —*v.i.* **11.** to bend; curve. [1125–75; ME *crok(e)* < ON *krāka* hook]

crook² (kro͝ok), *adj. Australian.* **1.** sick or feeble. **2.** ill-humored; angry. **3.** out of order; functioning improperly. **4.** unsatisfactory; disappointing. [1875–80; perh. alter. of CRONK]

crook•back (kro͝ok′bak′), *n.* a hunchback. [1400–50; late ME. See CROOK¹, BACK¹] —**crook′backed′,** *adj.*

crook•ed (kro͝ok′id *for 1-4, 6;* kro͝okt *for 5*), *adj.* **1.** not straight; bending; curved: *a crooked path.* **2.** askew; awry: *The picture on the wall seems to be crooked.* **3.** deformed: *a man with a crooked back.* **4.** not straightforward; dishonest. **5.** bent and often raised or moved to one side, as a finger or neck. **6.** (of a coin) polygonal: *a crooked sixpence.* [1200–50; ME *croked;* see CROOK¹, -ED²] —**crook′ed•ly,** *adv.* —**crook′ed•ness,** *n.*
—**Syn. 1.** winding, devious, sinuous, flexuous, tortuous, spiral, twisted. **3.** misshapen. **4.** unscrupulous, knavish, tricky, fraudulent.

Crookes (kro͝oks), *n.* **Sir William,** 1832–1919, English chemist and physicist: discovered the element thallium and the cathode ray.

Crookes′ dark′ space′, *Physics.* the dark space between the cathode glow and the negative glow in a vacuum tube, occurring when the pressure is low. Also called **Crookes′ space′.** [1890–95; after Sir W. CROOKES]

crookes•ite (kro͝ok′sīt), *n.* a rare mineral, selenide of copper, thallium, and silver, $(Cu, Tl, Ag)_2Se$, occurring in steel-gray, compact masses. [1865–70; after Sir W. CROOKES; see -ITE¹]

Crookes′ radiom′eter, *Optics.* radiometer (def. 1). [1880–85; after Sir W. CROOKES]

Crookes′ tube′, *Electronics.* a form of cathode-ray tube. [1880–85; after Sir W. CROOKES]

crook•neck (kro͝ok′nek′), *n.* **1.** any of several varieties of squash having a long, recurved neck. **2.** any plant bearing such fruit. [1750–60, *Amer.;* CROOK¹ + NECK]

crook′ raft′er. See **knee rafter.**

croon (kro͞on), *v.i.* **1.** to sing or hum in a soft, soothing voice: *to croon to a baby.* **2.** to sing in an evenly modulated, slightly exaggerated manner: *Popular singers began crooning in the 1930's.* **3.** to utter a low murmuring sound. **4.** *Scot. and North Eng.* **a.** to bellow; low. **b.** to lament; mourn. —*v.t.* **5.** to sing (a song) in a crooning manner. **6.** to lull by singing or humming to in a soft, soothing voice: *to croon a child to sleep.* —*n.* **7.** the act or sound of crooning. [1350–1400; ME *cronen* < MD: to lament] —**croon′er,** *n.* —**croon′ing•ly,** *adv.*

crop (krop), *n., v.,* **cropped** or (*Archaic*) **cropt; crop•ping.** —*n.* **1.** the cultivated produce of the ground, while growing or when gathered: *the wheat crop.* **2.** the yield of such produce for a particular season. **3.** the yield of some other product in a season: *the crop of diamonds.* **4.** a supply produced. **5.** a collection or group of persons or things appearing or occurring together: *this year's crop of students.* **6.** the stock or handle of a whip. **7.** Also called **riding crop.** a short riding whip consisting of a stock without a lash. **8.** Also called **craw.** *Zool.* **a.** a pouch in the esophagus of many birds, in which food is held for later digestion or for regurgitation to nestlings. **b.** a chamber or pouch in the foregut of arthropods and annelids for holding and partly crushing food. **9.** the act of cropping. **10.** a mark produced by clipping the ears, as of cattle. **11.** a close-cropped hair style. **12.** a head of hair so cut. **13.** an entire tanned hide of an animal. **14.** *Mining.* an outcrop of a vein or seam. —*v.t.* **15.** to cut off or remove the head or top of (a plant, grass, etc.). **16.** to cut off the ends or a part of: *to crop the ears of a dog.* **17.** to cut short. **18.** to clip the ears, hair, etc., of. **19.** *Photog.* to cut off or mask the unwanted parts of (a print or negative). **20.** to cause to bear a crop or crops. **21.** to graze off (the tops of plants, grass, etc.): *The sheep cropped the lawn.* —*v.i.* **22.** to bear or yield a crop or crops. **23.** to feed by cropping or grazing. **24. crop out, a.** *Geol., Mining.* to rise to the surface of the ground: *Veins of quartz crop out in the canyon walls.* **b.** to become evident or visible; occur: *A few cases of smallpox still crop out every now and then.* **25. crop up,** to appear, esp. suddenly or unexpectedly: *A new problem cropped up.* [bef. 900; ME, OE: sprout, ear of corn, paunch, crown of a tree; c. G *Kropf;* see CROUP²] **—crop′less,** *adj.*

—Syn. 1. CROP, HARVEST, PRODUCE, YIELD refer to the return in food obtained from land at the end of a season of growth. CROP, the term common in agricultural and commercial use, denotes the amount produced at one cutting or for one particular season: *the potato crop.* HARVEST denotes either the time of reaping and gathering, or the gathering, or that which is gathered: *the season of harvest; to work in a harvest; a ripe harvest.* PRODUCE esp. denotes household vegetables: *Produce from the fields and gardens was taken to market.* YIELD emphasizes what is given by the land in return for expenditure of time and labor: *There was a heavy yield of grain this year.*

crop-dust (krop′dust′), *v.t.* to subject (a field) to crop-dusting.

crop′ dust′er, 1. a pilot employed in crop-dusting from an airplane. **2.** an airplane used in crop-dusting. [1935–40]

crop-dust•ing (krop′dus′ting), *n.* the spraying of powdered fungicides or insecticides on crops, usually from an airplane.

crop-eared (krop′ērd′), *adj.* **1.** having the ears cropped. **2.** having the hair cropped short, so that the ears are conspicuous. [1520–30]

crop•land (krop′land′), *n.* land suitable for or used for the cultivation of crops. [1840–50; CROP + LAND]

crop′ milk′, a liquid secreted in the crop of certain adult pigeons and fed to their newly hatched young. Also called **pigeon milk.**

crop•per (krop′ər), *n.* **1.** a person or thing that crops. **2.** a person who raises a crop. **3.** a person who cultivates land for its owner in return for part of the crop; sharecropper. **4.** a plant that furnishes a crop. **5.** a cloth-shearing machine. **6. come a cropper,** *Informal.* **a.** to fail; be struck by some misfortune: *His big deal came a cropper.* **b.** to fall headlong, esp. from a horse. [1475–85; CROP + -ER¹]

crop•pie (krop′ē), *n., pl.* **-pies,** (*esp. collectively*) **-pie.** crappie.

crop′ rota′tion, the system of varying successive crops in a definite order on the same ground, esp. to avoid depleting the soil and to control weeds, diseases, and pests. [1905–10]

cropt (kropt), *v. Archaic.* a pt. and pp. of **crop.** [sp. var. of CROPPED]

cro•quem•bouche (krō′kəm bo͞osh′; *Fr.* krô kän-bo͞osh′), *n., pl.* **-bouches** (-bo͞o′shiz; *Fr.* -bo͞osh′). *French Cookery.* a pyramid of bite-size cream puffs coated and held in place with caramelized sugar. [< F, assimilated form of *croque en bouche* (it) crunches in (the) mouth]

cro•quet (krō kā′; *Brit.* krō′kā, -kē), *n., v.,* **-queted** (-kād′; *Brit.* -kād, -kēd), **-quet•ing** (-kā′ing; *Brit.* -kā-ing, -kē ing). **—n. 1.** a game played by knocking wooden balls through metal wickets with mallets. **2.** (in croquet) the act of driving away an opponent's ball by striking one's own when the two are in contact. **—v.t. 3.** to drive away (a ball) by a croquet. [1855–60; < F (dial.): hockey stick, lit., little hook; see CROCKET]

cro•quette (krō ket′), *n.* a small cake or ball of minced meat, poultry, or fish, or of rice, potato, or other food, often coated with beaten egg and bread crumbs, and fried in deep fat. [1700–10; < F, equiv. to *croqu(er)* to crunch (OF *crokier* to break, of expressive orig.) + *-ette* -ETTE]

cro•qui•gnole (krō′kə nōl′, -kin yōl′), *n.* a method of waving the hair by curling it around metal rods from the ends inward toward the scalp. Also called **cro′quignole wave′.** [1930–35; < F: light blow on the head or nose, small crunchy biscuit, appar. deriv. of *croquer* to crunch (see CROQUETTE), though formation is unclear]

cro•quis (krō kē′; *Fr.* krô kē′), *n., pl.* **-quis** (-kēz′; *Fr.* -kē′). a rough preliminary drawing; sketch. [1800–10; < F, equiv. to *croqu(er)* to make a quick sketch of, rough out, (earlier) know (a subject) superficially (appar. to be identified with *croquer* to crunch; see CROQUETTE) + *-is* n. suffix (see PENTHOUSE)]

crore (krôr, krōr), *n.* (in India) the sum of ten million, esp. of rupees; one hundred lacs. [1600–10; < Hindi *kroṛ, karoṛ*]

Cros•by (krôz′bē, kroz′-), *n.* **Bing** (*Harry Lillis Crosby*), 1904–77, U.S. singer and actor.

cros•ette (kro set′, kro-), *n.* crossette.

cro•sier (krō′zhər), *n.* **1.** a ceremonial staff carried by a bishop or an abbot, hooked at one end like a shepherd's crook. See illus. under **cope².** **2.** *Bot.* the circinate young frond of a fern. Also, **crozier.** [1350–1400; short for *crosier-staff;* ME *crosier* staff-bearer < MF; r. ME *crocer* < AF. See CROSSE, -ER²] **—cro′siered,** *adj.*

cross (krôs, kros), *n., v., adj.,* **-er, -est.** **—n. 1.** a structure consisting essentially of an upright and a transverse piece, upon which persons were formerly put to death. **2.** any object, figure, or mark resembling a cross, as two intersecting lines. **3.** a mark resembling a cross, usually an *X,* made instead of a signature by a person unable to write. **4. the Cross,** the cross upon which Jesus died. **5.** a figure of the Cross as a Christian emblem, badge, etc. **6.** the Cross as the symbol of Christianity. **7.** a small cross with a human figure attached to it, as a representation of Jesus crucified; crucifix. **8.** a sign made with the right hand by tracing the figure of a cross in the air or by touching the forehead, chest, and shoulders, as an act of devotion. **9.** a structure or monument in the form of a cross, set up for prayer, as a memorial, etc. **10.** any of various conventional representations or modifications of the Christian emblem used symbolically or for ornament, as in heraldry or art: *a Latin cross; a Maltese cross.* **11.** the crucifixion of Jesus as the culmination of His redemptive mission. **12.** any suffering endured for Jesus' sake. **13.** the teaching of redemption gained by Jesus' death. **14.** the Christian religion, or those who accept it; Christianity; Christendom. **15.** an opposition; thwarting; frustration. **16.** any misfortune; trouble. **17.** a crossing of animals or plants; a mixing of breeds. **18.** an animal, plant, breed, etc., produced by crossing; crossbreed. **19.** a person or thing that is intermediate in character between two others. **20.** *Boxing.* a punch thrown across and over the lead of an opponent. **21.** *Slang.* a contest the result of which is dishonestly arranged beforehand. **22.** a crossing. **23.** a place of crossing. **24.** *Plumbing.* a four-way joint or connection. **25.** *Theat.* an actor's movement from one area of a stage to another. **26.** Also called **cross-trade.** *Stock Exchange.* an arrangement for the simultaneous sale and purchase of a block of stock handled by a single broker. **27.** *Mach.* spider (def. 6b). **28.** (*cap.*) *Astron.* See **Southern Cross. 29. bear one's cross,** to accept trials or troubles patiently. **30. take the cross,** to make the vows of a crusader.

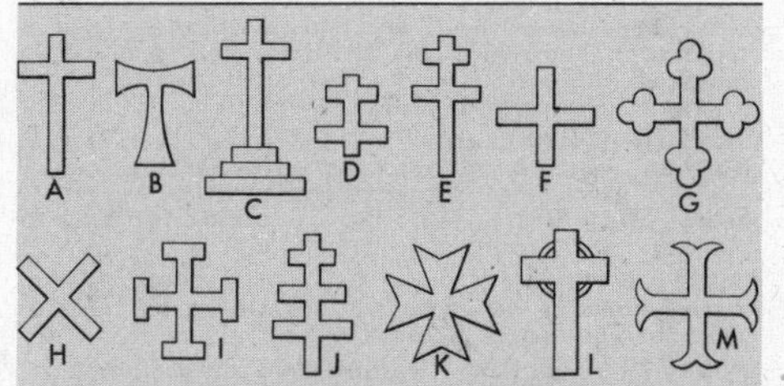

crosses (def. 10)
A, Latin cross; B, tau cross or St. Anthony's cross; C, cross of Calvary; D, cross of Lorraine; E, patriarchal cross; F, Greek cross; G, botonée; H, St. Andrew's cross; I, cross potent; J, papal cross; K, Maltese cross; L, Celtic cross; M, moline

—v.t. 31. to move, pass, or extend from one side to the other side of (a street, river, etc.). **32.** to put or draw (a line, lines, etc.) across. **33.** to cancel by marking with a cross or with a line or lines (often fol. by *off* or *out*). **34.** to mark with a cross. **35.** to lie or pass across; intersect. **36.** to meet and pass. **37.** to transport across something. **38.** to assist or guide (a person) across a street or intersection: *The guard crossed the child at the traffic light.* **39.** to place in the form of a cross or crosswise. **40.** *Biol.* to cause (members of different genera, species, breeds, varieties, or the like) to interbreed. **41.** to oppose openly; thwart; frustrate. **42.** *Slang.* to betray; double-cross. **43.** to make the sign of a cross upon or over, as in devotion: *to cross oneself.* **44.** *Naut.* to set (a yard) in proper position on a mast. **45.** *Obs.* to confront in a hostile manner.

—v.i. 46. to lie or be athwart; intersect. **47.** to move, pass, or extend from one side or place to another: *Cross at the intersection.* **48.** to meet and pass. **49.** to interbreed. **50.** *Theat.* to move from one side of the stage to the other, esp. by passing downstage of another actor. **51. cross one's heart.** See **heart** (def. 22). **52. cross one's mind.** See **mind** (def. 21). **53. cross one's path.** See **path** (def. 6). **54. cross over, a.** *Biol.* (of a chromosome segment) to undergo crossing over. **b.** to switch allegiance, as from one political party to another. **c.** to change successfully from one field of endeavor, genre, etc., to another: *to cross over from jazz to rock.* **d.** Also, **cross over to the other side.** to die; pass away. **55. cross someone's palm.** See **palm¹** (def. 11). **56. cross up, a.** to change arrangements made with; deceive: *He crossed me up after we had agreed to tell the police the same story.* **b.** to confuse: *I was supposed to meet him at the station, but got crossed up.*

—adj. 57. angry and annoyed; ill-humored; snappish: *Don't be cross with me.* **58.** lying or passing crosswise or across each other; athwart; transverse: *cross timbers.* **59.** involving a reciprocal action, interchange, or the like: *a cross-endorsement of political candidates; cross-marketing of related services.* **60.** contrary; opposite: *They were at cross purposes with each other.* **61.** adverse; unfavorable. **62.** crossbred; hybrid. [bef. 1000; ME, late OE *cros* < ON *kross* < OIr *cros* (< British Celtic) < L *crux;* see CRUX] **—cross′a•ble,** *adj.* **—cross′a•bil′i•ty,** *n.*

—Syn. 31, 35. traverse, span, bridge. **41.** baffle, foil, contradict. **57.** petulant, fractious, irascible, waspish, crabbed, churlish, sulky, cantankerous, cranky, ill-tempered, impatient, irritable, fretful, touchy, testy. CROSS, ILL-NATURED, PEEVISH, SULLEN refer to being in a bad mood or ill temper. CROSS means temporarily in an irritable or fretful state, and somewhat angry: *a cross reply.* ILL-NATURED implies a more permanent condition, without definite cause, and means unpleasant, unkind, inclined to snarl or be spiteful: *an ill-natured dog; ill-natured spite.* PEEVISH means complaining and snappish: *a peevish child.* SULLEN suggests a kind of glowering silent gloominess and means refusing to speak because of bad humor, anger, or a sense of injury or resentment: *sullen and vindictive.* **—Ant. 41.** aid. **57.** good-natured, agreeable.

Cross (krôs, kros), *n.* **Wilbur Lucius,** 1862–1948, U.S. educator: governor of Connecticut 1931–39.

cross-, a combining form of **cross.**

cross-ac•tion (krôs′ak′shən, kros′-), *n. Law.* an action brought within the same lawsuit by one defendant against another defendant or against the plaintiff. [1865–70]

cross-ad•dict•ed (krôs′ə dik′tid, kros′-), *adj.* addicted to two or more substances simultaneously.

cros•san•dra (krə san′drə, -sän′-, krō-), *n.* any of several plants of the genus *Crossandra,* native to Africa and Asia, esp. *C. infundibuliformis,* having glossy leaves and red-orange flowers and sometimes cultivated as a houseplant. Also called **firecracker flower.** [< NL (1806) < Gk *kross(oí)* tassels, fringe + *-andra,* fem. of *-andros,* adj. deriv. of *anḗr* man, male; hence, "having a fringed stamen"]

cross•band (krôs′band′, kros′-), *n. Zool., Bot.* a band or stripe that encircles horizontally. [CROSS- + BAND²] **—cross′band′ed,** *adj.*

cross•bar (krôs′bär′, kros′-), *n.* **1.** a horizontal bar, line, or stripe. **2.** the horizontal bar forming part of the goal posts, as in football and soccer. **3.** a horizontal bar used for gymnastics. **4.** a horizontal bar that rests on uprights and that an athlete must clear in performing the pole vault or high jump. **5.** a horizontal line in some letters of the alphabet, as in capital *H.* **6.** the horizontal top bar on the frame of a man's bicycle. [1550–60; CROSS- + BAR¹]

cross•beam (krôs′bēm′, kros′-), *n.* a transverse beam in a structure, as a joist. [1585–95; CROSS- + BEAM]

cross-bear•er (krôs′bâr′ər, kros′-), *n.* a person who carries or holds a cross, esp. in a religious procession. [1530–40; CROSS + BEARER]

cross-bed•ded (krôs′bed′id, kros′-), *adj. Geol.* having irregular laminations, as strata of sandstone, inclining in various directions not coincident with the general stratification. [CROSS- + *bedded* (see BED, -ED²)] **—cross′-bed′ding,** *n.*

cross•bill (krôs′bil′, kros′-), *n.* any bird belonging to the genus *Loxia,* of the finch family, characterized by mandibles curved so that the tips cross each other when the bill is closed. [1665–75; CROSS- + BILL²]

cross•birth (krôs′bûrth′, kros′-), *n. Obstet.* See **transverse presentation.** [CROSS- + BIRTH]

cross′bolt lock′ (krôs′bōlt′, kros′-), a lock controlling two bolts moving in opposite directions, as to the top and bottom of a doorframe. [CROSS- + BOLT¹] **—cross′•bolt′ed,** *adj.*

cross•bones (krôs′bōnz′, kros′-), *n.pl.* a representation of two bones placed crosswise, usually below a skull, to symbolize death. [1790–1800; CROSS- + BONE + -S³]

cross-bor•der (krôs′bôr′dər, kros′-), *adj.* crossing an international border: *cross-border tourist traffic.* [1890–95, for an earlier sense]

cross•bow (krôs′bō′, kros′-), *n.* a medieval weapon consisting of a bow fixed transversely on a stock having a trigger mechanism to release the bowstring, and often incorporating or accompanied by a mechanism for bending the bow. [1400–50; late ME *crossbowe.* See CROSS, BOW²]

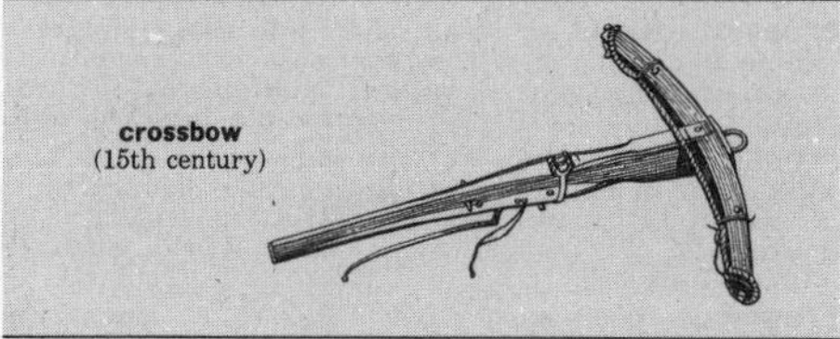

crossbow (15th century)

cross•bow•man (krôs′bō′mən, -bō′-, kros′-), *n., pl.* **-men. 1.** (in medieval warfare) a soldier armed with a crossbow. **2.** a person equipped with or skilled in the use of a crossbow. [1490–1500; CROSSBOW + -MAN]

cross•bred (krôs′bred′, kros′-), *adj.* **1.** produced by crossbreeding. **—n. 2.** an animal or group of animals produced by hybridization; hybrid. [1855–60; CROSS- + BRED]

cross•breed (krôs′brēd′, kros′-), *v.,* **-bred, -breed•ing,** *n.* **—v.t. 1.** to produce (a hybrid); hybridize. **—v.i. 2.** to undertake or engage in hybridizing; hybridize. **—n. 3.** a crossbred. [1665–75; CROSS- + BREED]

cross′ bridg′ing, *Carpentry.* bridging composed of crisscross pieces of wood. Also called **herringbone bridging, herringbone strutting.**

cross′ buck′, *Football.* an offensive play in which two running backs cross paths and charge into the line on opposite sides, one back receiving the ball from the quarterback and the other back faking possession.

crossbuck

cross•buck (krôs′buk′, kros′-), *n.* an X-shaped warning symbol for vehicular traffic at a railroad grade crossing. [CROSS- + BUCK³]

cross-check (*v.* krôs′chek′, kros′-; *n.* krôs′chek′, -chek′, kros′-), *v.t.* **1.** to determine the accuracy of (something) by checking it with various sources. **2.** *Ice Hockey.* to execute a cross-check on (an opponent). **—n. 3.** the act of cross-checking. **4.** a means of cross-checking: *I examined contemporary newspaper reports as a cross-check on his account.* **5.** *Ice Hockey.* an obstructing or impeding of the movement or progress of an opponent by placing the stick, with both hands, across the opponent's body or face. Cf. **check** (def. 42). [1935–40] —**cross′-check′er,** *n.*

cross-com•pound (krôs′kom′pound, kros′-), *adj.* (of a compound engine or turbine) having the high-pressure and low-pressure units side by side. Cf. **tandem-compound.**

cross-coun•try (*adj.* krôs′kun′trē, kros′-; *n.* krôs′-kun′trē, -kun′-, kros′-), *adj., n., pl.* **tries.** —*adj.* **1.** directed or proceeding over fields, through woods, etc., rather than on a road or path: *a cross-country race.* **2.** from one end of the country to the other: *a cross-country flight.* —*n.* **3.** a cross-country sport or race. [1760–70]

cross′-country ski′ing, the sport of skiing across the countryside, often through woods and usually on relatively flat terrain, using narrow skis with boots that can be raised off the ski at the heel when striding. Also called **ski touring.** —**cross′-country ski′er.**

cross-country skier

cross•court (krôs′kôrt′, -kōrt′, kros′-), *adj.* **1.** (in racket games) directed to the diagonally opposite side of the court. **2.** *Basketball.* directed to the opposite end of the court. —*adv.* **3.** (in racket games) to or toward the diagonally opposite side of the court. **4.** *Basketball.* to or toward the opposite end of the court. [1910–15; CROSS- + COURT]

cross-cous•in (krôs′kuz′ən, kros′-), *n.* a cousin who is the child either of one's mother's brother or one's father's sister. Cf. **parallel cousin.** [1930–35]

cross′-cousin mar′riage, marriage between the children of a brother and sister. Cf. **parallel cousin marriage.** [1885–90]

cross-cul•tur•al (krôs′kul′chər əl, kros′-), *adj.* combining, pertaining to, or contrasting two or more cultures or cultural groups: *cross-cultural studies; cross-cultural communication.* [1940–45] —**cross′-cul′tur•al•ly,** *adv.*

cross•cur•rent (krôs′kûr′ənt, -kur′-, kros′-), *n.* **1.** a current, as in a stream, moving across the main current. **2.** Often, **crosscurrents.** a conflicting tendency or movement. [1590–1600; CROSS- + CURRENT] —**cross′•cur′rent•ed,** *adj.*

cross•cut (krôs′kut′, kros′-), *adj., n., v.,* **-cut, -cut•ting.** —*adj.* **1.** made or used for cutting crosswise. **2.** cut across the grain or on the bias. —*n.* **3.** a transverse cut or course. **4.** a shortcut by way of an area not ordinarily traversed, as grass or open country; a route that cuts diagonally across a road or path network. **5.** *Mining.* an underground passageway, usually from a shaft to a vein of ore or crosswise of a vein of ore. **6.** *Motion Pictures, Television.* an act or instance of crosscutting. **7.** a crosscut saw. —*v.t.* **8.** to cut or go across. **9.** *Motion Pictures, Television.* to insert into a scene or sequence (portions of another scene), as to heighten suspense or suggest simultaneous action. —*v.i.* **10.** *Motion Pictures, Television.* to employ the technique of crosscutting. [1580–90; CROSS- + CUT] —**cross′cut′ter,** *n.*

cross′cut saw′, a saw for cutting wood perpendicular to the grain. [1635–45, *Amer.*]

cross•cut•ting (krôs′kut′ing, kros′-), *n. Motion Pictures, Television.* the technique of intercutting a scene with portions of another scene, esp. to heighten suspense by showing simultaneous action. [CROSS- + CUTTING]

cross-dis•ci•pli•nar•y (krôs′dis′ə plə ner′ē, kros′-), *adj.* involving two or more academic disciplines; interdisciplinary: *cross-disciplinary studies in Biblical archaeology.*

cross-dis•solve (krôs′di zolv′, kros′-) *n. Motion Pictures.* dissolve (def. 17).

cross-dress (krôs′dres′, kros′-), *v.i.* to dress in clothing typically worn by members of the opposite sex. —**cross′-dress′er,** *n.*

crosse (krôs, kros), *n.* a long-handled racket used in the game of lacrosse. [1865–70; < F: lit., hooked stick, OF *croce* < Gmc; see CRUTCH, CROOK[1]]

crossed (krôst, krost), *adj. Math.* (of partial derivatives) mixed, esp. of order two. [CROSS + -ED[2]]

crossed′ eyes′, strabismus, esp. the form in which one or both eyes turn inward. Also, **cross-eye.**

cross•ette (krô set′, kro-), *n. Archit.* a projection at a corner of a door or window architrave. Also, **croisette, crosette.** Also called **dog-ear, dog's-ear, elbow.** [1720–30; < F, dim. of *crosse.* See CROSSE, -ETTE]

cross-ex•am•ine (krôs′ig zam′in, kros′-), *v.t.,* **-ined, -in•ing. 1.** to examine by questions intended to check a previous examination; examine closely or minutely. **2.** *Law.* to examine (a witness called by the opposing side), as for the purpose of discrediting the witness's testimony. Cf. **direct-examine.** [1655–65] —**cross′-ex•am′i•na′tion,** *n.* —**cross′-ex•am′in•er,** *n.*

cross-eye (krôs′ī′, kros′ī′), *n.* See **crossed eyes.** [1785–95]

cross-eyed (krôs′īd′, kros′-), *adj.* having crossed eyes. [1785–95] —**cross′-eyed′ness,** *n.*

cross-fade (*v.* krôs′fād′, kros′-; *n.* krôs′fād′, kros′-), *v.,* **-fad•ed, -fad•ing,** *n. Motion Pictures, Television.* —*v.t.* **1.** to fade out (an image or sound) while simultaneously fading in a different image or sound. —*n.* **2.** an act or instance of cross-fading. [1935–40]

cross-fer•tile (krôs′fûr′tl, kros′-), *adj.* capable of cross-fertilization. [1925–30]

cross-fer•ti•li•za•tion (krôs′fûr′tl ə zā′shən, kros′-), *n.* **1.** *Biol.* the fertilization of an organism by the fusion of an egg from one individual with a sperm or male gamete from a different individual. **2.** *Bot.* fertilization of the flower of one plant by a gamete from the flower of a closely related plant (opposed to *self-fertilization*). **3.** (not in technical use) cross-pollination. **4.** interaction or interchange, as between two or more cultures, fields of activity or knowledge, or the like, that is mutually beneficial and productive: *a cross-fertilization of scientific and technical disciplines.* [1875–80]

cross-fer•ti•lize (krôs′fûr′tl īz′, kros′-), *v.,* **-lized, -liz•ing.** —*v.t.* **1.** to cause the cross-fertilization of. —*v.i.* **2.** to undergo cross-fertilization. Also, *esp. Brit.,* **cross′-fer′ti•lise′.** [1875–80] —**cross′-fer′ti•liz′a•ble,** *adj.*

cross-file (krôs′fīl′, kros′-), *v.i., v.t.,* **-filed, -fil•ing.** to register as a candidate in the primary elections of more than one party. [1870–75]

cross′ fire′, 1. lines of gunfire from two or more positions or combatants crossing one another, or a single one of such lines. **2.** a brisk exchange of words or opinions. **3.** a situation involving conflicting claims, forces, etc. Also, **cross′fire′.** [1855–60]

cross•foot (krôs′fo͝ot′, kros′-), *v.i. Accounting.* to total figures horizontally across columns instead of vertically. [CROSS- + FOOT] —**cross′foot′ing,** *n.*

cross′ fox′, a red fox in the color phase in which the fur is reddish brown with a dark stripe down the back and another over the shoulders. [1765–75]

cross-gar•net (krôs′gär′nit, kros′-), *n.* a T-shaped strap hinge with the crosspiece as the stationary member. See illus. under **hinge.** Also called **T hinge.** [1650–60]

cross-gar•tered (krôs′gär′tərd, kros′-), *adj.* (in Elizabethan and other costumes) wearing garters crisscrossed on the leg.

cross-grained (krôs′grānd′, kros′-), *adj.* **1.** having the grain running transversely or diagonally, or having an irregular or gnarled grain, as timber. **2.** stubborn; perverse. [1640–50] —**cross′-grained′ly,** *adv.* —**cross′-grained′ness,** *n.*

cross′ hairs′, 1. Also called **cross wires.** fine wires or fibers, strands of spider web, or the like, crossing in a focal plane of an optical instrument to center a target or object or to define a line of sight. **2.** marks for aiding in the positioning of overlaying images for correct registration in printing. Cf. **register** (def. 11b). [1880–85]

cross•hatch (krôs′hach′, kros′-), *v.t.* **1.** to mark or shade with two or more intersecting series of parallel lines. —*n.* **2.** a pattern or mark made with such lines. [1815–25; CROSS- + HATCH[3]] —**cross′hatch′ing,** *n.*

cross•head (krôs′hed′, kros′-), *n.* **1.** *Print.* a title or heading filling a line or group of lines the full width of the column. **2.** *Mach.* a sliding member of a reciprocating engine for keeping the motion of the joint between a piston rod and a connecting rod in a straight line. **3.** *Naut.* a crosspiece on a rudderpost by which the rudder is turned. **4.** *Engin., Building Trades.* a transverse timber for transmitting the lifting effort of two or more jackscrews supporting it to the foot of a shore that it supports. Cf. **shore[2]** (def. 1). [1835–45; CROSS- + HEAD]

cross′ in′dex, a note or group of notes referring the reader to material elsewhere.

cross-in•dex (krôs′in′deks, kros′-), *v.t.* **1.** to provide with cross references or with a cross-referenced index. —*v.i.* **2.** to refer by a note or indication of location to related material, as in an index, book, or article; contain cross references: *Footnotes cross-index to the appendix and bibliography.* [1890–95]

cross•ing (krô′sing, kros′ing), *n.* **1.** the act of a person or thing that crosses. **2.** a place where lines, streets, tracks, etc., cross each other. **3.** a place at which a road, railroad track, river, etc., may be crossed. **4.** hybridization; crossbreeding. **5.** the act of opposing or thwarting; frustration; contradiction. **6.** the intersection of nave and transept in a cruciform church. **7.** *Railroads.* a track structure composed of four connected frogs, permitting two tracks to cross each other at grade with sufficient clearance for wheel flanges. [1375–1425; late ME. See CROSS, -ING[1]]

cross′ing guard′, an auxiliary police officer, community volunteer, etc., who directs traffic and assists children in crossing a street near a school.

cross′ing o′ver, *Genetics.* the interchange of corresponding chromatid segments of homologous chromosomes with their linked genes. [1910–15]

cross•jack (krôs′jak′, kros′-; *Naut.* krô′jik, kroj′ik), *n. Naut.* the lowermost square sail set on the mizzenmast of a ship or of a bark with four or more masts; mizzen course. See diag. under **ship.** [1620–30; CROSS- + JACK[1]]

cross-leg•ged (krôs′leg′id, -legd′, kros′-), *adj.* having the legs crossed; having one leg placed across the other. [1520–30] —**cross′-leg′ged•ly,** *adv.* —**cross′-leg′ged•ness,** *n.*

cross•let (krôs′lit, kros′-), *n.* a small cross, as one used as a heraldic charge. [1350–1400; ME *croslet.* See CROSS, -LET] —**cross′let•ed,** *adj.*

cross•light (krôs′līt′, kros′-), *n.* **1.** a light shone across the path of another to illuminate an area left dark by the first light. **2.** light originating from sources not facing each other, as from windows in two adjacent walls. **3.** light originating from counterlights. [1850–55; CROSS- + LIGHT[1]] —**cross′light′ed,** *adj.*

cross•line (krôs′līn′, kros′-), *n.* **1.** a line crossing another line or connecting two separated points: *The main lines are linked at intervals by crosslines.* **2.** *Journalism.* a headline or bank consisting of a single line running across a column of type, usually centered and sometimes full width. —*adj.* **3.** of or pertaining to the offspring produced by crossbreeding two linebred individuals. [1350–1400; ME. See CROSS-, LINE[1]]

cross-link (*n.* krôs′lingk′, kros′-; *v.* krôs′lingk′, kros′-), *Chem.* —*n.* **1.** a bond, atom, or group linking the chains of atoms in a polymer, protein, or other complex organic molecule. —*v.t.* **2.** to attach by a cross-link. [1935–40] —**cross′-link′ing,** *n.* —**cross′-link′a•ble,** *adj.*

cross-link•er (krôs′lingk′kər, kros′-), *n. Chem.* a substance or agent, such as radiation, that induces the formation of cross-links. [1980–85; CROSS-LINK + -ER[1]]

cross′-lot brac′ing (krôs′lot′, kros′-), *Engin., Building Trades.* bracing extending from one side of an excavation to the opposite to retain the earth on both sides.

cross•ly (krôs′lē, kros′-), *adv.* in a cross or angry manner. [1585–95; CROSS + -LY]

cross-match (krôs′mach′, kros′-), *v.t.* **1.** to match (related items from two or more lists or groups). **2.** *Med.* to subject (blood) to cross matching. [1925–30]

cross′ match′ing, *Med.* the testing for compatibility of a donor's and a recipient's blood prior to transfusion, in which serum of each is mixed with red blood cells of the other and observed for hemagglutination. Also, **cross•match** (krôs′mach′, kros′-). [1935–40]

cross-mate (krôs′māt′, kros′-), *v.t., v.i.,* **-mat•ed, -mat•ing.** to crossbreed.

cross-mo•dal•i•ty (krôs′mō dal′i te, kros′-), *n.* the ability to integrate information acquired through separate senses. —**cross-mod•al** (krôs′mōd′l, kros′-), *adj.*

cross′ mul′tiply, *Math.* to remove fractions from an equation by multiplying each side by the common multiple of the denominators of the fractions of the opposite side. [1950–55] —**cross′ multiplica′tion.**

cross•ness (krôs′nis, kros′-), *n.* the quality or state of being cross or angry; irritability; snappishness. [1590–1600; CROSS + -NESS]

cross′ of Cal′vary, a Latin cross with a representation of steps beneath it. See illus. under **cross.**

cross′ of Lorraine′, a cross having two crosspieces, the upper shorter than the lower. See illus. under **cross.** [1890–95]

cros•sop•te•ryg•i•an (kro sop′tə rij′ē ən), *n.* **1.** any fish of the group Crossopterygii, extinct except for the coelacanth, regarded as being ancestral to amphibians and other land vertebrates. —*adj.* **2.** pertaining to or resembling a crossopterygian. [1860–65; < NL *Crossopterygi(i)* group name (< Gk *kross(oi)* tassels, fringe + *-o-* -O- + *pterýgi(on)* little wing or fin, equiv. to *pteryg-* (s. of *ptéryx*) wing, fin + *-ion* dim. suffix) + -AN]

cross-out (krôs′out′, kros′-), *n.* a word, line, etc., that has been crossed out. [n. use of v. phrase *cross out*]

cross•o•ver (krôs′ō′vər, kros′-), *n.* **1.** a bridge or other structure for crossing over a river, highway, etc. **2.** *Genetics.* **a.** See **crossing over. b.** a genotype resulting from crossing over. **3.** *Popular Music.* **a.** the act of crossing over in style, usually with the intention of broadening the commercial appeal to a wider audience. **b.** music that crosses over in style, occasionally sharing attributes with several musical styles and therefore often appealing to a broader audience. **4.** Also called **cross′•over vot′er.** *U.S. Politics.* a member of one political party who votes for the candidate of another party in a primary. **5.** See **crossover network. 6.** *Railroads.* a track structure composed of two or more turnouts, permitting movement of cars from either of two parallel and adjacent tracks to the other. **7.** *Dance.* **a.** a step in which dancers exchange places. **b.** a step involving partners in which the woman moves from one side of her partner to the other, crossing in front of him. **8.** *Bowling.* a ball that strikes the side of the head pin opposite to the bowling hand of the bowler. **9.** (in plumbing) a U-shaped pipe for bypassing another pipe. [1785–95; n. use of v. phrase *cross over*]

cross′over distor′tion, distortion that sometimes occurs at a frequency **(cross′over fre′quency)** at which a crossover network switches signals from one speaker to another.

cross′over net′work, an audio circuit device that sorts the impulses received and channels them into high- or low-frequency loudspeakers. Also called **crossover.**

cross-own•er•ship (krôs′ō′nər ship′, kros′-), *n.* ownership of two or more similar or related businesses, as communications media, esp. in the same locality: *to forbid cross-ownership of newspapers and TV or radio stations in the same city.* [1970–75]

cross•patch (krôs′pach′, kros′-), *n. Informal.* a bad-tempered or irritable person. [1690–1700; CROSS- + PATCH[1]]

cross•piece (krôs′pēs′, kros′-), *n.* a piece placed across something; transverse or horizontal piece. [1600–10; CROSS- + PIECE]

cross′-ply tire′ (krôs′plī′, kros′-). See **bias-ply tire.** [1960–65; CROSS- + PLY[2]]

cross-pol•li•nate (krôs′pol′ə nāt′, kros′-), *v.t.,* **-nat•ed, -nat•ing.** to subject to cross-pollination. [1895–1900]

cross-pol•li•na•tion (krôs′pol′ə nā′shən, kros′-), *n.*

CONCISE ETYMOLOGY KEY: <, descended or borrowed from; >, whence; b., blend of, blended; c., cognate with; cf., compare; deriv., derivative; equiv., equivalent; imit., imitative; obl., oblique; r., replacing; s., stem; sp., spelling, spelled; resp., respelling, respelled; trans., translation; ?, origin unknown; *, unattested; ‡, probably earlier than. See the full key inside the front cover.

1. *Bot.* the transfer of pollen from the flower of one plant to the flower of a plant having a different genetic constitution. Cf. **self-pollination. 2.** a sharing or interchange of knowledge, ideas, etc., as for mutual enrichment; cross-fertilization. [1880–85]

cross′ prod′uct, *Math.* a vector perpendicular to two given vectors, *u* and *v*, and having magnitude equal to the product of the magnitudes of the two given vectors multiplied by the sine of the angle between the two given vectors, usually represented by *u* × *v*. Also called **outer product, vector product.** [1925–30]

cross-pur·pose (krôs′pûr′pəs, kros′-), *n.* **1.** an opposing or contrary purpose. **2. at cross-purposes,** in a way that involves or produces mutual misunderstanding or frustration, usually unintentionally. [1660–70]

cross-ques·tion (krôs′kwes′chən, kros′-), *v.t.* **1.** to cross-examine. —*n.* **2.** a question asked by way of cross-examination. [1685–95]

cross·rail (krôs′rāl′, kros′-), *n.* a horizontal slat forming part of the back of a chair. [1875–80; CROSS- + RAIL[1]]

cross′ ra′tio, *Geom.* a ratio relating four points in the real or complex plane. Also called **anharmonic ratio.** [1880–85] —**cross′-ra′ti·o′,** *adj.*

cross-re·act (krôs′rē akt′, kros′-), *v.i. Immunol.* (of an antigen, antibody, or lymphocyte) to participate in a cross-reaction.

cross-re·ac·tion (krôs′rē ak′shən kros′-), *n.* an immunologic reaction between a given antigen and an antibody or lymphokine that is specific for a different antigen resembling the first one. [1945–50] —**cross′-re·ac′tive,** *adj.* —**cross′-re·ac·tiv′i·ty,** *n.*

cross-re·fer (krôs′ri fûr′, kros′-), *v.t., v.i.,* **-ferred, -fer·ring.** to refer by a cross reference. [1905–10]

cross′ ref′erence, a reference from one part of a book, index, or the like, to related material, as a word or illustration, in another part. [1825–35]

cross-ref·er·ence (krôs′ref′ər əns, -ref′rəns, kros′-), *v.t., v.i.,* **-enced, -enc·ing. 1.** to provide with cross references: *The new encyclopedia is completely cross-referenced.* **2.** cross-refer. [1900–05]

cross-re·sist·ance (krôs′ri zis′təns, kros′-), *n. Biol.* **1.** immunologic resistance to the pathogenic effects of a microorganism because of previous exposure to another species or type having cross-reactive antigens. **2.** resistance to the effects of a substance, as that of an insect population to an insecticide or a bacterial strain to an antibiotic, stimulated by exposure and adaptation to a similar or related substance. [1945–50]

cross·road (krôs′rōd′, kros′-), *n.* **1.** a road that crosses another road, or one that runs transversely to main roads. **2.** a by-road. **3.** Often, **crossroads.** (*used with a singular or plural v.*) **a.** the place where roads intersect. **b.** a point at which a vital decision must be made. **c.** a main center of activity. [1710–20; CROSS- + ROAD]

cross·ruff (*n.* krôs′ruf′, -ruf′, kros′-; *v.* krôs′ruf′, kros′-), *Bridge, Whist.* —*n.* **1.** a play in which each hand of a partnership alternately trumps a different suit in consecutive plays. —*v.t., v.i.* **2.** to play by means of a crossruff. [1585–95; CROSS- + RUFF[2]]

cross′ sea′, *Oceanog., Naut.* a sea with a choppy surface produced by the intersection of waves from different storms. [1865–70]

cross′ sec′tion, 1. a section made by a plane cutting anything transversely, esp. at right angles to the longest axis. **2.** a piece so cut off. **3.** a photograph, diagram, or other pictorial representation of such a section. **4.** the act of cutting anything across. **5.** a typical selection; a sample showing all characteristic parts, relationships, etc.: *a cross section of American opinion.* **6.** *Survey.* a vertical section of the ground surface taken at right angles to a survey line. **7.** Also called **nuclear cross section.** *Physics.* a quantity expressing the effective area that a given nucleus presents as a target to a bombarding particle, giving a measure of the probability that the particle will induce a reaction. [1825–35]

cross-sec·tion (krôs′sek′shən, kros′-), *adj.* **1.** Also, **cross′-sec′tion·al.** of or pertaining to a cross section. —*v.t.* **2.** to make or divide into a cross section. [1875–80]

cross-staff (krôs′staf′, -stäf′, kros′-), *n., pl.* **-staffs, -staves.** *Astron.* an instrument for measuring the angle of elevation of heavenly bodies, consisting of a calibrated staff with another shorter staff perpendicular to and sliding on it. Also called **forestaff, Jacob's staff.** [1400–50, for an earlier sense; late ME]

cross-ster·ile (krôs′ster′əl *or, esp. Brit.,* -īl, kros′-), *adj.* incapable of reproducing due to hybridization. [1945–50] —**cross′-ste·ril′i·ty,** *n.*

cross-stitch (krôs′stich′, kros′-), *n.* **1.** a stitch in which pairs of diagonal stitches of the same length cross each other in the middle to form an X. **2.** embroidery or needlepoint done with this stitch. —*v.t., v.i.* **3.** to work in cross-stitch. [1700–10]

cross′ street′, 1. a street crossing another street. **2.** a short street connecting main streets. [1815–25]

cross-string (krôs′string′, kros′-), *v.t.,* **-strung; -strung** or (*Rare*) **-stringed; -string·ing.** overstring.

cross′ stroke′, *Typography.* the horizontal line through the vertical of a *t* or *f.*

cross′ talk′, 1. interference heard on a telephone or radio because of unintentional coupling to another communication channel. **2.** incidental conversation; chatter, as opposed to formal discussion: *The meeting was slowed by cross talk between board members.* **3.** *Brit.* witty, fast-paced dialogue, esp. in a play, comic act, etc.; repartee. Also, **cross′-talk′, cross′talk′.** [1885–90]

cross·tie (krôs′tī′, kros′-), *n.* **1.** *Railroads.* a tie. **2.** a transverse timber forming a foundation or support. [1805–15, *Amer.*; CROSS- + TIE] —**cross′tied′,** *adj.*

cross-tol·er·ance (krôs′tol′ər əns, kros′-), *n. Physiol.* the resistance to one or more effects of a substance because of tolerance to a pharmacologically similar substance: *a cross-tolerance of some alcoholics to anesthetics.* [1920–25]

cross·town (krôs′toun′, kros′-), *adj.* **1.** situated or traveling in a direction extending across a town or city: *a crosstown street; a crosstown bus.* —*adv.* **2.** in a direction extending across a town or city: *The car sped crosstown.* —*n.* **3.** *Informal.* a bus running primarily in a crosstown direction. [1885–90; CROSS- + TOWN]

cross-trade (krôs′trād′, kros′-), *n. Stock Exchange.* cross (def. 26).

cross-train (krôs′trān′, kros′-), *v.t.* to train (a worker, athlete, etc.) to be proficient at different, usually related, skills, tasks, jobs, etc. [1980–85]

cross·tree (krôs′trē′, kros′-), *n.* **1.** *Naut.* either of a pair of timbers or metal bars placed athwart the trestletrees at a masthead to spread the shrouds leading to the mast above, or on the head of a lower mast to support the platform or top. **2.** *Carpentry.* a heavy crossbeam. [1620–30; CROSS- + TREE]

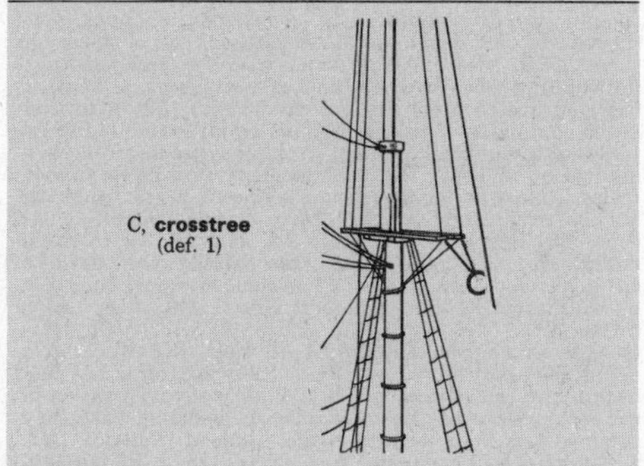

C, **crosstree** (def. 1)

cross-u·ti·lize (krôs′yōōt′l īz′, kros′-), *v.t.,* **-lized, -liz·ing.** to make use of in an additional or different way. Also, *esp. Brit.,* **cross′-u′ti·lise′.** —**cross′-u′ti·li·za′tion,** *n.*

cross-val·i·da·tion (krôs′val′i dā′shən, kros′-), *n. Statistics.* a process by which a method that works for one sample of a population is checked for validity by applying the method to another sample from the same population.

cross-vein (krôs′vān′, kros′-), *n. Zool.* a transverse vein that connects adjacent longitudinal veins in the wing of an insect.

cross·vine (krôs′vīn′, kros′-), *n.* a climbing or creeping woody vine, *Bignonia capreolata,* of the bignonia family, having yellow-red trumpet-shaped flowers and a stem that shows a crosslike arrangement in cross section. [1775–85, *Amer.*]

cross·walk (krôs′wôk′, kros′-), *n.* a lane marked off for pedestrians to use when crossing a street, as at an intersection. [1735–45; CROSS- + WALK]

cross·way (krôs′wā′, kros′-), *n.* a crossroad. [1375–1425; late ME *crosswey.* See CROSS, WAY[1]]

cross·ways (krôs′wāz′, kros′-), *adv.* crosswise.

cross′ wind′ (wind), a wind blowing across the course or path of a ship, aircraft, etc. Also, **cross′wind′.** [1915–20]

cross′ wires′, *Optics.* See **cross hairs** (def. 1). [1865–70]

cross·wise (krôs′wīz′, kros′-), *adv.* **1.** across; transversely. **2.** contrarily. **3.** *Archaic.* in the form of a cross. —*adj.* **4.** forming a cross; transverse. Also, **crossways.** [1350–1400; ME *a cross wise* in the form of a cross. See A-[1], CROSS, WISE[2]]

cross·word (krôs′wûrd′, kros′-), *n.* a crossword puzzle. [1910–15]

cross′word puz′zle, a puzzle in which words corresponding to numbered clues or definitions are supplied and fitted into correspondingly numbered sets of squares, one letter per square, the words being arranged horizontally or vertically so that most letters form part of two words. [1910–15; CROSS- + WORD, allegedly for earlier *word cross*]

cro·ta·lin (krōt′l in), *n. Biochem.* a protein in the venom of pit vipers, used as an antigen in the preparation of snake antivenins. [< NL *Crotal*(*us*) a genus of rattlesnakes, from whose venom the protein was extracted (< L *crotalum* < Gk *krótalon* rattle) + -IN[2]]

crotch (kroch), *n.* **1.** a forking or place of forking, as of the human body between the legs. **2.** the part of a pair of trousers, panties, or the like, formed by the joining of the two legs. **3.** a piece of material serving to form a juncture between the legs of trousers, panties, etc. **4.** a forked piece, part, support, etc., as a staff with a forked top. **5.** *Billiards.* **a.** an area 4½ in. (11.4 cm) square at each corner of a billiard table. **b.** the situation in which both balls to be struck by the cue ball are within this area. **6.** *Naut.* crutch (def. 6). **7.** the area of a tree at which a main branch joins the trunk. **8.** the wood from such an area; crotchwood. [1530–40; var. of CRUTCH] —**crotched** (krocht), *adj.*

crotch·et (kroch′it), *n.* **1.** an odd fancy or whimsical notion. **2.** a small hook. **3.** a hooklike device or part. **4.** *Entomol.* a small, hooklike process. **5.** *Music. Chiefly Brit.* a quarter note. See illus. under **note. 6.** a curved surgical instrument with a sharp hook. [1350–1400; ME *crochet* hook, staff with hook at end < MF (see CROCHET); doublet of CROCKET]
—**Syn. 1.** caprice, whimsy, eccentricity, quirk, oddity.

crotch·et·y (kroch′i tē), *adj.* **1.** given to odd notions, whims, grouchiness, etc. **2.** of the nature of a crotchet. [1815–25; CROTCHET + -Y[1]] —**crotch′et·i·ness,** *n.*
—**Syn. 1.** fussy, eccentric, grouchy.

crotch·wood (kroch′wo͝od′), *n.* wood from a tree crotch, characterized by a swirling, irregular figure and used for furniture and veneers. Also called **crotch.** [CROTCH + WOOD[1]]

cro·ton (krōt′n), *n.* **1.** any of numerous chiefly tropical plants constituting the genus *Croton,* of the spurge family, several species of which, as *C. tiglium,* have important medicinal properties. **2.** (among florists) any plant of the related genus *Codiaeum* (or *Phyllaurea*) cultivated for its ornamental foliage. [1745–55; < NL < Gk *krotṓn* a tick, also the castor-oil plant, which has berries likened to ticks]

cro·ton·al·de·hyde (krōt′n al′də hīd′), *n. Chem.* a whitish liquid with pungent and suffocating odor, C_4H_6O, soluble in water, used as a solvent, in tear gas, and in organic synthesis. Also called **betamethyl acrolein, croton′ic al′dehyde.** [croton(ic) (see CROTONIC ACID) + ALDEHYDE]

cro·ton·bug (krōt′n bug′), *n.* See **German cockroach.** Also, **Cro′ton bug′.** [1855–60, *Amer.*; allegedly after the *Croton* Reservoir in Westchester Co., N.Y.; its opening in 1842 was supposedly coincident with a rise in New York City's cockroach population; see BUG[1]]

cro·ton′ic ac′id (krō ton′ik, -tō′nik), *Chem.* a colorless, crystalline, water-soluble solid, $C_4H_6O_2$, used chiefly in organic synthesis. [1830–40; CROTON + -IC]

cro′ton oil′, a brownish-yellow oil, expressed from the seeds of the croton, *Croton tiglium,* that is a drastic purgative and counterirritant. [1870–75]

crouch (krouch), *v.i.* **1.** to stoop or bend low. **2.** to bend close to the ground, as an animal preparing to spring or shrinking with fear. **3.** to bow or stoop servilely; cringe. —*v.t.* **4.** to bend low. —*n.* **5.** the act of crouching. [1175–1225; ME *crouchen,* perh. b. *couchen* to lie down (see COUCH) and *croken* to CROOK[1]] —**crouch′er,** *n.* —**crouch′ing·ly,** *adv.*

croup[1] (kro͞op), *n. Pathol.* any condition of the larynx or trachea characterized by a hoarse cough and difficult breathing. [1755–65; n. use of *croup* to cry hoarsely (now dial.), b. CROAK and WHOOP]

croup[2] (kro͞op), *n.* the highest part of the rump of a quadruped, esp. a horse. See diag. under **horse.** [1250–1300; ME *croupe* < MF, AF *crupe,* OF *crope* < Gmc; see CROP]

crou·pade (kro͞o päd′, kro͞o′päd), *n. Dressage.* a movement in which a horse jumps up from a pesade with all four legs drawn up under it and lands on four legs in the same place. [1840–50; < F (trans. of It *groppata*), equiv. to *croupe* CROUP[2] + *-ade* -ADE[1]]

crou·pi·er (kro͞o′pē ər, -pē ā′; *Fr.* kro͞o pyā′), *n., pl.* **-pi·ers** (-pē ərz, -pē āz′; *Fr.* -pyā′). **1.** an attendant in a gambling casino who rakes in money or chips and pays winners at a gaming table. **2.** an assistant chairperson at a public dinner. [1700–10; < F: lit., one who sits behind another on horseback, equiv. to *croupe* rump (see CROUP[2]) + *-ier* -IER[2]]

croup·y (kro͞o′pē), *adj.,* **croup·i·er, croup·i·est. 1.** pertaining to or resembling croup. **2.** affected with croup. [1825–35; CROUP[1] + -Y[1]] —**croup′i·ly,** *adv.* —**croup′i·ness,** *n.*

crouse (kro͞os), *adj. Scot. and North Eng.* brisk; lively. [1250–1300; ME *crus, crous* fierce, bold, violent < MLG or Fris *krūs* crisp; c. G *kraus*] —**crouse′ly,** *adv.*

Crouse (krous), *n.* **Russel,** 1893–1966, U.S. dramatist.

crous·tade (kro͞o städ′), *n.* a shell of bread or pastry, sometimes of noodles, rice, or mashed potatoes, baked or fried and filled with ragout or the like. [1835–45; < F < Pr *crustado* < L *crustātus,* ptp. of *crustāre* to encrust, deriv. of *crusta* CRUST]

croûte (kro͞ot), *n.* crust. [< F; see CRUST]

crou·ton (kro͞o′ton, kro͞o ton′), *n.* a small piece of fried or toasted bread, sometimes seasoned, used as a garnish for soups, salads, and other dishes. [1800–10; < F, equiv. to *croûte* CRUST + *-on* dim. suffix]

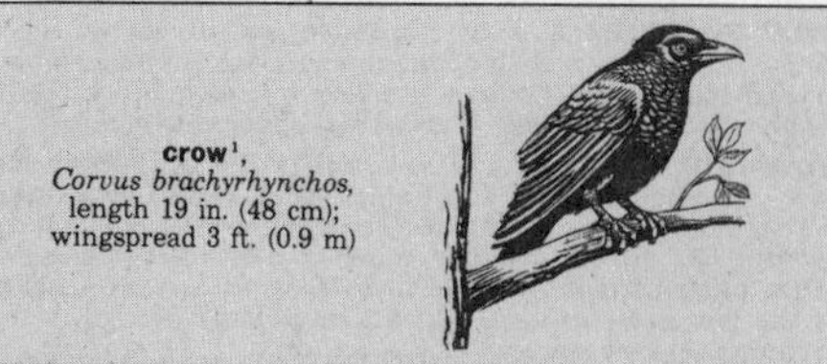
crow[1], *Corvus brachyrhynchos,* length 19 in. (48 cm); wingspread 3 ft. (0.9 m)

crow[1] (krō), *n.* **1.** any of several large oscine birds of the genus *Corvus,* of the family Corvidae, having a long, stout bill, lustrous black plumage, and a wedge-shaped tail, as the common *C. brachyrhynchos,* of North America. **2.** any of several other birds of the family Corvidae. **3.** any of various similar birds of other families. **4.** (*cap.*) *Astron.* the constellation Corvus. **5.** crowbar (def. 1). **6. as the crow flies,** in a straight line; by the most direct route: *The next town is thirty miles from here, as the crow flies.* **7. eat crow,** *Informal.* to be forced to admit to having made a mistake, as by retracting an emphatic statement; suffer humiliation: *His prediction was completely wrong, and he had to eat crow.* **8. have a crow to pick** or **pluck with someone,** *Midland and Southern U.S.* to have a reason to disagree or argue with someone. [bef. 900; ME *crowe,* OE *crāwe, crāwa;* c. OHG *krāwa;* akin to D *kraai,* G *Krähe*]

CONCISE PRONUNCIATION KEY: act, cāpe, dâre, pärt; set, ēqual; if, īce; ox, ōver, ôrder, oil, bo͝ok, bo͞ot, out; up, ûrge; child; sing; shoe; thin, *that;* zh as in *treasure.* ə = *a* as in *alone, e* as in *system, i* as in *easily, o* as in *gallop, u* as in *circus;* ᵊ as in *fire* (fīᵊr), *hour* (ouᵊr). l and n can serve as syllabic consonants, as in *cradle* (krād′l), and *button* (but′n). See the full key inside the front cover.

crow[2] (krō), *v.*, **crowed** or, for 1, (*esp. Brit.*), **crew; crowed; crow•ing;** *n.* —*v.i.* **1.** to utter the characteristic cry of a rooster. **2.** to gloat, boast, or exult (often fol. by *over*). **3.** to utter an inarticulate cry of pleasure, as an infant does. —*n.* **4.** the characteristic cry of a rooster. **5.** an inarticulate cry of pleasure. [bef. 1000; ME *crowen,* OE *crāwan;* c. D *kraaien,* G *krähen;* see CROW[1]] —**crow′er,** *n.* —**crow′ing•ly,** *adv.*
—**Syn. 2.** vaunt, brag.

Crow (krō), *n.* **1.** a member of a Siouan people of eastern Montana. **2.** a Siouan language closely related to Hidatsa. [1795–1805; trans. of North American F (*gens des) Corbeaux* Raven (people), literal trans. of Crow *apsáloke* a Crow Indian]

crow•bait (krō′bāt′), *n. Chiefly Northern, North Midland, and Western U.S.* an emaciated, worn-out horse or cow. [1855–60, *Amer.*; CROW[1] + BAIT]

crow•bar (krō′bär′), *n., v.t.,* **-barred, -bar•ring.** —*n.* **1.** Also called **crow.** a steel bar, usually flattened and slightly bent at one or both ends, used as a lever. —*v.t.* **2.** to pry open, loosen, etc., with a crowbar: *We had to crowbar a window to get in.* [1740–50, *Amer.*; CROW[1] + BAR[1]; so called because one end was beak-shaped]

crow•ber•ry (krō′ber′ē, -bə rē), *n., pl.* **-ries. 1.** the black or reddish berry of a heathlike, evergreen shrub, *Empetrum nigrum,* of northern regions. **2.** the plant itself. **3.** any of certain other fruits or the plants bearing similar berries, as the bearberry. [1590–1600; CROW[1] + BERRY, prob. trans. of G *Krähenbeere*]

crow′ black′bird, any of several North American grackles, esp. purple grackles of the genus *Quiscalus.* [1770–80, *Amer.*]

crow•boot (krō′bo͞ot′), *n. Canadian Dial.* a moccasinlike boot made of soft leather. [1960–65; appar. CROW[1] + BOOT[1], though literal sense unclear]

crowd[1] (kroud), *n.* **1.** a large number of persons gathered closely together; throng: *a crowd of angry people.* **2.** any large number of persons. **3.** any group or set of persons with something in common: *The restaurant attracts a theater crowd.* **4.** audience; attendance: *Opening night drew a good crowd.* **5.** the common people; the masses: *He feels superior to the crowd.* **6.** a large number of things gathered or considered together. **7.** *Sociol.* a temporary gathering of people responding to common stimuli and engaged in any of various forms of collective behavior. —*v.i.* **8.** to gather in large numbers; throng; swarm. **9.** to press forward; advance by pushing. —*v.t.* **10.** to press closely together; force into a confined space; cram: *to crowd clothes into a suitcase.* **11.** to push; shove. **12.** to fill to excess; fill by pressing or thronging into. **13.** to place under pressure or stress by constant solicitation: *to crowd a debtor for payment; to crowd someone with embarrassing questions.* **14. crowd on sail,** *Naut.* to carry a press of sail. [bef. 950; ME *crowden,* OE *crūden* to press, hurry; c. MD *crūden* to push (D *kruien*)] —**crowd′er,** *n.*
—**Syn. 1.** CROWD, MULTITUDE, SWARM, THRONG refer to large numbers of people. CROWD suggests a jostling, uncomfortable, and possibly disorderly company: *A crowd gathered to listen to the speech.* MULTITUDE emphasizes the great number of persons or things but suggests that there is space enough for all: *a multitude of people at the market on Saturdays.* SWARM as used of people is usually contemptuous, suggesting a moving, restless, often noisy, crowd: *A swarm of dirty children played in the street.* THRONG suggests a company that presses together or forward, often with some common aim: *The throng pushed forward to see the cause of the excitement.* **5.** proletariat, plebeians, populace. **8.** assemble, herd.
—**Usage.** See **collective noun.**

crowd[2] (kroud), *n.* an ancient Celtic musical instrument with the strings stretched over a rectangular frame, played with a bow. Also, **crwth.** [1275–1325; ME *crowd(e),* var. of *crouth* < Welsh *crwth* CRWTH]

crowd•ed (krou′did), *adj.* **1.** filled to excess; packed. **2.** filled with a crowd: *crowded streets.* **3.** uncomfortably close together: *crowded passengers on a bus.* [1605–15; CROWD[1] + -ED[2]] —**crowd′ed•ly,** *adv.*

crowd′er pea′, any variety of cowpea bearing pods with closely spaced seeds. [1780–90, *Amer.*]

crow•dy (kro͞o′dē, krō′-, kro͝od′ē), *n., pl.* **-dies.** *Scot. and North Eng.* a dish of meal, esp. oatmeal and water, or sometimes milk, stirred together; gruel; brose; porridge. Also, **crow′die.** [1490–1500; of obscure orig.]

crow•foot (krō′fo͝ot′), *n., pl.* **-foots** for 1, 2, **-feet** for 3–6. **1.** any plant of the genus *Ranunculus,* esp. one with divided leaves suggestive of a crow's foot; buttercup. **2.** any of various other plants with leaves or other parts suggestive of a bird's foot, as certain species of the genus *Geranium.* **3.** caltrop (def. 1). **4.** *Naut.* an arrangement of several bridlelike ropes rove through a suspended euphroe to support the backbone of an awning at a number of points. **5.** *Motion Pictures, Television.* a three-legged device placed under a tripod to keep the camera from slipping. **6.** (on an architectural or engineering drawing) a V-shaped mark the apex of which is a reference point. [1400–50; late ME *crowefote.* See CROW[1], FOOT]

crow•hop (krō′hop′), *n.* **1.** a short hop. **2.** a hop made by a horse with its legs stiffened and its back arched. [1895–1900, *Amer.*; CROW[1] + HOP[1]] —**crow′hop′per,** *n.*

Crow•ley (krou′lē), *n.* a city in S Louisiana. 16,036.

crown (kroun), *n.* **1.** any of various types of headgear worn by a monarch as a symbol of sovereignty, often made of precious metal and ornamented with valuable gems. **2.** a similar ornamental headgear worn by a person designated king or queen in a pageant, contest, etc. **3.** an ornamental wreath or circlet for the head, conferred by the ancients as a mark of victory, athletic or military distinction, etc. **4.** the distinction that comes from a great achievement. **5.** the power or dominion of a sovereign. **6.** (*often cap.*) the sovereign as head of the state, or the supreme governing power of a state under a monarchical government. **7.** any crownlike emblem or design, as in a heraldic crest. **8.** the top or highest part of anything, as of a hat or a mountain. **9.** the top of the head: *Jack fell down and broke his crown.* **10.** *Dentistry.* **a.** the part of a tooth that is covered by enamel. See diag. under **tooth. b.** an artificial substitute, as of gold or porcelain, for the crown of a tooth. **11.** the highest point of any construction of convex section or outline, as an arch, vault, deck, or road. **12.** the highest or most nearly perfect state of anything. **13.** an exalting or chief attribute. **14.** the acme or supreme source of honor, excellence, beauty, etc. **15.** something having the form of a crown, as the corona of a flower. **16.** *Bot.* **a.** the leaves and living branches of a tree. **b.** the point at which the root of a seed plant joins the stem. **c.** a circle of appendages on the throat of the corolla; corona. **17.** the crest, as of a bird. See diag. under **bird. 18.** *Archit.* **a.** a termination of a tower consisting of a lanternlike steeple supported entirely by a number of flying buttresses. **b.** any ornamental termination of a tower or turret. **19.** Also called **button.** *Horol.* a knurled knob for winding a watch. **20.** any of various coins bearing the figure of a crown or crowned head. **21.** a former silver coin of the United Kingdom, equal to five shillings: retained in circulation equal to 25 new pence after decimalization in 1971. **22.** the monetary unit of Denmark, Iceland, Norway, or Sweden: a krona or krone. **23.** the koruna of Czechoslovakia. **24.** a crimped metal bottle cap. **25.** See **crown glass. 26.** *Cookery.* See **crown roast. 27.** Also called **bezel, top.** *Jewelry.* the part of a cut gem above the girdle. **28.** a drill bit consisting of a metal matrix holding diamond chips. **29.** Also called **head.** *Naut.* the part of an anchor at which the arms join the shank. See diag. under **anchor. 30.** *Mach.* **a.** a slight convexity given to a pulley supporting a flat belt in order to center the belt. **b.** a slight convexity given to the outer faces of the teeth of two gears so that they mesh toward their centers rather than at the ends. **31.** a size of printing paper, 15 × 20 in. (38 × 51 cm). Cf. **double crown. 32.** *Naut., Mach.* swallow[1] (def. 12). **33.** *Knots.* a knot made by interweaving the strands at the end of a rope, often made as the beginning of a back splice or as the first stage in tying a more elaborate knot. **34.** a crownpiece.
—*v.t.* **35.** to invest with a regal crown, or with regal dignity and power. **36.** to place a crown or garland upon the head of. **37.** to honor or reward; invest with honor, dignity, etc. **38.** to be at the top or highest part of. **39.** to complete worthily; bring to a successful or triumphant conclusion: *The award crowned his career.* **40.** *Informal.* to hit on the top of the head: *She crowned her brother with a picture book.* **41.** to give to (a construction) an upper surface of convex section or outline. **42.** to cap (a tooth) with a false crown. **43.** *Checkers.* to change (a checker) into a king after having safely reached the last row. **44.** *Knots.* to form a crown on (the end of a rope).
—*v.i.* **45.** *Med.* (of a baby in childbirth) to reach a stage in delivery where the largest diameter of the fetal head is emerging from the pelvic outlet. [1125–75; ME *coroune, cr(o)une* < AF *coroune* < L *corōna* wreath; see CORONA] —**crown′less,** *adj.*

crowns of British royalty and nobility: A, sovereign; B, duke; C, earl; D, viscount

crown′ ant′ler, the topmost prong of a stag's antler. See diag. under **antler.** Also called **sur-royal.**

crown•beard (kroun′bērd′), *n.* any of various American composite plants constituting the genus *Verbesina,* having clustered, usually yellow flower heads. [1855–60, *Amer.*; CROWN + BEARD]

crown′ can′opy. canopy (def. 4).

crown′ col′ony, a British colony in which the crown has the entire control of legislation and administration, as distinguished from one having a constitution and representative government. [1835–45]

Crown′ corpora′tion, *Canadian.* a commercial company owned by the government and controlled and partially operated by civil servants. [1960–65]

crown′ cut′ter, a hollow, thin-walled cylinder having teeth formed radially on the end and used for cutting round holes out of thin, flat stock. Cf. **crown saw.**

crown′ dai′sy, a garden plant, *Chrysanthemum coronarium,* of the composite family, native to southern Europe, having numerous yellowish-white flower heads. [1880–85]

crowned (kround), *adj.* **1.** characterized by or having a crown (often used in combination): *a crowned signet ring; a low-crowned fedora.* **2.** originating from or founded on the royal crown or its associated dignity, sovereignty, etc.: *crowned despotism.* [1200–50; ME *crouned.* See CROWN, -ED[2]]

crown•er[1] (krou′nər), *n.* **1.** a person or thing that crowns. **2.** a crowning event or occurrence. [1400–50; late ME; see CROWN, -ER[1]]

crown•er[2] (krou′nər, kro͞o′-), *n. Brit. Dial.* coroner. [1300–50; ME; see CROWN, -ER[2]]

crown•et (krou′net, -nit), *n. Archaic.* a coronet. [1350–1400; ME; see CROWN, -ET]

crown′ fire′, a forest fire that spreads along treetops, often at great speeds. [1920–25, *Amer.*]

crown′ gall′, *Plant Pathol.* **1.** a disease of peaches, apples, roses, grapes, etc., characterized by the formation of galls on the roots or stems usually at or below ground level, caused by a bacterium, *Agrobacterium tumefaciens.* **2.** the gall itself. [1895–1900]

crown′ glass′, 1. an optical glass of low dispersion and generally low index of refraction. **2.** an old form of window glass formed by blowing a globe and whirling it into a disk. [1700–10]

crown′ graft′, *Hort.* a graft in which the scion is inserted at the crown of the stock. [1720–30] —**crown′ graft′ing.**

crown′ impe′rial, an Iranian plant, *Fritillaria imperialis,* of the lily family, having a purple-spotted stem and a whorl of usually reddish-orange flowers hanging beneath a tuft of leaves, grown as an ornamental. [1535–45]

crown•ing (krou′ning), *adj.* **1.** representing a level of surpassing achievement, attainment, etc.; supreme: *crowning accomplishment.* **2.** forming or providing a crown, top, or summit: *a crowning star on a Christmas tree.* [CROWN + -ING[2]]

crown′ land′, 1. land belonging to the crown, the revenue of which goes to the reigning sovereign. **2.** Also, **crown′land′.** one of the administrative divisions of the former empire of Austria-Hungary. [1615–25]

crown′ lens′, *Optics.* a lens made of crown glass, usually used as the converging lens component of an achromatic lens. [1825–35]

crown′ octa′vo, a size of book, about 5 × 7½ in. (13 × 19 cm), untrimmed. *Abbr.:* crown 8vo

crown-of-jew•els (kroun′əv jo͞o′əlz), *n., pl.* **-jew•els.** an annual herb, *Lopezia coronata,* of Mexico, having lilac-colored flowers with a red base.

crown′ of thorns′, 1. a climbing spurge, *Euphorbia milii splendens,* of Madagascar, having stems covered with spines. **2.** See **crown of thorns starfish. 3.** a painful burden, as of suffering, guilt, anxiety, etc.: from the wreath of thorns placed on Jesus' head to mock Him before He was crucified. Matt. 27:29; Mark 15:17; John 19:2, 5. [bef. 950; ME; OE]

crown′-of-thorns′ star′fish (kroun′əv thôrnz′), a starfish, *Acanthaster planci,* that feeds on living coral polyps, causing erosion and destruction of coral reefs. Also called **crown of thorns.** [1960–65]

crown•piece (kroun′pēs′), *n.* the strap of a bridle that fits across the head of a horse. See illus. under **harness.** [1640–50; CROWN + PIECE]

Crown′ Point′, 1. a village in NE New York, on Lake Champlain: the site of a strategic fort in the French and Indian and the Revolutionary wars. 1837. **2.** a town in NW Indiana. 16,455.

crown′ post′, any vertical member in a roof truss, esp. a king post. [1695–1705]

crown′ prince′, a male heir apparent to a throne. [1785–95]

crown′ prin′cess, 1. the wife of a crown prince. **2.** a female heir presumptive or heir apparent to a throne. [1860–65]

crown′ quar′to, *Chiefly Brit.* a size of book, about 7½ × 10 in. (19 × 25 cm), untrimmed. *Abbr.:* crown 4to

crown′ roast′, *Cookery.* a cut of meat, esp. lamb, veal, or pork, that is made by tying two rib roasts together in a circle. Also called **crown.** [1905–10]

crown′ rot′, *Plant Pathol.* a disease of plants, characterized by the rotting of the stem at ground level, caused by any of several fungi. [1920–25]

crown′ rust′, *Plant Pathol.* a disease of oats and other grasses, characterized by the formation, on the leaves, of orange or black spores, caused by a rust fungus, *Puccinia coronata.* [1895–1900]

crown′ saw′, a rotary saw consisting of a hollow cylinder with teeth formed on one end or edge, as a trephine or trepanning saw. Also called **cylinder saw, hole saw.** [1860–65]

crown′ vetch′, a plant, *Coronilla varia,* of the legume family, native to the Old World, having clusters of pink flowers and used to prevent erosion on banked roadsides. Also called **axseed.** [1895–1900]

crown′ wart′, *Plant Pathol.* a disease of alfalfa and clover, characterized by galls around the base of the stem, caused by several fungi of the genus *Urophlyctis.*

crown′ wheel′, *Horol.* **1.** a wheel next to the winding knob, having two sets of teeth, one at right angles to its plane. **2.** any of various wheels having the form of a hoop or short cylinder with a serrated edge, as the escape wheel in a verge escapement. [1640–50]

crown•work (kroun′wûrk′), *n. Fort.* an outwork containing a central bastion with a curtain and demibastions, usually designed to cover some advantageous position. [1670–80; CROWN + WORK]

crow-pheas•ant (krō′fez′ənt), *n.* a large coucal, *Centropus sinensis,* of Asia, having black and brown plumage and a long tail.

crow's-foot (krōz′fo͝ot′), *n., pl.* **-feet. 1.** Usually, **crow's-feet.** any of the tiny wrinkles at the outer corners of the eyes resulting from age or constant squinting. **2.** *Aeron.* an arrangement of ropes in which one main rope exerts pull at several points simultaneously through a group of smaller ropes, as in balloon or airship rigging. **3.** (in tailoring) a three-pointed embroidered design used as a finish, as at the end of a seam or opening. **4.** crowfoot (def. 1). [1350–1400; ME; so called because likened to a crow's foot or footprint]

crow's-nest (krōz′nest′), *n.* **1.** *Naut.* a platform or shelter for a lookout at or near the top of a mast. **2.** any

CONCISE ETYMOLOGY KEY: <, descended or borrowed from; >, whence; b., blend of, blended; c., cognate with; cf., compare; deriv., derivative; equiv., equivalent; imit., imitative; obl., oblique; r., replacing; s., stem; sp., spelling, spelled; resp., respelling, respelled; trans., translation; ?, origin unknown; *, unattested; ‡, probably earlier than. See the full key inside the front cover.

similar platform raised high above the ground, as a lookout or a station for a traffic officer. Also, **crow's′ nest′.** [1595–1605]

crow•step (krō′step′), *n.* corbiestep. [1815–25; CROW[1] + STEP]

Croy•don (kroid′n), *n.* a borough of Greater London, England: airport. 324,900.

croze (krōz), *n.* **1.** the groove at either end of the staves of a barrel, cask, etc., into which the edge of the head fits. **2.** a tool used by a cooper for cutting such a groove. [1605–15; perh. special use of *crose, croze* (var. of CROSS) in sense "cross groove"]

cro•zier (krō′zhər), *n.* crosier.

CRP, *Biochem.* See **C-reactive protein.**

crs., 1. creditors. **2.** credits.

CRT, 1. cathode-ray tube. **2.** a computer terminal or monitor that includes a cathode ray tube.

cru (kro͞o; *Fr.* KRY), *n., pl.* **crus** (kro͞oz; *Fr.* KRY). (in France) a vineyard producing wine of high quality, sometimes classified by the government as either a Great Growth **(Grand Cru)** or a First Growth **(Premier Cru).** [1815–25; < F, n. use of *crû,* ptp. of *croître* to grow < L *crēscere*]

cru•ces (kro͞o′sēz), *n.* a pl. of **crux.**

cru•cial (kro͞o′shəl), *adj.* **1.** involving an extremely important decision or result; decisive; critical: *a crucial experiment.* **2.** severe; trying. **3.** of the form of a cross; cross-shaped. [1700–10; < L *cruci-* (s. of *crux*) CROSS + -AL[1]] **—cru•ci•al•i•ty** (kro͞o′shē al′i tē, kro͞o shal′-), *n.* **—cru′cial•ly,** *adv.*
—Syn. 1. momentous, vital, essential, significant.

cru′cian carp′ (kro͞o′shən), a common cyprinid, *Carassius carassius,* that closely resembles the wild form of goldfish, occurring in streams in most parts of Europe and northern Asia. [1755–65; earlier *crusion,* prob. < LG (with pl. ending *-en* interpreted as sing.) *Krunsch, Kruutsch,* MLG *Karūsse* (cf. D *Karuts,* G *Karausche*), perh. ult. < L *coracīnus* < Gk *korakînos* a fish of the Nile]

cru•ci•ate (kro͞o′shē it, -āt′), *adj.* **1.** cross-shaped. **2.** *Bot.* having the form of a cross with equal arms, as the flowers of mustard. **3.** *Entomol.* crossing diagonally when at rest, as the wings of certain insects. [1675–85; < NL *cruciātus,* equiv. to L *cruci-* (s. of *crux*) CROSS + *-ātus* -ATE[1]] **—cru′ci•ate•ly,** *adv.*

cru•ci•ble (kro͞o′sə bəl), *n.* **1.** a container of metal or refractory material employed for heating substances to high temperatures. **2.** *Metall.* a hollow area at the bottom of a furnace in which the metal collects. **3.** a severe, searching test or trial. [1400–50; late ME *crusible, corusible* < ML *crucibulum;* cf. AF *crusil,* OF *croisuel, croisol* night lamp, crucible < Gallo-Rom **croceolus* (of uncert. orig.), prob. Latinized on the model of *tūribulum* THURIBLE]

cru′cible steel′, steel made in a crucible, esp. a high-grade steel prepared by melting selected materials. [1875–80]

cru•ci•fer (kro͞o′sə fər), *n.* **1.** a person who carries a cross, as in ecclesiastical processions. **2.** *Bot.* a cruciferous plant. [1565–75; < LL, equiv. to L *cruci-* (s. of *crux*) CROSS + *-fer* -FER]

cru•cif•er•ous (kro͞o sif′ər əs), *adj.* **1.** bearing a cross. **2.** *Bot.* belonging to the Cruciferae, the mustard family of plants. Cf. **mustard family.** [1650–60; < LL *crucifer* CRUCIFER; see -OUS]

cru•ci•fix (kro͞o′sə fiks), *n.* **1.** a cross with the figure of Jesus crucified upon it. **2.** any cross. **3.** *Gymnastics.* a stunt performed on the parallel rings in which the athlete holds himself or herself rigid with arms extended horizontally from the shoulders. [1175–1225; ME < LL *crucifixus* the crucified one (i.e., Christ), n. use of masc. of ptp. of L *crucifīgere* to CRUCIFY; see FIX] **—cru•ci•fi•cial** (kro͞o′sə fish′əl), *adj.*

cru•ci•fix•ion (kro͞o′sə fik′shən), *n.* **1.** the act of crucifying. **2.** the state of being crucified. **3.** (*cap.*) the death of Jesus upon the Cross. **4.** a picture or other representation of this. **5.** severe and unjust punishment or suffering; persecution. [1375–1425; late ME < LL *crucifixiōn-* (s. of *crucifixiō*). See CRUCIFIX, -ION]

cru•ci•form (kro͞o′sə fôrm′), *adj.* **1.** cross-shaped. *—n.* **2.** a cross. [1655–65; < L *cruci-* (s. of *crux*) cross + -FORM] **—cru′ci•for′mi•ty,** *n.* **—cru′ci•form′ly,** *adv.*

cru•ci•fy (kro͞o′sə fī′), *v.t.,* **-fied, -fy•ing. 1.** to put to death by nailing or binding the hands and feet to a cross. **2.** to treat with gross injustice; persecute; torment; torture. **3.** to subdue (passion, sin, etc.). [ME *crucifien* < AF, OF *crucifier* < L *crucifīgere,* equiv. to L *cruci-* (s. of *crux*) CROSS + *fīgere* to fix, bind fast] **—cru′ci•fi′er,** *n.*

Cru•cis (kro͞o′sis), *n. Astron.* gen. of **Crux.** [< L]

cru•ci•ver•bal•ist (kro͞o′sə vûr′bə list), *n.* a designer or aficionado of crossword puzzles. [1975–80; < L *cruci-,* s. of *crux* CROSS + VERBALIST]

cruck (kruk), *n.* (in old English building) one of a pair of naturally curved timbers forming one of several rigid arched frames supporting the roof of a cottage or farm building. [1885–90; var. of CROOK[1]]

crud (krud), *n., v.,* **crud•ded, crud•ding.** *—n.* **1.** *Slang.* **a.** a deposit or coating of refuse or of an impure or alien substance; muck. **b.** a filthy, repulsive, or contemptible person. **c.** something that is worthless, objectionable, or contemptible. **d.** prevarication, exaggeration, or flattery. **e.** a nonspecific, imaginary, or vaguely defined disease or disorder of the body: *jungle crud.* **f.** any unpleasant external ailment, disorder, or the like, as a skin rash. **g.** venereal disease, esp. syphilis. **h.** *Vulgar.* dried semen. **2.** *Dial.* curd. **3.** *Dial.* clabber. *—v.t., v.i.* **4.** *Dial.* to curd. [1325–75; ME; earlier form of CURD]
—Regional Variation. 3. See **clabber.**

crud•dy (krud′ē), *adj.,* **-di•er, -di•est.** *Slang.* **1.** covered, encrusted, or saturated with dirt, grease, or other objectionable substance; filthy: *It gets the cruddiest work clothes clean.* **2.** worthless or useless; inferior in quality; lousy: *a cruddy, broken-down car.* **3.** extremely disagreeable in character; nasty; contemptible; low-down: *Keep your cruddy remarks to yourself.* [1945–50; CRUD + -Y[1]]

crude (kro͞od), *adj.,* **crud•er, crud•est,** *n. —adj.* **1.** in a raw or unprepared state; unrefined or natural: *crude sugar.* **2.** lacking in intellectual subtlety, perceptivity, etc.; rudimentary; undeveloped. **3.** lacking finish, polish, or completeness: *a crude summary.* **4.** lacking culture, refinement, tact, etc.: *crude behavior.* **5.** undisguised; blunt: *a crude answer.* **6.** *Obs.* unripe; not mature. *—n.* **7.** See **crude oil.** [1350–1400; ME < L *crūdus* uncooked, raw, bleeding, rough, akin to *cruor* blood from a wound; see RAW] **—crude′ly,** *adv.* **—crude′ness,** *n.*
—Syn. 1. unfinished, coarse. See **raw. 4.** uncouth, rough, rude, coarse, clumsy. **—Ant. 1, 4.** refined.

crude′ oil′, petroleum as it comes from the ground, before refining. Also called **crude, crude′ petro′leum.** [1860–65]

cru•di•tés (kro͞o′di tā′; *Fr.* KRY dē tā′), *n.* (*used with singular or plural v.*) *French Cookery.* an appetizer consisting of a variety of raw vegetables, usually cut into strips or bite-size pieces, and served with a dip. [1965–70; < F, pl. of *crudité* lit., rawness, CRUDITY]

cru•di•ty (kro͞o′di tē), *n., pl.* **-ties** for 2. **1.** the state or quality of being crude. **2.** something crude. [1375–1425; late ME *crudite* < L *crūditās.* See CRUDE, -ITY]

cru•el (kro͞o′əl), *adj.,* **-er, -est. 1.** willfully or knowingly causing pain or distress to others. **2.** enjoying the pain or distress of others: *the cruel spectators of the gladiatorial contests.* **3.** causing or marked by great pain or distress: *a cruel remark; a cruel affliction.* **4.** rigid; stern; strict; unrelentingly severe. [1175–1225; ME < AF, OF < L *crūdēlis,* equiv. to *crūd(us)* (see CRUDE) + *-ēlis* adj. suffix] **—cru′el•ly,** *adv.* **—cru′el•ness,** *n.*
—Syn. 1. bloodthirsty, ferocious, merciless, relentless. CRUEL, PITILESS, RUTHLESS, BRUTAL, SAVAGE imply readiness to cause pain to others. CRUEL implies willingness to cause pain, and indifference to suffering: *a cruel stepfather.* PITILESS adds the idea of refusal to show compassion: *pitiless to captives.* RUTHLESS implies cruelty and unscrupulousness, letting nothing stand in one's way: *ruthless greed.* BRUTAL implies cruelty that takes the form of physical violence: *a brutal master.* SAVAGE suggests fierceness and brutality: *savage battles.*

cru•el•heart•ed (kro͞o′əl här′tid), *adj.* having a cruel heart; lacking kindness, compassion, etc. [1585–95; CRUEL + HEARTED]

cru•el•ty (kro͞o′əl tē), *n., pl.* **-ties** for 3. **1.** the state or quality of being cruel. **2.** cruel disposition or conduct. **3.** a cruel act. **4.** *Law.* conduct by a spouse that causes grievous bodily harm or mental suffering. [1175–1225; ME *cruelte* < AF, OF < L *crūdēlitāt-* (s. of *crūdēlitās*). See CRUEL, -ITY]
—Syn. 1. harshness, brutality, ruthlessness, barbarity, inhumanity, atrocity. **—Ant. 2, 3.** kindness.

cru•et (kro͞o′it), *n.* a glass bottle, esp. one for holding vinegar, oil, etc., for the table. [1250–1300; ME < AF, equiv. to OF *cru(i)e* pitcher (< Frankish **krūka;* cf. OE *crūce* pot) + *-et* -ET]

Cruik•shank (kro͝ok′shangk′), *n.* **George,** 1792–1878, English illustrator, caricaturist, and painter.

cruise (kro͞oz), *v.,* **cruised, cruis•ing,** *n. —v.i.* **1.** to sail about on a pleasure trip. **2.** to sail about, as a warship patrolling a body of water. **3.** to travel about without a particular purpose or destination. **4.** to fly, drive, or sail at a constant speed that permits maximum operating efficiency for sustained travel. **5.** to travel at a moderately fast, easily controllable speed: *cruising along the highway enjoying the scenery.* **6.** to travel about slowly, looking for customers or for something demanding attention: *Taxis and police cars cruise in the downtown area.* **7.** to go or travel (often fol. by *over*): *Let's cruise over to my house after the concert.* **8.** *Informal.* to go about on the streets or in public areas in search of a sexual partner. *—v.t.* **9.** to cruise in (a specified area): *patrol cars cruising the neighborhood; to cruise the Caribbean.* **10.** *Informal.* **a.** to move slowly through or visit (a street, park, bar, etc.) in search of a sexual partner. **b.** to make sexual overtures to; attempt to arouse the sexual interest of. **11.** to inspect (a tract of forest) for the purpose of estimating lumber potential. *—n.* **12.** the act of cruising. **13.** a pleasure voyage on a ship, usually with stops at various ports. [1645–55; < D *kruisen* to cross, cruise, deriv. of *kruis* CROSS] **—cruis′•ing•ly,** *adv.*

cruise′ car′. See **squad car.**

cruise′ control′, a system, available for some automobiles, motorcycles, etc., that automatically maintains a vehicle's speed by taking control of the accelerator.

cruise′ miss′ile, a winged guided missile designed to deliver a conventional or nuclear warhead by flying at low altitudes to avoid detection by radar.

cruis•er (kro͞o′zər), *n.* **1.** a person or thing that cruises. **2.** one of a class of warships of medium tonnage, designed for high speed and long cruising radius. **3.** See **squad car. 4.** a vessel, esp. a power-driven one, intended for cruising. **5.** See **cabin cruiser. 6.** Also called **timber cruiser.** a person who estimates the value of the timber in a tract of forest. **7.** *Slang.* a prostitute who walks the street soliciting customers. [1670–80; < D *kruiser,* equiv. to *kruis(en)* to CRUISE + *-er* -ER[1]]

cruis•er•weight (kro͞o′zər wāt′), *n. Brit.* a light-heavyweight boxer. [1915–20; so called by metaphor, since a cruiser is the second heaviest naval ship]

cruise′ ship′, a passenger ship built or used for pleasure cruises, usually taking passengers on an extended cruise with occasional calls in various places of interest. [1715–25]

cruise•way (kro͞oz′wā′), *n. Brit.* an inland waterway or canal for pleasure cruising. [1965–70; CRUISE + WAY]

cruis′ing ra′dius, the maximum distance that an aircraft or ship can traverse and then return to its starting point at cruising speed without refueling. [1925–30]

crul•ler (krul′ər), *n.* **1.** a rich, light cake cut from a rolled dough and deep-fried, usually having a twisted oblong shape and sometimes topped with sugar or icing. **2.** Also called **French cruller.** a rich, light, raised doughnut, often with a ridged surface and sometimes topped with white icing. Also, **kruller.** [1795–1805, *Amer.;* < D *krul* CURL + -ER[1]]

crumb (krum), *n.* **1.** a small particle of bread, cake, etc., that has broken off. **2.** a small particle or portion of anything; fragment; bit. **3.** the soft inner portion of a bread (distinguished from *crust*). **4. crumbs,** a cake topping made of sugar, flour, butter, and spice, usually crumbled on top of the raw batter and baked with the cake. **5.** *Slang.* a contemptibly objectionable or worthless person. *—v.t.* **6.** *Cookery.* to dress or prepare with crumbs. **7.** to break into crumbs or small fragments. **8.** to remove crumbs from: *The waiter crumbed the table.* [bef. 1000; ME *crome, crume,* OE *cruma;* akin to D *kruim,* G *Krume* crumb, L *grūmus* heap of earth] **—crumb′a•ble,** *adj.* **—crumb′er,** *n.*
—Syn. 2. scrap, shred, morsel, sliver, speck.

crum•ble (krum′bəl), *v.,* **-bled, -bling,** *n. —v.t.* **1.** to break into small fragments or crumbs. *—v.i.* **2.** to fall into small pieces; break or part into small fragments. **3.** to decay or disintegrate gradually: *The ancient walls had crumbled.* *—n.* **4.** a crumbly or crumbled substance. **5. crumbles,** bits of crisp bacon, bread, etc., added to other foods, esp. as a topping. **6.** *Brit. Dial.* crumb; particle; fragment. [1375–1425; earlier *crymble, crimble;* late ME *kremelen,* akin to *crome* CRUMB; see -LE] **—crum′bling•ness,** *n.*
—Syn. 1. mash, shatter. **2.** disintegrate.

crum•blings (krum′blingz), *n.pl.* crumbs; crumbled bits. [CRUMBLE + -ING[1] + -S[3]]

crum•bly (krum′blē), *adj.,* **-bli•er, -bli•est.** apt to crumble; friable. [1515–25; CRUMBLE + -Y[1]] **—crum′•bli•ness,** *n.*

crum•bum (krum′bum′), *n. Slang.* crumb (def. 5). [1950–55; playful variation]

crumb•y[1] (krum′ē), *adj.,* **crumb•i•er, crumb•i•est. 1.** full of crumbs. **2.** soft. [1725–35; CRUMB + -Y[1]]

crumb•y[2] (krum′ē), *adj.,* **crumb•i•er, crumb•i•est.** crummy[1] (def. 1).

crum•horn (krum′hôrn′), *n.* a Renaissance musical reed instrument having a cylindrical tube curved at the end. Also, **cromorne, krumhorn.** [1950–55; < G *Krummhorn,* equiv. to *krumm* crooked, bent + *Horn* HORN]

crum•mie (krum′ē, kro͝om′ē), *n. Chiefly Scot.* a cow with crooked horns. Also, **crummy.** [1715–25; obs. *crum* crooked (OE *crumb;* c. G *krumm*) + -IE]

crum•my[1] (krum′ē), *adj.,* **-mi•er, -mi•est,** *n., pl.* **-mies.** *—adj.* **1.** Also, **crumby.** *Slang.* **a.** dirty and run-down; shabby; seedy: *a crummy fleabag of a hotel.* **b.** of little or no value; cheap; worthless: *crummy furniture that falls apart after a month of use.* **c.** wretchedly inadequate; miserable; lousy: *They pay crummy salaries.* *—n.* **2.** *Railroads Slang.* a caboose. [1855–60; perh. obs. *crum* crooked (see CRUMMIE) + -Y[1]; sense "caboose" of unclear derivation and perh. a distinct word] **—crum′•mi•ly,** *adv.* **—crum′mi•ness,** *n.*

crum•my[2] (krum′ē, kro͝om′ē), *n., pl.* **-mies.** *Chiefly Scot.* crummie.

crump (krump, kro͝omp), *v.t.* **1.** to crunch or make a crunching sound, as with the teeth. *—v.i.* **2.** (of an artillery shell) to land and explode with a heavy, muffled sound. **3.** to make a crunching sound, as in walking over snow, or as snow when trodden on. *—n.* **4.** a crunching sound. **5.** a large explosive shell or bomb. **6.** Also called **bump.** *Mining.* a sudden ground movement in underground workings. [1640–50; imit.]

crum•pet (krum′pit), *n.* *Chiefly Brit.* **1.** a round soft unsweetened bread resembling a muffin, cooked on a griddle or the like, and often toasted. **2.** *Brit. Slang.* a sexually attractive woman. [1350–1400; short for *crumpetcake* curled cake, equiv. to ME *crompid* (ptp. of *crumpen,* var. of *crampen* to bend, curl (see CRAMP[1]) + CAKE]

crum•ple (krum′pəl), *v.,* **-pled, -pling,** *n. —v.t.* **1.** to press or crush into irregular folds or into a compact mass; bend out of shape; rumple; wrinkle. **2.** to cause to collapse or give way suddenly: *That right hook to the midsection crumpled him.* *—v.i.* **3.** to contract into wrinkles; shrink; shrivel. **4.** to give way suddenly; collapse. *—n.* **5.** an irregular fold or wrinkle produced by crumpling. [1400–50; late ME; var. of CRIMPLE] **—crum′ply,** *adj.*

crum•pled (krum′pəld), *adj.* **1.** rumpled; wrinkled; crushed. **2.** bent in a spiral curve: *a crumpled ram's horn.* [1275–1325; ME; var. of *crimpled,* ptp. of CRIMPLE]

crunch (krunch), *v.t.* **1.** to crush with the teeth; chew with a crushing noise. **2.** to crush or grind noisily. **3.** to tighten or squeeze financially: *The administration's policy seems to crunch the economy in order to combat inflation.* *—v.i.* **4.** to chew with a crushing sound. **5.** to produce, or proceed with, a crushing noise. **6. crunch numbers,** *Computers.* **a.** to perform a great many numerical calculations or extensive manipulations of numerical data. **b.** to process a large amount of data. *—n.* **7.** an act or sound of crunching. **8.** a shortage or reduction of something needed or wanted: *the energy crunch.* **9.** distress or depressed conditions due to such a shortage or reduction: *a budget crunch.* **10.** a critical or dangerous situation: *When the crunch comes, just do your best.* Also, **craunch.** [1795–1805; b. CRAUNCH and CRUSH] **—crunch′a•ble,** *adj.*

crunch•er (krun′chər), *n.* **1.** a person or thing that crunches. **2.** *Informal.* a decisive blow, argument, event, or the like. [1945–50; CRUNCH + -ER[1]]

crunch·y (krun′chē), *adj.*, **crunch·i·er, crunch·i·est.** crisp; brittle. [1890–95; CRUNCH + -Y[1]] —**crunch′i·ly,** *adv.* —**crunch′i·ness,** *n.*

cru·or (kro͞o′ôr), *n.* coagulated blood, or the portion of the blood that forms the clot. [1650–60; < L: blood (that flows from a wound), gore; akin to CRUDE]

crup·per (krup′ər, kro͝op′-), *n.* **1.** a leather strap fastened to the saddle of a harness and looping under the tail of a horse to prevent the harness from slipping forward. See illus. under **harness. 2.** the rump or buttocks of a horse. **3.** armor for the rump of a horse. [1250–1300; ME *cro(u)per,* var. of *cruper* < AF. See CROUP[2], -ER[2]]

cru·ral (kro͝or′əl), *adj.* **1.** of or pertaining to the leg or the hind limb. **2.** *Anat., Zool.* of or pertaining to the leg proper, or crus. [1590–1600; < L *crūrālis* belonging to the legs, equiv. to *crūr-* (s. of *crūs*) leg + *-ālis* -AL[1]]

crus (krus, kro͞os), *n., pl.* **cru·ra** (kro͝or′ə). *Anat., Zool.* **1.** the part of the leg or hind limb between the femur or thigh and the ankle or tarsus; shank. **2.** a limb or process, as of a bone or other structure. **3.** any of various parts likened to a leg or to a pair of legs. [1680–90; < L: leg, shank]

cru·sade (kro͞o sād′), *n., v.,* **-sad·ed, -sad·ing.** —*n.* **1.** (*often cap.*) any of the military expeditions undertaken by the Christians of Europe in the 11th, 12th, and 13th centuries for the recovery of the Holy Land from the Muslims. **2.** any war carried on under papal sanction. **3.** any vigorous, aggressive movement for the defense or advancement of an idea, cause, etc.: *a crusade against child abuse.* —*v.i.* **4.** to go on or engage in a crusade. [1570–80; earlier *crusada* < Sp *cruzada;* r. *croisade* < MF. See CROSS, -ADE[1]] —**cru·sad′er,** *n.*

cru·sa·do (kro͞o sā′dō, -zā′-), *n., pl.* **-does, -dos.** an early Portuguese coin of gold or silver, bearing the figure of a cross. Also, **cruzado.** [1535–45; < Pg *cruzado* crossed, marked with a cross. See CROSS, -ATE[1]]

cruse (kro͞oz, kro͞os), *n.* an earthen pot, bottle, etc., for liquids. [1225–75; ME *crouse* (OE *crūse;* c. G *Krause* pot with lid), conflated with *croo* (OE *crōg, crōh;* c. G *Krug* jug)]

crush (krush), *v.t.* **1.** to press or squeeze with a force that destroys or deforms. **2.** to squeeze or pound into small fragments or particles, as ore, stone, etc. **3.** to force out by pressing or squeezing; extract: *to crush cottonseeds in order to produce oil.* **4.** to rumple; wrinkle; crease. **5.** to smooth or flatten by pressure: *to crush leather.* **6.** to hug or embrace forcibly or strongly: *He crushed her in his arms.* **7.** to destroy, subdue, or suppress utterly: *to crush a revolt.* **8.** to overwhelm with confusion, chagrin, or humiliation, as by argumentation or a slighting action or remark; squelch. **9.** to oppress grievously. **10.** *Archaic.* to finish drinking (wine, ale, etc.). —*v.i.* **11.** to become crushed. **12.** to advance with crushing; press or crowd forcibly. —*n.* **13.** the act of crushing; state of being crushed. **14.** a great crowd: *a crush of shoppers.* **15.** *Informal.* **a.** an intense but usually short-lived infatuation. **b.** the object of such an infatuation: *Who is your latest crush?* [1300–50; ME *cruschen* < MF *cruisir* < Gmc; cf. OSw *krusa, krosa,* MLG *krossen* to crush] —**crush′a·ble,** *adj.* —**crush′a·bil′i·ty,** *n.* —**crush′a·bly,** *adv.* —**crush′er,** *n.*
—**Syn. 1.** crumple, rumple. **2.** pulverize, powder, mash, crumble. See **break. 7.** quell, overcome, quash.

crushed′ vel′vet, velvet processed to have an uneven, slightly wrinkled surface.

crush·proof (krush′pro͞of′), *adj.* resistant to being crushed: *a crushproof box.* [CRUSH + -PROOF]

Cru·soe (kro͞o′sō), *n.* **Robinson.** See **Robinson Crusoe.**

crust (krust), *n.* **1.** the brown, hard outer portion or surface of a loaf or slice of bread (distinguished from *crumb*). **2.** a slice of bread from the end of a loaf, consisting chiefly of this. **3.** the pastry covering the outside of a pie or other dish. **4.** a piece of stale bread. **5.** any more or less hard external covering or coating: *a crust of snow.* **6.** *Geol.* the outer layer of the earth, about 22 mi. (35 km) deep under the continents and 6 mi. (10 km) deep under the oceans. Cf. **mantle** (def. 3), **core**[1] (def. 10). **7.** a scab or eschar. **8.** *Slang.* unabashed self-assertiveness; nerve; gall: *He had a lot of crust going to the party without an invitation.* **9.** deposit from wine, as it ripens during aging, on the interior of bottles, consisting of tartar and coloring matter. **10.** the hard outer shell or covering of an animal. **11.** *Australian Slang.* a living or livelihood: *What do you do for a crust?* —*v.t.* **12.** to cover with or as with a crust; encrust. **13.** to form (something) into a crust. —*v.i.* **14.** to form or contract a crust. **15.** to form into a crust. [1275–1325; ME < AF, OF *cruste, croste* < L *crusta* hard coating, crust] —**crust′less,** *adj.*

crus·ta·cean (kru stā′shən), *n.* **1.** any chiefly aquatic arthropod of the class Crustacea, typically having the body covered with a hard shell or crust, including the lobsters, shrimps, crabs, barnacles, and wood lice. —*adj.* **2.** belonging or pertaining to the crustaceans. [1825–35; < NL *Crustace(a)* (neut. pl.) hard-shelled ones (see CRUST, -ACEA) + -AN]

crus·ta·ceous (kru stā′shəs), *adj.* **1.** of the nature of or pertaining to a crust or shell. **2.** crustacean. **3.** having a hard covering or crust. [1640–50; < NL *crūstāceus* (adj.) hard-shelled. See CRUSTACEAN, -ACEOUS]

crus·tal (krus′tl), *adj.* of or pertaining to a crust, as of the earth. [1855–60; < L *crūst(a)* shell, crust + -AL[1]]

crus′tal plate′, *Geol.* a large block or tabular section of the lithosphere that reacts to tectonic forces as a unit and moves as such. Also called **plate.**

crust·ed (krus′tid), *adj.* **1.** having a crust; encrusted. **2.** (of a wine) containing a hardened deposit accumulated during aging in the bottle: *crusted port.* **3.** having the accruals of age; antique. [1350–1400; ME; see CRUST, -ED[3]] —**crust′ed·ly,** *adv.*

crus·tose (krus′tōs), *adj. Bot., Mycol.* forming a crusty, tenaciously fixed mass that covers the surface on which it grows, as certain lichens. Cf. **foliose, fruticose.** [1875–80; < L *crustōsus* covered with a crust, equiv. to *crust(a)* CRUST + *-ōsus* -OSE[1]]

crust·y (krus′tē), *adj.,* **crust·i·er, crust·i·est. 1.** having a crisp or thick crust: *a loaf of crusty French bread.* **2.** of the nature of or resembling a crust. **3.** harsh; surly; rude: *a crusty remark.* [1350–1400; ME; see CRUST, -Y[1]] —**crust′i·ly,** *adv.* —**crust′i·ness,** *n.*
—**Syn. 3.** testy, prickly, touchy; curt, brusque.

crut (krut), *n. Slang.* crud (def. 1). [1920–25, *Amer.;* perh. back formation from CRUDDY, with *t* assumed to be the underlying consonant]

crutch (kruch), *n.* **1.** a staff or support to assist a lame or infirm person in walking, now usually with a crosspiece at one end to fit under the armpit. **2.** any of various devices resembling this in shape or use. **3.** anything that serves as a temporary and often inappropriate support, supplement, or substitute; prop: *He uses liquor as a psychological crutch.* **4.** a forked support or part. **5.** the crotch of the human body. **6.** Also, **crotch.** *Naut.* **a.** a forked support for a boom or spar when not in use. **b.** a forked support for an oar on the sides or stern of a rowboat. **c.** a horizontal knee reinforcing the stern frames of a wooden vessel. **7.** a forked device on the left side of a sidesaddle, consisting of two hooks, one of which is open at the bottom and serves to clamp the left knee and the other of which is open at the top and serves to support the right knee. —*v.t.* **8.** to support on crutches; prop; sustain. [bef. 900; ME *crucche,* OE *cryce* (obl. *crycce*); c. Norw *krykkja,* Dan *krykke,* G *Krücke,* D *kruk.* See CROOK[1]] —**crutch′like′,** *adj.*

crux (kruks), *n., pl.* **crux·es, cru·ces** (kro͞o′sēz). **1.** a vital, basic, decisive, or pivotal point: *The crux of the trial was his whereabouts at the time of the murder.* **2.** a cross. **3.** something that torments by its puzzling nature; a perplexing difficulty. [1635–45; < L: stake, scaffold, or cross used in executions, torment; figurative senses perh. < NL *crux (interpretum)* (commentators') torment, a difficult passage in a text; cf. CRUCIAL]
—**Syn. 1.** essence, heart, core, gist.

Crux (kruks), *n., gen.* **Cru·cis** (kro͞o′sis). *Astron.* See **Southern Cross.** [< L: a cross]

Cruz (kro͞oz; *Sp.* kro͞oth), *n.* **San Juan de la** (sän hwän de lä). See **John of the Cross, Saint.**

cru·za·do (kro͞o zä′dō; *Port.* kro͞o zä′do͞o), *n., pl.* **-does, -dos.** crusado.

Cruz Al·ta (kro͞oz äl′tə), a city in S Brazil. 54,447.

Cru·zan (kro͞o zan′, kro͞o′zan), *n.* **1.** a native or inhabitant of St. Croix. —*adj.* **2.** of or pertaining to St. Croix, its natives, or its inhabitants. [< AmerSp *(Santa) Cruz* St. Croix + -AN]

cru·zei·ro (kro͞o zâr′ō; *Port.* kro͞o ze′ro͞o), *n., pl.* **-zei·ros** (-zâr′ōz; *Port.* -ze′ro͞os). a monetary unit of Brazil equal to 100 centavos. [1925–30; < Pg, equiv. to *cruz* CROSS + *-eiro* < L *-ārius* -ARY]

crwth (kro͞oth), *n. Music.* crowd[2]. [1830–40; < Welsh; c. Ir *cruit* harp, lyre]

cry (krī), *v.,* **cried, cry·ing,** *n., pl.* **cries.** —*v.i.* **1.** to utter inarticulate sounds, esp. of lamentation, grief, or suffering, usually with tears. **2.** to weep; shed tears, with or without sound. **3.** to call loudly; shout; yell (sometimes fol. by *out*). **4.** to demand resolution or strongly indicate a particular disposition: *The rise in crime cried out for greater police protection.* **5.** to give forth vocal sounds or characteristic calls, as animals; yelp; bark. **6.** (of a hound or pack) to bay continuously and excitedly in following a scent. **7.** (of tin) to make a noise, when bent, like the crumpling of paper. —*v.t.* **8.** to utter or pronounce loudly; call out. **9.** to announce publicly as for sale; advertise: *to cry one's wares.* **10.** to beg or plead for; implore: *to cry mercy.* **11.** to bring (oneself) to a specified state by weeping: *The infant cried itself to sleep.* **12. cry down,** to disparage; belittle: *Those people cry down everyone who differs from them.* **13. cry havoc.** See **havoc** (def. 2). **14. cry off,** to break a promise, agreement, etc.: *We made arrangements to purchase a house, but the owner cried off at the last minute.* **15. cry one's eyes** or **heart out,** to cry excessively or inconsolably: *The little girl cried her eyes out when her cat died.* **16. cry over spilled** or **spilt milk.** See **milk** (def. 4). **17. cry up,** to praise; extol: *to cry up one's profession.* —*n.* **18.** the act or sound of crying; any loud utterance or exclamation; a shout, scream, or wail. **19.** clamor; outcry. **20.** a fit of weeping: *to have a good cry.* **21.** the utterance or call of an animal. **22.** a political or party slogan. **23.** See **battle cry. 24.** an oral proclamation or announcement. **25.** a call of wares for sale, services available, etc., as by a street vendor. **26.** public report. **27.** an opinion generally expressed. **28.** an entreaty; appeal. **29.** *Fox Hunting.* **a.** a pack of hounds. **b.** a continuous baying of a hound or a pack in following a scent. **30. a far cry, a.** quite some distance; a long way. **b.** only remotely related; very different: *This treatment is a far cry from that which we received before.* **31. in full cry,** in hot pursuit: *The pack followed in full cry.* [1175–1225; (v.) ME *crien* < AF, OF *crier* < VL **critāre* for L *quirītāre* to cry out in protest, make a public cry; associated by folk etym. with *Quirītēs* QUIRITES; (n.) < AF, OF *cri,* n. deriv. of the v.]
—**Syn. 1.** wail, keen, moan. **2.** sob, bawl, whimper. **3.** yowl, bawl, clamor, vociferate, exclaim, ejaculate, scream. CRY, SHOUT, BELLOW, ROAR refer to kinds of loud articulate or inarticulate sounds. CRY is the general word: *to cry out.* To SHOUT is to raise the voice loudly in uttering words or other articulate sounds: *He shouted to his companions.* BELLOW refers to the loud, deep cry of a bull, moose, etc., or, somewhat in deprecation, to human utterance that suggests such a sound: *The speaker bellowed his answer.* ROAR refers to a deep, hoarse, rumbling or vibrant cry, often of tumultuous volume: *The crowd roared approval.*

cry·ba·by (krī′bā′bē), *n., pl.* **-bies,** *v.,* **-bied, -by·ing.** —*n.* **1.** a person, esp. a child, who cries readily for very little reason. **2.** a person who complains too much, usually in a whining manner. —*v.i.* **3.** Also, **cry′-ba′by.** to cry or complain easily or often. [1850–55, *Amer.;* CRY + BABY]

cry·ing (krī′ing), *adj.* **1.** demanding attention or remedy; critical; severe: *a crying evil.* **2.** reprehensible; odious; notorious: *a crying shame.* [1300–50; ME *cryenge.* See CRY, -ING[2]] —**cry′ing·ly,** *adv.*

cry·mo·ther·a·py (krī′mō ther′ə pē), *n. Med.* cryotherapy. [< Gk *krȳmó(s)* frost, cold + THERAPY]

cryo-, a combining form meaning "icy cold," "frost," used in the formation of compound words: *cryogenics.* [comb. form repr. Gk. *krýos*]

cry·o·bi·ol·o·gy (krī′ō bī ol′ə jē), *n.* the study of the effects of very low temperatures on living organisms and biological systems. [1955–60; CRYO- + BIOLOGY] —**cry·o·bi·o·log·i·cal** (krī′ō bī′ə loj′i kəl), *adj.* —**cry′o·bi·ol′o·gist,** *n.*

cry·o·e·lec·tron·ics (krī′ō i lek tron′iks, -ē′lek-), *n.* (*used with a singular v.*) the branch of electronics dealing with the application of low-temperature behavior, esp. superconductivity, to electronic devices. [1970–75; CRYO- + ELECTRONICS] —**cry′o·e·lec·tron′ic,** *adj.*

cry·o·ex·trac·tion (krī′ō ik strak′shən), *n.* the surgical removal of a cataract with a cryoprobe. [CRYO- + EXTRACTION]

cry·o·gen (krī′ə jən, -jen′), *n.* a substance for producing low temperatures; freezing mixture. [1870–75; CRYO- + -GEN]

cry·o·gen·ic (krī′ə jen′ik), *adj.* **1.** of or pertaining to the production or use of very low temperatures: *cryogenic storage.* **2.** of or pertaining to cryogenics. [1900–05; CRYO- + -GENIC] —**cry′o·gen′i·cal·ly,** *adv.* —**cry·og·e·nist** (krī oj′ə nist), *n.*

cry·o·gen·ics (krī′ə jen′iks), *n.* (*used with a singular v.*) the branch of physics that deals with very low temperatures. [1955–60; CRYO- + -GENICS]

cry·og·en·ized (krī oj′ə nīzd′), *adj.* treated with or stored in a cryogen. [CRYOGEN + -IZE + -ED[2]]

cry·o·hy·drate (krī′ō hī′drāt), *n.* a mixture of ice and another substance in definite proportions such that a minimum melting or freezing point is attained. [1870–75; CRYO- + HYDRATE] —**cry·o·hy·dric** (krī′ō hī′drik), *adj.*

cry·o·lathe (krī′ə lāth′), *n., v.,* **-lathed, -lath·ing.** *Ophthalm.* —*n.* **1.** an instrument for reshaping the cornea to correct severe nearsightedness or farsightedness: the cornea is removed from the eye, rapidly frozen, reshaped, and reinserted. —*v.i.* **2.** to reshape the cornea with the aid of this instrument. [CRYO- + LATHE]

cry·o·lite (krī′ə līt′), *n.* a mineral, sodium aluminum fluoride, Na_3AlF_6, occurring in white masses, used as a flux in the electrolytic production of aluminum. Also called **Greenland spar.** [1795–1805; CRYO- + -LITE]

cry·ol·o·gy (krī ol′ə jē), *n.* the study of snow and ice. [1945–50; CRYO- + -LOGY]

cry·om·e·ter (krī om′i tər), *n.* a thermometer for measuring low temperatures. [CRYO- + -METER] —**cry·om′e·try,** *n.*

cry·on·ics (krī on′iks), *n.* (*used with a singular v.*) the deep-freezing of human bodies at death for preservation and possible revival in the future. [1965–70, *Amer.;* CRYO- + *-nics,* on the model of BIONICS, ELECTRONICS, etc.] —**cry·on′ic,** *adj.*

cry·o·phil·ic (krī′ō fil′ik), *adj.* preferring or thriving at low temperatures. [1940–45; CRYO- + -PHILIC]

cry·o·phyte (krī′ə fīt′), *n.* **1.** any plant, as certain algae, mosses, fungi, and bacteria, that grows on ice or snow. **2.** any low-growing, succulent, blooming plant of the genus *Cryophytum* (or *Mesembryanthemum*), certain species of which form extensive mats along the southwestern coasts of the U.S. [1905–10; CRYO- + -PHYTE]

cry·o·plank·ton (krī′ō plangk′tən), *n.* plankton that live in the icy waters and meltwaters of glacial or polar areas. [1930–35; CRYO- + PLANKTON]

cry·o·probe (krī′ə prōb′), *n.* an instrument used in cryosurgery, having a supercooled tip for applying extreme cold to diseased tissue in order to remove or destroy it. [1960–65; CRYO- + PROBE]

cry·o·scope (krī′ə skōp′), *n.* an instrument for determining the freezing point of a liquid or solution. [CRYO- + -SCOPE]

cry·os·co·py (krī os′kə pē), *n., pl.* **-pies. 1.** *Chem.* a technique for determining the molecular weight of a substance by dissolving it and measuring the freezing point of the solution. **2.** *Med.* the determination of the freezing points of certain bodily fluids, as urine, for diagnosis. [1895–1900; CRYO- + -SCOPY] —**cry·o·scop·ic** (krī′ə skop′ik), *adj.*

cry·o·stat (krī′ə stat′), *n.* an apparatus, usually automatic, maintaining a very low constant temperature. [1910–15; CRYO- + STAT] —**cry′o·stat′ic,** *adj.*

cry·o·sur·ger·y (krī′ō sûr′jə rē), *n.* the use of extreme cold to destroy tissue for therapeutic purposes. [1960–65; CRYO- + SURGERY] —**cry′o·sur′gi·cal,** *adj.*

cry·o·ther·a·py (krī′ō ther′ə pē), *n. Med.* treatment by means of applications of cold. Also, **crymotherapy.** [1925–30; CRYO- + THERAPY]

cry·o·tron (krī′ə tron′), *n. Electronics, Computers.* a cryogenic device that uses the principle that a varying magnetic field can cause the resistance of a superconducting element to change rapidly between its high normal and low superconductive values: used as a switch and as a computer-memory element. [1955–60; CRYO- + -TRON]

crypt (kript), *n.* **1.** a subterranean chamber or vault, esp. one beneath the main floor of a church, used as a burial place, a location for secret meetings, etc. **2.** *Anat.* a slender pit or recess; a small glandular cavity. [1375–

1425 for sense "grotto"; 1555–65 for current senses; late ME *cripte* < L *crypta* < Gk *kryptḗ* hidden place, n. use of fem. of *kryptós* hidden, verbid of *krýptein* to hide; r. earlier *crypta* < L, as above]

crypt·a·nal·y·sis (krip′tə nal′ə sis), *n.* **1.** the procedures, processes, methods, etc., used to translate or interpret secret writings, as codes and ciphers, for which the key is unknown. **2.** the science or study of such procedures. Cf. **cryptography** (def. 1). [1920–25, *Amer.*; CRYPT(OGRAM) + ANALYSIS] —**crypt·an·a·lyt·ic** (krip′tan l it′ik), *adj.* —**crypt′an·a·lyt′i·cal·ly,** *adv.* —**crypt·an·a·lyst** (krip tan′l ist), *n.*

crypt·an·a·lyt·ics (krip′tan l it′iks), *n.* (*used with a singular v.*) cryptanalysis (def. 1). [CRYPTANALY(SIS) + (ANALY)TICS]

crypt·an·a·lyze (krip tan′l īz′), *v.t.*, **-lyzed, -lyz·ing.** to study (a cryptogram) for the purpose of discovering the clear meaning; break (a code, cipher, etc.). Also, *esp. Brit.*, **crypt·an′a·lyse′.** [see CRYPTANALYSIS, ANALYZE]

crypt·es·the·sia (krip′təs thē′zhə, -zhē ə, -zē ə), *n. Psychol.* allegedly paranormal perception, as clairvoyance or clairaudience. [1920–25; CRYPT(O)- + ESTHESIA]

cryp·tic (krip′tik), *adj.* Also, **cryp′ti·cal. 1.** mysterious in meaning; puzzling; ambiguous: *a cryptic message.* **2.** abrupt; terse; short: *a cryptic note.* **3.** secret; occult: *a cryptic writing.* **4.** involving or using cipher, code, etc. **5.** *Zool.* fitted for concealing; serving to camouflage. —*n.* **6.** a cryptogram, esp. one designed as a puzzle. [1595–1605; < LL *crypticus* < Gk *kryptikós* hidden. See CRYPT, -IC] —**cryp′ti·cal·ly,** *adv.*
—**Syn. 1.** enigmatic, perplexing. See **ambiguous.**

cryp·to (krip′tō), *n., pl.* **-tos,** *adj.* —*n.* **1.** a person who secretly supports or adheres to a group, party, or belief. —*adj.* **2.** secret or hidden; not publicly admitted: *a crypto Nazi.* [1945–50; prob. independent use of CRYPTO-; cf -O]

crypto-, a combining form meaning "hidden," "secret," used in the formation of compound words: *cryptograph.* [comb. form repr. Gk *kryptós* hidden. See CRYPT]

cryp·to·a·nal·y·sis (krip′tō ə nal′ə sis), *n.* cryptanalysis. [CRYPTO- + ANALYSIS] —**cryp·to·an·a·lyt·ic** (krip′tō an′l it′ik), *adj.* —**cryp′to·an′a·lyt′i·cal·ly,** *adv.* —**cryp·to·an·a·lyst** (krip′tō an′l ist), *n.*

cryp·to·cli·mate (krip′tō klī′mit), *n.* See under **microclimate.** [CRYPTO- + CLIMATE]

cryp·to·cli·ma·tol·o·gy (krip′tō klī′mə tol′ə jē), *n.* See under **microclimatology.** [CRYPTO- + CLIMATOLOGY]

cryptococ′cal meningi′tis, a form of meningitis resulting from opportunistic infection by a cryptococcus fungus, occurring in persons who are immunodeficient.

cryp·to·coc·co·sis (krip′tō ko kō′sis), *n. Pathol.* a disease caused by the fungus *Cryptococcus neoformans,* chiefly found in soil contaminated by pigeon droppings, and characterized by lesions, esp. of the nervous system and lungs. Also called **European blastomycosis, torulosis.** [1935–40; < NL; see CRYPTOCOCCUS, -OSIS]

cryp·to·coc·cus (krip′tə kok′əs), *n.* any yeastlike fungus of the genus *Cryptococcus,* including *C. neoformans,* the causative agent of cryptococcosis. [1833; < NL; see CRYPTO-, -COCCUS] —**cryp′to·coc′cal,** *adj.*

cryp·to·crys·tal·line (krip′tō kris′tl in, -īn′), *adj. Mineral.* having a microscopic crystalline structure. [1860–65; CRYPTO- + CRYSTALLINE]

cryp·to·gam (krip′tə gam′), *n. Bot.* any of the Cryptogamia, a former primary division of plants that have no true flowers or seeds and that reproduce by spores, as the ferns, mosses, fungi, and algae. [1840–50; < NL *Cryptogamia.* See CRYPTO-, -GAMY] —**cryp′to·gam′ic, cryp·tog·a·mous** (krip tog′ə məs), **cryp′to·gam′i·cal,** *adj.* —**cryp·tog′a·mist,** *n.* —**cryp·tog′a·my,** *n.*

cryp·to·gen·ic (krip′tə jen′ik), *adj.* of obscure or unknown origin, as a disease. [1905–10; CRYPTO- + -GENIC]

cryp·to·gram (krip′tə gram′), *n.* **1.** a message or writing in code or cipher; cryptograph. **2.** an occult symbol or representation. [1875–80; CRYPTO- + -GRAM[1]] —**cryp′to·gram′mic, cryp·to·gram·mat·ic** (krip′tə grə mat′ik), **cryp′to·gram·mat′i·cal,** *adj.* —**cryp′to·gram′ma·tist,** *n.*

cryp·to·graph (krip′tə graf′, -gräf′), *n.* **1.** cryptogram (def. 1). **2.** a system of secret writing; cipher. **3.** a device for translating clear text into cipher. [1635–45; CRYPTO- + -GRAPH]

cryp·tog·ra·phy (krip tog′rə fē), *n.* **1.** the science or study of the techniques of secret writing, esp. code and cipher systems, methods, and the like. Cf. **cryptanalysis** (def. 2). **2.** the procedures, processes, methods, etc., of making and using secret writing, as codes or ciphers. **3.** anything written in a secret code, cipher, or the like. [1635–45; CRYPTO- + -GRAPHY] —**cryp·tog′ra·pher, cryp·tog′ra·phist,** *n.* —**cryp·to·graph·ic** (krip′tə graf′ik), **cryp′to·graph′i·cal, cryp·tog′ra·phal,** *adj.* —**cryp′to·graph′i·cal·ly,** *adv.*

cryp·tol·o·gy (krip tol′ə jē), *n.* **1.** cryptography. **2.** the science and study of cryptanalysis and cryptography. [1635–45; < NL *cryptologia.* See CRYPTO-, -LOGY] —**cryp·tol′o·gist,** *n.* —**cryp·to·log·ic** (krip′tl oj′ik), **cryp′to·log′i·cal,** *adj.*

cryp·tom·o·nad (krip tom′ə nad′), *n. Biol.* any of various protozoalike algae of the phylum Cryptophyta usually having two flagella, common in both marine and freshwater environments where they appear along the shore as algal blooms, some also occurring as intestinal parasites. Also called **cryptophyte.** [< NL *Cryptomonad-*, s. of *Cryptomonas,* a typical genus; see CRYPTO-, MONAD]

cryp·to·phyte (krip′tə fīt′), *n.* **1.** *Bot.* a plant that forms its reproductive structures, as corms or bulbs, underground or underwater. **2.** *Biol.* cryptomonad. [1900–05; CRYPTO- + -PHYTE] —**cryp·to·phyt·ic** (krip′tə fit′ik), *adj.*

cryp·to·por·ti·cus (krip′tə pôr′ti kəs, -pōr′-), *n., pl.* **-cus. 1.** a covered passage, as one underground, lighted on one side. **2.** a portico at the entrance to a crypt. [1675–85; < L: covered passage; see CRYPTO-, PORTICO]

cryp·tor·chi·dism (krip tôr′ki diz′əm), *n. Pathol.* failure of one or both testes to descend into the scrotum. Also, **cryp·tor·chism** (krip tôr′kiz əm). [1880–85; < NL *cryptorchidismus,* equiv. to *crypt-* CRYPTO- + *orchid-* (< Gk *orchid-*; see ORCHID) + *-ismus* -ISM] —**cryp·tor′·chid,** *adj.*

cryp·to·sys·tem (krip′tō sys′təm), *n.* a system for encoding and decoding secret messages. Also, **cryp′to sys′tem.** [1965–70; CRYPTO- + SYSTEM]

cryp·to·vol·can·ic (krip′tō vol kan′ik), *adj. Geol.* of or pertaining to a rock structure providing indirect or incomplete evidence of volcanism. [1920–25; CRYPTO- + VOLCANIC]

cryp·to·zo·ic (krip′tə zō′ik), *adj.* **1.** (*cap.*) *Geol.* of or pertaining to that part of Precambrian time whose stratigraphic record yields only sparse, primitive fossils. **2.** *Zool.* living in concealed or secluded places. —*n.* **3.** (*cap.*) *Geol.* the part of Precambrian time whose stratigraphic record yields only sparse, primitive fossils. [1890–95; CRYPTO- + ZO- + -IC]

cryp·to·zo·ite (krip′tə zō′īt), *n.* a malarial parasite in the stage of development during which it lives in tissue cells prior to invading the blood cells. [1945–50; CRYPTO- + ZO- + -ITE[1]]

cryp·to·zo·ol·o·gy (krip′tō zō ol′ə jē), *n.* the study of evidence tending to substantiate the existence of, or the search for, creatures whose reported existence is unproved, as the Abominable Snowman or the Loch Ness monster. [CRYPTO- + ZOOLOGY] —**cryp′to·zo·ol′o·gist,** *n.* —**cryp·to·zo·o·log·i·cal** (krip′tō zō′ə loj′i kəl), *adj.*

Cryp·to·zo·on (krip′tə zō′on), *n.* an extinct genus of algae from Precambrian and Cambrian times, forming irregularly hemispherical fossil colonies composed of layers of limy precipitate. [1883; < NL; see CRYPTO-, -ZOON]

cryp·to·zy·gous (krip′tə zī′gəs), *adj. Craniom.* having the skull broad and the face narrow. [1875–80; CRYPTO- + ZYG- (as in ZYGOMA) + -OUS] —**cryp′to·zy′gy,** *n.*

cryst., 1. crystalline. **2.** crystallized. **3.** crystallography.

crys·tal (kris′tl), *n., adj., v.,* **-taled, -tal·ing** or (*esp. Brit.*) **-talled, -tal·ling.** —*n.* **1.** a clear, transparent mineral or glass resembling ice. **2.** the transparent form of crystallized quartz. **3.** *Chem., Mineral.* a solid body having a characteristic internal structure and enclosed by symmetrically arranged plane surfaces, intersecting at definite and characteristic angles. **4.** anything made of or resembling such a substance. **5.** a single grain or mass of a crystalline substance. **6.** glass of fine quality and a high degree of brilliance. **7.** articles, esp. glassware for the table and ornamental objects, made of such a glass. **8.** the glass or plastic cover over the face of a watch. **9.** *Radio.* **a.** the piece of germanium, silicon, galena, or the like forming the essential part of a crystal detector. **b.** the crystal detector itself. **10.** *Electronics.* a quartz crystal ground in the shape of a rectangular parallelepiped, which vibrates strongly at one frequency when electric voltages of that frequency are placed across opposite sides: used to control the frequency of an oscillator (**crystal oscillator**), as of a radio transmitter. **11.** *Slang.* any stimulant drug in powder form, as methamphetamine or PCP. —*adj.* **12.** composed of crystal. **13.** resembling crystal; clear; transparent. **14.** *Radio.* pertaining to or employing a crystal detector. **15.** indicating the fifteenth event of a series, as a wedding anniversary. See table under **wedding anniversary.** —*v.t.* **16.** to make into crystal; crystallize. **17.** to cover or coat with, or as if with, crystal (usually fol. by *over*). [bef. 1000; ME *cristal(le),* OE *cristalla* < ML *cristallum,* L *crystallum* < Gk *krýstallos* clear ice, rock crystal, deriv. of *krystaínein* to freeze; see CRYO-] —**crys′tal·like′,** *adj.*

Crys·tal (kris′tl), *n.* **1.** a city in SE Minnesota, near Minneapolis. 25,543. **2.** a female given name.

crys′tal ball′, 1. a ball of clear crystal, glass, or the like, used in crystal gazing. **2.** a method or means of predicting the future. [1850–55]

crys·tal-clear (kris′tl klēr′), *adj.* absolutely clear; transparent; lucid. [1510–20]

crys′tal de′fect, *Crystall.* defect (def. 3).

crys′tal detec′tor, *Radio.* a device for rectifying a modulated radio-frequency signal, consisting of a crystal of germanium, silicon, galena, or the like with a cat whisker contact, permitting a high-frequency current to pass freely in one direction only: one of the two principal components of a crystal set. [1905–10]

crys′tal gaz′ing, 1. the practice of staring into a crystal ball, as by a fortuneteller, to see distant happenings, future events, etc. **2.** speculation about the future. [1885–90] —**crys′tal gaz′er.**

crystall-, var. of **crystallo-** before a vowel: *crystallite.*

crystall., crystallography.

Crys′tal Lake′, a town in NE Illinois. 18,590.

crys′tal lat′tice, lattice (def. 4). [1925–30]

crystalli-, var. of **crystallo-** before an element of Latin origin: *crystalliferous.*

crys·tal·lif·er·ous (kris′tl if′ər əs), *adj.* bearing, containing, or yielding crystals. Also, **crys·tal·lig·er·ous** (kris′tl ij′ər əs). [1880–85; CRYSTALLI- + -FEROUS]

crys·tal·line (kris′tl in, -in′, -ēn′), *adj.* **1.** of or like crystal; clear; transparent. **2.** formed by crystallization. **3.** composed of crystals. **4.** pertaining to crystals or their formation. [1350–1400; ME *cristal(l)yn(e)* < L *crystallinus* < Gk *krystállinos.* See CRYSTAL, -INE[1]] —**crys·tal·lin·i·ty** (kris′tl in′i tē), *n.*

crys′talline lens′, *Anat.* a doubly convex, transparent body in the eye, situated behind the iris, that focuses incident light on the retina. See diag. under **eye.** [1785–95]

crys·tal·lite (kris′tl īt′), *n. Mineral.* a minute body in glassy igneous rock, showing incipient crystallization. [1795–1805; CRYSTALL- + -ITE[1]] —**crys·tal·lit·ic** (kris′tl it′ik), *adj.*

crys·tal·li·za·tion (kris′tl ə zā′shən), *n.* **1.** the act or process of crystallizing. **2.** a crystallized body or formation. [1655–65; CRYSTALL- + -IZATION]

crys·tal·lize (kris′tl īz′), *v.,* **-lized, -liz·ing.** —*v.t.* **1.** to form into crystals; cause to assume crystalline form. **2.** to give definite or concrete form to: *to crystallize an idea.* **3.** to coat with sugar. —*v.i.* **4.** to form crystals; become crystalline in form. **5.** to assume definite or concrete form. Also, *esp. Brit.,* **crys′tal·lise′.** [1590–1600; CRYSTALL- + -IZE] —**crys′tal·liz′a·bil′i·ty,** *n.* —**crys′tal·liz′a·ble,** *adj.* —**crys′tal·liz′er,** *n.*

crystallo-, a combining form meaning "crystal," used in the formation of compound words: *crystallography.* Also, **crystall-, crystalli-.** [< Gk *krystallo-,* comb. form of *krýstallos* CRYSTAL]

crys·tal·lo·graph·ic (kris′tl ə graf′ik), *adj.* of, pertaining to, or dealing with crystals or crystallography. Also, **crys′tal·lo·graph′i·cal.** [1790–1800; CRYSTALLO- + -GRAPHIC] —**crys′tal·lo·graph′i·cal·ly,** *adv.*

crys′tallograph′ic ax′is, *Crystall.* one of the imaginary reference lines passing through the center of an ideal crystal, designated *a, b,* or *c.* [1855–60]

crys·tal·log·ra·phy (kris′tl og′rə fē), *n.* the science dealing with crystallization and the forms and structure of crystals. [1795–1805; CRYSTALLO- + -GRAPHY] —**crys′tal·log′ra·pher,** *n.*

crys·tal·loid (kris′tl oid′), *n.* **1.** a usually crystallizable substance that, when dissolved in a liquid, will diffuse readily through vegetable or animal membranes. **2.** *Bot.* one of certain minute crystallike granules of protein, found in the tissues of various seeds. —*adj.* **3.** resembling a crystal. **4.** of the nature of a crystalloid. [1860–65; < Gk *krystalloeidḗs.* See CRYSTALL-, -OID] —**crys′tal·loi′dal,** *adj.*

Crys·tal·lose (kris′tl ōs′), *Trademark.* a brand of saccharin sodium.

crys′tal os′cillator, *Electronics.* See under **crystal** (def. 10).

Crys′tal Pal′ace, a structure of prefabricated iron units, glass, and wood, built in London to house the Exhibition of 1851: destroyed by fire 1936.

crys′tal pick′up, a phonograph pickup that generates an electric current as the stylus applies pressure to a piezoelectric crystal. Cf. **magnetic pickup.**

crys′tal pleat′, any of a line of narrow, corrugated pleats pressed into a fabric, esp. one that is lightweight. [1975–80] —**crys′tal pleat′ed.**

crys′tal set′, an early, tubeless radio receiver using a crystal detector.

crys′tal sys′tem, *Crystall.* any of the six main classifications of crystals and of crystal lattices according to their symmetry: isometric, hexagonal, tetragonal, orthorhombic, monoclinic, and triclinic.

crys′tal tea′. See **wild rosemary.**

crys′tal vi′olet. See **gentian violet.** [1890–95]

Cs, *Symbol, Chem.* cesium.

cS, centistoke; centistokes. Also, **cs**

cs., case; cases.

C/S, cycles per second.

C.S., 1. chief of staff. **2.** Christian Science. **3.** Christian Scientist. **4.** Civil Service. **5.** Confederate States.

c.s., 1. capital stock. **2.** civil service.

CSA, See **Community Services Administration.**

C.S.A., Confederate States of America.

csar·das (chär′däsh), *n.* czardas.

CSC, Civil Service Commission.

csc, *Trig.* cosecant.

CSCE, See **Conference on Security and Cooperation in Europe.**

C-scroll (sē′skrōl′), *n.* an ornamental motif in the shape of a C, used chiefly on furniture.

CSEA, Civil Service Employees Association.

C-sec·tion (sē′sek′shən), *n. Informal.* See **Cesarean section.**

CSF, *Physiol.* cerebrospinal fluid.

csk., cask.

C.S.O., 1. Chief Signal Officer. **2.** Chief Staff Officer. Also, **CSO**

CST, Central Standard Time. Also, **C.S.T., c.s.t.**

C star, *Astron.* See **carbon star.**

C supply, *Electronics.* a battery or other source of power for supplying a constant voltage bias to a control electrode of a vacuum tube. Also called **C power supply.** Cf. **A supply, B supply.**

CT, 1. Central time. **2.** computed tomography. **3.** Connecticut (approved esp. for use with zip code).

Ct., 1. Connecticut. **2.** Count.

ct., 1. carat; carats. **2.** cent; cents. **3.** centum. **4.** certificate. **5.** county. **6.** court.

C.T., Central time.

CTA, commodities trading adviser.

C.T.A., *Law.* with the will annexed: *an administrator C.T.A.* [< L *cum testāmentō annexō*]

CTC, Citizens' Training Corps.

cte•nid•i•um (ti nid′ē əm), *n., pl.* **-nid•i•a** (-nid′ē ə). *Zool.* any of various comblike or featherlike structures, as the row of stiff bristles on the legs of a psocid. [1880–85; < NL; see CTENO-, -IDIUM] —**cte•nid′i•al,** *adj.*

cten•i•zid (ten′ə zid), *n.* **1.** a spider of the family Ctenizidae, comprising the trap-door spiders. —*adj.* **2.** belonging or pertaining to the ctenizids. [< NL *Ctenizidae* name of the family, equiv. to *Ctениz(a)* a genus (appar. irreg. < Gk *ktenízein* to comb; see CTENO-) + NL *-idae* -ID²]

cteno-, a combining form meaning "comb," used in the formation of compound words: *Ctenophora.* [< Gk *kteno-,* comb. form of *kteís* comb (gen. *ktenós*)]

cte•noid (tē′noid, ten′oid), *adj. Zool.* **1.** comblike or pectinate; rough-edged. **2.** having rough-edged scales. [1830–40; < Gk *ktenoeidḗs* like a comb. See CTENO-, -OID]

Cte•noph•o•ra (ti nof′ər ə), *n.* the phylum comprising the comb jellies. [< NL, neut. pl. of *ctenophorus* CTENOPHORE]

cte•noph•o•ran (ti nof′ər ən), *n.* **1.** ctenophore. —*adj.* **2.** Also, **cten•o•phor•ic** (ten′ə fôr′ik, -for′-), **cte•noph•o•rous** (ti nof′ər əs). belonging or pertaining to the Ctenophora. [1875–80; CTENOPHOR(A) + -AN]

cten•o•phore (ten′ə fôr′, -fōr′, tē′nə-), *n.* any gelatinous marine invertebrate of the phylum Ctenophora; a comb jelly. [1880–85; < NL *ctenophorus.* See CTENO-, -PHORE]

C terminus, *Biochem.* the carboxyl end of a protein molecule. Also, **C terminal.** [*C,* abbr. for *carboxyl*] —**C-ter•mi•nal** (sē′tûr′mə nl), *adj.*

Ctes•i•phon (tes′ə fon′), *n.* a ruined city in Iraq, on the Tigris, near Baghdad: an ancient capital of Parthia.

ctf, certificate.

ctg., **1.** Also, **ctge.** cartage. **2.** cartridge.

ctn, *Trig.* cotangent.

ctn., *pl.* **ctns.** carton.

ctr., center.

cts., **1.** centimes. **2.** cents. **3.** certificates.

CT scan. See **CAT scan.**

CT scanner. See **CAT scanner.**

CU, close-up.

Cu, *Symbol, Chem.* copper. [< L *cuprum*]

cu, cubic.

Cu., cumulus.

cu., **1.** cubic. **2.** cumulus.

cua•dril•la (kwä drē′yə, -drēl′yə; *Sp.* kwä t͟hrē′lyä, -t͟hrē′yä), *n., pl.* **-dril•las** (-drē′yəz, -drēl′yəz; *Sp.* -t͟hrē′lyäs, -t͟hrē′yäs). the group of assistants serving a matador in a bullfight, consisting of three banderilleros and two picadors. [1835–45; < Sp: group, gang (orig. one of four groups), dim. of *cuadra* < L *quadra* side of a square]

cub (kub), *n., v.* **cubbed, cub•bing.** —*n.* **1.** the young of certain animals, as the bear, lion, or tiger. **2.** a young shark. **3.** a young and inexperienced person, esp. a callow youth or young man. **4.** a young person serving as an apprentice. **5.** See **cub reporter. 6.** See **cub scout. 7.** (*cap.*) *Trademark. Aeron.* any small, light monoplane with a high wing, a single engine, and an enclosed cabin. —*v.i.* **8.** to work as a cub reporter. **9.** (of a female bear, lion, tiger, etc.) to give birth to a cub or cubs. **10.** to hunt fox cubs. [1520–30; perh. < Scand; cf. ON *kobbi* young seal, *kubbr* stump, hence, short, thick-set person] —**cub′bish,** *adj.*

cub., cubic.

Cu•ba (kyo͞o′bə; *Sp.* ko͞o′vä), *n.* a republic in the Caribbean, S of Florida: largest island in the West Indies. 9,405,000; 44,218 sq. mi. (114,525 sq. km). *Cap.:* Havana. —**Cu′ban,** *adj., n.*

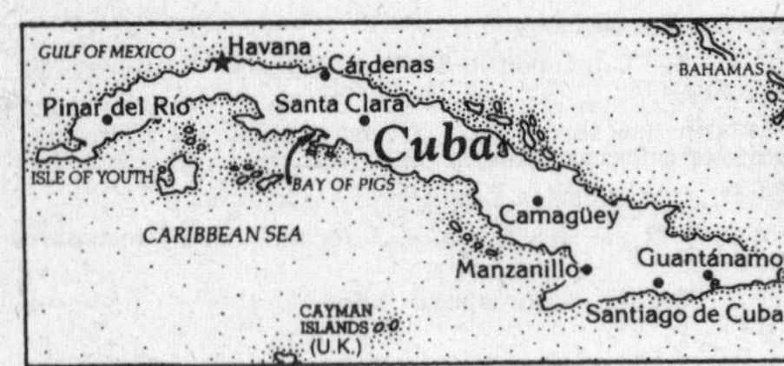

Cu•ba (ko͞o′bä), *n.* Cubba.

cub•age (kyo͞o′bij), *n.* cubic content, displacement, or volume. [1830–40; CUBE¹ + -AGE]

Cu•ba li•bre (kyo͞o′bə lē′brə), a drink of rum and cola. [1895–1900; < Sp: lit., free Cuba (a toast used in the uprising against Spain in 1895)]

Cu•ban•go (ko͝o bän′go͞o), *n.* Portuguese name of **Okavango.**

Cu′ban heel′, a broad heel of medium height, straight in front and slightly tapered toward the bottom in the rear, used on women's shoes. [1905–10]

Cu′ban roy′al palm′, a feather palm, *Roystonea regia,* of tropical America, having a trunk that is swollen in the middle, drooping leaves from 10 to 15 ft. (3 to 5 m) long, and small, round fruit.

Cu′ban sand′wich, *Chiefly Southern Florida and New York City.* a hero sandwich, esp. with ham, pork, cheese, and pickles, often grilled. [1975–80]
—**Regional Variation.** See **hero sandwich.**

CONCISE ETYMOLOGY KEY: <, descended or borrowed from; >, whence; b., blend of, blended; c., cognate with; cf., compare; deriv., derivative; equiv., equivalent; imit., imitative; obl., oblique; r., replacing; s., stem; sp., spelling, spelled; resp., respelling, respelled; trans., translation; ?, origin unknown; *, unattested; ‡, probably earlier than. See the full key inside the front cover.

cu•ba•ture (kyo͞o′bə chər), *n.* **1.** the determination of the cubic contents of something. **2.** cubic contents. [1670–80; CUBE¹ + *-ature,* after QUADRATURE]

Cub•ba (ko͞o′bä), *n.* a female day name for Wednesday. See under **day name.** Also, **Cuba.**

Cub•be•na (ko͞o′bə nä′), *n.* a male day name for Tuesday. See under **day name.**

cub•by (kub′ē), *n., pl.* **-bies. 1.** a cubbyhole. **2.** any of a group of small boxlike enclosures or compartments, open at the front, in which children can keep their belongings, as at a nursery school. [1835–45; dial. *cub* stall, shed (akin to COVE¹) + -Y²]

cub•by•hole (kub′ē hōl′), *n.* **1.** pigeonhole. **2.** a small, snug place. [1835–45; CUBBY + HOLE]

cube¹ (kyo͞ob), *n., v.,* **cubed, cub•ing.** —*n.* **1.** a solid bounded by six equal squares, the angle between any two adjacent faces being a right angle. **2.** an object, either solid or hollow, having this form or a form approximating it: *a cube of cheese; plastic storage cubes.* **3.** sugar cube. **4.** flashcube. **5.** *Math.* the third power of a quantity, expressed as $a^3 = a \cdot a \cdot a$. **6.** *Informal.* cubic inch, esp. as a measure of the displacement of an automotive engine: *a new sports car with 350 cubes.* **7.** *Slang.* one of a pair of dice; die. **8.** *Slang.* a person who is unaware of or unfamiliar with current ideas, opinions, trends, etc.; square. —*v.t.* **9.** to make into a cube or cubes. **10.** to cut into cubes. **11.** *Math.* to raise to the third power. **12.** to measure the cubic contents of. **13.** to tenderize (a thin cut or slice of meat) by scoring the fibers in a pattern of squares. [1350–1400; ME *cubus* < L < Gk *kýbos* cube, die] —**cub′er,** *n.*

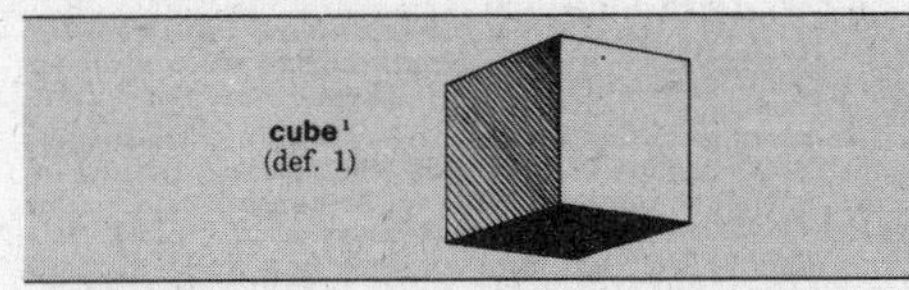
cube¹ (def. 1)

cu•be² (kyo͞o′bā), *n.* any of several tropical plants of the legume family that are used in making fish poisons and insecticides. Also, **cu•bé** (kyo͞o bā′). [1920–25; orig. uncert.]

cu•beb (kyo͞o′beb), *n.* the spicy fruit or drupe of an East Indian climbing shrub, *Piper cubeba,* of the pepper family. [1250–1300; < ML *cubēba* < Ar *kubābah* (classical Ar *kabābah*); r. ME *cucube, quibibe* < AF, MF < ML, as above]

cube′ root′, *Math.* a quantity of which a given quantity is the cube: *The cube root of 64 is 4.* [1690–1700]

cube′ steak′, a thin, square or round cut of beef tenderized by cubing. Also, **cubed′ steak′.** [1925–30]

cu•bic (kyo͞o′bik), *adj.* **1.** having three dimensions; solid. **2.** having the form of a cube; cubical. **3.** pertaining to the measurement of volume: *the cubic contents of a vessel.* **4.** pertaining to a unit of linear measure that is multiplied by itself twice to form a unit of measure for volume: *cubic foot; cubic centimeter; cubic inch; cubic meter.* **5.** *Math.* of or pertaining to the third degree. **6.** *Crystall.* belonging or pertaining to the isometric system of crystallization. —*n.* **7.** *Math.* a cubic polynomial or equation. [1490–1500; earlier *cubik* < L *cubicus* < Gk *kybikós.* See CUBE¹, -IC] —**cu•bic•i•ty** (kyo͞o bis′i tē), *n.*

cu•bi•cal (kyo͞o′bi kəl), *adj.* **1.** having the form of a cube. **2.** of or pertaining to volume. [1490–1500; CUBIC + -AL¹] —**cu′bi•cal•ly,** *adv.* —**cu′bi•cal•ness,** *n.*

cu•bi•cle (kyo͞o′bi kəl), *n.* **1.** a small space or compartment partitioned off. **2.** carrel (def. 1). **3.** a bedroom, esp. one of a number of small ones in a divided dormitory, as in English public schools. [1400–50; late ME < L *cubiculum* bedroom, equiv. to *cub(āre)* to lie down + *-i-* -I- + *-culum* -CLE²]

cu′bic meas′ure, 1. the measurement of volume or space by means of cubic units. **2.** a system of such units, esp. that in which 1728 cubic inches = 1 cubic foot and 27 cubic feet = 1 cubic yard, or that in which 1000 cubic millimeters = 1 cubic centimeter, 1000 cubic centimeters = 1000 cubic decimeters, and 1000 cubic decimeters = 1 cubic meter. [1650–60]

cu•bic•u•lum (kyo͞o bik′yə ləm), *n., pl.* **-la** (-lə). *Archaeol.* a burial chamber, as in catacombs. [1825–35; < L: bedroom. See CUBICLE]

cu′bic zir•co′ni•a (zûr kō′nē ə), *pl.* **-ni•as.** an artificial crystal resembling a diamond in refraction, dispersion, hardness, and color, used in jewelry. *Abbr.:* CZ Sometimes, **cu•bic zir•co′ni•um** (zûr kō′nē əm).

cu•bi•form (kyo͞o′bə fôrm′), *adj.* shaped like a cube. [1720–30; CUBE¹ + -I- + -FORM]

cub•ism (kyo͞o′biz əm), *n.* (*sometimes cap.*) *Fine Arts.* a style of painting and sculpture developed in the early 20th century, characterized chiefly by an emphasis on formal structure, the reduction of natural forms to their geometrical equivalents, and the organization of the planes of a represented object independently of representational requirements. [< F *cubisme* (1908); see CUBE¹, -ISM] —**cub′ist,** *n.* —**cub•is′tic,** *adj.*

cu•bit (kyo͞o′bit), *n.* an ancient linear unit based on the length of the forearm, from elbow to the tip of the middle finger, usually from 17 to 21 in. (43 to 53 cm). [1325–75; ME, OE < L *cubitum* elbow, cubit; perh. akin to *cubāre* to lie down]

cu•bi•tal (kyo͞o′bi tl), *adj.* **1.** *Anat., Zool.* pertaining to, involving, or situated near the cubitus. —*n.* **2.** *Ornith. Now Rare.* a secondary feather. [1375–1425 for an earlier sense; late ME < L *cubitālis.* See CUBIT, -AL¹]

cu′bital fur′row, (in certain insects) a crease, between the cubital and anal veins, along which the wing folds.

cu•bi•tus (kyo͞o′bi təs), *n., pl.* **-ti** (-tī′). **1.** a longitudinal vein in the rear portion of the wing of an insect. **2.** *Anat.* **a.** the forearm. **b.** *Now Rare.* the ulna. [1820–30; < NL, L, var. of *cubitum* CUBIT]

cu•boid (kyo͞o′boid), *adj.* Also, **cu•boi′dal. 1.** resembling a cube in form. **2.** *Anat.* noting or pertaining to the outermost bone of the distal row of tarsal bones. —*n.* **3.** *Math.* a rectangular parallelepiped. **4.** *Anat.* the cuboid bone. [1700–10; < Gk *kyboeidḗs* cubelike. See CUBE¹, -OID]

cuboi′dal epithe′lium, *Biol.* epithelium consisting of one or more layers of cells of cuboid or polyhedral shape.

cub′ report′er, a young and rather inexperienced newspaper reporter. [1895–1900]

cub′ scout′, (*sometimes caps.*) a member of the junior division (ages 8–10) of the Boy Scouts.

cub′ shark′. See **bull shark.**

Cu•chul•ainn (ko͞o kul′in, ko͞o′KHo͝o lin), *n. Irish Legend.* a hero of Ulster and the subject of many legends.

cuck′ing stool′ (kuk′ing), a former instrument of punishment consisting of a chair in which an offender was strapped, to be mocked and pelted or ducked in water. [1175–1225; ME *cucking stol,* lit., defecating stool, equiv. to *cucking,* prp. of *cukken* to defecate (< Scand; cf. dial Sw *kukka*) + *stol* STOOL]

cuck•old (kuk′əld), *n.* **1.** the husband of an unfaithful wife. —*v.t.* **2.** to make a cuckold of (a husband). [1200–50; ME *cukeweld,* later *cok(k)ewold, cukwold* < AF **cucuald* (cf. MF *cucuault*), equiv. to OF *cocu* CUCKOO + *-ald, -alt* pejorative suffix (see RIBALD); appar. orig. applied to an adulterer, in allusion to the cuckoo's habit of laying its eggs in other birds' nests] —**cuck′old•ly,** *adv.*

cuck•old•ry (kuk′əl drē), *n.* **1.** the act of making someone's husband a cuckold. **2.** the state or quality of being a cuckold. [1520–30; CUCKOLD + -RY]

cuck′old's knot′, *Naut.* a hitch, as for holding a spar, consisting of a single loop with the overlapping parts of the rope seized together. Also called **cuck′old's neck′, ring seizing, throat seizing.** [1840–50; so called because the noose so made is insecure]

cuck•oo (ko͞o′ko͞o, ko͝ok′o͞o), *n., pl.* **-oos,** *v.,* **-ooed, -oo•ing,** *adj.* —*n.* **1.** a common European bird, *Cuculus canorus,* of the family Cuculidae, noted for its characteristic call and its brood parasitism. **2.** any of several other birds of the family Cuculidae. **3.** the call of the cuckoo, or an imitation of it. **4.** *Slang.* a crazy, silly, or foolish person; simpleton. —*v.i.* **5.** to utter the call of the cuckoo or an imitation of it. —*v.t.* **6.** to repeat monotonously. —*adj.* **7.** *Slang.* crazy; silly; foolish. **8.** of, pertaining to, or like a cuckoo. [1200–50; ME *cuc(c)u, cuccuk(e)* (imit.); cf. L *cucūlus,* F *coucou,* G *Kuckuk,* D *koekoek,* ModGk *koûko*]

cuck′oo clock′, a wall or shelf clock, often carved and decorated, that announces the hours by a sound like the call of the cuckoo, usually accompanied by the appearance of an imitation bird through a little door. [1775–85]

cuck•oo•flow•er (ko͞o′ko͞o flou′ər, ko͝ok′o͞o-), *n.* any of various plants, as the lady's-smock or the ragged robin. [1570–80; CUCKOO + FLOWER, so called because it is found in bloom when the cuckoo is heard]

cuck•oo•pint (ko͞o′ko͞o pīnt′, ko͝ok′o͞o-), *n.* a common European arum, *Arum maculatum.* Also called **lords-and-ladies.** [1545–55; apocopated var. of obs. *cuckoopintle,* late ME *cokkupyntel* (see CUCKOO, PINTLE); its spadix is pintle-shaped]

cuck•oo-shrike (ko͞o′ko͞o shrīk′, ko͝ok′o͞o-), *n.* any of numerous Old World passerine birds of the family Campephagidae, certain species of which superficially resemble cuckoos and have hooked bills like shrikes.

cuck•oo-spit (ko͞o′ko͞o spit′, ko͝ok′o͞o-), *n.* **1.** Also called **frog spit.** a frothy secretion found on plants, exuded by the young of certain insects, as the froghoppers, and serving as a protective covering. **2.** an insect that produces this secretion. [1350–1400; ME *cokkowespitle* cuckoopint; so called from the spitlike secretion found on the plant and thought to be left by the bird]

cuck′oo wasp′, any of several small, metallic-green or -blue wasps of the family Chrysididae that deposit their eggs in nests of other wasps.

cu cm, cubic centimeter; cubic centimeters. Also, **cu. cm.**

cu•cul•late (kyo͞o′kə lāt′, kyo͞o kul′āt), *adj.* resembling a cowl or hood. Also, **cu•cul•lat•ed** (kyo͞o′kə lā′tid, kyo͞o kul′ā-). [1785–95; < LL *cucullātus* having a hood, equiv. to L *cucull(us)* a covering, hood + *-ātus* -ATE¹]

cu•cum•ber (kyo͞o′kum bər), *n.* **1.** a creeping plant, *Cucumis sativus,* of the gourd family, occurring in many cultivated forms. **2.** the edible, fleshy fruit of this plant, of a cylindrical shape with rounded ends and having a green, warty skin. **3.** any of various allied or similar plants. **4.** the fruit of any such plant. [1350–1400; ME *cucumbre* < AF, OF *co(u)combre* < L *cucumer-,* s. of *cucumis;* r. ME, OE *cucumer* < L, as above]

cu′cumber bee′tle, any leaf beetle of the genus *Diabrotica* and related genera that feeds on cucumbers and other plants of the gourd family and is a vector of cucurbit wilt. [1835–45, *Amer.*]

cu′cumber mosa′ic, *Plant Pathol.* a viral disease of cucumbers and many other plants, characterized by a mosaic pattern and distortion of leaves and fruits. [1915–20]

cu′cumber root′. See **Indian cucumber root.** [1400–50; late ME]

cu′cumber tree′, 1. any of several American magnolias, esp. *Magnolia acuminata,* having ovate leaves, yellowish-green bell-shaped flowers, and dark red, cone-like fruit. **2.** any of certain other trees, as an East Indian tree of the genus *Averrhoa.* [1775–85, *Amer.;* so called from the resemblance of its fruit to cucumbers]

cu•cur•bit (kyo͞o kûr′bit), *n.* **1.** a gourd. **2.** any plant of the gourd family. **3.** *Chem.* the gourd-shaped portion of an alembic, a vessel formerly used in distilling. [1350–1400; ME *cucurbite* < AF, OF < L *cucurbita;* cf. GOURD, COURGETTE]

cu•cur•bi•ta•ceous (kyo͞o kûr′bi tā′shəs), *adj.* belonging to the Cucurbitaceae, the gourd family of plants.

Cf. **gourd family.** [1850–55; < NL *Cucurbitace(ae)* (see CUCURBIT, -ACEAE) + -OUS]

cucur′bit wilt′, *Plant Pathol.* a disease of cucumbers and other plants of the gourd family, characterized by wilted leaves, caused by a bacterium, *Erwinia tracheiphila.*

Cú•cu•ta (ko͞o′ko͞o tä′), *n.* a city in E Colombia. 219,772.

cud (kud), *n.* **1.** the portion of food that a ruminant returns from the first stomach to the mouth to chew a second time. **2.** *Dial.* quid[1]. **3. chew one's** or **the cud,** *Informal.* to meditate or ponder; ruminate. [bef. 1000; ME; OE *cudu,* var. of *cwiodu, cwidu;* akin to OHG *quiti* glue, Skt *jatu* resin, gum. See QUID[1]]

cu•da (ko͞o′də), *n. Slang.* a barracuda. [by aphesis]

Cud•a•hy (kud′ə hē), *n.* **1.** a city in SE Wisconsin, near Milwaukee. 19,547. **2.** a city in SW California. 17,984.

cud•bear (kud′bâr′), *n.* a violet coloring matter obtained from various lichens, esp. *Lecanora tartarea.* [1760–70; coinage by Dr. *Cuthbert* Gordon, 18th-century Scottish chemist, based on his own name]

cud•dle (kud′l), *v.,* **-dled, -dling,** *n.* —*v.t.* **1.** to hold close in an affectionate manner; hug tenderly; fondle. —*v.i.* **2.** to lie close and snug; nestle. **3.** to curl up in going to sleep. —*n.* **4.** act of cuddling; hug; embrace. [1510–20; perh. back formation from ME *cudliche* intimate, affectionate, OE *cūthlic,* or from ME *cuthlechen,* OE *cūthlǣcan* to make friends with; see COUTH[2], -LY]

cud•dly (kud′lē), *adj.,* **-dli•er, -dli•est.** suitable for or inviting cuddling: *a cuddly teddy bear.* Also, **cud•dle•some** (kud′l səm). [1860–65; CUDDLE + -Y[1]]

cud•dy[1] (kud′ē), *n., pl.* **-dies. 1.** *Naut.* **a.** a small room, cabin, or enclosed space at the bow or stern of a boat, esp. one under the poop. **b.** a galley or pantry in a small boat. **c.** a small locker in an open boat, esp. one at the bow. **d.** (on a fishing boat) a platform on which a net is coiled when not in use. **2.** a small room, cupboard, or closet. [1650–60; of uncert. orig.]

cud•dy[2] (kud′ē, ko͝od′ē), *n., pl.* **-dies.** *Chiefly Scot.* **1.** a donkey. **2.** a stupid person. [1705–15; perh. generic use of *Cuddy,* short for *Cuthbert,* man's name]

cudg•el (kuj′əl), *n., v.,* **-eled, -el•ing,** or (*esp. Brit.*) **-elled, -el•ling.** —*n.* **1.** a short, thick stick used as a weapon; club. **2. take up the cudgels,** to come to the defense or aid of someone or something. —*v.t.* **3.** to strike with a cudgel; beat. **4. cudgel one's brains,** to try to comprehend or remember: *I cudgeled my brains to recall her name.* [bef. 900; ME *cuggel,* OE *cycgel;* akin to G *Kugel* ball] —**cudg′el•er;** *esp. Brit.,* **cud′gel•ler,** *n.*

Cud•jo (kuj′ō), *n.* a male day name for Monday. See under **day name.** Also, **Cud′joe.**

cud•weed (kud′wēd′), *n.* **1.** any of the woolly, composite plants of the genus *Gnaphalium,* having simple leaves and tubular flowers. **2.** any of various plants of allied genera. [1540–50; CUD + WEED[1]]

cue[1] (kyo͞o), *n., v.,* **cued, cu•ing.** —*n.* **1.** anything said or done, on or off stage, that is followed by a specific line or action: *An off-stage door slam was his cue to enter.* **2.** anything that excites to action; stimulus. **3.** a hint; intimation; guiding suggestion. **4.** the part a person is to play; a prescribed or necessary course of action. **5.** a sensory signal used to identify experiences, facilitate memory, or organize responses. **6.** *Archaic.* frame of mind; mood. **7. miss a cue, a.** to fail to respond to a cue. **b.** *Informal.* to miss the point: *You could tell by his expression that he had missed a cue.* —*v.t.* **8.** to provide with a cue or indication; give a cue to; prompt: *Will you cue me on my lines?* **9.** to insert, or direct to come in, in a specific place in a musical or dramatic performance (usually fol. by *in* or *into*): *to cue in a lighting effect.* **10.** to search for and reach (a specific track on a recording) (sometimes fol. by *up*). **11. cue (someone) in,** *Informal.* to inform; give instructions, information, news, etc., to: *Cue him in on the plans for the dance.* [1545–55; spelled name of the letter *q* as an abbreviation (found in acting scripts) of L *quandō* when]
—**Syn. 1.** signal. **3.** sign, clue, key, tip, inkling.

cue[2] (kyo͞o), *n., v.,* **cued, cu•ing.** —*n.* **1.** a long, tapering rod, tipped with a soft leather pad, used to strike the ball in billiards, pool, etc. **2.** a long, usually wooden stick with a concave head, used to propel the disks in shuffleboard. **3.** a queue of hair. **4.** a queue or file, as of persons awaiting their turn. —*v.t.* **5.** to tie into a queue. **6.** to strike with a cue. [1725–35; < F *queue* tail, OF *coue* < L *cōda,* earlier *cauda* tail; cf. COWARD, QUEUE]

cue[3] (kyo͞o), *n.* the letter Q, *q.* [1400–50; late ME *cu;* conventional adaptation in spelling of the letter name]

cue′ ball′, *Billiards, Pool.* the ball a player strikes with the cue, as distinguished from the other balls on the table. [1880–85; CUE[2] + BALL[1]]

cue′ bid′, *Bridge.* a bid in a suit showing control of the suit, as having an assured winner or a void. [1930–35]

cue-bid (kyo͞o′bid′), *v.,* **-bid, -bid•den** or **-bid, -bid•ding.** —*v.t.* **1.** to show control of (a suit) by a cue bid. —*v.i.* **2.** to make a cue bid. [1960–65]

cue′ card′, *Television.* a large card, out of range of the camera, on which words or phrases have been printed in large letters for the speaker or performer to read or use as a memory aid during a program.

cued′ speech′, (*sometimes caps.*) a method of communication in which a speaker uses a system of manual cues to aid a lipreader by clarifying potentially ambiguous mouth movements with hand gestures. [1970–75]

cue•ist (kyo͞o′ist), *n.* a billiard player. [1865–70; CUE[2] + -IST]

Cuen•ca (kweng′kä), *n.* a city in SW Ecuador. 104,470.

Cuer•na•va•ca (kwer′nə vä′kə; *Sp.* kwer′nä vä′kä), *n.* a city in and the capital of Morelos, in central Mexico. 357,600.

cue′ sheet′, a detailed listing of cues for use by a stage manager or the technicians during the production of a play or broadcast. [1925–30]

cues•ta (kwes′tə), *n.* a long, low ridge with a relatively steep face or escarpment on one side and a long, gentle slope on the other. [1810–20, *Amer.;* < Sp: shoulder, sloping land < L *costa* side (of a hill), rib; see COAST]

Cue•vas (kwā′vəs; *Sp.* kwe′väs), *n.* **Jo•sé Luis** (hō zā′ lwēs; *Sp.* hô se′ lwēs), born 1934, Mexican painter, graphic artist, and illustrator.

cuff[1] (kuf), *n.* **1.** a fold or band serving as a trimming or finish for the bottom of a sleeve. **2.** a turned-up fold, as at the bottom of a trouser leg. **3.** the part of a gauntlet or long glove that extends over the wrist. **4.** a separate or detachable band or piece of fabric worn about the wrist, inside or outside of the sleeve. **5.** an elasticized, ribbed, or reinforced band at the top of a sock or stocking. **6.** a band of leather or other material, wider than a collar, sewed around the outside of the top of a shoe or boot to serve as a trimming or finish. **7.** a handcuff. **8.** *Anat.* a bandlike muscle or group of muscles encircling a body part. **9.** *Furniture.* a horizontal strip of veneer used as an ornament on a leg. **10.** *Med.* an inflatable wrap placed around the upper arm and used in conjunction with a device for recording blood pressure. **11. off the cuff,** *Informal.* **a.** extemporaneously; on the spur of the moment. **b.** unofficially or informally: *I'm telling you this strictly off the cuff.* **12. on the cuff,** *Slang.* **a.** with the promise of future payment; on credit. **b.** without charge; with no payment expected: *He enjoyed his meal the more because it was on the cuff.* —*v.t.* **13.** to make a cuff or cuffs on: *to cuff a pair of trousers.* **14.** to put handcuffs on. [1350–1400; ME *cuffe* mitten; perh. akin to OE *cuffie* cap < ML *cuphia* COIF]

cuff[2] (kuf), *v.t.* **1.** to strike with the open hand; beat; buffet. —*n.* **2.** a blow with the fist or the open hand; buffet. [1520–30; perh. < Scand; cf. LG *kuffen,* Norw, Sw dial. *kuffa* to push, shove]

cuff′ but′ton, the button for a shirt cuff.

Cuf•fe (kuf′ē), *n.* **Paul,** 1759–1817, U.S. merchant, seaman, and philanthropist: advocated U.S. black emigration to Africa.

Cuf•fee (kuf′ē), *n.* a male day name for Friday. See under **day name.** Also, **Cuf′fy.**

cuff′ link′, one of a pair of linked ornamental buttons or buttonlike devices for fastening a shirt cuff. Also, **cuff′link′.** [1895–1900]

Cu•fic (kyo͞o′fik), *adj., n.* Kufic.

cu. ft., cubic foot; cubic feet.

Cu•i (kwē; *Fr.* kʏ ē′), *n.* **Cé•sar** (*Fr.* sā zar′) **An•to•no•vich** (*Russ.* un tô′nə vyich), 1835–1918, Russian composer.

Cu•ia•bá (ko͞o′yə bä′), *n.* **1.** a river in SW Brazil. ab. 300 mi. (485 km) long. **2.** a port in W Brazil, on the Cuiabá River. 219,262. Also, **Cuyabá.**

cu•i bo•no (ko͞oi bō′nō; *Eng.* kwē′ bō′nō, kī′-), *Latin.* **1.** for whose benefit? **2.** for what use? of what good?

cu. in., cubic inch; cubic inches.

cui•rass (kwi ras′), *n.* **1.** Also called **corselet.** defensive armor for the torso comprising a breastplate and backplate, originally made of leather. **2.** either of the plates forming such armor. **3.** any similar covering, as the protective armor of a ship. **4.** *Zool.* a hard shell or other covering forming an indurated defensive shield. —*v.t.* **5.** to equip or cover with a cuirass. [1425–75; < F *cuirasse* < LL *coriācea,* n. use of fem. of *coriāceus* (adj.) leather, equiv. to L *cori(um)* leather + *-āceus* -ACEOUS; r. late ME *curas* < MF *curasse,* var. of *cuirasse*]

cui•ras•sier (kwēr′ə sēr′), *n.* a cavalry soldier wearing a cuirass. [1545–55; < F; see CUIRASS, -IER[2]]

cuir•ie (kwēr′ē), *n. Armor.* a hardened leather piece for protecting the breast, worn over mail. [1225–75; ME *quirre* < OF *quiree, quirie, cuirie;* see CUIRASS]

Cui•se•naire′ rod′ (kwē′zə nâr′, kwē′zə nâr′), *Trademark.* one of a set of 10 colored rods from 1 to 10 cm (0.4 to 4 in.) in length, used in a method of teaching the basics of arithmetic to children.

Cui•si•nart (kwē′zə närt′, kwē′zə närt′), *Trademark.* a brand of food processor.

cui•sine (kwi zēn′), *n.* **1.** a style or quality of cooking; cookery: *Italian cuisine; This restaurant has an excellent cuisine.* **2.** *Archaic.* the kitchen or culinary department of a house, hotel, etc. [1475–85; < F: lit., kitchen < VL **cocīna,* for L *coquīna;* see KITCHEN]

cui•si•nier (kwē zē nyā′), *n., pl.* **-niers** (-nyā′). *French.* a male cook or chef.

cui•si•nière (kwē zē nyer′), *n., pl.* **-nières** (-nyer′). *French.* a female cook or chef.

cuisse (kwis), *n. Armor.* a piece of armor or padding for protecting the thigh. Also, **cuish** (kwish). See diag. under **armor.** [1275–1325; earlier also *cush,* pl. *cushies* (the pl. *cush(i)e-s* misanalyzed as *cush-(i)es*), ME *quysheu, kusheu,* pl. *quyssewes, cusschewis* < OF *quisseuz, cuisseus,* pl. of *cuissel,* equiv. to *cuisse* thigh (< L *coxa* hipbone) + *-el* n. suffix]

cuit•tle (kʏ′tl), *v.t.,* **-tled, -tling.** *Scot.* to wheedle, cajole, or coax. [1555–65; orig. uncert.]

cui-ui (kwē′wē), *n.* a freshwater sucker, *Chasmistes cujus,* of Nevada, having a thin-lipped mouth. [1875–80, *Amer.;* < Northern Paiute *kuyui*]

cuj., (in prescriptions) of which; of any. [< L *cūjus*]

cuke (kyo͞ok), *n. Informal.* cucumber. [1900–05; by shortening and resp.]

Cu•kor (ko͞o′kər, -kôr, kyo͞o′-), *n.* **George,** 1899–1983, U.S. film director.

Cul•bert•son (kul′bərt sən), *n.* **E•ly** (ē′lē), 1893–1955, U.S. authority on contract bridge.

culch (kulch), *n.* **1.** the stones, old shells, etc., forming an oyster bed and furnishing points of attachment for the spawn of oysters. **2.** the spawn of oysters. **3.** Also, sculch. *Eastern New Eng.* rubbish; refuse. —*v.t.* **4.** to prepare (an oyster bed) with culch. Also, **cultch.** [1660–70; perh. metathetic var. of CLUTCH; but note OF *culche* COUCH]

cul-de-sac (kul′də sak′, -sak′, ko͝ol′-; *Fr.* kʏdᵊ sak′), *n., pl.* **culs-de-sac** (kulz′də sak′, -sak′, ko͝olz′-; *Fr.* kʏdᵊ sak′). **1.** a street, lane, etc., closed at one end; blind alley; dead-end street. **2.** any situation in which further progress is impossible. **3.** the hemming in of a military force on all sides except behind. **4.** *Anat.* a saclike cavity, tube, or the like, open only at one end, as the cecum. [1730–40; < F: lit., bottom of the sack]

-cule[1], var. of **-cle**[1]: *animalcule; molecule; reticule.* [(< F) < L *-culus, -cula, -culum;* see -CLE[1]]

-cule[2], var. of **-cle**[2]: *ridicule.* [(< F) < L *-culum, -cula;* see -CLE[2]]

Cu•le′bra Cut′ (ko͞o lā′brə; *Sp.* ko͞o le′vrä), former name of **Gaillard Cut.**

cu•let (kyo͞o′lit), *n.* **1.** *Jewelry.* a small face forming the bottom of a faceted gem. **2.** *Armor.* a piece below the backplate, composed of lames and corresponding to the fauld in front. [1670–80; < F (obs.), equiv. to *cul* bottom (< L *cūlus* buttocks) + *-et* -ET]

cu•lex (kyo͞o′leks), *n., pl.* **-li•ces** (-lə sēz′). any of numerous mosquitoes constituting the widespread genus *Culex,* distinguished by the habit in the adult of holding the body parallel to the feeding or resting surface, as the common house mosquito, *C. pipiens.* Cf. **anopheles.** —**cu•li•cine** (kyo͞o′lə sīn′, -sin), *adj.* [< NL (Linnaeus); L: gnat, midge]

Cu•lia•cán (ko͞o′lyä kän′), *n.* a city in and capital of Sinaloa state, in NW Mexico. 358,800.

cu•lic•id (kyo͞o lis′id), *n.* **1.** any of numerous dipterous insects of the family Culicidae, comprising the mosquitoes. —*adj.* **2.** belonging or pertaining to the culicids. [< NL *Culicidae,* equiv. to *Culic-,* s. of *Culex* CULEX + *-idae* -ID[2]]

cul•i•nar•i•an (kyo͞o′lə nâr′ē ən, kul′ə-), *n.* a cook or chef. [1605–15; CULINARY + -AN]

cu•li•nar•y (kyo͞o′lə ner′ē, kul′ə-), *adj.* of, pertaining to, or used in cooking or the kitchen. [1630–40; < L *culīnārius* of the kitchen, equiv. to *culīn(a)* kitchen, food + *-ārius* -ARY] —**cu′li•nar′i•ly,** *adv.*

Cu•lion (ko͞o lyôn′), *n.* an island of the Philippines, in the W part of the group, N of Palawan. 150 sq. mi. (389 sq. km).

cull (kul), *v.t.* **1.** to choose; select; pick. **2.** to gather the choice things or parts from. **3.** to collect; gather; pluck. —*n.* **4.** act of culling. **5.** something culled, esp. something picked out and put aside as inferior. [1300–50; ME *coilen, cuilen, cullen* < AF, OF *cuillir* < L *colligere* to gather; see COLLECT[1]] —**cull′er,** *n.*
—**Syn. 2.** glean, extract. **3.** garner, winnow.

Cul•len (kul′ən), *n.* **Coun•tee** (koun tā′, -tē′), 1903–46, U.S. poet.

cul•len•der (kul′ən dər), *n.* colander.

cul•let (kul′it), *n.* broken or waste glass suitable for remelting. [1810–20; var. of *collet* < It *colletto* glass blower's term, lit., little neck. See COL, -ET]

cul•lion (kul′yən), *n. Archaic.* a base or vile fellow. [1350–1400; ME *culyon, coil(i)on* < AF, MF *coillon* worthless fellow, lit., testicle < VL **cōleōnem,* acc. of **cōleō,* for L *cōleī* (pl.) testicles, scrotum]

cul•lis (kul′is), *n.* a gutter, as at the eaves of a roof. [1830–40; < F *coulisse* COULISSE; cf. PORTCULLIS]

Cull•man (kul′mən), *n.* a city in N Alabama. 13,084.

cul•ly (kul′ē), *n., pl.* **-lies,** *v.,* **-lied, -ly•ing.** —*n.* **1.** *Archaic.* a dupe. **2.** *Slang.* fellow; companion. —*v.t.* **3.** to trick; cheat; dupe. [1655–65; perh. shortening of CULLION]

culm[1] (kulm), *n.* **1.** coal dust; slack. **2.** anthracite, esp. of inferior grade. [1300–50; ME *colme,* prob. equiv. to *col* COAL + *-m* suffix of uncert. meaning (cf. *-m* in OE *fæthm* fathom, *wæstm* growth)]

culm[2] (kulm), *n.* **1.** a stem or stalk, esp. the jointed and usually hollow stem of grasses. —*v.i.* **2.** to grow or develop into a culm. [1650–60; < L *culmus* stalk; akin to CALAMUS, HAULM]

cul•mic•o•lous (kul mik′ə ləs), *adj.* (of a fungus) growing on grass culms. [CULM[2] + -I- + -COLOUS]

cul•mif•er•ous (kul mif′ər əs), *adj.* having or producing culms. [1695–1705; CULM[2] + -I- + -FEROUS]

cul•mi•nant (kul′mə nənt), *adj.* culminating; topmost. [1595–1605; < ML *culminant-* (s. of *culmināns*), prp. of *culmināre* to come to a peak. See CULMINATE, -ANT]

cul•mi•nate (kul′mə nāt′), *v.,* **-nat•ed, -nat•ing.** —*v.i.* **1.** to reach the highest point, summit, or highest development (usually fol. by *in*). **2.** to end or arrive at a final stage (usually fol. by *in*): *The argument culminated in a fistfight.* **3.** to rise to or form an apex; terminate (usually fol. by *in*): *The tower culminates in a tall spire.* **4.** *Astron.* (of a celestial body) to be on the meridian, or reach the highest or the lowest altitude. —*v.t.* **5.** to bring to a close; complete; climax: *A rock song culminates the performance.* [1640–50; < LL *culminātus* (ptp. of *culmināre* to come to a peak), equiv. to L *culmin-* (s. of *culmen*) peak, top + *-ātus* -ATE[1]]

cul•mi•na•tion (kul′mə nā′shən), *n.* **1.** the act or fact of culminating. **2.** that in which anything culminates; the culminating position or stage; highest point; acme. **3.** *Astron.* the position of a celestial body when it is on the meridian. [1625–35; < ML *culminātiōn-,* s. of *culminātiō;* see CULMINATE, -ION]
—**Syn. 2.** climax, zenith, peak, summit.

CONCISE PRONUNCIATION KEY: *act, cāpe, dâre, pärt; set, ēqual; if, īce; ox, ōver, ôrder, oil, bo͝ok, bo͞ot, out; up, ûrge; child; sing; shoe; thin, that;* zh as in *treasure.* ə = *a* as in *alone, e* as in *system, i* as in *easily, o* as in *gallop, u* as in *circus;* ᵊ as in *fire* (fīᵊr), *hour* (ouᵊr). l and n can serve as syllabic consonants, as in *cradle* (krād′l), and *button* (but′n). See the full key inside the front cover.

cul·mi·na·tive (kul′mə nā′tiv), *adj. Ling.* (of stress or tone accent) serving to indicate the number of independent words or the important points in an utterance by assigning prominence to one syllable in each word or close-knit group of words. [CULMINATE + -IVE]

cu·lottes (ko͞o lots′, kyo͞o-), *n.pl.* women's trousers, usually knee-length or calf-length, cut full to resemble a skirt. Also, **cu·lotte′.** [1835–45; < F: lit., breeches, equiv. to *cul* rump + *-ottes,* pl. of *-otte,* fem. of *-ot* n. suffix. See CULET]

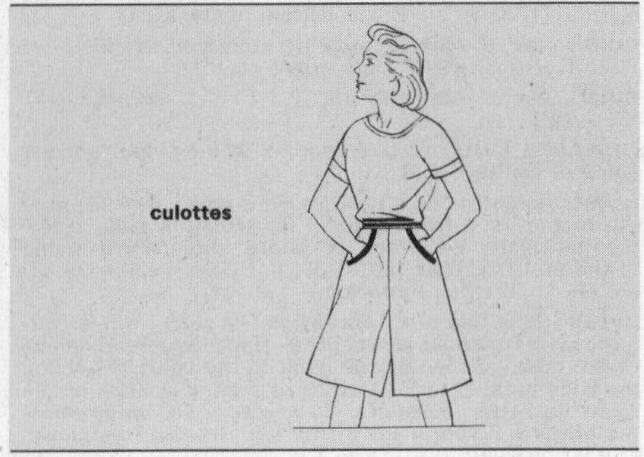
culottes

cul·pa (kul′pə; *Lat.* ko͝ol′pä), *n., pl.* **-pae** (-pē; *Lat.* -pī). **1.** *Roman and Civil Law.* negligence; neglect (distinguished from *dolus*): *One is not always liable before law for culpa resulting in damages.* **2.** guilt; sin. [1250–1300; OE < L: fault, liability, blame]

cul·pa·ble (kul′pə bəl), *adj.* deserving blame or censure; blameworthy. [1275–1325; ME < L *culpābilis,* equiv. to *culpā(re)* to hold liable (deriv. of *culpa* blame) + *-bilis* -BLE; r. ME *coupable* < MF < L as above] **—cul′pa·bil′i·ty, cul′pa·ble·ness,** *n.* **—cul′pa·bly,** *adv.*
—Syn. reprehensible.

Cul·pep·er (kul′pep′ər), *n.* **Thomas** (*2nd Baron Culpeper of Thoresway*), 1635–89, English colonial governor of Virginia 1680–83.

cul·prit (kul′prit), *n.* **1.** a person or other agent guilty of or responsible for an offense or fault. **2.** a person arraigned for an offense. [1670–80; traditionally explained as *cul* (repr. L *culpābilis* guilty) + *prit* (repr. AF *prest* ready), marking the prosecution as ready to prove the defendant's guilt. See CULPABLE, PRESTO]

cult (kult), *n.* **1.** a particular system of religious worship, esp. with reference to its rites and ceremonies. **2.** an instance of great veneration of a person, ideal, or thing, esp. as manifested by a body of admirers: *the physical fitness cult.* **3.** the object of such devotion. **4.** a group or sect bound together by veneration of the same thing, person, ideal, etc. **5.** *Sociol.* a group having a sacred ideology and a set of rites centering around their sacred symbols. **6.** a religion or sect considered to be false, unorthodox, or extremist, with members often living outside of conventional society under the direction of a charismatic leader. **7.** the members of such a religion or sect. **8.** any system for treating human sickness that originated by a person usually claiming to have sole insight into the nature of disease, and that employs methods regarded as unorthodox or unscientific. *—adj.* **9.** of or pertaining to a cult. **10.** of, for, or attracting a small group of devotees: *a cult movie.* [1610–20; < L *cultus* habitation, tilling, refinement, worship, equiv. to *cul-,* var. s. of *colere* to inhabit, till, worship + *-tus* suffix of v. action] **—cul′tic, cul·tu·al** (kul′cho͞o əl), *adj.* **—cult′ish,** *adj.*

cultch (kulch), *n., v.t.* culch.

cul·tel·lus (kul tel′əs), *n., pl.* **-tel·li** (-tel′ī). *Zool.* a sharp, knifelike structure, as the mouthparts of certain bloodsucking flies. [1895–1900; < L: dim. of *culter* knife, COLTER; for formation, see CASTELLUM]

cul·ti·gen (kul′tə jən, -jen′), *n.* a cultivated plant of unknown or obscure taxonomic origin. [1920–25; CULTI(VATED) + -GEN]

cult·ism (kul′tiz əm), *n.* the practices and devotions of a cult. [1830–40; CULT + -ISM] **—cult′ist,** *n.*

cul·ti·va·ble (kul′tə və bəl), *adj.* capable of being cultivated. Also, **cul·ti·vat·a·ble** (kul′tə vā′tə bəl). [1675–85; CULTIV(ATE) + -ABLE] **—cul′ti·va·bil′i·ty,** *n.* **—cul′ti·va·bly,** *adv.*

cul·ti·var (kul′tə vär′, -vər), *n.* a variety of plant that originated and persisted under cultivation. [1920–25; b. CULTIVATED and VARIETY]

cul·ti·vate (kul′tə vāt′), *v.t.,* **-vat·ed, -vat·ing. 1.** to prepare and work on (land) in order to raise crops; till. **2.** to use a cultivator on. **3.** to promote or improve the growth of (a plant, crop, etc.) by labor and attention. **4.** to produce by culture: *to cultivate a strain of bacteria.* **5.** to develop or improve by education or training; train; refine: *to cultivate a singing voice.* **6.** to promote the growth or development of (an art, science, etc.); foster. **7.** to devote oneself to (an art, science, etc.). **8.** to seek to promote or foster (friendship, love, etc.). **9.** to seek the acquaintance or friendship of (a person). [1610–20; < ML *cultivātus* (ptp. of *cultivāre* to till), equiv. to *cultiv(us)* (L *cult(us),* ptp. of *colere* to care for, till (cf. CULT) + *-īvus* -IVE) + *-ātus* -ATE[1]]

cul·ti·vat·ed (kul′tə vā′tid), *adj.* **1.** prepared and used for raising crops; tilled: *cultivated land.* **2.** produced or improved by cultivation, as a plant. **3.** educated; refined; cultured: *cultivated tastes.* [1655–65; CULTIVATE + -ED[2]]

cul·ti·va·tion (kul′tə vā′shən), *n.* **1.** the act or art of cultivating. **2.** the state of being cultivated. **3.** culture; refinement. [1690–1700; CULTIVATE + -ION]
—Syn. 3. gentility, breeding, taste.

cul·ti·va·tor (kul′tə vā′tər), *n.* **1.** a person or thing that cultivates. **2.** an implement drawn between rows of growing plants to loosen the earth and destroy weeds. [1655–65; CULTIVATE + -OR[2]]

cult′ of personal′ity, a cult promoting adulation of a living national leader or public figure, as one encouraged by Stalin to extend his power. [‡1965–70; trans. of Russ *kul't lichnosti*]

cul·trate (kul′trāt), *adj.* sharp-edged and pointed, as a leaf. Also, **cul′trat·ed.** [1855–60; < L *cultrātus* knife-shaped, equiv. to *cultr-* (s. of *culter*) knife + *-ātus* -ATE[1]]

cul·tur·al (kul′chər əl), *adj.* of or pertaining to culture or cultivation. [1865–70; CULTURE + -AL[1]] **—cul′tur·al·ly,** *adv.*

cul′tural anthropol′ogy, the branch of anthropology dealing with the origins, history, and development of human culture, and including in its scope the fields of archaeology, ethnology, and ethnography. Also called **social anthropology.** Cf. **physical anthropology.** [1920–25] **—cul′tural anthropol′ogist.**

cul′tural exchange′, an exchange of students, artists, athletes, etc., between two countries to promote mutual understanding.

cul·tur·al·ize (kul′chər ə līz′), *v.t.,* **-ized, -iz·ing.** *Anthropol.* to expose or subject to the influence of culture. Also, *esp. Brit.,* **cul′tur·al·ise′.** [CULTURAL + -IZE] **—cul′tur·al·i·za′tion,** *n.*

cul′tural lag′, *Sociol.* slowness in the rate of change of one part of a culture in relation to another part, resulting in a maladjustment within society, as from the failure of the nonmaterial culture to keep abreast of developments in the material culture. Also, **culture lag.**

cul′tural plu′ralism, *Sociol.* **1.** a condition in which minority groups participate fully in the dominant society, yet maintain their cultural differences. **2.** a doctrine that a society benefits from such a condition.

cul′tural relativ′ity, *Sociol.* a concept that cultural norms and values derive their meaning within a specific social context. Also called **cul′tural rel′ativism.** Cf. **ethnocentrism** (def. 2).

Cul′tural Revolu′tion, a radical sociopolitical movement in China c1966–71, led by Mao Zedong and characterized by military rule, terrorism, purges, restructuring of the educational system, etc. Cf. **Gang of Four, Red Guard.** Also called **Great Proletarian Cultural Revolution.** [trans. of Chin *wénhuà gémìng*]

cul′tural sociol′ogy, the study of the origins and development of societal institutions, norms, and practices.

cul′tural univer′sal, a cultural pattern extant in every known society.

cul·tu·ra·ti (kul′chə rä′tē, -rā′tī), *n.pl.* people deeply interested in cultural and artistic matters. [1970–75; CULTURE + *-ati,* patterned on LITERATI]

cul·ture (kul′chər), *n., v.,* **-tured, -tur·ing.** *—n.* **1.** the quality in a person or society that arises from a concern for what is regarded as excellent in arts, letters, manners, scholarly pursuits, etc. **2.** that which is excellent in the arts, manners, etc. **3.** a particular form or stage of civilization, as that of a certain nation or period: *Greek culture.* **4.** development or improvement of the mind by education or training. **5.** the behaviors and beliefs characteristic of a particular social, ethnic, or age group: *the youth culture; the drug culture.* **6.** *Anthropol.* the sum total of ways of living built up by a group of human beings and transmitted from one generation to another. **7.** *Biol.* **a.** the cultivation of microorganisms, as bacteria, or of tissues, for scientific study, medicinal use, etc. **b.** the product or growth resulting from such cultivation. **8.** the act or practice of cultivating the soil; tillage. **9.** the raising of plants or animals, esp. with a view to their improvement. **10.** the product or growth resulting from such cultivation. *—v.t.* **11.** to subject to culture; cultivate. **12.** *Biol.* **a.** to grow (microorganisms, tissues, etc.) in or on a controlled or defined medium. **b.** to introduce (living material) into a culture medium. [1400–50; late ME: tilling, place tilled (< AF) < L *cultūra.* See CULT, -URE]
—Syn. 4. See **education.**

cul′ture ar′ea, *Anthropol.* a region having a distinct pattern of culture.

cul′ture cen′ter, *Anthropol.* the part of a culture area in which the most distinctive traits of the area are concentrated.

cul′ture com′plex, *Sociol.* a group of culture traits all interrelated and dominated by one essential trait: *Nationalism is a culture complex.*

cul·tured (kul′chərd), *adj.* **1.** enlightened; refined. **2.** artificially nurtured or grown: *cultured bacteria.* **3.** cultivated; tilled. [1735–45; CULTURE + -ED[2]]
—Syn. 1. polished, sophisticated, elegant, genteel.

cul′ture diffu′sion, *Anthropol., Sociol.* the spreading out of culture, culture traits, or a cultural pattern from a central point. Cf. **diffusionism.** [1965–70]

cul′tured pearl′, a pearl induced to form by placement of a grain of sand or another irritating object within the shell of a pearl oyster or mussel. Also, **cul′ture pearl′.** [1920–25]

cul′ture fac′tor, *Anthropol., Sociol.* culture as a causative agent, esp. in contrast to biological factors.

cul′ture he′ro, 1. a mythical or mythicized historical figure who embodies the aspirations or ideals of a society. **2.** a mythical figure considered by a people to have furnished it the means of existence or survival, as by inventing their alphabet, teaching them husbandry, or stealing fire from the gods for them.

cul′ture lag′. See **cultural lag.**

cul′ture me′dium, *Bacteriol.* medium (def. 9). [1880–85]

cul′ture pat′tern, *Anthropol.* a group of interrelated culture traits of some continuity. [1930–35]

cul′ture shock′, a state of bewilderment and distress experienced by an individual who is suddenly exposed to a new, strange, or foreign social and cultural environment. [1955–60] **—cul′ture-shocked′,** *adj.*

cul′ture specif′ic syn′drome, *Psychiatry.* a behavioral disturbance in a specific cultural setting that is identified and named by the cultural group itself.

cul′ture trait′, *Anthropol.* any trait of human activity acquired in social life and transmitted by communication.

cul′ture vul′ture, *Slang.* a person with an excessive or pretentious interest in the arts. [1945–50]

cul·tur·ist (kul′chər ist), *n.* **1.** a cultivator. **2.** an advocate or devotee of culture. [1820–30; CULTURE + -IST]

cul·tur·ol·o·gy (kul′chə rol′ə jē), *n.* a branch of anthropology concerned with the study of cultural institutions as distinct from the people who are involved in them. [1935–40, *Amer.*; CULTURE + -O- + -LOGY]

cul·tus[1] (kul′təs), *n., pl.* **-tus·es, -ti** (-tī). a cult. [1630–40; < L; see CULT]

cul·tus[2] (kul′təs), *n., pl.* **-tus·es,** (*esp. collectively*) **-tus.** lingcod. Also called **cul′tus cod′.** [1850–55, *Amer.*; < Chinook Jargon *kə́ltəs* worthless, bad, < Lower Chinook *kə́ltas* in vain, only (but perh. itself < Chinook Jargon)]

cul·tus coo·lee (kul′təs ko͞o′lē), *Chiefly Western Canadian.* a purposeless or recreational stroll or ride. [1890–95; < Chinook Jargon; see CULTUS[2], COULEE]

cul·ver (kul′vər), *n. Brit. Dial.* a dove or pigeon. [bef. 900; ME; OE *culfer, culfre* < VL **columbra,* for L *columbula,* equiv. to *columb(a)* dove + *-ula* -ULE]

Cul′ver Cit′y (kul′vər), a city in SW California, W of Los Angeles. 38,139.

cul′ver hole′, *Masonry.* a hole for receiving a timber. [1555–65]

cul·ver·in (kul′vər in), *n.* **1.** medieval form of musket. **2.** a kind of heavy cannon used in the 16th and 17th centuries. [1400–50; late ME < MF *coulevrine* < L *colubrīna,* fem. of *colubrinus* COLUBRINE]

Cul′ver's root′, 1. the root of a tall plant, *Veronicastrum virginicum,* of the figwort family, having spikelike clusters of small, white, tubular flowers, used in medicine as a cathartic and emetic. **2.** the plant. [1710–20, *Amer.*; named after Dr. *Culver,* 17th–18th-century American physician]

cul·vert (kul′vərt), *n.* a drain or channel crossing under a road, sidewalk, etc.; sewer; conduit. [1765–75; orig. uncert.]

cum[1] (kum, ko͝om), *prep.* with; combined with; along with (usually used in combination): *My garage-cum-workshop is well equipped.* [1580–90; < L: with, together with (prep.)]

cum[2] (kum), *n. Slang (vulgar).* come (def. 62).

cum., cumulative.

Cu·mae (kyo͞o′mē), *n.* an ancient city in SW Italy, on the coast of Campania: believed to be the earliest Greek colony in Italy or in Sicily. **—Cu·mae′an,** *adj.*

Cu·ma·ná (ko͞o′mä nä′), *n.* a seaport in N Venezuela. 119,751.

cu·ma·rin (ko͞o′mə rin), *n. Chem.* coumarin.

cu·ma·rone (ko͞o′mə rōn′, kyo͞o′-), *n. Chem.* coumarone.

cum·ber (kum′bər), *v.t.* **1.** to hinder; hamper. **2.** to overload; burden. **3.** to inconvenience; trouble. *—n.* **4.** a hindrance. **5.** something that cumbers. **6.** *Archaic.* embarrassment; trouble. [1250–1300; ME *cumbre* (n.), *cumbren* (v.), aph. var. of *acumbren* to harass, defeat; see ENCUMBER] **—cum′ber·er,** *n.* **—cum′ber·ment,** *n.*

Cum·ber·land (kum′bər lənd), *n.* **1.** a former county in NW England, now part of Cumbria. **2.** a town in N Rhode Island. 27,069. **3.** a city in NW Maryland, on the Potomac River. 25,933. **4.** a river flowing W from SE Kentucky through N Tennessee into the Ohio River. 687 mi. (1106 km) long.

Cum′berland Gap′, a pass in the Cumberland Mountains at the junction of the Virginia, Kentucky, and Tennessee boundaries. 1315 ft. (401 m) high.

Cum′berland Moun′tains, a plateau largely in Kentucky and Tennessee, a part of the Appalachian Mountains: highest point, ab. 4000 ft. (1220 m). Also called **Cum′berland Plateau′.**

cum·ber·some (kum′bər səm), *adj.* **1.** burdensome; troublesome. **2.** unwieldy; clumsy. [1325–75; ME *cummyrsum.* See CUMBER, -SOME[1]] **—cum′ber·some·ly,** *adv.* **—cum′ber·some·ness,** *n.*
—Syn. 1. heavy, weighty, onerous. **2.** awkward.

cum·brance (kum′brəns), *n.* **1.** trouble; bother. **2.** burden; encumbrance. [1275–1325; ME *combraunce,* aph. var. of *acombraunce* defeat, harassment; see ENCUMBRANCE]

Cum·bri·a (kum′brē ə), *n.* a county in NW England. 473,800; 2659 sq. mi. (6886 sq. km).

cum·brous (kum′brəs), *adj.* cumbersome. [1325–75; ME *cumberous.* See CUMBER, -OUS] **—cum′brous·ly,** *adv.* **—cum′brous·ness,** *n.*

cum′ div′idend, *Stock Exchange.* with a previously declared dividend included in the price of a stock (distinguished from *ex dividend*). *Abbr.:* cum d, cum div [1875–80]

cu·mene (kyo͞o′mēn), *n. Chem.* a colorless and toxic liquid, C_9H_{12}, soluble in alcohol: used as a solvent and in the production of phenol and acetone. Also called **isopropylbenzene.** [< F *cumène;* see CUMIN, -ENE]

CONCISE ETYMOLOGY KEY: <, descended or borrowed from; >, whence; b., blend of, blended; c., cognate with; cf., compare; deriv., derivative; equiv., equivalent; imit., imitative; obl., oblique; r., replacing; s., stem; sp., spelling, spelled; resp., respelling, respelled; trans., translation; ?, origin unknown; *, unattested; ‡, probably earlier than. See the full key inside the front cover.

cum•in (kum′ən, kŏŏm′- *or, often,* ko͞o′mən, kyo͞o′-), *n.* **1.** a small plant, *Cuminum cyminum,* of the parsley family, bearing aromatic, seedlike fruit, used in cookery and medicine. **2.** the fruit or seeds of this plant. [bef. 900; ME *comyn, cumin* (< OF *comin*) < L *cuminum* < Gk *kýminon* < Sem (cf. Ar *kammūn,* Heb *kammōn* cumin); r. OE *cymen* < L, as above]

cum lau•de (kŏŏm lou′dä, -də, -dē; kum lô′dē), with honor: used in diplomas to grant the lowest of three special honors for grades above the average. Cf. **magna cum laude, summa cum laude.** [1890–95, *Amer.*; < L: with praise]

cum•mer (kum′ər), *n. Scot.* **1.** a godmother. **2.** a girl or woman. [1275–1325; ME *commare* godmother < AF, MF *commere* < LL *commāter,* equiv. to L *com-* COM- + *māter* MOTHER]

C, cummerbund

cum•mer•bund (kum′ər bund′), *n.* a wide sash worn at the waist, esp. a horizontally pleated one worn with a tuxedo. Also, **kummerbund.** [1610–20; < Hindi *kamarband* loin-band < Pers]

Cum•mings (kum′ingz), *n.* **Edward Est•lin** (est′lin), (*"e e cummings"*), 1894–1962, U.S. poet.

cum•ming•ton•ite (kum′ing tə nīt′), *n.* an amphibole mineral, magnesium-iron silicate, similar in composition to anthophyllite but richer in iron. [named after *Cummington,* Mass., where it is found; see -ITE¹]

cum•quat (kum′kwot), *n.* kumquat.

cum•shaw (kum′shô), *n.* a present; gratuity; tip. [1810–20; < dial. Chin (Xiamen) *kam siā,* equiv. to Chin *gǎn xiè* grateful thanks]

cu•mu•late (*v.* kyo͞o′myə lāt′; *adj.* kyo͞o′myə lit, -lāt′), *v.,* **-lat•ed, -lat•ing,** *adj.* —*v.t.* **1.** to heap up; amass; accumulate. —*adj.* **2.** heaped up. [1525–35; < L *cumulātus* (ptp. of *cumulāre* to heap up, pile up, accumulate), equiv. to *cumul(us)* a heap, pile, mass, CUMULUS + *-ātus* -ATE¹] —**cu′mu•late•ly,** *adv.*

cu•mu•la•tion (kyo͞o′myə lā′shən), *n.* **1.** the act of cumulating; accumulation. **2.** a heap; mass. [1610–20; CUMULATE + -ION]

cu•mu•la•tive (kyo͞o′myə lə tiv, -lā′tiv), *adj.* **1.** increasing or growing by accumulation or successive additions: *the cumulative effect of one rejection after another.* **2.** formed by or resulting from accumulation or the addition of successive parts or elements. **3.** of or pertaining to interest or dividends that, if not paid when due, become a prior claim for payment in the future: *cumulative preferred stocks.* [1595–1605; CUMULATE + -IVE] —**cu′mu•la•tive•ly,** *adv.* —**cu′mu•la•tive•ness,** *n.*

cu′mulative ev′idence, 1. evidence of which the parts reinforce one another, producing an effect stronger than any part by itself. **2.** *Chiefly Law.* **a.** testimony repetitive of testimony given earlier. **b.** evidence that confirms or adds to previous evidence. [1840–50]

cu′mulative scor′ing, *Duplicate Bridge.* a method of scoring in which the score of a partnership is taken as the sum of their scores on all hands played.

cu′mulative vot′ing, a system that gives each voter as many votes as there are persons to be elected from one representative district, allowing the voter to accumulate them on one candidate or to distribute them. [1850–55]

cu•mu•li•form (kyo͞o′myə lə fôrm′), *adj.* having the appearance or character of cumulus clouds. [1880–85; < NL *cumuli-,* comb. form of CUMULUS + -FORM]

cumulo-, a combining form representing **cumulus** in compound words. [see CUMULUS, -O-]

cu•mu•lo•nim•bus (kyo͞o′myə lō nim′bəs), *n., pl.* **-bus.** a cloud of a class indicative of thunderstorm conditions, characterized by large, dense towers that often reach altitudes of 30,000 ft. (9000 m) or more, cumuliform except for their tops, which appear fibrous because of the presence of ice crystals: occurs as a single cloud or as a group with merged bases and separate tops. Also called **thundercloud, thunderclouds, thunderhead.** [1885–90; CUMULO- + NIMBUS]

cu•mu•lus (kyo͞o′myə ləs), *n., pl.* **-lus. 1.** a heap; pile. **2.** a cloud of a class characterized by dense individual elements in the form of puffs, mounds, or towers, with flat bases and tops that often resemble cauliflower: as such clouds develop vertically, they form cumulonimbus. [1650–60; < NL (L: mass, pile)]

Cu•na (ko͞o′nə), *n., pl.* **-nas,** (*esp. collectively*) **-na** for 1. **1.** a member of a group of American Indian people inhabiting settlements on the Isthmus of Panama and islands in the Gulf of San Blas. **2.** the Chibchan language spoken by the Cuna.

Cu•nax•a (kyo͞o nak′sə), *n.* an ancient town in Babylonia, near the Euphrates: famous battle between Cyrus the Younger and Artaxerxes II in 401 B.C.

cunc•ta•tion (kungk tā′shən), *n.* delay; tardiness. [1575–85; < L *cunctātiōn-* (s. of *cunctātiō*) delay, equiv. to *cunctāt(us)* (ptp. of *cunctārī* to delay) + *-iōn-* -ION] —**cunc•ta′tious, cunc•ta•to•ry** (kungk′tə tôr′ē, -tōr′ē), **cunc•ta•tive** (kungk′tə tiv), *adj.*

cunc•ta•tor (kungk tā′tər), *n.* a procrastinator; delayer. [1645–55; < L, equiv. to *cunctā(rī)* to delay + *-tor* -TOR] —**cunc•ta′tor•ship′,** *n.*

cu•ne•al (kyo͞o′nē əl), *adj.* wedgelike; wedge-shaped. [1570–80; < L *cune(us)* a wedge + -AL¹]

cu•ne•ate (kyo͞o′nē it, -āt′), *adj.* **1.** wedge-shaped. **2.** (of leaves) triangular at the base and tapering to a point. Also, **cu′ne•at′ed.** [1800–10; < L *cuneātus,* equiv. to *cuneā(re)* to wedge, secure by wedging, become wedge-shaped + *-tus* ptp. suffix; see -ATE¹] —**cu′ne•ate•ly,** *adv.*

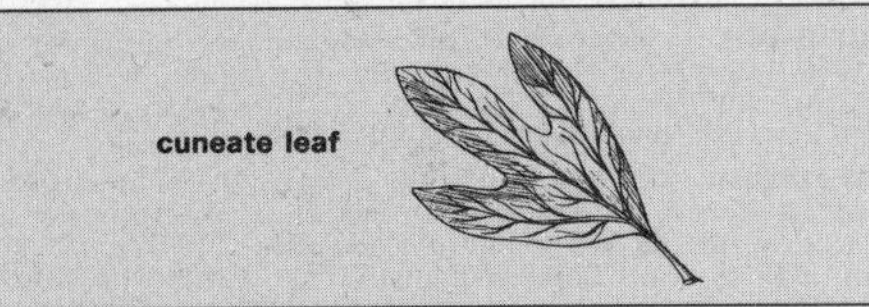
cuneate leaf

cu•ne•at•ic (kyo͞o′nē at′ik), *adj.* cuneiform; cuneate. [1850–55; CUNEATE + -IC]

cu•ne•i•form (kyo͞o nē′ə fôrm′, kyo͞o′nē ə-), *adj.* **1.** having the form of a wedge; wedge-shaped. **2.** composed of slim triangular or wedge-shaped elements, as the characters used in writing by the ancient Akkadians, Assyrians, Babylonians, Persians, and others. **3.** written in cuneiform characters: *cuneiform inscription.* **4.** *Anat.* noting or pertaining to any of various wedge-shaped bones, as of the tarsus. —*n.* **5.** cuneiform characters or writing. **6.** a cuneiform bone. Also, **cuniform.** [1670–80; < L *cune(us)* a wedge + -I- + -FORM]

cuneiform inscription
(Persian)

cu•ne•i•form•ist (kyo͞o nē′ə fôr′mist, kyo͞o′nē ə-), *n.* a person who studies or deciphers cuneiform writing. [1880–85; CUNEIFORM + -IST]

Cu•ne•o (ko͞o′ne ô), *n.* a city in NW Italy. 56,057.

cu•ne•us (kyo͞o′nē əs), *n., pl.* **-ne•i** (-nē ī′). **1.** *Anat.* a wedge-shaped convolution on the medial surface of the occipital lobe of the cerebrum. **2.** *Entomol.* a wedge-shaped segment of the corium of certain hemipterous insects. [< L: wedge]

cu•nic•u•lus (kyo͞o nik′yə ləs), *n., pl.* **-li** (-lī′). **1.** a small conduit or burrow, as an underground drain or rabbit hole. **2.** a low tunnel, as to a burial chamber. **3.** *Pathol.* a burrow in the skin caused by the itch mite. [1660–70; < L: rabbit, burrow; see CONY] —**cu•nic′u•lar,** *adj.*

cu•ni•form (kyo͞o′nə fôrm′), *adj., n.* cuneiform.

cun•ner (kun′ər), *n.* a small wrasse, *Tautogolabrus adspersus,* common in North Atlantic coastal waters of the U.S. Also called **bergall.** [1595–1605; orig. uncert.]

cun•ni•lin•gus (kun′l ing′gəs), *n.* the act or practice of orally stimulating the female genitals. Also, **cun•ni•linc•tus** (kun′l ingk′təs). [1885–90; < NL, L: one who licks the vulva, equiv. to *cunni-* (comb. form of *cunnus* vulva) + *-lingus* (deriv. of *lingere* to LICK)] —**cun′ni•lin′gual,** *adj.*

cun•ning (kun′ing), *n.* **1.** skill employed in a shrewd or sly manner, as in deceiving; craftiness; guile. **2.** adeptness in performance; dexterity: *The weaver's hand lost its cunning.* —*adj.* **3.** showing or made with ingenuity. **4.** artfully subtle or shrewd; crafty; sly. **5.** *Informal.* charmingly cute or appealing: *a cunning little baby.* **6.** *Archaic.* skillful; expert. —*v.* **7.** *Obs.* ppr. of **can¹.** [1275–1325; (n.) ME; OE *cunnung,* equiv. to *cunn(an)* to know (see CAN¹) + *-ung* -ING¹; (adj., v.) ME, prp. of *cunnan* to know (see CAN¹, -ING²)] —**cun′ning•ly,** *adv.* —**cun′ning•ness,** *n.*
—**Syn. 1.** shrewdness, artfulness, wiliness, trickery, finesse, intrigue, slyness, deception. CUNNING, ARTIFICE, CRAFT imply an inclination toward deceit, slyness, and trickery. CUNNING implies a shrewd, often instinctive skill in concealing or disguising the real purposes of one's actions: *not intelligence but a low kind of cunning.* An ARTIFICE is a clever, unscrupulous ruse, used to mislead others: *a successful artifice to conceal one's motives.* CRAFT suggests underhand methods and the use of deceptive devices and tricks to attain one's ends: *craft and deceitfulness in every act.* **2.** adroitness. **3.** ingenious, skillful. **4.** artful, wily, tricky, foxy.

Cun•ning•ham (kun′ing ham′), *n.* **1. Glenn** (*"Kansas Ironman"*), born 1909, U.S. track-and-field athlete. **2. Merce** (mûrs), born 1919?, U.S. dancer and choreographer.

cunt (kunt), *n. Slang* (*vulgar*). **1.** the vulva or vagina. **2.** *Disparaging and Offensive.* **a.** a woman. **b.** a contemptible person. **3.** sexual intercourse with a woman. [1275–1325; ME *cunte;* c. ON *kunta,* OFris, MLG, MD *kunte*]

Cuo•mo (kwō′mō), *n.* **Mario (Matthew),** born 1932, U.S. political leader: governor of New York since 1982.

cup (kup), *n., v.,* **cupped, cup•ping.** —*n.* **1.** a small, open container made of china, glass, metal, etc., usually having a handle and used chiefly as a receptable from which to drink tea, soup, etc. **2.** the bowllike part of a goblet or the like. **3.** a cup with its contents. **4.** the quantity contained in a cup. **5.** a unit of capacity, equal to 8 fluid ounces (237 milliliters) or 16 tablespoons; half-pint. **6.** an ornamental bowl, vase, etc., esp. of precious metal, offered as a prize for a contest. **7.** any of various beverages, as a mixture of wine and various ingredients: *claret cup.* **8.** the chalice used in the Eucharist. **9.** the wine of the Eucharist. **10.** something to be partaken of or endured; one's portion, as of joy or suffering. **11. cups,** the drinking of intoxicating liquors. **12.** any cuplike utensil, organ, part, cavity, etc. **13.** either of the two forms that cover and usually support the breasts in a brassiere or other garment, as a bathing suit. **14.** an athletic supporter reinforced with rigid plastic or metal for added protection. **15.** *Golf.* **a.** the metal receptacle within the hole. **b.** the hole itself. **16.** (*cap.*) *Astron.* the constellation Crater. **17.** See **cupping glass. 18.** *Metalworking.* a cylindrical shell closed at one end, esp. one produced in the first stages of a deep-drawing operation. **19.** *Math.* the cuplike symbol ∪, used to indicate the union of two sets. Cf. **union** (def. 10a). **20. in one's cups,** intoxicated; drunk. —*v.t.* **21.** to take or place in, or as in, a cup: *He cupped his ear with the palm of his hand.* **22.** to form into a cuplike shape: *He cupped his hands.* **23.** to use a cupping glass on. **24.** *Metalworking.* to form (tubing, containers, etc.) by punching hot strip or sheet metal and drawing it through a die. Cf. **deep-draw.** [bef. 1000; ME, OE *cuppe* < L *cuppa,* var. of *cūpa* tub, cask] —**cup′like′,** *adj.*

cup′ and cov′er, *Eng. Furniture.* a turning used in Elizabethan and Jacobean furniture and resembling a goblet with a domed cover.

cup′-and-sau′cer vine′ (kup′ən sô′sər), a woody, Mexican vine, *Cobaea scandens,* of the phlox family, having bell-shaped, violet-colored or greenish-purple flowers with an inflated, leaflike calyx and long, curved stamens. Also called **Mexican ivy.**

cup′ barom′eter, *Meteorol.* See **cistern barometer.**

cup•bear•er (kup′bâr′ər), *n.* a servant who fills and serves wine cups, as in a royal palace or at an elaborate banquet. [1375–1425; ME *cuppe-berer.* See CUP, BEARER]

cup•board (kub′ərd), *n.* **1.** a closet with shelves for dishes, cups, etc. **2.** *Chiefly Brit.* any small closet or cabinet, as for clothes, food, or the like. [1275–1325; ME *cuppebord.* See CUP, BOARD]

cup′board love′, a personal attachment that appears to be motivated by love but in fact stems from the hope of gain. [1750–60] —**cup′board lov′er.**

cup•cake (kup′kāk′), *n.* **1.** a small cake, the size of an individual portion, baked in a cup-shaped mold. **2.** *Older Slang.* **a.** a sexually attractive young woman. **b.** a beloved girl or woman. [1820–30, *Amer.*; CUP + CAKE]

cup′ cor′al, any of several species of coral in which the polyp forms and houses itself in a cup-shaped depression in the skeleton.

cu•pel (kyo͞o′pəl, kyo͞o pel′), *n., v.,* **-peled, -pel•ing** or (*esp. Brit.*) **-pelled, -pel•ling.** —*n.* **1.** a small, cuplike, porous container, usually made of bone ash, used in assaying, as for separating gold and silver from lead. **2.** a receptacle or furnace bottom in which silver is refined. —*v.t.* **3.** to heat or refine in a cupel. [1595–1605; < ML *cūpella,* equiv. to L *cūp(a)* tub + *-ella* dim. suffix] —**cu•pel•er** (kyo͞o′pə lər), **cu•pel•ler** (kyo͞o pel′ər), *n.* —**cu′pel•la′tion,** *n.*

Cu•per•ti•no (ko͞o′pər tē′nō, kyo͞o′-), *n.* a town in W California. 25,770.

cup•fer•ron (kup′fə ron′, kyo͞op′-, ko͞op′-), *n.* a creamy-white crystalline substance, $C_6H_9N_3O_2$, used as a reagent in analytical chemistry for the detection of copper. Also called **copperon.** [< G (1909) < L *cup(rum)* COPPER¹ + *fer(rum)* iron + G *-on* -ON¹]

cup•flow•er (kup′flou′ər), *n.* any of various plants belonging to the genus *Nierembergia,* of the nightshade family, having showy tubular or bell-shaped flowers. [CUP + FLOWER]

cup•ful (kup′fŏŏl), *n., pl.* **-fuls. 1.** the amount a cup can hold. **2.** *Cookery.* a volumetric measure equal to 8 fluid ounces (237 milliliters); half pint. [1350–1400; ME *cuppefulle.* See CUP, -FUL]
—**Usage. 1.** See **-ful.**

cup′ fun′gus, any small, often brightly colored mushroom of the family Pezizaceae, characterized by a fruiting body resembling a cup. [1905–10]

cu•phe•a (kyo͞o′fē ə), *n.* any of various New World plants belonging to the genus *Cuphea,* of the loosestrife family, having tubular, usually reddish or purple flowers. [< NL (1756), irreg. < Gk *kŷph(os)* hump (from the protuberance at the base of the calyx tube) + NL *-ea* -EA]

cup•hold•er (kup′hōl′dər), *n.* a competitor who has won or successfully defended a specific cup, trophy, championship, etc.; champion. [CUP + HOLDER]

Cu•pid (kyo͞o′pid), *n.* **1.** Also called **Amor.** the ancient Roman god of love and the son of either Mars or Mercury and Venus, identified with Eros and commonly represented as a winged, naked, infant boy with a bow and arrows. **2.** (*l.c.*) a similar winged being, or a representation of one, esp. as symbolic of love. [< L *Cupīdō* Cupid, the personification of *cupīdō* desire, love, equiv. to *cup(ere)* to long for, desire + *-īdō* n. suffix (cf. LIBIDO)]

cu•pid•i•ty (kyo͞o pid′i tē), *n.* eager or excessive desire, esp. to possess something; greed; avarice. [1400–50; late ME *cupidite* (< MF) < L *cupiditās,* equiv. to *cupid(us)* eager, desirous (*cup(ere)* to desire + *-idus* -ID⁴) + *-itās* -ITY] —**cu•pid•i•nous** (kyo͞o pid′n əs), *adj.*
—**Syn.** covetousness, avidity, hunger, acquisitiveness.

Cu′pid's ar′rows. See **love arrows.** [1880–85]

Cu′pid's bow′ (bō), **1.** a classical bow Cupid is traditionally pictured as bearing. **2.** a line or shape resembling this, esp. the line of the upper lip. [1855–60]

CONCISE PRONUNCIATION KEY: act, cāpe, dâre, pärt; set, ēqual; if, īce; ox, ōver, ôrder, oil, bŏŏk, bo͞ot, out; up, ûrge; child; sing; shoe; thin, *th*at; zh as in *treasure.* ə = *a* as in *alone, e* as in *system, i* as in *easily, o* as in *gallop, u* as in *circus;* ə as in *fire* (fīər), *hour* (ouər). l and n can serve as syllabic consonants, as in *cradle* (krād′l), and *button* (but′n). See the full key inside the front cover.

Cu·pid's-dart (kyo͞o′pidz därt′, -därt′), *n.* See **blue succory.**

cup′ of Eli′jah. See **Elijah's cup.**

cup′ of tea′, a task, topic, person, or object well-suited to a person's experience, taste, or liking. [1905–10]

cu·po·la (kyo͞o′pə lə), *n.* **1.** *Archit.* **a.** a light structure on a dome or roof, serving as a belfry, lantern, or belvedere. **b.** a dome, esp. one covering a circular or polygonal area. **2.** any of various domelike structures. **3.** *Metall.* a vertical furnace for melting iron to be cast. [1540–50; < It < L *cūpula,* equiv. to *cūp(a)* tub + *-ula* -ULE. Cf. CUP]

cupola (def. 1a)

cu·po·lat·ed (kyo͞o′pə lā′tid), *adj.* **1.** having a cupola or cupolas. **2.** having the form of a cupola. [1635–45; CUPOL(A) + -ATE[1] + -ED[2]]

cup·pa (kup′ə), *n. Brit. Informal.* a cup of tea. [1920–25; reduced form of *cup of (tea)*]

cupped (kupt), *adj.* hollowed out like a cup; cup-shaped. [1790–1800; CUP + -ED[3]]

cup·per (kup′ər), *n.* a person who performs the procedure of cupping. [1400–50 for an earlier sense; 1560–70 for current sense; late ME; see CUP, -ER[1]]

cup·ping (kup′ing), *n.* the process of drawing blood from the body by scarification and the application of a cupping glass, or by the application of a cupping glass without scarification, as for relieving internal congestion. [1350–1400; ME *cuppinge.* See CUP, -ING[1]]

cup′ping glass′, a glass vessel, used in cupping, in which a partial vacuum is created, as by heat. [1535–45]

cup′ plant′, a hardy composite plant, *Silphium perfoliatum,* of eastern North America, having large yellow flower heads and opposite leaves that envelop the stem, forming a cup. [1840–50, *Amer.*]

cup·py (kup′ē), *adj.* **-pi·er, -pi·est. 1.** cup-shaped; hollow. **2.** having indentations or depressions. [1880–85; CUP + -Y[1]]

cupr-, var. of **cupri-** before a vowel: *cupreous.*

cu·pram·mo·ni·um (kyo͞o′prə mō′nē əm, -mōn′yəm, ko͞o′-), *n. Chem.* any cation containing copper and ammonia. [1860–65; CUPR- + AMMONIUM]

cu·pre·ous (kyo͞o′prē əs, ko͞o′-), *adj.* **1.** copper-colored; metallic reddish-brown. **2.** consisting of or containing copper; copperlike. [1660–70; < LL *cupreus,* equiv. to *cupr(um)* COPPER[1] + *-eus* -EOUS]

cupri-, a combining form meaning "copper," used in the formation of compound words: *cupriferous.* Also, **cupr-, cupro-.** [comb. form of LL *cuprum* COPPER[1]]

cu·pric (kyo͞o′prik, ko͞o′-), *adj.* of or containing copper, esp. in the bivalent state, as cupric oxide, CuO. [1790–1800; CUPR- + -IC]

cu′pric hydrox′ide, *Chem.* See **copper hydroxide.**

cu′pric sul′fate, *Chem.* See **blue vitriol.**

cu·prif·er·ous (kyo͞o prif′ər əs, ko͞o-), *adj.* containing or yielding copper. [1775–85; CUPRI- + -FEROUS]

cu·prite (kyo͞o′prīt, ko͞o′-), *n.* a mineral, cuprous oxide, Cu_2O, occurring in red crystals and brown to black granular masses: an ore of copper. [1840–50; CUPR- + -ITE[1]]

cupro-, var. of **cupri-:** *cupronickel.*

cu·pro·nick·el (kyo͞o′prə nik′əl, ko͞o′-), *n.* **1.** any of various alloys of copper containing up to 40 percent nickel. —*adj.* **2.** containing copper and nickel. [1900–05; CUPRO- + NICKEL]

cu·prous (kyo͞o′prəs, ko͞o′-), *adj.* containing copper in the univalent state, as cuprous oxide, Cu_2O. [1660–70; CUPR- + -OUS]

cu′prous cy′anide, a creamy-white, highly poisonous, water-insoluble powder, CuCN, used chiefly in electroplating and in organic synthesis. Also called **copper cyanide.**

cu·prum (kyo͞o′prəm, ko͞o′-), *n. Chem.* copper. [< LL; see COPPER[1]]

cup′ shake′. See **wind shake.** [1785–95; so called because wood so damaged separates into concentric, cup-like pieces]

cup′ tow′el, *South Midland and Southern, esp. Texas, U.S.* a dishtowel. [1895–1900, *Amer.*]

cu·pu·late (kyo͞o′pyə lāt′, -lit), *adj.* shaped like a cupule. Also, **cu·pu·lar** (kyo͞o′pyə lər). [1825–35; CUPULE + -ATE[1]]

cu·pule (kyo͞o′pyo͞ol), *n.* **1.** *Bot.* **a.** a cup-shaped whorl of hardened, cohering bracts, as in the acorn. See illus. under **acorn. b.** a cup-shaped outgrowth of the thallus of certain liverworts. **c.** the apothecium of a cup fungus. **2.** *Zool.* a small cup-shaped sucker or similar organ or part. [1820–30; < NL *cūpula,* LL: small tub; see CUPOLA]

CONCISE ETYMOLOGY KEY: <, descended or borrowed from; >, whence; b., blend of, blended; c., cognate with; cf., compare; deriv., derivative; equiv., equivalent; imit., imitative; obl., oblique; r., replacing; s., stem; sp., spelling, spelled; resp., respelling, respelled; trans., translation; ?, origin unknown; *, unattested; ‡, probably earlier than. See the full key inside the front cover.

cur (kûr), *n.* **1.** a mongrel dog, esp. a worthless or unfriendly one. **2.** a mean, cowardly person. [1175–1225; ME *curre,* appar. shortened from *curdogge.* See CUR DOG] —**cur′like′,** *adj.*
—**Syn. 2.** blackguard, cad, heel.

cur., 1. currency. **2.** current.

cur·a·ble (kyo͝or′ə bəl), *adj.* capable of being cured. [1350–1400; ME (< MF) < L *cūrābilis,* equiv. to *cūrā(re)* to care for (deriv. of *cūra* care) + *-bilis* -BLE] —**cur′a·bil′i·ty, cur′a·ble·ness,** *n.* —**cur′a·bly,** *adv.*

Cu·ra·çao (ko͝or′ə sou′, -sō′, kyo͝or′-; ko͝or′ə sou′, -sō′, kyo͝or′-), *n.* **1.** the main island of the Netherlands Antilles, off the NW coast of Venezuela. 159,072; 173 sq. mi. (448 sq. km). *Cap.:* Willemstad. **2.** See **Netherlands Antilles. 3.** (*l.c.*) Also, **cu·ra·çao** (kyo͝or′ə sō′, -sō′ə). a cordial or liqueur flavored with the peel of the sour orange.

cu·ra·cy (kyo͝or′ə sē), *n., pl.* **-cies.** the office or position of a curate. [1675–85; CURA(TE) + -CY, modeled on pairs like *primate, primacy*]

cur·agh (kur′əKH, kur′ə), *n. Scot., Irish.* currach.

cu·ran·de·ra (ko͞o′rän de′Rä), *n., pl.* ***-ras*** (-Räs). *Spanish.* a woman folk healer.

cu·ran·de·ris·mo (ko͞o Rän′de Rēs′mô; *Eng.* ko͞o-rän′də riz′mō), *n. Spanish.* the use of folk medicine, esp. as practiced by a curandero.

cu·ran·de·ro (ko͞o′Rän de′Rô; *Eng.* ko͝or′ən dâr′ō), *n., pl.* ***-de·ros*** (-de′Rôs; *Eng.* -dâr′ōz). *Spanish.* a folk healer or medicine man who uses herbs or hallucinogenic plants, magic, and spiritualism to treat illness, induce visions, impart traditional wisdom, etc.

cu·ra·re (kyo͝o rär′ē, ko͞o-), *n.* **1.** a blackish, resinlike substance derived from tropical plants of the genus *Strychnos,* esp. *S. toxifera,* and from the root of pareira, used by certain South American Indians for poisoning arrows and employed in physiological experiments, medicine, etc., for arresting the action of motor nerves. **2.** a plant yielding this substance. Also, **cu·ra′ri.** [1770–80; < Pg < Carib *kurari*]

cu·ra·rize (kyo͝o rär′īz, ko͞o-, kyo͝or′ə rīz′, ko͝or′-), *v.t.,* **-rized, -riz·ing.** to administer curare to, as in vivisection. Also, *esp. Brit.,* **cu′ra·rise′.** [1870–75; CURAR(E) + -IZE] —**cu·ra′ri·za′tion,** *n.*

cu·ras·sow (kyo͝or′ə sō′, kyo͝o ras′ō), *n.* any of several large, arboreal, gallinaceous birds of the family Cracidae, of South and Central America. [1675–85; after CURAÇAO]

cu·rate (*n.* kyo͝or′it; *v.* kyo͝o rāt′, kyo͝or′āt), *n., v.,* **-rat·ed, -rat·ing.** —*n.* **1.** *Chiefly Brit.* a member of the clergy employed to assist a rector or vicar. **2.** any ecclesiastic entrusted with the cure of souls, as a parish priest. —*v.t.* **3.** to serve as curator for: *to curate an art exhibition.* [1300–50; ME *curat* (< AF) < ML *cūrātus,* equiv. to L *cūr(a)* care + *-ātus* -ATE[1]] —**cu·rat·ic** (kyo͝o rat′ik), **cu·rat′i·cal,** *adj.* —**cu′rate·ship′,** *n.*

cu′rate's egg′, *Brit.* something discreetly declared to be partly good but in fact thoroughly bad. [after a cartoon by G. du Maurier in the English humor weekly *Punch* (Nov. 9, 1895): a meek curate, when served a bad egg at the bishop's table, replies that "parts of it are excellent"]

cur·a·tive (kyo͝or′ə tiv), *adj.* **1.** serving to cure or heal; pertaining to curing or remedial treatment; remedial. —*n.* **2.** a curative agent; remedy. [1375–1425; late ME < MF *curatif* < ML *cūrātivus,* equiv. to LL *cūrāt(us)* (ptp. of *cūrāre* to care for, attend to; see CURE); see -IVE] —**cur′a·tive·ly,** *adv.*

cu·ra·tor (kyo͝o rā′tər, kyo͝or′ā- *for 1, 2;* kyo͝or′ə tər *for 3*), *n.* **1.** the person in charge of a museum, art collection, etc. **2.** a manager; superintendent. **3.** *Law.* a guardian of a minor, lunatic, or other incompetent, esp. with regard to his or her property. [1325–75; < L, equiv. to *cūrā(re)* to care for, attend to (see CURE) + *-tor* -TOR; r. ME *curatour* < AF < L as above] —**cu·ra·to·ri·al** (kyo͝or′ə tôr′ē əl, -tōr′-), *adj.* —**cu·ra′tor·ship′,** *n.*

curb (kûrb), *n.* **1.** a rim, esp. of joined stones or concrete, along a street or roadway, forming an edge for a sidewalk. **2.** anything that restrains or controls; a restraint; check. **3.** an enclosing framework or border. **4.** Also called **curb′ bit′.** a bit used with a bridoon for control of a horse, to which a chain (**curb′ chain′**) is hooked. **5.** Also called **curb market;** *Brit.,* **kerb market, kerbstone market.** a market, originally on the sidewalk or street, for the sale of securities not listed on a stock exchange. Cf. **American Stock Exchange. 6.** the framework around the top of a well. **7.** the arris between an upper and a lower slope on a gambrel or mansard roof. **8.** a belt of metal, masonry, etc., for abutting a dome at its base. **9.** (in a windmill) the track on which the cap turns. **10.** *Vet. Pathol.* a swelling on the lower part of the back of the hock of a horse, often causing lameness. **11.** *Engin.* the cutting edge at the bottom of a caisson. **12.** *Carpentry.* See **purlin plate.** —*v.t.* **13.** to control as with a curb; restrain; check. **14.** to cause to keep near the curb: *Curb your dog.* **15.** to furnish with or protect by a curb. **16.** to put a curb on (a horse). Also, *Brit.,* **kerb** (for defs. 1, 15). [1250–1300; ME *curb, courbe* curved piece of wood (n.), stooped, hunchbacked (adj.) < AF *curb, courb* curved, bowed; OF < L *curvus* crooked, bent, curved. See CURVE] —**curb′a·ble,** *adj.* —**curb′less,** *adj.* —**curb′like′,** *adj.*
—**Syn. 13.** bridle, repress. See **check.** —**Ant. 13.** encourage.

curb′ ball′, stoop ball played off a street curb.

Curb′ Exchange′, *Informal.* See **American Stock Exchange.**

curb·ing (kûr′bing), *n.* **1.** the material forming a curb, as along a street. **2.** curbstones collectively. **3.** a curb, or a section of a curb. Also, *Brit.,* **kerbing.** [1585–95; CURB + -ING[1]]

curb′ mar′ket, curb (def. 5).

curb′ roof′, a roof divided on each side of the ridge into two or more slopes, as a gambrel or mansard. [1725–35]

curb′ serv′ice, service given to customers in parked cars, as at a drive-in restaurant. [1930–35, *Amer.*]

curb·side (kûrb′sīd′), *n.* **1.** a side of a pavement or street bordered by a curb. —*adj.* **2.** being adjacent to a curb: *The car's curbside door is stuck.* Also, *Brit.,* **kerbside.** [1945–50; CURB + SIDE[1]]

curb·stone (kûrb′stōn′), *n.* one of the stones, or a range of stones, forming a curb, as along a street. Also, *Brit.,* **kerbstone.** [1785–95; CURB + STONE]

curb′ weight′, the weight of an automotive vehicle including fuel, coolant, and lubricants but excluding occupants and cargo. [1945–50]

curch (kûrch), *n.* **1.** a simple, close-fitting cap worn by women in colonial America. **2.** a kerchief worn by Scottish women. [1400–50; late ME *kerche, c(o)urche,* back formation from *courche(i)s* (pl.) < MF *couvrech(i)es,* pl. of *couvrechef* KERCHIEF; the final *e* of the sing. form, orig. long, was later lost]

cur·cu·li·o (kûr kyo͞o′lē ō′), *n., pl.* **-li·os.** any of several weevils, esp. one of the genus *Conotrachelus,* as *C. nenuphar* **(plum curculio),** which feeds on plums, cherries, and other fruits. [1750–60; < L: weevil, corn worm]

cur·cu·ma (kûr′kyo͝o mə), *n.* any of various chiefly Old World plants belonging to the genus *Curcuma,* of the ginger family, as *C. domestica,* yielding turmeric, or *C. zedoaria,* yielding zedoary. [1610–20; < NL < Ar *kurkum* saffron, turmeric; cf. CROCUS]

curd (kûrd), *n.* **1.** Often, **curds.** a substance consisting mainly of casein and the like, obtained from milk by coagulation, and used as food or made into cheese. **2.** any substance resembling this. **3.** Also called **curd′ cheese′.** *Chiefly Northeastern and Southern U.S.* cottage cheese. **4.** the edible flower heads of cauliflower, broccoli, and similar plants. —*v.t., v.i.* **5.** to turn into curd; coagulate; congeal. [1325–75; ME *curden* (v.), var. of *crudden* to CRUD, congeal; see CROWD[1]]
—**Regional Variation. 3.** See **cottage cheese.**

cur·dle (kûr′dl), *v.t., v.i.,* **-dled, -dling. 1.** to change into curd; coagulate; congeal. **2.** to spoil; turn sour. **3.** to go wrong; turn bad or fail: *Their friendship began to curdle as soon as they became business rivals.* **4. curdle the** or **one's blood,** to fill a person with horror or fear; terrify: *a scream that curdled the blood.* [1580–90; CURD + -LE] —**cur′dler,** *n.*

cur′ dog′, *South Midland and Southern U.S.* a worthless dog; mongrel. [1200–50; ME *cur dogge;* see CURR, DOG]

curd·y (kûr′dē), *adj.,* **curd·i·er, curd·i·est.** like curd; full of or containing curd; coagulated. [1500–10; CURD + -Y[1]] —**curd′i·ness,** *n.*

cure (kyo͝or), *n., v.,* **cured, cur·ing.** —*n.* **1.** a means of healing or restoring to health; remedy. **2.** a method or course of remedial treatment, as for disease. **3.** successful remedial treatment; restoration to health. **4.** a means of correcting or relieving anything that is troublesome or detrimental: *to seek a cure for inflation.* **5.** the act or a method of preserving meat, fish, etc., by smoking, salting, or the like. **6.** spiritual or religious charge of the people in a certain district. **7.** the office or district of a curate or parish priest.
—*v.t.* **8.** to restore to health. **9.** to relieve or rid of something detrimental, as an illness or a bad habit. **10.** to prepare (meat, fish, etc.) for preservation by salting, drying, etc. **11.** to promote hardening of (fresh concrete or mortar), as by keeping it damp. **12.** to process (rubber, tobacco, etc.) as by fermentation or aging.
—*v.i.* **13.** to effect a cure. **14.** to become cured. [1250–1300; (v.) ME *curen* < MF *curer* < L *cūrāre* to take care of, deriv. of *cūra* care; (n.) ME < OF *cure* < L *cūra*] —**cure′less,** *adj.* —**cure′less·ly,** *adv.* —**cur′er,** *n.*
—**Syn. 2.** remedy, restorative, specific, antidote. **9.** CURE, HEAL, REMEDY imply making well, whole, or right. CURE is applied to the eradication of disease or sickness: *to cure a headache.* HEAL suggests the making whole of wounds, sores, etc.: *to heal a burn.* REMEDY applies esp. to making wrongs right: *to remedy a mistake.*

cu·ré (kyo͝o rā′, kyo͝or′ā; *Fr.* KY RĀ′), *n., pl.* **cu·rés** (kyo͝o rāz′, kyo͝or′āz; *Fr.* KY RĀ′). (in France) a parish priest. [1645–55; < F, OF; modeled on ML *cūrātus* parish priest; see CURATE]

cure-all (kyo͝or′ôl′), *n.* panacea. [1785–95]

cu·ret (kyo͝o ret′), *n., v.t.,* **-ret·ted, -ret·ting.** curette.

cu·ret·tage (kyo͝or′i täzh′, kyo͝o ret′ij), *n. Surg.* the process of curetting. Cf. **D and C.** [1895–1900; < F, equiv. to *curette* CURETTE + *-age* -AGE]

cu·rette (kyo͝o ret′), *n., v.,* **-ret·ted, -ret·ting.** —*n.* **1.** a scoop-shaped surgical instrument for removing tissue from body cavities, as the uterus. —*v.t.* **2.** to scrape with a curette. Also, **curet.** [1745–55; < F, equiv. to *cur(er)* to cleanse + *-ette* -ETTE. See CURE]

cur·few (kûr′fyo͞o), *n.* **1.** an order establishing a specific time in the evening after which certain regulations apply, esp. that no civilians or other specified group of unauthorized persons may be outdoors or that places of public assembly must be closed. **2.** a regulation requiring a person to be home at a certain prescribed time, as imposed by a parent on a child. **3.** the time at which a daily curfew starts. **4.** the period during which a curfew is in effect. **5.** a signal, usually made with a bell, announcing the start of the time of restrictions under a curfew. **6.** a bell for sounding a curfew. **7.** (in medieval Europe) the ringing of a bell at a fixed hour in the evening as a signal for covering or extinguishing fires. **8.** a metal cover for shielding a banked or unattended fire. [1250–1300; ME < AF *coverfeu,* OF *covrefeu* lit., (it) covers (the) fire. See COVER, FOCUS]

cu•ri•a (kyŏŏr′ē ə), *n., pl.* **cu•ri•ae** (kyŏŏr′ē ē′). **1.** one of the political subdivisions of each of the three tribes of ancient Rome. **2.** the building in which such a division or group met, as for worship or public deliberation. **3.** the senate house in ancient Rome. **4.** the senate of an ancient Italian town. **5.** (*sometimes cap.*) See **Curia Romana. 6.** the papal court. **7.** the administrative aides of a bishop. [1590–1600; < L *cūria,* perh. < **coviria,* equiv. to *co-* CO- + *vir* man + *-ia* -IA] —**cu′•ri•al,** *adj.*

Cu•ri•a Re•gis (kyŏŏr′ē ə rē′jis), (*often l.c.*) *Eng. Hist.* **1.** a small, permanent council, composed chiefly of officials in the household of a Norman king, that served in an advisory and administrative capacity. **2.** See **great council** (def. 1). [< ML: lit., (the) king's curia]

Cu′ria Ro•ma′na (rō mā′nə, -mä′-), *Roman Cath. Ch.* the body of congregations, offices, permanent commissions, etc., that assist the pope in the government and administration of the church. [< ML, L: lit., (the) Roman curia]

cu•rie (kyŏŏr′ē, kyŏŏ rē′), *n. Physics, Chem.* a unit of activity of radioactive substances equivalent to 3.70 × 10^{10} disintegrations per second: it is approximately the amount of activity produced by 1 g of radium-226. *Abbr.:* Ci [1910; named in memory of Pierre CURIE]

Cu•rie (kyŏŏr′ē, kyŏŏ rē′; *Fr.* KY RĒ′), *n.* **1. I•rène** (*Fr.* ē REN′). See **Joliot-Curie, Irène. 2. Ma•rie** (mə rē′; *Fr.* MA RĒ′), 1867–1934, Polish physicist and chemist in France: codiscoverer of radium 1898; Nobel prize for physics 1903, for chemistry 1911. **3.** her husband, **Pierre** (pē âr′; *Fr.* PYER), 1859–1906, French physicist and chemist: codiscoverer of radium; Nobel prize for physics 1903.

Cu′rie point′, *Physics.* the temperature beyond that at which a ferromagnetic substance exhibits paramagnetism. Also called **Cu′rie tem′perature.** [1920–25; named after Pierre CURIE]

Cu′rie's law′, *Physics.* the law that the susceptibility of a paramagnetic substance is inversely proportional to its absolute temperature. [named after Pierre CURIE]

Cu′rie-Weiss′ law′ (kyŏŏr′ē wīs′, -vīs′), *Physics.* the law that the susceptibility of a paramagnetic substance is inversely proportional to the difference of its temperature and the Curie point and that the substance ceases to be paramagnetic below the Curie point. [named after P. CURIE and Pierre *Weiss* (1865–1940), French physicist]

cu•ri•o (kyŏŏr′ē ō′), *n., pl.* **-ri•os.** any unusual article, object of art, etc., valued as a curiosity. [1850–55; shortened from CURIOSITY]

cu•ri•o•sa (kyŏŏr′ē ō′sə), *n.pl.* **1.** books, pamphlets, etc., dealing with unusual subjects. **2.** (in selling and collecting books) books, pamphlets, etc., containing pornographic literature or art; erotica. [1880–85; < NL: unusual things, special use of neut. pl. of L *cūriōsus* careful, inquisitive. See CURIOUS]

cu•ri•os•i•ty (kyŏŏr′ē os′i tē), *n., pl.* **-ties. 1.** the desire to learn or know about anything; inquisitiveness. **2.** a curious, rare, or novel thing. **3.** a strange, curious, or interesting quality. **4.** *Archaic.* carefulness; fastidiousness. [1350–1400; ME *curiosite* (< AF) < L *cūriōsitās.* See CURIOUS, -ITY]

cu•ri•ous (kyŏŏr′ē əs), *adj.* **1.** eager to learn or know; inquisitive. **2.** prying; meddlesome. **3.** arousing or exciting speculation, interest, or attention through being inexplicable or highly unusual; odd; strange: *a curious sort of person; a curious scene.* **4.** *Archaic.* **a.** made or prepared skillfully. **b.** done with painstaking accuracy or attention to detail: *a curious inquiry.* **c.** careful; fastidious. **d.** marked by intricacy or subtlety. [1275–1325; ME < L *cūriōsus* careful, inquisitive, equiv. to *cūri-* (comb. form of *cūra* care) + *-ōsus* -OUS. See CURE] —**cu′ri•ous•ly,** *adv.* —**cu′ri•ous•ness,** *n.*
—**Syn. 1.** inquiring, interested. **2.** spying, peeping. CURIOUS, INQUISITIVE, MEDDLESOME, PRYING refer to taking an undue (and petty) interest in others' affairs. CURIOUS implies a desire to know what is not properly one's concern: *curious about a neighbor's habits.* INQUISITIVE implies asking impertinent questions in an effort to satisfy curiosity: *inquisitive about a neighbor's habits.* MEDDLESOME implies thrusting oneself into and taking an active part in other people's affairs entirely unasked and unwelcomed: *a meddlesome cousin who tries to run the affairs of a family.* PRYING implies a meddlesome and persistent inquiring into others' affairs: *a prying reporter inquiring into the secrets of a business firm.* **3.** singular, novel, rare. —**Ant. 1, 2.** indifferent.

cu•rite (kyŏŏr′īt), *n.* a radioactive uranium mineral, $Pb_2U_5O_{17}·4H_2O$, with adamantine luster, occurring as reddish-brown to deep-yellow needle-shaped crystals, formed by alteration of uraninite. [< F (1921), after Pierre CURIE; see -ITE[1]]

Cu•ri•ti•ba (kŏŏ′RĒ tē′bə; *Eng.* kŏŏr′i tē′bə), *n.* a city in and the capital of Paraná, in SE Brazil. 1,052,147. Also, **Cu′ri•ty′ba.**

cu•ri•um (kyŏŏr′ē əm), *n.* a radioactive element not found in nature but discovered in 1944 among the products of plutonium after bombardment by high-energy helium ions. *Symbol:* Cm; *at. no.:* 96. [1946; < NL; named after M. and P. CURIE; see -IUM]

curl (kûrl), *v.t.* **1.** to form into coils or ringlets, as the hair. **2.** to form into a spiral or curved shape; coil. **3.** to adorn with, or as with, curls or ringlets. —*v.i.* **4.** to grow in or form curls or ringlets, as the hair. **5.** to become curved or undulated. **6.** to coil. **7.** to play at the game of curling. **8.** to progress in a curving direction or path; move in a curving or spiraling way: *The ball curled toward the plate.* **9. curl one's** or **the hair,** to fill with horror or fright; shock: *Some of his stories about sailing across the Atlantic are enough to curl one's hair.* **10. curl one's lip,** to assume or display an expression of contempt: *He curled his lip in disdain.* **11. curl up,** to sit or lie down cozily: *to curl up with a good book.* —*n.* **12.** a coil or ringlet of hair. **13.** anything of a spiral or curved shape, as a lettuce leaf, wood shaving, etc. **14.** a coil. **15.** the act of curling or state of being curled. **16.** *Plant Pathol.* **a.** the distortion, fluting, or puffing of a leaf, resulting from the unequal development of its two sides. **b.** a disease so characterized. **17.** Also called **rotation.** *Math.* **a.** a vector obtained from a given vector by taking its cross product with the vector whose coordinates are the partial derivative operators with respect to each coordinate. **b.** the operation that produces this vector. **18.** *Weight Lifting.* **a.** an underhand forearm lift in which the barbell, held against the thighs, is raised to the chest and then lowered while keeping the legs, upper arms, and shoulders taut. **b.** a similar forearm lift using a dumbbell or dumbbells, usually from the side of the body to the shoulders. [1400–50; late ME, appar. back formation from *curled,* metathetic var. of ME *crulled* (ptp.) *crul* (adj.); cf. MD *crullen* to curl, CRULLER] —**curl•ed•ly** (kûr′lid lē, kûrld′-), *adv.* —**curl′ed•ness,** *n.*

curl•er (kûr′lər), *n.* **1.** a person or thing that curls. **2.** any of various pins, clasps, rollers, or appliances on which locks of hair are wound or clamped for curling. **3.** a player at the game of curling. [1630–40; CURL + -ER[1]]

cur•lew (kûr′lo͞o), *n.* **1.** any of several shorebirds of the genus *Numenius,* having a long, slender, down-curved bill, as the common *N. arquata,* of Europe. **2.** any of various similar birds. [1300–50; ME < AF *curleu,* c. MF *corleu;* perh. imit.]

curlew, *Numenius arquata,* length 23 in. (58 cm); wingspread 3¼ ft. (0.9 m)

Cur•ley (kûr′lē), *n.* **James M(ichael),** 1874–1958, U.S. politician.

curl•i•cue (kûr′li kyo͞o′), *n.* an ornamental, fancy curl or twist, as in a signature. Also, **curlycue.** [1835–45; CURLY + CUE[2]]

curl•ing (kûr′ling), *n.* a game played on ice in which two teams of four players each compete in sliding large stones toward a mark in the center of a circle. Cf. **house** (def. 20). [1610–20; perh. CURL + -ING[1], from the motion imparted to the sliding stones]

curl′ing i′ron, a rod, usually of metal, used when heated for curling the hair, which is twined around it. Also, **curl′ing i′rons.** Also called **curl′ing tongs′.** [1625–35]

curl′ing stone′, a large, heavy, ellipsoidal stone or a similar object made of iron, usually having one rough side and one smooth side with a hole in the center of each for screwing in a handle by which the stone is released, for use in the game of curling. [1610–20]

curling stone

curl•pa•per (kûrl′pā′pər), *n.* a piece of paper on which a lock of hair is rolled up tightly, to remain until the hair is fixed in a curl. [1810–20; CURL + PAPER]

curl•y (kûr′lē), *adj.,* **curl•i•er, curl•i•est. 1.** curling or tending to curl: *curly blond hair.* **2.** having curls (usually used in combination): *curlyheaded.* **3.** having a rippled or undulating appearance, as cut and finished wood: *curly maple.* [1720–30; CURL + -Y[1]] —**curl′i•ness,** *n.*

curl′y clem′atis. See **blue jasmine.**

curl′y-coat•ed retriev′er (kûr′lē kō′tid), one of an English breed of large sporting dogs having a dense, tightly curled, black or liver-colored coat, small, low-set ears, and a moderately short tail carried fairly straight, used as a land or water retriever. [1880–85]

curl•y•cue (kûr′li kyo͞o′), *n.* curlicue.

curl•y•head (kûr′lē hed′), *n.* **1.** a person whose hair is curly. **2. curlyheads,** (*used with a singular or plural v.*) a shrubby clematis, *Clematis ochroleuca,* of the eastern U.S. [1850–55, *Amer.;* CURLY + HEAD]

curl′y palm′, a feather palm, *Howea belmoreana,* of Lord Howe Island, having plumy leaves about 7 ft. (2.1 m) long.

curl′y top′, *Plant Pathol.* a disease of plants, esp. beets, characterized by puckered or cupped leaves and stunting or distortion, caused by a virus, *Ruga verrucosans.* [1900–05, *Amer.*]

cur•mudg•eon (kər muj′ən), *n.* a bad-tempered, difficult, cantankerous person. [1570–80; unexplained; perh. *cur-* repr. CUR] —**cur•mudg′eon•ly,** *adj.*
—**Syn.** grouch, crank, bear, sourpuss, crosspatch.

curn (kûrn), *n. Scot.* **1.** a grain. **2.** a small quantity or number. [1300–50; ME; akin to CORN[1], KERNEL]

curr (kûr), *v.i.* to make a low, purring sound, as a cat. [1670–80; akin to ON *kurra* to grumble, murmur, MHG *kurren,* MD *curren* to growl]

cur•rach (kur′əKH, kur′ə), *n. Scot., Irish.* a coracle. Also, **curagh, cur′ragh.** [1400–50; late ME *currok* < ScotGael *curach,* Ir *currach* boat; cf. CORACLE]

cur•ra•jong (kûr′ə jong′), *n.* kurrajong.

cur•rant (kûr′ənt, kur′-), *n.* **1.** a small seedless raisin, produced chiefly in California and in the Levant, and used in cookery and confectionery. **2.** the small, edible, acid, round fruit or berry of certain wild or cultivated shrubs of the genus *Ribes.* **3.** the shrub itself. **4.** any of various similar fruits or shrubs. [1300–50; shortened from ME *raysons of Coraunte* raisins of CORINTH, the port in Greece from which they orig. came]

cur′rant bor′er, the larva of a clearwing moth, *Ramosia tipuliformis,* that bores into the stems of currants. [1865–70]

cur′rant toma′to, a Peruvian plant, *Lycopersicum pimpinellifolium,* of the nightshade family, having numerous bell-shaped, yellow flowers and small, currant-like, red fruit.

cur•rant•worm (kûr′ənt wûrm′, kur′-), *n.* the larva of any of several insects, as a sawfly, *Nematus ribesii* **(imported currantworm),** which infests and feeds on the leaves and fruit of currants. [1865–70; CURRANT + WORM]

cur•ra•wong (kur′ə wông′, -wong′), *n.* any of several large black-and-white passerine birds of the genus *Strepera,* of Australia, having a resounding bell-like voice. [1925–30; < Dharuk *gu-ra-wa-ruŋ*]

cur•ren•cy (kûr′ən sē, kur′-), *n., pl.* **-cies. 1.** something that is used as a medium of exchange; money. See table on next page. **2.** general acceptance; prevalence; vogue. **3.** a time or period during which something is widely accepted and circulated. **4.** the fact or quality of being widely accepted and circulated from person to person. **5.** circulation, as of coin. [1650–60; < ML *currentia.* See CURRENT, -ENCY]

cur′rency bond′, a bond payable in legal tender.

cur′rency prin′ciple, the principle that banks should be permitted to issue notes only against bullion or coin. Also called **cur′rency doc′trine.**

cur•rent (kûr′ənt, kur′-), *adj.* **1.** passing in time; belonging to the time actually passing: *the current month.* **2.** prevalent; customary: *the current practice.* **3.** popular; in vogue: *current fashions.* **4.** new; present; most recent: *the current issue of a publication.* **5.** publicly reported or known: *a rumor that is current.* **6.** passing from one to another; circulating, as a coin. **7.** *Archaic.* running; flowing. **8.** *Obs.* genuine; authentic. —*n.* **9.** a flowing; flow, as of a river. **10.** something that flows, as a stream. **11.** a large portion of air, large body of water, etc., moving in a certain direction. **12.** the speed at which such flow moves; velocity of flow. **13.** *Elect.* See **electric current. 14.** a course, as of time or events; the main course; the general tendency. [1250–1300; < L *current-* (s. of *currēns*) running (prp. of *currere*); r. ME *curraunt* < AF < L as above; see -ENT] —**cur′rent•ly,** *adv.*
—**Syn. 2.** common, widespread, popular, rife. CURRENT, PRESENT, PREVAILING, PREVALENT refer to something generally or commonly in use. That which is CURRENT is in general circulation or a matter of common knowledge or acceptance: *current usage in English.* PRESENT refers to that which is in use now; it always has the sense of time: *present customs.* That which is PREVAILING is that which has superseded others: *prevailing fashion.* That which is PREVALENT exists or is spread widely: *a prevalent idea.* **3.** stylish, fashionable, modish. **10.** See **stream.** —**Ant. 2.** obsolete. **3.** old-fashioned.

cur′rent account′, 1. Also called **open account.** an account of credits, debits, receipts, and expenditures between two individuals or companies, usually providing for settlement at the end of specified accounting periods. **2.** (in certain foreign countries) a checking account. [1840–50]

cur′rent as′sets, *Com.* assets that are readily convertible into cash, usually within one year, without loss in value. [1905–10]

cur′rent bal′ance, *Elect.* an instrument for measuring electric currents, in which the magnetic force between two current-carrying coils is balanced against a weight.

cur′rent cost′, a cost based on the prevailing price paid for material, labor, etc.

cur′rent den′sity, *Elect.* the amount of current flowing through a given cross-sectional area in a given time interval: usually measured in amperes per square centimeter.

cur′rent expens′es, regularly continuing expenditures for the maintenance of business.

cur′rent liabil′ities, *Com.* indebtedness maturing within one year.

cur′rent lim′iter, *Elect.* a device, as a resistor or fuse, that limits the flow of current to a prescribed amount, independent of the voltage applied.

cur•rent•ly (kûr′ənt lē, kur′-), *adv.* at the present

SELECTED CURRENCIES OF THE WORLD

Country	Basic Monetary Unit	Intnl. Abbr. or Symbol	Principal Subdivision
Albania	lek	L	100 qintars
Algeria	dinar	DA	100 centimes
Argentina	austral	₳	100 centavos
Australia	dollar	A$	100 cents
Austria	schilling	S	100 groschen
Bahamas	dollar	B$	100 cents
Barbados	dollar	BDS$	100 cents
Belgium	franc	BF	100 centimes
Belize	dollar	BZ$	100 cents
Bermuda	dollar	Ber$	100 cents
Bolivia	peso	$b	100 centavos
Brazil	cruzado	Cz	1000 cruzeiros
Britain	pound	£	100 pence
Bulgaria	lev	LV	100 stotinki (sing., *stotinka*)
Canada	dollar	C$	100 cents
Chile	peso	Ch$	100 centavos
China	yuan	RMB	100 fen
Colombia	peso	Col$	100 centavos
Congo	CFA franc	CFAF	100 centimes
Costa Rica	colon	₡	100 centimos
Cuba	peso	$	100 centavos
Czech Republic	koruna	Kčs	100 halers
Denmark	krone	Dkr	100 öre
Dominican Republic	peso	RD$	100 centavos
Ecuador	sucre	S/	100 centavos
Egypt	pound	£E	100 piasters
El Salvador	colon	₡	100 centavos
Ethiopia	birr	EB	100 cents
Finland	markka	Fmk	100 pennia (sing., *penni*)
France	franc	F	100 centimes
Germany	mark	DM	100 pfennigs
Greece	drachma	Dr	100 lepta (sing., *lepton*)
Guatemala	quetzal	Q	100 centavos
Guyana	dollar	G$	100 cents
Haiti	gourde	G	100 centimes
Honduras	lempira	L	100 centavos
Hong Kong	dollar	HK$	100 cents
Hungary	forint	Ft	100 fillér
Iceland	krona	IKr	100 aurar (sing., *eyrir*)
India	rupee	Re	100 paise (sing., *paisa*)
Indonesia	rupiah	Rp	100 sen
Iran	rial	Rl	100 dinars
Ireland	pound (or punt)	IR£	100 pence
Israel	shekel	IS	100 agorot (sing., *agora*)
Italy	lira	Lit	100 centesimi (sing., *centesimo*)
Ivory Coast	CFA franc	CFAF	100 centimes
Jamaica	dollar	J$	100 cents
Japan	yen		100 sen

Country	Basic Monetary Unit	Intnl. Abbr. or Symbol	Principal Subdivision
Jordan	dinar	JD	1000 fils
Kenya	shilling	KSh	100 cents
Kuwait	dinar	KD	1000 fils
Lebanon	pound	LL	100 piasters
Libya	dinar	LD	1000 dirhams
Luxembourg	franc	LFr	100 centimes
Malawi	kwacha	K	100 tambala
Malaysia	ringgit	M$	100 cents
Mali	franc	MF	100 centimes
Mexico	peso	Mex$	100 centavos
Morocco	dirham	DH	100 centimes
Netherlands	guilder	f	100 cents
New Zealand	dollar	NZ$	100 cents
Nicaragua	cordoba	C$	100 centavos
Nigeria	naira	₦	100 kobo
North Korea	won	W	100 chon
Norway	krone	NKr	100 öre
Pakistan	rupee	PRe	100 paise (sing., *paisa*)
Panama	balboa	B	100 centesimos
Paraguay	guarani	₡	100 centimos
Peru	inti	I/	100 cents
Philippines	peso	₱	100 centavos
Poland	zloty	Zl	100 groszy (sing., *grosz*)
Portugal	escudo	Esc	100 centavos
Rumania	leu	L	100 bani (sing., *ban*)
Russia	ruble	Rbl	100 kopecks
Saudia Arabia	riyal	SRI	100 halalas
Singapore	dollar	S$	100 cents
South Africa	rand	R	100 cents
South Korea	won	W	100 chon
Spain	peseta	Pta	100 centimos
Sweden	krona	Skr	100 öre
Switzerland	franc	SwF	100 centimes
Syria	pound	£S	100 piasters
Taiwan	dollar (or yuan)	NT$	100 cents
Thailand	baht	B	100 satangs
Trinidad and Tobago	dollar	TT$	100 cents
Turkey	lira	TL	100 kurus
United Arab Emirates	dirham	Dh	100 fils
United States	dollar	US$	100 cents
Uruguay	peso	NUr$	100 centesimos
Venezuela	bolivar	Bs	100 centimos
Vietnam	dong	D	100 hao
Yemen	rial	YRI	100 cents
Yugoslavia	dinar	Din	100 paras
Zaire	zaire	Z	100 makuta (sing., *likuta*)
Zimbabwe	dollar	Z$	100 cents

time; now: *She is currently working as a lab technician.* [1570–80; CURRENT + -LY]

cur•rent•ness (kûr′ənt nis, kur′-), *n.* the state or quality of being current; currency. [1575–85; CURRENT + -NESS]

cur′rent ra′tio, the ratio between current assets and current liabilities.

cur′rent yield′, the ratio of the annual interest or dividend to the actual market price of a bond or stock. Also called **cur′rent return′.**

cur•ri•cle (kûr′i kəl), *n.* a light, two-wheeled, open carriage drawn by two horses abreast. [1675–85; < L *curriculum;* see CURRICULUM]

cur•ric•u•lum (kə rik′yə ləm), *n., pl.* **-la** (-lə), **-lums.** **1.** the aggregate of courses of study given in a school, college, university, etc.: *The school is adding more science courses to its curriculum.* **2.** the regular or a particular course of study in a school, college, etc. [1625–35; < L: action of running, course of action, race, chariot, equiv. to *curr(ere)* to run + *-i-* -I- + *-culum* -CULE[2]] —**cur•ric′u•lar,** *adj.*

cur•ric•u•lum vi•tae (kə rik′yə ləm vī′tē, vē′tī; *Lat.* KŌŌR rik′ŏŏ lŏŏm′ wē′tī), *pl.* **cur•ric•u•la vi•tae** (kə rik′yə lə vī′tē, vē′tī; *Lat.* KŌŌR RIK′ŏŏ lä′ wē′tī). **1.** Also called **vita, vitae.** a brief biographical résumé of one's career and training, as prepared by a person applying for a job. **2.** (*italics*) *Latin.* the course of one's life or career. [1900–05]

cur•rie (kûr′ē, kur′ē), *n., v.t.,* **-ried, -ry•ing.** curry[1].

cur•ri•er (kûr′ē ər, kur′-), *n.* **1.** a person who dresses and colors leather after it is tanned. **2.** a person who curries horses. [1350–1400; CURRY[2] + -ER[1]; r. ME *cur(r)iour, cor(r)iour* < AF < L *coriārius,* equiv. to *cori(um)* leather + *-ārius* -ARY]

Cur•ri•er (kûr′ē ər, kur-), *n.* **Nathaniel,** 1813–88, U.S. lithographer. Cf. **Ives** (def. 4).

Cur′rier and Ives′, the lithography firm of Nathaniel Currier and James Merritt Ives, founded originally by Currier (1835), which produced prints of American history, life, and manners.

cur•ri•er•y (kûr′ē ə rē, kur′-), *n., pl.* **-er•ies.** **1.** the occupation or business of a currier of leather. **2.** the place where it is carried on. [1885–90; CURRY[2] + -ERY]

cur•ri•jong (kur′i jong′), *n.* kurrajong.

cur•rish (kûr′ish), *adj.* **1.** of or pertaining to a cur. **2.** curlike; snarling; quarrelsome. **3.** contemptible; base. [1425–75; late ME *kuresshe.* See CUR, -ISH[1]] —**cur′rish•ly,** *adv.* —**cur′rish•ness,** *n.*

cur•ry[1] (kûr′ē, kur′ē), *n., pl.* **-ries,** *v.,* **-ried, -ry•ing.** —*n.* **1.** *East Indian Cookery.* a pungent dish of vegetables, onions, meat or fish, etc., flavored with various spices or curry powder, and often eaten with rice. **2.** any dish flavored with curry powder or the like: *a lamb curry.* **3.** See **curry powder.** **4. give (someone) a bit of curry,** *Australian.* to rebuke, discipline, or criticize; harass. —*v.t.* **5.** to cook or flavor (food) with curry powder or a similar combination of spices: *to curry eggs.* Also, **currie.** [1590–1600; < Tamil *kari* sauce]

cur•ry[2] (kûr′ē, kur′ē), *v.t.,* **-ried, -ry•ing.** **1.** to rub and clean (a horse) with a currycomb. **2.** to dress (tanned hides) by soaking, scraping, beating, coloring, etc. **3.** to beat; thrash. **4. curry favor,** to seek to advance oneself through flattery or fawning: *His fellow workers despised him for currying favor with the boss.* [1250–1300; ME *cor(r)ayen, cor(r)eyen* < AF *curreier,* c. OF *correer,* earlier *conreer* to make ready < VL **conrēdāre;* see CORODY]

Cur•ry (kûr′ē, kur′ē), *n.* **1. John (Anthony),** 1949–94, British figure skater. **2. John Steu•art** (stōō′ərt, styōō′-), 1897–1946, U.S. painter.

cur•ry•comb (kûr′ē kōm′, kur′-), *n.* **1.** a comb, usually with rows of metal teeth, for currying horses. —*v.t.* **2.** to rub or clean with such a comb. [1565–75; CURRY[2] + COMB[1]]

cur′ry pow′der, a powdered preparation of spices and other ingredients, usually including turmeric and coriander, used for making curry or for seasoning food. [1800–10; CURRY[1] + POWDER[1]]

curse (kûrs), *n., v.,* **cursed** or **curst, curs•ing.** —*n.* **1.** the expression of a wish that misfortune, evil, doom, etc., befall a person, group, etc. **2.** a formula or charm intended to cause such misfortune to another. **3.** the act of reciting such a formula. **4.** a profane oath; curse word. **5.** an evil that has been invoked upon one. **6.** the cause of evil, misfortune, or trouble. **7.** something accursed. **8.** *Slang.* the menstrual period; menstruation (usually prec. by *the*). **9.** an ecclesiastical censure or anathema. —*v.t.* **10.** to wish or invoke evil, calamity, injury, or destruction upon. **11.** to swear at. **12.** to blaspheme. **13.** to afflict with great evil. **14.** to excommunicate. —*v.i.* **15.** to utter curses; swear profanely. [bef. 1050; ME *curs* (n.), *cursen* (v.), OE *curs* (n.), *cursian* (v.), of disputed orig.] —**curs′er,** *n.*

—**Syn. 1, 9.** imprecation, execration, fulmination, malediction. **5.** misfortune, calamity, trouble. **5, 6.** bane, scourge, plague, affliction, torment. **10-12.** CURSE, BLASPHEME, SWEAR are often interchangeable in the sense of using profane language. However, CURSE is the general word for the heartfelt invoking or angry calling down of evil on another: *They called down curses on their enemies.* To BLASPHEME is to speak contemptuously or with abuse of God or of sacred things: *to blaspheme openly.* To SWEAR is to use the name of God or of some holy person or thing as an exclamation to add force or show anger: *to swear in every sentence.* **13.** plague, scourge, afflict, doom. —**Ant. 1, 9.** blessing, benediction. **10.** bless.

curs•ed (kûr′sid, kûrst), *adj.* **1.** under a curse; damned. **2.** deserving a curse; hateful; abominable. [1250–1300; ME; see CURSE, -ED[2]] —**curs′ed•ly,** *adv.* —**curs′ed•ness,** *n.*

—**Syn. 1.** accursed. **2.** damnable, execrable.

curse′ word′, **1.** a profane or obscene word, esp. as used in anger or for emphasis. **2.** any term conceived of as offensive. [1870–75]

cur•sive (kûr′siv), *adj.* **1.** (of handwriting) in flowing strokes with the letters joined together. **2.** *Print.* in flowing strokes resembling handwriting. —*n.* **3.** a cursive letter or character. **4.** *Print.* a style of typeface simulating handwriting. [1775–85; < ML *cursīvus* flowing (said of penmanship), equiv. to L *curs(us)* (ptp. of *currere* to run) + *-īvus* -IVE] —**cur′sive•ly,** *adv.* —**cur′sive•ness,** *n.*

cur•sor (kûr′sər), *n.* **1.** *Computers.* a movable, sometimes blinking, symbol that indicates the position on a CRT or other type of display where the next character entered from the keyboard will appear, or where user action is needed, as in the correction of an erroneous character already displayed. **2.** a sliding object, as the lined glass on a slide rule, that can be set at any point on a scale. [1250–1300; ME: courier (def. 2 from late 16th century) < L: a runner, racer, courier, equiv. to *cur(rere)* to run + *-sor,* for *-tor* -TOR; cf. COURSE]

cur•so•ri•al (kûr sôr′ē əl, -sōr′-), *adj. Zool.* **1.** adapted for running, as the feet and skeleton of dogs, horses, etc. **2.** having limbs adapted for running, as certain birds, insects, etc. [1830–40; < LL *cursōri(us)* of running (see CURSORY) + -AL[1]]

cur•so•ry (kûr′sə rē), *adj.* going rapidly over something, without noticing details; hasty; superficial: *a cursory glance at a newspaper article.* [1595–1605; < LL *cursōrius* running, equiv. to L *cur(rere)* to run + *-sōrius,* for *-tōrius* -TORY[1]; cf. COURSE] —**cur′so•ri•ly,** *adv.* —**cur′so•ri•ness,** *n.*

—**Syn.** quick, brief, passing, haphazard.

curst (kûrst), *v.* **1.** a pt. and pp. of **curse.** —*adj.* **2.** cursed. —**curst′ly,** *adv.* —**curst′ness,** *n.*

curt (kûrt), *adj.,* **-er, -est.** **1.** rudely brief in speech or abrupt in manner. **2.** brief; concise; terse; laconic. **3.** short; shortened. [1620–30; < L *curtus* shortened, short, cut short] —**curt′ly,** *adv.* —**curt′ness,** *n.*

—**Syn. 1.** snappish, sharp. **2.** See **blunt.** **3.** abbreviated.

Curt (kûrt), *n.* a male given name, form of **Curtis.**

cur•tail[1] (kər tāl′), *v.t.* to cut short; cut off a part of; abridge; reduce; diminish. [1425–75; late ME *curtailen* to restrict (said of royal succession or inheritance), prob. a conflation of MF *courtau(l)d* (see CURTAL) and ME *taillen* to cut (see TAILLE, TAILOR)] —**cur•tailed′ly,** *adv.* —**cur•tail′er,** *n.* —**cur•tail′ment,** *n.*

—**Syn.** lessen, dock. See **shorten.**

cur•tail[2] (kûr′tāl′), *n. Archit.* **1.** a horizontal, spiral termination to the lower end of a stair railing. **2.** Also called **cur′tail step′.** a starting step having a scroll termination to one or both ends of the tread. [prob. alter., by folk etym., of CURTAL]

cur•tain (kûr′tn), *n.* **1.** a hanging piece of fabric used

CONCISE ETYMOLOGY KEY: <, descended or borrowed from; >, whence; b., blend of, blended; c., cognate with; cf., compare; deriv., derivative; equiv., equivalent; imit., imitative; obl., oblique; r., replacing; s., stem; sp., spelling, spelled; resp., respelling, respelled; trans., translation; ?, origin unknown; *, unattested; ‡, probably earlier than. See the full key inside the front cover.

to shut out the light from a window, adorn a room, increase privacy, etc. **2.** a movable or folding screen used for similar purposes. **3.** *Chiefly New Eng.* a window shade. **4.** *Theat.* **a.** a set of hanging drapery for concealing all or part of the stage or set from the view of the audience. **b.** the act or time of raising or opening a curtain at the start of a performance: *an 8:30 curtain.* **c.** the end of a scene or act indicated by the closing or falling of a curtain: *first-act curtain.* **d.** an effect, line, or plot solution at the conclusion of a performance: *a strong curtain; weak curtain.* **e.** music signaling the end of a radio or television performance. **f.** (used as a direction in a script of a play to indicate that a scene or act is concluded.) **5.** anything that shuts off, covers, or conceals: *a curtain of artillery fire.* **6.** *Archit.* a relatively flat or featureless extent of wall between two pavilions or the like. **7.** *Fort.* the part of a wall or rampart connecting two bastions, towers, or the like. **8. curtains,** *Slang.* the end; death, esp. by violence: *It looked like curtains for another mobster.* **9. draw the curtain on** or **over, a.** to bring to a close: *to draw the curtain on a long career of public service.* **b.** to keep secret. **10. lift the curtain on, a.** to commence; start. **b.** to make known or public; disclose: *to lift the curtain on a new scientific discovery.* —*v.t.* **11.** to provide, shut off, conceal, or adorn with, or as if with, a curtain. [1250–1300; ME *co(u)rtine* < AF, OF < LL *cortina,* prob. equiv. to *co(ho)rt-* (s. of *cohors;* see COURT) + *-īna* -INE[1], as calque of Gk *aulaía* curtain, deriv. of *aulḗ* courtyard] —**cur′tain·less,** *adj.*

—**Syn. 1.** drapery, portiere, lambrequin, valance. **1, 3.** CURTAIN, BLIND, SHADE, SHUTTER agree in being covers for a window, to shut out light or keep persons from looking in. CURTAIN, BLIND, and SHADE may mean a cover, usually of cloth, which can be rolled up and down inside the window. CURTAIN, however, may also refer to a drapery at a window; and a Venetian BLIND consists of slats mounted on tapes for drawing up or down and varying the pitch of the slats. BLIND and SHUTTER may mean a cover made of two wooden frames with movable slats, attached by hinges outside a window and pulled together or opened at will. SHUTTERS may mean also a set of panels (wooden or iron) put up outside small shops or stores at closing time.

—**Regional Variation. 3.** See **window shade.**

cur′tain call′, **1.** the appearance of the performers at the conclusion of a theatrical or other performance in response to the applause of the audience. **2.** each individual appearance of a performer at the end of a performance in response to prolonged applause. [1880–85]

cur′tain lec′ture, *Older Use.* a scolding administered in private by a wife to her husband. [1625–35]

cur′tain line′, *Theat.* the last line of a scene, act, etc., as in a play; tag line. [1935–40]

cur′tain rais′er, **1.** a short play preceding a main play. **2.** any preliminary event or performance. [1885–90]

cur′tain shut′ter, *Photog.* a focal-plane shutter consisting of a curtain on two rollers, moved at a constant speed past the lens opening so as to expose the film to one of several slots in the curtain, the width of which determines the length of exposure. Also called **roller-blind shutter.**

cur′tain speech′, *Theat.* **1.** the final speech of an act, scene, or play. **2.** a brief speech by an actor, producer, author, or the like, immediately following a performance, usually delivered in front of the closed curtains on the stage.

cur′tain time′, the time at which a play or other performance is scheduled to begin.

cur′tain wall′, (in a framed building) an exterior wall having no structural function. [1850–55]

cur·tal (kûr′tl), *adj.* **1.** *Archaic.* wearing a short frock: *a curtal friar.* **2.** *Obs.* brief; curtailed. —*n.* **3.** a 16th-century bassoon. **4.** *Obs.* an animal with a docked tail. [1500–10; earlier *courtault* < MF, equiv. to *court* short (see CURT) + *-ault,* var. of *-ald* n. suffix; see RIBALD]

cur·tal·ax (kûr′tl aks′), *n. Archaic.* cutlass. Also, **curtle ax.** [1570–80; var. (by folk etym.) of earlier *curtilace,* appar. < dial. It *cortelazo,* assimilated var. of It *coltellaccio* hunting knife, equiv. to *coltell(o)* (< L; see CULTELLUS) + *-accio* n. suffix. See CUTLASS]

cur·tate (kûr′tāt), *adj.* shortened; reduced; abbreviated. [1670–80; < L *curtātus* ptp. of *curtāre* to shorten, deriv. of *curtus.* See CURT, -ATE[1]]

cur·ti·lage (kûr′tl ij), *n. Law.* the area of land occupied by a dwelling and its yard and outbuildings, actually enclosed or considered as enclosed. [1250–1300; ME *courtelage* < AF; OF *cortillage,* equiv. to *cortil* yard (*cort* COURT + *-il* dim. suffix) + *-age* -AGE]

Cur·tin (kûr′tin), *n.* **John,** 1885–1945, Australian statesman: prime minister 1941–45.

Cur·tis (kûr′tis), *n.* **1. Benjamin Robbins,** 1809–74, U.S. jurist: associate justice of the U.S. Supreme Court 1851–57; resigned in dissent over Dred Scott case. **2. Charles,** 1860–1936, vice president of the U.S. 1929–33. **3. Cyrus Her·mann Kotzsch·mar** (hûr′mən koch′mär), 1850–1933, U.S. publisher. **4. George Tick·nor** (tik′nər), 1812–94, U.S. attorney and writer. **5. George William,** 1824–92, U.S. essayist, editor, and reformer. **6.** a male given name: from an Old French word meaning "courteous."

Cur·tiss (kûr′tis), *n.* **Glenn Hammond,** 1878–1930, U.S. inventor: pioneer in the field of aviation.

Cur·ti·us (ko͝or′tsē o͞os′), *n.* **Ernst** (ernst), 1814–96, German archaeologist and historian.

cur′tle ax′ (kûr′tl), curtalax.

curt·sey (kûrt′sē), *n., pl.* **-seys,** *v.i.,* **-seyed, -sey·ing.** curtsy.

curt·sy (kûrt′sē), *n., pl.* **-sies,** *v.,* **-sied, -sy·ing.** —*n.* **1.** a respectful bow made by women and girls, consisting of bending the knees and lowering the body. —*v.i.* **2.** to make a curtsy. [1520–30; var. of COURTESY]

cu·rule (kyo͝or′o͞ol), *adj.* **1.** privileged to sit in a curule chair. **2.** of the highest rank. [1590–1600; < L *curūlis*]

cu′rule chair′, (in ancient Rome) a folding seat with curved legs and no back, often ornamented with ivory, used only by certain high officials. [1775–85]

cur·va·ceous (kûr vā′shəs), *adj. Informal.* (of a woman) having a well-shaped figure with voluptuous curves. Also, **cur·va′cious.** [1935–40, *Amer.;* CURVE + -ACEOUS] —**cur·va′ceous·ly, cur·va′cious·ly,** *adv.* —**cur·va′ceous·ness, cur·va′cious·ness,** *n.*

cur·va·ture (kûr′və chər, -cho͝or′), *n.* **1.** the act of curving or the state of being curved. **2.** a curved condition, often abnormal: *curvature of the spine.* **3.** the degree of curving of a line or surface. **4.** *Geom.* **a.** (at a point on a curve) the derivative of the inclination of the tangent with respect to arc length. **b.** the absolute value of this derivative. **5.** something curved. [1375–1425; late ME < L *curvātūra,* equiv. to *curvāt(us)* ptp. of *curvāre* to bend, CURVE + *-ūra* -URE. See -ATE[1]]

cur′vature of field′, *Optics.* a monochromatic aberration of a lens or other optical system in which the focal surface is curved, the refracted image of an object oriented perpendicular to the axis of the lens lying on a curved surface rather than in a plane perpendicular to the axis.

cur′vature of space′, *Physics, Astron.* **1.** (in relativity) a property of space near massive bodies in which their gravitational field causes light to travel along curved paths. **2.** (in cosmology) a large-scale property of the universe that has an algebraic sign that depends upon whether the density of matter and radiation of the universe exceeds, equals, or is less than the critical density, leading, respectively, to a closed universe with a positive sign, a flat universe with value zero, or an open universe with a negative sign. [1915–20]

curve (kûrv), *n., v.,* **curved, curv·ing,** *adj.* —*n.* **1.** a continuously bending line, without angles. **2.** the act or extent of curving. **3.** any curved outline, form, thing, or part. **4.** a curved section of a road, path, hallway, etc. **5.** *Railroads.* a curved section of track: in the U.S. the curve is often expressed as the central angle, measured in degrees, of a curved section of track subtended by a chord 100 ft. (30 m) long **(degree of curve). 6.** Also called **curve′ ball′.** *Baseball.* **a.** a pitch delivered with a spin that causes the ball to veer from a normal straight path, away from the side from which it was thrown. **b.** the course of such a pitched ball. **7.** a graphic representation of the variations effected in something by the influence of changing conditions; graph. **8.** *Math.* a collection of points whose coordinates are continuous functions of a single independent variable. **9.** a misleading or deceptive trick; cheat; deception. **10.** *Educ.* a grading system based on the scale of performance of a group, so that those performing better, regardless of their actual knowledge of the subject, receive high grades: *The new English professor marks on a curve.* Cf. **absolute** (def. 10). **11.** a curved guide used in drafting. **12. throw (someone) a curve, a.** to take (someone) by surprise, esp. in a negative way. **b.** to mislead or deceive. —*v.t.* **13.** to bend in a curve; cause to take the course of a curve. **14.** to grade on a curve. **15.** *Baseball.* to pitch a curve to. —*v.i.* **16.** to bend in a curve; take the course of a curve. —*adj.* **17.** curved. [1565–75; (< MF) < L *curvus* crooked, bent, curved] —**curv·ed·ly** (kûr′vid lē), *adv.* —**curv′ed·ness,** *n.* —**curve′less,** *adj.*

curve′ fit′ting, *Statistics.* the determination of a curve that fits a specified set of points: *The method of least squares is commonly used for curve fitting.* [1920–25] —**curve′-fit′ting,** *adj.*

cur·vet (*n.* kûr′vit; *v.* kər vet′, kûr′vit), *n., v.,* **-vet·ted** or **-vet·ed, -vet·ting** or **-vet·ing.** —*n.* **1.** *Dressage.* a leap of a horse from a rearing position, in which it springs up with the hind legs outstretched as the forelegs descend. —*v.i.* **2.** to leap in a curvet, as a horse; cause one's horse to do this. **3.** to leap and frisk. —*v.t.* **4.** to cause to make a curvet. [1565–75; earlier *curvetto* < It *corvetta* < F *courbette,* equiv. to *courb(er)* to bend, curve (<< L *curvāre;* cf. CURVE) + *-ette* -ETTE]

cur·vette (kûr vet′), *n. Jewelry.* cuvette (def. 1).

cur·vi·lin·e·ar (kûr′və lin′ē ər), *adj.* **1.** consisting of or bounded by curved lines: *a curvilinear figure.* **2.** forming or moving in a curved line. **3.** formed or characterized by curved lines. Also, **cur′vi·lin′e·al.** [1700–10; < L *curv(us)* CURVE + -I- + LINEAR] —**cur·vi·lin·e·ar·i·ty** (kûr′və lin′ē ar′i tē), *n.* —**cur′vi·lin′e·ar·ly,** *adv.*

curvilin′ear coor′dinate sys′tem, *Math.* a system of coordinates in which the coordinates are determined by three families of surfaces, usually perpendicular.

curvilin′ear trac′ery, *Archit.* tracery, esp. of the 14th and 15th centuries, characterized by a pattern of irregular, boldly curved forms. Also called **flowing tracery.**

curv·y (kûr′vē), *adj.,* **curv·i·er, curv·i·est. 1.** curved. **2.** *Informal.* curvaceous. Also, **curv′ey.** [1900–05; CURVE + -Y[1]]

Cur·zon (kûr′zən), *n.* **1. Sir Clifford,** 1907–82, British pianist. **2. George Nathaniel, 1st Marquis Curzon of Ked·le·ston** (ked′l stən), 1859–1925, British statesman: viceroy of India 1899–1905.

Cus·co (*Sp.* ko͞os′kô), *n.* Cuzco.

cu·sec (kyo͞o′sek), *n.* a unit of flow of one cubic foot per second. [1910–15; *cu(bic foot per) sec(ond)*]

cush (ko͝osh), *n. Slang.* money, esp. when reserved for some special use. [orig. uncert.; perh. to be identified with *cush* sweetened and fried cornmeal (cf. Gullah *cush, cushcush,* ult. < Ar *kuskus* COUSCOUS); or a back formation from CUSHY]

Cush (ko͝osh, kush), *n.* **1.** the eldest son of Ham. Gen. 10:6. **2.** an area mentioned in the Bible, sometimes identified with Upper Egypt. **3. Kingdom of,** an ancient African state in this area; part of the region of Nubia (1000 B.C.–A.D. 350). Also, **Kush.**

cush·at (kush′ət, ko͝osh′-), *n. Brit. Dial.* the ringdove, *Colomba palumbus.* [bef. 900; ME *couschot,* OE *cūscote* wood pigeon]

cu·shaw (kə shô′, ko͞o′shô), *n.* any of several squashes having long, curved necks, esp. varieties of *Cucurbita mixta.* [1580–90, *Amer.;* orig. obscure; alleged AmerInd etymologies unsubstantiated]

cush-cush (ko͝osh′ko͝osh′), *n.* yampee. [1870–75; orig. obscure]

Cush·ing (ko͝osh′ing), *n.* **1. Caleb,** 1800–79, U.S. statesman and diplomat. **2. Harvey (Williams),** 1869–1939, U.S. surgeon and author. **3. Richard James,** 1895–1970, U.S. Roman Catholic clergyman: cardinal 1958–70; archbishop of Boston 1944–70.

Cush′ing's disease′, *Pathol.* a disease characterized by abnormal accumulations of facial and trunk fat, fatigue, hypertension, and osteoporosis, caused by hyperfunction of the adrenal cortex or administration of adrenal cortical hormones. Also called **Cush′ing's syn′·drome.** [1935–40; after H. W. CUSHING, who first described it]

cush·ion (ko͝osh′ən), *n.* **1.** a soft bag of cloth, leather, or rubber, filled with feathers, air, foam rubber, etc., on which to sit, kneel, or lie. **2.** anything similar in form, used to dampen shocks or to prevent excessive pressure or chafing. **3.** something to absorb or counteract a shock, jar, or jolt, as a body of air or steam. **4.** something that lessens the effects of hardship, distress, or the like: *His inheritance was a cushion against unemployment.* **5.** *Anat., Zool.* any part or structure resembling a cushion. **6.** the resilient raised rim encircling the top of a billiard table. **7.** a pad worn under the hair by women. **8.** a portion of a radio or television script that can be adjusted in length or cut out altogether in order to end the program on time. **9.** *Ice Hockey, Canadian.* the iced surface of a rink. **10.** a pillow used in lacemaking. **11.** a leather pad on which gold leaf is placed preparatory to gilding. —*v.t.* **12.** to place on or support by a cushion. **13.** to furnish with a cushion or cushions. **14.** to cover or conceal with, or as if with, a cushion. **15.** to lessen or soften the effects of: *to cushion the blow to his pride.* **16.** to suppress (complaints, lamentations, etc.) by quietly ignoring. **17.** to check the motion of (a piston or the like) by a cushion, as of steam. **18.** to form (steam or the like) into a cushion. [1300–50; ME *cuisshin* < AF; MF *coussin* << L *cox(a)* hip + *-inus* -INE[1]; see COXA] —**cush′ion·less,** *adj.* —**cush′ion·like′,** *adj.*

—**Syn. 1.** pad. CUSHION, PILLOW, BOLSTER agree in being cases filled with a material more or less resilient, intended to be used as supports for the body or parts of it. A CUSHION is a soft pad used to sit, lie, or kneel on, or to lean against: *cushions on a sofa; cushions on pews in a church.* A PILLOW is a bag or case filled with feathers, down, or other soft material, usually to support the head: *to sleep with a pillow under one's head.* A BOLSTER is a firm pillow, long enough to extend the width of a bed and used as head support, with or without a pillow. **3.** shock absorber.

cush′ion cut′, *Jewelry.* a variety of brilliant cut in which the girdle has the form of a square with rounded corners.

cush′ion pink′, a low-growing mountain plant, *Silene acaulis,* of Europe and North America, having deep pink to purplish, solitary flowers and forming mosslike patches on rocky or barren ground. Also called **moss campion.** [1860–65]

cush′ion raft′er. See **auxiliary rafter.** [1810–20]

cush·ion·y (ko͝osh′ə nē), *adj.* **1.** soft and comfortable like a cushion. **2.** having or provided with cushions. **3.** used as a cushion. [1830–40; CUSHION + -Y[1]]

Cush·it·ic (kə shit′ik), *n.* **1.** a subfamily of the Afroasiatic family of languages, including Somali, Oromo, and other languages of Somalia and Ethiopia. —*adj.* **2.** of or pertaining to Cushitic. Also, **Kushitic.** [1905–10; *Cushite* (see CUSH, -ITE[1]) + -IC]

Cush·man (ko͝osh′mən), *n.* **Charlotte Saun·ders** (sôn′dərz, sän′-), 1816–76, U.S. actress.

cush·y (ko͝osh′ē), *adj.,* **cush·i·er, cush·i·est.** *Informal.* **1.** involving little effort for ample rewards; easy and profitable: *a cushy job.* **2.** soft and comfortable; cushiony: *a cushy chair.* [1910–15; prob. CUSH(ION) + -Y[1]; also adduced, but less likely: < Hindi *ḳhūsh* pleasant (allegedly via Anglo-Indian, but unattested) or < F *couchée* bed, sleeping place; cf. CUSH] —**cush′i·ly,** *adv.* —**cush′i·ness,** *n.*

cusk (kusk), *n., pl.* **cusks,** (*esp. collectively*) **cusk. 1.** an edible marine fish, *Brosme brosme,* of North Atlantic coastal waters. **2.** the burbot. [1610–20, *Amer.;* prob. var. of *tusk* kind of fish < Scand; cf. Norw *tosk,* var. of *torsk,* c. ON *thorskr* codfish]

cusk-eel (kusk′ēl′), *n., pl.* (*esp. collectively*) **-eel,** (*esp. referring to two or more kinds or species*) **-eels.** any of several eellike, marine fishes of the family Ophidiidae, having the ventral fins located under the throat and so modified as to resemble barbels.

cusp (kusp), *n.* **1.** a point or pointed end. **2.** *Anat., Zool., Bot.* a point, projection, or elevation, as on the crown of a tooth. **3.** Also called **spinode.** *Geom.* a point where two branches of a curve meet, end, and are tangent. **4.** *Archit.* a decorative device, used esp. in Gothic architecture to vary the outlines of intradoses or to form architectural foils, consisting of a pair of curves tangent to the real or imaginary line defining the area decorated and meeting at a point within the area. **5.** *Astron.* a point of a crescent, esp. of the moon. **6.** *Astrol.* **a.** the zodiacal degree that marks the beginning of a house or a sign. **b.** *Informal.* a person born on the first day of a sign. **7.** a point that marks the beginning of a change:

CONCISE PRONUNCIATION KEY: *act, cāpe, dâre, pärt; set, ēqual; if, ice; ox, ōver, ôrder, oil, bo͝ok, bo͞ot, out; up, ûrge; child; sing; shoe; thin, that;* zh as in *treasure.* ə = *a* as in *alone, e* as in *system, i* as in *easily, o* as in *gallop, u* as in *circus;* ᵊ as in *fire* (fīᵊr), *hour* (ouᵊr). l and n can serve as syllabic consonants, as in *cradle* (krād′l), and *button* (but′n). See the full key inside the front cover.

on the cusp of a new era. [1575–85; < L *cuspis* a point] —**cusp′al,** *adj.*

cusped (kuspt), *adj.* having a cusp or cusps; cusplike. Also, **cus·pate** (kus′pit, -pāt), **cus′pat·ed.** [1815–25; CUSP + -ED[3]]

cus·pid (kus′pid), *n.* (in humans) a tooth with a single projection point or elevation; canine. [1735–45; < L *cuspid-* (s. of *cuspis*) point]

cus·pi·dal (kus′pi dl), *adj.* of, like, or having a cusp; cuspidate. [1640–50; < L *cuspid-* (s. of *cuspis*) point + -AL[1]]

cus·pi·date (kus′pi dāt′), *adj.* **1.** having a cusp or cusps. **2.** furnished with or ending in a sharp and stiff point or cusp: *cuspidate leaves; a cuspidate tooth.* Also, **cus′pi·dat′ed.** [1685–95; < NL *cuspidātus,* equiv. to L *cuspid-* (see CUSPID) + *-ātus* -ATE[1]]

cus·pi·da·tion (kus′pi dā′shən), *n.* decoration with cusps, as in architecture. [1840–50; CUSPIDATE + -ION]

cus·pi·dor (kus′pi dôr′), *n.* a large bowl, often of metal, serving as a receptacle for spit, esp. from chewing tobacco: in wide use during the 19th and early 20th centuries. [1770–80; < Pg: lit., spitter, equiv. to *cusp(ir)* to spit (<< L *conspuere* to cover with spit; *con-* CON- + *spuere* to SPIT) + *-idor* < L *-i-tōrium;* see -I-, -TORY[2]]

cuss (kus), *Informal.* —*v.i.* **1.** to use profanity; curse; swear. —*v.t.* **2.** to swear at; curse: *He cussed the pedestrian for getting in his way.* **3.** to criticize or reprimand in harsh terms (often fol. by *out*): *The coach cussed out the team for losing.* —*n.* **4.** curse word; oath. **5.** a person or animal: *a strange but likable cuss.* [1765–75, *Amer.;* var. of CURSE, with loss of *r* and shortening of vowel, as in ASS[2], BASS[2], PASSEL, etc.] —**cuss′er,** *n.*

cuss·ed (kus′id), *adj. Informal.* **1.** cursed. **2.** obstinate; stubborn; perverse. [1830–40; CUSS + -ED[3]] —**cuss′ed·ly,** *adv.* —**cuss′ed·ness,** *n.*

cuss·word (kus′wûrd′), *n. Informal.* See **curse word.** [1870–75, *Amer.;* CUSS + WORD]

cus·tard (kus′tərd), *n.* a dessert made of eggs, sugar, and milk, either baked, boiled, or frozen. [1400–50; late ME, metathetic var. of earlier *crustade* kind of pie. See CRUST, -ADE[1]; cf. Pr *croustado*]

cus′tard ap′ple, **1.** any of several trees of the genus *Annona,* as the cherimoya. **2.** any of several other trees, as the pawpaw, *Asimina triloba,* bearing fruit with soft, edible pulp. **3.** the fruit of any of these trees. [1650–60]

cus′tard cup′, a heat-resistant porcelain or glass cup in which an individual custard is baked. [1815–25]

cus·tard-pie (kus′tərd pī′), *adj.* characteristic of a type of slapstick comedy in which a performer throws a pie in another's face: popular esp. in the era of vaudeville and early silent films. [1930–35]

Cus·ter (kus′tər), *n.* **George Arm·strong** (ärm′strông, -strong), 1839–76, U.S. general and Indian fighter.

cus·to·des (ku stō′dēz; *Lat.* ko͝os tō′des), *n.* pl. of **custos.**

cus·to·di·al (ku stō′dē əl), *adj.* **1.** of or pertaining to custody. **2.** of, pertaining to, or appropriate to a custodian: *a building superintendent's custodial duties.* **3.** responsible for or providing protective supervision and guardianship rather than seeking to improve or cure: *Overcrowding forces many mental hospitals to provide only custodial care.* —*n.* **4.** a container or receptacle for something sacred, as the Host. [1765–75; < L *custōdi(a)* CUSTODY + -AL[1]] —**cus·to′di·al·ism,** *n.*

cus·to·di·an (ku stō′dē ən), *n.* **1.** a person who has custody; keeper; guardian. **2.** a person entrusted with guarding or maintaining a property; janitor. [1775–85; < L *custōdi(a)* watchman (see CUSTODY) + -AN] —**cus·to′di·an·ship′,** *n.*

cus·to·dy (kus′tə dē), *n., pl.* **-dies. 1.** keeping; guardianship; care. **2.** the keeping or charge of officers of the law: *The car was held in the custody of the police.* **3.** imprisonment; legal restraint: *He was taken into custody.* **4.** Also called **child custody.** *Law.* the right of determining the residence, protection, care, and education of a minor child or children, esp. in a divorce or separation. Cf. **joint custody, sole custody.** [1400–50; late ME *custodye* < L *custōdia* a watching, watchman, equiv. to *custōd-* (s. of *custōs*) keeper + *-ia* -Y[3]]
—**Syn. 1.** safekeeping, charge, watch. CUSTODY, KEEPING, POSSESSION imply a guardianship or care for something. CUSTODY denotes a strict keeping, as by a formally authorized and responsible guardian or keeper: *in the custody of the sheriff.* KEEPING denotes having in one's care or charge, as for guarding or preservation: *I left the package in my mother's keeping.* POSSESSION means holding, ownership, or mastery: *Leave it in possession of its owner.*

cus·tom (kus′təm), *n.* **1.** a habitual practice; the usual way of acting in given circumstances. **2.** habits or usages collectively; convention. **3.** a practice so long established that it has the force of law. **4.** such practices collectively. **5.** *Sociol.* a group pattern of habitual activity usually transmitted from one generation to another. **6.** toll; duty. **7. customs, a.** (*used with a singular or plural v.*) duties imposed by law on imported or, less commonly, exported goods. **b.** (*used with a singular v.*) the government department that collects these duties. **c.** (*used with a singular v.*) the section of an airport, station, etc., where baggage is checked for contraband and for goods subject to duty. **8.** regular patronage of a particular shop, restaurant, etc. **9.** the customers or patrons of a business firm, collectively. **10.** the aggregate of customers. **11.** (in medieval Europe) a customary tax, tribute, or service owed by peasants to their lord. —*adj.* **12.** made specially for individual customers: *custom shoes.* **13.** dealing in things so made, or doing work to order: *a custom tailor.* [1150–1200; ME *custume* < AF; OF *costume* < VL **co(n)s(ue)tūmin-,* r. L *consuētūdin-* (s. of *consuētūdō*), equiv. to *consuēt(us)* accustomed, ptp. of *consuēscere* (*con-* CON- + *suē-* (akin to *suus* one's own) + *-tus* ptp. suffix) + *-ūdin-* n. suffix; cf. COSTUME]
—**Syn. 1, 2.** CUSTOM, HABIT, PRACTICE mean an established way of doing things. CUSTOM, applied to a community or to an individual, implies a more or less permanent continuance of a social usage: *It is the custom to give gifts at Christmas time.* HABIT, applied particularly to an individual, implies such repetition of the same action as to develop a natural, spontaneous, or rooted tendency or inclination to perform it: *to make a habit of reading the newspapers.* PRACTICE applies to a set of fixed habits or an ordered procedure in conducting activities: *It is his practice to verify all statements.*

cus·tom·a·ble (kus′tə mə bəl), *adj.* subject to customs or duties; dutiable. [1275–1325; ME < AF *c(o)ustumable.* See CUSTOM, -ABLE] —**cus′tom·a·ble·ness,** *n.*

cus·tom·ar·y (kus′tə mer′ē), *adj., n., pl.* **-ar·ies.** —*adj.* **1.** according to or depending on custom; usual; habitual. **2.** of or established by custom rather than law. **3.** *Law.* defined by long-continued practices: *the customary service due from land in a manor.* —*n.* **4.** a book or document containing the legal customs or customary laws of a locality. **5.** any body of such customs or laws. [1375–1425; 1515–25 for current senses; late ME < ML *custumārius, customārius,* equiv. to *costum(i)a* custom (also in VL; see CUSTOM) + *-ārius* -ARY] —**cus·tom·ar·i·ly** (kus′tə mer′ə lē; *for emphasis,* kus′tə mâr′ə lē), *adv.*
—**Syn. 1.** wonted, accustomed, conventional, common, regular. See **usual.** —**Ant. 1.** uncommon.

cus·tom-build (kus′təm bild′), *v.t.,* **-built, -build·ing.** to build to individual order: *The company will custom-build a kitchen cabinet to your specifications.* [1955–60]

cus·tom-built (kus′təm bilt′), *adj.* built to individual order: *a custom-built limousine.* [1920–25]

cus·tom·er (kus′tə mər), *n.* **1.** a person who purchases goods or services from another; buyer; patron. **2.** *Informal.* a person one has to deal with: *a tough customer; a cool customer.* [1400–50; late ME; see CUSTOM, -ER[1]; cf. ME *customer* collector of customs < AF; OF *costumier,* c. ML *custumārius;* see CUSTOMARY]

cus′tomer's man′, *Stock Exchange.* See **registered representative.** [1930–35, *Amer.*]

cus′tom house′, a government building or office, as at a seaport, for collecting customs, clearing vessels, etc. Also, **cus′tom·house′, cus′toms house′, cus′toms·house′.** [1480–90]

cus·tom·ize (kus′tə mīz′), *v.t.,* **-ized, -iz·ing.** to modify or build according to individual or personal specifications or preference: *to customize an automobile.* Also, *esp. Brit.,* **cus′tom·ise′.** [1930–35, *Amer.;* CUSTOM + -IZE] —**cus′tom·iz′a·ble,** *adj.* —**cus′tom·i·za′tion,** *n.* —**cus′tom·iz′er,** *n.*

cus·tom-made (kus′təm mād′), *adj.* **1.** made to individual order: *custom-made shoes.* —*n.* **2.** a custom-made item, esp. of apparel. [1850–55, *Amer.*]

cus·tom-make (kus′təm māk′), *v.t.,* **-made, -mak·ing.** to make to individual order.

cus·tom-or·der (kus′təm ôr′dər), *v.t.* to obtain by special or individual order: *These wide doors have to be custom-ordered.*

cus′toms bro′ker, a person or firm that clears goods or merchandise through customs for a consignee or shipper. Also called **cus′tomhouse bro′ker.**

cus′toms un′ion, an association of independent nations or tariff areas created to remove customs barriers between them and to adopt a uniform tariff policy toward nonmember nations.

cus·tom-tai·lor (kus′təm tā′lər), *v.t.* to modify to fit a specific use or need; tailor-make. [1890–95]

cus·tos (kus′tos; *Lat.* ko͝os′tōs), *n., pl.* **cus·to·des** (ku stō′dēz; *Lat.* ko͝os tō′des). **1.** (*italics*) *Latin.* a custodian. **2.** a superior in the Franciscan order. [1425–75; late ME < ML]

cus·tos mo·rum (ko͝os′tōs mō′ro͝om; *Eng.* kus′tos môr′əm, mōr′-), *pl.* **cus·to·des mo·rum** (ko͝os tō′des mō′ro͝om; *Eng.* ku stō′dēz môr′əm, mōr′-). *Latin.* a custodian or guardian of morals; censor. [lit., guardian of established usages, laws, etc.]

cus·tu·mal (kus′cho͞o məl), *n.* a customary. [1375–1425; 1560–70 for current sense; late ME (as adj.) < ML *custumālis,* a Latinization of OF *costumel* customary, usual, equiv. to *costume* CUSTOM + *-el* -AL[1]]

cut (kut), *v.,* **cut, cut·ting,** *adj., n.* —*v.t.* **1.** to penetrate with or as if with a sharp-edged instrument or object: *He cut his finger.* **2.** to divide with or as if with a sharp-edged instrument; sever; carve: *to cut a rope.* **3.** to detach with or as if with a sharp-edged instrument; separate from the main body; lop off: *to cut a slice from a loaf of bread.* **4.** to hew or saw down; fell: *to cut timber.* **5.** to trim by clipping, shearing, paring, or pruning: *to cut hair.* **6.** to mow; reap; harvest: *to cut grain.* **7.** to abridge or shorten; edit by omitting a part or parts: *to cut a speech.* **8.** to lower, reduce, diminish, or curtail (sometimes fol. by *down*): *to cut prices.* **9.** to dilute; make less thick: *to cut wine.* **10.** to dissolve: *That detergent cuts grease effectively.* **11.** to intersect; cross: *One line cuts another at right angles.* **12.** *Informal.* to cease; discontinue (often fol. by *out*): *Cut the kidding. Let's cut out the pretense.* **13.** to stop; halt the running of, as a liquid or an engine (often fol. by *off*): *The pilot cut the engines and glided in for a landing. Cut off the hot water.* **14.** to dilute or adulterate (a drug) by mixing it with other substances. **15.** to grow (a tooth or teeth) through the gum: *The baby is cutting his teeth.* **16.** to type, write, or draw on (a stencil) for mimeographing. **17.** to make or fashion by cutting, as a statue, jewel, or garment. **18.** *Glassmaking.* to produce a pattern (in glass) by grinding and polishing. **19.** to refuse to recognize socially; shun ostentatiously: *Her friends began to cut her as the season progressed.* **20.** to strike sharply, as with a whip. **21.** to absent oneself from: *allowed to cut three classes per semester.* **22.** *Motion Pictures, Television.* **a.** to stop (a scene or shot being filmed). **b.** to edit (a film). **23.** to wound the feelings of severely. **24.** *Cards.* **a.** to divide (a pack of cards) at random into two or more parts, by removing cards from the top. **b.** to take (a card) from a deck. **25.** to record a selection on (a phonograph record or tape); make a recording of. **26.** to castrate or geld. **27.** *Sports.* to hit (a ball) with either the hand or some instrument so as to change its course and often to cause it to spin. **28.** to hollow out; excavate; dig: *to cut a trench.* **29.** *Cricket.* to strike and send off (a ball) in front of the batsman, and parallel to the wicket. **30.** *Slang.* to be a nonplaying dealer, manager, or supervisor of (a card game, crap game, or other gambling game) in return for a percentage of the money bet or sometimes for a fee.
—*v.i.* **31.** to penetrate or divide something, as with a sharp-edged instrument; make an incision: *The scissors cut well.* **32.** to admit of being cut: *Butter cuts easily.* **33.** to pass, go, or come, esp. in the most direct way (usually fol. by *across, through, in,* etc.): *to cut across an empty lot.* **34.** *Motion Pictures, Television.* **a.** to shift suddenly from one shot to another: *Cut to the barroom interior.* **b.** to stop the action of a scene: used as a command by a director. **35.** to make a sudden or sharp turn in direction; change direction suddenly; swerve: *We cut to the left to avoid hitting the child.* **36.** to strike a person, animal, etc., sharply, as with a whip. **37.** to wound the feelings severely: *His criticism cut deep.* **38.** (of the teeth) to grow through the gums. **39.** *Cards.* to cut the cards. **40.** *Informal.* to leave hastily: *to cut for the hills.* **41.** (of a horse) to interfere. **42. cut a caper** or **figure,** to perform a spirited, brief, outlandish dance step, esp. as a result of euphoria. **43. cut across,** to precede or go beyond considerations of; transcend: *The new tax program cuts across party lines.* **44. cut a figure, a.** See **cut a caper. b.** to give a certain impression of oneself: *He cut a distinguished figure in his tuxedo.* **45. cut and run, a.** *Naut.* to cut the anchor cable and set sail, as in an emergency. **b.** to leave as hurriedly as possible; flee. **46. cut back, a.** to shorten by cutting off the end. **b.** to curtail or discontinue: *Steel production has been cut back in recent months.* **c.** to return to an earlier episode or event, as in the plot of a novel. **d.** *Football.* to reverse direction suddenly by moving in the diagonally opposite course. **47. cut both ways,** to have, produce, or result in advantages as well as disadvantages: *This decision will inevitably cut both ways.* **48. cut down, a.** Also, **cut down on.** to lessen; decrease: *to cut down on between-meal snacks.* **b.** to strike and cause to fall: *The first force to attempt an advance was swiftly cut down.* **c.** to destroy, kill, or disable: *The hurricane cut down everything in its path.* **d.** to remodel, remake, or reduce in size, as a garment: *She had her old coat cut down to fit her daughter.* **49. cut** or **chop down to size,** to reduce the stature or importance of: *The novelist had a big ego until the critics cut him down to size.* **50. cut in, a.** to move or thrust oneself, a vehicle, etc., abruptly between others: *A speeding car cut in and nearly caused an accident.* **b.** to interpose; interrupt: *to cut in with a remark.* **c.** *Informal.* to interrupt a dancing couple in order to dance with one of them. **d.** to blend (shortening) into flour by means of a knife. **51. cut it,** *Informal.* **a.** to achieve or maintain a desired level of performance: *The aging football player decided he couldn't cut it any longer and retired.* **b.** to be effective or successful; satisfy a need. **52. cut it out,** *Informal.* to stop doing something: *That hurts! Cut it out!* **53. cut no ice.** See **ice** (def. 10). **54. cut off, a.** to intercept. **b.** to interrupt. **c.** to stop suddenly; discontinue. **d.** to halt the operation of; turn off. **e.** to shut off or shut out. **f.** to disinherit. **g.** to sever; separate. **55. cut out, a.** to omit; delete; excise. **b.** to oust and replace a rival; supplant. **c.** to part an animal from a herd. **d.** to plan; arrange: *He has his work cut out for him.* **e.** to move out of one's lane of traffic. **f.** Also, **cut on out.** *Slang.* to leave suddenly. **g.** *Informal.* to refrain from; stop: *to cut out smoking.* **h.** (of an engine, machine, etc.) to stop running. **56. cut up, a.** to cut into pieces or sections. **b.** to lacerate; wound. **c.** to distress mentally; injure. **d.** *Informal.* to play pranks; misbehave: *They got scolded for cutting up in church.*
—*adj.* **57.** that has been subjected to cutting; divided into pieces by cutting; detached by cutting: *cut flowers.* **58.** fashioned by cutting; having the surface shaped or ornamented by grinding, polishing, or the like: *cut diamonds.* **59.** reduced by or as if by cutting: *cut whiskey; cut prices.* **60.** *Bot.* incised; cleft. **61.** castrated; gelded. **62.** *Slang.* drunk. **63. cut out for,** fitted for; capable of: *He wasn't cut out for military service.*
—*n.* **64.** the act of cutting; a stroke or a blow, as with a knife, whip, etc. **65.** the result of cutting, as an incision, wound, passage, or channel. **66.** a piece cut off: *a cut of a pie.* **67.** *Informal.* a share, esp. of earnings or profits: *His agent's cut is 20 percent.* **68.** a haircut, often with a styling. **69.** a reduction in price, salary, etc. **70.** the manner or fashion in which anything is cut: *the cut of a dress.* **71.** style; manner; kind: *We need a man of his cut in this firm.* **72.** a passage or course straight across or through: *a cut through the woods.* **73.** an excision or omission of a part. **74.** a part or quantity of text deleted or omitted. **75.** a quantity cut, esp. of lumber. **76.** a refusal to recognize an acquaintance. **77.** an act, speech, etc., that wounds the feelings. **78.** an engraved plate or block of wood used for printing. **79.** a printed picture or illustration. **80.** an absence, as from a school class, at which attendance is required. **81.** *Butchering.* part of an animal usually cut as one piece. **82.** *Cards.* a cutting of the cards. **83.** *Sports.* **a.** the act of cutting a ball. **b.** the spin imparted. **84.** *Fencing.* a blow with the edge of the blade instead of the tip. **85.** one of several pieces of straw, paper, etc., used in drawing lots. **86.** *Motion Pictures, Television.* **a.** the instantaneous or gradual transition from one shot or scene to another in an edited film. **b.** an edited version of a film. Cf. **rough cut, final cut. c.** an act or instance of editing a film. **87.** an individual song, musical piece, or other similar material on a record or tape. **88.** any product of the fractional distillation of

petroleum. **89. a cut above,** somewhat superior to another (thing, person, etc.) in some respect: *Her work is a cut above anyone else's.* [1175–1225; ME *cutten, kytten, kitten,* OE **cyttan;* akin to OSw *kotta* to cut, ON *kuti* little knife]
—Syn. 1. gash, slash, slit, lance. **2.** cleave, sunder, bisect. CUT, CHOP, HACK, HEW refer to giving a sharp blow or stroke. CUT is a general word for this: *to cut the grass.* To CHOP is to cut by giving repeated blows with something sharp, as an ax. To CHOP and to HEW are practically interchangeable, but HEW suggests keeping to a definite purpose: *to chop or hew down a tree; to hew out a clearing.* To HACK is to cut or chop roughly and unevenly: *to hack off a limb.* **7.** abbreviate, curtail.

cut·a·bil·i·ty (kut′ə bil′i tē), *n.* the lean yield of a beef carcass: the carcass of highest cutability, or top yield, has the largest proportion of lean meat within its grade. [1960–65; CUT + -ABILITY; due to noninitial stress, irreg. sp. with single rather than double *t*]

cut-and-cov·er (kut′n kuv′ər), *n.* a method for digging a tunnel, laying pipe, etc., by cutting a trench, constructing the tunnel or laying the pipe in it, and covering with the excavated material. [1830–40]

cut-and-dried (kut′n drīd′), *adj.* **1.** prepared or settled in advance; not needing much thought or discussion: *a cut-and-dried decision.* **2.** lacking in originality or spontaneity; routine; boring: *a lecture that was cut-and-dried.* Also, **cut′-and-dry′.** [1700–10]

cut′ and fill′, *Geol.* a process of localized gradation whereby material eroded from one place is deposited a short distance away.

cut-and-paste (kut′n pāst′), *adj.* assembled or produced from various existing bits and pieces: *The book purports to be a history but is just a cut-and-paste job of old essays and newspaper clippings.*

cut-and-try (kut′n trī′), *adj.* marked by a procedure of trial and error; empirical: *Many scientific advances are achieved with a cut-and-try approach.* [1900–05]

cu·ta·ne·ous (kyōō tā′nē əs), *adj.* of, pertaining to, or affecting the skin. [1570–80; < ML *cutāneus,* equiv. to L *cut(is)* the skin + *-āneus* (-*ān(us)* -AN + *-eus* -EOUS). See CUTIS] **—cu·ta′ne·ous·ly,** *adv.*

cuta′neous quit′tor, *Vet. Pathol.* a purulent infection of horses and other hoofed animals, characterized by an acute inflammation of soft tissue above the hoof and resulting in suppuration and sloughing of the skin and usually lameness.

cut·a·way (kut′ə wā′), *n.* **1.** Also called **cut′away coat′.** a man's formal daytime coat having the front portion of the skirt cut away from the waist so as to curve or slope to the tails at the back. **2.** *Motion Pictures, Television.* **a.** a switch from one scene to another for showing simultaneous or related action, creating suspense, etc. **b.** Also called **cut′away shot′.** a shot that abruptly introduces content, scenery, etc., away from the central action. **3.** an illustration or scale model having the outer section removed to display the interior. *—adj.* **4.** having a part cut away, as an outer section of something being illustrated so that the inside may be shown. [1835–45; adj., n. use of v. phrase *cut away*]

cutaway (def. 1)

cut′away dive′, a back dive in which the diver rotates the body to enter the water headfirst facing the springboard.

cut·back (kut′bak′), *n.* **1.** a reduction in rate, quantity, etc.: *a cutback in production.* **2.** a return in the course of a story, motion picture, etc., to earlier events. **3.** *Football.* a play in which the ball-carrier abruptly reverses direction, esp. by starting to make an end run and then turning suddenly to run toward the middle of the line. **4.** a maneuver in surfing of heading the surfboard back toward a wave's crest. [1895–1900; n. use of v. phrase *cut back*]

cut·bank (kut′bangk′), *n.* a nearly vertical cliff produced by erosion of the banks of a stream. [1810–20, *Amer.*; CUT + BANK[1]]

cut′-card′ work′ (kut′kärd′), silver leaf cut in shapes and soldered to a silver vessel. [1915–20]

cutch (kuch), *n.* catechu.

Cutch (kuch), *n.* Kutch.

cut·cha (kuch′ə), *adj.* kutcha.

cut·cher·ry (kə cher′ē, kuch′ə rē), *n., pl.* **-ries. 1.** (in India) a public administrative or judicial office. **2.** any administrative office. Also, **cut·cher′y.** [1600–10; < Hindi *kacerī,* var. of *kacahrī* audience house, courthouse, office]

cut·down (kut′doun′), *n.* **1.** reduction; decrease; diminution: *a cutdown in sales.* **2.** *Surg.* the incision of a superficial vein in order to effect direct insertion of a catheter. *—adj.* **3.** reduced in size. **4.** abridged or condensed: *They televised a cutdown version of the movie.* [1885–90; n. use of v. phrase *cut down*]

cut′ drop′, *Theat.* a drop scene cut to reveal part of the upstage area. [1960–65]

cute (kyōōt), *adj.,* **cut·er, cut·est,** *adv., n.* *—adj.* **1.** attractive, esp. in a dainty way; pleasingly pretty: *a cute child; a cute little apartment.* **2.** affectedly or mincingly pretty or clever; precious: *The child has acquired some intolerably cute mannerisms.* **3.** mentally keen; clever; shrewd. *—adv.* **4.** *Informal.* in a cute, charming, or amusing way; cutely: *In this type of movie the boy and girl always meet cute.* *—n.* **5. the cutes,** *Informal.* self-consciously cute mannerisms or appeal; affected coyness: *The young actress has a bad case of the cutes.* [1615–25; aph. var. of ACUTE] **—cute′ly,** *adv.* **—cute′ness,** *n.*

cute·sy (kyōōt′sē), *adj.,* **-si·er, -si·est.** *Informal.* forcedly and consciously cute; coyly mannered: *cutesy greeting cards, with animals peeking from behind flowers.* Also, **cute′sie.** [1910–15; CUTE + -SY] **—cute′·si·ness,** *n.*

cute′sy pie′, *Informal.* See **cutie pie.** **—cute′sy-pie′,** *adj.*

cute·sy-poo (kyōōt′sē pōō′), *adj. Informal.* embarrassingly or sickeningly cute. [*poo* perh. var. of *pie* (as in CUTIE PIE), altered to rhyme with *u* of CUTESY]

cut·ey (kyōō′tē), *n., pl.* **-eys.** cutie.

cut′ glass′, glass ornamented or shaped by cutting or grinding with abrasive wheels. [1835–45] **—cut′-glass′,** *adj.*

cut-grass (kut′gras′, -gräs′), *n.* any of several grasses having blades with rough edges, esp. grasses of the genus *Leersia.* [1830–40]

Cuth·bert (kuth′bərt), *n.* **Saint,** A.D. c635–687, English monk and bishop.

cu·ti·cle (kyōō′ti kəl), *n.* **1.** the nonliving epidermis that surrounds the edges of the fingernail or toenail. **2.** the epidermis. **3.** a superficial integument, membrane, or the like. **4.** Also called **cuticula.** *Zool.* the outer, noncellular layer of the arthropod integument, composed of a mixture of chitin and protein and commonly containing other hardening substances as well. **5.** *Bot.* a very thin hyaline film covering the surface of plants, derived from the outer surfaces of the epidermal cells. [1605–15; < L *cuticula* the skin, equiv. to *cuti(s)* skin, CUTIS + *-cula* -CLE[1]] **—cu·tic·u·lar** (kyōō tik′yə lər), *adj.*

cu·ti·col·or (kyōō′ti kul′ər), *adj.* of the color of flesh. [< NL, equiv. to L *cuti(s)* skin, CUTIS + *color* COLOR]

cu·tic·u·la (kyōō tik′yə lə), *n., pl.* **-lae** (-lē′). *Zool.* cuticle (def. 4). [1615–25; < NL, L; see CUTICLE]

cut·ie (kyōō′tē), *n.* **1.** *Informal.* a charmingly attractive or cute person, esp. a girl or a young woman (often used as a form of address): *Hi, cutie.* **2.** *Slang.* **a.** a person who tries to outsmart an opponent, as an athlete who outmaneuvers an opposing player: *The tackle was a real cutie when blocking on trap plays.* **b.** a clever or cunning maneuver: *He pulled a cutie.* [1760–70, *Amer.*; CUTE + -IE]

cut′ie pie′, *Informal.* **1.** darling; sweetheart; sweetie (often used as a term of endearment). **2.** cutie (def. 1). Also, **cutesy pie.** [1930–35] **—cut′ie-pie′,** *adj.*

cut-in (kut′in′), *n.* **1.** *Motion Pictures.* a still, as of a scene or an object, inserted in a film and interrupting the action or continuity: *We will insert a cut-in of the letter as she reads it.* **2.** *Radio and Television.* a commercial or other announcement inserted by a local station into a network broadcast. **3.** the act of cutting in, as on a dancing couple. [1880–85; n. use of v. phrase *cut in*]

cu·tin (kyōō′tin), *n.* a transparent, waxy substance constituting, together with cellulose, the cuticle of plants. [1860–65; < L *cut(is)* skin, CUTIS + -IN[2]]

cu·tin·ize (kyōōt′n īz′), *v.t., v.i.,* **-ized, -iz·ing.** to make into or become cutin. Also, *esp. Brit.,* **cu′tin·ise′.** [1885–90; CUTIN + -IZE] **—cu′tin·i·za′tion,** *n.*

cu·tis (kyōō′tis), *n., pl.* **-tes** (-tēz), **-tis·es.** the true skin, consisting of the dermis and the epidermis. [1595–1605; < L: skin; akin to Gk *skŷtos* HIDE[2]]

cu′tis an·se·ri′na (an′sə rī′nə), *Med.* See **goose flesh.** [< NL: goose flesh; see CUTIS, ANSERINE]

cu·tis ve·ra (kyōō′tis vēr′ə), *pl.* **cu·tes ve·rae** (kyōō′tēz vēr′ē). cutis. [< L: lit., true skin]

cut·lass (kut′ləs), *n.* a short, heavy, slightly curved sword with a single cutting edge, formerly used by sailors. Also, **cut′las.** [1585–95; earlier *coutelace* < MF *coutelas,* equiv. to *coutel* knife (F *couteau*) (< L *cultellus;* see CULTELLUS) + *-as* aug. suffix; c. It *coltellaccio* big knife; cf. CURTALAX]

cutlass

cut·lass·fish (kut′ləs fish′), *n., pl.* (*esp. collectively*) **-fish,** (*esp. referring to two or more kinds or species*) **-fish·es.** any compressed, ribbonlike fish of the genus *Trichiurus,* having daggerlike teeth. Also called **frostfish.** [1880–85; CUTLASS + FISH]

cut·ler (kut′lər), *n.* a person who makes, sells, or repairs knives and other cutting instruments. [1350–1400; ME *cuteler* < AF, c. MF *coutelier* < LL *cultellārius,* equiv. to L *cultell(us)* knife (see CULTELLUS) + *-ārius* -ARY; see -ER[2]]

Cut·ler (kut′lər), *n.* **Manasseh,** 1742–1823, U.S. Congregational clergyman and scientist: promoted settlement of Ohio; congressman 1801–05.

cut·ler·y (kut′lə rē), *n.* **1.** cutting instruments collectively, esp. knives for cutting food. **2.** utensils, as knives, forks, and spoons, used at the table for serving and eating food. **3.** the trade or business of a cutler. [1300–50; ME *cutellerie* < MF *coutelerie;* see CUTLER, -Y[3]]

cut·let (kut′lit), *n.* **1.** a slice of meat, esp. of veal, for broiling or frying. **2.** a flat croquette of minced chicken, lobster, or the like. [1700–10; < F *côtelette,* OF *costelette* double dim. of *coste* rib < L *costa.* See -LET]

cut·line (kut′līn′), *n.* a caption or legend accompanying a cut or illustration in a publication. [1910–15; CUT + LINE[1]]

cut′lips min′now (kut′lips′), a cyprinid fish, *Exoglossum maxillingua,* of northeastern U.S. coastal waters, having a three-lobed lower lip. [so called from the shape of its lower lip]

cut′ nail′, a nail having a tapering rectangular form with a blunt point, made by cutting from a thin rolled sheet of iron or steel. See illus. under **nail.** [1785–95, *Amer.*]

cut·off (kut′ôf′, -of′), *n.* **1.** an act or instance of cutting off. **2.** something that cuts off. **3.** a road, passage, etc., that leaves another, usually providing a shortcut: *Let's take the cutoff to Baltimore.* **4.** a new and shorter channel formed in a river by the water cutting across a bend in its course. **5.** a point, time, or stage serving as the limit beyond which something is no longer effective, applicable, or possible. **6. cutoffs,** Also, **cut′-offs′.** shorts made by cutting the legs off a pair of trousers, esp. jeans, above the knees and often leaving the cut edges ragged. **7.** *Accounting.* a selected point at which records are considered complete for the purpose of settling accounts, taking inventory, etc. **8.** *Baseball.* an infielder's interception of a ball thrown from the outfield in order to relay it to home plate or keep a base runner from advancing. **9.** *Mach.* arrest of the steam moving the pistons of an engine, usually occurring before the completion of a stroke. **10.** *Electronics.* (in a vacuum tube) the minimum grid potential preventing an anode current. **11.** *Rocketry.* the termination of propulsion, either by shutting off the propellant flow or by stopping the combustion of the propellant. *—adj.* **12.** being or constituting the limit or ending: *a cutoff date for making changes.* [1735–45; n. use of v. phrase *cut off*]

cut·out (kut′out′), *n.* **1.** something cut out from something else, as a pattern or figure cut out or intended to be cut out of paper, cardboard, or other material. **2.** a valve in the exhaust pipe of an internal-combustion engine, which when open permits the engine to exhaust directly into the air ahead of the muffler. **3.** an act or instance of cutting out. **4.** *Slang.* a trusted intermediary between two espionage agents or agencies. **5.** *Elect.* a device for the manual or automatic interruption of electric current. [1790–1800; n. use of v. phrase *cut out*]

cut·o·ver (kut′ō′vər), *adj.* **1.** (esp. of timberland) cleared of trees. *—n.* **2.** land, esp. timberland, cleared of trees. [1895–1900, *Amer.* adj., n. use of v. phrase *cut over*]

cut-pile (kut′pīl′), *adj.* having a pile with yarns that are cut instead of looped: *a cut-pile carpet.*

cut′ plug′, compressed chewing tobacco in a portion-sized cake. [1895–1900, *Amer.*]

cut·purse (kut′pûrs′), *n.* **1.** *Older Use.* a pickpocket. **2.** (formerly) a person who steals by cutting purses from the belt. [1325–75; ME *cutte-purs.* See CUT, PURSE]

cut′ rate′, a price, fare, or rate below the standard charge. [1880–85, *Amer.*] **—cut′-rate′,** *adj.*

cut-rat·er (kut′rā′tər), *n.* a person or company that offers goods or services at cut-rate prices. [CUT RATE + -ER[1]]

cut′ square′, *Philately.* a stamp cut from the envelope on which it has been printed so as to leave a square margin.

cut′ stone′, *Masonry.* a stone or stonework dressed to a relatively fine finish with tools other than hammers. [1800–10]

cut·ta·ble (kut′ə bəl), *adj.* that can be cut. [1400–50; late ME. See CUT, -ABLE]

Cut·tack (kut′ək), *n.* a city in E Orissa, in NE India. 194,036.

cut·tage (kut′ij), *n.* the process of propagating plants from separate vegetative parts. [1895–1900; CUT + -AGE]

cut·ter (kut′ər), *n.* **1.** a person who cuts, esp. as a job, as one who cuts fabric for garments. **2.** a machine, tool, or other device for cutting. **3.** *Naut.* **a.** a single-masted sailing vessel, very similar to a sloop but having its mast set somewhat farther astern, about two-fifths of the way aft measured on the water line. **b.** a ship's boat having double-banked oars and one or two lugsails. **4.** Also called **revenue cutter.** a lightly armed government vessel used to prevent smuggling and enforce the customs regulations. **5.** a person employed as a film editor. **6.** a small, light sleigh, usually single-seated and pulled by one horse. **7.** Also called **rubber.** a brick suitable for cutting and rubbing. **8.** (in U.S. government grading of beef) **a.** a low-quality grade of beef between utility and canner. **b.** beef of this grade, mostly used in processed beef products, as sausage. *—adj.* **9.** (in U.S. government grading of beef) graded between utility and canner. [1375–1425; ME *kittere, cuttere.* See CUT, -ER[1]]

CONCISE PRONUNCIATION KEY: act, cāpe, dâre, pärt; set, ēqual; if, īce; ox, ōver, ôrder, oil, bŏŏk, bōōt, out; up, ûrge; child; sing; shoe; thin, *th*at; zh as in *treasure.* ə = *a* as in *alone, e* as in *system, i* as in *easily, o* as in *gallop, u* as in *circus;* ᵊ as in *fire* (fīᵊr), *hour* (ouᵊr). l and n can serve as syllabic consonants, as in *cradle* (krād′l), and *button* (but′n). See the full key inside the front cover.

cut′ter bar′, 1. Also called **sickle bar.** (in a mower, binder, or combine) a bar with triangular guards along which a knife or blade runs. 2. a bar holding the cutting tool in a boring machine or lathe. [1865–70]

cut′ter deck′, the blade housing on a power mower. Also called **deck, mower deck.**

Cut′ter num′ber (kut′ər), *Library Science.* a code combining decimal numbers with letters from an author's surname, used in an alphabetizing system. [after Charles A. *Cutter* (1837–1903), U.S. librarian, whose classification system had a similar feature]

cut·ter-rigged (kut′ər rigd′), *adj.* fore-and-aft-rigged on one mast in the manner of a cutter. [1790–1800]

cut·throat (kut′thrōt′), *n.* 1. a person who cuts throats; murderer. —*adj.* 2. murderous. 3. ruthless: *cutthroat competition.* 4. pertaining to a game, as of cards, in which each of three or more persons acts and scores as an individual. [1525–35; CUT + THROAT]

cut′throat con′tract, *Bridge.* 1. a form of contract bridge for four persons in which partners are decided by the bidding. 2. any of a variety of contract bridge games for three persons. [1940–45]

cut′throat trout′, a spotted trout, *Salmo clarkii,* of coastal streams of western North America, having a reddish streak on each side of the throat. [1890–95, *Amer.*]

cut′ time′, *Music.* See **alla breve.**

cut·ting (kut′ing), *n.* 1. the act of a person or thing that cuts. 2. something cut, cut off, or cut out. 3. *Hort.* a piece, as a root, stem, or leaf, cut from a plant and used for propagation. 4. something made by cutting, as a recording. 5. *Chiefly Brit.* a clipping from a newspaper, magazine, etc. 6. *Brit.* a trenchlike excavation, esp. through a hill, as one made in constructing a highway. —*adj.* 7. that cuts; penetrating or dividing by, or as if by, a cut. 8. piercing, as a wind. 9. wounding the feelings severely; sarcastic. [1350–1400; ME; see CUT, -ING[1], -ING[2]] —**cut′ting·ly,** *adv.* —**cut′ting·ness,** *n.*

cut′ting board′, a board used as a firm surface for cutting food, cloth, leather, etc. [1815–25]

cut′ting edge′, 1. the sharp edge of a cutting implement. 2. forefront; lead: *on the cutting edge of computer technology.* [1950–55] —**cut′ting-edge′,** *adj.*

cut′ting flu′id, a liquid or gas for cooling or lubricating a cutting tool and a piece of work at their point of contact.

cut′ting gar′den, a household flower garden planted solely for growing flowers that are to be cut and displayed indoors.

cut′ting horse′, a saddle horse trained to separate calves, steers, etc., from a herd. [1880–85]

cut′ting oil′, a specially prepared oil used as a cutting fluid. [1915–20]

cut′ting room′, *Motion Pictures.* a film-editing room. [1830–40, for earlier sense]

cut′ting sty′lus, stylus (def. 2a).

cut·tle[1] (kut′l), *n.* 1. cuttlefish. 2. cuttlebone. [bef. 1000; late ME *codel,* OE *cudele* (replaced in the 16th century by CUTTLEFISH and subsequently reshortened)]

cut·tle[2] (kut′l), *v.t.,* **-tled, -tling.** *Textiles.* 1. to fold (cloth) face to face after finishing. 2. to allow (cloth) to lie without further treatment after fulling, milling, scouring, etc. [1535–45; orig. uncert.]

cut·tle·bone (kut′l bōn′), *n.* the calcareous internal shell of cuttlefishes, used to make powder for polishing and fed to canaries and other pet birds to supply their diet with lime. [1805–15; CUTTLE(FISH) + BONE]

cut·tle·fish (kut′l fish′), *n., pl.* (*esp. collectively*) **-fish,** (*esp. referring to two or more kinds or species*) **-fish·es.** any of several cephalopods, esp. of the genus *Sepia,* having eight arms with suckers and two tentacles, and ejecting a black, inklike fluid when in danger. [1400–50; late ME *codel,* OE *cudele* cuttlefish + FISH]

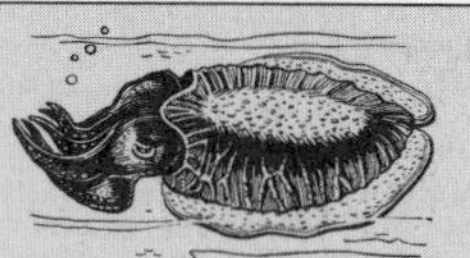

cuttlefish, *Sepia officinalis,* length to 10 in. (25 cm)

cut·ty (kut′ē), *adj., n., pl.* **-ties.** *Chiefly Scot.* —*adj.* 1. cut short; short; stubby. 2. irritable; impatient; short-tempered. —*n.* 3. a short spoon. 4. a short-stemmed tobacco pipe. 5. *Informal.* an immoral or worthless woman. [1650–60; CUT + -Y[1], -Y[2]]

cut·ty·hunk (kut′ē hungk′), *n.* a twisted, linen fishline, esp. one laid by hand. [1915–20, *Amer.*; named after *Cuttyhunk* Island, Massachusetts]

cut′ty stool′, *Scot.* 1. a low stool. 2. (formerly) a seat in churches where offenders against chastity, or other delinquents, received public rebuke. [1765–75]

cut·up (kut′up′), *n. Informal.* a prankster or show-off. [1775–85; n. use of v. phrase *cut up*]

cut′-up po′em (kut′up′), a poem created from parts of the works of various authors combined to form one composition. Also called **aleatory poem.**

cut′ vel′vet, 1. a fabric in which the looped pile has been cut. Cf. **velvet.** 2. a fabric having a pattern of figured velvet with a backing of chiffon or voile.

CONCISE ETYMOLOGY KEY: <, descended or borrowed from; >, whence; b., blend of, blended; c., cognate with; cf., compare; deriv., derivative; equiv., equivalent; imit., imitative; obl., oblique; r., replacing; s., stem; sp., spelling, spelled; resp., respelling, respelled; trans., translation; ?, origin unknown; *, unattested; ‡, probably earlier than. See the full key inside the front cover.

cut·ware (kut′wâr′), *n.* tools used in cutting, as knives or blades. [CUT + WARE[1]]

cut·wa·ter (kut′wô′tər, -wot′ər), *n.* 1. *Naut.* a. the forward edge of the stem of a vessel, dividing the water as the vessel advances. b. a vertical timber construction set forward of and following the stem of a wooden vessel below the water line, usually curving forward above the water line to support a beak-head or figurehead. 2. *Civ. Engin.* a sharply pointed upstream face of a bridge pier, for resisting the effects of moving water or ice. [1635–45; CUT + WATER]

cut·work (kut′wûrk′), *n.* 1. openwork embroidery in which the ground fabric is cut out about the pattern. 2. fretwork formed by perforation or cut in low relief. 3. ornamental needlework in which spaces are cut from a ground material into which are inserted decorative figures that were made separately. 4. See **point coupé** (def. 1). [1425–75; late ME *cut werk.* See CUT, WORK]

cut′work lace′. See **point coupé** (def. 2).

cut·worm (kut′wûrm′), *n.* the caterpillar of any of several noctuid moths, which feeds at night on the stems of young plants, cutting them off at the ground. [1800–10; CUT + WORM]

cuve (kyv), *n., pl.* ***cuves*** (kyv). *French.* a wine vat.

cu·vée (ko͞o vā′; *Fr.* ky vā′), *n.* 1. wine in vats or casks, blended, often from different vintages, for uniform quality. 2. a blend resulting from the mixing of wines, esp. of champagnes produced by several vineyards in the same district. [1825–35; < F, equiv. to *cuve* cask, vat (<< L *cūpa;* cf. CUP) + *-ée* ptp. suffix; see -EE]

cu·vette (ko͞o vet′, kyo͞o-), *n.* 1. Also, **curvette.** Also called **chevee.** a gemstone with a raised, cameolike figure or design carved on its hollowed surface. 2. *Chem.* a tube or vessel used in laboratory experimentation. [1670–80; < F, dim. of *cuve* vat << L *cūpa.* See CUP, -ETTE]

Cu·vi·er (kyo͞o′vē ā′, ko͞ov yā′; *Fr.* ky vyā′), *n.* **Georges Lé·o·pold Chré·tien Fré·dé·ric Da·go·bert** (zhôrzh lā ô pôld′ krā tyaN′ frā dā rēk′ dA gô beR′), **Baron,** 1769–1832, French naturalist: pioneer in the fields of paleontology and comparative anatomy.

Cux·ha·ven (ko͝oks′hä′fən), *n.* a seaport in NW Germany, at the mouth of the Elbe River. 60,200.

Cu·ya·bá (ko͞o′yä bä′), *n.* Cuiabá.

Cuy′a·hog′a Falls′ (kī′ə hog′ə; *older* kī′ə hō′gə), a city in NE Ohio, near Akron. 43,710.

Cuyp (koip), *n.* **Ael·bert** (äl′beRt), 1620–91, Dutch painter. Also, **Kuyp.**

Cuz·co (ko͞os′kō; *Sp.* ko͞os′kô), *n.* a city in S Peru: ancient Inca ruins. 121,464. Also, **Cusco.**

CV, 1. cardiovascular. 2. Also, **C.V.** curriculum vitae.

cv, convertible. Also, **cvt.**

CVA, 1. *Pathol.* cerebrovascular accident. See **stroke.** 2. Columbia Valley Authority.

CVD, *Com.* countervailing duty.

C.V.O., Commander of the Royal Victorian Order.

CVT, See **continuously variable transmission.**

CW, 1. chemical warfare. 2. *Radio.* continuous wave.

cw, clockwise.

CWA, 1. Civil Works Administration. 2. Communications Workers of America.

cwm (ko͞om), *n.* cirque (def. 1). [1850–55; < Welsh: valley. See COMBE]

Cwm·bran (ko͝om brän′), *n.* a town in Gwent, in SE Wales. 31,614.

CWO, *Mil.* chief warrant officer.

c.w.o., cash with order.

CWP, 1. Also, **C.W.P.** Communist Workers Party. 2. crossword puzzle.

CWPS, Council on Wage and Price Stability.

cwt, hundredweight; hundredweights.

Cy (sī), *n.* a male given name, form of **Cyrus.**

CY, calendar year.

cy, cycle; cycles.

-cy, 1. a suffix used to form abstract nouns from adjectives with stems in *-t, -te, -tic,* and esp. *-nt* (*democracy; accuracy; expediency; stagnancy; lunacy*), and sometimes used to form action nouns (*vacancy; occupancy*). 2. a suffix of nouns denoting rank or office, sometimes attached to the stem of a word rather than to the word itself: *captaincy; magistracy.* [repr. F *-cie, -tie,* L *-cia, -tia,* Gk *-kia, -keia, -tia, -teia;* in most cases to be analyzed as consonant + -Y[3]: the consonant making the whole or the last member of the preceding morpheme]

Cy., county.

cy., 1. capacity. 2. currency. 3. cycle; cycles.

CYA, *Slang* (*sometimes vulgar*). cover your ass.

cy·an (sī′an, sī′ən), *n.* See **cyan blue.** [1885–90; < Gk *kýanos* dark blue]

cyan-[1], var. of **cyano-**[1], usually before a vowel or *h: cyanamide.*

cyan-[2], var. of **cyano-**[2], before a vowel.

cyan-[3], var. of **cyano-**[3], before a vowel.

cy·an·a·mide (sī an′ə mid, -mīd′, sī′ə nam′id, -id), *n. Chem.* 1. a white, crystalline, unstable, deliquescent solid, CH_2N_2, usually produced by the action of ammonia on cyanogen chloride or by the action of sulfuric acid on calcium cyanamide. 2. (not in technical use) See **calcium cyanamide.** Also, **cy·an·a·mid** (sī an′ə mid, sī′ə nam′id). [1830–40; CYAN-[2] + AMIDE]

cy·a·nate (sī′ə nāt′, -nit), *n. Chem.* a salt or ester of cyanic acid. [1835–45; CYAN(IC ACID) + -ATE[2]]

cy′an blue′, a moderate greenish-blue to bluish-green color. [1875–80]

cy·an·e·ous (sī an′ē əs), *adj.* deep blue; cerulean. [1680–90; < L *cyaneus* < Gk *kyáneos.* See CYAN-[1], -EOUS]

cy·an·ic (sī an′ik), *adj.* 1. blue: applied esp. to a series of colors in flowers, including the blues and colors tending toward blue. 2. *Chem.* containing or pertaining to the cyano group. [1825–35; CYAN-[1] + -IC]

cyan′ic ac′id, *Chem.* an unstable, poisonous, liquid acid, HOCN, isomeric with fulminic acid. [1825–35]

cy·a·nide (sī′ə nīd′, -nid), *n., v.,* **-nid·ed, -nid·ing.** —*n.* 1. Also, **cy·a·nid** (sī′ə nid). *Chem.* a. a salt of hydrocyanic acid, as potassium cyanide, KCN. b. a nitrile, as methyl cyanide, C_2H_3N. —*v.t.* 2. to treat with a cyanide, as an ore in order to extract gold. [1820–30; CYAN-[3] + -IDE]

cy′anide proc′ess, a process for extracting gold or silver from ore by dissolving the ore in an alkaline solution of sodium cyanide or potassium cyanide and precipitating the gold or silver from the solution. [1885–90]

cy·a·nine (sī′ə nēn′, -nin), *n.* any of several groups of dyes that make silver halide photographic plates sensitive to a wider color range. Also, **cy·a·nin** (sī′ə nin). [1870–75; CYAN-[1] + -INE[2]]

cy·a·nite (sī′ə nīt′), *n. Mineral.* kyanite. [1785–95; CYAN-[1] + -ITE[1]] —**cy·a·nit·ic** (sī′ə nit′ik), *adj.*

cy·a·no (sī′ə nō′, sī an′ō), *adj. Chem.* containing the cyano group. [1960–65; independent use of CYANO-[3]]

cyano-[1], a combining form meaning "blue, dark blue," used in the formation of compound words: *cyanotype.* Also, *esp. before a vowel,* **cyan-**[1]. [< Gk *kýano(s)* dark blue (adj.), dark-blue substance (n.)]

cyano-[2], a combining form representing **cyanide** in the formation of compound words: *cyanogen.* Also, *esp. before a vowel,* **cyan-**[2].

cyano-[3], a combining form used in the names of chemical compounds in which the cyano group is present: *cyanohydrin.* Also, *esp. before a vowel,* **cyan-**[3]. [comb. form repr. CYANOGEN]

cy·a·no·ac·ry·late (sī′ə nō ak′rə lāt′, -lit, sī an′ō-), *n. Chem.* a colorless liquid acrylate monomer that is easily polymerized and used as a powerful, fast-acting adhesive. [1960–65; CYANO-[2] + ACRYLATE]

cy·a·no·bac·te·ri·a (sī′ə nō bak tēr′ē ə, sī an′ō-), *n.pl., sing.* **-te·ri·um** (-tēr′ē əm). *Biol.* blue-green algae. [1975–80; CYANO-[1] + BACTERIA]

cy·a·no·co·bal·a·min (sī′ə nō kō bal′ə min, sī an′ō-), *n. Biochem.* See **vitamin B_{12}.** [1945–50; CYANO-[3] + COBAL(T) + (VIT)AMIN]

cy·an·o·gen (sī an′ə jən, -jen′), *n.* 1. a colorless, poisonous, flammable, water-soluble gas, C_2N_2, having an almondlike odor: used chiefly in organic synthesis. 2. See **cyano group.** [1820–30; CYANO-[1] + -GEN]

cyan′ogen bro′mide, a colorless, slightly water-soluble, poisonous, volatile, crystalline solid, BrCN, used chiefly as a fumigant and a pesticide.

cyan′ogen chlo′ride, a colorless, volatile, poisonous liquid, CNCl, used chiefly in the synthesis of compounds containing the cyano group.

cy·a·no·gen·ic (sī′ə nō jen′ik, sī an′ə-), *adj. Biol., Chem.* capable of producing hydrogen cyanide. Also, **cy·a·no·ge·net·ic** (sī′ə nō jə net′ik, sī an′ō-). [CYANOGEN + -IC] —**cy′a·no·gen′e·sis,** *n.*

cy′ano group′, *Chem.* the univalent group CN; cyanogen.

cy·a·no·guan·i·dine (sī′ə nō gwä′ni dēn′, -din, sī an′ō-), *n. Chem.* dicyandiamide. [CYANO-[2] + GUANIDINE]

cy·a·no·hy·drin (sī′ə nō hī′drin, sī an′ō-), *n.* any of a class of organic chemical compounds that contains both the CN and the OH group, usually linked to the same carbon atom. [1920–25; CYANO-[3] + HYDR-[2] + -IN[2]]

cy·a·nom·e·ter (sī′ə nom′i tər), *n. Optics.* an instrument for measuring the amount and intensity of blue in light, as of the sky. [1820–30; CYANO-[1] + -METER]

Cy·a·noph·y·ta (sī′ə nof′i tə), *n. Biol.* a phylum, or subkingdom, in the kingdom Monera, comprising the blue-green algae. [< NL; see CYANO-[1], -PHYTA]

cy·a·no·phyte (sī′ə nō fīt′, sī an′ə-), *Biol.* —*n.* 1. any member of the phylum Cyanophyta. —*adj.* 2. belonging or pertaining to the Cyanophyta. [see CYANOPHYTA, -PHYTE]

cy·a·no·plat·i·nite (sī′ə nō plat′n īt′, sī an′ō-), *n. Chem.* platinocyanide. [CYANO-[2] + PLATINITE]

cy·a·no·sis (sī′ə nō′sis), *n. Pathol.* blueness or lividness of the skin, as from imperfectly oxygenated blood. [1825–35; < NL < Gk *kyánōsis* dark-blue color. See CYAN-[1], -OSIS] —**cy·a·not·ic** (sī′ə not′ik), *adj.*

cy·an·o·type (sī an′ə tīp′), *n.* 1. a process of photographic printing, used chiefly in copying architectural and mechanical drawings, that produces a blue line on a white background. 2. a print made by this process. [1835–45; CYANO-[1] + -TYPE]

cy·a·nu·rate (sī′ə no͝or′āt, -it, -nyo͝or′-), *n.* the salt or ester of cyanuric acid. [CYANUR(IC ACID) + -ATE[2]]

cy·a·nu·ric (sī′ə no͝or′ik, -nyo͝or′-), *adj.* of or derived from cyanuric acid. [1875–80; CYAN-[3] + URIC]

cy′anu′ric ac′id, a white, crystalline, water-soluble solid, $C_3H_3O_3N_3 \cdot 2H_2O$, used chiefly in organic synthesis. Also called **tricyanic acid.** [1875–80]

cy·ath·i·form (sī ath′ə fôrm′), *adj. Bot., Zool.* shaped like a cup. [1770–80; CYATH(IUM) + -I- + -FORM]

cy·ath·i·um (sī ath′ē əm), *n., pl.* **-ath·i·a** (-ath′ē ə). *Bot.* an inflorescence consisting of a cup-shaped involucre enclosing an apetalous, pistillate flower surrounded by several staminate flowers. [< NL < Gk *kyáthion,* dim. of *kýathos* ladle]

cy·a·thus (sī′ə thəs), *n., pl.* **-thi** (-thī′). kyathos. [< L < Gk *kýathos* KYATHOS]

Cyb·e·le (sib′ə lē′), *n.* a mother goddess of Phrygia and Asia Minor, identified by the Greeks with Rhea and by the Romans with Ops. Also, **Cy·be·be** (si bē′bē). Also called **Berecyntia, Dindymene.**

cy•ber•nate (sī′bər nāt′), *v.t.*, **-nat•ed, -nat•ing.** to control by cybernation. [1960–65; back formation from CYBERNATION]

cy•ber•na•tion (sī′bər nā′shən), *n.* the use of computers to control automatic processes, esp. in manufacturing. [1960–65; CYBERN(ETIC) + -ATION]

cy•ber•net•ics (sī′bər net′iks), *n.* (*used with a singular v.*) the study of human control functions and of mechanical and electronic systems designed to replace them, involving the application of statistical mechanics to communication engineering. [< Gk *kybernḗt(ēs)* helmsman, steersman (*kybernē-*, var. s. of *kybernân* to steer + *-tēs* agent suffix) + -ICS; term introduced by Norbert Wiener in 1948] —**cy′ber•net′ic, cy′ber•net′i•cal,** *adj.* —**cy′ber•net′i•cal•ly,** *adv.* —**cy′ber•net′i•cist, cy•ber•ne•ti•cian** (sī′bər ni tish′ən), *n.*

cy•ber•pho•bi•a (sī′bər fō′bē ə), *n. Psychiatry.* an abnormal fear of working with computers. [CYBER(NETIC) + -PHOBIA] —**cy′ber•phobe′,** *n.* —**cy′ber•pho′bic,** *adj.*

cy•ber•punk (sī′bər pungk′), *n.* **1.** science fiction featuring extensive human interaction with supercomputers and a punk ambiance. **2.** *Slang.* a computer hacker. [1985–90; CYBER(NETIC) + PUNK²]

cy•ber•space (sībər spās′), *n.* See **virtual reality.** [1985–90; CYBER(NETIC) + SPACE]

cy•borg (sī′bôrg), *n.* a person whose physiological functioning is aided by or dependent upon a mechanical or electronic device. [1960–65; *cyb(ernetic) org(anism)*]

cyc (sīk), *n. Informal.* cyclorama (def. 2). [shortened form]

CYC, cyclophosphamide.

cyc., cyclopedia.

cy•cad (sī′kad), *n.* any gymnospermous plant of the order Cycadales, intermediate in appearance between ferns and the palms, many species having a thick, unbranched, columnar trunk bearing a crown of large, leathery, pinnate leaves. [1835–45; < NL *Cycad-* (s. of *Cycas*) genus name < Gk *kýkas*, misspelling of *kóïkas*, acc. pl. of *kóïx* kind of palm] —**cy′cad•like′,** *adj.*

cy•ca•da•ceous (sī′kə dā′shəs, sik′ə), *adj.* belonging or pertaining to the order Cycadales. [1830–40; < NL *Cycad-* (see CYCAD) + -ACEOUS]

cy•cas (sī′kas, -kəs), *n.* any of several palmlike Old World tropical plants of the genus *Cycas*, some species of which are cultivated as ornamentals in warm climates. [< NL; see CYCAD]

cy•ca•sin (sī′kə sin), *n.* a naturally occurring toxic glucoside, $C_8H_{16}N_2O_7$, obtained from the seeds of cycad plants, carcinogenic in humans and other mammals. [appar. CYCAS + -IN²]

cycl-, var. of **cyclo-,** before a vowel: *cycloid.*

cy•cla•ble (sī′klə bəl), *adj.* fit or designed for bicycle riding: *a cyclable road.* [CYCLE + -ABLE]

Cyc•la•des (sik′lə dēz′), *n.* a group of Greek islands in the S Aegean. 86,337; 1023 sq. mi. (2650 sq. km).

Cy•clad•ic (si klad′ik, sī-), *adj.* **1.** of or pertaining to the Cyclades. **2.** of or pertaining to the Bronze Age culture of the Cyclades, c3000–c1100 B.C. [1910–15; CY-CLAD(ES) + -IC]

cy•cla•mate (sī′klə māt′, sik′lə-), *n.* any of several chemical compounds used as a noncaloric sweetening agent in foods and beverages: banned by the FDA in 1970 as a possible carcinogen. [1950–55; CYCLAM(IC ACID) + -ATE²]

cy•cla•men (sī′klə mən, -men′, sik′lə-), *n.* any plant of the genus *Cyclamen*, belonging to the primrose family, having nodding white, purple, pink, or crimson flowers with reflexed petals. [1540–50; < NL, ML < Gk *kykláminos* bulbous plant, akin to *kýklos* CYCLE]

cy′clamen al′dehyde, a colorless to light-yellow alcohol-soluble, synthetic liquid, $C_{13}H_{18}O$, having a strong floral odor, used chiefly in perfumes, esp. those of soap.

cy′cla•mic ac′id (sī′klə mik, sik′lə-), a white crystalline solid, $C_6H_{13}NSO_3$, the salts of which are referred to as cyclamates: used as an acidulant. Also called **cyclohexylsulfamic acid.** [CYCL(OHEXYLSULF)AMIC ACID]

cy•clan•de•late (sī klan′dl āt′, -it), *n. Pharm.* a vasodilator, $C_{17}H_{24}O_3$, used to treat certain vascular diseases. [CYCL- + (M)ANDEL(IC ACID) + -ATE²]

cyc•las (sik′ləs), *n., pl.* **-la•des** (-lə dēz′). **1.** a tunic or surcoat, longer in back than in front, worn over armor in the Middle Ages. **2.** a similar, full-length garment worn by women. **3.** a round robe with an elaborately ornamented border, worn by women in ancient Rome. [1825–35; < ML, L < Gk *kyklás*, n. use of *kyklás* encircling, akin to *kýklos* CYCLE]

cy•clase (sī′klās, -klāz), *n. Biochem.* an enzyme, as adenyl cyclase, that catalyzes the formation of a cyclic compound. [1940–45; CYCL(IC) + -ASE]

cy•claz•o•cine (sī klaz′ə sēn′, -sin, sī′klə zō′sēn, -sin), *n. Pharm.* a synthetic nonnarcotic and nonaddictive analgesic, $C_{18}H_{25}NO$, that blocks the effects of morphine or morphinelike drugs: used to treat heroin or morphine addiction. [contr. and alter. of the chemical name]

cy•cle (sī′kəl), *n., v.,* **-cled, -cling.** —*n.* **1.** any complete round or series of occurrences that repeats or is repeated. **2.** a round of years or a recurring period of time, esp. one in which certain events or phenomena repeat themselves in the same order and at the same intervals. **3.** any long period of years; age. **4.** a bicycle, motorcycle, tricycle, etc. **5.** a group of poems, dramas, prose narratives, songs etc., about a central theme, figure, or the like: *the Arthurian cycle.* **6.** *Physics.* **a.** a sequence of changing states that, upon completion, produces a final state identical to the original one. **b.** one of a succession of periodically recurring events. **c.** a complete alteration in which a phenomenon attains a maximum and minimum value, returning to a final value equal to the original one. **7.** *Math.* a permutation of a set of elements that leaves the original cyclic order of the elements unchanged. **8.** *Computers.* **a.** the smallest interval of time required to complete an operation in a computer. **b.** a series of computer operations repeated as a unit. **9. hit for the cycle,** *Baseball.* (of one player) to hit a single, double, triple, and home run in one game. —*v.i.* **10.** to ride or travel by bicycle, motorcycle, tricycle, etc. **11.** to move or revolve in cycles; pass through cycles. [1350–1400; ME *cicle* < LL *cyclus* < Gk *kýklos* cycle, circle, wheel, ring, disk, orb; see WHEEL]

cy′cle bill′ing, a method of billing customers at monthly intervals in which statements are prepared on each working day of the month and mailed to a designated fraction of the total number of customers.

cy•cle•car (sī′kəl kär′), *n.* a light automobile, open like a motorcycle but having three or four wheels. [1910–15; (MOTOR)CYCLE + CAR¹]

cy′cle of indic′tion, indiction (def. 3).

cy•cle•ry (sī′kəl rē, -klə-), *n., pl.* **-ries.** a shop that sells, rents, or services bicycles. Also called **cy′cle shop′.** [1895–1900, *Amer.*; CYCLE + -(E)RY]

cy•clic (sī′klik, sik′lik), *adj.* **1.** revolving or recurring in cycles; characterized by recurrence in cycles. **2.** of, pertaining to, or constituting a cycle or cycles. **3.** *Chem.* of or pertaining to a compound that contains a closed chain or ring of atoms (contrasted with *acyclic*). **4.** *Bot.* **a.** arranged in whorls, as the parts of a flower. **b.** (of a flower) having the parts so arranged. **5.** *Math.* **a.** pertaining to an algebraic system in which all the elements of a group are powers of one element. **b.** (of a set of elements) arranged as if on a circle, so that the first element follows the last. [1785–95; < L *cyclicus* < Gk *kyklikós* circular. See CYCLE, -IC] —**cy•clic•i•ty** (sī klis′i tē), *n.*

cy•cli•cal (sī′kli kəl, sik′li-), *adj.* **1.** cyclic. **2.** of or denoting a business or stock whose income, value, or earnings fluctuate widely according to variations in the economy or the cycle of the seasons. —*n.* **3.** Usually, **cyclicals.** stocks of cyclical companies. [1810–20; CYCLIC + -AL¹] —**cy′cli•cal•ly,** *adv.* —**cy′cli•cal′i•ty,** *n.*

cy′clical unemploy′ment, periodic unemployment caused by fluctuations in the business cycle.

cyclic AMP, *Biochem.* a cyclic anhydride of adenosine monophosphate formed from adenosine triphosphate by the action of adenylate cyclase: in cellular metabolism, it acts as an intracellular amplifier or second messenger of signals derived from hormones or neurotransmitters. Also called **cAMP, adenosine cyclic monophosphate.** [1965–70]

cyclic GMP, *Biochem.* a cyclic anhydride of guanosine monophosphate formed from guanosine triphosphate by the action of guanylate cyclase: in cellular metabolism, it acts as a second messenger associated with increased cell division and growth. Also called **cGMP, guanosine cyclic monophosphate, guanosine 3′,5′-cyclic monophosphate.** [1970–75]

cy′clic shift′, *Computers.* a transfer of digits from one end of a machine word to the other, retaining the same order in both places.

cy•cling (sī′kling), *n.* **1.** the act or sport of riding or traveling by bicycle, motorcycle, etc. **2.** Also called **bicycle race, bicycle racing.** *Sports.* a race on lightweight bicycles with low handlebars, conducted for specified distances or against time on a dirt or board track or over public roads between cities. [1935–40; CYCLE + -ING¹]

cy•clist (sī′klist), *n.* a person who rides a bicycle, motorcycle, etc. Also, **cy′cler.** [1880–85; CYCLE + -IST]

cy•cli•za•tion (sī′klə zā′shən, sik′lə-), *n. Chem.* the formation of a ring or rings. [1905–10; CYCLIZE + -ATION]

cy•clize (sī′klīz, sik′līz), *v.,* **-clized, -cliz•ing.** *Chem.* —*v.t.* **1.** to cause cyclization. —*v.i.* **2.** to undergo cyclization. Also, *esp. Brit.,* **cy′clise.** [1905–10; CYCLE + -IZE]

cy•cli•zine (sī′klə zēn′), *n. Pharm.* a substance, $C_{18}H_{22}N_2$, used primarily to prevent and treat motion sickness. [appar. CYCL- + -I- + (PIPERA)ZINE]

cy•clo (sē′klō, sī-), *n., pl.* **-clos.** *n.* a three-wheeled pedaled or motorized taxi in southeast Asia; rickshaw. [< F *cyclo(-pousse)*, equiv. to *cyclo-* comb. form repr. *cycle* motorized or pedaled bicycle or tricycle (see CY-CLO-) + *pousse* appar. short for *pousse-pousse* rickshaw (redupl. of *pousse*, n. deriv. of *pousser* to PUSH)]

cyclo-, a combining form meaning "cycle," used in the formation of compound words: *cyclohexane.* Also, *esp. before a vowel,* **cycl-.** [< Gk *kyklo-*, comb. form of *kýklos* circle, ring; c. Skt *cakra*, WHEEL]

cy•clo•ad•di•tion (sī′klō ə dish′ən, sik′lō-), *n. Chem.* the formation of a cyclic compound by the addition reaction of unsaturated molecules. [1960–65; CYCLO- + ADDITION]

cy•clo•al•i•phat•ic (sī′klō al′ə fat′ik, sik′lō-), *n. Chem.* alicyclic. [1935–40; CYCLO- + ALIPHATIC]

cy•clo-cross (sī′klō krôs′, -kros′), *n.* a bicycle race over a cross-country course, featuring steep hills, turns, and sometimes muddy terrain, that occasionally requires a rider to carry the bicycle over fences and up stairs. [1950–55; CYCLE + -O- + CROSS(COUNTRY); cf. MOTOCROSS]

cy•clo•di•ene (sī′klə dī′ēn, -dī ēn′), *n. Chem.* any of several organic chemicals having a chlorinated methylene group bonded to two carbon atoms of a 6-membered carbon ring, used commercially in insecticides. [1940–45; CYCLO- + DIENE]

cy•clo•gen•e•sis (sī′klə jen′ə sis, sik′lə-), *n. Meteorol.* the intensification or development of a cyclone. Cf. **cyclolysis.** [1935–40; CYCLO(NE) + GENESIS]

cy•clo•hex•ane (sī′klə hek′sān, sik′lə-), *n. Chem.* a colorless, pungent, flammable liquid, C_6H_{12}, composed of a ring of six methylene groups, derived from crude petroleum by distillation or from benzene by hydrogenation: used chiefly as a solvent and in the manufacture of adipic acid. Also called **hexahydrobenzene, hexamethylene, hexanaphthene.** [1920–25; CYCLO- + HEXANE]

cy•clo•hex•a•none (sī′klō hek′sə nōn′, sik′lō-), *n. Chem.* an oily liquid, $C_6H_{10}O$, with an acetone and peppermintlike odor, a cyclic butone used in organic synthesis and as an industrial solvent. [1905–10; see CYCLO-HEXANE, -ONE]

cy•clo•hex•i•mide (sī′klō hek′sə mīd′, -mid), *n. Pharm.* an antibiotic substance, $C_{15}H_{23}NO_4$, isolated from the bacterium *Streptomyces griseus*, used experimentally to block protein synthesis. [1945–50; CY-CLOHEX(ANE) + IMIDE]

cy•clo•hex•yl•a•mine (sī′klō hek sil′ə mēn′, -min, -hek′sə lə-, sik′lō-), *n. Chem.* a colorless liquid with an unpleasant odor, $C_6H_{11}NH_2$, a strong organic base used in the manufacture of plastics and rubber and as a corrosion inhibitor. Also called **aminocyclohexane, hexahydroaniline.** [1940–45; CYCLO- + HEXYL + AMINE]

cy′clo•hex′yl•sul•fam′ic ac′id (sī′klə hek′səl-sul fam′ik, sik′lə-), *Chem.* See **cyclamic acid.** [CYCLO- + HEXYL + *sulfamic acid* (appar. (*chloro*)*sulf*(*onic*) + AM(MONIA) + -IC)]

cy•cloid (sī′kloid), *adj.* **1.** resembling a circle; circular. **2.** (of the scale of a fish) smooth-edged, more or less circular in form, and having concentric striations. **3.** (of a fish) having such scales. **4.** *Psychiatry.* of or noting a personality type characterized by wide fluctuation in mood within the normal range. —*n.* **5.** a cycloid fish. **6.** *Geom.* a curve generated by a point on the circumference of a circle that rolls, without slipping, on a straight line. [1655–65; < Gk *kykloeidḗs* like a circle. See CYCL-, -OID] —**cy•cloi′dal,** *adj.* —**cy•cloi′dal•ly,** *adv.*

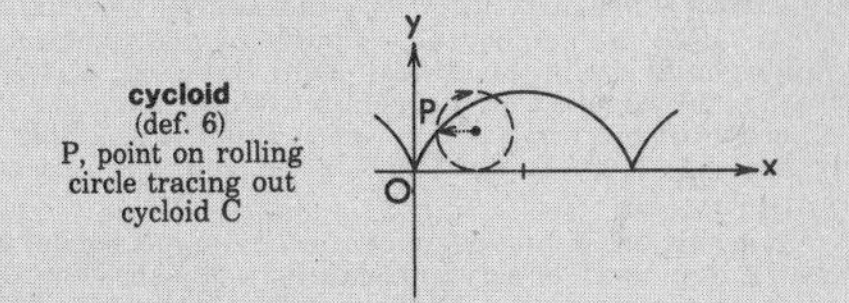

cycloid (def. 6) P, point on rolling circle tracing out cycloid C

cycloi′dal propul′sion, *Naut.* propulsion of a vessel by propellers of controllable pitch that steer as well as propel.

cy•clol•y•sis (sī klol′ə sis), *n. Meteorol.* the weakening or extinction of a cyclone. Cf. **cyclogenesis.** [CY-CLO(NE) + -LYSIS]

cy•clom•e•ter (sī klom′i tər), *n.* **1.** an instrument that measures circular arcs. **2.** a device for recording the revolutions of a wheel and hence the distance traversed by a wheeled vehicle; odometer. [1805–15; CYCLO- + -METER] —**cy•clo•met•ric** (sī′klə me′trik), *adj.*

cy•clo•nal (sī klōn′l), *adj.* of or like a cyclone. [1880–85; CYCLONE + -AL¹]

cy•clone (sī′klōn), *n.* **1.** a large-scale, atmospheric wind-and-pressure system characterized by low pressure at its center and by circular wind motion, counterclockwise in the Northern Hemisphere, clockwise in the Southern Hemisphere. Cf. **anticyclone, extratropical cyclone, tropical cyclone. 2.** (not in technical use) tornado. **3.** Also called **cy′clone collec′tor, cy′clone sep′arator.** *Mach.* a device for removing small or powdered solids from air, water, or other gases or liquids by centrifugal force. [term introduced by British meteorologist Henry Piddington (1797–1858) in 1848, perh. < Gk *kyklôn* revolving (prp. of *kykloûn* to revolve, v. deriv. of *kýklos*; see CYCLE); appar. confused by Piddington with *kýklōma* wheel, snake's coil]

cy′clone cel′lar, a cellar or other underground place for shelter from cyclones and tornadoes. Also called **storm cellar.** [1885–90, *Amer.*]

Cy′clone fence′, *Trademark.* a brand of chain-link fence.

cy′clone fur′nace, a furnace burning liquid or pulverized fuel in a whirling air column.

cy•clon•ic (sī klon′ik), *adj. Meteorol.* **1.** of or pertaining to a cyclone. **2.** describing a direction of rotation that is counterclockwise in the Northern Hemisphere, clockwise in the Southern Hemisphere. Also, **cy•clon′i•cal.** [1855–60; CYCLONE + -IC] —**cy•clon′i•cal•ly,** *adv.*

cy•clo•nite (sī′klə nīt′, sik′lə-), *n. Chem.* See **RDX.** [1920–25; CYCLO- + (TRI)NIT(RO-) + (AMIN)E]

cy•clo•oc•ta•tet•ra•ene (sī′klō ok′tə te′trə ēn′), *n. Chem.* a colorless, flammable liquid cyclic hydrocarbon, C_8H_8, used in organic research. [CYCLO- + OCTA- + TETRA- + -ENE]

cy•clo•o•le•fin (sī′klō ō′lə fin, sik′lō-), *n. Chem.* any of the homologous series of unsaturated, alicyclic hydrocarbons, as cyclooctatetraene and cyclopentadiene, containing one double bond in the ring and having the general formula $C_{11}H_{2n-2}$. [1920–25; CYCLO- + OLEFIN]

cy•clo•par•af•fin (sī′klə par′ə fin, sik′lə-), *n. Chem.* any of the homologous series of saturated, alicyclic hydrocarbons having the general formula C_nH_{2n}. [1895–1900; CYCLO- + PARAFFIN]

Cy•clo•pe•an (sī′klə pē′ən, sī klop′ē ən), *adj.* **1.** of or characteristic of the Cyclops. **2.** (*sometimes l.c.*) gigantic; vast. **3.** (*usually l.c.*) *Archit., Building Trades.* formed with or containing large, undressed stones fitted closely together without the use of mortar: *a cyclopean wall.* [1635–45; < L *Cyclōpē(us)* (< Gk *Kyklṓpeios*, equiv. to *Kyklōp(s)* CYCLOPS + -*eios* -EOUS) + -AN]

cy′clope′an con′crete, concrete containing stones larger than 6 in. (15 cm).

cy•clo•pe•di•a (sī′klə pē′dē ə), *n.* an encyclopedia. Also, **cy′clo•pae′di•a.** [1630–40; by aphesis] —**cy′clo•pe′dist, cy′clo•pae′dist,** *n.*

CONCISE PRONUNCIATION KEY: *act, cāpe, dâre, pärt; set, ēqual; if, īce; ox, ōver, ôrder, oil, bo͝ok, bo͞ot, out; up, ûrge; child; sing; shoe; thin,* t͟hat; zh *as in treasure.* ə = *a as in alone, e as in system, i as in easily, o as in gallop, u as in circus;* ᵊ *as in fire* (fīᵊr), *hour* (ouᵊr). l and n can serve as syllabic consonants, as in *cradle* (krād′l), and *button* (but′n). See the full key inside the front cover.

cy•clo•pe•dic (sī′klə pē′dik), *adj.* like a cyclopedia in character or contents; broad and varied; exhaustive. Also, **cy′clo•pae′dic.** [1835–45; aph. var. of ENCYCLOPEDIC] —**cy′clo•pe′di•cal•ly, cy′clo•pae′di•cal•ly,** *adv.*

cy•clo•pen•ta•di•ene (sī′klə pen′tə dī′ēn, sik′lə-), *n.* a colorless liquid, C_5H_6, derived by the distillation of coal tar: used chiefly in the manufacture of insecticides and resins. [CYCLO- + PENTA- + -DIENE]

cy•clo•pen•tane (sī′klə pen′tān, sik′lə-), *n.* a colorless, water-insoluble liquid, C_5H_{10}, obtained from petroleum and used chiefly as a solvent. Also called **pentamethylene.** [1955–60; CYCLO- + PENTANE]

cy•clo•phos•pha•mide (sī′klə fos′fə mīd′, -mid, sik′lə-), *n. Pharm.* a synthetic, crystalline, toxic substance, $C_7H_{15}Cl_2N_2O_2P$, related to nitrogen mustard, used in the treatment of Hodgkin's disease, lymphoma, and certain leukemias. *Abbr.:* CYC [1955–60; CYCLO- + PHOSPH- + AMIDE]

cy•clo•pi•a (sī klō′pē ə), *n. Pathol.* a congenital defect characterized by fusion of the orbits into a single cavity containing one eye. Also called **synophthalmia.** [1830–40; < NL < Gk *Kýklōp*(s) CYCLOPS + *-ia* -IA]

cy•clo•ple•gi•a (sī′klə plē′jē ə, -jə, sik′lə-), *n. Pathol.* paralysis of the intraocular muscles. [1900–05; CYCLO- + -PLEGIA] —**cy′clo•ple′gic,** *adj., n.*

cy•clo•pro•pane (sī′klə prō′pān, sik′lə-), *n. Chem., Pharm.* a colorless, flammable gas, C_3H_6, used in organic synthesis and in medicine as an anesthetic. Also called **trimethylene.** [1890–95; CYCLO- + PROPANE]

Cy•clops (sī′klops), *n., pl.* **Cy•clo•pes** (sī klō′pēz). **1.** *Class. Myth.* a member of a family of giants having a single round eye in the middle of the forehead. **2.** (*l.c.*) a freshwater copepod of the genus *Cyclops,* having a median eye in the front of the head. [< Gk *Kýklōps,* lit., round-eye, equiv. to *kýkl(os)* a circle, round + *ōps* EYE]

cy•clo•ram•a (sī′klə ram′ə, -rä′mə), *n.* **1.** a pictorial representation, in perspective, of a landscape, battle, etc., on the inner wall of a cylindrical room or hall, viewed by spectators occupying a position in the center. **2.** *Theat.* a curved wall or drop at the back of a stage, used for creating an illusion of unlimited space or distance in the background of exterior scenes or for obtaining lighting effects. [1830–40; CYCL- + Gk (*h*)*órāma* view; cf. PANORAMA] —**cy′clo•ram′ic,** *adj.*

cy•clo•sil•i•cate (sī′klə sil′i kit, -kāt′), *n. Mineral.* any silicate in which the SiO_4 tetrahedra are linked to form rings. Cf. **inosilicate, nesosilicate, sorosilicate, tektosilicate.** [CYCLO- + SILICATE]

cy•clo•sis (sī klō′sis), *n., pl.* **-ses** (-sēz). *Biol.* the movement of protoplasm within a cell. [1825–35; < Gk *kýklōsis* an encircling. See CYCL-, -OSIS]

cy•clo•spo•rine (sī′klə spôr′ēn, -in, -spōr′-, sik′lə-), *n. Pharm.* a substance, synthesized by certain soil fungi, that suppresses the immune response by disabling helper T cells, used to minimize rejection of foreign tissue transplants. Also, **cy•clo•spo•rin** (sī′klə spôr′in, -spōr′-, sik′lə-). [1975–80; < NL *Cyclospor(eae)* a class of brown algae (see CYCLO-, -SPORE, -EAE) + -IN[2]]

cy•clo•stom•a•tous (sī′klə stom′ə təs, -stō′mə-, sik′lə-), *adj.* **1.** having a circular mouth. **2.** belonging or pertaining to the cyclostomes. Also, **cy•clos•to•mate** (sī klos′tə mit, -māt′). [CYCLO- + STOMATOUS]

cy•clo•stome (sī′klə stōm′, sik′lə-), *adj.* **1.** belonging or pertaining to the Cyclostomata, a subclass of jawless, eellike, marine vertebrates of the class Agnatha, comprising the lampreys and hagfishes. **2.** having a circular mouth. —*n.* **3.** a cyclostome vertebrate; a lamprey or hagfish. [1825–35; CYCLO- + -STOME]

cy•clo•stroph•ic (sī′klə strof′ik, -strō′fik, sik′le-), *adj. Meteorol.* pertaining to atmospheric motion in which the centripetal acceleration exactly balances the horizontal pressure force. [1915–20; CYCLO- + LGk *strophikós* turned, equiv. to Gk *stroph-* (var. s. of *stréphein* to turn) + *-ikos* -IC; see STROPHE]

cy•clo•style[1] (sī′klə stīl′, sik′lə-), *n.* a manifolding device consisting of a kind of pen with a small toothed wheel at the end that cuts minute holes in a specially prepared paper stretched over a smooth surface: used to produce a stencil from which copies are printed. [1880–85; formerly trademark; cf. CYCLO-, STYLUS]

cy•clo•style[2] (sī′klə stīl′, sik′lə-), *n. Archit.* a circular colonnade or columned building open at the center. [CYCLO- + -STYLE[2]] —**cy′clo•sty′lar,** *adj.*

cy•clo•thy•mi•a (sī′klə thī′mē ə, sik′lə-), *n. Psychiatry.* a mild bipolar disorder characterized by instability of mood and a tendency to swing between mild euphorias and depressions. [1920–25; CYCLO- + -THYMIA] —**cy′clo•thy′mic,** *adj.*

cy•clo•tome (sī′klə tōm′, sik′lə-), *n. Surg.* a type of scalpel for performing a cyclotomy. [CYCLO- + -TOME]

cy•clo•tom•ic (sī′klə tom′ik, sik′lə-), *adj.* **1.** of or pertaining to cyclotomy. **2.** *Math.* (of a polynomial) irreducible and of the form $x^{p-1} + x^{p-2} \pm \ldots \pm 1$, where p is a prime number. [1875–80; CYCLOTOM(Y) + -IC]

cy•clot•o•my (sī klot′ə mē), *n., pl.* **-mies. 1.** *Surg.* incision of the ciliary muscle. **2.** *Geom.* the process of dividing a circle into a specific number of equal parts. [1875–80; CYCLO- + -TOMY]

cy•clo•tri•meth•yl•ene•tri•ni•tra•mine (sī′klō trī-meth′ə lēn′trī nī′trə mēn′, -nī tram′in, sik′lō-), *n. Chem.* See **RDX.** [CYCLO- + TRI- + METHYLENE + TRI- + NITR- + AMINE]

cy•clo•tron (sī′klə tron′, sik′lə-), *n. Physics.* an accelerator in which particles are propelled in spiral paths by the use of a constant magnetic field. [1930–35; CYCLO- + -TRON]

CONCISE ETYMOLOGY KEY: <, descended or borrowed from; >, whence; b., blend of, blended; c., cognate with; cf., compare; deriv., derivative; equiv., equivalent; imit., imitative; obl., oblique; r., replacing; s., stem; sp., spelling, spelled; resp., respelling, respelled; trans., translation; ?, origin unknown; *, unattested; ‡, probably earlier than. See the full key inside the front cover.

Cyd (sid), *n.* a female given name.

cy•der (sī′dər), *n. Brit.* cider.

Cyd•nus (sid′nəs), *n.* a river in SE Asia Minor, in Cilicia.

cy•e•sis (sī ē′sis), *n., pl.* **-ses** (-sēz). pregnancy. [< NL < Gk *kýēsis* pregnancy, equiv. to *kyē-* (var. s. of *kyeîn* to be pregnant) + *-sis* -SIS] —**cy•et•ic** (sī et′ik), *adj.*

cyg•net (sig′nit), *n.* a young swan. [1400–50; late ME *signet* < L *cygnus,* var. of *cycnus* < Gk *kýknos* swan; see -ET]

Cyg•nus (sig′nəs), *n., gen.* **-ni** (-nī). *Astron.* the Swan, a northern constellation southwest of Draco, containing the bright star Deneb. [< L: swan; see CYGNET]

Cygnus A, *Astron.* a strong radio source in the constellation Cygnus associated with a distant peculiar galaxy.

Cygnus X-1 (eks′wun′), *Astron.* a strong x-ray source in the constellation Cygnus, consisting of a binary system of which one component may be a black hole.

cyke (sīk), *n. Informal.* cyclorama (def. 2). [by shortening]

cyl., cylinder.

cyl•in•der (sil′in dər), *n.* **1.** *Geom.* a surface or solid bounded by two parallel planes and generated by a straight line moving parallel to the given planes and tracing a curve bounded by the planes and lying in a plane perpendicular or oblique to the given planes. **2.** any cylinderlike object or part, whether solid or hollow. **3.** the rotating part of a revolver, containing the chambers for the cartridges. **4.** (in a pump) a cylindrical chamber in which a piston slides to move or compress a fluid. **5.** (in an engine) a cylindrical chamber in which the pressure of a gas or liquid moves a sliding piston. **6.** (in certain printing presses) **a.** a rotating cylinder that produces the impression and under which a flat form to be printed from passes. **b.** either of two cylinders, one carrying a curved form or plate to be printed from, that rotate against each other in opposite directions. **7.** (in certain locks) a cylindrical device for retaining the bolt until tumblers have been pushed out of its way. **8.** (in a screw or cylindrical gear) an imaginary cylindrical form, concentric to the axis, defining the pitch or the inner or outer ends of the threads or teeth. **9.** *Computers.* the tracks of a magnetic disk that are accessible from a single radial position of the access mechanism. **10.** *Textiles.* the main roller on a carding machine, esp. the roller covered with card clothing that works in combination with the worker and stripper rollers in carding fibers. **11.** *Archaeol.* a cylindrical or somewhat barrel-shaped stone or clay object bearing a cuneiform inscription or a carved design, worn by the Babylonians, Assyrians, and kindred peoples as a seal and amulet. —*v.t.* **12.** to furnish with a cylinder or cylinders. **13.** to subject to the action of a cylinder or cylinders. [1560–70; < L *cylindrus* < Gk *kýlindros* roller, cylinder, akin to *kylíndein* to roll] —**cyl′in•der•like′,** *adj.*

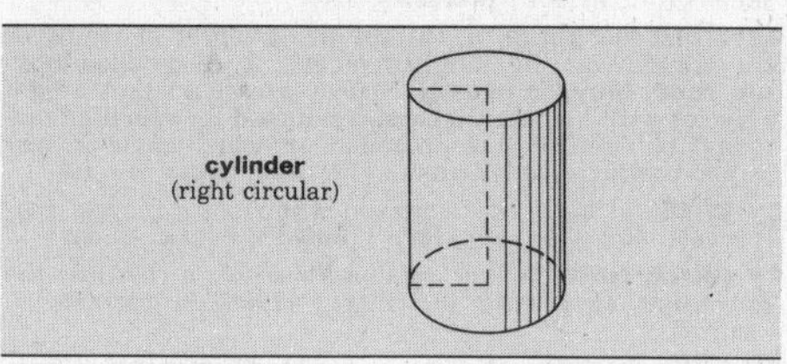
cylinder (right circular)

cyl′inder block′, *Auto.* the metal casting in which the cylinders of an internal-combustion engine are bored. Also called **block, engine block.** [1920–25]

cyl′inder desk′, a desk having a cylinder front, usually a tambour but occasionally of solid wood.

cyl′inder front′, *Furniture.* a front cover for a desk or the like, consisting either of a solid piece or of a tambour sliding up and back in quadrantal grooves.

cyl′inder glass′, a sheet of glass formed originally in the shape of a cylinder and then divided lengthwise and flattened. Also called **broad glass.** [1810–20, *Amer.*]

cyl′inder head′, (in a reciprocating engine or pump) a detachable plate or cover on the end opposite to that from which the piston rod or connecting rod projects. [1880–85]

cyl′inder press′, a printing press in which a flat bed holding the printing form moves against a rotating cylinder that carries the paper. Also called **flat-bed press.** Cf. **rotary press.** [1850–55, *Amer.*]

cyl′inder saw′. See **crown saw.** [1850–55]

cyl′inder seal′, a small carved cylinder used esp. by the ancient Mesopotamians to impress a design in wet clay. [1885–90]

cyl•in•dra•ceous (sil′in drā′shəs), *adj.* resembling a cylinder. [1670–80; CYLIND(E)R + -ACEOUS]

cy•lin•dri•cal (si lin′dri kəl), *adj.* of, pertaining to, or having the form of a cylinder. Also, **cy•lin′dric.** [1640–50; < NL *cylindric(us)* (< Gk *kylindrikós;* see CYLINDER, -IC) + -AL[1]] —**cy•lin′dri•cal′i•ty, cy•lin′dri•cal•ness,** *n.* —**cy•lin′dri•cal•ly,** *adv.*

cylin′drical coor′dinates, *Math.* a system of coordinates for locating a point in space by its polar coordinates and its perpendicular distance to the polar plane. [1930–35]

cyl•in•droid (sil′in droid′), *n.* **1.** a solid having the form of a cylinder, esp. one with an elliptical, as opposed to a circular, cross section. —*adj.* **2.** resembling a cylinder. [1655–65; < Gk *kylindroeidḗs* cylinderlike. See CYLINDER, -OID]

cy•lix (sī′liks, sil′iks), *n., pl.* **cyl•i•ces** (sil′ə sēz′). kylix.

Cyl•le•ni•an (si lē′nē ən), *adj.* of or pertaining to Mount Cyllene in Arcadia, Greece, or to the god Hermes, reputed to have been born there. [1730–40; < LL *Cyllēni(us)* (< Gk *Kyllḗnios,* equiv. to *Kyllḗn(ē)* + *-ios* -IOUS) + -AN]

Cym., Cymric.

cy•ma (sī′mə), *n., pl.* **-mae** (-mē), **-mas. 1.** *Archit.* either of two moldings having a partly convex and partly concave curve for an outline: used esp. in classical architecture. Cf. **cyma recta, cyma reversa. 2.** *Bot.* a cyme. [1555–65; < NL < Gk *kŷma* something swollen, a wave, wavy molding, sprout, equiv. to *ký(ein)* to be pregnant + *-ma* n. suffix]

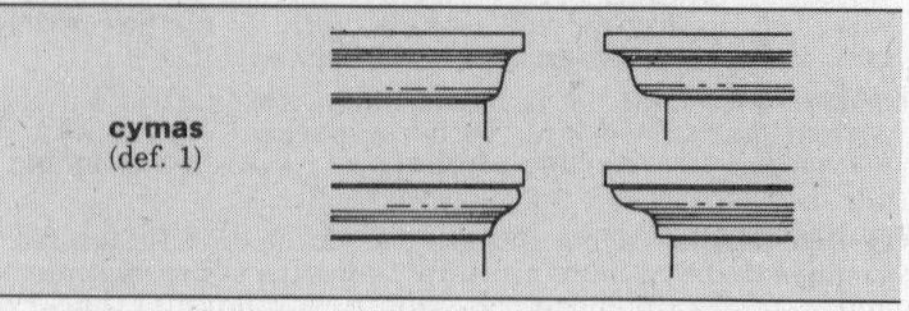
cymas (def. 1)

cy•maise (sē mez′), *n.* a pewter wine jar having a spout, a fixed handle on the side opposite the spout, and a bail for carrying. Also, **cimaise, semaise.** [1650–60; < F < L *cymatium* an ogee; see CYMATIUM]

cy•mar (si mär′), *n.* simar (def. 1).

cy′ma rec′ta (rek′tə), *Archit.* a cyma whose concave part projects beyond the convex part. See illus. under **molding.** [1695–1705; < NL: lit., straight cyma]

cy′ma re•ver′sa (ri vûr′sə), *Archit.* a cyma whose convex part projects beyond the concave part. Also called **Lesbian cyma, Lesbian cymatium.** See illus. under **molding.** [1555–65; < NL: lit., reversed cyma]

cy•ma•ti•on (si mā′shē on′, sī-), *n., pl.* **-ti•a** (-shē ə). cymatium.

cy•ma•ti•um (si mā′shē əm, sī-), *n., pl.* **-ti•a** (-shē ə). *Archit.* **1.** the uppermost member of a classical cornice or of a cornice of similar form: usually a cyma recta in classical examples. Cf. **sima[2]. 2.** echinus (def. 2c). [1555–65; < L < Gk *kymátion,* equiv. to *kŷmat-* (s. of *kŷma* wave; see CYMA) + *-ion* dim. suffix]

cymbals

cym•bal (sim′bəl), *n.* a concave plate of brass or bronze that produces a sharp, ringing sound when struck: played either in pairs, by being struck together, or singly, by being struck with a drumstick or the like. [bef. 900; ME; OE *cymbala* < ML, var. of *cymbalum* < L < Gk *kýmbalon,* var. of *kýmbos, kýmbē* hollow object] —**cym′bal•er, cym′bal•eer′, cym′bal•ist,** *n.* —**cym′bal•like′,** *adj.*

cym•ba•lom (sim′bə ləm), *n.* a complex zither played esp. in Hungary. Also, **cym•ba•lon** (sim′bə lən), **cimbalom, zimbalon.** [< Hungarian *cimbalom* < L *cymbalum* CYMBAL]

Cym•be•line (sim′bə lēn′), *n.* a romantic drama (1610?) by Shakespeare.

cym•bid•i•um (sim bid′ē əm), *n.* any of various orchids of the genus *Cymbidium,* native to Asia and Australia, having long clusters of numerous showy, variously colored flowers. [1799; < NL < Gk *kýmb(ē)* (see CYMBIFORM) + *-idion* -IDIUM]

cym•bi•form (sim′bə fôrm′), *adj. Bot., Zool.* boat-shaped. [1700–10; < L *cymb(a)* (< Gk *kýmbē* hollow object) + -I- + -FORM]

cym•bo•ceph•a•ly (sim′bō sef′ə lē), *n. Med.* scaphocephaly. [< Gk *kýmbo(s)* hollow object + -CEPHALY] —**cym•bo•ce•phal•ic** (sim′bō sə fal′ik), **cym′bo•ceph′a•lous,** *adj.*

cyme (sīm), *n.* **1.** an inflorescence in which the primary axis bears a single central or terminal flower that blooms first. See illus. under **inflorescence. 2.** a flat or convex inflorescence of this type. [1595–1605; < L *cȳma* cabbage sprout < Gk *kŷma;* see CYMA]

cy•mene (sī′mēn), *n.* a colorless, pleasant-smelling benzene derivative, $C_{10}H_{14}$, occurring in the volatile oil of the common cumin, *Cuminum cyminum,* and existing in three forms, the ortho, meta, and para isomers. Cf. **para-cymene.** [1860–65; < Gk *kým(inon)* CUMIN + -ENE]

cym•ling (sim′ling), *n.* See **pattypan squash.** [1770–80, *Amer.;* also *sim(b)lin,* earlier *symnel,* from its resemblance to a SIMNEL CAKE]

cymo-, a combining form meaning "wave," used in the formation of compound words: *cymometer.* [< Gk *kymo-,* comb. form of *kŷma* wave. See CYMA]

cy•mo•gene (sī′mə jēn′), *n. Chem.* a volatile, flammable petroleum distillate containing a large percentage of butane. [1885–90; CYM(ENE) + -O- + -GENE]

cy•mo•graph (sī′mə graf′, -gräf′), *n.* kymograph. —**cy•mo•graph•ic** (sī′mə graf′ik), *adj.*

cy•moid (sī′moid), *adj.* **1.** resembling a cyma. **2.** resembling a cyme. [1805–15; CYME + -OID]

cy•mo•phane (sī′mə fān′), *n. Mineral.* chrysoberyl. [1795–1805; CYMO- + -PHANE]

cy•mose (sī′mōs, sī mōs′), *adj. Bot.* **1.** bearing a cyme or cymes. **2.** of or of the nature of a cyme. [1800–10; < L *cȳmōsus* full of shoots. See CYME, -OSE[1]] **—cy′mose·ly,** *adv.*

cy·mot·ri·chous (sī mo′trə kəs), *adj.* having wavy hair. [1905–10; CYMO- + *-trichous* < Gk *-trichos* having hair (of the given sort); see TRICHO-, -OUS] **—cy·mot′ri·chy,** *n.*

Cym·ric (kim′rik, sim′-), *adj.* **1.** of or pertaining to the Cymry. —*n.* **2.** Welsh (def. 3). Also, **Kymric.** [CYMR(Y) + -IC]

Cym·ry (kim′rē), *n.* (*used with a plural v.*) the Welsh, or the branch of the Celtic people to which the Welsh belong, comprising also the Cornish people and the Bretons. Also, **Kymry.** [< Welsh *Cymry* Welshmen, pl. of *Cymro* < British Celtic **combrogos,* presumably "fellow countryman," equiv. to **com-* (c. L *com-* COM-) + **-brogos,* deriv. of **brogā* > Welsh, Cornish, Breton *bro* country, district; cf. *Allobrogēs* a Gaulish tribe, OIr *mruig* piece of inhabited or cultivated land]

Cyn·e·wulf (kin′ə wo͝olf′), *n.* fl. 9th century A.D., Anglo-Saxon poet. Also, **Cynwulf.**

cyn·ic (sin′ik), *n.* **1.** a person who believes that only selfishness motivates human actions and who disbelieves in or minimizes selfless acts or disinterested points of view. **2.** (*cap.*) one of a sect of Greek philosophers, 4th century B.C., who advocated the doctrines that virtue is the only good, that the essence of virtue is self-control, and that surrender to any external influence is beneath human dignity. **3.** a person who shows or expresses a bitterly or sneeringly cynical attitude. —*adj.* **4.** cynical. **5.** (*cap.*) Also, **Cynical.** of or pertaining to the Cynics or their doctrines. **6.** *Med. Now Rare.* resembling the actions of a snarling dog. [1540–50; < L *Cynicus* < Gk *Kynikós* Cynic, lit., doglike, currish, equiv. to *kyn-* (s. of *kýōn*) dog + *-ikos* -IC]
—Syn. 1, 3. skeptic, pessimist, misanthrope.

cyn·i·cal (sin′i kəl), *adj.* **1.** like or characteristic of a cynic; distrusting or disparaging the motives of others. **2.** showing contempt for accepted standards of honesty or morality by one's actions, esp. by actions that exploit the scruples of others. **3.** bitterly or sneeringly distrustful, contemptuous, or pessimistic. **4.** (*cap.*) cynic (def. 5). [1580–90; CYNIC + -AL[1]] **—cyn′i·cal·ly,** *adv.* **—cyn′i·cal·ness,** *n.*
—Syn. 1, 3. CYNICAL, PESSIMISTIC, SARCASTIC, SATIRICAL imply holding a low opinion of humanity. CYNICAL suggests a disbelief in the sincerity of human motives: *cynical about honesty.* PESSIMISTIC implies a more or less habitual disposition to look on the dark side of things, and to believe that the worst will happen: *pessimistic as to the future.* SARCASTIC refers to sneering or making cutting jibes: *sarcastic about a profession of faith.* SATIRICAL suggests expressing scorn or ridicule by saying the opposite of what one means: *a satirical attack on his political promises.* **—Ant. 1, 3.** optimistic.

cyn·i·cism (sin′ə siz′əm), *n.* **1.** cynical disposition, character, or belief. **2.** a cynical remark. **3.** (*cap.*) any of the doctrines or practices of the Cynics. [1665–75; CYNIC + -ISM]

cy·no·sure (sī′nə sho͝or′, sin′ə-), *n.* **1.** something that strongly attracts attention by its brilliance, interest, etc.: *the cynosure of all eyes.* **2.** something serving for guidance or direction. [1590–1600; < L *Cynosūra* < Gk *Kynósoura* the constellation Ursa Minor, equiv. to *kynós* dog's (gen. of *kýōn*) + *ourá* tail] **—cy′no·sur′al,** *adj.*

Cyn·thi·a (sin′thē ə), *n.* **1.** Artemis: so called from her birth on Mt. Cynthus, on Delos. **2.** *Literary.* the moon, the emblem of Artemis. **3.** a female given name.

Cyn·wulf (kin′wo͝olf), *n.* Cynewulf.

CYO, Catholic Youth Organization.

cy·per·a·ceous (sī′pə rā′shəs, sip′ə-), *adj.* belonging to the Cyperaceae, the sedge family of plants. Cf. **sedge family.** [1850–55; < NL *Cypēr(us)* the typical genus (L: kind of rush < Gk *kýpeiros* a marsh plant) + -ACEOUS]

cy·pher (sī′fər), *n., v.i., v.t. Chiefly Brit.* cipher.

cy pres (sē′ prā′), *Law.* **1.** as near as possible. **2.** the doctrine, applied esp. to cases of charitable trusts or donations, that, in place of an impossible or illegal condition, limitation, or object, allows the nearest practicable one to be substituted. Also, **cy′pres′.** [1475–85; < AF: lit., as near (cf. F *si près*)]

cy·press[1] (sī′prəs), *n.* **1.** any of several evergreen coniferous trees constituting the genus *Cupressus,* having dark-green, scalelike, overlapping leaves. **2.** any of various other coniferous trees of allied genera, as the bald cypress. **3.** any of various unrelated plants resembling the true cypress. **4.** the wood of these trees or plants. [bef. 1000; ME, OE *cypresse* < LL *cypressus,* appar. b. L *cupressus* and *cyparissus* < Gk *kypárissos;* r. ME *cipres* < AF, OF < LL, as above]

cy·press[2] (sī′prəs), *n. Obs.* a fine, thin fabric resembling lawn or crepe, formerly used in black for mourning garments and trimmings. Also, **cyprus.** [1350–1400; ME *cipre(s), cyprus,* after CYPRUS]

Cy·press (sī′prəs), *n.* a city in SW California. 40,391.

cy′press knee′, one of the woody growths that project above water from the roots of the bald cypress. [1775–85, *Amer.*]

cy′press spurge′, a perennial herb, *Euphorbia cyparissias,* of Eurasia, having small, greenish-yellow flowers in dense clusters. [1700–10]

cy′press vine′, a tropical American vine, *Ipomoea quamoclit* (or *Quamoclit pennata*), of the morning glory family, having finely divided leaves and tubular scarlet flowers. [1810–20, *Amer.*]

Cyp·ri·an (sip′rē ən), *adj.* **1.** noting or pertaining to the worship of Aphrodite or to conduct inspired by Aphrodite. **2.** lewd; licentious. **3.** Cypriot. —*n.* **4.** Cypriot. **5.** a lewd or licentious person, esp. a prostitute. **6. the Cyprian,** Aphrodite: so called because her cult was centered on Cyprus. [1590–1600; < L *Cypri(us)* of Cyprus (< Gk *Kýprios,* deriv. of *Kýpros* CYPRUS) + -AN]

Cyp·ri·an (sip′rē ən), *n.* **Saint** (*Thascius Caecillus Cyprianus*), A.D. c200–258, early church father, bishop, and martyr.

cy·pri·nid (si prī′nid, sip′rə-), *n.* **1.** any fish belonging to the Cyprinidae, or minnow family. —*adj.* **2.** carplike in form or structure. [1890–95; < NL *Cyprinidae* name of family, equiv. to *Cyprīn(us)* genus name (< L < Gk *kyprînos* carp) + *-idae* -ID[2]]

cy·prin·o·dont (si prin′ə dont′, si prī′nə-), *n.* **1.** any small, soft-rayed fish of the order Cyprinodontes, of warm, fresh or brackish waters in North America, including the killifishes, topminnows, and guppies. —*adj.* **2.** of, pertaining to, or resembling the cyprinodonts. [1855–60; < L *cyprīn(us)* (< Gk *kyprînos* carp) + -ODONT]

cyp·ri·noid (sip′rə noid′, si prī′noid), *adj.* **1.** resembling a carp; belonging to the Cyprinoidea, a group of fishes including the carps, suckers, and loaches. —*n.* **2.** a cyprinoid fish. [1840–50; < L *cyprīn(us)* (< Gk *kyprînos* carp) + -OID]

Cyp·ri·ot (sip′rē ət), *n.* **1.** a native or inhabitant of Cyprus. **2.** the Greek dialect of Cyprus. —*adj.* **3.** of, pertaining to, or characteristic of Cyprus, its people, or their language. Also, **Cyp·ri·ote** (sip′rē ōt′, -ət). [1590–1600; < Gk *Kypriṓtēs*]

Cyp′riot syl′labary, a syllabic script in use on Cyprus in the first millennium B.C., used for the writing of Greek and of an unknown language.

cyp·ri·pe·di·um (sip′rə pē′dē əm), *n.* any orchid of the genus *Cypripedium,* comprising the lady's-slippers. [1765–75; < NL, equiv. to L *Cypri(a)* Venus + *-pedi-* -PED + *-um* neut. ending]

Cyp·ris (sip′ris), *n.* an epithet of Aphrodite, meaning "Lady of Cyprus." Also, **Kypris.**

Cypro-, a combining form of **Cyprian:** *Cypro-Minoan.*

cy·pro·hep·ta·dine (sī′prō hep′tə dēn′), *n. Pharm.* a phenothiazine analogue, $C_{21}H_{21}N$, with antihistaminic action, used in the symptomatic treatment of hay fever and itching. [1970–75; CY(CLO-) + PRO(PYL) + HEPTA- + (PIPERI)DINE]

cy·prus (sī′prəs), *n. Obs.* cypress[2].

Cy·prus (sī′prəs), *n.* an island republic in the Mediterranean, S of Turkey: formerly a British colony; independent since 1960. 639,000; 3572 sq. mi. (9250 sq. km). *Cap.:* Nicosia.

cyp·se·la (sip′sə lə), *n., pl.* **-lae** (-lē′). *Bot.* an achene with an adherent calyx, as in the composite plants. [1865–70; < NL < Gk *kypsélē* hollow vessel, chest, box]

Cyr·a·no de Ber·ge·rac (sir′ə nō′ də bûr′jə rak′, -zhə-, bâr′-; *Fr.* sē RA nô də beR zhə RAK′), **1.** See **Bergerac, Savinien Cyrano de. 2.** (*italics*) a play in verse (1897) by Edmond Rostand.

Cyr·e·na·ic (sir′ə nā′ik, sī′rə-), *adj.* **1.** of or pertaining to Cyrenaica, or its chief city, Cyrene. **2.** noting or pertaining to a school of philosophy founded by Aristippus of Cyrene, who taught that pleasure is the only rational aim of life. —*n.* **3.** a native or inhabitant of Cyrenaica. **4.** a disciple of the Cyrenaic school of philosophy. [1580–90; < L *Cyrēnaicus* < Gk *Kyrēnaïkós,* equiv. to *Kyrēna-* (comb. form of *Kyrḗnē* CYRENE) + *-ikos* -IC]

Cyr·e·na·i·ca (sir′ə nā′i kə, sī′rə-), *n.* **1.** Also called **Barca.** an ancient district in N Africa. **2.** the E part of Libya. Also, **Cirenaica.**

Cy·re·ne (sī rē′nē), *n.* an ancient Greek city and colony in N Africa, in Cyrenaica.

Cyr·il (sir′əl), *n.* **1. Saint** ("*Apostle of the Slavs*"), A.D. 827–869, Greek missionary to the Moravians. **2.** a male given name.

Cy·ril·lic (si ril′ik), *adj.* **1.** noting or pertaining to a script derived from Greek uncials and traditionally supposed to have been invented by St. Cyril, first used for the writing of Old Church Slavonic and adopted with minor modifications for the writing of Russian, Bulgarian, Serbian, and some non-Slavic languages of Central Asia. **2.** of or pertaining to St. Cyril. —*n.* **3.** Cyrillic script. [1835–45; < NL *Cyrillicus,* equiv. to *Cyril-l(us)* Saint CYRIL + *-icus* -IC]

cyr·to·sis (sər tō′sis), *n.* **1.** *Pathol.* any abnormal curvature of the spine or of the extremities. **2.** *Plant Pathol.* a viral disease of the cotton plant, characterized by stunted and distorted growth. [< NL < Gk *kyrt(ós)* curved, arched, round + *-ōsis* -OSIS]

cyr·to·style (sûr′tə stil′), *n.* a convex portico, as at an entrance. [< Gk *kyrtó(s)* curved + -STYLE[2]]

Cy·rus (sī′rəs), *n.* **1.** ("*the Elder*" or "*the Great*") c600–529 B.C., king of Persia 558?–529: founder of the Persian empire. **2.** ("*the Younger*") 424?–401 B.C., Persian prince and satrap: leader of the armed conspiracy against his brother King Artaxerxes II. **3.** a male given name: from an Old Persian word meaning "throne."

Cys, *Biochem.* cysteine.

cyst (sist), *n.* **1.** *Pathol.* a closed, bladderlike sac formed in animal tissues, containing fluid or semifluid matter. **2.** a bladder, sac, or vesicle. **3.** *Bot., Mycol.* **a.** a sporelike cell with a resistant, protective wall. **b.** a cell or cavity enclosing reproductive bodies. **4.** *Zool.* **a.** a sac, usually spherical, surrounding an animal that has passed into a dormant condition. **b.** such a sac plus the contained animal. **c.** a capsule or resistant covering. [1705–15; < NL *cystis* < Gk *kýstis* bag, pouch, the bladder; akin to *kŷma* CYMA]

cyst-, var. of **cysto-,** before a vowel: *cystectomy.*

-cyst, var. of **cysto-,** as final element in a compound word: *statocyst.*

cys·ta·thi·o·nine (sis′tə thī′ə nēn′, -nin), *n. Biochem.* an amino acid, $C_7H_{14}O_4N_2S$, that is an intermediate in the transfer of sulfur from methionine to cysteine. [CYST(EINE) + *-a-* + (ME)THIONINE]

cys·tec·to·my (si stek′tə mē), *n., pl.* **-mies.** *Surg.* excision of a cyst or bladder, usually the urinary bladder. [1890–95; CYST- + -ECTOMY]

cys·te·ine (sis′tē ēn′, -in), *n. Biochem.* a crystalline amino acid, $C_3H_7O_2NS$, a component of nearly all proteins, obtained by the reduction of cystine. *Abbr.:* Cys; *Symbol:* C [1880–85; alter. of CYSTINE] **—cys′te·in′ic,** *adj.*

cysti-, var. of **cysto-:** *cysticercus.*

cys·tic (sis′tik), *adj.* **1.** pertaining to, of the nature of, or having a cyst or cysts; encysted. **2.** *Anat.* belonging or pertaining to the urinary bladder or gall bladder. [1625–35; CYST + -IC]

cys·ti·cer·co·sis (sis′tə sər kō′sis), *n. Pathol.* infestation with the larval form of beef or pork tapeworm, producing fever, malaise, muscle pain, and other symptoms depending on the area of the body affected. [1900–05; CYSTICERC(US) + -OSIS]

cys·ti·cer·cus (sis′tə sûr′kəs), *n., pl.* **-cer·ci** (-sûr′sī). the larva of certain tapeworms, having the head retracted into a bladderlike structure; a bladder worm. [1835–45; < NL < Gk *kýsti(s)* bladder, CYST + *kérkos* tail]

cys′tic fibro′sis, *Pathol.* a hereditary chronic disease of the exocrine glands, characterized by the production of viscid mucus that obstructs the pancreatic ducts and bronchi, leading to infection and fibrosis. [1950–55]

cys′tic masti′tis. See **fibrocystic disease.**

cys·tid·i·um (si stid′ē əm), *n., pl.* **cys·tid·i·a** (si stid′ē ə). *Mycol.* (in certain basidiomycetous fungi) one of the large, inflated, sterile cells growing between the basidia and usually projecting beyond them. [1855–60; < NL; see CYST-, -IDIUM]

cys·tine (sis′tēn, -tin), *n. Biochem.* a crystalline amino acid, $C_6H_{12}O_4N_2S_2$, occurring in most proteins, esp. the keratins in hair, wool, and horn, and yielding cysteine on reduction. [1835–45; CYST- + -INE[2]; so called because found in the bladder]

cys·ti·nu·ri·a (sis′tə no͝or′ē ə, -nyo͝or′-), *n. Pathol.* an inherited metabolic disorder that results in the excessive excretion of certain amino acids, esp. cystine, in the urine. [1850–55; CYSTINE + -URIA]

cys·ti·tis (si stī′tis), *n. Pathol.* inflammation of the urinary bladder. [1770–80; CYST- + -ITIS]

cysto-, a combining form representing **cyst** in the formation of compound words: *cystolith.* Also, **cyst-, -cyst, cysti-.**

cys·to·carp (sis′tə kärp′), *n.* the mass of carpospores formed in red algae as a result of fertilization. [1870–75; CYSTO- + -CARP] **—cys′to·car′pic,** *adj.*

cys·to·cele (sis′tə sēl′), *n. Pathol.* a herniation of the urinary bladder into the vagina. [1805–15; CYSTO- + -CELE[1]]

cyst·oid (sis′toid), *adj.* **1.** resembling a cyst. —*n.* **2.** a cystlike structure or formation. [1870–75; CYST + -OID]

cys·to·lith (sis′tl ith), *n. Bot.* a mass of calcium carbonate on the cellulose wall. [1840–50; CYSTO- + -LITH] **—cys′to·lith′ic,** *adj.*

cys·to·ma (si stō′mə), *n., pl.* **-mas, -ma·ta** (-mə tə). *Pathol.* a cystic tumor. [1870–75; CYST- + -OMA] **—cys·tom·a·tous** (si stom′ə təs), *adj.*

cys·tom·e·ter (si stom′i tər), *n. Med.* a device for determining the reaction of the urinary bladder to increased internal pressure. [CYSTO- + -METER]

cys·to·scope (sis′tə skōp′), *n. Med.* a slender, cylindrical instrument for examining the interior of the urinary bladder and for the introduction of medication therein. [1885–90; CYSTO- + -SCOPE] **—cys·to·scop·ic** (sis′tə skop′ik), *adj.* **—cys·tos·co·pist** (si stos′kə pist), *n.*

cys·tos·co·py (si stos′kə pē), *n., pl.* **-pies.** *Med.* an examination by means of a cystoscope. [1905–10; CYSTO- + -SCOPY]

cys·tos·to·my (si stos′tə mē), *n., pl.* **-mies.** *Surg.* **1.** the construction of an artificial opening from the bladder through the abdominal wall, permitting the drainage of urine. **2.** the opening so constructed. [1905–10; CYSTO- + -STOMY]

cy·tar·a·bine (sī tar′ə bēn′), *n. Pharm.* a toxic synthetic nucleoside, $C_9H_{13}N_3O_5$, used as an immunosuppressive and cytotoxic agent in the treatment of certain leukemias. Also **cytosine arabinoside, ara-C.** [CYT(OSINE) + ARAB(INOSIDE) + -INE[2]]

cy·tas·ter (sī tas′tər, sī′tas-), *n. Biol.* aster. [1890–95; CYT(O)- + -ASTER[2]]

-cyte, var. of **cyto-** as final element in a compound word: *leucocyte.*

Cyth·er·a (sith′ər ə, si thēr′ə), *n.* Cerigo.

Cyth·er·e·a (sith′ə rē′ə), *n.* Aphrodite: so called because of her birth in the sea near Cythera.

Cyth·er·ean (sith′ə rē′ən), *adj.* **1.** of or pertaining to Cytherea. **2.** of or pertaining to the planet Venus. [< L *Cytherē(a)* (< Gk *Kythéreia* CYTHEREA) + -AN]

cyt·i·dine (sit′i dēn′, -din, sī′ti-), *n. Biochem.* a white crystalline powder, $C_9H_{13}N_3O_5$, that is a ribonucleoside consisting of D-ribose and cytosine. [< G *Cytidin* (1910), equiv. to *cyt-* CYTO- + *-idin* suffix of organic compounds] **—cyt·i·dyl·ic** (sit′i dil′ik, sī′ti-), *adj.*

cyt′idine monophos′phate, *Biochem.* a nucleotide constituent of ribonucleic acids; a phosphoric acid ester of cytidine. *Abbr.:* **CMP** Also called **cyt′idyl′ic ac′id.**

cyto-, a combining form meaning "cell," used in the formation of compound words: *cytoplasm.* Also, **-cyte.** [< Gk *kyto-*, comb. form of *kýtos* container, receptacle, body]

cy·to·an·a·lyz·er (sī′tō an′l ī′zər), *n.* an electronic optical device for screening smears of cells suspected of being malignant. [CYTO- + ANALYZER]

cy·to·chem·is·try (sī′tə kem′ə strē), *n.* the branch of cell biology dealing with the detection of cell constituents by means of biochemical analysis and visualization techniques. [1900–05; CYTO- + CHEMISTRY] **—cy·to·chem·i·cal** (sī′tə kem′i kəl), *adj.*

cy·to·chrome (sī′tə krōm′), *n. Biochem.* any of several carrier molecules in the mitochondria of plant and animal cells, consisting of a protein and an iron-containing porphyrin ring and participating in the stepwise transfer of electrons in oxidation reactions: each cytochrome alternately accepts and releases an electron at a slightly lower energy level in the order designated *b*, c_1, *c*, *a*, and a_3. Cf. **electron transport.** [1895–1900; CYTO- + -CHROME]

cy·to·cid·al (sī′tə sīd′l), *adj.* capable of killing cells. [CYTO- + -CIDAL]

cy·toc·la·sis (sī tok′lə sis, sī′tə klā′sis), *n. Pathol.* destruction of cells. [CYTO- + Gk *klásis* a breaking]

cy·to·clas·tic (sī′tə klas′tik), *adj. Pathol.* **1.** of or pertaining to cytoclasis. **2.** destructive to cells. [CYTO- + CLASTIC]

cy·to·gen·e·sis (sī′tə jen′ə sis), *n. Cell Biol.* the origin and development of cells. [1855–60; CYTO- + -GENESIS]

cy·to·ge·net·ics (sī′tō jə net′iks), *n.* (*used with a singular v.*) the branch of biology linking the study of genetic inheritance with the study of cell structure, esp. for human chromosome analysis for the detection of inheritable diseases. [1930–35; CYTO- + GENETICS] **—cy′to·ge·net′ic, cy′to·ge·net′i·cal,** *adj.* **—cy′to·ge·net′i·cal·ly,** *adv.* **—cy′to·ge·net′i·cist,** *n.*

cy·to·ki·ne·sis (sī′tō ki nē′sis, -kī-), *n. Cell Biol.* the division of the cell cytoplasm that usually follows mitotic or meiotic division of the nucleus. [1915–20; CYTO- + -KINESIS] **—cy·to·ki·net·ic** (sī′tō ki net′ik, -kī-), *adj.*

cy·to·ki·nin (sī′tə kī′nin), *n. Biochem.* any of a class of plant hormones, produced by the roots and traveling upward through the xylem, that promote tissue growth and budding and, on application, retard plant senescence. Cf. **kinetin, zeatin.** [1960–65; CYTO- + -KININ]

cy·tol·o·gy (sī tol′ə jē), *n.* the study of the microscopic appearance of cells, esp. for the diagnosis of abnormalities and malignancies. [1885–90; CYTO- + -LOGY] **—cy·to·log·ic** (sīt′l oj′ik), **cy′to·log′i·cal,** *adj.* **—cy′·to·log′i·cal·ly,** *adv.* **—cy·tol′o·gist,** *n.*

cy·tol·y·sin (sī tol′ə sin, sīt′l ī′sin), *n. Biochem.* any substance that produces cytolysis. [1900–05; CYTOLYS(IS) + -IN[1]]

cy·tol·y·sis (sī tol′ə sis), *n. Physiol.* the dissolution or degeneration of cells. [1905–10; CYTO- + -LYSIS] **—cy·to·lyt·ic** (sīt′l it′ik), *adj.*

cy·to·me·gal·ic (sī′tō mi gal′ik), *adj. Pathol.* of, relating to, or distinguished by enlarged cells. [1950–55; *cytomegal(ia)* a cytomegalic condition (see CYTO-, -MEGALIA) + -IC]

cy·to·meg·a·lo·vi·rus (sī′tō meg′ə lō vī′rəs), *n., pl.* **-rus·es.** a common virus of the herpesvirus family, usually harmless or causing mild colds but capable of producing severe systemic damage in infected newborns and immunosuppressed persons. *Abbr.:* CMV [1960–65; *cytomegal(ia)* (see CYTOMEGALIC) + -O- + VIRUS]

cy·to·mem·brane (sī′tə mem′brān), *n.* See **cell membrane.** [1960–65; CYTO- + MEMBRANE]

cy·to·path·ic (sī′tə path′ik), *adj. Pathol.* of, pertaining to, or characterized by a pathological change in the function or form of a cell, leading to its death. [1960–65; CYTO- + -PATHIC]

cy·to·path·o·gen·ic (sī′tō path′ə jen′ik), *adj.* **1.** of or pertaining to a substance or microorganism that is pathologic for or destructive to cells. **2.** of or pertaining to such cellular changes. [1955–60; CYTO- + PATHOGENIC] **—cy·to·path·o·ge·nic·i·ty** (sī′tō path′ə jə nis′i tē), *n.*

cy·to·pa·thol·o·gy (sī′tō pə thol′ə jē), *n. Pathol.* the science dealing with the study of the diseases of cells. [1935–40; CYTO- + PATHOLOGY] **—cy·to·path·o·log·ic** (sī′tō path′ə loj′ik), **cy′to·path′o·log′i·cal,** *adj.* **—cy′·to·path′o·log′i·cal·ly,** *adv.* **—cy′to·pa·thol′o·gist,** *n.*

cy·to·pe·ni·a (sī′tə pē′nē ə), *n. Pathol.* the condition of having a decreased number of cellular elements in the blood; hypocytosis. [CYTO- + Gk *penía* poverty, want]

cy·toph·a·gy (sī tof′ə jē), *n.* the ingestion of cells by other cells. [CYTO- + -PHAGY] **—cy·to·phag·ic** (sī′tə-faj′ik, -fā′jik), **cy·toph·a·gous** (sī tof′ə gəs), *adj.*

cy·to·phar·ynx (sī′tə far′ingks), *n., pl.* **-to·pha·ryn·ges** (-tō fə rin′jēz), **-to·phar·ynx·es.** the gullet of a protozoan. [CYTO- + PHARYNX]

cy·to·pho·tom·e·ter (sī′tō fō tom′i tər), *n. Cytol.* an instrument for examining cells by determining the intensity or wavelengths of light transmitted through them. [CYTO- + PHOTOMETER] **—cy′to·pho·tom′e·try,** *n.*

cy·to·plasm (sī′tə plaz′əm), *n. Cell Biol.* the cell substance between the cell membrane and the nucleus, containing the cytosol, organelles, cytoskeleton, and various particles. See diag. under **cell.** [1870–75; CYTO- + -PLASM] **—cy′to·plas′mic,** *adj.* **—cy′to·plas′mi·cal·ly,** *adv.*

cy·to·plast (sī′tə plast′), *n. Cell Biol.* the intact, cytoplasmic content of a cell. [1890–95; CYTO- + -PLAST] **—cy′to·plas′tic,** *adj.*

cy·to·sine (sī′tə sēn′, -zēn′, -sin), *n. Biochem.* a pyrimidine base, $C_4H_5N_3O$, that is one of the fundamental components of DNA and RNA, in which it forms a base pair with guanine. *Symbol:* C Cf. **cytidine, cytidine monophosphate.** [< G *Cytosin* (1894); see CYTO-, -OSE[2], -INE[2]]

cy′tosine ar·a·bin′o·side (ar′ə bin′ə sīd′, ə rab′ə-nō-), *Pharm.* cytarabine.

cy·to·skel·e·ton (sī′tə skel′i tn), *n. Cell Biol.* a shifting lattice arrangement of structural and contractile components distributed throughout the cell cytoplasm, composed of microtubules, microfilaments, and larger filaments, functioning as a structural support and transport mechanism. [CYTO- + SKELETON] **—cy′to·skel′e·tal,** *adj.*

cy·to·sol (sī′tə sôl′, -sol′), *n. Cell Biol.* the water-soluble components of cell cytoplasm, constituting the fluid portion that remains after removal of the organelles and other intracellular structures. [1965–70; CYTO- + SOL(UTION), on the model of HYDROSOL, etc.] **—cy·to·sol·ic** (sī′tə sol′ik), *adj.*

cy·to·some (sī′tə sōm′), *n. Biol.* the cytoplasmic part of a cell. [CYTO- + -SOME[3]]

cy·tost (sī′tost), *n. Biochem.* any cellular substance liberated because of injury to the cell or cells. [CYT(O)- + Gk *ost(éon)* bone]

cy·to·sta·sis (sī′tə stā′sis, -stas′is), *n. Pathol.* arrest of cellular growth and division. [CYTO- + STASIS]

cy·to·stat·ic (sī′tə stat′ik), *adj.* **1.** inhibiting cell growth and division. **—***n.* **2.** any substance that inhibits cell growth and division. [CYTO- + STATIC]

cy·to·stome (sī′tə stōm′), *n.* the mouth of a protozoan. [1885–90; CYTO- + -STOME] **—cy′to·sto′mal,** *adj.*

cy·to·tax·is (sī′tə tak′sis), *n. Biol.* the mutual attraction or repulsion of cells or groups of motile cells. [CYTO- + -TAXIS] **—cy·to·tac·tic** (sī′tə tak′tik), *adj.*

cy·to·tax·on·o·my (sī′tō tak son′ə mē), *n.* a branch of taxonomy in which characteristics of cellular structures, particularly of somatic chromosomes, are used to classify organisms. [1925–30; CYTO- + TAXONOMY]

cy·to·tech·nol·o·gist (sī′tō tek nol′ə jist), *n.* a technician who specializes in identifying cells and cellular abnormalities. [1960–65; CYTO- + TECHNOLOGIST]

cy·to·tech·nol·o·gy (sī′tō tek nol′ə jē), *n.* the study of human cells to detect signs of cancer or other abnormalities. [CYTO- + TECHNOLOGY] **—cy·to·tech·no·log·ic** (sī′tō tek′nə loj′ik), *adj.* **—cy′to·tech·nol′o·gist,** *n.*

cy·to·tox·ic·i·ty (sī′tō tok sis′i tē), *n.* cell destruction caused by a cytotoxic substance. [CYTOTOXIC + -ITY]

cytotoxic T cell, *Immunol.* See **killer T cell.** Also called **cytotoxic T lymphocyte.**

cy·to·tox·in (sī′tə tok′sin), *n. Immunol., Pharm.* a substance that has a toxic effect on certain cells. [1900–05; CYTO- + TOXIN] **—cy′to·tox′ic,** *adj.*

cy·to·trop·ic (sī′tə trop′ik, -trō′pik), *adj. Biol.* **1.** (of cells or groups of cells) growing or moving toward or away from each other. **2.** having an affinity for cells, as certain viruses. [CYTO- + -TROPIC]

cy·tot·ro·pism (sī to′trə piz′əm), *n.* cytotropic tendency or behavior. [1905–10; CYTO- + -TROPISM]

cy·to·zo·on (sī′tə zō′on, -ən), *n., pl.* **-zo·a** (-zō′ə). a parasite, esp. a protozoon, living within a cell. [CYTO- + -ZOON] **—cy′to·zo′ic,** *adj.*

cy·wydd (ku′wiᵺ), *n. Pros.* a form of meter in Welsh poetry consisting of rhyming couplets, each line having seven syllables: first used in the 14th century. [1950–55; < Welsh; OWelsh *couid* song, metrical composition; c. OIr *cubaid* harmonious, rhyming]

Cyz·i·cus (siz′i kəs), *n.* an ancient city in NW Asia Minor, in Mysia, on a peninsula in the Sea of Marmara.

CZ, Canal Zone (approved esp. for use with zip code).

C.Z., Canal Zone.

czar (zär, tsär), *n.* **1.** an emperor or king. **2.** (*often cap.*) the former emperor of Russia. **3.** an autocratic ruler or leader. **4.** any person exercising great authority or power in a particular field: *a czar of industry.* Also, **tsar, tzar.** [1545–55; < Russ *tsar′*, ORuss *tsĭsarĭ* emperor, king (akin to OCS *tsěsarĭ*) < Goth *kaisar* emperor (< Gk or L); Gk *kaîsar* < L *Caesar* CAESAR]

czar·das (chär′däsh), *n.* a Hungarian national dance in two movements, one slow and the other fast. Also, **csardas.** [1855–60; < Hungarian *csárdás*, equiv. to *csárda* wayside tavern (< Serbo-Croatian *čardak* orig., watchtower < Turk < Pers *chārtāk* four-cornered room; *chār* FOUR + *tāk* vault) + *-s* adj. suffix; earlier *csárdák* was analyzed as *csárda* + *-k* pl. suffix]

czar·dom (zär′dəm, tsär′-), *n.* **1.** the domain of a czar. **2.** the power, authority, or position of a czar. Also, **tsardom, tzardom.** [1835–45; CZAR + -DOM]

czar·e·vitch (zär′ə vich, tsär′-), *n.* the son of a czar. Also, **tsarevitch, tzarevitch.** [1700–10; < Russ *tsarévich*, equiv. to *tsar′* CZAR + *-evich* masc. patronymic suffix]

cza·rev·na (zä rev′nə, tsä-), *n.* **1.** a daughter of a czar. **2.** the wife of the son of a czar. Also, **tsarevna, tzarevna.** [1875–80; < Russ *tsarévna*, equiv. to *tsar′* CZAR + *-evna* fem. patronymic suffix]

cza·ri·na (zä rē′nə, tsä-), *n.* the wife of a czar; Russian empress. Also, **tsarina, tzarina.** [1710–20; CZAR + *-ina* fem. suffix (as in *Christina*), modeled on G *Zarin* empress, equiv. to *Zar* Czar + *-in* fem. suffix]

czar·ism (zär′iz əm, tsär′-), *n.* **1.** dictatorship; despotic or autocratic government. **2.** the system of government in Russia under the czars. Also, **tsarism, tzarism.** [1850–55; CZAR + -ISM]

czar·ist (zär′ist, tsär′-), *adj.* Also, **czar·is·tic** (zä ris′-tik, tsä-), **tsaristic, tzaristic. 1.** of, pertaining to, or characteristic of a czar or the system and principles of government under a czar. **2.** autocratic; dictatorial. **—***n.* **3.** an adherent of a czar or of czarism. Also, **tsarist, tzarist.** [CZAR + -IST]

cza·rit·za (zä rit′sə, tsä-), *n.* a czarina. Also, **tsaritza, tzaritza.** [1690–1700; < Russ *tsarítsa*]

Czech (chek), *n.* **1.** a member of the most westerly branch of the Slavs, comprising the Bohemians, or Czechs proper, and, sometimes, the Moravians. **2.** the language of Bohemia and Moravia, a Slavic language similar to Slovak. **3.** (loosely) Czechoslovak. **—***adj.* **4.** Also, **Czech′ish.** of or pertaining to Czechoslovakia, its people, or their language.

Czech., Czechoslovakia. Also, **Czechosl.**

Czech·o·slo·vak (chek′ə slō′vak, -väk), *n.* **1.** a member of the branch of the Slavic peoples comprising the Czechs proper, the Moravians, and the Slovaks. **2.** a native or inhabitant of Czechoslovakia. **—***adj.* **3.** of or pertaining to Czechoslovakia, its people, or their language. Also, **Czech′o-Slo′vak.**

Czech·o·slo·va·ki·a (chek′ə slə vä′kē ə, -vak′ē ə), *n.* a former republic in central Europe: formed after World War I; comprised Bohemia, Moravia, Slovakia, and part of Silesia; a federal republic 1968–92. 49,383 sq. mi. (127,903 sq. km). *Cap.:* Prague. Formerly (1990–92), **Czech and Slo′vak Fed′erative Repub′lic;** (1948–89), **Czech′oslo′vak So′cialist Repub′lic. —Czech′·o·slo·va′ki·an, Czech′o-Slo·va′ki·an,** *adj., n.*

Czech′ Repub′lic, a republic in central Europe: includes the regions of Bohemia, Moravia, and part of Silesia; formerly part of Czechoslovakia; independent since 1993. 10,311,831; 30,449 sq. mi. (78,864 sq. km). *Cap.:* Prague.

Czer·no·witz (cheʀ′nô vits), *n.* German name of **Cernăuţi.**

Czer·ny (cher′nē), *n.* **Carl,** 1791–1857, Austrian composer, esp. of exercises in piano technique.

Czę·sto·cho·wa (cheɴ′stô hô′vä), *n.* a city in S Poland. 200,000.

CONCISE ETYMOLOGY KEY: <, descended or borrowed from; >, whence; b., blend of, blended; c., cognate with; cf., compare; deriv., derivative; equiv., equivalent; imit., imitative; obl., oblique; r., replacing; s., stem; sp., spelling, spelled; resp., respelling, respelled; trans., translation; ?, origin unknown; *, unattested; ‡, probably earlier than. See the full key inside the front cover.

DEVELOPMENT OF MAJUSCULE								
NORTH SEMITIC	GREEK		ETR.	LATIN		MODERN		
						GOTHIC	ITALIC	ROMAN
Δ	Δ	Δ	D	D	D	𝔇	*D*	D

D

DEVELOPMENT OF MINUSCULE					
ROMAN CURSIVE	ROMAN UNCIAL	CAROL. MIN.	MODERN		
			GOTHIC	ITALIC	ROMAN
d	δ	d	d	*d*	d

The fourth letter of the English alphabet developed from North Semitic *daleth* and Greek *delta*. The capital (D) corresponds generally to the North Semitic *daleth* and Greek *delta* (Δ), arriving at its present form in Latin. The minuscule (d) corresponds closely to the Greek *delta* (δ), acquiring its present form from the Roman cursive *d*.

D, d (dē), *n., pl.* **D's** or **Ds, d's** or **ds.** **1.** the fourth letter of the English alphabet, a consonant. **2.** any spoken sound represented by the letter *D* or *d*, as in *dog, ladder, ladle,* or *pulled.* **3.** something having the shape of a D. **4.** a written or printed representation of the letter *D* or *d*. **5.** a device, as a printer's type, for reproducing the letter *D* or *d*.

D-, *Symbol, Biochem.* (of a molecule) having a configuration resembling the dextrorotatory isomer of glyceraldehyde: always printed as a small capital, roman character (distinguished from L-). Cf. ***d-***.

d-, *Symbol, Chem., Biochem.* dextrorotatory; dextro- (distinguished from *l-*). Cf. **D-.**

d'[1]**,** *prep.* **1.** de (used in French names as an elided form of *de*): *Charles Louis d'Albert.* **2.** di (used in Italian names as an elided form of *di*): *Gabriele d'Annunzio.*

d'[2]**,** *Pron. Spelling.* contraction of *do* or *did* before *you: How d'you like your eggs cooked? D'you go to the movies last night?*

1. contraction of *had: I was glad they'd gone.* **2.** contraction of *did: Where'd they go?* **3.** contraction of *should* or *would: He'd like to go. I'd like to remind you of your promise.* **4.** contraction of *-ed: She OK'd the plan.*

D, **1.** *Elect.* debye. **2.** deep. **3.** depth. **4.** *Optics.* diopter. **5.** divorced. **6.** Dutch.

D, *Symbol.* **1.** the fourth in order or in a series. **2.** (*sometimes l.c.*) (in some grading systems) a grade or mark, as in school or college, indicating the quality of a student's work as poor or barely passing. **3.** (*sometimes l.c.*) a classification, rating, or the like, indicating poor quality. **4.** *Music.* **a.** the second tone in the scale of C major, or the fourth tone in the relative minor scale, A minor. **b.** a string, key, or pipe tuned to this tone. **c.** a written or printed note representing this tone. **d.** (in the fixed system of solmization) the second tone of the scale of C major, called *re.* **e.** the tonality having D as the tonic note. **5.** (*sometimes l.c.*) the Roman numeral for 500. Cf. **Roman numerals.** **6.** *Chem.* deuterium. **7.** *Elect.* **a.** electric displacement. **b.** a battery size for 1.5 volt dry cells: diameter, 1.3 in. (3.3 cm); length, 2.4 in. (6 cm). **8.** *Biochem.* aspartic acid. **9.** a symbol for a shoe width size narrower than E and wider than C. **10.** a proportional brassiere cup size larger than C.

D., **1.** day. **2.** December. **3.** Democrat. **4.** Democratic. **5.** *Physics.* density. **6.** Deus. **7.** Deuteronomy. **8.** Doctor. **9.** dose. **10.** Dutch.

d., **1.** (in prescriptions) give. [< L *dā*] **2.** date. **3.** daughter. **4.** day. **5.** deceased. **6.** deep. **7.** degree. **8.** delete. **9.** *Brit.* pence. [< L *denārii*] **10.** *Brit.* penny. [< L *denārius*] **11.** *Physics.* density. **12.** depth. **13.** deputy. **14.** dialect. **15.** dialectal. **16.** diameter. **17.** died. **18.** dime. **19.** dividend. **20.** dollar; dollars. **21.** dose. **22.** drachma.

da (də; *It.* dä; *Port.* də, dä), *prep.* from; of (used in Italian and Portuguese personal names, originally to indicate place of origin): *Lorenzo da Ponte; Vasco da Gama.* Also, **Da.** [< It *da* << L *dē* about, concerning + *ab, ā* from; < Pg *da*, contr. of *de* of, from (< L *dē*) + *a* fem. sing. definite article (<< L *illa* that)]

da (dä), *adv., n. Russian.* yes.

DA, **1.** Department of Agriculture. **2.** Dictionary of Americanisms.

DA (dē′ā′), *n., pl.* **DAs, DA's.** a male hairstyle, esp. of the 1950's, in which the hair is slicked back on both sides to overlap at the back of the head. [euphemistic abbr. of *duck's ass*]

DA., (in Algeria) dinar; dinars.

da., **1.** daughter. **2.** day; days.

D/A, **1.** (*sometimes l.c.*) days after acceptance. **2.** deposit account. **3.** documents against acceptance. **4.** documents for acceptance.

D.A., **1.** delayed action. **2.** direct action. **3.** District Attorney. **4.** documents against acceptance. **5.** documents for acceptance. **6.** doesn't answer; don't answer.

dab[1] (dab), *v.,* **dabbed, dab•bing,** *n.* —*v.t.* **1.** to pat or tap gently, as with something soft or moist: *The child dabbed his eyes with the handkerchief.* **2.** to apply (a substance) by light strokes: *He dabbed the ointment on the rash.* **3.** to strike, esp. lightly, as with the hand. **4.** *Masonry.* to dress (stonework) with a pointed tool. **5.** *Western U.S.* to throw (a rope or line) in an effort to lasso or catch something: *Joe dabbed his rope on the steer.* —*v.i.* **6.** to strike lightly; make a dab; pat: *She dabbed at the stain on her dress.* —*n.* **7.** a quick or light blow; a pat, as with the hand or something soft. **8.** a small moist lump or mass: *a dab of butter.* **9.** a small quantity: *a dab of powder.* [1250–1300; ME *dabben;* cf. Norw *dabbe* shuffle along, walk slowly, G *Tappe* pat, *tappen* to feel along, grope]
—**Syn. 8.** pat, bit; dollop, smidgen.

dab[2] (dab), *n.* any of several flatfishes of the genus *Limanda,* esp. the European flatfish, *L. limanda.* [1570–80; perh. special use of DAB[1]]

dab[3] (dab), *Slang.* —*n.* **1.** Also called **dab′ hand′.** a person skilled in something; an expert. **2.** an excellent or extraordinary person or thing. —*adj.* **3.** expert; excellent; extraordinary. [1685–95; of uncert. orig.]

DAB, Dictionary of American Biography.

dab•ber (dab′ər), *n.* **1.** a person or thing that dabs. **2.** a cushionlike article used for applying ink, as by printers and engravers. [1780–90; DAB[1] + -ER[1]]

dab•ble (dab′əl), *v.,* **-bled, -bling.** —*v.i.* **1.** to play and splash in or as if in water, esp. with the hands. **2.** to work at anything in an irregular or superficial manner: *to dabble in literature.* **3.** (of a duck) to feed on shallow-water vegetation with rapid, splashing movements of the bill. —*v.t.* **4.** to wet slightly in or with a liquid; splash; spatter. **5.** *Chiefly South Midland U.S.* to wash or rinse off lightly. [1550–60; prob. DAB[1] + -LE; cf. D *dabbelen, dabben*] —**dab′bler,** *n.* —**dab′bling•ly,** *adv.*
—**Syn. 2.** putter, fiddle, toy, dally.

dab′bling duck′, any of numerous shallow-water ducks, esp. of the genus *Anas,* that typically feed by upending and dabbling (contrasted with *diving duck*).

dab•chick (dab′chik′), *n.* any of various small grebes, esp. the little grebe. [1565–75; earlier *dapchick* (see DAP, CHICK); cf. *doppened* moorhen (lit., dipping duck)]

dab•ster (dab′stər), *n.* **1.** *Slang.* an expert. **2.** *Informal.* a person who works in a superficial or clumsy manner; dabbler. [1700–10; DAB[3] + -STER]

da ca•po (dä kä′pō; *It.* dä kä′pô), repeated from the beginning (used as a musical direction). [1715–25; < It: lit., from the head; see DA, CHIEF]

da•car•ba•zine (də kär′bə zēn′), *n. Pharm.* a toxic, light-sensitive powder, $C_6H_{10}N_6O$, used in the treatment of Hodgkin's disease and metastatic malignant melanoma. [1960–65; contr. and rearrangement of the chemical name]

Dac•ca (dak′ə, dä′kə), *n.* Dhaka.

dace (dās), *n., pl.* (*esp. collectively*) **dace,** (*esp. referring to two or more kinds or species*) **dac•es.** **1.** a small, freshwater cyprinoid fish, *Leuciscus leuciscus,* of Europe, having a stout, fusiform body. **2.** any of several similar or related fishes of the U.S. [1400–50; late ME *darce, darse* < OF *dars* < LL *darsus*]

da•cha (dä′chə), *n.* a Russian country house or villa. Also, **datcha.** [1895–1900; < Russ *dácha,* orig., allotment of land; c. Serbo-Croatian *dȁća,* Slovene *dáča* tribute < Slavic **datja;* akin to L *dōs,* s. *dōt-* DOWRY, DOT[2]]

Da•chau (dä′kou; *Ger.* dä′KHOU), *n.* a city in S Germany, near Munich: site of Nazi concentration camp. 33,200.

Da•ché (da shā′; *Fr.* dA shā′), *n.* **Lilly,** born 1914?, U.S. hat designer, born in France.

dachs•hund (däks′ho͝ont′, -ho͝ond′, -ənd, daks′-, dash′-), *n.* one of a German breed of dogs having short legs, a long body and ears, and a usually tan or black-and-tan coat. [1840–50; < G, equiv. to *Dachs* badger + *Hund* dog]

dachshund
8 in. (20 cm) high at shoulder

Da•ci•a (dā′shē ə, -shə), *n.* an ancient kingdom and later a Roman province in S Europe between the Carpathian Mountains and the Danube, corresponding generally to modern Rumania and adjacent regions.

dack•er (dak′ər, dä′kər), *v.i. Scot. and North Eng.* **1.** to totter or stagger. **2.** to waver or shake. **3.** to saunter; move slowly or idly. **4.** to vacillate; act irresolutely or indecisively. Also, **daiker.** [1625–35; perh. < early D *daeckeren* to flutter, vibrate, MD *dakeren* to wave, flutter]

Dack•o (dak′ō, dä′kō), *n.* **David,** born 1930, African statesman: president of the Central African Republic (now Central African Empire) 1960–66.

da•coit (də koit′), *n.* (in India and Burma) a member of a class of criminals who engage in organized robbery and murder. Also, **dakoit.** [1800–10; < Hindi *ḍakait*]

da•coit•y (də koi′tē), *n., pl.* **-coit•ies.** (in India and Burma) gang robbery; robbery by dacoits. Also, **dakoity.** [1810–20; < Hindi *ḍakaitī,* deriv. of *ḍakait* DACOIT]

dac•quoise (*Fr.* dA KWAZ′), *n.* a dessert consisting of baked layers of nut-flavored meringue with a cream filling, sometimes with the addition of fruit, served chilled. [< F, fem. of *dacquois* pertaining to DAX]

Da•cron (dā′kron, dak′ron), *Trademark.* a brand of polyester textile fiber that is wrinkle-resistant and strong.

dacryo-, a combining form meaning "tear," used in the formation of compound words; *dacryorrhea.* Also, *esp. before a vowel,* **dacry-.** [< Gk *dakryo-,* comb. form repr. *dákry* or *dákryon* TEAR[1]]

dac•ry•on (dak′rē on′), *n., pl.* **-ry•a** (-rē ə). *Anat.* the point of junction of the maxillary, lacrimal, and frontal bones. [1875–80; < NL < Gk *dákryon* a tear (var. of *dákry*); see DACRYO-]

dac•ry•or•rhe•a (dak′rē ə rē′ə), *n. Med.* excessive flow of tears. [DACRYO- + -RRHEA]

dac•ti•no•my•cin (dak′tə nō mī′sin), *n. Pharm.* a cytotoxic polypeptide, $C_{62}H_{86}N_{12}O_{16}$, isolated from the bacterium *Streptomyces parvullus,* used in the treatment of certain cancers. Also called **actinomycin D.** [reversal of *actinomycin D;* see ACTINOMYCIN]

dac•tyl (dak′til), *n.* **1.** *Pros.* a foot of three syllables, one long followed by two short in quantitative meter, or one stressed followed by two unstressed in accentual meter, as in *gently* and *humanly.* **2.** a finger or toe. [1350–1400; ME < L *dactylus* < Gk *dáktylos* finger, a dactyl, referring to the three joints of the finger]

Dac•tyl (dak′til), *n., pl.* **-tyls, -tyl•i** (-ti lī′). *Class. Myth.* any of a number of beings dwelling on Mount Ida

CONCISE PRONUNCIATION KEY: act, cāpe, dâre, pärt; set, ēqual; if, īce; ox, ōver, ôrder, oil, bo͝ok, bo͞ot, out; up, ûrge; child; sing; shoe; thin, t͟hat; zh as in *treasure.* ə = *a* as in *alone, e* as in *system, i* as in *easily, o* as in *gallop, u* as in *circus;* ə as in *fire* (fīər), *hour* (ouər). l and n can serve as syllabic consonants, as in *cradle* (krād′l), and *button* (but′n). See the full key inside the front cover.

and working as metalworkers and magicians. Also, **Dak·tyl.** [< Gk *Dáktyloi* (*Idaîoi*) (Idaean) craftsmen or wizards (pl. of *dáktylos;* see DACTYL)]

-dactyl, var. of **-dactylous,** esp. with nouns: *pterodactyl.*

dac·tyl·ic (dak til′ik), *adj.* **1.** of, containing, or characterized by dactyls: *dactylic hexameter; a dactylic line.* **2.** of a dactyl. —*n.* **3.** a dactylic verse. [1580–90; < L *dactylicus* < Gk *daktylikós.* See DACTYL, -IC] —**dac·tyl′i·cal·ly,** *adv.*

dactylo-, a combining form meaning "finger," "toe," used in the formation of compound words: *dactylomegaly.* Also, **dactyl-.** [< Gk, comb. form repr. *dáktylos* finger, toe]

dac·tyl·o·gram (dak til′ə gram′), *n.* a fingerprint. [1910–15; DACTYLO- + -GRAM[1]]

dac·ty·log·ra·phy (dak′tə log′rə fē), *n.* the study of fingerprints for purposes of identification. [1880–85; DACTYLO- + -GRAPHY] —**dac′ty·log′ra·pher,** *n.* —**dac·ty·lo·graph·ic** (dak′tə lə graf′ik), *adj.*

dac·ty·lol·o·gy (dak′tə lol′ə jē), *n., pl.* **-gies.** the technique of communicating by signs made with the fingers, esp. in the manual alphabets used by the deaf. [1650–60; DACTYLO- + -LOGY]

dac·ty·lo·meg·a·ly (dak′tə lō meg′ə lē), *n. Med.* abnormal enlargement of the fingers or toes. [DACTYLO- + -MEGALY]

dac·ty·los·co·py (dak′tə los′kə pē), *n.* a method of studying fingerprints to establish identification. [1905–10; DACTYLO- + -SCOPY]

-dactylous, a combining form meaning "fingered, possessing fingers," or "toed, possessing toes," used to form compound words in which the initial element specifies the type or number of fingers or toes: *tridactylous.* [< Gk *-daktylos,* adj. deriv. of *dáktylos* finger, toe; see -OUS]

dac·ty·lus (dak′tə ləs), *n., pl.* **-li** (-lī′, -lē′). an enlarged portion of the leg after the first joint in some insects, as the pollen-carrying segment in the hind leg of certain bees. [NL < Gk; see DACTYL]

-dactyly, a combination of **-dactyl** and **-y**[3], used to form nouns to stems in **-dactyl:** *hyperdactyly.* [< NL *-dactylia.* See -DACTYL, -Y[3]]

dad[1] (dad), *n. Informal.* father. [1490–1500; prob. orig. nursery word]

dad[2] (dad), *interj. Informal.* God (used in combination in mild oaths): *dad-blamed; dad-gummed.* [1670–80; euphemism for *God*]

dad[3] (dad), *n. Scot. and North Eng.* **1.** a solid blow or knock. **2.** a large slice, lump, or portion. [1710–20; prob. var. of DAB[1]]

ḍad (däd), *n.* the 15th letter of the Arabic alphabet. [< Ar]

da·da (dä′dä), *n.* (*sometimes cap.*) the style and techniques of a group of artists, writers, etc., of the early 20th century who exploited accidental and incongruous effects in their work and who programmatically challenged established canons of art, thought, morality, etc. [1915–20; < F: hobby horse, childish redupl. of *da* giddyap] —**da′da·ism,** *n.* —**da′da·ist,** *n.* —**da′da·is′tic,** *adj.* —**da′da·is′ti·cal·ly,** *adv.*

dad-blamed (dad′blāmd′), *adj., adv.* damned (used as a euphemism in expressions of surprise, disgust, anger, etc.): *The dad-blamed car got stuck in a snowdrift. He's so dad-blamed sure of himself.* [1835–45]

dad-blast·ed (dad′blas′tid, -bläs′-), *adj., adv.* damned (used as a euphemism in expressions of surprise, disgust, anger, etc.): *The dad-blasted door won't lock. What makes you so dad-blasted stubborn?* [1835–45]

dad-burned (dad′bûrnd′), *adj., adv.* damned (used as a euphemism in expressions of surprise, disgust, anger, etc.): *I ruined the whole dad-burned batch. You're dad-burned right I do!* [1825–35]

Dad·dah (dad′ə, dä′dä), *n.* **Mokh·tar Ould** (mōkʜ tär′ ould), born 1924, Mauritanian statesman: president of the Republic of Mauritania 1961–78.

dad·dy (dad′ē), *n., pl.* **-dies,** *v.,* **-died, -dy·ing.** —*n.* **1.** a diminutive of **dad**[1]. **2.** *Slang.* See **sugar daddy.** —*v.t.* **3.** *Chiefly Appalachian.* to father or sire. [1490–1500; DAD[1] + -Y[2]]

dad·dy-long·legs (dad′ē lông′legz′, -long′-), *n.* (*used with a singular or plural v.*) **1.** Also called **harvestman.** any of numerous spiderlike arachnids of the order Opiliones, having a compact rounded body and extremely long, slender legs. **2.** *Brit.* a crane fly. Also, **dad′dy long′legs.** [1805–15; DADDY + LONG[1] + LEG + -S[3]]

daddy-longlegs, *Phalangium opilio,* body length to ¾ in. (2 cm); legs to 6 in. (15 cm)

dad-gummed (dad′gumd′), *adj., adv.* damned (used as a euphemism to express anger, irritation, surprise, etc.). Also, **dad′-gum′.** [1940–45, *Amer.*; euphemistic alter. of GODDAMNED]

da·do (dā′dō), *n., pl.* **-does, -dos,** *v.* —*n.* **1.** Also called **die.** *Archit.* the part of a pedestal between the base and the cornice or cap. See diag. under **column. 2.** the lower broad part of an interior wall finished in wallpaper, a fabric, paint, etc. **3.** *Carpentry.* a groove or rectangular section for receiving the end of a board. —*v.t.* **4.** to provide with a dado. **5. dado in,** to insert (a board or the like) into a dado. [1655–65; < It: die, cube, pedestal, perh. < Ar *dad* game]

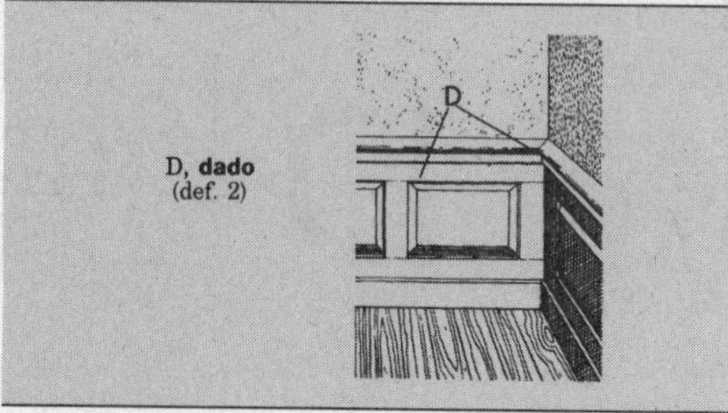

D, **dado** (def. 2)

da′do head′, a rotary cutter composed of several sawlike blades side by side, for cutting dadoes in wood.

D.A.E., Dictionary of American English. Also, **DAE**

dae·dal (dēd′l), *adj.* **1.** skillful; ingenious. **2.** cleverly intricate. **3.** diversified. [1580–90; < L *daedalus* skillful < Gk *daídalos,* equiv. to *daidál*(*lein*) to work with skill + *-os* adj. suffix]

Dae·da·la (dēd′l ə), *n.* (*sometimes used with a plural v.*) either of two festivals held in ancient Boeotia in honor of the reconciliation of Hera with Zeus, one (**Little Daedala**) being held every 6 years, the other (**Great Daedala**), every 59 years. [< Gk *Daídala* (neut. pl.), n. use of *daídalos* DAEDAL]

Daed·a·lid (ded′l id *or, esp. Brit.,* dēd′l id), *adj.* **1.** pertaining to or designating a style of vase painting developed in Attica from the middle to the end of the 7th century B.C., characterized chiefly by the use of the black-figure style in painting and a narrative treatment of subject matter. **2.** pertaining to or designating a style of terra-cotta sculpture developed in Greece during the 7th century B.C. [DAEDAL + -ID[2]]

Dae·da·li·on (dē dā′lē on′), *n. Class. Myth.* a son of Lucifer who, despondent over the death of his daughter Chione, leaped off Parnassus: Apollo changed him into a hawk.

Daed·a·lus (ded′l əs *or, esp. Brit.,* dēd′l əs), *n. Class. Myth.* an Athenian architect who built the labyrinth for Minos and made wings for himself and his son Icarus to escape from Crete. [< L < Gk *Daídalos;* see DAEDAL] —**Dae·da·li·an, Dae·da·le·an** (di dā′lē ən, -dāl′yən), **Dae·dal·ic** (di dal′ik), *adj.*

dae·mon (dē′mən), *n.* **1.** *Class. Myth.* **a.** a god. **b.** a subordinate deity, as the genius of a place or a person's attendant spirit. **2.** a demon. Also, **daimon.** [< L *daemōn* a spirit, an evil spirit < Gk *daímōn* a deity, fate, fortune, cf. *daíesthai* to distribute] —**dae·mon·ic** (dimon′ik), **dae·mon·is·tic** (dē′mə nis′tik), *adj.*

dae·mo·ni·an (di mō′nē ən), *n.* demonian.

dae·mon·ol·o·gy (dē′mə nol′ə jē), *n.* demonology.

daff[1] (daf), *v.i. Scot. and North Eng.* to make sport; dally; play. [1525–35; v. use of *daff* (obs.) a fool, ME *daffe* (n.); see DAFT]

daff[2] (daf), *v.t.* **1.** *Archaic.* to turn or thrust aside. **2.** *Obs.* to doff. [1590–1600; alter. of DOFF]

daf·fa·dil·ly (daf′ə dil′ē), *n., pl.* **-lies.** *Chiefly Brit. Dial.* daffodil. Also, **daf′fo·dil′ly.** [by alter.; see -Y[2]]

daf·fa·down·dil·ly (daf′ə doun′dil′ē), *n., pl.* **-lies.** *Chiefly Brit. Dial.* daffodil. Also, **daf′fo·down′dil′ly.** [1565–75; by alter.]

daf·fing (daf′ing), *n. Scot. and North Eng.* **1.** merriment; playful behavior; foolishness. **2.** *Archaic.* insanity. [1525–35; DAFF[1] + -ING[1]]

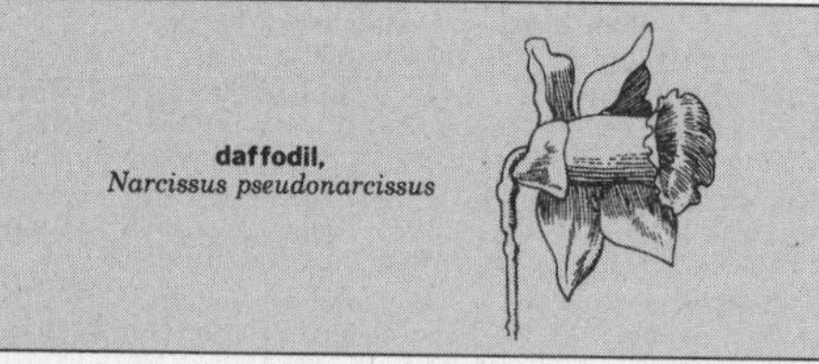
daffodil, *Narcissus pseudonarcissus*

daf·fo·dil (daf′ə dil), *n.* **1.** a bulbous plant, *Narcissus pseudonarcissus,* of the amaryllis family, having solitary, yellow, nodding flowers that bloom in the spring. **2.** (formerly) any plant of the genus *Narcissus.* **3.** clear yellow; canary. —*adj.* **4.** of the color daffodil. [1530–40; unexplained var. of ME *affodile* < VL *affodillus,* var. of *asphodelus* < Gk *asphódelos* ASPHODEL]

daf·fy (daf′ē), *adj.,* **-fi·er, -fi·est.** *Informal.* silly; weak-minded; crazy. [1880–85; *daff* (obs.; see DAFF[1]) + -Y[1]] —**daf′fi·ly,** *adv.* —**daf′fi·ness,** *n.*

daft (daft, däft), *adj.,* **-er, -est. 1.** senseless, stupid, or foolish. **2.** insane; crazy. **3.** *Scot.* merry; playful; frolicsome. [bef. 1000; ME *dafte* uncouth, awkward; earlier, gentle, meek, OE *dæfte;* cf. DEFT] —**daft′ly,** *adv.* —**daft′ness,** *n.*

Da·fydd ap Gwi·lym (dä′viᵺ äp gwi′lim), c1340–c1400, Welsh poet.

dag[1] (dag), *n., v.,* **dagged, dag·ging.** —*n.* **1.** one of a series of decorative scallops or foliations along the edge of a garment, cloth, etc. **2.** *Scot.* daglock. —*v.t.* **3.** to edge (a garment, cloth, etc.) with decorative scallops or the like. [1350–1400; ME *dagge* < ?; cf. OF *dague* dagger]

dag[2] (dag), *n. Australian and New Zealand Informal.* an amusing, unusual person. [1885–90; orig. uncert.]

Dag (däg, dag), *n.* a male given name.

dag, dekagram; dekagrams.

da Ga·ma (də gam′ə; *Port.* də gä′mə), **Vas·co** (vas′kō; *Port.* väsh′ko͞o). See **Gama, Vasco da.**

Da·gan (dä′gän), *n.* the Mesopotamian god of agriculture and the earth: a counterpart of the Phoenician and Philistine Dagon.

Dag·da (däg′də), *n. Irish Myth.* a god, the chief of the Tuatha De Danann, the father of Angus Og and Brigit, and the leader of the battle against the Fomorians. Also, **Daghda.**

Dag·en·ham (dag′ə nəm), *n.* a former borough in Greater London, now a part of Barking and Redbridge.

Da·ge·stan (dä′gə stän′, dag′ə stan′; *Russ.* də gyi-stän′), *n.* **1.** an autonomous republic in the SW Russian Federation on the W shore of the Caspian Sea. 1,800,000; 19,421 sq. mi. (50,300 sq. km). *Cap.:* Makhachkala. Formerly, **Dagestan′ Auton′omous So′viet So′cialist Repub′lic. 2.** a closely woven carpet of this region having a floral design and a zigzag border, usually in pastel shades.

dag·ga (dag′ə), *n. South African.* marijuana. [1670–75; < Afrik, first sp. *da*(*c*)*cha,* lit., hemp, orig. a similar indigenous plant of the genus *Leontis* < Khoikhoi; cf. Nama *daxa-b*]

dag·ger (dag′ər), *n.* **1.** a short, swordlike weapon with a pointed blade and a handle, used for stabbing. **2.** Also called **obelisk.** *Print.* a mark (†) used esp. for references. **3. look daggers at,** to look at angrily, threateningly, or with hate. —*v.t.* **4.** to stab with or as if with a dagger. **5.** *Print.* to mark with a dagger. [1350–1400; ME, prob. alter. of OF *dague,* of obscure orig.; cf. DAG[1]]

dagger (def. 1) with scabbard

dag·ger·board (dag′ər bôrd′, -bōrd′), *n. Naut.* a removable board on a small sailboat, typically of small dimension fore and aft, lowered into the water through a trunk to serve as a keel. Cf. **centerboard.** [DAGGER + BOARD]

dag′ger fern′. See **Christmas fern.**

dag·gle (dag′əl), *v.t., v.i.,* **-gled, -gling.** *Archaic.* to drag or trail through mud, water, etc.; draggle; bemire. [1520–30; *dag* to bemire + -LE]

Dagh·da (däg′də), *n. Irish Myth.* Dagda.

dag·lock (dag′lok′), *n. Scot.* a dangling, matted lock of wool on a sheep. [1615–25; DAG[1] + LOCK[2]]

Dag·mar (dag′mär), *n.* a female given name: fro Danish, meaning "day" and "glory."

da·go (dā′gō), *n., pl.* **-gos, -goes.** (*often cap.*) *Sl* (*disparaging and offensive*). a person of Italian or so times Spanish origin or descent. [1715–25, *Amer.*; alt of *Diego* < Sp: a given name]

Dag·ö (däg′œ′), *n.* Danish name of **Hiiumaa.**

da·go·ba (dä′gə bə), *n.* a dome-shaped memorial al leged to contain relics of Buddha or a Buddhist saint; stupa; chaitya. [1800–10; < Sinhalese *dāgoba* < Pali *dhātugabbha* < Skt *dhātugarbha,* equiv. to *dhātu* relics + *garbha* womb, inside]

Dag·o·bert I (dag′ə bərt; *Fr.* dᴀ gô bᴇʀ′), A.D. 602?–639, Merovingian king of the Franks 628–639.

Da·gon (dā′gon), *n.* a Phoenician and Philistine god of agriculture and the earth: the national god of the Philistines. [< L < Gk < Heb *dāghōn*]

Da′go red′, *Slang* (*offensive*). a cheap red wine, esp. a jug wine of Italian origin. [1895–1900]

D.Agr., Doctor of Agriculture.

Da·gu (dä′gʏ′), *n. Pinyin.* a fortified city in E Hebei province, in NE China, E of Tianjin: battles 1860, 1900. Also, **Taku.**

Da·guerre (də gâr′; *Fr.* dᴀ gᴇʀ′), *n.* **Louis Jacques Man·dé** (lwē zhäk män dā′), 1789–1851, French painter and inventor of the daguerreotype.

da·guerre·o·type (də gâr′ə tīp′, -ē ə tīp′), *n., v.,* **-typed, -typ·ing.** —*n.* **1.** an obsolete photographic process, invented in 1839, in which a picture made on a silver surface sensitized with iodine was developed by exposure to mercury vapor. **2.** a picture made by this process. —*v.t.* **3.** to photograph by this process. [1830–40; named after L. J. M. DAGUERRE; see -O-, -TYPE] —**da·guerre′o·typ′er, da·guerre′o·typ′ist,** *n.* —**da·guerre·o·typ·ic** (də gâr′ə tip′ik, -ē ə tip′-), *adj.* —**da·guerre′o·typ′y,** *n.*

Dag′wood sand′wich (dag′wo͝od), a thick sandwich filled with a variety of meats, cheeses, dressings, and condiments. Also called **Dag′wood.** [named after *Dagwood* Bumstead, a character in the comic strip *Blondie,* who makes and eats such sandwiches]

dah (dä), *n.* an echoic word, the referent of which is a tone interval approximately three times the length of the dot, used to designate the dash of Morse code, International Morse code, etc. Cf. **dit.** [1935–40]

da·ha·be·ah (dä′hə bē′ə), *n.* a large boat used on the Nile as a houseboat or for conveying passengers. Also, **da′ha·bee′yah, da′ha·bi′ah.** [1840–50; < Egyptian Ar *dahabīyah*]

Dahl·gren (dal′grən), *n.* **John Adelphus Bernard,** 1809–70, U.S. naval officer and inventor.

dahl·ia (dal′yə, däl′- *or, esp. Brit.,* dāl′-), *n.* **1.** any composite plant of the genus *Dahlia,* native to Mexico and Central America and widely cultivated for its showy, variously colored flower heads. **2.** the flower or tuberous root of a dahlia. **3.** a pale violet or amethyst color.

—*adj.* **4.** of the color dahlia. [1791; < NL, named after Anders *Dahl* (d. 1789), Swedish botanist; see -IA]

Dah•na (dä′nə, -hə nə), *n.* **1.** an area in the NE Rub' al Khali desert, comprising a region of E central Saudi Arabia. **2.** See **Rub' al Khali.**

Da•ho•mey (də hō′mē; *Fr.* dA ô mā′), *n.* former name of **Benin** (def. 1). —**Da•ho′me•an, Da•ho•man** (də hō′-mən), *adj., n.*

da•hoon (də ho͞on′), *n.* an evergreen shrub, *Ilex cassine,* of the southern U.S., having flat, leathery, dark green leaves and red or yellow fruits in large clusters. [1720–30, *Amer.*; orig. uncert.]

dai•but•su (dī bo͝ot′so͞o, -bo͝ot′-; *Japn.* dī′bo͞o tso͞o), *n.* a large representation of the Buddha. [< Japn, equiv. to *dai* (< MChin, equiv. to Chin *dà* big, great) + *butsu* BUTSU]

dai•ker (dā′kər), *v.i. Scot. and North Eng.* dacker.

dai•kon (dī′kən, -kon), *n.* a large, elongated, white winter radish, *Raphanus sativus longipinnatus,* used esp. in Asian cuisine and sometimes pickled. Also called **Chinese radish.** [1890–95; < Japn < MChin, equiv. to Chin *dà* big + *gēn* root]

Dáil Éir•eann (doil′ âr′ôn, -on; *Irish* dol′yᵊ ā′rʏən), the lower house of the parliament of the Republic of Ireland. Also called **Dail.** Cf. **Oireachtas.** [< Ir: assembly of Eire]

dai•ly (dā′lē), *adj., n., pl.* **-lies,** *adv.* —*adj.* **1.** of, done, occurring, or issued each day or each weekday: *daily attendance; a daily newspaper.* **2.** computed or measured by the day: *daily quota; a daily wage.* —*n.* **3.** a newspaper appearing each day or each weekday. **4. dailies,** *Motion Pictures.* a series of hastily printed shots from the previous day's shooting, selected by the director to be viewed for possible inclusion in the final version of the film; rushes. **5.** *Brit.* **a.** a nonresident servant who comes to work every day; a permanently employed servant who sleeps out. **b.** a person employed to do cleaning or other household work by the day. —*adv.* **6.** every day; day by day: *She phoned the hospital daily.* [bef. 1000; late ME; OE *dæglīc.* See DAY, -LY] —**dai′li•ness,** *n.*

dai•ly-bread•er (dā′lē bred′ər), *n. Brit.* a commuter. [1905–10; from the phrase *daily bread* + -ER[1]]

dai′ly dou′ble, a betting system in horse racing and dog racing in which the bettor makes one bet on the winners of two races, usually the first and second, and collects only if both choices win. [1940–45]

dai′ly doz′en, *Informal.* a set of calisthenic exercises to be done each day, originally a set of 12 or more such exercises. [1915–20, *Amer.*]

dai•men (dā′min), *adj. Scot.* rare; occasional. [1775–85; orig. uncert.]

Daim•ler (dīm′lər; *Ger.* dīm′lər), *n.* **Gott•lieb (Wil•helm)** (got′lēb wil′helm; *Ger.* gôt′lēp vil′helm), 1834–1900, German automotive engineer, inventor, and manufacturer.

dai•mon (dī′mōn), *n., pl.* **-mo•nes** (-mə nēz′), **-mons.** daemon. —**dai•mon•ic** (dī mon′ik), **dai•mon•is•tic** (dī′mə nis′tik), *adj.*

dai•myo (dī′myō), *n., pl.* **-myo, -myos.** *Japanese Hist.* one of the great feudal lords who were vassals of the shogun. [1830–40; < Japn, equiv. to *dai* big, great (< Chin) + *myō* name (< Chin)]

dain•ty (dān′tē), *adj.,* **-ti•er, -ti•est,** *n., pl.* **-ties.** —*adj.* **1.** of delicate beauty; exquisite: *a dainty lace handkerchief.* **2.** pleasing to the taste and, often, temptingly served or delicate; delicious: *dainty pastries.* **3.** of delicate discrimination or taste; particular; fastidious: *a dainty eater.* **4.** overly particular; finicky. —*n.* **5.** something delicious to the taste; a delicacy. [1175–1225; ME *deinte* worthiness, happiness, delicacy < AF (OF *deint(i)e*) < L *dignitāt-* (s. of *dignitās*); see DIGNITY] —**dain′ti•ly,** *adv.* —**dain′ti•ness,** *n.*
—**Syn. 1.** fine. See **delicate. 2.** tender, delectable. **3.** See **particular. 4.** overnice. **5.** tidbit, sweetmeat.

dai•qui•ri (dī′kə rē, dak′ə-), *n., pl.* **-ris.** a cocktail of rum, lemon or lime juice, and sugar, often with the addition of fruit and ice and mixed in an electric blender: *a frozen banana daiquiri.* [1915–20; named after *Daiquirí,* town on the east coast of Cuba]

Dai•ren (dī′ren′), *n.* former Japanese name of **Dalian** (def. 2).

dair•y (dâr′ē), *n., pl.* **dair•ies,** *adj.* —*n.* **1.** an establishment, as a room, building, or buildings, where milk and cream are kept and butter and cheese are made. **2.** a shop or company that sells milk, butter, etc. **3.** the business of a dairy farm, concerned with the production and treatment of milk and cream and the manufacture of butter and cheese. **4.** See **dairy farm. 5.** (in Jewish dietary law) dairy products. —*adj.* **6.** of or pertaining to a dairy or a dairy farm. **7.** of, for, or pertaining to milk, cream, butter, cheese, etc.: *dairy products; the dairy case at a supermarket.* **8.** (in Jewish dietary law) of or pertaining to those foods, including all milk products, eggs, fish, vegetables, etc., that may be eaten at a meal in which milk is served, in contrast to meat and meat products, which may not. [1250–1300; ME *daierie,* equiv. to *daie, deie* dairymaid (OE *dǣge* bread maker; c. ON *deigja*; see LADY) + *-erie* -ERY]

dair′y breed′, any of several breeds of cattle developed primarily for production of milk rather than meat, as Ayrshire, Guernsey, Holstein, and Jersey breeds. [1855–60]

dair′y cat′tle, cows raised mainly for their milk, esp. cows of a dairy breed. [1890–95]

dair′y farm′, a farm devoted chiefly to the production of milk and the manufacture of butter and cheese. [1775–85].

dair•y•ing (dâr′ē ing), *n.* the business of a dairy. [1640–50; DAIRY + -ING[1]]

dair•y•land (dâr′ē land′), *n.* **1.** an area or region specializing in dairy production, as Wisconsin and Minnesota in the U.S. **2.** land suitable for growing forage crops for dairy cattle. [DAIRY + -LAND]

dair•y•maid (dâr′ē mād′), *n.* a girl or woman employed in a dairy. [1590–1600; DAIRY + MAID]

dair•y•man (dâr′ē mən), *n., pl.* **-men. 1.** an owner or manager of a dairy. **2.** an employee in a dairy. [1775–85; DAIRY + -MAN]
—**Usage.** See **-man.**

dair•y•wom•an (dâr′ē wo͝om′ən), *n., pl.* **-wom•en.** a woman who owns, manages, or works in a dairy. [1600–10; DAIRY + -WOMAN]
—**Usage.** See **-woman.**

da•is (dā′is, dī′-, dās), *n.* a raised platform, as at the front of a room, for a lectern, throne, seats of honor, etc. [1225–75; ME *deis* < AF (OF *dois*) < L *discus* quoit; see DISCUS]

dai•shi•ki (dī shē′kē), *n., pl.* **-kis.** dashiki.

dai•sy (dā′zē), *n., pl.* **-sies. 1.** any of various composite plants the flowers of which have a yellow disk and white rays, as the English daisy and the oxeye daisy. **2.** Also called **daisy ham.** a small section of pork shoulder, usually smoked, boned, and weighing from two to four pounds. Cf. **picnic** (def. 3). **3.** *Slang.* someone or something of first-rate quality: *That new car is a daisy.* **4.** a cheddar cheese of cylindrical shape, weighing about 20 pounds. **5. push up daisies,** *Informal.* to be dead and buried. [bef. 1000; ME *dayesye,* OE *dægesēge* the day's eye] —**dai′sied,** *adj.*

Dai•sy (dā′zē), *n.* a female given name.

dai′sy chain′, 1. a string of daisies linked together to form a chain. **2.** such a chain used as a garland or carried on festive days by a group of women college students. **3.** a series of interconnected or related things or events: *a daisy chain of legislative delays and stalemates.* **4.** *Slang.* a group sexual activity in which the participants serve as active and passive partners to different people simultaneously. **5.** *Com.* a series of transactions designed to create the appearance of active trading, as in a particular stock, in order to manipulate the price. [1835–45]

dai•sy-cut•ter (dā′zē kut′ər), *n.* **1.** *Sports Slang.* a batted or served ball that skims along near the ground. **2.** *Mil. Slang.* an antipersonnel fragmentation bomb. [1785–95]

dai′sy flea′bane, a North American composite plant, *Erigeron annuus,* having hairy stems and numerous, small, daisylike flowers with narrow white rays. [1840–50, *Amer.*]

dai′sy ham′, daisy (def. 2). [1935–40]

dai′sy wheel′, a small metal or plastic wheel with raised, fully formed letters, numbers, and symbols on the tips of petallike spokes: used as the printing element in a type of electronic typewriter or computer printer (**dai′sy wheel′ print′er**). Also called **printwheel.** [1975–80]

dak (dôk, däk), *n.* **1.** transportation by relays of people or horses, esp. in the East Indies. **2.** mail delivered by such transportation. Also, **dauk, dawk.** [1820–30; < Hindi *ḍāk*]

Dak., Dakota.

Da•kar (dä kär′), *n.* a seaport in and the capital of Senegal; capital of former French West Africa. 600,000; 68 sq. mi. (176 sq. km).

Dakh•la (däkн′lä), *n.* **1.** an oasis in S Egypt: source of ocher. **2.** Formerly, **Villa Cisneros.** a seaport and town in Western Sahara: former capital of Río de Oro in the former Spanish Sahara, on the NW coast of Africa. 7000.

dakh•ma (däk′mə), *n.* See **tower of silence.** [1860–65; < Pers; MPers *dakhmak,* Avestan *daxma-* funeral site]

da•koit (də koit′), *n.* dacoit.

da•koit•y (də koi′tē), *n., pl.* **-koit•ies.** dacoity.

Da•ko•ta (də kō′tə), *n.* **1.** a former territory in the United States: divided into the states of North Dakota and South Dakota 1889. **2.** North Dakota or South Dakota. **3. the Dakotas,** North Dakota and South Dakota. **4.** Also called **Sioux.** a member of the largest tribe of the Siouan stock of North American Indians, who originally occupied Minnesota and Wisconsin and later migrated westward to the Great Plains. **5.** Santee (defs. 3, 4). **6.** a Siouan language spoken by the Dakota and Assiniboin Indians. —**Da•ko′tan,** *adj., n.*

Dak•tyl (dak′til), *n., pl.* **-tyls, -tyl•i** (-ti lī′). Dactyl.

dal (däl), *n. East Indian Cookery.* a sauce made from lentils and spices, usually served with rice. Also **dhal.** [< Hindi *dāl* split pulse, cooked pulse; cf. Skt *dal-* to split]

dāl (däl), *n.* the eighth letter of the Arabic alphabet. [< Ar]

Dal (däl), *n.* a river in S Sweden, flowing SE from the W border to the Gulf of Bothnia. ab. 250 mi. (405 km) long.

dal, dekaliter; dekaliters.

Da•la•dier (dA lA dyā′), *n.* **É•douard** (ā dwAʀ′), 1884–1970, premier of France 1933, 1934, 1938–40.

Da•lai La•ma (dä′lī lä′mə), (formerly) the ruler and chief monk of Tibet, believed to be a reincarnation of Avalokitesvara and sought for among newborn children after the death of the preceding Dalai Lama. Cf. **Tashi Lama.** [< Mongolian, equiv. to *dalai* ocean + *lama* a celibate priest]

da•lan (də län′), *n.* (in Persian and Indian architecture) a veranda or open hall for reception of visitors. Also, **dallan.** [< Pers *dālān*]

dal•a•pon (dal′ə pon′), *n. Chem.* a selective herbicide, $C_3H_4Cl_2O_2$, used to eradicate certain grass weeds in sugarcane and other crops. [1950–55; prob. *d(i)-al(ph)a-(dichloropro)p(i)on(ic acid),* an alternate chemical name; see DI-[1], ALPHA, CHLORO-, PROPIONIC]

da•la•si (dä lä′sē), *n., pl.* **-si, -sis.** a paper money, cupronickel coin, and monetary unit of Gambia, equal to 100 bututs.

d'Al•bert (dal′bərt; *Ger.* däl′bеʀt), *n.* **Eu•gen** (oi gān′) (or **Eugene**) **Francis Charles.** See **Albert, d', Eugen** (or **Eugene**) **Francis Charles.**

Dal•croze (*Fr.* dAl kʀôz′), *n.* Jaques-Dalcroze.

dale (dāl), *n.* a valley, esp. a broad valley. [bef. 900; ME *dal,* OE *dæl;* c. G *Tal,* ON *dalr,* Goth *dals*]

Dale (dāl), *n.* **1. Sir Henry Hal•lett** (hal′it), 1875–1968, English physiologist: Nobel prize for medicine 1936. **2. Sir Thomas,** died 1619, British colonial administrator in America: governor of Virginia 1614–16. **3.** a male or female given name.

Da•lén (də län′, da-), *n.* **Gus•taf** (go͝os′täf), 1869–1937, Swedish inventor: Nobel prize for physics 1912.

dales•man (dālz′mən), *n., pl.* **-men.** a person living in a dale or valley, esp. in the northern counties of England. [1760–70; DALE + 'S[1] + MAN[1]]

da•leth (dä′ləd, -ləth, -lət; *Seph. Heb.* dä′let), *n.* **1.** the fourth letter of the Hebrew alphabet. **2.** the consonant sound represented by this letter. Also, **da′let, da•les** (*Ashk. Heb.* dä′ləs). [< Heb *dāleth,* akin to *dālāh* door]

Da•ley (dā′lē), *n.* **Richard J(oseph),** 1902–76, U.S. politician: mayor of Chicago 1955–76.

Dal•hou•sie (dal ho͞o′zē, -hou′-), *n.* **1. George Ramsay, Earl of,** 1770–1838, British general: governor of the Canadian colonies 1819–28. **2. James Andrew Broun Ramsay, 1st Marquis and 10th Earl of,** 1812–60, British statesman: viceroy of India 1848–56.

Da•li (dä′lē), *n.* **Sal•va•dor** (sal′və dôr′; *Sp.* säl′vä-ᴛʜôʀ′), 1904–89, Spanish painter and illustrator.

Da•lian (dä′lyän′), *n. Pinyin.* **1.** Formerly, **Lüda.** an urban municipality in S Liaoning province, in NE China, on the southern tip of the Liaodong peninsula: comprises the old cities of Dalian and Lüshun, and five adjacent counties. 7,000,000; ab. 1300 sq. mi. (3367 sq. km). **2.** Formerly, *Japanese,* **Dairen;** *Russian,* **Dalny.** an old city in S Liaoning province, in NE China: one of the finest harbors on the E Asian coast; now part of the urban area of Dalian. 4,000,000. Also, **Talien.**

Da•li•esque (dä′lē esk′), *adj.* of, pertaining to, resembling, or characteristic of the surrealist art of Salvador Dali: *giant advertising posters depicting Daliesque distortions of everyday objects.* [1940–45; DALI + -ESQUE]

Dal•i•la (dal′ə lə), *n. Douay Bible.* Delilah (def. 1).

Dal′kon Shield′ (dal′kon), *Pharm., Trademark.* a brand name for an intrauterine contraceptive device withdrawn from the market in 1974, having been associated with an increased risk of pelvic inflammatory disease and spontaneous abortion in women who used it.

dal•lan (də län′), *n.* dalan.

Dal•la•pic•co•la (dä′lä pē′kō lə; *It.* däl′lä pēk′kô lä), *n.* **Lu•i•gi** (lo͞o ē′jē), 1904–75, Italian composer.

Dal•las (dal′əs), *n.* **1. George Miff•lin** (mif′lin), 1792–1864, U.S. diplomat: vice-president of the U.S. 1845–49. **2.** a city in NE Texas. 904,078. —**Dal′las•ite′,** *n.*

dalles (dalz), *n.pl.* the rapids of a river running between the walls of a canyon or gorge. Also, **dells.** [1825–35, *Amer.*; < CanF, pl. of F dial. (Normandy) *dalle* lit., sink << Gmc; cf. OE *dæl* DALE]

Dalles (dalz), *n.* **The,** a city in N Oregon. 10,820. Also called **City of the Dalles.**

dal•li•ance (dal′ē əns, dal′yəns), *n.* **1.** a trifling away of time; dawdling. **2.** amorous toying; flirtation. [1300–50; ME *daliaunce.* See DALLY, -ANCE]

Dal•lin (dal′in), *n.* **Cyrus Earle,** 1861–1944, U.S. sculptor.

Dal′lis grass′ (dal′is), a pasture grass, *Paspalum dilatatum,* native to South America and naturalized in the southern U.S. [1905–10; after A. T. *Dallis* (or Dallas), a farmer who cultivated the grass successfully near La Grange, Georgia, in the late 19th century]

Dall's′ sheep′ (dôlz), a white-haired wild sheep, *Ovis dalli,* of mountainous regions of northwestern North America, having curved horns. Also, **Dall′ sheep′.** [1905–10; named after William H. *Dall* (1845–1927), American naturalist]

dal•ly (dal′ē), *v.,* **-lied, -ly•ing.** —*v.i.* **1.** to waste time; loiter; delay. **2.** to act playfully, esp. in an amorous or flirtatious way. **3.** to play mockingly; trifle: *to dally with danger.* —*v.t.* **4.** to waste (time) (usually fol. by *away*). [1250–1300; ME *dalien* < AF *dalier* to chat, of uncert. orig.] —**dal′li•er,** *n.* —**dal′ly•ing•ly,** *adv.*
—**Syn. 1.** See **loiter. 2.** flirt, tease, trifle. **3.** toy.

Dal•mane (dal′mān), *Pharm., Trademark.* a brand of flurazepam.

Dal•ma•tia (dal mā′shə), *n.* **1.** a historic region along the Adriatic coast of Croatia: a former Austrian crownland. **2.** a Roman province formed by Emperor Tiberius and called after the tribe inhabiting the area.

CONCISE PRONUNCIATION KEY: act, cāpe, dâre, pärt; set, ēqual; *if,* īce; ox, ōver, ôrder, oil, bo͞ok, bo͞ot, out; up, ûrge; child; sing; shoe; thin, tħat; zh as in *treasure.* ə = *a* as in *alone, e* as in *system, i* as in *easily, o* as in *gallop, u* as in *circus;* ᵊ as in *fire* (fīᵊr), *hour* (ouᵊr). l and n can serve as syllabic consonants, as in *cradle* (krād′l), and *button* (but′n). See the full key inside the front cover.

Dal•ma•tian (dal mā′shən), *adj.* **1.** of or pertaining to Dalmatia or its people. —*n.* **2.** an inhabitant of Dalmatia, esp. a member of the native Slavic-speaking people of Dalmatia. **3.** Also called **coach dog, Dalma′tian dog′.** one of a breed of short-haired dogs having a white coat marked with black or brown spots. **4.** a Romance language of Dalmatia, extinct since 1898. [1575–85; DALMATI(A) + -AN]

Dalmatian (def. 3) 21 in. (53 cm) high at shoulder

dal•mat•ic (dal mat′ik), *n.* **1.** *Eccles.* a vestment worn over the alb by the deacon, as at the celebration of the Mass, and worn by bishops on some occasions, as at a coronation. **2.** a similar vestment worn by a sovereign of England at his or her coronation. [1400–50; late ME < AF *dalmatike* < LL *Dalmatica* (*vestis*) Dalmatian (garment). See DALMATIA, -IC]

Dal•ny (däl′nē), *n.* former Russian name of **Dalian** (def. 2).

Dal•rym•ple (dal rim′pəl, dal′rim-), *n.* **Sir James, 1st Viscount Stair,** 1619–95, Scottish jurist.

dal se•gno (däl sän′yō; *It.* däl se′nyô), go back to the sign marking the beginning of a repeat (used as a musical direction). [1850–55; < It: from the sign; see SIGN]

dal•ton (dôl′tn), *n. Physics.* See **atomic mass unit.** [1935–40; named after J. DALTON]

Dal•ton (dôl′tn), *n.* **1. John,** 1766–1844, English chemist and physicist. **2. Robert,** 1867–92, U.S. outlaw in the West. **3.** a city in NW Georgia. 20,743. **4.** a male given name.

Dal•to•ni•an (dôl tō′nē ən), *adj.* **1.** of John Dalton or his atomic theory. **2.** of or pertaining to daltonism. [1805–15; J. DALTON + -IAN]

dal•ton•ism (dôl′tn iz′əm), *n.* (*sometimes cap.*) *Pathol.* color blindness, esp. the inability to distinguish red from green. [1835–45; J. DALTON + -ISM] —**dal•ton•ic** (dôl-ton′ik), *adj.*

Dal′ton's law′, *Physics, Chem.* the law that the total pressure exerted by a mixture of gases is equal to the sum of the partial pressures of the gases of the mixture. Also called **Dal′ton's law′ of par′tial pres′sures, law of partial pressures.** [named after J. DALTON]

Dal′ton Sys′tem, a method of progressive education whereby students contract to carry through on their own responsibility the year's work as divided up into monthly assignments. Also called **Dal′ton Plan′.** [named after *Dalton,* Massachusetts, where it was first used in the high schools]

Da•ly (dā′lē), *n.* **(John) Au•gus•tin** (ô gus′tin), 1838–99, U.S. playwright, critic, and theatrical manager.

Da′ly Cit′y, a city in central California, S of San Francisco. 78,519.

dam[1] (dam), *n., v.,* **dammed, dam•ming.** —*n.* **1.** a barrier to obstruct the flow of water, esp. one of earth, masonry, etc., built across a stream or river. **2.** a body of water confined by a dam. **3.** any barrier resembling a dam. —*v.t.* **4.** to furnish with a dam; obstruct or confine with a dam. **5.** to stop up; block up. [1275–1325; ME < MD, MLG, *dam;* akin to OE *for-demman* to stop up, block]
—**Syn. 5.** impede, clog, check, choke.

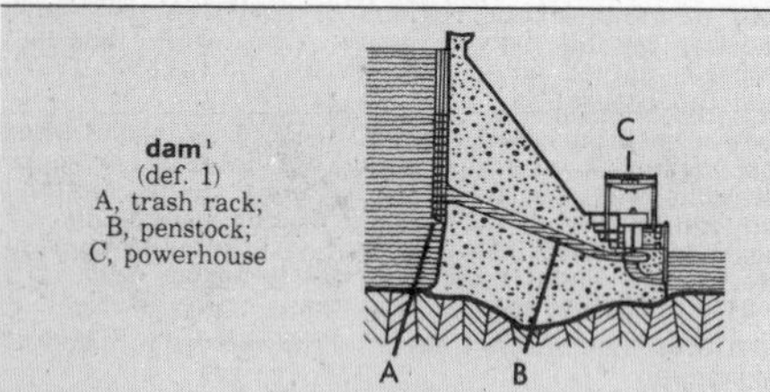

dam[1] (def. 1) A, trash rack; B, penstock; C, powerhouse

dam[2] (dam), *n.* a female parent (used esp. of four-footed domestic animals). [1250–1300; ME; var. of DAME]

Dam (dam, däm), *n.* **(Carl Pe•ter) Hen•rik** (kärl pē′tər hen′rik; *Dan.* kärl pā′tər hen′rik), 1895–1976, Danish biochemist: Nobel prize for medicine 1943.

dam, dekameter; dekameters.

dam•age (dam′ij), *n., v.,* **-aged, -ag•ing.** —*n.* **1.** injury or harm that reduces value or usefulness: *The storm did considerable damage to the crops.* **2. damages,** *Law.* the estimated money equivalent for detriment or injury sustained. **3.** Often, **damages.** *Informal.* cost; expense; charge: *What are the damages for the lubrication job on my car?* —*v.t.* **4.** to cause damage to; injure or harm; reduce the value or usefulness of: *He damaged the saw on a nail.* —*v.i.* **5.** to become damaged: *Soft wood damages easily.* [1250–1300; ME < OF, equiv. to *dam* (< L *damnum* damage, fine) + *-age* -AGE; see DAMN] —**dam′age•a•ble,** *adj.* —**dam′age•a•ble•ness, dam′age•a•bil′i•ty,** *n.* —**dam′ag•er,** *n.*
—**Syn. 1.** loss. DAMAGE, DETRIMENT, HARM, MISCHIEF refer to injuries of various kinds. DAMAGE is the kind of injury or the effect of injury that directly impairs appearance, value, usefulness, soundness, etc.: *Fire causes damage to property.* DETRIMENT is a falling off from an original condition as the result of damage, depreciation, devaluation, etc.: *Overeating is a detriment to health.* HARM may denote either physical hurt or mental, moral, or spiritual injury: *bodily harm; harm to one's self-confidence.* MISCHIEF may be damage, harm, trouble, or misfortune caused by a person, esp. if maliciously: *an enemy who would do one mischief.* **4.** impair, hurt.

dam′age control′, **1.** a department or group, as aboard a naval vessel, responsible for taking action to control damage caused by fire, collision, etc. **2.** any efforts, as by a company, to curtail losses, counteract unfavorable publicity, etc. —**dam′age-con•trol′,** *adj.*

dam•ag•ing (dam′i jing), *adj.* causing or capable of causing damages; harmful; injurious. [1850–55; DAMAGE + -ING[2]] —**dam′ag•ing•ly,** *adv.*

dam•an (dam′ən), *n.* **1.** a hyrax, *Procavia syriaca,* of Syria, Palestine, etc.: the cony of the Bible. **2.** any hyrax. [1730–40; < Ar *damān* (*Isrā′īl*), lit., lamb (of Israel)]

Da•man (də män′), *n.* **1.** a district in W India, part of the union territory of Goa, Daman, and Diu: formerly a Portuguese colony. **2.** the chief town of this district. Portuguese, **Da•mão** (dä moun′). See **Goa, Daman, and Diu.**

Da•man•hur (dä′män hōōr′), *n.* a city in N Egypt, near Alexandria. 175,900.

dam•ar (dam′är, -ər, də mär′), *n.* dammar.

Da•ma•ra•land (də mär′ə land′, dam′ər ə-), *n.* a region in the central part of Namibia.

Da•mas (dA mä′), *n.* French name of **Damascus.**

Dam•a•scene (dam′ə sēn′, dam′ə sēn′), *adj., n., v.,* **-scened, -scen•ing.** —*adj.* **1.** of or pertaining to the city of Damascus. **2.** (*l.c.*) of or pertaining to the art of damascening. —*n.* **3.** an inhabitant of Damascus. **4.** (*l.c.*) work or patterns produced by damascening. —*v.t.* **5.** (*l.c.*) Also, **dam•a•skeen** (dam′ə skēn′, dam′ə skēn′). to produce wavy lines on (Damascus steel). [1350–1400; ME < L *Damascēnus* of Damascus < Gk *Damaskēnós,* equiv. to *Damask(ós)* DAMASCUS + *-ēnos* -ENE]

Dam•a•sce•nus (dam′ə sē′nəs), *n.* **Jo•han•nes** (jō-han′ēz, -is). See **John of Damascus, Saint.**

Da•mas•cus (də mas′kəs), *n.* a city in and the capital of Syria, in the SW part: reputed to be the oldest continuously existing city in the world. 936,567. French, **Damas.**

Damas′cus steel′, hand-wrought steel, made in various Asian countries, from parts of a bloom of heterogeneous composition, repeatedly folded over and welded and finally etched to reveal the resulting grain: used esp. for sword blades. Also called **damask, damask steel.** [1720–30]

dam•ask (dam′əsk), *n.* **1.** a reversible fabric of linen, silk, cotton, or wool, woven with patterns. **2.** napery of this material. **3.** *Metall.* **a.** Also called **dam′ask steel′.** See **Damascus steel. b.** the pattern or wavy appearance peculiar to the surface of such steel. **4.** the pink color of the damask rose. —*adj.* **5.** made of or resembling damask: *damask cloth.* **6.** of the pink color of the damask rose. —*v.t.* **7.** to damascene. **8.** to weave or adorn with elaborate design, as damask cloth. [1200–50; ME *damaske* < ML *damascus,* named after DAMASCUS where fabrics were first made]

dam′ask rose′, a fragrant, pink rose, *Rosa damascena.* [1530–40]

Da•mas•tes (də mas′tēz), *n. Class. Myth.* Procrustes.

Dam•a•sus I (dam′ə səs), **Saint,** pope A.D. 366–384.

Damasus II, died 1048, pope 1048.

d'Am•boise (*Fr.* dän bwaz′), *n.* **Jacques** (*Fr.* zhäk) **(Joseph),** born 1934, U.S. ballet dancer and choreographer.

dame (dām), *n.* **1.** (*cap.*) (in Britain) **a.** the official title of a female member of the Order of the British Empire, equivalent to that of a knight. **b.** the official title of the wife of a knight or baronet. **2.** (formerly) a form of address to any woman of rank or authority. **3.** a matronly woman of advanced age; matron. **4.** *Slang* (*sometimes offensive*). a woman; female. **5.** *Eccles.* a title of a nun in certain orders. **6.** a mistress of a dame-school. **7.** *Archaic.* the mistress of a household. **8.** *Archaic.* a woman of rank or authority, esp. a female ruler. [1175–1225; ME < OF < L *domina,* fem. of *dominus* lord, master]

dame-school (dām′skōōl′), *n.* (formerly) a school in which the rudiments of reading, writing, and arithmetic were taught to neighborhood children by a woman in her own home. [1810–20]

dame's′ rock′et, a Eurasian plant, *Hesperis matronalis,* of the mustard family, having loose clusters of fourpetalled purple or white fragrant flowers. Also called **dame's′ vi′olet.**

dam•fool (dam′fōōl′), *Informal.* —*n.* **1.** a person who is exceptionally stupid or foolish. —*adj.* **2.** Also, **dam•fool•ish** (dam′fōō′lish). extraordinarily stupid or foolish. [1880–85; alter. of *damned fool* or *foolish*]

Dam•i•a (dam′ē ə), *n. Class. Myth.* a spirit of fertility.

dam•i•an•a (dam′ē an′ə), *n.* the dried leaves of a Mexican plant, *Turnera diffusa,* formerly used as a laxative and a tonic, and purported to be effective in the treatment of sexual impotence. [< AmerSp]

Da•mien (dā′mē ən; *Fr.* dA myaN′), *n.* **Father (Jo•seph de Veu•ster)** (*Fr.* zhô zef′ də vœ ster′), 1840–89, Belgian Roman Catholic missionary to the lepers of Molokai.

Dam•i•et•ta (dam′ē et′ə), *n.* a city in NE Egypt, in the Nile delta. 110,000. Arabic, **Dumyat.**

da•min•o•zide (də min′ə zīd′), *n. Chem.* a plant-growth retardant, $C_6H_{12}N_2O_3$, used commercially on apples. [*d*(*imethyl*) + *amino-* + (*hydra*)*zide* components of the chemical name]

dam•mar (dam′är, -ər, də mär′), *n.* **1.** Also called **gum dammar.** a copallike resin derived largely from dipterocarpaceous trees of southern Asia, esp. Malaya and Sumatra, and used chiefly for making colorless varnish. **2.** any of various similar resins from trees of other families. Also, **damar, dam•mer** (dam′ər). [1690–1700; < Malay *damar*]

dam•mit (dam′it), *interj. Eye Dialect.* damn it (used as a mild expletive). [1905–10]

damn (dam), *v.t.* **1.** to declare (something) to be bad, unfit, invalid, or illegal. **2.** to condemn as a failure: *to damn a play.* **3.** to bring condemnation upon; ruin. **4.** to doom to eternal punishment or condemn to hell. **5.** to swear at or curse, using the word "damn": *Damn the torpedoes! Full speed ahead!* —*v.i.* **6.** to use the word "damn"; swear. **7. damn with faint praise,** to praise so moderately as, in effect, to condemn: *The critic damned the opera with faint praise when he termed the production adequate.* —*interj.* **8.** (used as an expletive to express anger, annoyance, disgust, etc.) —*n.* **9.** the utterance of "damn" in swearing or for emphasis. **10.** something of negligible value: *not worth a damn.* **11. give a damn,** *Informal.* to care; be concerned; consider as important: *You shouldn't give a damn about their opinions.* Also, **give a darn.** —*adj.* **12.** damned (defs. 2, 3). —*adv.* **13.** damned. **14. damn well,** *Informal.* See **damned** (def. 7). [1250–1300; ME *dam*(*p*)*nen* < OF *dam*(*p*)*ner* < L *damnāre* to condemn, deriv. of *damnum* damage, fine, harm] —**damn′er,** *n.*
—**Syn. 2.** berate, censure, denounce, disparage, blast.

dam•na•ble (dam′nə bəl), *adj.* **1.** worthy of condemnation. **2.** detestable, abominable, or outrageous. [1275–1325; ME *dam*(*p*)*nable* < MF *damnable* < LL *damnābilis,* equiv. to L *damn*(*āre*) (see DAMN) + *-ābilis* -ABLE] —**dam′na•ble•ness, dam′na•bil′i•ty,** *n.* —**dam′na•bly,** *adv.*

dam•na•tion (dam nā′shən), *n.* **1.** the act of damning or the state of being damned. **2.** a cause or occasion of being damned. **3.** *Theol.* condemnation to eternal punishment as a consequence of sin. **4.** an oath expressing anger, disappointment, etc. —*interj.* **5.** (used in exclamatory phrases to express anger, disappointment, etc.) [1250–1300; ME *dam*(*p*)*nacioun* < OF *damnation* < L *damnātiōn-* (s. of *damnātiō*), equiv. to *damnāt*(*us*) (ptp. of *damnāre;* see DAMN, -ATE[1]) + *-iōn-* -ION]

dam•na•to•ry (dam′nə tôr′ē, -tōr′ē), *adj.* conveying, expressing, or causing condemnation; damning. [1675–85; < L *damnātōrius,* equiv. to *damnā*(*re*) (see DAMN) + *-tōrius* -TORY[1]]

damned (damd), *adj., superl.* **damned•est, damnd•est,** *n., adv.* —*adj.* **1.** condemned or doomed, esp. to eternal punishment: *the wailing of damned souls.* **2.** detestable; loathsome: *Get that damned dog out of here!* **3.** complete; absolute; utter: *a damned nuisance; a damned fool.* **4.** *Informal.* extraordinary; amazing: *It was the damnedest thing I'd ever seen.* —*n.* **5. the damned,** those condemned to suffer eternal punishment. —*adv.* **6.** extremely; very; absolutely: *a damned good singer; too damned lazy.* **7. damned well,** *Informal.* certainly or without doubt; emphatically: *You damned well better say you're sorry!* Also, **damn well.** [1350–1400; ME *dam*(*p*)*ned.* See DAMN, -ED[2]]

damned•est (dam′dist), *n. Informal.* best; utmost: *They did their damnedest to finish on time.* [1820–30; DAMNED + -EST[1]]

dam•ni•fy (dam′nə fī′), *v.t.,* **-fied, -fy•ing.** *Law.* to cause loss or damage to. [1505–15; < MF *damnifier,* OF < LL *damnificāre,* deriv. of L *damnific*(*us*) harmful, equiv. to *damn*(*um*) damage + *-ificus* (see -I-, -FIC); see -IFY]

damn•ing (dam′ing, dam′ning), *adj.* causing incrimination: *damning evidence.* [1590–1600; DAMN + -ING[2]] —**damn′ing•ly,** *adv.* —**damn′ing•ness,** *n.*

damn•yan•kee (dam′yang′kē), *n. Informal.* damyankee. [1805–15]

Dam•o•cles (dam′ə klēz′), *n.* **1.** a flatterer who, having extolled the happiness of Dionysius, tyrant of Syracuse, was seated at a banquet with a sword suspended over his head by a single hair to show him the perilous nature of that happiness. **2. sword of Damocles,** any situation threatening imminent harm or disaster. —**Dam•o•cle•an** (dam′ə klē′ən), *adj.*

dam•oi•selle (dam′ə zel′), *n. Archaic.* damsel. Also, **dam′o•sel′, dam′o•zel′.**

Da•mon (dā′mən), *n.* a male given name.

Da′mon and Pyth′ias, *Gk. Legend.* two friends whose mutual loyalty was shown by Damon's offer of his life as pledge that Pythias would return from settling his affairs to be executed for rebelling against Dionysius: Pythias returned, and Dionysius relented and pardoned them both.

damp (damp), *adj.,* **-er, -est,** *n., v.* —*adj.* **1.** slightly wet; moist: *damp weather; a damp towel.* **2.** unenthusiastic; dejected; depressed: *The welcoming committee gave them a rather damp reception.* —*n.* **3.** moisture; humidity; moist air: *damp that goes through your warmest clothes.* **4.** a noxious or stifling vapor or gas, esp. in a mine. **5.** depression of spirits; dejection. **6.** a restraining or discouraging force or factor. —*v.t.* **7.** to make damp; moisten. **8.** to check or retard the energy, action, etc., of; deaden; dampen: *A series of failures damped her enthusiasm.* **9.** to stifle or suffocate; extinguish: *to damp a furnace.* **10.** *Acoustics, Music.* to check or retard the action of (a vibrating string); dull; deaden. **11.** *Physics.* to cause a decrease in amplitude of (successive oscillations or waves). **12. damp off,** to undergo damping-off. [1300–50; ME (in sense of def. 4); cf. MD *damp,*

MHG *dampf* vapor, smoke] —**damp′ish,** *adj.* —**damp′ish·ly,** *adv.* —**damp′ish·ness,** *n.* —**damp′ly,** *adv.* —**damp′ness,** *n.*
—**Syn. 1.** dank, steamy. DAMP, HUMID, MOIST mean slightly wet. DAMP usually implies slight and extraneous wetness, generally undesirable or unpleasant unless the result of intention: *a damp cellar; to put a damp cloth on a patient's forehead.* HUMID is applied to unpleasant dampness in the air: *The air is oppressively humid today.* MOIST denotes something that is slightly wet, naturally or properly: *moist ground; moist leather.* **3.** dankness, dampness, fog, vapor. **7.** humidify. **8.** slow, inhibit.

damp′ box′, *Ceram.* a box that is lined with moist material for keeping clay in a plastic state.

damp-dry (damp′drī′, -drī′), *v.,* **-dried, -dry·ing,** *adj.* —*v.i.* **1.** (of laundry) to dry partially so that some moisture remains, as for ease in ironing. —*v.t.* **2.** to cause (laundry) to damp-dry. —*adj.* **3.** of or pertaining to laundry so dried. [1955–60]

damp·en (dam′pən), *v.t.* **1.** to make damp; moisten: *to dampen a sponge.* **2.** to dull or deaden; depress: *to dampen one's spirits.* **3.** damp (def. 10). —*v.i.* **4.** to become damp. [1620–30; DAMP + -EN[1]] —**damp′en·er,** *n.*

damp·er (dam′pər), *n.* **1.** a person or thing that damps or depresses: *His glum mood put a damper on their party.* **2.** a movable plate for regulating the draft in a stove, furnace, etc. **3.** *Music.* **a.** a device in stringed keyboard instruments to deaden the vibration of the strings. **b.** the mute of a brass instrument, as a horn. **4.** *Elect.* an attachment to keep the indicator of a measuring instrument from oscillating excessively, as a set of vanes in a fluid or a short-circuited winding in a magnetic field. **5.** *Mach.* a shock absorber. **6.** *Australian.* **a.** a round, flat cake made of flour and water, and cooked over a campfire. **b.** the dough for such cakes. [1740–50; DAMP + -ER[1]]

damp′er ped′al, *Music.* a pedal on a piano that when depressed with the foot raises the dampers and permits the strings to vibrate and sustain the tone. Also called **loud pedal.**

Dam·pi·er (dam′pē ər, damp′yər), *n.* **William,** 1652–1715, English navigator, explorer, buccaneer, and writer.

damp·ing-off (dam′ping ôf′, -of′), *n. Plant Pathol.* a disease of seedlings, occurring either before or immediately after emerging from the soil, characterized by rotting of the stem at soil level and eventual collapse of the plant, caused by any of several soil fungi. [1895–1900]

damp-mop (damp′mop′, -mop′), *v.i., v.t.,* **-mopped, -mop·ping.** to clean with a mop that has been slightly moistened or soaked in water and wrung out.

damp·proof (damp′pro͞of′), *adj.* **1.** resistant to dampness or the effects of dampness. —*v.t.* **2.** to make dampproof. [1880–85; DAMP + -PROOF]

damp′ squib′, *Brit. Informal.* something meant but failing to impress or succeed. [1965–70]

Dam·rosch (dam′rosh; *for 1 also Ger.* däm′rôsh), *n.* **1. Le·o·pold** (lē′ə pōld′; *Ger.* lā′ô pôlt′) 1832–85, German conductor and violinist, in the U.S. after 1871. **2.** his son, **Walter Jo·han·nes** (jō han′is), 1862–1950, U.S. conductor, born in Germany.

dam·sel (dam′zəl), *n. Literary.* a young woman or girl; a maiden, originally one of gentle or noble birth. [1150–1200; ME *damisel* < AF (OF *damoisele*) < VL **dominicella,* equiv. to L *domin(a)* lady (see DAME) + *-i-* -I- + *-cella* fem. dim. suffix]

dam′sel bug′, any of various small predaceous bugs of the family Nabidae.

dam·sel·fish (dam′zəl fish′), *n., pl.* (*esp. collectively*) **-fish,** (*esp. referring to two or more kinds or species*) **-fish·es.** any of several chiefly tropical, brilliantly colored, marine fishes of the family Pomacentridae, living among coral reefs. Also called **demoiselle.** [1900–05; DAMSEL + FISH]

dam·sel·fly (dam′zəl flī′), *n., pl.* **-flies.** any of numerous slender, nonstinging insects of the order Odonata (suborder Zygoptera), distinguished from the dragonflies by having the wings folded back in line with the body when at rest. [1805–15; DAMSEL + FLY[2]]

dam·son (dam′zən, -sən), *n.* **1.** Also called **dam′son plum′.** the small, dark-blue or purple fruit of a plum, *Prunus insititia,* of the rose family, introduced into Europe from Asia Minor. **2.** a medium to dark violet. —*adj.* **3.** of the color damson. [1350–1400; ME *damascene, damson* < L (*prūnum*) *Damascēnum* (plum) of Damascus; see DAMASCENE]

dam·yan·kee (dam′yang′kē), *n. Informal.* (in the southern U.S.) a person native to the northern states of the U.S., esp. one who is disliked or regarded with suspicion. Also, **damnyankee.** [alter. of *damned Yankee*]

dan (dän, dan), *n. Martial Arts.* a degree of expertise in karate, judo, tae kwon do, etc., usually signified by the wearing of a cloth belt of a particular color; level: *a sixth-degree dan.* [1940–45; < Japn < MChin, equiv. to Chin *duàn* step, grade]

Dan (dan), *n.* **1.** a son of Jacob and Bilhah. Gen. 30:6. **2.** one of the 12 tribes of Israel, traditionally descended from him. **3.** the northernmost city of ancient Palestine. **4. from Dan to Beersheba,** from one outermost extreme or limit to the other. Judges 20:1. **5.** a male given name; form of **Daniel.**

Dan (dan), *n. Archaic.* a title of honor equivalent to *master* or *sir: Dan Chaucer.* [1275–1325; ME < OF *danz* < ML *domnus,* contr. of L *dominus* lord, master]

Dan., **1.** *Bible.* Daniel (def. 1). **2.** Also, **Dan** Danish.

Da·na (dā′nə), *n.* **1. Charles Anderson,** 1819–97, U.S. journalist, editor, and publisher. **2. Edward Salisbury,** 1849–1935, U.S. mineralogist and physicist. **3.** his father, **James Dwight,** 1813–95, U.S. geologist and mineralogist. **4. Richard Henry, Jr.,** 1815–82, U.S. jurist, author, and sailor: specialist in admiralty law. **5.** a male or female given name.

Da·na (dä′nə), *n. Irish Myth.* Danu.

Dan·a·ë (dan′ə ē′), *n. Class. Myth.* a daughter of the king of Argos and mother, by Zeus disguised as a shower of gold, of Perseus. —**Dan·a·än** (dan′ē ən), *adj.*

Dan·a·i (dan′ā ī′), *n.pl. Class. Myth.* **1.** the Argives. **2.** the Greeks.

Da·na·i·des (də nā′i dēz′), *n.pl. Class. Myth.* the 50 daughters of Danaus, 49 of whom were condemned to pour water forever into a leaky vessel for having murdered their husbands. Also, **Da·na·i·dae** (də nā′i dē′), **Da·na·ids** (də nā′idz). —**Dan·a·id·e·an** (dan′ē id′ē ən, dan′ē i dē′ən), *adj.*

da·na·ite (dā′nə īt′), *n. Mineral.* a variety of arsenopyrite having cobalt in place of some of the iron. [1825–35, *Amer.*; named after J. F. *Dana* (1793–1827), American chemist; see -ITE[1]]

Da·na·kil (dan′ə kil, -kēl′, də nä′kēl), *n., pl.* **-kils,** (*esp. collectively*) **-kil.** Afar.

Da·nang (də näng′, -nang′, dä-), *n.* a seaport in central Vietnam. 500,000. Also, **Da′ Nang′.** Formerly, **Tourane.**

Dan·a·us (dan′ā əs), *n. Class. Myth.* a ruler of Argos who ordered his 50 daughters to kill their husbands on their wedding night. Cf. **Danaides.**

Da·na·va (dä′nə və), *n. Hinduism.* one of the Vedic demons. Cf. **Asura, Vrita.**

da·na·zol (dä′nə zôl′, -zol′), *n. Pharm.* a synthetic androgenic steroid, $C_{22}H_{27}NO_2$, used in the treatment of endometriosis that is responsive to hormonal management. [contr. of the chemical name]

dan′ bu′oy (dan), a temporary buoy having a staff for carrying a flag or light. [1680–90; orig. uncert.]

dan·bur·ite (dan′bə rīt′), *n.* a rare mineral, calcium borosilicate, $CaB_2Si_2O_8$, occurring in pegmatite in yellow or colorless crystals resembling topaz. [*Amer.*; after DANBURY, where it was discovered in 1839; see -ITE[1]]

Dan·bur·y (dan′ber′ē, -bə rē), *n.* a city in SW Connecticut. 60,470.

dance (dans, däns), *v.,* **danced, danc·ing,** *n.* —*v.i.* **1.** to move one's feet or body, or both, rhythmically in a pattern of steps, esp. to the accompaniment of music. **2.** to leap, skip, etc., as from excitement or emotion; move nimbly or quickly: *to dance with joy.* **3.** to bob up and down: *The toy sailboats danced on the pond.* —*v.t.* **4.** to perform or take part in (a dance): *to dance a waltz.* **5.** to cause to dance: *He danced her around the ballroom.* **6.** to cause to be in a specified condition by dancing: *She danced her way to stardom.* **7. dance attendance.** See **attendance** (def. 4). **8. dance on air,** *Slang.* to be hanged. **9. dance to another tune,** to change one's behavior, attitudes, etc. —*n.* **10.** a successive group of rhythmical steps or bodily motions, or both, usually executed to music. **11.** an act or round of dancing; set: *May I have this dance?* **12.** the art of dancing: *to study dance.* **13.** a social gathering or party for dancing; ball: *Was he invited to the dance?* **14.** a piece of music suited in rhythm or style to a particular form of dancing: *He liked the composer's country dances.* **15.** *Animal Behav.* a stylized pattern of movements performed by an animal, as a bird in courtship display, or an insect, as a honeybee in indicating a source of nectar. **16. the dance,** ballet, interpretive dancing, and other dancing of an artistic nature performed by professional dancers before an audience. [1250–1300; (v.) ME *da(u)ncen* < AF *dancer, dauncer,* OF *dancier,* perh. < OHG **dansjan* to lead (someone) to a dance; (n.) ME *da(u)nce* < AF; OF *dance,* deriv. of *dancier*] —**danc′ing·ly,** *adv.*

dance·a·ble (dan′sə bəl, dän′-), *adj.* appropriate for or conducive to dancing: *danceable music.* [1855–60; DANCE + -ABLE] —**dance′a·bil′i·ty,** *n.*

dance′ band′, a musical group that specializes in playing music for social dancing. [1925–30]

dance′ card′, a card listing, in order, the names of the partners with whom a woman has agreed to dance at a formal ball or party. [1890–95, *Amer.*]

dance′ dra′ma, drama performed through dance movements, frequently with dialogue. [1920–25]

dance′ form′, *Music.* the binary form used in most of the movements of the 18th-century suite.

dance′ hall′, a public establishment that, for an admission fee, provides its patrons with music and space for dancing and, sometimes, dancing partners and refreshments. [1855–60, *Amer.*]

dance′ of death′, **1.** a symbolic dance in which Death, represented as a skeleton, leads people or skeletons to their grave. **2.** a representation of this theme in art. Also called **danse macabre.** [1470–80]

danc·er (dan′sər, dän′-), *n.* **1.** a person who dances. **2.** a person who dances professionally, as on the stage. [1250–1300; ME *dauncer;* see DANCE, -ER[1]]

Dan·cer (dan′sər, dän′-), *n.* **Stanley,** born 1927, U.S. harness racer and trainer.

danc·er·cise (dan′sər sīz′, dän′-), *n.* vigorous dancing done as an exercise for physical fitness. [1980–85; DANCE + (EXER)CISE]

dan·cette (dan set′), *n. Archit.* an ornamental zigzag, as in a molding. [1830–40; var. of *dancetté,* heraldry term denoting a zigzag line, prob. alter. (see -ETTE) of F *denché* indented < LL *denticātus,* deriv. of L *dēns* TOOTH (see -IC, -ATE[1])]

danc′ing·la′dy or′chid (dan′sing lā′dē, dän′-), any of numerous epiphytic orchids of the genus *Oncidium,* often grown as houseplants.

danc′ing step′. See **balanced step.** Also called **danc′ing wind′er.**

D and C, *Med.* a surgical method for the removal of diseased tissue or an early embryo from the lining of the uterus by means of scraping. [*d(ilation) and c(urettage)*]

D&D, Dungeons and Dragons.

dan·de·li·on (dan′dl ī′ən), *n.* **1.** a weedy composite plant, *Taraxacum officinale,* having edible, deeply toothed or notched leaves, golden-yellow flowers, and rounded clusters of white, hairy seeds. **2.** any other plant of the genus *Taraxacum.* [1505–15; < MF, alter. of *dent de lion,* lit., tooth of (a) lion, trans. of ML *dēns leōnis,* in allusion to the toothed leaves]

dan·der[1] (dan′dər), *n.* **1.** loose scales formed on the skin and shed from the coat or feathers of various animals, often causing allergic reactions in susceptible persons. **2.** *Informal.* anger; temper: *Don't get your dander up over such a trifle.* [1825–35; alter. of DANDRUFF]

dan·der[2] (dan′dər), *n.* **1.** *Scot.* a stroll; saunter. **2.** *Brit. Dial.* a fit of shivering. [1590–1600; orig. uncert.]

Dan·die Din·mont (dan′dē din′mont), one of a breed of small terriers having short legs, pendulous ears, and a long, wiry, pepper- or mustard-colored coat. [1840–50; after a character in Scott's novel, *Guy Mannering*]

dan·di·fy (dan′də fī′), *v.t.,* **-fied, -fy·ing.** to make into or cause to resemble a dandy or fop. [1815–25; DANDY + -FY] —**dan′di·fi·ca′tion,** *n.*

dan·di·prat (dan′dē prat′), *n.* **1.** a silver coin of 16th-century England, equal to about twopence. **2.** *Archaic.* **a.** a diminutive person; a dwarf, pygmy, or midget. **b.** a person of small or childish mind; a silly, finicky, or puerile person. **c.** a child. [1510–20; orig. uncert.]

dan·dle (dan′dl), *v.t.,* **-dled, -dling.** **1.** to move (a baby, child, etc.) lightly up and down, as on one's knee or in one's arms. **2.** to pet; pamper. [1520–30; *dand-* (obscurely akin to the base of F *dandiner* to dandle, *se dandiner* to waddle, and related Romance words) + -LE] —**dan′dler,** *n.*

Dan·dong (dän′dông′), *n.* a seaport in SE Liaoning province, in NE China, at the mouth of the Yalu River. 450,000. Formerly, **Antung.**

dan·druff (dan′drəf), *n.* a seborrheic scurf that forms on the scalp and comes off in small scales. Also, **dan·driff** (dan′drif). [1535–45; orig. uncert.] —**dan′druff·y, dan′driff·y,** *adj.*

dan·dy (dan′dē), *n., pl.* **-dies,** *adj.,* **-di·er, -di·est.** —*n.* **1.** a man who is excessively concerned about his clothes and appearance; a fop. **2.** *Informal.* something or someone of exceptional or first-rate quality: *Your reply was a dandy.* —*adj.* **3.** characteristic of a dandy; foppish. **4.** *Informal.* fine; excellent; first-rate: *a dandy vacation spot.* [1770–80; orig. uncert.] —**dan′di·ly, dan′dy·ish·ly, dan·di·a·cal·ly** (dan dī′ək lē), *adv.* —**dan′dy·ish, dan·di′a·cal,** *adj.* —**dan′dy·ism,** *n.*

dan′dy brush′, a brush with stiff, short bristles that is used for grooming animals, esp. horses. [1835–45]

dan′dy fe′ver, *Pathol.* (in the West Indies) dengue. [1820–30; prob. < West Indian Creole, of Afr orig.]

dan′dy roll′, *Papermaking.* a light, open cylinder of wire gauze in a papermaking machine, for smoothing wet pulp and for impressing a watermark. Also called **dan′dy roll′er.** [1830–40]

Dane (dān), *n.* **1.** a native or inhabitant of Denmark. **2.** a person of Danish descent. **3.** See **Great Dane. 4.** a male given name. [bef. 950; ME *Dan,* OE *Dene* (pl.), influenced by ON *Danir* (pl.)]

Dane·geld (dān′geld′), *n.* (in medieval England) an additional tax on land believed to have been levied originally as a tribute to the Danish invaders but later continued for other purposes. Also, **dane′geld′, Dane·gelt, dane·gelt** (dān′gelt′). [bef. 1150; ME *denegeld, danegeld,* OE (Domesday Book) *Danegeld.* See DANE, GELD[2]]

Dane·law (dān′lô′), *n.* **1.** the body of laws in force in the northeast of England where the Danes settled in the 9th century A.D. **2.** the part of England under this law. Also, **Dane·la·ge** (dān′lä′gə, dä′nə lä′gə), **Dane·lagh** (dān′lô′). [bef. 1050; ME *Dene-lawe,* earlier *Dene-lawe,* OE *Dena lagu.* See DANE, LAW[1]]

dang (dang), *v.t., adj., n.* damn (used euphemistically). [1780–90]

danged (dangd), *adj., adv.* damned (used euphemistically). [1870–75]

dan·ger (dān′jər), *n.* **1.** liability or exposure to harm or injury; risk; peril. **2.** an instance or cause of peril; menace. **3.** *Obs.* power; jurisdiction; domain. [1175–1225; ME *da(u)nger* < AF; OF *dangier,* alter. of *dongier* (by influence of *dam* DAMAGE) < VL **domniārium,* equiv. to L *domini(um)* DOMINION + *-ārium,* neut. of *-ārius* -ARY] —**dan′ger·less,** *adj.*
—**Syn. 1.** DANGER, HAZARD, PERIL, JEOPARDY imply harm that one may encounter. DANGER is the general word for liability to all kinds of injury or evil consequences, either near at hand and certain, or remote and doubtful: *to be in danger of being killed.* HAZARD suggests a danger that one can foresee but cannot avoid: *A mountain climber is exposed to many hazards.* PERIL usually denotes great and imminent danger: *The passengers on the disabled ship were in great peril.* JEOPARDY, a less common word, has essentially the same meaning as PERIL, but emphasizes exposure to the chances of a situation: *To save his friend he put his life in jeopardy.*

dan′ger an′gle, *Navig.* a horizontal or vertical angle, subtended by two points on shore, that provides a maximum or minimum angle between the points as observed from a vessel if it is to steer a safe course. [1890–95]

Dan′ger Cave′, a deep, stratified site in the eastern Great Basin, in Utah, occupied by Amerindian cultures from at least 7000 B.C. to historic times.

dan·ger·ous (dān′jər əs, dānj′rəs), *adj.* **1.** full of danger or risk; causing danger; perilous; risky; hazardous; unsafe. **2.** able or likely to cause physical injury: *a dangerous criminal.* [1175–1225; ME *da(u)ngerous* domineering, fraught with danger < OF *dangereus* threatening, difficult, equiv. to *dangier* (see DANGER) + *-eus* -OUS] —**dan′ger·ous·ly,** *adv.* —**dan′ger·ous·ness,** *n.*

dan•gle (dang′gəl), *v.*, **-gled, -gling,** *n.* —*v.i.* **1.** to hang loosely, esp. with a jerking or swaying motion: *The rope dangled in the breeze.* **2.** to hang around or follow a person, as if seeking favor or attention. **3.** *Gram.* to occur as a modifier without a head or as a participle without an implied subject, as *leaving the tunnel* in *The daylight was blinding, leaving the tunnel.* —*v.t.* **4.** to cause to dangle; hold or carry swaying loosely. **5.** to offer as an inducement. **6. keep someone dangling,** to keep someone in a state of uncertainty. —*n.* **7.** the act of dangling. **8.** something that dangles. [1580–90; expressive word akin to Norw, Sw *dangla,* Dan *dangle* dangle] —**dan′gler,** *n.* —**dan′gling•ly,** *adv.*
—**Syn. 1.** swing, sway, flap.

dan•gle•ber•ry (dang′gəl ber′ē), *n., pl.* **-ries.** tangleberry. [1825–35, *Amer.*]

dan′gling par′ticiple, *Gram.* a participle or participial phrase, often found at the beginning of a sentence, that appears from its position to modify an element of the sentence other than the one it was intended to modify, as *plunging* in *Plunging hundreds of feet into the gorge, we saw Yosemite Falls.* Cf. **misplaced modifier.**
—**Usage.** Most usage guides warn against the DANGLING PARTICIPLE and usually suggest revising any sentence that has one. The example *Plunging hundreds of feet into the gorge, we saw Yosemite Falls* would, by such guidelines, be recast as *We saw Yosemite Falls plunging hundreds of feet into the gorge.* Constructions that may technically be classified as DANGLING PARTICIPLES have, however, long been a feature of standard literary English and are today commonplace in speech and edited writing: *Looking to the west, a deep river valley can be seen in the distance.* Obviously, it is not the river valley that is looking to the west, but the sentence is nonetheless immediately clear and stylistically unexceptionable. Modern British writers are much less timid than their American counterparts about the use of such phrases.
Some participial constructions are never felt to be dangling or unattached. Some of these are simply independent phrases: *Generally speaking, the report is true.* Others have come to function as conjunctions or prepositions: *Considering she has been through so much illness, she looks wonderful. Owing to the weather, the performance was canceled. Assuming congressional approval, the bill will go to the President on Friday.* Despite many criticisms, DANGLING PARTICIPLES continue to appear in edited prose. Only when an unintentionally ridiculous meaning is suggested (*Having finished our breakfast, the boat was loaded and launched*) are DANGLING PARTICIPLES deliberately avoided. See also **misplaced modifier.**

Da•ni•a (dā′nē ə), *n.* a town in S Florida. 11,811.

Dan•iel (dan′yəl), *n.* **1.** *Bible.* **a.** a prophet living in Babylon during the Captivity. **b.** the book of the Bible bearing his name. *Abbr.:* Dan. **2. Samuel,** 1562–1619, English poet and historian: poet laureate 1599–1619. **3.** a male given name: from a Hebrew word meaning "the Lord is my judge."

Dan•ielle (dan yel′), *n.* a female given name.

Dan•iels (dan′yəlz), *n.* **1. Jonathan Worth,** 1902–81, U.S. journalist, editor, and author. **2.** his father, **Jo•se•phus** (jō sē′fəs), 1862–1948, U.S. editor and statesman.

Da•ni•lo•va (də nē′lə və, -lō-; *Russ.* du nyē′lə və), *n.* **Al•ex•an•dra** (al′ig zan′drə, -zän′-; *Russ.* u lyi ksän′drə), born 1904?, Russian ballet dancer.

dan•i•o (dā′nē ō′), *n., pl.* **-i•os.** any of several cyprinid fishes of the genera *Danio* and *Brachydanio,* of India and Sri Lanka, often kept in aquariums. [1880–85; < NL]

Dan•ish (dā′nish), *adj.* **1.** of or pertaining to the Danes, their country, or their language. —*n.* **2.** a North Germanic language, the language of Denmark, closely related to Norwegian, Swedish, and Icelandic. *Abbr.:* Dan., Dan **3.** (*sometimes l.c.*) See **Danish pastry.** [bef. 900; ME, alter. of *Denish* (by influence of *Dan* DANE), OE *Denisc* < Gmc **danisk-;* see DANE, -ISH[1]]

Dan′ish oil′, a furniture oil, based on synthetic resins, that gives a soft luster.

Dan′ish pas′try, a light, rich, flaky pastry, esp. a puff paste, leavened with yeast and often filled with cheese, nuts and raisins, custard, or fruit. [1930–35]

Dan′ish West′ In′dies, former name of the **Virgin Islands of the United States.** Also called **Dan′ish Vir′gin Is′lands.**

Dan•ite (dan′īt), *n.* **1.** a member of the tribe of Dan. **2.** a member of an alleged secret order of Mormons supposed to have been formed about 1837. [1525–35; DAN + -ITE[1]]

dank (dangk), *adj.,* **-er, -est.** unpleasantly moist or humid; damp and, often, chilly: *a dank cellar.* [1350–1400; ME (adj. and n.), prob. < Scand; cf. dial. Sw *dänka,* Norw *dynke* moisten, c. ON *døkk* water hole] —**dank′ly,** *adv.* —**dank′ness,** *n.*
—**Syn.** wet, clammy, muggy, sticky, soggy.

dan•ke (däng′kə), *interj. German.* thank you.

dan•ke schön (däng′kə shœn′), *German.* thank you very much.

Danl., Daniel.

D'An•nun•zio (də nōōn′sē ō′; *It.* dän nōōn′tsyô), *n.* **Ga•bri•e•le** (*It.* gä′brē e′le), (*Duca Minimo*), 1863–1938, Italian soldier, novelist, and poet.

Dan•ny (dan′ē), *n.* a male given name, form of **Daniel.**

Da•no-Nor•we•gian (dā′nō nôr wē′jən), *n.* Bokmål. [< LL *Dan(i)* DANES + -O- + NORWEGIAN]

dan•sant (dän sän′), *n., pl.* **-sants** (-sän′). *French.* See ***thé dansant.***

danse du ven•tre (*Fr.* däns dy vän′trᵊ), *pl.* **danses du ven•tre** (*Fr.* däns dy vän′trᵊ). See **belly dance.** [1890–95; < F]

danse ma•ca•bre (*Fr.* däns mA kA′brᵊ). See **dance of death.** [< F]

dan•seur (*Fr.* dän sœr′), *n., pl.* **-seurs** (*Fr.* -sœr′). a male ballet dancer. [1820–30; < F: lit., dancer. See DANCE, -EUR]

dan•seur no•ble (*Fr.* dän sœr nô′blᵊ), *pl.* **dan•seurs no•bles** (*Fr.* dän sœr nô′blᵊ). a male dancer who is the partner of a ballerina, as in a pas de deux. [1940–45; < F; lit., noble dancer]

dan•seuse (*Fr.* dän sœz′), *n., pl.* **-seuses** (*Fr.* -sœz′). a female ballet dancer. [1835–45; < F; fem. of DANSEUR; see -EUSE]

Dan•te (dan′tē, dän′tā; *It.* dän′te), *n.* (*Dante Alighieri*), 1265–1321, Italian poet: author of the *Divine Comedy.*

Dan•te•an (dan′tē ən, dan tē′ən), *adj.* **1.** of or pertaining to Dante or his writings. **2.** Dantesque. —*n.* **3.** a person who is an expert on the writings of Dante. [1825–35; DANTE + -AN]

Dan′te chair′, *Italian Furniture.* a chair of the Renaissance having two transverse pairs of curved legs crossing beneath the seat and rising to support the arms and back. Also called **Dan•tes′ca chair′** (dan tes′kə, dän tes′kä). Cf. **Savonarola chair.** [named after DANTE]

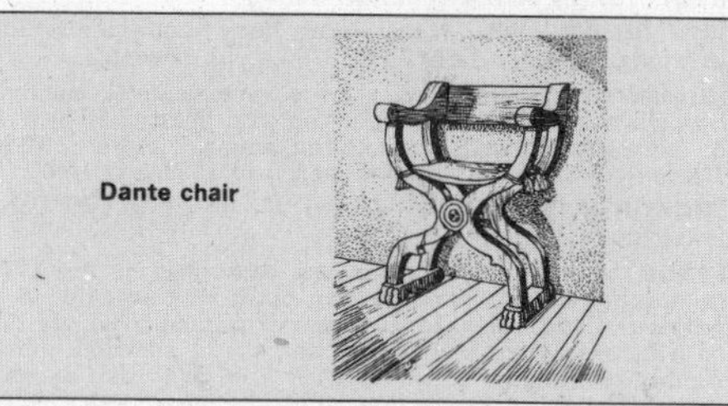
Dante chair

Dan•tesque (dan tesk′), *adj.* in the style of Dante; characterized by impressive elevation of style with deep solemnity or somberness of feeling. [1825–35; DANT(E) + -ESQUE; cf. F *dantesque,* It *dantesco*]

Dan•ton (dan′tn; *Fr.* dän tôn′), *n.* **Georges Jacques** (zhôrzh zhäk), 1759–94, French Revolutionary leader.

dan•tro•lene (dan′trə lēn′), *n. Pharm.* a toxic orange powder, $C_{14}H_{10}N_4O_5$, used to control muscle spasms, as in the treatment of local trauma, multiple sclerosis, cerebral palsy, or other neurological disorders. [*dantrol-,* contracted from letters of the chemical name + -ENE]

Da•nu (dä′nōō), *n. Irish Myth.* the mother of the Tuatha De Danann: identified with the Welsh Don. Also, **Dana.**

Dan•ube (dan′yōōb), *n.* a river in central and SE Europe, flowing E from southern Germany to the Black Sea. 1725 mi. (2775 km) long. German, **Donau.** Hungarian, **Duna.** Czech and Slovak, **Dunaj.** Rumanian, **Dunărea.**

Dan•u•bi•an (dan yōō′bē ən), *adj.* of, pertaining to, or characteristic of a Neolithic culture of the Danube basin. [1925–30; DANUBE + -IAN]

Dan•vers (dan′vərz), *n.* a town in NE Massachusetts, near Boston. 24,100.

Dan•ville (dan′vil), *n.* **1.** a city in S Virginia. 45,642. **2.** a city in E Illinois. 38,985. **3.** a town in W California. 26,446. **4.** a town in central Kentucky. 12,942.

Dan•zig (dan′sig; *Ger.* dän′tsik), *n.* **1.** German name of **Gdańsk. 2. Free City of,** a former self-governing territory including the seaport of Danzig: constituted by the treaty of Versailles 1920; a part of Germany 1939–45; now in Poland. 754 sq. mi. (1955 sq. km). **3. Gulf of,** an inlet of the Baltic Sea, in N Poland. ab. 60 mi. (95 km) wide.

dap (dap), *v.,* **dapped, dap•ping,** *n.* —*v.i.* **1.** to fish by letting the bait fall lightly on the water. **2.** to dip lightly or suddenly into water: *The bird dapped for the fish.* **3.** to bounce or skip, as on the surface of a body of water: *The stone dapped along the surface of the pond.* —*v.t.* **4.** to cause to dip in and out of water: *to dap one's bait.* **5.** to cause to skip along the surface of water: *to dap stones across the river.* **6.** *Carpentry.* to notch (a timber) to receive part of another timber. —*n.* **7.** *Carpentry.* a notch in a timber for receiving part of another timber. [1575–85; prob. var. of DAB[1]]

Daph•ne (daf′nē), *n.* **1.** *Class. Myth.* a nymph who, when pursued by Apollo, was saved by being changed into a laurel tree. **2.** (*l.c.*) *Bot.* any Eurasian shrub belonging to the genus *Daphne,* certain species of which, as *D. mezereum,* are cultivated for their fragrant flowers. **3.** a female given name. [< L *Daphnē* < Gk *dáphnē* laurel]

Daph•ne•pho•ri•a (daf′nə fôr′ē ə, -fōr′-), *n.* an ancient Greek festival in honor of Apollo.

Daph•ni•a (daf′nē ə), *n.* a genus of tiny, freshwater crustaceans having a transparent body, used in biological research and as food for tropical fish. Cf. **water flea.** [1840–50; < NL, perh. after DAPHNE; see -IA]

Daph•nis (daf′nis), *n. Class. Myth.* a son of Hermes: the originator of pastoral poetry.

Daph′nis and Chlo′e, 1. two lovers in pastoral literature, esp. in a Greek romance attributed to Longus. **2.** (*italics*) a ballet (1912) with music by Maurice Ravel and scenario and choreography by Michel Fokine. **3.** (*italics*) either of two orchestral suites by Ravel based on the music of this ballet.

Da Pon•te (də pon′tē; *It.* dä pôn′te), **Lo•ren•zo** (lə ren′zō, lō-, lō-; *It.* lô ren′dzō), (*Emanuele Conegliano*), 1749–1838, Italian librettist and teacher of Italian, in the U.S. after 1805.

dap•per (dap′ər), *adj.* **1.** neat; trim; smart: *He looked very dapper in his new suit.* **2.** lively and brisk: *to walk with a dapper step.* **3.** small and active. [1400–50; late ME *daper* < MD *dapper* nimble, stalwart; c. G *tapfer* brave] —**dap′per•ly,** *adv.* —**dap′per•ness,** *n.*
—**Syn. 1.** spruce, modish, jaunty, natty.

dap•ple (dap′əl), *n., adj., v.,* **-pled, -pling.** —*n.* **1.** a spot or mottled marking, usually occurring in clusters. **2.** an animal with a mottled skin or coat. —*adj.* **3.** dappled; spotted: *a dapple horse.* —*v.t., v.i.* **4.** to mark or become marked with spots. [1545–55; prob. back formation from DAPPLED]

dap•pled (dap′əld), *adj.* having spots of a different shade, tone, or color from the background; mottled. [1350–1400; ME, prob. < Scand; akin to ON *depill* spot]

dap•ple-gray (dap′əl grā′), *adj.* gray with ill-defined mottling of a darker shade. [1350–1400; ME, perh. **appelgrei,* with *d-* from DAPPLED; cf. ON *apalgrār, apli* dapple-gray horse]

Dap•sang (dəp sung′), *n.* See **K2.**

dap•sone (dap′sōn), *n. Pharm.* an antibacterial substance, $C_{12}H_{12}N_2O_2S$, used to treat leprosy and certain forms of dermatitis. Also called **DDS** [1965–70; *d(i)a(minodi)p(henyl) sulfone*]

DAR, Defense Aid Reports.

D.A.R., See **Daughters of the American Revolution.**

dar•bies (där′bēz), *n.pl. Brit. Slang.* handcuffs; manacles. [1565–75; prob. from the phrase *Darby's bonds* a rigid bond, perh. named after a noted 16th-century usurer]

dar•by (där′bē), *n., pl.* **-bies.** *Building Trades.* a float having two handles, used by plasterers. [1565–75; perh. after a proper name or DERBY, England]

Dar•by (där′bē), *n.* a city in SE Pennsylvania. 11,513.

Dar′by and Joan′ a happily married elderly couple who lead a placid, uneventful life. [named after a couple mentioned in an 18th-century song]

Dar′by and Joan′ settee′, a settee having a back resembling two chair backs.

Dar•by•ite (där′bē īt′), *n.* a member of the Plymouth Brethren. [1880–85; after John N. *Darby* (1800–82), English theologian; see -ITE[1]]

dar•cy (där′sē), *n., pl.* **-cies.** *Physics.* a unit of permeability, representing the flow, at 1 atmosphere, of 1 cubic centimeter of fluid with 1 centipoise viscosity in 1 second through a 1-square-centimeter cross section of porous medium 1 centimeter long. [after Henri-Philibert-Gaspard *Darcy* (1803–58), French engineer]

Dar•cy (där′sē), *n.* a male given name.

Dard (därd), *n.* **1.** Also, **Dard′ic.** a group of Indic languages spoken in Kashmir, northern Pakistan, and eastern Afghanistan, and including Kashmiri. **2.** a member of the peoples who speak these languages.

Dar•dan (där′dn), *adj., n.* Trojan. Also, **Dar•da•ni•an** (där dā′nē ən). [1600–10]

Dar•da•nelles (där′dn elz′), *n.* (*used with a plural v.*) the strait between European and Asian Turkey, connecting the Aegean Sea with the Sea of Marmara. 40 mi. (64 km) long; 1–5 mi. (1.6–8 km) wide. Ancient, **Hellespont.**

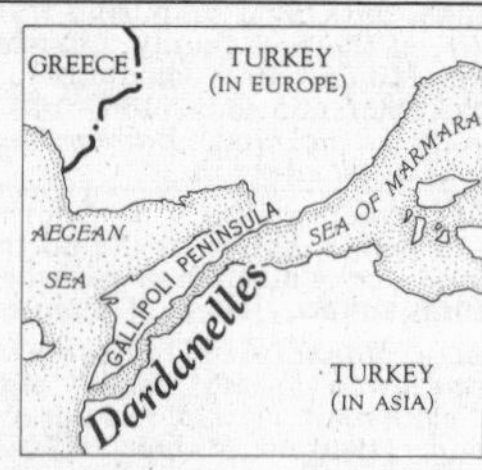

Dar•da•nus (där′dn əs), *n. Class. Myth.* the ancestor of the Trojans.

dare (dâr), *v.,* **dared** or (*Archaic*) **durst; dared; daring;** *pres. sing. 3rd pers.* **dares** or **dare,** *n.* —*v.i.* **1.** to have the necessary courage or boldness for something; be bold enough: *You wouldn't dare!* —*v.t.* **2.** to have the boldness to try; venture; hazard. **3.** to meet defiantly; face courageously. **4.** to challenge or provoke (a person) into a demonstration of courage; defy: *to dare a man to fight.* **5. dare say,** daresay. —*auxiliary v.* **6.** to have the necessary courage or boldness to (used chiefly in questions and negatives): *How dare you speak to me like that? He dare not mention the subject again.* —*n.* **7.** an act of daring or defiance; challenge. [bef. 900; ME *dar* (v.), OE *dear(r),* 1st and 3rd person sing. pres. indic. of *durran;* akin to OHG *gitarran*] —**dar′er,** *n.*
—**Syn. 1.** DARE, VENTURE imply involvement in risks and dangers. DARE emphasizes the state of mind that makes one willing to meet danger: *He dared to do what he knew was right.* VENTURE emphasizes the act of doing

something that involves risk: *He ventured into deep water.* **2.** hazard, risk, brave.

Dare (dâr), *n.* **Virginia,** 1587–?, first child born of English parents in the Western Hemisphere.

DARE, Dictionary of American Regional English.

dare•dev•il (dâr′dev′əl), *n.* **1.** a recklessly daring person. —*adj.* **2.** recklessly daring. [1785–95; DARE + DEVIL]

dare•dev•il•try (dâr′dev′əl trē), *n.* reckless daring; venturesome boldness. Also, **dare•dev•il•ry** (dâr′dev′əl rē). [1870–75, *Amer.*; DAREDEVIL + *-try,* as in DEVILTRY]

dare•ful (dâr′fəl), *adj. Obs.* daring. [1595–1605; DARE + -FUL]

dare•n't (dâr′ənt), contraction of *dare not.*

dare•say (dâr′sā′), *v.i., v.t.* to venture to say (something); assume (something) as probable (used only in pres. sing. 1st pers.): *I daresay we will soon finish.* Also, **dare′ say′.** [1250–1300; ME *dar sayen* I dare to say]

Dar es Sa•laam (där′ es sə läm′), a seaport in Tanzania, on the Indian Ocean: the former capital. 757,346. Also, **Dar′-es-Sa•laam′.**

Dar•fur (där fo͝or′), *n.* a province in the W Sudan. 1,869,000; 191,650 sq. mi. (496,374 sq. km). *Cap.:* El Fasher.

darg (därg), *n.* **1.** *Scot. and North Eng.* a day's work. **2.** *Australian.* a fixed or definite amount of work; a work quota. [1375–1425; late ME *dawerk, daiwerk,* OE *dægweorc,* equiv. to *dæg* DAY + *weorc* WORK]

Da•ri (där′ē), *n.* a form of Persian, spoken in Afghanistan.

dar•ic (dar′ik), *n.* a gold coin and monetary unit of ancient Persia. [1560–70; < Gk *Dāreikós* (*statḗr*) Persian stater (of DARIUS)]

Dar•i•en (dâr′ē en′, -ən, dar′-, dâr′ē en′, dar′-), *n.* **1. Gulf of,** an arm of the Caribbean between NE Panama and NW Colombia. **2. Isthmus of,** former name of the Isthmus of Panama. **3.** a town in SW Connecticut. 18,892. **4.** a city in NE Illinois. 14,968. Spanish, **Da•rién** (dä ʀyen′) (for defs. 1, 2).

dar•ing (dâr′ing), *n.* **1.** adventurous courage; boldness. —*adj.* **2.** bold or courageous; fearless or intrepid; adventurous. [1575–85; DARE + -ING[1], -ING[2]] —**dar′ing•ly,** *adv.* —**dar′ing•ness,** *n.*

—**Syn. 1.** audacity, bravery. **2.** dauntless, undaunted.

Da•rí•o (dä ʀē′ô), *n.* **Ru•bén** (ro͞o ven′), (*Félix Rubén García Sarmiento*), 1867–1916, Nicaraguan poet and diplomat.

dar•i•ole (dar′ē ōl′), *n. French Cookery.* a small round mold. [1350–1400; ME < OF *dariole*]

Da•ri•us I (də rī′əs), (*Darius Hystaspes*) ("*the Great*") 558?–486? B.C., king of Persia 521–486.

Darius II, (*Ochus*) died 404 B.C., king of Persia 424–404 (son of Artaxerxes I).

Darius III, (*Codomannus*) died 330 B.C., king of Persia 336–330.

Dar•jee•ling (där jē′ling), *n.* **1.** a town in West Bengal, in NE India: mountain resort. 42,700. **2.** Also called **Darjee′ling tea′.** a type of tea grown in mountainous areas around the town of Darjeeling.

dark (därk), *adj.,* **-er, -est,** *n., v.* —*adj.* **1.** having very little or no light: *a dark room.* **2.** radiating, admitting, or reflecting little light: *a dark color.* **3.** approaching black in hue: *a dark brown.* **4.** not pale or fair; swarthy: *a dark complexion.* **5.** brunette; dark-colored: *dark eyebrows.* **6.** having brunette hair: *She's dark but her children are blond.* **7.** (of coffee) containing only a small amount of milk or cream. **8.** gloomy; cheerless; dismal: *the dark days of World War II.* **9.** sullen; frowning: *a dark expression.* **10.** evil; iniquitous; wicked: *a dark plot.* **11.** destitute of knowledge or culture; unenlightened. **12.** hard to understand; obscure. **13.** hidden; secret. **14.** silent; reticent. **15.** (of a theater) offering no performances; closed: *The theaters in this town are dark on Sundays.* **16.** *Phonet.* **a.** (of an *l*-sound) having back-vowel resonance; situated after a vowel in the same syllable. Cf. **clear** (def. 24a). **b.** (of a speech sound) of dull quality; acoustically damped. **17. keep dark,** to keep as a secret; conceal: *They kept their political activities dark.* —*n.* **18.** the absence of light; darkness: *I can't see well in the dark.* **19.** night; nightfall: *Please come home before dark.* **20.** a dark place. **21.** a dark color. **22. in the dark, a.** in ignorance; uninformed: *He was in the dark about their plans for the evening.* **b.** in secrecy; concealed; obscure. —*v.t.* **23.** to make dark; darken. —*v.i.* **24.** *Obs.* to grow dark; darken. [bef. 1000; (adj.) ME *derk,* OE *deorc;* (n. and v.) ME, deriv. of the adj.; cf. MHG *terken* to darken, hide]

—**Syn. 1.** DARK, DIM, OBSCURE, GLOOMY, MURKY refer to absence or insufficiency of light. DARK implies a more or less complete absence of light: *a dark night.* DIM implies faintness of light or indistinctness of form (resulting from the lack of light or from imperfect vision): *a dim outline.* OBSCURE implies dimness that may arise also from factors that interfere with light or vision: *obscure because of haze.* GLOOMY means cloudy, ill-lighted, dusky: *a gloomy hall.* MURKY implies a thick or misty darkness: *murky water.* **4.** dusky, black. **12.** recondite.

dark′ adapta′tion, *Ophthalm.* the reflex adaptation of the eye to dim light, consisting of a dilatation of the pupil and an increase in the number of functioning rods accompanied by a decrease in the number of functioning cones (opposed to *light adaptation*). [1905–10] —**dark′-a•dapt′ed,** *adj.*

Dark′ Ag′es, 1. the period in European history from about A.D. 476 to about 1000. **2.** the whole of the Middle Ages, from about A.D. 476 to the Renaissance. **3.** (*often l.c.*) a period or stage marked by repressiveness, a lack of enlightenment or advanced knowledge, etc. [1720–30]

dark′ choc′olate, chocolate to which little or no milk has been added.

Dark′ Con′tinent, The, Africa: so called, esp. during the 19th century, because little was known about it. [1875–80]

dark•en (där′kən), *v.t.* **1.** to make dark or darker. **2.** to make obscure. **3.** to make less white or clear in color. **4.** to make gloomy; sadden: *He darkened the festivities by his presence.* **5.** to make blind. —*v.i.* **6.** to become dark or darker. **7.** to become obscure. **8.** to become less white or clear in color. **9.** to grow clouded, as with gloom or anger. **10.** to become blind. **11. darken someone's door,** to come to visit; make an appearance: *Never darken my door again!* [1250–1300; ME *derknen.* See DARK, -EN[1]] —**dark′en•er,** *n.*

—**Syn. 4.** depress, dispirit, blacken, deject.

dark′-eyed jun′co (därk′īd′), a common North American junco, *Junco hyemalis,* having a pink bill, gray and brown body plumage, white belly and outer tail feathers, and differing from other species of junco in having a dark brown rather than yellow iris. Cf. **slate-colored junco.**

dark-field (därk′fēld′), *adj. Optics.* of or pertaining to the illumination of an object by which it is seen, through a microscope, as bright against a dark background. [1860–65]

dark′ horse′, 1. a racehorse, competitor, etc., about whom little is known or who unexpectedly wins. **2.** a candidate who is unexpectedly nominated at a political convention. [1825–35]

dark•ie (där′kē), *n.* darky.

dark•ish (där′kish), *adj.* slightly dark: *a darkish color.* [1350–1400; ME; see DARK, -ISH[1]] —**dark′ish•ness,** *n.*

dark′ lan′tern, a lantern having an opening with a shutter that can be slid across the opening to obscure the light. [1640–50]

dar•kle (där′kəl), *v.i.,* **-kled, -kling. 1.** to appear dark; show indistinctly. **2.** to grow dark, gloomy, etc. [1790–1800; back formation from DARKLING, adv. taken as prp.]

dark•ling (därk′ling), *adv.* **1.** in the dark. —*adj.* **2.** growing dark. **3.** being or occurring in the dark; dark; obscure. **4.** vaguely threatening or menacing. [1400–50; late ME *derkeling.* See DARK, -LING[2]]

dark′ling bee′tle, any brown or black beetle of the family Tenebrionidae, the larvae of which feed on dead or decaying plant material, fungi, stored grain, etc. Also called **tenebrionid.** [1810–20]

dark•ly (därk′lē), *adv.* **1.** so as to appear dark. **2.** vaguely; mysteriously. **3.** in a vaguely threatening or menacing manner: *He hinted darkly that we had not heard the last of the matter.* **4.** imperfectly; faintly. [bef. 1000; ME *derkly,* OE *deorclīce* (in fig. sense only). See DARK, -LY]

dark′ mat′ter, a hypothetical form of matter invisible to electromagnetic radiation, postulated to account for gravitational forces observed in the universe. [1985–90]

dark′ meat′, 1. meat that is dark in appearance after cooking, esp. a leg or thigh of chicken or turkey (distinguished from *white meat*). **2.** *Slang* (*vulgar*). a black person, considered as a sexual partner. [1855–60, *Amer.*]

dark′ min′eral, *Geol.* any rock-forming mineral that has a specific gravity greater than 2.8 and that is generally dark in color. Cf. **light mineral.**

dark′ neb′ula, *Astron.* a cloud of interstellar gas and dust that absorbs and thus obscures the light from stars behind it, appearing as a dark patch in front of a bright nebula or in an otherwise bright area of sky. Also called **absorption nebula.** [1930–35]

dark•ness (därk′nis), *n.* **1.** the state or quality of being dark: *The room was in total darkness.* **2.** absence or deficiency of light: *the darkness of night.* **3.** wickedness or evil: *Satan, the prince of darkness.* **4.** obscurity; concealment: *The darkness of the metaphor destroyed its effectiveness.* **5.** lack of knowledge or enlightenment: *heathen darkness.* **6.** lack of sight; blindness. [bef. 1050; ME *derknesse,* OE *deorcnysse.* See DARK, -NESS]

dark′ of the moon′, the period during which the moon is not visible. [1645–55]

dark′ reac′tion, the phase of photosynthesis, not requiring light, in which carbohydrates are synthesized from carbon dioxide.

dark•room (därk′ro͞om′, -ro͝om′), *n. Photog.* a room in which film or the like is made, handled, or developed and from which the actinic rays of light are excluded. [1835–45; DARK + ROOM]

dark′ slide′, *Photog.* **1.** Also called **draw slide.** a black plastic, metal, or fabric sheet that is inserted into a film holder to protect the film from light. **2.** a lightproof holder for sheet film or a photographic plate.

dark•some (därk′səm), *adj.* dark; darkish. [1520–30; DARK + -SOME[1]] —**dark′some•ness,** *n.*

dark′ star′, *Astron.* an invisible member of a binary or multiple star system.

dark•town (därk′toun′), *n. Usually Offensive Older Use.* a part of a town or city inhabited largely by blacks. [1880–85, *Amer.;* DARK + TOWN]

dark•y (där′kē), *n., pl.* **dark•ies.** *Offensive.* a black person. Also, **darkie.** [1765–75; DARK + -Y[2]]

Dar•lan (dar län′), *n.* **Jean Louis Xa•vier Fran•çois** (zhän lwē gza vyā′ frän swa′), 1881–1942, French naval officer and politician.

Dar•lene (där lēn′), *n.* a female given name: from the Old English word meaning "darling." Also, **Dar•leen′.**

dar•ling (där′ling), *n.* **1.** a person very dear to another; one dearly loved. **2.** (*sometimes cap.*) an affectionate or familiar term of address. **3.** a person or thing in great favor; a favorite: *She was the darling of café society.* —*adj.* **4.** very dear; dearly loved: *my darling child.* **5.** favorite; cherished. **6.** *Informal.* charming; cute; lovable: *What a darling baby!* [bef. 900; ME *derling,* OE *dēorling.* See DEAR, -LING[1]] —**dar′ling•ly,** *adv.* —**dar′ling•ness,** *n.*

Dar•ling (där′ling), *n.* **Jay Nor•wood** (nôr′wo͝od), ("*Ding*"), 1876–1962, U.S. political cartoonist.

Dar′ling Range′, a range of low mountains along the SE coast of Australia. Highest peak, Mt. Cooke, 1910 ft. (580 m).

Dar′ling Riv′er, a river in SE Australia, flowing SW into the Murray River. 1160 mi. (1870 km). long.

Dar•ling•ton (där′ling tən), *n.* a city in S Durham, in NE England. 97,800.

Darm•stadt (därm′stat; *Ger.* däʀm′shtät′), *n.* a city in SW central Germany, S of Frankfort: former capital of Hesse. 136,200.

darn[1] (därn), *v.t.* **1.** to mend, as torn clothing, with rows of stitches, sometimes by crossing and interweaving rows to span a gap. —*n.* **2.** a darned place, as in a garment: *an old sock full of darns.* [1590–1600; perh. to be identified with ME *dernen* to keep secret, conceal, OE (Anglian) *dernan*]

—**Syn. 1.** See **mend.**

darn[2] (därn), *Informal.* —*adj., adv.* **1.** darned. —*v.t.* **2.** to curse; damn: *Darn that pesky fly!* —*n.* **3. give a darn.** See **damn** (def. 11). [1775–85; see DARNED]

darned (därnd), *Informal.* —*adj.* **1.** irritating; damned; confounded: *Get that darned bicycle out of the driveway!* —*adv.* **2.** very; extremely; remarkably: *She's a darned good tennis player.* [1800–10; euphemism for DAMNED, perh. by construing *dern* dark, dreary (now obs.) as an intensifier in phrases such as *dern and dreary, dern and doleful*]

dar•nel (där′nl), *n.* any of several grasses of the genus *Lolium,* having simple stems, flat leaves, and terminal spikes. [1275–1325; ME; cf. F (Walloon) *darnelle,* prob. < Gmc]

darn•er (där′nər), *n.* **1.** a person or thing that darns. **2.** any of numerous odonate insects of the family Aeshnidae, comprising the largest dragonflies. [1605–15; DARN[1] + -ER[1]]

darn•ing (där′ning), *n.* **1.** the act of a person or thing that darns. **2.** the result produced. **3.** articles darned or to be darned. [1605–15; DARN[1] + -ING[1]]

darn′ing egg′, a smooth, egg-shaped piece of wood, ivory, marble, jade, or the like, for holding under a hole or tear to serve as a backing while darning. [1895–1900]

darn′ing nee′dle, 1. a long needle with a long eye used in darning. **2.** *Chiefly Northern and Western U.S.* a dragonfly. [1755–65]

—**Regional Variation. 2.** See **dragonfly.**

Darn•ley (därn′lē), *n.* **Lord Henry Stewart** or **Stuart,** 1545–67, Scottish nobleman: second husband of Mary Queen of Scots (father of James I of England).

Dar•ren (dar′ən), *n.* a male given name.

Dar•row (dar′ō), *n.* **Clarence (Seward),** 1857–1938, U.S. lawyer, lecturer, and author.

dar•shan (där′shən; *Seph. Heb.* där shän′; *Ashk. Heb.* däʀ′shən), *n., pl.* **dar•sha•nim** (*Seph. Heb.* däʀ′shä-nēm′; *Ashk. Heb.* däʀ shô′nim), **dar•shans.** *Judaism.* a preacher or teacher of Aggadah or Halakhah in a synagogue. [1915–20; < Heb *darshān,* akin to *dārash* interpret, expound]

dar•sha•na (dur′shə nə), *n. Hinduism.* any of the six principal systems of philosophy. [< Skt *darśana* act of seeing]

D'Ar′son•val galvanom′eter (där′sən vôl′, -val′), *Elect.* a galvanometer consisting of a large, fixed magnet and a light coil that swings in the magnetic field. Also, **d'Ar′sonval galvanom′eter.** [named after Jacques A. *D'Arsonval* (1851–1940), French physicist]

dart (därt), *n.* **1.** a small, slender missile that is pointed at one end and usually feathered at the other and is propelled by hand, as in the game of darts, or by a blowgun when used as a weapon. **2.** something similar in function to such a missile, as the stinging member of an insect. **3. darts,** (*used with a singular v.*) a game in which darts are thrown at a target usually marked with concentric circles divided into segments and with a bull's-eye in the center. **4.** an act of darting; a sudden swift movement. **5.** a tapered seam of fabric for adjusting the fit of a garment. —*v.i.* **6.** to move swiftly; spring or start suddenly and run swiftly: *A mouse darted out of the closet and ran across the room.* —*v.t.* **7.** to thrust or move suddenly or rapidly: *He darted his eyes around the room.* [1275–1325; ME < AF, OF < Old Low Franconian; cf. OE *daroth,* OHG *tart,* ON *darrathr* spear, lance] —**dart′ing•ly,** *adv.* —**dart′ing•ness,** *n.*

—**Syn. 1.** arrow, barb. **6.** dash, bolt, shoot.

dart•board (därt′bôrd′, -bōrd′), *n.* the target used in the game of darts. [1900–05; DART + BOARD]

dart•er (där′tər), *n.* **1.** a person or thing that darts or moves swiftly. **2.** anhinga. **3.** any of several small, darting, freshwater fishes of the perch family, inhabiting streams of eastern North America. [1555–65; DART + -ER[1]]

dar•tle (där′tl), *v.t., v.i.,* **-tled, -tling.** to dart or shoot forth repeatedly. [1850–55; DART + -LE]

Dart•moor (därt′mo͝or, -môr, -mōr), *n.* **1.** a rocky plateau in SW England, in Devonshire. ab. 20 mi. (30 km) long. **2.** a prison on this plateau. **3.** one of an English breed of sheep having coarse, long wool. **4.** one of an English breed of pony originating in Devon, noted for sure-footedness and longevity.

Dart•mouth (därt′məth), *n.* **1.** a coastal city in S Nova Scotia, in SE Canada, on Halifax harbor, across from Halifax. 65,341. **2.** a city in SE Massachusetts. 23,966.

da•ru•ma (də ro͞o′mə; *Japn.* dä ʀo͞o′mä), *n.* a large red papier-mâché Japanese doll in the form of a seated potbellied Buddhist monk: considered a bringer of luck and prosperity. [1960–65; < Japn < Chin, transliteration of Skt *dharma* DHARMA]

Dar•von (där′von), *Pharm., Trademark.* a brand of propoxyphene.

Dar′von Com′pound, *Pharm., Trademark.* a combination of Darvon, phenacetin, aspirin, and caffeine used chiefly in the treatment of pain.

Dar•win (där′win), *n.* **1. Charles (Robert),** 1809–82, English naturalist and author. **2.** his grandfather, **Erasmus,** 1731–1802, English naturalist and poet. **3.** a seaport in and the capital of Northern Territory, in N Australia. 56,482.

Dar•win•i•an (där win′ē ən), *adj.* **1.** (*sometimes l.c.*) pertaining to Charles Darwin or his doctrines. —*n.* **2.** a follower of Charles Darwin; a person who accepts or advocates Darwinism. [1855–60; DARWIN + -IAN]

Darwin′ian fit′ness, fitness (def. 3).

Dar•win•ism (där′wə niz′əm), *n.* the Darwinian theory that species originate by descent, with variation, from parent forms, through the natural selection of those individuals best adapted for the reproductive success of their kind. [1855–60; DARWIN + -ISM] —**Dar′win•ist, Dar•win•ite** (där′wə nīt′), *n., adj.* —**Dar′win•is′tic,** *adj.*

Dar′win's finch′es, a group of Galapagos Island finches, observed by Charles Darwin, that provide striking evidence of speciation. [1945–50]

Dar′win tu′lip, a class of tulips having a tall stem and broad, bright-colored flowers with a flat, rectangular base. [1885–90; named after C. R. DARWIN]

das (das, däs), *n., pl.* **das•es, das•ses.** hyrax. [< Afrik; cf. D, MD *das* badger, c. G *Dachs;* cf. Norw *svintoks*]

DASD, (däz′dē), *n. Computers.* an external storage device, as a magnetic disk storage unit, in which the access mechanism and storage medium can be positioned directly at the addresses sought to read or write specific data items. [*d*(*irect*-)*a*(*ccess*) *s*(*torage*) *d*(*evice*)]

Da•se•hra (dus′ər ə), *n.* a Hindu festival symbolizing the triumph of good over evil, celebrated for ten days in October. Also, **Da•sa•ha•ra** (dus′ə hur′ə). Also called **Durga Puja.** [< Skt *daśaharā* lit., (goddess) who takes away the ten major sins]

dash[1] (dash), *v.t.* **1.** to strike or smash violently, esp. so as to break to pieces: *He dashed the plate into smithereens against the wall.* **2.** to throw or thrust violently or suddenly: *to dash one stone against another.* **3.** to splash, often violently; bespatter (with water, mud, etc.): *He recovered consciousness when they dashed water in his face.* **4.** to apply roughly, as by splashing: *to dash paint here and there on the wall.* **5.** to mix or adulterate by adding another substance: *to dash wine with water.* **6.** to ruin or frustrate (hopes, plans, etc.): *The rain dashed our hopes for a picnic.* **7.** to depress; dispirit: *The failure dashed his spirits.* **8.** to confound or abash: *His rejection dashed and humiliated him.* —*v.i.* **9.** to strike with violence: *The waves dashed against the cliff.* **10.** to move with violence; rush: *The horses dashed out of the burning stable.* **11. dash off, a.** to hurry away; leave: *I must dash off now.* **b.** Also, **dash down.** to write, make, accomplish, etc., hastily: *We dashed off a letter to announce the news. He dashed down a memo.* —*n.* **12.** a small quantity of anything thrown into or mixed with something else: *a dash of salt.* **13.** a hasty or sudden movement; a rush or sudden onset: *They all made a dash for the door.* **14.** the mark or sign (—) used to note an abrupt break or pause in a sentence or hesitation in an utterance, to begin and end a parenthetic word, phrase, or clause, to indicate the omission of letters or words, to divide a line, to substitute for certain uses of the colon, and to separate any of various elements of a sentence or series of sentences, as a question from its answer. **15.** the throwing or splashing of liquid against something: *the dash of the waves against the dock.* **16.** the sound of such splashing: *The dash of the waves on the beach could be heard from afar.* **17.** spirited action; élan; vigor in action or style: *The dancer performed with spirit and dash.* **18.** *Track.* a short race: *a 100-yard dash.* **19.** dashboard (def. 1). **20.** *Telegraphy.* a signal of longer duration than a dot, used in groups of dots, dashes, and spaces to represent letters, as in Morse code. **21.** a hasty stroke, esp. of a pen. **22.** *Archaic.* a violent and rapid blow or stroke. **23. cut a dash,** to make a striking impression; be ostentatious or showy. [1250–1300; (v.) ME *dasshen,* perh. < ON; cf. Dan *daske* slap, flap, Sw *daska;* (n.) ME: blow, clash, deriv. of the v.]
—**Syn. 10.** dart, bolt. See **rush**[1]. **12.** pinch, bit; touch.

dash[2] (dash), *v.t. Chiefly Brit.* to damn (usually used interjectionally). [1790–1800; euphemism based on *d—n,* printed form of DAMN]

dash[3] (dash), (in West Africa) —*n.* **1.** a tip, bribe, or recompense. **2.** bribery. —*v.t.* **3.** to give a tip or bribe to (esp. a government employee). [1780–1790; perh. first recorded in D as *dache, dasche* (1602); orig. uncert., but often alleged to be < Pg *das* (you) give (2d sing. pres. indic. of *dar* to give)]

dash•board (dash′bôrd′, -bōrd′), *n.* **1.** (in an automobile or similar vehicle) a panel beneath the front window having various gauges and accessories for the use of the driver; instrument panel. **2.** a board or panel at the front of an open carriage or the like to protect the occupants from mud or dirt cast up by the hoofs of the animals drawing the vehicle. [1840–50; DASH[1] + BOARD]

dashed[1] (dasht), *adj.* made up of dashes: *a dashed line down the middle of the road.* [1640–50; DASH[1] + -ED[2]]

dashed[2] (dasht), *adj., adv. Chiefly Brit.* (used as a euphemism) damned: *dashed impudence; dashed bad luck.* [1640–50; DASH[2] + -ED[2]] —**dash•ed•ly** (dash′id lē), *adv.*

da•sheen (da shēn′), *n.* the taro plant, *Colocasia esculenta,* native to tropical Asia, now cultivated in the southern U.S. for its edible tubers. [1895–1900; repr. F *de Chine* of China]

dash•er (dash′ər), *n.* **1.** a person or thing that dashes. **2.** a kind of plunger with paddles at one end, for stirring and mixing liquids or semisolids in a churn, ice-cream freezer, or the like. **3.** a person of dashing appearance or manner. [1780–90; DASH[1] + -ER[1]]

dash′er block′, *Naut.* See **jewel block.**

da•shi•ki (də shē′kē, dä-), *n., pl.* **-kis.** a loose, often colorfully patterned, pullover garment originating in Africa and worn chiefly by men. Also, **daishiki.** [< Yoruba *dàńṣíkí* < Hausa *dàn cikì* (with imploded *d*)]

dashiki

dash•ing (dash′ing), *adj.* **1.** energetic and spirited; lively: *a dashing hero.* **2.** elegant and gallant in appearance and manner: *a dashing young cavalry officer.* **3.** showy; stylish. [1800–05; DASH[1] + -ING[2]] —**dash′ing•ly,** *adv.*

dash′ light′, *Auto.* a light built into the dashboard of an automobile for the purpose of illuminating the gauges and accessories.

dash•pot (dash′pot′), *n.* a device for cushioning, damping, or reversing the motion of a piece of machinery, consisting of a cylinder in which a piston operates to create a pressure or vacuum on an enclosed gas or to force a fluid in or out of the chamber through narrow openings. [1860–65; DASH[1] + POT[1]]

Dasht-i-Ka•vir (däsht′ē kä vēr′; *Eng.* däsht′ē kə vēr′), *n.* a salt desert in N central Iran. 200 mi. (320 km) wide. ab. 18,000 sq. mi. (46,620 sq. km). Also called **Kavir Desert, Great Salt Desert.**

Dasht-i-Lut (däsht′ē lo͞ot′), *n.* a desert in E central Iran. 200 mi. (320 km) long; 100 mi. (160 km) wide. ab. 20,000 sq. mi. (52,000 sq. km). Also called **Lut Desert.**

dash•y (dash′ē), *adj.,* **dash•i•er, dash•i•est.** showy; stylish; dashing. [1815–25; DASH[1] + -Y[1]]

Das Ka•pi•tal (*Ger.* däs kä′pi täl′), a work (1867) by Karl Marx, dealing with economic, social, and political relations within society and containing the tenets on which modern communism is based.

das•sie (das′ē, dä′sē), *n.* hyrax. [1780–90; < Afrik, dim. of *das;* see DAS]

Das•sin (das′in, da sin′; *Fr.* dA saN′), *n.* **Jules** (jo͞olz; *Fr.* zhyl), born 1911, French motion-picture director, born in the U.S.

dass•n't (das′ənt), *Chiefly Northern U.S.* contraction of *dare not.* Also, **das′n't.**

dast (dast), *v.i. Older Use.* dare (def. 1).

das•tard (das′tərd), *n.* **1.** a mean, sneaking coward. —*adj.* **2.** of or befitting a dastard; mean, sneaky, and cowardly. [1400–50; late ME < ?.]

das•tard•ly (das′tərd lē), *adj.* cowardly; meanly base; sneaking: *a dastardly act.* [1560–70; DASTARD + -LY] —**das′tard•li•ness,** *n.*

da•stur (də sto͝or′), *n.* a Parsee chief priest. Also, **dustoor, dustour.** [1885–90; < Pers *dastur*]

dasy-, a combining form meaning "hairy," "shaggy," "dense," used in the formation of compound words: *dasyphyllous.* [< Gk, comb. form repr. *dasýs;* see DENSE]

da•sym•e•ter (da sim′i tər), *n.* an instrument for determining the density of a gas. [1870–75; DASY- + -METER]

das•y•phyl•lous (das′ə fil′əs), *adj. Bot.* having very hairy leaves. [DASY- + -PHYLLOUS]

Das•yu (dus′yo͞o), *n. Hinduism.* a member of the Asuras, survivors of the ancient culture of Harappa: defeated by Indra. [< Skt *dasyu*]

das•y•ure (das′ē yo͝or′), *n.* **1.** any of several nocturnal, carnivorous marsupials of the genus *Dasyurus* and related genera, of Australia, Tasmania, and nearby islands, typically having a reddish or olive-brown coat marked with white spots. **2.** Also called **ursine dasyure.** any of several related animals, as the Tasmanian devil. [1830–40; < NL *Dasyurus* name of the genus < Gk *dasy-* DASY- + *-ouros* -tailed, adj. deriv. of *ourá* tail] —**das•y•u•rine** (das′i yo͝or′in, -in), *adj.* —**das′y•u′roid,** *adj., n.*

DAT, digital audiotape.

dat., dative.

da•ta (dā′tə, dat′ə, dä′tə), *n.* **1.** a pl. of **datum. 2.** (*used with a plural v.*) individual facts, statistics, or items of information: *These data represent the results of our analyses. Data are entered by terminal for immediate processing by the computer.* **3.** (*used with a singular v.*) a body of facts; information: *Additional data is available from the president of the firm.*
—**Usage.** DATA is a plural of DATUM, which is originally a Latin noun meaning "something given." Today, DATA is used in English both as a plural noun meaning "facts or pieces of information" (*These data are described more fully elsewhere*) and as a singular mass noun meaning "information": *Not much data is available on flood control in Brazil.* It is almost always treated as a plural in scientific and academic writing. In other types of writing it is either singular or plural. The singular DATUM meaning "a piece of information" is now rare in all types of writing. In surveying and civil engineering, where DATUM has specialized senses, the plural form is DATUMS.

da′ta bank′, **1.** a fund of information on a particular subject or group of related subjects, usually stored in and used via a computer system. **2.** database. Also, **da′ta•bank′.** [1965–70]

da•ta•base (dā′tə bās′), *n.* **1.** a comprehensive collection of related data organized for convenient access, generally in a computer. **2.** See **data bank.** Also, **da′•ta-base′, da′ta base′.** [1965–70; DATA + BASE[1]]

da•ta•cen•ter (dā′tə sen′tər), *n.* a facility equipped with or connected to one or more computers, used for processing or transmitting data. Also, **da′ta cen′ter.** Also called **da′ta proc′essing cen′ter.** [DATA + CENTER]

da′ta communica′tion, *Telecommunications.* electronic transmission of information that has been encoded for storage and processing by computers.

da′ta proc′essing, processing of information, esp. the handling of information by computers in accordance with strictly defined systems of procedure. Also called **information processing.** [1950–55] —**da′ta proc′essor.**

da•ta•ry (dā′tə rē), *n., pl.* **-ries.** *Rom. Cath. Ch.* **1.** the office of the Curia Romana that investigates candidates for papal benefices. **2.** the cardinal who heads this office. [1520–30; < ML **datāria* the office (where documents were dated); *datārius* the officer (who gave the dates), equiv. to LL *dat*(*a*) DATE[1] + L *-āria, -ārius* -ARY]

da′ta set′, *Computers.* **1.** a collection of data records for computer processing. **2.** modem. [1970–75]

dat•cha (dä′chə), *n.* dacha.

date[1] (dāt), *n., v.,* **dat•ed, dat•ing.** —*n.* **1.** a particular month, day, and year at which some event happened or will happen: *July 4, 1776 was the date of the signing of the Declaration of Independence.* **2.** the day of the month: *Is today's date the 7th or the 8th?* **3.** an inscription on a writing, coin, etc., that shows the time, or time and place, of writing, casting, delivery, etc.: *a letter bearing the date January 16.* **4.** the time or period to which any event or thing belongs; period in general: *at a late date.* **5.** the time during which anything lasts; duration: *The pity is that childhood has so short a date.* **6.** an appointment for a particular time: *They have a date with their accountant at ten o'clock.* **7.** a social appointment, engagement, or occasion arranged beforehand with another person: *to go out on a date on Saturday night.* **8.** a person with whom one has such a social appointment or engagement: *Can I bring a date to the party?* **9.** an engagement for an entertainer to perform. **10. dates,** the birth and death dates, usually in years, of a person: *Dante's dates are 1265 to 1321.* **11. to date,** up to the present time; until now: *This is his best book to date.* **12. up to date,** in agreement with or inclusive of the latest information; modern: *Bring us up to date on the news.* —*v.i.* **13.** to have or bear a date: *The letter dates from 1873.* **14.** to belong to a particular period; have its origin: *That dress dates from the 19th century. The architecture dates as far back as 1830.* **15.** to reckon from some point in time: *The custom dates from the days when women wore longer skirts.* **16.** to go out socially on dates: *She dated a lot during high school.* —*v.t.* **17.** to mark or furnish with a date: *Please date the check as of today.* **18.** to ascertain or fix the period or point in time of; assign a period or point in time to: *The archaeologist dated the ruins as belonging to the early Minoan period.* **19.** to show the age of; show to be old-fashioned. **20.** to make a date with; go out on dates with: *He's been dating his best friend's sister.* [1275–1325; (n.) ME < MF < LL *data,* n. use of *data* (fem. of *datus,* ptp. of *dare* to give), from the phrase *data* (*Romae*) written, given (at Rome); (v.) ME *daten* to sign or date a document, deriv. of the n.] —**dat′a•ble, date′a•ble,** *adj.* —**dat′a•ble•ness, date′a•ble•ness,** *n.* —**dat′er,** *n.*

date[2] (dāt), *n.* the oblong, fleshy fruit of the date palm, a staple food in northern Africa, Arabia, etc., and an important export. [1250–1300; ME < AF; OF *dade, date* < ML *datil*(*l*)*us* (> OPr, Catalan, Sp *datil*) < L *dactylus;* see DACTYL]

date•book (dāt′bo͝ok′), *n.* a printed notebook for listing appointments, making entries of events, etc., often with printed headings or lines for each day of the year and for the hours of the day. [DATE[1] + BOOK]

dat•ed (dā′tid), *adj.* **1.** having or showing a date: *a dated record of all meetings.* **2.** out-of-date; old-fashioned: *a nostalgic program of dated songs.* [1580–90; DATE[1] + -ED[3]] —**dat′ed•ly,** *adv.* —**dat′ed•ness,** *n.*
—**Syn. 2.** outmoded, passé, unfashionable.

date•less (dāt′lis), *adj.* **1.** without a date; undated. **2.** endless; limitless. **3.** so old as to be undatable: *a dateless rock formation.* **4.** of permanent interest regardless of age: *a dateless work of art.* **5.** having no social engagement. [1585–95; DATE[1] + -LESS]

date′ line′. See **International Date Line.** [1875–80]

date•line (dāt′līn′), *n., v.,* **-lined, -lin•ing.** —*n.* **1.** a line giving the place of origin and usually the date of a news dispatch or the like. —*v.t.* **2.** to furnish (a news story) with a dateline: *He datelines his reports Damascus.* [1885–90; DATE[1] + LINE[1]]

date′ mus′sel, any brown, date-sized marine mussel, genus *Lithophaga,* that bores into rock or coral.

date′ of rec′ord, the final date a registered stockholder of a corporation has the right to receive a dividend or other benefit.

date′ palm′, any of several date-bearing palms of the genus *Phoenix,* esp. *P. dactylifera,* having a stem reaching a height of 60 ft. (18 m) and terminating in a crown of pinnate leaves. [1830–40]

date′ rape′, sexual intercourse forced by a man upon the woman with whom he has a date. [1980–85]

date′ stamp′, **1.** a device for stamping dates and often the place of origin or receipt, as on postal matter. **2.** the information stamped by this device. [1855–60]

date-stamp (dāt′stamp′), *v.t.* to stamp the date on, as with a date stamp: *He date-stamped every letter received.* [1925–30]

dat′ing bar′. See **singles bar.** [1965–70]

dat′ing nail′, a nail driven into a wooden tie, pole, etc., bearing on its head the date of installation or last treatment of the timber.

da•tive (dā′tiv), *Gram.* —*adj.* **1.** (in certain inflected languages, as Latin, Greek, and German) noting a case having as a distinctive function indication of the indirect object of a verb or the object of certain prepositions. —*n.* **2.** the dative case. **3.** a word or form in that case, as Latin *regi* in *regi haec dicite* meaning "tell this to the king." [1400–50; late ME *datif* < L *datīvus* (*casus*) dative (case), equiv. to *dat*(*us*) given (see DATE¹) + *-īvus* -IVE; trans. of Gk *dotikḗ* (*ptôsis*)] —**da•ti•val** (dā ti′vəl), *adj.* —**da′tive•ly,** *adv.*

da′tive bond′, *Chem.* See **coordinate bond.**

da•to (dä′tō; *Sp.* dä′tô), *n., pl.* **-tos** (-tōz; *Sp.* -tôs), **1.** (in the Philippines) a native chief. **2.** the headman of a barrio or of a Malay tribe. Also, **datu.** [1835–45; < Sp or Pg < Malay *datuk* war chief]

dat•o•lite (dat′l īt′), *n.* a mineral, calcium and boron silicate, $CaB(SiO_4)(OH)$, usually occurring in rock cavities in the form of colorless, prismatic crystals. [1800–10; < G *Datolith,* equiv. to Gk *dat*(*eîsthai*) to divide, share out + -o- + G *-lith;* see -LITE] —**dat•o•lit•ic** (dat′l it′ik), *adj.*

Da•tong (dä′tông′), *n. Pinyin.* a city in N Shanxi province, in NE China. 300,000. Also, **Tatung.**

da•tu (dä′to͞o), *n.* dato.

da•tum (dā′təm, dat′əm, dä′təm), *n., pl.* **da•ta** (dā′tə, dat′ə, dä′tə) for 1–3, **da•tums** for 4, 5. **1.** a single piece of information, as a fact, statistic, or code; an item of data. **2.** *Philos.* **a.** any fact assumed to be a matter of direct observation. **b.** any proposition assumed or given, from which conclusions may be drawn. **3.** Also called **sense datum.** *Epistemology.* the object of knowledge as presented to the mind. Cf. **ideatum. 4.** *Survey., Civ. Eng.* any level surface, line, or point used as a reference in measuring elevations. **5.** *Survey.* a basis for horizontal control surveys, consisting of the longitude and latitude of a certain point, the azimuth of a certain line from this point, and two constants used in defining the terrestrial spheroid. [1640–50; < L: a thing given, neut. ptp. of *dare* to give]
—**Usage.** See **data.**

da•tu•ra (də to͝or′ə, -tyo͝or′ə), *n.* any of several plants belonging to the genus *Datura,* of the nightshade family, including some species grown as ornamentals and usually having funnel-shaped flowers and prickly pods: the leaves and seeds are the source of hallucinogenic alkaloids. Cf. **angel's-trumpet, jimson weed.** [1655–65; < NL < Hindi *dhatūra* jimson weed < Skt *dhattūra*] —**da•tu′ric,** *adj.*

dau (dou), *n.* dhow.

dau., daughter.

daub (dôb), *v.t.* **1.** to cover or coat with soft, adhesive matter, as plaster or mud: *to daub a canvas with paint; to daub stone walls with mud.* **2.** to spread (plaster, mud, etc.) on or over something: *to daub plaster on a brick wall.* **3.** to smear, soil, or defile. **4.** to apply, as paint or colors, unskillfully. —*v.i.* **5.** to daub something. **6.** to paint unskillfully. —*n.* **7.** material, esp. of an inferior kind, for daubing walls. **8.** something daubed on. **9.** an act of daubing. **10.** a crude, inartistic painting. [1275–1325; (v.) ME *dauben* < AF, OF *dauber* to whiten, paint < L *dealbāre,* equiv. to *de-,* prevocalic var. of *dē-* DE- + *albāre* to whiten, deriv. of *albus* white; (n.) late ME, deriv. of the v.] —**daub′er,** *n.* —**daub′ing•ly,** *adv.* —**daub′y,** *adj.*

daube (dōb), *n.* **1.** a stew of braised meat, vegetables, herbs, and seasonings. **2.** the pot or casserole in which such a stew is cooked. [1715–25; < F (sp. by assoc. with *dauber* to DAUB) < It *dobba* < Catalan (*a la*) *adoba* stewed, deriv. of *adobar* to spice, orig. to prepare, arrange, ult. < Gmc **dubban* to strike; see DUB¹]

daub•er•y (dô′bə rē), *n.* unskillful painting or work. Also, **daub•ry** (dô′brē). [1540–50; DAUB + -ERY]

Dau•bi•gny (dō bē nyē′), *n.* **Charles Fran•çois** (shȧrl fräɴ swȧ′), 1817–78, French painter.

Dau•det (dō dā′, dō-; *Fr.* dō de′), *n.* **1. Al•phonse** (al fôɴs′), 1840–97, French novelist and short-story writer. **2.** his son, **Lé•on** (lā ôɴ′), 1867–1942, French journalist and novelist.

dau•er•schlaf (dou′ər shläf′), *n.* a form of therapy, now rarely used, that involves the use of drugs to induce long periods of deep sleep. [< G, equiv. to *dauer* long lasting + *Schlaf* sleep]

Dau•ga•va (dou′gä vä′), *n.* Latvian name of **Dvina.**

Dau•gav•pils (dou′gäf pēls′), *n.* a city in SE Latvia, on the Dvina. 128,200. German, **Dünaburg.** Russian, **Dvinsk.**

daugh•ter (dô′tər), *n.* **1.** a female child or person in relation to her parents. **2.** any female descendant. **3.** a person related as if by the ties binding daughter to parent: *daughter of the church.* **4.** anything personified as female and considered with respect to its origin: *The United States is the daughter of the 13 colonies.* **5.** *Chem., Physics.* an isotope formed by radioactive decay of another isotope. —*adj.* **6.** *Biol.* pertaining to a cell or other structure arising from division or replication: *daughter cell; daughter DNA.* [bef. 950; ME *doughter,* OE *dohtor;* c. G *Tochter,* Gk *thygátēr,* Skt *duhitā́*] —**daugh′ter•less,** *adj.* —**daugh′ter•like′,** *adj.*

daugh•ter-in-law (dô′tər in lô′), *n., pl.* **daugh•ters-in-law.** the wife of one's son. [1350–1400; ME *doughter in lawe*]

daugh′ter lan′guage, a language that has evolved from another specified language.

daugh•ter•ly (dô′tər lē), *adj.* pertaining to, befitting, or like a daughter. [1525–35; DAUGHTER + -LY] —**daugh′ter•li•ness,** *n.*

Daugh′ters of the Amer′ican Revolu′tion, a patriotic society of women descended from Americans of the Revolutionary period, organized in 1890. *Abbr.:* D.A.R.

dauk (dôk), *n.* dak.

Dau•mier (dō myā′), *n.* **Ho•no•ré** (ô nô rā′), 1808–79, French painter, cartoonist, and lithographer.

daun•cy (dôn′sē, dän′-), *adj.* donsie.

daunt (dônt, dänt), *v.t.* **1.** to overcome with fear; intimidate: *to daunt one's adversaries.* **2.** to lessen the courage of; dishearten: *Don't be daunted by the amount of work still to be done.* [1250–1300; ME *da*(*u*)*nten* < AF *da*(*u*)*nter,* OF *danter,* alter. of *donter* (prob. by influence of *dangier* power, authority; see DANGER) < L *domitāre* to tame, deriv. of *domitus,* ptp. of *domāre* to tame] —**daunt′ing•ly,** *adv.* —**daunt′ing•ness,** *n.*
—**Syn. 1.** overawe, subdue, dismay, frighten. **2.** discourage, dispirit. —**Ant. 2.** encourage.

daunt•less (dônt′lis, dänt′-), *adj.* **1.** not to be daunted or intimidated; fearless; intrepid; bold: *a dauntless hero.* —*n.* **2.** (*cap.*) Also called **Douglas SBD.** the principal U.S. Navy fleet bomber of early World War II, capable of carrying bombs or depth charges and particularly successful as a dive bomber. [1585–95; DAUNT + -LESS] —**daunt′less•ly,** *adv.* —**daunt′less•ness,** *n.*
—**Syn. 1.** undaunted, daring, brave, courageous.

Dau•nus (dô′nəs), *n. Rom. Legend.* father of Euippe, second wife of Diomedes.

dau•phin (dô′fin; *Fr.* dō faɴ′), *n., pl.* **-phins** (-finz; *Fr.* -faɴ′). the eldest son of a king of France, used as a title from 1349 to 1830. [1475–85; < F; MF *dalphin,* after DAUPHINÉ, from an agreement to thus honor the province after its cession to France]

dau•phine (dô′fēn; *Fr.* dō fēn′), *n., pl.* **-phines** (-fēnz; *Fr.* -fēn′). the wife of a dauphin. Also, **dauphiness.** [1860–65; < F; MF *dalfine,* fem. of *dalphin* DAUPHIN]

Dau•phi•né (dō fē nā′), *n.* a historical region and former province of SE France.

dau•phin•ess (dô′fi nis), *n.* dauphine. [1540–50; earlier *daulphiness.* See DAUPHIN, -ESS]
—**Usage.** See **-ess.**

daut (dôt, dät), *v.t. Scot.* to caress. [1490–1500; orig. uncert.]

daut•ie (dô′tē, dä′-), *n. Scot.* a darling. [1670–80; DAUT + -IE]

D.A.V., Disabled American Veterans. Also, **DAV**

Da•vao (dä vou′, dä′vou), *n.* a seaport on SE Mindanao, in the S Philippines. 610,375.

Davao′ Gulf′, a gulf of the Pacific Ocean on the SE coast of Mindanao, Philippines.

Dave (dāv), *n.* a male given name, form of **David.**

da•ven (dä′vən), *v.i., v.t. Yiddish.* to pray. Also, ***doven.***

D'Av•e•nant (dav′ə nənt), *n.* **Sir William,** 1606–68, English dramatist and producer: poet laureate 1638–68. Also, **Dav′e•nant.**

dav•en•port (dav′ən pôrt′, -pōrt′), *n.* **1.** a large sofa, often one convertible into a bed. **2.** *Chiefly Brit.* a small writing desk. [1850–55; the desk is said to be named after a Captain *Davenport* who first commissioned it]

Dav•en•port (dav′ən pôrt′, -pōrt′), *n.* **1. John,** 1597–1670, Puritan clergyman: one of the founders of New Haven. **2.** a city in E Iowa, on the Mississippi River. 103,264.

dav′enport ta′ble. See **sofa table.**

Da•vid (dā′vid *for 1, 2, 5; Fr.* dȧ vēd′ *for 3, 5; Sp.* dä vēth′ *for 4, 5*), *n.* **1.** died c970 B.C., the second king of Israel, reigned c1010–c970, successor to Saul: slayer of the Philistine giant Goliath. **2. Saint.** Also called **Dewi Sant.** A.D. c510–601?, Welsh bishop: patron saint of Wales. **3. Jacques Louis** (zhäk lwē), 1748–1825, French painter. **4.** a city in SW Panama. 70,700. **5.** a male given name: from a Hebrew word meaning "beloved."

Da•vid I (dā′vid), 1084–1153, king of Scotland 1124–53.

Da•vid Cop•per•field (dā′vid kop′ər fēld′), a novel (1850) by Charles Dickens.

Da•vid•ic (də vid′ik), *adj.* of or pertaining to the Biblical David or his descendants. [1820–30; DAVID + -IC]

Da•vid•son (dā′vid sən), *n.* **Jo** (jō), 1883–1952, U.S. sculptor.

Da′vidson Cur′rent, a winter countercurrent that flows N along the W coast of the U.S. [after George *Davidson* (1825–1911), U.S. astronomer and geodesist]

Da•vie (dā′vē), *n.* a town in SE Florida. 20,877.

Da•vies (dā′vēz), *n.* **1. Arthur Bow•en** (bō′ən), 1862–1928, U.S. painter. **2. Joseph Edward,** 1876–1958, U.S. lawyer and diplomat. **3. (William) Robertson,** born 1913, Canadian novelist, playwright, and essayist.

da Vin•ci (də vin′chē; *It.* dä vēn′chē), **Le•o•nar•do** (lē′ə när′dō, lā′-; *It.* le′ô när′dô). See **Leonardo da Vinci.**

Da•vis (dā′vis), *n.* **1. Alexander Jackson,** 1803–92, U.S. architect. **2. Benjamin Oliver,** 1877–1970, U.S. military officer: first black Army brigadier general. **3.** his son, **Benjamin Oliver, Jr.,** born 1912, U.S. military officer: first black Air Force lieutenant general. **4. Bet•te** (bet′ē), (*Ruth Elizabeth Davis*), 1908–89, U.S. film actress. **5. Dwight F(il•ley)** (fil′ē), 1879–1945, U.S. tennis player and public official: donor of the Davis Cup (1900), an international tennis trophy; Secretary of War 1925–29. **6. Elmer (Holmes),** 1890–1958, U.S. radio commentator and author. **7. Jefferson,** 1808–89, U.S. statesman: president of the Confederate States of America 1861–65. **8. John.** Also, **Davys.** c1550–1605, English navigator and explorer. **9. John William,** 1873–1955, U.S. lawyer, politician, and diplomat. **10. Miles (Dewey, Jr.),** 1926–91, U.S. jazz trumpeter. **11. Owen,** 1874–1956, U.S. playwright. **12. Richard Harding,** 1864–1916, U.S. journalist, novelist, and playwright. **13. Stuart,** 1894–1964, U.S. painter and illustrator. **14.** a town in central California. 36,640.

Da•vis•son (dā′və sən), *n.* **Clinton Joseph,** 1881–1958, U.S. physicist: Nobel prize 1937.

Da′vis•son-Ger′mer exper′iment (dā′və sən gûr′mər), *Physics.* an experiment that verified the wave properties of matter by showing that a beam of electrons is diffracted by a crystal at an angle dependent upon the velocity of the electrons. [named after C. J. DAVISSON and Lester Halbert *Germer* (1896–1971), American physicists]

Da′vis Strait′, a strait between Canada and Greenland, connecting Baffin Bay and the Atlantic. 200–500 mi. (320–800 km) wide.

dav•it (dav′it, dā′vit), *n.* any of various cranelike devices used singly or in pairs for supporting, raising, and lowering esp. boats, anchors, and cargo over a hatchway or side of a ship. [1325–75; ME *daviot* < AF, appar. dim. of *Davi* David]

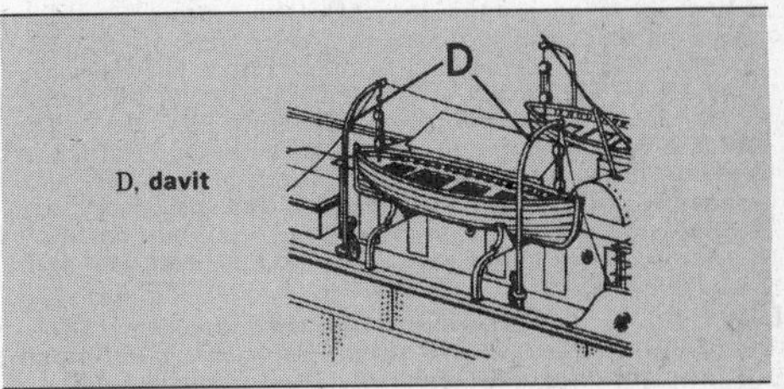

D, davit

Da•vout (dȧ vo͞o′), *n.* **Louis Ni•co•las** (lwē nē kô lä′), **Duke of Au•er•stadt** (ou′ər stat′), **Prince of Eck•mühl** (ek′myo͞ol), 1770–1823, marshal of France: one of Napoleon's leading generals.

Da•vy (dā′vē), *n.* **Sir Humphry,** 1778–1829, English chemist.

Da′vy Jones′ (jōnz), the personification of the sea. [1745–55; orig. uncert.]

Da′vy Jones′s lock′er, (jōn′ziz, jōnz), the ocean's bottom, esp. when regarded as the grave of all who perish at sea. [1795–1805]

Da′vy lamp′, a safety lamp formerly used by miners. [1810–20; named after Sir H. DAVY]

Da•vys (dā′vis), *n.* **John.** See **Davis, John.**

daw (dô), *n.* **1.** jackdaw. **2.** *Obs.* simpleton; fool. [1400–50; late ME *dawe;* cf. OHG *taha*]

daw•dle (dôd′l), *v.,* **-dled, -dling.** —*v.i.* **1.** to waste time; idle; trifle; loiter: *Stop dawdling and help me with these packages!* **2.** to move slowly, languidly, or dilatorily; saunter. —*v.t.* **3.** to waste (time) by or as if by trifling (usually fol. by *away*): *He dawdled away the whole morning.* [1650–60; var. of *daddle* to toddle] —**daw′dler,** *n.* —**daw′dling•ly,** *adv.*
—**Syn. 1, 2.** See **loiter. 3.** fritter, putter, idle, trifle.

Dawes (dôz), *n.* **Charles Gates,** 1865–1951, U.S. financier and diplomat: vice president of the U.S. 1925–29; Nobel peace prize 1925.

Dawes′ plan′, a plan to ensure payments of reparations by Germany after World War I, devised by an international committee headed by Charles Gates Dawes and put into effect in 1924. Cf. **Young plan.**

dawk¹ (dôk, däk), *n.* dak.

dawk² (dôk), *n.* a person who advocates neither a conciliatory nor a belligerent national attitude. [1965–70; D(OVE)¹ + (H)AWK¹] —**dawk′ish,** *adj.*

dawn (dôn), *n.* **1.** the first appearance of daylight in the morning: *Dawn broke over the valley.* **2.** the beginning or rise of anything; advent: *the dawn of civilization.* —*v.i.* **3.** to begin to grow light in the morning: *The day dawned with a cloudless sky.* **4.** to begin to open or develop. **5.** to begin to be perceived (usually fol. by *on*): *The idea dawned on him.* [bef. 1150; ME *dawen* (v.), OE *dagian,* deriv. of *dæg* DAY; akin to ON *daga,* MD, MLG *dagen,* OHG *tagēn*] —**dawn′like′,** *adj.*
—**Syn. 1.** daybreak, sunrise. **5.** appear, occur, break.
—**Ant. 1.** sunset.

Dawn (dôn), *n.* a female given name.

dawn′ horse′, eohippus. [1200–50]

dawn•ing (dô′ning), *n.* **1.** daybreak; dawn. **2.** beginning; start: *the dawning of the space age.* [ME; see DAWN, -ING¹]

dawn′ patrol′, a flight, esp. during the early days of military aviation, undertaken at dawn or early morning in order to reconnoiter enemy positions. [1910–15]

dawn′ red′wood, metasequoia.

Daw•son (dô′sən), *n.* **1. Sir John William,** 1820–99,

CONCISE PRONUNCIATION KEY: act, cāpe, dâre, pärt; set, ēqual; *if,* īce; ox, ōver, ôrder, oil, bo͝ok, bo͞ot, out; up, ûrge; child; sing; shoe; thin, *that;* zh as in *treasure.* ə = a as in *alone,* e as in *system,* i as in *easily,* o as in *gallop,* u as in *circus;* ᵊ as in *fire* (fīᵊr), *hour* (ouᵊr). l and n can serve as syllabic consonants, as in *cradle* (krād′l), and *button* (but′n). See the full key inside the front cover.

Canadian geologist and educator. **2. William Levi,** born 1899, U.S. composer and conductor. **3.** a town in NW Canada, at the confluence of the Yukon and Klondike rivers: former capital of the Yukon Territory. 838.

Daw′son Creek′, a village in NE British Columbia, Canada, at the SE terminus of the Alaska Highway. 10,528.

daw·son·ite (dô′sə nīt′), *n.* an orthorhombic mineral, hydrous sodium aluminum carbonate, $NaAlCO_3(OH)_2$, with a vitreous luster, occurring as white blade-shaped crystals: mined as an ore of aluminum. [named after J.W. DAWSON; see -ITE[1]]

Dax (däks), *n.* a city in SW France: mineral hot springs. 20,294.

day (dā), *n.* **1.** the interval of light between two successive nights; the time between sunrise and sunset: *Since there was no artificial illumination, all activities had to be carried on during the day.* **2.** the light of day; daylight: *The owl sleeps by day and feeds by night.* **3.** *Astron.* **a.** Also called **mean solar day.** a division of time equal to 24 hours and representing the average length of the period during which the earth makes one rotation on its axis. **b.** Also called **solar day.** a division of time equal to the time elapsed between two consecutive returns of the same terrestrial meridian to the sun. **c.** Also called **civil day.** a division of time equal to 24 hours but reckoned from one midnight to the next. Cf. **lunar day, sidereal day. 4.** an analogous division of time for a planet other than the earth: *the Martian day.* **5.** the portion of a day allotted to work: *an eight-hour day.* **6.** a day on which something occurs: *the day we met.* **7.** (*often cap.*) a day assigned to a particular purpose or observance: *New Year's Day.* **8.** a time considered as propitious or opportune: *His day will come.* **9.** a day of contest or the contest itself: *to win the day.* **10.** Often, **days.** a particular time or period: *the present day; in days of old.* **11.** Usually, **days.** period of life or activity: *His days are numbered.* **12.** period of existence, power, or influence: *in the day of the dinosaurs.* **13.** light[1] (def. 19a). **14. call it a day,** to stop one's activity for the day or for the present; quit temporarily: *After rewriting the paper, she decided to call it a day.* **15. day in, day out,** every day without fail; regularly: *They endured the noise and dirt of the city day in, day out.* Also, **day in and day out.** [bef. 950; ME; OE *dæg;* c. G *Tag*]

Day (dā), *n.* **1. Clarence (Shep·ard)** (shep′ərd), 1874–1935, U.S. author. **2. Dorothy,** 1897–1980, U.S. Roman Catholic social activist, journalist, and publisher.

Day·ak (dī′ak, -ək), *n., pl.* **-aks,** (*esp. collectively*) **-ak.** a member of any of several indigenous, Austronesian-speaking tribal peoples of Sarawak and Indonesian Borneo. Also, **Dyak.** [1830–40]

da·yan (*Seph.* dä yän′; *Ashk.* dä yôn′), *n., pl.* ***da·ya·nim*** (*Seph.* dä′yä nēm′; *Ashk.* dä yô′nim). *Hebrew.* **1.** a judge in a Jewish religious court. **2.** a person knowledgeable in Talmudic law whose advice on religious questions is often sought by rabbis. [*dayyān* judge]

Da·yan (dä yän′), *n.* **Mo·she** (mô she′; *Eng.* mō′shə), 1915–81, Israeli politician and military leader: defense minister 1967–74, foreign minister 1977–79.

day·bea·con (dā′bē′kən), *n.* an unlighted navigational beacon used as a daymark. [DAY + BEACON]

day·bed (dā′bed′), *n.* **1.** a couch that can be used as a sofa by day and a bed by night. **2.** a couch, esp. of the 17th or 18th century, in the form of a usually armless chair, with a greatly elongated seat supported by extra legs and a slanted, sometimes hinged, back, used for reclining or sleeping during the day. [1585–95; DAY + BED]

day′ blind′ness, hemeralopia (def. 1). [1825–35]

day·book (dā′bo͝ok′), *n.* **1.** *Bookkeeping.* a book in which the transactions of the day are entered in the order of their occurrence. **2.** a diary; journal. **3.** datebook. [1570–80; DAY + BOOK]

day′ boy′, *Chiefly Brit.* a male boarding-school student who lives at home. [1840–50]

day·break (dā′brāk′), *n.* the first appearance of daylight in the morning; dawn. [1520–30; DAY + BREAK]

day-by-day (dā′bī dā′), *adj.* taking place each day; daily: *a day-by-day account.* [1350–1400; ME]

day′ camp′, a camp for children providing no sleeping facilities and attended only during the day on weekdays. Cf. **summer camp.**

day′ care′, supervised daytime care for preschool children, the elderly, or those with chronic disabilities, usually provided at a center outside the home. [1940–45]

day-care (dā′kâr′), *adj.* of, pertaining to, or providing day care: *day-care center; day-care program.* [1960–65]

day′ coach′, **1.** an ordinary railroad passenger car, as distinguished from a sleeping car, parlor car, or other deluxe accommodations. **2.** the class of airline coach for daytime flight at regular fare. Cf. **night coach.** Also, **day′coach′.** [1870–75, *Amer.*]

day′ cruis′er, a motorboat too small to have any accommodations for sleeping.

day·dream (dā′drēm′), *n.* **1.** a reverie indulged in while awake. —*v.i.* **2.** to indulge in such a reverie. [1675–85; DAY + DREAM] **—day′dream′er,** *n.* **—day′·dream′y,** *adj.*
—Syn. 2. fantasize, dream, muse, woolgather.

day·flow·er (dā′flou′ər), *n.* any plant of the genus *Commelina,* usually bearing clusters of small, blue flowers that bloom for only one day. [1680–90; DAY + FLOWER]

CONCISE ETYMOLOGY KEY: <, descended or borrowed from; >, whence; b., blend of, blended; c., cognate with; cf., compare; deriv., derivative; equiv., equivalent; imit., imitative; obl., oblique; r., replacing; s., stem; sp., spelling, spelled; resp., respelling, respelled; trans., translation; ?, origin unknown; *, unattested; ‡, probably earlier than. See the full key inside the front cover.

day·fly (dā′flī′), *n., pl.* **-flies.** a mayfly. [1595–1605; DAY + FLY[2]]

Day-Glo (dā′glō′), *Trademark.* a brand of pigments and other products that exhibit fluorescence in daylight.

day·glow (dā′glō′), *n.* See under **airglow.** [1955–60; DAY + GLOW]

day′ in court′, **1.** the day on which one involved in a lawsuit is to be afforded the opportunity to appear and be heard in court. **2.** a chance to present one's defense or argument.

day′ jas′mine, a West Indian shrub, *Cestrum diurnum,* of the nightshade family, having clusters of white flowers that are very fragrant by day.

day′ la′bor, **1.** workers hired on a daily basis only, esp. unskilled labor. **2.** work done by a day laborer. [1400–50; late ME]

day′ la′borer, an unskilled worker paid by the day. [1540–50]

day′ let′ter, a telegram having a limited number of words and sent slower and cheaper than a regular telegram. [1920–25]

Day-Lew·is (dā′lo͞o′is), *n.* **C(ecil).** See **Lewis, C(ecil) Day.**

day·light (dā′līt′), *n., adj., v.,* **-light·ed** or **-lit, -light·ing.** —*n.* **1.** the light of day: *At the end of the tunnel they could see daylight.* **2.** public knowledge or awareness; openness: *The newspaper article brought the scandal out into the daylight.* **3.** the period of day; daytime. **4.** daybreak; dawn. **5.** a clear space between any two parts that should be close together, as between the jambs of the opening of a doorway or the knees of a horseback rider and a saddle. **6. daylights,** mental soundness; consciousness; wits: *The noise scared the daylights out of us.* **7. see daylight,** to progress to a point where completion of a difficult task seems possible or probable. —*adj.* **8.** *Photog.* of, pertaining to, or being film made for exposure by the natural light of day. —*v.t.* **9.** to suffuse (an interior space) with artificial light or with daylight filtered through translucent materials, as roofing panels. [1175–1225; ME; see DAY, LIGHT[1]]

day′light sav′ing, the practice of advancing standard time by one hour in the spring of each year and of setting it back by one hour in the fall in order to gain an extra period of daylight during the early evening. Also, **day′light sav′ings.** [1905–10]

day′light-sav′ing time′ (dā′līt′sā′ving), the civil time observed when daylight saving is adopted in a country or community. Also, **day′light sav′ing time′.** [1905–10]

day·lil·y (dā′lil′ē), *n.* any lily of the genus *Hemerocallis,* having yellow, orange, or red flowers that commonly last only for a day. Also, **day′ lil′y.** [1590–1600]

day·lin·er (dā′lī′nər), *n.* **1.** a train, boat, etc., having a regularly scheduled route during daylight hours. **2.** a passenger on a day-liner. [1830–40]

day′ loan′, a bank loan to finance the purchase of securities which is repayable within the calendar day on which it is made. Also called **clearing loan, morning loan.**

day·long (dā′lông′, -long′), *adj.* during the entire day; lasting all day: *a daylong trip.* [1850–55; DAY + LONG[1]]

day′ man′, **1.** a seaman who is a member of a deck gang. **2.** Also called **idler.** a member of a ship's company who does not stand watch and who ordinarily works only during the day, as a carpenter or sailmaker. [1875–80]

day·mare (dā′mâr′), *n.* **1.** a distressing experience, similar to a bad dream, occurring while one is awake. **2.** an acute anxiety attack. [1730–40; DAY + (NIGHT)MARE]

day·mark (dā′märk′), *n.* a navigational aid distinctively marked for visibility by day. [DAY + MARK[1]]

day′ name′, (formerly, esp. in creole-speaking cultures) a name given at birth to a black child, in accordance with African customs, indicating the child's sex and the day of the week on which he or she was born, as the male and female names for Sunday **(Quashee** and **Quasheba),** Monday **(Cudjo** or **Cudjoe** and **Juba),** Tuesday **(Cubbena** and **Beneba),** Wednesday **(Quaco** and **Cuba** or **Cubba),** Thursday **(Quao** and **Abba),** Friday **(Cuffee** or **Cuffy** and **Pheba** or **Phibbi),** and Saturday **(Quamin** or **Quame** and **Mimba).**

day-neu·tral (dā′no͞o′trəl, -nyo͞o′-), *adj.* of or pertaining to plants that mature or flower regardless of the length of their exposure to alternate periods of darkness and light. [1940–45]

day′ nurs′ery, a center for the care of small children during the day, esp. while their parents are at work. [1835–45]

Day′ of Atone′ment, *Judaism.* See **Yom Kippur.** [1810–20]

Day′ of In′famy, December 7, 1941, on which Japan attacked Pearl Harbor, bringing the United States into World War II: so referred to by President Franklin D. Roosevelt in his speech to Congress the next day, asking for a declaration of war on Japan.

Day′ of Judg′ment. See **Judgment Day.** [1525–35]

day′ of reck′oning, the time when one is called to account for one's actions, to pay one's debts, or to fulfill one's promises or obligations.

Day′ of the Lord′, **1.** Also called **Day′ of Yah′weh.** (in Old Testament eschatology) a day of final judgment. Amos 5:18–21; Ezek. 30. **2.** Also called **Day′ of Christ′, Day of Je′sus Christ′.** the day of the Second Advent. II Peter 3:10; I Cor. 1:8; Phil. 1:10, 2:16. [1350–1400; ME]

day′ one′, (*often caps.*) the very first day or beginning of something. [1975–80]

day·pack (dā′pak′), *n.* a relatively small backpack, with shoulder straps, used for day hikes, carrying books, or the like. [DAY + PACK[1]]

day′ room′, **1.** a room at an institution, as on a military base, providing facilities for leisure activities. **2.** (in a hospital) a recreation room for ambulatory patients. Also, **day′room′.** [1815–25]

days (dāz), *adv.* in or during the day regularly: *They slept days rather than nights.* [1125–75; ME *daies;* see DAY, -S[1]]

day·sail (dā′sāl′), *v.i.* to go boating in a day sailer. [back formation from DAY SAILER]

day′ sail′er, a small sailboat without sleeping accommodations, suitable for short trips. [1960–65]

day′ school′, **1.** a school open for instruction on weekdays only, usually from 9 A.M. until 3 P.M. **2.** a school conducted in the daytime (distinguished from *night school*). **3.** a private school for pupils living outside the school (distinguished from *boarding school*). [1775–85]

day′ shift′, **1.** the work force, as of a factory, scheduled to work during the daytime. **2.** the scheduled period of labor for this work force. [1870–75]

day·side (dā′sīd′), *n.* **1.** *Journalism.* the day shift of a newspaper. **2.** *Astron.* the side of a planet or moon illuminated by the sun. Cf. **nightside.** [1960–65; DAY + SIDE[1]]

days·man (dāz′mən), *n., pl.* **-men.** *Archaic.* an umpire; mediator. [1480–90; DAY + 'S[1] + -MAN; cf. *day* to submit for arbitration, appar. v. use of DAY]

days′ of grace′, days, usually three, allowed by law or custom for payment after a bill or note falls due. [1840–50; trans. of L *diēs grātiae*]

days′ of wine′ and ros′es, a period of happiness and prosperity.

day·spring (dā′spring′), *n. Archaic.* dawn; daybreak. [1250–1300; ME; see DAY, SPRING]

day·star (dā′stär′), *n.* **1.** a morning star. **2.** the sun. [bef. 1000; ME *daysterre,* OE *dægsteorra.* See DAY, STAR]

day′ stu′dent, a student who attends regular classes at a preparatory school or college but who does not reside at the institution.

day·time (dā′tīm′), *n.* **1.** the time between sunrise and sunset. —*adj.* **2.** occurring, done, presented, etc., during the day: *daytime television.* Cf. **nighttime.** [1525–35; DAY + TIME]

day-to-day (dā′tə dā′), *adj.* **1.** occurring each day; daily: *day-to-day chores; day-to-day worries.* **2.** concerned only with immediate needs or desires without preparation for the future. [1150–1200; ME]

Day·ton (dāt′n), *n.* **1. Jonathan,** 1760–1824, U.S. politician, Speaker of the House 1795–99. **2.** a city in SW Ohio. 203,588.

Day·to′na Beach′ (dā tō′nə), a city in NE Florida: seashore resort. 54,176.

day-trade (dā′trād′), *v.i.,* **-trad·ed, -trad·ing.** to buy and sell a listed security or commodity on the same day, usually on margin, for a quick profit. **—day′-trad′·er,** *n.*

day-trip (dā′trip′), *v.i.,* **-tripped, -trip·ping,** to travel as a day-tripper. [back formation from DAY-TRIPPER]

day-trip·per (dā′trip′ər), *n.* a person who goes on a trip, esp. an excursion, lasting all or part of a day but not overnight. [1895–1900; *day trip* + -ER[1]]

day·wear (dā′wâr′), *n.* **1.** clothing, makeup, etc., suitable for wear or use during the day. —*adj.* **2.** suitable as or used for daywear: *daywear dresses.* [DAY + WEAR]

day·work (dā′wûrk′), *n.* work done and paid for by the day. [bef. 1000; ME *dai-werk* the amount of land worked by a team in one day, OE *dæg-weorc* day's work. See DAY, WORK] **—day′work′er,** *n.*

daze (dāz), *v.,* **dazed, daz·ing,** *n.* —*v.t.* **1.** to stun or stupefy with a blow, shock, etc.: *He was dazed by a blow on the head.* **2.** to overwhelm; dazzle: *The splendor of the palace dazed her.* —*n.* **3.** a dazed condition; state of bemusement: *After meeting the author, I was in a daze for a week.* [1275–1325; ME *dasen* (v.) < ON *dasa-* (as in *dasask* to become weary); cf. Dan *dase* to doze, mope] **—daz·ed·ly** (dā′zid lē), *adv.* **—daz′ed·ness,** *n.*
—Syn. 2. amaze, astound, dumbfound, flabbergast.

da·zi·bao (dä′dzē′bou′), *n., pl.* **-baos.** (in China) a wallposter. [1970–75; < Chin *dàzì bào* lit., big-letter newspaper]

daz·zle (daz′əl), *v.,* **-zled, -zling,** *n.* —*v.t.* **1.** to overpower or dim the vision of by intense light: *He was dazzled by the sudden sunlight.* **2.** to impress deeply; astonish with delight: *The glorious palace dazzled him.* —*v.i.* **3.** to shine or reflect brilliantly: *gems dazzling in the sunlight.* **4.** to be overpowered by light: *Her eyes dazzled in the glare.* **5.** to excite admiration by brilliance: *The old palace no longer dazzles.* —*n.* **6.** an act or instance of dazzling: *the dazzle of the spotlights.* **7.** something that dazzles. [1475–85; DAZE + -LE] **—daz′·zler,** *n.* **—daz′zling·ly,** *adv.*
—Syn. 2. awe, overwhelm, overpower, stupefy.

dB, *Physics.* decibel; decibels. Also, **db**

DB, *Radio and Television.* delayed broadcast.

D.B., **1.** Bachelor of Divinity. **2.** Domesday Book.

d.b., daybook.

d/b/a, doing business as. Also, **d.b.a.**

DBA, doing business as. Also, **dba, d.b.a.**

dBa, decibels above reference noise, adjusted. Also, **dba**

D.B.A., Doctor of Business Administration.

D.B.E., Dame Commander of the Order of the British Empire.

D.Bib., Douay Bible.

dbl., double.

DBMS, *Computers.* Data Base Management System: software that mediates access to, additions and deletions of, and changes in data contained in a database, so as to store and access data efficiently and control which data particular programs or individuals are allowed to use.

DBS, *Television.* direct broadcast satellite: a satellite that transmits television signals that can be picked up directly by a home viewer with a dish antenna.

DC, 1. dental corps. 2. *Elect.* direct current. 3. District of Columbia (approved esp. for use with zip code).

D.C., 1. *Music.* da capo. 2. Dictionary of Canadianisms. 3. *Elect.* direct current. 4. See **District of Columbia.** 5. Doctor of Chiropractic.

dc, *Elect.* direct current. Also, **d.c.**

D.Ch.E., Doctor of Chemical Engineering.

DCHP, Dictionary of Canadianisms on Historical Principles.

D.C.L., Doctor of Civil Law.

D.C.M., *Brit.* Distinguished Conduct Medal.

D.Cn.L., Doctor of Canon Law.

DCPA, Defense Civil Preparedness Agency.

D.Crim., Doctor of Criminology.

D.C.S., 1. Deputy Clerk of Sessions. 2. Doctor of Christian Science. 3. Doctor of Commercial Science.

DD, dishonorable discharge.

dd, 1. *Law.* today's date. [< L *dē datō*] 2. degree-day. 3. delayed delivery. 4. delivered. 5. demand draft. 6. double deck. 7. *Shipbuilding.* dry dock.

dd., delivered.

D/D, *Com.* days after date.

D.D., 1. demand draft. 2. Doctor of Divinity.

D-day (dē′dā′), *n.* 1. *Mil.* the day, usually unspecified, set for the beginning of a planned attack. 2. June 6, 1944, the day of the invasion of western Europe by Allied forces in World War II. 3. *Informal.* any day of special significance, as one marking an important event or goal. Also, **D-Day.** [D (for *day*) + DAY; the same pattern as H-HOUR]

DDP, *Computers.* See **distributed data processing.**

DDR, German Democratic Republic. [< G *D(eutsche) D(emokratische) R(epublik)*]

DDS, *Pharm.* dapsone. [*d(iamino)d(iphenyl) s(ulfone)*]

D.D.S., 1. Doctor of Dental Science. 2. Doctor of Dental Surgery.

D.D.Sc., Doctor of Dental Science.

DDT, *Chem.* a white, crystalline, water-insoluble solid, $C_{14}H_9Cl_5$, usually derived from chloral by reaction with chlorobenzene in the presence of fuming sulfuric acid: used as an insecticide and as a scabicide and pediculicide: agricultural use prohibited in the U.S. since 1973. Also called **dichlorodiphenyltrichloroethane, chlorophenothane.** [*d(ichloro)d(iphenyl)t(richloroethane)*]

de (də; *Fr.* də; *Sp.* de; *Port.* di), *prep.* from; of (used in French, Spanish, and Portuguese personal names, originally to indicate place of origin): *Comte de Rochambeau; Don Ricardo de Aragón.* [< F, Sp, Pg < L *dē*]

de-, a prefix occurring in loanwords from Latin (*decide*); also used to indicate privation, removal, and separation (*dehumidify*), negation (*demerit; derange*), descent (*degrade; deduce*), reversal (*detract*), intensity (*decompound*). Cf. **di-²**, **dis-¹**. [ME < L *dē-*, prefixal use of *dē* (prep.) from, away from, of, out of; in some words, < F < L *dē-* or *dis-* DIS-¹]

—**Note.** The lists at the bottom of this and following pages provide the spelling, syllabification, and stress for words whose meanings may be easily inferred by combining the meanings of DE- and an attached base word, or base word plus a suffix. Appropriate parts of speech are also shown. Words prefixed by DE- that have special meanings or uses are entered in the main vocabulary or as derived forms run on at the end of a main vocabulary entry.

DE, 1. Delaware (approved esp. for use with zip code). 2. destroyer escort.

de′ (də; *It.* de), *prep.* dei (used in Italian names as an elided form of *dei*): *de′ Medici.*

D.E., 1. Doctor of Engineering. 2. driver education.

DEA, 1. Drug Enforcement Administration.

Dea., Deacon.

de·ac·cel·er·ate (dē′ak sel′ə rāt′), *v.i., v.t.,* **-at·ed, -at·ing.** to decelerate. [DE- + ACCELERATE] —**de′ac·cel′er·a′tion,** *n.*

de·ac·ces·sion (dē′ak sesh′ən), *v.t.* 1. to sell (a work of art) from a museum's or gallery's collections, esp. with a view to acquiring funds for the purchase of other works. —*v.i.* 2. to deaccession a work of art from a museum's or gallery's collections. —*n.* 3. a deaccessioned work of art. [1970–75; DE- + ACCESSION] Also, **de′-ac·ces′sion.**

de·a·cet·y·late (dē′ə set′l āt′), *v.t.,* **-lat·ed, -lat·ing.** *Chem.* to remove the acetyl group from (an organic compound). [DE- + ACETYLATE] —**de′a·cet′y·la′tion,** *n.*

de·a·cid·i·fy (dē′ə sid′ə fī′), *v.t., v.i.,* **-fied, -fy·ing.** *Chem.* 1. to remove acid from (a substance). 2. to reduce the acidity of (a substance). [DE- + ACIDIFY] —**de′a·cid′i·fi·ca′tion,** *n.*

dea·con (dē′kən), *n.* 1. (in hierarchical churches) a member of the clerical order next below that of a priest. 2. (in other churches) an appointed or elected officer having variously defined duties. 3. (in Freemasonry) either of two officers in a masonic lodge. —*v.t.* 4. to pack (vegetables or fruit) with only the finest pieces or the most attractive sides visible. 5. to falsify (something); doctor. 6. to castrate (a pig or other animal). 7. to read aloud (a line of a psalm, hymn, etc.) before singing it. [bef. 900; ME *deken,* OE *diacon* < LL *diāconus* < Gk *diākonos* servant, minister, deacon, equiv. to *diā-* DIA- + *-konos* service] —**dea′con·ship′,** *n.*

dea·con·ess (dē′kə nis), *n.* 1. (in certain Protestant churches) a woman belonging to an order or sisterhood dedicated to the care of the sick or poor or who is engaging in other social-service duties, as teaching or missionary work. 2. a woman elected by a church to assist the clergy. [1530–40; earlier *deaconisse,* part trans., part adoption of LL *diāconissa,* fem. of *diāconus* DEACON; see -ESS]

—**Usage.** See **-ess.**

dea·con·ry (dē′kən rē), *n., pl.* **-ries.** 1. the office of a deacon. 2. deacons collectively. [1425–75; late ME *dekenry.* See DEACON, -RY]

dea′con seat′, a bench running most of the length of a bunkhouse in a lumbering camp. [1850–55, *Amer.*]

de-ac·qui·si·tion (dē ak′wə zish′ən), *v.t., v.i., n.* deaccession. [1970–75; DE- + ACQUISITION]

de·ac·ti·vate (dē ak′tə vāt′), *v.,* **-vat·ed, -vat·ing.** —*v.t.* 1. to cause to be inactive; remove the effectiveness of. 2. to demobilize or disband (a military unit). 3. to render (a bomb, shell, or the like) inoperative, esp. by disconnecting, removing, or otherwise interfering with the action of the fuze. 4. *Chem.* to render (a chemical, enzyme, catalyst, etc.) inactive. —*v.i.* 5. *Physical Chem.* to lose radioactivity. [1900–05; DE- + ACTIVATE] —**de·ac′ti·va′tion,** *n.* —**de·ac′ti·va′tor,** *n.*

dead (ded), *adj.,* **-er, -est,** *n., adv.* —*adj.* 1. no longer living; deprived of life: *dead people; dead flowers; dead animals.* 2. brain-dead. 3. not endowed with life; inanimate: *dead stones.* 4. resembling death; deathlike: *a dead sleep; a dead faint.* 5. bereft of sensation; numb: *He was half dead with fright. My leg feels dead.* 6. lacking sensitivity of feeling; insensitive: *dead to the needs of others.* 7. incapable of being emotionally moved; unresponsive: *dead to the nuances of the music.* 8. (of an emotion) no longer felt; ended; extinguished: *a dead passion; dead affections.* 9. no longer current or prevalent, as in effect, significance, or practice; obsolete: *a dead law; a dead controversy.* 10. no longer functioning, operating, or productive: *a dead motor; a dead battery.* 11. not moving or circulating; stagnant; stale: *dead water; dead air.* 12. utterly tired; exhausted: *They felt dead from the six-hour trip.* 13. (of a language) no longer in use as a sole means of oral communication among a people: *Latin is a dead language.* 14. without vitality, spirit, enthusiasm, or the like: *a dead party.* 15. lacking the customary activity; dull; inactive: *a dead business day.* 16. complete; absolute: *dead silence; The plan was a dead loss.* 17. sudden or abrupt, as the complete stoppage of an action: *The bus came to a dead stop.* 18. put out; extinguished: *a dead cigarette.* 19. without resilience or bounce: *a dead tennis ball.* 20. infertile; barren: *dead land.* 21. exact; precise: *the dead center of a circle.* 22. accurate; sure; unerring: *a dead shot.* 23. direct; straight: *a dead line.* 24. tasteless or flat, as a beverage: *a dead soft drink.* 25. flat rather than glossy, bright, or brilliant: *The house was painted dead white.* 26. without resonance; anechoic: *dead sound; a dead wall surface of a recording studio.* 27. not fruitful; unproductive: *dead capital.* 28. *Law.* deprived of civil rights so that one is in the state of civil death, esp. deprived of the rights of property. 29. *Sports.* out of play: *a dead ball.* 30. (of a golf ball) lying so close to the hole as to make holing on the next stroke a virtual certainty. 31. (of type or copy) having been used or rejected. 32. *Elect.* **a.** free from any electric connection to a source of potential difference and from electric charge. **b.** not having a potential different from that of the earth. 33. *Metall.* (of steel) **a.** fully killed. **b.** unresponsive to heat treatment. 34. (of the mouth of a horse) no longer sensitive to the pressure of a bit. 35. noting any rope in a tackle that does not pass over a pulley or is not rove through a block. 36. **dead in the water,** completely inactive or inoperable; no longer in action or under consideration: *Our plans to expand the business have been dead in the water for the past two months.* 37. **dead to rights,** in the very act of committing a crime, offense, or mistake; red-handed. —*n.* 38. the period of greatest darkness, coldness, etc.: *the dead of night; the dead of winter.* 39. **the dead,** dead persons collectively: *Prayers were recited for the dead.* —*adv.* 40. absolutely; completely: *dead right; dead tired.* 41. with sudden and total stoppage of motion, action, or the like: *He stopped dead.* 42. directly; exactly; straight: *The island lay dead ahead.* [bef. 950; ME *deed,* OE *dēad;* c. Goth *dauths,* G *tot,* ON *daudhr;* orig. ptp. See DIE¹] —**dead′ness,** *n.*

—**Syn.** 1. DEAD, DECEASED, EXTINCT, LIFELESS refer to something that does not have or appear to have life. DEAD is usually applied to something that had life but from which life is now gone: *dead trees.* DECEASED, a more formal word than DEAD, is applied to human beings who no longer have life: *a deceased member of the church.* EXTINCT is applied to a race, species, or the like, no member of which is any longer alive: *Mastodons are now extinct.* LIFELESS is applied to something that may or may not have had life but that does not have it or appear to have it now: *The lifeless body of a child was taken out of the water. Minerals consist of lifeless materials.* 6. unfeeling, indifferent, callous, cold. 10. inert, inoperative. 11. still, motionless. 16. utter, entire, total. 20. sterile. —**Ant.** 1. living, alive.

dead′ air′, the loss or suspension of the video or audio signal during a television or radio transmission. [1940–45]

dead′-air′ space′ (ded′âr′), an unventilated air space in which the air does not circulate. [1900–05]

dead′-ball line′ (ded′bôl′), *Rugby.* the line at each end of the field parallel to and not over 25 yards (23 m) behind the goal line. [1890–95]

dead·beat (*n.* ded′bēt′; *adj.* ded′bēt′), *n.* 1. a person who deliberately avoids paying debts. 2. a loafer; sponger. —*adj.* 3. *Horol.* noting any of various escapements acting without recoil of the locking parts from the shock of contact. See diag. under **escapement.** 4. *Elect.* (of the indicator of an electric meter and the like) coming to a stop with little or no oscillation. [1760–70; DEAD + BEAT]

dead·bolt (ded′bōlt′), *n.* a lock bolt that is moved into position by the turning of a knob or key rather than by spring action. Also called **deadlock.** [DEAD + BOLT¹]

dead′ cen′ter, *Mach.* 1. Also called **dead point.** (in a reciprocating engine) either of two positions at which the crank cannot be turned by the connecting rod, occurring at each end of a stroke when the crank and connecting rod are in the same line. 2. See under **center** (def. 19a). [1870–75] —**dead′-cen′ter,** *adj.*

dead′ drop′, a prearranged secret spot where one espionage agent leaves a message or material for another agent to pick up.

dead′ duck′, a person or thing that is beyond help, redemption, or hope: *One more missed opportunity and this whole enterprise is a dead duck.* [1820–30, *Amer.*; orig., in political slang, a person who has lost influence or power and is therefore useless; perh. from the proverb "never waste powder on a dead duck"]

dead·en (ded′n), *v.t.* 1. to make less sensitive, active, energetic, or forcible; weaken: *to deaden sound; to deaden the senses; to deaden the force of a blow.* 2. to lessen the velocity of; retard: *to deaden the headway of a ship.* 3. to make impervious to sound, as a floor. —*v.i.* 4. to become dead. [1655–65; DEAD + -EN¹] —**dead′en·er,** *n.*

—**Syn.** 1. blunt, diminish, lessen, numb, dull.

dead′ end′, 1. something, as a street or water pipe, that has no exit. 2. a position that offers no hope of progress; blind alley; cul-de-sac: *His theory led him to a dead end.* [1885–90]

dead-end (ded′end′), *adj.* 1. terminating in a dead end: *a dead-end street.* 2. Also, **dead′-end′ed.** having no possibility for or hope of progress, advancement, etc.: *a low-level, dead-end job.* 3. leading a life in the slums: *growing up as a tough dead-end kid.* —*v.i.* 4. to come to a dead end: *The road dead-ends at the lake.* [1885–90]

dead·en·ing (ded′n ing), *n.* 1. a device or material employed to deaden or render dull. 2. a device or material preventing the transmission of sound. 3. a woodland in which the trees are killed by girdling prior to being cleared. [1775–85; DEADEN + -ING¹]

dead·eye (ded′ī′), *n., pl.* **-eyes.** 1. *Naut.* either of a pair of disks of hardwood having holes through which a lanyard is rove: used to tighten shrouds and stays. 2. an expert marksman. [1740–50; DEAD + EYE; as nautical term, prob. ellipsis from *deadman's eye,* ME *dedmaneseye* deadeye]

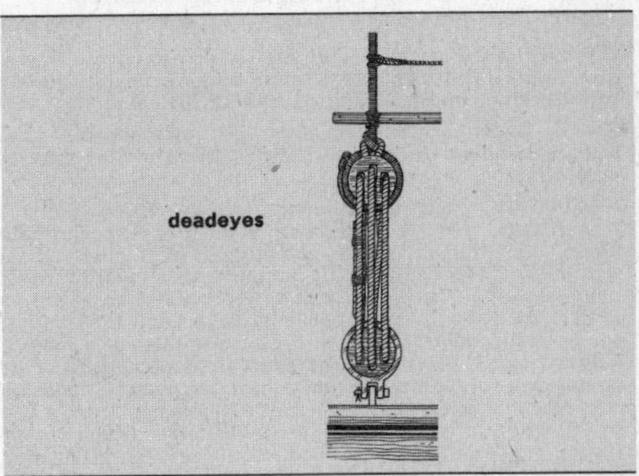

dead·fall (ded′fôl′), *n.* 1. a trap, esp. for large game, in which a weight falls on and crushes the prey. 2. a mass of brush and fallen trees. [1605–15; DEAD + FALL]

dead′ fir′ing, firing of a furnace or boiler at less than normal operating temperature in order to maintain conditions desirable during a period of idleness.

dead′ freight′, *Com.* 1. an amount owed by a contractor who charters space in a ship but fails to occupy it fully. 2. the unoccupied space of such a ship. 3. heavy or unwieldy nonperishable freight.

dead′ hand′, *Law.* mortmain.

dead·head (ded′hed′), *Informal.* —*n.* 1. a person who attends a performance, sports event, etc., or travels on a train, airplane, etc., without having paid for a ticket, esp. a person using a complimentary ticket or free pass. 2. a train, railroad car, airplane, truck, or other commercial vehicle while operating empty, as when returning to a terminal. 3. a stupid or boring person; dullard. 4. *Metall.* excess metal in the riser of a mold. 5. a

CONCISE PRONUNCIATION KEY: act, cāpe, dâre, pärt; set, ēqual; *if,* ice; ox, ōver, ôrder, oil, bo͝ok, bo͞ot, out; up, ûrge; child; sing; shoe; thin, *th*at; zh as in *treasure.* ə = *a* as in *alone,* *e* as in *system,* *i* as in *easily,* *o* as in *gallop,* *u* as in *circus;* ᵊ as in *fire* (fīᵊr), *hour* (ouᵊr). l and n can serve as syllabic consonants, as in *cradle* (krād′l), and *button* (but′n). See the full key inside the front cover.

de·ac′tu·ate′, *v.t.,* **-at·ed, -at·ing.**
de·al′lo·cate′, *v.t.,* **-cat·ed, -cat·ing.**
de·al′lo·ca′tion, *n.*
de′-A·mer′i·can·i·za′tion, *n.*
de′-A·mer′i·can·ize′, *v.,* **-ized, -iz·ing.**
de′a·nath′e·ma·tize′, *v.t.,* **-tized, -tiz·ing.**
de-An′gli·cize′, *v.t.,* **-cized, -ciz·ing.**
de′an·nex·a′tion, *n.*
de′a·ro′ma·tize′, *v.t.,* **-tized, -tiz·ing.**
de-A′sian·ize′, *v.,* **-ized, -iz·ing.**
de·au′thor·i·za′tion, *n.*
de·au′thor·ize′, *v.t.,* **-ized, -iz·ing.**
de·au′to·mate′, *v.,* **-mat·ed, -mat·ing.**
de·bar′ba·rize′, *v.t.,* **-rized, -riz·ing.**
de′bu·reauc′ra·tize′, *v.t.,* **-tized, -tiz·ing.**
de·cal′o·rize′, *v.t.,* **-rized, -riz·ing.**
de·cap′, *v.t.,* **-capped, -cap·ping.**

sunken or partially sunken log. —*v.t.* **6.** to transport (someone) as a deadhead. **7.** to move (an empty commercial vehicle) along a route. **8.** *Hort.* to remove faded blooms from (ornamental plants), esp. in flower gardens, often to help continued blooming. —*v.i.* **9.** to act or serve as a deadhead. **10.** (of a commercial vehicle) to travel without cargo or paying passengers: *The train carried coal to Pittsburgh and then deadheaded back to Virginia to pick up another load.* [1570–80; DEAD + HEAD]

dead′ heat′, **1.** a race in which two or more competitors finish in a tie. **2.** the result of such a race; tie. [1790–1800]

dead′ horse′, **1.** something that has ceased to be useful or relevant. **2. beat** or **flog a dead horse,** to persist in pursuing or trying to revive interest in a project or subject that has lost its usefulness or relevance. [1820–30, *Amer.*]

dead′ let′ter, **1.** a law, ordinance, etc., that has lost its force but has not been formally repealed or abolished. **2.** a letter that cannot reach the addressee or be returned to the sender, usually because of incorrect address, and that is sent to and handled in a special division or department **(dead′-let′ter of′fice)** of a general post office. [1570–80] —**dead′-let′ter,** *adj.*

dead′ lift′, **1.** a direct lifting without any mechanical assistance. **2.** a situation that requires all one's strength or ingenuity. [1545–55]

dead•light (ded′līt′), *n. Naut.* **1.** a strong shutter able to be screwed against the interior of a porthole in heavy weather. **2.** a thick pane of glass set in the hull or deck to admit light. [1720–30; DEAD + LIGHT[1]]

dead•line (ded′līn′), *n.* **1.** the time by which something must be finished or submitted; the latest time for finishing something: *a five o'clock deadline.* **2.** a line or limit that must not be passed. **3.** (formerly) a boundary around a military prison beyond which a prisoner could not venture without risk of being shot by the guards. [1855–60; DEAD + LINE[1]]

dead′ load′, *Engin.* See under **load** (def. 11). [1865–70, *Amer.*]

dead•lock (ded′lok′), *n.* **1.** a state in which progress is impossible, as in a dispute, produced by the counteraction of opposing forces; standstill; stalemate: *The union and management reached a deadlock over fringe benefits.* **2.** deadbolt. **3.** a maximum-security cell for the solitary confinement of a prisoner. —*v.t., v.i.* **4.** to bring or come to a deadlock. [1770–80; DEAD + LOCK[1]]
—**Syn. 1.** standoff, impasse, draw.

dead•ly (ded′lē), *adj.*, **-li•er, -li•est,** *adv.* —*adj.* **1.** causing or tending to cause death; fatal; lethal: *a deadly poison.* **2.** aiming to kill or destroy; implacable: *a deadly enemy.* **3.** like death: *a deadly pallor.* **4.** excruciatingly boring: *The dinner party was absolutely deadly.* **5.** excessive; inordinate: *deadly haste.* **6.** extremely accurate: *Annie Oakley was a deadly shot.* —*adv.* **7.** in a manner resembling or suggesting death: *deadly pale.* **8.** excessively; completely: *deadly dull.* [bef. 900; ME *deedli(ch),* OE *dēadlīce.* See DEAD, -LY] —**dead′li•ness,** *n.*
—**Syn. 1.** See **fatal. 4.** dull, tedious, tiresome.

dead′ly night′shade, belladonna (def. 1). [1570–80]

dead′ly sins′, the seven sins of pride, covetousness, lust, anger, gluttony, envy, and sloth. Also called **seven deadly sins, capital sins.** [1300–50; ME *deedly synnes*]

dead′ mail′, undeliverable and unreturnable mail that is handled in the dead-letter office of the general post office.

dead•man (ded′man′, -mən), *n., pl.* **-men** (-men′, -mən), *adj.* —*n.* **1.** *Building Trades.* a log, concrete block, etc., buried in the ground as an anchor. **2.** a crutchlike prop temporarily supporting a pole or mast being erected. **3.** *Naut.* **a.** an object fixed on shore to hold a mooring line temporarily. **b.** a rope for hauling the boom of a derrick inboard after discharge of a load of cargo. —*adj.* **4.** Also, **dead-man's.** *Mach., Auto.* of or pertaining to a control or switch on a powered machine or vehicle that disengages a blade or clutch, applies the brake, shuts off the engine, etc., when the driver or operator ceases to press a pedal, squeeze a throttle, etc.: *deadman throttle; dead-man's control.* [DEAD + MAN[1]]

dead′-man's fin′gers (ded′manz′, -mənz), any of various fungi, sponges, plant roots, animal parts, etc., having fingerlike projections and a pale or dull color, as the gray-black woodland fungus *Xylaria polymorpha* or the whitish spongy gills of a food crab. [1595–1605]

dead′-man's float′, *Swimming.* a prone floating position, used esp. by beginning swimmers, with face downward, legs extended backward, and arms stretched forward. Also called **prone float.** [1945–50]

dead′ man's′ hand′, *Poker.* a hand containing the two pairs of two aces and two eights.

dead′ march′, a piece of solemn music for a funeral procession, esp. one played at a military funeral. [1595–1605]

dead′ mat′ter, *Print.* **1.** type that has been set and used for printing or platemaking and is of no further use. **2.** See **foul matter.** [1875–80]

dead-melt (ded′melt′), *v.t. Metall.* to melt (steel) until killed. [1875–80]

CONCISE ETYMOLOGY KEY: <, descended or borrowed from; >, whence; b., blend of, blended; c., cognate with; cf., compare; deriv., derivative; equiv., equivalent; imit., imitative; obl., oblique; r., replacing; s., stem; sp., spelling, spelled; resp., respelling, respelled; trans., translation; ?, origin unknown; *, unattested; ‡, probably earlier than. See the full key inside the front cover.

dead′ met′al, *Print.* furniture (def. 4).

dead′ net′tle, any of various plants belonging to the genus *Lamium,* of the mint family, native to the Old World, having opposite leaves and clusters of small reddish or white flowers. [1350–1400; ME]

dead-on (ded′on′, -ôn′), *adj. Informal.* exactly right, accurate, or pertinent: *The film director has a dead-on feel for characterization.* [1885–90]

dead•pan (ded′pan′), *adj., adv., v.,* **-panned, -pan•ning,** *n.* —*adj.* **1.** marked by or accomplished with a careful pretense of seriousness or calm detachment; impassive or expressionless: *deadpan humor.* **2.** displaying no emotional or personal involvement: *a deadpan style.* —*adv.* **3.** in a deadpan manner: *He spoke his lines utterly deadpan.* —*v.i., v.t.* **4.** to behave or perform in a deadpan manner. —*n.* Also, **dead′ pan′. 5.** a face showing no expression. **6.** a style of comedy that relies on the comedian's maintaining such a face. [1925–30, *Amer.*; DEAD + PAN[1]] —**dead′ pan′ner.**

dead′ point′. *Mach.* See **dead center** (def. 1). [1820–30]

dead-reck•on (ded′rek′ən), *v.t. Navig.* to calculate (one's position) by means of dead reckoning. [by back formation] —**dead′-reck′on•er,** *n.*

dead′ reck′oning, *Navig.* **1.** calculation of one's position on the basis of distance run on various headings since the last precisely observed position, with as accurate allowance as possible being made for wind, currents, compass errors, etc. **2.** one's position as so calculated. [1605–15]

dead′ ring′er, *Slang.* a person or thing that closely resembles another; ringer: *That old car is a dead ringer for the one we used to own.* [1890–95]

dead•rise (ded′rīz′), *n. Naut.* the angle with the horizontal made by the outboard rise of the bottom of a vessel at the widest frame. Also, **dead′-rise′.** [1655–65; DEAD + RISE]

dead′ run′, a steady run at top speed: *The centerfielder caught the ball on the dead run.* [1885–90]

Dead′ Sea′, a salt lake between Israel and Jordan: the lowest lake in the world. 46 mi. (74 km) long; 10 mi. (16 km) wide; 1293 ft. (394 m) below sea level.

Dead′ Sea′ fruit′, something that appears to be beautiful or full of promise but is in reality nothing but illusion and disappointment. [1810–20]

Dead′ Sea′ Scrolls′, a number of leather, papyrus, and copper scrolls dating from c100 B.C. to A.D. 135, containing partial texts of some of the books of the Old Testament and some non-Biblical scrolls, in Hebrew and Aramaic, and including apocryphal writings, commentaries, hymns, and psalms: found in caves near the NW coast of the Dead Sea beginning in 1947.

dead set (ded′ set′ *for 1; 2;* ded′ set′ *for 3*), **1.** firmly decided or determined; resolved: *His family was dead set against the marriage.* **2.** a serious or determined attempt; firm effort: *He made a dead set at winning the championship.* **3.** *Hunting.* the stiff posture assumed by a hunting dog in indicating the presence and location of game. [1840–50, *Amer.*]

dead′ slow′, *Naut.* as slow as possible without losing steerageway.

dead-smooth (ded′smōōth′), *adj.* **1.** noting a double-cut metal file having the minimum commercial grade of coarseness. **2.** extremely smooth. [1870–75]

dead′ sol′dier, *Slang.* an empty beer, liquor, or wine bottle or empty beer can. [1915–20]

dead′ spin′dle, *Metalworking.* See under **spindle** (def. 6).

dead′ spot′. See **blind spot** (def. 4).

dead′-stick land′ing (ded′stik′), *Aeron., Aerospace.* a landing of an airplane or space vehicle with the engine cut off. [1930–35]

dead′ stor′age, the storage of furniture, files, or other unused or seldom used items in a warehouse or other location for an indefinite period of time.

dead′ time′, **1.** downtime. **2.** *Electronics.* an interval during which an actuating signal produces no response. [1905–10]

dead′ wa′ter, **1.** water eddying beside a moving hull, esp. directly astern. **2.** a part of a stream where there is a slack current. [1555–65]

dead′ weight′, **1.** the heavy, unrelieved weight of anything inert: *The dead weight of the bear's body was over 300 pounds.* **2.** a heavy or oppressive burden or responsibility. **3.** the weight of a railroad car, truck, etc., as distinct from its load or contents. Also, **dead′weight′.** [1650–60]

dead′weight ton′nage, *Naut.* the capacity in long tons of cargo, passengers, fuel, stores, etc. **(dead′weight tons′),** of a vessel: the difference between the loaded and light displacement tonnage of the vessel. Also called **dead′weight capac′ity.**

dead•wood (ded′wŏŏd′), *n.* **1.** the dead branches on a tree; dead branches or trees. **2.** useless or burdensome persons or things: *He cut the deadwood from his staff.* **3.** (in writing) unnecessary words, phrases, or exposition; expendable verbiage. **4.** *Naut.* a solid construction, serving only as reinforcement, located between the keel of a vessel and the stem or sternpost. **5.** *Bowling.* pins remaining on the alley after having been knocked down by the ball. **6.** *Cards.* **a.** *Rummy.* cards in a hand that have not been included in sets and are usually counted as points against the holder. **b.** *Poker.* cards that have been discarded. [1720–30; DEAD + WOOD[1]]

dead•work (ded′wûrk′), *n. Mining.* work necessary to expose an orebody, as the removal of overburden. [1645–55; DEAD + WORK]

de•aer•ate (dē âr′āt, -ā′ə rāt′), *v.t.*, **-at•ed, -at•ing. 1.** to remove air or gas from. **2.** to remove bubbles from (a liquid, as boiler feedwater), as by mechanical agitation in a vacuum or by heating at atmospheric pressure. Also, **de-aer′ate.** [1785–95; DE- + AERATE] —**de′aer•a′tion,** *n.* —**de•aer•a•tor** (dē âr′ā tər, -ā′ə rā′-), *n.*

deaf (def), *adj.*, **-er, -est,** *n.* —*adj.* **1.** partially or wholly lacking or deprived of the sense of hearing; unable to hear. **2.** refusing to listen, heed, or be persuaded; unreasonable or unyielding: *deaf to all advice.* —*n.* **3.** (*used with a plural v.*) deaf persons collectively (usually prec. by *the*). [bef. 900; ME *deef,* OE *dēaf;* c. MLG *dōf,* D *doof,* OHG *toub*] —**deaf′ly,** *adv.* —**deaf′•ness,** *n.*
—**Pronunciation.** DEAF is usually pronounced (def), with the vowel of *left.* In uneducated speech the pronunciation (dēf), to rhyme with *leaf,* is heard, though it is becoming less common.

deaf-and-dumb (def′ən dum′), *adj. Often Offensive.* deaf-mute (def. 1). [1150–1200; ME *def and doumb*]

deaf-blind (def′blīnd′), *adj.* of or pertaining to a person who is both deaf and blind.

deaf•en (def′ən), *v.t.* **1.** to make deaf: *The accident deafened him for life.* **2.** to stun or overwhelm with noise: *The pounding of the machines deafened us.* **3.** deaden (def. 3). **4.** *Obs.* to render (a sound) inaudible, esp. by a louder sound. [1590–1600; DEAF + -EN[1]] —**deaf′en•ing•ly,** *adv.*

deaf•en•ing (def′ə ning), *n.* deadening (def. 2). [1590–1600; DEAFEN + -ING[1]]

deaf-mute (def′myōōt′), *Often Offensive.* —*adj.* **1.** unable to hear and speak. —*n.* **2.** a person who is unable to hear and speak, esp. one in whom inability to speak is due to congenital or early deafness. [1830–40; trans. of F *sourd-muet*] —**deaf′-mute′ness,** **deaf′-mut′ism,** *n.*

Dea•kin (dē′kin), *n.* **Alfred,** 1856–1919, Australian statesman: prime minister 1903–04; 1905–08; 1909–10.

deal[1] (dēl), *v.,* **dealt, deal•ing,** *n.* —*v.i.* **1.** to occupy oneself or itself (usually fol. by *with* or *in*): *Botany deals with the study of plants. He deals in generalities.* **2.** to take action with respect to a thing or person (fol. by *with*): *Law courts must deal with lawbreakers.* **3.** to conduct oneself toward persons: *He deals fairly.* **4.** to be able to handle competently or successfully; cope (fol. by *with*): *I can't deal with your personal problems.* **5.** to trade or do business (fol. by *with* or *in*): *to deal with a firm; to deal in used cars.* **6.** to distribute, esp. the cards in a game (often fol. by *out*): *to deal out five hands of six cards each; your turn to deal.* **7.** *Slang.* to buy and sell drugs illegally. **8.** *Archaic.* to have dealings or commerce, often in a secret or underhand manner (often fol. by *with*): *to deal with the Devil.* —*v.t.* **9.** to give to one as a share; apportion: *Deal me in.* **10.** to distribute among a number of recipients, as the cards required in a game: *Deal five cards to each player.* **11.** *Cards.* to give a player (a specific card) in dealing: *You dealt yourself four aces.* **12.** to deliver; administer: *to deal a blow.* **13.** *Slang.* to buy and sell (drugs) illegally. **14.** *Slang.* to trade (an athlete) to another team. **15. deal off, a.** *Poker.* to deal the final hand of a game. **b.** *Slang.* to get rid of or trade (something or someone) in a transaction. **16. deal someone in,** *Slang.* to include: *He was making a lot of dough in the construction business so I got him to deal me in.* —*n.* **17.** a business transaction: *They closed the deal after a week of negotiating.* **18.** a bargain or arrangement for mutual advantage: *the best deal in town.* **19.** a secret or underhand agreement or bargain: *His supporters worked a number of deals to help his campaign.* **20.** *Informal.* treatment received in dealing with another: *He got a raw deal.* **21.** an indefinite but large quantity, amount, extent, or degree (usually prec. by *good* or *great*): *a good deal of work; a great deal of money.* **22.** *Cards.* **a.** the distribution of cards to the players in a game. **b.** the set of cards in one's hand. **c.** the turn of a player to deal. **d.** the period of time during which a deal is played. **23.** an act of dealing or distributing. **24.** (*cap.*) an economic and social policy pursued by a political administration: *the Fair Deal; the New Deal.* **25.** *Obs.* portion; share. **26. cut a deal,** *Informal.* to make an agreement, esp. a business agreement: *Networks have cut a deal with foreign stations for an international hookup.* [bef. 900; (v.) ME *delen,* OE *dǣlan* (c. G *teilen*), deriv. of *dǣl* part (c. G *Teil*); (n.) in part deriv. of the v.; (in defs. 21 and 25) ME *deel, del(e),* OE *dǣl*]
—**Syn. 3.** act, behave. **5.** traffic. **10.** allot, assign, dole; mete, dispense. **18.** pact, contract.

deal[2] (dēl), *n.* **1.** a board or plank, esp. of fir or pine, cut to any of various standard sizes. **2.** such boards collectively. **3.** fir or pine wood. —*adj.* **4.** made of deal. [1375–1425; late ME *dele* < MLG or MD; see THILL]

de•car′tel•i•za′tion, *n.*
de•car′tel•ize′, *v.t.,* **-ized, -iz•ing.**
de•cat′e•go•ri•za′tion, *n.*
de•cat′e•go•rize′, *v.t.,* **-rized, -riz•ing.**
de•cer′e•mo′ni•al•i•za′tion, *n.*
de-Chris′tian•ize′, *v.,* **-ized, -iz•ing.**
de•civ′i•li•za′tion, *n.*
de•civ′i•lize′, *v.t.,* **-lized, -liz•ing.**
de•claw′, *v.t.*
de•cler′gi•fy′, *v.t.,* **-fied, -fy•ing.**
de•cler′i•cal•ize′, *v.t.,* **-ized, -iz•ing.**
de•clog′ger, *n.*
de•clot′, *v.,* **-clot•ted, -clot•ting.**
de′col•lec′ti•vize′, *v.t.,* **-vized, -viz•ing.**
de•col′or•a′tion, *n.*
de′com•mer′cial•i•za′tion, *n.*
de′com•mer′cial•ize, *v.t.,* **-ized, iz•ing.**
de•com′mu•nize′, *v.t.,* **-ized, -iz•ing.**
de′com•part•men′tal•i•za′tion, *n.*
de′com•part•men′tal•ize′, *v.t.,* **-ized, -iz•ing.**

de•a•late (dē′ā lāt′, -lit), *Entomol.* —*adj.* **1.** Also, **de•a•lat•ed** (dē′ā lā′tid). (of certain ants and termites after nuptial flights) having no wings as a result of having bitten or rubbed them off. —*n.* **2.** a dealate insect. [DE- + ALATE] —**de′a•la′tion,** *n.*

deal•er (dē′lər), *n.* **1.** a person who buys and sells articles without altering their condition; trader or merchant, esp. a wholesaler: *I got a dealer's discount on this coat.* **2.** *Cards.* the player distributing the cards. **3.** a person who behaves or acts toward another or others in a specified manner: *a plain dealer.* **4.** *Slang.* a person who buys and sells drugs illegally. **5.** a person who buys securities for his or her account and retains them until sold to another. Cf. **stockbroker.** [bef. 1000; ME *delere,* OE *dǣlere.* See DEAL[1], -ER[1]]

deal′er's choice′, a card game, as poker, in which the dealer decides what particular game is to be played, often depending on the number of players, and designates any special variations or unusual rules, including setting the stakes.

deal•er•ship (dē′lər ship′), *n.* **1.** authorization to sell a commodity: *He got the dealership for the area after a long investigation into his credit status.* **2.** a sales agency or distributor having such authorization. [1915–20; DEALER + -SHIP]

deal•fish (dēl′fish′), *n., pl.* **-fish•es,** (*esp. collectively*) **-fish.** a ribbonfish, esp. *Trachipterus arcticus.* [1835–45; DEAL[2] + FISH]

deal•ing (dē′ling), *n.* **1.** Usually, **dealings.** relations; business: *frequent dealings; commercial dealings.* **2.** conduct in relations to others; treatment: *honest dealing.* [1250–1300; ME *deling.* See DEAL[1], -ING[1]]

deal′ing box′, a box that holds a deck or decks of cards, allowing them to be dealt only one at a time, often used in casino games such as blackjack or chemin de fer. Also called **shoe.** [1925–30]

dealt (delt), *v.* pt. and pp. of **deal**[1].

de•am•bu•la•to•ry (dē am′byə lə tôr′ē, -tōr′ē), *n., pl.* **-ries.** ambulatory (def. 6). [1400–50; late ME < ML *deambulātōrium,* equiv. to L *deambulā(re)* to go for a walk (see DE-, AMBLE) + *-tōrium* -TORY[2]]

de•am•i•dase (dē am′i dās′, -dāz′), *n. Biochem.* an enzyme that releases the amido group from a compound. [DE- + AMIDASE]

de•am•i•nase (dē am′ə nās′, -nāz′), *n. Biochem.* an enzyme that releases the amino group from a compound. [1915–20; DE- + AMIN(O)- + -ASE]

de•am•i•nate (dē am′ə nāt′), *v.t.,* **-nat•ed, -nat•ing.** *Chem.* to remove the amino group from (a compound). [1910–15; DE- + AMINATE] —**de•am′i•na′tion,** *n.*

de•am•i•nize (dē am′ə nīz′), *v.t.,* **-nized, -niz•ing.** deaminate. Also, *esp. Brit.,* **de•am′i•nise′.** [1920–25; DE- + AMIN(O)- + -IZE] —**de•am′i•ni•za′tion,** *n.*

dean[1] (dēn), *n.* **1.** *Educ.* **a.** the head of a faculty, school, or administrative division in a university or college: *the dean of admissions.* **b.** an official in an American college or secondary school having charge of student personnel services, such as counseling or discipline: *the dean of men.* **c.** the official in charge of undergraduate students at an English university. **2.** *Eccles.* **a.** the head of the chapter of a cathedral or a collegiate church. **b.** Also called **vicar forane.** a priest in the Roman Catholic Church appointed by a bishop to take care of the affairs of a division of a diocese. **3.** the senior member, in length of service, of any group, organization, profession, etc.: *the dean of lexicographers.* [1300–50; ME *deen* < AF *deen, dean,* OF *deien* < LL *decānus* chief of ten, equiv. to L *dec(em)* ten + *-ānus* -AN] —**dean′ship,** *n.*

dean[2] (dēn), *n. Brit.* dene.

Dean (dēn), *n.* **1. Jay Hanna** (*"Dizzy"*), 1911–74, U.S. baseball pitcher. **2.** a male given name: from the Old English family name meaning "valley."

dean•er•y (dē′nə rē), *n., pl.* **-er•ies.** **1.** the office, jurisdiction, district, or residence of an ecclesiastical dean. [1250–1300; ME *denerie.* See DEAN[1], -ERY]

De•an•na (dē an′ə), *n.* a female given name, form of **Diana.**

dean's′ list′, a list of students of high scholastic standing, compiled by a college or university usually at the end of each semester or academic year. Cf. **honor roll** (def. 1). [1925–30]

de•an•thro•po•mor•phism (dē an′thrə pə môr′fiz-əm), *n.* the ridding of philosophy or religion of anthropomorphic beliefs and doctrines. [1885–90; DE- + ANTHROPOMORPHISM] —**de•an′thro•po•mor′phic,** *adj.*

dear[1] (dēr), *adj.,* **-er, -est,** *n., adv., interj.* —*adj.* **1.** beloved or loved: *a dear friend.* **2.** (used in the salutation of a letter as an expression of affection or respect or as a conventional greeting): *Dear Sir.* **3.** precious in one's regard; cherished: *our dearest possessions.* **4.** heartfelt; earnest: *one's dearest wish.* **5.** high-priced; expensive: *The silk dress was too dear.* **6.** charging high prices: *That shop is too dear for my budget.* **7.** excessive; high: *a dear price to pay for one's independence.* **8.** *Obs.* difficult to get; scarce. **9.** *Obs.* worthy; honorable. —*n.* **10.** a person who is good, kind, or generous: *You're a dear to help me with the work.* **11.** a beloved one. **12.** (*sometimes cap.*) an affectionate or familiar term of address. —*adv.* **13.** dearly; fondly. **14.** at a high price: *That painting cost me dear.* —*interj.* **15.** (used as an exclamation of surprise, distress, etc.): *Oh dear, what a disappointment! Dear me! What's all that noise?* [bef. 900; ME *dere,* OE *dēore;* c. OHG *tiuri,* ON *dȳrr*] —**dear′ly,** *adv.* —**dear′ness,** *n.*
—**Syn. 1.** darling, cherished. **5.** See **expensive.**

dear[2] (dēr), *adj.,* **-er, -est.** *Archaic.* hard; grievous. Also, **dere.** [bef. 1000; ME *dere,* OE *dēor* brave, bold, severe]

Dear•born (dēr′bərn, -bôrn), *n.* **1. Henry,** 1751–1829, U.S. soldier and diplomat: Secretary of War 1801–09. **2.** a city in SE Michigan, near Detroit. 90,660. **3.** See **Fort Dearborn.**

Dear′born Heights′, a city in SE Michigan, near Detroit. 67,706.

Dear′ John′, *Informal.* **1.** a letter from a woman informing her boyfriend or fiancé that she is ending their relationship or informing her husband that she wants a divorce: *Nothing is worse for a soldier's morale than getting a Dear John.* **2.** any letter terminating a relationship. Also called **Dear′ John′ let′ter.** [1940–45]

dearth (dûrth), *n.* **1.** an inadequate supply; scarcity; lack: *There is a dearth of good engineers.* **2.** scarcity and dearness of food; famine. [1200–50; ME *derthe.* See DEAR[1], -TH[1]]
—**Syn. 1.** shortage, want, paucity, insufficiency.

dear•y (dēr′ē), *n., pl.* **dear•ies.** *Informal* (*sometimes facetious*). darling. Also, **dear′ie.** [1675–85; DEAR[1] + -Y[2]]

dea•sil (dē′zəl), *adv. Chiefly Scot.* clockwise or in a direction following the apparent course of the sun: considered as lucky or auspicious. Cf. **withershins.** [1765–75; < ScotGael, Ir *deiseal,* MIr *dessel,* equiv. to *dess* right, south + *sel* turn, time; opposed in Ir to *túaithbel*]

death (deth), *n.* **1.** the act of dying; the end of life; the total and permanent cessation of all the vital functions of an organism. Cf. **brain death.** **2.** an instance of this: *a death in the family; letters published after his death.* **3.** the state of being dead: *to lie still in death.* **4.** extinction; destruction: *It will mean the death of our hopes.* **5.** manner of dying: *a hero's death.* **6.** (*usually cap.*) the agent of death personified, usually represented as a man or a skeleton carrying a scythe. Cf. **Grim Reaper.** **7.** Also called **spiritual death.** loss or absence of spiritual life. **8.** *Christian Science.* the false belief that life comes to an end. **9.** bloodshed or murder: *Hitler was responsible for the death of millions.* **10.** a cause or occasion of death: *You'll be the death of me yet!* **11.** *Archaic.* pestilence; plague. Cf. **Black Death.** **12. at death's door,** in serious danger of death; gravely ill: *Two survivors of the crash are still at death's door.* **13. be death on,** *Informal.* **a.** to be excessively strict about: *That publisher is death on sloppily typed manuscripts.* **b.** to be snobbish about or toward. **c.** to be able to cope with easily and successfully: *The third baseman is death on pop flies.* **14. do to death, a.** to kill, esp. to murder. **b.** to repeat too often, to the point of becoming monotonous and boring: *That theme has been done to death.* **15. in at the death, a.** *Fox Hunting.* present at the kill. **b.** present at the climax or conclusion of a situation. **16. put to death,** to kill; execute. **17. to death,** to an extreme degree; thoroughly: *sick to death of the heat.* [bef. 900; ME *deeth,* OE *dēath;* c. G *Tod,* Goth *dauthus;* akin to ON *deyja* to DIE[1]; see -TH]
—**Syn. 1.** decease, demise, passing, departure.

death′ ad′der, either of two highly venomous elapid snakes of the genus *Acanthophis,* of Australia and New Guinea, having a stout body and broad head. [1855–60]

death′ an′gel, Azrael. [1785–95]

death•bed (deth′bed′), *n.* **1.** the bed on which a person dies: *The museum contains Lincoln's deathbed.* **2. on one's deathbed,** in the last few hours before death. —*adj.* **3.** of, pertaining to, said, or done during the last few hours of a person's life: *a deathbed confession.* [1350–1400; ME *deethbed.* See DEATH, BED]

death′ bell′, the bell that announces a death. [1730–40]

death′ ben′efit, the amount of money to be paid under the terms of an insurance policy to the designated beneficiary upon the death of the insured. [1920–25]

death•blow (deth′blō′), *n.* a blow causing death. [1785–95; DEATH + BLOW[1]]

death′ cam′ass, **1.** any of several North American plants belonging to the genus *Zigadenus,* of the lily family, having narrow leaves and clusters of flowers. **2.** the root of any of these plants, poisonous to sheep and other animals. [1885–90, *Amer.*]

death′ camp′, a concentration camp in which the inmates are unlikely to survive or to which they have been sent to be executed. [1940–45]

death′ certif′icate, a certificate signed by a doctor, giving pertinent identifying information, as age and sex, about a deceased person and certifying the time, place, and cause of death.

death′ chair′. See **electric chair.** [1885–90, *Amer.*]

death′ cham′ber, **1.** a room in which a person is dying or has died. **2.** a place, as in a prison, in which executions take place.

death′ cup′, **1.** a poisonous mushroom of the genus *Amanita.* **2.** the part of this mushroom that persists around the base of the stalk as a membranous cup. [1900–05]

death•day (deth′dā′), *n.* the day or the anniversary of the day of a person's death. [bef. 900; ME *deth day,* OE *deothdæge.* See DEATH, DAY]

death′ du′ty, *Brit.* See **inheritance tax.** [1880–85]

death•ful (deth′fəl), *adj.* **1.** deadly; fatal. **2.** resembling death; deathlike. [1200–50; ME *deethful.* See DEATH, -FUL]

death′ house′, a building or part of a prison in which persons condemned to death await execution. [1915–20]

death′ in′stinct, **1.** suicidal tendency or inclination; predisposition to self-destruction. **2.** *Psychoanal.* an impulse to withdraw or destroy, working in opposition to forces urging survival and creation (**life instinct**). [1915–20]

Death′ in Ven′ice, (German, *Der Tod in Venedig*), a novella (1913) by Thomas Mann.

death′ knell′, **1.** a harbinger of the end, death, or destruction of something. **2.** See **passing bell.**

death•less (deth′lis), *adj.* **1.** not subject to death; immortal: *the belief that the human soul is deathless.* **2.** unceasing; perpetual: *his deathless devotion to the cause.* **3.** likely to endure because of superior quality, timelessness, etc. (sometimes used ironically): *deathless prose.* [1590–1600; DEATH + -LESS] —**death′less•ly,** *adv.* —**death′less•ness,** *n.*

death•like (deth′līk′), *adj.* resembling death. [1540–50; DEATH + -LIKE; cf. OE *dēathlīc* DEATHLY]

death•ly (deth′lē), *adj.* **1.** causing death; deadly; fatal. **2.** like death: *a deathly silence.* **3.** of, pertaining to, or indicating death; morbid: *a deathly odor from the sepulcher.* —*adv.* **4.** in the manner of death. **5.** very; utterly: *deathly afraid.* [bef. 1000; ME *dethlich,* OE *dēathlīc.* See DEATH, -LY] —**death′li•ness,** *n.*

death′ mask′, a cast taken of a person's face after death. Cf. **life mask.** [1875–80]

death′ met′al, a type of speed metal music featuring violent or Satanic imagery. [1985–1990]

Death′ of a Sales′man, a play (1949) by Arthur Miller.

Death′ of I•van′ Il′yich′, The, (ē vän′ ē lyēch′, ī′vən il′yich), a short novel (1884) by Leo Tolstoy.

death•place (deth′plās′), *n.* the place at which a person dies: *Lincoln is buried in Illinois, but his deathplace was Washington, D.C.* [1820–30; DEATH + PLACE]

death′ rate′, the number of deaths per unit, usually 1000, of population in a given place and time. [1855–60]

death′ rat′tle, a sound produced by a person immediately preceding death, resulting from the passage of air through the mucus in the throat. [1820–30]

death′ ray′, a hypothetical ray that destroys life from a distance. [1915–20]

death′ row′, a row of prison cells for prisoners awaiting execution. [1950–55]

death′ seat′, the passenger seat next to the driver in an automobile, regarded as dangerous in the event of a collision. [1940–45]

death′ sen′tence, a sentence condemning a convicted felon to execution by the state. Cf. **life sentence.**

death's-head (deths′hed′), *n.* a human skull, esp. as a symbol of mortality. [1590–1600]

death's′-head moth′, a European hawk moth, *Acherontia atropos,* having markings on the back of the thorax that resemble a human skull. [1775–85]

deaths•man (deths′mən), *n., pl.* **-men.** *Archaic.* an executioner. [1580–90; DEATH + -'S[1] + MAN[1]]

death′ spi′ral, (in pair skating) a dramatic movement in which the man spins his partner around him in a gradually increasing radius while he spins in place, holding the extended arm of the woman, who revolves around him on one skate with the other leg stretched out and gradually lowers herself backward until she is just above the ice surface.

death′ squad′, any of various groups of assassins, esp. in Central America, whose members murder political dissidents, petty criminals, etc., usually with the tacit approval of the government. [1965–70]

death′ tax′, **1.** See **estate tax.** **2.** See **inheritance tax.** [1935–40]

death•trap (deth′trap′), *n.* a structure, place, or situation where there is imminent risk of death: *They escaped from the deathtrap just before it exploded.* [1825–35; DEATH + TRAP[1]]

Death′ Val′ley, an arid basin in E California and S Nevada: lowest land in North America. ab. 1500 sq. mi. (3900 sq. km); 280 ft. (85 m) below sea level.

Death′ Val′ley Na′tional Mon′ument, a national monument in E California, including most of Death Valley: site of Badwater, lowest point in the U.S., 282 ft. (86 m) below sea level. 2980 sq. mi. (7718 sq. km).

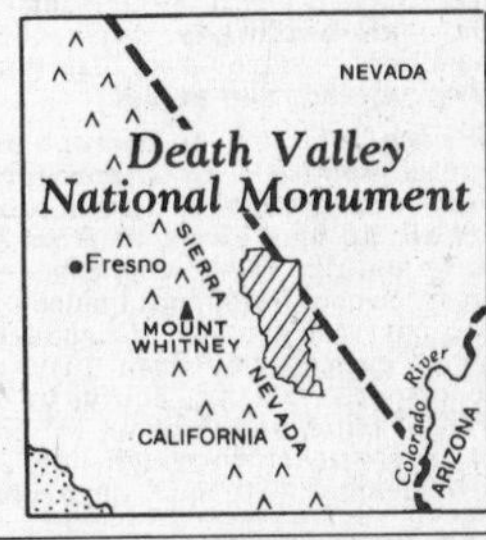

CONCISE PRONUNCIATION KEY: act, cāpe, dâre, pärt; set, ēqual; if, īce; ox, ōver, ôrder, oil, bo͝ok, bo͞ot, out; up, ûrge; child; sing; shoe; thin, *th*at; zh as in *treasure.* ə = *a* as in *alone,* *e* as in *system,* *i* as in *easily,* *o* as in *gallop,* *u* as in *circus;* ᵊ as in *fire* (fīᵊr), *hour* (ouᵊr). l and n can serve as syllabic consonants, as in *cradle* (krād′l), and *button* (but′n). See the full key inside the front cover.

de′con•glom′er•ate′, *v.,* **-at•ed, -at•ing.**
de•con′gre•gate′, *v.,* **-gat•ed, -gat•ing.**
de•con′se•crate′, *v.t.,* **-crat•ed, -crat•ing.**
de•con′se•cra′tion, *n.*
de′con•vert′, *v.t.*
de•crumb′, *v.t.*
de•cul′tur•al, *adj.*
de•cul′tur•al•ize′, *v.t.,* **-ized, -iz•ing.**
de•cu′mu•late′, *v.t.,* **-lat•ed, -lat•ing.**
de•cu′mu•la′tion, *n.*
de′-de•moc′ra•ti•za′tion, *n.*
de′-de•moc′ra•tize′, *v.,* **-tized, -tiz•ing.**
de•dep′u•tize′, *v.t.,* **-tized, -tiz•ing.**
de•des′ig•nate′, *v.t.,* **-nat•ed, -nat•ing.**
de′des•ig•na′tion, *n.*
de′-e•mo′tion•al•i•za′tion, *n.*
de′-e•mo′tion•al•ize′, *v.t.,* **-ized, -iz•ing.**
de′-em•ployed′, *adj.*
de′-ev•o•lu′tion, *n.*
de′-ex•pro′pri•a′tion, *n.*
de•fat′, *v.t.,* **-fat•ted, -fat•ting.**

death′ war′rant, 1. an official order authorizing the execution of the sentence of death. 2. anything that ends hope, expectation, etc. [1685–95]

death·watch (deth′woch′, -wôch′), *n.* 1. a vigil beside a dying or dead person. 2. a guard set over a condemned person before execution. 3. Also called **death′·watch bee′tle.** any of several beetles of the family Anobiidae that make a ticking sound as they bore through wood: the sound was once believed to be an omen of death. [1660–70; DEATH + WATCH]

death′ wish′, 1. desire for one's own death or for the death of another. 2. *Psychiatry.* a suicidal desire, manifested by passivity, withdrawal, and absorption in nihilistic thoughts, that may eventually lead to suicidal behavior. [1910–15]

death·y (deth′ē), *adj., adv. Archaic.* deathly. [1790–1800; DEATH + -Y[1]] —**death′i·ness,** *n.*

Deau·ville (dō′vil; *Fr.* dō vēl′), *n.* a coastal resort in NW France, S of Le Havre. 5232.

deave (dēv), *v.t.,* **deaved, deav·ing.** *Chiefly Scot.* to make deaf; deafen. [bef. 1050; ME *deven,* OE *-dēafian* (in *ādēafian* to grow DEAF; see A-[3])]

deb (deb), *n. Informal.* a debutante. [1915–20, *Amer.*; by shortening]

deb., debenture.

de·ba·cle (dā bä′kəl, -bak′əl, də-), *n.* 1. a general breakup or dispersion; sudden downfall or rout: *The revolution ended in a debacle.* 2. a complete collapse or failure. 3. a breaking up of ice in a river. Cf. **embacle.** 4. a violent rush of waters or ice. [1795–1805; < F *débâcle,* deriv. of *débâcler* to unbar, clear, equiv. to *dé-* DIS-[1] + *bâcler* to bar << L *baculum* stick, rod]
—**Syn.** 2. disaster, ruin, fiasco, catastrophe, calamity.

de·bag (dē bag′), *v.t.,* **-bagged, -bag·ging.** *Brit. Slang.* 1. to depants. 2. to debunk. [1910–15; DE- + BAG]

De Ba·key (də bā′kē), **Michael Ellis,** born 1908, U.S. physician: pioneer in heart surgery.

de·bar (di bär′), *v.t.,* **-barred, -bar·ring.** 1. to shut out or exclude from a place or condition: *to debar all those who are not members.* 2. to hinder or prevent; prohibit: *to debar an action.* [1400–50; late ME < MF, OF *desbarrer* to lock out, bar. See DE-, BAR[1]] —**de·bar′ment,** *n.*
—**Syn.** 2. interdict. —**Ant.** 1. admit. 2. permit.

de·bark[1] (di bärk′), *v.t., v.i.* to disembark. [1645–55; < F *débarquer,* equiv. to *dé-* DIS-[1] + *barque* BARK[3] + *-er* inf. suffix] —**de·bar·ka·tion** (dē′bär kā′shən), *n.*

de·bark[2] (dē bärk′), *v.t.* to remove the bark from (a log). [1735–45; DE- + BARK[2]] —**de·bark′er,** *n.*

de·base (di bās′), *v.t.,* **-based, -bas·ing.** 1. to reduce in quality or value; adulterate: *They debased the value of the dollar.* 2. to lower in rank, dignity, or significance: *He wouldn't debase himself by doing manual labor.* [1555–65; DE- + BASE[2]; cf. ABASE] —**de·bas·ed·ness** (di bā′sid nis, -bāst′-), *n.* —**de·base′ment,** *n.* —**de·bas′·er,** *n.* —**de·bas′ing·ly,** *adv.*
—**Syn.** 1. lower, vitiate, corrupt; contaminate, pollute, defile. 2. degrade, abase, demean, reduce.

de·bat·a·ble (di bā′tə bəl), *adj.* 1. open to question; in dispute; doubtful: *Whether or not he is qualified for the job is debatable.* 2. capable of being debated. [1425–75; late ME < MF. See DEBATE, -ABLE]
—**Syn.** 1. questionable, dubious, arguable, disputable.

de·bate (di bāt′), *n., v.,* **-bat·ed, -bat·ing.** —*n.* 1. a discussion, as of a public question in an assembly, involving opposing viewpoints: *a debate in the Senate on farm price supports.* 2. a formal contest in which the affirmative and negative sides of a proposition are advocated by opposing speakers. 3. deliberation; consideration. 4. *Archaic.* strife; contention. —*v.i.* 5. to engage in argument or discussion, as in a legislative or public assembly: *When we left, the men were still debating.* 6. to participate in a formal debate. 7. to deliberate; consider: *I debated with myself whether to tell them the truth or not.* 8. *Obs.* to fight; quarrel. —*v.t.* 9. to argue or discuss (a question, issue, or the like), as in a legislative or public assembly: *They debated the matter of free will.* 10. to dispute or disagree about: *The homeowners debated the value of a road on the island.* 11. to engage in formal argumentation or disputation with (another person, group, etc.): *Jones will debate Smith. Harvard will debate Princeton.* 12. to deliberate upon; consider: *He debated his decision in the matter.* 13. *Archaic.* to contend for or over. [1250–1300; (v.) ME *debaten* < OF *debatre,* equiv. to *de-* DE- + *batre* to beat < L *battere,* earlier *battuere;* (n.) ME *debat* < OF, deriv. of *debatre*] —**de·bat′er,** *n.* —**de·bat′ing·ly,** *adv.*
—**Syn.** 1. argument, controversy, disputation, contention. 5. dispute, contend. See **argue.**

de·bauch (di bôch′), *v.t.* 1. to corrupt by sensuality, intemperance, etc.; seduce. 2. to corrupt or pervert; sully: *His honesty was debauched by the prospect of easy money.* 3. *Archaic.* to lead away, as from allegiance or duty. —*v.i.* 4. to indulge in debauchery. —*n.* 5. a period of wanton or sensual self-indulgence. 6. an uninhibited spree or party; orgy: *a wild debauch.* [1585–95; < F *débaucher* to entice away from duty, debauch, OF *desbauchier* to disperse, scatter, equiv. to *des-* DIS-[1] + *-bauchier,* deriv. of *bauc, bauch* beam (< Gmc; see BALCONY, BALK; cf. F *ébaucher* to rough-hew); hence, presumably, to hew (beams) > to split, separate > to separate from work or duty] —**de·bauch′er,** *n.* —**de·bauch′·ment,** *n.*
—**Syn.** 1. See **debase.**

CONCISE ETYMOLOGY KEY: <, descended or borrowed from; >, whence; b., blend of, blended; c., cognate with; cf., compare; deriv., derivative; equiv., equivalent; imit., imitative; obl., oblique; r., replacing; s., stem; sp., spelling, spelled; resp., respelling, respelled; trans., translation; ?, origin unknown; *, unattested; ‡, probably earlier than. See the full key inside the front cover.

de·bauched (di bôcht′), *adj.* 1. displaying the effect of excessive indulgence in sensual pleasure: *a flabby and debauched face.* 2. corrupted; debased: *debauched morals.* [1590–1600; DEBAUCH + -ED[2]] —**de·bauch·ed·ly** (di bô′chid lē), *adv.* —**de·bauch′ed·ness,** *n.*
—**Syn.** 2. depraved, dissipated, profligate; immoral.

deb·au·chee (deb′ô chē′, -shē′), *n.* a person addicted to excessive indulgence in sensual pleasures; one given to debauchery. [1655–65; < F *débauché* (ptp. of *débaucher*). See DEBAUCH, -EE]

de·bauch·er·y (di bô′chə rē), *n., pl.* **-er·ies.** 1. excessive indulgence in sensual pleasures; intemperance. 2. *Archaic.* seduction from duty, allegiance, or virtue. [1635–45; DEBAUCH + -ERY]

Deb·bie (deb′ē), *n.* a female given name, form of **Deborah.** Also, **Deb′by.**

Deb·bo·ra (deb′ər ə, deb′rə), *n. Douay Bible.* Deborah (def. 1).

de·beak (dē bēk′), *v.t. Vet. Med.* to remove the upper beak from (a bird) to prevent egg eating or attacks on other birds. [1935–40; DE- + BEAK] —**de·beak′er,** *n.*

de Beau·voir (də bōv wär′; *Fr.* də bō vwar′), **Simone** (sē môn′) (*Lucie Ernestine Marie Bertrand*), 1908–86, French playwright, novelist, and essayist.

de be·ne es·se (di bē′nē es′ē, dē, dā bā′nā es′ā), *Law.* of validity for the time being but subject to objection or nullification at a later date; provisionally: *to take evidence de bene esse to ensure against its loss.* [1595–1605; < ML *dē bene esse* of well-being]

de·ben·ture (di ben′chər), *n.* 1. See **certificate of indebtedness.** 2. a certificate of drawback issued at a custom house. [1425–75; late ME *debentur* < L *dēbentur* (*mihi*) there are owing (to me), 3rd person pl. pass. indic. of *dēbēre* to owe (see DEBT)] —**de·ben′tured,** *adj.*

deben′ture bond′, a corporate bond unsecured by any mortgage, dependent on the credit of the issuer. [1865–70]

de·bil·i·tate (di bil′i tāt′), *v.t.,* **-tat·ed, -tat·ing.** to make weak or feeble; enfeeble: *The siege of pneumonia debilitated her completely.* [1525–35; < L *dēbilitātus* (ptp. of *dēbilitāre*), equiv. to *dēbilit-,* s. of *dēbilis* weak + *-ātus* -ATE[1]] —**de·bil′i·tant,** *n.* —**de·bil′i·ta′tion,** *n.* —**de·bil′i·ta′tive,** *adj.*
—**Syn.** weaken, deplete, enervate, devitalize.

de·bil·i·ty (di bil′i tē), *n., pl.* **-ties.** 1. a weakened or enfeebled state; weakness: *Debility prevented him from getting out of bed.* 2. a particular mental or physical handicap; disability. [1425–75; late ME *debylite* < MF *debilite* < L *dēbilitās,* equiv. to *dēbil(is)* weak + *-itās* -ITY]

De·bir (dē′bər), *n.* a royal city in the vicinity of Hebron, conquered by Othniel.

deb·it (deb′it), *n.* 1. the recording or an entry of debt in an account. 2. *Bookkeeping.* a. that which is entered in an account as a debt; a recorded item of debt. b. any entry or the total shown on the debit side. c. the left-hand side of an account on which such entries are made (opposed to *credit*). 3. an undesirable or disadvantageous feature. —*v.t.* 4. to charge with a debt: *The store debited her account for the purchase.* 5. to charge as a debt: *The store debited the purchase to her account.* 6. *Bookkeeping.* to enter upon the debit side of an account. [1400–50; late ME < OF < L *dēbitum* something owed; see DEBT]

deb·it·age (deb′i tij), *n. Archaeol.* lithic debris and discards found at the sites where stone tools and weapons were made. [< F *débitage,* equiv. to *débit(er)* to cut up, saw up (< *dé-* DE- + *-biter,* v. deriv. of *bitte* bitt) + *-age* -AGE]

deb′it card′, a plastic card that resembles a credit card but functions like a check and through which payments for purchases or services are made electronically to the bank accounts of participating retailing establishments directly from those of card holders. [1975–80]

deb·i·tor (deb′i tər), *n. Obs.* a debtor. [1475–85; < OF < L *dēbitor;* see DEBTOR]

deb′it pol′icy, *Insurance.* a policy for industrial life insurance sold door to door by an agent who collects the premiums.

dé·boî·té (*Fr.* dā bwa tā′), *n., pl.* **-tés** (*Fr.* -tā′). *Ballet.* a step in which the dancer stands on the toes with legs together and then springs up, swinging one foot out and around to the back of the other. Cf. **emboîté.** [< F: dislocated (n. use of ptp.)]

deb·o·nair (deb′ə nâr′), *adj.* 1. courteous, gracious, and having a sophisticated charm: *a debonair gentleman.* 2. jaunty; carefree; sprightly. Also, **deb′o·naire′, deb′on·naire′.** [1175–1225; ME *debone(i)re* < AF; OF *debonaire,* orig. phrase *de bon aire* of good lineage] —**deb′o·nair′ly,** *adv.* —**deb′o·nair′ness,** *n.*
—**Syn.** 1. urbane, suave, elegant, polished.

de·bone (dē bōn′), *v.t.,* **-boned, -bon·ing.** to remove the bones from (meat, fish, or fowl); bone: *Before cooking, the chicken breasts should be deboned with a small, sharp knife.* [1940–45; DE- + BONE] —**de·bon′er,** *n.*

de bo·nis non ad·min·i·stra·tis (di bō′nis non ad min′ə strā′tis, dē, dā), *Law.* of the part of the estate of a deceased person that has not been administered: *administration or an administrator de bonis non administratis.* Also, **de′bo′nis non′.** [< L *dē bonis nōn administrātis*]

Deb·o·rah (deb′ər ə, deb′rə), *n.* 1. a prophetess and judge of Israel. Judges 4, 5. 2. Also, **Deb′o·ra.** a female given name: from a Hebrew word meaning "bee."

de·boss (di bôs′, -bos′), *v.t.* to indent (a figure or design) into a surface: *The design on the book's cover is debossed.* [DE- + BOSS[2]]

de·bouch (di bo͞osh′, -bouch′), *v.i.* 1. to march out from a narrow or confined place into open country, as a body of troops: *The platoon debouched from the defile into the plain.* 2. *Physical Geog.* a. to emerge from a relatively narrow valley upon an open plain: *A river or glacier debouches on the plains.* b. to flow from a small valley into a larger one. 3. to come forth; emerge. —*n.* 4. débouché. [1655–65; < F *déboucher,* equiv. to *dé-* DIS-[1] + *-boucher,* v. deriv. of *bouche* mouth < L *bucca* cheek, jaw]

dé·bou·ché (dā bo͞o shā′), *n.* 1. *Fort.* a passage or opening through which troops may debouch. 2. an outlet; an exit. [1750–60; < F, n. use of ptp. of *déboucher* to DEBOUCH]

de·bouch·ment (di bo͞osh′mənt, -bouch′-), *n.* 1. an act or instance of debouching. 2. Also, **de·bou·chure** (di bo͞o′sho͝or, di bo͞o sho͝or′). *Physical Geog.* a mouth or outlet, as of a river or pass. [1820–30; < F *débouchement.* See DEBOUCH, -MENT]

dé·bou·lés (*Fr.* dā bo͞o lā′), *n.pl. Ballet.* small, very quick half-turns executed alternately on each foot, usually in a series in a straight line. [< F, n. use of pl. ptp. of *débouler* to bolt, make a quick start, equiv. to *dé-* DE- + *bouler* to roll (transit.)]

Deb·ra (deb′rə), *n.* a female given name, form of **Deborah.**

De·bre·cen (de′bre tsen′), *n.* a city in E Hungary. 187,103.

de·bride (di brēd′, dā-), *v.t.,* **-brid·ed, -brid·ing.** to clean (a wound) by debridement. [by back formation]

de·bride·ment (di brēd′mənt, dā-), *n.* surgical removal of foreign matter and dead tissue from a wound. [1835–45; < F *débridement,* equiv. to *débride(r)* to take away the bridle, MF *desbrider* (*des-* DE- + *brider,* deriv. of *bride* BRIDLE) + *-ment* -MENT]

de·brief (dē brēf′), *v.t.* 1. to interrogate (a soldier, astronaut, diplomat, etc.) on return from a mission in order to assess the conduct and results of the mission. 2. to question formally and systematically in order to obtain useful intelligence or information: *Political and economic experts routinely debrief important defectors about conditions in their home country.* 3. to subject to prohibitions against revealing or discussing classified information, as upon separation from a position of military or political sensitivity. 4. *Psychol.* (after an experiment) to disclose to the subject the purpose of the experiment and any reasons for deception or manipulation. [1940–45; DE- + BRIEF] —**de·brief′er,** *n.* —**de·brief′ing,** *n.*

de·bris (də brē′, dā′brē *or, esp. Brit.,* deb′rē), *n.* 1. the remains of anything broken down or destroyed; ruins; rubble: *the debris of buildings after an air raid.* 2. *Geol.* an accumulation of loose fragments of rock. Also, **dé·bris′.** [1700–10; < F *débris,* MF *debris,* deriv. of *debriser* to break up (in pieces), OF *debrisier* (*de-* DE- + *brisier* to break; see BRUISE)]
—**Syn.** 1. detritus, litter, trash.

de Bro·glie (də brō glē′, brō′glē, broi; *Fr.* də brô glē′), **Louis Vic·tor** (*Fr.* lwē vēk tôr′). 1892–1987, French physicist: Nobel prize 1929.

de Bro′glie equa′tion, *Physics.* the postulate of wave mechanics that a particle of mass *m* moving at a velocity *v* will have the properties of a wave of wavelength h/mv (**de Bro′glie wave′length**), where *h* is Planck's constant. [named after L.V. DE BROGLIE]

de Bro′glie wave′, *Physics.* a hypothetical wave associated with the motion of a particle of atomic or subatomic size that describes effects such as the diffraction of beams of particles by crystals. Also called **matter wave.** [1925–30; named after L.V. DE BROGLIE]

dé·brouil·lard (dā bro͞o yar′), *adj., n., pl.* ***-brouil·lards*** (-bro͞o yar′). *French.* —*adj.* 1. skilled at adapting to any situation; resourceful. —*n.* 2. a resourceful person who can act independently or cope with any development.

de·bruise (də bro͞oz′, dē-), *v.t.,* **-bruised, -bruis·ing.** *Heraldry.* to overlay (a charge) other than an ordinary with an ordinary. [1250–1300; ME *debrusen, debrisen* to break down, crush < OF *debr(u)isier,* equiv to *de-* DE- + *bruisier* to break; see BRUISE]

Debs (debz), *n.* **Eugene Victor,** 1855–1926, U.S. labor leader: Socialist candidate for president 1900–20.

debt (det), *n.* 1. something that is owed or that one is bound to pay to or perform for another: *a debt of $50.* 2. a liability or obligation to pay or render something: *My debt to her for advice is not to be discharged easily.* 3. the condition of being under such an obligation: *His gambling losses put him deeply in debt.* 4. *Theol.* an offense requiring reparation; a sin; a trespass. [1175–1225; ME *dette* < OF < L *dēbita* (neut. pl., taken in VL as fem. sing.), n. use of *dēbitus,* ptp. of *dēbēre* to owe, contr. of **dēhabēre,* equiv. to *dē-* DE- + *habēre* to have, possess] —**debt′less,** *adj.*
—**Syn.** 1. obligation, duty, due.

debt′ is′sue, any fixed corporate obligations, as bonds or debentures.

debt′ lim′it, (in public finance) the legal maximum debt permitted a municipal, state, or national government.

de·fem′i·ni·za′tion, *n.*
de·fem′i·nize′, *v.t.,* **-nized, -niz·ing.**
de·feu′dal·ize′, *v.t.,* **-ized, -iz·ing.**
de·fla′vor, *v.t.*
de·fluor′i·date′, *v.t.,* **-dat·ed, -dat·ing.**
de·fluor′i·da′tion, *n.*
de·foam′, *v.t.*
de·fo′cal·i·za′tion, *n.*
de·frame′, *v.t.,* **-framed, -fram·ing.**
de·freeze′, *v.t.,* **-froze, -fro·zen, -freez·ing.**
de·fu′el, *v.t.,* **-eled, -el·ing** or (*esp. Brit.*) **-elled, -el·ling.**
de·func′tion·al·ize′, *v.t.,* **-ized, -iz·ing.**
de·gel′, *v.t.,* **-gelled, -gel·ling.**
de-Ger′man·ize′, *v.,* **-ized, -iz·ing.**
de·ghost′, *v.t.*
de·glo′ri·fi·ca′tion, *n.*
de·glo′ri·fy′, *v.t.,* **-fied, -fy·ing.**
de·hair′, *v.t.*
de-Hel′len·ize′, *v.,* **-ized, -iz·ing.**
de·hex′, *v.t.*
de·hos′pi·tal·i·za′tion, *n.*

debt′ of hon′or, a gambling debt. [1640–50]

debt·or (det′ər), *n.* a person who is in debt or under financial obligation to another (opposed to *creditor*). [1250–1300; ME *detto(u)r* < AF *dett(o)ur, de(b)tour,* OF *det(t)or* < L *dēbitōr-,* s. of *dēbitor,* equiv. to *dēbi-,* var. s. of *dēbēre* (see DEBT) + *-tor* -TOR]

debt′ serv′ice, the amount set aside annually in a fund to pay the interest and the part of the principal due on a debt. **—debt′ serv′icing.**

de·bug (dē bug′), *v.t.,* **-bugged, -bug·ging.** *Informal.* **1.** to detect and remove defects or errors from. **2.** to remove electronic bugs from (a room or building). **3.** *Computers.* to detect and remove errors from (a computer program). **4.** to rid (a garden, plant, etc.) of insect pests, as by the application of a pesticide. [1940–45; DE- + BUG[1]] **—de·bug′ger,** *n.*

de·bunk (di bungk′), *v.t.* to expose or excoriate (a claim, assertion, sentiment, etc.) as being pretentious, false, or exaggerated: *to debunk advertising slogans.* [1920–25, *Amer.*; DE- + BUNK[2]] **—de·bunk′er,** *n.* **—Syn.** disparage, ridicule, lampoon.

de·burr (dē bûr′), *v.t.* **1.** to remove burrs from (a piece of machined work); burr. —*v.i.* **2.** to remove burrs from a piece of machined work. [DE- + BURR[1]]

de·bus (dē bus′), *v.t., v.i.,* **-bused** or **-bussed, -bus·ing** or **-bus·sing.** to get out of a bus; alight from a bus. [1910–15; DE- + BUS]

De·bus·sy (deb′yŏŏ sē′, dā′byŏŏ-, də byŏŏ′sē; *Fr.* də bʏ sē′), *n.* **Claude A·chille** (klōd ə shēl′; *Fr.* klōd A shēl′), 1862–1918, French composer. **—De·bus·sy·an** (di byŏŏ′sē ən), *adj.*

de·but (dā byŏŏ′, di-, dā′byŏŏ, deb′yŏŏ), *n.* **1.** a first public appearance on a stage, on television, etc. **2.** the first appearance of something, as a new product. **3.** (of a young woman) a formal introduction and entrance into society, as at an annual ball. **4.** the beginning of a profession, career, etc. —*v.i.* **5.** to make a debut, as in society or in a performing art: *She decided to debut with several other violinists.* **6.** to appear for the first time, as on the market: *A new product will debut next month.* —*v.t.* **7.** to perform (something) for the first time before an audience: *He didn't know when the orchestra would debut his new symphony.* **8.** to place on the market for the first time; introduce. —*adj.* **9.** of, pertaining to, or constituting a first appearance: *a debut performance; a debut record album.* Also, **dé·but′.** [1745–55; < F *début,* deriv. of *débuter* to make the first stroke in a game, make one's first appearance, equiv. to *dé-* DE- + *-buter,* v. deriv. of *but* goal; see BUTT[2]]

deb·u·tant (deb′yŏŏ tänt′, -yə-), *n.* a person who makes a debut into a professional career or before the public. Also, **déb′u·tant′.** [1815–25; < F *débutant,* prp. of *débuter.* See DEBUT, -ANT]

deb·u·tante (deb′yŏŏ tänt′, -tant′), *n.* a young woman making a debut into society. Also, **déb′u·tante′.** [1795–1805; < F; fem. of *débutant* DEBUTANT]

de·bye (di bī′), *n. Elect.* a unit of measure for electric dipole moments, equal to 10^{-18} statcoulomb-centimeters. *Abbr.:* D [1930–35; named after P. J. W. DEBYE]

De·bye (di bī′), *n.* **Pe·ter Jo·seph Wil·helm** (pā′tər yō′sef vil′helm), 1884–1966, Dutch physicist, in the U.S. after 1940: Nobel prize for chemistry 1936.

dec-, var. of **deca-** before a vowel: *decathlon.*

Dec., December.

dec., **1.** (in prescriptions) pour off. [< L *dēcantā*] **2.** deceased. **3.** decimeter. **4.** declension. **5.** decrease. **6.** *Music.* decrescendo.

deca-, a combining form meaning "ten," used in the formation of compound words: *decapod.* Also, *esp. before a vowel,* **dec-.** Cf. **deci-, deka.** [< Gk *deka-,* comb. form of *déka* TEN; c. L *decem*]

dec·a·dal (dek′ə dl), *adj.* of or pertaining to a decade. [1745–55; DECADE + -AL[1]] **—dec′a·dal·ly,** *adv.*

dec·ade (dek′ād; *Brit. also* də kād′), *n.* **1.** a period of ten years: *the three decades from 1776 to 1806.* **2.** a period of ten years beginning with a year whose last digit is zero: *the decade of the 1980's.* **3.** a group, set, or series of ten. [1425–75; late ME < MF < LL *decad-* (s. of *decas*) < Gk *dekad-* (s. of *dekás*) group of ten, equiv. to *dék(a)* TEN + *-ad-* -ADE[2]]

dec·a·dence (dek′ə dəns, di kād′ns), *n.* **1.** the act or process of falling into an inferior condition or state; deterioration; decay: *Some historians hold that the fall of Rome can be attributed to internal decadence.* **2.** moral degeneration or decay; turpitude. **3.** unrestrained or excessive self-indulgence. **4.** (*often cap.*) the decadent movement in literature. Also, **dec·a·den·cy** (dek′ə dən sē, di kād′n-). [1540–50; < MF < ML *dēcadentia,* equiv. to LL *dēcadent-* (s. of *dēcadēns*), prp. of *dēcadere* to fall away (*dē-* DE- +*cad(ere)* to fall + *-ent-* -ENT) + *-ia* n. suffix; see -ENCE] **—Syn. 1.** degeneration, retrogression, decline.

dec·a·dent (dek′ə dənt, di kād′nt), *adj.* **1.** characterized by decadence, esp. culturally or morally: *a decadent life of excessive money and no sense of responsibility.* **2.** (*often cap.*) of or like the decadents. —*n.* **3.** a person who is decadent. **4.** (*often cap.*) one of a group of French and English writers of the latter part of the 19th century whose works were characterized by aestheticism, great refinement or subtlety of style, and a marked tendency toward the artificial and abnormal in content. [1830–40; back formation from DECADENCE; see -ENT] **—dec·a·dent·ly** (dek′ə dənt lē, di kād′nt-), *adv.* **—Syn. 1.** corrupt, immoral, degenerate, debased, debauched, self-indulgent.

dec·a·drachm (dek′ə dram′), *n.* a silver coin of ancient Greece equal to 10 drachmas. Also, **dekadrachm, dec·a·drach·ma** (dek′ə drak′mə). [1855–60; DECA- + DRACHM]

Dec·a·dron (dek′ə dron′), *Pharm., Trademark.* a brand of dexamethasone.

de·caf (dē′kaf′), *Informal.* —*n.* **1.** decaffeinated coffee or tea. —*adj.* **2.** decaffeinated. [by shortening]

de·caf·fein·ate (dē kaf′ə nāt′, -kaf′ē ə-), *v.t.,* **-at·ed, -at·ing.** to extract caffeine from: *to decaffeinate coffee.* [1925–30; DE- + CAFFEIN + -ATE[1]] **—de·caf′fein·a′·tion,** *n.* **—de·caf′fein·a′tor,** *n.*

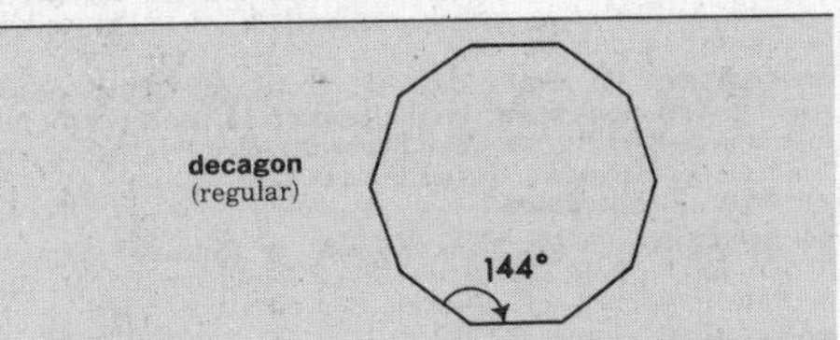

decagon (regular)

dec·a·gon (dek′ə gon′), *n. Geom.* a polygon having ten angles and ten sides. [1565–75; < ML *decagōnum.* See DECA-, -GON] **—de·cag·o·nal** (də kag′ə nl), *adj.*

dec·a·gram (dek′ə gram′), *n.* dekagram.

dec·a·he·dron (dek′ə hē′drən), *n., pl.* **-drons, -dra** (-drə). *Geom.* a solid figure having ten faces. [1820–30; < NL; see DECA-, -HEDRON] **—dec·a·he·dral** (dek′ə-hē′drəl), *adj.*

dec·a·hy·drate (dek′ə hī′drāt, -drāt), *n. Chem.* a hydrate that contains ten molecules of water, as washing soda, $Na_2CO_3 \cdot 10H_2O$. [1900–05; DECA- + HYDRATE] **—dec′a·hy′drat·ed,** *adj.*

dec·a·hy·dro·naph·tha·lene (dek′ə hī′drō naf′thə-lēn′, -nap′-), *n. Chem.* a colorless, aromatic liquid, $C_{10}H_{18}$, insoluble in water and soluble in alcohol and ether: used as a solvent for oils, fats, etc., in cleaning fluids, lubricants, etc. [1875–80; DECA- + HYDRO-[2] + NAPHTHALENE]

de·cal (dē′kal, di kal′), *n., v.,* **-caled** or **-called, -cal·ing** or **-cal·ling.** —*n.* **1.** a specially prepared paper bearing a picture or design for transfer to wood, metal, glass, etc. **2.** the picture or design itself. —*v.t.* **3.** to apply decals on. [1950–55; shortened form of DECALCOMANIA]

de·cal·ci·fi·ca·tion (dē kal′sə fi kā′shən), *n.* **1.** the act or process of decalcifying. **2.** the loss of calcium or calcium compounds, as from bone or soil. [1855–60; DECALCI(FY) + -FICATION]

de·cal·ci·fy (dē kal′sə fī′), *v.,* **-fied, -fy·ing.** —*v.t.* **1.** to deprive of lime or calcareous matter, as a bone. —*v.i.* **2.** to become decalcified. [1840–50; DE- + CALCIFY] **—de·cal′ci·fi′er,** *n.*

de·cal·co·ma·ni·a (di kal′kə mā′nē ə, -mān′yə), *n.* **1.** the art or process of transferring pictures or designs from specially prepared paper to wood, metal, glass, etc. **2.** decal (defs. 1, 2). [1860–65; < F *décalcomanie,* equiv. to *décalc-* (repr. *décalquer* to transfer a tracing of, equiv. to *dé-* DE- + *calquer* to trace) + *-o-* -O- + *-manie* -MANIA]

de·ca·les·cence (dē′kə les′əns), *n. Metall.* absorption of heat without a corresponding increase in temperature when a metal has been heated to a critical point. [1890–95; < L *dēcalēsc(ent-)* (s. of *dēcalēscēns*) becoming warm (see DE-, CALESCENT) + -ENCE] **—de′ca·les′cent,** *adj.*

Dec·a·lin (dek′ə lin), *Chem., Trademark.* a brand of decahydronaphthalene.

dec·a·li·ter (dek′ə lē′tər), *n.* dekaliter.

Dec·a·logue (dek′ə lôg′, -log′), *n.* See **Ten Commandments.** Ex. 20:2–17. Also, **dec′a·logue′, Dec′a·log′, dec′a·log′.** [1350–1400; ME *decalog* < LL *decalogus* < MGk, Gk *dekálogos.* See DECA-, -LOGUE]

De·cam·er·on, The (di kam′ər ən), a collection of 100 tales (1353) by Boccaccio. **—De·cam·er·on·ic** (di-kam′ə ron′ik), *adj.*

de·cam·er·ous (di kam′ər əs), *adj.* consisting of ten parts or divisions. [1880–85; DECA- + -MEROUS]

dec·a·me·ter (dek′ə mē′tər), *n.* dekameter.

dec·a·met·ric (dek′ə me′trik), *adj.* (of a radio wave) having a wavelength between 10 and 100 meters: *decametric wave.* Also, **dekametric.** [DECA- + -METRIC]

de·camp (di kamp′), *v.i.* **1.** to depart from a camp; to pack up equipment and leave a camping ground: *We decamped before the rain began.* **2.** to depart quickly, secretly, or unceremoniously: *The band of thieves decamped in the night.* [1670–80; < F *décamper,* equiv. to *dé-* DIS-[1] + *camper* to encamp; see CAMP[1]] **—de·camp′·ment,** *n.*

dec·an (dek′ən), *n. Astrol.* any of three divisions of 10° within a sign of the zodiac. [1400–50; late ME < LL *decānus* chief of ten; see DEAN[1]]

dec·a·nal (dek′ə nl, di kān′l), *adj.* of or pertaining to a dean or deanery: *decanal responsibilities.* [1700–10; < LL *decān(us)* DEAN[1] + -AL[1]] **—dec′a·nal·ly, de·can·i·cal·ly** (di kan′ik lē), *adv.*

dec·ane (dek′ān), *n. Chem.* a hydrocarbon, $C_{10}H_{22}$, of the methane series, occurring in several isomeric forms. [1870–75; DEC- + -ANE]

de·ca·ni (di kā′nī), *adj.* of or pertaining to the epistle or liturgical south side of a church (opposed to *cantoris*). [1750–60; < ML *decānī* of the dean (gen. of *decānus*); see DEAN[1]]

dec′a·no′ic ac′id (dek′ə nō′ik, dek′-), *Chem.* See **capric acid.** [DECANE + -O- + -IC]

dec·a·nol (dek′ə nôl′, -nol′), *n. Chem.* a colorless liquid, $C_{10}H_{22}O$, insoluble in water and soluble in alcohol: used as a plasticizer, detergent, and in perfumes and flavorings. Also called **decatyl alcohol, decyl alcohol.** [DECANE + -OL]

dec·a·nor·mal (dek′ə nôr′məl), *adj. Chem.* (of a solution) containing ten equivalent weights of solute per liter of solution. [DECA- + NORMAL]

de·cant (di kant′), *v.t.* **1.** to pour (wine or other liquid) gently so as not to disturb the sediment. **2.** to pour (a liquid) from one container to another. [1625–35; < ML *dēcanthāre,* equiv. to L *dē-* DE- + ML *canth(us)* spout, rim of a vessel (L: iron band round a wheel < Gk *kánthos* corner of the eye, tire) + *-āre* inf. suffix] **—de·can·ta·tion** (dē′kan tā′shən), *n.*

de·cant·er (di kan′tər), *n.* **1.** a vessel, usually an ornamental glass bottle, for holding and serving wine, brandy, or the like. **2.** a bottle used for decanting. [1705–15; DECANT + -ER[1]]

decanter (def. 1)

de·cap·i·tal·ize (dē kap′i tl īz′), *v.t.,* **-ized, -iz·ing.** to deprive of capital; discourage capital formation; withdraw capital from: *The government decapitalized industry with harsh tax policies.* Also, *esp. Brit.,* **de·cap′i·tal·ise′.** [1870–75; DE- + CAPITALIZE] **—de·cap′i·tal·i·za′·tion,** *n.*

de·cap·i·tate (di kap′i tāt′), *v.t.,* **-tat·ed, -tat·ing.** to cut off the head of; behead: *Many people were decapitated during the French Revolution.* [1605–15; < LL *dēcapitātus,* ptp. of *dēcapitāre,* equiv. to *dē-* DE- + *capit-* (s. of *caput*) head + *-ātus* -ATE] **—de·cap′i·ta′tion,** *n.* **—de·cap′i·ta′tor,** *n.*

dec·a·pod (dek′ə pod′), *n.* **1.** any crustacean of the order Decapoda, having five pairs of walking legs, including the crabs, lobsters, crayfish, prawns, and shrimps. **2.** any dibranchiate cephalopod having ten arms, as the cuttlefish or squid. **3.** (*cap.*) a steam locomotive having a two-wheeled front truck, ten driving wheels, and no rear truck. See table under **Whyte classification.** —*adj.* **4.** belonging or pertaining to the decapods. **5.** having ten feet or legs. [1825–35; < NL *Decapoda* name of the order. See DECA-, -POD] **—de·cap·o·dan** (də kap′ə dn), *adj., n.* **—de·cap′o·dous,** *adj.*

De·cap·o·lis (di kap′ə lis), *n.* a region in the NE part of ancient Palestine: confederacy of ten cities in the 1st century B.C.

de·car·bon·ate (dē kär′bə nāt′), *v.t.,* **-at·ed, -at·ing.** to remove carbon dioxide from. [1825–35; DE- + CARBONATE] **—de·car′bon·a′tion,** *n.*

de·car·bon·ize (dē kär′bə nīz′), *v.t.,* **-ized, -iz·ing.** decarburize. Also, *esp. Brit.,* **de·car′bon·ise′.** [1815–25; DE- + CARBONIZE] **—de·car′bon·i·za′tion,** *n.* **—de·car′bon·iz′er,** *n.*

de·car·bo·ny·late (dē kär′bə nl āt′), *v.t.,* **-lat·ed, -lat·ing.** *Chem.* to remove the carbonyl group from (an organic compound). [DE- + CARBONYLATE] **—de′car·bon′yl·a′tion,** *n.*

de·car·box·yl·ase (dē′kär bok′sə lās′, -lāz′), *n. Biochem.* any of the class of enzymes that catalyze the release of carbon dioxide from the carboxyl group of certain organic acids. Also called **carboxylase.** [1935–40; DECARBOXYL(ATE) + -ASE]

de·car·box·yl·ate (dē′kär bok′sə lāt′), *v.t.,* **-at·ed, -at·ing.** *Chem.* to remove the carboxyl group from (an organic compound). [1920–25; DE- + CARBOXYLATE] **—de′car·box′yl·a′tion,** *n.*

de·car·bu·rize (dē kär′bə rīz′, -byə-), *v.t.,* **-rized, -riz·ing.** to remove carbon from (molten steel, automobile cylinders, etc.). Also, *esp. Brit.,* **de·car′bu·rise′.** [1855–60; DE- + CARBURIZE] **—de·car′bu·ri·za′tion, de·car′·bu·ra′tion,** *n.*

dec·a·style (dek′ə stīl′), *adj. Archit.* **1.** having ten columns. **2.** (of a classical temple) having ten columns on one front or on each front. Also, **dec′a·styl′ar.** [1720–30; < L *decastylos* < Gk *dekástȳlos,* equiv. to *déka* DECA- + *-stȳlos* -STYLE[2]]

dec·a·sty·los (dek′ə stī′los), *n.* a decastyle building, as a classical temple. [< L; see DECASTYLE]

de·cas·u·al·ize (dē kazh′ŏŏ ə līz′), *v.t.,* **-ized, -iz·ing.** to reduce or eliminate the employment of (casual labor). Also, *esp. Brit.,* **de·cas′u·al·ise′.** [1890–95; DE- + CASUAL + -IZE] **—de·cas′u·al·i·za′tion,** *n.*

CONCISE PRONUNCIATION KEY: act, cāpe, dâre, pärt; set, ēqual; *if,* ice; ox, ōver, ôrder, oil, bŏŏk, bōōt, out; up, ûrge; child; sing; shoe; thin, *th*at; zh as in *treasure.* ə = a as in *alone,* e as in *system,* i as in *easily,* o as in *gallop,* u as in *circus;* ᵊ as in *fire* (fīᵊr), *hour* (ouᵊr). l and n can serve as syllabic consonants, as in *cradle* (krād′l), and *button* (but′n). See the full key inside the front cover.

de·hy′phen, *v.t.*
de·in′di·vid′u·a′tion, *n.*
de·in′te·grate′, *v.,* **-grat·ed, -grat·ing.**
de′-in·te·gra′tion, *n.*
de′-in·ten′si·fy′, *v.,* **-fied, -fy·ing.**
de′in·ter·na′tion·al·ize′, *v.t.,* **-ized, -iz·ing.**
de′ju·di′cial·i·za′tion, *n.*
de-Lat′in·i·za′tion, *n.*
de·law′yer, *v.t.*
de·law′yer·i·za′tion, *n.*
de′le·git′i·mate′, *v.t.,* **-mat·ed, -mat·ing.**
de′le·git′i·ma′tion, *n.*
de·li′cense, *v.t.,* **-censed, -cens·ing.**
de·lint′, *v.t.*
de·lit′ter, *v.t.*
de·mas′cu·lin·i·za′tion, *n.*
de·mas′cu·lin·ize′, *v.t.,* **-ized, -iz·ing.**
de·med′i·cate′, *v.t.,* **-cat·ed, -cat·ing.**

dec·a·syl·lab·ic (dek′ə si lab′ik), *adj.* having ten syllables: *a decasyllabic verse.* [1765–75; DECA- + SYLLABIC; cf. F *décasyllabique*]

dec·a·syl·la·ble (dek′ə sil′ə bəl), *n.* a word or line of verse of ten syllables. [1830–40; DECA- + SYLLABLE]

de·ca·thect (dē′kə thekt′), *v.t.* to withdraw one's feelings of attachment from (a person, idea, or object), as in anticipation of a future loss: *He decathected from her in order to cope with her impending death.* [DE- + CATHECT] —**de·ca·thex·is** (dē′kə thek′sis), *n.*

de·cath·lete (di kath′lēt), *n.* an athlete who takes part in or trains chiefly for a decathlon. [1965–70; b. DECATHLON and ATHLETE]

de·cath·lon (di kath′lon), *n.* an athletic contest comprising ten different track-and-field events and won by the contestant amassing the highest total score. [1910–15; DEC- + Gk *âthlon* prize, contest]

dec·at·ing (dek′ə ting), *n.* a finishing process for making fabric more lustrous, for improving the tactile quality of the nap, and for setting the material to reduce shrinkage. Also, **dec·a·tiz·ing** (dek′ə ti′zing). [< F *décat(ir)* to sponge, remove gloss (*dé-* DE- + *catir* to press, add gloss to < VL **coāctīre* to drive together, equiv. to L *coāct(us)*, ptp. of *coagere* (*co-* CO- + *ag(ere)* to drive, set in motion + *-tus* ptp. suffix) + *-īre* inf. suffix) + -ING[1]]

De·ca·tur (di kā′tər), *n.* **1. Stephen,** 1779–1820, U.S. naval officer. **2.** a city in central Illinois. 94,081. **3.** a city in N Alabama. 42,002. **4.** a city in N Georgia, near Atlanta. 18,404.

dec′a·tyl al′cohol (dek′ə tl), *Chem.* decanol. [< Gk *dékat(os)* tenth (see DECA-, -TH[2]) + -YL]

de·cay (di kā′), *v.i.* **1.** to become decomposed; rot: *vegetation that was decaying.* **2.** to decline in excellence, prosperity, health, etc.; deteriorate. **3.** *Physics.* (of a radioactive nucleus) to change spontaneously into one or more different nuclei in a process in which atomic particles, as alpha particles, are emitted from the nucleus, electrons are captured or lost, or fission takes place. —*v.t.* **4.** to cause to decay or decompose; rot: *The dampness of the climate decayed the books.* —*n.* **5.** decomposition; rot: *Decay made the wood unsuitable for use.* **6.** a gradual falling into an inferior condition; progressive decline: *the decay of international relations; the decay of the Aztec civilizations.* **7.** decline in or loss of strength, health, intellect, etc.: *His mental decay is distressing.* **8.** Also called **disintegration, radioactive decay.** *Physics.* a radioactive process in which a nucleus undergoes spontaneous transformation into one or more different nuclei and simultaneously emits radiation, loses electrons, or undergoes fission. **9.** *Aerospace.* the progressive, accelerating reduction in orbital parameters, particularly apogee and perigee, of a spacecraft due to atmospheric drag. [1425–75; (v.) late ME *decayen* < ONF *decair*, equiv. to *de-* DE- + *cair* to fall < VL **cadēre*, for L *cadere;* (n.) late ME, deriv. of the v.] —**de·cay′a·ble,** *adj.* —**de·cayed·ness** (di kād′nis, -kā′id-), *adj.* —**de·cay′less,** *adj.*
—**Syn. 1.** degenerate, wither; putrefy. DECAY, DECOMPOSE, DISINTEGRATE, ROT imply a deterioration or falling away from a sound condition. DECAY implies either entire or partial deterioration by progressive natural changes: *Teeth decay.* DECOMPOSE suggests the reducing of a substance to its component elements: *Moisture makes some chemical compounds decompose.* DISINTEGRATE emphasizes the breaking up, going to pieces, or wearing away of anything, so that its original wholeness is impaired: *Rocks disintegrate.* ROT is a stronger word than DECAY and is esp. applied to decaying vegetable matter, which may or may not emit offensive odors: *Potatoes rot.* **5.** putrefaction. **7.** deterioration, decadence, impairment, dilapidation, degeneration.

decay′ con′stant, *Physics.* the reciprocal of the decay time. Also called **decay rate, disintegration constant.** [1930–35]

decay′ se′ries, *Physics.* See **radioactive series.**

decay′ time′, *Physics.* the time required for a collection of atoms of a particular radionuclide to decay to a fraction of the initial number equal to 1/*e*. Cf. **e** (symbol) (def. 1). Also called **mean life.**

Dec·ca (dek′ə), *n.* a British radio navigational aid by which a fix is obtained by determining phase difference between continuous-wave signals from two synchronized fixed signals. Cf. **loran.** [1945–50]

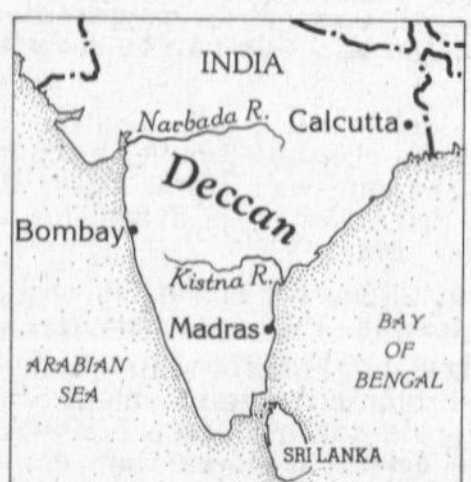

CONCISE ETYMOLOGY KEY: <, descended or borrowed from; >, whence; b., blend of, blended; c., cognate with; cf., compare; deriv., derivative; equiv., equivalent; imit., imitative; obl., oblique; r., replacing; s., stem; sp., spelling, spelled; resp., respelling, respelled; trans., translation; ?, origin unknown; *, unattested; ‡, probably earlier than. See the full key inside the front cover.

Dec·can (dek′ən), *n.* **1.** the entire peninsula of India S of the Narbada River. **2.** a plateau region in S India between the Narbada and Krishna rivers.

dec′can hemp′ (dek′ən), kenaf.

decd., deceased.

dece (dēs), *adj. Slang.* great, wonderful. Also, **dees.** [shortening of DECENT]

de·cease (di sēs′), *n., v.,* **-ceased, -ceas·ing.** —*n.* **1.** the act of dying; departure from life; death. —*v.i.* **2.** to depart from life; die. [1300–50; (n.) ME *deces* < OF < L *dēcessus* departure, death, equiv. to *dēced-*, var. s. of *dēcēdere* to go away (*dē-* DE- + *cēdere* to go; see CEDE) + *-tus* suffix of v. action, with *dt* > *s;* (v.) late ME *decesen*, deriv. of the n.]

de·ceased (di sēst′), *adj.* **1.** no longer living; dead. —*n.* **2. the deceased, a.** the particular dead person or persons referred to. **b.** dead persons collectively: *to speak well of the deceased.* [1480–90; DECEASE + -ED[2]]
—**Syn. 1.** See **dead.**

de·ce·dent (di sēd′nt), *n. Law.* a deceased person. [1590–1600; < L *dēcēdent-* (s. of *dēcēdēns*) departing, withdrawing, prp. of *dēcēdere.* See DECEASE, -ENT]

dece′dent estate′, *Law.* the estate left by a decedent.

de·ceit (di sēt′), *n.* **1.** the act or practice of deceiving; concealment or distortion of the truth for the purpose of misleading; duplicity; fraud; cheating: *Once she exposed their deceit, no one ever trusted them again.* **2.** an act or device intended to deceive; trick; stratagem. **3.** the quality of being deceitful; duplicity; falseness: *a man full of deceit.* [1225–75; ME *deceite* < AF, OF, n. use of fem. of *deceit*, ptp. of *deceivre* to DECEIVE]
—**Syn. 1.** deception, dissimulation. **1, 3.** DECEIT, GUILE, HYPOCRISY, DUPLICITY, FRAUD, TRICKERY refer either to practices designed to mislead or to the qualities that produce those practices. DECEIT is the quality that prompts intentional concealment or perversion of truth for the purpose of misleading: *honest and without deceit.* The quality of GUILE leads to craftiness in the use of deceit: *using guile and trickery to attain one's ends.* HYPOCRISY is the pretense of possessing qualities of sincerity, goodness, devotion, etc.: *It was sheer hypocrisy for him to go to church.* DUPLICITY is the form of deceitfulness that leads one to give two impressions, either or both of which may be false: *the duplicity of a spy working for two governments.* FRAUD refers usually to the practice of subtle deceit or duplicity by which one may derive benefit at another's expense: *an advertiser convicted of fraud.* TRICKERY is the quality that leads to the use of tricks and habitual deception: *notorious for his trickery in business deals.* —**Ant. 3.** honesty, sincerity.

de·ceit·ful (di sēt′fəl), *adj.* **1.** given to deceiving: *A deceitful person cannot keep friends for long.* **2.** intended to deceive; misleading; fraudulent: *a deceitful action.* [1400–50; late ME; see DECEIT, -FUL] —**de·ceit′ful·ly,** *adv.* —**de·ceit′ful·ness,** *n.*
—**Syn. 1.** insincere, disingenuous, false, hollow, designing, tricky, wily. **2.** illusory, fallacious. —**Ant. 1.** honest. **2.** genuine.

de·ceiv·a·ble (di sē′və bəl), *adj.* **1.** capable of being deceived; gullible. **2.** *Archaic.* misleading; deceptive. [1350–1400; ME; see DECEIVE, ABLE]

de·ceive (di sēv′), *v.,* **-ceived, -ceiv·ing.** —*v.t.* **1.** to mislead by a false appearance or statement; delude: *They deceived the enemy by disguising the destroyer as a freighter.* **2.** to be unfaithful to (one's spouse or lover). **3.** *Archaic.* to while away (time). —*v.i.* **4.** to mislead or falsely persuade others; practice deceit: *an engaging manner that easily deceives.* [1250–1300; ME *deceiven* < OF *deceivre* < L *dēcipere*, lit., to ensnare, equiv. to *dē-* DE- + *-cipere*, comb. form of *capere* to take] —**de·ceiv′a·ble·ness, de·ceiv′a·bil′i·ty,** *n.* —**de·ceiv′a·bly,** *adv.* —**de·ceiv′er,** *n.* —**de·ceiv′ing·ly,** *adv.*
—**Syn. 1.** cozen, dupe, fool, gull, hoodwink, trick, defraud, outwit, entrap, ensnare, betray. See **cheat.**

de·cel·er·ate (dē sel′ə rāt′), *v.,* **-at·ed, -at·ing.** —*v.t.* **1.** to decrease the velocity of: *He decelerates the bobsled when he nears a curve.* **2.** to slow the rate of increase of: *efforts to decelerate inflation.* —*v.i.* **3.** to slow down: *The plane decelerated just before landing.* [1895–1900; DE- + (AC)CELERATE] —**de·cel′er·a′tion,** *n.* —**de·cel′er·a′tor,** *n.*

de·cel·er·om·e·ter (dē sel′ə rom′i tər), *n.* a device that measures the rate of deceleration, as of a vehicle. [1920–25; DECELER(ATION) + -O- + -METER]

de·cel·er·on (dē sel′ə ron′), *n. Aeron.* an aileron that acts as a brake. [b. DECELERATE and AILERON]

de·cem (de′kem; *Eng.* des′em), *adj. Latin.* ten.

De·cem·ber (di sem′bər), *n.* the twelfth month of the year, containing 31 days. *Abbr.:* Dec. [bef. 1000; ME *decembre* < OF < L *december* (s. *decembr-*) the tenth month of the early Roman year, appar. < **dec(em)-membri-*, equiv. to *decem* TEN + **-membri-* < *mens-* month + *-ri-* suffix (with *-sr-* > *-br-* and assimilation of nasal)]

De·cem·brist (di sem′brist), *n. Russ. Hist.* a participant in the conspiracy and insurrection against Nicholas I on his accession in December, 1825. [1880–85; trans. of Russ *dekabrist.* See DECEMBER, -IST]

de·cem·vir (di sem′vər), *n., pl.* **-virs, -vi·ri** (-və rī′). **1.** a member of a permanent board or a special commission of ten members in ancient Rome, esp. the commission that drew up Rome's first code of law. **2.** a member of any council or ruling body of ten. [1570–80; < L, orig. pl. *decemvirī*, equiv. to *decem* TEN + *virī* men] —**de·cem′vi·ral,** *adj.*

de·cem·vi·rate (di sem′vər it, -və rāt′), *n.* **1.** a board or group of decemvirs. **2.** the office or government of decemvirs. [1610–20; < L *decemvirātus.* See DECEMVIR, -ATE[3]]

de·cen·cy (dē′sən sē), *n., pl.* **-cies. 1.** the state or quality of being decent. **2.** conformity to the recognized standard of propriety, good taste, modesty, etc. **3. decencies, a.** the recognized standards of decent or proper behavior; proprieties: *The least you can expect from them is some respect for the decencies.* **b.** the requirements or amenities for decent or comfortable living: *to be able to afford the decencies.* [1560–70; < L *decentia* comeliness, decency, equiv. to *decent-* (s. of *decēns*) fitting (see DECENT) + *-ia* n. suffix]
—**Syn. 2.** decorum, respectability, gentility.

de·cen·na·ry (di sen′ə rē), *n., pl.* **-ries,** *adj.* —*n.* **1.** a decennium. —*adj.* **2.** pertaining to a period of ten years; decennial. [1815–25; < L *decenn(is)* of ten years (*dec(em)* TEN + *-ennis*, comb. form of *annus* a year) + -ARY]

de·cen·ni·al (di sen′ē əl), *adj.* **1.** of or for ten years. **2.** occurring every ten years. —*n.* **3.** a decennial anniversary. **4.** its celebration. [1650–60; < L *decenni(um)* a period of ten years (*decenn(is)* DECENNARY + *-ium* -IUM) + -AL[1]] —**de·cen′ni·al·ly,** *adv.*

de·cen·ni·um (di sen′ē əm), *n., pl.* **-cen·ni·ums, -cen·ni·a** (-sen′ē ə). a period of ten years; a decade. [1675–85; < L; see DECENNIAL]

de·cent (dē′sənt), *adj.* **1.** conforming to the recognized standard of propriety, good taste, modesty, etc., as in behavior or speech. **2.** respectable; worthy: *a decent family.* **3.** adequate; fair; passable: *a decent wage.* **4.** kind; obliging; generous: *It was very decent of him to lend me his watch.* **5.** suitable; appropriate: *She did not have a decent coat for the cold winter.* **6.** of fairly attractive appearance: *a decent face.* **7.** *Informal.* wearing enough clothing to appear in public. **8.** *Slang.* great; wonderful. [1485–95; < L *decent-* (s. of *decēns*) fitting (prp. of *decēre* to be fitting; see -ENT), akin to *decus* honor] —**de′cent·ly,** *adv.* —**de′cent·ness,** *n.*
—**Syn. 1.** seemly, proper, decorous. **5.** apt, fit, becoming. —**Ant. 1.** unseemly. **5.** inappropriate.

de·cen·ter (dē sen′tər), *v.t.* **1.** to put out of center. **2.** to make eccentric. Also, *esp. Brit.,* **decentre.** [1885–90; DE- + CENTER]

de·cen·tral·ize (dē sen′trə līz′), *v.,* **-ized, -iz·ing.** —*v.t.* **1.** to distribute the administrative powers or functions of (a central authority) over a less concentrated area: *to decentralize the national government.* **2.** to disperse (something) from an area of concentration: *to decentralize the nation's industry.* —*v.i.* **3.** to undergo decentralization: *The city government is looking for ways to decentralize.* Also, *esp. Brit.,* **de·cen′tral·ise′.** [1850–55; DE- + CENTRALIZE] —**de·cen′tral·ist,** *n.* —**de·cen′tral·i·za′tion,** *n.*

de·cen·tre (dē sen′tər), *v.t.,* **-tred, -tring.** *Chiefly Brit.* decenter.

de·cep·tion (di sep′shən), *n.* **1.** the act of deceiving; the state of being deceived. **2.** something that deceives or is intended to deceive; fraud; artifice. [1400–50; late ME *decepcioun* < OF < LL *dēceptiōn-* (s. of *dēceptiō*), equiv. to L *dēcept(us)* (ptp. of *dēcipere;* see DECEIVE) + *-iōn-* -ION]
—**Syn. 2.** trick, stratagem, ruse, wile, hoax, imposture.

decep′tion bed′, any of various kinds of concealed or disguised beds designed in the 18th century.

decep′tion ta′ble, a table of the 18th century made so as to conceal its true function, as in serving as a cabinet for a chamber pot.

de·cep·tive (di sep′tiv), *adj.* **1.** apt or tending to deceive: *The enemy's peaceful overtures may be deceptive.* **2.** perceptually misleading: *It looks like a curved line, but it's deceptive.* [1605–15; < ML *dēceptīvus*, equiv. to L *dēcept(us)* (see DECEPTION) + *-īvus* -IVE] —**de·cep′tive·ly,** *adv.* —**de·cep′tive·ness,** *n.*
—**Syn. 1.** delusive, fallacious, specious.

decep′tive ca′dence, *Music.* a cadence consisting of a dominant harmony followed by a resolution to a harmony other than the tonic.

de·cer·e·brate (*v.* dē ser′ə brāt′; *n.* dē ser′ə brāt′, -brit), *v.,* **-brat·ed, -brat·ing,** *n.* —*v.t.* **1.** *Surg.* to remove the cerebrum. —*n.* **2.** a decerebrated animal. **3.** a person who, because of brain injury, exhibits behavior characteristic of a decerebrated animal. [1895–1900; DE- + CEREBR- + -ATE[1]] —**de·cer′e·bra′tion,** *n.*

de·cern (di sûrn′), *v.i.* **1.** *Scots Law.* to enter a judicial decree. —*v.t.* **2.** *Archaic.* to discern. [1400–50; late ME *decernen* to decide < OF *decerner* < L *dēcernere*, equiv. to *dē-* DE- + *cernere* to separate, decide]

de·cer·ti·fy (dē sûr′tə fī′), *v.t.,* **-fied, -fy·ing.** to withdraw certification from. [1915–20; DE- + CERTIFY] —**de·cer·ti·fi·ca·tion** (dē sûr′tə fə kā′shən, dē′sər-tif′ə-), *n.*

de·chlo·ri·nate (dē klôr′ə nāt′, -klōr′-), *v.t.,* **-at·ed, -at·ing.** *Chem.* to remove the chlorine from (a substance, as water): *to dechlorinate tap water for use in an aquarium.* [1940–45; DE- + CHLORINATE] —**de·chlo′ri·na′tion,** *n.*

deci-, a combining form meaning "tenth," used in words denoting units of the metric system (*deciliter*); on this model, extended to other systems (*decibel*). Cf. **deca-.** [< F *déci-* < L *decimus* tenth]

dec·i·bar (des′ə bär′), *n. Physics.* a centimeter-gram-second unit of pressure, equal to $^1/_{10}$ bar or 100,000 dynes per square centimeter. [1905–10; DECI- + BAR[1]]

dec·i·bel (des′ə bel′, -bəl), *n. Physics.* **1.** a unit used to express the intensity of a sound wave, equal to 20 times the common logarithm of the ratio of the pressure pro-

de·merge′, *v.t.,* **-merged, -merg·ing.**
de·merg′er, *n.*
de·met′ro·pol′i·tan·i·za′tion, *n.*
de·mist′, *v.t.*
de·mois′tur·ize′, *v.t.,* **-ized, -iz·ing.**
de·mois′tur·iz′er, *n.*
de·moth′, *v.t.*
de·mo′ti·vate′, *v.t.,* **-vat·ed, -vat·ing.**
de·mo′ti·va′tion, *n.*
de·mo′ti·va′tor, *n.*
de·myth′i·ci·za′tion, *n.*
de·myth′i·cize′, *v.t.,* **-cized, -ciz·ing.**
de·myth′i·fi·ca′tion, *n.*
de·myth′i·fy, *v.t.,* **-fied, -fy·ing.**
de·nic′o·tin·ize′, *v.t.,* **-ized, -iz·ing.**
de·nor′mal·i·za′tion, *n.*
de·num′ber, *v.t.*
de′-ob·jec′ti·fi·ca′tion, *n.*

duced by the sound wave to a reference pressure, usually 0.0002 microbar. **2.** a unit of power ratio, the number of units being equal to a constant times the logarithm to the base 10 of the intensities of two sources. **3.** a unit used to compare two voltages or currents, equal to 20 times the common logarithm of the ratio of the voltages or currents measured across equal resistances. *Abbr.:* dB, db [1925–30; DECI- + BEL]

de•cid•a•ble (di sī′də bəl), *adj.* **1.** capable of being decided. **2.** *Logic.* (of an axiom, proposition, etc.) having the property that its consistency or inconsistency with the axioms of a given logical system is determinable. [1585–95; DECIDE + -ABLE] —**de•cid′a•bil′i•ty,** *n.*

de•cide (di sīd′), *v.,* **-cid•ed, -cid•ing.** —*v.t.* **1.** to solve or conclude (a question, controversy, or struggle) by giving victory to one side: *The judge decided the case in favor of the plaintiff.* **2.** to determine or settle (something in dispute or doubt): *to decide an argument.* **3.** to bring (a person) to a decision; persuade or convince: *The new evidence decided him.* —*v.i.* **4.** to settle something in dispute or doubt: *The judge decided in favor of the plaintiff.* **5.** to make a judgment or determine a preference; come to a conclusion. [1350–1400; ME *deciden* < MF *decider* < L *dēcīdere* lit., to cut off, equiv. to *dē-* DE- + *-cīdere* (comb. form of *caedere* to cut)] —**de•cid′er,** *n.*
—**Syn. 1.** DECIDE, RESOLVE, DETERMINE imply settling upon a purpose and being able to adhere to it. To DECIDE is to make up one's mind as to what shall be done and the way to do it: *He decided to go today.* To RESOLVE is to show firmness of purpose: *He resolved to ask for a promotion.* To DETERMINE is to make up one's mind and then to stick to a fixed or settled purpose: *determined to maintain his position at all costs.*

de•cid•ed (di sī′did), *adj.* **1.** in no way uncertain or ambiguous; unquestionable; unmistakable: *a decided victory.* **2.** free from hesitation or wavering; resolute; determined: *a decided approach to a problem.* [1780–90; DECIDE + -ED[2]] —**de•cid′ed•ly,** *adv.* —**de•cid′ed•ness,** *n.*
—**Syn. 1.** undeniable, indisputable, positive, certain, pronounced, definite, sure, indubitable. **2.** resolved, unhesitating, unwavering. —**Ant. 1, 2.** uncertain.

de•cid•ing (di sī′ding), *adj.* that settles a question or dispute or leads to a final decision; determining; decisive: *the deciding vote; The weather will be the deciding factor as to whether we have the picnic or not.* [1650–60; DECIDE + -ING[2]] —**de•cid′ing•ly,** *adv.*

de•cid•u•a (di sij′o͞o ə), *n., pl.* **-cid•u•as, -cid•u•ae** (-sij′o͞o ē′). *Embryol.* the endometrium of a pregnant uterus that in many of the higher mammals is cast off at parturition. [1775–85; < NL, n. use of fem. of L *dēciduus* falling; see DECIDUOUS] —**de•cid′u•al,** *adj.*

de•cid•u•ate (di sij′o͞o it), *adj. Anat., Zool.* **1.** having or characterized by a decidua. **2.** (of a placenta) partly formed from the decidua. **3.** deciduous (def. 2). [1865–70; < NL *dēciduātus,* equiv. to *dēcidua* DECIDUA + L *-ātus* -ATE[1]]

de•cid•u•i•tis (di sij′o͞o ī′tis), *n. Pathol.* inflammation of the decidua. [< NL; see DECIDUA, -ITIS]

de•cid•u•ous (di sij′o͞o əs), *adj.* **1.** shedding the leaves annually, as certain trees and shrubs. **2.** falling off or shed at a particular season, stage of growth, etc., as leaves, horns, or teeth. **3.** not permanent; transitory. [1650–60; < L *dēciduus* tending to fall, falling, equiv. to *dēcid(ere)* to fall off, down (*dē-* DE- + *-cidere,* comb. form of *cadere* to fall) + *-uus* deverbal adj. suffix; see -OUS] —**de•cid′u•ous•ly,** *adv.* —**de•cid′u•ous•ness,** *n.*

decid′uous tooth′. See **milk tooth.**

dec•i•gram (des′i gram′), *n.* a unit of mass or weight equal to 1/10 gram (1.543 grains). *Abbr.:* dg Also, *esp. Brit.,* **dec′i•gramme′.** [1800–10; < F *décigramme.* See DECI-, -GRAM[2]]

dec•ile (des′il, -īl), *n. Statistics.* one of the values of a variable that divides the distribution of the variable into ten groups having equal frequencies. [1880–85; DEC- + -ILE]

dec•i•li•ter (des′ə lē′tər), *n.* a unit of capacity equal to 1/10 liter (6.102 cu. in., or 3.381 U.S. fluid ounces). *Abbr.:* dl Also, *esp. Brit.,* **dec′i•li′tre.** [1795–1805; < F *décilitre.* See DECI-, LITER]

de•cil•lion (di sil′yən), *n.* **1.** a cardinal number represented in the U.S. by 1 followed by 33 zeros, and in Great Britain by 1 followed by 60 zeros. —*adj.* **2.** amounting to one decillion in number. [1835–45; < L *dec(em)* TEN + *-illion,* as in *million*] —**de•cil′lionth,** *adj., n.*

dec•i•mal (des′ə məl, des′məl), *adj.* **1.** pertaining to tenths or to the number 10. **2.** proceeding by tens: *a decimal system.* —*n.* **3.** See **decimal fraction.** [1600–10; < ML *decimālis* of tenths, equiv. to L *decim(a)* tenth (deriv. of *decem* TEN) + *-ālis* -AL[1]] —**dec′i•mal•ly,** *adv.*

dec′imal classifica′tion. See **Dewey decimal classification.** [1875–80]

dec′imal frac′tion, *Arith.* a fraction whose denominator is some power of 10, usually indicated by a dot (**dec′imal point′** or **point**) written before the numerator: as 0.4 = 4/10; 0.126 = 126/1000. Cf. **common fraction, nonterminating decimal, terminating decimal.** [1650–60]

dec•i•mal•ize (des′ə mə līz′, des′mə-), *v.t.,* **-ized, -iz•ing.** to reduce to a decimal system. Also, *esp. Brit.,* **dec′i•mal•ise′.** [1855–60; DECIMAL + -IZE] —**dec′i•mal•i•za′tion,** *n.*

dec′imal sys′tem, a system of counting or measurement, the units of which are powers of 10: the numerical system in common worldwide use. [1835–45]

dec•i•mate (des′ə māt′), *v.t.,* **-mat•ed, -mat•ing.** **1.** to destroy a great number or proportion of: *The population was decimated by a plague.* **2.** to select by lot and kill every tenth person of. **3.** *Obs.* to take a tenth of or from. [1590–1600; < L *decimātus,* ptp. of *decimāre* to punish every tenth man chosen by lot, v. deriv. of *decimus* tenth, deriv. of *decem* TEN; see -ATE[1]] —**dec′i•ma′tion,** *n.* —**dec′i•ma′tor,** *n.*
—**Usage.** The earliest English sense of DECIMATE is "to select by lot and execute every tenth soldier of (a unit)." The extended sense "destroy a great number or proportion of" developed in the 19th century: *Cholera decimated the urban population.* Because the etymological sense of one-tenth remains to some extent, DECIMATE is not ordinarily used with exact fractions or percentages: *Drought has destroyed* (not *decimated*) *nearly 80 percent of the cattle.*

dé•cime (dā sēm′), *n., pl.* ***-cimes*** (-sēm′). *French.* a former copper or bronze coin of France issued from 1795 to 1801 and from 1814 to 1815, the 10th part of a franc, equal in value to 10 centimes.

dec•i•me•ter (des′ə mē′tər), *n.* a unit of length equal to 1/10 meter. *Abbr.:* dm Also, *esp. Brit.,* **dec′i•me′tre.** [1800–10; < F *décimètre.* See DECI-, METER[1]]

dec•i•mus (des′ə məs; *Lat.* dek′i mo͞os′), *adj.* (in prescriptions) tenth. [< L]

dec•i•nor•mal (des′ə nôr′məl), *adj. Chem.* (of a solution) containing 1/10 the equivalent weight of solute per liter of solution. [1860–65; DECI- + NORMAL]

de•ci•pher (di sī′fər), *v.t.* **1.** to make out the meaning of (poor or partially obliterated writing, etc.): *to decipher a hastily scribbled note.* **2.** to discover the meaning of (anything obscure or difficult to trace or understand): *to decipher hieroglyphics.* **3.** to interpret by the use of a key, as something written in cipher: *to decipher a secret message.* **4.** *Obs.* to depict; portray. [1520–30; trans. of MF *déchiffrer.* See DE-, CIPHER] —**de•ci′pher•a•ble,** *adj.* —**de•ci′pher•a•bil′i•ty,** *n.* —**de•ci′pher•er,** *n.* —**de•ci′pher•ment,** *n.*
—**Syn. 2.** comprehend, solve, unravel, explain.

de•ci•sion (di sizh′ən), *n.* **1.** the act or process of deciding; determination, as of a question or doubt, by making a judgment: *They must make a decision between these two contestants.* **2.** the act of or need for making up one's mind: *This is a difficult decision.* **3.** something that is decided; resolution: *He made a poor decision.* **4.** a judgment, as one formally pronounced by a court. **5.** the quality of being decided; firmness: *He spoke with decision.* **6.** the final score in any sport or contest: *The decision was 5 to 4 in favor of the home team.* **7.** *Boxing.* the awarding of a victory in a match not decided by a knockout or technical knockout, usually through a vote of the referee and judges. —*v.t.* **8.** *Boxing.* to win a victory over (one's opponent) by a point score rather than a knockout. [1425–75; late ME *decisioun* < MF < L *dēcīsiōn-* (s. of *dēcīsiō*) lit., a cutting off, equiv. to *dēcīs(us)* (ptp. of *dēcīdere;* see DECIDE) + *-iōn-* -ION] —**de•ci′sion•al,** *adj.*
—**Syn. 4.** ruling, verdict, finding, decree.

deci′sion proce′dure, *Logic.* a procedure, as an algorithm, for determining in a finite number of steps the validity of any of a certain class of propositions. [1940–45]

deci′sion the′ory, *Statistics.* the theory of making decisions based on assigning probabilities to various factors and assigning numerical consequences to the outcome. [1960–65]

deci′sion tree′, *Logic.* a tree diagram in which the selection of each branch requires that some type of logical decision be made. [1965–70] —**de•ci′sion-tree′,** *adj.*

de•ci•sive (di sī′siv), *adj.* **1.** having the power or quality of deciding; putting an end to controversy; crucial or most important: *Your argument was the decisive one.* **2.** characterized by or displaying no or little hesitation; resolute; determined: *The general was known for his decisive manner.* **3.** indisputable; definite: *a decisive defeat.* **4.** unsurpassable; commanding: *a decisive lead in the voting.* [1605–15; < ML *dēcīsīvus,* equiv. to L *dēcīs(us)* (see DECISION) + *-īvus* -IVE] —**de•ci′sive•ly,** *adv.* —**de•ci′sive•ness,** *n.*
—**Syn. 1.** conclusive, final. **2.** firm.

De•cius (dē′shəs, desh′əs), *n.* (*Gaius Messius Quintus Trajanus Decius*) A.D. c201–251, emperor of Rome 249–251.

deck (dek), *n.* **1.** *Naut.* **a.** a floorlike surface wholly or partially occupying one level of a hull, superstructure, or deckhouse, generally cambered, and often serving as a member for strengthening the structure of a vessel. **b.** the space between such a surface and the next such surface above: *Our stateroom was on B deck.* **2.** any open platform suggesting an exposed deck of a ship. **3.** an open, unroofed porch or platform extending from a house or other building. Cf. **sun deck.** **4.** any level, tier, or vertical section, as of a structure or machine. **5.** See **flight deck** (def. 2). **6.** a flat or nearly flat watertight surface, as at the top of a French roof. **7.** a floor or roof surface composed of decking units. **8.** *Meteorol.* cloud deck. See **cloud layer.** **9.** *Slang.* a small packet of a narcotic, esp. heroin. **10.** a pack of playing cards. **11.** *Print.* bank[3] (def. 8). **12.** Also called **rear deck.** the cover of a space behind the backseat of an automobile or the space itself. **13.** *Library Science.* a level of book shelving and associated facilities in the stacks of a library, as one of a series of floors or tiers. **14.** See **cutter deck.** **15.** a cassette deck or tape deck. **16. clear the decks, a.** to prepare for combat, as by removing all unnecessary gear. **b.** to prepare for some activity or work, as by getting rid of hindrances. **17. hit the deck,** *Slang.* **a.** *Naut.* to rise from bed. **b.** to fall, drop, or be knocked to the ground or floor. **18. on deck, a.** *Baseball.* next at bat; waiting one's turn to bat. **b.** *Informal.* next in line; coming up; scheduled. **c.** *Informal.* prepared to act or work; ready. **19. play with** or **have a full deck,** *Slang.* to be sane, rational, or reasonably intelligent: *Whoever dreamed up this scheme wasn't playing with a full deck.* **20. stack the deck.** See **stack** (def. 23). —*adj.* **21.** *Civ. Engin.* (of a bridge truss) having a deck or floor upon or above the structure. Cf. **through** (def. 23). —*v.t.* **22.** to clothe or attire (people) or array (rooms, houses, etc.) in something ornamental or decorative (often fol. by *out*): *We were all decked out in our Sunday best. The church was decked with holly for the holiday season.* **23.** to furnish with a deck. **24.** *Informal.* to knock down; floor: *The champion decked the challenger in the first round.* [1425–75; (n.) late ME *dekke* material for covering < MD *dec* covering, roof; (v.) < D *dekken* to cover; c. G *decken;* cf. THATCH]
—**Syn. 22.** bedeck, garnish, trim, bedizen, adorn, embellish; dress.

deck′ bolt′, *Shipbuilding.* a flat-headed bolt for fastening down deck planking.

deck′ chair′, a folding chair, usually with arms and a full-length leg rest, commonly used for lounging on the decks of passenger ships. Also called **steamer chair.** [1880–85]

deck•el (dek′əl), *n. Papermaking.* deckle.

deck•er (dek′ər), *n.* something, as a ship or bed, having a specified number of decks, floors, levels, or the like (used in combination): *The cruise ship is a five-decker.* [1785–95; DECK + -ER[1]]

Deck•er (dek′ər), *n.* **Thomas.** See **Dekker, Thomas.**

deck′ gang′, *Naut.* **1.** (on a ship) the sailors who are on duty but not on watch. **2.** the longshoremen working on board a ship during loading and unloading.

deck′ hand′, *Naut.* a sailor whose duties are performed on deck. [1835–45, *Amer.*]

deck•head (dek′hed′), *n. Naut.* the undersurface of a deck. [1880–85; DECK + HEAD]

deck′ hook′, *Naut.* hook (def. 16). [1840–50]

deck•house (dek′hous′), *n., pl.* **-hous•es** (-hou′ziz). *Naut.* any enclosed structure projecting above the weather deck of a vessel and, usually, surrounded by exposed deck area on all sides. Cf. **superstructure** (def. 4). [1855–60; DECK + HOUSE]

deck•ing (dek′ing), *n.* **1.** material, as paper or fiberboard, treated in various ways as a waterproof covering for a deck or roof. **2.** material of concrete, asbestos, steel, or the like, in the form of self-supporting flooring or roofing units laid between joists or rafters. [1525–35; DECK + -ING[1]]

deck•le (dek′əl), *n. Papermaking.* **1.** a board, usually of stainless steel, fitted under part of the wire in a Fourdrinier machine for supporting the pulp stack before it is sufficiently formed to support itself on the wire. **2.** See **deckle edge.** Also, **deckel.** [1800–10; < G *Deckel* cover, lid, equiv. to *deck(en)* to cover (see DECK) + *-el* n. suffix]

deck′le edge′, the irregular, untrimmed edge of handmade paper, often used for ornamental effect in fine books and stationery, now often produced artificially on machine-made paper. Also called **deckle.** [1870–75]

deck•le-edged (dek′əl ejd′), *adj.* having a deckle edge: *deckle-edged paper for stationery.* [1885–90]

deck′ lid′, the hinged lid forming the upper surface of an automobile deck. Also, **deck′lid′.**

deck′ light′, *Naut.* **1.** a skylight for a 'tween deck, built flush with the upper deck. **2.** any light for illuminating the deck of a ship. [1840–50]

deck′ load′, *Naut.* cargo carried on an open deck of a ship. [1750–60]

deck′ log′, *Naut.* a log filled in by the officer of the watch at the end of each watch, giving details of weather, navigation, unusual happenings, etc.

deck′ of′ficer, *Naut.* any officer whose responsibilities include navigation, cargo handling, etc.

deck′ pas′sage, overnight accommodation on a vessel other than in a regular sleeping space. [1820–30, *Amer.*] —**deck′ pas′senger.**

deck′ plate′, *Carpentry.* a purlin plate at the edge of a deck. [1870–75]

deck′ ten′nis, a game played on a small court, usually on the deck of a ship, in which a ring, generally of rubber or Manila rope, is alternately thrown and caught, using only one hand, by two opponents standing on opposite sides of a net. [1925–30]

deck′ watch′, (on a ship) a precision watch used on deck for navigational purposes to avoid disturbing the chronometer. [1855–60]

decl., declension.

de•claim (di klām′), *v.i.* **1.** to speak aloud in an oratorical manner; make a formal speech: *Brutus declaimed from the steps of the Roman senate building.* **2.** to inveigh (usually fol. by *against*): *He declaimed against the high rents in slums.* **3.** to speak or write for oratorical effect, as without sincerity or sound argument. —*v.t.* **4.** to utter aloud in an oratorical manner: *to declaim a speech.* [1350–1400; ME *declamen* < L *dēclāmāre,* equiv. to *dē-* DE- + *clāmāre* to cry, shout; see CLAIM] —**de•claim′er,** *n.*

dec•la•ma•tion (dek′lə mā′shən), *n.* **1.** the act or art

CONCISE PRONUNCIATION KEY: *act, cāpe, dâre, pärt; set, ēqual; if, īce; ox, ōver, ôrder, oil, bo͝ok, bo͞ot, out; up, ûrge; child; sing; shoe; thin, that;* zh as in *treasure.* ə = *a* as in *alone, e* as in *system, i* as in *easily, o* as in *gallop, u* as in *circus;* [ə] as in *fire* (fī[ə]r), *hour* (ou[ə]r). l and n can serve as syllabic consonants, as in *cradle* (krād′l), and *button* (but′n). See the full key inside the front cover.

de′-pa•ro′chi•al•ize′, *v.t.,* **-ized, -iz•ing.**
de•pest′, *v.t.*
de•po′lar•i•za′tion, *n.*
de•po′lar•ize′, *v.t.,* **-ized, -iz•ing.**
de•po′lar•iz′er, *n.*
de•pol′ish, *v.t.*
de′po•lit′i•cal•i•za′tion, *n.*
de′po•lit′i•cal•ize′, *v.t.,* **-ized, -iz•ing.**
de′po•lit′i•ci•za′tion, *n.*
de′po•lit′i•cize′, *v.t.,* **-cized, -ciz•ing.**
de•pop′u•lar•ize′, *v.t.,* **-ized, -iz•ing.**
de•pot′, *v.t.,* **-pot•ted, -pot•ting.**
de•pow′er, *v.t.*
de′pro•vin′cial•i•za′tion, *n.*
de′pro•vin′cial•ize′, *v.t.,* **-ized, -iz•ing.**
de•pulp′, *v.t.*
de•re′gal•ize′, *v.t.,* **-ized, -iz•ing.**
de•reg′u•la′tion•ist, *n.*
de′re•strict′, *v.t.*

of declaiming. **2.** exercise in oratory or elocution, as in the recitation of a classic speech. **3.** speech or writing for oratorical effect. **4.** *Music.* the proper enunciation of the words, as in recitative. [1350–1400; < L *dēclāmātiōn-* (s. of *dēclāmātiō*), equiv. to *dēclāmāt(us)* (ptp. of *dēclāmāre* to DECLAIM; see -ATE[1]) + *-iōn-* -ION]

de•clam•a•to•ry (di klam′ə tôr′ē, -tōr′ē), *adj.* **1.** pertaining to or characterized by declamation. **2.** merely oratorical or rhetorical; stilted: *a pompous, declamatory manner of speech.* [1575–85; < L *dēclāmātōrius,* equiv. to *dēclāmā(re)* (see DECLAIM) + *-tōrius* -TORY[1]]

de•clar•ant (di klâr′ənt), *n.* **1.** a person who declares or makes a declaration or statement. **2.** *Law.* an alien who has formally declared his or her intention before a court of record to become a citizen of the U.S. [1675–85; DECLARE + -ANT]

dec•la•ra•tion (dek′lə rā′shən), *n.* **1.** the act of declaring; announcement: *a declaration of a dividend.* **2.** a positive, explicit, or formal statement; proclamation: *a declaration of war.* **3.** something that is announced, avowed, or proclaimed. **4.** a document embodying or displaying an announcement or proclamation: *He posted the declaration in a public place.* **5.** *Law.* **a.** a formal statement presenting the plaintiff's claim in an action. **b.** a complaint. **c.** a statement, esp. by a witness. **d.** a statement made to an official. **6.** *Cards.* **a.** *Bridge.* a bid, esp. the successful bid. **b.** the statement during the game of the points earned by a player, in bezique or other games. **7.** a statement of goods, income, etc., esp. for the assessment of duty, tax, or the like. [1300–50; ME *declaracioun* (< AF) < L *dēclārātiōn-* (s. of *dēclārātiō*) explanation, equiv. to *dēclārāt(us)* (ptp. of *dēclārāre* to explain, DECLARE; see -ATE[1]) + *-iōn-* -ION]
—Syn. 4. notice, bulletin; manifesto, edict.

Declara′tion of Indepen′dence, 1. the public act by which the Second Continental Congress, on July 4, 1776, declared the Colonies to be free and independent of England. **2.** the document embodying it.

de•clar•a•tive (di klar′ə tiv), *adj.* serving to declare, make known, or explain: *a declarative statement.* Also, **de•clar•a•to•ry** (di klar′ə tôr′ē, -tōr′ē). [1530–40; < L *dēclārātīvus* explanatory, equiv. to *dēclārāt(us)* (see DECLARATION) + *-īvus* -IVE] **—de•clar′a•tive•ly,** *adv.*

declar′atory judg′ment, *Law.* a judgment that merely decides the rights of parties in a given transaction, situation, or dispute but does not order any action or award damages.

de•clare (di klâr′), *v.,* **-clared, -clar•ing.** *—v.t.* **1.** to make known or state clearly, esp. in explicit or formal terms: *to declare one's position in a controversy.* **2.** to announce officially; proclaim: *to declare a state of emergency; to declare a winner.* **3.** to state emphatically: *He declared that the allegation was a lie.* **4.** to manifest; reveal; show: *Her attendance at the rally declared her political allegiance.* **5.** to make due statement of, esp. goods for duty or income for taxation. **6.** to make (a dividend) payable. **7.** *Bridge.* to bid (a trump suit or no-trump). *—v.i.* **8.** to make a declaration. **9.** to proclaim oneself (usually fol. by *for* or *against*): *He declared against the proposal.* **10.** *Cricket.* (of a team) to surrender a turn at bat in an innings before ten players are put out. [1275–1325; ME *declaren* < L *dēclārāre* to explain, equiv. to *dē-* DE- + *clārāre* to make clear (*clār(us)* CLEAR + *-āre* inf. suffix)] **—de•clar′a•ble,** *adj.*
—Syn. 3. aver, asseverate, state. DECLARE, AFFIRM, ASSERT, PROTEST imply making something known emphatically, openly, or formally. To DECLARE is to make known, sometimes in the face of actual or potential contradiction: *to declare someone the winner of a contest.* To AFFIRM is to make a statement based on one's reputation for knowledge or veracity, or so related to a generally recognized truth that denial is not likely: *to affirm the necessity of high standards.* To ASSERT is to state boldly, usually without other proof than personal authority or conviction: *to assert that the climate is changing.* To PROTEST is to affirm publicly, as if in the face of doubt: *to protest that a newspaper account is misleading.* **4.** disclose, publish. **—Ant. 3.** deny.

de•clared (di klârd′), *adj.* publicly avowed or professed; self-confessed: *a declared liberal.* [1645–55; DECLARE + -ED[2]] **—de•clar•ed•ly** (di klâr′id lē), *adv.*

de•clar•er (di klâr′ər), *n.* **1.** a person or thing that declares. **2.** *Bridge.* the player who plays the contract; dummy's partner. [1520–30; DECLARE + -ER[1]]

de•class (dē klas′, -kläs′), *v.t.* to remove or degrade from one's social class, position, or rank; lower in status. [1885–90; < F *déclasser.* See DE-, CLASS]

dé•clas•sé (dā′kla sā′, -klä-; *Fr.* dā klä sā′), *adj.* **1.** reduced to or having low or lower status: *a once-chic restaurant that had become completely déclassé.* **2.** reduced or belonging to a lower or low social class, position, or rank. [1885–1890; < F, ptp. of *déclasser.* See DE-, CLASS]

de•clas•si•fy (dē klas′ə fī′), *v.t.,* **-fied, -fy•ing.** to remove the classification from (information, a document, etc.) that restricts access in terms of secrecy, confidentiality, etc. Cf. **classification** (def. 5). [1860–65; DE- + CLASSIFY] **—de•clas′si•fi′a•ble,** *adj.* **—de•clas•si•fi•ca•tion** (dē klas′ə fi kā′shən), *n.*

de•clen•sion (di klen′shən), *n.* **1.** *Gram.* **a.** the inflection of nouns, pronouns, and adjectives for categories such as case and number. **b.** the whole set of inflected forms of such a word, or the recital thereof in a fixed order. **c.** a class of such words having similar sets of inflected forms: *the Latin second declension.* **2.** an act or instance of declining. **3.** a bending, sloping, or moving downward: *land with a gentle declension toward the sea.* **4.** deterioration; decline. **5.** deviation, as from a standard. [1400–50; late ME *declenson, declynson* (with suffix later assimilated to -SION), by stress retraction and syncope < OF *declinaison* < L *dēclīnātiō* DECLINATION]

de•clen•sion•al (di klen′shə nl), *adj.* of or pertaining to grammatical declension. [1855–60; DECLENSION + -AL[1]] **—de•clen′sion•al•ly,** *adv.*

de•clin•a•ble (di klī′nə bəl), *adj. Gram.* able to be declined. [1520–30; < MF, equiv. to *decliner* to DECLINE + *-able* -ABLE; or DECLINE + -ABLE]

dec•li•nate (dek′lə nāt′, -nit), *adj.* having a downward curve or slope; bending away, as from the horizontal: *a declinate flower.* [1800–10; < L *dēclīnātus,* ptp. of *dēclīnāre.* See DECLINE, -ATE[1]]

dec•li•na•tion (dek′lə nā′shən), *n.* **1.** a bending, sloping, or moving downward. **2.** deterioration; decline. **3.** a swerving or deviating, as from a standard. **4.** a polite refusal. **5.** *Astron.* the angular distance of a heavenly body from the celestial equator, measured on the great circle passing through the celestial pole and the body. **6.** variation (def. 8). **7.** the formal refusal by a nominee of a nomination to public office. [1350–1400; ME *declinacioun* < OF *declinacion* < L *dēclīnātiōn-* (s. of *dēclīnātiō*), equiv. to *dēclīnāt(us),* lit., turned aside (ptp. of *dēclīnāre;* see DECLINE, -ATE[1]) + *-iōn-* -ION] **—dec′li•na′tion•al,** *adj.*

N
A
B
D
E
C
S

declination (def. 5) A, star; B, Earth; angle ABC, declination of star; N, north celestial pole; S, south celestial pole; DE, celestial equator

de•clin•a•to•ry (di klī′nə tôr′ē, -tōr′ē), *adj.* expressing refusal; implying declination. [1665–75; < ML *dēclīnātōrius,* equiv. to L *dēclīnā(re)* (see DECLINE) + *-tōrius* -TORY[1]]

de•clin•a•ture (di klī′nə chər, -chŏŏr′), *n.* the act of refusing. [1630–40; alter. of earlier *declinatour,* influenced by L *dēclīnātūra.* See DECLINATION, -URE]

de•cline (di klīn′), *v.,* **-clined, -clin•ing,** *n.* *—v.t.* **1.** to withhold or deny consent to do, enter into or upon, etc.; refuse: *He declined to say more about it.* **2.** to express inability or reluctance to accept; refuse with courtesy: *to decline an invitation; to decline an offer.* **3.** to cause to slope or incline downward. **4.** *Gram.* **a.** to inflect (a noun, pronoun, or adjective), as Latin *puella,* declined *puella, puellae, puellae, puellam, puella* in the five cases of the singular. **b.** to recite or display all or some subset of the inflected forms of a noun, pronoun, or adjective in a fixed order. *—v.i.* **5.** to express courteous refusal; refuse: *We sent him an invitation but he declined.* **6.** to bend or slant down; slope downward; descend: *The hill declines to the lake.* **7.** (of pathways, routes, objects, etc.) to follow a downward course or path: *The sun declined in the skies.* **8.** to draw toward the close, as the day. **9.** to fail in strength, vigor, character, value, etc.; deteriorate. **10.** to fail or dwindle; sink or fade away: *to decline in popularity.* **11.** to descend, as to an unworthy level; stoop. **12.** *Gram.* to be characterized by declension. *—n.* **13.** a downward slope; declivity. **14.** a downward movement, as of prices or population; diminution: *a decline in the stock market.* **15.** a failing or gradual loss, as in strength, character, power, or value; deterioration: *the decline of the Roman Empire.* **16.** a gradual deterioration of the physical powers, as in later life or in disease: *After his seventieth birthday he went into a decline.* **17.** progress downward or toward the close, as of the sun or the day. **18.** the later years or last part: *He became an editor in the decline of his life.* [1275–1325; (v.) ME *declinen* < OF: to inflect, turn aside, sink < L *dēclīnāre* to slope, incline, bend; cf. Gk *klī́nein* to LEAN[1]; (n.) ME *declin* < OF, deriv. of *decliner*] **—de•clin′er,** *n.*
—Syn. 1. reject. See **refuse**[1]. **9.** degenerate, decay, weaken, diminish, languish. **13.** hill. **15.** retrogression, degeneration, enfeeblement, weakening. **—Ant. 6.** rise. **9.** improve.

Decline′ and Fall′ of the Ro′man Em′pire, The, a history in six volumes (1776–88) by Edward Gibbon.

dec•li•nom•e•ter (dek′lə nom′i tər), *n.* an instrument for measuring magnetic declination. [1855–60; DECLIN(ATION) + -O- + -METER]

de•clive (di klīv′), *adj. Obs.* declivous. [1625–35; < L *dēclīvis* sloping downward; see DECLIVITY]

de•cliv•i•tous (di kliv′i təs), *adj.* having a somewhat steep downward slope. [1790–1800; DECLIVIT(Y) + -OUS] **—de•cliv′i•tous•ly,** *adv.*

de•cliv•i•ty (di kliv′i tē), *n., pl.* **-ties.** a downward slope, as of ground (opposed to *acclivity*). [1605–15; < L *dēclīvitās* a slope, hill, equiv. to *dēclīvi(s)* sloping downward (*dē-* DE- + *clīv(us)* slope, hill + *-is* adj. suffix) + *-tās* -TY]

de•cli•vous (di klī′vəs), *adj.* sloping downward. Also, **de•cli′vent.** [1675–85; < L *dēclīv(is)* (see DECLIVITY) + -OUS]

Dec•lo•my•cin (dek′lō mī′sin), *Pharm., Trademark.* a brand of demeclocycline.

de•clutch (dē kluch′), *v.i.* to release a clutch. [DE- + CLUTCH[1]]

dec•o (dek′ō, dā′kō, dā kō′), *n.* **1.** See **art deco.** *—adj.* **2.** of, pertaining to, or suggestive of art deco design: *The new wallpaper gives the foyer a deco look.* Also, **Dec′o.** [1970–75; by shortening]

de•coct (di kokt′), *v.t.* to extract the flavor or essence of by boiling. [1375–1425; late ME *decocten* < L *dēcoctus* boiled down; see DECOCTION]

de•coc•tion (di kok′shən), *n.* **1.** the act of decocting. **2.** *Pharm.* **a.** an extract obtained by decocting. **b.** water in which a crude vegetable drug has been boiled and which therefore contains the constituents or principles of the substance soluble in boiling water. [1350–1400; ME *decoccioun* < OF *decoction* < LL *dēcoctiōn-* (s. of *dēcoctiō*) a boiling down, equiv. to *dēcoct(us),* ptp. of *dēcoquere* (*dē-* DE- + *coc-,* for *coquere* to COOK + *-tus* ptp. suffix) + *-iōn-* -ION] **—de•coc′tive,** *adj.*

de•code (dē kōd′), *v.,* **-cod•ed, -cod•ing.** *—v.t.* **1.** to translate (data or a message) from a code into the original language or form. **2.** to extract meaning from (spoken or written symbols). **3.** *Television.* to unscramble (an electronic signal) so as to provide a video picture for cable subscribers. *—v.i.* **4.** to work at decoding. [1895–1900; DE- + CODE]

de•cod•er (dē kō′dər), *n.* **1.** a person who decodes messages or the like. **2.** a device for decoding cryptograms, codes, or the like, as an electric or electronic apparatus that transforms arbitrary input signals into letters, words, etc. **3.** *Navig.* an electronic circuit designed to respond only to certain signals and to reject others. **4.** *Computers.* a circuit designed to produce a single output when actuated by a certain combination of inputs. **5.** *Television.* a box attached to a television set containing circuitry to unscramble encoded signals, as cable-television programs or closed captions, so that the signals can be displayed on the screen. [1915–20; DECODE + -ER[1]]

de•co′ic ac′id (di kō′ik), *Chem.* See **capric acid.** [DEC(ANE) + -O- + -IC]

de•col•late[1] (di kol′āt), *v.t.,* **-lat•ed, -lat•ing.** to behead; decapitate. [1590–1600; < L *dēcollātus* (ptp. of *dēcollāre* to behead, equiv. to *dē-* DE- + *coll(āre)* (see COLLAR) + *-ātus* -ATE[1]] **—de•col•la•tion** (dē′kə lā′shən), *n.* **—de′col•la′tor,** *n.*

de•col•late[2] (dek′ə lāt′, dē′kə lāt′, dē kō′lāt, -kol′āt), *v.t.,* **-lat•ed, -lat•ing.** to separate (the copies of multiply paper, continuous forms, or computer printout) into individual sets or sheets. [DE- + COLLATE] **—de′col•la′tor,** *n.*

de•col′late snail′ (dē kol′it, dek′ə lit), a cone-shaped, burrowing snail, *Rumina decollata,* that feeds on common brown garden snails. Also called **decol′lated awl′ snail′.** [< NL *decollata,* the specific epithet; see DECOLLATE[1]]

dé•colle•tage (dā′kol täzh′, -kol ə-, dek′ə lə-; *Fr.* dā kôl tazh′), *n.* **1.** the neckline of a dress cut low in the front or back and often across the shoulders. **2.** a décolleté garment or costume. Also, **de′colle•tage′.** [1890–95; < F, equiv. to *décollet(er)* (see DÉCOLLETÉ) + *-age* -AGE]

dé•colle•té (dā′kol tā′, -kol ə-, dek′ə lə-; *Fr.* dā kôl tā′), *adj.* **1.** (of a garment) low-necked. **2.** wearing a low-necked garment. Also, **de′colle•te′.** [1825–35; < F: ptp. of *décolleter* to bare the neck, equiv. to *dé-* DE- + *collet* COLLAR (see -ET) + *-er* inf. suffix]

de•co•lo•ni•al•ize (dē′kə lō′nē ə līz′), *v.t.,* **-ized, -iz•ing.** to decolonize. Also, *esp. Brit.,* **de′co•lo′ni•al•ise′.** [DE- + COLONIALIZE] **—de′co•lo′ni•al•i•za′tion,** *n.*

de•col•o•nize (dē kol′ə nīz′), *v.,* **-nized, -niz•ing.** *—v.t.* **1.** to release from the status of a colony. **2.** to allow (a colony) to become self-governing or independent. *—v.i.* **3.** to free a colony to become self-governing or independent. Also, *esp. Brit.,* **de•col′o•nise′.** [DE- + COLONIZE] **—de•col′o•ni•za′tion,** *n.*

de•col•or (dē kul′ər), *v.t.* to remove the color from; deprive of color; bleach. Also, *esp. Brit.,* **de•col′our.** [1400–50; late ME *decolouren* < L *dēcolōrāre,* equiv. to *dē-* DE- + *colōrāre* to COLOR] **—de′col•or•a′tion,** *n.*

de•col•or•ant (dē kul′ər ənt), *adj.* **1.** having the property of removing color; bleaching. *—n.* **2.** a decolorant substance or agent. Also, *esp. Brit.,* **de•col′our•ant.** [1860–65; DECOLOR + -ANT]

de•col•or•ize (dē kul′ə rīz′), *v.t.,* **-ized, -iz•ing.** to decolor. Also, *esp. Brit.,* **de•col′or•ise′.** [1830–40; DE- + COLORIZE] **—de•col′or•i•za′tion,** *n.* **—de•col′or•iz′er,** *n.*

de•com•mis•sion (dē′kə mish′ən), *v.t.* **1.** to remove or retire (a ship, airplane, etc.) from active service. **2.** to deactivate; shut down: *to decommission a nuclear power plant.* [1925–30; DE- + COMMISSION]

de•com•pen•sa•tion (dē′kom pən sā′shən), *n. Med.* **1.** the inability of a diseased heart to compensate for its defect. **2.** *Psychol.* a loss of ability to maintain normal or appropriate psychological defenses, sometimes resulting in depression, anxiety, or delusions. [1900–05; DE- + COMPENSATION]

de•com•pose (dē′kəm pōz′), *v.,* **-posed, -pos•ing.** *—v.t.* **1.** to separate or resolve into constituent parts or elements; disintegrate: *The bacteria decomposed the milk into its solid and liquid elements.* *—v.i.* **2.** to rot; putrefy: *The egg began to decompose after a day in the sun.* [1745–55; < F *décomposer,* equiv. to *dé-* DIS-[1] + *composer* to COMPOSE] **—de′com•pos′a•ble,** *adj.* **—de′•com•pos′a•bil′i•ty,** *n.*
—Syn. 1. distill, fractionate, analyze. **2.** See **decay.**

CONCISE ETYMOLOGY KEY: <, descended or borrowed from; >, whence; b., blend of, blended; c., cognate with; cf., compare; deriv., derivative; equiv., equivalent; imit., imitative; obl., oblique; r., replacing; s., stem; sp., spelling, spelled; resp., respelling, respelled; trans., translation; ?, origin unknown; *, unattested; ‡, probably earlier than. See the full key inside the front cover.

de•rit′u•al•ize′, *v.,* **-ized, -iz•ing.**
de•rust′, *v.t.*
de•sat′u•rate′, *v.t.,* **-rat•ed, -rat•ing.**
de•sat′u•ra′tion, *n.*
de•scale′, *v.t.,* **-scaled, -scal•ing.**
de•seed′, *v.t.*
de•sen′sa•tion•al•ize′, *v.t.,* **-ized, -iz•ing.**
de•sex′i•fy′, *v.t.,* **-fied, -fy•ing.**
de•sex′u•al•ize′, *v.t.,* **-ized, -iz•ing.**
de•shell′, *v.t.*
de•silt′, *v.t.*
de•sludge′, *v.t.,* **-sludged, -sludg•ing.**
de•slum′, *v.t.,* **-slummed, -slum•ming.**
de•smog′, *v.t.,* **-smogged, -smog•ging.**
de•sod′, *v.t.,* **-sod•ded, -sod•ding.**
de•sol′der, *v.t.*

de·com·posed (dē′kəm pōzd′), *adj.* **1.** having undergone decomposition. **2.** (of a feather) having the barbs separate, hanging loosely, and not interconnected by barbules. [1840–50; DECOMPOSE + -ED[2]]

de·com·pos·er (dē′kəm pō′zər), *n.* **1.** a person or thing that decomposes. **2.** *Ecology.* an organism, usually a bacterium or fungus, that breaks down the cells of dead plants and animals into simpler substances. [1815–25; DECOMPOSE + -ER[1]]

de·com·po·si·tion (dē′kom pə zish′ən), *n.* **1.** the act or process of decomposing. **2.** the state of being decomposed; decay. [1650–60; prob. < F *décomposition,* deriv. of *décomposer* to DECOMPOSE; see COMPOSITION]

de·com·pound (*v.* dē′kəm pound′; *adj.* dē kom′-pound, dē′kom pound′, -kəm-), *v.t.* **1.** to decompose. **2.** *Obs.* to compound a second or further time. —*adj.* **3.** *Bot.* divided into compound divisions. **4.** composed of compounds the parts of which are also compounds, as a bipinnate leaf. [1605–15; DE- + COMPOUND[1]]

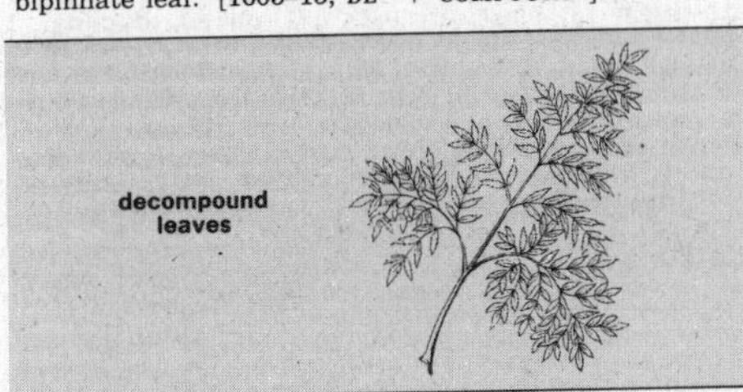

de·com·press (dē′kəm pres′), *v.t.* **1.** to cause to undergo decompression. —*v.i.* **2.** to undergo decompression. **3.** *Informal.* to relax; unwind. [1900–05; trans. of F *décomprimer.* See DE-, COMPRESS] —**de′com·pres′·sive,** *adj.*

de·com·pres·sion (dē′kəm presh′ən), *n.* **1.** the gradual reduction in atmospheric pressure experienced by divers, construction workers, etc., after working in deep water or breathing compressed air. **2.** the act or process of releasing from pressure. **3.** *Surg.* the procedure of relieving increased cranial, cardiac, or orbital pressure. **4.** a state of relief from pressure; a return to normalcy after a stressful period or situation. [1900–05; prob. < F *décompression.* See DE-, COMPRESSION]

decompres′sion cham′ber. See **hyperbaric chamber.** [1930–35]

decompres′sion sick′ness, *Pathol.* aeroembolism (def. 2). [1940–45]

decompres′sion ta′bles. See **dive tables.**

de·con·cen·trate (dē kon′sən trāt′), *v.t.,* **-trat·ed, -trat·ing.** to reduce the power or control of (a corporation, industry, etc.); decentralize. [1885–90; DE- + CONCENTRATE] —**de·con′cen·tra′tion,** *n.*

de·con·di·tion (dē′kən dish′ən), *v.t.* **1.** to diminish the physical strength, stamina, or vitality of; weaken. **2.** to diminish or eliminate the conditioned responses or behavior patterns of. [1935–40; DE- + CONDITION]

de·con·gest (dē′kən jest′), *v.t.* to diminish or end the congestion of. [1955–60; DE- + CONGEST, or by back formation from DECONGESTANT] —**de′con·ges′tion,** *n.*

de·con·ges·tant (dē′kən jes′tənt), *Pharm.* —*adj.* **1.** of or pertaining to a substance that relieves mucus congestion of the upper respiratory tract. —*n.* **2.** any such substance. [1945–50; DE- + CONGEST + -ANT]

de·con·ges·tive (dē′kən jes′tiv), *adj. Med.* relieving or tending to relieve congestion. [1900–05; DE- + CONGESTIVE]

de·con·struct (dē′kən strukt′), *v.t.* to break down into constituent parts; dissect; dismantle. [appar. back formation from DECONSTRUCTION]

de·con·struc·tion (dē′kən struk′shən), *n.* a philosophical and critical movement, starting in the 1960's and esp. applied to the study of literature, that questions all traditional assumptions about the ability of language to represent reality and emphasizes that a text has no stable reference or identification because words essentially only refer to other words and therefore a reader must approach a text by eliminating any metaphysical or ethnocentric assumptions through an active role of defining meaning, sometimes by a reliance on new word construction, etymology, puns, and other word play. [DE- + CONSTRUCTION] —**de′con·struc′tion·ist,** *adj., n.* —**de′con·struc′tive,** *adj.*

de·con·tam·i·nate (dē′kən tam′ə nāt′), *v.t.,* **-nated, -nat·ing. 1.** to make (an object or area) safe for unprotected personnel by removing, neutralizing, or destroying any harmful substance, as radioactive material or poisonous gas. **2.** to make free of contamination; purify: *to decontaminate a sickroom.* [1935–40; DE- + CONTAMINATE] —**de′con·tam′i·na′tion,** *n.* —**de′con·tam′i·na′tive,** *adj.* —**de′con·tam′i·na′tor,** *n.*

de·con·trol (dē′kən trōl′), *v.,* **-trolled, -trol·ling,** *n.* —*v.t.* **1.** to remove controls, esp. government or other official controls, from: *to decontrol prices or rents.* —*n.* **2.** the removal of control. [1915–20; DE- + CONTROL]

dé·cor (dā kôr′, di-, dā′kôr), *n.* **1.** style or mode of decoration, as of a room, building, or the like: *modern office décor; a bedroom having a Spanish décor.* **2.** decoration in general; ornamentation: *beads, baubles, and other décor.* **3.** *Theat.* scenic decoration; scenery. Also, **de·cor′.** [1650–60; < F, deriv. of *décorer* to DECORATE]

dec·o·rate (dek′ə rāt′), *v.t.,* **-rat·ed, -rat·ing. 1.** to furnish or adorn with something ornamental or becoming; embellish: *to decorate walls with murals.* **2.** to plan and execute the design, furnishings, and ornamentation of the interior of (a house, office, apartment, etc.), esp. by selecting colors, fabrics, and style of furniture, by making minor structural changes, etc.: *Their house is decorated in French Provincial style.* **3.** to confer distinction upon by a badge, a medal of honor, etc.: *to decorate a soldier for valor.* [1375–1425; late ME (adj.) < L *decorātus* (ptp. of *decorāre*), equiv. to *decor-* (s. of *decus*) an ornament, splendor, honor (see DECENT) + *-ātus* -ATE[1]]
—**Syn. 1.** ornament, bedeck, trim, garnish, festoon.

dec·o·rat·ed (dek′ə rā′tid), *adj.* (*often cap.*) of pertaining to, or characteristic of the English gothic architecture of the late 13th through the late 14th centuries, characterized by curvilinear tracery, elaborate ornamental sculpture and vaulting, and refinement of stonecutting techniques. [1720–30; DECORATE + -ED[2]]

dec′orated shed′, *Archit.* a contemporary design concept characterized by buildings generally of purely utilitarian design but with fronts intended to give them more grandeur or to announce their functions.

dec·o·ra·tion (dek′ə rā′shən), *n.* **1.** something used for decorating; adornment; embellishment: *The gymnasium was adorned with posters and crepe-paper decorations for the dance.* **2.** the act of decorating. **3.** See **interior decoration. 4.** a badge, medal, etc., conferred and worn as a mark of honor: *a decoration for bravery.* [1575–85; < LL *decorātiōn-* (s. of *decorātiō*) an ornament. See DECORATE, -ION]

Decora′tion Day′. See **Memorial Day** (def. 1).

dec·o·ra·tive (dek′ər ə tiv, dek′rə-, dek′ə rā′-), *adj.* **1.** serving or tending to decorate. **2.** *Fine Arts.* serving only to decorate, in contrast to providing a meaningful experience. [1785–95; DECORATE + -IVE] —**dec′o·ra·tive·ly,** *adv.* —**dec′o·ra·tive·ness,** *n.*

dec·o·ra·tor (dek′ə rā′tər), *n.* **1.** See **interior designer. 2.** a person who decorates. —*adj.* **3.** harmonizing with or suitable for a scheme of interior decoration: *appliances in decorator colors.* [1745–55; DECORATE + -OR[2]]

dec·o·rous (dek′ər əs, di kôr′əs, -kōr′-), *adj.* characterized by dignified propriety in conduct, manners, appearance, character, etc. [1655–65; < L *decōrus* seemly, becoming, deriv. of *decus;* see DECORATE, -OUS] —**dec′o·rous·ly,** *adv.* —**dec′o·rous·ness,** *n.*
—**Syn.** proper, becoming. —**Ant.** undignified.

de·cor·ti·cate (dē kôr′ti kāt′), *v.t.,* **-cat·ed, -cat·ing. 1.** to remove the bark, husk, or outer covering from. **2.** *Surg.* to remove the cortex from (an organ or structure). [1605–15; < L *dēcorticātus* (ptp. of *dēcorticāre* to peel), equiv. to *dē-* DE- + *corticātus* having bark, shell; see CORTICATE] —**de·cor′ti·ca′tor,** *n.*

de·cor·ti·ca·tion (dē kôr′ti kā′shən), *n.* **1.** the act or process of decorticating. **2.** Also, **de·cor·ti·za·tion** (dē-kôr′tə zā′shən). *Surg.* the removal of the cortex, the enveloping membrane, or a fibrinous covering from an organ or structure. [1615–25; < L *dēcorticātiōn-* (s. of *dēcorticātiō*) the act of peeling off bark. See DECORTICATE, -ION]

de·co·rum (di kôr′əm, -kōr′-), *n.* **1.** dignified propriety of behavior, speech, dress, etc. **2.** the quality or state of being decorous; orderliness; regularity. **3.** Usually, **decorums.** an observance or requirement of polite society. [1560–70; < L *decōrum,* n. use of neut. of *decōrus* DECOROUS]
—**Syn. 1.** politeness, manners, dignity. See **etiquette.**

de·cou·page (dā′ko͞o päzh′), *n., v.,* **-paged, -pag·ing.** —*n.* Also, **dé·cou·page** (dā′ko͞o päzh′; *Fr.* dā ko͞o-pazh′). **1.** the art or technique of decorating something with cut-outs of paper, linoleum, plastic, or other flat material over which varnish or lacquer is applied. **2.** work produced by the art or technique of decoupage. —*v.t.* **3.** to decorate by decoupage: *walls decoupaged with photographs of movie stars.* **4.** to apply or use as decoupage or by decoupage technique: *Let's decoupage these maps onto the tabletops.* [1955–60; < F *découpage* a cutting out, equiv. to MF *decoup(er)* to cut out (*de-* DE- + *couper* to cut; see COUPÉ, COUP) + *-age* -AGE]

de·cou·ple (dē kup′əl), *v.,* **-pled, -pling.** —*v.t.* **1.** to cause to become separated, disconnected, or divergent; uncouple. **2.** to absorb the shock of (a nuclear explosion): *a surrounding mass of earth and rock can decouple a nuclear blast.* **3.** *Electronics.* to loosen or eliminate the coupling of (a signal between two circuits). —*v.i.* **4.** to separate or diverge from an existing connection; uncouple. [1595–1605; DE- + COUPLE] —**de·cou′pler,** *n.*

de·coy (*n.* dē′koi, di koi′; *v.* di koi′), *n.* **1.** a person who entices or lures another person or thing, as into danger, a trap, or the like. **2.** anything used as a lure. **3.** a trained bird or other animal used to entice game into a trap or within gunshot. **4.** an artificial bird, as a painted wooden duck, used for the same purpose. **5.** a pond into which wild fowl are lured for capture. **6.** an object capable of reflecting radar waves, used as a spurious aircraft, missile, chaff, etc., for the deception of radar detectors. —*v.t.* **7.** to lure by or as if by a decoy: *They decoyed the ducks to an area right in front of the blind.* —*v.i.* **8.** to become decoyed: *Ducks decoy more easily than most other waterfowl.* [1610–20; var. of *coy* (now dial.) < D (*de*) *kooi* (the) cage, MD *côie* < L *cavea* CAGE] —**de·coy′er,** *n.*
—**Syn. 2.** enticement, bait, inducement, allurement.

de·crease (*v.* di krēs′; *n.* dē′krēs, di krēs′), *v.,* **-creased, -creas·ing,** *n.* —*v.i.* **1.** to diminish or lessen in extent, quantity, strength, power, etc.: *During the ten-day march across the desert their supply of water decreased rapidly.* —*v.t.* **2.** to make less; cause to diminish: *to decrease one's work load.* —*n.* **3.** the act or process of decreasing; condition of being decreased; gradual reduction: *a decrease in sales; a decrease in intensity.* **4.** the amount by which a thing is lessened: *The decrease in sales was almost 20 percent.* [1350–1400; ME *decres* (n.), *decresen* (v.) < OF *decreiss-,* long s. of *decreistre* < L *dēcrēscere* (*dē-* DE- + *crēscere* to grow); see CRESCENT]
—**Syn. 1.** wane, lessen, fall off, decline, contract, abate. DECREASE, DIMINISH, DWINDLE, SHRINK imply becoming smaller or less in amount. DECREASE commonly implies a sustained reduction in stages, esp. of bulk, size, volume, or quantity, often from some imperceptible cause or inherent process: *The swelling decreased daily.* DIMINISH usually implies the action of some external cause that keeps taking away: *Disease caused the number of troops to diminish steadily.* DWINDLE implies an undesirable reduction by degrees, resulting in attenuation: *His followers dwindled to a mere handful.* SHRINK esp. implies contraction through an inherent property under specific conditions: *Many fabrics shrink in hot water.* **3.** abatement, decline, subsidence, shrinking, dwindling, ebbing. —**Ant. 1.** increase, expand.

de·creas·ing (di krē′sing), *adj.* **1.** becoming less or fewer; diminishing. **2.** *Math.* (of a function) having the property that for any two points in the domain such that one is larger than the other, the image of the larger point is less than or equal to the image of the smaller point; nonincreasing. Cf. **increasing** (def. 2). [1350–1400; ME; see DECREASE, -ING[2]] —**de·creas′ing·ly,** *adv.*

decreas′ing term′ insur′ance, a life insurance policy providing a death benefit that decreases throughout the term of the contract, reaching zero at the end of the term.

de·cree (di krē′), *n., v.,* **-creed, -cree·ing.** —*n.* **1.** a formal and authoritative order, esp. one having the force of law: *a presidential decree.* **2.** *Law.* a judicial decision or order. **3.** *Theol.* one of the eternal purposes of God, by which events are foreordained. —*v.t., v.i.* **4.** to command, ordain, or decide by decree. [1275–1325; (n.) ME *decre* < AF *decre, decret* < L *dēcrētum,* n. use of neut. of *dēcrētus,* ptp. of *dēcernere;* see DECERN; (v.) ME *decreen,* deriv. of the n.]

de·cree-law (di krē′lô′), *n.* an executive decree made pursuant to a delegation from the legislature and having the full force of legislation. [1925–30]

decree′ ni′si (nī′sī), *Law.* a decree, esp. of divorce, that will become absolute at a later date. [1890–95]

dec·re·ment (dek′rə mənt), *n.* **1.** the act or process of decreasing; gradual reduction. **2.** the amount lost by reduction. **3.** *Math.* a negative increment. **4.** *Physics.* the ratio of amplitudes of a damped harmonic motion in the course of two successive oscillations. [1475–85; < L *dēcrēmentum,* equiv. to *dēcrē(tus)* (see DECREASE) + *-mentum* -MENT] —**dec·re·men·tal** (dek′rə men′tl), *adj.*

dec·re·me·ter (dek′rə mē′tər, di krem′i tər), *n.* an instrument for measuring the damping of an electromagnetic wave train. [1910–15; DECRE(MENT) + -METER]

de·cre·o·lize (dē krē′ə līz′), *v.t.,* **-lized, -liz·ing.** *Ling.* to modify (a creole language) in the direction of a standard form of the language on which most of the vocabulary of the creole is based. Also, *esp. Brit.,* **de·cre′o·lise′.** [DE- + CREOLIZE] —**de·cre′o·li·za′tion,** *n.*

de·crep·it (di krep′it), *adj.* **1.** weakened by old age; feeble; infirm: *a decrepit man who can hardly walk.* **2.** worn out by long use; dilapidated: *a decrepit stove.* [1400–50; late ME < L *dēcrepitus,* lit., broken down, equiv. to *dē-* DE- + *crep(āre)* to crack + *-i-* -I- + *-tus* ptp. suffix] —**de·crep′it·ly,** *adv.* —**de·crep′it·ness,** *n.*
—**Syn. 1.** enfeebled. See **weak.** —**Ant. 1.** vigorous.

de·crep·i·tate (di krep′i tāt′), *v.,* **-tat·ed, -tat·ing.** —*v.t.* **1.** to roast or calcine (salt, minerals, etc.) so as to cause crackling or until crackling ceases. —*v.i.* **2.** to break up when exposed to heat. [1640–50; < NL *dēcrepitātus* crackled, ptp. of *dēcrepitāre,* equiv. to L *dē-* DE- + *crepitāre* to crackle (freq. of *crepāre* to crack); see -ATE[1]] —**de·crep′i·ta′tion,** *n.*

de·crep·i·tude (di krep′i to͞od′, -tyo͞od′), *n.* decrepit condition; dilapidated state; feebleness, esp. from old age. [1595–1605; < F *décrépitude,* deriv. of *décrépit* DECREPIT; see -TUDE]

decresc., *Music.* decrescendo.

de·cre·scen·do (dē′kri shen′dō, dā′-; *It.* de′kre-shen′dô), *adj., adv., n., pl.* **-dos,** *It.* **-di** (dē). *Music.* —*adj., adv.* **1.** gradually reducing force or loudness; diminuendo (opposed to *crescendo*). —*n.* **2.** a gradual reduction in force or loudness. **3.** a decrescendo passage. [1800–10; < It, ger. of *decrescere;* see DECREASE]

de·cres·cent (di kres′ənt), *adj.* **1.** diminishing; decreasing. **2.** waning, as the moon. [1600–10; < L *dēcrēscent-* (s. of *dēcrēscēns*), prp. of *dēcrēscere* to DECREASE; see -ENT] —**de·cres′cence,** *n.*

de·cre·tal (di krēt′l), *adj.* **1.** pertaining to, of the nature of, or containing a decree or decrees. —*n.* **2.** a papal decree authoritatively determining some point of doctrine or church law. **3. Decretals,** the body or collection of such decrees as a part of the canon law. [1350–1400; ME < OF < LL *dēcrētālis* fixed by decree, equiv. to *dēcrēt(um)* DECREE + *-ālis* -AL[1]]

de·cre·tist (di krē′tist), *n.* (in medieval universities) **1.** a student in the faculty of law. **2.** a student of the Decretals; expert in the canon law. [1350–1400; < ML *dēcrētista,* equiv. to L *dēcrēt(um)* DECREE + *-ista* -IST]

CONCISE PRONUNCIATION KEY: *act, cāpe, dâre, pärt; set, ēqual; if, īce; ox, ōver, ôrder, oil, bo͝ok, bo͞ot, out; up, ûrge; child; sing; shoe; thin, that;* zh as in *treasure.* ə = *a* as in *alone, e* as in *system, i* as in *easily, o* as in *gallop, u* as in *circus;* ᵊ as in *fire* (fīᵊr), *hour* (ouᵊr). l and n can serve as syllabic consonants, as in *cradle* (krād′l), and *button* (but′n). See the full key inside the front cover.

de·spe′cial·i·za′tion, *n.*
de·spir′it·u·al·i·za′tion, *n.*
de·spir′it·u·al·ize′, *v.t.,* **-ized, -iz·ing.**
de·stain′er, *n.*
de·stig′ma·tize′, *v.t.,* **-tized, -tiz·ing.**
de·stock′, *v.t.*
de·strat′i·fy′, *v.t.,* **-fied, -fy·ing.**
de·stress′, *v.t.*
de·struc′ture, *v.t.,* **-tured, -tur·ing.**
de·sub′li·mate′, *v.t.,* **-mat·ed, -mat·ing.**
de·sub′si·di·za′tion, *n.*
de·sub′si·dize′, *v.t.,* **-dized, -diz·ing.**
de·syn′chro·ni·za′tion, *n.*
de·syn′chro·nize′, *v.t.,* **-nized, -niz·ing.**
de·tan′gle, *v.,* **-gled, -gling.**
de·tar′, *v.t.,* **-tarred, -tar·ring.**
de·tas′sel, *v.t.,* **-seled, -sel·ing** or (*esp. Brit.*) **-selled, -sel·ling.**
de·wire′, *v.t.,* **-wired, -wir·ing.**

de•cre•tive (di krē′tiv), *adj.* having the force of a decree; pertaining to a decree. [1600–10; < L *dēcrēt(um)* DECREE + -IVE] —**de•cre′tive•ly,** *adv.*

dec•re•to•ry (dek′ri tôr′ē, -tōr′ē), *adj.* **1.** pertaining to or following a decree. **2.** established by a decree; judicial. [1570–80; < L *dēcrētōrius* decisive, crucial, equiv. to *dēcrē-*, var. s. of *dēcernere* (see DECERN, DECREE) + *-tōrious* -TORY[1]]

de•cri•al (di krī′əl), *n.* the act of decrying; noisy censure. [1705–15; DECRY + -AL[2]]

de•crim•i•nal•ize (dē krim′ə nl īz′), *v.t.*, **-ized, -iz•ing.** to eliminate criminal penalties for or remove legal restrictions against: *to decriminalize marijuana.* Also, *esp. Brit.,* **de•crim′i•nal•ise′.** [1965–70, *Amer.*; DE- + CRIMINAL + -IZE] —**de•crim′i•nal•i•za′tion,** *n.*

de•cry (di krī′), *v.t.*, **-cried, -cry•ing. 1.** to speak disparagingly of; denounce as faulty or worthless; express censure of: *She decried the lack of support for the arts in this country.* **2.** to condemn or depreciate by proclamation, as foreign or obsolete coins. [1610–20; < F *décrier,* OF *descrier.* See DIS-[1], CRY] —**de•cri′er,** *n.*
—**Syn. 1.** belittle, disparage, discredit, depreciate, minimize. DECRY, DENIGRATE, DEPRECATE, DEROGATE all involve the expression of censure or disapproval. DECRY means to express one's vigorous disapproval of or to denounce: *to decry all forms of discrimination.* DENIGRATE means to speak damagingly of, to criticize in derogative terms: *denigrating his works as trifling and poorly executed.* DEPRECATE implies the expression of earnest, thoughtful disapproval: *to deprecate a plan because of possible environmental damage.* DEROGATE means to speak in such a way as to decrease the status, high quality, or good reputation of someone or something, making the person or object seem of less value: *Fear of change makes them derogate every proposal put forth.*

de•crypt (dē kript′, di-), *v.t.* to decode or decipher. [1935–40; DE- + CRYPT(OGRAM)] —**de•cryp′tion,** *n.*

de•cub•i•tus (di kyōō′bi təs), *n., pl.* **-tus.** *Med.* any position assumed by a patient when lying in bed. [1865–70; < NL, equiv. to L *dēcubi-*, var. s. of *dēcumbere* to lie down, take to one's bed (*dē-* DE- + *-cumbere,* telic v., with nasal infix, corresponding to *cubāre* to lie) + *-tus* suffix of verbal action] —**de•cu′bi•tal,** *adj.*

decu′bitus ul′cer, *Pathol.* bedsore.

de•cul•tur•ate (dē kul′chə rāt′), *v.t.*, **-at•ed, -at•ing.** to cause the loss or abandonment of culture or cultural characteristics of (a people, society, etc.). [DE- + CULTURE + -ATE[1]] —**de•cul′tur•a′tion,** *n.*

de•cul•ture (dē kul′chər), *v.t.*, **-tured, -tur•ing.** to deculturate. [DE- + CULTURE]

dec•u•man (dek′yōō mən), *adj.* **1.** large or immense, as a wave. **2.** (in ancient Rome) of or pertaining to the tenth cohort of a legion. —*n.* **3.** Also called **dec′uman gate′.** (in ancient Rome) the main gate of a military camp, facing away from the enemy and near which the tenth cohort of the legion was usually stationed. [1650–60; < L *decumānus, decimānus* of the tenth, large, equiv. to *decim(us)* tenth (see DECIMATE) + *-ānus* -AN]

de•cum•bent (di kum′bənt), *adj.* **1.** lying down; recumbent. **2.** *Bot.* (of stems, branches, etc.) lying or trailing on the ground with the extremity tending to ascend. [1635–45; < L *dēcumbent-* (s. of *dēcumbēns*), prp. of *dēcumbere.* See DECUBITUS, -ENT] —**de•cum′bence, de•cum′ben•cy,** *n.* —**de•cum′bent•ly,** *adv.*

dec•u•ple (dek′yōō pəl), *adj., n., v.*, **-pled, -pling.** —*adj.* **1.** ten times as great; tenfold. —*n.* **2.** a tenfold quantity or multiple. —*v.t.* **3.** to make ten times as great. [1375–1425; late ME < MF < L *decuplus* tenfold, equiv. to *dec(em)* ten + *-uplus,* as in *quadruplus* QUADRUPLE]

de•cu•ri•on (di kyŏŏr′ē ən), *n. Rom. Hist.* **1.** the head of a decury. **2.** a member of the senate of an ancient Roman colony or municipality. [1350–1400; ME < L *decuriōn-* (s. of *decuriō*), equiv. to *decuri(a)* a division of ten (*dec(em)* TEN + *-uria* -URE) + *-iōn-* -ION]

de•cur•rent (di kûr′ənt, -kur′-), *adj. Bot.* extending down the stem below the place of insertion, as certain leaves. [1745–55; < L *dēcurrent-* (s. of *dēcurrēns*) running down (prp. of *dēcurrere,* equiv. to *dē-* DE- + *currere* to run); see CURRENT] —**de•cur′rence, de•cur′ren•cy,** *n.* —**de•cur′rent•ly,** *adv.*

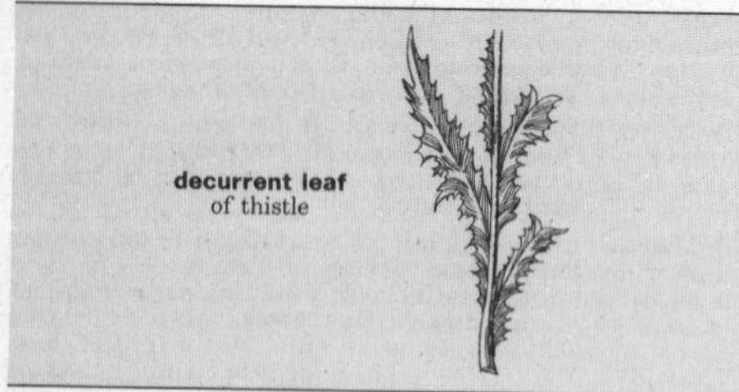
decurrent leaf of thistle

de•curved (dē kûrvd′), *adj.* curved downward, as the bill of a bird. [1825–35; DE- + CURVED]

dec•u•ry (dek′yōō rē), *n., pl.* **-ries.** *Rom. Hist.* **1.** a division, company, or body of ten men. **2.** any larger body of men, esp. the curiae. [1525–35; < L *decuria* a company of ten. See DECURION, -Y[3]]

de•cus•sate (*v.* di kus′āt, dek′ə sāt′; *adj.* di kus′āt, -it), *v.*, **-sat•ed, -sat•ing,** *adj.* —*v.t., v.i.* **1.** to cross in the form of an X; intersect. —*adj.* **2.** in the form of an X; crossed; intersected. **3.** *Bot.* arranged along the stem in pairs, each pair at right angles to the pair next above or below, as leaves. [1650–60; < ML *decussātus* divided in the form of an X (ptp. of *decussāre*), equiv. to L *decussis* the numeral ten, orig., a ten-as weight (*dec(em)* TEN + *-ussis,* comb. form of *as* AS[2]) + *-ātus* -ATE[1]] —**de•cus′sate•ly,** *adv.*

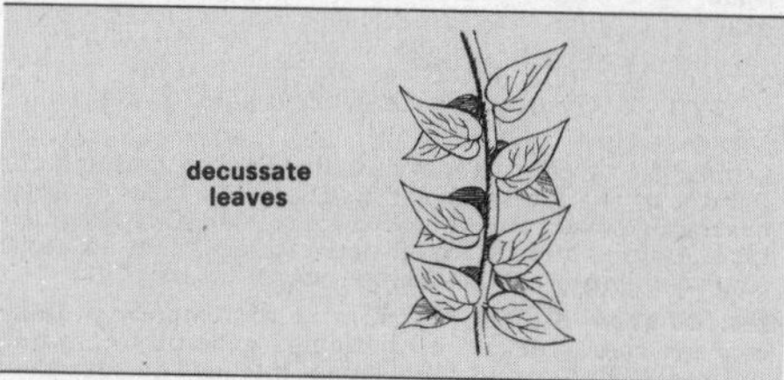
decussate leaves

de•cus•sa•tion (dē′kə sā′shən, dek′ə-), *n.* **1.** a process of becoming or condition of being crossed in the form of an X. **2.** *Anat.* a nerve or tract of nerve fibers that crosses from one side of the central nervous system to the other. [1650–60; DECUSSATE + -ION]

dec•yl (des′əl), *n. Chem.* a group of isomeric univalent radicals, $C_{10}H_{21}$, derived from the decanes by removing one hydrogen atom. [DEC(ANE) + -YL]

dec′yl al′cohol, *Chem.* decanol.

de•cyl′ic ac′id (di sil′ik), *Chem.* See **capric acid.** [DECYL + -IC]

D.Ed., Doctor of Education.

de•dal (dēd′l), *adj. Archaic.* daedal.

de•dans (də däN′), *n., pl.* **-dans** (-däN′). (*used with a singular v.*) *Court Tennis.* **1.** a netted winning opening of rectangular shape at the service side of the court. Cf. **grille** (def. 5), **winning gallery. 2.** the body of spectators behind this opening at a court-tennis match. [1700–10; < F: (the) inside, MF (adv. and prep.), OF *dedenz,* equiv. to *de* of (< L *dē*) + *denz* in (< LL *deintus,* equiv. to L *dē-* DE- + *intus* inside (adv.))]

De•de Ag•ach (*Turk.* de′de ä äch′), former name of **Alexandroupolis.** Also, **De′de Ağ•aç.**

De•de•kind (dā′di kind; *Ger.* dā′də kint), *n.* **Ju•li•us Wil•helm Rich•ard** (jōōl′yəs wil′helm rich′ərd; *Ger.* yōō′lē ŏŏs′ vil′helm rikh′ärt), 1831–1916, German mathematician.

De′dekind cut′, *Math.* two nonempty subsets of an ordered field, as the rational numbers, such that one subset is the collection of upper bounds of the second and the second is the collection of lower bounds of the first: can be used to define the real numbers in terms of the rational numbers. [named after J.W.R. DEDEKIND]

de•den•dum (di den′dəm), *n., pl.* **-da** (-də). *Mach.* (on a gear or rack) the radial distance between the pitch circle or line and the root circle or line. Cf. **addendum** (def. 3a). [1900–05; < L: to be given up, ger. of *dēdere,* equiv. to *dē-* DE- + *-dere* comb. form of *dare* to give; see ADDENDUM]

Ded•ham (ded′əm), *n.* a town in E Massachusetts, near Boston. 25,298.

ded•i•cate (*v.* ded′i kāt′; *adj.* ded′i kit), *v.*, **-cat•ed, -cat•ing,** *adj.* —*v.t.* **1.** to set apart and consecrate to a deity or to a sacred purpose: *The ancient Greeks dedicated many shrines to Aphrodite.* **2.** to devote wholly and earnestly, as to some person or purpose: *He dedicated his life to fighting corruption.* **3.** to offer formally (a book, piece of music, etc.) to a person, cause, or the like in testimony of affection or respect, as on a prefatory page. **4.** (loosely) to inscribe a personal signature on (a book, drawing, etc., that is one's own work), usually with a salutation addressing the recipient. **5.** to mark the official completion or opening of (a public building, monument, highway, etc.), usually by formal ceremonies. **6.** to set aside for or assign to a specific function, task, or purpose: *The county health agency has dedicated one inspector to monitor conditions in nursing homes.* —*adj.* **7.** dedicated. [1375–1425; late ME (v. and adj.) < L *dēdicātus* ptp. of *dēdicāre* to declare, devote, equiv. to *dē-* DE- + *dicāre* to indicate, consecrate, akin to *dīcere* to say, speak (see DICTATE)] —**ded′i•ca′tor,** *n.*
—**Syn. 1.** See **devote. 2.** commit, pledge, consecrate.

ded•i•cat•ed (ded′i kā′tid), *adj.* **1.** wholly committed to something, as to an ideal, political cause, or personal goal: *a dedicated artist.* **2.** set apart or reserved for a specific use or purpose: *We don't need a computer but a dedicated word processor.* **3.** (of machine parts, electrical components, hardware, etc.) made or designed to interconnect exclusively with one model or a limited range of models in a manufacturer's line: *The new tractors use only high-priced dedicated accessories.* [1590–1600; DEDICATE + -ED[2]] —**ded′i•cat′ed•ly,** *adv.*

ded•i•ca•tee (ded′i kə tē′), *n.* a person to whom something is dedicated. [1750–60; DEDICATE + -EE]

ded•i•ca•tion (ded′i kā′shən), *n.* **1.** the act of dedicating. **2.** the state of being dedicated: *Her dedication to medicine was so great that she had time for little else.* **3.** a formal, printed inscription in a book, piece of music, etc., dedicating it to a person, cause, or the like. **4.** a personal, handwritten inscription in or on a work, as by an author to a friend. **5.** a ceremony marking the official completion or opening of a public building, institution, monument, etc. [1350–1400; ME *dedicacioun* < L *dēdicātiōn-* (s. of *dēdicātiō*), equiv. to *dēdicāt(us)* (see DEDICATE) + *-iōn-* -ION] —**ded′i•ca′tion•al,** *adj.*

ded•i•ca•to•ry (ded′i kə tôr′ē, -tōr′ē), *adj.* of or pertaining to dedication; serving as a dedication. Also, **ded•i•ca•tive** (ded′i kā′tiv). [1555–65; DEDICATE + -ORY[1]] —**ded′i•ca•to′ri•ly,** *adv.*

de•dif•fer•en•ti•ate (dē′dif ə ren′shē āt′), *v.i.*, **-at•ed, -at•ing.** *Biol.* to undergo dedifferentiation. [1915–20; back formation from DEDIFFERENTIATION]

de•dif•fer•en•ti•a•tion (dē dif′ə ren′shē ā′shən), *n. Biol.* a process by which structures or behaviors that were specialized for a specific function lose their specialization and become simplified or generalized. [1915–20; DE- + DIFFERENTIATION]

de d in d, (in prescriptions) from day to day. [< L *dē diē in diem*]

de do•lo ma•lo (di dō′lō mal′ō), *Law.* with evil intention; with intent to defraud. [< L *dē dolō malō*]

de•do•lo•mit•i•za•tion (dē dō′lə mī′tə zā′shən, -mi-, -dol′ə-), *n. Geol., Petrol.* a metamorphic process in which the magnesium in dolomitic rock forms new minerals, as brucite and forsterite, and the calcium forms calcite. [DE- + DOLOMITIZATION]

de•do•lo•mit•ize (dē dō′lə mī tīz′, -mi-, -dol′ə-), *v.t.*, **-ized, -iz•ing.** to transform (dolomite or dolomitic limestone) by separating the dolomite into calcium carbonate and magnesium carbonate. Also, *esp. Brit.,* **de•do′lo•mit•ise′.** [1900–05; DE- + DOLOMITE + -IZE]

de•duce (di dōōs′, -dyōōs′), *v.t.*, **-duced, -duc•ing. 1.** to derive as a conclusion from something known or assumed; infer: *From the evidence the detective deduced that the gardener had done it.* **2.** to trace the derivation of; trace the course of: *to deduce one's lineage.* [1520–30; < L *dēdūcere* to lead down, derive, equiv. to *dē-* DE- + *dūcere* to lead, bring] —**de•duc′i•ble,** *adj.* —**de•duc′i•bil′i•ty, de•duc′i•ble•ness,** *n.* —**de•duc′i•bly,** *adv.*
—**Syn. 1.** conclude, reason, gather, determine.

de•duct (di dukt′), *v.t.* **1.** to take away, as from a sum or amount: *Once you deduct your expenses, there is nothing left.* —*v.i.* **2.** detract; abate (usually fol. by *from*): *The rocky soil deducts from the value of his property.* [1375–1425; late ME < L *dēductus* brought down, withdrawn, ptp. of *dēdūcere;* see DEDUCE]
—**Syn. 1.** See **subtract.** —**Ant.** add.

de•duct•i•ble (di duk′tə bəl), *adj.* **1.** capable of being deducted. **2.** allowable as a tax deduction: *Charitable contributions are deductible expenses.* —*n.* **3.** the amount for which the insured is liable on each loss, injury, etc., before an insurance company will make payment: *The deductible on our medical coverage has been raised from $50 to $100 per illness.* [1855–60; DEDUCT + -IBLE] —**de•duct′i•bil′i•ty,** *n.*

deduct′ible clause′, a clause in an insurance policy stipulating that the insured will be liable for a specified initial amount of each loss, injury, etc., and that the insurance company will be liable for any additional costs up to the insured amount. Cf. **franchise clause.**

de•duc•tion (di duk′shən), *n.* **1.** the act or process of deducting; subtraction. **2.** something that is or may be deducted: *She took deductions for a home office and other business expenses from her taxes.* **3.** the act or process of deducing. **4.** something that is deduced: *His astute deduction was worthy of Sherlock Holmes.* **5.** *Logic.* **a.** a process of reasoning in which a conclusion follows necessarily from the premises presented, so that the conclusion cannot be false if the premises are true. **b.** a conclusion reached by this process. Cf. **induction** (def. 4). [1400–50; late ME *deduccioun* (< AF) < L *dēductiōn-* (s. of *dēductiō*) a leading away. See DEDUCT, -ION]

de•duc•tive (di duk′tiv), *adj.* based on deduction from accepted premises: *deductive argument; deductive reasoning.* [1640–50; < L *dēductīvus* derivative. See DEDUCT, -IVE] —**de•duc′tive•ly,** *adv.*
—**Syn.** DEDUCTIVE and INDUCTIVE refer to two distinct logical processes. DEDUCTIVE reasoning is a logical process in which a conclusion drawn from a set of premises contains no more information than the premises taken collectively. *All dogs are animals; this is a dog; therefore, this is an animal:* The truth of the conclusion is dependent only on the method. *All men are apes; this is a man; therefore, this is an ape:* The conclusion is logically true, although the premise is absurd. INDUCTIVE reasoning is a logical process in which a conclusion is proposed that contains more information than the observations or experience on which it is based. *Every crow ever seen was black; all crows are black:* The truth of the conclusion is verifiable only in terms of future experience and certainty is attainable only if all possible instances have been examined. In the example, there is no certainty that a white crow will not be found tomorrow, although past experience would make such an occurrence seem unlikely.

de Du•ve (də dy′və), **Chris•tian Re•né** (krēs tyäN′ rə nā′). See **Duve, Christian René de.**

dee (dē), *n.* **1.** a metal loop attached to tack, for fastening gear: *to hang wire cutters from a dee on a saddle.* **2.** *Physics.* a hollow electrode for accelerating particles in a cyclotron. [1785–95; so called from its shape, which resembles the letter *D*]

Dee (dē), *n.* **1. John,** 1527–1608, English mathematician and astrologer. **2.** a river in NE Scotland, flowing E into the North Sea at Aberdeen. 90 mi. (145 km) long. **3.** a river in N Wales and W England, flowing E and N into the Irish Sea. ab. 70 mi. (110 km) long. **4.** a male or female given name.

deed (dēd), *n.* **1.** something that is done, performed, or accomplished; an act: *Do a good deed every day.* **2.** an exploit or achievement; feat: *brave deeds.* **3.** Often, **deeds.** an act or gesture, esp. as illustrative of intentions, one's character, or the like: *Her deeds speak for themselves.* **4.** *Law.* a writing or document executed under seal and delivered to effect a conveyance, esp. of real estate. —*v.t.* **5.** to convey or transfer by deed. [bef. 900; ME *dede,* OE *dēd,* var. of *dǣd;* c. G *Tat,* Goth *gadēths;* see DO[1]] —**deed′less,** *adj.*
—**Syn. 1.** See **action.**

deed′ of trust′. See **trust deed.**

deed′ poll′ (pōl), *Law.* a deed signed and executed only by the grantor. [1580–90]

dee•jay (dē′jā′), *n. Informal.* See **disc jockey.** [1940–45; pron. of initials D.J.]

deel•ie (dē′lē), *n. Northwestern U.S.* (*chiefly Seattle*). a thing whose name is unknown or forgotten; thingumbob. [DEAL[1] + -IE]

CONCISE ETYMOLOGY KEY: <, descended or borrowed from; >, whence; b., blend of, blended; c., cognate with; cf., compare; deriv., derivative; equiv., equivalent; imit., imitative; obl., oblique; r., replacing; s., stem; sp., spelling, spelled; resp., respelling, respelled; trans., translation; ?, origin unknown; *, unattested; ‡, probably earlier than. See the full key inside the front cover.

deem (dēm), *v.i.* **1.** to form or have an opinion; judge; think: *He did not deem lightly of the issue.* —*v.t.* **2.** to hold as an opinion; think; regard: *He deemed it wise to refuse the offer.* [bef. 900; ME *demen,* OE *dēman;* c. Goth *dōmjan,* OHG *tuomen;* see DOOM]
—Syn. 2. consider, hold, believe.

de•em•pha•sis (dē em′fə sis), *n., pl.* **-ses** (-sēz′). **1.** a reduction in emphasis: *There has been de-emphasis on athletic activities at the school.* **2.** the act or process of de-emphasizing. **3.** *Electronics.* a process of reducing the relative amplitude of certain frequencies in a signal that have been exaggerated by preemphasis, restoring the signal to its original form. Also, **de•em′pha•sis.** [1935–40; DE- + EMPHASIS]

de•em•pha•size (dē em′fə sīz′), *v.t.,* **-sized, -siz•ing.** to place less emphasis upon; reduce in importance, size, scope, etc.: *The university de-emphasized intercollegiate football.* Also, *esp. Brit.,* **de•em′pha•sise′.** [1935–40; DE- + EMPHASIZE]

deem•ster (dēm′stər), *n.* a judge of the Isle of Man. Also, **dempster.** [1250–1300; ME *demestre;* see DEEM, -STER] **—deem′ster•ship′,** *n.*

de•en•er•gize (dē en′ər jīz′), *v.t.,* **-gized, -giz•ing.** to deprive of electrical energy or exhaust the electrical energy from: *Turning off the ignition de-energizes the spark plugs.* Also, *esp. Brit.,* **de•en′er•gise′.**

deep (dēp), *adj.* **-er, -est,** *n., adv.,* **-er, -est.** —*adj.* **1.** extending far down from the top or surface: *a deep well; a deep valley.* **2.** extending far in or back from the front or from an edge, surface, opening, etc., considered as the front: *a deep shelf.* **3.** extending far in width; broad: *deep lace; a deep border.* **4.** ranging far from the earth and sun: *a deep space probe.* **5.** having a specified dimension in depth: *a tank 8 feet deep.* **6.** covered or immersed to a specified depth (often used in combination): *standing knee-deep in water.* **7.** having a specified width or number of items from front to back (often used in combination): *shelves that are 10 inches deep; cars lined up at the entrance gates three-deep.* **8.** extending or cutting far down relative to the surface of a given object: *The knife made a deep scar in the table.* **9.** situated far down, in, or back: *deep below the surface; deep in the woods.* **10.** reaching or advancing far down: *a deep dive.* **11.** coming from far down: *a deep breath.* **12.** made with the body bent or lowered to a considerable degree: *a deep bow.* **13.** immersed or submerged in or heavily covered with (fol. by *in*): *a road deep in mud.* **14.** difficult to penetrate or understand; abstruse: *a deep allegory.* **15.** not superficial; profound: *deep thoughts.* **16.** grave or serious: *deep disgrace.* **17.** heartfelt; sincere: *deep affections.* **18.** absorbing; engrossing: *deep study.* **19.** great in measure; intense; extreme: *deep sorrow.* **20.** sound and heavy; profound: *deep sleep.* **21.** (of colors) dark and vivid: *a deep red.* **22.** low in pitch, as sound, a voice, or the like: *deep, sonorous tones.* **23.** having penetrating intellectual powers: *a deep scholar.* **24.** profoundly cunning or artful: *a deep and crafty scheme.* **25.** mysterious; obscure: *deep, dark secrets.* **26.** immersed or involved; enveloped: *a man deep in debt.* **27.** absorbed; engrossed: *deep in thought.* **28.** *Baseball.* relatively far from home plate: *He hit the ball into deep center field.* **29.** *Ling.* belonging to an early stage in the transformational derivation of a sentence; belonging to the deep structure. **30. go off the deep end, a.** to enter upon a course of action with heedless or irresponsible indifference to consequences. **b.** to become emotionally overwrought. **31. in deep water, a.** in difficult or serious circumstances; in trouble. **b.** in a situation beyond the range of one's capability or skill: *You're a good student, but you'll be in deep water in medical school.* —*n.* **32.** the deep part of a body of water, esp. an area of the ocean floor having a depth greater than 18,000 ft. (5400 m). **33.** a vast extent, as of space or time. **34.** the part of greatest intensity, as of winter. **35.** *Naut.* any of the unmarked levels, one fathom apart, on a deep-sea lead line. Cf. **mark**[1] (def. 20). **36. the deep,** *Chiefly Literary.* the sea or ocean: *He was laid to rest in the deep.* —*adv.* **37.** to or at a considerable or specified depth: *The boat rode deep in the water.* **38.** far on in time: *He claimed he could see deep into the future.* **39.** profoundly; intensely. **40.** *Baseball.* at or to a deep place or position: *Outfielders play deep when the batter is a slugger.* **41. in deep, a.** inextricably involved. **b.** having made or committed oneself to make a large financial investment. [bef. 900; ME *dep,* OE *dēop;* akin to Goth *diups,* ON *djupr,* OHG *tiof*] **—deep′ness,** *n.*
—Syn. 14. recondite, mysterious, obscure, profound. **23.** sagacious, wise, profound, shrewd.

deep-chest•ed (dēp′ches′tid), *adj.* **1.** having a large, broad chest: *a deep-chested man.* **2.** coming from deep in the chest: *a deep-chested cough.* [1830–40]

deep′ dis′count, a discount far larger than normally offered.

deep-dish (dēp′dish′), *adj. Cookery.* baked in a deep dish, often with a pastry top: *a deep-dish peach pie.* [1935–40]

deep-draw (dēp′drô′), *v.t.,* **-drew, -drawn, -draw•ing.** *Metalworking.* to form (tubing, containers, etc.) by pulling strip or sheet metal between suitably formed and spaced dies. Cf. **cup** (def. 23). [1920–25]

deep-dyed (dēp′dīd′), *adj.* thorough; unmitigated: *a deep-dyed villain.* [1810–20]

deep•en (dē′pən), *v.t., v.i.* **1.** to make or become deep or deeper: *Larger ships will be able to navigate the river after the main channel is deepened. The shadows deepened toward late afternoon.* **2.** *Meteorol.* to decrease in atmospheric pressure: *a deepening cyclone.* [1595–1605; DEEP + -EN[1]] **—deep′en•er,** *n.* **—deep′en•ing•ly,** *adv.*

deep′-etch plate′ (dēp′ech′), an offset printing plate with an intaglio image filled with a substance that attracts ink to make it planographic. Cf. **albumen plate.**

deep′ fat′, hot fat used for deep-frying food. [1950–55]

deep′ floor′, *Naut.* any of the floors toward the ends of a vessel, deeper than those of standard depth amidships.

deep′ fo′cus, *Cinematog.* **1.** the focusing of a filmed scene so as to make near and distant objects equally clear. **2.** a shot utilizing a large depth of field.

deep′ freeze′, **1.** a state or period of halted or suspended activity or progress: *High interest rates created a deep freeze in housing construction.* **2.** suspended animation. **3. put in** or **into the deep freeze,** *Informal.* to stop or suspend the activity or progress of: *A series of quarrels put their romance into the deep freeze.* [1940–45, *Amer.*]

Deep•freeze (dēp′frēz′, -frēz′), *Trademark.* a brand of deep freezer.

deep-freeze (dēp′frēz′), *v.t.,* **-freezed** or **-froze, -freezed** or **-fro•zen, -freez•ing. 1.** to quick-freeze (food). **2.** to store in a frozen state. [1945–50, *Amer.;* DEEP + FREEZE]

deep′ freez′er, freezer (def. 1). [1945–50, *Amer.*]

deep-fry (dēp′frī′), *v.t.,* **-fried, -fry•ing.** to fry in a quantity of fat sufficient to cover the food being cooked. [1930–35]

deep′ fry′er, a deep pan or pot with a basket, usually of mesh, inside, for deep-frying. [1950–55]

deep′ kiss′. See **soul kiss.** [1945–50]

deep-kiss (dēp′kis′), *v.t., v.i.* to soul-kiss. [1945–50]

deep-laid (dēp′lād′), *adj.* carefully, cunningly, or secretly made: *a deep-laid plot.* [1760–70]

deep•ly (dēp′lē), *adv.* **1.** at or to a considerable extent downward; well within or beneath a surface. **2.** to a thorough extent or profound degree: *deeply pained; deeply committed.* **3.** with depth of color, tone, sound, etc. **4.** with great cunning, skill, and subtlety. [bef. 900; ME *deply,* OE *dēoplice,* deriv. of *dēoplic* (adj.), equiv. to *dēop* DEEP + *-lic(e)* -LY]
—Syn. 2. greatly, thoroughly, intensely, acutely.

deep′ mourn′ing, completely black mourning clothes made of a drab material: *After her brother died, she was in deep mourning for a year.* [1715–25]

deep′ pock′ets, an abundance of money or wealth. [1975–80]

deep-root•ed (dēp′rōō′tid, -ro͝ot′id), *adj.* deeply rooted; firmly implanted or established: *a deep-rooted patriotism; deep-rooted suspicions.* [1660–70] **—deep′-root′ed•ness,** *n.*

deep′ scat′tering lay′er, *Oceanog.* a zone of biological origin within the ocean, at a depth of 900–1200 ft. (270–360 m), which scatters sounding echoes.

deep-sea (dēp′sē′), *adj.* of, pertaining to, in, or associated with the deeper parts of the sea: *deep-sea fishing; deep-sea diver.* [1620–30]

deep′-sea core′ (dēp′sē′), *Oceanog.* an intact sample of sediment extracted from the ocean floor by drilling with a long hollow tube.

deep-seat•ed (dēp′sē′tid), *adj.* firmly implanted or established: *a deep-seated sense of loyalty.* [1735–45]

deep-set (dēp′set′), *adj.* placed far in: *a face with deep-set eyes under bushy brows.* [1830–35]

deep′ six′, *Slang.* **1.** burial or discarding at sea. **2.** complete rejection or ruin. [1940–45]

deep-six (dēp′siks′), *v.t. Slang.* **1.** to throw overboard. **2.** to get rid of; abandon; discard. **3.** to reject, negate, or ruin: *The team deep-sixed the manager's attempt to call Sunday practice.* [1950–55; v. use of DEEP SIX]

Deep′ South′, the southeastern part of the U.S., including esp. South Carolina, Georgia, Alabama, Mississippi, and Louisiana.

deep′ space′, space beyond the limits of the solar system. Also called **outer space.** [1950–55] **—deep′-space′,** *adj.*

deep′ struc′ture, *Ling.* (in transformational-generative grammar) the underlying semantic or syntactic representation of a sentence, from which the surface structure may be derived. Cf. **surface structure.** [1960–65, *Amer.*]

deep-voiced (dēp′voist′), *adj.* having a voice that is low in pitch: *a deep-voiced young man.* [1840–50]

deep•wa•ter (dēp′wô′tər, -wot′ər), *adj.* having, requiring, or operating in deep water: *deepwater shipping; deepwater drilling for oil.* [1785–95; DEEP + WATER]

deer (dēr), *n., pl.* **deer,** *(occasionally)* **deers. 1.** any of several ruminants of the family Cervidae, most of the males of which have solid, deciduous antlers. **2.** any of the smaller species of this family, as distinguished from the moose, elk, etc. [bef. 900; ME *der,* OE *dēor* beast; akin to Goth *dius* beast, OHG *tior*]

white-tailed deer, *Odocoileus virginianus,* 3½ ft. (1 m) high at shoulder; length 6½ ft. (2 m)

deer•ber•ry (dēr′ber′ē, -bə rē), *n., pl.* **-ries. 1.** either of two shrubs, *Vaccinium stamineum* or *V. caesium,* of the heath family, native to the eastern U.S., having clusters of small, white or greenish flowers and blue or greenish berries. **2.** the fruit of either of these shrubs. Also called **squaw huckleberry.** [1805–15, *Amer.;* DEER + BERRY; alleged to be a source of winter food for deer]

Deere (dēr), *n.* **John,** 1804–86, U.S. inventor and manufacturer of farm implements.

deer′ fern′, an evergreen fern, *Blechnum spicant,* of Eurasia and western North America, having densely clustered fronds. [so called because it is often cultivated for deer]

Deer•field (dēr′fēld′), *n.* a city in NE Illinois. 17,430.

Deer′field Beach′, a town in S Florida. 39,193.

deer′ fly′, any of several tabanid flies of the genus *Chrysops,* the female of which is a vector of tularemia in deer, livestock, and humans. [1850–55, *Amer.*]

deer′ fly′ fe′ver, *Med., Vet. Med.* tularemia. [1935–40]

deer′ grass′. See **meadow beauty.** [1775–85]

deer•hound (dēr′hound′), *n.* See **Scottish deerhound.** [1805–15; DEER + HOUND[1]]

deer′ lick′, a spot of ground, naturally or artificially salty, where deer come to lick. [1735–45]

deer′ mouse′. See **white-footed mouse.** [1825–35]

Deer′ Park′, 1. a town on central Long Island, in SE New York. 30,394. **2.** a town in S Texas. 22,648.

deer•skin (dēr′skin′), *n.* **1.** the skin of a deer. **2.** leather made from this. **3.** a garment made of such leather. —*adj.* **4.** made of deerskin: *a deerskin jacket.* [1350–1400; ME *dereskin,* var. of *deres skin.* See DEER, SKIN]

deer•stalk•er (dēr′stô′kər), *n.* **1.** a person who stalks deer. **2.** Also called **fore-and-after.** a close-fitting woolen cap having a visor in front and in back, with earflaps usually raised and tied on top of the crown, worn as a hunting cap: esp. associated with Sherlock Holmes. [1810–20; DEER + STALKER] **—deer′stalk′ing,** *n.*

deer's-tongue (dērz′tung′), *n.* See **green gentian.** [1860–65]

deer•weed (dēr′wēd′), *n.* any of several shrubby Californian plants belonging to the genus *Lotus,* of the legume family, esp. *L. scoparious,* having pinnate leaves and clusters of yellow flowers. Also, **deer′ weed′.** [1910–15, *Amer.;* DEER + WEED[1]]

deer•yard (dēr′yärd′), *n.* an area where deer gather in winter. [1840–50, *Amer.;* DEER + YARD[2]]

dees (dēs), *adj. Slang.* dece.

de•es•ca•late (dē es′kə lāt′), *v.t., v.i.,* **-lat•ed, -lat•ing.** to decrease in intensity, magnitude, etc.: *to de-escalate a war.* Also, **de•es′ca•late′.** [1960–65; DE- + ESCALATE] **—de-es′ca•la′tion, de•es′ca•la′tion,** *n.* **—de-es•ca•la•to•ry, de•es•ca•la•to•ry** (dē es′kə lə tôr′ē, -tōr′ē), *adj.*

de•e•sis (dē ē′sis), *n., pl.* **-ses** (-sēz). a representation in Byzantine art of Christ enthroned and flanked by the Virgin Mary and St. John the Baptist, often found on an iconostasis. [< Gk *déēsis* entreaty, equiv. to *deē-,* var. s. of *déesthai* to beg + *-sis* -SIS]

Deet (dēt), *Chem., Trademark.* a brand of diethyltoluamide.

de•ex•cite (dē′ik sīt′), *v.,* **-cit•ed, -cit•ing.** *Physics.* —*v.t.* **1.** to cause (an atom) to fall from an excited energy level to a lower energy level. —*v.i.* **2.** to become de-excited. Also, **de′ex•cite′.** [1960–65] **—de′-ex•ci•ta′tion, de′ex•ci•ta′tion,** *n.*

def[1] (def), *adv. Informal.* definitely: *Going to Europe this summer? But def!* [by shortening]

def[2] (def), *adj. Slang.* excellent: *That hip-hop record is def!* [1980–85, *Amer.;* of uncert. orig.]

def., 1. defective. **2.** defendant. **3.** defense. **4.** deferred. **5.** defined. **6.** definite. **7.** definition.

de•face (di fās′), *v.t.,* **-faced, -fac•ing. 1.** to mar the surface or appearance of; disfigure: *to deface a wall by writing on it.* **2.** to efface, obliterate, or injure the surface of, as to make illegible or invalid: *to deface a bond.* [1275–1325; ME *defacen* < OF *desfacier,* equiv. to *des-* DIS-[1] + *facier* (*face* FACE + *-ier* inf. suffix)] **—de•face′•a•ble,** *adj.* **—de•face′ment,** *n.* **—de•fac′er,** *n.*
—Syn. 1. spoil. See **mar.**

de fac•to (dē fak′tō, dā), **1.** in fact; in reality: *Although his title was prime minister, he was de facto president of the country. Although the school was said to be open to all qualified students, it still practiced de facto segregation.* **2.** actually existing, esp. when without lawful authority (distinguished from *de jure*). **3.** *Australian.* a person who lives in an intimate relationship with but is not married to a person of the opposite sex; lover. [1595–1605; < L *dē factō* lit., from the fact]

de•fal•cate (di fal′kāt, -fôl′-), *v.i.,* **-cat•ed, -cat•ing.** *Law.* to be guilty of defalcation. [1530–40; < ML *dēfalcātus* (ptp. of *dēfalcāre* to cut off), equiv. to *dē-* DE- + *falcātus;* see FALCATE] **—de•fal′ca•tor,** *n.*

de•fal•ca•tion (dē′fal kā′shən, -fôl-), *n. Law.* **1.** misappropriation of money or funds held by an official, trustee, or other fiduciary. **2.** the sum misappropriated. [1425–75; late ME: deduction from wages (< MF) < ML *dēfalcātiōn-* (s. of *dēfalcātiō*) a taking away, equiv. to *dēfalcāt(us)* (see DEFALCATE) + *-iōn-* -ION]

def•a•ma•tion (def′ə mā′shən), *n.* the act of defaming; false or unjustified injury of the good reputation of another, as by slander or libel; calumny: *She sued the magazine for defamation of character.* [1275–1325; ME r. (by analogy with DEFAME) ME *diffamacioun* < ML *diffāmātiōn-* (s. of *diffāmātiō*), equiv. to L *diffāmāt(us)* (ptp. of *diffāmāre;* see DEFAME) + *-iōn-* -ION]

de•fam•a•to•ry (di fam′ə tôr′ē, -tōr′ē), *adj.* containing defamation; injurious to reputation; slanderous or libelous: *She claimed that the article in the magazine was defamatory.* [1585–95; < ML *diffāmātōrius,* equiv. to L *diffāmā(re)* (see DEFAME) + *-tōrius* -TORY[1]]

de•fame (di fām′), *v.t.,* **-famed, -fam•ing. 1.** to attack

CONCISE PRONUNCIATION KEY: *act, cāpe, dâre, pärt; set, ēqual; if, ice; ox, ōver, ôrder, oil, bo͝ok, bo͞ot, out; up, ûrge; child; sing; shoe; thin, that;* zh as in *treasure.* ə = *a* as in *alone, e* as in *system, i* as in *easily, o* as in *gallop, u* as in *circus;* ° as in *fire* (fī°r), *hour* (ou°r). l and n can serve as syllabic consonants, as in *cradle* (krād′l), and *button* (but′n). See the full key inside the front cover.

the good name or reputation of, as by uttering or publishing maliciously or falsely anything injurious; slander or libel; calumniate: *The newspaper editorial defamed the politician.* **2.** *Archaic.* to disgrace; bring dishonor upon. **3.** *Archaic.* to accuse. [1275–1325; ME *defamen* (< AF *defamer*) < ML *dēfāmāre,* by-form of ML, L *diffāmāre* (*dē-* DE- for *dif-*; cf. L *dēfāmātus* infamous) to spread the news of, slander, equiv. to *dif-* DIF- + *-fāmāre* v. deriv. of *fāma* news, rumor, slander (see FAME); r. ME *diffamen* (< AF, OF *diffamer*) < ML, L, as above] **—de•fam′er,** *n.* **—de•fam′ing•ly,** *adv.*
—Syn. 1. malign, disparage, discredit, vilify, derogate, revile, denigrate, backbite.

de•fang (dē fang′), *v.t.* **1.** to remove the fangs of: *to defang a snake.* **2.** to cause to become less powerful or threatening; render harmless. [1950–55; DE- + FANG]

de•fault (di fôlt′), *n.* **1.** failure to act; inaction or neglect: *They lost their best client by sheer default.* **2.** failure to meet financial obligations. **3.** *Law.* failure to perform an act or obligation legally required, esp. to appear in court or to plead at a time assigned. **4.** *Sports.* failure to arrive in time for, participate in, or complete a scheduled match. **5.** lack; want; absence. **6.** *Computers.* a value that a program or operating system assumes, or a course of action that a program or operating system will take, when the user or programmer specifies no overriding value or action. *—v.i.* **7.** to fail in fulfilling or satisfying an engagement, claim, or obligation. **8.** to fail to meet financial obligations or to account properly for money in one's care: *When he defaulted in his payments, the bank foreclosed on the car.* **9.** *Law.* to fail to appear in court. **10.** *Sports.* **a.** to fail to participate in or complete a match. **b.** to lose a match by default. *—v.t.* **11.** to fail to perform or pay: *to default a debt.* **12.** to declare to be in default, esp. legally: *The judge defaulted the defendant.* **13.** *Sports.* **a.** to fail to compete in (a scheduled game, race, etc.). **b.** to lose by default. **14.** *Law.* to lose by failure to appear in court. [1175–1225; ME *defau(l)te* < AF *defalte,* OF *defaute,* deriv. of *defaillir,* after *faute, faillir.* See DE-, FAULT, FAIL]

de•fault•er (di fôl′tər), *n.* **1.** a person who defaults or fails to fulfill an obligation, esp. a legal or financial one. **2.** *Brit.* a soldier convicted by court-martial. [1660–70; DEFAULT + -ER[1]]

DEFCON (def′kon), *n.* any of several alert statuses for U.S. military forces, ranked numerically from normal, 5, to maximum readiness, 1. [*def(ense readiness) con(dition)*]

de•fea•sance (di fē′zəns), *n. Law.* **1.** a rendering null and void. **2.** a condition on the performance of which a deed or other instrument is defeated or rendered void. **3.** a collateral deed or other writing embodying such a condition. [1400–50; late ME *defesance* < AF *defesaunce,* OF *defesance,* equiv. to *desfes-* (ptp. s. of *desfaire* to undo; see DEFEAT) + *-ance* -ANCE]

de•fease (di fēz′), *v.t.,* **-feased, -feas•ing.** to defeat or annul (a contract, deed, etc.). [1470–80; back formation from DEFEASANCE]

de•fea•si•ble (di fē′zə bəl), *adj.* capable of being annulled or terminated. [1580–90; < AF *defesible.* See DEFEASANCE, -IBLE] **—de•fea′si•ble•ness, de•fea′si•bil′i•ty,** *n.*

de•feat (di fēt′), *v.t.* **1.** to overcome in a contest, election, battle, etc.; prevail over; vanquish: *They defeated the enemy. She defeated her brother at tennis.* **2.** to frustrate; thwart. **3.** to eliminate or deprive of something expected: *The early returns defeated his hopes of election.* **4.** *Law.* to annul. *—n.* **5.** the act of overcoming in a contest: *an overwhelming defeat of all opposition.* **6.** an instance of defeat; setback: *He considered his defeat a personal affront.* **7.** an overthrow or overturning; vanquishment: *the defeat of a government.* **8.** a bringing to naught; frustration: *the defeat of all his hopes and dreams.* **9.** the act or event of being bested; losing: *Defeat is not something she abides easily.* **10.** *Archaic.* undoing; destruction; ruin. [1325–75; ME *defeten* (v.) < AF, OF *desfait,* ptp. of *desfaire* to undo, destroy < ML *disfacere,* equiv. to L *dis-* DIS-[1] + *facere* to do] **—de•feat′er,** *n.*
—Syn. 1. overwhelm, overthrow, rout, check. DEFEAT, CONQUER, OVERCOME, SUBDUE imply gaining a victory or control over an opponent. DEFEAT suggests beating or frustrating: *to defeat an enemy in battle.* CONQUER implies finally gaining control over, usually after a series of efforts or against systematic resistance: *to conquer a country, one's inclinations.* OVERCOME emphasizes surmounting difficulties in prevailing over an antagonist: *to overcome opposition, bad habits.* SUBDUE means to conquer so completely that resistance is broken: *to subdue a rebellious spirit.* **2.** foil, baffle, balk. **7.** downfall.

de•feat•ism (di fē′tiz əm), *n.* the attitude, policy, or conduct of a person who admits, expects, or no longer resists defeat, as because of a conviction that further struggle or effort is futile; pessimistic resignation. [1915–20; DEFEAT + -ISM, modeled on F *défaitisme*]

de•feat•ist (di fē′tist), *n.* **1.** a person who surrenders easily or is subject to defeatism. **2.** an advocate or follower of defeatism as a public policy. *—adj.* **3.** marked by defeatism. [1915–20; DEFEAT + -IST, modeled on F *défaitiste*]

de•fea•ture[1] (di fē′chər), *n. Archaic.* disfigurement. [1580–90; DE- + FEATURE]

de•fea•ture[2] (di fē′chər), *n. Obs.* defeat; ruin. [1580–90; DEFEAT + -URE]

def•e•cate (def′i kāt′), *v.,* **-cat•ed, -cat•ing.** *—v.i.* **1.** to void excrement from the bowels through the anus; have a bowel movement. **2.** to become clear of dregs, impurities, etc. *—v.t.* **3.** to clear of dregs, impurities, etc.; purify; refine. [1565–75; < L *dēfaecātus* (ptp. of *dēfaecāre* to cleanse, refine), equiv. to *dē-* DE- + *faec-* (s. of *faex* dregs, sediment) + *-ātus* -ATE[1]] **—def′e•ca′tion,** *n.*

de•fect (*n.* dē′fekt, di fekt′; *v.* di fekt′), *n.* **1.** a shortcoming, fault, or imperfection: *a defect in an argument; a defect in a machine.* **2.** lack or want, esp. of something essential to perfection or completeness; deficiency: *a defect in hearing.* **3.** Also called **crystal defect, lattice defect.** *Crystall.* a discontinuity in the lattice of a crystal caused by missing or extra atoms or ions, or by dislocations. *—v.i.* **4.** to desert a cause, country, etc., esp. in order to adopt another (often fol. by *from* or *to*): *He defected from the U.S.S.R to the West.* [1375–1425; late ME < L *dēfectus* failure, weakness, equiv. to *dēfec-* var. s. of *dēficere* to run short, fail, weaken (see DEFICIENT) + *-tus* suffix of v. action] **—de•fect′i•ble,** *adj.* **—de•fect′i•bil′i•ty,** *n.* **—de•fect′less,** *adj.*
—Syn. 1. DEFECT, BLEMISH, FLAW refer to faults that detract from perfection. DEFECT is the general word for any kind of shortcoming or imperfection, whether literal or figurative: *a defect in eyesight, in a plan.* A BLEMISH is usually a defect on a surface, which mars the appearance: *a blemish on her cheek.* FLAW is applied to a defect in quality, caused by imperfect structure (as in a diamond) or brought about during manufacture (as in texture of cloth, in clearness of glass, etc.).

de•fec•tion (di fek′shən), *n.* **1.** desertion from allegiance, loyalty, duty, or the like; apostasy: *His defection to East Germany was regarded as treasonable.* **2.** failure; lack; loss: *He was overcome by a sudden defection of courage.* [1535–45; < L *dēfectiōn-* (s. of *dēfectiō*), equiv. to *dēfect(us)* (see DEFECT) + *-iōn-* -ION]
—Ant. 1. loyalty.

de•fec•tive (di fek′tiv), *adj.* **1.** having a defect or flaw; faulty; imperfect: *a defective machine.* **2.** *Psychol.* characterized by subnormal intelligence or behavior. **3.** *Gram.* (of an inflected word or its inflection) lacking one or more of the inflected forms proper to most words of the same class in the language, as English *must,* which occurs only in the present tense. *—n.* **4.** a defective person or thing. [1375–1425; < LL *dēfectīvus,* equiv. to *dēfectus* (see DEFECT) + *-īvus* -IVE; r. ME *defectif* < MF < LL, as above] **—de•fec′tive•ly,** *adv.* **—de•fec′tive•ness,** *n.*
—Syn. 1. incomplete, deficient. **—Ant. 1.** perfect, complete.

defec′tive num′ber, *Math.* See **deficient number.**

defec′tive year′. See under **Jewish calendar.** [1905–10]

de•fec•tor (di fek′tər), *n.* a person who defects from a cause, country, alliance, etc. [1655–65; < L *dēfector* renegade, rebel, equiv. to *dēfec-* (var. s. of *dēficere* to become disaffected, revolt, lit., to fail; see DEFECT) + *-tor* -TOR]

de•fed•er•al•ize (dē fed′ər ə līz′), *v.t.,* **-ized, -iz•ing.** to shift the functions or powers of (an agency, service, etc.) from the jurisdiction of the federal government to that of state or local government: *to defederalize construction loans.* Also, *esp. Brit.,* **de•fed′er•al•ise′.** [DE- + FEDERALIZE] **—de•fed′er•al•i•za′tion,** *n.*

de•fence (di fens′), *n., v.t.,* **-fenced, -fenc•ing.** *Chiefly Brit.* defense. **—de•fence′a•ble,** *adj.* **—de•fence′less,** *adj.* **—de•fence′less•ly,** *adv.* **—de•fence′less•ness,** *n.*

de•fend (di fend′), *v.t.* **1.** to ward off attack from; guard against assault or injury (usually fol. by *from* or *against*): *The sentry defended the gate against sudden attack.* **2.** to maintain by argument, evidence, etc.; uphold: *She defended her claim successfully.* **3.** to contest (a legal charge, claim, etc.). **4.** *Law.* to serve as attorney for (a defendant): *He has defended some of the most notorious criminals.* **5.** to support (an argument, theory, etc.) in the face of criticism; prove the validity of (a dissertation, thesis, or the like) by answering arguments and questions put by a committee of specialists. **6.** to attempt to retain (a championship title, position, etc.), as in a competition against a challenger. *—v.i.* **7.** *Law.* to enter or make a defense. [1200–50; ME *defenden* < OF *defendre* < L *dēfendere* to ward off, equiv. to *dē-* DE- + *-fendere* to strike] **—de•fend′a•ble,** *adj.* **—de•fend′er,** *n.*
—Syn. 1. shelter, screen, shield; garrison, fortify. DEFEND, GUARD, PRESERVE, PROTECT all mean to keep safe. To DEFEND is to strive to keep safe by resisting attack: *to defend one's country.* To GUARD is to watch over in order to keep safe: *to guard a camp.* To PRESERVE is to keep safe in the midst of danger, either in a single instance or continuously: *to preserve a spirit of conciliation.* To PROTECT is to keep safe by interposing a shield or barrier: *to protect books by means of heavy paper covers.* **2.** vindicate. **—Ant. 1.** attack.

de•fend•ant (di fen′dənt *or, esp. in court for 1,* -dant), *n.* **1.** *Law.* a person, company, etc., against whom a claim or charge is brought in a court (opposed to *plaintiff*). **2.** *Obs.* defender. *—adj.* **3.** making one's defense; defending: *a defendant corporation.* **4.** *Obs.* defensive. [1275–1325; ME *defendaunt* < AF (MF, OF *defendant*). See DEFEND, -ANT]

defend′er of the bond′, *Rom. Cath. Ch.* an official appointed in each diocese to uphold marriages of disputed validity. Also called **defend′er of the mar′riage bond′.**

Defend′er of the Faith′, a title conferred on Henry VIII by Pope Leo X in 1521, later withdrawn but restored by Parliament and used ever since by English sovereigns. [trans. of NL *Fidei dēfēnsor*]

de•fen•es•tra•tion (dē fen′ə strā′shən), *n.* the act of throwing a thing or esp. a person out of a window: *the defenestration of the commissioners at Prague.* [1610–20; DE- + L *fenestr(a)* window + -ATION]

de•fense (di fens′ *or, esp. for 7, 9,* dē′fens), *n., v.,* **-fensed, -fens•ing.** *—n.* **1.** resistance against attack; protection: *Two more regiments are needed for the defense of the city.* **2.** something that defends, as a fortification, physical or mental quality, or medication: *This fort was once the main defense of the island.* **3.** the defending of a cause or the like by speech, argument, etc.: *He spoke in defense of the nation's foreign policy.* **4.** a speech, argument, etc., in vindication: *She delivered a defense of free enterprise.* **5.** *Law.* **a.** the denial or pleading of the defendant in answer to the claim or charge that has been made. **b.** the proceedings adopted by a defendant, or the defendant's legal agents, for defending against the charges that have been made. **c.** a defendant and his or her counsel. **6.** *Psychol.* See **defense mechanism** (def. 2). **7.** *Sports.* **a.** the practice or art of defending oneself or one's goal against attack, as in fencing, boxing, soccer, or football. **b.** the team attempting to thwart the attack of the team having the ball or puck. **c.** the players of a team who line up in their own defensive zone. **d.** the positions on the field, ice, etc., taken by such players. **8.** (*cap.*) Also called **Defense′ Depart′ment.** *Informal.* the Department of Defense. *—v.t.* **9.** *Sports.* to defend against (an opponent, play, or tactic). Also, *esp. Brit.,* **defence.** [1250–1300; ME < OF < LL *dēfēnsa* a forbidding, n. use of fem. of ptp. of L *dēfendere* to DEFEND; r. ME *defens* < AF, OF < ML *dēfēnsum* (thing) forbidden, neut. ptp. of L *dēfendere*] **—de•fense′less,** *adj.* **—de•fense′less•ly,** *adv.* **—de•fense′less•ness,** *n.*
—Syn. 1. security, preservation, safeguard. **3.** support, advocacy, justification.

de•fense•man (di fens′mən, -man′), *n., pl.* **-men** (-mən, -men′). *Sports.* a player in certain games, as ice hockey or lacrosse, who lines up in a defensive zone or position. [1890–95; DEFENSE + MAN[1]]

defense′ mech′anism, 1. *Physiol.* the defensive reaction of an organism, as against a pathogenic microorganism. **2.** *Psychol.* an unconscious process, as denial, that protects an individual from unacceptable or painful ideas or impulses. [1890–95]

de•fen•si•ble (di fen′sə bəl), *adj.* **1.** capable of being defended against assault or injury: *The troops were bivouacked in a defensible position.* **2.** that can be defended in argument; justifiable. [1250–1300; ME < LL *dēfēnsibilis,* equiv. to L *dēfēns(us)* (see DEFENSE) + *-ibilis* -IBLE; r. ME *defensable* < OF < LL *dēfēnsābilis,* equiv. to *dēfēnsā(re)* (freq. of *dēfendere* to DEFEND) + *-bilis* -BLE] **—de•fen′si•bil′i•ty, de•fen′si•ble•ness,** *n.* **—de•fen′si•bly,** *adv.*
—Syn. 2. suitable, fit, tenable, allowable, warrantable.

de•fen•sive (di fen′siv), *adj.* **1.** serving to defend; protective: *defensive armament.* **2.** made or carried on for the purpose of resisting attack: *defensive treaty; a defensive attitude.* **3.** of or pertaining to defense. **4.** (of stocks, securities, etc.) **a.** able to provide moderately steady growth with minimal risk: *The bank has put a large percentage of its assets in defensive rather than growth stocks.* **b.** considered stable and relatively safe for investment, esp. during a decline in the economy. **5.** excessively concerned with guarding against the real or imagined threat of criticism, injury to one's ego, or exposure of one's shortcomings. *—n.* **6.** a position or attitude of defense: *to be on the defensive about one's mistakes.* **7.** *Obs.* something that serves to defend. [1350–1400; < ML *dēfēnsīvus* (see DEFENSE, -IVE); r. ME *defensif* < MF < ML, as above] **—de′fen′sive•ly,** *adv.* **—de•fen′sive•ness,** *n.*

defen′sive back′, *Football.* a defender positioned off the line of scrimmage for the purpose of covering pass receivers and tackling runners who elude linemen and linebackers.

defen′sive med′icine, the practice by a physician of ordering many tests or consultations as a means of self-protection against charges of malpractice in the event of an unfavorable outcome of treatment. [1965–70]

de•fer[1] (di fûr′), *v.,* **-ferred, -fer•ring.** *—v.t.* **1.** to put off (action, consideration, etc.) to a future time: *The decision has been deferred by the board until next week.* **2.** to exempt temporarily from induction into military service. *—v.i.* **3.** to put off action; delay. [1325–75; ME *deferren,* var. of *differren* to DIFFER] **—de•fer′rer,** *n.*
—Syn. 1. DEFER, DELAY, POSTPONE imply keeping something from occurring until a future time. To DEFER is to decide to do something later on: *to defer making a payment.* To DELAY is sometimes equivalent to DEFER, but usually it is to act in a dilatory manner and thus lay something aside: *to delay one's departure.* To POSTPONE a thing is to put it off to (usually) some particular time in the future, with the intention of beginning or resuming it then: *to postpone an election.* **3.** procrastinate.

de•fer[2] (di fûr′), *v.,* **-ferred, -fer•ring.** *—v.i.* **1.** to yield respectfully in judgment or opinion (usually fol. by *to*): *We all defer to him in these matters.* *—v.t.* **2.** to submit for decision; refer: *We defer questions of this kind to the president.* [1400–50; late ME *deferren* < L *dēferre* to carry from or down, report, accuse, equiv. to *dē-* DE- + *ferre* to BEAR[1]]
—Syn. 1. accede, submit, acquiesce, capitulate.

de•fer•a•ble (di fûr′ə bəl), *adj., n.* deferrable.

def•er•ence (def′ər əns), *n.* **1.** respectful submission or yielding to the judgment, opinion, will, etc., of another. **2.** respectful or courteous regard: *in deference to his wishes.* [1640–50; < F *déférence,* MF, equiv. to *defer(er)* to DEFER[2] + *-ence* -ENCE]

def•er•ent[1] (def′ər ənt), *adj.* marked by or showing deference: *She was always deferent to her elders.* [1815–25; DEFER[2] + -ENT]

def•er•ent[2] (def′ər ənt), *adj. Anat.* **1.** conveying away; efferent. **2.** of or pertaining to the vas deferens. *—n.* **3.** *Astron.* (in the Ptolemaic system) the circle around the earth in which a celestial body or the center of the epicycle of its orbit was thought to move. [1375–1425; late ME < L *dēferent-* (s. of *dēferēns*), prp. of *dēferre.* See DEFER[2], -ENT]

def•er•en•tial (def′ə ren′shəl), *adj.* showing deference; deferent; respectful. [1815–25; after DEFERENCE, by analogy with such pairs as *residence: residential*] **—def′er•en′tial•ly,** *adv.*
—Syn. courteous, regardful, dutiful, obedient, reverential.

de•fer•ment (di fûr′mənt), *n.* **1.** the act of deferring or putting off; postponement. **2.** a temporary exemption from induction into military service. [1605–15; DEFER[1] + -MENT]

de•fer•ra•ble (di fûr′ə bəl), *adj.* **1.** capable of being deferred or postponed: *a deferrable project.* **2.** qualified or eligible to receive a military deferment. —*n.* **3.** a person eligible for deferment from compulsory military service. Also, **deferable.** [1940–45; DEFER[1] + -ABLE]

de•fer•ral (di fûr′əl), *n.* deferment. [DEFER[1] + -AL[2]]

de•ferred (di fûrd′), *adj.* **1.** postponed or delayed. **2.** suspended or withheld for or until a certain time or event: *a deferred payment; deferred taxes.* **3.** classified as temporarily exempt from induction into military service. [1645–55; DEFER[1] + -ED[2]]

deferred′ annu′ity, an annuity that starts at the end of a specified period or after the annuitant reaches a certain age. Cf. **immediate annuity.**

deferred′ charge′, an expenditure shown as a cost of operation carried forward and written off in one or more future periods.

deferred′ share′, *Chiefly Brit.* a share of stock on which a dividend is not paid until some fixed date or until some conditional event. [1880–85]

de•fer•vesce (dē′fər ves′, def′ər-), *v.i.,* **-vesced, -vesc•ing.** to undergo defervescence. [1855–60; back formation from DEFERVESCENCE]

de•fer•ves•cence (dē′fər ves′əns, def′ər-), *n. Med.* abatement of fever. [1715–25; < G *Deferveszenz* < L *dēfervēsc(ent-)* (s. of *dēfervēscēns,* prp. of *dēfervēscere,* equiv. to *dē-* DE- + *fervēscere* to begin to boil) + -ENCE; see EFFERVESCENT] —**de′fer•ves′cent,** *adj.*

de•fi•ance (di fī′əns), *n.* **1.** a daring or bold resistance to authority or to any opposing force. **2.** open disregard; contempt (often fol. by *of*): *defiance of danger; His refusal amounted to defiance.* **3.** a challenge to meet in combat or in a contest. **4. bid defiance to,** to offer resistance; defy. **5. in defiance of,** in spite of; notwithstanding: *There was a splendid audience in defiance of the rainstorm.* [1250–1300; ME < OF, equiv. to *defi(er)* to DEFY + *-ance* -ANCE]

De•fi•ance (di fī′əns), *n.* a city in NW Ohio. 16,810.

de•fi•ant (di fī′ənt), *adj.* characterized by defiance; boldly resistant or challenging: *a defiant attitude.* [1830–40; < F *défiant,* OF, prp. of *defier* to DEFY; see -ANT] —**de•fi′ant•ly,** *adv.* —**de•fi′ant•ness,** *n.*
—**Syn.** insubordinate, contumacious, refractory.

de•fi•ber (dē fī′bər), *v.t.* defibrate. [DE- + FIBER]

de•fi•bered (dē fī′bərd), *adj.* (of food) having little or no natural fiber, typically as the result of commercial refining or processing. [DE- + FIBER + -ED[2]]

de•fi•ber•ize (dē fī′bə rīz′), *v.t.,* **-ized, -iz•ing.** defibrate. Also, *esp. Brit.,* **de•fi′ber•ise′.** [DE- + FIBER + -IZE]

de•fi•brate (dē fī′brāt), *v.t.,* **-brat•ed, -brat•ing.** to break (wood, paper, garbage, etc.) into fibrous components; reduce to fibers. [DE- + FIBR- + -ATE[1]]

de•fib•ril•late (dē fib′rə lāt′, -fī′brə-), *v.t.,* **-lat•ed, -lat•ing.** *Med.* to arrest the fibrillation of (heart muscle) by applying electric shock across the chest, thus depolarizing the heart cells and allowing normal rhythm to return. [1930–35; DE- + *fibrillate,* back formation from FIBRILLATION] —**de•fib′ril•la′tion,** *n.*

de•fib•ril•la•tor (dē fib′rə lā′tər, -fī′brə-), *n. Med.* an agent or device for arresting fibrillation of the atrial or ventricular muscles of the heart. [1955–60; DE- + FIBRILL(ATION) + -ATOR]

de•fi•bri•nate (dē fī′brə nāt′), *v.t.,* **-nat•ed, -nat•ing.** *Med.* to remove fibrin from (blood). [1835–45; DE- + FIBRIN + -ATE[1]] —**de•fi′bri•na′tion,** *n.*

de•fi•cience (di fish′əns), *n. Obs.* deficiency.

de•fi•cien•cy (di fish′ən sē), *n., pl.* **-cies. 1.** the state of being deficient; lack; incompleteness; insufficiency. **2.** the amount lacked; a deficit. [1625–35; < LL *dēficientia,* L *dēficient-* (s. of *dēficiēns*). See DEFICIENT, -ENCY]
—**Syn. 1.** shortage, inadequacy, paucity, scarcity.

defi′ciency account′, an account summarizing the financial condition of an individual or company in danger of bankruptcy. Also called **defi′ciency state′ment.**

defi′ciency disease′, *Pathol.* any illness associated with an insufficient supply of one or more essential dietary constituents. [1910–15]

defi′ciency judg′ment, *Law.* a judgment in favor of a creditor who has not satisfied the full amount of a claim against a debtor.

de•fi•cient (di fish′ənt), *adj.* **1.** lacking some element or characteristic; defective: *deficient in taste.* **2.** insufficient; inadequate: *deficient knowledge.* —*n.* **3.** a person who is deficient, esp. one who is mentally defective. [1575–85; < L *dēficient-* (s. of *dēficiēns,* prp. of *dēficere* to fail, run short, lack, weaken), equiv. to *dē-* DE- + *fic-,* comb. form of *facere* to make, DO[1] + thematic *-i-* + *-ent-* -ENT] —**de•fi′cient•ly,** *adv.*

defi′cient num′ber, *Math.* a positive number that is greater than the sum of all positive integers that are submultiples of it, as 10, which is greater than the sum of 1, 2, and 5. Also called **defective number.** Cf. **abundant number, perfect number.** [1720–30]

def•i•cit (def′ə sit; *Brit. also* di fis′it), *n.* **1.** the amount by which a sum of money falls short of the required amount. **2.** the amount by which expenditures or liabilities exceed income or assets. **3.** a lack or shortage; deficiency. **4.** a disadvantage or handicap: *The team's major deficit is its poor pitching.* **5.** a loss, as in the operation of a business. [1775–85; < L *dēficit* (it) lacks, 3rd pers. sing. pres. indic. of *dēficere;* see DEFICIENT]

def′icit finan′cing, (esp. of a government) expenditures in excess of public revenues, made possible typically by borrowing.

def′icit spend′ing, the practice of spending funds in excess of income, esp. by a government. [1935–40]

de fi•de (de fē′de; *Eng.* dē fī′dē), *Latin.* of the faith: a phrase used in the Roman Catholic Church to qualify certain teachings as being divinely revealed, belief in them therefore being obligatory.

de•fi•er (di fī′ər), *n.* a person who defies. [1575–85; DEFY + -ER[1]]

def•i•lade (def′ə lād′), *n., v.,* **-lad•ed, -lad•ing.** —*n.* **1.** protection or shielding from hostile ground observation and flat projecting fire provided by an artificial or natural obstacle, as a hill. —*v.t.* **2.** to shield from enemy fire by using natural or artificial obstacles. [1820–30; < F *défil(er),* orig. to unthread (equiv. to *dé-* DIS-[1] + *(en)filer* to thread << L *fīlum* thread) + F *-ade* -ADE[1]]

de•file[1] (di fīl′), *v.t.,* **-filed, -fil•ing. 1.** to make foul, dirty, or unclean; pollute; taint; debase. **2.** to violate the chastity of. **3.** to make impure for ceremonial use; desecrate. **4.** to sully, as a person's reputation. [1275–1325; ME *defilen, defelen,* alter. of *defoilen* (by assoc. with *filen* to FILE[3]) < AF, OF *defouler* to trample on, violate; cf. OE *befȳlan* to befoul] —**de•fil′a•ble,** *adj.* —**de•file′ment,** *n.* —**de•fil′er,** *n.* —**de•fil′ing•ly,** *adv.*

de•file[2] (di fīl′, dē′fīl), *n., v.,* **-filed, -fil•ing.** —*n.* **1.** any narrow passage, esp. between mountains. —*v.i.* **2.** to march in a line or by files. [1675–85; < F *défilé,* n. use of ptp. of *défiler* to file off; see DEFILADE]

de•fine (di fīn′), *v.,* **-fined, -fin•ing.** —*v.t.* **1.** to state or set forth the meaning of (a word, phrase, etc.): *They disagreed on how to define "liberal."* **2.** to explain or identify the nature or essential qualities of; describe: *to define judicial functions.* **3.** to fix or lay down definitely; specify distinctly: *to define one's responsibilities.* **4.** to determine or fix the boundaries or extent of: *to define property with stakes.* **5.** to make clear the outline or form of: *The roof was boldly defined against the sky.* —*v.i.* **6.** to set forth the meaning of a word, phrase, etc.; construct a definition. [1325–75; ME *def(f)inen* < AF, OF *definer* to put an end to < L *dēfīnīre* to limit, define, equiv. to *dē-* DE- + *fīnīre;* see FINISH] —**de•fin′a•ble,** *adj.* —**de•fin′a•bil′i•ty,** *n.* —**de•fin′a•bly,** *adv.* —**de•fine′ment,** *n.* —**de•fin′er,** *n.*
—**Syn. 3.** state, name, describe, detail, enumerate.

de•fin•i•en•dum (di fin′ē en′dəm), *n., pl.* **-da** (-də). **1.** something that is or is to be defined, esp. the term at the head of a dictionary entry. **2.** *Logic.* an expression to be defined in terms of another expression previously defined. Cf. **definiens.** [1870–75; < L *dēfīniendum,* neut. ger. of *dēfīnīre;* see DEFINE]

de•fin•i•ens (di fin′ē ənz), *n., pl.* **de•fin•i•en•tia** (di fin′ē en′shə, -shē ə). **1.** something that defines, esp. the defining part of a dictionary entry. **2.** *Logic.* an expression in terms of which another may be adequately defined. Cf. **definiendum.** [1870–75; < L *dēfīniēns,* prp. of *dēfīnīre;* see DEFINE]

defin′ing mo′ment, a point at which the essential nature or character of a person, group, etc., is revealed or identified. [1980–85]

def•i•nite (def′ə nit), *adj.* **1.** clearly defined or determined; not vague or general; fixed; precise; exact: *a definite quantity; definite directions.* **2.** having fixed limits; bounded with precision: *a definite area.* **3.** positive; certain; sure: *It is definite that he will take the job.* **4.** defining; limiting. **5.** *Bot.* (of an inflorescence) determinate. [1520–30; < L *dēfīnītus* limited, precise, ptp. of *dēfīnīre;* see DEFINE, -ITE[2]] —**def′i•nite•ness,** *n.*
—**Syn. 1.** specific, particular. **2.** well-defined.

def′inite ar′ticle, *Gram.* an article, as English *the,* that classes as identified or definite the noun it modifies. [1755–65]

def′inite in′tegral, *Math.* the representation, usually in symbolic form, of the difference in values of a primitive of a given function evaluated at two designated points. Cf. **indefinite integral.** [1875–80]

def•i•nite•ly (def′ə nit lē), *adv.* **1.** in a definite manner; unambiguously. **2.** unequivocally; positively. —*interj.* **3.** (used to express complete agreement or strong affirmation): *Are you starting your diet tomorrow? Definitely!* [1575–85; DEFINITE + -LY]
—**Syn. 1.** See **clearly. 2.** absolutely, certainly.

def′inite rel′ative clause′, a relative clause with a definite relative pronoun as subordinating word, as *that they said* in *We heard the things that they said.*

def′inite rel′ative pro′noun, a relative pronoun that refers to an antecedent, as *who* in *It was I who told you.*

def•i•ni•tion (def′ə nish′ən), *n.* **1.** the act of defining or making definite, distinct, or clear. **2.** the formal statement of the meaning or significance of a word, phrase, etc. **3.** the condition of being definite, distinct, or clearly outlined. **4.** *Optics.* sharpness of the image formed by an optical system. **5.** *Radio and Television.* the accuracy of sound or picture reproduction. [1350–1400; ME *diffinicioun* < OF *diffinition* < L *dēfīnītiōn-* (s. of *dēfīnītiō*), equiv. to *dēfīnīt(us)* (see DEFINITE) + *-iōn-* -ION] —**def′i•ni′tion•al,** *adj.* —**def′i•ni′tion•al•ly,** *adv.*

de•fin•i•tive (di fin′i tiv), *adj.* **1.** most reliable or complete, as of a text, author, criticism, study, or the like: *the definitive biography of Andrew Jackson.* **2.** serving to define, fix, or specify definitely: *to clarify with a definitive statement.* **3.** having its fixed and final form; providing a solution or final answer; satisfying all criteria: *the definitive treatment for an infection; a definitive answer to a dilemma.* **4.** *Biol.* fully developed or formed; complete. —*n.* **5.** a defining or limiting word, as an article, a demonstrative, or the like. **6.** *Philately.* a stamp that is a regular issue and is usually on sale for an extended period of time. Cf. **commemorative** (def. 2). [1350–1400; ME < OF < L *dēfīnītīvus,* equiv. to *dēfīnīt(us)* (see DEFINITE) + *-īvus* -IVE] —**de•fin′i•tive•ly,** *adv.* —**de•fin′i•tive•ness,** *n.*
—**Syn. 3.** complete, absolute, ultimate, supreme.

defin′itive host′, *Zool.* the host in or on which a parasite spends the sexual stage of its life cycle. [1900–05]

defin′itive plum′age, *Ornith.* the plumage of a bird that, once attained, does not change significantly in color or pattern for the rest of the bird's life.

def•i•nit•ize (def′ə ni tīz′, di fin′i-), *v.t.,* **-ized, -iz•ing.** to cause to become definite; crystallize. Also, *esp. Brit.,* **def′i•nit•ise′.** [1875–80; DEFINITE + -IZE]

de•fin•i•tude (di fin′i to͞od′, -tyo͞od′), *n.* definiteness; exactitude; precision. [1830–40; DEFINITE + -TUDE]

def•la•grate (def′lə grāt′), *v.t., v.i.,* **-grat•ed, -grat•ing.** to burn, esp. suddenly and violently. [1720–30; < L *dēflagrātus* (ptp. of *dēflagrāre* to burn down), equiv. to *dē-* DE- + *flagr(āre)* to burn + *-ātus* -ATE[1]] —**def′la•gra•ble,** *adj.* —**def′la•gra•bil′i•ty,** *n.* —**def′la•gra′tion,** *n.*

de•flate (di flāt′), *v.,* **-flat•ed, -flat•ing.** —*v.t.* **1.** to release the air or gas from (something inflated, as a balloon): *They deflated the tires slightly to allow the truck to drive under the overpass.* **2.** to depress or reduce (a person or a person's ego, hopes, spirits, etc.); puncture; dash: *Her rebuff thoroughly deflated me.* **3.** to reduce (currency, prices, etc.) from an inflated condition; to affect with deflation. —*v.i.* **4.** to become deflated. [1890–95; < L *dēflātus* blown off, away (ptp. of *dēflāre*), equiv. to *dē-* DE- + *fl(āre)* to blow + *-ātus* -ATE[1]] —**de•fla′tor,** *n.*

de•fla•tion (di flā′shən), *n.* **1.** the act of deflating or the state of being deflated. **2.** *Econ.* a fall in the general price level or a contraction of credit and available money (opposed to *inflation*). Cf. **disinflation. 3.** the erosion of sand, soil, etc., by the action of the wind. [1890–95; DEFLATE + -ION] —**de•fla′tion•ar′y,** *adj.* —**de•fla′tion•ism,** *n.* —**de•fla′tion•ist,** *n., adj.*

defla′tionary spi′ral. See under **spiral** (def. 7).

de•flect (di flekt′), *v.t., v.i.* to bend or turn aside; turn from a true course or straight line; swerve. [1545–55; < L *dēflectere* to bend down, turn aside, equiv. to *dē-* DE- + *flectere* to bend, turn] —**de•flect′a•ble,** *adj.* —**de•flec′tor,** *n.*

de•flect•ed (di flek′tid), *adj. Biol.* **1.** curved or bent downward. **2.** deflexed. [1820–30; DEFLECT + -ED[2]]

deflect′ing force′, *Physics.* See **Coriolis effect.**

de•flec•tion (di flek′shən), *n.* **1.** the act or state of deflecting or the state of being deflected. **2.** amount of deviation. **3.** the deviation of the indicator of an instrument from the position taken as zero. **4.** *Optics.* deviation (def. 5a). **5.** *Mil.* the angle formed by the line of sight to the target and the line of sight to the point at which a gun is aimed so as to strike the target. **6.** *Electronics.* (in a cathode-ray tube) the bending by a magnetic field of the beam of electrons leaving the electron gun. Also, *Brit.,* **de•flex′ion.** [1595–1605; < LL *dēflexiōn-* (s. of *dēflexiō*), equiv. to L *dēflex(us)* (ptp. of *dēflectere;* see DEFLECT) + *-iōn-* -ION]

deflec′tion yoke′, *Electronics.* an assembly of one or more coils through which a controlled current is passed to produce a magnetic field for deflecting a beam of electrons, as in a picture tube. Also called **yoke.**

de•flec•tive (di flek′tiv), *adj.* causing deflection. [1805–15; DEFLECT + -IVE]

de•flexed (di flekst′), *adj. Biol.* **1.** bent abruptly downward. **2.** deflected. [1820–30; < L *dēflex(us)* bent down (see DEFLECTION) + -ED[2]]

de•floc•cu•lant (dē flok′yə lənt), *n. Ceram.* a chemical added to slip to increase fluidity. [1925–30; DEFLOCCUL(ATE) + -ANT]

de•floc•cu•late (dē flok′yə lāt′), *v.t.,* **-lat•ed, -lat•ing.** *Physical Chem.* to reduce from a flocculent state by dispersing the flocculated particles. [1905–10; DE- + FLOCCULATE] —**de•floc′cu•la′tion,** *n.*

def•lo•ra•tion (def′lə rā′shən, dē′flə-), *n.* the act of deflowering. [1350–1400; ME *defloracioun* < OF *defloracion* < LL *dēflōrātiōn-* (s. of *dēflōrātiō*) a plucking of flowers, equiv. to *dēflōrāt(us)* (ptp. of *dēflōrāre* to DEFLOWER) + *-iōn-* -ION]

de•flow•er (di flou′ər), *v.t.* **1.** to deprive (a woman) of virginity. **2.** to despoil of beauty, freshness, sanctity, etc. **3.** to deprive or strip of flowers: *The deer had deflowered an entire section of the garden.* [1350–1400; ME *deflouren* < OF *desflorer* < L *dēflōrāre,* equiv. to *dē-* DE- + *flōr-,* s. of *flōs* FLOWER + *-āre* inf. suffix] —**de•flow′er•er,** *n.*

de•flux•ion (di fluk′shən), *n. Pathol.* a copious discharge of fluid matter, as in catarrh. [1540–50; < LL *dēfluxiōn-* (s. of *dēfluxiō*) a flowing down, discharge, equiv. to L *dē-* DE- + *fluxiōn-* FLUXION]

de•fo•cus (dē fō′kəs), *v.,* **-cused, -cus•ing** or (*esp. Brit.*) **-cussed, -cus•sing,** *n., pl.* **-cus•es.** —*v.t.* **1.** to cause loss of focus of: *The slightest movement will defocus the microscope.* **2.** to interrupt or disturb (concentration, attention, etc.). **3.** to disturb the concentration or awareness of (someone). —*v.i.* **4.** to lose or go out of focus. **5.** to lose concentration or awareness; become distracted. —*n.* **6.** the result of defocusing, as a blurred photographic image. [1930–35; DE- + FOCUS]

De•foe (di fō′), *n.* **Daniel** 1659?–1731, English novelist and political journalist. Also, **De Foe′.**

de•fog (dē fog′, -fôg′), *v.t.,* **-fogged, -fog•ging. 1.** to remove the fog or moisture from (a car window, mirror, etc.). **2.** *Informal.* to make intelligible, specific, or obvious; clarify: *In a lengthy interview the mayor defogged the issues in the transit strike.* [1900–05; DE- + FOG[1]]

de•fog•ger (dē fog′ər, -fô′gər), *n.* defroster (def. 2). [DEFOG + -ER[1]]

de•fo•li•ant (dē fō′lē ənt), *n.* a preparation for defoliating plants. [1940–45; DEFOLI(ATE) + -ANT]

CONCISE PRONUNCIATION KEY: act, cāpe, dâre, pärt; set, ēqual; *if,* īce; ox, ōver, ôrder, oil, bo͝ok, bo͞ot, out; up, ûrge; child; sing; shoe; thin, *th*at; zh as in *treasure.* ə = *a* as in *alone, e* as in *system, i* as in *easily, o* as in *gallop, u* as in *circus;* ° as in *fire* (fī°r), *hour* (ou°r). l and n can serve as syllabic consonants, as in *cradle* (krād′l), and *button* (but′n). See the full key inside the front cover.

de•fo•li•ate (*v.* dē fō′lē āt′; *adj.* dē fō′lē it, -āt′), *v.*, **-at•ed, -at•ing,** *adj.* —*v.t.* **1.** to strip (a tree, bush, etc.) of leaves. **2.** to destroy or cause widespread loss of leaves in (an area of jungle, forest, etc.), as by using chemical sprays or incendiary bombs, in order to deprive enemy troops or guerrilla forces of concealment. —*v.i.* **3.** to lose leaves. —*adj.* **4.** (of a tree) having lost its leaves, esp. by a natural process. [1785–1795; < ML *dēfoliātus,* ptp. of *dēfoliāre,* equiv. to L *dē-* DE- + *foli(um)* leaf + *-ātus* -ATE[1]] —**de•fo′li•a′tion,** *n.* —**de•fo′li•a′tor,** *n.*

de•force (di fôrs′, -fōrs′), *v.t.,* **-forced, -forc•ing.** *Law.* **1.** to withhold (property, esp. land) by force or violence, as from the rightful owner. **2.** to eject or evict by force. [1250–1300; ME < AF *deforcer,* OF *de(s)forcier,* equiv. to *de(s)-* DE- + *forc(i)er* to FORCE] —**de•force′ment,** *n.* —**de•forc′er,** *n.*

de•for•ciant (di fôr′shənt, -fōr′-), *n. Law.* a person who deforces the rightful owner. [1250–1300; ME *deforciaunt* < AF, prp. of *deforcer.* See DEFORCE, -ANT]

De For•est (di fôr′ist, for′-), **Lee,** 1873–1961, U.S. inventor of radio, telegraphic, and telephonic equipment.

de•for•est (dē fôr′ist, -for′-), *v.t.* to divest or clear of forests or trees: *Poor planning deforested the area in ten years.* [1530–40; DE- + FOREST] —**de•for′est•a′tion,** *n.* —**de•for′est•er,** *n.*

de•form[1] (di fôrm′), *v.t.* **1.** to mar the natural form or shape of; put out of shape; disfigure: *In cases where the drug was taken during pregnancy, its effects deformed the infants.* **2.** to make ugly, ungraceful, or displeasing; mar the beauty of; spoil: *The trees had been completely deformed by the force of the wind.* **3.** to change the form of; transform. **4.** *Geol., Mech.* to subject to deformation: *The metal was deformed under stress.* —*v.i.* **5.** to undergo deformation. [1350–1400; ME *deformen* < L *dēfōrmāre,* equiv. to *dē-* DE- + *fōrmāre* to FORM] —**de•form′a•ble,** *adj.* —**de•form′a•bil′i•ty,** *n.* —**de•form′a•tive,** *adj.* —**de•form′er,** *n.*
—**Syn. 1.** misshape. See **mar. 2.** ruin.

de•form[2] (di fôrm′), *adj. Archaic.* deformed; ugly. [1350–1400; ME *defo(u)rme* < L *dēfōrmis,* equiv. to *dē-* DE- + *-formis* -FORM]

de•for•mal•ize (dē fôr′mə līz′), *v.t.,* **-ized, -iz•ing.** to make less formal; reduce the strictness, preciseness, etc., of. Also, *esp. Brit.,* **de•for′mal•ise′.** [1875–80; DE- + FORMALIZE] —**de•for′mal•i•za′tion,** *n.*

de•for•ma•tion (dē′fôr mā′shən, def′ər-), *n.* **1.** the act of deforming; distortion; disfigurement. **2.** the result of deforming; change of form, esp. for the worse. **3.** an altered form. **4.** *Geol., Mech.* a change in the shape or dimensions of a body, resulting from stress; strain. [1400–50; late ME *deformacioun* < L *dēfōrmātiōn-* (s. of *dēfōrmātiō*), equiv. to *dēfōrmāt(us)* (ptp. of *dēfōrmāre;* see DEFORM[1]) + *-iōn-* -ION] —**de′for•ma′tion•al,** *adj.*

de•formed (di fôrmd′), *adj.* **1.** having the form changed, esp. with loss of beauty; misshapen; disfigured: *After the accident his arm was permanently deformed.* **2.** hateful; offensive: *a deformed personality.* [1350–1400; ME; see DEFORM[1], -ED[2]] —**de•form•ed•ly** (di fôr′mid lē), *adv.* —**de•form′ed•ness,** *n.*
—**Syn. 1.** malformed, crippled.

deformed′ bar′, a rod for reinforcing concrete, having surface irregularities, as transverse ridges, to improve the bond.

de•for•me•ter (di fôr′mē tər), *n.* a gauge used to determine stresses in a structure by tests on a model of the structure. [1925–30; DEFOR(MATION) + -METER]

de•form•i•ty (di fôr′mi tē), *n., pl.* **-ties. 1.** the quality or state of being deformed, disfigured, or misshapen. **2.** *Pathol.* an abnormally formed part of the body. **3.** a deformed person or thing. **4.** hatefulness; ugliness. [1350–1400; ME *deformite* < OF < L *dēfōrmitās,* equiv. to *dēfōrm(is)* DEFORM[2] + *-itās* -ITY]

de•fraud (di frôd′), *v.t.* to deprive of a right, money, or property by fraud: *Dishonest employees defrauded the firm of millions of dollars.* [1325–75; ME *defrauden* < OF *defrauder* < L *dēfraudāre,* equiv. to *dē-* DE- + *fraudāre* to cheat; see FRAUD] —**de•frau•da•tion** (dē′frô dā′shən), **de•fraud′ment,** *n.* —**de•fraud′er,** *n.*
—**Syn.** bilk, swindle, fleece, rip off, gyp, rook, cheat.

de•fray (di frā′), *v.t.* to bear or pay all or part of (the costs, expenses, etc.): *The grant helped defray the expenses of the trip.* [1535–45; < MF *défrayer,* OF *deffroier* to pay costs, equiv. to *de-* DIS-[1] + *frayer* to bear the costs, deriv. of *frais, fres* (pl.) costs, prob. < L *frācta* things broken (see FRACTURE), hence, expense incurred from breakage] —**de•fray′a•ble,** *adj.* —**de•fray′er,** *n.*

de•fray•al (di frā′əl), *n.* payment of some or all charges or expenses. Also, **de•fray′ment.** [1810–20; DEFRAY + -AL[2]]

de•frock (dē frok′), *v.t.* to unfrock. [1575–85; < F *défroquer,* equiv. to *dé-* DIS-[1] + *froque* FROCK + *-er* inf. suffix]

de•frost (di frôst′, -frost′), *v.t.* **1.** to remove the frost or ice from: *to defrost a refrigerator; to defrost the windshield of a car.* **2.** to thaw or partially thaw (frozen food). —*v.i.* **3.** to become free of ice or frost: *The refrigerator defrosted quickly.* **4.** to thaw, as frozen food: *The meat took two hours to defrost.* [1890–95; DE- + FROST]

de•frost•er (di frô′stər, -fros′tər), *n.* **1.** a person or thing that defrosts. **2.** Also called **defogger;** *esp. Brit.,* **demister.** a device for melting frost, ice, or condensation on a windshield or other window of an automobile, airplane, etc., by warming the window. [1925–30; DEFROST + -ER[1]]

defs., definitions.

CONCISE ETYMOLOGY KEY: <, descended or borrowed from; >, whence; b., blend of, blended; c., cognate with; cf., compare; deriv., derivative; equiv., equivalent; imit., imitative; obl., oblique; r., replacing; s., stem; sp., spelling, spelled; resp., respelling, respelled; trans., translation; ?, origin unknown; *, unattested; ‡, probably earlier than. See the full key inside the front cover.

deft (deft), *adj.,* **-er, -est.** dexterous; nimble; skillful; clever: *deft hands; a deft mechanic.* [1175–1225; ME; var. of DAFT] —**deft′ly,** *adv.* —**deft′ness,** *n.*
—**Syn.** See **dexterous.**

de•funct (di fungkt′), *adj.* **1.** no longer in effect or use; not operating or functioning: *a defunct law; a defunct organization.* **2.** no longer in existence; dead; extinct: *a defunct person; a defunct tribe of Indians.* —*n.* **3. the defunct,** the dead person referred to: *the survivors of the defunct.* [1540–50; < L *dēfunctus* discharged, dead (ptp. of *dēfungī*), equiv. to *dē-* DE- + *functus* performed; see FUNCTION] —**de•funct′ness,** *n.*

de•func•tive (di fungk′tiv), *adj.* of or pertaining to the dead; funereal. [1595–1605; < L *dēfunct(us)* DEFUNCT + -IVE]

de•fund (dē fund′), *v.t.* **1.** to deplete the financial resources of: *The cost of the lawsuit defunded the company's operating budget.* **2.** to withdraw financial support from: *Many university programs were defunded by the recent government cutbacks.* [DE- + FUND]

de•fuse (dē fyo͞oz′), *v.,* **-fused, -fus•ing.** —*v.t.* **1.** to remove the fuze from (a bomb, mine, etc.). **2.** to make less dangerous, tense, or embarrassing: *to defuse a potentially ugly situation.* —*v.i.* **3.** to grow less dangerous; weaken. Also, **defuze.** [1940–45; DE- + FUSE[1]] —**de•fus′er,** *n.*

de•fu•sion (dē fyo͞o′zhən), *n. Psychoanal.* separation of the life instinct from the death instinct, a process often accompanying maturity. [1925–30; DE- + FUSION]

de•fuze (dē fyo͞oz′), *v.t., v.i.,* **-fuzed, -fuz•ing.** defuse. —**de•fuz′er,** *n.*

de•fy (*v.* di fī′; *n.* di fī′, dē′fī), *v.,* **-fied, -fy•ing,** *n., pl.* **-fies.** —*v.t.* **1.** to challenge the power of; resist boldly or openly: *to defy parental authority.* **2.** to offer effective resistance to: *a fort that defies attack.* **3.** to challenge (a person) to do something deemed impossible: *They defied him to dive off the bridge.* **4.** *Archaic.* to challenge to a combat or contest. —*n.* **5.** a challenge; a defiance. [1250–1300; ME *defien* < OF *desfier,* equiv. to *des-* DIS-[1] + *fier* to trust < VL **fīdāre,* var. of L *fīdere*] —**de•fi′a•ble,** *adj.* —**de•fy′ing•ly,** *adv.*
—**Syn. 1.** dare, brave, flout, scorn.

deg., degree; degrees.

dé•ga•gé (dā′gä zhā′; *Fr.* dā GA zhā′), *adj.* **1.** unconstrained; easy, as in manner or style. **2.** without emotional involvement; detached. [< F, ptp. of *dégager* to release, free, redeem, OF *desg(u)agier;* see DE-, GAGE[1]; cf. ENGAGE]

de•ga•me (də gä′mā), *n.* lemonwood. [said to be < AmerSp *degame, dagame*]

de•gas (dē gas′), *v.t.,* **-gassed, -gas•sing. 1.** to free from gas. **2.** *Electronics.* to complete the evacuation of gases in (a vacuum tube). [1915–20; DE- + GAS]

De•gas (dā gä′; *Fr.* də gä′), *n.* **Hi•laire Ger•main Ed•gar** (ē leR′ zheR maN′ ed gaR′), 1834–1917, French impressionist painter.

De Gas•pe•ri (de gäs′pe rē), **Al•ci•de** (äl chē′de), 1881–1954, Italian statesman: premier 1945–53.

de Gaulle (də gōl′, gôl′), **Charles An•dré Jo•seph Ma•rie** (chärlz än′drā jō′zəf mə rē′; *Fr.* shaRl äN dRā′ zhō zef′ mA Rē′), 1890–1970, French general and statesman: president 1959–69.

de Gaull•ism (də gō′liz əm, gô′-), Gaullism.

de Gaull•ist (də gō′list, gô′-), Gaullist.

de•gauss (dē gous′), *v.t.* to demagnetize (a ship's hull, electrical equipment, etc.) by means of electric coils. Cf. **deperm.** [1935–40; DE- + GAUSS]

de•gauss•er (dē gou′sər), *n.* **1.** something that degausses. **2.** a device, esp. one used in filmmaking, that can erase a whole roll of magfilm, audiotape, etc., so that it can be used again. [DEGAUSS + -ER[1]]

de•gen•der•ize (dē jen′də rīz′), *v.t.,* **-ized, -iz•ing. 1.** to free from any association with or dependence on gender: *to degenderize employment policies.* **2.** to rid of unnecessary reference to gender or of prejudice toward a specific sex: *to degenderize textbooks; to degenderize one's vocabulary.* Also, **de•gen′der;** *esp. Brit.,* **de•gen′der•ise′.** [DE- + GENDER + -IZE]

de•gen•er•a•cy (di jen′ər ə sē), *n.* **1.** degenerate state or character. **2.** the process of degenerating; decline. **3.** degenerate behavior, esp. behavior considered sexually deviant. **4.** *Physics.* the number of distinct quantum states of a system that have a given energy. [1655–65; DEGENER(ATE) + -ACY]

de•gen•er•ate (*v.* di jen′ə rāt′; *adj., n.* di jen′ər it), *v.,* **-at•ed, -at•ing,** *adj., n.* —*v.i.* **1.** to fall below a normal or desirable level in physical, mental, or moral qualities; deteriorate: *The morale of the soldiers degenerated, and they were unable to fight.* **2.** to diminish in quality, esp. from a former state of coherence, balance, integrity, etc.: *The debate degenerated into an exchange of insults.* **3.** *Pathol.* to lose functional activity, as a tissue or organ. **4.** *Evolution.* (of a species or any of its traits or structures) to revert to a simple, less highly organized, or less functionally active type, as a parasitic plant that has lost its taproot or the vestigial wings of a flightless bird. —*v.t.* **5.** to cause degeneration in; bring about a decline, deterioration, or reversion in. —*adj.* **6.** having fallen below a normal or desirable level, esp. in physical or moral qualities; deteriorated; degraded: *a degenerate king.* **7.** having lost, or become impaired with respect to, the qualities proper to the race or kind: *a degenerate vine.* **8.** characterized by or associated with degeneracy: *degenerate times.* **9.** *Math.* pertaining to a limiting case of a mathematical system that is more symmetrical or simpler in form than the general case. **10.** *Physics.* **a.** (of modes of vibration of a system) having the same frequency. **b.** (of quantum states of a system) having equal energy. —*n.* **11.** a person who has declined, as in morals or character, from a type or standard considered normal. **12.** a person or thing that reverts to an earlier stage of culture, development, or evolution. **13.** a sexual deviate. [1485–95; < L *dēgenerātus* (ptp. of *dēgenerāre* to decline from an ancestral standard), equiv. to *dē* DE- + *gener-,* s. of *genus* race (see GENUS) + *-ātus* -ATE[1]; see GENERATE] —**de•gen′er•ate•ly,** *adv.* —**de•gen′er•ate•ness,** *n.*
—**Syn. 1.** worsen, decline, backslide, retrogress.

degen′erate mat′ter, *Physics.* matter consisting of atoms that have lost their orbital electrons.

degen′erate state′, Usually, **degenerate states.** *Physics.* a quantum state of a system, having the same energy level as, but a different wave function from, another state of the system. [1925–30]

de•gen•er•a•tion (di jen′ə rā′shən), *n.* **1.** the process of degenerating. **2.** the condition or state of being degenerate. **3.** *Pathol.* **a.** a process by which a tissue deteriorates, loses functional activity, and may become converted into or replaced by other kinds of tissue. **b.** the condition produced by such a process. [1475–85; < LL *dēgenerātiōn-* (s. of *dēgenerātiō*). See DE-, GENERATION]

de•gen•er•a•tive (di jen′ər ə tiv, -ə rā′tiv), *adj.* **1.** tending to degenerate. **2.** characterized by degeneration. [1840–50; DEGENERATE + -IVE]

degen′erative joint′ disease′, *Pathol.* osteoarthritis.

de•germ (dē jûrm′), *v.t.* **1.** to rid of germs. **2.** to remove the germ or embryo from (a kernel of grain), usually through milling. [DE- + GERM]

de•ger•mi•nate (dē jûr′mə nāt′), *v.t.,* **-nat•ed, -nat•ing.** degerm (def. 2). [DE- + GERMINATE]

de Ghel•de•rode (də gel də rōd′), **Mi•chel** (mē shel′), 1898–1962, Belgian dramatist.

de•gla•ci•a•tion (dē glā′shē ā′shən, -sē-), *n. Geol.* the gradual melting away of a glacier from the surface of a landmass. [1890–95; DE- + GLACIATION]

de•glam•or•ize (dē glam′ə rīz′), *v.t.,* **-ized, -iz•ing.** to take away the glamor of; treat so as to reduce the attractiveness or status of. Also, **de•glam′our•ize′;** *esp. Brit.,* **de•glam′o•rise′.** [1935–40; DE- + GLAMORIZE] —**de•glam′or•i•za′tion, de•glam′our•i•za′tion,** *n.*

de•glaze (dē glāz′), *v.t.,* **-glazed, -glaz•ing. 1.** to remove the glaze from (porcelain or the like), so as to impart a dull finish. **2.** to add wine or other liquid to (a pan in which meat has been roasted or sauteed) so as to make a sauce that incorporates the cooking juices. [1885–90; DE- + GLAZE]

de•gloss (dē glos′, -glôs′), *v.t.* **1.** to remove the gloss from (a surface), esp. in order to roughen: *The old paint needs to be deglossed before new paint can be applied.* —*n.* **2.** Also, **de•gloss′er.** a substance used to remove the gloss from a surface. [DE- + GLOSS[1]]

deglut., (in prescriptions) may be swallowed; let it be swallowed. [< L *dēglutiātur*]

de•glu•ti•nate (dē glo͞ot′n āt′), *v.t.,* **-nat•ed, -nat•ing.** to extract the gluten from. [1600–10; < L *dēglūtinātus* (ptp. of *dēglūtināre* to unglue), equiv. to *dē-* DE- + *glūtinātus* glued (*glūtin-* (see GLUTEN) + *-ātus* -ATE[1])] —**de•glu′ti•na′tion,** *n.*

de•glu•ti•tion (dē′glo͞o tish′ən), *n. Physiol.* the act or process of swallowing. [1640–50; < F *déglutition* < L *dēglūtīt(us)* (ptp. of *dēglūtīre* to swallow down, equiv. to *dē-* DE- + *glūtī(re)* to swallow (see GLUTTON[1]) + *-tus* ptp. suffix) + F *-ion* -ION] —**de′glu•ti′tious,** *adj.*

de•gorg•er (dē gôr′jər), *n.* a device for removing a fishhook from the throat of a fish. [DE- + GORGE[1] + -ER[1]]

de•grad•a•ble (di grā′də bəl), *adj.* susceptible to chemical breakdown. Cf. **biodegradable.** [1960–65; DEGRADE + -ABLE] —**de•grad′a•bil′i•ty,** *n.*

deg•ra•da•tion (deg′rə dā′shən), *n.* **1.** the act of degrading. **2.** the state of being degraded. **3.** *Physical Geog.* the wearing down of the land by the erosive action of water, wind, or ice. **4.** *Chem.* the breakdown of an organic compound. [1525–35; < LL *dēgradātiōn-* (s. of *dēgradātiō*), equiv. to *dēgradāt(us)* (ptp. of *dēgradāre* to DEGRADE) + *-iōn-* -ION] —**deg′ra•da′tion•al,** *adj.* —**deg′ra•da′tive,** *adj.*
—**Syn. 2.** humiliation, disgrace, dishonor, debasement.

degrada′tion of en′ergy, *Thermodynamics.* the principle that during any irreversible process the total energy available to do work decreases.

de•grade (di grād′ *or, for 3,* dē grād′), *v.,* **-grad•ed, -grad•ing.** —*v.t.* **1.** to lower in dignity or estimation; bring into contempt: *He felt they were degrading him by making him report to the supervisor.* **2.** to lower in character or quality; debase. **3.** to reduce (someone) to a lower rank, degree, etc.; deprive of office, rank, status, or title, esp. as a punishment: *degraded from director to assistant director.* **4.** to reduce in amount, strength, intensity, etc. **5.** *Physical Geog.* to wear down by erosion, as hills. Cf. **aggrade. 6.** *Chem.* to break down (a compound, esp. an organic hydrocarbon). —*v.i.* **7.** to become degraded; weaken or worsen; deteriorate. **8.** *Chem.* (esp. of an organic hydrocarbon compound) to break down or decompose. [1275–1325; ME *degraden* < LL *dēgradāre,* equiv. to L *dē-* DE- + *grad(us)* GRADE + *-āre* inf. suffix] —**de•grad′er,** *n.*
—**Syn. 1.** disgrace, dishonor, discredit. See **humble. 2.** abase, vitiate. **3.** demote, depose, downgrade, lower, cashier, break. —**Ant. 1, 2.** exalt. **3.** promote.

de•grad•ed (di grā′did), *adj.* **1.** reduced in rank, position, reputation, etc.: *He felt degraded by the trivial tasks assigned to him.* **2.** reduced in quality or value; debased; vulgarized: *the degraded level of the modern novel.* [1400–50; late ME; see DEGRADE, -ED[2]] —**de•grad′ed•ly,** *adv.* —**de•grad′ed•ness,** *n.*

de•grad•ing (di grā′ding), *adj.* that degrades; debasing; humiliating: *degrading submission.* [1675–85; DEGRADE + -ING[2]] —**de•grad′ing•ly,** *adv.* —**de•grad′ing•ness,** *n.*

de•gran•u•la•tion (dē gran′yə lā′shən), *n.* the loss or elimination of granules. [1940–45; DE- + GRANULATION]

de gra·ti·a (di grā′shē ə; *Lat.* de grä′tē ä′), *Law.* by favor or grace. [< L *dē gratiā*]

de·grease (dē grēs′, -grēz′), *v.t.*, **-greased, -greas·ing.** to remove grease, oil, or the like, from, esp. by treating with a chemical. [1885–90; DE- + GREASE] —**de·greas′er,** *n.*

de·gree (di grē′), *n.* **1.** any of a series of steps or stages, as in a process or course of action; a point in any scale. **2.** a stage or point in or as if in progression or retrogression: *We followed the degrees of her recovery with joy.* **3.** a stage in a scale of intensity or amount: *a high degree of mastery.* **4.** extent, measure, scope, or the like: *To what degree will he cooperate?* **5.** a stage in a scale of rank or station; relative standing in society, business, etc.: *His uncouth behavior showed him to be a man of low degree.* **6.** *Educ.* an academic title conferred by universities and colleges as an indication of the completion of a course of study, or as an honorary recognition of achievement. **7.** a unit of measure, as of temperature or pressure, marked off on the scale of a measuring instrument: *This thermometer shows a scale of degrees between only 20° and 40° C.* **8.** *Geom.* the 360th part of a complete angle or turn, often represented by the sign °, as in 45°, which is read as 45 degrees. Cf. **angle**[1] (def. 1c). **9.** the distinctive classification of a crime according to its gravity: *murder in the first degree.* **10.** *Gram.* one of the parallel formations of adjectives and adverbs used to express differences in quality, quantity, or intensity. In English, *low* and *careful* are the positive degree, *lower* and *more careful* are the comparative degree, *lowest* and *most careful* are the superlative degree. **11.** *Math.* **a.** the sum of the exponents of the variables in an algebraic term: x^3 *and* $2x^2y$ *are terms of degree three.* **b.** the term of highest degree of a given equation or polynomial: *The expression* $3x^2y + y^2 + 1$ *is of degree three.* **c.** the exponent of the derivative of highest order appearing in a given differential equation. **12.** *Music.* a tone or step of the scale. **13.** *Astrol.* any of the 360 equal divisions of the ecliptic measured counterclockwise from the vernal equinox. Each of the 12 signs of the zodiac contains 30 degrees. **14.** a certain distance or remove in the line of descent, determining the proximity of relationship: *a cousin of the second degree.* **15.** *Archaic.* a line or point on the earth or the celestial sphere, as defined by degrees of latitude. **16.** *Obs.* a step, as of a stair. **17. by degrees,** by easy stages; gradually: *She grew angrier by degrees.* **18. to a degree, a.** to a considerable extent; exceedingly. **b.** to a small extent; somewhat: *He is to a degree difficult to get along with.* [1200–50; ME *degre* < AF, OF < VL **dēgradus*; see DE-, GRADE] —**de·greed′,** *adj.* —**de·gree′less,** *adj.*
—**Syn. 2.** step, mark, grade, level, phase.

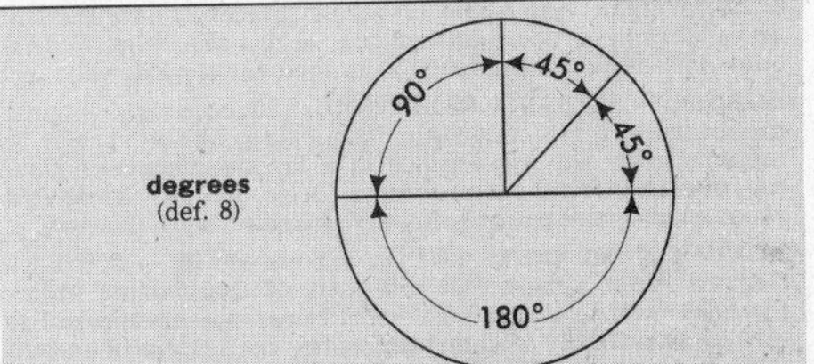

degrees (def. 8)

de·gree-day (di grē′dā′), *n. Engin.* one degree of departure, on a single day, of the daily mean temperature from a given standard temperature. *Abbr.:* dd Also, **degree′ day′.** Cf. **cooling degree-day, growing degree-day, heating degree-day.** [1925–1930]

degree′ mill′. See **diploma mill.**

degree′ of curve′, *Railroads.* See under **curve** (def. 5).

degree′ of free′dom, 1. *Statistics.* any of the statistically independent values of a sample that are used to determine a property of the sample, as the mean or variance. **2.** *Physical Chem.* any of the independent variables required to specify the energy of a molecule or atom. [1900–05]

de·gres·sion (di gresh′ən), *n.* **1.** a downward movement; descent. **2.** the decrease in rate in degressive taxation. [1375–1425; late ME < ML *dēgressiōn-* (s. of *dēgressiō*) descent, equiv. to L *degred-* (s. of *dēgredī* to go down, descend; *dē-* DE- + *-gredī,* comb. form of *gradī* to step, walk) + *-tiōn-* -TION]

de·gres·sive (di gres′iv), *adj.* pertaining to a form of taxation in which the rate diminishes gradually on sums below a certain fixed amount. [1905–10; DEGRESS(ION) + -IVE] —**de·gres′sive·ly,** *adv.*

dé·grin·go·lade (dā gran gô lad′; *Eng.* dā grang′gə läd′), *n., pl.* **-lades** (-lad′; *Eng.* -lädz′). *French.* a quick deterioration or breakdown, as of a situation or circumstance.

de Groot (də khrōt′), **Huig** (hœikh). See **Grotius, Hugo.**

de·gu (dā′go͞o), *n.* a rat-sized New World burrowing rodent, *Octodon degus,* having long, smooth fur and a black-tipped, tufted tail. [1835–45; AmerSp < Araucanian *deuñ*]

de·gum (dē gum′), *v.t.*, **-gummed, -gum·ming. 1.** to free from gum. **2.** to remove sericin from (silk filaments or yarn) by boiling in a soap solution; boil off. [1885–90; DE- + GUM[1]] —**de·gum′mer,** *n.*

de·gust (di gust′), *v.t.* to taste or savor carefully or appreciatively. Also, **de·gus·tate** (di gus′tāt). [1615–25; < L *dēgustāre* to taste, try, equiv. to *dē-* DE- + *gustāre* to taste (*gust*(*us*) a tasting + *-āre* inf. suffix)] —**de·gus·ta·tion** (dē′gu stā′shən), *n.*

de gus·ti·bus non est dis·pu·tan·dum (de go͞os′ti bo͞os′ nōn est dis′po͞o tän′do͞om; *Eng.* dē gus′tə bəs non est dis′pyo͞o tan′dəm), *Latin.* there is no disputing about tastes.

de·gut (dē gut′), *v.t.*, **-gut·ted, -gut·ting. 1.** to remove the entrails of; disembowel; gut. **2.** to divest of essential character, strength, force, etc.: *The leading lady's poor performance degutted the play of its vitality.* Also, **de-gut′.** [1930–35; DE- + GUT]

de Haas (də häz′), **Jacob,** 1872–1937, English Zionist leader, in U.S. after 1902.

de haut en bas (də ō tän bä′), *French.* **1.** from top to bottom; from head to foot. **2.** in a haughty, disdainful manner; condescendingly.

de·hire (dē hīər′), *v.t.*, **-hired, -hir·ing.** to discharge from employment; fire, esp. at the executive level and generally with an attempt to be tactful. Also, **de-hire′.** [1965–70; DE- + HIRE]

de·hisce (di his′), *v.i.*, **-hisced, -hisc·ing.** to burst open, as capsules of plants; gape. [1650–60; < L *dēhiscere* to gape, part, equiv. to *dē-* DE- + *hiscere* to gape, yawn (*hi*(*āre*) to yawn + *-scere* inchoative suffix)]

de·his·cence (di his′əns), *n.* **1.** *Biol.* the release of materials by the splitting open of an organ or tissue. **2.** *Bot.* the natural bursting open of capsules, fruits, anthers, etc., for the discharge of their contents. **3.** *Surg.* the bursting open of a surgically closed wound. [1820–30; < NL *dēhiscentia,* equiv. to L *dēhiscent-* s. of *dēhiscēns,* prp. of *dēhiscere* (see DEHISCE) + *-ia;* see -ENCE] —**de·his′cent,** *adj.*

De·hi·wa·la-Mount La·vin·i·a (de′hi wä′lə mount′ lə vin′ē ə), a city in SW Sri Lanka, on the Indian Ocean. 136,000.

de·horn (dē hôrn′), *v.t.* **1.** to remove the horns of (cattle). **2.** to prevent the formation or growth of horns in (cattle), as by cauterization. **3.** *Hort.* to prune (a tree, shrub, etc.) by shortening major branches to an extreme degree. [1885–90, *Amer.;* DE- + HORN] —**de·horn′er,** *n.*

de·hort (di hôrt′), *v.t. Archaic.* to try to dissuade. [1525–35; < L *dēhortārī* to dissuade, equiv. to *dē-* DE- + *hortārī* to urge (*hor*(*īrī*) to urge + *-t-* freq. suffix + *-ārī* inf. suffix)] —**de·hor·ta·tion** (dē′hôr tā′shən), *n.* —**de·hor·ta·tive, de·hor·ta·to·ry** (di hôr′tə tôr′ē, -tōr′ē), *adj., n.* —**de·hort′er,** *n.*

Deh·ra Dun (dā′rə do͞on′), a city in NW Uttar Pradesh, in N India. 199,443.

de·hull (dē hul′), *v.t.* to remove the hulls from (beans, seeds, etc.); hull. [DE- + HULL[1]]

de·hu·man·ize (dē hyo͞o′mə nīz′ *or, often,* -yo͞o′-), *v.t.*, **-ized, -iz·ing.** to deprive of human qualities or attributes; divest of individuality: *Conformity dehumanized him.* Also, *esp. Brit.,* **de·hu′man·ise′.** [1810–20; DE- + HUMANIZE] —**de·hu′man·i·za′tion,** *n.*

de·hu·mid·i·fi·er (dē′hyo͞o mid′ə fī′ər, *or, often,* -yo͞o-), *n.* an appliance for removing moisture from the air, as for lowering the humidity in a storage room. [1920–25; DE- + HUMIDIFIER]

de·hu·mid·i·fy (dē′hyo͞o mid′ə fī′ *or, often,* -yo͞o-), *v.t.*, **-fied, -fy·ing.** to remove moisture from. [1920–25; DE- + HUMIDIFY] —**de′hu·mid′i·fi·ca′tion,** *n.*

de·hy·drate (dē hī′drāt), *v.*, **-drat·ed, -drat·ing.** —*v.t.* **1.** to deprive (a chemical compound) of water or the elements of water. **2.** to free (fruit, vegetables, etc.) from moisture for preservation; dry. **3.** to remove water from (the body or a tissue). **4.** to deprive of spirit, force, or meaning; render less interesting or effectual. —*v.i.* **5.** to lose water or moisture: *Milk dehydrates easily.* [1850–55; DE- + HYDRATE]
—**Syn. 2.** See **evaporate.**

de·hy·dra·tion (dē′hī drā′shən), *n.* **1.** the act or process of dehydrating. **2.** an abnormal loss of water from the body, esp. from illness or physical exertion. [1850–55; DEHYDRATE + -ION]

de·hy·dra·tor (dē hī′drā tər), *n.* **1.** a person or thing that dehydrates. **2.** a device, apparatus, or appliance that dehydrates food for preservation. [DEHYDRATE + -OR[2]]

dehydro-, a combining form meaning "dehydrogenated," used in the formation of compound words: *dehydrochlorinate.*

de·hy·dro·chlo·ri·nase (dē hī′drə klôr′ə nās′, -nāz′, -klōr′-), *n. Biochem.* an enzyme that catalyzes the removal of hydrogen and chlorine atoms or ions from chlorinated hydrocarbons. [1955–60; DEHYDROCHLORIN(ATE) + -ASE]

de·hy·dro·chlo·ri·nate (dē hī′drə klôr′ə nāt′, -klōr′-), *v.t.*, **-nat·ed, -nat·ing.** *Chem.* to remove hydrogen chloride or chlorine and hydrogen from (a substance). [DEHYDRO- + CHLORINATE] —**de·hy′dro·chlo′ri·na′tion,** *n.*

de·hy·dro·freeze (dē hī′drə frēz′), *v.t.*, **-froze, -fro·zen, -freez·ing.** to subject (food) to partial dehydration and quick-freezing. [DE- + HYDRO-[1] + FREEZE]

de·hy·dro·gen·ase (dē hī′drə jə nās′, -nāz′), *n. Biochem.* an oxidoreductase enzyme that catalyzes the removal of hydrogen. [1920–25; DEHYDROGEN(ATE) + -ASE]

de·hy·dro·gen·ate (dē hī′drə jə nāt′, dē′hī droj′ə-), *v.t.*, **-at·ed, -at·ing.** *Chem.* to remove hydrogen from (a compound). [1840–50; DE- + HYDROGENATE] —**de·hy′dro·gen·a′tion,** *n.*

de·hy·dro·gen·ize (dē hī′drə jə nīz′, dē′hī droj′ə-), *v.t.*, **-ized, -iz·ing.** *Chem.* dehydrogenate. Also, *esp. Brit.,* **de·hy′dro·gen·ise′.** [1875–80; DE- + HYDROGENIZE] —**de·hy′dro·gen·i·za′tion,** *n.* —**de·hy′dro·gen·iz′er,** *n.*

de·hyp·no·tize (dē hip′nə tīz′), *v.t.*, **-tized, -tiz·ing.** to bring out of the hypnotic state. Also, *esp. Brit.,* **de·hyp′no·tise′.** [DE- + HYPNOTIZE]

D.E.I., Dutch East Indies.

De·ia·ni·ra (dē′yə nī′rə), *n. Class. Myth.* a sister of Meleager and wife of Hercules, whom she killed unwittingly by giving him a shirt that had been dipped in the poisoned blood of Nessus. Also, **De′ia·nei′ra.**

de·ice (dē īs′), *v.t.*, **-iced, -ic·ing.** to free of ice; prevent or remove ice formation on, as the wing of an airplane. Also, **de-ice′.** [1930–35; DE- + ICE]

de·ic·er (dē ī′sər), *n.* a device or a chemical substance for preventing or removing ice. Also, **de-ic′er.** [1930–35; DEICE + -ER[1]]

de·i·cide (dē′ə sīd′), *n.* **1.** a person who kills a god. **2.** the act of killing a god. [1605–15; < NL *deicīda* (def. 1), *deicīdium* (def. 2), equiv. to L *dei-* (comb. form of *deus* god) + *-cīda, -cīdium* -CIDE] —**de′i·cid′al,** *adj.*

deic·tic (dīk′tik), *adj.* **1.** *Logic.* proving directly. **2.** *Gram.* specifying identity or spatial or temporal location from the perspective of one or more of the participants in an act of speech or writing, in the context of either an external situation or the surrounding discourse, as *we, you, here, there, now, then, this, that, the former,* or *the latter.* —*n.* **3.** *Gram.* a deictic element. [1820–30; < Gk *deiktikós* demonstrative, equiv. to *deikt*(*ós*) able to be proved, v. adj. of *deiknýnai* to show, prove, point + *-ikos* -IC] —**deic′ti·cal·ly,** *adv.*

de·if·ic (dē if′ik), *adj.* making divine; deifying. [1480–90; < LL *deificus,* equiv. to L *dei-* (comb. form of *deus* god) + *-ficus* -FIC]

de·i·fi·ca·tion (dē′ə fi kā′shən), *n.* **1.** the act of deifying. **2.** the state of being deified. **3.** the result of deifying: *Their gods were deifications of their ancient kings.* [1350–1400; ME *deificacion* < LL *deificātiōn-* (s. of *deificātiō*), equiv. to *deificāt*(*us*) (ptp. of *deificāre; deific*(*us*) DEIFIC + *-ātus* -ATE[1]) + *-iōn-* -ION]

de·i·form (dē′ə fôrm′), *adj.* godlike or divine in form or nature. [1635–45; < ML *deiformis,* equiv. to L *dei-* (comb. form of *deus* god) + *-formis* -FORM] —**de′i·form′i·ty,** *n.*

de·i·fy (dē′ə fī′), *v.t.*, **-fied, -fy·ing. 1.** to make a god of; exalt to the rank of a deity; personify as a deity: *to deify a beloved king.* **2.** to adore or regard as a deity: *to deify wealth.* [1300–50; ME *deifien* < OF *deifier* < LL *deificāre.* See DEIFICATION, -IFY] —**de′i·fi′er,** *n.*

deign (dān), *v.i.* **1.** to think fit or in accordance with one's dignity; condescend: *He would not deign to discuss the matter with us.* —*v.t.* **2.** to condescend to give or grant: *He deigned no reply.* **3.** *Obs.* to condescend to accept. [1250–1300; ME *deinen* < OF *deignier* < L *dignārī* to judge worthy, equiv. to *dign*(*us*) worthy + *-ārī* inf. suffix]

De·i gra·ti·a (de′ē grä′tē ä′; *Eng.* dē′ī grā′shē ə, dē′ē), *Latin.* by the grace of God.

deil (dēl), *n. Scot.* devil.

Dei·mos (dī′mos), *n.* **1.** an ancient Greek personification of terror, a son of Ares and Aphrodite. **2.** *Astron.* one of the two moons of Mars.

de·in·dex (dē in′deks), *v.t.* to remove from an index or any system of indexing, esp. to stop adjusting compensation according to the cost of living: *to deindex wages.* [1975–80; DE- + INDEX]

de·in·dus·tri·al·ize (dē′in dus′trē ə līz′), *v.*, **-ized, -iz·ing.** —*v.t.* **1.** to cause to lose industrial capability or strength; make less industrial in character or emphasis. **2.** to deprive (a conquered nation) of the means or potential for industrial growth. —*v.i.* **3.** to lose industrial capability or character; become deindustrialized. Also, **de′-in·dus′tri·al·ize;** *esp. Brit.,* **de′in·dus′tri·al·ise′.** [1880–85; DE- + INDUSTRIALIZE] —**de′in·dus′tri·al·i·za′tion,** *n.*

dei·non·y·chus (dī non′i kəs), *n.* a small bipedal dinosaur, genus *Deinonychus,* of the Cretaceous Period, characterized by having a large, curved claw on each hind foot. [< NL (1969) < Gk *dein*(*ós*) fearful, terrible (see DINOSAUR) + *-onychos* -clawed, adj. deriv. of *ónyx* claw, nail; see ONYX]

de·in·sti·tu·tion·al·ize (dē in′sti to͞o′shə nl īz′, -tyo͞o′-, dē′in-), *v.*, **-ized, -iz·ing.** —*v.t.* **1.** to release (a mentally or physically handicapped person) from a hospital, asylum, home, or other institution with the intention of providing treatment, support, or rehabilitation primarily through community resources under the supervision of health-care professionals or facilities. **2.** to remove (care, therapy, etc.) from the confines of an institution by providing treatment, support, or the like through community facilities. **3.** to free from the confines or limitations of an institution. **4.** to free from the bureaucracy and complex procedures associated with institutions. —*v.i.* **5.** to give up or lose institutional character or status; become deinstitutionalized. Also, **de·in′sti·tu′tion·al·ize′;** *esp. Brit.,* **de·in′sti·tu′tion·al·ise′.** [1960–65; DE- + INSTITUTIONALIZE] —**de·in′sti·tu′tion·al·i·za′tion,** *n.*

de·i·on·ize (dē ī′ə nīz′), *v.t.*, **-ized, -iz·ing.** *Chem.* **1.** to remove ions from. **2.** to reassociate the ions of (an ionized gas). Also, *esp. Brit.,* **de·i′on·ise′.** [1905–10; DE- + IONIZE] —**de·i′on·i·za′tion,** *n.* —**de·i′on·iz′er,** *n.*

deip·nos·o·phist (dīp nos′ə fist), *n.* a person who is an adept conversationalist at table. [1650–60; after a literary work by Athenaeus, *Deipnosophistés,* an expert in affairs of the kitchen, equiv. to Gk *deîpno*(*n*) meal + *sophistés* SOPHIST]

Deir·dre (dēr′drə, -drē; *Irish* dâr′dRə), *n.* **1.** *Irish Legend.* the wife of Naoise, who killed herself after her husband had been murdered by his uncle, King Conchobar. **2.** a female given name.

de·ism (dē′iz əm), *n.* **1.** belief in the existence of a God on the evidence of reason and nature only, with rejection of supernatural revelation (distinguished from *theism*). **2.** belief in a God who created the world but has since remained indifferent to it. [1675–85; < F *déisme* < L *de*(*us*) god + F *-isme* -ISM]

CONCISE PRONUNCIATION KEY: *act, cāpe, dâre, pärt; set, ēqual; if, īce; ox, ōver, ôrder, oil, bo͝ok, bo͞ot, out; up, ûrge; child; sing; shoe; thin, that;* zh as in *treasure.* ə = *a* as in *alone, e* as in *system, i* as in *easily, o* as in *gallop, u* as in *circus;* ə as in *fire* (fīər), *hour* (ouər). l and n can serve as syllabic consonants, as in *cradle* (krād′l), and *button* (but′n). See the full key inside the front cover.

de·i·so·late (dē ī′sə lāt′, -is′ə-), *v.t.*, **-lat·ed, -lat·ing.** to remove from isolation. [1965–70; DE- + ISOLATE] —**de·i′so·la′tion,** *n.*

de·ist (dē′ist), *n.* a person who believes in deism. [1555–65; < MF *déiste* < L *de(us)* god + F *-iste* -IST] —**de·is′tic, de·is′ti·cal,** *adj.* —**de·is′ti·cal·ly,** *adv.*

de·i·ty (dē′i tē), *n., pl.* **-ties. 1.** a god or goddess. **2.** divine character or nature, esp. that of the Supreme Being; divinity. **3.** the estate or rank of a god: *The king attained deity after his death.* **4.** a person or thing revered as a god or goddess: *a society in which money is the only deity.* **5. the Deity,** God; Supreme Being. [1250–1300; ME *deite* < OF < LL *deitāt-* (s. of *deitās*), equiv. to L *dei-* (comb. form of *deus* god) + *-tāt-* -TY, formed after L *dīvīnitās* DIVINITY]

deix·is (dīk′sis), *n. Gram.* the operation or function of deictic elements. [1945–50; < Gk *deîxis* lit., proof, display, equiv. to *deik(nýnai)* to show, prove, point + *-sis* -SIS]

dé·jà vu (dā′zhä vo͞o′, vyo͞o′; *Fr.* dā zhA vY′), **1.** *Psychol.* the illusion of having previously experienced something actually being encountered for the first time. **2.** disagreeable familiarity or sameness: *The new television season had a sense of déjà vu about it—the same old plots and characters with new names.* [1900–05; < F: lit., already seen]

de·ject (di jekt′), *v.t.* **1.** to depress the spirits of; dispirit; dishearten: *Such news dejects me.* —*adj.* **2.** *Archaic.* dejected; downcast. [1375–1425; late ME *dejecten* (v.) < L *dējectus* (ptp. of *dējicere* to throw down), equiv. to *dē-* DE- + *-jec-*, comb. form of *jacere* to throw + *-tus* ptp. suffix]

de·jec·ta (di jek′tə), *n.* (*used with a plural v.*) waste discharged from the body; excrement. [1885–90; < NL, neut. pl. of L *dējectus;* see DEJECT]

de·ject·ed (di jek′tid), *adj.* depressed in spirits; disheartened; low-spirited: *The dejected expression on the face of the loser spoiled my victory.* [1575–85; DEJECT + -ED²] —**de·ject′ed·ly,** *adv.* —**de·ject′ed·ness,** *n.* —**Syn.** discouraged, despondent, dispirited.

de·jec·tion (di jek′shən), *n.* **1.** depression or lowness of spirits. **2.** *Med., Physiol.* **a.** evacuation of the bowels; fecal discharge. **b.** excrement. [1400–50; late ME *deieccioun* < L *dējectiōn-* (s. of *dējectiō*) a throwing down, equiv. to *dēject(us)* (see DEJECT) + *-iōn-* -ION]

dé·jeu·ner (dā zhœ nā′; *Eng.* dā′zhə nā′, dā′zhə nā′), *n., pl.* **-ners** (-nā′; *Eng.* -nāz′, -nāz′). *French.* lunch; luncheon.

dé·jeu·ner à la four·chette (dā zhœ nā A lA fo͞or shet′), *pl.* **dé·jeu·ners à la four·chette** (dā zhœ nā A lA fo͞or shet′). *French.* a luncheon or light meal, esp. one at which eggs, meat, etc., are served. Cf. **petit déjeuner.** [lit., lunch with the fork]

de ju·re (di jo͝or′ē, dā jo͝or′ā; *Lat.* de yo͞o′re), by right; according to law (distinguished from *de facto*). [< L *dē jūre*]

deka-, a combining form meaning "ten," used in the names of metric units which are ten times the size of the unit denoted by the base word: *dekaliter.* Also, esp. before a vowel, **dek-.** Cf. **deci-.** [< Gk *deka-*, comb. form of *déka* TEN]

dek·a·drachm (dek′ə dram′), *n.* decadrachm.

dek·a·gram (dek′ə gram′), *n.* a unit of mass or weight equal to 10 grams (0.3527 ounce avoirdupois). *Abbr.:* dag Also, **decagram;** *esp. Brit.,* **dek′a·gramme′.** [1800–10; < F *décagramme.* See DEKA-, -GRAM²]

de Kalb (di kalb′), **1. Baron.** See **Kalb, Johann. 2.** a city in N Illinois. 33,099.

dek·a·li·ter (dek′ə lē′tər), *n.* a unit of capacity equal to 10 liters (9.08 quarts U.S. dry measure or 2.64 gallons U.S. liquid measure). *Abbr.:* dal Also, **decaliter;** *esp. Brit.,* **dek′a·li′tre.** [1800–10; < F *décalitre.* See DEKA-, LITER]

dek·a·me·ter (dek′ə mē′tər), *n.* a unit of length equal to 10 meters (32.81 ft.). *Abbr.:* dam Also, **decameter;** *esp. Brit.,* **dek′a·me′tre.** [1800–10; < F *décamètre.* See DEKA-, METER¹]

dek·a·met·ric (dek′ə me′trik), *adj. Radio.* decametric.

deke (dēk), *v.,* **deked, dek·ing,** *n. Ice Hockey.* —*v.t.* **1.** to deceive (an opponent) by a fake. —*n.* **2.** a fake or feint intended to deceive a defensive player, often drawing that player out of position. [1955–60; orig. Canadian E shortening of DECOY]

Dek·ker (dek′ər), *n.* **Thomas,** 1572?–1632?, English dramatist. Also, **Decker.**

dek·ko (dek′ō), *n., pl.* **-kos.** *n. Brit. Slang.* a look or glance. [1890–95; < Hindi *dēkhō* look (impv.)]

de Klerk (də klârk′), **Frederik Willem,** born 1936, South African political leader: president 1989–94.

de Koo·ning (də ko͞o′ning), **Wil·lem** (vil′əm, wil′-), 1904–97, U.S. painter, born in the Netherlands.

De Ko·ven (di kō′vən), **(Henry Louis) Reginald,** 1861–1920, U.S. composer, conductor, and music critic.

de Kruif (də krīf′), **Paul,** 1890–1971, U.S. bacteriologist and author.

del¹ (del), **1.** (in names of Spanish derivation) a contraction of *de* and the article *el: Estanislao del Campo.* **2.** (in names of Italian derivation) a contraction of *di* and the article *il: Giovanni del Monte.*

del² (del), *n. Math.* a differential operator. *Symbol:* ∇ Cf. **gradient** (def. 4), **Laplace operator.** [1900–05; short form of DELTA]

Del., Delaware.

CONCISE ETYMOLOGY KEY: <, descended or borrowed from; >, whence; b., blend of, blended; c., cognate with; cf., compare; deriv., derivative; equiv., equivalent; imit., imitative; obl., oblique; r., replacing; s., stem; sp., spelling, spelled; resp., respelling, respelled; trans., translation; ?, origin unknown; *, unattested; ‡, probably earlier than. See the full key inside the front cover.

del., **1.** delegate; delegation. **2.** delete; deletion. **3.** delineavit.

de·la·bi·a·li·za·tion (dē lā′bē ə lə zā′shən), *n. Phonet.* **1.** the result or process of delabializing. **2.** the historical progression in which labial sounds delabialize, as the *kw*-sound in Latin words in *quin-* "five" becoming a *k*-sound as in Spanish *quince* "fifteen." [1905–10; DE- + LABIALIZATION]

de·la·bi·al·ize (dē lā′bē ə līz′), *v.,* **-ized, -iz·ing.** *Phonet.* —*v.t.* **1.** to deprive (a sound) of labial character, as in unrounding a vowel. —*v.i.* **2.** (of a speech sound) to lose its labial character. [1870–75; DE- + LABIALIZE]

De·la·croix (də lA krwä′), *n.* **(Fer·di·nand Vic·tor) Eu·gène** (fer dē näN′ vēk tôr′ œ zhen′), 1798–1863, French painter.

Del′a·go′a Bay′ (del′ə gō′ə, del′-), an inlet of the Indian Ocean, in S Mozambique. 55 mi. (89 km) long.

de·laine (də lān′), *n.* **1.** (*cap.*) See **Delaine Merino. 2.** a high-quality wool of combing length often used in worsteds. **3.** a high-grade worsted dress goods formerly in use. [1830–40; < F (*mousseline*) *de laine* (muslin) of wool]

Delaine′ Meri′no, one of an American strain of Merino sheep.

de la Ma·drid Hur·ta·do (də lä mə drid′ hər tä′dō; *Sp.* de lä mä thrēth′ o͞or tä′thō), **Mi·guel** (mē gel′), born 1934, Mexican political leader: president since 1982.

de la Mare (də lə mâr′, del′ə mâr′), **Walter (John),** 1873–1956, English poet, novelist, playwright, and short-story writer.

Del·a·ma·ter (del′ə mä′tər, del′ə mā′tər), *n.* **Cornelius Henry,** 1821–89, U.S. mechanical engineer and shipbuilder.

de·lam·i·nate (dē lam′ə nāt′), *v.i.,* **-nat·ed, -nat·ing.** to split into laminae or thin layers. [1875–80; DE- + LAMINATE]

de·lam·i·na·tion (dē lam′ə nā′shən), *n.* **1.** a splitting apart into layers. **2.** *Embryol.* the separation of a primordial cell layer into two layers by a process of cell migration. [1875–80; DE- + LAMINATION]

De Lan·cey (də lan′sē), **James,** 1703–60, American jurist and politician in New York.

De Land (də land′), a city in E Florida. 15,354.

De·land (də land′), *n.* **Margaret** (*Margaretta Wade Campbell Deland*), 1857–1945, U.S. novelist.

De·la′ney Amend′ment (də lā′nē), an amendment to the U. S. Food, Drug and Cosmetic Act banning the use of carcinogenic food additives, as certain artificial sweeteners and food colorings. Also called **Dela′ney clause′.**

De·lan·noy (də lA nwA′), *n.* **Mar·cel** (mAR sel′), born 1898, French composer.

De·la·no (də lā′nō), *n.* a city in S California. 16,491.

De·la·ny (də lā′nē), *n.* **Martin Robinson,** 1812–85, U.S. physician, army officer, and political reformer: leader of the black nationalist movement.

de la Ren·ta (də lə ren′tə, del′ə, dē′ lə), **Oscar,** born 1932, U.S. fashion designer, born in the Dominican Republic.

de la Roche (də lə rôsh′), **Ma·zo** (mā′zō), 1885–1961, Canadian novelist.

De·la·roche (də lA rôsh′), *n.* **(Hip·po·lyte) Paul** (ē pô lēt′ pôl), 1797–1856, French historical and portrait painter.

de la Rue (del′ə ro͞o′, del′ə ro͞o′), **Warren,** 1815–89, English astronomer and inventor.

de·late (di lāt′), *v.t.,* **-lat·ed, -lat·ing. 1.** *Chiefly Scot.* to inform against; denounce or accuse. **2.** *Archaic.* to relate; report: *to delate an offense.* [1505–15; < L *dēlātus* (suppletive ptp. of *dēferre* to bring down, report, accuse), equiv. to *dē-* DE- + *lā-* carry (ptp. s. of *ferre*) + *-tus* ptp. suffix] —**de·la′tion,** *n.* —**de·la′tor, de·lat′er,** *n.* —**de·la·to·ri·an** (del′ə tôr′ē ən, -tōr′-), *adj.*

de·la·tive (di lā′tiv), *Gram.* —*adj.* **1.** noting a case whose distinctive function is to indicate place down from which. —*n.* **2.** the delative case. [< L *dēlāt(us)* (see DELATE) + -IVE]

De·lau·nay (də lō ne′), *n.* **Ro·bert** (Rō beR′), 1885–1941, French painter.

De·la·vigne (də lA vēn′yᵊ), *n.* **(Jean Fran·çois) Ca·si·mir** (zhäN fRäN swA′ kA zē mēR′), 1793–1843, French poet and dramatist.

Del·a·ware (del′ə wâr′), *n., pl.* **-wares,** (*esp. collectively*) **-ware** for 5. **1. Baron.** See **De La Warr, 12th Baron. 2.** a state in the eastern United States, on the Atlantic coast. 595,225; 2057 sq. mi. (5330 sq. km). *Cap.:* Dover. *Abbr.:* DE (for use with zip code), Del. **3.** a city in central Ohio. 18,780. **4.** a river flowing S from SE New York, along the boundary between Pennsylvania and New Jersey into Delaware Bay. 296 mi. (475 km) long. **5.** a member of a grouping of North American Indian peoples, comprising the Munsee, Unami, and Unalachtigo, formerly occupying the drainage basin of the Delaware River, the lower Hudson River valley, and the intervening area. **6.** the Eastern Algonquian language of any of the Delaware peoples. **7.** *Hort.* **a.** a red viniferа grape grown for table use that yields a white wine. **b.** the vine bearing this fruit.

Del·a·war·e·an (del′ə wâr′ē ən), *n.* **1.** a native or inhabitant of Delaware. —*adj.* **2.** of or pertaining to Delaware of Delawareans. [DELAWARE + -AN]

Del′aware Bay′, an inlet of the Atlantic between E Delaware and S New Jersey. ab. 70 mi. (115 km) long.

Del′aware Jar′gon, a jargon based on Unami Delaware, now extinct but formerly used as a lingua franca in Pennsylvania, New Jersey, and New York.

Del′aware Wa′ter Gap′, a gorge on the boundary between E Pennsylvania and NW New Jersey.

De La Warr (del′ə wâr′; *Brit.* del′ə wər), **12th Baron** (*Thomas West*), 1577–1618, 1st English colonial governor of Virginia. Also, **Delaware.**

de·lay (di lā′), *v.t.* **1.** to put off to a later time; defer; postpone: *The pilot delayed the flight until the weather cleared.* **2.** to impede the process or progress of; retard; hinder: *The dense fog delayed the plane's landing.* —*v.i.* **3.** to put off action; linger; loiter: *He delayed until it was too late.* —*n.* **4.** the act of delaying; procrastination; loitering. **5.** an instance of being delayed: *There were many delays during the train trip.* **6.** the period or amount of time during which something is delayed: *The ballet performance began after a half-hour delay.* [1225–75; ME *delaien* (v.), *delai(e)* (n.) < OF *delaier* (v.), *delai* (n.)] —**de·lay′a·ble,** *adj.* —**de·lay′er,** *n.* —**de·lay′ing·ly,** *adv.*
—**Syn. 1.** See **defer¹. 2.** slow, detain. **3.** procrastinate, tarry. **4.** tarrying, dawdling. **5.** deferment, postponement, respite.

de·layed (di lād′), *adj. Physics.* of or pertaining to a particle, as a neutron or alpha particle, that is emitted from an excited nucleus formed in a nuclear reaction, the emission occurring some time after the reaction is completed.

de·layed-ac·tion (di lād′ak′shən), *adj.* (of an explosive projectile) exploding some time after hitting the target. Also, **de·lay-ac·tion** (di lā′ak′shən). [1890–95]

delayed′ speech′, *Speech Pathol.* a speech disorder of children in which the levels of intelligibility, vocabulary, complexity of utterance, etc., are significantly below the levels considered standard for a particular age.

delayed′ stress′ reac′tion, *Psychiatry.* a post-traumatic stress disorder occurring more than six months after the experience of a traumatic event. Also, **de·layed′-stress′ reac′tion.** Also called **delayed′ stress′ syn′drome, de·layed′-stress′ syn′drome.**

delay′ing ac′tion, *Mil.* a maneuver in which a defensive force delays the advance of a superior enemy force by withdrawing while inflicting the maximum destruction possible without engaging in decisive combat.

delay′ screen′, *Electronics.* (in a cathode-ray tube) a sensitized screen with a phosphorescent coating that retains the image formed by the electron beam for an appreciable time.

Del·bert (del′bərt), *n.* a male given name, form of **Albert.**

Del·brück (del′bro͝ok; *Ger.* del′bRYk), *n.* **Max** (maks; *Ger.* mäks), 1906–81, U.S. biologist, born in Germany: Nobel prize for medicine 1969.

Del·cas·sé (del kA sā′), *n.* **Thé·o·phile** (tā ô fēl′), 1852–1923, French statesman.

Del′ Cit′y, a city in central Oklahoma. 28,424.

de·le (dē′lē), *v.,* **de·led, de·le·ing,** *n. Print.* —*v.t.* **1.** to delete. —*n.* **2.** a mark, as ℘ or ₰, used to indicate matter to be deleted. [1695–1705; < L *dēlē* (2nd pers. sing. impv. of *dēlēre*), equiv. to *dēl-* destroy + *-ē* impv. ending]

de·lead (dē led′), *v.t. Metalworking.* to remove lead adhering to (a metal object) after cold-drawing through a die in which the lead served as a lubricant. [DE- + LEAD²]

de·lec·ta·ble (di lek′tə bəl), *adj.* **1.** delightful; highly pleasing; enjoyable: *a delectable witticism.* **2.** delicious: *a delectable dinner.* —*n.* **3.** an especially appealing or appetizing food or dish: *a buffet table spread with delectables.* [1350–1400; ME < L *dēlectābilis* delightful, equiv. to *dēlectā(re)* to delight (freq. of *dēlicere* to entice) + *-bilis* -BLE] —**de·lec′ta·ble·ness, de·lec′ta·bil′i·ty,** *n.* —**de·lec′ta·bly,** *adv.*
—**Syn. 1.** pleasurable, gratifying, agreeable; amusing, entertaining. —**Ant. 1, 2.** disagreeable, distasteful.

de·lec·tate (di lek′tāt), *v.t.,* **-tat·ed, -tat·ing.** to please; charm; delight. [1705–1805; < L *dēlectātus* delighted, ptp. of *dēlectāre.* See DELECTABLE, -ATE¹]

de·lec·ta·tion (dē′lek tā′shən), *n.* delight; enjoyment. [1350–1400; ME *delectacioun* < L *dēlectātiōn-* (s. of *dēlectātiō*), equiv. to *dēlectāt(us)* (see DELECTATE) + *-iōn-* -ION]

De·led·da (de led′dä), *n.* **Gra·zia** (grä′tsyä), 1875–1936, Italian novelist.

del·e·ga·ble (del′i gə bəl), *adj.* capable of being delegated: *delegable authority.* [1650–60; DELEG(ATE) + -ABLE]

del·e·ga·cy (del′i gə sē), *n., pl.* **-cies. 1.** the position or commission of a delegate. **2.** the appointing or sending of a delegate. **3.** a body of delegates; delegation. **4.** (at Oxford University) a permanent committee charged with certain duties. [1525–35; DELEG(ATE) + -ACY]

de·le·gal·ize (dē lē′gə līz′), *v.t.,* **-ized, -iz·ing.** to revoke the statutory authorization of. Also, *esp. Brit.,* **de·le′gal·ise′.** [DE- + LEGALIZE]

del·e·gate (*n.* del′i git, -gāt′; *v.* del′i gāt′), *n., v.,* **-gat·ed, -gat·ing.** —*n.* **1.** a person designated to act for or represent another or others; deputy; representative, as in a political convention. **2.** (formerly) the representative of a Territory in the U.S. House of Representatives. **3.** a member of the lower house of the state legislature of Maryland, Virginia, or West Virginia. —*v.t.* **4.** to send or appoint (a person) as deputy or representative. **5.** to commit (powers, functions, etc.) to another as agent or deputy. [1350–1400; ME (n.) < ML *dēlēgātus,* n. use of L: ptp. of *dēlēgāre* to assign, equiv. to *dē-* DE- + *lēgātus* deputed; see LEGATE] —**del·e·ga·tee** (del′i gə tē′), *n.* —**del·e·ga·tor** (del′i gā′tər), *n.*
—**Syn. 5.** entrust, assign, transfer.

del·e·ga·tion (del′i gā′shən), *n.* **1.** a group or body of delegates: *Our club sent a delegation to the rally.* **2.** the body of delegates chosen to represent a political unit, as a state, in an assembly: *the New Jersey delegation in Congress.* **3.** the act of delegating. **4.** the state of being delegated. [1605–15; < L *dēlēgātiōn-* (s. of *dēlēgātiō*), equiv. to *dēlēgāt(us)* (see DELEGATE) + *-iōn-* -ION]
—**Syn. 2.** commission.

del·e·ga·to·ry (del′i gə tôr′ē, -tōr′ē), *adj.* of or pertaining to the delegation or assignment of authority, power, or responsibility. [1590–1600; DELEGATE + -ORY[1]]

de·le·git·i·ma·tize (dē′li jit′ə mə tīz′), *v.t.,* **-tized, -tiz·ing.** delegitimize. Also, *esp. Brit.,* **de′le·git′i·ma·tise′.** [DE- + LEGITIMATIZE]

de·le·git·i·mize (dē′li jit′ə mīz′), *v.t.,* **-mized, -miz·ing.** to remove the legitimate or legal status of. Also, *esp. Brit.,* **de′le·git′i·mise′.** [DE- + LEGITIMIZE] —**de′le·git′i·mi·za′tion,** *n.*

de Les·seps (də les′eps; *Fr.* də le seps′), **Vicomte Fer·di·nand Ma·rie** (fûr′dn and′ mə rē′; *Fr.* fer dē-näN′ ma rē′). See **Lesseps, Ferdinand Marie, Vicomte de.**

de·lete (di lēt′), *v.t.,* **-let·ed, -let·ing.** to strike out or remove (something written or printed); cancel; erase; expunge. [1485–95; < L *dēlētus* (ptp. of *dēlēre* to destroy), equiv. to *dēl-* destroy + *-ē-* thematic vowel + *-tus* ptp. suffix] —**de·let′a·ble,** *adj.*
—**Syn.** eradicate. See **cancel.**

del·e·te·ri·ous (del′i tēr′ē əs), *adj.* **1.** injurious to health: *deleterious gases.* **2.** harmful; injurious: *deleterious influences.* [1635–45; < Gk *dēlētḗrios* destructive, adj. deriv. of *dēlētḗr* destroyer, equiv. to *dēlē-* var. s. of *dēleîsthai* to hurt, injure + *-tēr* agent suffix + *-ios* adj. suffix; see -IOUS] —**del′e·te′ri·ous·ly,** *adv.* —**del′e·te′ri·ous·ness,** *n.*
—**Syn. 2.** pernicious, hurtful, destructive; noxious.
—**Ant. 2.** beneficial.

de·le·tion (di lē′shən), *n.* **1.** an act or instance of deleting. **2.** the state of being deleted. **3.** a deleted word, passage, etc. **4.** *Genetics.* a type of chromosomal aberration in which a segment of the chromosome is removed or lost. [1580–90; < L *dēlētiōn-* (s. of *dēlētiō*) a destroying, equiv. to *dēlēt(us)* (see DELETE) + *-iōn-* -ION]

delft (delft), *n.* **1.** earthenware having an opaque white glaze with an overglaze decoration, usually in blue. **2.** any pottery resembling this. Also, **delf** (delf). Also called **delft′ ware′.** [1705–15; after DELFT]

Delft (delft), *n.* a city in W Netherlands. 84,129.

Del·ga·do (del gä′dō), *n.* **Cape,** a cape at the NE extremity of Mozambique.

Del·hi (del′ē), *n.* **1.** a union territory in N India. 4,065,698; 574 sq. mi. (1487 sq. km). **2.** Also called **Old Delhi.** a city in and the capital of this territory: former capital of the old Mogul Empire; administrative headquarters of British India 1912–29. 3,647,023. Cf. **New Delhi.**

Del′hi bel′ly, *Slang.* diarrhea experienced by travelers in a foreign country, who are not accustomed to the local food and water. [1960–65; after DELHI, India]

del·i (del′ē), *n., pl.* **del·is** (del′ēz). *Informal.* **1.** a delicatessen. **2.** food typically sold at a delicatessen, as cold cuts, salads, and pickles. [1960–65; by shortening]

De·li·an (dē′lē ən, dēl′yən), *adj.* **1.** pertaining to Delos. —*n.* **2.** a native or inhabitant of Delos. [1615–25; < L *Dēli(us)* (< Gk *Dḗlios*) + -AN]

de·lib·er·ate (*adj.* di lib′ər it; *v.* di lib′ə rāt′), *adj., v.,* **-at·ed, -at·ing.** —*adj.* **1.** carefully weighed or considered; studied; intentional: *a deliberate lie.* **2.** characterized by deliberation; careful or slow in deciding: *a deliberate decision.* **3.** leisurely and steady in movement or action; slow and even; unhurried: *a deliberate step.* —*v.t.* **4.** to weigh in the mind; consider: *to deliberate a question.* —*v.i.* **5.** to think carefully or attentively; reflect: *She deliberated for a long time before giving her decision.* **6.** to consult or confer formally: *The jury deliberated for three hours.* [1350–1400; ME < L *dēlīberātus* (ptp. of *dēlīberāre* to consider), equiv. to *dē-* DE- + *līber(āre)* to balance, weigh (deriv. of *lībra* balance, scales) + *-ātus* -ATE[1]] —**de·lib′er·ate·ly,** *adv.* —**de·lib′er·ate·ness,** *n.* —**de·lib′er·a′tor,** *n.*
—**Syn. 1.** purposeful; willful. DELIBERATE, INTENTIONAL, PREMEDITATED, VOLUNTARY refer to something not happening by chance. DELIBERATE is applied to what is done not hastily but with full realization of what one is doing: *a deliberate attempt to evade justice.* INTENTIONAL is applied to what is definitely intended or done on purpose: *an intended omission.* PREMEDITATED is applied to what has been planned in advance: *a premeditated crime.* VOLUNTARY is applied to what is done by a definite exercise of the will and not because of outward pressure: *a voluntary enlistment.* **2.** methodical, thoughtful, circumspect, cautious. **3.** See **slow. 4.** ponder. **5.** cogitate, ruminate. —**Ant. 1.** accidental. **2.** impulsive, precipitate.

de·lib·er·a·tion (di lib′ə rā′shən), *n.* **1.** careful consideration before decision. **2.** formal consultation or discussion. **3.** deliberate quality; leisureliness of movement or action; slowness. [1325–75; ME *deliberacion* < L *dēlīberātiōn-* (s. of *dēlīberātiō*), equiv. to *dēlīberāt(us)* (see DELIBERATE) + *-iōn-* -ION]
—**Syn. 1.** reflection, forethought.

de·lib·er·a·tive (di lib′ər ə tiv, -ə rā′tiv), *adj.* **1.** having the function of deliberating, as a legislative assembly: *a deliberative body.* **2.** having to do with policy; dealing with the wisdom and expediency of a proposal: *a deliberative speech.* [1545–55; < L *dēlīberātīvus,* equiv. to *dēlīberāt(us)* (see DELIBERATE) + *-īvus* -IVE] —**de·lib′er·a·tive·ly,** *adv.* —**de·lib′er·a·tive·ness,** *n.*

De·libes (də lēb′), *n.* **(Clé·ment Phi·li·bert) Lé·o** (klā-mäN′ fē lē ber′ lā ō′), 1836–91, French composer, esp. of operas, operettas, and ballets.

del·i·ca·cy (del′i kə sē), *n., pl.* **-cies.** **1.** fineness of texture, quality, etc.; softness; daintiness: *the delicacy of lace.* **2.** something delightful or pleasing, esp. a choice food considered with regard to its rarity, costliness, or the like: *Caviar is a great delicacy.* **3.** the quality of being easily broken or damaged; fragility. **4.** the quality of requiring or involving great care or tact: *negotiations of great delicacy.* **5.** extreme sensitivity; precision of action or operation; minute accuracy: *the delicacy of a skillful surgeon's touch; a watch mechanism of unusual delicacy.* **6.** fineness of perception or feeling; sensitiveness: *the delicacy of the pianist's playing.* **7.** fineness of feeling with regard to what is fitting, proper, etc.: *Delicacy would not permit her to be rude.* **8.** sensitivity with regard to the feelings of others: *She criticized him with such delicacy that he was not offended.* **9.** bodily weakness; liability to sickness; frailty. **10.** *Ling.* (esp. in systemic linguistics) the degree of minuteness pursued at a given stage of analysis in specifying distinctions in linguistic description. **11.** *Obs.* sensuous indulgence; luxury. [1325–75; ME *delicasie.* See DELICATE, -CY]
—**Syn. 5.** sensitivity, discrimination; prudence, consideration, circumspection. —**Ant. 1, 6.** coarseness.

del·i·cate (del′i kit), *adj.* **1.** fine in texture, quality, construction, etc.: *a delicate lace collar.* **2.** fragile; easily damaged; frail: *delicate porcelain; a delicate child.* **3.** so fine as to be scarcely perceptible; subtle: *a delicate flavor.* **4.** soft or faint, as color: *a delicate shade of pink.* **5.** fine or precise in action or execution; capable of responding to the slightest influence: *a delicate instrument.* **6.** requiring great care, caution, or tact: *a delicate international situation.* **7.** distinguishing subtle differences: *a delicate eye; a delicate sense of smell.* **8.** exquisite or refined in perception or feeling; sensitive. **9.** regardful of what is becoming, proper, etc.: *a delicate sense of propriety.* **10.** mindful of or sensitive to the feelings of others: *a delicate refusal.* **11.** dainty or choice, as food: *delicate tidbits.* **12.** primly fastidious; squeamish: *not a movie for the delicate viewer.* **13.** *Obs.* sensuous; voluptuous. —*n.* **14.** *Archaic.* a choice food; delicacy. **15.** *Obs.* a source of pleasure; luxury. [1325–75; ME *delicat* < L *dēlicātus* delightful, dainty; akin to DELICIOUS] —**del′i·cate·ly,** *adv.* —**del′i·cate·ness,** *n.*
—**Syn. 1.** DELICATE, DAINTY, EXQUISITE imply beauty such as belongs to rich surroundings or which needs careful treatment. DELICATE, used of an object, suggests fragility, small size, and often very fine workmanship: *a delicate piece of carving.* DAINTY, in concrete references, suggests a smallness, gracefulness, and beauty that forbid rough handling: *a dainty handkerchief;* of persons, it refers to fastidious sensibilities: *dainty in eating habits.* EXQUISITE suggests an outstanding beauty and elegance, or a discriminating sensitivity and ability to perceive fine distinctions: *an exquisite sense of humor.* **2.** tender, slight, weak. **5.** exact, accurate. **6.** critical, precarious. **7.** discriminating, careful. —**Ant. 1, 2.** coarse. **3.** hard, crude.

del·i·ca·tes·sen (del′i kə tes′ən), *n.* **1.** a store selling foods already prepared or requiring little preparation for serving, as cooked meats, cheese, salads, and the like. **2.** *Informal.* the food products sold in such a store or at a counter: *We're having delicatessen for dinner.* [1885–90, *Amer.;* < G, pl. of *Delikatesse* dainty < F *délicatesse*]

De·li·cia (də lish′ə), *n.* a female given name.

de·li·cious (di lish′əs), *adj.* **1.** highly pleasing to the senses, esp. to taste or smell: *a delicious dinner; a delicious aroma.* **2.** very pleasing; delightful: *a delicious sense of humor.* —*n.* **3.** (*cap.*) a red or yellow variety of apple, cultivated in the U.S. [1250–1300; ME < OF < LL *dēliciōsus,* equiv. to L *dēliciae* delight + *-ōsus* -OUS] —**de·li′cious·ly,** *adv.* —**de·li′cious·ness,** *n.*
—**Syn. 1.** palatable, savory, delectable, dainty, delicate. DELICIOUS, LUSCIOUS refer to that which is especially agreeable to the senses. That which is DELICIOUS is highly agreeable to the taste or sometimes to the smell: *a delicious meal.* LUSCIOUS implies such a luxuriant fullness or ripeness as to make an object rich: *a luscious banana; a luscious beauty; luscious music.* —**Ant. 1.** unpleasant.

de·lict (di likt′), *n.* **1.** *Law.* a misdemeanor; offense. **2.** *Roman and Civil Law.* a civil wrong permitting compensation. [1515–25; < L *dēlictum* a fault, n. use of neut. of *dēlictus* (ptp. of *dēlinquere* to do wrong; see DELINQUENCY), equiv. to *dēlic-* fail + *-tus* ptp. suffix]

de·light (di līt′), *n.* **1.** a high degree of pleasure or enjoyment; joy; rapture: *She takes great delight in her job.* **2.** something that gives great pleasure: *The dance was a delight to see.* —*v.t.* **3.** to give great pleasure, satisfaction, or enjoyment to; please highly: *The show delighted everyone.* —*v.i.* **4.** to have great pleasure; take pleasure (fol. by *in* or an infinitive): *She delights in going for long walks in the country.* [1175–1225; (v.) resp., after LIGHT[1], of earlier *delite,* ME *deliten* < AF *deliter,* OF *delitier* < L *delectāre* (see DELECTABLE); (n.) resp. (as above) of ME *delit* < AF, OF, deriv. of v.] —**de·light′er,** *n.* —**de·light′ing·ly,** *adv.* —**de·light′less,** *adj.*
—**Syn. 1.** transport, delectation. See **pleasure. 3.** charm, enrapture. —**Ant. 1.** distress. **2.** disappointment.

de·light·ed (di lī′tid), *adj.* **1.** highly pleased. **2.** *Obs.* delightful. [1595–1605; DELIGHT + -ED[2]] —**de·light′ed·ly,** *adv.* —**de·light′ed·ness,** *n.*
—**Syn. 1.** captivated, enraptured, enchanted, ecstatic.

de·light·ful (di līt′fəl), *adj.* giving great pleasure or delight; highly pleasing: *a delightful surprise.* [1520–30; DELIGHT + -FUL] —**de·light′ful·ly,** *adv.* —**de·light′ful·ness,** *n.*
—**Syn.** pleasant, pleasurable, enjoyable; charming, enchanting, delectable, agreeable. —**Ant.** disagreeable.

de·light·some (di līt′səm), *adj. Literary.* highly pleasing; delightful. [1490–1500; DELIGHT + -SOME[1]] —**de·light′some·ly,** *adv.* —**de·light′some·ness,** *n.*

De·li·lah (di lī′lə), *n.* **1.** Samson's mistress, who betrayed him to the Philistines. Judges 16. **2.** a seductive and treacherous woman. **3.** a female given name: from a Hebrew word meaning "delicate."

de·lim·it (di lim′it), *v.t.* to fix or mark the limits or boundaries of; demarcate: *A ravine delimited the property on the north.* [1850–55; < F *délimiter* < L *dēlīmitāre,* equiv. to *dē-* DE- + *līmitāre* to LIMIT]

de·lim·i·tate (di lim′i tāt′), *v.t.,* **-tat·ed, -tat·ing.** delimit. [1880–85; < L *dēlīmitātus,* ptp. of *dēlīmitāre.* See DELIMIT, -ATE[1]] —**de·lim′i·ta′tion,** *n.* —**de·lim′i·ta′tive,** *n., adj.*

de·lim·it·er (di lim′i tər), *n. Computers.* a blank space, comma, or other character or symbol that indicates the beginning or end of a character string, word, or data item. [1960–65; DELIMIT + -ER[1]]

de·lin·e·ate (di lin′ē āt′), *v.t.,* **-at·ed, -at·ing.** **1.** to trace the outline of; sketch or trace in outline; represent pictorially: *He delineated the state of Texas on the map with a red pencil.* **2.** to portray in words; describe or outline with precision: *In her speech she delineated the city plan with great care.* [1550–60; < L *dēlīneātus,* equiv. to *dē-* DE- + *līneātus* LINEATE] —**de·lin·e·a·ble** (di lin′ē ə bəl), *adj.*

de·lin·e·a·tion (di lin′ē ā′shən), *n.* **1.** the act or process of delineating. **2.** a chart or diagram; sketch; rough draft. **3.** a description. [1560–70; < LL *dēlīneātiōn-* (s. of *dēlīneātiō*) a sketch, equiv. to L *dēlīneāt(us)* (see DELINEATE) + *-iōn-* -ION] —**de·lin·e·a·tive** (di lin′ē ā′tiv, -ē ə tiv), *adj.*

de·lin·e·a·tor (di lin′ē ā′tər), *n.* **1.** a person or thing that delineates. **2.** a tailor's pattern that can be adjusted for cutting garments of different sizes. [1765–75; DELINEATE + -OR[2]]

de·li·ne·a·vit (de lin′e ä′wit; *Eng.* di lin′ē ā′vit), *Latin.* he drew (this); she drew (this). *Abbr.:* del.

de·link (dē lingk′), *v.t.* to make independent; dissociate; separate: *The administration has delinked human rights from economic aid to underdeveloped nations.* [DE- + LINK[1]] —**de·link′age,** *n.*

de·lin·quen·cy (di ling′kwən sē), *n., pl.* **-cies.** **1.** failure in or neglect of duty or obligation; dereliction; default: *delinquency in payment of dues.* **2.** wrongful, illegal, or antisocial behavior. Cf. **juvenile delinquency. 3.** any misdeed, offense, or misdemeanor. **4.** something, as a debt, that is past due or otherwise delinquent. [1630–40; < LL *dēlinquentia* fault, crime, equiv. to L *dēlinquent-* (s. of *dēlinquēns,* prp. of *dēlinquere* to do wrong, equiv. to *dē-* DE- + *linquere* to leave) + *-ia* n. suffix; see -ENCY]

de·lin·quent (di ling′kwənt), *adj.* **1.** failing in or neglectful of a duty or obligation; guilty of a misdeed or offense. **2.** (of an account, tax, debt, etc.) past due; overdue. **3.** of or pertaining to delinquents or delinquency: *delinquent attitudes.* —*n.* **4.** a person who is delinquent. **5.** See **juvenile delinquent.** [1475–85; < L *dēlinquent-;* see DELINQUENCY] —**de·lin′quent·ly,** *adv.*

del·i·quesce (del′i kwes′), *v.i.,* **-quesced, -quesc·ing.** **1.** to become liquid by absorbing moisture from the air, as certain salts. **2.** to melt away. **3.** *Bot.* to form many small divisions or branches. [1750–60; < L *dēliquēscere* to become liquid, equiv. to *dē-* DE- + *liquēscere;* see LIQUESCENT]

del·i·ques·cence (del′i kwes′əns), *n.* **1.** the act or process of deliquescing. **2.** the substance produced when something deliquesces. [1750–60; DELIQUESCE + -ENCE] —**del′i·ques′cent,** *adj.*

del·i·ra·tion (del′ə rā′shən), *n. Archaic.* mental derangement; raving; delirium. [1590–1600; (< F) < L *dēlīrātiōn-* (s. of *dēlīrātiō*) folly, equiv. to *dēlīr(āre)* to be silly, lit., go out of the furrow (*dē-* DE- + *līr(a)* furrow + *-āre* inf. ending) + *-ātiōn-* -ATION]

de·lir·i·ant (di lēr′ē ənt), *adj.* **1.** involving or causing delirium. —*n.* **2.** a substance, as a compound or drug, that causes delirium. [1880–85; DELIRI(UM) + -ANT]

de·lir·i·ous (di lēr′ē əs), *adj.* **1.** *Pathol.* affected with or characteristic of delirium. **2.** wild with excitement, enthusiasm, etc.: *She was delirious with joy at the news.* [1590–1600; DELIRI(UM) + -OUS] —**de·lir′i·ous·ly,** *adv.* —**de·lir′i·ous·ness,** *n.*
—**Syn. 2.** thrilled, excited, ecstatic.

de·lir·i·um (di lēr′ē əm), *n., pl.* **-lir·i·ums, -lir·i·a** (-lēr′ē ə). **1.** *Pathol.* a more or less temporary disorder of the mental faculties, as in fevers, disturbances of consciousness, or intoxication, characterized by restlessness, excitement, delusions, hallucinations, etc. **2.** a state of violent excitement or emotion. [1590–1600; < L *dēlīrium* frenzy, equiv. to *dēlīr(āre)* (see DELIRATION) + *-ium* -IUM]

delir′ium tre′mens (trē′mənz, -menz), *Pathol.* a withdrawal syndrome occurring in persons who have developed physiological dependence on alcohol, characterized by tremor, visual hallucinations, and autonomic instability. *Abbr.:* d.t. Also called **the d.t.'s.** [1813; < NL: trembling delirium]

de·list (dē list′), *v.t.* **1.** to delete from a list, as one that indicates acceptability, legitimacy, or the like. **2.** to withdraw or remove (a security) from the group listed with a particular stock exchange. [1930–35; DE- + LIST[1]]

del•i•tes•cent (del′i tes′ənt), *adj.* concealed; hidden; latent. [1675–85; < L *dēlitēscent-* (s. of *dēlitēscēns*) (prp. of *dēlitēscere* to hide away); see DE-, LATESCENT] —**del′i•tes′cence, del′i•tes′cen•cy,** *n.*

De•li•um (dē′lē əm), *n.* an ancient seaport in Greece, in Boeotia: the Boeotians defeated the Athenians here 424 B.C.

De•li•us (dē′lē əs, dēl′yəs), *n.* **Frederick,** 1862–1934, English composer.

de•liv•er (di liv′ər), *v.t.* **1.** to carry and turn over (letters, goods, etc.) to the intended recipient or recipients: *to deliver mail; to deliver a package.* **2.** to give into another's possession or keeping; surrender: *to deliver a prisoner to the police; to deliver a bond.* **3.** to bring (votes) to the support of a candidate or a cause. **4.** to give forth in words; utter or pronounce: *to deliver a verdict; to deliver a speech.* **5.** to give forth or emit: *The oil well delivers 500 barrels a day.* **6.** to strike or throw: *to deliver a blow.* **7.** to set free or liberate: *The Israelites were delivered from bondage.* **8.** to rescue or save: *Deliver me from such tiresome people!* **9.** to assist (a female) in bringing forth young: *The doctor delivered her of twins.* **10.** to assist at the birth of: *The doctor delivered the baby.* **11.** to give birth to: *She delivered twins at 4 A.M.* **12.** to disburden (oneself) of thoughts, opinions, etc. **13.** to make known; assert. —*v.i.* **14.** to give birth. **15.** to provide a delivery service for goods and products: *The store delivers free of charge.* **16.** to do or carry out as promised: *an ad agency known for delivering when a successful campaign is needed.* —*adj.* **17.** *Archaic.* agile; quick. [1175–1225; ME *deliveren* < OF *delivrer* < LL *dēliberāre* to set free, equiv. to *dē-* DE- + *liberāre* to LIBERATE] —**de•liv′er•er,** *n.*
—**Syn. 1.** hand over, transfer, cede, yield. **4.** communicate, announce, proclaim. **7.** emancipate, release.

de•liv•er•a•ble (di liv′ər ə bəl), *adj.* **1.** capable of delivery. —*n.* **2.** something that can be done, esp. something that is a realistic expectation: *The corporation says that making a profit this year is a deliverable.* **3.** something, as merchandise, that is or can be delivered, esp. to fulfill a contract: *All deliverables are to be shipped within 30 days.* [1745–55; DELIVER + -ABLE] —**de•liv′er•a•bil′i•ty,** *n.*

de•liv•er•ance (di liv′ər əns), *n.* **1.** an act or instance of delivering. **2.** salvation. **3.** liberation. **4.** a thought or judgment expressed; a formal or authoritative pronouncement. [1250–1300; ME *deliveraunce* < OF *delivrance,* equiv. to *delivr(er)* to DELIVER + *-ance* -ANCE]

deliv′ered price′, a quoted price of merchandise, as steel, that includes freight charges from the basing point to the point of delivery, usually f.o.b.

de•liv•er•ly (di liv′ər lē), *adv. Archaic.* quickly; deftly. [1300–50; ME; see DELIVER, -LY]

de•liv•er•y (di liv′ə rē), *n., pl.* **-er•ies. 1.** the carrying and turning over of letters, goods, etc., to a designated recipient or recipients. **2.** a giving up or handing over; surrender. **3.** the utterance or enunciation of words. **4.** vocal and bodily behavior during the presentation of a speech: *a speaker's fine delivery.* **5.** the act or manner of giving or sending forth: *the pitcher's fine delivery of the ball.* **6.** the state of being delivered of or giving birth to a child; parturition. **7.** something delivered: *The delivery is late today.* **8.** *Com.* a shipment of goods from the seller to the buyer. **9.** *Law.* a formal act performed to make a transfer of property legally effective: *a delivery of deed.* **10.** *Print.* Also called **deliv′ery end′.** the part of a printing press where the paper emerges in printed form. **11.** *Archaic.* release or rescue; liberation; deliverance. [1400–50; late ME *delyvere, delyvery* < AF *delivrée,* n. use of fem. ptp. of *delivrer* to DELIVER, with suffix assimilated to -ERY]

deliv′ery boy′, a boy or youth employed by a store to deliver customers' purchases. [1915–20]

de•liv•er•y•man (di liv′ə rē man′, -mən), *n., pl.* **-men** (-men′, -mən). a person employed to make deliveries of merchandise to purchasers, usually by means of a truck. [1915–20; DELIVERY + MAN[1]]

deliv′ery room′, 1. an area in a hospital equipped for delivering babies. **2.** a room or area in which deliveries are made or received, as the section of a public library where books are taken out or returned. [1945–50]

dell (del), *n.* a small, usually wooded valley; vale. [bef. 1000; ME *delle,* OE *dell;* akin to DALE]

Dell (del), *n.* a male or female given name.

dell′ (del), (in names of Italian derivation) an elided form of *della: Giovanni dell' Anguillara.*

del•la (del′lä), (in names of Italian derivation) a contraction of *di* and the article *la: Andrea della Robbia.*

Del•la (del′ə), *n.* a female given name, form of **Delia.**

del•la Rob•bia (del′ə rō′bē ə; *It.* del′lä Rôb′byä), **Lu•ca** (lo͞o′kä). See **Robbia, Luca della.**

Del•lo Joi•o (del′ō joi′ō), **Norman,** born 1913, U.S. composer and pianist.

dells (delz), *n.pl.* dalles. [by construal as a pl. of DELL]

Del•mar′va Penin′sula (del mär′və), a peninsula between Chesapeake and Delaware bays including most of Delaware and those parts of Maryland and Virginia E of Chesapeake Bay. Cf. **Eastern shore.**

Del•mon•i•co (del mon′i kō′), *n., pl.* **-cos.** See **club steak.** Also called **Delmon′ico steak′.** [after L. DELMONICO]

Del•mon•i•co (del mon′i kō′), *n.* **Lorenzo,** 1813–81, U.S. restaurateur, born in Switzerland.

CONCISE ETYMOLOGY KEY: <, descended or borrowed from; >, whence; b., blend of, blended; c., cognate with; cf., compare; deriv., derivative; equiv., equivalent; imit., imitative; obl., oblique; r., replacing; s., stem; sp., spelling, spelled; resp., respelling, respelled; trans., translation; ?, origin unknown; *, unattested; ‡, probably earlier than. See the full key inside the front cover.

de•lo•cal•ize (dē lō′kə līz′), *v.t.,* **-ized, -iz•ing. 1.** to remove from the proper or usual locality. **2.** to free or remove from the restrictions of locality; free of localism, provincialism, or the like: *to delocalize a person's accent.* Also, *esp. Brit.,* **de•lo′cal•ise′.** [1850–55; DE- + LOCALIZE] —**de•lo′cal•i•za′tion,** *n.*

De•lo•res (də lôr′is, -lōr′-), *n.* a female given name.

De•lorme (də lôrm′), *n.* **Phi•li•bert** (fē lē ber′), 1515?–70, French architect.

De•los (dē′los, del′ōs), *n.* a Greek island in the Cyclades, in the SW Aegean: site of an oracle of Apollo.

de los An•ge•les (dā lôs an′jə ləs, -lēz′, los; *Sp.* de lôs än′he les), **Vic•to•ria** (vik tôr′ē ə, -tōr′-; *Sp.* bēk tô′ryä), born 1923?, Spanish operatic soprano.

de•louse (dē lous′, -louz′), *v.t.,* **-loused, -lous•ing.** to free of lice; remove lice from. [1915–20; DE- + LOUSE] —**de•lous′er,** *n.*

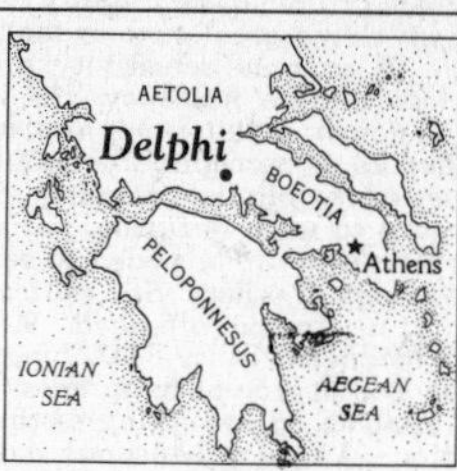

Del•phi (del′fī), *n.* an ancient city in central Greece, in Phocis: site of an oracle of Apollo.

Del•phi•an (del′fē ən), *n.* **1.** a native or inhabitant of Delphi. —*adj.* **2.** Delphic. [1615–25; DELPHI + -AN]

Del•phic (del′fik), *adj.* **1.** of or pertaining to Delphi. **2.** of or pertaining to Apollo, or to his temples or oracles. **3.** (*often l.c.*) oracular; obscure; ambiguous: *She was known for her Delphic pronouncements.* [1590–1600; < L *Delphicus* < Gk *Delphikós,* equiv. to *Delph(oí)* DELPHI + *-ikos* -IC] —**del′phi•cal•ly,** *adv.*

Del′phic or′acle, the oracle of Apollo at Delphi, noted for giving ambiguous answers.

Del•phin•i•a (del fin′ē ə), *n.* **1.** an ancient Greek festival in honor of Apollo. **2.** Also, **Del•phine** (del fēn′). a female given name: from a Greek word meaning "dolphin."

del•phi•nin (del′fə nin), *n. Chem.* a violet anthocyanin, $C_{41}H_{38}O_{21}$, found in the flowers of the larkspur, *Delphinium consolida.* [DELPHIN(IUM) + -IN[2]]

del•phi•nine (del′fə nēn′, -nin), *n. Chem.* a bitter, poisonous, crystalline alkaloid, $C_{33}H_{45}NO_9$, obtained from various species of larkspur, esp. *Delphinium staphisagria.* [1820–30; DELPHIN(IUM) + -INE[2]]

del•phin•i•um (del fin′ē əm), *n., pl.* **-i•ums, -i•a** (-ē ə). any of numerous plants of the genus *Delphinium,* esp. any of various tall, cultivated species having usually blue, pink, or white flowers. Cf. **larkspur.** [1655–65; < NL < Gk *delphínion* larkspur, deriv. of *delphís* (s. *delphīn-*) DOLPHIN; so called from the shape of the nectary]

Del•phi•nus (del fī′nəs), *n., gen.* **-ni** (-nī). *Astron.* the Dolphin, a northern constellation between Aquila and Pegasus. [< L *delphīnus* dolphin < Gk *delphís* DOLPHIN, s. *delphīn-*]

Del′ray Beach′ (del′rā), a city in SE Florida. 34,325.

Del Ri•o (del rē′ō), a city in S Texas, on the Rio Grande. 30,034.

Del•sarte (del särt′; *Fr.* del sart′), *n.* **Fran•çois** (fran swä′; *Fr.* fräɴ swa′), 1811–71, French musician and teacher.

Delsarte′ meth′od, a theory or system devised by François Delsarte for improving musical and dramatic expression through the mastery of various bodily attitudes and gestures. Also called **Delsarte′ sys′tem.**

Del•sar•ti•an (del sär′tē ən), *adj.* of, pertaining to, or characteristic of François Delsarte or the Delsarte method. [DELSARTE + -IAN]

del Sar•to (del sär′tō; *It.* del sär′tô), **An•dre•a** (än drā′ə; *It.* än dre′ä). See **Andrea del Sarto.**

del•ta (del′tə), *n.* **1.** the fourth letter of the Greek alphabet (Δ, δ). **2.** the consonant sound represented by this letter. **3.** the fourth in a series of items. **4.** anything triangular, like the Greek capital delta (Δ). **5.** *Math.* an incremental change in a variable, as Δ or δ. **6.** a nearly flat plain of alluvial deposit between diverging branches of the mouth of a river, often, though not necessarily, triangular: *the Nile delta.* **7.** (*usually cap.*) a word used in communications to represent the letter *D.* **8.** (*cap.*) *Astron.* a star that is usually the fourth brightest of a constellation: *The fourth brightest star in the Southern Cross is Delta Crucis.* [1350–1400; ME *deltha* < L *delta* < Gk *délta;* akin to Heb *dāleth*]

Del•ta (del′tə), *n. Mil.* the NATO name for a class of Soviet nuclear-powered ballistic missile submarine armed with 16 multi-warhead missiles.

Del′ta Aq′uarids, *Astron.* See under **Aquarids.**

del′ta connec′tion, *Elect.* the series connection of three elements in a three-phase circuit forming a triangle. [1900–05]

del′ta func′tion, *Physics, Math.* a generalized function having the value 0 except at 0, the value infinity at 0, and an integral from minus infinity to plus infinity of 1, used in thermodynamics and quantum mechanics. Also called **Dirac delta function.**

del′ta hepati′tis, *Immunol.* See **hepatitis delta.**

del•ta•ic (del tā′ik), *adj.* **1.** pertaining to or like a delta. **2.** forming or having a delta. [DELTA + -IC]

del′ta i′ron, *Metall.* an allotrope of iron, stable above 1400°C, having a body-centered cubic lattice structure.

del′ta par′ticle, *Physics.* any of a family of baryon resonances having strangeness 0, isotopic spin $^3/_2$, and either a single or double positive electric charge, a single negative charge, or no charge. *Symbol:* Δ

del′ta ray′, *Physics.* a low-energy electron emitted by a substance after bombardment by higher-energy particles, as alpha particles. [1905–10]

del′ta rhythm′, *Physiol.* a pattern of slow brain waves, having a frequency of less than 6 cycles per second and as recorded by an electroencephalograph, associated with deep sleep. [1935–40]

Del′ta team′, an assault unit of highly trained and specialized U.S. troops that can be quickly dispatched to deal with terrorist action.

del′ta vi′rus. See under **hepatitis delta.**

del′ta wave′, *Physiol.* any of the slow brain waves constituting delta rhythm. [1935–40]

del′ta wing′, a triangularly shaped surface that serves as both wing and horizontal stabilizer of a space vehicle and some supersonic aircraft. [1945–50]

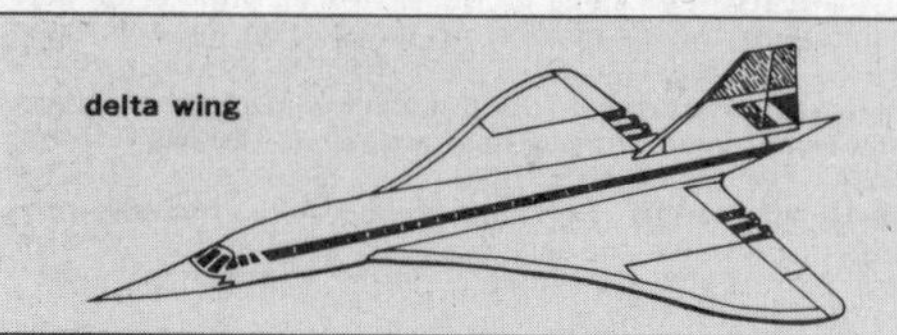

del•ti•ol•o•gy (del′tē ol′ə jē), *n.* the hobby of collecting post cards. [1945–50; < Gk *deltí(on),* dim. of *déltos* writing tablet + -O- + -LOGY] —**del•ti•o•log•i•cal** (del′tē ə loj′i kəl), *adj.* —**del′ti•ol′o•gist,** *n.*

del•toid (del′toid), *n.* **1.** *Anat.* a large, triangular muscle covering the joint of the shoulder, the action of which raises the arm away from the side of the body. —*adj.* **2.** *Anat.* pertaining to or involving the deltoid. **3.** Also, **deltoidal.** in the shape of a Greek capital delta (Δ); triangular. [1675–85; < Gk *deltoeidḗs* delta-shaped, equiv. to *délt(a)* DELTA + *-oeidēs* -OID]

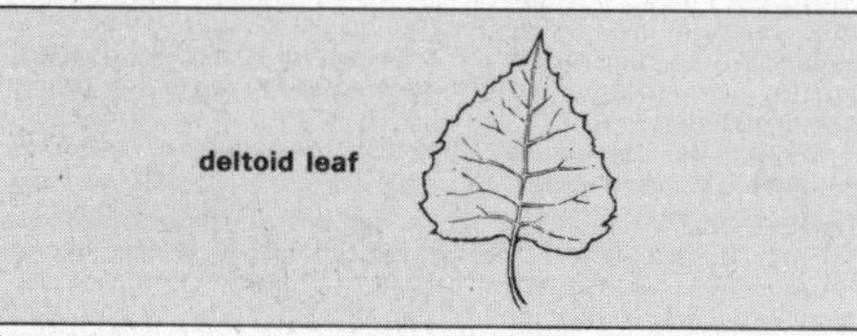

del•toi•dal (del toid′l), *adj.* **1.** of or pertaining to a river delta. **2.** deltoid (def. 3). [1830–40; DELTOID + -AL[1]]

delts (delts), *n.pl. Informal.* deltoid muscles. [1965–70; by shortening]

de•lu•brum (də lo͞o′brəm), *n., pl.* **-bra** (-brə). (in ancient Rome) a temple, shrine, or sanctuary. [1655–65; < L *dēlūbrum,* appar. equiv. to *dēlu(ere)* to wash off (*dē-* DE- + *-luere,* comb. form of *lavere* to wash) + *-brum* instrumental suffix]

de•lude (di lo͞od′), *v.t.,* **-lud•ed, -lud•ing. 1.** to mislead the mind or judgment of; deceive: *His conceit deluded him into believing he was important.* **2.** *Obs.* to mock or frustrate the hopes or aims of. **3.** *Obs.* to elude; evade. [1400–50; late ME *deluden* < L *dēlūdere* to play false, equiv. to *dē-* DE- + *lūdere* to play] —**de•lud′er,** *n.* —**de•lud′ing•ly,** *adv.*
—**Syn. 1.** beguile, cozen, dupe, cheat, defraud, gull.

del•uge (del′yo͞oj, -yo͞ozh, del′o͞oj, -o͞ozh, di lo͞oj′, -lo͞ozh′), *n., v.,* **-uged, -ug•ing.** —*n.* **1.** a great flood of water; inundation; flood. **2.** a drenching rain; downpour. **3.** anything that overwhelms like a flood: *a deluge of mail.* **4. the Deluge.** See **flood** (def. 3). —*v.t.* **5.** to flood; inundate. **6.** to overrun; overwhelm: *She was deluged with congratulatory letters.* [1325–75; ME < OF < L *dīluvium* flood, equiv. to *diluv-,* base of *diluere* to wash away, dissolve (*di-* DI[2] + *-luere,* comb. form of *lavere* to wash) + *-ium* -IUM]
—**Syn. 1.** See **flood. 3.** cataclysm, catastrophe.

de•lu•sion (di lo͞o′zhən), *n.* **1.** an act or instance of deluding. **2.** the state of being deluded. **3.** a false belief or opinion: *delusions of grandeur.* **4.** *Psychiatry.* a fixed false belief that is resistant to reason or confrontation with actual fact: *a paranoid delusion.* [1375–1425; late ME < L *dēlūsiōn-* (s. of *dēlūsiō*), equiv. to *dēlūs(us)* (ptp. of *dēlūdere;* see DELUDE) + *-iōn-* -ION] —**de•lu′sion•al, de•lu′sion•ar′y,** *adj.*
—**Syn. 1.** deception. See **illusion.**

de•lu•sive (di lo͞o′siv), *adj.* **1.** tending to delude; misleading; deceptive: *a delusive reply.* **2.** of the nature of a delusion; false; unreal: *a delusive belief.* Also, **de•lu•so•ry** (di lo͞o′sə rē). [1595–1605; DELUS(ION) + -IVE] —**de•lu′sive•ly,** *adv.* —**de•lu′sive•ness,** *n.*

de•lus•ter•ant (dē lus′tər ənt), *n.* a chemical agent, as titanium dioxide, used in reducing the sheen of a yarn or fabric. Also, **de•lus•trant** (dē lus′trənt). [DE- + LUSTER[1] + -ANT]

de•lust•er•ing (dē lus′tər ing), *n.* a chemical process for reducing the luster of rayon yarns by adding a finely divided pigment to the spinning solution. [1925–30; DE- + LUSTER[1] + -ING[1]]

de•luxe (də luks′, -lo͝oks′), *adj.* **1.** of special elegance, sumptuousness, or fineness; high or highest in quality, luxury, etc.: *a deluxe hotel; a deluxe edition of Shakespeare bound in leather..* —*adv.* **2.** in a luxurious or sumptuous manner: *We always travel deluxe.* Also, **de luxe′.** [1810–20; < F *de luxe* of luxury]

delve (delv), *v.,* **delved, delv•ing.** —*v.i.* **1.** to carry on intensive and thorough research for data, information, or the like; investigate: *to delve into the issue of prison reform.* **2.** *Archaic.* to dig, as with a spade. —*v.t.* **3.** *Archaic.* to dig; excavate. [bef. 900; ME *delven,* OE *delfan;* c. D *delven,* OHG *telban*] —**delv′er,** *n.*
—**Syn. 1.** research, inquire, probe, examine, explore.

dely., delivery.

Dem (dem), *n. Informal.* **1.** a member of the Democratic party. **2. the Dems,** the Democratic party. [1830–40, *Amer.;* shortening of DEMOCRAT]

Dem., 1. Democrat. **2.** Democratic.

dem., 1. demonstrative. **2.** demurrage.

de•mag•net•ize (dē mag′ni tīz′), *v.t.,* **-ized, -iz•ing.** to remove magnetization from. Also, *esp. Brit.,* **de•mag′•net•ise′.** [1830–40; DE- + MAGNETIZE] —**de•mag′net•iz′a•ble,** *adj.* —**de•mag′net•i•za′tion,** *n.* —**de•mag′•net•iz′er,** *n.*

dem•a•gog•ic (dem′ə goj′ik, -gog′-, -gō′jik), *adj.* of, pertaining to, or characteristic of a demagogue. Also, **dem′a•gog′i•cal.** [1825–35; < Gk *dēmagōgikós,* equiv. to *dēmagōg(ós)* (see DEMAGOGUE) + *-ikos* -IC] —**dem′a•gog′i•cal•ly,** *adv.*

dem•a•gogue (dem′ə gog′, -gôg′), *n., v.,* **-gogued, -gogu•ing.** —*n.* **1.** a person, esp. an orator or political leader, who gains power and popularity by arousing the emotions, passions, and prejudices of the people. **2.** (in ancient times) a leader of the people. —*v.t.* **3.** to treat or manipulate (a political issue) in the manner of a demagogue; obscure or distort with emotionalism, prejudice, etc. —*v.i.* **4.** to speak or act like a demagogue. Also, **dem′a•gog′.** [1640–50; < Gk *dēmagōgós* a leader of the people, popular leader, equiv. to *dêm(os)* people + *agōgós* leading, guiding; see -AGOGUE]

dem•a•gogu•er•y (dem′ə gog′ə rē, -gôg′gə-), *n.* the methods or practices of a demagogue. [1850–55, *Amer.;* DEMAGOGUE + -RY]

dem•a•gogu•ism (dem′ə gog′iz əm, -gô′giz-), *n.* demagoguery. Also, **dem′a•gog′ism.** [1835–45; DEMAGOGUE + -ISM]

dem•a•go•gy (dem′ə gō′jē, -gô′jē, -goj′ē), *n.* **1.** *Chiefly Brit.* demagoguery. **2.** the character of a demagogue. **3.** a body of demagogues. [1645–55; < Gk *dēmagōgía* leadership of the people, equiv. to *dēmagō-g(ós)* DEMAGOGUE + *-ia* -Y[3]]

de•mand (di mand′, -mänd′), *v.t.* **1.** to ask for with proper authority; claim as a right: *He demanded payment of the debt.* **2.** to ask for peremptorily or urgently: *He demanded sanctuary. She demanded that we let her in.* **3.** to call for or require as just, proper, or necessary: *This task demands patience. Justice demands objectivity.* **4.** *Law.* **a.** to lay formal legal claim to. **b.** to summon, as to court. —*v.i.* **5.** to make a demand; inquire; ask. —*n.* **6.** the act of demanding. **7.** something that is demanded. **8.** an urgent or pressing requirement: *demands upon one's time.* **9.** *Econ.* **a.** the desire to purchase, coupled with the power to do so. **b.** the quantity of goods that buyers will take at a particular price. **10.** a requisition; a legal claim: *The demands of the client could not be met.* **11.** the state of being wanted or sought for purchase or use: *an article in great demand.* **12.** *Archaic.* inquiry; question. **13. on demand,** upon presentation or request for payment: *The fee is payable on demand.* [1250–1300; ME *demaunden* < AF *demaunder* < ML *dēmandāre* to demand, L to entrust, equiv. to *dē-* DE- + *mandāre* to commission, order; see MANDATE] —**de•mand′a•ble,** *adj.* —**de•mand′er,** *n.*
—**Syn. 3.** exact. DEMAND, CLAIM, REQUIRE imply making an authoritative request. To DEMAND is to ask in a bold, authoritative way: *to demand an explanation.* To CLAIM is to assert a right to something: *He claimed it as his due.* To REQUIRE is to ask for something as being necessary; to compel: *The Army requires absolute obedience of its soldiers.*

de•mand•ant (di man′dənt, -män′-), *n. Law.* **1.** the plaintiff in a real action. **2.** any plaintiff. [1300–50; ME < AF *demaundant,* n. use of prp. of *demaunder* to DEMAND; see -ANT]

demand′ bid′, *Bridge.* a bid to which one's partner is obliged to respond.

demand′ bill′, a bill payable upon presentation.

demand′ depos′it, *Banking.* a deposit subject to withdrawal at the demand of the depositor without prior notice. [1925–30]

de•mand•ing (di man′ding, -män′-), *adj.* **1.** requiring or claiming more than is generally felt by others to be due: *a demanding teacher.* **2.** calling for intensive effort or attention; taxing: *a demanding job.* [1520–30; DEMAND + -ING[2]] —**de•mand′ing•ly,** *adv.*

demand′ loan′. See **call loan.** [1910–15]

demand′ note′, a note payable upon presentation. [1860–65]

de•mand′-pull infla′tion (di mand′po͝ol′, -mänd′-), inflation in which rising demand results in a rise in prices. Also called **buyers' inflation.** Cf. **cost-push inflation.**

de•mand-side (di mand′sīd′, -mänd′-), *adj. Econ.* of or pertaining to an economic policy that treats consumer demand as the chief determinant of the economy. Cf. **supply-side.** —**de•mand′-sid′er,** *n.*

de•man•toid (di man′toid), *n. Mineral.* a brilliant green variety of andradite garnet, used as a gem. Also called **Uralian emerald.** [1890–95; < G, equiv. to (obs.) *Demant* DIAMOND (< MHG *diemant* < OF *diamant*) + *-oid* -OID]

de•mar•cate (di mär′kāt, dē′mär kāt′), *v.t.,* **-cat•ed, -cat•ing.** **1.** to determine or mark off the boundaries or limits of: *to demarcate a piece of property.* **2.** to separate distinctly: *to demarcate the lots with fences.* [1810–20; back formation from DEMARCATION] —**de•mar′ca•tor,** *n.*

de•mar•ca•tion (dē′mär kā′shən), *n.* **1.** the determining and marking off of the boundaries of something. **2.** separation by distinct boundaries: *line of demarcation.* Also, **de′mar•ka′tion.** [1720–30; Latinization of Sp *demarcación* (in *línea de demarcación* line of demarcation, dividing the world between Spain and Portugal) deriv. of *demarcar* to mark out the bounds of, equiv. to *de-* DE- + *marcar* < It *marcare* < Gmc; see MARK[1], -ATION]

de•mar•ca•tive (di mär′kā tiv, dē′mär kā′-), *adj. Ling.* (of a phonological feature) serving to indicate the beginning or end of each successive word in an utterance, as word-initial stress in Hungarian or penultimate stress in Polish. Also, **de′mar•ca′tion•al.** [1950–55; DEMARCATE + -IVE]

dé•marche (dā märsh′), *n., pl.* **-marches** (-märsh′). *French.* **1.** an action or gesture by a diplomat, esp. a formal appeal, protest, or the like. **2.** a statement, protest, or the like presented to public officials by private citizens, interest groups, etc. **3.** a procedure or step; move; maneuver. [lit., gait]

de•mark (di märk′), *v.t.* demarcate. [1825–35; DE- + MARK[1]]

de•mar•ket•ing (dē mär′ki ting), *n.* advertising that urges the public to limit the consumption of a product, as at a time of shortage. [1970–75; DE- + MARKETING]

de•mas•si•fy (dē mas′ə fī′), *v.t.,* **-fied, -fy•ing.** **1.** to cause (society or a social system) to become less uniform or centralized; diversify or decentralize: *to demassify the federal government.* **2.** to break (something standardized or homogeneous) into elements that appeal to individual tastes or special interests: *to demassify the magazine industry into special-interest periodicals.* Also, **de•mas′si•fy′.** [DE- + MASS + -IFY] —**de•mas′si•fi•ca′tion,** *n.* —**de•mas′si•fi′er,** *n.*

de•ma•te•ri•al•ize (dē′mə tēr′ē ə līz′), *v.t., v.i.,* **-ized, -iz•ing.** to deprive of or lose material character. Also, *esp. Brit.,* **de′ma•te′ri•al•ise′.** [1880–85; DE- + MATERIALIZE] —**de′ma•te′ri•al•i•za′tion,** *n.*

Dem•a•vend (dem′ə vend′), *n.* a mountain in N Iran, in the Elburz Mountains. 18,606 ft. (5670 m).

deme (dēm), *n.* **1.** one of the administrative divisions of ancient Attica and of modern Greece. **2.** *Biol.* a local population of organisms of the same kind, esp. one in which the genetic mix is similar throughout the group. [1620–30; < Gk *dêmos* a district, the people, commons] —**dem•ic** (dem′ik, dē′mik), *adj.*

de•mean[1] (di mēn′), *v.t.* to lower in dignity, honor, or standing; debase: *He demeaned himself by accepting the bribe.* [1595–1605; DE- + MEAN[2], modeled on *debase*]
—**Syn.** degrade, humble, humiliate, mortify. —**Ant.** dignify, honor.

de•mean[2] (di mēn′), *v.t.* **1.** to conduct or behave (oneself) in a specified manner. —*n.* **2.** *Archaic.* demeanor. [1250–1300; ME *deme(i)nen* < AF, OF *demener,* equiv. to *de-* DE- + *mener* to lead, conduct < L *mināre* to drive, *minārī* to threaten]

de•mean•ing (di mē′ning), *adj.* that demeans; debasing; degrading: *Being forced to apologize when I had done nothing wrong was a demeaning task.* [1875–80; DEMEAN[1] + -ING[2]]

de•mean•or (di mē′nər), *n.* **1.** conduct; behavior; deportment. **2.** facial appearance; mien. Also, *esp. Brit.,* **de•mean′our.** [1425–75; late ME *demenure.* See DEMEAN[2], -OR[1]]
—**Syn.** manner, comportment, bearing.

dem•e•clo•cy•cline (dem′ə klō sī′klēn), *n. Pharm.* a broad-spectrum antibiotic, $C_{21}H_{21}ClN_2O_8$, derived from a mutant strain of the bacterium *Streptomyces aureofaciens:* used against a wide range of susceptible microorganisms. [contr. and rearrangement of *7-chloro-6-demethyltetracycline,* an alternate name]

de•ment (di ment′), *v.t. Obs.* to make mad or insane. [1535–45; < LL *dēmentāre* to deprive of mind, equiv. to L *dēment-* (s. of *dēmēns*) out of one's mind (*dē-* DE- + *ment-* (s. of *mēns*) mind) + *-āre* inf. suffix]

de•ment•ed (di men′tid), *adj.* **1.** crazy; insane; mad. **2.** affected with dementia. [1635–45; DEMENT + -ED[2]] —**de•ment′ed•ly,** *adv.* —**de•ment′ed•ness,** *n.*
—**Syn. 1.** lunatic, crazed, deranged, unbalanced.

dé•men•ti (dā män tē′; *Fr.* dā mäN tē′), *n., pl.* **-tis** (-tēz′; *Fr.* -tē′). an official denial by a government of actions, aims, etc., ascribed to it. [1585–95; < F: lit., contradiction, ptp. of *démentir* to deny, OF *desmentir,* equiv. to *des-* DIS-[1] + *mentir* to lie < L *mentīrī*]

de•men•tia (di men′shə, -shē ə), *n. Psychiatry.* severe impairment or loss of intellectual capacity and personality integration, due to the loss of or damage to neurons in the brain. [1800–10; < L *dēmentia* madness, equiv. to *dēment-* out of one's mind (see DEMENT) + *-ia* n. suffix] —**de•men′tial,** *adj.*

demen′tia prae′cox (prē′koks), *Psychiatry.* schizophrenia. [1895–1900; < NL: precocious dementia]

de•ment•o (di men′tō), *n., pl.* **-ment•os.** *Slang.* a deranged, mentally disturbed, or fanatic person; lunatic; nut. [DEMENT(ED) + -O]

dem•e•ra•ra (dem′ə rär′ə, -râr′ə), *n.* (*often cap.*) a light brown raw sugar grown in Guyana and used esp. in the country's rum-making industry. [after the DEMERARA River] —**dem′e•ra′ran,** *adj.*

Dem•e•ra•ra (dem′ə rär′ə, -râr′ə), *n.* a river in E Guyana flowing S to N and emptying into the Atlantic Ocean at Georgetown. 215 mi. (346 km) long.

de•mer•it (di mer′it), *n.* **1.** a mark against a person for misconduct or deficiency: *If you receive four demerits during a term, you will be expelled from school.* **2.** the quality of being censurable or punishable; fault; culpability. **3.** *Obs.* merit or desert. [1350–1400; ME (< OF *demerite*) < ML *dēmeritum* fault, n. use of neut. ptp. of L *dēmerēre* to earn, win the favor of (*dē-* taken in ML as privative, hence pejorative). See DE-, MERIT] —**de•mer•i•to•ri•ous** (di mer′i tôr′ē əs, -tōr′-), *adj.* —**de•mer′i•to′ri•ous•ly,** *adv.*

Dem•e•rol (dem′ə rôl′, -rol′), *Pharm., Trademark.* a brand of meperidine.

de•mesne (di mān′, -mēn′), *n.* **1.** possession of land as one's own: *land held in demesne.* **2.** an estate or part of an estate occupied and controlled by, and worked for the exclusive use of, the owner. **3.** land belonging to and adjoining a manor house; estate. **4.** the dominion or territory of a sovereign or state; domain. **5.** a district; region. [1250–1300; ME *demeine* < AF *demesne,* OF *demein;* see DOMAIN] —**de•mesn′i•al,** *adj.*

De•me•ter (di mē′tər), *n.* the ancient Greek chthonian goddess of agriculture and the protector of marriage and the social order, identified by the Romans with Ceres. She presided over the Eleusinian mysteries.

De•me•tri•as (di mē′trē əs), *n.* an ancient city in NE Greece, in Thessaly.

De•me•tri•us I (di mē′trē əs) (*Poliorcetes*) 337?–283 B.C., king of Macedonia 294–286 (son of Antigonus I).

demi-, a combining form appearing in loanwords from French meaning "half" (*demilune*), "lesser" (*demitasse*), or sometimes used with a pejorative sense (*demimonde*); on this model, also prefixed to words of English origin (*demigod*). [< F, comb. form repr. *demi* (adj.; also n. and adv.) < VL **dimedius,* for L *dimidius* half, equiv. to *di-* DI-[2] + *medius* middle]

dem•i•bas•tion (dem′ē bas′chən), *n. Fort.* a work consisting of half a bastion, and hence having one face and one flank. [1685–95; DEMI- + BASTION] —**dem′i•bas′tioned,** *adj.*

dem•i•can•non (dem′ē kan′ən), *n.* a large cannon of the 16th century, having a bore of about 6½ in. (17 cm) and firing a shot of from 30 to 36 lb. (14 to 16 kg). [1550–60; < MF; see DEMI-, CANNON]

dem•i•can•ton (dem′ē kan′tən, -ton, -kan ton′), *n.* either of the two political divisions in Switzerland into which the cantons of Basel, Appenzell, and Unterwalden are each divided. [< F *demi-canton.* See DEMI-, CANTON]

dem•i•cul•ver•in (dem′ē kul′vər in), *n.* a culverin having a bore of about 4½ in. (11 cm) and firing a shot of about 10 lb. (5 kg). Also, **dem′i•cul′ver•in.** [1580–90; < F *demi-coulevrine.* See DEMI-, CULVERIN]

dem•i-dé•tour•né (dem′ē dā′to͝or nā′; *Fr.* də mē dā-to͞or nā′), *n., pl.* **-nés** (-nāz′; *Fr.* -nā′). *Ballet.* a turn in which the dancer on pointe or demi-pointe completes a half turn toward the back foot and lowers the heels, with the back foot finishing in front. [< F, equiv. to *demi-* DEMI- + *détourné,* ptp. of *détourner* to turn away; see DE-, TURN]

dem•i•god (dem′ē god′), *n.* **1.** a mythological being who is partly divine and partly human; an inferior deity. **2.** a deified mortal. [1520–30; trans. of L *sēmideus.* See DEMI-, GOD]

dem•i•god•dess (dem′ē god′is), *n.* **1.** a female mythological being who is partly divine and partly human. **2.** a deified woman. [1595–1605; DEMI- + GODDESS]

dem•i•hunt•er (dem′ē hun′tər), *n.* a watch having a hinged case with a hole in the lid permitting the time to be seen even when the lid is closed. [1880–85]

dem•i•john (dem′i jon′), *n.* a large bottle having a short, narrow neck, and usually being encased in wickerwork. [1760–70; by folk etym. < F *dame-jeanne,* appar. special use of proper name]

de•mil•i•ta•rize (dē mil′i tə rīz′), *v.t.,* **-rized, -riz•ing.** **1.** to deprive of military character; free from militarism. **2.** to place under civil instead of military control. **3.** to forbid military use of (a border zone). Also, *esp. Brit.,* **de•mil′i•ta•rise′.** [1880–85; DE- + MILITARIZE] —**de•mil′i•ta•ri•za′tion,** *n.*

demil′itarized zone′, 1. an area in which it is forbidden to station military forces or maintain military installations. **2.** *Informal.* any area, place, or circumstance in which conflicts or hostilities are held in abeyance. *Abbr.:* DMZ [1930–35]

de Mille (də mil′), **Agnes (George),** 1908–93, U.S. choreographer and dancer.

De Mille (də mil′), **Cecil B(lount)** (blunt), 1881–1959, U.S. motion-picture producer and director (uncle of Agnes de Mille).

dem•i•lune (dem′i lo͞on′), *n.* **1.** a crescent. **2.** *Fort.* an outwork resembling a bastion with a crescent-shaped gorge. **3.** a crescent or half-moon shape, as of the top of a piece of furniture. —*adj.* **4.** shaped like a crescent. [1720–30; < F: half moon. See DEMI-, LUNE[1]]

dem•i•met•o•pe (dem′ē met′ə pē′, -met′ōp), *n.* the space between the end of a Doric frieze and the first triglyph. [DEMI- + METOPE]

dem•i•mon•daine (dem′ē mon dān′; *Fr.* də mē môN-den′), *n., pl.* **-daines** (-dānz′; *Fr.* -den′), *adj.* —*n.* **1.** a woman of the demimonde. —*adj.* **2.** of or pertaining to the demimonde. [1890–95; < F, equiv. to *demimonde* DEMIMONDE + *-aine* fem. adj. suffix < L *-āna* -AN]

dem•i•monde (dem′ē mond′; *Fr.* də mē môNd′), *n.* **1.** (esp. during the last half of the 19th century) a class of women who have lost their standing in respectable society because of indiscreet behavior or sexual promiscuity. **2.** a demimondaine. **3.** prostitutes or courtesans in general. **4.** a group whose activities are ethically or legally questionable: *a demimonde of investigative journalists writing for the sensationalist tabloids.* **5.** a group characterized by lack of success or status: *the literary demimonde.* [1850–55; < F, equiv. to *demi-* DEMI- + *monde* world (< L *mundus*)]

de•min•er•al•ize (dē min′ər ə līz′), *v.,* **-ized, -iz•ing.** —*v.t.* **1.** to remove minerals from; deprive of mineral

CONCISE PRONUNCIATION KEY: act, cāpe, dâre, pärt; set, ēqual; *if,* īce; ox, ōver, ôrder, oil, bo͝ok, bo͞ot, out; up, ûrge; child; sing; shoe; thin, *th*at; zh as in *treasure.* ə = *a* as in *alone, e* as in *system, i* as in *easily, o* as in *gallop, u* as in *circus;* ᵊ as in *fire* (fīᵊr), *hour* (ouᵊr). l and n can serve as syllabic consonants, as in *cradle* (krād′l), and *button* (but′n). See the full key inside the front cover.

content. —*v.i.* **2.** to lose mineral content; become demineralized. Also, *esp. Brit.,* **de·min′er·al·ise′.** [1930–35; DE- + MINERALIZE] —**de·min′er·al·i·za′tion,** *n.*

de·min·er·al·iz·er (dē min′ər ə lī′zər), *n.* an instrument, apparatus, or chemical used to remove minerals from water. [1955–60; DE- + MINERALIZE + -ER[1]]

de·mi-pen·sion (də mē pän syôN′), *n. French.* **1.** an arrangement whereby a guest or resident pays, usually at a fixed rate, for room, breakfast, and one other daily meal offered in a hotel or boardinghouse; half board. Cf. **modified American plan. 2.** an arrangement whereby a student takes the midday meal offered at a school.

dem·i·pique (dem′i pēk′), *n.* an 18th-century military saddle with a low pommel. [1685–95; DEMI- + *pique* (pseudo-F sp. of PEAK[1])]

dem·i-pli·é (dem′ē plē ā′; *Fr.* də mē plē ā′), *n., pl.* **-pli·és** (-plē āz′; *Fr.* -plē ā′). *Ballet.* a movement done in any of the five positions, in which the dancer bends the knees halfway, keeping the heels securely on the ground. [< F: lit., half-plié; see DEMI-, PLIÉ]

dem·i-pointe (dem′ē point′; *Fr.* də mē pwaNt′), *n., pl.* **-pointes** (-points′; *Fr.* -pwaNt′). *Ballet.* a position on the balls of the feet. [< F *demi-pointe (des pieds)* lit., half-tiptoe; see DEMI-, POINTE]

dem·i·qua·ver (dem′ē kwā′vər), *n. Music.* a sixteenth note; semiquaver. [1650–60; DEMI- + QUAVER]

dem·i·re·lief (dem′ē ri lēf′), *n.* mezzo-relievo. [1870–75; DEMI- + RELIEF[2]]

dem·i·rep (dem′ē rep′), *n.* a demimondaine. [1740–50; short for *demi-reputation*]

de·mise (di mīz′), *n., v.,* **-mised, -mis·ing.** —*n.* **1.** death or decease. **2.** termination of existence or operation: *the demise of the empire.* **3.** *Law.* **a.** a death or decease occasioning the transfer of an estate. **b.** a conveyance or transfer of an estate. **4.** *Govt.* transfer of sovereignty, as by the death or deposition of the sovereign. —*v.t.* **5.** *Law.* to transfer (an estate or the like) for a limited time; lease. **6.** *Govt.* to transfer (sovereignty), as by the death or abdication of the sovereign. —*v.i.* **7.** *Law.* to pass by bequest, inheritance, or succession. [1400–50; late ME *dimis(s)e, demise* < OF *demis* (ptp. of *desmetre*) < L *dimissum* (ptp. of *dimittere*); see DEMIT[1], DISMISS] —**de·mis′a·bil′i·ty,** *n.* —**de·mis′a·ble,** *adj.*

dem·i-sec (dem′ē sek′), *adj.* (of wines) semidry; sweeter than sec but drier than doux. [1930–35; < F; see DEMI-, SEC[1]]

dem·i·sem·i·qua·ver (dem′ē sem′ē kwā′vər), *n. Music, Chiefly Brit.* a thirty-second note. See illus. under **note.** [1700–10; DEMI- + SEMIQUAVER]

de·mis·sion (di mish′ən), *n.* **1.** abdication. **2.** dismissal. [1400–50; late ME < AF < L *dimissiōn-* (s. of *dimissiō*), equiv. to *dimiss(us)* (see DISMISS) + *-iōn* -ION]

de·mist·er (dē mis′tər), *n.* **1.** *Chiefly Brit.* defroster (def. 2). **2.** a type of defroster for the side window of an automobile. [1935–40; DE- + MIST + -ER[1]]

de·mit[1] (di mit′), *v.,* **-mit·ted, -mit·ting,** *n.* —*v.t.* **1.** to resign (a job, public office, etc.); relinquish. **2.** *Archaic.* to dismiss; fire. —*v.i.* **3.** to resign. —*n.* **4.** Also, **dimit.** (esp. in Freemasonry) a written certification of honorable withdrawal or resignation, as from membership. [1520–30; < MF *demettre,* OF *demetre* < L *dēmittere* to DEMIT[2] (but also with some senses of L *dimittere* send away, dismiss, equiv. to *di-* DI-[2] + *mittere* to send)]

de·mit[2] (di mit′), *v.t.,* **-mit·ted, -mit·ting. 1.** to put in or send to a lower place. **2.** *Obs.* to lower in status, rank, or esteem; humble. [1550–60; < L *dēmittere* to let fall, send down, equiv. to *dē-* DE- + *mittere* to send]

dem·i·tasse (dem′i tas′, -täs′), *n.* **1.** a small cup for serving strong black coffee after dinner. **2.** the coffee contained in such a cup. [1835–45; < F: lit., half-cup]

dem·i·urge (dem′ē ûrj′), *n.* **1.** *Philos.* **a.** *Platonism.* the artificer of the world. **b.** (in the Gnostic and certain other systems) a supernatural being imagined as creating or fashioning the world in subordination to the Supreme Being, and sometimes regarded as the originator of evil. **2.** (in many states of ancient Greece) a public official or magistrate. [1590–1600; < Gk *dēmiourgós* a worker for the people, skilled worker, equiv. to *dēmio(s)* of the people (deriv. of *dêmos* the people) + *-ergos* a worker, deriv. of *érgon* work, with *oe* > *ou*] —**dem·i·ur·geous** (dem′ē ûr′jəs), **dem′i·ur′gic, dem′i·ur′gi·cal,** *adj.* —**dem′i·ur′gi·cal·ly,** *adv.*

de·mi-vierge (dem′ē vē ârzh′; *Fr.* də mē vyerzh′), *n., pl.* **-vierges** (-vē âr′zhiz; *Fr.* -vyerzh′). a girl or woman who behaves in a sexually provocative and permissive way without yielding her virginity. Also called **dem·i-vir·gin** (dem′ē vûr′jin, dem′ē vûr′-). [< F: lit., half-virgin; after *Les demi-vierges* (1894), a novel by French writer Marcel Prévost (1862–1940)]

dem·i·volt (dem′ē vōlt′), *n.* a half turn made by a horse with forelegs raised. Also, **dem′i·volte′.** [< F *demi-volte.* See DEMI-, VOLT[1]]

dem·i·world (dem′ē wûrld′), *n.* demimonde (defs. 4, 5). [1860–65; partial trans. of DEMIMONDE; see DEMI-, WORLD]

dem·o (dem′ō), *n., pl.* **dem·os.** *Informal.* **1.** demonstration (defs. 4,6). **2.** demonstrator (def. 5). **3.** a phonograph record or tape recording of a new song or of one performed by an unknown singer or singing group, distributed to disc jockeys, recording companies, etc., to demonstrate the merits of the song or performer. [1935–40; by shortening; see -O]

Dem·o (dem′ō), *n., pl.* **Dem·os.** *Informal.* a member of the Democratic party; Democrat. [1785–95, *Amer.*]

CONCISE ETYMOLOGY KEY: <, descended or borrowed from; >, whence; b., blend of, blended; c., cognate with; cf., compare; deriv., derivative; equiv., equivalent; imit., imitative; obl., oblique; r., replacing; s., stem; sp., spelling, spelled; resp., respelling, respelled; trans., translation; ?, origin unknown; *, unattested; ‡, probably earlier than. See the full key inside the front cover.

demo-, a combining form occurring in loanwords from Greek, where it meant "people" (*democratic*); on this model, used in the formation of compound words (*demography*). [< Gk *dēmo-,* comb. form of *dêmos*]

de·mob (dē mob′), *n., v.,* **-mobbed, -mob·bing.** *Chiefly Brit. Informal.* —*n.* **1.** demobilization. **2.** a person who has been demobilized. —*v.t.* **3.** to discharge (a person) from the armed forces; demobilize. [1915–20; orig. short for DEMOBILIZE]

de·mo·bi·lize (dē mō′bə līz′), *v.t.,* **-lized, -liz·ing. 1.** to disband (troops, an army, etc.). **2.** to discharge (a person) from military service. Also, *esp. Brit.,* **de·mo′bi·lise′.** [1865–70; DE- + MOBILIZE] —**de·mo′bi·li·za′tion,** *n.*

de·moc·ra·cy (di mok′rə sē), *n., pl.* **-cies. 1.** government by the people; a form of government in which the supreme power is vested in the people and exercised directly by them or by their elected agents under a free electoral system. **2.** a state having such a form of government: *The United States and Canada are democracies.* **3.** a state of society characterized by formal equality of rights and privileges. **4.** political or social equality; democratic spirit. **5.** the common people of a community as distinguished from any privileged class; the common people with respect to their political power. [1525–35; < MF *démocratie* < LL *dēmocratia* < Gk *dēmokratía* popular government, equiv. to *dēmo-* DEMO- + *-kratia* -CRACY]

Democ′racy in Amer′ica, (French, *Démocracie en Amérique*), a study (1835) by Alexis de Tocqueville of American political institutions.

dem·o·crat (dem′ə krat′), *n.* **1.** an advocate of democracy. **2.** a person who believes in the political or social equality of all people. **3.** (*cap.*) *Politics.* **a.** a member of the Democratic party. **b.** a member of the Democratic-Republican party. **4.** Also called **dem′ocrat wag′on.** a high, lightweight, horse-drawn wagon, usually having two seats. [1780–90; < F *démocrate,* back formation from *démocratie* DEMOCRACY. See DEMO-, -CRAT]

dem·o·crat·ic (dem′ə krat′ik), *adj.* **1.** pertaining to or of the nature of democracy or a democracy. **2.** pertaining to or characterized by the principle of political or social equality for all: *democratic treatment.* **3.** advocating or upholding democracy. **4.** (*cap.*) *Politics.* **a.** of, pertaining to, or characteristic of the Democratic party. **b.** of, pertaining to, or belonging to the Democratic-Republican party. Also, **dem′o·crat′i·cal.** [1595–1605; < F *démocratique* or ML *democraticus,* both < Gk *dēmokratikós,* equiv. to *dēmokrat(ía)* (see DEMOCRACY) + *-ikos* -IC] —**dem′o·crat′i·cal·ly,** *adv.*

Dem′ocrat′ic par′ty, one of the two major political parties in the U.S., founded in 1828.

Democrat′ic-Repub′lican par′ty, *U.S. Hist.* a political party opposed to the Federalist party.

de·moc·ra·tize (di mok′rə tīz′), *v.t., v.i.,* **-tized, -tiz·ing.** to make or become democratic. Also, *esp. Brit.,* **de·moc′ra·tise′.** [1790–1800; < F *démocratiser,* equiv. to *démocrate* DEMOCRAT + *-iser* -IZE] —**de·moc′ra·ti·za′tion,** *n.* —**de·moc′ra·tiz′er,** *n.*

De·moc·ri·tus (di mok′ri təs), *n.* (*"the Laughing Philosopher"*) c460–370 B.C., Greek philosopher.

Democ′ritus Jun′ior, pen name of Robert Burton.

dé·mo·dé (dā mô dā′), *adj. French.* no longer in fashion; out of date; outmoded.

de·mod·ed (dē mō′did), *adj.* out of date; outmoded. [1885–90; partial trans. of F *démodé*]

de·mod·u·late (dē moj′ə lāt′), *v.t.,* **-lat·ed, -lat·ing.** *Telecommunications.* to extract the original information-bearing signal from a modulated carrier wave or signal; detect. —**de·mod′u·la′tor,** *n.* [1920–25; DE- + MODULATE]

de·mod·u·la·tion (dē moj′ə lā′shən), *n. Telecommunications.* detection (def. 4b). [1920–25; DE- + MODULATION]

De·mo·gor·gon (dē′mə gôr′gən, dem′ə-), *n.* a vague, mysterious, infernal power or divinity mistakenly thought to belong to ancient mythology. [1580–90; < LL *Dēmogorgōn,* of uncert. orig.]

dem·o·graph·ic (dem′ə graf′ik, dē′mə-), *adj.* of or pertaining to demography. Also, **dem′o·graph′i·cal.** [1880–85; DEMO- + -GRAPHIC] —**dem′o·graph′i·cal·ly,** *adv.*

dem·o·graph·ics (dem′ə graf′iks, dē′mə-), *n.* (*used with a plural v.*) the statistical data of a population, esp. those showing average age, income, education, etc. [1965–70; see DEMOGRAPHIC, -ICS]

de·mog·ra·phy (di mog′rə fē), *n.* the science of vital and social statistics, as of the births, deaths, diseases, marriages, etc., of populations. [1875–80; DEMO- + -GRAPHY] —**de·mog′ra·pher, de·mog′ra·phist,** *n.*

dem·oi·selle (dem′wə zel′, dem′ə-; *Fr.* də mwa zel′), *n., pl.* **-selles** (-zelz′; *Fr.* -zel′). **1.** an unmarried girl or young woman. **2.** See **demoiselle crane. 3.** a damselfly, esp. of the genus *Agrion.* **4.** damselfish. **5.** *Furniture.* a lady's wig stand of the 18th century, in the form of a pedestal table. [1760–70; < F; see DAMSEL]

demoiselle′ crane′, a gray crane, *Anthropoides virgo,* of northern Africa, Europe, and Asia, having long, white plumes behind each eye. [1680–90]

de Moi·vre (də mwäv′, mwä′vrə, moi′vər; *Fr.* de mwä′vr′), **A·bra·ham** (A BRA AM′), 1667–1754, French mathematician in England.

de Moi′vre's the′orem, *Math.* the theorem that a complex number raised to a given positive integral power is equal to the modulus of the number raised to the power and multiplied by the amplitude times the given power. [named after A. DE MOIVRE]

de·mol·ish (di mol′ish), *v.t.* **1.** to destroy or ruin (a building or other structure), esp. on purpose; tear down; raze. **2.** to put an end to; destroy; explode: *The results of his research demolished many theories.* **3.** to lay waste to; ruin utterly: *The fire demolished the area.* **4.** *Informal.* to devour completely: *We simply demolished that turkey.* [1560–70; < MF *démoliss-,* s. of *démolir* < L *dēmōlīrī* to destroy, equiv. to *dē-* DE- + *mōlīrī* to set in motion, struggle (*mōl(ēs)* mass, bulk + *-īrī* inf. suffix)] —**de·mol′ish·er,** *n.* —**de·mol′ish·ment,** *n.*
—**Syn. 1.** level, wreck, bulldoze. See **destroy.**

dem·o·li·tion (dem′ə lish′ən, dē′mə-), *n.* **1.** an act or instance of demolishing. **2.** the state of being demolished; destruction. **3.** destruction or demolishment by explosives. **4. demolitions,** explosives, esp. as used in war. —*adj.* **5.** of, pertaining to, or working with explosives: *A demolition squad attempted to blow up the bridge before the enemy captured it.* **6.** of or pertaining to tearing down or demolishing: *Demolition work had begun on the old building.* [1540–50; < L *dēmōlītiōn-* (s. of *dēmōlītiō*), equiv. to *dēmōlīt(us)* (ptp. of *dēmōlīrī;* see DEMOLISH) + *-iōn-* -ION] —**dem′o·li′tion·ist,** *n.*

demoli′tion bomb′, a bomb containing a relatively large charge, used esp. to destroy structures.

dem′oli′tion der′by, 1. a contest in which drivers deliberately and repeatedly crash old cars into each other, on a racetrack or in an enclosed area, with the winner being the last vehicle still moving after all others have been disabled. **2.** *Informal.* any event or circumstance having the chaotically destructive character of such a competition. [1950–55]

de·mon (dē′mən), *n.* **1.** an evil spirit; devil or fiend. **2.** an evil passion or influence. **3.** a person considered extremely wicked, evil, or cruel. **4.** a person with great energy, drive, etc.: *He's a demon for work.* **5.** a person, esp. a child, who is very mischievous: *His younger son is a real little demon.* **6.** daemon. **7.** *Australian Slang.* a policeman, esp. a detective. —*adj.* **8.** of, pertaining to, characteristic of, or noting a demon. **9.** possessed or controlled by a demon. [1350–1400; ME < L *daemonium* < Gk *daimónion,* thing of divine nature (in Jewish and Christian writers, evil spirit), neut. of *daimónios,* deriv. of *daímōn;* (def. 6) < L; see DAEMON]

demon-, var. of **demono-** before a vowel: *demonism.*

de·mon·e·tize (dē mon′i tīz′, -mun′-), *v.t.,* **-tized, -tiz·ing. 1.** to divest (a monetary standard or the like) of value. **2.** to withdraw (money or the like) from use. **3.** to deprive (an issue of postage stamps) of validity by legal methods and without marking the stamps themselves. Also, *esp. Brit.,* **de·mon′e·tise′.** [1850–55; < F *démonétiser.* See DE-, MONETIZE] —**de·mon′e·ti·za′tion,** *n.*

de·mo·ni·ac (di mō′nē ak′, dē′mə nī′ak), *adj.* Also, **de·mo·ni·a·cal** (dē′mə nī′ə kəl). **1.** of, pertaining to, or like a demon; demonic: *demoniac laughter.* **2.** possessed by or as by an evil spirit; raging; frantic. —*n.* **3.** a person seemingly possessed by a demon or evil spirit. [1350–1400; ME < LL *daemoniacus* < Gk *daimoniakós,* equiv. to *daimóni(os)* pertaining to a DAEMON + *-akos* -AC] —**de·mo·ni·a·cal·ly** (dē′mə nī′ik lē), *adv.*
—**Ant. 1.** angelic.

de·mo·ni·an (di mō′nē ən), *adj.* demoniac (def. 1). Also, **daemonian.** [DEMON + -IAN]

de·mon·ic (di mon′ik), *adj.* **1.** inspired as if by a demon, indwelling spirit, or genius. **2.** demoniac (def. 1). Also, **daemonic, de·mon′i·cal.** [1655–65; < LL *daemonicus* < Gk *daimonikós,* equiv. to *daimon-* DEMON- + *-ikos* -IC] —**de·mon′i·cal·ly,** *adv.*
—**Syn. 1.** frantic, frenzied, obsessed, possessed.

de·mon·ism (dē′mə niz′əm), *n.* **1.** belief in demons. **2.** the study of demons; demonology. [1690–1700; DEMON- + -ISM] —**de′mon·ist,** *n.*

de·mon·ize (dē′mə nīz′), *v.t.,* **-ized, -iz·ing. 1.** to turn into a demon or make demonlike. **2.** to subject to the influence of demons. Also, *esp. Brit.,* **de′mon·ise′.** [1815–25; < ML *daemonizāre,* equiv. to LL *daemon* DEMON + *-izāre* -IZE] —**de′mon·i·za′tion,** *n.*

demono-, a combining form representing **demon** in compound words: *demonology.* Also, *esp. before a vowel,* **demon-.**

de·mon·og·ra·phy (dē′mə nog′rə fē), *n., pl.* **-phies.** a treatise on demons. [1885–90; DEMONO- + -GRAPHY] —**de′mon·og′ra·pher,** *n.*

de·mon·ol·a·ter (dē′mə nol′ə tər), *n.* a person who worships demons. [1875–80; back formation from DEMONOLATRY]

de·mon·ol·a·try (dē′mə nol′ə trē), *n.* the worship of demons. [1660–70; DEMONO- + -LATRY] —**de′mon·ol′a·trous,** *adj.* —**de′mon·ol′a·trous·ly,** *adv.*

de·mon·ol·o·gy (dē′mə nol′ə jē), *n.* **1.** the study of demons or of beliefs about demons. **2.** belief in demons. **3.** a group of persons or things regarded as evil or pernicious. Also, **daemonology.** [1590–1600; DEMONO- + -LOGY] —**de·mon·o·log·ic** (dē′mə nl oj′ik), **de′mon·o·log′i·cal,** *adj.* —**de′mon·o·log′i·cal·ly,** *adv.* —**de′mon·ol′o·gist,** *n.*

De′mon Star′, *Astron.* Algol. [1890–95; trans. of Ar *ghūl* GHOUL]

de·mon·stra·ble (di mon′strə bəl, dem′ən-), *adj.* **1.** capable of being demonstrated or proved. **2.** clearly evident; obvious: *a demonstrable lack of concern for the general welfare.* [1350–1400; ME < OF < LL *dēmonstrābilis,* equiv. to L *dēmonstrā(re)* (see DEMONSTRATE) + *-bilis* -BLE] —**de·mon′stra·bil′i·ty, de·mon′stra·ble·ness,** *n.* —**de·mon′stra·bly,** *adv.*

de·mon·strant (də mon′strənt), *n.* demonstrator (def. 2). [1865–70; < L *dēmonstrant-* (s. of *dēmonstrāns*), prp. of *dēmonstrāre* to show. See DEMONSTRATE, -ANT]

dem·on·strate (dem′ən strāt′), *v.,* **-strat·ed, -strat·ing.** —*v.t.* **1.** to make evident or establish by arguments or reasoning; prove: *to demonstrate a philosophical principle.* **2.** to describe, explain, or illustrate by examples, specimens, experiments, or the like: *to demonstrate the force of gravity by dropping an object.* **3.** to manifest or exhibit; show: *He demonstrated his courage by his actions in battle.* **4.** to display openly or publicly, as feelings: *to demonstrate one's anger by slamming a door.* **5.** to exhibit the operation or use of (a device, process, product, or the like), usually to a purchaser or prospect: *to demonstrate an automobile.* —*v.i.* **6.** to make, give,

or take part in, a demonstration: *The pickets required a license to demonstrate.* **7.** *Mil.* to attack or make a show of force to deceive an enemy. [1545–55; < L *dēmonstrātus,* ptp. of *dēmonstrāre* to show, point out, equiv. to *dē-* DE- + *monstrāre* to show, v. deriv. of *monstrum* sign, portent] —**dem′on·strat′ed·ly,** *adv.*
—**Syn. 1.** show, confirm, verify, corroborate.

dem·on·stra·tion (dem′ən strā′shən), *n.* **1.** the act or circumstance of proving or being proved conclusively, as by reasoning or a show of evidence: *a belief incapable of demonstration.* **2.** something serving as proof or supporting evidence: *They sent a check as a demonstration of their concern.* **3.** a description or explanation, as of a process, illustrated by examples, specimens, or the like: *a demonstration of methods of refining ore.* **4.** the act of exhibiting the operation or use of a device, machine, process, product, or the like, as to a prospective buyer. **5.** an exhibition, as of feeling; display; manifestation: *His demonstration of affection was embarrassing.* **6.** a public exhibition of the attitude of a group of persons toward a controversial issue, or other matter, made by picketing, parading, etc. **7.** a show of military force or of offensive operations made to deceive an enemy. **8.** *Math.* a logical presentation of the way in which given assumptions imply a certain result; proof. [1325–75; ME *demonstracioun* < L *dēmonstrātiōn-* (s. of *dēmonstrātiō,* equiv. to *dēmonstrāt(us)* (see DEMONSTRATE) + *-iōn-* -ION] —**dem′on·stra′tion·al,** *adj.* —**dem′on·stra′·tion·ist,** *n.*

de·mon·stra·tive (də mon′strə tiv), *adj.* **1.** characterized by or given to open exhibition or expression of one's emotions, attitudes, etc., esp. of love or affection: *She wished her fiancé were more demonstrative.* **2.** serving to demonstrate; explanatory or illustrative. **3.** serving to prove the truth of anything; indubitably conclusive. **4.** *Gram.* indicating or singling out the thing referred to. *This* is a demonstrative pronoun. —*n.* **5.** *Gram.* a demonstrative word, as *this* or *there.* [1350–1400; ME *demonstratif* (< MF) < L *dēmonstrātīvus,* equiv. to *dēmonstrāt(us)* (see DEMONSTRATE) + *-īvus* -IVE] —**de·mon′stra·tive·ly,** *adv.* —**de·mon′stra·tive·ness,** *n.*

dem·on·stra·tor (dem′ən strā′tər), *n.* **1.** a person or thing that demonstrates. **2.** Also, **demonstrant.** a person who takes part in a public demonstration, as by marching or picketing. **3.** a person who explains or teaches by practical demonstrations. **4.** a person who exhibits the use and application of (a product, service, etc.) to a prospective customer. **5.** the product, device, machine, etc., actually used in demonstrations to purchasers or prospective customers: *They sold the demonstrator at half price.* [1605–15; < L *dēmonstrātor,* equiv. to *dēmonstrā(re)* (see DEMONSTRATE) + *-tor* -TOR]

de·mor·al·ize (di môr′ə līz′, -mor′-), *v.t.,* **-ized, -iz·ing. 1.** to deprive (a person or persons) of spirit, courage, discipline, etc.; destroy the morale of: *The continuous barrage demoralized the infantry.* **2.** to throw (a person) into disorder or confusion; bewilder: *We were so demoralized by that one wrong turn that we were lost for hours.* **3.** to corrupt or undermine the morals of. Also, *esp. Brit.,* **de·mor′al·ise′.** [1785–95; < F *démoraliser.* See DE-, MORAL, -IZE] —**de·mor′al·i·za′tion,** *n.* —**de·mor′al·iz′er,** *n.* —**de·mor′al·iz′ing·ly,** *adv.*

De Mor·gan (di môr′gən), **1. Augustus,** 1806–71, English mathematician and logician. **2. William Frend** (frend), 1839–1917, English novelist and ceramist.

De Mor′gan's laws′, 1. *Logic.* two laws, one stating that the denial of the conjunction of a class of propositions is equivalent to the disjunction of the denials of a proposition, and the other stating that the denial of the disjunction of a class of propositions is equivalent to the conjunction of the denials of the propositions. **2.** *Math.* **a.** the theorem of set theory that the complement of the union of two sets is equal to the intersection of the complements of the sets. **b.** the theorem of set theory that the complement of the intersection of two sets is equal to the union of the complements of the sets. [1915–20; named after A. DE MORGAN]

de·mos (dē′mos), *n.* **1.** the common people of an ancient Greek state. **2.** the common people; populace. **3.** *Sociol.* a people viewed as a political unit. [1770–80; < Gk *dêmos* district, people; cf. DEMO-]

De·mos·the·nes (di mos′thə nēz′), *n.* 384?–322 B.C., Athenian statesman and orator.

de·mote (di mōt′), *v.t.,* **-mot·ed, -mot·ing.** to reduce to a lower grade, rank, class, or position (opposed to *promote*): *They demoted the careless waiter to busboy.* [1890–95, *Amer.*; DE- + (PRO)MOTE] —**de·mo′tion,** *n.*

de·moth·ball (dē môth′bôl′, -moth′-), *v.t.* to remove (naval or military equipment) from storage or reserve, usually for active duty; reactivate. [DE- + MOTHBALL]

de·mot·ic (di mot′ik), *adj.* **1.** of or pertaining to the ordinary, everyday, current form of a language; vernacular: *a poet with a keen ear for demotic rhythms.* **2.** of or pertaining to the common people; popular. **3.** of, pertaining to, or noting the simplified form of hieratic writing used in ancient Egypt between 700 B.C. and A.D. 500. —*n.* **4.** demotic script. **5.** (*cap.*) Also called **Romaic.** the Modern Greek vernacular (distinguished from *Katharevusa*). [1815–25; < Gk *dēmotikós* popular, plebeian, equiv. to *dēmót(ēs)* a plebeian (deriv. of *dêmos;* see DEMO-) + *-ikos* -IC]

de·mount (dē mount′), *v.t.* **1.** to remove from a mounting, setting, or place of support, as a gun. **2.** to take apart; disassemble. [1930–35; DE- + MOUNT[1]] —**de·mount′a·ble,** *adj.* —**de·mount′a·bil′i·ty,** *n.*

Demp·sey (demp′sē), *n.* **Jack** (*William Harrison Dempsey*), 1895–1983, U.S. boxer: world heavyweight champion 1919–26.

demp·ster (demp′stər, dem′-), *n.* deemster.

Demp·ster (demp′stər, dem′-), *n.* **Arthur Jeffrey,** 1886–1950, U.S. physicist.

de·mul·cent (di mul′sənt), *adj.* **1.** soothing or mollifying, as a medicinal substance. —*n.* **2.** a demulcent substance or agent, often mucilaginous, as for soothing or protecting an irritated mucous membrane. [1725–35; < L *dēmulcent-* (s. of *dēmulcēns,* prp. of *dēmulcere* to stroke down, soften), equiv. to *dē-* DE- + *mulc(ere)* to soothe + *-ent-* -ENT]

de·mul·si·fy (dē mul′sə fī′), *v.t.,* **-fied, -fy·ing.** *Physical Chem.* to break down (an emulsion) into separate substances incapable of re-forming the emulsion that was broken down. [DE- + (E)MULSIFY] —**de·mul′si·fi·ca′tion,** *n.* —**de·mul′si·fi′er,** *n.*

de·mur (di mûr′), *v.,* **-murred, -mur·ring,** *n.* —*v.i.* **1.** to make objection, esp. on the grounds of scruples; take exception; object: *They wanted to make him the treasurer, but he demurred.* **2.** *Law.* to interpose a demurrer. **3.** *Archaic.* to linger; hesitate. —*n.* **4.** the act of making objection. **5.** an objection raised. **6.** hesitation. **7.** *Law. Obs.* a demurrer. [1175–1225; ME *demuren* < AF *demurer,* OF *demorer* < L *dēmorārī* to linger, equiv. to *dē-* DE- + *morārī* to delay, deriv. of *mora* delay] —**de·mur′ra·ble,** *adj.*
—**Syn. 5.** scruple, qualm, misgiving. —**Ant. 1.** agree, accede.

de·mure (di myŏŏr′), *adj.,* **-mur·er, -mur·est. 1.** characterized by shyness and modesty; reserved. **2.** affectedly or coyly decorous, sober, or sedate. [1350–1400; ME *dem(e)ur(e)* well-mannered, grave < AF *demuré,* ptp. of *demurer* to DEMUR; perh. influenced by OF *mur, mëur* grave, mature (< L *matūrus*)] —**de·mure′·ly,** *adv.* —**de·mure′ness,** *n.*
—**Syn. 1.** retiring. See **modest.** —**Ant. 1, 2.** indecorous.

de·mur·rage (di mûr′ij), *n. Com.* **1.** the detention in port of a vessel by the shipowner, as in loading or unloading, beyond the time allowed or agreed upon. **2.** the similar undue detention of a railroad car, truck, etc. **3.** a charge for such undue detention. [1635–45; DEMUR + -AGE]

de·mur·ral (di mûr′əl), *n.* an act or instance of demurring; demur. [1800–10; DEMUR + -AL[2]]

de·mur·rer[1] (di mûr′ər), *n.* a person who demurs; objector. [DEMUR + -ER[1]]

de·mur·rer[2] (di mûr′ər), *n.* **1.** *Law.* a pleading in effect that even if the facts are as alleged by the opposite party, they do not sustain the contention based on them. **2.** an objection raised; demur. [1525–35; < AF *demur(r)er.* See DEMUR, -ER[3]]
—**Syn. 2.** dissent, challenge, protest, qualm, misgiving.

De·muth (di mo͞oth′), *n.* **Charles,** 1883–1935, U.S. painter and illustrator.

de·mu·tu·al·ize (dē myo͞o′cho͞o ə līz′), *v.t.,* **-ized, -iz·ing.** to convert (a mutual life-insurance company) to a stockholder-owned corporation. Also, *esp. Brit.,* **de·mu′·tu·al·ise′.** [DE- + MUTUALIZE]

de·my (di mī′), *n., pl.* **-mies. 1.** a foundation scholar at Magdalen College, Oxford: so called because such a scholar originally received half the allowance of a fellow. **2.** (in England) a size of printing paper, 17½ × 22½ in. (44 × 57 cm). **3.** a size of drawing or writing paper, 15½ (39 cm) or 15 × 20 in. (38 × 51 cm) in England, 16 × 21 in. (41 × 53 cm) in the U.S. **4.** Also called **demy′ octa′·vo.** a size of book, about 5½ × 8¾ in. (14 × 48 cm), untrimmed. *Abbr.:* demy 8vo **5.** Also called **demy′ quar′to.** *Chiefly Brit.* a size of book, about 8¾ × 11 in. (22 × 28 cm), untrimmed. *Abbr.:* demy 4to [1400–50; late ME *demi, demy;* see DEMI-]

de·my·e·li·nate (di mī′ə lə nāt′), *v.t.,* **-nat·ed, -nat·ing.** to obliterate or remove the myelin sheath from (a nerve or nerves). [1960–65; DE- + MYELIN + -ATE[1]]

de·my·e·li·na·tion (dē′mī ə lə nā′shən), *n.* loss of myelin from the nerve sheaths, as in multiple sclerosis. [1930–35; DE- + MYELINATION]

de·mys·ti·fy (dē mis′tə fī′), *v.t.,* **-fied, -fy·ing.** to rid of mystery or obscurity; clarify: *to demystify medical procedures.* [1960–65; DE- + MYSTIFY] —**de·mys′ti·fi·ca′tion,** *n.* —**de·mys′ti·fi′er,** *n.*

de·my·thol·o·gize (dē′mi thol′ə jīz′), *v.,* **-gized, -giz·ing.** —*v.t.* **1.** to divest of mythological or legendary attributes or forms, as in order to permit clearer appraisal and understanding: *to demythologize the music dramas of Richard Wagner for modern listeners.* **2.** to make less mysterious or mythical so as to give a more human character to: *to demythologize the presidency.* —*v.i.* **3.** to separate mythological, legendary, or apocryphal elements from a writing, work of art, historical figure, etc. Also, *esp. Brit.,* **de′my·thol′o·gise′.** [1945–50; DE- + MYTHOLOGIZE] —**de′my·thol′o·gi·za′tion,** *n.* —**de′·my·thol′o·giz′er,** *n.*

den (den), *n., v.,* **denned, den·ning.** —*n.* **1.** the lair or shelter of a wild animal, esp. a predatory mammal. **2.** a room, often secluded, in a house or apartment, designed to provide a quiet, comfortable, and informal atmosphere for conversation, reading, writing, etc. **3.** a cave used as a place of shelter or concealment. **4.** a squalid or vile abode or place: *dens of misery.* **5.** one of the units of a cub scout pack, analogous to a patrol in the Boy Scouts. —*v.t.* **6.** to drive or pursue (an animal) into its den. **7.** to kill (an animal) inside its den. —*v.i.* **8.** to live in or as if in a den. [bef. 1000; ME; OE *denn;* cf. early D *denne* floor, cave, den, G *Tenne* floor]

Den., Denmark.

De·na′li Na′tional Park′ (də nä′lē), a national park in S central Alaska, including Mount McKinley. 3030 sq. mi. (7850 sq. km). Formerly, **Mount McKinley National Park.**

de·nar·i·us (di nâr′ē əs), *n., pl.* **-nar·i·i** (-nâr′ē ī′). **1.** a silver coin and monetary unit of ancient Rome, first issued in the latter part of the 3rd century B.C., that fluctuated in value and sometimes appeared as a bronze coin. **2.** a gold coin of ancient Rome equal to 25 silver denarii; aureus. [< L *dēnārius,* orig. adj.: containing ten (asses). See DENARY]

den·a·ry (den′ə rē, dē′nə-), *adj.* **1.** containing ten; tenfold. **2.** proceeding by tens; decimal. [1570–80; < L *dēnārius* containing ten, equiv. to *dēn(ī)* ten at a time (deriv. of *decem* TEN) + *-ārius* -ARY]

de·na·sal·ize (dē nā′zə līz′), *v.t.,* **-ized, -iz·ing.** *Phonet.* to diminish the nasal resonance of (speech or a speech sound). Also, *esp. Brit.,* **de·na′sal·ise′.** [DE- + NASALIZE]

de·na·tion·al·ize (dē nash′ə nl īz′), *v.t.,* **-ized, -iz·ing. 1.** to remove (an industry or the like) from government ownership or control. **2.** to deprive of national status, attachments, or characteristics. Also, *esp. Brit.,* **de·na′·tion·al·ise′.** [1800–10; DE- + NATIONALIZE] —**de·na′·tion·al·i·za′tion,** *n.*

de·nat·u·ral·ize (dē nach′ər ə līz′), *v.t.,* **-ized, -iz·ing. 1.** to deprive of proper or true nature; make unnatural. **2.** to deprive of the rights and privileges of citizenship or of naturalization. Also, *esp. Brit.* **de·nat′u·ral·ise′.** [1790–1800; DE- + NATURALIZE] —**de·nat′u·ral·i·za′·tion,** *n.*

de·na·ture (dē nā′chər), *v.t.,* **-tured, -tur·ing. 1.** to deprive (something) of its natural character, properties, etc. **2.** to render (any of various alcohols) unfit for drinking by adding an unwholesome substance that does not alter usefulness for other purposes. **3.** *Biochem.* to treat (a protein or the like) by chemical or physical means so as to alter its original state. **4.** to make (fissionable material) unsuitable for use in an atomic weapon by mixing it with unfissionable material. [1675–85; DE- + NATURE] —**de·na′tur·ant,** *n.* —**de·na′tur·a′tion,** *n.*

dena′tured al′cohol, *Chem.* alcohol, esp. ethyl alcohol, that has been denatured: used chiefly as a solvent and in chemical synthesis.

de·na·tur·ize (dē nā′chə rīz′), *v.t.,* **-ized, -iz·ing.** denature. [1895–1900; DE- + NATURE + -IZE] Also, *esp. Brit.,* **de·na′tur·ise′.** —**de·na′tur·i·za′tion,** *n.* —**de·na′tur·iz′er,** *n.*

de·na·zi·fy (dē nä′tsə fī′, -nat′sə-), *v.t.,* **-fied, -fy·ing.** to rid of Nazism or Nazi influences. [1940–45; DE- + NAZI + -FY] —**de·na′zi·fi·ca′tion,** *n.*

Den·bigh·shire (den′bē shēr′, -shər), *n.* a historic county in Clywd in N Wales. Also called **Den′bigh.**

den′ chief′, (in the Boy Scouts) a boy scout who supervises a cub scout den in cooperation with a den mother or den father.

dendr-, var. of **dendro-** before a vowel: *dendrite.*

den·dra (den′drə), *n.* a pl. of **dendron.**

dendri-, var. of **dendro-** before elements of Latin origin: *dendriform.*

den·dri·form (den′drə fôrm′), *adj.* treelike in form. [1840–50; DENDRI- + -FORM]

den·drite (den′drīt), *n.* **1.** *Petrol., Mineral.* **a.** a branching figure or marking, resembling moss or a shrub or tree in form, found on or in certain stones or minerals due to the presence of a foreign material. **b.** any arborescent crystalline growth. **2.** *Anat.* the branching process of a neuron that conducts impulses toward the cell. See diag. under **neuron.** [1720–30; < Gk *dendrítēs* pertaining to a tree, equiv. to *dendr-* DENDR- + *-ītēs* -ITE[1]]

dendrite (def. 1a)

den·drit·ic (den drit′ik), *adj.* **1.** formed or marked like a dendrite. **2.** of a branching form; arborescent. Also, **den·drit′i·cal.** [1795–1805; DENDRITE + -IC] —**den·drit′i·cal·ly,** *adv.*

dendrit′ic cell′, a branching cell of the lymph nodes, blood, and spleen that functions as a network trapping foreign protein.

dendro-, a combining form meaning "tree," used in the formation of compound words: *dendrology.* Also, **dendr-, dendri-, -dendron.** [< Gk, comb. form of *déndron*]

den·dro·bi·um (den drō′bē əm), *n.* any of numerous epiphytic orchids of the genus *Dendrobium,* native to tropical and subtropical regions of the Eastern Hemisphere, having variously colored, often showy flowers. [< NL (1799), equiv. to Gk *dendro-* DENDRO- + NL *-bium* < Gk *-bion,* neut. of *-bios* -lived, having such a life, living on (adj. deriv. of *bíos* life; see BIO-)]

den·dro·chro·nol·o·gy (den′drō krə nol′ə jē), *n.* the science dealing with the study of the annual rings of trees in determining the dates and chronological order of past events. [1925–30; DENDRO- + CHRONOLOGY] —**den·dro·chron·o·log·i·cal** (den′drō kron′l oj′i kəl), *adj.* —**den′dro·chron′o·log′i·cal·ly,** *adv.* —**den′dro·chro·nol′o·gist,** *n.*

den·dro·gram (den′drə gram′), *n. Biol.* a treelike diagram depicting evolutionary changes from ancestral to descendant forms, based on shared characteristics. Cf. **cladogram, phenogram.** [DENDRO- + -GRAM[1]]

den·droid (den′droid), *adj.* treelike; branching like a tree; arborescent. Also, **den·droi′dal.** [1840–50; < Gk *dendroeidḗs* treelike, equiv. to *dendr-* DENDR- + *-oeidēs* -OID]

den·drol·o·gy (den drol′ə jē), *n.* the branch of botany dealing with trees and shrubs. [1700–10; DENDRO- + -LOGY] —**den·dro·log·i·cal** (den′drə loj′i kəl), **den′dro·**

CONCISE PRONUNCIATION KEY: act, cāpe, dâre, pärt; set, ēqual; if, īce; ox, ōver, ôrder, oil, bo͝ok, bo͞ot, out; up, ûrge; child; sing; shoe; thin, *th*at; zh as in *treasure.* ə = a as in *alone,* e as in *system,* i as in *easily,* o as in *gallop,* u as in *circus;* ᵊ as in *fire* (fīᵊr), *hour* (ouᵊr). l and n can serve as syllabic consonants, as in *cradle* (krād′l), and *button* (but′n). See the full key inside the front cover.

log′ic, den·drol·o·gous (den drol′ə gəs), *adj.* **—den·drol·o·gist** (den drol′ə jist), *n.*

den·dron (den′dron), *n., pl.* **-drons, -dra** (-drə). *Anat.* a dendrite. [1890–95; < NL < Gk *déndron* tree] **—den′dric,** *adj.*

-dendron, var. of **dendro-** as final element of a compound word: *rhododendron.*

den·droph·a·gous (den drof′ə gəs), *adj.* feeding on the wood of trees, as certain insects. [DENDRO- + -PHAGOUS]

den·droph·i·lous (den drof′ə ləs), *adj. Zool.* living in or on trees; arboreal. [1885–90; DENDRO- + -PHILOUS]

dene (dēn), *n. Brit.* a bare, sandy tract or low sand hill near the sea. Also, **dean.** [1815–20; earlier *den,* in same sense, ME (in phrase *den and strond*); perh. to be identified with ME *dene,* OE *denu, dænu* valley]

Den·eb (den′eb), *n. Astron.* a first-magnitude star in the constellation Cygnus. [1865–70; < Ar *dhanab* a tail]

den·e·ga·tion (den′i gā′shən), *n.* denial; contradiction. [1480–90; < LL *dēnegātiōn-* (s. of *dēnegātiō*). See DE-, NEGATION]

de·ner·vate (dē nûr′vāt), *v.t.,* **-vat·ed, -vat·ing.** *Surg.* to cut off the nerve supply from (an organ or body part) by surgery or anesthetic block. [1900–05; DE- + NERVE + -ATE[1]] **—de′ner·va′tion,** *n.*

den′ fa′ther, 1. (in the Boy Scouts) a man who serves as an adult leader or supervisor of a cub scout den. **2.** *Informal.* a man who serves as an adviser or protector to a group of people. Cf. **den mother.**

D.Eng., Doctor of Engineering.

D.Eng.S., Doctor of Engineering Science.

den·gue (deng′gā, -gē), *n. Pathol.* an infectious, eruptive fever of warm climates, usually epidemic, characterized esp. by severe pains in the joints and muscles. Also called **den′gue fe′ver.** [1820–30, *Amer.;* < AmerSp]

Deng Xiao·ping (dung′ shou′ping′; *Chin.* dœng′ shyou′ping′), born 1904, Chinese Communist leader: chairman of the Central Advisory Commission since 1982, China's de facto leader.

Den Haag (den häkh′), a Dutch name of The Hague.

Den·ham (den′əm), *n.* **Sir John,** 1615–69, English poet and architect.

de·ni·a·bil·i·ty (di nī′ə bil′ə tē), *n.* the ability to deny something, as knowledge of or connection with an illegal activity. [1970–75; DENIABLE + -ITY]

de·ni·a·ble (di nī′ə bəl), *adj.* capable of being or liable to be denied or contradicted. [1540–50; DENY + -ABLE]

de·ni·al (di nī′əl), *n.* **1.** an assertion that something said, believed, alleged, etc., is false: *Despite his denials, we knew he had taken the purse. The politician issued a denial of his opponent's charges.* **2.** refusal to believe a doctrine, theory, or the like. **3.** disbelief in the existence or reality of a thing. **4.** the refusal to satisfy a claim, request, desire, etc., or the refusal of a person making it. **5.** refusal to recognize or acknowledge; a disowning or disavowal: *the traitor's denial of his country; Peter's denial of Christ.* **6.** *Law.* refusal to acknowledge the validity of a claim, suit, or the like; a plea that denies allegations of fact in an adversary's plea: *Although she sued for libel, he entered a general denial.* **7.** sacrifice of one's own wants or needs; self-denial. **8.** *Psychol.* an unconscious defense mechanism used to reduce anxiety by denying thoughts, feelings, or facts that are consciously intolerable. [1520–30; DENY + -AL[2]]
—Syn. 1. disavowal, disclaimer, repudiation. **—Ant. 1.** admission, acknowledgment, confession.

de·ni·er[1] (di nī′ər), *n.* a person who denies. [1350–1400; ME; see DENY, -ER[1]]

de·nier[2] (də nēr′ *or, esp. for 1,* den′yər; *Fr.* də nyā′), *n.* **1.** a unit of weight indicating the fineness of fiber filaments and yarns, both silk and synthetic, and equal to a yarn weighing one gram per each 9000 meters: used esp. in indicating the fineness of women's hosiery. **2.** any of various coins issued in French-speaking regions, esp. a coin of France, originally of silver but later of copper, introduced in the 8th century and continued until 1794. [1375–1425; late ME < OF < L *dēnārius* DENARIUS]

den·i·grate (den′i grāt′), *v.t.,* **-grat·ed, -grat·ing. 1.** to speak damagingly of; criticize in a derogatory manner; sully; defame: *to denigrate someone's character.* **2.** to treat or represent as lacking in value or importance; belittle; disparage: *to denigrate someone's contributions to a project.* **3.** to make black; blacken: *rain clouds denigrating the sky.* [1520–30; < L *dēnigrātus* (ptp. of *dēnigrāre* to blacken), equiv. to *dē-* DE- + *nigr(āre)* to make black + *-ātus* -ATE[1]] **—den′i·gra′tion,** *n.* **—den′i·gra′tive,** *adj.* **—den′i·gra′tor,** *n.* **—den·i·gra·to·ry** (den′i grə tôr′ē, -tōr′ē), *adj.*
—Syn. 1. malign, besmirch, slander, traduce, disparage, vilify. See **decry.**

De·ni·ker (de nē kĕr′), *n.* **Jo·seph** (zhô zef′), 1852–1918, French anthropologist and naturalist.

den·im (den′əm), *n.* **1.** a heavy, Z-twist, twill cotton for jeans, overalls, and other work and leisure garments. **2.** a similar fabric of finer quality, for covering cushions, furniture, etc. **3. denims,** (*used with a plural v.*) a garment, esp. trousers or overalls, made of denim. [1685–95; < F: short for *serge de Nîmes* serge of NÎMES]

den·imed (den′əmd), *adj.* wearing garments made of denim. [1965–70; DENIM + -ED[3]]

Den·is (den′is), *n.* a male given name.

Den·îs (den′is; *Fr.* də nē′), *n.* **Saint,** died A.D. c280, 1st bishop of Paris: patron saint of France.

CONCISE ETYMOLOGY KEY: <, descended or borrowed from; >, whence; b., blend of, blended; c., cognate with; cf., compare; deriv., derivative; equiv., equivalent; imit., imitative; obl., oblique; r., replacing; s., stem; sp., spelling, spelled; resp., respelling, respelled; trans., translation; ?, origin unknown; *, unattested; ‡, probably earlier than. See the full key inside the front cover.

De·nise (də nēs′, -nēz′), *n.* a female given name: derived from *Denis.*

Den·i·son (den′ə sən), *n.* a city in NE Texas. 23,884.

de·ni·trate (dē nī′trāt), *v.t.,* **-trat·ed, -trat·ing.** *Chem.* to free from nitric acid or nitrates; remove oxides of nitrogen from. [1860–65; DE- + NITRATE] **—de′ni·tra′tion,** *n.*

de·ni·tri·fy (dē nī′trə fī′), *v.t.,* **-fied, -fy·ing.** *Chem.* **1.** to remove nitrogen or nitrogen compounds from. **2.** to reduce (nitrates) to nitrites, ammonia, and free nitrogen, as in soil by microorganisms. [1890–95; DE- + NITRIFY] **—de·ni′tri·fi·ca′tion,** *n.* **—de·ni′tri·fi′er, de·ni′tri·fi·ca′tor,** *n.*

den·i·zen (den′ə zən), *n.* **1.** an inhabitant; resident. **2.** a person who regularly frequents a place; habitué: *the denizens of a local bar.* **3.** *Brit.* an alien admitted to residence and to certain rights of citizenship in a country. **4.** anything adapted to a new place, condition, etc., as an animal or plant not indigenous to a place but successfully naturalized. **—*v.t.* 5.** to make a denizen of. [1425–75; late ME *denisein* < AF, equiv. to *deinz* within (OF; see DEDANS) + *-ein* -AN] **—den′i·za′tion, den′i·zen·a′tion,** *n.* **—den′i·zen·ship′,** *n.*

Den·mark (den′märk), *n.* a kingdom in N Europe, on the Jutland peninsula and adjacent islands. 5,079,000; 16,576 sq. mi. (42,930 sq. km). *Cap.:* Copenhagen.

Den′mark Strait′, a strait between Iceland and Greenland. 130 mi. (210 km) wide.

den′ moth′er, 1. (in the Boy Scouts) a woman who serves as an adult leader or supervisor of a cub scout den. **2.** *Informal.* a woman who serves as an adviser or protector to a group of people. Cf. **den father.** [1945–50]

Den·nis (den′is), *n.* **1. John,** 1657–1734, English dramatist and critic. **2.** a town in SE Massachusetts. 12,360. **3.** a male given name: from the Greek word meaning "of Dionysus."

Den·ny (den′ē), *n.* a male given name, form of **Dennis.**

denom., denomination.

de·nom·i·nal (di nom′ə nl), *adj.* **1.** denominative (def. 2). **—*n.* 2.** denominative (def. 3). [1930–35; DE- + NOMINAL]

de·nom·i·nate (di nom′ə nāt′), *v.t.,* **-nat·ed, -nat·ing.** to give a name to; denote; designate. [1545–55; < L *dēnōminātus* (ptp. of *dēnōmināre*), equiv. to *dē-* DE- + *nōminātus;* see NOMINATE]

de·nom′i·nate num′ber (di nom′ə nit, -nāt′), a number associated with a unit of measurement. Cf. **abstract number.** [1570–80]

de·nom·i·na·tion (di nom′ə nā′shən), *n.* **1.** a religious group, usually including many local churches, often larger than a sect: *the Lutheran denomination.* **2.** one of the grades or degrees in a series of designations of quantity, value, measure, weight, etc.: *He paid $500 in bills of small denomination.* **3.** a name or designation, esp. one for a class of things. **4.** a class or kind of persons or things distinguished by a specific name. **5.** the act of naming or designating a person or thing. [1350–1400; ME *denominacioun* < LL *dēnōminātiōn-* (s. of *dēnōminātiō*), in L: metonymy, equiv. to *dēnōmināt(us)* (see DENOMINATE) + *-iōn-* -ION]

de·nom·i·na·tion·al (di nom′ə nā′shə nl), *adj.* **1.** of or pertaining to a denomination or denominations. **2.** founded, sponsored, or controlled by a particular religious denomination or sect: *denominational schools.* **3.** limited, conditioned, originating in, or influenced by the beliefs, attitudes, or interests of a religious sect, political party, etc.: *denominational prejudice.* [1830–40; DENOMINATION + -AL[1]] **—de·nom′i·na′tion·al·ly,** *adv.*

de·nom·i·na·tion·al·ism (di nom′ə nā′shə nl iz′əm), *n.* denominational or sectarian spirit or policy; the tendency to divide into denominations or sects. [1850–55; DENOMINATIONAL + -ISM] **—de·nom′i·na′tion·al·ist,** *n.*

de·nom·i·na·tive (di nom′ə nā′tiv, -nə tiv), *adj.* **1.** conferring or constituting a distinctive designation or name. **2.** *Gram.* (esp. of verbs) formed from a noun, as English *to man* from the noun *man.* **—*n.* 3.** *Gram.* a denominative verb or other word. [1580–90; < LL *dēnōminātīvus,* equiv. to *dēnōmināt(us)* (see DENOMINATE) + *-īvus* -IVE] **—de·nom·i·na·tive·ly** (di nom′ə-nā′tiv lē, -nə tiv-), *adv.*

de·nom·i·na·tor (di nom′ə nā′tər), *n.* **1.** *Arith.* that term of a fraction, usually written under the line, that indicates the number of equal parts into which the unit is divided; divisor. Cf. **numerator** (def. 1). **2.** something shared or held in common; standard. **3.** *Archaic.* a person or thing that denominates. [1535–45; < ML *dēnōminātor,* equiv. to L *dēnōmina(re)* (see DENOMINATE) + *-tor* -TOR]

de·no·ta·tion (dē′nō tā′shən), *n.* **1.** the explicit or direct meaning or set of meanings of a word or expression, as distinguished from the ideas or meanings associated with it or suggested by it; the association or set of associations that a word usually elicits for most speakers of a language, as distinguished from those elicited for any individual speaker because of personal experience. Cf. **connotation. 2.** a word that names or signifies something specific: *"Wind" is the denotation for air in natural motion. "Poodle" is the denotation for a certain breed of dog.* **3.** the act or fact of denoting; indication. **4.** something that denotes; mark; symbol. **5.** *Logic.* **a.** the class of particulars to which a term is applicable. **b.** that which is represented by a sign. [1525–35; < L *dēnotātiōn-* (s. of *dēnotātiō*) a marking out, equiv. to *dēnotāt(us)* (ptp. of *dēnotāre;* see DENOTE) + *-iōn-* -ION]

de·no·ta·tive (dē′nō tā′tiv, di nō′tə tiv), *adj.* **1.** having power to denote. **2.** denoting or tending to denote: *the denotative meaning of a word.* [1605–15; DENOTATE + -IVE] **—de′no·ta′tive·ly,** *adv.* **—de′no·ta′tive·ness,** *n.*

de·note (di nōt′), *v.t.,* **-not·ed, -not·ing. 1.** to be a mark or sign of; indicate: *A fever often denotes an infection.* **2.** to be a name or designation for; mean. **3.** to represent by a symbol; stand as a symbol for. [1585–95; < MF *dénoter,* L *dēnotāre* to mark out, equiv. to *dē-* DE- + *notāre* to mark; see NOTE] **—de·not′a·ble,** *adj.* **—de·note′ment,** *n.*
—Syn. 1. mark, signal, signify, evidence.

de·no·tive (di nō′tiv), *adj.* used or serving to denote; denotative. [1820–30; DENOTE + -IVE]

de·noue·ment (dā′no͞o män′), *n.* **1.** the final resolution of the intricacies of a plot, as of a drama or novel. **2.** the place in the plot at which this occurs. **3.** the outcome or resolution of a doubtful series of occurrences. Also, **dé′noue·ment′.** [1745–55; < F: lit., an untying, equiv. to *dénouer* to untie, OF *desnoer* (*des-* DE- + *noer* to knot < L *nōdāre,* deriv. of *nōdus* knot) + *-ment* -MENT]
—Syn. 3. solution, conclusion, end, upshot.

de·nounce (di nouns′), *v.t.,* **-nounced, -nounc·ing. 1.** to condemn or censure openly or publicly: *to denounce a politician as morally corrupt.* **2.** to make a formal accusation against, as to the police or in a court. **3.** to give formal notice of the termination or denial of (a treaty, pact, agreement, or the like). **4.** *Archaic.* to announce or proclaim, esp. as something evil or calamitous. **5.** *Obs.* to portend. [1250–1300; ME *denouncen* < OF *denoncier* to speak out < L *dēnuntiāre* to threaten (*dē-* DE- + *nuntiāre* to announce, deriv. of *nuntius* messenger)] **—de·nounce′ment,** *n.* **—de·nounc′er,** *n.*
—Syn. 1. attack, stigmatize, blame, brand. **—Ant. 1.** praise, commend.

de no·vo (de nō′wō; *Eng.* dē nō′vō, dā), *Latin.* anew; afresh; again; from the beginning.

Den·pa·sar (den pä′sär), *n.* a city on S Bali, in S Indonesia. 98,000. Also, **Den Pa′sar.**

dens (denz), *n., pl.* **den·tes** (den′tēz). *Zool.* a tooth or toothlike part. [< L *dēns;* see TOOTH]

dense (dens), *adj.,* **dens·er, dens·est. 1.** having the component parts closely compacted together; crowded or compact: *a dense forest; dense population.* **2.** stupid; slow-witted; dull. **3.** intense; extreme: *dense ignorance.* **4.** relatively opaque; transmitting little light, as a photographic negative, optical glass, or color. **5.** difficult to understand or follow because of being closely packed with ideas or complexities of style: *a dense philosophical essay.* **6.** *Math.* of or pertaining to a subset of a topological space in which every neighborhood of every point in the space contains at least one point of the subset. [1590–1600; < L *dēnsus* thick; c. Gk *dasýs*] **—dense′ly,** *adv.* **—dense′ness,** *n.*
—Syn. 1. congested, crammed, teeming; impenetrable.

den·si·fy (den′sə fī′), *v.t.,* **-fied, -fy·ing.** to impregnate (wood) with additives under heat and pressure in order to achieve greater density and hardness. [1810–20; DENSE + -IFY] **—den′si·fi·ca′tion,** *n.* **—den′si·fi′·er,** *n.*

den·sim·e·ter (den sim′i tər), *n. Chem., Physics.* any instrument for measuring density. [1860–65; < L *dēns(us)* DENSE + -I- + -METER] **—den·si·met·ric** (den′sə-me′trik), *adj.* **—den′si·met′ri·cal·ly,** *adv.* **—den·sim′e·try,** *n.*

den·si·tom·e·ter (den′si tom′i tər), *n.* **1.** *Photog.* an instrument for measuring the density of negatives. **2.** a densimeter. [1900–05; DENSIT(Y) + -O- + -METER] **—den·si·to·met·ric** (den′si tə me′trik), *adj.* **—den′si·tom′e·try,** *n.*

den·si·ty (den′si tē), *n., pl.* **-ties. 1.** the state or quality of being dense; compactness; closely set or crowded condition. **2.** stupidity; slow-wittedness; obtuseness. **3.** the number of inhabitants, dwellings, or the like, per unit area: *The commissioner noted that the population density of certain city blocks had fallen dramatically.* **4.** *Physics.* mass per unit volume. **5.** *Elect.* **a.** the quantity of electricity per unit of volume at a point in space, or the quantity per unit of area at a point on a surface. **b.** See **current density. 6.** the degree of opacity of a substance, medium, etc., that transmits light. **7.** *Photog.* the relative degree of opacity of an area of a negative or transparency, often expressed logarithmically. **8.** *Computers.* a measure of the compactness of data stored on an external storage medium, as disk or tape, or displayed on a CRT or other screen. [1595–1605; < L *dēnsitās,* equiv. to *dēns(us)* DENSE + *-itās* -ITY]

den′sity cur′rent, *Geol., Oceanog.* See **turbidity current.**

dent[1] (dent), *n.* **1.** a hollow or depression in a surface, as from a blow. **2.** a noticeable effect, esp. of reduction: *to leave a dent in one's savings; a dent in one's pride.* **3. make a dent,** *Informal.* to cause a person to take heed; make an impression: *The doctor told him to stop smoking, but it didn't make a dent.* **4. make a dent in,** to show initial progress; pass an initial stage of (work, thought, solving a problem, etc.): *I haven't even made a dent in this pile of work.* **—*v.t.* 5.** to make a dent in or on; indent: *The impact dented the car's fender.* **6.** to have the effect of reducing or slightly injuring: *The caustic remark dented his ego.* —*v.i.* **7.** to show dents; become indented: *Tin dents more easily than steel.* **8.** to sink in, making a dent: *Nails dent into metal.* [1250–1300; ME *dente,* var. of DINT]

dent[2] (dent), *n.* **1.** a toothlike projection, as a tooth of a gearwheel. **2.** *Textiles.* the space between two wires through which the warp ends are drawn in the reed of a loom. [1545–55; < MF < L *dent-* (s. of *dēns*) TOOTH]

dent-, var. of **denti-** before a vowel: *dentin.*

dent., **1.** dental. **2.** dentist. **3.** dentistry.

den•tal (den′tl), *adj.* **1.** of or pertaining to the teeth. **2.** of or pertaining to dentistry or a dentist. **3.** *Phonet.* **a.** (of a speech sound) articulated with the tongue tip touching the back of the upper front teeth or immediately above them, as French *t.* **b.** alveolar, as English *t.* **c.** interdental (def. 2). —*n.* **4.** *Phonet.* a dental sound. [1585–95; < ML *dentālis,* equiv. to L *dent-* (s. of *dēns*) TOOTH + *-ālis* -AL[1]] —**den•tal′i•ty,** *n.* —**den′tal•ly,** *adv.*

den′tal car′ies, cavity formation in teeth caused by bacteria that attach to teeth and form acids in the presence of sucrose, other sugars, and refined starches; tooth decay. Also called **caries.**

den′tal floss′, a soft, strong, waxed or unwaxed thread, usually made of nylon, for drawing between the teeth to remove food particles and prevent the buildup of plaque. Also called **floss.** [1905–10, *Amer.*]

den′tal hy′giene. See **oral hygiene.**

den′tal hygien′ist, a person who is trained and licensed to clean teeth, take dental x-rays, and provide related dental services and care, usually under the supervision of a dentist. [1920–25; DENTAL HYGIENE + -IST]

den•ta•li•um (den tā′lē əm), *n., pl.* **-li•ums, -li•a.** any tooth shell of the genus *Dentalium.* [1860–65; < NL < ML *dentāl(is)* DENTAL + *-ium* -IUM]

den•tal•ize (den′tl īz′), *v.t.,* **-ized, -iz•ing.** *Phonet.* to change into or pronounce as a dental sound. Also, *esp. Brit.,* **den′tal•ise′.** [1860–65; DENTAL + -IZE] —**den′tal•i•za′tion,** *n.*

den′tal lisp′, *Phonet.* See under **lisp** (def. 2).

den•tal•man (den′tl mən), *n., pl.* **-men.** *U.S. Navy.* an enlisted person working as a dental assistant. [DENTAL + -MAN]

den′tal plate′, a dental prosthesis; denture.

den′tal pulp′, pulp (def. 4).

den′tal techni′cian, a skilled worker who makes dentures, bridges, etc., as specified by dentists for their patients. [1960–65]

den•ta•ry (den′tə rē), *n., pl.* **-ries.** *Zool.* one of a pair of membrane bones that in lower vertebrates form the distal part of the lower jaws and in mammals comprise the mandible. [1820–30; < L *dentārius* of the teeth, equiv. to *dent-* (s. of *dēns*) TOOTH + *-ārius* -ARY]

den•tate (den′tāt), *adj. Bot., Zool.* having a toothed margin or toothlike projections or processes. [1800–10; < L *dentātus,* equiv. to *dent-* (s. of *dēns*) TOOTH + *-ātus* -ATE[1]] —**den′tate•ly,** *adv.*

den•ta•tion (den tā′shən), *n. Bot., Zool.* **1.** the state or form of being dentate. **2.** an angular or toothlike projection of a margin. [1795–1805; DENTATE + -ION]

dent′ corn′, a variety of field corn, *Zea mays indentata,* having yellow or white kernels that become indented as they ripen. [1870–75]

den•telle (den tel′, dän-), *n.* **1.** lace (def. 1). **2.** a lacelike, tooled pattern used in decorating book covers. [1840–50; < F: lace, lit., little tooth < OF *dentele,* dim. of *dent* TOOTH < L *dent-* (s. of *dēns*)]

den•tes (den′tēz), *n.* pl. of **dens.**

denti-, a combining form meaning "tooth," used in the formation of compound words: *dentiform.* Also, *esp. before a vowel,* **dent-.** Cf. **odonto-.** [< L, comb. form of *dēns,* s. *dent-;* see TOOTH]

den•ti•cle (den′ti kəl), *n.* a small tooth or toothlike part. [1350–1400; ME < L *denticulus,* equiv. to *denti-* DENTI- + *-culus* -CLE[1]]

den•tic•u•late (den tik′yə lit, -lāt′), *adj.* **1.** *Bot., Zool.* finely dentate, as a leaf. **2.** *Archit.* having dentils. Also, **den•tic′u•lat′ed.** [1655–65; < L *denticulātus* having small teeth, equiv. to *denticul(us)* DENTICLE + *-ātus* -ATE[1]] —**den•tic′u•late•ly,** *adv.*

den•tic•u•la•tion (den tik′yə lā′shən), *n.* **1.** the state or form of being denticulate. **2.** a denticle. **3.** a series of denticles. [1675–85; DENTICULATE + -ION]

den•ti•form (den′tə fôrm′), *adj.* having the form of a tooth; tooth-shaped. [1570–80; DENTI- + -FORM]

den•ti•frice (den′tə fris), *n.* a paste, powder, liquid, or other preparation for cleaning the teeth. [1550–60; < MF < L *dentifricium* tooth powder, equiv. to *denti-* DENTI- + *fric(āre)* to rub + *-ium* -IUM]

den•tig•er•ous (den tij′ər əs), *adj. Anat.* having teeth. [1830–40; DENTI- + -GEROUS]

den•til (den′tl, -til), *n. Archit.* any of a series of closely spaced, small, rectangular blocks, used esp. in classical architecture beneath the coronas of Ionic, Corinthian, and Composite cornices. [1655–65; < F *dentille* (obs.), fem. dim. of *dent* TOOTH] —**den′tiled,** *adj.*

den′til band′, (in classical architecture) a molding occupying the position of a row of dentils and often cut to resemble one. [1815–25]

den•ti•lin•gual (den′ti ling′gwəl), *Phonet.* —*adj.* **1.** articulated with the tongue near or touching the front teeth; interdental. —*n.* **2.** a dentilingual sound. [1870–75; DENTI- + LINGUAL]

den•tin (den′tn, -tin), *n. Dentistry.* the hard, calcareous tissue, similar to but denser than bone, that forms the major portion of a tooth, surrounds the pulp cavity, and is situated beneath the enamel and cementum. See diag. under **tooth.** Also, **den•tine** (den′tēn). [1830–40; DENT- + -IN[2]] —**den′tin•al,** *adj.*

den•ti•ros•tral (den′ti ros′trəl), *adj. Ornith.* having a toothlike projection on the cutting edge of the bill, as falcons and shrikes. [1835–45; DENTI- + ROSTRAL]

den•tist (den′tist), *n.* a person whose profession is dentistry. [1750–60; < F *dentiste,* equiv. to *dent* TOOTH (see DENT[2]) + *-iste* -IST]

den•tist•ry (den′tə strē), *n.* the profession or science dealing with the prevention and treatment of diseases and malformations of the teeth, gums, and oral cavity, and the removal, correction, and replacement of decayed, damaged, or lost parts, including such operations as the filling and crowning of teeth, the straightening of teeth, and the construction of artificial dentures. [1830–40; DENTIST + -RY]

den•ti•tion (den tish′ən), *n.* **1.** the makeup of a set of teeth including their kind, number, and arrangement. **2.** the eruption or cutting of the teeth; teething; odontiasis. [1605–15; < L *dentitiōn-* (s. of *dentitiō*), equiv. to *dentīt(us)* (ptp. of *dentīre* to cut teeth, teethe) + *-iōn-* -ION]

den•toid (den′toid), *adj.* resembling a tooth; toothlike. [1820–30; DENT- + -OID]

Den•ton (den′tn), *n.* a city in N Texas. 48,063.

den•to•sur•gi•cal (den′tō sûr′ji kəl), *adj.* of or pertaining to surgery performed in the oral cavity. [*dento-* (irreg. for DENTI-; see -O-) + SURGICAL]

D'Entre•cas•teaux′ Is′lands (dän trə ka stō′), a group of islands in Papua New Guinea, off the E tip of New Guinea.

den•tu•lous (den′chə ləs), *adj.* possessing or bearing teeth. [1925–30; back formation from EDENTULOUS]

den•ture (den′chər), *n.* **1.** an artificial replacement of one or several of the teeth **(partial denture),** or all of the teeth **(full denture)** of either or both jaws; dental prosthesis. **2.** a set of teeth. [1870–75; < F, equiv. to *dent* TOOTH (see DENT[2]) + *-ure* -URE]

den•tur•ism (den′chə riz′əm), *n.* the practice by denturists of making artificial dentures and fitting them to patients. [DENTURE + -ISM]

den•tur•ist (den′chər ist), *n.* a dental technician in Canada and some states of the U.S. who is licensed to make and fit artificial dentures without the cooperation or supervision of a dentist. [DENTURE + -IST]

de•nu•cle•ar•ize (dē no͞o′klē ə rīz′, -nyo͞o′- *or, by metathesis,* -kyə lə-), *v.t.,* **-ized, -iz•ing.** **1.** to remove nuclear weapons from (a country, region, etc.). **2.** to prohibit the deployment or construction of nuclear weapons in (a country, region, etc.). Also, *esp. Brit.,* **de•nu′cle•ar•ise′.** [1955–60; DE- + NUCLEAR + -IZE] —**de•nu′cle•ar•i•za′tion,** *n.*

—**Pronunciation.** See **nuclear.**

den•u•date (*v.* den′yo͝o dāt′, di no͞o′dāt, -nyo͞o′-; *adj.* di no͞o′dāt, -nyo͞o′-, den′yo͝o dāt′), *v.,* **-dat•ed, -dat•ing,** *adj.* —*v.t.* **1.** to make bare; strip; denude. —*adj.* **2.** denuded; bare. [1620–30; < L *dēnūdātus,* ptp. of *dēnūdāre* to DENUDE; see -ATE[1]]

den•u•da•tion (den′yo͝o dā′shən, dē′no͝o-, -nyo͝o-), *n.* **1.** the act of denuding. **2.** the state of being denuded. **3.** *Geol.* the exposing or laying bare of rock by erosive processes. [1575–85; < LL *dēnūdātiōn-* (s. of *dēnūdātiō*), equiv. to L *dēnūdāt(us)* (see DENUDATE) + *-iōn-* -ION] —**den′u•da′tion•al,** *adj.* —**de•nu•da•tive** (di no͞o′də tiv, -nyo͞o′-), *adj.*

de•nude (di no͞od′, -nyo͞od′), *v.t.,* **-nud•ed, -nud•ing.** **1.** to make naked or bare; strip: *The storm completely denuded the trees.* **2.** *Geol.* to subject to denudation. [1505–15; < L *dēnūdāre,* equiv. to *dē-* DE- + *nūdāre* to lay bare; see NUDE] —**de•nud′er,** *n.*

de•nu•mer•a•ble (di no͞o′mər ə bəl, -nyo͞o′-), *adj.* countable (def. 2b). [1900–05; DE- + NUMERABLE] —**de•nu′mer•a•bil′i•ty,** *n.* —**de•nu′mer•a•bly,** *adv.*

de•nun•ci•ate (di nun′sē āt′, -shē-), *v.t., v.i.,* **-at•ed, -at•ing.** to denounce; condemn openly. [1585–95; < L *dēnuntiātus* (ptp. of *dēnuntiāre* to declare). See DENOUNCE, -ATE[1]] —**de•nun′ci•a•ble,** *adj.* —**de•nun′ci•a′tor,** *n.*

de•nun•ci•a•tion (di nun′sē ā′shən, -shē-), *n.* **1.** an act or instance of denouncing; public censure or condemnation. **2.** an accusation of crime before a public prosecutor or tribunal. **3.** notice of the termination or the renouncement of an international agreement or part thereof. **4.** *Archaic.* warning of impending evil; threat. [1540–50; < L *dēnuntiātiōn-* (s. of *dēnuntiātiō*), equiv. to *dēnuntiāt(us)* (see DENUNCIATE) + *-iōn-* -ION]

de•nun•ci•a•to•ry (di nun′sē ə tôr′ē, -tōr′ē, -shē-), *adj.* characterized by or given to denunciation. Also, **de•nun•ci•a•tive** (di nun′sē ā′tiv, -ə tiv, -shē-) [1720–30; DENUNCIATE + -ORY[1]] —**de•nun′ci•a′tive•ly,** *adv.*

Den•ver (den′vər), *n.* a city in and the capital of Colorado, in the central part. 491,396.

Den′ver boot′, boot[1] (def. 11). [after DENVER, Colorado, one of the first large communities to adopt the device]

de•ny (di nī′), *v.t.,* **-nied, -ny•ing.** **1.** to state that (something declared or believed to be true) is not true: *to deny an accusation.* **2.** to refuse to agree or accede to: *to deny a petition.* **3.** to withhold the possession, use, or enjoyment of: *to deny access to secret information.* **4.** to withhold something from, or refuse to grant a request of: *to deny a beggar.* **5.** to refuse to recognize or acknowledge; disown; disavow; repudiate: *to deny one's gods.* **6.** to withhold (someone) from accessibility to a visitor: *The secretary denied his employer to all those without appointments.* **7.** *Obs.* to refuse to take or accept. **8. deny oneself,** to refrain from satisfying one's desires or needs; practice self-denial. [1250–1300; ME *denien* < OF *denier* < L *dēnegāre.* See DENEGATION] —**de•ny′ing•ly,** *adv.*

—**Syn. 1.** dispute, controvert, oppose, gainsay. DENY, CONTRADICT both imply objecting to or arguing against something. To DENY is to say that something is not true: *to deny an allegation.* To CONTRADICT is to declare that the contrary is true: *to contradict a statement.* **5.** renounce, abjure. —**Ant. 1.** admit, accept. **3.** allow.

Den•ys (den′is; *Fr.* də nē′), *n.* **Saint.** See **Denis, Saint.**

de•o•dand (dē′ə dand′), *n. Eng. Law.* (before 1846) an animal or article that, having been the immediate cause of the death of a human being, was forfeited to the crown to be applied to pious uses. [1520–30; < ML *deōdandum* (a thing) to be given to God < L *deō* to God (dat. sing. of *deus*) + *dandum* to be given (neut. ger. of *dare* to give)]

de•o•dar (dē′ə där′), *n.* a large Himalayan cedar, *Cedrus deodara,* yielding a durable wood. [1795–1805; < Hindi *deodār* < Skt *devadāru* wood of the gods, equiv. to *deva* god + *dāru* wood]

de•o•dor•ant (dē ō′dər ənt), *n.* **1.** an agent for destroying odors. **2.** a substance, often combined with an antiperspirant, for inhibiting or masking perspiration or other bodily odors. —*adj.* **3.** capable of destroying odors: *a deodorant cream.* [1865–70; DE- + ODOR + -ANT]

de•o•dor•ize (dē ō′də rīz′), *v.t.,* **-ized, -iz•ing.** to rid of odor, esp. of unpleasant odor. Also, *esp. Brit.,* **de•o′dor•ise′.** [1855–60; DE- + ODOR + -IZE] —**de•o′dor•i•za′tion,** *n.* —**de•o′dor•iz′er,** *n.*

De•o gra•ti•as (dā′ō grä′tsē äs′), *Latin.* thanks to God.

deon′tolog′ical eth′ics, the branch of ethics dealing with right action and the nature of duty, without regard to the goodness or value of motives or the desirability of the ends of any act. Cf. **axiological ethics.**

de•on•tol•o•gy (dē′on tol′ə jē), *n.* ethics, esp. that branch dealing with duty, moral obligation, and right action. [1820–30; < Gk *deont-* that which is binding (s. of *déon,* neut. prp. of *deîn* to bind), equiv. to *de-* bind + *-ont-* prp. suffix + -O- + -LOGY] —**de•on•to•log•i•cal** (dē on′tl oj′i kəl), *adj.* —**de′on•tol′o•gist,** *n.*

de•or•bit (dē ôr′bit), *Aerospace.* —*v.i.* **1.** to depart deliberately from orbit, usually to enter a descent phase. —*v.t.* **2.** to cause to deliberately depart from orbit. [1960–65; DE- + ORBIT]

de•ox•i•dant (dē ok′si dənt), *n. Chem.* an agent that deoxidizes. [DEOXID(IZE) + -ANT]

de•ox•i•dize (dē ok′si dīz′), *v.t.,* **-dized, -diz•ing.** *Chem.* to remove oxygen from, esp. by reducing an oxide. Also, *esp. Brit.,* **de•ox′i•dise′.** [1760–70; DE- + OXIDIZE] —**de•ox′i•di•za′tion,** *n.* —**de•ox′i•diz′er,** *n.*

deoxy-, a combining form meaning "deoxygenated," used in the formation of compound words: *deoxyribose.* Also, **desoxy-.**

de•ox•y•cor•ti•cos•ter•one (dē ok′si kôr′ti kos′tə rōn′, -kō′stə rōn′), *n.* **1.** *Biochem.* a steroid hormone, $C_{21}H_{30}O_3$, secreted by the adrenal cortex, related to corticosterone and involved in regulating the water and electrolyte balance. **2.** *Pharm.* a preparation of deoxycorticosterone used to treat symptoms of adrenal insufficiency. [DEOXY- + CORTICOSTERONE]

de•ox•y•gen•ate (dē ok′si jə nāt′), *v.t.,* **-at•ed, -at•ing.** *Chem.* to remove oxygen from (a substance, as blood or water). [1790–1800; DE- + OXYGENATE] —**de•ox′y•gen•a′tion,** *n.*

de•ox•y•gen•ize (dē ok′si jə nīz′), *v.t.,* **-ized, -iz•ing.** *Chem.* to deoxygenate. Also, *esp. Brit.,* **de•ox′y•gen•ise′.** [1880–85; DE- + OXYGENIZE] —**de•ox′y•gen•i•za′tion,** *n.*

de•ox•y•he•mo•glo•bin (dē ok′si hē′mə glō′bin, -hem′ə-), *n. Biochem.* See under **hemoglobin.** [DEOXY- + HEMOGLOBIN]

de•ox•y•man•nose (dē ok′si man′ōs), *n. Biochem.* rhamnose. [DEOXY- + MANNOSE]

de•ox•y•ri•bo•nu•cle•ase (dē ok′si rī′bō no͞o′klē ās′, -āz′, -nyo͞o′-), *n. Biochem.* See **DNase.** [1945–50; DEOXY- + RIBONUCLEASE]

de•ox′y•ri′bo•nu•cle′ic ac′id (dē ok′si rī′bō no͞o klē′ik, -nyo͞o-, -ok′si rī′-), *Genetics.* See **DNA.** [1930–35; DEOXY- + RIBONUCLEIC ACID]

de•ox•y•ri•bo•nu•cle•o•pro•tein (dē ok′si rī′bō no͞o′klē ō prō′tēn, -tē in, -nyo͞o′-), *n. Biochem.* any of a class of nucleoproteins that yield DNA upon partial hydrolysis. [1940–45; DEOXYRIBONUCLE(IC ACID) + -O- + PROTEIN]

de•ox•y•ri•bo•nu•cle•o•side (dē ok′si rī′bō no͞o′klē ə sīd′, -nyo͞o′-), *n. Biochem.* a compound composed of deoxyribose and either a purine or a pyrimidine. [1965–70; DEOXYRIBO(NUCLEIC ACID) + NUCLEOSIDE]

de•ox•y•ri•bo•nu•cle•o•tide (dē ok′si rī′bō no͞o′klē ə tīd′, -nyo͞o′-), *n. Biochem.* an ester of a deoxyribonucleoside and phosphoric acid; a constituent of DNA. [1945–50; DEOXYRIBO(NUCLEIC ACID) + NUCLEOTIDE]

de•ox•y•ri•bose (dē ok′si rī′bōs), *n. Biochem.* **1.** any of certain carbohydrates derived from ribose by the replacement of a hydroxyl group with a hydrogen atom.

2. the sugar, $HOCH_2(CHOH)_2CH_2CHO$, obtained from DNA by hydrolysis. [1930–35; DEOXY- + RIBOSE]

dep., **1.** depart. **2.** department. **3.** departs. **4.** departure. **5.** deponent. **6.** deposed. **7.** deposit. **8.** depot. **9.** deputy.

de•paint (di pānt′), *v.t. Archaic.* to depict; portray. [1175–1225; ME *depeinten* < OF *depeint,* ptp. of *depeindre* < L *dēpingere* to DEPICT]

de•pants (dē pants′), *v.t. Slang.* to remove the trousers from, as a joke or punishment. [DE- + PANTS]

de•part (di pärt′), *v.i.* **1.** to go away; leave: *She departed from Paris today. The train departs at 10:52.* **2.** to diverge or deviate (usually fol. by *from*): *The new method departs from the old in several respects.* **3.** to pass away, as from life or existence; die. —*v.t.* **4.** to go away from; leave: *to depart this life.* —*n.* **5.** *Archaic.* departure; death. [1175–1225; ME *departen* < OF *departir,* equiv. to *de-* DE- + *partir* to go away; see PART (v.)]
—**Syn. 1.** DEPART, RETIRE, RETREAT, WITHDRAW imply leaving a place. DEPART is a somewhat literary word for going away from a place: *to depart on a journey.* RETIRE emphasizes absenting oneself or drawing back from a place: *to retire from a position in battle.* RETREAT implies a necessary withdrawal, esp. as a result of adverse fortune in war: *to retreat to secondary lines of defense.* WITHDRAW suggests leaving some specific place or situation, usually for some definite and often unpleasant reason: *to withdraw from a hopeless task.* **4.** quit. —**Ant. 1.** arrive.

de•part•ed (di pär′tid), *adj.* **1.** deceased; dead. **2.** gone; past. —*n.* **3. the departed, a.** the dead person referred to. **b.** dead persons collectively. [1550–60; DEPART + -ED[2]]

de•part•ee (di pär tē′, dē′-), *n.* a person who leaves an area, country, etc. [1945–50; DEPART + -EE]

dé•par•te•ment (dā PAR tə mäN′), *n., pl.* ***-ments*** (mäN′). *French.* department (def. 7).

de•part•ment (di pärt′mənt), *n.* **1.** a distinct part of anything arranged in divisions; a division of a complex whole or organized system. **2.** one of the principal branches of a governmental organization: *the sanitation department.* **3.** (*cap.*) one of the principal divisions of the U.S. federal government, headed by a Secretary who is a member of the President's cabinet. **4.** a division of a business enterprise dealing with a particular area of activity: *the personnel department.* **5.** a section of a retail store selling a particular class or kind of goods: *the sportswear department.* **6.** one of the sections of a school or college dealing with a particular field of knowledge: *the English department.* **7.** one of the large districts into which certain countries, as France, are divided for administrative purposes. **8.** a division of official business, duties, or functions: *judicial departments.* **9.** a sphere or province of activity, knowledge, or responsibility: *Paying the bills is not my department.* **10.** (*usually cap.*) *U.S. Army.* (formerly) a large geographical division of the U.S. or its possessions as divided for military and defense purposes: *the Hawaiian Department.* [1730–35; < F *département,* equiv. to *départ(ir)* (see DEPART) + *-ment* -MENT] —**de•part•men•tal** (di pärt men′tl, dē′pärt-), *adj.* —**de•part•men′tal•ly,** *adv.*
—**Syn. 1.** branch, bureau, section, unit, segment.

de•part•men•tal•ism (di pärt men′tl iz′əm, dē′pärt-), *n.* **1.** division into departments, as in a university. **2.** advocacy of or partiality for such division. [1885–90; DEPARTMENTAL + -ISM]

de•part•men•tal•ize (di pärt men′tl īz′, dē′pärt-), *v.t.,* **-ized, -iz•ing.** to divide into departments. Also, *esp. Brit.,* **de•part•men′tal•ise′.** [1895–1900; DEPARTMENTAL + -IZE] —**de′part•men′tal•i•za′tion,** *n.*

departmen′tal store′, *Brit.* a department store.

Depart′ment of Ag′riculture, the department of the U.S. federal government that institutes and administers all federal programs dealing with agriculture. *Abbr.:* USDA [1890–95, *Amer.*]

Depart′ment of Com′merce, the department of the U.S. federal government that promotes and administers domestic and foreign commerce. *Abbr.:* DOC

Depart′ment of Defense′, the department of the U.S. federal government charged with ensuring that the military capacity of the U.S. is adequate to safeguard the national security. *Abbr.:* DOD

Depart′ment of Educa′tion, the department of the U.S. federal government that administers federal programs dealing with education: created in 1979, largely by transfer from part of the former Department of Health, Education, and Welfare. *Abbr.:* ED

Depart′ment of En′ergy, the department of the U.S. federal government that sets forth and maintains the national energy policy, including energy conservation, environmental protection, etc. *Abbr.:* DOE

Depart′ment of Health′ and Hu′man Serv′ices, the department of the U.S. government that administers federal programs dealing with public health, welfare, and income security: created in 1979 from the reorganized Department of Health, Education, and Welfare. *Abbr.:* HHS

Depart′ment of Health′, Educa′tion, and Wel′fare, a former department of the U.S. government (1953–79) that administered federal programs dealing with health, education, welfare, and income security. *Abbr.:* HEW

Depart′ment of Hous′ing and Ur′ban Devel′opment, the department of the U.S. federal government that institutes and administers all federal programs dealing with better housing, urban renewal, and metropolitan planning. *Abbr.:* HUD

Depart′ment of Jus′tice, the department of the U.S. federal government charged with the responsibility for the enforcement of federal laws. *Abbr.:* DOJ

Depart′ment of La′bor, the department of the U.S. federal government that promotes and improves the welfare, opportunities, and working conditions of wage earners. *Abbr.:* DOL

Depart′ment of State′, the department of the U.S. federal government that sets forth and maintains the foreign policy of the U.S., esp. in negotiations with foreign governments and international organizations. *Abbr.:* DOS

Depart′ment of the Inte′rior, the department of the U.S. federal government charged with the conservation and development of the natural resources of the U.S. and its possessions. *Abbr.:* DOI

Depart′ment of the Treas′ury, the department of the U.S. federal government that collects revenue and administers the national finances. *Abbr.:* TD

Depart′ment of Transporta′tion, the department of the U.S. federal government that coordinates and institutes national transportation programs. *Abbr.:* DOT

depart′ment store′, a large retail store carrying a wide variety of merchandise and organized into various departments for sales and administrative purposes. [1885–90, *Amer.*]

de•par•ture (di pär′chər), *n.* **1.** an act or instance of departing: *the time of departure; a hasty departure.* **2.** divergence or deviation, as from a standard, rule, etc.: *a departure from accepted teaching methods.* **3.** *Navig.* **a.** the distance due east or west traveled by a vessel or aircraft. **b.** See **point of departure. 4.** *Survey.* the length of the projection, on the east-west reference line, of a survey line. **5.** *Archaic.* death. [1375–1425; late ME < OF *departeüre;* cf. AF *departir* (n. use of inf.). See DEPART, -URE]
—**Syn. 1.** leaving, going, exit, leave-taking.

de•pau•per•ate (di pô′pər it), *adj. Biol.* poorly or imperfectly developed. [1425–75; late ME < LL *dēpauperātus* (ptp. of *dēpauperāre* to make poor), equiv. to *dē-* DE- + *pauper(āre)* to make poor (*pauper-* poor (see PAUPER) + *-ātus* -ATE[1])] —**de•pau•per•a•tion** (di pô′pə rā′shən), *n.*

de•pend (di pend′), *v.i.* **1.** to rely; place trust (usually fol. by *on* or *upon*): *You may depend on the accuracy of the report.* **2.** to rely for support, maintenance, help, etc. (usually fol. by *on* or *upon*): *Children depend on their parents.* **3.** to be conditioned or contingent (usually fol. by *on* or *upon*): *His success here depends upon effort and ability.* **4.** to be undetermined or pending: *I may go to Europe or I may not, it all depends.* **5.** *Gram.* (of a word or other linguistic form) to be subordinate to another linguistic form in the same construction; to form a part of a construction other than the head. **6.** to hang down; be suspended (usually fol. by *from*): *The chandelier depends from the ceiling of the ballroom.* [1375–1425; late ME *dependen* < OF *dependre* < L *dēpendere* to hang down, equiv. to *dē-* DE- + *pendere* to hang]

de•pend•a•ble (di pen′də bəl), *adj.* capable of being depended on; worthy of trust; reliable: *a dependable employee.* [1725–35; DEPEND + -ABLE] —**de•pend′a•bil′i•ty, de•pend′a•ble•ness,** *n.* —**de•pend′a•bly,** *adv.*
—**Syn.** trustworthy, trusty, trusted, steadfast, faithful, responsible.

de•pend•ant (di pen′dənt), *adj., n.* dependent. —**de•pend′ant•ly,** *adv.*

de•pend•ence (di pen′dəns), *n.* **1.** the state of relying on or needing someone or something for aid, support, or the like. **2.** reliance; confidence; trust: *Her complete reliability earned her our dependence.* **3.** an object of reliance or trust. **4.** the state of being conditional or contingent on something, as through a natural or logical sequence: *the dependence of an effect upon a cause.* **5.** the state of being psychologically or physiologically dependent on a drug after a prolonged period of use. **6.** subordination or subjection: *the dependence of Martinique upon France.* Also, **de•pend′ance.** [1400–50; late ME *dependaunce* < OF *dependance,* equiv. to *depend(re)* (see DEPEND) + *-ance* -ENCE]

de•pend•en•cy (di pen′dən sē), *n., pl.* **-cies. 1.** the state of being dependent; dependence. **2.** something dependent or subordinate; appurtenance. **3.** an outbuilding or annex. **4.** a subject territory that is not an integral part of the ruling country. Also, **de•pend′an•cy.** [1585–95; DEPENDENCE + -Y[3]]

de•pend•en•cy-prone (di pen′dən sē prōn′), *adj.* tending to become psychologically or physiologically dependent on a drug. [1965–70]

de•pend•ent (di pen′dənt), *adj.* **1.** relying on someone or something else for aid, support, etc. **2.** conditioned or determined by something else; contingent: *Our trip is dependent on the weather.* **3.** subordinate; subject: *a dependent territory.* **4.** *Gram.* not used in isolation; used only in connection with other forms. In *I walked out when the bell rang, when the bell rang* is a dependent clause. Cf. **independent** (def. 14), **main**[1] (def. 4). **5.** hanging down; pendent. **6.** *Math.* **a.** (of a variable) having values determined by one or more independent variables. **b.** (of an equation) having solutions that are identical to those of another equation or to those of a set of equations. **7.** *Statistics.* (of an event or a value) not statistically independent. —*n.* **8.** a person who depends on or needs someone or something for aid, support, favor, etc. **9.** a child, spouse, parent, or certain other relative to whom one contributes all or a major amount of necessary financial support: *She listed two dependents on her income-tax form.* **10.** *Archaic.* a subordinate part. Also, **dependant.** [1375–1425; late ME *dependaunt.* See DEPEND, -ENT] —**de•pend′ent•ly,** *adv.*

depend′ent var′iable, 1. *Math.* a variable in a functional relation whose value is determined by the values assumed by other variables in the relation, as *y* in the relation $y = 3x^2$. **2.** *Statistics.* (in an experiment) the event studied and expected to change when the independent variable is changed. [1850–55]

de•peo•ple (dē pē′pəl), *v.t.,* **-pled, -pling.** to depopulate. [1605–15; DE- + PEOPLE]

De Pere (də pēr′), a city in E Wisconsin. 14,892.

de•perm (dē pûrm′), *v.t. Naut.* to reduce the permanent magnetism of (a vessel) by wrapping an electric cable around it vertically athwartships and energizing the cable. Cf. **degauss.** [1945–50; DE- + PERM(ANENT)]

de•per•son•a•li•za•tion (dē pûr′sə nl ə zā′shən), *n.* **1.** the act of depersonalizing. **2.** the state of being depersonalized. **3.** *Psychiatry.* a state in which one no longer perceives the reality of one's self or one's environment. [1905–10; DEPERSONALIZE + -ATION]

de•per•son•al•ize (dē pûr′sə nl īz′), *v.t.,* **-ized, -iz•ing. 1.** to make impersonal. **2.** to deprive of personality or individuality: *a mechanistic society that is depersonalizing its members.* Also, *esp. Brit.,* **de•per′son•al•ise′.** [1865–70; DE- + PERSONALIZE]

De•pew (də pyōō′), *n.* **1. Chauncey Mitchell,** 1834–1928, U.S. lawyer, legislator, and orator. **2.** a town in W New York. 19,819.

de•phos•pho•ryl•ate (dē fos′fər ə lāt′), *v.i.,* **-at•ed, -at•ing.** *Biochem.* to undergo dephosphorylation. [DE- + PHOSPHORYLATE]

de•phos•pho•ryl•a•tion (dē fos′fər ə lā′shən), *n. Biochem.* **1.** the removal of a phosphate group from an organic compound, as in the changing of ATP to ADP. **2.** the resulting state or condition. [DEPHOSPHORYLATE + -ION]

de•pict (di pikt′), *v.t.* **1.** to represent by or as if by painting; portray; delineate. **2.** to represent or characterize in words; describe. [1625–35; < L *dēpictus* (ptp. of *dēpingere*), equiv. to *dē-* DE- + *pic-* ptp. s. of *pingere* to PAINT + *-tus* ptp. suffix] —**de•pict′er, de•pic′tor,** *n.* —**de•pic′tion,** *n.* —**de•pic′tive,** *adj.*
—**Syn. 1.** reproduce, draw, paint, limn. **1, 2.** DEPICT, PORTRAY, SKETCH imply a representation of an object or scene by colors or lines, or by words. DEPICT emphasizes vividness of detail: *to depict the confusion of departure.* PORTRAY emphasizes faithful representation: *We could not portray the anguish of the exiles.* SKETCH suggests the drawing of the outlines of the most prominent features or details, often in a preparatory way: *to sketch the plans for a community development.*

de•pig•men•ta•tion (dē pig′mən tā′shən), *n. Pathol.* loss of pigment. [1885–90; DE- + PIGMENTATION]

dep•i•late (dep′ə lāt′), *v.t.,* **-lat•ed, -lat•ing.** to remove the hair from (hides, skin, etc.). [1550–60; < L *dēpilātus* (ptp. of *dēpilāre* to pluck), equiv. to *dē-* DE- + *pil(āre)* to deprive of hair (deriv. of *pilus* a hair) + *-ātus* -ATE[1]] —**dep′i•la′tion,** *n.* —**dep′i•la′tor,** *n.*

de•pil•a•to•ry (di pil′ə tôr′ē, -tōr′ē), *adj., n., pl.* **-ries.** —*adj.* **1.** capable of removing hair. —*n.* **2.** a depilatory agent. **3.** such an agent in a mild liquid or cream form for temporarily removing unwanted hair from the body. [1595–1605; < ML *dēpilātōrius* < L *dēpilā(re)* (see DEPILATE) + *-tōrius* -TORY[1]]

de•plane (dē plān′), *v.i.,* **-planed, -plan•ing.** to disembark from an airplane. [1920–25; DE- + PLANE[1]]

de pla•no (dē plā′nō, dē, dā), *Chiefly Law.* **1.** without argument. **2.** by manifest right; plainly. [< L *dē plānō*]

de•plete (di plēt′), *v.t.,* **-plet•ed, -plet•ing.** to decrease seriously or exhaust the abundance or supply of: *The fire had depleted the game in the forest. Extravagant spending soon depleted his funds.* [1800–10; < L *dēplētus* empty (ptp. of *dēplēre* to empty out), equiv. to *dē-* DE- + *plē(re)* to FILL + *-tus* ptp. suffix] —**de•plet′a•ble,** *adj.* —**de•ple′tion,** *n.* —**de•ple′tive, de•ple•to•ry** (di plē′tə rē), *adj.*
—**Syn.** use up, drain, reduce, consume, lessen.

deple′tion allow′ance, a tax reduction allowed on income from exhaustible resources, as oil or timber.

de•plor•a•ble (di plôr′ə bəl, -plōr′-), *adj.* **1.** causing or being a subject for grief or regret; lamentable: *the deplorable death of a friend.* **2.** causing or being a subject for censure, reproach, or disapproval; wretched; very bad: *This room is in deplorable order. You have deplorable manners!* [1605–15; < F *déplorable* < MF, equiv. to *deplor(er)* (see DEPLORE) + *-able* -ABLE] —**de•plor′a•ble•ness, de•plor′a•bil′i•ty,** *n.* —**de•plor′a•bly,** *adv.*

de•plore (di plôr′, -plōr′), *v.t.,* **-plored, -plor•ing. 1.** to regret deeply or strongly; lament: *to deplore the present state of morality.* **2.** to disapprove of; censure. **3.** to feel or express deep grief for or in regard to: *The class deplored the death of their teacher.* [1550–60; < L *dēplōrāre* to weep bitterly, complain, equiv. to *dē-* DE- + *plōrāre* to wail, prob. of imit. orig.] —**dep•lo•ra•tion** (dep′lə rā′shən, dē′plə-), *n.* —**de•plor′er,** *n.* —**de•plor′ing•ly,** *adv.*
—**Syn. 1.** bemoan, bewail. **3.** mourn.

de•ploy (di ploi′), *v.t.* **1.** *Mil.* to spread out (troops) so as to form an extended front or line. **2.** to arrange in a position of readiness, or to move strategically or appropriately: *to deploy a battery of new missiles.* —*v.i.* **3.** to spread out strategically or in an extended front or line. **4.** to come into a position ready for use: *the plane can't land unless the landing gear deploys.* [1470–80; < F *déployer,* equiv. to *dé-* DIS-[1] + *ployer* to fold; see PLOY] —**de•ploy′a•ble,** *adj.* —**de•ploy′a•bil′i•ty,** *n.* —**de•ploy′ment,** *n.*

de•plume (dē plōōm′), *v.t.,* **-plumed, -plum•ing. 1.** to deprive of feathers; pluck. **2.** to strip of honor, wealth, etc. [1375–1425; late ME *deplumen* < ML *dēplūmāre,* equiv. to L *dē-* DE- + *plūm(a)* feather (see PLUME) + *-āre* inf. suffix] —**de′plu•ma′tion,** *n.*

de•po•lar•iz•er (dē pō′lə rī′zər), *n.* a substance added to the electrolyte of an electric cell or battery to remove gas collected at the electrodes.

de•pol•lute (dē′pə lōōt′), *v.t.,* **-lut•ed, -lut•ing.** to eliminate, clean up, or decrease pollution in (an area). [1965–70; DE- + POLLUTE] —**de′pol•lu′tion,** *n.*

CONCISE ETYMOLOGY KEY: <, descended or borrowed from; >, whence; b., blend of, blended; c., cognate with; cf., compare; deriv., derivative; equiv., equivalent; imit., imitative; obl., oblique; r., replacing; s., stem; sp., spelling, spelled; resp., respelling, respelled; trans., translation; ?, origin unknown; *, unattested; ‡, probably earlier than. See the full key inside the front cover.

de•po•lym•er•ize (dē′pə lim′ə rīz′, dē pol′ə mə-), *v.t.*, **-ized, -iz•ing.** *Chem.* to break down (a polymer) into monomers. Also, *esp. Brit.,* **de′po•lym′er•ise′.** [1890–95; DE- + POLYMERIZE] —**de′po•lym′er•i•za′tion,** *n.*

de•pone (di pōn′), *v.t., v.i.,* **-poned, -pon•ing.** to testify under oath; depose. [1525–35; < L *dēpōnere* to put away, down, aside (ML: to testify), equiv. to *dē-* DE- + *pōnere* to put]

de•po•nent (di pō′nənt), *adj.* **1.** *Class. Gk. and Latin Gram.* (of a verb) appearing only in the passive or Greek middle-voice forms, but with active meaning. —*n.* **2.** *Law.* a person who testifies under oath, esp. in writing. **3.** *Class. Gk. and Latin Gram.* a deponent verb, as Latin *loquor.* [1520–30; < L *dēpōnent-* (s. of *dēpōnēns*) putting away (ML: testifying), prp. of *dēpōnere.* See DEPONE, -ENT]

Dep•o-Pro•ve•ra (dep′ō prō vâr′ə), *Pharm., Trademark.* a brand of medroxyprogesterone.

de•pop•u•late (*v.* dē pop′yə lāt′; *adj.* dē pop′yə lit, -lāt′), *v.,* **-lat•ed, -lat•ing,** *adj.* —*v.t.* **1.** to remove or reduce the population of, as by destruction or expulsion. —*adj.* **2.** *Archaic.* depopulated. [1525–35; < L *dēpopulātus* devastated (ptp. of *dēpopulārī*), equiv. to *dē-* DE- + *populātus;* see POPULATE] —**de•pop′u•la′tion,** *n.* —**de•pop′u•la′tive,** *adj.* —**de•pop′u•la′tor,** *n.*

de•port (di pôrt′, -pōrt′), *v.t.* **1.** to expel (an alien) from a country; banish. **2.** to send or carry off; transport, esp. forcibly: *The country deported its criminals.* **3.** to bear, conduct, or behave (oneself) in a particular manner. [1475–85; < MF *déporter* < L *dēportāre* to carry away, banish oneself, equiv. to *dē-* DE- + *portāre* to carry; see PORT[5]] —**de•port′a•ble,** *adj.* —**de′por•tee′,** *n.* —**de•port′er,** *n.*

de•por•ta•tion (dē′pôr tā′shən, -pōr-), *n.* **1.** the lawful expulsion of an undesired alien or other person from a state. **2.** an act or instance of deporting. [1585–95; < L *dēportātiōn-* (s. of *dēportātiō*), equiv. to *dēportāt(us)* (ptp. of *dēportāre;* see DEPORT, -ATE[1]) + *-iōn-* -ION]

de•port•ment (di pôrt′mənt, -pōrt′-), *n.* **1.** demeanor; conduct; behavior. **2.** the conduct or obedience of a child in school, as graded by a teacher. [1595–1605; < F *déportement,* equiv. to *déporte(r)* (see DEPORT) + *-ment* -MENT]
—**Syn.** See **behavior.**

de•pos•al (di pō′zəl), *n.* an act of deposing. [1350–1400; ME; see DEPOSE, -AL[2]]

de•pose (di pōz′), *v.,* **-posed, -pos•ing.** —*v.t.* **1.** to remove from office or position, esp. high office: *The people deposed the dictator.* **2.** to testify or affirm under oath, esp. in a written statement: *to depose that it was true.* —*v.i.* **3.** to give sworn testimony, esp. in writing. [1250–1300; ME *deposen* < OF *deposer* to put down, equiv. to *de-* DE- + *poser* < VL **posāre,* LL *pausāre;* see POSE[1]] —**de•pos′a•ble,** *adj.* —**de•pos′er,** *n.*

de•pos•it (di poz′it), *v.t.* **1.** to place for safekeeping or in trust, esp. in a bank account: *He deposited his paycheck every Friday.* **2.** to give as security or in part payment. **3.** to deliver and leave (an item): *Please deposit your returned books with the librarian.* **4.** to insert (a coin) in a coin-operated device: *Deposit a quarter and push the button.* **5.** to put, place, or set down, esp. carefully or exactly: *She deposited the baby in the crib.* **6.** to lay or throw down by a natural process; precipitate: *The river deposited soil at its mouth.* —*v.i.* **7.** to be placed, inserted, precipitated, left for safekeeping, given as security or in partial payment, etc. —*n.* **8.** money placed in a bank account or an instance of placing money in a bank account. **9.** anything given as security or in part payment: *The boy returned the bottle and got his five-cent deposit back. They made a deposit on the house and signed a ten-year mortgage.* **10.** anything laid away or entrusted to another for safekeeping: *A large deposit of jewels was stolen from the hotel safe.* **11.** a place for safekeeping; depository. **12.** something precipitated, delivered and left, or thrown down, as by a natural process: *a deposit of soil.* **13.** the natural sediment of wine in a bottle. **14.** a coating of metal deposited on something, usually by an electric current. **15.** a natural accumulation or occurrence, esp. of oil or ore: *a mountain range with many rich deposits of gold.* [1615–25; < L *dēpositus* laid down, ptp. of *dēpōnere;* see DEPONE]
—**Syn. 1.** bank, save, store. **15.** lode, vein, pocket.

de•pos•i•tar•y (di poz′i ter′ē), *n., pl.* **-tar•ies. 1.** one to whom anything is given in trust. **2.** depository (def. 1). —*adj.* **3.** depository (def. 3). [1595–1605; < LL *dēpositārius* a trustee, equiv. to L *dēposit(us)* (see DEPOSIT) + *-ārius* -ARY]

dep•o•si•tion (dep′ə zish′ən, dē′pə-), *n.* **1.** removal from an office or position. **2.** the act or process of depositing: *deposition of the documents with the Library of Congress.* **3.** the state of being deposited or precipitated: *deposition of soil at the mouth of a river.* **4.** something that is deposited. **5.** *Law.* **a.** the giving of testimony under oath. **b.** the testimony so given. **c.** a statement under oath, taken down in writing, to be used in court in place of the spoken testimony of the witness. **6.** *Eccles.* **a.** the interment of the body of a saint. **b.** the reinterment of the body or the relics of a saint. **7.** (*cap.*) a work of art depicting Christ being lowered from the Cross. [1350–1400; ME (< AF) < LL *dēpositiōn-* (s. of *dēpositiō*) a putting aside, testimony, burial, equiv. to L *dēposit(us)* laid down (see DEPOSIT) + *-iōn-* -ION] —**dep′o•si′tion•al,** *adj.*

depos′it mon′ey, *Banking.* checks, letters of credit, etc., that circulate and are payable on demand. [1815–25]

de•pos•i•tor (di poz′i tər), *n.* **1.** a person or thing that deposits. **2.** a person who deposits money in a bank or who has a bank account. [1555–65; < LL, equiv. to L *dēposi-,* var. s. of *dēpōnere* (see DEPONE) + *-tor* -TOR]

de•pos•i•to•ry (di poz′i tôr′ē, -tōr′ē), *n., pl.* **-ries. 1.** a place where something is deposited or stored, as for safekeeping: *the night depository of a bank.* **2.** a depositary; trustee. —*adj.* **3.** of or pertaining to a depository or depositories: *the depository role of a bank.* [1650–60; (def. 1) < ML *dēpositōrium;* (def. 2) DEPOSIT + -ORY[1] (n. use of adj. suffix)]

depos′itory li′brary, a library designated by law to receive without charge all or a selection of the official publications of a government. [1925–30]

depos′it slip′, a slip for listing deposits made to a bank account. Also called **credit slip.** [1900–05]

de•pot (dē′pō; *Mil. or Brit.* dep′ō), *n.* **1.** a railroad station. **2.** a bus station. **3.** *Mil.* **a.** a place in which supplies and materials are stored for distribution. **b.** (formerly) a place where recruits are assembled for classification, initial training, and assignment to active units. **4.** a storehouse or warehouse, as a building where freight is deposited. **5.** *Physiol.* a place where body products not actively involved in metabolic processes are accumulated, deposited, or stored. [1785–95; < F *dépôt* < L *dēpositum,* n. use of neut. of *dēpositus;* see DEPOSIT]
—**Syn. 1, 2.** terminal.

depr., **1.** depreciation. **2.** depression.

de•prave (di prāv′), *v.t.,* **-praved, -prav•ing. 1.** to make morally bad or evil; vitiate; corrupt. **2.** *Obs.* to defame. [1325–75; ME *depraven* (< AF) < L *dēprāvāre* to pervert, corrupt, equiv. to *dē-* DE- + *prāv(us)* crooked + *-āre* inf. suffix] —**dep•ra•va•tion** (dep′rə vā′shən), *n.* —**de•prav′er,** *n.* —**de•prav′ing•ly,** *adv.*

de•praved (di prāvd′), *adj.* corrupt, wicked, or perverted. [1585–95; DEPRAVE + -ED[2]] —**de•praved•ly** (di-prāvd′lē, -prā′vid-), *adv.* —**de•praved′ness,** *n.*
—**Syn.** evil, sinful, debased, reprobate, degenerate; dissolute, profligate; licentious, lewd. See **immoral.**

de•prav•i•ty (di prav′i tē), *n., pl.* **-ties** for 2. **1.** the state of being depraved. **2.** a depraved act or practice. [1635–45; DEPRAVE + -ITY]

dep•re•cate (dep′ri kāt′), *v.t.,* **-cat•ed, -cat•ing. 1.** to express earnest disapproval of. **2.** to urge reasons against; protest against (a scheme, purpose, etc.). **3.** to depreciate; belittle. **4.** *Archaic.* to pray for deliverance from. [1615–25; < L *dēprecātus* prayed against, warded off (ptp. of *dēprecārī*), equiv. to *dē-* DE- + *prec(ārī)* to PRAY + *-ātus* -ATE[1]] —**dep′re•cat′ing•ly,** *adv.* —**dep′re•ca′tion,** *n.* —**dep′re•ca′tor,** *n.*
—**Syn. 1.** condemn, denounce, disparage. See **decry.**
—**Usage.** An early and still the most current sense of DEPRECATE is "to express disapproval of." In a sense development still occasionally criticized by a few, DEPRECATE has come to be synonymous with the similar but etymologically unrelated word DEPRECIATE in the sense "belittle": *The author modestly deprecated the importance of his work.* In compounds with *self-,* DEPRECATE has almost totally replaced DEPRECIATE in modern usage: *Her self-deprecating account of her career both amused and charmed the audience.*

dep•re•ca•tive (dep′ri kā′tiv, -kə tiv), *adj.* serving to deprecate; deprecatory. [1480–90; (< AF) < LL *dēprecātīvus,* equiv. to *dēprecāt(us)* (see DEPRECATE) + *-īvus* -IVE] —**dep′re•ca′tive•ly,** *adv.*

dep•re•ca•to•ry (dep′ri kə tôr′ē, -tōr′ē), *adj.* **1.** of the nature of or expressing disapproval, protest, or depreciation. **2.** apologetic; making apology. [1580–90; < LL *dēprecātōrius,* equiv. to L *dēprecā(rī)* (see DEPRECATE) + *-tōrius* -TORY[1]] —**dep′re•ca•to′ri•ly,** *adv.* —**dep′re•ca•to′ri•ness,** *n.*

de•pre•ci•a•ble (di prē′shē ə bəl, -shə bəl), *adj.* **1.** capable of depreciating or being depreciated in value. **2.** capable of being depreciated for tax purposes. [DEPRECI(ATE) + -ABLE]

de•pre•ci•ate (di prē′shē āt′), *v.,* **-at•ed, -at•ing.** —*v.t.* **1.** to reduce the purchasing value of (money). **2.** to lessen the value or price of. **3.** to claim depreciation on (a property) for tax purposes. **4.** to represent as of little value or merit; belittle. —*v.i.* **5.** to decline in value. [1640–50; < LL *dēpretiātus* undervalued (ptp. of *dēpretiāre,* in ML sp. *depreciāre*), equiv. to L *dē-* DE- + *preti(um)* PRICE + *-ātus* -ATE[1]] —**de•pre′ci•at′ing•ly,** *adv.* —**de•pre′ci•a′tor,** *n.*
—**Syn. 4.** disparage, decry, minimize.
—**Usage. 4.** See **deprecate.**

de•pre•ci•a•tion (di prē′shē ā′shən), *n.* **1.** decrease in value due to wear and tear, decay, decline in price, etc. **2.** such a decrease as allowed in computing the value of property for tax purposes. **3.** a decrease in the purchasing or exchange value of money. **4.** a lowering in estimation. [1730–40, *Amer.*; DEPRECIATE + -ION]

de•pre•ci•a•to•ry (di prē′shē ə tôr′ē, -tōr′ē, -prē′-shə-), *adj.* tending to depreciate. Also, **de•pre•ci•a•tive** (di prē′shē ā′tiv, -shə tiv). [1795–1805; DEPRECIATE + -ORY[1]] —**de•pre′ci•a•tive•ly,** *adv.*

dep•re•date (dep′ri dāt′), *v.,* **-dat•ed, -dat•ing.** —*v.t.* **1.** to plunder or lay waste to; prey upon; pillage; ravage. —*v.i.* **2.** to plunder; pillage. [1620–30; < LL *dēpraedātus* plundered (ptp. of *depraedārī*), equiv. to L *dē-* DE- + *praed(ārī)* to plunder (see PREY) + *-ātus* -ATE[1]] —**dep′re•da′tor,** *n.* —**dep•re•da•to•ry** (dep′ri dā′tə rē, di-pred′ə tôr′ē, -tōr′ē), *adj.*

dep•re•da•tion (dep′ri dā′shən), *n.* the act of preying upon or plundering; robbery; ravage. [1475–85; < LL *dēpraedātiōn-* (s. of *dēpraedātiō*) a plundering, equiv. to *dēpraedāt(us)* (see DEPREDATE) + *-iōn-* -ION] —**dep′re•da′tion•ist,** *n.*

de•press (di pres′), *v.t.* **1.** to make sad or gloomy; lower in spirits; deject; dispirit. **2.** to lower in force, vigor, activity, etc.; weaken; make dull. **3.** to lower in amount or value. **4.** to put into a lower position: *to depress the muzzle of a gun.* **5.** to press down. **6.** *Music.* to lower in pitch. [1275–1325; ME *depressen* < AF, OF *depresser* < L *dēpressus* pressed down (ptp. of *dēprimere,* equiv. to *dē-* DE- + *-primere,* comb. form of *premere* to press); see PRESSURE] —**de•press′i•ble,** *adj.* —**de•press′i•bil′i•ty,** *n.*
—**Syn. 1.** dishearten, discourage, sadden. See **oppress. 3.** devalue, cheapen. —**Ant. 4.** raise, elevate.

de•pres•sant (di pres′ənt), *adj.* **1.** *Med.* having the quality of depressing or lowering the vital activities; sedative. **2.** causing a lowering in spirits; dejecting. **3.** causing a drop in value; economically depressing. —*n.* **4.** *Med.* a sedative. Cf. **stimulant** (def. 1). **5.** *Chem.* any agent capable of diminishing a specific property of a substance. [1875–80; DEPRESS + -ANT]

de•pressed (di prest′), *adj.* **1.** sad and gloomy; dejected; downcast. **2.** pressed down, or situated lower than the general surface. **3.** lowered in force, amount, etc. **4.** undergoing economic hardship, esp. poverty and unemployment. **5.** being or measured below the standard or norm. **6.** *Bot., Zool.* flattened down; greater in width than in height. **7.** *Psychiatry.* suffering from depression. [1375–1425; late ME; see DEPRESS, -ED[2]]
—**Syn. 1.** saddened, morose, despondent, miserable; blue; morbid. —**Ant. 1.** happy.

depressed′ ar′ea, a region where unemployment and a low standard of living prevail. [1925–30]

de•press•ing (di pres′ing), *adj.* serving to depress; inducing a state of depression: *depressing news.* [1780–90; DEPRESS + -ING[2]] —**de•press′ing•ly,** *adv.*

de•pres•sion (di presh′ən), *n.* **1.** the act of depressing. **2.** the state of being depressed. **3.** a depressed or sunken place or part; an area lower than the surrounding surface. **4.** sadness; gloom; dejection. **5.** *Psychiatry.* a condition of general emotional dejection and withdrawal; sadness greater and more prolonged than that warranted by any objective reason. Cf. **clinical depression. 6.** dullness or inactivity, as of trade. **7.** *Econ.* a period during which business, employment, and stock-market values decline severely or remain at a very low level of activity. **8. the Depression.** See **Great Depression. 9.** *Pathol.* a low state of vital powers or functional activity. **10.** *Astron.* the angular distance of a celestial body below the horizon; negative altitude. **11.** *Survey.* the angle between the line from an observer or instrument to an object below either of them and a horizontal line. **12.** *Phys. Geog.* an area completely or mostly surrounded by higher land, ordinarily having interior drainage and not conforming to the valley of a single stream. **13.** *Meteorol.* an area of low atmospheric pressure. [1350–1400; ME (< AF) < ML *dēpressiōn-* (s. of *dēpressiō*), LL: a pressing down, equiv. to L *dēpress(us)* (see DEPRESS) + *-iōn-* -ION]
—**Syn. 4.** discouragement, despondency.

Depres′sion glass′, inexpensive, machine-pressed, usually translucent glassware, including dishware, vases, etc., mass-produced in the U.S. from the late 1920's to the 1940's and often used as giveaways, as to induce customers to buy goods or movie tickets.

de•pres•sive (di pres′iv), *adj.* **1.** tending to depress. **2.** characterized by depression, esp. mental depression. —*n.* **3.** a person suffering from a depressive illness. [1610–20; DEPRESS + -IVE] —**de•pres′sive•ly,** *adv.* —**de•pres′sive•ness,** *n.*

de•pres•so•mo•tor (di pres′ō mō′tər), *adj. Physiol., Med.* causing a retardation of motor activity: *depressomotor nerves.* [DEPRESS + -O- + MOTOR]

de•pres•sor (di pres′ər), *n.* **1.** a person or thing that depresses. **2.** *Surg.* an instrument for pressing down a protruding part, as a tongue depressor. **3.** *Anat.* **a.** a muscle that draws down a part of the body, as the corner of the mouth. Cf. **levator. b.** Also called **depres′sor nerve′.** a nerve that, when stimulated, induces a decrease in activity, as a slowed heartbeat. [1605–15; < LL, deriv. of L *dēprimere* (see DEPRESS, -TOR)]

de•pres•sur•ize (dē presh′ə rīz′), *v.,* **-ized, -iz•ing.** —*v.t.* **1.** to remove the air pressure from (a pressurized compartment of an aircraft or spacecraft). **2.** to relieve the tensions of; cause to relax: *A week's vacation should depressurize me.* —*v.i.* **3.** to lose air pressure: *The airplane cabin depressurized almost instantly.* Also, *esp. Brit.,* **de•pres′sur•ise′.** [1940–45; DE- + PRESSURIZE] —**de•pres′sur•i•za′tion,** *n.* —**de•pres′sur•iz′er,** *n.*

dep•ri•va•tion (dep′rə vā′shən), *n.* **1.** the act of depriving. **2.** the fact of being deprived. **3.** dispossession; loss. **4.** removal from ecclesiastical office. **5.** privation. [1525–35; < ML *dēprīvātiōn-* (s. of *dēprīvātiō*), equiv. to *dēprīvāt(us)* deprived (ptp. of *dēprīvāre;* see DEPRIVE, -ATE[1]) + *-iōn-* -ION]

de•prive (di prīv′), *v.t.,* **-prived, -priv•ing. 1.** to remove or withhold something from the enjoyment or possession of (a person or persons): *to deprive a man of life; to deprive a baby of candy.* **2.** to remove from ecclesiastical office. [1275–1325; ME *depriven* < AF, OF *depriver* < ML *dēprīvāre,* equiv. to L *dē-* DE- + *prīvāre* to deprive (*prīv(us)* PRIVATE + *-āre* inf. suffix)] —**de•priv′a•ble,** *adj.* —**de•priv′al,** *n.* —**de•priv•a•tive** (di priv′ə-tiv), *adj.* —**de•priv′er,** *n.*
—**Syn. 1.** See **strip.**

de•prived (di prīvd′), *adj.* marked by deprivation; lacking the necessities of life, as adequate food and shelter: *a deprived childhood.* [1545–55; DEPRIVE + -ED[2]]

de•pro•fes•sion•al•ize (dē′prə fesh′ə nl īz′), *v.t.,* **-ized, -iz•ing. 1.** to remove from professional control, influence, manipulation, etc. **2.** to cause to appear or become unprofessional; discredit or deprive of professional status: *a campaign to deprofessionalize the nation's doctors.* Also, *esp. Brit.,* **de′pro•fes′sion•al•ise′.** [1880–85; DE- + PROFESSIONALIZE]

de pro•fun•dis (dā prō fo͝on′dis), *Latin.* out of the depths (of sorrow, despair, etc.).

de•pro•gram (dē prō′gram), *v.t.,* **-grammed** or **-gramed, -gram•ming** or **-gram•ing. 1.** to free a convert) from the influence of a religious cult, political indoctrination, etc., by intensive persuasion or reeducation. **2.** to retrain, as for the purpose of eliminating or replacing a learned or acquired behavior pattern or habit that is undesirable or unsuitable. [1970–75, *Amer.*; DE- + PROGRAM] —**de•pro′gram•mer, de•pro′gram•er,** *n.*

dep•side (dep′sīd, -sid), *n. Chem.* any of a group of

CONCISE PRONUNCIATION KEY: *act, cāpe, dâre, pärt; set, ēqual; if, īce; ox, ōver, ôrder, oil, bo͝ok, bo͞ot, out; up, ûrge; child; sing; shoe; thin, that;* zh *as in treasure.* ə = *a* as in *alone, e* as in *system, i* as in *easily, o* as in *gallop, u* as in *circus;* ᵊ as in *fire* (fīᵊr), *hour* (ouᵊr). l and n can serve as syllabic consonants, as in *cradle* (krād′l), and *button* (but′n). See the full key inside the front cover.

esters formed from two or more phenol carboxylic acid molecules. [1905–10; < Gk *déps(ein)* to tan, soften + -IDE]

dept., **1.** department. **2.** deponent. **3.** deputy.

Dept·ford (det′fərd), *n.* a former borough of London, England, now part of Lewisham, S of the Thames River.

Dept′ford pink′, a plant, *Dianthus armeria,* of the pink family, native to Eurasia, having slender, erect stems and leaves and clusters of small, bright pink flowers. [1655–65; appar. after DEPTFORD]

depth (depth), *n.* **1.** a dimension taken through an object or body of material, usually downward from an upper surface, horizontally inward from an outer surface, or from top to bottom of something regarded as one of several layers. **2.** the quality of being deep; deepness. **3.** complexity or obscurity, as of a subject: *a question of great depth.* **4.** gravity; seriousness. **5.** emotional profundity: *the depth of someone's feelings.* **6.** intensity, as of silence, color, etc. **7.** lowness of tonal pitch: *the depth of a voice.* **8.** the amount of knowledge, intelligence, wisdom, insight, feeling, etc., present in a person's mind or evident either in some product of the mind, as a learned paper, argument, work of art, etc., or in the person's behavior. **9.** a high degree of such knowledge, insight, etc. **10.** Often, **depths.** a deep part or place: *from the depths of the ocean.* **11.** an unfathomable space; abyss: *the depth of time.* **12.** Sometimes, **depths.** the farthest, innermost, or extreme part or state: *the depth of space; the depths of the forest; the depths of despair.* **13.** Usually, **depths.** a low intellectual or moral condition: *How could he sink to such depths?* **14.** the part of greatest intensity, as of night or winter. **15.** *Sports.* the strength of a team in terms of the number and quality of its substitute players: *With no depth in the infield, an injury to any of the regulars would be costly.* **16. in depth,** extensively or thoroughly: *Make a survey in depth of the conditions.* **17. out of** or **beyond one's depth. a.** in water deeper than one's height or too deep for one's safety. **b.** beyond one's knowledge or capability: *The child is being taught subjects that are beyond his depth.* [1350–1400; ME *depthe,* equiv. to *dep* (OE *dēop* DEEP) + *-the* -TH[1]] —**depth′less,** *adj.*
—**Ant. 2.** shallowness. **9.** superficiality.

depth′ charge′, an explosive device that is used against submarines and other underwater targets, and is usually set to detonate at a predetermined depth. Also called **depth′ bomb′.** [1915–20]

depth′ of field′, *Optics, Photog.* the range of distances along the axis of an optical instrument, usually a camera lens, through which an object will produce a relatively distinct image. Also called **depth′ of fo′cus.** [1910–15]

depth′ percep′tion, the ability of an observer to judge the spatial relationships of objects, esp. their relative distance from the observer and from one another. [1905–10]

depth′ psychol′ogy, any approach to psychology that postulates and studies personality from the standpoint of dynamic and unconscious motivation. [1925–30]

dep·u·rate (dep′yə rāt′), *v.t., v.i.,* **-rat·ed, -rat·ing.** to make or become free from impurities. [1610–20; < ML *dēpūrātus* purified (ptp. of *dēpūrāre*), equiv. to L *dē-* DE- *pūr(us)* PURE + *-ātus* -ATE[1]] —**dep′u·ra′tion,** *n.* —**dep′u·ra′tor,** *n.*

dep·u·ra·tive (dep′yə rā′tiv), *adj.* **1.** serving to depurate; purifying. —*n.* **2.** a depurative agent or substance. [1675–85; DEPURATE + -IVE]

dep·u·ta·tion (dep′yə tā′shən), *n.* **1.** the act of appointing a person or persons to represent or act for another or others. **2.** the person or body of persons so appointed or authorized. [1350–1400; ME *deputacioun* < ML *dēputātiōn-* (s. of *dēputātiō*), LL: delegation, equiv. to *dēputāt(us)* (ptp. of *dēputāre;* see DEPUTE, -ATE[1]) + *-iōn-* -ION]

de·pute (də pyōōt′), *v.t.,* **-put·ed, -put·ing. 1.** to appoint as one's substitute, representative, or agent. **2.** to assign (authority, a function, etc.) to a deputy. [1350–1400; ME *deputen* < AF, OF *deputer* to assign < LL *dēputāre* to allot, L: to consider, equiv. to *dē-* DE- + *putāre* to think] —**dep·u·ta·ble** (dep′yə tə bəl, də pyōō′-), *adj.*

dep·u·tize (dep′yə tīz′), *v.,* **-tized, -tiz·ing.** —*v.t.* **1.** to appoint as deputy. —*v.i.* **2.** to act as a deputy; substitute. Also, *esp. Brit.,* **dep′u·tise′.** [1720–30; DEPUT(Y) + -IZE] —**dep′u·ti·za′tion,** *n.*

dep·u·ty (dep′yə tē), *n., pl.* **-ties. 1.** a person appointed or authorized to act as a substitute for another or others. **2.** See **deputy sheriff. 3.** a person appointed or elected as assistant to a public official, serving as successor in the event of a vacancy. **4.** a person representing a constituency in certain legislative bodies. —*adj.* **5.** appointed, elected, or serving as an assistant or second-in-command. [1375–1425; late ME *depute* < OF, n. use of ptp. of *deputer* to DEPUTE] —**dep′u·ty·ship′,** *n.*
—**Syn. 1.** agent, representative, surrogate, envoy, emissary, proxy.

dep′uty sher′iff, a peace officer subordinate to a sheriff. [1665–75]

De Quin·cey (di kwin′sē), **Thomas,** 1785–1859, English essayist.

der., 1. derivation. **2.** derivative. **3.** derive. **4.** derived.

de·rac·in·ate (di ras′ə nāt′), *v.t.,* **-nat·ed, -nat·ing. 1.** to pull up by the roots; uproot; extirpate; eradicate. **2.** to isolate or alienate (a person) from a native or customary culture or environment. [1590–1600; < F *déracin(er)* (equiv. to *dé-* DIS-[1] + *-raciner,* v. deriv. of *racine* root < LL *rādīcīna* for L *rādīc-,* s. of *rādix*) + -ATE[1]] —**de·rac′i·na′tion,** *n.*

de·rad·i·cal·ize (dē rad′i kə līz′), *v.t.,* **-ized, -iz·ing.** to free from radical ideas, goals, or elements: *The more conservative politicians were trying to deradicalize the liberation movement.* Also, *esp. Brit.,* **de·rad′i·cal·ise′.** [1970–75; DE- + RADICAL + -IZE] —**de·rad′i·cal·i·za′tion,** *n.*

de·rail (dē rāl′), *v.t.* **1.** to cause (a train, streetcar, etc.) to run off the rails of a track. **2.** to cause to fail or become deflected from a purpose; reduce or delay the chances for success or development of: *Being drafted into the army derailed his career for two years.* —*v.i.* **3.** (of a train, streetcar, etc.) to run off the rails of a track. **4.** to become derailed; go astray. —*n.* **5.** a track device for derailing rolling stock in an emergency. [1840–50; < F *dérailler,* equiv. to *dé-* DIS-[1] + *-railler,* v. deriv. of *rail* RAIL[1] (< E)]

de·rail·leur (di rā′lər), *n.* a gear-shifting mechanism on a bicycle that shifts the drive chain from one sprocket wheel to another. [1945–50; < F *dérailleur* lit., a device causing disengagement or derailing, equiv. to *déraill(er)* to DERAIL + *-eur* -EUR]

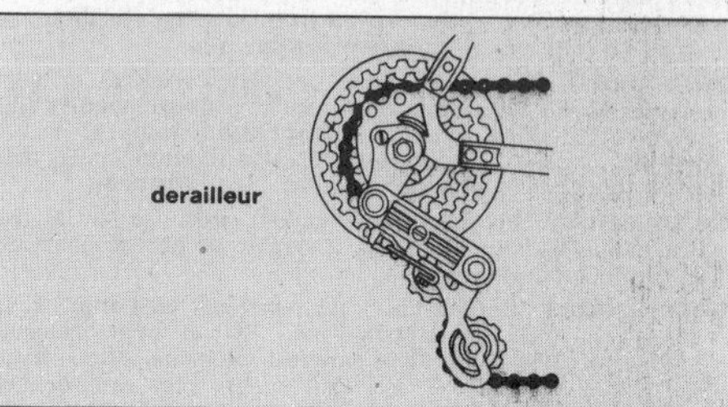

de·rail·ment (dē rāl′mənt), *n.* **1.** the act or process of derailing. **2.** *Psychiatry.* See **loosening of associations.** [1940–45; DERAIL + -MENT, or < F *déraillement*]

De·rain (də RAN′), *n.* **An·dré** (äN drā′), 1880–1954, French painter.

de·range (di rānj′), *v.t.,* **-ranged, -rang·ing. 1.** to throw into disorder; disarrange. **2.** to disturb the condition, action, or function of. **3.** to make insane. [1770–80; < F *déranger,* OF *desrengier,* equiv. to *des-* DIS-[1] + *rengier;* see RANGE] —**de·range′a·ble,** *adj.* —**de·rang′er,** *n.*

de·ranged (di rānjd′), *adj.* **1.** insane. **2.** disordered; disarranged. [1780–90; DERANGE + -ED[2]]

de·range·ment (di rānj′mənt), *n.* **1.** the act of deranging. **2.** insanity. **3.** disarrangement; disorder. [1730–40; < F *dérangement.* See DERANGE, -MENT]

de·ra·tion (dē rā′shən), *v.t.* to discontinue the rationing of (something). [1915–20; DE- + RATION]

de·rat·i·za·tion (dē rat′ə zā′shən), *n.* extermination of rats, esp. aboard a merchant vessel. [1910–15; DERATIZE + -ATION]

de·rat·ize (dē rat′īz), *v.t.,* **-ized, -izing.** to carry out the deratization of. Also, *esp. Brit.,* **de·rat′ise.** [DE- + RAT + -IZE]

Der·bent (dər bent′; *Russ.* dyiʀ byent′), *n.* a seaport in the SW RSFSR in the S Soviet Union in Europe, on the Caspian Sea. 69,000.

Der·by (dûr′bē; *Brit.* där′bē), *n., pl.* **-bies. 1.** a race for three-year-old horses that is run annually at Epsom Downs, near London, England: first run in 1780. **2.** any of certain other important annual horse races, usually for three-year-old horses, esp. the Kentucky Derby. **3.** (*l.c.*) a race or contest, usually one open to all who wish to enter and offering a prize for the winner. **4.** (*l.c.*) any endeavor or venture regarded as a competition: *to win the gubernatorial derby.* **5.** (*l.c.*) Also called **bowler.** a stiff felt hat with rounded crown and narrow brim, worn chiefly by men. [1830–40; after Edward Stanley, 12th Earl of *Derby* (d. 1834), who instituted the race]

Der·by (dûr′bē; *for 1, 2 also Brit.* där′bē), *n.* **1.** a city in Derbyshire, in central England. 215,200. **2.** Derbyshire. **3.** a city in S Connecticut. 12,346.

Der·by·shire (dûr′bē shēr′, -shər; *Brit.* där′bi shēr′, -shər), *n.* a county in central England. 887,400; 1060 sq. mi. (2630 sq. km). Also called **Derby.**

Der′byshire chair′, *Eng. Furniture* a chair of the mid-17th century, made of oak, usually without arms, and having a back of two carved rails between square uprights. Also called **Yorkshire chair.**

dere (dēr), *adj.* dear[2].

de·re·al·i·za·tion (dē rē′ə lə zā′shən), *n. Psychiatry.* an alteration in perception leading to the feeling that the reality of the world has been changed or lost. [1940–45; DE- + REALIZATION, orig. in the phrase *feeling of derealization,* as trans. of G *Entfremdungsgefühl* (Freud)]

de·rec·og·nize (dē rek′əg nīz′), *v.t.,* **-nized, -niz·ing.** to withdraw diplomatic recognition from: *to derecognize a foreign government.* Also, *esp. Brit.,* **de·rec′og·nise′.** [1945–50; DE- + RECOGNIZE]

de·reg·u·late (dē reg′yə lāt′), *v.,* **-lat·ed, -lat·ing.** —*v.t.* **1.** to remove government regulatory controls from (an industry, a commodity, etc.): *to deregulate the trucking industry; to deregulate oil prices.* —*v.i.* **2.** to undergo deregulation: *Some banks have already started to deregulate.* [1960–65, *Amer.;* DE- + REGULATE] —**de·reg′u·la′tion,** *n.* —**de·reg′u·la′tor,** *n.* —**de·reg·u·la·to·ry** (dē reg′yə lə tôr′ē, -tōr′ē), *adj.*

de·re·ism (dē rē′iz əm, dā rā′-), *n. Psychol.* autism. [< L *dē rē,* lit., away from the matter + -ISM] —**de′re·is′tic,** *adj.* —**de′re·is′ti·cal·ly,** *adv.*

Der·ek (der′ik), *n.* a male given name.

der·e·lict (der′ə likt), *adj.* **1.** left or deserted, as by the owner or guardian; abandoned: *a derelict ship.* **2.** neglectful of duty; delinquent; negligent. —*n.* **3.** a person abandoned by society, esp. a person without a permanent home and means of support; vagrant; bum. **4.** *Naut.* a vessel abandoned in open water by its crew without any hope or intention of returning. **5.** personal property abandoned or thrown away by the owner. **6.** one guilty of neglect of duty. **7.** *Law.* land left dry by a change of the water line. [1640–50; < L *dērelictus* forsaken (ptp. of *dērelinquere*), equiv. to *dē-* DE- + *relictus* ptp. of *relinquere* to leave, abandon; see RELINQUISH] —**der′e·lict·ly,** *adv.* —**der′e·lict·ness,** *n.*
—**Syn. 2.** remiss, careless, heedless.

der·e·lic·tion (der′ə lik′shən), *n.* **1.** deliberate or conscious neglect; negligence; delinquency: *dereliction of duty.* **2.** the act of abandoning something. **3.** the state of being abandoned. **4.** *Law.* a leaving dry of land by recession of the water line. [1590–1600; < L *dērelictiōn-* (s. of *dērelictiō*) an abandoning, equiv. to *dērelict(us)* (see DERELICT) + *-iōn-* -ION]
—**Syn. 1.** See **neglect. 2.** desertion.

de·re·press (dē′ri pres′), *v.t. Genetics.* induce (def. 5). [1960–65; DE- + REPRESS] —**de·re·pres·sion** (dē′ri presh′ən), *n.*

de·req·ui·si·tion (dē rek′wə zish′ən), *Brit.* —*n.* **1.** a freeing of requisitioned property, esp. from military to civilian control. —*v.i.* **2.** to free requisitioned property. —*v.t.* **3.** to return (something that has been requisitioned by the military) to civilian control. [1940–45; DE- + REQUISITION]

De Rid·der (də rid′ər), a town in W Louisiana. 11,057.

de·ride (di rīd′), *v.t.,* **-rid·ed, -rid·ing.** to laugh at in scorn or contempt; scoff or jeer at; mock. [1520–30; < L *dērīdēre* to mock, equiv. to *dē-* DE- + *rīdēre* to laugh] —**de·rid′er,** *n.* —**de·rid′ing·ly,** *adv.*
—**Syn.** taunt, flout, gibe, banter, rally. See **ridicule.**

de ri·gueur (də ri gûr′; *Fr.* də ʀē gœʀ′), strictly required, as by etiquette, usage, or fashion. [1825–35; < F]

der·in·ger (der′in jər), *n.* derringer.

de·ri·sion (di rizh′ən), *n.* **1.** ridicule; mockery: *The inept performance elicited derision from the audience.* **2.** an object of ridicule. [1350–1400; ME *derisioun* < OF *derision* < LL *dērīsiōn-* (s. of *dērīsiō*), equiv. to L *dērī-s(us)* mocked (ptp. of *dērīdēre;* see DERIDE) + *-iōn-* -ION] —**de·ris·i·ble** (di riz′ə bəl), *adj.*

de·ri·sive (di rī′siv), *adj.* characterized by or expressing derision; contemptuous; mocking: *derisive heckling.* Also, **de·ri·so·ry** (di rī′sə rē, -zə-). [1655–65; DERIS(ION) + -IVE] —**de·ri′sive·ly,** *adv.* —**de·ri′sive·ness,** *n.*

deriv., 1. derivation. **2.** derivative. **3.** derive. **4.** derived.

der·i·va·tion (der′ə vā′shən), *n.* **1.** the act or fact of deriving or of being derived. **2.** the process of deriving. **3.** the source from which something is derived; origin. **4.** something that is or has been derived; derivative. **5.** *Math.* **a.** development of a theorem. **b.** differentiation. **6.** *Gram.* **a.** the process or device of adding affixes to or changing the shape of a base, thereby assigning the result to a form class that may undergo further inflection or participate in different syntactic constructions, as in forming *service* from *serve, song* from *sing,* and *hardness* from *hard* (contrasted with *inflection*). **b.** the systematic description of such processes in a given language. **7.** *Ling.* **a.** a set of forms, including the initial form, intermediate forms, and final form, showing the successive stages in the generation of a sentence as the rules of a generative grammar are applied to it. **b.** the process by which such a set of forms is derived. [1375–1425; late ME *derivacioun* < L *dērīvātiōn-* (s. of *dērīvātiō*) a turning away, equiv. to *dērīvāt(us)* (ptp. of *dērīvāre;* see DERIVE, -ATE[1]) + *-iōn-* -ION] —**der′i·va′tion·al,** *adj.* —**der′i·va′tion·al·ly,** *adv.*

de·riv·a·tive (di riv′ə tiv), *adj.* **1.** derived. **2.** not original; secondary. —*n.* **3.** something derived. **4.** Also called **derived form.** *Gram.* a form that has undergone derivation from another, as *atomic* from *atom.* **5.** *Chem.* a substance or compound obtained from, or regarded as derived from, another substance or compound. **6.** Also called **differential quotient;** *esp. Brit.,* **differential coefficient.** *Math.* the limit of the ratio of the increment of a function to the increment of a variable in it, as the latter tends to 0; the instantaneous change of one quantity with respect to another, as velocity, which is the instantaneous change of distance with respect to time. Cf. **first derivative, second derivative.** [1400–50; late ME *derivatif* < LL *dērīvātīvus,* equiv. to L *dērīvāt(us)* (see DERIVATION) + *-īvus* -IVE] —**de·riv′a·tive·ly,** *adv.* —**de·riv′a·tive·ness,** *n.*

de·rive (di rīv′), *v.,* **-rived, -riv·ing.** —*v.t.* **1.** to receive or obtain from a source or origin (usually fol. by *from*). **2.** to trace from a source or origin. **3.** to reach or obtain by reasoning; deduce; infer. **4.** *Chem.* to produce or obtain (a substance) from another. —*v.i.* **5.** to come from a source or origin; originate (often fol. by *from*). [1350–1400; ME *diriven, deriven* to flow, draw from, spring < AF, OF *deriver* < L *dērīvāre* to lead off, equiv. to *dē-* DE- + *rīv(us)* a stream + *-āre* inf. suffix] —**de·riv′a·ble,** *adj.* —**de·riv′er,** *n.*
—**Syn. 1.** gain, attain, glean, gather, reap, net.

derived′ curve′, *Math.* a curve whose equation is the derivative of the equation of a given curve.

derived′ form′, derivative (def. 4).

derived′ u′nit, (in physics, chemistry, etc.) a unit derived from fundamental units of length, mass, and time.

Der·leth (dûr′leth, -ləth), *n.* **August (William),** 1909–71, U.S. novelist, poet, and short-story writer.

derm (dûrm), *n.* a navigational device for making a nearby object conspicuous on a radarscope. [*d(elayed) e(cho) r(adar) m(arker)*]

derm-, var. of **dermato-** before a vowel: *dermoid.*

-derm, var. of **-dermatous,** usually with nouns (*melanoderm; pachyderm*), or var. of **-dermis** (*blastoderm; ectoderm; mesoderm*). [prob. < F *-derme* (< Gk *-dermos*

CONCISE ETYMOLOGY KEY: <, descended or borrowed from; >, whence; b., blend of, blended; c., cognate with; cf., compare; deriv., derivative; equiv., equivalent; imit., imitative; obl., oblique; r., replacing; s., stem; sp., spelling, spelled; resp., respelling, respelled; trans., translation; ?, origin unknown; *, unattested; ‡, probably earlier than. See the full key inside the front cover.

-skinned, adj. deriv. of *dérma* skin; or < *-dermis* -DERMIS); or directly < Gk *-dermos*]

der·ma[1] (dûr′mə), *n. Anat., Zool.* dermis. [1825–35; NL < Gk *dérma* skin, equiv. to *dér(ein)* to skin + *-ma* n. suffix]

der·ma[2] (dûr′mə), *n.* **1.** beef or fowl intestine used as a casing in preparing certain savory dishes, esp. kishke. **2.** kishke. [< Yiddish *derme,* pl. of *darm* intestine < MHG; akin to OE *thearm* gut]

-derma, a combining form of **derma**[1], used esp. in the names of disorders of the skin: *scleroderma; xeroderma.*

derm·a·bra·sion (dûr′mə brā′zhən), *n.* the removal of acne scars, dermal nevi, or the like, by abrading. Also called **skin planing.** [1950–55; DERM- + ABRASION]

der·mal (dûr′məl), *adj.* of or pertaining to the skin. Also, **dermic.** [1795–1805; DERM(A)[1] + -AL[1]]

der·map·ter·an (dər map′tər ən), *adj.* **1.** Also, **der·map′ter·ous.** belonging or pertaining to the insect order Dermaptera, comprising the earwigs. —*n.* **2.** any of numerous brown to black, small to medium-sized nocturnal insects of the order Dermaptera, widely distributed in warm, moist areas, characterized by a slender, elongated, flattened body with pincerlike appendages at the tail end of the abdomen. [1860–65; < NL *Dermapter(a)* (irreg. < Gk *dermóptera* (see DERMOPTERAN), or a deliberate alter. of *Dermoptera* to keep the taxa distinct) + -AN]

dermat-, var. of **dermato-** before a vowel: *dermatitis.*

der·ma·therm (dûr′mə thûrm′), *n. Med.* an instrument for measuring skin temperature. Also, **dermotherm.** [DERMA[1] + -THERM]

der·ma·ti·tis (dûr′mə tī′tis), *n. Pathol.* inflammation of the skin. [1875–80; DERMAT- + -ITIS]

dermato-, a combining form meaning "skin," used in the formation of compound words: *dermatology.* Also, **dermo-.** Also, *esp. before a vowel,* **derm-, dermat-.** [< Gk, comb. form of *dermat-,* s. of *dérma*]

der·mat·o·gen (dər mat′ə jən, -jen′, dûr′mə tə-), *n. Bot.* protoderm. [1880–85; DERMATO- + -GEN]

der·mat·o·glyph·ics (dər mat′ə glif′iks, dûr′mə tə-), *n.* **1.** (*used with a plural v.*) the patterns of ridges on the inner surface of the hands and feet. **2.** (*used with a singular v.*) the science dealing with the study of these patterns. [1925–30; DERMATO- + Gk *glýph(ein)* to carve + -ICS] —**der·mat′o·glyph′ic,** *adj.*

der·mat·o·graph·i·a (dər mat′ə graf′ē ə, dûr′mə-tə-), *n. Med.* a condition in which touching or lightly scratching the skin causes raised, reddish marks. Also, **der·ma·tog·ra·phism** (dûr′mə tog′rə fiz′əm), **dermographia, dermographism.** [1850–55; < NL; see DERMATO-, -GRAPHY] —**der·mat′o·graph′ic,** *adj.*

der·ma·toid (dûr′mə toid′), *adj.* resembling skin; skinlike. [1850–55; DERMAT- + -OID]

der·ma·tol·o·gist (dûr′mə tol′ə jist), *n.* a specialist in dermatology, esp. a doctor who specializes in the treatment of diseases of the skin. [1860–65; DERMATOLOG(Y) + -IST]

der·ma·tol·o·gy (dûr′mə tol′ə jē), *n.* the branch of medicine dealing with the skin and its diseases. [1810–20; DERMATO- + -LOGY] —**der·ma·to·log·i·cal** (dûr′mə-tl oj′i kəl), **der′ma·to·log′ic,** *adj.*

der·ma·tome (dûr′mə tōm′), *n.* **1.** *Anat.* an area of skin that is supplied with the nerve fibers of a single, posterior, spinal root. **2.** *Surg.* a mechanical instrument for cutting thin sections of skin for grafting. **3.** *Embryol.* the part of a mesodermal somite contributing to the development of the dermis. [1925–30; DERMA[1] + -TOME] —**der·ma·tom·ic** (dûr′mə tom′ik), **der′ma·to′mal,** *adj.*

der·mat·o·my·co·sis (dər mat′ə mī kō′sis, dûr′mə-tō-), *n. Pathol.* a superficial fungal infection of the skin. [DERMATO- + MYCOSIS]

der·mat·o·my·o·si·tis (dər mat′ə mī′ə sī′tis, dûr′-mə tō-), *n. Pathol.* an inflammatory disease of connective tissues, manifested by skin inflammation and muscle weakness. [1895–1900; DERMATO- + *myositis* inflammation of muscle tissue, irreg. < Gk *myós* (gen. of *mŷs* MUSCLE, mouse) + -ITIS]

der·mat·o·phyte (dər mat′ə fīt′, dûr′mə tə-), *n. Pathol.* any fungus parasitic on the skin and causing a skin disease, as ringworm. [1880–85; DERMATO- + -PHYTE] —**der·mat·o·phyt·ic** (dər mat′ə fit′ik, dûr′mə-tə-), *adj.* —**der·mat′o·phy·to′sis,** *n.*

der·ma·to·plas·ty (dər mat′ə plas′tē, dûr′mə tə-), *n. Surg.* See **skin grafting.** [DERMATO- + -PLASTY] —**der·mat′o·plas′tic,** *adj.*

der·ma·to·sis (dûr′mə tō′sis), *n., pl.* **-to·ses** (-tō′sēz). *Pathol.* any disease of the skin. [1865–70; < NL; see DERMAT-, -OSIS]

-dermatous, a combining form meaning "skinned," "possessing skin," used to form compound words in which the initial element specifies the type of skin: *xerodermatous.* Cf. **-derm.** [< Gk *-dermatos,* adj. deriv. of *dérma,* s. *dermat-* skin; see -OUS]

der·mat·o·zo·on (dər mat′ə zō′on, dûr′mə tə-), *n., pl.* **-zo·a** (-zō′ə). *Biol.* any microscopic animal or protozoan living as a parasite on or in the skin of the host. [DERMATO- + -ZOON]

der·ma·trop·ic (dûr′mə trop′ik, -trō′pik), *adj.* (esp. of viruses) in, attracted toward, or affecting the skin. Also, **dermotropic, der·mat·o·trop·ic** (dər mat′ə trop′-ik, dûr′mə tə-). [DERMA[1] + -TROPIC]

der·mic (dûr′mik), *adj.* dermal. [1835–45; DERM(A)[1] + -IC]

der·mis (dûr′mis), *n. Anat., Zool.* the dense inner layer of skin beneath the epidermis, composed of connective tissue, blood and lymph vessels, sweat glands, hair follicles, and an elaborate sensory nerve network. Also called **corium.** [1820–30; < NL; abstracted from EPIDERMIS]

-dermis, a combining form meaning "skin," "layer of tissue," used in the formation of compound words: *exodermis; gastrodermis.* Cf. **-derm.** [on the model of EPIDERMIS; cf. DERMIS]

dermo-, var. of **dermato-**: *dermographic.*

der·mo·graph·i·a (dûr′mə graf′ē ə), *n. Med.* dermatographia. Also, **der·mog·ra·phism** (dər mog′rə fiz′-əm). [1850–55; < NL; see DERMO-, -GRAPHY] —**der′mo·graph′ic,** *adj.*

der·moid (dûr′moid), *adj.* skinlike; dermatoid. [1810–20; DERM- + -OID]

der·mo·plas·ty (dûr′mə plas′tē), *n.* See **skin grafting.** [DERMO- + -PLASTY]

der·mop·ter·an (dər mop′tər ən, -trən), *n.* **1.** any member of the order Dermoptera, comprising the flying lemurs. —*adj.* **2.** of or pertaining to the dermopterans. [< NL *Dermopter(a)* (< Gk, neut. pl. of *dermópteros* having wings of skin (term used by Aristotle to describe bats); see DERMO-, -PTEROUS) + -AN]

der·mo·therm (dûr′mə thûrm′), *n. Med.* dermatherm.

der·mo·trop·ic (dûr′mə trop′ik, -trō′pik), *adj.* dermatropic.

dern (dûrn), *adj., adv., v.t. Dial.* darn[2].

der·nier cri (dern′yā krē′, dûrn′-; *Fr.* dɛʀ nyā kʀē′), the latest fashion; last word. [1895–1900; < F: lit., last cry]

der·o·gate (*v.* der′ə gāt′; *adj.* der′ə git, -gāt′), *v.,* **-gat·ed, -gat·ing,** *adj.* —*v.i.* **1.** to detract, as from authority, estimation, etc. (usually fol. by *from*). **2.** to stray in character or conduct; degenerate (usually fol. by *from*). —*v.t.* **3.** to disparage or belittle. **4.** *Archaic.* to take away (a part) so as to impair the whole. —*adj.* **5.** *Archaic.* debased. [1375–1425; late ME < L *dērogātus* repealed, restricted (ptp. of *dērogāre*), equiv. to *dē-* DE- + *rog(āre)* to ask + *-ātus* -ATE[1]] —**der′o·ga′tion,** *n.*
—**Syn. 1.** See **decry.**

de·rog·a·tive (di rog′ə tiv), *adj.* lessening; belittling; derogatory. [1470–80; < OF *derogatif* < LL *dērogātīvus.* See DEROGATE, -IVE] —**de·rog′a·tive·ly,** *adv.*

de·rog·a·to·ry (di rog′ə tôr′ē, -tōr′ē), *adj.* tending to lessen the merit or reputation of a person or thing; disparaging; depreciatory: *a derogatory remark.* [1495–1505; < LL *dērogātōrius* cursing, equiv. to *dērogā(re)* (see DEROGATE) + *-tōrius* -TORY[1]] —**de·rog′a·to′ri·ly,** *adv.* —**de·rog′a·to′ri·ness,** *n.*
—**Syn.** belittling, uncomplimentary, denigrating.

de·ro·man·ti·cize (dē′rō man′tə sīz′), *v.t.,* **-cized, -ciz·ing.** to remove the romantic, ideal, or heroic aura from. Also, *esp. Brit.,* **de′ro·man′ti·cise′.** [DE- + ROMANTICIZE]

der·rick (der′ik), *n.* **1.** *Mach.* a jib crane having a boom hinged near the base of the mast so as to rotate about the mast, for moving a load toward or away from the mast by raising or lowering the boom. **2.** Also called **oil derrick.** the towerlike framework over an oil well or the like. **3.** a boom for lifting cargo, pivoted at its inner end to a ship's mast or kingpost, and raised and supported at its outer end by topping lifts. —*v.t., v.i.* **4.** *Mach.* luff. [orig. a hangman, the gallows, after the surname of a well-known Tyburn hangman, ca. 1600]

der·ri·ère (der′ē âr′; *Fr.* de ʀyɛʀ′), *n.* the buttocks; rump. Also, **der′ri·ere′.** [1765–75; < F (prep., n.); OF *deriere* < VL **dē retrō,* for L *retrō* towards the rear, backwards; cf. ARREAR]

der·ring-do (der′ing do͞o′), *n.* daring deeds; heroic daring. [1325–75; ME *durring-do* lit., daring to do, erroneously taken as n. phrase. See DARE, DO[1]]

der·rin·ger (der′in jər), *n.* an early short-barreled pocket pistol. Also, **deringer.** [1850–55, *Amer.*; named after Henry Deringer, mid-19th-century American gunsmith who invented it]

derringer

der·ris (der′is), *n.* any East Indian plant belonging to the genus *Derris,* of the legume family, esp. *D. elliptica,* the roots of which contain rotenone and are used as an insecticide. [1855–60; NL < Gk: a covering, deriv. of *déros* skin, hide; see DERMA[1]]

der·ry (der′ē), *n., pl.* **-ries.** a meaningless refrain or chorus in old songs. Also called **der·ry-down** (der′ē doun′). [1545–55; of obscure orig.]

Der·ry (der′ē), *n.* **1.** Londonderry (defs. 1, 2). **2.** a town in SE New Hampshire. 18,875.

der·trum (dûr′trəm), *n., pl.* **-tra** (-trə). *Ornith.* the extremity of the maxilla of a bird's bill, esp. when hooked or differentiated from the rest of the bill, as in pigeons and plovers. [1885–90; < NL < Gk *dértron* membrane, deriv. of *dérein* to skin; cf. *dérma* DERMA[1]]

der·vish (dûr′vish), *n.* a member of any of various Muslim ascetic orders, as the Sufis, some of which carry on ecstatic observances, such as energetic dancing and whirling or vociferous chanting or shouting. [1575–85; < Turk < Pers *darvīsh* poor man, beggar]

Der·went (dûr′wənt), *n.* **1.** a river flowing N and W into Solway Firth, in N England. ab. 33 mi. (53 km) long. **2.** a river flowing S and SE past Derby to the Trent, in central England. ab. 60 mi. (95 km) long. **3.** a river flowing into the Ouse, in Yorkshire in NE England. ab. 57 mi. (91 km) long. **4.** a river flowing NE to the Tyne, in N England. ab. 30 mi. (48 km) long. **5.** a river in S Australia, in S Tasmania, flowing SE to the Tasman Sea. 107 mi. (170 km) long.

des (dā), *prep.* used in French names as a contraction of *de* and the article *les: François des Adrets.*

DES, See **diethylstilbestrol.**

-des, a plural suffix appearing in loanwords from Greek: *proboscides.* [< Gk, nom. pl. of *d*-stem nouns]

de·sa·cral·ize (dē sā′krə līz′, -sak′rə-), *v.t.,* **-ized, -iz·ing.** to remove the aura of sacredness from; secularize. [DE- + SACRAL[1] + -IZE] —**de·sa′cral·i·za′tion,** *n.*

De·saix de Vey·goux (də ze′ də vā go͞o′), **Louis Charles An·toine** (lwē sharl äɴ twaɴ′), 1768–1800, French general.

de·sal·i·nate (dē sal′ə nāt′), *v.t.,* **-nat·ed, -nat·ing.** desalt. [1945–50; DE- + SALINE + -ATE[1]] —**de·sal′i·na′tion,** *n.* —**de·sal′i·na′tor,** *n.*

de·sal·in·ize (dē sal′ə nīz′, -sā′lə-, -lī-), *v.t.,* **-ized, -iz·ing.** desalt. Also, *esp. Brit.,* **de·sal′in·ise′.** [1960–65; DE- + SALINE + -IZE] —**de·sal′in·i·za′tion,** *n.*

de·sal·i·vate (dē sal′ə vāt′), *v.t.,* **-vat·ed, -vat·ing.** to arrest the flow of saliva in (a human or other animal). [1970–75; DE- + SALIV(A) + -ATE[1]]

de·salt (dē sôlt′), *v.t.* to remove the salt from (esp. sea water), usually to make it drinkable. Also, **desalinate, desalinize.** [1905–10; DE- + SALT] —**de·salt′er,** *n.*

de·sa·pa·re·ci·do (*Sp.* de′sä pä′ʀe sē′t͟hô; *Port.* de′-zä pä′ʀi sē′do͞o; *Eng.* des′ə pär′ə sē′dō), *n., pl.* **-dos** (*Sp.* -t͟hôs; *Port.* -do͞os; *Eng.* -dōz). *Spanish, Portuguese.* one who has disappeared: used, esp. in Latin America, in referring to a person who has been secretly imprisoned or killed during a government's program of political suppression.

De·sargues (dā zarg′, *Eng.* dā zärg′), *n.* **Gé·rard** (zhā ʀaʀ′), 1593–1662, French mathematician.

Desargues′'s the′orem, *Geom.* the theorem that if two triangles are so related that the lines joining corresponding vertices meet in a point, then the extended corresponding lines of the two triangles meet in three points, all on the same line. [named after G. DESARGUES]

de·sat·u·rat·ed (dē sach′ə rā′tid), *adj.* (of a color) formed by mixing a color of the spectrum with white. [1910–15; DE- + SATURATE + -ED[2]]

desc., descendant.

des·ca·mi·sa·do (des′kam ə sä′dō; *Sp.* des′kä mē-sä′t͟hô), *n., pl.* **-dos** (-dōz; *Sp.* -t͟hôs). **1.** an extreme liberal of the Spanish revolution 1820–23. **2.** (in Argentina) a worker, esp. a poor laborer or factory worker. [1815–25; < Sp: lit., shirtless]

des·cant (*n., adj.* des′kant; *v.* des kant′, dis-), *n.* **1.** *Music.* **a.** a melody or counterpoint accompanying a simple musical theme and usually written above it. **b.** (in part music) the soprano. **c.** a song or melody. **2.** a variation upon anything; comment on a subject. —*adj.* **3.** *Music, Chiefly Brit.* **a.** soprano: *a descant recorder.* **b.** treble: *a descant viol.* —*v.i.* **4.** *Music.* to sing. **5.** to comment or discourse at great length. Also, **discant.** [1350–1400; ME *discant, descaunt* < AF < ML *discanthus,* equiv. to L *dis-* DIS-[1] + *cantus* song; see CHANT] —**des·cant′er,** *n.*

Des·cartes (dā kärt′; *Fr.* dā kaʀt′), *n.* **Re·né** (rə nā′; *Fr.* ʀə nā′), 1596–1650, French philosopher and mathematician.

Descartes′ law′, *Optics.* See **Snell's law.** [named after René DESCARTES]

de·scend (di send′), *v.i.* **1.** to go or pass from a higher to a lower place; move or come down: *to descend from the mountaintop.* **2.** to pass from higher to lower in any scale or series. **3.** to go from generals to particulars, as in a discussion. **4.** to slope, tend, or lead downward: *The path descends to the pond.* **5.** to be inherited or transmitted, as through succeeding generations of a family: *The title descends through eldest sons.* **6.** to have a specific person or family among one's ancestors (usually fol. by *from*): *He is descended from Cromwell.* **7.** to be derived from something remote in time, esp. through continuous transmission: *This festival descends from a druidic rite.* **8.** to approach or pounce upon, esp. in a greedy or hasty manner (fol. by *on* or *upon*): *Thrill-seekers descended upon the scene of the crime.* **9.** to settle, as a cloud or vapor. **10.** to appear or become manifest, as a supernatural being, state of mind, etc.: *Jupiter descended to humankind.* **11.** to attack, esp. with violence and suddenness (usually fol. by *on* or *upon*): *to descend upon enemy soldiers.* **12.** to sink or come down from a certain intellectual, moral, or social standard: *He would never descend to baseness.* **13.** *Astron.* to move toward the horizon, as the sun or a star. —*v.t.* **14.** to move downward upon or along; go or climb down (stairs, a hill, etc.). **15.** to extend or lead down along: *The path descends the hill.* [1250–1300; ME *descenden* < OF *descendre* < L *dēscendere,* equiv. to *dē-* DE- + *-scendere,* comb. form of *scandere* to climb; cf. SCANSION] —**de·scend′ing·ly,** *adv.*

de·scend·ant (di sen′dənt), *n.* **1.** a person or animal that is descended from a specific ancestor; an offspring. **2.** something deriving in appearance, function, or general character from an earlier form. **3.** an adherent who follows closely the teachings, methods, practices, etc., of an earlier master, as in art, music, philosophy, etc.; disciple. **4.** *Astrol.* **a.** the point opposite the ascendant. **b.** the point of the ecliptic or the sign and degree of the zodiac setting below the western horizon at the time of a birth or of an event. **c.** the cusp of the seventh house. —*adj.* **5.** descending; descendent. [1425–75; late ME *descendaunt* (adj.) < OF *descendant,* prp. of *descendre.* See DESCEND, -ANT]

de·scend·ent (di sen′dənt), *adj.* **1.** descending; going or coming down. **2.** deriving or descending from an ancestor. [1565–75; < L *dēscendent-* (s. of *dēscendēns*), prp. of *dēscendere.* See DESCEND, -ENT]

de•scend•er (di sen′dər), *n.* **1.** a person or thing that descends. **2.** *Print.* **a.** the part of a lowercase letter that goes below the body. **b.** a letter having such a part, as *p, q, j,* or *y.* [1660–70; DESCEND + -ER[1]]

de•scend•i•ble (di sen′də bəl), *adj.* **1.** capable of being transmitted by inheritance. **2.** permitting descent: *a descendible hill.* Also, **de•scend′a•ble.** [1425–75; late ME *descendable* < OF, equiv. to *descend(re)* to DESCEND + *-able* -ABLE; sp. later Latinized] —**de•scend′i•bil′i•ty, de•scend′a•bil′i•ty,** *n.*

descend′ing co′lon (kō′lən), *Anat.* the last portion of the colon, beginning at the upper left abdomen in the region of the spleen and continuing downward along the left posterior wall to the sigmoid flexure. See diag. under **intestine.**

descend′ing node′, *Astron.* the node through which an orbiting body passes as it moves to the south (opposed to *ascending node*). [1690–1700]

descend′ing rhythm′. See **falling rhythm.**

de•scen•sion (di sen′shən), *n.* **1.** *Astrol.* the part of the zodiac in which the influence of a planet is weakest. Cf. **exaltation** (def. 6). **2.** descent. [1350–1400; ME *descensioun* < OF *descension* < L *dēscēnsiōn-* (s. of *dēscēnsiō*), equiv. to *dēscēns(us)* (ptp. of *dēscendere* to DESCEND) + *-iōn-* -ION]

de•scent (di sent′), *n.* **1.** the act, process, or fact of descending. **2.** a downward inclination or slope. **3.** a passage or stairway leading down. **4.** derivation from an ancestor; lineage; extraction. **5.** any passing from higher to lower in degree or state; decline. **6.** a sudden raid or hostile attack. **7.** *Law.* transmission of real property by intestate succession. [1300–50; ME < AF, OF *descente,* deriv. of *descendre* to DESCEND, modeled on such pairs as *vente, vendre*]
—**Syn. 1.** falling, sinking. **2.** decline, grade, declivity. **4.** ancestry, parentage. **6.** assault, foray.

de•school (dē skōōl′), *v.t.* to abolish or phase out traditional schools from, so as to replace them with alternative methods and forms of education. [DE- + SCHOOL[1]]

Des•chutes (dā shōōt′), *n.* a river flowing N from the Cascade Range in central Oregon to the Columbia River. 250 mi. (400 km) long.

des•cloi•zite (dā kloi′zit, di-), *n.* a mineral, lead zinc vanadate. [1850–55; < F, named after A.L.O. *Des Cloizeaux* (1817–97), French mineralogist; see -ITE[1]]

de•scram•ble (dē skram′bəl), *v.t.,* **-bled, -bling.** unscramble (def. 2). [DE- + SCRAMBLE]

de•scram•bler (dē skram′blər), *n.* unscrambler (def. 2). [DESCRAMBLE + -ER[1]]

de•scribe (di skrīb′), *v.t.,* **-scribed, -scrib•ing. 1.** to tell or depict in written or spoken words; give an account of: *He described the accident very carefully.* **2.** to pronounce, as by a designating term, phrase, or the like; label: *There are few people who may be described as geniuses.* **3.** to indicate; be a sign of; denote: *Conceit, in many cases, describes a state of serious emotional insecurity.* **4.** to represent or delineate by a picture or figure. **5.** *Geom.* to draw or trace the outline of: *to describe an arc.* [1400–50; late ME *describen* < L *dēscrībere,* equiv. to *dē-* DE- + *scrībere* to write] —**de•scrib′a•bil′i•ty,** *n.* —**de•scrib′a•ble,** *adj.* —**de•scrib′a•bly,** *adv.* —**de•scrib′er,** *n.*
—**Syn. 1.** portray, characterize, represent; recount, tell, relate. DESCRIBE, NARRATE agree in the idea of giving an account of something. To DESCRIBE is to convey in words the appearance, nature, attributes, etc., of something. The word often implies vividness of personal observation: *to describe a scene, an event.* To NARRATE is to recount the occurrence of something, usually by giving the details of an event or events in the order of their happening. NARRATE thus applies only to that which happens in time: *to narrate an incident.*

de•scrip•tion (di skrip′shən), *n.* **1.** a statement, picture in words, or account that describes; descriptive representation. **2.** the act or method of describing. **3.** sort; kind; variety: *dogs of every description.* **4.** *Geom.* the act or process of describing a figure. [1300–50; ME *descripcioun* < L *dēscrīptiōn-* (s. of *dēscrīptiō*), equiv. to *dēscrīpt(us)* (ptp. of *dēscrībere* to DESCRIBE) + *-iōn-* -ION]
—**Syn. 3.** species; nature, character, condition; ilk.

de•scrip•tive (di skrip′tiv), *adj.* **1.** having the quality of describing; characterized by description: *a descriptive passage in an essay.* **2. a.** *Gram.* (of an adjective or other modifier) expressing a quality of the word it modifies, as *fresh* in *fresh milk.* Cf. **limiting. b.** (of a clause) nonrestrictive. Cf. **restrictive** (def. 4). **3.** noting, concerned with, or based upon the fact or experience. **4.** characterized by or based upon the classification and description of material in a given field: *descriptive botany.* [1745–55; < LL *dēscrīptīvus,* equiv. to L *dēscrīpt(us)* (see DESCRIPTION) + *-īvus* -IVE] —**de•scrip′tive•ly,** *adv.* —**de•scrip′tive•ness,** *n.*

descrip′tive bibliog′raphy, *Library Science.* **1.** the aspect of bibliography concerned with the close physical study and description of books and other works. **2.** a record of such description of a given number of related works.

descrip′tive cat′aloging, *Library Science.* the aspect of cataloging concerned with the bibliographic and physical description of a book, recording, or other work, accounting for such items as author or performer, title, edition, and imprint as opposed to subject content. [1900–05]

descrip′tive clause′. See **nonrestrictive clause.**

descrip′tive geom′etry, 1. the theory of making projections of any accurately defined figure such that its projective as well as its metrical properties can be deduced from them. **2.** geometry in general, treated by means of projections. [1815–25]

descrip′tive gram′mar, 1. an approach to grammar that is concerned with reporting the usage of native speakers without reference to proposed norms of correctness or advocacy of rules based on such norms. **2.** a set of grammatical descriptions based on such an approach.

descrip′tive linguis′tics, the study of the grammar, classification, and arrangement of the features of a language at a given time, without reference to the history of the language or comparison with other languages. Also called **synchronic linguistics.** [1925–30]

de•scrip•tiv•ist (di skrip′tə vist), *n.* **1.** a writer, teacher, or supporter of descriptive grammar or descriptive linguistics. —*adj.* **2.** of, pertaining to, or based on descriptive grammar or descriptive linguistics. [1950–55; DESCRIPTIVE + -IST] —**de•scrip′tiv•ism,** *n.*

de•scrip•tor (di skrip′tər), *n.* **1.** a significant word or phrase used to categorize or describe text or other material, esp. when indexing or in an information retrieval system. **2.** *Computers.* a data item that stores the attributes of some other datum: *a task descriptor.* [1930–35, for an earlier sense; DESCRIBE + -TOR, with vowel change and devoicing by analogy with similar L derivatives]

de•scry (di skrī′), *v.t.,* **-scried, -scry•ing. 1.** to see (something unclear or distant) by looking carefully; discern; espy: *The lookout descried land.* **2.** to discover; perceive; detect. [1250–1300; ME *descrien* < OF *de(s)crier* to proclaim, decry. See DIS-[1], CRY] —**de•scri′er,** *n.*
—**Syn. 1.** notice.

Des•de•mo•na (dez′də mō′nə), *n.* (in Shakespeare's *Othello*) Othello's wife, murdered by her husband as a result of jealousy instilled by Iago.

des•e•crate (des′i krāt′), *v.t.,* **-crat•ed, -crat•ing. 1.** to divest of sacred or hallowed character or office. **2.** to divert from a sacred to a profane use or purpose. **3.** to treat with sacrilege; profane. [1665–75; DE- + *-secrate,* modeled on *consecrate*] —**des′e•crat′er, des′e•cra′•tor,** *n.* —**des′e•cra′tion,** *n.*
—**Syn. 3.** defile, violate, dishonor, pollute, outrage.

de•seg•re•gate (dē seg′ri gāt′), *v.,* **-gat•ed, -gat•ing.** —*v.t.* **1.** to eliminate racial segregation in: *to desegregate all schools.* —*v.i.* **2.** to eliminate racial segregation. [1950–55; DE- + SEGREGATE]

de•seg•re•ga•tion (dē′seg ri gā′shən, dē seg′-), *n.* the elimination of laws, customs, or practices under which different races, groups, etc., are restricted to specific or separate public facilities, neighborhoods, schools, organizations, or the like. [1950–55; DE- + SEGREGATION] —**de′seg•re•ga′tion•ist,** *n.*

de•se•lect (dē′si lekt′), *v.t.* to discharge (a trainee) from a program of training. [1960–65; DE- + SELECT]

de•sen•si•ti•za•tion (dē sen′si tə zā′shən), *n.* **1.** the act or process of desensitizing. **2.** *Physiol., Med.* the elimination or reduction of natural or acquired reactivity or sensitivity to an external stimulus, as an allergen. **3.** *Psychiatry.* a behavior modification technique, used esp. in treating phobias, in which panic or other undesirable emotional response to a given stimulus is reduced or extinguished, esp. by repeated exposure to that stimulus. [1920–25; DESENSITIZE + -ATION]

de•sen•si•tize (dē sen′si tīz′), *v.t.,* **-tized, -tiz•ing. 1.** to lessen the sensitiveness of. **2.** to make indifferent, unaware, or the like, in feeling. **3.** *Photog.* to make less sensitive or wholly insensitive to light, as the emulsion on a film. **4.** *Print.* to treat (the design on a lithographic plate) with an etch in order to increase the capacity to retain moisture, and to remove traces of grease. **5.** *Chem.* to reduce the sensitivity of (an explosive) to those stimuli capable of detonating it. Also, *esp. Brit.,* **de•sen′si•tise′.** [1900–05; DE- + SENSITIZE] —**de•sen′si•tiz′er,** *n.*

Des•er•et (dez′ə ret′), *n.* **1.** a territory established by the Mormons in 1849 as a proposed state of the Union: was refused admission to the Union by Congress and incorporated in the newly organized Territory of Utah 1850. **2.** *Informal.* the state of Utah.

de•ser•pi•dine (di sûr′pi dēn′), *n. Pharm.* a purified alkaloid derived from rauwolfia, $C_{32}H_{38}N_2O_8$, used as an antihypertensive in mild cases of essential hypertension and also as a major tranquilizer for the symptomatic relief of agitated psychotic states. [perh. D(I)-[1] + (R)ESERP(INE) + *-idine* suffix of derivative compounds]

des•ert[1] (dez′ərt), *n.* **1.** a region so arid because of little rainfall that it supports only sparse and widely spaced vegetation or no vegetation at all: *The Sahara is a vast sandy desert.* See table on next page. **2.** any area in which few forms of life can exist because of lack of water, permanent frost, or absence of soil. **3.** an area of the ocean in which it is believed no marine life exists. **4.** (formerly) any unsettled area between the Mississippi and the Rocky Mountains thought to be unsuitable for human habitation. **5.** any place lacking in something: *The town was a cultural desert.* —*adj.* **6.** of, pertaining to, or like a desert; desolate; barren. **7.** occurring, living, or flourishing in the desert: *a desert tribe; a desert palm.* **8.** designed or suitable for wear in the desert, as cool, protective clothing: *a big, wide-brimmed desert hat.* [1175–1225; ME < AF < LL *dēsertum* (neut.), n. use of ptp. of L *dēserere* to abandon, forsake, equiv. to *dē-* DE- + *serere* to join together (in a line); cf. SERIES] —**de•ser•tic** (di zûr′tik), *adj.* —**des′ert•like′,** *adj.*
—**Syn. 1.** DESERT, WASTE, WILDERNESS refer to areas that are largely uninhabited. DESERT emphasizes lack of water; it refers to a dry, barren, treeless region, usually sandy: *an oasis in a desert.* WASTE emphasizes lack of inhabitants and of cultivation; it is used of wild, barren land: *a desolate waste.* WILDERNESS emphasizes the difficulty of finding one's way, whether because of barrenness or of dense vegetation: *a trackless wilderness.*

de•sert[2] (di zûrt′), *v.t.* **1.** to leave (a person, place, etc.) without intending to return, esp. in violation of a duty, promise, or the like: *He deserted his wife.* **2.** (of military personnel) to leave or run away from (service, duty, etc.) with the intention of never returning. **3.** to fail (someone) at a time of need: *None of his friends had deserted him.* —*v.i.* **4.** to forsake or leave one's duty, obligations, etc. (sometimes fol. by *from, to,* etc.): *Many deserted during the food shortage.* **5.** (of military personnel) to leave service, duty, etc., with no intention of returning: *Troops were deserting to the enemy.* [1470–80; < MF *déserter* < LL *dēsertāre,* freq. of L *dēserere;* see DESERT[1]] —**de•sert′ed•ly,** *adv.* —**de•sert′ed•ness,** *n.* —**de•sert′er,** *n.*
—**Syn. 1.** DESERT, ABANDON, FORSAKE mean to leave behind persons, places, or things. DESERT implies intentionally violating an oath, formal obligation, or duty: *to desert campaign pledges.* ABANDON suggests giving up wholly and finally, whether of necessity, unwillingly, or through shirking responsibilities: *to abandon a hopeless task; abandon a child.* FORSAKE has emotional connotations, since it implies violating obligations of affection or association: *to forsake a noble cause.*

de•sert[3] (di zûrt′), *n.* **1.** Often, **deserts.** reward or punishment that is deserved: *to get one's just deserts.* **2.** the state or fact of deserving reward or punishment. **3.** the fact of deserving well; merit; virtue. [1275–1325; ME < OF *deserte,* n. use of fem. ptp. of *deservir* to DESERVE]
—**Syn. 3.** See **merit.**

Des′ert boot′, *Trademark.* a brand of laced ankle-high boot of soft suede with a crepe sole.

Des′ert Cul′ture, the nomadic hunting, fishing, and gathering preagricultural post-Pleistocene phase in the American West, characterized by an efficient exploitation of varied natural resources that was continued by Amerindian cultures into historic times.

de•sert•ed (di zûr′tid), *adj.* **1.** abandoned; forsaken: *the problems of deserted wives and children.* **2.** untenanted: without inhabitants: *a deserted village; a deserted farmhouse.* **3.** unfrequented; lonely: *The victim was lured to a deserted spot.* [1620–30; DESERT[2] + -ED[2]]

des′ert fa′thers, monks, as Saint Anthony or Saint Pachomius, who lived as hermits in the deserts of Egypt and founded the first Christian monasteries.

des′ert fe′ver, *Pathol.* coccidioidomycosis.

des•er•tic•o•lous (dez′ər tik′ə ləs), *adj. Biol.* living or growing in a desert. [DESERT[1] + -I- + -COLOUS]

de•sert•i•fi•ca•tion (di zûr′tə fi kā′shən), *n. Ecol.* **1.** the processes by which an area becomes a desert. **2.** the rapid depletion of plant life and the loss of topsoil at desert boundaries and in semiarid regions, usually caused by a combination of drought and the overexploitation of grasses and other vegetation by people. Also, **des•ert•i•za•tion** (dez′ər tə zā′shən). Cf. **aridification.** [1970–75; DESERT[1] + -I- + -FICATION]

des′ert igua′na, a long-tailed iguanid lizard, *Dipsosaurus dorsalis,* of arid areas in the southwestern U.S. and northwestern Mexico, having a row of enlarged scales down the back. Also called **crested lizard.**

de•ser•tion (di zûr′shən), *n.* **1.** the act of deserting or the state of being deserted. **2.** *Law.* willful abandonment, esp. of one's wife or husband without consent, in violation of legal or moral obligations. **3.** an act of leaving military service or duty without the intention of returning. Cf. **AWOL.** [1585–95; < LL *dēsertiōn-* (s. of *dēsertiō*) < L *dēsert(us)* (see DESERT[1]) + *-iōn-* -ION]

des′ert lo′cust, a migratory locust, *Schistocerca gregaria,* of North Africa and Asia, associated with the plagues described in the Old Testament. [1940–45]

des′ert rat′, 1. any of various small rodents, as the kangaroo rat, inhabiting arid regions. **2.** *Chiefly Western U.S.* one who lives in the desert, esp. in order to prospect for gold or other valuable minerals. **3.** *Informal.* a soldier fighting in the N African desert in World War II, esp. a British soldier. [1905–10, *Amer.*]

des′ert var′nish, the dark, lustrous coating or crust, usually of manganese and iron oxides, that forms on rocks, pebbles, etc., when exposed to weathering in the desert. Also called **des′ert pol′ish.** [1900–05]

de•serve (di zûrv′), *v.,* **-served, -serv•ing.** —*v.t.* **1.** to merit, be qualified for, or have a claim to (reward, assistance, punishment, etc.) because of actions, qualities, or situation: *to deserve exile; to deserve charity; a theory that deserves consideration.* —*v.i.* **2.** to be worthy of, qualified for, or have a claim to reward, punishment, recompense, etc.: *to reward him as he deserves; an idea deserving of study.* [1250–1300; ME *deserven* < AF, OF *deservir,* L *dēservīre* to devote oneself to the service of, equiv. to *dē-* DE- + *servīre* to SERVE] —**de•serv′er,** *n.*
—**Syn. 1.** rate, warrant, justify.

de•served (di zûrvd′), *adj.* justly or rightly earned; merited: *a deserved increase in salary.* [1545–55; DESERVE + -ED[2]] —**de•serv•ed•ness** (di zûr′vid nis), *n.*

de•serv•ed•ly (di zûr′vid lē), *adv.* according to desert; justly; rightly. [1540–50; DESERVED + -LY]

de•serv•ing (di zûr′ving), *adj.* **1.** qualified for or having a claim to reward, assistance, etc., because of one's actions, qualities, or situation: *the deserving poor; a deserving applicant.* **2.** meriting; worthy: *a criminal deserving of a lifetime sentence.* [1570–80; DESERVE + -ING[2]] —**de•serv′ing•ly,** *adv.* —**de•serv′ing•ness,** *n.*

De Se•ver•sky (də sə ver′skē), **Alexander Procofieff.** See **Seversky, Alexander Procofieff de.**

de•sex (dē seks′), *v.t.* **1.** *Vet. Surg.* to castrate or spay. **2.** to deprive of sex, sex appeal, or sexual interest. **3.** to remove elements of sexism from; degenderize: *a campaign to desex business writing.* [1910–15; DE- + SEX]

des•ha•bille (dez′ə bēl′, -bē′), *n.* dishabille.

De Si•ca (də sē′kə; *It.* de sē′kä), **Vit•to•rio** (vi tôr′ē ō′, -tōr′-; *It.* vēt tô′ryō), 1901–74, Italian motion-picture director, producer, and actor.

des•ic•cant (des′i kənt), *adj.* **1.** desiccating or drying, as a medicine. —*n.* **2.** a desiccant substance or agent.

NOTABLE DESERTS OF THE WORLD

Name	Location	Approximate Area sq. mi.	sq. km
Sahara	N Africa	3,500,000	9,065,000
Great Australian	Interior of Australia	1,480,000	3,830,000
Libyan	E part of Sahara Desert	650,000	1,683,500
Great Arabian	Arabian Peninsula, SW Asia	500,000	1,295,000
Gobi	Central Asia, Mongolia, and Inner Mongolia	500,000	1,295,000
Rub' al Khali	S Arabian Peninsula	250,000	647,500
Kalahari	S Botswana	200,000	518,000
Great Sandy	NW Australia	160,000	414,400
Nubian	NE Sudan	157,000	406,600
Great Victoria	SW central Australia	125,000	324,000
Syrian	N Saudi Arabia, SE Syria, W Iraq, and NE Jordan	125,000	324,000
Taklamakan	S central Xinjiang Uygur, China	125,000	324,000
Kara Kum	Turkmenistan	110,000	284,900
Thar	NW India and adjacent Pakistan	100,000	259,000
Kyzyl Kum	Uzbekistan and S Kazakhstan, SE of Aral Sea	90,000	233,100
Atacama	N Chile	70,000	181,300
Namib	W Namibia	50,000	129,500
Nefud	N Saudi Arabia	50,000	129,500
Dasht-i-Kavir	N central Iran	18,000	46,620
Sinai	Sinai Peninsula, E Egypt	17,000	44,000
Mojave	S California	15,000	38,850
Negev	S Israel	5000	12,950
Painted	NE Arizona	5000	12,950
Great Salt Lake	NW Utah	4000	10,360
Death Valley	E California and S Nevada	1500	3900

[1670–80; < L *dēsiccant-*, s. of *dēsiccāns*, prp. of *dēsiccāre* to dry up. See DESICCATE, -ANT]

des•ic•cate (des′i kāt′), *v.*, **-cat•ed, -cat•ing.** —*v.t.* **1.** to dry thoroughly; dry up. **2.** to preserve (food) by removing moisture; dehydrate. —*v.i.* **3.** to become thoroughly dried or dried up. [1565–75; < L *dēsiccātus* dried up, ptp. of *dēsiccāre,* equiv. to *dē-* DE- + *siccāre,* deriv. of *siccus* dry; see -ATE[1]] —**des′ic•ca′tion,** *n.* —**des′ic•ca′tive,** *adj.*

des•ic•cat•ed (des′i kā′tid), *adj.* dehydrated or powdered: *desiccated coconut.* [1670–80; DESICCATE + -ED[2]]

des•ic•ca•tor (des′i kā′tər), *n.* **1.** an apparatus for drying fruit, milk, etc. **2.** *Chem.* **a.** an apparatus for absorbing the moisture present in a chemical substance. **b.** an airtight, usually glass container containing calcium chloride or some other drying agent for absorbing the moisture of another substance placed in the container. [1830–40; DESICCATE + -OR[2]]

de•sid•er•a•ta (di sid′ə rā′tə, -rä′-, -zid′-), *n.* pl. of **desideratum.**

de•sid•er•ate (di sid′ə rāt′), *v.t.*, **-at•ed, -at•ing.** to wish or long for. [1635–45; < L *dēsīderātus* (ptp. of *dēsīderāre* to long for, require), equiv. to *dē-* DE- + *sīder-* (s. of *sīdus*) heavenly body, constellation + *-ātus* -ATE[1]] —**de•sid′er•a′tion,** *n.*

de•sid•er•a•tive (di sid′ər ə tiv, -ə rā′tiv), *adj.* **1.** having or expressing desire. **2.** *Gram.* (of a verb derived from another verb) expressing desire to perform the action denoted by the underlying verb, as Sanskrit *pi-pa-tiṣ-ati* "he wishes to fly" from *pát-ati,* "he flies." —*n.* **3.** *Gram.* a desiderative verb. [1545–55; < LL *dēsīderātīvus.* See DESIDERATE, -IVE]

de•sid•er•a•tum (di sid′ə rā′təm, -rä′-, -zid′-), *n., pl.* **-ta** (-tə). something wanted or needed. [1645–55; < L, n. use of neut. ptp. of *dēsīderāre;* see DESIDERATE]

des•i•der•i•um (des′i dēr′ē əm), *n., pl.* **-der•i•a** (-dēr′ē ə). an ardent longing, as for something lost. [1705–15; < L; see DESIDERATE, -IUM]

de•sign (di zīn′), *v.t.* **1.** to prepare the preliminary sketch or the plans for (a work to be executed), esp. to plan the form and structure of: *to design a new bridge.* **2.** to plan and fashion artistically or skillfully. **3.** to intend for a definite purpose: *a scholarship designed for foreign students.* **4.** to contrive or plan: *The prisoner designed an intricate escape.* **5.** to have as one's purpose. **6.** *Obs.* to mark out, as by a sign; indicate. —*v.i.* **7.** to make drawings, preliminary sketches, or plans. **8.** to plan and fashion the form and structure of an object, work of art, decorative scheme, etc. —*n.* **9.** an outline, sketch, or plan, as of the form and structure of a work of art, an edifice, or a machine to be executed or constructed. **10.** organization or structure of formal elements in a work of art; composition. **11.** the combination of details or features of a picture, building, etc.; the pattern or motif of artistic work: *the design on a bracelet.* **12.** the art of designing: *a school of design.* **13.** a plan or project: *a design for a new process.* **14.** a plot or intrigue, esp. a deceitful one: *His political rivals formulated a design to unseat him.* **15. designs,** a hostile or aggressive project or scheme having evil or selfish motives: *He had designs on his partner's stock.* **16.** intention; purpose; end. **17.** adaptation of means to a preconceived end. [1350–1400; ME *designen* < L *dēsignāre* to mark out. See DE-, SIGN]
—**Syn. 5.** See **intend. 13.** See **plan.**

des•ig•nate (*v.* dez′ig nāt′; *adj.* dez′ig nit, -nāt′), *v.*, **-nat•ed, -nat•ing,** *adj.* —*v.t.* **1.** to mark or point out; indicate; show; specify. **2.** to denote; indicate; signify. **3.** to name; entitle; style. **4.** to nominate or select for a duty, office, purpose, etc.; appoint; assign. —*adj.* **5.** named or selected for an office, position, etc., but not yet installed (often used in combination following the noun it modifies): *ambassador-designate.* [1640–50; < L *dēsignātus,* ptp. of *dēsignāre.* See DESIGN, -ATE[1]] —**des′ig•na′tive, des•ig•na•to•ry** (dez′ig nə tôr′ē, -tōr′ē, dez′ig nā′tə rē), *adj.* —**des′ig•na′tor,** *n.* —**des′ig•nee′,** *n.*

des′ignated driv′er, a person who abstains from alcoholic beverages at a gathering in order to be fit to drive companions home safely.

des′ignated hit′ter, *Baseball.* a hitter selected prior to the start of the game to bat for the starting pitcher and all subsequent pitchers without otherwise affecting the status of the pitchers in the game. *Abbr.:* DH, dh [1970–75, *Amer.*]

des•ig•na•tion (dez′ig nā′shən), *n.* **1.** an act of designating. **2.** the fact of being designated. **3.** something that designates; a distinctive name or title; appellation. **4.** nomination, appointment, or election to an office, position, etc.: *His designation as treasurer has been confirmed.* [1350–1400; ME *designacioun* < L *dēsignātiōn-* (s. of *dēsignātiō*) a marking out, equiv. to *dēsignāt(us)* (see DESIGNATE) + *-iōn-* -ION]

de•signed (di zīnd′), *adj.* made or done intentionally; intended; planned. [1580–90; DESIGN + -ED[2]] —**de•sign•ed•ness** (di zī′nid nis), *n.*

de•sign•ed•ly (di zī′nid lē), *adv.* intentionally; purposely; deliberately. [1650–60; DESIGNED + -LY]

de•sign•er (di zī′nər), *n.* **1.** a person who devises or executes designs, esp. one who creates forms, structures, and patterns, as for works of art or machines. **2.** a schemer, intriguer, or plotter. —*adj.* **3.** designed or created by or carrying a label or identification of a designer, esp. a fashion designer, but often mass-produced: *designer jeans.* [1640–50; DESIGN + -ER[1]]

design′er drug′, a drug produced by a minor modification in the chemical structure of an existing drug, resulting in a new substance with similar pharmacologic effects, esp. one created to achieve the same effect as a controlled or illegal drug. [1980–85]

design′er gene′, a gene altered or created by genetic engineering, esp. for use in gene therapy. [1980–85]

de•sign•ing (di zī′ning), *adj.* **1.** scheming; intriguing; artful; crafty. **2.** showing or using forethought. —*n.* **3.** the act or art of making designs. [1610–20; DESIGN + -ING[2], -ING[1]] —**de•sign′ing•ly,** *adv.*
—**Syn. 1.** wily, cunning, tricky, sly.

de•sign•ment (di zīn′mənt), *n. Obs.* design; plan. [1560–70; DESIGN + -MENT]

de•sil•ver (dē sil′vər), *v.t.* to remove silver from (lead in the form of base bullion). [1860–65; DE- + SILVER]

de•sil•ver•ize (dē sil′və rīz′), *v.t.*, **-ized, -iz•ing.** to desilver. Also, *esp. Brit.,* **de•sil′ver•ise′.** [1865–70; DESILVER + -IZE]

des•i•nence (des′ə nəns), *n.* **1.** a termination or ending, as the final line of a verse. **2.** *Gram.* a termination, ending, or suffix of a word. [1590–1600; < F < ML *dēsinentia,* equiv. to L *dēsinent-* (s. of *dēsinēns*), prp. of *dēsinere* to put down, leave (*dē-* DE- + *sinere* to leave) + *-ia* -IA; see -ENCE] —**des′i•nent, des•i•nen•tial** (des′ə nen′shəl), *adj.*

de•si•pra•mine (də zip′rə mēn′, dez′ə pram′in), *n. Pharm.* a tricyclic antidepressant, $C_{18}H_{22}N_2$, used for symptomatic relief in a variety of depressive states. [shortening of *desmethylimipramine,* contracted from the chemical name]

de•sir•a•ble (di zīᵊr′ə bəl), *adj.* **1.** worth having or wanting; pleasing, excellent, or fine: *a desirable apartment.* **2.** arousing desire or longing: *a desirable man or woman.* **3.** advisable; recommendable: *a desirable law.* —*n.* **4.** a person or thing that is desirable. [1350–1400; ME < OF. See DESIRE, -ABLE] —**de•sir′a•bil′i•ty, de•sir′a•ble•ness,** *n.* —**de•sir′a•bly,** *adv.*

de•sire (di zīᵊr′), *v.*, **-sired, -sir•ing,** *n.* —*v.t.* **1.** to wish or long for; crave; want. **2.** to express a wish to obtain; ask for; request: *The mayor desires your presence at the next meeting.* —*n.* **3.** a longing or craving, as for something that brings satisfaction or enjoyment: *a desire for fame.* **4.** an expressed wish; request. **5.** something desired. **6.** sexual appetite or a sexual urge. [1200–50; ME *desiren* < OF *desirer* < L *dēsīderāre;* see DESIDERATE] —**de•sir•ed•ly** (di zīᵊr′id lē, -zīᵊrd′-), *adv.* —**de•sired′ness,** *n.* —**de•sire′less,** *adj.* —**de•sir′er,** *n.* —**de•sir′ing•ly,** *adv.*
—**Syn. 1.** covet, fancy. See **wish. 2.** solicit. **3.** aspiration, hunger, appetite, thirst. DESIRE, CRAVING, LONGING, YEARNING suggest feelings that impel one to the attainment or possession of something. DESIRE is a strong feeling, worthy or unworthy, that impels one to attain something that is seemingly within reach: *a desire for success.* CRAVING implies a deep and imperative wish for something, based on a sense of need and hunger: *a craving for food, companionship.* A LONGING is an intense wish for something that is momentarily beyond reach: *a longing to visit Europe.* YEARNING suggests persistent, uneasy, and sometimes wistful or tender longing: *a yearning for one's native land.*

de•sired (di zīᵊrd′), *adj.* **1.** yearned or wished for; coveted. **2.** deemed correct or proper: *Add water to the desired level.* [1250–1300; ME; see DESIRE, -ED[2]]

Desire′ Un′der the Elms′, a play (1924) by Eugene O'Neill.

de•sir•ous (di zīᵊr′əs), *adj.* having or characterized by desire; desiring: *desirous of high political office.* [1250–1300; ME < OF *desireus.* See DESIRE, -OUS] —**de•sir′ous•ly,** *adv.* —**de•sir′ous•ness,** *n.*

de•sist (di zist′, -sist′), *v.i.* to cease, as from some action or proceeding; stop. [1425–75; late ME < OF *desister* < L *dēsistere* to leave off, equiv. to *dē-* DE- + *sistere* to stand, place, akin to *stāre* to STAND] —**de•sist′ance, de•sist′ence,** *n.*

de Sit•ter (də sit′ər), **Wil•lem** (wil′əm). See **Sitter, Willem de.**

desk (desk), *n.* **1.** an article of furniture having a broad, usually level, writing surface, as well as drawers or compartments for papers, writing materials, etc. **2.** a frame for supporting a book from which the service is read in a church. **3.** a pulpit. **4.** the section of a large organization, as a governmental bureau or newspaper, having authority over and responsibility for particular operations within the organization: *city desk; foreign desk.* **5.** a table or counter, as in a library or office, at which a specific job is performed or a service offered: *an information desk; reception desk.* **6.** a stand used to support sheet music; music stand. **7.** (in an orchestra) a seat or position assigned by rank (usually used in combination): *a first-desk flutist.* —*adj.* **8.** of or pertaining to a writing desk: *a desk drawer.* **9.** of a size or form suitable for use on a desk: *desk dictionary.* **10.** done at or based on a desk, as in an office or schoolroom: *He used to be a traveling salesman, but now he has a desk job.* [1350–1400; ME *deske* < ML *desca, descus* desk, lectern, prob. < a Romance-influenced form of L *discus* DISCUS; cf. DAIS, DISH, ML *discus* refectory table]

desk•bound (desk′bound′), *adj.* **1.** doing sedentary work; working exclusively at a desk. **2.** unfamiliar with actualities or practical matters outside one's own job: *deskbound executives who can't grasp production problems.* **3.** noncombatant: *deskbound generals.* [1940–45; DESK + -BOUND[1]]

desk′ cal′endar, a loose-leaf calendar containing one or two pages for each day, with spaces for notes. [1905–10]

desk′ cop′ier, a photocopier compact enough to fit on a desk, table, or similar surface.

de•skill (dē skil′), *v.t.* to remove any need of skill, judgment, or initiative in: *jobs being deskilled by automation.* [DE- + SKILL[1]]

desk′ job′ber. See **drop shipper.**

desk•man (desk′man′, -mən), *n., pl.* **-men** (-men′, -mən). **1.** *Journalism.* a member of a newspaper staff who processes news and prepares copy, usually from information telephoned in by reporters. **2.** a person who works at a desk. [1890–95; DESK + MAN[1]]

desk′ pad′, a cushioned pad, often topped with a blotter, for the surface of a desk.

desk-size (desk′sīz′), *adj.* of a size suitable for use on a desk: *a desk-size dictionary.* Also, **desk′-sized′.**

desk•top (desk′top′), *adj.* small or compact enough to fit or be used on a desk: *a desktop computer.* [1925–30; DESK + TOP[1]]

desk′top pub′lishing, *Computers.* the design and production of publications by means of specialized software enabling a microcomputer to generate typeset-quality text and graphics. Also called **computer-aided publishing.**

desk′ work′, **1.** work done at a desk. **2.** habitual writing, as that of a clerk. [1860–65]

D. ès L., Doctor of Letters. [< F *Docteur ès Lettres*]

des•man (des′mən), *n., pl.* **-mans.** either of two aquatic, insectivorous mammals, *Myogale moschata,* of southeastern Russia, or *M. pyrenaica,* of the Pyrenees, related to shrews. [1765–75; < Sw, short for *desmanrätta* muskrat]

des•mid (dez′mid), *n.* any single-celled freshwater algae of the family Desmidiaceae, characterized by a division of the body into mirror-image halves joined by a bridge containing the nucleus, and having a spiny or bristly exterior: sometimes forming into colonies or branching filaments. [1860–65; < NL *Desmidium* a genus of the family < Gk *desm(ós)* a band, chain (cf. *deîn* to fasten) + NL *-idium* -IDIUM] —**des•mid′i•an,** *adj.*

des•mi•tis (dez mī′tis), *n. Pathol.* inflammation of a ligament. [< NL < Gk *desm(ós)* (see DESMID) + *-ītis* -ITIS]

des•moid (dez′moid), *adj. Anat., Zool.* **1.** resembling a fascia or fibrous sheet. **2.** resembling a ligament; ligamentous. —*n.* **3.** *Pathol.* a firm and tough tumor of nonmetastasizing, fibrous tissue. [1840–50; < Gk *desm(ós)* (see DESMID) + -OID]

Des Moines (də moin′), **1.** a city in and the capital of Iowa, in the central part, on the Des Moines River. 191,003. **2.** a river flowing SE from SW Minnesota

CONCISE PRONUNCIATION KEY: act, cāpe, dâre, pärt; set, ēqual; if, īce; ox, ōver, ôrder, oil, bŏŏk, bŏŏt, out; up, ûrge; child; sing; shoe; thin, *th*at; zh as in *treasure.* ə = *a* as in *alone, e* as in *system, i* as in *easily, o* as in *gallop, u* as in *circus;* ᵊ as in *fire* (fīᵊr), *hour* (ouᵊr). l and n can serve as syllabic consonants, as in *cradle* (krād′l), and *button* (but′n). See the full key inside the front cover.

through Iowa to the Mississippi River. ab. 530 mi. (850 km) long. —**Des Moines·i·an** (də moi′nē ən).

Des·mond (dez′mənd), *n.* a male given name.

des′mo·pres′sin ac′etate (dez′mə pres′in, dez′-), *Pharm.* a vasopressin analogue, $C_{46}H_{84}N_{14}O_{12}S_2$, used in the treatment of diabetes insipidus. [*des(a)m(in)o-*, a component of its chemical name + (VASO)PRESSIN]

des·mo·some (dez′mə sōm′), *n. Cell Biol.* a plaquelike site on a cell surface that functions in maintaining cohesion with an adjacent cell. [1930–35; < Gk *desm(ós)* band, chain (see DESMID) + -O- + -SOME[2]]

Des·mou·lins (de mo͞o laN′), *n.* **(Lu·cie Sim·plice) Ca·mille (Be·noit)** (lʏ sē′ saN plēs′ ka mē′yᵊ bə nwa′), 1760–94, journalist, pamphleteer, and leader in the French Revolution.

De·sna (də snä′; *Russ.* dyi snä′), *n.* a river in the W Russian Federation flowing S to join the Dnieper River near Kiev in Ukraine. ab. 500 mi. (800 km) long.

de·so·cial·ize (dē sō′shə līz′), *v.t.*, **-ized, -iz·ing.** to remove from a customary social environment: *Imprisonment desocializes the inmates.* Also, *esp. Brit.,* **de·so′·cial·ise′.** [1885–90; DE- + SOCIALIZE] —**de·so′cial·i·za′tion,** *n.*

des·o·late (*adj.* des′ə lit; *v.* des′ə lāt′), *adj., v.,* **-lat·ed, -lat·ing.** —*adj.* **1.** barren or laid waste; devastated: *a treeless, desolate landscape.* **2.** deprived or destitute of inhabitants; deserted; uninhabited. **3.** solitary; lonely: *a desolate place.* **4.** having the feeling of being abandoned by friends or by hope; forlorn. **5.** dreary; dismal; gloomy: *desolate prospects.* —*v.t.* **6.** to lay waste; devastate. **7.** to deprive of inhabitants; depopulate. **8.** to make disconsolate. **9.** to forsake or abandon. [1325–75; ME < L *dēsōlātus* forsaken, ptp. of *dēsōlāre,* equiv. to *dē-* DE- + *sōlāre* to make lonely, deriv. of *sōlus* SOLE[1]; see -ATE[1]] —**des′o·late·ly,** *adv.* —**des′o·late·ness,** *n.* —**des′o·lat′er, des′o·la′tor,** *n.*
—**Syn. 1.** ravaged. **2.** desert. **4.** lonesome, lost; miserable, wretched, woebegone, woeful, inconsolable, cheerless, hopeless. DESOLATE, DISCONSOLATE, FORLORN suggest one who is in a sad and wretched condition. The DESOLATE person is deprived of human consolation, relationships, or presence: *desolate and despairing.* The DISCONSOLATE person is aware of the efforts of others to console and comfort, but is unable to be relieved or cheered by them: *She remained disconsolate even in the midst of friends.* The FORLORN person is lost, deserted, or forsaken by friends: *wretched and forlorn in a strange city.* **6.** ravage, ruin. **8.** sadden, depress. **9.** desert. —**Ant. 4.** delighted, happy.

des·o·la·tion (des′ə lā′shən), *n.* **1.** an act or instance of desolating. **2.** the state of being desolated. **3.** devastation; ruin. **4.** depopulation. **5.** dreariness; barrenness. **6.** deprivation of companionship; loneliness. **7.** sorrow; grief; woe. **8.** a desolate place. [1350–1400; ME < LL *dēsōlātiōn-* (s. of *dēsōlātiō*) abandonment, equiv. to *dēsōlāt(us)* (see DESOLATE) + *-iōn-* -ION]

de·sorb (dē sôrb′, -zôrb′), *v.t. Physical Chem.* to remove an absorbate or adsorbate from (an absorbent or adsorbent). [1920–25; DE- + *-sorb,* modeled on ABSORB] —**de·sorp·tion** (dē sôrp′shən, -zôrp′-), *n.*

De So·to (də sō′tō; *Sp.* de sô′tô), **1. Her·nan·do** (hər nan′dō; *Sp.* er nän′dō) or **Fer·nan·do** (fər nan′dō; *Sp.* fer nän′dō), c1500–42, Spanish soldier and explorer in America. **2.** a city in NE Texas. 15,538.

desoxy-, older form of **deoxy-.**

de·spair (di spâr′), *n.* **1.** loss of hope; hopelessness. **2.** someone or something that causes hopelessness: *He is the despair of his mother.* —*v.i.* **3.** to lose, give up, or be without hope (often fol. by *of*): *to despair of humanity.* —*v.t.* **4.** *Obs.* to give up hope of. [1275–1325; ME *despeir* (n.), *despeiren* (v.) < AF *despeir,* OF *despoir* (n.), *despeir-,* tonic s. of *desperer* (v.) < L *dēspērāre* to be without hope, equiv. to *dē-* DE- + *spērāre* to hope, deriv. of *spēs* hope] —**de·spair′er,** *n.*
—**Syn. 1.** gloom, disheartenment. DESPAIR, DESPERATION, DESPONDENCY, DISCOURAGEMENT, HOPELESSNESS refer to a state of mind caused by circumstances that seem too much to cope with. DESPAIR suggests total loss of hope, which may be passive or may drive one to furious efforts, even if at random: *in the depths of despair; courage born of despair.* DESPERATION is usually an active state, the abandonment of hope impelling to a furious struggle against adverse circumstances, with utter disregard of consequences: *an act of desperation when everything else had failed.* DESPONDENCY is a state of deep gloom and disheartenment: *a spell of despondency.* DISCOURAGEMENT is a loss of courage, hope, and ambition because of obstacles, frustrations, etc.: *His optimism yielded to discouragement.* HOPELESSNESS is a loss of hope so complete as to result in a more or less permanent state of passive despair: *a state of hopelessness and apathy.* —**Ant. 1.** hope.

de·spair·ing (di spâr′ing), *adj.* **1.** given to despair or hopelessness. **2.** indicating despair: *a despairing look.* [1585–95; DESPAIR + -ING[2]] —**de·spair′ing·ly,** *adv.*
—**Syn. 1.** See **hopeless.** —**Ant. 1.** hopeful.

des·patch (di spach′), *v.t., v.i., n.* dispatch.

des·per·a·do (des′pə rä′dō, -rā′-), *n., pl.* **-does, -dos.** a bold, reckless criminal or outlaw, esp. in the early days of the American West. [1600–10; prob. pseudo-Sp alter. of DESPERATE (as n., now obs.), in same sense]

des·per·ate (des′pər it, -prit), *adj.* **1.** reckless or dangerous because of despair or urgency: *a desperate killer.* **2.** having an urgent need, desire, etc.: *desperate for attention.* **3.** leaving little or no hope; very serious or dangerous: *a desperate illness.* **4.** extremely bad; intolerable or shocking: *clothes in desperate taste.* **5.** extreme or excessive. **6.** making a final, ultimate effort; giving all: *a desperate attempt to save a life.* **7.** actuated by a feeling of hopelessness. **8.** having no hope; giving in to despair. —*n.* **9.** *Obs.* a desperado. [1350–1400; ME < L *dēspērātus,* ptp. of *dēspērāre* to DESPAIR; see -ATE[1]] —**des′per·ate·ly,** *adv.* —**des′per·ate·ness,** *n.*
—**Syn. 1.** rash, frantic. **3.** grave. See **hopeless. 8.** forlorn, desolate. —**Ant. 1.** careful. **3, 8.** hopeful.

des·per·a·tion (des′pə rā′shən), *n.* **1.** the state of being desperate or of having the recklessness of despair. **2.** the act or fact of despairing; despair. [1325–75; ME *desperacioun* < L *dēspērātiōn-* (s. of *dēspērātiō*). See DESPERATE, -ION]
—**Syn. 1.** See **despair.**

des·pi·ca·ble (des′pi kə bəl, di spik′ə-), *adj.* deserving to be despised; contemptible: *a mean, despicable man.* [1545–55; < LL *dēspicābilis,* equiv. to L *dēspic(āri)* to despise or *dēspic(ere)* to look down (*dē-* DE- + *-spic-* look, comb. form of *specere*) + *-ābilis* -ABLE] —**des′pi·ca·bil′i·ty, des′pi·ca·ble·ness,** *n.* —**des′pi·ca·bly,** *adv.*
—**Syn.** vile, mean, detestable. —**Ant.** admirable.

de·spise (di spīz′), *v.t.,* **-spised, -spis·ing.** to regard with contempt, distaste, disgust, or disdain; scorn; loathe. [1250–1300; ME *despisen* < OF *despis-,* s. of *despire* < L *dēspicere;* see DESPICABLE] —**de·spis′a·ble,** *adj.* —**de·spis′a·ble·ness,** *n.* —**de·spis′er,** *n.* —**de·spis′ing·ly,** *adv.*
—**Syn.** contemn, detest. —**Ant.** admire.

de·spite (di spīt′), *prep., n., v.,* **-spit·ed, -spit·ing.** —*prep.* **1.** in spite of; notwithstanding. —*n.* **2.** contemptuous treatment; insult. **3.** malice, hatred, or spite. **4. in despite of,** in spite of; notwithstanding: *He was tolerant in despite of his background and education.* —*v.t.* **5.** *Obs.* to anger or annoy (someone) out of spite. [1250–1300; orig. *in despite of;* ME *despit* < OF < L *dēspectus* view from a height, scorn, equiv. to *dēspec-,* var. s. of *dēspicere* (see DESPICABLE) + *-tus* suffix of v. action]
—**Syn. 1.** See **notwithstanding.**

de·spite·ful (di spīt′fəl), *adj.* **1.** malicious; spiteful. **2.** *Obs.* contemptuous; insolent. [1400–50; late ME. See DESPITE, -FUL] —**de·spite′ful·ly,** *adv.* —**de·spite′ful·ness,** *n.*

des·pit·e·ous (di spit′ē əs), *adj. Archaic.* **1.** malicious; spiteful. **2.** contemptuous. [1350–1400; var. of ME *despitous* < AF; OF *despiteus,* equiv. to *despit* DESPITE + *-eus* -EOUS] —**des·pit′e·ous·ly,** *adv.*

Des Plaines (des plānz′), a city in NE Illinois, near Chicago. 53,568.

de·spoil (di spoil′), *v.t.* to strip of possessions, things of value, etc.; rob; plunder; pillage. [1175–1225; ME *despoilen* < OF *despoillier* < L *dēspoliāre* to strip, rob, plunder, equiv. to *dē-* DE- + *spoliāre* to plunder; see SPOIL] —**de·spoil′er,** *n.* —**de·spoil′ment,** *n.*
—**Syn.** dispossess, divest; rifle, sack; fleece.

de·spo·li·a·tion (di spō′lē ā′shən), *n.* **1.** the act of plundering. **2.** the fact or circumstance of being plundered. [1650–60; < LL *dēspoliātiōn-* (s. of *dēspoliātiō*), equiv. to L *dēspoliāt(us)* (ptp. of *dēspoliāre;* see DESPOIL) + *-iōn-* -ION]

de·spond (di spond′ *or, esp. for 2,* des′pond), *v.i.* **1.** to be depressed by loss of hope, confidence, or courage. —*n.* **2.** despondency. [1670–80; < L *dēspondēre* to give up, lose heart, promise, equiv. to *dē-* DE- + *spondēre* to promise] —**de·spond′er,** *n.* —**de·spond′ing·ly,** *adv.*

de·spond·en·cy (di spon′dən sē), *n.* state of being despondent; depression of spirits from loss of courage or hope; dejection. Also, **de·spond′ence.** [1645–55; DESPOND + -ENCY]
—**Syn.** melancholy, gloom. See **despair.** —**Ant.** joy.

de·spond·ent (di spon′dənt), *adj.* feeling or showing profound hopelessness, dejection, discouragement, or gloom: *despondent about failing health.* [1690–1700; < L *dēspondent-* (s. of *dēspondēns*), prp. of *dēspondēre.* See DESPOND, -ENT] —**de·spond′ent·ly,** *adv.*
—**Syn.** disheartened, downhearted, melancholy, blue. See **hopeless.** —**Ant.** happy, hopeful.

des·pot (des′pət, -pot), *n.* **1.** a king or other ruler with absolute, unlimited power; autocrat. **2.** any tyrant or oppressor. **3.** *Hist.* an honorary title applied to a Byzantine emperor, afterward to members of his family, and later to Byzantine vassal rulers and governors. [1555–65; < Gk *despótēs* master < **dems-pot-* presumably, "master of the house," equiv. to **dems-,* akin to *dómos* house + *pot-,* base of *pósis* husband, spouse; cf. HOSPODAR, HOST[1]]

des·pot·ic (di spot′ik), *adj.* of, pertaining to, or of the nature of a despot or despotism; autocratic; tyrannical. Also, **des·pot′i·cal.** [1640–50; < F *despotique* < Gk *despotikós.* See DESPOT, -IC] —**des·pot′i·cal·ly,** *adv.*

despot′ic mon′archy. See **absolute monarchy.** —**despot′ic mon′arch.**

des·pot·ism (des′pə tiz′əm), *n.* **1.** the rule of a despot; the exercise of absolute authority. **2.** absolute power or control; tyranny. **3.** an absolute or autocratic government. **4.** a country ruled by a despot. [1720–30; < F *despotisme.* See DESPOT, -ISM]

Des Prés (də prā′; *Fr.* dā prā′), **Jos·quin** (zhus′kan; *Fr.* zhôs kaN′), c1445–1521, Flemish composer.

des·qua·mate (des′kwə māt′), *v.i.,* **-mat·ed, -mat·ing.** *Pathol.* to come off in scales, as the skin in certain diseases; peel off. [1720–30; < L *dēsquāmātus* (ptp. of *dēsquāmāre* to remove scales from). See DE-, SQUAMATE] —**des′qua·ma′tion,** *n.*

D. ès S., Doctor of Sciences. [< F *Docteur ès Sciences*]

Des·sa·lines (dā sa lēn′), *n.* **Jean Jacques** (zhäN zhäk), 1758–1806, Haitian revolutionary: emperor of Haiti as Jacques I 1804–06.

Des·sau (des′ou), *n.* a city in NE central Germany, SW of Berlin: formerly the capital of Anhalt. 102,000.

des·sert (di zûrt′), *n.* **1.** cake, pie, fruit, pudding, ice cream, etc., served as the final course of a meal. **2.** *Brit.* a serving of fresh fruit after the main course of a meal. [1780–90; < F, deriv. of *desservir* to clear the table. See DIS-[1], SERVE]

dessert′ fork′, a fork used for eating certain desserts, usually somewhat smaller than a dinner fork.

dessert′ knife′, a knife used during the dessert course, usually somewhat smaller than a dinner knife. [1785–95]

des·sert·spoon (di zûrt′spo͞on′), *n.* a spoon intermediate in size between a tablespoon and a teaspoon, used in eating certain desserts. [1800–10; DESSERT + SPOON]

des·sert·spoon·ful (di zûrt′spo͞on fo͝ol′), *n., pl.* **-fuls.** as much as a dessertspoon can hold: 2½ fluid drams. [1870–75; DESSERTSPOON + -FUL]
—**Usage.** See **-ful.**

dessert′ wine′, a sweet wine served with dessert or sometimes after a meal. [1765–75]

des·sia·tine (des′yə tēn′), *n.* a Russian unit of land measure equal to 2.7 U.S. acres (1.1 hectare). [1790–1800; < Russ *desyatína* lit., tithe, tenth, deriv. of *désyat′* ten]

de·sta·bi·lize (dē stā′bə līz′), *v.t.,* **-lized, -liz·ing.** to make unstable; rid of stabilizing attributes: *conflicts that tend to destabilize world peace.* Also, *esp. Brit.,* **de·sta′·bi·lise′.** [1930–35; DE- + STABILIZE] —**de·sta′bi·li·za′·tion,** *n.*

de·stain (dē stān′), *v.t. Histol.* to remove stain (from a specimen) to enhance visibility and contrast of parts. [1925–30; DE- + STAIN]

de-Sta·lin·i·za·tion (dē stä′lə nə zā′shən, -stal′ə-), *n.* the policy, pursued in most Communist areas and among most Communist groups after 1956, of eradicating the memory or influence of Stalin and Stalinism, as by alteration of governmental policies or the elimination of monuments, place names, etc., named for Stalin. Also, **de·sta′lin·i·za′tion.** [1955–60; DE-STALINIZE + -ATION]

de-Sta·lin·ize (dē stä′lə nīz′, -stal′ə-), *v.,* **-ized, -iz·ing.** —*v.i.* **1.** (of a Communist country) to engage in de-Stalinization. —*v.t.* **2.** to subject to de-Stalinization. Also, **de·sta′lin·ize′;** *esp. Brit.,* **de-Sta′lin·ise′, de·sta′·lin·ise′.** [1955–60; DE- + STALIN + -IZE]

de·stem (dē stem′), *v.t.,* **-stemmed, -stem·ming.** to remove the stem from (a fruit or vegetable); stem. [DE- + STEM[1]] —**de·stem′mer,** *n.*

de·ster·i·lize (dē ster′ə līz′), *v.t.,* **-lized, -liz·ing.** to utilize an idle fund or commodity, as when a nation issues currency against gold previously unused. Also, *esp. Brit.,* **de·ster′i·lise′.** [DE- + STERILIZE] —**de·ster′i·li·za′tion,** *n.*

Des·ter·ro (*Port.* des ter′ro͞o), *n.* former name of **Florianópolis.**

de Stijl (də stīl′), a school of art that was founded in the Netherlands in 1917, embraced painting, sculpture, architecture, furniture, and the decorative arts, and was marked esp. by the use of black and white with the primary colors, rectangular forms, and asymmetry. Also, **De Stijl′.** [1930–35; < D: lit., the style, the name of a magazine published by participants in the movement]

des·ti·na·tion (des′tə nā′shən), *n.* **1.** the place to which a person or thing travels or is sent: *Her destination was Rome.* **2.** the purpose for which something is destined. [1350–1400; ME < L *dēstinātiōn-* (s. of *dēstinātiō*) an establishing, purpose, equiv. to *dēstināt(us)* (ptp. of *dēstināre;* see DESTINE) + *-iōn-* -ION]

des·tine (des′tin), *v.t.,* **-tined, -tin·ing.** **1.** to set apart for a particular use, purpose, etc.; design; intend. **2.** to appoint or ordain beforehand, as by divine decree; foreordain; predetermine. [1250–1300; ME *destinen* < OF *destiner* < L *dēstināre* to establish, determine, equiv. to *dē-* DE- + **stanāre,* deriv. of *stāre* to STAND]

des·tined (des′tind), *adj.* **1.** bound for a certain destination: *a freighter destined for the Orient.* **2.** ordained, appointed, or predetermined to be or do something. **3.** liable, planning, or intending to be or do something. [1590–1600; DESTINE + -ED[2]]

des·ti·ny (des′tə nē), *n., pl.* **-nies.** **1.** something that is to happen or has happened to a particular person or thing; lot or fortune. **2.** the predetermined, usually inevitable or irresistible, course of events. **3.** the power or agency that determines the course of events. **4.** (*cap.*) this power personified or represented as a goddess. **5. the Destinies,** the Fates. [1275–1325; ME *destinee* < OF (n. use of ptp. of *destiner*) < L *dēstināta,* fem. ptp. of *dēstināre.* See DESTINE, -EE]
—**Syn. 1.** fate, karma, kismet. **2.** future. See **fate.**

des·ti·tute (des′ti to͞ot′, -tyo͞ot′), *adj., v.,* **-tut·ed, -tut·ing.** —*adj.* **1.** without means of subsistence; lacking food, clothing, and shelter. **2.** deprived of, devoid of, or lacking (often fol. by *of*): *destitute of children.* —*v.t.* **3.** to leave destitute. [1350–1400; ME < L *dēstitūtus* (ptp. of *dēstituere* to abandon, deprive of support), equiv. to *dē-* DE- + *stit-* place, put (comb. form of *statuere;* see STATUTE) + *-ū-* thematic vowel + *-tus* ptp. suffix] —**des′ti·tute′ly,** *adv.* —**des′ti·tute′ness,** *n.*
—**Syn. 1.** needy, poor, indigent, necessitous, penniless, impoverished. **2.** deficient. —**Ant. 1.** affluent.

des·ti·tu·tion (des′ti to͞o′shən, -tyo͞o′-), *n.* **1.** lack of the means of subsistence; utter poverty. **2.** deprivation, lack, or absence. [1400–50; late ME < L *dēstitūtiōn-* (s. of *dēstitūtiō*) an abandoning, equiv. to *dēstitūt(us)* (see DESTITUTE) + *-iōn-* -ION]
—**Syn. 1.** See **poverty.** —**Ant. 1.** affluence.

de·stool (dē sto͞ol′), *v.t.* to remove (a West African ruler) from office. [1925–30; DE- + STOOL]

des·tri·er (des′trē ər, de strēr′), *n. Archaic.* a war-horse; charger. [1250–1300; ME *destrer* < AF, var. of OF *destrier,* lit., (horse) led at the right hand < VL **dextrārius (equus),* equiv. to L *dext(e)r* right-hand (see DEXTER) + *-ārius* -ARY]

de·stroy (di stroi′), *v.t.* **1.** to reduce (an object) to useless fragments, a useless form, or remains, as by rending, burning, or dissolving; injure beyond repair or renewal; demolish; ruin; annihilate. **2.** to put an end to; extin-

CONCISE ETYMOLOGY KEY: <, descended or borrowed from; >, whence; b., blend of, blended; c., cognate with; cf., compare; deriv., derivative; equiv., equivalent; imit., imitative; obl., oblique; r., replacing; s., stem; sp., spelling, spelled; resp., respelling, respelled; trans., translation; ?, origin unknown; *, unattested; ‡, probably earlier than. See the full key inside the front cover.

guish. **3.** to kill; slay. **4.** to render ineffective or useless; nullify; neutralize; invalidate. **5.** to defeat completely. —*v.i.* **6.** to engage in destruction. [1175–1225; ME *destroyen* < OF *destruire* < VL **dēstrūgere,* for L *dēstruere* (*dē-* DE- + *struere* to pick up, build)] —**de·stroy′a·ble,** *adj.*
—**Syn. 1.** smash, level, waste, ravage, devastate. DESTROY, DEMOLISH, RAZE imply reducing a thing to uselessness. To DESTROY is to reduce something to nothingness or to take away its powers and functions so that restoration is impossible: *Fire destroys a building. Disease destroys tissues.* To DEMOLISH is to destroy something organized or structured: *to demolish a machine.* To RAZE is to level down to the ground: *to raze a fortress.* **2.** extirpate, annihilate, uproot. —**Ant. 1, 2.** create.

de·stroy·er (di stroi′ər), *n.* **1.** a person or thing that destroys. **2.** a fast, relatively small, warship armed mainly with 5-in. (13-cm) guns. [1350–1400; ME *destroiere* (cf. OF *destruiere*). See DESTROY, -ER[1]]

destroy′er es′cort, a warship somewhat smaller than a destroyer, designed esp. for antisubmarine action. *Abbr.:* DE [1940–45]

destroy′ing an′gel, any of several deadly poisonous mushrooms of the genus *Amanita,* having a white cap and stem, white spores, and a conspicuous volva at the base of the stem. [1905–10]

de·struct (di strukt′), *adj.* **1.** serving or designed to destroy: *a destruct mechanism on a missile.* —*n.* **2.** the act or process of intentional destruction: *One out of ten launchings ended in destructs.* —*v.t.* **3.** to destroy. —*v.i.* **4.** to be destroyed. [1630–40; back formation from DESTRUCTION]

de·struct·i·ble (di struk′tə bəl), *adj.* capable of being destroyed; liable to destruction. [1745–55; < LL *dēstructibil(is),* equiv. to L *dēstruct(us)* pulled down (see DESTRUCTION) + *-ibilis* -IBLE] —**de·struct′i·bil′i·ty, de·struct′i·ble·ness,** *n.*

de·struc·tion (di struk′shən), *n.* **1.** the act of destroying: *wanton destruction of a town.* **2.** the condition of being destroyed; demolition; annihilation. **3.** a cause or means of destroying. [1275–1325; ME (< AF) < L *dēstructiōn-* (s. of *dēstructiō*), equiv. to *dēstruct(us)* (ptp. of *dēstruere;* see DESTROY) + *-iōn-* -ION]
—**Syn. 1.** See **ruin.**

de·struc·tion·ist (di struk′shə nist), *n.* an advocate of the destruction of an existing political institution or the like. [1800–10; DESTRUCTION + -IST]

de·struc·tive (di struk′tiv), *adj.* **1.** tending to destroy; causing destruction or much damage (often fol. by *of* or *to*): *a very destructive windstorm.* **2.** tending to overthrow, disprove, or discredit (opposed to *constructive*): *destructive criticism.* [1480–90; < MF < LL *dēstructīvus,* equiv. to L *dēstruct(us)* (see DESTRUCTION) + *-īvus* -IVE] —**de·struc′tive·ly,** *adv.* —**de·struc′tive·ness, de·struc·tiv·i·ty** (dē′struk tiv′i tē), *n.*
—**Syn. 1.** ruinous, deleterious. **2.** unfavorable, adverse, negative. —**Ant. 1.** creative. **2.** constructive.

destruc′tive distilla′tion, *Chem.* the decomposition of a substance, as wood or coal, by heating with a minimal exposure to air, and the collection of the volatile products formed. [1825–35]

destruc′tive interfer′ence, *Physics.* the interference of two waves of equal frequency and opposite phase, resulting in their cancellation where the negative displacement of one always coincides with the positive displacement of the other. Cf. **constructive interference.**

de·struc·tor (di struk′tər), *n.* **1.** *Brit.* a furnace for the burning of refuse; incinerator. **2.** *Rocketry.* a destruct mechanism or device for destroying an off-course airborne missile or launch vehicle. [1685–95; < LL *dēstructor,* equiv. to L *dēstruc-* var. s. of *dēstruere* (see DESTRUCTION) + *-tor* -TOR]

des·ue·tude (des′wi to͞od′, -tyo͞od′), *n.* the state of being no longer used or practiced. [1425–75; late ME < L *dēsuētūdo,* equiv. to *dēsuē-,* base of *dēsuēscere* to become disaccustomed to, unlearn (*dē-* DE- + *suēscere* to become accustomed to) + *-tūdō* -TUDE]

de·sul·fur (dē sul′fər), *v.t.* to free from sulfur; desulfurize. Also, **de·sul·phur.** [1870–75; DE- + SULFUR]

de·sul·fu·rate (dē sul′fyə rāt′, -fə-), *v.t.,* **-rat·ed, -rat·ing.** *Chem.* to desulfurize. Also, **de·sul′phu·rate′.** [1750–60; DE- + SULFURATE] —**de·sul′fu·ra′tion,** *n.*

de·sul·fu·rize (dē sul′fyə rīz′, -fə-), *v.t.,* **-rized, -riz·ing.** to free from sulfur. Also, **de·sul′phu·rize′;** *esp. Brit.,* **de·sul′fu·rise.** [1860–65; DE- + SULFURIZE] —**de·sul′fu·ri·za′tion,** *n.* —**de·sul′fu·riz′er,** *n.*

des·ul·to·ry (des′əl tôr′ē, -tōr′ē), *adj.* **1.** lacking in consistency, constancy, or visible order, disconnected; fitful: *desultory conversation.* **2.** digressing from or unconnected with the main subject; random: *a desultory remark.* [1575–85; < L *dēsultōrius* pertaining to a *dēsultor* (a circus rider who jumps from one horse to another), equiv. to *dēsul-,* var. s. of *dēsilīre* to jump down (*dē-* DE- + *-silīre,* comb. form of *salīre* to leap) + *-tōrius* -TORY[1]] —**des′ul·to′ri·ly,** *adv.* —**des′ul·to′ri·ness,** *n.*
—**Syn. 1.** See **haphazard.**

DET, 1. Also, **Det** *Ling.* determiner. **2.** *Pharm.* diethyltryptamine.

det., 1. detach. **2.** detachment. **3.** detail. **4.** determine. **5.** (in prescriptions) let it be given. [< L *dētur*]

de·tach (di tach′), *v.t.* **1.** to unfasten and separate; disengage; disunite. **2.** *Mil.* to send away (a regiment, ship, etc.) on a special mission. [1470–80; < MF *détacher,* OF *destachier;* see DIS-[1], ATTACH] —**de·tach′a·ble,** *adj.* —**de·tach′a·bil′i·ty,** *n.* —**de·tach′a·bly,** *adv.* —**de·tach′er,** *n.*

de·tached (di tacht′), *adj.* **1.** not attached; separated: *a detached ticket stub.* **2.** having no wall in common with another building (opposed to *attached*): *a detached house.* **3.** impartial or objective; disinterested; unbiased: *a detached judgment.* **4.** not involved or concerned; aloof. [1700–10; DETACH + -ED[2]] —**de·tach·ed·ly** (di tach′id lē, -tacht′lē), *adv.* —**de·tach′ed·ness,** *n.*
—**Syn. 3.** uninvolved, neutral, evenhanded, dispassionate, unprejudiced. —**Ant. 1, 2.** attached.

de·tach·ment (di tach′mənt), *n.* **1.** the act of detaching. **2.** the condition of being detached. **3.** aloofness, as from worldly affairs or from the concerns of others. **4.** freedom from prejudice or partiality. **5.** the act of sending out a detached force of troops or naval ships. **6.** the body of troops or ships so detached. [1660–70; < F *détachement.* See DETACH, -MENT]
—**Syn. 3.** coolness, indifference, unconcern.

de·tail (*n.* di tāl′, dē′tāl; *v.* di tāl′), *n.* **1.** an individual or minute part; an item or particular. **2.** particulars collectively; minutiae. **3.** attention to or treatment of a subject in individual or minute parts: *to postpone detail and concentrate on a subject as a whole.* **4.** intricate, finely wrought decoration. **5.** *Engin.* See **detail drawing. 6.** any small section of a larger structure or whole, considered as a unit. **7.** *Mil.* **a.** an appointment or assignment, as of a small group or an officer, for a special task. **b.** the party or person so selected: *the kitchen detail.* **c.** a particular assignment of duty. **8.** the property of an image or of a method of image production to make small, closely spaced image elements individually distinguishable. **9. in detail,** item by item; with particulars: *The résumé stated his qualifications in detail.* —*v.t.* **10.** to relate or report with complete particulars; tell fully and distinctly. **11.** to mention one by one; specify; list: *He detailed the events leading up to the robbery.* **12.** *Mil.* to appoint or assign for some particular duty: *We were detailed to patrol the border.* **13.** to provide with intricate, finely wrought decoration: *lingerie detailed with lace and embroidery.* [1595–1605; < F *détail,* OF, n. deriv. of *detailler* to cut in pieces, equiv. to *de-* DIS-[1] + *tailler* to cut < VL **tāliāre;* see TAILOR]
—**Syn. 11.** itemize, enumerate, catalog.

de′tail draw′ing, *Engin.* a drawing, at relatively large scale, of a part of a building, machine, etc., with dimensions or other information for use in construction. Also called **detail.**

de·tailed (di tāld′, dē′tāld), *adj.* **1.** having many details: *a detailed problem.* **2.** thorough in the treatment of details; minute: *a detailed report.* [1730–40; DETAIL + -ED[2]] —**de·tailed·ly** (di tāld′lē, -tā′lid-), *adv.* —**de·tailed′ness,** *n.*
—**Syn. 1.** involved, complex, complicated. **2.** itemized, particularized; exhaustive, thorough, comprehensive.

de·tail·er (dē′tā lər), *n.* a manufacturer's representative who calls on customers to supply information on products and visits stores to monitor sales and replenish stock. Also called **de′tail man′.** [1785–95, for an earlier sense; DETAIL + -ER[1]]

de·tain (di tān′), *v.t.* **1.** to keep from proceeding; keep waiting; delay. **2.** to keep under restraint or in custody. **3.** *Obs.* to keep back or withhold, as from a person. [1480–90; *detainen* < AF, OF *detenir* < VL **dētenīre,* for L *dētinēre,* equiv. to *dē-* DE- + *-tinēre,* comb. form of *tenēre* to hold] —**de·tain′a·ble,** *adj.* —**de·tain′ment,** *n.*
—**Syn. 1.** retard, stop, slow, stay, check.

de·tain·ee (di tā′nē, dē′tā nē′), *n.* a person held in custody, esp. for a political offense or for questioning. [1925–30; DETAIN + -EE]

de·tain·er (di tā′nər), *n. Law.* **1.** a writ for the further detention of a person already in custody. **2.** the wrongful detaining or withholding of what belongs to another. [1610–20; < AF *detener* (n. use of inf.), var. of OF *detenir;* see DETAIN]

de·tect (di tekt′), *v.t.* **1.** to discover or catch (a person) in the performance of some act: *to detect someone cheating.* **2.** to discover the existence of: *to detect the odor of gas.* **3.** to find out the true character or activity of: *to detect a spy.* **4.** *Telecommunications.* **a.** to rectify alternating signal currents in a radio receiver. **b.** to demodulate. [1400–50; late ME < L *dētectus* (ptp. of *dētegere*), equiv. to *dē-* DE- + *teg(ere)* to cover + *-tus* ptp. suffix] —**de·tect′a·ble, de·tect′i·ble,** *adj.* —**de·tect′a·bil′i·ty, de·tect′i·bil′i·ty,** *n.*
—**Syn. 2.** See **learn.**

de·tec·tion (di tek′shən), *n.* **1.** the act of detecting. **2.** the fact of being detected. **3.** discovery, as of error or crime: *chance detection of smuggling.* **4.** *Telecommunications.* **a.** rectification of alternating signal currents in a radio receiver. **b.** Also called **demodulation.** the conversion of an alternating, modulated carrier wave or current into a direct, pulsating current equivalent to the transmitted information-bearing signal. [1425–75; late ME < LL *dētectiōn-* (s. of *dētectiō*), equiv. to L *dētect(us)* (see DETECT) + *-iōn-* -ION]

de·tec·tive (di tek′tiv), *n.* **1.** a member of the police force or a private investigator whose function is to obtain information and evidence, as of offenses against the law. —*adj.* **2.** of or pertaining to detection or detectives: *a detective story.* **3.** serving to detect; detecting: *various detective devices.* [1830–40; DETECT + -IVE]

de·tec·tor (di tek′tər), *n.* **1.** a person or thing that detects. **2.** a device for detecting smoke, fire, or some other hazardous condition. **3.** a device for detecting the presence of metal, contraband, or other items that might be hidden or concealed. **4.** *Telecommunications.* **a.** a device for detecting electric oscillations or waves. **b.** a device, as a crystal detector or a vacuum tube, that rectifies the alternating current in a radio receiver. [1535–45; < LL *dētector* revealer, equiv. to L *dēteg(ere)* to uncover, reveal (see DETECT) + *-tor* -TOR]

de·tent (di tent′), *n. Mach.* a mechanism that temporarily keeps one part in a certain position relative to that of another, and can be released by applying force to one of the parts. [1680–90; < F *détente,* OF *destente,* deriv. of *destendre* to relax, equiv. to *des-* DIS-[1] + *tendre* to stretch; see TENDER[2]]

dé·tente (dā tänt′; *Fr.* dā tänt′), *n., pl.* **-tentes** (-tänts′; *Fr.* -tänt′). a relaxing of tension, esp. between nations, as by negotiations or agreements. Also, **de·tente′.** [1905–10; < F; see DETENT]

de·ten·tion (di ten′shən), *n.* **1.** the act of detaining. **2.** the state of being detained. **3.** maintenance of a person in custody or confinement, esp. while awaiting a court decision. **4.** the withholding of what belongs to or is claimed by another. —*adj.* **5.** of or pertaining to detention or used to detain: *the detention room of a police station.* [1400–50; late ME < L *dētentiōn-* (s. of *dētentiō*), equiv. to *dētent(us)* detained (ptp. of *dētinēre;* see DETAIN) + *-iōn-* -ION]

deten′tion camp′, a compound where prisoners are detained temporarily, as pending determination of their legal status under immigration laws. [1915–20]

deten′tion home′, a house of correction or detention for juvenile offenders or delinquents, usually under the supervision of a juvenile court. [1925–30]

de·ter (di tûr′), *v.t.,* **-terred, -ter·ring. 1.** to discourage or restrain from acting or proceeding: *The large dog deterred trespassers.* **2.** to prevent; check; arrest: *timber treated with creosote to deter rot.* [1570–80; < L *dēterrēre* to prevent, hinder, equiv. to *dē-* DE- + *terrēre* to frighten] —**de·ter′ment,** *n.* —**de·ter′ra·ble,** *adj.* —**de·ter′ra·bil′i·ty,** *n.* —**de·ter′rer,** *n.*

de·terge (di tûrj′), *v.t.,* **-terged, -terg·ing. 1.** to wipe or wash away; cleanse. **2.** to cleanse of impurities or undesirable matter, as a wound. [1615–25; (< F) < L *dētergēre* to wipe off, equiv. to *dē-* DE- + *tergēre* to wipe] —**de·ter′gen·cy,** *n.*

de·ter·gent (di tûr′jənt), *n.* **1.** any of a group of synthetic, organic, liquid or water-soluble cleaning agents that, unlike soap, are not prepared from fats and oils, are not inactivated by hard water, and have wetting-agent and emulsifying-agent properties. **2.** a similar substance that is oil-soluble and capable of holding insoluble foreign matter in suspension, used in lubricating oils, dry-cleaning preparations, etc. **3.** any cleansing agent, including soap. Cf. **anionic detergent, cationic detergent, synthetic detergent.** —*adj.* **4.** cleansing; purging. [1610–20; (< F) < L *dētergent-* (s. of *dētergēns*) wiping off (prp. of *dētergēre*). See DETERGE, -ENT]

de·te·ri·o·rate (di tēr′ē ə rāt′), *v.t., v.i.,* **-rat·ed, -rat·ing. 1.** to make or become worse or inferior in character, quality, value, etc. **2.** to disintegrate or wear away. [1565–75; < LL *dēteriōrātus* made worse (ptp. of *dēteriōrāre*), equiv. to L *dēterior* worse (*dē* from + *-ter-* formative in adjs. of spatial orientation (cf. EXTERIOR, INTERIOR) + *-ior* comp. suffix) + *-ātus* -ATE[1]] —**de·te′ri·o·ra′tive,** *adj.*
—**Syn. 1.** degenerate, decline, worsen.

de·te·ri·o·ra·tion (di tēr′ē ə rā′shən), *n.* **1.** the act or process of deteriorating. **2.** the state or condition of having deteriorated. **3.** a gradual decline, as in quality, serviceability, or vigor. [1650–60; < LL *dēteriōrātiōn-* (s. of *dēteriōrātiō*), equiv. to *dēteriōrāt(us)* (see DETERIORATE) + *-iōn-* -ION]

de·ter·mi·na·ble (di tûr′mə nə bəl), *adj.* **1.** capable of being determined. **2.** *Law.* subject to termination. [1275–1325; ME: fixed < OF < LL *dēterminābilis,* equiv. to L *dētermin(āre)* to bound, DETERMINE + *-ābilis* -ABLE] —**de·ter′mi·na·bil′i·ty, de·ter′mi·na·ble·ness,** *n.* —**de·ter′mi·na·bly,** *adv.*

de·ter·mi·na·cy (di tûr′mə nə sē), *n.* **1.** the quality of being determinate. **2.** the condition of being determined or mandated. [1870–75; DETERMIN(ATE) + -ACY]

de·ter·mi·nant (di tûr′mə nənt), *n.* **1.** a determining agent or factor. **2.** *Math.* an algebraic expression of the sum of products of elements, each with an appropriate algebraic sign, usually written in a square array and used in the solution of systems of linear equations. **3.** Also called **antigenic determinant, epitope.** *Immunol.* any site on an antigen molecule at which an antibody can bind, the chemical structure of the site determining the specific combining antibody. **4.** *Genetics Archaic.* a gene. [1600–10; < L *dēterminant-* (s. of *dēterminans*), prp. of *dēterminare.* See DETERMINE, -ANT]

deter′minant rank′, *Math.* rank[1] (def. 14).

de·ter·mi·nate (*adj.* di tûr′mə nit; *v.* di tûr′mə nāt′), *adj., v.,* **-nat·ed, -nat·ing.** —*adj.* **1.** having defined limits; definite. **2.** settled; positive. **3.** conclusive; final. **4.** resolute. **5.** *Bot.* (of an inflorescence) having the primary and each secondary axis ending in a flower or bud, thus preventing further elongation. **6.** *Engin.* **a.** (of a structure) able to be analyzed completely by means of the principles of statics. **b.** (of a member of a structure) subject only to definite, known stresses. **c.** (of a stress) able to be determined through the principles of statics. —*v.t.* **7.** to make certain of. **8.** to identify. [1350–1400; ME < L *dēterminātus,* ptp. of *dēterminare.* See DETERMINE, -ATE[1]] —**de·ter′mi·nate·ly,** *adv.* —**de·ter′mi·nate·ness,** *n.*

de·ter·mi·na·tion (di tûr′mə nā′shən), *n.* **1.** the act of coming to a decision or of fixing or settling a purpose. **2.** ascertainment, as after observation or investigation: *determination of a ship's latitude.* **3.** the information ascertained; solution. **4.** the settlement of a dispute, question, etc., as by authoritative decision. **5.** the decision or settlement arrived at or pronounced. **6.** the quality of being resolute; firmness of purpose. **7.** a fixed purpose or intention: *It is my determination to suppress vice.* **8.** the fixing or settling of amount, limit, character, etc.: *the determination of a child's allowance.* **9.** fixed direction or tendency toward some object or end. **10.** *Chiefly Law.* conclusion or termination. **11.** *Embryol.* the fixation of the fate of a cell or group of cells, esp. before actual morphological or functional differentiation occurs. **12.** *Logic.* **a.** the act of rendering a notion more precise by the addition of differentiating characteristics. **b.** the definition of a concept in terms of its constituent elements. [1350–1400; ME (< AF) < L *dēterminātiōn-* (s. of *dēterminātiō*) a boundary, conclusion, equiv. to *dētermindruāt(us)* (see DETERMINATE) + *-iōn-* -ION]

de·ter·mi·na·tive (di tûr′mə nā′tiv, -nə tiv), *adj.* **1.**

serving to determine; determining. —*n.* **2.** something that determines. **3.** a graphic symbol used in ideographic writing to denote a semantic class and written next to a word to indicate in what semantic category that word is to be understood, thus at times distinguishing homographs. [1645–55; prob. < ML *dēterminātīvus* fixed, LL: crucial (of a disease), equiv. to L *dētermināt(us)* (see DETERMINATE) + *-īvus* -IVE] —**de•ter′mi•na′tive•ly,** *adv.* —**de•ter′mi•na′tive•ness,** *n.*

de•ter•mi•na•tor (di tûr′mə nā′tər), *n.* determiner (def. 1). [1550–60; DETERMINE + -ATOR]

de•ter•mine (di tûr′min), *v.,* **-mined, -min•ing.** —*v.t.* **1.** to settle or decide (a dispute, question, etc.) by an authoritative or conclusive decision. **2.** to conclude or ascertain, as after reasoning, observation, etc. **3.** *Geom.* to fix the position of. **4.** to cause, affect, or control; fix or decide causally: *Demand for a product usually determines supply.* **5.** to give direction or tendency to; impel. **6.** *Logic.* to limit (a notion) by adding differentiating characteristics. **7.** *Chiefly Law.* to put an end to; terminate. **8.** to lead or bring (a person) to a decision. **9.** to decide upon. —*v.i.* **10.** to come to a decision or resolution; decide. **11.** *Chiefly Law.* to come to an end. [1325–75; ME *determinen* < AF, OF *determiner* < L *dēterminare,* equiv. to *dē-* DE- + *termināre* to bound, limit; see TERMINATE]
—**Syn. 1.** resolve, adjust. See **decide. 2.** verify. **4.** influence. **5.** induce, lead, incline.

de•ter•mined (di tûr′mind), *adj.* **1.** resolute; staunch: *the determined defenders of the Alamo.* **2.** decided; settled; resolved. **3.** *Gram.* (of a phonetic feature) predictable from its surrounding context. [1490–1500; DETERMINE + -ED[2]] —**de•ter•mined•ly** (di tûr′mind lē, -mə nid lē), *adv.* —**de•ter′mined•ness,** *n.*
—**Syn. 1.** inflexible, unfaltering, unwavering.

de•ter•min•er (di tûr′mə nər), *n.* **1.** a person or thing that determines. **2.** *Gram.* a member of a subclass of English limiting adjectival words that usually precede descriptive adjectives and include the articles *the, a,* and *an,* and any words that may substitute for them, as *your, their, some,* and *each.* [1520–30; DETERMINE + -ER[1]]

de•ter•min•ism (di tûr′mə niz′əm), *n.* **1.** the doctrine that all facts and events exemplify natural laws. **2.** the doctrine that all events, including human choices and decisions, have sufficient causes. [1840–50; DETERMINE + -ISM] —**de•ter′min•ist,** *n., adj.* —**de•ter′min•is′tic,** *adj.* —**de•ter′min•is′ti•cal•ly,** *adv.*

de•ter•rence (di tûr′əns, -tur′-, -ter′-), *n.* the act of deterring, esp. deterring a nuclear attack by the capacity or threat of retaliating. [1860–65; DETERR(ENT) + -ENCE]

de•ter•rent (di tûr′ənt, -tur′-, -ter′-), *adj.* **1.** serving or tending to deter. —*n.* **2.** something that deters: *a deterrent to crime.* **3.** military strength or an ability to defend a country or retaliate strongly enough to deter an enemy from attacking. [1820–30; < L *dēterrent-* (s. of *dēterrēns*), prp. of *dēterrēre.* See DETER, -ENT] —**de•ter′rent•ly,** *adv.*
—**Syn. 2.** restraint, curb, check, hindrance.

de•ter•sive (di tûr′siv), *adj.* **1.** cleansing; detergent. —*n.* **2.** a detersive agent or medicine. [1580–90; < MF *détersif* < L *dēters(us)* (ptp. of *dētergēre;* see DETERGE) + *-if* -IVE] —**de•ter′sive•ly,** *adv.* —**de•ter′sive•ness,** *n.*

de•test (di test′), *v.t.* to feel abhorrence of; hate; dislike intensely. [1525–35; < MF *detester* < L *dētestārī* to call down a curse upon, loathe, equiv. to *dē-* DE- + *testārī* to bear witness; see TESTATE] —**de•test′er,** *n.*
—**Syn.** abhor, loathe, abominate, execrate, despise. See **hate.** —**Ant.** love, like.

de•test•a•ble (di tes′tə bəl), *adj.* deserving to be detested; abominable; hateful. [1375–1425; late ME < MF < L *dētestābilis,* equiv. to *dētest(ārī)* to DETEST + *-ābilis* -ABLE] —**de•test′a•bil′i•ty, de•test′a•ble•ness,** *n.* —**de•test′a•bly,** *adv.*
—**Syn.** execrable, abhorrent, loathsome, odious, vile.

de•tes•ta•tion (dē′te stā′shən), *n.* **1.** abhorrence; hatred. **2.** a person or thing detested. [1375–1425; late ME (< MF) < L *dētestātiōn-* (s. of *dētestātiō*), equiv. to *dētestāt(us)* (ptp. of *dētestārī* to DETEST; see -ATE[1]) + *-iōn-* -ION]

de•thatch (dē thach′), *v.t. Hort.* thatch (def. 7). [DE- + THATCH]

de•throne (dē thrōn′), *v.t.,* **-throned, -thron•ing. 1.** to remove from a throne; depose. **2.** to remove from any position of power or authority. [1600–10; DE- + THRONE] —**de•throne′ment,** *n.* —**de•thron′er,** *n.*

de•tick (dē tik′), *v.t.* to free (as livestock) of ticks, as by a chemical dip, spray, or dust. [1920–25; DE- + TICK[2]]

det. in dup., (in prescriptions) let twice as much be given. [< L *dētur in duplō*]

det•i•nue (det′n ōō′, -yōō′), *n. Law.* an old common-law form of action to recover possession of personal property wrongfully detained. [1425–75; late ME *detenu* < AF *detenue, detinue* detention, orig. fem. ptp. of *detenir* to DETAIN]

det•o•nate (det′n āt′), *v.,* **-nat•ed, -nat•ing.** —*v.i.* **1.** to explode with suddenness and violence. —*v.t.* **2.** to cause (something explosive) to explode. [1720–30; < L *dētonātus* thundered forth (ptp. of *dētonāre*), equiv. to *dē-* DE- + *ton(āre)* to THUNDER + *-ātus* -ATE[1]] —**det•o•na•ble** (det′n ə bəl), **det′o•nat′a•ble,** *adj.* —**det′o•na•bil′i•ty, det′o•nat′a•bil′i•ty,** *n.*

det•o•na•tion (det′n ā′shən), *n.* **1.** the act of detonating. **2.** an explosion. **3.** *Mach.* the premature spontaneous burning of a fuel–air mixture in an internal-combustion engine due to the high temperature of air compressed in a cylinder. [1670–80; < ML *dētonātiōn-* (s. of *dētonātiō*), equiv. to L *dētonāt(us)* (see DETONATE) + *-iōn-* -ION] —**det′o•na′tive,** *adj.*

det•o•na•tor (det′n ā′tər), *n.* **1.** a device, as a percussion cap, used to make another substance explode. **2.** something that explodes. [1815–25; DETONATE + -OR[2]]

de•tour (dē′tŏŏr, di tŏŏr′), *n.* **1.** a roundabout or circuitous way or course, esp. one used temporarily when the main route is closed. **2.** an indirect or roundabout procedure, path, etc. —*v.i.* **3.** to make a detour; go by way of a detour. —*v.t.* **4.** to cause to make a detour. **5.** to make a detour around: *We detoured Birmingham.* [1730–40 < F *détour,* OF *destor,* deriv. of *destorner* to turn aside, equiv. to *des-* DE- + *torner* to TURN]

de•tox (*n.* dē′toks; *v.* dē toks′), *Informal.* —*n.* **1.** detoxification. —*v.t., v.i.* **2.** to detoxify. [1970–75, *Amer.;* by shortening]

de•tox•i•cate (dē tok′si kāt′), *v.t.,* **-cat•ed, -cat•ing.** to detoxify. [1865–70; DE- + L *toxic(um)* poison (see TOXIC) + -ATE[1]] —**de•tox•i•cant** (dē tok′si kənt), *adj., n.* —**de•tox′i•ca′tor,** *n.*

de•tox•i•fi•ca•tion (dē tok′sə fi kā′shən), *n.* **1.** *Biochem.* the metabolic process by which toxins are changed into less toxic or more readily excretable substances. **2.** the act of detoxifying. **3.** the state of being detoxified. **4.** a period of medical treatment, usually including counseling, during which a person is helped to overcome physical and psychological dependence on alcohol or drugs. Also, **de•tox′i•ca′tion.** [1900–05; DETOXI(CATE) + -FICATION]

de•tox•i•fy (dē tok′sə fī′), *v.,* **-fied, -fy•ing.** —*v.t.* **1.** to rid of poison or the effect of poison. **2.** to treat (a person addicted to alcohol or drugs) under a program of detoxification. —*v.i.* **3.** to undergo detoxification. [1900–05; DETOXI(CATE) + -FY]

de•tract (di trakt′), *v.i.* **1.** to take away a part, as from quality, value, or reputation (usually fol. by *from*). —*v.t.* **2.** to draw away or divert; distract: *to detract another's attention from more important issues.* **3.** *Archaic.* to take away (a part); abate: *The dilapidated barn detracts charm from the landscape.* [1400–50; late ME (< MF *detracter*) < L *dētractus* drawn away (ptp. of *dētrahere*), equiv. to *dē-* DE- + *tractus* drawn; see TRACT[1]] —**de•tract′ing•ly,** *adv.* —**de•trac′tor,** *n.*

de•trac•tion (di trak′shən), *n.* the act of disparaging or belittling the reputation or worth of a person, work, etc. [1300–50; ME (< AF) < LL *dētractiōn-* (s. of *dētractiō*), equiv. to L *dētract(us)* (see DETRACT) + *-iōn-* -ION]

de•trac•tive (di trak′tiv), *adj.* tending or seeking to detract. Also, **de•trac•to•ry** (di trak′tə rē). [1480–90; < MF *detractif.* See DETRACT, -IVE] —**de•trac′tive•ly,** *adv.* —**de•trac′tive•ness,** *n.*

de•train (dē trān′), *v.i.* **1.** to alight from a railway train; arrive by train. **2.** *Meteorol.* to transfer air from an organized air current to the surrounding atmosphere (opposed to *entrain*). [1880–85; DE- + TRAIN] —**de•train′ment,** *n.*

de•trib•al•ize (dē trī′bə līz′), *v.t.,* **-ized, -iz•ing.** to cause to lose tribal allegiances and customs, chiefly through contact with another culture. Also, *esp. Brit.,* **de•trib′al•ise′.** [1915–20; DE- + TRIBAL + -IZE] —**de•trib′al•i•za′tion,** *n.*

det•ri•ment (de′trə mənt), *n.* **1.** loss, damage, disadvantage, or injury. **2.** a cause of loss or damage. [1400–50; late ME (< MF) < L *dētrīmentum* loss, damage, equiv. to *dētrī-* (see DETRITUS) + *-mentum* -MENT]
—**Syn. 1.** See **damage.**

det•ri•men•tal (de′trə men′tl), *adj.* **1.** causing detriment; damaging; harmful. —*n.* **2.** a detrimental person or thing. [1650–60; DETRIMENT + -AL[1]] —**det′ri•men•tal′i•ty, det′ri•men′tal•ness,** *n.* —**det′ri•men′tal•ly,** *adv.*

de•tri•tion (di trish′ən), *n.* the act of wearing away by rubbing. [1665–75; < ML *dētrītiōn-* (s. of *dētrītiō*), equiv. to L *dētrīt(us)* (ptp. of *dēterere;* see DETRITUS) + *-iōn-* -ION]

de•tri•ti•vore (di trī′tə vôr′, -vōr′), *n. Ecol.* an organism that uses organic waste as a food source, as certain insects. [1975–80; DETRIT(US) + -I- + -VORE] —**det•ri•tiv•or•ous** (de′trə tiv′ər əs), **de•triv•or•ous** (di triv′ər əs), *adj.*

de•tri•tus (di trī′təs), *n.* **1.** rock in small particles or other material worn or broken away from a mass, as by the action of water or glacial ice. **2.** any disintegrated material; debris. [1785–95; < F *détritus* < L: a rubbing away, equiv. to *dētrī-,* var. s. of *dēterere* to wear down, rub off (*de-* DE- + *terere* to rub) + *-tus* suffix of v. action] —**de•tri′tal,** *adj.*

De•troit (di troit′), *n.* **1.** a city in SE Michigan, on the Detroit River. 1,203,339. **2.** a river in SE Michigan, flowing S from Lake St. Clair to Lake Erie, forming part of the boundary between the U.S. and Canada. ab. 32 mi. (52 km) long. **3.** the U.S. automobile industry.

de trop (də trō′), **1.** too much; too many. **2.** in the way; not wanted. [1950–55; < F]

de•trude (di trōōd′), *v.t.,* **-trud•ed, -trud•ing. 1.** to thrust out or away. **2.** to thrust or force down. [1425–75; late ME < L *dētrūdere* to thrust down, drive away, equiv. to *dē-* DE- + *trūdere* to thrust, drive, force]

de•trun•cate (di trung′kāt), *v.t.,* **-cat•ed, -cat•ing.** to reduce by cutting off a part; cut down. [1615–25; < L *dētruncātus* (ptp. of *dētruncāre*). See DE-, TRUNCATE] —**de′trun•ca′tion,** *n.*

de•tru•sion (di trōō′zhən), *n.* the act of detruding. [1610–20; < LL *dētrūsiōn-* (s. of *dētrūsiō*) a thrusting down, equiv. to L *dētrūs(us)* (ptp. of *dētrūdere;* see DETRUDE) + *-iōn-* -ION] —**de•tru•sive** (di trōō′siv), *adj.*

de•tu•mes•cence (dē′tōō mes′əns, -tyōō-), *n.* reduction or subsidence of swelling. [1670–80; < L *dētumēsc(ere)* to cease swelling (*dē-* DE- + *tumēscere* to swell) + -ENCE; see TUMESCENCE] —**de′tu•mes′cent,** *adj.*

Deu•ca•li•on (dōō kā′lē ən, dyōō-), *n. Class. Myth.* a son of Prometheus who survived the Deluge to regenerate the human race.

deuce[1] (dōōs, dyōōs), *n.* **1.** *Cards.* a card having two pips; a two, or two-spot. **2.** *Dice.* **a.** the face of a die having two pips. **b.** a cast or point of two. **3.** *Tennis.* a situation, as a score of 40–40 in a game or 5–5 in a match, in which a player must score two successive points to win the game or two successive games to win the set. **4.** *Slang.* **a.** a two-dollar bill. **b.** the sum of two dollars. —*adj.* **5.** (esp. in games, sports, and gambling) two. [1425–75; late ME *deus* < AF, MF: two < L *duōs* (masc. acc. of *duo*)]

deuce[2] (dōōs, dyōōs), *n.* devil; dickens (used as a mild oath): *Where the deuce did they hide it?* [1645–55; appar. to be identified with DEUCE[1]]

deuce′ court′, *Tennis.* the receiver's right-hand service court, into which the ball is served when the score is deuce.

deuc•ed (dōō′sid, dyōō′-; dōōst, dyōōst), *Chiefly Brit.* —*adj.* **1.** devilish; confounded; damned. —*adv.* **2.** deucedly. [1775–1785; DEUCE[2] + -ED[3]]

deuc•ed•ly (dōō′sid lē, dyōō′-), *adv. Chiefly Brit.* devilishly; damnably. [1810–20; DEUCED + -LY]

deuc′es wild′, *Cards.* a variety or method of playing certain poker and other games in which a deuce represents any suit or denomination that the holder chooses: *We're playing five-card stud, deuces wild.* [1910–15]

de•un•ion•ize (dē yōōn′yə nīz′), *v.t.,* **-ized, -iz•ing.** to eliminate labor unions from (a company, industry, etc.). Also, *esp. Brit.,* **de•un′ion•ise′.** [DE- + UNIONIZE] —**de•un′ion•i•za′tion,** *n.*

de•ur•ban•ize (dē ûr′bə nīz′), *v.t.,* **-ized, -iz•ing.** to divest (a city or locality) of urban characteristics. Also, *esp. Brit.,* **de•ur′ban•ise′.** [1920–25; DE- + URBANIZE] —**de•ur′ban•i•za′tion,** *n.*

De•us (dē′əs, dā′-; *Lat.* de′ōōs), *n.* God. *Abbr.:* D. [1250–1300; < L: god, earlier *deiuos;* c. Skt *deva,* Lith *diẽvas,* OIr *día*]

De•us•ded•it (dē′əs ded′it, -dē′dit), *n.* **Saint,** died A.D. 618, Italian ecclesiastic: pope 615–618. Also called **Adeodatus I.**

de•us ex ma•chi•na (dā′əs eks mä′kə nə, dē′əs eks mak′ə nə), **1.** (in ancient Greek and Roman drama) a god introduced into a play to resolve the entanglements of the plot. **2.** any artificial or improbable device resolving the difficulties of a plot. [1690–1700; < NL lit., god from a machine (i.e., stage machinery from which a deity's statue was lowered), as trans. of Gk *apò mēchanês theós* (Demosthenes), *theòs ek mēchanês* (Menander), etc.]

De•us Ra•mos (de′ōōsh rä′mōōsh), **Jo•ão de** (zhwoun də), 1830–96, Portuguese poet.

De•us vo•bis•cum (de′ōōs vō bis′kōōm), *Latin.* God (be) with you.

De•us vult (de′ōōs vōōlt′), *Latin.* God wills (it): cry of the Crusaders.

Deut., Deuteronomy.

deuter-, var. of **deutero-** before a vowel: *deuteranopia.*

deu•ter•ag•o•nist (dōō′tə rag′ə nist, dyōō′-), *n.* (in ancient Greece) the actor next in importance to the protagonist. [1850–55; < Gk *deuteragōnistḗs.* See DEUTER-, AGONIST]

deu•ter•a•no•pia (dōō′tər ə nō′pē ə, dyōō′-), *n. Ophthalm.* a defect of vision in which the retina fails to respond to the color green. [1900–05; < NL; see DEUTER-, ANOPIA] —**deu•ter•an•op•ic** (dōō′tər ə nop′ik, dyōō′-), *adj.*

deu•ter•ate (dōō′tə rāt′, dyōō′-), *v.t.,* **-at•ed, -at•ing.** *Chem.* to add deuterium to (a chemical compound). [DEUTER(IUM) + -ATE[1]] —**deu′ter•a′tion,** *n.*

deu•ter•ide (dōō′tə rīd′, -tər id, dyōō′-), *n. Chem.* a hydride in which deuterium takes the place of ordinary hydrogen. [DEUTER(IUM) + -IDE]

deu•te•ri•um (dōō tēr′ē əm, dyōō-), *n. Chem.* an isotope of hydrogen, having twice the mass of ordinary hydrogen; heavy hydrogen. *Symbol:* D; *at. wt.:* 2.01; *at. no.:* 1. [1933; < Gk *deúter(os)* second (see DEUTERO-) + -IUM]

deute′rium ox′ide, *Chem.* See **heavy water.** [1930–35]

deutero-, a combining form meaning "second," used in the formation of compound words: *deuterocanonical.* Also, *esp. before a vowel,* **deuter-.** [< Gk, comb. form of *deúteros*]

deu′ter•o•ca•non′ical books′ (dōō′tə rō kə non′i kəl, dyōō′-, dōō′-, dyōō′-), the books of the Bible regarded by the Roman Catholic Church as canonical but not universally acknowledged as such in the early church, including, in the Old Testament, most of the Protestant Apocrypha. [1720–30; DEUTERO- + CANONICAL]

deu•ter•og•a•my (dōō′tə rog′ə mē, dyōō′-), *n.* digamy. [1650–60; < Gk *deuterogamía* a second marriage. See DEUTERO-, -GAMY] —**deu′ter•og′a•mist,** *n.*

deu•ter•o•my•cete (dōō′tə rō mī′sēt, -mī sēt′, dyōō′-), *n.* any fungus of the class Fungi Imperfecti. [< NL *Deuteromycetes;* see DEUTERO-, -MYCETE]

deu•ter•on (dōō′tə ron′, dyōō′-), *n. Physics.* a positively charged particle consisting of a proton and a neutron, equivalent to the nucleus of an atom of deuterium. Cf. **triton.** [1933; < Gk *deúter(os)* second + -ON[1]]

Deu•ter•o•nom•ic (dōō′tər ə nom′ik, dyōō′-), *adj.* of, pertaining to, or resembling Deuteronomy, esp. the laws contained in that book. [1855–60; DEUTERONOM(Y) + -IC]

Deu•ter•on•o•mist (dōō′tə ron′ə mist, dyōō′-), *n.* one of the writers of material used in the early books of the Old Testament. [1860–65; DEUTERONOM(Y) + -IST] —**Deu′ter•on′o•mis′tic,** *adj.*

Deu•ter•on•o•my (dōō′tə ron′ə mē, dyōō′-), *n.* the fifth book of the Pentateuch, containing a second statement of the Mosaic law. *Abbr.:* Deut. [< LL

CONCISE ETYMOLOGY KEY: <, descended or borrowed from; >, whence; b., blend of, blended; c., cognate with; cf., compare; deriv., derivative; equiv., equivalent; imit., imitative; obl., oblique; r., replacing; s., stem; sp., spelling, spelled; resp., respelling, respelled; trans., translation; ?, origin unknown; *, unattested; ‡, probably earlier than. See the full key inside the front cover.

Deuteronomium < Gk *Deuteronómion* (see DEUTERO-, -NOMY); earlier *Deutronome,* ME *Deutronomie* < LL]

deu·ter·op·a·thy (do͞o′tə rop′ə thē, dyo͞o′-), *n. Pathol.* any abnormality that is secondary to another pathological condition. [1645–55; DEUTERO- + -PATHY] —**deu·ter·o·path·ic** (do͞o′tər ə path′ik, dyo͞o′-), *adj.*

deu·ter·o·stome (do͞o′tər ə stōm′, dyo͞o′-), *n.* **1.** *Embryol.* a mouth that develops separately from the blastopore. **2.** *Taxonomy.* any member of the phyla (Chordata, Hemichordata, Echinodermata, Chaetognatha) in which the anus appears first, developing at or near the blastopore, cleavage is radial and indeterminate, and the mesoderm and coelom form from outgrowths of the primitive gut. Cf. **protostome.** [1945–50; DEUTERO- + -STOME]

deu·ter·ot·o·ky (do͞o′tə rot′ə kē, dyo͞o′-), *n.* production of both males and females parthenogenetically. [1890–95; DEUTERO- + Gk *-tokia,* equiv. to *-tok(os)* child (akin to *tiktein* to bear) + *-ia* -y[3]]

deu·ton (do͞o′ton, dyo͞o′-), *n. Physics Now Rare.* deuteron. [1930–35]

deu·to·plasm (do͞o′tə plaz′əm, dyo͞o′-), *n. Embryol.* the reserve nutritive material, as a yolk granule, in the ovarian cytoplasm. [1880–85; < Gk *deút(eros)* second + -O- + -PLASM] —**deu′to·plas′mic,** *adj.*

Deutsch (doich), *n.* **Babette,** 1895–1982, U.S. poet, novelist, and critic.

Deut′sche mark′ (doi′chə, doich), a cupronickel coin, the monetary unit of Germany, equal to 100 pfennigs: replaced the reichsmark in 1948. *Abbr.:* DM Also, **Deut′sche·mark′.** Cf. **ostmark.** [1945–50; < G: German mark]

Deut·scher (doi′chər), *n.* **Isaac,** 1907–1967, English journalist and author, born in Poland.

Deut·sches Reich (doi′chəs RĪKH′), former German name of **Germany.**

Deutsch·land (doich′länt′), *n.* German name of **Germany.**

deut·zi·a (do͝ot′sē ə, dyo͝ot′-, doit′-), *n.* any of various shrubs belonging to the genus *Deutzia,* of the saxifrage family, having showy white, pink, or lavender flowers, grown as an ornamental. [< NL (1781), named after Jean *Deutz,* 18th-century Dutch botanical patron; see -IA]

Deux-Sè·vres (dœ se′VRᵊ), *n.* a department in W France. 326,462; 2338 sq. mi. (6055 sq. km). *Cap.:* Niort.

dev., **1.** development. **2.** deviation.

de·va (dā′və), *n.* **1.** *Hinduism, Buddhism.* a god or divinity. **2.** *Zoroastrianism.* one of an order of evil spirits. [< Skt]

De Va·le·ra (dev′ə lâr′ə, -lēr′ə), **Ea·mon** (ā′mən), 1882–1975, Irish political leader and statesman, born in the U.S.: prime minister of the Republic of Ireland 1932–48, 1951–54, 1957–59; president 1959–73.

de Val·ois (də val′wä), **Dame Ni·nette** (ni net′), (*Edris Stannus*), born 1898, British ballet dancer, choreographer, teacher, and director: founder of the Royal Ballet (originally the Sadler's Wells Ballet).

de·val·u·ate (dē val′yo͞o āt′), *v.t., v.i.,* **-at·ed, -at·ing.** to devalue. [1895–1900; DE- + VALUE + -ATE[1]]

de·val·u·a·tion (dē val′yo͞o ā′shən), *n.* **1.** an official lowering of the exchange value of a country's currency relative to gold or other currencies. **2.** a reduction of a value, status, etc. [1910–15; DEVALUATE + -ION]

de·val·u·a·tion·ist (dē val′yo͞o ā′shə nist), *n.* a person, as an economist, who advocates the devaluation of a currency. [1930–35; DEVALUATION + -IST]

de·val·ue (dē val′yo͞o), *v.,* **-val·ued, -val·u·ing.** —*v.t.* **1.** to deprive of value; reduce the value of. **2.** to fix a lower value on (a currency). —*v.i.* **3.** to undergo devaluation: *The currency has devalued at a rapid rate.* Also, **devaluate.** [1915–20; DE- + VALUE]

De·va·na·ga·ri (dā′və nä′gə rē′), *n.* an alphabetical script with some syllabic features derived from Brahmi, used for the writing of Hindi and many other languages of India including Sanskrit. Also called **Nagari.** [1775–85; < Skt *devanāgarī*]

dev·as·tate (dev′ə stāt′), *v.t.,* **-tat·ed, -tat·ing. 1.** to lay waste; render desolate: *The invaders devastated the city.* **2.** to overwhelm. [1625–35; < L *dēvastātus* laid waste (ptp. of *dēvastāre*), equiv. to *dē-* DE- + *vast(āre)* to lay waste (akin to *vastus* empty) + *-ātus* -ATE[1]] —**dev′·as·ta′tive,** *adj.* —**dev′as·ta′tor,** *n.*

—**Syn. 1.** destroy, sack, despoil. See **ravage.**

dev·as·tat·ing (dev′ə stā′ting), *adj.* **1.** tending or threatening to devastate: *a devastating fire.* **2.** satirical, ironic, or caustic in an effective way: *a devastating portrayal of society.* [1625–35; DEVASTATE + -ING[2]] —**dev′·as·tat′ing·ly,** *adv.*

dev·as·ta·tion (dev′ə stā′shən), *n.* **1.** the act of devastating; destruction. **2.** devastated state; desolation. [1425–75; late ME < LL *dēvastātiōn-* (s. of *dēvastātiō*), equiv. to L *dēvastāt(us)* (see DEVASTATE) + *-iōn-* -ION]

de Ve·ga (də vā′gə; *Sp.* de be′gä), *n.* **Lo·pe** (lō′pā, -pe; *Sp.* lô′pe), (*Lope Félix de Vega Carpio*), 1562–1635, Spanish dramatist and poet.

de·vein (dē vān′), *v.t.* to remove the dark dorsal vein of (a shrimp). [DE- + VEIN]

devel., development.

de·vel·op (di vel′əp), *v.t.* **1.** to bring out the capabilities or possibilities of; bring to a more advanced or effective state: *to develop natural resources; to develop one's musical talent.* **2.** to cause to grow or expand: *to develop one's muscles.* **3.** to elaborate or expand in detail: *to develop a theory.* **4.** to bring into being or activity; generate; evolve. **5.** *Drafting.* to transfer the details of (a more or less two-dimensional design, pattern, or the like) from one surface, esp. one that is prismatic or cylindrical, onto another, usually planar, in such a way that the distances between points remain the same. **6.** *Biol.* **a.** to reach sexual maturity. **b.** to cause to go through the process of natural evolution from a previous and lower stage. **c.** to progress from an embryonic to an adult form. **d.** to undergo growth and differentiation in ontogeny or progress in phylogeny. **7.** *Math.* to express in an extended form, as in a series. **8.** *Music.* to unfold, by various technical means, the inherent possibilities of (a theme). **9.** *Photog.* **a.** to render visible (the latent image on an exposed film or the like). **b.** to treat (an exposed film or the like) with chemicals so as to render the latent image visible. **10.** *Chess.* to bring (a piece) into effective play, esp. during the initial phase of a game when pieces are moved from their original position on the board: *He developed his rook by castling.* **11.** *Mining.* to prepare (a new mine) for working by digging access openings and building necessary structures. —*v.i.* **12.** to grow into a more mature or advanced state; advance; expand: *She is developing into a good reporter.* **13.** to come gradually into existence or operation; be evolved. **14.** to be disclosed; become evident or manifest: *The plot of the novel developed slowly.* **15.** to undergo developing, as a photographic film. [1585–95; < MF *développer,* OF *desveloper,* equiv. to *des-* DIS-[1] + *voloper* to wrap up; see ENVELOP] —**de·vel′op·a·ble** *adj.* —**de·vel′op·a·bil′i·ty,** *n.*

devel′opable sur′face, *Math.* a surface that can be flattened onto a plane without stretching or compressing any part of it, as a circular cone.

de·vel·op·er (di vel′ə pər), *n.* **1.** a person or thing that develops. **2.** *Photog.* a reducing agent or solution for developing a film or the like. **3.** a person who invests in and develops the urban or suburban potentialities of real estate, esp. by subdividing the land into home sites and then building houses and selling them. **4.** *Shipbuilding.* a person who lays out at full size the lines of a vessel and prepares templates from them. [1825–35; DEVELOP + -ER[1]]

de·vel·op·ing (di vel′ə ping), *adj.* **1.** undergoing development; growing; evolving. **2.** (of a nation or geographical area) having a standard of living or level of industrial production well below that possible with financial or technical aid; not yet highly industrialized. [1765–75; DEVELOP + -ING[2]]

de·vel′op·ing-out′ pa′per (di vel′ə ping out′, -vel′-), *Photog.* a sensitized printing paper requiring development in order to bring out the image. *Abbr.:* D.O.P. Cf. **print-out paper.** [1915–20]

de·vel·op·ment (di vel′əp mənt), *n.* **1.** the act or process of developing; growth; progress: *child development; economic development.* **2.** a significant consequence or event: *recent developments in the field of science.* **3.** a developed state or form: *Drama reached its highest development in the plays of Shakespeare.* **4.** *Music.* the part of a movement or composition in which a theme or themes are developed. **5.** a large group of private houses or of apartment houses, often of similar design, constructed as a unified community, esp. by a real-estate developer or government organization. **6.** *Chess.* the act or process of developing chess pieces. **7.** *Mining.* the work of digging openings, as tunnels, raises, and winzes, to give access to new workings, and of erecting necessary structures. [1745–55; DEVELOP + -MENT, or < F *développement*] —**de·vel′op·men′tal, de·vel′·op·men′ta·ry,** *adj.* —**de·vel′op·men′tal·ly,** *adv.*

—**Syn. 1.** expansion, elaboration, growth, evolution; unfolding, opening, maturing, maturation. **3.** maturity, ripeness. **5.** community, subdivision. —**Ant. 1.** deterioration, disintegration.

developmen′tal biol′ogy, the branch of biology dealing with the processes of growth and change that transform an organism from a fertilized egg or asexual reproductive unit, as a spore or gemmule, to an adult. [1970–75]

developmen′tal disabil′ity, a disability, as mental retardation or cerebral palsy, that begins at an early age and continues indefinitely, leading to substantial handicap. —**developmen′tally disa′bled.**

de·vel·op·men·tal·ist (di vel′əp men′tl ist), *n.* an expert in or advocate of developmental psychology. [1860–65; DEVELOPMENTAL + -IST]

developmen′tal psychol′ogy, a branch of psychology that studies changes in human behavior from early life to death. —**developmen′tal psychol′ogist.**

devel′opment rights′, rights to use real property, such as farmland, in ways that differ from the current use.

de·vel·op·pé (di vel′ə pā′; *Fr.* devᵊ lô pā′), *n., pl.* **-pés** (-pāz′; *Fr.* -pā′). a movement in ballet in which the free leg is drawn up beside the working leg and then extended into the air. [1910–15; < F, ptp. of *développer* to DEVELOP]

De·ven·ter (dā′vən tər), *n.* a city in E Netherlands. 64,824.

de·verb·al (dē vûr′bəl), *adj., n.* deverbative. [1930–35; DE- + VERBAL]

de·verb·a·tive (dē vûr′bə tiv), *Gram.* —*adj.* **1.** (esp. of nouns) derived from a verb, as the noun *driver* from the verb *drive.* **2.** indicating derivation from a verb, as the suffix *-er* in *driver* or *-ment* in *development.* —*n.* **3.** a deverbative word. [1910–15; DE- + VERB + -ATIVE, by analogy with DENOMINATIVE]

Dev·e·reux (dev′ə ro͞o′), *n.* **Robert, 2nd Earl of Essex,** 1566–1601, British statesman, soldier, and courtier of Queen Elizabeth I.

de·vest (di vest′), *v.t.* **1.** *Law.* to divest. **2.** *Obs.* to remove the clothes from; undress. [1555–65; < MF *desvester,* OF *desvestir,* equiv. to *des-* DIS-[1] + *vestir* to clothe < L *vestīre;* see DIVEST]

De·vi (dā′vē), *n. Hinduism.* **1.** a mother goddess of which Durga, Kali, etc., are particular forms. **2.** Also called **Annapurna, Parvati.** the consort of Shiva, identified with Shakti and Kali as a goddess of love, maternity, and death. [< Skt, fem. of *deva* DEVA]

de·vi·ance (dē′vē əns), *n.* **1.** deviant quality or state. **2.** deviant behavior. Also, **de′vi·an·cy.** [1940–45; DEVI(ANT) + -ANCE]

de·vi·ant (dē′vē ənt), *adj.* **1.** deviating or departing from the norm; characterized by deviation: *deviant social behavior.* —*n.* **2.** a person or thing that deviates or departs markedly from the accepted norm. [1350–1400; ME < LL *dēviant-* (s. of *dēviāns,* prp. of *dēviāre* to DEVIATE), equiv. to L *dē-* DE- + *vi(a)* road, way + *-ant-* -ANT]

de·vi·ate (*v.* dē′vē āt′; *adj., n.* dē′vē it), *v.,* **-at·ed, -at·ing,** *adj., n.* —*v.i.* **1.** to turn aside, as from a route, way, course, etc. **2.** to depart or swerve, as from a procedure, course of action, or acceptable norm. **3.** to digress, as from a line of thought or reasoning. —*v.t.* **4.** to cause to swerve; turn aside. —*adj.* **5.** characterized by deviation or departure from an accepted norm or standard, as of behavior. —*n.* **6.** a person or thing that departs from the accepted norm or standard. **7.** a person whose sexual behavior departs from the norm in a way that is considered socially or morally unacceptable. **8.** *Statistics.* a variable equal to the difference between a variate and some fixed value, often the mean. [1625–35; < LL *dēviātus* turned from the straight road, ptp. of *dēviāre.* See DEVIANT, -ATE[1]] —**de′vi·a·ble,** *adj.* —**de·vi·a·bil·i·ty** (dē′vē ə bil′i tē), *n.* —**de′vi·a′tor,** *n.*

—**Syn. 1.** veer, wander, stray. DEVIATE, DIGRESS, DIVERGE, SWERVE imply turning or going aside from a path. To DEVIATE is to turn or wander, often by slight degrees, from what is considered the most direct or desirable approach to a given physical, intellectual, or moral end: *Fear caused him to deviate from the truth.* To DIGRESS is primarily to wander from the main theme or topic in writing or speaking: *Some authors digress to relate entertaining episodes.* Two paths DIVERGE when they proceed from a common point in such directions that the distance between them increases: *The sides of an angle diverge from a common point. Their interests gradually diverged.* To SWERVE is to make a sudden or sharp turn from a line or course: *The car swerved to avoid striking a pedestrian.*

de·vi·a·tion (dē′vē ā′shən), *n.* **1.** the act of deviating. **2.** departure from a standard or norm. **3.** *Statistics.* the difference between one of a set of values and some fixed value, usually the mean of the set. **4.** *Navig.* the error of a magnetic compass, as that of a ship, on a given heading as a result of local magnetism. Cf. **variation** (def. 8). **5.** *Optics.* **a.** Also called **deflection.** the bending of rays of light away from a straight line. **b.** See **angle of deviation. 6.** departure or divergence from an established dogma or ideology, esp. a Communist one. [1375–1425; late ME (< MF) < ML *dēviātiōn-* (s. of *dēviātiō*), equiv. to LL *dēviāt(us)* (see DEVIATE) + *-iōn-* -ION] —**de·vi·a·to·ry** (dē′vē ə tôr′ē, -tōr′ē), **de′vi·a′·tive,** *adj.*

de·vi·a·tion·ism (dē′vē ā′shə niz′əm), *n.* **1.** (in Communist ideology) departure from accepted party policies or practices. **2.** any deviation from official policy. [1935–40; DEVIATION + -ISM] —**de′vi·a′tion·ist,** *n.*

de·vice (di vīs′), *n.* **1.** a thing made for a particular purpose; an invention or contrivance, esp. a mechanical or electrical one. **2.** a plan or scheme for effecting a purpose. **3.** a crafty scheme; trick. **4.** a particular word pattern, figure of speech, combination of word sounds, etc., used in a literary work to evoke a desired effect or arouse a desired reaction in the reader: *rhetorical devices.* **5.** something elaborately or fancifully designed. **6.** a representation or design used as a heraldic charge or as an emblem, badge, trademark, or the like. **7.** a motto. **8.** *Archaic.* devising; invention. [1375–1425; b. late ME *devis* division, discourse and *devise* heraldic device, will; both < AF, OF < L *dīvīsa,* fem. of *dīvīsus;* see DIVISION] —**de·vice′ful,** *adj.* —**de·vice′ful·ly,** *adv.* —**de·vice′ful·ness,** *n.*

—**Syn. 1.** gadget. **2.** project, design. **3.** wile, ruse, artifice, stratagem, maneuver. **7.** slogan, legend.

dev·il (dev′əl), *n., v.,* **-iled, -il·ing** or (*esp. Brit.*) **-illed, -il·ling.** —*n.* **1.** *Theol.* **a.** (*sometimes cap.*) the supreme spirit of evil; Satan. **b.** a subordinate evil spirit at enmity with God, and having power to afflict humans both with bodily disease and with spiritual corruption. **2.** an atrociously wicked, cruel, or ill-tempered person. **3.** a person who is very clever, energetic, reckless, or mischievous. **4.** a person, usually one in unfortunate or pitiable circumstances: *The poor devil kept losing jobs through no fault of his own.* **5.** Also called **printer's devil.** *Print.* a young worker below the level of apprentice in a printing office. **6.** any of various mechanical devices, as a machine for tearing rags, a machine for manufacturing wooden screws, etc. **7.** *Naut.* (in deck or hull planking) any of various seams difficult to caulk because of form or position. **8.** any of various portable furnaces or braziers used in construction and foundry work. **9. between the devil and the deep (blue) sea,** between two undesirable alternatives; in an unpleasant dilemma. **10. devil of a,** extremely difficult or annoying; hellish: *I had a devil of a time getting home through the snow.* **11. give the devil his due,** to give deserved credit even to a person one dislikes: *To give the devil his due, you must admit that she is an excellent psychologist.* **12. go to the devil, a.** to fail completely; lose all hope or chance of succeeding. **b.** to become depraved. **c.** (an expletive expressing annoyance, disgust, impatience, etc.) **13. let the devil take the hindmost,** to leave the least able or fortunate persons to suffer adverse consequences; leave behind or to one's fate: *They ran from the pursuing mob and let the devil take the hindmost.* **14. play the devil with,** to ruin completely; spoil: *The financial crisis played the devil with our investment plans.* **15. raise the devil, a.** to cause a commotion or disturbance. **b.** to celebrate wildly; revel. **c.** to make an emphatic protest or take drastic measures. **16. the devil,** (used as an emphatic expletive or mild oath to express disgust, anger, astonishment, negation, etc.): *What the devil do you mean by that?* **17. the devil to pay,**

trouble to be faced; mischief in the offing: *If conditions don't improve, there will be the devil to pay.* —*v.t.* **18.** to annoy; harass; pester: *to devil Mom and Dad for a new car.* **19.** to tear (rags, cloth, etc.) with a devil. **20.** *Cookery.* to prepare (food, usually minced) with hot or savory seasoning: *to devil eggs.* [bef. 900; ME *devel,* OE *dēofol* < LL *diabolus* < Gk *diábolos* Satan (Septuagint, NT), lit., slanderer (n.), slanderous (adj.), verbal of *diabállein* to assault someone's character, lit., to throw across, equiv. to *dia-* DIA- + *bállein* to throw]

dev′il dog′, *Informal.* a United States Marine. [1915–20]

dev•il•fish (dev′əl fish′), *n., pl.* (*esp. collectively*) **-fish,** (*esp. referring to two or more kinds or species*) **-fish•es. 1.** manta. **2.** octopus. [1700–10; DEVIL + FISH]

dev•il•ish (dev′ə lish, dev′lish), *adj.* **1.** of, like, or befitting a devil; diabolical; fiendish. **2.** extreme; very great: *a devilish mess.* —*adv.* **3.** excessively; extremely: *He's devilish proud.* [1400–50; late ME. See DEVIL, -ISH[1]] —**dev′il•ish•ly,** *adv.* —**dev′il•ish•ness,** *n.*
—**Syn. 1.** satanic, demoniac, infernal.

dev•il•kin (dev′əl kin), *n.* a little devil; imp. [1500–10; DEVIL + -KIN]

dev•il-may-care (dev′əl mā kâr′), *adj.* reckless; careless; rollicking. [1785–95]

dev•il•ment (dev′əl mənt), *n.* devilish action or conduct; deviltry. [1765–75; DEVIL + -MENT]

dev′il ray′, manta.

dev•il•ry (dev′əl rē), *n., pl.* **-ries.** deviltry. [1325–75; ME; see DEVIL, -RY]

dev′il's ad′vocate, 1. a person who advocates an opposing or unpopular cause for the sake of argument or to expose it to a thorough examination. **2.** Also called **promoter of the faith.** *Rom. Cath. Ch.* an official appointed to present arguments against a proposed beatification or canonization of a beatus. [1750–60; trans. of NL *advocātus diaboli*]

dev•il's-bit (dev′əlz bit′), *n.* an eastern North American plant, *Chamaelirium luteum,* of the lily family, having a dense, drooping spike of small white flowers. Also called **fairy wand.** [1400–50; late ME]

dev′il's club′, a spiny shrub, *Oplopanax horridus,* of northwestern North America, having broad palmate leaves, greenish flowers, and clusters of bright red berries. [1880–85, *Amer.*]

dev′il's darn′ing nee′dle. *Chiefly Northern and Western U.S.* a dragonfly. [1800–10]
—**Regional Variation.** See **dragonfly.**

dev′il's dung′, asafetida. [1595–1605]

dev′il's food′ cake′, a rich chocolate cake. [1900–05, *Amer.*; modeled on ANGEL FOOD CAKE]

dev′il's grip′, *Pathol.* pleurodynia (def. 2). [1885–90]

Dev′il's Is′land, one of the Safety Islands, off the coast of French Guiana: former French penal colony. French, **Île du Diable.**

dev′il's mark′, (in witchcraft) a mark, as a scar or blemish, on the body of a person who has made a compact with a devil. Also called **witch's mark.**

dev′il's paint′brush. See **orange hawkweed.** [1895–1900]

dev•il's-tongue (dev′əlz tung′), *n.* a foul-smelling, fleshy plant, *Amorphophallus rivieri,* of the Old World tropics, having flowers on a spike surrounded by a dark-red spathe. Also called **snake palm.**

Dev′il's Tri′angle. See **Bermuda Triangle.**

dev•il's-walk•ing-stick (dev′əlz wô′king stik′), *n.* Hercules'-club (def. 2). [1925–30, *Amer.*]

dev′il tree′, jelutong (def. 3). [1865–70]

dev•il•try (dev′əl trē), *n., pl.* **-tries. 1.** reckless or unrestrained mischievous behavior. **2.** extreme or utter wickedness. **3.** an act or instance of mischievous or wicked behavior. **4.** diabolic magic or art. **5.** demonology. Also, **devilry.** [1780–90; var. of DEVILRY]

dev•il•wood (dev′əl wo͝od′), *n.* a small olive tree, *Osmanthus americanus,* of the U.S., yielding a hard wood. [1810–20; DEVIL + WOOD[1]]

de•vi•ous (dē′vē əs), *adj.* **1.** departing from the most direct way; circuitous; indirect: *a devious course.* **2.** without definite course; vagrant: *a devious current.* **3.** departing from the proper or accepted way; roundabout: *a devious procedure.* **4.** not straightforward; shifty or crooked: *a devious scheme to acquire wealth.* [1590–1600; < L *dēvius* out-of-the way, erratic, equiv. to *dē-* DE- + *-vius* adj. deriv. of *via* way; see -OUS] —**de′vi•ous•ly,** *adv.* —**de′vi•ous•ness,** *n.*
—**Syn. 1.** roundabout, tortuous, involved. **4.** subtle, cunning, crafty, artful, sly.

de•vis•a•ble (di vī′zə bəl), *adj.* **1.** capable of being devised, invented, or contrived. **2.** *Law.* capable of being transferred. [1250–1300; ME < AF: assignable by will, OF: that which may be divided, equiv. to *devis(er)* (see DEVISE) + *-able* -ABLE]

de•vis•al (di vī′zəl), *n.* the act of devising; contrivance. [1850–55; DEVISE + -AL[2]]

de•vise (di vīz′), *v.,* **-vised, -vis•ing,** *n.* —*v.t.* **1.** to contrive, plan, or elaborate; invent from existing principles or ideas: *to devise a method.* **2.** *Law.* to assign or transmit (property) by will. **3.** *Archaic.* to imagine; suppose. —*v.i.* **4.** to form a plan; contrive. —*n.* **5.** *Law.* **a.** the act of disposing of property, esp. real property, by will. **b.** a will or clause in a will disposing of property, esp. real property. **c.** the property so disposed of. [1150–1200; (v.) ME *devisen* to inspect, design, compose < OF *deviser* < VL **dēvisāre,* for **divisāre,* freq. of L *dividere* to DIVIDE; (n.) see DEVICE] —**de•vis′er,** *n.*
—**Syn. 1.** See **prepare.**

CONCISE ETYMOLOGY KEY: <, descended or borrowed from; >, whence; b., blend of, blended; c., cognate with; cf., compare; deriv., derivative; equiv., equivalent; imit., imitative; obl., oblique; r., replacing; s., stem; sp., spelling, spelled; resp., respelling, respelled; trans., translation; ?, origin unknown; *, unattested; ‡, probably earlier than. See the full key inside the front cover.

de•vi•see (di vī zē′, dev′ə zē′), *n. Law.* a person to whom a devise is made. [1535–45; DEVISE + -EE]

de•vi•sor (di vī′zər), *n. Law.* a person who makes a devise. [1400–50; late ME (in general sense "one who devises") < AF *devisour* (OF *deviseur*). See DEVISE, -OR[2]]

de•vi•tal•ize (dē vīt′l īz′), *v.t.,* **-ized, -iz•ing.** to deprive of vitality or vital properties; make lifeless; weaken. Also, *esp. Brit.,* **de•vi′tal•ise′.** [1840–50; DE- + VITALIZE] —**de•vi′tal•i•za′tion,** *n.*

de•vit•ri•fy (dē vi′trə fī′), *v.,* **-fied, -fy•ing.** —*v.t.* **1.** *Chem.* to deprive, wholly or partly, of vitreous character or properties. —*v.i.* **2.** *Petrol.* (of a volcanic rock or particle) to undergo a change in texture from glassy to crystalline. [1825–35; DE- + VITRIFY] —**de•vit′ri•fi′a•ble,** *adj.* —**de•vit′ri•fi•ca′tion,** *n.*

de•vo•cal•ize (dē vō′kə līz′), *v.t.,* **-ized, -iz•ing.** *Phonet.* **1.** to devoice. **2.** to convert (a speech sound) from a vowel to a glide. Also, *esp. Brit.,* **de•vo′cal•ise′.** [1875–80; DE- + VOCALIZE] —**de•vo′cal•i•za′tion,** *n.*

de•voice (dē vois′), *v.,* **-voiced, -voic•ing.** *Phonet.* —*v.t.* **1.** to pronounce (an ordinarily voiced speech sound) without vibration of the vocal cords; make voiceless. —*v.i.* **2.** to devoice a speech sound. Also, **unvoice.** [1930–35; DE- + VOICE]

de•void (di void′), *adj.* **1.** not possessing, untouched by, void, or destitute (usually fol. by *of*). —*v.t.* **2.** to deplete or strip of some quality or substance: *imprisonment that devoids a person of humanity.* [1350–1400; ME, orig. ptp. < AF, for OF *desvuidier* to empty out, equiv. to *des-* DIS-[1] + *vuidier* to empty, VOID]
—**Syn. 1.** lacking, wanting, destitute, bereft, barren.

de•voir (də vwär′, dev′wär; *Fr.* də VWAR′), *n., pl.* **de•voirs** (də vwärz′, dev′wärz; *Fr.* də VWAR′). **1.** an act of civility or respect. **2. devoirs,** respects or compliments. **3.** something for which a person is responsible; duty. [1250–1300; ME *devoir, deveir, dever* < OF *devoir* (AF *deveir, dever*) < L *dēbēre* to owe; cf. DEBT]

de•vol•a•til•ize (dē vol′ə tl īz′), *v.,* **-ized, -iz•ing.** *Chem.* —*v.t.* **1.** to cause (a vapor) to liquefy. —*v.i.* **2.** (of a vapor) to liquefy. Also, *esp. Brit.,* **de•vol′a•til•ise′.** [1860–65; DE- + VOLATILIZE] —**de•vol′a•til•i•za′tion,** *n.*

dev•o•lu•tion (dev′ə lo͞o′shən *or, esp. Brit.,* dē′və-), *n.* **1.** the act or fact of devolving; passage onward from stage to stage. **2.** the passing on to a successor of an unexercised right. **3.** *Law.* the passing of property from one to another, as by hereditary succession. **4.** *Biol.* degeneration. **5.** the transfer of power or authority from a central government to a local government. [1535–45; (< MF) < ML *dēvolūtiōn-* (s. of *dēvolūtiō*) a rolling down, equiv. to L *dēvolūt(us)* rolled down (ptp. of *dēvolvere;* see DEVOLVE) + *-iōn-* -ION] —**dev′o•lu′tion•ar′y,** *adj., n.,* —**dev′o•lu′tion•ist,** *n.*

de•volve (di volv′), *v.,* **-volved, -volv•ing.** —*v.t.* **1.** to transfer or delegate (a duty, responsibility, etc.) to or upon another; pass on. **2.** *Obs.* to cause to roll downward. —*v.i.* **3.** to be transferred or passed on from one to another: *The responsibility devolved on me.* **4.** *Archaic.* to roll or flow downward. [1375–1425; late ME *devolven* < L *dēvolvere* to roll down, equiv. to *dē-* DE- + *volvere* to roll] —**de•volve′ment,** *n.*

Dev•on (dev′ən), *n.* **1.** Devonshire. **2.** one of an English breed of red cattle, bred for beef and milk. **3.** one of an English breed of sheep, bred for its long, coarse wool.

Dev′on cream′, *Brit.* See **clotted cream.**

De•vo•ni•an (də vō′nē ən), *adj.* **1.** *Geol.* noting or pertaining to a period of the Paleozoic Era, 405 to 345 million years ago, characterized by the dominance of fishes and the advent of amphibians and ammonites. See table under **geologic time. 2.** of or pertaining to Devonshire, England. —*n.* **3.** *Geol.* the Devonian Period or System. [1605–15; < ML *Devoni(a)* Devon + -AN]

Dev•on•port (dev′ən pôrt′, -pōrt′), *n.* a city in N Tasmania. 21,424.

Dev•on•shire (dev′ən shēr′, -shər), *n.* a county in SW England. 936,300; 2591 sq. mi. (6710 sq. km). Also called **Devon.**

Dev′onshire cream′. See **clotted cream.** [1815–25]

de•vote (di vōt′), *v.t.,* **-vot•ed, -vot•ing. 1.** to give up or appropriate to or concentrate on a particular pursuit, occupation, purpose, cause, etc.: *to devote one's time to reading.* **2.** to appropriate by or as if by a vow; set apart or dedicate by a solemn or formal act; consecrate: *She devoted her life to God.* **3.** to commit to evil or destruction; doom. [1580–90; < L *dēvōtus* vowed (ptp. of *dēvovēre*), equiv. to *dē-* DE- + *vōtus;* see VOTE, VOW]
—**Syn. 1.** assign, apply, consign. **2.** DEVOTE, DEDICATE, CONSECRATE share the sense of assigning or applying someone or something to an activity, function, or end. DEVOTE, though it has some overtones of religious dedication, is the most general of the three terms: *He devoted his free time to mastering the computer.* DEDICATE is more solemn and carries an ethical or moral tone: *We are dedicated to the achievement of equality for all.* CONSECRATE, even in nonreligious contexts, clearly implies a powerful and sacred dedication: *consecrated to the service of humanity.*

de•vot•ed (di vō′tid), *adj.* zealous or ardent in attachment, loyalty, or affection: *a devoted friend.* [1585–95; DEVOTE + -ED[2]] —**de•vot′ed•ly,** *adv.* —**de•vot′ed•ness,** *n.*
—**Syn.** faithful, constant, loyal, devout.

dev•o•tee (dev′ə tē′, -tā′), *n.* **1.** a person who is greatly devoted to something. **2.** a person who is extremely devoted to a religion; a follower. **3.** an enthusiastic follower or fan: *He's a devotee of jazz.* [1635–45; DEVOTE + -EE]
—**Syn. 1, 3.** See **fanatic.**

de•vo•tion (di vō′shən), *n.* **1.** profound dedication; consecration. **2.** earnest attachment to a cause, person, etc. **3.** an assignment or appropriation to any purpose, cause, etc.: *the devotion of one's wealth and time to scientific advancement.* **4.** Often, **devotions.** *Eccles.* religious observance or worship; a form of prayer or worship for special use. [1150–1200; ME *devocioun* (< AF) < LL *dēvōtiōn-* (s. of *dēvōtiō*), equiv. to L *dēvōt(us)* (see DEVOTE) + *-iōn-* -ION]
—**Syn. 2.** zeal, ardor. See **love.**

de•vo•tion•al (di vō′shə nl), *adj.* **1.** characterized by devotion. **2.** used in devotions: *devotional prayers.* —*n.* **3.** Often, **devotionals.** a short religious service. [1640–50; DEVOTION + -AL[1]] —**de•vo′tion•al′i•ty, de•vo′tion•al•ness,** *n.* —**de•vo′tion•al•ly,** *adv.*

De Vo•to (də vō′tō), **Bernard (Augustine),** 1897–1955, U.S. novelist and critic.

de•vour (di vour′), *v.t.* **1.** to swallow or eat up hungrily, voraciously, or ravenously. **2.** to consume destructively, recklessly, or wantonly: *Fire devoured the old museum.* **3.** to engulf or swallow up. **4.** to take in greedily with the senses or intellect: *to devour the works of Freud.* **5.** to absorb or engross wholly: *a mind devoured by fears.* [1275–1325; ME *devouren* < AF, OF *devourer* < L *dēvorāre* to swallow down, equiv. to *dē-* DE- + *vorāre* to eat up] —**de•vour′er,** *n.* —**de•vour′ing•ly,** *adv.* —**de•vour′ing•ness,** *n.*

de•vout (di vout′), *adj.,* **-er, -est. 1.** devoted to divine worship or service; pious; religious: *a devout Catholic.* **2.** expressing devotion or piety: *devout prayer.* **3.** earnest or sincere; hearty: *He had a devout allegiance to the political regime.* [1175–1225; ME < AF, OF *devo(u)t* < LL *dēvōtus,* L: devoted; see DEVOTE] —**de•vout′ly,** *adv.* —**de•vout′ness,** *n.*
—**Syn. 1.** worshipful; holy, saintly. See **religious. 3.** intense, serious, fervent, ardent. —**Ant. 1.** irreverent.

De Vries (də vrēs′; *Du.* də VRĒS′), **Hu•go** (hyo͞o′gō; *Du.* HY′gō), 1848–1935, Dutch botanist and student of organic heredity: developed the concept of mutation as a factor in the process of evolution.

dew (do͞o, dyo͞o), *n.* **1.** moisture condensed from the atmosphere, esp. at night, and deposited in the form of small drops upon any cool surface. **2.** something like or compared to such drops of moisture, as in purity, delicacy, or refreshing quality. **3.** moisture in small drops on a surface, as tears or perspiration. **4.** *Informal.* **a.** See **Scotch whisky. b.** See **mountain dew.** —*v.t.* **5.** to wet with or as with dew. [bef. 900; ME; OE *dēaw;* c. G *Tau,* ON *dǫgg*] —**dew′less,** *adj.*

DEW (do͞o, dyo͞o), distant early warning. Cf. **DEW line.**

De•wa•li (də wä′lē), *n.* Diwali.

de•wan (di wän′, -wôn′), *n.* (in India) any of certain officials, as a financial minister or prime minister of a native colony. Also, **diwan.** [1680–90; < Hindi: minister (of state) < Pers *dēvan* register; see DIVAN]

Dew•ar (do͞o′ər, dyo͞o′-), *n.* **1. Sir James,** 1842–1923, Scottish chemist and physicist. **2.** See **Dewar vessel.**

Dew′ar ves′sel, a container with an evacuated space between two walls that are highly reflective, capable of maintaining its contents at a near-constant temperature over relatively long periods of time; thermos. Also called **Dewar, Dew′ar flask′.** [1900–05; named after Sir James DEWAR, its inventor]

de•wa•ter (dē wô′tər, -wot′ər), *v.t.* to remove the water from; drain; dehydrate. [1905–10; DE- + WATER] —**de•wa′ter•er,** *n.*

dew•ber•ry (do͞o′ber′ē, -bə rē, dyo͞o′-), *n., pl.* **-ries. 1.** (in North America) the fruit of any of several trailing blackberries of the genus *Rubus.* **2.** (in England) the fruit of a bramble, *Rubus caesius.* **3.** a plant bearing either fruit. [1570–80; DEW + BERRY]

dew′ cell′, an electrical instrument for measuring the dew point.

dew•claw (do͞o′klô′, dyo͞o′-), *n.* **1.** a functionless claw of some dogs, not reaching the ground in walking. **2.** an analogous false hoof of deer, hogs, etc. [1570–80; DEW + CLAW; cf. DEWLAP] —**dew′clawed′,** *adj.*

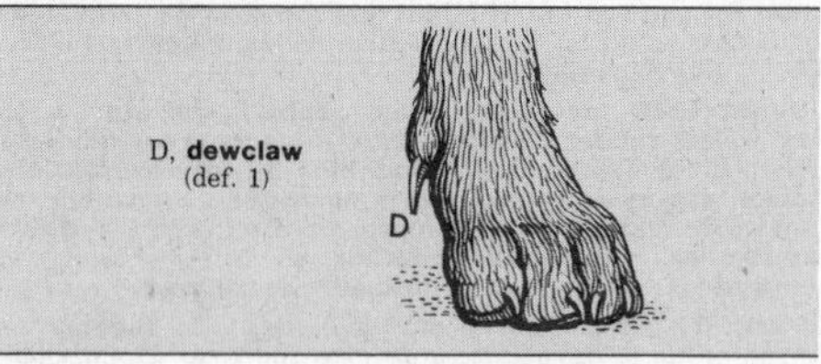

D, **dewclaw** (def. 1)

dew•drop (do͞o′drop′, dyo͞o′-), *n.* a drop of dew. [1150–1200; ME. See DEW, DROP]

De Wet (də wet′), **Chris•ti•an Ru•dolph** (kris′chən ro͞o′dolf, -dôlf; *Du.* KRIS′tē än′ RY′dolf), 1854–1922, Boer general and politician.

Dew•ey (do͞o′ē, dyo͞o′ē), *n.* **1. George,** 1837–1917, U.S. admiral: defeated Spanish fleet in Manila Bay during the Spanish-American War. **2. John,** 1859–1952, U.S. philosopher and educator. **3. Mel•vil** (mel′vil), (*Melville Louis Kossuth Dewey*), 1851–1931, U.S. educator, administrator, and innovator in the field of library science. **4. Thomas E(dmund),** 1902–71, U.S. lawyer and political leader. **5.** a male given name, form of **David.**

Dew′ey dec′imal classifica′tion, *Trademark.* a system of classifying books and other works into ten main classes of knowledge with further subdivision in these classes by use of the numbers of a decimal system: devised by Melvil Dewey, published in 1876, and used in many libraries in the U.S. and elsewhere. [1880–85]

dew•fall (do͞o′fôl′, dyo͞o′-), *n.* **1.** formation of dew. **2.** the time at which dew begins to form. [1615–25; DEW + FALL]

De•wi (dā′wē), *n.* **Saint.** See **David, Saint.**

De Witt (də wit′), **1. Jan** (yän), 1625–72, Dutch statesman. **2.** a male given name: from the Flemish family name meaning "white."

dew•lap (do͞o′lap′, dyo͞o′-), *n.* **1.** a pendulous fold of skin under the throat of a bovine animal. **2.** any similar part in other animals, as the wattle of fowl or the inflatable loose skin under the throat of some lizards. [1350–1400; ME *dew(e)lappe,* appar. *dewe* DEW + *lappe* LAP[1]; cf. Dan *dog-læp,* D (dial.) *dauw-zwengel;* literal sense is unclear] **—dew′lapped′,** *adj.*

DEW′ line′ (do͞o, dyo͞o), a 3000-mi. (4800-km)-long network of radar stations north of the Arctic Circle, maintained by the U.S. and Canada for providing advance warning of the approach of hostile planes, missiles, etc. [1955–60; *D(istant) E(arly) W(arning)*]

de•worm (dē wûrm′), *v.t.* worm (def. 19). [1925–30; DE- + WORM]

dew′ plant′, sundew. [1825–35]

dew′ point′, the temperature to which air must be cooled, at a given pressure and water-vapor content, for it to reach saturation; the temperature at which dew begins to form. Also called **dew′-point tem′perature.** Cf. **absolute humidity, mixing ratio, relative humidity, specific humidity.** [1825–35]

dew′-point spread′ (do͞o′point′, dyo͞o′-), the number of degrees of difference between the air temperature and the dew point. Also called **dew′-point def′icit, dew′-point depres′sion.**

dew-worm (do͞o′wûrm′, dyo͞o′-), *n. Chiefly Inland North and Canadian.* the common earthworm. Also, **dew′ worm′.** [bef. 1000; OE *dēaw-wyrm* (not recorded in ME); see DEW, WORM]
—Regional Variation. See **earthworm.**

dew•y (do͞o′ē, dyo͞o′ē), *adj.* **dew•i•er, dew•i•est. 1.** moist with or as if with dew. **2.** having the quality of dew: *dewy tears.* [bef. 1000; ME; OE *dēawig;* see DEW, -Y[1]] **—dew′i•ly,** *adv.* **—dew′i•ness,** *n.*

dew•y-eyed (do͞o′ē īd′, dyo͞o′-), *adj.* romantically naive or credulous; sentimental, innocent, and trusting: *dewy-eyed, aspiring young actresses.* [1935–40]

dex•a•meth•a•sone (dek′sə meth′ə sōn′, -zōn′), *n. Pharm.* a crystalline, water-soluble steroid, $C_{22}H_{29}FO_5$, used in the treatment of certain allergic or inflammatory conditions, as rheumatoid arthritis, bronchial asthma, or dermatosis. [1955–60; perh. DEXA(MYL) + METH(YL) + -a- (of unclear orig.) (CORTI)SONE]

Dex•a•myl (dek′sə mil), *Pharm., Trademark.* a brand name for a mixture of dextroamphetamine and amobarbital that curbs appetite and elevates mood, used in the treatment of obesity or mental depression.

Dex•e•drine (dek′si drēn′, -drin), *Pharm., Trademark.* a brand of dextroamphetamine.

dex•ie (dek′sē), *n. Slang.* Dexedrine, esp. in tablet form. [1955–60; DEX(EDRINE) + -IE]

dex•i•o•car•di•a (dek′sē ō kär′dē ə), *n. Pathol.* dextrocardia. [1865–70; < Gk *dexió(s)* on the right hand or side + -CARDIA]

dex•i•o•trop•ic (dek′sē ō trop′ik, -trō′pik), *adj.* dextral (def. 3). [1880–85; < Gk *dexi(ós)* right (side) + -o- + -TROPIC]

dex•ter (dek′stər), *adj.* **1.** on the right side; right. **2.** noting the side of a heraldic shield that is to the right of one who bears it (opposed to *sinister*). [1555–65; < L: right, favorable; akin to Goth *taihswa,* OIr *dess,* Gk *dexiós,* Lith *dẽšinas,* Skt *dakṣina*]

Dex•ter (dek′stər), *n.* **1.** Also, **Dex•ter-Ker•ry** (dek′stər ker′ē). one of a breed of small, hardy, usually black dual-purpose cattle, derived from the Kerry breed of Ireland. **2.** a male given name.

dex•ter•i•ty (dek ster′i tē), *n.* **1.** skill or adroitness in using the hands or body; agility. **2.** mental adroitness or skill; cleverness. [1520–30; < L *dexteritās* readiness, equiv. to *dexter-* (s. of *dexter*) skillful + *-itās* -ITY]

dex•ter•ous (dek′strəs, -stər əs), *adj.* **1.** skillful or adroit in the use of the hands or body. **2.** having mental adroitness or skill; clever. **3.** done with skill or adroitness. **4.** right-handed. Also, **dextrous.** [1595–1605; < L *dexter* right-hand, skillful + -OUS] **—dex′ter•ous•ly,** *adv.* **—dex′ter•ous•ness,** *n.*
—Syn. 1. deft, nimble, handy. **1, 2.** expert, apt, able, quick. DEXTEROUS, ADROIT, DEFT, SKILLFUL, HANDY all imply facility and ease in performance. DEXTEROUS and ADROIT both referred originally to right-handedness. DEXTEROUS is still most often used to refer to manual or physical ability but can also refer to mental or social agility: *a dexterous wood carver; dexterous management of a potentially embarrassing situation.* ADROIT implies cleverness or mental acuity, occasionally complex physical skill: *an adroit politician; an adroit juggler.* DEFT suggests a light and assured touch, either physical or mental: *deft manipulation of the sensitive controls, of public opinion.* SKILLFUL is the most general of these synonyms and can be substituted in most contexts for any of the foregoing, sacrificing only the overtones or connotations of each: *a skillful performer.* HANDY applies mainly to physical skill, often achieved without formal training: *handy with tools.* **—Ant. 1.** clumsy. **2.** inept. **3.** awkward.

dextr-, var. of **dextro-** before a vowel: *dextral.*

dex•tral (dek′strəl), *adj.* **1.** of, pertaining to, or on the right side; right (opposed to *sinistral*). **2.** right-handed. **3.** Also, **dexiotropic.** *Zool.* (of certain gastropod shells) coiling clockwise, as seen from the apex. [1640–50; < L *dext(e)r* DEXTER + -AL[1]] **—dex′tral•ly,** *adv.*

dex•tral•i•ty (dek stral′i tē), *n.* **1.** the state or quality of having the right side or its parts or members different from and, usually, more efficient than the left side or its parts or members; right-handedness. **2.** preference for using the right hand or side. Cf. **sinistrality. 3.** *Zool.* the state of being dextral. [1640–50; DEXTRAL + -ITY]

dex•tran (dek′strən), *n. Chem., Pharm.* a viscous polysaccharide, composed of dextrose, produced by bacterial action on sucrose: used in confections and lacquers and in medicine chiefly as an extender for blood plasma. [1875–80; DEXTR(OSE) + -AN(HYDRIDE)]

dex•tran•ase (dek′strə nās′, -nāz′), *n. Biochem.* an enzyme that hydrolyzes dextran to smaller oligosaccharides: used in dentifrices to dissolve dental plaque. [1945–50; DEXTRAN + -ASE]

dex•trin (dek′strin), *n. Biochem., Chem.* a soluble, gummy substance, formed from starch by the action of heat, acids, or ferments, occurring in various forms and having dextrorotatory properties: used chiefly as a thickening agent in printing inks and food, as a mucilage, and as a substitute for gum arabic and other natural substances. Also, **dex•trine** (dek′strin, -strēn). Also called **British gum.** [1825–35; < F *dextrine.* See DEXTR-, -IN[2]]

dex•tro (dek′strō), *adj. Optics.* dextrorotatory. [by shortening]

dextro-, 1. a combining form meaning "right," used in the formation of compound words: *dextrorotatatory.* **2.** *Chem.* a combining form meaning "turning clockwise": *dextroglucose.* Also, *esp. before a vowel,* **dextr-.** [< L *dextr-,* s. of *dexter* right-hand + -o-, on the model of RETRO-]

dex•tro•am•phet•a•mine (dek′strō am fet′ə mēn′, -min), *n. Pharm.* a white, crystalline, water-soluble solid, $C_9H_{13}N$, that stimulates the central nervous system: used in medicine as an antidepressive and appetite suppressant. [1945–50; DEXTRO- + AMPHETAMINE]

dex•tro•car•di•a (dek′strō kär′dē ə), *n. Pathol.* **1.** an abnormal condition in which the heart is displaced to the right side of the chest. **2.** dextral displacement of the heart with complete transposition of the cardiac chambers, the right chambers being on the left side and the left chambers being on the right side. Also, **dexiocardia.** [< NL; see DEXTRO-, -CARDIA] **—dex′tro•car′di•al,** *adj.*

dex•troc•u•lar (dek strok′yə lər), *adj. Ophthalm.* favoring the right eye, rather than the left, by habit or for effective vision (opposed to *sinistrocular*). [DEXTR- + OCULAR] **—dex•troc•u•lar•i•ty** (dek strok′yə lar′i tē), *n.*

dex•tro•glu•cose (dek′strō glo͞o′kōs), *n. Biochem.* See under **glucose** (def. 1). [DEXTRO- + GLUCOSE]

dex•tro•ro•ta•to•ry (dek′strō rō′tə tôr′ē, -tōr′ē), *adj. Optics.* turning to the right, as the rotation to the right of the plane of polarization of light in certain crystals and the like. *Symbol: d-* Also, **dex•tro•ro•ta•ry** (dek′strō rō′tə rē). [1875–80; DEXTRO- + ROTATORY] **—dex•tro•ro•ta•tion** (dek′strō rō tā′shən), *n.*

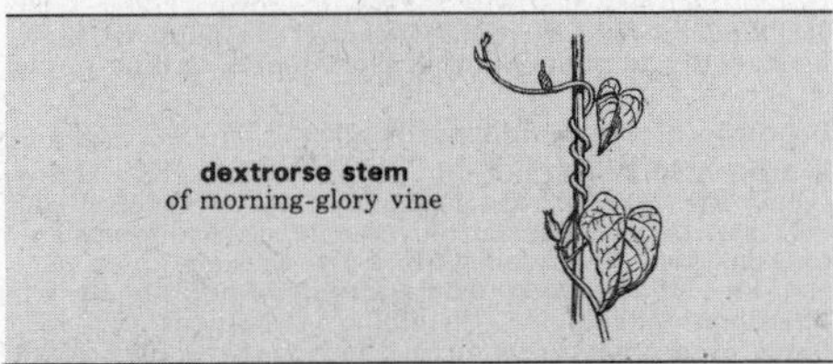
dextrorse stem
of morning-glory vine

dex•trorse (dek′strôrs, dek strôrs′), *adj. Bot.* (of a climbing plant) rising helically from right to left, as seen from outside the helix (opposed to *sinistrorse*). Also, **dex•tror′sal.** [1860–65; < L *dextrorsum* toward the right, earlier *dextrōvorsum,* equiv. to *dextrō-* to the right (see DEXTER) + *vorsum,* acc. of *vorsus,* var. of *versus,* ptp. of *vertere* to turn] **—dex′trorse•ly,** *adv.*

dex•trose (dek′strōs), *n. Biochem.* dextroglucose, commercially obtainable from starch by acid hydrolysis. Also called **corn sugar, grape sugar.** [1865–70; DEXTR- + -OSE[2]]

dex•tro•sin•is•tral (dek′strō sin′ə strəl), *adj.* **1.** passing or extending from the right to the left. **2.** left-handed, but having the right hand trained for writing. [DEXTRO- + SINISTRAL] **—dex′tro•sin′is•tral•ly,** *adv.*

dex•trous (dek′strəs), *adj.* dexterous. **—dex′trous•ly,** *adv.* **—dex′trous•ness,** *n.*

dey (dā), *n.* **1.** the title of the governor of Algiers before the French conquest in 1830. **2.** a title sometimes used by the former rulers of Tunis and Tripoli. [1650–60; < F < Turk *dayı* orig., maternal uncle]

De•zhnev (dezh′nef, -ne ôf′; *Russ.* dyi zhnyôf′), *n.* **Cape,** a cape in the NE Russian Federation in Asia, on the Bering Strait: the northeasternmost point of Asia. Also called **East Cape.**

de•zinc•i•fi•ca′tion (dē zing′kə fi kā′shən), *n. Metall.* **1.** removal of zinc. **2.** loss of zinc by corrosion. [1870–75; DE- + ZINCIFICATION]

D/F, direction finding. Also, **DF**

D.F., 1. Defender of the Faith. [< NL *Dēfēnsor Fideī*] **2.** Distrito Federal. **3.** Doctor of Forestry.

D.F.A., Doctor of Fine Arts.

D.F.C., See **Distinguished Flying Cross.**

D.F.M., Distinguished Flying Medal.

dg, decigram; decigrams.

D.G., 1. by the grace of God. [< L *Deī grātiā*] **2.** Director General.

d-glu•cose (dē′glo͞o′kōs), *n. Biochem.* See under **glucose** (def. 1). [1935–40]

DH, 1. *Racing.* See **dead heat. 2.** *Baseball.* See **designated hitter.** Also, **dh**

DH., (in Morocco) dirham; dirhams.

D.H., 1. Doctor of Humanics. **2.** Doctor of Humanities.

DHA, *Biochem.* docosahexaenoic acid: an omega-3 fatty acid present in fish oils.

Dhah•ran (dä rän′), *n.* a city in E Saudi Arabia: oil center. 12,500.

Dha•ka (dak′ə, dä′kə), *n.* a city in and the capital of Bangladesh, in the central part. 2,365,695. Also, **Dacca.**

dhal (däl), *n. East Indian Cookery.* dal.

dhāl (thäl), *n.* the ninth letter of the Arabic alphabet. [< Ar]

dha•man (dä′mən), *n.* a large, harmless, colubrid snake, *Ptyas mucosus,* of southern Asia, the skin of which is used in making shoes, purses, and other items. [1875–80; < Hindi *dhāman;* cf. Skt *dharmaṇa* a kind of snake]

dhar•ma (där′mə, dur′-), *n. Hinduism, Buddhism.* **1.** essential quality or character, as of the cosmos or one's own nature. **2.** conformity to religious law, custom, duty, or one's own quality or character. **3.** virtue. **4.** religion. **5.** law, esp. religious law. **6.** the doctrine or teaching of the Buddha. Pali, **dham•ma** (dum′ə). [1790–1800; < Skt: custom, duty, akin to *dhārayati* holds, maintains] **—dhar′mic,** *adj.*

dhar•na (där′nə, dur′-), *n.* (in India) the practice of exacting justice or compliance with a just demand by sitting and fasting at the doorstep of an offender until death or until the demand is granted. Also, **dhurna.** [1785–95; < Hindi: placing]

Dha•ruk (där′o͝ok), *n.* an Australian aboriginal language, now extinct, spoken in the area of the first European settlement at Port Jackson.

Dhau•la•gi•ri (dou′lə gēr′ē), *n.* a mountain in W central Nepal: a peak of the Himalayas. 26,826 ft. (8180 m).

Dhe•gi•ha (dā′gē hä′), *n.* a division of the Siouan language family, comprising the dialects spoken by the Omaha, Osage, Kansa, Ponca, and Quapaw.

dhikr (dik′ər), *n., pl.* **dhikrs, dhikr.** *Islam.* **1.** a meeting of dervishes at which a phrase containing a name of God is chanted rhythmically to induce a state of ecstasy. **2.** each set of passages from the Koran so chanted, with its accompanying ritual. Also, **zikr.** [< Ar: recitation]

D.H.L., 1. Doctor of Hebrew Letters. **2.** Doctor of Hebrew Literature.

dhole (dōl), *n.* a wild Asian dog, *Cuon alpinus,* that hunts in packs: an endangered species. [1827; said to be the indigenous name of the animal, though appar. not attested in Indo-Aryan or Dravidian languages]

dhoo•ly (do͞o′lē), *n., pl.* **-lies.** dooly.

dho•ti (dō′tē), *n., pl.* **-tis. 1.** a long loincloth worn by many Hindu men in India. **2.** the cotton fabric, sometimes patterned, of which the loincloth is made. Also, **dhoo•ti, dhoo•tie, dhu•ti** (do͞o′tē). [1615–25; < Hindi]

dhow (dou), *n.* any of various types of sailing vessels used by Arabs on the east African, Arabian, and Indian coasts, generally lateen-rigged on two or three masts. Also, **dau, dow.** [1795–1805; < Ar *dāwa*]

dhow

Dhu 'l-hij•jah (do͞ol hij′ə), *Islam.* the twelfth month of the Muslim calendar, in leap year containing one extra day. Also, **Dhu 'l-hij′ja, Zu 'l-hijjah.** Cf. **Muslim calendar.** [1760–70; < Ar *dhū al-ḥijjah*]

Dhu 'l-Qa•'da (do͞ol kä′də), *Islam.* the eleventh month of the Muslim calendar. Also, **Zu 'l-kadah.** Cf. **Muslim calendar.** [1760–70; < Ar *dhū al-qa'dah*]

dhur•rie (dûr′ē), *n.* a thick, nonpile cotton rug of India. Also, **durrie.** [1875–80; < Hindi *darī*]

di[1] (dē), *prep.* from; of: used in Italian personal names, originally to indicate place of origin: *Conte di Savòia.* Also, **Di.** [< It < L *dē*]

di[2] (dē), *n. Music.* a tone in the ascending chromatic scale between do and re. [perh. alter. of DO[2]]

Di (dī), *n.* a female given name, form of **Diana.**

DI, 1. Department of the Interior. **2.** drill instructor.

Di, *Symbol, Chem.* didymium.

di-[1], a prefix occurring in loanwords from Greek, where it meant "two," "twice," "double" (*diphthong*); on this model, freely used in the formation of compound words (*dicotyledon; dipolar*) and in chemical terms (*diatomic; disulfide*). Also, **dis-**[2]. Cf. **mono-.** [ME << L < Gk, comb. form repr. *dís* twice, double, akin to *dýo* TWO. See BI-, TWI-]

di-[2], var. of **dis-**[1] before *b, d, l, m, n, r, s, v,* and sometimes *g* and *j: digest; divide.*

di-[3], var. of **dia-** before a vowel: *diorama.*

di., diameter. Also, **dia.**

dia-, a prefix occurring in loanwords from Greek (*diabetes; dialect*) and used, in the formation of compound words, to mean "passing through" (*diathermy*), "thoroughly," "completely" (*diagnosis*), "going apart" (*dialysis*), and "opposed in moment" (*diamagnetism*). Also, *esp. before a vowel,* **di-.** [< Gk, comb. form repr. *diá* (prep.) through, between, across, by, of, akin to *dýo* TWO and *di-* DI-[1]]

dia., diameter.

di·a·base (dī′ə bās′), *n. Petrol.* **1.** a fine-grained gabbro occurring as minor intrusions. **2.** *Brit.* a dark igneous rock consisting essentially of augite and feldspar; an altered dolerite. [1810–20; < F, equiv. to *dia-* (error for *di-* two) + *base* BASE[1]] **—di′a·ba′sic,** *adj.*

di·a·bat·ic (dī′ə bat′ik), *adj.* occurring with an exchange of heat (opposed to *adiabatic*): *a diabatic process.* [< Gk *diabat(ós)* able to be crossed, fordable (equiv. to *dia-* DIA- + *batós* passable, verbal adj. of *baínein* to walk, go) + -IC]

Dia·bel·li (dē′ä bel′ē), *n.* **An·to·ni·o** (än tô′nē ō′), 1781–1858, Austrian composer and music publisher.

di·a·be·tes (dī′ə bē′tis, -tēz), *n. Pathol.* **1.** any of several disorders characterized by increased urine production. **2.** Also called **diabe′tes mel′li·tus** (mel′i təs, mə lī′-). a disorder of carbohydrate metabolism, usually occurring in genetically predisposed individuals, characterized by inadequate production or utilization of insulin and resulting in excessive amounts of glucose in the blood and urine, excessive thirst, weight loss, and in some cases progressive destruction of small blood vessels leading to such complications as infections and gangrene of the limbs or blindness. **3.** Also called **Type I diabetes, insulin-dependent diabetes, juvenile diabetes.** a severe form of diabetes mellitus in which insulin production by the beta cells of the pancreas is impaired, usually resulting in dependence on externally administered insulin, the onset of the disease typically occurring before the age of 25. **4.** Also called **Type II diabetes, non-insulin-dependent diabetes, adult-onset diabetes, maturity-onset diabetes.** a mild, sometimes asymptomatic form of diabetes mellitus characterized by diminished tissue sensitivity to insulin and sometimes by impaired beta cell function, exacerbated by obesity and often treatable by diet and exercise. **5.** Also called **diabe′tes in·sip′i·dus** (in sip′i dəs). increased urine production caused by inadequate secretion of vasopressin by the pituary gland. [1555–65; < NL, L < Gk, equiv. to *diabē-* (var. s. of *diabaínein* to go through, pass over, equiv. to *dia-* DIA- + *baínein* to pass) + *-tēs* agent suffix]

di·a·bet·ic (dī′ə bet′ik). *adj.* **1.** of or pertaining to diabetes or persons having diabetes. **2.** having or resulting from diabetes. *—n.* **3.** a person who has diabetes. [1790–1800; DIABET(ES) + -IC]

diabet′ic retinop′athy, *Pathol.* a disorder of the blood vessels of the retina occurring as a complication of poorly controlled diabetes mellitus and often leading to blindness.

di·a·be·tol·o·gist (dī′ə bi tol′ə jist), *n.* a physician, usually an internist or endocrinologist, who specializes in the treatment of diabetes mellitus. [1960–65; DIABET(ES) + -O- + -LOGY]

di·a·ble·rie (dē ä′blə rē; *Fr.* dyA blə Rē′), *n., pl.* **-ries** (-rēz; *Fr.* -Rē′). **1.** diabolic magic or art; sorcery; witchcraft. **2.** the domain or realm of devils. **3.** the lore of devils; demonology. **4.** reckless mischief; deviltry. [1745–55; < F, OF, equiv. to *diable* DEVIL + *-erie* -ERY]

di·a·bol·ic (dī′ə bol′ik), *adj.* **1.** having the qualities of a devil; devilish; fiendish; outrageously wicked: *a diabolic plot.* **2.** pertaining to or actuated by a devil. Also, **di′a·bol′i·cal.** [1350–1400; ME *diabolik* (< MF) < LL *diabolicus* < Gk *diabolikós,* equiv. to *diábol(os)* DEVIL + *-ikos* -IC] **—di′a·bol′i·cal·ly,** *adv.* **—di′a·bol′i·cal·ness,** *n.*

di·ab·o·lism (dī ab′ə liz′əm), *n.* **1.** *Theol.* **a.** action aided or caused by the devil; sorcery; witchcraft. **b.** the character or condition of a devil. **c.** a doctrine concerning devils. **d.** a belief in or worship of devils. **2.** action befitting the devil; deviltry. [1600–10; < Gk *diábol(os)* DEVIL + -ISM] **—di·ab′o·list,** *n.*

di·ab·o·lize (dī ab′ə līz′), *v.t.,* **-lized, -liz·ing.** **1.** to make diabolical or devilish. **2.** to represent as diabolical. **3.** to subject to diabolical influences. Also, *esp. Brit.,* **di·ab′o·lise′.** [1695–1705; < Gk *diábol(os)* DEVIL + -IZE] **—di·ab′o·li·za′tion,** *n.*

di·ab·o·lo (dē ab′ə lō′), *n., pl.* **-los** for 2. **1.** a game in which a toplike object is spun, thrown, and caught by or balanced on and whirled along a string the ends of which are fastened to the ends of two sticks that are manipulated by hand. **2.** the top used in this game. Cf. **yoyo.** [1905–10; < It: lit., DEVIL]

di·a·caus·tic (dī′ə kô′stik), *Math., Optics.* *—adj.* **1.** noting a caustic surface or curve formed by the refraction of light. *—n.* **2.** a diacaustic surface or curve. Cf. **catacaustic.** [1695–1705; DIA- + CAUSTIC]

di′a·ce′tic ac′id (dī′ə sē′tik, -set′ik, dī′-), *Chem.* See **acetoacetic acid.** [1880–85; DI-[1] + ACETIC ACID]

di·ac′e·tone al′cohol (dī as′i tōn′), *Chem.* a colorless, flammable liquid with a pleasant odor, $C_6H_{12}O_2$: used as a solvent for lacquers, dyes, cellulose nitrate, and resins. [DI-[1] + ACETONE]

di·a·ce·tyl (dī′ə sēt′l, -set′l, dī as′i tl), *n. Chem.* biacetyl. [1870–75; DI-[1] + ACETYL]

di·a·ce·tyl·mor·phine (dī′ə sēt′l môr′fēn, -set′-, dī as′i tl-), *n. Pharm.* heroin. [1870–75; DIACETYL + MORPHINE]

di·a·chron·ic (dī′ə kron′ik), *adj. Ling.* of or pertaining to the changes in a linguistic system between successive points in time; historical: *diachronic analysis.* Cf. **synchronic.** [1925–30; < F *diachronique* (term introduced by F. de Saussure); see DIA-, CHRONIC] **—di′a·chron′i·cal·ly,** *adv.* **—di′a·chron′ic·ness,** *n.*

diachron′ic linguis′tics. See **historical linguistics.** [1925–30]

di·ach·ro·ny (dī ak′rə nē), *n., pl.* **-nies.** **1.** *Ling.* **a.** a diachronic approach to language study. **b.** change or development in a linguistic system over a period of time. **2.** historical change. [1955–60; DIACHRON(IC) + -Y[3]]

di·ach·y·lon (dī ak′ə lon′), *n. Med.* an adhesive plaster consisting chiefly of litharge and oil, used in the treatment of wounds and excoriations. Also, **di·ach·y·lum** (dī ak′ə ləm). [1275–1325; < L < Gk *diáchylōn* (something) made of juices, equiv. to *dia-* DIA- + *chylós* juice (also Latinized as *diachȳlum* whence E sp. with *-um*); r. ME *diaculon* < ML, and ME *diaquilon* < MF, both < LL *diachȳlōn*]

di·ac·id (dī as′id), *adj. Chem.* **1.** capable of combining with two molecules of a monobasic acid. **2.** (of an acid or a salt) having two replaceable hydrogen atoms. [1865–70; DI-[1] + ACID]

di·ac·o·nal (dī ak′ə nl), *adj.* pertaining to a deacon. [1605–15; < LL *diāconālis.* See DEACON, -AL[1]]

di·ac·o·nate (dī ak′ə nit, -nāt′), *n.* **1.** the office or dignity of a deacon. **2.** a body of deacons. [1720–30; < LL *diāconātus.* See DEACON, -ATE[3]]

di·a·con·i·con (dī′ə kon′i kon′, -kən), *n., pl.* **-ca** (-kə). a sacristy in an Eastern or early Christian church, usually on the south side of the bema. [1720–30; < LGk *diākonikón* (> LL *diāconicum*), neut. of *diākonikós* of a DEACON; see -IC]

di·a·crit·ic (dī′ə krit′ik), *n.* **1.** Also called **diacrit′ical mark′.** a mark, point, or sign added or attached to a letter or character to distinguish it from another of similar form, to give it a particular phonetic value, to indicate stress, etc., as a cedilla, tilde, circumflex, or macron. *—adj.* **2.** diacritical. **3.** diagnostic. [1670–80; < Gk *diakritikós* distinctive, equiv. to *dia-* DIA- + *kritikós;* see CRITIC]

di·a·crit·i·cal (dī′ə krit′i kəl), *adj.* **1.** serving to distinguish; distinctive. **2.** capable of distinguishing. **3.** *Phonet.* serving as a diacritic. [1740–50; DIACRITIC + -AL[1]] **—di′a·crit′i·cal·ly,** *adv.*

di·ac·tin·ic (dī′ak tin′ik), *adj. Physics.* capable of transmitting actinic rays. [1865–70; DI-[3] + ACTINIC] **—di·ac′tin·ism,** *n.*

di·ad (dī′ad), *n., adj.* dyad.

di·a·del·phous (dī′ə del′fəs), *adj. Bot.* **1.** (of stamens) united into two sets by their filaments. **2.** (of plants) having the stamens so united. [1800–10; DI-[1] + -ADELPHOUS]

di·a·dem (dī′ə dem′), *n.* **1.** a crown. **2.** a cloth headband, sometimes adorned with jewels, formerly worn by Oriental kings. **3.** royal dignity or authority. *—v.t.* **4.** to adorn with or as if with a diadem; crown. [1250–1300; ME *diademe* (< AF) < L *diadēma* < Gk *diádēma* fillet, band, equiv. to *diadē-* (verbid s. of *diadeîn* to bind round + *-ma* n. suffix]

di·ad·ic (dī ad′ik), *adj., n.* dyadic.

di·ad·o·cho·ki·ne·sia (dī ad′ə kō ki nē′zhə, -zhē ə, -zē ə, -kī-), *n. Med.* the normal ability to perform rapidly alternating muscular movements, as flexion and extension. Also, **di·ad·o·cho·ki·ne·sis** (dī ad′ə kō ki nē′sis, -kī-), **di·ad′oko·ki·ne′sia, di·ad′o·ko·ki·ne′sis.** Cf. **adiadochokinesia.** [< Gk *diádocho(s)* succeeding, verbid of *diadéchesthai* to succeed (*dia-* DIA- + *déchesthai* to take up) + -KINESIA]

di·ad·o·chy (dī ad′ə kē), *n. Crystall.* the ability of certain different elements to exist in place of each other in certain points of a space lattice; isomorphism. [irreg. < Gk *diadochḗ* succession; see DIADOCHOKINESIA] **—di·a·doch·ic** (dī′ə dok′ik), *adj.*

di·ad·ro·mous (dī ad′rə məs), *adj.* **1.** *Bot.* (of a leaf) having a fanlike arrangement of veins. **2.** (of fish) migrating between fresh and salt waters. Cf. **anadromous, catadromous.** [1945–50; DIA- + -DROMOUS]

di·aer·e·sis (dī er′ə sis), *n., pl.* **-ses** (-sēz′). dieresis. **—di·ae·ret·ic** (dī′ə ret′ik), *adj.*

diag., **1.** diagonal; diagonally. **2.** diagram.

di·a·gen·e·sis (dī′ə jen′ə sis), *n. Geol.* the physical and chemical changes occurring in sediments between the times of deposition and solidification. [1885–90; < NL; see DIA-, -GENESIS] **—di·a·ge·net·ic** (dī′ə jə net′ik), *adj.*

di·a·ge·o·trop·ic (dī′ə jē′ə trop′ik, -trō′pik), *adj. Bot.* (of a plant part) growing at a right angle to the direction of gravity. [1875–80; DIA- + GEOTROPIC]

di·a·ge·ot·ro·pism (dī′ə jē o′trə piz′əm), *n. Bot.* diageotropic tendency or growth. [1875–80; DIA- + GEOTROPISM]

Dia·ghi·lev (dē ä′gə lef′; *Russ.* dyä′gyi lyif), *n.* **Ser·gei Pa·vlo·vich** (sûr gā′ pav lō′vich; *Russ.* syir gyā′ pu vlô′vyich), 1872–1929, Russian ballet producer.

di·ag·nose (dī′əg nōs′, -nōz′, dī′əg nōs′, -nōz′), *v.,* **-nosed, -nos·ing.** *—v.t.* **1.** to determine the identity of (a disease, illness, etc.) by a medical examination: *The doctor diagnosed the illness as influenza.* **2.** to ascertain the cause or nature of (a disorder, malfunction, problem, etc.) from the symptoms: *The mechanic diagnosed the trouble that caused the engine knock.* **3.** to classify or determine on the basis of scientific examination. *—v.i.* **4.** to make a diagnosis. [1860–65; back formation from DIAGNOSIS] **—di′ag·nos′a·ble,** *adj.*

di·ag·no·sis (dī′əg nō′sis), *n., pl.* **-ses** (-sēz). **1.** *Med.* **a.** the process of determining by examination the nature and circumstances of a diseased condition. **b.** the decision reached from such an examination. *Abbr.:* Dx **2.** *Biol.* scientific determination; a description that classifies a group or taxon precisely. **3.** a determining or analysis of the cause or nature of a problem or situation. **4.** an answer or solution to a problematic situation. [1675–85; < NL < Gk *diágnōsis* a distinguishing. See DIA-, -GNOSIS]

di·ag·nos·tic (dī′əg nos′tik), *adj.* **1.** of, pertaining to, or used in diagnosis. **2.** serving to identify or characterize; being a precise indication. *—n.* **3.** diagnosis (def. 1). **4.** a symptom or characteristic of value in diagnosis. **5.** *Med.* a device or substance used for the analysis or detection of diseases or other medical conditions. **6.** *Computers.* **a.** a message output by a computer diagnosing an error in a computer program, computer system, or component device. **b.** a program or subroutine that produces such messages. [1615–25; < Gk *diagnōstikós,* equiv. to *diagnōst(ós)* distinguished (akin to *diágnōsis;* see DIAGNOSIS) + *-ikos* -IC] **—di′ag·nos′ti·cal·ly,** *adv.*

di·ag·nos·ti·cate (dī′əg nos′ti kāt′), *v.t., v.i.,* **-cat·ed, -cat·ing.** to diagnose. [1840–50; DIAGNOSTIC + -ATE[1]] **—di′ag·nos′ti·ca′tion,** *n.*

di·ag·nos·ti·cian (dī′əg no stish′ən), *n.* an expert in making diagnoses, esp. a medical doctor. [1865–70; DIAGNOSTIC + -IAN]

di·ag·nos·tics (dī′əg nos′tiks), *n.* (*used with a singular v.*) *Med.* the discipline or practice of diagnosis. [1660–70; see DIAGNOSTIC, -ICS]

di·ag·o·nal (dī ag′ə nl, -ag′nl), *adj.* **1.** *Math.* **a.** connecting two nonadjacent angles or vertices of a polygon or polyhedron, as a straight line. **b.** extending from one edge of a solid figure to an opposite edge, as a plane. **2.** having an oblique direction. **3.** having oblique lines, ridges, markings, etc. *—n.* **4.** a diagonal line or plane. **5.** virgule. **6.** a diagonal row, part, pattern, etc. **7.** *Manège.* (of a horse at a trot) the foreleg and the hind leg, diagonally opposite, which move forward simultaneously. **8.** See **diagonal cloth.** **9.** *Math.* a set of entries in a square matrix running either from upper left to lower right **(main diagonal** or **principal diagonal)** or lower left to upper right **(secondary diagonal).** **10.** *Chess.* one of the oblique lines of squares on a chessboard: *He advanced his bishop along the open diagonal.* [1535–45; < L *diagōnālis* < Gk *diagṓn(ios)* from angle to angle (see DIA-, -GON) + L *-ālis* -AL[1]] **—di·ag′o·nal·ly,** *adv.*

diag′onal cloth′, a twilled fabric woven with distinctly diagonal lines. Also called **diagonal.** [1860–65]

di·ag·o·nal·ize (dī ag′ə nl īz′, -ag′nl-), *v.t.,* **-ized, -iz·ing.** *Math.* to transform (a matrix) to a diagonal matrix. Also, *esp. Brit.,* **di·ag′o·nal·ise′.** [1880–85; DIAGONAL + -IZE]

diag′onal ma′trix, *Math.* a square matrix in which all the entries except those along the diagonal from upper left to lower right are zero. [1925–30]

di·a·gram (dī′ə gram′), *n., v.,* **-gramed** or **-grammed, -gram·ing** or **-gram·ming.** *—n.* **1.** a figure, usually consisting of a line drawing, made to accompany and illustrate a geometrical theorem, mathematical demonstration, etc. **2.** a drawing or plan that outlines and explains the parts, operation, etc., of something: *a diagram of an engine.* **3.** a chart, plan, or scheme. *—v.t.* **4.** to represent by a diagram; make a diagram of. [1610–20; < L *diagramma* < Gk: that which is marked out by lines. See DIA-, -GRAM[1]] **—di′a·gram′ma·ble,** *adj.*

di·a·gram·mat·ic (dī′ə grə mat′ik), *adj.* **1.** in the form of a diagram; graphic; outlined. **2.** pertaining to diagrams. Also, **di′a·gram·mat′i·cal.** [1850–55; DIAGRAM + *-atic* as in *problem, problematic*] **—di′a·gram·mat′i·cal·ly,** *adv.*

di·a·graph (dī′ə graf′, -gräf′), *n.* **1.** a device for drawing, used in reproducing outlines, plans, etc., mechanically on any desired scale. **2.** a combined protractor and scale. [1840–50; < F *diagraphe* < Gk *diagráphein* to draw. See DIA-, -GRAPH]

di·a·ki·ne·sis (dī′ə ki nē′sis, -kī-), *n. Cell Biol.* the last stage in prophase, in which the nucleolus and nuclear envelope disappear, spindle fibers form, and the chromosomes shorten in preparation for anaphase. [Latinization of G *Diakinese* (1897); see DIA-, -KINESIS]

di·al (dī′əl, dīl), *n., v.,* **di·aled, di·al·ing** or (*esp. Brit.*) **di·alled, di·al·ling,** *adj.* *—n.* **1.** a plate, disk, face, or other surface containing markings or figures upon which the time of day is indicated by hands, pointers, or shadows, as of a clock or sundial. **2.** a plate or disk with markings or figures for indicating or registering some measurement or number, as of pressure, number of revolutions, the frequency to which a radio is tuned, etc., usually by means of a pointer. **3.** a rotatable plate, disk, or knob used for regulating a mechanism, making and breaking electrical connections, etc., as in tuning a radio or television station in or out. **4.** Also called **rotary dial.** a rotatable plate or disk on a telephone, fitted with finger holes that are marked with letters or numbers, used in making calls through an automatic switchboard. **5.** any mechanism on the face of a telephone by which the caller places a call, as push buttons. **6.** Also called **miner's dial.** *Mining.* a compass used for underground surveying. *—v.t.* **7.** to indicate or register on or as if on a dial. **8.** to measure with or as if with a dial. **9.** to regulate, select, or tune in by means of a dial, as on a radio: *to dial my favorite program.* **10.** to make a telephone call to: *Dial me at home.* *—v.i.* **11.** to use a telephone dial; to dial a telephone: *I keep dialing, but the line seems dead.* **12.** to tune in or regulate by means of a dial: *to dial into the opera broadcast.* **13. dial up,** to obtain, reach, or contact by telephone: *to dial up stock-market information; to dial up Chicago and do some business.* *—adj.* **14.** (of a telephone) having a rotary dial mechanism. [1400–50; late ME: instrument for telling time by the sun's shadow, presumably < ML *diālis* daily (L *di(ēs)* day + *-ālis* -AL[1])]

dial., **1.** dialect. **2.** dialectal. **3.** dialectic. **4.** dialectical.

di·a·lect (dī′ə lekt′), *n.* **1.** *Ling.* a variety of a language that is distinguished from other varieties of the same language by features of phonology, grammar, and vocabulary, and by its use by a group of speakers who are set off from others geographically or socially. **2.** a provincial, rural, or socially distinct variety of a language that differs from the standard language, esp. when considered as substandard. **3.** a special variety of a language: *The literary dialect is usually taken as the standard language.* **4.** a language considered as one of a group that have a common ancestor: *Persian, Latin, and English are Indo-European dialects.* **5.** jargon or cant. [1545–55; < L *dialectus* < Gk *diálektos* discourse, lan-

CONCISE ETYMOLOGY KEY: <, descended or borrowed from; >, whence; b., blend of, blended; c., cognate with; cf., compare; deriv., derivative; equiv., equivalent; imit., imitative; obl., oblique; r., replacing; s., stem; sp., spelling, spelled; resp., respelling, respelled; trans., translation; ?, origin unknown; *, unattested; ‡, probably earlier than. See the full key inside the front cover.

guage, dialect, equiv. to *dialég(esthai)* to converse (*dia-* DIA- + *légein* to speak) + *-tos* v. adj. suffix]
—Syn. 2. idiom, patois. See **language.**

di•a•lec•tal (dī′ə lek′tl), *adj.* **1.** of a dialect. **2.** characteristic of a dialect. Also, **dialectic, dialectical.** [1825–35; DIALECT + -AL[1]] **—di′a•lec′tal•ly,** *adv.*
—Usage. In linguistics DIALECTAL, not DIALECTICAL, is the term more commonly used to denote regional or social language variation: *Dialectal variation is more marked in the South than elsewhere in the United States.* In general writing either term may be found.

di′alect at′las, *Ling.* a collection of maps of a certain area indicating the distribution of various phonological, morphological, lexical, or other features of the dialects of that area. [1930–35]

di′alect geog′raphy, *Ling.* the study of regional dialect variation. [1925–30] **—di′alect geog′rapher.**

di•a•lec•tic (dī′ə lek′tik), *adj.* Also, **dialectical. 1.** of, pertaining to, or of the nature of logical argumentation. **2.** dialectal. *—n.* **3.** the art or practice of logical discussion as employed in investigating the truth of a theory or opinion. **4.** logical argumentation. **5.** Often, **dialectics. a.** logic or any of its branches. **b.** any formal system of reasoning or thought. **6.** See **Hegelian dialectic. 7. dialectics,** (*often used with a singular v.*) the arguments or bases of dialectical materialism, including the elevation of matter over mind and a constantly changing reality with a material basis. **8.** (in Kantian epistemology) a fallacious metaphysical system arising from the attribution of objective reality to the perceptions by the mind of external objects. Cf. **transcendental dialectic. 9.** the juxtaposition or interaction of conflicting ideas, forces, etc. [1350–1400; ME (< AF) < L *dialectica* < Gk *dialektikḗ (téchnē)* argumentative (art). See DIALECT, -IC] **—di′a•lec′ti•cal•ly,** *adv.*

di•a•lec•ti•cal (dī′ə lek′ti kəl), *adj.* **1.** dialectic. **2.** of or characteristic of a dialect; dialectal. [1520–30; DIALECTIC + -AL[1]]
—Usage. See **dialectal.**

dialec′tical mate′rialism, a form of materialism, developed chiefly by Karl Marx, noted esp. for the application of the Hegelian dialectic in its philosophy of history. [1925–30] **—dialec′tical mate′rialist.**

dialec′tical theol′ogy, a form of neoorthodox theology emphasizing the infinite tensions, paradoxes, and basic ambiguities inherent in Christian existence, and holding, against rationalism, that God is unknowable to humans except through divine grace and revelation.

di•a•lec•ti•cian (dī′ə lek tish′ən), *n.* **1.** a person skilled in dialectic; logician. **2.** a dialectologist. [1685–95; < F *dialecticien* < L *dialectic(us)* DIALECTIC + F *-ien* -IAN]

di•a•lec•ti•cism (dī′ə lek′tə siz′əm), *n.* **1.** dialectal speech or influence. **2.** a dialectal word or expression. [1885–90; DIALECTIC + -ISM]

di•a•lec•tol•o•gist (dī′ə lek tol′ə jist), *n.* a specialist in dialectology. [1880–85; DIALECTOLOG(Y) + -IST]

di•a•lec•tol•o•gy (dī′ə lek tol′ə jē), *n., pl.* **-gies** for 2. **1.** *Ling.* the study dealing with dialects and dialect features. **2.** the linguistic features of a dialect or of the dialects of a language. [1875–80; DIALECT + -O- + -LOGY] **—di•a•lec•to•log•ic** (dī′ə lek′tl oj′ik), **di′a•lec′to•log′i•cal,** *adj.*

di•al•er (dī′ə lər, dī′lər), *n.* **1.** a person or thing that dials. **2.** an electronic device attached to a telephone to call preselected numbers automatically when activated. Also, *esp. Brit.,* **di′al•ler.** [1740–50; DIAL+ ER[1]]

di•al•lage (dī′ə lij), *n. Mineral.* a variety of diopside with a laminated structure, found in gabbro and other igneous rocks. [1795–1805; < F < Gk *diallagḗ* interchange, change, n. deriv. from base of *diallássein* make an exchange, equiv. to *di-* DI-[3] + *allássein* to change, exchange]

di•al′lyl sul′fide (dī al′il), *Chem.* See **allyl sulfide.** [DI[1] + ALLYL]

di•a•log•ic (dī′ə loj′ik), *adj.* **1.** of, pertaining to, or characterized by dialogue. **2.** participating in dialogue. Also, **di′a•log′i•cal.** [1825–35; < ML *dialogicus* < Gk *dialogikós,* equiv. to *diálog(os)* DIALOGUE + *-ikos* -IC] **—di′a•log′i•cal•ly,** *adv.*

di•al•o•gist (dī al′ə jist), *n.* **1.** a speaker in a dialogue. **2.** a writer of dialogue. [1650–60; < LL *dialogista* < Gk *dialogistḗs,* equiv. to *diálog(os)* DIALOGUE + *-istēs* -IST] **—di•a•lo•gis•tic** (dī′ə lō jis′tik), *adj.* **—di′a•lo•gis′ti•cal•ly,** *adv.*

di•al•o•gite (dī al′ə jīt′), *n. Mineral.* rhodocrosite. [1820–30; < Gk *dialog(ḗ)* selection, deriv. of *dialégein* to select (*dia-* DIA- + *légein* to speak) + -ITE[1]]

di•al•o•gize (dī al′ə jīz′), *v.i.,* **-gized, -giz•ing.** to carry on a dialogue. Also, *esp. Brit.,* **di•al′o•gise′.** [1595–1605; < Gk *dialogízesthai* to converse; see DIALOGUE, -IZE]

di•a•logue (dī′ə lôg′, -log′), *n., v.* **-logued, -logu•ing.** *—n.* **1.** conversation between two or more persons. **2.** the conversation between characters in a novel, drama, etc. **3.** an exchange of ideas or opinions on a particular issue, esp. a political or religious issue, with a view to reaching an amicable agreement or settlement. **4.** a literary work in the form of a conversation: *a dialogue of Plato.* *—v.i.* **5.** to carry on a dialogue; converse. **6.** to discuss areas of disagreement frankly in order to resolve them. *—v.t.* **7.** to put into the form of a dialogue. Also, **di′a•log′.** [1175–1225; ME < OF *dïalogue,* L *dialogus* < Gk *diálogos.* See DIA-, -LOGUE] **—di′a•logu′er,** *n.*

di′al tone′, (in a telephone) a tone that indicates the line is ready for dialing. [1890–95]

di′al train′, *Horol.* the part of a going train that drives the minute and hour hands.

di•al-up (dī′əl up′, dīl′-), *adj. Computers.* of or pertaining to a terminal that links to a computer by dialing a telephone number. [adj. use of v. phrase *dial up*]

di•al•y•sis (dī al′ə sis), *n., pl.* **-ses** (-sēz′). **1.** *Physical Chem.* the separation of crystalloids from colloids in a solution by diffusion through a membrane. **2.** *Biochem.* the separation of large molecules, as proteins, from small molecules and ions in a solution by allowing the latter to pass through a semipermeable membrane. **3.** *Med.* (in kidney disease) the process by which uric acid and urea are removed from circulating blood by means of a dialyzer. [1580–90; < LL < Gk *diálysis* a separation. See DIA-, -LYSIS]

di•a•lyt•ic (dī′ə lit′ik), *adj.* **1.** of or pertaining to dialysis. **2.** characterized by or displaying dialysis. [1840–50; < Gk *dialytikós;* see DIA-, -LYTIC] **—di′a•lyt′i•cal•ly,** *adv.*

di•al•y•zate (dī al′ə zāt′), *n.* (in dialysis) **1.** the remaining, or colloidal, portion of a solution. **2.** the solution or the crystalline material that passes into it through the semipermeable membrane; diffusate. [1865–70; DIALYZE + -ATE[1]]

di•a•lyze (dī′ə līz′), *v.,* **-lyzed, -lyz•ing.** *—v.t.* **1.** to subject to dialysis; separate or procure by dialysis. *—v.i.* **2.** to undergo dialysis. Also, *esp. Brit.,* **di′a•lyse′.** [1860–65; DIA- + -LYZE] **—di′a•lyz′a•ble,** *adj.* **—di′a•lyz′a•bil′i•ty,** *n.* **—di′a•ly•za′tion,** *n.*

di•a•lyz•er (dī′ə lī′zər), *n.* Also, **di•al•y•za•tor** (dī al′i-zā′tər). an apparatus containing a semipermeable membrane for dialysis. [1860–65; DIALYZE + -ER[1]]

diam., diameter.

di•a•mag•net (dī′ə mag′nit), *n. Physics.* a diamagnetic substance. [1860–65; back formation from DIAMAGNETIC]

di•a•mag•net•ic (dī′ə mag net′ik), *adj. Physics.* of or pertaining to a class of substances, as bismuth and copper, whose permeability is less than that of a vacuum: in a magnetic field, their induced magnetism is in a direction opposite to that of iron. Cf. **antiferromagnetic, ferrimagnetic, ferromagnetic, paramagnetic.** [1840–50; DIA- + MAGNETIC] **—di′a•mag•net′i•cal•ly,** *adv.* **—di•a•mag•net•ism** (dī′ə mag′ni tiz′əm), *n.*

di•a•man•té (dē′ə män tā′), *n.* **1.** a sequin, rhinestone, or other glittery ornamentation on a garment. **2.** fabric covered or patterned with such ornamentation. [1900–05; < F *diamanté* ornamented with diamonds, ptp. of *diamanter,* v. deriv. of *diamant* DIAMOND]

di•a•man•tif•er•ous (dī′ə man tif′ər əs), *adj. Mining.* diamondiferous. [1875–80; < F *diamantifère,* equiv. to *diamant* DIAMOND + *-ifère;* see -I-, -FEROUS]

di•am•e•ter (dī am′i tər), *n.* **1.** *Geom.* **a.** a straight line passing through the center of a circle or sphere and meeting the circumference or surface at each end. **b.** a straight line passing from side to side of any figure or body, through its center. **2.** the length of such a line. **3.** the width of a circular or cylindrical object. [1350–1400; ME *diametre* < OF < L *diametros* < Gk *diámetros* diagonal, diameter, equiv. to *dia-* DIA- + *-metros,* deriv. of *métron* METER[1]]

di•am•e•tral (dī am′i trəl), *adj.* **1.** of a diameter. **2.** forming a diameter. [1350–1400; ME < ML *diametrālis* < L *diametr(os)* DIAMETER + *-ālis* -AL[1]] **—di•am′e•tral•ly,** *adv.*

di•a•met•ri•cal (dī′ə me′tri kəl), *adj.* **1.** of, pertaining to, or along a diameter. **2.** in direct opposition; being at opposite extremes; complete: *diametrical opposites; a diametrical difference.* Also, **di′a•met′ric.** [1545–55; < Gk *diametrik(ós)* (*diámetr(os)* DIAMETER + *-ikos* -IC) + -AL[1]] **—di′a•met′ri•cal•ly,** *adv.*

di•a•mide (dī′ə mīd′, dī am′id), *n. Chem.* a compound containing two amide groups. [1865–70; DI-[1] + AMIDE]

di•am•ine (dī′ə mēn′, dī am′in), *n. Chem.* **1.** a compound containing two amino groups. **2.** hydrazine (def. 1). [1865–70; DI-[1] + AMINE]

di′am•mo′ni•um phos′phate, (dī′ə mō′nē əm, dī′-), *Chem.* a white, crystalline, water-soluble compound, $(NH_4)_2HPO_4$, used as fertilizer, in fire extinguishers, etc. [DI-[1] + AMMONIUM]

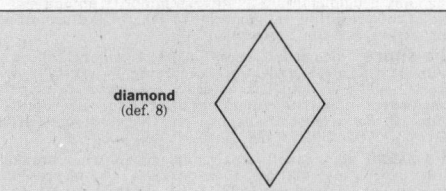

diamond
(def. 8)

di•a•mond (dī′mənd, dī′ə-), *n.* **1.** a pure or nearly pure, extremely hard form of carbon, naturally crystallized in the isometric system. **2.** a piece of this stone. **3.** a transparent, flawless or almost flawless piece of this stone, esp. when cut and polished, valued as a precious gem. **4.** a ring or other piece of jewelry containing such a precious stone, esp. an engagement ring. **5.** a piece of this stone used in a drill or cutting tool. **6.** a tool provided with such an uncut stone, used for cutting glass. **7.** crystallized carbon, or a piece of it, artificially produced. **8.** an equilateral quadrilateral, esp. as placed with its diagonals vertical and horizontal; a lozenge or rhombus. **9.** any rhombus-shaped figure or object oriented with its diagonals vertical and horizontal. **10.** a red rhombus-shaped figure on a playing card. **11.** a card of the suit bearing such figures. **12. diamonds,** (*used with a singular or plural v.*) the suit so marked: *Diamonds is trump. Diamonds are trump.* **13.** *Baseball.* **a.** the space enclosed by home plate and the three bases; infield. **b.** the entire playing field. **14.** *Print.* a 4½-point type of a size between brilliant and pearl. **15. diamond in the rough,** a person of fine character but lacking refined manners or graces. *—adj.* **16.** made of or set with a diamond or diamonds. **17.** having the shape of a diamond: *a dress with a diamond print.* **18.** indicating the 75th, or sometimes the 60th, event of a series, as a wedding anniversary. See table under **wedding anniversary.** *—v.t.* **19.** to adorn with or as if with diamonds. [1275–1325; ME *diamant* < OF < VL **diamant-,* s. of **diamas,* perh. alter. of **adimas* (> F *aimant* magnet, OPr *aziman* diamond, magnet), for L *adamas* ADAMANT, diamond] **—dia′mond•like′,** *adj.*

Di•a•mond (dī′mənd, dī′ə-), *n.* **Cape,** a hill in Canada, in S Quebec, on the St. Lawrence River.

di•a•mond•back (dī′mənd bak′, dī′ə-), *adj.* **1.** bearing diamond-shaped marks, designs, or configurations on the back. *—n.* **2.** See **diamondback rattlesnake. 3.** See **diamondback terrapin. 4.** See **diamondback moth.** [1810–20; DIAMOND + BACK[1]]

dia′mondback moth′, a moth, *Plutella maculipennis,* having brownish wings marked with diamond-shaped, yellow spots in the male, the larvae of which feed on the leaves of cabbages and other cruciferous plants. Also called **cabbage moth.**

dia′mondback rat′tlesnake, either of two large, highly venomous rattlesnakes of the genus *Crotalus,* having diamond-shaped markings on the back. Cf. **eastern diamondback rattlesnake, western diamondback rattlesnake.** [1890–95]

dia′mondback ter′rapin, any of several edible turtles of the genus *Malaclemys,* found in tidewaters of the eastern and southern U.S., having diamond-shaped markings on the back. [1875–80]

Dia′mond Bar′, a city in SW California. 28,045.

dia′mond bird′, pardalote. Also, **dia′mond-bird′.**

dia′mond drill′, a drill having a hollow, cylindrical bit set with diamonds, used for obtaining cores of rock samples. [1820–30]

dia′mond dust′, pulverized diamonds, used as an abrasive. [1695–1705]

Dia′mond Head′, a promontory on SE Oahu Island, in central Hawaii. 761 ft. (232 m) high.

dia•mond•if•er•ous (dī′mən dif′ər əs, dī′ə-), *adj.* containing or yielding diamonds for mining. Also, **diamantiferous.** [1865–70; DIAMOND + -I- + -FEROUS]

dia′mond jubilee′. See under **jubilee** (def. 1).

dia′mond lane′, a highway or street lane for buses and passenger vans marked with a large diamond shape on the pavement. [1985–90]

dia′mond-leaf lau′rel (dī′mənd lēf′, dī′ə-), an ornamental tree, *Pittosporum rhombifolium,* of Australia, having coarsely toothed, oval or diamond-shaped leaves and white flowers.

dia′mond point′, 1. *Furniture.* a faceted, low-relief ornamental motif giving the effect of a cut gem. **2.** an acute, pyramidal point on a nail or spike. [1870–75]

dia′mond-point spoon′ (dī′mənd point′, dī′ə-), a spoon having a handle terminating in a polygonal, pointed knob. Also called **spear-head spoon.**

dia′mond ring′ effect′, *Astron.* a phenomenon, sometimes observed immediately before and after a total eclipse of the sun, in which one of Baily's beads is much brighter than the others, resembling a diamond ring around the moon.

dia′mond skin′ disease′, *Vet. Pathol.* a form of swine erysipelas in which diamond-shaped skin inflammations appear, often accompanied by swollen joints.

Dia′mond State′, Delaware (used as a nickname).

dia′mond wil′low, 1. a small willow tree or shrub, *Salix bebbiana,* of northern North America, having a gray bark often with diamond-shaped furrows caused by fungi. **2.** the slender stems of this tree, often carved into furniture, walking sticks, and other decorative objects.

di•a•mor•phine (dī′ə môr′fēn), *n. Pharm.* heroin. [1910–15; DIA(CETYL) + MORPHINE]

Di•a•mox (dī′ə moks′), *Pharm., Trademark.* a brand of acetazolamide.

di•am′yl sul′fide (dī am′əl), *Chem.* a yellow liquid consisting of a mixture of isomers having the formula $(C_5H_{11})_2S$, used chiefly in the preparation of organic sulfur compounds. Also called **amyl sulfide.** [DI-[1] + AMYL]

Di•an•a (dī an′ə), *n.* **1.** (*Princess of Wales*) (*Lady Diana Spencer*), born 1961, wife of Charles, Prince of Wales. **2.** an ancient Roman deity, virgin goddess of the moon and of hunting, identified with the Greek Artemis. **3.** the moon personified as a goddess. **4.** Also, **Di•ane** (dī an′). a female given name.

Diana
(def. 2)

di•an•drous (dī an′drəs), *adj. Bot.* **1.** (of a flower) having two stamens. **2.** (of a plant) having flowers with two stamens. [1760–70; < NL *diandrus.* See DI-[1], -ANDROUS]

di•a•no•et•ic (dī′ə nō et′ik), *adj.* pertaining to dianoia. [1670–80; < Gk *dianoētik(ós),* equiv. to *diáno(ia)*

CONCISE PRONUNCIATION KEY: act, cāpe, dâre, pärt; set, ēqual; if, ice; ox, ōver, ôrder, oil, bŏŏk, bōōt, out; up, ûrge; child; sing; shoe; thin, *th*at; zh as in *treasure.* ə = *a* as in *alone, e* as in *system, i* as in *easily, o* as in *gallop, u* as in *circus;* ᵊ as in *fire* (fīᵊr), *hour* (ouᵊr). l and n can serve as syllabic consonants, as in *cradle* (krād′l), and *button* (but′n). See the full key inside the front cover.

DIANOIA + *-ē-* thematic vowel + *-tikos* -TIC] —**di′a·no·et′i·cal·ly,** *adv.*

di·a·noi·a (dī′ə noi′ə), *n. Greek Philos.* the mental faculty used in discursive reasoning. [< Gk *diánoia* the intellect, a thought, notion, belief, equiv. to *dia-* DIA- + *no(eîn)* to think + *-ia* -IA]

di·an·thus (dī an′thəs), *n., pl.* **-thus·es.** any of numerous plants belonging to the genus *Dianthus,* of the pink family, as the carnation or sweet william. [< NL (Linnaeus) < Gk *Di(ós)* of Zeus (gen. of *Zeús*) + *ánthos* flower]

di·a·pa·son (dī′ə pā′zən, -sən), *n. Music.* **1.** a full, rich outpouring of melodious sound. **2.** the compass of a voice or instrument. **3.** a fixed standard of pitch. **4.** either of two principal timbres or stops of a pipe organ, one of full, majestic tone **(open diapason)** and the other of strong, flutelike tone **(stopped diapason). 5.** any of several other organ stops. **6.** a tuning fork. [1350–1400; ME *diapasoun* < L *diapāsōn* the whole octave < Gk *dià pāsôn (chordôn)* through all (the notes), short for *hē dià pāsôn chordôn symphōnía* the concord through all the notes of the scale] —**di′a·pa′son·al,** *adj.*

diapa′son nor′mal pitch′, *Music.* a standard of pitch in which A above middle C is established at 435 vibrations per second. Also called **French pitch, international pitch, low pitch.**

di·a·pause (dī′ə pôz′), *n., v.,* **-paused, -paus·ing.** *Zool.* —*n.* **1.** a period of hormonally controlled quiescence, esp. in immature insects, characterized by cessation of growth and reduction of metabolic activity, often occurring seasonally or when environmental conditions are unfavorable. —*v.i.* **2.** to undergo diapause. [1890–95; < Gk *diápausis;* see DIA-, PAUSE]

di·a·pe·de·sis (dī′ə pi dē′sis), *n. Physiol.* the passage of blood cells, esp. leukocytes, through the unruptured walls of the capillaries into the tissues. [1615–25; < NL < Gk *diapḗdēsis* a leaping through, equiv. to *diapēdē-* (verbid s. of *diapēdân* to leap through) + *-sis* -SIS] —**di·a·pe·det·ic** (dī′ə pi det′ik), *adj.*

di·a·per (dī′pər, dī′ə pər), *n.* **1.** a piece of cloth or other absorbent material folded and worn as underpants by a baby not yet toilet-trained. **2.** Also called **dia′per cloth′.** a linen or cotton fabric with a woven pattern of small, constantly repeated figures, as diamonds. **3.** Also called **dia′per pat′tern.** such a pattern, originally used in the Middle Ages in weaving silk and gold. —*v.t.* **4.** to put a diaper on. **5.** to ornament with a diaperlike pattern. [1300–50; ME *diapre* < AF *dia(s)p(r)e* < ML *diasprus* made of diaper < MGk *díaspros* pure white, equiv. to Gk *di-* DI[3] + MGk *áspros* white]

dia′per rash′, a reddish inflammation of the buttocks occurring in infants usually as a result of irritation by ammonia formed as a breakdown product of urine.

di·aph·a·ne·i·ty (dī af′ə nē′i tē, dī′ə fə-), *n.* the quality of being diaphanous; transparency. [1650–60; < Gk *diaphanḗ(s)* showing through + -ITY]

di·aph·a·nom·e·ter (dī af′ə nom′i tər), *n.* an instrument for measuring the transparency of a solid, liquid, or gas. [1780–90; DIAPHAN(OUS) + -O- + -METER] —**di·aph·a·no·met·ric** (dī af′ə nə me′trik), *adj.* —**di·aph′a·nom′e·try,** *n.*

di·aph·a·nous (dī af′ə nəs), *adj.* **1.** very sheer and light; almost completely transparent or translucent. **2.** delicately hazy. [1605–15; < ML *diaphanus* < Gk *diaphan(ḗs)* transparent (equiv. to *diaphan-,* s. of *diaphaínein* to show through (see DIA-, -PHANE) + *-ēs* adj. suffix) + -OUS] —**di·aph′a·nous·ly,** *adv.* —**di·aph′a·nous·ness,** *n.*

di·a·phone (dī′ə fōn′), *n.* **1.** a foghorn producing a low-pitched, penetrating signal of two tones. **2.** *Phonet.* **a.** a phoneme in one dialect corresponding to a similar but phonetically different phoneme in a related dialect. **b.** a group of sounds comprising all the phonetically different dialectal variants of a given phoneme in a language: *The broad* a *and flat* a *of "half" are members of a single diaphone.* [1905–10; DIA- + -PHONE]

di·aph·o·rase (dī af′ə rās′), *n. Biochem.* a flavoprotein, found in mitochondria, that acts as an enzyme in catalyzing the oxidation of reduced NAD. [< G *Diaphorase* (1938) < Gk *diáphor(os)* different, unlike (see DIA-, -PHORE) + G *-ase* -ASE]

di·a·pho·re·sis (dī′ə fə rē′sis), *n. Med.* perspiration, esp. when artificially induced. [1675–85; < LL < Gk: a sweating, equiv. to *diaphorē-* (verbid s. of *diaphoreîn* to carry off or through) + *-sis* -SIS]

di·a·pho·ret·ic (dī′ə fə ret′ik), *Med.* —*adj.* **1.** producing perspiration. —*n.* **2.** a diaphoretic medicine. [1555–65; < LL *diaphorēticus* < Gk *diaphorētikós* promoting perspiration, equiv. to *diaphorē-* (see DIAPHORESIS) + *-tikos* -TIC]

di·a·phragm (dī′ə fram′), *n.* **1.** *Anat.* **a.** a muscular, membranous or ligamentous wall separating two cavities or limiting a cavity. **b.** the partition separating the thoracic cavity from the abdominal cavity in mammals. **2.** *Physical Chem.* **a.** a porous plate separating two liquids, as in a galvanic cell. **b.** a semipermeable membrane. **3.** a thin disk that vibrates when receiving or producing sound waves, as in a telephone, microphone, speaker, or the like. **4.** Also called **pessary.** a thin, dome-shaped device, usually of rubber, for wearing over the uterine cervix during sexual intercourse to prevent conception. **5.** a plate with a hole in the center or a ring that is placed on the axis of an optical instrument, as a camera, and that controls the amount of light entering the instrument. **6.** a plate or web for stiffening metal-framed constructions. —*v.t.* **7.** to furnish with a diaphragm. **8.** to reduce the aperture of (a lens, camera, etc.) by means of a diaphragm. [1350–1400; ME *diafragma* < LL *diaphragma* < Gk *diáphragma* the diaphragm, midriff, equiv. to *dia-* DIA- + *phrágma* a fence]

di·a·phrag·mat·ic (dī′ə frag mat′ik), *adj.* **1.** of the diaphragm. **2.** like a diaphragm. [1650–60; < Gk *diaphragmat-* (s. of *diáphragma* DIAPHRAGM) + -IC] —**di′a·phrag·mat′i·cal·ly,** *adv.*

di′aphragm shut′ter, *Photog.* See **iris shutter.**

di·aph·y·sis (dī af′ə sis), *n., pl.* **-ses** (-sēz′). *Anat.* the shaft of a long bone. [1825–35; < NL < Gk, equiv. to *diaphý(esthai)* to grow between + *-sis* -SIS] —**di·a·phys·i·al, di·a·phys·e·al** (dī′ə fiz′ē əl), *adj.*

di·a·pir (dī′ə pēr′), *n. Geol.* a dome or anticline, the upper regions of which have been ruptured and penetrated by material squeezed up from below. Cf. **plume** (def. 10), **salt dome.** [1915–20; < F, said to be < Gk *diapeírein* to drive through, pierce; *dia-* DIA- + *peírein* to pierce] —**di·a·pir·ic** (dī′ə pir′ik), *adj.*

di·a·poph·y·sis (dī′ə pof′ə sis), *n., pl.* **-ses** (-sēz′). *Anat., Zool.* the part of the transverse process of a thoracic vertebra that articulates with its corresponding rib. [1854; < NL; see DI-[3], APOPHYSIS] —**di·ap·o·phys·i·al** (dī′ap ə fiz′ē əl), *adj.*

di·a·pos·i·tive (dī′ə poz′i tiv), *n.* a positive photographic image produced on a transparent film or glass base. [1890–95; DIA- + POSITIVE]

di·ap·sid (dī ap′sid), *adj.* **1.** (of reptiles) having two openings in the skull behind each eye, characteristic of the subclasses Lepidosauria and Archosauria, including all living reptiles except turtles. —*n.* **2.** a diapsid reptile. Cf. **anapsid.** [< NL *Diapsida* (1903); see DI-[1], ANAPSID]

Di·ar·bek·r (*Turk.* dē är′buk ər), *n.* Diyarbakir.

di·ar·chy (dī′är kē), *n., pl.* **-chies.** government in which power is vested in two rulers or authorities. Also, **dyarchy.** [1825–35; DI-[1] + -ARCHY] —**di·ar′chi·al, di·ar′chic,** *adj.*

di·a·rist (dī′ə rist), *n.* a person who keeps a diary. [1810–20; DIAR(Y) + -IST] —**di′a·ris′tic,** *adj.*

di·ar·rhe·a (dī′ə rē′ə), *n. Pathol.* an intestinal disorder characterized by abnormal frequency and fluidity of fecal evacuations. Also, **di′ar·rhoe′a.** [1350–1400; ME *diaria* < LL *diarrhoea* < Gk *diárrhoia* a flowing through, equiv. to *diarrho-* (var. s. of *diarrheîn* to flow through) + *-ia* -IA] —**di′ar·rhe′al, di′ar·rhe′ic, di·ar·rhet·ic** (dī′ə ret′ik), **di′ar·rhoe′al, di′ar·rhoe′ic, di′ar·rhoet′ic,** *adj.*

di·ar·thro·sis (dī′är thrō′sis), *n., pl.* **-ses** (-sēz). *Anat.* a form of articulation that permits maximal motion, as the knee joint. [1570–80; < NL < Gk; see DI-[3], ARTHROSIS] —**di·ar·thro·di·al** (dī′är thrō′dē əl), *adj.*

di·a·ry (dī′ə rē), *n., pl.* **-ries. 1.** a daily record, usually private, esp. of the writer's own experiences, observations, feelings, attitudes, etc. **2.** a book for keeping such a record. **3.** a book or pad containing pages marked and arranged in calendar order, in which to note appointments and the like. [1575–85; < L *diārium* daily allowance, journal, equiv. to *di(ēs)* day + *-ārium* -ARY] —**Syn. 1, 2.** journal, daybook, log, chronicle.

Di·as (dē′əs; *Port.* dē′əsh), *n.* **Bar·tho·lo·me·u** (bär′-to͞o lo͞o me′o͞o), c1450–1500, Portuguese navigator: discoverer of the Cape of Good Hope. Also, **Diaz.**

di·as·chi·sis (dī as′kə sis), *n. Med.* a disturbance or loss of function in one part of the brain due to a localized injury in another part. [1910–15; < NL < Gk *diáschisis* a division; see DIA-, SCHI(ZO)-, -SIS]

Di·as·po·ra (dī as′pər ə), *n.* **1.** the scattering of the Jews to countries outside of Palestine after the Babylonian captivity. **2.** (*often l.c.*) the body of Jews living in countries outside Palestine or modern Israel. **3.** such countries collectively: *the return of the Jews from the Diaspora.* **4.** (*l.c.*) any group migration or flight from a country or region; dispersion. **5.** (*l.c.*) any group that has been dispersed outside its traditional homeland. **6.** (*l.c.*) any religious group living as a minority among people of the prevailing religion. [1875–80; < Gk *diasporá* a dispersion. See DIA-, SPORE]

di·a·spore (dī′ə spôr′, -spōr′), *n.* **1.** a mineral, aluminum oxyhydroxide, $AlO(OH)$, occurring in crystals, or more usually in lamellar or scaly masses: a principal constituent of bauxite and an important source of aluminum. **2.** *Bot.* a disseminule, esp. one that undergoes dispersal. [1795–1805; < Gk *diasporá;* see DIASPORA]

di·a·stase (dī′ə stās′, -stāz′), *n.* an enzyme that breaks down starch into maltose, then dextrose, and is present in malt. [< F *diastase* (1833) < Gk *diástasis;* see DIASTASIS, -ASE]

di·as·ta·sis (dī as′tə sis), *n., pl.* **-ses** (-sēz′). **1.** *Med.* the separation of normally joined parts, as in the dislocation of bones, without fracture. **2.** *Physiol.* the diastolic rest period immediately preceding systole. [1735–45; < NL < Gk *diástasis* a separation. See DIA-, STASIS]

di·a·stat·ic (dī′ə stat′ik), *adj.* **1.** *Biochem.* **a.** of or pertaining to diastase. **b.** having the properties of diastase: *diastatic action.* **2.** *Med., Physiol.* of or pertaining to diastasis. Also, **di·a·sta·sic** (dī′ə stā′sik). [1880–85; < Gk *diastatikós* separative. See DIA-, STATIC]

di·a·stem (dī′ə stem′), *n. Geol.* a minor hiatus in an orderly succession of sedimentary rocks. Cf. **unconformity.** [1850–55; < Gk *diástēma* interval; see DIASTEMA] —**di′a·stem′ic,** *adj.*

di·a·ste·ma (dī′ə stē′mə), *n., pl.* **-ma·ta** (-mə tə). **1.** *Cell Biol.* the modified protoplasm at the equator of a cell, existing before mitotic division. **2.** *Dentistry.* a space between two teeth, esp. a space between a canine and an incisor of the upper jaw into which a lower canine occludes. [1350–1400; ME < LL < Gk: interval, equiv. to *diastē,* var. s. of *diastánai* to stand apart + *-ma* n. suffix denoting the result of action]

di·as·ter (dī as′tər), *n. Cell Biol.* the stage in mitosis at which the chromosomes, after their division and separation, are grouped near the poles of the spindle. [1880–85; DI-[1] + -ASTER[2]] —**di·as′tral,** *adj.*

di·a·ster·e·o·mer (dī′ə ster′ē ə mər, -stēr′-), *n. Chem.* either of a pair of stereoisomers that are not mirror images of each other. Also called **di·a·ster·e·o·i·so·mer** (dī′ə ster′ē ō ī′sə mər, -stēr′-). Cf. **enantiomer.** [1935–40; DIA- + STEREO(ISO)MER]

di·as·to·le (dī as′tl ē′, -tl ē), *n.* **1.** *Physiol.* the normal rhythmical dilatation of the heart during which the chambers are filling with blood. Cf. **systole** (def. 1). **2.** *Pros.* the lengthening of a syllable regularly short, esp. before a pause or at the ictus. [1570–80; < LL *diastolē* < Gk *diastolḗ* a putting asunder, dilation, lengthening; cf. *diastéllein* to set apart, equiv. to *dia-* DIA- + *stéllein* to put, place]

di·as·tol·ic (dī′ə stol′ik), *adj.* **1.** pertaining to or produced by diastole. **2.** (of blood pressure) indicating the arterial pressure during the interval between heartbeats. Cf. **systolic.** [1685–95; DIASTOLE + -IC]

di·as·tro·phism (dī as′trə fiz′əm), *n. Geol.* **1.** Also called **tectonism.** the action of the forces that cause the earth's crust to be deformed, producing continents, mountains, changes of level, etc. **2.** any such resulting deformation. [1880–85; < Gk *diastroph(ḗ)* a distortion (see DIA-, STROPHE) + -ISM] —**di·a·stroph·ic** (dī′ə strof′ik, -strō′fik), *adj.* —**di′a·stroph′i·cal·ly,** *adv.*

di·a·style (dī′ə stīl′), *adj. Archit.* having an intercolumniation of three diameters. See illus. under **intercolumniation.** [1555–65; < L *diastȳlos* < Gk *diástȳlos* with columns far apart, equiv. to *dia-* DIA- + *-stȳlos* -STYLE[2]]

di·a·sys·tem (dī′ə sis′təm), *n. Gram.* a linguistic system forming a common denominator for a group or set of dialects. [DIA(LECT) + SYSTEM]

di·a·ther·man·cy (dī′ə thûr′mən sē), *n., pl.* **-cies.** the property of transmitting heat as electromagnetic radiation. [1830–40; < F *diathermansie* < Gk *dia-* DIA- + *thérmansis* heating, equiv. to *therman-* (var. s. of *thermaínein* to warm, heat, deriv. of *thermós* hot) + *-sis* -SIS] —**di′a·ther′ma·nous,** *adj.*

di·a·ther·mic (dī′ə thûr′mik), *adj.* **1.** of or pertaining to diathermy. **2.** capable of conducting heat. [1830–40; < F *diathermique;* see DIA-, THERM-, -IC]

di·a·ther·my (dī′ə thûr′mē), *n. Med.* the production of heat in body tissues by electric currents, for therapeutic purposes. Also, **di·a·ther·mi·a** (dī′ə thûr′mē ə). [< G *Diathermie* (1909). See DIA-, -THERMY]

di·ath·e·sis (dī ath′ə sis), *n., pl.* **-ses** (-sēz′). *Pathol.* a constitutional predisposition or tendency, as to a particular disease or affection. [1645–55; < NL < Gk *diáthesis* arrangement, disposition. See DIA-, THESIS] —**di·a·thet·ic** (dī′ə thet′ik), *adj.*

di·a·tom (dī′ə təm -tom′), *n.* any of numerous microscopic, unicellular, marine or freshwater algae of the phylum Chrysophyta, having cell walls containing silica. [1835–45; < NL *Diatoma* orig. a genus name, fem. n. based on Gk *diátomos* cut in two. See DIA-, -TOME]

di·a·to·ma·ceous (dī′ə tə mā′shəs), *adj.* consisting of or containing diatoms or their fossil remains. [1840–50; < NL *Diatomace(ae)* an order name (see DIATOM, -ACEAE) + -OUS]

di′atoma′ceous earth′, a fine siliceous earth composed chiefly of the cell walls of diatoms: used in filtration, as an abrasive, etc. Also called **di·at·o·mite** (dī at′-ə mīt′), **kieselguhr.** [1880–85]

di·a·tom·ic (dī′ə tom′ik), *adj. Chem.* **1.** having two atoms in the molecule. **2.** containing two replaceable atoms or groups; binary. [1865–70; DI-[1] + ATOMIC] —**di·at·o·mic·i·ty** (dī′at ə mis′i tē), *n.*

di·a·ton·ic (dī′ə ton′ik), *adj. Music.* **1.** noting those scales that contain five whole tones and two semitones, as the major, minor, and certain modal scales. **2.** of or pertaining to the tones, intervals, or harmonies of such scales. [1590–1600; < LL *diatonicus* < Gk *diatonikós;* see DIA-, TONIC] —**di′a·ton′i·cal·ly,** *adv.*

di·a·ton·i·cism (dī′ə ton′ə siz′əm), *n.* the use of diatonic harmony; composition in a diatonic idiom. [1930–35; DIATONIC + -ISM]

di·a·treme (dī′ə trēm′), *n. Geol.* a volcanic vent produced in a solid rock structure by the explosive energy of gases in magmas. [1930–35; DIA- + Gk *trêma* hole]

di·a·tribe (dī′ə trīb′), *n.* a bitter, sharply abusive denunciation, attack, or criticism: *repeated diatribes against the senator.* [1575–85; < L *diatriba* < Gk *diatribḗ* pastime, study, discourse, deriv. of *diatríbein* to rub away (*dia-* DIA- + *tríbein* to rub)] —**Syn.** tirade, harangue.

di·at·ro·pism (dī a′trə piz′əm), *n. Bot.* the tendency of some plant organs to take a transverse position to the line of action of an outside stimulus. [DIA- + TROPISM] —**di·a·trop·ic** (dī′ə trop′ik, -trō′pik), *adj.*

Di·az (dē′əs; *Port.* dē′əsh), *n.* **Bar·tho·lo·me·u** (bär′-to͞o lo͞o me′o͞o). See **Dias, Bartholomeu.**

Dí·az (dē′äs), *n.* **(Jo·sé de la Cruz) Por·fi·rio** (hô se′ the lä kro͞os′ pôr fē′ryô), 1830–1915, president of Mexico 1877–80, 1884–1911.

diaz-, var. of **diazo-** before a vowel: *diazine.*

Dí·az de Bi·var (dē′äth the vē vär′), **Ro·dri·go** (rô-thrē′gô) or **Ruy** (rwē). See **Cid, The.** Also, **Dí·az de Vi·var** (dē′äth the vē vär′).

Dí·az del Cas·til·lo (dē′äth thel käs tē′lyô), **Ber·nal** (ber näl′), 1492–1581, Spanish soldier-historian of the conquest of Mexico.

di·az·e·pam (dī az′ə pam′), *n. Pharm.* a benzodiazepine, $C_{16}H_{13}ClN_2O$, used for alleviation of anxiety and tension, as a hypnotic, a muscle relaxant, and an anticonvulsant, and in alcohol withdrawal. [appar. (BENZO)DIAZEP(INE) + *-am,* of unexplained orig.]

di·a·zine (dī′ə zēn′, -zin, dī az′ēn, -in), *n. Chem.* any of three isomeric compounds having the formula $C_4H_4N_2$, containing a ring of four carbon atoms and two nitrogen atoms. [DIAZ- + -INE[2]]

CONCISE ETYMOLOGY KEY: <, descended or borrowed from; >, whence; b., blend of, blended; c., cognate with; cf., compare; deriv., derivative; equiv., equivalent; imit., imitative; obl., oblique; r., replacing; s., stem; sp., spelling, spelled; resp., respelling, respelled; trans., translation; ?, origin unknown; *, unattested; ‡, probably earlier than. See the full key inside the front cover.

Dí·az Mi·rón (dē′äs mē rôn′), **Sal·va·dor** (säl′vä thôr′), 1853–1928, Mexican poet.

di·az·o (dī az′ō, -ā′zō), *adj. Chem.* containing the diazo group. [1855–60; independent use of DIAZO-]

diazo-, *Chem.* a combining form with the meaning "diazo group," used in the formation of compound words: *diazomethane.* Also, *esp. before a vowel,* **diaz-.** [DI-[1] + AZO-]

di·az·o·al·kane (dī az′ō al′kān, -ā′zō-), *n. Chem.* any diazo compound having the general formula R_2CN_2, where R is hydrogen or any saturated organic group, as diazomethane, CH_2N_2. [DIAZO- + ALKANE]

di·az·o·a·mi·no (dī az′ō ə mē′nō, -am′ə nō′, -ā′zō-), *adj. Chem.* containing the diazoamino group. [DIAZO- + AMINO]

diazoami′no group′, *Chem.* the divalent group $-N{=}NNH-$. Also called **diazoami′no rad′ical.**

diaz′o group′, *Chem.* the bivalent group $-N{=}N-$ united with one hydrocarbon group and another atom or group, as in benzenediazo hydroxide, $C_6H_5N{=}NOH$, or the bivalent group $=N{=}N$ united with one hydrocarbon group, as in diazomethane, $CH_2{=}N{=}N$. Also called **diazo radical.**

di·a·zole (dī′ə zōl′, dī az′ōl), *n. Chem.* any of a group of organic compounds containing three carbon atoms and two nitrogen atoms arranged in a ring. [DIAZ- + -OLE]

di·az·o·meth·ane (dī az′ō meth′ān, -ā′zō-), *n. Chem.* a yellow, odorless, toxic, explosive gas, CH_2N_2, used chiefly as a methylating agent and in organic synthesis. [DIAZO- + METHANE]

di·a·zo·ni·um (dī′ə zō′nē əm), *adj. Chem.* of or derived from a diazonium compound. [1890–95; DIAZ- + *-onium,* as in AMMONIUM]

diazo′nium com′pound, *Chem.* any of a series of compounds that contain the group ArN_2-, in which Ar represents an aryl group. [1890–95]

diazo′nium salt′, *Chem.* any of a group of salts of the general formula ArN_2X, in which Ar represents an aryl group and X an anion, as benzenediazonium chloride, $C_6H_5N(N)Cl$, many of which are important intermediates in the manufacture of azo dyes. [1905–10]

diaz′o proc′ess, *Photog.* a method for printing on paper treated with a diazo compound that disintegrates upon exposure to light and developing the unexposed areas by the use of diazo dyes. [1945–50]

diaz′o rad′ical. See **diazo group.**

Dí·az Or·daz (dē′äs ôr thäs′), *n.* **Gus·ta·vo** (go͞os tä′vō), 1911–79, Mexican teacher, jurist, and public official: president 1964–70.

di·az·o·ti·za·tion (dī az′ə tə zā′shən), *n. Chem.* the preparation of a diazonium salt by treatment of an arylamine with nitrous acid. [1890–95; DIAZOTIZE + -ATION]

di·az·o·tize (dī az′ə tīz′), *v.t.,* **-tized, -tiz·ing.** *Chem.* to cause diazotization. Also, *esp. Brit.,* **di·az′o·tise′.** [1885–90; DI-[1] + AZOTE + -IZE] **—di·az′o·tiz′a·ble,** *adj.* **—di·az′o·tiz′a·bil′i·ty,** *n.*

di·az·o·type (dī az′ə tīp′), *n. Photog.* a print produced by the diazo process. [1885–90; DIAZO- + -TYPE]

di·az·ox·ide (dī′az ok′sīd), *n. Pharm.* a substance, $C_8H_7ClN_2O_2S$, having potent antihypertensive action and used to reduce blood pressure in hypertensive crisis. [DIAZ- + OXIDE, components of the chemical name]

Dí·az Ro·drí·guez (dē′äs rô thrē′ges), **Ma·nuel** (mä nwel′), 1868–1927, Venezuelan author.

dib (dib), *v.i.,* **dibbed, dib·bing.** to fish by letting the bait bob lightly on the water. [1600–10; expressive word akin to DAB[1], DIP[1], BOB[1], etc.]

Di·bai (di bī′), *n.* Dubai.

di·ba·sic (dī bā′sik), *adj. Chem.* **1.** containing two replaceable or ionizable hydrogen atoms: *dibasic acid.* **2.** having two univalent, basic atoms, as dibasic sodium phosphate, Na_2HPO_4. [1865–70; DI-[1] + BASIC] **—di·ba·sic·i·ty** (dī′bā sis′i tē), *n.*

diba′sic potas′sium phos′phate, *Chem.* potassium monophosphate. See under **potassium phosphate.**

diba′sic so′dium phos′phate, *Chem.* See **sodium phosphate** (def. 2).

dib·a·tag (dib′ə tag′), *n.* a small gazelle, *Ammodorcas clarkei,* of Somaliland, having a long neck: now rare. Also called **Clarke's gazelle.** [1890–95; < Somali *dibtáag,* equiv. to *dib* tail + *táag* strong]

dib·ble (dib′əl), *n., v.,* **-bled, -bling.** —*n.* **1.** Also, **dibber** (dib′ər). a small, hand-held, pointed implement for making holes in soil for planting seedlings, bulbs, etc. —*v.t.* **2.** to make a hole (in the ground) with or as if with a dibble. **3.** to set (plants) in holes made with a dibble. —*v.i.* **4.** to work with a dibble. [1325–75; late ME, perh. akin to DIB] **—dib′bler,** *n.*

dib·buk (*Seph. Heb.* dē bo͝ok′; *Ashk. Heb.* dib′ək), *n., pl.* **dib·buks, dib·buk·im** (*Seph. Heb.* dē bo͞o kēm′; *Ashk. Heb.* di bo͝ok′im). *Jewish Folklore.* dybbuk.

Di·be·li·us (di bā′lē əs, -bāl′yəs; *Ger.* dē bā′lē o͞os′), *n.* **Mar·tin** (mär′tn; *Ger.* mär′tēn), 1883–1947, German theologian.

D'I·ber·ville (dī′bər vil′), *n.* a town in SE Mississippi. 13,369.

di·bo·rane (dī bôr′ān, -bōr′-), *n. Chem.* a colorless gas with an unpleasant odor, B_2H_6, used in the synthesis of organic boron compounds as a dope to introduce boron and as a polymerization catalyst for ethylene. [DI-[1] + BORANE]

di·brach (dī′brak), *n. Pros.* pyrrhic[1] (def. 3). [< L *dibrachys* < Gk *díbrachys* a foot of two short syllables, equiv. to *di-* DI-[1] + *brachýs* short; see BRACHY-]

di·bran·chi·ate (dī brang′kē it, -kē āt′), *adj.* **1.** belonging or pertaining to the Dibranchiata, a subclass or order of cephalopods with two gills, including the decapods and octopods. —*n.* **2.** a dibranchiate cephalopod. [1825–35; < NL *Dibranchiata;* see DI-[1], BRANCHIATE]

Di·brom (dī′brom), *Chem., Trademark.* a brand of naled.

di·bro·mide (dī brō′mīd, -mid), *n. Chem.* a compound containing two bromine atoms, as ethylene dibromide, $C_2H_4Br_2$. [1865–70; DI-[1] + BROMIDE]

dibs (dibz), *n. Informal.* **1.** money in small amounts. **2.** rights; claims: *I have dibs on the car when Jimmy brings it back.* [1720–30; shortening of earlier *dibstones* a children's game; see DIB]

di·bu·caine (dī byo͞o′kān), *n. Pharm.* a compound, $C_{20}H_{29}N_3O_2$, used as a local and spinal anesthetic. [DI-[1] + BU(TYL) + (CO)CAINE]

dibu′tyl phthal′ate (thal′āt, fthal′-), *Chem.* a colorless oily liquid, $C_{16}H_{22}O_4$, insoluble in water, used as a solvent, insect repellent, and plasticizer. [1920–25; DI-[1] + BUTYL]

dical′cium sil′icate (dī kal′sē əm), *Chem.* a component of cement, $2CaO·SiO_2$, also used to neutralize acid soils. [DI-[1] + CALCIUM]

dicar′box·yl′ic ac′id (dī kär′bok sil′ik, -kär′-), *Chem.* any of the organic compounds that contain two carboxyl groups. [DI-[1] + CARBOXYLIC ACID]

di·cast (dī′kast, dik′ast), *n.* (in ancient Athens) a citizen eligible to sit as a judge. [1700–10; < Gk *dikastḗs* a juryman, equiv. to **dikad-,* base of *dikázein* to judge, determine (deriv. of *díkē* right, law, order) + *-tēs* agentive suffix]

dice (dīs), *n.pl., sing.* **die,** *v.,* **diced, dic·ing.** —*n.* **1.** small cubes of plastic, ivory, bone, or wood, marked on each side with one to six spots, usually used in pairs in games of chance or in gambling. **2.** See **poker dice. 3.** any of various games, esp. gambling games, played by shaking and throwing from two to six dice or poker dice onto a flat surface. Cf. **craps. 4.** any small cubes. **5.** *Auto Racing.* a jockeying for lead position between two or more drivers in which tactics are used to pass or keep from being passed. **6. no dice,** *Informal.* of no use or help; ineffective. —*v.t.* **7.** to cut into small cubes. **8.** to decorate with cubelike figures. **9.** to lose by gambling with dice (often fol. by *away*). —*v.i.* **10.** to play at dice. **11.** to cause or bring about by gambling with dice. **12.** *Auto Racing.* to duel with another car or cars in a dice. [1300–50; ME *dees, dis, dyce* (sing. and pl.), *dyces* (pl.) < OF *de(i)z, dés* (pl.); see DIE[2]] **—dic′er,** *n.*

dice′ cup′, a container, usually cylindrical and open at the top, in which dice are shaken to give them a random position and from which they are then thrown or rolled.

di·cen·tra (dī sen′trə), *n.* any of several plants belonging to the genus *Dicentra,* of the fumitory family, having long clusters of drooping flowers, as the Dutchman's-breeches or the bleeding heart. [1833; < NL < Gk *díkentr(os)* with two stings or spurs, equiv. to *di-* DI-[1] + *-kentros,* deriv. of *kéntron* a spur, point, sting (deriv. of *kenteîn* to prick, sting) + L *-a* -A[2]]

di·cen·tric (dī sen′trik), *adj.* (of a chromosome or chromatid) having two centromeres. [1935–40; DI-[1] + -CENTRIC]

di·ceph·a·lous (dī sef′ə ləs), *adj.* having two heads; two-headed. [1800–10; < Gk *diképhalos* two-headed. See DI-[1], -CEPHALOUS] **—di·ceph′a·lism,** *n.*

dic·ey (dī′sē), *adj.,* **dic·i·er, dic·i·est.** *Informal.* unpredictable; risky; uncertain. [1935–40; DICE + -EY[1]]

di·cha·sium (dī kā′zhəm, -zhē əm, -zē əm), *n., pl.* **-si·a** (-zhē ə, -zē ə). *Bot.* a form of cymose inflorescence in which each axis produces a pair of lateral axes. [1870–75; < NL < Gk *dichasís* a division, deriv. of *dicházein* to cleave (deriv. of *dícha* apart) + L *-ium* -IUM] **—di·cha′sial,** *adj.*

di·chla·myd·e·ous (dī′klə mid′ē əs), *adj.* (of a flower) having both a calyx and a corolla. [1820–30; DI-[1] + CHLAMYDEOUS]

di·chlo·be·nil (dī klō′bə nil), *n.* a nonselective preemergence herbicide, $C_7H_3Cl_2N$, used primarily as a weed and grass killer. Also, **di·chlor·be·nil** (dī klôr′bə nil, -klōr′-). Also called **2,6-dichlorobenzonitrile.** [DI-[1] + CHLO(RO)-[2] + BEN(ZONITR)IL(E)]

di·chlo·ride (dī klôr′īd, -id, -klōr′-), *n.* a compound in which two atoms of chlorine are combined with another element or group. Also called **bichloride.** [1815–25; DI-[1] + CHLORIDE]

di·chlo·ro·ben·zene (dī klôr′ə ben′zēn, -ben zēn′, -klōr′-), *n. Chem.* any of three isomers consisting of benzene in which two of the hydrogen atoms are replaced by chlorine atoms: ortho-, meta-, and paradichlorobenzene. [DI-[1] + CHLORO-[2] + BENZENE]

di·chlo′ro·di·eth′yl sul′fide (dī klôr′ō dī eth′əl, -klōr′-, -klôr′-, -klōr′-), *Chem.* See **mustard gas.** [DI-[1] + CHLORO-[2] + DI-[1] + ETHYL + SULFIDE]

di·chlo·ro·di·fluor·o·meth·ane (dī klôr′ō dī flo͝or′ō meth′ān, -flôr′-; dī klōr′ō dī flo͝or′ō meth′ān; -flōr′-), *n. Chem.* a colorless, slightly water-soluble, nonflammable gas, CCl_2F_2, that boils at −29°C: used chiefly as a propellant in aerosols and as a refrigerant. [1955–60; DI-[1] + CHLORO-[2] + DI-[1] + FLUORO-[1] + METHANE]

di·chlo·ro·di·phen·yl·tri·chlor·o·eth·ane (dī klôr′ō dī fen′l trī klôr′ō eth′ān, dī klōr′ō dī fen′l trī klōr′-), *n. Chem.* See **DDT.** [DI-[1] + CHLORO-[2] + DI-[1] + PHENYL + TRI- + CHLORO-[2] + ETHANE]

di·chlo·ro·eth·ane (dī klôr′ō eth′ān, -klōr′-), *n. Chem.* See **ethylene dichloride.** [DI-[1] + CHLORO-[2] + ETHANE]

di·chlo·ro·eth′yl for′mal (dī klôr′ō eth′əl, -klōr′-), *Chem.* a colorless liquid, $C_5H_{10}O_2Cl_2$, used chiefly as a solvent and in the manufacture of certain synthetic rubbers. Also, **dichlo′rodieth′yl for′mal.** [DI- + CHLORO-[2] + ETHYL]

di·chlo·ro·meth·ane (dī klôr′ə meth′ān, -klōr′-), *n. Chem.* See **methylene chloride.** [DI-[1] + CHLORO-[2] + METHANE]

di·chlo′ro·phe·nox′y·a·ce′tic ac′id (dī klôr′ō fī nok′sē ə sē′tik, -ə set′ik, dī klôr′-, dī klôr′ō fī nok′-, dī klōr′-), *Chem.* a white to yellow, crystalline powder, $C_8H_6O_3Cl_2$, slightly soluble in water: used for killing weeds. Also called **2, 4-D.** [DI-[1] + CHLORO-[2] + PHEN- + OXY-[2] + ACETIC ACID]

dicho-, a combining form meaning "in two parts," "in pairs," used in the formation of compound words: *dichogamy.* [< Gk, comb. form of *dícha* in two, asunder]

di·chog·a·mous (dī kog′ə məs), *adj. Bot.* having the stamens and pistils maturing at different times, thereby preventing self-pollination, as a monoclinous flower (opposed to *homogamous*). Also, **di·cho·gam·ic** (dī′kō gam′ik). [1855–60; DICHO- + -GAMOUS]

di·chog·a·my (dī kog′ə mē), *n.* a dichogamous condition. [1860–65; < G *Dichogamie.* See DICHO-, -GAMY]

di·chon·dra (dī kon′drə), *n.* any of several prostrate, creeping, tropical vines belonging to the genus *Dichondra,* of the morning glory family, esp. *D. micrantha,* often used as a grass substitute for lawns. [< NL (1776), equiv. to *di-* DI-[1] + *-chondra* (< Gk *chóndr(os)* grain, granule (see CHONDRIA-) + *-a* -A[2])]

di·chot·o·mize (dī kot′ə mīz′), *v.,* **-mized, -miz·ing.** —*v.t.* **1.** to divide or separate into two parts, kinds, etc. —*v.i.* **2.** to become divided into two parts; form a dichotomy. Also, *esp. Brit.,* **di·chot′o·mise′.** [1600–10; < LL *dichotom(os)* DICHOTOMOUS + -IZE] **—di·chot·o·mist** (dī kot′ə mist), *n.* **—di·chot′o·mis′tic,** *adj.* **—di·chot′o·mi·za′tion,** *n.*

di·chot·o·mous (dī kot′ə məs), *adj.* **1.** divided or dividing into two parts. **2.** of or pertaining to dichotomy. [1680–90; < LL *dichotomos* < Gk *dichótomos.* See DICHO-, -TOME, -OUS] **—di·chot′o·mous·ly,** *adv.* **—di·chot′o·mous·ness,** *n.*

di·chot·o·my (dī kot′ə mē), *n., pl.* **-mies. 1.** division into two parts, kinds, etc.; subdivision into halves or pairs. **2.** division into two mutually exclusive, opposed, or contradictory groups: *a dichotomy between thought and action.* **3.** *Bot.* a mode of branching by constant forking, as in some stems, in veins of leaves, etc. **4.** *Astron.* the phase of the moon or of an inferior planet when half of its disk is visible. [1600–10; < Gk *dichotomía.* See DICHO-, -TOMY] **—di·cho·tom·ic** (dī′kə tom′ik), *adj.* **—di′cho·tom′i·cal·ly,** *adv.*

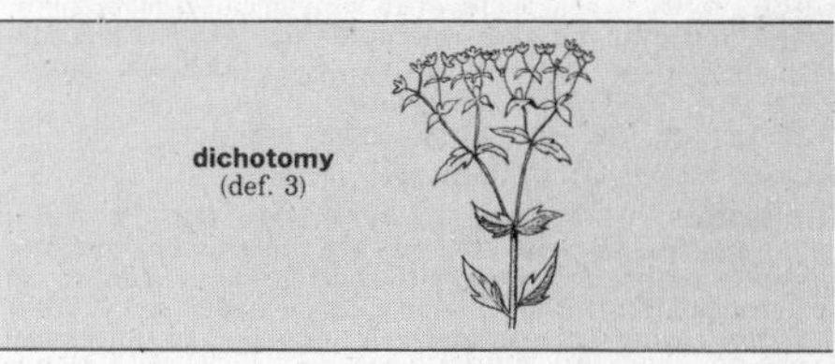
dichotomy (def. 3)

di·chro·ic (dī krō′ik), *adj.* **1.** characterized by dichroism: *dichroic crystal.* **2.** dichromatic. Also, **di·chro·it·ic** (dī′krō it′ik). [1860–65; < Gk *díchro(os)* of two colors + -IC; see DI-[1], -CHROIC]

di·chro·ism (dī′krō iz′əm), *n.* **1.** *Crystall.* pleochroism of a uniaxial crystal such that it exhibits two different colors when viewed from two different directions under transmitted light. **2.** *Chem.* the exhibition of essentially different colors by certain solutions in different degrees of dilution or concentration. [1810–20; < Gk *díchro(os)* (see DICHROIC) + -ISM]

di·chro·ite (dī′krō īt′), *n. Mineral.* cordierite. [1800–10; < F < Gk *díchro(os)* (see DICHROIC) + F *-ite* -ITE[1]]

di·chro·mate (dī krō′māt), *n. Chem.* a salt of the hypothetical acid $H_2Cr_2O_7$, as potassium dichromate, $K_2Cr_2O_7$. Also, **bichromate.** [1860–65; DI-[1] + CHROMATE]

di·chro·mat·ic (dī′krō mat′ik, -krə-), *adj.* **1.** Also, **dichroic.** having or showing two colors; dichromic. **2.** *Zool.* exhibiting two color phases within a species not due to age or season. [1840–50; DI-[1] + CHROMATIC]

di·chro·ma·tism (dī krō′mə tiz′əm), *n.* **1.** the quality or state of being dichromatic. **2.** Also called **di·chro·ma·top·si·a** (dī krō′mə top′sē ə). *Ophthalm.* a defect of vision in which the retina responds to only two of the three primary colors. Cf. **monochromatism** (def. 2), **trichromatism** (def. 3). [1880–85; DICHROMAT(IC) + -ISM]

di·chro·mic[1] (dī krō′mik), *adj.* pertaining to or involving two colors only: *dichromic vision.* [1850–55; DI-[1] + CHROMIC]

di·chro·mic[2] (dī krō′mik), *adj. Chem.* (of a compound) containing two atoms of chromium. [DI-[1] + CHROM(IUM) + -IC]

dichro′mic ac′id, *Chem.* the hypothetical acid $H_2Cr_2O_7$, from which dichromates are derived.

dic·ing (dī′sing), *n.* **1.** gambling or playing with dice. **2.** ornamentation, esp. of leather, with squares or diamonds. [1425–75; late ME; see DICE, -ING[1]]

dick (dik), *n. Slang.* **1.** a detective. **2.** *Vulgar.* penis. [1545–55; generic use of the proper name]

Dick (dik), *n.* **1. George Frederick,** 1881–1967, U.S. internist. **2.** a male given name, form of **Richard.**

dick·cis·sel (dik sis′əl), *n.* a bunting, *Spiza americana,* of the eastern and central U.S., having a brownish back streaked with black and a yellowish breast and in the male a black patch on the throat. [1885–90; said to be imit. of its call]

dick·ens (dik′inz), *n.* devil; deuce (usually prec. by *the* and often used in exclamations and as a mild imprecation): *The dickens you say! What the dickens does he*

CONCISE PRONUNCIATION KEY: act, cāpe, dâre, pärt; set, ēqual; *if,* īce; ox, ōver, ôrder, oil, bo͝ok, bo͞ot, out; up, ûrge; child; sing; shoe; thin, *that;* zh as in *treasure.* ə = a as in *alone,* e as in *system,* i as in *easily,* o as in *gallop,* u as in *circus;* ᵊ as in *fire* (fīᵊr), *hour* (ouᵊr). l and n can serve as syllabic consonants, as in *cradle* (krād′l), and *button* (but′n). See the full key inside the front cover.

want? [1590–1600; appar. a fanciful use of *Dicken,* form of *Dick,* proper name]

Dick·ens (dik′inz), *n.* **Charles (John Huf·fam)** (huf′əm), ("*Boz*"), 1812–70, English novelist. —**Dick·en·si·an** (di ken′zē ən), *adj.*

dick·er[1] (dik′ər), *v.i.* **1.** to deal, swap, or trade with petty bargaining; bargain; haggle. **2.** to barter. **3.** to try to arrange matters by mutual bargaining: *They dickered for hours over some of the finer points of the contract.* —*n.* **4.** a petty bargain. **5.** a barter or swap. **6.** an item or goods bartered or swapped. **7.** a deal, esp. a political deal. [1795–1805; perh. v. use of DICKER[2]]

dick·er[2] (dik′ər), *n.* the number or quantity ten, esp. a lot of ten hides or skins. [1225–75; ME *diker* < OF *dacre,* ML *dikeria;* cf. L *decuria* DECURY]

dick·ey[1] (dik′ē), *n., pl.* **-eys.** **1.** an article of clothing made to look like the front or collar of a shirt, blouse, vest, etc., worn as a separate piece under another garment, as a jacket or dress. Cf. **vest** (def. 2), **vestee. 2.** a detachable linen shirt collar. **3.** a bib or pinafore worn by a child. **4.** a small bird. **5.** a donkey, esp. a male. **6.** an outside seat on a carriage. **7.** *Brit.* See **rumble seat** (def. 1). Also, **dicky, dick′ie.** [1745–55; generic use of *Dicky,* dim. of *Dick,* proper name]

dick·ey[2] (dik′ē), *adj. Slang.* faulty: *I'm fed up with this dickey air conditioner.* [1805–15; orig. uncert.]

Dick·ey (dik′ē), *n.* **James,** born 1923, U.S. poet and novelist.

dick·ey·bird (dik′ē bûrd′), *n.* dickey[1] (def. 4). [1775–85; DICKEY[1] + BIRD]

Dick·in·son (dik′in sən), *n.* **1. Edwin (Walter),** 1891–1978, U.S. landscape and still-life painter. **2. Emily (Elizabeth),** 1830–86, U.S. poet. **3. John,** 1732–1808, U.S. statesman and publicist. **4.** a town in W North Dakota. 15,942.

dick·ite (dik′īt), *n. Mineral.* a polymorph of kaolinite. [named after A. B. Dick (d. 1926), English mineralogist + -ITE[1]]

Dick·son (dik′sən), *n.* **Leonard Eugene,** 1874–1954, U.S. mathematician.

Dick′ test′, *Med.* a test for determining immunity or susceptibility to scarlet fever in which scarlet fever toxin is injected into the skin, susceptibility being characterized by redness at the injection area. [1920–25; named after G. F. DICK, who devised it]

dick·ty (dik′tē), *adj.,* **-ti·er, -ti·est.** dicty.

dick·y (dik′ē), *n., pl.* **dick·ies.** dickey[1].

di·cli·nous (dī′klə nəs, dī klī′-), *adj. Bot.* **1.** (of a plant species, variety, etc.) having the stamens and the pistils in separate flowers, either on the same plant or on different plants; either monoecious or dioecious. **2.** (of a flower) having only stamens or only pistils; unisexual. [1820–30; DI-[1] + Gk *klín(ē)* couch, bed + -OUS] —**di′cli·nism,** *n.*

di·co·fol (dī kō′fôl, -fol), *n.* a white crystalline solid, $C_{14}H_9Cl_5O$, derived from DDT and used to protect crops from mites. [laboratory coinage of unexplained orig.]

di·cot (dī′kot), *n. Bot.* a dicotyledon. Also, **di·cot·yl** (dī kot′l). [by shortening]

di·cot·y·le·don (dī kot′l ēd′n, dī′kot l-), *n. Bot.* any angiospermous plant of the class (or subclass) Dicotyledoneae, producing seeds with two cotyledons and having an exogenous manner of growth. Cf. **monocotyledon.** [1720–30; < NL *Dicotyledones* a pre-Linnean grouping of such plants. See DI-[1], COTYLEDON]

di·cot·y·le·don·ous (dī kot′l ēd′n əs, dī′kot l-), *adj.* belonging or pertaining to the Dicotyledoneae; having two cotyledons. [1785–95; DICOTYLEDON + -OUS]

di·cou·ma·rin (dī ko͞o′mər in, kyo͞o′-), *n. Pharm.* dicumarol. [1885–90; DI-[1] + COUMARIN]

di·cou·ma·rol (dī ko͞o′mə rôl′, -rol′, -kyo͞o′-) *n. Pharm.* dicumarol.

di·crot·ic (dī krot′ik), *adj. Physiol.* having or pertaining to a double beat of the pulse for each beat of the heart. [1700–10; < Gk *díkrot(os)* double beating (*di-* DI-[1] + *krótos* a clapping, rattling noise) + -IC] —**di·cro·tism** (dī′krə tiz′əm), *n.*

dict., **1.** dictation. **2.** dictator. **3.** dictionary.

dic·ta (dik′tə), *n.* a pl. of **dictum.**

Dic·ta·phone (dik′tə fōn′), *Trademark.* a brand name for a dictating machine.

dic·tate (*v.* dik′tāt, dik tāt′; *n.* dik′tāt), *v.,* **-tat·ed, -tat·ing,** *n.* —*v.t.* **1.** to say or read (something) aloud for another person to transcribe or for a machine to record: *to dictate some letters to a secretary.* **2.** to prescribe or lay down authoritatively or peremptorily; command unconditionally: *to dictate peace terms to a conquered enemy.* —*v.i.* **3.** to say or read aloud something to be written down by a person or recorded by a machine. **4.** to give orders. —*n.* **5.** an authoritative order or command. **6.** a guiding or governing principle, requirement, etc.: *to follow the dictates of one's conscience.* [1585–95; < L *dictātus,* ptp. of *dictāre* to say repeatedly, prescribe, order, freq. of *dicere* to say] —**dic′tat·ing·ly,** *adv.*
—**Syn. 6.** bidding, urging, prompting.

dic′tat·ing machine′ (dik′tā ting), a machine for recording dictation, as on cassettes or disks, for subsequent transcription. [1935–40]

dic·ta·tion (dik tā′shən), *n.* **1.** the act or manner of dictating for reproduction in writing. **2.** the act or manner of transcribing words uttered by another. **3.** words that are dictated or that are reproduced from dictation. **4.** the playing or singing of music to be notated by a listener, esp. as a technique of training the ear. **5.** music notated from dictation. **6.** the act of commanding arbitrarily. **7.** something commanded. [1650–60; < LL *dictātiōn-* (s. of *dictātiō*) a dictating < L *dictāt(us)* (see DICTATE) + *-iōn-* -ION] —**dic·ta′tion·al,** *adj.*

dic·ta·tor (dik′tā tər, dik tā′tər), *n.* **1.** a person exercising absolute power, esp. a ruler who has absolute, unrestricted control in a government without hereditary succession. **2.** (in ancient Rome) a person invested with supreme authority during a crisis, the regular magistracy being subordinated to him until the crisis was met. **3.** a person who authoritatively prescribes conduct, usage, etc.: *a dictator of fashion.* **4.** a person who dictates, as to a secretary. [1350–1400; ME < L *dictātor,* equiv. to *dictā(re)* (see DICTATE) + *-tor* -TOR]

dic·ta·to·ri·al (dik′tə tôr′ē əl, -tōr′-), *adj.* **1.** of or pertaining to a dictator or dictatorship. **2.** appropriate to, or characteristic of, a dictator; absolute; unlimited: *dictatorial powers in wartime.* **3.** inclined to dictate or command; imperious; overbearing: *a dictatorial attitude.* [1695–1705; < L *dictātōri(us)* (equiv. to *dictā(re)* (see DICTATE) + *-tōrius* -TORY[1]) + -AL[1]] —**dic′ta·to′ri·al·ly,** *adv.* —**dic′ta·to′ri·al·ness,** *n.*
—**Syn. 2.** totalitarian. **3.** despotic, tyrannical, autocratic.

dic·ta·tor·ship (dik tā′tər ship′, dik′tā-), *n.* **1.** a country, government, or the form of government in which absolute power is exercised by a dictator. **2.** absolute, imperious, or overbearing power or control. **3.** the office or position held by a dictator. [1580–90; DICTATOR + -SHIP]

dic·tion (dik′shən), *n.* **1.** style of speaking or writing as dependent upon choice of words: *good diction.* **2.** the accent, inflection, intonation, and speech-sound quality manifested by an individual speaker, usually judged in terms of prevailing standards of acceptability; enunciation. [1400–50; late ME *diccion* < LL *dictiōn-* (s. of *dictiō*) word, L: rhetorical delivery, equiv. to *dict(us)* said, spoken (ptp. of *dicere*) + *-iōn-* -ION] —**dic′tion·al,** *adj.* —**dic′tion·al·ly,** *adv.*
—**Syn. 1.** usage, language. DICTION, PHRASEOLOGY, WORDING refer to the means and the manner of expressing ideas. DICTION usually implies a high level of usage; it refers chiefly to the choice of words, their arrangement, and the force, accuracy, and distinction with which they are used: *The speaker was distinguished for his excellent diction; poetic diction.* PHRASEOLOGY refers more to the manner of combining the words into related groups, and esp. to the peculiar or distinctive manner in which certain technical, scientific, and professional ideas are expressed: *legal phraseology.* WORDING refers to the exact words or phraseology used to convey thought: *the wording of a will.*

dic·tion·ar·y (dik′shə ner′ē), *n., pl.* **-ar·ies.** **1.** a book containing a selection of the words of a language, usually arranged alphabetically, giving information about their meanings, pronunciations, etymologies, inflected forms, etc., expressed in either the same or another language; lexicon; glossary: *a dictionary of English; a Japanese-English dictionary.* **2.** a book giving information on particular subjects or on a particular class of words, names, or facts, usually arranged alphabetically: *a biographical dictionary; a dictionary of mathematics.* **3.** *Computers.* **a.** a list of codes, terms, keys, etc., and their meanings, used by a computer program or system. **b.** a list of words used by a word-processing program as the standard against which to check the spelling of text entered. [1520–30; < ML *dictiōnārium, dictiōnārius* < LL *dictiōn-* word (see DICTION) + *-ārium, -ārius* -ARY]

dic′tionary cat′alog, a library catalog having all its entries, including authors, titles, subjects, etc., in one general alphabetical sequence. [1875–80, *Amer.*]

Dic·to·graph (dik′tə graf′, -gräf′), *Trademark.* a brand name for a telephonic device with a highly sensitive transmitter obviating the necessity of a mouthpiece: used for listening to conversations secretly or obtaining a record of them.

dic·tum (dik′təm), *n., pl.* **-ta** (-tə), **-tums.** **1.** an authoritative pronouncement; judicial assertion. **2.** a saying; maxim. **3.** See **obiter dictum.** [1660–70; < L: something said, a saying, command, word, n. use of neut. ptp. of *dicere* to say, speak; cf. INDEX]
—**Syn. 1.** edict, decree, fiat, order, declaration. **2.** adage, proverb, truism, saw.

dic·ty (dik′tē), *adj.* **-ti·er, -ti·est.** *Slang.* **1.** high-class or stylish. **2.** snobbish or haughty. Also, **dickty.** [1925–30; of obscure orig.]

Dic·tyn·na (dik tin′ə), *n.* an ancient Cretan goddess of the sea.

dic·ty·o·some (dik′tē ə sōm′), *n. Cell Biol.* the set of flattened membranes in a Golgi body, resembling a stack of plates. [1925–30; < Gk *díkty(on)* net + -o- + -SOME[3]]

di·cu·ma·rol (dī ko͞o′mə rôl′, -rol′, -kyo͞o′-), *Pharm.* a synthetic coumarin derivative, $C_{19}H_{12}O_6$, used chiefly to prevent blood coagulation and in the treatment of arterial thrombosis. Also, **dicoumarin, dicoumarol.** [resp. of DI-[1] + COUMAR(IN) + -OL]

di·cy·an·di·am·ide (dī sī′ən dī am′īd), *n. Chem.* a white, crystalline, rather sparingly water-soluble solid, $C_2H_4N_4$, produced from cyanamide by polymerization: used in the manufacture of plastics and pharmaceuticals. Also, **di·cy·an·o·di·am·ide** (dī sī′ə nō′dī am′īd). Also called **cyanoguanidine.** [DI-[1] + CYAN(O)-[2] + DI-[1] + AMIDE]

di·cy·clo·pen·ta·di·en·yl·i·ron (dī sī′klō pen′tə dī-en′l ī′ərn), *n. Chem.* ferrocene (def. 1). [DI-[1] + CYCLOPENTADIENE + -YL + IRON]

di·cy·clo·pen·ta·di·en′yl met′al (dī sī′klō pen′tə-dī en′l), *Chem.* ferrocene (def. 2). [DI-[1] + CYCLOPENTADIENE + -YL]

did (did), *v.* pt. of **do**[1].

di·dact (dī′dakt), *n.* a didactic person; one overinclined to instruct others. [1950–55; prob. back formation from DIDACTIC; cf. AUTODIDACT]

di·dac·tic (dī dak′tik), *adj.* **1.** intended for instruction; instructive: *didactic poetry.* **2.** inclined to teach or lecture others too much: *a boring, didactic speaker.* **3.** teaching or intending to teach a moral lesson. **4. didactics,** (*used with a singular v.*) the art or science of teaching. Also, **di·dac′ti·cal.** [1635–45; < Gk *didaktikós* apt at teaching, instructive, equiv. to *didakt(ós)* that may be taught + *-ikos* -IC] —**di·dac′ti·cal·ly,** *adv.* —**di·dac′ti·cism,** *n.*
—**Syn. 2.** pedantic, preachy, donnish, pedagogic.

di·dap·per (dī′dap′ər), *n.* a dabchick. [1400–50; late ME *dydoppar;* shortened form of *dive-dapper;* see DAP]

did·di·kai (did′i kī′), *n.* a person of partial Gypsy extraction. [1850–55; < Romany]

did·dle[1] (did′l), *v.t.,* **-dled, -dling.** *Informal.* to cheat; swindle; hoax. [1800–10; perh. special use of DIDDLE[2]] —**did′dler,** *n.*

did·dle[2] (did′l), *v.,* **-dled, -dling.** —*v.i.* **1.** *Informal.* to toy; fool (usually fol. by *with*): *The kids have been diddling with the controls on the television set again.* **2.** to waste time; dawdle (often fol. by *around*): *You would be finished by now if you hadn't spent the morning diddling around.* **3.** *Informal.* to move back and forth with short rapid motions. —*v.t.* **4.** *Informal.* to move back and forth with short rapid motions; jiggle: *Diddle the switch and see if the light comes on.* **5.** *Slang.* **a.** to copulate with. **b.** to practice masturbation upon. [1800–10; expressive coinage, perh. orig. in the Siamese twins *diddle-diddle, diddle-daddle;* cf. DODDER[1], DOODLE[1]] —**did′dler,** *n.*

Did·dley (did′lē), *n.* **Bo** (bō), (*Elias McDaniel*), born 1928, U.S. rock-'n'-roll singer, guitarist, and composer.

did·dly (did′lē), *n., pl.* **-dlies** for 2. *Slang.* **1.** a thing of little or no value; naught: *Your excuses aren't worth diddly to me.* **2.** a flaw; malfunction. [perh. euphemistic shortening of DIDDLYSHIT]

did·dly·shit (did′lē shit′), *n. Slang* (*vulgar*). diddly (def. 1). [‡1960–65, *Amer.; diddly* (perh. DIDDLE[2] + -Y[2]) + SHIT]

did·dly-squat (did′lē skwot′), *n. Slang.* doodly-squat. [prob. euphemistic var. of DIDDLYSHIT]

Di·de·rot (dē′də rō′; *Fr.* dēdə RŌ′), *n.* **De·nis** (də nē′), 1713–84, French philosopher, critic, and encyclopedist.

did·n't (did′nt), contraction of *did not.*
—**Usage.** See **contraction.**

di·do (dī′dō), *n., pl.* **-dos, -does.** Usually, **didos, didoes.** *Informal.* **1.** a mischievous trick; prank; antic. **2.** a bauble or trifle. [1800–10; orig. uncert.]

Di·do (dī′dō), *n.* **1.** Phoenician, **Elissa.** *Class. Myth.* a queen of Carthage who killed herself when abandoned by Aeneas. **2.** a female given name.

Di·dot′ point′ sys′tem (dē dō′), *Print.* a Continental system of measurement for type, based on a unit of 0.0148 in. (0.3759 mm). [named after François Ambrose Didot (1730–1804), French printer who devised it]

di·drachm (dī′dram′), *n.* a silver coin of ancient Greece equal to two drachmas. Also, **di·drach·ma** (dī drak′mə). [1540–50; < LL *didrachmon* < Gk *dídrachmon* worth two drachms. See DI-[1], DRACHMA]

Did·rik·son (did′rik sən), *n.* **Mildred.** See **Zaharias, Mildred Didrikson.**

didst (didst), *v. Archaic.* 2nd pers. sing. pt. of **do**[1].

di·dy (dī′dē), *n., pl.* **-dies.** *Baby Talk.* diaper (def. 1). Also, **di′die.** [1900–05; by alter.]

di·dym·i·um (dī dim′ē əm, di-), *n. Chem.* a mixture of neodymium and praseodymium, formerly thought to be an element. *Symbol:* Di [< NL < Gk *dídym(os)* twin (see DIDYMOUS) + -IUM; so named by Swedish chemist Carl Mosander (1797–1858), who discovered it in 1843, from its close association with lanthanum]

did·y·mous (did′ə məs), *adj. Bot.* occurring in pairs; paired; twin. [1785–95; < Gk *dídymos* twin, double, (akin to *dís* twice, double); see -OUS]

di·dyn·a·mous (dī din′ə məs), *adj.* (of a flower) having four stamens in two pairs of different length. [1785–95; < NL *Didynam(ia)* name of the class (equiv. to *di-* DI-[1] + Gk *dýnam(is)* power (see DYNAMIC) + *-ia* -IA) + -OUS] —**di·dyn′a·my,** *n.*

die[1] (dī), *v.i.,* **died, dy·ing.** **1.** to cease to live; undergo the complete and permanent cessation of all vital functions; become dead. **2.** (of something inanimate) to cease to exist: *The laughter died on his lips.* **3.** to lose force, strength, or active qualities: *Superstitions die slowly.* **4.** to cease to function; stop: *The motor died.* **5.** to be no longer subject; become indifferent: *to die to worldly matters.* **6.** to pass gradually; fade or subside gradually (usually fol. by *away, out,* or *down*): *The storm slowly died down.* **7.** *Theol.* to lose spiritual life. **8.** to faint or languish. **9.** to suffer as if fatally: *I'm dying of boredom!* **10.** to pine with desire, love, longing, etc.: *I'm dying to see my home again.* **11.** to desire or want keenly or greatly: *I'm dying for a cup of coffee.* **12. die away,** (of a sound) to become weaker or fainter and then cease: *The hoofbeats gradually died away.* **13. die down,** to become calm or quiet; subside. **14. die hard, a.** to die only after a bitter struggle. **b.** to give way or surrender slowly or with difficulty: *Childhood beliefs die hard.* **15. die off,** to die one after another until the number is greatly reduced: *Her friends are dying off.* **16. die out, a.** to cease to exist; become extinct: *Both lines of the family died out before the turn of the century.* **b.** to die away; fade; subside: *The roar of the engines died out as the rocket vanished into the clouds.* **17. die standing up,** *Theat.* (of a performance) to be received with silence rather than applause. **18. never say die,** never give up hope; never abandon one's efforts. [1150–1200; ME *dien, deien* < ON *deyja.* Cf. DEAD, DEATH]
—**Syn. 1.** expire, depart. DIE, PASS AWAY (PASS ON), PERISH mean to relinquish life. TO DIE is to become dead from any cause and in any circumstances. It is the simplest, plainest, and most direct word for this idea, and is used figuratively of anything that has once displayed activity: *An echo, flame, storm, rumor dies.* PASS AWAY (or PASS ON) is a commonly used euphemism implying a con-

tinuation of life after death: *Grandfather passed away (passed on).* PERISH, a more literary term, implies death under harsh circumstances such as hunger, cold, neglect, etc.; figuratively, PERISH connotes utter extinction: *Hardship caused many pioneers to perish. Ancient Egyptian civilization has perished.*

die[2] (dī), *n., pl.* **dies** for 1, 2, 4, **dice** for 3; *v.,* **died, die·ing.** —*n.* **1.** *Mach.* **a.** any of various devices for cutting or forming material in a press or a stamping or forging machine. **b.** a hollow device of steel, often composed of several pieces to be fitted into a stock, for cutting the threads of bolts or the like. **c.** one of the separate pieces of such a device. **d.** a steel block or plate with small conical holes through which wire, plastic rods, etc., are drawn. **2.** an engraved stamp for impressing a design upon some softer material, as in coining money. **3.** sing. of **dice. 4.** *Archit.* dado (def. 1). **5. the die is cast,** the irrevocable decision has been made; fate has taken charge: *The die is cast—I can't turn back.* —*v.t.* **6.** to impress, shape, or cut with a die. [1300–50; ME *de* (in early modern E taking the vowel of the pl. form DICE) < OF *de(i),* presumbly < L *datum* given (neut. ptp. of *dare* to give), perh. in the deriv. sense "put, placed," hence "played, cast"]

die[2] (def. 2) A, Greek drachma, 4th century B.C.; B, die

die·back (dī′bak′), *n. Plant Pathol.* a condition in a plant in which the branches or shoots die from the tip inward, caused by any of several bacteria, fungi, or viruses or by certain environmental conditions. [1885–90, *Amer.;* DIE[1] + BACK[2]]

dieb. alt., (in prescriptions) every other day. [< L *diēbus alternīs*]

dieb. secund., (in prescriptions) every second day. [< L *diēbus secundīs*]

dieb. tert., (in prescriptions) every third day. [< L *diēbus tertiīs*]

die′ cast′, to shape or form by die casting. [1905–10]

die-cast (dī′kast′, -käst′), *adj.* formed by die casting. [1905–10]

die′ cast′ing, *Metall.* **1.** a process in which molten metal is forced into metallic molds under hydraulic pressure to shape it, form objects, etc. **2.** an article made by this process. [1910–15] —**die′-cast′ing,** *adj.*

di·e·cious (dī ē′shəs), *adj. Biol.* dioecious. —**di·e′·cious·ly,** *adv.*

Die·fen·ba·ker (dē′fən bā′kər), *n.* **John George,** 1895–1979, prime minister of Canada 1957–63.

dief·fen·bach·i·a (dē′fən bak′ē ə, -bä′kē ə), *n.* any of various plants belonging to the genus *Dieffenbachia,* of the arum family, native to tropical America, often cultivated as houseplants for their decorative foliage. Cf. **dumb cane.** [< NL (1829), named after Ernst *Dieffenbach* (1811–55), German naturalist; see -IA]

Dié·go-Sua·rez (dyā′gō swär′es), *n.* a seaport on N Madagascar. 46,000. Also called **Antsirane.**

die-hard (dī′härd′), *n.* **1.** a person who vigorously maintains or defends a seemingly hopeless position, outdated attitude, lost cause, or the like. —*adj.* **2.** resisting vigorously and stubbornly to the last; stubborn. Also, **die′hard′.** [1835–45; n., adj. use of v. phrase *die hard*] —**die′-hard′ism,** *n.*

di·el (dī′əl, dē′-), *adj. Biol.* of or pertaining to a 24-hour period, esp. a regular daily cycle, as of the physiology or behavior of an organism. [1930–35; appar. < L *di(ēs)* day + -AL[1], sp. with *e* to avoid identity with DIAL]

diel·drin (dēl′drin), *n. Chem.* a light tan, crystalline, water-insoluble, poisonous solid, $C_{12}H_8OCl_6$, used as an insecticide: manufacture and use have been discontinued in the U.S. [1945–50; DIEL(S-AL)D(E)R (REACTION) + -IN[2]]

di·e·lec·tric (dī′i lek′trik), *Elect.* —*n.* **1.** a nonconducting substance; insulator. **2.** a substance in which an electric field can be maintained with a minimum loss of power. —*adj.* **3.** of or pertaining to a dielectric substance. [1830–40; DI-[3] + ELECTRIC] —**di′e·lec′tri·cal·ly,** *adv.*

di′elec′tric con′stant, *Elect.* permittivity. [1870–75]

di′elec′tric heat′ing, *Elect.* the heating of a nonconducting substance caused by dielectric loss when the material is placed in a variable electric field. [1940–45]

di′elec′tric loss′, *Elect.* the loss of power in a dielectric caused by the loss of energy in the form of heat generated by an electric field.

di′elec′tric strength′, *Elect.* the maximum voltage that can be applied to a given material without causing it to break down, usually expressed in volts or kilovolts per unit of thickness. Cf. **breakdown voltage.**

Diels (dēlz; *Ger.* dēls), *n.* **Ot·to** (ot′ō; *Ger.* ôt′ō), 1876–1954, German chemist: Nobel prize 1950.

Diels′-Al′der reac′tion (dēlz′äl′dər), *Chem.* the reaction in which a conjugated diene combines with a double or triple bond of a given compound to form a ring of six carbon atoms. [named after O. DIELS and K. ALDER]

Dien Bien Phu (dyen′ byen′ fo͞o′), a town in NW Vietnam: site of defeat of French forces by Vietminh 1954, bringing to an end the French rule of Indochina.

di·en·ceph·a·lon (dī′en sef′ə lon′), *n., pl.* **-lons, -la** (-lə). *Anat.* the posterior section of the forebrain. [1880–85; < NL; see DI-[3], ENCEPHALON] —**di·en·ce·phal·ic** (dī′en sə fal′ik), *adj.*

di·ene (dī′ēn, dī ēn′), *n. Chem.* any compound, as 1,3-butadiene, $CH_2{=}CH{-}CH{=}CH_2$, that contains two double bonds. Also called **diolefin.** [1915–20; DI-[1] + -ENE]

die-off (dī′ôf′, -of′), *n.* a sudden, natural perishing of large numbers of a species, population, or community. [1935–40; n. use of v. phrase *die off*]

Di·eppe (dē ep′; *Fr.* dyep), *n.* a seaport in N France, on the English Channel: raided by an Allied expeditionary force August 1942. 26,111.

di·er·e·sis (dī er′ə sis), *n., pl.* **-ses** (-sēz′). **1.** the separation of two adjacent vowels, dividing one syllable into two. **2.** a sign (¨) placed over the second of two adjacent vowels to indicate separate pronunciation, as in one spelling of the older forms *naïve* and *coöperate:* no longer widely used in English. **3.** *Pros.* the division made in a line or verse by coincidence of the end of a foot and the end of a word. Also, **diaeresis.** [1605–15; < L *diaeresis* < Gk *diaíresis* lit., distinction, division, equiv. to *diaire-,* s. of *diaireîn* to divide (*di-* DI-[3] + *haireîn* to take) + *-sis* -SIS] —**di·o·ret·ic** (dī′ə ret′ik), *adj.*

Dies (dīz), *n.* **Martin,** 1901–72, U.S. politician.

Dies′ Commit′tee, *U.S. Hist.* an early, informal name for the House Un-American Activities Committee. [named after Martin DIES, its first chairman]

die·sel (dē′zəl, -səl), *adj.* **1.** noting a machine or vehicle powered by a diesel engine: *diesel locomotive.* **2.** of or pertaining to a diesel engine: *diesel fuel.* —*n.* **3.** See **diesel engine. 4.** a vehicle powered by a diesel engine. **5.** See **diesel fuel.** Also, **Diesel.** [after R. DIESEL, the engine's inventor]

Die·sel (dē′zəl, -səl), *n.* **Ru·dolf** (ro͞o′dolf, -dôlf; *Ger.* RO͞O′dôlf), 1858–1913, German automotive engineer.

die′sel cy′cle, *Mach.* a theoretical heat cycle for an engine in which combustion occurs at a constant pressure and cooling at a constant volume.

die·sel-e·lec·tric (dē′zəl i lek′trik, -səl-), *adj.* having an electric motor powered directly by an electric generator or by batteries charged by the generator, with the generator being driven by a diesel engine: *a diesel-electric locomotive.* Also, **Die′sel-e·lec′tric.** [1920–25]

die′sel en′gine, a compression-ignition engine in which a spray of fuel, introduced into air compressed to a temperature of approximately 1000° F (538° C), ignites at a virtually constant pressure. Also called **diesel.** [1890–95]

die′sel fu′el, a combustible petroleum distillate used as fuel for diesel engines. Also called **die′sel oil′.**

die·sel·ing (dē′zə ling, -sə-), *n. Auto.* after-run. [1950–55; DIESEL + -ING[1]]

die·sel·ize (dē′zə līz′, -sə-), *v.,* **-ized, -iz·ing.** —*v.t.* **1.** to equip with diesel machinery. —*v.i.* **2.** to become equipped with diesel machinery or vehicles, as a railroad. Also, *esp. Brit.* **die′sel·ise′.** [1945–50; DIESEL + -IZE] —**die′sel·i·za′tion,** *n.*

die·sink·er (dī′sing′kər), *n.* an engraver of dies for stamping or embossing. [1805–15; DIE[2] + SINKER]

Di·es I·rae (dē′äs ēr′ā), a Latin hymn on the Day of Judgment, commonly sung in a Requiem Mass.

di·e·sis (dī′ə sis), *n., pl.* **-ses** (-sēz′). *Print.* See **double dagger.** [1350–1400; orig., any of several musical intervals smaller than a tone (for which a double dagger was used as a symbol); ME < L *di(h)esis* < Gk *díesis* lit., a sending through, equiv. to *die-,* base of *diiénai* to send through (*di-* DI-[3] + *hiénai* to send) + *-sis* -SIS]

di·es non (dī′ēz non′, dē′äs nōn′), *Law.* a day on which no courts can be held. [1600–10; short for L *diēs nōn jūridicus* a day not juridical (for legal business)]

di·es·ter (dī′es′tər), *n. Chem.* an organic compound that contains two ester groups. [1930–35; DI-[1] + ESTER]

die·stock (dī′stok′), *n.* a frame for holding a number of standard threaded dies for cutting screw threads. [1860–65; DIE[2] + STOCK]

di·es·trus (dī es′trəs), *n.* (in female mammals) an interval of sexual inactivity between periods of estrus. Also, *Brit.* **dioestrus.** [1940–45; DI-[3] + ESTRUS] —**di·es′trous,** *adj.*

di·et[1] (dī′it), *n., v.,* **-et·ed, -et·ing,** *adj.* —*n.* **1.** food and drink considered in terms of its qualities, composition, and its effects on health: *Milk is a wholesome article of diet.* **2.** a particular selection of food, esp. as designed or prescribed to improve a person's physical condition or to prevent or treat a disease: *a diet low in sugar.* **3.** such a selection or a limitation on the amount a person eats for reducing weight: *No pie for me, I'm on a diet.* **4.** the foods eaten, as by a particular person or group: *The native diet consists of fish and fruit.* **5.** food or feed habitually eaten or provided: *The rabbits were fed a diet of carrots and lettuce.* **6.** anything that is habitually provided or partaken of: *Television has given us a steady diet of game shows and soap operas.* —*v.t.* **7.** to regulate the food of, esp. in order to improve the physical condition. **8.** to feed. —*v.i.* **9.** to select or limit the food one eats to improve one's physical condition or to lose weight: *I've dieted all month and lost only one pound.* **10.** to eat or feed according to the requirements of a diet. —*adj.* **11.** suitable for consumption with a weight-reduction diet; dietetic: *diet soft drinks.* [1175–1225; (n.) ME *diete* < AF, OF < L *diaeta* < Gk *díaita* way of living, diet, equiv. to *dia-* DIA- + *-aita* (akin to *aîsa* share, lot); (v.) ME *dieten* (transit.) < AF, OF *dieter,* deriv. of the n.] —**di′et·er,** *n.*

di·et[2] (dī′it), *n.* **1.** the legislative body of certain countries, as Japan. **2.** the general assembly of the estates of the former Holy Roman Empire. [1400–50; late ME < ML *diēta* public assembly, appar. the same word as L *diaeta* (see DIET[1]) with sense affected by L *diēs* day]

di·e·tar·y (dī′i ter′ē), *adj., n., pl.* **-tar·ies.** —*adj.* **1.** of or pertaining to diet: *a dietary cure.* —*n.* **2.** a regulated allowance of food. **3.** *Obs.* a system or course of diet. [1400–50; late ME *dietarie* system of diet. See DIET[1], -ARY] —**di′e·tar′i·ly,** *adv.*

di′etary fi′ber, fiber (def. 9). [1975–80]

di′etary law′, *Judaism.* law dealing with foods permitted to be eaten, food preparation and combinations, and the utensils and dishes coming into contact with food. Cf. **kashruth.** [1925–30]

di·e·tet·ic (dī′i tet′ik), *adj.* Also, **di′e·tet′i·cal. 1.** pertaining to diet or to regulation of the use of food. **2.** prepared or suitable for special diets, esp. those requiring a restricted sugar intake: *a jar of dietetic jelly.* —*n.* **3. dietetics,** (*used with a singular v.*) the science concerned with the nutritional planning and preparation of foods. [1535–45; < L *diaeteticus* < Gk *diaitētikós,* equiv. to *diaitē-,* var. s. of *diaitân* to treat, regulate (deriv. of *díaita* DIET[1]) + *-tikos* -TIC] —**di′e·tet′i·cal·ly,** *adv.*

di·eth·yl·ac·e·tal (dī eth′əl as′i tal′), *n. Chem.* acetal (def. 1). [DI-[1] + ETHYL + ACETAL]

di·eth·yl·am·i·no·eth·a·nol (dī eth′əl ə mē′nō eth′ə nôl′, -nol′, -am′ə nō-), *n. Chem.* a colorless, hygroscopic, water-soluble liquid, $C_6H_{15}NO$, used for the synthesis of local anesthetics, in antirust compounds, and in photographic emulsions. Also, **di·eth·yl·eth·a·nol·a·mine** (dī eth′əl eth′ə nô′lə mēn′, -nol′ə-). [DI-[1] + ETHYL + AMINO- + ETHANOL]

di·eth·yl·car·bam·a·zine (dī eth′əl kär bam′ə zēn′), *n. Pharm.* an anthelmintic, $C_{10}H_{21}N_3O$, used in the treatment of various filarial worm infestations, esp. those of the genera *Wuchereria, Loa,* and *Onchocerca.* [1965–70; DI-[1] + ETHYL + CARBAM(YL) + (PIPER)AZINE]

di·eth′yl·ene gly′col (dī eth′ə lēn′), *Chem.* a syrupy colorless liquid, $C_4H_{10}O_3$, used as a solvent for cellulose nitrate and as a fabric softener. Also called **diglycol.** [DI-[1] + ETHYLENE]

di·eth′yl e′ther (dī eth′əl), *Chem.* ether (def. 1). [1925–30; DI-[1] + ETHYL]

dieth′yl ox′ide, *Chem.* ether (def. 1).

di·eth·yl·pro·pi·on (dī eth′əl prō′pē ən), *n. Pharm.* a sympathomimetic substance, $C_{13}H_{19}NO{\cdot}HCl$, used as an appetite suppressor and a short-term adjunct in the management of certain kinds of obesity. [appar. DI-[1] + ETHYL + PROPION(IC)]

di·eth·yl·stil·bes·trol (dī eth′əl stil bes′trôl, -trol), *n. Pharm.* a nonsteroidal synthetic estrogen, $C_{18}H_{20}O_2$, used in medicine chiefly in the treatment of menopausal symptoms and in animal feeds for chemical caponization: formerly used during pregnancy for the prevention of miscarriage but discontinued owing to its association with an increased risk of vaginal and cervical cancers in women having had fetal exposure. *Abbr.:* DES Also, **di·eth′yl·stil·boes′trol.** [1935–40; DI-[1] + ETHYL + STILBESTROL]

di·eth·yl·tol·u·a·mide (dī eth′əl tol′yo͞o ə mīd′, -mid), *n. Chem.* a liquid, $C_{12}H_{17}NO$, used as an insect repellent and resin solvent. Cf. **Deet.** [DI-[1] + ETHYL + TOLU + AMIDE]

di·eth·yl·tryp·ta·mine (dī eth′əl trip′tə mēn′, -min), *n. Pharm.* a synthetic derivative of tryptamine with hallucinogenic and psychotogenic effects. *Abbr.:* DET [DI-[1] + ETHYL + TRYPTAMINE]

di·e·ti·tian (dī′i tish′ən), *n.* a person who is an expert in nutrition or dietetics. Also, **di′e·ti′cian.** [1840–50; DIET[1] + *-itian;* see -ICIAN]

di′et kitch′en, a kitchen, as in a hospital, where special food is prepared for those requiring it. [1865–70, *Amer.*]

di′et pill′, a tablet or capsule containing chemical substances that aid in reducing or controlling body weight, usually by suppressing the appetite. [1965–70]

Die·trich (dē′trik, -triкн), *n.* **Mar·le·ne** (mär lā′nə), 1904–92, U.S. actress and singer, born in Germany.

Die·trich von Bern (dē′triкн fən bern′), Theodoric of Verona: the name of the eastern Gothic emperor Theodoric as it appears in German legends.

Dieu et mon droit (dyœ′ ā môɴ drwa′), *French.* God and my right: motto on the royal arms of England.

Dieu vous garde (dyœ′ vo͞o gard′), *French.* God keep you.

dif (dif), *n. Informal.* difference: *What's the dif where you buy it, as long as you get it?* [1910–15; by shortening]

dif-, var. of **dis-**[1] before *f: differ.*

dif., 1. difference. **2.** different.

diff., 1. difference. **2.** different.

dif·fe·o·mor·phism (dif′ē ō môr′fiz əm), *n. Math.* a differentiable homeomorphism. [by contr.]

dif·fer (dif′ər), *v.i.* **1.** to be unlike, dissimilar, or distinct in nature or qualities (often fol. by *from*): *The two writers differ greatly in their perceptions of the world. Each writer's style differs from that of another.* **2.** to disagree in opinion, belief, etc.; be at variance; disagree (often fol. by *with* or *from*): *His business partner always differs with him.* **3.** *Obs.* to dispute; quarrel. [1325–75; ME *differren* to distinguish < MF *differer* to put off, distinguish, L *differre* to bear apart, put off, delay (see DEFER[1]) be different, equiv. to *dif-* DIF- + *ferre* to bear]

dif·fer·ence (dif′ər əns, dif′rəns), *n., v.,* **-enced, -enc·ing.** —*n.* **1.** the state or relation of being different; dissimilarity: *There is a great difference between the two.* **2.** an instance or point of unlikeness or dissimilarity: *What accounts for the differences in their behavior?* **3.** a significant change in or effect on a situation: *His tact makes a difference in the way people accept his sugges-*

CONCISE PRONUNCIATION KEY: act, cāpe, dâre, pärt; set, ēqual; *if,* īce; ox, ōver, ôrder, oil, bo͝ok, bo͞ot, out; up, ûrge; child; sing; shoe; thin, *that;* zh as in *treasure.* ə = *a* as in *alone, e* as in *system, i* as in *easily, o* as in *gallop, u* as in *circus;* ᵊ as in *fire* (fīᵊr), *hour* (ouᵊr). l and n can serve as syllabic consonants, as in *cradle* (krād′l), and *button* (but′n). See the full key inside the front cover.

tions. **4.** a distinguishing characteristic; distinctive quality, feature, etc.: *The difference in the two products is quality.* **5.** the degree to which one person or thing differs from another. **6.** the act of distinguishing; discrimination; distinction. **7.** a disagreement in opinion. **8.** a dispute or quarrel. **9.** Also called **finite distance.** *Math.* **a.** the amount by which one quantity is greater or less than another. **b.** See **relative complement. c.** (of a function f) an expression of the form $f(x + h) - f(x)$. **10.** a differentia. **11. split the difference, a.** to compromise, esp. to make equal concessions. **b.** to divide the remainder equally: *Let's take half of the cake and let the three of them split the difference.* —*v.t.* **12.** to cause or constitute a difference in or between; make different. **13.** to perceive the difference in or between; discriminate. [1300–50; ME (< AF) < L *differentia,* equiv. to *different-* carrying different ways (see DIFFERENT) + *-ia* -IA; see -ENCE]

—Syn. 1. inconsistency, variation, diversity, imbalance, inequality, divergence, contrast, contrariety. DIFFERENCE, DISCREPANCY, DISPARITY, DISSIMILARITY imply perceivable unlikeness, variation, or diversity. DIFFERENCE refers to a lack of identity or a degree of unlikeness: *a difference of opinion; a difference of six inches.* DISCREPANCY usually refers to an inconsistency between things that should agree, balance, or harmonize: *a discrepancy between the statements of two witnesses.* DISPARITY implies inequality, often where a greater equality might reasonably be expected: *a great disparity between the ages of husband and wife.* DISSIMILARITY indicates an essential lack of resemblance between things in some respect comparable: *a dissimilarity between social customs in Asia and America.* **6.** See **distinction. —Ant. 1.** similarity, agreement.

dif′ference ring′, *Math.* See **quotient ring.**

dif•fer•ent (dif′ər ənt, dif′rənt), *adj.* **1.** not alike in character or quality; differing; dissimilar: *The two are different.* **2.** not identical; separate or distinct: *three different answers.* **3.** various; several: *Different people told me the same story.* **4.** not ordinary; unusual. [1350–1400; ME < AF < L *different-* (s. of *differēns*), prp. of *differre.* See DIFFER, -ENT] **—dif′fer•ent•ly,** *adv.* **—dif′fer•ent•ness,** *n.*

—Syn. 1. unlike, diverse, divergent, contrary. **3.** sundry, divers, miscellaneous. See **various.**

—Usage. Although it is frequently claimed that DIFFERENT should be followed only by FROM, not by THAN, in actual usage both words occur and have for at least 300 years. FROM is more common today in introducing a phrase, but THAN is also used: *New York speech is different from* (or *than*) *that of Chicago.* THAN is used to introduce a clause: *The stream followed a different course than the map showed.* In sentences of this type, FROM is sometimes used instead of THAN; when it is, more words are necessary: *a different course from the one the map showed.* Regardless of the sentence construction, both FROM and THAN are standard after DIFFERENT in all varieties of spoken and written American English. In British English TO frequently follows DIFFERENT: *The early illustrations are very different to the later ones.* The use of DIFFERENT in the sense "unusual" is well established in all but the most formal American English: *The décor in the new restaurant is really different.*

dif•fer•en•ti•a (dif′ə ren′shē ə, -shə), *n., pl.* **-ti•ae** (-shē ē′). **1.** the character or attribute by which one species is distinguished from all others of the same genus. **2.** the character or basic factor by which one entity is distinguished from another. [1820–30; < L; see DIFFERENCE]

dif•fer•en•ti•a•ble (dif′ə ren′shē ə bəl, -shə bəl), *adj.* capable of being differentiated. [1860–65; DIFFERENTI(ATE) + -ABLE] **—dif′fer•en′ti•a•bil′i•ty,** *n.*

dif′feren′tiable man′ifold, *Math.* a manifold having the property that any two overlapping open sets are homeomorphic to locally Euclidean spaces whose coordinates are related by differentiable functions, a property with wide applications in mathematical physics and differential geometry.

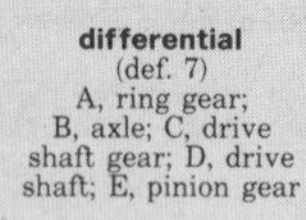

differential
(def. 7)
A, ring gear;
B, axle; C, drive
shaft gear; D, drive
shaft; E, pinion gear

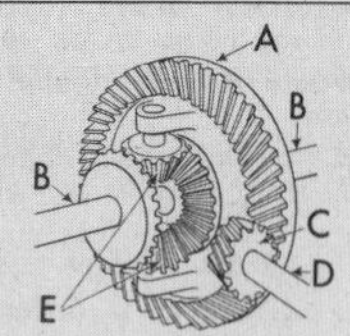

dif•fer•en•tial (dif′ə ren′shəl), *adj.* **1.** of or pertaining to difference or diversity. **2.** constituting a difference; distinguishing; distinctive: *a differential feature.* **3.** exhibiting or depending upon a difference or distinction. **4.** *Physics, Mach.* pertaining to or involving the difference of two or more motions, forces, etc. **5.** *Math.* pertaining to or involving a derivative or derivatives. —*n.* **6.** a difference or the amount of difference, as in rate, cost, quantity, degree, or quality, between things that are comparable. **7.** Also called **differential gear.** *Mach.* an epicyclic train of gears designed to permit two or more shafts to rotate at different speeds, as a set of gears in an automobile permitting the rear wheels to be driven at different speeds when the car is turning. **8.** *Math.* **a.** a function of two variables that is obtained from a given function, $y = f(x)$, and that expresses the approximate increment in the given function as the derivative of the function times the increment in the independent variable, written as $dy = f'(x)dx$. **b.** any generalization of this function to higher dimensions. **9.** *Com.* **a.** the difference involved in a differential rate. **b.** See **differential rate. 10.** *Physics.* the quantitative difference between two or more forces, motions, etc.: *a pressure differential.* [1640–50; < ML *differentiālis,* equiv. to *differenti(a)* DIFFERENCE + *-ālis* -AL] **—dif′fer•en′tial•ly,** *adv.*

differen′tial an′alyzer, an analog computer designed for solving certain differential equations. [1930–35]

differen′tial associa′tion, a theory that criminal and deviant behavior is learned through close and frequent association with criminal or deviant behavior patterns, norms, and values.

dif′feren′tial cal′culus, the branch of mathematics that deals with differentials and derivatives. [1700–05]

differen′tial coeffic′ient, *Chiefly Brit.* derivative (def. 6). [1810–20]

differen′tial compac′tion, *Geol.* differences in the extent to which sediment is compacted owing to topographic irregularities of the surface on which it is deposited.

differen′tial equa′tion, *Math.* an equation involving differentials or derivatives. [1755–65]

dif′feren′tial gear′, *Mach.* **1.** differential (def. 7). **2.** any of various comparable arrangements of gears, as an epicyclic train. [1885–90]

differen′tial geom′etry, *Math.* the branch of mathematics that deals with the application of the principles of differential and integral calculus to the study of curves and surfaces.

dif′feren′tial op′erator, *Math.* a function, usually expressed as a polynomial, that indicates linear combinations of the derivatives of the expression on which it operates.

differen′tial psychol′ogy, the branch of psychology dealing with the study of characteristic differences or variations of groups or individuals, esp. through the use of analytic techniques and statistical methods.

dif′feren′tial quo′tient, derivative (def. 6).

dif′feren′tial rate′, a special lower rate, as one charged by one of two or more competing businesses.

differen′tial topol′ogy, *Math.* the branch of topology that studies the properties of differentiable manifolds that remain invariant under diffeomorphisms.

dif′feren′tial weath′ering, *Geol.* the difference in degree of discoloration, disintegration, etc., of rocks of different kinds exposed to the same environment.

dif′feren′tial wind′lass, a pair of hoisting drums of different diameter turning at the same rate, such that a pulley suspended below them on a line wound on the larger drum and unwound from the smaller drum is raised with mechanical advantage. Also called **Chinese windlass.**

dif•fer•en•ti•ate (dif′ə ren′shē āt′), *v.,* **-at•ed, -at•ing.** —*v.t.* **1.** to form or mark differently from other such things; distinguish. **2.** to change; alter. **3.** to perceive the difference in or between. **4.** to make different by modification, as a biological species. **5.** *Math.* to obtain the differential or the derivative of. —*v.i.* **6.** to become unlike or dissimilar; change in character. **7.** to make a distinction. **8.** *Biol.* (of cells or tissues) to change from relatively generalized to specialized kinds, during development. [1810–20; < ML *differentiātus* distinguished (ptp. of *differentiāre*), equiv. to L *different(ia)* DIFFERENCE + *-ātus* -ATE[1]]

—Syn. 1. set off. See **distinguish. 3.** separate.

dif•fer•en•ti•a•tor (dif′ə ren′shē ā′tər), *n.* **1.** a person or thing that differentiates. **2.** *Computers.* an electronic device whose output signal is proportional to the derivative of its input signal. **3.** *Electricity, Electronics.* a transducer or circuit **(differen′tiator cir′cuit)** whose output is proportional to the rate of change of the input signal. [1885–90; DIFFERENTIATE + -OR[2]]

dif•fi•cile (dif′i sēl′; *Fr.* dē fē sēl′), *adj.* **1.** hard to deal with, satisfy, or please. **2.** hard to do; difficult. [1470–80; < F < L *difficilis* difficult; see DIF-, FACILE]

dif•fi•cult (dif′i kult′, -kəlt), *adj.* **1.** not easily or readily done; requiring much labor, skill, or planning to be performed successfully; hard: *a difficult job.* **2.** hard to understand or solve: *a difficult problem.* **3.** hard to deal with or get on with: *a difficult pupil.* **4.** hard to please or satisfy: *a difficult employer.* **5.** hard to persuade or induce; stubborn: *a difficult old man.* **6.** disadvantageous; trying; hampering: *The operation was performed under the most difficult conditions.* **7.** fraught with hardship, esp. financial hardship: *We saw some difficult times during the depression years.* [1350–1400; ME, back formation from DIFFICULTY] **—dif′fi•cult′ly,** *adv.*

—Syn. 1. arduous. See **hard. 2.** intricate, perplexing, involved, knotty. **4.** particular, finical, fussy. **5.** obdurate, uncompromising. **—Ant. 1.** easy. **2.** simple.

dif•fi•cul•ty (dif′i kul′tē, -kəl tē), *n., pl.* **-ties. 1.** the fact or condition of being difficult. **2.** Often, **difficulties.** an embarrassing situation, esp. of financial affairs. **3.** a trouble or struggle. **4.** a cause of trouble, struggle, or embarrassment. **5.** a disagreement or dispute. **6.** reluctance; unwillingness. **7.** a demur; objection. **8.** something that is hard to do, understand, or surmount; an impediment or obstacle. [1350–1400; ME *difficulte* (< AF) < L *difficultās,* equiv. to *difficil(is)* DIFFICILE + *-tās* -TY[2]]

—Syn. 2. dilemma, predicament, quandary, plight, fix, exigency, strait. **3.** problem.

dif•fi•dence (dif′i dəns), *n.* the quality or state of being diffident. [1350–1400; ME < L *diffidentia* mistrust, want of confidence. See DIFFIDENT, -ENCE]

dif•fi•dent (dif′i dənt), *adj.* **1.** lacking confidence in one's own ability, worth, or fitness; timid; shy. **2.** restrained or reserved in manner, conduct, etc. **3.** *Archaic.* distrustful. [1425–75; late ME < L *diffident-* (s. of *diffidēns* mistrusting, despairing prp. of *diffidere*), equiv. to *dif-* DIF- + *fīd-* trust + *-ent-* -ENT] **—dif′fi•dent•ly,** *adv.* **—dif′fi•dent•ness,** *n.*

—Syn. 1. self-conscious, self-effacing, abashed, embarrassed, modest, unassuming, unconfident. See **shy**[1].

dif•flu•ence (dif′lo͞o əns), *n.* **1.** the act of flowing off or away. **2.** the act or process of dissolving into a liquid; liquefaction; deliquescence. **3.** the rate at which fluid flow diverges along an axis perpendicular to the direction of flow at a given point. Cf. **divergence.** [1625–35; DIFFLU(ENT) + -ENCE]

dif•flu•ent (dif′lo͞o ənt), *adj.* **1.** tending to flow off or away. **2.** easily dissolving. [1610–20; < L *diffluent-* (s. of *diffluēns,* prp. of *diffluere*), equiv. to *dif-* DIF- + *fluent-* flowing; see FLUENT]

Dif•flu•gi•a (di flo͞o′jē ə), *n.* a genus of ameboid protozoans that construct a shell of cemented sand grains. [< NL (1816), equiv. to L *difflu(ere)* to flow away (see DIFFLUENT) + *-g-* (unexplained) + *-ia* -IA]

dif•fract (di frakt′), *v.t.* to break up or bend by diffraction. [1795–1805; back formation from DIFFRACTION]

dif•frac•tion (di frak′shən), *n. Physics.* **1.** the phenomenon exhibited by wave fronts that, passing the edge of an opaque body, are modulated, thereby causing a redistribution of energy within the front: it is detectable in light waves by the presence of a pattern of closely spaced dark and light bands **(diffrac′tion pat′tern)** at the edge of a shadow. **2.** the bending of waves, esp. sound and light waves, around obstacles in their path. [1665–75; < NL *diffractiōn-* (s. of *diffractiō*) a breaking up, equiv. to L *diffract(us)* broken up (ptp. of *diffringere*) + *-iōn-* -ION. See DIF-, FRACTION]

diffrac′tion grat′ing, *Physics.* a band of equidistant, parallel lines, usually more than 5000 per inch (2000 per centimeter), ruled on a glass or polished metal surface for diffracting light to produce optical spectra. Also called **grating.** [1865–70]

dif•frac•tive (di frak′tiv), *adj.* causing or pertaining to diffraction. [1820–30; DIFFRACT + -IVE] **—dif•frac′•tive•ly,** *adv.* **—dif•frac′tive•ness,** *n.*

dif•frac•tom•e•ter (di frak tom′i tər, dif′rak-), *n. Physics.* an instrument that is used to study atomic crystal structure by measuring the angles at which x-rays, neutrons, or electrons are diffracted by matter. [1905–10; DIFFRACT + -O- + -METER]

dif•fu•sate (di fyo͞o′zāt), *n. Physical Chem.* (in dialysis) the solution or the crystalline material that passes into it through the semipermeable membrane; dialyzate. [1840–50; DIFFUS(ION) + -ATE[1]]

dif•fuse (*v.* di fyo͞oz′; *adj.* di fyo͞os′), *v.,* **-fused, -fusing,** *adj.* —*v.t.* **1.** to pour out and spread, as a fluid. **2.** to spread or scatter widely or thinly; disseminate. **3.** *Physics.* to spread by diffusion. —*v.i.* **4.** to spread. **5.** *Physics.* to intermingle by diffusion. —*adj.* **6.** characterized by great length or discursiveness in speech or writing; wordy. **7.** widely spread or scattered; dispersed. **8.** *Bot.* widely or loosely spreading. **9.** *Optics.* (of reflected light) scattered, as from a rough surface (opposed to *specular*). [1350–1400; ME (< AF) < L *diffūsus* spread, poured forth. See DIF-, FUSE[2]] **—dif•fuse•ly** (di-fyo͞os′lē), *adv.* **—dif•fuse′ness,** *n.*

diffuse′ neb′ula, *Astron.* nebula (def. 1a).

dif•fuse-po•rous (di fyo͞os′pôr′əs, -pōr′-), *adj. Bot.* having annual rings in which the size of pores is approximately the same in wood formed in spring and summer. Cf. **ring-porous.** [1900–05]

dif•fus•er (di fyo͞o′zər), *n.* **1.** a person or thing that diffuses. **2.** (in various machines or mechanical systems, as centrifugal pumps or compressors) a device for utilizing part of the kinetic energy of a fluid passing through a machine by gradually increasing the cross-sectional area of the channel or chamber through which it flows so as to decrease its speed and increase its pressure. **3.** (in a lighting fixture) any of a variety of translucent materials for filtering glare from the light source. **4.** a pierced plate or similar device for distributing compressed air for aeration of sewage. Also, **diffusor.** [1670–80; DIFFUSE + -ER[1]]

dif•fus•i•ble (di fyo͞o′zə bəl), *adj.* capable of being diffused. [1775–85; DIFFUSE + -IBLE] **—dif•fus′i•bil′i•ty, dif•fus′i•ble•ness,** *n.* **—dif•fus′i•bly,** *adv.*

dif•fu•sion (di fyo͞o′zhən), *n.* **1.** act of diffusing; state of being diffused. **2.** prolixity of speech or writing; discursiveness. **3.** *Physics.* **a.** Also called **migration.** an intermingling of molecules, ions, etc., resulting from random thermal agitation, as in the dispersion of a vapor in air. **b.** a reflection or refraction of light or other electromagnetic radiation from an irregular surface or an erratic dispersion through a surface; scattering. **4.** *Motion Pictures.* a soft-focus effect resulting from placing a gelatin or silk plate in front of a studio light or a camera lens, or through the use of diffusion filters. **5.** *Meteorol.* the spreading of atmospheric constituents or properties by turbulent motion as well as molecular motion of the air. **6.** *Anthropol., Sociol.* the transmission of elements or features of one culture to another. [1325–75; ME < L *diffūsiōn-* (s. of *diffūsiō*) a spreading out, equiv. to *diffūs(us)* (see DIFFUSE) + *-iōn-* -ION]

dif•fu•sion•ism (di fyo͞o′zhə niz′əm), *n. Anthropol.* the theory or principle that diffusion is the main force in cultural innovation and change. [1935–40; DIFFUSION + -ISM] **—dif•fu′sion•ist,** *n., adj.*

dif•fu•sive (di fyo͞o′siv), *adj.* tending to diffuse; characterized by diffusion. [1605–15; DIFFUSE + -IVE] **—dif•fu′sive•ly,** *adv.* **—dif•fu′sive•ness,** *n.*

dif•fu•siv•i•ty (dif′yo͞o siv′i tē), *n. Physics.* the property of a substance indicative of the rate at which a thermal disturbance, as a rise in temperature, will be transmitted through the substance. [1875–80; DIFFUSIVE + -ITY]

dif•fu•sor (di fyo͞o′zər), *n.* diffuser.

dif•lu•ence (dif′lo͞o əns), *n.* diffluence. [DI-[2] + *-fluence* (as in *confluence*). See DIFFLUENT]

di•flu•ni•sal (di flo͞o′nə sal′), *n. Pharm.* a substance,

CONCISE ETYMOLOGY KEY: <, descended or borrowed from; >, whence; b., blend of, blended; c., cognate with; cf., compare; deriv., derivative; equiv., equivalent; imit., imitative; obl., oblique; r., replacing; s., stem; sp., spelling, spelled; resp., respelling, respelled; trans., translation; ?, origin unknown; *, unattested; ‡, probably earlier than. See the full key inside the front cover.

$C_{13}H_8F_2O_3$, used as an analgesic, antipyretic, and anti-inflammatory drug in the treatment of rheumatoid diseases and other musculoskeletal disorders. [shortening and resp. of *5-(2, 4-difluorophenyl)salicylic acid*]

dig[1] (dig), *v.*, **dug** or (*Archaic*) **digged, dig·ging,** *n.* —*v.i.* **1.** to break up, turn over, or remove earth, sand, etc., as with a shovel, spade, bulldozer, or claw; make an excavation. **2.** to make one's way or work by or as by removing or turning over material: *to dig through the files.* —*v.t.* **3.** to break up, turn over, or loosen (earth, sand, etc.), as with a shovel, spade, or bulldozer (often fol. by *up*). **4.** to form or excavate (a hole, tunnel, etc.) by removing material. **5.** to unearth, obtain, or remove by digging (often fol. by *up* or *out*). **6.** to find or discover by effort or search. **7.** to poke, thrust, or force (usually fol. by *in* or *into*): *He dug his heel into the ground.* **8. dig in, a.** to dig trenches, as in order to defend a position in battle. **b.** to maintain one's opinion or position. **c.** to start eating. **9. dig into,** *Informal.* to attack, work, or apply oneself voraciously, vigorously, or energetically: *to dig into one's work; to dig into a meal.* **10. dig out, a.** to remove earth or debris from by digging. **b.** to hollow out by digging. **c.** to find by searching: *to dig out facts for a term paper.* **11. dig up, a.** to discover in the course of digging. **b.** to locate; find: *to dig up information.* —*n.* **12.** thrust; poke: *He gave me a dig in the ribs with his elbow.* **13.** a cutting, sarcastic remark. **14.** an archaeological site undergoing excavation. **15. digs,** *Informal.* living quarters; lodgings. [1275–1325; ME *diggen,* perh. repr. an OE deriv. of *dīc* DITCH; MF *diguer* to dig (< MD) is attested later and appar. not the immediate source]

dig[2] (dig), *v.t.*, **dug, dig·ging.** *Slang.* **1.** to understand: *Can you dig what I'm saying?* **2.** to take notice of: *Dig those shoes he's wearing.* **3.** to like, love, or enjoy: *She digs that kind of music. We really dig each other.* [1935–40; perh. < Ir *(an) dtuig(eann tú mé?)* do you understand me? and parallel expressions with *tuigim* I understand (see TWIG[2])]

dig., digest.

Di·gam·ba·ra (di gum′bər ə), *n.* the earlier of the two principal Jain sects, whose members went naked. Cf. **Svetambara.** [< Skt: naked]

di·gam·ma (dī gam′ə), *n.* a letter of the early Greek alphabet that generally fell into disuse in Attic Greek before the classical period and that represented a sound similar to English *w.* [1545–55; < L < Gk *dígamma,* equiv. to *di-* DI-[1] + *gámma* GAMMA; from its resemblance to two gammas placed one over the other, similar to Roman F, which is a descendant of digamma] —**di·gam·mat·ed** (dī gam′ā tid), *adj.*

dig·a·my (dig′ə mē), *n.* a second marriage, after the death or divorce of the first husband or wife; deuterogamy. Cf. **monogamy** (def. 3). [1625–35; < LL *digamia* < Gk *digamía,* equiv. to *di-* DI-[1] + *-gamia* -GAMY] —**dig′a·mous,** *adj.*

di·gas·tric (dī gas′trik), *Anat.* —*adj.* **1.** (of a muscle) having two bellies with an intermediate tendon. —*n.* **2.** a muscle of the lower jaw, the action of which assists in lowering the jaw. [1690–1700; < NL *digastricus.* See DI-[1], GASTRIC]

Dig·by (dig′bē), *n.* **Sir Kenelm,** 1603–65, English writer, naval commander, and diplomat.

Dig′by chick′en, *Canadian (chiefly the Maritime Provinces).* a smoked herring. [1915–20; after *Digby,* a port in Nova Scotia]

di·gen·e·sis (dī jen′ə sis), *n. Zool.* See **alternation of generations.** [1875–80; < NL; see DI-[1], GENESIS] —**di·ge·net·ic** (dī′jə net′ik), *adj.*

di·gest (*v.* di jest′, dī-; *n.* dī′jest), *v.t.* **1.** to convert (food) in the alimentary canal into absorbable form for assimilation into the system. **2.** to promote the digestion of (food). **3.** to obtain information, ideas, or principles from; assimilate mentally: *to digest a pamphlet on nuclear waste.* **4.** to arrange methodically in the mind; think over: *to digest a plan.* **5.** to bear with patience; endure. **6.** to arrange in convenient or methodical order; reduce to a system; classify. **7.** to condense, abridge, or summarize. **8.** *Chem.* to soften or disintegrate (a substance) by means of moisture, heat, chemical action, or the like. —*v.i.* **9.** to digest food. **10.** to undergo digestion, as food. —*n.* **11.** a collection or compendium, usually of literary, historical, legal, or scientific matter, esp. when classified or condensed. **12.** *Law.* **a.** a systematic abstract of some body of law. **b. the Digest,** a collection in fifty books of excerpts, esp. from the writings of the Classical Roman jurists, compiled by order of Justinian in the 6th century A.D.; the Pandects. **13.** *Biochem.* the product of the action of an enzyme on food or other organic material. [1350–1400; (v.) ME *digesten* < L *digestus* separated, dissolved (ptp. of *dīgerere*), equiv. to *dī-* DI-[2] + *ges-* carry, bear (base of *gerere*) + *-tus* ptp. suffix; (n.) ME: collection of laws < LL *dīgesta* (pl.), L: collection of writings, neut. pl. of *dīgestus,* as above] —**di·gest′ed·ly,** *adv.* —**di·gest′ed·ness,** *n.*
—**Syn. 4.** understand; study, ponder. **6.** systematize, codify. **11.** epitome, abridgment. See **summary.**

di·gest·ant (di jes′tənt, dī-), *n. Pharm.* a substance that promotes digestion. [1870–75; DIGEST + -ANT]

di·gest·er (di jes′tər, dī-), *n.* **1.** a person or thing that digests. **2.** Also, **digestor.** *Chem.* an apparatus in which substances are softened or disintegrated, esp. by moisture, heat, or chemical action. [1570–80; DIGEST + -ER[1]]

di·gest·i·ble (di jes′tə bəl, dī-), *adj.* capable of being digested; readily digested. [1350–1400; ME < LL *dīgestibilis* < L *dīgest(us)* (see DIGEST) + *-ibilis* -IBLE] —**di·gest′i·bil′i·ty,** *n.* —**di·gest′i·bly,** *adv.*

di·ges·tif (dē zhe stēf′), *n. French.* a drink of brandy, liqueur, etc., taken after a meal to aid the digestion.

di·ges·tion (di jes′chən, dī-), *n.* **1.** the process in the alimentary canal by which food is broken up physically, as by the action of the teeth, and chemically, as by the action of enzymes, and converted into a substance suitable for absorption and assimilation into the body. **2.** the function or power of digesting food: *My digestion is bad.* **3.** the act of digesting or the state of being digested. [1350–1400; ME *digestioun* < AF, MF < L *dīgestiōn-* (s. of *dīgestiō*), equiv. to *dīgest(us)* (see DIGEST) + *-iōn-* -ION] —**di·ges′tion·al,** *adj.*

di·ges·tive (di jes′tiv, dī-), *adj.* **1.** serving for or pertaining to digestion; having the function of digesting food: *the digestive tract.* **2.** promoting digestion. —*n.* **3.** a substance promoting digestion. [1350–1400; ME < MF *digestif* < L *dīgestīvus,* equiv. to *dīgest(us)* (see DIGEST) + *-īvus* -IVE] —**di·ges′tive·ly,** *adv.*

diges′tive gland′, any gland having ducts that pour secretions into the digestive tract, as the salivary glands, liver, and pancreas. [1935–40]

diges′tive sys′tem, the system by which ingested food is acted upon by physical and chemical means to provide the body with absorbable nutrients and to excrete waste products; in mammals the system includes the alimentary canal extending from the mouth to the anus, and the hormones and enzymes assisting in digestion. [1950–55]

di·ges·tor (di jes′tər, dī-), *n. Chem.* digester (def. 2).

digged (digd), *v. Archaic.* a pt. of **dig**[1].

dig·ger (dig′ər), *n.* **1.** a person or an animal that digs. **2.** a tool, part of a machine, etc., for digging. **3.** (*cap.*) Also called **Dig′ger In′dian.** a member of any of several Indian peoples of western North America, esp. of a tribe that dug roots for food. **4.** an Australian or New Zealand soldier of World War I. **5.** (*cap.*) *Eng. Hist.* a member of a group that advocated the abolition of private property and began in 1649 to cultivate certain common lands. **6.** *Slang.* a person hired by a scalper to buy tickets to a show or performance for resale by the scalper at inflated prices. [1400–50; late ME; see DIG[1], -ER[1]]

Dig′ger pine′, a pine, *Pinus sabiniana,* of California, having drooping, grayish-green needles and large, heavy cones with edible seeds. [1880–85, *Amer.*; after the DIGGER Indians, who used the tree as a food source]

dig′ger wasp′, any of numerous solitary wasps of the family Sphecidae, which excavate nests in soil, wood, etc., and provision them with prey paralyzed by stinging. [1840–50]

dig·gings (dig′ingz *for 1–3;* dig′ənz *for 4*), *n.* **1.** (*usually used with a singular v.*) a place where digging is carried on. **2.** (*used with a plural v.*) a mining operation or locality. **3.** (*used with a plural v.*) something that is removed from an excavation. **4.** *Brit. Informal.* dig[1] (def. 15). [1530–40; DIG[1] + -ING[1] + -S[3]]

dig′ging stick′, a pointed or spatulate wooden stick, sometimes having a stone weight or crossbar attached and used in primitive societies for loosening the ground to extract buried wild plant foods and for tilling the soil.

dight (dīt), *v.t.*, **dight** or **dight·ed, dight·ing.** *Archaic.* to dress; adorn. [bef. 1000; ME *dighten,* OE *dihtan* to arrange, compose < L *dictāre* (see DICTATE); c. G *dichten*]

dig·it (dij′it), *n.* **1.** a finger or toe. **2.** the breadth of a finger used as a unit of linear measure, usually equal to ¾ in. (2 cm). **3.** any of the Arabic figures of 1 through 9 and 0. **4.** any of the symbols of other number systems, as 0 or 1 in the binary. **5.** index (def. 6). **6.** *Astron.* the twelfth part of the sun's or moon's diameter: used to express the magnitude of an eclipse. [1350–1400; ME < L *digitus* finger, toe]

dig·it·al (dij′i tl), *adj.* **1.** of or pertaining to a digit or finger. **2.** resembling a digit or finger. **3.** manipulated with a finger or the fingertips: *a digital switch.* **4.** displaying a readout in digital form: *a digital speedometer.* **5.** having digits or digitlike parts. **6.** of, pertaining to, or using data in the form of numerical digits. **7.** *Computers.* involving or using numerical digits expressed in a scale of notation to represent discretely all variables occurring in a problem. **8.** of, pertaining to, or using numerical calculations. —*n.* **9.** one of the keys or finger levers of keyboard instruments. [1400–50; late ME < L *digitālis,* equiv. to *digit(us)* (see DIGIT) + *-ālis* -AL[1]] —**dig′it·al·ly,** *adv.*

dig′ital au′diodisk, a compact disk containing an audio program.

dig′ital au′diotape, magnetic tape on which sound is digitally recorded with high fidelity for playback.

dig′ital clock′, a clock that displays the time in numerical digits rather than by hands on a dial. Cf. **analog clock.** [1975–80]

dig′ital comput′er, a computer that processes information in digital form. Cf. **analog computer.** [1940–45]

dig·i·tal·in (dij′i tal′in, -tā′lin), *n. Pharm.* **1.** a glucoside obtained from digitalis. **2.** any of several extracts of mixtures of glucosides obtained from digitalis. [1830–40; DIGITAL(IS) + -IN[2]]

dig·i·tal·is (dij′i tal′is, -tā′lis), *n.* **1.** any plant belonging to the genus *Digitalis,* of the figwort family, esp. the common foxglove, *D. purpurea.* **2.** the dried leaves of the foxglove, *Digitalis purpurea,* used in medicine as a heart stimulant. [1655–65; < NL *digitālis,* a name appar. suggested by the G name for the foxglove, *Fingerhut* lit., thimble; see DIGITAL]

dig·i·tal·ism (dij′i tl iz′əm), *n. Pathol.* the abnormal condition resulting from an overconsumption of digitalis. [DIGITAL(IS) + -ISM]

dig·i·tal·i·za·tion (dij′i tl ə zā′shən), *n. Med.* **1.** (in the treatment of heart disease) the administration of digitalis, usually in a regimen, to produce a desired physiological effect. **2.** the effect produced. [1880–85; DIGITALIZE + -ATION]

dig·i·tal·ize (dij′i tl īz′, dij′i tal′īz), *v.t.*, **-ized, -iz·ing.** **1.** *Med.* to treat (a person) with a regimen of digitalis. **2.** *Computers.* to digitize. Also, *esp. Brit.,* **dig′i·tal·ise′.** [1925–30; DIGITAL(IS) + -IZE]

dig′ital photog′raphy, the manipulation of photographs by computer.

dig′ital record′ing, 1. a method of sound recording in which an input audio waveform is sampled at regular intervals, usually between 40,000 and 50,000 times per second, and each sample is assigned a numerical value, usually expressed in binary notation. **2.** a record or tape made by this method. Cf. **analog recording. 3.** *Computers.* a system of recording information on magnetic tape for processing by a digital computer.

dig′ital subtrac′tion angiog′raphy, a computerized x-ray technique in which arteries are visualized following injection of dye into a vein. *Abbr.:* DSA

dig′ital watch′, a watch that displays the time in numerical digits rather than by hands on a dial. Cf. **analog watch.** [1970–75]

dig·i·tate (dij′i tāt′), *adj.* **1.** *Zool.* having digits or digitlike processes. **2.** *Bot.* having radiating divisions or leaflets resembling the fingers of a hand. See illus. under **palmate. 3.** like a digit or finger. Also, **dig′i·tat′ed.** [1655–65; < L *digitātus.* See DIGIT, -ATE[1]] —**dig′i·tate′·ly,** *adv.*

dig·i·ta·tion (dij′i tā′shən), *n. Biol.* **1.** digitate formation. **2.** a digitlike process or division. [1650–60; DIGITATE + -ION]

digiti-, a combining form meaning "finger," used in the formation of compound words: *digitinervate.* [comb. form repr. L *digitus*]

dig·i·ti·form (dij′i tə fôrm′), *adj.* like a finger. [1840–50; DIGITI- + -FORM]

dig·i·ti·grade (dij′i ti grād′), *adj.* **1.** walking on the toes, as most quadruped mammals. —*n.* **2.** a digitigrade animal. [1825–35; < F; see DIGITI-, -GRADE]

dig·i·ti·nerv·ate (dij′i tə nûr′vāt), *adj. Bot.* (of a leaf) having veins that radiate from the petiole like the fingers of a hand. Also, **dig·i·ti·nerved** (dij′i tə nûrvd′). [1880–85; DIGITI- + NERVATE]

dig·i·ti·pin·nate (dij′i tə pin′āt), *adj. Bot.* (of a compound leaf) digitate with pinnate leaflets. [1880–85; DIGITI- + PINNATE]

dig·i·tize (dij′i tīz′), *v.t.*, **-tized, -tiz·ing.** *Computers.* **1.** to convert (data) to digital form for use in a computer. **2.** to convert (analogous physical measurements) to digital form. Also, **digitalize;** *esp. Brit.,* **dig′i·tise′.** [1950–55; DIGIT + -IZE] —**dig′i·ti·za′tion,** *n.* —**dig′i·tiz′er,** *n.*

dig·i·tox·in (dij′i tok′sin), *n. Pharm.* a white, crystalline, water-insoluble cardiac glycoside, $C_{41}H_{64}O_{13}$, or a mixture of cardiac glycosides of which this is the chief constituent, obtained from digitalis and used in the treatment of congestive heart failure. [1880–85; DIGI(TALIS) + TOXIN]

di·glos·si·a (dī glos′ē ə, -glô′sē ə), *n.* **1.** the widespread existence within a society of sharply divergent formal and informal varieties of a language each used in different social contexts or for performing different functions, as the existence of Katharevusa and Demotic in modern Greece. **2.** *Pathol.* the presence of two tongues or of a single tongue divided into two parts by a cleft. [1955–60; Latinization of F *diglossie,* equiv. to Gk *díglōss(os)* speaking two languages (see DIGLOT) + F *-ie* -Y[3]] —**di·glos·sic** (dī glos′ik), *adj.*

di·glot (dī′glot), *adj.* **1.** bilingual. —*n.* **2.** a bilingual book or edition. [1860–65; < Gk *diglōttos,* equiv. to *di-* DI-[1] + *-glōttos,* adj. deriv. of *glôssa, glôtta* tongue, language; see GLOSS[2]] —**di·glot′tic,** *adj.*

di·glyc·er·ide (dī glis′ə rīd′, -ər id), *n. Chem.* an ester obtained from glycerol by the esterification of two hydroxyl groups with fatty acids. Cf. **glyceride.** [DI-[1] + GLYCERIDE]

di·gly·col (dī glī′kôl, -kol), *n. Chem.* See **diethylene glycol.**

di′gly·col′ic ac′id (dī′glī kol′ik, dī′-), *Chem.* a white, crystalline, water-soluble solid, $C_4H_6O_5$, used chiefly in the manufacture of resins and plasticizers. Also, **di′glycol′lic ac′id.** [1870–75; DI-[1] + GLYCOLIC]

dig·ni·fied (dig′nə fīd′), *adj.* characterized or marked by dignity of aspect or manner; stately; decorous: *dignified conduct.* [1660–70; DIGNIFY + -ED[2]] —**dig·ni·fied·ly** (dig′nə fīd′lē, -fī′id-), *adv.* —**dig′ni·fied′·ness,** *n.*
—**Syn.** grave, august, noble.

dig·ni·fy (dig′nə fī′), *v.t.*, **-fied, -fy·ing. 1.** to confer honor or dignity upon; honor; ennoble. **2.** to give a high-sounding title or name to; confer unmerited distinction upon: *to dignify pedantry by calling it scholarship.* [1375–1425; late ME *dignifien* < OF *dignefier* < ML *dignificāre,* equiv. to L *dign(us)* worthy + *-ificāre* -IFY]

dig·ni·tar·y (dig′ni ter′ē), *n., pl.* **-tar·ies.** a person who holds a high rank or office, as in the government or church. [1665–75; DIGNIT(Y) + -ARY] —**dig·ni·tar·i·al** (dig′ni târ′ē əl), *adj.*

dig·ni·ty (dig′ni tē), *n., pl.* **-ties. 1.** bearing, conduct, or speech indicative of self-respect or appreciation of the formality or gravity of an occasion or situation. **2.** nobility or elevation of character; worthiness: *dignity of sentiments.* **3.** elevated rank, office, station, etc. **4.** relative standing; rank. **5.** a sign or token of respect: *an impertinent question unworthy of the dignity of an answer.* **6.** *Archaic.* **a.** person of high rank or title. **b.** such persons collectively. [1175–1225; ME *dignite* < AF, OF < L *dignitās* worthiness, equiv. to *dign(us)* worthy + *-itās* -ITY]

dig·ox·in (dij ok′sin), *n. Pharm.* a cardiac glycoside of purified digitalis, $C_{41}H_{64}O_{14}$, derived from the plant leaves of *Digitalis lanata* and widely used in the treatment of congestive heart failure. [1930; DIG(ITALIS) + (T)OXIN]

di·gram (dī′gram), *n.* a sequence of two adjacent letters or symbols. [1860–65; DI-[1] + -GRAM[1]]

di·graph (dī′graf, -gräf), *n.* a pair of letters represent-

CONCISE PRONUNCIATION KEY: act, cāpe, dâre, pärt; set, ēqual; if, īce; ox, ōver, ôrder, oil, bo͝ok, bo͞ot, out; up, ûrge; child; sing; shoe; thin, *th*at; zh as in *treasure.* ə = *a* as in *alone, e* as in *system, i* as in *easily, o* as in *gallop, u* as in *circus;* ə as in *fire* (fīər), *hour* (ouər). l and n can serve as syllabic consonants, as in *cradle* (krād′l), and *button* (but′n). See the full key inside the front cover.

ing a single speech sound, as *ea* in *meat* or *th* in *path.* [1780–90; DI-[1] + -GRAPH] **—di·graph·ic** (dī graf′ik), *adj.* **—di·graph′i·cal·ly,** *adv.*

di·gress (di gres′, dī-), *v.i.* **1.** to deviate or wander away from the main topic or purpose in speaking or writing; depart from the principal line of argument, plot, study, etc. **2.** *Archaic.* to turn aside. [1520–30; < L *digressus,* ptp. of *digredī* to go off, depart, digress, equiv. to *dī-* DI-[2] + *-gredī,* comb. form of *gradī* to go; cf. GRADE] **—di·gress′er,** *n.* **—di·gress′ing·ly,** *adv.*
—Syn. 1. ramble, stray. See **deviate.**

di·gres·sion (di gresh′ən, dī-), *n.* **1.** the act of digressing. **2.** a passage or section that deviates from the central theme in speech or writing. [1325–75; ME < AF < L *digressiōn-* (s. of *digressiō*) a going away, aside, equiv. to *digress(us)* (see DIGRESS) + *-iōn-* -ION] **—di·gres′sion·al, di·gres′sion·ar′y,** *adj.*
—Syn. 1, 2. deviation, divergence.

di·gres·sive (di gres′iv, dī-), *adj.* tending to digress; departing from the main subject. [1605–15; < L *digressīvus.* See DIGRESS, -IVE] **—di·gres′sive·ly,** *adv.* **—di·gres′sive·ness,** *n.*

di·he·dral (dī hē′drəl), *adj.* **1.** having or formed by two planes. **2.** of or pertaining to a dihedron. **—***n.* **3.** dihedron. **4.** *Aeron.* the angle at which the right and left wings or the halves of any other horizontal surface of an airplane or the like are inclined upward or downward. [1790–1800; DI-[1] + -HEDRAL]

dihe′dral an′gle, *Geom.* **1.** the angle between two planes in a dihedron. **2.** dihedron. [1820–30]

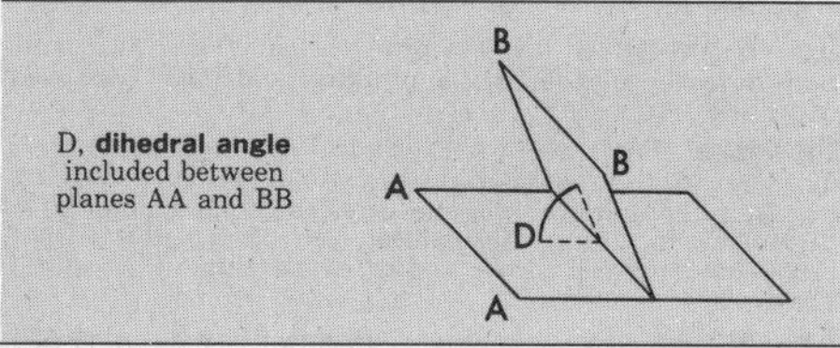

D, **dihedral angle** included between planes AA and BB

di·he·dron (dī hē′drən), *n. Geom.* a figure formed by two intersecting planes. Also called **dihedral, dihedral angle.** [1820–30; DI-[1] + -HEDRON]

Di·hua (*Chin.* dē′hwä′), *n. Pinyin.* former name of **Ürümqi.** Also, **Tihua.**

di·hy·brid (dī hī′brid), *Biol.* **—***n.* **1.** the offspring of parents differing in two specific pairs of genes. **—***adj.* **2.** of or pertaining to such an offspring. [1905–10; DI-[1] + HYBRID] **—di·hy′brid·ism,** *n.*

di·hy·drate (dī hī′drāt), *n. Chem.* a hydrate that contains two molecules of water, as potassium sulfite, $K_2SO_3 \cdot 2H_2O$. [DI-[1] + HYDRATE] **—di·hy′drat·ed,** *adj.*

di·hy·dric (dī hī′drik), *adj. Chem.* (esp. of alcohols and phenols) dihydroxy. [1875–80; DI-[1] + -HYDRIC]

di·hy·dro·er·got·a·mine (dī hī′drō ûr got′ə mēn′, -min, -ûr′gə tam′ēn, -in), *n. Pharm.* an ergot alkaloid, $C_{33}H_{37}N_5O_5$, used in the treatment of various types of migraine headache. [1940–45; DI-[1] + HYDRO-[2] + ERGOTAMINE]

di·hy·dro·mor·phi·none (dī hī′drō môr′fə nōn′), *n. Pharm.* a narcotic compound, $C_{17}H_{19}O_3N$, prepared from morphine and used chiefly as an analgesic. [DI-[1] HYDRO-[2] + MORPHINE + -ONE]

di·hy·dro·strep·to·my·cin (dī hī′drō strep′tə mī′sin), *n. Pharm.* an antibiotic, $C_{21}H_{41}N_7O_{12}$, derived by organic synthesis from and believed to be less toxic than streptomycin: used in the form of its sulfate chiefly in the treatment of tuberculosis. [1945–50; DI-[1] + HYDRO-[2] + STREPTOMYCIN]

di·hy·dro·ta·chys·ter·ol (dī hī′drō tə kis′tə rôl′, -rol′), *n. Pharm.* a white, crystalline, water-insoluble sterol, $C_{28}H_{46}O$, derived from ergosterol: used chiefly in the treatment of hypoparathyroidism. [DI-[1] + HYDRO-[2] + TACHY- + STEROL]

di·hy·drox·y (dī′hī drok′sē), *adj. Chem.* (of a molecule) containing two hydroxyl groups. [DI-[1] + HYDROXY]

di·hy·drox·y·phen·yl·al·a·nine (dī′hī drok′si fen′l al′ə nēn′, -nin, -fēn′l-), *n. Biochem.* dopa. [DIHYDROXY + PHENYLALANINE]

di·i·o·do·meth·ane (dī ī′ə dō meth′ān), *n. Chem.* See **methylene iodide.** [DI-[1] + IODO- + METHANE]

di·i·so·bu·tyl phthal·ate (dī ī′sō byo͞ot′l thal′āt, fthal′-, -ī′sō-), *Chem.* a clear, colorless liquid, $C_{14}H_{20}O_4$, used chiefly as a plasticizer for nitrocellulose. [DI-[1] + ISO- + BUTYL; PHTHAL(IC ACID) + -ATE[2]]

Di·jon (dē zhôɴ′), *n.* a city in and the capital of Côte d'Or, in E central France. 156,787.

Di′jon mus′tard (dē′zhon; *Fr.* dē zhôɴ′), a medium-hot mustard, originally made in Dijon.

dik-dik (dik′dik′), *n.* any antelope of the genus *Madoqua* or *Rhynchotragus,* of eastern and southwestern Africa, growing only to 14 in. (36 cm) high at the shoulder. [1880–85; said to be a name imit. of the animal's cry, but language of orig. not ascertained]

dike[1] (dīk), *n., v.,* **diked, dik·ing.** **—***n.* **1.** an embankment for controlling or holding back the waters of the sea or a river: *They built a temporary dike of sandbags to keep the river from flooding the town.* **2.** a ditch. **3.** a bank of earth formed of material being excavated. **4.** a causeway. **5.** *Brit. Dial.* a low wall or fence, esp. of earth or stone, for dividing or enclosing land. **6.** an obstacle; barrier. **7.** *Geol.* **a.** a long, narrow, cross-cutting mass of igneous rock intruded into a fissure in older rock. **b.** a similar mass of rock composed of other kinds of material, as sandstone. **8.** *Chiefly Australian Slang.* a urinal. **—***v.t.* **9.** to furnish or drain with a dike. **10.** to enclose, restrain, or protect by a dike: *to dike a tract of land.* Also, **dyke.** [bef. 900; ME *dik(e),* OE *dīc* < ON *díki;* akin to DITCH] **—dik′er,** *n.*

dike[2] (dīk), *n. Slang (often disparaging and offensive).* dyke[2]. **—dike′y,** *adj.*

di·ke·tone (dī kē′tōn), *n. Chem.* a compound containing two C=O groups, as $CH_3COCOCH_3$. [1895–1900; DI-[1] + KETONE]

dik·tat (dik tät′), *n.* a harsh, punitive settlement or decree imposed unilaterally on a defeated nation, political party, etc. [1930–35; < G: lit., something dictated < L *dictātus,* ptp. of *dictāre* to DICTATE]

dil, **1.** dilute. **2.** diluted.

di·lac·er·ate (di las′ə rāt′, dī-), *v.t.,* **-at·ed, -at·ing.** to tear apart or to pieces. [1375–1425; late ME (adj.) < L *dīlacerātus* torn to pieces (ptp. of *dīlacerāre*), equiv. to *dī-* DI-[2] + *lacerātus* torn; see LACERATE]

di·lac·er·a·tion (di las′ə rā′shən, dī-), *n.* **1.** the act of dilacerating. **2.** the state of being dilacerated. **3.** *Dentistry.* displacement in the position of a developing tooth, resulting in angulation or distortion. [1375–1425; late ME < LL *dīlacerātiōn-* (s. of *dīlacerātiō*) a tearing to pieces, equiv. to *dīlacerāt(us)* (see DILACERATE) + *-iōn-* -ION]

Di·lan·tin (dī lan′tn, -tin, di-), *Pharm., Trademark.* a brand of diphenylhydantoin.

di·lap·i·date (di lap′i dāt′), *v.,* **-dat·ed, -dat·ing.** **—***v.t.* **1.** to cause or allow (a building, automobile, etc.) to fall into a state of disrepair, as by misuse or neglect (often used passively): *The house had been dilapidated by neglect.* **2.** *Archaic.* to squander; waste. **—***v.i.* **3.** to fall into ruin or decay. [1560–70; < ML *dīlapidātus,* ptp. of *dīlapidāre* to squander (cf. *dīlapidātiō* disrepair), L: to pelt with stones; see DI-[2], LAPIDATE] **—di·lap′i·da′tion,** *n.* **—di·lap′i·da′tor,** *n.*

di·lap·i·dat·ed (di lap′i dā′tid), *adj.* reduced to or fallen into partial ruin or decay, as from age, wear, or neglect. [1800–10; DILAPIDATE + -ED[2]]
—Syn. run-down, tumbledown, ramshackle, rickety.

di·lat·ant (dī lāt′nt, di-), *adj.* **1.** dilating; expanding. **2.** *Physical Chem.* exhibiting an increase in volume on being changed in shape, owing to a wider spacing between particles. **3.** *Petrol.* (of rock) exhibiting an increase in volume owing to rearrangement and recrystallization of constituent grains. [1835–45; < L *dīlātant-* (s. of *dīlātāns*), prp. of *dīlātāre* to DILATE; see -ANT] **—di·lat′an·cy,** *n.*

di·lat·ate (dī lā′tāt, dil′ə tāt′), *adj.* dilated; broadened. [1375–1425; late ME < L *dīlātātus,* ptp. of *dīlātāre* to DILATE; see -ATE[1]]

dil·a·ta·tion (dil′ə tā′shən, dī′lə-), *n.* **1.** a dilated formation or part. **2.** *Pathol.* an abnormal enlargement of an aperture or a canal of the body. **3.** *Surg.* **a.** an enlargement made in a body aperture or canal for surgical or medical treatment. **b.** a restoration to normal patency of an abnormally small body opening or passageway, as of the anus or esophagus. **4.** *Mech.* the increase in volume per unit volume of a homogeneous substance. Also, **dilation.** [1350–1400; ME (< OF) < L *dīlātātiōn-* (s. of *dīlātātiō*), equiv. to *dīlātāt(us)* spread out (ptp. of *dīlātāre* to DILATE) + *iōn-* -ION] **—dil′a·ta′tion·al,** *adj.*

di·late (dī lāt′, di-, dī′lāt), *v.,* **-lat·ed, -lat·ing.** **—***v.t.* **1.** to make wider or larger; cause to expand. **2.** *Archaic.* to describe or develop at length. **—***v.i.* **3.** to spread out; expand. **4.** to speak or write at length; expatiate (often fol. by *on* or *upon*). [1350–1400; ME *dilaten* < MF *dilater,* L *dīlātāre* to spread out, equiv. to *dī-* DI-[2] + *lāt-* (*us*) broad + *-āre* inf. suffix] **—di·lat′a·bil′i·ty,** *n.* **—di·lat′a·ble,** *adj.*
—Syn. 1. See **expand.**

di·la·tion (dī lā′shən, di-), *n.* **1.** the act of dilating; state of being dilated. **2.** dilatation. [1590–1600; DILATE + -ION]

di·la·tive (dī lā′tiv, di-, dī′lā-), *adj.* serving or tending to dilate. [1520–30; DILATE + -IVE]

dil·a·tom·e·ter (dil′ə tom′i tər), *n. Physics.* a device for measuring expansion caused by changes in temperature in substances. [1880–85; DILATE + -O- + -METER] **—dil·a·to·met·ric** (dil′ə tə me′trik), *adj.* **—dil′a·to·met′ri·cal·ly,** *adv.* **—dil′a·tom′e·try,** *n.*

di·la·tor (dī lā′tər, di-, dī′lā-), *n.* **1.** *Anat.* a muscle that dilates some cavity of the body. **2.** *Surg.* an instrument for dilating body canals, orifices, or cavities. Also, **di·lat′er.** [1595–1605; DILATE + -OR[2]]

dil·a·to·ry (dil′ə tôr′ē, -tōr′ē), *adj.* **1.** tending to delay or procrastinate; slow; tardy. **2.** intended to cause delay, gain time, or defer decision: *a dilatory strategy.* [1250–1300; ME (< AF) < L *dīlātōrius,* equiv. to *dīlā-,* suppletive s. of *differre* to postpone (see DIFFER) + *-tōrius* -TORY[1]] **—dil′a·to′ri·ly,** *adv.* **—dil′a·to′ri·ness,** *n.*

Di·lau·did (dī lô′did, di-), *Pharm., Trademark.* a brand name for the hydrochloride salt of dihydromorphinone.

dil·do (dil′dō), *n., pl.* **-dos.** *Slang.* an artificial erect penis, used as a sexual aid. [1585–95; of obscure orig.]

di·lem·ma (di lem′ə), *n.* **1.** a situation requiring a choice between equally undesirable alternatives. **2.** any difficult or perplexing situation or problem. **3.** *Logic.* a form of syllogism in which the major premise is formed of two or more hypothetical propositions and the minor premise is a disjunctive proposition, as "If A, then B; if C then D. Either A or C. Therefore, either B or D." [1515–25; < LL < Gk *dílēmma,* equiv. to *di-* DI-[1] + *lêmma* an assumption, premise, deriv. of *lambánein* to take] **—dil·em·mat·ic** (dil′ə mat′ik), **dil′em·mat′i·cal, di·lem′·mic,** *adj.* **—dil′em·mat′i·cal·ly,** *adv.*
—Syn. 1. See **predicament. 2.** question, difficulty.

dil·et·tante (dil′i tänt′, dil′i tänt′, -tän′tä, -tan′tē), *n., pl.* **-tantes, -tan·ti** (-tän′tē), *adj.* **—***n.* **1.** a person who takes up an art, activity, or subject merely for amusement, esp. in a desultory or superficial way; dabbler. **2.** a lover of an art or science, esp. of a fine art. **—***adj.* **3.** of or pertaining to dilettantes. [1725–35; < It, n. use of prp. of *dilettare* < L *dēlectāre* to DELIGHT] **—dil′et·tan′tish, dil′et·tan′te·ish,** *adj.*
—Syn. 1. amateur.

dil·et·tant·ism (dil′i tän tiz′əm, -tan-), *n.* the practices or characteristics of a dilettante. Also, **dil·et·tan·te·ism** (dil′i tän′tē iz′əm, -tan′-). [1800–10; DILETTANTE + -ISM]

Di·li (dil′ē), *n.* a city on NE Timor, in S Indonesia. 52,158. Also, **Dilli, Dilly.**

dil·i·gence[1] (dil′i jəns), *n.* **1.** constant and earnest effort to accomplish what is undertaken; persistent exertion of body or mind. **2.** *Law.* the degree of care and caution required by the circumstances of a person. **3.** *Obs.* care; caution. [1300–50; ME *deligence* (< AF) < L *dīligentia,* equiv. to *dīligent-* (s. of *dīligēns*) DILIGENT + *-ia;* see -ENCE]

dil·i·gence[2] (dil′i jəns; *Fr.* dē lē zhäns′), *n., pl.* **-gen·ces** (-jən siz; *Fr.* -zhäns′). a public stagecoach, esp. as formerly used in France. [1735–45; short for F *carosse de diligence* speed coach]

diligence[2]

dil·i·gent (dil′i jənt), *adj.* **1.** constant in effort to accomplish something; attentive and persistent in doing anything: *a diligent student.* **2.** done or pursued with persevering attention; painstaking: *a diligent search of the files.* [1300–50; ME (< AF) < L *dīligent-* (s. of *dīligēns*), prp. of *dīligere* to choose, like, equiv. to *dī-* DI-[2] + *-ligere* (comb. form of *legere* to choose, read); see -ENT] **—dil′i·gent·ly,** *adv.* **—dil′i·gent·ness,** *n.*
—Syn. 1. industrious, assiduous, sedulous. See **busy. 2.** indefatigable, untiring, tireless, unremitting.

dill (dil), *n.* **1.** a plant, *Anethum graveolens,* of the parsley family, having aromatic seeds and finely divided leaves, both of which are used for flavoring food. **2.** dillweed. **3.** See **dill pickle.** [bef. 900; ME *di(l)le,* OE *dile;* akin to G *Dill,* Sw *dill*] **—dilled,** *adj.*

Dil·li (dil′ē), *n.* Dili. Also, **Dil′ly.**

Dil·lin·ger (dil′in jər), *n.* **John,** 1902–34, U.S. bank robber and murderer.

Dil·lon (dil′ən), *n.* **1. C(larence) Douglas,** born 1909, U.S. lawyer and government official, born in Switzerland: Secretary of the Treasury 1961–65. **2. John Forrest,** 1831–1914, U.S. jurist and legal scholar.

dill′ pick′le, a cucumber pickle flavored with dill. [1900–05]

dill·weed (dil′wēd′), *n.* the leaves of the dill plant, esp. when used dried and as a food flavoring. [DILL + WEED[1]]

dil·ly (dil′ē), *n., pl.* **-lies.** *Informal.* something or someone regarded as remarkable, unusual, etc.: *a dilly of a movie.* [1930–35; *Amer.;* earlier as adj.: wonderful, appar. a shortening of DELIGHTFUL or DELICIOUS, with -Y[1] (now taken as -Y[2])]

dil′ly bag′ (dil′ē), *Australian.* a bag made from reeds, grasses, or hair. [1840–50; *dilly* < Waga (Australian Aboriginal language spoken around Kingaroy, S Queensland) *dila*]

dil·ly·dal·ly (dil′ē dal′ē, -dal′-), *v.i.,* **-lied, -ly·ing.** to waste time, esp. by indecision; vacillate; trifle; loiter. [1735–45; gradational redupl. of DALLY]

dil·ti·a·zem (dil tī′ə zem′), *n. Pharm.* a white to whitish crystalline powder, $C_{22}H_{26}N_2O_4S$, used as a calcium blocker in the treatment of angina pectoris. [presumably from isolated and rearranged letters of the chemical name]

dil·u·ent (dil′yo͞o ənt), *adj.* **1.** serving to dilute; diluting. **—***n.* **2.** a diluting substance. [1715–25; < L *dīluent-* (s. of *dīluēns*), prp. of *dīluere* to DILUTE; see -ENT]

di·lute (di lo͞ot′, dī-; *adj. also* dī′lo͞ot), *v.,* **-lut·ed, -lut·ing,** *adj.* **—***v.t.* **1.** to make (a liquid) thinner or weaker by the addition of water or the like. **2.** to make fainter, as a color. **3.** to reduce the strength, force, or efficiency of by admixture. **—***v.i.* **4.** to become diluted. **—***adj.* **5.** reduced in strength, as a chemical by admixture; weak: *a dilute solution.* [1545–55; < L *dīlūtus* washed away, dissolved (ptp. of *dīluere*), equiv. to *dī-* DI-[2] + *-lūtus,* comb. form of *lautus* (*lav(ere)* to wash + *-tus* ptp. suffix)] **—di·lut′er, di·lu′tor,** *n.* **—di·lu′tive,** *adj.*
—Syn. 3. weaken, temper, mitigate, diminish.

di·lu·tion (di lo͞o′shən, dī-), *n.* **1.** the act of diluting or the state of being diluted. **2.** something diluted. [1640–50; DILUTE + -ION]

di·lu·vi·al (di lo͞o′vē əl), *adj.* **1.** pertaining to or caused by a flood or deluge. **2.** *Geol. Now Rare.* pertaining to or consisting of diluvium. Also, **di·lu′vi·an.** [1650–60; < LL *dīluviālis,* equiv. to *dīluvi(um)* flood (see DELUGE) + *-ālis* -AL[1]]

di·lu·vi·um (di lo͞o′vē əm), *n., pl.* **-vi·a** (-vē ə), **-vi·ums.** *Geol. Now Rare.* a coarse surficial deposit formerly attributed to a general deluge but now regarded as glacial drift. Also, **di·lu′vi·on.** [1810–20; < L *dīluvium* flood; see DELUGE]

dim (dim), *adj.,* **dim·mer, dim·mest,** *v.,* **dimmed, dim·ming.** **—***adj.* **1.** not bright; obscure from lack of light or

CONCISE ETYMOLOGY KEY: <, descended or borrowed from; >, whence; b., blend of, blended; c., cognate with; cf., compare; deriv., derivative; equiv., equivalent; imit., imitative; obl., oblique; r., replacing; s., stem; sp., spelling, spelled; resp., respelling, respelled; trans., translation; ?, origin unknown; *, unattested; ‡, probably earlier than. See the full key inside the front cover.

emitted light: *a dim room; a dim flashlight.* **2.** not seen clearly or in detail; indistinct: *a dim object in the distance.* **3.** not clear to the mind; vague: *a dim idea.* **4.** not brilliant; dull in luster: *a dim color.* **5.** not clear or distinct to the senses; faint: *a dim sound.* **6.** not seeing clearly: *eyes dim with tears.* **7.** tending to be unfavorable; not likely to happen, succeed, be favorable, etc.: *a dim chance of winning.* **8.** not understanding clearly. **9.** rather stupid; dim-witted. **10. take a dim view of,** to regard with disapproval, skepticism, or dismay: *Her mother takes a dim view of her choice of friends.* —*v.t.* **11.** to make dim or dimmer. **12.** to switch (the headlights of a vehicle) from the high to the low beam. —*v.i.* **13.** to become or grow dim or dimmer. **14. dim out,** (in wartime) to reduce the night illumination of (a city, ship, etc.) to make it less visible from the air or sea, as a protection from enemy aircraft or ships. [bef. 1000; ME, OE *dim(me),* c. OFris *dim,* ON *dimmr*] —**dim′ly,** *adv.* —**dim′ma•ble,** *adj.* —**dim′ness,** *n.*
—**Syn. 1.** See **dark. 3.** unclear, faint, indefinite, indistinct, fuzzy, hazy. **11.** darken, cloud. **13.** dull, fade.

dim., 1. dimension. **2.** (in prescriptions) one-half. [< L *dīmidius*] **3.** diminish. **4.** diminuendo. **5.** diminutive.

Di•Mag•gi•o (də mä′jē ō′, -maj′ē ō′), *n.* **Joseph Paul** (*Joe*), born 1914, U.S. baseball player.

dim•bulb (dim′bulb′, -bulb′), *n. Slang.* a stupid person; dimwit. [1930–35, *Amer.*; DIM + BULB]

dime (dīm), *n.* **1.** a cupronickel-clad coin of the U.S. and Canada, the 10th part of a dollar, equal to 10 cents. **2.** *Slang.* **a.** ten dollars. **b.** a 10-year prison sentence. **c.** See **dime bag. 3. a dime a dozen,** *Informal.* so abundant that the value has decreased; readily available. [1350–1400; ME < AF, OF *di(s)me* < L *decima* tenth part, tithe, n. use of fem. of *decimus* tenth, deriv. of *decem* TEN]

dime′ bag′, *Slang.* a packet containing an amount of an illegal drug selling for ten dollars. Also called **dime.**

di•men•hy•dri•nate (dī′men hī′drə nāt′), *n. Pharm.* a synthetic, crystalline, antihistamine powder, $C_{17}H_{22}NO \cdot C_7H_6ClN_4O_2$, used in the treatment of allergic disorders and as a preventive for seasickness and airsickness. [1945–50; DIME(THYL) + (AMI)N(E) + HYDR(AM)INE + -ATE[2]]

dime′ nov′el, a cheap melodramatic or sensational novel, usually in paperback and selling for ten cents, esp. such an adventure novel popular c1850 to c1920. [1860–65, *Amer.*]

di•men•sion (di men′shən, dī-), *n.* **1.** *Math.* **a.** a property of space; extension in a given direction: *A straight line has one dimension, a parallelogram has two dimensions, and a parallelepiped has three dimensions.* **b.** the generalization of this property to spaces with curvilinear extension, as the surface of a sphere. **c.** the generalization of this property to vector spaces and to Hilbert space. **d.** the generalization of this property to fractals, which can have dimensions that are noninteger real numbers. **e.** extension in time: *Space-time has three dimensions of space and one of time.* **2.** Usually, **dimensions. a.** measurement in length, width, and thickness. **b.** scope; importance: *the dimensions of a problem.* **3.** unit (def. 6). **4.** magnitude; size: *Matter has dimension.* **5.** *Topology.* **a.** a magnitude that, independently or in conjunction with other such magnitudes, serves to define the location of an element within a given set, as of a point on a line, an object in a space, or an event in space-time. **b.** the number of elements in a finite basis of a given vector space. **6.** *Physics.* any of a set of basic kinds of quantity, as mass, length, and time, in terms of which all other kinds of quantity can be expressed; usually denoted by capital letters, with appropriate exponents, placed in brackets: *The dimensions of velocity are* [LT^{-1}]. Cf. **dimensional analysis. 7. dimensions,** *Informal.* the measurements of a woman's bust, waist, and hips, in that order: *The chorus girl's dimensions were 38-24-36.* **8.** See **dimension lumber.** —*v.t.* **9.** to shape or fashion to the desired dimensions: *Dimension the shelves so that they fit securely into the cabinet.* **10.** to indicate the dimensions of an item, area, etc., on (a sketch or drawing). [1375–1425; late ME *dimensioun* (< AF) < L *dīmēnsiōn-* (s. of *dīmēnsiō*) a measuring, equiv. to *dīmēns(us)* measured out (ptp. of *dīmētīrī,* equiv. to *dī-* DI-[2] + *mētīrī* to measure) + *-iōn-* -ION] —**di•men′sion•al,** *adj.* —**di•men′sion•al′i•ty,** *n.* —**di•men′sion•al•ly,** *adv.* —**di•men′sion•less,** *adj.*
—**Syn. 2b.** range, extent, magnitude.

dimen′sional anal′ysis, *Physics.* a method for comparing the dimensions of the physical quantities occurring in a problem to find relationships between the quantities without having to solve the problem completely. Cf. **dimension** (def. 6). [1920–25]

dimen′sion lum′ber, 1. building lumber cut to standard or specified sizes. **2.** sawed lumber from 2 to 5 in. (5 to 12.7 cm) thick and from 4 to 12 in. (10.2 to 30.5 cm) wide. Also called **dimension.** [1870–75]

dimen′sion stone′, quarried and squared stone 2 ft. (0.6 m) or more in length and width and of specified thickness.

di•mer (dī′mər), *n. Chem.* **1.** a molecule composed of two identical, simpler molecules. **2.** a polymer derived from two identical monomers. Cf. **oligomer.** [1905–10; DI-[1] + -MER] —**di•mer•ic** (dī mer′ik), *adj.*

di•mer•cap•rol (dī′mər kap′rôl, -rol), *n. Chem.* a colorless, oily, viscous liquid, $C_3H_8OS_2$, originally developed as an antidote to lewisite and now used in treating bismuth, gold, mercury, and arsenic poisoning. Also called **BAL, British Anti-Lewisite.** [1945–50; contr. of *di-mercapto-propanol* (*mercapto-* comb. form of MERCAPTAN)]

di•mer•ize (dī′mə rīz′), *v.i., v.t.* **-ized, -iz•ing.** *Chem.* to form (a dimer), as in polymerization. Also, *esp. Brit.,* **di′mer•ise′.** [1850–55; back formation from *dimerization;* see DIMER, -IZE] —**di′mer•i•za′tion,** *n.*

dim•er•ous (dim′ər əs), *adj.* **1.** consisting of or divided into two parts. **2.** *Bot.* (of flowers) having two members in each whorl. [1820–30; < NL *dimerus* < Gk *dimerés* bipartite. See DI-[1], -MEROUS] —**dim′er•ism,** *n.*

dimerous flower

dime′ store′, 1. five-and-ten (def. 1). **2.** *Bowling.* a split in which the five and ten pins remain standing. [1925–30, *Amer.*]

dim•e•ter (dim′i tər), *n. Pros.* a verse or line of two measures or feet, as *He is gone on the mountain,/He is lost to the forest.* [1580–90; < LL *dimeter* < Gk *dímetros* of two measures, a dimeter, equiv. to *di-* DI-[1] + *-metros,* adj. deriv. of *métron* METER[1]]

di•meth•o•ate (dī meth′ō āt′), *n. Chem.* a highly toxic crystalline compound, $C_5H_{12}NO_3PS_2$, used as an insecticide. [1955–60; prob. *dimeth(yl)* + *-(thi)oate,* components of the chemical name]

di•me•thox•y•meth•ane (dī′mə thok′sē meth′ān), *n. Chem.* methylal. [DI-[1] + METH(YL) + OXY-[2] + METHANE]

di•meth•yl (dī meth′əl), *n. Chem.* ethane. [1865–70; DI-[1] + METHYL]

di•meth•yl•an•thran•i•late (dī meth′əl an thran′l āt′, -it, -an′thrə nl āt′), *n. Chem.* a colorless or pale-yellow liquid, $C_9H_{11}NO_2$, having a grape odor: used chiefly in perfumes, flavorings, and drugs. [DIMETHYL + ANTHR(ACENE) + ANIL(INE) + -ATE[2]]

di•meth•yl•ben•zene (dī meth′əl ben′zēn, -ben zēn′), *n. Chem.* xylene. [1865–70; DI-[1] + METHYL + BENZENE]

di•meth•yl•car•bi•nol (dī meth′əl kär′bə nôl′, -nol′), *n. Chem.* See **isopropyl alcohol.** [1865–70; DI- + METHYL + CARBINOL]

di•meth•yl•hy•dra•zine (dī meth′əl hī′drə zēn′, -zin), *n. Chem.* a flammable, highly toxic, and colorless liquid, $C_2H_8N_2$, used as a component in jet and rocket fuels. [DIMETHYL + HYDRAZINE]

di•meth•yl•ke•tol (dī meth′əl kē′tôl, -tol), *n. Chem.* acetoin. [DI-[1] + METHYL + KET(ONE) + -OL[1]]

di•meth•yl•ke•tone (dī meth′əl kē′tōn), *n. Chem.* acetone. [DIMETHYL + KETONE]

di•meth•yl•meth•ane (dī meth′əl meth′ān), *n. Chem.* propane. [DI-[1] + METHYL + METHANE]

di•meth•yl•ni•tros•a•mine (dī meth′əl nī trō′sə mēn′, -nī′trōs am′in), *n. Chem.* a yellow, water-soluble carcinogenic liquid, $C_2H_6N_2O$, found in tobacco smoke and certain foods: known to be a potent carcinogen. *Abbr.:* DMN, DMNA [1960–65; DIMETHYL + NITROSAMINE]

dimeth′yl sul′fate, *Chem.* a colorless or yellow, slightly water-soluble, poisonous liquid, $(CH_3)_2SO_2$, used chiefly in organic synthesis. Also, **methyl sulfate.**

dimeth′yl sulf•ox′ide (sul fok′sīd), *Chem.* See **DMSO.** [1960–65]

di•meth•yl•tryp•ta•mine (dī meth′əl trip′tə mēn′, -min), *n. Pharm.* a hallucinogenic drug, $C_{12}H_{16}N_2$, with an action of short duration. *Abbr.:* DMT [1965–70; DIMETHYL + TRYPTAMINE]

di•met•ro•don (dī me′trə don′), *n.* an extinct carnivorous mammallike reptile of the genus *Dimetrodon,* dominant in North America during the Permian Period, up to 10 ft. (3.1 m) long and usually bearing spinal sails. [< NL (1878), equiv. to Gk *dímetr(os)* having two measures (see DIMETER) + *odṓn* tooth; appar. so named in reference to the large size of the anterior incisors relative to the other teeth]

dimin., 1. diminish. **2.** diminuendo. **3.** diminutive.

di•min•ish (di min′ish), *v.t.* **1.** to make or cause to seem smaller, less, less important, etc.; lessen; reduce. **2.** *Archit.* to give (a column) a form tapering inward from bottom to top. **3.** *Music.* to make (an interval) smaller by a chromatic half step than the corresponding perfect or minor interval. **4.** to detract from the authority, honor, stature, or reputation of; disparage. —*v.i.* **5.** to lessen; decrease. [1400–50; late ME; b. *diminuen* (< AF *diminuer* < ML *diminuere* for L *dēminuere* to make smaller) and *minishen* MINISH] —**di•min′ish•a•ble,** *adj.* —**di•min′ish•ment,** *n.*
—**Syn. 5.** See **decrease.**

dimin′ishing returns′, 1. any rate of profit, production, benefits, etc., that beyond a certain point fails to increase proportionately with added investment, effort, or skill. **2.** Also called **law of diminishing returns.** *Econ.* the fact, often stated as a law or principle, that when any factor of production, as labor, is increased while other factors, as capital and land, are held constant in amount, the output per unit of the variable factor will eventually diminish. [1805–15]

di•min•u•en•do (di min′yōō en′dō), *adj., adv., n., pl.* **-does.** *Music.* —*adj., adv.* **1.** gradually reducing in force or loudness; decrescendo (opposed to *crescendo*). —*n.* **2.** a gradual reduction of force or loudness. **3.** a diminuendo passage. *Symbol:* > [1765–75; < It, prp. of *diminuire;* see DIMINISH]

dim•i•nu•tion (dim′ə nōō′shən, -nyōō′-), *n.* **1.** the act, fact, or process of diminishing; lessening; reduction. **2.** *Music.* the repetition or imitation of a subject or theme in notes of shorter duration than those first used. [1275–1325; ME *diminucion* < AF *diminuciun* < L *dīminūtiōn-* (s. of *dīminūtiō*), for *dēminūtiōn-* (s. of *dēminūtiō*) (by influence of *dimunuere;* see DIMINISH), equiv. to *dēminūt(us)* (ptp. of *dēminuere,* equiv. to *dē-* DE- + *minuere* to lessen) + *-iōn-* -ION]

di•min•u•tive (di min′yə tiv), *adj.* **1.** small; little; tiny: *a diminutive building for a model-train layout.* **2.** *Gram.* pertaining to or productive of a form denoting smallness, familiarity, affection, or triviality, as the suffix *-let,* in *droplet* from *drop.* —*n.* **3.** a small thing or person. **4.** *Gram.* a diminutive element or formation. **5.** *Heraldry.* a charge, as an ordinary, smaller in length or breadth than the usual. [1350–1400; ME < ML *dīminūtīvus,* equiv. to L *dīminūt(us)* lessened (for *dēminūtus;* see DIMINUTION) + *-īvus* -IVE] —**di•min′u•tive•ly,** *adv.* —**di•min′u•tive•ness,** *n.*
—**Syn. 1.** See **little.**

dim•is•so•ry (dim′ə sôr′ē, -sōr′ē), *adj.* dismissing or giving permission to depart. [1425–75; late ME: a dimissory letter < LL *dīmissōrius,* equiv. to L *dīmitt(ere)* to send away, release (see DEMIT) + *-tōrius* -TORY[1]]

Di•mi•tri•os I (di mē′trē əs), (*Dimitrios Papadopoulos*), 1914–91, Archbishop of Constantinople and Ecumenical Patriarch of the Eastern Orthodox Church 1972–91.

Di•mi•trov (di mē′trôf), *n.* **Ge•or•gi** (ge ôr′gi), 1882–1949, Bulgarian political leader: premier 1946–49.

Di•mi•tro•vo (di mē′trô vo), *n.* a city in W Bulgaria, near Sofia. 79,300. Formerly, **Pernik.**

dim•i•ty (dim′i tē), *n., pl.* **-ties.** a thin cotton fabric, white, dyed, or printed, woven with a stripe or check of heavier yarn. [1400–50; earlier *dimite,* late ME *demyt* < ML *dimettum* < Gk *dímiton,* n. use of neut. of *dímitos* double-threaded, equiv. to *di-* DI-[1] + *mít(os)* warp thread + *-os* adj. suffix; source of final syll. unclear]

dim•mer (dim′ər), *n.* **1.** a person or thing that dims. **2.** Also called **dim′mer switch′.** a rheostat or similar device by which the intensity of an electric light may be varied. **3. dimmers, a.** the low-beam headlights of an automobile or truck. **b.** the small, parking lights of an automobile. [1815–25; DIM + -ER[1]]

di•morph (dī′môrf), *n. Crystall.* either of the two forms assumed by a mineral or other chemical substance exhibiting dimorphism. [< Gk *dímorphos* having two shapes; see DI-[1], -MORPH]

di•mor•phism (dī môr′fiz əm), *n.* **1.** *Zool.* the occurrence of two forms distinct in structure, coloration, etc., among animals of the same species. Cf. **sexual dimorphism. 2.** *Bot.* the occurrence of two different forms of flowers, leaves, etc., on the same plant or on different plants of the same species. **3.** *Crystall.* the property of some substances of crystallizing in two chemically identical but crystallographically distinct forms. [1825–35; DIMORPH + -ISM]

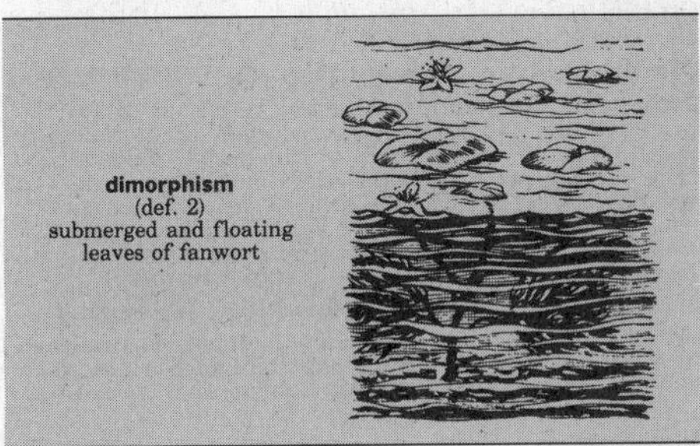
dimorphism (def. 2) submerged and floating leaves of fanwort

di•mor•phite (dī môr′fīt), *n.* a mineral, arsenic sulfide, As_4S_3, yellow-orange in color and similar in its properties to orpiment. [1850–55; DIMORPH + -ITE[1]]

di•mor•phous (dī môr′fəs), *adj.* having two forms. Also, **di•mor′phic.** [1825–35; < Gk *dímorphos.* See DI-MORPH, -OUS]

dim-out (dim′out′), *n.* **1.** a reduction or concealment of night lighting in wartime to make the source less visible to an enemy from the air or sea. **2.** a reduction of night lighting caused by a failure in an electric generating system or a reduction in its output. Also, **dim′out′.** Cf. **blackout** (def. 2), **brownout.** [1940–45; DIM + (BLACK)OUT]

dim•ple (dim′pəl), *n., v.,* **-pled, -pling.** —*n.* **1.** a small, natural hollow area or crease, permanent or transient, in some soft part of the human body, esp. one formed in the cheek in smiling. **2.** any similar slight depression. —*v.t.* **3.** to mark with or as if with dimples; produce dimples in: *A smile dimpled her face.* **4.** *Metalworking.* **a.** to dent (a metal sheet) so as to permit use of bolts or rivets with countersunk heads. **b.** to mark (a metal object) with a drill point as a guide for further drilling. —*v.i.* **5.** to form or show dimples. [1350–1400; ME *dimpel,* OE **dympel;* c. G *Tümpel* pool] —**dim′ply,** *adj.*

dim sum (dim′ sum′), *Chinese Cookery.* small dumplings, usually steamed or fried and filled with meat, seafood, vegetables, condiments, etc. [1965–70; < Chin dial. (Guangdong) *dim sàm,* equiv. to Chin *diǎnxīn* (*diǎn* dot, speck + *xīn* heart)]

dim•wit (dim′wit′), *n. Slang.* a stupid or slow-thinking person. [1920–25, *Amer.*; DIM + WIT[1]] —**dim′wit′ted,** *adj.* —**dim′wit′ted•ly,** *adv.* —**dim′wit′ted•ness,** *n.*
—**Syn.** dummy, nitwit, numskull, booby, dumbbell.

din[1] (din), *n., v.,* **dinned, din•ning.** —*n.* **1.** a loud, confused noise; a continued loud or tumultuous sound; noisy clamor. —*v.t.* **2.** to assail with din. **3.** to sound or utter with clamor or persistent repetition. —*v.i.* **4.** to make a din. [bef. 900; ME *din(e)* (n.), OE *dyne, dynn;* c. ON *dynr* noise, OHG *tuni,* Skt *dhuni* roaring]
—**Syn. 1.** uproar. See **noise.**

din[2] (din), *n.* (*used with a plural v.*) *Islam.* religion, esp. the religious observances of a Muslim. Cf. **Ibada, Pillars of Islam.** [< Ar *din* religion < Pers *dēn*]

CONCISE PRONUNCIATION KEY: act, cāpe, dâre, pärt; set, ēqual; *if,* īce; ox, ōver, ôrder, oil, bŏŏk, bōōt, out; up, ûrge; child; sing; shoe; thin, *th*at; zh as in *treasure.* ə = *a* as in *alone, e* as in *system, i* as in *easily, o* as in *gallop, u* as in *circus;* ᵊ as in *fire* (fīᵊr), *hour* (ouᵊr). l and n can serve as syllabic consonants, as in *cradle* (krād′l), and *button* (but′n). See the full key inside the front cover.

DIN, *Photog.* a designation, originating in Germany, of the speed of a particular film emulsion. [< G *D(eutsche) I(ndustrie) N(ormen)* German industrial standards (later construed as *Das ist Norm* that is (the) standard), registered mark of the German Institute for Standardization]

Din., (in Yugoslavia) dinar; dinars.

Di•nah (dī′nə), *n.* **1.** Also, *Douay Bible,* **Di′na.** the daughter of Jacob and Leah. Gen. 30:21. **2.** a female given name: from a Hebrew word meaning "vindicated."

di•nar (di när′), *n.* **1.** any of various former coins of the Near East, esp. gold coins issued by Islamic governments. **2.** a money of account of Iran, the 100th part of a rial. **3.** an aluminum coin and monetary unit of Yugoslavia, equal to 100 paras. *Abbr.:* Din. **4.** a paper money, silver or nickel coin, and monetary unit of Iraq, equal to 1000 fils or 20 dirhams. *Abbr.:* ID. **5.** a paper money and monetary unit of Jordan, equal to 1000 fils. *Abbr.:* JD. **6.** a paper money and monetary unit of Kuwait, equal to 10 dirhams or 1000 fils. *Abbr.:* KD. **7.** a paper money and monetary unit of Tunisia, equal to 10 dirhams or 1000 millimes. **8.** a paper money, cupronickel coin, and monetary unit of Algeria, equal to 100 centimes. *Abbr.:* DA. **9.** a paper money and monetary unit of Bahrain, equal to 1000 fils. *Abbr.:* BD. **10.** a paper money and monetary unit of Libya, equal to 1000 dirham: replaced the pound in 1971. *Abbr.:* LD. **11.** (formerly) a paper money and monetary unit of the People's Democratic Republic of Yemen, equal to 1000 fils. *Abbr.:* YD. [1625–35; < Ar, Pers *dīnār* < LGk *dēnárion* < L *dēnārius* a ten-as coin; see DENARY]

din•ar•chy (din′är kē), *n., pl.* **-chies.** duarchy. [1650–60; < F (obs.) *dinarchie,* equiv. to *din-* erroneous for DI-¹ (after *bi-, bin-*) + *-archie* -ARCHY]

Di•nard (dē NAR′), *n.* a city in W France: seaside resort. 9068.

Di•nar•ic (di nar′ik), *adj.* **1.** of or pertaining to the Alpine region of Yugoslavia. **2.** of, pertaining to, or characteristic of a Caucasoid subracial type with a long face and round, often flattened head, found chiefly in eastern Europe, esp. in Yugoslavia and Albania: no longer in technical use.

Dinar′ic Alps′, a range of the Alps paralleling the E Adriatic coast from Slovenia to N Albania: extends across W Croatia, and most of Bosnia and Herzegovina, and the Yugoslav republic of Montenegro. Higest peak, 8714 ft. (2656 m).

din-din (din′din′), *n. Baby Talk.* dinner. [1900–05; by shortening and redupl.]

d'In•dy (daN dē′), **Vin•cent** (VAN säN′). See **Indy, d'.**

dine (dīn), *v.,* **dined, din•ing,** *n.* —*v.i.* **1.** to eat the principal meal of the day; have dinner. **2.** to take any meal. —*v.t.* **3.** to entertain at dinner. **4. dine out,** to take a meal, esp. the principal or more formal meal of the day, away from home, as in a hotel or restaurant. —*n.* **5.** *Scot.* dinner. [1250–1300; ME *dinen* < AF, OF *di(s)ner* < VL **disjējūnāre* to break one's fast, equiv. to L *dis-* DIS-¹ + LL *jējūnāre* to fast; see JEJUNE]

Dine (dīn), *n.* **James** *(Jim),* born 1935, U.S. painter.

din•er (dī′nər), *n.* **1.** a person who dines. **2.** a railroad dining car. **3.** a restaurant built like such a car. **4.** a small, informal, and usually inexpensive restaurant. [1800–10; DINE + -ER¹]

di•ner•gate (dī nûr′git), *n.* a soldier ant. [DIN(O)- + ERGATE]

di•ner•ic (dī ner′ik, di-), *adj. Physics.* of or pertaining to the face of separation of two immiscible liquid phases. [1900–05; DI-¹ + LGk *nēr(on)* water + -IC]

di•ne•ro (di nâr′ō; *Sp.* dē ne′RÔ), *n., pl.* **-ne•ros** (-nâr′ōz; *Sp.* -ne′RÔs). **1.** a former silver coin of Peru, the 10th part of a sol. **2.** any of various billon or copper coins of Spain, issued from the 11th to the 16th centuries. **3.** *Slang.* money. [1825–35; < Sp: money, treasure, dinero < L *dēnārius;* see DENARIUS, DENARY]

din•er-out (dī′nər out′), *n., pl.* **din•ers-out.** a person who dines out. [1800–10; *dine out* + -ER¹]

Din•e•sen (din′ə sən dē′nə-), *n.* **I•sak** (ē′säk), (pen name of *Baroness Karen Blixen*), 1885–1962, Danish author.

di•nette (dī net′), *n.* **1.** a small space or alcove, often in or near the kitchen, serving as an informal dining area. **2.** Also called **dinette′ set′.** a small table and set of matching chairs for such a space or alcove. [1925–30; *Amer.;* DINE + -ETTE]

ding¹ (ding), *v.t.* **1.** to cause to make a ringing sound. **2.** to speak about insistently. —*v.i.* **3.** to make a ringing sound. **4.** to talk insistently. —*n.* **5.** a ringing sound. [1575–85; see DING-DONG]

ding² (ding), *Informal.* —*v.t.* **1.** to cause surface damage to; dent: *Flying gravel had dinged the car's fenders.* **2.** to strike with force; hit: *The catcher was dinged on the shoulder by a wild throw.* **3.** to blackball: *Only one freshman was dinged by the fraternity.* —*n.* **4.** dent; nick: *The surfboard has a few dings in it from scraping over rocks.* [1250–1300; ME *dingen, dengen,* prob. OE **dingan;* akin to OE *dencgan,* ON *dengja*]

ding-a-ling (ding′ə ling′), *n. Slang.* a stupid, foolish, or eccentric person. [1930–35; rhyming compound imit. of a bell]

ding an sich (ding′ än ziKH′), *pl.* ***ding•e an sich*** (ding′ə än ziKH′). *German.* thing-in-itself.

ding•bat (ding′bat′), *n.* **1.** *Slang.* an eccentric, silly, or empty-headed person. **2.** dingus. **3.** *Print.* an ornamental piece of type for borders, separators, decorations, etc. **4.** an object, as a brick, serving as a missile. [1830–40; orig. uncert.]

ding-dong (ding′dông′, -dong′), *n.* **1.** the sound of a bell. **2.** any similar sound of repeated strokes. **3.** *Slang.* ding-a-ling. —*adj.* **4.** characterized by or resembling the sound of a bell. **5.** marked by rapid alternation of retaliatory action: *a ding-dong struggle.* [1550–60; gradational compound based on *ding,* appar. b. DIN¹ and RING²]

dinge (dinj), *n.* **1.** the condition of being dingy. **2.** *Slang (disparaging and offensive).* a black person. [1840–50; back formation from DINGY]

ding•er (ding′ər), *n. Slang.* **1.** humdinger. **2.** *Baseball.* See **home run.** [1800–10; perh. DING¹ + -ER¹]

din•ghy (ding′gē), *n., pl.* **-ghies.** **1.** any small boat designed as a tender or lifeboat, esp. a small ship's boat, rowed, sailed, or driven by a motor. **2.** a boat used by warships, having four single-banked oars and a spritsail. **3.** any of various rowing or sailing boats used in sheltered waters along the Indian coasts to transport passengers and freight. **4.** an inflatable life raft. [1785–95; < Bengali *diṅgi,* Hindi *ḍiṅgī,* dim. of *ḍiṅgā* boat]

din•gle (ding′gəl), *n.* a deep, narrow cleft between hills; shady dell. [1200–50; ME: a deep dell, hollow; akin to OE *dung* dungeon, OHG *tunc* cellar]

din•gle•ber•ry (ding′gəl ber′ē), *n., pl.* **-ries.** *Slang.* a small clot of dung, as clinging to the hindquarters of an animal. [1920–25; perh. DINGLE + BERRY; perh. by assoc. with DANGLE]

Ding Ling (ding′ ling′), *(Jiang Bingzhi)* 1904–86, Chinese author.

dingo, *Canis familiaris dingo,* 21 in. (53 cm) high at shoulder; head and body 2 ft. (0.6 m); tail 14 in. (36 cm)

din•go (ding′gō), *n., pl.* **-goes.** **1.** a wolflike, wild dog, *Canis familiaris dingo,* of Australia, having a reddish- or yellowish-brown coat. **2.** *Australian.* a coward or sneak. [1789; < Dharuk *din-gu* tame dingo]

ding•us (ding′əs), *n., pl.* **-us•es.** *Informal.* a gadget, device, or object whose name is unknown or forgotten. [1870–75; < D *dinges* or its source, G *Dinges,* prob. orig. gen., with partitive value, of *Ding* THING¹]

din•gy (din′jē), *adj.,* **-gi•er, -gi•est.** **1.** of a dark, dull, or dirty color or aspect; lacking brightness or freshness. **2.** shabby; dismal. [1730–40; orig. uncert.] —**din′gi•ly,** *adv.* —**din′gi•ness,** *n.*

din′ing car′, a railroad car equipped with tables and chairs, in which meals are served. Also, *esp. Brit.,* **restaurant car.** Also called **diner.** [1830–40, *Amer.*]

din′ing hall′, a large room in which meals are served to members of a special group and their guests, as to the students and faculty of a college. [1660–70]

din′ing room′, **1.** a room in which meals are eaten, as in a home or hotel, esp. the room in which the major or more formal meals are eaten. **2.** *Informal.* the furniture usually used in a dining room and sometimes sold as a matching set; dining room suite. [1595–1605]

din′ing ta′ble, a table, esp. one seating several persons, where meals are served and eaten. [1585–95]

di•ni•tro•ben•zene (dī nī′trə ben′zēn, -ben zēn′), *n. Chem.* any of three isomeric benzene derivatives having the formula $C_6H_4NO_2$, made by nitration of benzene or nitrobenzene, the most important of which is the meta form: used chiefly in the manufacture of dyes. [1870–75; DI-¹ + NITROBENZENE]

di•ni•tro•phe•nol (dī nī′trə fē′nôl, -nol), *n. Chem., Pharm.* any of the six isomers consisting of phenol where two hydrogen atoms are substituted by nitro groups, $C_6H_4N_2O_5$, used in dyes and wood preservatives, and in biochemistry to uncouple oxidative phosphorylation. [1895–1900; DI-¹ + NITROPHENOL]

dink¹ (dingk), *n.* dinghy. [1900–05; by apocope and devoicing]

dink² (dingk), *n. Tennis, Volleyball.* a softly hit ball that falls just over the net. [1935–40; imit., prob. influenced by DINKY¹]

dink³ (dingk), *n. Slang (disparaging).* an Asian, esp. a Vietnamese. [1915–20; cf. Australian slang *dink* Chinese person; perh. back formation from DINKY, reinforced by rhyme with CHINK]

dink⁴ (dingk), *n. Informal.* either partner of a married couple having two incomes and no children. [1985–90; *d(ouble) i(ncome), n(o) k(ids)*]

Din•ka (ding′kə), *n., pl.* **-kas,** *(esp. collectively)* **-ka.** **1.** a member of a tall, pastoral, Negroid people of Sudan. **2.** the language of the Dinka, a Nilotic language closely related to Shilluk.

dink•ey (ding′kē), *n., pl.* **-eys.** a small locomotive, esp. with a switch engine. Also, **dinky.** [1840–50; n. use of DINKY; see -EY²]

din•kum (ding′kəm), *adj. Australian.* genuine; authentic. [1890–95; of obscure orig.]

dink•y (ding′kē), *adj.,* **dink•i•er, dink•i•est,** *n., pl.* **dink•ies.** —*adj.* **1.** *Informal.* small, unimportant, unimpressive, or shabby: *We stayed in a dinky old hotel.* **2.** *Brit. Informal.* fashionable; well dressed; smart. —*n.* **3.** dinkey. [1780–90; cf. Scots *dink* neatly dressed, trim (of obscure orig.); sense shift perh.: trim >dainty >small >insignificant; see -Y¹]

din•ner (din′ər), *n.* **1.** the main meal of the day, eaten in the evening or at midday. **2.** a formal meal in honor of some person or occasion. **3.** See **table d'hôte.** [1250–1300; ME *diner* < OF *disner* (n. use of v.); see DINE] —**din′ner•less,** *adj.*

din′ner clothes′, formal or semiformal clothing worn for formal dinners or similar social occasions.

din′ner dance′, a formal social gathering that includes a dinner followed by dancing. [1900–05]

din′ner dress′, a dress, often long and having sleeves or a jacket, more elaborate than one designed for daytime wear but less formal than an evening gown. [1805–15]

din′ner fork′, a fork used to eat the main course of a meal.

din′ner jack′et, tuxedo (def. 1). [1890–95]

din′ner knife′, a knife used in eating the main course of a meal.

din′ner plate′, a plate for holding an individual serving of the main course of a meal.

din′ner ring′, a woman's ring, usually with a large, ornate setting.

din′ner ta′ble. See **dining table.** [1800–10]

din′ner the′ater, **1.** a restaurant in which a stage production is performed during or after dinner. **2.** stage productions performed in dinner theaters. [1965–70]

din•ner•time (din′ər tīm′), *n.* the period set aside for eating dinner. [1325–75; ME. See DINNER, TIME]

din•ner•ware (din′ər wâr′), *n.* china, glasses, and silver used for table service. [1890–95; DINNER + WARE¹]

dino-, a combining form meaning "terrifying, frightful," used in the formation of compound words: *dinothere.* [< Gk *deino-,* comb. form of *deinós*]

din•o•flag•el•late (din′ə flaj′ə lāt′), *n.* any of numerous chiefly marine plankton of the phylum Pyrrophyta (or, in some classification schemes, the order Dinoflagellata), usually having two flagella, one in a groove around the body and the other extending from its center. [1900–05; DINO- + FLAGELLATE]

di•no•saur (dī′nə sôr′), *n.* **1.** any chiefly terrestrial, herbivorous or carnivorous reptile of the extinct orders Saurischia and Ornithischia, from the Mesozoic Era, certain species of which are the largest known land animals. **2.** something that is unwieldy in size, anachronistically outmoded, or unable to adapt to change: *The old steel mill was a dinosaur that cost the company millions to operate.* [< NL *Dinosaurus* (1841), orig. a genus name. See DINO-, -SAUR]

dinosaur, *Tyrannosaurus rex,* height 20 ft. (6 m); length 50 ft. (15 m)

di•no•sau•ri•an (dī′nə sôr′ē ən), *adj.* **1.** pertaining to or of the nature of a dinosaur. —*n.* **2.** a dinosaur. [< NL *Dinosauri(a)* (1841), orig. a name for a suborder or tribe (see DINO-, SAURIAN) + -AN]

Di′nosaur Na′tional Mon′ument, a national monument in NE Utah and NW Colorado: site of prehistoric animal fossils. 322 sq. mi. (834 sq. km).

di•no•there (dī′nə thēr′), *n.* any elephantlike mammal of the extinct genus *Dinotherium,* from the later Tertiary Period of Europe and Asia, having large, outwardly curving tusks. Also, **di•no•the•ri•um** (dī′nə-thēr′ē əm). [< NL *Dinotherium* (1829); see DINO-, -THERE]

d. in p. aeq., (in prescriptions) let it be divided into equal parts. [< L *dividātur in partēs aequālēs*]

dint (dint), *n.* **1.** force; power: *By dint of hard work she became head of the company.* **2.** a dent. **3.** *Archaic.* a blow; stroke. —*v.t.* **4.** to make a dent or dents in. **5.** to impress or drive in with force. [bef. 900; ME; OE *dynt;* c. ON *dyntr*] —**dint′less,** *adj.*
—**Syn. 1.** effort, strain, exertion, struggle.

di•nu•cle•o•tide (dī no͞o′klē ə tīd′, -nyo͞o′-), *n. Biochem.* a molecule composed of two nucleotide subunits. [1925–30; DI-¹ + NUCLEOTIDE]

Din•wid•die (din wid′ē, din′wid ē), *n.* **Robert,** 1693–1770, British colonial administrator in America: lieutenant governor of Virginia 1751–58.

dioc., **1.** diocesan. **2.** diocese.

di•oc•e•san (dī os′ə sən), *adj.* **1.** of or pertaining to a diocese. —*n.* **2.** one of the clergy or people of a diocese. **3.** the bishop in charge of a diocese. [1400–50; late ME (< AF) < ML *dioecēsānus.* See DIOCESE, -AN]

di•o•cese (dī′ə sis, -sēz′, -sēs′), *n.* an ecclesiastical district under the jurisdiction of a bishop. [1300–50; ME *diocise, diocese* < AF < LL *diocēsis,* var. of LL, L *dioecēsis,* < Gk *dioíkēsis* housekeeping, administration, province, diocese, equiv. to *dioikē-,* var. s. of *dioikeîn* to keep house, administer, govern (*di-* DI-³ + *oikeîn* to dwell, occupy, manage, deriv. of *oîkos* house) + *-sis* -SIS]

Di•o•cle•tian (dī′ə klē′shən), *n.* (*Gaius Aurelius Valerius Diocletianus*), A.D. 245–316, Illyrian soldier: emperor of Rome 284–305.

Di′ocle′tian win′dow. See **Palladian window.**

di•ode (dī′ōd), *n. Electronics.* a device, as a two-element electron tube or a semiconductor, through which current can pass freely in only one direction. [1919; DI-¹ + -ODE²]

CONCISE ETYMOLOGY KEY: <, descended or borrowed from; >, whence; b., blend of, blended; c., cognate with; cf., compare; deriv., derivative; equiv., equivalent; imit., imitative; obl., oblique; r., replacing; s., stem; sp., spelling, spelled; resp., respelling, respelled; trans., translation; ?, origin unknown; *, unattested; ‡, probably earlier than. See the full key inside the front cover.

Di•o•do•rus Sic•u•lus (dī′ō dôr′əs sik′yə ləs, -dōr′-), late 1st century B.C., Greek historian.

di•oe•cious (dī ē′shəs), *adj. Biol.* (esp. of plants) having the male and female organs in separate and distinct individuals; having separate sexes. Also, **diecious.** [1740–50; < NL *Dioeci(a)* a class name (*di-* DI-[1] + Gk *oikía* a house, dwelling, sp. var. of *oîkos*) + -OUS] —**di•oe′cious•ly,** *adv.* —**di•oe′cious•ness,** *n.* —**di•oe•cism** (dī ē′siz əm), *n.*

di•oes•trus (dī es′trəs, -ē′strəs), *n. Brit.* diestrus.

Di•og•e•nes (dī oj′ə nēz′), *n.* 412?–323 B.C., Greek Cynic philosopher. —**Di•o•gen•ic** (dī′ə jen′ik), **Di•og′e•ne′an,** *adj.*

di•ol (dī′ôl, -ol), *n. Chem.* glycol (def. 2). [1920–25; DI-[1] + -OL]

di•o•le•fin (dī ō′lə fin), *n. Chem.* diene. [1905–10; DI-[1] + OLEFIN]

Di′o•mede Is′lands (dī′ə mēd′), two islands in the Bering Strait, one belonging to the Russian Federation (**Big Diomede**), ab. 15 sq. mi. (39 sq. km), and one belonging to the U.S. (**Little Diomede**), ab. 4 sq. mi. (10 sq. km): separated by the International Date Line.

Di•o•me•des (dī′ə mē′dēz), *n. Class. Myth.* **1.** a Greek hero in the Trojan War. **2.** a Thracian king who fed his wild mares on human flesh and was himself fed to them by Hercules.

di•o•nae•a (dī′ə nē′ə), *n.* the Venus's-flytrap. [< NL *Dionaea* (1773), the genus name < Gk *Diōnaía*, fem. of *Diōnaîos* pertaining to *Diṓnē* a metronymic name for Aphrodite; see DIONE]

Di•o•ne (dī ō′nē), *n.* **1.** *Class. Myth.* a Titan and a consort of Zeus. **2.** *Astron.* a moon of the planet Saturn.

Di•o•ny•si•a (dī′ə nish′ē ə, -nis′-), *n.pl.* the orgiastic and dramatic festivals held periodically in honor of Dionysus, esp. those in Attica, from which Greek comedy and tragedy developed. Cf. **Greater Dionysia, Lesser Dionysia.** [1890–95; < L < Gk]

Di•o•nys•i•ac (dī′ə nis′ē ak′, -nī′sē-), *adj.* **1.** of or pertaining to the Dionysia or to Dionysus; Bacchic. **2.** Dionysian (def. 2). [1820–30; < L *Dionȳsiacus* < Gk *Dionȳsiakós*, equiv. to *Diónȳs(os)* DIONYSUS + *-i-* deriv. s. vowel + *-akos* -AC] —**Di•o•ny•si•a•cal•ly** (dī′ə ni sī′ik lē), *adv.*

Di•o•ny•sian (dī′ə nish′ən, -nis′ē ən, -nī′sē-), *adj.* **1.** of, pertaining to, or honoring Dionysus or Bacchus. **2.** recklessly uninhibited; unrestrained; undisciplined; frenzied; orgiastic. [1600–10; DIONYS(US) + -IAN]

Di•o•ny•si•us (dī′ə nish′ē əs, -nis′-, -nish′əs, -nī′sē-əs), *n.* **1.** *("the Elder")* 431?–367 B.C., Greek soldier: tyrant of Syracuse 405–367. **2. Saint,** died A.D. 268, pope 259–268.

Diony′sius Ex•ig′u•us (eg zig′yo͞o əs, ek sig′-), died A.D. 556?, Scythian monk and chronologist: devised the current system of reckoning the Christian era.

Diony′sius of Alexan′dria, Saint *("the Great")*, A.D. c190–265, patriarch of Alexandria 247?–265?.

Diony′sius of Halicarnas′sus, died 7? B.C., Greek rhetorician and historian in Rome.

Diony′sius the Areop′agite, 1st century A.D., Athenian scholar: converted to Christianity by Saint Paul c50.

Diony′sius Thrax′ (thraks), c100 B.C., Greek grammarian.

Di•o•ny•sus (dī′ə nī′səs), *n. Class. Myth.* the god of fertility, wine, and drama; Bacchus. Also, **Di′o•ny′sos.**

di•o•on (dī′ō on′), *n.* any of several Mexican and Central American palmlike plants belonging to the genus *Dioon*, of the cycad family, having a crown of stiff, pinnate leaves. [< NL (1843) < Gk *di-* DI-[1] + *ōión* egg; so named because the seeds are borne in pairs]

di•o•phan′tine equa′tion (dī′ə fan′tīn, -tēn, -fan′-tn), *Math.* an equation involving more than one variable in which the coefficients of the variables are integers and for which integral solutions are sought. [1925–30; named after *Diophantus*, 3rd-century A.D. Greek mathematician; see -INE[1]]

di•op•side (dī op′sīd, -sid), *n. Mineral.* a monoclinic pyroxene mineral, calcium magnesium silicate, $CaMg(SiO_3)_2$, occurring in various colors, usually in crystals. [1800–10; DI-[3] + Gk *óps(is)* appearance + -IDE]

di•op•sim•e•ter (dī′op sim′i tər), *n. Ophthalm.* an instrument for measuring the field of vision. [DI-[3] + Gk *ops-* (s. of *ópsis*) sight, vision + -I- + -METER]

di•op•tase (dī op′tās), *n.* a mineral, hydrous copper silicate, $CuSiO_3{\cdot}H_2O$, occurring in emerald-green crystals. [1795–1805; < F, equiv. to *di-* DI-[3] + Gk *optasía* view]

di•op•ter (dī op′tər), *n.* **1.** *Optics.* a unit of measure of the refractive power of a lens, having the dimension of the reciprocal of length and a unit equal to the reciprocal of one meter. *Abbr.:* D **2.** an instrument, invented by Hipparchus, to measure the apparent diameter of the sun or moon or to estimate the size or elevation of distant objects. Also, *esp. Brit.,* **di•op′tre.** [1585–95; < L *dioptra* < Gk: instrument for measuring height or levels, equiv. to *di-* DI-[3] + *op-* (for *ópsesthai* to see) + *-tra* n. suffix of means] —**di•op′tral,** *adj.*

di•op•tom•e•ter (dī′op tom′i tər), *n. Ophthalm.* an instrument for measuring the refraction of the eye. [DI-[3] + OPT(IC) + -O- + -METER]

di•op•tric (dī op′trik), *adj.* **1.** *Optics.* pertaining to dioptrics: *dioptric images.* **2.** *Optics, Ophthalm.* noting or pertaining to refraction or refracted light. Also, **di•op′tri•cal.** [1625–35; < Gk *dioptrikós.* See DIOPTER, -IC] —**di•op′tri•cal•ly,** *adv.*

di•op•trics (dī op′triks), *n.* (*used with a singular v.*) the branch of geometrical optics dealing with the formation of images by lenses. [1635–45; SEE DIOPTRIC, -ICS]

Di•or (dē ôr′; *Fr.* dē ôʀ′), *n.* **Chris•tian** (kris′chən; *Fr.* krēs tyäɴ′), 1905–57, French fashion designer.

di•o•ram•a (dī′ə ram′ə, -rä′mə), *n.* **1.** a scene, often in miniature, reproduced in three dimensions by placing objects, figures, etc., in front of a painted background. **2.** a life-size display representing a scene from nature, a historical event, or the like, using stuffed wildlife, wax figures, real objects, etc., in front of a painted or photographed background. **3.** a spectacular picture, partly translucent, for exhibition through an aperture, made more realistic by various illuminating devices. **4.** a building or room, often circular, for exhibiting such a scene or picture, esp. as a continuous unit along or against the walls. [1815–25; < F, equiv. to *di-* DI-[3] + Gk *(h)órāma* view (*horā-*, var. s. of *horân* to see, look + *-ma* n. suffix denoting the result of action)] —**di′o•ram′ic,** *adj.*

di•o•rite (dī′ə rīt′), *n.* a granular igneous rock consisting essentially of plagioclase feldspar and hornblende. [1820–30; < F < Gk *dior(ízein)* to distinguish (see DI-[3], HORIZON) + F *-ite* -ITE[1]] —**di•o•rit•ic** (dī′ə rit′ik), *adj.*

di•os•cin (dī os′in), *n. Biochem.* a saponin, found in Mexican yams, that on hydrolysis produces diosgenin, glucose, and rhamnose. [< NL *Diosc(orea)* (see DIOSGENIN) + -IN[2]]

Di•os•cu•ri (dī′ə skyo͝or′ī), *n.pl. Class. Myth.* Castor and Pollux, the twin sons of Zeus and Leda.

di•os•gen•in (dī′oz jen′in, dī oz′jə nin), *n. Biochem.* a crystalline compound, $C_{27}H_{42}O_3$, the aglycone of dioscin: used in the synthesis of steroidal hormones, as of progesterone. [< G *Diosgenin* (1936), equiv to NL *Dios(corea)* the yam genus from which it was first extracted, irreg. after *Dioscorides* 1st-century A.D. Greek physician + G *-genin;* see -GEN, -IN[2]]

di•os•mose (dī os′mōs, -oz′-), *v.t.,* **-mosed, -mos•ing.** *Physical Chem.* osmose. [DI-[1] + OSMOSE] —**di•os•mo•sis** (dī′os mō′sis, -oz-), *n.*

di•o•tic (dī ō′tik, -ot′ik), *adj. Med.* pertaining to or affecting both ears; binaural. [DI-[1] + OTIC]

Diouf (dyo͞of), *n.* **Ab•dou** (ab do͞o′), born 1935, president of Senegal since 1981.

di•ox•ane (dī ok′sān), *n. Chem.* a colorless, flammable, liquid cyclic ether, $C_4H_8O_2$, having a faint, pleasant odor: used chiefly in the varnish and silk industries and as a dehydrator in histology. [1910–15; DI-[1] + OX(Y)-[2] + -ANE]

di•ox•ide (dī ok′sīd, -sid), *n. Chem.* an oxide containing two atoms of oxygen, each of which is bonded directly to an atom of a second element, as manganese dioxide, MnO_2, or nitrogen dioxide, NO_2. [1840–50; DI-[1] + OXIDE]

di•ox•in (dī ok′sin), *n. Chem.* a general name for a family of chlorinated hydrocarbons, $C_{12}H_4Cl_4O_2$, typically used to refer to one isomer, TCDD, a by-product of pesticide manufacture: a toxic compound that is carcinogenic and teratogenic in certain animals. Also called **TCDD** Cf. **Agent Orange.** [1965–70; DI-[1] + OX- + -IN[2]]

dip[1] (dip), *v.,* **dipped** or (*Archaic*) **dipt; dip•ping;** *n.* —*v.t.* **1.** to plunge (something, as a cloth or sponge) temporarily into a liquid, so as to moisten it, dye it, or cause it to take up some of the liquid: *He dipped the brush into the paint bucket.* **2.** to raise or take up by a bailing, scooping, or ladling action: *to dip water out of a boat; to dip ice cream from a container.* **3.** to lower and raise: *to dip a flag in salutation.* **4.** to immerse (a sheep, hog, etc.) in a solution to destroy germs, parasites, or the like. **5.** to make (a candle) by repeatedly plunging a wick into melted tallow or wax. **6.** *Naut.* to lower and rehoist (a yard of a lugsail) when coming about in tacking. **7.** *Archaic.* to baptize by immersion. **8.** *Obs.* to moisten or wet as if by immersion. —*v.i.* **9.** to plunge into water or other liquid and emerge quickly: *The boat dipped into the waves.* **10.** to put the hand, a dipper, etc., down into a liquid or a container, esp. in order to remove something (often fol. by *in* or *into*): *He dipped into the jar for an olive.* **11.** to withdraw something, esp. in small amounts (usually fol. by *in* or *into*): *to dip into savings.* **12.** to sink or drop down: *The sun dipped below the horizon.* **13.** to incline or slope downward: *At that point the road dips into a valley.* **14.** to decrease slightly or temporarily: *Stock-market prices often dip on Fridays.* **15.** to engage slightly in a subject (often fol. by *in* or *into*): *to dip into astronomy.* **16.** to read here and there in a book, subject, or author's work (often fol. by *in* or *into*): *to dip into Plato.* **17.** *South Midland and Southern U.S.* to take snuff. —*n.* **18.** the act of dipping. **19.** that which is taken up by dipping. **20.** a quantity taken up by dipping; the amount that a scoop, ladle, dipper, etc., will hold. **21.** a scoop of ice cream. **22.** *Chiefly Northern U.S.* a liquid or soft substance into which something is dipped. **23.** a creamy mixture of savory foods for scooping with potato chips, crackers, and the like, often served as an hors d'oeuvre, esp. with cocktails. **24.** a momentary lowering; a sinking down. **25.** a moderate or temporary decrease: *a dip in stock-market prices.* **26.** a downward extension, inclination, slope, or course. **27.** the amount of such extension. **28.** a hollow or depression in the land. **29.** a brief swim: *She took a dip in the ocean and then sat on the beach for an hour.* **30.** *Geol., Mining.* the downward inclination of a vein or stratum with reference to the horizontal. **31.** the angular amount by which the horizon lies below the level of the eye. **32.** Also called **angle of dip, inclination, magnetic dip, magnetic inclination.** the angle that a freely rotating magnetic needle makes with the plane of the horizon. **33.** a short, downward plunge, as of an airplane. **34.** a candle made by repeatedly dipping a wick into melted tallow or wax. **35.** *Gymnastics.* an exercise on the parallel bars in which the elbows are bent until the chin is on a level with the bars, and then the body is elevated by straightening the arms. **36.** *Slang.* a pickpocket. **37. at the dip,** *Naut.* not fully raised; halfway up the halyard: *an answering pennant flown at the dip.* Cf. **close** (def. 65b). [bef. 1000; ME *dippen* (v.), OE *dyppan;* akin to G *taufen* to baptize, and to DEEP] —**dip′pa•ble,** *adj., n.*

—**Syn. 1.** duck. DIP, IMMERSE, PLUNGE refer to putting something into liquid. To DIP is to put down into a liquid quickly or partially and lift out again: *to dip a finger into water to test the temperature.* IMMERSE denotes a lowering into a liquid until covered by it: *to immerse meat in salt water.* PLUNGE adds a suggestion of force or suddenness to the action of dipping: *to plunge a chicken into boiling water before stripping off the feathers.* **2.** scoop. **9.** dive.

dip[2] (dip), *n. Slang.* dipsomaniac. [by shortening]

dip[3] (dip), *n. Slang.* a naive, foolish, or obnoxious person. [prob. back formation from DIPPY]

DIP (dip), *n. Computers.* a packaged chip that connects to a circuit board by means of pins. [*d(ual) i(n-line) p(ackage)*]

di•pep•ti•dase (dī pep′ti dās′, -dāz′), *n. Biochem.* any enzyme that catalyzes the hydrolysis of dipeptides. [DIPEPTIDE + -ASE]

di•pep•tide (dī pep′tīd, dī-), *n. Biochem.* a peptide that yields two amino acids on hydrolysis. [1900–05; DI-[1] + PEPTIDE]

di•pet•al•ous (dī pet′l əs), *adj. Bot.* bipetalous. [1700–10; < NL *dipetalus;* see DI-[1], PETALOUS]

di•phase (dī′fāz′), *adj. Elect.* having two phases; two-phase. Also, **di•phas•ic** (dī fā′zik). [1895–1900; DI-[1] + PHASE]

di•phen•a•mid (dī fen′ə mid), *n.* a selective preemergence herbicide, $C_{16}H_{17}ON$, used to control weed growth on lawns and various croplands. [DIPHEN(YL) + (ACET)-AMID(E)]

di•phen•hy•dra•mine (dī′fen hī′drə mēn′), *n. Pharm.* a white, crystalline, antihistaminic compound, $C_{17}H_{21}NO$, used orally, topically, and parenterally, esp. for allergies. [1945–50; DIPHEN(YL) + HYDR-[2] + AMINE]

di•phen•ox•y•late (dī′fen ok′sə lāt′), *n. Pharm.* a substance, $C_{30}H_{32}N_2O_2$, used in the form of its hydrochloride in the treatment of diarrhea. [DIPHEN(YL) + OX- + -YL + -ATE[2]]

di•phen•yl (dī fen′l, -fēn′l), *n. Chem.* biphenyl. [1860–65]

di•phen•yl•a•cet•y•lene (dī fen′l ə set′l ēn′, -fēn′-), *n. Chem.* tolan. [DIPHENYL + ACETYLENE]

di•phen•yl•a•mine (dī fen′l ə mēn′, -am′in, -fēn′-), *n. Chem.* a colorless, crystalline, slightly water-soluble benzene derivative, $C_{12}H_{11}N$, used chiefly in the preparation of various dyes, as a stabilizer for nitrocellulose propellants, and for the detection of oxidizing agents in analytical chemistry. [1860–65; DIPHENYL + AMINE]

di•phen•yl•a•mine•chlo•rar•sine (dī fen′l ə mēn′-klō rär′sēn, -klō-, -am′ən-, -fēn′-), *n. Chem.* adamsite. [DIPHENYLAMINE + CHLOR-[2] + ARSINE]

di•phen•yl•hy•dan•to•in (dī fen′l hī dan′tō in, -fēn′-), *n. Pharm.* a white, slightly water-soluble powder, $C_{15}H_{11}N_2O_2$, used in the form of its sodium salt to prevent or arrest convulsions in epilepsy. [1935–40; DIPHENYL + HYDANTOIN]

diphen′yl ke′tone, *Chem.* benzophenone.

di•pho•ni•a (dī fō′nē ə), *n. Pathol.* diplophonia.

di•phos•gene (dī fos′jēn), *n. Chem.* a colorless liquid, $C_2Cl_4O_2$, usually derived from methyl formate or methyl chloroformate by chlorination: a World War I poison gas now used chiefly in organic synthesis. Also called **trichloromethyl chloroformate.** [1920–25; DI-[1] + PHOSGENE]

di•phos•phate (dī fos′fāt), *n. Chem.* **1.** a pyrophosphate. **2.** a phosphate containing two phosphate groups. [1820–30; DI-[1] + PHOSPHATE]

di•phos•pho•glyc•er•ate (dī fos′fō glis′ə rāt′), *n. Biochem.* an ester of phosphoric acid and glyceric acid that occurs in the blood and that promotes the release of hemoglobin-bound oxygen. [DIPHOSPH(ATE) + -O- + GLYCER(IC ACID) + -ATE[2]]

diph•the•ri•a (dif thēr′ē ə, dip-), *n. Pathol.* a febrile, infectious disease caused by the bacillus *Corynebacterium diphtheriae*, and characterized by the formation of a false membrane in the air passages, esp. the throat. [1850–55; < NL < F *diphthérie* < Gk *diphthér(a)* skin, leather + *-ia* -IA]

diph•the•rit•ic (dif′thə rit′ik, dip′-), *adj. Pathol.* **1.** pertaining to diphtheria. **2.** affected by diphtheria. Also, **diph•the•ri•al** (dif thēr′ē əl, dip-), **diph•ther•ic** (dif-ther′ik, dip-). [1840–50; earlier *diphtherit(is)* (see DIPHTHERIA, -ITIS) + -IC] —**diph′the•rit′i•cal•ly,** *adv.*

diph•the•roid (dif′thə roid′, dip′-), *adj. Pathol.* **1.** resembling diphtheria, esp. in the formation of a false membrane in the throat. —*n.* **2.** any bacterium, esp. of the genus *Corynebacterium*, that resembles the diphtheria bacillus but does not produce diphtheria toxin. [1860–65; DIPHTHER(IA) + -OID]

diph•thong (dif′thông, -thong, dip′-), *n.* **1.** *Phonet.* an unsegmentable, gliding speech sound varying continuously in phonetic quality but held to be a single sound or phoneme and identified by its apparent beginning and ending sound, as the *oi*-sound of *toy* or *boil.* **2.** (not in technical use) **a.** a digraph, as the *ea* of *meat.* **b.** a ligature, as æ. —*v.t., v.i.* **3.** to diphthongize. [1425–75; late ME *diptonge* < LL *diphthongus* < Gk *díphthongos* lit., having two sounds (*di-* DI-[1] + *phthóngos* voice, sound)] —**diph•thon•gal** (dif thông′gəl, -thong′-, dip-), **diph•thon′gic, diph•thon′gous,** *adj.*

diph•thon•gi•a (dif thông′ē ə, -gē ə, -thong′-, dip-), *n. Pathol.* diplophonia. [DIPHTHONG + -IA]

diph•thong•ize (dif′thông īz′, -gīz′, -thong-, dip′-), *v.,* **-ized, -iz•ing.** *Phonet.* —*v.t.* **1.** to change into or pronounce as a diphthong. —*v.i.* **2.** to become a diphthong. Also, *esp. Brit.,* **diph′thong•ise′.** [1865–70; DIPHTHONG + -IZE] —**diph′thong•i•za′tion,** *n.*

diph•y•cer•cal (dif′ə sûr′kəl), *adj. Ichthyol.* having a tail or caudal fin with the spinal column extending horizontally to the end of the tail, characteristic of lungfish, several other primitive fishes, and the juvenile stage of modern bony fishes. Cf. **homocercal, heterocercal.** [*diphy-* double (see DIPHYODONT) + CERCAL]

di·phy·let·ic (dī′fī let′ik), *adj. Biol.* of or pertaining to a taxonomic group of organisms derived from two separate ancestral lines. [1900–05; DI-[1] + PHYLETIC]

di·phyl·lous (dī fil′əs), *adj. Bot.* having two leaves. [1780–90; < NL *diphyllus.* See DI-[1], -PHYLLOUS]

diph·y·o·dont (dif′ē ə dont′), *adj. Zool.* having two successive sets of teeth, as most mammals. [1850–55; < Gk *diphy(ḗs)* double, twofold (*di-* DI-[1] + *-phyēs,* deriv. of *phyḗ* growth, nature, deriv. of *phýein* to produce, grow) + -ODONT]

dipl., **1.** diplomat. **2.** diplomatic.

dip·la·cu·sis (dip′lə kyōō′sis), *n., pl.* **-ses** (-sēz). *Pathol.* a difference in hearing by the two ears so that one sound is heard as two. [< NL, equiv. to *dipl(o)-* DIPLO- + Gk *akoúsis* hearing (*akoú(ein)* to hear, listen to + *-sis* -SIS)]

di·ple·gia (dī plē′jə, -jē ə), *n. Pathol.* paralysis of the identical part on both sides of the body. [1880–85; < NL; see DI-[1], -PLEGIA] **—di·ple′gic,** *adj.*

di·plex (dī′plex), *adj.* pertaining to the simultaneous operation of two radio transmitters or to the simultaneous reception and transmission of radio signals over a single antenna through the use of two frequencies. Cf. **multiplex.** [1875–80; DI-[1] + -PLEX]

diplo-, a combining form meaning "double," "in pairs," used in the formation of compound words: *diplococcus.* [< Gk, comb. form of *diplóos* TWOFOLD]

dip·lo·ba·cil·lus (dip′lō bə sil′əs), *n., pl.* **-cil·li** (-sil′ī). *Bact.* a double bacillus; two bacilli linked end to end. [1900–05; DIPLO- + BACILLUS]

dip·lo·blas·tic (dip′lə blas′tik), *adj.* having two germ layers, the ectoderm and endoderm, as the embryos of sponges and coelenterates. [1880–85; DIPLO- + -BLAST + -IC]

dip·lo·car·di·ac (dip′lə kär′dē ak′), *adj. Zool.* having the right and left sides of the heart somewhat or completely divided, as in birds and mammals. [1850–55; DIPLO- + CARDIAC]

dip·lo·coc·cus (dip′lə kok′əs), *n., pl.* **-coc·ci** (-kok′sī, -sē), *Bacteriol.* any of several spherical bacteria occurring in pairs, as *Diplococcus pneumoniae.* [1886; < NL; see DIPLO-, COCCUS] **—dip′lo·coc′cal, dip·lo·coc·cic** (dip′lə kok′sik), *adj.*

di·plod·o·cus (di plod′ə kəs), *n., pl.* **-cus·es.** a huge herbivorous dinosaur of the genus *Diplodocus,* from the Late Jurassic Epoch of western North America, growing to a length of about 87 ft. (26.5 m). [< NL (1878), equiv. to *diplo-* DIPLO- + Gk *dokós* beam, bar, shaft]

dip·lo·ë (dip′lō ē′), *n. Anat.* the cancellate bony tissue between the hard inner and outer walls of the bones of the cranium. [1690–1700; < Gk *diplóē* lit., a fold, n. use of fem. of *diplóos* double] **—di·plo·ic** (di plō′ik), **di·plo·et·ic** (dip′lō et′ik), *adj.*

dip·loid (dip′loid), *adj.* **1.** double; twofold. **2.** *Biol.* having two similar complements of chromosomes. **—***n.* **3.** *Biol.* an organism or cell having double the basic haploid number of chromosomes. **4.** *Crystall.* a solid belonging to the isometric system and having 24 trapezoidal planes. [1905–10; DIPL(O)- + -OID] **—dip·loi′dic,** *adj.*

di·plo·ma (di plō′mə), *n., pl.* **-mas,** *Lat.* **-ma·ta** (-mə tə), *v.,* **-maed, -ma·ing.** **—***n.* **1.** a document given by an educational institution conferring a degree on a person or certifying that the person has satisfactorily completed a course of study. **2.** a document conferring some honor, privilege, or power. **3.** a public or official document, esp. one of historical interest: *a diploma from Carolingian times.* **—***v.t.* **4.** to grant or award a diploma to. [1635–45; < L *diplōma* a letter of recommendation, an official document < Gk *díplōma* a letter folded double, equiv. to *diplō-,* var. s. of *diploûn* to double (deriv. of *diplóos;* see DIPLO-) + *-ma* suffix of result]

di·plo·ma·cy (di plō′mə sē), *n.* **1.** the conduct by government officials of negotiations and other relations between nations. **2.** the art or science of conducting such negotiations. **3.** skill in managing negotiations, handling people, etc., so that there is little or no ill will; tact: *Seating one's dinner guests often calls for considerable diplomacy.* [1790–1800; < F *diplomatie* (with *t* pronounced as *s*), equiv. to *diplomate* DIPLOMAT + *-ie* -Y[3]]

diplo′ma mill′, **1.** an organization claiming to be an institution of higher learning but existing for profit only and granting degrees without demanding proper qualifications of the recipients. **2.** a college or university having such a large number of students that none receives individual attention from the teachers. Also called **degree mill.** [1925–30]

dip·lo·mat (dip′lə mat′), *n.* **1.** a person appointed by a national government to conduct official negotiations and maintain political, economic, and social relations with another country or countries. **2.** a person who is tactful and skillful in managing delicate situations, handling people, etc. [1805–15; < F *diplomate,* back formation from *diplomatique* DIPLOMATIC]

dip·lo·mate (dip′lə māt′), *n.* a person who has received a diploma, esp. a doctor, engineer, etc., who has been certified as a specialist by a board within the appropriate profession. [1875–80; DIPLOM(A) + -ATE[1]]

dip·lo·mat·ic (dip′lə mat′ik), *adj.* **1.** of, pertaining to, or engaged in diplomacy: *diplomatic officials.* **2.** skilled in dealing with sensitive matters or people; tactful. **3.** of or pertaining to diplomatics. [1705–15; < F *diplomatique* < NL *diplōmaticus,* equiv. to L *diplōmat-* (s. of *diplōma*) DIPLOMA + *-icus* -IC] **—dip′lo·mat′i·cal·ly,** *adv.*

—Syn. 2. DIPLOMATIC, POLITIC, TACTFUL imply ability to avoid offending others or hurting their feelings, esp. in situations where this ability is important. DIPLOMATIC suggests a smoothness and skill in handling others, usually in such a way as to attain one's own ends and yet avoid any unpleasantness or opposition: *By diplomatic conduct he avoided antagonizing anyone.* POLITIC emphasizes expediency or prudence in looking out for one's own interests, thus knowing how to treat people of different types and on different occasions: *a truth which it is not politic to insist on.* TACTFUL suggests a nice touch in the handling of delicate matters or situations, and, unlike the other two, often suggests a sincere desire not to hurt the feelings of others: *a tactful way of correcting someone.* **—Ant. 2.** blunt, blundering, tactless.

diplomat′ic corps′, the entire body of diplomats accredited to and resident at a court or capital. Also called **diplomat′ic bod′y.**

diplomat′ic immu′nity, exemption from taxation, searches, arrest, etc., enjoyed by diplomatic officials and their dependent families under international law, and usually on a reciprocal basis. [1910–15]

dip′lomat′ic pouch′, a sealed mailbag containing diplomatic correspondence that is sent free of inspection between a foreign office and its diplomatic or consular post abroad or from one such post to another.

dip·lo·mat·ics (dip′lə mat′iks), *n.* (*used with a singular v.*) the science of deciphering old official documents, as charters, and of determining their authenticity, age, or the like. [1785–95; see DIPLOMATIC, -ICS]

dip′lomat′ic secr′etary, secretary (def. 5).

di·plo·ma·tist (di plō′mə tist), *n.* **1.** *Brit. Older Use.* a Foreign Office employee officially engaged as a diplomat. **2.** a person who is astute and tactful in any negotiation or relationship. [1805–15; DIPLOMAT(IC) + -IST]

di·plo·ma·tize (di plō′mə tīz′), *v.,* **-tized, -tiz·ing.** **—***v.i.* **1.** to use diplomacy or tact. **—***v.t.* **2.** to use the techniques of diplomacy on. Also, *esp. Brit.,* **di·plo′ma·tise′.** [1660–70; DIPLOMAT + -IZE] **—di·plo′ma·ti·za′·tion,** *n.*

dip·lont (dip′lont), *n. Biol.* **1.** the diploid individual in a life cycle that has a diploid and a haploid phase. **2.** an organism having two sets of chromosomes in its somatic cells and a single, haploid set of chromosomes in its gametes. [1920–25; DIPL(O)- + *-ont* < Gk *ont-,* s. of *ṓn* being, prp. of *eînai* to be (cf. ONTO-)]

dip·lo·phase (dip′lə fāz′), *n. Biol.* the diploid part of an organism's life cycle. [1920–25; DIPLO- + PHASE]

dip·lo·pho·ni·a (dip′lə fō′nē ə), *n. Pathol.* a condition in which the voice simultaneously produces two sounds of different pitch. Also called **diphonia, diphthongia.** [< NL, equiv. to *diplo-* DIPLO- + Gk *phōn(ḗ)* sound, tone, voice + L *-ia* -IA] **—dip·lo·phon·ic** (dip′lə fon′ik), *adj.*

di·plo·pi·a (di plō′pē ə), *n. Ophthalm.* a pathological condition of vision in which a single object appears double (opposed to *haplopia*). Also called **double vision.** [1805–15; < NL; see DIPLO-, -OPIA] **—di·plop·ic** (di-plop′ik, -plō′pik), *adj.*

dip·lo·pod (dip′lə pod′), *adj.* **1.** belonging or pertaining to the class Diplopoda. **—***n.* **2.** any arthropod of the class Diplopoda, comprising the millipedes. [1860–65; < NL *Diplopoda.* See DIPLO-, -POD]

di·plo·sis (di plō′sis), *n. Cell Biol.* the doubling of the chromosome number by the union of the haploid sets in the union of gametes. [< Gk *díplōsis* a doubling, equiv. to *diplō-* (see DIPLOMA) + *-sis* -SIS]

dip·lo·ste·mo·nous (dip′lə stē′mə nəs, -stem′ə-), *adj. Bot.* having two whorls of stamens, with the outer whorl opposite the sepals and the inner whorl opposite the petals. [1865–70; DIPLO- + Gk *stḗmon-* (s. of *stḗmōn*) the warp (see STAMEN) + -OUS] **—dip′lo·ste′mo·ny,** *n.*

dip·lo·tene (dip′lə tēn′), *n. Cell Biol.* a late stage of prophase during meiosis, in which the chromatid pairs of the tetrads begin to separate and chiasmata can be seen. [< F *diplotène* (1900); see DIPLO-, -TENE]

dip′ nee′dle, an early form of magnetometer, consisting of a magnetic needle pivoted through its center of gravity and having its axis through the vertical plane of the earth's magnetic meridian so as to point in the direction of maximum magnetic intensity. Also called **inclinometer.**

dip·no·an (dip′nō ən), *adj.* **1.** belonging or pertaining to the order Dipnoi, comprising the lungfishes. **—***n.* **2.** a dipnoan fish. [1880–85; < NL *Dipno(i)* name of the order, pl. of *dipnous* < Gk *dípnoos* double-breathing (*di-* DI-[1] + *-pnoos,* deriv. of *pnoḗ* breathing, breath, air, deriv. of *pneîn* to breathe) + -AN]

dip·o·dy (dip′ə dē), *n., pl.* **-dies.** *Pros.* a group of two feet, esp., in accentual verse, in which one of the two accented syllables bears primary stress and the other bears secondary stress. [1835–45; < LL *dipodia* < Gk: the quality of having two feet, equiv. to *dipod-* (s. of *dípous*) two-footed (see DI-[1], -POD) + *-ia* -Y[3]] **—di·pod·ic** (dī pod′ik), *adj.*

di·pole (dī′pōl′), *n.* **1.** *Physics, Elect.* a pair of electric point charges or magnetic poles of equal magnitude and opposite signs, separated by an infinitesimal distance. **2.** *Physical Chem.* a polar molecule. **3.** Also called **di′pole anten′na.** *Radio, Television.* an antenna of a transmitter or receiving set consisting of two equal rods extending in opposite direction from the connection to the lead-in wire. [1910–15; DI-[1] + POLE[2]] **—di·po′lar,** *adj.*

di′pole mo′ment, **1.** See **electric dipole moment. 2.** See **magnetic moment.** [1930–35]

dip·per (dip′ər), *n.* **1.** a person or thing that dips. **2.** a cuplike container with a long handle, used for dipping liquids. **3.** (*cap.*) *Astron.* **a.** See **Big Dipper. b.** See **Little Dipper. 4.** *Ornith.* Also called **water ouzel.** any small, stocky diving bird of the family Cinclidae, related to the thrushes, esp. *Cinclus aquaticus* of Europe and *C. mexicanus* of western North America, having dense, oily plumage and frequenting rapid streams and rivers. **5.** *South Midland and Southern U.S.* a person who uses snuff. [1350–1400; ME: diving bird; see DIP, -ER[1]]

dip·py (dip′ē), *adj.,* **-pi·er, -pi·est.** *Slang.* somewhat mad or foolish: *dippy with love.* [1900–05; orig. uncert.]

di·prot·ic (dī prot′ik), *adj. Chem.* (of an acid) having two transferable protons. [DI-[1] + PROT(ON) + -IC]

dip·sa·ca·ceous (dip′sə kā′shəs), *adj.* belonging to the Dipsacaceae, the teasel family of plants. Cf. **teasel family.** [1840–50; < NL *Dipsacace(ae)* name of the family (*Dipsac(us)* the typical genus < Gk *dípsakos* teasel (deriv. of *dípsa* thirst) + NL *-aceae* -ACEAE) + -OUS]

dip·so (dip′sō), *n., pl.* **-sos.** *Slang.* a dipsomaniac; habitual drunk. [1875–80; by shortening; cf. -O]

dip·so·ma·ni·a (dip′sə mā′nē ə, -sō-), *n.* an irresistible, typically periodic craving for alcoholic drink. [1835–45; < NL < Gk *díps(a)* thirst + *-o-* -O- + *mania* -MANIA]

dip·so·ma·ni·ac (dip′sə mā′nē ak′, -sō-), *n.* a person with an irresistible craving for alcoholic drink. [1855–60; DIPSOMANI(A) + -AC] **—dip·so·ma·ni·a·cal** (dip′sə-mə nī′ə kəl, -sō-), *adj.*

—Syn. See **drunkard.**

dip·stick (dip′stik′), *n.* **1.** a rod for measuring the depth of a liquid; esp., a thin metal rod used to measure the oil level in the crankcase of an automotive engine. **2.** *Slang.* fool; jerk. [1925–30; DIP[1] + STICK[1]]

dip′stick test′, a test for detecting the presence of sugar in the urine, as in diabetes.

dip·sy-doo·dle (dip′sē dōōd′l), *n. Slang.* **1.** a quick dipping, sliding motion of the body, as made by ball carriers in football to evade tacklers. **2.** an act, movement, etc., to confuse, evade, or distract the attention of an opponent or competitor. **3.** shady dealings; chicanery. [1940–45; see DIP[1], -SY, DOODLE[1]]

dipt (dipt), *v.* a pt. of **dip.**

Dip·ter·a (dip′tər ə, -trə), *n.* **1.** the order comprising the dipterous insects. **2.** (*l.c.*) pl. of **dipteron.** [1810–20; < NL < Gk, neut. pl. of *dípteros* two-winged, equiv. to *di-* DI-[1] + *-pteros* -PTEROUS]

dip·ter·al (dip′tər əl), *adj. Entomol., Bot.* dipterous. [1805–15; < L *dipter(us)* (< Gk *dípteros;* see DIPTERA) + -AL[1]]

dip·ter·an (dip′tər ən), *adj.* **1.** dipterous (def. 1). **—***n.* **2.** a dipterous insect. [1835–45; DIPTER(A) + -AN]

dip·ter·on (dip′tə ron′), *n., pl.* **-ter·a** (-tər ə). a dipterous insect. [1890–95; < Gk, neut. of *dípteros;* see DIPTERA]

dip·ter·ous (dip′tər əs), *adj.* **1.** *Entomol.* belonging or pertaining to the order Diptera, comprising the houseflies, mosquitoes, and gnats, characterized by a single, anterior pair of membranous wings with the posterior pair reduced to small, knobbed structures. **2.** *Bot.* having two winglike appendages, as seeds or stems. [1765–75; < NL *dipterus* < Gk *dípteros;* see DIPTERA, -OUS]

dip·tote (dip′tōt), *n.* a substantive declined in only two cases, esp. when occurring in a language in which this is less than the normal number. [1605–15; < LL *diptōtos* noun with only two cases < Gk, equiv. to *di-* DI-[1] + *-ptōtos,* verbid of *píptein* to fall; cf. *ptōsis* accidence, lit., falling]

dip·tych (dip′tik), *n.* **1.** a hinged two-leaved tablet used in ancient times for writing on with a stylus. **2.** Usually, **diptychs. a.** a similar tablet of wood or metal containing on one leaf the names of those among the living, and on the other those among the dead, for whom prayers and Masses are said. **b.** the lists of such persons. **c.** the intercession in the course of which these names were introduced. **3.** a pair of pictures or carvings on two panels, usually hinged together. [1615–25; < LL *diptycha* writing tablet with two leaves < Gk *díptycha,* neut. pl. of *díptychos* folded together, equiv. to *di-* DI-[1] + *-ptychos,* verbid of *ptýssein* to fold]

di·pyr·a·mid (dī pir′ə mid), *n. Crystall.* bipyramid. **—di·py·ram·i·dal** (dī′pi ram′i dl), *adj.*

di·pyr·id·a·mole (dī pir′i də mōl′, -pə rid′ə-), *n. Pharm.* a yellow crystalline powder, $C_{24}H_{40}N_8O_4$, used prophylactically for angina pectoris and in combination with other drugs to reduce thrombus formation. [DI-[1] + PYRI(MI)D(INE) + AM(INO)- + *-ole,* perh. -OLE[2]]

di·quat (dī′kwot), *n.* a yellow crystalline substance, $C_{12}H_{12}Br_2N_2$, used as a selective postemergence herbicide to control weeds on noncrop land and for aquatic weed control. [1955–60; DI-[1] + QUAT(ERNARY)]

dir., **1.** director. **2.** direxit.

Di·rac (di rak′), *n.* **Paul Adrien Maurice,** 1902–84, British physicist, in the U.S. after 1971: Nobel prize 1933.

Dirac′ del′ta func′tion, *Physics, Math.* See **delta function.** Also called **Dirac′ func′tion.** [named after P.A.M. DIRAC]

di·rad·i·cal (dī rad′i kəl), *n. Chem.* an atom or molecule having two unpaired electrons. Also called **biradical.** Cf. **free radical.** [DI-[1] + RADICAL]

Di·rae (dī′rē), *n. pl. Rom. Myth.* the Furies. See **fury** (def. 3).

dir·dum (dir′dəm, dûr′-), *n. Scot.* blame. [1400–50; Scots: blame, scolding, (earlier) altercation, uproar, late ME (north) *durdan* uproar, din < ScotGael; cf. Ir *deardan,* MIr *dertan* storm, rough weather]

dire (dīᵊr), *adj.,* **dir·er, dir·est.** **1.** causing or involving great fear or suffering; dreadful; terrible: *a dire calamity.* **2.** indicating trouble, disaster, misfortune, or the like: *dire predictions about the stock market.* **3.** urgent; desperate: *in dire need of food.* [1560–70; < L *dirus* fearful, unlucky] **—dire′ly,** *adv.* **—dire′ness,** *n.*

direc. prop., (in prescriptions) with a proper direction. [< L *directiōne propriā*]

di·rect (di rekt′, dī-), *v.t.* **1.** to manage or guide by advice, helpful information, instruction, etc.: *He directed the company through a difficult time.* **2.** to regulate the

CONCISE ETYMOLOGY KEY: <, descended or borrowed from; >, whence; b., blend of, blended; c., cognate with; cf., compare; deriv., derivative; equiv., equivalent; imit., imitative; obl., oblique; r., replacing; s., stem; sp., spelling, spelled; resp., respelling, respelled; trans., translation; ?, origin unknown; *, unattested; ‡, probably earlier than. See the full key inside the front cover.

course of; control: *History is directed by a small number of great men and women.* **3.** to administer; manage; supervise: *She directs the affairs of the estate.* **4.** to give authoritative instructions to; command; order or ordain: *I directed him to leave the room.* **5.** to serve as a director in the production or performance of (a musical work, play, motion picture, etc.). **6.** to guide, tell, or show (a person) the way to a place: *I directed him to the post office.* **7.** to point, aim, or send toward a place or object: *to direct radio waves around the globe.* **8.** to channel or focus toward a given result, object, or end (often fol. by *to* or *toward*): *She directed all her energies toward the accomplishment of the work.* **9.** to address (words, a speech, a written report, etc.) to a person or persons: *The secretary directed his remarks to two of the committee members.* **10.** to address (a letter, package, etc.) to an intended recipient. —*v.i.* **11.** to act as a guide. **12.** to give commands or orders. **13.** to serve as the director of a play, film, orchestra, etc. —*adj.* **14.** proceeding in a straight line or by the shortest course; straight; undeviating; not oblique: *a direct route.* **15.** proceeding in an unbroken line of descent; lineal rather than collateral: *a direct descendant.* **16.** *Math.* **a.** (of a proportion) containing terms of which an increase (or decrease) in one results in an increase (or decrease) in another: a term is said to be in direct proportion to another term if one increases (or decreases) as the other increases (or decreases). **b.** (of a function) the function itself, in contrast to its inverse. Cf. **inverse** (def. 2). **17.** without intervening persons, influences, factors, etc.; immediate; personal: *direct contact with the voters; direct exposure to a disease.* **18.** straightforward; frank; candid: *the direct remarks of a forthright individual.* **19.** absolute; exact: *the direct opposite.* **20.** consisting exactly of the words originally used; verbatim: *direct quotation.* **21.** *Govt.* of or by action of voters, which takes effect without any intervening agency such as representatives. **22.** inevitable; consequential: *War will be a direct result of such political action.* **23.** allocated for or arising from a particular known agency, process, job, etc.: *The new machine was listed by the accountant as a direct cost.* **24.** *Elect.* of or pertaining to direct current. **25.** *Astron.* **a.** moving in an orbit in the same direction as the earth in its revolution around the sun. **b.** appearing to move on the celestial sphere in the direction of the natural order of the signs of the zodiac, from west to east. Cf. **retrograde** (def. 4). **26.** *Survey.* (of a telescope) in its normal position; not inverted or transited. **27.** (of dye colors) working without the use of a mordant; substantive. —*adv.* **28.** in a direct manner; directly; straight: *Answer me direct.* [1325–75; ME *direct* (adj., adv.), *directen* (v.) (< AF) < L *dīrēctus, dērēctus* (the latter prob. the orig. form, later reanalyzed as *dī-* DI-[2]), ptp. of *dērigere* to align, straighten, guide (*dē-* DE- + *-rigere*, comb. form of *regere* to guide, rule)] —**di·rect′a·ble,** *adj.* —**di·rect′·ness,** *n.*
—**Syn. 1.** See **guide. 4.** DIRECT, ORDER, COMMAND mean to issue instructions. DIRECT suggests also giving explanations or advice; the emphasis is not on the authority of the director, but on steps necessary for the accomplishing of a purpose. ORDER connotes a personal relationship in which one in a superior position imperatively instructs a subordinate to do something. COMMAND, less personal and, often, less specific in detail, suggests greater formality and, sometimes, a more fixed authority on the part of the superior. **18.** open, sincere, outspoken.

di·rect-ac·cess (di rekt′ak′ses, -ak′-, dī-), *adj. Computers.* pertaining to the ability to obtain data from, or place data in, external storage without the need to sequentially scan other data contained there. Also, **random-access.** Cf. **sequential-access.**

direct′-access stor′age device′, *Computers.* See **DASD.**

di·rect-act·ing (di rekt′ak′ting, dī-), *adj.* (of a steam pump) having the steam pistons connected directly to the pump pistons without a crankshaft or flywheel. [1855–60]

direct′ ac′tion, any action seeking to achieve an immediate or direct result, esp. an action against an established authority or powerful institution, as a strike or picketing. [1835–45] —**direct′ ac′tionist.**

direct′ address′, **1.** *Gram.* the use of a term or name for the person spoken to, as in securing the attention of that person; use of a vocative form. **2.** *Computers.* See under **indirect address.**

direct′ broad′cast sat′ellite, *Television.* See **DBS.**

direct′ cin′ema, a rigorous form of cinéma vérité, esp. as practiced by some American cinematographers in the late 1950's, in which only indigenous sound is used.

direct′ cost′, a cost that can be related directly to the production of a product or to a particular function or service. Cf. **indirect cost.** [1895–1900]

direct′ cur′rent. *Elect.* an electric current of constant direction, having a magnitude that does not vary or varies only slightly. *Abbr.:* dc Cf. **alternating current.** [1885–90] —**di·rect′-cur′rent,** *adj.*

direct′ depos′it, a plan in which salaries or other payments are transferred by the paying agency directly to the accounts of the recipients.

di·rect-di·al (di rekt′dī′əl, -dīl′, dī-), *v.i., v.t.* **1.** to make a telephone call outside the local area without the assistance of an operator. —*adj.* **2.** being a telephone or telephone system enabling long-distance calls to be direct-dialed. **3.** of or pertaining to direct dialing. Also, **direct′ di′al.**

direct′ dis′course, quotation of a speaker in which the speaker's exact words are repeated. Cf. **indirect discourse.**

direct′ dis′tance di′aling, a telephone network service feature enabling customers to direct-dial their long-distance calls.

di·rect·ed (di rek′tid, dī-), *adj.* **1.** guided, regulated, or managed: *a carefully directed program.* **2.** subject to direction, guidance, regulation, etc. **3.** *Math.* having positive or negative direction or orientation assigned. [1530–40; DIRECT + -ED[2]] —**di·rect′ed·ness,** *n.*

di·rect′ed-en′er·gy device′ (di rek′tid en′ər jē, dī-). See **beam weapon.**

direct′ed ver′dict, an order by a judge to a jury to find a verdict because the facts proved are indisputable.

direct′ ev′idence, evidence of a witness who testifies to the truth of the fact to be proved (contrasted with *circumstantial evidence*).

direct′ examina′tion, *Law.* the first interrogation of a witness by the side that has called that witness.

di·rect-ex·am·ine (di rekt′ig zam′in, dī-), *v.t.,* **-ined, -in·ing.** *Law.* to subject to direct examination. Cf. **cross-examine** (def. 2).

direct′ free′ kick′, *Soccer.* a free kick awarded to a team as the result of a foul by an opposing player and from which a goal can be scored directly, without the ball being touched by another player.

di·rec·tion (di rek′shən, dī′-), *n.* **1.** the act or an instance of directing. **2.** the line along which anything lies, faces, moves, etc., with reference to the point or region toward which it is directed: *The storm moved in a northerly direction.* **3.** the point or region itself: *The direction is north.* **4.** a position on a line extending from a specific point toward a point of the compass or toward the nadir or the zenith. **5.** a line of thought or action or a tendency or inclination: *the direction of contemporary thought.* **6.** Usually, **directions.** instruction or guidance for making, using, etc.: *directions for baking a cake.* **7.** order; command. **8.** management; control; guidance; supervision: *a company under good direction.* **9.** a directorate. **10.** the name and address of the intended recipient as written on a letter, package, etc. **11.** decisions in a stage or film production as to stage business, speaking of lines, lighting, and general presentation. **12.** the technique, act, or business of making such decisions, managing and training a cast of actors, etc. **13.** the technique, act, or business of directing an orchestra, concert, or other musical presentation or group. **14.** *Music.* a symbol or phrase that indicates in a score the proper tempo, style of performance, mood, etc. **15.** a purpose or orientation toward a goal that serves to guide or motivate; focus: *He doesn't seem to have any direction in life.* [1375–1425; late ME *direccioun* (< MF) < L *dīrēctiōn-* (s. of *dīrēctiō*) arranging in line, straightening. See DIRECT, -ION] —**di·rec′tion·less,** *adj.*
—**Syn. 5.** See **tendency.**

di·rec·tion·al (di rek′shə nl, dī-), *adj.* **1.** of, pertaining to, or indicating direction in space. **2.** *Radio.* adapted for determining the direction of signals received, or for transmitting signals in a given direction: *a directional antenna.* **3.** of, pertaining to, or providing guidance or leadership. [1605–15; DIRECTION + -AL[1]] —**di·rec′tion·al′i·ty,** *n.* —**di·rec′tion·al·ly,** *adv.*

direc′tional deriv′ative, *Math.* the limit, as a function of several variables moving along a given line from one specified point to another on the line, of the difference in the functional values at the two points divided by the distance between the points.

direc′tional mi′crophone, a microphone that has a greater sensitivity to sounds coming from a particular area in front of it: used to eliminate unwanted sounds.

direc′tional sig′nal. See **turn signal.**

direc′tion an′gle, *Math.* an angle made by a given vector and a coordinate axis. Cf. **direction cosine.** [1930–35]

direc′tion co′sine, *Math.* the cosine of the angle made by a given vector and a coordinate axis. Cf. **direction angle.** [1890–95]

direc′tion find′er, *Radio.* a receiver with a loop antenna rotating on a vertical axis, used to ascertain the direction of incoming radio waves. —**direc′tion find′·ing.** [1910–15]

direc′tion num′ber, *Math.* the component of a vector along a given line; any number proportional to the direction cosines of a given line.

di·rec·tive (di rek′tiv, dī-), *adj.* **1.** serving to direct; directing: *a directive board.* **2.** *Psychol.* pertaining to a type of psychotherapy in which the therapist actively offers advice and information rather than dealing only with information supplied by the patient. —*n.* **3.** an authoritative instruction or direction; specific order: *a new directive by the President on foreign aid.* [1425–75; late ME < ML *dīrēctīvus.* See DIRECT, -IVE]

direct′ la′bor, labor performed, as by workers on a production line, and considered in computing costs per unit of production. Cf. **indirect labor.**

direct′ light′ing, lighting in which most of the light is cast directly from the fixture or source to the illumined area. [1925–30]

di·rect·ly (di rekt′lē, dī-), *adv.* **1.** in a direct line, way, or manner; straight: *The path leads directly to the lake.* **2.** at once; without delay; immediately: *Do that directly.* **3.** shortly; soon: *They will be here directly.* **4.** exactly; precisely: *directly opposite the store.* **5.** without intervening space; next in order: *The truck was parked directly behind my car.* **6.** openly or frankly; candidly: *He didn't hesitate to speak directly about his debts.* **7.** *Math.* in direct proportion. —*conj.* **8.** as soon as: *Directly he arrived, he mentioned the subject.* [1350–1400; ME *directli.* See DIRECT, -LY]
—**Syn. 2.** See **immediately. 6.** straightforwardly, freely, plainly, unreservedly.

direct′ mail′, mail, usually consisting of advertising matter, appeals for donations, or the like, sent simultaneously to large numbers of possible individual customers or contributors. *Abbr.:* DM [1925–30] —**di·rect′-mail′,** *adj.*

di·rect-mail·er (di rekt′mā′lər, dī-), *n.* **1.** a person or firm engaged in direct-mail advertising. **2.** a letter, advertisement, or other item sent out in direct mail.

direct′ mar′keting, marketing direct to the consumer, as by direct mail or coupon advertising.

direct′ meth′od, a technique of foreign-language teaching in which only the target language is used, little instruction is given concerning formal rules of grammar, and language use is often elicited in situational contexts. [1900–05]

direct′ ob′ject, a word or group of words representing the person or thing upon which the action of a verb is performed or toward which it is directed: in English, generally coming after the verb, without a preposition. In *He saw it* the pronoun *it* is the direct object of *saw.* [1900–05]

Di·rec·toire (dē rek twär′), *adj.* **1.** noting or pertaining to the style of French furnishings and decoration of the mid-1790's, characterized by an increasing use of Greco-Roman forms along with an introduction, toward the end, of Egyptian motifs: usually includes the Consulate period. **2.** (of costume) in the style of the period of the French Directory. —*n.* **3.** *Fr. Hist.* directory (def. 5). [< F; see DIRECTORY]

di·rec·tor (di rek′tər, dī-), *n.* **1.** a person or thing that directs. **2.** one of a group of persons chosen to control or govern the affairs of a company or corporation: *a board of directors.* **3.** the person responsible for the interpretive aspects of a stage, film, or television production; the person who supervises the integration of all the elements, as acting, staging, and lighting, required to realize the writer's conception. Cf. **producer** (def. 3). **4.** the musical conductor of an orchestra, chorus, etc. **5.** the manager or chief executive of certain schools, institutes, government bureaus, etc. **6.** *Mil.* a mechanical or electronic device that continuously calculates firing data for use against an airplane or other moving target. [1470–80; < LL; see DIRECT, -TOR] —**di·rec′tor·ship′,** *n.*
—**Syn. 1, 2, 5.** supervisor, head, manager, leader, administrator, chief, boss.

di·rec·to·rate (di rek′tər it, dī-), *n.* **1.** the office of a director. **2.** a body of directors. [1830–40; < F *directorat* < LL *dīrēctor* DIRECTOR + F *-at* -ATE[3]]

direc′tor gen′eral, *pl.* **directors general.** the executive head of an organization or of a major subdivision, as a branch or agency, of government. [1875–80]

di·rec·to·ri·al (di rek tôr′ē əl, -tōr′-, dī′rek-), *adj.* pertaining to a director or directorate. [1760–70; < LL *dīrēctōri(us)* (see DIRECT, -TORY[1]) + -AL[1]]

direc′tor of photog′raphy, *Motion Pictures.* the person who is responsible for all operations concerning camera work and lighting during the production of a film. Also called **cinematographer.**

direc′tor's chair′, a lightweight folding armchair with transversely crossed legs and having a canvas seat and back panel, as traditionally used by motion-picture directors. [1950–55]

di·rec·to·ry (di rek′tə rē, -trē, dī-), *n., pl.* **-ries,** *adj.* —*n.* **1.** a book containing an alphabetical index of the names and addresses of persons in a city, district, organization, etc., or of a particular category of people. **2.** a board or tablet on a wall of a building listing the room and floor numbers of the occupants. **3.** a book of directions. **4.** *Computers.* **a.** a list of files contained in external storage. **b.** a description of characteristics of a particular file, as the layout of fields within each record. **5. the Directory,** *Fr. Hist.* the body of five directors forming the executive power of France from 1795 to 1799. —*adj.* **6.** serving to direct; directing; directive. [1400–50; late ME < ML *dīrēctōrium,* n. use of LL *dīrēctōrius* DIRECTORIAL; in def. 5, trans. of F *Directoire* < ML, as above]

Direc′tory Assis′tance, a telephone company service that furnishes telephone directory information over the telephone. Also called **information.**

direct′ pos′itive, *Photog.* a positive obtained from another positive without an intermediate step.

direct′ pri′mary, *U.S. Politics.* a primary in which members of a party nominate its candidates by direct vote. Cf. **indirect primary.** [1895–1900]

direct′ prod′uct, *Math.* a group, or other such system, every element of which can be written uniquely as the product of elements of disjoint groups, with each group contributing one element to the product. [1920–25]

di·rec·tress (di rek′tris, dī-), *n.* a woman who is a director. [1570–80; DIRECT(O)R + -ESS]
—**Usage.** See **-ess.**

di·rec·trix (di rek′triks, dī-), *n., pl.* **di·rec·trix·es, di·rec·tri·ces** (di rek′tri sēz′, dī-, dī′rek tri′sēz). **1.** *Geom.* a fixed line used in the description of a curve or surface. See diag. under **parabola. 2.** *Archaic.* a directress. [1615–25; < NL; see DIRECT, -TRIX]
—**Usage.** See **-trix.**

direct′ sum′, *Math.* a composition of two disjoint sets, as vector spaces, such that every element in the composition can be written uniquely as the sum of two elements, one from each of the given sets. [1925–30]

direct′ tax′, *Govt.* a tax exacted directly from the persons who will bear the burden of it (without reimbursement to them at the expense of others), as a poll tax, a general property tax, or an income tax. [1785–90, *Amer.*]

di·rect′-vi′sion prism′ (di rekt′vizh′ən, dī-), *Optics.* See **Amici prism.** [‡1960–65]

direct′-vi′sion spec′troscope, *Optics.* a simple spectroscope consisting of a collimating lens and an Amici prism. [1875–80]

Di·re·da·wa (dē′rä də wä′), *n.* a city in E Ethiopia. 76,800. Also, **Di′re Da·wa′.**

dire·ful (dīᵊr′fəl), *adj.* **1.** dreadful; awful; terrible. **2.**

CONCISE PRONUNCIATION KEY: act, cāpe, dâre, pärt; set, ēqual; if, īce; ox, ōver, ôrder, oil, bo͝ok, bo͞ot, out; up, ûrge; child; sing; shoe; thin, *th*at; zh as in *treasure*. ə = *a* as in *alone*, *e* as in *system*, *i* as in *easily*, *o* as in *gallop*, *u* as in *circus*; ᵊ as in *fire* (fīᵊr), *hour* (ouᵊr). l and n can serve as syllabic consonants, as in *cradle* (krād′l), and *button* (but′n). See the full key inside the front cover.

indicating trouble: *direful forecasts.* [1575–85; DIRE + -FUL] **—dire′ful·ly,** *adv.* **—dire′ful·ness,** *n.*

di·remp·tion (di remp′shən), *n.* a sharp division into two parts; disjunction; separation. [1615–25; < L *diremptiōn-* (s. of *diremptiō*), equiv. to *dirempt(us)* (ptp. of *dirimere* to separate, equiv. to *dis-* DIS-[1] + *-imere,* comb. form of *emere* to take, buy) + *-iōn-* -ION]

dire′ wolf′, an extinct wolf, *Canis dirus,* widespread in North America during the Pleistocene Epoch, having a larger body and a smaller brain than the modern wolf. [1920–25; from the NL specific epithet *dirus* inspiring dread; cf. DIRE]

di·rex·it (dē REK′sit; *Eng.* dī rek′sit), *Latin.* he supervised (this); she supervised (this). *Abbr.:* dir., direx.

dirge (dûrj), *n.* **1.** a funeral song or tune, or one expressing mourning in commemoration of the dead. **2.** any composition resembling such a song or tune in character, as a poem of lament for the dead or solemn, mournful music: *Tennyson's dirge for the Duke of Wellington.* **3.** a mournful sound resembling a dirge: *The autumn wind sang the dirge of summer.* **4.** *Eccles.* the office of the dead, or the funeral service as sung. [1175–1225; ME *dir(i)ge* < L: DIRECT, syncopated var. of *dirige* (impv. of *dirigere*), first word of the antiphon sung in the Latin office of the dead (Psalm V, 8)]

dir·ham (dir ham′, di ram′, dir′əm), *n.* **1.** a money of account of Iraq, the 20th part of a dinar, equal to 50 fils. **2.** a money of account of Kuwait, the 10th part of a dinar, equal to 100 fils. **3.** a brass-clad steel coin and monetary unit of Libya, the 1000th part of a dinar: replaced the millieme in 1971. **4.** a cupronickel coin and monetary unit of Morocco, equal to 100 centimes. *Abbr.:* DH. **5.** a bronze or cupronickel coin of Qatar, the 100th part of a riyal. **6.** a money of account of Tunisia, the 10th part of a dinar, equal to 100 millimes. **7.** a cupronickel coin and monetary unit of the United Arab Emirates, equal to 100 fils. [1965–70; < Ar *dirham* < Gk *drachma;* see DRACHMA]

dir·hem (dir hem′, di rem′, dir′əm), *n.* any of various fractional silver coins issued in Islamic countries at different periods. [1780–90; var. of DIRHAM]

di·rhin·ous (dī rī′nəs), *adj. Zool.* having paired nostrils. [DI-[1] + RHIN- + -OUS]

Di·ri·chlet (dir′i klā′; *Ger.* dē′RĒ klā′), *n.* **Pe·ter Gus·tav Le·jeune** (pā′tər go͞os′täf lə zhœn′), 1805–59, German mathematician.

dir·i·gi·ble (dir′i jə bəl, di rij′ə-), *n.* **1.** an airship. *—adj.* **2.** designed for or capable of being directed, controlled, or steered. [1575–85; 1905–10 for n.; < L *dirig(ere)* to DIRECT + -IBLE] **—dir′i·gi·bil′i·ty,** *n.*

di·ri·go (dē′RI gō′; *Eng.* dir′i gō′), *Latin.* I direct: motto of Maine.

dir·i·ment (dir′ə mənt), *adj.* causing to become wholly void; nullifying. [1840–50; < L *diriment-,* s. of *dirimēns,* prp. of *dirimere;* see DIREMPTION]

dir′iment imped′iment, *Law.* a fact or circumstance that renders a marriage void from the beginning.

dirk (dûrk), *n.* **1.** a dagger, esp. of the Scottish Highlands. *—v.t.* **2.** to stab with a dirk. [1595–1605; orig. Scots; of obscure etym.]

Dirk (dûrk), *n.* a male given name, form of **Derek.**

dirl (dirl, dûrl), *v.i. Scot.* to vibrate; shake. [1505–15; akin to DRILL]

dirn·dl (dûrn′dl), *n.* **1.** a woman's dress with a close-fitting bodice and full skirt, commonly of colorful and strikingly patterned material, fashioned after Tyrolean peasant wear. **2.** a full, gathered skirt attached to a waistband or hip yoke. **3.** any skirt with gathers at the waistband. [1935–40; < G *Dirndl,* short for *Dirndlkleid,* equiv. to *Dirndl* young woman (orig. Bavarian, Austrian dial., dim. of *Dirne* young woman, MHG *dierne,* OHG *thiorna;* akin to THANE) + *Kleid* dress (see CLOTH)]

dirt (dûrt), *n.* **1.** any foul or filthy substance, as mud, grime, dust, or excrement. **2.** earth or soil, esp. when loose. **3.** something or someone vile, mean, or worthless: *After that last outburst of hers I thought she was dirt.* **4.** moral filth; vileness; corruption. **5.** obscene or lewd language: *to talk dirt.* **6.** *Informal.* gossip, esp. of a malicious, lurid, or scandalous nature: *Tell me all the latest dirt.* **7.** private or personal information which if made public would create a scandal or ruin the reputation of a person, company, etc. **8.** *Mining.* **a.** crude, broken ore or waste. **b.** (in placer mining) the material from which gold is separated by washing. **9. do (someone) dirt.** See **dirty** (def. 15). **10. eat dirt,** *Informal.* to accept blame, guilt, criticism, or insults without complaint; humble or abase oneself: *The prosecutor seemed determined to make the defendant eat dirt.* [1250–1300; ME *dirt, drit;* c. ON *drit* excrement; cf. OE *drītan*]
—Syn. 6. scandal, slander, rumor, scuttlebutt.

dirt′ bike′. *Informal.* See **trail bike.**

dirt-cheap (dûrt′chēp′), *adj.* **1.** very inexpensive: *The house may need a lot of work, but it was dirt-cheap.* *—adv.* **2.** cheaply: *They got it dirt-cheap.* [1815–25]

dirt′ daub′er, *South Midland and Southern U.S.* mud dauber.

dirt′ farm′, a tract of land on which a dirt farmer works.

dirt′ farm′er, a farmer who works on the soil, distinguished from one who operates a farm with hired hands or tenants. [1920–25, *Amer.*] **—dirt′ farm′ing.**

dirt′ poor′, lacking nearly all material means or resources for living. [1935–40, *Amer.*]

dirt′ road′, an unpaved road. [1850–55, *Amer.*]

dirt·y (dûr′tē), *adj.,* **dirt·i·er, dirt·i·est,** *v.,* **dirt·ied, dirt·y·ing,** *adv.* *—adj.* **1.** soiled with dirt; foul; unclean: *dirty laundry.* **2.** spreading or imparting dirt; soiling: *dirty smoke.* **3.** vile; mean; sordid; contemptible: *to play a dirty trick on someone.* **4.** obscene; pornographic; lewd: *a dirty joke.* **5.** undesirable or unpleasant; thankless: *He left the dirty work for me.* **6.** very unfortunate or regrettable: *That's a dirty shame!* **7.** not fair or sportsmanlike; unscrupulous: *a dirty fighter.* **8.** hostile, insulting, contemptuous, or resentful: *She gave me a dirty look. He made a dirty crack about the cooking.* **9.** (of a nuclear weapon) producing a relatively large amount of radioactive fallout. **10.** (of the weather) stormy; squally: *It looks dirty to windward.* **11.** *Informal.* obtained through illegal or disreputable means: *dirty money.* **12.** appearing as if soiled; dark-colored; dingy; murky. **13.** *Slang.* using or in possession of narcotics. **14.** *Foreign Exchange.* (of currency floats) manipulated, as by a central bank influencing or changing exchange rates (opposed to *clean*). **15. do (someone) dirty,** *Slang.* to treat unfairly or reprehensibly, as by cheating or slandering. *—v.t., v.i.* **16.** to make or become dirty. *—adv.* **17.** *Informal.* in a mean, unscrupulous, or underhand way: *to play dirty.* **18.** *Informal.* in a lewd manner: *to talk dirty.* [1520–30; DIRT + -Y[1]] **—dirt′i·ly,** *adv.* **—dirt′i·ness,** *n.*
—Syn. 1. grimy, defiled. DIRTY, FILTHY, FOUL, SQUALID refer to that which is not clean. DIRTY is applied to that which is filled or covered with dirt so that it is unclean or defiled: *dirty clothes.* FILTHY is an emphatic word suggesting something that is excessively soiled or dirty: *filthy streets.* Both DIRTY and FILTHY can refer to obscenity: *a dirty mind, a filthy novel.* FOUL implies an uncleanness that is grossly offensive to the senses: *a foul odor.* SQUALID, applied usually to dwellings or surroundings, implies dirtiness that results from the slovenly indifference often associated with poverty: *a squalid tenement.* **3.** base, vulgar, low, shabby, groveling. **4.** nasty, lascivious, lecherous. **10.** rainy, foul, sloppy, disagreeable, nasty. **12.** dull, dark, sullied, clouded. **16.** soil.

dirt′y bomb′, a nuclear warhead designed to produce a great amount of radioactive debris by use of a fusion core, fission trigger, and casing of uranium-238.

dirt′y lin′en, personal or private matters that could cause embarrassment if made public: *You didn't have to air our dirty linen to all your friends!* Also called **dirt′y laun′dry.** [1945–50]

dirt·y-mind·ed (dûr′tē mīn′did), *adj.* tending to have vulgar, obscene, or lewd thoughts, interpretations, etc. [1885–90]

dirt′y old′ man′, *Informal.* a mature or elderly man with lewd or obscene preoccupations. [1930–35]

dirt′y pool′, *Informal.* unethical, unfair, or unsportsmanlike conduct.

dirt′y rice′, a Cajun dish of rice cooked with herbs and often chicken livers.

dirt′y tricks′, *Informal.* **1.** *Politics.* unethical or illegal campaign practices or pranks intended to disrupt or sabotage the campaigns of opposing candidates. **2.** any similar practices carried out against rival countries or corporations for espionage or commercial purposes. [1970–75] **—dirt·y·trick·er·y** (dûr′tē trik′ə rē), *n.* **—dirt′y-tricks′,** *adj.* **—dirt·y-trick·ster** (dûr′tē trik′stər), *n.*

dirt′y war′, a war conducted by the military or secret police of a regime against revolutionary and terrorist insurgents and often marked by the kidnapping, torture, and murder of civilians.

dirt′y word′, **1.** a vulgar or taboo word; obscenity. **2.** any word, name, or concept considered reprehensible or unmentionable; anathema: *"Lose" is a dirty word to this team.* [1835–45]

dirt′y work′, **1.** disagreeable, often tedious tasks. **2.** any illegal or dishonest dealing.

dis[1] (dēs), *n., pl.* **dis·ir** (dē′sir). *Scand. Myth.* **1.** lady; woman. **2.** female deity, esp. one promoting fertility: often used as a suffix on names: *Freydis; Hjordis; Thordis.* [< ON *dīs,* pl. *dīsir;* orig. uncert.]

dis[2] (dis), *v.,* **dissed, dis·sing,** *n. Slang.* *—v.t.* **1.** to show disrespect for; affront. **2.** to disparage; belittle. *—n.* **3.** insult or disparagement; criticism. [1980–85, *Amer.;* from DIS-[1] extracted from such words as *disrespect* and *disparage*]

Dis (dis), *n. Class. Myth.* a god of the underworld. Also called **Dis Pater.** Cf. **Pluto.**

dis-[1], a Latin prefix meaning "apart," "asunder," "away," "utterly," or having a privative, negative, or reversing force (see **de-, un-**[2]); used freely, esp. with these latter senses, as an English formative: *disability; disaffirm; disbar; disbelief; discontent; dishearten; dislike; disown.* Also, **di-.** [< L (akin to *bis,* Gk *dís* twice); before *f, dif-;* before some consonants, *di-;* often r. obs. *des-* < OF]

dis-[2], var. of **di-**[1] before *s: dissyllable.*

dis., **1.** distance. **2.** distant. **3.** distribute.

dis·a·bil·i·ty (dis′ə bil′i tē), *n., pl.* **-ties** for 2. **1.** lack of adequate power, strength, or physical or mental ability; incapacity. **2.** a physical or mental handicap, esp. one that prevents a person from living a full, normal life or from holding a gainful job. **3.** anything that disables or puts one at a disadvantage. **4.** the state or condition of being disabled. **5.** legal incapacity; legal disqualification. **6.** See **disability insurance.** [1570–80; DIS-[1] + ABILITY]
—Syn. 1. disqualification, incompetence, incapability, impotence. DISABILITY, INABILITY imply a lack of power or ability. A DISABILITY is some disqualifying deprivation or loss of power, physical or other: *excused because of a physical disability.* INABILITY is a lack of ability, usually because of an inherent lack of talent, power, etc.: *inability to talk, to do well in higher mathematics.*

disabil′ity clause′, *Insurance.* a clause in a life-insurance policy providing for waiver of premium and sometimes payment of monthly income if the policyholder becomes totally and permanently disabled.

disabil′ity insur′ance, insurance providing income to a policyholder who is disabled and cannot work.

dis·a·ble (dis ā′bəl), *v.t.,* **-bled, -bling.** **1.** to make unable or unfit; weaken or destroy the capability of; cripple; incapacitate: *He was disabled by blindness.* **2.** to make legally incapable; disqualify. [1475–85; DIS-[1] + ABLE] **—dis·a′ble·ment,** *n.* **—dis·a′bler,** *n.*
—Syn. 1. enfeeble, paralyze. See **cripple.**

dis·a·bled (dis ā′bəld), *adj.* **1.** crippled; injured; incapacitated. *—n.* **2.** (*used with a plural v.*) persons who are crippled, injured, or incapacitated (usually prec. by *the*): *Ramps have been installed at the entrances to accommodate the disabled.* [1625–35; DISABLE + -ED[2]]

dis·a·buse (dis′ə byo͞oz′), *v.t.,* **-bused, -bus·ing.** to free (a person) from deception or error. [1605–15; < F *désabuser.* See DIS-[1], ABUSE] **—dis′a·bus′al,** *n.*

di·sac·cha·ri·dase (dī sak′ər i dās′, -dāz′), *n. Biochem.* an enzyme that catalyzes the hydrolysis of disaccharides, as sucrose or lactose, to produce monosaccharides, as fructose or glucose. [1960–65; DISACCHARIDE + -ASE]

di·sac·cha·ride (dī sak′ə rīd′, -rid), *n. Chem.* any of a group of carbohydrates, as sucrose or lactose, that yield monosaccharides on hydrolysis. Also called **double sugar.** [1890–95; DI-[1] + SACCHARIDE]

dis·ac·cord (dis′ə kôrd′), *v.i.* **1.** to be out of accord; disagree. *—n.* **2.** disagreement: *grave disaccords among nations.* [1350–1400; ME < AF, OF *desac(c)order,* deriv. of *desacort.* See DIS-[1], ACCORD]

dis·ac·cred·it (dis′ə kred′it), *v.t.* to take away the accreditation or authorization of: *to disaccredit a diplomat.* [DIS-[1] + ACCREDIT] **—dis′ac·cred′i·ta′tion,** *n.*

dis·ac·cus·tom (dis′ə kus′təm), *v.t.* to cause to lose a habit: *In the country I was quickly disaccustomed of sleeping late.* [1475–85; < AF *desacustumer;* MF, OF. See DIS-[1], ACCUSTOM]

dis·ad·van·tage (dis′əd van′tij, -vän′-), *n., v.,* **-taged, -tag·ing.** *—n.* **1.** absence or deprivation of advantage or equality. **2.** the state or an instance of being in an unfavorable circumstance or condition: *to be at a disadvantage.* **3.** something that puts one in an unfavorable position or condition: *His bad temper is a disadvantage.* **4.** injury to interest, reputation, credit, profit, etc.; loss: *Your behavior is a disadvantage to your family's good name.* *—v.t.* **5.** to subject to disadvantage: *I was disadvantaged by illness.* [1350–1400; ME *disavauntage* < AF; OF *desavantage.* See DIS-[1], ADVANTAGE]
—Syn. 1. drawback, inconvenience, hindrance. **4.** detriment, hurt, harm, damage.

dis·ad·van·taged (dis′əd van′tijd, -vän′-), *adj.* **1.** lacking the normal or usual necessities and comforts of life, as proper housing, educational opportunities, job security, adequate medical care, etc.: *The government extends help to disadvantaged minorities.* *—n.* **2.** (*used with a plural v.*) disadvantaged persons collectively (usually prec. by *the*): *The Senator advocates increased funding for federal programs that aid the disadvantaged.* [1930–35; DISADVANTAGE + -ED[2]] **—dis′ad·van′·taged·ness,** *n.*
—Syn. 1. poor, underprivileged, impoverished, deprived; handicapped, impaired, disabled.

dis·ad·van·ta·geous (dis ad′vən tā′jəs, dis′ad-), *adj.* characterized by or involving disadvantage; unfavorable; detrimental. [1595–1605; DIS-[1] + ADVANTAGEOUS] **—dis·ad′van·ta′geous·ly,** *adv.* **—dis·ad′van·ta′geous·ness,** *n.*

dis·af·fect (dis′ə fekt′), *v.t.* to alienate the affection, sympathy, or support of; make discontented or disloyal: *The dictator's policies had soon disaffected the people.* [1615–25; DIS-[1] + AFFECT[2]]
—Syn. See **estrange.**

dis·af·fect·ed (dis′ə fek′tid), *adj.* discontented and disloyal, as toward the government or toward authority. [1625–35; DISAFFECT + -ED[2]] **—dis′af·fect′ed·ly,** *adv.* **—dis′af·fect′ed·ness,** *n.*

dis·af·fec·tion (dis′ə fek′shən), *n.* the absence or alienation of affection or goodwill; estrangement; disloyalty: *Disaffection often leads to outright treason.* [1595–1605; DIS-[1] + AFFECTION[1]]

dis·af·fil·i·ate (dis′ə fil′ē āt′), *v.,* **-at·ed, -at·ing.** *—v.t.* **1.** to sever affiliation with; disassociate: *He disaffiliated himself from the political group he had once led.* *—v.i.* **2.** to sever an affiliation. [1865–70; DIS-[1] + AFFILIATE] **—dis′af·fil′i·a′tion,** *n.*

dis·af·firm (dis′ə fûrm′), *v.t.* **1.** to deny; contradict. **2.** *Law.* to annul; reverse; repudiate. [1525–35; DIS-[1] + AFFIRM] **—dis·af·fir·ma·tion** (dis′af ər mā′shən), **dis′·af·fir′mance,** *n.*

dis·ag·gre·gate (dis ag′ri gāt′), *v.,* **-gat·ed, -gat·ing.** *—v.t.* **1.** to separate (an aggregate or mass) into its component parts. *—v.i.* **2.** to become separated from an aggregate or mass. [1820–30; DIS- + AGGREGATE] **—dis·ag′gre·ga′tion,** *n.* **—dis·ag′gre·ga′tive,** *adj.*

dis·a·gree (dis′ə grē′), *v.i.,* **-greed, -gree·ing.** **1.** to fail to agree; differ: *The conclusions disagree with the facts. The theories disagree in their basic premises.* **2.** to differ in opinion; dissent: *Three of the judges disagreed with the verdict.* **3.** to quarrel: *They disagreed violently and parted company.* **4.** to cause physical discomfort or ill effect (usually fol. by *with*): *The oysters disagreed with her. Cold weather disagrees with me.* [1425–75; late ME < AF, MF *desagreer.* See DIS-[1], AGREE]

dis·a·gree·a·ble (dis′ə grē′ə bəl), *adj.* **1.** contrary to one's taste or liking; unpleasant; offensive; repugnant. **2.** unpleasant in manner or nature; unamiable: *a thoroughly disagreeable person.* *—n.* **3.** an unpleasant or repugnant circumstance, attribute, thing, etc.: *Bent on being cheerful, he suppressed any mention of the disagreeable in our conversation.* **4. disagreeables,** the disagreeable aspects of a situation, course of action, etc.: *The pleasant features of the arrangement far outweigh the disagreeables.* [1350–1400; ME < MF *desagreable.* See DIS-[1], AGREEABLE] **—dis′a·gree′a·ble·ness, dis′a·gree′a·bil′i·ty,** *n.* **—dis′a·gree′a·bly,** *adv.*
—Syn. 2. cross, grouchy, surly, testy.

dis·a·gree·ment (dis′ə grē′mənt), *n.* **1.** the act,

CONCISE ETYMOLOGY KEY: <, descended or borrowed from; >, whence; b., blend of, blended; c., cognate with; cf., compare; deriv., derivative; equiv., equivalent; imit., imitative; obl., oblique; r., replacing; s., stem; sp., spelling, spelled; resp., respelling, respelled; trans., translation; ?, origin unknown; *, unattested; ‡, probably earlier than. See the full key inside the front cover.

state, or fact of disagreeing. **2.** lack of agreement; diversity; unlikeness: *a disagreement of colors.* **3.** difference of opinion; dissent. **4.** quarrel; dissension; argument. [1485–95; < AF, MF *desagrement.* See DISAGREE, -MENT]

dis a·li·ter vi·sum (dēs ä′li teʀ′ wē′so͝om; *Eng.* dis al′i tər vī′səm), *Latin.* the gods have deemed otherwise.

dis·al·low (dis′ə lou′), *v.t.* **1.** to refuse to allow; reject; veto: *to disallow a claim for compensation.* **2.** to refuse to admit the truth or validity of: *to disallow the veracity of a report.* [1350–1400; ME < OF *desallouer.* See DIS-[1], ALLOW] **—dis′al·low′a·ble,** *adj.* **—dis′al·low′a·ble·ness,** *n.* **—dis′al·low′ance,** *n.*

dis·am·big·u·ate (dis′am big′yo͞o āt′), *v.t.*, **-at·ed, -at·ing.** to remove the ambiguity from; make unambiguous: *In order to disambiguate the sentence "She lectured on the famous passenger ship," you'll have to write either "lectured on board" or "lectured about."* [1960–65; DIS-[1] + AMBIGU(OUS) + -ATE[1]] **—dis′am·big′u·a′·tion,** *n.*

dis·an·nul (dis′ə nul′), *v.t.*, **-nulled, -nul·ling.** to annul utterly; make void: *to disannul a contract.* [1485–95; DIS-[1] + ANNUL] **—dis′an·nul′ler,** *n.* **—dis′an·nul′·ment,** *n.*

dis·ap·pear (dis′ə pēr′), *v.i.* **1.** to cease to be seen; vanish from sight. **2.** to cease to exist or be known; pass away; end gradually: *One by one the symptoms disappeared.* [1520–30; DIS-[1] + APPEAR]
—Syn. 1. DISAPPEAR, FADE, VANISH suggest that something passes from sight. DISAPPEAR is used of whatever suddenly or gradually goes out of sight: *We watched him turn down a side street and then disappear.* FADE suggests a (complete or partial) disappearance that proceeds gradually and often by means of a blending into something else: *Colors in the sky at sunrise quickly fade.* VANISH suggests complete, generally rapid, and often mysterious disappearance: *A mirage can vanish as suddenly as it appears.*

dis·ap·pear·ance (dis′ə pēr′əns), *n.* the act or an instance of disappearing; a ceasing to be seen or to exist. [1705–15; DISAPPEAR + -ANCE]

dis·ap·point (dis′ə point′), *v.t.* **1.** to fail to fulfill the expectations or wishes of: *His gross ingratitude disappointed us.* **2.** to defeat the fulfillment of (hopes, plans, etc.); thwart; frustrate: *to be disappointed in love.* —*v.i.* **3.** to bring or cause disappointment. [1400–50; late ME < MF *desappointer.* See DIS-[1], APPOINT] **—dis′ap·point′er,** *n.*
—Syn. 1. sadden, disillusion, dishearten, disenchant.

dis·ap·point·ed (dis′ə poin′tid), *adj.* **1.** depressed or discouraged by the failure of one's hopes or expectations: *a disappointed suitor.* **2.** *Obs.* inadequately appointed; ill-equipped. [1545–55; DISAPPOINT + -ED[2]] **—dis′ap·point′ed·ly,** *adv.*

dis·ap·point·ing (dis′ə poin′ting), *adj.* failing to fulfill one's hopes or expectations: *a disappointing movie; a disappointing marriage.* [1520–30; DISAPPOINT + -ING[2]] **—dis′ap·point′ing·ly,** *adv.*

dis·ap·point·ment (dis′ə point′mənt), *n.* **1.** the act or fact of disappointing: *All of his efforts only led to the disappointment of his supporters.* **2.** the state or feeling of being disappointed: *Her disappointment was very great when she didn't get the job.* **3.** a person or thing that disappoints: *The play was a disappointment.* [1605–15; DISAPPOINT + -MENT]
—Syn. 1. failure, defeat, frustration.

dis·ap·pro·ba·tion (dis′ap rə bā′shən), *n.* disapproval; condemnation. [1640–50; DIS-[1] + APPROBATION]

dis·ap·prov·al (dis′ə pro͞o′vəl), *n.* the act or state of disapproving; a condemnatory feeling, look, or utterance; censure: *stern disapproval.* [1655–65; DIS-[1] + APPROVAL]
—Syn. disapprobation, dislike, condemnation.

dis·ap·prove (dis′ə pro͞ov′), *v.*, **-proved, -prov·ing.** —*v.t.* **1.** to think (something) wrong or reprehensible; censure or condemn in opinion. **2.** to withhold approval from; decline to sanction: *The Senate disapproved the nominations.* —*v.i.* **3.** to have an unfavorable opinion; express disapproval (usually fol. by *of*). [1475–85; DIS-[1] + APPROVE] **—dis′ap·prov′er,** *n.* **—dis′ap·prov′ing·ly,** *adv.*
—Syn. 1. deplore, decry, criticize. **—Ant. 1.** praise.

dis·arm (dis ärm′), *v.t.* **1.** to deprive of a weapon or weapons. **2.** to remove the fuze or other actuating device from: *to disarm a bomb.* **3.** to deprive of the means of attack or defense: *The lack of logic disarmed his argument.* **4.** to divest or relieve of hostility, suspicion, etc.; win the affection or approval of; charm: *His smile disarmed us.* —*v.i.* **5.** to lay down one's weapons. **6.** (of a country) to reduce or limit the size, equipment, armament, etc., of the army, navy, or air force. [1325–75; ME < OF *desarmer.* See DIS-[1], ARM[2]] **—dis·arm′er,** *n.*

dis·ar·ma·ment (dis är′mə mənt), *n.* **1.** the act or an instance of disarming. **2.** the reduction or limitation of the size, equipment, armament, etc., of the army, navy, or air force of a country. [1785–95; DISARM + *-ament,* after ARMAMENT]

dis·arm·ing (dis är′ming), *adj.* removing or capable of removing hostility, suspicion, etc., as by being charming: *a disarming smile.* [1540–50; DISARM + -ING[2]] **—dis·arm′ing·ly,** *adv.*
—Syn. winning, engaging, winsome.

dis·ar·range (dis′ə rānj′), *v.t.*, **-ranged, -rang·ing.** to disturb the arrangement of; disorder; unsettle. [1735–45; DIS-[1] + ARRANGE] **—dis′ar·range′ment,** *n.* **—dis′ar·rang′er,** *n.*

dis·ar·ray (dis′ə rā′), *v.t.* **1.** to put out of array or order; throw into disorder. **2.** to undress. —*n.* **3.** disorder; confusion: *The army retreated in disarray.* **4.** disorder of apparel. [1350–1400; (n.) late ME; ME *disrai, d(e)rai* < AF *dissairay,* OF *desroi;* (v.) ME *disarayen* < AF *desaraier,* OF *desareer;* see DIS-[1], ARRAY]

dis·ar·tic·u·late (dis′är tik′yə lāt′), *v.t., v.i.*, **-lat·ed, -lat·ing.** to make or become disjointed, as the bones of a body or stems of a plant. [1820–30; DIS-[1] + ARTICULATE] **—dis′ar·tic′u·la′tion,** *n.* **—dis′ar·tic′u·la′tor,** *n.*

dis·as·sem·ble (dis′ə sem′bəl), *v.*, **-bled, -bling.** —*v.t.* **1.** to take apart. —*v.i.* **2.** to come apart: *These shelves disassemble quickly for easy moving.* [1605–15; DIS-[1] + ASSEMBLE] **—dis′as·sem′bly,** *n.*

dis·as·so·ci·ate (dis′ə sō′shē āt′, -sē-), *v.t.*, **-at·ed, -at·ing.** to dissociate. [1595–1605; DIS-[1] + ASSOCIATE] **—dis′as·so′ci·a′tion,** *n.*

dis·as·sort′a·tive mat′ing (dis′ə sôr′tə tiv), *Animal Behav., Psychol.* the reproductive pairing of individuals that have traits more dissimilar than would likely be the case if mating were random (contrasted with *assortative mating*). Cf. **panmixia.** [DIS-[1] + ASSORT + -ATIVE]

dis·as·ter (di zas′tər, -zä′stər), *n.* **1.** a calamitous event, esp. one occurring suddenly and causing great loss of life, damage, or hardship, as a flood, airplane crash, or business failure. **2.** *Obs.* an unfavorable aspect of a star or planet. [1585–95; < MF *desastre* < It *disastro,* equiv. to *dis-* DIS-[1] + *astro* star < L *astrum* < Gk *ástron*]
—Syn. 1. mischance, misfortune, misadventure, mishap, accident, blow, reverse, adversity, affliction. DISASTER, CALAMITY, CATASTROPHE, CATACLYSM refer to adverse happenings often occurring suddenly and unexpectedly. A DISASTER may be caused by carelessness, negligence, bad judgment, or the like, or by natural forces, as a hurricane or flood: *a railroad disaster.* CALAMITY suggests great affliction, either personal or general; the emphasis is on the grief or sorrow caused: *the calamity of losing a child.* CATASTROPHE refers esp. to the tragic outcome of a personal or public situation; the emphasis is on the destruction or irreplaceable loss: *the catastrophe of a defeat in battle.* CATACLYSM, physically an earth-shaking change, refers to a personal or public upheaval of unparalleled violence: *a cataclysm that turned his life in a new direction.*

disas′ter ar′ea, 1. a region or locality in which the population is generally affected by the occurrence of a major disaster, as a widespread flood, an explosion causing extensive damage, or the like. **2.** such a region or locality officially determined to be eligible, under statutory provisions, for emergency governmental relief. [1955–60]

dis·as·trous (di zas′trəs, -zä′strəs), *adj.* **1.** causing great distress or injury; ruinous; very unfortunate; calamitous: *The rain and cold proved disastrous to his health.* **2.** *Archaic.* foreboding disaster. [1580–90; < MF *desastreux,* It *disastroso.* See DISASTER, -OUS] **—dis·as′trous·ly,** *adv.* **—dis·as′trous·ness,** *n.*

dis·a·vow (dis′ə vou′), *v.t.* to disclaim knowledge of, connection with, or responsibility for; disown; repudiate: *He disavowed the remark that had been attributed to him.* [1350–1400; ME *disavouen, desavouen* < AF, OF *desavouer.* See DIS-[1], AVOW] **—dis′a·vow′ed·ly,** *adv.* **—dis′a·vow′er,** *n.*
—Syn. deny, reject, disclaim.

dis·a·vow·al (dis′ə vou′əl), *n.* a disowning; repudiation; denial. [1740–50; DISAVOW + -AL[2]]

dis·band (dis band′), *v.t.* **1.** to break up or dissolve (an organization): *They disbanded the corporation.* —*v.i.* **2.** to disperse. [1585–95; < MF *desbander,* equiv. to *des-* DIS-[1] + *-bander,* deriv. of *bande* troop, BAND[1]] **—dis·band′ment,** *n.*

dis·bar (dis bär′), *v.t.*, **-barred, -bar·ring.** to expel from the legal profession or from the bar of a particular court. [1625–35; DIS-[1] + BAR[1]] **—dis·bar′ment,** *n.*
—Syn. debar, suspend, exclude.

dis·be·lief (dis′bi lēf′), *n.* **1.** the inability or refusal to believe or to accept something as true. **2.** amazement; astonishment: *We stared at the Taj Mahal in disbelief.* [1665–75; DIS-[1] + BELIEF]

dis·be·lieve (dis′bi lēv′), *v.*, **-lieved, -liev·ing.** —*v.t.* **1.** to have no belief in; refuse or reject belief in: *to disbelieve reports of UFO sightings.* —*v.i.* **2.** to refuse or reject belief; have no belief. [1635–45; DIS-[1] + BELIEVE] **—dis′be·liev′er,** *n.* **—dis′be·liev′ing·ly,** *adv.*

dis·bos·om (dis bo͝oz′əm, -bo͞o′zəm), *v.t.* to reveal; confess. [1835–45; DIS-[1] + BOSOM]

dis·bound (dis bound′), *adj.* (of a book) having the binding torn or loose. [1965–70; DIS- + BOUND[1]]

dis·bud (dis bud′), *v.t.*, **-bud·ded, -bud·ding.** *Hort.* **1.** to remove leaf buds or shoots from (a plant) to produce a certain shape or effect. **2.** to remove certain flower buds from (a plant) to improve the quality and size of the remaining flowers. **3.** to dehorn (livestock) by removing the horn bud or preventing its further development. [1715–25; DIS-[1] + BUD[1]]

dis·bur·den (dis bûr′dn), *v.t.* **1.** to remove a burden from; rid of a burden. **2.** to relieve of anything oppressive or annoying: *Confession disburdened his mind of anxiety.* **3.** to get rid of (a burden); discharge. —*v.i.* **4.** to unload a burden. [1525–35; DIS-[1] + BURDEN[1]] **—dis·bur′den·ment,** *n.*

dis·burse (dis bûrs′), *v.t.*, **-bursed, -burs·ing. 1.** to pay out (money), esp. for expenses; expend. **2.** to distribute or scatter: *Our troops were disbursed over a wide area. She disbursed the flowers to the children.* [1520–30; < MF *desbourser,* OF *desborser,* equiv. to *des-* DIS-[1] + *-borser,* deriv. of *borse* PURSE < LL *bursa* bag] **—dis·burs′a·ble,** *adj.* **—dis·burs′er,** *n.*
—Syn. 1. lay out. See **spend.**

dis·burse·ment (dis bûrs′mənt), *n.* **1.** the act or an instance of disbursing. **2.** money paid out or spent. [1590–1600; < MF *desboursement.* See DISBURSE, -MENT]

disc (disk), *n.* **1.** a phonograph record. **2.** disk (defs. 1, 2, 4–9). —*v.t.* **3.** *Informal.* to make (a recording) on a phonograph disc. **4.** disk (defs. 11, 12). Also, **disk** (for defs. 1, 3). [see DISK]

disc., 1. discount. **2.** discovered.

dis·calced (dis kalst′), *adj.* (chiefly of members of certain religious orders) without shoes; unshod; barefoot. Also, **dis·cal·ce·ate** (dis kal′sē it, -āt′). Cf. **calced.** [1625–35; part trans. of L *discalceātus,* equiv. to *dis-* DIS-[1] + *calceātus,* ptp. of *calceāre* to fit with shoes (*calce(us)* a shoe, deriv. of *calc-* (s. of *calx*) heel + *-ātus* -ATE[1])]

dis·cant (*n.* dis′kant; *v.* dis kant′), *n.* **1.** Also, **dis·can·tus** (dis kan′təs). *Music.* a 13th-century polyphonic style with strict mensural meter in all the voice parts, in contrast to the metrically free organum of the period. **2.** descant. —*v.i.* **3.** descant. [1400–50; late ME < ML *discanthus;* see DESCANT] **—dis·cant′er,** *n.*

dis·card (*v.* di skärd′; *n.* dis′kärd), *v.t.* **1.** to cast aside or dispose of; get rid of: *to discard an old hat.* **2.** *Cards.* **a.** to throw out (a card or cards) from one's hand. **b.** to play (a card, not a trump, of a different suit from that of the card led). —*v.i.* **3.** *Cards.* to discard a card or cards. —*n.* **4.** the act of discarding. **5.** a person or thing that is cast out or rejected. **6.** *Cards.* A card or cards discarded. [1580–90; DIS-[1] + CARD[1]] **—dis·card′a·ble,** *adj.* **—dis·card′er,** *n.*
—Ant. 1. retain.

dis·car·nate (dis kär′nit, -nāt), *adj.* without a physical body; incorporeal. [1655–65; DIS[1] + *-carnate,* as in INCARNATE] **—dis′car·na′tion,** *n.*

dis·case (dis kās′), *v.t.*, **-cased, -cas·ing.** to take the case or covering from; uncase. [1590–1600; DIS-[1] + CASE[2]]

disc′ brake′, *Auto.* a brake system in which a disc attached to a wheel is slowed by the friction of brake pads being pressed against the disc by a caliper. Also, **disk brake.** [1900–05]

disc brake
A, caliper;
B, brake pad;
C, disc

disc′ cam′era, a camera that accepts a film cartridge in the form of a rotatable disc with film frames mounted around the outer edge.

dis·cern (di sûrn′, -zûrn′), *v.t.* **1.** to perceive by the sight or some other sense or by the intellect; see, recognize, or apprehend: *They discerned a sail on the horizon.* **2.** to distinguish mentally; recognize as distinct or different; discriminate: *He is incapable of discerning right from wrong.* —*v.i.* **3.** to distinguish or discriminate. [1300–50; ME (< OF) < L *discernere* to separate, equiv. to *dis-* DIS-[1] + *cernere* to separate] **—dis·cern′er,** *n.*
—Syn. 1. discover, descry, espy. See **notice. 2, 3.** differentiate, judge.

dis·cern·i·ble (di sûr′nə bəl, -zûr′-), *adj.* capable of being discerned; distinguishable. Also, **dis·cern′a·ble.** [1555–65; < L *discernibilis* (see DISCERN, -IBLE); r. earlier *discernable* < MF, equiv. to *discern(er)* to discern + *-able* -ABLE] **—dis·cern′i·ble·ness, dis·cern′a·ble·ness,** *n.* **—dis·cern′i·bly, dis·cern′a·bly,** *adv.*

dis·cern·ing (di sûr′ning, -zûr′-), *adj.* showing good or outstanding judgment and understanding: *a discerning critic of French poetry.* [1600–10; DISCERN + -ING[2]] **—dis·cern′ing·ly,** *adv.*
—Syn. perceptive, keen, sharp, discriminating.

dis·cern·ment (di sûrn′mənt, -zûrn′-), *n.* **1.** the faculty of discerning; discrimination; acuteness of judgment and understanding. **2.** the act or an instance of discerning. [1580–90; < MF *discernement,* equiv. to *discern(er)* to DISCERN + *-ment* -MENT]
—Syn. 1. judgment, perspicacity, penetration, insight.

dis·cerp·ti·ble (di sûrp′tə bəl, -zûrp′-), *adj.* capable of being torn apart; divisible. [1730–40; < L *discerpt(us)* torn to pieces (ptp. of *discerpere;* see DIS-[1], EXCERPT) + -IBLE] **—dis·cerp′ti·bil′i·ty, dis·cerp′ti·ble·ness,** *n.*

disc′ film′, film used in a disc camera.

dis·charge (*v.* dis chärj′; *n.* dis′chärj, dis chärj′), *v.*, **-charged, -charg·ing,** *n.* —*v.t.* **1.** to relieve of a charge or load; unload: *to discharge a ship.* **2.** to remove or send forth: *They discharged the cargo at New York.* **3.** to fire or shoot (a firearm or missile): *to discharge a gun.* **4.** to pour forth; emit: *to discharge oil; to discharge a stream of invective.* **5.** to relieve oneself of (an obligation, burden, etc.). **6.** to relieve of obligation, responsibility, etc. **7.** to fulfill, perform, or execute (a duty, function, etc.). **8.** to relieve or deprive of office, employment, etc.; dismiss from service. **9.** to release, send away, or allow to go (often fol. by *from*): *The children were discharged early from school. They discharged him from prison.* **10.** to pay (a debt). **11.** *Law.* **a.** to release (a defendant, esp. one under confinement). **b.** to release (a bankrupt) from former debts. **c.** to cancel (a contract). **d.** to release (bail). **12.** (in a legislative body) to order (a committee) to cease further consideration of a bill so that it can be voted on. **13.** *Elect.* to rid (a battery, capacitor, etc.) of a charge of electricity. **14.** *Dyeing.* to free from a dye, as by chemical bleaching. —*v.i.* **15.** to get rid of a burden or load. **16.** to deliver a charge or load. **17.** to pour forth. **18.** to go off or fire, as a firearm or missile. **19.** to blur or run, as a color or dye. **20.** *Elect.* to lose or give up a charge of electricity. —*n.* **21.** the act of discharging a ship, load, etc. **22.** the act of firing a weapon, as an arrow by drawing and releasing the string of the bow, or a gun by exploding the charge of powder.

23. a sending or coming forth, as of water from a pipe; ejection; emission. 24. the rate or amount of such issue. 25. something sent forth or emitted. 26. a relieving, ridding, or getting rid of something of the nature of a charge. 27. *Law.* **a.** an acquittal or exoneration. **b.** an annulment, as of a court order. **c.** the freeing of one held under legal process. 28. a relieving or being relieved of obligation or liability; fulfillment of an obligation. 29. the payment of a debt. 30. a release or dismissal, as from prison, an office, or employment. 31. a certificate of such a release or a certificate of release from obligation or liability. 32. the act or process of ordering a legislative committee to cease further consideration of a bill so that it can be voted on. 33. *Mil.* **a.** the separation of a person from military service. **b.** a certificate of such separation. 34. *Elect.* **a.** the removal or transference of an electric charge, as by the conversion of chemical energy to electrical energy. **b.** the equalization of a difference of potential, as between two terminals. [1300–50; ME *deschargen* < AF *descharger,* OF < LL *discarricāre,* equiv. to *dis-* DIS-[1] + *carricāre* to load; see CHARGE] —**dis•charge′a•ble,** *adj.* —**dis•charg′er,** *n.*
—**Syn. 1.** unburden, disburden. **4.** expel, eject, exude. **6.** See **release. 7.** See **perform. 8.** cashier, fire, remove. **9.** dismiss, expel. **10.** settle, liquidate. **22.** detonation, shooting. **28.** execution, performance.

dis•char•gee (dis′chär jē′), *n.* a person who has been discharged, as from military service. [1890–95; DISCHARGE + -EE]

dis′charge lamp′, a lamp in which light is produced by an electric discharge in a gas-filled glass enclosure. [1935–40]

dis′charge print′ing, a fabric-printing method in which the material is dyed and then certain areas are discharged so as to permit the original hue or its color replacement to act as a pattern against the colored ground. Also called **extract printing.** Cf. **resist printing.**

dis′charge tube′, *Electronics.* See **gas tube.** [1895–1900]

discharg′ing arch′, an arch for taking some of the weight from a structural member beneath it. Also called **relieving arch.** [1810–20]

dis•ci•flo•ral (dis′i flôr′əl, -flōr′-), *adj. Bot.* having flowers in which the receptacle is expanded into a conspicuous disk, as in composite plants. [1870–75; DISC + -I- + FLORAL]

dis•ci•ple (di sī′pəl), *n., v.,* **-pled, -pling.** —*n.* **1.** *Relig.* **a.** one of the 12 personal followers of Christ. **b.** one of the 70 followers sent forth by Christ. Luke 10:1. **c.** any other professed follower of Christ in His lifetime. **2.** any follower of Christ. **3.** (*cap.*) a member of the Disciples of Christ. **4.** a person who is a pupil or an adherent of the doctrines of another; follower: *a disciple of Freud.* —*v.t.* **5.** *Archaic.* to convert into a disciple. **6.** *Obs.* to teach; train. [bef. 900; ME < AF, OF < L *discipulus,* equiv. to *dis-* DIS-[1] + *-cip(ere),* comb. form of *capere* to take + *-ulus* -ULE; r. ME *deciple* < AF *de(s)ciple;* r. OE *discipul* < L, as above] —**dis•ci′ple•like′,** *adj.* —**dis•ci′ple•ship′,** *n.*
—**Syn. 4.** See **pupil**[1].

Disci′ples of Christ′, a Christian denomination, founded in the U.S. by Alexander Campbell in the early part of the 19th century, that rejects all creeds, holds the Bible as a sufficient rule of faith and practice, administers baptism by immersion, celebrates the Lord's Supper every Sunday, and has a congregational polity.

dis•ci•plin•a•ble (dis′ə plin′ə bəl), *adj.* **1.** subject to or meriting disciplinary action: *a disciplinable breach of rules.* **2.** capable of being instructed. [1425–75; late ME < MF < LL *disciplīnābilis.* See DISCIPLINE, -ABLE]

dis•ci•pli•nar•i•an (dis′ə plə nâr′ē ən), *n.* **1.** a person who enforces or advocates discipline: *The teacher was a formidable disciplinarian.* —*adj.* **2.** disciplinary. [1575–85; DISCIPLINE + -ARIAN]

dis•ci•pli•nar•y (dis′ə plə ner′ē), *adj.* of, for, or constituting discipline; enforcing or administering discipline: *disciplinary action.* [1575–85; DISCIPLINE + -ARY]

dis•ci•pline (dis′ə plin), *n., v.,* **-plined, -plin•ing.** —*n.* **1.** training to act in accordance with rules; drill: *military discipline.* **2.** activity, exercise, or a regimen that develops or improves a skill; training: *A daily stint at the typewriter is excellent discipline for a writer.* **3.** punishment inflicted by way of correction and training. **4.** the rigor or training effect of experience, adversity, etc.: *the harsh discipline of poverty.* **5.** behavior in accord with rules of conduct; behavior and order maintained by training and control: *good discipline in an army.* **6.** a set or system of rules and regulations. **7.** *Eccles.* the system of government regulating the practice of a church as distinguished from its doctrine. **8.** an instrument of punishment, esp. a whip or scourge, used in the practice of self-mortification or as an instrument of chastisement in certain religious communities. **9.** a branch of instruction or learning: *the disciplines of history and economics.* —*v.t.* **10.** to train by instruction and exercise; drill. **11.** to bring to a state of order and obedience by training and control. **12.** to punish or penalize in order to train and control; correct; chastise. [1175–1225; ME < AF < L *disciplina* instruction, tuition, equiv. to *discipul(us)* DISCIPLE + *-ina* -INE[2]] —**dis•ci•pli•nal** (dis′ə plə nl, -plin′l, dis′ə plin′l), *adj.* —**dis′ci•plin′er,** *n.*
—**Syn. 3.** chastisement, castigation. **12.** See **punish.**

dis•ci•plined (dis′ə plind), *adj.* having or exhibiting discipline; rigorous: *paintings characterized by a disciplined technique.* [1350–1400; ME. See DISCIPLINE, -ED[2]]

dis•cis•sion (di sish′ən), *n. Ophthalm.* an incision of the lens of the eye, as for removal of cataract. [1640–50; < LL *discissiōn-* (s. of *discissiō*) division, separation, equiv. to L *disciss(us)* torn apart, ptp. of *discindere* (*di-* DI-[2] + *scissus* torn) + *-iōn-* -ION; see SCISSION]

disc′ jock′ey. 1. a person who conducts a radio broadcast consisting of recorded music, informal talk, commercial announcements, etc. **2.** a person who selects, plays, and announces records at a discotheque. Also, **disk jockey.** [1940–45, *Amer.*]

dis•claim (dis klām′), *v.t.* **1.** to deny or repudiate interest in or connection with; disavow; disown: *disclaiming all participation.* **2.** *Law.* to renounce a claim or right to. **3.** to reject the claims or authority of. —*v.i.* **4.** *Law.* to renounce or repudiate a legal claim or right. **5.** *Obs.* to disavow interest. [1400–50; late ME < AF *disclaimer, desclamer.* See DIS-[1], CLAIM]

dis•claim•er (dis klā′mər), *n.* **1.** the act of disclaiming; the renouncing, repudiating, or denying of a claim; disavowal. **2.** a person who disclaims. **3.** a statement, document, or assertion that disclaims responsibility, affiliation, etc.; disavowal; denial. [1400–50; late ME < AF: to DISCLAIM]

dis•cla•ma•tion (dis′klə mā′shən), *n.* the act of disclaiming; renunciation; disavowal. [1585–95; < ML *disclamāt(us)* (ptp. of *disclamāre* to DISCLAIM, prob. < AF *disclaimer;* see -ATE[1]) + -ION] —**dis•clam•a•to•ry** (dis klam′ə tôr′ē, -tōr′ē), *adj.*

dis•cli•max (dis klī′maks), *n. Ecol.* a stable community that has replaced the normal climax in a given area, owing to disturbance by humans or domestic animals. [1935–40; DIS-[1] + CLIMAX]

dis•close (di sklōz′), *v.,* **-closed, -clos•ing,** *n.* —*v.t.* **1.** to make known; reveal or uncover: *to disclose a secret.* **2.** to cause to appear; allow to be seen; lay open to view: *In spring the violets disclose their fragrant petals.* **3.** *Obs.* to open up; unfold. —*n.* **4.** *Obs.* disclosure. [1350–1400; ME *disclosen, desclosen* < OF *desclos-,* s. of *desclore,* equiv. to *des-* DIS-[1] + *clore* to close < L *claudere;* see CLOSE] —**dis•clos′er,** *n.*
—**Syn. 1.** show, tell, unveil. See **reveal. 2.** expose. —**Ant. 1.** conceal.

dis•clos•ing (di sklō′zing), *adj.* indicating or involving a substance used to reveal the presence of plaque on the teeth by staining the plaque. [DISCLOSE + -ING[2]]

dis•clo•sure (di sklō′zhər), *n.* **1.** the act or an instance of disclosing; exposure; revelation. **2.** that which is disclosed; a revelation. **3.** *Patent Law.* (in a patent application) the descriptive information imparted by the specification claims, drawings, and models submitted. [1590–1600; DISCLOSE + -URE]

dis•co (dis′kō), *n., pl.* **-cos,** *adj., v.* —*n.* **1.** discotheque. **2.** a style of popular music for dancing, usually recorded and with complex electronic instrumentation, in which simple, repetitive lyrics are subordinated to a heavy, pulsating, rhythmic beat. **3.** any of various forms of dance, often improvisational, performed to such music. —*adj.* **4.** of or pertaining to a disco or disco music. **5.** intended for a disco or its patrons. —*v.i.* **6.** to dance disco, esp. at a discotheque. [1960–65, *Amer.;* by shortening]

dis•cog•ra•pher (di skog′rə fər), *n.* a person who compiles discographies. [1940–45; DISCOGRAPH(Y) + -ER[1]]

dis•cog•ra•phy (di skog′rə fē), *n., pl.* **-phies. 1.** a selective or complete list of phonograph recordings, typically of one composer, performer, or conductor. **2.** the analysis, history, or classification of phonograph recordings. **3.** the methods of analyzing or classifying phonograph recordings. Also, **diskography.** [1930–35; < F *discographie.* See DISC, -O-, -GRAPHY] —**dis•co•graph•i•cal** (dis′kə graf′i kəl), **dis′co•graph′ic,** *adj.* —**dis′co•graph′i•cal•ly,** *adv.*

dis•coid (dis′koid), *adj.* Also, **dis•coi′dal. 1.** having the form of a discus or disk; flat and circular. **2.** *Bot.* (of a composite flower) consisting of a disk only, without rays. —*n.* **3.** something in the form of a disk. **4.** *Dentistry.* an excavator with a disklike blade. [1785–95; < LL *discoīdēs* < Gk *diskoeidḗs* quoit-shaped. See DISCUS, -OID]

dis•col•or (dis kul′ər), *v.t.* **1.** to change or spoil the color of; fade or stain. —*v.i.* **2.** to change color; become faded or stained. [1350–1400; ME *discolouren* < OF *descolorer* < LL *discolōrāri* to change color, deriv. of L *discolor* of another color. See DIS-[1], COLOR]

dis•col•or•a•tion (dis kul′ə rā′shən), *n.* **1.** the act or fact of discoloring or the state of being discolored. **2.** a discolored marking or area; stain. Also called **dis•col′or•ment.** [1635–45; DISCOLOR + -ATION]

dis•com•bob•u•late (dis′kəm bob′yə lāt′), *v.t.,* **-lat•ed, -lat•ing.** to confuse or disconcert; upset; frustrate: *The speaker was completely discombobulated by the hecklers.* [1825–35, *Amer.;* fanciful alter. of DISCOMPOSE or DISCOMFORT] —**dis′com•bob′u•la′tion,** *n.*

dis•com•fit (dis kum′fit), *v.t.* **1.** to confuse and deject; disconcert: *to be discomfited by a question.* **2.** to frustrate the plans of; thwart; foil. **3.** *Archaic.* to defeat utterly; rout: *The army was discomfited in every battle.* —*n.* **4.** *Archaic.* rout; defeat. [1175–1225; ME < AF *descunfit,* OF *desconfit,* ptp. of *desconfire,* equiv. to *des-* DIS-[1] + *confire* to make, accomplish < L *conficere;* see CONFECT] —**dis•com′fit•er,** *n.*
—**Syn. 1.** discompose, embarrass, disturb.

dis•com•fi•ture (dis kum′fi chər), *n.* **1.** disconcertion; confusion; embarrassment. **2.** frustration of hopes or plans. **3.** *Archaic.* defeat in battle; rout. [1300–50; ME *desconfiture* < AF: defeat. See DISCOMFIT, -URE]

dis•com•fort (dis kum′fərt), *n.* **1.** an absence of comfort or ease; uneasiness, hardship, or mild pain. **2.** anything that is disturbing to or interferes with comfort. —*v.t.* **3.** to disturb the comfort or happiness of; make uncomfortable or uneasy. [1300–50; (v.) ME *discomforten* to discourage, pain < AF *descomforter* to sadden, grieve; see DIS-[1], COMFORT; (n.) ME < AF, deriv. of v.] —**dis•com•fort•a•ble** (dis kum′fər tə bəl, -kumf′tə-), *adj.* —**dis•com′fort•ing•ly,** *adv.*

dis•com•mend (dis′kə mend′), *v.t.* **1.** to express disapproval of; belittle; disparage. *The diners discommended the wine.* **2.** to bring into disfavor: *He was discommended for his negligence.* [1485–95; DIS-[1] + COMMEND] —**dis′com•mend′er,** *n.*

dis•com•mode (dis′kə mōd′), *v.t.,* **-mod•ed, -mod•ing.** to cause inconvenience to; disturb, trouble, or bother. [1715–25; < F *discommoder,* equiv. to *dis-* DIS-[1] + *-commoder,* v. deriv. of *commode* convenient; see COMMODE] —**dis′com•mo′di•ous,** *adj.* —**dis′com•mo′di•ous•ly,** *adv.* —**dis′com•mo′di•ous•ness,** *n.*

dis•com•mod•i•ty (dis′kə mod′i tē), *n., pl.* **-ties.** *Archaic.* **1.** inconvenience; disadvantageousness. **2.** a source of inconvenience or trouble; disadvantage. [1505–15; DIS-[1] + COMMODITY]

dis•com•mon (dis kom′ən), *v.t.* **1.** (at Oxford and Cambridge) to prohibit (tradespeople or townspeople who have violated the regulations of the university) from dealing with the undergraduates. **2.** *Law.* to deprive of the character of a common, as by enclosing a piece of land. [1470–80; DIS-[1] + obs. *common* to participate, associate]

dis•com•pose (dis′kəm pōz′), *v.t.,* **-posed, -pos•ing. 1.** to upset the order of; disarrange; disorder; unsettle: *The breeze discomposed the bouquet.* **2.** to disturb the composure of; agitate; perturb: *The bad news discomposed us.* [1475–85; DIS-[1] + COMPOSE] —**dis′com•pos′ed•ly,** *adv.* —**dis′com•pos′ing•ly,** *adv.*
—**Syn. 2.** discomfit, disconcert.

dis•com•po•sure (dis′kəm pō′zhər), *n.* the state of being discomposed; disorder; agitation; perturbation. [1635–45; DIS-[1] + COMPOSURE]

dis•co•my•cete (dis′kō mī′sēt, -mī sēt′), *n. Mycol.* any of a group of fungi considered as belonging to the class Ascomycetes of the kingdom Plantae, including cup fungi, morels, and truffles, characterized by a cup-shaped or disk-shaped fruiting body. [< NL *Discomycetes;* see DISK, -O-, -MYCETE]

dis•co•my•co•ta (dis′kō mī kō′tə), *n.pl. Mycol.* the discomycetes considered as belonging to the phylum Ascomycota of the kingdom Fungi. [< NL; see DISCOMYCETE, -OTE]

dis•con•cert (dis′kən sûrt′), *v.t.* **1.** to disturb the self-possession of; perturb; ruffle: *Her angry reply disconcerted me completely.* **2.** to throw into disorder or confusion; disarrange: *He changed his mind and disconcerted everybody's plans.* [1680–90; < obs. F *disconcerter.* See DIS-[1], CONCERT] —**dis′con•cert′ed,** *adj.* —**dis′con•cert′ing•ly,** *adv.* —**dis′con•cert′ing•ness,** *n.* —**dis′con•cer′tion, dis′con•cert′ment,** *n.*
—**Syn. 1.** discompose, perplex, bewilder, abash, discomfit. See **confuse.** —**Ant. 1.** calm. **2.** arrange.

dis•con•firm (dis′kən fûrm′), *v.t.* to prove to be invalid. [1935–40; DIS- + CONFIRM] —**dis•con•fir•ma•tion** (dis kon′fər mā′shən, dis′kon-), *n.*

dis•con•form•a•ble (dis′kən fôr′mə bəl), *adj. Geol.* of or pertaining to a disconformity. [1900–05; DIS-[1] + CONFORMABLE]

dis•con•form•i•ty (dis′kən fôr′mi tē), *n., pl.* **-ties. 1.** *Geol.* the surface of a division between parallel rock strata, indicating interruption of sedimentation: a type of unconformity. **2.** *Archaic.* nonconformity. [1595–1605; DIS-[1] + CONFORMITY]

dis•con•gru•i•ty (dis′kən grōō′i tē, -kəng-), *n., pl.* **-ties.** *Obs.* incongruity. [1615–25; DIS-[1] + CONGRUITY]

dis•con•nect (dis′kə nekt′), *v.t.* **1.** to sever or interrupt the connection of or between; detach: *They disconnected the telephone. We were disconnected.* —*v.i.* **2.** to sever or terminate a connection, as of a telephone; hang up: *State your business and disconnect.* **3.** to withdraw into one's private world: *When social pressures become too great, she simply disconnects.* —*n.* **4.** an act or instance of disconnecting, esp. the suspension of telephone or cable TV service for nonpayment of service charges. [1760–70; DIS-[1] + CONNECT] —**dis′con•nect′er,** *n.* —**dis′con•nec′tive,** *adj.* —**dis′con•nec′tive•ness,** *n.*

dis•con•nect•ed (dis′kə nek′tid), *adj.* **1.** disjointed; broken. **2.** not coherent; seemingly irrational: *a disconnected argument.* [1775–85; DISCONNECT + -ED[2]] —**dis′con•nect′ed•ly,** *adv.* —**dis′con•nect′ed•ness,** *n.*
—**Syn. 2.** confused, rambling, incoherent, disjointed. —**Ant. 2.** cogent, logical, coherent.

dis•con•nec•tion (dis′kə nek′shən), *n.* **1.** the act of disconnecting. **2.** the state of being disconnected; lack of connection. Also, *Brit.,* **dis′con•nex′ion.** [1725–35; DIS-[1] + CONNECTION]

dis•con•so•late (dis kon′sə lit), *adj.* **1.** without consolation or solace; hopelessly unhappy; inconsolable: *Loss of her pet dog made her disconsolate.* **2.** characterized by or causing dejection; cheerless; gloomy: *disconsolate prospects.* [1325–75; ME < ML *disconsōlātus,* equiv. to L *dis-* DIS-[1] + *consōlātus* consoled, ptp. of *consōlārī* to CONSOLE; see -ATE[1]] —**dis•con′so•late•ly,** *adv.* —**dis•con•so•la•tion** (dis kon′sə lā′shən), **dis•con′so•late•ness,** *n.*
—**Syn. 1.** heartbroken, dejected. **1, 2.** sad, melancholy, sorrowful, miserable. See **desolate.**

dis•con•tent (dis′kən tent′), *adj.* **1.** not content; dissatisfied; discontented. —*n.* **2.** Also, **dis′con•tent′ment.** lack of content; dissatisfaction. **3.** a restless desire or craving for something one does not have. **4.** a malcontent. —*v.t.* **5.** to make discontented; dissatisfy; displease. [1485–95; DIS-[1] + CONTENT[2]]
—**Syn. 2.** uneasiness, inquietude, restlessness, displeasure. See **dissatisfaction.**

dis•con•tent•ed (dis′kən ten′tid), *adj.* not content or satisfied; dissatisfied; restlessly unhappy: *For all their wealth, or perhaps because of it, they were discontented.* [1485–95; DISCONTENT + -ED[2]] —**dis′con•tent′ed•ly,** *adv.* —**dis′con•tent′ed•ness,** *n.*

dis•con•tin•u•ance (dis′kən tin′yōō əns), *n.* **1.** the act or state of discontinuing or the state of being discontinued; cessation: *the discontinuance of a business.* **2.** *Law.* the termination of a suit by the act of the plaintiff,

CONCISE ETYMOLOGY KEY: <, descended or borrowed from; >, whence; b., blend of, blended; c., cognate with; cf., compare; deriv., derivative; equiv., equivalent; imit., imitative; obl., oblique; r., replacing; s., stem; sp., spelling, spelled; resp., respelling, respelled; trans., translation; ?, origin unknown; *, unattested; ‡, probably earlier than. See the full key inside the front cover.

as by notice in writing, or by neglect to take the proper adjournments to keep it pending. [1350–1400; ME < AF; see DIS-[1], CONTINUANCE]

dis·con·tin·u·a·tion (dis′kən tin′yo͞o ā′shən), *n.* a breach or interruption of continuity or unity: *Progress was delayed by repeated discontinuations of work.* [1605–15; < MF < ML *discontinuātiōn-* (s. of *discontinuātiō*), equiv. to *discontinuāt(us)* (ptp. of *discontinuāre* to DISCONTINUE; see -ATE[1]) + -*iōn-* -ION]

dis·con·tin·ue (dis′kən tin′yo͞o), *v.*, **-tin·ued, -tin·u·ing.** —*v.t.* **1.** to put an end to; stop; terminate: *to discontinue nuclear testing.* **2.** to cease to take, use, subscribe to, etc.: *to discontinue a newspaper.* **3.** *Law.* to terminate or abandon (a suit, claim, or the like). —*v.i.* **4.** to come to an end or stop; cease; desist. [1400–50; late ME < AF *discontinuer* < ML *discontinuāre.* See DIS-[1], CONTINUE] —**dis′con·tin′u·er,** *n.*
—**Syn. 1.** See **interrupt.** —**Ant. 1.** resume.

dis·con·ti·nu·i·ty (dis′kon tn o͞o′i tē, -yo͞o′-), *n., pl.* **-ties. 1.** lack of continuity; irregularity: *The plot of the book was marred by discontinuity.* **2.** a break or gap: *The surface of the moon is characterized by major discontinuities.* **3.** *Math.* a point at which a function is not continuous. **4.** *Geol.* a zone deep within the earth where the velocity of earthquake waves changes radically. [1560–70; < ML *discontinuitās.* See DISCONTINUOUS, -ITY]

dis·con·tin·u·ous (dis′kən tin′yo͞o əs), *adj.* **1.** not continuous; broken; interrupted; intermittent: *a discontinuous chain of mountains; a discontinuous argument.* **2.** *Math.* (of a function at a point) not continuous at the point. [1660–70; < ML *discontinuus.* See DIS-[1], CONTINUOUS] —**dis′con·tin′u·ous·ly,** *adv.* —**dis′con·tin′u·ous·ness,** *n.*

dis·co·phile (dis′kə fīl′), *n.* a person who studies and collects phonograph records, esp. those of a rare or specialized nature. [1935–40; DISC + -O- + -PHILE]

dis·cord (*n.* dis′kôrd; *v.* dis kôrd′), *n.* **1.** lack of concord or harmony between persons or things: *marital discord.* **2.** disagreement; difference of opinion. **3.** strife; dispute; war. **4.** *Music.* an inharmonious combination of musical tones sounded together. **5.** any confused or harsh noise; dissonance. —*v.i.* **6.** to disagree; be at variance. [1200–50; (n.) ME *descorde, discorde* < AF; OF *descort* (deriv. of *descorder*), *descorde* < L *discordia,* deriv. of *discord-* (s. of *discors*) discordant (*dis-* DIS-[1] + *cord-,* s. of *cors* heart); (v.) ME *discorden* < AF, OF *descorder* < L *discordāre* deriv. of *discord-,* as above]
—**Syn. 1–3.** conflict, struggle, controversy, antagonism, argument, contention, quarreling.

dis·cord·ance (dis kôr′dns), *n.* **1.** a discordant state; disagreement; discord. **2.** an instance of this. **3.** dissonance. **4.** *Geol.* lack of parallelism between adjacent strata, as in an angular unconformity. **5.** (in genetic studies) the degree of dissimilarity in a pair of twins with respect to the presence or absence of a disease or trait. [1300–50; ME < AF *discordaunce, descordance;* see DISCORD, -ANCE]

dis·cor·dan·cy (dis kôr′dn sē), *n., pl.* **-cies.** discordance (defs. 1–3). [1600–10; DISCORDANCE + -Y[3]]

dis·cord·ant (dis kôr′dnt), *adj.* **1.** being at variance; disagreeing; incongruous: *discordant opinions.* **2.** disagreeable to the ear; dissonant; harsh. **3.** *Geol.* (of strata) structurally unconformable. [1250–1300; ME *discordaunt* < AF < L *discordant-* (s. of *discordāns*), prp. of *discordāre.* See DISCORD, -ANT] —**dis·cord′ant·ly,** *adv.*

Dis·cor·di·a (dis kôr′dē ə), *n.* the ancient Roman goddess of discord, identified with the Greek goddess Eris. [< L: DISCORD]

dis·co·theque (dis′kə tek′, dis′kə tek′), *n.* a nightclub for dancing to live or recorded music and often featuring sophisticated sound systems, elaborate lighting, and other effects. Also, **dis′co·thèque′.** Also called **disco.** [1950–55; < F *discothèque.* See DISC, -O-, -THECA]

dis·count (*v.* dis′kount, dis kount′; *n., adj.* dis′kount), *v.t.* **1.** to deduct a certain amount from (a bill, charge, etc.): *All bills that are paid promptly will be discounted at two percent.* **2.** to offer for sale or sell at a reduced price: *The store discounted all clothing for the sale.* **3.** to advance or lend money with deduction of interest on (commercial paper not immediately payable). **4.** to purchase or sell (a bill or note) before maturity at a reduction based on the interest for the time it still has to run. **5.** to leave out of account; disregard: *Even if we discount the irrelevant material, the thesis remains mediocre.* **6.** to allow for exaggeration in (a statement, opinion, etc.): *Knowing his political bias they discounted most of his story.* **7.** to take into account in advance, often so as to diminish the effect of: *They had discounted the effect of a decline in the stock market.* —*v.i.* **8.** to advance or lend money after deduction of interest. **9.** to offer goods or services at a reduced price. —*n.* **10.** the act or an instance of discounting. **11.** an amount deducted from the usual list price. **12.** any deduction from the nominal value. **13.** a payment of interest in advance upon a loan of money. **14.** the amount of interest obtained by one who discounts. **15.** an allowance made for exaggeration or bias, as in a report, story, etc.: *Even after all the discounts are taken, his story sounds phony.* **16. at a discount, a.** *Com.* below par. **b.** below the usual list price. **c.** in low esteem or regard: *His excuses were taken at a discount by all who knew him.* **d.** not in demand; unwanted: *Such ancient superstitions are at a discount in a civilized society.* —*adj.* **17.** selling or offered at less than the usual or established price: *discount theater tickets.* **18.** selling goods at a discount: *a discount drugstore.* [1615–25; DIS-[1] + COUNT[1], modeled on F *décompter,* OF *desconter* < ML *discomputāre*] —**dis′count·a·ble,** *adj.*

dis′count bro′ker, 1. an agent who discounts commercial paper. **2.** a stockbroker who charges discount commission fees. [1860–65] —**dis′count bro′kerage.**

dis·coun·te·nance (dis koun′tn əns), *v.,* **-nanced, -nanc·ing,** *n.* —*v.t.* **1.** to disconcert, embarrass, or abash: *With his composure, he survived every attempt to discountenance him.* **2.** to show disapproval of: *The teachers discountenanced smoking by the students.* —*n.* **3.** disapproval; disapprobation. [1570–80; DIS-[1] + COUNTENANCE] —**dis·coun′te·nanc·er,** *n.*

dis·count·er (dis′koun tər), *n.* **1.** a person who discounts. **2.** a person who operates a discount house or business. **3.** *Informal.* a discount house. **4.** See **discount broker.** [1725–35; DISCOUNT + -ER[1]]

dis′count house′, 1. Also called **dis′count store′.** a store that sells much of its merchandise at a price below the usual price. **2.** *Brit.* See **bill broker.** [1945–50]

dis′count mar′ket, a trading market in which notes, bills, and other negotiable instruments are discounted. [1890–95]

dis′count rate′, *Finance.* **1.** the rate of interest charged in discounting commercial paper. **2.** the interest rate charged by Federal Reserve Banks on loans to their member banks, usually against government securities as collateral. **3.** the rediscount rate. [1925–30]

dis·cour·age (di skûr′ij, -skur′-), *v.,* **-aged, -ag·ing.** —*v.t.* **1.** to deprive of courage, hope, or confidence; dishearten; dispirit. **2.** to dissuade (usually fol. by *from*). **3.** to obstruct by opposition or difficulty; hinder: *Low prices discourage industry.* **4.** to express or make clear disapproval of; frown upon: *to discourage the expression of enthusiasm.* —*v.i.* **5.** to become discouraged: *a person who discourages easily.* [1400–50; late ME *discoragen* < MF *descorager,* OF *descoragier.* See DIS-[1], COURAGE] —**dis·cour′ag·er,** *n.* —**dis·cour′age·a·ble,** *adj.* —**dis·cour′ag·ing·ly,** *adv.*
—**Syn. 1.** daunt, depress, deject, overawe, cow, abash. DISCOURAGE, DISMAY, INTIMIDATE mean to dishearten or frighten. To DISCOURAGE is to dishearten by expressing disapproval or by suggesting that a contemplated action or course will probably fail: *He was discouraged from going into business.* To DISMAY is to dishearten completely: *Her husband's philandering dismayed her.* To INTIMIDATE is to frighten, as by threats of force, violence, or dire consequences: *to intimidate a witness.* —**Ant. 1.** encourage.

dis·cour·age·ment (di skûr′ij mənt, -skur′-), *n.* **1.** an act or instance of discouraging. **2.** the state of being discouraged. **3.** something that discourages: *Poor health and poverty are grave discouragements.* [1555–65; < MF *descouragement,* OF *descoragement.* See DISCOURAGE, -MENT]
—**Syn. 2.** depression, dejection, hopelessness. See **despair. 3.** deterrent, damper, impediment, obstacle, obstruction. —**Ant. 1–3.** encouragement.

dis·course (*n.* dis′kôrs, -kōrs, dis kôrs′, -kōrs′; *v.* dis kôrs′, -kōrs′), *n., v.,* **-coursed, -cours·ing.** —*n.* **1.** communication of thought by words; talk; conversation: *earnest and intelligent discourse.* **2.** a formal discussion of a subject in speech or writing, as a dissertation, treatise, sermon, etc. **3.** *Ling.* any unit of connected speech or writing longer than a sentence. —*v.i.* **4.** to communicate thoughts orally; talk; converse. **5.** to treat of a subject formally in speech or writing. —*v.t.* **6.** to utter or give forth (musical sounds). [1325–75; ME *discours* < ML *discursus* (sp. by influence of ME *cours* course), LL: conversation, L: a running to and fro, equiv. to *discur(rere)* to run about (*dis-* DIS-[1] + *currere* to run) + -*sus* for -*tus* suffix of v. action] —**dis·cours′er,** *n.*
—**Syn. 1.** discussion, colloquy, dialogue, chat, parley.

dis′course anal′ysis, *Ling.* **1.** the study of the rules or patterns characterizing units of connected speech or writing longer than a sentence. **2.** the study of the rules governing appropriate language use in communicative situations.

dis·cour·te·ous (dis kûr′tē əs), *adj.* not courteous; impolite; uncivil; rude: *a discourteous salesman.* [1570–80; DIS-[1] + COURTEOUS] —**dis·cour′te·ous·ly,** *adv.* —**dis·cour′te·ous·ness,** *n.*

dis·cour·te·sy (dis kûr′tə sē), *n., pl.* **-sies. 1.** lack or breach of courtesy; incivility; rudeness. **2.** a discourteous or impolite act. [1545–55; DIS-[1] + COURTESY]

dis·cov·er (di skuv′ər), *v.t.* **1.** to see, get knowledge of, learn of, find, or find out; gain sight or knowledge of (something previously unseen or unknown): *to discover America; to discover electricity.* **2.** to notice or realize: *I discovered I didn't have my credit card with me when I went to pay my bill.* **3.** *Archaic.* to make known; reveal; disclose. [1250–1300; ME < AF *discoverir, descovrir,* OF *descovrir* < LL *discooperīre.* See DIS-[1], COVER] —**dis·cov′er·a·ble,** *adj.* —**dis·cov′er·a·bly,** *adv.*
—**Syn. 1.** detect, espy, descry, discern, ascertain, unearth, ferret out, notice. DISCOVER, INVENT, ORIGINATE suggest bringing to light something previously unknown. To DISCOVER may be to find something that had previously existed but had hitherto been unknown: *to discover a new electricity;* it may also refer to devising a new use for something already known: *to discover how to make synthetic rubber.* To INVENT is to make or create something new, esp. something ingeniously devised to perform mechanical operations: *to invent a device for detecting radioactivity.* To ORIGINATE is to begin something new, esp. new ideas, methods, etc.: *to originate a political movement, the use of assembly-line techniques.* See also **learn.**

discov′ered check′, *Chess.* a check that is effected by moving an intervening piece from the line of attack of a queen, rook, or bishop. [1840–50]

dis·cov·er·er (di skuv′ər ər), *n.* **1.** a person who discovers. **2.** (*cap.*) *U.S. Aerospace.* one of an early series of polar-orbiting reconnaissance satellites. [1250–1300; ME < OF *descovreur.* See DISCOVER, -ER[1]]

dis·cov·er·ist (di skuv′ər ist), *adj. Educ.* advocating or using the discovery method. [DISCOVER(Y) + -IST]

dis·cov·ert (dis kuv′ərt), *adj. Law.* (of a woman) not covert; not under the protection of a husband. [1250–1300; ME < AF *discoverte, descoverte* (fem. adj.). See DIS-[1], COVERT]

dis·cov·er·ture (dis kuv′ər chər), *n. Law.* the state of being discovert; freedom from coverture. [1810–20; DISCOVERT + -URE]

dis·cov·er·y (di skuv′ə rē), *n., pl.* **-er·ies. 1.** the act or an instance of discovering. **2.** something discovered. **3.** *Law.* compulsory disclosure, as of facts or documents. **4.** (*cap., italics*) *U.S. Aerospace.* the third space shuttle to orbit and return to earth. [1545–55; DISCOVER + -Y[3]]

Discov′ery Club′, a division of Camp Fire, Inc., for members who are 12 or 13 years of age.

Discov′ery Day′. See **Columbus Day.**

Discov′ery In′let, an inlet of the Ross Sea, Antarctica.

discov′ery meth′od, *Educ.* a largely unstructured, situational method or philosophy of teaching whereby students are permitted to find solutions to problems on their own or at their own pace, often jointly in group activities, either independent of or under the guidance of a teacher. [1970–75]

discov′ery proce′dure, *Ling.* any rigorous method by the application of which a grammar might be constructed from a corpus of utterances in a language; an algorithm leading from the data to a formulation.

disc′ play′er. See **videodisc player.**

dis·cre·ate (dis′krē āt′), *v.t.,* **-at·ed, -at·ing.** to reduce to nothing; annihilate. [1560–70; DIS[1]- + CREATE] —**dis′cre·a′tion,** *n.*

dis·cred·it (dis kred′it), *v.t.* **1.** to injure the credit or reputation of; defame: *an effort to discredit honest politicians.* **2.** to show to be undeserving of trust or belief; destroy confidence in: *Later research discredited earlier theories.* **3.** to give no credence to; disbelieve: *There was good reason to discredit the witness.* —*n.* **4.** loss or lack of belief or confidence; disbelief; distrust: *His theories met with general discredit.* **5.** loss or lack of repute or esteem; disrepute. **6.** something that damages a good reputation: *This behavior will be a discredit to your good name.* [1550–60; DIS-[1] + CREDIT]
—**Syn. 1.** disparage, disgrace, tarnish, undermine.

dis·cred·it·a·ble (dis kred′i tə bəl), *adj.* bringing or liable to bring discredit. [1630–40; DISCREDIT + -ABLE] —**dis·cred′it·a·bil′i·ty,** *n.* —**dis·cred′it·a·bly,** *adv.*

dis·creet (di skrēt′), *adj.* **1.** judicious in one's conduct or speech, esp. with regard to respecting privacy or maintaining silence about something of a delicate nature; prudent; circumspect. **2.** showing prudence and circumspection; decorous: *a discreet silence.* **3.** modestly unobtrusive; unostentatious: *a discreet, finely wrought gold necklace.* [1325–75; ME *discret* < AF, OF < ML *discrētus,* L: separated (ptp. of *discernere;* see DISCERN), equiv. to *dis-* DIS-[1] + *crē-* separate, distinguish (var. s. of *cernere*) + -*tus* ptp. suffix] —**dis·creet′ly,** *adv.* —**dis·creet′ness,** *n.*
—**Syn. 1.** See **careful.** —**Ant. 1.** indiscreet.

dis·crep·an·cy (di skrep′ən sē), *n., pl.* **-cies** for 2. **1.** the state or quality of being discrepant; difference; inconsistency. **2.** an instance of difference or inconsistency: *There are certain discrepancies between the two versions of the story.* Also, **dis·crep′ance.** [1615–25; < L *discrepantia,* equiv. to *discrepant-* (see DISCREPANT) + -*ia;* see -ANCY]
—**Syn. 1.** incongruity, disagreement, discordance, contrariety, variance. See **difference. 2.** variation.

dis·crep·ant (di skrep′ənt), *adj.* (usually of two or more objects, accounts, findings etc.) differing; disagreeing; inconsistent: *discrepant accounts.* [1400–50; late ME < L *discrepant-* (s. of *discrepāns*), prp. of *discrepāre* to sound discordant, equiv. to *dis-* DIS-[1] + *crepāre* to crack, creak; see -ANT] —**dis·crep′ant·ly,** *adv.*

dis·crete (di skrēt′), *adj.* **1.** apart or detached from others; separate; distinct: *six discrete parts.* **2.** consisting of or characterized by distinct or individual parts; discontinuous. **3.** *Math.* **a.** (of a topology or topological space) having the property that every subset is an open set. **b.** defined only for an isolated set of points: *a discrete variable.* **c.** using only arithmetic and algebra; not involving calculus: *discrete methods.* [1350–1400; ME < L *discrētus* separated; see DISCREET] —**dis·crete′ly,** *adv.* —**dis·crete′ness,** *n.*
—**Syn. 1.** different, individual, unconnected.

dis·cre·tion (di skresh′ən), *n.* **1.** the power or right to decide or act according to one's own judgment; freedom of judgment or choice: *It is entirely within my discretion whether I will go or stay.* **2.** the quality of being discreet, esp. with reference to one's own actions or speech; prudence or decorum: *Throwing all discretion to the winds, he blurted out the truth.* **3. at discretion,** at one's option or pleasure: *They were allowed to work overtime at discretion.* [1250–1300; ME *discrecioun* < AF < LL *discrētiōn-* (s. of *discrētiō*). See DISCREET, -ION]
—**Syn. 2.** judgment, wisdom, discrimination, sense.

dis·cre·tion·al (di skresh′ə nl), *adj.* discretionary. [1650–60; DISCRETION + -AL[1]] —**dis·cre′tion·al·ly,** *adv.*

dis·cre·tion·ar·y (di skresh′ə ner′ē), *adj.* **1.** subject or left to one's own discretion. **2.** for any use or purpose one chooses; not earmarked for a particular purpose: *discretionary income; a discretionary fund.* [1690–1700; DISCRETION + -ARY] —**dis·cre′tion·ar′i·ly,** *adv.*

discre′tionary account′, an account in which the stockbroker is allowed complete control over the purchase and sale of securities on the customer's behalf. [1915–20]

dis·crim·i·na·ble (di skrim′ə nə bəl), *adj.* capable of being discriminated or distinguished. [1720–30; DISCRIMIN(ATE) + -ABLE] —**dis·crim′i·na·bil′i·ty,** *n.* —**dis·crim′i·na·bly,** *adv.*

dis·crim·i·nant (di skrim′ə nənt), *n. Math.* a relatively simple expression that determines some of the properties, as the nature of the roots, of a given equation or function. [1830–40; < L *discrīminant-* (s. of *discrīmināns*) separating, prp. of *discrīmināre* to divide up, sep-

CONCISE PRONUNCIATION KEY: act, cāpe, dâre, pärt; set, ēqual; if, īce; ox, ōver, ôrder, oil, bo͝ok, bo͞ot, out; up, ûrge; child; sing; shoe; thin, *th*at; zh as in *treasure.* ə = *a* as in *alone, e* as in *system, i* as in *easily, o* as in *gallop, u* as in *circus;* ᵊ as in *fire* (fīᵊr), *hour* (ouᵊr). l and n can serve as syllabic consonants, as in *cradle* (krād′l), and *button* (but′n). See the full key inside the front cover.

arate, v. deriv. of *discrīmen,* s. *discrīmin-* separating line, distinction, equiv. to *discri-,* var. s. of *discernere* (see DISCERN) + *-men* n. suffix; see -ANT] **—dis·crim·i·nan·tal** (dis krim′ə nan′tl), *adj.*

discrim′inant func′tion, *Statistics.* a linear function of measurements of different properties of an object or event that is used to assign the object or event to one population or another **(discriminant analysis).** [1935–40]

dis·crim·i·nate (*v.* di skrim′ə nāt′; *adj.* di skrim′ə-nit), *v.,* **-nat·ed, -nat·ing,** *adj.* **—***v.i.* **1.** to make a distinction in favor of or against a person or thing on the basis of the group, class, or category to which the person or thing belongs rather than according to actual merit; show partiality: *The new law discriminates against foreigners. He discriminates in favor of his relatives.* **2.** to note or observe a difference; distinguish accurately: *to discriminate between things.* **—***v.t.* **3.** to make or constitute a distinction in or between; differentiate: *a mark that discriminates the original from the copy.* **4.** to note or distinguish as different: *He can discriminate minute variations in tone.* **—***adj.* **5.** marked by discrimination; making or evidencing nice distinctions: *discriminate people; discriminate judgments.* [1620–30; < L *discrimi-nātus* separated, ptp. of *discrimināre.* See DISCRIMINANT, -ATE[1]] **—dis·crim′i·nate·ly,** *adv.*
—Syn. 3. See **distinguish.**

dis·crim·i·nat·ing (di skrim′ə nā′ting), *adj.* **1.** differentiating; analytical. **2.** noting differences or distinctions with nicety; discerning; perspicacious: *a discriminating interpreter of events.* **3.** having excellent taste or judgment: *a discriminating interior designer.* **4.** differential, as a tariff. **5.** possessing distinctive features; capable of being differentiated; discriminative. [1640–50; DISCRIMINATE + -ING[2]] **—dis·crim′i·nat′ing·ly,** *adv.*

dis·crim·i·na·tion (di skrim′ə nā′shən), *n.* **1.** an act or instance of discriminating. **2.** treatment or consideration of, or making a distinction in favor of or against, a person or thing based on the group, class, or category to which that person or thing belongs rather than on individual merit: *racial and religious intolerance and discrimination.* **3.** the power of making fine distinctions; discriminating judgment: *She chose the colors with great discrimination.* **4.** *Archaic.* something that serves to differentiate. [1640–50; < L *discrīminātiōn-* (s. of *discrīminātiō*) a distinguishing. See DISCRIMINATE, -ION] **—dis·crim′i·na′tion·al,** *adj.*
—Syn. 3. discernment, taste, acumen, perception.

dis·crim·i·na·tive (di skrim′ə nā′tiv, -nə tiv), *adj.* **1.** constituting a particular quality, trait, or difference; characteristic; notable. **2.** making distinctions; discriminating. **3.** discriminatory (def. 1). [1630–40; DISCRIMINATE + -IVE] **—dis·crim′i·na′tive·ly,** *adv.*

dis·crim·i·na·tor (di skrim′ə nā′tər), *n.* **1.** a person or thing that discriminates. **2.** *Electronics.* a circuit in which the output is a function of some variation of an input signal from a fixed characteristic. [1820–30; < LL; see DISCRIMINATE, -TOR]

dis·crim·i·na·to·ry (di skrim′ə nə tôr′ē, -tōr′ē), *adj.* **1.** characterized by or showing prejudicial treatment, esp. as an indication of racial, religious, or sexual bias: *discriminatory practices in housing; a discriminatory tax.* **2.** discriminative (defs. 1, 2). [1820–30; DISCRIMINATE + -ORY[1]] **—dis·crim′i·na·to′ri·ly,** *adv.*

dis·crown (dis kroun′), *v.t.* to deprive of a crown; dethrone; depose. [1580–90; DIS-[1] + CROWN]

dis·cur·sion (di skûr′shən), *n.* **1.** an instance of discursive writing, speech, etc.; a wandering or logically unconnected statement. **2.** the quality or characteristic of ranging from topic to topic; discursiveness; digressiveness. **3.** the process or procedure of rigorous formal analysis or demonstration, as distinguished from immediate or intuitive formulation. [1525–35; < LL *discursiōn-* (s. of *discursiō*) a running to and fro. See DISCOURSE, -ION]

dis·cur·sive (di skûr′siv), *adj.* **1.** passing aimlessly from one subject to another; digressive; rambling. **2.** proceeding by reasoning or argument rather than intuition. [1590–1600; < ML *discursīvus.* See DISCOURSE, -IVE] **—dis·cur′sive·ly,** *adv.* **—dis·cur′sive·ness,** *n.*
—Syn. 1. wandering, long-winded, prolix.

dis·cus (dis′kəs), *n., pl.* **dis·cus·es, dis·ci** (dis′ī). **1.** a circular disk more than 7 in. (18 cm) in diameter and 2.2 lb. (1 kg) in weight, usually wooden with a metal rim and thicker in the center than at the edge, for throwing for distance in athletic competition. **2.** the sport of throwing this disk for distance. [1650–60; < L < Gk *dískos* a quoit, discus, disk, deriv. of *diskeîn* to throw]

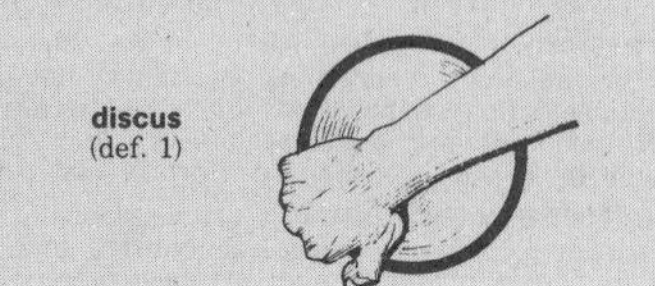
discus (def. 1)

dis·cuss (di skus′), *v.t.* **1.** to consider or examine by argument, comment, etc.; talk over or write about, esp. to explore solutions; debate: *to discuss the proposed law on taxes.* **2.** *Civil Law.* **a.** to collect a debt from (the person primarily liable) before proceeding against the person secondarily liable. **b.** to execute against the movable property of (a debtor) before proceeding against the debtor's immovable property, as land. **3.** *Rare.* to consume (food or drink) enthusiastically. **4.** *Obs.* to make known; reveal. [1300–50; ME (< AF *discusser*) < L *discussus* struck asunder, shaken, scattered, ptp. of *discutere,* equiv. to *dis-* DIS-[1] + *-cutere* (comb. form of *quatere* to shake, strike)] **—dis·cuss′er,** *n.* **—dis·cuss′a·ble, dis·cuss′i·ble,** *adj.*
—Syn. 1. reason, deliberate. See **argue.**

dis·cus·sant (di skus′ənt), *n.* a person who participates in a formal discussion or symposium and is responsible for a specific topic. [1925–30, *Amer.*; DISCUSS + -ANT]

dis·cus·sion (di skush′ən), *n.* an act or instance of discussing; consideration or examination by argument, comment, etc., esp. to explore solutions; informal debate. [1300–50; ME < AF < LL *discussiōn-* (s. of *discussiō*) inquiry, examination, L: a shaking. See DISCUSS, -ION] **—dis·cus′sion·al,** *adj.*

dis·dain (dis dān′, di stān′), *v.t.* **1.** to look upon or treat with contempt; despise; scorn. **2.** to think unworthy of notice, response, etc.; consider beneath oneself: *to disdain replying to an insult.* **—***n.* **3.** a feeling of contempt for anything regarded as unworthy; haughty contempt; scorn. [1300–50; (v.) ME *disdainen* < AF *de(s)deigner* (see DIS-[1], DEIGN); (n.) ME *disdeyn* < AF *desdai(g)n,* deriv. of the verb]
—Syn. 1. contemn, spurn. **3.** haughtiness, arrogance. See **contempt.** **—Ant. 1.** accept. **3.** admiration.

dis·dain·ful (dis dān′fəl, di stān′-), *adj.* full of or showing disdain; scornful. [1535–45; DISDAIN + -FUL] **—dis·dain′ful·ly,** *adv.* **—dis·dain′ful·ness,** *n.*
—Syn. contemptuous, haughty, contumelious.

dis·ease (di zēz′), *n., v.,* **-eased, -eas·ing.** **—***n.* **1.** a disordered or incorrectly functioning organ, part, structure, or system of the body resulting from the effect of genetic or developmental errors, infection, poisons, nutritional deficiency or imbalance, toxicity, or unfavorable environmental factors; illness; sickness; ailment. **2.** any abnormal condition in a plant that interferes with its vital physiological processes, caused by pathogenic microorganisms, parasites, unfavorable environmental, genetic, or nutritional factors, etc. **3.** any harmful, depraved, or morbid condition, as of the mind or society: *His fascination with executions is a disease.* **4.** decomposition of a material under special circumstances: *tin disease.* **—***v.t.* **5.** to affect with disease; make ill. [1300–50; ME *disese* < AF *dese(a)se, disaise;* see DIS-[1], EASE] **—dis·eas′ed·ly,** *adv.* **—dis·eas′ed·ness,** *n.*
—Syn. 1. morbidity, complaint, derangement, distemper, indisposition, infirmity, disorder, malady. **—Ant. 1.** health. **5.** cure.

dis·eased (di zēzd′), *adj.* having or affected with disease. [1425–75; late ME *disesed;* cf. AF *disease.* See DISEASE, -ED[2]]

dis·e·con·o·my (dis′i kon′ə mē), *n., pl.* **-mies** for 2. **1.** a lack of economy. **2.** something that adds costs, as opposed to something that contributes to economy or efficiency. [1935–40; DIS-[1] + ECONOMY]

di·se·gno (dē se′nyô), *n. Italian.* drawing or design: a term used during the 16th and 17th centuries to designate the formal discipline required for the representation of the ideal form of an object in the visual arts, esp. as expressed in the linear structure of a work of art.

dis·em·bar·go (dis′em bär′gō), *v.t.,* **-goed, -go·ing.** to remove an embargo from. [1875–80; DIS-[1] + EMBARGO]

dis·em·bark (dis′em bärk′), *v.i.* **1.** to go ashore from a ship. **2.** to leave an aircraft or other vehicle. **—***v.t.* **3.** to remove or unload (cargo or passengers) from a ship, aircraft, or other vehicle. [1575–85; < MF *desembarquer,* equiv. to *des-* DIS-[1] + *embarquer* to EMBARK] **—dis·em·bar·ka·tion** (dis em′bär kā′shən), **dis′em·bark′ment,** *n.*

dis·em·bar·rass (dis′em bar′əs), *v.t.* **1.** to disentangle or extricate from something troublesome, embarrassing, or the like. **2.** to relieve; rid. **3.** to free from embarrassment. [1720–30; DIS-[1] + EMBARRASS] **—dis′em·bar′rass·ment,** *n.*

dis·em·bod·y (dis′em bod′ē), *v.t.,* **-bod·ied, -bod·y·ing.** to divest (a soul, spirit, etc.) of a body. [1705–15; DIS-[1] + EMBODY] **—dis′em·bod′i·ment,** *n.*

dis·em·bogue (dis′em bōg′), *v.,* **-bogued, -bogu·ing.** **—***v.i.* **1.** to discharge contents by pouring forth. **2.** to discharge water, as at the mouth of a stream: *a river that disembogues into the ocean.* **—***v.t.* **3.** to discharge; cast forth. [1585–95; earlier *disemboque, disemboke* < Sp *desembocar,* equiv. to *des-* DIS-[1] + *embocar* to enter by the mouth (*en-* in (< L *in-* IN-[2]) + *boc(a)* mouth (< L *bucca*) + *-ar* inf. suffix)] **—dis′em·bogue′ment,** *n.*

dis·em·bos·om (dis′em bo͝oz′əm, -bo͞o′zəm), *v.t.* **1.** to reveal; divulge. **2.** to unburden (oneself) of a secret. [1735–45; DIS-[1] + EMBOSOM]

dis·em·bow·el (dis′em bou′əl), *v.t.,* **-eled, -el·ing** or (*esp. Brit.*) **-elled, -el·ling.** **1.** to remove the bowels or entrails from; eviscerate. **2.** to cut or slash open the abdomen of, as by bayoneting, so as to expose or remove the viscera. [1595–1605; DIS-[1] + EMBOWEL] **—dis′em·bow′el·ment,** *n.*

dis·em·broil (dis′em broil′), *v.t.* to free from embroilment, entanglement, or confusion. [1615–25; DIS-[1] + EMBROIL]

dis·em·ploy (dis′em ploi′), *v.t.* to put out of work; cause to become unemployed. [1610–20; DIS- + EMPLOY] **—dis′em·ploy′ment,** *n.*

dis·em·pow·er (dis′em pou′ər), *v.t.* to deprive of influence, importance, etc.: *Voters feel they have become disempowered by recent political events.* [1805–15; DIS-[1] + EMPOWER] **—dis′em·pow′er·ment,** *n.*

dis·en·a·ble (dis′en ā′bəl), *v.t.,* **-bled, -bling.** to deprive of ability; make unable; prevent. [1595–1605; DIS-[1] + ENABLE]

dis·en·am·or (dis′i nam′ər), *v.t.* to disillusion; disenchant (usually used in the passive and fol. by *of* or *with*): *He was disenamored of working in the city.* Also, *esp. Brit.,* **dis′en·am′our.** [1590–1600; DIS-[1] + ENAMOR]

dis·en·chant (dis′en chant′, -chänt′), *v.t.* to rid of or free from enchantment, illusion, credulity, etc.; disillusion: *The harshness of everyday reality disenchanted him of his idealistic hopes.* [1580–90; < MF *desenchanter,* equiv. to *des-* DIS-[1] + *enchanter* to ENCHANT] **—dis′en·chant′er,** *n.* **—dis′en·chant′ing,** *adj.* **—dis′en·chant′ing·ly,** *adv.* **—dis′en·chant′ment,** *n.*

dis·en·cum·ber (dis′en kum′bər), *v.t.* to free from a burden or other encumbrance; disburden. [1590–1600; < MF *desencombrer,* equiv. to *des-* DIS-[1] + *encombrer* to ENCUMBER]
—Syn. disentangle, disembarrass, unburden.

dis·en·dow (dis′en dou′), *v.t.* to deprive (a church, school, etc.) of endowment. [1860–65; DIS-[1] + ENDOW] **—dis′en·dow′er,** *n.* **—dis′en·dow′ment,** *n.*

dis·en·fran·chise (dis′en fran′chīz), *v.t.,* **-chised, -chis·ing.** to disfranchise. [1620–30; DIS-[1] + ENFRANCHISE] **—dis·en·fran·chise·ment** (dis′en fran′chiz-mənt, -chīz-), *n.*

dis·en·gage (dis′en gāj′), *v.,* **-gaged, -gag·ing.** **—***v.t.* **1.** to release from attachment or connection; loosen; unfasten: *to disengage a clutch.* **2.** to free (oneself) from an engagement, pledge, obligation, etc.: *He accepted the invitation, but was later forced to disengage himself.* **3.** *Mil.* to break off action with (an enemy). **—***v.i.* **4.** to become disengaged; free oneself. [1605–15; < MF *desengager,* equiv. to *des-* DIS-[1] + *engager* to ENGAGE] **—dis·en·gag·ed·ness** (dis′en gā′jid nis, -gājd′-), *n.*

dis·en·gage·ment (dis′en gāj′mənt), *n.* **1.** the act or process of disengaging or the state of being disengaged. **2.** freedom from obligation or occupation; leisure. **3.** *Obstet.* (during childbirth) the emergence of the head or the presenting part of the fetus from the vulva. [1640–50; DISENGAGE + -MENT]

dis·en·roll (dis′en rōl′), *v.t.* to dismiss or cause to become removed from a program of training, care, etc.: *The academy disenrolled a dozen cadets.* [1625–35; DIS-[1] + ENROLL] **—dis′en·roll′ment,** *n.*

dis·en·tail (dis′en tāl′), *v.t. Law.* to free (an estate) from entail. [1635–45; DIS-[1] + ENTAIL] **—dis′en·tail′ment,** *n.*

dis·en·tan·gle (dis′en tang′gəl), *v.t., v.i.,* **-gled, -gling.** to free or become free from entanglement; untangle; extricate (often fol. by *from*). [1590–1600; DIS-[1] + ENTANGLE] **—dis′en·tan′gle·ment,** *n.* **—dis′en·tan′gler,** *n.*
—Syn. disembarrass, disencumber.

dis·en·thral (dis′en thrôl′), *v.t.,* **-thralled, -thralling.** disenthrall. **—dis′en·thral′ment,** *n.*

dis·en·thrall (dis′en thrôl′), *v.t.* to free from bondage; liberate: *to be disenthralled from morbid fantasies.* [1635–45; DIS-[1] + ENTHRALL] **—dis′en·thrall′ment,** *n.*

dis·en·throne (dis′en thrōn′), *v.t.,* **-throned, -throning.** to dethrone. [1600–10; DIS-[1] + ENTHRONE] **—dis′en·throne′ment,** *n.*

dis·en·ti·tle (dis′en tīt′l), *v.t.,* **-tled, -tling.** to deprive of title or right. [1645–55; DIS-[1] + ENTITLE] **—dis′en·ti′tle·ment,** *n.*

dis·en·tomb (dis′en to͞om′), *v.t.* to remove from the tomb; disinter. [1620–30; DIS-[1] + ENTOMB] **—dis′en·tomb′ment,** *n.*

dis·en·trance (dis′en trans′, -träns′), *v.t.,* **-tranced, -tranc·ing.** to bring out of an entranced condition; disenchant. [1655–65; DIS-[1] + ENTRANCE[2]] **—dis′en·trance′ment,** *n.*

dis·en·twine (dis′en twīn′), *v.t., v.i.,* **-twined, -twin·ing.** to bring or come out of an entwined or intertwined state; untwine. [1805–15; DIS-[1] + ENTWINE]

di·sep·a·lous (dī sep′ə ləs), *adj. Bot.* having two sepals. [1835–45; DI-[1] + -SEPALOUS]

dis·e·quil·i·brate (dis′i kwil′ə brāt′, dis ē′kwə lī′-brāt), *v.t.,* **-brat·ed, -brat·ing.** to put out of equilibrium; unbalance: *A period of high inflation could disequilibrate the monetary system.* [1895–1900; DIS- + EQUILIBRATE] **—dis′e·quil′i·bra′tion,** *n.*

dis·e·qui·lib·ri·um (dis ē′kwə lib′rē əm, dis′ē-), *n.* lack of equilibrium; imbalance. [1830–40; DIS-[1] + EQUILIBRIUM]

dis·es·tab·lish (dis′i stab′lish), *v.t.* **1.** to deprive of the character of being established; cancel; abolish. **2.** to withdraw exclusive state recognition or support from (a church). [1590–1600; DIS-[1] + ESTABLISH] **—dis′es·tab′lish·ment,** *n.*

dis·es·tab·lish·men·tar·i·an (dis′i stab′lish mən-târ′ē ən), *n.* **1.** a person who favors the separation of church and state, esp. the withdrawal of special rights, status, and support granted an established church by a state; an advocate of disestablishing a state church. **—***adj.* **2.** of, pertaining to, or favoring the disestablishment of a state church. [1880–85; DIS-[1] + ESTABLISHMENT + -ARIAN] **—dis′es·tab′lish·men·tar′i·an·ism,** *n.*

dis·es·teem (dis′i stēm′), *v.t.* **1.** to hold in low regard; think unfavorably of. **—***n.* **2.** lack of esteem; disfavor; low regard. [1585–95; DIS-[1] + ESTEEM]

di·seur (dē zûr′; *Fr.* dē zœʀ′), *n., pl.* **-seurs** (-zûrz′; *Fr.* -zœʀ′). a male professional entertainer who performs monologues. [< F: lit., speaker, OF, equiv. to *dis-* (s. of *dire* < L *dīcere;* see DICTION) + *-eur* -EUR]

di·seuse (*Fr.* dē zœz′), *n., pl.* **-seuses** (-zœz′). a female professional entertainer who performs monologues. [1895–1900; < F, fem. of *diseur* DISEUR; see -EUSE]

dis·fa·vor (dis fā′vər), *n.* **1.** unfavorable regard; displeasure; disesteem; dislike: *The prime minister incurred the king's disfavor.* **2.** the state of being regarded unfavorably; disrepute: *The fashions of one year are in disfavor the next.* **3.** a disadvantageous or detrimental act; disservice: *The pianist did himself a disfavor in trying to sing.* **—***v.t.* **4.** to regard or treat with disfavor. Also, *esp. Brit.,* **dis·fa′vour.** [1525–35; DIS-[1] + FAVOR] **—dis·fa′vor·er;** *esp. Brit.,* **dis·fa′vour·er,** *n.*

dis·fea·ture (dis fē′chər), *v.t.,* **-tured, -tur·ing.** to mar the features of; disfigure. [1650–60; DIS-[1] + FEATURE] **—dis·fea′ture·ment,** *n.*

CONCISE ETYMOLOGY KEY: <, descended or borrowed from; >, whence; b., blend of, blended; c., cognate with; cf., compare; deriv., derivative; equiv., equivalent; imit., imitative; obl., oblique; r., replacing; s., stem; sp., spelling, spelled; resp., respelling, respelled; trans., translation; ?, origin unknown; *, unattested; ‡, probably earlier than. See the full key inside the front cover.

dis•fel•low•ship (dis fel′ō ship′), *n., v.,* **-shiped, -ship•ing** or (*esp. Brit.*) **-shipped, -ship•ping.** —*n.* **1.** (in some Protestant religions) the status of a member who, because of some serious infraction of church policy, has been denied the church's sacraments and any post of responsibility and is officially shunned by other members. —*v.t.* **2.** to place in the status of disfellowship. [1600–10; DIS-[1] + FELLOWSHIP]

dis•fig•ure (dis fig′yər; *Brit.* dis fig′ər), *v.t.,* **-ured, -ur•ing. 1.** to mar the appearance or beauty of; deform; deface: *Our old towns are increasingly disfigured by tasteless new buildings.* **2.** to mar the effect or excellence of: *His reputation was disfigured by instances of political favoritism.* [1325–75; ME *disfiguren* < AF, OF *desfigurer,* equiv. to *des-* DIS-[1] + *-figurer,* v. deriv. of *figure* FIGURE] —**dis•fig′ur•er,** *n.*
—**Syn. 1.** spoil, blemish. See **mar.** —**Ant. 1.** beautify.

dis•fig•ure•ment (dis fig′yər mənt; *Brit.* dis fig′ər mənt), *n.* **1.** an act or instance of disfiguring. **2.** a disfigured condition. **3.** something that disfigures, as a scar. Also called **dis•fig′ur•a′tion.** [1625–35; DISFIGURE + -MENT]

dis•flu•en•cy (dis flōō′ən sē), *n., pl.* **-cies** for 2. **1.** *Pathol.* impairment of the ability to produce smooth, fluent speech. **2.** an interruption in the smooth flow of speech, as by a pause or the repetition of a word or syllable. Also, **dysfluency.** [1975–80; DIS-[1] + FLUENCY]

dis•fran•chise (dis fran′chīz), *v.t.,* **-chised, -chis•ing. 1.** to deprive (a person) of a right of citizenship, as of the right to vote. **2.** to deprive of a franchise, privilege, or right. Also, **disenfranchise.** [1425–75; late ME; see DIS-[1], FRANCHISE] —**dis•fran•chise•ment** (dis fran′chīz mənt, -chiz-), *n.* —**dis•fran′chis•er,** *n.*

dis•frock (dis frok′), *v.t. Eccles.* to unfrock. [1830–40; DIS-[1] + FROCK]

dis•func•tion (dis fungk′shən), *n.* dysfunction. [by confusion of DYS- with DIS-[1]] —**dis•func′tion•al,** *adj.*

dis•fur•nish (dis fûr′nish), *v.t.* to deprive of something with which a person or thing is furnished; divest of possessions; strip. [1525–35; < MF *desfourniss-,* s. of *desfournir,* equiv. to des- DIS-[1] + *fournir* to FURNISH] —**dis•fur′nish•ment,** *n.*

dis•gav•el (dis gav′əl), *v.t.,* **-eled, -el•ing** or (*esp. Brit.*) **-elled, -el•ling.** *Eng. Law.* to free from the tenure of gavelkind: *to disgavel an estate.* [1675–85; DIS-[1] + GAVEL[2]]

dis•gorge (dis gôrj′), *v.,* **-gorged, -gorg•ing.** —*v.t.* **1.** to eject or throw out from the throat, mouth, or stomach; vomit forth. **2.** to surrender or yield (something, esp. something illicitly obtained). **3.** to discharge forcefully or as a result of force. —*v.i.* **4.** to eject, yield, or discharge something. [1470–80; < MF *desgorger,* equiv. to *des-* DIS-[1] + *-gorger,* deriv. of *gorge* throat; see GORGE] —**dis•gorge′ment,** *n.* —**dis•gorg′er,** *n.*

dis•grace (dis grās′), *n., v.,* **-graced, -grac•ing.** —*n.* **1.** the loss of respect, honor, or esteem; ignominy; shame: *the disgrace of criminals.* **2.** a person, act, or thing that causes shame, reproach, or dishonor or is dishonorable or shameful. **3.** the state of being out of favor; exclusion from favor, confidence, or trust: *courtiers and ministers in disgrace.* —*v.t.* **4.** to bring or reflect shame or reproach upon: *to be disgraced by cowardice.* **5.** to dismiss with discredit; put out of grace or favor; rebuke or humiliate: *to be disgraced at court.* [1540–50; (n.) < MF < It *disgrazia,* equiv. to *dis-* DIS-[1] + *grazia* < L *gratia* (see GRACE); (v.) < MF *disgracier* < It *disgraziare,* deriv. of *disgrazia*] —**dis•grac′er,** *n.*
—**Syn. 1.** disapproval, disapprobation, notoriety, taint. DISGRACE, DISHONOR, IGNOMINY, INFAMY imply a very low position in the opinion of others. DISGRACE implies the disfavor of others: *to be in disgrace.* DISHONOR implies a stain on honor or honorable reputation; it relates esp. to the person's own conduct: *He preferred death to dishonor.* IGNOMINY is disgrace in which one's situation invites contempt: *the ignominy of being discovered cheating.* INFAMY is shameful notoriety, or baseness of action or character that is widely known and recognized: *The children never outlived the father's infamy.* **3.** disfavor, odium, obloquy. **4.** dishonor, defame, stain, sully, taint. **5.** degrade, disapprove. —**Ant. 1.** honor.

dis•grace•ful (dis grās′fəl), *adj.* bringing or deserving disgrace; shameful; dishonorable; disreputable. [1585–95; DISGRACE + -FUL] —**dis•grace′ful•ly,** *adv.* —**dis•grace′ful•ness,** *n.*

dis•gre•gate (dis′gri gāt′), *v.t., v.i.,* **-gat•ed, -gat•ing.** to separate; disintegrate; scatter. [1375–1425; late ME < LL *disgregātus* separated (ptp. of *disgregāre*), equiv. to L *dis-* DIS-[1] + *greg(āre)* to assemble, collect, deriv. of *greg-* (s. of *grex*) flock, herd, crowd + *-ātus* -ATE[1]] —**dis′gre•ga′tion,** *n.*

dis•grun•tle (dis grun′tl), *v.t.,* **-tled, -tling.** to put into a state of sulky dissatisfaction; make discontent. [1675–85; DIS-[1] + *gruntle,* freq. of GRUNT] —**dis•grun′tle•ment,** *n.*

dis•grun•tled (dis grun′tld), *adj.* displeased and discontented; sulky; peevish: *Her disgruntled husband refused to join us.* [DISGRUNTLE + -ED[2]]
—**Syn.** grouchy, testy, sullen, grumpy, dissatisfied.

dis•guise (dis gīz′, di skīz′), *v.,* **-guised, -guis•ing,** *n.* —*v.t.* **1.** to change the appearance or guise of so as to conceal identity or mislead, as by means of deceptive garb: *The king was disguised as a peasant.* **2.** to conceal or cover up the truth or actual character of by a counterfeit form or appearance; misrepresent: *to disguise one's intentions.* —*n.* **3.** that which disguises; something that serves or is intended for concealment of identity, character, or quality; a deceptive covering, condition, manner, etc.: *Noble words can be the disguise of base intentions.* **4.** the makeup, mask, costume, or overall changed appearance of an entertainer: *a clown's disguise.* **5.** the act of disguising: *to speak without disguise.* **6.** the state of being disguised; masquerade: *The gods appeared in disguise.* [1275–1325; ME *disg(u)isen* < AF, OF *de(s)guiser,* equiv. to *des-* DIS-[1] + *-guiser,* deriv. of *guise* GUISE] —**dis•guis′a•ble,** *adj.* —**dis•guis′ed•ly,** *adv.* —**dis•guis′ed•ness,** *n.* —**dis•guis′er,** *n.* —**dis•guise′ment,** *n.*
—**Syn. 2.** cloak, mask, hide, dissemble.

dis•gust (dis gust′, di skust′), *v.t.* **1.** to cause loathing or nausea in. **2.** to offend the good taste, moral sense, etc., of; cause extreme dislike or revulsion in: *Your vulgar remarks disgust me.* —*n.* **3.** a strong distaste; nausea; loathing. **4.** repugnance caused by something offensive; strong aversion: *He left the room in disgust.* [1590–1600; (v.) < MF *desgouster,* equiv. to *des-* DIS-[1] + *gouster* to taste, relish, deriv. of *goust* taste < L *gusta* (see CHOOSE); (n.) < MF *desgoust,* deriv. of the v.] —**dis•gust′ed•ly,** *adv.* —**dis•gust′ed•ness,** *n.*
—**Syn. 1.** sicken, nauseate. **2.** repel, revolt. **4.** abhorrence, detestation, antipathy. See **dislike.** —**Ant. 1.** delight. **4.** relish.

dis•gust•ful (dis gust′fəl, di skust′-), *adj.* causing disgust; nauseous; offensive. [1605–15; DISGUST + -FUL] —**dis•gust′ful•ly,** *adv.*

dis•gust•ing (dis gus′ting, di skus′-), *adj.* causing disgust; offensive to the physical, moral, or aesthetic taste. [1745–55; DISGUST + -ING[2]] —**dis•gust′ing•ly,** *adv.* —**dis•gust′ing•ness,** *n.*
—**Syn.** loathsome, sickening, nauseous, repulsive, revolting, repugnant, abhorrent, detestable.

dish (dish), *n.* **1.** an open, relatively shallow container of pottery, glass, metal, wood, etc., used for various purposes, esp. for holding or serving food. **2.** any container used at table: *dirty dishes.* **3.** the food served or contained in a dish: *The meal consisted of several dishes.* **4.** a particular article, type, or preparation of food: *Rice is an inexpensive dish.* **5.** the quantity held by a dish; dishful: *a dish of applesauce.* **6.** anything like a dish in form or use. **7.** concavity or the degree of concavity, as of a wheel. **8.** Also called **dish′ anten′na.** a concave, dish-shaped reflector serving to focus electromagnetic energy as part of a transmitter or receiver of radio, television, or microwave signals. **9.** *Slang* (*sometimes offensive*). an attractive girl or woman: *The receptionist is quite a dish.* **10.** *Slang.* an item of gossip. —*v.t.* **11.** to put into or serve in a dish, as food: *to dish food onto plates.* **12.** to fashion like a dish; make concave. **13.** *Slang.* to gossip about: *They talked all night, dishing their former friends.* **14.** *Slang.* to defeat; frustrate; cheat. —*v.i.* **15.** *Slang.* to talk together informally, esp., to gossip. **16. dish it out,** *Informal.* to dispense abusive language, punishment, or praise, enthusiastic approval, etc.: *When it comes to flattery, he can really dish it out.* **17. dish out,** *Informal.* **a.** to serve (food) from a serving dish, pot, etc. **b.** to deal out; distribute: *She dished out our pay in silver dollars.* [bef. 900; ME; OE *disc* dish, plate, bowl (akin to G *Tisch* table) < L *discus* dish, DISCUS]

dis•ha•bille (dis′ə bēl′, -bē′), *n.* **1.** the state of being dressed in a careless, disheveled, or disorderly style or manner; undress. **2.** a garment worn in undress. **3.** a loose morning dress. **4.** a disorderly or disorganized state of mind or way of thinking. Also, **des•habille.** [1665–75; < F *déshabillé,* n. use of ptp. of *déshabiller* to undress, equiv. to *dés-* DIS-[1] + *habiller* to dress; see HABILIMENT]

dis•ha•bit•u•ate (dis′hə bich′ōō āt′), *v.t.,* **-at•ed, -at•ing.** to cause to be no longer habituated or accustomed. [1865–70; DIS-[1] + HABITUATE]

dis•hal•low (dis hal′ō), *v.t.* to profane; desecrate. [1545–55; DIS-[1] + HALLOW[1]]

dis•har•mon•ic (dis′här mon′ik), *adj.* **1.** lacking harmony; disharmonious; discordant. **2.** without symmetry in physical form. [1885–90; DISHARMON(Y) + -IC]

dis•har•mo•ni•ous (dis′här mō′nē əs), *adj.* inharmonious; discordant. [1650–60; DIS-[1] + HARMONIOUS]

dis•har•mo•nize (dis här′mə nīz′), *v.t., v.i.,* **-nized, -niz•ing.** to make or be inharmonious. Also, *esp. Brit.,* **dis•har′mo•nise′.** [1795–1805; DIS-[1] + HARMONIZE] —**dis•har•mo•nism** (dis här′mə niz′əm), *n.*

dis•har•mo•ny (dis här′mə nē), *n., pl.* **-nies. 1.** lack of harmony; discord. **2.** something discordant. [1595–1605; DIS-[1] + HARMONY]

dish•cloth (dish′klôth′, -kloth′), *n., pl.* **-cloths** (-klôthz′, -klothz′, -klôths′, -kloths′). a cloth for use in washing dishes; dishrag. Also, *Brit.,* **dish•clout** (dish′klout′). [1820–30; DISH + CLOTH]

dish′cloth gourd′, loofah (def. 1). [1895–1900]

dis•heart•en (dis här′tn), *v.t.* to depress the hope, courage, or spirits of; discourage. [1590–1600; DIS-[1] + HEARTEN] —**dis•heart′en•er,** *n.* —**dis•heart′en•ing•ly,** *adv.* —**dis•heart′en•ment,** *n.*
—**Syn.** dismay, daunt, deject, dispirit.

dished (disht), *adj.* **1.** concave: *a dished face.* **2.** *Older Slang.* exhausted; worn out. **3.** (of a parallel pair of vehicle wheels) farther apart at the top than at the bottom. [1580–90; DISH + -ED[2]]

dis•helm (dis helm′), *v.t.* to deprive of a helmet. [1470–80; DIS-[1] + HELM[2]]

dis•her•i•son (dis her′ə sən, -zən), *n.* disinheritance. [1250–1300; ME < OF *desheriteison,* deriv. of *deseriter* to disinherit; see DISHERIT]

dis•her•it (dis her′it), *v.t.* to disinherit. [1250–1300; ME *deseriten* < AF, OF *deseriter,* equiv. to *des-* DIS-[1] + *heriter* to INHERIT] —**dis•her′i•tor,** *n.*

di•shev•el (di shev′əl), *v.t.,* **-eled, -el•ing** or (*esp. Brit.*) **-elled, -el•ling. 1.** to let down, as hair, or wear or let hang in loose disorder, as clothing. **2.** to cause untidiness and disarray in: *The wind disheveled the papers on the desk.* [1590–1600; back formation from DISHEVELED] —**di•shev′el•ment,** *n.*

di•shev•eled (di shev′əld), *adj.* **1.** hanging loosely or in disorder; unkempt: *disheveled hair.* **2.** untidy; disarranged: *a disheveled appearance.* Also, *esp. Brit.,* **di•shev′elled.** [1375–1425; late ME *discheveled* < OF *deschevele,* ptp. of *descheveler* to dishevel the hair, equiv. to *des-* DIS-[1] + *-cheveler,* deriv. of *chevel* a hair < L *capillus*]
—**Syn. 2.** rumpled, messy, slovenly, sloppy.

dish•ful (dish′fo͝ol), *n., pl.* **-fuls.** the amount that a dish will hold. [1275–1325; ME; see DISH, -FUL]
—**Usage.** See **-ful.**

dish′ gra′vy, meat juices, as from a roast, served as a gravy without seasoning or thickening. Cf. **pan gravy.**

dish′ night′, (formerly) a night, usually held weekly, when a movie theater distributed a free dish or piece of chinaware to each patron as an inducement to visit the theater. [1930–35]

dis•hon•est (dis on′ist), *adj.* **1.** not honest; disposed to lie, cheat, or steal; not worthy of trust or belief: *a dishonest person.* **2.** proceeding from or exhibiting lack of honesty; fraudulent: *a dishonest advertisement.* [1350–1400; ME *dishoneste* < AF, OF *deshoneste,* equiv. to *des-* DIS-[1] + *honeste* HONEST] —**dis•hon′est•ly,** *adv.*
—**Syn. 1.** unscrupulous, knavish, deceitful, perfidious. See **corrupt. 2.** false. —**Ant. 1, 2.** honest.

dis•hon•es•ty (dis on′ə stē), *n., pl.* **-ties. 1.** lack of honesty; a disposition to lie, cheat, or steal. **2.** a dishonest act; fraud. [1350–1400; ME *deshonestee.* See DIS-[1], HONESTY]

dis•hon•or (dis on′ər), *n.* **1.** lack or loss of honor; disgraceful or dishonest character or conduct. **2.** disgrace; ignominy; shame: *His arrest brought dishonor to his family.* **3.** an indignity; insult: *to do someone a dishonor.* **4.** a cause of shame or disgrace: *He is a dishonor to his family.* **5.** *Com.* failure or refusal of the drawee or intended acceptor of a bill of exchange or note to accept it or, if it is accepted, to pay and retire it. —*v.t.* **6.** to deprive of honor; disgrace; bring reproach or shame on. **7.** *Com.* to fail or refuse to honor or pay (a draft, check, etc.). **8.** to rape or seduce. Also, *esp. Brit.,* **dis•hon′our.** [1250–1300; ME *dishonour* (n.), *dishonouren* (v.) < AF, OF; see DIS-[1], HONOR] —**dis•hon′or•er,** *n.*
—**Syn. 1, 2.** See **disgrace.**

dis•hon•or•a•ble (dis on′ər ə bəl), *adj.* **1.** showing lack of honor or integrity; ignoble; base; disgraceful; shameful: *Cheating is dishonorable.* **2.** having no honor or good repute; unprincipled; disreputable: *a dishonorable man.* Also, *esp. Brit.,* **dis•hon′our•a•ble.** [1525–35; DIS-[1] + HONORABLE] —**dis•hon′or•a•ble•ness,** *n.* —**dis•hon′or•a•bly,** *adv.*
—**Syn. 1.** shameless, false. **2.** infamous, unscrupulous, disgraceful, scandalous, ignominious.

dishon′orable dis′charge, *Mil.* **1.** the discharge of a person from military service for an offense more serious than one for which a bad-conduct discharge is given. **2.** a certificate of such a discharge.

dish•pan (dish′pan′), *n.* a large pan in which dishes, pots, etc., are washed. [1870–75, *Amer.*; DISH + PAN[1]]

dish′pan hands′, hands, esp. of one who does housework, that are red and rough, as from washing dishes and exposure to strong cleaning agents. [1940–45]

dish•rag (dish′rag′), *n.* a dishcloth. [1830–40, *Amer.*; DISH + RAG[1]]

dish′ top′, a circular table top upturned at the edge.

dish•tow•el (dish′tou′əl), *n.* a towel for drying dishes. [1865–70; DISH + TOWEL]

dish•ware (dish′wâr′), *n.* dishes used for food; tableware. [1945–50; DISH + WARE[1]]

dish•wash•er (dish′wosh′ər, -wô′shər), *n.* **1.** a person who washes dishes. **2.** a machine for washing dishes, kitchen utensils, etc., automatically. [1520–30; DISH + WASHER]

dish•wash•er•proof (dish′wosh′ər prōōf′, -wô′shər-), *adj.* (of dishes, cooking utensils, etc.) able to withstand washing in an automatic dishwasher without breaking, chipping, fading, etc. [DISHWASHER + -PROOF]

dish•wa•ter (dish′wô′tər, -wot′ər), *n.* **1.** water in which dishes are, or have been, washed. **2. dull as dishwater** or **ditchwater,** extremely dull; boring. [1475–85; DISH + WATER]

dish•y (dish′ē), *adj.,* **dish•i•er, dish•i•est.** *Slang.* **1.** *Chiefly Brit.* very attractive; pretty or beautiful: *a couple of dishy fashion models.* **2.** gossipy; full of gossip: *a dishy book about Hollywood.* [1960–65; DISH + -Y[1]]

dis•il•lu•sion (dis′i lōō′zhən), *v.t.* **1.** to free from or deprive of illusion, belief, idealism, etc.; disenchant. —*n.* **2.** a freeing or a being freed from illusion or conviction; disenchantment. [1590–1600; DIS-[1] + ILLUSION] —**dis′il•lu′sion•ment,** *n.* —**dis•il•lu•sive** (dis′i lōō′siv), *adj.*
—**Syn. 1.** disabuse, disenthrall, undeceive, disappoint.

dis•il•lu•sion•ize (dis′i lōō′zhə nīz′), *v.t.,* **-ized, -iz•ing.** to disillusion. Also, *esp. Brit.,* **dis′il•lu′sion•ise′.** [1860–65; DISILLUSION + -IZE] —**dis′il•lu′sion•iz′er, dis′il•lu′sion•ist,** *n.*

dis•im•pas•sioned (dis′im pash′ənd), *adj.* calm; dispassionate. [1860–65; DIS-[1] + IMPASSIONED]

dis•im•pris•on (dis′im priz′ən), *v.t.* to release from imprisonment. [1605–15; DIS-[1] + IMPRISON] —**dis′im•pris′on•ment,** *n.*

dis•in•cen•tive (dis′in sen′tiv), *n.* something that discourages or deters; deterrent: *High interest rates and government regulations are disincentives to investment.* [1945–50; DIS- + INCENTIVE]

dis•in•cli•na•tion (dis in′klə nā′shən, dis′in-), *n.* the absence of inclination; reluctance; unwillingness. [1640–50; DIS-[1] + INCLINATION]

dis•in•cline (dis′in klīn′), *v.t., v.i.,* **-clined, -clin•ing.** to make or be averse or unwilling: *Your rudeness disinclines me to grant your request.* [1640–50; DIS-[1] + INCLINE]

dis•in•clined (dis′in klīnd′), *adj.* lacking desire or

willingness; unwilling; averse: *I'm disinclined to go to the movies tonight.* [1640–50; DISINCLINE + -ED[2]]
—Syn. reluctant, loath.

dis•in•cor•po•rate (dis′in kôr′pə rāt′), *v.*, **-rat•ed, -rat•ing.** —*v.t.* **1.** to remove from an incorporated state or status. —*v.i.* **2.** to become removed from an incorporated state or status. **—dis′in•cor′po•ra′tion,** *n.* [1690–1700; DIS-[1] + INCORPORATE[1]]

dis•in•fect (dis′in fekt′), *v.t.* to cleanse (rooms, wounds, clothing, etc.) of infection; destroy disease germs in. [1590–1600; < MF *desinfecter,* equiv. to *des-* DIS-[1] + *infecter* to INFECT] **—dis′in•fec′tion,** *n.* **—dis′in•fec′•tive,** *adj.* **—dis′in•fec′tor,** *n.*

dis•in•fect•ant (dis′in fek′tənt), *n.* **1.** any chemical agent used chiefly on inanimate objects to destroy or inhibit the growth of harmful organisms. —*adj.* **2.** serving as a disinfectant. [1830–40; < F *désinfectant,* n. use of prp. of *désinfecter,* MF. See DISINFECT, -ANT]

dis•in•fest (dis′in fest′), *v.t.* to rid of insects, rodents, etc. [1915–20; DIS-[1] + INFEST] **—dis•in′fes•ta′tion,** *n.*

dis•in•flate (dis′in flāt′), *v.*, **-flat•ed, -flat•ing.** *Econ.* —*v.i.* **1.** (of an economy) to slow down the rate of inflation. —*v.t.* **2.** to slow down the rate of inflation in (an economy). [1945–50; DIS-[1] + INFLATE]

dis•in•fla•tion (dis′in flā′shən), *n. Econ.* a period or process of slowing the rate of inflation. [1875–80; DIS-[1] + INFLATION] **—dis′in•fla′tion•ar′y,** *adj.*

dis•in•form (dis′in fôrm′), *v.t.* to give or supply disinformation to. [1975–80; back formation from DISINFORMATION] **—dis′in•form′er,** *n.*

dis•in•for•ma•tion (dis in′fər mā′shən, dis′in-), *n.* false information, as about a country's military strength or plans, publicly announced or planted in the news media, esp. of other countries. [1965–70; DIS-[1] + INFORMATION, as trans. of Russ *dezinformátsiya* < F *désinform(er)* to misinform + Russ *-atsiya* << L *-ātiō* (see -ATION)]

dis•in•gen•u•ous (dis′in jen′yo͞o əs), *adj.*, lacking in frankness, candor, or sincerity; falsely or hypocritically ingenuous; insincere: *Her excuse was rather disingenuous.* [1645–55; DIS-[1] + INGENUOUS] **—dis′in•gen′u•ous•ly,** *adv.* **—dis′in•gen′u•ous•ness,** *n.*

dis•in•her•it (dis′in her′it), *v.t.* **1.** *Law.* to exclude from inheritance (an heir or a next of kin). **2.** to deprive of a heritage, country, right, privilege, etc.: *the disinherited peoples of the earth.* [1525–35; DIS-[1] + INHERIT] **—dis′in•her′i•tance,** *n.*

dis•in•hi•bi•tion (dis in′i bish′ən, -in′hi-, dis′in-), *n.* **1.** *Psychol.* a temporary loss of inhibition caused by an outside stimulus. **2.** *Chem.* removal of an inhibitor. [1925–30; DIS-[1] + INHIBITION]

dis•in•hume (dis′in hyo͞om′ *or, often,* -yo͞om′), *v.t.*, **-humed, -hum•ing.** to disinter. [1815–25; DIS-[1] + INHUME]

dis•in•te•grate (dis in′tə grāt′), *v.*, **-grat•ed, -grat•ing.** —*v.i.* **1.** to separate into parts or lose intactness or solidness; break up; deteriorate: *The old book is gradually disintegrating with age.* **2.** *Physics.* **a.** to decay. **b.** (of a nucleus) to change into one or more different nuclei after being bombarded by high-energy particles, as alpha particles or gamma rays. —*v.t.* **3.** to reduce to particles, fragments, or parts; break up or destroy the cohesion of: *Rocks are disintegrated by frost and rain.* [1790–1800; DIS-[1] + INTEGRATE] **—dis•in•te•gra•ble** (dis in′tə grə bəl), *adj.* **—dis•in′te•gra′tive, dis•in•te•gra•to•ry** (dis in′tə grə tôr′ē, -tōr′ē, -grā′tə rē), *adj.* **—dis•in′te•gra′tor,** *n.*
—Syn. 1, 3. See **decay.**

dis•in•te•gra•tion (dis in′tə grā′shən), *n.* **1.** the act or process of disintegrating. **2.** *Physics.* decay (def. 8). [1790–1800; DISINTEGRATE + -ION]

disintegra′tion con′stant, *Physics.* See **decay constant.** [1925–30]

dis•in•ter (dis′in tûr′), *v.t.*, **-terred, -ter•ring.** **1.** to take out of the place of interment; exhume; unearth. **2.** to bring from obscurity into view: *The actor's autobiography disinterred a past era.* [1605–15; DIS-[1] + INTER] **—dis′in•ter′ment,** *n.*

dis•in•ter•est (dis in′tər ist, -trist), *n.* **1.** absence of interest; indifference. —*v.t.* **2.** to divest of interest or concern. [1605–15; DIS-[1] + INTEREST]

dis•in•ter•est•ed (dis in′tə res′tid, -tri stid), *adj.* **1.** unbiased by personal interest or advantage; not influenced by selfish motives: *a disinterested decision by the referee.* **2.** not interested; indifferent. [1605–15; DIS-[1] + INTERESTED] **—dis•in′ter•est′ed•ly,** *adv.* **—dis•in′ter•est′ed•ness,** *n.*
—Syn. 1. impartial, neutral, unprejudiced, dispassionate. See **fair**[1]. **—Ant. 1.** partial, biased.
—Usage. DISINTERESTED and UNINTERESTED share a confused and confusing history. DISINTERESTED was originally used to mean "not interested, indifferent"; UNINTERESTED in its earliest use meant "impartial." By various developmental twists, DISINTERESTED is now used in both senses. UNINTERESTED is used mainly in the sense "not interested, indifferent." It is occasionally used to mean "not having a personal or property interest."
Many object to the use of DISINTERESTED to mean "not interested, indifferent." They insist that DISINTERESTED can mean only "impartial": *A disinterested observer is the best judge of behavior.* However, both senses are well established in all varieties of English, and the sense intended is almost always clear from the context.

dis•in•ter•me•di•a•tion (dis′in tər mē′dē ā′shən), *n.* the act of removing funds from savings banks and placing them into short-term investments on which the interest-rate yields are higher. [1965–70; DIS-[1] + INTERMEDIATION]

dis•in•tox•i•ca•tion (dis′in tok′si kā′shən), *n.* detoxification (def. 4). [1925–30; DIS-[1] + INTOXICATION]

dis•in•vest (dis′in vest′), *v.i.* **1.** to engage in disinvestment. —*v.t.* **2.** to subject (capital goods) to disinvestment. [1620–30; DIS-[1] + INVEST]

dis•in•vest•ment (dis′in vest′mənt), *n.* the withdrawal of invested funds or the cancellation of financial aid, subsidies, or investment plans, as in a property, neighborhood, or foreign country. [1935–40; DISINVEST + -MENT]

dis•in•vite (dis′in vīt′), *v.t.*, **-vit•ed, -vit•ing.** to withdraw an invitation to. [1570–80; DIS-[1] + INVITE]

dis•in•volve•ment (dis′in volv′mənt), *n.* the action or process of withdrawing from an obligation or commitment, esp. from a political or military involvement: *The Secretary of State promised disinvolvement from the alliance.* [DIS-[1] + INVOLVE + -MENT]

dis•jas•ked (dis jas′kit), *adj. Scot.* dilapidated; decayed; broken. Also, **dis•jas′ket, dis•jas′kit.** [1810–20; perh. alter. of DEJECTED]

dis•ject (dis jekt′), *v.t.* to scatter; disperse. [1575–85; < L *disjectus,* ptp. of *disicere,* equiv. to *dis-* DIS-[1] + *-icere* (comb. form of *jacere* to throw); see JET[1]] **—dis•jec′tion,** *n.*

dis•jec•ta mem•bra (dis jek′tə mem′brə), scattered members; disjointed portions or parts: applied to fragments of poetry or fragmentary quotations. [< L, alter. of *disjecti membra poētae* limbs of a dismembered poet, a phrase in Horace]

dis•join (dis join′), *v.t.* **1.** to undo or prevent the junction or union of; disunite; separate. —*v.i.* **2.** to become disunited; separate. [1475–85; ME *disjoinen* < OF *desjoindre* < L *disjungere,* equiv. to *dis-* DIS-[1] + *jungere* to JOIN] **—dis•join′a•ble,** *adj.*

dis•joined (dis joind′), *adj.* **1.** separated; disunited. **2.** *Entomol.* disjunct (def. 3). [1565–75; DISJOIN + -ED[2]]

dis•joint (dis joint′), *v.t.* **1.** to separate or disconnect the joints or joinings of. **2.** to put out of order; derange. —*v.i.* **3.** to come apart. **4.** to be dislocated; be out of joint. —*adj.* **5.** *Math.* **a.** (of two sets) having no common elements. **b.** (of a system of sets) having the property that every pair of sets is disjoint. **6.** *Obs.* disjointed; out of joint. [1400–50; late ME *disjointen* to destroy < AF, OF *desjoint,* ptp. of *desjoindre* to DISJOIN]

dis•joint•ed (dis join′tid), *adj.* **1.** having the joints or connections separated: *a disjointed fowl.* **2.** disconnected; incoherent: *a disjointed discourse.* **3.** *Entomol.* disjunct (def. 3). [1580–90; DISJOINT + -ED[2]] **—dis•joint′ed•ly,** *adv.* **—dis•joint′ed•ness,** *n.*
—Syn. 2. rambling, confused, chaotic, disordered.

dis•junct (*adj.* dis jungkt′; *n.* dis′jungkt), *adj.* **1.** disjoined; separated. **2.** *Music.* progressing melodically by intervals larger than a second. **3.** *Entomol.* having the head, thorax, and abdomen separated by deep constrictions; disjoined; disjointed. —*n.* **4.** See **sentence adverb.** [1375–1425; late ME < L *disjunctus* separated, ptp. of *disjungere* to DISJOIN; see JUNCTION]

dis•junc•tion (dis jungk′shən), *n.* **1.** the act of disjoining or the state of being disjoined: *a disjunction between thought and action.* **2.** *Logic.* **a.** Also called **disjunctive, inclusive disjunction.** a compound proposition that is true if and only if at least one of a number of alternatives is true. **b.** Also called **exclusive disjunction.** a compound proposition that is true if and only if one and only one of a number of alternatives is true. **c.** the relation among the components of such propositions, usually expressed by OR or V. [1350–1400; ME *disjunccioun* < L *disjunctiōn-* (s. of *disjunctiō*) separation, equiv. to *disjunct(us)* (see DISJUNCT) + *-iōn-* -ION]

dis•junc•tive (dis jungk′tiv), *adj.* **1.** serving or tending to disjoin; separating; dividing; distinguishing. **2.** *Gram.* **a.** syntactically setting two or more expressions in opposition to each other, as *but* in *poor but happy,* or expressing an alternative, as *or* in *this or that.* **b.** not syntactically dependent upon some particular expression. **3.** *Logic.* **a.** characterizing propositions that are disjunctions. **b.** (of a syllogism) containing at least one disjunctive proposition as a premise. —*n.* **4.** a statement, course of action, etc., involving alternatives. **5.** *Logic.* disjunction (def. 2a). **6.** *Gram.* a disjunctive word. [1400–50; late ME < LL *disjunctīvus* placed in opposition, equiv. to L *disjunct(us)* (see DISJUNCT) + *-īvus* -IVE] **—dis•junc′tive•ly,** *adv.*

dis•junc•ture (dis jungk′chər), *n.* the act of disjoining or the state of being disjoined; disjunction. [1350–1400; ME (< AF) < ML *disjunctūra,* equiv. to L *disjunct(us)* (see DISJUNCT) + *-ūra* -URE]

dis•june (dis jo͞on′), *n. Scot. Obs.* breakfast. [1485–95; late ME (Scots) *disione* < OF *desjeun,* deriv. of *desjeuner* to break one's fast; see DINE]

disk (disk), *n.* **1.** any thin, flat, circular plate or object. **2.** any surface that is flat and round, or seemingly so: *the disk of the sun.* **3.** disc (def. 1). **4.** *Computers.* any of several types of media consisting of thin, round plates of plastic or metal, used for external storage: *magnetic disk; floppy disk; optical disk.* **5.** *Bot., Zool.* any of various roundish, flat structures or parts. **6.** See **intervertebral disk.** **7.** *Bot.* (in the daisy and other composite plants) the central portion of the flower head, composed of tubular florets. **8.** any of the circular steel blades that form the working part of a disk harrow. **9.** *Math.* the domain bounded by a circle. **10.** *Archaic.* discus. —*v.t.* **11.** *Informal.* disc (def. 3). **12.** to cultivate (soil) with a disk harrow. Also, **disc** (for defs. 1, 2, 4–9, 12). [1655–65; < L *discus* DISCUS; cf. DISH] **—disk′like′,** *adj.*

disk′ brake′, *Auto.* See **disc brake.**

disk′ crank′, *Mach.* a crank having the form of a disk with a crankpin mounted off-center. See diag. under **crankpin.** [1885–90]

disk′ drive′, *Computers.* a device that, using an access mechanism under program control, enables data to be read from or written on a spinning magnetic disk, magnetic disk pack, floppy disk, or optical disk. [1970–75]

disk•ette (di sket′), *n. Computers.* See **floppy disk.** [1970–75; DISK + -ETTE]

disk′ flow′er, *Bot.* one of a number of small tubular flowers composing the disk of certain composite plants. Also called **disk′ flo′ret.** Cf. **ray flower.** [1865–70]

disk′ har′row, a harrow having a number of sharp-edged, concave disks set at such an angle that as the harrow is drawn along the ground they turn the soil, pulverize it, and destroy weeds. [1880–85]

disk′ jock′ey. See **disc jockey.**

dis•kog•ra•phy (di skog′rə fē), *n., pl.* **-phies.** discography.

disk′ op′erating sys′tem, *Computers.* See **DOS.**

disk′ pack′, *Computers.* a cylinder containing several magnetic disks that can be installed in or removed from a disk drive as a unit: used for data storage and retrieval. [1965–70]

disk′ sand′er, a sander that uses a revolving abrasive disk driven by an electric motor. Cf. **belt sander, orbital sander.**

disk′ wheel′, a spokeless vehicular wheel, esp. on automobiles, having a heavy circular pressed-steel disk mounted on the wheel hub and supporting the tire rim on its outer edge. [1905–10]

dis•like (dis līk′), *v.*, **-liked, -lik•ing,** *n.* —*v.t.* **1.** to regard with displeasure, antipathy, or aversion: *I dislike working. I dislike oysters.* —*n.* **2.** a feeling of aversion; antipathy: *a strong dislike for Bach.* [1545–55; DIS-[1] + LIKE[2]] **—dis•lik′a•ble, dis•like′a•ble,** *adj.*
—Syn. 2. disrelish. DISLIKE, DISGUST, DISTASTE, REPUGNANCE imply antipathy toward something. DISLIKE is a general word, sometimes connoting an inherent or permanent feeling of antipathy for something: *to have a dislike for crowds.* DISGUST connotes a feeling of loathing for what is offensive to the feelings and sensibilities: *He felt disgust at seeing such ostentation.* DISTASTE implies a more or less settled dislike: *to have distaste for spicy foods, for hard work.* REPUGNANCE is a strong feeling of aversion for, and antagonism toward, something: *to feel repugnance for* (or *toward*) *low criminals.*

dis•limn (dis lim′), *v.t. Archaic.* to cause to become dim or indistinct. [1600–10; DIS-[1] + LIMN]

dis•lo•cate (dis′lō kāt′, dis lō′kāt), *v.*, **-cat•ed, -cat•ing** *n.* —*v.t.* **1.** to put out of place; put out of proper relative position; displace: *The glacier dislocated great stones. The earthquake dislocated several buildings.* **2.** to put out of joint or out of position, as a limb or an organ. **3.** to throw out of order; upset; disorder: *Frequent strikes dislocated the economy.* —*n.* **4.** *Gymnastics.* a maneuver on the rings in which a gymnast in an inverted pike position turns over to swing down while pushing the arms out and turning them so that the palms are facing out when the body turns over. [1595–1605; < ML *dislocātus* (ptp. of *dislocāre*), equiv. to L *dis-* DIS-[1] + *locātus* placed; see LOCATE]

dis•lo•ca•tion (dis′lō kā′shən), *n.* **1.** an act or instance of dislocating. **2.** the state of being dislocated. **3.** *Crystall.* (in a crystal lattice) a line about which there is a discontinuity in the lattice structure. Cf. **defect** (def. 3). [1350–1400; ME *dislocaciou*n; see DISLOCATE, -ION]

dis•lodge (dis loj′), *v.*, **-lodged, -lodg•ing.** —*v.t.* **1.** to remove or force out of a particular place: *to dislodge a stone with one's foot.* **2.** to drive out of a hiding place, a military position, etc. —*v.i.* **3.** to go from a place of lodgment. [1400–50; late ME *disloggen* < OF *desloger,* equiv. to *des-* DIS-[1] + *loger* to LODGE] **—dis•lodg′ment;** *esp. Brit.,* **dis•lodge′ment,** *n.*

dis•loy•al (dis loi′əl), *adj.* false to one's obligations or allegiances; not loyal; faithless; treacherous. [1470–80; < MF *desloial,* OF *desleal,* equiv. to *des-* DIS-[1] + *leal* LOYAL] **—dis•loy′al•ist,** *n.* **—dis•loy′al•ly,** *adv.*
—Syn. unfaithful, perfidious, traitorous, treasonable.

dis•loy•al•ty (dis loi′əl tē), *n., pl.* **-ties.** **1.** the quality of being disloyal; lack of loyalty; unfaithfulness. **2.** violation of allegiance or duty, as to a government. **3.** a disloyal act. [1400–50; late ME < MF *desloiaute,* OF *desleaute,* equiv. to *desleal* DISLOYAL + *-te* -TY[2]]
—Syn. 1. faithlessness, subversion. DISLOYALTY, PERFIDY, TREACHERY, TREASON imply betrayal of trust. DISLOYALTY applies to any violation of loyalty, whether to a person, a cause, or one's country, and whether in thought or in deeds: *to suspect disloyalty in a friend.* PERFIDY implies deliberate breaking of faith or of one's pledges and promises, on which others are relying: *It is an act of perfidy to cheat innocent people.* TREACHERY implies being secretly traitorous but seeming friendly and loyal: *In treachery deceit is added to disloyalty.* TREASON is performing overt acts to help the enemies of one's country or government: *Acting to aid a hostile power is treason.*

dis•mal (diz′məl), *adj.* **1.** causing gloom or dejection; gloomy; dreary; cheerless; melancholy: *dismal weather.* **2.** characterized by ineptness or lack of skill, competence, effectiveness, imagination, or interest; pitiful: *Our team played a dismal game.* **3.** *Obs.* **a.** disastrous; calamitous. **b.** unlucky; sinister. —*n.* **4.** *Southern U.S.* a tract of swampy land, usually along the coast. [1275–1325; ME *dismale* unlucky time, *dismol day* one of two days in each month considered unlucky (hence later taken as adj.) < AF *dis mal* < ML *diēs mali* lit., evil days] **—dis′mal•ly,** *adv.* **—dis′mal•ness, dis•mal′i•ty,** *n.*
—Syn. 2. hopeless, abysmal, dreadful. **—Ant. 1.** cheerful.

Dis′mal Swamp′, a swamp in SE Virginia and NE North Carolina. ab. 30 mi. (48 km) long; ab. 600 sq. mi. (1500 sq. km).

dis•man•tle (dis man′tl), *v.t.*, **-tled, -tling.** **1.** to de-

CONCISE ETYMOLOGY KEY: <, descended or borrowed from; >, whence; b., blend of, blended; c., cognate with; cf., compare; deriv., derivative; equiv., equivalent; imit., imitative; obl., oblique; r., replacing; s., stem; sp., spelling, spelled; resp., respelling, respelled; trans., translation; ?, origin unknown; *, unattested; ‡, probably earlier than. See the full key inside the front cover.

prive or strip of apparatus, furniture, equipment, defenses, etc.: *to dismantle a ship; to dismantle a fortress.* **2.** to disassemble or pull down; take apart: *They dismantled the machine and shipped it in pieces.* **3.** to divest of dress, covering, etc.: *The wind dismantled the trees of their leaves.* [1570–80; < MF *desmanteler.* See DIS-[1], MANTLE] **—dis•man′tle•ment,** *n.* **—dis•man′tler,** *n.*

dis•mast (dis mast′, -mäst′), *v.t.* to deprive (a ship) of masts; break off the masts of. [1740–50; DIS-[1] + MAST[1]] **—dis•mast′ment,** *n.*

dis•may (dis mā′), *v.t.* **1.** to break down the courage of completely, as by sudden danger or trouble; dishearten thoroughly; daunt: *The surprise attack dismayed the enemy.* **2.** to surprise in such a manner as to disillusion: *She was dismayed to learn of their disloyalty.* **3.** to alarm; perturb: *The new law dismayed some of the more conservative politicians.* **—***n.* **4.** sudden or complete loss of courage; utter disheartenment. **5.** sudden disillusionment. **6.** agitation of mind; perturbation; alarm. [1275–1325; ME *desmay* (n.), *de(s)mayen, dismayen* (v.) < presumed AF alter., by prefix change, of OF *esmaier* to trouble, frighten < VL **exmagāre* to disable, deprive of strength, equiv. to *ex-* EX- + **magāre* < Gmc **magan* to be able to; see MAY[1]] **—dis•mayed•ness** (dis mād′nis, -mā′id-), *n.* **—dis•may′ing•ly,** *adv.*
—Syn. 1. appall, terrify, frighten, scare, intimidate, disconcert. See **discourage. 4.** consternation, terror, panic, horror, fear. **—Ant. 1.** hearten. **4.** confidence.

disme (dīm), *n.* a former coin of the U.S., equal to 10 cents, issued in 1792: early form of the dime. [earlier or archaized sp. of DIME]

dis•mem•ber (dis mem′bər), *v.t.* **1.** to deprive of limbs; divide limb from limb: *The ogre dismembered his victims before he ate them.* **2.** to divide into parts; cut to pieces; mutilate. **3.** to reduce, reorganize, or discontinue the services or parts of (a company, government agency, etc.): *Our business was dismembered by the conglomerate that bought it.* [1250–1300; ME *dismembren* < AF, OF *desmembrer,* equiv. to *des-* DIS-[1] + *-membrer,* v. deriv. of *membre* MEMBER] **—dis•mem′ber•er,** *n.* **—dis•mem′ber•ment,** *n,*

dis•miss (dis mis′), *v.t.* **1.** to direct (an assembly of persons) to disperse or go: *I dismissed the class early.* **2.** to bid or allow (a person) to go; give permission or a request to depart. **3.** to discharge or remove, as from office or service: *to dismiss an employee.* **4.** to discard or reject: *to dismiss a suitor.* **5.** to put off or away, esp. from consideration; put aside; reject: *She dismissed the story as mere rumor.* **6.** to have done with (a subject) after summary treatment: *After a perfunctory discussion, he dismissed the idea.* **7.** *Law.* to put out of court, as a complaint or appeal. [1400–50; late ME < ML *dismissus* (for L *dimissus,* ptp. of *dimittere* to send away), equiv. to L *dis-* DIS-[1] + *mitt(ere)* to send + *-tus* ptp. suffix] **—dis•miss′i•ble,** *adj.*
—Syn. 2. See **release. 3.** fire. **—Ant. 2.** recall. **3.** hire. **4.** accept.

dis•miss•al (dis mis′əl), *n.* **1.** an act or instance of dismissing. **2.** the state of being dismissed. **3.** a spoken or written order of discharge from employment, service, enrollment, etc. Also, **dis•mis•sion** (dis mish′ən). [1800–10; DISMISS + -AL[2]]

dis•mis•sive (dis mis′iv), *adj.* **1.** indicating dismissal or rejection; having the purpose or effect of dismissing, as from one's presence or from consideration: *a curt, dismissive gesture.* **2.** indicating lack of interest or approbation; scornful; disdainful. [1635–45; DISMISS + -IVE] **—dis•mis′sive•ly,** *adv.*

dis•mount (*v.* dis mount′; *n.* dis mount′, dis′mount′), *v.i.* **1.** to get off or alight from a horse, bicycle, etc. **—***v.t.* **2.** to bring or throw down, as from a horse; unhorse; throw: *The horse twisted and bucked and finally dismounted its rider.* **3.** to remove (a thing) from its mounting, support, setting, etc.: *to dismount a picture.* **4.** to take (a mechanism) to pieces. **—***n.* **5.** an act or process of dismounting. **6.** *Gymnastics.* a move by which a gymnast gets off an apparatus or finishes a floor exercise, usually landing upright on the feet. [1525–35; prob. modeled on ML *dismontāre* or MF *desmonter.* See DIS-[1], MOUNT[1]] **—dis•mount′a•ble,** *adj.*

dis•na•ture (dis nā′chər), *v.t.,* **-tured, -tur•ing.** to deprive (something) of its proper nature or appearance; make unnatural. [1400–50; late ME < AF, MF *desnaturer,* equiv. to *des-* DIS-[1] + *-naturer,* v. deriv. of *nature* NATURE]

Dis•ney (diz′nē), *n.* **Walt(er E.),** 1901–66, U.S. creator and producer of animated cartoons, motion pictures, etc.

Dis•ney•land (diz′nē land′), **1.** *Trademark.* a large amusement park in Anaheim, Calif.: prototypical theme park. **—***n.* **2.** any large, bustling place noted for its colorful attractions: *The new shopping center has become an after-hours Disneyland.* **3.** a land or place of make-believe; fantasyland.

dis•o•be•di•ence (dis′ə bē′dē əns), *n.* lack of obedience or refusal to comply; disregard or transgression. [1350–1400; ME < OF *desobedience,* equiv. to *des-* DIS-[1] + *obedience* OBEDIENCE]

dis•o•be•di•ent (dis′ə bē′dē ənt), *adj.* neglecting or refusing to obey; not submitting; refractory. [1400–50; late ME < OF *desobedient,* equiv. to *des-* DIS-[1] + *obedient* OBEDIENT] **—dis′o•be′di•ent•ly,** *adv.*
—Syn. insubordinate, contumacious, defiant, rebellious, unsubmissive, uncompliant. **—Ant.** obedient.

dis•o•bey (dis′ə bā′), *v.t., v.i.* to neglect or refuse to obey. [1350–1400; ME *disobeien* < OF *desobeir,* equiv. to *des-* DIS-[1] + *obeir* to OBEY] **—dis′o•bey′er,** *n.*
—Syn. defy, disregard, resist, ignore, oppose.

dis•o•blige (dis′ə blīj′), *v.t.,* **-bliged, -blig•ing. 1.** to refuse or neglect to oblige; act contrary to the desire or convenience of; fail to accommodate. **2.** to give offense to; affront: *to be disobliged by a tactless remark.* **3.** to cause inconvenience to; incommode: *to be disobliged by an uninvited guest.* [1595–1605; < MF *desobliger,* equiv. to *des-* DIS-[1] + *obliger* to OBLIGE] **—dis′o•blig′ing•ly,** *adv.* **—dis′o•blig′ing•ness,** *n.*

di•so′di•um phos′phate (dī sō′dē əm), *Chem.* See **sodium phosphate** (def. 2). [DI-[1] + SODIUM]

di•so•pyr•a•mide (dī′sō pir′ə mīd′), *n. Pharm.* a substance, $C_{21}H_{29}N_3O$, used in its phosphate form in the symptomatic and prophylactic treatment of certain cardiac arrhythmias. [contr. of the chemical name]

dis•or•der (dis ôr′dər), *n.* **1.** lack of order or regular arrangement; confusion: *Your room is in utter disorder.* **2.** an irregularity: *a disorder in legal proceedings.* **3.** breach of order; disorderly conduct; public disturbance. **4.** a disturbance in physical or mental health or functions; malady or dysfunction: *a mild stomach disorder.* **—***v.t.* **5.** to destroy the order or regular arrangement of; disarrange. **6.** to derange the physical or mental health or functions of. [1470–80; DIS-[1] + ORDER]
—Syn. 1. disorderliness, disarray, jumble, litter, clutter. **3.** riot, turbulence. DISORDER, BRAWL, DISTURBANCE, UPROAR are disruptions or interruptions of a peaceful situation. DISORDER refers to civil unrest or to any scene in which there is confusion or fighting: *The police went to the scene of the disorder.* A BRAWL is a noisy, unseemly quarrel, usually in a public place: *a tavern brawl.* A DISTURBANCE is disorder of a size as to inconvenience people: *to cause a disturbance.* An UPROAR is a tumult, a bustle and clamor of many voices, often because of a disturbance: *a mighty uproar.* **4.** ailment, malady, illness, complaint, sickness, indisposition. **5.** disarray, mess up, disorganize. **6.** disturb, upset, confuse.

dis•or•dered (dis ôr′dərd), *adj.* **1.** lacking organization or in confusion; disarranged. **2.** suffering from or afflicted with a physical or mental disorder: *a disordered liver.* [1540–50; DISORDER + -ED[2]] **—dis•or′dered•ly,** *adv.* **—dis•or′dered•ness,** *n.*
—Syn. 1. confused, disarrayed, haphazard.

dis•or•der•ly (dis ôr′dər lē), *adj.* **1.** characterized by disorder; irregular; untidy; confused: *a disorderly desk.* **2.** unruly; turbulent; tumultuous: *a disorderly mob.* **3.** *Law.* contrary to public order or morality. **—***adv.* **4.** in a disorderly manner. [1555–65; DIS-[1] + ORDERLY] **—dis•or′der•li•ness,** *n.*

disor′derly con′duct, *Law.* any of various petty misdemeanors, generally including nuisances, breaches of the peace, offensive or immoral conduct in public, etc. [1885–90]

disor′derly house′, 1. a house of prostitution; brothel. **2.** a gambling place. [1800–10]

disor′derly per′son, *Law.* a person guilty of disorderly conduct. [1735–45]

dis•or•gan•i•za•tion (dis ôr′gə nə zā′shən), *n.* **1.** a breaking up of order or system; disunion or disruption of constituent parts. **2.** the absence of organization or orderly arrangement; disarrangement; disorder. [1785–95; < F *désorganisation,* equiv. to *désorganis(er)* to DISORGANIZE + *-ation* -ATION]

dis•or•gan•ize (dis ôr′gə nīz′), *v.t.,* **-ized, -iz•ing.** to destroy the organization, systematic arrangement, or orderly connection of; throw into confusion or disorder. Also, *esp. Brit.,* **dis•or′gan•ise′.** [1785–95; < F *désorganiser,* equiv. to *dés-* DIS-[1] + *organiser* to ORGANIZE] **—dis•or′gan•iz′er,** *n.*

dis•or•gan•ized (dis ôr′gə nīzd′), *adj.* **1.** functioning without adequate order, systemization, or planning; uncoordinated: *a woefully disorganized enterprise.* **2.** careless or undisciplined; sloppy: *too disorganized a person to be an agreeable roommate.* [1805–15; DISORGANIZE + -ED[2]]
—Syn. muddled, confused, disorderly, unsystematic.

dis•o•ri•ent (dis ôr′ē ent′, -ōr′-), *v.t.* **1.** to cause to lose one's way: *The strange streets disoriented him.* **2.** to confuse by removing or obscuring something that has guided a person, group, or culture, as customs, moral standards, etc.: *Society has been disoriented by changing values.* **3.** *Psychiatry.* to cause to lose perception of time, place, or one's personal identity. [1645–55; < F *désorienter,* equiv. to *dés-* DIS-[1] + *orienter* to ORIENT]

dis•o•ri•en•tate (dis ôr′ē ən tāt′, -ōr′-), *v.t.,* **-tat•ed, -tat•ing.** to disorient. [1695–1705; DIS-[1] + ORIENTATE] **—dis•o′ri•en•ta′tion,** *n.*

dis•o•ri•ent•ed (dis ôr′ē en′tid, -ōr′-), *adj.* confused as to time or place; out of touch: *therapy for disoriented patients.* [DISORIENT + -ED[2]]
—Syn. distracted, mixed up, unstable, unhinged.

dis•own (dis ōn′), *v.t.* to refuse to acknowledge as belonging or pertaining to oneself; deny the ownership of or responsibility for; repudiate; renounce: *to disown one's heirs; to disown a published statement.* [1610–20; DIS-[1] + OWN] **—dis•own′ment,** *n.*
—Syn. disclaim, disavow, reject, abjure.

dis•par•age (di spar′ij), *v.t.,* **-aged, -ag•ing. 1.** to speak of or treat slightingly; depreciate; belittle: *Do not disparage good manners.* **2.** to bring reproach or discredit upon; lower the estimation of: *Your behavior will disparage the whole family.* [1250–1300; ME < AF, OF *desparag(i)er* to match unequally, equiv. to *des-* DIS-[1] *-parag(i)er,* deriv. of *parage* equality, equiv. to *par(er)* to equalize (< L *parāre;* see PEER[1]) + *-age* -AGE] **—dis•par′ag•er,** *n.*
—Syn. 1. ridicule, discredit, mock, demean, denounce, derogate.

dis•par•age•ment (di spar′ij mənt), *n.* **1.** the act of disparaging. **2.** something that derogates or casts in a bad light, as a remark or censorious essay. [1480–90; < AF, MF *desparagement,* equiv. to *desparag(ier)* to DISPARAGE + *-ment* -MENT]

dis•par•ag•ing (di spar′i jing), *adj.* that disparages; tending to belittle or bring reproach upon: *disparaging remarks.* [1635–45; DISPARAGE + -ING[2]] **—dis•par′ag•ing•ly,** *adv.*

dis•pa•rate (dis′pər it, di spar′-), *adj.* distinct in kind; essentially different; dissimilar: *disparate ideas.* [1580–90; < L *disparātus* separated (ptp. of *disparāre*), equiv. to *dis-* DIS-[1] + *par(āre)* to prepare (see PARE) + *-ātus* -ATE[1]] **—dis′pa•rate•ly,** *adv.* **—dis′pa•rate•ness,** *n.*
—Syn. separate, divergent, incommensurable, unlike.

dis•par•i•ty (di spar′i tē), *n., pl.* **-ties.** lack of similarity or equality; inequality; difference: *a disparity in age; disparity in rank.* [1545–55; < MF *desparite* < LL *disparitās;* see DIS-[1], PARITY[1]]
—Syn. See **difference.**

dis•part (dis pärt′), *v.t., v.i.* to divide into parts; separate; sunder. [1580–90; appar. < It *dispartire* < L *dispartire* to part, separate, divide, equiv. to *dis-* DIS-[1] + *partire* to share out, deriv. of *part-* PART] **—dis•part′•ment,** *n.*

dis•pas•sion (dis pash′ən), *n.* the state or quality of being unemotional or emotionally uninvolved. [1685–95; DIS-[1] + PASSION]

dis•pas•sion•ate (dis pash′ə nit), *adj.* free from or unaffected by passion; devoid of personal feeling or bias; impartial; calm: *a dispassionate critic.* [1585–95; DIS-[1] + PASSIONATE] **—dis•pas′sion•ate•ly,** *adv.* **—dis•pas′•sion•ate•ness,** *n.*
—Syn. cool, unemotional, uninvolved; fair, just.

dis•patch (di spach′), *v.t.* **1.** to send off or away with speed, as a messenger, telegram, body of troops, etc. **2.** to dismiss (a person), as after an audience. **3.** to put to death; kill: *The spy was promptly dispatched.* **4.** to transact or dispose of (a matter) promptly or speedily. **—***v.i.* **5.** *Archaic.* to hasten; be quick. **—***n.* **6.** the sending off of a messenger, letter, etc., to a destination. **7.** the act of putting to death; killing; execution. **8.** prompt or speedy transaction, as of business. **9.** expeditious performance; promptness or speed: *Proceed with all possible dispatch.* **10.** *Com.* **a.** a method of effecting a speedy delivery of goods, money, etc. **b.** a conveyance or organization for the expeditious transmission of goods, money, etc. **11.** a written message sent with speed. **12.** an official communication sent by special messenger. **13.** *Journalism.* a news story transmitted to a newspaper, wire service, or the like, by one of its reporters, or by a wire service to a newspaper or other news agency. **14. mentioned in dispatches,** *Brit.* honored by being named in official military reports for special bravery or acts of service. Also, **despatch.** [1510–20; < It *dispacciare* to hasten, speed, or < Sp *despachar* both ult. < OF *despeechier* to unshackle, equiv. to *des-* DIS-[1] + *-peechier* < LL *-pedicāre* to shackle; see IMPEACH]
—Syn. 9. rapidity, haste, alacrity, celerity.

dispatch′ boat′, *Naut.* a small, fast boat used for delivering dispatches. [1785–95]

dispatch′ case′. See **attaché case.** [1915–20]

dis•patch•er (di spach′ər), *n.* **1.** a person who dispatches. **2.** a person who oversees the departure of trains, airplanes, buses, etc., as for a transportation company or railroad. **3. dispatchers,** *Slang.* a fraudulently made pair of dice; loaded dice. [1540–50; DISPATCH + -ER[1]]

Dis Pa•ter (dis pā′tər), *Class. Myth.* Dis.

dis•pau•per (dis pô′pər), *v.t. Law.* to divest of the status of a person having the privileges of a pauper, as of public support or of legal rights as a pauper. [1625–35; DIS-[1] + PAUPER]

dis•pel (di spel′), *v.t.,* **-pelled, -pel•ling. 1.** to drive off in various directions; disperse; dissipate: *to dispel the dense fog.* **2.** to cause to vanish; alleviate: *to dispel her fears.* [1625–35; < L *dispellere* to drive asunder, equiv. to *dis-* DIS-[1] + *pellere* to drive] **—dis•pel′la•ble,** *adj.* **—dis•pel′ler,** *n.*
—Syn. 1, 2. See **scatter. —Ant. 1.** gather.

dis•pend (di spend′), *v.t. Obs.* to pay out; expend; spend. [1250–1300; ME *dispenden* < AF, OF *despendre* < L *dispendere* to weigh out; see DISPENSE]

dis•pen•sa•ble (di spen′sə bəl), *adj.* **1.** capable of being dispensed with or done without; not necessary or essential. **2.** capable of being dispensed or administered: *The money is not dispensable at present.* **3.** *Rom. Cath. Ch.* capable of being permitted or forgiven, as an offense or sin. [1525–35; < ML *dispēnsābilis,* equiv. to L *dispēns(āre)* to distribute by weight (see DISPENSE) + *-ābilis* -ABLE] **—dis•pen′sa•bil′i•ty, dis•pen′sa•ble•ness,** *n.*
—Syn. 1. expendable, unnecessary; unessential, unimportant, extraneous.

dis•pen•sa•ry (di spen′sə rē), *n., pl.* **-ries. 1.** a place where something is dispensed, esp. medicines. **2.** a charitable or public facility where medicines are furnished and free or inexpensive medical advice is available. [1690–1700; < ML *dispēnsāria* storeroom, equiv. to L *dispēns(āre)* to DISPENSE + *-āria* -ARY]

dis•pen•sa•tion (dis′pən sā′shən, -pen-), *n.* **1.** an act or instance of dispensing; distribution. **2.** something that is distributed or given out. **3.** a certain order, system, or arrangement; administration or management. **4.** *Theol.* **a.** the divine ordering of the affairs of the world. **b.** an appointment, arrangement, or favor, as by God. **c.** a divinely appointed order or age: *the old Mosaic, or Jewish, dispensation; the new gospel, or Christian, dispensation.* **5.** a dispensing with, doing away with, or doing without something. **6.** *Rom. Cath. Ch.* **a.** a relaxation of law in a particular case granted by a competent superior or the superior's delegate in laws that the superior has the power to make and enforce: *a dispensation regarding the Lenten fast.* **b.** an official document authorizing such a relaxation of law. [1325–75; ME *dispensacioun* < ML *dispēnsātiōn-* (s. of *dispēnsātiō*) a pardon, relaxation, LL: order, system, divine grace, L: distribution, equiv. to *dispēnsāt(us)* (ptp. of *dispēnsāre* to DISPENSE; see -ATE[1]) + *-iōn-* -ION] **—dis′pen•sa′tion•al,** *adj.* **—dis•pen•sa•to•ri•ly** (di spen′sə tôr′ə lē, -tōr′-), *adv.*
—Syn. 1. dispersion, meting out, apportioning, dissemination, bestowal.

dis•pen•sa•tion•al•ism (dis′pən sā′shə nl iz′əm,

-pen-), *n.* the interpreting of history as a series of divine dispensations. [DISPENSATIONAL + -ISM]

dis·pen·sa·tor (dis′pən sā′tər, -pen-), *n. Obs.* a person who dispenses; distributor; administrator. [1350–1400; ME *dispensatour* < ML *dispēnsātor,* L: manager, steward, equiv. to *dispēnsā(re)* (see DISPENSE) + *-tor* -TOR]

dis·pen·sa·to·ry (di spen′sə tôr′ē, -tōr′ē), *n., pl.* **-ries.** **1.** a book in which the composition, preparation, and uses of medicinal substances are described; a nonofficial pharmacopoeia. **2.** a dispensary. [1560–70; < ML *dispēnsātōrium,* LL *dispēnsātōrius* of management, equiv. to L *dispēnsā(re)* (see DISPENSE) + *-tōrium* -TORY[2]]

dis·pense (di spens′), *v.,* **-pensed, -pens·ing,** *n.* —*v.t.* **1.** to deal out; distribute: *to dispense wisdom.* **2.** to administer: *to dispense the law without bias.* **3.** *Pharm.* to make up and distribute (medicine), esp. on prescription. **4.** *Rom. Cath. Ch.* to grant dispensation. —*v.i.* **5.** to grant dispensation. **6. dispense with, a.** to do without; forgo: *to dispense with preliminaries.* **b.** to do away with; rid of. **c.** to grant exemption from a law or promise. —*n.* **7.** *Obs.* expenditure. [1275–1325; ME *dispensen* < ML *dispēnsāre* to pardon, exempt, L: to pay out, distribute, equiv. to *dis-* DIS-[1] + *pēnsāre,* freq. of *pendere* to weigh]
—Syn. 1. apportion, allot, dole. See **distribute.**

dis·pens·er (di spen′sər), *n.* **1.** a person or thing that dispenses. **2.** a container, package, device, or vending machine for holding and dispensing something in small amounts, as facial tissue, paper cups, or candy. [1250–1300; ME; see DISPENSE, -ER[1]]

dis·pen·si·ble (di spen′sə bəl), *adj. Obs.* dispensable.

dis·peo·ple (dis pē′pəl), *v.t.,* **-pled, -pling.** to deprive of people; depopulate. [1480–90; DIS-[1] + PEOPLE] **—dis·peo′ple·ment,** *n.* **—dis·peo′pler,** *n.*

di·sper·mous (dī spûr′məs), *adj. Bot.* having two seeds. [1720–30; DI-[1] + SPERMOUS]

di·sper·my (dī′spûr′mē), *n.* the fertilization of an ovum by two spermatozoa. Cf. **monospermy, polyspermy.** [1895–1900; DI-[1] + *-spermy* < Gk *-spermía.* See -SPERM, -Y[3]] **—di·sper′mic,** *adj.*

dis·per·sal (di spûr′səl), *n.* dispersion (def. 1). [1815–25; DISPERSE + -AL[2]]

dis·per·sant (di spûr′sənt), *n.* **1.** something that disperses. **2.** *Physical Chem.* any admixture to a dispersion capable of maintaining the dispersed particles in suspension. —*adj.* **3.** acting as a dispersant. [1940–45; DISPERSE + -ANT]

dis·perse (di spûrs′), *v.,* **-persed, -pers·ing,** *adj.* —*v.t.* **1.** to drive or send off in various directions; scatter: *to disperse a crowd.* **2.** to spread widely; disseminate: *to disperse knowledge.* **3.** to dispel; cause to vanish: *The wind dispersed the fog.* **4.** *Physical Chem.* to cause (particles) to separate uniformly throughout a solid, liquid, or gas. **5.** *Optics.* to subject (light) to dispersion. —*v.i.* **6.** to separate and move apart in different directions without order or regularity; become scattered: *The crowd dispersed.* **7.** to be dispelled; be scattered out of sight; vanish: *The smoke dispersed into the sky.* —*adj.* **8.** *Physical Chem.* noting the dispersed particles in a dispersion. [1350–1400; ME *dispersen, disparsen* (< MF *disperser*) < L *dispersus* (ptp. of *dispergere*), equiv. to *di-* DI-[2] + *-sper(g)-* scatter (s. of *-spergere,* comb. form of *spargere* to scatter, strew) + *-sus* ptp. suffix] **—dis·pers′ed·ly** (di spûr′sid lē), *adv.* **—dis·pers′er,** *n.* **—dis·pers′i·bil′i·ty,** *n.* **—dis·pers′i·ble,** *adj.*
—Syn. 1. See **scatter. 2.** sow, broadcast. **7.** disappear, evanesce. **—Ant. 1.** combine, collect.

disperse′ dye′, *Chem.* any of the class of slightly water-soluble dyes dispersed in aqueous solution for dyeing synthetic textile fibers.

dis·per·sion (di spûr′zhən, -shən), *n.* **1.** Also, **dispersal.** an act, state, or instance of dispersing or of being dispersed. **2.** *Optics.* **a.** the variation of the index of refraction of a transparent substance, as glass, with the wavelength of light, with the index of refraction increasing as the wavelength decreases. **b.** the separation of white or compound light into its respective colors, as in the formation of a spectrum by a prism. **3.** *Statistics.* the scattering of values of a variable around the mean or median of a distribution. **4.** *Mil.* a scattered pattern of hits of bombs dropped under identical conditions or of shots fired from the same gun with the same firing data. **5.** Also called **disperse′ sys′tem.** *Physical Chem.* a system of dispersed particles suspended in a solid, liquid, or gas. **6.** (*cap.*) Diaspora (def. 1). [1350–1400; ME *dispersio(u)n* (< AF) < L *dispersiōn-* (s. of *dispersiō*), equiv. to *dispers(us)* (see DISPERSE) + *-iōn-* -ION]

dis·per·sive (di spûr′siv), *adj.* serving or tending to disperse. [1620–30; DISPERSE + -IVE] **—dis·per′sive·ly,** *adv.* **—dis·per′sive·ness,** *n.*

disper′sive pow′er, *Optics.* a measure of the ability of a substance to disperse light, equal to the quotient of the difference in refractive indices of the substance for two representative wavelengths divided by the difference of the refractive index for an intermediate wavelength and 1. Cf. **Abbe number.**

dis·per·soid (di spûr′soid), *n. Physical Chem.* the suspended particles in a dispersion. [1910–15; DISPERSE + -OID]

di·sphe·noid (dī sfē′noid), *n. Crystall.* bisphenoid. [1890–95]

dis·pir·it (di spir′it), *v.t.* to deprive of spirit, hope, enthusiasm, etc.; depress; discourage; dishearten. [1635–45; DI-[2] + SPIRIT]

dis·pir·it·ed (di spir′i tid), *adj.* discouraged; dejected; disheartened; gloomy. [1640–50; DISPIRIT + -ED[2]] **—dis·pir′it·ed·ly,** *adv.* **—dis·pir′it·ed·ness,** *n.*

dis·pit·e·ous (dis pit′ē əs), *adj. Archaic.* malicious; cruel; pitiless. [1795–1805; earlier *despiteous,* alter., after PITEOUS, of *dispitous, despitous,* ME < AF, OF; see DESPITE, -OUS; later taken as DIS-[1] + PITEOUS] **—dis·pit′e·ous·ly,** *adv.* **—dis·pit′e·ous·ness,** *n.*

dis·place (dis plās′), *v.t.,* **-placed, -plac·ing.** **1.** to compel (a person or persons) to leave home, country, etc. **2.** to move or put out of the usual or proper place. **3.** to take the place of; replace; supplant: *Fiction displaces fact.* **4.** to remove from a position, office, or dignity. **5.** *Obs.* to rid oneself of. [1545–55; DIS-[1] + PLACE, perh. modeled on MF *desplacer*] **—dis·place′a·ble,** *adj.*
—Syn. 2. relocate. DISPLACE, MISPLACE mean to put something in a different place from where it should be. To DISPLACE often means to shift something solid and comparatively immovable, more or less permanently from its place: *The flood displaced houses from their foundations.* To MISPLACE is to put an object in a wrong place so that it is difficult to find: *Papers belonging in the safe were misplaced and temporarily lost.* **4.** depose, oust, dismiss.

dis·placed (dis plāst′), *adj.* **1.** lacking a home, country, etc. **2.** moved or put out of the usual or proper place. —*n.* **3.** (*used with a plural v.*) persons who lack a home, as through political exile, destruction of their previous shelter, or lack of financial resources (usually prec. by *the*): *After the earthquake, the displaced were temporarily housed in armories.* [1565–75; DISPLACE + -ED[2]]

displaced′ home′maker, a woman recently divorced, separated, or widowed after many years as a homemaker. [1975–80]

displaced′ per′son, a person driven or expelled from his or her homeland by war, famine, tyranny, etc. *Abbr.:* DP, D.P. [1940–45]

dis·place·ment (dis plās′mənt), *n.* **1.** the act of displacing. **2.** the state of being displaced or the amount or degree to which something is displaced. **3.** *Physics.* **a.** the displacing in space of one mass by another. **b.** the weight or the volume of fluid displaced by a floating or submerged body. Cf. **Archimedes' principle. c.** the linear or angular distance in a given direction between a body or point and a reference position. **d.** the distance of an oscillating body from its central position or point of equilibrium at any given moment. **4.** *Mach., Auto.* **a.** the volume of the space through which a piston travels during a single stroke in an engine, pump, or the like. **b.** the total volume of the space traversed by all the pistons. **5.** *Naut.* the amount of water that a vessel displaces, expressed in displacement tons. **6.** *Geol.* the offset of rocks caused by movement along a fault. **7.** *Psychoanal.* the transfer of an emotion from its original focus to another object, person, or situation. **8.** See **electric displacement.** [1605–15; DISPLACE + -MENT]

displace′ment activ′ity, *Animal Behav.* a behavior performed out of its usual context and apparently irrelevant to the prevailing situation, as eating when an unknown individual approaches, tending to occur when appropiate behaviors, as attacking or fleeing, are in conflict or obstructed. [1945–50]

displace′ment cur′rent, *Elect.* the rate of change, at any point in space, of electric displacement with time. [1890–95]

displace′ment en′gine. See **reciprocating engine.**

displace′ment hull′, *Naut.* a hull that displaces a significant volume of water when under way. Cf. **planing hull.**

displace′ment ton′, *Naut.* a unit for measuring the displacement of a vessel, equal to a long ton of 2240 lb. (1016 kg) or 35 cu. ft. (1 cu. m) of seawater.

displace′ment ton′nage, *Naut.* the number of long tons of water displaced by a vessel, light or load displacement being specified.

dis·plac·er (dis plā′sər), *n.* **1.** a person or thing that displaces. **2.** plum (def. 10). [1580–90; DISPLACE + -ER[1]]

dis·plant (dis plant′, -plänt′), *v.t. Obs.* **1.** to dislodge. **2.** to transplant. [1485–95; DIS-[1] + PLANT, modeled on MF *desplanter*]

dis·play (di splā′), *v.t.* **1.** to show or exhibit; make visible: *to display a sign.* **2.** to reveal; betray: *to display fear.* **3.** to unfold; open out; spread out: *to display a sail.* **4.** to show ostentatiously; flaunt. **5.** *Print.* to give special prominence to (words, captions, etc.) by choice, size, and arrangement of type. **6.** *Computers.* to output (data) on a CRT or other screen. —*v.i.* **7.** (of animals) to engage in a stereotyped behavior that conveys information to individuals of the same or another species. —*n.* **8.** an act or instance of displaying; exhibition: *a display of courage.* **9.** an ostentatious show: *a vulgar display of wealth.* **10.** *Print.* **a.** the giving of prominence to particular words, sentences, etc., by the choice, size, and arrangement of types and position, as in an advertisement, headline, or news story. **b.** printed matter thus displayed. **11.** an arrangement, as of merchandise, art objects, or flowers, designed to please the eye, attract buyers, etc. **12.** the visual representation of the output of an electronic device, as the screen of a cathode ray tube. **13.** *Animal Behav.* **a.** a pattern of behavior, as posturing, calling, or exposing a color patch, that conveys information to individuals of the same or another species: *a threat display.* **b.** an instance of such behavior. [1250–1300; ME *desplayen* < AF, OF *despleier* < LL *displicāre* to unfold. See DIS-[1], PLICATE] **—dis·play′er,** *n.*
—Syn. 1, 2. DISPLAY, EVINCE, EXHIBIT, MANIFEST mean to show or bring to the attention of another or others. To DISPLAY is literally to spread something out so that it may be most completely and favorably seen: *to display goods for sale.* To EXHIBIT is to display something in a show: *to exhibit the best flowers.* They may both be used for showing (off) one's qualities or feelings: *He displayed his wit. He exhibited great surprise.* To EVINCE and to MANIFEST also mean to show feelings or qualities: *to evince or manifest surprise, interest.* **4.** flourish, parade, air. **8.** See **show. —Ant. 1, 2.** conceal.

display′ ad′, an advertisement, in a newspaper or other publication, often using special attention-getting devices, as large size, display type, and illustrations. [1915–20]

display′ ad′vertising, display ads taken collectively.

dis·played (di splād′), *adj. Heraldry.* (of a bird) represented with wings and legs spread: *an eagle displayed.* [1350–1400; ME; see DISPLAY, -ED[2]]

display′ type′, *Print.* type larger than body type, used in headings, advertisements, etc. Cf. **body type.** [1860–65]

dis·please (dis plēz′), *v.,* **-pleased, -pleas·ing.** —*v.t.* **1.** to incur the dissatisfaction, dislike, or disapproval of; offend; annoy: *His reply displeased the judge.* —*v.i.* **2.** to be unpleasant; cause displeasure: *Bad weather displeases.* [1300–50; ME *desplesen* < AF, MF *desplaisir.* See DIS-[1], PLEASE] **—dis·pleas′ing·ly,** *adv.* **—dis·pleas′ing·ness,** *n.*

dis·pleas·ure (dis plezh′ər), *n., v.,* **-ured, -ur·ing.** —*n.* **1.** dissatisfaction, disapproval, or annoyance. **2.** discomfort, uneasiness, or pain. **3.** *Archaic.* a cause of offense, annoyance, or injury. —*v.t.* **4.** *Archaic.* to displease. [1400–50; DIS-[1] + PLEASURE; r. late ME *desplaisir* < MF (n. use of inf.); see DISPLEASE] **—dis·pleas′ure·a·ble,** *adj.* **—dis·pleas′ure·a·bly,** *adv.*
—Syn. 1. distaste, dislike; indignation, vexation. See **dissatisfaction. —Ant. 1.** pleasure.

dis·plode (dis plōd′), *v.t., v.i.,* **-plod·ed, -plod·ing.** *Archaic.* to explode. [1660–70; < L *displōdere,* equiv. to *dis-* DIS-[1] + *-plōdere,* comb. form of *plaudere* to clap] **—dis·plo·sion** (dis plō′zhən), *n.*

dis·plume (dis plo͞om′), *v.t.,* **-plumed, -plum·ing.** **1.** to strip of plumes; deplume. **2.** to strip of honors. [1470–80; DIS-[1] + PLUME; cf. DEPLUME]

dis·plu·vi·ate (dis plo͞o′vē āt′), *adj.* (of the atrium of an ancient Roman house) having roofs sloping downward and outward from a central opening. [< L *displuviātus,* equiv. to *dis-* DIS-[1] + *pluvi(a)* rain + *-ātus* -ATE[1]]

dis·port (di spôrt′, -spōrt′), *v.t.* **1.** to divert or amuse (oneself). **2.** to display (oneself) in a sportive manner: *The picnickers disported themselves merrily on the beach.* —*v.i.* **3.** to divert oneself; sport. —*n.* **4.** diversion; amusement; play; sport. [1275–1325; (v.) ME *disporten, desporten* < AF *desporter,* equiv. to *des-* DIS-[1] + *porter* lit., to carry (see PORT[5]); (n.) ME < AF, deriv. of the v.] **—dis·port′ment,** *n.*

dis·pos·a·ble (di spō′zə bəl), *adj.* **1.** designed for or capable of being thrown away after being used or used up: *disposable plastic spoons; a disposable cigarette lighter.* **2.** free for use; available: *Every disposable vehicle was sent.* —*n.* **3.** something disposable after a single use, as a paper cup, plate, or napkin. [1645–55; DISPOSE + -ABLE] **—dis·pos′a·bil′i·ty, dis·pos′a·ble·ness,** *n.* **—dis·pos′a·bly,** *adv.*

dispos′able in′come, **1.** the part of a person's income remaining after deducting personal income taxes. **2.** (in national income accounting) the total disposable income of all consumers. [1945–50]

dis·pos·al[1] (di spō′zəl), *n.* **1.** an act or instance of disposing; arrangement: *the disposal of the troops.* **2.** a disposing of or getting rid of something: *the disposal of waste material.* **3.** a disposing or allotting of, as by gift or sale; bestowal or assignment: *She left no will to indicate the disposal of her possessions.* **4.** power or right to dispose of a thing; control: *left at his disposal.* [1620–30; DISPOSE + -AL[2]]
—Syn. 4. command, direction, management.

dis·pos·al[2] (di spō′zəl), *n.* an electrical device in the drain of a sink, for grinding up garbage to be washed down the drain. Also called **disposer.** [short for *garbage-disposal;* see DISPOSAL[1]]

dis·pose (di spōz′), *v.,* **-posed, -pos·ing,** *n.* —*v.t.* **1.** to give a tendency or inclination to; incline: *His temperament disposed him to argue readily with people.* **2.** to put in a particular or the proper order or arrangement; adjust by arranging the parts. **3.** to put in a particular or suitable place: *The lamp was disposed on a table nearby.* **4.** to make fit or ready; prepare: *Your words of cheer dispose me for the task.* —*v.i.* **5.** to arrange or decide matters: *to do as God disposes.* **6.** *Obs.* to make terms. **7. dispose of, a.** to deal with conclusively; settle. **b.** to get rid of; discard. **c.** to transfer or give away, as by gift or sale. **d.** to do away with; destroy. —*n.* **8.** *Archaic.* disposition; habit. **9.** *Obs.* arrangement; regulation; disposal. [1300–50; ME < MF *disposer,* equiv. to *dis-* DIS-[1] + *poser* to place (see POSE[1]), on the model of L *dispōnere*] **—dis·pos′ing·ly,** *adv.*

dis·posed (di spōzd′), *adj.* having a certain inclination or disposition; inclined (usually fol. by *to* or an infinitive): *a man disposed to like others.* [1300–50; ME. See DISPOSE, -ED[2]] **—dis·pos′ed·ly,** *adv.* **—dis·pos′ed·ness,** *n.*

dis·pos·er (di spō′zər), *n.* **1.** a person or thing that disposes. **2.** disposal[2]. [1520–30; DISPOSE + -ER[1]]

dis·po·si·tion (dis′pə zish′ən), *n.* **1.** the predominant or prevailing tendency of one's spirits; natural mental and emotional outlook or mood; characteristic attitude: *a girl with a pleasant disposition.* **2.** state of mind regarding something; inclination: *a disposition to gamble.* **3.** physical inclination or tendency: *the disposition of ice to melt when heated.* **4.** arrangement or placing, as of troops or buildings. **5.** final settlement of a matter. **6.** bestowal, as by gift or sale. **7.** power to dispose of a thing; control: *funds at one's disposition.* **8.** regulation; management; dispensation: *the disposition of God.* [1325–75; ME *disposicioun* (< AF) < L *dispositiōn-* (s. of *dispositiō*), equiv. to *disposit(us)* (ptp. of *dispōnere* to distribute; *dispos-* (see DISPOSE) + *-itus* ptp. suffix) + *-iōn-* -ION] **—dis′po·si′tion·al,** *adj.*
—Syn. 1. nature, character, humor. DISPOSITION, TEMPER, TEMPERAMENT refer to the aspects and habits of mind and emotion that one displays over a length of time. DISPOSITION is the natural or prevailing aspect of

one's mind as shown in behavior and in relationships with others: *a happy disposition; a selfish disposition.* TEMPER sometimes denotes the essential quality of one's nature: *a glacial temper;* usually it has to do with propensity toward anger: *an even temper; a quick* or *hot temper.* TEMPERAMENT refers to the particular balance of emotions determining a person's character: *an artistic temperament.* **2.** bent, tendency, predisposition, proclivity. **4.** order, grouping, location, placement. **5.** outcome, result. **7.** control, direction. **—Ant. 2.** unwillingness.

dis·pos·i·tive (di spoz′i tiv), *adj.* involving or affecting disposition or settlement: *a dispositive clue in a case of embezzlement.* [1475–85; DISPOSE + -ITIVE, on the model of POSITIVE]

dis·pos·sess (dis′pə zes′), *v.t.* **1.** to put (a person) out of possession, esp. of real property; oust. **2.** to banish. **3.** to abandon ownership of (a building), esp. as a bad investment: *Landlords have dispossessed many old tenement buildings.* [1425–75; DIS-[1] + POSSESS; r. ME *dis-posseden,* equiv. to DIS-[1] + *posseden* (< OF *posseder*) < L *possidēre;* see POSSESS] **—dis′pos·ses′sion,** *n.* **—dis′·pos·ses′sor,** *n.* **—dis·pos·ses·so·ry** (dis′pə zes′ə rē), *adj.*
—Syn. 1. See **strip**[1].

dis·pos·sessed (dis′pə zest′), *adj.* **1.** evicted, as from a dwelling, land, etc.; ousted. **2.** without property, status, etc., as wandering or displaced persons; rootless; disfranchised. **3.** having suffered the loss of expectations, prospects, relationships, etc.; disinherited; disaffiliated; alienated: *The modern city dweller may feel spiritually dispossessed.* [1590–1600; DISPOSSESS + -ED[2]]

dis·po·sure (di spō′zhər), *n. Archaic.* disposal; disposition. [1560–70; DISPOSE + -URE]

dis·praise (dis prāz′), *v.,* **-praised, -prais·ing,** *n.* —*v.t.* **1.** to speak of as undeserving or unworthy; censure; disparage. —*n.* **2.** an act or instance of dispraising; censure. [1300–50; ME < AF, OF *despreis(i)er,* equiv. to *des-* DIS-[1] + *preis(i)er* to PRAISE] **—dis·prais′·er,** *n.* **—dis·prais′ing·ly,** *adv.*

dis·pread (di spred′), *v.t., v.i.,* **-pread, -pread·ing.** to spread out; extend. Also, **disspread.** [1580–90; DI-[2] + SPREAD] **—dis·pread′er,** *n.*

dis·prize (dis prīz′), *v.t.,* **-prized, -priz·ing.** to hold in small esteem; disdain. [1425–75; late ME *disprisen* < AF, MF *despriser,* late var. of *despreis(i)er* to DISPRAISE]

dis·proof (dis pro͞of′), *n.* **1.** the act of disproving. **2.** proof to the contrary; refutation. [1525–35; DIS-[1] + PROOF]

dis·pro·por·tion (dis′prə pôr′shən, -pōr′-), *n.* **1.** lack of proportion; lack of proper relationship in size, number, etc.: *architectural disproportions.* **2.** something out of proportion: *the disproportions of an awkward body.* —*v.t.* **3.** to make disproportionate. [1545–55; DIS-[1] + PROPORTION; cf. MF *disproportion*] **—dis′pro·por′tion·a·ble,** *adj.* **—dis′pro·por′tion·a·ble·ness,** *n.* **—dis′·pro·por′tion·a·bly,** *adv.*

dis·pro·por·tion·al (dis′prə pôr′shə nl, -pōr′-), *adj.* not in proportion; disproportionate. [1600–10; DIS-[1] + PROPORTIONAL] **—dis′pro·por′tion·al′i·ty, dis′pro·por′tion·al·ness,** *n.* **—dis′pro·por′tion·al·ly,** *adv.*

dis·pro·por·tion·ate (dis′prə pôr′shə nit, -pōr′-), *adj.* not proportionate; out of proportion, as in size or number. [1544–55; DIS-[1] + PROPORTIONATE] **—dis′pro·por′tion·ate·ly,** *adv.* **—dis′pro·por′tion·ate·ness,** *n.*

dis·pro·por·tion·a·tion (dis′prə pôr′shə nā′shən, -pōr′-), *n. Chem.* the simultaneous oxidation and reduction of a substance reacting with itself, thereby forming two dissimilar molecules, as $2C_2H_4 \rightarrow C_2H_6 + C_2H_2$. [1925–30; DISPROPORTION + -ATION]

dis·prove (dis pro͞ov′), *v.t.,* **-proved, -prov·ing.** to prove (an assertion, claim, etc.) to be false or wrong; refute; invalidate: *I disproved his claim.* [1350–1400; ME < AF, OF *desprover,* equiv. to *des-* -DIS-[1] + *prover* to PROVE] **—dis·prov′a·ble,** *adj.* **—dis·prov′er,** *n.*
—Syn. discredit, contradict, negate, confute.

dis·put·a·ble (di spyo͞o′tə bəl, dis′pyo͞o-), *adj.* capable of being disputed; debatable; questionable. [1540–50; < L *disputābilis,* equiv. to *disput-* (see DISPUTE) + *-ābilis* -ABLE] **—dis·put′a·bil′i·ty, dis·put′a·ble·ness,** *n.* **—dis·put′a·bly,** *adv.*
—Syn. controvertible, doubtful, dubious, uncertain.

dis·pu·tant (di spyo͞ot′nt), *n.* **1.** a person who disputes; debater. —*adj.* **2.** engaged in dispute; disputing. [1605–15; < L *disputant-* (s. of *disputāns,* prp. of *disputāre*), equiv. to *disput-* (see DISPUTE) + *-ant-* -ANT]

dis·pu·ta·tion (dis′pyo͞o tā′shən), *n.* **1.** the act of disputing or debating; verbal controversy; discussion or debate. **2.** an academic exercise consisting of the arguing of a thesis between its maintainer and its opponents. **3.** *Obs.* conversation. [1350–1400; ME *disputacioun* < L *disputātiōn-* (s. of *disputātiō*), equiv. to *disputāt(us)* (ptp. of *disputāre; disput-* (see DISPUTE) + *-ātus* -ATE[1]) + *-iōn-* -ION; r. *desputisoun* < OF]

dis·pu·ta·tious (dis′pyo͞o tā′shəs), *adj.* fond of or given to disputation; argumentative; contentious: *disputatious litigants.* Also, **dis·put·a·tive** (di spyo͞o′tə tiv). [1650–60; DISPUTATI(ON) + -OUS] **—dis′pu·ta′tious·ly,** *adv.* **—dis′pu·ta′tious·ness,** *n.*

dis·pute (di spyo͞ot′), *v.,* **-put·ed, -put·ing,** *n.* —*v.i.* **1.** to engage in argument or debate. **2.** to argue vehemently; wrangle or quarrel. —*v.t.* **3.** to argue or debate about; discuss. **4.** to argue against; call in question: *to dispute a proposal.* **5.** to quarrel or fight about; contest. **6.** to strive against; oppose: *to dispute an advance of troops.* —*n.* **7.** a debate, controversy, or difference of opinion. **8.** a wrangling argument; quarrel. [1275–1325; ME (< AF, OF *desputer*) < L *disputāre* to argue a point, equiv. to *dis-* DIS-[1] + *putāre* to reckon, consider; see PUTATIVE] **—dis·pute′less,** *adj.* **—dis·put′er,** *n.*
—Syn. 2. bicker, squabble. **8.** disputation, altercation, wrangle, bickering, squabble. See **argument.**

dis·qual·i·fi·ca·tion (dis kwol′ə fi kā′shən), *n.* **1.** an act or instance of disqualifying. **2.** the state of being disqualified. **3.** something that disqualifies. [1705–15; DISQUALI(FY) + -FICATION]

dis·qual·i·fy (dis kwol′ə fī′), *v.t.,* **-fied, -fy·ing. 1.** to deprive of qualification or fitness; render unfit; incapacitate. **2.** to deprive of legal, official, or other rights or privileges; declare ineligible or unqualified. **3.** *Sports.* to deprive of the right to participate in or win a contest because of a violation of the rules. [1710–20; DIS-[1] + QUALIFY] **—dis·qual′i·fi′a·ble,** *adj.*

dis·quan·ti·ty (dis kwon′ti tē), *v.t.,* **-tied, -ty·ing.** *Obs.* to diminish in quantity; make less. [1595–1605; DIS- + QUANTITY]

dis·qui·et (dis kwī′it), *n.* **1.** lack of calm, peace, or ease; anxiety; uneasiness. —*v.t.* **2.** to deprive of calmness, equanimity, or peace; disturb; make uneasy: *The news disquieted him.* —*adj.* **3.** *Archaic.* uneasy; disquieted. [1520–30; DIS-[1] + QUIET] **—dis·qui′et·ed·ly,** *adv.* **—dis·qui′et·ed·ness,** *n.* **—dis·qui′et·ly,** *adv.*

dis·qui·et·ing (dis kwī′i ting), *adj.* causing anxiety or uneasiness; disturbing: *disquieting news.* [1570–80; DISQUIET + -ING[2]] **—dis·qui′et·ing·ly,** *adv.*

dis·qui·e·tude (dis kwī′i to͞od′, -tyo͞od′), *n.* the state of disquiet; uneasiness. [1700–10; DIS-[1] + QUIETUDE]

dis·qui·si·tion (dis′kwə zish′ən), *n.* a formal discourse or treatise in which a subject is examined and discussed; dissertation. [1595–1605; < L *disquīsītiōn-* (s. of *disquīsītiō*), equiv. to *disquīsīt(us)* (ptp. of *disquīrere* to investigate; *dis-* DIS-[1] + *quaerere* to seek, ask) + *-iōn-* -ION] **—dis′qui·si′tion·al,** *adj.*

Dis·rae·li (diz rā′lē), *n.* **Benjamin, 1st Earl of Beaconsfield** (*"Dizzy"*), 1804–81, British statesman and novelist: prime minister 1868, 1874–80.

dis·rate (dis rāt′), *v.t.,* **-rat·ed, -rat·ing.** to reduce to a lower rating or rank. [1805–15; DIS-[1] + RATE[1]]

dis·re·gard (dis′ri gärd′), *v.t.* **1.** to pay no attention to; leave out of consideration; ignore: *Disregard the footnotes.* **2.** to treat without due regard, respect, or attentiveness; slight: *to disregard an invitation.* —*n.* **3.** lack of regard or attention; neglect. **4.** lack of due or respectful regard. [1635–45; DIS-[1] + REGARD] **—dis′re·gard′a·ble,** *adj.* **—dis′re·gard′er,** *n.*
—Syn. 1. ignore. **2.** insult. See **slight. 3.** inattention, oversight. **4.** disrespect, slight. **—Ant. 1.** notice.

dis·re·gard·ful (dis′ri gärd′fəl), *adj.* neglectful; careless. [1630–40; DIS-[1] + REGARDFUL] **—dis′re·gard′ful·ly,** *adv.* **—dis′re·gard′ful·ness,** *n.*

dis·re·lat·ed (dis′ri lā′tid), *adj.* lacking relation or connection; unrelated. [1890–95; DIS-[1] + RELATED] **—dis′re·la′tion,** *n.*

dis·rel·ish (dis rel′ish), *v.t.* **1.** to have a distaste for; dislike. —*n.* **2.** distaste; dislike. [1540–50; DIS-[1] + RELISH]

dis·re·mem·ber (dis′ri mem′bər), *v.t. Southern and South Midland U.S.* to fail to remember; forget. [1805–15; DIS-[1] + REMEMBER]

dis·re·pair (dis′ri pâr′), *n.* the condition of needing repair; an impaired or neglected state. [1790–1800; DIS-[1] + REPAIR]

dis·rep·u·ta·ble (dis rep′yə tə bəl), *adj.* **1.** not reputable; having a bad reputation: *a disreputable barroom.* **2.** discreditable; dishonorable. **3.** shabby or shoddy; of poor quality or condition: *disreputable clothes.* [1765–75; DIS-[1] + REPUTABLE] **—dis·rep′u·ta·bil′i·ty, dis·rep′u·ta·ble·ness,** *n.* **—dis·rep′u·ta·bly,** *adv.*
—Syn. 2. disgraceful, ignoble, unprincipled, objectionable, low, shameful, debased.

dis·rep·u·ta·tion (dis rep′yə tā′shən), *n. Archaic.* disrepute. [1595–1605; DIS-[1] + REPUTATION]

dis·re·pute (dis′ri pyo͞ot′), *n.* bad repute; low regard; disfavor (usually prec. by *in* or *into*): *Some literary theories have fallen into disrepute.* [1645–55; DIS-[1] + REPUTE]
—Syn. disfavor, disgrace.

dis·re·spect (dis′ri spekt′), *n.* **1.** lack of respect; discourtesy; rudeness. —*v.t.* **2.** to regard or treat without respect; regard or treat with contempt or rudeness. [1605–15; DIS-[1] + RESPECT]
—Syn. 1. contempt, disregard, irreverence.

dis·re·spect·a·ble (dis′ri spek′tə bəl), *adj.* not respectable. [1805–15; DIS-[1] + RESPECTABLE] **—dis′re·spect′a·bil′i·ty,** *n.*

dis·re·spect·ful (dis′ri spekt′fəl), *adj.* characterized by, having, or showing disrespect; lacking courtesy or esteem: *a disrespectful remark about teachers.* [1670–80; DIS-[1] + RESPECTFUL] **—dis′re·spect′ful·ly,** *adv.* **—dis′re·spect′ful·ness,** *n.*
—Syn. impolite, rude, impertinent, irreverent.

dis·robe (dis rōb′), *v.t., v.i.,* **-robed, -rob·ing.** to undress. [1575–85; DIS-[1] + ROBE; cf. MF *desrober*] **—dis·robe′ment,** *n.* **—dis·rob′er,** *n.*

dis·root (dis ro͞ot′, -ro͝ot′), *v.t.* to uproot; dislodge. [1605–15; DIS-[1] + ROOT[1]]

dis·rupt (dis rupt′), *v.t.* **1.** to cause disorder or turmoil in: *The news disrupted their conference.* **2.** to destroy, usually temporarily, the normal continuance or unity of; interrupt: *Telephone service was disrupted for hours.* **3.** to break apart: *to disrupt a connection.* —*adj.* **4.** broken apart; disrupted. [1650–60; < L *disruptus* (var. of *dīruptus,* ptp. of *dirumpere; di-* DI-[2] + *rumpere* to break), equiv. to *dis-* DIS-[1] + *rup-* break + *-tus* ptp. suffix] **—dis·rupt′er, dis·rup′tor,** *n.*

dis·rup·tion (dis rup′shən), *n.* **1.** forcible separation or division into parts. **2.** a disrupted condition: *The state was in disruption.* [1640–50; < L *disruptiōn-* (s. of *disruptiō*), equiv. to *disrupt-* (see DISRUPT) + *-iōn-* -ION]

dis·rup·tive (dis rup′tiv), *adj.* causing, tending to cause, or caused by disruption; disrupting: *the disruptive effect of their rioting.* [1835–45; DISRUPT + -IVE] **—dis·rup′tive·ly,** *adv.* **—dis·rup′tive·ness,** *n.*

disrup′tive dis′charge, *Elect.* the sudden, large increase in current through an insulating medium resulting from complete failure of the medium under electrostatic stress.

dis·rup·ture (dis rup′chər), *n.* interruption; disruption. [1775–85; DISRUPT + -URE]

dis·sat·is·fac·tion (dis′sat is fak′shən, dis sat′-), *n.* **1.** the state or attitude of not being satisfied; discontent; displeasure. **2.** a particular cause or feeling of displeasure or disappointment: *many dissatisfactions with the plan.* [1630–40; DIS-[1] + SATISFACTION]
—Syn. 1. disappointment, disapproval, uneasiness. DISSATISFACTION, DISCONTENT, DISPLEASURE imply a sense of dislike for, or unhappiness in, one's surroundings. DISSATISFACTION results from contemplating what falls short of one's wishes or expectations: *dissatisfaction with the results of an afternoon's work.* DISCONTENT is a sense of lack and a general feeling of uneasy dislike for the conditions of one's life: *feeling a continual vague discontent.* DISPLEASURE suggests a certain amount of anger as well as dissatisfaction: *displeasure at being kept waiting.* **—Ant.** satisfaction.

dis·sat·is·fac·to·ry (dis′sat is fak′tə rē, dis sat′-), *adj.* causing dissatisfaction; unsatisfactory: *dissatisfactory service.* [1600–10; DIS-[1] + SATISFACTORY] **—dis′sat·is·fac′to·ri·ness,** *n.*

dis·sat·is·fied (dis sat′is fīd′), *adj.* **1.** not satisfied or pleased; discontented. **2.** showing dissatisfaction: *a dissatisfied look.* [1665–75; DISSATISFY + -ED[2]] **—dis·sat′·is·fied′ly,** *adv.* **—dis·sat′is·fied′ness,** *n.*
—Syn. displeased, unhappy, disgruntled.

dis·sat·is·fy (dis sat′is fī′), *v.t.,* **-fied, -fy·ing.** to cause to be displeased, esp. by failing to provide something expected or desired. [1660–70; DIS-[1] + SATISFY]

dis·save (dis sāv′), *v.i.,* **-saved, -sav·ing. 1.** to withdraw or spend savings, esp. to meet increased living expenses. **2.** to save little or nothing or to go into debt, esp. because of increased spending or inflation. [1935–40; DIS-[1] + SAVE[1]] **—dis·sav′er,** *n.*

dis·seat (dis sēt′), *v.t. Archaic.* to unseat. [1605–1615; DIS-[1] + SEAT]

dis·sect (di sekt′, dī-), *v.t.* **1.** to cut apart (an animal body, plant, etc.) to examine the structure, relation of parts, or the like. **2.** to examine minutely part by part; analyze: *to dissect an idea.* [1600–10; < L *dissectus* (ptp. of *dissecāre* to cut up), equiv. to *dis-* DIS-[1] + *sec-* cut + *-tus* ptp. suffix] **—dis·sec′ti·ble,** *adj.* **—dis·sec′tor,** *n.*
—Syn. 1, 2. anatomize.

dis·sect·ed (di sek′tid, dī-), *adj.* **1.** *Bot.* deeply divided into numerous segments, as a leaf. **2.** *Phys. Geog.* separated, by erosion, into many closely spaced crevices or gorges, as the surface of a plateau. [1625–35; DISSECT + -ED[2]]

dis·sec·tion (di sek′shən, dī-), *n.* **1.** the act of dissecting. **2.** something that has been dissected. **3.** a detailed, part-by-part analysis. [1575–85; < L *dissectiōn-* (s. of *dissectiō*), equiv. to *dissect-* (see DISSECT) + *-iōn-* -ION]

dissec′tor tube′, *Electronics.* See **image dissector.**

dis·seize (dis sēz′), *v.t.,* **-seized, -seiz·ing.** *Law.* to deprive (a person) of seizin, or of the possession, of a freehold interest in land, esp. wrongfully or by force; oust. [1250–1300; ME *disseise* < AF *disseisir,* equiv. to *dis-* DIS-[1] + *seisir* to SEIZE] **—dis·sei′zor,** *n.*

dis·sei·zee (dis′sē zē′, dis sē zē′), *n.* a person who is disseized. [1535–40; DISSEIZE + -EE]

dis·sei·zin (dis sē′zin), *n. Law.* **1.** the act of disseizing. **2.** the state of being disseized. [1250–1300; ME *disseisine* < AF. See DIS-[1], SEIZIN]

dis·sem·blance[1] (di sem′bləns), *n.* dissimilarity; unlikeness. [1425–75; late ME < MF *dessemblance.* See DIS-[1], SEMBLANCE]

dis·sem·blance[2] (di sem′bləns), *n.* dissembling; dissimulation. [1550–60; DISSEMBLE + -ANCE]

dis·sem·ble (di sem′bəl), *v.,* **-bled, -bling.** —*v.t.* **1.** to give a false or misleading appearance to; conceal the truth or real nature of: *to dissemble one's incompetence in business.* **2.** to put on the appearance of; feign: *to dissemble innocence.* **3.** *Obs.* to let pass unnoticed; ignore. —*v.i.* **4.** to conceal one's true motives, thoughts, etc., by some pretense; speak or act hypocritically. [1490–1500; alter. (by assoc. with obs. *semble* to RESEMBLE) of ME *dissimulen* < L *dissimulāre.* See DIS-[1], SIMULATE] **—dis·sem′bler,** *n.* **—dis·sem′bling·ly,** *adv.*
—Syn. 1. mask, hide, camouflage, dissimulate.

dis·sem·i·nate (di sem′ə nāt′), *v.t.,* **-nat·ed, -nat·ing.** to scatter or spread widely, as though sowing seed; promulgate extensively; broadcast; disperse: *to disseminate information about preventive medicine.* [1595–1605; < L *dissēminātus* (ptp. of *dissēmināre; dis-* DIS-[1] + *sēmināre* to sow), equiv. to *dis-* + *sēmin-* (s. of *sēmen* seed) + *-ātus* -ATE[1]] **—dis·sem′i·na′tion,** *n.* **—dis·sem′i·na′tive,** *adj.* **—dis·sem′i·na′tor,** *n.*

dis·sem·i·nule (di sem′ə nyo͞ol′), *n. Bot.* any propagative part of a plant, as a bud, seed, or spore, that is capable of disseminating the plant. [1900–05; prob. DISSEMIN(ATE) + -ULE]

dis·sen·sion (di sen′shən), *n.* **1.** strong disagreement; a contention or quarrel; discord. **2.** difference in sentiment or opinion; disagreement. [1300–50; ME *dissenciun, dissensio(u)n* < AF < L *dissēnsiōn-* (s. of *dissēnsiō*), equiv. to *dissēns(us)* (ptp. of *dissentīre; dissent-* (see DISSENT) + *-tus* ptp. suffix) + *-iōn-* -ION]
—Syn. 1. strife. See **quarrel**[1].

dis·sent (di sent′), *v.i.* **1.** to differ in sentiment or opinion, esp. from the majority; withhold assent; disagree (often fol. by *from*): *Two of the justices dissented from the majority decision.* **2.** to disagree with the methods, goals, etc., of a political party or government;

CONCISE PRONUNCIATION KEY: act, cāpe, dâre, pärt; set, ēqual; if, ice; ox, ōver, ôrder, oil, bo͝ok, bo͞ot, out; up, ûrge; child; sing; shoe; thin, *th*at; zh as in *treasure.* ə = *a* as in *alone, e* as in *system, i* as in *easily, o* as in *gallop, u* as in *circus;* ᵊ as in *fire* (fīᵊr), *hour* (ouᵊr). l and n can serve as syllabic consonants, as in *cradle* (krād′l), and *button* (but′n). See the full key inside the front cover.

take an opposing view. **3.** to disagree with or reject the doctrines or authority of an established church. **—n. 4.** difference of sentiment or opinion. **5.** See **dissenting opinion. 6.** disagreement with the philosophy, methods, goals, etc., of a political party or government. **7.** separation from an established church, esp. the Church of England; nonconformity. [1400–50; late ME *dissenten* (< MF *dissentir*) < L *dissentīre,* equiv. to *dis-* DIS-[1] + *sentīre* to feel] **—dis•sent′ing•ly,** *adv.*
—Syn. 4, 6. disagreement, dissatisfaction, opposition. DISSENT, DISSIDENCE mean disagreement with the majority opinion. DISSENT may express either withholding of agreement or open disagreement. DISSIDENCE, formerly much the same as DISSENT, has come to suggest not only strong dissatisfaction but a determined opposition.

dis•sent•er (di sen′tər), *n.* **1.** a person who dissents, as from an established church, political party, or majority opinion. **2.** (*sometimes cap.*) an English Protestant who dissents from the Church of England. [1630–40; DISSENT + -ER[1]]

dis•sen•tient (di sen′shənt), *adj.* **1.** dissenting, esp. from the opinion of the majority. **—n. 2.** a person who dissents. [1615–25; < L *dissentient-* (s. of *dissentiēns,* prp. of *dissentīre*), equiv. to *dissenti-* (see DISSENT) + *-ent-* -ENT] **—dis•sen′tience, dis•sen′tien•cy,** *n.* **—dis•sen′tient•ly,** *adv.*

dissent′ing opin′ion, *Law.* (in appellate courts) an opinion filed by a judge who disagrees with the majority decision of a case. Also called **dissent.**

dis•sen•tious (di sen′shəs), *adj.* contentious; quarrelsome. [1550–60; DISSENT + -IOUS]

dis•sep•i•ment (di sep′ə mənt), *n.* **1.** *Anat., Zool.* a partition or septum in a tissue. **2.** *Bot.* one of the partitions formed within ovaries and fruits by the coherence of the sides of the constituent carpels. [1720–30; < L *dissaepimentum,* equiv. to *dis-* DIS-[1] + *saepimentum* hedge (*saepī(re)* to fence + *-mentum* -MENT)] **—dis•sep′i•men′tal,** *adj.*

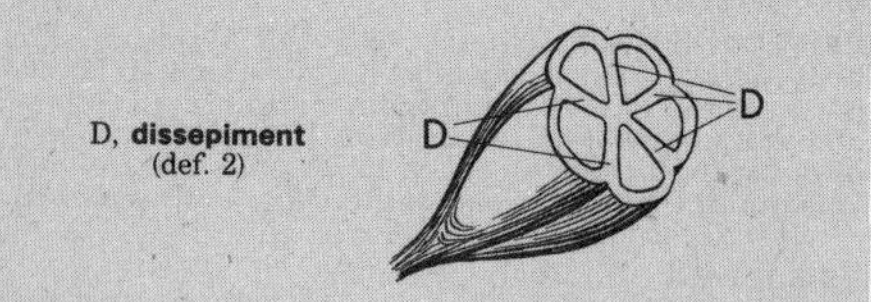

D, **dissepiment** (def. 2)

dis•sert (di sûrt′), *v.i.* to discourse on a subject. [1615–25; < L *dissertāre* to set forth at length (freq. of *disserere* to arrange in order), equiv. to *dis-* DIS-[1] + *ser-* put together + freq. *-t-* + *-āre* inf. suffix]

dis•ser•tate (dis′ər tāt′), *v.i.,* **-tat•ed, -tat•ing.** to discuss a subject fully and learnedly; discourse. [1760–70; prob. back formation from DISSERTATION] **—dis′ser•ta′tor,** *n.*

dis•ser•ta•tion (dis′ər tā′shən), *n.* **1.** a written essay, treatise, or thesis, esp. one written by a candidate for the degree of Doctor of Philosophy. **2.** any formal discourse in speech or writing. [1605–15; < L *dissertātiōn-* (s. of *dissertātiō*), equiv. to *dissertāt(us)* (ptp. of *dissertāre; dissert-* (see DISSERT) + *-ātus* -ATE[1]) + *-iōn-* -ION] **—dis′ser•ta′tion•al,** *adj.* **—dis′ser•ta′tion•ist,** *n.*

dis•serve (dis sûrv′), *v.t.,* **-served, -serv•ing.** to be a disservice to; serve harmfully or injuriously. [1610–20; DIS-[1] + SERVE]

dis•serv•ice (dis sûr′vis), *n., v.,* **-iced, -ic•ing. —n. 1.** harmful or injurious service; an ill turn. **—v.t. 2.** to provide inadequate or faulty service to: *Small shippers are most often disserviced by transportation breakdowns.* [1590–1600; DIS-[1] + SERVICE]
—Syn. 1. wrong, hurt, harm, injury, unkindness.

dis•sev•er (di sev′ər), *v.t.* **1.** to sever; separate. **2.** to divide into parts. **—v.i. 3.** to part; separate. [1250–1300; ME *des(s)everen* < OF *dessevrer* < LL *dissēparāre,* equiv. to L *dis-* DIS-[1] + *sēparāre* to SEPARATE] **—dis•sev′er•ance, dis•sev′er•ment, dis•sev′er•a′tion,** *n.*

dis•si•dence (dis′i dəns), *n.* disagreement: *political dissidence.* [1650–60; < L *dissidentia,* equiv. to *dissid-* (see DISSIDENT) + *-entia* -ENCE]
—Syn. See **dissent.**

dis•si•dent (dis′i dənt), *n.* **1.** a person who dissents. **—adj. 2.** disagreeing or dissenting, as in opinion or attitude: *a ban on dissident magazines.* [1525–35; < L *dissident-* (s. of *dissidēns,* prp. of *dissidēre* to sit apart), equiv. to *dis-* DIS-[1] + *-sid-* (comb. form of *sed-* SIT) + *-ent-* -ENT] **—dis′si•dent•ly,** *adv.*

dis•sil•i•ent (di sil′ē ənt), *adj.* bursting apart; bursting open. [1650–60; < L *dissilient-* (s. of *dissiliēns,* prp. of *dissilīre* to leap apart), equiv. to *dis-* DIS-[1] + *-sili-* (comb. form of *sali-* leap; see SALLY) + *-ent-* -ENT] **—dis•sil′i•en•cy, dis•sil′i•ence,** *n.*

dis•sim•i•lar (di sim′ə lər, dis sim′-), *adj.* not similar; unlike; different. [1615–25; DIS-[1] + SIMILAR] **—dis•sim′i•lar•ly,** *adv.*
—Syn. distinct, disparate, diverse, individual.

dis•sim•i•lar•i•ty (di sim′ə lar′i tē, dis sim′-), *n., pl.* **-ties. 1.** unlikeness; difference. **2.** a point of difference: *There are dissimilarities in our outlooks.* [1695–1705; DIS-[1] + SIMILARITY]
—Syn. 1. See **difference.**

dis•sim•i•late (di sim′ə lāt′), *v.t.,* **-lat•ed, -lat•ing.** *Phonet.* to modify by dissimilation. [1835–45; DIS-[1] + (AS)SIMILATE] **—dis•sim′i•la′tive,** *adj.* **—dis•sim•i•la•to•ry** (di sim′ə lə tôr′ē, -tōr′ē), *adj.*

CONCISE ETYMOLOGY KEY: <, descended or borrowed from; >, whence; b., blend of, blended; c., cognate with; cf., compare; deriv., derivative; equiv., equivalent; imit., imitative; obl., oblique; r., replacing; s., stem; sp., spelling, spelled; resp., respelling, respelled; trans., translation; ?, origin unknown; *, unattested; ‡, probably earlier than. See the full key inside the front cover.

dis•sim•i•la•tion (di sim′ə lā′shən), *n.* **1.** the act of making or becoming unlike. **2.** *Phonet.* the process by which a speech sound becomes different from or less like a neighboring sound, as *pilgrim* (pil′grim) from Latin *peregrinus* (peʀ′e gʀē′nōōs), and *purple* (pûr′pəl) from Old English *purpure* (pōōʀ′pōō ʀe), or disappears entirely because of a like sound in another syllable, as in the pronunciation (guv′ə nər) for *governor.* Cf. **assimilation** (def. 5). **3.** *Biol.* catabolism. [1820–30; DIS-[1] + (AS)SIMILATION]

dis•si•mil•i•tude (dis′si mil′i tōōd′, -tyōōd′), *n.* **1.** unlikeness; difference; dissimilarity. **2.** a point of difference; dissimilarity. [1525–35; < L *dissimilitūdō,* equiv. to *dis-* DIS-[1] + *similitūdō* SIMILITUDE]

dis•sim•u•late (di sim′yə lāt′), *v.,* **-lat•ed, -lat•ing. —v.t. 1.** to disguise or conceal under a false appearance; dissemble: *to dissimulate one's true feelings about a rival.* **—v.i. 2.** to conceal one's true motives, thoughts, etc., by some pretense; speak or act hypocritically. [1525–35; < L *dissimulātus* (ptp. of *dissimulāre* to feign). See DIS-[1], SIMULATE] **—dis•sim′u•la′tive,** *adj.* **—dis•sim′u•la′tor,** *n.*

dis•sim•u•la•tion (di sim′yə lā′shən), *n.* the act of dissimulating; feigning; hypocrisy. [1350–1400; ME *dissimulacioun* (< AF) < L *dissimulātiōn-* (s. of *dissimulātiō* a feigning); see DIS-[1], SIMULATION]

dis•si•pate (dis′ə pāt′), *v.,* **-pat•ed, -pat•ing. —v.t. 1.** to scatter in various directions; disperse; dispel. **2.** to spend or use wastefully or extravagantly; squander; deplete: *to dissipate one's talents; to dissipate a fortune on high living.* **—v.i. 3.** to become scattered or dispersed; be dispelled; disintegrate: *The sun shone and the mist dissipated.* **4.** to indulge in extravagant, intemperate, or dissolute pleasure. [1525–35; < L *dissipātus* (ptp. of *dissipāre, dissupāre* to scatter); see -ATE[1]] **—dis′si•pat′er, dis′si•pa′tor,** *n.* **—dis′si•pa′tive,** *adj.* **—dis•si•pa•tiv•i•ty** (dis′ə pə tiv′i tē), *n.*
—Syn. 1. See **scatter. 3.** disappear, vanish. **—Ant. 1, 3.** unite.

dis•si•pat•ed (dis′ə pā′tid), *adj.* indulging in or characterized by excessive devotion to pleasure; intemperate; dissolute. [1600–10; DISSIPATE + -ED[2]] **—dis′si•pat′ed•ly,** *adv.* **—dis′si•pa′ted•ness,** *n.*

dis•si•pa•tion (dis′ə pā′shən), *n.* **1.** the act of dissipating. **2.** the state of being dissipated; dispersion; disintegration. **3.** a wasting by misuse: *the dissipation of a fortune.* **4.** mental distraction; amusement; diversion. **5.** dissolute way of living, esp. excessive drinking of liquor; intemperance. **6.** *Physics, Mech.* a process in which energy is used or lost without accomplishing useful work, as friction causing loss of mechanical energy. [1535–45; < L *dissipātiōn-* (s. of *dissipātiō*), equiv. to *dissipāt(us)* (see DISSIPATE) + *-iōn-* -ION]

dissipa′tion trail′, a clear rift left behind an aircraft flying through a thin cloud layer. Also called **distrail.**

dis•so•ci•a•ble (di sō′shē ə bəl, -shə bəl *or, for 1,* -sē ə-), *adj.* **1.** capable of being dissociated; separable: *Worthy and unworthy motives are often not dissociable.* **2.** not sociable; unsociable. **3.** incongruous; not reconcilable. [1595–1605; < L *dissociābilis,* equiv. to *dis-* DIS-[1] + *sociābilis* SOCIABLE] **—dis•so′ci•a•bil′i•ty, dis•so′ci•a•ble•ness,** *n.*

dis•so•cial (di sō′shəl), *adj.* disinclined to or unsuitable for society; unsocial. [1755–65; < LL *dissociālis* irreconcilable, equiv. to *dis-* DIS-[1] + *sociālis* sociable (see SOCIAL)] **—dis•so′ci•al′i•ty,** *n.*

dis•so•ci•ate (di sō′shē āt′, -sē-), *v.,* **-at•ed, -at•ing. —v.t. 1.** to sever the association of (oneself); separate: *He tried to dissociate himself from the bigotry in his past.* **2.** to subject to dissociation. **—v.i. 3.** to withdraw from association. **4.** to undergo dissociation. [1605–15; DIS-[1] + (AS)SOCIATE, modeled on L *dissociātus,* ptp. of *dissociāre* to divide, sever] **—dis•so′ci•a′tive,** *adj.*

dis•so•ci•a•tion (di sō′sē ā′shən, -shē ā′-), *n.* **1.** an act or instance of dissociating. **2.** the state of being dissociated; disjunction; separation: *the dissociation of church and state.* **3.** *Physical Chem.* **a.** the reversible resolution or decomposition of a complex substance into simpler constituents caused by variation in physical conditions, as when water gradually decomposes into hydrogen and oxygen under great heat in such a way that when the temperature is lowered the liberated elements recombine. **b.** See **electrolytic dissociation. 4.** *Psychiatry.* the splitting off of a group of mental processes from the main body of consciousness, as in amnesia or certain forms of hysteria. [1605–15; DIS-[1] + (AS)SOCIATION, modeled on L *dissociātiō* separation]

disso′ciative disor′der, *Psychiatry.* a mental disorder, as multiple personality, characterized by sudden temporary alteration in consciousness, identity, or motor behavior.

dis•sog•e•ny (di soj′ə nē), *n. Zool.* the condition in ctenophores in which an individual has two periods of sexual maturity, one in the larval and one in the adult stage. Also, **dis•sog•o•ny** (di sog′ə nē). [1895–1900; < Gk *dissó(s)* twofold + -GENY]

dis•sol•u•ble (di sol′yə bəl), *adj.* **1.** capable of being dissolved: *tablets dissoluble in water.* **2.** capable of being destroyed, as through disintegration or decomposition. [1525–35; < L *dissolūbilis,* equiv. to *dissolū-,* s. of *dissolvere* to DISSOLVE + *-bilis* -BLE. See DIS-[1], SOLUBLE] **—dis•sol′u•bil′i•ty, dis•sol′u•ble•ness,** *n.*

dis•so•lute (dis′ə lōōt′), *adj.* indifferent to moral restraints; given to immoral or improper conduct; licentious; dissipated. [1350–1400; ME (< AF) < L *dissolūtus* (ptp. of *dissolvere* to DISSOLVE). See DIS-[1], SOLUTE] **—dis′so•lute′ly,** *adv.* **—dis′so•lute′ness,** *n.*
—Syn. corrupt, loose, debauched, wanton, abandoned.

dis•so•lu•tion (dis′ə lōō′shən), *n.* **1.** the act or process of resolving or dissolving into parts or elements. **2.** the resulting state. **3.** the undoing or breaking of a bond, tie, union, partnership, etc. **4.** the breaking up of an assembly or organization; dismissal; dispersal. **5.** *Govt.* an order issued by the head of a state terminating a parliament and necessitating a new election. **6.** death; decease. **7.** a bringing or coming to an end; disintegration; decay; termination. **8.** legal termination, esp. of business activity, with the final distribution of assets, the fixing of liabilities, etc. **9.** *Chem.* the process by which a solid, gas, or liquid is dispersed homogeneously in a gas, solid, or, esp., a liquid. [1350–1400; ME *dissolucioun* (< AF) < L *dissolūtiōn-* (s. of *dissolūtiō*). See DIS-[1], SOLUTION] **—dis′so•lu′tive,** *adv.*

dis•solve (di zolv′), *v.,* **-solved, -solv•ing,** *n.* **—v.t. 1.** to make a solution of, as by mixing with a liquid; pass into solution: *to dissolve salt in water.* **2.** to melt; liquefy: *to dissolve sugar into syrup.* **3.** to undo (a tie or bond); break up (a connection, union, etc.). **4.** to break up (an assembly or organization); dismiss; disperse. **5.** *Govt.* to order the termination of (a parliament or other legislative body). **6.** to bring to an end; terminate; destroy: *to dissolve one's hopes.* **7.** to separate into parts or elements; disintegrate. **8.** to destroy the binding power or influence of: *to dissolve a spell.* **9.** *Law.* to deprive of force; abrogate; annul: *to dissolve a marriage.* **—v.i. 10.** to become dissolved, as in a solvent. **11.** to become melted or liquefied. **12.** to disintegrate, break up, or disperse. **13.** to lose force, intensity, or strength. **14.** to disappear gradually; fade away. **15.** to break down emotionally; lose one's composure: *The poor child dissolved in tears.* **16.** *Motion Pictures, Television.* to fade out one shot or scene while simultaneously fading in the next, overlapping the two during the process. **—n. 17.** Also called **lap dissolve, cross-dissolve.** *Motion Pictures, Television.* a transition from one scene to the next made by dissolving. [1350–1400; ME < L *dissolvere,* equiv. to *dis-* DIS-[1] + *solvere* to SOLVE] **—dis•solv′a•bil′i•ty, dis•solv′a•ble•ness,** *n.* **—dis•solv′a•ble,** *adj.* **—dis•solv′er,** *n.* **—dis•solv′ing•ly,** *adv.*
—Syn. 1. See **melt. 3.** sever, loosen. **5.** adjourn.

dis•sol•vent (di zol′vənt), *adj.* **1.** capable of dissolving another substance. **—n. 2.** a solvent. [1640–50; < L *dissolvent-* (s. of *dissolvēns,* prp. of *dissolvere*). See DIS-[1], SOLVENT]

dissolv′ing view′, an effect created by the projection of slides on a screen in such a way that each picture seems to dissolve into the succeeding one without an interval in between. [1840–50]

dis•so•nance (dis′ə nəns), *n.* **1.** inharmonious or harsh sound; discord; cacophony. **2.** *Music.* **a.** a simultaneous combination of tones conventionally accepted as being in a state of unrest and needing completion. **b.** an unresolved, discordant chord or interval. Cf. **consonance** (def. 3). See illus. under **resolution. 3.** disagreement or incongruity. [1565–75; < LL *dissonantia,* equiv. to *disson-* (see DISSONANT) + *-antia* -ANCE]

dis•so•nan•cy (dis′ə nən sē), *n., pl.* **-cies.** dissonance.

dis•so•nant (dis′ə nənt), *adj.* **1.** disagreeing or harsh in sound; discordant. **2.** out of harmony; incongruous; at variance. **3.** *Music.* characterized by dissonance. [1400–50; late ME *dissonaunte* (< AF) < L *dissonant-* (s. of *dissonāns,* prp. of *dissonāre* to sound harsh), equiv. to *disson-* (deriv. of *dissonus* discordant; see DIS-[1], SOUND) + *-ant-* -ANT] **—dis′so•nant•ly,** *adv.*
—Syn. 2. incompatible, incongruent, inconsistent.

dis•spir•it (di spir′it, dis-), *v.t. Obs.* dispirit.

dis•spread (di spred′), *v.t., v.i.,* **-spread, -spread•ing.** dispread.

dis•suade (di swād′), *v.t.,* **-suad•ed, -suad•ing. 1.** to deter by advice or persuasion; persuade not to do something (often fol. by *from*): *She dissuaded him from leaving home.* **2.** *Archaic.* to advise or urge against: *to dissuade an action.* [1505–15; < L *dissuādēre,* equiv. to *dis-* DIS-[1] + *suādēre* to recommend, urge, deriv. of *suād-,* base of *suāvis* tasting agreeable; see SUAVE] **—dis•suad′a•ble,** *adj.* **—dis•suad′er,** *n.*

dis•sua•sion (di swā′zhən), *n.* an act or instance of dissuading. [1520–30; < L *dissuāsiōn-* (s. of *dissuāsiō*) a speaking against, equiv. to *dissuās(us)* (ptp. of *dissuādēre; dissuād-* (see DISSUADE) + *-tus* ptp. suffix) + *-iōn-* -ION]

dis•sua•sive (di swā′siv), *adj.* tending or liable to dissuade. [1600–10; DISSUAS(ION) + -IVE] **—dis•sua′sive•ly,** *adv.* **—dis•sua′sive•ness,** *n.*

dis•syl•la•bize (di sil′ə bīz′, dis sil′-, dī sil′-), *v.t.,* **-bized, -biz•ing.** disyllabize. Also, *esp. Brit.,* **dis•syl′la•bise′. —dis•syl•la•bism** (di sil′ə biz′əm, dis sil′-, dī sil′-), *n.*

dis•syl•la•ble (di sil′ə bəl, dis sil′-, dī′sil-), *n.* disyllable. **—dis•syl•lab•ic** (dis′i lab′ik, dis′si-, dī′si-), *adj.*

dis•sym•me•try (di sim′i trē, dis sim′-), *n.* absence or lack of symmetry. [1835–45; DIS-[1] + SYMMETRY] **—dis•sym•met•ric** (dis′i me′trik, dis′si-), **dis′sym•met′ri•cal,** *adj.* **—dis′sym•met′ri•cal•ly,** *adv.*

dist., 1. distance. **2.** distant. **3.** distinguish. **4.** distinguished. **5.** district.

di•stad (dis′tad), *adv.* toward or at the distal end or part. [1795–1805; DIST(ANT) + -AD[3]]

dis•taff (dis′taf, -täf), *n.* **1.** a staff with a cleft end for holding wool, flax, etc., from which the thread is drawn in spinning by hand. **2.** a similar attachment on a spinning wheel. **3.** *Archaic.* **a.** a woman or women collectively. **b.** woman's work. **—adj. 4.** *Sometimes Offensive.* noting, pertaining to, characteristic of, or suitable for a woman; female. [bef. 1000; ME *distaf,* OE *distæf,* equiv. to *dis-* (c. LG *diesse* bunch of flax on a distaff; cf. DIZEN) + *stæf* STAFF]

dis•taff•er (dis′taf ər, -tä fər), *n. Sometimes Offensive.* a woman, esp. in a field or place usually or generally dominated by men: *the first distaffer to have a seat on the stock exchange.* [DISTAFF + -ER[1], with play on STAFFER]

dis′taff side′, the female side of a family (opposed to *spear side*). [1885–90]

dis•tain (di stān′), *v.t. Archaic.* to discolor; stain; sully. [1350–1400; ME *desteignen* < AF, MF *desteign-,* s. of *desteindre,* equiv. to *des-* DIS-[1] + *teindre* < L *tingere* to dye, TINGE]

dis·tal (dis′tl), *adj.* **1.** situated away from the point of origin or attachment, as of a limb or bone; terminal. Cf. **proximal. 2.** *Dentistry.* directed away from the sagittal plane or midline of the face, along the dental arch. Cf. **buccal** (def. 3), **mesial** (def. 2). [1800–10; DIST(ANT) + -AL¹] —**dis′tal·ly,** *adv.*

dis·tance (dis′təns), *n., v.,* **-tanced, -tanc·ing.** —*n.* **1.** the extent or amount of space between two things, points, lines, etc. **2.** the state or fact of being apart in space, as of one thing from another; remoteness. **3.** a linear extent of space: *Seven miles is a distance too great to walk in an hour.* **4.** an expanse; area: *A vast distance of water surrounded the ship.* **5.** the interval between two points of time; an extent of time: *His vacation period was a good distance away.* **6.** remoteness or difference in any respect: *Our philosophies are a long distance apart.* **7.** an amount of progress: *We've come a long distance on the project.* **8.** a distant point, place, or region. **9.** the distant part of a field of view: *a tree in the distance.* **10.** absence of warmth; reserve: *Their first meeting in several years was hampered by a certain distance between them.* **11.** *Music.* interval (def. 6). **12.** See **aesthetic distance. 13.** *Horse Racing.* (in a heat race) the space measured back from the winning post that a horse must reach by the time the winner passes the winning post or be eliminated from subsequent heats. **14.** *Math.* the greatest lower bound of differences between points, one from each of two given sets. **15.** *Obs.* disagreement or dissension; a quarrel. **16. go the distance, a.** (in horse racing) to be able to run well in a long race. **b.** *Informal.* to finish or complete something, esp. something difficult, challenging, or requiring sustained effort. **17. keep at a distance,** to treat coldly or in an unfriendly manner. **18. keep one's distance,** to avoid becoming familiar or involved; remain cool or aloof. —*v.t.* **19.** to leave behind at a distance, as at a race; surpass. **20.** to place at a distance. **21.** to cause to appear distant. [1250–1300; ME < L *distantia,* equiv. to *distant-* (see DISTANT) + *-ia* -Y³; r. ME *destaunce* < AF] —**dis′tance·less,** *adj.*
—**Syn. 10.** remoteness, restraint, coolness, aloofness.

dis′tance med′ley, *Track.* a medley relay in which the first member of a team runs 440 yd. (402 m), the second runs 880 yd. (805 m), the third runs 1320 yd. (1207 m), and the fourth runs 1760 yd. (1609 m). Cf. **sprint medley.**

dis′tance univer′sity, *Canadian.* a degree-granting institution operating wholly or mainly by correspondence courses for students not resident on or within commuting distance of the campus.

dis·tant (dis′tənt), *adj.* **1.** far off or apart in space; not near at hand; remote or removed (often fol. by *from*): *a distant place; a town three miles distant from here.* **2.** apart or far off in time: *distant centuries past.* **3.** remote or far apart in any respect: *a distant relative.* **4.** reserved or aloof; not familiar or cordial: *a distant greeting.* **5.** arriving from or going to a distance, as a communication, journey, etc.: *I have here a distant letter from Japan.* [1350–1400; ME *dista(u)nt* (< AF) < L *distant-* (s. of *distāns,* prp. of *distāre* to stand apart), equiv. to *di-* DI-² + *stā-* STAND + *-nt-* prp. suffix] —**dis′tant·ly,** *adv.* —**dis′tant·ness,** *n.*
—**Syn. 4.** cool, withdrawn.

dis·taste (dis tāst′), *n., v.,* **-tast·ed, -tast·ing.** —*n.* **1.** dislike; disinclination. **2.** dislike for food or drink. —*v.t.* **3.** *Archaic.* to dislike. [1580–90; DIS-¹ + TASTE]
—**Syn. 1.** aversion, repugnance, disgust. See **dislike.**

dis·taste·ful (dis tāst′fəl), *adj.* **1.** unpleasant, offensive, or causing dislike: *a distasteful chore.* **2.** unpleasant to the taste: *a distasteful medicine.* **3.** showing distaste or dislike. [1600–10; DISTASTE + -FUL] —**dis·taste′ful·ly,** *adv.* —**dis·taste′ful·ness,** *n.*
—**Syn. 1.** disagreeable, displeasing; repugnant, repulsive. **2.** unpalatable, unsavory.

Dist. Atty., district attorney.

Dist. Ct., District Court.

dis·tel·fink (dis′tl fingk′), *n.* a stylized bird motif traditional in Pennsylvania German art. [standard G sp. for PaG *dischdelfink* goldfinch (*Carduelis carduelis*), equiv. to *dischdel* THISTLE + *fink* FINCH]

dis·tem·per¹ (dis tem′pər), *n.* **1.** *Vet. Pathol.* **a.** Also called **canine distemper.** an infectious disease chiefly of young dogs, caused by an unidentified virus and characterized by lethargy, fever, catarrh, photophobia, and vomiting. **b.** Also called **colt distemper, equine distemper, strangles.** an infectious disease of horses, caused by the bacillus *Streptococcus equi* and characterized by catarrh of the upper air passages and the formation of pus in the submaxillary and other lymphatic glands. **c.** Also called **cat distemper, feline agranulocytosis, feline distemper, feline infectious enteritis, feline panleukopenia.** a usually fatal viral disease of cats, characterized by fever, vomiting, and diarrhea, leading to severe dehydration. **2.** a deranged condition of mind or body; a disorder or disease: *a feverish distemper.* **3.** disorder or disturbance, esp. of a political nature. —*v.t.* **4.** *Obs.* to derange physically or mentally. [1300–50; ME *distemp(e)ren, destempren* (v.) (< MF *destemper*) < ML *distemperāre,* equiv. to L *dis-* DIS-¹ + *temperāre* to TEMPER] —**dis·tem′pered·ly,** *adv.* —**dis·tem′pered·ness,** *n.*

dis·tem·per² (dis tem′pər), *n.* **1.** *Art.* **a.** a technique of decorative painting in which glue or gum is used as a binder or medium to achieve a mat surface and rapid drying. **b.** (formerly) the tempera technique. **2.** a painting executed by this method. **3.** *Brit.* whitewash; calcimine. —*v.t.* **4.** to paint in distemper. **5.** *Brit.* to whitewash a wall, cottage, etc.; calcimine. [1350–1400; ME *distemperen* (v.) (< AF *distemprer*) < ML *distemperāre* to dissolve, dilute, equiv. to L *dis-* DIS-¹ + *temperāre* to blend, TEMPER]

dis·tem·per·a·ture (dis tem′pər ə chər), *n.* a distempered or disordered condition; disturbance of health, mind, or temper. [1525–35; obs. *distemperate* (DIS-¹ + TEMPERATE) + -URE]

dis·tem·per·oid (dis tem′pə roid′), *adj. Vet. Pathol.* **1.** resembling distemper. **2.** of or pertaining to a weakened strain of canine distemper virus used to make dogs and other susceptible animals immune to distemper infection. [DISTEMPER¹ + -OID]

dis·tend (di stend′), *v.t., v.i.* **1.** to expand by stretching, as something hollow or elastic: *Habitual overeating had distended his stomach.* **2.** to spread in all directions; expand; swell: *The sea distended about them.* [1375–1425; late ME (< AF *destendre*) < L *distendere,* equiv. to *dis-* DIS-¹ + *tendere* to stretch] —**dis·tend′er,** *n.*
—**Syn. 1.** See **expand. 1, 2.** enlarge, bloat. —**Ant. 1, 2.** shrink, contract.

dis·tend·ed (di sten′did), *adj.* **1.** increased, as in size, volume, etc.; expanded; dilated: *the distended nostrils of the terrified horse.* **2.** swollen, by or as by internal pressure, out of normal size or shape; protuberant: *distended wineskins; the distended arteries of his neck.* [1590–1600; DISTEND + -ED²] —**dis·tend′ed·ly,** *adv.* —**dis·tend′ed·ness,** *n.*

dis·ten·si·ble (di sten′sə bəl), *adj.* capable of being distended. [1820–30; < L *distēns(us)* (ptp. of *distendere; distend-* DISTEND + *-tus* ptp. suffix) + -IBLE] —**dis·ten′si·bil′i·ty,** *n.*

dis·ten·sile (di sten′sil), *adj.* **1.** distensible. **2.** serving to distend. [1730–40; < L *distēns(us)* (ptp. of *distendere* to DISTEND) + -ILE]

dis·tent (di stent′), *adj. Obs.* distended. [1580–90; < L *distentus* distended (var. of *distēnsus* ptp. of *distendere* to DISTEND)]

dis·ten·tion (di sten′shən), *n.* the act of distending or the state of being distended. Also, **dis·ten′sion.** [1375–1425; late ME *distensioun* < L *distentiōn-* (s. of *distentiō*), equiv. to *distent(us)* DISTENT + *-iōn-* -ION]

dis·tich (dis′tik), *n. Pros.* **1.** a unit of two lines of verse, usually a self-contained statement; couplet. **2.** a rhyming couplet. [1545–55; < L *distichon,* n. use of neut. of Gk *dístichos* having two lines, equiv. to *di-* DI-¹ + *stíchos* row] —**dis′ti·chal,** *adj.*

dis·ti·chous (dis′ti kəs), *adj.* **1.** *Bot.* arranged alternately in two vertical rows on opposite sides of an axis, as leaves. **2.** *Zool.* divided into two parts. [1745–55; < L *distichus* (< Gk *dístichos* (adj.); see DISTICH), with -OUS for L *-us* adj. suffix] —**dis′ti·chous·ly,** *adv.*

dis·til (di stil′), *v.t., v.i.* **-tilled, -til·ling.** *Chiefly Brit.* distill.

dis·till (di stil′), *v.t.* **1.** to subject to a process of vaporization and subsequent condensation, as for purification or concentration. **2.** to extract the volatile components of by distillation; transform by distillation. **3.** to concentrate, purify, or obtain by or as by distillation: *to distill whiskey from mash.* **4.** to remove by distillation (usually fol. by *off* or *out*): *to distill out impurities.* **5.** to extract the essential elements of; refine; abstract: *She managed to distill her ideas into one succinct article.* **6.** to let fall in drops; give forth in or as in drops: *The cool of the night distills the dew.* —*v.i.* **7.** to undergo or perform distillation. **8.** to become vaporized and then condensed in distillation. **9.** to drop, pass, or condense as a distillate. **10.** to fall in drops; trickle; exude. [1325–75; ME *distillen* (< AF *distiller*) < L *distillāre,* var. of *dēstillāre,* equiv. to *dē-* DE- + *stillāre* to drip] —**dis·till′a·ble,** *adj.*

dis·til·land (dis′tl and′), *n.* a substance that undergoes distillation. Cf. **distillate** (def. 1). [< L *distillandum,* neut. ger. of *distillāre* to DISTILL]

dis·til·late (dis′tl it, -āt′, di stil′it), *n.* **1.** the product obtained from the condensation of vapors in distillation. **2.** any concentration, essence, or abstraction. [1860–65; < L *distillātus* (ptp. of *distillāre* to trickle down), equiv. to *distill-* DISTILL + *-ātus* -ATE¹]

dis·til·la·tion (dis′tl ā′shən), *n.* **1.** the volatilization or evaporation and subsequent condensation of a liquid, as when water is boiled in a retort and the steam is condensed in a cool receiver. **2.** the purification or concentration of a substance, the obtaining of the essence or volatile properties contained in it, or the separation of one substance from another, by such a process. **3.** a product of distilling; distillate. **4.** the act or fact of distilling or the state of being distilled. [1350–1400; ME *distillacioun* (< AF) < L *distillātiōn-* (s. of *distillātiō*), equiv. to *distillāt(us)* DISTILLATE + *-iōn-* -ION] —**dis·til·la·to·ry** (di stil′ə tôr′ē, -tōr′ē), **dis·til·la·tive** (di stil′ə tiv), *adj.*

distilla′tion col′umn, *Chem.* a type of still fitted with interior baffles, used for fractional distillation. Cf. **still²** (def. 1).

dis·tilled (di stild′), *adj.* obtained or produced by distillation. [1425–75; late ME. See DISTILL, -ED²]

distilled′ wa′ter, water from which impurities, as dissolved salts and colloidal particles, have been removed by one or more processes of distillation; chemically pure water. [1495–1505]

dis·till·er (di stil′ər), *n.* **1.** an apparatus for distilling, as a condenser; still. **2.** a person or company whose business it is to extract alcoholic liquors by distillation. [1570–80; DISTILL + -ER¹]

dis·till·er·y (di stil′ə rē), *n., pl.* **-er·ies.** a place or establishment where distilling, esp. the distilling of liquors, is done. [1670–80; DISTILL + -ERY]

dis·till·ment (di stil′mənt), *n. Archaic.* distillation. Also, *esp. Brit.,* **dis·til′ment.** [1595–1605; DISTILL + -MENT]

dis·tinct (di stingkt′), *adj.* **1.** distinguished as not being the same; not identical; separate (sometimes fol. by *from*): *His private and public lives are distinct.* **2.** different in nature or quality; dissimilar (sometimes fol. by *from*): *Gold is distinct from iron.* **3.** clear to the senses or intellect; plain; unmistakable: *The ship appeared as a distinct silhouette.* **4.** distinguishing or perceiving clearly: *distinct vision.* **5.** unquestionably exceptional or notable: *a distinct honor.* **6.** *Archaic.* distinctively decorated or adorned. [1350–1400; ME < L *distinctus,* ptp. of *disting(u)ere* to divide off, pick out, distinguish (*di-* DI-² + **sting(u)ere* presumably, to prick, mark by pricking; cf. INSTINCT¹, INSTIGATE)] —**dis·tinct′ness,** *n.*
—**Syn. 1.** individual. See **various. 3.** well-defined, unconfused. —**Ant. 3, 4.** indistinct.

dis·tinc·tion (di stingk′shən), *n.* **1.** a marking off or distinguishing as different: *His distinction of sounds is excellent.* **2.** the recognizing or noting of differences; discrimination: *to make a distinction between right and wrong.* **3.** a discrimination made between things as different; special regard or favoritism: *Death comes to all without distinction.* **4.** condition of being different; difference: *There is a distinction between what he says and what he does.* **5.** a distinguishing quality or characteristic: *It has the distinction of being the oldest house in the town.* **6.** a distinguishing or treating with special honor, attention, or favor. **7.** an act of bestowing, or a mark of, honor or favor. **8.** marked superiority; note; eminence. **9.** distinguished appearance. **10.** *Obs.* division; separation. [1175–1225; ME *distinccioun* (< AF) < L *distinctiōn-* (s. of *distinctiō*), equiv. to *distinct(us)* (see DISTINCT) + *-iōn-* -ION] —**dis·tinc′tion·less,** *adj.*
—**Syn. 3.** DISTINCTION and DIFFERENCE may both refer to perceivable dissimilarities and, in this meaning, may be used interchangeably: *There is a distinction (difference) between the two.* DISTINCTION, however, usually suggests the perception of dissimilarity, as the result of analysis and discrimination: *a carefully made distinction between two treatments of the same theme;* whereas DIFFERENCE refers only to the condition of being dissimilar: *the difference between Gothic and Roman architecture.* "A distinction without a difference" is a way of referring to an artificial or false discrimination. **7.** See **honor. 8.** renown, importance. —**Ant. 4.** resemblance.

dis·tinc·tive (di stingk′tiv), *adj.* **1.** serving to distinguish; characteristic; distinguishing: *the distinctive stripes of the zebra.* **2.** having a special quality, style, attractiveness, etc.; notable. [1575–85; < ML *distinctīvus,* equiv. to L *distinct(us)* DISTINCT + *-īvus* -IVE] —**dis·tinc′tive·ly,** *adv.* —**dis·tinc′tive·ness,** *n.*
—**Syn. 1.** individual.

distinc′tive fea′ture, *Ling.* **1.** a feature of the sound system of a language that serves as the crucial distinguishing mark between two phonemes, as the distinctive feature of voicing, which distinguishes *b* from *p* in English, or nasality, which distinguishes *m* from *b* and *p.* **2.** any of a set of phonetic properties, as coronal, nasal, or strident, serving as a basic unit of phonological analysis by which the sounds that are significant in a language can be characterized and distinguished from one another. **3.** a component or phonetic feature characterizing a phoneme. [1925–30]

dis·tinct·ly (di stingkt′lē), *adv.* **1.** in a distinct manner; clearly: *Speak more distinctly.* **2.** without doubt; unmistakably. [1350–1400; ME. See DISTINCT, -LY]
—**Syn. 1.** See **clearly.**

dis·tin·gué (dis′tang gā′, di stang′gā; *Fr.* dē staN gā′), *adj.* having an air of distinction; distinguished. [1805–15; < F, adj. use of ptp. of *distinguer* to DISTINGUISH]

dis·tin·guée (dis′tang gā′, di stang′gā; *Fr.* dē staN gā′), *adj.* (of a woman) having an air of distinction; distinguished. [< F, fem. of *distingué* DISTINGUÉ]

dis·tin·guish (di sting′gwish), *v.t.* **1.** to mark off as different (often fol. by *from* or *by*): *He was distinguished from the other boys by his height.* **2.** to recognize as distinct or different; recognize the salient or individual features or characteristics of: *It is hard to distinguish her from her twin sister.* **3.** to perceive clearly by sight or other sense; discern; recognize: *He could not distinguish many of the words.* **4.** to set apart as different; be a distinctive characteristic of; characterize: *It is his Italian accent that distinguishes him.* **5.** to make prominent, conspicuous, or eminent: *to distinguish oneself in battle.* **6.** to divide into classes; classify: *Let us distinguish the various types of metaphor.* **7.** *Archaic.* to single out for or honor with special attention. —*v.i.* **8.** to indicate or show a difference (usually fol. by *between*). **9.** to recognize or note differences; discriminate. [1555–65; extension, by -ISH², of ME *disting(u)en* (< AF, MF *distinguer*) < L *distinguere;* see DISTINCT] —**dis·tin′guish·a·ble,** *adj.* —**dis·tin′guish·a·ble·ness, dis·tin′guish·a·bil′i·ty,** *n.* —**dis·tin′guish·a·bly,** *adv.* —**dis·tin′guish·er,** *n.* —**dis·tin′guish·ment,** *n.*
—**Syn. 2.** DISTINGUISH, DIFFERENTIATE, DISCRIMINATE suggest an attempt to analyze characteristic features or qualities of things. To DISTINGUISH is to recognize the characteristic features belonging to a thing: *to distinguish a light cruiser from a heavy cruiser.* To DISCRIMINATE is to perceive the particular, nice, or exact differences between things, to determine wherein these differences consist, and to estimate their significance: *to discriminate prejudiced from unprejudiced testimony.* To DIFFERENTIATE is to point out exactly and in detail the differences between (usually) two things: *The symptoms of both diseases are so similar that it is hard to differentiate one from another.* —**Ant. 2.** confuse.

dis·tin·guished (di sting′gwisht), *adj.* **1.** made conspicuous by excellence; noted; eminent; famous: *a distinguished scholar.* **2.** having an air of distinction, dignity, or eminence: *a distinguished old gentleman.* **3.** conspicuous; marked. [1600–10; DISTINGUISH + -ED²] —**dis·tin′guished·ly,** *adv.*
—**Syn. 1.** renowned, illustrious. See **famous.**

Distin′guished Con′duct Med′al, *Brit. Mil.* a decoration awarded for distinguished conduct in operations in the field against an enemy. *Abbr.:* D.C.M.

Distin′guished Fly′ing Cross′, 1. *Mil.* a decoration awarded for heroic or extraordinary achievement while on aerial duty. **2.** *Brit. Mil.* a decoration awarded for similar achievement while in flying operations against an enemy. *Abbr.:* D.F.C.

Distin′guished Serv′ice Cross′, *U.S. Army.* a bronze medal awarded for extraordinary heroism in military action against an armed enemy. *Abbr.:* D.S.C.

Distin′guished Serv′ice Med′al, 1. *U.S. Mil.* a decoration awarded for exceptionally meritorious performance of a duty of great responsibility. **2.** *Brit. Mil.* a decoration awarded for distinguished conduct in war. *Abbr.:* D.S.M.

Distin′guished Serv′ice Or′der, *Brit. Mil.* a decoration awarded for distinguished service in action. *Abbr.:* D.S.O.

dis•tin•guish•ing (di sting′gwi shing), *adj.* distinctive; characteristic, as a definitive feature of an individual or group: *Intricate rhyming is a distinguishing feature of her poetry.* [1660–70; DISTINGUISH + -ING[2]] **—dis•tin′guish•ing•ly,** *adv.*

di•sto•ma•to•sis (di stō′mə tō′sis), *n. Vet. Pathol.* liver-rot. [1890–95; < NL *Distomat(a)* name of a suborder of trematode worms (see DI-[1], STOMATA) + -OSIS]

dis•tort (di stôrt′), *v.t.* **1.** to twist awry or out of shape; make crooked or deformed: *Arthritis had distorted his fingers.* **2.** to give a false, perverted, or disproportionate meaning to; misrepresent: *to distort the facts.* **3.** *Electronics.* to reproduce or amplify (a signal) inaccurately by changing the frequencies or unequally changing the delay or amplitude of the components of the output wave. [1580–90; < L *distortus* (ptp. of *distorquēre* to distort), equiv. to *dis-* DIS-[1] + *tor(qu)-* (s. of *torquēre* to twist) + *-tus* ptp. suffix] **—dis•tort′er,** *n.* **—dis•tor′tive,** *adj.*
—Syn. 2. pervert, misconstrue, twist, falsify, misstate. See **misrepresent.**

dis•tort•ed (di stôr′tid), *adj.* **1.** not truly or completely representing the facts or reality; misrepresented; false: *She has a distorted view of life.* **2.** twisted; deformed; misshapen. **3.** mentally or morally twisted, as with an aberration or bias: *He has a distorted sense of values.* [1625–35; DISTORT + -ED[2]] **—dis•tort′ed•ly,** *adv.* **—dis•tort′ed•ness,** *n.*

dis•tor•tion (di stôr′shən), *n.* **1.** an act or instance of distorting. **2.** the state of being distorted or the relative degree or amount by which something is distorted or distorts. **3.** anything that is distorted, as a sound, image, fact, etc. **4.** *Optics.* an aberration of a lens or system of lenses in which the magnification of the object varies with the lateral distance from the axis of the lens. Cf. **barrel distortion, pincushion distortion.** [1575–85; < L *distortiōn-* (s. of *distortiō*). See DISTORT, -ION] **—dis•tor′tion•al, dis•tor′tion•ar′y,** *adj.*

distr., 1. distribute. **2.** distribution. **3.** distributor.

dis•tract (di strakt′), *v.t.* **1.** to draw away or divert, as the mind or attention: *The music distracted him from his work.* **2.** to disturb or trouble greatly in mind; beset: *Grief distracted him.* **3.** to provide a pleasant diversion for; amuse; entertain: *I'm bored with bridge, but golf still distracts me.* **4.** to separate or divide by dissension or strife. *—adj.* **5.** *Obs.* distracted. [1350–1400; ME < L *distractus* (ptp. of *distrahere* to draw apart), equiv. to *dis-* DIS-[1] + *trac-* (var. s. of *trahere* to draw) + *-tus* ptp. suffix] **—dis•tract′er,** *n.* **—dis•tract′i•ble,** *adj.* **—dis•tract′ing•ly,** *adv.*
—Syn. 2. bewilder, agitate, pain, torment, distress.

dis•tract•ed (di strak′tid), *adj.* **1.** having the attention diverted: *She tossed several rocks to the far left and slipped past the distracted sentry.* **2.** rendered incapable of behaving, reacting, etc., in a normal manner, as by worry, remorse, or the like; irrational; disturbed. [1580–90; DISTRACT + -ED[2]] **—dis•tract′ed•ly,** *adv.* **—dis•tract′ed•ness,** *n.*

dis•tract•i•bil•i•ty (di strak′tə bil′i tē), *n. Psychiatry.* inability to sustain one's attention or attentiveness, which is rapidly diverted from one topic to another: a symptom of a variety of mental disorders, as manic disorder, schizophrenia, or anxiety states. [1900–05; DISTRACT + -IBILITY]

dis•trac•tion (di strak′shən), *n.* **1.** the act of distracting. **2.** the state of being distracted. **3.** mental distress or derangement: *That child will drive me to distraction.* **4.** that which distracts, divides the attention, or prevents concentration: *The distractions of the city interfere with my studies.* **5.** that which amuses, entertains, or diverts; amusement; entertainment: *Fishing is his major distraction.* **6.** division or disorder caused by dissension; tumult. [1425–75; late ME (< AF) < L *distractiōn-* (s. of *distractiō*) separation. See DISTRACT, -ION]
—Syn. 3. madness, lunacy, insanity, craziness.

dis•trac•tive (di strak′tiv), *adj.* tending to distract. [1625–35; DISTRACT + -IVE] **—dis•trac′tive•ly,** *adv.*

dis•trail (dis′trāl′), *n. Aeron.* See **dissipation trail.** [by shortening]

dis•train (di strān′), *Law.* *—v.t.* **1.** to constrain by seizing and holding goods, etc., in pledge for rent, damages, etc., or in order to obtain satisfaction of a claim. **2.** to levy a distress upon. *—v.i.* **3.** to levy a distress. [1250–1300; ME *distreinen* < AF, OF *destreindre* < L *distringere* to stretch out, equiv. to *di-* DI-[2] + *stringere* to draw tight; see STRAIN[1]] **—dis•train′a•ble,** *adj.* **—dis•train•ee′,** *n.* **—dis•train′ment,** *n.* **—dis•trai′nor, dis•train′er,** *n.*

dis•traint (di strānt′), *n. Law.* the act of distraining; a distress. [1720–30; DISTRAIN + *-t,* modeled on CONSTRAINT, RESTRAINT]

dis•trait (di strā′; *Fr.* dēs tre′), *adj.* inattentive because of distracting worries, fears, etc.; absent-minded. [1740–50; < F < L *distractus;* see DISTRACT]

dis•traite (di strāt′; *Fr.* dēs tret′), *adj.* (of a woman) inattentive because of distracting worries, fears, etc.; absent-minded. [1840–50; < F, fem. of *distrait* DISTRAIT]

dis•traught (di strôt′), *adj.* **1.** distracted; deeply agitated. **2.** mentally deranged; crazed. [1350–1400; ME var. of obs. *distract* distracted, by assoc. with *straught,* old ptp. of STRETCH] **—dis•traught′ly,** *adv.*

dis•tress (di stres′), *n.* **1.** great pain, anxiety, or sorrow; acute physical or mental suffering; affliction; trouble. **2.** a state of extreme necessity or misfortune. **3.** the state of a ship or airplane requiring immediate assistance, as when on fire in transit. **4.** that which causes pain, suffering, trouble, danger, etc. **5.** liability or exposure to pain, suffering, trouble, etc.; danger: *a damsel in distress.* **6.** *Law.* **a.** the legal seizure and detention of the goods of another as security or satisfaction for debt, etc.; the act of distraining. **b.** the thing seized in distraining. **7.** to dent, scratch, or stain (furniture, lumber, or the like) so as to give an appearance of age. *—adj.* **8.** afflicted with or suffering distress: *distress livestock; distress wheat.* **9.** caused by or indicative of distress or hardship: *distress prices; distress borrowing.* *—v.t.* **10.** to afflict with great pain, anxiety, or sorrow; trouble; worry; bother. **11.** to subject to pressure, stress, or strain; embarrass or exhaust by strain: *to be distressed by excessive work.* **12.** to compel by pain or force of circumstances: *His suffering distressed him into committing suicide.* [1250–1300; (n.) ME *destresse* < AF *distresse, destresse,* OF < VL **districtia,* equiv. to L *district(us)* (see DISTRICT) + *-ia* -Y[3]; (v.) ME *destressen* < AF *destresser* (OF *destrecier*), deriv. of the n.] **—dis•tress′ing•ly,** *adv.*
—Syn. 1. agony, anguish, adversity, tribulation. See **sorrow. 2.** need, destitution. **—Ant. 1.** comfort.

distress′ call′, 1. a prearranged communication code sign indicating that the sender is in a situation of peril, distress, or the like, as SOS, Mayday, etc. Cf. **distress signal** (def. 1). **2.** a communication prompted by or indicating distress: *The hospital sent out distress calls for all available stocks of the antitoxin.* [1910–15]

dis•tressed (di strest′), *adj.* **1.** affected with or suffering from distress. **2.** (of merchandise or property for sale) damaged, out-of-date, or used. **3.** (of real estate) foreclosed and offered for sale. **4.** (of furniture) purposely blemished or marred so as to give an antique appearance. **5.** (of fabric) made or processed to appear faded or wrinkled, as if from long, steady use: *Our best-selling jeans are the ones in distressed denim.* [1580–90; DISTRESS + -ED[2]] **—dis•tress•ed•ly** (di stres′id lē, -strest′lē), *adv.* **—dis•tress′ed•ness,** *n.*

distressed′ ar′ea, 1. a region so severely damaged by a flood, hurricane, or other natural catastrophe that its inhabitants need food, clothing, shelter, and economic aid from national charities or the federal government. **2.** See **depressed area.** [1925–30]

distress′ flag′, any flag flown by a vessel to show that it is in distress, as an ensign flown at half-mast or upside down.

distress′ fre′quency, a radio frequency band reserved for emergency signals from aircraft or ships in distress.

dis•tress•ful (di stres′fəl), *adj.* **1.** causing or involving distress: *the distressful circumstances of poverty and sickness.* **2.** full of, feeling, or indicating distress: *a distressful cry.* [1585–95; DISTRESS + -FUL] **—dis•tress′ful•ly,** *adv.* **—dis•tress′ful•ness,** *n.*

distress′ gun′, *Naut.* a gun fired at one-minute intervals as a signal of distress. [1815–25]

distress′ mer′chandise, *Com.* **1.** goods sold below the prevailing price in order to raise cash quickly or to meet some other financial emergency. **2.** damaged goods sold below fair-trade prices. Also, **distressed′ mer′chandise.** Also called **distressed′ goods′.**

distress′ sale′, a sale held for the purpose of raising money to meet emergency expenses and usually offering goods at a substantial discount for the payment of cash. [1880–85]

distress′ sig′nal, 1. a signal used, or designed to be used, by persons in peril, for the purpose of summoning aid, indicating their position, etc., as a radio code sign, aerial flare, flag hoist, or the like. Cf. **distress call** (def. 1). **2.** an indication, esp. a nonverbal one, that assistance, cooperation, or the like, is needed: *He correctly interpreted the host's upturned eyes as a distress signal and hastily changed the subject.* [1870–75]

dis•trib•u•tar•y (di strib′yo͞o ter′ē), *n., pl.* **-tar•ies.** an outflowing branch of a stream or river, typically found in a delta (opposed to *tributary*). [1535–45; DISTRIBUTE + -ARY]

dis•trib•ute (di strib′yo͞ot), *v.t.,* **-ut•ed, -ut•ing. 1.** to divide and give out in shares; deal out; allot. **2.** to disperse through a space or over an area; spread; scatter. **3.** to promote, sell, and ship or deliver (an item or line of merchandise) to individual customers, esp. in a specified region or area. **4.** to pass out or deliver (mail, newspapers, etc.) to intended recipients. **5.** to divide into distinct phases: *The process was distributed into three stages.* **6.** to divide into classes: *These plants are distributed into 22 classes.* **7.** *Logic.* to employ (a term) in a proposition so as to refer to all individuals denoted by the term. **8.** *Physical Chem.* to dissolve uniformly in a solvent consisting of layers of immiscible or partially miscible substances. **9.** *Print.* **a.** to roll out (ink) on the table to attain the proper consistency. **b.** to return (type) to the proper place after printing. [1400–50; late ME < L *distribūtus,* ptp. of *distribuere* to divide up. See DIS-[1], TRIBUTE] **—dis•trib′ut•a•ble,** *adj.*
—Syn. 1. assign, mete, apportion. DISTRIBUTE, DISPENSE apply to giving out something. DISTRIBUTE implies apportioned, individualized giving, esp. of something that is definite or limited in amount or number: *The prizes were distributed among ten winners.* DISPENSE formerly implied indiscriminate, general, and liberal giving, esp. of something that was more or less indefinite or unmeasured in amount: *to dispense largess.* It now applies chiefly to giving according to need or deserts, from an organized and official source: *to dispense medicines and food to the victims.* **6.** dispose, sort, arrange, categorize.

dis•trib•ut•ed (di strib′yo͞o tid), *adj. Ling.* (in distinctive feature analysis) characterized by relatively extensive contact or constriction between the articulating organs, as the (sh) in *show* in contrast to the (s) in *so.* [DISTRIBUTE + -ED[2]]

distrib′uted da′ta proc′essing, *Computers.* a method of organizing data processing that uses a central computer in combination with smaller local computers or terminals, which communicate with the central computer and perhaps with one another. Also called **DDP.**

dis•trib•u•tee (di strib′yo͞o tē′), *n.* **1.** *Law.* a person who shares in a decedent estate. **2.** a person to whom something is distributed. [1865–70, *Amer.;* DISTRIBUTE + -EE]

dis•trib•ut•er (di strib′yə tər), *n.* distributor.

dis•tri•bu•tion (dis′trə byo͞o′shən), *n.* **1.** an act or instance of distributing. **2.** the state or manner of being distributed. **3.** arrangement; classification. **4.** something that is distributed. **5.** the frequency of occurrence or the natural geographic range or place where any item or category of items occurs: *What is the distribution of coniferous forests in the world?* **6.** placement, location, arrangement, or disposition: *The distribution of our troops is a military secret.* **7.** apportionment: *The court decided the distribution of the property among the heirs.* **8.** the delivery or giving out of an item or items to the intended recipients, as mail or newspapers. **9.** the total number of an item delivered, sold, or given out: *The distribution of our school paper is now 800.* **10.** the marketing, transporting, merchandising, and selling of any item. **11.** (in bridge and other card games) the way in which the suits of a deck of cards are, or one specific suit is, divided or apportioned in one player's hand or among the hands of all the players: *My distribution was six spades, four hearts, two clubs, and a singleton diamond.* **12.** *Econ.* **a.** the division of the aggregate income of any society among its members, or among the factors of production. **b.** the system of dispersing goods throughout a community. **13.** *Statistics.* a set of values or measurements of a set of elements, each measurement being associated with an element. **14.** *Math.* a generalized function used esp. in solving differential equations. [1375–1425; late ME (< AF) < L *distribūtiōn-* (s. of *distribūtiō*). See DISTRIBUTE, -ION] **—dis′tri•bu′tion•al,** *adj.*

distribu′tion curve′, *Statistics.* the curve or line of a graph in which cumulative frequencies are plotted as ordinates and values of the variate as abscissas.

distribu′tion func′tion, *Statistics.* (of any random variable) the function that assigns to each number the probability that the random variable takes a value less than or equal to the given number. [1905–10]

dis•trib•u•tive (di strib′yə tiv), *adj.* **1.** serving to distribute, assign, allot, or divide; characterized by or pertaining to distribution. **2.** *Gram.* referring to the members of a group individually, as the adjectives *each* and *every.* **3.** *Logic.* (of a term) distributed in a given proposition. **4.** *Math.* **a.** (of a binary operation) having the property that terms in an expression may be expanded in a particular way to form an equivalent expression, as $a(b + c) = ab + ac$. **b.** having reference to this property: *distributive law for multiplication over addition.* **c.** (of a lattice) having the property that for any three elements, the intersection of the first element with the union of the others is equal to the intersection of the first element with each of the others. *—n.* **5.** a distributive word or expression. [1425–75; late ME *distributif* < MF < LL *distribūtīvus* (see DISTRIBUTE, -IVE)] **—dis•trib′u•tive•ly,** *adv.* **—dis•trib′u•tive•ness,** *n.*

distrib′utive educa′tion, a special program of vocational education at the high-school level in which a student is employed part-time, receiving on-the-job training, and also attends classes, most of which pertain directly to the student's vocational field. [1945–50]

dis•trib•u•tor (di strib′yə tər), *n.* **1.** a person or thing that distributes. **2.** *Com.* **a.** a person, firm, etc., engaged in the general distribution or marketing of some article or class of goods. **b.** a wholesaler who has exclusive rights to market, within a given territory, the goods of a manufacturer or company. **3.** *Auto., Mach.* a device in a multicylinder engine that distributes the igniting voltage to the spark plugs in a definite sequence. **4.** *Print.* **a.** (in a press) one of the rollers for spreading ink on the table, rolling it to a proper consistency, and transferring it to rollers that ink the form or plate. **b.** Also called **distrib′utor bar′.** (in a Linotype) a bar with keylike cuts along its length, for sorting matrices into their proper magazines after type has been cast. Also, **distributer.** [1520–30; < LL *distribūtor.* See DISTRIBUTE, -TOR]

dis•trib•u•tor•ship (di strib′yə tər ship′), *n. Com.* a franchise held by a distributor. [1815–25; DISTRIBUTOR + -SHIP]

dis•trict (dis′trikt), *n.* **1.** a division of territory, as of a country, state, or county, marked off for administrative, electoral, or other purposes. **2.** a region or locality: *the theater district; the Lake District.* **3.** *Brit.* a subdivision of a county or a town. **4. the District,** the District of Columbia; Washington, D.C. *—v.t.* **5.** to divide into districts. [1605–15; (< F) < ML *districtus* exercise of justice, (area of) jurisdiction, deriv. of L *distringere* to stretch out (see DISTRAIN), equiv. to *di-* DI-[2] + *strig-* (base of *stringere* to bind, tie) + *-tus* suffix of verbal action]

dis′trict attor′ney, an officer who acts as attorney for the people or government within a specified district. [1780–90, *Amer.*]

dis′trict coun′cil, *Brit.* the local ruling body of an urban or rural district. [1890–95]

dis′trict court′, *U.S. Law.* **1.** (in many states) the court of general jurisdiction. **2.** the federal trial court sitting in each district of the United States. [1780–90, *Amer.*]

CONCISE ETYMOLOGY KEY: <, descended or borrowed from; >, whence; b., blend of, blended; c., cognate with; cf., compare; deriv., derivative; equiv., equivalent; imit., imitative; obl., oblique; r., replacing; s., stem; sp., spelling, spelled; resp., respelling, respelled; trans., translation; ?, origin unknown; *, unattested; ‡, probably earlier than. See the full key inside the front cover.

dis′trict judge′, any judge of a federal district court. [1780–90, *Amer.*]

dis′trict man′, a legman who covers a beat for a newspaper.

Dis′trict of Colum′bia, a federal area in the E United States, on the Potomac, coextensive with the federal capital, Washington. 637,651; 69 sq. mi. (179 sq. km). *Abbr.:* DC (for use with zip code), D.C.

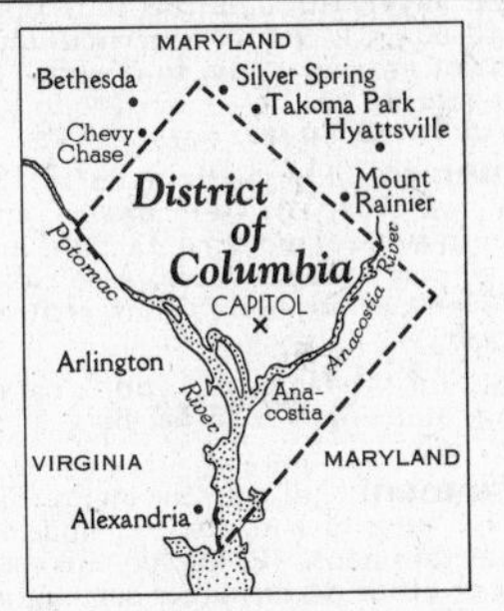

Dis·tri·to Fe·de·ral (dēs tʀē′tô fe′the ʀäl′), *Spanish.* See **Federal District.** *Abbr.:* D.F.

dis·trust (dis trust′), *v.t.* **1.** to regard with doubt or suspicion; have no trust in. —*n.* **2.** lack of trust; doubt; suspicion. [1505–15; DIS-[1] + TRUST] —**dis·trust′er,** *n.*
—**Syn. 2.** See **suspicion.**

dis·trust·ful (dis trust′fəl), *adj.* unable or unwilling to trust; doubtful; suspicious: *An alert scientist is distrustful of coincidences.* [1585–95; DISTRUST + -FUL] —**dis·trust′ful·ly,** *adv.* —**dis·trust′ful·ness,** *n.*

dis·turb (di stûrb′), *v.t.* **1.** to interrupt the quiet, rest, peace, or order of; unsettle. **2.** to interfere with; interrupt; hinder: *Please do not disturb me when I'm working.* **3.** to interfere with the arrangement, order, or harmony of; disarrange: *to disturb the papers on her desk.* **4.** to perplex; trouble: *to be disturbed by strange behavior.* —*v.i.* **5.** to cause disturbance to someone's sleep, rest, etc.: *Do not disturb.* [1175–1225; ME *disto(u)rben, disturben* < AF *disto(u)rber, desturber* < L *disturbāre* to demolish, upset, equiv. to *dis-* DIS-[1] + *turbāre* to confuse] —**dis·turb′er,** *n.*
—**Syn. 1.** bother, annoy, trouble, pester.

dis·turb·ance (di stûr′bəns), *n.* **1.** the act of disturbing. **2.** the state of being disturbed. **3.** an instance of this; commotion. **4.** something that disturbs. **5.** an outbreak of disorder; a breach of public peace: *Political disturbances shook the city.* **6.** *Meteorol.* any cyclonic storm or low-pressure area, usually a small one. **7.** *Geol.* a crustal movement of moderate intensity, somewhat restricted in area. [1250–1300; ME *disto(u)rbance* < AF, OF. See DISTURB, -ANCE]
—**Syn. 2.** perturbation, confusion. See **agitation. 5.** confusion, tumult, riot. See **disorder.** —**Ant. 3.** order.

dis·turbed (di stûrbd′), *adj.* **1.** marked by symptoms of mental illness: *a disturbed personality.* **2.** agitated or distressed; disrupted: *disturbed seas; a disturbed situation.* —*n.* **3.** (*used with a plural v.*) persons who exhibit symptoms of neurosis or psychosis (usually prec. by *the*). [1585–95; DISTURB + -ED[2]]

dis·turb·ing (di stûr′bing), *adj.* upsetting or disquieting; dismaying: *a disturbing increase in the crime rate.* [1585–95; DISTURB + -ING[2]] —**dis·turb′ing·ly,** *adv.*

disty., distillery.

dis·tyle (dis′tīl, dī′stīl), *adj. Archit.* **1.** having two columns. **2.** (of a classical temple or building in the style of one) having two columns on one or either front. Also, **di·sty·lar** (dī stī′lər), **dyostyle.** [1830–40; DI-[1] + -STYLE[2]]

di·sub·sti·tut·ed (dī sub′sti to͞o′tid, -tyo͞o′-), *adj. Chem.* containing two substituents. [1885–90; DI-[1] + SUBSTITUTED]

di·sul·fate (dī sul′fāt), *n. Chem.* a salt of pyrosulfuric acid, as sodium disulfate, $Na_2S_2O_7$. Also, **disulphate.** [1830–40; DI-[1] + SULFATE]

di·sul·fide (dī sul′fīd, -fid), *n. Chem.* **1.** (in inorganic chemistry) a sulfide containing two atoms of sulfur, as carbon disulfide, CS_2. **2.** (in organic chemistry) a sulfide containing the bivalent group –SS–, as diethyl disulfide, $C_4H_{10}S_2$. Also, **di·sul′phide.** [1860–65; DI-[1] + SULFIDE]

di·sul·fir·am (dī′sul fēr′əm), *n. Pharm.* a cream-colored, water-insoluble solid, $C_{10}H_{20}N_2S_4$, used chiefly in the treatment of chronic alcoholism, producing highly unpleasant symptoms when alcohol is taken following its administration. Also called **tetraethylthiuram disulfide.** [1950–55; DISULFI(DE) + (*thiu*)*ram;* see THIO-, UREA, AMYL]

di·sul·fo·ton (dī sul′fə ton′), *n. Chem.* a pale-yellow, highly toxic liquid, $C_8H_{19}O_2PS_3$, used as an insecticide and miticide. [1960–65; perh. DI-[1] + SULFO- + T(HI)ON-(ATE)]

di·sul·fu·ric (dī′sul fyo͝or′ik), *adj. Chem.* pyrosulfuric. Also, **di′sul·phu′ric.** [1870–75; DI-[1] + SULFURIC]

di·sul·phate (dī sul′fāt), *n. Chem.* disulfate.

dis·u·ni·fy (dis yo͞o′nə fī′), *v.t.,* **-fied, -fy·ing.** to destroy the unity of. [1890–95; DIS-[1] + UNIFY]

dis·un·ion (dis yo͞on′yən), *n.* **1.** a severance of union; separation; disjunction. **2.** lack of unity; dissension. [1590–1600; DIS-[1] + UNION]

dis·un·ion·ist (dis yo͞on′yə nist), *n.* **1.** a person who advocates or causes disunion. **2.** *U.S. Hist.* a secessionist during the period of the Civil War. [1825–35, *Amer.;* DISUNION + -IST] —**dis·un′ion·ism,** *n.*

dis·u·nite (dis′yo͞o nīt′), *v.,* **-nit·ed, -nit·ing.** —*v.t.* **1.** to sever the union of; separate; disjoin. **2.** to set at variance; alienate: *The issue disunited the party members.* —*v.i.* **3.** to part; fall apart. [1550–60; DIS-[1] + UNITE] —**dis′u·nit′er,** *n.*

dis·u·nity (dis yo͞o′ni tē), *n., pl.* **-ties.** lack of unity or accord. [1625–35; DIS-[1] + UNITY]

dis·use (*n.* dis yo͞os′; *v.* dis yo͞oz′), *n., v.,* **-used, -us·ing.** —*n.* **1.** discontinuance of use or practice: *Traditional customs are falling into disuse.* —*v.t.* **2.** to cease to use. [1375–1425; late ME. See DIS-[1], USE]

dis·u·til·i·ty (dis′yo͞o til′i tē), *n.* the quality of causing inconvenience, harm, distress, etc. [1875–80; DIS-[1] + UTILITY]

dis·val·ue (dis val′yo͞o), *n., v.,* **-ued, -u·ing.** —*n.* **1.** disesteem; disparagement. —*v.t.* **2.** *Archaic.* to depreciate; disparage. [1595–1605; DIS-[1] + VALUE]

di·syl·lab·ic (dī′si lab′ik, dis′i-), *adj.* consisting of or pertaining to two syllables. Also, **dissyllabic.** [1630–40; DI-[1] + SYLLABIC]

di·syl·la·bism (dī sil′ə biz′əm, di-), *n.* the state of being disyllabic. Also, **dissyllabism.** [1880–85; DI-[1] + SYLLABISM]

di·syl·la·bize (dī sil′ə bīz′, di-), *v.t.,* **-bized, -biz·ing.** to make disyllabic. Also, **dissyllabize;** *esp. Brit.,* **di·syl′la·bise′.** [1865–70; DISYLLABLE + -IZE]

di·syl·la·ble (dī′sil′ə bəl, dī sil′-, di-), *n.* a word of two syllables. Also, **dissyllable.** [1580–90; DI-[1] + SYLLABLE; cf. Gk *disýllabos* of two syllables; var. *dissyllable* has *ss* < MF *dissilabe*]

dis·yoke (dis yōk′), *v.t.,* **-yoked, -yok·ing.** to free from or as from a yoke. [1840–50; DIS-[1] + YOKE]

dit (dit), *n.* an echoic word, the referent of which is a click or brief tone interval, used to designate the dot of Morse code, International Morse code, etc. Cf. **dah.** [1935–40]

di·tat De·us (dē′tät de′o͝os; *Eng.* dī′tat dē′əs, dā′əs), *Latin.* God enriches: motto of Arizona.

ditch (dich), *n.* **1.** a long, narrow excavation made in the ground by digging, as for draining or irrigating land; trench. **2.** any open passage or trench, as a natural channel or waterway. —*v.t.* **3.** to dig a ditch or ditches in or around. **4.** to derail (a train) or drive or force (an automobile, bus, etc.) into a ditch. **5.** to crash-land on water and abandon (an airplane). **6.** *Slang.* **a.** to get rid of: *I ditched that old hat of yours.* **b.** to escape from: *He ditched the cops by driving down an alley.* **c.** to absent oneself from (school or a class) without permission or an acceptable reason. —*v.i.* **7.** to dig a ditch. **8.** (of an aircraft or its crew) to crash-land in water and abandon the sinking aircraft. **9.** *Slang.* to be truant; play hooky. [bef. 900; 1940–45 for def. 5, 1885–90 for def. 6, 1955–60 for def. 9; ME *dich,* OE *dīc;* c. G *Teich.* See DIKE[1]] —**ditch′less,** *adj.*

ditch·dig·ger (dich′dig′ər), *n.* **1.** a worker whose occupation is digging ditches, esp. with pick and shovel. **2.** a person engaged in exhausting manual work, esp. work that requires little or no originality. **3.** Also called **ditcher, trencher.** a power excavating machine designed to remove earth in a continuous line and to a predetermined width and depth, as by means of a rotating belt equipped with scoops. [1895–1900; DITCH + DIGGER] —**ditch′dig′ging,** *n., adj.*

ditch·er (dich′ər), *n.* **1.** a person who digs ditches. **2.** a person who ditches. **3.** ditchdigger (def. 3). [1350–1400; ME *dicher.* See DITCH, -ER[1]]

ditch-moss (dich′môs′, -mos′), *n.* elodea. [1830–40; *Amer.*]

ditch·wa·ter (dich′wô′tər, -wot′ər), *n.* **1.** water, esp. stagnant and dirty water, that has collected in a ditch. **2. dull as ditchwater.** See **dishwater** (def. 2). [1275–1325; ME. See DITCH, WATER]

dite (dīt), *n. Brit. Dial.* a bit (usually used in negative constructions): *I don't care a dite.* [1905–10; reflecting regional pron. of DOIT, in the sense "trifle"]

di·the·ism (dī′thē iz′əm), *n.* **1.** the doctrine of or belief in two equally powerful gods. **2.** belief in the existence of two independent antagonistic principles, one good and the other evil, as in Zoroastrianism. [1670–80; DI-[1] + THEISM] —**di′the·ist,** *n.* —**di′the·is′tic, di′the·is′ti·cal,** *adj.*

dith·er (dith′ər), *n.* **1.** a trembling; vibration. **2.** a state of flustered excitement or fear. —*v.i.* **3.** to act irresolutely; vacillate. **4.** *North Eng.* to tremble with excitement or fear. [1640–50; var. of *didder* (late ME *diddere*); cf. DODDER] —**dith′er·er,** *n.* —**dith′er·y,** *adj.*

di·thi·o·nate (dī thī′ə nāt′, -nit), *n. Chem.* a salt of dithionic acid. [1865–70; DITHION(IC ACID) + -ATE[2]]

di·thi·on·ic (dī′thī on′ik, dith′ē-), *adj. Chem.* of or derived from dithionic acid. [1850–55; DI-[1] + THIONIC]

di′thion′ic ac′id, *Chem.* a strong, unstable acid, $H_2S_2O_6$, known only in solution and in the form of its salts. [1850–55]

dith·y·ramb (dith′ə ram′, -ramb′), *n.* **1.** a Greek choral song or chant of vehement or wild character and of usually irregular form, originally in honor of Dionysus or Bacchus. **2.** any poem or other composition having similar characteristics, as an impassioned or exalted theme or irregular form. **3.** any wildly enthusiastic speech or writing. [1595–1605; < L *dithyrambus* < Gk *dithýrambos*]

dith·y·ram·bic (dith′ə ram′bik), *adj.* **1.** of, pertaining to, or of the nature of a dithyramb. **2.** wildly irregular in form. **3.** wildly enthusiastic. [1595–1605; < L *dithyrambicus* < Gk *dithyrambikós.* See DITHYRAMB, -IC] —**dith′y·ram′bi·cal·ly,** *adv.*

Dit·mars (dit′märz), *n.* **Raymond Lee,** 1876–1942, U.S. zoologist and author.

dit·o·kous (dit′ə kəs), *adj.* **1.** producing two young or laying two eggs at a time. **2.** producing two kinds of young, as certain worms. [< Gk *ditókos* twin-bearing, equiv. to *di-* DI-[1] + *-tókos* childbearing; see -OUS]

di·tri·glyph (dī trī′glif′), *n.* (in Doric architecture) **1.** the distance, on centers, between a metope and the second one distant. **2.** an intercolumniation having two whole triglyphs. [1720–30; < F *ditriglyphe.* See DI-[1], TRIGLYPH] —**di′tri·glyph′ic,** *adj.*

di·tro·chee (dī′trō′kē), *n. Pros.* a form of poetic meter in which two trochees constitute one metrical unit. [1700–10; < L *ditrochaeus* < Gk *ditróchaios,* equiv. to *di-* DI-[1] + *trochaîos* TROCHEE]

dit·sy (dit′sē), *adj.,* **-si·er, -si·est.** *Slang.* flighty and easily confused; mildly or harmlessly eccentric. Also, **ditzy.** [1975–80; expressive coinage, perh. with elements of DOTTY[1] and DIZZY; cf. -SY]

dit·ta·ny (dit′n ē), *n., pl.* **-nies. 1.** a Cretan plant, *Origanum dictamnus,* of the mint family, having spikes of purple flowers and formerly believed to have medicinal qualities. **2.** Also called **stone mint.** a North American plant, *Cunila origanoides,* of the mint family, bearing clusters of purplish flowers. **3.** See **gas plant.** [1350–1400; ME *ditane, detany* < OF *dita(i)n* < L *dictamnus, dictamnum* < Gk *díktamnon,* perh. akin to *Díktē,* a mountain in Crete where the herb abounded]

Dit·ters·dorf (dit′ərz dôrf′; *Ger.* dit′əʀs dôʀf′), *n.* **Karl Dit·ters von** (kärl dit′əʀs fən), 1739–99, Austrian violinist and composer.

dit·to (dit′ō), *n., pl.* **-tos,** *adv., v.,* **-toed, -to·ing.** —*n.* **1.** the aforesaid; the above; the same (used in accounts, lists, etc., to avoid repetition). *Abbr.:* do. *Symbol:* ″. Cf. **ditto mark. 2.** another of the same. **3.** *Informal.* a duplicate; copy. —*adv.* **4.** as already stated; likewise. —*v.t.* **5.** to make a copy of, using a Ditto machine. **6.** to duplicate or repeat the action or statement of (another person). [1615–25; < It, var. of *detto* < L *dictus* said, ptp. of *dicere* to say; see DICTUM]

dit·to·graph (dit′ə graf′, -gräf′), *n.* an instance of dittography; a passage containing reduplicated syllables, etc. [1870–75; back formation from DITTOGRAPHY]

dit·tog·ra·phy (di tog′rə fē), *n.* reduplication of letters or syllables in writing, printing, etc., usually through error. Cf. **haplography.** [1870–75; < Gk *dittographía,* dial. var. of *dissographía,* equiv. to *dissó(s)* double + *-graphia* -GRAPHY] —**dit·to·graph·ic** (dit′ə graf′ik), *adj.*

Dit′to machine′, *Trademark.* a brand of machine that copies typed or written material, drawings, etc., esp. by an ink-transfer process.

dit′to mark′, Often, **ditto marks.** two small marks (″) indicating the repetition of something, usually placed beneath the thing repeated.

dit·ty (dit′ē), *n., pl.* **-ties,** *v.,* **-tied, -ty·ing.** —*n.* **1.** a poem intended to be sung. **2.** a short, simple song. —*v.i.* **3.** *Obs.* to sing. —*v.t.* **4.** *Obs.* to set to or celebrate in music. [1250–1300; ME *dite* < AF, OF *dit(i)e* poem, n. use of ptp. of *ditier* to compose < L *dictāre;* see DICTATE]

dit′ty bag′, a small bag used esp. by sailors to hold sewing implements, toiletries, etc. [1855–60; of obscure orig.]

dit′ty box′, a small box used like a ditty bag. [1880–85; *Amer.*]

ditz (dits), *n. Slang.* airhead[2]. [1980–85; back formation from DITZY]

dit·zy (dit′sē), *adj.,* **-zi·er, -zi·est.** ditsy.

Di·u (dē′o͞o), *n.* part of the union territory of Goa, Daman, and Diu, in W India: a former Portuguese colony, comprising a small island and seaport at the extremity of Kathiawar peninsula. See **Goa, Daman, and Diu.**

di·u·re·sis (dī′ə rē′sis), *n.* increased discharge of urine. [1675–85; < NL < Gk *diourē-* (verbal s. of *diourein* to urinate) + *-sis* -SIS; see DIURETIC]

di·u·ret·ic (dī′ə ret′ik), *adj.* **1.** increasing the volume of the urine excreted, as by a medicinal substance. —*n.* **2.** a diuretic medicine or agent. [1375–1425; ME *d(i)uretik* < LL *diūrēticus* < Gk *diourētikós,* equiv. to *di-* DI-[3] + *ourē-* (verbid s. of *ourein* to urinate) + *-tikos* -TIC] —**di′u·ret′i·cal·ly,** *adv.* —**di′u·ret′i·cal·ness,** *n.*

Di·ur·il (dī′ər il), *Pharm., Trademark.* a brand of chlorothiazide.

di·ur·nal (dī ûr′nl), *adj.* **1.** of or pertaining to a day or each day; daily. **2.** of or belonging to the daytime (opposed to *nocturnal*). **3.** *Bot.* showing a periodic alteration of condition with day and night, as certain flowers that open by day and close by night. **4.** active by day, as certain birds and insects (opposed to *nocturnal*). —*n.* **5.** *Liturgy.* a service book containing offices for the daily hours of prayer. **6.** *Archaic.* a diary. **7.** *Archaic.* a newspaper, esp. a daily one. [1400–50; late ME < L *diurnālis,* equiv. to *diurn(us)* daily + *-ālis* -AL[1]] —**di·ur′nal·ly,** *adv.* —**di·ur′nal·ness,** *n.*

diur′nal arc′, *Astron.* the portion of the diurnal circle that is above the horizon at a given point. Cf. **nocturnal arc.**

diur′nal cir′cle, *Astron.* the apparent circle described by a heavenly body as a result of one rotation by the earth.

diur′nal mo′tion, *Astron.* the apparent daily motion, caused by the earth's rotation, of celestial bodies across the sky.

diur′nal par′allax, *Astron.* See under **parallax** (def. 2).

di·u·ron (dī′ə ron′), *n.* a white crystalline substance, $C_9H_{10}Cl_2N_2O$, used as a weed-killer. [1955–60; *di*(*chlorophenyl*) + (*dimethyl*)*ur*(*ea*) + -ON[1]]

Div., **1.** divine. **2.** divinity.

div, **1.** *Math., Mech.* divergence. **2.** *Music.* divisi.

div., **1.** divide. **2.** divided. **3.** dividend. **4.** division. **5.** divisor. **6.** divorced.

di·va (dē′və, -vä), *n., pl.* **-vas, -ve** (-ve). a distinguished female singer; prima donna. [1880–85; < It < L *dīva,* fem. of *dīvus* god; cf. DIVINE]

di·va·gate (dī′və gāt′), *v.i.,* **-gat·ed, -gat·ing. 1.** to wander; stray. **2.** to digress in speech. [1590–1600; < L *dīvagātus* (ptp. of *dīvagārī* to wander off), equiv. to *dī-* DI-[2] + *vag-* (s. of *vagārī* to wander) + *-ātus* -ATE[1]] **—di′va·ga′tion,** *n.*

di·va·lent (dī vā′lənt), *adj. Chem.* having a valence of two, as the ferrous ion, Fe^{++}. [1865–70; DI-[1] + -VALENT] **—di·va′lence,** *n.*

Di·va·li (di vä′lē), *n.* Diwali.

di·van[1] (di van′, -vän′ *or, esp. for 1,* dī′van), *n.* **1.** a sofa or couch, usually without arms or back, often usable as a bed. **2.** a long, cushioned seat, usually without arms or back, placed against a wall, as in Oriental countries. **3.** a council of state in Turkey and other countries of the Middle East. **4.** any council, committee, or commission. **5.** (in the Middle East) **a.** a council chamber, judgment hall, audience chamber, or bureau of state. **b.** a large building used for some official or public purpose, as a custom house. **6.** a smoking room, as in connection with a tobacco shop. **7.** a collection of poems, esp. a collection in Arabic or Persian of poems by one poet. [1580–90; < Turk < Pers *dīwān,* orig. *dēvan* booklet (whence account book, office, council, bench)]

di·van[2] (di van′), *adj.* (esp. of chicken or turkey breast) sliced and baked in a casserole with broccoli and hollandaise sauce. [of uncert. orig.; perh. a representation in E sp. of F *divin* DIVINE]

di·var·i·cate (*v.* dī var′i kāt′, di-; *adj.* dī var′ə kit, -kāt′, di-), *v.,* **-cat·ed, -cat·ing,** *adj.* **—***v.i.* **1.** to spread apart; branch; diverge. **2.** *Bot., Zool.* to branch at a wide angle. **—***adj.* **3.** spread apart; widely divergent. **4.** *Bot., Zool.* branching at a wide angle. [1615–25; < L *dīvāricātus* (ptp. of *dīvāricāre*), equiv. to *dī* DI-[2] + *vāric-* (base of *vāricāre* to straddle; see PREVARICATE) + *-ātus* -ATE[1]] **—di·var′i·cate·ly,** *adv.* **—di·var′i·cat′ing·ly,** *adv.* **—di·var′i·ca′tion,** *n.* **—di·var′i·ca′tor,** *n.*

dive (dīv), *v.,* **dived** or **dove, dived, div·ing,** *n.* **—***v.i.* **1.** to plunge into water, esp. headfirst. **2.** to go below the surface of the water, as a submarine. **3.** to plunge, fall, or descend through the air, into the earth, etc.: *The acrobats dived into nets.* **4.** *Aeron.* (of an airplane) to descend rapidly. **5.** to penetrate suddenly into something, as with the hand: *to dive into one's purse.* **6.** to dart: *to dive into a doorway.* **7.** to enter deeply or plunge into a subject, activity, etc. **—***v.t.* **8.** to cause to plunge, submerge, or descend. **9.** to insert quickly; plunge: *He dived his hand into his pocket.* **—***n.* **10.** an act or instance of diving. **11.** a jump or plunge into water, esp. in a prescribed way from a diving board. **12.** the vertical or nearly vertical descent of an airplane at a speed surpassing the possible speed of the same plane in level flight. **13.** a submerging, as of a submarine or skindiver. **14.** a dash, plunge, or lunge, as if throwing oneself at or into something: *He made a dive for the football.* **15.** a sudden or sharp decline, as in stock prices. **16.** *Informal.* a dingy or disreputable bar or nightclub. **17.** *Boxing.* a false show of being knocked out, usually in a bout whose result has been prearranged: *to take a dive in an early round.* [bef. 900; ME *diven* to dive, dip, OE *dȳfan* to dip (causative of *dūfan* to dive, sink); c. ON *dȳfa* dip, G *taufen* to baptize; akin to DIP]
—Usage. Both DIVED and DOVE are standard as the past tense of DIVE. DIVED, historically the older form, is somewhat more common in edited writing, but DOVE occurs there so frequently that it also must be considered standard: *The rescuer dove into 20 feet of icy water.* DOVE is an Americanism that probably developed by analogy with alternations like *drive, drove* and *ride, rode.* It is the more common form in speech in the northern United States and in Canada, and its use seems to be spreading. The past participle of DIVE is always DIVED.

dive-bomb (dīv′bom′), *v.i., v.t.* to attack with or as if with a dive bomber. [1930–35]

dive′ bomb′er, an airplane of the fighter-bomber type that drops its bombs while diving at the enemy. [1935–40]

dive′ bomb′ing, *Mil.* a technique of bombing in which the bomb load is released when the aircraft is in a steep dive, usually at an angle of 60 degrees or more from horizontal. [1930–35]

dive′ brake′, *Aeron.* a flap deployed from the wings or fuselage of an aircraft, as a dive bomber or sailplane, that increases drag to permit a relatively steep angle of descent without a dangerous buildup in speed. [1935–40]

dive·mas·ter (dīv′mas′tər, -mä′stər), *n.* a professional qualified to oversee scuba diving operations, as in salvage work or at a resort, and responsible for procedures and safety, monitoring the whereabouts of divers underwater or at the surface, and making rescues when necessary. [DIVE + MASTER]

div·er (dī′vər), *n.* **1.** a person or thing that dives. **2.** a person who makes a business of diving, as for pearl oysters or to examine sunken vessels. **3.** *Brit.* a loon. **4.** any of several other birds noted for their skill in diving. [1500–10; DIVE + -ER[1]]

di·ver·bi·um (dī vûr′bē əm), *n., pl.* **-bi·a** (-bē ə). the spoken part of an ancient Roman drama. Cf. **canticum.** [< L; var. of *dēverbium,* equiv. to *dē-* DE- + *verb(um)* word, verb + *-ium* -IUM]

di·verge (di vûrj′, dī-), *v.,* **-verged, -verg·ing.** **—***v.i.* **1.** to move, lie, or extend in different directions from a common point; branch off. **2.** to differ in opinion, character, form, etc.; deviate. **3.** *Math.* (of a sequence, series, etc.) to have no unique limit; to have infinity as a limit. **4.** to turn aside or deviate, as from a path, practice, or plan. **—***v.t.* **5.** to deflect or turn aside. [1655–65; < ML *dīvergere,* equiv. to L *dī-* DI-[2] + *vergere* to incline]
—Syn. 1. separate, deviate, fork. **4.** See **deviate.**

di·ver·gence (di vûr′jəns, dī-), *n.* **1.** the act, fact, or amount of diverging: *a divergence in opinion.* **2.** (in physics, meteorology, etc.) the total amount of flux escaping an infinitesimal volume at a point in a vector field, as the net flow of air from a given region. **3.** *Ophthalm.* a turning motion of the eyeballs outward in relation to each other. **4.** *Electronics.* the spreading of a stream of electrons resulting from their mutual electrostatic repulsion. [1650–60; < ML *dīvergentia.* See DIVERGE, -ENCE]
—Syn. 1. separation, division, variation, deviation. **—Ant. 1.** convergence.

di·ver·gen·cy (di vûr′jən sē, dī-), *n., pl.* **-cies.** divergence; deviation. [1700–10; < ML *dīvergentia.* See DIVERGE, -ENCY]

di·ver·gent (di vûr′jənt, dī-), *adj.* **1.** diverging; differing; deviating. **2.** pertaining to or causing divergence. **3.** (of a mathematical expression) having no finite limits. [1690–1700; < ML *dīvergent-* (s. of *dīvergēns,* prp. of *dīvergere*). See DIVERGE, -ENT] **—di·ver′gent·ly,** *adv.*

diverg′ing lens′, *Optics.* a lens that causes a beam of parallel rays to diverge after refraction, as from a virtual image; a lens that has a negative focal length. Also called **negative lens.** Cf. **converging lens.**

di·vers (dī′vərz), *adj.* **1.** several; various; sundry: *divers articles.* **—***pron.* **2.** (*used with a plural v.*) an indefinite number more than one: *He chose divers of them, who were asked to accompany him.* [1200–50; ME < AF, OF < L *dīversus* DIVERSE]

di·verse (di vûrs′, dī-, dī′vûrs), *adj.* **1.** of a different kind, form, character, etc.; unlike: *a wide range of diverse opinions.* **2.** of various kinds or forms; multiform. [1275–1325; ME < L *dīversus* (ptp. of *dīvertere* to DIVERT), equiv. to *dī-* DI-[2] + *vert-* (base of *vertere* to turn) + *-tus* ptp. suffix] **—di·verse′ly,** *adv.* **—di·verse′·ness,** *n.*
—Syn. 1. varied, manifold, divergent. **2.** dissimilar, separate. See **various.**

di·ver·si·fi·ca·tion (di vûr′sə fi kā′shən, dī-), *n.* **1.** the act or process of diversifying; state of being diversified. **2.** the act or practice of manufacturing a variety of products, investing in a variety of securities, selling a variety of merchandise, etc., so that a failure in or an economic slump affecting one of them will not be disastrous. [1595–1605; < ML *dīversificātiōn-* (s. of *dīversificātiō*). See DIVERSIFY, -FICATION]

di·ver·si·fied (di vûr′sə fīd′, dī-), *adj.* **1.** distinguished by various forms or by a variety of objects: *diversified activity.* **2.** distributed among or producing several types; varied: *diversified investments.* [1605–15; DIVERSIFY + -ED[2]]

diver′sified farm′ing, the practice of producing a variety of crops or animals, or both, on one farm, as distinguished from specializing in a single commodity.

di·ver·si·form (di vûr′sə fôrm′, dī-), *adj.* differing in form; of various forms. [1650–60; < L *dīvers(us)* DIVERSE + -I- + -FORM]

di·ver·si·fy (di vûr′sə fī′, dī-), *v.,* **-fied, -fy·ing.** **—***v.t.* **1.** to make diverse, as in form or character; give variety or diversity to; variegate. **2.** to invest in different types of (securities, industries, etc.). **3.** to produce different types of (manufactured products, crops, etc.). **—***v.i.* **4.** to invest in different types of industries, securities, etc. **5.** to add different types of manufactured products, crops, etc., esp. to a business. [1400–50; late ME < AF *diversifier* < ML *dīversificāre,* equiv. to L *dīvers(us)* DIVERSE + *-ificāre* -IFY] **—di·ver′si·fi′a·ble,** *adj.* **—di·ver′si·fi′a·bil′i·ty,** *n.* **—di·ver′si·fi′er,** *n.*

di·ver·sion (di vûr′zhən, -shən, dī-), *n.* **1.** the act of diverting or turning aside, as from a course or purpose: *a diversion of industry into the war effort.* **2.** a channel made to divert the flow of water from one course to another or to direct the flow of water draining from a piece of ground. **3.** *Brit.* a detour on a highway or road. **4.** distraction from business, care, etc.; recreation; amusement; a pastime: *Movies are his favorite diversion.* **5.** *Mil.* a feint intended to draw off attention from the point of main attack. [1590–1600; < ML *dīversiōn-* (s. of *dīversiō*), equiv. to L *dīvers(us)* DIVERSE + *-iōn-* -ION]

di·ver·sion·al (di vûr′zhə nl, -shə-, dī-), *adj.* offering diversion or recreation; diverting. [DIVERSION + -AL[1]]

di·ver·sion·ar·y (di vûr′zhə ner′ē, -shə-, dī-), *adj.* tending to divert or distract the attention: *diversionary tactics of the guerrilla fighters.* [1840–50; DIVERSION + -ARY]

di·ver·sion·ist (di vûr′zhə nist, -shə-, dī-), *n.* **1.** a person engaged in activities that divert attention from a primary focus. **2.** a person who deviates politically. [1935–40; DIVERSION + -IST] **—di·ver′sion·ism,** *n.*

di·ver·si·ty (di vûr′si tē, dī-), *n., pl.* **-ties. 1.** the state or fact of being diverse; difference; unlikeness. **2.** variety; multiformity. **3.** a point of difference. [1300–50; ME *diversite* < AF < L *dīversitās.* See DIVERSE, -ITY]
—Syn. 2. change, difference, variation, dissimilarity.

di·vert (di vûrt′, dī-), *v.t.* **1.** to turn aside or from a path or course; deflect. **2.** *Brit.* to route (traffic) on a detour. **3.** to draw off to a different course, purpose, etc. **4.** to distract from serious occupation; entertain or amuse. **—***v.i.* **5.** to turn aside; veer: *It is sad to see so much talent divert to trivial occupations.* [1400–50; late ME < L *dīvertere,* equiv. to *dī-* DI-[2] + *vertere* to turn] **—di·vert′ed·ly,** *adv.* **—di·vert′er,** *n.* **—di·vert′i·ble,** *adj.*
—Syn. 4. delight. See **amuse.** **—Ant. 4.** bore.

di·ver·tic·u·li·tis (dī′vər tik′yə lī′tis), *n. Pathol.* inflammation of one or more diverticula, characterized by abdominal pain, fever, and changes in bowel movements. [1895–1900; DIVERTICUL(UM) + -ITIS]

di·ver·tic·u·lo·sis (dī′vər tik′yə lō′sis), *n. Pathol.* the presence of saclike herniations of the mucosal layer of the colon through the muscular wall, common among older persons and usually producing no symptoms except occasional rectal bleeding. [1915–20; DIVERTICUL(UM) + -OSIS]

di·ver·tic·u·lum (dī′vər tik′yə ləm), *n., pl.* **-la** (-lə). *Anat.* a blind, tubular sac or process branching off from a canal or cavity, esp. an abnormal, saclike herniation of the mucosal layer through the muscular wall of the colon. [1640–50; < L, var. of *dēverticulum* byway, tributary, means of escape, equiv. to *dēverti-* (comb. form of *dēvertere,* equiv. to *dē-* DE- + *vertere* to turn) + *-culum* -CULE[2]] **—di′ver·tic′u·lar,** *adj.*

di·ver·ti·men·to (di vûr′tə men′tō; *It.* dē veʀ′tē-men′tô), *n., pl.* **-tos, -ti** (-tē). *Music.* an instrumental composition in several movements, light and diverting in character, similar to a serenade. Also called **divertissement.** [1750–60; < It, equiv. to *diverti(re)* to DIVERT + *-mento* -MENT]

di·vert·ing (di vûr′ting, dī-), *adj.* serving to divert; entertaining; amusing. [1645–55; DIVERT + -ING[2]] **—di·vert′ing·ly,** *adv.*

di·ver·tisse·ment (di vûr′tis mənt; *Fr.* dē veʀ tēs-mäN′), *n., pl.* **-ments** (-mənts; *Fr.* -mäN′). **1.** a diversion or entertainment. **2.** *Music.* divertimento. **3.** a short ballet or other performance serving as an interlude in a play, opera, etc. **4.** a program consisting of such performances. [1720–30; < F, equiv. to *divertisse-* (s. of *divertir* to DIVERT) + *-ment* -MENT]

di·ver·tive (di vûr′tiv, dī-), *adj.* diverting; amusing. [1590–1600; DIVERT + -IVE]

Di·ves (dī′vēz), *n.* **1.** the rich man of the parable in Luke 16:19–31. **2.** any rich man. [< L *dīves* rich, rich man]

di·vest (di vest′, dī-), *v.t.* **1.** to strip of clothing, ornament, etc.: *The wind divested the trees of their leaves.* **2.** to strip or deprive (someone or something), esp. of property or rights; dispossess. **3.** to rid of or free from: *He divested himself of all responsibility for the decision.* **4.** *Law.* to take away or alienate (property, rights, etc.). **5.** *Com.* **a.** to sell off: *to divest holdings.* **b.** to rid of through sale: *The corporation divested itself of its subsidiaries.* [1595–1605; < ML *dīvestīre,* equiv. to *dī-* DI-[2] + *vestīre* to dress, VEST]
—Syn. 1. unclothe, denude. **2.** See **strip**[1].

di·ves·ti·ble (di ves′tə bəl, dī-), *adj.* capable of being divested, as an estate in land. [1640–50; DIVEST + -IBLE]

di·vest·i·ture (di ves′ti chər, -cho͝or′, dī-), *n.* **1.** the act of divesting. **2.** the state of being divested. **3.** something, as property or investments, that has been divested: *to reexamine the company's acquisitions and divestitures.* **4.** Also, **di·ves·ture** (di ves′chər, -cho͝or, dī-). the sale of business holdings or part of a company, esp. under legal compulsion. Also, **di·vest′ment.** [1595–1605; DI-[2] + (IN)VESTITURE]

dive′ ta′bles, numerical tables used by scuba divers to determine time limits of dives, according to depth, as well as possible decompression delays during ascent and requisite surface intervals between dives. Also called **decompression tables.**

divid., (in prescriptions) divide. [< L *dīvide*]

di·vid·a·ble (di vī′də bəl), *adj.* capable of being divided; divisible. [1580–90; DIVIDE + -ABLE] **—di·vid′a·ble·ness,** *n.*

di·vide (di vīd′), *v.,* **-vid·ed, -vid·ing,** *n.* **—***v.t.* **1.** to separate into parts, groups, sections, etc. **2.** to separate or part from something else; sunder; cut off. **3.** to deal out in parts; distribute in shares; apportion. **4.** to cleave; part. **5.** to separate in opinion or feeling; cause to disagree: *The issue divided the senators.* **6.** to distinguish the kinds of; classify. **7.** *Math.* **a.** to separate into equal parts by the process of mathematical division; apply the mathematical process of division to: *Eight divided by four is two.* **b.** to be a divisor of, without a remainder. **8.** to mark a uniform scale on (a ruler, thermometer, etc.). **9.** *Brit. Govt.* to separate (a legislature, assembly, etc.) into two groups in ascertaining the vote on a question. **—***v.i.* **10.** to become divided or separated. **11.** to share something with others. **12.** to diverge; branch; fork: *The road divides six miles from here.* **13.** to perform the mathematical process of division: *He could add and subtract but hadn't learned to divide.* **14.** *Brit. Govt.* to vote by separating into two groups. **—***n.* **15.** a division: *a divide in the road.* **16.** *Physical Geog.* the line or zone of higher ground between two adjacent streams or drainage basins. **17.** *Archaic.* the act of dividing. [1325–75; ME (< AF *divider*) < L *dīvidere* to separate, divide]
—Syn. 1. See **separate. 2.** sever, shear. **3.** partition, portion. **5.** alienate, estrange. **6.** sort, arrange, distribute. **—Ant. 1.** unite.

di·vid·ed (di vī′did), *adj.* **1.** separated; separate. **2.** disunited. **3.** shared; apportioned. **4.** (of a leaf) cut into distinct portions by incisions extending to the midrib or base. [1555–65; DIVIDE + -ED[2]] **—di·vid′ed·ly,** *adv.* **—di·vid′ed·ness,** *n.*

divid′ed high′way, a superhighway with a broad median strip, designed to prevent collisions, headlight glare, etc., between vehicles moving in opposite directions, and usually having limited or cloverleaf access. Also called **dual highway.** Cf. **autobahn.**

div·i·dend (div′i dend′), *n.* **1.** *Math.* a number that is to be divided by a divisor. **2.** *Law.* a sum out of an insolvent estate paid to creditors. **3.** *Finance.* **a.** a pro-rata share in an amount to be distributed. **b.** a sum of money paid to shareholders of a corporation out of earnings. **4.** *Insurance.* (in participating insurance) a distribution to a policyholder of a portion of the premium not needed by the company to pay claims or to meet expenses. **5.** a share of anything divided. **6.** anything received as a bonus, reward, or in addition to or beyond what is expected: *Swimming is fun, and gives you the*

dividend of better health. [1470–80; < L *dividendum* thing to be divided, neut. ger. of *dividere* to DIVIDE]
—Syn. 5. allotment, portion.

div′idend on′, *Stock Exchange.* cum dividend.

di•vi•den•dus (dĭ′vi den′dəs), *adj.* (in prescriptions) meant to be divided. [< L]

di•vid•er (di vī′dər), *n.* **1.** a person or thing that divides. **2. dividers,** a pair of compasses, as used for dividing lines, measuring, etc. **3.** a partition between two areas or dividing one area into two, as a piece of cardboard in a box or a bookcase jutting out from a wall. **4.** See **room divider. 5.** *Mining.* bunton. [1520–30; DIVIDE + -ER¹]

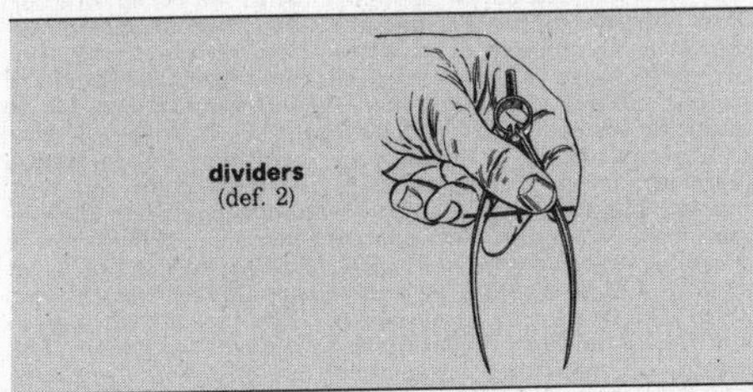

div•i•div•i (div′ē div′ē), *n., pl.* **div•i•div•is, div•i•div•i. 1.** a tropical American shrub or small tree, *Caesalpinia coriaria,* of the legume family, the astringent pods of which are used in tanning and dyeing. **2.** the related species *C. spinosa.* **3.** the pods of either plant. [1825–35; < Sp < Carib]

di•vid•u•al (di vij′o͞o əl), *adj. Archaic.* **1.** divisible or divided. **2.** separate; distinct. **3.** distributed; shared. [1590–1600; < L *dīvidu(us)* divisible (*divid(ere)* to DIVIDE + *-uus* deverbal adj. suffix) + -AL¹] **—di•vid′u•al•ly,** *adv.*

div•i•na•tion (div′ə nā′shən), *n.* **1.** the practice of attempting to foretell future events or discover hidden knowledge by occult or supernatural means. **2.** augury; prophecy: *The divination of the high priest was fulfilled.* **3.** perception by intuition; instinctive foresight. [1350–1400; ME *divinacioun* (< AF) < L *dīvīnātiōn-* (s. of *dīvīnātiō*), equiv. to *dīvīnāt(us),* ptp. of *dīvīnāre* to soothsay (*dīvīn-* DIVINE + *-ātus* -ATE¹) + *-iōn-* -ION] **—di•vin•a•to•ry** (di vin′ə tôr′ē, -tōr′ē), *adj.*

di•vine (di vīn′), *adj.,* **-vin•er, -vin•est,** *n., v.,* **-vined, -vin•ing.** *—adj.* **1.** of or pertaining to a god, esp. the Supreme Being. **2.** addressed, appropriated, or devoted to God or a god; religious; sacred: *divine worship.* **3.** proceeding from God or a god: *divine laws.* **4.** godlike; characteristic of or befitting a deity: *divine magnanimity.* **5.** heavenly; celestial: *the divine kingdom.* **6.** *Informal.* extremely good; unusually lovely: *He has the most divine tenor voice.* **7.** being a god; being God: *a divine person.* **8.** of superhuman or surpassing excellence: *Beauty is divine.* **9.** *Obs.* of or pertaining to divinity or theology. *—n.* **10.** a theologian; scholar in religion. **11.** a priest or member of the clergy. **12. the Divine, a.** God. **b.** (*sometimes l.c.*) the spiritual aspect of humans; the group of attributes and qualities of humankind regarded as godly or godlike. *—v.t.* **13.** to discover or declare (something obscure or in the future) by divination; prophesy. **14.** to discover (water, metal, etc.) by means of a divining rod. **15.** to perceive by intuition or insight; conjecture. **16.** *Archaic.* to portend. *—v.i.* **17.** to use or practice divination; prophesy. **18.** to have perception by intuition or insight; conjecture. [1275–1325; ME < L *dīvīnus,* equiv. to *dīv(us)* god + *-īnus* -INE¹; r. ME *devin(e)* < OF *devin* < L, as above] **—di•vin′a•ble,** *adj.* **—di•vine′ly,** *adv.* **—di•vine′ness,** *n.*
—Syn. 13, 17. foretell, predict, foresee, forecast. **15, 18.** discern, understand. **—Ant. 5.** worldly, mundane.

Divine′ Com′edy, (Italian, *Divina Commedia*), a narrative epic poem (14th century) by Dante.

divine′ heal′ing, 1. healing through divine intervention as in response to prayer or because of faith. **2.** a method employing prayer or faith in the hope of receiving such healing.

Divine′ Lit′urgy, *Chiefly Eastern Ch.* liturgy (def. 5). [1865–70]

Divine′ Mind′, *Christian Science.* mind (def. 18).

Divine′ Moth′er, *Hinduism.* the creative, dynamic aspect of the Godhead, the consort or Shakti of Brahma, Vishnu, or Shiva, variously known as Devi, Durga, Kali, Shakti, etc.

divine′ of′fice, (*sometimes caps.*) *Eccles.* office (def. 12c). [1350–1400; ME]

di•vin•er (di vī′nər), *n.* **1.** a person who divines; soothsayer; prophet. **2.** a person skilled in using a divining rod. [1300–50; DIVINE + -ER¹; r. ME *divinour* < AF < LL *dīvīnātor* soothsayer, equiv. to L *dīvīnā(re)* to DIVINE + *-tor* -TOR]

divine′ right′ of kings′, the right to rule derived directly from God, not from the consent of the people. [1735–45]

divine′ serv′ice, service¹ (def. 15). [1350–1400; ME]

div′ing bee′tle, any of numerous predaceous water beetles of the family Dytiscidae, having the body adapted for swimming.

div′ing bell′, a chamber with an open bottom in which persons can go underwater without special apparatus, water being excluded from the upper part by compressed air fed in by a hose. [1655–65]

div′ing board′, a springboard. [1890–95]

div′ing boat′, a boat used as a tender for divers or others working under water. [1795–1805]

div′ing duck′, any of numerous ducks, common in coastal bays and river mouths, that typically dive from the water's surface for their food (contrasted with *dabbling duck*). [1805–15]

div′ing pet′rel, any of several small seabirds of the family Pelecanoididae, of Southern Hemisphere seas, having compact bodies, tubelike processes near the nostrils, and usually drab plumage.

div′ing re′flex, *Physiol.* a reflex of humans, other mammals, reptiles, and birds, triggered by immersion in cold water, that slows the heart rate and diverts blood flow to the brain, heart, and lungs: serves to conserve oxygen until breathing resumes and to delay potential brain damage. [1975–80]

div′ing suit′, any of various waterproof garments for underwater swimming or diving, esp. one that is weighted, hermetically sealed, and supplied with air under pressure through a hose attached to a removable helmet. [1905–10]

divin′ing rod′, a rod, esp. a forked stick, commonly of hazel, supposed to be useful in locating underground water, metal deposits, etc. Also called **dowsing rod.** [1745–55]

di•vin•i•ty (di vin′i tē), *n., pl.* **-ties. 1.** the quality of being divine; divine nature. **2.** deity; godhood. **3.** a divine being; God. **4. the Divinity,** (*sometimes l.c.*) the Deity. **5.** a being having divine attributes, ranking below God but above humans: *minor divinities.* **6.** the study or science of divine things; theology. **7.** godlike character; supreme excellence. **8.** Also called **divin′ity fudge′.** a fluffy white or artificially tinted fudge made usually of sugar, corn syrup, egg whites, and flavoring, often with nuts. [1275–1325; ME *divinite* < AF < L *dīvīnitās.* See DIVINE, -ITY]

divin′ity cir′cuit. See **circuit binding.**

divin′ity school′, a Protestant seminary. [1545–55]

div•i•nize (div′ə nīz′), *v.t.,* **-nized, -niz•ing.** to make divine; deify. Also, *esp. Brit.,* **div′i•nise′.** [1650–60; DIVINE + -IZE; cf. F *diviniser*] **—div′i•ni•za′tion,** *n.*

div. in par. aeq., (in prescriptions) let it be divided into equal parts. [< L *dīvidātur in partēs aequālēs*]

di•vi•nyl•ben•zene (dī vīn′l ben′zēn, -ben zēn′), *n. Chem.* a clear liquid, $C_{10}H_{10}$, easily polymerized, used in the manufacture of rubbers, drying oils, ion-exchange resins, and polyesters. Also called **vinylstyrene.** [DI-¹ + VINYL + BENZENE]

di•vi′nyl e′ther (dī vīn′l), *Pharm.* See **vinyl ether.** [DI-¹ + VINYL]

di•vi•si (di vē′zē), *adj. Music.* divided; separated (used as a musical direction for two or more performers reading a part to begin reading two or more parts). [1730–40; < It, pl. of *diviso* divided, ptp. of *dividere* to DIVIDE]

di•vis•i•bil•i•ty (di viz′ə bil′i tē), *n.* **1.** the capacity of being divided. **2.** *Math.* the capacity of being evenly divided, without remainder. [1635–45; < LL *dīvīsibil(is)* DIVISIBLE + -ITY]

di•vis•i•ble (di viz′ə bəl), *adj.* **1.** capable of being divided. **2.** *Math.* **a.** capable of being evenly divided, without remainder. **b.** of or pertaining to a group in which given any element and any integer, there is a second element that when raised to the integer equals the first element. [1545–55; (< AF) < LL *dīvīsibilis,* equiv. to L *dīvīs(us),* ptp. of *dividere* to DIVIDE (*di-* DI-² + *vid-* (var. s.) + *-tus* ptp. suffix) + *-ibilis* -IBLE] **—di•vis′i•ble•ness,** *n.* **—di•vis′i•bly,** *adv.*

di•vi•sion (di vizh′ən), *n.* **1.** the act or process of dividing; state of being divided. **2.** *Arith.* the operation inverse to multiplication; the finding of a quantity, the quotient, that when multiplied by a given quantity, the divisor, gives another given quantity, the dividend; the process of ascertaining how many times one number or quantity is contained in another. **3.** something that divides or separates; partition. **4.** something that marks a division; dividing line or mark. **5.** one of the parts into which a thing is divided; section. **6.** separation by difference of opinion or feeling; disagreement; dissension. **7.** *Govt.* the separation of a legislature, or the like, into two groups, in taking a vote. **8.** one of the parts into which a country or an organization is divided for political, judicial, military, or other purposes. **9.** *Mil.* **a.** (in the army) a major administrative and tactical unit, larger than a regiment or brigade and smaller than a corps: it is usually commanded by a major general. **b.** (in the navy) a number of ships, usually four, forming a tactical group that is part of a fleet or squadron. **10.** a major autonomous or semi-independent but subordinate administrative unit of an industrial enterprise, government bureau, transportation system, or university: *the sales division of our company; the Division of Humanities.* **11.** (in sports) a category or class containing all the teams or competitors grouped together according to standing, skill, weight, age, or the like: *a team in the first division; the heavyweight division in boxing.* **12.** *Bot.* a major primary subdivision of the plant kingdom, consisting of one or more classes; plant phylum. **13.** *Zool.* any subdivision of a classificatory group or category. **14.** *Hort.* a type of propagation in which new plants are grown from segments separated from the parent plant. **15.** the ornamentation of a melodic line in 17th- and 18th-century music. [1325–75; ME *divisioun, devisioun* (< AF) < L *dīvīsiōn-* (s. of *dīvīsiō*), equiv. to *dīvīs(us)* (see DIVISIBLE) + *-iōn-* -ION] **—di•vi′sion•al, di•vi′sion•ar′y,** *adj.* **—di•vi′sion•al•ly,** *adv.*
—Syn. 1. separation, apportionment, allotment, distribution. DIVISION, PARTITION suggest dividing into parts. DIVISION usually means marking off or separating a whole into parts. PARTITION often adds the idea of allotting or assigning parts following division: *partition of an estate, of a country.* **4.** boundary, demarcation. **5.** compartment, segment. **6.** breach, rift, disunion, rupture, estrangement, alienation. **—Ant. 6.** accord, union.

divi′sion al′gebra, *Math.* a linear algebra in which each element of the vector space has a multiplicative inverse.

divi′sion al′gorithm, *Math.* **1.** the theorem that an integer can be written as the sum of the product of two integers, one a given positive integer, added to a positive integer smaller than the given positive integer. Cf. **Euclidean algorithm. 2.** any systematic process for calculating the quotient of two numbers.

di•vi•sion•ism (di vizh′ə niz′əm), *n.* (*sometimes cap.*) pointillism. [1900–05; DIVISION + -ISM] **—di•vi′sion•ist,** *n., adj.*

divi′sion of la′bor, *Econ.* a production process in which a worker or group of workers is assigned a specialized task in order to increase efficiency. [1770–80]

divi′sion ring′, *Math.* a ring in which the set of nonzero elements is a group with the operation of multiplication.

divi′sion sign′, *Arith.* the symbol (÷) or (/) placed between two expressions and denoting division of the first by the second. [1930–35]

di•vi•sive (di vī′siv), *adj.* **1.** forming or expressing division or distribution. **2.** creating dissension or discord. [1590–1600; < LL *dīvīsīvus,* equiv. to L *dīvīs(us)* (see DIVISIBLE) + *-īvus* -IVE] **—di•vi′sive•ly,** *adv.* **—di•vi′sive•ness,** *n.*

di•vi•sor (di vī′zər), *n. Math.* **1.** a number by which another number, the dividend, is divided. **2.** a number contained in another given number a certain integral number of times, without a remainder. [1425–75; late ME < L *dīvīsor,* one who divides, equiv. to *dīvīd-* (var. s. of *dīvidere* to DIVIDE) + *-tor* -TOR]

di•vorce (di vôrs′, -vōrs′), *n., v.* **-vorced, -vorc•ing.** *—n.* **1.** a judicial declaration dissolving a marriage in whole or in part, esp. one that releases the husband and wife from all matrimonial obligations. Cf. **judicial separation. 2.** any formal separation of husband and wife according to established custom. **3.** total separation; disunion: *a divorce between thought and action.* *—v.t.* **4.** to separate by divorce: *The judge divorced the couple.* **5.** to break the marriage contract between oneself and (one's spouse) by divorce: *She divorced her husband.* **6.** to separate; cut off: *Life and art cannot be divorced.* *—v.i.* **7.** to get a divorce. [1350–1400; ME < AF < L *dīvortium* separation, equiv. to *dīvort(ere),* var. of *dīvertere* to DIVERT + *-ium* -IUM] **—di•vorce′a•ble,** *adj.* **—di•vorc′er,** *n.* **—di•vor′cive,** *adj.*
—Syn. 6. dissociate, divide, disconnect, split, disjoin.

di•vor•cé (di vôr sā′, -vōr-, -vôr′sā, -vōr′-), *n.* a divorced man. [1805–15; < F, n. use of masc. ptp. of *divorcer* < ML *dīvortiāre* to divorce, deriv. of L *dīvortium* DIVORCE]

divorce′ court′, a court having jurisdiction over termination of marital relations, as actions for divorce or annulment.

di•vor•cée (di vôr sā′, -sē′, -vōr-, -vôr′sā, -vōr′-), *n.* a divorced woman. Also, **di•vor•cee′.** [1805–15; < F *divorcée,* fem. of *divorcé* DIVORCÉ]

di•vorce•ment (di vôrs′mənt, -vōrs′-), *n.* divorce; separation. [DIVORCE + -MENT]

divorce′ mill′, *Informal.* a divorce court, esp. such a court in a state or country that does not impose difficult requirements, as a long period of residence or humiliating grounds, on those who wish to dissolve their marriage.

div•ot (div′ət), *n.* **1.** *Golf.* a piece of turf gouged out with a club in making a stroke. **2.** *Scot.* a piece of turf. [1530–40; orig. Scots, earlier *deva(i)t, diffat, duvat,* of obscure orig.]

di•vul•gate (di vul′gāt), *v.t.,* **-gat•ed, -gat•ing.** *Archaic.* to make publicly known; publish. [1375–1425; late ME < L *dīvulgātus* made common property (ptp. of *dīvulgāre*), equiv. to *divulg-* (see DIVULGE) + *-ātus* -ATE¹] **—di•vul′ga•tor, di•vul′gat•er,** *n.* **—di•vul•ga•tion** (div′əl gā′shən), *n.* **—di•vul•ga•to•ry** (di vul′gə tôr′ē, -tōr′ē), *adj.*

di•vulge (di vulj′, dī-), *v.t.,* **-vulged, -vulg•ing.** to disclose or reveal (something private, secret, or previously unknown). [1425–75; late ME (< AF) < L *dīvulgāre,* equiv. to *dī-* DI-² + *vulgāre* to make general or common, to spread (*vulg(us)* the masses + *-āre* inf. suffix)] **—di•vulge′ment,** *n.* **—di•vulg′er,** *n.*
—Syn. See **reveal.**

di•vul•gence (di vul′jəns, dī-), *n.* a divulging. [1850–55; DIVULGE + -ENCE]

di•vulse (dī vuls′, di-), *v.t.,* **-vulsed, -vuls•ing.** *Surg.* to tear away or apart, as distinguished from cut or dissect. [1595–1605; < L *dīvulsus* (ptp. of *dīvellere*), equiv. to *dī-* DI-² + *vulsus* plucked (ptp. of *vellere*)]

di•vul•sion (di vul′shən, dī-), *n. Surg.* a tearing apart; violent separation. [1595–1605; < L *dīvulsiōn-* (s. of *dīvulsiō*), equiv. to *dīvuls(us)* (see DIVULSE) + *-iōn-* -ION] **—di•vul•sive** (di vul′siv), *adj.*

div•vy (div′ē), *v.,* **-vied, -vy•ing,** *n., pl.* **-vies.** *Informal.* *—v.t., v.i.* **1.** to divide; distribute (often fol. by *up*): *The thieves divvied up the loot.* *—n.* **2.** a distribution or sharing. [1870–75; DIV(IDE) or DIV(IDEND) + -Y²]

Di•wa•li (di wä′lē), *n.* the Hindu festival of lights, celebrated as a religious holiday throughout India in mid-November. Also, **Dewali, Divali.**

di•wan (di wän′, -wôn′), *n.* dewan.

Dix (diks), *n.* **Dorothea Lynde** (lind), (*Dorothy*), 1802–87, U.S. educator and social reformer.

dix•ie (dik′sē), *n. Anglo-Indian.* a large iron pot, esp. a 12-gallon camp kettle used by the British Army. [1895–1900; < Hindi *degcī,* dim. of *degcā* pot]

Dix•ie (dik′sē), *n.* **1.** Also called **Dixieland, Dixie Land.** the southern states of the United States, esp. those that were formerly part of the Confederacy. **2.** (*italics*) any of several songs with this name, esp. the minstrel song (1859) by D. D. Emmett, popular as a Con-

CONCISE PRONUNCIATION KEY: act, cāpe, dâre, pärt; set, ēqual; *if,* īce; ox, ōver, ôrder, oil, bo͝ok, bo͞ot, out; up, ûrge; child; sing; shoe; thin, *that;* zh as in *treasure.* ə = *a* as in *alone, e* as in *system, i* as in *easily, o* as in *gallop, u* as in *circus;* ᵊ as in *fire* (fīᵊr), *hour* (ouᵊr). l and n can serve as syllabic consonants, as in *cradle* (krād′l), and *button* (but′n). See the full key inside the front cover.

federate war song. **3.** a female given name. **4. whistle Dixie,** to indulge in unrealistically optimistic fantasies. —*adj.* **5.** of, from, or characteristic of the southern states of the United States. [1855–60, *Amer.;* often said to be (MASON-)DIX(ON LINE) + -IE]

Dix·ie·crat (dik′sē krat′), *n.* a member of a faction of southern Democrats stressing states' rights and opposed to the civil-rights programs of the Democratic party, esp. a southern Democrat who bolted the party in 1948 and voted for the candidates of the States' Rights Democratic party. [1945–50, *Amer.;* DIXIE + (DEMO)CRAT] —**Dix′ie·crat′ic,** *adj.*

Dix′iecrat par′ty. See **States' Rights Democratic party.**

Dix′ie Cup′, **1.** *Trademark.* a brand of disposable paper cup, as for beverages. **2.** *Navy Slang.* a round, white, brimmed hat worn by U.S. sailors.

Dix·ie·land (dik′sē land′), *n.* **1.** (*sometimes l.c.*) a style of jazz, originating in New Orleans, played by a small group of instruments, as trumpet, trombone, clarinet, piano, and drums, and marked by strongly accented four-four rhythm and vigorous, quasi-improvisational solos and ensembles. **2.** Also, **Dix′ie Land′.** Dixie (def. 1). [1925–30; DIXIE + LAND]

Dix·ie·land·er (dik′sē lan′dər), *n.* a musician specializing in Dixieland jazz. [1930–35; DIXIELAND + -ER[1]]

dix·it (dik′sit), *n.* an utterance. [1620–30; < L: he has said]

Dix·on (dik′sən), *n.* **1. Jeremiah,** died 1777, English astronomer and surveyor. Cf. **Mason-Dixon line. 2.** a city in N Illinois. 15,659. **3.** a male given name.

dix·y (dik′sē), *n., pl.* **dix·ies.** *Anglo-Indian.* dixie.

DIY, *Brit.* do-it-yourself: *DIY house decorating.* Also, **D.I.Y., d.i.y.**

Di·yar·ba·kir (dē yär′bук ər), *n.* a city in SE Turkey in Asia, on the Tigris River. 169,746. Also, **Diarbekr, Di·yar′bek·ir.**

DIYer (dē′ī′wī′ər), *Brit.* do-it-yourselfer. Also, **DIY′er.**

di·zain (di zān′; *Fr.* dē zaN′), *n. Pros.* a French poem or stanza of ten lines, employing eight or ten syllables to the line and having a specific rhyming pattern, as *ababbccdcd.* [1565–75; < F; OF *dezen, dizain,* tenth, tenth part, equiv. to *dix* ten (< L *decem*) + *-ain* (prob. < L *-ānum* -AN, r. L distributive suffix *-ēnum*)]

di·zen (dī′zən, diz′ən), *v.t. Archaic.* to deck with clothes or finery; bedizen. [1520–30; *dis-* bunch of flax on a DISTAFF + -EN[1]] —**di′zen·ment,** *n.*

di·zy·got·ic (dī′zī got′ik), *adj.* developed from two fertilized ova, as fraternal twins. Also, **di·zy·gous** (dī zī′gəs). [1925–30; DI-[1] + ZYGOTIC] —**di·zy·gos·i·ty** (dī′zī gos′i tē), *n.*

diz·zy (diz′ē), *adj.,* **-zi·er, -zi·est,** *v.,* **-zied, -zy·ing.** —*adj.* **1.** having a sensation of whirling and a tendency to fall; giddy; vertiginous. **2.** bewildered; confused. **3.** causing giddiness or confusion: *a dizzy height.* **4.** heedless; thoughtless. **5.** *Informal.* foolish; silly. —*v.t.* **6.** to make dizzy. [bef. 900; ME *dysy,* OE *dysig* foolish; c. LG *düsig* stupefied] —**diz′zi·ly,** *adv.* —**diz′zi·ness,** *n.*

diz·zy·ing (diz′ē ing), *adj.* making or tending to make one dizzy: *The tower rose to dizzying heights.* [1795–1805; DIZZY + -ING[2]] —**diz′zy·ing·ly,** *adv.*

D.J., **1.** Also, **DJ, d.j.** See **disc jockey. 2.** District Judge. **3.** Doctor of Law. [< L *Doctor Jūris*]

Dja·ja·pu·ra (jä′yə po͝or′ə), *n.* Jayapura. Also, **Jajapura.**

Dja·kar·ta (jə kär′tə), *n.* Jakarta.

Djam·bi (jäm′bē), *n.* Jambi.

djeb·el (jeb′əl), *n.* (chiefly in Arabic-speaking countries) a mountain: often used as part of a placename: *the Djebel Druze of southern Syria.* Also, **jebel.** [< F < dial. Ar *jebel*]

Djeb·el Druze (jeb′əl dro͞oz′), See **Jebel ed Druz.**

djel·la·bah (jə lä′bə), *n.* a loose-fitting hooded gown or robe worn by men in North Africa. Also, **djel·la′ba, jellaba.** [1915–20; < Ar *jallabah*]

Djer·ba (jer′bə), *n.* an island off the SE coast of Tunisia: Roman ruins. 65,533; 197 sq. mi. (510 sq. km). Also, **Jerba.**

Djer·ma (jûr′mə, jâr′-), *n., pl.* **-mas,** (*esp. collectively*) **-ma** for 1. **1.** a member of a people living in southwestern Niger, closely related to the Songhai. **2.** the Nilo-Saharan language, a dialect of Songhai, spoken by the Djermas. Also, **Dyerma.**

djib·bah (jib′ə), *n.* jibba.

Dji·bou·ti (ji bo͞o′tē), *n.* **1.** Formerly, **French Somaliland, French Territory of the Afars and Issas.** a republic in E Africa, on the Gulf of Aden: a former overseas territory of France; gained independence 1977. 286,000; 8492 sq. mi. (21,994 sq. km). *Cap.:* Djibouti. **2.** a seaport in and the capital of this republic, in the SE part. 200,000. Also, **Jibuti.** —**Dji·bou′ti·an,** *adj., n.*

Dji·las (ji′läs), *n.* **Mi·lo·van** (mē′lô vän), born 1911, Yugoslavian political leader and author.

djin (jin), *n., pl.* **djins,** (*esp. collectively*) **djin.** *Islam.* jinn. Also, **djinn, djin·ni** (jin′ē).

Djok·ja·kar·ta (jōk′yä kär′tä), *n.* Dutch name of **Jogjakarta.**

D.Journ., Doctor of Journalism.

D.J.S., Doctor of Juridical Science.

D.J.T., Doctor of Jewish Theology.

DK, *Real Estate.* deck.

dk., **1.** dark. **2.** deck. **3.** dock.

CONCISE ETYMOLOGY KEY: <, descended or borrowed from; >, whence; b., blend of, blended; c., cognate with; cf., compare; deriv., derivative; equiv., equivalent; imit., imitative; obl., oblique; r., replacing; s., stem; sp., spelling, spelled; resp., respelling, respelled; trans., translation; ?, origin unknown; *, unattested; ‡, probably earlier than. See the full key inside the front cover.

dkg, dekagram; dekagrams.

dkl, dekaliter; dekaliters.

dkm, dekameter; dekameters.

DL, diesel.

dl, deciliter; deciliters.

D/L, demand loan.

D layer, the lowest region of the ionosphere, characterized by mounting electron and ion density: exists, during the day only, from about 43 to 50 mi. (70 to 80 km) altitude. Cf. **D region.** [1930–35]

D. Lit., Doctor of Literature.

D. Litt., Doctor of Letters. [< L *Doctor Litterārum*]

D.L.O., dead letter office.

dlr., **1.** dealer. **2.** Also, **dlr** dollar.

dlrs., dollars. Also, **dlrs**

D.L.S., Doctor of Library Science.

dlvy., delivery.

DM, See **Deutsche mark.**

dm, decimeter; decimeters.

DM., See **direct mail.**

Dm., See **Deutsche mark.**

DMA, *Computers.* direct memory access: a technique for transferring data to and from external storage.

D-mark (dē′märk′). See **Deutsche mark.** Also, **D-Mark.**

D.M.D., Doctor of Dental Medicine. [< NL *Dentāriae Medicīnae Doctor* or *Doctor Medicīnae Dentālis*]

DMDT, *Chem.* methoxychlor. [*d(i)m(ethoxy)d(iphenyl) t(richloroethane)*]

D meson, *Physics.* a meson with charm +1 or −1, strangeness 0, and isotopic spin ½. Also called **D particle.**

D.M.L., Doctor of Modern Languages.

DMN, *Chem.* dimethylnitrosamine. Also, **DMNA**

D.M.S., **1.** Director of Medical Services. **2.** Doctor of Medical Science.

DMSO, dimethyl sulfoxide: a liquid substance, C_2H_6OS, used in industry as a solvent and paint and varnish remover; proposed as an analgesic and anti-inflammatory in musculoskeletal disorders. [1960–65; *d(i)m(ethyl) s(ulf)o(xide)*]

DMT, dimethyltryptamine.

D. Mus., Doctor of Music.

DMV, Department of Motor Vehicles.

DMZ, demilitarized zone.

dn., down.

DNA, *Genetics.* deoxyribonucleic acid: an extremely long macromolecule that is the main component of chromosomes and is the material that transfers genetic characteristics in all life forms, constructed of two nucleotide strands coiled around each other in a ladderlike arrangement with the sidepieces composed of alternating phosphate and deoxyribose units and the rungs composed of the purine and pyrimidine bases adenine, guanine, cytosine, and thymine: the genetic information of DNA is encoded in the sequence of the bases and is transcribed as the strands unwind and replicate. Cf. **base pair, gene, genetic code, RNA.** [1930–35; *d(eoxyribo)n(ucleic) a(cid)*]

DNA fingerprinting, the use of a DNA probe for the identification of an individual, as for the matching of genes from a forensic sample with those of a criminal suspect. Also called **genetic fingerprinting.** [1985–90] —**DNA fingerprint.**

DNA polymerase, any of a class of enzymes involved in the synthesis of DNA from its deoxyribonucleoside triphosphate precursors. [1960–65; POLYMER + -ASE]

DNA probe, *Biotech.* a technique for identifying a segment of DNA, using a known sequence of nucleotide bases from a DNA strand to detect a complementary sequence in the sample by means of base pairing.

DNase (dē′en′ās, -āz), deoxyribonuclease: any of several enzymes that break down the double-stranded or single-stranded DNA molecule into its component nucleotides. Also, **DNAase.**

DNA virus, any virus containing DNA.

D.N.B., *Brit.* Dictionary of National Biography.

Dnepr (dnyepʀ), *n.* Russian name of **Dnieper.**

Dne·pro·dzer·zhinsk (nep′rō dər zhinsk′; *Russ.* dnyi prə dzyir zhinsk′), *n.* a city in E central Ukraine, in the SW Russian Federation in Europe, on the Dnieper River. 250,000.

Dne·pro·pe·trovsk (nep′rō pi trôfsk′; *Russ.* dnyi prə pyi trôfsk′), *n.* a city in E central Ukraine, in the SW Russian Federation in Europe, on the Dnieper River. 1,066,000. Formerly, **Ekaterinoslav, Yekaterinoslav.**

Dnes·tr (dnyestʀ), *n.* Russian name of **Dniester.**

Dnie·per (nē′pər; *Russ.* dnyepʀ), *n.* a river rising in the W Russian Federation, flowing S through Byelorussia (Belarus) and Ukraine to the Black Sea. 1400 mi. (2250 km) long. Russian, **Dnepr.**

Dnies·ter (nē′stər; *Russ.* dnyestʀ), *n.* a river in the SW Russian Federation in Europe, flowing SE from the Carpathian Mountains to the Black Sea. ab. 875 mi. (1410 km) long. Russian, **Dnestr.** Rumanian, **Nistru.**

D-no·tice (dē′nō′tis), *n. Brit.* a government notice sent to newspapers or other publications requesting them to withhold information for reasons of state security. Also, **D notice.** [1960–65; *D(efence) notice*]

DNR, **1.** *Med.* do not resuscitate (used in hospitals and other health-care facilities to indicate to the staff the decision of a patient's doctors and family, or of the patient by a living will, to avoid extraordinary means of prolonging life). **2.** Also, **D.N.R.** do not return.

do[1] (do͞o; *unstressed* do͝o, də), *v.* and *auxiliary v., pres. sing. 1st pers.* **do,** *2nd* **do** or (*Archaic*) **do·est** or **dost,** *3rd* **does** or (*Archaic*) **do·eth** or **doth,** *pres. pl.* **do;** *past sing. 1st pers.* **did,** *2nd* **did** or (*Archaic*) **didst,** *3rd* **did,** *past pl.* **did;** *past part.* **done;** *pres. part.* **do·ing;** *n., pl.* **dos, do's.** —*v.t.* **1.** to perform (an act, duty, role, etc.): *Do nothing until you hear the bell.* **2.** to execute (a piece or amount of work): *to do a hauling job.* **3.** to accomplish; finish; complete: *He has already done his homework.* **4.** to put forth; exert: *Do your best.* **5.** to be the cause of (good, harm, credit, etc.); bring about; effect. **6.** to render, give, or pay (homage, justice, etc.). **7.** to deal with, fix, clean, arrange, move, etc., (anything) as the case may require: *to do the dishes.* **8.** to travel; traverse: *We did 30 miles today.* **9.** to serve; suffice for: *This will do us for the present.* **10.** to condone or approve, as by custom or practice: *That sort of thing simply isn't done.* **11.** to travel at the rate of (a specified speed): *He was doing 80 when they arrested him.* **12.** to make or prepare: *I'll do the salad.* **13.** to serve (a term of time) in prison, or, sometimes, in office. **14.** to create, form, or bring into being: *She does wonderful oil portraits.* **15.** to translate into or change the form or language of: *MGM did the book into a movie.* **16.** to study or work at or in the field of: *I have to do my math tonight.* **17.** to explore or travel through as a sightseer: *They did Greece in three weeks.* **18.** (used with a pronoun, as *it* or *that,* or with a general noun, as *thing,* that refers to a previously mentioned action): *You were supposed to write thank-you letters; do it before tomorrow, please.* **19.** *Informal.* to wear out; exhaust; tire: *That last set of tennis did me.* **20.** *Informal.* to cheat, trick, or take advantage of: *That crooked dealer did him for $500 at poker.* **21.** *Informal.* to attend or participate in: *Let's do lunch next week.* **22.** *Slang.* to use (a drug or drugs), esp. habitually: *The police report said he was doing cocaine.*
—*v.i.* **23.** to act or conduct oneself; be in action; behave. **24.** *Slang.* to rob; steal from: *The law got him for doing a lot of banks.* **25.** to proceed: *to do wisely.* **26.** to get along; fare; manage: *to do without an automobile.* **27.** to be in health, as specified: *Mother and child are doing fine.* **28.** to serve or be satisfactory, as for the purpose; be enough; suffice: *Will this do?* **29.** to finish or be finished. **30.** to happen; take place; transpire: *What's doing at the office?* **31.** (used as a substitute to avoid repetition of a verb): *I think as you do.*
—*auxiliary verb.* **32.** (used in interrogative, negative, and inverted constructions): *Do you like music? I don't care. Seldom do we witness such catastrophes.* **33.** *Archaic.* (used in imperatives with *you* or *thou* expressed; and occasionally as a metric filler in verse): *Do thou hasten to the king's side. The wind did blow, the rain did fall.* **34.** (used to lend emphasis to a principal verb): *Do visit us!* **35. do a number on (someone).** See **number** (def. 27). **36. do away with, a.** to put an end to; abolish. **b.** to kill. **37. do by,** to deal with; treat: *He had always done well by his family.* **38. do for, a.** to cause the defeat, ruin, or death of. **b.** *Chiefly Brit.* to cook and keep house for; manage or provide for. **39. do in,** *Informal.* **a.** to kill, esp. to murder. **b.** to injure gravely or exhaust; wear out; ruin: *The tropical climate did them in.* **c.** to cheat or swindle: *He was done in by an unscrupulous broker.* **40. do one proud.** See **proud** (def. 11). **41. do one's number.** See **number** (def. 28). **42. do one's (own) thing.** See **thing[1]** (def. 17). **43. do or die,** to make a supreme effort. **44. do out of,** *Informal.* to swindle; cheat: *A furniture store did me out of several hundred dollars.* **45. do over,** to redecorate. **46. do time,** *Informal.* to serve a term in prison: *It's hard to get a decent job once you've done time.* **47. do to death.** See **death** (def. 15). **48. do up,** *Informal.* **a.** to wrap and tie up. **b.** to pin up or arrange (the hair). **c.** to renovate; launder; clean. **d.** to wear out; tire. **e.** to fasten: *Do up your coat.* **f.** to dress: *The children were all done up in funny costumes.* **49. do with,** to gain advantage or benefit from; make use of: *I could do with more leisure time.* **50. do without, a.** to forgo; dispense with. **b.** to dispense with the thing mentioned: *The store doesn't have any, so you'll have to do without.* **51. have to do with.** See **have** (def. 36). **52. make do,** to get along with what is at hand, despite its inadequacy: *I can't afford a new coat so I have to make do with this one.*
—*n.* **53.** *Informal.* a burst of frenzied activity; action; commotion. **54.** *Informal.* a hairdo or hair styling. **55.** *Brit. Slang.* a swindle; hoax. **56.** *Chiefly Brit.* a festive social gathering; party. **57. dos and don'ts,** customs, rules, or regulations: *The dos and don'ts of polite manners are easy to learn.* [bef. 900; ME, OE *dōn;* c. D *doen,* G *tun;* akin to L *-dere* to put, *facere* to make, do, Gk *tithénai* to set, put, Skt *dadhāti* (he) puts]
—**Syn. 1, 25.** act. **3.** Do, ACCOMPLISH, ACHIEVE mean to bring some action to a conclusion. Do is the general word: *He did a great deal of hard work.* ACCOMPLISH and ACHIEVE both connote successful completion of an undertaking. ACCOMPLISH emphasizes attaining a desired goal through effort, skill, and perseverance: *to accomplish what one has hoped for.* ACHIEVE emphasizes accomplishing something important, excellent, or great: *to achieve a major breakthrough.*

do[2] (dō), *n., pl.* **dos.** *Music.* **1.** the syllable used for the first tone or keynote of a diatonic scale. **2.** (in the fixed system of solmization) the tone C. Cf. **sol-fa** (def. 1), **ut.** [1745–55; < It, inverted var. of *ut;* see GAMUT]

do., ditto.

D/O, delivery order. Also, **d.o.**

D.O., **1.** Also, **DO, d.o.** direct object. **2.** Doctor of Optometry. **3.** Doctor of Osteopathy.

DOA, dead on arrival. Also, **D.O.A.**

do·a·ble (do͞o′ə bəl), *adj.* capable of being done. [1400–50; late ME; see DO[1], -ABLE]

do-all (do͞o′ôl′), *n.* a person employed as a factotum. [1625–35]

doat (dōt), *v.i.* dote.

doat·er[1] (dō′tər), *n.* doter.

doa·ter[2] (dō′tər), *n. Newfoundland.* a fully mature harp seal. Also, **dotard.** [1785–95]

DOB, date of birth. Also, **D.O.B., d.o.b.**

dob·ber (dob′ər), *n.* a float for a fishing line; bob. [1800–10, *Amer.*; < D: float, buoy]

dob·bin (dob′in), *n.* **1.** a horse, esp. a quiet, plodding horse for farm work or family use. **2.** a drinking vessel of the 18th century holding a gill. [1590–1600; alter. of *Robin,* hypocoristic form of *Robert*]

Dobbs′ Fer′ry (dobz), a town in SE New York. 10,053.

dob·by (dob′ē), *n., pl.* **-bies. 1.** *Brit. Dial.* a fatuous person; fool. **2.** *Textiles.* **a.** an attachment on a loom, used in weaving small patterns. **b.** Also called **dob′by weave′.** a small geometric or floral pattern produced by this attachment. **c.** a fabric having such a pattern. [1685–95; akin to dial. *dovie* stupid, imbecile, deriv. of *dove* to doze, dote, OE *dofian, dobian;* c. G *toben* to rage; cf. OE *dobende* decrepit]

dob′by loom′, a loom equipped with a dobby for weaving small, geometric patterns.

Do′bell's solu′tion (dō′belz), *Pharm.* a clear, yellowish, aqueous solution of sodium borate, sodium bicarbonate, phenol, and glycerol, used chiefly as an antiseptic and astringent for the nose and throat. [named after H. B. *Dobell* (1828–1917), English physician]

do·ber·man (dō′bər mən), *n., pl.* **-mans.** *Informal.* See **Doberman pinscher.**

Do′berman pin′scher, one of a German breed of medium-sized, short-haired dogs having a black, brown, or blue coat with rusty brown markings. [1915–20; named after Ludwig *Dobermann,* 19th-century German, original breeder; *pinscher* terrier, a pseudo-G coinage, perh. based on G *Pinzgau* Austrian district noted for its breeding farms]

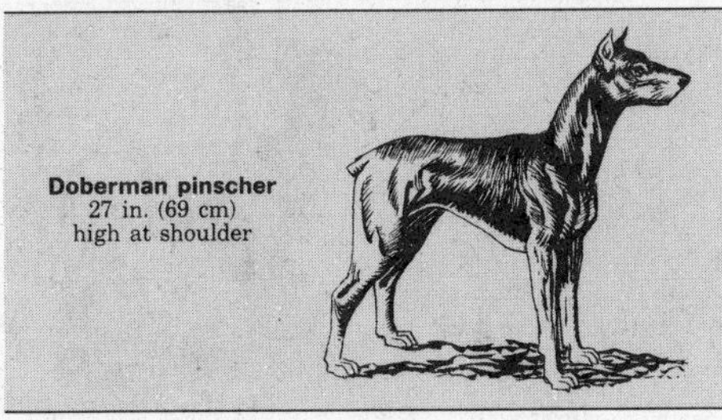

Doberman pinscher
27 in. (69 cm)
high at shoulder

do·bie (dō′bē), *n.* **1.** *Chiefly Southwestern U.S.* adobe. **2.** a playing marble, esp. one made of clay. [1830–40, *Amer.*; aph. form]

Do·bie (dō′bē), *n.* **(James) Frank,** 1888–1964, U.S. folklorist, educator, and author.

do·bla (dō′blä), *n.* a former gold coin of Spain. [1590–1600; < Sp < L *dupla,* fem. of *duplus* DOUBLE]

Dö·blin (dœ′blēn), *n.* **Al·fred** (äl′frät), 1878–1957, German physician and novelist.

do·blón (də blōn′; *Sp.* dô vlôn′), *n., pl.* **-blon·es** (-blō′nēz; *Sp.* -vlô′nes). a former gold coin of Spain and Spanish America, equal to two gold escudos. [< Sp: DOUBLOON]

do·bra (dō′brə), *n.* any of various former Portuguese coins, esp. a gold coin of John V equal to two johannes. [< Pg < L *dupla;* see DOBLA]

Do·bro (dō′brō), *pl.* **-bros** for 2. **1.** *Trademark.* a brand of acoustic guitar commonly used in country music, usually played on the lap and having a raised bridge and a metal resonator cone that produces a tremulous, moaning sound. —*n.* **2.** (*l.c.*) any guitar of this type.

Do·bru·ja (dō′brŏŏ jə; *Bulg.* dô′brŏŏ jə), *n.* a region in SE Rumania and NE Bulgaria, between the Danube River and the Black Sea. 2970 sq. mi. (7690 sq. km). Rumanian, **Do·bro·gea** (dô′bro jä′).

Do·bry·nin (dō brē′nin, -brin′; *Russ.* du brĭ′nyin), *n.* **A·na·to·ly F(e·do·ro·vich)** (an′ə tō′lē fyô′də rō′-vich; *Russ.* u nu tô′lyĕ fyô′də rə vyich), born 1919, Russian diplomat.

dob·son (dob′sən), *n.* **1.** dobsonfly. **2.** hellgrammite. [1880–85, *Amer.*; by shortening]

Dob·son (dob′sən), *n.* **(Henry) Austin,** 1840–1921, English poet, biographer, and essayist.

dob·son·fly (dob′sən flī′), *n., pl.* **-flies.** a large, soft-bodied insect, *Corydalus cornutus,* having four distinctly veined membranous wings, biting mouthparts, and, in the male, huge mandibles that jut out from the head. Cf. **hellgrammite.** [1900–05; after surname *Dobson;* see FLY[2]]

Dob·so′ni·an tel′escope (dob sō′nē ən), a relatively inexpensive Newtonian telescope, suitable for visual but not photographic use, in which the tube assembly slips freely in the lower base. [after John *Dobson,* U.S. astronomer, its inventor; see -IAN]

Do·bu (dō′bŏŏ), *n., pl.* **-bus,** (*esp. collectively*) **-bu. 1.** a member of a Melanesian people who inhabit the settlement of Dobu, in Papua New Guinea. **2.** the Austronesian language of the Dobu. Also, **Dobuan.**

Do·bu·an (dō′bŏŏ ən, dō bŏŏ′ən), *n.* **1.** Dobu. —*adj.* **2.** of or pertaining to the Dobu or their language. [DOBU + -AN]

do·by (dō′bē), *n., pl.* **-bies.** *Chiefly Southwestern U.S.* adobe. [aph. form]

Dob·zhan·sky (dob zhän′skē), *n.* **Theodosius (Gri·go·ri·e·vich)** (gri gôr′ē ə vich, -gōr′-), 1900–75, U.S. geneticist, born in Russia.

doc (dok), *n. Informal.* **1.** doctor. **2.** a casual, impersonal term of address used to a man. [1845–50; by shortening]

DOC, See **Department of Commerce.**

doc., *pl.* **docs.** document.

do·cent (dō′sənt; *Ger.* dō tsent′), *n.* **1.** privatdocent. **2.** a college or university lecturer. **3.** a person who is a knowledgeable guide, esp. one who conducts visitors through a museum and delivers a commentary on the exhibitions. [1630–40; < G *Dozent* < L *docent-* (s. of *docēns,* prp. of *docēre*), equiv. to *doc-* teach + *-ent* -ENT] —**do′cent·ship′,** *n.*

Do·ce·tae (dō sē′tē), *n.pl.* early Christian adherents of Docetism. [1810–20; < LGk *dokētaí,* pl. of *dokētḗs* one who professes the heresy of appearance, equiv. to Gk *dokē-* (var. s. of *dokeîn* to seem, appear; cf. DOGMA) + *-tēs* agent n. suffix]

Do·ce·tism (dō sē′tiz əm, dō′si tiz′-), *n.* **1.** an early Christian doctrine that the sufferings of Christ were apparent and not real and that after the crucifixion he appeared in a spiritual body. **2.** *Rom. Cath. Ch.* an ancient heresy asserting that Jesus lacked full humanity. [1840–50; DOCET(AE) + -ISM] —**Do·ce′tic,** *adj.* —**Do·ce′tist,** *n., adj.*

doch-an-dor·rach (dokн′ən dor′əkн), *n. Scot., Irish.* a stirrup cup. Also, **doch′-an-dor′roch, doch-an-dor·ris** (dokн′ən dor′is). [1675–85; cf. Ir *deoch an dorais* drink of the door]

doc·ile (dos′əl; *Brit.* dō′sīl), *adj.* **1.** easily managed or handled; tractable: *a docile horse.* **2.** readily trained or taught; teachable. [1475–85; < L *docilis* readily taught, equiv. to *doc(ēre)* to teach + *-ilis* -ILE] —**doc′ile·ly,** *adv.* —**do·cil·i·ty** (do sil′i tē, dō-), *n.*
—**Syn. 1.** manageable, malleable; obedient.

dock[1] (dok), *n.* **1.** a landing pier. **2.** the space or waterway between two piers or wharves, as for receiving a ship while in port. **3.** such a waterway, enclosed or open, together with the surrounding piers, wharves, etc. **4.** See **dry dock. 5.** a platform for loading and unloading trucks, railway freight cars, etc. **6.** an airplane hangar or repair shed. **7.** Also called **scene dock.** a place in a theater near the stage or beneath the floor of the stage for the storage of scenery. —*v.t.* **8.** to bring (a ship or boat) into a dock; lay up in a dock. **9.** to place in dry dock, as for repairs, cleaning, or painting. **10.** to join (a space vehicle) with another or with a space station in outer space. —*v.i.* **11.** to come or go into a dock or dry dock. **12.** (of two space vehicles) to join together in outer space. [1505–15; < MD *doc(ke)*]

dock[2] (dok), *n.* **1.** the solid or fleshy part of an animal's tail, as distinguished from the hair. **2.** the part of a tail left after cutting or clipping. —*v.t.* **3.** to cut off the end of; cut short: *to dock a tail.* **4.** to cut short the tail of: *to dock a horse.* **5.** to deduct from the wages of, usually as a punishment: *The boss docked him a day's pay.* **6.** to deduct from (wages): *The boss docked his paycheck $20.* [1300–50; ME *dok,* OE *-docca,* in *fingirdoccana* (gen. pl.) finger muscles; c. Fris *dok,* LG *docke* bundle, Icel *dokkur* stumpy tail, MHG *tocke* bundle, sheaf]

dock[3] (dok), *n.* **1.** the place in a courtroom where a prisoner is placed during trial. **2. in the dock,** being tried in a court, esp. a criminal court; on trial. [1580–90; perh. < D *dok* (dial. sense) cage, poultry pen, rabbit hutch]

dock[4] (dok), *n.* **1.** any of various weedy plants belonging to the genus *Rumex,* of the buckwheat family, as *R. obtusifolius* **(bitter dock)** or *R. acetosa* **(sour dock),** having long taproots. **2.** any of various other plants, mostly coarse weeds. [bef. 1000; ME *dokke,* OE *docce;* c. MD *docke,* MHG *tocke*]

dock·age[1] (dok′ij), *n.* **1.** a charge for the use of a dock. **2.** docking accommodations. **3.** the act of docking a ship. [1700–10; DOCK[1] + -AGE]

dock·age[2] (dok′ij), *n.* **1.** a curtailment; deduction, as from wages. **2.** waste material in wheat and other grains that is easily removed. [1885–90; DOCK[2] + -AGE]

dock·er[1] (dok′ər), *n.* a laborer on shipping docks; longshoreman. [1755–65; DOCK[1] + -ER[1]]

dock·er[2] (dok′ər), *n.* a person or thing that docks or cuts short. [1800–10; DOCK[2] + -ER[1]]

dock·et (dok′it), *n., v.,* **-et·ed, -et·ing.** —*n.* **1.** Also called **trial docket.** a list of cases in court for trial, or the names of the parties who have cases pending. **2.** *Chiefly Brit.* **a.** an official memorandum or entry of proceedings in a legal cause. **b.** a register of such entries. **c.** any of various certificates or warrants giving the holder right to obtain, buy, or move goods that are controlled by the government, as a custom-house docket certifying duty has been paid. **3.** the list of business to be transacted by a board, council, legislative assembly, or the like. **4.** *Brit.* a writing on a letter or document stating its contents; any statement of particulars attached to a package, envelope, etc.; a label or ticket. —*v.t.* **5.** *Law.* to enter in the docket of the court. **6.** *Law.* to make an abstract or summary of the heads of, as a document; abstract and enter in a book: *judgments regularly docketed.* **7.** to endorse (a letter, document, etc.) with a memorandum. [1475–85; earlier *dogget,* of obscure orig.]

dock·hand (dok′hand′), *n.* a dockworker. [1915–20; DOCK[1] + HAND]

dock′ing bridge′, *Naut.* a raised platform running from one side to the other of a ship toward the stern, used by officers for supervising docking operations.

dock′ing keel′, *Naut.* one of two keellike projections for bracing a hull of a ship against bilge blocks when the ship is in dry dock.

dock·land (dok′land′), *n. Brit.* the land or area surrounding a commercial port. [1900–05; DOCK[1] + LAND]

dock·mack·ie (dok′mak′ē), *n.* a North American shrub, *Viburnum acerifolium,* of the honeysuckle family, having long stemmed clusters of white flowers and ovoid, almost black berries. [1810–20, *Amer.*; < New York D, perh. < a Mahican word (with a reflex of Proto-Algonquian *-a·xkw tree) + D *-je* dim. suffix]

dock·mas·ter (dok′mas′tər, -mä′stər), *n. Naut.* a person who supervises the dry-docking of ships. [1730–40; DOCK[1] + MASTER]

dock·o·min·i·um (dok′ə min′ē əm), *n.* a dock or boat slip bought and sold as real property. [1980–85; DOCK[1] + (COND)OMINIUM]

dock·side (dok′sīd′), *n.* **1.** land or area adjoining a dock: *We were at the dockside to greet them.* —*adj.* **2.** pertaining to or located at or near a dockside: *dockside warehouses; a dockside fire.* [1885–90; DOCK[1] + SIDE[1]]

dock·wal·lop·er (dok′wol′ə pər), *n. Slang.* a casual laborer about docks or wharves. [1830–40, *Amer.*; DOCK[1] + WALLOPER] —**dock′-wal′lop·ing,** *n.*

dock·work·er (dok′wûr′kər), *n.* a person employed on the docks of a port, as in loading and unloading vessels. [1920–25; DOCK[1] + WORKER]

dock·yard (dok′yärd′), *n.* **1.** a waterside area containing docks, workshops, warehouses, etc., for building, outfitting, and repairing ships, for storing naval supplies, etc. **2.** *Brit.* a navy yard. [1695–1705; DOCK[1] + YARD[2]]

doc′o·sa·hex·a·e·no′ic ac′id (dok′ə sə hek′sə i-nō′ik, dok′-), *Biochem.* See **DHA.** [see DOCOSANOIC, HEXA-]

doc·o·sa·no·ic (dok′ə sə nō′ik), *adj. Chem.* behenic. [*do-* (< Gk, comb. form of *dúo* two) + *-cos-* (extracted from Gk *eíkosi* twenty) + -ANE + -O- + -IC]

doc·tor (dok′tər), *n.* **1.** a person licensed to practice medicine, as a physician, surgeon, dentist, or veterinarian. **2.** a person who has been awarded a doctor's degree: *He is a Doctor of Philosophy.* **3.** See **Doctor of the Church. 4.** *Older Slang.* a cook, as at a camp or on a ship. **5.** *Mach.* any of various minor mechanical devices, esp. one designed to remedy an undesirable characteristic of an automatic process. **6.** *Angling.* any of several artificial flies, esp. the silver doctor. **7.** an eminent scholar and teacher. —*v.t.* **8.** to give medical treatment to: *He feels he can doctor himself for just a common cold.* **9.** to treat (an ailment): *He doctored his cold at home.* **10.** to repair or mend: *She was able to doctor the chipped vase with a little plastic cement.* **11.** to tamper with; falsify: *He doctored the birthdate on his passport.* **12.** to add a foreign substance to; adulterate: *Someone had doctored the drink.* **13.** to revise, alter, or adapt (a photograph, manuscript, etc.) in order to serve a specific purpose or to improve the material: *to doctor a play.* **14.** to award a doctorate to: *He did his undergraduate work in the U.S. and was doctored at Oxford.* —*v.i.* **15.** to practice medicine. **16.** *Older Use.* to take medicine; receive medical treatment. **17.** *Metall.* (of an article being electroplated) to receive plating unevenly. [1275–1325; ME *docto(u)r* (< AF) < L, equiv. to *doc(ēre)* to teach + *-tor* -TOR] —**doc′tor·al, doc·to·ri·al** (dok-tôr′ē əl, -tōr′-), *adj.* —**doc′tor·al·ly, doc·to′ri·al·ly,** *adv.* —**doc′tor·less,** *adj.* —**doc′tor·ship′,** *n.*

doc·tor·ate (dok′tər it), *n.* **1.** See **Doctor of Philosophy** (def. 1). **2.** See **doctor's degree** (defs. 1, 2). [1670–80; < ML *doctorātus* degree of doctor. See DOCTOR, -ATE[3]]

Doc′tor Faus′tus, (*The Tragical History of Doctor Faustus*) a play (c1588) by Christopher Marlowe, based on the medieval legend of Faust.

doc·tor·fish (dok′tər fish′), *n., pl.* **-fish·es,** (*esp. collectively*) **-fish.** a surgeonfish, esp. *Acanthurus chirurgus,* of the West Indies, having a bluish body and black tail. [1825–35; so named from the knifelike rays on its tail]

Doc′tor of Philos′ophy, 1. Also called **doctorate.** the highest degree awarded by a graduate school, usually to a person who has completed at least three years of graduate study and a dissertation approved by a board of professors. **2.** a person who has been awarded this degree. *Abbr.:* Ph.D.

Doc′tor of the Church′, a title conferred on an ecclesiastic for great learning and saintliness.

doc′tor's degree′, 1. any of several academic degrees of the highest rank, as the Ph.D. or Ed.D., awarded by universities and some colleges for completing advanced work in graduate school or a professional school. **2.** an honorary degree conferring the title of doctor upon the recipient, as with the LL.D. degree. **3.** a degree awarded to a graduate of a school of medicine, dentistry, or veterinary science. Also called **doctorate** (for defs. 1, 2).

doc·tri·naire (dok′trə nâr′), *n.* **1.** a person who tries to apply some doctrine or theory without sufficient regard for practical considerations; an impractical theorist. —*adj.* **2.** dogmatic about others' acceptance of one's

CONCISE PRONUNCIATION KEY: act, cāpe, dâre, pärt; set, ēqual; *if,* ice; ox, ōver, ôrder, oil, bŏŏk, bōōt, out; up, ûrge; child; sing; shoe; thin, *that;* zh as in *treasure.* ə = *a* as in *alone, e* as in *system, i* as in *easily, o* as in *gallop, u* as in *circus;* ᵊ as in *fire* (fīᵊr), *hour* (ouᵊr). l and n can serve as syllabic consonants, as in *cradle* (krād′l), and *button* (but′n). See the full key inside the front cover.

ideas; fanatical: *a doctrinaire preacher.* **3.** merely theoretical; impractical. **4.** of, pertaining to, or characteristic of a doctrinaire. [1810–20; < F; see DOCTRINE, -AIRE] —**doc′tri·nair′ism,** *n.*
—**Syn. 2.** authoritarian, uncompromising, inflexible, unyielding. —**Ant. 2.** reasonable, flexible.

doc·tri·nal (dok′trə nl; *Brit. also* dok trīn′l), *adj.* of, pertaining to, or concerned with doctrine: *a doctrinal dispute.* [1400–50; late ME < LL *doctrīnālis,* equiv. to L *doctrīn(a)* (see DOCTRINE) + *-ālis* -AL[1]] —**doc′tri·nal′i·ty,** *n.* —**doc′tri·nal·ly,** *adv.*

doc′trinal theol′ogy, dogmatics.

doc·trine (dok′trin), *n.* **1.** a particular principle, position, or policy taught or advocated, as of a religion or government: *Catholic doctrines; the Monroe Doctrine.* **2.** something that is taught; teachings collectively: *religious doctrine.* **3.** a body or system of teachings relating to a particular subject: *the doctrine of the Catholic Church.* [1350–1400; ME < AF < L *doctrīna* teaching, equiv. to *doct(o)r* DOCTOR + *-ina* -INE[2]]
—**Syn. 1.** tenet, dogma, theory, precept, belief.

doc·u·dra·ma (dok′yə drä′mə, -dram′ə), *n. Television.* a fictionalized drama based primarily on actual events. [1960–65; DOCU(MENTARY) + DRAMA] —**doc·u·dram·a·tist** (dok′yə dram′ə tist, -drä′mə-), *n.*

doc·u·ment (*n.* dok′yə mənt; *v.* dok′yə ment′), *n.* **1.** a written or printed paper furnishing information or evidence, as a passport, deed, bill of sale, or bill of lading; a legal or official paper. **2.** any written item, as a book, article, or letter, esp. of a factual or informative nature. **3.** *Archaic.* evidence; proof. —*v.t.* **4.** to furnish with documents. **5.** to furnish with references, citations, etc., in support of statements made: *a carefully documented biography.* **6.** to support by documentary evidence: *to document a case.* **7.** *Naut.* to provide (a vessel) with a certificate giving particulars concerning nationality, ownership, tonnage, dimensions, etc. **8.** *Obs.* to instruct. [1400–50; late ME (< AF) < L *documentum* example (as precedent, warning, etc.), equiv. to *doc-* (s. of *docēre* to teach) + *-u-* (var. of *-i-* -I- before labials) + *-mentum* -MENT] —**doc·u·ment·a·ble** (dok′yə men′tə bəl, dok′yə men′-), *adj.* —**doc′u·ment′er,** *n.*
—**Syn. 6.** corroborate, verify, substantiate, validate.

doc·u·men·tar·i·an (dok′yə men târ′ē ən, -mən-), *n.* **1.** *Motion Pictures, Television.* a filmmaker, producer, etc., who specializes in documentaries. **2.** a writer, photographer, or other artist whose work constitutes a document or documentary of an aspect of life. Also, **doc·u·men·ta·rist** (dok′yə men′tər ist). [1940–45; DOCUMENT(ARY) + -ARIAN]

doc·u·men·ta·ry (dok′yə men′tə rē, -trē), *adj., n., pl.* **-ries.** —*adj.* **1.** Also, **doc·u·men·tal** (dok′yə men′tl). pertaining to, consisting of, or derived from documents: *a documentary history of France.* **2.** *Motion Pictures, Television.* based on or re-creating an actual event, era, life story, etc., that purports to be factually accurate and contains no fictional elements: *a documentary life of Gandhi.* —*n.* **3.** *Motion Pictures, Television.* a documentary film, radio or television program, etc. [1795–1805; DOCUMENT + -ARY] —**doc′u·men·tar′i·ly,** *adv.*

doc·u·men·ta·tion (dok′yə men tā′shən, -mən-), *n.* **1.** the use of documentary evidence. **2.** a furnishing with documents, as to substantiate a claim or the data in a book or article. **3.** *Computers.* manuals, listings, diagrams, and other hard- or soft-copy written and graphic materials that describe the use, operation, maintenance, or design of software or hardware: *The documentation for the driver program is displayed on the screen.* [1745–55; DOCUMENT + -ATION] —**doc′u·men·ta′tion·al,** *adj.*

DOD, See **Department of Defense.**

do·dad (do͞o′dad′), *n.* doodad.

Dodd (dod), *n.* **William Edward,** 1869–1940, U.S. historian and diplomat.

dod·der[1] (dod′ər), *v.i.* to shake; tremble; totter. [1610–20; cf. DITHER, TOTTER, TEETER, etc.] —**dod′der·er,** *n.*

dod·der[2] (dod′ər), *n.* a leafless parasitic plant, *Cuscuta gronovii,* having dense clusters of small, white, bell-shaped flowers on orange-yellow stems that twine about clover or flax. Also called **love vine.** [1225–75; ME *doder;* c. D, Dan *dodder,* MLG *dod(d)er,* MHG *toter,* G *Dotter*]

dod·dered (dod′ərd), *adj.* **1.** infirm; feeble. **2.** (of a tree) having lost most of its branches owing to decay or age. [1690–1700; DODDER[1] + -ED[2]]

dod·der·ing (dod′ər ing), *adj.* shaky or trembling, as from old age; tottering: *a doddering old man.* Also, **dod·der·y** (dod′ə rē). [‡1735–45; DODDER[1] + -ING[2]]

dod·die (dod′ē), *n.* a cow or bull having no horns, esp. an Aberdeen Angus. Also, **doddy.** [1580–90; *dod* to poll (ME *dodden*) + -IE]

Dodds (dodz), *n.* **Warren** (*"Baby"*), 1898–1959, U.S. jazz drummer.

dod·dy (dod′ē), *n., pl.* **-dies.** doddie.

dodeca-, a combining form meaning "twelve," used in the formation of compound words: *dodecasyllabic.* Also, *esp. before a vowel,* **dodec-.** [< Gk *dōdeka-,* comb. form of *dōdekás* twelve, equiv. to *dō-* TWO + *-dekas* TEN]

do·dec·a·gon (dō dek′ə gon′, -gən), *n. Geom.* a polygon having 12 angles and 12 sides. Also, **duodecagon.** [1650–60; DODECA- + -GON] —**do·de·cag·o·nal** (dō′də kag′ə nl), *adj.*

do·dec·a·he·dron (dō dek′ə hē′drən, dō′dek-), *n., pl.* **-drons, -dra** (-drə). *Geom., Crystall.* a solid figure having 12 faces. [1560–70; DODECA- + -HEDRON] —**do·dec′a·he′dral,** *adj.*

CONCISE ETYMOLOGY KEY: <, descended or borrowed from; >, whence; b., blend of, blended; c., cognate with; cf., compare; deriv., derivative; equiv., equivalent; imit., imitative; obl., oblique; r., replacing; s., stem; sp., spelling, spelled; resp., respelling, respelled; trans., translation; ?, origin unknown; *, unattested; ‡, probably earlier than. See the full key inside the front cover.

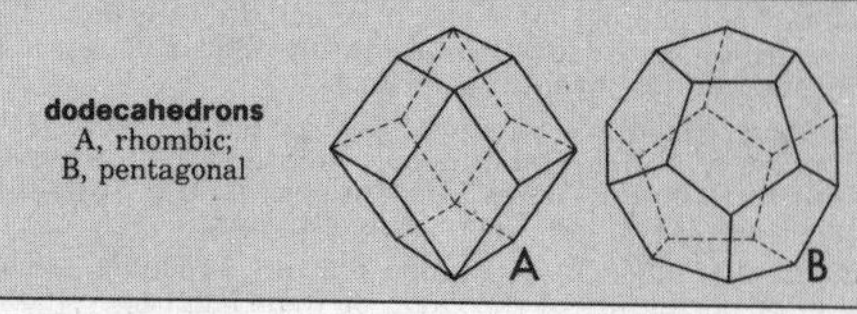

dodecahedrons
A, rhombic;
B, pentagonal

do·dec·a·nal (dō dek′ə nal′, -nôl′), *n. Chem.* See **lauric aldehyde.** [*dodecane* (DODEC- + -ANE) + -AL[3]]

Do·dec·a·nese (dō dek′ə nēs′, -nēz′, dō′dek ə-), *n.* a group of 12 Greek islands in the Aegean, off the SW coast of Turkey: belonged to Italy 1911–45. 121,017; 1035 sq. mi. (2680 sq. km).

do·dec′a·no′ic ac′id (dō dek′ə nō′ik, dō′dek-, dō′dek′-, dō′dek-), *Chem.* See **lauric acid.** [DODEC- + -ANE + -O- + -IC]

do·dec·a·pho·nism (dō dek′ə fə niz′əm, dō′di kaf′ə-), *n.* musical composition using the 12-tone technique. Also, **do·dec·a·pho·ny** (dō dek′ə fō′nē, dō′di kaf′ə nē). [1950–55;. DODECA- + -PHONE + -ISM] —**do·dec·a·phon·ic** (dō dek′ə fon′ik), *adj.* —**do·dec′a·phon′i·cal·ly,** *adv.* —**do·dec′a·phon·ist,** *n.*

do·dec·a·style (dō dek′ə stīl′), *adj. Archit.* **1.** having 12 columns. **2.** (of a classical temple or building in the style of one) having 12 columns on one or either front. Also, **do·dec′a·sty′lar, duodecastyle.** [1815–25; < Gk *dōdekástylos;* see DODECA-, -STYLE[2]]

do·dec·a·sty·los (dō dek′ə stī′ləs, -los, dō′dek-), *n.* a dodecastyle building, as a classical temple. [< Gk *dōdekástylos.* See DODECASTYLE]

do·dec·a·syl·lab·ic (dō dek′ə si lab′ik, dō′dek-), *adj.* **1.** consisting of or pertaining to 12 syllables. —*n.* **2.** a dodecasyllable. [1880–85; DODECA- + SYLLABIC]

do·dec·a·syl·la·ble (dō dek′ə sil′ə bəl, dō′dek-), *n.* a word or line of verse containing 12 syllables. [1745–55; DODECA- + SYLLABLE]

do′de·cyl al′dehyde (dō′də sil), *Chem.* See **lauric aldehyde.** [DODEC- + -YL]

do·de·cyl·phen·ol (dō′də sil fē′nôl, -nol), *n. Chem.* a thick, straw-colored, water-insoluble liquid mixture of isomers having the formula $C_{18}H_{30}O$, used chiefly as a solvent and as an intermediate for surface-active agents. [DODECYL + PHENOL]

dodge (doj), *v.,* **dodged, dodg·ing,** *n.* —*v.t.* **1.** to elude or evade by a sudden shift of position or by strategy: *to dodge a blow; to dodge a question.* **2.** Also, **hold back.** *Photog.* (in printing) to shade (an area of a print) from exposure for a period, while exposing the remainder of the print in order to lighten or eliminate the area (sometimes fol. by *out*). Cf. **burn**[1] (def. 36). —*v.i.* **3.** to move aside or change position suddenly, as to avoid a blow or get behind something. **4.** to use evasive methods; prevaricate: *When asked a direct question, he dodges.* —*n.* **5.** a quick, evasive movement, as a sudden jump away to avoid a blow or the like. **6.** an ingenious expedient or contrivance; shifty trick. [1560–70; of obscure orig.]
—**Syn. 1.** avoid. **4.** equivocate, quibble.

Dodge (doj), *n.* **Mary Elizabeth,** 1831–1905, U.S. editor and author of children's books.

dodge′ ball′, a circle game in which players throw an inflated ball at opponents within the circle who try to avoid being hit, and therefore eliminated, the winner being the one who remains unhit. [1920–25]

Dodge′ Cit′y, a city in SW Kansas, on the Arkansas River: important frontier town and railhead on the old Santa Fe route. 18,001.

Dodg·em (doj′əm), *n.* an attraction at amusement parks, carnivals, or the like, consisting of small electrically powered automobiles that the patrons drive, trying to bump other cars while avoiding being bumped by them. [DODGE + 'EM; formerly a trademark]

dodg·er (doj′ər), *n.* **1.** a person who dodges. **2.** a shifty person, esp. one who persistently evades a responsibility, as specified: *tax dodger; draft dodger.* **3.** a leafhopper. **4.** a small handbill; throwaway. **5.** *Chiefly South Midland and Southern U.S.* See **corn dodger. 6.** *Naut.* a shield, as of canvas, erected on a flying bridge to protect persons on watch from wind, flying spray, etc. **7.** *Australian.* a large slice, lump, or portion of food, esp. of bread. [1560–70; DODGE + -ER[1]]

dodg·er·y (doj′ə rē), *n., pl.* **-er·ies.** the use of a dodge or dodges; trickery; duplicity. [1660–70; DODGER + -Y[3]]

Dodg·son (doj′sən), *n.* **Charles Lut·widge** (lut′wij), (*"Lewis Carroll"*), 1832–98, English mathematician and writer of books for children.

dodg·y (doj′ē), *adj.,* **dodg·i·er, dodg·i·est. 1.** inclined to dodge. **2.** evasively tricky: *a dodgy manner of dealing with people.* **3.** *Chiefly Brit.* risky; hazardous; chancy. [1860–65; DODGE + -Y[1]]

do·do (dō′dō), *n., pl.* **-dos, -does. 1.** any of several clumsy, flightless, extinct birds of the genera *Raphus* and *Pezophaps,* related to pigeons but about the size of a turkey, formerly inhabiting the islands of Mauritius, Réunion, and Rodriguez. **2.** *Slang.* a dull-witted, slow-reacting person. **3.** a person with old-fashioned, conservative, or outmoded ideas. **4.** a thing that is outmoded or obsolete. [1620–30; < Pg *doudo,* fool, madman (of uncert. orig.); the bird appar. so called from its clumsy appearance] —**do′do·ism,** *n.*

dodo,
Raphus solitarius,
length 3 ft. (0.9 m)

Do·do·ma (dō′dō mä, dō′də-), *n.* a city in and the capital of Tanzania, in the central part. 45,703.

Do·do·na (də dō′nə), *n.* an ancient town in NW Greece, in Epirus: the site of a famous oracle of Zeus. —**Do·do·nae·an, Do·do·ne·an, Do·do·ni·an** (dōd′n ē′ən, də dō′nē ən), *adj.*

do′do split′, *Bowling Slang.* a split in which the head pin and the seven or ten pin remain standing.

doe (dō), *n., pl.* **does,** (*esp. collectively*) **doe.** the female of the deer, antelope, goat, rabbit, and certain other animals. [bef. 1000; ME *do,* OE *dā;* c. Dan *daa;* akin to OE *dēon* to suck]

doe
of white-tailed deer,
Odocoileus virginianus

DOE, 1. See **Department of Energy. 2.** Also, **d.o.e.** depends on experience; depending on experience: used in stating a salary range in help-wanted ads.

Doe·nitz (dœ′nits), *n.* **Karl** (kärl), 1891–1980, German admiral.

do·er (do͞o′ər), *n.* **1.** a person or thing that does something, esp. a person who gets things done with vigor and efficiency. **2.** a person characterized by action, as distinguished from one given to contemplation. **3.** *Australian.* an amusing or eccentric person; character. [1300–50; ME. See DO[1], -ER[1]]

does[1] (dōz), *n.* a pl. of **doe.**

does[2] (duz), *v.* a 3rd pers. sing. pres. indic. of **do**[1].

doe·skin (dō′skin′), *n.* **1.** the skin of a doe. **2.** leather made from this. **3. doeskins,** soft leather gloves made of sheepskin. **4.** a closely woven woolen cloth made with a satin or a small twill weave. —*adj.* **5.** made of doeskin. [1425–75; late ME *doskin.* See DOE, SKIN]

does·n't (duz′ənt), contraction of *does not.*
—**Usage.** See **contraction.**
—**Pronunciation.** See **isn't.**

do·est (do͞o′ist), *v. Archaic.* 2nd pers. sing. pres. ind. of **do**[1].

do·eth (do͞o′ith), *v. Archaic.* 3rd pers. sing. pres. ind. of **do**[1].

doff (dof, dôf), *v.t.* **1.** to remove or take off, as clothing. **2.** to remove or tip (the hat), as in greeting. **3.** to throw off; get rid of: *Doff your stupid ideas and join our side!* **4.** *Textiles.* **a.** to strip (carded fiber) from a carding machine. **b.** to remove (full bobbins, material, etc.) from a textile machine. —*n.* **5.** *Textiles.* **a.** the act of removing bobbins, material, etc., and stripping fibers from a textile machine. **b.** the material so doffed. [1300–50; ME, contr. of *do off;* cf. DON[1]]

doff·er (dof′ər, dô′fər), *n.* **1.** a person or thing that doffs. **2.** *Textiles.* **a.** a wire-clothed roller on a carding machine, esp. the roller to which the carded fibers are transferred from the cylinder and then prepared for conversion into sliver. **b.** any roller that removes the fibers from another roller. [1815–25; DOFF + -ER[1]]

dog (dôg, dog), *n., v.,* **dogged, dog·ging.** —*n.* **1.** a domesticated canid, *Canis familiaris,* bred in many varieties. See illus. on next page. **2.** any carnivore of the dog family Canidae, having prominent canine teeth and, in the wild state, a long and slender muzzle, a deep-chested muscular body, a bushy tail, and large, erect ears. Cf. **canid. 3.** the male of such an animal. **4.** any of various animals resembling a dog. **5.** a despicable man or youth. **6.** *Informal.* a fellow in general: *a lucky dog.* **7. dogs,** *Slang.* feet. **8.** *Slang.* **a.** something worthless or of extremely poor quality: *That used car you bought is a dog.* **b.** an utter failure; flop: *Critics say his new play is a dog.* **9.** *Slang.* an ugly, boring, or crude person. **10.** *Slang.* See **hot dog. 11.** (*cap.*) *Astron.* either of two constellations, Canis Major or Canis Minor. **12.** *Mach.* **a.** any of various mechanical devices, as for gripping or holding something. **b.** a projection on a moving part for moving steadily or for tripping another part with which it engages. **13.** Also called **gripper, nipper.** *Metalworking.* a device on a drawbench for drawing the work through the die. **14.** a cramp binding together two timbers. **15.** an iron bar driven into a stone or timber to provide a means of lifting it. **16.** an andiron; firedog. **17.** *Meteo-*

rol. a sundog or fogdog. **18.** a word formerly used in communications to represent the letter D. **19. go to the dogs,** *Informal.* to deteriorate; degenerate morally or physically: *This neighborhood is going to the dogs.* **20. lead a dog's life,** to have an unhappy or harassed existence: *He maintained that he led a dog's life in the army.* **21. let sleeping dogs lie,** to refrain from action that would alter an existing situation for fear of causing greater problems or complexities. **22. put on the dog,** *Informal.* to assume an attitude of wealth or importance; put on airs. —*v.t.* **23.** to follow or track like a dog, esp. with hostile intent; hound. **24.** to drive or chase with a dog or dogs. **25.** *Mach.* to fasten with dogs. **26. dog it,** *Informal.* **a.** to shirk one's responsibility; loaf on the job. **b.** to retreat, flee, renege, etc.: *a sponsor who dogged it when needed most.* [bef. 1050; ME *dogge,* OE *docga*] —**dog′less,** *adj.* —**dog′like′,** *adj.*

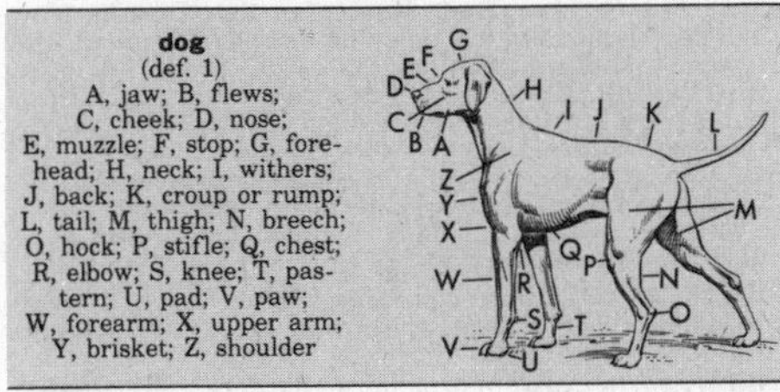

dog (def. 1) A, jaw; B, flews; C, cheek; D, nose; E, muzzle; F, stop; G, forehead; H, neck; I, withers; J, back; K, croup or rump; L, tail; M, thigh; N, breech; O, hock; P, stifle; Q, chest; R, elbow; S, knee; T, pastern; U, pad; V, paw; W, forearm; X, upper arm; Y, brisket; Z, shoulder

dog′ and po′ny show′, *Informal.* an elaborate sales, advertising, or publicity presentation or campaign. [1965–70]

dog′ ape′, baboon. [1590–1600]

dog·bane (dôg′bān′, dog′-), *n.* any of several plants of the genus *Apocynum,* esp. *A. androsaemifolium,* yielding an acrid milky juice and having an intensely bitter root. [1590–1600; DOG + BANE]

dog′bane fam′ily, the plant family Apocynaceae, characterized by shrubs, trees, and herbaceous plants having milky and often poisonous juice, simple opposite leaves, often showy flowers, and fruit usually in dry pods, and including the dogbane, oleander, periwinkle, and plumeria.

dog·ber·ry (dôg′ber′ē, -bə rē, dog′-), *n., pl.* **-ries. 1.** the berry or fruit of any of various plants, as the European dogwood, *Cornus sanguinea,* the chokeberry, *Aronia arbutifolia,* or the mountain ash, *Sorbus americana.* **2.** the plant itself. **3.** any of several plants, esp. the dog rose, bearberry, and guelder rose. [1545–55; DOG + BERRY]

Dog·ber·ry (dôg′ber′ē, -bə rē, dog′-), *n., pl.* **-rys** for 2. **1.** a foolish constable in Shakespeare's *Much Ado About Nothing.* **2.** any foolish, blundering, or stupid official.

dog′ bis′cuit, 1. a hard biscuit for dogs, usually containing ground meat, bones, etc. **2.** *Mil.* a hard dry biscuit used as an emergency ration. [1855–60]

dog·cart (dôg′kärt′, dog′-), *n.* **1.** a light, two-wheeled, horse-drawn vehicle for ordinary driving, with two transverse seats back to back, and originally having a box under the rear seat for carrying a dog. **2.** a cart drawn by a dog or dogs. [1660–70; DOG + CART]

dog·catch·er (dôg′kach′ər, dog′-), *n.* a person employed by a municipal pound, humane society, or the like, to find and impound stray or homeless dogs, cats, etc. [1825–35, *Amer.;* DOG + CATCHER]

dog-cheap (dôg′chēp′, dog′-), *Informal.* —*adj.* **1.** very inexpensive. —*adv.* **2.** very inexpensively. [1520–30]

dog′ clutch′, *Mach.* a clutch in which projections of one of the engaging parts fit into recesses of the other.

dog′ col′lar, 1. a collar used to restrain or identify a dog. **2.** *Informal.* a close-fitting necklace, as a wide band covered with or composed of precious or semiprecious stones; choker. **3.** *Slang.* a collar of the type worn by some clergymen, priests, etc., having the opening at the back; clerical collar. [1515–25]

dog′ cur′tain, *Naut.* a flap on a canvas cover for a binnacle, affording a view of the compass when raised.

dog′-day cica′da (dôg′dā′, dog′-), any of several cicadas of the genus *Tibicen,* that have distinctive songs commonly heard during July and August. Also called **harvest fly.**

dog′ days′, 1. the sultry part of the summer, supposed to occur during the period that Sirius, the Dog Star, rises at the same time as the sun: now often reckoned from July 3 to August 11. **2.** a period marked by lethargy, inactivity, or indolence. [1530–40; trans. of L *diēs caniculārēs;* see CANICULAR] —**dog′-day′,** *adj.*

dog·dom (dôg′dəm, dog′-), *n.* **1.** the category of all dogs. **2.** the state of being a dog. **3.** those people, collectively, who are interested in dogs. [1850–55; DOG + -DOM]

dog-doo (dôg′do͞o′, dog′-), *n. Informal.* dog excrement. [DOG + (DOO)-DOO]

doge (dōj), *n.* the chief magistrate in the former republics of Venice and Genoa. [1540–50; < Upper It (Venetian) < L *ducem,* acc. of *dux* leader; cf. DUCE, DUKE, DUX] —**doge′dom,** *n.* —**doge′ship,** *n.*

dog-ear (dôg′ēr′, dog′-), *n.* **1.** (in a book) a corner of a page folded over like a dog's ear, as by careless use, or to mark a place. **2.** *Archit.* crossette. —*v.t.* **3.** to fold down the corner of (a page in a book). Also, **dog′ear′, dog's-ear.** [1650–60]

dog-eared (dôg′ērd′, dog′-), *adj.* **1.** having dog-ears: *a dog-eared book.* **2.** shabby; worn: *dog-eared furniture.* Also, **dog′eared′.** [1775–85]

dog-eat-dog (dôg′ēt dôg′, dog′ēt dog′), *adj.* **1.** marked by destructive or ruthless competition; without self-restraint, ethics, etc.: *It's a dog-eat-dog industry.* —*n.* **2.** complete egotism; action based on utter cynicism: *The only rule of the marketplace was dog-eat-dog.* [1930–35]

do·gey (dō′gē), *n., pl.* **-geys.** dogie.

dog·face (dôg′fās′, dog′-), *n. Older Slang.* an enlisted man in the U.S. Army, esp. an infantryman in World War II. [1940–45; DOG + FACE]

dog′ fen′nel, mayweed. [1515–25]

dog·fight (dôg′fīt′, dog′-), *n., v.,* **-fought, -fight·ing.** —*n.* **1.** a violent fight between dogs. **2.** a fight between warring fighter planes. **3.** any rough-and-tumble physical battle. —*v.t.* **4.** to engage in a dogfight with. —*v.i.* **5.** to engage in a dogfight. [1650–60; 1915 for def. 2; DOG + FIGHT]

dog·fish (dôg′fish′, dog′-), *n., pl.* (*esp. collectively*) **-fish,** (*esp. referring to two or more kinds or species*) **-fish·es. 1.** any of several small sharks, esp. of the genera *Mustelus* and *Squalus,* that are destructive to food fishes. **2.** any of various other fishes, as the bowfin. [1425–75; earlier *dokefyche;* late ME. See DOG, FISH]

dog′ flea′, See under **flea.** [1835–45]

dog′ fox′, a male fox. [1570–80]

dog·ged[1] (dô′gid, dog′id), *adj.* persistent in effort; stubbornly tenacious: *a dogged worker.* [1275–1325; ME: having characteristics of a dog; see DOG, -ED[3]] —**dog′ged·ly,** *adv.* —**dog′ged·ness,** *n.*
—**Syn.** mulish, inflexible, unyielding. See **stubborn.**

dogged[2] (dôgd, dogd), *adj. Southern U.S.* doggoned; damned; confounded: *Well, I'll be dogged!*

dog·ger[1] (dô′gər, dog′ər), *n.* a two-masted Dutch fishing vessel with a blunt bow, used in the North Sea. [1325–75; ME < MD *dogge* fishing boat + *-er* -ER[1]]

dog·ger[2] (dô′gər, dog′ər), *n. Metalworking.* an assistant at a drawbench. [DOG + -ER[1]]

Dog′ger Bank′ (dô′gər, dog′ər), a shoal in the North Sea, between N England and Denmark: fishing grounds; naval battle 1915.

dog·ger·el (dô′gər əl, dog′ər-), *adj.* **1.** (of verse) **a.** comic or burlesque, and usually loose or irregular in measure. **b.** rude; crude; poor. —*n.* **2.** doggerel verse. Also, **dog·grel** (dô′grəl, dog′rəl). [1350–1400; ME; see DOG, -REL; cf. DOG LATIN]

dog·ger·y (dô′gə rē, dog′ə-), *n., pl.* **-ger·ies. 1.** dog-like behavior or conduct, esp. when surly. **2.** dogs collectively. **3.** rabble; mob. **4.** *Older Slang.* a place where liquor is sold; saloon. [1605–15; DOG + -ERY]

dog·gish (dô′gish, dog′ish), *adj.* **1.** like a dog; canine: *doggish affection.* **2.** surly; mean: *a doggish temper.* **3.** stylish and showy. [1350–1400; ME; see DOG, -ISH[1]] —**dog′gish·ly,** *adv.* —**dog′gish·ness,** *n.*

dog·go (dô′gō, dog′ō), *adv.* **1.** *Informal.* in concealment; out of sight. **2. lie doggo,** *Brit. Slang.* to keep out of sight; hide: *Lie doggo until the excitement blows over.* [1890–95; appar. DOG + -O]

dog·gone (dôg′gôn′, -gon′, dog′-), *v.t.,* **-goned, -gon·ing,** *adj., superl.* **-gon·est,** *adv. Informal.* —*v.t.* **1.** to damn: *Doggone your silly advice!* —*adj.* **2.** Also, **doggoned.** damned; confounded: *a doggone fool; Well, I'll be doggoned.* —*adv.* **3.** Also, **doggoned.** damned: *He's a doggone poor sport.* [1850–55, *Amer.;* perh. from *dog on it!* euphemistic alter. of *God damned*]

dog·goned (dôg′gônd′, -gond′, dog′-), *adj., superl.* **-goned·est,** *adv.* doggone.

dog·gy[1] (dô′gē, dog′ē), *n., pl.* **-gies. 1.** a little dog or a puppy. **2.** a pet term for any dog. Also, **dog′gie.** [1815–25; DOG + -Y[2]]

dog·gy[2] (dô′gē, dog′ē), *adj.,* **-gi·er, -gi·est. 1.** of or pertaining to a dog: *a doggy smell.* **2.** fond of dogs: *tweedy, doggy people.* **3.** pretentious; ostentatious. Also, **dog′gie.** [1350–1400; ME; see DOG, -Y[1]]

dog′gy bag′, a small bag provided on request by a restaurant for a customer to carry home leftovers of a meal, ostensibly to feed a dog or other pet. [1965–70, *Amer.*]

dog′ hook′, an iron hook used for handling logs in lumbering. [1565–75]

dog·house (dôg′hous′, dog′-), *n., pl.* **-hous·es** (-hou′ziz). **1.** a small shelter for a dog. **2.** (on a yacht) a small cabin that presents a relatively high profile and gives the appearance of a box. Cf. **trunk cabin. 3.** *Rocketry Slang.* a bulge on the surface of a rocket or missile, for scientific instruments. **4. in the doghouse,** *Slang.* in disfavor or disgrace. [1605–15; DOG + HOUSE]

D, doghouse (def. 2) C, cabin

do·gie (dō′gē), *n. Western U.S.* a motherless calf in a cattle herd. Also, **dogey, dogy.** [1885–90, *Amer.;* orig. obscure; alleged to be *doughg(uts)* + -IE]

dog′ in the man′ger, a person who selfishly keeps something that he or she does not really need or want so that others may not use or enjoy it. [1555–65] —**dog′-in-the-man′ger,** *adj.*

dog′ i′ron, *South Midland and Southern U.S.* an andiron.

dog′ Lat′in, 1. mongrel or spurious Latin. **2.** a jargon imitating Latin. [1760–70]

dog·leg (dôg′leg′, dog′-), *n., adj., v.,* **-legged, -leg·ging.** —*n.* **1.** a route, way, or course that turns at a sharp angle. —*adj.* **2.** dog-legged. —*v.i.* **3.** to proceed around a sharp angle or along an angular or zigzag course: *The road doglegged through the mountains.* [1885–90; DOG + LEG]

dog′leg fence′. See **snake fence.** [1885–90]

dog-leg·ged (dôg′leg′id, -legd′, dog′-), *adj.* bent like the hind leg of a dog; zigzag. Also, **dogleg.** [1695–1705]

dog′-leg stair′ (dôg′leg′, dog′-), a half-turn stair, the successive flights of which are immediately side by side and connected by an intervening platform. Also, **dog′-legged stair′.** [1890–95]

dog·like (dôg′līk′, dog′-), *adj.* **1.** similar to a dog; having the appearance, traits, etc., of a dog. **2.** uncritical; unshakeable, as the attachment of a dog for its owner: *doglike devotion.* [1595–1605; DOG + -LIKE]

dog·ma (dôg′mə, dog′-), *n., pl.* **-mas, -ma·ta** (-mə tə). **1.** a system of principles or tenets, as of a church. **2.** a specific tenet or doctrine authoritatively laid down, as by a church: *the dogma of the Assumption.* **3.** prescribed doctrine: *political dogma.* **4.** a settled or established opinion, belief, or principle. [1590–1600; < L < Gk, equiv. to *dok(eîn)* to seem, think, seem good + *-ma* n. suffix]

dog·mat·ic (dôg mat′ik, dog-), *adj.* **1.** of, pertaining to, or of the nature of a dogma or dogmas; doctrinal. **2.** asserting opinions in a doctrinaire or arrogant manner; opinionated. Also, **dog·mat′i·cal.** [1595–1605; < LL *dogmaticus* < Gk *dogmatikós,* equiv. to *dogmat-* (s. of *dógma* DOGMA) + *-ikos* -IC] —**dog·mat′i·cal·ly,** *adv.* —**dog·mat′i·cal·ness,** *n.*
—**Syn. 2.** arbitrary, imperious, dictatorial.

dog·mat·ics (dôg mat′iks, dog-), *n.* (*used with a singular v.*) the study of the arrangement and statement of religious doctrines, esp. of the doctrines received in and taught by the Christian church. Also called **dogmat′ic theol′ogy, doctrinal theology.** [1835–45; see DOGMATIC, -ICS]

dog·ma·tism (dôg′mə tiz′əm, dog′-), *n.* dogmatic character; unfounded positiveness in matters of opinion; arrogant assertion of opinions as truths. [1595–1605; < LL *dogmatismus,* equiv. to L *dogmat(icus)* DOGMATIC + *-ismus* -ISM; r. *dogmatisme* < F]

dog·ma·tist (dôg′mə tist, dog′-), *n.* **1.** a person who asserts his or her opinions in an unduly positive or arrogant manner; a dogmatic person. **2.** a person who lays down dogmas. [1535–45; < ML *dogmatista,* equiv. to *dogmat(izāre)* to DOGMATIZE + *-ista* -IST]

dog·ma·tize (dôg′mə tīz′, dog′-), *v.,* **-tized, -tiz·ing.** —*v.i.* **1.** to make dogmatic assertions; speak or write dogmatically. —*v.t.* **2.** to assert or deliver as a dogma. Also, esp. *Brit.,* **dog′ma·tise′.** [1605–15; < LL *dogmatizāre,* equiv. to L *dogmat(icus)* DOGMATIC + *-izāre* -IZE] —**dog′ma·ti·za′tion,** *n.* —**dog′ma·tiz′er,** *n.*

dog′ nail′, a nail having a head projecting to one side. [1695–1705]

dog·nap (dôg′nap, dog′-), *v.t.,* **-napped** or **-naped, -nap·ping** or **-nap·ing.** to steal (a dog), esp. for the purpose of selling it for profit. [1945–50, *Amer.;* DOG + -NAP] —**dog′nap·per, dog′nap·er,** *n.*

Do·gon (dō′gon), *n., pl.* **-gons,** (*esp. collectively*) **-gon** for 1. **1.** a member of a group of indigenous people of the mountains of central Mali. **2.** the Gur language of the Dogon.

do-good (do͞o′go͝od′), *adj.* of or befitting a do-gooder. [1965–70; back formation from DO-GOODER]

do-good·er (do͞o′go͝od′ər, -go͝od′-), *n.* a well-intentioned but naive and often ineffectual social or political reformer. [1925–30, *Amer.; do good* + -ER[1]]

do-good·ism (do͞o′go͝od iz′əm), *n.* the actions or principles of a do-gooder. Also, **do-good·er·ism** (do͞o′go͝od′ə riz′əm). [1950–55; DO-GOOD(ER) + -ISM]

dog′ pad′dle, a simple swimming stroke mainly used to stay afloat while remaining almost stationary in the water, executed by paddling both arms underwater while kicking the legs, with the body in a crouching position and the head above water. [1900–05]

dog-pad·dle (dôg′pad′l, dog′-), *v.i.,* **-dled, -dling.** to swim or keep afloat by use of the dog paddle. [1900–05]

dog-poor (dôg′po͝or′, dog′-), *adj.* very poor. [1885–90]

dog′ rose′, an Old World wild rose, *Rosa canina,* having pink or white flowers. [1590–1600]

dog's′ age′, *Northern U.S.* quite a long time: *I haven't seen you in a dog's age!* [1830–40, *Amer.*]

dog′ salm′on. See **chum salmon.** [1865–70, *Amer.*]

dogs·bod·y (dôgz′bod′ē, dogz′-), *n., pl.* **-bod·ies.** *Chiefly Brit. Slang.* a menial worker; drudge. [1810–20; orig. a junior naval officer, earlier a sailor's term for soaked sea biscuits or pease pudding]

dog's′ break′fast, *Chiefly Canadian Slang.* a disorderly mixture; hodgepodge. [1935–40]

dog's′ chance′, *Slang.* little likelihood; small chance (usually used in the negative): *That project didn't have a dog's chance of succeeding.* [1900–05]

dog's′ disease′, *Australian Slang.* influenza. [1925–30]

dog's-ear (dôgz′ēr′, dogz′-), *n., v.t.* dog-ear. —**dog's′-eared′,** *adj.*

dog′ shift′, *Informal.* See **graveyard shift.**

dog·shore (dôg′shôr′, -shōr′, dog′-), *n. Shipbuilding.* any of several shores for holding the hull of a small or moderate-sized vessel in place after keel blocks and other shores are removed and until the vessel is launched. [1795–1805; DOG + SHORE[2]]

dog′ show′, a competitive event in which dogs are ex-

CONCISE PRONUNCIATION KEY: act, cāpe, dâre, pärt; set, ēqual; if, īce; ox, ōver, ôrder, oil, bo͝ok, bo͞ot, out; up, ûrge; child; sing; shoe; thin, *th*at; zh as in *treasure.* ə = *a* as in *alone, e* as in *system, i* as in *easily, o* as in *gallop, u* as in *circus;* ᵊ as in *fire* (fīᵊr), *hour* (ouᵊr). l and n can serve as syllabic consonants, as in *cradle* (krād′l), and *button* (but′n). See the full key inside the front cover.

hibited and judged by an established standard or set of ideals prescribed for each breed. [1855–60]

dog·sled (dôg′sled′, dog′-), *n., v.,* **-sled·ded, -sled·ding.** —*n.* **1.** Also, **dog′ sledge′.** a sled pulled by dogs, esp. one used by Arctic peoples, as the Eskimos. —*v.i.* **2.** to travel by dogsled. [1800–10, *Amer.*; DOG + SLED]

dog's′ let′ter, the letter *r,* esp. when representing a trill. [1585–95; trans. of L *littera canīna,* from the resemblance of the sound of the trill to a dog's snarl]

Dog′ Star′, **1.** the bright star Sirius, in Canis Major. **2.** the bright star Procyon, in Canis Minor. [1570–80]

dog′ tag′, **1.** a small disk or strip attached to a dog's harness or collar stating owner, home, etc. **2.** See **identification tag.** **3.** *Informal.* **a.** any tag for a suitcase, camera, or other personal possession with the owner's name or address. **b.** a tag or card with a person's name or affiliation, worn at conventions, large meetings, etc. [1915–20]

dog′ tick′, any of a variety of ticks, as the American dog tick, that commonly infest dogs and may transmit Rocky Mountain spotted fever or tularemia to humans. See illus. under **tick.** [1545–55]

dog-tired (dôg′tīᵊrd′, dog′-), *adj.* utterly exhausted; worn out. [1800–10]

dog·tooth (dôg′to͞oth′, dog′-), *n.* **1.** Also, **dog′ tooth′.** a canine tooth. **2.** *Archit.* any of a series of small pyramidal ornaments, usually formed by a radiating arrangement of four sculptured leaves, set close together in a concave molding, used esp. in England in the 13th century. [1545–55; DOG + TOOTH]

dog′tooth vi′olet, **1.** Also called **adder's-tongue, trout lily.** any of several North American lilies of the genus *Erythronium,* having nodding flowers and usually mottled leaves. **2.** a related Old World plant, *E. denscanis,* having purplish flowers. [1620–30]

dog·trot (dôg′trot′, dog′-), *n., v.,* **-trot·ted, -trot·ting.** —*n.* **1.** a gentle trot, like that of a dog. **2.** *South Midland and Southern U.S.* a covered passage or porch linking two parts of a house; breezeway. —*v.i.* **3.** to go or move at a gentle trot or a dogtrot. [1655–65; DOG + TROT]

dog·vane (dôg′vān′, dog′-), *n. Naut.* a small vane that shows the direction of the wind, mounted in a position visible to a helmsman. [1760–70; DOG + VANE]

dog-walk·er (dôg′wô′kər, dog′-), *n.* a person who walks other people's dogs, esp. for a fee.

dog′ war′den, dogcatcher.

dog·watch (dôg′woch′, -wôch′, dog′-), *n.* **1.** *Naut.* either of two two-hour watches, the first from 4 to 6 P.M., the latter from 6 to 8 P.M. **2.** Also called **lobster shift, lobster trick, sunrise watch.** *Journalism Slang.* the period, after the regular editions of a newspaper have gone to press, during which staff personnel remain on duty to await any new developments that may warrant an extra issue. **3.** *Informal.* any night shift, esp. the last or latest one. Also, **dog′ watch′.** [1690–1700; DOG + WATCH]

dog′ whelk′, any of several carnivorous, marine gastropods of the family Nassidae. Also called **dog·win·kle** (dôg′wing′kəl, dog′-). [1855–60]

dog·wood (dôg′wo͝od′, dog′-), *n.* **1.** any tree or shrub of the genus *Cornus,* esp. *C. sanguinea,* of Europe, or *C. florida,* of America. **2.** the wood of any such tree. **3.** a light to medium brown or a medium yellowish-brown color. —*adj.* **4.** having the color dogwood. [1610–20; DOG + WOOD[1]]

dog′wood fam′ily, the plant family Cornaceae, characterized by trees and shrubs having simple opposite leaves, small flowers often surrounded by showy, petallike bracts, and berrylike fruit, including the bunchberry, cornelian cherry, and dogwood.

dog′wood win′ter, *South Midland and Southern U.S.* a short period of cold weather in the spring. [1905–10, *Amer.*]

dog′ work′, *Informal.* tedious labor; drudgery.

do·gy (dō′gē), *n., pl.* **-gies.** dogie.

Do·ha (dō′hä), *n.* a city in and the capital of the state of Qatar, on the Persian Gulf. 100,000.

DOHC, *Auto.* See **double overhead camshaft.**

Doh·ná·nyi (dôh′nä nyi), *n.* **Ernst von** (ernst fən) or **Er·nő** (ɛʀ′nœ), 1877–1960, Hungarian pianist and composer in the U.S.

DOI, See **Department of the Interior.**

doiled (doild), *adj. Scot.* stupid; foolish; crazed. [1505–15; cf. ME *deolen, dolen* to grieve < AF, OF *duel-,* tonic s. of *doleir* < L *dolēre* to grieve; see DOLE[2]]

doi·ly (doi′lē), *n., pl.* **-lies.** **1.** any small, ornamental mat, as of embroidery or lace. **2.** *Archaic.* a small napkin, as one used during a dessert course. Also, **doyley.** [1670–80; named after a London draper of the late 17th century]

do·ing (do͞o′ing), *n.* **1.** action; performance; execution: *Your misfortune is not of my doing.* **2. doings,** deeds; proceedings; happenings; events. [1275–1325; ME; see DO[1], -ING[1]]

Doi·sy (doi′zē), *n.* **Edward Ad·el·bert** (ad′l bərt, ə del′-), born 1893, U.S. biochemist: Nobel prize for medicine 1943.

doit (doit), *n.* **1.** Also, **duit.** an old small copper coin of the Netherlands and Dutch colonies, first issued in the 17th century. **2.** a bit or trifle. [1585–95; < D *duit*]

doit·ed (doi′tid, -tit), *adj. Scot.* childish or feebleminded, esp. because of advanced age; senile. [1375–1425; late ME (Scots), appar. a form of ME *doted,* ptp. of *doten* to DOTE]

do-it-your·self (do͞o′i chər self′, -it yər-), *adj.* **1.** of or designed for construction or use by amateurs without special training: *a do-it-yourself kit for building a radio.* —*n.* **2.** the practice or hobby of building or repairing things for oneself, usually in one's own home. [1950–55] —**do′-it-your·self′er,** *n.*

DOJ, See **Department of Justice.**

do·jo (dō′jō), *n., pl.* **-jos.** a school or practice hall where karate, judo, or other martial arts are taught. [1940–45; < Japn *dōjō* Buddhist seminary, drill hall < MChin transliteration of Skt *bodhi-maṇḍa* lit., seat of wisdom (equiv. to Chin *dàochǎng*)]

dol (dōl), *n.* a unit for measuring the intensity of pain. Cf. **dolorimetry.** [1945–50; < L *dol(or)* pain]

DOL, See **Department of Labor.**

dol., **1.** *Music.* dolce. **2.** dollar.

do·lab·ri·form (dō lab′rə fôrm′), *adj. Bot., Zool.* shaped like an ax or a cleaver. [1745–55; < L *dolābr(a)* mattock, pickax + -I- + -FORM]

Dol·by (dōl′bē, dôl′-), *Trademark.* a brand of system for reducing high-frequency noise in audiotape using various electronic devices during recording and playback.

dol·ce (dōl′chā; *It.* dôl′che), *Music.* —*adj.* **1.** sweet; soft. —*n.* **2.** an instruction to the performer that the music is to be executed softly and sweetly. **3.** a soft-toned organ stop. [1840–50; < It < L *dulcis* savory, sweet; see DULCET]

dol·ce far nien·te (dôl′che fär nyen′te), *Italian.* pleasing inactivity. [lit., (it is) sweet to do nothing]

dol·ce vi·ta (dôl′che vē′tä; *Eng.* dōl′chā vē′tə), *Italian.* sweet life; the good life perceived as one of physical pleasure and self-indulgence (usually prec. by *la*).

dol·drums (dōl′drəmz, dol′-, dôl′-), *n.* (*used with a plural v.*) **1.** a state of inactivity or stagnation, as in business or art: *August is a time of doldrums for many enterprises.* **2. the doldrums, a.** a belt of calms and light baffling winds north of the equator between the northern and southern trade winds in the Atlantic and Pacific oceans. **b.** the weather prevailing in this area. **3.** a dull, listless, depressed mood; low spirits. [1795–1805; obs. *dold* stupid (see DOLT) + *-rum(s)* (pl.) n. suffix (see TANTRUM)]
—**Syn. 3.** depression, gloom, melancholy, dejection.

dole[1] (dōl), *n., v.,* **doled, dol·ing.** —*n.* **1.** a portion or allotment of money, food, etc., esp. as given at regular intervals by a charity or for maintenance. **2.** a dealing out or distributing, esp. in charity. **3.** a form of payment to the unemployed instituted by the British government in 1918. **4.** any similar payment by a government to an unemployed person. **5.** *Archaic.* one's fate or destiny. **6. on the dole,** receiving payment from the government, as relief: *They couldn't afford any luxuries while living on the dole.* —*v.t.* **7.** to distribute in charity. **8.** to give out sparingly or in small quantities (usually fol. by *out*): *The last of the water was doled out to the thirsty crew.* [bef. 1000; ME *dol,* OE *gedāl* sharing; cf. DEAL[1]]
—**Syn. 1.** share, pittance. **8.** ration.

dole[2] (dōl), *n. Archaic.* grief or sorrow; lamentation. [1200–50; ME *do(e)l* < AF, OF < LL *dolus,* for L *dolor* DOLOR]

Dole (dōl), *n.* **1. Robert J(oseph),** born 1923, U.S. politician: senator 1969–96. **2. Sanford Ballard,** 1844–1926, U.S. politician and jurist in Hawaii: president of Republic of Hawaii 1894–98; first territorial governor 1900–03.

dole′ bludg′er, *Australian Slang.* a person who collects unemployment benefits but makes no serious effort to get work. [see BLUDGE]

dole′ cup′board, a livery cupboard formerly used in churches for holding bread to be distributed to the poor. [1905–10]

dole·ful (dōl′fəl), *adj.* sorrowful; mournful; melancholy: *a doleful look on her face.* [1225–75; ME *dolful.* See DOLE[2], -FUL] —**dole′ful·ly,** *adv.* —**dole′ful·ness,** *n.*

dol·er·ite (dol′ə rīt′), *n. Petrol.* **1.** a coarse-grained variety of basalt. **2.** any of various other igneous rocks, as diabase. **3.** any basaltlike igneous rock whose composition can be determined only by microscopic examination. [1830–40; < F *dolérite* < Gk *doler(ós)* deceitful (deriv. of *dólos* wile) + F *-ite* -ITE[1]] —**dol·er·it·ic** (dol′ə rit′ik), *adj.*

dole·some (dōl′səm), *adj. Literary.* doleful. [1525–35; DOLE[2] + -SOME[1]]

dolicho-, a combining form meaning "long" or "narrow": *dolichocephalic.* [< Gk, comb. form of *dolichós*]

dol·i·cho·ce·phal·ic (dol′i kō sə fal′ik), *adj. Cephalom.* long-headed; having a cephalic index of 75 and under. Also, **dol·i·cho·ceph·a·lous** (dol′i kō sef′ə ləs). [1840–50; DOLICHO- + CEPHALIC] —**dol·i·cho·ceph·a·lism** (dol′i kō sef′ə liz′əm), **dol′i·cho·ceph′a·ly,** *n.*

dol·i·cho·cra·nic (dol′i kō krā′nik), *adj. Craniom.* dolichocephalic. [DOLICHO- + CRAN(IO)- + -IC]

Do·lin (dō′lin), *n.* **Sir An·ton** (an′ton), (*Patrick Healey-Kay*), 1904–83, English ballet dancer.

do·li·um (dō′lē əm), *n., pl.* **-li·a** (-lē ə). a large earthenware jar used by the ancient Romans. [1475–85; < L *dōlium*]

doll (dol), *n.* **1.** a small figure, esp. a child's toy, representing a baby or other human being. **2.** *Slang.* **a.** a pretty but expressionless or unintelligent woman. **b.** a girl or woman, esp. one who is considered attractive. **c.** a boy or man who is considered attractive. **d.** (*sometimes cap.*) an affectionate term of address (often offensive when used indiscriminately, esp. by a male to a female). **3.** *Informal.* a generous or helpful person: *You're a doll for lending me your car.* —*v.t., v.i.* **4. doll up,** *Informal.* to dress in an elegant or ostentatiously stylish manner: *We got all dolled up for the opera.* [1550–60; generic use of DOLL] —**doll′ish, doll′-like′,** *adj.* —**doll′ish·ly,** *adv.* —**doll′ish·ness,** *n.*

Doll (dol), *n.* a female given name, form of **Dorothy.**

dol·lar (dol′ər), *n.* **1.** a paper money, silver or cupronickel coin, and monetary unit of the United States, equal to 100 cents. *Symbol:* $ **2.** a silver or nickel coin and monetary unit of Canada, equal to 100 cents. *Symbol:* $ **3.** any of the monetary units of various other nations, as Australia, the Bahamas, Barbados, Belize, Bermuda, Fiji, Guyana, Hong Kong, Jamaica, Liberia, New Zealand, Singapore, the Solomon Islands, Trinidad and Tobago, and Zimbabwe, equal to 100 cents. **4.** Also called **ringgit.** a cupronickel coin and monetary unit of Brunei, equal to 100 sen. **5.** ringgit (def. 1). **6.** a thaler. **7.** a peso. **8.** See **Levant dollar.** **9.** yuan (def. 1). **10.** *Brit. Slang.* (formerly) **a.** five-shilling piece; crown. **b.** the sum of five shillings. [1545–55; earlier *daler* < LG, D *daler;* c. G *Taler,* short for *Joachimsthaler* coin minted in Joachimsthal in Bohemia]

dol′lar ar′ea, those countries among which trade is conducted in U.S. dollars or in freely convertible currencies. [1945–50]

dol·lar-av·er·age (dol′ər av′ər ij, -av′rij), *v.i.,* **-aged, -ag·ing.** to engage in dollar averaging.

dol′lar av′eraging, a system of buying securities at regular intervals, using the same amount of cash for each purchase, over a considerable period of time regardless of the prevailing prices of the securities, resulting in having bought the total at an average cost. Also called **dol′lar cost′ av′eraging.** [1925–30]

dol′lar-a-year′ man′ (dol′ər ə yēr′), a federal appointee serving for a token annual salary, usually of one dollar. [1915–20, *Amer.*]

dol·lar·bird (dol′ər bûrd′), *n.* a common roller, *Eurystomus orientalis,* of Asia and Australia, having on its wings a silvery spot the size of a dollar. [1840–50; DOLLAR + BIRD]

dol′lar day′, a sale day on which retail merchandise is reduced to a dollar or very low price. [1945–50]

Dol·lard-des-Or·meaux (*Fr.* dô lar dā zôr mō′), *n.* a town in S Quebec, in E Canada: suburb of Montreal. 39,940.

dol′lar diplo′macy, **1.** a government policy of promoting the business interests of its citizens in other countries. **2.** diplomacy or foreign relations strengthened by the power of a nation's financial resources. [1905–10, *Amer.*]

dol·lar·fish (dol′ər fish′), *n., pl.* (*esp. collectively*) **-fish,** (*esp. referring to two or more kinds or species*) **-fish·es.** **1.** butterfish. **2.** moonfish. [1840–50; so called because of its roundish shape and silvery color]

dol′lar gap′, the difference, measured in U.S. dollars, between the earnings of a foreign country through sales and investments in the U.S. and the payments made by that country to the U.S. Also called **dol′lar short′age, dol′lar def′icit.** [1945–50]

dol·lar·i·za·tion (dol′ər ə zā′shən), *n.* the conversion of a country's currency system into U.S. dollars. [1985–90]

dol·lars-and-cents (dol′ərz ən sents′), *adj.* considered strictly in terms of money: *from a dollars-and-cents viewpoint.* [1835–45, *Amer.*]

dol′lar sign′, the symbol $ before a number indicating that the number represents dollars. [1855–60, *Amer.*]

dol·lar·spot (dol′ər spot′), *n. Plant Pathol.* a turf disease caused by the fungus *Sclerotinia* or related genera, characterized by small, brown to straw-colored, round patches of dead grass that gradually spread and coalesce. [1910–15; DOLLAR + SPOT]

dol·lar·wise (dol′ər wīz′), *adv.* **1.** as expressed in dollars; in dollars and cents: *How much does a million francs amount to, dollarwise?* **2.** on a monetary basis; financially: *The plan has disadvantages, but we will come out ahead dollarwise.* [DOLLAR + -WISE]

doll·face (dol′fās′), *n.* a person having a smooth, unblemished complexion and small, regular features. [1880–85; DOLL + FACE] —**doll′faced′,** *adj.*

Doll·fuss (dôl′fo͞os), *n.* **Eng·el·bert** (eng′əl bert′), 1892–1934, Austrian statesman: premier 1932–34.

doll·house (dol′hous′), *n., pl.* **-hous·es** (-hou′ziz). **1.** a miniature house the scale of children's dolls. **2.** a small cottage or housetrailer. Also, *esp. Brit.,* **doll's′ house′.** [1775–85; DOLL + HOUSE]

dol·lop (dol′əp), *n.* **1.** a lump or blob: *dollops of mud.* **2.** a small quantity: *Add a dollop of soda water to the mixture.* —*v.t.* **3.** to dispense in dollops. [1565–75; cf. Icel *dölpur* fat man, Norw (dial.) *dolp* lump]

Doll's′ House′, A, a play (1879) by Henrik Ibsen.

dol·ly (dol′ē), *n., pl.* **dol·lies,** *v.,* **dol·lied, dol·ly·ing.** —*n.* **1.** *Informal.* a doll. **2.** a low truck or cart with small wheels for moving loads too heavy to be carried by hand. **3.** *Motion Pictures, Television.* a small wheeled platform, usually having a short boom, on which a camera can be mounted for making moving shots. **4.** *Mach.* a tool for receiving and holding the head of a rivet while the other end is being headed. **5.** a block placed on the head of a pile being driven to receive the shock of the blows. **6.** a small locomotive operating on narrow-gauge tracks, esp. in quarries, construction sites, etc. **7.** a short, wooden pole with a hollow dishlike base for stirring clothes while laundering them. **8.** *Slang.* a tablet of Dolophine. **9.** Also called **dol′ly bird′.** *Brit. Informal.* an attractive girl or young woman. **10.** (*sometimes cap.*) *Slang.* an affectionate or familiar term of address (sometimes offensive when used to strangers, casual acquaint-

CONCISE ETYMOLOGY KEY: <, descended or borrowed from; >, whence; b., blend of, blended; c., cognate with; cf., compare; deriv., derivative; equiv., equivalent; imit., imitative; obl., oblique; r., replacing; s., stem; sp., spelling, spelled; resp., respelling, respelled; trans., translation; ?, origin unknown; *, unattested; ‡, probably earlier than. See the full key inside the front cover.

ances, subordinates, etc., esp. by a male to a female). —*v.t.* **11.** to transport or convey (a camera) by means of a dolly. —*v.i.* **12.** to move a camera on a dolly, esp. toward or away from the subject being filmed or televised (often fol. by *in* or *out*): *to dolly in for a close-up.* [1600–10; 1900–05 for def. 9; DOLL + -Y[2]]

Dol·ly (dol′ē), *n.* a female given name, form of **Doll.** Also, **Dol′lie.**

dol·ly·man (dol′ē mən), *n., pl.* **-men.** *Motion Pictures, Television.* a technician who moves or pushes the camera dolly during or between shots. [1850–55, for an earlier sense; DOLLY + MAN[1]]

dol′ly shot′, *Motion Pictures, Television.* a camera shot taken from a moving dolly. Also called **track shot, tracking shot, trucking shot.** [1930–35]

Dol·ly Var·den (dol′ē vär′dn), **1.** a woman's costume of the late 19th century, including a flower-trimmed, broad-brimmed hat and a dress consisting of a tight bodice and bouffant panniers in a flower print over a calf-length quilted petticoat. **2.** the hat of this costume. **3.** the dress of this costume. **4.** *Ichthyol.* Also called **bull trout, Dol′ly Var′den trout′.** a char, *Salvelinus malma,* inhabiting fresh and marine waters of western North America and eastern Asia. **5.** *Newfoundland.* a large earthenware drinking cup used on fishing vessels. [1870–75; costume named after a colorfully dressed character in Dickens' *Barnaby Rudge* (1841); applied to fish in allusion to its coloring]

Dol′ly Var′den pat′tern, a fabric print consisting of bouquets of flowers.

dol·ma (dôl′mə, -mä), *n. Near Eastern Cookery.* a dish of tomatoes, green peppers, vine leaves, or eggplants stuffed with a mixture of meat, rice, and spices. [1885–90; < Turk *dolma* lit., something filled, filling, equiv. to *dol-* fill + *-ma* suffix of deverbal nouns]

dol·man (dōl′mən, dol′-), *n., pl.* **-mans. 1.** a woman's mantle with capelike arm pieces instead of sleeves. **2.** a long outer robe worn by Turks. [1575–85; syncopated var. of *doliman, dolyman* < Turk *dolaman* (obs.), deriv. of *dolamak* to wind round]

dol′man sleeve′, a sleeve tapered from a very large armhole to fit closely at the wrist, used on women's garments. [1930–35]

dol·men (dōl′men, -mən, dol′-), *n. Archaeol.* a structure usually regarded as a tomb, consisting of two or more large, upright stones set with a space between and capped by a horizontal stone. Cf. **chamber tomb.** [1855–60; < F < Cornish, lenited form of *tolmen* hole of stone (taken by French archeologists to mean CROMLECH)] —**dol·men·ic** (dōl men′ik, dol-), *adj.*

dolmen

Dol·ní Vě·sto·ni·ce (dôl′nyē vye′stô nyi tse), a camping site of Upper Paleolithic mammoth hunters c23,000 B.C. in southern Moravia, Czech Republic, characterized chiefly by Venus figures, ornaments of mammoth ivory, and animal figures of baked clay.

do·lo·mite (dō′lə mīt′, dol′ə-), *n.* **1.** a very common mineral, calcium magnesium carbonate, $CaMg(CO_3)_2$, occurring in crystals and in masses. **2.** a rock consisting essentially or largely of this mineral. [1785–95; < F, named after D. de *Dolom(ieu)* (1750–1801), French mineralogist; see -ITE[1]] —**dol·o·mit·ic** (dol′ə mit′ik), *adj.*

dol′omite mar′ble, coarse-grained dolomite. [1790–1800]

Do·lo·mites (dō′lə mīts′, dol′ə-), *n.* (*used with a plural v.*) a mountain range in N Italy: a part of the Alps. Highest peak, Marmolada, 10,965 ft. (3340 m). Also called **Do′lomite Alps′.**

do·lo·mit·i·za·tion (dō′lə mi′tə zā′shən, -mi-, dol′ə-), *n. Geol.* the conversion of limestone into dolomite. [1860–65; DOLOMITIZE + -ATION]

do·lo·mit·ize (dō′lə mi tīz′, -mi-, dol′ə-), *v.t.,* **-ized, -iz·ing.** *Geol.* to convert (limestone) into dolomite. Also, *esp. Brit.,* **do′lo·mit·ise′.** [1860–65; DOLOMITE + -IZE]

Do·lon (dō′lon), *n.* (in the *Iliad*) a son of Eumedes who was killed by Diomedes and Odysseus even though he had given them valuable information about the Trojans.

do·lor (dō′lər), *n.* sorrow; grief. Also, *esp. Brit.,* **do·lour.** [1275–1325; ME *dolour* (< AF) < L *dolor,* equiv. to *dol(ēre)* to feel pain + *-or* -OR[1]]

Do·lo·res (də lôr′is, -lōr′-), *n.* a female given name: from a Latin word meaning "sorrows."

do·lo·rim·e·ter (dō′lə rim′i tər), *n. Med.* an instrument used in dolorimetry. [1945–50; DOLOR + -I- + -METER]

do·lo·rim·e·try (dō′lə rim′i trē, dol′ə-), *n. Med.* a technique for measuring the sensitivity to pain produced by heat rays focused on an area of skin and recorded in dols. [DOLOR + -I- + -METRY] —**do·lo·ri·met·ric** (dō′lər ə me′trik, dol′ər-), *adj.* —**do′lo·ri·met′ri·cal·ly,** *adv.*

do·lo·ro·so (dō′lə rō′sō; *It.* dô′lô Rô′sô), *adj.* plaintive, as if expressing sorrow (used as a musical direction). [1800–10; < It; see DOLOR, -OSE[1]]

dol·or·ous (dol′ər əs, dō′lər-), *adj.* full of, expressing, or causing pain or sorrow; grievous; mournful: *a dolorous melody; dolorous news.* [1375–1425; ME *dolorous, dolerous* < AF, OF; see DOLOR, -OUS] —**dol′or·ous·ly,** *adv.* —**dol′or·ous·ness,** *n.*

dol·phin (dol′fin, dôl′-), *n.* **1.** any of several chiefly marine, cetacean mammals of the family Delphinidae, having a fishlike body, numerous teeth, and the front of the head elongated into a beaklike projection. **2.** Also called **dolphinfish, mahimahi.** either of two large, slender fishes, *Coryphaena hippurus* or *C. equisetis,* of warm and temperate seas. **3.** *Naut.* **a.** a pile, cluster of piles, or buoy to which a vessel may be moored in open water. **b.** a cluster of piles used as a fender, as at the entrance to a dock. **c.** a pudding fender at the nose of a tugboat or on the side of a vessel. **4.** (*cap.*) *Astron.* the constellation Delphinus. [1300–50; ME *dolphyn* < OF *daulphin* < OPr *dalfin* < VL **dalfīnus,* L *delphīnus* < Gk *delphī́n*]

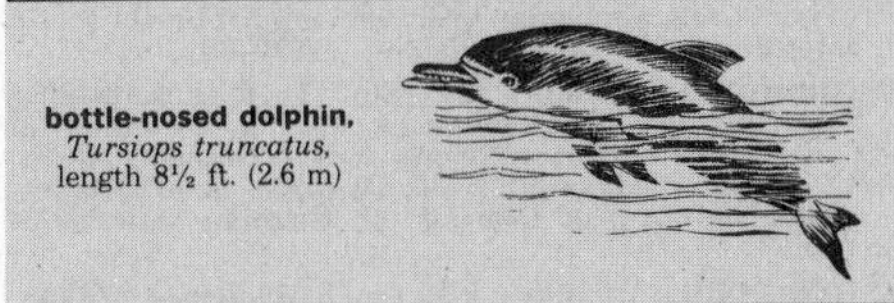
bottle-nosed dolphin, *Tursiops truncatus,* length 8½ ft. (2.6 m)

dol·phin·fish (dol′fin fish′, dôl′-), *n., pl.* (*esp. collectively*) **-fish,** (*esp. referring to two or more kinds or species*) **-fishes.** dolphin (def. 2). [1505–15; DOLPHIN + FISH]

dol′phin kick′, *Swimming.* (in the butterfly stroke) a kick in which the legs move up and down together, with the knees bent on the upswing.

dols., dollars.

dolt (dōlt), *n.* a dull, stupid person; blockhead. [1535–45; var. of obs. *dold* stupid, orig. ptp. of ME *dollen, dullen* to DULL] —**dolt′ish,** *adj.* —**dolt′ish·ly,** *adv.* —**dolt′ish·ness,** *n.*
—**Syn.** idiot, fool, clod, nitwit, dummy.

Dol·ton (dōl′tn), *n.* a city in NE Illinois, near Chicago. 24,766.

do·lus (dō′ləs), *n. Roman and Civil Law.* fraud; deceit, esp. involving or evidencing evil intent (distinguished from *culpa*): *One is always liable for dolus resulting in damages.* [< L]

dom (dom; *for 2 also Port.* dôɴ), *n.* **1.** (*sometimes cap.*) a title of a monk in the Benedictine, Carthusian, Cistercian, and other monastic orders. **2.** (*usually cap.*) a Portuguese title affixed to a man's given name; Sir. [1710–20; short for L *dominus* lord, master]

Dom (dom), *n.* a male given name, form of **Dominic.**

-dom, a suffix forming nouns which refer to domain (*kingdom*), collection of persons (*officialdom*), rank or station (*earldom*), or general condition (*freedom*). [ME; OE *-dōm;* c. ON *-dōmr,* G *-tum;* see DOOM]

Dom., **1.** Dominica. **2.** Dominican.

dom., **1.** domain. **2.** domestic. **3.** dominant. **4.** dominion.

D.O.M., to God, the Best, the Greatest. [< L *Deō Optimō Maximō*]

d.o.m., *Slang.* dirty old man.

Do·magk (dō′mäk), *n.* **Ger·hard** (ger′härt), 1895–1964, German physician: declined 1939 Nobel prize at demand of Nazi government.

do·main (dō mān′), *n.* **1.** a field of action, thought, influence, etc.: *the domain of science.* **2.** the territory governed by a single ruler or government; realm. **3.** a realm or range of personal knowledge, responsibility, etc. **4.** a region characterized by a specific feature, type of growth or wildlife, etc.: *We entered the domain of the pine trees.* **5.** *Law.* land to which there is superior title and absolute ownership. **6.** *Math.* **a.** the set of values assigned to the independent variables of a function. **b.** region (def. 11a). **7.** *Physics.* one of many regions of magnetic polarity within a ferromagnetic body, each consisting of a number of atoms having a common polarity, and collectively determining the magnetic properties of the body by their arrangement. **8.** *Crystall.* a connected region with uniform polarization in a twinned ferroelectric crystal. [1595–1605; < F *domaine,* alter., by assoc. with L *dominium* DOMINIUM, of OF *demeine* < LL *dominicum,* n. use of neut. of L *dominicus* of a master, equiv. to *domin(us)* lord + *-icus* -IC] —**do·ma′ni·al,** *adj.*

dom·al (dō′məl), *adj.* **1.** of or like a dome. **2.** *Phonet.* retroflex (def. 2). —*n.* **3.** *Phonet.* a domal sound. [1710–20; DOME + -AL[1]]

dome (dōm), *n., v.,* **domed, dom·ing.** —*n.* **1.** *Archit.* **a.** a vault, having a circular plan and usually in the form of a portion of a sphere, so constructed as to exert an equal thrust in all directions. **b.** a domical roof or ceiling. **c.** a polygonal vault, ceiling, or roof. **2.** any covering thought to resemble the hemispherical vault of a building or room: *the great dome of the sky.* **3.** anything shaped like a hemisphere. **4.** (in a dam) a semidome having its convex surface toward the impounded water. **5.** *Crystall.* a form having planes that intersect the vertical axis and are parallel to one of the lateral axes. **6.** *Geol.* upwarp. **7.** Also called **vistadome.** *Railroads.* a raised, glass-enclosed section of the roof of a passenger car, placed over an elevated section of seats to afford passengers a full view of scenery. **8.** *Horol.* an inner cover for the works of a watch, which snaps into the rim of the case. **9.** a mountain peak having a rounded summit. **10.** *Slang.* a person's head. —*v.t.* **11.** to cover with or as if with a dome. **12.** to shape like a dome. —*v.i.* **13.** to rise or swell as a dome. [1505–15; < MF *dome* < It *duomo* < ML *domus* (*Deī*) house (of God), church; akin to TIMBER] —**dome′like′,** *adj.*

dome′ car′, a railroad passenger car having a dome in its roof. Cf. **dome** (def. 7).

domed (dōmd), *adj.* **1.** shaped like a dome: *a domed forehead.* **2.** having a dome: *a domed roof.* [1765–75; DOME + -ED[3]]

dome′ light′, **1.** a small light under the roof of an automobile or boat. **2.** a flashing light on the roof of an emergency vehicle, as a police car or ambulance. Also, **dome′light′.** [1955–60]

Dom·e·nic (dom′ə nik), *n.* a male given name.

Dome′ of the Rock′, *Islam.* a shrine in Jerusalem at the site from which Muhammad ascended through the seven heavens to the throne of God: built on the site of the Jewish Temple. Cf. **Isra′, Mi′raj.**

domes·day (do͞omz′dā′, dōmz′-), *n. Archaic.* doomsday.

Domes′day Book′ (do͞omz′dā′, dōmz′-), a record of a survey of the lands of England made by order of William the Conqueror about 1086, giving ownership, extent, value, etc., of the properties. Also, ***Doomsday Book.***

do·mes·tic (də mes′tik), *adj.* **1.** of or pertaining to the home, the household, household affairs, or the family: *domestic pleasures.* **2.** devoted to home life or household affairs. **3.** tame; domesticated. **4.** of or pertaining to one's own or a particular country as apart from other countries: *domestic trade.* **5.** indigenous to or produced or made within one's own country; not foreign; native: *domestic goods.* —*n.* **6.** a hired household servant. **7.** something produced or manufactured in one's own country. **8. domestics,** household items made of cloth, as sheets, towels, and tablecloths. [1515–25; < L *domesticus,* deriv. of *domus* house (see DOME); r. *domestique* < MF] —**do·mes′ti·cal·ly,** *adv.*

domes′tic an′imal, an animal, as the horse or cat, that has been tamed and kept by humans as a work animal, food source, or pet, esp. a member of those species that have, through selective breeding, become notably different from their wild ancestors. [1850–55]

do·mes·ti·cate (də mes′ti kāt′), *v.,* **-cat·ed, -cat·ing.** —*v.t.* **1.** to convert (animals, plants, etc.) to domestic uses; tame. **2.** to tame (an animal), esp. by generations of breeding, to live in close association with human beings as a pet or work animal and usually creating a dependency so that the animal loses its ability to live in the wild. **3.** to adapt (a plant) so as to be cultivated by and beneficial to human beings. **4.** to accustom to household life or affairs. **5.** to take (something foreign, unfamiliar, etc.) for one's own use or purposes; adopt. **6.** to make more ordinary, familiar, acceptable, or the like: *to domesticate radical ideas.* —*v.i.* **7.** to be domestic. [1635–45; < ML *domesticātus* (ptp. of *domesticāre*), equiv. to *domestic-* DOMESTIC + *-ātus* -ATE[1]] —**do·mes·ti·ca·ble** (də mes′ti kə bəl), *adj.* —**do·mes′ti·ca′tion,** *n.* —**do·mes′ti·ca′tive,** *adj.* —**do·mes′ti·ca′tor,** *n.*

domes′tic com′merce. See under **commerce** (def. 1).

domes′tic fowl′, **1.** a chicken. **2.** poultry.

do·mes·tic·i·ty (dō′me stis′i tē), *n., pl.* **-ties. 1.** the state of being domestic; domestic or home life. **2.** a domestic or household act, activity, duty, or chore. [1715–25; DOMESTIC + -ITY]

domes′tic part′ner, either member of an unmarried, cohabiting, and esp. homosexual couple that seeks benefits usu. available only to spouses. [1975–80] —**domes′tic part′nership.**

domes′tic prel′ate, *Rom. Cath. Ch.* an honorary distinction conferred by the Holy See upon clergy, entitling them to some of the privileges of a bishop. [1925–30]

do·mes′tic-re·la′tions court′ (də mes′tik ri lā′shənz). See **court of domestic relations.** [1935–40]

domes′tic sci′ence. See **home economics.**

domes′tic sys′tem, a manufacturing system whereby workers make products in their own homes with materials supplied by entrepreneurs.

dome′ top′, *Furniture.* a top to a desk, secretary, or the like having the form of a semicircular pediment. Cf. **bonnet top, hooded top.**

Dom·ett (dom′it), *n.* **Alfred,** 1811–87, British government official and poet: prime minister of New Zealand 1862.

dom·i·cal (dō′mi kəl, dom′i-), *adj.* **1.** domelike. **2.** having a dome. Also, **dom′ic.** [1840–50; DOME + -ICAL] —**dom′i·cal·ly,** *adv.*

dom·i·cile (dom′ə sīl′, -səl, dō′mə-), *n., v.,* **-ciled, -cil·ing.** —*n.* **1.** a place of residence; abode; house or home. **2.** *Law.* a permanent legal residence. —*v.t.* **3.** to establish in a domicile. Also, **dom′i·cil.** [1470–80; < MF < L *domicilium,* perh. equiv. to **domicol(a)* (*domi-,* comb. form of *domus* house + *-cola* dweller; see COLONUS) + *-ium* -IUM]

dom·i·cil·i·ar (dom′ə sil′ē ər, dō′mə-), *n. Eccles. Obs.* a canon of a minor order. [1645–55; < L *domicili(um)* DOMICILE + -AR[1]]

dom·i·cil·i·ar·y (dom′ə sil′ē er′ē), *adj., n., pl.* **-ar·ies.** —*adj.* **1.** of or pertaining to a domicile. —*n.* **2.** an institutional home for aged and disabled veterans who cannot care for themselves. [1780–90; < L *domicili(um)* DOMICILE + -ARY]

dom·i·cil·i·ate (dom′ə sil′ē āt′), *v.,* **-at·ed, -at·ing.** —*v.t.* **1.** to domicile. —*v.i.* **2.** to establish a residence for oneself or one's family. [1770–80; < L *domicili(um)* DOMICILE + -ATE[1]] —**dom′i·cil′i·a′tion,** *n.*

dom·i·nance (dom′ə nəns), *n.* **1.** rule; control; authority; ascendancy. **2.** the condition of being dominant. **3.** *Psychol.* the disposition of an individual to assert control in dealing with others. **4.** *Animal Behav.* high status in a social group, usually acquired as the result of aggression, that involves the tendency to take priority in access to limited resources, as food, mates, or space. **5.** *Neurol.* the normal tendency for one side of the brain to be more important than the other in controlling certain functions, as speech and language. Also, **dom′i•nan•cy.** [1810–20; DOMIN(ANT) + -ANCE]

dom′inance hi′erarchy, *Animal Behav.* a system or set of relationships in animal groups that is based on a hierarchical ranking, usually established and maintained by behavior in aggressive encounters: one or a few members hold the highest rank and the others are submissive to those ranking higher and dominant to those ranking lower. [1970–75]

dom•i•nant (dom′ə nənt), *adj.* **1.** ruling, governing, or controlling; having or exerting authority or influence: *dominant in the chain of command.* **2.** occupying or being in a commanding or elevated position. **3.** predominant; main; major; chief: *Corn is the dominant crop of Iowa.* **4.** *Genetics.* of or pertaining to a dominant. **5.** *Music.* pertaining to or based on the dominant: *the dominant chord.* —*n.* **6.** *Genetics.* **a.** the one of a pair of alternative alleles that masks the effect of the other when both are present in the same cell or organism. **b.** the trait or character determined by such an allele. Cf. **recessive** (defs. 4, 5). **7.** *Music.* the fifth tone of a diatonic scale. **8.** *Ecol.* any of one or more types of plants, or sometimes animals, that by virtue of abundance, size, or habits exert so important an influence on the conditions of an area as to determine, to a great extent, what other organisms can live there. [1525–35; < L *dominant-* (s. of *dominān̄s*, prp. of *dominārī* to DOMINATE), equiv. to *domin(us)* master + *-ant-* -ANT] —**dom′i•nant•ly,** *adv.*
—**Syn. 1.** prevailing, principal. DOMINANT, PREDOMINANT, PARAMOUNT, PREEMINENT describe something outstanding. DOMINANT describes something that is most influential or important: *the dominant characteristics of monkeys.* PREDOMINANT describes something that is dominant over all others, or is more widely prevalent: *Curiosity is the predominant characteristic of monkeys.* PARAMOUNT applies to something that is first in rank or order: *Safety is of paramount importance.* PREEMINENT applies to a prominence based on recognition of excellence: *His work was of preeminent quality.*

dom′inant ten′ement, *Law.* land in favor of which an easement or other servitude exists over another's land. Also called **dom′inant estate′.** Cf. **servient tenement.** [1870–75]

dom•i•nate (dom′ə nāt′), *v.,* **-nat•ed, -nat•ing.** —*v.t.* **1.** to rule over; govern; control. **2.** to tower above; overlook; overshadow: *A tall pine dominated the landscape.* **3.** to predominate, permeate, or characterize. **4.** *Math.* (of a series, vector, etc.) to have terms or components greater in absolute value than the corresponding terms or components of a given series, vector, etc. **5.** *Ling.* (of a node in a tree diagram) to be connected with (a subordinate node) either directly by a single downward branch or indirectly by a sequence of downward branches. —*v.i.* **6.** to rule; exercise control; predominate. **7.** to occupy a commanding or elevated position. [1605–15; < L *dominātus* (ptp. of *dominārī* to master, control), equiv. to *domin-* (s. of *dominus*) master + *-ātus* -ATE[1]] —**dom′i•nat′ing•ly,** *adv.* —**dom′i•na′tor,** *n.*

dom•i•na•tion (dom′ə nā′shən), *n.* **1.** an act or instance of dominating. **2.** rule or sway; control, often arbitrary. **3. dominations,** *Theol.* one of the nine orders of celestial attendants of God. Cf. **angel** (def. 1). [1350–1400; ME < L *dominātiōn-* (s. of *dominātiō*), equiv. to *domindruat(us)* (see DOMINATE) + *-iōn-* -ION; r. ME *dominacioun* < AF]

dom•i•na•tive (dom′ə nā′tiv, -nə tiv), *adj.* dominating; controlling. [1590–1600; < ML *dominātīvus.* See DOMINATE, -IVE]

dom•i•na•trix (dom′ə nā′triks), *n., pl.* **-na•tri•ces** (-nā′trə sēz′, -nə trī′sēz). **1.** a woman who plays the dominant role in a sado-masochistic sexual relationship or encounter. **2.** a woman who dominates. [1555–65; < L; see DOMINATE, -TRIX]
—**Usage.** See **-trix.**

dom•i•ne (dom′ə nē′, dō′mə-), *n. Obs.* lord; master (used as a title of address). [voc. of L *dominus* master, lord]

dom•i•ne, di•ri•ge nos (dō′mi ne′, dē′ri ge′ nōs′; *Eng.* dom′ə nē′, dir′ə jē nōs′), *Latin.* Master, guide us: motto of the city of London.

dom•i•nee (dom′ə nē, dō′mə-), *n. South African.* dominie (def. 2).

dom•i•neer (dom′ə nēr′), *v.t., v.i.* **1.** to rule arbitrarily or despotically; tyrannize. **2.** to tower; to tower over or above: *The castle domineers the town.* [1585–95; < D *domineren* < F *dominer* < L *dominārī*, equiv. to *domin(us)* lord + *-ārī* inf. suffix]

dom•i•neer•ing (dom′ə nēr′ing), *adj.* inclined to rule arbitrarily or despotically; overbearing; tyrannical: *domineering parents.* [1580–90; DOMINEER + -ING[2]] —**dom′i•neer′ing•ly,** *adv.* —**dom′i•neer′ing•ness,** *n.*
—**Syn.** arrogant; despotic, oppressive.

Do•min•go (də ming′gō; *Sp.* dô mēng′gô), *n.* **Pla•ci•do** (plä′si dō′; *Sp.* plä′thē thô, -sē-), born 1941, Spanish operatic tenor, in the U.S.

Do•min•guín (dō′mēng gēn′), *n.* **Luis Mi•guel** (lwēs mē gel′), (*Luis Miguel González Lucas*), born 1926, Spanish bullfighter.

Dom•i•nic (dom′ə nik), *n.* **1. Saint,** 1170–1221, Spanish priest: founder of the Dominican order. **2.** a male given name: from the Latin word meaning "of the Lord."

Dom•i•ni•ca (dom′ə nē′kə, də min′i kə), *n.* **1.** one of the Windward Islands, in the E West Indies. **2.** an independent republic comprising this island: a former British colony; gained independence 1978. 78,000; 290 sq. mi. (751 sq. km). *Cap.:* Roseau. **3.** a female given name.

do•min•i•cal (də min′i kəl), *adj.* **1.** of or pertaining to Jesus Christ as Lord. **2.** of or pertaining to the Lord's Day, or Sunday. [1530–40; < LL *dominicālis*, equiv. to L *dominic(us)* of a lord or the Lord (*dominus* lord, Lord + *-icus* -IC) + *-ālis* -AL[1]]

domin′ical al′tar, *Eccles.* a high altar.

do•min•i•ca•le (də min′i kā′lē), *n.* a veil formerly worn by women during divine service. [< It, var. of *domenicale* DOMINICAL]

domin′ical let′ter, any one of the letters from *A* to *G* used in church calendars to mark the Sundays throughout any particular year, serving primarily to aid in determining the date of Easter. [1570–80]

Do•min•i•can (də min′i kən), *adj.* **1.** of or pertaining to St. Dominic or the Dominicans. —*n.* **2.** a member of one of the mendicant religious orders founded by St. Dominic; Black Friar. [1625–35; *Dominic-* (s. of *Dominicus* Latinized form of *Domingo* de Guzman, founder of the order) + -AN]

Do•min•i•can (də min′i kən *for 1, 3;* dom′ə nē′kən, də min′i- *for 2, 4*), *adj.* **1.** of or pertaining to the Dominican Republic. **2.** of or pertaining to the Commonwealth of Dominica. —*n.* **3.** a native or inhabitant of the Dominican Republic. **4.** a native or inhabitant of the Commonwealth of Dominica. [< Sp *dominicano;* (defs. 2, 4) DOMINIC(A) + -AN]

Domin′ican Repub′lic, a republic in the West Indies, occupying the E part of the island of Hispaniola. 4,835,000; 19,129 sq. mi. (49,545 sq. km). *Cap.:* Santo Domingo. Formerly, **Santo Domingo, San Domingo.**

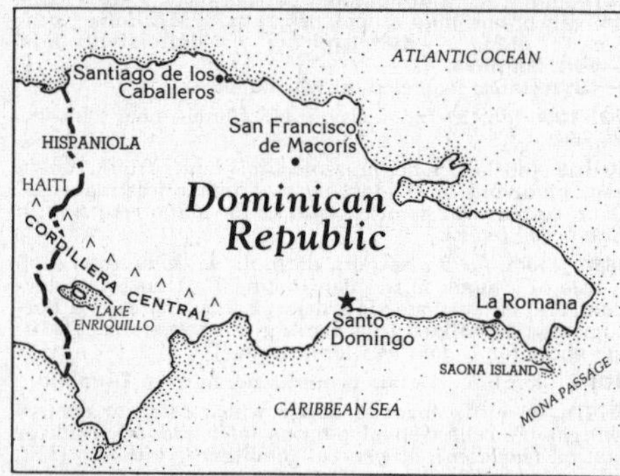

Dom•i•nick (dom′ə nik), *n.* **1.** *Animal Husb.* Dominique. **2.** a male given name.

dom•i•nie (dom′ə nē, dō′mə-), *n.* **1.** *Chiefly Scot.* a schoolmaster. **2.** a pastor in the Dutch Reformed Church. **3.** *Chiefly Hudson Valley.* a pastor or minister. [1605–15; var. of DOMINE]

do•min•ion (də min′yən), *n.* **1.** the power or right of governing and controlling; sovereign authority. **2.** rule; control; domination. **3.** a territory, usually of considerable size, in which a single rulership holds sway. **4.** lands or domains subject to sovereignty or control. **5.** *Govt.* a territory constituting a self-governing commonwealth and being one of a number of such territories united in a community of nations, or empire: formerly applied to self-governing divisions of the British Empire, as Canada and New Zealand. **6. dominions,** *Theol.* domination (def. 3). [1400–50; late ME < MF < ML **dominiōn-* (s. of **dominiō*) lordship, equiv. to L *domin(ium)* DOMINIUM + *-iōn-* -ION]

Domin′ion Day′, former name of **Canada Day.** [1890–95]

Dom•i•nique (dom′ə nēk′), *n. Animal Husb.* one of an American breed of chicken, having slate-colored plumage crossed by light and dark bars, raised for its meat and brown eggs. Also, **Dominick.** [1800–10, *Amer.*; named after F *Dominique* DOMINICA]

Dom•i•nique (dom′ə nēk′), *n.* a female given name: from a Latin word meaning "of the Lord."

do•min•i•um (də min′ē əm), *n. Law.* complete power to use, to enjoy, and to dispose of property at will. [1815–25; < L, equiv. to *domin(us)* lord, master + *-ium* -IUM]

dom•i•no[1] (dom′ə nō′), *n., pl.* **-noes. 1.** a flat, thumb-sized, rectangular block, the face of which is divided into two parts, each either blank or bearing from one to six pips or dots: 28 such pieces form a complete set. **2. dominoes,** (*used with a singular v.*) any of various games played with such pieces, usually by matching the ends of pieces and laying the dominoes down in lines and angular patterns. [1710–20; perh. special use of DOMINO[2]]

dom•i•no[2] (dom′ə nō′), *n., pl.* **-noes, -nos. 1.** a large, hooded cloak with a mask covering the eyes, worn at masquerades. **2.** the mask. **3.** a person wearing such dress. [1710–20; < It: hood and mask costume < ML or MF: black hood worn by priests in winter; obscurely akin to L *dominus* lord]

Dom•i•no (dom′ə nō′), *n.* **Antoine** ("*Fats*"), born 1928, U.S. rhythm-and-blues pianist, singer, and composer.

dom′ino effect′, the cumulative effect that results when one event precipitates a series of like events. Also called **dom′ino reac′tion.** [1965–70]

dom′ino pa′per, a marbleized or figured decorative paper, used for wallpaper, end papers, etc., printed from wood blocks and colored by hand. [1920–25]

dom′ino the′ory, a theory that if one country is taken over by an expansionist, esp. Communist, neighbor, party, or the like, the nearby nations will be taken over one after another. [1960–65]

Do•mi•nus (dō′mi nōōs′, dom′i-), *n. Latin.* God; the Lord.

Do•mi•nus vo•bis•cum (dō′mi nōōs′ vō bis′kōōm, dom′i-), *Latin.* the Lord be with you.

do•mi•tae na•tu•rae (dom′i tē′ nə tōōr′ē), *Law.* tamed or domesticated animals (distinguished from *ferae naturae*). [< L: lit., of a tamed nature]

Do•mi•tian (də mish′ən, -ē ən), *n.* (*Titus Flavius Domitianus Augustus*) A.D. 51–96, Roman emperor 81–96.

Dom′nus (dom′nəs), *n.* Donus.

Dom•re•my-la-Pu•celle (dôn rə mē lä py sel′), *n.* a village in NE France, SW of Nancy: birthplace of Joan of Arc. Also called **Dom•re•my′.**

Dom. Rep., Dominican Republic.

don[1] (don; *Sp., It.* dôn), *n.* **1.** (*cap.*) Mr.; Sir: a Spanish title prefixed to a man's given name. **2.** (in Spanish-speaking countries) a lord or gentleman. **3.** (*cap.*) an Italian title of address, esp. for a priest. **4.** a person of great importance. **5.** (in the English universities) a head, fellow, or tutor of a college. **6.** (in the Mafia) a head of a family or syndicate. [1515–25; < Sp, It < L *dominus*]

don[2] (don), *v.t.,* **donned, don•ning.** to put on or dress in: *to don one's clothes.* [1560–70; contr. of DO[1] + ON; cf. DOFF]

don[3] (dōn), *conj.* (in prescriptions) donec. [by shortening]

Don (don; *for 1 also Russ.* dôn), *n.* **1.** a river flowing generally S from Tula in the Russian Federation in Europe, to the Sea of Azov. ab. 1200 mi. (1930 km) long. **2.** a river in NE Scotland, flowing E from Aberdeen county to the North Sea. 62 mi. (100 km) long. **3.** a river in central England, flowing NE from S Yorkshire to the Humber estuary. 60 mi. (97 km) long. **4.** a male given name, form of **Donald.**

Don (dôn), *n. Welsh Myth.* a goddess, the mother of Gwydion and Arianrod: corresponds to the Irish Danu.

do•na (dô′nä), *n.* **1.** (*cap.*) Madam; Lady: a Portuguese title prefixed to a woman's given name. **2.** (in Portuguese-speaking countries) a lady or gentlewoman. [1615–25; < Pg < L *domina*, fem. of *dominus*]

do•ña (dô′nyä), *n.* **1.** (*cap.*) Madam; Lady: a Spanish title prefixed to a woman's given name. **2.** (in Spanish-speaking countries) a lady or gentlewoman. [1615–25; < Sp < L *domina*, fem. of *dominus*]

do•na•ble (dō′nə bəl), *adj.* available free from government surpluses: *Needy people in the program were eligible for donable foods such as beans and peas.* [1720–30; DON(ATE) + -ABLE]

Don•ald (don′ld), *n.* a male given name: from Celtic words meaning "world" and "power."

Do•nar (dō′när), *n. Germanic Myth.* the god of thunder, corresponding to Thor. [< OHG *thonar, donar;* c. OE *Thunor,* ON *Thōrr;* see THUNDER, THURSDAY]

do•nate (dō′nāt, dō nāt′), *v.,* **-nat•ed, -nat•ing.** —*v.t.* **1.** to present as a gift, grant, or contribution; make a donation of, as to a fund or cause: *to donate used clothes to the Salvation Army.* —*v.i.* **2.** to make a gift, grant, or contribution of something; give; contribute: *They donate to the Red Cross every year.* [1775–85, *Amer.*; prob. back formation from DONATION] —**do′na•tor,** *n.*
—**Syn. 1.** contribute, bestow, present, bequeath.

Don•a•tel•lo (don′ə tel′ō; *It.* dô′nä tel′lô), *n.* (*Donato di Niccolo di Betto Bardi*) 1386?–1466, Italian sculptor. Also, **Do•na•to** (də nä′tō; *It.* dô nä′tô).

do•na•tion (dō nā′shən), *n.* **1.** an act or instance of presenting something as a gift, grant, or contribution. **2.** a gift, as to a fund; contribution. [1375–1425, for an earlier sense; late ME < L *dōnātiōn-* (s. of *dōnātiō*), equiv. to *dōnāt(us)*, ptp. of *dōnāre* to give (*dōn-*, s. of *dōnum* gift, + *-ātus* -ATE[1]) + *-iōn-* -ION]
—**Syn. 2.** offering, benefaction, gratuity. See **present.**

dona′tion land′, (in the U.S.) land given free or sold on liberal terms by a state or the federal government, esp. to encourage settlement in undeveloped areas. [1775–85, *Amer.*]

Don•a•tist (don′ə tist, dō′nə-), *n.* a member of a Christian sect that developed in northern Africa in A.D. 311 and maintained that it alone constituted the whole and only true church and that baptisms and ordinations of the orthodox clergy were invalid. [1350–1400; ME < ML *Dōnātista;* see DONATUS, -IST] —**Don′a•tism,** *n.* —**Don′a•tis′tic, Don′a•tis′ti•cal,** *adj.*

don•a•tive (don′ə tiv, dō′nə-), *n.* a gift or donation. [1400–50; late ME < L *dōnātīvum,* n. use of neut. of *dōnātīvus* gratuitous, equiv. to *dōnāt(us)* (see DONATION) + *-īvus* -IVE]

don•a•to•ry (don′ə tôr′ē, -tōr′ē, dō′nə-), *n., pl.* **-ries.** *Chiefly Scots Law.* a donee of the king, esp. one given the right by the king to property obtained by escheat or forfeit. [1610–20; < ML *dōnātōrius,* equiv. to L *dōnā(re)* (see DONATION) + *-tōrius* -TORY[1]]

Do•na•tus (dō nā′təs), *n.* **1.** early-4th-century bishop of Casae Nigrae in northern Africa: leader of a heretical Christian group. Cf. **Donatist. 2. Aelius.** 4th century A.D., Roman grammarian.

Do•nau (dō′nou), *n.* German name of **Danube.**

Don•cas•ter (dong′kas tər; *Brit.* dong′kə stər), *n.* a city in South Yorkshire, in N England. 285,000.

done (dun), *v.* **1.** pp. of **do**[1]. **2.** *Nonstandard.* a pt. of **do**[1]. —*auxiliary verb.* **3.** *South Midland and Southern U.S. Nonstandard.* (used with a principal verb in the past or, sometimes, present tense to indicate completed action): *I done told you so. He done eat his lunch.* **4. be** or **have done with,** to break off relations or connections with; stop. —*adj.* **5.** completed; finished; through: *Our work is done.* **6.** cooked sufficiently. **7.** worn out; exhausted; used up. **8.** in conformity with fashion, good taste, or propriety; acceptable: *It isn't done.* **9. done for,** *Informal.* **a.** tired; exhausted. **b.** deprived of one's means, position, etc. **c.** dead or close to death. **10. done in,** *Informal.* very tired; exhausted: *He was really done in after a close race.*
—**Usage. 5.** In the adjectival sense "completed,

finished, through," DONE dates from the 14th century and is entirely standard: *Is your portrait done yet?*

do•nec (dō′nek), *conj.* (in prescriptions) until. Also, **don.** [< L]

do•nee (dō nē′), *n. Law.* **1.** a person to whom a gift is made. **2.** a person who has a power of appointment in property. [1515–25; DON(OR) + -EE]

Don•e•gal (don′i gôl′, don′i gôl′), *n.* **1.** a county in the N Republic of Ireland. 124,783; 1865 sq. mi. (4830 sq. km). *Co. seat:* Lifford. **2.** Also called **Don′egal tweed′.** a plain or herringbone tweed with colored slubs.

Don•el•son, Fort (don′l sən). See **Fort Donelson.**

done•ness (dun′nis), *n.* the condition of being cooked to a desired degree. [1925–30; DONE + -NESS]

Do•nets (də nets′; *Russ.* du nyets′), *n.* **1.** a river rising in the SW Russian Federation near Belgorod, flowing SE through Ukraine to the Don River. ab. 650 mi. (1045 km) long. **2.** Also called **Donets′ Ba′sin.** an area S of this river, in E Ukraine: important coal mining region and recently developed industrial area. 9650 sq. mi. (24,995 sq. km).

Do•netsk (də netsk′; *Russ.* du nyetsk′), *n.* a city in E Ukraine, in the Donets Basin. 1,021,000. Formerly, **Stalin, Stalino, Yuzovka.**

dong[1] (dông, dong), *n.* a deep sound like that of a large bell. [1580–90; imit.; see DING-DONG]

dong[2] (dông, dong), *n., pl.* **dong.** a monetary unit of Vietnam, equal to 100 hao: replaced the southern piaster and the northern dong in 1978. [< Vietnamese *đồng*]

dong[3] (dông, dong), *n. Slang (vulgar).* penis. [1925–30; orig. uncert.]

don•ga (dong′gə, dông′gə), *n.* **1.** (in an ice shelf) a small ravine with steep sides. **2.** (in South Africa) an eroded ravine; a dry watercourse. [1875–80; < Nguni (cf. Zulu *u(lu)donga*); perh. directly < a pidginized form with loss of the class prefix, as Fanagalo *donga*]

Dong•en (dong′ən; *Du.* dông′ən, dông′ə), *n.* **Kees van** (kās van; *Du.* kās vän). See **van Dongen, Kees.**

Dong Hai (dông′ hī′), *Pinyin.* See **East China Sea.**

Don Gio•van•ni (don′ jō vä′nē, jē ə-; *It.* dôn′ jô vän′nē), an opera (1787) by Wolfgang Amadeus Mozart.

Don•go•la (dong′gə lə), *n.* a former province in the N Sudan, now part of Northern Province.

Don′gola leath′er, a leather similar to kid, made from goatskin, sheepskin, or calfskin. Also called **Don′gola kid′.** [1885–90; after DONGOLA]

don•ick•er (don′i kər), *n. Older Slang.* bathroom; toilet. [prob. alter. (with -ER[1]) of dial. *dunnekin* outhouse or open cesspool; see DUNNY, -KIN]

Don•i•zet•ti (don′i zet′ē; *It.* dô′nē dzet′tē), *n.* **Ga•e•ta•no** (gä′e tä′nô), 1797–1848, Italian operatic composer.

don•jon (dun′jən, don′-), *n.* the inner tower, keep, or stronghold of a castle. [var. of DUNGEON]

Don Juan (don wän′ *or, Sp.,* dôn hwän′ *for 1, 2; esp. for 4* don jo͞o′ən), **1.** a legendary Spanish nobleman famous for his many seductions and dissolute life. **2.** a libertine or rake. **3.** a ladies' man; womanizer. **4.** (*italics*) an unfinished epic satire (1819–24) by Byron.

Don Juan•ism (don wä′niz əm), *Psychiatry.* a syndrome, occurring in males, of excessive preoccupation with sexual gratification or conquest and leading to persistently transient and sometimes exploitative relationships. Also called **satyriasis.** Cf. **nymphomania.** [1880–85; DON JUAN + -ISM]

don•key (dong′kē, dông′-, dung′-), *n., pl.* **-keys,** *adj.* —*n.* **1.** the domestic ass, *Equus asinus.* **2.** (since 1874) a representation of this animal as the emblem of the U.S. Democratic party. **3.** a stupid, silly, or obstinate person. **4.** a woodworking apparatus consisting of a clamping frame and saw, used for cutting marquetry veneers. —*adj.* **5.** *Mach.* auxiliary: *donkey engine; donkey pump; donkey boiler.* [1775–85; perh. alter. of *Dunkey,* hypocoristic form of *Duncan,* man's name]

don′key's tail′. See **burro's tail.**

don′key's years′, *Informal.* a very long time; eons. [1895–1900; prob. orig. *donkey('s) ears,* as rhyming slang for *years,* with *years* replacing *ears* once rhyming orig. was forgotten]

don′key top′sail, *Naut.* a four-sided gaff topsail, used above a gaff sail or lugsail, having its head laced to a small spar.

don′key work′, *Informal.* tedious, repetitious work; drudgery. Also, **don•key•work** (dong′kē wûrk′, dông′-, dung′-). [1915–20]

don•na (don′ä), *n.* **1.** (*cap.*) Madam; Lady: an Italian title of respect prefixed to the given name of a woman. **2.** an Italian lady. [1660–70; < It < L *domina,* fem. of *dominus*]

Don•na (don′ə), *n.* a female given name.

don•nard (don′ərd), *adj. Chiefly Scot.* stunned; dazed. Also, **don′nered.** [1715–25; ptp. of Scots *donnar, donner* to daze, stun, freq. of ME *donen, dinen,* OE *dynian* to make a DIN]

Donn-Byrne (don′bûrn′), *n.* **Brian Oswald** ("Donn Byrne"), 1889–1928, U.S. novelist and short-story writer.

Donne (dun), *n.* **John,** 1573–1631, English poet and clergyman.

don•née (do nā′), *n.* a set of artistic or literary premises or assumptions. [1875–80; < F: lit., given, n. use of fem. ptp. of *donner* to give < L *dōnāre;* see DONATE]

Don′ner Pass′ (don′ər), a mountain pass in the Sierra Nevada, in E California. 7135 ft. (2175 m) high.

don•nish (don′ish), *adj.* resembling or characteristic of a university don; bookish; pedantic. [1825–35; DON[1] + -ISH[1]] —**don′nish•ly,** *adv.* —**don′nish•ness,** *n.* —**don′nism,** *n.*

don•ny•brook (don′ē bro͝ok′), *n.* (*often cap.*) an inordinately wild fight or contentious dispute; brawl; free-for-all. Also called **Donnybrook Fair.** [1850–55; after DONNYBROOK (FAIR)]

Don′ny•brook Fair′ (don′ē bro͝ok′), **1.** a fair which until 1855 was held annually at Donnybrook, County Dublin, Ireland, and which was famous for rioting and dissipation. **2.** donnybrook.

do•nor (dō′nər), *n.* **1.** a person who gives or donates. **2.** *Med.* a person or animal providing blood, an organ, bone marrow cells, or other biological tissue for transfusion or transplantation. **3.** *Law.* a person who gives property by gift, legacy, or devise, or who confers a power of appointment. —*adj.* **4.** of or pertaining to the biological tissue of a donor: *donor organ.* [1400–50; late ME *donour* < AF (OF *doneur*) < L *dōnātor,* equiv. to *dōnā(re)* (see DONATION) + *-tor* -TOR] —**do′nor•ship′,** *n.*
—**Syn. 1.** supporter, contributor, sponsor, patron.

do′nor card′, a signed and witnessed card, meant to be carried in a wallet, purse, etc., specifying a person's wish to offer body organs or parts for transplantation or scientific use in case of death.

do-noth•ing (do͞o′nuth′ing), *n.* **1.** a person who chooses to do nothing; a lazy or worthless person. —*adj.* **2.** characterized by inability or unwillingness to initiate action, work toward a goal, assume responsibility, or the like: *a do-nothing government.* [1570–80]

do-noth•ing•ism (do͞o′nuth′ing iz′əm), *n.* the policy or practice of opposing a specific measure or change simply by refusing to consider or act on proposals; deliberate obstructionism. [1830–40; DO-NOTHING + -ISM]

Don•o•van (don′ə vən), *n.* **William Joseph** ("Wild Bill"), 1883–1959, U.S. lawyer and military officer: organizer and director of the OSS 1942–45.

Don Quix•o•te (don′ kē hō′tē, don kwik′sət; *Sp.* dôn kē hō′te), **1.** the hero of a novel by Cervantes who was inspired by lofty and chivalrous but impractical ideals. **2.** (*italics*) (*Don Quixote de la Mancha*) the novel itself (1605 and 1615).

don•sie (don′sē, dôn′-), *adj.* **1.** *Midland U.S.* somewhat sick, weak, or lacking in vitality; not completely well. **2.** *Scot.* unfortunate; ill-fated; unlucky. **3.** *Brit. Dial.* fastidious; neat; tidy. Also, **don′sy.** [1710–20; < ScotGael *donas* harm, ill + -IE]

don't (dōnt), *v.* **1.** contraction of *do not.* **2.** *Nonstandard (except in some dialects).* contraction of *does not.* —*n.* **3. don'ts,** customs, rules, or regulations that forbid something: *The boss has a long list of don'ts that you had better observe if you want a promotion.* Cf. **do**[1] (def. 56).
—**Usage.** DON'T is the standard contraction for *do not.* As a contraction for *does not,* DON'T first appeared in writing in the latter half of the 17th century, about the same time as the first written appearance of other contracted forms with *not,* like *mayn't* and *can't.* DON'T remained the standard contraction for *does not* in both speech and writing through the 18th century. During the 19th century, under pressure from those who thought it illogical, DON'T for *does not* gradually became less frequent in writing but continued to be common in speech. DON'T for *does not* still occurs in the informal speech and writing of many Americans. It does not occur in edited writing or formal speech.

don't-know (dōnt′nō′), *n.* a person who has no opinion or is undecided, as in answering an item on a public-opinion poll. [1885–90]

Do•nus (dō′nəs), *n.* died A.D. 678, pope 676–678. Also, **Domnus.**

do•nut (dō′nət, -nut′), *n.* doughnut.

don•zel (don′zəl), *n. Archaic.* a young gentleman not yet knighted; squire; page. [1585–95; < It *donzello* < OPr *donzel* < VL **dom(i)nicellus,* equiv. to L *domin(us)* lord + *-cellus* dim. suffix; cf. DAMSEL]

doo•bie (do͞o′bē), *n. Slang.* a marijuana cigarette. [1975–80; orig. unknown]

doo•dad (do͞o′dad′), *n. Informal.* **1.** a decorative embellishment; trinket; bauble: *a dress covered with doodads.* **2.** a gadget; device: *a kitchen full of the latest doodads.* Also, **do-dad.** [1900–05; gradational compound based on dial. *dad* piece, flake]

doo•dle[1] (do͞od′l), *v.,* **-dled, -dling,** *n.* —*v.t., v.i.* **1.** to draw or scribble idly: *He doodled during the whole lecture.* **2.** to waste (time) in aimless or foolish activity. **3.** *Dial.* to deceive; cheat. —*n.* **4.** a design, figure, or the like, made by idle scribbling. **5.** *Archaic.* a foolish or silly person. [1935–40, *Amer.;* orig. sense, fool (n.)] —**doo′dler,** *n.*

doo•dle[2] (do͞od′l), *n. Chiefly North Midland U.S.* a small pile of hay; haystack. Also called **hay doodle.** [prob. extracted from COCK-A-DOODLE-DO; a euphemism for COCK[3], to avoid assoc. with COCK[1], in sense "penis"]

doo•dle•bug[1] (do͞od′l bug′), *n.* the larva of an antlion. [1865–70, *Amer.;* DOODLE[1] + BUG[1]]

doo•dle•bug[2] (do͞od′l bug′), *n.* **1.** any of various small, squat vehicles. **2.** a divining rod or similar device supposedly useful in locating underground water, oil, minerals, etc. **3.** *Brit. Informal.* See **buzz bomb.** [1865–70; special use of DOODLEBUG[1]]

doo•dle•sack (do͞od′l sak′), *n.* bagpipe (def. 1). Also, **dudelsack.** [1840–50; < G *Dudelsack,* equiv. to *Dudel* (bag)pipe + *Sack* SACK[1]]

doo•dly-squat (do͞od′lē skwot′), *n. Slang.* a minimum amount; the least bit (usually used in the negative): *This stock isn't worth doodly-squat in today's market.* Also, **diddly-squat.** [prob. euphemistic var. of *doodly-shit,* DIDDLYSHIT; see DOODLE[1], DIDDLE[2], -Y[2]]

doo-doo (do͞o′do͞o′), *n. Baby Talk.* feces; bowel movement.

doo•fus (do͞o′fəs), *n., pl.* **-fus•es.** *Slang.* a foolish or inept person. Also, **dufus.** [1960–65, *Amer.;* prob. alter. of earlier *goofus* in same sense; cf. GOOF]

doo•hick•ey (do͞o′hik′ē), *n., pl.* **-eys.** *Informal.* a gadget; dingus; thingumbob. [1910–15, *Amer.;* DOO(DAD) + HICKEY]

dook (do͝ok), *n.* plug (def. 17). [1800–10; orig. uncert.]

doo•lie[1] (do͞o′lē), *n. Slang.* a first-year cadet in the U.S. Air Force Academy. [orig. uncert.]

doo•lie[2] (do͞o′lē), *n.* dooly.

Doo•lit•tle (do͞o′lit′l), *n.* **1. Hilda** ("*H.D.*"), 1886–1961, U.S. poet. **2. James Harold,** born 1896, U.S. aviator and general.

doo•ly (do͞o′lē), *n., pl.* **-lies.** (in India) a simple litter, often used to transport sick or wounded persons. Also, **doolie, dhooly.** [1615–25; < Hindi *ḍolī* litter]

doom (do͞om), *n.* **1.** fate or destiny, esp. adverse fate; unavoidable ill fortune: *In exile and poverty, he met his doom.* **2.** ruin; death: *to fall to one's doom.* **3.** a judgment, decision, or sentence, esp. an unfavorable one: *The judge pronounced the defendant's doom.* **4.** the Last Judgment, at the end of the world. **5.** *Obs.* a statute, enactment, or legal judgment. —*v.t.* **6.** to destine, esp. to an adverse fate. **7.** to pronounce judgment against; condemn. **8.** to ordain or fix as a sentence or fate. [bef. 900; ME *dome, dōm,* OE *dōm* judgment, law; c. ON *dōmr,* Goth *dōms;* cf. Skt *dhā́man,* Gk *thémis* law; see DO[1], DEEM] —**doom′y,** *adj.*
—**Syn. 1.** See **fate. 3.** condemnation. **6.** predestine.

doom•ful (do͞om′fəl), *adj.* foreshadowing doom; portentously direful; ominous. [1580–90; DOOM + -FUL] —**doom′ful•ly,** *adv.*

doom′ palm′, an African fan palm, *Hyphaene thebaica,* bearing an edible, gingerbread-flavored fruit. Also, **doum palm.** Also called **gingerbread palm.** [1820–30; < dial. Ar *dōm*]

dooms (do͞omz), *adv. Scot. and North Eng.* very; extremely: used as a euphemism for *damned.* [1805–15; DOOM + -S[1]]

doom•say•er (do͞om′sā′ər), *n.* a person who predicts impending misfortune or disaster. [1950–55; DOOM + SAY + -ER[1]; cf. NAYSAYER, SOOTHSAYER] —**doom′say′ing,** *adj., n.*

dooms•day (do͞omz′dā′), *n.* **1.** the day of the Last Judgment, at the end of the world. **2.** any day of judgment or sentence. **3.** nuclear destruction of the world. —*adj.* **4.** given to or marked by forebodings or predictions of impending calamity; esp. concerned with or predicting future universal destruction: *the doomsday issue of all-out nuclear war.* **5.** capable of causing widespread or total destruction: *doomsday weapons.* [bef. 1000; ME *domes dai,* OE *dōmesdæg* Judgment Day. See DOOM, DAY]

Dooms′day Book′ (do͞omz′dā′). See ***Domesday Book.***

dooms•day•er (do͞omz′dā′ər), *n.* a doomsayer. [1970–75; DOOMSDAY + -ER[1]]

dooms•man (do͞omz′mən), *n., pl.* **-men.** *Archaic.* a judge. [1150–1200; early ME *domes man* man of judgment; see DOOM, 'S[1], -MAN]

doom•ster (do͞om′stər), *n.* **1.** a doomsayer. **2.** *Archaic.* a judge. [1400–50; late ME *domster,* prob. alt. of *demester* DEEMSTER, by assoc. with *dome* DOOM; def. 1 prob. a new formation with DOOM, -STER]

Doon (do͞on), *n.* a river in SW Scotland, flowing NW from Ayr County to the Firth of Clyde. ab. 30 mi. (48 km) long.

door (dôr, dōr), *n.* **1.** a movable, usually solid, barrier for opening and closing an entranceway, cupboard, cabinet, or the like, commonly turning on hinges or sliding in grooves. **2.** a doorway: *to go through the door.* **3.** the building, house, etc., to which a door belongs: *My friend lives two doors down the street.* **4.** any means of approach, admittance, or access: *the doors to learning.* **5.** any gateway marking an entrance or exit from one place or state to another: *at heaven's door.* **6. lay at someone's door,** to hold someone accountable for; blame; impute. **7. leave the door open,** to allow the possibility of accommodation or change; be open to reconsideration: *The boss rejected our idea but left the door open for discussing it again next year.* **8. lie at someone's door,** to be the responsibility of; be imputable to: *One's mistakes often lie at one's own door.* **9. show someone the door,** to request or order someone to leave; dismiss: *She resented his remark and showed him the door.* [bef. 900; ME *dore,* OE *duru* door, *dor* gate; akin to G *Tür,* ON *dyrr,* Gk *thýra,* L *foris,* OIr *dorus,* OCS *dvĭrĭ*] —**door′less,** *adj.*

door•bell (dôr′bel′, dōr′-), *n.* **1.** a bell chime, or the like, at a door or connected with a door, rung by persons outside wanting someone inside to open the door. —*v.i.* **2.** to canvass or solicit from door to door, esp. for votes or contributions. [1805–15; DOOR + BELL[1]]

door•brand (dôr′brand′, dōr′-), *n.* a hinge having a long strap holding together the planks of a door. [alter. of obs. *doorband,* ME *dorband,* equiv. to *dor* DOOR + *band* BAND[2]]

door′ buck′, buck[3] (def. 4).

door•case (dôr′kās′, dōr′-), *n.* the finish frame of a doorway. [1590–1600; DOOR + CASE[2]]

door′ chain′, a short chain with a removable slide fitting that can be attached between the inside of a door and the doorjamb to prevent the door from being opened more than a few inches without the chain being removed. [1830–40]

door′ charge′, an entrance fee.

door′ check′, a device, usually hydraulic or pneumatic, for controlling the closing of a door and preventing it from slamming. Also called **door′ clos′er.**

do-or-die (do͞o′ər dī′), *adj.* **1.** reflecting or characterized by an irrevocable decision to succeed at all costs; desperate; all-out: *a do-or-die attempt to halt the invaders.* **2.** involving a potentially fatal crisis or crucial emergency. [1875–80]

door•frame (dôr′frām′, dōr′-), *n.* the frame of a doorway, including two jambs and a lintel, or head. [1850–55; DOOR + FRAME]

door′ han′dle, *Chiefly Brit.* doorknob. [1825–35]

door′ jack′, a frame for holding a door while its edge is being planed.

door•jamb (dôr′jam′, dōr′-), *n.* either of the two sidepieces of a doorframe. Also called **doorpost.** [1830–40; DOOR + JAMB[1]]

door•keep•er (dôr′kē′pər, dōr′-), *n.* **1.** a person who guards the entrance of a building. **2.** *Brit.* a janitor; hall porter. **3.** *Rom. Cath. Ch.* ostiary (def. 1). [1525–35; DOOR + KEEPER]

door′-key child′ (dôr′kē′, dōr′-), *Older Use.* See **latch-key child.**

door•knob (dôr′nob′, dōr′-), *n.* the handle or knob by which a door is opened or closed. [1840–50; DOOR + KNOB]

door•man (dôr′man′, ′-mən, dōr′-), *n., pl.* **-men** (-men′, -mən). the door attendant of an apartment house, night club, etc., who acts as doorkeeper and performs minor services for entering and departing residents or guests. [1855–60; DOOR + MAN[1]]

door•mat (dôr′mat′, dōr′-), *n.* **1.** a mat, usually placed before a door or other entrance, for people arriving to wipe their shoes on before entering. **2.** a person who is the habitual object of abuse or humiliation by another. [1655–65; DOOR + MAT[1]]

door′ mon′ey, admission fee to a place of entertainment or recreation. [1800–10]

door•nail (dôr′nāl′, dōr′-), *n.* **1.** a large-headed nail formerly used for strengthening or ornamenting doors. **2. dead as a doornail,** stone-dead: *After midnight, the town is dead as a doornail.* [1300–50; ME *dornail.* See DOOR, NAIL]

door′ o′pener, **1.** a mechanism that automatically opens a door, as of a garage, when actuated by a radio transmitter, electric eye, or other device. **2.** *Informal.* something that is effective in leading to opportunity or success: *Sales experience can be a door opener for young executives.* Also, **door′-o′pener.**

door•piece (dôr′pēs′, dōr′-), *n.* an architecturally treated doorframe. [1605–15; DOOR + PIECE]

door•plate (dôr′plāt′, dōr′-), *n.* a small identification plate on the outside door of a house or room, bearing the occupant's name, the apartment or house number, or the like. [1815–25; DOOR + PLATE[1]]

door•post (dôr′pōst′, dōr′-), *n.* doorjamb. [1525–35; DOOR + POST[1]]

door′ prize′, a prize awarded at a dance, party, or the like, either by chance through a drawing or as a reward, as for having the best costume. [1950–55]

door•sill (dôr′sil′, dōr′-), *n.* the sill of a doorway. [1555–65; DOOR + SILL]

door•stead (dôr′sted′, dōr′-), *n. Chiefly Brit.* the structure of a doorway. [1600–10; DOOR + STEAD]

door•step (dôr′step′, dōr′-), *n.* **1.** a step or one of a series of steps leading from the ground to a door. **2.** *Brit. Slang.* a thick slice of bread. [1800–10; DOOR + STEP]

door•stone (dôr′stōn′, dōr′-), *n.* a stone serving as the sill of a doorway. [1755–65; DOOR + STONE]

door•stop (dôr′stop′, dōr′-), *n.* **1.** a device for holding a door open, as a wedge or small weight. **2.** Also called **slamming stile, stop.** (in a doorframe) a strip or projecting surface against which the door closes. **3.** a device for preventing a door from striking a wall or an object on a wall, as a small rubber-covered projection. [1870–75, *Amer.*; DOOR + STOP]

door-to-door (dôr′tə dôr′, dōr′tə dōr′), *adj.* **1.** calling, selling, canvassing, etc., at each house or apartment in an area, town, or the like: *a door-to-door poll.* **2.** sent direct from the point of pickup to the point of delivery, as a shipment or order of merchandise. **3.** covering the complete route of a door-to-door shipment, delivery, etc.: *door-to-door carrying charges; door-to-door insurance.* —*adv.* **4.** in a door-to-door manner. [1900–05]

door•way (dôr′wā′, dōr′-), *n.* **1.** the passage or opening into a building, room, etc., commonly closed and opened by a door; portal. **2.** a means of access: *a doorway to success.* [1790–1800; DOOR + WAY]

door•yard (dôr′yärd′, dōr′-), *n.* a yard in front of the door of a house. [1755–65, *Amer.*; DOOR + YARD[2]]

doo•ver (do͞o′vər), *n. Australian Slang.* thingumbob; thingumajig. [1940–45; prob. to be identified with *doofer, doofah* in same sense, perh. repr. *do for,* as in *that will do for now*]

doo-wop (do͞o′wop′), *n. Popular Music.* a style of small-group vocal harmonizing, commercialized as a type of so-called street singing in the 1950's, in which words and nonsense syllables are chanted in rhythmic harmony to support the stylized melody of the lead singer. [repr. the chanted syllables]

doo•zie (do͞o′zē), *n., v.,* **-zied, -zi•ing.** *Informal.* —*n.* **1.** Also, **doo•zer** (do͞o′zər). something that is extraordinary or outstanding of its kind: *The storm was a doozie, with winds of fifty miles an hour.* —*v.i.* **2. doozie up,** to make more attractive or appealing, as by adding features or ornaments, cleaning or repairing, or clothing brightly: *You'll have to doozie up the house before you can sell it.* [1925–30, *Amer.*; of uncert. orig.; sometimes associated with the *Duesenburg,* a luxury auto, though the var. *dozy* precedes the appearance of the car in 1920]

doo•zy (do͞o′zē), *n., pl.* **-zies,** *v.,* **-zied, -zy•ing.** *Informal.* doozie.

dop (dop), *n.* a tool for holding gemstones for cutting or polishing. [1690–1700; < D: shell, pod, cover]

D.O.P., *Photog.* See **developing-out paper.**

do•pa (dō′pə), *n. Biochem.* an amino acid, $C_9H_{11}NO_4$, formed from tyrosine in the liver during melanin and epinephrine biosynthesis: the L-dopa isomer is converted in the brain to dopamine. Cf. **levodopa.** [< G *Dopa* (1917), contr. of *3, 4- Dioxyphenylalanin;* see DI-[1], OXY-, PHENYLALININE]

do•pa•mine (dō′pə mēn′), *n.* **1.** *Biochem.* a catecholamine neurotransmitter in the central nervous system, retina, and sympathetic ganglia, acting within the brain to help regulate movement and emotion: its depletion may cause Parkinson's disease. Cf. **dopa. 2.** *Pharm.* a dopamine preparation used to increase the force of contraction of the heart in the treatment of shock. Cf. **levodopa.** [1955–60; see DOPA, AMINE]

do•pa•mi•ner•gic (dō′pə mi nûr′jik), *adj. Biochem.* activated by or sensitive to dopamine. [1970–75; DOPAMINE + -ERGIC]

dop•ant (dō′pənt), *n. Electronics.* an impurity added intentionally in a very small, controlled amount to a pure semiconductor to change its electrical properties: *Arsenic is a dopant for silicon.* [1960–65; DOPE + -ANT]

do•pat•ta (dō put′ə), *n.* a silk or muslin shawl, often interwoven with gold or silver threads, worn by men and women in India. [< Hindi]

dope (dōp), *n., v.,* **doped, dop•ing.** —*n.* **1.** any thick liquid or pasty preparation, as a lubricant, used in preparing a surface. **2.** an absorbent material used to absorb and hold a liquid, as in the manufacture of dynamite. **3.** *Aeron.* **a.** any of various varnishlike products for coating a fabric, as of airplane wings, in order to make it waterproof, stronger, etc. **b.** a similar product used to coat the fabric of a balloon to reduce gas leakage. **4.** *Slang.* **a.** any narcotic or narcoticlike drug taken to induce euphoria or satisfy addiction. **b.** any illicit drug. **5.** *Slang.* a narcotic preparation given surreptitiously to a horse to improve or retard its performance in a race. **6.** *Slang.* information, data, or news: *What's the latest dope on the strike?* **7.** *Informal.* a stupid or unresponsive person. **8.** *Southern U.S.* (*chiefly South Atlantic States*) soda pop, esp. cola-flavored. **9.** *North Central U.S.* (*chiefly Ohio*). syrup used as a topping for ice cream. —*v.t.* **10.** *Slang.* to affect with dope or drugs. **11.** to apply or treat with dope. **12.** *Electronics.* to add or treat (a pure semiconductor) with a dopant. —*v.i.* **13.** *Slang.* to take drugs. **14. dope out,** *Slang.* **a.** to figure out; calculate; devise: *to dope out a plan.* **b.** to deduce or infer from available information: *to dope out a solution to a problem.* [1840–50, 1885–90 for def. 4, 1900–05 for def. 6; < D *doop* (dial.) sauce, deriv. of *dopen* to DIP]
—**Regional Variation. 8.** See **soda pop.**

dope′ ad′dict, *Slang.* a drug addict. [1930–35]

doped-out (dōpt′out′), *adj. Slang.* under the influence of dope; drugged. Also, **doped-up** (dōpt′up′).

dope′ fiend′, *Slang.* a drug addict. [1890–95]

dope•head (dōp′hed′), *n. Slang.* a drug addict. [DOPE + HEAD] —**dope′head′ed,** *adj.*

dope′ push′er, pusher (def. 2). Also called **dope′ ped′dler.**

dop•er (dō′pər), *n. Slang.* **1.** a drug addict. **2.** pusher (def. 2). [1910–15; DOPE + -ER[1]]

dope•sheet (dōp′shēt′), *n.* a bulletin or list including the names of entries in various horse races, and including information on each entry, as the name, jockey, and past performances. [1900–05, *Amer.*; DOPE + SHEET[1]]

dope•ster (dōp′stər), *n.* a person who undertakes to predict the outcome of elections, sports events, or other contests that hold the public interest. [1905–10, *Amer.*; DOPE + -STER]

dope′ sto′ry. See **think piece.**

dope•y (dō′pē), *adj.,* **dop•i•er, dop•i•est.** *Informal.* **1.** stupid; inane: *It was rather dopey of him to lock himself out.* **2.** sluggish or befuddled from or as from the use of narcotics or alcohol. Also, **dop′y.** [1895–1900, *Amer.*; DOPE + -Y[1]] —**dop′i•ness, dop′ey•ness,** *n.*

dop•ing (dō′ping), *n. Electronics.* a method of adding a dopant to a pure semiconductor to change its electrical properties. [1950–55; DOPE + -ING[1]]

Dop•pel•gäng•er (dop′əl gang′ər; *Ger.* dô′pəl geng′ər), *n.* a ghostly double or counterpart of a living person. Also called **doubleganger.** [1850–55; < G: lit., double-walker]

Dop′pler effect′ (dop′lər), *Physics.* (*often l.c.*) the shift in frequency **(Dop′pler shift′)** of acoustic or electromagnetic radiation emitted by a source moving relative to an observer as perceived by the observer: the shift is to higher frequencies when the source approaches and to lower frequencies when it recedes. [1900–05; named after C. J. *Doppler* (1803–53), Austrian physicist]

Dop′pler ra′dar, *Electronics.* a radar tracking system that determines the velocity of a moving object by measuring the Doppler shift of the frequency of a radar signal reflected by the object. Cf. **DOVAP.** [1955–60]

dor[1] (dôr), *n.* **1.** Also, **dor•bee•tle** (dôr′bēt′l). a common European dung beetle, *Geotrupes stercorarius.* **2.** any of several insects, as the June bug, that make a buzzing noise in flight. Also, **dorr.** [bef. 900; ME *dor(r)e,* OE *dora;* cf. MLG *dorte* drone]

dor[2] (dôr), *n. Archaic.* mockery; scorn. [1545–55; < ON *dār* mockery; cf. G *Tor* fool]

Dor., **1.** Dorian. **2.** Doric.

Do•ra (dôr′ə, dōr′ə), *n.* a female given name: from a Greek word meaning "gift."

do•rab (dôr′ab, də rab′), *n.* See **wolf herring.** [orig. uncert.]

do•ra•do (də rä′dō), *n., pl.* **-dos,** (*esp. collectively*) **-do.** dolphin (def. 2). [1595–1605; < Sp < LL *deaurātus,* ptp. of *deaurāre* to gild. See DE-, AURUM, -ATE[1]]

Do•ra•do (də rä′dō; *for 1 also Sp.* dô rä′thô), *n., gen.* **-dus** (-dəs) for 2. **1.** a city in N Puerto Rico. 10,203. **2.** the Swordfish, a small southern constellation between Volans and Horologium. [1595–1605; < Sp; see DORADO]

do-rag (do͞o′rag′), *n. Slang.* a kerchief or scarf worn on the head to protect the hairdo, esp. after kinky hair has been straightened. [1960–65; *do* hairdo + RAG]

DORAN (dôr′an, dōr′-), *n.* an electronic device for determining range and assisting navigation, employing the principle of the Doppler effect. [*Do(ppler) ran(ge)*]

Do•ra•ti (dô rä′tē, dō-; *Hung.* dô′rô ti), *n.* **An•tal** (än′täl; *Hung.* on′tol), born 1906, Hungarian conductor, in the U.S.

Dor•cas (dôr′kəs), *n.* a Christian woman at Joppa who made clothing for the poor. Acts 9:36–41.

Dor′cas soci′ety, a society of women of a church whose work it is to provide clothing for the poor. [1825–35; named after DORCAS]

Dor•ches•ter (dôr′ches′tər, -chə stər), *n.* a town in S Dorsetshire, in S England, on the Frome River: named *Casterbridge* in Thomas Hardy's novels. 13,737.

Dor•dogne (dôr dôn′yᵊ), *n.* **1.** a river in SW France, flowing W to the Gironde estuary. 300 mi. (485 km) long. **2.** a department in SW central France. 373,149; 3561 sq. mi. (9225 sq. km). *Cap.:* Périgueux.

Dor•drecht (dôr′drekht), *n.* a city in SW Netherlands, on the Waal River. 108,041. Also called **Dort.**

Dore (dôr), *n.* **Monts** (môn), a group of mountains in central France: highest peak, 6188 ft. (1885 m).

do•ré[1] (dô rā′), *n. Canadian Dial.* the walleye or pike perch of North America. [1765–75; < CanF: lit., gilded, F < LL *deaurātus;* see DORADO]

do•ré[2] (dô rā′), *n. Mining.* a mixture of gold and silver in cast bars, as bullion. [< F: lit., gilded; see DORÉ[1]]

Do•ré (dô rā′; *Fr.* dô rā′), *n.* **(Paul) Gus•tave** (pôl gystav′), 1832?–83, French painter, illustrator, and sculptor.

Do•reen (dô rēn′, dō-, dôr′ēn, dōr′-), *n.* a female given name. Also, **Do•rene′.**

do-re-mi (dō′rā′mē′), *n. Slang.* money. [1920–25; pun on DOUGH (money); see DO[2], RE[1], MI]

Do•ri•an (dôr′ē ən, dōr′-), *adj.* **1.** of or pertaining to the ancient Greek region of Doris or to the Dorians. —*n.* **2.** a member of a people who entered Greece about the 12th century B.C., conquered the Peloponnesus, and destroyed the Mycenaean culture: one of the four main divisions of the prehistoric Greeks. Cf. **Achaean** (def. 5), **Aeolian** (def. 2), **Ionian** (def. 4). [1595–1605; < L *Dōri(us)* (< Gk *Dṓrios* Dorian) + -AN]

Do•ri•an (dôr′ē ən, dōr′-), *n.* a male or female given name.

Do′rian mode′, *Music.* an authentic church mode represented on the white keys of a keyboard instrument by an ascending scale from D to D.

Dor•ic (dôr′ik, dor′-), *adj.* **1.** of or pertaining to Doris, its inhabitants, or their dialect. **2.** rustic, as a dialect. **3.** *Archit.* noting or pertaining to one of the five classical orders, developed in Greece and altered by the Romans. The Greek Doric order consists typically of a channeled column without a base, having as a capital a circular echinus supporting a square abacus, above which come a plain architrave, a frieze of triglyphs and metopes, and a cornice, the corona of which has mutules on its soffit. In the Roman Doric order, the columns usually have bases, the channeling is sometimes altered or omitted, and the capital usually consists of three parts: a thick, bandlike necking, an echinus with an ovolo outline, and a molded abacus. Cf. **composite** (def. 2), **Corinthian** (def. 2), **Ionic** (def. 1), **Tuscan** (def. 2). See illus. under **order.** —*n.* **4.** a dialect of ancient Greek spoken on Rhodes and other islands of the Dodecanese, in Crete, in Syracuse, and in all of the Peloponnesus except Arcadia. **5.** rustic English speech. [1555–65; < L *Dōricus* < Gk *Dōrikós* Dorian]

Dor•i•den (dôr′i dn, -den′), *Pharm., Trademark.* a brand of glutethimide.

Do•ris (dôr′is, dōr′-, dor′-), *n.* **1.** an ancient region in central Greece: the earliest home of the Dorians. **2.** a region in SW Asia Minor, on the coast of Caria: Dorian settlements.

Do•ris (dôr′is, dōr′-, dor′-), *n.* **1.** *Class. Myth.* the wife of Nereus and mother of the Nereids. **2.** a female given name: from a Greek word meaning "bountiful."

dor•je (dôr′jə), *n. Lamaism.* a small trident symbolizing power. [1880–85; < Tibetan *rdo rje* (the initial *r* is absent in Tibetan pron.)]

dork (dôrk), *n. Slang.* **1.** a stupid or ridiculous person; jerk; nerd. **2.** *Vulgar.* penis. [1960–65; expressive coinage; cf. similar phonetic elements in DOLT, DONG[3], JERK[1], etc.]

Dor•king (dôr′king), *n.* one of an English breed of chicken, having five toes on each foot instead of the usual four. [1830–40; named after *Dorking,* town in Surrey, England]

dork•y (dôr′kē), *adj.* **dork•i•er, dork•i•est.** *Slang.* stupid, inept, or unfashionable. [DORK + -Y[1]]

dorm (dôrm), *n. Informal.* dormitory. [1895–1900; by shortening]

dor•man•cy (dôr′mən sē), *n.* the state of being dormant. [1780–90; DORM(ANT) + -ANCY]

dor•mant (dôr′mənt), *adj.* **1.** lying asleep or as if asleep; inactive, as in sleep; torpid: *The lecturer's sudden shout woke the dormant audience.* **2.** in a state of rest or inactivity; inoperative; in abeyance: *The project is dormant for the time being.* **3.** *Biol.* in a state of minimal metabolic activity with cessation of growth, either as

CONCISE ETYMOLOGY KEY: <, descended or borrowed from; >, whence; b., blend of, blended; c., cognate with; cf., compare; deriv., derivative; equiv., equivalent; imit., imitative; obl., oblique; r., replacing; s., stem; sp., spelling, spelled; resp., respelling, respelled; trans., translation; ?, origin unknown; *, unattested; ‡, probably earlier than. See the full key inside the front cover.

a reaction to adverse conditions or as part of an organism's normal annual rhythm. **4.** undisclosed; unasserted: *dormant musical talent.* **5.** (of a volcano) not erupting. **6.** *Bot.* temporarily inactive: *dormant buds; dormant seeds.* **7.** (of a pesticide) applied to a plant during a period of dormancy: *a dormant spray.* **8.** *Heraldry.* (of an animal) represented as lying with its head on its forepaws, as if asleep. [1350–1400; ME *dorma(u)nt* < AF, prp. of *dormir* < L *dormīre* to sleep; see -ANT] —**Syn. 1, 2.** quiescent. See **inactive. 4.** latent. —**Ant. 1.** awake, active.

dor·mer (dôr′mər), *n.* **1.** Also called **dor′mer win′·dow.** a vertical window in a projection built out from a sloping roof. **2.** the entire projecting structure. [1585–95; < MF *dormoir* DORMITORY] —**dor′mered,** *adj.*

dormer (def. 1)

dor·meuse (*Fr.* dôR mœz′), *n.* **1.** mobcap. **2.** *Obs.* a nightcap. [1725–35; < F; fem. of *dormeur* sleeper; see DORMANT, -EUSE]

dor·mie (dôr′mē), *adj. Golf.* (of a player or side in match play) being in the lead by as many holes as are still to be played. Also, **dor′my.** [1885–90; orig. uncert.]

dor·mi·ent (dôr′mē ənt), *adj.* sleeping; dormant. [1635–45; < L *dormient-* (s. of *dormiēns,* prp. of *dormīre*), equiv. to *dormi-* sleep + *-ent-* -ENT]

dor·mi·to·ry (dôr′mi tôr′ē, -tōr′ē), *n., pl.* **-ries. 1.** a building, as at a college, containing a number of private or semiprivate rooms for residents, usually along with common bathroom facilities and recreation areas. **2.** a room containing a number of beds and serving as communal sleeping quarters, as in an institution, fraternity house, or passenger ship. [1475–85; < L *dormītōrium* bedroom, equiv. to *dormī(re)* to sleep + *-tōrium* -TORY[2]]

dor′mitory sub′urb, a suburb occupied mainly by the homes of commuters. Also called **bedroom suburb.** [1945–50]

Dor·mont (dôr′mont), *n.* a city in SW Pennsylvania. 11,275.

dor·mouse (dôr′mous′), *n., pl.* **-mice** (-mīs′). any small, furry-tailed, Old World rodent of the family Gliridae, resembling small squirrels in appearance and habits. [1400–50; late ME *dormowse, dormoūse;* etym. obscure; perh. AF deriv. of OF *dormir* to sleep (see DORMANT), with final syll. reanalyzed as MOUSE, but no such AF word is known]

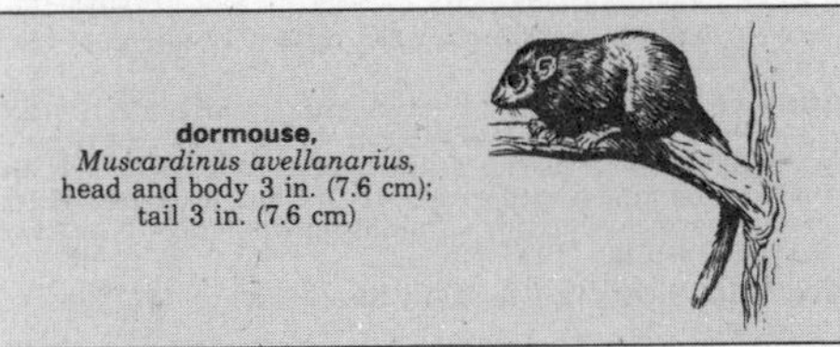
dormouse, *Muscardinus avellanarius,* head and body 3 in. (7.6 cm); tail 3 in. (7.6 cm)

dor·nick[1] (dôr′nik), *n.* a stout linen cloth, esp. one of a damask linen. Also, **dor′neck.** [1400–50; late ME *dornyk,* after *Doornik* (F *Tournai*), where the cloth was first made]

dor·nick[2] (dôr′nik), *n.* a small stone that is easy to throw. [1830–40, *Amer.;* < Ir *dornóg* small casting stone (lit., fistful)]

Do·ro·bo (də rō′bō), *n., pl.* **-bos,** (*esp. collectively*) **-bo.** a member of a tribal people living in the uplands of Kenya and Tanzania. Also called **Wandorobo.**

do·ron·i·cum (də ron′ə kəm), *n.* any composite plant of the genus *Doronicum,* comprising the leopard's-banes. [1600–10; < NL < Ar *dārūn(aj)* (< Pers *darūnak*) + L *-icum,* neut. of *-icus* -IC]

Dor·o·the·a (dôr′ə thē′ə, dor′-), *n.* a female given name: from a Greek word meaning "gift of God."

Dor·o·thy (dôr′ə thē, dor′-), *n.* a female given name, form of **Dorothea.**

dorp (dôrp), *n.* a village; hamlet. [1560–70; < D; c. THORP]

Dor·pat (dôR′pät), *n.* German name of **Tartu.**

dor·per (dôr′pər), *n.* one of a breed of sheep having a black face and white body, developed in South Africa from the Dorset Horn and black-headed Persian breeds and raised for meat. [1945–50; DOR(SET HORN) + *Per(sian)*]

dorr (dôr), *n.* dor[1].

Dorr's′ Rebel′lion (dôrz), an insurrection in Rhode Island (1842) that grew out of dissatisfaction with the existing state constitution, which restricted suffrage to landholders or their eldest sons. [named after Thomas W. *Dorr* (1805–54), state legislator and leader of the insurrection]

dor·sad (dôr′sad), *adv. Anat., Zool.* toward the back or dorsum; dorsally. [1795–1805; < L *dors(um)* back + -AD[3]]

dor·sal[1] (dôr′səl), *adj.* **1.** of, pertaining to, or situated at the back, or dorsum. **2.** *Anat., Zool.* **a.** situated on or toward the upper side of the body, equivalent to the back, or posterior, in humans. **b.** situated on or toward the posterior plane in humans or toward the upper plane in quadrupeds. **3.** *Bot.* pertaining to the surface away from the axis, as of a leaf; abaxial. **4.** *Phonet.* (of a speech sound) articulated with the dorsum of the tongue. —*n.* **5.** *Phonet.* a dorsal speech sound. **6.** *Anat.* a dorsal structure. [1535–45; < ML *dorsālis,* equiv. to L *dors(um)* back + *-ālis* -AL[1]] —**dor′sal·ly,** *adv.*

dor·sal[2] (dôr′səl), *n.* dossal (def. 1).

dor′sal fin′, the fin or finlike integumentary expansion generally developed on the back of aquatic vertebrates. See diag. under **fish.** [1760–70]

dor·sal·is (dôr sal′is, -sā′lis), *adj., n., pl.* **-sal·es** (-sal′ēz, -sā′lēz). *Anat.* —*adj.* **1.** dorsal[1]. —*n.* **2.** a blood vessel or nerve serving the back of the part with which it is associated. [< NL; see DORSAL[1]]

dor′sal lip′, *Embryol.* the dorsal marginal region of the blastopore, which acts as a center of differentiation: as cells move through this region to the interior of the embryo during gastrulation, they acquire the ability to induce the overlying ectoderm to develop into a variety of tissues. [1935–40]

dor′sal root′. See under **nerve root.** [1930–35]

dorse (dôrs), *n.* **1.** the back of a book or folded document. **2.** *Eccles. Obs.* dossal (def. 1). [1515–25; < L *dorsum* back]

dor·ser (dôr′sər), *n.* dosser[1].

Dor·set (dôr′sit), *n.* **1. 1st Earl of.** See **Sackville, Thomas. 2.** Dorsetshire.

Dor·set (dôr′sit), *n.* an Eskimo culture that flourished from A.D. 100–1000 in the central and eastern regions of arctic North America. [after Cape *Dorset* in northern Canada]

Dor′set Horn′, one of an English breed of sheep having a close-textured, medium-length wool. [1890–95; after DORSET]

Dor·set·shire (dôr′sit shēr′, -shər), *n.* a county in S England. 572,900; 1024 sq. mi. (2650 sq. km). Also called **Dorset.**

dorsi-, a combining form representing **dorsum** or **dorsal** in compound words: *dorsispinal.* Also, **dorso-.**

dor·sif·er·ous (dôr sif′ər əs), *adj. Bot.* borne on the back, as the sori on most ferns. [1720–30; DORSI- + -FEROUS]

dor·si·flex·ion (dôr′sə flek′shən), *n. Anat.* flexion toward the back. [1815–25; *dorsiflex* to bend backward (DORSI- + FLEX) + -ION]

dor·si·flex·or (dôr′sə flek′sər), *n. Anat.* a muscle causing dorsiflexion. [DORSI- + FLEXOR]

dor·si·spi·nal (dôr′sə spīn′l), *adj. Anat.* of or pertaining to the back and the spine. [1835–45; DORSI- + SPINAL]

dor·si·ven·tral (dôr′sə ven′trəl), *adj.* **1.** *Bot.* having distinct dorsal and ventral sides, as most foliage leaves. **2.** *Zool.* dorsoventral. [1880–85; DORSI- + VENTRAL] —**dor′si·ven·tral′i·ty,** *n.* —**dor′si·ven′tral·ly,** *adv.*

dorso-, var. of **dorsi-:** *dorsoventral.*

dor·so·lat·er·al (dôr′sō lat′ər əl), *adj. Anat., Zool.* of, pertaining to, or affecting the back and the side. [1825–35; DORSO- + LATERAL]

dor·so·lum·bar (dôr′sō lum′bər, -bär), *adj. Anat.* of, pertaining to, or affecting the back in the region of the lumbar vertebrae. [1850–55; DORSO- + LUMBAR]

dor·so·ven·tral (dôr′sō ven′trəl), *adj.* **1.** *Zool.* pertaining to the dorsal and ventral aspects of the body; extending from the dorsal to the ventral side: *the dorsoventral axis.* **2.** *Bot.* dorsiventral. [1865–70; DORSO- + VENTRAL] —**dor′so·ven·tral′i·ty,** *n.* —**dor′so·ven′·tral·ly,** *adv.*

dor·sum (dôr′səm), *n., pl.* **-sa** (-sə). *Anat., Zool.* **1.** the back, as of the body. **2.** the back or outer surface of an organ, part, etc. [1775–85; < L]

Dort (dôrt), *n.* Dordrecht.

dor·ter (dôr′tər), *n.* a dormitory, esp. in a monastery. Also, **dor′tour.** [1250–1300; ME *dortour* < OF < L *dormitōrium* DORMITORY]

Dor·ti·cós (dôR′tē kôs′), *n.* **Os·val·do** (ôs väl′dô), (*Osvaldo Dorticós Torrado*), 1919–83, Cuban lawyer and statesman: president 1959–76.

Dort·mund (dôrt′mənd; *Ger.* dôRt′mo͝ont′), *n.* a city in W Germany. 583,600.

dort·y (dôr′tē), *adj. Scot.* sullen; sulky. [1505–15; *dort* sulkiness (< ?) + -Y[1]] —**dor′ti·ness,** *n.*

Dor·val (dôr val′; *Fr.* dôR VAL′), *n.* a city in S Quebec, in E Canada: suburb of Montreal. 17,722.

do·ry[1] (dôr′ē, dōr′ē), *n., pl.* **-ries.** a boat with a narrow, flat bottom, high bow, and flaring sides. [1700–10, *Amer.;* alleged to be < Miskito *dóri, dúri* (if this word is itself not < E)]

dory[1]

do·ry[2] (dôr′ē, dōr′ē), *n., pl.* **-ries.** See **John Dory.** [1400–50; late ME *dorre, dorray* < MF *doree* (fem. ptp. of *dorer* to gild) < LL *deaurāta;* see DORADO]

do·ry·man (dôr′ē mən, dōr′-), *n., pl.* **-men.** a person who uses a dory, esp. a person who engages in fishing, lobstering, etc. [1960–65; DORY[1] + MAN[1]]

do′ry skiff′, *Naut.* an open boat similar to but smaller than a dory.

DOS (dôs, dos), *n. Computers.* any of several single-user, command-driven operating systems for microcomputers, esp. MS DOS. [*d(isk) o(perating) s(ystem)*]

DOS, See **Department of State.**

dos-à-dos (dō′sē dō′, -zi- *for 1, 2; Fr.* dō ZA dō′ *for 3*), *n., pl.* **-dos** (-dōz′), *v.,* **-dosed** (-dōd′), **-dos·ing** (-dō′ing), *adv.* —*n.* **1.** do-si-do. —*v.t., v.i.* **2.** to do-si-do. —*adv.* **3.** *Archaic.* back to back. [1830–40; < F: back to back]

dos·age (dō′sij), *n.* **1.** the administration of medicine in doses. **2.** the amount of medicine to be given. **3.** *Physics.* dose. **4.** the process of adding a sugar solution to champagne and other sparkling wines before final corking. [1840–50; DOSE + -AGE]

dose (dōs), *n., v.,* **dosed, dos·ing.** —*n.* **1.** a quantity of medicine prescribed to be taken at one time. **2.** a substance, situation, or quantity of anything analogous to medicine, esp. of something disagreeable: *Failing the exam was a hard dose to swallow.* **3.** an amount of sugar added in the production of champagne. **4.** *Physics.* **a.** Also called **absorbed dose.** the quantity of ionizing radiation absorbed by a unit mass of matter, esp. living tissue: measured in gray or rad. **b.** See **exposure dose. 5.** *Slang.* a case of gonorrhea or syphilis. —*v.t.* **6.** to administer in or apportion for doses. **7.** to give a dose of medicine to. **8.** to add sugar to (champagne) during production. —*v.i.* **9.** to take a dose of medicine. [1590–1600; earlier *dos* < LL *dosis* < Gk *dósis* a giving] —**dos′er,** *n.*

dose′ equiv′alent, *Physics.* a unit that quantifies the biological effectiveness of an absorbed dose of ionizing radiation, obtained by multiplying the absorbed dose by dimensionless factors that account for the kind of radiation, its energy, and the nature of the absorber: measured in Sievert or rem.

dose′-re·sponse curve′ (dōs′ri spons′), a curve plotting the relationship between the dose of a drug administered and its pharmacological effect. [1970–75]

do-si-do (dō′sē dō′), *n., pl.* **-dos,** *v.,* **-doed, -do·ing.** —*n.* **1.** a figure in square-dancing, in which two persons advance, pass around each other back to back, and return to their places. —*v.t.* **2.** to dance this figure around (one's partner). —*v.i.* **3.** to execute a do-si-do. [see DOS-À-DOS]

do·sim·e·ter (dō sim′i tər), *n.* a device carried on the person for measuring the quantity of ionizing radiation, as gamma rays, to which one has been exposed. [1880–85; < Gk *dósi(s)* DOSE + -METER]

do·sim·e·try (dō sim′i trē), *n.* **1.** the process or method of measuring the dosage of ionizing radiation. **2.** the measurement of the doses of medicines. [1940–45; < Gk *dósi(s)* DOSE + -METRY] —**do·si·met·ric** (dō′sə me′trik), *adj.* —**do·si·me·tri·cian** (dō′sə mi trish′ən), **do·sim′e·trist,** *n.*

Dos Pas·sos (dōs pas′ōs), **John (Rod·er·i·go)** (ro drē′gō), 1896–1970, U.S. novelist.

doss (dos), *Chiefly Brit.* —*n.* **1.** a place to sleep, esp. in a cheap lodging house. **2.** sleep. —*v.i.* **3.** to sleep or lie down in any convenient place. [1775–85; orig. obscure]

dos·sal (dos′əl), *n.* **1.** Also, **dorsal.** an ornamental hanging placed at the back of an altar or at the sides of the chancel. **2.** *Archaic.* dosser[1] (def. 2). Also, **dos′sel.** [1650–60; < ML *dossale,* for L *dorsale,* neut. of *dorsālis,* equiv. to *dors(um)* back + *-ālis* -AL[1]]

dos·ser[1] (dos′ər), *n.* **1.** a basket for carrying objects on the back; pannier. **2.** an ornamental covering for the back of a seat, esp. a throne or the like. **3.** dossal (def. 1). Also, **dorser.** [1300–50; ME < AF; MF *dossier* < ML *dosserium,* var. of *dorserium,* equiv. to *dors(um)* back + *-erium* -ERY; r. ME *dorser* < ML *dorserium*]

dos·ser[2] (dos′ər), *n. Chiefly Brit.* a person who sleeps in a doss house. [1865–70; DOSS + -ER[1]]

dos·se·ret (dos′ə ret′), *n. Archit.* a supplementary capital or thickened abacus, as in Byzantine architecture. Also called **impost block.** [1860–65; < F, dim. of *dossier* DOSSER[1]]

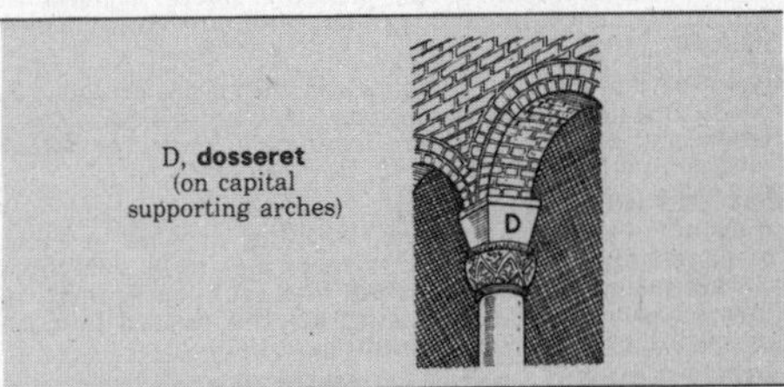

D, **dosseret** (on capital supporting arches)

doss′ house′, *Chiefly Brit.* flophouse. [1885–90]

dos·si·er (dos′ē ā′, -ē ər, dô′sē ā′, -sē ər; *Fr.* dô syā′), *n., pl.* **dos·si·ers** (dos′ē āz′, -ē ərz, dô′sē āz′, -sē ərs; *Fr.* dô syā′). a collection or file of documents on the same subject, esp. a complete file containing detailed information about a person or topic. [1875–80; < F: bundle of documents with a label attached to the back or spine, equiv. to *dos* (< L *dorsum*) back + *-ier* -IER[2]] —**Syn.** record, report, folder.

dos·sil (dos′əl), *n. Engraving.* a cloth roll for removing excess ink from a plate before printing. [1250–1300; ME *dosil* < MF < ML *duciculus,* equiv. to L *duci-* (s. of *dux*) leader + *-culus* -CULE[1]]

dost (dust), *v. Archaic.* 2nd pers. sing. pres. ind. of **do**[1].

Do·sto·ev·sky (dos′tə yef′skē, dus′-; *Russ.* du stuyef′skyē), *n.* **Fyo·dor Mi·khai·lo·vich** (fyō′dər mi kī′lə vich; *Russ.* fyô′dəR myi KHĪ′lə vyich), 1821–81, Russian

CONCISE PRONUNCIATION KEY: act, cāpe, dâre, pärt; set, ēqual; if, ice; ox, ōver, ôrder, oil, bo͝ok, bo͞ot, out; up, ûrge; child; sing; shoe; thin, that; zh as in *treasure.* ə = *a* as in *alone, e* as in *system, i* as in *easily, o* as in *gallop, u* as in *circus;* ᵊ as in *fire* (fīᵊr), *hour* (ouᵊr). l and n can serve as syllabic consonants, as in *cradle* (krād′l), and *button* (but′n). See the full key inside the front cover.

novelist. Also, **Do′sto·yev′sky, Do′sto·ev′ski, Do′sto·yev′ski, Do′stoi·ev′ski.**

dot[1] (dot), *n., v.,* **dot·ted, dot·ting.** —*n.* **1.** a small, roundish mark made with or as if with a pen. **2.** a minute or small spot on a surface; speck: *There were dots of soot on the window sill.* **3.** anything relatively small or specklike. **4.** a small specimen, section, amount, or portion: *a dot of butter.* **5.** *Music.* **a.** a point placed after a note or rest, to indicate that the duration of the note or rest is to be increased one half. A double dot further increases the duration by one half the value of the single dot. **b.** a point placed under or over a note to indicate that it is to be played staccato. **6.** *Teleg.* a signal of shorter duration than a dash, used in groups along with groups of dashes and spaces to represent letters, as in Morse code. **7.** *Print.* an individual element in a halftone reproduction. **8. on the dot,** *Informal.* precisely; exactly at the time specified: *The guests arrived at eight o'clock on the dot.* **9. the year dot,** *Brit. Informal.* very long ago. —*v.t.* **10.** to mark with or as if with a dot or dots. **11.** to stud or diversify with or as if with dots: *Trees dot the landscape.* **12.** to form or cover with dots: *He dotted a line across the page.* **13.** *Cookery.* to sprinkle with dabs of butter, margarine, or the like: *Dot the filling with butter.* —*v.i.* **14.** to make a dot or dots. **15. dot one's i's and cross one's t's,** to be meticulous or precise, even to the smallest detail. [bef. 1000; perh. to be identified with OE *dott* head of a boil, though not attested in ME; cf. DOTTLE, *dit,* deriv. of OE *dyttan* to stop up (prob. deriv. of *dott*); c. OHG *tutta* nipple] —**dot′like′,** *adj.* —**dot′ter,** *n.*

dot[2] (dot, dôt), *n. Civil Law.* dowry (def. 1). [1850–55; < F < L *dōtem,* acc. of *dōs* dowry, akin to *dāre* to give] —**do·tal** (dōt′l), *adj.*

Dot (dot), *n.* a female given name, form of **Dorothea** and **Dorothy.**

DOT, 1. See **Department of Transportation. 2.** Dictionary of Occupational Titles.

dot·age (dō′tij), *n.* **1.** a decline of mental faculties, esp. as associated with old age; senility. **2.** excessive fondness; foolish affection. [1300–50; ME; see DOTE, -AGE]

do·tard (dō′tərd), *n.* **1.** a person, esp. an old person, exhibiting a decline in mental faculties; a weak-minded or foolish old person. **2.** doater[2]. [1350–1400; ME; see DOTE, -ARD] —**do′tard·ly,** *adv.*

do·ta·tion (dō tā′shən), *n.* an endowment. [1350–1400; < L *dōtātiōn-* (s. of *dōtātiō*), equiv. to *dōtāt(us),* ptp. of *dōtāre* to provide a dowry for (deriv. of *dōs* dowry; cf. DOT[2]) + *-iōn-* -ION; r. ME *dotacioun* < AF]

dote (dōt), *v.,* **dot·ed, dot·ing,** *n.* —*v.i.* Also, **doat. 1.** to bestow or express excessive love or fondness habitually (usually fol. by *on* or *upon*): *They dote on their youngest daughter.* **2.** to show a decline of mental faculties, esp. associated with old age. —*n.* **3.** decay of wood. [1175–1225; ME *doten* to behave foolishly, become feeble-minded; c. MD *doten.*] —**dot′er,** *n.*

dot′ etch′ing, *Print.* a method of making corrections in halftone positives or negatives by using chemicals to reduce the size of halftone dots. [1945–50]

doth (duth), *v. Archaic.* 3rd pers. sing. pres. ind. of **do**[1].

Do·than (dō′thən), *n.* a city in SE Alabama. 48,750.

dot·ing (dō′ting), *adj.* **1.** excessively fond: *doting parents.* **2.** showing a decline of mental faculties, esp. associated with old age; weak-minded; senile. [1480–90; DOTE + -ING[2]] —**dot′ing·ly,** *adv.* —**dot′ing·ness,** *n.*

dot′ ma′trix, *Computers.* a method of forming characters and graphics, used by CRTs and other screens, some printers **(dot′-ma′trix print′ers),** and some plotters, by creating the desired pattern using dots from a dense matrix. [1960–65]

dot′ prod′uct, *Math.* See **inner product** (def. 1).

dot-se·quen·tial (dot′si kwen′shəl), *adj. Television.* of, relating to, or being a color television system that sends and reproduces the primary colors as dots in proper sequence on each scanned line to produce a color picture. [1950–55]

dot·ted (dot′id), *adj.* **1.** marked with a dot or dots. **2.** consisting or constructed of dots. **3.** having objects scattered or placed in a random manner: *a landscape dotted with small houses.* [1765–75; DOT[1] + -ED[3]]

dot′ted line′, 1. a line on a contract or similar document for a party's signature. **2.** a line at which a sheet of paper is perforated or a piece of it is to be detached. **3. signature on the dotted line,** full agreement to terms and conditions. **4. sign on the dotted line,** to agree fully to terms or conditions. [1770–75]

dot′ted swiss′. See under **Swiss muslin.** [1920–25]

dot·ter·el (dot′ər əl), *n.* **1.** any of several plovers usually inhabiting upland areas, esp. *Eudromias morinellus,* of Europe and Asia. **2.** *Brit. Dial.* a silly, stupid person, esp. one who is easily duped. Also, **dot·trel** (do′trəl). [1400–50; late ME *dotrelle.* See DOTE, -REL]

Dot·tie (dot′ē), *n.* a female given name, form of **Dorothea** and **Dorothy.** Also, **Dot′ty.**

dot·tle (dot′l), *n.* the plug of half-smoked tobacco in the bottom of a pipe after smoking. Also, **dot′tel.** [1815–25; dial. *dot* small lump (prob. identical with DOT[1]) + -LE]

dot·ty[1] (dot′ē), *adj.,* **-ti·er, -ti·est.** *Informal.* **1.** crazy or eccentric. **2.** feeble or unsteady in gait. **3.** very enthusiastic or infatuated (usually fol. by *about* or *over*). [1805–15; perh. *dott(ard)* var. of DOTARD + -Y[1]] —**dot′ti·ly,** *adv.* —**dot′ti·ness,** *n.*

dot·ty[2] (dot′ē), *adj.,* **-ti·er, -ti·est.** marked with dots; dotted. [1805–15; DOT[1] + -Y[1]] —**dot′ti·ness,** *n.*

CONCISE ETYMOLOGY KEY: <, descended or borrowed from; >, whence; b., blend of, blended; c., cognate with; cf., compare; deriv., derivative; equiv., equivalent; imit., imitative; obl., oblique; r., replacing; s., stem; sp., spelling, spelled; resp., respelling, respelled; trans., translation; ?, origin unknown; *, unattested; ‡, probably earlier than. See the full key inside the front cover.

dot·y (dō′tē), *adj.,* **dot·i·er, dot·i·est.** *Southern U.S.* (of wood) decayed. [1880–85; DOTE + -Y[1]]

Dou (dou), *n.* **Ge·rard** (gä′RÄRT), 1613–75, Dutch painter: pupil of Rembrandt. Also, **Douw, Dow.**

Dou·ai (do͞o ā′; *Fr.* dwe), *n.* a city in N France, SE of Calais. 47,570. Also, **Dou·ay′.**

Dou·a·la (do͝o ä′lä), *n.* a seaport in W Cameroon. 340,000. Also, **Duala.**

douane (dwAN), *n., pl.* ***douanes*** (dwAN). *French.* a custom house; customs.

doua·nier (dwA nyā′), *n., pl.* ***-niers*** (-nyā′). *French.* a customs officer or official.

Dou′ay Bi′ble (do͞o′ā), an English translation of the Bible, prepared by Roman Catholic scholars from the Vulgate. The New Testament was published at Rheims in 1582 and the Old Testament was published at Douai in 1609–10. Also called **Dou′ay Ver′sion, Dou′ay-Rheims′ Bi′ble** (do͞o′ā rēmz′), **Rheims-Douay Bible.** Cf. **New American Bible.**

dou·ble (dub′əl), *adj., n., v.,* **-bled, -bling,** *adv.* —*adj.* **1.** twice as large, heavy, strong, etc.; twofold in size, amount, number, extent, etc.: *a double portion; a new house double the size of the old one.* **2.** composed of two like parts or members; twofold in form; paired: *double doors; a double sink.* **3.** of, pertaining to, or suitable for two persons: *a double room.* **4.** twofold in character, meaning, or conduct; dual or ambiguous: *a double interpretation.* **5.** deceitful; hypocritical; insincere. **6.** (of musical instruments) producing a tone an octave lower than the notes indicate. **7.** duple, as time or rhythm. **8.** folded in two; having one half folded over the other. **9.** (of a bed or bedclothes) full-size: *a double blanket.* **10.** *Bot.* (of flowers) having many more than the normal number of petals: *double petunias; double hollyhocks.* —*n.* **11.** anything that is twofold in size or amount or twice the usual size, quantity, strength, etc. **12.** a duplicate or counterpart; something exactly or closely resembling another: *This dress is the double of that. He is the double of his cousin.* **13.** Also called **double room.** a type of hotel accommodation with two beds, or sometimes a double bed, for occupancy by two persons. Cf. **twin** (def. 4). **14.** a fold or plait. **15.** an alcoholic drink containing twice the usual amount of alcohol. **16.** a sudden backward turn or bend, as of a fox on the run in fox hunting; reversal. **17.** a trick or artifice, as of argument in a formal debate. **18.** a substitute actor or singer ready to take another's place; understudy. **19.** *Motion Pictures, Television.* a substitute who performs feats or actions too hazardous or difficult for a star. **20.** *Baseball.* See **two-base hit. 21.** *Mil.* double time. **22. doubles,** (*used with a singular v.*) a game or match in which there are two players on each side, as in tennis. **23.** (in bridge or other card games) **a.** a challenge by an opponent that the declarer cannot fulfill the designated contract, increasing the points to be won or lost. **b.** a hand that warrants such a challenge. **24.** *Bridge.* a conventional bid informing one's partner that a player's hand is of a certain strength. **25.** *Bowling.* two strikes in succession: *He needed a double in the tenth frame to win.* **26.** See **daily double. 27.** any of certain feasts in the Roman Catholic Church, marked by a doubled antiphon and taking precedence over lesser feasts. **28.** *Music. Rare.* a variation. **29.** a former coin of France, the sixth part of a sol, issued in silver in the 14th century, later made of copper. **30. at the double,** *Brit. Informal.* on the double. **31. on the double,** *Informal.* **a.** without delay; rapidly: *The fire engines came on the double.* **b** in double time, as marching troops. —*v.t.* **32.** to make double or twice as great; to add an equal amount to: *The baby doubled its weight in a year.* **33.** to bend or fold with or as with one part over another (often fol. by *over, up, back,* etc.): *Double the edge over before sewing.* **34.** to clench: *He doubled his fists.* **35.** to be or have twice as much as: *Income doubled expenditure.* **36.** *Naut.* **a.** to sail around (a projecting area of land): *to double Cape Horn.* **b.** to add a new layer of planking or ceiling to (an old wooden hull). **37.** to pair; couple: *The players were doubled for the tournament.* **38.** *Music.* to reduplicate by means of a tone in another part, either at the unison or at an octave above or below. **39.** (in bridge and other card games) **a.** to challenge (the bid of an opponent) by making a call that increases the value of tricks to be won or lost. **b.** to challenge the bid of (an opponent): *He doubled me into game.* **40.** *Baseball.* **a.** to cause the advance of (a base runner) by a two-base hit: *He doubled him to third.* **b.** to cause (a run) to be scored by a two-base hit (often fol. by *in*): *He doubled in the winning run.* **c.** to put out (a base runner) as the second out of a double play (often fol. by *up*). —*v.i.* **41.** to become double: *My money doubled in three years.* **42.** to bend or fold (often fol. by *up* or *over*): *to double over with pain.* **43.** to turn back on a course or reverse direction (often fol. by *back*): *He doubled back by another road and surprised us.* **44.** *Mil.* to march at the double-time pace. **45.** to serve in two capacities or in an additional capacity: *She doubles as producer and director.* **46.** to act as a double in a play, motion picture, or the like. **47.** *Music.* to play an instrument besides one's regular instrument (usually followed by *on*): *The saxophonist doubles on drums.* **48.** (in bridge and other card games) to double the bid of an opponent. **49.** *Baseball.* to make a two-base hit. **50.** to double-date. **51. double in brass,** *Informal.* to serve in two capacities; be able to do work different from one's own: *It is a small firm, and everyone doubles in brass when emergencies arise.* **52. double or nothing,** a bet having as its outcome either the doubling of a previous loss or debt or the canceling of that loss or debt. Also, **double or quits. 53. double up, a.** to share quarters planned for only one person or family: *Because of the room shortage, we had to double up.* **b.** to bend over, as from pain: *He doubled up in agony.* —*adv.* **54.** to twice the amount, number, extent, etc.; twofold; doubly. **55.** two together: *There are only a few beds, so some of the children will have to sleep double for the night.* [1175–1225; ME < OF < L *duplus,* equiv. to *du(o)* TWO + *-plus* -FOLD] —**dou′ble·ness,** *n.* —**dou′bler,** *n.*

dou′ble achieve′ment, *Heraldry.* a representation of the arms of a husband beside those of his wife such that a difference of rank between them is shown.

dou·ble-act·ing (dub′əl ak′ting), *adj.* **1.** (of a reciprocating engine, pump, etc.) having pistons accomplishing work in both directions, fluid being admitted alternately to opposite ends of the cylinders. Cf. **single-acting. 2.** (of a hinge of a door or the like) permitting movement in either direction from the normal, or closed, position. **3.** having twice the usual effectiveness, strength, use, etc. [1835–45]

dou·ble-ac·tion (dub′əl ak′shən), *adj.* (of a firearm) requiring only one pull of the trigger to cock and fire it. [1850–55]

dou′ble a′gent, 1. a person who spies on a country while pretending to spy for it. **2.** a spy in the service of two rival countries, companies, etc. [1930–35]

dou′ble al′tar, an altar on which the Eucharist may be celebrated from either the liturgical east or the liturgical west side.

dou′ble ax′, an ax with a double-edged blade, frequently depicted in prehistoric decorative designs of the eastern Mediterranean region. [1890–95]

dou·ble-bank (dub′əl bangk′), *v.t. Naut.* **1.** to have two rowers pull (each of a number of oars). **2.** to have people pull (a rope) from both sides. **3.** to row (a boat) with rowers for both sides on each thwart. [1825–35]

dou′ble bar′, *Music.* a double vertical line on a staff indicating the conclusion of a piece of music or a subdivision of it. See illus. under **bar**[1]. [1665–75]

dou·ble-bar·reled (dub′əl bar′əld), *adj.* **1.** having two barrels mounted side by side, as a shotgun. **2.** serving a double purpose or having two parts or aspects: *a double-barreled attack on corruption.* [1700–10]

dou′ble bass′ (bās), the largest instrument of the violin family, having three or, usually, four strings, rested vertically on the floor when played. Also called **bass fiddle, bass viol, contrabass, string bass.** [1720–30] —**dou′ble bass′ist.**

dou′ble bassoon′, a bassoon an octave lower in pitch than the ordinary bassoon: the largest and deepest-toned instrument of the oboe class; contrabassoon. [1875–80]

dou′ble bat′ten, *Theat.* two wooden battens screwed together for holding the edge of a drop between them. Also called **sandwich batten.**

dou′ble bed′, a bed large enough for two adults, esp. a bed measuring 54 in. (137 cm) wide; full-size bed. [1790–1800]

dou′ble bill′. See **double feature.** [1925–30]

dou·ble-bill (dub′əl bil′), *v.t.* **1.** to bill (different accounts) for the same charge: *He double-billed different clients for the same business trip.* **2.** to place (a motion picture) on a double bill: *The film is being double-billed in some theaters.* —*v.i.* **3.** to bill different accounts for the same charge. [1925–30]

dou′ble bind′, 1. *Psychol.* a situation in which a person is given conflicting cues, esp. by a parent, such that to obey one cue is to disobey the other. **2.** dilemma (def. 1). [1955–60, *Amer.*]

dou·ble-blind (dub′əl blīnd′), *adj.* of or pertaining to an experiment or clinical trial in which neither the subjects nor the researchers know which subjects are receiving the active medication, treatment, etc., and which are not: a technique for eliminating subjective bias from the test results. [1935–40]

dou′ble block′, *Mach.* a block having two sheaves or pulleys.

dou′ble blos′som, *Plant Pathol.* a disease of blackberries and dewberries, characterized by witches'-brooms and flower malformations, caused by a fungus, *Cercosporella rubi.*

dou′ble bo′gey, *Golf.* a score of two strokes over par on a hole.

dou′ble boil′er, a utensil consisting of two pots, one of which fits partway into the other: water is boiled in the lower pot to cook or warm food or melt a substance in the upper. [1875–80, *Amer.*]

dou′ble bond′, *Chem.* a chemical linkage consisting of two covalent bonds between two atoms of a molecule, represented in chemical formulas by two lines, two dots, or four dots, as $CH_2{=}CH_2$; $CH_2{:}CH_2$; $CH_2{::}CH_2$. [1885–90]

dou·ble-book (dub′əl bo͝ok′), *v.t.* **1.** to overbook by accepting more than one reservation for the same hotel room, airplane seat, etc. **2.** to make reservations for (more than one hotel accommodation, seat on a plane, etc.) so as to be certain of obtaining at least one of them. —*v.i.* **3.** to make double reservations for passenger space, a hotel room, etc. [1965–70]

dou·ble-bot·tom (dub′əl bot′əm), *n.* See **tandem trailer** (def. 1).

dou′ble-breast·ed (dub′əl bres′tid), *adj.* **1.** (of a coat, jacket, etc.) overlapping sufficiently in front to allow for two rows of buttons. **2.** (of a suit) having a coat or jacket that so overlaps. Cf. **single-breasted.** [1695–1700]

dou·ble-breast·ing (dub′əl bres′ting), *n.* the practice of employing nonunion workers, esp. in a separate division, to supplement the work of higher-paid union workers. [1975–80]

dou′ble cen′tering, *Survey.* a method of extending a survey line by taking the average of two foresights, one with the telescope direct and one with it inverted, made each time by transiting the telescope after a backsight.

dou′ble check′, *Chess.* a simultaneous check by two pieces in which the moving of one piece to give check also results in discovering a check by another piece.

dou′ble-check (dub′əl chek′), *v.t., v.i.* **1.** to check twice or again; recheck. —*n.* **2.** a second examination or verification to assure accuracy, proper functioning, or the like. [1950–55, *Amer.*]

dou′ble chin′, a fold of fat beneath the chin. [1825–35] —**dou′ble-chinned′,** *adj.*

dou′ble cloth′, a cloth used in overcoating, blankets, brocade, etc., made by interweaving two physically discrete fabrics at various points in the pattern by bringing warp and fill yarns from each through the other to be worked on the opposite face of the compound fabric.

dou•ble-clutch[1] (dub′əl kluch′), *v.i. Auto.* to downshift by shifting gears in an automotive vehicle first into neutral and then into the desired gear, releasing the clutch twice, once for each shift.

dou•ble-clutch[2] (dub′əl kluch′), *v.i.* (of a bird) to produce a second clutch of eggs after the first has been removed, usually for hatching in an incubator.

dou′ble coat′, an outer coat of hair on a dog serving as protection against underbrush and resistant to weather, combined with an undercoat of softer hair for warmth and waterproofing.

dou′ble co′conut, 1. a tall, stout, fan palm, *Lodoicea maldivica,* of the Seychelles Islands, having nuts that are the largest seeds of any plant, often weighing 50 lb. (22.6 kg): populations are declining. **2.** the seed of this tree. Also called **coco-de-mer.** [1820–30]

dou′ble coun′terpoint, *Music.* invertible counterpoint using two transposable voices.

dou′ble cream′, (in France) a fresh, soft cheese with at least 60 percent fat, made from cow's milk enriched with cream. Also, **dou′ble crème′.** Cf. **triple cream.** [1875–80]

dou′ble-crest•ed cor′morant (dub′əl kres′tid), a North American cormorant, *Phalacrocorax auritus,* having tufts of black and white feathers on the sides of the head. [1825–35, *Amer.*]

dou•ble-crop (dub′əl krop′), *v.,* **-cropped, -crop•ping.** —*v.i.* **1.** to raise two consecutive crops on the same land within a single growing season. —*v.t.* **2.** to raise two crops per year on (an area of land).

dou′ble cross′, 1. a betrayal or swindle of a colleague. **2.** an attempt to win a contest that one has agreed beforehand to lose. Cf. **cross** (def. 21). **3.** *Genetics.* a cross in which both parents are first-generation hybrids from single crosses, thus involving four inbred lines. [1825–35]

dou•ble-cross (dub′əl krôs′, -kros′), *v.t. Informal.* to prove treacherous to; betray or swindle, as by a double cross. [1900–05] —**dou′ble-cross′er,** *n.*

Dou•ble-Cros•tic (dub′əl krô′stik, -kros′tik), *Trademark.* a word game in which the player suits word definitions to numbered spaces to produce a quotation, the first letters of the definitions forming the name of the author and of the work from which the quote comes.

dou′ble crown′, *Chiefly Brit.* a size of printing paper, 20 × 30 in. (51 × 76 cm).

dou′ble cup′, (in Renaissance art) a matched pair of metal cups, made so that one can be placed inverted on top of the other.

dou•ble-cut (dub′əl kut′), *adj.* noting a file having parallel cutting ridges crisscrossing in two directions. Cf. **single-cut.**

dou′ble dag′ger, *Print.* a mark (‡) used for references, as footnotes. Also called **diesis.** [1700–10]

dou′ble date′, *Informal.* a date on which two couples go together. [1920–25]

dou•ble-date (dub′əl dāt′), *v.,* **-dat•ed, -dat•ing.** *Informal.* —*v.i.* **1.** to take part in a double date. —*v.t.* **2.** to accompany (someone) on a double date: *They double-dated the two sisters.* [1945–50]

Dou•ble•day (dub′əl dā′), *n.* **Abner,** 1819–93, U.S. army officer; sometimes credited with inventing the modern game of baseball.

dou•ble-deal (dub′əl dēl′), *v.i.,* **-dealt** (-delt′), **-deal•ing.** to practice double-dealing. [1965–70] —**dou′•ble-deal′er,** *n.*

dou•ble-deal•ing (dub′əl dē′ling), *n.* **1.** duplicity; treachery; deception. —*adj.* **2.** using duplicity; treacherous. [1520–30]

dou•ble-deck (dub′əl dek′), *adj.* **1.** Also, **dou′•ble-decked′.** having two decks, tiers, or levels: *a double-deck bunk; a double-deck bus.* —*v.t.* **2.** to add a second deck to (a bridge) or a second level to (a road). [1865–70, *Amer.*]

dou•ble-deck•er (dub′əl dek′ər), *n.* **1.** something with two decks, tiers, or the like, as two beds one above the other, a ship with two decks above the water line, or a bus with two decks. **2.** a food item consisting of two main layers, as a sandwich made with three slices of bread and two layers of filling. [1825–35, *Amer.*]

dou′ble decomposi′tion, *Chem.* a reaction whose result is the interchange of two parts of two substances to form two new substances, as $AgNO_3 + NaCl \rightarrow AgCl + NaNO_3$. Also called **metathesis.** [1865–70]

dou′ble dem′y, a size of printing paper, 22½ × 35 in. (57 × 89 cm).

dou•ble-dig•it (dub′əl dij′it), *adj.* of or denoting a percentage greater than ten. [1970–75]

dou′ble dip′, 1. a complement equal to the original; a double measure: *a double dip of protection through both insurance and Social Security.* **2.** something that happens twice in a cycle, esp. on a downturn: *a double dip of recession.*

dou•ble-dip (dub′əl dip′), *v.,* **-dipped, -dip•ping,** *adj.* —*v.i.* **1.** *Informal.* to earn a salary from one position while collecting a pension from the same employer or organization, esp. to be a wage earner on the federal payroll while receiving a military retiree's pension. —*adj.* **2.** of, pertaining to, or of the nature of a double dip. [1960–65] —**dou′ble-dip′per,** *n.*

dou•ble-dip•ping (dub′əl dip′ing), *n.* the act or practice of receiving more than one income or collecting double benefits from the same employer or organization. [1970–75]

dou•ble-dome (dub′əl dōm′), *n. Informal.* an intellectual; egghead. [1935–40] —**dou′ble-domed′,** *adj.*

dou′ble dress′er, *Furniture.* a dresser having two long drawers across its width for most of its height.

dou′ble drib′ble, *Basketball.* **1.** an infraction, resulting in loss of possession of the ball, occurring either when a player uses both hands simultaneously when dribbling or when a player interrupts a dribble by holding the ball momentarily in one or both hands. **2.** to commit a double dribble.

dou′ble drift′, *Navig.* a method of calculating wind direction and velocity by observing the direction of drift of an aircraft on two or more headings.

dou′ble dum′my, *Cards.* a variety of bridge for two players in which two hands are kept face down until the end of the bidding when both hands are exposed. [1900–05]

dou′ble Dutch′, *Slang.* unintelligible or garbled speech or language: *She could have been talking double Dutch for all we understood of it.* [1875–80]

Dou′ble Dutch′, (*sometimes l.c.*) a form of the game of jump rope in which two persons, holding the respective ends of two long jump ropes, swing them in a synchronized fashion, usually directed inward so the ropes are going in opposite directions, for one or two others to jump over.

dou•ble-du•ty (dub′əl do͞o′tē, -dyo͞o′-), *adj.* designed to fill two functions: *double-duty tools.*

dou′ble ea′gle, 1. a gold coin of the U.S., issued from 1849 to 1933, equal to 2 eagles or 20 dollars. **2.** *Golf.* a score of three strokes under par on a hole. [1840–50, *Amer.*]

dou•ble-edged (dub′əl ejd′), *adj.* **1.** having two cutting edges, as a razor blade. **2.** capable of acting two ways or having opposite effects: *a double-edged argument.* [1545–55]

dou•ble-end•ed (dub′əl en′did), *adj.* **1.** having the two ends alike. **2.** *Naut.* **a.** operating equally well with either end as the bow, as a ferryboat. **b.** noting a vessel having a stern curved or pointed so as to resemble or suggest a bow. **3.** noting any of various vehicles, as certain streetcars, designed to be operated with either end serving as the front. [1870–75]

dou′ble-ended bolt′, a headless bolt threaded at both ends.

dou′ble end′er, *Naut.* a double-ended vessel. Also, **dou′ble-end′er.** [1860–65, *Amer.*]

dou•ble en•ten•dre (dub′əl än tän′drə, -tänd′; *Fr.* do͞o blän tän′drᵊ), *pl.* **dou•ble en•ten•dres** (dub′əl än-tän′drəz, -tändz′; *Fr.* do͞o blän tän′drᵊ). **1.** a double meaning. **2.** a word or expression used in a given context so that it can be understood in two ways, esp. when one meaning is risqué. [1665–75; < obs. F; see DOUBLE, INTEND]

dou•ble en•tente (do͞o blän tänt′), *pl.* ***dou•bles en•tentes*** (do͞o blə zän tänt′). *French.* a double meaning; ambiguity.

dou′ble en′try, *Bookkeeping.* a method in which each transaction is entered twice in the ledger, once to the debit of one account, and once to the credit of another. Cf. **single entry.** [1715–25] —**dou′ble-en′try,** *adj.*

dou′ble expo′sure, *Photog.* **1.** the act of exposing the same film, frame, plate, etc., twice. **2.** the picture resulting from such exposure. [1890–95]

dou•ble-faced (dub′əl fāst′), *adj.* **1.** practicing duplicity; hypocritical. **2.** having two faces or aspects. **3.** having two usable sides, esp. two sides designed to be used in the same manner: *double-faced adhesive tape.* [1565–75] —**dou•ble-fac•ed•ly** (dub′əl fā′sid lē, -fāst′-), *adv.* —**dou′ble-fac′ed•ness,** *n.*

dou′ble fault′, (in tennis, squash, handball, etc.) two faults in succession, resulting in the loss of the point, the loss of the serve, or both. [1905–10]

dou′ble fea′ture, a motion-picture program consisting of two films shown one after the other for the price of a single ticket. Also called **double bill.** [1930–35, *Amer.*]

dou′ble fertiliza′tion, the fertilization process characteristic of flowering plants, in which one sperm cell of a pollen grain fertilizes an egg cell while a second fuses with two polar nuclei to produce a triploid body that gives rise to the endosperm. [1905–10]

dou•ble-fig•ure (dub′əl fig′yər; *Brit.* dub′əl fig′ər), *adj. Brit.* double-digit. [1855–60]

dou′ble first′, *Brit. Univ.* **1.** a first in two subjects. **2.** a student who earns a first in two subjects.

dou′ble flat′, *Music.* **1.** a symbol (♭♭) that lowers the pitch of the note following it by two semitones. **2.** a note or tone marked or affected by such a symbol.

dou′ble fugue′, *Music.* **1.** a fugue with two subjects developed simultaneously. **2.** a fugue having two subjects that are developed at first independently and then together.

dou•ble•gang•er (dub′əl gang′ər), *n.* Doppelgänger. [1820–30; half-trans. of G *Doppelgänger*]

dou′ble gen′itive. See **double possessive.**

dou•ble-glazed (dub′əl glāzd′), *adj.* of, having, or provided with double glazing: *double-glazed windows and doors.*

dou′ble glaz′ing, *Building Trades.* glazing consisting of two thicknesses of glass with a dead air space between them.

dou′ble har′ness, 1. harness for a pair of horses. **2.** **in double harness,** *Informal.* married. [1865–70, *Amer.*]

dou•ble•head•er (dub′əl hed′ər), *n.* **1.** *Sports.* **a.** two games, as of baseball, between the same teams on the same day in immediate succession. **b.** two games, as of basketball, between two different pairs of teams on the same day in immediate succession. **2.** two performances or two events occurring one after the other or within a short time of each other. **3.** a railroad train pulled by two locomotives. [1895–1900, *Amer.*; DOUBLE + HEAD + -ER[1]]

dou′ble-hel•i•cal gear′ (dub′əl hel′i kəl). See **herringbone gear.**

dou′ble he′lix, *Biochem., Genetics.* the spiral arrangement of the two complementary strands of DNA. [1953; term introduced by J.D. Watson and F.H.C. Crick]

dou′ble hitch′, a Blackwall hitch with an extra upper loop passed around the hook.

dou•ble-hung (dub′əl hung′), *adj.* **1.** (of a window) having two vertically sliding sashes, each closing a different part of the opening. **2.** (of a window sash) sliding vertically, with a counterweight on each side. [1815–25]

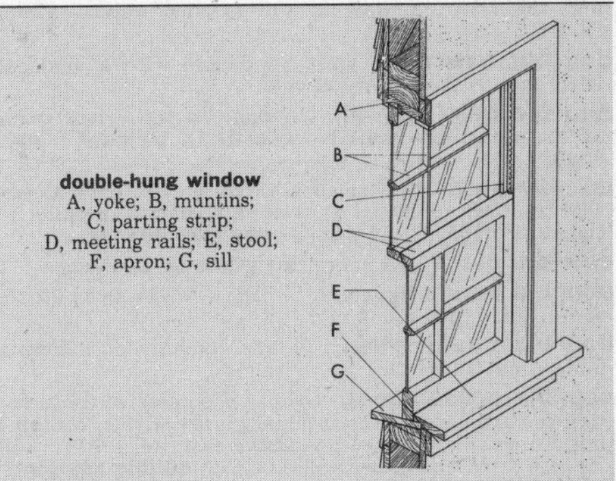

double-hung window
A, yoke; B, muntins; C, parting strip; D, meeting rails; E, stool; F, apron; G, sill

dou′ble i′kat. See under **ikat.**

dou′ble indem′nity, a clause in a life-insurance or accident-insurance policy providing for payment of twice the face value of the policy in the event of accidental death. Cf. **accidental death benefit.** [1920–25, *Amer.*]

dou′ble in′tegral, *Math.* an integral in which the integrand involves a function of two variables and that requires two applications of the integration process to evaluate.

dou′ble jeop′ardy, *Law.* the subjecting of a person to a second trial or punishment for the same offense for which the person has already been tried or punished. [1905–10]

dou•ble-joint•ed (dub′əl join′tid), *adj.* (of particular people or animals) having unusually flexible joints that can bend in unusual ways or to abnormally great extent. [1825–35]

dou′ble jump′, 1. *Chess.* the advance of a pawn, in its original move only, from its initial position on the second rank to the fourth without stopping at the intervening square. **2.** *Checkers.* the capturing of two of the opponent's checkers in two uninterrupted jumps, constituting a single move by one piece.

doub•le-knit (dub′əl nit′, -nit′), *n.* **1.** a weft-knit fabric that consists of two single-knit fabrics intimately interlooped. **2.** a garment made of such a fabric. Also, **dou′ble knit′, dou′ble•knit′.** [1890–95]

dou•ble-lock (dub′əl lok′), *v.t.* **1.** to lock with two turns of a key, so that a second bolt is engaged. **2.** to fasten with particular care. [1585–95]

dou′ble mag′num, Jeroboam (def. 2).

dou•ble-mind•ed (dub′əl mīn′did), *adj.* wavering or undecided in mind. [1545–55] —**dou′ble-mind′ed•ly,** *adv.* —**dou′ble-mind′ed•ness,** *n.*

dou′ble mod′al, a syntactic construction in which two modal auxiliaries occur consecutively within a clause, as *might could* in *I might could help you.*

dou′ble mon′astery, a religious community of both men and women who live in separate establishments under the same superior and who worship in a common church.

dou′ble neg′ative, a syntactic construction in which two negative words are used in the same clause to express a single negation. [1820–30]

—Usage. Double or multiple negation was standard in English through the time of Shakespeare. An oft-quoted line from Chaucer's *Canterbury Tales* (c1390) exemplifies the practice in earlier English: *"He never yet no vileynye ne sayde"* (*He never said anything discourteous*). Similar uses of double or multiple negation to reinforce or strengthen a negative are universally considered nonstandard in modern English: *They never paid me no money. He didn't have nothing to do with it.* They do not occur in educated speech or writing, where *any* and *anything* would be substituted for *no* and *nothing* in such examples.

Other uses of double negatives are fully standard. Occasionally a double negative strongly suggests an affirmative alternative: *We cannot just say nothing about the problem* (*We must say something about the problem*). The use of a negative before an adjective or adverb having a negative sense or with a negative prefix is also standard and is the figure of speech known as litotes, in which something is affirmed by denying its opposite: *In the not unlikely event that the bill passes, prices will certainly rise.* St. Paul said that he was *"a citizen of no mean city*" (Tarsus in Cilicia; Acts 21:39), meaning that the city was important. See also **hardly.**

dou•ble•ness (dub′əl nis), *n.* **1.** the quality or condition of being double. **2.** deception or dissimulation. [1325–75; ME; see DOUBLE, -NESS]

dou•ble-nick•el (dub′əl nik′əl), *n. Slang.* the national speed limit of 55 miles per hour as established in 1974 on U.S. highways. [1975–80]

dou•ble-O (dub′əl ō′), *n., pl.* **-Os.** *Older Slang.* careful scrutiny or close inspection. [1915–20; after the two o's in ONCE-OVER]

dou′ble oc′cupancy, a type of travel accommodation, as in a hotel, for two persons sharing the same room: *The rate is $35 per person, double occupancy, or $65, single occupancy.* Cf. **single occupancy. —dou′•ble-oc′cu•pan•cy,** *adj.*

dou′ble o′verhead cam′shaft, *Auto.* a pair of overhead camshafts, one to operate the intake valves and the other to operate the exhaust valves. *Abbr.:* DOHC

dou′ble pad′dle, *Naut.* a paddle with a blade at each end, as that of the kayak.

dou′ble pair′ roy′al, *Cribbage.* a set of four cards of the same denomination, worth 12 points. Cf. **pair royal.**

dou•ble-park (dub′əl pärk′), *v.t., v.i.* to park alongside another vehicle that is already parked parallel to the curb. [1930–35, *Amer.*] **—dou′ble-park′er,** *n.*

dou′ble piece′, *Armor.* See **piece of exchange.**

dou′ble play′, *Baseball.* a play in which two putouts are made. [1865–70, *Amer.*]

dou′ble pneumo′nia, *Pathol.* pneumonia affecting both lungs. [1890–95]

dou′ble posses′sive, *Gram.* a possessive construction consisting of a prepositional phrase with *of* containing a substantive in the possessive case, as *of father's* in *He is a friend of father's.* Also called **double genitive.**

dou′ble preci′sion, *Computers.* using twice the normal amount of storage, as two words rather than one, to represent a number.

dou′ble predestina′tion, *Theol.* the doctrine that God has foreordained both those who will be saved and those who will be damned.

dou′ble quat′refoil, *Heraldry.* a charge having the form of a foil with eight leaves, used esp. as the cadency mark of a ninth son. Also called **octofoil.**

dou•ble-quick (*adj., adv.* dub′əl kwik′; *n., v.* dub′əl kwik′), *adj.* **1.** very quick or rapid. *—adv.* **2.** in a very quick or rapid manner. *—n.* **3.** a very quick marching pace: double time. *—v.t., v.i.* **4.** to double-time. [1815–25]

dou′ble quotes′, quotation marks (" "), as usually appear around quoted material. Cf. **single quotes.**

dou•ble-reed (dub′əl rēd′), *adj. Music.* of or pertaining to wind instruments producing sounds through two reeds fastened and beating together, as the oboe. [1875–80]

dou′ble refrac′tion, *Optics.* the separation of a ray of light into two unequally refracted, plane-polarized rays of orthogonal polarizations, occurring in crystals in which the velocity of light rays is not the same in all directions. Also called **birefringence.** [1870–75]

dou′ble rhyme′. See under **feminine rhyme.**

dou•ble-ring (dub′əl ring′), *adj.* being or pertaining to a marriage ceremony in which the bride and groom give rings to one another. [1955–60]

dou•ble-rip•per (dub′əl rip′ər), *n. New Eng.* bobsled (def. 2). Also called **dou•ble-run•ner** (dub′əl run′ər). [1875–80, *Amer.*]

dou′ble room′, double (def. 13). [1930–35]

dou′ble run′, *Cribbage.* a set of four cards consisting of a three-card run plus a fourth card of the same denomination as one of the others, as 2, 3, 4, 4, worth eight points.

dou′ble salt′, *Chem.* a salt that crystallizes as a single substance but ionizes as two distinct salts when dissolved, as carnallite, $KMgCl_3 \cdot 6H_2O$. [1840–50]

dou′ble sculls′, a race for sculls rowed by two rowers, each using a pair of oars. Cf. **single sculls.**

dou′ble sharp′, *Music.* **1.** a symbol (× or ※) that raises by two semitones the pitch of the following note. **2.** a note or tone marked or affected by such a symbol.

dou•ble-sid•ed (dub′əl sī′did), *adj.* double-faced (defs. 2, 3). [1860–65]

dou′ble sol′itaire, *Cards.* a game of solitaire for two persons, each player usually having a pack and layout but pooling foundations with the opponent.

dou•ble-space (dub′əl spās′), *v.,* **-spaced, -spac•ing.** *—v.t.* **1.** to type (text, copy, etc.) leaving a full space between lines: *Always double-space a term paper.* *—v.i.* **2.** to type leaving a full space between lines: *I can never remember to double-space.* [1895–1900]

dou′ble Span′ish bur′ton, a tackle having one standing block and two running blocks, giving a mechanical advantage of five, neglecting friction. See diag. under **tackle.**

dou•ble-speak (dub′əl spēk′), *n.* evasive, ambiguous language that is intended to deceive or confuse. [1950–55; DOUBLE + SPEAK, by analogy with DOUBLETHINK] **—dou′ble-speak′er,** *n.*

CONCISE ETYMOLOGY KEY: <, descended or borrowed from; >, whence; b., blend of, blended; c., cognate with; cf., compare; deriv., derivative; equiv., equivalent; imit., imitative; obl., oblique; r., replacing; s., stem; sp., spelling, spelled; resp., respelling, respelled; trans., translation; ?, origin unknown; *, unattested; ‡, probably earlier than. See the full key inside the front cover.

dou′ble spread′, **1.** any pair of facing pages in a completed book, magazine, etc. **2.** a picture, advertisement, etc., occupying two facing pages. [1955–60]

dou′ble stand′ard, **1.** any code or set of principles containing different provisions for one group of people than for another, esp. an unwritten code of sexual behavior permitting men more freedom than women. Cf. **single standard** (def. 1). **2.** *Econ.* bimetallism. [1950–55]

dou′ble star′, *Astron.* two stars that appear as one if not viewed through a telescope with adequate magnification, such as two stars that are separated by a great distance but are nearly in line with each other and an observer **(optical double star),** or those that are relatively close together and comprise a single physical system **(physical double star).** Cf. **binary star.** [1775–85]

dou′ble steal′, *Baseball.* a play in which two base runners steal a base each. [1895–1900, *Amer.*]

dou′ble stop′, *Music.* two or more notes bowed simultaneously on a stringed instrument, as the violin. [1875–80]

dou•ble-stop (dub′əl stop′), *v.,* **-stopped, -stop•ping.** *Music. —v.t.* **1.** to play a double stop on (a stringed instrument). *—v.i.* **2.** to play a double stop. [1875–80]

dou′ble sug′ar, *Chem.* disaccharide. [1955–60]

dou•blet (dub′lit), *n.* **1.** a close-fitting outer garment, with or without sleeves and sometimes having a short skirt, worn by men in the Renaissance. **2.** an undergarment, quilted and reinforced with mail, worn beneath armor. **3.** a pair of like things; couple. **4.** one of a pair of like things; duplicate. **5.** *Ling.* one of two or more words in a language that are derived from the same source, esp. when one is learned while the other is popular, as *coy* and *quiet,* both taken from the same Latin word, *quiet* directly, and *coy* by way of Old French. **6.** *Print.* an unintentional repetition in printed matter or proof. **7. doublets,** a throw of a pair of dice in which the same number of spots turns up on each die. **8.** *Jewelry.* a counterfeit gem made of two pieces, either of smaller gemstones, inferior stones, or glass. Cf. **imitation doublet, triplet** (def. 6). **9.** *Optics.* a compound lens made of two thin lenses shaped so as to reduce chromatic and spherical aberrations. [1300–50; ME < MF. See DOUBLE, -ET]

doublets (def. 1) of the Elizabethan period

dou′ble tack′le, a pulley system using blocks having two grooved wheels.

dou•ble-tailed (dub′əl tāld′), *adj. Heraldry.* (of a lion) represented with two tails joined together next to the body. Cf. **queue fourché.**

dou′ble take′, a rapid or surprised second look, either literal or figurative, at a person or situation whose significance had not been completely grasped at first: *His friends did a double take when they saw how much weight he had lost.* [1935–40, *Amer.*]

dou•ble-talk (dub′əl tôk′), *n.* **1.** speech using nonsense syllables along with words in a rapid patter. **2.** deliberately evasive or ambiguous language: *When you try to get a straight answer, he gives you double-talk.* *—v.i.* **3.** to engage in double-talk. *—v.t.* **4.** to accomplish or persuade by double-talk. Also, **dou′ble-talk′.** [1935–40, *Amer.*] **—dou′ble-talk′er,** *n.*

dou′ble tape′. See under **magnetic tape.**

dou•ble-team (dub′əl tēm′), *v.t.* **1.** to defend against or block (an opposing player) by using two players, as in football or basketball: *By double-teaming the end the safety men left the other receiver in the open.* **2.** to use two people in the handling of: *The company is double-teaming the more complicated jobs with both a scientist and a group manager.* [1835–45, *Amer.*]

dou•ble•think (dub′əl thingk′), *n.* the acceptance of two contradictory ideas or beliefs at the same time. [DOUBLE + THINK[1]; coined by George Orwell in his novel *1984* (1949)]

dou′ble tide′, agger (def. 1).

dou′ble time′, **1.** *U.S. Army.* the fastest rate of marching troops, a slow jog in which 180 paces, each of 3 ft. (0.9 m), are taken in a minute. **2.** a slow run by troops in step. **3.** a rate of overtime pay that is twice the regular wage rate. [1850–55]

dou•ble-time (dub′əl tīm′), *v.,* **-timed, -tim•ing.** *—v.t.* **1.** to cause to move in double time: *Double-time the troops to the mess hall.* *—v.i.* **2.** to move in double-time. [1850–55]

dou•ble•ton (dub′əl tən), *n. Chiefly Bridge.* a set of only two cards of the same suit in a hand as dealt: *The other player held a doubleton.* [1905–10; modeled on SINGLETON]

dou•ble-tongue (dub′əl tung′), *v.i.,* **-tongued, -tongu•ing.** *Music.* to interrupt the wind flow by moving the tongue as if pronouncing *t* and *k* alternately, esp. in playing rapid passages or staccato notes on a brass instrument. Cf. **triple-tongue.**

dou•ble-tongued (dub′əl tungd′), *adj.* deceitful; hypocritical. [1350–1400; ME *dowble tungid*]

dou′blet pat′tern, *Fine Arts.* a pattern, as on a fabric, in which a figure or group is duplicated in reverse order on the opposite side of a centerline.

dou′ble-trail•er truck′ (dub′əl trā′lər). See **tandem trailer** (def. 1).

dou•ble•tree (dub′əl trē′), *n.* a pivoted bar with a whiffletree attached to each end, used in harnessing two horses abreast. See illus. under **whiffletree.** [1840–50, *Amer.*; modeled on SINGLETREE]

dou′ble truck′, **1.** *Typesetting.* a chase for holding the type for a center spread, esp. for a newspaper. **2.** *Journalism.* matter occupying a center spread, esp. advertising matter.

dou•ble-u (dub′əl yo͞o′), *n.* the letter *w.* [1830–40]

dou′ble vi′sion, diplopia. [1855–60]

dou′ble whip′. See under **whip** (def. 28).

dou′ble wick′et, cricket in which two wickets are used, being the usual form of the game.

dou•ble-wide (dub′əl wīd′), *adj.* twice the usual width: *double-wide mobile homes consisting of two sections bolted together.* Also, **dou•ble-width** (dub′əl-width′, -witth′ *or, often,* -with′).

dou′ble wing′back forma′tion, *Football.* an offensive formation in which two backs line up at opposite ends of the backfield about one yard outside of the ends and about one yard behind the line of scrimmage. Also called **dou′ble wing′.** Cf. **single wingback formation.** [1925–30, *Amer.*]

dou•bling (dub′ling), *n. Naut.* the part of the upper or lower end of one spar of a mast that is overlapped by another spar above or below it. [1350–1400; ME; see DOUBLE, -ING[1]]

dou•bloon (du blo͞on′), *n.* a former gold coin of Spain and Spanish America, originally equal to two escudos but fluctuating in value. [1615–25; < Sp *doblón,* equiv. to *dobl(a)* DOBLA + *-ón* aug. suffix]

dou•blure (də blo͝or′, do͞o-; *Fr.* do͞o blyʀ′), *n., pl.* **-blures** (-blo͝orz′; *Fr.* -blyʀ′). an ornamental lining of a book cover. [1885–90; < F: a lining, equiv. to *doubl(er)* to line (lit., to DOUBLE) + *-ure* -URE]

dou•bly (dub′lē), *adv.* **1.** to a double measure or degree: *to be doubly cautious.* **2.** in a double manner. **3.** *Obs.* with duplicity. [1350–1400; ME; see DOUBLE, -LY]

Doubs (do͞o), *n.* **1.** a river in E France, flowing into the Saône River. ab. 260 mi. (420 km) long. **2.** a department in E France. 471,082; 2031 sq. mi. (5260 sq. km). *Cap.:* Besançon.

doubt (dout), *v.t.* **1.** to be uncertain about; consider questionable or unlikely; hesitate to believe. **2.** to distrust. **3.** *Archaic.* to fear; be apprehensive about. *—v.i.* **4.** to be uncertain about something; be undecided in opinion or belief. *—n.* **5.** a feeling of uncertainty about the truth, reality, or nature of something. **6.** distrust. **7.** a state of affairs such as to occasion uncertainty. **8.** *Obs.* fear; dread. **9. beyond the shadow of a doubt,** with certainty; definitely. Also, **beyond a doubt, beyond doubt. 10. in doubt,** in a state of uncertainty or suspense: *His appointment to the position is still in doubt.* **11. no doubt, a.** probably. **b.** certainly: *There is no doubt an element of truth in what you say.* **12. without doubt,** unquestionably; certainly. [1175–1225; (v.) ME *douten* < AF, OF *douter* < L *dubitāre* to waver, hesitate, be uncertain (freq. of OL *dubāre*), equiv. to *dub-* doubt + *-it-* freq. suffix + *-āre* inf. suffix; (n.) ME *doute* < AF, OF, deriv. of the v.] **—doubt′a•ble,** *adj.* **—doubt′a•bly,** *adv.* **—doubt′er,** *n.* **—doubt′ing•ly,** *adv.* **—doubt′ing•ness,** *n.*

—Syn. 1, 2. mistrust, suspect, question. **5.** indecision, irresolution.

—Usage. DOUBT and DOUBTFUL may be followed by a subordinate clause beginning with *that, whether,* or *if: I doubt that* (or *whether* or *if*) *the story is true. It is doubtful that* (or *whether* or *if*) *the story is true. There is some doubt that* (or *whether* or *if*) *the story is true.* In negative or interrogative sentences, *that* almost always introduces the subordinate clause: *I do not doubt that the story is true. Is it doubtful that the story is true? Is there any doubt that the story is true?*

The expressions DOUBT BUT and DOUBT BUT THAT occur in all varieties of standard speech and writing: *I don't doubt but she is sincere. There is no doubt but that the charges will affect his career.* DOUBT BUT WHAT occurs mainly in informal speech and writing: *There is no doubt but what the rainy weather will hurt the crops.*

doubt•ful (dout′fəl), *adj.* **1.** of uncertain outcome or result. **2.** admitting of or causing doubt; uncertain; ambiguous. **3.** unsettled in opinion or belief; undecided; hesitating. **4.** of equivocal or questionable character: *His tactics are highly doubtful.* [1350–1400; ME *douteful.* See DOUBT, -FUL] **—doubt′ful•ly,** *adv.* **—doubt′•ful•ness,** *n.*

—Syn. 1. undetermined, unsettled, indecisive, dubious, problematic. **2.** unsure, indeterminate. **3.** irresolute, vacillating, hesitant. DOUBTFUL, DUBIOUS, INCREDULOUS, SKEPTICAL imply reluctance or unwillingness to be convinced. To be DOUBTFUL about something is to feel that it is open to question or that more evidence is needed to prove it: *to be doubtful about the statements of witnesses.* DUBIOUS implies vacillation, unsureness, or suspicion: *dubious about suggested methods of manufacture.* INCREDULOUS means unwilling or reluctant to believe: *incredulous at the good news.* SKEPTICAL implies a general disposition to doubt or question: *skeptical of human progress.* **4.** shady. **—Ant. 1, 2.** certain.

—Usage. See **doubt.**

doubt′ing Thom′as, a person who refuses to believe without proof; skeptic. John 20:24–29.

doubt•less (dout′lis), *adv.* Also, **doubt′less•ly. 1.** without doubt; certainly; surely; unquestionably. **2.** probably or presumably. *—adj.* **3.** free from doubt or uncertainty; certain, sure. [1300–50; ME *douteles.* See DOUBT, -LESS] **—doubt′less•ness,** *n.*

—Syn. 1, 2. DOUBTLESS, UNDOUBTEDLY, INDUBITABLY, UNQUESTIONABLY are adverbs that express certainty. DOUBTLESS, although it sometimes denotes an absolute degree of certainty, more often means "probably," "presumably," or "no doubt": *She will doubtless accept the offer.* UNDOUBTEDLY means "beyond doubt": *undoubtedly the most prolific and popular composer of his time.* INDUBITABLY and UNQUESTIONABLY both affirm an unassailable conviction; they differ only in tone, INDUBITABLY being appropriate to more formal or learned discourse and UNQUESTIONABLY appropriate in a wider range of contexts and styles: *an indubitably* (or *unquestionably*) *accurate transliteration of the hieroglyphic text; unquestionably the hottest running back in the league.*

douce (do͞os), *adj. Scot. and North Eng.* sedate; modest; quiet. [1275–1325; ME < MF (fem.) < L *dulcis* sweet; see DULCET] **—douce′ly,** *adv.* **—douce′ness,** *n.*

douce·peres (do͞os′pērz′, do͞o′sə-), *n.pl., sing.* **-per** (-pēr′). douzepers.

dou·ceur (do͞o sûr′; *Fr.* do͞o sœʀ′), *n., pl.* **-ceurs** (-sûrz′; *Fr.* -sœʀ′). **1.** a gratuity; tip. **2.** a conciliatory gift or bribe. **3.** *Archaic.* sweetness or agreeableness. [1350–1400; ME < MF: sweetness < LL *dulcor,* with initial syll. reshaped under influence of F *doux, douce;* see DOUCE, -EUR]

douche (do͞osh), *n., v.,* **douched, douch·ing.** **—***n.* **1.** a jet or current of water, sometimes with a dissolved medicating or cleansing agent, applied to a body part, organ, or cavity for medicinal or hygienic purposes. **2.** the application of such a jet. **3.** an instrument, as a syringe, for administering it. **4.** a bath administered by such a jet. **—***v.t.* **5.** to apply a douche to. **—***v.i.* **6.** to use a douche or douches; undergo douching. [1675–85; < F < It *doccia* water pipe, back formation from *doccione* drainpipe (where *-one* was taken as aug. suffix) < L *ductiōn-* (s. of *ductiō*) drawing off, conveying (water), equiv. to *duct(us),* ptp. of *dūcere* (see DUCTILE) + *-iōn-* -ION]

douche′ bag′, a small syringe having detachable nozzles for fluid injections, used chiefly for vaginal lavage and for enemas. [1930–35]

Doug (dug), *n.* a male given name, form of **Douglas.**

dough (dō), *n.* **1.** flour or meal combined with water, milk, etc., in a mass for baking into bread, cake, etc.; paste of bread. **2.** any similar soft, pasty mass. **3.** *Slang.* money. [bef. 1000; ME *do(u)gh, do(u)h, dou(e),* OE *dāg, dāh;* c. D *deeg,* ON *deig,* Goth *daigs,* G *Teig*] **—dough′like′,** *adj.*

dough·bel·ly (dō′bel′ē), *n., pl.* **-lies.** stoneroller (def. 1). [DOUGH + BELLY]

dough′ bird′, the Eskimo curlew. [1825–35, *Amer.*]

dough·boy (dō′boi′), *n.* **1.** *Informal.* an American infantryman, esp. in World War I. **2.** a rounded mass of dough, boiled or steamed as a dumpling or deep-fried and served as a hot bread. [1675–85; DOUGH + BOY; sense "infantryman," from mid-1860's, is obscurely derived; two plausible, but unsubstantiated claims: *doughboy* orig. referred to the globular brass buttons on infantry uniforms, likened to the pastry; *dough* referred to a clay used to clean the white uniform belts]

Dough′er·ty wag′on (dô′ər tē, dä′-, dôr′ə-, där′ə-), a horse- or mule-drawn passenger wagon having doors on the side, transverse seats, and canvas sides that can be rolled down. [1900–05, *Amer.*; orig. obscure]

dough·face (dō′fās′), *n. U.S. Hist.* **1.** a Northerner who sympathized with the South during the controversies over new territories and slavery before the Civil War. **2.** a congressman from a northern state not opposed to slavery in the South. [1785–95, *Amer.*; DOUGH + FACE]

dough·foot (dō′fo͝ot′), *n., pl.* **-feet** (-fēt′), **-foots.** *Informal.* an infantryman in the U.S. Army, esp. in World War II. [1940–45; DOUGH + FOOT, perh. b. DOUGHBOY and FOOT SOLDIER]

dough′ hook′, an attachment for a food processor or electric mixer, for kneading dough.

dough·nut (dō′nət, -nut′), *n.* **1.** a small cake of sweetened or, sometimes, unsweetened dough fried in deep fat, typically shaped like a ring or, when prepared with a filling, a ball. **2.** anything shaped like a thick ring; an annular object; toroid. Also, **donut.** [1795–1805; DOUGH + NUT]

dought (dout), *v.* a pt. of **dow.**

dough·ty (dou′tē), *adj.,* **-ti·er, -ti·est.** steadfastly courageous and resolute; valiant. [bef. 1000; ME; OE *dohtig* worthy, equiv. to **doht* worth (c. OHG *toht;* see DOW[1], -TH[1]) + *-ig* -Y[1]; r. OE *dyhtig,* c. G *tüchtig*] **—dough′ti·ly,** *adv.* **—dough′ti·ness,** *n.*
—Syn. brave, bold, intrepid, fearless, dauntless.

Dough·ty (dou′tē), *n.* **Charles Mon·ta·gu** (mon′tə gyo͞o′), 1843–1926, English traveler and writer.

dough·y (dō′ē), *adj.,* **dough·i·er, dough·i·est.** of or like dough, esp. in being soft and heavy or pallid and flabby: *a doughy consistency; a fat, doughy face.* [1595–1605; DOUGH + -Y[1]] **—dough′i·ness,** *n.*

Doug·las (dug′ləs), *n.* **1. Sir James** ("*the Black Douglas*"), 1286–1330, Scottish military leader. **2. James, 2nd Earl of,** 1358?–88, Scottish military leader. **3. Lloyd C(as·sel)** (kas′əl), 1877–1951, U.S. novelist and clergyman. **4. Stephen A(rnold),** 1813–61, U.S. political leader and statesman. **5. William O(r·ville)** (ôr′vil), 1898–1980, Associate Justice of the U.S. Supreme Court 1939–75. **6.** a city on and the capital of the Isle of Man: resort. 19,897. **7.** a city in SE Arizona. 13,058. **8.** a town in central Georgia. 10,980. **9.** a male given name: from a Scottish word meaning "black water."

Doug′las bag′, an airtight bag used to collect expired air for analysis of oxygen consumption. [1960–65; named after Claude G. *Douglas* (1882–1963), British physiologist]

Doug′las fir′, a coniferous tree, *Pseudotsuga menziesii,* of western North America, often more than 200 ft. (60 m) high, having reddish-brown bark, flattened needles, and narrow, light-brown cones, and yielding a strong, durable timber: the state tree of Oregon. Also called **Doug′las pine′, Doug′las spruce′, Oregon fir, Oregon pine.** [1855–60; named after David *Douglas* (1798–1834), Scottish botanist and traveler in America]

Doug·las-Home (dug′ləs hyo͞om′), *n.* **Alexander Frederick,** (Baron Home of the Hirsel), born 1903, British statesman and politician: prime minister 1963–64.

Doug·lass (dug′ləs), *n.* **1. Frederick,** 1817–95, U.S. ex-slave, abolitionist, and orator. **2.** a male given name.

Douglas SBD, dauntless (def. 2).

Dou·kho·bor (do͞o′kō bôr′), *n.* a member of an independent religious sect originating in Russia in the 18th century, believing in the supreme authority of the inner voice and in the transmigration of souls, rejecting the divinity of Christ and the establishing of churches, and expressing opposition to civil authority by refusing to pay taxes, do military service, etc. Also, **Dukhobor.** [1875–80; < Russ *dukhobór, dukhobórets,* ORuss *dukhoborĭtsĭ* lit., one who fights against the Holy Ghost, a calque of LGk *pneumatomáchos* (cf. Russ *dukh* spirit, *boréts* wrestler); orig. a derisive term, later adopted by the sect itself]

dou·ma (do͞o′mä), *n.* duma.

Dou·mergue (do͞o merg′), *n.* **Gas·ton** (gas tôn′), 1863–1937, French statesman: president of France 1924–31.

doum′ palm′ (do͞om). See **doom palm.**

doup (doup), *n. Scot.* **1.** the bottom, end, or butt of something. **2.** the buttocks. [1505–15; cf. ON *daup*]

doup·pi·o·ni (do͞o′pē ō′nē), *n.* an irregular silk thread reeled from two or more entangled cocoons and producing a coarse yarn generally used in fabrics such as shantung or pongee. Also, **dou·pi·on** (do͞o′pē on′), **dou′pi·o′·ni, dupion, dupioni.** [< It *doppione;* see DUPION]

dour (do͝or, douər, dou′ər), *adj.* **1.** sullen; gloomy: *The captain's dour look depressed us all.* **2.** severe; stern: *His dour criticism made us regret having undertaken the job.* **3.** *Scot.* (of land) barren; rocky, infertile, or otherwise difficult or impossible to cultivate. [1325–75; ME < L *dūrus* DURE[1]] **—dour′ly,** *adv.* **—dour′ness,** *n.*
—Syn. 1. morose, sour, moody. See **glum.**

dou·ra (do͝or′ə), *n.* durra. Also, **dou′rah.**

dou·rine (do͝o rēn′), *n. Vet. Pathol.* an infectious disease of horses, affecting the genitals and hind legs, caused by a protozoan parasite, *Trypanosoma equiperdum.* [1880–85; < F; cf. Ar *darin* scabby]

Dou·ro (*Port.* dō′ʀo͝o), *n.* a river in SW Europe, flowing W from N Spain through N Portugal to the Atlantic. ab. 475 mi. (765 km) long. Spanish, **Duero.**

dou·rou·cou·li (do͝or′ə ko͞o′lē), *n.* a small, nocturnal South American monkey of the genus *Aotus,* having large, owllike eyes: in danger of extinction. Also, **dou·ri·cou·li** (do͝or′i ko͞o′lē). Also called **night monkey, owl monkey.** [< F; recorded by A. von Humboldt as the animal's name in the language of a Río Negro tribe (S Venezuela)]

douse (dous), *v.,* **doused, dous·ing,** *n.,* **—***v.t.* **1.** to plunge into water or the like; drench: *She doused the clothes in soapy water.* **2.** to splash or throw water or other liquid on: *The children doused each other with the hose.* **3.** to extinguish: *She quickly doused the candle's flame with her fingertips.* **4.** *Informal.* to remove; doff. **5.** *Naut.* **a.** to lower or take in (a sail, mast, or the like) suddenly. **b.** to slacken (a line) suddenly. **c.** to stow quickly. **—***v.i.* **6.** to plunge or be plunged into a liquid. **—***n.* **7.** *Brit. Dial.* a stroke or blow. Also, **dowse.** [1590–1600; orig. uncert.]

dous·er (dou′sər), *n.* **1.** a person or thing that douses. **2.** dowser. [1880–85; DOUSE + -ER[1]]

dout·er (dou′tər, do͞o′-), *n.* an implement for snuffing out candles, consisting either of a scissorlike device with two broad flat blades or of a cone at the end of a handle. [1615–25; dial. *dout* (v.) (contr. of DO[1] + OUT; cf. DOFF, DON[2]) + -ER[1]]

Douw (*Du.* dou), *n.* **Ger·rard** (*Du.* gä′ʀäʀt). See **Dou, Gerard.**

doux (do͞o), *adj.* (of champagne) very sweet. [1940–45; < F < L *dulcis* savory, sweet]

dou·zaine (do͞o zen′), *n., pl.* ***-zaines*** (-zen′). *French.* a bet in roulette on 12 numbers simultaneously so as to share in any that win. [lit., dozen]

douze·pers (do͞oz′pērz′), *n.pl., sing.,* **-per** (-pēr′). **1.** *Fr. Legend.* the 12 peers or paladins represented in old romances as attendants of Charlemagne. **2.** *Fr. Hist.* the 12 great spiritual and temporal peers of France, taken to represent those of Charlemagne. Also, **douceperes.** [1175–1225; ME *dusze pers* (pl.) < OF *douze pers* (pl.) twelve equals. See DOZEN[1], PEER[1]]

dou·zi·ème (do͞o′zē em′; *Fr.* do͞o zyem′), *n., pl.* **-zi·èmes** (-zē emz′; *Fr.* -zyem′). (in Swiss watchmaking) the 12th part of a ligne, used mainly to gauge the thickness of a movement. [< F: lit., twelfth]

DOVAP (dō′vap), *n. Electronics.* a system for plotting the trajectory of a missile or other rapidly moving long-range object by means of the Doppler effect exhibited by radio waves bounced off the object. Cf. **Doppler radar.** [*Do(ppler) V(elocity) a(nd) P(osition)*]

dove[1] (duv), *n.* **1.** any bird of the family Columbidae, esp. the smaller species with pointed tails. Cf. **pigeon** (def. 1). **2.** a pure white member of this species, used as a symbol of innocence, gentleness, tenderness, and peace. **3.** (*cap.*) a symbol for the Holy Ghost. **4.** an innocent, gentle, or tender person. **5.** Also called **peace dove.** a person, esp. one in public office, who advocates peace or a conciliatory national attitude. Cf. **hawk**[1] (def. 4). **6.** See **dove color. 7.** (*cap.*) *Astron.* the constellation Columba. [1150–1200; ME; OE *dūfe-* (in *dūfedoppa* dipdiver); c. D *duif,* G *Taube,* ON *dūfa,* Goth *dūbo,* orig. a diver] **—dove′like′, dov′ish,** *adj.* **—dov′ish·ness,** *n.*

dove[2] (dōv), *v.* a pt. of **dive.**

dove′ col′or (duv), warm gray with a slight purplish or pinkish tint. [1590–1600] **—dove′-col′ored,** *adj.*

dove·cote (duv′kōt′), *n.* **1.** a structure, usually at a height above the ground, for housing domestic pigeons. **2. flutter the dovecotes,** to cause a stir in a quiet or conservative institution or group: *The flamboyant manner of the tourists fluttered the dovecotes of the sleepy New England town.* Also, **dove·cot** (duv′kot). [1375–1425; late ME; see DOVE[1], COTE]

dove·kie (duv′kē), *n.* **1.** a small, short-billed, black and white auk, *Alle alle,* of northern Atlantic and Arctic oceans. **2.** *Brit.* the black guillemot. Also, **dove′key.** [1815–25; DOVE[1] + *-kie* compound suffix (see -OCK, -IE)]

do·ven (dä′vən), *v.i., v.t. Yiddish.* daven.

Dove′ prism′ (duv), *Optics.* a prism that inverts a beam of light, often used in a telescope to produce an erect image. Also called **erecting prism, reversing prism, rotating prism.** [named after Heinrich W. *Dove* (1803–79), German physicist]

Do·ver (dō′vər), *n.* **1.** a seaport in E Kent, in SE England: point nearest the coast of France. 101,700. **2. Strait of.** French, **Pas de Calais.** a strait between England and France, connecting the English Channel and the North Sea: least width 20 mi. (32 km). **3.** a city in and the capital of Delaware, in the central part. 23,512. **4.** a city in SE New Hampshire. 22,377. **5.** a town in N New Jersey. 14,681. **6.** a city in E Ohio. 11,526.

Do′ver's pow′der, *Pharm.* a powder containing ipecac and opium, used as an anodyne, diaphoretic, and antispasmodic. [1795–1805; named after T. *Dover* (1660–1742), English physician]

dove·tail (duv′tāl′), *n. Carpentry.* **1.** a tenon broader at its end than at its base; pin. **2.** a joint formed of one or more such tenons fitting tightly within corresponding mortises. **—***v.t., v.i.* **3.** *Carpentry.* to join or fit together by means of a dovetail or dovetails. **4.** to join or fit together compactly or harmoniously. [1555–65; so named from its shape] **—dove′tail′er,** *n.*

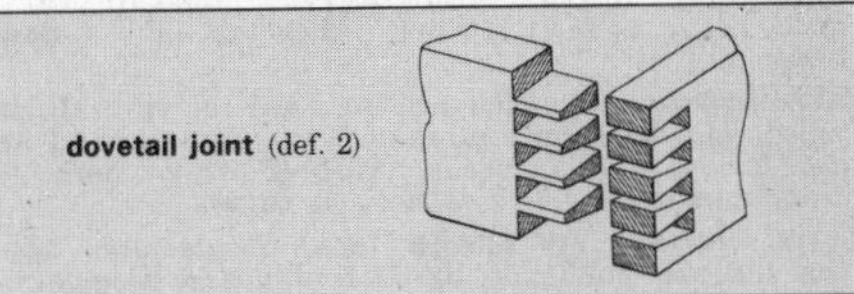

dovetail joint (def. 2)

dove·tailed (duv′tāld′), *adj. Heraldry.* noting a partition line or a charge, as an ordinary, having a series of indentations suggesting dovetails. [1715–25; DOVETAIL + -ED[3]]

dove′tail hinge′, a strap hinge having leaves which are narrower at their junction than at their other extremities.

dove′tail plane′, *Carpentry.* a plane for cutting tongues and grooves with parallel or inclined sides.

dove′tail saw′, a backsaw for fine woodworking, as dovetailing. [1805–15]

Dov·zhen·ko (dəv zheng′kō; *Russ.* duv zhen′kə), *n.* **A·le·xan·der P.** (u lyi ksändʀ′), 1894–1956, Russian motion-picture director.

dow[1] (dou, dō), *v.i.,* **dowed** or **dought** (dout), **dow·ing.** *Scot. and North Eng.* **1.** to be able. **2.** to thrive; prosper; do well. [bef. 900; ME *dowen, doghen,* OE *dugan* to be worthy; c. G *taugen;* cf. DOUGHTY]

dow[2] (dou), *n.* dhow.

Dow (dou), *n.* **1. Ger·rard** (*Du.* gä′ʀäʀt). See **Dou, Gerard. 2. Herbert Henry,** 1866–1930, U.S. chemist, inventor, and industrialist.

Dow., dowager.

dow·a·ble (dou′ə bəl), *adj. Law.* **1.** subject to the provision of a dower: *dowable land.* **2.** entitled to dower. [1425–75; late ME < AF; see ENDOW, -ABLE]

dow·a·ger (dou′ə jər), *n.* **1.** a woman who holds some title or property from her deceased husband, esp. the widow of a king, duke, etc. (often used as an additional title to differentiate her from the wife of the present king, duke, etc.): *a queen dowager; an empress dowager.* **2.** an elderly woman of stately dignity, esp. one of elevated social position: *a wealthy dowager.* **—***adj.* **3.** noting, pertaining to, or characteristic of a dowager: *the dowager duchess; to prefer a dowager style of dress.* [1520–30; < MF *douag(i)ere,* equiv. to *douage* dower (see ENDOW, -AGE) + *-iere,* fem. of *-ier* -IER[2]] **—dow′a·ger·ism,** *n.*

dow′ager's hump′, a type of kyphosis, common in older women, in which the shoulders become rounded and the upper back develops a hump: caused by osteoporosis resulting in skeletal deformity. Cf. **lordosis.**

Dow·den (doud′n), *n.* **Edward,** 1843–1913, Irish critic and poet.

dow·dy[1] (dou′dē), *adj.,* **-di·er, -di·est,** *n., pl.* **-dies.** **—***adj.* **1.** not stylish; drab; old-fashioned: *Why do you always wear those dowdy old dresses?* **2.** not neat or tidy; shabby. **—***n.* **3.** a dowdy woman. [1300–50; ME *doude* unattractive woman (of uncert. orig.) + -Y[1] or -Y[2]] **—dow′di·ly,** *adv.* **—dow′di·ness,** *n.* **—dow′dy·ish,** *adj.* **—dow′dy·ism,** *n.*
—Syn. 1. frumpy. **—Ant. 1.** fashionable, stylish.

dow·dy[2] (dou′dē), *n., pl.* **-dies.** See **apple pandowdy.** [1935–40; short form]

dow·el (dou′əl), *n., v.,* **-eled, -el·ing** or (*esp. Brit.*) **-elled, -el·ling.** **—***n.* **1.** Also called **dow′el pin′.** *Carpentry.* a pin, usually round, fitting into holes in two adjacent pieces to prevent their slipping or to align them. See illus. on next page. **2.** a piece of wood driven into a hole drilled in a masonry wall to receive nails, as for fas-

CONCISE PRONUNCIATION KEY: act, cāpe, dâre, pärt; set, ēqual; *if,* ice; ox, ōver, ôrder, oil, bo͝ok, bo͞ot, out; up, ûrge; child; sing; shoe; thin, *th*at; zh as in *treasure.* ə = *a* as in *alone, e* as in *system, i* as in *easily, o* as in *gallop, u* as in *circus;* ə as in *fire* (fīər), *hour* (ouər). l and n can serve as syllabic consonants, as in *cradle* (krād′l), and *button* (but′n). See the full key inside the front cover.

tening woodwork. **3.** a round wooden rod of relatively small diameter. **4.** *Dentistry.* a peg, usually of metal, set into the root canal of a natural tooth to give additional support to an artificial crown. —*v.t.* **5.** to reinforce or furnish with a dowel or dowels. [1300–50; ME *dowle* < MLG *dovel* plug; cf. G *Döbel, Dübel,* OHG *tubili*]

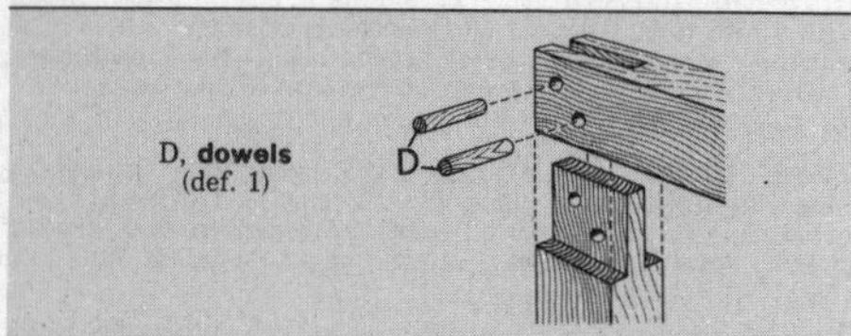
D, **dowels** (def. 1)

dow·er (dou′ər), *n.* **1.** *Law.* the portion of a deceased husband's real property allowed to his widow for her lifetime. **2.** dowry (def. 1). **3.** a natural gift or endowment. —*v.t.* **4.** to provide with a dower or dowry. **5.** to give as a dower or dowry. [1250–1300; ME *dowere* < OF *do(u)aire* < ML *dōtārium.* See DOT[2], -ARY] —**dow′er·less,** *adj.*

dow′er chest′, a Pennsylvania Dutch hope chest bearing the initials of the owner. [1880–85]

dow′er house′, *Brit.* the dwelling that is intended for or occupied by the widowed mother of the owner of an ancestral estate. [1860–65]

dow·er·y (dou′ə rē, dou′rē), *n., pl.* **-er·ies.** dowry.

dowf (douf, do͞of), *adj. Scot. and North Eng.* dull; stupid. [1475–85; < ON *daufr* DEAF, dull]

dow·ie (dou′ē, dō′ē), *adj. Scot. and North Eng.* dull; melancholy; dismal. Also, **dowy.** [1500–10; var. of *dolly,* equiv. to DULL + -LY] —**dow′i·ly,** *adv.* —**dow′i·ness,** *n.*

dow·itch·er (dou′ich ər), *n.* any of several long-billed, snipelike shore birds of North America and Asia, esp. *Limnodromus griseus.* [1835–45, *Amer.*; perh. < N Iroquoian; cf. Mohawk *tawístawis* snipe]

Dow′ Jones′ Av′erage (dou), *Trademark.* any of the indexes published by Dow Jones & Company, a financial publishing firm in New York City, showing the average closing prices of the representative common stocks of 30 industrials, 20 transportation companies, or 15 utilities.

Dow·land (dou′lənd), *n.* **John,** 1563–1626, English lutenist and composer.

dow·las (dou′ləs), *n.* a coarse linen or cotton cloth. [1485–95; after *Daoulas* in Brittany; r. late ME *douglas,* popular substitution for *dowlas*]

Dow′ met′al, *Trademark.* a brand name applied to any of various magnesium alloys containing more than 85 percent magnesium, characterized by extreme lightness.

down[1] (doun), *adv.* **1.** from higher to lower; in descending direction or order; toward, into, or in a lower position: *to come down the ladder.* **2.** on or to the ground, floor, or bottom: *He fell down.* **3.** to or in a sitting or lying position. **4.** to or in a position, area, or district considered lower, esp. from a geographical or cartographic standpoint, as to the south, a business district, etc.: *We drove from San Francisco down to Los Angeles.* **5.** to or at a lower value or rate. **6.** to a lesser pitch or volume: *Turn down the radio.* **7.** in or to a calmer, less active, or less prominent state: *The wind died down.* **8.** from an earlier to a later time: *from the 17th century down to the present.* **9.** from a greater to a lesser strength, amount, etc.: *to water down liquor.* **10.** in an attitude of earnest application: *to get down to work.* **11.** on paper or in a book: *Write down the address.* **12.** in cash at the time of purchase; at once: *We paid $50 down and $20 a month.* **13.** to the point of defeat, submission, inactivity, etc.: *They shouted down the opposition.* **14.** in or into a fixed or supine position: *They tied down the struggling animal.* **15.** to the source or actual position: *The dogs tracked down the bear.* **16.** into a condition of ill health: *He's come down with a cold.* **17.** in or into a lower status or condition: *kept down by lack of education.* **18.** *Naut.* toward the lee side, so as to turn a vessel to windward: *Put the helm down!* **19.** *Slang.* on toast (as used in ordering a sandwich at a lunch counter or restaurant): *Give me a tuna down.* **20. down with! a.** away with! cease!: *Down with tyranny!* **b.** on or toward the ground or into a lower position: *Down with your rifles!*
—*prep.* **21.** in a descending or more remote direction or place on, over, or along: *They ran off down the street.*
—*adj.* **22.** downward; going or directed downward: *the down escalator.* **23.** being at a low position or on the ground, floor, or bottom. **24.** toward the south, a business district, etc. **25.** associated with or serving traffic, transportation, or the like, directed toward the south, a business district, etc.: *the down platform.* **26.** downcast; depressed; dejected: *You seem very down today.* **27.** ailing, esp., sick and bedridden: *He's been down with a bad cold.* **28.** being the portion of the full price, as of an article bought on the installment plan, that is paid at the time of purchase or delivery: *a payment of $200 down.* **29.** *Football.* (of the ball) not in play. **30.** behind an opponent or opponents in points, games, etc.: *The team won the pennant despite having been down three games in the final week of play.* **31.** *Baseball.* out. **32.** losing or having lost the amount indicated, esp. at gambling: *After an hour at poker, he was down $10.* **33.** having placed one's bet: *Are you down for the fourth race?* **34.** finished, done, considered, or taken care of: *five down and one to go.* **35.** out of order: *The computer has been down all day.* **36. down and out,** down-and-out. **37. down cold** or **pat,** mastered or learned perfectly: *Another hour of studying and I'll have the math lesson down cold.* **38. down in the mouth,** discouraged; depressed; sad. **39. down on,** *Informal.* hostile or averse to: *Why are you so down on sports?*
—*n.* **40.** a downward movement; descent. **41.** a turn for the worse; reverse: *The business cycle experienced a sudden down.* **42.** *Football.* **a.** one of a series of four plays during which a team must advance the ball at least 10 yd. (9 m) to keep possession of it. **b.** the declaring of the ball as down or out of play, or the play immediately preceding this. **43.** *Slang.* an order of toast at a lunch counter or restaurant. **44.** *Slang.* downer (defs. 1a, b).
—*v.t.* **45.** to put, knock, or throw down; subdue: *He downed his opponent in the third round.* **46.** to drink down, esp. quickly or in one gulp: *to down a tankard of ale.* **47.** *Informal.* to defeat in a game or contest: *The Mets downed the Dodgers in today's game.* **48.** to cause to fall from a height, esp. by shooting: *Antiaircraft guns downed ten bombers.*
—*v.i.* **49.** to go down; fall.
—*interj.* **50.** (used as a command to a dog to stop attacking, to stop jumping on someone, to get off a couch or chair, etc.): *Down, Rover!* **51.** (used as a command or warning to duck, take cover, or the like): *Down! They're starting to shoot!* [bef. 1100; ME *doune,* OE *dūne,* aph. var. of *adūne* for *of dūne* off (the) hill; see A-[2], DOWN[3]]

down[2] (doun), *n.* **1.** the soft, first plumage of many young birds. **2.** the soft under plumage of birds as distinct from the contour feathers. **3.** the under plumage of some birds, as geese and ducks, used for filling in quilts, clothing, etc., chiefly for warmth. **4.** a growth of soft, fine hair or the like. **5.** *Bot.* **a.** a fine, soft pubescence on plants and some fruits. **b.** the light, feathery pappus or coma on seeds by which they are borne on the wind, as on the dandelion and thistle. —*adj.* **6.** filled with down: *a down jacket.* [1325–75; ME *downe* < ON *dūnn*] —**down′less,** *adj.* —**down′like′,** *adj.*

down[3] (doun), *n.* **1.** Often, **downs.** (used esp. in southern England) open, rolling, upland country with fairly smooth slopes usually covered with grass. **2.** (*cap.*) any sheep of several breeds, raised originally in the downs of southern England, as the Southdown, Suffolk, etc. **3.** *Archaic.* a hill, esp. a sand hill or dune. [bef. 1000; ME; OE *dūn* hill; c. D *duin* DUNE; not related to Ir, OIr *dún* (see TOWN)]

Down (doun), *n.* **1.** a county in SW Northern Ireland. 311,876; 952 sq. mi. (2466 sq. km). *Co. seat:* Downpatrick. **2.** an administrative district in this county. 49,500; 253 sq. mi. (654 sq. km).

down-and-dirt·y (doun′ən dûr′tē), *adj. Informal.* **1.** unscrupulous; nasty: *a down-and-dirty election campaign.* **2.** earthy; funky. [1985–90]

down-and-out (doun′ənd out′, -ən), *adj.* **1.** without any money, or means of support, or prospects; destitute; penniless. **2.** without physical strength or stamina; disabled; incapacitated. **3.** too physically weakened by repeated defeats to qualify as a competent professional boxer. —*n.* **4.** Also, **down′-and-out′er.** a person who is down-and-out. [1885–90, *Amer.*]

down-at-heel (doun′ət hēl′), *adj.* of a shabby, rundown appearance; seedy: *He is rapidly becoming a down-at-heel drifter and a drunk.* Also, **down′-at-the-heel′, down′-at-heels′, down′-at-the-heels′.** [1695–1705]

down·beat (doun′bēt′), *n. Music.* **1.** the downward stroke of a conductor's arm or baton indicating the first or accented beat of a measure. **2.** the first beat of a measure. —*adj.* **3.** gloomy or depressing; pessimistic: *Hollywood movies seldom have downbeat endings.* [1875–80; DOWN[1] + BEAT (n.)]

down-bow (doun′bō′), *n. Music.* (in bowing on a stringed instrument) a stroke bringing the tip of the bow toward the strings, indicated in scores by the symbol ⊓ (opposed to *up-bow*). [1890–95; DOWN[1] + BOW[2]]

down·burst (doun′bûrst′), *n.* a strong downward current of air from a cumulonimbus cloud, often associated with intense thunderstorms. [DOWN[1] + BURST]

down′ card′, *Cards.* a card that is dealt and played face down, as in blackjack and stud poker.

down·cast (doun′kast′, -käst′), *adj.* **1.** directed downward, as the eyes. **2.** dejected in spirit; depressed. —*n.* **3.** overthrow or ruin. **4.** a downward look or glance. **5.** a shaft down which air passes, as into a mine (opposed to *upcast*). [1250–1300; ME *douncasten.* See DOWN[1], CAST] —**down′cast′ly,** *adv.* —**down′cast′·ness,** *n.*
—**Syn. 2.** sad, desolate, disconsolate; low, blue.

down·come (doun′kum′), *n.* **1.** a downcomer. **2.** *Archaic.* descent or downfall; comedown; humiliation. [1505–15; DOWN[1] + COME]

down·com·er (doun′kum′ər), *n.* a pipe, tube, or passage for conducting fluid materials downward. [1865–70; DOWN[1] + COMER]

down·court (doun′kôrt′, -kōrt′), *Basketball.* —*adv.* **1.** to or into the opposite end of the court. —*adj.* **2.** directed to or into the opposite end of the court. [1950–55; DOWN[1] + COURT]

down·curved (doun′kûrvd′), *adj.* curved downward at the edges or end: *his downcurved mouth conveyed his disappointment; downcurved beak.* [DOWN[1] + CURVED]

down·cy·cle (doun′sī′kəl), *n.* a downward course in the business cycle. [1975–80; DOWN[1] + CYCLE]

down·draft (doun′draft′, -dräft′), *n.* **1.** a downward current, as of air: *a downdraft in a mine shaft.* **2.** a downward movement, as of the stock market. [1780–90; DOWN[1] + DRAFT]

down′ East′, **1.** in, to, or into New England. **2.** New England. **3.** in, to, or into the state of Maine. **4.** the state of Maine. **5.** *Canadian.* **a.** in, to, or into the Maritime Provinces. **b.** the Maritime Provinces. [1810–20, *Amer.*]

down·east·er (doun′ē′stər), *n.* **1.** a full-rigged ship built in New England in the late 19th century, usually of wood and relatively fast. **2.** a native or inhabitant of Maine. **3.** a native or inhabitant of New England. **4.** *Canadian.* a native or resident of the Maritime Provinces. [1810–20, *Amer.* DOWN EAST + -ER[1]]

down·er (dou′nər), *n.* **1.** *Informal.* **a.** a depressant or sedative drug, esp. a barbiturate. **b.** a depressing experience, person, or situation. **2.** *Animal Husb.* an old or diseased animal, esp. one that cannot stand up. [1910–15, *Amer.*, for an earlier sense; 1965–70, for def. 1; DOWN[1] + -ER[1]]

Dow′ners Grove′ (dou′nərz), a city in NE Illinois, near Chicago. 39,274.

Dow·ney (dou′nē), *n.* a city in SW California, near Los Angeles. 82,602.

down·fall (doun′fôl′), *n.* **1.** descent to a lower position or standing; overthrow; ruin. **2.** something causing ruin, failure, etc.: *Liquor was his downfall.* **3.** a fall, as of rain, snow, or the like, often sudden or heavy. **4.** a trap using a falling weight for killing, injuring, or imprisoning the prey. [1250–1300; ME; see DOWN[1], FALL] —**down′fall′en,** *adj.*

down·field (doun′fēld′), *adv., adj. Football.* past the line of scrimmage and at or toward the goal line of the defensive team. [1940–45; DOWN[1] + FIELD]

down·grade (doun′grād′), *n., adj., adv., v.,* **-grad·ed, -grad·ing.** —*n.* **1.** a downward slope, esp. of a road. **2. on the downgrade,** in a decline toward an inferior state or position: *His career has been on the downgrade.* —*adj., adv.* **3.** downhill. —*v.t.* **4.** to assign to a lower status with a smaller salary. **5.** to minimize the importance of; denigrate: *She tried to downgrade the findings of the investigation.* **6.** to assign a lower security classification to (information, a document, etc.). [1855–60, *Amer.*; DOWN[1] + GRADE] —**down′grad′er,** *n.*

down·growth (doun′grōth′), *n.* something that grows or has grown in a downward direction: *The posterior pituitary is a downgrowth of the brain.* [DOWN[1] + GROWTH]

down·haul (doun′hôl′), *n. Naut.* any of various lines for pulling down a sail or a yard, as for securing in a lowered position when not in use. [1660–70; DOWN[1] + HAUL]

down·heart·ed (doun′här′tid), *adj.* dejected; depressed; discouraged. [1645–55; DOWN[1] + HEARTED] —**down′heart′ed·ly,** *adv.* —**down′heart′ed·ness,** *n.*
—**Syn.** downcast, despondent, disheartened, dispirited.

down·hill (*adv., adj.* doun′hil′; *n.* doun′hil′), *adv.* **1.** down the slope of a hill; downward. **2.** into a worse or inferior condition: *The business has been going downhill.* —*adj.* **3.** going or tending downward on or as on a hill. **4.** free of problems or obstacles; easy: *After the initial setbacks on the project, it was downhill all the way.* **5.** of or pertaining to skiing downhill. —*n.* **6.** a timed ski race on a steep slope in which competitors take the most direct route to the finish line following a course with relatively few turns and attaining very high speeds. Cf. **slalom.** [1585–95; DOWN[1] + HILL]

down·hill·er (doun′hil′ər), *n.* **1.** a skier who competes in downhill races, esp. in the downhill. **2.** a downhill skier (contrasted with *cross-country skier*). [1965–70; DOWNHILL + -ER[1]]

down′hill ski′ing, the sport of skiing down a slope, usually making turns and various maneuvers. Cf. **cross-country skiing.** —**down′hill ski′er.**

downhill skier

down·hold (doun′hōld′), *n.* the act of keeping spending, expenses, losses, inflation, etc., as low as possible or advisable. [DOWN[1] + HOLD[1]]

down·hole (doun′hōl′), *n.* **1.** a hole dug or drilled downward, as in a mine or a petroleum or gas well. —*adj.* **2.** occurring or situated in such a hole. [DOWN[1] + HOLE]

down-home (doun′hōm′), *adj.* of, pertaining to, or exhibiting the simple, familiar, or folksy qualities associated with one's family or with rural areas, esp. of the southern U.S.: *down-home cooking; down-home hospitality.* [1820–30, *Amer.*]

Down·ing (dou′ning), *n.* **Andrew Jackson,** 1815–52, U.S. landscape architect.

Down′ing Street′, **1.** a street in W central London, England: cabinet office; residence of the prime minister. **2.** the British prime minister and cabinet.

down·light (doun′līt′), *n.* a lamp, often a light bulb set in a metal cylinder, mounted on or recessed into the ceiling so that a beam of light is directed downward. [DOWN[1] + LIGHT[1]]

down·link (doun′lingk′), *n.* **1.** a transmission path for data or other signals from a communications satellite or airborne platform to an earth station. —*adj.* **2.** pertaining to such transmission. Cf. **uplink.** [1965–70; DOWN[1] + LINK]

down·load (doun′lōd′), *v.t. Computers.* to transfer (software, data, character sets, etc.) from a distant to a nearby computer, from a larger to a smaller computer, or from a computer to a peripheral device. [DOWN[1] + LOAD]

down-mar·ket (doun′mär′kit), *Chiefly Brit.* —*adj.* **1.** appealing or catering to lower-income consumers;

widely affordable or accessible. —*adv.* **2.** in a down-market way. [1970–75]

down′ pay′ment, **1.** an initial amount paid at the time of purchase, in installment buying, time sales, etc. **2.** any initial or partial payment, gift, favor, or recompense, as to reduce one's indebtedness or express one's obligation or gratitude: *This gift is just a down payment for all the favors I owe you.* Also, **down′-pay′ment.** [1925–30]

down•pipe (doun′pīp′), *n. Brit.* downspout. [1855–60; DOWN[1] + PIPE[1]]

down•play (doun′plā′), *v.t.* to treat or speak of (something) so as to reduce emphasis on its importance, value, strength, etc.: *The press has downplayed the president's role in the negotiations.* [1950–55; DOWN[1] + PLAY, from v. phrase *play down*]

down•pour (doun′pôr′, -pōr′), *n.* a heavy, drenching rain. [1805–15; DOWN[1] + POUR]

down′ quark′, *Physics.* the quark having electric charge −⅓ times the elementary charge, with strangeness, charm, and other quark quantum numbers equal to 0. Also called **d quark.** [1975–80]

down•range (*adj.* doun′rānj′; *adv.* doun′rānj′), *adj., adv. Rocketry.* being in the designated path from a launch pad to the point on a course generally taken as the target: *The signal was picked up by a downrange radar station.* [1950–55; DOWN[1] + RANGE]

down•rate (doun′rāt′), *v.t.,* **-rat•ed, -rat•ing.** to lower the rate of: *to downrate the speed of an economic recovery.* [DOWN[1] + RATE[1]]

down•right (doun′rīt′), *adj.* **1.** thorough; absolute; out-and-out: *a downright falsehood.* **2.** frankly direct; straightforward: *a downright person.* **3.** *Archaic.* directed straight downward: *a downright blow.* —*adv.* **4.** completely or thoroughly: *I'm not just upset—I'm downright angry.* [1175–1225; ME; see DOWN[1], RIGHT] —**down′right′ly,** *adv.* —**down′right′ness,** *n.*
—**Syn. 2.** candid, forthright, open, frank, blunt.

down•riv•er (doun′riv′ər), *adv., adj.* with or in the direction of the current of a river: *logs floating downriver.* [1885–90; DOWN[1] + RIVER[1]]

Downs, The (dounz), **1.** a range of low ridges in S and SW England. **2.** a roadstead in the Strait of Dover, between SE England and Goodwin Sands.

down•scale (doun′skāl′), *adj., v.,* **-scaled, -scal•ing.** —*adj.* **1.** located at, moving toward, or of or for the middle or lower end of a social or economic scale: *The discount store caters mainly to downscale customers.* **2.** plain, practical, or inexpensive; not luxurious: *downscale clothing.* —*v.t.* **3.** downsize (def. 1). **4.** to make less luxurious or expensive. [DOWN[1] + SCALE[3]]

down•shift (doun′shift′), *v.i.* **1.** to shift an automotive transmission or vehicle into a lower gear. **2.** to become less active; slow down: *The economy seems to be downshifting.* —*v.t.* **3.** to shift (an automotive transmission or vehicle) into a lower gear. —*n.* **4.** an act or instance of downshifting. [1950–55; DOWN[1] + SHIFT]

down•side (doun′sīd′), *n.* **1.** the lower side or part. **2.** a downward trend, esp. in stock prices. —*adj.* **3.** of or involving a decline, esp. in stock prices: *The downside risk on this stock is considered far greater than the potential for gain.* [1675–85; DOWN[1] + SIDE[1]]

down•size (doun′sīz′), *v.,* **-sized, -siz•ing,** *adj.* —*v.t.* **1.** to design or manufacture a smaller version or type of: *The automotive industry downsized its cars for improved fuel economy.* **2.** to reduce in number; cut back. —*adj.* **3.** Also, **down′sized′.** being of a smaller size or version: *a downsize car.* [1970–75, *Amer.*; DOWN[1] + SIZE[1]]

down•slide (doun′slīd′), *n.* a decline or downward trend, as of prices. [1925–30; DOWN[1] + SLIDE]

down•spin (doun′spin′), *n.* spin (def. 22). [DOWN[1] + SPIN]

down•spout (doun′spout′), *n.* a pipe for conveying rain water from a roof or gutter to the ground or to a drain. Also called **drainspout;** *Brit.,* **downpipe.** [1895–1900; DOWN[1] + SPOUT]

Down's′ syn′drome, *Pathol.* See **Down syndrome.**

down•stage (*adv., n.* doun′stāj′; *adj.* doun′stāj′), *Theat.* —*adv.* **1.** at or toward the front of the stage. —*adj.* **2.** of or pertaining to the front of the stage. —*n.* **3.** the front half of the stage. [1895–1900; DOWN[1] + STAGE]

down•stairs (*adv., n.* doun′stârz′; *adj.* doun′stârz′), *adv.* **1.** down the stairs. **2.** to or on a lower floor. —*adj.* **3.** Also, **down′stair′.** pertaining to or situated on a lower floor, esp. the ground floor. —*n.* **4.** (*used with a singular v.*) the lower floor or floors of a building: *The downstairs is being painted.* **5.** the stairway designated for use by people descending: *Don't try to go up the downstairs.* [1590–1600; DOWN[1] + STAIR + -S[3]]

down•state (*n., adv.* doun′stāt′; *adj.* doun′stāt′), —*n.* **1.** the southern part of a U.S. state. —*adj.* **2.** located in or characteristic of this part: *The downstate precincts reported early.* —*adv.* **3.** in, to, or into the downstate area: *We're going downstate for the holidays.* [1905–10, *Amer.*; DOWN[1] + STATE] —**down′stat′er,** *n.*

down•stream (doun′strēm′), *adv.* **1.** with or in the direction of the current of a stream. —*adj.* **2.** of or pertaining to the latter part of a process or system. **3.** *Genetics.* with or in the direction of transcription, translation, or synthesis of a DNA, RNA, or protein molecule. [1700–10; DOWN[1] + STREAM]

down•stroke (doun′strōk′), *n.* **1.** a downward stroke, as of a machine part, piston, or the like. **2.** a downward stroke in writing, often heavier and darker than an upward stroke. [1850–55; DOWN[1] + STROKE[1]]

down•swing (doun′swing′), *n.* **1.** a downward swing, as of a golf club in driving a ball. **2.** a downward trend or decrease, as of business or a nation's birth rate. [1895–1900; DOWN[1] + SWING[1]]

Down′ syn′drome, *Pathol.* a genetic disorder, associated with the presence of an extra chromosome 21, characterized by mild to severe mental retardation, weak muscle tone, a low nasal bridge, and epicanthic folds at the eyelids. Also, **Down's syndrome.** Formerly, **mongolism.** Also called **trisomy 21.** [1960–65; after John L. H. *Down* (1828–96), British physician]

down•take (doun′tāk′), *n.* a pipe or passage for conducting smoke, a current of air, or the like downward from a furnace, opening, etc. [DOWN[1] + TAKE]

down-the-line (doun′thə līn′), *adj.* **1.** complete, full, unreserved, or whole-hearted: *a down-the-line endorsement.* —*adv.* **2.** fully; completely; whole-heartedly: *Will you support it down-the-line?* [1895–1900]

down•throw (doun′thrō′), *n.* a throwing down or being thrown down; overthrow. [1605–15; n. use of v. phrase *throw down*]

down•tick (doun′tik′), *n.* **1.** a decline or deterioration in business activity, in mood, etc. **2.** Also called **minus tick.** *Stock Exchange.* a slight downward trend in price. Cf. **uptick.** [DOWN[1] + TICK[1]]

down•time (doun′tīm′), *n.* **1.** a time during a regular working period when an employee is not actively productive. **2.** an interval during which a machine is not productive, as during repair, malfunction, maintenance. Also called **dead time.** [1925–30; DOWN[1] + TIME]

down-to-earth (doun′tōō ûrth′, -tə-), *adj.* practical and realistic: *a down-to-earth person.* [1925–30]
—**Syn.** hard-headed, sensible, sober, pragmatic.

down•town (doun′toun′), *adv.* **1.** to or in the main business section of a city. —*adj.* **2.** of, pertaining to, or situated in the main business section of a city. —*n.* **3.** the main business section of a city. [1825–35, *Amer.*; DOWN[1] + TOWN] —**down′town′er,** *n.*

down•trend (doun′trend′), *n.* a downward or decreasing tendency, movement, or shift: *a downtrend in gasoline consumption; a downtrend in stock prices.* [1925–30; DOWN[1] + TREND]

down•trod•den (doun′trod′n), *adj.* **1.** tyrannized over; oppressed: *the downtrodden plebeians of ancient Rome.* **2.** trodden down; trampled upon. Also, **down′•trod′.** [1560–70; DOWN[1] + TRODDEN] —**down′trod′•den•ness,** *n.*

down•turn (doun′tûrn′), *n.* **1.** an act or instance of turning down or the state of being turned down: *the downturn of a lower lip in a permanent pout.* **2.** a turn or trend downward; decrease or decline: *The new year brought a downturn in the cost of living.* [1925–30; n. use of v. phrase *turn down*]

down′ un′der, **1.** Australia or New Zealand. **2.** in, to, or into Australia or New Zealand. [1895–1900]

down•ward (doun′wərd), *adv.* **1.** Also, **down′wards.** from a higher to a lower place or condition. **2.** down from a source or beginning: *As the river flows downward, it widens.* **3.** from a past time, predecessor, or ancestor: *The estate was handed downward from generation to generation.* —*adj.* **4.** moving or tending to a lower place or condition. **5.** descending from a source or beginning. [1150–1200; ME *dounward,* aph. var. of *adounward,* OE *adūnweard.* See DOWN[1], -WARD] —**down′ward•ly,** *adv.* —**down′ward•ness,** *n.*

down′ward mobil′ity. See under **vertical mobility** (def. 1). —**down′wardly mo′bile.**

down•wash (doun′wosh′, -wôsh′), *n. Aeron.* a deflection of air downward relative to an airfoil that causes the deflection. [1910–15; DOWN[1] + WASH]

down•well•ing (doun′wel′ing), *n. Oceanog.* a downward current of surface water in the ocean, usually caused by differences in the density of seawater. [1965–70; DOWN[1] + WELL[2] + -ING[1]]

down•wind (doun′wind′), *adv.* **1.** in the direction toward which the wind is blowing: *We coasted downwind.* **2.** on or toward the lee side: *The lion was running downwind of us and caught our scent.* —*adj.* **3.** moving downwind: *a downwind current.* **4.** situated on or toward the lee side: *The downwind halyard blew outboard.* Cf. **upwind.** [1850–55; DOWN[1] + WIND[1]]

down•y (dou′nē), *adj.,* **down•i•er, down•i•est.** **1.** of the nature of or resembling down; fluffy; soft. **2.** made of down. **3.** covered with down. **4.** soft; soothing. [1540–50; DOWN[2] + -Y[1]] —**down′i•ly,** *adv.* —**down′i•ness,** *n.*

down′y mil′dew, **1.** Also called **false mildew.** any fungus of the family Peronosporaceae, causing many plant diseases and producing a white, downy mass of conidiophores, usually on the under surface of the leaves of the host plant. **2.** *Plant Pathol.* a disease of plants, characterized by mildewed, distorted, and yellowed foliage, caused by any of several fungi of the family Peronosporaceae, as of the genera *Peronospora* and *Phytophthora.* [1885–90]

down′y wood′pecker, a small, North American woodpecker, *Picoides pubescens,* having black and white plumage. [1800–10, *Amer.*]

down•zone (doun′zōn′), *v.,* **-zoned, -zon•ing.** —*v.t.* **1.** to change the zoning designation on (property) to restrict high-density development. —*v.i.* **2.** to downzone development. Also, **down′-zone′.** [DOWN[1] + ZONE]

dow•ry (dou′rē), *n., pl.* **-ries.** **1.** Also, **dower.** the money, goods, or estate that a wife brings to her husband at marriage. **2.** *Archaic.* a widow's dower. **3.** a natural gift, endowment, talent, etc. Also, **dowery.** [1250–1300; ME *dowerie* < AF *douarie* < ML *dōtārium.* See DOT[2], -ARY]

dow•sa•bel (dou′sə bel′), *n. Obs.* sweetheart. [1575–85; << L *Dulcibella* woman's name. See DULCET, BELLE]

dowse[1] (dous), *v.t., v.i.,* **dowsed, dows•ing,** *n.* douse.

dowse[2] (douz), *v.,* **dowsed, dows•ing.** —*v.i.* **1.** to search for underground supplies of water, metal, etc., by the use of a divining rod. —*v.t.* **2.** to search for (as water) by or as if by dowsing. [1685–95; orig. dial. (SW England); orig. obscure]

dows•er (dou′zər), *n.* **1.** Also called **dows′ing rod′** (dou′zing). See **divining rod.** **2.** a person skilled in its use. [1830–40; DOWSE[2] + -ER[1]]

Dow•son (dou′sən), *n.* **Ernest (Christopher),** 1867–1900, English poet.

dow•y (dou′ē, dō′ē), *adj. Scot. and North Eng.* dowie.

dox•e•pin (dok′sə pin), *n. Pharm.* a tricyclic antidepressant, $C_{19}H_{21}NO$, used primarily to treat depression or anxiety. [a contr. of the chemical name]

dox•ol•o•gy (dok sol′ə jē), *n., pl.* **-gies.** **1.** a hymn or form of words containing an ascription of praise to God. **2. the Doxology,** the metrical formula beginning "Praise God from whom all blessings flow." [1640–50; < ML *doxologia* < Gk, equiv. to *doxo-* (comb. form of *dóxa* honor, glory) + *-logia* -LOGY] —**dox•o•log•i•cal** (dok′sə loj′i kəl), *adj.* —**dox′o•log′i•cal•ly,** *adv.*

dox•o•ru•bi•cin (dok′sə rōō′bə sin), *n. Pharm.* a cytotoxic antibiotic, $C_{27}H_{29}NO_{11}$, derived from a variety of the bacterium *Streptomyces peucetius* and used in the treatment of sarcoma, malignant lymphoma, acute leukemia, and other cancers. [D(E)OX(Y)- + -O- + L *rub(er)* red (alluding to its color; see RUBRIC, RED) + -I- + -(MY)-CIN]

dox•y[1] (dok′sē), *n., pl.* **dox•ies.** **1.** opinion; doctrine. **2.** religious views. Also, **dox′ie.** [1720–30; extracted from HETERODOXY, ORTHODOXY]

dox•y[2] (dok′sē), *n., pl.* **dox•ies.** **1.** an immoral woman; prostitute. **2.** *Archaic.* a mistress. [1520–30; of obscure orig.]

dox•y•cy•cline (dok′sē sī′klēn, -klin), *n. Pharm.* a synthetic analog of a broad-spectrum antibiotic tetracycline drug, $C_{22}H_{24}N_2O_8$, used against a wide range of susceptible Gram-positive and Gram-negative organisms. [contr. of *deoxytetracycline*]

doy•en (doi en′, doi′ən; *Fr.* dwA yaN′), *n., pl.* **doy•ens** (doi enz′, doi′ənz; *Fr.* dwA yaN′). the senior member, as in age, rank, or experience, of a group, class, profession, etc. [1665–75; < F; OF *deien* < L *decānus* DEAN[1]]

doy•enne (doi en′; *Fr.* dwA yen′), *n., pl.* **doy•ennes** (doi enz′; *Fr.* dwA yen′). a woman who is the senior member, as in age or rank, of a group, class, profession, etc. [1900–05; < F, fem. of *doyen* DOYEN]
—**Usage.** See **-enne.**

Doyle (doil), *n.* **Sir Arthur Co•nan** (kô′nən, kō′-), 1859–1930, British physician, novelist, and detective-story writer.

doy•ley (doi′lē), *n., pl.* **-leys.** doily.

D'Oy•ly Carte (doi′lē kärt′), **1. Richard,** 1844–1901, English theatrical producer. **2.** an English light opera company founded in London in 1881 by Richard D'Oyly Carte primarily for the presentation of the works of Gilbert and Sullivan.

doz., dozen; dozens.

doze[1] (dōz), *v.,* **dozed, doz•ing,** *n.* —*v.i.* **1.** to sleep lightly or fitfully. **2.** to fall into a light sleep unintentionally (often fol. by *off*): *He dozed off during the sermon.* **3.** to sleep for a short time; nap. **4.** to be dull or half asleep. —*v.t.* **5.** to pass or spend (time) in drowsiness (often fol. by *away*): *He dozed away the afternoon.* —*n.* **6.** a light or fitful sleep; nap. [1640–50; orig. (now obs.) to stupefy, make drowsy; cf. Scots, N England dial. *dozened,* ME (Scots) *dosnyt, dosinnit* stupefied, dazed; akin to ON *dūsa* rest, Sw dial. *dusa* doze, slumber, MLG *dusen* to be thoughtless; cf. DAZE]
—**Syn. 6.** snooze, siesta, catnap, forty winks.

doze[2] (dōz), *v.t., v.i.,* **dozed, doz•ing.** *Informal.* to clear or level with a bulldozer. [1940–45; shortened form of BULLDOZE]

doz•en[1] (duz′ən), *n., pl.* **doz•ens,** (*as after a numeral*) **doz•en,** *adj.* —*n.* **1.** a group of 12. **2. the dozens,** *Slang.* a ritualized game typically engaged in by two persons each of whom attempts to outdo the other in insults directed against members of the other's family (usually used in the phrase *play the dozens*). —*adj.* **3.** twelve. [1250–1300; ME *dozeine* < OF *do(u)zaine,* equiv. to *do(u)ze* (< L *duodecim*) + *-aine* (< L *-āna*) -AN]

doz•en[2] (dō′zən), *v.t. Scot.* to stun. [1325–75; ME (Scots); see DOZE[1]]

doz•enth (duz′ənth), *adj.* twelfth. [1700–10; DOZEN[1] + -TH[2]]

doz•er[1] (dō′zər), *n.* a person who dozes. [1700–10; DOZE[1] + -ER[1]]

doz•er[2] (dō′zər), *n.* bulldozer (def. 1). [by shortening]

doz•y (dō′zē), *adj.,* **doz•i•er, doz•i•est.** **1.** drowsy; half asleep. **2.** decayed, as timber. [1685–95; DOZE[1] + -Y[1]] —**doz′i•ly,** *adv.* —**doz′i•ness,** *n.*

DP, **1.** data processing. **2.** displaced person.

dp, **1.** data processing. **2.** *Baseball.* double play.

D/P, documents against payment.

D.P., **1.** data processing. **2.** displaced person.

d.p., (in prescriptions) with a proper direction. [< L *dirēctiōne propriā*]

D.P.A., Doctor of Public Administration.

D particle, *Physics.* See **D meson.** [1975–80]

DPC, Defense Plant Corporation.

D. Ph., Doctor of Philosophy.

D.P.H., Doctor of Public Health.

DPL, diplomat.

D.P.M., Doctor of Podiatric Medicine.

D.P.P., *Insurance.* deferred payment plan.

CONCISE PRONUNCIATION KEY: act, cāpe, dâre, pärt; set, ēqual; if, īce; ox, ōver, ôrder, oil, bŏŏk, bōōt, out; up, ûrge; child; sing; shoe; thin, *th*at; zh as in *treasure.* ə = *a* as in *alone, e* as in *system, i* as in *easily, o* as in *gallop, u* as in *circus;* ᵊ as in *fire* (fīᵊr), *hour* (ouᵊr). l and n can serve as syllabic consonants, as in *cradle* (krād′l), and *button* (but′n). See the full key inside the front cover.

D.P.S., Doctor of Public Service.

DPT, diphtheria, pertussis, and tetanus: a mixed vaccine of formalin-inactivated diphtheria and tetanus toxoids and pertussis vaccine, used for primary immunization. Also, **DTP**

dpt., **1.** department. **2.** deponent.

D.P.W., Department of Public Works.

DQ, disqualify.

d quark, *Physics.* See **down quark.**

DR, *Real Estate.* dining room.

Dr, *Chiefly Brit.* Doctor.

dr, **1.** door. **2.** dram; drams.

Dr., **1.** Doctor. **2.** Drive (used in street names).

dr., **1.** debit. **2.** debtor. **3.** drachma; drachmas. **4.** dram; drams. **5.** drawer. **6.** drum.

D.R., **1.** Daughters of the (American) Revolution. **2.** *Navig.* See **dead reckoning.** **3.** Dutch Reformed.

drab[1] (drab), *adj.*, **drab·ber, drab·best,** *n.* —*adj.* **1.** dull; cheerless; lacking in spirit, brightness, etc. **2.** having the color drab. —*n.* **3.** dull gray; dull brownish or yellowish gray. **4.** any of several fabrics of this color, esp. of thick wool or cotton. [1535–45; < MF *drap* < LL *drappus* piece of cloth] **—drab′ly,** *adv.* **—drab′·ness,** *n.*

drab[2] (drab), *n.*, *v.*, **drabbed, drab·bing.** —*n.* **1.** a dirty, untidy woman; slattern. **2.** a prostitute. —*v.i.* **3.** to associate with drabs. [1505–15; perh. akin to D *drab* dregs, lees, obs. D *drablen* to run or tramp about; cf. DRABBLE, DRAFF]

drab·ble (drab′əl), *v.t., v.i.*, **-bled, -bling.** to draggle; make or become wet and dirty. [1350–1400; ME *drabelen* < MLG *drabbeln* to wade in liquid mud, bespatter, equiv. to *drabbe* liquid mud + *-eln* freq. v. suffix; see DRAB[2], DRAFF]

dra·cae·na (drə sē′nə), *n.* **1.** any treelike tropical plant of the genus *Dracaena,* many species of which are cultivated as ornamentals for their showy leaves. **2.** any plant of the closely related genus *Cordyline.* Also, **dra·ce′na.** [< NL (Linnaeus) < Gk *drákaina,* fem. of *drákōn* DRAGON]

drachm[1] (dram), *n. Brit.* a dram in apothecaries' and troy weights, and sometimes in avoirdupois weights. [learned sp. of DRAM]

drachm[2] (dram), *n.*, drachma.

drach·ma (drak′mə, dräk′-), *n., pl.* **-mas, -mae** (-mē). **1.** a cupronickel coin and monetary unit of modern Greece, equal to 100 lepta. *Abbr.:* dr., drch. **2.** the principal silver coin of ancient Greece. **3.** a small unit of weight in ancient Greece, approximately equivalent to the U.S. and British apothecaries' dram. **4.** any of various modern weights, esp. a dram. Also, **drachm.** [1520–30; < L < Gk *drachmḗ,* prob. equiv. to *drach-* base of *drássesthai* to grasp + *-mē* n. suffix (hence lit., handful)] **—drach′mal,** *adj.*

Dra·co (drā′kō), *n., gen.* **Dra·co·nis** (drā kō′nis, drə-). *Astron.* the Dragon, a northern circumpolar constellation between Ursa Major and Cepheus. [< L < Gk *drákōn* DRAGON]

Dra·co (drā′kō), *n.* a late 7th-century B.C. Athenian statesman noted for the severity of his code of laws. Also, **Dra·con** (drā′kon).

Dra·co·ni·an (drā kō′nē ən, drə-), *adj.* **1.** of, pertaining to, or characteristic of Draco or his code of laws. **2.** (*often l.c.*) rigorous; unusually severe or cruel: *Draconian forms of punishment.* Also, **Draconic.** [1810–20; < L *Dracōn-* (s. of DRACO) + -IAN] **—Dra·co′ni·an·ism,** *n.*

dra·con·ic (drā kon′ik, drə-), *adj.* of or like a dragon. [1670–80; < L *dracōn-* (s. of *dracō*) DRAGON + -IC] **—dra·con′i·cal·ly,** *adv.*

Dra·con·ic (drā kon′ik, drə-), *adj.* (*often l.c.*) Draconian. [< L *Dracōn-* (see DRACO) + -IC] **—Dra·con′i·cal·ly,** *adv.*

dracon′ic month′. See under **month** (def. 5).

Drac·o·nid (drak′ə nid), *n. Astron.* any of several unrelated meteor showers whose radiants are in the constellation Draco. [< Gk *Drákōn* DRACO + -ID[1]]

Drac·u·la (drak′yə lə), *n.* **1.** (*italics*) a novel (1897) by Bram Stoker. **2. Count,** the central character in this novel: the archetype of a vampire. [<< LG *Dracol, Dracole, Dracle* a by-name of the Wallachian prince Vlad II, "the Impaler" (1431–76); orig. of the name is disputed, but it has long been popularly associated with Rum *dracul* the devil (*drac* devil (< L *dracō* DRAGON) + *-ul* definite article)]

Dra·cut (drā′kət), *n.* a city in NE Massachusetts. 21,249.

drae·ger·man (drā′gər mən), *n., pl.* **-men.** *Mining.* a miner, usually a member of a special crew, trained in underground rescue work and other emergency procedures. [1915–20; after Alexander B. *Dräger* (d. 1928), German scientist and inventor of rescue equipment; see MAN[1]]

draff (draf), *n.* dregs, as in a brewing process; lees; refuse. [1175–1225; ME *draf;* c. Icel, D *draf;* akin to D *drab* (see DRAB[2]), G *Treber* draff] **—draff′y,** *adj.*

draft (draft, dräft), *n.* **1.** a drawing, sketch, or design. **2.** a first or preliminary form of any writing, subject to revision, copying, etc. **3.** act of drawing; delineation. **4.** a current of air in any enclosed space, esp. in a room, chimney, or stove. **5.** a current of air moving in an upward or downward direction. **6.** a device for regulating the current of air in a stove, fireplace, etc. **7.** an act of drawing or pulling loads. **8.** something that is drawn or pulled; a haul. **9.** an animal or team of animals used to pull a load. **10.** the force required to pull a load. **11.** the taking of supplies, forces, money, etc., from a given source. **12.** a selection or drawing of persons, by lot or otherwise, from the general body of the people for military service; levy; conscription. **13.** the persons so selected. **14.** *Sports.* a selecting or drawing of new players from a choice group of amateur players by professional teams, esp. a system of selecting new players so that each team in a professional league receives some of the most promising players. **15.** *Brit.* a selection of persons already in military service to be sent from one post or organization to another; detachment. **16.** a written order drawn by one person upon another; a writing directing the payment of money on account of the drawer; bill of exchange. **17.** a drain or demand made on anything. **18.** See **draft beer. 19.** an act of drinking or inhaling. **20.** something that is taken in by drinking or inhaling; a drink; dose. **21.** a quantity of fish caught. **22.** *Naut.* the depth to which a vessel is immersed when bearing a given load. **23.** Also called **leave.** *Metall.* the slight taper given to a pattern so that it may be drawn from the sand without injury to the mold. **24.** *Metalworking.* **a.** the change in sectional area of a piece of work caused by a rolling or drawing operation. **b.** a taper on a die or punch permitting it to be withdrawn readily from the work. **25.** *Masonry.* a line or border chiseled at the edge of a stone, to serve as a guide in leveling the surfaces. **26.** *Textiles.* **a.** the degree of attenuation produced in fibers during yarn processing, expressed either by the ratio of the weight of raw to the weight of processed fiber, or by the ratio between the varying surface speeds of the rollers on the carding machine. **b.** the act of attenuating the fibers. **27.** an allowance granted to a buyer for waste of goods sold by weight. **28. on draft,** available to be drawn from a cask rather than from a sealed bottle: *imported beer on draft.* —*v.t.* **29.** to draw the outlines or plan of; sketch. **30.** to draw up in written form; compose. **31.** to draw or pull. **32.** to take or select by draft, esp. for military service. **33.** *Masonry.* to cut a draft on. —*v.i.* **34.** to do drafting; work as a draftsman. **35.** (in an automobile race) to drive or ride close behind another car so as to benefit from the reduction in air pressure created behind the car ahead. —*adj.* **36.** used or suited for drawing loads: *a draft horse.* **37.** drawn or available to be drawn from a cask rather than served from a sealed bottle: *draft ale.* **38.** being a tentative or preliminary outline, version, design, or sketch. Also, *esp. Brit.,* **draught** (for defs. 1, 3–10, 18–25, 28–34, 36–38). [later sp. of DRAUGHT (since 16th century)] **—draft′a·ble,** *adj.* **—draft′er,** *n.*

draft′ an′imal, an animal used for pulling heavy loads.

draft′ beer′, beer drawn or available to be drawn from a cask or barrel. [1780–90]

draft′ board′, a board of civilians charged with registering, classifying, and selecting persons for U.S. military service. [1950–55]

draft′ chair′, a chair so designed as to fend off drafts from behind, as a wing chair.

draft′ dodg′er, a person who evades or attempts to evade compulsory military service. [1935–40]

draft·ee (draf tē′, dräf-), *n.* a person who is drafted into military service. Cf. **enlistee** (def. 1). [1860–65; DRAFT + -EE]

draft·ing (draf′ting, dräf′-), *n.* See **mechanical drawing.** [1875–80; DRAFT + -ING[1]]

draft′ing board′. See **drawing board.**

draft′ing yard′, *Australian.* a yard fenced into compartments for the holding and sorting of livestock. [1860–65]

draft′ mark′, *Naut.* any of a series of figures or marks at the stem or stern of a vessel indicating the distance vertically from the lowermost part of the hull.

draft′ mill′, smokejack.

drafts·man (drafts′mən, dräfts′-), *n., pl.* **-men. 1.** a person employed in making mechanical drawings, as of machines, structures, etc. **2.** a person who draws sketches, plans, or designs. **3.** an artist exceptionally skilled in drawing: *Matisse was a superb draftsman.* **4.** a person who draws up documents. **5.** draughtsman (def. 1). Also, *Brit.,* **draughtsman** (for defs. 1–4). [1655–65; DRAFT + 's[1] + MAN[1]] **—drafts′man·ship′,** *n.*
—Usage. See **-man.**

drafts·per·son (drafts′pûr′sən, dräfts′-), *n.* a person employed in making mechanical drawings, esp. in an architectural or engineering firm. [DRAFTS(MAN) + -PERSON]
—Usage. See **-person.**

draft′ tube′, the flared passage leading vertically from a water turbine to its tailrace. [1840–50]

draft·y (draf′tē, dräf′-), *adj.*, **draft·i·er, draft·i·est.** characterized by or admitting currents of air, usually uncomfortable. Also, *esp. Brit.,* **draughty.** [1840–50; DRAFT + -Y[1]] **—draft′i·ly,** *adv.* **—draft′i·ness,** *n.*

drag (drag), *v.*, **dragged, drag·ging,** *n., adj.* —*v.t.* **1.** to draw with force, effort, or difficulty; pull heavily or slowly along; haul; trail: *They dragged the carpet out of the house.* **2.** to search with a drag, grapnel, or the like: *They dragged the lake for the body of the missing man.* **3.** to level and smooth (land) with a drag or harrow. **4.** to introduce; inject; insert: *He drags his honorary degree into every discussion.* **5.** to protract (something) or pass (time) tediously or painfully (often fol. by *out* or *on*): *They dragged the discussion out for three hours.* —*v.i.* **6.** to be drawn or hauled along. **7.** to trail on the ground. **8.** to move heavily or with effort. **9.** to proceed or pass with tedious slowness: *The parade dragged by endlessly.* **10.** to feel listless or apathetic; move listlessly or apathetically (often fol. by *around*): *This heat wave has everyone dragging around.* **11.** to lag behind. **12.** to use a drag or grapnel; dredge. **13.** to take part in a drag race. **14.** to take a puff: *to drag on a cigarette.* **15. drag one's feet** or **heels,** to act with reluctance; delay: *The committee is dragging its feet coming to a decision.* —*n.* **16.** *Naut.* **a.** a designed increase of draft toward the stern of a vessel. **b.** resistance to the movement of a hull through the water. **c.** any of a number of weights dragged cumulatively by a vessel sliding down ways to check its speed. **d.** any object dragged in the water, as a sea anchor. **e.** any device for dragging the bottom of a body of water to recover or detect objects. **17.** *Agric.* a heavy wooden or steel frame drawn over the ground to smooth it. **18.** *Slang.* someone or something tedious; a bore: *It's a drag having to read this old novel.* **19.** a stout sledge or sled. **20.** *Aeron.* the aerodynamic force exerted on an airfoil, airplane, or other aerodynamic body that tends to reduce its forward motion. **21.** a four-horse sporting and passenger coach with seats inside and on top. **22.** a metal shoe to receive a wheel of heavy wagons and serve as a brake on steep grades. **23.** something that retards progress. **24.** an act of dragging. **25.** slow, laborious movement or procedure; retardation. **26.** a puff or inhalation on a cigarette, pipe, etc. **27.** *Hunting.* **a.** the scent left by a fox or other animal. **b.** something, as aniseed, dragged over the ground to leave an artificial scent. **c.** Also called **drag hunt.** a hunt, esp. a fox hunt, in which the hounds follow an artificial scent. **28.** *Angling.* **a.** a brake on a fishing reel. **b.** the sideways pull on a fishline, as caused by a crosscurrent. **29.** clothing characteristically associated with one sex when worn by a person of the opposite sex: *a Mardi Gras ball at which many of the dancers were in drag.* **30.** clothing characteristic of a particular occupation or milieu: *Two guests showed up in gangster drag.* **31.** Also called **comb.** *Masonry.* a steel plate with a serrated edge for dressing a stone surface. **32.** *Metall.* the lower part of a flask. Cf. **cope**[2] (def. 5). **33.** *Slang.* influence: *He claims he has drag with his senator.* **34.** *Slang.* a girl or woman that one is escorting; date. **35.** *Informal.* a street or thoroughfare, esp. a main street of a town or city. **36.** See **drag race. 37.** *Eastern New Eng.* a sledge, as for carrying stones from a field. —*adj.* **38.** marked by or involving the wearing of clothing characteristically associated with the opposite sex; transvestite. [1350–1400; 1920–25 for def. 18; ME; both n. and v. prob. < MLG *draggē* grapnel, *draggen* to dredge, deriv. of *drag-* DRAW; defs. 29-30, 38, obscurely related to other senses and perh. a distinct word of independent orig.]
—Syn. 1. See **draw. 11.** linger, loiter.

drag′ bunt′, *Baseball.* an in-motion bunt for a base hit usually attempted by a left-handed batter, who starts for first base while trailing the bat to meet the ball, without squaring around, in order to catch the infield by surprise. Cf. **sacrifice** (def. 6). [1945–50]

drag′ chain′, *Shipbuilding.* one of a number of chains attached to a hull about to be launched in restricted waters in order to slow its motion by dragging along the bottom. [1785–95]

drag′ coeffi′cient, *Aerodynamics.* the ratio of the drag on a body moving through air to the product of the velocity and surface area of the body. Also called **coefficient of drag.**

dra·gée (dra zhā′), *n.* **1.** a sugarcoated nut or candy. **2.** a small, beadlike piece of candy, usually silver-colored and used for decorating cookies, cake, and the like. **3.** a sugarcoated medication. [1850–55; < F; OF *dragee, dragie* < ML *drageia* < MGk **dragéa,* for Gk *tragḗma* sweetmeat, dried fruit]

drag·ger (drag′ər), *n.* **1.** any of various small motor trawlers operating off the North Atlantic coast of the U.S. **2.** a person or thing that drags. [1490–1500; DRAG + -ER[1]]

drag·ging (drag′ing), *adj.* **1.** extremely tired or slow, as in movement; lethargic; sluggish: *He was annoyed by their dragging way of walking and talking.* **2.** used in dragging, hoisting, etc.: *dragging ropes.* [1765–75; DRAG + -ING[2]] **—drag′ging·ly,** *adv.*

drag′ging piece′, (in a hipped roof) a short beam holding the foot of a hip rafter to counteract its thrust. Also called **drag′ging beam′, dragon beam, dragon piece.**

drag·gle (drag′əl), *v.*, **-gled, -gling.** —*v.t.* **1.** to soil by dragging over damp ground or in mud. —*v.i.* **2.** to trail on the ground; be or become draggled. **3.** to follow slowly; straggle. [1490–1500; DRAG + -LE]

drag·gle-tail (drag′əl tāl′), *n.* slut; slattern. [1590–1600; DRAGGLE + TAIL[1]]

drag·gle-tailed (drag′əl tāld′), *adj.* **1.** untidy; bedraggled; slovenly. [1645–55; DRAGGLE-TAIL + -ED[3]]

drag·gy (drag′ē), *adj.*, **-gi·er, -gi·est. 1.** moving or developing very slowly. **2.** boring; dull. [1885–90; DRAG + -Y[1]]

drag·hound (drag′hound′), *n.* a hound for use in following a hunting drag, specifically bred for speed and stamina rather than subtlety of sense of smell. [1880–85; DRAG + HOUND[1]]

drag′ hunt′, drag (def. 27c). [1850–55]

drag·line (drag′līn′), *n.* **1.** a rope dragging from something; dragrope. **2.** See **dragline crane.** [1915–20, *Amer.;* DRAG + LINE[1]]

drag′line crane′, an excavating crane having a bucket that is dropped from a boom and dragged toward the crane base by a cable. Also called **dragline.**

drag′ link′, *Mach.* a link connecting cranks on parallel shafts. [1840–50]

drag·net (drag′net′), *n.* **1.** a net to be drawn along the bottom of a river, pond, etc., or along the ground, to catch fish, small game, etc. **2.** a system or network for finding or catching someone, as a criminal wanted by the police. [1535–45; ME; see DRAG, NET[1], DRAY]

Dra·go (drä′gō; *Sp.* drä′gô), *n.* **Lu·is Ma·rí·a** (lo͞o′is mə rē′ə; *Sp.* lo͞o ēs′ mä rē′ä), 1859–1921, Argentine jurist and statesman.

drag·o·man (drag′ə mən), *n., pl.* **-mans, -men.** (in the Near East) a professional interpreter. [1300–50; < F; r. ME *drogman* interpreter < MF *drog(o)man, dragoman* < MGk *drago(u)mános* < Sem; cf. Ar *tarjumān,*

CONCISE ETYMOLOGY KEY: <, descended or borrowed from; >, whence; b., blend of, blended; c., cognate with; cf., compare; deriv., derivative; equiv., equivalent; imit., imitative; obl., oblique; r., replacing; s., stem; sp., spelling, spelled; resp., respelling, respelled; trans., translation; ?, origin unknown; *, unattested; ‡, probably earlier than. See the full key inside the front cover.

Akkadian *targumannu*] **—drag·o·man·ic** (drag′ə man′ik), **drag′o·man·ish,** *adj.*

drag·on (drag′ən), *n.* **1.** a mythical monster generally represented as a huge, winged reptile with crested head and enormous claws and teeth, and often spouting fire. **2.** *Archaic.* a huge serpent or snake. **3.** *Bible.* a large animal, possibly a large snake or crocodile. **4. the dragon,** Satan. **5.** a fierce, violent person. **6.** a very watchful and strict woman. **7.** See **flying dragon. 8.** *Bot.* any of several araceous plants, as *Arisaema dracontium* **(green dragon** or **dragonroot),** the flowers of which have a long, slender spadix and a green, shorter spathe. **9.** a short musket carried by a mounted infantryman in the 16th and 17th centuries. **10.** a soldier armed with such a musket. **11.** (*cap.*) *Astron.* the constellation Draco. [1175–1225; ME < OF < L *dracōn-* (s. of *dracō*) < Gk *drákōn* kind of serpent, prob. orig. epithet, the (sharp-)sighted one, akin to *dérkesthai* to look] **—drag′on·ish,** *adj.* **—drag′on·like′,** *adj.*

drag′on beam′. See **dragging piece.** [1695–1705]

drag·on·et (drag′ə net′. drag′ə nit), *n.* any fish of the genus *Callionymus,* the species of which are small and usually brightly colored. [1300–50; ME < MF; see DRAGON, -ET]

drag·on·fish (drag′ən fish′), *n., pl.* (*esp. collectively*) **-fish,** (*esp. referring to two or more kinds or species*) **-fish·es. 1.** any marine fish of the family Bathydraconidae, of Antarctic seas, having an elongated body and flattened head and being biochemically adapted to extremely low temperatures. **2.** Also called **seamoth.** any fish of the family Pegasidae, of tropical Indo-Pacific waters, having armor of bony rings and large, horizontal, fanlike pectoral fins. [1685–95; DRAGON + FISH]

drag·on·fly (drag′ən flī′), *n., pl.* **-flies. 1.** any of numerous stout-bodied, nonstinging insects of the order Odonata (suborder Anisoptera), the species of which prey on mosquitoes and other insects and are distinguished from the damselflies by having the wings outstretched rather than folded when at rest. **2.** (*cap.*) *Mil.* a two-seat, twin-turbojet U.S. attack aircraft in service since 1967, armed with a Minigun and capable of carrying nearly 5700 lb. (2585 kg) of ordnance. [1620–30; DRAGON + FLY[2]]

—Regional Variation. 1. The DRAGONFLY is also called a DARNING NEEDLE and a DEVIL'S DARNING NEEDLE in the Northern and Western U.S. In the Northern U.S. it is also called a SEWING NEEDLE. In the Midland U.S. it is called a SNAKE FEEDER, in the Southern U.S. a SNAKE DOCTOR, and in Southern Coastal areas, it is called a MOSQUITO HAWK or a SKEETER HAWK. SPINDLE is also in use, chiefly in New Jersey and in the Delaware Valley. EAR SEWER is in older use in some regional areas.

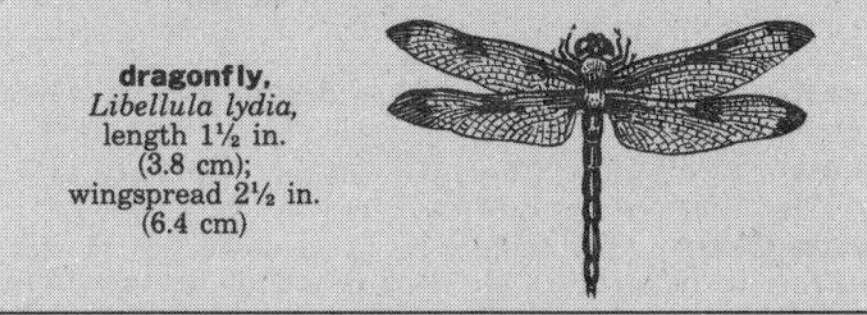
dragonfly, *Libellula lydia,* length 1½ in. (3.8 cm); wingspread 2½ in. (6.4 cm)

drag·on·head (drag′ən hed′), *n.* any of several mints of the genus *Dracocephalum* having spikes of double-lipped flowers. Also, **dragon's head.** [1500–10; trans. of NL *Dracocephalum*]

drag′on la′dy (*often caps.*) a woman of somewhat sinister glamour often perceived as wielding ruthless or corrupt power. [after the villainous Oriental woman in the cartoon strip *Terry and the Pirates* (1934–1973) created by U.S. cartoonist Milton Caniff (born 1907)]

drag′on liz′ard. See **Komodo dragon.** [1925–30]

drag·on·nade (drag′ə nād′), *n.* **1.** one of a series of persecutions of French Protestants, under Louis XIV, by dragoons quartered upon them. **2.** any persecution with the aid of troops. [1705–15; < F, equiv. to *dragonne* pertaining to a DRAGOON + *-ade* -ADE]

drag′on piece′. See **dragging piece.**

drag·on·root (drag′ən ro͞ot′, -ro͝ot′), *n.* See under **dragon** (def. 8). [1615–25; DRAGON + ROOT[1]]

drag′on's blood′, 1. a deep-red, water-insoluble resin exuding from the fruit of a palm, *Daemonorops draco,* of the Malay Archipelago, used chiefly in the preparation of varnishes and in photoengraving for protecting certain areas of the metal plate from the acid. **2.** any of various similar resins from other trees. **3.** See **Pompeian red.** [1590–1600]

drag′on's head′, 1. dragonhead. **2.** *Astron.* (formerly) the ascending node of the moon or a planet. [1500–10]

drag′on's mouth′. See **arethusa** (def. 1). [1930–35]

drag′on's tail′, *Astron.* (formerly) the descending node of the moon or a planet. [1595–1605]

drag′on tree′, 1. a tall, treelike plant, *Dracaena draco,* of the Canary Islands, scarce in the wild but common in cultivation, yielding a variety of dragon's blood. **2.** any of several other plants of the genus *Dracaena,* as *D. marginata,* having long, sword-shaped, variously colored leaves, cultivated as ornamentals. [1605–15]

dra·goon (drə go͞on′), *n.* **1.** (esp. formerly) a European cavalryman of a heavily armed troop. **2.** a member of a military unit formerly composed of such cavalrymen, as in the British army. **3.** (formerly) a mounted infantryman armed with a short musket. —*v.t.* **4.** to set dragoons or soldiers upon; persecute by armed force; oppress. **5.** to force by oppressive measures; coerce: *The authorities dragooned the peasants into leaving their farms.* [1615–25; < F *dragon,* special use of *dragon* DRAGON, applied first to a pistol hammer (so named because of its shape), then to the firearm, then to the troops so armed] **—dra·goon′age,** *n.*

drag′ par′achute. See **drogue parachute** (def. 2).

drag′ queen′, a male transvestite. [1960–65]

drag′ race′, a race between two or more automobiles starting from a standstill, the winner being the car that can accelerate the fastest. Also called **drag.** [1940–45] **—drag′ rac′er. —drag′ rac′ing.**

drag′ rake′, a heavy rake with closely set, hooklike teeth, for use in digging for clams. [1750–60]

drag·rope (drag′rōp′), *n.* **1.** a rope for dragging something, as a piece of artillery. **2.** a rope dragging from something, as the guide rope from a balloon. [1760–70; DRAG + ROPE]

drag′ sail′, *Naut.* a sea anchor made of canvas. Also called **drag′ sheet′.**

drag·saw (drag′sô′), *n.* a large power saw having a reciprocating blade, as a power hacksaw for metals or a lumbermill saw. [1865–70, *Amer.*; DRAG + SAW[1]] **—drag′saw′ing,** *n.*

drag·ster (drag′stər), *n.* **1.** an automobile designed and built specifically for drag racing, esp. on a ¼-mi. (402-m) or ⅛-mi. (201-m) drag strip. **2.** a person who races such an automobile. [1945–50; DRAG + -STER]

drag′ strip′, a straight, paved area or course where drag races are held, as a section of road or airplane runway. Also, **drag′strip′, drag·way** (drag′wā′). [1950–55, *Amer.*]

drags·ville (dragz′vil), *n. Slang.* something unpleasantly boring or tedious. [1965–70; DRAG + 's[1] + *-ville,* a final element in place names]

Dra·gui·gnan (dRA gē nyäN′), *n.* a town in and the capital of Var, in SE France. 22,406.

draht·haar (drät′här), *n.* one of a German breed of wirehaired pointing dogs. [< G, equiv. to *Draht* wire + *Haar* hair]

drail (drāl), *Angling.* *n.* **1.** a hook with a lead-covered shank used in trolling. —*v.i.* **2.** to fish by trolling with a drail. [1625–35; *Amer.*; special use of obs. E, ME *drail* to drag along, appar. alter. of TRAIL under influence of DRAG, DRAW, etc.]

drain (drān), *v.t.* **1.** to withdraw or draw off (a liquid) gradually; remove slowly or by degrees, as by filtration: *to drain oil from a crankcase.* **2.** to withdraw liquid gradually from; make empty or dry by drawing off liquid: *to drain a crankcase.* **3.** to exhaust the resources of: *to drain the treasury.* **4.** to deprive of strength; tire. —*v.i.* **5.** to flow off gradually. **6.** to become empty or dry by the gradual flowing off of liquid or moisture: *This land drains into the Mississippi.* —*n.* **7.** something, as a pipe or conduit, by which a liquid drains. **8.** *Surg.* a material or appliance for maintaining the opening of a wound to permit free exit of fluids. **9.** gradual or continuous outflow, withdrawal, or expenditure. **10.** something that causes a large or continuous outflow, expenditure, or depletion: *Medical expenses were a major drain on his bank account.* **11.** an act of draining. **12.** *Physical Geog.* **a.** an artificial watercourse, as a ditch or trench. **b.** a natural watercourse modified to increase its flow of water. **13. go down the drain, a.** to become worthless or profitless. **b.** to go out of existence; disappear. [bef. 1000; ME *dreynen,* OE *drēhnian, drēahnian* to strain, filter; akin to DRY] **—drain′a·ble,** *adj.* **—drain′er,** *n.*

drain·age (drā′nij), *n.* **1.** the act or process of draining. **2.** a system of drains, artificial or natural. **3.** See **drainage basin. 4.** something that is drained off. **5.** *Surg.* the drainage of fluids, as bile, urine, etc., from the body, or of pus and other diseased products from a wound. [1645–55; DRAIN + -AGE]

drain′age ba′sin, the area drained by a river and all its tributaries. Also called **catchment area, drain′age ar′ea.** Cf. **watershed** (def. 2). [1880–85, *Amer.*]

drain·age·way (drā′nij wā′), *n.* a conduit, ditch, or the like, for draining water from an area. [DRAINAGE + WAY]

drain′age wind′ (wind), *Meteorol.* See **gravity wind.**

drain·board (drān′bôrd′, -bōrd′), *n.* a working surface beside or on a kitchen sink, formed and inclined to drain into the sink. [1900–05, *Amer.*; DRAIN + BOARD]

drain·field (drān′fēld′), *n.* an open area, the soil of which absorbs the contents of a septic tank. [DRAIN + FIELD]

drain·less (drān′lis), *adj.* inexhaustible. [1810–20; DRAIN + -LESS]

drain·pipe (drān′pīp′), *n.* a large pipe that carries away the discharge of waste pipes, soil pipes, etc. [1855–60; DRAIN + PIPE[1]]

drain·spout (drān′spout′), *n.* downspout. [DRAIN + SPOUT]

Draize′ test′ (drāz), *Pharm.* a test assessing the potential of drugs, chemicals, cosmetics, and other commercial products to produce irritation, pain, or damage to the human eye by studying its effect on a rabbit's eye. [1975–80; after John H. *Draize* (born 1900), U.S. pharmacologist, who devised it]

drake[1] (drāk), *n.* a male duck. Cf. **duck**[1] (def. 2). [1250–1300; ME; c. LG *drake,* dial. G *drache;* cf. OHG *antrahho, anutrehho* male duck]

drake[2] (drāk), *n.* **1.** a small cannon, used esp. in the 17th and 18th centuries. **2.** drake fly. **3.** *Archaic.* a dragon. [bef. 900; ME; OE *draca* < L *dracō* DRAGON]

Drake (drāk), *n.* **1. Sir Francis,** c1540–96, English admiral and buccaneer: sailed around the world 1577–80. **2. Joseph Rod·man** (rod′mən), 1795–1820, U.S. poet.

drake′ fly′, *Angling.* See **May fly.** Also called **drake.** [1400–50; perh. late ME *drake flye* artificial fly dressed with drake feathers]

drake′ foot′, *Furniture.* See **trifid foot.**

Dra·kens·berg (drä′kənz bûrg′), *n.* a mountain range in the E Republic of South Africa: highest peak, 10,988 ft. (3350 m). Also called **Quathlamba.**

Drake′ Pas′sage, a strait between S South America and the South Shetland Islands, connecting the Atlantic and Pacific oceans.

dram (dram), *n., v.,* **drammed, dram·ming.** —*n.* **1.** *Meas.* **a.** a unit of apothecaries' weight, equal to 60 grains, or ⅛ ounce (3.89 grams). **b.** 1/16 ounce, avoirdupois weight (27.34 grains; 1.77 grams). *Abbr.:* dr., dr **2.** See **fluid dram. 3.** a small drink of liquor. **4.** a small quantity of anything. —*v.i.* **5.** *Archaic.* to drink drams; tipple. —*v.t.* **6.** *Archaic.* to ply with drink. [1400–50; late ME *dramme,* assimilated var. of *dragme* < OF < LL *dragma,* L *drachma* DRACHMA]

dra·ma (drä′mə, dram′ə), *n.* **1.** a composition in prose or verse presenting in dialogue or pantomime a story involving conflict or contrast of character, esp. one intended to be acted on the stage; a play. **2.** the branch of literature having such compositions as its subject; dramatic art. **3.** the art dealing with the writing and production of plays. **4.** any situation or series of events having vivid, emotional, or conflicting interest or results: *the drama of a murder trial.* **5.** the quality of being dramatic. [1505–15; < LL < Gk *drâma* action (of a play), equiv. to *drâ(n)* to do + *-ma* n. suffix]

dra·ma·dy (drä′mə dē, dram′ə-), *n., pl.* **-dies.** dramedy.

Dram·a·mine (dram′ə mēn′), *Pharm., Trademark.* a brand of dimenhydrinate.

dra·mat·ic (drə mat′ik), *adj.* **1.** of or pertaining to the drama. **2.** employing the form or manner of the drama. **3.** characteristic of or appropriate to the drama, esp. in involving conflict or contrast; vivid; moving: *dramatic colors; a dramatic speech.* **4.** highly effective; striking. [1580–90; < LL *drāmaticus* < Gk *drāmatikós,* equiv. to *drāmat-* (s. of *drâma*) DRAMA + *-ikos* -IC] **—dra·mat′i·cal·ly,** *adv.*

—Syn. 1. theatrical. **4.** startling, sensational.

dramat′ic i′rony, irony inherent in the speeches or situation of a drama that is understood by the audience but not by the characters in the play. [1905–10]

dramat′ic mon′ologue, a poetic form in which a single character, addressing a silent auditor at a critical moment, reveals himself or herself and the dramatic situation. Also called **dramat′ic lyr′ic.** [1930–35]

dra·mat·ics (drə mat′iks), *n.* **1.** (*used with a singular or plural v.*) the art of producing or acting dramas. **2.** (*used with a plural v.*) dramatic productions, esp. by amateurs. **3.** (*used with a plural v.*) dramatic, overly emotional, or insincere behavior: *His friends are tired of all his phony dramatics.* [1675–85; see DRAMATIC, -ICS]

dramat′ic u′nities, the three unities of time, place, and action observed in classical drama as specified by Aristotle in his *Poetics.* [1920–25]

dram·a·tis per·so·nae (dram′ə tis pər sō′nē, drä′mə-), **1.** (*used with a plural v.*) the characters in a play. **2.** (*used with a singular v.*) a list of the characters preceding the text of a play. [1720–30; < L: characters of the play]

dram·a·tist (dram′ə tist, drä′mə-), *n.* a writer of dramas or dramatic poetry; playwright. [1670–80; < Gk *drāmat-* (see DRAMATIC) + -IST]

dram·a·ti·za·tion (dram′ə tə zā′shən, drä′mə-), *n.* **1.** the act of dramatizing. **2.** construction or representation in dramatic form. **3.** a dramatized version of a novel, historic incident, etc. [1790–1800; DRAMATIZE + -ATION]

dram·a·tize (dram′ə tīz′, drä′mə-), *v.,* **-tized, -tiz·ing.** —*v.t.* **1.** to put into a form suitable for acting on a stage. **2.** to express or represent vividly or emotionally. —*v.i.* **3.** to express oneself in a dramatic or exaggerated way. Also, *esp. Brit.,* **dram′a·tise′.** [1770–80; < Gk *drāmat-* (see DRAMATIC) + -IZE] **—dram′a·tiz′a·ble,** *adj.* **—dram′a·tiz′er,** *n.*

dram·a·turge (dram′ə tûrj′, drä′mə-), *n.* a specialist in dramaturgy, esp. one who acts as a consultant to a theater company, advising them on possible repertory. Also, **dram′a·turg′.** [1855–60; perh. back formation from DRAMATURGY, but cf. F *dramaturge,* G *Dramaturg*]

dram·a·tur·gy (dram′ə tûr′jē, drä′mə-), *n.* the craft or the techniques of dramatic composition. [1795–1805; < Gk *drāmatourgía* dramatic composition, equiv. to *drāmaturg(ós)* playwright + *-ia* -Y[3]. See DRAMATIC, -URGY] **—dram′a·tur′gic, dram′a·tur′gi·cal,** *adj.* **—dram′a·tur′gi·cal·ly,** *adv.*

Dram·bu·ie (dram bo͞o′ē), *Trademark.* a brand of liqueur combining Scotch whisky with heather honey and herbs.

dra·me·dy (drä′mə dē, dram′ə-), *n., pl.* **-dies.** a television program or series using both serious and comic subjects, usu. without relying on conventional plots, laugh tracks, etc. Also, **dramady.** [b. DRAMA and COMEDY]

dram′ glass′. See **joey glass.** [1710–20]

dram·mock (dram′ək), *n. Chiefly Scot.* an uncooked mixture of meal, usually oatmeal, and cold water. Also, **dram·mach** (dram′əKH), **drummock.** [1555–65; cf. ScotGael *dramag* foul mixture]

dram. pers., dramatis personae.

dram·shop (dram′shop′), *n.* bar; barroom; saloon. [1715–25; DRAM + SHOP]

drang (drang), *n. Newfoundland.* a narrow lane or alleyway. Also, **drung.** [cf., in SW England, *drang, drong,* with same sense; dial. form of THRONG]

drank (drangk), *v.* a pt. and pp. of **drink.**

drape (drāp), *v.,* **draped, drap·ing,** *n.* —*v.t.* **1.** to cover or hang with cloth or other fabric, esp. in graceful folds; adorn with drapery. **2.** to adjust (curtains, clothes, etc.) into graceful folds, attractive lines, etc. **3.** to arrange, hang, or let fall carelessly: *Don't drape your feet over the chair!* **4.** *Med., Surg.* to place cloth so as to surround (a part to be examined, treated, or operated upon). **5.** (in reinforced-concrete construction) to hang (reinforcement) in a certain form between two points before pouring the concrete. **6.** to put a black cravat on (a flagstaff) as a token of mourning. —*v.i.* **7.** to hang, fall, or become arranged in folds, as drapery: *This silk drapes well.* —*n.* **8.** a curtain or hanging of heavy fabric and usually considerable length, esp. either of a pair for covering a window and drawn open and shut horizontally. **9.** either of a pair of similar curtains extending or draped at the sides of a window, French doors, or the like as decoration. **10.** manner or style of hanging: *the drape of a skirt.* [1400–50; late ME < MF *draper,* deriv. of *drap* cloth (see DRAB[1])] —**drap′a•ble, drape′a•ble,** *adj.* —**drap′a•bil′i•ty, drape′a•bil′i•ty,** *n.*

Dra•peau (dra pō′; *Fr.* DRA pō′), *n.* **Jean** (zhäN), born 1916, Canadian lawyer and politician: mayor of Montreal 1954–57 and 1960–86.

drape′ form′ing, thermoforming of plastic sheeting over an open mold by a combination of gravity and a vacuum. [1960–65]

drap•er (drā′pər), *n. Brit.* **1.** a dealer in cloth; a retail merchant or clerk who sells piece goods. **2.** a retail merchant or clerk who sells clothing and dry goods. [1325–75; ME < AF; OF *drapier,* equiv. to *drap* cloth + *-ier* -IER[2]; see -ER[2]]

Dra•per (drā′pər), *n.* **1. Henry,** 1837–82, U.S. astronomer. **2.** his father, **John William,** 1811–82, U.S. chemist, physiologist, historian, and writer; born in England. **3. Ruth,** 1884–1956, U.S. diseuse and writer of character sketches.

dra•per•y (drā′pə rē), *n., pl.* **-per•ies. 1.** coverings, hangings, clothing, etc., of fabric, esp. as arranged in loose, graceful folds. **2.** Often, **draperies.** long curtains, usually of heavy fabric and often designed to open and close across a window. **3.** the draping or arranging of hangings, clothing, etc., in graceful folds. **4.** *Art.* hangings, clothing, etc., as represented in sculpture or painting. **5.** cloths or textile fabrics collectively. **6.** *Brit.* **a.** See **dry goods. b.** the stock, shop, or business of a draper. [1250–1300; ME *draperie* < OF, equiv. to *drap* cloth + *-erie* -ERY] —**dra′per•ied,** *adj.*

dras•tic (dras′tik), *adj.* **1.** acting with force or violence; violent. **2.** extremely severe or extensive: *a drastic tax-reduction measure.* [1685–95; < Gk *drastikós* active, equiv. to *drast(ós)* (verbal adj. of *drân* to do) + *-ikos* -IC] —**dras′ti•cal•ly,** *adv.*

drat (drat), *v.,* **drat•ted, drat•ting,** *interj.* —*v.t.* **1.** to damn; confound: *Drat your interference.* —*interj.* **2.** (used to express mild disgust, disappointment, or the like): *Drat, there goes another button off my shirt.* [1805–15; alter. of (*o*)*d rot* God rot (i.e., may God rot him, her, it)]

drat•ted (drat′id), *adj.* damned; confounded (used as a mild oath): *This dratted car won't start.* [1855–60; DRAT + -ED[2]]

draught (draft, dräft), *n.* **1. draughts,** (*used with a singular v.*) *Brit.* the game of checkers. **2.** *Chiefly Brit.* draft (defs. 1, 3–10, 18–25, 28). —*v.t.* **3.** *Chiefly Brit.* draft (defs. 29–33). —*v.i.* **4.** *Chiefly Brit.* draft (def. 34). —*adj.* **5.** *Chiefly Brit.* draft (defs. 36–38). [1150–1200; ME *draht* (c. D *dracht,* G *Tracht,* ON *drāttr*); akin to OE *dragan* to DRAW, *drōht* a pull (at the oars)] —**draught′•er,** *n.*

—**Pronunciation.** DRAUGHT is a variant spelling of *draft* and is normally pronounced the same way, as (draft) or (dräft) or with a vowel somewhere between (a) and (ä). A pronunciation (drôt) is sometimes heard for DRAUGHT, perhaps because *-aught* is frequently pronounced (-ôt) elsewhere, as in *caught* and *taught.*

draught•board (draft′bôrd′, -bōrd′, dräft′-), *n. Brit.* checkerboard (def. 1). Also, **draughts•board** (drafts′bôrd′, -bōrd′, dräfts′-). [1720–30; DRAUGHT + BOARD]

draughts•man (drafts′mən, dräfts′-), *n., pl.* **-men.** *Brit.* **1.** a checker, as used in the game of checkers. **2.** draftsman (defs. 1–4). [1655–65; DRAUGHT + -S[3] + MAN[1]]

draught•y (draf′tē, dräf′-), *adj.,* **draught•i•er, draught•i•est.** *Chiefly Brit.* drafty. —**draught′i•ly,** *adv.* —**draught′i•ness,** *n.*

Dra•va (drä′və), *n.* a river in S central Europe, flowing E and SE from the Alps in S Austria, through NE Slovenia, along a part of the border between Hungary and Croatia into the Danube in Yugoslavia. 450 mi. (725 km) long. **Dra′ve.** German, **Drau** (DROU).

drave (drāv), *v. Archaic.* a pt. of **drive.**

Dra•vid•i•an (drə vid′ē ən), *n.* **1.** a family of languages, wholly distinct from Indo-European, spoken mostly in southern India and Sri Lanka and including Tamil, Telugu, Kannada, Malayalam, and, in Pakistan, Brahui. **2.** a member of the aboriginal population occupying much of southern India and parts of Sri Lanka. —*adj.* **3.** Also, **Dra•vid′ic.** of or pertaining to this people or their language. [1855–60; < Skt *Draviḍ(a)* ethnonym + -IAN]

dra•vite (drä′vīt), *n.* a brown variety of magnesium tourmaline. [< G *Dravit.* See DRAVA, -ITE[1]]

draw (drô), *v.,* **drew, drawn, draw•ing,** *n.* —*v.t.* **1.** to cause to move in a particular direction by or as if by a pulling force; pull; drag (often fol. by *along, away, in, out,* or *off*). **2.** to bring, take, or pull out, as from a receptacle or source: *to draw water from a well.* **3.** to bring toward oneself or itself, as by inherent force or influence; attract: *The concert drew a large audience.* **4.** to sketch (someone or something) in lines or words; delineate; depict: *to draw a vase with charcoal; to draw the comedy's characters with skill.* **5.** to compose or create (a picture) in lines. **6.** to mark or lay out; trace: *to draw perpendicular lines.* **7.** to frame or formulate: *to draw a distinction.* **8.** to write out in legal form (sometimes fol. by *up*): *Draw up the contract.* **9.** to inhale or suck in: *to draw liquid through a straw.* **10.** to derive or use, as from a source: *to draw inspiration from Shakespeare.* **11.** to deduce; infer: *to draw a conclusion.* **12.** to get, take, or receive, as from a source: *to draw interest on a savings account; to draw a salary of $600 a week.* **13.** to withdraw funds from a drawing account, esp. against future commissions on sales. **14.** to produce; bring in: *The deposits draw interest.* **15.** to disembowel: *to draw a turkey.* **16.** to drain: *to draw a pond.* **17.** to pull out to full or greater length; make by attenuating; stretch: *to draw filaments of molten glass.* **18.** to bend (a bow) by pulling back its string in preparation for shooting an arrow. **19.** to choose or to have assigned to one at random, by or as by picking an unseen number, item, etc.: *Let's draw straws to see who has to wash the car.* **20.** *Metalworking.* to form or reduce the sectional area of (a wire, tube, etc.) by pulling through a die. **21.** to wrinkle or shrink by contraction. **22.** *Med.* to cause to discharge: *to draw an abscess by a poultice.* **23.** to obtain (rations, clothing, equipment, weapons, or ammunition) from an issuing agency, as an army quartermaster. **24.** *Naut.* (of a vessel) to need (a specific depth of water) to float: *She draws six feet.* **25.** to leave (a contest) undecided; finish with neither side winning, as in a tie. **26.** *Cards.* **a.** to take or be dealt (a card or cards) from the pack. **b.** *Bridge.* to remove the outstanding cards in (a given suit) by leading that suit: *He had to draw spades first in order to make the contract.* **27.** *Billiards.* to cause (a cue ball) to recoil after impact by giving it a backward spin on the stroke. **28.** *Northeastern U.S.* (*chiefly New Eng.*). to haul; cart. **29.** *Hunting.* to search (a covert) for game. **30.** *Cricket.* to play (a ball) with a bat held at an angle in order to deflect the ball between the wicket and the legs. **31.** *Curling.* to slide (the stone) gently. **32.** to steep (tea) in boiling water. **33.** to form or shape (glass) as it comes from the furnace by stretching.

—*v.i.* **34.** to exert a pulling, moving, or attracting force: *A sail draws by being properly trimmed and filled with wind.* **35.** to move or pass, esp. slowly or continuously, as under a pulling force (often fol. by *on, off, out,* etc.): *The day draws near.* **36.** to take out a sword, pistol, etc., for action. **37.** to hold a drawing, lottery, or the like: *to draw for prizes.* **38.** to sketch or to trace figures; create a picture or depict by sketching. **39.** to be skilled in or practice the art of sketching: *I can't paint, but I can draw.* **40.** to shrink or contract (often fol. by *up*). **41.** to make a demand (usually fol. by *on* or *upon*): *to draw on one's imagination.* **42.** *Med.* **a.** to act as an irritant; cause blisters. **b.** to cause blood, pus, or the like to gather at a specific point. **43.** to produce or permit a draft, as a pipe or flue. **44.** to leave a contest undecided; tie. **45.** *Hunting.* (of a hound) **a.** to search a covert for game. **b.** to follow a game animal by its scent. **46.** to attract customers, an audience, etc.: *Our newspaper advertisement drew very well.* **47.** to pull back the string of a bow in preparation for shooting an arrow. **48. draw ahead, a.** to gradually pass something moving in the same direction. **b.** *Naut.* (of the wind) to blow from a direction closer to that in which a vessel is moving; haul forward. Cf. **veer**[1] (def. 2b). **49. draw away, a.** to move or begin to move away: *He drew his hand away from the hot stove.* **b.** to move farther ahead: *The lead runner gradually drew away from his competitor.* **50. draw down,** to deplete or be depleted through use or consumption: *to draw down crude-oil supplies.* **51. draw in, a.** to cause to take part or enter, esp. unwittingly: *I heard them debating the point, but I avoided being drawn in.* **b.** to make a rough sketch of: *to draw in a person's figure against the landscape background.* **52. draw off,** to move back or away. **53. draw on, a.** to come nearer; approach: *He sensed winter drawing on.* **b.** to clothe oneself in: *She drew on her cape and gloves.* **c.** *Naut.* (of a vessel) to gain on (another vessel). **d.** to utilize or make use of, esp. as a source: *The biography has drawn heavily on personal interviews.* **54. draw oneself up,** to assume an erect posture. **55. draw out, a.** to pull out; remove. **b.** to prolong; lengthen. **c.** to persuade to speak: *You'll find she's quite interesting if you take the trouble to draw her out.* **d.** *Naut.* (of a vessel) to move away from (sometimes fol. by *from*): *The boat drew out from the wharf.* **e.** to take (money) from a place of deposit: *She drew her money out of the bank and invested it in bonds.* **56. draw up, a.** to devise or formulate; draft, esp. in legal form or as a formal proposal: *to draw up a will.* **b.** to put into position; arrange in order or formation: *The officer drew up his men.* **c.** to bring or come to a stop; halt: *Their car drew up at the curb.*

—*n.* **57.** an act of drawing. **58.** something that attracts customers, an audience, etc. **59.** something that is moved by being drawn, as the movable part of a drawbridge. **60.** something that is chosen or drawn at random, as a lot or chance. **61.** drawing (defs. 5, 6). **62.** a contest that ends in a tie; an undecided contest. **63.** Also called **draw play.** *Football.* a play in which the quarterback fades as if to pass and then hands the ball to a back, usually the fullback, who is running toward the line of scrimmage. **64.** *Poker.* **a.** a card or cards taken or dealt from the pack. **b.** See **draw poker. 65.** *Physical Geog.* **a.** a small, natural drainageway with a shallow bed; gully. **b.** the dry bed of a stream. **c.** *Chiefly Western U.S.* a coulee; ravine. **66.** the pull necessary to draw a bow to its full extent. **67.** an amount regularly drawn, as from a drawing account. **68.** a fund, as an expense account or credit line, from which money may be withdrawn when needed. **69.** *Horol.* the tendency of a tooth of an escape wheel to force toward the center of the wheel a pallet engaging with it. **70. beat to the draw,** to react quicker than an opponent. **71. luck of the draw.** See **luck** (def. 7). [bef. 900; ME *drawen,* OE *dragan;* c. ON *draga* to draw, G *tragen* to carry; cf. DRAG] —**draw′a•ble,** *adj.*

—**Syn. 1.** tug, tow. DRAW, DRAG, HAUL, PULL imply causing movement of an object toward one by exerting force upon it. To DRAW is to move by a force, in the direction from which the force is exerted: *A magnet draws iron to it.* To DRAG is to draw with the force necessary to overcome friction between the object drawn and the surface on which it rests: *to drag a sled to the top of a hill.* To HAUL is to transport a heavy object slowly by mechanical force or with sustained effort: *to haul a large boat across a portage.* To PULL is to draw or tug, exerting varying amounts of force according to the effort needed: *to pull out an eyelash; to pull fighting dogs apart.*

draw•a•bil•i•ty (drô′ə bil′i tē), *n. Metalworking.* the degree to which a metal can be drawn. [DRAW(ABLE) + -ABILITY]

draw•back (drô′bak′), *n.* **1.** a hindrance or disadvantage; an undesirable or objectionable feature. **2.** *Com.* an amount paid back from a charge made. **3.** *Govt.* a refund of tariff or other tax, as when imported goods are reexported. [1610–20; n. use of v. phrase *draw back*]

draw•bar (drô′bär′), *n.* a heavy bar, often made of steel, attached to the rear of a tractor and used as a hitch for pulling machinery, as a plow or mower. [1660–70, *Amer.,* for an earlier sense; DRAW + BAR[1]]

draw′bar pull′, the force, measured in pounds, available to a locomotive for pulling rolling stock after overcoming its own tractive resistance.

draw•bench (drô′bench′), *n. Metalworking.* a bench having apparatus for cold-drawing wires, tubes, etc. [1855–60; DRAW + BENCH]

draw•bore (drô′bôr′, -bōr′), *n., v.,* **-bored, -bor•ing.** *Carpentry.* —*n.* **1.** a hole in a tenon made eccentric with the corresponding holes to the mortise so that the two pieces being joined will be forced tightly together when the pin (**draw′bore pin′**) is hammered into place. —*v.t.* **2.** to make a drawbore in (a tenon). [1815–25; DRAW + BORE[1]]

draw•boy (drô′boi′), *n.* **1.** an apparatus for controlling and manipulating the harness cords on a power loom. **2.** a boy who operates and controls the harness cords of a draw-loom. [1725–35; DRAW + BOY]

draw•bridge (drô′brij′), *n.* a bridge of which the whole or a section may be drawn up, let down, or drawn aside, to prevent access or to leave a passage open for boats, barges, etc. [1300–50; ME *drawebrigge.* See DRAW, BRIDGE[1]]

drawbridge

draw•card (drô′kärd′), *n.* See **drawing card.** [1955–60; DRAW + CARD[1]]

draw′ cur′tain, *Theat.* a curtain, opening at the middle, that can be drawn to the sides of a stage.

draw•down (drô′doun′), *n.* **1.** a lowering of water surface level, as in a well. **2.** a reduction or depletion: *a drawdown of weapons in an arms-limitation plan.* [1780–90, for literal sense; DRAW + DOWN[1]]

draw•ee (drô ē′), *n. Finance.* a person on whom an order, draft, or bill of exchange is drawn. [1760–70; DRAW + -EE]

draw•er (drôr *for 1, 2;* drô′ər *for 3–6*), *n.* **1.** a sliding, lidless, horizontal compartment, as in a piece of furniture, that may be drawn out in order to gain access to it. **2. drawers,** (*used with a plural v.*) an undergarment, with legs, that covers the lower part of the body. **3.** a person or thing that draws. **4.** *Finance.* a person who draws an order, draft, or bill of exchange. **5.** *Metalworking.* a person who operates a drawbench. **6.** a tapster. [1300–50, 1580–90 for def. 1, 1560–70 for def. 2; ME; see DRAW, -ER[1]]

draw•er•ful (drôr′fo͝ol), *n., pl.* **-fuls.** an amount sufficient to fill a drawer: *a drawerful of socks.* [1820–30; DRAWER + -FUL]

—**Usage.** See **-ful.**

draw′ game′, *Dominoes.* a game in which a player must keep drawing pieces from the boneyard until a playable one is drawn. [1815–25]

draw•hole (drô′hōl′), *n. Mining.* a funnel-shaped vertical opening cut at the bottom of a stope, which permits the loading of ore into conveyances in the passageways below. Also called **glory hole, mill hole.** [DRAW + HOLE]

draw•ing (drô′ing), *n.* **1.** the act of a person or thing that draws. **2.** a graphic representation by lines of an object or idea, as with a pencil; a delineation of form without reference to color. **3.** a sketch, plan, or design, esp. one made with pen, pencil, or crayon. **4.** the art or technique of making these. **5.** something decided by drawing lots; lottery. **6.** the selection, or time of selection, of the winning chance or chances sold by lottery or raffle. [1275–1325; ME; see DRAW, -ING[1]]

draw′ing account′, *Com.* **1.** an account used by a partner or employee for cash withdrawals. **2.** an account that is charged with advances of money for expenses, on salaries, against earnings, etc., esp. for sales representatives. [1825–35]

draw′ing board′, 1. a rectangular board on which paper is placed or mounted for drawing or drafting. **2. back to the drawing board,** back to the original or an earlier stage of planning or development: *Our plan didn't work out, so it's back to the drawing board.* **3. on the drawing board,** in the planning or design stage: *The shopping center is still on the drawing board.* [1715–25]

draw′ing card′, a person who or thing that attracts attention or patrons. [1885–90, *Amer.*]

draw′ing chis′el, an obliquely edged wood chisel for working across grain, as in forming the ends of tenons.

draw′ing frame′, *Textiles.* a machine used to attenuate and straighten fibers by having them pass, in sliver form, through a series of double rollers, each pair of which revolves at a slightly greater speed than the preceding pair and reduces the number of strands originally fed into the machine to one extended fibrous strand doubled or redoubled in length. [1825–35]

draw·ing-in (drô′ing in′), *n., pl.* **draw·ings-in.** the act or process of threading warp ends through the heddle eyes of the harness and the dents of the reed according to a given plan for weaving a fabric. [1835–45; *draw in* + -ING[1]]

draw′ing pin′, *Brit.* a thumbtack. [1855–60]

draw′ing room′, **1.** a formal reception room, esp. in an apartment or private house. **2.** (in a railroad car) a private room for two or three passengers. **3.** *Brit.* a formal reception, esp. at court. [1635–45; as shortening of now obs. *withdrawing room*] —**draw′ing-room′,** *adj.*

draw′ing-room com′edy (drô′ing ro͞om′, -ro͝om′), *Theat.* a light, sophisticated comedy typically set in a drawing room with characters drawn from polite society. [1880–85]

draw′ing ta′ble, a table having a surface consisting of a drawing board adjustable to various heights and angles. Also called **architect's table.** [1905–10]

draw·knife (drô′nīf′), *n., pl.* **-knives.** *Carpentry.* a knife with a handle at each end at right angles to the blade, used by drawing over a surface. Also called **draw′ing knife′, drawshave.** [1630–40; DRAW + KNIFE]

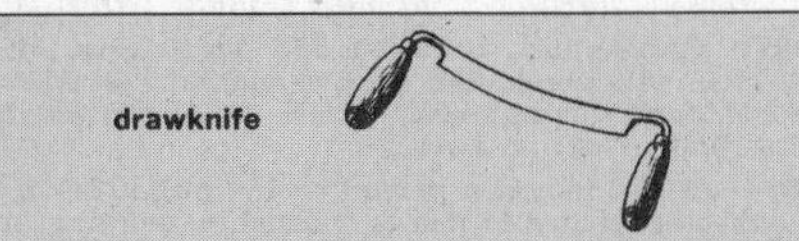

drawl (drôl), *v.t., v.i.* **1.** to say or speak in a slow manner, usually prolonging the vowels. —*n.* **2.** an act or utterance of a person who drawls. [1590–1600; < D or LG *dralen* to linger] —**drawl′er,** *n.* —**drawl′ing·ly,** *adv.* —**drawl′ing·ness,** *n.* —**drawl′y,** *adj.*

draw-loom (drô′lo͞om′), *n.* an early handloom used for producing figured fabrics. [1825–35]

drawn (drôn), *v.* **1.** pp. of **draw.** —*adj.* **2.** tense; haggard. **3.** eviscerated, as a fowl. **4.** *Glassmaking.* **a.** of or pertaining to the stem of a drinking glass that has been formed by stretching from a small mass of molten metal left at the base of the bowl of the vessel. **b.** of or pertaining to glass that is drawn over a series of rollers as it comes from the furnace.

drawn′ but′ter, **1.** melted butter, clarified and often seasoned with herbs or lemon juice. **2.** a sauce of melted butter, flour, vegetable or fish stock, and lemon juice. [1820–30, *Amer.*]

drawn-out (drôn′out′), *adj.* long-drawn-out. [1885–90]

drawn′ work′, ornamental work done by drawing threads from a fabric, the remaining portions usually being formed into lacelike patterns by needlework. [1585–95]

draw′-out ta′ble (drô′out′). See **draw table.**

draw′ play′, *Football.* draw (def. 63). [1950–55]

draw′ pok′er, a variety of poker in which a player is dealt five cards and, after an initial bet, may discard usually up to three of these cards and receive replacements from the dealer. [1855–60, *Amer.*]

draw′ run′ner, *Furniture.* loper. Also called **draw′ slip′.**

draw·shave (drô′shāv′), *n. Carpentry.* drawknife. [1820–30; DRAW + SHAVE]

draw·sheet (drô′shēt′), *n.* a narrow sheet, often used on hospital beds, placed under a patient's buttocks and often over a rubber sheet, that can easily be removed if soiled. [1865–70; DRAW + SHEET[1]]

draw′ shot′, *Billiards, Pool.* a stroke that imparts a backward spin to the cue ball, causing it to roll back after striking the object ball. Cf. **follow shot** (def. 2). [1895–1900]

draw′ slide′, *Photog.* See **dark slide** (def. 1).

draw·string (drô′string′), *n.* a string or cord that tightens or closes an opening, as of a bag, clothing, or the like, when one or both ends are pulled. Also, **draw′string′.** [1825–35; DRAW + STRING]

draw′ ta′ble, a table having one or more sliding leaves that may be drawn out as an extension. Also called **draw-out table, draw′-top ta′ble** (drô′top′). [1900–05]

draw′ top′, *Furniture.* a tabletop that can be extended by drawing out and raising leaves suspended from either end. [1900–05]

draw·tube (drô′to͞ob′, -tyo͞ob′), *n.* a tube sliding within another tube, as the tube carrying the eyepiece in a microscope. [1890–95; DRAW + TUBE]

draw′ weight′, the measured force, in foot-pounds, stored by an archery bow when fully drawn.

dray (drā), *n.* **1.** a low, strong cart without fixed sides, for carrying heavy loads. **2.** a sledge or sled. **3.** any vehicle, as a truck, used to haul goods, esp. one used to carry heavy loads. —*v.t.* **4.** to convey on a dray. —*v.i.* **5.** to drive or operate a dray, esp. as an occupation. **6.** to convey goods by dray, esp. locally or for short distances. [1325–75; ME *draye* sledge; cf. OE *draeg-* (in *drægnet* dragnet), akin to *dragan* to DRAW]

dray·age (drā′ij), *n.* **1.** conveyance by dray. **2.** a charge made for it. [1785–95, *Amer.*; DRAY + -AGE]

dray′ horse′, a draft horse used for pulling a dray.

dray·ing (drā′ing), *n.* the business, occupation, or activities of driving a dray. [1855–60; DRAY + -ING[1]]

dray·man (drā′mən), *n., pl.* **-men.** a person who drives a dray. [1575–85; DRAY + MAN[1]]

Dray·ton (drāt′n), *n.* **1. Michael,** 1563–1631, English poet. **2. William Henry,** 1742–1779, American member of Continental Congress, 1778–79.

drch., drachma; drachmas. Also, **dr.**

D.R.E., **1.** Director of Religious Education. **2.** Doctor of Religious Education.

dread (dred), *v.t.* **1.** to fear greatly; be in extreme apprehension of: *to dread death.* **2.** to be reluctant to do, meet, or experience: *I dread going to big parties.* **3.** *Archaic.* to hold in respectful awe. —*v.i.* **4.** to be in great fear. —*n.* **5.** terror or apprehension as to something in the future; great fear. **6.** a person or thing dreaded. **7.** *Archaic.* deep awe or reverence. —*adj.* **8.** greatly feared; frightful; terrible. **9.** held in awe or reverential fear. [1125–75; ME *dreden* (v.), OE *drǣdan,* aph. var. of *adrǣdan, ondrǣdan;* c. OHG *intrātan* to fear] —**dread′a·ble,** *adj.* —**dread′ness,** *n.*
—**Syn.** **5.** See **fear.** **8.** dire, dreadful, horrible. —**Ant.** **1.** welcome.

dread·ful (dred′fəl), *adj.* **1.** causing great dread, fear, or terror; terrible: *a dreadful storm.* **2.** inspiring awe or reverence. **3.** extremely bad, unpleasant, or ugly: *dreadful cooking; a dreadful hat.* —*n. Brit.* **4.** See **penny dreadful.** **5.** a periodical given to highly sensational matter. [1175–1225; ME *dredful.* See DREAD, -FUL] —**dread′ful·ness,** *n.*
—**Syn.** **1.** frightful, dire.

dread·ful·ly (dred′fə lē), *adv.* **1.** in a dreadful way: *The pain has increased dreadfully.* **2.** very; extremely: *Sorry to be so dreadfully late.* [1275–1325; ME. See DREADFUL, -LY]

dread·locks (dred′loks′), *n.* (*used with a plural v.*) a hair style, esp. among Rastafarians, in which the hair is worn in long, ropelike locks. [1955–60; DREAD + LOCK[2] + -S[3]]

dread·nought (dred′nôt′), *n.* **1.** a type of battleship armed with heavy-caliber guns in turrets: so called from the British battleship *Dreadnought,* launched in 1906, the first of its type. **2.** an outer garment of heavy woolen cloth. **3.** a thick cloth with a long pile. Also, **dread′naught′.** [1800–10; DREAD + NOUGHT]

dream (drēm), *n., v.,* **dreamed** or **dreamt, dream·ing,** *adj.* —*n.* **1.** a succession of images, thoughts, or emotions passing through the mind during sleep. **2.** the sleeping state in which this occurs. **3.** an object seen in a dream. **4.** an involuntary vision occurring to a person when awake. **5.** a vision voluntarily indulged in while awake; daydream; reverie. **6.** an aspiration; goal; aim: *A trip to Europe is his dream.* **7.** a wild or vain fancy. **8.** something of an unreal beauty, charm, or excellence. —*v.i.* **9.** to have a dream. **10.** to indulge in daydreams or reveries: *He dreamed about vacation plans when he should have been working.* **11.** to think or conceive of something in a very remote way (usually fol. by *of*): *I wouldn't dream of asking them.* —*v.t.* **12.** to see or imagine in sleep or in a vision. **13.** to imagine as if in a dream; fancy; suppose. **14.** to pass or spend (time) in dreaming (often fol. by *away*): *to dream away the afternoon.* **15. dream up,** to form in the imagination; devise: *They dreamed up the most impossible plan.* —*adj.* **16.** most desirable; ideal: *a dream vacation.* [1200–50; ME *dreem,* OE *drēam* joy, mirth, gladness, c. OS *drōm* mirth, dream, ON *draumr,* OHG *troum* dream; modern sense first recorded in ME but presumably also current in OE, as in OS] —**dream′ful,** *adj.* —**dream′ful·ly,** *adv.* —**dream′ful·ness,** *n.* —**dream′ing·ly,** *adv.* —**dream′like′,** *adj.*
—**Syn.** **1.** DREAM, NIGHTMARE, and VISION refer to the kinds of mental images that form during sleep. DREAM is the general term for any such succession of images. A NIGHTMARE is a dream that brings fear or anxiety: *frightened by a nightmare.* VISION refers to a series of images of unusual vividness, clarity, order, and significance, sometimes seen in a dream.

dream′ anal′ysis, *Psychoanal.* the analysis of dreams as a means of gaining access to the unconscious mind, typically involving free association.

dream·boat (drēm′bōt′), *n. Slang.* **1.** a highly attractive or desirable person. **2.** anything considered as highly desirable of its kind: *His new car is a dreamboat.* [1935–40; DREAM + BOAT]

dream′ book′, a book, pamphlet, etc., that lists common dreams and purports to interpret them, esp. in regard to their meaning for the future. [1785–95]

dream·er (drē′mər), *n.* **1.** a person who dreams. **2.** a person who lives in a world of fantasy; one who is impractical and unrealistic. **3.** a person whose ideas or projects are considered audacious or highly speculative; visionary. [1250–1300; ME. See DREAM, ER[1]]

dream·land (drēm′land′), *n.* **1.** a pleasant, lovely land that exists only in dreams or the imagination; the region of reverie. **2.** a state of sleep. [1825–35; DREAM + LAND]

dream·less (drēm′lis), *adj.* undisturbed by dreams: *a sound and dreamless sleep.* [1595–1605; DREAM + -LESS] —**dream′less·ly,** *adv.* —**dream′less·ness,** *n.*

dream′ mer′chant, a person, as a moviemaker or advertiser, who panders to or seeks to develop the public's craving for luxury, romance, or escapism.

Dream′ of the Red′ Cham′ber, The, (Chinese, *Hung Lou Mêng* or *Hong Lou Meng*) an 18th-century Chinese novel by Ts'ao Hsüeh-ch'in, completed by Kao E, in 120 chapters.

dream·scape (drēm′skāp′), *n.* **1.** a dreamlike, often surrealistic scene. **2.** a painting depicting such a scene. [1965–70; DREAM + -SCAPE]

dreamt (dremt), *v.* a pt. and pp. of **dream.**

dream·time (drēm′tīm′), *n.* the ancient time of the creation of all things by sacred ancestors, whose spirits continue into the present, as conceived in the mythology of the Australian Aborigines. Also called **alcheringa, the dreaming.** [1905–10; DREAM + TIME]

dream′ vi′sion, a conventional device used in narrative verse, employed esp. by medieval poets, that presents a story as told by one who falls asleep and dreams the events of the poem: *Dante's* Divine Comedy *exemplifies the dream vision in its most developed form.* Also called **dream′ al′legory.** [1905–10]

dream·work (drēm′wûrk′), *n. Psychoanal.* the processes that cause the transformation of unconscious thoughts into the content of dreams, as displacement, distortion, condensation, and symbolism. Also, **dream′ work′.** [1910–15]

dream′ world′, the world of imagination or illusion rather than of objective reality. Also, **dream′world′.** [1810–20]

dream·y (drē′mē), *adj.,* **dream·i·er, dream·i·est.** **1.** of the nature of or characteristic of dreams; visionary. **2.** vague; dim. **3.** soothing; restful; quieting: *dreamy music.* **4.** given to daydreaming or reverie. **5.** abounding in dreams; characterized by or causing dreams. **6.** *Informal.* wonderful; marvelous: *He has a dreamy new convertible.* [1560–70; DREAM + -Y[1]] —**dream′i·ly,** *adv.* —**dream′i·ness,** *n.*

drear (drēr), *adj. Literary.* dreary. [1620–30; back formation from DREARY]

drear·y (drēr′ē), *adj.,* **drear·i·er, drear·i·est.** **1.** causing sadness or gloom. **2.** dull; boring. **3.** sorrowful; sad. [bef. 900; ME *drery,* OE *drēorig* gory, cruel, sad, equiv. to *drēor* gore + *-ig* -Y[1]; akin to ON *dreyrigr* bloody, G *traurig* sad] —**drear′i·ly,** *adv.* —**drear′i·ness,** *n.* —**drear′i·some,** *adj.*
—**Syn.** **1.** gloomy, dismal, drear, cheerless, depressing, comfortless. **2.** tedious, monotonous, wearisome, tiresome. —**Ant.** **1.** cheerful. **2.** interesting.

dreck (drek), *n. Slang.* **1.** excrement; dung. **2.** worthless trash; junk. Also, **drek.** [1920–25; < Yiddish *drek;* c. G *Dreck* filth; cf. OE *threax,* ON *threkkr* excrement]

dredge[1] (drej), *n., v.,* **dredged, dredg·ing.** —*n.* **1.** Also called **dredging machine.** any of various powerful machines for dredging up or removing earth, as from the bottom of a river, by means of a scoop, a series of buckets, a suction pipe, or the like. **2.** a barge on which such a machine is mounted. **3.** a dragnet or other contrivance for gathering material or objects from the bottom of a river, bay, etc. —*v.t.* **4.** to clear out with a dredge; remove sand, silt, mud, etc., from the bottom of. **5.** to take, catch, or gather with a dredge; obtain or remove by a dredge. —*v.i.* **6.** to use a dredge. **7. dredge up, a.** to unearth or bring to notice: *We dredged up some old toys from the bottom of the trunk.* **b.** to locate and reveal by painstaking investigation or search: *Biographers excel at dredging up little known facts.* [1425–75; late ME (Scots) *dreg-,* OE **drecg(e);* see DRAY, DRAW]

dredge[2] (drej), *v.t.,* **dredged, dredg·ing.** *Cookery.* to sprinkle or coat with some powdered substance, esp. flour. [1590–1600; v. use of *dredge* (now obs. or dial.) mixture of grains, late ME *dragge, dregge,* appar. to be identified with ME *drag(g)e, dragie* (disyllabic) sweetmeat, confection < AF *drag(g)é, dragee,* OF (see DRAGÉE); cf. similar dual sense of ML *dragētum, dragium*]

dredg·er[1] (drej′ər), *n.* **1.** dredge[1] (def. 1). **2.** a person who uses a dredge. [1500–10; DREDGE[1] + -ER[1]]

dredg·er[2] (drej′ər), *n.* a container with a perforated top for sprinkling flour, sugar, etc., on food for cooking. [1660–70; DREDGE[2] + -ER[1]]

dredg′ing machine′, dredge[1] (def. 1). [1820–30]

Dred′ Scott′ Deci′sion (dred). See under **Scott** (def. 2).

dree (drē), *adj., v.,* **dreed, dree·ing.** *Scot. and North Eng.* —*adj.* **1.** tedious; dreary. —*v.t.* **2.** to suffer; endure. Also, **dreegh** (drēKH), **dreigh, driech, driegh.** [bef. 1000; ME; OE *drēogan* to endure; c. Goth *driugan* to serve (in arms)]

dreg (dreg), *n.* **1. dregs,** the sediment of liquids; lees; grounds. **2.** Usually, **dregs.** the least valuable part of anything: *the dregs of society.* **3.** a small remnant; any small quantity. [1250–1300; ME < ON *dregg* yeast (pl. *dreggjar* dregs); c. OSw *dräg* dregs]

dreg·gy (dreg′ē), *adj.,* **-gi·er, -gi·est.** abounding in or like dregs; filthy; muddy. [1400–50; late ME. See DREG, -Y[1]] —**dreg′gi·ness,** *n.*

D region, the lowest region of the ionosphere, in which the D layer develops. [1925–30]

drei·del (drād′l), *n., pl.* **-dels, -del.** a four-sided top bearing the Hebrew letters *nun, gimel, he,* and *shin,* one on each side, used chiefly in a children's game traditionally played on the Jewish festival of Hanukkah. [1925–30; < Yiddish *dreydl,* equiv. to *drey(en)* to rotate, turn (< MHG *dræ(je)n, dræhen;* cf. G. *drehen*) + *-dl* n. suffix]

dreigh (drēKH), *adj., v.t. Scot. and North Eng.* dree. [var. of DRIEGH]

drei·kan·ter (drī′kän′tər), *n., pl.* **-ters, -ter.** a pebble or boulder having three faces formed by the action of windblown sand. [1900–05; < G, equiv. to *drei* THREE + *Kante* edge + *-er* -ER[1]]

Drei·ser (drī′sər, -zər), *n.* **Theodore,** 1871–1945, U.S. novelist.

drek (drek), *n.* dreck.

drench (drench), *v.t.* **1.** to wet thoroughly; soak. **2.** to saturate by immersion in a liquid; steep. **3.** to cover or fill completely; bathe: *trees drenched with sunlight.* **4.** *Vet. Med.* to administer a draft of medicine to (an animal), esp. by force: *to drench a horse.* **5.** *Archaic.* to cause to drink. —*n.* **6.** the act of drenching. **7.** something that drenches: *a drench of rain.* **8.** a preparation for drenching or steeping. **9.** a solution, esp. one of fermenting bran, for drenching hides or skins. **10.** a large drink or draft. **11.** a draft of medicine, esp. one administered to an animal by force. **12.** *Hort.* a mixture of pesticide and water applied to the soil surrounding a plant. [bef. 900; ME *drenchen,* OE *drencan,* causative of *drincan* to DRINK; c. D *drenken,* G *tränken* to water, give to drink] —**drench′er,** *n.* —**drench′ing·ly,** *adv.*
—**Syn. 1.** See **wet.**

Dren·the (dren′tə), *n.* a province in E Netherlands. 423,311; 1011 sq. mi. (2620 sq. km). Also, **Dren′te.**

Dres·den (drez′dən; *Ger.* drās′dən), *n.* the capital of Saxony in E Germany, on the Elbe River. 518,057.

Dres′den chi′na, porcelain ware produced at Meissen, Germany, near Dresden, after 1710. Also called **Dres′den por′celain, Dres′den ware′, Meissen porcelain.** [1725–35]

dress (dres), *n., adj., v.,* **dressed** or **drest, dress·ing.** —*n.* **1.** an outer garment for women and girls, consisting of bodice and skirt in one piece. **2.** clothing; apparel; garb: *The dress of the 18th century was colorful.* **3.** formal attire. **4.** a particular form of appearance; guise. **5.** outer covering, as the plumage of birds. —*adj.* **6.** of or for a dress or dresses. **7.** of or for a formal occasion. **8.** requiring formal dress. —*v.t.* **9.** to put clothing upon. **10.** to put formal or evening clothes on. **11.** to trim; ornament; adorn: *to dress a store window; to dress a Christmas tree.* **12.** to design clothing for or sell clothes to. **13.** to comb out and do up (hair). **14.** to cut up, trim, and remove the skin, feathers, viscera, etc., from (an animal, meat, fowl, or flesh of a fowl) for market or for cooking (often fol. by *out* when referring to a large animal): *We dressed three chickens for the dinner. He dressed out the deer when he got back to camp.* **15.** to prepare (skins, fabrics, timber, stone, ore, etc.) by special processes. **16.** to apply medication or a dressing to (a wound or sore). **17.** to make straight; bring (troops) into line: *to dress ranks.* **18.** to make (stone, wood, or other building material) smooth. **19.** to cultivate (land, fields, etc.). **20.** *Theat.* to arrange (a stage) by effective placement of properties, scenery, actors, etc. **21.** to ornament (a vessel) with ensigns, house flags, code flags, etc.: *The bark was dressed with masthead flags only.* **22.** *Angling.* **a.** to prepare or bait (a fishhook) for use. **b.** to prepare (bait, esp. an artificial fly) for use. **23.** *Print.* to fit (furniture) around and between pages in a chase prior to locking it up. **24.** to supply with accessories, optional features, etc.: *to have one's new car fully dressed.* —*v.i.* **25.** to clothe or attire oneself; put on one's clothes: *Wake up and dress, now!* **26.** to put on or wear formal or fancy clothes: *to dress for dinner.* **27.** to come into line, as troops. **28.** to align oneself with the next soldier, marcher, dancer, etc., in line. **29. dress down, a.** to reprimand; scold. **b.** to thrash; beat. **c.** to dress informally or less formally: *to dress down for the shipboard luau.* **30. dress ship, a.** to decorate a ship by hoisting lines of flags running its full length. **b.** *U.S. Navy.* to display the national ensigns at each masthead and a larger ensign on the flagstaff. **31. dress up, a.** to put on one's best or fanciest clothing; dress relatively formally: *They were dressed up for the Easter parade.* **b.** to dress in costume or in another person's clothes: *to dress up in Victorian clothing; to dress up as Marie Antoinette.* **c.** to embellish or disguise, esp. in order to make more appealing or acceptable: *to dress up the facts with colorful details.* [1275–1325; ME *dressen* < AF *dresser, dresc(i)er,* to arrange, prepare, OF *drecier* < VL **dīrēctiāre,* deriv. of L *dīrēctus* DIRECT; n. use of v. in sense "attire" from ca. 1600]
—**Syn. 1.** frock. DRESS, COSTUME, GOWN refer to garments for women. DRESS is the general term for a garment: *a black dress.* COSTUME is used of the style of dress appropriate to some occasion, purpose, period, or character, esp. as used on the stage, at balls, at court, or the like, and may apply to men's garments as well: *an 18th-century costume.* GOWN is usually applied to a dress more expensive and elegant than the ordinary, usually long, to be worn on a special occasion: *a wedding gown.* **2.** raiment, attire, clothes, habit, garments, vestments, habiliments. **9.** clothe, robe, garb.

dres·sage (drə säzh′; *Fr.* dʀe sazh′), *n.* **1.** See ***haute école*** (def. 1). **2.** the art or method of training a horse in obedience and in precision of movement. [1935–40; < F, equiv. to *dress(er)* to DRESS + *-age* -AGE]

dress′ cir′cle, a circular or curving division of seats in a theater, opera house, etc., usually the first gallery, originally set apart for spectators in evening dress. [1815–25]

dress′ coat′. See **tail coat.** [1760–70] —**dress′-coat′ed,** *adj.*

dress′ code′, a set of rules specifying the garb or type of clothing to be worn by a group or by people under specific circumstances: *a military dress code; The restaurant's dress code requires men to wear jackets and ties at dinner.*

dress·er[1] (dres′ər), *n.* **1.** a person who dresses. **2.** a person employed to dress actors, care for costumes, etc., at a theater, television studio, or the like. **3.** *Chiefly Brit.* a surgeon's assistant. **4.** a person who dresses in a particular manner, as specified: *a fancy dresser; a careful and distinctive dresser.* **5.** any of several tools or devices used in dressing materials. **6.** *Metalworking.* **a.** a block, fitting into an anvil, on which pieces are forged. **b.** a mallet for shaping sheet metal. **7.** a tool for truing the surfaces of grinding wheels. [1400–50; late ME: guide. See DRESS, -ER[1]]

dress·er[2] (dres′ər), *n.* **1.** a dressing table or bureau. **2.** a sideboard or set of shelves for dishes and cooking utensils. **3.** *Obs.* a table or sideboard on which food is dressed for serving. [1375–1425; ME *dresso(u)r* sideboard < AF; MF *dresseur,* OF *dreceor(e),* equiv. to *dreci(er)* to DRESS + *-ore* -ORY[2] (F *dressoir*)]

dress′er set′, a set of toilet articles, as comb, brush, mirror, etc., usually of matching design, for arrangement and use on a dresser or vanity. [1930–35]

dress′ goods′, cloth or material for dresses. [1870–75, *Amer.*]

dress·ing (dres′ing), *n.* **1.** the act of a person or thing that dresses. **2.** a sauce for food: *salad dressing.* **3.** stuffing for a fowl: *turkey dressing.* **4.** material used to dress or cover a wound. **5.** manure, compost, or other fertilizers. **6.** the ornamental detail of a building, esp. that around openings. [1400–50; late ME; see DRESS, -ING[1]]

dress′ing case′, a small piece of luggage for carrying toilet articles, medicine, etc. [1780–90]

dress·ing-down (dres′ing doun′), *n.* a severe reprimand; scolding. [1860–65, *Amer.*; n. use (with -ING[1]) of v. phrase *dress down*]

dress′ing glass′, a small, adjustable mirror designed to stand on a dressing table. [1705–15]

dress′ing gown′, a tailored robe worn for lounging or for grooming, applying makeup, etc. [1770–80]

dress′ing room′, a room for use in getting dressed, esp. one for performers backstage in a theater, television studio, etc. [1665–75]

dress′ing sack′, a woman's dressing gown. [1860–65, *Amer.*]

dress′ing sta′tion, *Mil.* a post or center that gives first aid to the wounded, located near a combat area. [1890–95]

dress′ing ta′ble, a table or stand, usually surmounted by a mirror, in front of which a person sits while dressing, applying makeup, etc. [1790–1800]

Dress·ler (dres′lər), *n.* **Marie** (*Leila Koerber*), 1869–1934, U.S. actress, born in Canada.

dress·mak·er (dres′mā′kər), *n.* **1.** a person whose occupation is the making or alteration of women's dresses, coats, etc. —*adj.* **2.** (of women's clothing) having soft lines or elaborate detail. Cf. **man-tailored, tailored.** [1795–1805; DRESS + MAKER] —**dress′mak′·ing,** *n.*

dres·soir (dʀes waʀ′), *n., pl.* **dres·soirs** (dʀes waʀ′). *Fr. Furniture.* a cabinet of the 18th century, having a number of shallow shelves for dishes over a base with drawers and closed cupboards. [< F; see DRESSER[2]]

dress′ rehears′al, a rehearsal of a play or other performance in costume and with scenery, properties, and lights arranged and operated as for a performance: often the final rehearsal. [1820–30]

dress′ shield′, a fabric or plastic pad for attaching to the inside of the underarm of a woman's garment to protect the garment from being soiled by perspiration. Also called **shield.** [1880–85]

dress′ shirt′, **1.** a man's shirt worn for formal or semiformal evening dress, usually having French cuffs and a stiff or pleated front to be fastened with studs. **2.** a man's shirt, buttoning down the front and typically having long sleeves with barrel or French cuffs, and a soft or starched collar, worn with a necktie. Cf. **sport shirt.** [1890–95]

dress′ suit′, a man's suit for formal evening dress, with tail coat and open-front waistcoat. [1800–10]

dress′ u′niform, **1.** *U.S. Air Force.* a uniform consisting of the coat and trousers of the service uniform, with a white shirt and black bow tie, worn for formal occasions. **2.** *U.S. Army.* a blue uniform worn for formal occasions. **3.** *U.S. Navy.* a dark blue uniform worn in cool seasons or climates. [1895–1900]

dress-up (dres′up′), *adj.* **1.** being an occasion, situation, etc., for which one must be somewhat formally well-dressed: *the first dress-up dance of the season.* —*n.* **2.** *Informal.* Usually, **dress-ups. a.** a person's best clothes: *Wear your dress-ups for the reception.* **b.** accessories or other added features: *a car with custom dress-ups.* [1665–75; n., adj. use of v. phrase *dress up*]

dress·y (dres′ē), *adj.,* **dress·i·er, dress·i·est. 1.** appropriate to somewhat formal occasions: *an outfit that's a little too dressy for office wear.* **2.** showy in dress; stylish: *a rather dressy reception.* [1760–70; DRESS + -Y[1]] —**dress′i·ly,** *adv.* —**dress′i·ness,** *n.*

drest (drest), *v. Obs.* a pt. and pp. of **dress.**

drew (dro͞o), *v.* pt. of **draw.**

Drew (dro͞o), *n.* **1. Charles Richard,** 1904–50, U.S. physician: developer of blood-bank technique. **2. John,** 1827–62, U.S. actor, born in Ireland. **3.** his son, **John,** 1853–1927, U.S. actor. **4.** a male given name: from a Germanic word meaning "trusty."

Drey·fus (drā′fəs, drī′-; *Fr.* dʀā fys′), *n.* **Al·fred** (al′frid; *Fr.* al fʀed′), 1859–1935, French army officer of Jewish descent: convicted of treason 1894, 1899; acquitted 1906.

Drey·fu·sard (drī′fə särd′, -zärd′, drā′-; drī′fə särd′, -zärd′, drā′-), *n.* a defender or supporter of Alfred Dreyfus. [1895–1900; DREYFUS + -ARD]

drib (drib), *n.* a small or minute quantity; bit. [1720–30; back formation from DRIBLET]

drib·ble (drib′əl), *v.,* **-bled, -bling,** *n.* —*v.i.* **1.** to fall or flow in drops or small quantities; trickle. **2.** to drivel; slaver. **3.** *Sports.* to advance a ball or puck by bouncing it or giving it a series of short kicks or pushes. —*v.t.* **4.** to let fall in drops. **5.** *Sports.* **a.** *Basketball.* to bounce (the ball) as in advancing or keeping control of it. **b.** (esp. in ice hockey and soccer) to move (the ball or puck) along by a rapid succession of short kicks or pushes. —*n.* **6.** a small trickling stream or a drop. **7.** a small quantity of anything: *a dribble of revenue.* **8.** *Sports.* an act or instance of dribbling a ball or puck. **9.** *Scot.* a drizzle; a light rain. [1555–65; freq. of obs. *drib* (v.), prob. var. of DRIP] —**drib′bler,** *n.*

drib·let (drib′lit), *n.* **1.** a small portion or part. **2.** a small or petty sum. Also, **drib′blet.** [1590–1600; obs. *drib* (v.) (see DRIBBLE) + -LET]

dribs′ and drabs′, small and usually irregular amounts: *He repaid the loan in dribs and drabs.*

driech (drēкн), *adj., v.t. Scot. and North Eng.* dree. [var. of DRIEGH]

dried (drīd), *v.* pt. and pp. of **dry.**

dried′-fruit′ bee′tle (drīd′fro͞ot′), a small beetle, *Carpophilus hemipterus,* of worldwide distribution, that infests ripe, dried, and fermenting fruits, esp. figs and dates. [1915–20]

dried′ milk′. See **dry milk.**

dried-up (drīd′up′), *adj.* **1.** depleted of water or moisture; gone dry: *a dried-up water hole.* **2.** shriveled with age; wizened: *a dried-up old mule skinner.* [1810–20]

driegh (drēкн), *adj., v.t. Scot. and North Eng.* dree. [bef. 1150; ME *dregh,* OE *gedrēog* patient, serious (of persons), tame (of animals); c. ON *drjūgr* substantial, lasting, ample; akin to DREE]

dri·er[1] (drī′ər), *n.* **1.** a person or thing that dries. **2.** any substance added to paints, varnishes, printing inks, etc., to make them dry quickly. **3.** dryer (def. 1). [1300–50; ME *dreyere* (as surname). See DRY, -ER[1]]

dri·er[2] (drī′ər), *adj.* comparative of **dry.**

dries (drīz), *n.* a pl. of **dry.**

dri·est (drī′ist), *adj.* superlative of **dry.**

drift (drift), *n.* **1.** a driving movement or force; impulse; impetus; pressure. **2.** *Navig.* (of a ship) the component of the movement that is due to the force of wind and currents. **3.** *Oceanog.* a broad, shallow ocean current that advances at the rate of 10 to 15 mi. (16 to 24 km) a day. **4.** *Naut.* **a.** the flow or the speed in knots of an ocean current. **b.** the distance between the end of a rope and the part in use. **c.** the distance between two blocks in a tackle. **d.** the difference in diameter between two parts, one of which fits within the other, as a mast and its mast hoops, or a treenail and its hole. **5.** *Aeron.* the deviation of an aircraft from a set course due to cross winds. **6.** the course along which something moves; tendency; aim: *The drift of political events after the war was toward chaos.* **7.** a meaning; intent; purport: *the drift of a statement.* **8.** something driven, as animals, rain, etc. **9.** a heap of any matter driven together. **10.** a snowdrift. **11.** *Geol.* See **glacial drift. 12.** the state or process of being driven. **13.** overbearing power or influence. **14.** *Mil.* a tool used in charging an ordnance piece. **15.** *Electronics.* **a.** a gradual change in some operating characteristic of a circuit, tube, or other electronic device, either during a brief period as an effect of warming up or during a long period as an effect of continued use. **b.** the movement of charge carriers in a semiconductor due to the influence of an applied voltage. **16.** *Ling.* gradual change in the structure of a language. **17.** *Mach.* **a.** Also called **driftpin.** a round, tapering piece of steel for enlarging holes in metal, or for bringing holes in line to receive rivets or bolts. **b.** a flat, tapered piece of steel used to drive tools with tapered shanks, as drill bits, from their holders. **18.** *Civ. Engin.* a secondary tunnel between two main tunnels or shafts. **19.** *Mining.* an approximately horizontal passageway in underground mining. **20.** *Physics.* the movement of charged particles under the influence of an electric field. **21.** *Aerospace.* the gradual deviation of a rocket or guided missile from its intended trajectory. **22.** *Mech.* displacement of the gimbals of a gyroscope due to friction on bearings, unbalance of the gyroscope's mass or other imperfections. **23.** the thrust of an arched structure. **24.** *Dentistry.* a shift of the teeth from their normal position in the dental arch. **25.** *Western U.S.* a flock of animals or birds.
—*v.i.* **26.** to be carried along by currents of water or air, or by the force of circumstances. **27.** to wander aimlessly: *He drifts from town to town.* **28.** to be driven into heaps, as by the wind: *drifting sand.* **29.** to deviate or vary from a set course or adjustment.
—*v.t.* **30.** to carry along: *The current drifted the boat to sea.* **31.** to drive into heaps: *The wind drifted the snow.* **32.** *Mach.* **a.** to enlarge (a punched or drilled hole) with a drift. **b.** to align or straighten (holes, esp. rivet holes) with a drift. [1250–1300; ME *drift,* n. deriv. of OE *drīfan* to DRIVE; c. D *drift* herd, flock, G *Trift* herd, pasturage, road to pasture] —**drift′ing·ly,** *adv.* —**drift′·less,** *adj.* —**drift′less·ness,** *n.*
—**Syn. 7.** tenor. See **tendency.**

drift·age (drif′tij), *n.* **1.** the action or an amount of drifting. **2.** drifted matter. **3.** *Navig.* the amount of drift away from a set course as a result of wind and currents. **4.** windage. [1760–70; DRIFT + -AGE]

drift′ an′chor, a sea anchor or drag. [1870–75]

drift′ an′gle, *Naut.* the angle made by the path of a drifting vessel with its heading. [1880–85]

drift·bolt (drift′bōlt′), *n.* **1.** Also called **driftpin.** a spike having a round shank and used for fastening heavy timbers together. —*v.t.* **2.** to fasten (timbers) together with a driftbolt. [1865–70; DRIFT + BOLT[1]]

drift·er (drif′tər), *n.* **1.** a person or thing that drifts. **2.** a person who goes from place to place, job to job, etc., remaining in each for a short period, esp. a hobo. **3.** Also called **drift′ boat′.** a boat used in fishing with a drift net. [1860–65; DRIFT + -ER[1]]

CONCISE ETYMOLOGY KEY: <, descended or borrowed from; >, whence; b., blend of, blended; c., cognate with; cf., compare; deriv., derivative; equiv., equivalent; imit., imitative; obl., oblique; r., replacing; s., stem; sp., spelling, spelled; resp., respelling, respelled; trans., translation; ?, origin unknown; *, unattested; ‡, probably earlier than. See the full key inside the front cover.

drift•fish (drift′fish′), *n., pl.* (*esp. collectively*) **-fish,** (*esp. referring to two or more kinds or species*) **-fish•es.** any of several butterfishes, esp. of the genus *Psenes,* inhabiting tropical waters. [1860–65; DRIFT + FISH]

drift′ ice′, detached floating ice in masses that drift with the wind or ocean currents, as in the polar seas. [1590–1600]

drift′ in′dicator, *Aeron.* an instrument that indicates the amount of drift of an aircraft. Also called **drift′ me′ter, drift′ sight′.** [1915–20]

Drift′ing Cloud′, The, (Japanese, *Uki Gumo*) a novel (1887–89) by Shimei Futabatei. Also called ***The Floating Cloud.***

drift′ lead′ (led), *Naut.* a lead indicating, by the angle its line makes with the perpendicular, the movement of a supposedly stationary ship or the movement of water past a stationary ship.

drift′less ar′ea, a tract of land that was once surrounded but never covered by a continental glacier, consequently having no glacial deposits.

drift′ mine′, **1.** a mine the opening of which is dug into an outcrop of coal or ore. **2.** an underground placer mine. [1885–90, *Amer.*]

drift′ net′, a fishing net supported upright in the water by floats attached along the upper edge and sinkers along the lower, so as to be carried with the current or tide. [1840–50]

drift′ net′ter, a person who uses a drift net in fishing. [1885–90]

drift•pin (drift′pin′), *n.* **1.** driftbolt (def. 1). **2.** drift (def. 17a). [1870–75; DRIFT + PIN]

drift′ tube′, *Radio.* a conducting enclosure, usually cylindrical, held at a constant potential so that electrons or charged particles within will experience no force, and therefore no change in velocity. Cf. **Klystron** (def. 1).

drift•wood (drift′wo͝od′), *n.* **1.** wood floating on a body of water or cast ashore by it. **2.** such wood adapted for use in interior decoration. —*adj.* **3.** of, pertaining to, or made of driftwood: *a driftwood lamp.* [1605–15; DRIFT + WOOD[1]]

drift•y (drif′tē), *adj.,* **drift•i•er, drift•i•est.** of the nature of or characterized by drifts. [1565–75; DRIFT + -Y[1]]

drill[1] (dril), *n.* **1.** *Mach., Building Trades.* **a.** a shaftlike tool with two or more cutting edges for making holes in firm materials, esp. by rotation. **b.** a tool, esp. a hand tool, for holding and operating such a tool. **2.** *Mil.* **a.** training in formal marching or other precise military or naval movements. **b.** an exercise in such training: *gun drill.* **3.** any strict, methodical, repetitive, or mechanical training, instruction, or exercise: *a spelling drill.* **4.** the correct or customary manner of proceeding. **5.** a gastropod, *Urosalpinx cinera,* that bores holes in shellfish, as oysters. —*v.t.* **6.** to pierce or bore a hole in (something). **7.** to make (a hole) by boring. **8.** *Mil.* to instruct and exercise in formation marching and movement, in the carrying of arms during formal marching, and in the formal handling of arms for ceremonies and guard work. **9.** to impart (knowledge) by strict training, discipline, or repetition. —*v.i.* **10.** to pierce or bore something with or as with a drill. **11.** to go through exercise in military or other training. [1605–15; < D *dril* (n.), *drillen* (v.)] —**drill′a•ble,** *adj.* —**drill′a•bil′i•ty,** *n.* —**drill′er,** *n.*
—**Syn. 3.** See **exercise.**

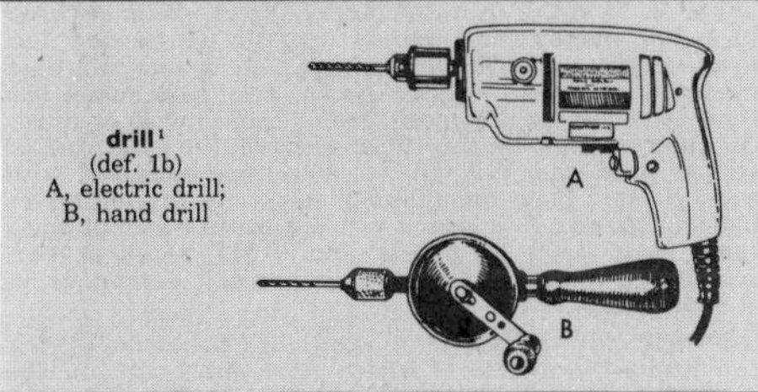

drill[1] (def. 1b) A, electric drill; B, hand drill

drill[2] (dril), *n.* **1.** a small furrow made in the soil in which to sow seeds. **2.** a row of seeds or plants thus sown. **3.** a machine for sowing in rows and for covering the seeds when sown. —*v.t.* **4.** to sow (seed) in drills. **5.** to sow or plant (soil, a plot of ground, etc.) in drills. —*v.i.* **6.** to sow seed in drills. [1720–30; cf. *drill* rill, G *Rille* furrow, *rillen* to groove] —**drill′er,** *n.*

drill[3] (dril), *n.* a strong, twilled cotton fabric. [1735–45; short for DRILLING[2]]

drill[4] (dril), *n.* a large, baboonlike monkey, *Mandrillus leucophaeus,* of western Africa, similar to the related mandrill but smaller and less brightly colored: now endangered. [1635–45; of obscure orig.; cf. MANDRILL]

drill′ bit′, bit[1] (defs. 1a, b).

drill′ chuck′, a chuck for holding a drill bit. [1870–75]

drill′ corps′. See **drill team.** [1955–60]

drill•ing[1] (dril′ing), *n.* the act of a person or thing that drills. [1615–25; DRILL[1] + -ING[1]]

drill•ing[2] (dril′ing), *n.* drill[3]. [1630–40; alter. of G *Drillich,* itself alter. of L *trilix* triple-twilled (G *dri-* three- r. L *tri-*)]

drill′ing mud′, a water-based or oil-based suspension of clays pumped into an oil well during drilling in order to seal off porous rock layers, equalize the pressure, cool the bit, and flush out the cuttings. Also called **drill′ing flu′id.**

drill•mas•ter (dril′mas′tər, -mä′stər), *n.* **1.** a person who trains others in something, esp. routinely or mechanically. **2.** *Mil.* a person who instructs in marching drill. [1865–70; DRILL[1] + MASTER]

drill′ pipe′, (in oil-well drilling or the like) any of several coupled tubes for rotating the bit and supplying drilling mud.

drill′ press′, a drilling machine having a single vertical spindle. [1860–65, *Amer.*]

drill′ rig′, rig[1] (def. 9). Also called **drill′ing rig′.** [1910–15, *Amer.*]

drill•ship (dril′ship′), *n.* a ship equipped with a drill rig and engaged in offshore oil and gas exploration, oceanographic research, etc. [1860–65; DRILL[1] +SHIP]

drill•stock (dril′stok′), *n.* a device for holding a drill. [1770–80; DRILL[1] + STOCK]

drill′ string′, (on a drill rig) the assemblage of drill pipes that link the drill bit to the mechanism that imparts rotary or reciprocating motion. [1695–1705]

drill′ team′, a group trained, esp. for exhibition purposes, in precision marching, the manual of arms, etc. Also called **drill corps.** [1925–30]

drill′ tow′er, a structure, usually of concrete and steel, that resembles a building and is used by firefighters for practicing and improving firefighting techniques.

dri•ly (drī′lē), *adv.* dryly.

Drin (drēn), *n.* a river in S Europe, flowing generally NW from SW Macedonia through N Albania into the Adriatic. 180 mi. (290 km) long.

Dri•na (drē′nə, -nä), *n.* a river in S Europe, flowing N along part of the border between Serbia and Bosnia and Herzegovina to the Sava River. 285 mi. (459 km) long.

D-ring (dē′ring′), *n.* a D-shaped, usually metal ring of various sizes, used on clothing or other articles as a closure, a means of securing straps or objects, or a decoration. Also, **D ring.**

drink (dringk), *v.,* **drank** or (*Nonstandard*) **drunk, drunk** or, often, **drank, drink•ing;** *n.* —*v.i.* **1.** to take water or other liquid into the mouth and swallow it; imbibe. **2.** to imbibe alcoholic drinks, esp. habitually or to excess; tipple: *He never drinks. They won't find jobs until they stop drinking.* **3.** to show one's respect, affection, or hopes with regard to a person, thing, or event by ceremoniously taking a swallow of wine or some other drink (often fol. by *to*): *They drank to his victory.* **4.** to be savored or enjoyed by drinking: *a wine that will drink deliciously for many years.* —*v.t.* **5.** to take (a liquid) into the mouth and swallow. **6.** to take in (a liquid) in any manner; absorb. **7.** to take in through the senses, esp. with eagerness and pleasure (often fol. by *in*): *He drank in the beauty of the scene.* **8.** to swallow the contents of (a cup, glass, etc.). **9.** to propose or participate in a toast to (a person, thing, or event): *to drink one's health.* —*n.* **10.** any liquid that is swallowed to quench thirst, for nourishment, etc.; beverage. **11.** liquor; alcohol. **12.** excessive indulgence in alcohol: *Drink was his downfall.* **13.** a swallow or draft of liquid; potion: *She took a drink of water before she spoke.* **14.** *Informal.* a large body of water, as a lake, ocean, river, etc. (usually prec. by *the*): *His teammates threw him in the drink.* [bef. 900; ME *drinken,* OE *drincan;* c. D *drinken,* G *trinken,* Goth *drinkan,* ON *drekka*]
—**Syn. 2.** tope. **5.** quaff. DRINK, IMBIBE, SIP refer to swallowing liquids. DRINK is the general word: *to drink coffee.* IMBIBE is formal in reference to actual drinking; it is used more often in the sense to absorb: *to imbibe culture.* SIP implies drinking little by little: *to sip a cup of broth.* **9.** toast.
—**Usage.** As with many verbs of the pattern *sing, sang, sung* and *ring, rang, rung,* there is some confusion about the forms for the past tense and past participle of DRINK. The historical reason for this confusion is that originally verbs of this class in Old English had a past-tense singular form in *a* but a past-tense plural form in *u.* Generally the form in *a* has leveled out to become the standard past-tense form: *We drank our coffee.* However, the past-tense form in *u,* though considered nonstandard, occurs often in speech: *We drunk our coffee.*
The standard and most frequent form of the past participle of DRINK in both speech and writing is DRUNK: *Who has drunk all the milk?* However, perhaps because of the association of DRUNK with intoxication, DRANK is widely used as a past participle in speech by educated persons and must be considered an alternate standard form: *I'd drank my fill of scenery.* See also **drunk.**

drink•a•ble (dring′kə bəl), *adj.* suitable for drinking. [1605–15; DRINK + -ABLE] —**drink′a•bil′i•ty, drink′a•ble•ness,** *n.* —**drink′a•bly,** *adv.*

drink•er (dring′kər), *n.* **1.** a person who drinks. **2.** a person who drinks alcohol habitually or to excess. [bef. 950; ME *drinkere,* OE *drincere.* See DRINK, -ER[1]]

drink•er•y (dring′kə rē), *n., pl.* **-er•ies.** barroom; tavern. [1830–40, *Amer.;* DRINK + -ERY]

drink•ing (dring′king), *adj.* **1.** suitable or safe to drink: *drinking water.* **2.** used in drinking: *a drinking glass.* **3.** addicted to or indulging excessively in alcohol: *Is he a drinking man?* **4.** of or pertaining to the act of drinking, esp. the drinking of alcohol: *a drinking companion.* —*n.* **5.** habitual and excessive consumption of alcohol: *His drinking caused him to lose his job.* [1125–75; ME; see DRINK, -ING[2], -ING[1]]

drink′ing foun′tain, a water fountain that ejects a jet of water for drinking without a cup. [1855–60]

drink′ing song′, a song of hearty character suitable for singing by a group engaged in convivial drinking. [1590–1600]

Drink•wa•ter (dringk′wô′tər, -wot′ər), *n.* **John,** 1882–1937, English poet, playwright, and critic.

drip (drip), *v.,* **dripped** or **dript, drip•ping,** *n.* —*v.i.* **1.** to let drops fall; shed drops: *This faucet drips.* **2.** to fall in drops, as a liquid. —*v.t.* **3.** to let fall in drops. —*n.* **4.** an act of dripping. **5.** liquid that drips. **6.** the sound made by falling drops: *the irritating drip of a faucet.* **7.** *Slang.* an unattractive, boring, or colorless person. **8.** (in house painting) the accumulation of solidified drops of paint at the bottom of a painted surface. **9.** *Archit., Building Trades.* any device, as a molding, for shedding rain water to keep it from running down a wall, falling onto the sill of an opening, etc. **10.** a pipe for draining off condensed steam from a radiator, heat exchanger, etc. **11.** *Med.* See **intravenous drip. 12.** *Slang.* maudlin sentimentality. [bef. 1000; ME *dryppe,* OE *dryppan;* cf. DROP]
—**Syn. 2.** trickle, dribble, leak, sprinkle, drizzle.

drip′ cap′, *Carpentry.* a molding over an opening for catching and shedding rain water.

drip′ cof′fee, 1. a beverage prepared in a vessel in which boiling water filters from a top compartment through the coffee into a pot below. **2.** See **drip grind.** [1880–85, *Amer.*]

drip-dry (*adj., n.* drip′drī′; *v.* drip′drī′, -drī′), *adj., v.,* **-dried, -dry•ing,** *n., pl.* **-dries.** —*adj.* **1.** wash-and-wear. —*v.i.* **2.** (of a cloth item) to dry into a desired form and shape when hung dripping wet after washing. —*v.t.* **3.** to hang (a cloth item) after washing while it is dripping wet and allow it to dry, esp. in anticipation of its assuming its desired form and shape during the drying process. —*n.* **4.** a garment or other cloth item that can be washed and drip-dried. [1950–55]

drip-feed (drip′fēd′), *n.* intravenous feeding. [1905–10, for earlier sense]

drip′ grind′, finely ground coffee beans, used in making drip coffee.

drip′ irriga′tion, a system of crop irrigation involving the controlled delivery of water directly to individual plants through a network of tubes or pipes. Also called **trickle irrigation.** [1970–75]

drip•less (drip′lis), *adj.* designed so that the substance, item, or its contents will not drip: *a dripless candle; a dripless pitcher.* [1885–90; DRIP (v.) + -LESS]

drip•page (drip′ij), *n.* **1.** a dripping, as of water from a faucet. **2.** an amount formed by dripping: *emptying the drippage from under the freezer.* [DRIP + -AGE]

drip′ paint′ing, a technique of abstract painting exemplified chiefly in the later works of Jackson Pollack and marked by the intricately executed dripping and pouring of the paint on a canvas placed on the floor. [1955–60]

drip′ pan′, 1. a pan for collecting liquid waste: *Put a drip pan under the crankcase.* **2.** See **dripping pan.**

drip•ping (drip′ing), *n.* **1.** the act of something that drips. **2.** Often, **drippings. a.** the liquid that drips. **b.** fat and juices exuded from meat in cooking, used for basting, for making gravy, or as a cooking fat. [1400–50; late ME; see DRIP, -ING[1]]

drip′ping pan′, a shallow metal pan used under roasting meat to receive the drippings. Also, **drip pan.** [1425–75]

drip•py (drip′ē), *adj.* **-pi•er, -pi•est. 1.** dripping or tending to drip: *a drippy faucet.* **2.** tending to be rainy, wet, or drizzly: *a hot, drippy country; drippy weather.* **3.** *Slang.* revoltingly sentimental; mawkish: *another drippy love story.* [1810–20; DRIP + -Y[1]]

drip•stone (drip′stōn′), *n.* **1.** *Archit.* a stone molding used as a drip. **2.** calcium carbonate occurring in the form of stalactites and stalagmites. [1785–95; DRIP + STONE]

dript (dript), *v.* a pt. and pp. of **drop.**

driv•a•bil•i•ty (drī′və bil′i tē), *n. Auto.* the degree of smoothness and steadiness of acceleration of an automotive vehicle: *The automatic transmission has been improved to give the new model better drivability.* Also, **drive′a•bil′i•ty.** [1970–75; DRIVE + -ABILITY]

driv•age (drī′vij), *n. Mining.* a horizontal or inclined heading or roadway in the process of construction. [DRIVE + -AGE]

drive (drīv), *v.,* **drove** or (*Archaic*) **drave, driv•en, driv•ing,** *n., adj.* —*v.t.* **1.** to send, expel, or otherwise cause to move by force or compulsion: *to drive away the flies; to drive back an attacking army; to drive a person to desperation.* **2.** to cause and guide the movement of (a vehicle, an animal, etc.): *to drive a car; to drive a mule.* **3.** to convey in a vehicle: *She drove them to the station.* **4.** to force to work or act: *He drove the workers until they collapsed.* **5.** to impel; constrain; urge; compel. **6.** to carry (business, an agreement, etc.) vigorously through: *He drove a hard bargain.* **7.** to keep (machinery) going. **8.** *Baseball.* **a.** to cause the advance of (a base runner) by a base hit or sacrifice fly: *He drove him home with a scratch single.* **b.** to cause (a run) to be scored by a base hit or sacrifice fly: *He drove in two runs.* **9.** *Golf.* to hit (a golf ball), esp. from the tee, as with a driver or driving iron: *She drove the ball within ten feet of the pin.* **10.** *Sports.* **a.** to hit or propel (a ball, puck, shuttlecock, etc.) very hard. **b.** to kick (a ball) with much force. **11.** *Hunting.* **a.** to chase (game). **b.** to search (a district) for game. **12.** to float (logs) down a river or stream. **13.** (in mining, construction, etc.) to excavate (a mine or tunnel heading).
—*v.i.* **14.** to cause and guide the movement of a vehicle or animal, esp. to operate an automobile. **15.** to go or travel in a driven vehicle: *He drives to work with me.* **16.** *Golf.* to hit a golf ball, esp. from the tee, as with a driver or driving iron: *He drove long and straight throughout the match.* **17.** to strive vigorously toward a goal or objective; to work, play, or try wholeheartedly and with determination. **18.** to go along before an impelling force; be impelled: *The ship drove before the wind.* **19.** to rush or dash violently. **20. drive at,** to attempt or intend to convey; allude to; suggest: *What are you driving at?* **21. let drive,** to aim a blow or missile at; attack: *He let drive at his pursuers.*
—*n.* **22.** the act of driving. **23.** a trip in a vehicle, esp. a short pleasure trip: *a Sunday drive in the country.* **24.** an impelling along, as of game, cattle, or floating logs, in a particular direction. **25.** the animals, logs, etc., thus

driven. **26.** *Psychol.* an inner urge that stimulates activity or inhibition; a basic or instinctive need: *the hunger drive; sex drive.* **27.** a vigorous onset or onward course toward a goal or objective: *the drive toward the goal line.* **28.** a strong military offensive. **29.** a united effort to accomplish some specific purpose, esp. to raise money, as for a charity. **30.** energy and initiative: *a person with great drive.* **31.** vigorous pressure or effort, as in business. **32.** a road for vehicles, esp. a scenic one, as in or along a park, or a short one, as an approach to a house. **33.** *Mach.* a driving mechanism, as of an automobile: *gear drive; chain drive.* **34.** *Auto.* the point or points of power application to the roadway: *front-wheel drive; four-wheel drive.* **35.** *Sports.* **a.** an act or instance of driving a ball, puck, shuttlecock, or the like. **b.** the flight of such a ball, puck, shuttlecock, or the like, that has been driven with much force. **36.** *Golf.* a shot, esp. with a driver or driving iron from the tee, that is intended to carry a great distance. **37.** a hunt in which game is driven toward stationary hunters. **38.** *Electronics.* excitation (def. 5).
—*adj.* **39.** noting or pertaining to a part of a machine or vehicle used for its propulsion. [bef. 900; ME *drīven,* OE *drīfan;* c. D *drijven,* ON *drīfa,* Goth *dreiban,* G *treiben*] —**driv′a•ble, drive′a•ble,** *adj.*
—**Syn. 1.** push, force. **2, 15.** DRIVE, RIDE are used interchangeably to mean traveling in an automobile or, formerly, in a horse-drawn vehicle. These two words are not synonyms in other connections. To DRIVE is to maneuver, guide, or steer the progress of a vehicle, animal, etc.: *to drive a bus, a horse.* To RIDE is to be carried about by an animal or be carried as a passenger in a vehicle: *to ride a horse, a train, a bus.* **30.** push; ambition, motivation.

drive•a•way (drīv′ə wā′), *n.* **1.** the delivery of a car to a buyer or to a specified destination by means of a hired driver. **2.** the action of moving forward in a vehicle from a stopped position: *How many seconds from ignition to driveaway?* [n. use of v. phrase *drive away*]

drive-by (drīv′bī′), *n., pl.* **-bys,** *adj.* —*n.* **1.** the action of driving by a specified locality, object, etc.: *a drive-by of Nelson's Monument.* —*adj.* **2.** consisting of or featuring a drive-by: *We boarded the sightseeing bus for a drive-by tour of the nation's capital.* [n., adj. use of v. phrase *drive by*]

drive′ fit′. See **press fit.**

drive-in (drīv′in′), *n.* **1.** a motion-picture theater, refreshment stand, bank, or other public facility designed to accommodate patrons in their automobiles. —*adj.* **2.** of, pertaining to, or characteristic of such an establishment: *Drive-in business far exceeded walk-in business.* [1925–30, *Amer.*; n., adj. use of v. phrase *drive in*]

driv•el (driv′əl), *n. v.,* **-eled, -el•ing** or (*esp. Brit.*) **-elled, -el•ling.** —*n.* **1.** saliva flowing from the mouth, or mucus from the nose; slaver. **2.** childish, silly, or meaningless talk or thinking; nonsense; twaddle. —*v.i.* **3.** to let saliva flow from the mouth or mucus from the nose; slaver. **4.** to talk childishly or idiotically. **5.** *Archaic.* to issue like spittle. —*v.t.* **6.** to utter childishly or idiotically. **7.** to waste foolishly. [bef. 1000; ME *dryvelen,* var. of *drevelen,* OE *dreflian;* akin to DRAFF] —**driv′el•er;** *esp. Brit.,* **driv′el•ler,** *n.* —**driv′el•ing•ly;** *esp. Brit.,* **driv′el•ling•ly,** *adv.*

drive•line (drīv′līn′), *n.* the components of the power train of an automotive vehicle that are between the transmission and the differential, and generally consisting of the drive shaft and universal joint. Cf. **drive train.** [1945–50; DRIVE + LINE[1]]

driv•en (driv′ən), *v.* **1.** pp. of **drive.** —*adj.* **2.** being under compulsion, as to succeed or excel: *a driven young man who was fiercely competitive.* —**driv′en•ness,** *n.*

driv•er (drī′vər), *n.* **1.** a person or thing that drives. **2.** a person who drives a vehicle; coachman, chauffeur, etc. **3.** a person who drives an animal or animals, as a drover or cowboy. **4.** Also called **number one wood.** *Golf.* a club with a wooden head whose face has almost no slope, for hitting long, low drives from the tee. **5.** *Mach.* **a.** a part that transmits force or motion. **b.** the member of a pair of connected pulleys, gears, etc., that is nearer to the power source. **6.** *Computers.* software or hardware that controls the interface between a computer and a peripheral device. **7.** *Railroads.* See **driving wheel** (def. 2). **8.** *Brit.* a locomotive engineer. **9.** *Audio.* **a.** the part of a loudspeaker that transforms the electrical signal into sound. **b.** the entire loudspeaker. **10.** *Naut.* **a.** a jib-headed spanker sail. **b.** a designation given to one of the masts abaft the mizzen on a sailing vessel having more than three masts, either the fifth or sixth from forward. Cf. **pusher** (def. 4), **spanker** (def. 1b). [1350–1400; ME *drivere.* See DRIVE, -ER[1]] —**driv′er•less,** *adj.*

driv′er ant′. See **army ant.** [1855–60]

driv′er ed′ (ed), *Informal.* See **driver education.** [by shortening]

driv′er educa′tion, a course of study, as for high-school students, that teaches the techniques of driving a vehicle, along with basic vehicle maintenance, safety precautions, and traffic regulations and laws.

driv′er's li′cense, a permit, as one issued by a state's motor vehicle bureau, that allows the holder to drive a motor vehicle on public roads. [1940–45]

driv′er's seat′, **1.** the seat from which a vehicle is operated. **2.** a position of power, dominance, control, or superiority: *After the election the Democrats were back in the driver's seat.* [1920–25]

drive′ screw′, a fastener with a helical thread of coarse pitch that can be driven into wood with a hammer and removed with a screwdriver. Also called **screw nail.** See illus. under **nail.** [1885–90]

drive′ shaft′, *Mach.* a shaft for imparting torque from a power source or prime mover to machinery. See diag. under **differential.** [1890–95]

drive-through (drīv′thro͞o′), *n.* **1.** the act of driving through a specified locality or place, esp. driving into a place of business, completing a transaction from one's car, and driving out: *a quick drive-through of Beverly Hills; The bank has outside tellers' windows to accept deposits by drive-through.* —*adj.* **2.** designed to accommodate or arranged for a drive-through: *a drive-through zoo; a drive-through car wash.* [1970–75; n., adj. use of v. phrase *drive through*]

drive′ time′. See **driving time.**

drive′ train′, the power train of an automotive vehicle consisting of all the components between the engine and driving wheels and including the clutch and axle, as well as the components of the driveline. Also, **drive′•train′.** [1950–55] —**drive′-train′,** *adj.*

drive-up (drīv′up′), *adj.* serving or accessible to customers who drive up in their cars: *a drive-up taco stand; a drive-up window at a bank.* [adj. use of v. phrase *drive up*]

drive•way (drīv′wā′), *n.* **1.** a road, esp. a private one, leading from a street or other thoroughfare to a building, house, garage, etc. **2.** any road for driving on. [1865–70, *Amer.*; DRIVE + WAY]

driv•ing (drī′ving), *adj.* **1.** demanding a high or unreasonable rate of work from subordinates. **2.** vigorously active; energetic: *a driving young executive.* **3.** having force and violence: *a driving storm.* **4.** relaying or transmitting power. **5.** used while operating a vehicle: *driving gloves.* [1250–1300; ME; see DRIVE, -ING[2]] —**driv′ing•ly,** *adv.*

driv′ing bar′rel, (in a weight-driven clock) the drum turned by the descent of the weight, which drives the clock mechanism.

driv′ing dog′, (on a lathe) a clamp securing a piece of work and engaging with a slot in a faceplate.

driv′ing i′ron, *Golf.* a club with a long shaft and an iron head the face of which has almost no slope, for hitting long, low drives. Also called **number one iron.** [1885–90]

driv′ing range′, *Golf.* a tract of land for practicing long golf shots, esp. drives, with clubs and balls available for rent from the management. [1945–50]

driv′ing sail′, *Naut.* a sail that, when filled, tends to force the hull of a vessel downward (opposed to *lifting sail*).

driv′ing time′, **1.** the time or estimated time to drive between two points or to one's destination. **2.** a period, as in early morning and late afternoon, when many people are driving to or from work and listening to car radios: *Many radio commercials are broadcast during driving time.* Also, **drive time.**

driv′ing wheel′, **1.** *Mach.* a main wheel that communicates motion to others. **2.** Also called **driver.** *Railroads.* one of the wheels of a locomotive that transmits the power of an engine or motor into tractive effort. [1830–40]

driz•zle (driz′əl), *v.,* **-zled, -zling,** *n.* —*v.i.* **1.** to rain gently and steadily in fine drops; sprinkle: *It drizzled throughout the night.* **2.** to fall in fine drops. —*v.t.* **3.** to rain or let fall in fine drops; sprinkle: *He drizzled honey over the fruit.* **4.** to pour in a fine stream: *Drizzle melted butter over the breadcrumb topping.* —*n.* **5.** a very light rain. **6.** *Meteorol.* precipitation consisting of numerous, minute droplets of water less than ¹⁄₅₀ in. (0.5 mm) in diameter. [1535–45; perh. back formation from *dryseling,* dissimilated var. of ME *drysning* fall (of dew); akin to OE *drēosan* to fall; c. OS *driosan,* Goth *driusan*] —**driz′zly,** *adv.*

Dr. Jekyll and Mr. Hyde, (*The Strange Case of Dr. Jekyll and Mr. Hyde*) a novel (1886) by Robert Louis Stevenson.

Drog•he•da (drô′i də), *n.* a seaport in the NE Republic of Ireland, near the mouth of the Boyne River: the town was captured by Cromwell in 1649 and its garrisons as well as many male inhabitants put to the sword. 23,173.

dro•gher (drō′gər), *n.* a freight barge of the West Indies, rigged as a cutter or schooner. [1775–85; < D *drog(h)er* ship for fishing and drying herring and mackerel, equiv. to *drog(en)* to DRY + *-er* -ER[1]]

drogue (drōg), *n.* **1.** a bucket or canvas bag used as a sea anchor. **2.** *Aeron.* **a.** a funnel-shaped device attached to the end of a hose on a tanker aircraft for connecting with the probe of another aircraft to be refueled in flight. **b.** See **drogue parachute** (def. 1). [1715–25; earlier *drug,* common dial. var. of DRAG]

drogue′ par′achute, **1.** Also called **drogue.** a small parachute that deploys first in order to pull a larger parachute from its pack. **2.** Also called **drag parachute.** a parachute used to slow a vehicle or aircraft. [1950–55]

droid (droid), *n. Informal.* android. [by shortening]

droit (droit; *Fr.* DRWA), *n., pl.* **droits** (droits; *Fr.* DRWA). **1.** a legal right or claim. **2. droits,** *Finance Rare.* customs duties. [1470–80; < F < LL *dirēctum* legal right, law (n. use of neut. of L *dirēctus* DIRECT)]

droit des gens (DRWA dā zhäN′), *pl.* ***droits des gens*** (DRWA dā zhäN′). *French.* law of nations; international law.

droit du sei•gneur (*Fr.* DRWA dʏ se nyœʀ′), the supposed right claimable by a feudal lord to have sexual relations with the bride of a vassal on her first night of marriage. [1815–25; < F: lit., right of the lord]

droi•tu•ral (droi′chər əl), *adj. Law.* pertaining to right of ownership as distinguished from right of possession. [1840–50; < F *droiture* equity, uprightness (see DROIT, -URE) + -AL[1]]

droke (drōk), *n. Canadian* (*chiefly Atlantic Provinces and Northwest Territories*). a valley with steeply sloping sides. [cf. dial. (W England) *droke* small watercourse, ditch, culvert; further relations unclear]

droll (drōl), *adj.,* **-er, -est,** *n., v.* —*adj.* **1.** amusing in an odd way; whimsically humorous; waggish. —*n.* **2.** a droll person; jester; wag. —*v.i.* **3.** *Archaic.* to jest; joke. [1615–25; < MF *drolle* pleasant rascal < MD *drol* a fat little man] —**droll′ness,** *n.* —**drol′ly,** *adv.*
—**Syn. 1.** diverting, odd, witty. See **amusing. 2, 3.** clown. —**Ant. 1.** serious.

droll•er•y (drō′lə rē), *n., pl.* **-er•ies. 1.** something whimsically amusing or funny. **2.** an oddly amusing story or jest. **3.** a droll quality or manner; whimsical humor. **4.** the action or behavior of a droll, waggish person; jesting. **5.** a comic picture. **6.** *Archaic.* a puppet show. [1590–1600; DROLL + -ERY; cf. F *drôlerie*]

Drôme (dʀōm), *n.* a department in SE France. 361,847; 2533 sq. mi. (6560 sq. km). *Cap.:* Valence.

-drome, a combining form meaning "running," "course," "racecourse" (*hippodrome*); on this model used to form words referring to other large structures (*airdrome*). [comb. form of Gk *drómos* DROMOS]

drom•e•dar•y (drom′i der′ē, drum′-), *n., pl.* **-dar•ies.** the single-humped camel, *Camelus dromedarius,* of Arabia and northern Africa. Cf. **Bactrian camel.** [1300–50; ME *dromedarie, -ary* (< AF) < LL *dromedārius* (*camēlus*) < Gk *dromad-* (s. of *dromás*) running + L *-ārius* -ARY]

dromedary, *Camelus dromedarius,* 6 ft. (1.8 m) high at shoulder; length 9½ ft. (2.9 m)

drom•ond (drom′ənd, drum′-), *n.* a large, fast-sailing ship of the Middle Ages. Also, **drom•on** (drom′ən, drum′-). [1300–50; ME *dromund* < AF *dromund, dromo(u)n* < LL *dromō,* s. *dromōn-* < Gk *drómōn* swift ship, deriv. of *drómos* a running]

drom•os (drom′əs, -os; drō′məs, -mos), *n., pl.* **drom•oi** (drom′oi, drō′moi). **1.** *Archaeol.* a passageway into an ancient subterranean tomb. **2.** a racetrack in ancient Greece. [1840–50; < Gk *drómos* a running, course, place for running]

-dromous, a combining form used to form adjectives corresponding to nouns ending in **-drome.** [-DROME + -OUS]

drone[1] (drōn), *n.* **1.** the male of the honeybee and other bees, stingless and making no honey. See illus. under **bee. 2.** a remote control mechanism, as a radio-controlled airplane or boat. **3.** a person who lives on the labor of others; parasitic loafer. **4.** a drudge. [bef. 1000; 1945–50 for def. 2; ME *drone, drane,* OE *dran, dron;* akin to OHG *treno,* G *Drohne*] —**dron′ish,** *adj.*

drone[2] (drōn), *v.,* **droned, dron•ing,** *n.* —*v.i.* **1.** to make a dull, continued, low, monotonous sound; hum; buzz. **2.** to speak in a monotonous tone. **3.** to proceed in a dull, monotonous manner (usually fol. by *on*): *The meeting droned on for hours.* —*v.t.* **4.** to say in a dull, monotonous tone. —*n.* **5.** *Music.* **a.** a continuous low tone produced by the bass pipes or bass strings of musical instruments. **b.** the pipes (esp. of the bagpipe) or strings producing this tone. **c.** a bagpipe equipped with such pipes. **6.** a monotonous low tone; humming or buzzing sound. **7.** a person who speaks in a monotonous tone. [1490–1500; see DRONE[1] and cf. ME *droun* to roar, Icel *drynja* to bellow, Goth *drunjus* noise] —**dron′er,** *n.* —**dron′ing•ly,** *adv.*

dron•go[1] (drong′gō), *n., pl.* **-gos.** any passerine bird of the family *Dicruridae,* of Africa, Asia, and Australia, the several species usually having black plumage and long, forked tails. [1835–45; < Malagasy]

dron•go[2] (drong′gō), *n., pl.* **-gos.** *Australian Slang.* a stupid or slow-witted person; simpleton. [1920–25; prob. to be identified with DRONGO[1], as a name for the Australian bird *Dicrurus bracteata;* though often popularly alleged to have originated from the name of an unsuccessful racehorse of the 1920's]

drool (dro͞ol), *v.i.* **1.** to water at the mouth, as in anticipation of food; salivate; drivel. **2.** to show excessive pleasure or anticipation of pleasure. **3.** to talk foolishly. —*n.* **4.** saliva running down from one's mouth; drivel. [1795–1805; var. of *driule,* itself var. of DRIVEL]

drool•y (dro͞o′lē), *adj.,* **drool•i•er, drool•i•est. 1.** drooling, tending to drool, or covered with drool. **2.** *Slang.* exceptionally pleasing. [DROOL + -Y[1]]

droop (dro͞op), *v.i.* **1.** to sag, sink, bend, or hang down, as from weakness, exhaustion, or lack of support. **2.** to fall into a state of physical weakness; flag; fail. **3.** to lose spirit or courage. **4.** to descend, as the sun; sink. —*v.t.* **5.** to let sink or drop: *an eagle drooping its wings.* —*n.* **6.** a sagging, sinking, bending, or hanging down, as from weakness, exhaustion, or lack of support. [1300–50; ME *drupen, drowpen* < ON *drūpa;* akin to DROP] —**droop′ing•ly,** *adv.*
—**Syn. 1.** flag, languish. **2.** weaken, decline, faint, wilt, wither, fade.

droop•y (dro͞o′pē), *adj.,* **droop•i•er, droop•i•est. 1.** hanging down; sagging. **2.** lacking in spirit or courage; disheartened; dejected. [1200–50; ME *drupi.* See DROOP, -Y[1]] —**droop′i•ness,** *n.*
—**Syn. 2.** dispirited, forlorn, despondent, discouraged, downhearted, downcast, doleful, subdued, depressed.

drop (drop), *n., v.,* **dropped** or **dropt, drop•ping.** —*n.* **1.** a small quantity of liquid that falls or is produced in a

more or less spherical mass; a liquid globule. **2.** the quantity of liquid contained in such a globule. **3.** a very small quantity of liquid: *I'll have a little more tea, just a drop.* **4.** a minute quantity of anything: *not even a drop of mercy.* **5.** Usually, **drops. a.** liquid medicine given in a dose or form of globules from a medicine dropper. **b.** a solution for dilating the pupils of the eyes, administered to the eyes in globules by a medicine dropper. **6.** a limited amount of an alcoholic beverage: *He occasionally takes a drop after dinner.* **7.** an act or instance of dropping; fall; descent. **8.** the distance or depth to which anything drops: *a ten-foot drop to the ground.* **9.** a steep slope: *a short drop to the lake.* **10.** a decline in amount, degree, quality, value, etc.: *a drop in prices.* **11.** a small, usually spherical, piece of candy; lozenge: *a lemon drop.* **12.** a central depository where items are left or transmitted: *a mail drop.* **13.** a predesignated place where secret letters or packages can be left to be picked up by another person without attracting attention, as in espionage or drug dealing. **14.** something resembling or likened to a liquid globule, as certain ornaments, a spherical earring, etc. **15.** a pendant. **16.** a descent by parachute. **17.** an instance of dropping supplies by parachute or an amount of supplies so dropped. **18.** something that drops or is used for dropping. **19.** a group of persons dropped by parachute, as the personnel dropped by parachute during one military action. **20.** *Theat.* **a.** See **drop curtain. b.** See **drop scene. 21.** See **trap door. 22.** a gallows. **23.** a slit or opening into which something can be dropped, as in a mailbox. **24.** (in a casino) the income from the sale of chips. **25.** a small flag, usually of enameled metal, that gives a visual signal in an annunciator. **26.** *Furniture.* an applied ornament resembling a pendant. **27.** *Archit.* gutta (def. 2). **28.** *Naut.* the vertical dimension amidships of any sail that is bent to a standing yard. Cf. **hoist** (def. 7a). **29.** Also called **drop panel.** (in reinforced-concrete-slab construction) a thickened portion of the ceiling around a column head. **30.** *Horol.* the free motion of an escape wheel between successive checks by the pallet. **31.** the newborn young of an animal. **32. at the drop of a hat,** at the slightest provocation or without delay: *He's ready to fight at the drop of a hat.* **33. drop in the bucket.** See **bucket** (def. 9). **34. get** or **have the drop on, a.** to aim and be ready to shoot a gun at an antagonist before the other person's gun can be drawn. **b.** to get or have at a disadvantage.
—*v.i.* **35.** to fall in globules or small portions, as water or other liquid: *Rain drops from the clouds.* **36.** to fall vertically; have an abrupt descent. **37.** to sink or fall to the ground, floor, or bottom as if inanimate. **38.** to fall lower in condition, degree, value, etc.; diminish or lessen; sink: *The prices dropped sharply.* **39.** to come to an end; cease; lapse: *There the matter dropped.* **40.** to fall or move to a position that is lower, farther back, inferior, etc.: *to drop back in line; to drop to the rear.* **41.** to withdraw; quit (often fol. by *out* or *from*): *to drop out of a race; to drop from a game.* **42.** to pass or enter without effort into some condition, activity, or the like: *to drop into sleep; to drop into a habit.* **43.** to make an unexpected or unannounced stop at a place; pay an informal visit or call (usually fol. by *in, by,* or *over*): *Since we're in the neighborhood, why don't we drop in at my brother's?* **44.** to cease to appear or be seen; vanish: *to drop from sight or notice.* **45.** to fall wounded, dead, etc.: *A thousand men dropped in the battle.* **46.** to squat or crouch, as a dog at the sight of game. **47.** to move gently, as with the tide or a light wind (usually fol. by *down*). **48.** *Slang.* to ingest an illicit drug orally; swallow.
—*v.t.* **49.** to let fall in drops or small portions: *to drop lemon juice into tea.* **50.** to let or cause to fall. **51.** to cause or allow to sink to a lower position. **52.** to cause to decrease in value, amount, quality, etc.; reduce. **53.** to utter or express casually or incidentally: *to drop a hint.* **54.** to write and send: *Drop me a note.* **55.** to bring to the ground by a blow or shot. **56.** to set down or unload, as from a ship, car, etc. (often fol. by *off*): *Drop me at the corner.* **57.** to omit (a letter or syllable) in pronunciation or writing: *He dropped his h's.* **58.** to lower (the voice) in pitch or loudness. **59.** to cease to keep up or have to do with: *I dropped the subject. Will you drop your old friends if you win the lottery?* **60.** to cease to employ, admit as a member, or include, as on a list; dismiss: *to drop an accountant from the payroll; to drop three members of the club who have not paid their dues.* **61.** to withdraw or cease to pursue: *The police dropped the charges against the suspect.* **62.** *Sports.* **a.** to throw, shoot, hit, kick, or roll (a ball, puck, etc.) through or into a basket, hole, or other goal: *He dropped the ball through the basket for two points.* **b.** to lose (a game or contest): *They dropped two games in a row and were eliminated from the tournament.* **63.** *Football.* **a.** to drop-kick (a ball). **b.** to score with a drop kick. **64.** (of animals) to give birth to: *The cat dropped a litter of six kittens.* **65.** to parachute (persons, supplies, etc.): *The Marines dropped 300 combat troops into the jungle battlefield.* **66.** to lengthen by lowering or letting out: *to drop the hem of a skirt.* **67.** to lower (the wheels) into position for landing an airplane. **68.** *Slang.* to take (esp. an illicit drug) by swallowing; ingest: *to drop LSD.* **69.** *Naut.* to pass out of sight of; outdistance. **70.** *Cookery.* to poach (an egg). **71. drop behind,** to fall short of the required pace or progress: *Her long illness caused her to drop behind the rest of the class.* **72. drop dead,** (used as an expression of contempt, disgust, impatience, etc.): *If that's the way you feel about it, drop dead!* **73. drop off, a.** to fall asleep. **b.** to decrease; decline: *Sales have dropped off drastically.* **74. drop out, a.** to withdraw from being a member or participant: *to drop out of a club; to drop out of society and become a wanderer.* **b.** to stop attending school or college. [bef. 1000; (n.) ME *drop(e)* drop of liquid, OE *dropa;* (v.) ME *droppen,* OE *droppian;* akin to DRIP, DROOP] **—drop′like′,** *adj.*

drop′ arch′, 1. a pointed arch having radii of length less than the span. **2.** Also called **surbased arch.** an arch having a rise of less than half its span. [1840–50]

drop•back (drop′bak′), *n.* a lowering, as of prices or standards, esp. to a previous level: *Auto manufacturers requested a dropback in emissions standards.* [n. use of v. phrase *drop back*]

drop′ bis′cuit, a biscuit made by dropping baking powder biscuit dough from a spoon onto a pan for baking. [1850–55, *Amer.*]

drop′ black′, *Chem.* carbon, as animal black or lampblack, formed into pellets by mixing with water or glue: used as a black pigment.

drop′ box′, *Textiles.* a box for holding shuttles on a loom, as a box loom, used on either side of the race plate in weaving cloth having a variety of colors in the filling. [1855–60]

drop′ cloth′, a sheet of cloth, paper, plastic, or the like laid over furniture and floors for protection while a room is being painted or laid over shrubbery while the exterior of a house is being painted. Also, **drop′cloth′.** [1925–30]

drop′ cook′ie, a cookie made by dropping batter from a spoon onto a cookie sheet for baking. [1825–35, *Amer.*]

drop′ cur′tain, *Theat.* a curtain that is lowered into position from the flies. [1825–35]

drop-dead (drop′ded′), *adj.* inspiring awe, astonishment, or envy: *a drop-dead guest list; a drop-dead sable coat.* [1965–70]

drop′ el′bow, *Plumbing.* an elbow having lugs for attaching it to a wall or joist. Also called **drop′ ell′.**

dro•per•i•dol (drō per′i dôl′, -dol′), *n. Pharm.* a phenothiazine, $C_{22}H_{22}FN_3O_2$, used as an anesthetic or antiemetic, or for emergency control of severe behavioral disturbance. [(*dehy*)*dro*(*benz*)*peridol*]

drop′ forge′, *Metalworking.* a device for making large forgings in which a heavy object is allowed to fall vertically upon a piece of work placed on an anvil or between dies. Also called **drop hammer, drop press.** [1895–1900]

drop-forge (drop′fôrj′, -fōrj′), *v.t.,* **-forged, -forg•ing.** *Metalworking.* to form in a drop forge. [1890–95] **—drop′-forg′er,** *n.*

drop′ forg′ing, *Metalworking.* a drop-forged object. [1880–85]

drop′ front′, *Furniture.* See **fall front.** [1930–35]

drop′ girt′, *Carpentry.* a girt running beneath the ends of joists and at right angles to them. Cf. **flush girt.**

drop′ ham′mer. See **drop forge.** [1860–65, *Amer.*]

drop-in (drop′in′), *n.* **1.** *Informal.* Also, **dropper-in.** a person or thing that pays an unexpected or uninvited visit: *a feeder for squirrels, raccoons, and other drop-ins.* **2.** *Informal.* a social gathering at which the guests are not expected to stay long: *Be sure to stop by our house for a glass of eggnog at our Christmas drop-in.* —*adj.* **3.** provided for short-term patronage: *a drop-in shelter for the homeless.* **4.** requiring only insertion to be ready for use: *a drop-in film cartridge.* [1810–20; n., adj. use of v. phrase *drop in*]

drop′ ini′tial, *Print.* See **inset initial.** [1950–55, *Amer.*]

drop′ keel′, *Naut.* centerboard. [1895–1900]

drop′ kick′, *Football.* a kick made by dropping a football to the ground and kicking it as it starts to bounce up. Cf. **place kick, punt**[1] (def. 1). [1835–45]

drop-kick (drop′kik′), *Football.* —*v.t.* **1.** to score (a field goal or point after touchdown) by a drop kick. **2.** to kick (the ball as dropped for a drop kick). —*v.i.* **3.** to make a drop kick. [1870–75] **—drop′-kick′er,** *n.*

drop′ leaf′, *Furniture.* a hinged leaf attached to the end or side of a table that can be raised to extend the tabletop or folded vertically downward when not in use. [1880–85] **—drop′-leaf′,** *adj.*

drop•let (drop′lit), *n.* a little drop. [1600–10; DROP + -LET]

drop′let infec′tion, infection spread by airborne droplets of secretions from the nose, throat, or lungs. [1905–10]

drop′ let′ter, a letter that is mailed to a local address at a post office without city delivery or a rural delivery service and must be picked up by the addressee. [1835–45, *Amer.*]

drop•light (drop′līt′), *n.* an electric or gas lamp suspended from the ceiling or wall by a flexible cord or tube. [1860–65, *Amer.;* DROP + LIGHT[1]]

drop•line (drop′līn′), *n. Journalism.* a headline or bank consisting of a top line set flush with the left margin, with each succeeding line indented on the left, and the final line flush with the right margin. Also called **stagger head, staggered head, stephead, stepped line.** [1880–85; DROP + LINE[1]]

drop-off (drop′ôf′, -of′), *n.* **1.** a vertical or very steep descent: *The trail has a drop-off of several hundred feet.* **2.** a decline; decrease: *Sales have shown a considerable drop-off this year.* **3.** a place where a person or thing can be left, received, accommodated, etc.: *a new drop-off for outpatients.* —*adj.* **4.** applied when a rented vehicle is left elsewhere than at the point of hire: *to pay a drop-off charge.* [1955–60; n., adj. use of v. phrase *drop off*]

drop•out (drop′out′), *n.* **1.** an act or instance of dropping out. **2.** a student who withdraws before completing a course of instruction. **3.** a student who withdraws from high school after having reached the legal age to do so. **4.** a person who withdraws from established society, esp. to pursue an alternate lifestyle. **5.** a person who withdraws from a competition, job, task, etc.: *the first dropout from the presidential race.* **6.** *Rugby.* a drop kick made by a defending team from within its own 25-yd. (23-m) line as a result of a touchdown or of the ball's having touched or gone outside of a touch-in-goal line or the dead-ball line. **7.** Also called **highlight halftone.** a halftone negative or plate in which dots have been eliminated from highlights by continued etching, burning in, opaquing, or the like. **8.** Also called **drop′-out er′ror.** the loss of portions of the information on a recorded magnetic tape due to contamination of the magnetic medium or poor contact with the tape heads. Also, **drop′-out′.** [1925–30, *Amer.*; n. use of v. phrase *drop out*]

drop•page (drop′ij), *n.* **1.** an amount dropped or wasted during application, installation, etc.: *Mix some extra plaster to allow for droppage.* **2.** the amount of fruit that falls from a tree before ripening: *Storms greatly increased the droppage of oranges this year.* **3.** the act or an instance of dropping: *glassware that is not insured against droppage.* [DROP + -AGE]

drop′ pan′el, drop (def. 29).

drop′ pass′, (in hockey and soccer) a pass in which a player in control of the ball or puck simply leaves it to be picked up by a trailing teammate and continues past it to draw off the defense. [1945–50]

dropped′ egg′, *New Eng.* a poached egg. [1820–25]

dropped′ seat′, a seat of a chair or the like, having a front dished so as to be lower than the sides or back. Also called **scoop seat.**

dropped′ waist′, the waistline of a dress, gown, or the like when it is placed at the hips rather than at the natural waist.

drop•per (drop′ər), *n.* **1.** a person or thing that drops. **2.** a glass tube with a hollow rubber bulb at one end and a small opening at the other, for drawing in a liquid and expelling it in drops; medicine dropper. **3.** a short-haired dog that is a cross between a pointer and a setter. [1690–1700; DROP + -ER[1]]

drop•per-in (drop′ər in′), *n., pl.* **drop•pers-in.** drop-in (def. 1). [1895–1900; v. phrase *drop in* + -ER[1], with particle postposed]

drop•ping (drop′ing), *n.* **1.** the act of a person or thing that drops. **2.** something that drops or falls in drops. **3. droppings,** dung, esp. in the form of pellets. [bef. 1000; ME; OE *droppung.* See DROP, -ING[1]]

drop′ping bot′tle, a bottle with correlated lengthwise grooves in the neck and in the stopper, permitting a controlled flow of the liquid contents in the form of drops. [1820–30]

drop′ press′, *Metalworking.* See **drop forge.** [1850–55, *Amer.*]

drop′ rud′der, *Naut.* a rudder that can be lowered beneath the level of the bottom of a boat.

drop′ scene′, *Theat.* **1.** a drop curtain, often of painted or dyed canvas, located downstage and used as the backdrop for a scene played while the set upstage is being changed. **2.** a scene or act played with less intensity than the preceding one. **3.** the last scene of an act or play. [1805–15]

drop′ seat′, 1. a hinged seat, as in a taxicab or bus, that may be pulled down for use when an additional seat is needed. **2.** a rear panel, as on long one-piece underwear or children's pajamas, that may be opened and lowered separately. [1925–30]

drop-ship (drop′ship′), *v.t.,* **-shipped, -ship•ping.** to ship (goods) as a drop shipment: *The books will be drop-shipped by the publisher to your home.* [back formation from DROP SHIPMENT]

drop′ ship′ment, a shipment of goods made directly from the manufacturer to the retailer or consumer but billed through the wholesaler or distributor.

drop′ ship′per, a wholesaler or distributor who conducts business in drop shipments. Also called **desk jobber.**

drop′ shot′, 1. (in tennis, badminton, etc.) a ball or shuttlecock so softly hit that it falls to the playing surface just after clearing the net. **2.** (in squash, handball, etc.) a ball so softly hit that it falls suddenly to the ground just after striking the front wall. **3.** shot made in a shot tower. [1630–40]

drop•si•cal (drop′si kəl), *adj.* of, like, or affected with dropsy. [1670–80; DROPS(Y) + -ICAL] **—drop′si•cal•ly,** *adv.* **—drop′si•cal•ness,** *n.*

drop′ sid′ing, weatherboarding having its upper edges narrowed to fit into grooves or rabbets in its lower edges, and its backs flat against the sheathing or studs of the wall. See illus. under **siding.** Also called **novelty siding.**

drops•ley (drop′slē), *n. Ontario.* a dish of very small dumplings made from a batter of butter, egg, flour, and seasoning dropped in small pieces into broth. [orig. undetermined]

drop•sonde (drop′sond′), *n. Meteorol.* an instrument similar to a radiosonde that is attached to a parachute and released from an aircraft. [1945–50; DROP + (RADI-O)SONDE]

drop•sy (drop′sē), *n.* **1.** (formerly) edema. **2.** an infectious disease of fishes, characterized by a swollen, spongelike body and protruding scales, caused by a variety of the bacterium *Pseudomonas punctata.* [1250–1300; ME *drop(e)sie,* aph. var. of *ydropesie* < OF < ML *(h)ydrōpisia,* equiv. to L *hydrōpis(is)* (< Gk *hydrōpi-,* s. of *hýdrōps* dropsy (*hydr-* HYDR- + *-ōpsi-* < ?) + *-sis* -SIS) + *-ia* -Y[3]] **—drop•sied** (drop′sēd), *adj.*

dropt (dropt), *v.* a pt. and pp. of **drop.**

drop′ ta′ble, a tabletop hinged to a wall, held in a horizontal position by a bracket while in use. [1860–65]

drop′ tee′, *Plumbing.* a tee having lugs for attaching it to a wall or joist.

drop′ the hand′kerchief, a children's game in which all the players but one stand in a circle facing inward, while that one player stealthily drops a handker-

CONCISE PRONUNCIATION KEY: *act, cāpe, dâre, pärt; set, ēqual; if, ice; ox, ōver, ôrder, oil, bŏŏk, bōōt, out; up, ûrge; child; sing; shoe; thin, that;* zh as in *treasure.* ə = *a* as in *alone, e* as in *system, i* as in *easily, o* as in *gallop, u* as in *circus;* ᵊ as in *fire* (fīᵊr), *hour* (ouᵊr). l and n can serve as syllabic consonants, as in *cradle* (krād′l), and *button* (but′n). See the full key inside the front cover.

chief behind a player in the circle who must pursue and attempt to catch the one who dropped the handkerchief before the latter reaches the vacated place.

drop′ valve′, a valve, as for a steam engine, that drops freely to close.

drop′ win′dow, a window with a sash that slides into a space below the sill. [1900–05]

drop•wort (drop′wûrt′, -wôrt′), *n.* a European plant, *Filipendula vulgaris,* of the rose family, bearing small, scentless, white or reddish flowers. [1530–40; DROP + WORT[2]]

drop′ zone′, an area into which paratroopers, soldiers, or supplies are landed from aircraft for a military operation. *Abbr.:* DZ [1940–45]

dros•er•a (dros′ər ə), *n.* any of several insectivorous plants of the genus *Drosera,* having leaves covered with sticky hairs, comprising the sundews. [< NL (Linnaeus), the genus name < Gk *droserá,* fem. of *droserós* dewy, equiv. to *drós(os)* dew + *-eros* adj. suffix]

drosh•ky (drosh′kē), *n., pl.* **-kies.** **1.** a light, low, four-wheeled, open vehicle used mainly in Russia, in which the passengers sit astride or sideways on a long, narrow bench. **2.** any of various other carriages, used mainly in Russia. [1800–10; < Russ *drózhki,* orig. dim. of *drógi* a long, bodyless wagon, pl. (functioning as sing.) of *drogá* one of the shafts joining the front and rear axles of a wagon]

dros•ky (dros′kē), *n., pl.* **-kies.** droshky.

dro•som•e•ter (drō som′i tər, drə-), *n.* an instrument for measuring the amount of dew formed on a given surface. [1815–25; < Gk *drós(os)* dew + -METER]

dro•soph•i•la (drō sof′ə lə, drə-), *n., pl.* **-las, -lae** (-lē′). a fly of the genus *Drosophila,* esp. *D. melanogaster,* used in laboratory studies of genetics and development. [< NL < Gk *dróso(s)* dew + NL *-phila* < Gk *-philē,* fem. of *-philos* -PHILE]

dross (drôs, dros), *n.* **1.** waste matter; refuse. **2.** *Metall.* a waste product taken off molten metal during smelting, essentially metallic in character. **3.** *Brit.* coal of little value. [bef. 1050; ME *dros(se),* OE *drōs;* c. MD *droes* dregs; cf. ME *drōsen,* OE *drōsna;* c. MHG *truosen* husks]

dross•y (drô′sē, dros′ē), *adj.,* **dross•i•er, dross•i•est.** **1.** containing dross. **2.** resembling dross; worthless. [1400–50; late ME; see DROSS, -Y[1]] —**dross′i•ness,** *n.*

Dro•ste-Hüls•hoff (drôs′tə hʏls′hôf′), *n.* **An•net•te E•li•sa•beth Frei•in von** (ä net′ə ä lē′zä bet′ frī′in fən), 1797–1848, German poet.

drought (drout), *n.* **1.** a period of dry weather, esp. a long one that is injurious to crops. **2.** an extended shortage: *a drought of good writing.* **3.** *Archaic.* thirst. Also, **drouth** (drouth). [bef. 1000; ME; OE *drūgath,* equiv. to *drūg-* (base of *drȳge* DRY) + *-ath* -TH[1]; c. D *droogte* dryness]

—**Syn. 2.** scarcity, lack, want, dearth, paucity, famine.

—**Pronunciation.** DROUGHT and DROUTH, nouns derived from the adjective *dry* plus a suffix, are spellings that represent two phonetic developments of the same Old English word, and are pronounced (drout) and (drouth) respectively. The latter pronunciation, therefore, is not a mispronunciation of DROUGHT. The now unproductive suffix *-th*[1] and its alternate form *-t* were formerly used to derive nouns from adjectives or verbs, resulting in such pairs as DROUTH—DROUGHT from *dry* and *highth* —*height* (the former now obsolete) from *high.*

In American English, DROUGHT with the pronunciation (drout) is common everywhere in educated speech, and is the usual printed form.

drought•y (drou′tē), *adj.,* **drought•i•er, drought•i•est.** **1.** dry. **2.** lacking rain. **3.** *Chiefly Brit. Dial.* thirsty. Also, **drouthy.** [1595–1605; DROUGHT + -Y[1]] —**drought′i•ness,** *n.*

drouk (dro͝ok), *v.t. Scot.* to wet thoroughly; drench. [1505–15; < ON *drukna* to be drowned; c. OE *druncnian* to drown]

drouth•y (drou′thē), *adj.,* **drouth•i•er, drouth•i•est.** droughty. —**drouth′i•ness,** *n.*

drove[1] (drōv), *v.* pt. of **drive.**

drove[2] (drōv), *n., v.,* **droved, drov•ing.** —*n.* **1.** a number of oxen, sheep, or swine driven in a group; herd; flock. **2.** Usually, **droves.** a large crowd of human beings, esp. in motion: *They came to Yankee Stadium in droves.* **3.** Also called **drove′ chis′el.** *Masonry.* a chisel, from 2 to 4 in. (5 to 10 cm) broad at the edge, for dressing stones to an approximately true surface. —*v.t., v.i.* **4.** to drive or deal in (cattle) as a drover; herd. **5.** *Masonry.* to work or smooth (stone) as with a drove. [bef. 950; ME; OE *drāf* that which is driven, i.e., herd, flock; akin to DRIVE]

—**Syn. 1.** See **flock**[1].

dro•ver (drō′vər), *n.* **1.** a person who drives cattle or sheep to market. **2.** a dealer in cattle. [1350–1400; ME. See DROVE[2], -ER[1]]

drown (droun), *v.i.* **1.** to die under water or other liquid of suffocation. —*v.t.* **2.** to kill by submerging under water or other liquid. **3.** to destroy or get rid of by, or as if by, immersion: *He drowned his sorrows in drink.* **4.** to flood or inundate. **5.** to overwhelm so as to render inaudible, as by a louder sound (often fol. by *out).* **6.** to add too much water or liquid to (a drink, food, or the like). **7.** to slake (lime) by covering with water and letting stand. **8. drown in, a.** to be overwhelmed by: *The company is drowning in bad debts.* **b.** to be covered with or enveloped in: *The old movie star was drowning in mink.* [1250–1300; ME *drounnen,* OE *druncnian,* perh. by loss of *c* between nasals and shift of length from *nn* to *ou]* —**drown′er,** *n.*

—**Syn. 4.** deluge, engulf, submerge, drench, soak.

drowned′ val′ley, a valley that, having been flooded by the sea, now exists as a bay or estuary. [1900–05]

drown•proof (droun′pro͞of′), *v.t.* to teach (a person) the technique of drownproofing. [1975–80; back formation from DROWNPROOFING]

drown•proof•ing (droun′pro͞o′fing), *n.* a survival technique, for swimmers or nonswimmers, in which the body is allowed to float vertically in the water, with the head submerged, the lungs filled with air, and the arms and legs relaxed, the head being raised to breathe every ten seconds or so. [1965–70; DROWN + -PROOF + -ING[1], modeled on WATERPROOFING, etc.]

drowse (drouz), *v.,* **drowsed, drows•ing,** *n.* —*v.i.* **1.** to be sleepy or half-asleep. **2.** to be dull or sluggish. —*v.t.* **3.** to pass or spend (time) in drowsing (often fol. by *away*): *He drowsed away the morning.* **4.** to make sleepy. —*n.* **5.** a sleepy condition; state of being half-asleep. [bef. 900; OE *drūsian* to droop, become sluggish (not recorded in ME); akin to OE *drēosan* to fall]

drow•si•head (drou′zē hed′), *n. Archaic.* drowsiness. [1580–90; DROWSY + HEAD]

drow•sy (drou′zē), *adj.,* **-si•er, -si•est.** **1.** half-asleep; sleepy. **2.** marked by or resulting from sleepiness. **3.** dull; sluggish. **4.** inducing lethargy or sleepiness: *drowsy spring weather.* [1520–30; DROWSE + -Y[1]] —**drow′si•ly,** *adv.* —**drow′si•ness,** *n.*

—**Syn. 1.** somnolent, dozy. **3.** lethargic, listless.

Dr. Strange•love (strānj′luv′), a person, esp. a military or government official, who advocates initiating nuclear warfare. Also called **Strangelove.** [after a character in a movie of the same name (1963) by U.S. director Stanley Kubrick]

drub (drub), *v.,* **drubbed, drub•bing,** *n.* —*v.t.* **1.** to beat with a stick or the like; cudgel; flog; thrash. **2.** to defeat decisively, as in a game or contest. **3.** to drive as if by flogging: *Latin grammar was drubbed into their heads.* **4.** to stamp (the feet). —*n.* **5.** a blow with a stick or the like. [1625–35; perh. by uncert. mediation < Ar *ḍarb* blow, beating] —**drub′ber,** *n.*

drub•bing (drub′ing), *n.* **1.** a beating; a sound thrashing. **2.** a decisive, humiliating defeat, as in a game or contest. [1640–50; DRUB + -ING[1]]

Dru•cil•la (dro͞o sil′ə), *n.* a female given name.

drudge (druj), *n., v.,* **drudged, drudg•ing.** —*n.* **1.** a person who does menial, distasteful, dull, or hard work. **2.** a person who works in a routine, unimaginative way. —*v.i.* **3.** to perform menial, distasteful, dull, or hard work. [1485–95; cf. OE man's name *Drycghelm* helmet maker, equiv. to *drycg* (akin to *drēogan* to work) + *helm* HELM[2]] —**drudg′er,** *n.* —**drudg′ing•ly,** *adv.*

—**Syn. 3.** toil, hack, grub, plod, slave.

drudg•er•y (druj′ə rē), *n., pl.* **-er•ies.** menial, distasteful, dull, or hard work. [1540–50; DRUDGE + -ERY]

—**Syn.** See **work.**

drug[1] (drug), *n., v.,* **drugged, drug•ging.** —*n.* **1.** *Pharm.* a chemical substance used in the treatment, cure, prevention, or diagnosis of disease or used to otherwise enhance physical or mental well-being. **2.** (in federal law) **a.** any substance recognized in the official pharmacopoeia or formulary of the nation. **b.** any substance intended for use in the diagnosis, cure, mitigation, treatment, or prevention of disease in humans or other animals. **c.** any article, other than food, intended to affect the structure or any function of the body of humans or other animals. **d.** any substance intended for use as a component of such a drug, but not a device or a part of a device. **3.** a habit-forming medicinal or illicit substance, esp. a narcotic. **4. drugs, a.** chemical substances prepared and sold as pharmaceutical items, either by prescription or over the counter. **b.** personal hygienic items sold in a drugstore, as toothpaste, mouthwash, etc. **5.** *Obs.* any ingredient used in chemistry, pharmacy, dyeing, or the like. **6. drug on the market,** a commodity that is overabundant or in excess of demand in the market. Also, **drug in the market.** —*v.t.* **7.** to administer a medicinal drug to. **8.** to stupefy or poison with a drug. **9.** to mix (food or drink) with a drug, esp. a stupefying, narcotic, or poisonous drug. **10.** to administer anything nauseous to. —*v.i.* **11. drug up,** to take a narcotic drug: *The addict prowled about for a place to drug up.* [1300–50; ME *drogges* (pl.) < MF *drogue,* of obscure orig.]

drug[2] (drug), *v. Chiefly Midland and Southern U.S. Nonstandard.* a pt. and pp. of **drag.**

Drug (dro͝og), *n. Zoroastrianism.* the cosmic principle of disorder and falsehood. Cf. **Asha.** [< Avestan *drauga*]

drug′ abuse′, **1.** addiction to drugs. **2.** substance abuse involving drugs. [1965–70] —**drug′ abus′er.**

drug′ ad′dict, a person who is addicted to a narcotic. Also called **dope addict.** [1915–20]

drugged-out (drugd′out′), *adj. Informal.* being under the influence of drugs, esp. a narcotic or an illicit drug.

drug•get (drug′it), *n.* **1.** Also called **India drugget.** a rug from India of coarse hair with cotton or jute. **2.** a fabric woven wholly or partly of wool, used for clothing. [1570–80; < MF *droguet* worthless stuff (textile), equiv. to *drogue* trash (cf. DRUG[1]) + *-et* -ET]

drug•gie (drug′ē), *n. Slang.* a habitual user of drugs, esp. a narcotic or illicit drug. Also, **druggy.** [1965–70; DRUG[1] + -IE]

drug•gist (drug′ist), *n.* **1.** a person who compounds or prepares drugs according to medical prescriptions; apothecary; pharmacist; dispensing chemist. **2.** the owner or operator of a drugstore. [1605–15; DRUG[1] + -IST; cf. F *droguiste*]

drug•gy[1] (drug′ē), *n., pl.* **-gies.** druggie. [1970–75; DRUG + -Y[2]]

drug•gy[2] (drug′ē), *adj.,* **-gi•er, -gi•est.** affected by a drug, esp. a narcotic or illicit drug: *playing to a druggy audience.* [DRUG + -Y[1]]

drug•less (drug′lis), *adj.* being without the use of drugs, as certain methods of medical treatment. [1875–80; DRUG[1] + -LESS]

drug•mak•er (drug′mā′kər), *n.* a person or company that manufactures pharmaceutical products. [1960–65; DRUG[1] + MAKER]

drug•push•er (drug′po͝osh′ər), *n.* a person who sells illicit drugs. [1965–70; DRUG[1] + PUSHER]

drug•store (drug′stôr′, -stōr′), *n.* the place of business of a druggist, usually also selling cosmetics, stationery, toothpaste, mouthwash, cigarettes, etc., and sometimes soft drinks and light meals. Also, **drug′ store′.** [1800–10, *Amer.*; DRUG[1] + STORE]

drug′store cow′boy, *Slang.* **1.** a young man who loafs around drugstores or on street corners. **2.** a person who dresses like a cowboy but has never worked as one. [1905–10]

Dru•id (dro͞o′id), *n.* (*often l.c.*) a member of a pre-Christian religious order among the ancient Celts of Gaul, Britain, and Ireland. [1555–65; < L *druidae* (pl.) < Gaulish; r. *druide* < F; cf. OIr *druí* (nom.), *druid* (dat., acc.) wizard] —**dru•id′ic, dru•id′i•cal,** *adj.*

Dru•id•ess (dro͞o′i dis), *n.* (*often l.c.*) a female member of the Druids. [1745–55; DRUID + -ESS]

—**Usage.** See **-ess.**

dru•id•ism (dro͞o′i diz′əm), *n.* the religion or rites of the Druids. [1705–15; DRUID + -ISM]

dru•i•dol•o•gy (dro͞o′i dol′ə jē), *n.* the study of the religion, customs, and practices of the Druids. [DRUID + -O- + -LOGY]

Dru′id stone′, sarsen. [1840–50]

drum[1] (drum), *n., pl.* **drums,** (*esp. collectively for 11*) **drum,** *v.,* **drummed, drum•ming.** —*n.* **1.** a musical percussion instrument consisting of a hollow, usually cylindrical, body covered at one or both ends with a tightly stretched membrane, or head, which is struck with the hand, a stick, or a pair of sticks, and typically produces a booming, tapping, or hollow sound. **2.** any hollow tree or similar object or device used in this way. **3.** the sound produced by such an instrument, object, or device. **4.** any rumbling or deep booming sound. **5.** a natural organ by which an animal produces a loud or bass sound. **6.** eardrum. **7.** any cylindrical object with flat ends. **8.** a cylindrical part of a machine. **9.** a cylindrical box or receptacle, esp. a large, metal one for storing or transporting liquids. **10.** Also called **tambour.** *Archit.* **a.** any of several cylindrical or nearly cylindrical stones laid one above the other to form a column or pier. **b.** a cylindrical or faceted construction supporting a dome. **11.** any of several marine and freshwater fishes of the family Sciaenidae that produce a drumming sound. **12.** *Computers.* See **magnetic drum.** **13.** *Archaic.* an assembly of fashionable people at a private house in the evening. **14.** a person who plays the drum. **15.** *Australian Informal.* reliable, confidential, or profitable information: *to give someone the drum.* **16. beat the drum,** to promote, publicize, or advertise: *The boss is out beating the drum for a new product.* —*v.i.* **17.** to beat or play a drum. **18.** to beat on anything rhythmically, esp. to tap one's fingers rhythmically on a hard surface. **19.** to make a sound like that of a drum; resound. **20.** (of ruffed grouse and other birds) to produce a sound resembling drumming. —*v.t.* **21.** to beat (a drum) rhythmically; perform by beating a drum: *to drum a rhythm for dancers.* **22.** to call or summon by, or as if by, beating a drum. **23.** to drive or force by persistent repetition: *to drum an idea into someone.* **24.** to fill a drum with; store in a drum: *to drum contaminated water and dispose of it.* **25. drum out, a.** (formerly) to expel or dismiss from a military service in disgrace to the beat of a drum. **b.** to dismiss in disgrace: *He was drummed out of the university for his gambling activities.* **26. drum up, a.** to call or summon by, or as if by, beating a drum. **b.** to obtain or create (customers, trade, interest, etc.) through vigorous effort: *They were unable to drum up enthusiasm for the new policies.* **c.** to concoct; devise: *to drum up new methods of dealing with urban crime.* [1535–45; back formation from *drumslade* drum, drummer, alter. of D or LG *trommelslag* drumbeat, equiv. to *trommel* drum + *slag* beat (akin to *slagen* to beat; c. SLAY)]

drum[2] (drum), *n. Scot., Irish Eng.* a long, narrow hill or ridge. [1715–25; < Ir and ScotGael *druim*]

drum′ and bu′gle corps′, a marching band of drum players and buglers.

drum•beat (drum′bēt′), *n.* the rhythmic sound of a drum. [1850–55; DRUM[1] + BEAT]

drum•beat•er (drum′bē′tər), *n.* a person who vigorously proclaims or publicizes the merits of a product, idea, movie, etc.; press agent. [DRUM[1] + BEATER]

drum′ brake′, *Auto.* a brake system in which a pair of brake shoes can be pressed against the inner surface of a shallow metal drum that is rigidly attached to a wheel. [1945–50]

drum′ corps′, a band, esp. a marching band, of drum players usually under the direction of a drum major. [1860–65, *Amer.*]

drum•fire (drum′fīᵊr′), *n.* gunfire so heavy and continuous as to sound like the beating of drums. [1915–20; DRUM[1] + FIRE]

drum•fish (drum′fish′), *n., pl.* (*esp. collectively*) **-fish,** (*esp. referring to two or more kinds or species*) **-fish•es.** drum[1] (def. 11). [1675–85; DRUM[1] + FISH]

drum•head (drum′hed′), *n.* **1.** the membrane stretched upon a drum. **2.** the top part of a capstan. —*adj.* **3.** characteristic of a drumhead court-martial; carried out in summary fashion: *a drumhead execution.* [1615–25; DRUM[1] + HEAD]

drum′head court′-martial, a court-martial held, usually on a battlefield, for the summary trial of charges of offenses committed during military operations. [1825–35; so called from the use of a drumhead as a table during the court-martial]

CONCISE ETYMOLOGY KEY: <, descended or borrowed from; >, whence; b., blend of, blended; c., cognate with; cf., compare; deriv., derivative; equiv., equivalent; imit., imitative; obl., oblique; r., replacing; s., stem; sp., spelling, spelled; resp., respelling, respelled; trans., translation; ?, origin unknown; *, unattested; ‡, probably earlier than. See the full key inside the front cover.

drum·lin (drum′lin), *n. Geol.* a long, narrow or oval, smoothly rounded hill of unstratified glacial drift. [1825–35; DRUM[2] + *-lin,* var. of -LING[1]]

drum·ly (drum′lē; *Scot.* dro͞om′lē), *adj.,* **-li·er, -li·est.** *Scot.* troubled; gloomy. [1505–15; nasalized var. of ME *drublie, droblie,* OE *drōflic,* equiv. to *drōf* turbid, troubled (c. G *trüb*) + *-lic* -LY]

drum′ ma′jor, the marching leader of a drum corps or a band. [1590–1600]

drum′ majorette′, **1.** a girl or woman who leads a marching band or drum corps. **2.** a girl or woman who twirls a baton with a marching band or drum corps. Also called **majorette.** [1935–40, *Amer.*]
—Usage. See **-ette.**

drum·mer (drum′ər), *n.* **1.** a person who plays a drum. **2.** a commercial traveler or traveling sales representative. **3. march to a different drummer,** to be motivated by a different set of values than the average person. [1565–75; DRUM[1] + -ER[1]]

drum·mock (drum′ək), *n. Chiefly Scot.* drammock.

Drum·mond (drum′ənd), *n.* **1. Henry,** 1851–97, Scottish clergyman and writer. **2. William,** 1585–1649, Scottish poet. **3. William Henry,** 1854–1907, Canadian poet, born in Ireland.

Drum′mond light′. See **calcium light.** [1835–45; named after Capt. T. *Drummond* (1797–1840), British engineer]

Drum·mond·ville (drum′ənd vil′), *n.* a city in S Quebec, in E Canada. 27,347.

drum′ pan′eling, flush paneling in a door.

drum′ print′er, *Computers.* a line printer that uses a rotating drum with raised characters, against which the paper is pressed. [1965–70]

drum·roll (drum′rōl′), *n.* **1.** a roll on a drum. **2.** the sound of a drumroll. [1885–90; DRUM[1] + ROLL]

drum·skin (drum′skin′), *n.* drumhead (def. 1). [DRUM[1] + SKIN]

drum·stick (drum′stik′), *n.* **1.** a stick for beating a drum. **2.** the meaty leg of a chicken, duck, turkey, or other fowl. [1580–90; DRUM[1] + STICK[1]]

drum′ ta′ble, a table having a cylindrical top with drawers or shelves in the skirt, rotating on a central post with three or four outwardly curving legs. Also called **capstan table.**

drung (drung), *n. Newfoundland.* drang.

drunk (drungk), *adj.* **1.** being in a temporary state in which one's physical and mental faculties are impaired by an excess of alcoholic drink; intoxicated: *The wine made him drunk.* **2.** overcome or dominated by a strong feeling or emotion: *drunk with power; drunk with joy.* **3.** pertaining to or caused by intoxication or intoxicated persons. —*n.* **4.** an intoxicated person. **5.** a spree; drinking party. —*v.* **6.** pp. and nonstandard pt. of **drink.** [1300–50; ME *drunken,* OE *druncen,* ptp. of *drincan* to DRINK]
—Syn. 1. drunken, inebriated. **—Ant. 1-3.** sober.
—Usage. Both DRUNK and DRUNKEN are used as modifiers before nouns naming persons: *a drunk customer; a drunken merrymaker.* Only DRUNK occurs after a linking verb: *He was not drunk, just jovial. The actor was drunk with success.* The modifier DRUNK in legal language describes a person whose blood contains more than the legally allowed percentage of alcohol: *Drunk drivers go to jail.* DRUNKEN, not DRUNK, is almost always the form used with nouns that do not name persons: *drunken arrogance; a drunken free-for-all.* In such uses it normally has the sense "pertaining to, caused by, or marked by intoxication." DRUNKEN is also idiomatic in such expressions as *drunken bum.* See also **drink.**

drunk·ard (drung′kərd), *n.* a person who is habitually or frequently drunk. [1400–50; late ME; see DRUNK, -ARD]
—Syn. toper, sot, tippler, drinker. DRUNKARD and INEBRIATE are terms for a person who drinks hard liquors habitually. DRUNKARD connotes willful indulgence to excess. INEBRIATE is a slightly more formal term than DRUNKARD. DIPSOMANIAC is the term for a person who, because of some psychological or physiological illness, has an irresistible craving for liquor. The DIPSOMANIAC is popularly called an ALCOHOLIC. **—Ant.** teetotaler.

drunk′ard's chair′, *Eng. Furniture.* a low, deep armchair of the 18th century.

drunk′ driv′ing, the operating of a motor vehicle while drunk. **—drunk′-driv′ing,** *adj.*

drunk·en (drung′kən), *adj.* **1.** intoxicated; drunk. **2.** given to drunkenness. **3.** pertaining to, caused by, or marked by intoxication: *a drunken quarrel.* [var. of DRUNK adj. and ptp.] **—drunk′en·ly,** *adv.* **—drunk′en·ness,** *n.*
—Syn. 1. inebriated, tipsy, fuddled, besotted. **—Ant. 1.** sober.
—Usage. See **drunk.**

drunk·om·e·ter (drung kom′i tər), *n.* a device for measuring the amount of alcohol in a person's breath to determine the amount of alcohol in the bloodstream. [1930–35, *Amer.*; DRUNK + -O- + -METER]

drunk′ tank′, *Informal.* a large jail cell where persons arrested for drunkenness are kept, usually overnight. [1940–45]

dru·pa·ceous (dro͞o pā′shəs), *adj. Bot.* **1.** resembling or relating to a drupe; consisting of drupes. **2.** producing drupes: *drupaceous trees.* [1815–25; DRUPE + -ACEOUS]

drupe (dro͞op), *n. Bot.* any fruit, as a peach, cherry, plum, etc., consisting of an outer skin, a usually pulpy and succulent middle layer, and a hard and woody inner shell usually enclosing a single seed. [1745–55; < L *drūpa, druppa* overripe olive < Gk *drýppa* olive]

drupe·let (dro͞op′lit), *n. Bot.* a little drupe, as one of the individual pericarps composing the blackberry. [1875–80; DRUPE + -LET]

Dru′ry Lane′ (dro͝or′ē), **1.** a street in London, England, formerly notable for its theaters, named after the house Sir William Drury built there in the reign of Henry VIII. **2.** a famous theater (founded 1661) on Drury Lane in London, England. **3.** the theatrical district located on or near this street.

druse (dro͞oz), *n.* an incrustation of small crystals on the surface of a rock or mineral. [1745–55; < G; cf. MHG, OHG *druos* gland, tumor, G *Drüse* gland (MHG *drües,* pl. of *druos*)]

Dru·sil·la (dro͞o sil′ə), *n.* a female given name.

Dru·sus (dro͞o′səs), *n.* **Nero Claudius** (*"Germanicus"*), 38–9 B.C., Roman general.

druth·ers (druth′ərz), *n. Informal.* one's own way, choice, or preference: *If I had my druthers, I'd dance all night.* [1870–75; pl. of *druther,* (*I, you,* etc.) *'d rather* (contr. of *would rather*)]

Druze (dro͞oz), *n. Islam.* a member of an independent religious sect living chiefly in Syria, Lebanon, and Israel, established in the 11th century as a branch of Isma'ili Shi'ism and containing elements of Christianity, Judaism, and Islam, and believing in the transmigration of souls and the ultimate perfection of humankind. Also, **Druse.** [1595–1605; < Ar *durūz,* pl. of *durzī* a Druze, deriv. of the name of one of the sect founders, *Muḥammad ibn Ismā'īl al-Darazī*] **—Dru′ze·an, Dru′zi·an,** *adj.*

D.R.V., (on food labels) Daily Reference Value: the amount of nutrients appropriate for one day.

dry (drī), *adj.,* **dri·er, dri·est,** *v.,* **dried, dry·ing,** *n., pl.* **drys, dries.** —*adj.* **1.** free from moisture or excess moisture; not moist; not wet: *a dry towel; dry air.* **2.** having or characterized by little or no rain: *a dry climate; the dry season.* **3.** characterized by absence, deficiency, or failure of natural or ordinary moisture. **4.** not under, in, or on water: *It was good to be on dry land.* **5.** not now containing or yielding water or other liquid; depleted or empty of liquid: *The well is dry.* **6.** not yielding milk: *a dry cow.* **7.** free from tears: *dry eyes.* **8.** drained or evaporated away: *a dry river.* **9.** desiring drink; thirsty: *He was so dry he could hardly speak.* **10.** causing thirst: *dry work.* **11.** served or eaten without butter, jam, etc.: *dry toast.* **12.** (of cooked food) lacking enough moisture or juice to be satisfying or succulent. **13.** (of bread and bakery products) stale. **14.** of or pertaining to nonliquid substances or commodities: *dry measure; dry provisions.* **15.** (of wines) not sweet. **16.** (of a cocktail) **a.** made with dry vermouth: *a dry Manhattan.* **b.** made with relatively little dry vermouth: *a dry martini.* **17.** characterized by or favoring prohibition of the manufacture and sale of alcoholic liquors for use in beverages: *a dry state.* **18.** (of British biscuits) not sweet. **19.** plain; bald; unadorned: *dry facts.* **20.** dull; uninteresting: *a dry subject.* **21.** expressed in a straight-faced, matter-of-fact way: *dry humor.* **22.** indifferent; cold; unemotional: *a dry answer.* **23.** unproductive: *The greatest of artists have dry years.* **24.** (of lumber) fully seasoned. **25.** *Building Trades.* **a.** (of masonry construction) built without fresh mortar or cement. **b.** (of a wall, ceiling, etc., in an interior) finished without the use of fresh plaster. **26.** *Ceram.* **a.** unglazed. **b.** insufficiently glazed. **27.** *Art.* hard and formal in outline, or lacking mellowness and warmth in color. **28. not dry behind the ears,** immature; unsophisticated: *Adult responsibilities were forced on him, although he was still not dry behind the ears.* —*v.t.* **29.** to make dry; free from moisture: *to dry the dishes.* —*v.i.* **30.** to become dry; lose moisture. **31. dry out, a.** to make or become completely dry. **b.** to undergo or cause to undergo detoxification from consumption of excessive amounts of alcohol. **32. dry up, a.** to make or become completely dry. **b.** to cease to exist; evaporate. **c.** *Informal.* to stop talking. **d.** (in acting) to forget one's lines or part. —*n.* **33.** a prohibitionist. **34.** a dry place, area, or region. [bef. 900; ME *drie,* OE *drȳge;* akin to D *droog,* G *trocken;* see DROUGHT] **—dry′a·ble,** *adj.* **—dry′ly,** *adv.* **—dry′ness,** *n.*
—Syn. 1. DRY, ARID both mean without moisture. DRY is the general word indicating absence of water or freedom from moisture: *a dry well; dry clothes.* ARID suggests great or intense dryness in a region or climate, esp. such as results in bareness or in barrenness: *arid tracts of desert.* **20.** tedious, barren, boring, tiresome, jejune. **29.** See **evaporate. 30.** dehydrate. **—Ant. 1.** wet. **20.** interesting.

dry·ad (drī′əd, -ad), *n., pl.* **-ads, -a·des** (-ə dēz′). (*often cap.*) *Class. Myth.* a deity or nymph of the woods. Cf. **hamadryad.** [1545–55; extracted from Gk *Dryádes,* pl. of *Dryás,* deriv. of *drȳ́(s)* tree, oak] **—dry·ad·ic** (drī ad′ik), *adj.*

dry·as (drī′əs), *n., pl.* **dry·as.** any creeping plant belonging to the genus *Dryas,* of the rose family, having solitary white or yellow flowers, comprising the mountain avens. [< NL, named after species of wood nymphs; see DRYAD]

dry-as-dust (drī′əz dust′), *adj.* dull and boring: *a dry-as-dust biography.* Also, **dry′as·dust′.** [1870–75; after Dr. *Dryasdust,* a fictitious pedant satirized in the prefaces of Sir Walter Scott's novels]

dry′ bat′tery, *Elect.* a dry cell or a voltaic battery consisting of a number of dry cells. [1880–85]

dry′-bone ore′ (drī′bōn′), *Mineral.* a porous variety of smithsonite found near the surface of the earth.

dry·brush (drī′brush′), *n.* a technique of drawing or painting in which a brush having a small quantity of pigment or medium is applied to or dragged across a surface. [1910–15; DRY + BRUSH[1]]

dry′-bulb thermom′eter (drī′bulb′), a thermometer having a dry bulb: used in conjunction with a wet-bulb thermometer in a psychrometer.

dry′ bulk′, a category of cargo stowed in bulk, consisting of grain, cotton, coal, etc. **—dry′-bulk′,** *adj.*

dry′ cell′, *Elect.* a cell in which the electrolyte exists in the form of a paste, is absorbed in a porous medium, or is otherwise restrained from flowing. Cf. **battery** (def. 1). [1890–95]

dry-clean (drī′klēn′), *v.t.* to clean (garments, draperies, rugs, etc.) with a liquid other than water, as benzine or gasoline. [1810–20; back formation from DRY CLEANING]

dry′ clean′er, **1.** a business that dry-cleans garments, draperies, etc. **2.** a person who owns or operates such an establishment. **3.** a liquid solvent used in dry cleaning. [1895–1900]

dry′ clean′ing, **1.** the cleaning of garments, fabrics, draperies, etc., with any of various chemicals rather than water. **2.** garments for cleaning in this way. [1810–20] **—dry′-clean′ing,** *adj.*

dry-cleanse (drī′klenz′), *v.t.,* **-cleansed, -cleans·ing.** to dry-clean.

dry′ com′pass, *Navig.* a compass having a compass card mounted on pivots. Cf. **wet compass.**

Dry·den (drīd′n), *n.* **John,** 1631–1700, English poet, dramatist, and critic. **—Dry·de·ni·an** (drī dē′nē ən, -dēn′yən), **Dry·den·ic** (drī den′ik), *adj.*

dry′ distilla′tion, *Chem.* See **destructive distillation.**

dry′ dock′, a structure able to contain a ship and to be drained or lifted so as to leave the ship free of water with all parts of the hull accessible for repairs, painting, etc. Cf. **floating dock, graving dock.** [1620–30]

dry-dock (drī′dok′), *v.t.* **1.** to place (a ship) in a dry dock. —*v.i.* **2.** (of a ship) to go into a dry dock. [1880–85]

dry-dock·age (drī′dok′ij), *n.* **1.** the act or fact of placing a ship in a dry dock. **2.** a charge for repairs in a dry dock: *Dry-dockage is the largest item in the ship's maintenance.* [DRY-DOCK + -AGE]

dry·er (drī′ər), *n.* **1.** Also, **drier.** a machine, appliance, or apparatus for removing moisture, as by forced ventilation or heat: *hair dryer; clothes dryer.* **2.** drier[1] (defs. 1, 2).

dry′ eye′, *Pathol.* an abnormal eye condition caused by an inadequate tear film, characterized by burning, itchy, and dry eyes and sometimes blurred vision.

dry-eyed (drī′īd′), *adj.* not weeping; unmoved. [1660–70]

dry-farm (drī′färm′), *v.i.* **1.** to engage in dryland farming. —*v.t.* **2.** to grow (a specified crop) by means of dryland farming. [1915–20, *Amer.*] **—dry′ farm′er.**

dry′ farm′ing. See **dryland farming.** [1875–80]

dry′ fly′, *Angling.* an artificial fly designed for use on the surface of the water. Cf. **wet fly.** [1840–50]

dry′ fog′, *Meteorol.* a fog that does not moisten exposed surfaces.

dry-foot·ing (drī′fo͝ot′ing), *n. Ceram.* removal of glaze from the rim at the bottom of a piece. [*dry foot* the base of the piece + -ING[1]]

dry′ freeze′, *Meteorol.* the occurrence of freezing temperatures without the formation of hoarfrost.

dry′ fres′co. See **fresco secco.**

dry′ gan′grene, death of tissue owing to arterial obstruction without subsequent bacterial decomposition and putrefaction. [1930–35]

Dry·gas (drī′gas′), *Chem., Trademark.* a brand of gasoline-line antifreeze consisting of methyl alcohol, isopropyl alcohol, or a mixture of these.

dry′ goods′, textile fabrics and related merchandise, as distinguished from groceries, hardware, etc. [1695–1705]

dry-gulch (drī′gulch′), *v.t. Informal.* **1.** to ambush with the intent of killing or severely mauling: *The riders were dry-gulched by bandits.* **2.** to betray by a sudden change of attitude or allegiance: *The party dry-gulched its chief candidate at the convention.* Also, **dry′gulch′.** [1865–70]

dry′ hole′, any well drilled for oil or gas that does not yield enough to be commercially profitable. Also called **duster.** [1880–85, *Amer.*]

Dry′ Ice′, *Chem., Trademark.* the solid form of carbon dioxide, which sublimes at −109.26°F (−78.48°C) and is used chiefly as a refrigerant.

dry·ing (drī′ing), *adj.* **1.** causing dryness: *a drying breeze.* **2.** designed to become or capable of becoming dry and hard on exposure to air. [1350–1400; ME; see DRY, -ING[2]]

dry′ing oil′, any of a group of oily, organic liquids occurring naturally, as linseed, soybean, or dehydrated castor oil, or synthesized, that when applied as a thin coating absorb atmospheric oxygen, forming a tough, elastic layer. [1860–65]

dry·ing-out (drī′ing out′), *n.* the process of detoxifying an alcoholic patient: *Drying-out takes time.* [1965–70; n. use (with -ING[1]) of v. phrase *dry out*]

dry′ kiln′, an oven for the controlled drying and seasoning of cut lumber. [1905–10]

dry′ lake′, a tract of land in a desert region over which a shallow lake is formed during the rainy season or after prolonged heavy rains. Cf. **playa.**

dry·land (drī′land′), *n.* Often, **drylands.** a tract of land having dry, often sandy soil, as on the floor of a valley: *Acres of the drylands have been reclaimed by irrigation.* [1175–1225; ME. See DRY, -LAND]

dry′land farm′ing, a mode of farming, practiced in regions of slight or insufficient rainfall, that relies mainly on tillage methods rendering the soil more receptive of moisture and on the selection of suitable crops. Also called **dry farming.** [1910–15, *Amer.*]

dry′ law′, a law prohibiting the manufacture or sale of alcoholic beverages.

dry′ lot′, *Agric.* a fenced-in area that is free of vegetation and is used for the containment, feeding, and fattening of livestock. [1920–25; DRY (implying a lack of vegetation, as opposed to pasture) + LOT]

dry′ meas′ure, the system of units of capacity ordinarily used in measuring dry commodities, as grain or fruit. In the U.S. 2 pints = 1 quart (1.101 liters); 8 quarts = 1 peck (8.810 liters); 4 pecks = 1 bushel (35.24 liters). In Great Britain 2 pints = 1 quart (1.136 liters); 4 quarts = 1 gallon (4.546 liters); 8 quarts = 1 peck (9.092 liters); 4 pecks = 1 bushel (36.37 liters); 8 bushels = 1 quarter (291.0 liters). [1680–90]

dry′ milk′, dehydrated milk from which about 95 percent of the moisture has been evaporated. Also called **dried milk, milk powder, powdered milk.**

dry′ mop′. See **dust mop.** [1930–35]

dry′ mount′ing, the technique of fastening a print, photograph, or the like to a board by using a heated thermoplastic tissue as an adhesive. [1900–05] —**dry′-mount′ed,** *adj.*

dry′ nurse′, **1.** a nurse who takes care of but does not breast-feed another's infant. Cf. **wet nurse. 2.** *Informal.* a person who tutors and guides an inexperienced person at work. [1590–1600]

dry-nurse (drī′nûrs′), *v.t.,* **-nursed, -nurs•ing.** to act as a dry nurse to. [1575–85]

dry′ off′set, *Print.* letterset. [1955–60]

dry•o•morph (drī′ə môrf′), *n.* any member of the extinct genus *Dryopithecus.* Cf. **Proconsul.** [DRYO(PITHECUS) + -MORPH]

dry•o•pith•e•cine (drī′ō pith′ə sēn′, -sīn′, -pə thē′-sin, -sīn), *n.* **1.** (*sometimes cap.*) an extinct ape of the genus *Dryopithecus,* known from Old World Miocene fossils. —*adj.* **2.** of or pertaining to this ape. [1945–50; DRYOPITHEC(US) + -INE[1]]

Dry•o•pith•e•cus (drī′ō pith′i kəs, -pə thē′-), *n.* **1.** an extinct genus of generalized hominoids that lived in Europe and Africa during the Miocene Epoch and whose members are characterized by small molars and incisors. **2.** one of the four subgenera of this genus, limited to Europe. Cf. **dryomorph, Proconsul.** [< NL (1856) < Gk *drŷ(s)* tree, oak + -o- -o- + *píthēkos* monkey]

dry•out (drī′out′), *n.* **1.** the process or an instance of drying out: *applying compost to the garden soil to retard dryout.* **2.** *Informal.* a facility for detoxifying alcoholic patients. [n. use of v. phrase *dry out*]

dry′ plate′, **1.** a glass photographic plate coated with a sensitive emulsion of silver bromide and silver iodide in gelatin. **2.** *Metall.* tin plate having patches of dull finish. [1855–60]

dry•point (drī′point′), *n.* **1.** a technique of engraving, esp. on copper, in which a sharp-pointed needle is used for producing furrows having a burr that is often retained in order to produce a print characterized by soft, velvety black lines. **2.** a print made by this technique. [1825–35; DRY + POINT]

dry′ pud′dling, *Metall.* puddling in a furnace with a bottom of sand. Cf. **wet puddling.**

dry′ rent′, *Law.* See **rent seck.**

dry-roast•ed (drī′rō′stid), *adj.* roasted with no oil, or less oil than is usually used in roasting, so that the product is drier, crisper, and less caloric: *dry-roasted peanuts.* Also, **dry′-roast′.**

dry′ rot′, **1.** *Plant Pathol.* **a.** a decay of seasoned timber, resulting in its becoming brittle and crumbling to a dry powder, caused by various fungi. **b.** any of various diseases of plants in which the rotted tissues are dry. **2.** any concealed or unsuspected inner decay. [1785–95]

dry-rot (drī′rot′), *v.i., v.t.,* **-rot•ted, -rot•ting.** to undergo or cause to undergo the action or effects of dry rot. [1865–70]

dry′ rot′ fun′gus, a fungus, *Merulius lacrymans,* that causes a common type of dry rot. Also called **house fungus.**

dry′ run′, **1.** a rehearsal or practice exercise. **2.** *Mil.* practice in firing arms without using live ammunition. [1940–45, *Amer.*] —**dry′-run′,** *adj.*

dry-salt (drī′sôlt′), *v.t.* to cure or preserve (meat, hides, etc.) by drying and salting. [1615–25]

dry•salt•er (drī′sôl′tər), *n. Brit.* a dealer in dry chemicals and dyes. [1700–10; DRY + SALTER]

dry-shod (drī′shod′), *adj.* having or keeping the shoes dry. [bef. 1000; ME *drye schodde,* OE *drȳgsceod,* equiv. to *drȳg-* DRY + *sc(e)od,* ptp. of *scōgan* to shoe, deriv. of *sc(e)ōh* SHOE]

dry′ sink′, a wooden kitchen sink, esp. of the 19th century, not connected to an external water supply, with a shallow zinc- or tin-lined well on top in which a dishpan can be placed, and usually a cupboard below. [1950–55]

dry′ sock′et, *Dentistry.* a painful inflammatory infection of the bone and tissues at the site of an extracted tooth.

dry′ spell′, **1.** a prolonged period of dry weather. **2.** a period of little or no productivity or activity, low income, etc. [1885–90]

dry′ suit′, a close-fitting, double-layered synthetic garment worn by a scuba diver in especially cold water, protecting the skin from contact with water and having an internal, warming layer of air that can be added to in order to equalize pressure during descent. [1950–55]

CONCISE ETYMOLOGY KEY: <, descended or borrowed from; >, whence; b., blend of, blended; c., cognate with; cf., compare; deriv., derivative; equiv., equivalent; imit., imitative; obl., oblique; r., replacing; s., stem; sp., spelling, spelled; resp., respelling, respelled; trans., translation; ?, origin unknown; *, unattested; ‡, probably earlier than. See the full key inside the front cover.

Dry′ Tor•tu′gas (tôr to͞o′gəz), a group of ten small islands at the entrance to the Gulf of Mexico W of Key West: a part of Florida; the site of Fort Jefferson.

dry′ wall′, *Building Trades.* **1.** Also, **dry′wall′. a.** an interior wall or partition finished in a dry material, usually in the form of prefabricated sheets or panels nailed to studs, as distinguished from one that is plastered. **b.** a material, as wallboard or plasterboard, used for such a wall. **2.** a masonry or stone wall laid up without mortar. [1770–80, for earlier sense]

dry-wall (drī′wôl′), *v.t.* **1.** to construct or renovate with dry wall: *to dry-wall the interior of a house.* —*adj.* **2.** of, pertaining to, or having dry wall. —**dry′-wall′er,** *n.*

dry′ wash′, **1.** clothes, curtains, etc., washed and dried but not yet ironed. Cf. **wet wash. 2.** wash (def. 46). [1870–75]

dry′ well′, **1.** a drainage pit lined with loose stonework for the leaching of liquid wastes. **2.** See **absorbing well.** [1760–70]

Dr. Zhi•va•go (zhi vä′gō), a novel (1958) by Boris Pasternak.

Ds, *Symbol, Chem.* (formerly) dysprosium.

ds, decistere; decisteres.

D.S., **1.** *Music.* from the sign. [< It *dal segno*] **2.** Doctor of Science.

d.s., **1.** daylight saving. **2.** *Com.* Also, **D/S** days after sight. **3.** document signed.

DSA, See **digital subtraction angiography.**

DSC, Defense Supplies Corporation.

D.Sc., Doctor of Science.

D.S.C., **1.** See **Distinguished Service Cross. 2.** Doctor of Surgical Chiropody.

D.S.M., **1.** See **Distinguished Service Medal. 2.** Doctor of Sacred Music.

DSNA, Dictionary Society of North America.

D.S.O., See **Distinguished Service Order.**

D.S.P., died without issue. [< L *dēcessit sine prōle*]

DSR, See **dynamic spatial reconstructor.**

D.S.S., Doctor of Social Science.

DST, daylight-saving time.

D.S.T, **1.** daylight-saving time. **2.** Doctor of Sacred Theology.

D. Surg., Dental Surgeon.

D.S.W., **1.** Doctor of Social Welfare. **2.** Doctor of Social Work.

DT, *Slang.* detective. Also, **D.T.**

d.t.d., (in prescriptions) give such doses. [< L *dentur tālēs dosēs*]

D.Th., Doctor of Theology. Also, **D.Theol.**

DTP, diphtheria, tetanus, and pertussis. See **DPT.**

d.t.'s (dē′tēz′), *n.* **the,** See **delirium tremens.**

du (do͞o, dyo͞o; *Fr.* dʏ), (in names of French derivation) a contraction of *de* and the article *le: Joachim du Bellay.*

Du., **1.** Duke. **2.** Dutch.

du•ad (do͞o′ad, dyo͞o′-), *n.* a group of two; couple; pair. [1650–60; < L *duo* TWO + -AD[1]]

du•al (do͞o′əl, dyo͞o′-), *adj.* **1.** of, pertaining to, or noting two. **2.** composed or consisting of two people, items, parts, etc., together; twofold; double: *dual ownership; dual controls on a plane.* **3.** having a twofold, or double, character or nature. **4.** *Gram.* being or pertaining to a member of the category of number, as in Old English, Old Russian, or Arabic, that denotes two of the things in question. —*n. Gram.* **5.** the dual number. **6.** a form in the dual, as Old English *git* "you two," as contrasted with *ge* "you" referring to three or more. [1535–45; < L *duālis* containing two, relating to a pair, equiv. to *du(o)* TWO + *-ālis* -AL[1]] —**du′al•ly,** *adv.*

Du•a•la (do͞o ä′lä), *n.* Douala.

Du′al Alli′ance, **1.** the alliance between France and Russia (1890), strengthened by a military convention (1892–93) and lasting until the Bolshevik Revolution in 1917. **2.** the alliance between Germany and Austria-Hungary against Russia 1879–1918.

du•al-carb (do͞o′əl kärb′, dyo͞o′-), *adj. Auto.* (of an engine) equipped with a pair of carburetors.

du′al car′riageway, *Brit.* See **divided highway.** [1930–35]

du′al cit′izen, a person who is a citizen or subject of two or more nations; one having dual citizenship.

du′al cit′izenship, **1.** Also called **du′al national′ity.** the status of a person who is a legal citizen of two or more countries. **2.** citizenship of both a state and a nation, in nations consisting of a federation of states, as the U.S. [1920–25]

du′al high′way. See **divided highway.** [1955–60]

du•al•ism (do͞o′ə liz′əm, dyo͞o′-), *n.* **1.** the state of being dual or consisting of two parts; division into two. **2.** *Philos.* **a.** the view that there are just two mutually irreducible substances. Cf. **monism, pluralism. b.** the view that substances are either material or mental. **3.** *Theol.* **a.** the doctrine that there are two independent divine beings or eternal principles, one good and the other evil. **b.** the belief that a human being embodies two parts, as body and soul. [1785–95; DUAL + -ISM] —**du′•al•ist,** *n., adj.*

du•al•is•tic (do͞o′ə lis′tik, dyo͞o′-), *adj.* **1.** of, pertaining to, or of the nature of dualism. **2.** dual; twofold. [1795–1805; DUAL + -ISTIC] —**du′al•is′ti•cal•ly,** *adv.*

du•al•i•ty (do͞o al′i tē, dyo͞o-), *n.* **1.** a dual state or quality. **2.** *Math.* a symmetry within a mathematical system such that a theorem remains valid if certain objects, relations, or operations are interchanged, as the interchange of points and lines in a plane in projective geometry. [1350–1400; ME *dualitie* < LL *duālitās.* See DUAL, -ITY]

dual′ity prin′ciple, *Math.* the principle that a mathematical duality exists under certain conditions. Also called **principle of duality.**

du•al•ize (do͞o′ə līz′, dyo͞o′-), *v.t.,* **-ized, -iz•ing. 1.** to make dual. **2.** to regard as dual. Also, *esp. Brit.,* **du′al•ise′.** [1830–40; DUAL + -IZE] —**du′al•i•za′tion,** *n.*

Du′al Mon′archy, the kingdom of Austria-Hungary 1867–1918.

du′al national′ity. See **dual citizenship** (def. 1).

du′al personal′ity, *Psychol.* a disorder in which an individual possesses two dissociated personalities. Cf. **multiple personality.** [1900–05]

du•al-pur•pose (do͞o′əl pûr′pəs, dyo͞o′-), *adj.* **1.** serving two functions. **2.** (of cattle) bred for two purposes, as to provide beef and milk. [1910–15]

du′al space′, *Math.* the set of all linear functionals whose domain is a given vector space.

Duane (dwān, do͞o ān′), *n.* a male given name.

du•ar•chy (do͞o′är kē, dyo͞o′-), *n., pl.* **-chies.** a government or form of government in which power is vested equally in two rulers. [1580–90; < L *du(o)* TWO + -ARCHY]

Duar•te (dwär′tē), *n.* a city in SW California. 16,766.

Duar•te Fuen•tes (dwäʀ′te fwen′tes), **Jo•sé Na•po•le•ón** (hô se′ nä pô le ôn′), 1926–90, Salvadoran political leader: president 1980–82, 1984–89.

dub[1] (dub), *v.,* **dubbed, dub•bing,** —*v.t.* **1.** to invest with any name, character, dignity, or title; style; name; call: *He was dubbed a hero.* **2.** to strike lightly with a sword in the ceremony of conferring knighthood; make, or designate as, a knight: *The king dubbed him a knight.* **3.** to strike, cut, rub, or make smooth, as leather or timber. **4. dub bright,** *Shipbuilding.* to shave off the outer surface of the planking of (a ship). [1175–1225; ME *dubben,* late OE **dubbian* (in phrase *dubbade tō ridere* dubbed to knight(hood)), < AF *dubber, dobber, douber,* aph. form of *ad(o)uber,* equiv. to *a-* A-[5] + *-do(u)ber* < Old Low Franconian **dubban* to strike, beat, c. LG *dubben,* DUB[3]; cf. DAUBE] —**dub′ber,** *n.*

dub[2] (dub), *n. Slang.* an awkward, unskillful person. [1885–90; of expressive orig., cf. FLUB, FLUBDUB, DUB[3]]

dub[3] (dub), *v.,* **dubbed, dub•bing,** *n.* —*v.t.* **1.** to thrust; poke. **2.** *Golf.* to hit (a ball) poorly; misplay (a shot). **3.** to execute poorly. —*v.i.* **4.** to thrust; poke. —*n.* **5.** a thrust; poke. **6.** a drumbeat. [1505–15; appar. same word (with older sense) as DUB[1]]

dub[4] (dub), *v.,* **dubbed, dub•bing,** *n.* —*v.t.* **1.** to furnish (a film or tape) with a new sound track, as one recorded in the language of the country of import. **2.** to add (music, speech, etc.) to a film or tape recording (often fol. by *in*). **3.** to copy (a tape or disc recording). —*v.i.* **4.** to copy program material from one tape recording onto another. **5. dub out,** to omit or erase (unwanted sound) on a tape or sound track: *to dub out background noise.* —*n.* **6.** the new sounds added to a film or tape. [1925–30; short for DOUBLE] —**dub′ber,** *n.*

dub[5] (dub), *n. Chiefly Scot.* a pool of water; puddle. [1490–1500; of obscure orig.; perh. akin to G *Tümpel* pond, puddle]

Du•bai (do͞o bī′), *n.* **1.** an emirate in the NE United Arab Emirates, on the Persian Gulf. 278,437. **2.** a seaport in and the capital of the emirate of Dubai. 206,861. Also, **Dibai.**

Du Bar•ry (do͞o bar′ē, dyo͞o; *Fr.* dʏ bᴀ ʀē′), **Comtesse** (*Marie Jeanne Bécu*), 1746–93, mistress of Louis XV.

dub•bel•tje (dub′əl chə, -tyə), *n.* a silver ten-cent piece of the Netherlands. [1815–25; < D, equiv. to *dubbel* DOUBLE + *-tje* dim. suffix; double the value of a 5-cent piece]

dub•bin (dub′in), *n.* a mixture of tallow and oil used in dressing leather. Also, **dubbing.** [1815–25; var. of DUBBING]

dub•bing[1] (dub′ing), *n.* **1.** the conferring of knighthood; accolade. **2.** *Angling.* the material used for the body of an artificial fly. **3.** dubbin. [1250–1300; ME; see DUB[1], -ING[1]]

dub•bing[2] (dub′ing), *n.* the act or process of furnishing a film or tape with a new sound track or adding music, sound effects, etc., to an existing one. [1925–30; DUB[4] + -ING[1]]

Dub•bo (dub′ō), *n.* a city in E Australia. 23,986.

Dub•ček (do͞ob′chek; *Czech.* do͝op′chek), *n.* **Alexander,** 1921–92, Czechoslovakian political leader: first secretary of the Communist party 1968–69.

du Bel•lay (do͞o bə lā′, dyo͞o; *Fr.* dʏ be lā′), **Jo•a•chim** (*Fr.* zhô ᴀ kēm′). See **Bellay, Joachim du.**

du•bi•e•ty (do͞o bī′i tē, dyo͞o-), *n., pl.* **-ties. 1.** doubtfulness; doubt. **2.** a matter of doubt. Also called **dubiosity.** [1740–50; < L *dubietās,* equiv. to *dubi(us)* DUBIOUS + *-etās,* var. of *-itās* after vocalic stems; see -ITY]
—**Syn. 1.** skepticism, mistrust, distrust, suspicion.

Du•bin•sky (do͞o bin′skē), *n.* **David,** 1892–1982, U.S. labor leader, born in Poland: president of the I.L.G.W.U. 1932–66.

du•bi•os•i•ty (do͞o′bē os′i tē, dyo͞o′-), *n., pl.* **-ties.** dubiety. [1640–50]

du•bi•ous (do͞o′bē əs, dyo͞o′-), *adj.* **1.** doubtful; marked by or occasioning doubt: *a dubious reply.* **2.** of doubtful quality or propriety; questionable: *a dubious compliment; a dubious transaction.* **3.** of uncertain outcome: *in dubious battle.* **4.** wavering or hesitating in opinion; inclined to doubt. [1540–50; < L *dubius;* see -OUS] —**du′bi•ous•ly,** *adv.* —**du′bi•ous•ness,** *n.*
—**Syn. 1.** equivocal, ambiguous, obscure, unclear. **4.** undecided, uncertain, hesitant, fluctuating. See **doubtful.**

du•bi•ta•ble (do͞o′bi tə bəl, dyo͞o′-), *adj.* open to doubt; doubtful; uncertain. [1615–25; < L *dubitābilis,* equiv. to *dubitā(re)* to doubt + *-bilis* -BLE] **—du′bi·ta·bly,** *adv.*

du·bi·ta·tion (do͞o′bi tā′shən, dyo͞o′-), *n. Archaic.* doubt. [1400–50; late ME (< MF, OF) < L *dubitātiōn-* (s. of *dubitātiō*), equiv. to *dubitāt(us)*, ptp. of *dubitāre* (*dubit-* DOUBT + *-ātus* -ATE[1]) + *-iōn-* -ION]

du·bi·ta·tive (do͞o′bi tā′tiv, dyo͞o′-), *adj.* **1.** doubting; doubtful. **2.** expressing doubt. [1605–15; < LL *dubitātivus*, equiv. to *dubitāt(us)* (see DUBITATION) + *-ivus* -IVE] **—du′bi·ta′tive·ly,** *adv.*

Dub·lin (dub′lin), *n.* **1.** Gaelic, **Baile Àtha Cliath.** a seaport in and the capital of the Republic of Ireland, in the E part, on the Irish Sea. 422,220. **2.** a county in E Republic of Ireland. 1,001,985; 356 sq. mi. (922 sq. km). *Co. seat:* Dublin. **3.** a city in central Georgia. 16,083.

Dub·lin·ers (dub′lə nərz), *n.* a collection of short stories (1914) by James Joyce.

Du Bois (do͞o bois′), **William Edward Burg·hardt** (bûrg′härd), 1868–1963, U.S. educator and writer.

Du·bois (dʏ bwä′), *n.* **(Ma·rie) Eu·gène (Fran·çois Tho·mas)** (mȧ rē′ œ zhen′ fräɴ swȧ′ tô mä′), 1858–1941, Dutch physical anthropologist and anatomist.

Du·bon·net (do͞o′bə nā′, dyo͞o′-), **1.** *Trademark.* a brand of sweet, red or white, aromatized wine, used chiefly as an apéritif. —*n.* **2.** (*l.c.*) a deep purple-red color. —*adj.* **3.** (*l.c.*) of the color dubonnet.

Du·bos (do͞o bōs′; *Fr.* dʏ bôs′), *n.* **Re·né Jules** (rə nā′ jo͞olz; *Fr.* rə nā′ zhʏl), 1901–82, U.S. bacteriologist, born in France: early advocate of ecological concern.

Du·brov·nik (do͞o′brôv nik), *n.* a seaport in S Croatia, on the Adriatic: resort. 58,920. Italian, **Ragusa.**

Du·buf·fet (do͞o′bə fā′, dyo͞o′-; *Fr.* dʏ bʏ fe′), *n.* **Jean** (zhäɴ), 1901–85, French painter.

Du·buque (də byo͞ok′), *n.* a city in E Iowa, on the Mississippi River. 62,321.

duc (dʏk), *n., pl.* ***ducs*** (dʏk). *French.* duke.

du·cal (do͞o′kəl, dyo͞o′-), *adj.* of or pertaining to a duke or dukedom. [1485–95; < LL *ducālis* of a leader. See DUKE, -AL[1]]

du·cal·ly (do͞o′kə lē, dyo͞o′-), *adv.* **1.** in the manner of or pertaining to a duke. **2.** *Heraldry.* with a ducal coronet: *a lion gules ducally gorged.* [1815–25; DUCAL + -LY]

Du·casse (dʏ kȧs′), *n.* **Jean Jules A·ma·ble Ro·ger-** (zhäɴ zhʏl ȧ mȧ′blə rô zhā′). See **Roger-Ducasse, Jean Jules Amable.**

duc·at (duk′ət), *n.* **1.** any of various gold coins formerly issued in various parts of Europe, esp. that first issued in Venice in 1284. Cf. **sequin** (def. 2). **2.** any of various silver coins formerly issued in various parts of Europe. **3.** *Slang.* a ticket to a public performance. **4.** **ducats,** *Slang.* money; cash. [1350–1400; ME < MF < OIt *ducato* < ML *ducātus* DUCHY; prob. so called from the L words *dux* or *ducātus*, which formed part of the legends of such coins]

duc·a·toon (duk′ə to͞on′, duk′ə to͞on′), *n.* a former silver coin of the Netherlands, used through the 17th and 18th centuries: equal to three gulden. Also, **duc·a·ton** (duk′ə ton′). [1605–15; < F *ducaton*, dim. of *ducat* DUCAT]

Duc·cio di Buo·nin·se·gna (do͞ot′chô dē bwô′nēnse′nyä), c1255–1319?, Italian painter.

du·ce (do͞o′chā; *It.* do͞o′che), *n., pl.* **-ces, -ci** (-chē). **1.** a leader or dictator. **2. il Duce,** the leader: applied esp. to Benito Mussolini as head of the fascist Italian state. [1920–25; < It < ML *dux* (gen. *ducis*), L: leader; cf. DUKE, DUX]

du Cer·ceau (*Fr.* dʏ ser sō′), **An·drou·et** (äɴ dro͞o e′). See **Androuet du Cerceau.**

du·ces te·cum (do͞o′sēz tē′kəm, do͞o′säz tā′kəm), *Law.* See **subpoena duces tecum.**

Du Chail·lu (do͞o shī′yo͞o, shal′-, dyo͞o; *Fr.* dʏ shȧyʏ′), **Paul Bel·lo·ni** (pôl bə lō′nē; *Fr.* pôl be lô nē′), 1835–1903, U.S. explorer in Africa, traveler, and writer; born in France.

Du·champ (dʏ shäɴ′), *n.* **Mar·cel** (mȧr sel′), 1887–1968, French painter, in U.S. after 1915 (brother of Raymond Duchamp-Villon and Jacques Villon).

Du·champ-Vil·lon (dʏ shäɴ vē yôɴ′), *n.* **Ray·mond** (re môɴ′), 1876–1918, French sculptor (brother of Jacques Villon and Marcel Duchamp).

duch·ess (duch′is), *n.* **1.** the wife or widow of a duke. **2.** a woman who holds in her own right the sovereignty or titles of a duchy. [1300–50; ME *duchesse* < AF, OF, fem. deriv. of *duc* DUKE; see -ESS] **—duch′ess·like′,** *adj.*
—Usage. See **-ess.**

du·chesse (*Fr.* dʏ shes′), *n., pl.* **du·chesses** (*Fr.* dʏshes′). *Fr. Furniture.* a daybed having a rounded, partially enclosed head and usually a similar foot, sometimes made in two or three pieces able to be used separately **(duchesse brisée).** [1785–95; < F; see DUCHESS]

duchesse′ bed′, *Fr. Furniture.* a bed having a suspended, full-length tester. Cf. **angel bed.**

du·chesse bri·sée (*Fr.* dʏ shes brē zā′), *pl.* **du·chesses bri·sées** (*Fr.* dʏ shes brē zā′). See under **duchesse.** [1935–40; < F: folding duchesse]

Duch′ess of Mal′fi, The (mal′fē), a tragedy (1614?) by John Webster.

duch′ess pota′toes, mashed potatoes mixed with cream, eggs, butter, and seasonings, piped onto a baking sheet or platter, sprinkled with grated cheese, and browned in the oven. [1925–30]

duch·y (duch′ē), *n., pl.* **duch·ies.** the territory ruled by a duke or duchess. [1350–1400; ME *duche* < MF *duche;* AF, OF *duchié* < ML *ducātus;* LL, L: the rank or functions of a DUX; see DUKE, -ATE[3]]

duck[1] (duk), *n., pl.* **ducks,** (*esp. collectively for 1, 2*) **duck. 1.** any of numerous wild or domesticated webfooted swimming birds of the family Anatidae, esp. of the genus *Anas* and allied genera, characterized by a broad, flat bill, short legs, and depressed body. **2.** the female of this bird, as distinguished from the male. Cf. **drake**[1]. **3.** the flesh of this bird, eaten as food. **4.** *Informal.* person; individual: *He's the queer old duck with the knee-length gaiters and walrus mustache.* **5.** a playing marble, esp. one that is not used as a shooter. **6.** **ducks,** (*used with a singular v.*) *Brit. Slang.* ducky[2]. **7.** *Cricket Slang.* **a.** failure of a batsman to score: *to be out for a duck.* **b.** a player's score of zero: *to be bowled for a duck.* Cf. **goose egg. 8. water off a duck's back,** something that has little or no effect: *Our criticisms of his talk rolled off him like water off a duck's back.* [bef. 1000; ME *duk, doke,* OE *dūce* diver, duck; akin to DUCK[2]]

duck[2] (duk), *v.i.* **1.** to stoop or bend suddenly; bob. **2.** to avoid or evade a blow, unpleasant task, etc.; dodge. **3.** to plunge the whole body or the head momentarily under water. **4.** *Cards Informal.* to play a card lower than the card led. —*v.t.* **5.** to lower suddenly: *Duck your head going through that low doorway.* **6.** to avoid or evade (a blow, unpleasant task, etc.); dodge: *to duck a hard right; to duck an embarrassing question.* **7.** to plunge or dip in water momentarily. **8.** *Cards Informal.* to play a card lower than (the card led). —*n.* **9.** an act or instance of ducking. [1250–1300; ME *duken, douken;* c. G *tauchen* to dive, *ducken* to duck]
—Syn. 1. bow, dodge. **3.** dive, dip, souse.

duck[3] (duk), *n.* **1.** a heavy, plain-weave cotton fabric for tents, clothing, bags, etc., in any of various weights and widths. **2. ducks,** (*used with a plural v.*) slacks or trousers made of this material. [1630–40; < D *doek* cloth; c. G *Tuch*]

duck[4] (duk), *n.* an amphibious military truck. [1940–45, *Amer.;* alter. of *DUKW*, code name]

duck′ and drake′. See **ducks and drakes** (def. 1). [1575–85]

duck·bill (duk′bil′), *n.* platypus. Also called **duck′bill plat′ypus, duck′-billed plat′ypus.** [1550–60; DUCK[1] + BILL[2]]

duck′-billed di′nosaur (duk′bild′), hadrosaur. [DUCK[1] + BILL[2] + -ED[3]]

duck·board (duk′bôrd′, -bōrd′), *n.* a board or boards laid as a track or floor over wet or muddy ground. [1915–20; DUCK[1] + BOARD]

duck-egg (duk′egg′), *n. Cricket.* duck[1] (def. 7). [1860–65]

duck·er (duk′ər), *n.* a person or thing that ducks. [1425–75; late ME; see DUCK[2], -ER[1]]

duck′ foot′, *Furniture.* See **web foot.**

duck·foot·ed (duk′fo͝ot′id), *adj.* afflicted with splayfoot. [1890–95; DUCK[1] + FOOTED]

duck′ hawk′, a peregrine falcon of the American subspecies *Falco peregrinus anatum*, noted for its especially swift flight. [1805–15, *Amer.*]

duck·ie (duk′ē), *adj.,* **duck·i·er, duck·i·est.** ducky[1].

duck′ing stool′, a former instrument of punishment consisting of a chair in which an offender was tied to be plunged into water. [1590–1600]

ducking stool

duck-leg·ged (duk′leg′id *or, esp. Brit.,* -legd′), *adj.* having legs that are unusually short: *He crept up in a half-crouch that made him look duck-legged.* [1640–50]

duck·ling (duk′ling), *n.* a young duck. [1400–50; late ME; see DUCK[1], -LING[1]]

duck′ on a rock′, a children's game in which one player stands guard over a stone on a rock while the other players attempt to knock it off by throwing another stone in turn: if the thrower is tagged by the guard while trying to recover the stone, the two players then change positions. Also called **duck′ on the rock′, duck′ on drake′.**

duck·pin (duk′pin′), *n.* **1.** *Bowling.* a short pin of relatively large diameter, used in a game resembling tenpins, and bowled at with small balls. **2. duckpins,** (*used with a singular v.*) the game played with such pins. [1905–10; so called from the pin's resemblance to the shape of a duck]

duck′ press′. See under **pressed duck.**

ducks′ and drakes′, 1. Also, **duck and drake.** a pastime in which flat stones or shells are thrown across water so as to skip over the surface several times before sinking. **2. play ducks and drakes with,** to handle recklessly; squander: *He played ducks and drakes with his fortune.* Also, **make ducks and drakes of.** [1575–85; from a fancied likeness to a waterfowl's movements]

duck's′ ass′, *Slang* (*vulgar*). DA. [1965–70]

duck′ soup′, something that is easy to do or accomplish: *Fixing the car will be duck soup for anyone with the right tools.* [1910–15, *Amer.*]

duck·tail (duk′tāl′), *n.* DA. Also called **duck′tail hair′cut.** [1950–55; DUCK[1] + TAIL[1]]

duck-walk (duk′wôk′), *v.i.* to walk like a duck, as with legs apart and feet turned outward.

duck·weed (duk′wēd′), *n.* any plant of the family Lemnaceae, esp. of the genus *Lemna*, comprising small aquatic plants that float free on still water. [1400–50; late ME *dockewede;* so called because eaten by ducks]

duck·wheat (duk′hwēt′, -wēt′), *n.* See **India wheat.** [1605–15; DUCK[1] + WHEAT]

duck·y[1] (duk′ē), *adj.,* **duck·i·er, duck·i·est.** *Informal.* **1.** fine; excellent; wonderful. **2.** darling; charming; cute. [1810–20; DUCK[1] + -Y[1]]

duck·y[2] (duk′ē), *n., pl.* **duck·ies.** *Brit. Slang.* (used as a term of endearment or familiarity) dear; sweetheart; darling; pet. [1530–40; DUCK[1] + -Y[2] (perh. alter. by folk etym. of MD *docke* doll)]

Du·com·mun (dʏ kô mœɴ′), *n.* **É·lie** (ā lē′), 1833–1906, Swiss author: Nobel peace prize 1902.

duct (dukt), *n.* **1.** any tube, canal, pipe, or conduit by which a fluid, air, or other substance is conducted or conveyed. **2.** *Anat., Zool.* a tube, canal, or vessel conveying a body fluid, esp. a glandular secretion or excretion. **3.** *Bot.* a cavity or vessel formed by elongated cells or by many cells. **4.** *Elect.* a single enclosed runway for conductors or cables. **5.** *Print.* (in a press) the reservoir for ink. —*v.t.* **6.** to convey or channel by means of a duct or ducts: *to duct heat to the outside.* [1640–50; < L *ductus* conveyance (of water), hence channel (in ML), equiv. to *duc-* (var. s. of *dūcere* to lead) + *-tus* suffix of verbal action] **—duct′less,** *adj.*

duc·tile (duk′tl, -til), *adj.* **1.** capable of being hammered out thin, as certain metals; malleable. **2.** capable of being drawn out into wire or threads, as gold. **3.** able to undergo change of form without breaking. **4.** capable of being molded or shaped; plastic. [1300–50; ME < L *ductilis*, equiv. to *duct(us)* (ptp. of *dūcere* to draw along) + *-ilis* -ILE] **—duc′tile·ly,** *adv.* **—duc·til′i·ty, duc′·tile·ness,** *n.*

duc′tile i′ron. See **nodular cast iron.**

duct·ing (duk′ting), *n.* **1.** ductwork. **2.** materials for making ducts. [1940–45; DUCT + -ING[1]]

duct′ keel′, *Naut.* See **box keel.**

duct′less gland′. See **endocrine gland.** [1840–50]

duc·tor (duk′tər), *n. Print.* the roller that conveys ink in a press from the ink reservoir to the distributor. [1540–50; < L: guide, equiv. to *duc-* (var. s. of *dūcere* to lead) + *-tor* -TOR]

duct′ tape′ (duk, dukt), a strongly adhesive silver-gray cloth tape, used in plumbing, household repairs, etc.

duc·tule (duk′to͞ol, -tyo͞ol), *n. Anat., Zool.* a small duct. [1880–85; DUCT + -ULE]

duc·tus ar·te·ri·o·sis (duk′təs är tēr′ē ō′sis), *Anat.* a fetal blood vessel that connects the left pulmonary artery directly to the descending aorta, normally closing after birth. [1805–15; < NL: lit., arterial channel]

duct·work (dukt′wûrk′), *n.* **1.** a system of ducts used for a particular purpose, as in a ventilation or heating system. **2.** the pipes, vents, etc., belonging to such a system. Also, **ducting.** [1930–35; DUCT + WORK]

dud (dud), *n.* **1.** a device, person, or enterprise that proves to be a failure. **2.** a shell or missile that fails to explode after being fired. [1815–25; special use of *dud*, sing. of DUDS]
—Syn. 1. fiasco, debacle, fizzle, miscarriage.

dud·dy (dud′ē), *adj. Scot.* ragged; tattered. Also, **dud′·die.** [1715–25; DUD(S) + -Y[1]]

dude (do͞od, dyo͞od), *n., v.,* **dud·ed, dud·ing.** —*n.* **1.** a man excessively concerned with his clothes, grooming, and manners. **2.** *Slang.* fellow; chap. **3.** a person reared in a large city. **4.** *Western U.S.* an urban Easterner who vacations on a ranch. —*v.* **5. dude up,** *Informal.* to dress in one's fanciest, best, or most stylish clothes; dress up. [1880–85, *Amer.;* orig. uncert.]

du·deen (do͞o dēn′), *n.* a short clay tobacco pipe. [1835–45; < Ir *dúidín*, equiv. to *dúd* pipe + *-ín* dim. suffix]

du·del·sack (do͞od′l sak′; *Ger.* do͞od′l zäk′), *n. Music.* doodlesack.

dude′ ranch′, a ranch operated primarily as a vacation resort. [1905–10]

Du·de·vant (*Fr.* dʏdə väɴ′), *n.* **Madame A·man·dine Lu·cile Au·rore** (*Fr.* ȧ mäɴ dēn′ lʏ sēl′ ō rôr′). See **Sand, George.**

dudg·eon[1] (duj′ən), *n.* a feeling of offense or resentment; anger: *We left in high dudgeon.* [1565–75; orig. uncert.]
—Syn. indignation, pique.

dudg·eon[2] (duj′ən), *n. Obs.* **1.** a kind of wood used esp. for the handles of knives, daggers, etc. **2.** a handle or hilt made of this wood. **3.** a dagger having such a hilt. [1400–50; late ME; cf. AF *digeon*]

dud·ish (do͞o′dish, dyo͞o′-), *adj.* resembling or characteristic of a dude, as in manner or appearance. [1880–85, *Amer.;* DUDE + -ISH[1]] **—dud′ish·ly,** *adv.*

Dud·ley (dud′lē), *n.* **1. Robert, 1st Earl of Leicester,** 1532?–88, British statesman and favorite of Queen Elizabeth. **2. Thomas,** 1576–1653, English governor of Massachusetts Bay Colony, 1634–35, 1640–41, 1645–46, 1650–51. **3.** a borough in West Midlands, central England, near Birmingham. 300,700. **4.** a male given name: from an Old English placename meaning "dry field."

dud·ley·a (dud′lē ə), any of several smooth succulents belonging to the genus *Dudleya*, of the stonecrop family, native to the western U.S. and Mexico, sometimes grown as an ornamental. [< NL, named in honor of William R. Dudley (1849–1911), U.S. botanist and taxonomist; see -A[2]]

duds (dudz), *n.pl. Informal.* **1.** clothes, esp. a suit of clothes. **2.** belongings in general. [1275–1325; ME *dudde;* perh. akin to LG *dudel* coarse sackcloth]

due (do͞o, dyo͞o), *adj.* **1.** owed at present; having reached the date for payment: *This bill is due.* **2.** owing or owed, irrespective of whether the time of payment has arrived: *This bill is due next month.* **3.** owing or observed as a moral or natural right. **4.** rightful; proper; fitting: *due care; in due time.* **5.** adequate; sufficient: *a due margin for delay.* **6.** under engagement as to time; expected to be ready, be present, or arrive; scheduled: *The plane is due at noon.* **7. due to, a.** attributable to; ascribable to: *The delay was due to heavy traffic.* **b.** because of; owing to: *All planes are grounded due to fog.* —*n.* **8.** something that is due, owed, or naturally belongs to someone. **9.** Usually, **dues.** a regular fee or charge payable at specific intervals, esp. to a group or organization: *membership dues.* **10. give someone his** or **her due, a.** to give what justice demands; treat fairly: *Even though he had once cheated me, I tried to give him his due.* **b.** to credit a disliked or dishonorable person for something that is likable, honorable, or the like. **11. pay one's dues,** to earn respect, a position, or a right by hard work, sacrifice, or experience: *She's a famous musician now, but she paid her dues with years of practice and performing in small towns.* —*adv.* **12.** directly or exactly: *a due east course.* **13.** *Obs.* duly. [1275–1325; ME < AF; MF *deu,* ptp. of *devoir* < L *dēbēre* to owe; see DEBT] —**due′ness,** *n.*

—**Usage. 7.** DUE TO as a prepositional phrase meaning "because of, owing to" has been in use since the 14th century: *Due to the sudden rainstorm, the picnic was moved indoors.* Some object to this use on the grounds that DUE is historically an adjective and thus should be used only predicatively in constructions like *The delay was due to electrical failure.* Despite such objections, DUE TO occurs commonly as a compound preposition and is standard in all varieties of speech and writing.
—**Pronunciation.** See **new.**

due′ bill′, a brief written acknowledgment of indebtedness, not payable to order. [1785–95, *Amer.*]

du·e·cen·to (do͞o′ə chen′tō, dyo͞o′-; *It.* do͞o′e chen′tô), *n.* (*often cap.*) the 13th century, with reference to Italy, esp. to its art or literature. Also, **dugento.** [< It, short for *mil duecento* 1200, used to refer to the period 1200–99] —**du′e·cen′tist,** *n.*

due′ course′ of law′. See **due process of law.**

du·el (do͞o′əl, dyo͞o′-), *n., v.,* **-eled, -el·ing** or (*esp. Brit.*) **-elled, -el·ling.** —*n.* **1.** a prearranged combat between two persons, fought with deadly weapons according to an accepted code of procedure, esp. to settle a private quarrel. **2.** any contest between two persons or parties. —*v.t., v.i.* **3.** to fight in a duel. [1585–95; earlier *duell* < ML *duellum,* L: earlier form of *bellum* war, prob. maintained and given sense "duel" by assoc. with L *duo* TWO] —**du′el·is′tic;** *esp. Brit.,* **du′el·lis′tic,** *adj.*

du·el·ist (do͞o′ə list, dyo͞o′-), *n.* a person who participates in a duel. Also, *esp. Brit.,* **du′el·list.** Also called **du′el·er;** *esp. Brit.,* **du′el·ler.** [1585–95; DUEL + -IST]

du·el·lo (do͞o el′ō, dyo͞o-; *It.* do͞o el′lô), *n.* **1.** the practice or art of dueling. **2.** the code of rules regulating dueling. [1580–90; < It; see DUEL]

duen·de (dwen′de; *Eng.* do͞o en′dā), *n., pl.* ***-des*** (-des; *Eng.* -dāz) for 1. *Spanish.* **1.** a goblin; demon; spirit. **2.** charm; magnetism.

du·en·na (do͞o en′ə, dyo͞o-), *n.* **1.** (in Spain and Portugal) an older woman serving as escort or chaperon of a young lady. **2.** a governess. [1660–70; < Sp *duenna* (now *dueña*) < L *domina,* fem. of *dominus* master] —**du·en′na·ship′,** *n.*

due′ proc′ess of law′, the regular administration of the law, according to which no citizen may be denied his or her legal rights and all laws must conform to fundamental, accepted legal principles, as the right of the accused to confront his or her accusers. Also called **due′ proc′ess, due course of law.** [1885–90]

Due·ro (dwe′rô), *n.* Spanish name of **Douro.**

dues-pay·ing (do͞oz′pā′ing, dyo͞oz′-), *adj.* **1.** gaining experience, esp. by hard and often unpleasant or uncongenial work: *He spent his dues-paying years as a cocktail pianist.* —*n.* **2.** the act or process of gaining experience, esp. slowly and laboriously: *She had many years of dues-paying before her abilities were recognized.*

du·et (do͞o et′, dyo͞o-), *n.* a musical composition for two voices or instruments. [1730–40; earlier *duett* < It *duetto,* equiv. to *du(o)* duet + *-etto* -ET] —**du·et′·tist,** *n.*

du·et·ting (do͞o et′ing, dyo͞o-), *n. Animal Behav.* turn-taking by two birds in the execution of a song pattern. [DUET + -ING[1]]

Du·fay (do͞o fī′; *Fr.* dʏ fā′), *n.* **Guil·laume** (gē yōm′), c1400–74, Flemish composer.

duff[1] (duf), *n. Slang.* the buttocks or rump: *If you don't like the way things are, get off your duff and do something about it!* [1885–90; expressive word, perh. akin to DOUP]

duff[2] (duf), *n.* a stiff flour pudding, boiled or steamed and often flavored with currants, citron, and spices. [1830–40; dial. var. (Scots, N England) of DOUGH]

duff[3] (duf), *v.t. Slang.* **1.** to give a deliberately deceptive appearance to; misrepresent; fake. **2.** *Brit.* (in golf) to misplay (a golf ball), esp. to misjudge one's swing so that the club strikes the ground behind the ball before hitting it. **3.** *Australian.* **a.** to steal (cattle). **b.** (formerly) to alter the brand on (stolen cattle). **4.** to cheat someone. [1830–40; back formation from DUFFER (def. 3)]

duff[4] (duf), *n.* **1.** organic matter in various stages of decomposition on the floor of the forest. **2.** fine, dry coal, esp. anthracite. [1835–45; orig. Scots dial.; perh. metaphorical use of DUFF[2], by assoc. with Scots *dowf* decayed, rotten (see DOWF), *deaf* (of soil) unproductive, springy to the tread]

duf·fel (duf′əl), *n.* **1.** a camper's clothing and equipment. **2.** a coarse woolen cloth having a thick nap, used for coats, blankets, etc. **3.** See **duffel bag.** Also, **duf′·fle.** [1640–50; after *Duffel,* a town near Antwerp]

duf′fel bag′, a large, cylindrical bag, esp. of canvas, for carrying personal belongings, orginally used by military personnel. [1915–20, *Amer.*]

duff·er (duf′ər), *n.* **1.** *Informal.* **a.** a plodding, clumsy, incompetent person. **b.** a person inept or inexperienced at a specific sport, as golf. **2.** *Northern U.S.* an old man, esp. a dull or indecisive one. **3.** *Slang.* **a.** anything inferior, counterfeit, or useless. **b.** a peddler, esp. one who sells cheap, flashy goods. [1835–45; perh. Scots dial. *duffar, dowfart* dull, stupid person, deriv. of DOWF; def. 3 perh. re-formation with DUFF[3] + -ER[1]]

duf′fle coat′, a hooded overcoat of sturdy wool, usually knee-length and with frog fasteners. Also, **duf′fel coat′.** [1675–85; var. of DUFFEL]

Duf·fy (duf′ē), *n.* **Sir Charles Gav·an** (gav′ən), 1816–1903, Irish and Australian politician.

Du Fu (do͞o′ fo͞o′), *Pinyin.* See **Tu Fu.**

du·fus (do͞o′fəs), *n., pl.* **-fus·es.** doofus.

Du·fy (dʏ fē′), *n.* **Ra·oul** (ʀᴀ o͞ol′), 1877–1953, French painter, lithographer, and decorator.

dug[1] (dug), *v.* a pt. and pp. of **dig.**

dug[2] (dug), *n.* the mamma or the nipple of a female mammal. [1520–30; orig. obscure; perh. < a Gmc base akin to Dan *dægge,* Norw *degge,* Sw *dägga* to suckle]

Du Gard (*Fr.* dʏ ɢᴀʀ′), **Ro·ger Mar·tin** (*Fr.* ʀô zhā′ ᴍᴀʀ ᴛᴀɴ′). See **Martin Du Gard, Roger.**

du·gen·to (do͞o jen′tō, dyo͞o-; *It.* do͞o jen′tô), *n.* duecento.

du·gong (do͞o′gong, -gông), *n.* an herbivorous, aquatic mammal, *Dugong dugon,* of the Red Sea and Indian Ocean, having a barrel-shaped body, flipperlike forelimbs, no hind limbs, and a triangular tail: widespread but rare. [1790–1800; < NL < G: first recorded as *dugung,* appar. misrepresentation of Malay *duyung,* or a cognate Austronesian word]

dugong, *Dugong dugong,* length 9 ft. (2.7 m)

dug·out (dug′out′), *n.* **1.** a boat made by hollowing out a log. **2.** *Baseball.* a roofed structure enclosed on three sides and with the fourth side open and facing the playing field, usually with the floor below ground level, where the players sit when not on the field. **3.** a rough shelter or dwelling formed by an excavation in the ground, in the face of a bank, in the side of a hill, etc., esp. one used by soldiers. [1715–25, *Amer.*; n. use of v. phrase *dug out*]

Du Gues·clin (dʏ ge klᴀɴ′), **Ber·trand** (beʀ ᴛʀäɴ′), ("*the Eagle of Brittany*"), c1320–80, French military leader: constable of France 1370–80.

Du·ha·mel (do͞o′ə mel′, dyo͞o′-; *Fr.* dʏ ᴀ mel′), *n.* **Georges** (zhôʀzh), (*Denis Thévenin*), 1884–1966, French novelist, physician, poet, and essayist.

dui·ker (dī′kər), *n., pl.* **-kers,** (*esp. collectively*) **-ker.** any of several small African antelopes of the *Cephalophus, Sylvicapra,* and related genera, the males and often the females having short, spikelike horns: some are endangered. [1770–80; < Afrik, D *duiker* diver, equiv. to *duiken* to dive (see DUCK[2]) + *-er* -ER[1]]

dui·ker·bok (dī′kər bok′), *n., pl.* **-boks,** (*esp. collectively*) **-bok.** duiker. [1780–90; < Afrik, equiv. to *duiker* DUIKER + *bok* BUCK[1]]

Dui′no El′egies (dwē′nō), (German, *Duineser Elegien*), a collection of ten poems (1923) by Rainer Maria Rilke.

Duis·burg (dʏs′bo͝oʀk), *n.* a city in W Germany, at the junction of the Rhine and Ruhr rivers: the largest river port in Europe; formed 1929 from the cities of Duisburg and Hamborn. 525,200. Formerly, **Duis·burg-Ham·born** (dʏs′bo͝oʀk′häm′bôʀn).

duit (doit, dit), *n.* doit (def. 1).

du jour (də zho͝or′, do͞o; *Fr.* dʏ zho͞oʀ′), as prepared on the particular day; of the kind being served today: *The soup du jour is split pea.* [< F: of the day]

Du·ka·kis (do͞o kä′kis), *n.* **Michael S.,** born 1933, U.S. politician: governor of Massachusetts since 1983.

Du·kas (dʏ ᴋᴀ′), *n.* **Paul (Ab·ra·ham)** (pôl ᴀ ʙʀᴀ ᴀᴍ′), 1865–1935, French composer.

duke (do͞ok, dyo͞ok), *n., v.,* **duked, duk·ing.** —*n.* **1.** (in Continental Europe) the male ruler of a duchy; the sovereign of a small state. **2.** a British nobleman holding the highest hereditary title outside the royal family, ranking immediately below a prince and above a marquis; a member of the highest rank of the British peerage. Cf. **royal duke. 3.** a nobleman of corresponding rank in certain other countries. **4.** a cultivated hybrid of the sweet and sour cherry. **5. dukes,** *Slang.* fists; hands: *Put up your dukes.* —*v.t.* **6.** *Slang.* to hit or thrash with the fists (sometimes fol. by *out*): *He duked me because he said I had insulted him. The bully said he was going to duke out anyone who disagreed.* **7. duke it out,** to fight, esp. with the fists; do battle. [1100–50; ME *duke, duc,* late OE *duc* < OF *duc, dus, dux* < ML *dux* ruler of a small state, L: leader; see DUX; *dukes* "fists" of unclear derivation and perh. of distinct orig.]

Duke (do͞ok, dyo͞ok), *n.* **1. Benjamin Newton,** 1855–1929, and his brother, **James Buchanan,** 1856–1925, U.S. industrialists. **2.** a male given name.

duke·dom (do͞ok′dəm, dyo͞ok′-), *n.* **1.** a duchy. **2.** the office or rank of a duke. [1425–75; late ME; see DUKE, -DOM]

duked′ up′, *Slang.* dressed up; ornamented; embellished: *an old car duked up with leather upholstery and wire wheels.* [perh. DUKE + -ED[2], though literal sense uncert.]

Du·kho·bor (do͞o′kə bôr′), *n., pl.* **Du·kho·bors, Du·kho·bor·tsy** (do͞o′kə bôrt′sē). Doukhobor.

duk·kha (do͞o′kə), *n. Buddhism.* the first of the Four Noble Truths, that all human experience is transient and that suffering results from excessive desire and attachment. [< Pali]

Dul·bec·co (dul bek′ō; *It.* do͞ol bek′kô), *n.* **Re·na·to** (rə nä′tō; *It.* ʀe nä′tô), born 1914, U.S. biologist, born in Italy: Nobel prize for medicine 1975.

dulc., (in prescriptions) sweet. [< L *dulcis*]

Dul·ce (dul′sē), *n.* a female given name: from the Latin word meaning "sweet." Also, **Dul·cie** (dul′sē).

dul·ce et de·co·rum est pro pa·tri·a mo·ri (do͞ol′ke et de kō′ʀo͞om est ᴘʀō pä′tʀē ä′ mō′ʀē; *Eng.* dul′sē et di kôr′əm est prō pä′trē ə môr′ī, mōr′ī, -kōr′əm), *Latin.* sweet and fitting it is to die for one's country.

Dul′ce Gulf′ (do͞ol′sā; *Sp.* do͞ol′se). See **Izabal, Lake.**

dul·cet (dul′sit), *adj.* **1.** pleasant to the ear; melodious: *the dulcet tones of the cello.* **2.** pleasant or agreeable to the eye or the feelings; soothing. **3.** *Archaic.* sweet to the taste or smell. —*n.* **4.** an organ stop resembling the dulciana but an octave higher. [1350–1400; obs. *dulce* (< L, neut. of *dulcis* sweet) + -ET; r. ME *doucet* < MF; see DOUCE] —**dul′cet·ly,** *adv.* —**dul′cet·ness,** *n.*
—**Syn. 1.** musical, tuneful, mellifluous, sweet-sounding.

dul·ci·an·a (dul′sē an′ə, -ä′nə), *n.* an organ stop having metal pipes and giving thin, incisive, somewhat stringlike tones. [1770–80; < ML, equiv. to L *dulci(s)* sweet + *-āna,* fem. of *-ānus* -AN]

dul·ci·fy (dul′sə fī′), *v.t.,* **-fied, -fy·ing. 1.** to make more agreeable; mollify; appease. **2.** to sweeten. [1590–1600; < LL *dulcificāre,* with -FY for *-ficāre*] —**dul′ci·fi·ca′tion,** *n.*

dul·ci·mer (dul′sə mər), *n.* **1.** a trapezoidal zither with metal strings that are struck with light hammers. **2.** a modern folk instrument related to the guitar and plucked with the fingers. [1560–70; alter. of ME *dowcemere* < MF *doulcemer,* dissimilated var. of *doulcemele* < OIt *dolcimelo, dolzemele* < L *dulce melos* sweet song. See DULCET, MELIC]

dulcimer (def. 1)

dul·cin·e·a (dul sin′ē ə, dul′sə nē′ə), *n.* a ladylove; sweetheart. [1740–50; after *Dulcinea* the ladylove of Don Quixote]

dul·ci·tol (dul′si tôl′, -tol′), *n. Biochem.* a water-soluble sugar alcohol, $C_6H_{14}O_6$, isomeric with sorbitol, that is found in many plant species and is prepared in the laboratory by galactose reduction. Also called **galactitol, dul·cite** (dul′sīt), **dul·cose** (dul′kōs). [1880–85; *dulcite* an earlier name (< L *dulc(is)* sweet + -ITE[1]) + OL[1]]

Dul·cy (dul′sē), *n.* a female given name, form of **Dulce.**

du·li·a (do͞o lī′ə, dyo͞o-), *n. Rom. Cath. Theol.* veneration and invocation given to saints as the servants of God. Cf. **hyperdulia, latria.** [1605–15; < ML *dūlia* service, work done < Gk *douleía* slavery, equiv. to *doûl(os)* slave + *-eia* -Y[3]]

dull (dul), *adj.,* **-er, -est,** *v.* —*adj.* **1.** not sharp; blunt: *a dull knife.* **2.** causing boredom; tedious; uninteresting: *a dull sermon.* **3.** not lively or spirited; listless. **4.** not bright, intense, or clear; dim: *a dull day; a dull sound.* **5.** having very little depth of color; lacking in richness or intensity of color. **6.** slow in motion or action; not brisk; sluggish: *a dull day in the stock market.* **7.** mentally slow; lacking brightness of mind; somewhat stupid; obtuse. **8.** lacking keenness of perception in the senses or feelings; insensible; unfeeling. **9.** not intense or acute: *a dull pain.* —*v.t., v.i.* **10.** to make or become dull. [1200–50; ME; akin to OE *dol* foolish, stupid; c. G *toll*] —**dull′ness, dul′ness,** *n.* —**dul′ly,** *adv.*
—**Syn. 1.** DULL, BLUNT refer to the edge or point of an instrument, tool, or the like. DULL implies a lack or a loss of keenness or sharpness: *a dull razor or saw.* BLUNT may mean the same or may refer to an edge or point not intended to be keen or sharp: *a blunt or stub pen; a blunt foil.* **2.** boring, tiresome, dreary, vapid. **3.** apathetic, torpid, inactive, inert. **7.** unimaginative, unintelligent, stolid. DULL, BLUNTED, SLOW, STUPID are applied to mental qualities. DULL implies obtuseness, lack of imagination: *a dull child.* BLUNTED implies loss of original keenness of intelligence through disease, sad experience, or the like: *blunted faculties.* SLOW applies to a sluggish intellect: *a slow mind.* STUPID implies slowness of mental processes, but also lack of intelligence, wisdom, prudence, etc.: *a stupid person.* **10.** blunt, deaden, benumb; depress, dishearten, discourage. —**Ant. 1.** sharp, keen. **2.** interesting. **7.** bright.

dull•ard (dul′ərd), *n.* a stupid, insensitive person. [1400–50; late ME; see DULL, -ARD]
—Syn. dunce, dolt, dumbbell, dummy.

Dul•les (dul′əs), *n.* **John Foster,** 1888–1959, U.S. statesman: secretary of state 1953–59.

Dul′les Interna′tional Air′port, airport in N Virginia, just west of Washington, D.C., used mainly for international flights.

dull•ish (dul′ish), *adj.* somewhat dull; tending to be dull. [1350–1400; ME; see DULL, -ISH[1]]

Dull′ Knife′, (*Tah-me-la-pash-me*), died 1883, leader of the Northern Cheyenne.

dulls•ville (dulz′vil), *n. Slang.* something boring or dull: *That movie was strictly dullsville.* [1960–65; DULL + *-s-* + *-ville,* by analogy with place names; see DRAGSVILLE]

dull-wit•ted (dul′wit′id), *adj.* mentally slow; stupid. [1350–1400; ME] **—dull′-wit′ted•ness,** *n.*

du•loc•ra•cy (do͞o lok′rə sē, dyo͞o-), *n.* rule by slaves. [1650–60; < Gk *doûlo(s)* slave + -CRACY]

du•lo•sis (do͞o lō′sis, dyo͞o-), *n.* the enslavement of an ant colony or its members by ants of a different species. [1900–05; < Gk *doúlōsis* enslavement, equiv. to *doulō-,* var. s. of *doulóun* to enslave (deriv. of *doûlos* slave + *-sis* -SIS] **—du•lot•ic** (do͞o lot′ik, dyo͞o-), *adj.*

dulse (duls), *n.* a coarse, edible, red seaweed, *Rhodymenia palmata.* [1540–50; Scots dial. < ScotGael *duileasg* (by syncope, as in SCOTS, etc.)]

Du•luth (də lo͞oth′; *for 1 also Fr.* dʏ lʏt′), *n.* **1. Da•niel Grey•so•lon** (dᴀ nyel′ ɢʀe sô lôɴ′), **Sieur,** 1636–1710, French trader and explorer in Canada and Great Lakes region. **2.** a port in E Minnesota, on Lake Superior. 92,811.

du•ly (do͞o′lē, dyo͞o′-), *adv.* **1.** in a due manner; properly; fittingly. **2.** in due season; punctually. [1350–1400; ME *duelich(e).* See DUE, -LY]

du•ma (do͞o′mə), *n.* **1.** (in Russia prior to 1917) a council or official assembly. **2.** (*cap.*) an elective legislative assembly, established in 1905 by Nicholas II, constituting the lower house of parliament. Also, **douma.** [1865–70; < Russ, ORuss *dúma* assembly, council (an early homonym with *dúma* thought); c. Bulg *dúma* word, Slovak *duma* meditation; Slav **dum-* prob. < Goth *dōms* judgment (see DOOM)]

Du•ma•gue•te (do͞o′mä ge′te), *n.* a city on S Negros, in the S central Philippines. 63,411.

Du•mas (dʏ mä′ *or, Eng.,* do͞o mä′, dyo͞o- *for 1, 2;* do͞o′məs, dyo͞o′- *for 3*), *n.* **1. A•le•xan•dre** (ᴀ lek sän′dʀᵊ), ("*Dumas père*"), 1802–70, and his son, **Alexandre** ("*Dumas fils*"), 1824–95, French dramatists and novelists. **2. Jean-Bap•tiste An•dré** (zhän bᴀ tēst′ äɴ dʀā′), 1800–84, French chemist. **3.** a town in N Texas. 12,194.

Du Mau•ri•er (do͞o môr′ē ā′, dyo͞o; *Fr.* dʏ mō ʀyā′), **1. Dame Daphne** (*Lady Browning*), born 1907, English novelist. **2.** her grandfather, **George Louis Pal•mel•la Bus•son** (pal mel′ə bo͞o sôn′; *Fr.* bʏ sôɴ′), 1834–96, English illustrator and novelist. **3.** her father, **Sir Gerald (Hubert Edward Bus•son)** (bʏ sôɴ′), 1873–1934, English actor and theatrical manager.

dumb (dum), *adj.,* **-er, -est. 1.** lacking intelligence or good judgment; stupid; dull-witted. **2.** lacking the power of speech (often offensive when applied to humans): *a dumb animal.* **3.** temporarily unable to speak: *dumb with astonishment.* **4.** refraining from any or much speech; silent. **5.** made, done, etc., without speech. **6.** lacking some usual property, characteristic, etc. **7.** performed in pantomime; mimed. **8.** *Computers.* pertaining to the inability to do processing locally: *A dumb terminal can input, output, and display data, but cannot process it.* Cf. **intelligent** (def. 4). **9.** *Naut.* **a.** (of a barge) without means of propulsion. **b.** (of any craft) without means of propulsion, steering, or signaling. [bef. 1000; OE; c. ON *dumbr,* Goth *dumbs,* OS *dumb,* OHG *tump,* G *dumm*] **—dumb′ly,** *adv.* **—dumb′ness,** *n.*
—Syn. 2, 3. DUMB, MUTE, SPEECHLESS, VOICELESS describe a condition in which speech is absent. DUMB was formerly used to refer to persons unable to speak; it is now used almost entirely of the inability of animals to speak: *dumb beasts of the field.* The term MUTE is applied to persons who, usually because of congenital deafness, have never learned to talk: *With training most mutes learn to speak well enough to be understood.* Either of the foregoing terms or SPEECHLESS may describe a temporary inability to speak, caused by emotion, etc.: *dumb with amazement; mute with terror; left speechless by surprise.* VOICELESS means literally having no voice, either from natural causes or from injury: *Turtles are voiceless. A laryngectomy leaves a person voiceless until he or she has learned esophageal speech.*

dumb′ a′gue, *Pathol.* an irregular form of intermittent malarial fever, lacking the usual chill. [1780–90]

Dum•bar•ton (dum bär′tn), *n.* **1.** Also, **Dunbarton.** Also called **Dum•bar•ton•shire** (dum bär′tn shēr′, -shər). a historic county in W Scotland. **2.** a city in W Scotland, near the Clyde River: shipbuilding. 80,105.

Dum′bar•ton Oaks′ (dum′bär tn), an estate in the District of Columbia: site of conferences held to discuss proposals for creation of the United Nations, August–October, 1944.

dumb-ass (dum′as′), *n. Slang* (*vulgar*). a thoroughly stupid person; blockhead. Also, **dumb′ass′.** [1970–75; *Amer.*]

dumb′ bar′ter, a form of barter practiced among some peoples, in which the goods for exchange are left at and taken from a preselected spot without the exchanging parties ever coming face-to-face. Also called **silent barter, silent trade.**

dumb•bell (dum′bel′), *n.* **1.** a gymnastic apparatus consisting of two wooden or metal balls connected by a short bar serving as a handle, used as a weight for exercising. **2.** a stupid person. [1705–15; DUMB + BELL[1]]
—Syn. 2. dunce, ignoramus, fool, blockhead, dimwit.

dumbbell (def. 1)

Dumb′bell neb′ula, *Astron.* the planetary nebula in the constellation Vulpecula, which in photographs appears to have the shape of a dumbbell. [1975–80]

dumb′ bid′, the undisclosed price set by the owner of something to be auctioned, below which no offer will be accepted.

dumb′ bun′ny, a stupid person. [1940–45]

dumb′ cane′, a West Indian foliage plant, *Dieffenbachia seguine,* of the arum family, having yellow-blotched leaves that cause temporary speechlessness when chewed. Also called **mother-in-law plant.** [1690–1700]

dumb′ cluck′, *Slang.* a stupid person. [1920–25]

dumb′ com′pass, *Navig.* pelorus.

dumb′ Do′ra, *Slang.* a foolishly simple, stupid, or scatterbrained woman. [1910–15]

dumb-dumb (dum′dum′), *n., adj.* dum-dum.

dumb•found (dum found′, dum′found′), *v.t.* to make speechless with amazement; astonish. Also, **dumb•found′er.** [1645–55; DUMB + (CON)FOUND] **—dumb•found′er•ment,** *n.*
—Syn. amaze, confound, astound, stagger.

dumb•head (dum′hed′), *n. Slang.* blockhead. [1815–25; DUMB + HEAD]

dum•bo (dum′bō), *n., pl.* **-bos,** *adj. Slang.* **—n. 1.** a stupid person: *a class full of dumbos.* **—adj. 2.** stupid or foolish: *What a dumbo idea!* [‡1955–60; DUMB + -O]

dumb′ sheave′, *Naut.* **1.** a block having no sheave or other part rolling with the movement of a line. **2.** a groove in a spar or other timber, through which a rope can slide. [1855–60]

dumb′ show′, 1. a part of a dramatic representation given in pantomime, common in early English drama. **2.** gestures without speech. [1555–65] **—dumb′-show′,** *adj.*

dumb•struck (dum′struk′), *adj.* temporarily deprived of the power of speech, as by surprise or confusion; dumbfounded. Also, **dumb•strick•en** (dum′strik′ən). [1885–90; DUMB + STRUCK]

dumb•wait•er (dum′wā′tər), *n.* **1.** a small elevator, manually or electrically operated, consisting typically of a box with shelves, used in apartment houses, restaurants, and large private dwellings for moving dishes, food, garbage, etc., between floors. **2.** *Brit.* **a.** an auxiliary serving table. **b.** a serving stand with tiers of revolving shelves. **c.** a serving cart. [1745–55; DUMB + WAITER]

dum-dum (dum′dum′), *Slang.* **—n. 1.** a silly, stupid person. **—adj. 2.** typical of a dum-dum: *another dum-dum idea.* Also, **dumb-dumb, dumdum.** [appar. redupl. and resp. of DUMB]

dum•dum[1] (dum′dum′), *n.* a hollow-nosed or soft-nosed bullet that expands on impact, inflicting a severe wound. Also called **dum′dum bul′let.** [1895–1900; named after *Dum-Dum,* town in India where the bullets were made]

dum•dum[2] (dum′dum′), *n., adj.* dum-dum.

Dum′dum fe′ver, *Pathol.* kala-azar.

dum•found (dum found′, dum′found′), *v.t.* to dumbfound. Also, **dum•found′er.** **—dum•found′er•ment,** *n.*

Dum•fries (dum frēs′), *n.* **1.** Also called **Dum•fries•shire** (dum frēs′shēr′, -shər). a historic county in S Scotland. **2.** a burgh of Dumfries and Galloway in S Scotland: burial place of Robert Burns. 29,259.

Dumfries′ and Gal′loway, a region in S Scotland. 143,667; 2460 sq. mi. (6371 sq. km).

dum•ka (do͝om′kə), *n., pl.* **-ky** (-kē). **1.** a Slavic folk song that alternates in character between sadness and gaiety. **2.** an instrumental composition or movement imitative of such a folk song. [1890–95; < Czech < Ukrainian *dúmka,* orig. dim. of *dúma* a genre of narrative folk poetry; see DUMA]

dumm•kopf (do͝om′kôf′, -kôpf′, dum′-), *n.* a stupid person; dumbbell; blockhead. [1800–10, *Amer.*; < G, equiv. to *dumm* DUMB + *Kopf* head]

dum•my (dum′ē), *n., pl.* **-mies,** *adj., v.,* **-mied, -my•ing.** **—n. 1.** a representation or copy of something, as for displaying to indicate appearance: *a display of lipstick dummies made of colored plastic.* **2.** a representation of a human figure, as for displaying clothes in store windows. **3.** *Informal.* a stupid person; dolt. **4.** a person who has nothing to say or who takes no active part in affairs. **5.** one put forward to act for others while ostensibly acting for oneself. **6.** *Slang* **a.** (*offensive*). a person who lacks the power of speech. **b.** a person who is characteristically and habitually silent. **7.** *Bridge.* **a.** the declarer's partner, whose hand is exposed and played by the declarer. **b.** the hand of cards so exposed. **c.** a game so played. **d.** an imaginary player represented by an exposed hand that is played by and serves as partner to one of the players. **8.** *Brit.* pacifier (def. 2). **9.** *Print.* sheets folded and made up to show the size, shape, form, sequence, and general style of a contemplated piece of printing. **10.** a rammer for pushing out dents in lead pipe. **11.** *Computers.* an artificial address, instruction, or other datum fed into a computer only to fulfill prescribed conditions and not affecting operations for solving problems. **12.** *Mil.* a nonexplosive bomb used for practice exercises. **13.** *Dentistry.* pontic. **—adj. 14.** noting or pertaining to an imitation, representation, or copy. **15.** counterfeit; sham; fictitious. **16.** put forward to act for others while ostensibly acting for oneself. **17.** *Cards.* played with a dummy. **—v.t. 18.** *Print.* to prepare a dummy of (often fol. by *up*): *The designer dummied up the book so that they could study the format.* **19.** to represent in a dummy (often fol. by *in*): *to dummy in an illustration.* **20. dummy up,** *Informal.* to keep silent; refuse to answer: *If anybody asks you, just dummy up.* [1590–1600; 1915–20, *Amer.* for def. 20; DUMB + -Y[3]]

dum′my block′, *Metalworking.* a freely moving cylinder for transmitting the pressure of a ram to a piece being extruded.

dum′my joint′, a slot cut into a concrete slab to prevent serious fractures.

Du•mont (do͞o′mont, dyo͞o′-), *n.* a city in NE New Jersey. 18,334.

Du•mont d'Ur•ville (dʏ môɴ dʏʀ vēl′), **Jules Sé•bas•tien Cé•sar** (zhʏl sā bᴀs tyaɴ′ sā zᴀʀ′), 1790–1842, French naval officer: explored South Pacific and Antarctic.

du•mor•ti•er•ite (do͞o môr′tē ə rīt′, dyo͞o-), *n.* a mineral, aluminum borosilicate. [1880–85; < F, named after Eugène *Dumortier,* 19th-century French paleontologist; see -ITE[1]]

dump (dump), *v.t.* **1.** to drop or let fall in a mass; fling down or drop heavily or suddenly: *Dump the topsoil here.* **2.** to empty out, as from a container, by tilting or overturning. **3.** to unload or empty out (a container), as by tilting or overturning. **4.** to be dismissed, fired, or released from a contract: *The first baseman was dumped from the team after hitting .210 for the first half of the season.* **5.** to transfer or rid oneself of suddenly and irresponsibly: *Don't dump your troubles on me!* **6.** *Boxing Slang.* **a.** to knock down: *The champion was dumped twice but won the fight.* **b.** to lose (a match) intentionally: *a bribe to dump a fight.* **7.** *Com.* **a.** to put (goods or securities) on the market in large quantities and at a low price without regard to the effect on market conditions. **b.** to sell (goods) into foreign markets below cost in order to promote exports or damage foreign competition. **8.** *Computers.* to print, display, or record on an output medium (the contents of a computer's internal storage or the contents of a file), often at the time a program fails. **9.** *Slang.* to kill; murder: *threats to dump him if he didn't pay up.* **—v.i. 10.** to fall or drop down suddenly. **11.** to throw away or discard garbage, refuse, etc. **12.** *Com.* **a.** to offer goods for sale in large quantities at a low price. **b.** to dump below-cost goods into foreign markets. **13.** to release contents: *a sewage pipe that dumps in the ocean.* **14.** *Slang.* to complain, criticize, gossip, or tell another person one's problems: *He calls me up just to dump.* **15.** *Slang* (*vulgar*). to defecate. **16. dump on (someone),** *Informal.* **a.** to attack with verbal abuse; criticize harshly: *Reporters never tired of dumping on certain public figures.* **b.** to unload one's problems onto (another person): *You never phone me without dumping on me.* **—n. 17.** an accumulation of discarded garbage, refuse, etc. **18.** Also called **dumpsite, dumping-ground.** a place where garbage, refuse, etc., is deposited. **19.** *Mil.* **a.** a collection of ammunition, stores, etc., deposited at some point, as near a battlefront, for distribution. **b.** the ammunition, stores, etc., so deposited. **20.** the act of dumping. **21.** *Mining.* **a.** a runway or embankment equipped with tripping devices, from which low-grade ore, rock, etc., are dumped. **b.** the pile of ore so dumped. **22.** *Informal.* a place, house, or town that is dilapidated, dirty, or disreputable. **23.** (in merchandising) a bin or specially made carton in which items are displayed for sale: *Fifty copies of the best-selling paperback novel were in a dump near the checkout counter.* **24.** *Computers.* a copy of the contents of a computer's internal storage or of the contents of a file at a given instant, that is printed, displayed, or stored on an output medium. [1250–1300; ME (in sense "to fall suddenly") < ON *dumpa* strike, bump; modern senses as transit. v. and n. (not known before 19th cent.) perh. < another source, or independent expressive formation] **—dump′er,** *n.*

dump•cart (dump′kärt′), *n.* a cart with a body that can be tilted or a bottom that can be opened downward to discharge the contents. [1865–70, *Amer.*; DUMP + CART]

dump•ing-ground (dum′ping ground′), *n.* dump (def. 18). [1855–60, *Amer.*]

dump′ish (dum′pish), *adj.* depressed; sad. [1535–45; DUMP(S) + -ISH[1]] **—dump′ish•ly,** *adv.* **—dump′ish•ness,** *n.*

dump•ling (dump′ling), *n.* **1.** a rounded mass of steamed and seasoned dough, often served in soup or with stewed meat. **2.** a dessert consisting of a wrapping of dough enclosing sliced apples or other fruit, boiled or baked. **3.** a short or stout person. [1590–1600; *dump* (of uncert. orig.) + -LING[1]]

dumps (dumps), *n.* a depressed state of mind (usually prec. by *in the*): *to be in the dumps over money problems.* [1515–25; cf. G *dumpf* dull, MD *domp* haze]

dump′ scow′. See **hopper barge.**

dump•site (dump′sīt′), *n.* dump (def. 18). [DUMP + SITE]

Dump•ster (dump′stər), *Trademark.* a brand of large metal bin for refuse designed to be hoisted onto a specially equipped truck for emptying or hauling away.

dump′ truck′, a usually open-topped truck having a body that can be tilted to discharge its contents, as sand or gravel, through an open tailgate. Also, **dump′truck′.** [1925–30, *Amer.*]

CONCISE PRONUNCIATION KEY: *act, cāpe, dâre, pärt; set, ēqual; if, ice; ox, ōver, ôrder, oil, bo͝ok, bo͞ot, out; up, ûrge; child; sing; shoe; thin, that;* zh as in *treasure.* ə = *a* as in *alone, e* as in *system, i* as in *easily, o* as in *gallop, u* as in *circus;* ᵊ as in *fire* (fīᵊr), *hour* (ouᵊr). l and n can serve as syllabic consonants, as in *cradle* (krād′l), and *button* (but′n). See the full key inside the front cover.

dump·y[1] (dum′pē), *adj.*, **dump·i·er, dump·i·est.** dumpish; dejected; sulky. [1610–20; DUMP(S) + -Y[1]]

dump·y[2] (dum′pē), *adj.*, **dump·i·er, dump·i·est.** short and stout; squat: *a dumpy figure.* [1740–50; perh. akin to DUMPLING] —**dump′i·ly,** *adv.* —**dump′i·ness,** *n.*

dump′y lev′el, *Survey.* an instrument consisting of a spirit level mounted under and parallel to a telescope, the latter being rigidly attached to its supports. [1830–40]

dum spi·ro, spe·ro (dŏŏm spē′rō, spā′rō; *Eng.* dum spī′rō, spēr′ō), *Latin.* while I breathe, I hope: a motto of South Carolina.

Du·mu·zi (do͞o′mŏŏ zē), *n.* the Sumerian god of pastures and vegetation: the consort of Inanna. Cf. **Tammuz.**

dum vi·vi·mus, vi·va·mus (dŏŏm wē′wi mŏŏs′, wiwä′mŏŏs; *Eng.* dum viv′i məs, vi vä′məs), *Latin.* while we are alive, let us live.

Dum·yat (dŏŏm yät′), *n.* Arabic name of **Damietta.**

dun[1] (dun), *v.,* **dunned, dun·ning,** *n.* —*v.t.* **1.** to make repeated and insistent demands upon, esp. for the payment of a debt. —*n.* **2.** a person, esp. a creditor, who duns another. **3.** a demand for payment, esp. a written one. [1620–30; orig. obscure]

dun[2] (dun), *adj.* **1.** dull, grayish brown. **2.** dark; gloomy. —*n.* **3.** a dun color. **4.** a dun-colored horse with a black mane and tail. **5.** mayfly. **6.** *Angling.* See **dun fly.** [bef. 1000; ME *dun(ne),* OE *dunn;* c. OS *dun*] —**dun′ness,** *n.*

Du·na (do͝o′no), *n.* Hungarian name of the **Danube.**

Dü·na (dʏ′nä), *n.* German name of the **Dvina.**

Dü·na·burg (dʏ′nä bo͝ork′), *n.* German name of **Daugavpils.**

Du·naj (do͝o′nī), *n.* Czech and Slovak name of the **Danube.**

Du·nant (*Fr.* dʏ nän′), *n.* **Jean Hen·ri** (*Fr.* zhän än rē′), 1828–1910, Swiss banker and philanthropist: founder of the Red Cross; Nobel peace prize 1901.

Du·nă·rea (do͝o′nə ryä), *n.* Rumanian name of the **Danube.**

Dun·bar (dun′bär *for 1;* dun bär′ *for 2, 3*), *n.* **1. Paul Laurence,** 1872–1906, U.S. poet. **2. William,** c1460–c1520, Scottish poet. **3.** a town in the Lothian region, in SE Scotland, at the mouth of the Firth of Forth: site of Cromwell's defeat of the Scots 1650. 4586.

Dun·bar·ton (dun bär′tn), *n.* Dumbarton (def. 1).

Dun·can (dung′kən), *n.* **1. Isadora,** 1878–1927, U.S. dancer: pioneer in modern dance. **2.** a city in S Oklahoma. 22,517. **3.** a male given name.

Duncan I, died 1040, king of Scotland 1030–40: murdered by Macbeth.

Dun·can Phyfe (dung′kən fīf′), of, pertaining to, or resembling the furniture made by Duncan Phyfe, esp. the earlier pieces in the Sheraton and Directoire styles.

Duncan Phyfe furniture
A, side table with carved legs; B, chair with lyre motif; C, banquet couch

Dun·can·ville (dung′kən vil′), *n.* a town in N Texas. 27,781.

dunce (duns), *n.* a dull-witted, stupid, or ignorant person; dolt. [1520–30; after John DUNS SCOTUS, whose writings were attacked by the humanists as foolish] —**dun′ci·cal, dunc′ish,** *adj.* —**dunc′ish·ly,** *adv.*
—**Syn.** dullard, numbskull, blockhead, ignoramus.

dunce′ cap′, a tall, cone-shaped hat formerly worn by slow or lazy students as a punishment in school. Also, **dunce′'s cap′.** Also called **fool's cap.** [1830–40]

Dun·ci·ad, The (dun′sē ad′), a poem (1728–42) by Pope, satirizing various contemporary writers.

Dun·dalk (dun′dôk *for 1;* dun dôk′, -dôlk′ *for 2*), *n.* **1.** a town in central Maryland, near Baltimore. 71,293. **2.** a seaport in NE Republic of Ireland. 25,610.

Dun·das (dun′dəs, dun das′), *n.* a town in SE Ontario, in S Canada, near Hamilton. 19,586.

Dun·dee (dun dē′, dun′dē), *n.* a seaport in E Scotland, on the Firth of Tay: administrative center of the Tayside. 194,732.

dun·der (dun′dər), *n.* the thick lees from boiled sugarcane juice used in the distillation of rum. [1785–95; alter. of Sp *redundar* to overflow]

dun·der·head (dun′dər hed′), *n.* a dunce; blockhead; numbskull. Also called **dun·der·pate** (dun′dər pāt′). [1615–25; appar. < D *dunder(kop)* numbskull (*dunder* THUNDER + *kop* head) + HEAD] —**dun′der·head′ed,** *adj.* —**dun′der·head′ed·ness,** *n.*

dun·drear·ies (dun drēr′ēz), *n.pl.* (*sometimes cap.*) long, full sideburns or muttonchop whiskers. Also called **dun·drear′y whisk′ers.** [1860–65; after the sideburns worn by actor Edward A. Sothern as Lord *Dundreary,* a character in the play *Our American Cousin* (1858) by Tom Taylor]

CONCISE ETYMOLOGY KEY: <, descended or borrowed from; >, whence; b., blend of, blended; c., cognate with; cf., compare; deriv., derivative; equiv., equivalent; imit., imitative; obl., oblique; r., replacing; s., stem; sp., spelling, spelled; resp., respelling, respelled; trans., translation; ?, origin unknown; *, unattested; ‡, probably earlier than. See the full key inside the front cover.

dune (do͞on, dyo͞on), *n.* a sand hill or sand ridge formed by the wind, usually in desert regions or near lakes and oceans. [1780–90; < F, OF < MD *dūna;* c. DOWN[3]]

dune′ bug′gy, a small, lightweight, open automotive vehicle equipped with oversize, low-pressure tires for traveling along sand beaches, over dunes, etc. Also called **beach buggy.** [1955–60]

dune-bug·gy (do͞on′bug′ē, dyo͞on′-), *v.i.,* **-gied, -gy·ing.** to drive or ride in a dune buggy.

Dun·e·din (dun ē′din), *n.* **1.** a seaport on SE South Island, in New Zealand. 120,426. **2.** a town in W Florida. 30,203.

dune′ grass′. See **sea lyme grass.**

dune·land (do͞on′land′, dyo͞on′-), *n.* a tract of land dominated by sand dunes, often bordering on a beach. [1920–25; DUNE + -LAND]

Dun·ferm·line (dun fûrm′lin, -ferm′-, dum-), *n.* **1.** an administrative district in E Scotland, in the Fife region. 120 sq. mi. (311 sq. km); 125,027. **2.** a city in this district, near the Firth of Forth. 51,738.

dun′ fly′, *Angling.* a dun-colored artificial fly that resembles the larval stage of certain real flies. [1400–50; late ME]

dung (dung), *n.* **1.** excrement, esp. of animals; manure. —*v.t.* **2.** to manure (ground) with or as if with dung. [bef. 1000; ME, OE; c. LG, G *dung;* cf. Icel *dyngja* heap, dung, Sw *dynga* dung, muck, OHG *tunga* manuring] —**dung′y,** *adj.*

dun·ga·ree (dung′gə rē′), *n.* **1. dungarees, a.** work clothes, overalls, etc., of blue denim. **b.** See **blue jeans. 2.** blue denim. [1605–15; < Hindi *dungrī* kind of coarse cloth]

dung′ bee′tle, any of various scarab beetles that feed on or breed in dung. [1625–35]

Dun′ge·ness crab′ (dun′jə nes′, dun′jə nes′), an edible crab, *Cancer magister,* of shallow Pacific coastal waters from northern California to Alaska. [1920–25; after *Dungeness,* village in NW Washington]

dun·geon (dun′jən), *n.* **1.** a strong, dark prison or cell, usually underground, as in a medieval castle. **2.** the keep or stronghold of a castle; donjon. [1250–1300; ME *dungeo(u)n, dongeoun, dungun* < MF *donjon* < VL **domniōn-* (s. of **domniō*) keep, mastery, syncopated var. of **dominiōn-* DOMINION]

Dun′geons and Drag′ons, *Trademark.* a role-playing game set in a fantasy world resembling the Middle Ages. *Abbr:* D&D

dung·hill (dung′hil′), *n.* **1.** a heap of dung. **2.** a repugnantly filthy or degraded place, abode, or situation. [1275–1325; ME; see DUNG, HILL]

Dun·ham (dun′əm), *n.* **Katherine,** born 1910?, U.S. dancer and choreographer.

dun·ie·was·sal (do͞o′nē wos′əl), *n.* a gentleman, esp. a cadet of a ranking family, among the Highlanders of Scotland. [1555–65; < ScotGael *duine uasal; duine* man, *uasal* noble, well-born (OIr *úasal* lit., high)]

du·nite (do͞o′nīt, dun′īt), *n.* a coarse-grained igneous rock composed almost entirely of olivine. [1865–70; named after Mt. *Dun* in New Zealand, where it is found; see -ITE[1]]

dunk (dungk), *v.t.* **1.** to dip (a doughnut, cake, etc.) into coffee, milk, or the like, before eating. **2.** to submerge in a liquid. **3.** *Basketball.* to attempt to thrust (a ball) through the basket using a dunk shot. —*v.i.* **4.** to dip or submerge something, oneself, etc., in a liquid: *Let's dunk in the pool before dinner.* **5.** *Basketball.* to execute or attempt a dunk shot. —*n.* **6.** any flavorful sauce, dip, gravy, etc., into which portions of food are dipped before eating. **7.** *Basketball.* See **dunk shot.** [1865–70, *Amer.;* < PaG *dunke* to dip, immerse; cf. G *tunken,* MHG *dunken, tunken,* OHG *thunkōn, dunkōn*] —**dunk′a·ble,** *adj., n.* —**dunk′er,** *n.*

Dunk·er (dung′kər), *n.* a member of the Church of the Brethren, a denomination of Christians founded in Germany in 1708 and later reorganized in the U.S., characterized by the practice of trine immersion, the celebration of a love feast accompanying the Lord's Supper, and opposition to the taking of oaths and to military service. Also, **Dunk·ard** (dung′kərd), **Tunker.** [1705–15, *Amer.;* < PaG; see DUNK, -ER[1]]

dunk·ing (dung′king), *n.* the action of plunging or being plunged into water or other liquid: *Learning to canoe cost me a dunking.* [1915–20; DUNK + -ING[1]]

Dun·kirk (dun′kûrk), *n.* **1.** French, **Dun·kerque** (dœn kerk′). a seaport in N France: site of the evacuation of a British expeditionary force of over 330,000 men under German fire May 29–June 4, 1940. 83,759. **2.** a period of crisis or emergency when drastic measures must be enforced: *The smaller nations were facing a financial Dunkirk.* **3.** a city in W New York, on Lake Erie. 15,310.

dunk′ shot′, *Basketball.* a shot in which a player near the basket jumps with the ball and attempts to thrust it through the basket with one hand or both hands held above the rim. Also called **dunk, stuff shot.** [1965–70]

Dun Laoghai·re (dun lâr′ə), a seaport in E Republic of Ireland, near Dublin. 54,405. Also, **Dun·lea′ry.**

Dun·lap (dun′lap), *n.* **William,** 1766–1839, U.S. dramatist, theatrical producer, and historian.

dun·lin (dun′lin), *n.* a common sandpiper, *Calidris alpina,* that breeds in the northern parts of the Northern Hemisphere. [1525–35; var. of *dunling.* See DUN[2], -LING[1]]

Dun·lop (dun lop′, dun′lop), *n.* **John Boyd,** 1840–1921, Scottish inventor of the pneumatic tire.

Dun·more (dun môr′, -mōr′; dun′môr, -mōr), *n.* **1. John Murray, 4th Earl of,** 1732–1809, Scottish colonial governor in America. **2.** a borough in NE Pennsylvania, near Scranton. 16,781.

dun·nage (dun′ij), *n., v.,* **-naged, -nag·ing.** —*n.* **1.** baggage or personal effects. **2.** loose material laid beneath or wedged among objects carried by ship or rail to prevent injury from chafing or moisture, or to provide ventilation. —*v.t.* **3.** to cover or pack with dunnage. [1615–25; earlier *dynnage;* cf. AL *dennagium* dunnage; of obscure orig.]

Dunne (dun), *n.* **Fin·ley Peter** (fin′lē), 1867–1936, U.S. humorist.

dunn·ite (dun′īt), *n.* an ammonium picrate explosive used as a bursting charge for armor-piercing projectiles and in high-explosive shells; explosive D. [named after Col. B. W. *Dunn* (1860–1936), U.S. Army, the inventor; see -ITE[1]]

dun·no (də nō′), *Pron. Spelling.* don't know: *Who did it? I dunno!* [1835–45]

dun·nock (dun′ək), *n. Brit.* See **hedge sparrow.** [1425–75; late ME *dunoke, donek.* See DUN[2], -OCK]

Dunn·ville (dun′vil), *n.* a town in SE Ontario, in S Canada. 11,353.

dun·ny (dun′ē), *n., pl.* **-nies.** *Australian Slang.* an outside privy; outhouse. [1870–90; shortening of earlier dial. and criminal argot *dunnekin* outhouse, of obscure orig.]

Du·nois (dʏ nwa′), *n.* **Jean** (zhän), **Comte de,** ("*Bastard of Orleans*"), 1403?–68; French military leader: relieved by Joan of Arc and her troops when besieged at Orleans.

Dun·sa·ny (dun sā′nē), *n.* **Edward John More·ton Drax Plun·kett** (môr′tn draks plung′ket, -kit, mōr′-), **18th Baron** ("*Lord Dunsany*"), 1878–1957, Irish dramatist, poet, and essayist.

Dun·si·nane (dun′sə nān′, dun′sə nān′), *n.* a hill NE of Perth, in central Scotland: a ruined fort on its summit is traditionally called Macbeth's Castle. 1012 ft. (308 m).

Duns Sco·tus (dunz skō′təs), **John** ("*Doctor Subtilis*"), 1265?–1308, Scottish scholastic theologian.

Dun·sta·ble (dun′stə bəl), *n.* **John,** c1390–1453, English composer. Also, **Dun·sta·ple** (dun′stə pəl).

Dun·stan (dun′stən), *n.* **Saint, 1.** A.D. c925–988, English statesman: archbishop of Canterbury 961–978. **2.** a male given name: from an Old English word meaning "stone hill."

dunt[1] (dunt, do͝ont), *Scot.* —*n.* **1.** a hard blow or hit, esp. one that makes a dull sound; thump. —*v.t.* **2.** to strike, esp. with a dull sound. [1375–1425; late ME; c. Sw *dunt* DINT]

dunt[2] (dunt), *v.i.* (of ceramic ware) to crack because of excessively rapid cooling. [orig. uncert.]

du·o (do͞o′ō, dyo͞o′ō), *n., pl.* **du·os. 1.** *Music.* duet. **2.** two persons commonly associated with each other; couple. **3.** two animals or objects of the same sort; two things ordinarily placed or found together; a pair: *a duo of lovebirds.* [1580–90; < It < L: TWO]

duo-, a combining form meaning "two," used in the formation of compound words: *duologue.* [comb. form of Gk *dýo,* L *duo* TWO]

du·o·dec·a·gon (do͞o′ə dek′ə gon′, dyo͞o′-), *n. Geom.* dodecagon.

du·o·dec·a·style (do͞o′ə dek′ə stil′, dyo͞o′-), *adj.* dodecastyle.

du·o·de·cil·lion (do͞o′ō di sil′yən, dyo͞o′-), *n., pl.* **-lions,** (*as after a numeral*) **-lion,** *adj.* —*n.* **1.** a cardinal number represented in the U.S. by 1 followed by 39 zeros, and in Great Britain by 1 followed by 72 zeros. —*adj.* **2.** amounting to one duodecillion in number. [1910–15; < L *duodec(im)* twelve + *-illion,* as in *million*] —**du′o·de·cil′lionth,** *n., adj.*

du·o·dec·i·mal (do͞o′ə des′ə məl, dyo͞o′-), *adj.* **1.** pertaining to twelfths or to the number 12. **2.** proceeding by twelves. —*n.* **3.** one of a system of numbers based on the number 12. **4.** one of 12 equal parts. [1705–15; < L *duodecim* twelve + -AL[1]] —**du′o·dec′i·mal′i·ty,** *n.* —**du′o·dec′i·mal·ly,** *adv.*

du·o·dec·i·mo (do͞o′ə des′ə mō′, dyo͞o′-), *n., pl.* **-mos,** *adj.* —*n.* **1.** Also called **twelvemo.** a book size of about 5 × 7½ in. (13 × 19 cm), determined by printing on sheets folded to form 12 leaves or 24 pages. *Symbol:* 12 mo, 12° **2.** a book of this size. —*adj.* **3.** in duodecimo; twelvemo. [1650–60; short for L *in duodecimō* in twelfth]

du·o·de·nal (do͞o′ə dēn′l, dyo͞o′-; do͞o od′n əl, dyo͞o-), *adj.* of or pertaining to the duodenum. [1835–45; DUODEN(UM) + -AL[1]]

duode′nal ul′cer, *Pathol.* a peptic ulcer located in the duodenum.

du·o·den·a·ry (do͞o′ə den′ə rē, -dē′nə rē, dyo͞o′-), *adj.* duodecimal. [1675–85; < L *duodēn(ī)* twelve each + -ARY]

du·o·de·ni·tis (do͞o′ō di nī′tis, dyo͞o′-; do͞o od′n ī′tis, dyo͞o-), *n. Pathol.* inflammation of the duodenum. [1850–55; DUODEN(UM) + -ITIS]

du•o•de•no•je•ju•nos•to•my (do͞o′ə dē′nō ji jo͞o-nos′tə mē, dyo͞o′-, do͞o od′n ō-, dyo͞o-), *n., pl.* **-mies.** *Surg.* the formation of an artificial connection between the duodenum and the jejunum. [DUODEN(UM) + -O- + JEJUNOSTOMY]

du•o•de•num (do͞o′ə dē′nəm, dyo͞o′-; do͞o od′n əm, dyo͞o-), *n., pl.* **du•o•de•na** (do͞o′ə dē′nə, dyo͞o′-; do͞o od′-n ə, dyo͞o-), **du•o•de•nums.** *Anat., Zool.* the first portion of the small intestine, from the stomach to the jejunum. See diag. under **intestine.** [1350–1400; ME < ML, by ellipsis from *intestinum duodēnum digitōrum* intestine of twelve fingerbreadths, with original gen. pl. construed as neut. sing.; L *duodēni* twelve each (here lacking distributive sense)]

du•o•logue (do͞o′ə lôg′, -log′, dyo͞o′-), *n.* **1.** a conversation between two persons; dialogue. **2.** a dramatic performance or piece in the form of a dialogue limited to two speakers. [1860–65; DUO- + (MONO)LOGUE]

duo•mo (dwō′mō), *n., pl.* **-mos, -mi** (-mē). cathedral, esp. in Italy. [1540–50; < It; see DOME]

du•op•o•ly (do͞o op′ə lē, dyo͞o-), *n., pl.* **-lies.** the market condition that exists when there are only two sellers. Cf. **monopoly** (def. 1), **oligopoly.** [1915–20; DUO- + (MONO)POLY]

du•op•so•ny (do͞o op′sə nē, dyo͞o-), *n., pl.* **-nies.** the market condition that exists when there are only two buyers. Cf. **monopsony, oligopsony.** [DU(O)- + *-opsony* < Gk *opsōnía* purchasing of food, equiv. to *óps(on)* viands + *ōn(eîsthai)* to buy + *-ia* -Y[3]]

du•o•tone (do͞o′ə tōn′, dyo͞o′-), *adj.* **1.** of two tones or colors. —*n.* **2.** a picture in two tones or colors. **3.** *Print.* **a.** a method of printing an illustration either in a dark and a tinted shade of the same color or in two different colors from two plates of a monochrome original made from negatives at different screen angles. **b.** an illustration printed by this method. [1905–10; DUO- + TONE]

du•o•type (do͞o′ə tīp′, dyo͞o′-), *n. Print.* two halftone plates made from a monochrome original but etched differently to create two values of intensity when superimposed in printing. [1910–15; DUO- + -TYPE]

dup (dup), *v.t.,* **dupped, dup•ping.** *Archaic.* to open. [1540–50; contr. of DO[1] + UP; cf. DOFF, DON[2]]

dup., duplicate.

dupe[1] (do͞op, dyo͞op), *n., v.,* **duped, dup•ing.** —*n.* **1.** a person who is easily deceived or fooled; gull. **2.** a person who unquestioningly or unwittingly serves a cause or another person: *a dupe of the opponents.* —*v.t.* **3.** to make a dupe of; deceive; delude; trick. [1675–85; < F; MF *duppe* for *(*tête*) *d'uppe* head of hoopoe, i.e., fool (cf. *tête de fou*) < VL **uppa,* L *upupa* hoopoe, a bird thought to be especially stupid; cf. HOOPOE] —**dup′a•ble,** *adj.* —**dup′a•bil′i•ty,** *n.* —**dup′er,** *n.*

dupe[2] (do͞op, dyo͞op), *n., v.,* **duped, dup•ing,** *adj. Informal.* —*n.* **1.** duplicate. **2.** *Motion Pictures.* **a.** a duplicate picture negative used for making additional release prints or for making special effects to be inserted in the release negative. **b.** the procedure for producing such a duplicate. **3.** *Television.* a duplicate videotape obtained by electronic printing of the original videotape. —*v.t., v.i.* **4.** to duplicate. —*adj.* **5.** duplicate. [1895–90; by shortening]

dup•er•y (do͞o′pə rē, dyo͞o′-), *n., pl.* **-er•ies** for 1. **1.** an act, practice, or instance of duping. **2.** the state of one who is duped. [1750–60; < F *duperie.* See DUPE[1], -ERY]

du•pi•on (do͞o′pē on′), *n.* **1.** a cocoon formed jointly by two silkworms. **2.** douppioni. Also, **du•pi•o•ni** (do͞o′pē-ō′nē). [1820–30; alter. of F *doupion* < It *doppione,* equiv. to *doppi(e)* DOUBLE + *-one* aug. suffix]

du•pla•tion (do͞o plā′shən, dyo͞o-), *n.* multiplication by two; doubling. [1375–1425; late ME < L *duplātiōn-,* s. of *duplātiō* a doubling, equiv. to *duplāt(us)* (*dupl(us)* DUPLE + *-ātus* -ATE[1]) + *-iōn-* -ION]

du•ple (do͞o′pəl, dyo͞o′-), *adj.* **1.** having two parts; double; twofold. **2.** *Music.* having two or sometimes a multiple of two beats in a measure: *duple meter.* [1535–45; < L *duplus* DOUBLE]

Du•pleix (dʏ pleks′), *n.* **Jo•seph Fran•çois** (zhō zef′ fräɴ swa′), **Marquis,** 1697–1763, French colonial governor of India 1724–54.

du′ple rhythm′, *Pros.* a rhythmic pattern created by a succession of disyllabic feet. [1880–85]

Du•ples•sis-Mor•nay (*Fr.* dʏ ple sē môr nā′), *n.* **Philippe** (fē lēp′). See **Mornay, Philippe de.**

du′ple time′, *Music.* characterized by two beats to the measure. Also called **du′ple meas′ure, two-part time.** [1715–25]

du•plex (do͞o′pleks, dyo͞o′-), *n.* **1.** See **duplex apartment. 2.** See **duplex house. 3.** paper or cardboard having different colors, finishes, or stocks on opposite sides. **4.** *Print.* **a.** a method of reproducing an illustration using two halftone plates, one black and the other in a color. **b.** a printing press equipped to print both sides of a sheet in one pass. **5.** *Genetics.* a double-stranded region of DNA. —*adj.* **6.** having two parts; double; twofold. **7.** (of a machine) having two identical working units, operating together or independently, in a single framework or assembly. **8.** pertaining to or noting a telecommunications system, as most telephone systems, permitting the simultaneous transmission of two messages in opposite directions over one channel. —*v.t.* **9.** to make duplex; make or change into a duplex: *Many owners are duplexing their old houses for extra income.* [1810–20; < L: twofold, double, equiv. to *du(o)* TWO + *-plex* -PLEX] —**du•plex′i•ty,** *n.*

du′plex apart′ment, an apartment with rooms on two connected floors. Also called **duplex.** [1935–40, *Amer.*]

du•plex•er (do͞o′plek sər, dyo͞o′-), *n. Electronics.* an automatic electronic switching device that permits the use of the same antenna for transmitting and receiving. [1950–55; DUPLEX + -ER[1]]

du′plex house′, a house having separate apartments for two families, esp. a two-story house having a complete apartment on each floor and two separate entrances. Also called **duplex.**

du′plex lock′, a lock capable of being opened either by a master key or a change key, each operating its own mechanism.

du′plex proc′ess, any of several methods for making steel in which the process is begun in one furnace and finished in another. [1900–05]

du′plex pump′, a pair of direct-acting steam pumps so arranged that each pump begins its working stroke just as the other finishes its working stroke, so that the rate of flow of the fluid is nearly continuous.

du•pli•ca•ble (do͞o′pli kə bəl, dyo͞o′-), *adj.* capable of being duplicated. Also, **du•pli•cat•a•ble** (do͞o′pli kā′tə-bəl, dyo͞o′-). [DUPLIC(ATE) + -ABLE] —**du′pli•ca•bil′i•ty, du′pli•cat′a•bil′i•ty,** *n.*

du•pli•cate (*n., adj.* do͞o′pli kit, dyo͞o′-; *v.* do͞o′pli kāt′, dyo͞o′-), *n., v.,* **-cat•ed, -cat•ing,** *adj.* —*n.* **1.** a copy exactly like an original. **2.** anything corresponding in all respects to something else. **3.** *Cards.* a duplicate game. **4. in duplicate,** in two copies, esp. two identical copies: *Please type the letter in duplicate.* —*v.t.* **5.** to make an exact copy of. **6.** to do or perform again; repeat: *He duplicated his father's way of standing with his hands in his pockets.* **7.** to double; make twofold. —*v.i.* **8.** to become duplicate. —*adj.* **9.** exactly like or corresponding to something else: *duplicate copies of a letter.* **10.** consisting of or existing in two identical or corresponding parts; double. **11.** *Cards.* noting a game in which each team plays a series of identical hands, the winner being the team making the best total score. [1400–50; late ME < L *duplicātus* (ptp. of *duplicāre* to make double), equiv. to *duplic-* (s. of *duplex*) DUPLEX + *-ātus* -ATE[1]] —**du′pli•ca′tive,** *adj.*
—**Syn. 1.** facsimile, replica, reproduction. **5.** See **imitate. 10.** twofold. —**Ant. 1.** original.

du′plicate bridge′, a form of contract bridge used in tournaments in which contestants play the identical series of deals, with each deal being scored independently, permitting individual scores to be compared. [1925–30]

du′plicating machine′, 1. a duplicator, esp. one for making identical copies of documents, letters, etc. **2.** profiler. [1890–95]

du•pli•ca•tion (do͞o′pli kā′shən, dyo͞o′-), *n.* **1.** an act or instance of duplicating. **2.** the state of being duplicated. **3.** a duplicate. **4.** *Genetics.* a type of chromosomal aberration in which a region of the chromosome is repeated. [1490–1500; (< AF) < L *duplicātiōn-* (s. of *duplicātiō*), equiv. to *duplicāt(us)* (see DUPLICATE) + *-iōn-* -ION]

duplica′tion of the cube′, *Geom.* the insoluble problem of constructing a cube having twice the volume of a given cube, using only a ruler and compass. [1650–60]

du•pli•ca•tor (do͞o′pli kā′tər, dyo͞o′-), *n.* a machine for making duplicates, as a mimeograph. [1890–95; DUPLICATE + -OR[2]]

du•pli•ca•ture (do͞o′pli kə cho͝or′, -kə chər, -kā′chər, dyo͞o′-), *n.* a folding or doubling of a part on itself, as a membrane. [1680–90; < NL *duplicātūra.* See DUPLICATE, -URE]

du•pli•ca•tus (do͞o′pli kā′təs, dyo͞o′-), *adj. Meteorol.* (of a cloud) consisting of superposed layers that sometimes partially merge. [< L: doubled; see DUPLICATE]

du•plic•i•tous (do͞o plis′i təs, dyo͞o-), *adj.* marked or characterized by duplicity. [1960–65; DUPLICIT(Y) + -OUS] —**du•plic′i•tous•ly,** *adv.*

du•plic•i•ty (do͞o plis′i tē, dyo͞o-), *n., pl.* **-ties** for 1. **1.** deceitfulness in speech or conduct; speaking or acting in two different ways concerning the same matter with intent to deceive; double-dealing. **2.** a twofold or double state or quality. [1400–50; late ME *duplicite* < MF < ML, LL *duplicitās,* with *-ite* r. *-itās;* see DUPLEX, -ITY]
—**Syn. 1.** deception, dissimulation. See **deceit.** —**Ant. 1.** straightforwardness.

du•pon•di•us (do͞o pon′dē əs, dyo͞o-), *n., pl.* **-di•i** (-dē-ī′). a coin of ancient Rome, equal to two asses. [1595–1605; < L, equiv. to *du(o)* TWO + *pond(us)* weight, POUND[2] + *-ius* adj. suffix]

Du•Pont (do͞o pont′, dyo͞o-, do͞o′pont, dyo͞o′-; *for 1, 2 also Fr.* dʏ pôɴ′), *n.* **1. E•leu•thère I•ré•née** (e lœ teʀ′ ē ʀä nā′), 1771–1834, U.S. industrialist, born in France. **2. Pierre Sam•u•el** (pē âr′ sam′yo͞o əl; *Fr.* pyeʀ sa-mʏ el′), 1739–1817, French economist and statesman (father of Eleuthère Irénée). **3. Samuel Francis,** 1803–65, Union admiral in the U.S. Civil War. Also, **Du Pont′.**

Du•pré (dʏ pʀā′), *n.* **1. Jules** (zhʏl), 1812–89, French painter. **2. Mar•cel** (maʀ sel′), 1886–1971, French organist and composer.

Du•que de Ca•xi•as (do͞o′ki di kä shē′äs), a city in SE Brazil: a suburb of Rio de Janeiro. 537,308.

Du•quesne (do͞o kān′, dyo͞o-; *for 1 also Fr.* dʏ ken′), *n.* **1. A•bra•ham** (a bʀa am′), 1610–88, French naval commander. **2.** a city in SW Pennsylvania, on the Monongahela River. 10,094. **3. Fort.** See **Fort Duquesne.**

Du Quoin (do͞o koin′), a town in SW Illinois: site of the Hambletonian. 6594.

dur (do͞oʀ), *adj. German.* (in music) written in a major key; major.

du•ra (do͝or′ə, dyo͝or′ə), *n.* See **dura mater.** [1880–85]

du•ra•ble (do͝or′ə bəl, dyo͝or′-), *adj.* **1.** able to resist wear, decay, etc., well; lasting; enduring. —*n.* **2. durables.** See **durable goods.** [1350–1400; ME < MF < L *dūrābilis.* See DURE[2], -ABLE] —**du′ra•bil′i•ty, du′ra•ble•ness,** *n.* —**du′ra•bly,** *adv.*
—**Syn. 1.** permanent. —**Ant. 1.** weak, transitory.

du′rable goods′, goods, as household appliances, machinery, or sports equipment, that are not consumed or destroyed in use and can be used for a period of time, usually three or more years. Also called **hard goods.** [1925–30]

du′rable press′. See **permanent press.** [1965–70, *Amer.*]

du•rain (do͝or′ān, dyo͝or′-), *n. Mineral.* the coal forming the dull layers in banded bituminous coal. Cf. **clarain, vitrain.** [1915–20; < L *dūr(us)* hard + *-ain,* from FUSAIN, by analysis as a suffix]

du•ral (do͝or′əl, dyo͝or′əl), *adj.* of or pertaining to the dura mater. [1885–90; DUR(A) + -AL[1]]

du•ral•u•min (do͝o ral′yə min, dyo͝o-), *n.* an alloy of aluminum that is 4 percent copper and contains small amounts of magnesium, manganese, iron, and silicon: used for applications requiring lightness and strength, as in airplane construction. [1905–10; < L *dūr(us)* hard + ALUMIN(UM)]

du′ra ma′ter (mā′tər), *Anat.* the tough, fibrous membrane forming the outermost of the three coverings of the brain and spinal cord. Also called **dura.** Cf. **arachnoid** (def. 6), **pia mater.** [1350–1400; ME < ML: lit., hard mother]

du•ra•men (do͝o rā′min, dyo͝o-), *n. Bot.* heartwood. [1830–40; < L *dūrāmen* hardness, hardened vine branch, equiv. to *dūrā(re)* to harden + *-men* n. suffix]

dur•ance (do͝or′əns, dyo͝or′-), *n.* **1.** incarceration or imprisonment (often used in the phrase *durance vile*). **2.** *Archaic.* endurance. [1400–50; late ME < MF. See DURE[2], -ANCE]

Du•rand (də rand′), *n.* **Asher Brown,** 1796–1886, U.S. engraver and landscape painter of the Hudson River School.

Du•ran•go (də rang′gō; *for 1, 2 also Sp.* do͞o räng′gô), *n.* **1.** a state in N Mexico. 1,122,000; 47,691 sq. mi. (123,520 sq. km). **2.** a city in and the capital of this state, in the S part. 209,000. **3.** a city in SW Colorado. 11,426.

Du•rant (də rant′), *n.* **1. Ariel,** 1898–1981, U.S. author and historian (wife of Will). **2. Will(iam James),** 1885–1981, U.S. author and historian. **3.** a city in S Oklahoma. 11,972.

Du•ran•te (də ran′tē), *n.* **James Francis** (*Jimmy*), 1893–1980, U.S. comedian.

du•ran•te vi•ta (do͞o rän′te wē′tä; *Eng.* do͝o ran′tē vī′tə, vē′tə, dyo͝o-), *Latin.* during life.

Du•ran•ty (də ran′tē), *n.* **Walter,** 1884–1957, English journalist and author in the U.S.

du•ra•tion (do͝o rā′shən, dyo͝o-), *n.* **1.** the length of time something continues or exists (often used with *the*). **2.** continuance in time. **3.** (in the philosophy of Bergson) a temporal continuum, intuitively known, within which the élan vital operates. [1350–1400; ME < ML *dūrātiōn-* (s. of *dūrātiō*), equiv. to L *dūrāt(us)* (ptp. of *dūrāre* to last; see DURE[2]) + *-iōn-* -ION] —**du•ra′tion•al,** *adj.*

dur•a•tive (do͝or′ə tiv, dyo͝or′-), *adj. Gram.* noting or pertaining to a verb aspect expressing incomplete or continued action. *Beat* and *walk* are durative in contrast to *strike* and *step.* [1885–90; DURAT(ION) + -IVE]

Du•raz•zo (də rät′sō; *It.* do͞o rät′tsô), *n.* Italian name of **Durrës.**

Dur•ban (dûr′bən), *n.* a seaport in SE Natal, in the E Republic of South Africa. 851,000.

dur•bar (dûr′bär), *n.* (in India) **1.** the court of a native ruler. **2.** a public audience or levee held by a native prince or by a British governor or viceroy; an official reception. **3.** the hall or place of audience. **4.** the audience itself. [1600–10; alter. of Urdu *darbār* court < Pers, equiv. to *dar* door + *bār* entry]

dure[1] (do͝or, dyo͝or), *adj. Archaic.* hard; severe. [1325–75; ME < MF < L *dūrus* hard]

dure[2] (do͝or, dyo͝or), *v.i., v.t.,* **dured, dur•ing.** *Archaic.* endure. [1225–75; ME < OF *durer* < L *dūrāre* to last; see DURE[1]]

Dü•rer (do͝or′ər, dyo͝or′-; *Ger.* dʏ′ʀəʀ), *n.* **Al•brecht** (äl′bʀeKHt), 1471–1528, German painter and engraver.

du•ress (do͝o res′, dyo͝o-, do͝or′is, dyo͝or′-), *n.* **1.** compulsion by threat or force; coercion; constraint. **2.** *Law.* such constraint or coercion as will render void a contract or other legal act entered or performed under its influence. **3.** forcible restraint, esp. imprisonment. [1275–1325; ME *duresse* < MF *duresse, -esce, -ece* < L *dūritia* hardness, harshness, oppression, equiv. to *dūr(us)* hard + *-itia* -ICE]
—**Syn. 1.** intimidation, pressure, bullying, browbeating.

du•res•sor (do͝o res′ər, dyo͝o-), *n. Law.* a person who subjects another to duress. [1620–30; DURESS + -OR[2]]

D'Ur•fey (dûr′fē), *n.* **Thomas,** 1653–1723, English dramatist.

Dur•ga (do͝or′gä), *n. Hinduism.* the sometimes malignant goddess of war: an aspect of Devi.

Dur•ga Pu•ja (do͝or′gə po͞o′jə), Dasehra.

Dur•ham (dûr′əm, dur′-), *n.* **1.** a county in NE England. 607,600; 940 sq. mi. (2435 sq. km). **2.** a city in this county. 86,500. **3.** a city in N North Carolina. 100,831. **4.** a town in SE New Hampshire. 10,652. **5.** *Animal Husb.* Shorthorn.

du•ri•an (do͝or′ē ən, -än′), *n.* **1.** the edible fruit of a tree, *Durio zibethinus,* of the bombax family, of southeastern Asia, having a hard, prickly rind, a highly flavored, pulpy flesh, and an unpleasant odor. **2.** the tree itself. Also, **du′ri•on.** [1580–90; < Malay: a fruit with spiky skin, equiv. to *duri* thorn + *-an* nominalizer suffix]

CONCISE PRONUNCIATION KEY: act, cāpe, dâre, pärt; set, ēqual; *if,* ice; ox, ōver, ôrder, oil, bo͝ok, bo͞ot, out; up, ûrge; child; sing; shoe; thin, *that;* zh as in *treasure.* ə = *a* as in *alone, e* as in *system, i* as in *easily, o* as in *gallop, u* as in *circus;* ᵊ as in *fire* (fīᵊr), *hour* (ouᵊr). l and n can serve as syllabic consonants, as in *cradle* (krād′l), and *button* (but′n). See the full key inside the front cover.

dur·i·crust (dŏŏr′i krust′, dyŏŏr′-), *n.* a hard crust that forms on or in soil in semiarid climates owing to cementation of soil particles. Cf. **caliche, hardpan** (defs. 1, 2). [< L *dūr(us)* hard + -I- + CRUST]

dur·ing (dŏŏr′ing, dyŏŏr′-), *prep.* **1.** throughout the duration, continuance, or existence of: *He lived in Florida during the winter.* **2.** at some time or point in the course of: *They departed during the night.* [1350–1400; ME; see DURE[2], -ING[2]]

Durk·heim (dûrk′hīm; *Fr.* dyʀ kem′), *n.* **É·mile** (ā mēl′), 1858–1917, French sociologist and philosopher.

dur·mast (dûr′mast′, -mäst′), *n.* a European oak, *Quercus petraea,* yielding a heavy, elastic wood used for furniture and in the construction of buildings. [1785–95; short for *durmast oak,* perh. erroneously for *dunmast oak;* see DUN[2], MAST[2]]

durn (dûrn), *adj., adv., v.t., n. Informal.* darn[2]. [resp. to reflect regional pron.]

durned (dûrnd), *adj., adv. Informal.* darned. [DURN + -ED[2]]

du·ro (dŏŏr′ō; *Sp.* dōō′rô), *n., pl.* **-ros** (-rōz; *Sp.* -rôs). a peso of Spain or Spanish America. [1825–35; < Sp, short for *peso duro* hard piastre; see DURE[1]]

Du·roc (dŏŏr′ok, dyŏŏr′-), *n.* one of an American breed of hardy red hogs having drooping ears. Also called **Du·roc-Jer·sey** (dŏŏr′ok jûr′zē, dyŏŏr′-). [1880–85, *Amer.*; named after a horse owned by breeder]

du·rom·e·ter (dŏŏ rom′i tər, dyŏŏ-), *n.* a device for measuring the hardness of materials, esp. metals. [1885–90; < L *dūr(us)* hard + -O- + -METER]

dur·ra (dŏŏr′ə), *n.* a type of grain sorghum with slender stalks, cultivated in Asia and Africa and introduced into the U.S. Also, **doura, dourah.** Also called **Indian millet, Guinea corn.** [1790–1800; < Ar *dhura(h)*]

Dur·rell (dŏŏr′əl, dur′-), *n.* **Lawrence (George),** 1912–90, English novelist and poet.

Dür·ren·matt (dŏŏr′ən mät′, dyŏŏr′-; *Ger.* dʏʀ′ən-mät′), *n.* **Frie·drich** (frē′drik; *Ger.* frē′dʀɪкн), 1921–90, Swiss dramatist and novelist.

Dur·rës (dŏŏr′əs; *Alb.* dōō′ʀəs), *n.* a seaport in W Albania, on the Adriatic: important ancient city. 80,000. Italian, **Durazzo.**

dur·rie (dûr′ē), *n.* dhurrie.

durst (dûrst), *v. Archaic.* pt. of **dare.**

du′rum wheat′ (dŏŏr′əm, dyŏŏr′-), a wheat, *Triticum turgidum,* the grain of which yields flour used in making pasta. Also called **du′rum, macaroni wheat.** [1905–10; < NL, the earlier specific epithet. See DURE[1]]

Dur·yea (dŏŏr′yā, dŏŏr′ē ā′), *n.* **Charles Edgar,** 1861–1938, U.S. inventor and manufacturer of automobiles and automotive devices.

Du Sa·ble (dōō sä′blə, säb′, dyōō; *Fr.* dy sa′blᵊ), **Jean Bap·tiste Pointe** (zhän bä tēst′ pwant), 1745?–1818, U.S. pioneer trader, born in Haiti: early settler of Chicago.

Du·se (dōō′zā; *It.* dōō′ze), *n.* **E·le·o·no·ra** (el′ē ə nôr′ə; *It.* e′le ô nô′rä), 1859–1924, Italian actress.

Du·shan·be (dōō shän′bə, -shäm′-, dyōō-; *Russ.* dōō-shun byě′), *n.* a city in and the capital of Tadzhikistan, in the SW Russian Federation in Asia, SW of Tashkent. 493,000. Formerly, **Dyushambe** (before 1929), **Stalinabad** (1929–61).

dusk[1] (dusk), *n.* **1.** the state or period of partial darkness between day and night; the dark part of twilight. **2.** partial darkness; shade; gloom: *She was barely visible in the dusk of the room.* [1615–25; back formation from DUSKY]

dusk[2] (dusk), *adj.* **1.** tending to darkness; dark. —*v.t., v.i.* **2.** to make or become dusk; darken. [bef. 1000; ME *duske* (adj.), *dusken* (v.); metathetic alter. of OE *dox* dusky, *doxian* to turn dark; c. L. *fuscus* dark] —**dusk′·ish,** *adj.*

dusk·y (dus′kē), *adj.,* **dusk·i·er, dusk·i·est.** **1.** somewhat dark; having little light; dim; shadowy. **2.** having dark skin. **3.** of a dark color. **4.** gloomy; sad. [1550–60; DUSK[2] + -Y[1]] —**dusk′i·ly,** *adv.* —**dusk′i·ness,** *n.*

dusk′y grouse′. See **blue grouse.** [1820–30; *Amer.*]

dusk′y sea′side spar′row. See under **seaside sparrow.** Also called **dusk′y spar′row.**

dusk′y shark′, a blue-gray shark, *Carcharinus obscurus,* of warm Atlantic and eastern Pacific seas, reaching a length of 12 ft. (3.7 m).

Düs·sel·dorf (dŏŏs′əl dôrf′; *Ger.* dʏs′əl dôʀf′), *n.* a port in and the capital of North Rhine-Westphalia, in W Germany, on the Rhine. 563,400.

dust (dust), *n.* **1.** earth or other matter in fine, dry particles. **2.** a cloud of finely powdered earth or other matter in the air. **3.** any finely powdered substance, as sawdust. **4.** the ground; the earth's surface. **5.** the substance to which something, as the dead human body, is ultimately reduced by disintegration or decay; earthly remains. **6.** *Brit.* **a.** ashes, refuse, etc. **b.** junk[1] (def. 1). **7.** a low or humble condition. **8.** anything worthless. **9.** disturbance; turmoil. **10.** See **gold dust. 11.** the mortal body of a human being. **12.** a single particle or grain. **13.** *Archaic.* money; cash. **14. bite the dust, a.** to be killed, esp. in battle; die. **b.** to suffer defeat; be unsuccessful; fail: *Another manufacturer has bitten the dust.* **15. leave one in the dust,** to overtake and surpass a competitor or one who is less ambitious, qualified, etc.: *Don't be so meek, they'll leave you in the dust.* **16. lick the dust, a.** to be killed; die. **b.** to humble oneself abjectly; grovel: *He will resign rather than lick the dust.* **17. make the dust fly,** to execute with vigor or speed: *We turned them loose on the work, and they made the dust fly.* **18. shake the dust from one's feet,** to depart in anger or disdain; leave decisively or in haste, esp. from an unpleasant situation: *As the country moved toward totalitarianism, many of the intelligentsia shook the dust from their feet.* **19. throw dust in someone's eyes,** to mislead; deceive: *He threw dust in our eyes by pretending to be a jeweler and then disappeared with the diamonds.* —*v.t.* **20.** to wipe the dust from: *to dust a table.* **21.** to sprinkle with a powder or dust: *to dust rosebushes with an insecticide.* **22.** to strew or sprinkle (a powder, dust, or other fine particles): *to dust insecticide on a rosebush.* **23.** to soil with dust; make dusty. —*v.i.* **24.** to wipe dust from furniture, woodwork, etc. **25.** to become dusty. **26.** to apply dust or powder to a plant, one's body, etc.: *to dust with an insecticide in late spring.* **27. dust off, a.** *Baseball.* (of a pitcher) to throw the ball purposely at or dangerously close to (the batter). **b.** to take out or prepare for use again, as after a period of inactivity or storage: *I'm going to dust off my accounting skills and try to get a job in the finance department.* **c.** to beat up badly: *The gang of hoodlums dusted off a cop.* [bef. 900; ME; OE *dūst;* c. G *Dunst* vapor] —**dust′·less,** *adj.*

dust′ ball′, *Chiefly Northern and North Midland U.S.* a ball or roll of dust and lint that accumulates indoors, as in corners or under furniture. Also called **dust′ curl′.** —**Regional Variation.** DUST BALL and DUST CURL are used chiefly in the North and North Midland U.S. DUST KITTEN and DUST KITTY are also in use in the Northern U.S., but there are many other terms that are in use in widely scattered local areas, such as DUST MOUSE, HOUSE MOSS, and WOOLLY.

dust-bathe (dust′bāth′), *v.i.,* **-bathed, -bath·ing.** *Animal Behav.* (of a bird) to squat in dusty soil and fluff dust through the plumage: probably performed to combat ectoparasites.

dust·bin (dust′bin′), *n. Chiefly Brit.* an ashcan; garbage can. Also, **dust′ bin′.** [1840–50; DUST + BIN]

Dust′ Bowl′, **1.** the region in the S central U.S. that suffered from dust storms in the 1930's. **2.** (*l.c.*) any similar dry region elsewhere. [1935–40, *Amer.*]

dust′ bowl′er, a person who is a native or resident of a dust bowl region. [DUST BOWL + -ER[1]]

dust′ cart′, *Brit.* a garbage truck. [1770–80]

dust·cloth (dust′klôth′, -kloth′), *n., pl.* **-cloths** (-klôthz′, -klothz′, -klôths′, -kloths′). a soft, absorbent cloth used for dusting. [1720–30; DUST + CLOTH]

dust′ count′er, any instrument used to measure the size and number of dust particles per unit volume in the atmosphere. Also called **nucleus counter.** [1890–95]

dust′ cov′er, **1.** a cloth or plastic covering used to protect furniture or equipment, as during a period of nonuse. **2.** See **book jacket.** [1900–05]

dust′ dev′il, a small whirlwind 10–100 ft. (3–30 m) in diameter and from several hundred to 1000 ft. (305 m) high, common in dry regions on hot, calm afternoons and made visible by the dust, debris, and sand it picks up from the ground. Also called **dust whirl.** [1890–95]

dust·er (dus′tər), *n.* **1.** a person or thing that removes or applies dust. **2.** a cloth, brush, etc., for removing dust. **3.** a lightweight housecoat. **4.** an apparatus or device for sprinkling dust, powder, insecticide, or the like, esp. on plants. **5.** a person employed in spreading insecticidal dusts or the like on crops from a low-flying plane. **6.** a long, light overgarment, worn esp. in the early days of open automobiles to protect the clothing from dust. **7.** a summer-weight coat for women that is loose-fitting and often unlined. **8.** See **dust storm. 9.** *Baseball.* a ball purposely thrown by a pitcher at or dangerously close to a batter. **10.** See **dry hole. 11.** (*cap.*) *Mil.* a self-propelled U.S. antiaircraft gun of the 1950's, armed with twin 40mm cannon. [1570–80; DUST + -ER[1]]

dust′ gun′, a hand-operated device for spraying pesticide or dusting plants.

dust′ head′, *Slang.* a habitual user of angel dust. Also, **dust′head′.** [1975–80]

dust·heap (dust′hēp′), *n.* **1.** a heap or pile of rubbish, refuse, or the like. **2.** oblivion; obscurity; disregard; disuse: *He was consigned to the dustheap after many years of public service.* [1645–55; DUST + HEAP]

Dus·tin (dus′tin), *n.* a male given name.

dust·ing (dus′ting), *n.* **1.** a light application: *a dusting of powder.* **2.** a beating; defeat: *He gave his opponent a good dusting.* [1615–25; DUST + -ING[1]]

dust′ing pow′der, a powder used on the skin, esp. to relieve irritation or absorb moisture. [1905–10]

dust′ jack′et. See **book jacket.** [1925–30]

dust′ kit′ten, *Northern U.S.* a dust ball. Also called **dust′ kit′ty.** —**Regional Variation.** See **dust ball.**

dust·man (dust′man′, -mən), *n., pl.* **-men** (-men′, -mən). *Brit.* a person employed to remove or cart away garbage, refuse, ashes, etc.; garbage collector. [1700–10; DUST + MAN[1]]

dust′ mop′, a long-handled mop of dry, absorbent material, used for dusting floors. Also called **dry mop.** [1950–55]

dust-mop (dust′mop′), *v.t.,* **-mopped, -mop·ping.** to clean with a dust mop.

dust′ mouse′, *Dial.* a dust ball. —**Regional Variation.** See **dust ball.**

dust·off (dust′ôf′, -of′), *n. Mil. Slang.* medevac (def. 1). [1965–70; DUST + (TAKE)OFF, with pun on v. phrase *dust off*]

du·stoor (də stŏŏr′), *n.* dastur. Also, **du·stour′.**

dust·pan (dust′pan′), *n.* a short-handled shovellike utensil into which dust is swept for removal. [1775–85; DUST + PAN[1]]

dust·proof (dust′prōōf′), *adj.* impervious to or free of dust. [1865–70; DUST + -PROOF]

dust′ ruf′fle, **1.** a ruffle attached to the inside hem of a full-length petticoat or skirt to protect the bottom edge of the garment against dirt and wear, popular in the 19th and early 20th centuries. **2.** a wide ruffle encircling the bottom perimeter of a bed and reaching to the floor, used decoratively or as protection against dust.

dust′ shot′, the smallest size of shot for use in a shotgun. [1790–1800]

dust′ storm′, a storm of strong winds and dust-filled air over an extensive area during a period of drought over normally arable land (distinguished from *sandstorm*). Also, **dust′storm′.** Also called **duster.** [1875–80]

dust·up (dust′up′), *n.* a quarrel; argument; row. [1895–1900; n. use of v. phrase *dust up*]

dust′ well′, a hollow in the surface of a glacier, formed by the melting action of dust or soil deposits.

dust′ whirl′. See **dust devil.** [1885–90]

dust·y (dus′tē), *adj.,* **dust·i·er, dust·i·est.** **1.** filled, covered, or clouded with or as with dust. **2.** of the nature of dust; powdery. **3.** of the color of dust; having a grayish cast. [1175–1225; ME; see DUST, -Y[1]] —**dust′i·ly,** *adv.* —**dust′i·ness,** *n.*

dust′y clo′ver, a bush clover, *Lespedeza capitata.*

dust′y mill′er, **1.** *Bot.* **a.** any of several composite plants, as *Centaurea cineraria, Senecio cineraria,* or the beach wormwood, having pinnate leaves covered with whitish pubescence. **b.** See **rose campion. 2.** *Angling.* a type of artificial fly used chiefly for trout and salmon. [1815–25]

dust·y·wing (dus′tē wing′), *n.* any of the rare, minute neuropterous insects of the family Coniopterygidae, characterized by a white, powdery body and wing cover, large eyes, long and slender antennae, and chewing mouthparts. [DUSTY + WING]

Dutch (duch), *adj.* **1.** of, pertaining to, or characteristic of the natives or inhabitants of the Netherlands or their country or language. **2.** pertaining to or designating the style of painting and subject matter developed in the Netherlands during the 17th century, chiefly characterized by the use of chiaroscuro, muted tones, naturalistic colors or forms, and of genre, landscape, or still-life subjects drawn from contemporary urban and rural life. **3.** of, pertaining to, or characteristic of the Pennsylvania Dutch. **4.** *Archaic.* German; Teutonic. **5. go Dutch,** to have each person pay his or her own expenses: *a dinner where everyone goes Dutch.* Also, **go dutch.** —*n.* **6.** the people of the Netherlands and their immediate descendants elsewhere, collectively. **7.** See **Pennsylvania Dutch. 8.** Also called **Netherlandic.** the Germanic language of the Netherlands and northern Belgium. *Abbr.:* D Cf. **Flemish. 9.** *Obs.* the German language. **10. in Dutch,** in trouble or disfavor (with someone): *in Dutch with the teacher for disturbing the class.* [1350–1400; ME *Duch* < MD *duutsch* Dutch, German(ic); c. OHG *diutisc* popular (language) (as opposed to learned Latin), trans. of L (*lingua*) *vulgāris* popular (language)]

Dutch 200, *Bowling.* a score of 200 in a game, made by bowling strikes and spares alternately.

Dutch′ auc′tion, a method of auction consisting in the offer of a property at a price above the actual value and then at gradually reduced prices until a buyer is found. [1860–65]

Dutch′ Belt′ed, one of a breed of black dairy cattle, raised originally in the Netherlands, having a broad white band encircling the body.

Dutch′ bob′, a hair style consisting of bangs cut straight across the forehead and the rest of the hair cut to a uniform length just below the ears. Also called **Dutch′boy bob′** (duch′boi′), **Dutch cut.**

Dutch′ bond′, *Masonry.* See **English cross bond.**

Dutch′ Bor′neo, the former name of the southern and larger part of the island of Borneo: now part of Indonesia.

Dutch′ chair′, *Eng. Furniture.* a chair of c1700, derived from Dutch models, having curved uprights, a wide splat joined to the seat rail, and cabriole legs. [1690–1700]

Dutch′ cheese′. *Inland North.* cottage cheese. [1690–1700]

Dutch′ clo′ver. See **white clover.** [1790–1800]

Dutch′ Colo′nial, **1.** of or pertaining to the domestic architecture of Dutch settlers in New York and New Jersey, often characterized by gambrel roofs having curved eaves over porches on the long sides. **2.** a house built in such a style. [1920–25]

Dutch′ cour′age, *Sometimes Offensive.* courage inspired by drunkenness or drinking liquor. [1805–15]

Dutch′ cup′board, a buffet with open upper shelves.

Dutch′ cut′. See **Dutch bob.** [1920–25]

Dutch′ door′, a door consisting of two units horizontally divided so that each half can be opened or closed separately. [1640–50]

Dutch door

CONCISE ETYMOLOGY KEY: <, descended or borrowed from; >, whence; b., blend of, blended; c., cognate with; cf., compare; deriv., derivative; equiv., equivalent; imit., imitative; obl., oblique; r., replacing; s., stem; sp., spelling, spelled; resp., respelling, respelled; trans., translation; ?, origin unknown; *, unattested; ‡, probably earlier than. See the full key inside the front cover.

Dutch′ East′ In′dies, a former name of the Republic of Indonesia.

Dutch′ elm′ disease′, a disease of elms characterized by wilting, yellowing, and falling of the leaves and caused by a fungus, *Ceratostomella ulmi,* transmitted by bark beetles. [1920–25]

Dutch′ gold′, an alloy of copper and zinc in the form of thin sheets, used as an imitation of gold leaf. Also called **Dutch′ foil′, Dutch′ leaf′.**

Dutch′ Guian′a, former name of **Suriname.**

Dutch′ Har′bor, a U.S. naval base on Unalaska Island, in the Aleutian Islands.

Dutch′ lap′, a method of laying shingles, slates, or the like, in which each shingle or slate overlaps those below and to one side and is itself overlapped by those above and to the other side.

Dutch′ lunch′, an individual portion or serving of cold cuts. Also, **dutch′ lunch′.** [1900–05, *Amer.*]

Dutch•man (duch′mən), *n., pl.* **-men. 1.** a native or inhabitant of the Netherlands. **2.** (*l.c.*) *Building Trades.* a piece or wedge inserted to hide the fault in a badly made joint, to stop an opening, etc. **3.** *Theat.* a narrow strip of canvas to conceal the join between two flats. **4.** *Slang (sometimes offensive).* a German. [1350–1400; ME; see DUTCH, MAN[1]]

Dutch•man's-breech•es (duch′mənz brich′iz), *n., pl.* **-breech•es.** a plant, *Dicentra cucullaria,* of the fumitory family, having long clusters of pale-yellow, two-spurred flowers. Also called **white eardrop.** [1830–40; so called from the shape of the flowers]

Dutch′man's log′, *Naut.* a method of gauging a ship's speed, in which the distance between two shipboard observation stations is divided by the time elapsing between the throwing overboard of an object by the first station and the sighting of it by the second.

Dutch•man's-pipe (duch′mənz pīp′), *n.* a climbing vine, *Aristolochia durior,* of the birthwort family, having large, heart-shaped leaves and brownish-purple flowers of a curved form suggesting a tobacco pipe. [1835–45, *Amer.*]

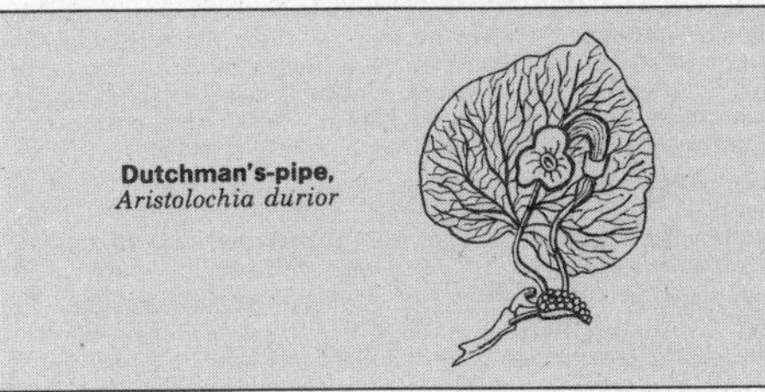
Dutchman's-pipe, *Aristolochia durior*

Dutch′ New′ Guin′ea, a former name of **Irian Jaya.**

Dutch′ ov′en, 1. a heavily constructed kettle with a close-fitting lid, used for pot roasts, stews, etc. **2.** a metal utensil, open in front, for roasting before an open fire. **3.** a brick oven in which the walls are preheated for cooking. [1760–70]

Dutch′ Reformed′, of or pertaining to a Protestant denomination **(Dutch′ Reformed′ Church′),** founded by Dutch settlers in New York in 1628 and renamed the Reformed Church in America in 1867. [1815–25, *Amer.*]

Dutch′ rush′. See **scouring rush.** [1820–30]

Dutch′ set′tle, a settle having a back so hinged that it can be lowered onto the arms to form a table.

Dutch′ straight′, *Poker.* See **skip straight.**

Dutch′ treat′, a meal or entertainment for which each person pays his or her own expenses. [1870–75]

Dutch′ un′cle, a person who criticizes or reproves with unsparing severity and frankness. [1820–30]

Dutch′ West′ In′dia Com′pany, a Dutch merchant company chartered in 1621 to carry on trade with Africa, the West Indies, North and South America, and Australia.

Dutch′ West′ In′dies, a former name of **Netherlands Antilles.**

Dutch′ wife′, (in tropical countries) an open framework used in bed as a rest for the limbs. [1875–80]

du•te•ous (do͞o′tē əs, dyo͞o′-), *adj.* dutiful; obedient. [1585–95; DUTY + -OUS] **—du′te•ous•ly,** *adv.* **—du′te•ous•ness,** *n.*

du•ti•a•ble (do͞o′tē ə bəl, dyo͞o′-), *adj.* subject to customs duty, as imported goods. [1765–75; DUTY + -ABLE] **—du′ti•a•bil′i•ty,** *n.*

du•ti•ful (do͞o′tə fəl, dyo͞o′-), *adj.* **1.** performing the duties expected or required of one; characterized by doing one's duty: *a dutiful child.* **2.** required by duty; proceeding from or expressive of a sense of duty. [1545–55; DUTY + -FUL] **—du′ti•ful•ly,** *adv.*
—Syn. 1. respectful, docile, submissive, duteous.

du•ty (do͞o′tē, dyo͞o′-), *n., pl.* **-ties. 1.** something that one is expected or required to do by moral or legal obligation. **2.** the binding or obligatory force of something that is morally or legally right; moral or legal obligation. **3.** an action or task required by a person's position or occupation; function: *the duties of a clergyman.* **4.** the respectful and obedient conduct due a parent, superior, elder, etc. **5.** an act or expression of respect. **6.** a task or chore that a person is expected to perform: *It's your duty to do the dishes.* **7.** *Mil.* **a.** an assigned task, occupation, or place of service: *He was on radar duty for two years.* **b.** the military service required of a citizen by a country: *After graduation, he began his duty.* **8.** *Com.* a specific or ad valorem tax imposed by law on the import or export of goods. **9.** a payment, service, etc., imposed and enforceable by law or custom. **10.** *Chiefly Brit.* tax: *income duty.* **11.** *Mach.* **a.** the amount of work done by an engine per unit amount of fuel consumed. **b.** the measure of effectiveness of any machine. **12.** *Agric.* the amount of water necessary to provide for the crop in a given area. **13.** *Baby Talk.* bowel movement. **14. do duty,** to serve the same function; substitute for: *bookcases that do duty as room dividers.* **15. off duty,** not at one's post or work; at liberty. **16. on duty,** at one's post or work; occupied; engaged. [1250–1300; ME *du(e)te* < AF *duete.* See DUE, -TY[2]]
—Syn. 1. DUTY, OBLIGATION refer to what one feels bound to do. DUTY is what one performs, or avoids doing, in fulfillment of the permanent dictates of conscience, piety, right, or law: *duty to one's country; one's duty to tell the truth.* An OBLIGATION is what one is bound to do to fulfill the dictates of usage, custom, or propriety, and to carry out a particular, and often personal agreement: *financial obligations.* **3.** responsibility. **4.** deference.

du•ty-free (do͞o′tē frē′, dyo͞o′-), *adj., adv.* **1.** free of customs duty: *duty-free cargo; merchandise shipped duty-free.* **2.** pertaining to or selling goods for import or export free of the usual customs duty: *a duty-free shop at the airport.* [1680–90]

du•um•vir (do͞o um′vər, dyo͞o-), *n., pl.* **-virs, -vi•ri** (-və rī′). *Rom. Hist.* one of two officers or magistrates jointly exercising the same public function. [1590–1600; < L, back formation from *duumvirōrum,* gen. pl. of *duovirī* two men, equiv. to *duo-* DUO- + *virī,* pl. of *vir* man, c. OE *wer* (see WEREWOLF)]

du•um•vi•rate (do͞o um′vər it, dyo͞o-), *n.* **1.** a coalition of two persons holding the same office, as in ancient Rome. **2.** the office or government of two such persons. [1650–60; < L *duumvirātus.* See DUUMVIR, -ATE[3]]

Du•va•lier (do͞o′väl yā′; *Fr.* dy va lyā′), *n.* **1. François** (fräN swa′), ("*Papa Doc*"), 1907–71, Haitian physician and dictator: president 1957–71. **2.** his son **Jean-Claude** (zhäN klōd′), ("*Baby Doc*"), born 1951, Haitian political leader: president 1971–86.

Du•ve (dy′və), *n.* **Chris•tian Re•né de** (krēs tyäN′ Rə nā′ də), born 1917, Belgian biologist, born in England: Nobel prize for medicine 1974.

Du•ve•neck (do͞o′və nek′), *n.* **Frank** (*Frank Decker*), 1848–1919, U.S. painter and teacher.

du•vet (do͞o vā′, dyo͞o-), *n.* a usually down-filled quilt, often with a removable cover; comforter. [1750–60; < F: down (plumage), MF, alter. of *dumet,* deriv. of OF *dum* << ON *dūnn* DOWN[2]]

du•ve•tyn (do͞o′vi tēn′, dyo͞o′-), *n.* a napped fabric, in a twilled or plain weave, of cotton, wool, silk, or rayon. Also, **du′ve•tine′, du′ve•tyne′.** [1910–15; < F *duvetine,* equiv. to *duvet* down (see DUVET) + *-ine* -INE[2]]

Du•vi•da (*Port.* do͞o′vē də), *n.* **Ri•o da** (*Port.* rē′o͝o də). former name of **Rio Roosevelt.**

du Vi•gneaud (do͞o vēn′yō, dyo͞o), **Vincent,** 1901–78, U.S. biochemist: Nobel prize for chemistry 1955.

dux (duks, do͝oks), *n., pl.* **du•ces** (do͞o′sēz, dyo͞o′-, do͞o′kās), **dux•es** (duk′siz, do͝ok′-). **1.** *Brit.* the pupil who is academically first in a class or school. **2.** (in the later Roman Empire) a military chief commanding the troops in a frontier province. [1800–10; < L: lit., leader, n. deriv. from base of *dūcere* to lead]

Dux•bur•y (duks′ber′ē, -bə rē), *n.* a city in SE Massachusetts. 11,807.

D.V., 1. Deo volente. **2.** Douay Version (of the Bible).

dvai•ta (dvī′tə), *n. Hinduism.* **1.** any of the pluralistic schools of philosophy. **2.** (*cap.*) (in Vedantic philosophy) one of the two principal schools, asserting that entities have a real existence apart from Brahman. Cf. **Advaita.** [< Skt; akin to TWO]

dvan•dva (dvän′dvä, dvun′dvə), *n. Gram.* a compound word neither element of which is subordinate to the other, as *bittersweet, Anglo-Saxon.* [1840–50; < Skt, nasalized redupl. of *dva* TWO]

Dva•pa•ra Yu•ga (dvä′pər ə yo͝og′ə), *Hinduism.* the third of the Yugas, not as good as the Treta Yuga but better than the Kali Yuga. [< Skt, equiv. to *dvāpara* third best (*dvā* TWO + *para* ahead) + *yuga* era (lit., YOKE)]

dvi•ja (dvē′jä), *n. Hinduism.* a person who is twice-born: a distinction made between the first three classes of society and the lowest class, the Shudra. Only the dvijas may study the Vedas. [< Skt]

Dvi•na (dvē′nə; *Russ.* dvyi nä′), *n.* **1.** Also called **Western Dvina.** Latvian, **Daugava.** a river rising in the Valdai Hills in the W Russian Federation, flowing W through Byelorussia (Belarus) and Latvia to the Baltic Sea at Riga. ab. 640 mi. (1030 km) long. **2.** Also called **Northern Dvina.** a river in the N Russian Federation in Europe, flowing NW into the White Sea. ab. 470 mi. (750 km) long.

Dvi′na Bay′, an arm of the White Sea, in the NW Russian Federation in Europe. Formerly, **Gulf of Archangel.**

Dvinsk (dvyēnsk), *n.* Russian name of **Daugavpils.**

D.V.M., Doctor of Veterinary Medicine. Also, **DVM**

D.V.M.S., Doctor of Veterinary Medicine and Surgery.

Dvo•řák (dvôr′zhäk, -zhak; *Czech* dvô′rzhäk), *n.* **Antonín** (än′tô nyēn), 1841–1904, Czech composer.

Dvo′rak Key′board (dvôr′ak), *Trademark.* a typewriter or computer keyboard designed to facilitate speed by having the most frequently used characters on the home row, with all the vowels on the left side. Cf. **QWERTY.** See illus. under **keyboard.**

D.V.S., Doctor of Veterinary Surgery.

DW, *Real Estate.* dishwasher (def. 2).

D/W, dock warrant.

dwarf (dwôrf), *n., pl.* **dwarfs, dwarves,** *adj., v.* **—n. 1.** a person of abnormally small stature owing to a pathological condition, esp. one suffering from cretinism or some other disease that produces disproportion or deformation of features and limbs. **2.** an animal or plant much smaller than the average of its kind or species. **3.** (in folklore) a being in the form of a small, often misshapen and ugly, man, usually having magic powers. **4.** *Astron.* See **dwarf star.** **—adj. 5.** of unusually small stature or size; diminutive. **—v.t. 6.** to cause to appear or seem small in size, extent, character, etc., as by being much larger or better: *He dwarfed all his rivals in athletic ability.* **7.** to make dwarf or dwarfish; prevent the due development of. **—v.i. 8.** to become stunted or smaller. [bef. 900; ME *dwerf,* OE *dweorh;* r. ME *dwerg,* OE *dweorg;* c. OHG *twerg,* ON *dvergr*] **—dwarf′like′,** *adj.* **—dwarf′ness,** *n.*
—Syn. 1. DWARF, MIDGET, PYGMY are terms for a very small person. A DWARF is someone checked in growth or stunted, or in some way not normally formed. A MIDGET (not in technical use) is someone perfect in form and normal in function, but diminutive. A PYGMY is properly a member of one of certain small-sized peoples of Africa and Asia, but the word is often used imprecisely to mean dwarf or midget. DWARF is a term often used to describe very small plants. PYGMY is used to describe very small animals. **2.** runt, miniature. **—Ant. 1, 5.** giant.

dwarf′ banan′a, a large southern Chinese plant, *Musa acuminata,* of the banana family, having blue-green leaves, yellowish-white flowers with reddish-brown bracts, and fragrant, edible, curved fruit from 4 to 5 in. (10 to 13 cm) long, often borne in clusters of 200. Also called **Chinese banana.**

dwarf′ buf′falo, anoa.

dwarf′ cher′ry. See **sand cherry.**

dwarf′ cor′nel, the bunchberry.

dwarf′ crest′ed i′ris, a low iris, *Iris cristata,* of the eastern and central U.S., having faintly fragrant, yellow-crested, lilac-dotted flowers. Also called **crested iris.**

dwarf′ door′, a door of approximately half normal height, as the lower half of a Dutch door.

dwarf′ fan′ palm′. See **parlor palm.**

dwarf′ gin′seng, a plant, *Panax trifolius,* of eastern North America, having globe-shaped clusters of small, white flowers and yellow fruit.

dwarf•ish (dwôr′fish), *adj.* like a dwarf, esp. in being abnormally small; diminutive. [1555–65; DWARF + -ISH[1]] **—dwarf′ish•ly,** *adv.* **—dwarf′ish•ness,** *n.*
—Syn. pygmy, tiny, stunted, runty.

dwarf•ism (dwôr′fiz əm), *n. Med.* the condition of being a dwarf or dwarfed. [1860–65; DWARF + -ISM]

dwarf′ Jap′anese quince′, a low, shrubby, Japanese flowering quince, *Chaenomeles japonica,* of the rose family, having salmon-to-orange flowers and yellow fruit.

dwarf′ lau′rel. See **sheep laurel.**

dwarf′ mal′low, cheese (def. 5).

dwarf′ palmet′to, an apparently stemless palm, *Sabal minor,* of the southeastern U.S., having stiff, bluish-green leaves, the leafstalks arising from the ground. Also called **bluestem.**

dwarf′ poincia′na. See **Barbados pride** (def. 2).

dwarf′ star′, *Astron.* any of the ordinary main sequence stars, as those of spectral types O, B, A, F, G, K, and M. Also called **dwarf.** Cf. **white dwarf.** [1910–15]

dwarf′ su′mac, a shrub or small tree, *Rhus copallina,* of the cashew family, native to the eastern U.S., having shiny, pinnate leaves, greenish flowers, and clusters of red, berrylike fruit.

dwarves (dwôrvz), *n.* a pl. of **dwarf.**

Dwayne (dwān), *n.* a male given name.

dweeb (dwēb), *n. Slang.* nerd; wimp. [1980–85] **—dweeb′ish,** *adj.*

dwell (dwel), *v.,* **dwelt** or **dwelled, dwell•ing,** *n.* **—v.i. 1.** to live or stay as a permanent resident; reside. **2.** to live or continue in a given condition or state: *to dwell in happiness.* **3.** to linger over, emphasize, or ponder in thought, speech, or writing (often fol. by *on* or *upon*): *to dwell on a particular point in an argument.* **4.** (of a moving tool or machine part) to be motionless for a certain interval during operation. **—n. 5.** *Mach.* **a.** a flat or cylindrical area on a cam for maintaining a follower in a certain position during part of a cycle. **b.** a period in a cycle in the operation of a machine or engine during which a given part remains motionless. [bef. 900; ME *dwellen* to lead astray, stun, abide, OE *dwellan* to lead or go astray, hinder; c. ON *dvelja*] **—dwell′er,** *n.*

dwell•ing (dwel′ing), *n.* a building or place of shelter to live in; place of residence; abode; home. [1250–1300; ME; see DWELL, -ING[1]]
—Syn. See **house.**

dwell′ing house′, a house occupied, or intended to be occupied, as a residence. [1400–50; late ME]

dwell′ing place′, a dwelling. [1350–1400; ME]

dwelt (dwelt), *v.* a pt. and pp. of **dwell.**

DWEM, *Slang.* dead white European male.

DWI, driving while intoxicated: often used as an official police abbreviation. [1965–70]

Dwight (dwīt), *n.* **1. Timothy,** 1826–1916, U.S. ecclesiastic: president of Yale University 1886–98. **2.** a male given name: from an Anglo-French surname meaning "of the Isle of Wight."

dwin•dle (dwin′dl), *v.,* **-dled, -dling.** **—v.i. 1.** to become smaller and smaller; shrink; waste away: *His vast fortune has dwindled away.* **2.** to fall away, as in quality; degenerate. **—v.t. 3.** to make smaller and smaller; cause to shrink. [1590–1600; *dwine* (now dial.) to waste away (ME; OE *dwīnan;* c. MD *dwīnen* to languish, ON *dvīna* to pine away) + -LE]

CONCISE PRONUNCIATION KEY: *act, cāpe, dâre, pärt; set, ēqual; if, īce; ox, ōver, ôrder, oil, bo͝ok, bo͞ot, out; up, ûrge; child; sing; shoe; thin, that;* zh as in *treasure.* ə = *a* as in *alone, e* as in *system, i* as in *easily, o* as in *gallop, u* as in *circus;* ° as in *fire* (fī°r), *hour* (ou°r). l and n can serve as syllabic consonants, as in *cradle* (krād′l), and *button* (but′n). See the full key inside the front cover.

—**Syn.** 1. diminish, decline, lessen, wane. See **decrease.** 3. lessen. —**Ant.** 1. increase. 3. magnify.

DWM, *Slang.* dead white male.

DWT, deadweight tons; deadweight tonnage.

dwt, 1. deadweight tons; deadweight tonnage. 2. pennyweight; pennyweights.

d.w.t., deadweight tons; deadweight tonnage.

dwy (dwī), *n. Newfoundland.* a gust or flurry of rain or snow. [cf. dial. (Isle of Wight) *dwyes* eddies, (Wiltshire, Hampshire) *twy* coastal squall; further relations unclear]

DX, *Radio.* distance (used esp. to designate difficult shortwave reception). Also, **D.X.**

Dx, diagnosis.

Dy, *Symbol, Chem.* dysprosium.

dy·ad (dī′ad), *n.* 1. a group of two; couple; pair. 2. *Biol.* **a.** a secondary morphological unit, consisting of two monads: *a chromosome dyad.* **b.** the double chromosomes resulting from the separation of the four chromatids of a tetrad. 3. *Chem.* an element, atom, or group having a valence of two. Cf. **monad, triad** (def. 2a). 4. *Math.* two vectors with no symbol connecting them, usually considered as an operator. 5. *Sociol.* **a.** two persons involved in an ongoing relationship or interaction. **b.** the relationship or interaction itself. —*adj.* 6. of two parts; dyadic. [1665–75; < Gk *dyad-* (s. of *dyás*) pair, equiv. to *dý(o)* two + *-ad-* -AD[1]]

dy·ad·ic (dī ad′ik), *adj.* 1. of or consisting of a dyad; being a group of two. 2. pertaining to the number 2. —*n.* 3. *Math.* two or more dyads added together. [1720–30; < Gk *dyadikós.* See DYAD, -IC]

dyad′ic sys′tem. See **binary system.**

Dy·ak (dī′ak), *n.* Dayak.

dy·ar·chy (dī′är kē), *n., pl.* **-chies.** diarchy. —**dy·ar′chic, dy·ar′chi·cal,** *adj.*

Dyaus (dyous), *n.* the Vedic god of the sky. Also called **Dyaus-pit·ar** (dyous′pit′ər).

Dy·a·zide (dī′ə zīd′), *Pharm., Trademark.* a brand name for a diuretic preparation used in the treatment of edema and hypertension.

dyb·buk (*Seph. Heb.* dē bo͝ok′; *Ashk. Heb., Eng.* dib′-ək), *n., pl.* **dyb·buks, dyb·bu·kim** (*Seph. Heb.* dē′bo͞o-kēm′; *Ashk. Heb.* di bo͝ok′im). *Jewish Folklore.* a demon, or the soul of a dead person, that enters the body of a living person and directs the person's conduct, exorcism being possible only by a religious ceremony. Also, **dibbuk.** [1900–05; < Yiddish *dibek* < Heb *dibbūq,* deriv. of *dābhaq* cleave (to); sp. *dybbuk* is a Pol transliteration of the Heb word]

Dyce (dīs), *n.* **Alexander,** 1798–1869, Scottish editor.

dye (dī), *n., v.,* **dyed, dye·ing.** —*n.* 1. a coloring material or matter. 2. a liquid containing coloring matter, for imparting a particular hue to cloth, paper, etc. 3. color or hue, esp. as produced by dyeing. 4. **of the deepest** or **blackest dye,** of the most extreme or the worst sort: *a prevaricator of the blackest dye.* —*v.t.* 5. to color or stain; treat with a dye; color (cloth, hair, etc.) with a substance containing coloring matter: *to dye a dress green.* 6. to impart (color) by means of a dye: *The coloring matter dyed green.* —*v.i.* 7. to impart color, as a dye: *This brand dyes well.* 8. to become colored or absorb color when treated with a dye: *This cloth dyes easily.* [bef. 1000; ME *dien,* OE *dēagian,* deriv. of *dēag* a dye] —**dy′a·ble, dye′a·ble,** *adj.* —**dy′er,** *n.*

dyed-in-the-wool (dīd′n *th*ə wo͝ol′), *adj.* 1. through and through; complete: *a dyed-in-the-wool reformer.* 2. dyed before weaving. [1570–80]

dye·ing (dī′ing), *n.* process of coloring fibers, yarns, or fabrics. [bef. 1000; ME; OE *dēagunge.* See DYE, -ING[1]]

dye·line (dī′līn′), *n. Photog.* a contact print of a line drawing, giving brown lines on an off-white background. [1950–55; DYE + LINE[1]]

Dy·er (dī′ər), *n.* 1. **John,** 1700–58, British poet. 2. **Mary,** died 1660, American Quaker religious martyr, born in England.

Dyer·ma (jûr′mə, jâr′-, dyâr′-), *n., pl.* **-mas,** (*esp. collectively*) **-ma.** Djerma.

dy·er's-broom (dī′ərz bro͞om′, -bro͝om′), *n.* woadwaxen. [1810–20]

Dy·ers·burg (dī′ərz bûrg′), *n.* a city in W Tennessee. 15,856.

dy′er's green′weed (grēn′wēd′), woadwaxen. [1590–1600]

dy′er's moss′, a lichen, *Roccella tinctoria,* from which the purple dye orchil can be prepared.

dy′er's rock′et, weld[2]. [1860–65; cultivated for a yellow dye]

dy·er's-weed (dī′ərz wēd′), *n.* any plant yielding a dye, as the weld, *Reseda luteola,* the dyeweed, *Genista tinctoria,* or the woad, *Isatis tinctoria.* [1570–80]

dy′er's wood′ruff, a European plant, *Asperula tinctoria,* of the madder family, having red or pinkish-white flowers and red roots.

dye′ sen′sitizing, *Photog.* the producing of panchromatic or orthochromatic film by treating it with an emulsion containing dyes that absorb light of all or certain colors.

dye·stuff (dī′stuf′), *n.* a material yielding or used as a dye. [1830–40; prob. trans. of G *Farbstoff*]

dye′ trans′fer, *Photog.* 1. a photographic printing method by which a full-color image is produced by the printing of separate cyan, magenta, and yellow images from individual gelatin relief matrices. 2. a print made by this process.

dye·wood (dī′wo͝od′), *n.* any wood yielding a coloring matter used for dyeing. [1690–1700; DYE + WOOD[1]]

Dy·fed (duv′id), *n.* a county in Wales. 321,700; 2227 sq. mi. (5767 sq. km).

dy·ing (dī′ing), *adj.* 1. ceasing to live; approaching death; expiring: *a dying man.* 2. of, pertaining to, or associated with death: *his dying hour.* 3. given, uttered, or manifested just before death: *her dying words.* 4. drawing to a close; ending: *the dying year.* —*n.* 5. the act or process of ceasing to live, ending, or drawing to a close. [1250–1300; ME. See DIE[1], -ING[2], -ING[1]]

dyke[1] (dīk), *n., v.,* **dyked, dyk·ing.** dike[1].

dyke[2] (dīk), *n. Slang (disparaging and offensive).* a female homosexual; lesbian. Also, **dike.** [1940–45; earlier in form *bulldike* (with a var. *bulldagger*); of obscure orig.; claimed to be a shortening of *morphodyke* (var. of *morphodite,* a reshaping of HERMAPHRODITE), though *morphodyke* is more likely a b. *morphodite* and a preexisting *dyke;* other hypothesized connections, such as with *diked out* or *dike* "ditch," are dubious on semantic grounds] —**dyke′y,** *adj.*

Dyl·an (dil′ən), *n.* 1. **Bob** (*Robert Zimmerman*), born 1941, U.S. folk-rock singer, guitarist, and composer. 2. a male given name.

dy·max·i·on (dī mak′sē ən), *adj.* noting or pertaining to R. Buckminster Fuller's concept of the use of technology and resources to maximum advantage, with minimal expenditure of energy and material. [1925–30]

dyn, *Physics.* dyne; dynes.

dyn., dynamics. Also, **dynam.**

dyna-, a combining form meaning "power," used in the formation of compound words: *dynamotor.* Also, **dynam-, dynamo-.** [comb. form of Gk *dýnamis* power, *dýnasthai* to be able]

dy·nam·e·ter (dī nam′i tər), *n. Optics.* an instrument for determining the magnifying power of telescopes. [1820–30; DYNA- + METER]

dy·nam·ic (dī nam′ik), *adj.* Also, **dy·nam′i·cal.** 1. pertaining to or characterized by energy or effective action; vigorously active or forceful; energetic: *the dynamic president of the firm..* 2. *Physics.* **a.** of or pertaining to force or power. **b.** of or pertaining to force related to motion. 3. pertaining to the science of dynamics. 4. of or pertaining to the range of volume of musical sound. 5. *Computers.* (of data storage, processing, or programming) affected by the passage of time or the presence or absence of power: *Dynamic memory must be constantly refreshed to avoid losing data.* 6. *Gram.* nonstative. —*n.* 7. a basic or dynamic force, esp. one that motivates, affects development or stability, etc. [1810–20; < F *dynamique* < Gk *dynamikós,* equiv. to *dýnam(is)* force, power + *-ikos* -IC] —**dy·nam′i·cal·ly,** *adv.*

dynam′ic brak′ing, *Railroads.* a braking system used on electric and diesel-electric locomotives in which the leads of the electric motors can be reversed so that the motors act as generators, offering resistance to the rotating wheel axles and dissipating kinetic energy, thereby retarding the locomotive. [1925–30]

dynam′ic head′room, *Audio.* the additional power output capability of an amplifier when producing short-term peak signals, compared with its continuous-signal power rating. Also called **headroom.**

dynam′ic meteorol′ogy, the branch of meteorology dealing with the study of atmospheric motion and its causal relation to other forces. Cf. **physical meteorology.**

dynam′ic psychi′atry, an approach to psychiatry that emphasizes emotional processes and their origins and mental mechanisms.

dynam′ic psychol′ogy, any approach to psychology that emphasizes drives and motives as determinants of behavior.

dynam′ic range′, *Audio.* the ratio of the loudest to faintest sounds reproduced without significant distortion, usually expressed in decibels. [1930–35]

dy·nam·ics (dī nam′iks), *n.* 1. (*used with a singular v.*) *Physics.* the branch of mechanics that deals with the motion and equilibrium of systems under the action of forces, usually from outside the system. 2. (*used with a plural v.*) the motivating or driving forces, physical or moral, in any field. 3. (*used with a plural v.*) the pattern or history of growth, change, and development in any field. 4. (*used with a plural v.*) variation and gradation in the volume of musical sound. 5. (*used with a singular v.*) psychodynamics. [1780–90; see DYNAMIC, -ICS]

dynam′ic similar′ity, a principle whereby model airplanes, ships, and hydraulic structures are operated for test purposes under conditions exactly simulating full-scale performance.

dynam′ic spa′tial reconstruc′tor, an x-ray machine that displays bodily organs in three-dimensional moving images. *Abbr.:* DSR

dynam′ic strength′, resistance of a structure to loads applied suddenly, as during an earthquake.

dynam′ic viscos′ity, *Physics.* See **coefficient of viscosity.**

dy·na·mism (dī′nə miz′əm), *n.* 1. any of various theories or philosophical systems that seek to explain phenomena of nature by the action of force. Cf. **mechanism** (def. 8), **vitalism** (def. 1). 2. great energy, force, or power; vigor: *the dynamism of the new governor.* 3. *Psychol.* a habitual mode of reducing or eliminating tension. [1825–35; DYNAM- + -ISM] —**dy′na·mist,** *n.* —**dy′na·mis′tic,** *adj.*

dy·na·mite (dī′nə mīt′), *n., v.,* **-mit·ed, -mit·ing,** *adj.* —*n.* 1. a high explosive, originally consisting of nitroglycerin mixed with an absorbent substance, now with ammonium nitrate usually replacing the nitroglycerin. 2. any person or thing having a spectacular effect. —*v.t.* 3. to blow up, shatter, or destroy with dynamite: *Saboteurs dynamited the dam.* 4. to mine or charge with dynamite. —*adj.* 5. *Informal.* creating a spectacular or optimum effect; great; topnotch: *a dynamite idea; a dynamite crew.* [1867; < Sw *dynamit,* introduced by A. B. Nobel, its inventor; see DYNAM-, -ITE[1]] —**dy′na·mit′er,** *n.* —**dy·na·mit·ic** (dī′nə mit′ik), *adj.* —**dy′na·mit′i·cal·ly,** *adv.*

dy·na·mize (dī′nə mīz′), *v.t.,* **-mized, -miz·ing.** to make more active, productive, or the like; energize: *an attempt to dynamize the local economy.* Also, *esp. Brit.,* **dy′na·mise′.** [1880–85; DYNAM(IC) + -IZE] —**dy′na·mi·za′tion,** *n.*

dy·na·mo (dī′nə mō′), *n., pl.* **-mos.** 1. an electric generator, esp. for direct current. 2. an energetic, hard-working, forceful person. [1882; short for DYNAMOELECTRIC]

dynamo-, var. of **dyna-:** *dynamometer.* Also, **dynam-.**

dy·na·mo·e·lec·tric (dī′nə mō i lek′trik), *adj.* pertaining to the conversion of mechanical energy into electric energy, or vice versa: *a dynamoelectric machine.* Also, **dy′na·mo·e·lec′tri·cal.** [1880–85; DYNAMO- + ELECTRIC]

dy·na·mo·gen·e·sis (dī′nə mō jen′ə sis), *n., pl.* **-ses** (-sēz′). *Psychol.* the correlation of changes in response with changes in sensory activity. [DYNAMO- + -GENESIS] —**dy′na·mo·gen′ic, dy·na·mog·e·nous** (dī′nə moj′ə-nəs), *adj.* —**dy′na·mog′e·nous·ly,** *adv.*

dy·na·mom·e·ter (dī′nə mom′i tər), *n.* 1. a device for measuring mechanical force, as a balance. 2. a device for measuring mechanical power, esp. one that measures the output or driving torque of a rotating machine. [1800–10; DYNAMO- + -METER]

dynamom′eter car′, *Railroads.* a car equipped with special instruments and coupled to a locomotive to record its energy output, fuel consumption, and other data continuously during a regularly scheduled run. [1875–80]

dy·na·mom·e·try (dī′nə mom′i trē), *n.* the act, method, or process of using a dynamometer. [1890–95; DYNAMO- + -METRY] —**dy·na·mo·met·ric** (dī′nə mō-me′trik), **dy′na·mo·met′ri·cal,** *adj.*

dy·na·mo·tor (dī′nə mō′tər), *n.* an electric machine for transforming direct current into alternating current or for altering the voltage of direct current, having two armature windings on the same core and a common magnetic field. [1905–10; DYNA- + MOTOR]

dy·nast (dī′nast, -nəst; *Brit. also* din′ast), *n.* a ruler or potentate, esp. a hereditary ruler. [1625–35; < L *dynastēs* < Gk *dynástēs,* equiv. to *dýnas(thai)* to rule + *-tēs* agent suffix]

dy·nas·tid (dī nas′tid), *n.* See **rhinoceros beetle.** [< NL *Dynastidae* the family which includes such beetles, equiv. to *Dynast(es)* a genus (see DYNAST) + *-idae* -ID[2]]

dy·nas·ty (dī′nə stē; *Brit. also* din′ə stē), *n., pl.* **-ties.** 1. a sequence of rulers from the same family, stock, or group: *the Ming dynasty.* 2. the rule of such a sequence. 3. a series of members of a family who are distinguished for their success, wealth, etc. [1425–75; late ME < LL *dynastia* < Gk *dynasteía.* See DYNAST, -Y[3]] —**dy·nas·tic** (dī nas′tik; *Brit. also* di nas′tik), **dy·nas′ti·cal,** *adj.* —**dy·nas′ti·cal·ly,** *adv.*

dy·na·tron (dī′nə tron′), *n. Electronics.* a tetrode, once frequently used as an oscillator in radio, in which an increase in the plate voltage results in a decrease in the plate current because of emission of electrons from the plate. [1915–20; DYNA- + -TRON]

dyne (dīn), *n. Physics.* the standard centimeter-gram-second unit of force, equal to the force that produces an acceleration of one centimeter per second per second on a mass of one gram. *Abbr.:* dyn [1835–45; < F < Gk *dýnamis* force, power]

Dy·nel (dī nel′), *Trademark.* 1. a brand of modacrylic fiber used in textiles, characterized chiefly by its strength, rapid drying rate, and noncombustibility. 2. yarn or fabric made of this fiber.

dy·no (dī′nō), *n., pl.* **-nos.** *Informal.* dynamometer (def. 2). [by shortening; see -O]

dy·node (dī′nōd), *n. Electronics.* an electrode for the emission of secondary electrons in a vacuum tube. [1935–40; DYN(A)- + -ODE[2]]

Dy·oph·y·site (dī of′ə sīt′), *n. Theol.* a person who maintains that Christ has two natures, one divine and the other human. Cf. **Monophysite.** [1855–60; < LGk *dyophysîtes,* equiv. to *dýo* two + *phýs(is)* nature + *-ītes* -ITE[1]] —**Dy·oph·y·sit·ic** (dī of′ə sit′ik), **Dy·oph′y·sit′i·cal,** *adj.*

dy·o·style (dī′ə stīl′), *adj.* distyle.

Dy·oth·e·lite (dī oth′ə līt′), *n. Theol.* a person who maintains that Christ has two wills, one divine and the other human. Cf. **Monothelite.** [1840–50; < Gk *dýo* two + *-thelite* as in *monothelite*] —**Dy·oth′e·lit·ism,** *n.*

dys-, a combining form meaning "ill," "bad," used in the formation of compound words: *dysfunction.* [< Gk; c. ON *tor-,* G *zer-,* Skt *dus-*]

dys·a·cou·sia (dis′ə ko͞o′zhə, -zhē ə, -zē ə), *n. Pathol.* a condition in which noise produces pain in the ear. Also, **dys·a·cous·ma** (dis′ə ko͞oz′mə), **dys·a·cu·sia** (dis′ə-kyo͞o′zhə, -zhē ə, -zē ə). [< NL, equiv. to *dys-* DYS- + *-acousia* < Gk *ákous(is)* ability to hear (*akoú(ein)* to hear + *-sis* -SIS) + *-ia* -IA]

dys·ad·ap·ta·tion (dis ad′əp tā′shən), *n. Ophthalm.* faulty adaptation of the iris and retina to light. Also, **dys·ap·ta·tion** (dis′ap tā′shən). [DYS- + ADAPTATION]

dys·an·ag·no·sia (dis an′əg nō′zhə, -zhē ə, -zē ə), *n. Pathol.* an inability to comprehend certain words. [DYS- + Gk *anagnōsía* ability to read (*ana-* ANA- + *gnōsía* knowledge; see GNOSIS)]

dys·a·phi·a (dis ā′fē ə, -af′ē ə), *n. Pathol.* a disorder of the sense of touch. Also, **dys·a′phe·a.** [DYS- + Gk *haph(ḗ)* touch + -IA]

dys·ar·thri·a (dis är′thrē ə), *n. Pathol.* any of certain disorders of articulation, as stammering or stuttering, caused by a nerve defect. [1875–80; < NL, equiv. to *dys-* DYS- + Gk *árthr(on)* joint + *-ia* -IA] **—dys·ar′thric,** *adj.*

dys·au·to·no·mi·a (dis ô′tə nō′mē ə), *n. Pathol.* a rare inherited disorder of the autonomic nervous system, occurring mostly in Ashkenazic Jews, characterized by lack of reflexes, abnormal sweating, defective lacrimation and sense perceptions, emotional instability, and motor incoordination. [1970–75; DYS- + Gk *autonomía* AUTONOMY]

dys·bar·ism (dis′bä riz′əm), *n. Med.* the condition resulting from a difference between the atmospheric pressure and the pressure of gases within the body. [DYS- + BAR(O)- + -ISM]

dys·cal·cu·li·a (dis′kal kyo͞o′lē ə), *n.* acalculia. [1950–55; DYS- + CALCUL(ATE) + -IA]

dys·chron·o·gen·ic (dis kron′ə jen′ik), *adj.* of or pertaining to an action causing the disruption of biorhythms. [DYS- + CHRONO- + -GENIC]

dys·cra·sia (dis krā′zhə, -zhē ə, -zē ə), *n. Pathol.* a malfunction or abnormal condition, esp. an imbalance of the constituents of the blood. [1350–1400; ME; < ML < Gk *dyskrasía* bad mixture, equiv. to *dys-* DYS- + *krâs(is)* a mixing + *-ia* -IA] **—dys·cra′si·al, dys·cras·ic** (dis-kraz′ik, -kras′-), **dys·crat′ic,** *adj.*

dys·en·ter·y (dis′ən ter′ē), *n.* **1.** *Pathol.* an infectious disease marked by inflammation and ulceration of the lower part of the bowels, with diarrhea that becomes mucous and hemorrhagic. **2.** diarrhea. [1350–1400; < ML *dysenteria* < Gk, equiv. to *dysénter(a)* bad bowels (see DYS-, ENTERON) + *-ia* -IA; r. ME *dissenterie* < OF] **—dys′en·ter′ic,** *adj.*

dys·er·gia (di sûr′jə, -jē ə), *n. Pathol.* lack of muscular coordination due to defective nerve conduction. [< NL < Gk *dysergía* difficulty in working, equiv. to *dys-* DYS- + *-ergia;* see ERG[1], -Y[3]]

dys·es·the·sia (dis′əs thē′zhə, -zhē ə, -zē ə), *n. Pathol.* **1.** any impairment of the senses, esp. of the sense of touch. **2.** a condition in which light physical contact of the skin causes pain. [< NL < Gk *dysaisthēsía.* See DYS-, ESTHESIA] **—dys·es·thet·ic** (dis′is thet′ik), **dys′·aes·thet′ic,** *adj.*

dys·flu·en·cy (dis flo͞o′ən sē), *n., pl.* **-cies.** disfluency. [by confusion of DYS- with DIS-[1]]

dys·func·tion (dis fungk′shən), *n.* **1.** *Med.* malfunctioning, as of an organ or structure of the body. **2.** any malfunctioning part or element: *the dysfunctions of the country's economy.* **3.** *Sociol.* a consequence of a social practice or behavior pattern that undermines the stability of a social system. [1915–20; DYS- + FUNCTION] **—dys·func′tion·al,** *adj.*

dys·gen·e·sis (dis jen′ə sis), *n. Pathol.* defective development of an organ, as of the gonads in Klinefelter's syndrome. [1880–85; DYS- + -GENESIS]

dys·gen·ic (dis jen′ik), *adj. Pathol.* pertaining to or causing degeneration in the type of offspring produced. Cf. **eugenic.** [1910–15; DYS- + -GENIC]

dys·gen·ics (dis jen′iks), *n.* (*used with a singular v.*) *Biol.* the study of the operation of factors that cause degeneration in offspring. [1915–20; see DYSGENIC, -ICS]

dys·geu·sia (dis gyo͞o′zhə, -zhē ə, -zē ə), *n. Pathol.* an impairment of the sense of taste. [DYS- + Gk *geûs(is)* taste + -IA]

dys·gno·sia (dis nō′zhə, -zhē ə, -zē ə), *n. Psychiatry.* any intellectual impairment. [< Gk *dysgnōsía.* See DYS-, -GNOSIS, -IA]

dys·gon·ic (dis gon′ik), *adj. Bacteriol.* growing poorly on artificial media, as certain bacteria (opposed to *eugonic*). [DYS- + Gk *gón(os)* offspring + -IC]

dys·graph·i·a (dis graf′ē ə), *n. Psychiatry.* inability to write, caused by cerebral lesion. [1930–35; DYS- + -GRAPH + -IA]

dys·ki·ne·sia (dis′ki nē′zhə, -zhē ə, -zē ə, -kī-), *n. Pathol.* difficulty or abnormality in performing voluntary muscular movements. Cf. **tardive dyskinesia** [1700–10; < NL < Gk *dyskīnēsía;* see DYS-, -KINESIA] **—dys·ki·net·ic** (dis′ki net′ik, -kī-), *adj.*

dys·la·li·a (dis lā′lē ə, -lal′ē ə), *n. Pathol.* an inability to speak due to a defect of the organs of speech. [1850–55; < NL; see DYS-, -LALIA]

dys·lex·i·a (dis lek′sē ə), *n. Pathol.* any of various reading disorders associated with impairment of the ability to interpret spatial relationships or to integrate auditory and visual information. [1885–90; < NL < Gk *dys-* DYS- + *léx(is)* word + *-ia* -IA]

dys·lex·ic (dis lek′sik), *n.* **1.** a person subject to or having dyslexia. **—***adj.* **2.** of or pertaining to dyslexia. [1960–65; DYSLEX(IA) + -IC]

dys·lo·gia (dis lō′jə, -jē ə), *n. Pathol.* inability to express ideas because of faulty reasoning or speech, due to a mental disorder. [1880–85; < NL < Gk *dys-* DYS- + *lóg(os)* speech + *-ia* -IA]

dys·lo·gis·tic (dis′lə jis′tik), *adj.* conveying disapproval or censure; not complimentary or eulogistic. [1795–1805; DYS- + (EU)LOGISTIC] **—dys′lo·gis′ti·cal·ly,** *adv.*

dys·me·li·a (dis mē′lē ə), *n. Pathol.* a congenital abnormality characterized by missing, shortened, or excessive development of extremities. [1970–75; DYS- + -MELIA]

dys·men·or·rhe·a (dis′men ə rē′ə), *n. Med.* painful menstruation. Also, **dys′men·or·rhoe′a.** [1800–10; < NL; see DYS-, MENORRHEA] **—dys′men·or·rhe′al,** *adj.*

dys·met·ri·a (dis me′trē ə), *n. Pathol.* the inability to conform muscular action to desired movements because of faulty judgment of distance. [1910–15; < NL < Gk *dys-* DYS- + *métr(on)* a measure + *-ia* -IA]

dys·mne·sia (dis nē′zhə, -zhē ə, -zē ə), *n. Psychiatry.* an impairment of memory. [DYS- + Gk *mnês(is)* a remembering + -IA]

dys·os·mi·a (dis oz′mē ə), *n. Pathol.* an impairment of the sense of smell. [DYS- + Gk *osm(ḗ)* smell + -IA]

dys·pa·reu·ni·a (dis′pə ro͞o′nē ə), *n. Med.* painful coitus. [1870–75; DYS- + Gk *páreun(os)* bedfellow + -IA]

dys·pa·thy (dis′pə thē), *n.* antipathy. [1930–35; DYS- + (SYM)PATHY] **—dys′pa·thet′ic,** *adj.*

dys·pep·sia (dis pep′shə, -sē ə), *n.* deranged or impaired digestion; indigestion (opposed to *eupepsia*). Also, **dys·pep·sy** (dis pep′sē). [1650–60; < L < Gk *dyspepsía,* equiv. to *dys-* DYS- + *péps(is)* digestion + *-ia* -IA]

dys·pep·tic (dis pep′tik), *adj.* Also, **dys·pep′ti·cal. 1.** pertaining to, subject to, or suffering from dyspepsia. **2.** gloomy, pessimistic, and irritable. **—***n.* **3.** a person subject to or suffering from dyspepsia. [1685–95; DYS- + Gk *peptikós* pertaining to digestion, equiv. to *pept(ós)* digested (*pep-* cook, digest + *-tos* ptp. suffix) + *-ikos* -IC] **—dys·pep′ti·cal·ly,** *adv.*

dys·pha·gia (dis fā′jə, -jē ə), *n. Pathol.* difficulty in swallowing. [1775–85; < NL < Gk *dys-* DYS- + *phag(eîn)* to eat, devour + *-ia* -IA] **—dys·phag·ic** (dis faj′-ik, -fā′jik), *adj.*

dys·pha·sia (dis fā′zhə, -zhē ə, -zē ə), *n. Pathol.* inability to speak or understand words because of a brain lesion. [1875–80; DYS- + (A)PHASIA] **—dys·pha·sic** (dis-fā′zik, -sik), *adj.*

dys·phe·mi·a (dis fē′mē ə), *n. Psychol.* any impairment in the ability to speak. [1890–95; < NL < Gk *dys-* DYS- + *phḗm(ē)* utterance + *-ia* -IA]

dys·phe·mism (dis′fə miz′əm), *n.* **1.** the substitution of a harsh, disparaging, or unpleasant expression for a more neutral one. **2.** an expression so substituted. [1880–85; DYS- + (EU)PHEMISM] **—dys′phe·mis′tic,** *adj.* **—Ant.** euphemism.

dys·pho·ni·a (dis fō′nē ə), *n.* any disturbance of normal vocal function. [1700–10; < NL < Gk *dysphōnía* roughness of sound, equiv. to *dys-* DYS- + *phōn(ḗ)* sound, voice + *-ia* -IA] **—dys·phon·ic** (dis fon′ik), *adj.*

dys·pho·ri·a (dis fôr′ē ə, -fōr′-), *n. Pathol.* a state of dissatisfaction, anxiety, restlessness, or fidgeting. [1835–45; < NL < Gk *dysphoría* malaise, discomfort, equiv. to *dys-* DYS- + *phor(ós)* bearing + *-ia* -IA] **—dys·phor·ic** (dis fôr′ik, -for′-), *adj.*

dys·pla·sia (dis plā′zhə, -zhē ə, -zē ə), *n. Pathol.* abnormal growth or development of cells, tissue, bone, or an organ. [1930–35; DYS- + -PLASIA] **—dys·plas·tic** (dis plas′tik), *adj.*

dysp·ne·a (disp nē′ə), *n. Pathol.* difficult or labored breathing. [1675–85; DYS- + -PNEA] **—dysp·ne′al, dysp·ne′ic,** *adj.*

dys·prax·i·a (dis prak′sē ə), *n. Pathol.* inability to perform coordinated movements. [< Gk: ill success, equiv. to *dys-* DYS- + *prâx(is)* action + *-ia* -IA]

dys·pro·si·um (dis prō′sē əm, -shē-), *n. Chem.* a rare-earth metallic element, highly reactive and paramagnetic, found in small amounts in various rare-earth minerals, as euxenite and monazite: used to absorb neutrons in nuclear reactors. *Symbol:* Dy; *at. wt.:* 162.50; *at. no.:* 66. [1885–90; < NL < Gk *dysprós(itos)* hard to get at (*dys-* DYS- + *pros-* to + *itós,* ptp. of *iénai* to go) + -IUM]

dys·rhyth·mi·a (dis rit͟h′mē ə), *n.* a disturbance of rhythm, as of speech or of brain waves recorded by an electroencephalograph. [1905–10; < NL < Gk *dys-* DYS- + *rhythm(ós)* RHYTHM + *-ia* -IA]

dys·tel·e·ol·o·gy (dis′tel ē ol′ə jē, -tē lē-), *n.* **1.** *Philos.* a doctrine denying the existence of a final cause or purpose. **2.** the assumed absence of purpose in life or nature. **3.** the evasion or frustration of a natural or normal function or purpose. [1870–75; < G *Dysteleologie;* see DYS-, TELEOLOGY] **—dys·tel·e·o·log·i·cal** (dis′tel ē-ə loj′i kəl, -tē lē-), *adj.* **—dys′tel·e·ol′o·gist,** *n.*

dys·thy·mi·a (dis thī′mē ə), *n.* depression; despondency or a tendency to be despondent. [1840–50; < NL < Gk *dysthymía;* see DYS-, -THYMIA] **—dys·thy′mic,** *adj.*

dys·to·ni·a (dis tō′nē ə), *n. Pathol.* abnormal tone of any tissue. [DYS- + -TONIA] **—dys·ton·ic** (dis ton′ik), *adj.*

dys·to·pi·a (dis tō′pē ə), *n.* a society characterized by human misery, as squalor, oppression, disease, and overcrowding. Cf. **utopia.** [1865–70; DYS- + (U)TOPIA] **—dys·to′pi·an,** *adj.* **—dys·to′pi·an·ism,** *n.*

dys·troph·ic (di strof′ik, -strō′fik), *adj.* **1.** *Med.* pertaining to or caused by dystrophy. **2.** *Ecol.* (of a lake) having too low an accumulation of dissolved nutrients to support abundant plant life; having highly acid, brownish waters filled with undecayed plant materials, and eventually developing into a peat bog or marsh. [1890–95; DYS- + TROPHIC]

dys·tro·phi·ca·tion (dis′trə fi kā′shən), *n. Ecol.* the process by which a body of water becomes dystrophic. [1965–70; DYSTROPHIC + -ATION]

dys·tro·phy (dis′trə fē), *n.* **1.** *Med.* faulty or inadequate nutrition or development. **2.** *Pathol.* any of a number of disorders characterized by weakening, degeneration, or abnormal development of muscle. **3.** *Ecol.* the state of being dystrophic. Also, **dys·tro·phi·a** (di-strō′fē ə). [1885–90; < NL *dystrophia.* See DYS-, -TROPHY]

dys·u·ri·a (dis′yo͝o rē′ə, dis yo͝or′ē ə), *n. Pathol.* difficult or painful urination. [1350–1400; < NL < Gk *dysouría.* See DYS- UR-[1], -IA; r. earlier *dysury,* ME *dissure, dissuria* (< MF) < ML < Gk] **—dys·u′ric,** *adj.*

Dyu·sham·be (dyo͝o shäm′bə), *n.* a former name of **Dushanbe.**

DZ, See **drop zone.**

dz., dozen; dozens.

Dzer·zhinsk (dər zhinsk′; *Russ.* dzɪʀ zhinsk′), *n.* a city in the central Soviet Union in Europe, ENE of Moscow. 257,000.

Dzham·bul (jäm bo͞ol′; *Russ.* jum bo͞ol′), *n.* a city in S Kazakhstan, in the SW Soviet Union in Asia, NE of Tashkent. 264,000. Formerly, **Aulie Ata.**

Dzhu·gash·vi·li (jo͞o′gəsh vē′lē; *Russ.* jo͞o gu shvyē′-lyi), *n.* **Io·sif Vis·sa·ri·o·no·vich** (*Russ.* yô′syif vyi sə-ʀyi ô′nə vyich). See **Stalin, Joseph.** Also, **Dzu′gash·vi′li.**

Dzi·bil·chal·tun (dzē bēl′chäl to͞on′), *n.* a large, ancient Mayan ceremonial and commercial center near Mérida, Mexico, founded perhaps as early as 3000 B.C. and in continuous use until the 16th century.

dzig·ge·tai (jig′i tī′), *n.* chigetai.

Dzun·ga·ri·a (dzo͝ong gâr′ē ə, zo͝ong-), *n.* a region in N Sinkiang, China: a Mongol kingdom during the 11th to 14th centuries.

CONCISE PRONUNCIATION KEY: *act, cāpe, dâre, pärt; set, ēqual; if, īce; ox, ōver, ôrder, oil, bo͝ok, bo͞ot, out; up, ûrge; child; sing; shoe; thin, that;* zh as in *treasure.* ə = *a* as in *alone, e* as in *system, i* as in *easily, o* as in *gallop, u* as in *circus;* ᵊ as in *fire* (fīᵊr), *hour* (ouᵊr). l and n can serve as syllabic consonants, as in *cradle* (krād′l), and *button* (but′n). See the full key inside the front cover.

DEVELOPMENT OF MAJUSCULE								
NORTH SEMITIC	GREEK		ETR	LATIN		MODERN		
						GOTHIC	ITALIC	ROMAN
		E			E	E	*E*	E

DEVELOPMENT OF MINUSCULE					
ROMAN CURSIVE	ROMAN UNCIAL	CAROL MIN	MODERN		
			GOTHIC	ITALIC	ROMAN
				e	e

The fifth letter of the English alphabet developed from North Semitic *he*. Originally a consonant with an *h*-sound, it was transformed into a vowel in Greek, although in Classical Greek and in certain local alphabets North Semitic *heth* (see **H**) was used to represent *eta* (long e). The minuscule (e) was derived from the capital (E) through the uncial form.

E, e (ē), *n., pl.* **E's** or **Es, e's** or **es. 1.** the fifth letter of the English alphabet, a vowel. **2.** any spoken sound represented by the letter *E* or *e*, as in *met, meet, mere,* etc. **3.** something having the shape of an E. **4.** a written or printed representation of the letter *E* or *e*. **5.** a device, as a printer's type, for reproducing the letter *E* or *e*.

E, 1. east. **2.** eastern. **3.** English. **4.** excellent. **5.** Expressway.

E, *Symbol.* **1.** the fifth in order or in a series. **2.** (*sometimes l.c.*) (in some grading systems) a grade or mark, as in school or college, indicating the quality of a student's work is in need of improvement in order to be passing. **3.** *Music.* **a.** the third tone in the scale of C major or the fifth tone in the relative minor scale, A minor. **b.** a string, key, or pipe tuned to this tone. **c.** a written or printed note representing this tone. **d.** (in the fixed system of solmization) the third tone of the scale of C major, called *mi*. **e.** the tonality having E as the tonic note. **4.** (*sometimes l.c.*) the medieval Roman numeral for 250. Cf. **Roman numerals. 5.** *Physics, Elect.* **a.** electric field. **b.** electric field strength. **6.** *Physics.* energy. **7.** *Biochem.* See **glutamic acid. 8.** *Logic.* See **universal negative. 9.** a proportional shoe width size narrower than EE and wider than D.

e, 1. electron. **2.** *Physics.* elementary charge.

e, *Symbol.* **1.** *Math.* a transcendental constant equal to 2.7182818 . . . , used as the base of natural logarithms; the limit of the expression $(1+1/n)^n$ as *n* approaches infinity. **2.** *Logic.* See **universal negative.**

e-, var. of **ex-**[1], occurring in words of Latin origin before consonants other than *c, f, p, q, s,* and *t*: *emit.*

E., 1. Earl. **2.** Earth. **3.** east. **4.** Easter. **5.** eastern. **6.** engineer. **7.** engineering. **8.** English.

e., 1. eldest. **2.** *Football.* end. **3.** engineer. **4.** engineering. **5.** entrance. **6.** *Baseball.* error; errors.

E·a (ā′ä), *n.* the Akkadian god of wisdom, the son of Apsu and father of Marduk: the counterpart of Enki.

-ea, a suffix occurring in loanwords from Latin: *cornea.* [< L *-ēa, -aea, -ea,* fem. sing. and neut. pl. of *-ēus, -aeus, -eus;* see -EAN]

ea., each.

E.A.A., Engineer in Aeronautics and Astronautics.

each (ēch), *adj.* **1.** every one of two or more considered individually or one by one: *each stone in a building; a hallway with a door at each end.* —*pron.* **2.** every one individually; each one: *Each had a different solution to the problem.* —*adv.* **3.** to, from, or for each; apiece: *They cost a dollar each.* [bef. 900; ME *eche,* OE *ælc,* equiv. to *ā* ever (see AY[1]) + *(ge)līc* ALIKE; c. OHG *ēogilīh,* OFris *ellik,* D, LG *elk*]
—Syn. 1. EACH, EVERY are alike in having a distributive meaning. Of two or more members composing an aggregate, EACH directs attention to the separate members in turn: *Each child* (of those considered and enumerated) *received a large apple.* EVERY emphasizes inclusiveness or universality: *Every child* (of all in existence) *likes to play.*
—Usage. The adjective EACH is always followed by a singular noun: *each person; each book.* When the adjective follows a plural subject, the verb agrees with the subject: *They each dress in different styles. The houses each have central heating.* When the pronoun EACH comes immediately before the verb, it always takes a singular verb: *Each comes* (not *come*) *from a different country.* When the pronoun is followed by an *of* phrase containing a plural noun or pronoun, there is a tendency for the verb to be plural: *Each of the candidates has* (or *have*) *spoken on the issue.* Some usage guides maintain that only the singular verb is correct, but plural verbs occur frequently even in edited writing.
It is also sometimes said that the pronoun EACH must always be referred to by a singular pronoun, but again actual usage does not regularly observe this stricture: *Each member of our garden club had their own special interests.* In the most formal speech and writing, singular verbs and pronouns occur more frequently than plural: *Each member . . . had his own special interests.* The use of plural forms, especially plural pronouns, has been increasing in the United States, partially because of the desire to avoid using *he* or *his* to refer to a female.
ANYONE, ANYBODY, EVERYONE, EVERYBODY, NO ONE, SOMEONE, and SOMEBODY follow the same general patterns of pronoun agreement as EACH. See also **they.**

each′ oth′er, each the other; one another (used as a compound reciprocal pronoun): *to strike at each other; to hold each other's hands; to love each other.* [bef. 1000; ME; OE. See EACH, OTHER]
—Usage. Although some insist that EACH OTHER be used only in reference to two (*The two candidates respected each other*) and ONE ANOTHER in reference to three or more (*The three nations threaten one another*), in standard practice they are interchangeable. EACH OTHER is not restricted to two, nor is ONE ANOTHER restricted to three or more.
The possessive of EACH OTHER is *each other's;* the possessive of ONE ANOTHER is *one another's.*

ead., (in prescriptions) the same. [< L *eādem*]

Ead·mund I (ed′mənd, ā′əd mo͝ond′). See **Edmund I.**

Eadmund II. See **Edmund II.**

Eads (ēdz), *n.* **James Buchanan,** 1820–87, U.S. engineer and inventor.

Ead·wine (ed′win, ā′əd win′ə), *n.* Edwin (def. 1).

-eae, plural of **-ea:** *tracheae.*

Ea·gan (ē′gən), *n.* a town in SE Minnesota. 20,532.

ea·ger[1] (ē′gər), *adj.* **1.** keen or ardent in desire or feeling; impatiently longing: *I am eager for news about them. He is eager to sing.* **2.** characterized by or revealing great earnestness: *an eager look.* **3.** *Obs.* keen; sharp; biting. [1250–1300; ME *egre* < AF, OF *egre, aigre* < VL **ācrus* for L *ācer* sharp] **—ea′ger·ly,** *adv.* **—ea′ger·ness,** *n.*
—Syn. 1. enthusiastic, desirous. See **avid. 2.** fervent, zealous, fervid, intent, intense, earnest. **—Ant. 1, 2.** indifferent, uninterested. **2.** heedless.

ea·ger[2] (ē′gər, ā′gər), *n. Chiefly Brit.* eagre.

ea′ger bea′ver (ē′gər), a person who is excessively diligent or overly zealous. [1940–45, *Amer.*]

ea·gle (ē′gəl), *n., v.,* **-gled, -gling.** **—***n.* **1.** any of several large, soaring birds of prey belonging to the hawk family Accipitridae, noted for their size, strength, and powers of flight and vision: formerly widespread in North America, eagles are mostly confined to Alaska and a few isolated populations. Cf. **bald eagle, golden eagle. 2.** a figure or representation of an eagle, much used as an emblem: *the Roman eagle.* **3.** a standard, seal, or the like bearing such a figure. **4.** one of a pair of silver insignia in the shape of eagles with outstretched wings worn by a colonel in the U.S. Army, Air Force, and Marine Corps and by a captain in the U.S. Navy. **5.** (*cap.*) a gold coin of the U.S., traded for investment, available in denominations of 5, 10, 25, and 50 dollars containing 1/10 to 1 troy ounce of gold, having on its reverse a picture of an eagle: first issued in 1986. **6.** a former gold coin of the U.S., issued until 1933, equal to 10 dollars, showing an eagle on its reverse. **7.** *Golf.* a score of two below par for any single hole. **8.** (*cap.*) *Astron.* the constellation Aquila. **9.** *Cards,* **a.** a representation in green of an eagle, used on playing cards to designate a suit in the pack additional to the four standard suits. **b.** a card of a suit so designated. **c. eagles,** the suit itself. **—***v.t.* **10.** *Golf.* to make an eagle on (a hole). [1350–1400; ME *egle* < AF, OF *egle, aigle* < L *aquila,* n. use of fem. of *aquilus* dark-colored]

ea′gle eye′, 1. unusually sharp visual powers; keen ability to watch or observe. **2.** a person who has sharp vision or who maintains a keen watchfulness. **3.** alert watchfulness. [1595–1605]

ea·gle-eyed (ē′gəl īd′), *adj.* having keen vision. [1595–1605]

ea′gle owl′, any of several large owls of the genus *Bubo,* having prominent tufts of feathers on each side of the head, esp. *B. bubo* of Europe and Asia. [1670–80]

Ea′gle Pass′, a city in S Texas, on the Rio Grande. 21,407.

ea′gle ray′, any of several rays of the family Myliobatidae, found in tropical seas and noted for the soaring movements by which they propel themselves through the water. [1855–60]

ea′gle scout′, a boy scout who has achieved the highest rank in U.S. scouting. [1910–15, *Amer.*]

ea·gle·stone (ē′gəl stōn′), *n.* a concretionary lump of ironstone about the size of a walnut, formerly believed to be carried by eagles to their nests as a magical aid in laying eggs. [1595–1605; EAGLE + STONE]

ea·glet (ē′glit), *n.* a young eagle. [1565–75; < MF *aiglette* (in heraldry). See EAGLE, -ET]

ea·gle·wood (ē′gəl wo͝od′), *n.* agalloch. [1510–20; trans. of Pg *pāo d'aguila* wood of agalloch, by confusion of Pg *águia* eagle with *aguila* < Malayalam *agil* agalloch]

ea·gre (ē′gər, ā′gər), *n. Chiefly Brit.* a tidal bore or flood. Also, **eager.** [1640–50; appar. repr. earlier *agar, ager,* obscurely akin to *hyger, higre;* (cf. AL (12th century) *higra* the tidal bore of the Severn); compared with OE *ēgor, eogor* flood, high tide, though preservation of *g* in modern forms is problematic]

Ea·kins (ā′kinz), *n.* **Thomas,** 1844–1916, U.S. painter.

eal·dor·man (ôl′dər mən), *n., pl.* **-men.** *Obs.* alderman. Also, **eal′der·man.**

Ea·ling (ē′ling), *n.* a borough of Greater London, England. 297,600.

EAM, National Liberation Front, a Greek underground resistance movement of World War II and political coalition of various leftist groups. [< ModGk *E(thnikō) A(pelevtherōtikò) M(étōpo)*]

Eames (ēmz), *n.* **Charles,** 1907–78, U.S. furniture designer and architect.

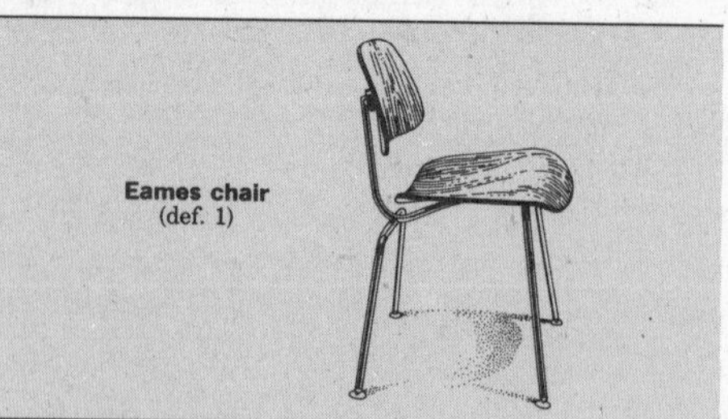
Eames chair (def. 1)

Eames′ chair′, 1. Also called **LCM chair.** a side chair designed by Charles Eames in 1946, having a slender tubular steel frame with a seat and back of molded plywood panels. **2.** Also called **Eames′ lounge′ chair′.** an armchair with matching ottoman designed by Charles Eames in 1956, having separate headrest, backrest, and seat sections of molded plywood fitted with leather cushions and mounted on a metal base that can swivel or tilt. [1945–50, *Amer.*]

-ean, an element used to form adjectives from nouns ending in **-ea:** *crustacean.* [< L *-ē(us)* (Gk *-eios*), *-ae(us)* (Gk *-aios*), *-e(us)* + -AN]

CONCISE ETYMOLOGY KEY: <, descended or borrowed from; >, whence; b., blend of, blended; c., cognate with; cf., compare; deriv., derivative; equiv., equivalent; imit., imitative; obl., oblique; r., replacing; s., stem; sp., spelling, spelled; resp., respelling, respelled; trans., translation; ?, origin unknown; *, unattested; ‡, probably earlier than. See the full key inside the front cover.

ean•ling (ēn′ling), *n. Obs.* a young lamb; kid. [1590–1600; var. of YEANLING]

EAP, employee assistance program.

ear[1] (ēr), *n.* **1.** the organ of hearing and equilibrium in vertebrates, in humans consisting of an external ear that gathers sound vibrations, a middle ear in which the vibrations resonate against the tympanic membrane, and a fluid-filled internal ear that maintains balance and that conducts the tympanic vibrations to the auditory nerve, which transmits them as impulses to the brain. **2.** the external ear alone: *The hat completely covers his ears.* **3.** the sense of hearing: *sounds that are pleasing to the ear.* **4.** keen or sensitive perception of the differences of sound, esp. sensitiveness to the quality and correctness of musical sounds: *an ear for music; a violinist with a good ear.* **5.** attention; heed: *to gain a person's ear.* **6.** any part that resembles or suggests an ear in position or form, as the handle of a teacup. **7.** *Archit.* crossette. **8.** *Journalism.* a small box in either upper corner of a newspaper page, usually the front page or split page, containing the name of or a symbol for the edition, a weather bulletin, a slogan, or the like. **9.** *Furniture.* **a.** a decorative feature at the upper end of a leg. **b.** one of the decorative features at each end of a crest rail. **10.** **ears,** *Slang.* earphones. **11.** **be all ears,** *Informal.* to give all one's attention; listen: *We were all ears as the scandal was revealed.* **12.** **bend an ear,** to listen attentively: *to bend an ear to a request for aid.* **13.** **bend someone's ear,** *Informal.* to talk to someone uninterruptedly and often so as to induce boredom: *He'll bend your ear for hours if given the chance.* **14.** **by ear,** without reference to written or printed music: *to play the piano by ear.* **15.** **fall on deaf ears,** to be disregarded; pass unheeded: *Their pleas for mercy fell on deaf ears.* **16.** **give ear,** to pay attention; listen carefully. Also, **lend an ear.** **17.** **go in one ear and out the other,** to be heard but ignored; be put out of mind: *My repeated warnings to her went in one ear and out the other.* **18.** **have one's ears on,** *Slang.* to be listening through earphones to a radio, cassette player, telephone communication, or the like. **19.** **have** or **keep one's ear to the ground,** to keep well-informed about current trends; be shrewd or astute: *Because she had her ear to the ground, she made a large fortune in stock speculation.* **20.** **pin someone's ears back,** *Slang.* to give a person a sound beating; defeat a person utterly: *If he doesn't behave himself, I'll pin his ears back.* **21.** **set by the ears,** to cause to dispute or quarrel: *He's a troublemaker who keeps trying to set the two other children by the ears.* **22.** **set on one's ear** or **ears,** to excite or stir up; shock; amaze: *The presence of the movie star set the whole town on its ear.* **23.** **turn a deaf ear to,** to refuse to listen to or consider (a request, petition, etc.): *He turns a deaf ear to requests for loans.* **24.** **up to one's ears,** deeply involved or occupied to full capacity: *We are up to our ears in work.* **25.** **wet behind the ears.** See **wet** (def. 11). [bef. 900; ME *ere,* OE *ēare;* c. ON *eyra,* G *Ohr,* Goth *auso,* L *auris,* Lith *ausis,* Gk *oûs*] —**ear′less,** *adj.* —**ear′like′,** *adj.*

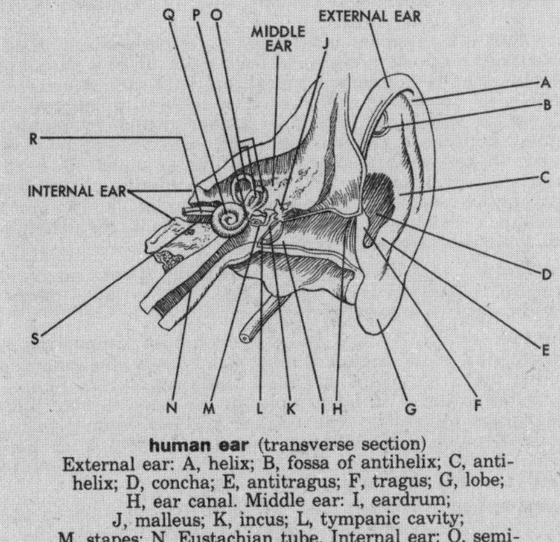

human ear (transverse section)
External ear: A, helix; B, fossa of antihelix; C, antihelix; D, concha; E, antitragus; F, tragus; G, lobe; H, ear canal. Middle ear: I, eardrum; J, malleus; K, incus; L, tympanic cavity; M, stapes; N, Eustachian tube. Internal ear: O, semicircular canals; P, vestibule; Q, cochlea; R, auditory nerve, S, internal auditory meatus

ear[2] (ēr), *n.* **1.** the part of a cereal plant, as corn, wheat, etc., that contains the flowers and hence the fruit, grains, or kernels. —*v.i.* **2.** to form or put forth ears. [bef. 900; ME *ere,* OE *ēar, æhher;* c. G *Ähre,* ON *ax,* Goth *ahs* ear, L *acus* husk]

ear[3] (ēr), *v.t. Brit. Dial.* to plow; cultivate. [bef. 900; ME *ere(n),* OE *erian;* c. ON *erja,* Goth *arjan,* L *arāre*]

ear•ache (ēr′āk′), *n.* pain in the ear; otalgia. [1650–60; EAR[1] + ACHE]

ear′ band′. See **ear wrap.**

ear•bob (ēr′bob′), *n. Southern and South Midland U.S.* an earring or eardrop. [1640–50; EAR[1] + BOB[2]]

ear′ can′dy, *Slang.* pleasant, melodic pop music. [1980–85]

ear•drop (ēr′drop′), *n.* an earring with a pendant. [1710–20; EAR[1] + DROP]

ear′ drops′, medicinal drops for use in the ears.

ear•drum (ēr′drum′), *n. Anat., Zool.* a membrane in the ear canal between the external ear and the middle ear; tympanic membrane. [1635–45; EAR[1] + DRUM[1]]

eared (ērd), *adj.* having ears or earlike appendages. [1350–1400; ME *ered,* OE *ēarede.* See EAR[1], -ED[3]]

eared′ seal′, any seal of the family Otariidae, comprising the sea lions and fur seals, having external ears and flexible hind flippers that are used when moving about on land: the front flippers are used in swimming. Cf. **earless seal.** [1880–85]

ear•flap (ēr′flap′), *n.* either of a pair of flaps attached to a cap, for covering the ears in cold weather. Also called **earlap.** [1855–60; EAR[1] + FLAP]

ear•ful (ēr′fo͝ol′), *n., pl.* **-fuls. 1.** an outpouring of oral information or advice, esp. when given without solicitation. **2.** a sharp verbal rebuke; a scolding. [1915–20; EAR[1] + -FUL] —**Usage.** See **-ful.**

ear′ fun′gus, a smooth, reddish-brown ear-shaped fungus, *Otidia smithii,* abundant in North America.

Ear•hart (âr′härt), *n.* **Amelia (Mary),** 1897–1937, U.S. aviator: vanished in flight over Pacific Ocean.

ear•ing (ēr′ing), *n. Naut.* a rope attached to a cringle and used for bending a corner of a sail to a yard, boom, or gaff or for reefing a sail. [1620–30; EAR[1] + -ING[1]]

earl (ûrl), *n.* **1.** a British nobleman of a rank below that of marquis and above that of viscount: called count for a time after the Norman conquest. The wife of an earl is a countess. **2.** (in Anglo-Saxon England) a governor of one of the great divisions of England, including East Anglia, Mercia, Northumbria, and Wessex. [bef. 900; ME *erl,* OE *eorl;* c. OS *erl* man, ON *jarl* chieftain]

Earl (ûrl), *n.* a male given name: from the old English word meaning "noble." Also, **Earle.**

ear•lap (ēr′lap′), *n.* **1.** earflap. **2.** the lobe of the ear. **3.** the whole external ear; pinna. [bef. 1000; ME *erelappe,* OE *ēarlæppa* external ear. See EAR[1], LAP[1]]

earl•dom (ûrl′dəm), *n.* **1.** Also called **earlship.** the rank or title of an earl. **2.** the territory or jurisdiction of an earl. [bef. 1150; ME *erldom,* OE *eorldōm.* See EARL, -DOM,]

ear′less liz′ard, any of several slender iguanid lizards of the genus *Holbrookia,* of the western U.S. and Mexico, that have no external ear opening.

ear′less seal′, any seal of the family Phocidae, comprising seals that lack external ears and that use the hind flippers for swimming: land locomotion is accomplished by wriggling and by propelling with the front flippers. Also called **true seal.** Cf. **eared seal.**

Ear′lier Han′, the Han dynasty before A.D. 9. Also called **Western Han.** Cf. **Han** (def. 1), **Later Han.**

ear•lobe (ēr′lōb′), *n.* the soft, pendulous lower part of the external ear. Also, **ear′ lobe′.** Also called **lobe.** See diag. under **ear.** [1855–60; EAR[1] + LOBE]

ear•lock (ēr′lok′), *n.* **1.** a lock of hair worn near or in front of the ear. **2.** *Judaism.* a lock of hair worn in front of each ear by Hasidic and Yemenite Jewish males in accordance with the Biblical prohibition against clipping the hair at the temples. Lev. 19:27. [1765–75; EAR[1] + LOCK[2]]

earl′ pal′atine, *pl.* **earls palatine.** See **count palatine** (def. 2).

earl•ship (ûrl′ship), *n.* earldom (def. 1). [bef. 1000; ME; OE *eorlscipe.* See EARL, -SHIP]

ear•ly (ûr′lē), *adv.,* **-li•er, -li•est,** *adj.,* **-li•er, -li•est,** *n., pl.* **-lies.** —*adv.* **1.** in or during the first part of a period of time, a course of action, a series of events, etc.: *early in the year.* **2.** in the early part of the morning: *to get up early.* **3.** before the usual or appointed time; ahead of time: *They came early and found their hosts still dressing.* **4.** far back in time: *The Greeks early learned to sail and navigate.* **5.** **early on,** with but little time elapsed; early in the course of a process, project, etc.; early in the game. —*adj.* **6.** occurring in the first part of a period of time, a course of action, a series of events, etc.: *an early hour of the day.* **7.** occurring before the usual or appointed time: *an early dinner.* **8.** belonging to a period far back in time: *early French architecture.* **9.** occurring in the near future: *I look forward to an early reply.* **10.** (of a fruit or vegetable) appearing or maturing before most others of its type: *early apples.* —*n.* **11.** a fruit or vegetable that appears before most others of its type. [bef. 950; ME *erlich* (adj.), *erliche* (adv.), OE *ærlic, ǣrlīce,* mutated var. of *ārlīc, ārlīce,* equiv. to *ār-* early (positive of *ǣr* ERE) + *līc(e)* -LY] —**ear′li•ness,** *n.*

Ear•ly (ûr′lē), *n.* **Ju•bal Anderson** (jo͞o′bəl), 1816–94, Confederate general in the U.S. Civil War.

Ear′ly Amer′ican, 1. (of furniture, buildings, utensils, etc.) built or made in the U.S. in the colonial period or somewhat later. **2.** built or made in imitation of works of this period. [1890–95]

ear′ly bird′, 1. a person who rises at an early hour. **2.** a person who arrives before others, as for the purpose of gaining some advantage: *The early birds got the best seats for the play.* **3.** *(caps.) Aerospace.* the first of the Intelsat series of communications satellites, orbited (1965) by Intelsat. [1885–90]

ear′ly blight′, *Plant Pathol.* a disease of plants characterized by leaf spotting, defoliation, and stunted growth, caused by any of several fungi, as *Alternaria solani* or *Cercospora apii.*

Ear′ly Eng′lish, pertaining to the first style of Gothic architecture in England, ending in the latter half of the 13th century, characterized by the use of lancet arches, plate tracery, and narrow openings. [1800–10]

Ear′ly He′brew, noting or pertaining to the alphabetical script used for the writing of Hebrew mainly from the 11th to the 6th centuries B.C.

Ear′ly Mod′ern Eng′lish, the English language represented in printed documents of the period starting with Caxton (1476) and ending with Dryden (1700).

Ear′ly Ren′aissance, a style of art developed principally in Florence, Italy, during the 15th century and characterized chiefly by the development of linear perspective, chiaroscuro, and geometrically based compositions. Cf. **High Renaissance.**

ear′ly sax′ifrage, an eastern North American plant, *Saxifraga virginiensis,* of the saxifrage family, having toothed basal leaves and branched clusters of small white flowers.

ear′ly-warn′ing sys′tem (ûr′lē wôr′ning), **1.** *Mil.* a network of radar installations designed to detect enemy aircraft or missiles in time for the effective deployment of defense systems. **2.** any series of steps established to spot potential problems. [1945–50]

ear′ly wood′, springwood. [1910–15]

ear•mark (ēr′märk′), *n.* **1.** any identifying or distinguishing mark or characteristic: *The mayor's statement had all the earmarks of dirty politics.* **2.** a mark of identification made on the ear of an animal to show ownership. —*v.t.* **3.** to set aside for a specific purpose, use, recipient, etc.: *to earmark goods for export.* **4.** to mark with an earmark. [1515–25; EAR[1] + MARK[1]]

ear•mind•ed (ēr′mīn′did), *adj.* tending to perceive one's environment in terms of sound and to recall sounds more vividly than sights, smells, etc. Cf. **eye-minded, motor-minded.** [1885–90] —**ear′-mind′ed•ness,** *n.*

ear•muff (ēr′muf′), *n.* either of a pair of often adjustable coverings for protecting the ears in cold weather. [1855–60, *Amer.;* EAR[1] + MUFF]

earn[1] (ûrn), *v.t.* **1.** to gain or get in return for one's labor or service: *to earn one's living.* **2.** to merit as compensation, as for service; deserve: *to receive more than one has earned.* **3.** to acquire through merit: *to earn a reputation for honesty.* **4.** to gain as due return or profit: *Savings accounts earn interest.* **5.** to bring about or cause deservedly: *His fair dealing earned our confidence.* —*v.i.* **6.** to gain income: *securities that earn on a quarterly basis.* [bef. 900; ME *ern(i)en,* OE *earnian;* akin to OHG *arnēn* to earn, harvest] —**earn′er,** *n.*
—**Syn. 1.** procure, make, receive, obtain. See **gain**[1].

earn[2] (ûrn), *v.i. Obs.* to grieve. [1570–80; perh. var. of YEARN]

earned′ in′come, income from wages, salaries, fees, or the like, accruing from labor or services performed by the earner. Cf. **unearned income.** [1880–85]

earned′ run′, *Baseball.* a run yielded by a pitcher in which no error by the pitcher or the pitcher's teammates and no passed ball by the catcher was involved. [1875–80, *Amer.*]

earned′ run′ av′erage, *Baseball.* a measure of the effectiveness of a pitcher, obtained by dividing the number of earned runs scored against the pitcher by the number of innings pitched and multiplying the result by nine. A pitcher yielding three earned runs in nine innings has an earned run average of 3.00. *Abbr.:* ERA, era [1945–50]

earned′ sur′plus. See **retained earnings.**

ear•nest[1] (ûr′nist), *adj.* **1.** serious in intention, purpose, or effort; sincerely zealous: *an earnest worker.* **2.** showing depth and sincerity of feeling: *earnest words; an earnest entreaty.* **3.** seriously important; demanding or receiving serious attention. —*n.* **4.** full seriousness, as of intention or purpose: *to speak in earnest.* [bef. 1000; ME *erneste,* OE *eornoste* (adj.); ME *ernest,* OE *eornost* (n.); c. D, G *ernest*] —**ear′nest•ly,** *adv.* —**ear′nest•ness,** *n.*
—**Syn. 1.** fervent, intent, purposeful, determined, industrious, ambitious. EARNEST, RESOLUTE, SERIOUS, SINCERE imply having qualities of depth and firmness. EARNEST implies having a purpose and being steadily and soberly eager in pursuing it: *an earnest student.* RESOLUTE adds a quality of determination: *resolute in defending the right.* SERIOUS implies having depth and a soberness of attitude that contrasts with gaiety and frivolity; it may include the qualities of both earnestness and resolution: *serious and thoughtful.* SINCERE suggests genuineness, trustworthiness, and absence of superficiality: *a sincere interest in music.* —**Ant. 1.** frivolous.

ear•nest[2] (ûr′nist), *n.* **1.** a portion of something, given or done in advance as a pledge of the remainder. **2.** *Law.* See **earnest money. 3.** anything that gives pledge, promise, or indication of what is to follow. [1175–1225; ME *ernes(t),* alter. of OF *erres,* pl. of *erre* earnest money < L *arr(h)a* short for *arr(h)abō* (perh. by taking *-bō* as a future tense ending) < Gk *arrhabṓn* < Sem (cf. Heb *'ērābhōn* security, pledge). Cf. ARRAS[2]]

ear′nest mon′ey, *Law.* money given by a buyer to a seller to bind a contract. [1550–60]

earn•ings (ûr′ningz), *n.* money earned; wages; profits. [bef. 1050; ME *erning,* OE *earning, earnung* merit, pay. See EARN, -ING[1], -S[3]]

earn′ings per share′, the net income of a corporation divided by the total number of shares of its common stock outstanding at a given time. *Abbr.:* EPS

Earp (ûrp), *n.* **Wy•att (Ber•ry Stapp)** (wī′ət ber′ē stap), 1848–1929, U.S. frontiersman, law officer, and gunfighter.

ear•phone (ēr′fōn′), *n.* **1.** a sound receiver that fits in or over the ear, as of a radio or telephone. **2.** Usually, **earphones.** a headset; headphone. [1920–25; EAR[1] + PHONE[1]]

ear•piece (ēr′pēs′), *n.* **1.** a piece that covers or passes over the ear, as on a cap or eyeglasses. **2.** an earphone. [1835–45; EAR[1] + PIECE]

ear-pierc•ing (ēr′pēr′sing), *adj.* extremely harsh and irritating to the ear: *ear-piercing noise.* [1595–1605]

ear•plug (ēr′plug′), *n.* a plug of soft, pliable material inserted into the opening of the outer ear, esp. to keep out water or noise. [1900–05; EAR[1] + PLUG]

ear•reach (ēr′rēch′), *n.* earshot. [1635–45; EAR[1] + REACH]

ear•ring (ēr′ring′, -ing), *n.* an ornament worn on or hanging from the lobe of the ear. [bef. 1000; ME *erering,* OE *ēarhring.* See EAR[1], RING[1]] —**ear′ringed,** *adj.*

CONCISE PRONUNCIATION KEY: *act, cāpe, dâre, pärt; set, ēqual; if, īce; ox, ōver, ôrder, oil, bo͝ok, bo͞ot, out; up, ûrge; child; sing; shoe; thin,* t͟hat; zh as in *treasure.* ə = *a* as in *alone, e* as in *system; i* as in *easily, o* as in *gallop, u* as in *circus;* ᵊ as in *fire* (fīᵊr), *hour* (ouᵊr). l and n can serve as syllabic consonants, as in *cradle* (krād′l), and *button* (but′n). See the full key inside the front cover.

ear′ sew′er (sō′ər), *Dial.* a dragonfly. **—Regional Variation.** See **dragonfly.**

ear•shot (ēr′shot′), *n.* the range or distance within which a sound, voice, etc., can be heard. Also called **ear-reach.** [1600–10; EAR[1] + SHOT[1]]

ear•split•ting (ēr′split′ing), *adj.* ear-piercing: *an ear-splitting explosion.* [1880–85; EAR[1] + SPLITTING]

ear′ stone′, an otolith. [1850–55]

ear′ tag′, an identification tag fastened to the ear of an animal.

earth (ûrth), *n.* **1.** (*often cap.*) the planet third in order from the sun, having an equatorial diameter of 7926 mi. (12,755 km) and a polar diameter of 7900 mi. (12,714 km), a mean distance from the sun of 92.9 million mi. (149.6 million km), and a period of revolution of 365.26 days, and having one satellite. See table under **planet. 2.** the inhabitants of this planet, esp. the human inhabitants: *The whole earth rejoiced.* **3.** this planet as the habitation of humans, often in contrast to heaven and hell: *to create a hell on earth.* **4.** the surface of this planet: *to fall to earth.* **5.** the solid matter of this planet; dry land; ground. **6.** soil and dirt, as distinguished from rock and sand; the softer part of the land. **7.** the hole of a burrowing animal; lair. **8.** *Chem.* any of several metallic oxides that are difficult to reduce, as alumina, zirconia, and yttria. Cf. **alkaline earth, rare earth. 9.** Also called **earth′ col′or.** *Fine Arts.* any of various pigments consisting chiefly of iron oxides and tending toward brown in hue. **10.** *Chiefly Brit. Elect.* a ground. **11.** *Archaic.* a land or country. **12. move heaven and earth.** See **heaven** (def. 7). **13. on earth,** in the world: *Where on earth have you been?* **14. run to earth, a.** *Hunting.* to chase (an animal) into its hole or burrow: *to run a fox to earth.* **b.** to search out; track down: *They ran the fugitive to earth in Algiers.* —*v.t.* **15.** *Chiefly Brit. Elect.* to ground. [bef. 950; ME *erthe,* OE *eorthe;* c. G *Erde,* D *aarde,* ON *jǫrth,* Dan *jord,* Goth *airtha*]
—Syn. 3. EARTH, GLOBE, WORLD are terms applied to the planet on which we dwell. EARTH is used esp. in speaking of a condition of existence contrasted with that in heaven or hell: *those who are yet on earth.* GLOBE formerly emphasized merely the roundness of the earth: *to circumnavigate the globe.* It is now used more like WORLD, with especial application to the inhabitants of the earth and their activities, interests, and concerns. In this sense, both GLOBE and WORLD are more inclusive than EARTH and are used more abstractly: *the politics of the globe; the future of the world; One World.*

Ear•tha (ûr′thə), *n.* a female given name.

earth′ al′mond, chufa. [1855–60]

earth′ art′, the artistic genre consisting of earthworks. Also called **land art.** [1965–70]

earth′ au′ger, a drill for boring holes in the ground, as to tap springs.

earth•born (ûrth′bôrn′), *adj.* **1.** born on or sprung from the earth; of earthly origin. **2.** mortal; human. [1595–1605; EARTH + BORN]

earth•bound[1] (ûrth′bound′), *adj.* **1.** firmly set in or attached to the earth. **2.** limited to the earth or its surface. **3.** having only earthly interests. **4.** lacking in imagination or sophistication: *earthbound prose.* Also, **earth′-bound′.** [1595–1605; EARTH + -BOUND[1]]

earth•bound[2] (ûrth′bound′), *adj.* headed for the earth: *an earthbound meteorite.* Also, **earth′-bound′.** [1930–35; EARTH + -BOUND[2]]

earth•en (ûr′thən), *adj.* **1.** composed of earth. **2.** worldly. [1175–1225; ME *erthen,* OE *eorthen.* See EARTH, -EN[2]]

earth•en•ware (ûr′thən wâr′), *n.* **1.** pottery of baked or hardened clay, esp. any of the coarse, opaque varieties. **2.** clay for making such pottery. [1640–50; EARTHEN + WARE[1]]

earth-god (ûrth′god′), *n.* a god of fertility and vegetation. Also, **earth′ god′.**

earth-god•dess (ûrth′god′is), *n.* a goddess of fertility and vegetation. Also, **earth′ god′dess.** [1875–80]

earth′ induc′tor com′pass, *Aeron.* a compass actuated by induction from the earth's magnetic field.

earth•light (ûrth′līt′), *n. Astron.* earthshine. [1825–35; EARTH + LIGHT[1]]

earth•ling (ûrth′ling), *n.* **1.** an inhabitant of earth; mortal. **2.** worldling. [1585–95; EARTH + -LING[1]]

earth′ lodge′, a circular, usually dome-shaped dwelling of certain North American Indians, made of posts and beams covered variously with branches, grass, sod, or earth and having a central opening in the roof, a tamped earth floor, and frequently a vestibule.

earth•ly (ûrth′lē), *adj.,* **-li•er, -li•est. 1.** of or pertaining to the earth, esp. as opposed to heaven; worldly. **2.** possible or conceivable: *an invention of no earthly use to anyone.* [bef. 1000; ME *erth(e)ly,* OE *eorthlic.* See EARTH, -LY] **—earth′li•ness,** *n.*
—Syn. 1. secular, temporal, mortal. EARTHLY, TERRESTRIAL, WORLDLY, MUNDANE refer to that which is concerned with the earth literally or figuratively. EARTHLY now almost always implies a contrast to that which is heavenly: *earthly pleasures; our earthly home.* TERRESTRIAL, from Latin, is the dignified equivalent of EARTHLY, and it applies to the earth as a planet or to the land as opposed to the water: *the terrestrial globe; terrestrial areas.* WORLDLY is commonly used in the sense of being devoted to the vanities, cares, advantages, or gains of this present life to the exclusion of spiritual interests or the life to come: *worldly success; worldly standards.* MUNDANE, from Latin, is a formal equivalent of WORLDLY and suggests that which is bound to the earth, is not exalted, and therefore is commonplace: *mundane pursuits.* **—Ant. 1.** spiritual, divine.

earth•man (ûrth′man′, -mən), *n., pl.* **-men** (-men′, -mən). a human inhabitant or native of the planet Earth. [1855–60; EARTH + MAN[1]]

earth′ moth′er, 1. the earth conceived of as the female principle of fertility and the source of all life. **2.** a female spirit or deity serving as a symbol of life or fertility. **3.** a sensuous, maternal woman. Also, **Earth′ Moth′er.** [1900–05]

earth•mov•er (ûrth′mo͞o′vər), *n.* a vehicle, as a bulldozer, for pushing or carrying excavated earth from place to place. [1940–45; EARTH + MOVER]

earth•mov•ing (ûrth′mo͞o′ving), *adj.* of or pertaining to earthmovers: *earthmoving machinery.* [1935–40; EARTH + MOVING]

earth•nut (ûrth′nut′), *n.* **1.** any of various roots, tubers, or underground growths, as the peanut and the truffle. **2.** any of the plants producing these. [bef. 900; ME *erthenote,* OE *eorthnutu.* See EARTH, NUT]

earth•pea (ûrth′pē′), *n.* the peanut. [EARTH + PEA[1]]

earth•per•son (ûrth′pûr′sən), *n.* a human inhabitant or native of the planet Earth. [EARTH + -PERSON]

earth′ pil′lar, *Geol.* a pillar of earthy matter left by erosion of the surrounding ground. [1865–70]

earth•quake (ûrth′kwāk′), *n.* **1.** a series of vibrations induced in the earth's crust by the abrupt rupture and rebound of rocks in which elastic strain has been slowly accumulating. **2.** something that is severely disruptive; upheaval. [1300–50; ME *erthequake* (see EARTH, QUAKE), r. OE *eorthdyne* (see DIN)]
—Syn. 1. quake, tremor, shock, seism, temblor.

Earth′ Re′sources Technol′ogy Sat′ellite, former name of **Landsat.** *Abbr.:* ERTS

earth•rise (ûrth′rīz′), *n. Astron.* the rising of the earth above the horizon of the moon or other celestial body, viewed from that body's surface or from a spacecraft orbiting it. [1965–70; EARTH + (SUN)RISE]

earth′ sci′ence, any of various sciences, as geography, geology, or meteorology, that deal with the earth, its composition, or any of its changing aspects. Also called **geoscience.** [1935–40] **—earth′ sci′entist.**

earth•shak•ing (ûrth′shā′king), *adj.* imperiling, challenging, or affecting basic beliefs, attitudes, relationships, etc. [1350–1400; ME. See EARTH, SHAKING] **—earth′shak′er,** *n.*

earth-shat•ter•ing (ûrth′shat′ər ing), *adj.* earthshaking.

earth•shine (ûrth′shīn′), *n. Astron.* the faint illumination of the part of the moon not illuminated by sunlight, as during a crescent phase, caused by the reflection of light from the earth. Also called **earthlight.** [1825–35; EARTH + SHINE]

earth′ sign′, any of the three astrological signs, Taurus, Virgo, or Capricorn, that are grouped together because of the shared attributes of practicality and interest in material things. Cf. **triplicity.**

earth•star (ûrth′stär′), *n.* **1.** a fungus of the genus *Geaster,* having an outer covering that splits into the form of a star. **2.** any of various bromeliads of the genus *Cryptanthus,* native to Brazil, having rosettes of stiff, prickly leaves. [1810–20; EARTH + STAR]

earth′ sta′tion, a terminal equipped to receive, or receive and transmit, signals from or to communications satellites. Also called **ground station.** [1965–70]

earth′ tone′, any of various warm, muted colors ranging basically from neutral to deep brown. [1970–75]

earth′ tongue′, any of a group of fungi of the phylum Ascomycota, characterized by a tongue-shaped fruiting body, found on decaying logs and damp soil.

earth•ward (ûrth′wərd), *adv.* **1.** Also, **earth′wards.** toward the earth. —*adj.* **2.** directed toward the earth. [1350–1400; ME *ertheward.* See EARTH, -WARD]

earth′ wave′, *Geol.* any elastic wave traveling through the material of the earth, as a wave caused by an earthquake.

earth•wom•an (ûrth′wo͝om′ən), *n., pl.* **-wom•en.** a female inhabitant or native of the planet Earth. [1900–05; EARTH(MAN) + WOMAN]

earth•work (ûrth′wûrk′), *n.* **1.** excavation and piling of earth in connection with an engineering operation. **2.** *Mil.* a construction formed chiefly of earth for protection against enemy fire, used in both offensive and defensive operations. **3.** an artistic work that consists of a large-scale alteration or modification of an area of land in a configuration designed by an artist or of an artist's sculptural installation, as in a museum or gallery, of soil, rock, or similar elemental materials. [1625–35; EARTH + WORK]

earth•worm (ûrth′wûrm′), *n.* **1.** any one of numerous annelid worms that burrow in soil and feed on soil nutrients and decaying organic matter. **2.** *Archaic.* a mean or groveling person. [1400–50; late ME *ertheworm.* See EARTH, WORM]
—Regional Variation. The EARTHWORM, a commonly used bait for angling, is also called an ANGLEWORM in the Northern U.S. and a FISHWORM in the Northern and Midland U.S. and in New England. It is called a FISHING WORM in parts of the Midland and Southern U.S., and a WIGGLER in the Southern U.S.
Because the worm often comes to the surface of the earth when the ground is cool or wet, it is also called a NIGHTWALKER in New England, a NIGHTCRAWLER, chiefly in the Northern, North Midland, and Western U.S., and a DEW WORM, chiefly in the Inland North and Canada. It is also called a RED WORM in the North Central, South Midland, and Southern U.S.

earth•y (ûr′thē), *adj.,* **earth•i•er, earth•i•est. 1.** of the nature of or consisting of earth or soil. **2.** characteristic of earth: *an earthy smell.* **3.** realistic; practical. **4.** coarse or unrefined: *an earthy sense of humor.* **5.** direct; robust; unaffected: *an earthy, generous woman.* **6.** (of a mineral) having a dull luster and rough to the touch. **7.** *Archaic.* worldly; pertaining to the earth. [1350–1400; ME *erthy.* See EARTH, -Y[1]] **—earth′i•ly,** *adv.* **—earth′i•ness,** *n.*
—Syn. 4. lusty, rough. **—Ant. 4.** genteel, refined.

ear′ trum′pet, a trumpet-shaped device held to the ear for collecting and intensifying sounds and once commonly used as an aid to hearing. [1770–80]

ear•wax (ēr′waks′), *n.* a yellowish, waxlike secretion from certain glands in the external auditory canal; cerumen. [1350–1400; ME *erewax.* See EAR[1], WAX[1]]

ear•wig (ēr′wig′), *n., v.,* **-wigged, -wig•ging.** —*n.* **1.** any of numerous elongate, nocturnal insects of the order Dermaptera, having a pair of large, movable pincers at the rear of the abdomen. —*v.t.* **2.** to fill the mind of with prejudice by insinuations. [bef. 1000; ME *erwigge,* OE *ēarwicga* ear insect; from the notion that it enters people's ears. See WIGGLE]

ear•wit•ness (ēr′wit′nis), *n. Law.* a person who testifies or can testify to what he or she has heard. [1585–95; EAR[1] + WITNESS]

ear wrap a small ornament worn on the rim of the ear, shaped so as to grip the rim gently instead of piercing or squeezing it. Also called **ear band.**

ease (ēz), *n., v.,* **eased, eas•ing.** —*n.* **1.** freedom from labor, pain, or physical annoyance; tranquil rest; comfort: *to enjoy one's ease.* **2.** freedom from concern, anxiety, or solicitude; a quiet state of mind: *to be at ease about one's health.* **3.** freedom from difficulty or great effort; facility: *It can be done with ease.* **4.** freedom from financial need; plenty: *a life of ease on a moderate income.* **5.** freedom from stiffness, constraint, or formality; unaffectedness: *ease of manner; the ease and elegance of her poetry.* **6. at ease.** *Mil.* a position of rest in which soldiers may relax but may not leave their places or talk. —*v.t.* **7.** to free from anxiety or care: *to ease one's mind.* **8.** to mitigate, lighten, or lessen: *to ease pain.* **9.** to release from pressure, tension, or the like. **10.** to move or shift with great care: *to ease a car into a narrow parking space.* **11.** to render less difficult; facilitate: *I'll help if it will ease your job.* **12.** to provide (an architectural member) with an easement. **13.** *Shipbuilding.* to trim (a timber of a wooden hull) so as to fair its surface into the desired form of the hull. **14.** *Naut.* **a.** to bring (the helm or rudder of a vessel) slowly amidships. **b.** to bring the head of (a vessel) into the wind. **c.** to slacken or lessen the hold upon (a rope). **d.** to lessen the hold of (the brake of a windlass). —*v.i.* **15.** to abate in severity, pressure, tension, etc. (often fol. by *off* or *up*). **16.** to become less painful, burdensome, etc. **17.** to move, shift, or be moved or be shifted with great care. **18. ease out,** to remove from a position of authority, a job, or the like, esp. by methods intended to be tactful: *He was eased out as division head to make way for the boss's nephew.* [1175–1225; (n.) ME *ese, eise* < AF *ese,* OF *aise, eise* comfort, convenience < VL **adjace(m),* acc. of **adjacēs* vicinity (cf. ML *in aiace* in (the) vicinity), the regular outcome of L *adjacēns* ADJACENT, taken in VL as a n. of the type *nūbēs,* acc. *nūbem* cloud; (v.) ME *esen* < AF *e(i)ser,* OF *aisier,* deriv. of the n.]
—Syn. 1. repose, contentment, effortlessness. EASE, COMFORT refer to a sense of relaxation or of well-being. EASE implies a relaxed condition with an absence of effort or pressure: *a life of ease.* COMFORT suggests a sense of well-being, along with ease, which produces a quiet happiness and contentment: *comfort in one's old age.* **2.** tranquillity, serenity, calmness, peace. **5.** naturalness, informality. **7.** comfort, relieve, disburden; tranquilize, soothe. **8.** alleviate, assuage, allay, abate, reduce. **—Ant. 1.** discomfort, effort. **2.** disturbance. **5.** stiffness, formality, tenseness.

ease•ful (ēz′fəl), *adj.* comfortable; quiet; peaceful; restful. [1325–75; ME *eisefull.* See EASE, -FUL] **—ease′ful•ly,** *adv.* **—ease′ful•ness,** *n.*

ea•sel (ē′zəl), *n.* **1.** a stand or frame for supporting or displaying at an angle an artist's canvas, a blackboard, a china plate, etc. **2.** Also called **masking frame.** *Photog.* a frame, often with adjustable masks, used to hold photographic paper flat and control borders when printing enlargements. [1625–35; < D *ezel* ass, easel (c. G *Esel,* OE *esol* ass) < VL **asilus,* for L *asellus,* dim. of *asinus* ASS[1]] **—ea′seled,** *adj.*

ease•ment (ēz′mənt), *n.* **1.** *Law.* a right held by one property owner to make use of the land of another for a limited purpose, as right of passage. **2.** an easing; relief. **3.** something that gives ease; a convenience. **4.** *Archit.* a curved joint. [1350–1400; ME *esement* < OF *aisement,* equiv. to *aise* EASE + *-ment* -MENT]

eas•i•er (ē′zē ər), *adj.* comparative of **easy.**

eas•i•est (ē′zē ist), *adj.* superlative of **easy.**

eas•i•ly (ē′zə lē, ēz′lē), *adv.* **1.** in an easy manner; with ease; without trouble: *The traffic moved along easily.* **2.** beyond question; by far: *easily the best.* **3.** likely; well: *He may easily change his mind.* [1250–1300; ME *esily.* See EASY, -LY]
—Syn. 2. certainly, surely, clearly, plainly.

eas•i•ness (ē′zē nis), *n.* **1.** the quality or condition of being easy. **2.** ease of manner; carelessness; indifference. [1350–1400; ME *esinesse.* See EASY, -NESS]

Eas•ley (ēz′lē), *n.* a town in NW South Carolina. 14,264.

east (ēst), *n.* **1.** a cardinal point of the compass, 90° to the right of north. *Abbr:* E **2.** the direction in which this point lies. **3.** (*usually cap.*) a quarter or territory situated in this direction. **4. the East, a.** the parts of Asia collectively lying east of Europe and including Asia Minor, Syria, Arabia, India, China, etc.; the Orient. **b.** the Far East. **c.** the Soviet Union and its allies. **d.** the part of the U.S. east of the Mississippi River. **e.** the part of the U.S. east of the Allegheny Mountains. **f.** New England. **g.** *Ancient and Medieval Hist.* the Eastern Roman Empire. —*adj.* **5.** directed or proceeding toward the east. **6.** coming from the east: *an east wind.* **7.** lying toward or situated in the east: *the east side.* **8.** *Eccles.* being at the end of the church where the high altar

CONCISE ETYMOLOGY KEY: <, descended or borrowed from; >, whence; b., blend of, blended; c., cognate with; cf., compare; deriv., derivative; equiv., equivalent; imit., imitative; obl., oblique; r., replacing; s., stem; sp., spelling, spelled; resp., respelling, respelled; trans., translation; ?, origin unknown; *, unattested; ‡, probably earlier than. See the full key inside the front cover.

is: *an east window.* —*adv.* **9.** to, toward, or in the east: *an island located east of Sumatra; He went east.* [bef. 900; ME *est,* OE *ēast;* c. G *ost,* ON *austr;* akin to L *aurōra,* Gk *aúōs* (dial. var. of *ēōs, héōs*) dawn. See EASTER] —**east′ness,** *n.*

East., eastern. Also, **east.**

East′ An′glia, an early English kingdom in SE Britain: modern Norfolk and Suffolk. See map under **Mercia.** —**East′ An′glian.**

East′ A′sia, the countries and land area of the People's Republic of China, Hong Kong, Japan, Korea, Macao, Mongolia, Taiwan, and the Russian Federation in Asia. —**East′ A′sian.**

East′ Austral′ia Cur′rent, the part of the South Equatorial Current flowing S along the E coast of Australia.

East′ Bengal′, formerly a part of the Indian province of Bengal; now coextensive with Bangladesh. Cf. **Bengal** (def. 1).

East′ Berlin′. See under **Berlin** (def. 2).

east•bound (ēst′bound′), *adj.* traveling, proceeding, or headed east: *an eastbound train.* [1875–80, *Amer.;* EAST + -BOUND[2]]

East•bourne (ēst′bôrn, -bōrn, -bərn), *n.* a seaport in East Sussex, in SE England. 72,700.

east′ by north′, *Navig., Survey.* a point on the compass 11°15′ north of east. *Abbr.:* EbN

east′ by south′, *Navig., Survey.* a point on the compass 11°15′ south of east. *Abbr.:* EbS

East′ Cape′. See **Dezhnev, Cape.**

East′ Chica′go, a port in NW Indiana, on Lake Michigan, near Chicago. 39,786.

East′ Chi′na Sea′, a part of the N Pacific, bounded by China, Japan, the Ryukyus, and Taiwan. 480,000 sq. mi. (1,243,200 sq. km). Also called **Dong Hai.**

East′ Cleve′land, a city in NE Ohio, near Cleveland. 36,957.

East′ Coast′, the region of the U.S. bordering on the Atlantic Ocean.

East′ Detroit′, a city in SE Michigan. 38,280.

East′ End′, a section of E London, England.

Eas•ter (ē′stər), *n.* **1.** an annual Christian festival in commemoration of the resurrection of Jesus Christ, observed on the first Sunday after the first full moon after the vernal equinox, as calculated according to tables based in Western churches on the Gregorian calendar and in Orthodox churches on the Julian calendar. **2.** Also called **Easter Sunday.** the day on which this festival is celebrated. **3.** the Easter season; the week following Easter. [bef. 900; ME *ester,* OE *ēastre;* c. G *Ostern;* orig. name of a goddess and her festival; akin to EAST]

Eas′ter cac′tus, an epiphytic cactus, *Rhipsalidopsis gaertneri,* native to Brazil, having oblong joints and red flowers.

Eas′ter can′dle, *Rom. Cath. Ch.* See **paschal candle.**

Eas′ter dai′sy, a nearly stemless composite plant, *Townsendia exscapa,* of the Rocky Mountain regions, having stalkless purplish or white flowers in a rosette of narrow leaves. [so called because its flowers appear at Easter time]

Eas′ter egg′, a chicken egg that is dyed and often given a figure or design, or an imitation of such an egg, as an egg-shaped candy or chocolate, used at Easter as a gift or decoration. [1795–1805]

Eas′ter egg′ chick′en, Araucana.

Eas′ter Is′land, an island in the S Pacific, W of and belonging to Chile. ab. 45 sq. mi. (117 sq. km): gigantic statues. Also called **Rapa Nui.** Spanish, **Isla de Pascua.**

Eas′ter lil′y, any of several white-flowered lilies that are artificially brought into bloom in early spring, esp. *Lilium longiflorum eximium,* native to Taiwan and widely cultivated. [1875–80]

east•er•ling (ē′stər ling), *n. Archaic.* a native of a country lying to the east, esp. a merchant from the Baltic. [1375–1425; late ME *esterling,* equiv. to *ester* eastern (perh. repr. OE *ēastra,* comp. of *ēast* adj.) + -LING[1]]

east•er•ly (ē′stər lē), *adj., adv., n., pl.* **-lies.** —*adj.* **1.** moving, directed, or situated toward the east: *an easterly course.* **2.** (esp. of a wind) coming from the east. —*adv.* **3.** toward the east. **4.** from the east. —*n.* **5.** a wind that blows from the east. [1540–50; obs. *easter* eastern (see EASTERLING) + -LY] —**east′er•li•ness,** *n.*

east′erly wave′, a westward-moving, wavelike disturbance of low atmospheric pressure embedded in tropical easterly winds.

Eas′ter Mon′day, the day after Easter, observed as a holiday in some places. [1350–1400; ME]

east•ern (ē′stərn), *adj.* **1.** lying toward or situated in the east: *the eastern half of the island.* **2.** directed or proceeding toward the east: *an eastern route.* **3.** coming from the east: *an eastern wind.* **4.** (*often cap.*) of or pertaining to the East in the U.S.: *an eastern Congressman.* **5.** (*cap.*) of or pertaining to the Eastern Church or to any of the churches comprising it. **6.** (*usually cap.*) Oriental. **7.** (*usually cap.*) of or pertaining to the Soviet Union and its allies. [bef. 1000; ME *esterne,* OE *ēasterne;* akin to ON *austroenn,* OHG *ōstrōni.* See EAST, -ERN]

East′ern A′den Protec′torate, a former British protectorate, now the E part of the People's Democratic Republic of Yemen: composed of the Arab sheikdoms of Hadhramaut and the island of Socotra.

East′ern Algon′quian, a subgroup of the Algonquian language family, comprising the languages spoken aboriginally from Nova Scotia to northeastern North Carolina.

East′ern Church′, **1.** any of the churches originating in countries formerly part of the Eastern Roman Empire, observing an Eastern rite and adhering to the Niceno-Constantinopolitan Creed; Byzantine Church. **2.** See **Orthodox Church** (def. 2). [1585–95]

east′ern cor′al snake′. See under **coral snake.**

east′ern di′amondback rat′tlesnake, an extremely venomous diamondback rattlesnake, *Crotalus adamanteus,* of the southeastern U.S.

East′ern Em′pire. See **Eastern Roman Empire.**

east•ern•er (ē′stər nər), *n.* (*often cap.*) a native or inhabitant of an eastern area, esp. of the eastern U.S. [1830–40, *Amer.;* EASTERN + -ER[1]]

East′ern Ghats′, a low mountain range in S India along the E margin of the Deccan plateau and parallel to the coast of the Bay of Bengal.

East′ern Hem′isphere, the eastern part of the terrestrial globe, including Asia, Africa, Australia, and Europe.

east′ern hem′lock, a hemlock, *Tsuga canadensis,* of eastern North America, having horizontal branches that often droop to the ground: the state tree of Pennsylvania. Also called **Canada hemlock.**

East′ern Hin′di, the vernacular of the eastern half of the Hindi-speaking area in India.

east•ern•ize (ē′stər nīz′), *v.t.,* **-ized, -iz•ing.** **1.** to influence with ideas, customs, etc., characteristic of the Orient. **2.** to influence with ideas, customs, etc., characteristic of the eastern U.S. Also, *esp. Brit.,* **east′ern•ise′.** [EASTERN + -IZE] —**east′ern•i•za′tion,** *n.*

east′ern king′bird. See under **kingbird.**

east′ern low′land goril′la. See under **gorilla.**

east′ern mead′owlark. See under **meadowlark.**

east•ern•most (ē′stərn mōst′ *or, esp. Brit.,* -məst), *adj.* farthest east. [1820–30; EASTERN + -MOST]

East′ern Or′thodox, of or pertaining to the Orthodox Church.

East′ern Or′thodox Church′. See **Orthodox Church** (def. 1).

East′ern Or′thodoxy, the faith, practice, membership, and government of the Eastern Orthodox Church.

east′ern red′ ce′dar. See **red cedar** (def. 1).

East′ern rite′, **1.** the rite of an Eastern church, usually observed in the national language of the country where the church is located. **2.** a Uniate church.

East′ern Ro′man Em′pire, the eastern part of the Roman Empire, esp. after the division in A.D. 395, having its capital at Constantinople: survived the fall of the Western Roman Empire in A.D. 476. Also called **Eastern Empire.** Cf. **Byzantine Empire.**

East′ern shore′, the eastern shore of Chesapeake Bay, including parts of Maryland, Delaware, and Virginia.

East′ern Slavs′. See under **Slav** (def. 1).

East′ern Sudan′ic, a group of languages belonging to the Nilo-Saharan family, spoken in eastern and central Africa and including the Nilotic languages.

East′ern Thrace′. See under **Thrace** (def. 2).

East′ern time′. See under **standard time.** Also called **East′ern Stand′ard Time′.** [1880–85, *Amer.*]

East′ern Tur′kestan. See under **Turkestan.**

Eas′ter sep′ulcher, sepulcher (def. 2).

Eas′ter Sun′day, Easter (def. 2).

Eas•ter•tide (ē′stər tīd′), *n.* **1.** Easter time. **2.** the week following Easter. **3.** the 50 days between Easter and Whitsuntide. [1100–50; ME *Estertyde,* late OE *Eastren tyde.* See EASTER, TIDE[1]]

East′ Flan′ders, a province in W Belgium. 1,325,419; 1150 sq. mi. (2980 sq. km). *Cap.:* Ghent.

East′ Fri′sian Is′lands. See under **Frisian Islands.**

East′ Gar′y, former name of **Lake Station.**

East′ German′ic, a branch of the Germanic languages no longer extant, comprising Gothic and probably others of which there are no written records. *Abbr.:* EGmc [1900–05]

East′ Ger′many, a former country in central Europe: created in 1949 from the Soviet zone of occupied Germany established in 1945: reunited with West Germany in 1990. 16,340,000; 41,827 sq. mi. (108,333 sq. km). *Cap.:* East Berlin. Official name, **German Democratic Republic.** Cf. **Germany.** —**East′ Ger′man.**

East′ Goth′, an Ostrogoth.

East′ Grand′ Rap′ids, a town in W central Michigan, near Grand Rapids. 10,914.

East′ Green′land cur′rent, a cold ocean current of low salinity flowing south along the east coast of Greenland.

East′ Green′wich (gren′ich), a town in central Rhode Island. 10,211.

East′ Gwil′lim•bur•y (gwil′əm ber′ē, -bə rē), *n.* a town in S Ontario, in S Canada. 12,565.

East′ Ham′, a former borough, now part of Newham, in SE England, near London.

East•hamp•ton (ēst′hamp′tən), *n.* a city in W Massachusetts. 15,580.

East′ Hart′ford, a town in central Connecticut. 52,563.

East′ Ha′ven, a town in S Connecticut, near New Haven. 25,028.

East′ In′dia Com′pany, **1.** the company chartered by the English government in 1600 to carry on trade in the East Indies: dissolved in 1874. **2.** any similar company, as one chartered by the Dutch (1602–1798), the French (1664–1769), or the Danes (1729–1801).

East′ In′dian lo′tus. See **Indian lotus.**

East′ In′dian wal′nut, lebbek.

East′ In′dies, **1.** Also called **the Indies, Indonesia.** SE Asia, including India, Indonesia, and the Malay Archipelago. **2.** the Malay Archipelago. Also called **East′ In′dia.** —**East′ In′dian.**

east•ing (ē′sting), *n.* **1.** *Navig.* the distance due east made good on any course tending eastward; easterly departure. **2.** a shifting eastward; easterly direction. **3.** *Survey.* a distance east from a north-south reference line. [1620–30; EAST + -ING[1]]

east′ing down′, *Naut.* **1.** the passage eastward from the Cape of Good Hope, as made by a sailing ship bound for Australia or the East Indies. **2.** the passage eastward from Australia, as made by a sailing ship bound for Cape Horn.

East′ I′slip, a town on the S shore of Long Island, in SE New York. 13,852.

East′ Kil•bride′ (kil brīd′), **1.** an administrative district in the Strathclyde region, in S Scotland. 83,441; 1300 sq. mi. (3367 sq. km). **2.** a town in this district. 32,000.

East•lake (ēst′lāk′), *n.* **1. Sir Charles Locke,** 1836–1906, English architect, designer, and author. **2.** a city in NE Ohio. 22,104.

East•land (ēst′lənd), *n.* **James O(liver),** 1904–86, U.S. politician: senator 1941, 1943–78.

East′ Lan′sing, a city in S Michigan. 43,309.

East′ Liv′erpool, a city in E Ohio, on the Ohio River. 16,687. —**East′ Liverpud′lian.**

East′ Lon′don, a seaport in the SE Cape of Good Hope province, in the S Republic of South Africa. 130,000. —**East′ Lon′doner.**

East′ Long′mead•ow (lông′med′ō, long′-), a city in SW Massachusetts. 12,905.

East′ Los′ An′geles, a city in SW California, near Los Angeles. 110,017.

East′ Lo′thi•an (lō′thē ən), a historic county in SE Scotland.

East′ Lyme′ (līm), a town in SE Connecticut. 13,870.

East•man (ēst′mən), *n.* **1. George,** 1854–1932, U.S. philanthropist and inventor in the field of photography. **2. Max For•res•ter** (fôr′ə stər, for′-), 1883–1969, U.S. editor and writer.

East′ Massape′qua, a town on SW Long Island, in SE New York. 13,987.

East′ Mead′ow, a town on W Long Island, in SE New York. 39,317.

East′ Moline′, a city in NW Illinois. 20,907.

east•most (ēst′mōst′ *or, esp. Brit.,* -məst), *adj.* easternmost. [1275–1325; ME *estmest,* OE *ēastmest.* See EAST, -MOST]

east-north•east (ēst′nôrth′ēst′; *Naut.* ēst′nôr′ēst′), *Navig., Survey.* —*n.* **1.** the point on a compass midway between east and northeast. —*adj.* **2.** coming from this point: *an east-northeast wind.* **3.** directed toward this point: *an east-northeast course.* —*adv.* **4.** toward this point: *sailing east-northeast. Abbr.:* ENE

East′ North′port, a town on NW Long Island, in SE New York. 20,187.

Eas•ton (ē′stən), *n.* **1.** a city in E Pennsylvania, on the Delaware River. 26,027. **2.** a city in SE Massachusetts. 16,623.

East′ Or′ange, a city in NE New Jersey, near Newark. 77,025.

East′ Pacif′ic Rise′, a long north-south elevation of the sea floor in the E Pacific Ocean extending southward from SW Mexico to the Antarctic Ocean.

East′ Pak′istan, former name of **Bangladesh.**

East′ Pal′o Al′to, a town in W central California, on the S shore of San Francisco Bay. 18,191.

East′ Pat′erson, former name of **Elmwood Park** (def. 2).

East′ Peo′ria, a city in central Illinois, near Peoria. 22,385.

East′ Point′, a city in N Georgia, near Atlanta. 37,486.

East′ Prov′idence, a town in NE Rhode Island, near Providence. 50,980.

East′ Prus′sia, a former province in NE Germany: an enclave separated from Germany by the Polish Corridor; now divided between Poland and the Russian Federation. 14,283 sq. mi. (36,993 sq. km). *Cap.:* Königsberg. German, **Ostpreussen.** —**East′ Prus′sian.**

East′ Punjab′, the eastern part of the former province of Punjab, in British India: now part of Punjab state, India. —**East′ Punjab′i.**

East′ Ridge′, a city in SE Tennessee, near Chattanooga. 21,236.

East′ Ri′ding, (rī′ding), a former administrative division of Yorkshire, in NE England, now part of Humberside.

East′ Riv′er, a strait in SE New York separating Manhattan Island from Long Island and connecting New York Bay and Long Island Sound.

East′ Rock′away, a town in SE New York. 10,917.

East′ Side′, **1.** the eastern section of Manhattan, in New York City, lying to the east of Fifth Avenue. **2.** of, pertaining to, or located in this section: *East Side shops.* Also, **East′side′.** [1880–85, *Amer.*]

East′ Sid′er (sī′dər), a native or resident of the East

Side of Manhattan, in New York City. Also, **East′sid′er.** [1900–05, *Amer.*; EAST SIDE + -ER[1]]

east-south•east (ēst′south′ēst′; *Naut.* ēst′sou′ēst′), *Navig., Survey.* —*n.* **1.** the point on a compass midway between east and southeast. —*adj.* **2.** coming from this point: *an east-southeast wind.* **3.** directed toward this point: *an east-southeast course.* —*adv.* **4.** toward this point: *sailing east-southeast. Abbr.:* ESE

East St. Louis, a city in SW Illinois, across the Mississippi River from St. Louis, Missouri. 55,200. —**East St. Louisan.**

East′ Suf′folk, a former administrative division of Suffolk county, in E England.

East′ Sus′sex, a county in SE England. 657,300; 693 sq. mi. (1795 sq. km).

east•ward (ēst′wərd), *adv.* **1.** Also, **east′wards.** toward the east. —*adj.* **2.** moving, bearing, facing, or situated toward the east. —*n.* **3.** the eastward part, direction, or point. [bef. 850; ME *estward,* OE *ēasteweard.* See EAST, -WARD]

east•ward•ly (ēst′wərd lē), *adj.* **1.** having an eastward direction or situation. **2.** coming from the east: *an eastwardly wind.* —*adv.* **3.** toward the east. **4.** from the east. [1660–70; EASTWARD + -LY]

East-West (ēst′west′), *adj.* occurring between the East and the West, esp. occurring between the Soviet Union and the U.S.: *East-West trade; East-West relations.* [1955–60]

eas•y (ē′zē), *adj.,* **eas•i•er, eas•i•est,** *adv., n.* —*adj.* **1.** not hard or difficult; requiring no great labor or effort: *a book that is easy to read; an easy victory.* **2.** free from pain, discomfort, worry, or care: *He led an easy life.* **3.** providing or conducive to ease or comfort; comfortable: *an easy stance; an easy relationship.* **4.** fond of or given to ease; easygoing: *an easy disposition.* **5.** not harsh or strict; lenient: *an easy master.* **6.** not burdensome or oppressive: *easy terms on a loan.* **7.** not difficult to influence or overcome; compliant: *an easy prey; an easy mark.* **8.** free from formality, constraint, or embarrassment: *He has an easy manner.* **9.** effortlessly clear and fluent: *an easy style of writing.* **10.** readily comprehended or mastered: *an easy language to learn.* **11.** not tight or constricting: *an easy fit.* **12.** not forced or hurried; moderate: *an easy pace.* **13.** not steep; gradual: *an easy flight of stairs.* **14.** *Com.* **a.** (of a commodity) not difficult to obtain; in plentiful supply and often weak in price. **b.** (of the market) not characterized by eager demand. **15.** *Naut.* **a.** (of a bilge) formed in a long curve so as to make a gradual transition between the bottom and sides of a vessel; slack. **b.** (of the run of a hull) having gently curved surfaces leading from the middle body to the stern; not abrupt. —*adv.* **16.** *Informal.* in an easy manner; comfortably: *to go easy; take it easy.* —*n.* **17.** a word formerly used in communications to represent the letter *E.* [1150–1200; ME *aisie, esy* < AF *(a)eisie,* OF *aisié, aised,* ptp. of *aisier* to EASE] —**eas′y•like′,** *adj.*
—**Syn. 2.** tranquil, untroubled, comfortable, contented, quiet. **8.** smooth, unconstrained. —**Ant. 1.** difficult. **2.** agitated. **3.** uncomfortable.

eas•y-care (ē′zē kâr′), *adj.* requiring little care or maintenance: *easy-care fabrics; easy-care furniture.* [1955–60]

eas′y chair′, 1. an upholstered armchair for lounging. **2.** *Obs.* See **wing chair.** [1700–10]

eas•y•go•ing (ē′zē gō′ing), *adj.* **1.** calm and unworried; relaxed and rather casual: *an easygoing person.* **2.** going easily, as a horse. Also, **eas′y-go′ing.** [1665–75; EASY + GOING] —**eas′y•go′ing•ness,** *n.*

eas′y lis′tening, middle-of-the-road (def. 3).

eas′y mon′ey, 1. money obtained with a minimum of effort. **2.** money obtained by deception, fraud, artifice, etc. [1895–1900, *Amer.*]

eas′y street′, a state of wealth, financial independence, or ease. Also, **Eas′y Street′.** [1900–05, *Amer.*]

eat (ēt), *v.,* **ate** (āt; *esp. Brit.* et) or (*Archaic*) **eat** (et, ēt); **eat•en** or (*Archaic*) **eat** (et, ēt); **eat•ing;** *n.* —*v.t.* **1.** to take into the mouth and swallow for nourishment; chew and swallow (food). **2.** to consume by or as if by devouring gradually; wear away; corrode: *The patient was eaten by disease and pain.* **3.** to make (a hole, passage, etc.), as by gnawing or corrosion. **4.** to ravage or devastate: *a forest eaten by fire.* **5.** to absorb wastefully; consume (often fol. by *up*): *Unexpected expenses have been eating up their savings.* **6.** *Slang (vulgar).* to perform cunnilingus or fellatio on. —*v.i.* **7.** to consume food; take a meal: *We'll eat at six o'clock.* **8.** to make a way, as by gnawing or corrosion: *Acid ate through the linoleum.* **9. be eating someone,** *Informal.* to worry, annoy, or bother: *Something seems to be eating him—he's been wearing a frown all day.* **10. eat away** or **into,** to destroy gradually, as by erosion: *For eons, the pounding waves ate away at the shoreline.* **11. eat crow.** See **crow**[1] (def. 7). **12. eat high off the hog.** See **hog** (def. 11). **13. eat humble pie.** See **humble pie** (def. 3). **14. eat in,** to eat or dine at home. **15. eat one's heart out.** See **heart** (def. 23). **16. eat one's terms.** See **term** (def. 16). **17. eat one's words.** See **word** (def. 14). **18. eat out,** to have a meal at a restaurant rather than at home. **19. eat out of one's hand.** See **hand** (def. 36). **20. eat someone out of house and home,** to eat so much as to strain someone's resources of food or money: *A group of hungry teenagers can eat you out of house and home.* **21. eat the wind out of,** *Naut.* to blanket (a sailing vessel sailing close-hauled) by sailing close on the weather side of. **22. eat up, a.** to consume wholly. **b.** to show enthusiasm for; take pleasure in: *The audience ate up everything he said.* **c.** to believe without question. —*n.* **23. eats,** *Informal.* food. [bef. 900; ME *eten,* OE *etan;* c. G *essen,* Goth *itan,* L *edere*] —**eat′er,** *n.*

eat•a•ble (ē′tə bəl), *adj.* **1.** edible. —*n.* **2.** Usually, **eatables.** articles of food. [1475–85; EAT + -ABLE]

eat•en (ēt′n), *v.* a pp. of **eat.**

eat•er•y (ē′tə rē), *n., pl.* **-er•ies.** *Informal.* a restaurant or other commercial establishment serving food. [1900–05, *Amer.*; EAT + -ERY]

eath (ēth, ēth), *adj., adv. Scot.* easy. [bef. 1000; ME *ethe, OE ēathe* (adv.); c. ON *auth-,* OHG *-ōdo;* akin to OE *ēadig,* Goth *audags* happy]

eat•ing (ē′ting), *n.* **1.** the act of a person or thing that eats. **2.** food with reference to its quality or tastiness when eaten: *This fish is delicious eating.* —*adj.* **3.** good or fit to eat, esp. raw (distinguished from *cooking*): *eating apples.* **4.** used in eating: *eating utensils.* [1125–75; ME; see EAT, -ING[1], -ING[2]]

Ea•ton (ēt′n), *n.* **1. Theophilus,** 1590–1658, English colonist and colonial administrator in America. **2.** a male given name.

Ea•ton•town (ēt′n toun′), *n.* a borough in E central New Jersey. 12,703.

Eau Claire (ō′ klâr′), a city in W Wisconsin. 51,509.

eau de Co•logne (ō′ də kə lōn′), cologne. [1795–1805]

eau de Ja•velle (ō′ də zha vel′, -zhə-; *Fr.* ōdᵊ zhavel′). See **Javel water.**

eau de toi•lette (ō′ də twä let′; *Fr.* ōdᵊ twa let′). See **toilet water.**

eau de vie (ōdᵊ vē′; *Eng.* ō′ də vē′), *French.* brandy, esp. a coarser and less purified variety. [lit., water of life; cf. AQUA VITAE]

eau de vie de marc (ōdᵊ vēdᵊ mar′; *Eng.* ō′ də vē′ də märk′), *French.* marc (def. 2).

eau mi•né•rale (ō mē nā ral′), *pl.,* **eaux mi•né•rales** (ō mē nā ral′). *French.* See **mineral water** (def. 1).

eave (ēv), *n.* Usually, **eaves.** the overhanging lower edge of a roof. [bef. 1000; ME *eves,* OE *efes;* c. OHG *obisa,* Goth *ubizwa* hall; cf. ABOVE, OVER] —**eaved,** *adj.*

eaves•drop (ēvz′drop′), *v.,* **-dropped, -drop•ping,** *n.* —*v.i.* **1.** to listen secretly to a private conversation. —*v.t.* **2.** *Archaic.* to eavesdrop on. —*n.* Also, **eaves•drip** (ēvz′drip′). **3.** water that drips from the eaves. **4.** the ground on which such water falls. [bef. 900; (n.) ME *evesdrope, evesdripe,* OE *yfesdrype;* as v., prob. back formation from *eavesdropper,* late ME *evisdroppyr,* appar. lit., one who stands on the *eavesdrop* in order to listen to conversations inside the house; see EAVE, DROP, DRIP] —**eaves′drop′per,** *n.*

eave′ spout′, *Chiefly New Eng.* waterspout (def. 1). Also, **eaves′ spout′.** [1885–90, *Amer.*]

eave′ trough′, *Northern U.S.* gutter (def. 3). Also, **eaves′ trough′, eaves′trough′.**

E•ban (ē′bən), *n.* **Ab•ba** (ä′bə), (*Aubrey Solomon Eban*), born 1915, Israeli political leader and diplomat, born in South Africa.

ebb (eb), *n.* **1.** the flowing back of the tide as the water returns to the sea (opposed to *flood, flow*). **2.** a flowing backward or away; decline or decay: *the ebb of a once great nation.* **3.** a point of decline: *His fortunes were at a low ebb.* —*v.i.* **4.** to flow back or away, as the water of a tide (opposed to *flow*). **5.** to decline or decay; fade away: *His life is gradually ebbing.* [bef. 1000; (n.) ME *eb(be),* OE *ebba;* c. OFris *ebba,* D *eb(be),* G *Ebbe* ebb, ON *efja* place where water backs up; (v.) ME *ebben,* OE *ebbian,* deriv. of the n.; akin to OFF]
—**Syn. 4.** subside, abate, recede, retire. **5.** dwindle, diminish, decrease.

ebb′ tide′, the reflux of the tide or the tide at ebb; ebb. [1830–40]

EBCDIC (eb′sē dik′), *n. Computers.* a code consisting of 256 8-bit characters and used for data representation and transfer. [1965–70; *e(xtended) b(inary-)c(oded) d(ecimal) i(nterchange) c(ode)*]

Eb•en•e•zer (eb′ə nē′zər), *n.* a male given name: from a Hebrew word meaning "stone of help."

E•ber•hart (ā′bər härt′, eb′ər-), *n.* **Richard,** born 1904, U.S. poet.

E•bert (ā′bərt; *Ger.* ā′bərt), *n.* **Frie•drich** (frē′drikh), 1871–1925, first president of Germany 1919–25.

Eb•la (eb′lə, ē′blə), *n.* an ancient city whose remains are located near Aleppo in present-day Syria, the site of the discovery in 1974–75 of cuneiform tablets **(Eb′la Tab′lets)** documenting a thriving culture of the third millennium B.C.

Eb•la•ite (eb′lə it′, ē′blə-), *n.* **1.** the Semitic language of the people of Ebla, believed to be closely related to Ugaritic, Phoenician, and Hebrew, but written in cuneiform characters borrowed from Sumerian: decoded from the Ebla Tablets. Cf. **Ebla. 2.** a member of these people. —*adj.* **3.** Also, **Eb•lan** (eb′lən, ē′blən). of or pertaining to Ebla, its people, or their language.

EbN, See **east by north.**

eb•on (eb′ən), *adj.* ebony (def. 6). [1350–1400; ME *eban, ebyn* ebony < AF *eban(ne),* OF *eban, ebaine* < ML *ebanus,* for L *(h)ebenus* < Gk *ébenos,* of Sem. orig.]

eb•on•ist (eb′ə nist), *n.* a worker in ebony. [1700–10; EBON(Y) + -IST]

eb•on•ite (eb′ə nīt′), *n.* vulcanite. [1860–65; EBON(Y) + -ITE[1]]

eb•on•ize (eb′ə nīz′), *v.t.,* **-ized, -iz•ing.** to stain or finish black in imitation of ebony. Also, *esp. Brit.,* **eb′on•ise′.** [1875–80; EBON(Y) + -IZE]

eb•on•y (eb′ə nē), *n., pl.* **-on•ies,** *adj.* —*n.* **1.** a hard, heavy, durable wood, most highly prized when black, from various tropical trees of the genus *Diospyros,* as *D. ebenum* of southern India and Sri Lanka, used for cabinetwork, ornamental objects, etc. **2.** any tree yielding such wood. **3.** any of various similar woods or trees. **4.** a deep, lustrous black. —*adj.* **5.** Also, **ebon.** made of ebony. **6.** of a deep, lustrous black. [1590–1600; earlier *hebeny;* -y perh. after IVORY]

eb′ony spleen′wort, a fern, *Asplenium platyneuron,* of woody areas of North America, having ladderlike leaves and shiny, dark brown stems. [1825–35, *Amer.*]

Eb•o•ra•cum (eb′ə rā′kəm), *n.* ancient name of **York, England.**

é•boule•ment (ā bo͞ol män′), *n., pl.* **-ments** (-män′) for 1. *French.* **1.** a collapse; cave-in. **2.** debris.

e•brac•te•ate (ē brak′tē āt′, -it), *adj. Bot.* having no bracts. [1820–30; < NL *ēbracteātus.* See E-, BRACTEATE]

E•bro (ē′brō; *Sp.* e′vrô), *n.* a river flowing SE from N Spain to the Mediterranean. ab. 470 mi. (755 km) long.

EbS, See **east by south.**

e•bul•lience (i bul′yəns, i bo͝ol′-), *n.* **1.** high spirits; exhilaration; exuberance. **2.** a boiling over; overflow. Also, **e•bul′lien•cy.** [1740–50; EBULLI(ENT) + -ENCE]

e•bul•lient (i bul′yənt, i bo͝ol′-), *adj.* **1.** overflowing with fervor, enthusiasm, or excitement; high-spirited: *The award winner was in an ebullient mood at the dinner in her honor.* **2.** bubbling up like a boiling liquid. [1590–1600; < L *ēbullient-* (s. of *ēbulliēns* boiling up, prp. of *ēbullīre*), equiv. to *ē-* E- + *bulli-* (deriv. of *bulla* a bubble) + *-ent-* -ENT] —**e•bul′lient•ly,** *adv.*

eb•ul•li•tion (eb′ə lish′ən), *n.* **1.** a seething or overflowing, as of passion or feeling; outburst. **2.** the state of being ebullient. **3.** the act or process of boiling up. **4.** a rushing forth of water, lava, etc., in a state of agitation. [1525–35; < L *ēbullītiōn-* (s. of *ēbullītiō*), equiv. to *ēbullīt(us)* (ptp. of *ēbullīre* to boil up *ēbulli-* (see EBULLIENT) + *-tus* ptp. suffix) + *-iōn-* -ION]

e•bur•na•tion (ē′bər nā′shən, eb′ər-), *n. Pathol.* an abnormal condition in which bone becomes hard and dense like ivory. [1830–40; < L *ebur*n*(us)* of ivory (equiv. to *ebur* IVORY + *-nus* adj. suffix) + -ATION]

EBV, See **Epstein-Barr virus.**

ec-, var. of **ex-**[3] before a consonant: *eccentric.*

EC, European Community.

E.C., 1. Engineering Corps. **2.** Established Church.

e.c., for the sake of example. [< L *exemplī causā*]

ECA, See **Economic Cooperation Administration.** Also, **E.C.A.**

e•cal•ca•rate (ē kal′kə rāt′), *adj. Bot., Zool.* having no spur or calcar. [1810–20; E- + CALCAR + -ATE[1]]

e•car•i•nate (ē kar′ə nāt′), *adj. Bot., Zool.* having no carina or keel. [E- + CARINATE]

é•car•té (ā′kär tā′; *Brit.* ā kär′tā; *Fr.* ā kar tā′), *n.* a card game for two players. [1815–25; < F]

e•cau•date (ē kô′dāt), *adj. Zool.* having no tail. [1840–50; < NL *ēcaudātus.* See E-, CAUDATE]

Ec•bat•a•na (ek bat′n ə), *n.* ancient name of **Hamadan.**

ec•bol•ic (ek bol′ik), *adj.* **1.** *Med.* promoting labor by increasing uterine contractions. —*n.* **2.** *Pharm.* an ecbolic drug. [1745–55; < Gk *ekbol(ḗ)* expulsion (equiv. to *ek-* EC- + *-bolē* a throwing) + -IC]

ec•ce ho•mo (ech′ā hō′mō, ek′ā *for 1;* ek′sē hō′mō, ek′ā *for 2*), *Latin.* **1.** "Behold the man!": the words with which Pilate presented Christ, crowned with thorns, to his accusers. John 19:5. **2.** *Art.* a painting, statue, or other representation of Christ crowned with thorns.

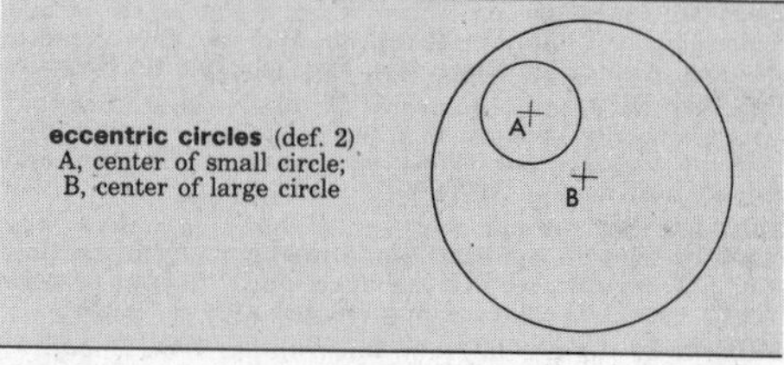

eccentric circles (def. 2)
A, center of small circle;
B, center of large circle

ec•cen•tric (ik sen′trik, ek-), *adj.* **1.** deviating from the recognized or customary character, practice, etc.; irregular; erratic; peculiar; odd: *eccentric conduct; an eccentric person.* **2.** *Geom.* not having the same center; not concentric: used esp. of two circles or spheres at least one of which contains the centers of both. **3.** (of an axis, axle, etc.) not situated in the center. **4.** *Mach.* having the axis or support away from the center: *an eccentric wheel.* **5.** *Astron.* deviating from a circular form, as an elliptic orbit. —*n.* **6.** a person who has an unusual, peculiar, or odd personality, set of beliefs, or behavior pattern. **7.** something that is unusual, peculiar, or odd. **8.** *Mach.* a device for converting circular motion into rectilinear motion, consisting of a disk fixed somewhat off-center to a revolving shaft, and working freely in a surrounding collar **(eccen′tric strap′),** to which a rod **(eccen′tric rod′)** is attached. Also, *esp. Brit.,* **excentric.** [1350–1400; < ML *eccentricus* < Gk *ékkentr(os)* out of center (see EC-, CENTER) + L *-icus* -IC] —**ec•cen′tri•cal,** *adj.* —**ec•cen′tri•cal•ly,** *adv.*
—**Syn. 1.** strange, weird, bizarre. —**Ant. 1.** normal, regular, ordinary, customary, conventional.

ec•cen•tric•i•ty (ek′sən tris′i tē, ek′sen-), *n., pl.* **-ties. 1.** an oddity or peculiarity, as of conduct: *an interesting man, known for his eccentricities.* **2.** the quality of being eccentric. **3.** the amount by which something is eccentric. **4.** *Mach.* the distance between the centers of two cylindrical objects one of which surrounds the other, as between an eccentric and the shaft on which it is mounted. **5.** *Math.* a constant expressed as the ratio of the distance from a point on a conic to a focus and the

CONCISE ETYMOLOGY KEY: <, descended or borrowed from; >, whence; b., blend of, blended; c., cognate with; cf., compare; deriv., derivative; equiv., equivalent; imit., imitative; obl., oblique; r., replacing; s., stem; sp., spelling, spelled; resp., respelling, respelled; trans., translation; ?, origin unknown; *, unattested; ‡, probably earlier than. See the full key inside the front cover.

distance from the point to the directrix. [1545–55; < ML *eccentricitās*, equiv. to *eccentric-* (see ECCENTRIC) + *-itās* -ITY]
—**Syn. 2.** queerness, strangeness, oddness, freakishness, aberration. ECCENTRICITY, PECULIARITY, QUIRK, IDIOSYNCRASY all refer to some noticeable deviation in behavior, style, or manner from what is normal or expected. ECCENTRICITY usually suggests a mildly amusing but harmless characteristic or style: *a whimsical eccentricity in choice of clothing.* PECULIARITY is the most general of these words, referring to almost any perceptible oddity or departure from any norm: *the peculiarity of his eyelashes, of the weather.* QUIRK often refers to a minor, unimportant kind of oddity: *Her one quirk was a habit of speaking to strangers in elevators.* Sometimes QUIRK has overtones of strangeness: *sexual quirks.* IDIOSYNCRASY refers to a variation in behavior or manner exclusive to or characteristic of a single individual: *idiosyncrasies of style that irritated editors but often delighted readers.*

ec•ce sig•num (ek′e sig′nŏŏm; *Eng.* ek′sē sig′nəm, ek′ā), *Latin.* behold the sign (or proof).

ec•chy•mo•sis (ek′ə mō′sis), *n., pl.* **-ses** (-sēz). *Pathol.* a discoloration due to extravasation of blood, as in a bruise. [1535–45; < NL < Gk *ekchýmōsis* extravasation, equiv. to *ek-* EC- + *chŷm(ós)* juice + *-ōsis* -OSIS] —**ec•chy•mot•ic** (ek′ə mot′ik), *adj.*

Eccl., Ecclesiastes. Also, **Eccles.**

eccl., **1.** ecclesiastic. **2.** ecclesiastical. Also, **eccles.**

Ec•cles (ek′əlz), *n.* **1. Sir John Ca•rew** (kə rōō′), born 1903, Australian physiologist: Nobel prize for medicine 1963. **2. Mar•ri•ner Stod•dard** (mar′ə nər stod′ərd), 1890–1977, U.S. economist and banker.

ec•cle•si•a (i klē′zhē ə, -zē ə), *n., pl.* **-si•ae** (-zhē ē′, -zē ē′). **1.** an assembly, esp. the popular assembly of ancient Athens. **2.** a congregation; church. [1570–80; < L < Gk *ekklēsía* assembly, equiv. to *ékklēt(os)* summoned (*ek-* EC- + *klē-*, var. of *kal-*, s. of *kaleîn* to call, + *-tos* ptp. suffix) + *-ia* -IA]

ec•cle•si•al (i klē′zē əl), *adj.* pertaining to a church or its functions, teachings, or organization. [1640–50; < L *ecclēsi(a)* ECCLESIA + -AL¹; cf. F *ecclésial*]

ec•cle•si•arch (i klē′zē ärk′), *n. Eastern Ch.* a sacristan, esp. of a monastery. [1775–85; < MGk *ekklēsiárchēs.* See ECCLESIA, -ARCH]

Ec•cle•si•as•tes (i klē′zē as′tēz), *n.* a book of the Bible. *Abbr.:* Eccl., Eccles. [< LL < Gk *ekklēsiastḗs* assemblyman, preacher, equiv. to *ekklēsí(a)* ECCLESIA + *-astēs*, var. of *-istēs* -IST after a vowel]

ec•cle•si•as•tic (i klē′zē as′tik), *n.* **1.** a member of the clergy or other person in religious orders. **2.** a member of the ecclesia in ancient Athens. —*adj.* **3.** ecclesiastical. [1475–85; < LL *ecclēsiasticus* < Gk *ekklēsiastikós.* See ECCLESIASTES, -IC]

ec•cle•si•as•ti•cal (i klē′zē as′ti kəl), *adj.* of or pertaining to the church or the clergy; churchly; clerical; not secular. [1375–1425; late ME; see ECCLESIASTES, -ICAL] —**ec•cle′si•as′ti•cal•ly,** *adv.*

eccle′sias′tical cal′endar, 1. a calendar based on the lunisolar cycle, used by many Christian churches in determining the dates for the movable feasts. **2.** Also called **church calendar.** a calendar of the Christian year, indicating the days and seasons for fasts and festivals.

eccle′sias′tical court′, a church court in ecclesiastical matters, presided over by members of the clergy and usually having no compulsory jurisdiction. Also called **court Christian.** [1675–85]

ecclesias′tical soci′ety, (in Congregational churches) a legal corporation with power to sue and be sued and to administer all of the temporalities of the church.

ec•cle•si•as•ti•cism (i klē′zē as′tə siz′əm), *n.* **1.** ecclesiastical principles, practices, or spirit. **2.** devotion, esp. excessive devotion, to the principles or interests of the church. [1860–65; ECCLESIASTIC + -ISM]

Ec•cle•si•as•ti•cus (i klē′zē as′ti kəs), *n.* a book of the Apocrypha. Also called **Wisdom of Jesus.** *Abbr.:* Ecclus.

ec•cle•si•ol•a•try (i klē′zē ol′ə trē), *n.* excessive reverence for churchly forms and traditions. [1840–50; ECCLESI(A) + -O- + -LATRY] —**ec•cle′si•ol′a•ter,** *n.*

ec•cle•si•ol•o•gy (i klē′zē ol′ə jē), *n.* **1.** the study of ecclesiastical adornments and furnishings. **2.** the study of church doctrine. [1830–40; ECCLESI(A) + -O- + -LOGY] —**ec•cle•si•o•log•ic** (i klē′zē ə loj′ik), **ec•cle′si•o•log′i•cal,** *adj.* —**ec•cle′si•o•log′i•cal•ly,** *adv.*

Ecclus., Ecclesiasticus.

ec•crine (ek′rin, -rīn, -rēn), *adj. Physiol.* **1.** of or pertaining to certain sweat glands, distributed over the entire body, that secrete a type of sweat important for regulating body heat (distinguished from *apocrine*). **2.** of or pertaining to secretions of these glands: *eccrine sweat.* **3.** exocrine. [1925–30; < Gk *ekkrínein* to secrete (see ECCRINOLOGY), as if with -INE¹; cf. APOCRINE, ENDOCRINE]

ec•cri•nol•o•gy (ek′rə nol′ə jē), *n.* the branch of physiology and anatomy dealing with secretions and the secretory glands. [< Gk *ekkrín(ein)* to secrete (*ek-* EC- + *krínein* to separate) + -O- + -LOGY]

ec•dem•ic (ek dem′ik), *adj. Pathol.* noting or pertaining to a disease that is observed far from the area in which it originates. Cf. **endemic, epidemic.** [EC- + (EPI)DEMIC]

ec•dys•i•ast (ek diz′ē ast′, -ist), *n.* stripper (def. 3). [ECDYSI(S) + *-ast*, var. of -IST after a vowel; coined by H. L. Mencken in 1940]

ec•dy•sis (ek′də sis), *n., pl.* **-ses** (-sēz′). the shedding or casting off of an outer coat or integument by snakes, crustaceans, etc. [1850–55; < NL < Gk *ékdysis* a getting out, equiv. to *ek-* EC- + *dý(ein)* to enter + *-sis* -SIS] —**ec•dys•i•al** (ek diz′ē əl, -dizh′-, -dizh′əl), *adj.*

ec•dy•sone (ek′də zōn′, -sōn′), *n.* an insect hormone that stimulates metamorphosis. [1955–60; ECDYS(IS) + -ONE]

e•ce•sis (i sē′sis), *n. Ecol.* the establishment of an immigrant plant in a new environment. [1900–05; < Gk *oíkēsis* an inhabiting, equiv. to *oikē-*, var. s. of *oikeîn* to inhabit (deriv. of *oîkos* house) + *-sis* -SIS] —**e•ce′sic,** *adj.*

E•ce•vit (e je vēt′), *n.* **Bü•lent** (bʏ lent′), born 1925, Turkish journalist and political leader: prime minister 1974, 1977, 1978–79.

ECF, extended-care facility.

ECG, 1. electrocardiogram. **2.** electrocardiograph.

é•chap•pé (ā′sha pā′, ā shap′ā; *Fr.* ā shA pā′), *n., pl.* **é•chap•pés** (ā′sha pāz′, ā shap′āz; *Fr.* ā shA pā′). a ballet movement in which the dancer jumps from the fifth position and lands on the toes or the balls of the feet in the second position. [< F, ptp. of *échapper* to ESCAPE]

échap•pée (ā′sha pā′, ā shap′ā; *Fr.* ā shA pā′), *n., pl.* **é•chap•pées** (ā′sha pāz′, ā shap′āz; *Fr.* ā shA pā′), *Music.* a melodic ornamental tone following a principal tone by a step above or below and proceeding by a skip. Cf. **cambiata.** [< F: lit., escaped (fem. ptp. of *échapper*). See ESCAPE]

E, échappées

E•che•ga•ray (e′che gä rī′), *n.* **Jo•sé** (hô se′), (*José Echegaray y Eizaguirre*), 1832–1916, Spanish dramatist and statesman: Nobel prize 1904.

ech•e•lette (esh′ə let′, ā′shə-), *n. Spectography.* a diffraction grating designed to reflect infrared radiation. Also called **echelette′ grat′ing.** [< F *échelette* rack, equiv. to *échelle* ladder (see ECHELON) + *-ette* -ETTE]

ech•e•lon (esh′ə lon′), *n.* **1.** a level of command, authority, or rank: *the top echelon of city officials.* **2.** a formation of troops, ships, airplanes, etc., in which groups of soldiers or individual vehicles or craft are arranged in parallel lines, each to the right or left of the one in front, so that the whole presents the appearance of steps. **3.** one of the groups of a formation so arranged. **4.** Also called **ech′elon grat′ing.** *Spectroscopy.* a diffraction grating that is used in the resolution of fine structure lines and consists of a series of plates of equal thickness stacked in staircase fashion. —*v.t., v.i.* **5.** to form in an echelon. [1790–1800; < F *échelon*, orig. rung of a ladder, OF *eschelon*, equiv. to *esch(i)ele* ladder (< L *scāla;* see SCALE³) + *-on* n. suffix] —**ech′e•lon′•ment,** *n.*
—**Syn. 1.** grade, position, rating.

ech•e•ve•ri•a (ech′ə və rē′ə), *n.* any of numerous succulent plants of the genus *Echeveria*, native to tropical America and having thick leaves characteristically forming rosettes. [< NL (1828), named after Atanasio *Echeverría* (fl. 1771), Mexican botanical illustrator]

E•che•ver•rí•a (e′che ver rē′ä), *n.* **Es•te•ban** (es te′vän), 1805–51, Argentine poet.

E•che•ver•rí•a Ál•va•rez (ech′ə və rē′ə al′və rez′; *Sp.* e′che ver rē′ä äl′vä res′), *n.* **Luis** (lwēs), born 1922, Mexican political leader: president 1970–76.

e•chid•na (i kid′nə), *n.* Also called **spiny anteater.** any of several insectivorous monotremes of the genera *Tachyglossus*, of Australia, Tasmania, and New Guinea, and *Zaglossus*, of New Guinea, that have claws and a slender snout and are covered with coarse hair and long spines. [< NL (1798), orig. a genus name; L: serpent, *Echidna* a mythical creature which gave birth to the Hydra and other monsters < Gk *échidna*, akin to *échis* viper]

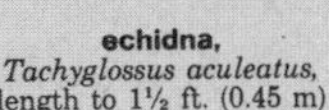

echidna, *Tachyglossus aculeatus,* length to 1½ ft. (0.45 m)

e•chi•nate (i kī′nāt, -nit, ek′ə nāt′, -nit), *adj.* bristly; prickly. Also, **ech′i•nat′ed.** [1660–70; < L *echinātus.* See ECHINUS, -ATE¹]

e•chi•no•derm (i kī′nə dûrm′, ek′ə nə-), *n.* any marine animal of the invertebrate phylum Echinodermata, having a radiating arrangement of parts and a body wall stiffened by calcareous pieces that may protrude as spines and including the starfishes, sea urchins, sea cucumbers, etc. [1825–35; taken as sing. of NL *Echinodermata*, neut. pl. of *echinodermatus* < Gk *echîn(os)* sea urchin + -o- -O- + *-dermatos* -DERMATOUS]

e•chi•no•der•ma•tous (i kī′nə dûr′mə təs, ek′ə nə-), *adj.* belonging or pertaining to the echinoderms. [1825–35; see ECHINODERM, -OUS]

e•chi•noid (i kī′noid, ek′ə noid′), *adj.* **1.** belonging or pertaining to the class Echinoidea, comprising mainly sea urchins and sand dollars. —*n.* **2.** any echinoderm of the Echinoidea. [1850–55; < NL *Echinoidea;* see ECHINUS, -OIDEA]

e•chin•u•late (i kin′yə lit, -lāt′, i kīn′-), *adj.* (of a plant or animal) having a covering of prickles or small spines. [appar. ECHIN(US) + -ULE + -ATE¹]

e•chi•nus (i kī′nəs), *n., pl.* **-ni** (-nī). **1.** any sea urchin of the genus *Echinus.* **2.** *Archit.* **a.** an ovolo molding, esp. one having an outline with several radii or one carved with an egg-and-dart pattern. See illus. under **molding. b.** the prominent circular molding supporting the abacus of a Doric or Tuscan capital. **c.** Also called **cymatium.** the circular molding, usually carved with an egg-and-dart pattern, forming part of an Ionic capital between the volutes and under the balteus. [1325–75; ME < L < Gk *echînos* hedgehog, sea urchin]

ech•i•u•rid (ek′ē yŏŏr′id), *n.* any of various unsegmented marine worms of the phylum Echiura, comprising the spoonworms. [< NL *Echiurida*, var. of *Echiura* < Gk *échi(s)* viper + *-oura* neut. pl. of *-ouros* -tailed (deriv. of *ourá* tail); cf. *Echiurus* a genus of the phylum; see -IDA]

ech•i•u•roid (ek′ē yŏŏr′oid), *n.* **1.** any wormlike invertebrate of the phylum Echiuroidea, found in sand and mud of tropical and subtropical seas, having at the mouth a ciliated, often elongated prostomium. —*adj.* **2.** belonging or pertaining to the Echiuroidea. [1885–90; < NL *Echiuroidea;* see ECHIURID, -OIDEA]

ech•o (ek′ō), *n., pl.* **ech•oes,** *v.,* **ech•oed, ech•o•ing.** —*n.* **1.** a repetition of sound produced by the reflection of sound waves from a wall, mountain, or other obstructing surface. **2.** a sound heard again near its source after being reflected. **3.** any repetition or close imitation, as of the ideas or opinions of another. **4.** a person who reflects or imitates another. **5.** a sympathetic or identical response, as to sentiments expressed. **6.** a lingering trace or effect. **7.** (*cap.*) *Class. Myth.* a mountain nymph who pined away for love of the beautiful youth Narcissus until only her voice remained. **8.** *Cards.* the play of a high card and then a low card in the suit led by one's partner as a signal to continue leading the suit, as in bridge, or to lead a trump, as in whist. **9.** *Electronics.* the reflection of a radio wave, as in radar or the like. **10.** (*cap.*) *U.S. Aerospace.* one of an early series of inflatable passive communications satellites. **11.** a word used in communications to represent the letter *E.* —*v.i.* **12.** to emit an echo; resound with an echo: *The hall echoed with cheers.* **13.** to be repeated by or as by an echo: *Shouts echoed through the street.* —*v.t.* **14.** to repeat by or as by an echo; emit an echo of: *The hall echoes the faintest sounds.* **15.** to repeat or imitate the words, sentiments, etc., of (a person). **16.** to repeat or imitate (words, sentiments, etc.). [1300–50; ME *ecco* < L *ēchō* < Gk, akin to *ēchḗ* sound] —**ech′o•er,** *n.* —**ech′•o•less,** *adj.*
—**Syn. 12, 13.** ring, reverberate.

ech•o•car•di•o•gram (ek′ō kär′dē ə gram′), *n.* a graphic record produced by an echocardiograph. [1975–80; ECHO + CARDIOGRAM]

ech•o•car•di•o•graph (ek′ō kär′dē ə graf′, -gräf′), *n. Med.* an instrument employing reflected ultrasonic waves to examine the structures and functioning of the heart. [ECHO + CARDIOGRAPH] —**ech•o•car•di•o•graph•ic** (ek′ō kär′dē ə graf′ik), **ech′o•car′di•o•graph′i•cal,** *adj.* —**ech′o•car′di•o•graph′i•cal•ly,** *adv.* —**ech•o•car•di•og•ra•phy** (ek′ō kär′dē og′rə fē), *n.*

ech′o cham′ber, a room or studio with resonant walls for broadcasting or recording echoes or hollow sound effects. [1935–40, *Amer.*]

ech•o•en•ceph•a•lo•gram (ek′ō en sef′ə lə gram′), *n. Med.* a graphic record produced by an echoencephalograph. [ECHO + ENCEPHALOGRAM]

ech•o•en•ceph•a•lo•graph (ek′ō en sef′ə lə graf′, -gräf′), *n. Med.* a device that employs reflected ultrasonic waves to examine the position of brain structures. [ECHO + ENCEPHALOGRAPH] —**ech•o•en•ceph•a•lo•graph•ic** (ek′ō en sef′ə lə graf′ik), **ech′o•en•ceph′a•lo•graph′i•cal,** *adj.* —**ech′o•en•ceph′a•lo•graph′i•cal•ly,** *adv.* —**ech•o•en•ceph•a•log•ra•phy** (ek′ō en sef′ə log′rə fē), *n.*

ech•o•gen•ic (ek′ō jen′ik), *adj.* capable of generating or reflecting sound waves. [ECHO + -GENIC]

ech•o•gram (ek′ō gram′), *n.* a record produced by the action of an echograph. [1935–40; ECHO + -GRAM¹]

ech•o•graph (ek′ō graf′, -gräf′), *n.* **1.** a device that records oceanic depths by means of sonic waves. **2.** a similar device used in ultrasonography to examine internal body structures or monitor fetal development. [1945–50; ECHO + -GRAPH] —**ech•o•graph•ic** (ek′ō-graf′ik), *adj.* —**ech′o•graph′i•cal•ly,** *adv.* —**e•chog•ra•phy** (e kog′rə fē), *n.*

e•cho•ic (e kō′ik), *adj.* **1.** resembling an echo. **2.** onomatopoeic. [1875–80; < L *ēchōicus.* See ECHO, -IC]

ech•o•ism (ek′ō iz′əm), *n.* onomatopoeia. [1875–80; ECHO + -ISM]

ech•o•la•li•a (ek′ō lā′lē ə), *n.* **1.** *Psychiatry.* the uncontrollable and immediate repetition of words spoken by another person. **2.** the imitation by a baby of the vocal sounds produced by others, occurring as a natural phase of childhood development. [1880–85; ECHO + -LALIA] —**ech•o•lal•ic,** (ek′ō lal′ik, -lā′lik), *adj.*

ech•o•lo•ca•tion (ek′ō lō kā′shən), *n.* **1.** the general method of locating objects by determining the time for an echo to return and the direction from which it returns, as by radar or sonar. **2.** *Zool.* the sonarlike system used by dolphins, bats, and other animals to detect and locate objects by emitting usually high-pitched sounds that reflect off the object and return to the animal's ears or other sensory receptors. [1944; ECHO + LOCATION]

ech•o•prax•i•a (ek′ō prak′sē ə), *n. Psychiatry.* the abnormal repetition of the actions of another person. [1900–05; < NL; see ECHO, PRAXIS, -IA] —**ech•o•prac•tic** (ek′ō prak′tik), *adj.*

ech′o ques′tion, *Gram.* a question uttered by a listener that in effect repeats a speaker's sentence, replacing an unclear or doubted portion of the sentence with a stressed interrogative word, as *You said WHAT to John?* or *He WHAT?* [1955–60]

CONCISE PRONUNCIATION KEY: *act, cāpe, dâre, pärt; set, ēqual; if, īce; ox, ōver, ôrder, oil, bŏŏk, bōōt, out; up, ûrge; child; sing; shoe; thin, that;* zh as in *treasure.* ə = *a* as in *alone, e* as in *system, i* as in *easily, o* as in *gallop, u* as in *circus;* ᵊ as in *fire* (fīᵊr), *hour* (ouᵊr). l and n can serve as syllabic consonants, as in *cradle* (krād′l), and *button* (but′n). See the full key inside the front cover.

ech·o·vi·rus (ek′ō vī′rəs), *n., pl.* **-rus·es.** any of numerous retroviruses of the picornavirus group, some harmless and others associated with various human disorders, as aseptic meningitis. Also, **ech′o vi′rus, ECHO virus.** [1950–55; *echo-* (acronym from *enteric cytopathogenic human orphan*) + VIRUS; orig. termed "orphan" because they were not known to be the cause of any disease]

echt (EKHT), *adj. German.* real; authentic; genuine.

Eck (ek), *n.* **Jo·hann** (yō′hän), (*Johann Mayer*), 1486–1543, German Roman Catholic theologian: opponent of Martin Luther.

Eck·er·mann (ek′əʀ män′), *n.* **Jo·hann Pe·ter** (yō′-hän pā′təʀ), 1792–1854, German writer and literary assistant to Goethe.

Eck·hart (ek′ärt), *n.* **Jo·han·nes** (yō hä′nəs), (*"Meister Eckhart"*), c1260–1327?, Dominican theologian and preacher: founder of German mysticism. Also, **Eck′ardt, Eck′art.**

é·clair (ā klâr′, i klâr′, ā′klâr), *n.* a finger-shaped cream puff, filled with whipped cream, custard, or pastry cream, often coated with icing. [1860–65; < F: lit., lightning (flash), OF *esclair,* n. deriv. of *esclairier* to light, flash < VL **exclariāre,* for L *exclārāre,* equiv. to *ex-* EX-[1] + *clārāre* to make bright, deriv. of *clārus* CLEAR]

é·clair·cisse·ment (ā kleʀ sēs mäɴ′), *n., pl.* ***-ments*** (-mäɴ′). *French.* **1.** clarification; explanation. **2.** (*cap.*) the Enlightenment.

ec·lamp·si·a (i klamp′sē ə), *n. Pathol.* a form of toxemia of pregnancy, characterized by albuminuria, hypertension, and convulsions. [1855–60; < NL < Gk *éklampsis* sudden development (*ek-* EC- + *lámp(ein)* to shine + *-sis* -SIS + *-ia* -IA] **—ec·lamp′tic,** *adj.*

é·clat (ā klä′; *Fr.* ā klᴀ′), *n.* **1.** brilliance of success, reputation, etc.: *the éclat of a great achievement.* **2.** showy or elaborate display: *a performance of great éclat.* **3.** acclamation; acclaim. [1665–75; < F: splinter, fragment, burst, flash, brilliance, OF *esclat,* n. deriv. of *esclater* to burst, break violently, prob. < Old Low Franconian **slaitan* to split, break (cf. OHG *sleizan* to tear), a causative of Gmc **slitan;* see SLIT]

ec·lec·tic (i klek′tik), *adj.* **1.** selecting or choosing from various sources. **2.** made up of what is selected from different sources. **3.** not following any one system, as of philosophy, medicine, etc., but selecting and using what are considered the best elements of all systems. **4.** noting or pertaining to works of architecture, decoration, landscaping, etc., produced by a certain person or during a certain period, that derive from a wide range of historic styles, the style in each instance often being chosen for its fancied appropriateness to local tradition, local geography, the purpose to be served, or the cultural background of the client. —*n.* **5.** Also, **ec·lec·ti·cist** (i klek′tə sist). a person who follows an eclectic method, as in philosophy or architecture. [1675–85; < Gk *eklektikós* selective, equiv. to *eklekt(ós)* chosen, select (*eklég(ein)* to pick out + *-tos* ptp. suffix; see EC-) + *-ikos* -IC] **—ec·lec′ti·cal·ly,** *adv.*

ec·lec·ti·cism (i klek′tə siz′əm), *n.* **1.** the use or advocacy of an eclectic method. **2.** a tendency in architecture and the decorative arts to mix various historical styles with modern elements with the aim of combining the virtues of many styles or increasing allusive content. [1825–35; ECLECTIC + -ISM]

e·clipse (i klips′), *n., v.,* **e·clipsed, e·clips·ing.** —*n.* **1.** *Astron.* **a.** the obscuration of the light of the moon by the intervention of the earth between it and the sun **(lunar eclipse)** or the obscuration of the light of the sun by the intervention of the moon between it and a point on the earth **(solar eclipse). b.** a similar phenomenon with respect to any other planet and either its satellite or the sun. **c.** the partial or complete interception of the light of one component of a binary star by the other. **2.** any obscuration of light. **3.** a reduction or loss of splendor, status, reputation, etc.: *Scandal caused the eclipse of his career.* —*v.t.* **4.** to cause to undergo eclipse: *The moon eclipsed the sun.* **5.** to make less outstanding or important by comparison; surpass: *a soprano whose singing eclipsed that of her rivals.* [1250–1300; ME *eclips(e), clips* < AF, OF *eclipse* < L *eclīpsis* < Gk *ékleipsis,* equiv. to *ekleíp(ein)* to leave out, forsake, fail to appear (see EC-) + *-sis* -SIS] **—e·clips′er,** *n.*

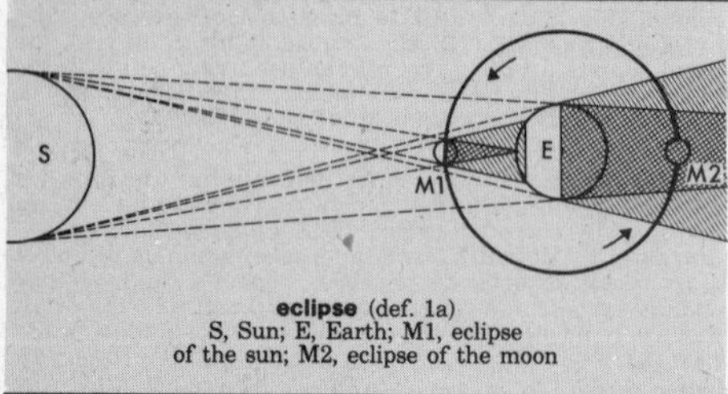

eclipse (def. 1a)
S, Sun; E, Earth; M1, eclipse of the sun; M2, eclipse of the moon

eclipse′ plum′age, *Ornith.* the dull plumage developed in some brightly colored birds after the breeding season. [1905–10]

eclips′ing var′iable, *Astron.* a variable star whose changes in brightness are caused by periodic eclipses of two stars in a binary system. Also called **eclips′ing bi′nary.** [1920–25; ECLIPSE + -ING[2]]

CONCISE ETYMOLOGY KEY: <, descended or borrowed from; >, whence; b., blend of, blended; c., cognate with; cf., compare; deriv., derivative; equiv., equivalent; imit., imitative; obl., oblique; r., replacing; s., stem; sp., spelling, spelled; resp., respelling, respelled; trans., translation; ?, origin unknown; *, unattested; ‡, probably earlier than. See the full key inside the front cover.

e·clip·tic (i klip′tik), *n.* **1.** *Astron.* **a.** the great circle formed by the intersection of the plane of the earth's orbit with the celestial sphere; the apparent annual path of the sun in the heavens. **b.** an analogous great circle on a terrestrial globe. **2.** *Astrol.* the great circle of the ecliptic, along which are located the 12 houses and signs of the zodiac. —*adj.* Also, **e·clip′ti·cal. 3.** pertaining to an eclipse. **4.** pertaining to the ecliptic. [1350–1400; ME < ML *eclīptica,* fem. of *eclīpticus* < Gk *ekleiptikós,* equiv. to *ekleíp(ein)* (see ECLIPSE) + *-tikos* -TIC] **—e·clip′ti·cal·ly,** *adv.*

ec·lo·gite (ek′lə jīt′), *n.* a rock consisting of a granular aggregate of green pyroxene and red garnet, often containing kyanite, silvery mica, quartz, and pyrite. [1815–25; < Gk *eklog(ḗ)* selection (see ECLOGUE) + -ITE[1]]

ec·logue (ek′lôg, -log), *n.* a pastoral poem, often in dialogue form. [1400–50; late ME *eclog* < L *ecloga* < Gk *eklogḗ* selection, akin to *eklégein* to select; see EC-]

Ec·logues (ek′lôgz, -logz), *n.* a collection of pastoral poems (42–37 B.C.) by Vergil. Also called ***Bucolics.***

e·clo·sion (i klō′zhən), *n. Entomol.* **1.** the emergence of an adult insect from its pupal case. **2.** the hatching of a larva from its egg. [1885–90; < F *éclosion,* equiv. to *éclos* (ptp. of *éclore* to hatch < VL **exclaudere,* for L *exclūdere* to hatch, EXCLUDE) + *-ion* -ION]

ECM, 1. electronic countermeasures. **2.** European Common Market.

eco-, a combining form representing **ecology** in the formation of compounds (*ecosystem; ecotype*); also with the more general sense "environment," "nature," "natural habitat" (*ecocide; ecolaw; ecopolitics*).

ec·o·ca·tas·tro·phe (ek′ō kə tas′trə fē, ē′kō-), *n. Ecol.* a disaster caused by changes in the environment. [1965–70; ECO- + CATASTROPHE]

ec·o·cide (ek′ə sīd′, ē′kə-), *n.* the destruction of large areas of the natural environment by such activity as nuclear warfare, overexploitation of resources, or dumping of harmful chemicals. [1965–70, *Amer.;* ECO- + -CIDE] **—ec′o·ci′dal,** *adj.*

ec·o·fal·low (ek′ə fal′ō, ē′kə-), *n.* a method of farming that diminishes weeds and conserves water by rotating crops and reducing or eliminating tillage. [1975–80; ECO- + FALLOW[1]]

ec·o·freak (ek′ō frēk′, ē′kō-), *n. Slang* (*often disparaging*). a zealous or overly zealous environmentalist or preservationist. [1965–70; ECO- + FREAK[1]]

ec·o·haz·ard (ek′ō haz′ərd, ē′kō-), *n.* any substance or activity that poses a threat to a habitat or an environment: *Off-the-road motorcycling is an ecohazard to fragile desert habitats.* [ECO- + HAZARD]

ecol., 1. ecological. **2.** ecology.

é·cole (ā kôl′), *n., pl.* ***é·coles*** (ā kôl′). *French.* school[1].

E. co·li (ē′ kō′lī). See ***Escherichia coli.***

ec′olog′ical niche′, niche (def. 3).

ecolog′ical succes′sion, succession (def. 6).

e·col·o·gy (i kol′ə jē), *n.* **1.** the branch of biology dealing with the relations and interactions between organisms and their environment, including other organisms. **2.** Also called **human ecology.** the branch of sociology concerned with the spacing and interdependence of people and institutions. Also, **oecology.** [1870–75; earlier *oecology* < G *Ökologie* < Gk *oîk(os)* + *-o-* -O- + G *-logie* -LOGY; term introduced by E. H. Haeckel] **—ec·o·log·i·cal** (ek′ə loj′i kəl, ē′kə-), **ec′o·log′ic,** *adj.* **—ec′·o·log′i·cal·ly,** *adv.* **—e·col′o·gist,** *n.*

econ., 1. economic. **2.** economics. **3.** economy.

ec·o·niche (ek′ō nich′, ē′kō-), *n.* niche (def. 3). [1975–80; ECO- + NICHE]

e·con·o·met·rics (i kon′ə me′triks), *n.* (*used with a singular v.*) *Econ.* the application of statistical and mathematical techniques in solving problems as well as in testing and demonstrating theories. [1930–35; see ECONOMY, METRIC[2], -ICS] **—e·con′o·met′ric, e·con′o·met′ri·cal,** *adj.* **—e·con·o·me·tri·cian** (i kon′ə mi-trish′ən), **e·con′o·met′rist,** *n.*

ec·o·nom·ic (ek′ə nom′ik, ē′kə-), *adj.* **1.** pertaining to the production, distribution, and use of income, wealth, and commodities. **2.** of or pertaining to the science of economics. **3.** pertaining to an economy, or system of organization or operation, esp. of the process of production. **4.** involving or pertaining to one's personal resources of money: *to give up a large house for economic reasons.* **5.** pertaining to use as a resource in the economy: *economic entomology; economic botany.* **6.** affecting or apt to affect the welfare of material resources: *weevils and other economic pests.* **7.** economical. [1585–95; (< MF *economique*) < L *oeconomicus* < Gk *oikonomikós* relating to household management, equiv. to *oikonóm(os)* steward (*oîko(s)* house + *nómos* manager) + *-ikos* -IC]

ec·o·nom·i·cal (ek′ə nom′i kəl, ē′kə-), *adj.* **1.** avoiding waste or extravagance; thrifty: *an economical meal; an economical use of interior space.* **2.** economic. [1570–80; ECONOMIC + -AL[1]]
—Syn. 1. saving, provident, sparing, parsimonious. ECONOMICAL, THRIFTY, FRUGAL imply careful and saving use of resources. ECONOMICAL implies prudent planning in the disposition of resources so as to avoid unnecessary waste or expense: *economical in budgeting household expenditures.* THRIFTY is a stronger word than economical, and adds to it the idea of industry and successful management: *a thrifty shopper looking for bargains.* FRUGAL emphasizes being saving, sometimes excessively saving, esp. in such matters as food or dress: *frugal almost to the point of being stingy.* **—Ant. 1.** wasteful, extravagant, spendthrift, prodigal, profligate.

ec·o·nom·i·cal·ly (ek′ə nom′ik lē, ē′kə-), *adv.* **1.** in a thrifty or frugal manner; with economy. **2.** as regards the efficient use of income and wealth: *economically feasible proposals.* **3.** as regards one's personal resources of money: *He's quite well off economically.* [1690–1700; ECONOMICAL + -LY]

Econom′ic Coopera′tion Administra′tion, the U.S. government agency that administered the European Recovery Program. *Abbr.:* ECA, E.C.A.

ec′onom′ic cy′cle. See **business cycle.**

econom′ic deter′minism, the doctrine that all social, cultural, political, and intellectual forms are determined by or result from such economic factors as the quality of natural resources, productive capability, technological development, or the distribution of wealth. **—econom′ic deter′minist.**

econom′ic geog′raphy, a branch of geography that deals with the relation of physical and economic conditions to the production and utilization of raw materials and their manufacture into finished products. [1910–15]

econom′ic geol′ogy, the branch of geology dealing with the location and exploitation of industrial materials obtained from the earth. [1920–25]

ec′onom′ic good′, a commodity or service that can be utilized to satisfy human wants and that has exchange value.

ec′onom′ic mod′el, *Econ.* model (def. 10).

ec′onom′ic rent′, the return on a productive resource, as land or labor, that is greater than the amount necessary to keep the resource producing or on a product in excess of what would have been the return except for some unique factor. Also called **Ricardian theory of rent.** [1885–90]

ec·o·nom·ics (ek′ə nom′iks, ē′kə-), *n.* **1.** (*used with a singular v.*) the science that deals with the production, distribution, and consumption of goods and services, or the material welfare of humankind. **2.** (*used with a plural v.*) financial considerations; economically significant aspects: *What are the economics of such a project?* [1785–95; see ECONOMIC, -ICS]

ec′onom′ic strike′, a strike called in protest over wages, hours, or working conditions.

e·con·o·mism (i kon′ə miz′əm), *n.* the theory or practice of assigning primary importance to the economy or to economic achievement. [1915–20; < F *économisme;* see ECONOMY, -ISM]

e·con·o·mist (i kon′ə mist), *n.* **1.** a specialist in economics. **2.** *Archaic.* a thrifty or frugal person. [1580–90; ECONOM(Y) + -IST]

e·con·o·mize (i kon′ə mīz′), *v.,* **-mized, -miz·ing.** —*v.i.* **1.** to practice economy; avoid waste or extravagance. —*v.t.* **2.** to manage economically; use sparingly or frugally. Also, *esp. Brit.,* **e·con′o·mise′.** [1640–50; ECONOM(Y) + -IZE]
—Syn. 1, 2. save, conserve, husband.

e·con·o·miz·er (i kon′ə mī′zər), *n.* **1.** a person who economizes. **2.** (in a boiler) a device for warming feed water with gases entering the chimney or stack. [1830–40; ECONOMIZE + -ER[1]]

e·con·o·my (i kon′ə mē), *n., pl.* **-mies,** *adj., adv.* —*n.* **1.** thrifty management; frugality in the expenditure or consumption of money, materials, etc. **2.** an act or means of thrifty saving; a saving: *He achieved a small economy by walking to work instead of taking a bus.* **3.** the management of the resources of a community, country, etc., esp. with a view to its productivity. **4.** the prosperity or earnings of a place: *Further inflation would endanger the national economy seriously.* **5.** the disposition or regulation of the parts or functions of any organic whole; an organized system or method. **6.** the efficient, sparing, or concise use of something: *an economy of effort; an economy of movement.* **7.** See **economy class. 8.** *Theol.* **a.** the divine plan for humanity, from creation through redemption to final beatitude. **b.** the method of divine administration, as at a particular time or for a particular race. **9.** *Obs.* the management of household affairs. —*adj.* **10.** intended to save money: *to reduce the staff in an economy move.* **11.** costing less to make, buy, or operate: *an economy car.* **12.** of or pertaining to economy class: *the economy fare to San Francisco.* —*adv.* **13.** in economy-class accommodations, or by economy-class conveyance: *to travel economy.* [1520–30; (< MF *economie*) < L *oeconomia* < Gk *oikonomía* household management, equiv. to *oîko(s)* house + *-nomia* -NOMY]
—Syn. 1. thriftiness, thrift, saving. **—Ant. 1.** lavishness, extravagance, wastefulness.

econ′omy class′, a low-priced type of accommodation for travel, esp. on an airplane. [1955–60] **—e·con′·o·my-class′,** *adj.*

e·con·o·my-size (i kon′ə mē sīz′), *adj.* **1.** larger in size and costing less per unit of measurement than a smaller size: *an economy-size box of soap flakes.* **2.** smaller in size and costing less: *economy-size cars.* Also, **e·con′o·my-sized′.** [1945–50]

ec·o·phys·i·ol·o·gy (ek′ō fiz′ē ol′ə jē, ē′kō-), *n.* the branch of physiology that deals with the physiological processes of organisms with respect to their environment. [1960–65; ECO- + PHYSIOLOGY] **—ec·o·phys·i·o·log·i·cal** (ek′ō fiz′ē ə loj′i kəl, ē′kō-), *adj.* **—ec′o·phys′i·ol′o·gist,** *n.*

ec·o·pol·i·tics[1] (ek′ō pol′i tiks, ē′kō-), *n.* (*used with a singular v.*) the study of politics as influenced by economic power. [1970–75; ECO(NOMIC) + POLITICS]

ec·o·pol·i·tics[2] (ek′ō pol′i tiks, ē′kō-), *n.* (*used with a singular v.*) the study of the interrelation between political and ecological issues and problems. [1970–75; ECO- + POLITICS]

E·corse (i kôrs′, ē′kôrs), *n.* a city in SE Michigan, near Detroit. 14,447.

ec·o·spe·cies (ek′ō spē′shēz, -sēz, ē′kō-), *n. Ecol.* a taxon consisting of one or more interbreeding ecotypes: equivalent to a taxonomic species. [1920–25; ECO- + SPECIES] **—ec·o·spe·cif·ic** (ek′ō spi sif′ik), *adj.* **—ec′·o·spe·cif′i·cal·ly,** *adv.*

ec•o•sphere (ek′ō sfēr′, ē′kō-), *n.* **1.** Also called **physiological atmosphere.** the part of the atmosphere in which it is possible to breathe normally without aid: the portion of the troposphere from sea level to an altitude of about 13,000 ft. (4000 m). **2.** *Ecol.* the planetary ecosystem, including all the earth's living organisms and their physical environment; biosphere. [1950–55; ECO- + SPHERE]

é•cos•saise (ā′kō sāz′; -kə-), *n.* a country-dance in quick duple meter. [1860–65; < F, fem. of *écossais* Scottish, equiv. to *Écosse* Scotland + *-ais* -ESE; trans. of G *schottisch*]

ec•o•sys•tem (ek′ō sis′təm, ē′kō-), *n. Ecol.* a system formed by the interaction of a community of organisms with their environment. [1930–35; ECO- + SYSTEM]

ec•o•tage (ek′ə täzh′, ē′kə-), *n.* sabotage aimed at polluters or destroyers of the natural environment. [1970–75; ECO- + (SABO)TAGE]

ec•o•ter•ror•ist (ek′ō ter′ər ist, ē′kō-), *n.* one who commits ecotage; monkey-wrencher. [1980–85] —**ec′o•ter′ror•ism,** *n.*

ec•o•tone (ek′ə tōn′, ē′kə-), *n. Ecol.* the transition zone between two different plant communities, as that between forest and prairie. [1900–05; ECO- + *tone* < Gk *tónos* tension] —**ec′o•ton′al,** *adj.*

ec•o•type (ek′ə tīp′, ē′kə-), *n. Ecol.* a subspecies or race that is especially adapted to a particular set of environmental conditions. [1920–25; ECO- + TYPE] —**ec•o•typ•ic** (ek′ə tip′ik, ē′kə-), *adj.* —**ec′o•typ′i•cal•ly,** *adv.*

ec•pho•ne•sis (ek′fə nē′sis), *n. Rhet.* the use of an exclamatory phrase, as in "O tempore! O mores!" [1580–90; < Gk *ekphṓnēsis,* equiv. to *ekphōnē-,* var. s. of *ekphōneîn* to cry out (see EC-, -PHONE) + *-sis* -SIS]

é•cra•sé (ā′krä zā′, -krə), *adj.* (of leather) crushed to produce a grained effect. [< F, ptp. of *écraser* to crush, bruise, MF, equiv. to *é-* EX-[1] + *-craser* < ME *crasen* to brake, shatter; see CRAZE]

é•cre•visse (ā krə vēs′), *n., pl.* **-visses** (-vēs′). *French.* crayfish.

ec•ru (ek′ro͞o, ā′kro͞o), *adj.* **1.** very light brown in color, as raw silk, unbleached linen, etc. —*n.* **2.** an ecru color. Also, **é•cru** (*Fr.* ā krʏ′). [1865–70; < F, equiv. to *é-* completely (< L *ex-* EX-[1]) + *cru* raw (< L *crūdus;* see CRUDE)]

ec•sta•sy (ek′stə sē), *n., pl.* **-sies. 1.** rapturous delight. **2.** an overpowering emotion or exaltation; a state of sudden, intense feeling. **3.** the frenzy of poetic inspiration. **4.** mental transport or rapture from the contemplation of divine things. [1350–1400; ME *extasie* < MF < ML *extasis* < Gk *ékstasis* displacement, trance, equiv. to *ek-* EC- + *stásis* STASIS]
—**Syn. 2.** delight, bliss, elation. ECSTASY, RAPTURE, TRANSPORT, EXALTATION share a sense of being taken or moved out of one's self or one's normal state, and entering a state of intensified or heightened feeling. ECSTASY suggests an intensification of emotion so powerful as to produce a trancelike dissociation from all but the single overpowering feeling: *an ecstasy of rage, grief, love.* RAPTURE shares the power of ecstasy but most often refers to an elevated sensation of bliss or delight, either carnal or spiritual: *the rapture of first love.* TRANSPORT, somewhat less extreme than either ECSTASY or RAPTURE, implies a strength of feeling that results in expression of some kind: *They jumped up and down in a transport of delight.* EXALTATION refers to a heady sense of personal well-being so powerful that one is lifted above normal emotional levels and above normal people: *wild exaltation at having finally broken the record.*

ec•stat•ic (ek stat′ik), *adj.* **1.** of, pertaining to, or characterized by ecstasy. **2.** subject to or in a state of ecstasy; rapturous. —*n.* **3.** a person subject to fits of ecstasy. [1620–30; (< MF *extatique*) < ML *ecstaticus* < Gk *ekstatikós,* equiv. to *ek-* EC- + *statikós* STATIC. See ECSTASY] —**ec•stat′i•cal•ly,** *adv.*

ECT, electroconvulsive therapy.

ect-, var. of **ecto-** before a vowel: *ectal.*

ec•tad (ek′tad), *adv. Anat., Zool.* outward. [1880–85; ECT- + -AD[3]]

ec•tal (ek′tl), *adj. Anat., Zool.* external; outer; on the surface of. [1880–85; ECT- + -AL[1]] —**ec′tal•ly,** *adv.*

ec•thlip•sis (ek thlip′sis), *n., pl.* **-ses** (-sēz). loss of a consonant, esp., in Latin, loss of a final *m* before a word beginning with a vowel or *h.* [1650–60; < LL < Gk *ékthlipsis,* equiv. to *ekthlī́b(ein)* to squeeze out (*ek-* EC- + *thlī́bein,* var. of *phlī́bein* to squeeze) + *-sis* -SIS]

ec•thy•ma (ek′thə mə, ek thī′-), *n. Vet. Pathol.* a contagious viral disease of sheep and goats and occasionally of humans, marked by vesicular and pustular lesions on the lips. Also called **contagious ecthyma, sore mouth.** [1825–35; < Gk *ékthyma* pustule, equiv. to *ek-* EC- + *thȳ́(ein)* to be angry + *-ma* n. suffix] —**ec•thym•a•tous** (ek thim′ə təs, -thī′mə-), *adj.*

ecto-, a combining form meaning "outer," "outside," "external," used in the formation of compound words: *ectoderm.* Also, *esp. before a vowel,* **ect-.** [comb. form of Gk *ektós* outside]

ec•to•blast (ek′tə blast′), *n. Embryol.* **1.** the ectoderm. **2.** epiblast. [1860–65; ECTO- + -BLAST] —**ec′to•blas′tic,** *adj.*

ec•to•com•men•sal (ek′tō kə men′səl), *adj.* **1.** *Biol.* (of an organism) living in a commensal relationship on the exterior of another organism. —*n.* **2.** an ectocommensal organism. [1935–40; ECTO- + COMMENSAL] —**ec′to•com•men′sal•ism, ec•to•com•men•sal•i•ty** (ek′tō kom′en sal′i tē), *n.*

ec•to•cor•ne•a (ek′tō kôr′nē ə), *n. Anat.* the outer layer of the cornea. [ECTO- + CORNEA]

ec•to•derm (ek′tə dûrm′), *n. Embryol.* the outer germ layer in the embryo of a metazoan. Also called **ectoblast.** [1860–65; ECTO- + -DERM] —**ec′to•der′mal, ec′to•der′mic,** *adj.* —**ec•to•der•moi•dal** (ek′tō dər moid′l), *adj.*

ec•to•en•zyme (ek′tō en′zīm), *n. Biochem.* exoenzyme. [ECTO- + ENZYME]

ec•to•gen•e•sis (ek′tō jen′ə sis), *n. Biol.* development outside the body, as of an embryo in an artificial environment. [1905–10; < NL; see ECTO-, -GENESIS] —**ec•to•ge•net•ic** (ek′tō jə net′ik), *adj.*

ec•tog•e•nous (ek toj′ə nəs), *adj.* growing outside the body of the host, as certain bacteria and other parasites. Also, **ec•to•gen•ic** (ek′tə jen′ik). [1880–85; ECTO- + -GENOUS]

ec•to•mere (ek′tə mēr′), *n. Embryol.* any of the blastomeres that participate in the development of the ectoderm. [1885–90; ECTO- + -MERE] —**ec•to•mer•ic** (ek′tə mer′ik), *adj.*

ec•to•morph (ek′tə môrf′), *n.* a person of the ectomorphic type. [1935–40; ECTO- + -MORPH]

ec•to•mor•phic (ek′tə môr′fik), *adj.* having a thin body build, roughly characterized by the relative prominence of structures developed from the embryonic ectoderm (contrasted with *endomorphic, mesomorphic*). [1935–40; ECTO- + -MORPHIC] —**ec′to•morph′y,** *n.*

-ectomy, a combining form meaning "excision" of the part specified by the initial element: *tonsillectomy.* [< NL *-ectomia.* See EC-, -TOMY]

ec•to•par•a•site (ek′tō par′ə sīt′), *n.* an external parasite (opposed to *endoparasite*). [1860–65; ECTO- + PARASITE] —**ec•to•par•a•sit•ic** (ek′tō par′ə sit′ik), *adj.*

ec•to•phyte (ek′tə fīt′), *n.* a parasitic plant growing on an animal or another plant. [1880–85; ECTO- + -PHYTE] —**ec•to•phyt•ic** (ek′tə fit′ik), *adj.*

ec•to•pi•a (ek tō′pē ə), *n. Med.* the usually congenital displacement of an organ or part. [1840–50; < NL < Gk *éktop(os)* out of place (*ek-* EC- + *tópos* place) + *-ia* -IA]

ec•top•ic (ek top′ik), *adj. Pathol.* occurring in an abnormal position or place; displaced. [1870–75; ECTOP(IA) + -IC]

ectop′ic preg′nancy, *Med.* the development of a fertilized ovum outside the uterus, as in a Fallopian tube. Also called **extrauterine pregnancy.** [1925–30]

ec•to•plasm (ek′tə plaz′əm), *n.* **1.** *Biol.* the outer portion of the cytoplasm of a cell. Cf. **endoplasm. 2.** *Spiritualism.* the supposed emanation from the body of a medium. [1880–85; ECTO- + -PLASM] —**ec′to•plas′mic, ec•to•plas•mat•ic** (ek′tə plaz mat′ik), *adj.*

ec•to•proct (ek′tə prokt′), *n.* bryozoan; formerly, one of two broad types of bryozoan. Cf. **entoproct.** [see ECTOPROCTA]

Ec•to•proc•ta (ek′tə prok′tə), *n.* the phylum Bryozoa, esp. as distinguished from the phylum Entoprocta by a body plan having the anus of the polyp outside the crown of tentacles. [< NL, equiv. to Gk *ekto-* ECTO- + *-prōkta,* neut. pl. of *-prōktos,* adj. deriv. of *prōktós* anus; see PROCTO-]

ec•to•sarc (ek′tə särk′), *n. Biol.* the ectoplasm of a protozoan (opposed to *endosarc*). [1875–80; ECTO- + -SARC] —**ec′to•sar′cous,** *adj.*

ec•tos•to•sis (ek′to stō′sis, -tə-), *n.* the ossification of cartilage that begins under the perichondrium and proceeds inward. [ECT- + OSTOSIS] —**ec•tos•te•al** (ek tos′tē əl), *adj.* —**ec•tos′te•al•ly,** *adv.*

ec•to•therm (ek′tə thûrm′), *n. Zool.* a cold-blooded animal. [1940–45; ECTO- + THERM] —**ec′to•ther′mic,** *adj.*

ec•to•troph•ic (ek′tə trof′ik, -trō′fik), *adj.* (of a mycorrhiza) growing outside the root or between the cells. Cf. **endotrophic.** [1925–30; ECTO- + -TROPHIC]

ec•to•zo•an (ek′tə zō′ən), *Biol.* —*n.* **1.** ectozoon. —*adj.* **2.** of or pertaining to an ectozoon.

ec•to•zo•ic (ek′tə zō′ik), *adj.* (of a parasitic animal) living on the surface of its host. [ECTOZO(ON) + -IC]

ec•to•zo•on (ek′tə zō′on, -ən), *n., pl.* **-zo•a** (-zō′ə). *Biol.* any animal parasite, as the louse, that lives on the surface of its host (opposed to *entozoon*). Also, **ectozoan.** [1855–60; ECTO- + -ZOON]

Ec•trin (ek′trin), *Vet. Med., Trademark.* a brand of fenvalerate.

ec•tro•dac•tyl•ism (ek′trō dak′tə liz′əm), *n. Med.* the congenital absence of part or all of one or more fingers or toes. Also, **ec•tro•dac•tyl•i•a** (ek′trō dak til′ē ə, -til′yə), **ec•tro•dac•ty•ly** (ek′trō dak′tə lē). [1880–85; < Gk *éktrō(sis)* miscarriage (*ektrō-,* base of *ektitrṓskein* to miscarry + *-sis* -SIS) + -DACTYL + -ISM] —**ec′tro•dac′ty•lous,** *adj.*

ec•tro•me•li•a (ek′trō mē′lē ə), *n.* **1.** *Med.* the congenital absence or imperfection of a limb or limbs. **2.** Also called **infectious ectromelia, mousepox.** *Vet. Pathol.* a viral disease of mice, characterized by gangrene of the extremities, swelling and loss of limbs, and mottling of the liver. [1905–10; *ectro-* (see ECTRODACTYLISM) + -MELIA] —**ec•tro•mel•ic** (ek′trō mel′ik), *adj.*

ec•type (ek′tīp), *n.* a reproduction; copy (opposed to *prototype*). [1640–50; < Gk *éktyp(os)* wrought in relief, equiv. to *ek-* EC- + *týp(os)* figure (on a wall) + *-os* adj. suffix; akin to TYPE] —**ec•ty•pal** (ek′tə pəl, -tī-), *adj.*

é•cu (ā kyo͞o′; *Fr.* ā kʏ′), *n., pl.* **é•cus** (ā kyo͞oz′; *Fr.* ā kʏ′). **1.** the shield carried by a mounted man-at-arms in the Middle Ages. **2.** any of various gold and silver coins of France, issued from the 13th through the 18th centuries, bearing the figure of a shield. [1695–1705; < F; OF *escu* < L *scūtum* shield]

ECU (ā ko͞o′ *or, sometimes,* ē′sē′yo͞o′), *n.* a money of account of the European Common Market used in international finance, based on the combined prorated values of the currencies of member nations. [*E(uropean) C(urrency) U(nit),* perh. with play on ÉCU]

E.C.U., English Church Union.

Ecua., Ecuador.

Ec•ua•dor (ek′wə dôr′), *n.* a republic in NW South America. 7,560,000; 109,483 sq. mi. (283,561 sq. km). *Cap.:* Quito. —**Ec′ua•do′ran, Ec′ua•dor′e•an, Ec′ua•do′ri•an,** *adj., n.*

ec•u•men•i•cal (ek′yo͝o men′i kəl *or, esp. Brit.,* ē′kyo͝o-), *adj.* **1.** general; universal. **2.** pertaining to the whole Christian church. **3.** promoting or fostering Christian unity throughout the world. **4.** of or pertaining to a movement (**ecumenical movement**), esp. among Protestant groups since the 1800's, aimed at achieving universal Christian unity through international interdenominational organizations. **5.** interreligious or interdenominational: *an ecumenical marriage.* **6.** including or containing a mixture of diverse elements or styles; mixed: *an ecumenical meal of Italian and Chinese dishes.* Also, **ec′u•men′ic, oecumenical, oecumenic.** [1835–45; < LL *oecumenicus* belonging to the whole inhabited world (< Gk *oikoumenikós,* equiv. to *oikoumen-* (s. of pass. prp. of *oikeîn* to inhabit) + *-ikos* -IC) + -AL[1]] —**ec′u•men′i•cal•ly,** *adv.*

ec′umen′ical coun′cil, a solemn assembly in the Roman Catholic Church, convoked and presided over by the pope and composed of cardinals, bishops, and certain other prelates whose decrees, when confirmed by the pope, become binding. Also, **Ec′umen′ical Coun′cil.**

ec•u•men•i•cal•ism (ek′yo͝o men′i kə liz′əm *or, esp. Brit.,* ē′kyo͝o-), *n.* the doctrines and practices of the ecumenical movement. Also, **ecumenicism.** [1945–50; ECUMENICAL + -ISM]

ecumen′ical move′ment. See under **ecumenical** (def. 4).

ecumen′ical pa′triarch, the patriarch of Constantinople, regarded as the highest dignitary of the Greek Orthodox Church. [1860–65] —**ecumen′ical pa′triarchate.**

ec•u•men•i•cism (ek′yo͝o men′ə siz′əm *or, esp. Brit.,* ē′kyo͝o-), *n.* ecumenicalism; ecumenism. [1960–65; ECUMENIC(AL) + -ISM]

ec•u•men•i•cist (ek′yo͝o men′ə sist *or, esp. Brit.,* ē′kyo͝o-), *n.* a person who advocates Christian ecumenicity. [ECUMENIC + -IST]

ec•u•me•nic•i•ty (ek′yo͝o mə nis′i tē, -me- *or, esp. Brit.,* ē′kyo͝o-), *n.* (in the Christian church) the state of being ecumenically united, esp. in furthering the aims of the ecumenical movement. [1830–40; ECUMENIC + -ITY]

ec•u•men•ics (ek′yo͝o men′iks *or, esp. Brit.,* ē′kyo͝o-), *n.* (*used with a singluar v.*) the study of the Christian church in its aspect as a worldwide Christian community. [1935–40; see ECUMENICAL, -ICS]

ec•u•me•nism (ek′yo͝o mə niz′əm, i kyo͞o′- *or, esp. Brit.,* ē′kyo͝o-), *n.* ecumenical doctrines and practices, esp. as manifested in the ecumenical movement. [1965–70; ECUMEN(IC) + -ISM] —**ec′u•me•nist,** *n.*

ec•ze•ma (ek′sə mə, eg′zə-, ig zē′-), *n. Pathol.* an inflammatory condition of the skin attended with itching and the exudation of serous matter. [1745–55; < NL < Gk *ékzema,* equiv. to *ek-* EC- + *ze-* (s. of *zeîn* to boil, ferment) + *-ma* n. suffix] —**ec•zem′a•tous** (ig zem′ə təs, -zē′mə-), *adj.*

ed (ed), *n. Informal.* education: *a course in driver's ed; adult ed.* [by shortening]

Ed (ed), *n.* a male given name, form of **Edgar** or **Edward.**

ED, See **Department of Education.**

ED_{50}, *Pharm.* effective dose for 50 percent of the group; the amount of a drug that is therapeutic in 50 percent of the persons or animals in which it is tested.

-ed[1], a suffix forming the past tense of weak verbs: *he crossed the river.* [OE *-de, -ede, -ode, -ade;* orig. disputed]

-ed[2], a suffix forming the past participle of weak verbs (*he had crossed the river*), and of participial adjectives indicating a condition or quality resulting from the action of the verb (*inflated balloons*). [OE *-ed, -od, -ad;* orig. disputed]

-ed[3], a suffix forming adjectives from nouns: *bearded; monied; tender-hearted.* [ME; OE *-ede*]

ed., 1. edited. **2.** *pl.* **eds.** edition. **3.** *pl.* **eds.** editor. **4.** education.

E.D., 1. Eastern Department. **2.** election district. **3.** ex dividend. **4.** executive director.

Ed•a (ed′ə), *n.* a female given name.

EDA, Economic Development Administration.

e•da•cious (i dā′shəs), *adj.* devouring; voracious; consuming. [1810–20; EDACI(TY) + -OUS]

e•dac•i•ty (i das′i tē), *n.* the state of being edacious;

voraciousness; appetite. [1620–30; < L *edācitās,* equiv. to *edāci-* (s. of *edāx*) gluttonous, equiv. to *ed-* EAT + *-āci-* adj. suffix + *-tās* -TY[2]]

E•dam (ē′dəm, ē′dam; *Du.* ā däm′), *n.* a mild, hard, yellow cheese, produced in a round shape and coated with red wax. Also called **E′dam cheese′.** [1830–40; after *Edam,* town in the Netherlands, where it originated]

e•daph•ic (i daf′ik), *adj.* related to or caused by particular soil conditions, as of texture or drainage, rather than by physiographic or climatic factors. [< G *edaphisch* (1898); see EDAPHON, -IC] **—e•daph′i•cal•ly,** *adv.*

edaph′ic cli′max, *Ecol.* a localized climax community that may differ from the surrounding climax vegetation by reason of slightly differing soil type, exposure to sun and wind, drainage, etc. [1945–50]

ed•a•phon (ed′ə fon′), *n.* the aggregate of organisms that live in the soil. [< G *Edaphon* (1913) < Gk *édaphos* ground, floor; *-on* prob. after PLANKTON]

EDB, *Chem.* ethylene dibromide: a colorless liquid, $C_2H_4Br_2$, used as an organic solvent, an additive in gasoline to prevent lead buildup, and a pesticide and soil fumigant, esp. by citrus and grain farmers.

Ed.B., Bachelor of Education.

EDC, European Defense Community.

Ed.D., Doctor of Education.

Ed•da (ed′ə), *n.* a female given name. Also, **Eda.**

Ed•da (ed′ə), *n.* either of two old Icelandic literary works, one a collection of poems on mythical and religious subjects (***Elder Edda*** or ***Poetic Edda***) erroneously attributed to Saemund Sigfusson (c1055–1133), the other a collection of ancient Scandinavian myths and legends, rules and theories of versification, poems, etc. (***Younger Edda*** or ***Prose Edda***), compiled and written in part by Snorri Sturluson (1179–1241). **—Ed′dic, Ed•da•ic** (e dā′ik), *adj.*

Ed•ding•ton (ed′ing tən), *n.* **Sir Arthur (Stanley),** 1882–1944, English astronomer, physicist, and writer.

ed•do (ed′ō), *n., pl.* **-does.** the edible root of the taro or of any of several related plants. [1765–75; < one or more WAfr languages; cf. Igbo *édè,* Fante *edwó(w)* yam]

ed•dy (ed′ē), *n., pl.* **-dies,** *v.,* **-died, -dy•ing.** **—***n.* **1.** a current at variance with the main current in a stream of liquid or gas, esp. one having a rotary or whirling motion. **2.** a small whirlpool. **3.** any similar current, as of air, dust, or fog. **4.** a current or trend, as of opinion or events, running counter to the main current. **—***v.t., v.i.* **5.** to move or whirl in eddies. [1425–75; late ME; OE *ed-* turning + *ēa* water; akin to ON *itha*]

Ed•dy (ed′ē), *n.* **1. Mary (Morse) Baker** (*Mrs. Glover; Mrs. Patterson*), 1821–1910, U.S. founder of the Christian Science Church. **2.** Also, **Ed′die.** a male given name, form of **Edgar** or **Edward.**

ed′dy cur′rent, an electric current in a conducting material that results from induction by a moving or varying magnetic field. [1590–1600, for an earlier sense]

Ed′dy•stone Rocks′ (ed′ə stən), a group of rocks near the W end of the English Channel, SW of Plymouth, England: celebrated lighthouse.

E•de (ā dā′, ā′dā *for 1;* ā′də *for 2*), *n.* **1.** a city in SW Nigeria. 182,000. **2.** a city in central Netherlands. 83,738.

Ed•el•man (ed′l mən), *n.* **Gerald Maurice,** born 1929, U.S. biochemist: Nobel prize for medicine 1972.

e•del•weiss (ād′l vīs′, -wīs′), *n.* **1.** a small composite plant, *Leontopodium alpinum,* having white woolly leaves and flowers, growing in the high altitudes of the Alps. **2.** a liqueur made in Italy, flavored with the extracts of alpine flowers. [1860–65; < G, equiv. to *edel* noble + *weiss* WHITE]

e•de•ma (i dē′mə), *n., pl.* **-mas, -ma•ta** (-mə tə). *Pathol.* **1.** effusion of serous fluid into the interstices of cells in tissue spaces or into body cavities. **2.** *Plant Pathol.* **a.** a small surface swelling of plant parts, caused by excessive moisture. **b.** any disease so characterized. Also, **oedema.** [1490–1500; < NL *oedēma* < Gk *oídēma* a swelling, equiv. to *oidē-* (var. s. of *oideîn* to swell) + *-ma* n. suffix] **—e•dem•a•tous** (i dem′ə təs, i dē′mə-), **e•dem•a•tose** (i dem′ə tōs′, i dē′mə-), *adj.*

E•den (ēd′n), *n.* **1.** the place where Adam and Eve lived before the Fall. Gen. 2:8–24. **2.** any delightful region or abode; paradise. **3.** a state of perfect happiness or bliss. Also called **Garden of Eden** (for defs. 1–3). **4.** a town in N North Carolina. 15,672. [< Heb *'ēden* delight, pleasure] **—E•den•ic** (ē den′ik), *adj.*

E•den (ēd′n), *n.* **(Robert) Anthony, Earl of Avon,** 1897–1977, British statesman: prime minister 1955–57.

E′den Prai′rie, a town in SE Minnesota. 16,263.

e•den•tate (ē den′tāt), *adj.* **1.** belonging or pertaining to the Edentata, an order of New World mammals characterized by the absence of incisors and canines in the arrangement of teeth and comprising the armadillos, the sloths, and the South American anteaters. **2.** toothless. **—***n.* **3.** an edentate mammal. [1820–30; < L *ēdentātus* deprived of teeth, equiv. to *ē-* E- + *dent-* (s. of *dēns*) TOOTH + *-ātus* -ATE[1]]

e•den•tu•lous (ē den′chə ləs), *adj.* lacking teeth; toothless. [1775–85; < L *ēdentulus,* equiv. to *ē-* E- + *dent-* (s. of *dēns* TOOTH) + *-ulus* -ULOUS]

E•der (ā′dər), *n.* a river in central Germany, mainly in Hesse and flowing E to Kassel. 110 mi. (177 km) long.

E•der•le (ā′dər lē), *n.* **Gertrude Caroline,** born 1907?, U.S. swimmer.

CONCISE ETYMOLOGY KEY: <, descended or borrowed from; >, whence; b., blend of, blended; c., cognate with; cf., compare; deriv., derivative; equiv., equivalent; imit., imitative; obl., oblique; r., replacing; s., stem; sp., spelling, spelled; resp., respelling, respelled; trans., translation; ?, origin unknown; *, unattested; ‡, probably earlier than. See the full key inside the front cover.

EDES, Hellenic National Democratic army, a Greek resistance coalition in World War II. [< ModGk *E(thnikós) D(ēmokratikós) E(llēnikós) S(yndésmos)*]

E•des•sa (i des′ə), *n.* an ancient city in NW Mesopotamia, on the modern site of Urfa: an early center of Christianity; the capital of a principality under the Crusaders. **—E•des′san, E•des•sene** (i des′ēn), *adj.*

ed′e•tate cal′cium diso′dium (ed′ə tāt′), *n. Pharm.* a chelating agent, $C_{10}H_{12}CaN_2Na_2O_8$, used in medicine to treat lead poisoning. [*edetate* appar. irreg. from EDTA + -ATE[2]]

Ed•gar (ed′gər), *n.* an award given annually in various categories of mystery writing. [1945–50; named after *Edgar* Allan Poe]

Ed•gar (ed′gər), *n.* a male given name: from Old English words meaning "rich, happy" and "spear."

edge (ej), *n., v.,* **edged, edg•ing.** **—***n.* **1.** a line or border at which a surface terminates: *Grass grew along the edges of the road. The paper had deckle edges.* **2.** a brink or verge: *the edge of a cliff; the edge of disaster.* **3.** any of the narrow surfaces of a thin, flat object: *a book with gilt edges.* **4.** a line at which two surfaces of a solid object meet: *an edge of a box.* **5.** the thin, sharp side of the blade of a cutting instrument or weapon. **6.** the sharpness proper to a blade: *The knife has lost its edge.* **7.** sharpness or keenness of language, argument, tone of voice, appetite, desire, etc.: *The snack took the edge off his hunger. Her voice had an edge to it.* **8.** *Brit. Dial.* a hill or cliff. **9.** an improved position; advantage: *He gained the edge on his opponent.* **10.** *Cards.* **a.** advantage, esp. the advantage gained by being the age or eldest hand. **b.** See **eldest hand.** **11.** *Ice Skating.* one of the two edges of a skate blade where the sides meet the bottom surface, made sharp by carving a groove on the bottom. **12.** *Skiing.* one of the two edges on the bottom of a ski that is angled into a slope when making a turn. **13. have an edge on,** *Informal.* to be mildly intoxicated with alcoholic liquor: *He had a pleasant edge on from the sherry.* **14. on edge, a.** (of a person or a person's nerves) acutely sensitive; nervous; tense. **b.** impatient; eager: *The contestants were on edge to learn the results.* **15. set one's teeth on edge.** See **tooth** (def. 18). **—***v.t.* **16.** to put an edge on; sharpen. **17.** to provide with an edge or border: *to edge a terrace with shrubbery; to edge a skirt with lace.* **18.** to make or force (one's way) gradually by moving sideways. **19.** *Metalworking.* **a.** to turn (a piece to be rolled) onto its edge. **b.** to roll (a piece set on edge). **c.** to give (a piece) a desired width by passing between vertical rolls. **d.** to rough (a piece being forged) so that the bulk is properly distributed for final forging. **—***v.i.* **20.** to move sideways: *to edge through a crowd.* **21.** to advance gradually or cautiously: *a car edging up to a curb.* **22. edge in,** to insert or work in or into, esp. in a limited period of time: *Can you edge in your suggestion before they close the discussion?* **23. edge out,** to defeat (rivals or opponents) by a small margin: *The home team edged out the visitors in an exciting finish.* [bef. 1000; ME *egge,* OE *ecg;* c. G *Ecke* corner; akin to L *aciēs,* Gk *akís* point] **—edge′less,** *adj.*
—Syn. 1. rim, lip. EDGE, BORDER, MARGIN refer to a boundary. An EDGE is the boundary line of a surface or plane: *the edge of a table.* BORDER is the boundary of a surface or the strip adjacent to it, inside or out: *a border of lace.* MARGIN is a limited strip, generally unoccupied, at the extremity of an area: *the margin of a page.*

edge•bone (ej′bōn′), *n.* aitchbone. [by folk etym.]

edged (ejd), *adj.* **1.** having an edge or edges (often used in combination): *dull-edged; a two-edged sword.* **2.** sarcastic; cutting: *an edged reply.* [1585–95; EDGE + -ED[3]]

edge′ effect′, *Ecol.* the tendency toward greater variety and density of plant and animal populations in an ecotone. [1930–35]

edge′ mold′ing, a convexly rounded molding having a fillet or concavity at or near its centerline. [1755–65]

edg•er (ej′ər), *n.* **1.** a person who puts an edge, esp. a finishing edge, on a garment, surface, lens, etc. **2.** a machine for finishing or making an edge, as for stitching, beveling, or trimming. **3.** a gardening tool with a rotary blade for cutting a neat border around a lawn, flower bed, or the like. [1585–95; EDGE + -ER[1]]

edg•er-feed•er (ej′ər fē′dər), *n.* a machine used to sort letters automatically according to envelope size.

edge′ tool′, a tool with a cutting edge. [1300–50; ME]

edge′ wave′, *Oceanog.* a wave aligned at right angles to the shoreline.

edge•wise (ej′wīz′), *adv.* **1.** with the edge forward; in the direction of the edge. **2.** sideways. **3. get a word in edgewise,** to succeed in entering a conversation or expressing one's opinion in spite of competition or opposition: *There were so many people talking at once that I couldn't get a word in edgewise.* Also, **edge•ways** (ej′wāz′). [1560–70; EDGE + -WISE]

Edge•wood (ej′wŏŏd′), *n.* a city in NE Maryland, near Baltimore. 19,455.

Edge•worth (ej′wûrth), *n.* **Maria,** 1767–1849, English novelist.

edg•ing (ej′ing), *n.* **1.** something that forms or is placed along an edge or border. **2.** *Skiing.* the tilting of a ski to the side so that one edge cuts into the snow. [1550–60; EDGE + -ING[1]] **—edg′ing•ly,** *adv.*

edg′ing lobel′ia, a trailing lobelia, *Lobelia erinus,* of southern Africa, having loose clusters of blue flowers.

edg•y (ej′ē), *adj.,* **edg•i•er, edg•i•est.** **1.** nervously irritable; impatient and anxious. **2.** sharp-edged; sharply defined, as outlines. [1765–75; EDGE + -Y[1]] **—edg′i•ly,** *adv.* **—edg′i•ness,** *n.*

edh (eth), *n.* eth.

ed•i•ble (ed′ə bəl), *adj.* **1.** fit to be eaten as food; eatable; esculent. **—***n.* **2.** Usually, **edibles.** edible substances; food. [1605–15; < LL *edibilis,* equiv. to *ed(ere)* to EAT + *-ibilis* -IBLE] **—ed′i•bil′i•ty, ed′i•ble•ness,** *n.*
—Syn. 1. comestible, consumable.

e•dict (ē′dikt), *n.* **1.** a decree issued by a sovereign or other authority. **2.** any authoritative proclamation or command. [1250–1300; ME < L *ēdictum,* n. use of neut. of *ēdictus* (ptp. of *ēdicere* to say out), equiv. to *ē-* E- + *dictus* said; see DICTUM] **—e•dic′tal,** *adj.* **—e•dic′tal•ly,** *adv.*
—Syn. 1. dictum, pronouncement.

ed•i•cule (ed′i kyŏŏl′), *n.* aedicule.

E•die (ē′dē), *n.* a female given name, form of **Edith.**

ed•i•fi•ca•tion (ed′ə fi kā′shən), *n.* **1.** an act of edifying. **2.** the state of being edified; uplift. **3.** moral improvement or guidance. [1350–1400; ME (< AF) < L *aedificātiōn-* (s. of *aedificātiō*), equiv. to *aedificāt(us)* (ptp. of *aedificāre*) built (*aedi-* s. of *aedēs* house + *-fic-,* comb. form of *facere* to make + *-ātus* -ATE[1]) + *-iōn-* -ION]

e•dif•i•ca•to•ry (i dif′i kə tôr′ē, -tōr′ē, ed′ə fi kā′tə-rē), *adj.* intended or serving to edify. [1640–50; < LL *aedificātōrius* edifying, equiv. to *aedificā(re)* to EDIFY + *-tōrius* -TORY[1]]

ed•i•fice (ed′ə fis), *n.* **1.** a building, esp. one of large size or imposing appearance. **2.** any large, complex system or organization. [1350–1400; ME < AF, MF < L *aedificium,* equiv. to *aedific(āre)* to build (see EDIFY) + *-ium* -IUM] **—ed•i•fi•cial** (ed′ə fish′əl), *adj.*
—Syn. 1. See **building.**

ed•i•fy (ed′ə fī), *v.t.,* **-fied, -fy•ing.** to instruct or benefit, esp. morally or spiritually; uplift: *religious paintings that edify the viewer.* [1300–50; ME *edifien* < AF, OF *edifier* < L *aedificāre* to build, equiv. to *aedi-* (s. of *aedes*) house, temple + *-ficāre* -FY] **—ed′i•fi′er,** *n.* **—ed′i•fy′ing•ly,** *adv.*

e•dile (ē′dīl), *n. Rom. Hist.* aedile.

E•di•na (i dī′nə), *n.* a city in SE Minnesota, near Minneapolis. 46,073.

Ed•in•burg (ed′n bûrg′), *n.* a city in S Texas. 24,075.

Ed•in•burgh (ed′n bûr′ə, -bur′ə *or, esp. Brit.,* -brə), *n.* **1. Duke of.** See **Philip** (def. 4). **2.** a city in and the capital of Scotland, in the SE part: administrative center of the Lothian region. 470,085.

E•dir•ne (e dēr′ne), *n.* a city in NW Turkey, in the European part. 54,885. Also called **Adrianople.** Formerly, **Adrianopolis.**

Ed•i•son (ed′ə sən), *n.* **1. Thomas Al•va** (al′və), 1847–1931, U.S. inventor, esp. of electrical devices. **2.** a township in central New Jersey. 70,193.

Ed′ison effect′, *Physics.* the phenomenon of the flow of electric current when an electrode sealed inside the bulb of an incandescent lamp is connected to the positive terminal of the lamp. [named after T. A. EDISON]

ed•it (ed′it), *v.t.* **1.** to supervise or direct the preparation of (a newspaper, magazine, book, etc.); serve as editor of; direct the editorial policies of. **2.** to collect, prepare, and arrange (materials) for publication. **3.** to revise or correct, as a manuscript. **4.** to expunge; eliminate (often fol. by *out*): *The author has edited out all references to his own family.* **5.** to add (usually fol. by *in*). **6.** to prepare (motion-picture film, video or magnetic tape) by deleting, arranging, and splicing, by synchronizing the sound record with the film, etc. **7.** *Genetics.* to alter the arrangement of (genes). **8.** *Computers.* to modify or add to (data or text). **—***n.* **9.** an instance of or the work of editing: *automated machinery that allows a rapid edit of incoming news.* [1785–95; 1915–20 for def. 6; partly back formation from EDITOR, partly < F *éditer* < L *ēditus* published (ptp. of *ēdere* to give out), equiv. to *ē-* E- + *-ditus* comb. form of *datus* given; cf. DATUM]

edit., **1.** edited. **2.** edition. **3.** editor.

E•dith (ē′dith), *n.* a female given name: from Old English words meaning "rich, happy" and "war." Also, **E′dithe.**

e•di•tion (i dish′ən), *n.* **1.** one of a series of printings of the same book, newspaper, etc., each issued at a different time and differing from another by alterations, additions, etc. (distinguished from *impression*). **2.** the format in which a literary work is published: *a one-volume edition of Shakespeare.* **3.** the whole number of impressions or copies of a book, newspaper, etc., printed from one set of type at one time. **4.** a version of anything, printed or not, presented to the public: *the newest edition of a popular musical revue.* [1545–55; (< MF) < L *ēditiōn-* (s. of *ēditiō*) publication, equiv. to *ēdit(us)* (ptp. of *ēdere;* see EDIT) + *-iōn-* -ION]

edi′tion bind′ing, a decorative binding for books, often of leather or simulated leather. Cf. **library binding.**

e•di•ti•o prin•ceps (e dit′i ō′ prıng′keps; *Eng.* i dish′ē ō′ prin′seps), *pl.* ***e•di•ti•o•nes prin•ci•pes*** (e dit′i ō′nes prıng′ki pes′; *Eng.* i dish′ē ō′nēz prin′sə pēz′). *Latin.* first edition.

ed•i•tor (ed′i tər), *n.* **1.** a person having managerial and sometimes policy-making responsibility for the editorial part of a publishing firm or of a newspaper, magazine, or other publication. **2.** the supervisor or conductor of a department of a newspaper, magazine, etc.: *the sports editor of a newspaper.* **3.** a person who edits material for publication, films, etc. **4.** a device for editing film or magnetic tape. [1640–50; < ML, LL: publisher; see EDIT, -TOR]

ed•i•to•ri•al (ed′i tôr′ē əl, -tōr′-), *n.* **1.** an article in a newspaper or other periodical presenting the opinion of the publisher, editor, or editors. **2.** a statement broadcast on radio or television that presents the opinion of the owner, manager, or the like, of the station or channel. **3.** something regarded as resembling such an article or statement, as a lengthy, dogmatic utterance. **—***adj.* **4.** of or pertaining to an editor or to editing: *editorial policies; editorial techniques.* **5.** of, pertaining to, or involved in the preparation of an editorial or editorials: *editorial page; editorial writer.* **6.** of or pertaining to the literary and artistic activities or contents of a publication, broadcasting organization, or the like, as distinguished from its business activities, advertisements, etc.: *an editorial employee; an editorial decision, not an ad-*

vertising one. [1735–45; EDITOR + -IAL] —**ed·i·to·ri·al·ist** (ed′i tôr′ē ə list, -tōr′-), *n.* —**ed′i·to′ri·al·ly,** *adv.*

ed·i·to·ri·al·ize (ed′i tôr′ē ə līz′, -tōr′-), *v.i.,* **-ized, -iz·ing. 1.** to set forth one's position or opinion on some subject in, or as if in, an editorial. **2.** to inject personal interpretations or opinions into an otherwise factual account. Also, *esp. Brit.,* **ed′i·to′ri·al·ise′.** [1855–60, *Amer.*; EDITORIAL + -IZE] —**ed′i·to′ri·al·i·za′tion,** *n.* —**ed′i·to′ri·al·iz′er,** *n.*

ed′ito′rial we′, we (def. 6).

ed′itor in chief′, *pl.* **editors in chief.** the policy-making executive or principal editor of a publishing house, publication, etc. [1870–75]

ed·i·tor·ship (ed′i tər ship′), *n.* **1.** the office or function of an editor. **2.** editorial direction. [1775–85; EDITOR + -SHIP]

ed·i·tress (ed′i tris), *n.* a woman employed in the work of editing. [1790–1800; EDIT(O)R + -ESS]
—**Usage.** See **-ess.**

ed′it trace′, (in electronic publishing) a record of editorial changes, additions, and deletions that can be displayed on a screen or printed out with edited copy.

Ed.M., Master of Education.

Ed·man (ed′mən), *n.* **Irwin,** 1896–1954, U.S. philosopher and essayist.

Ed·mond (ed′mənd), *n.* **1.** a town in central Oklahoma. 34,637. **2.** Also, **Ed′mund.** a male given name: from Old English words meaning "rich, happy" and "protection."

Ed·monds (ed′məndz), *n.* a town in NW Washington. 27,526.

Ed·mon·ton (ed′mən tən), *n.* a city in and the capital of Alberta, in the central part, in SW Canada. 461,361.

Edmund I, A.D. 921?–946, English king 940–946. Also, **Eadmund I.**

Edmund II, (*"Ironside"*) A.D. c980–1016, English king 1016: defeated by Canute. Also, **Eadmund II.**

Ed·mun·da (ed mun′də), *n.* a female given name. Also, **Ed·monde** (ed′mənd).

Ed·munds (ed′məndz), *n.* **George Franklin,** 1828–1919, U.S. lawyer and politician: senator 1866–91.

Ed·munds·ton (ed′mənd stən, -mən-), *n.* a city in NW New Brunswick, in SE Canada, on the upper part of the St. John River. 12,044.

Ed·na (ed′nə), *n.* a female given name: from a Hebrew word meaning "rejuvenation, rebirth."

Ed·nas (ed′nəs), *n. Douay Bible.* Adnah.

E·do (ed′ō; *Japn.* e′dô′), *n.* a former name of **Tokyo.**

E·do (ed′ō), *n., pl.* **E·dos,** (*esp. collectively*) **E·do** for 1. **1.** a member of an indigenous people of western Africa, in the Benin region of southern Nigeria. **2.** the Kwa language of the Edo people.

E·dom (ē′dəm), *n.* **1.** Esau, the brother of Jacob. **2.** Greek, **Idumaea, Idumea.** an ancient region between the Dead Sea and the Gulf of Aqaba, bordering ancient Palestine. See map under **Philistia. 3.** the kingdom of the Edomites located in this region.

E·dom·ite (ē′də mīt′), *n.* a descendant of Esau or Edom. Num. 20:14–21. [1350–1400; EDOM + -ITE[1]] —**E′dom·it′ish, E·dom·it·ic** (ē′də mit′ik), *adj.*

EDP, electronic data processing: the use of computers in the processing of data. Cf. **ADP, IDP.**

ed·ro·pho·ni·um (ed′rə fō′nē əm), *n. Pharm.* a substance, $C_{10}H_{16}BrNO$, used to reverse certain muscle-relaxing agents, such as tubocurarine, in surgical procedures: also used in the diagnosis of myasthenia gravis. [contr. of components of the chemical name]

eds., 1. editions. **2.** editors.

Ed.S., Education Specialist.

Ed·sel (ed′səl), *n.* a male given name: from Old English words meaning "rich" and "hall."

Ed′sel Ford′ Range′, a mountain range in Antarctica, E of the Ross Sea.

EDT, Eastern daylight-saving time. Also, **E.D.T.**

EDTA, *Chem., Pharm.* ethylenediaminetetraacetic acid: a colorless compound, $C_{10}H_{16}N_2O_8$, capable of chelating a variety of divalent metal cations: as a salt used as an anticoagulant, antioxidant, blood cholesterol reducer, food preservative; as a calcium-disodium salt used in the treatment of lead and other heavy-metal poisonings.

educ., 1. educated. **2.** education. **3.** educational.

ed·u·ca·ble (ej′o͝o kə bəl), *adj.* **1.** capable of being educated. **2.** of or pertaining to mildly retarded individuals who may achieve self-sufficiency. Also, **ed·u·cat·a·ble** (ej′o͝o kā′tə bəl). [1835–45; EDUC(ATE) + -ABLE] —**ed′u·ca·bil′i·ty,** *n.*

ed·u·cate (ej′o͝o kāt′), *v.,* **-cat·ed, -cat·ing.** —*v.t.* **1.** to develop the faculties and powers of (a person) by teaching, instruction, or schooling. **2.** to qualify by instruction or training for a particular calling, practice, etc.; train: *to educate someone for law.* **3.** to provide schooling or training for; send to school. **4.** to develop or train (the ear, taste, etc.): *to educate one's palate to appreciate fine food.* **5.** to inform: *to educate oneself about the best course of action.* —*v.i.* **6.** to educate a person or group: *A television program that educates can also entertain.* [1580–90; < L *ēducātus* brought up, taught (ptp. of *ēducāre*), equiv. to *ē-* E- + *-duc-* lead + *-ātus* -ATE[1]]
—**Syn. 1.** instruct, school, drill, indoctrinate. See **teach.**

ed·u·cat·ed (ej′o͝o kā′tid), *adj.* **1.** having undergone education: *educated people.* **2.** characterized by or displaying qualities of culture and learning. **3.** based on some information or experience: *an educated estimate of next year's sales.* [1660–70; EDUCATE + -ED[2]]

ed·u·cat·ee (ej′o͝o kā tē′), *n.* a person who receives instruction; student. [1805–15; EDUCATE + -EE]

ed·u·ca·tion (ej′o͝o kā′shən), *n.* **1.** the act or process of imparting or acquiring general knowledge, developing the powers of reasoning and judgment, and generally of preparing oneself or others intellectually for mature life. **2.** the act or process of imparting or acquiring particular knowledge or skills, as for a profession. **3.** a degree, level, or kind of schooling: *a university education.* **4.** the result produced by instruction, training, or study: *to show one's education.* **5.** the science or art of teaching; pedagogics. [1525–35; (< MF) < L *ēducātiōn-* (s. of *ēducātiō*), equiv. to *ēducāt(us)* (see EDUCATE) + *-iōn-* -ION]
—**Syn. 1.** instruction, schooling, learning. EDUCATION, TRAINING imply a discipline and development by means of study and learning. EDUCATION is the development of the abilities of the mind (learning to know): *a liberal education.* TRAINING is practical education (learning to do) or practice, usually under supervision, in some art, trade, or profession: *training in art, teacher training.* **4.** learning, knowledge, enlightenment. EDUCATION, CULTURE are often used interchangeably to mean the results of schooling. EDUCATION, however, suggests chiefly the information acquired. CULTURE is a mode of thought and feeling encouraged by education. It suggests an aspiration toward, and an appreciation of high intellectual and esthetic ideals: *The level of culture in a country depends upon the education of its people.*

ed·u·ca·tion·al (ej′o͝o kā′shə nl), *adj.* **1.** pertaining to education. **2.** tending or intended to educate, instruct, or inform: *an educational show on television.* [1645–55; EDUCATION + -AL[1]] —**ed′u·ca′tion·al·ly,** *adv.*

ed′uca′tional park′, a group of elementary and high schools, usually clustered in a parklike setting and having certain facilities shared by all grades, that often accommodates students from a large area. [1965–70]

educa′tional psychol′ogy, a branch of psychology concerned with developing effective educational techniques and dealing with psychological problems in schools. [1910–15] —**educa′tional psychol′ogist.**

educa′tional sociol′ogy, the application of sociological principles and methods to the solution of problems in an educational system. [1915–20]

ed′uca′tional tel′evision, television of informational or instructional content. [1950–55]

ed·u·ca·tion·ese (ej′o͝o kā′shə nēz′, -nēs′), *n.* the jargon associated with the field of education. [EDUCATION + -ESE]

ed·u·ca·tion·ist (ej′o͝o kā′shə nist), *n.* a specialist in the theory and methods of education. Also, **ed′u·ca′·tion·al·ist.** [1820–30; EDUCATION + -IST]

ed·u·ca·tive (ej′o͝o kā′tiv), *adj.* **1.** serving to educate: *educative knowledge.* **2.** pertaining to or productive of education. [1835–45; EDUCATE + -IVE]

ed·u·ca·tor (ej′o͝o kā′tər), *n.* **1.** a person or thing that educates, esp. a teacher, principal, or other person involved in planning or directing education. **2.** an educationist. [1560–70; < L *ēducātor,* equiv. to *ēducā(re)* (see EDUCATE) + *-tor* -TOR]

ed·u·ca·to·ry (ej′o͝o kə tôr′ē, -tōr′ē), *adj.* educative. [1835–45; EDUCATE + -ORY[1]]

e·duce (i do͞os′, i dyo͞os′), *v.t.,* **e·duced, e·duc·ing. 1.** to draw forth or bring out, as something potential or latent; elicit; develop. **2.** to infer or deduce. [1400–50; late ME < L *ēdūcere,* equiv. to *ē-* E- + *dūcere* to lead] —**e·duc′i·ble,** *adj.*

e·duct (ē′dukt), *n.* **1.** something educed; eduction. **2.** *Chem.* a substance extracted from a mixture, as distinguished from a product. [1790–1800; < L *ēductum* something educed, n. use of neut. of *ēductus* educed (ptp. of *ēdūcere* to EDUCE), equiv. to *ē-* E- + *-duc-* lead + *-tus* ptp. suffix]

e·duc·tion (i duk′shən), *n.* **1.** the act of educing. **2.** something educed. [1640–50; < L *ēductiōn-* (s. of *ēductiō*), equiv. to *ēduct(us)* (see EDUCT) + *-iōn-* -ION]

e·duc·tive (i duk′tiv), *adj.* educing; serving to educe. [1650–60; < L *ēduct(us)* (see EDUCT) + -IVE]

e·duc·tor (i duk′tər), *n.* ejector (def. 3). [1785–95; < LL: one who leads forth from. See EDUCE, -TOR]

e·dul·co·rate (i dul′kə rāt′), *v.t.,* **-rat·ed, -rat·ing.** *Chem.* to free from acids, salts, or impurities by washing; purify. [1800–10; < NL *ēdulcorātus,* equiv. to *ē-* E- + LL *dulcorātus* sweetened (ptp. of *dulcorāre*), equiv. to L *dulcor* sweetness (*dulc(is)* sweet + *-or* -OR[1]) + *-ātus* -ATE[1]] —**e·dul′co·ra′tion,** *n.* —**e·dul′co·ra′tive,** *adj.*

ed·u·tain·ment (ej′o͝o tān′mənt), *n.* a television program, movie, book, etc., that is both educational and entertaining, esp. one intended primarily for children in the elementary grades. Also called **infotainment.** [EDU(CATION) + (ENTER)TAINMENT]

Ed·ward (ed′wərd), *n.* **1. Prince of Wales** and **Duke of Cornwall** (*"The Black Prince"*), 1330–76, English military leader (son of Edward III). **2. Lake,** a lake in central Africa, between Uganda and Zaire: a source of the Nile. 830 sq. mi. (2150 sq. km). **3.** a male given name: from Old English words meaning "rich, happy" and "guardian."

Edward I, (*"Edward Longshanks"*) 1239–1307, king of England 1272–1307 (son of Henry III).

Edward II, 1284–1327, king of England 1307–27 (son of Edward I).

Edward III, 1312–77, king of England 1327–77 (son of Edward II).

Edward IV, 1442–83, king of England 1461–70, 1471–1483: 1st king of the house of York.

Edward V, 1470–83, king of England 1483 (son of Edward IV).

Edward VI, 1537–53, king of England 1547–53 (son of Henry VIII and Jane Seymour).

Edward VII, (*Albert Edward*) (*"the Peacemaker"*) 1841–1910, king of Great Britain and Ireland 1901–10 (son of Queen Victoria).

Edward VIII, (*Duke of Windsor*) 1894–1972, king of Great Britain 1936: abdicated (son of George V; brother of George VI).

Ed·ward·i·an (ed wôr′dē ən, -wär′-), *adj.* **1.** of or pertaining to the reign of Edward VII. **2.** reflecting the opulence or self-satisfaction characteristic of this reign. **3.** noting or pertaining to the castle architecture of Edward I. —*n.* **4.** a person who lived during the reign of Edward VII. [1860–65; EDWARD (VII, I) + -IAN] —**Ed·ward′i·an·ism,** *n.*

Ed·wards (ed′wərdz), *n.* **Jonathan,** 1703–58, American clergyman and theologian.

Ed·ward·si·an·ism (ed wôrd′zē ə niz′əm, -wärd′-), *n.* a modified form of Calvinism taught by Jonathan Edwards. [1880–85, *Amer.*; Jonathan EDWARDS + -IAN + -ISM] —**Ed·ward′si·an,** *adj., n.*

Ed′wards Plateau′, a highland area in SW Texas. 2000–5000 ft. (600–1500 m) high.

Ed·wards·ville (ed′wərdz vil′), *n.* a town in SW Illinois. 12,460.

Ed′ward the Confes′sor, Saint, 1002?–66, English king 1042–66: founder of Westminster Abbey.

Ed·win (ed′win), *n.* **1.** Also, **Eadwine.** A.D. 585?–633, king of Northumbria 617–633. **2.** a male given name: from Old English words meaning "rich, happy" and "friend."

Ed·wi·na (ed wē′nə, -win′ə), *n.* a female given name: derived from *Edwin.*

E·dyth (ē′dith), *n.* a female given name. Also, **E′dythe.**

-ee, a suffix forming from transitive verbs nouns which denote a person who is the object or beneficiary of the act specified by the verb (*addressee; employee; grantee*); recent formations now also mark the performer of an act, with the base being an intransitive verb (*escapee; returnee; standee*) or, less frequently, a transitive verb (*attendee*) or another part of speech (*absentee; refugee*). [< F *-é,* (masc.), *-ée* (fem.), ptp. endings < L *-ātus, -āta* -ATE[1]]

EE, a proportional shoe width size narrower than EEE and wider than E.

E.E., 1. Early English. **2.** electrical engineer. **3.** electrical engineering.

e.e., errors excepted.

E.E. & M.P., Envoy Extraordinary and Minister Plenipotentiary.

EEC, See **European Economic Community.**

EEE, the widest proportional shoe width size.

EEG, electroencephalogram.

eel (ēl), *n., pl.* (*esp. collectively*) **eel,** (*esp. referring to two or more kinds or species*) **eels. 1.** any of numerous elongated, snakelike marine or freshwater fishes of the order Apodes, having no ventral fins. **2.** any of several similar but unrelated fishes, as the lamprey. [bef. 1000; ME *ele,* OE *ēl, ǣl;* c. D *aal,* G *Aal,* ON *āll*] —**eel′like,** *adj.* —**eel′y,** *adj.*

eel, *Anguilla rostrata,* length to 6 ft. (1.8 m)

eel·blen·ny (ēl′blen′ē), *n., pl.* (*esp. collectively*) **-ny,** (*esp. referring to two or more kinds or species*) **-nies.** any of several eellike fishes of the genus *Lumpenus,* of the prickleback family, found in subarctic coastal waters. [EEL + BLENNY]

eel·grass (ēl′gras′, -gräs′), *n.* **1.** a grasslike marine plant, *Zostera marina,* having ribbonlike leaves. **2.** See **tape grass.** [1780–90, *Amer.*; EEL + GRASS]

eel·pout (ēl′pout′), *n.* **1.** any fish of the family Zoarcidae, esp. *Zoarces viviparus,* of Europe. **2.** the burbot. [bef. 1000; OE *ǣlepūte* (not recorded in ME); see EEL, POUT[2]]

eel·worm (ēl′wûrm′), *n.* any small nematode worm of the family Anguillulidae, including the minute vinegar eel, *Anguillula aceti.* [1885–90; EEL + WORM]

e'en (ēn), *adv. Chiefly Literary.* even[2].

een·sy-ween·sy (ēn′sē wēn′sē), *adj. Baby Talk.* tiny; small. Also, **een′sie-ween′sie.** [alter. of TEENSY-WEENSY, with *-weensy* taken as the basic shape and a new rhyme formed minus the initial consonant, as in ITTY-BITTY]

EENT, *Med.* eye, ear, nose, and throat.

EEO, equal employment opportunity.

EEOC, See **Equal Employment Opportunity Commission.**

EER, See **energy efficiency ratio.**

e'er (âr), *adv. Chiefly Literary.* ever.

-eer, a noun-forming suffix occurring originally in loanwords from French (*buccaneer; mutineer; pioneer*) and productive in the formation of English nouns denoting persons who produce, handle, or are otherwise significantly associated with the referent of the base word (*auctioneer; engineer; mountaineer; pamphleteer*); now frequently pejorative (*profiteer; racketeer*). Cf. **-ary, -er**[2],

CONCISE PRONUNCIATION KEY: *act, cāpe, dâre, pärt; set, ēqual; if, īce; ox, ōver, ôrder, oil, bo͝ok, bo͞ot, out; up, ûrge; child; sing; shoe; thin, that;* zh *as in treasure.* ə = *a* as in *alone, e* as in *system, i* as in *easily, o* as in *gallop, u* as in *circus;* ə as in *fire* (fīər), *hour* (ouər). l and n can serve as syllabic consonants, as in *cradle* (krād′l), and *button* (but′n). See the full key inside the front cover.

-ier[2]. [< F, MF *-ier* (OF < L *-ārius* -ARY as suffix of personal nouns); in some nouns r. earlier suffixes (see ENGINEER, CHARIOTEER) or the F suffix *-aire* -AIRE (see MUSKETEER, VOLUNTEER)]

ee•rie (ēr′ē), *adj.*, **-ri•er, -ri•est.** **1.** uncanny, so as to inspire superstitious fear; weird: *an eerie midnight howl.* **2.** *Chiefly Scot.* affected with superstitious fear. Also, **eery.** [1250–1300; ME *eri,* dial. var. of *argh,* OE *earg* cowardly; c. OFris *erg,* ON *argr* evil, G *arg* cowardly] **—ee′ri•ly,** *adv.* **—ee′ri•ness,** *n.*
—Syn. 1. See **weird.**

ee•ry (ēr′ē), *adj.*, **-ri•er, -ri•est.** eerie.

ef-, var. of **ex-**[1] (by assimilation) before *f: efficient.*

eff., efficiency.

ef•fa•ble (ef′ə bəl), *adj.* utterable; expressible. [1630–40; < F < L *effābilis,* equiv. to *eff(ārī)* to speak out (*ef-* EF- + *fārī* to speak) + *-ābilis* -ABLE]

ef•face (i fās′), *v.t.*, **-faced, -fac•ing.** **1.** to wipe out; do away with; expunge: *to efface one's unhappy memories.* **2.** to rub out, erase, or obliterate (outlines, traces, inscriptions, etc.). **3.** to make (oneself) inconspicuous; withdraw (oneself) modestly or shyly. [1480–90; < MF *effacer.* See EF-, FACE] **—ef•face′a•ble,** *adj.* **—ef•face′ment,** *n.* **—ef•fac′er,** *n.*

ef•fect (i fekt′), *n.* **1.** something that is produced by an agency or cause; result; consequence: *Exposure to the sun had the effect of toughening his skin.* **2.** power to produce results; efficacy; force; validity; influence: *His protest had no effect.* **3.** the state of being effective or operative; operation or execution; accomplishment or fulfillment: *to bring a plan into effect.* **4.** a mental or emotional impression produced, as by a painting or a speech. **5.** meaning or sense; purpose or intention: *She disapproved of the proposal and wrote to that effect.* **6.** the making of a desired impression: *We had the feeling that the big, expensive car was only for effect.* **7.** an illusory phenomenon: *a three-dimensional effect.* **8.** a real phenomenon (usually named for its discoverer): *the Doppler effect.* **9.** See **special effects.** **10. in effect, a.** for practical purposes; virtually: *His silence was in effect a confirmation of the rumor.* **b.** essentially; basically. **c.** operating or functioning; in force: *The plan is now in effect.* **11. take effect, a.** to go into operation; begin to function. **b.** to produce a result: *The prescribed medicine failed to take effect.* —*v.t.* **12.** to produce as an effect; bring about; accomplish; make happen: *The new machines finally effected the transition to computerized accounting last spring.* [1350–1400; ME < L *effectus* the carrying out (of a task, etc.), hence, that which is achieved, outcome, equiv. to *effec-* (var. s. of *efficere* to make, carry out; *ef-* EF- + *-ficere,* comb. form of *facere* to DO[1]) + *-tus* suffix of v. action] **—ef•fect′i•ble,** *adj.*
—Syn. 1. outcome, issue. EFFECT, CONSEQUENCE(S), RESULT refer to something produced by an action or a cause. An EFFECT is that which is produced, usually more or less immediately and directly: *The effect of morphine is to produce sleep.* A CONSEQUENCE, something that follows naturally or logically, as in a train of events or sequence of time, is less intimately connected with its cause than is an effect: *Punishment is the consequence of disobedience.* A RESULT may be near or remote, and often is the sum of effects or consequences as making an end or final outcome: *The English language is the result of the fusion of many different elements.* **12.** achieve, realize, fulfill, perform, consummate.
—Usage. See **affect**[1].

ef•fect•er (i fek′tər), *n.* effector (def. 1).

ef•fec•tive (i fek′tiv), *adj.* **1.** adequate to accomplish a purpose; producing the intended or expected result: *effective teaching methods; effective steps toward peace.* **2.** actually in operation or in force; functioning: *The law becomes effective at midnight.* **3.** producing a deep or vivid impression; striking: *an effective photograph.* **4.** prepared and available for service, esp. military service. —*n.* **5.** a member of the armed forces fit for duty or active service. **6.** the effective total of a military force. [1350–1400; ME < L *effectīvus* practical, equiv. to *effect(us),* ptp. of *efficere* (see EFFECT) + *-īvus* -IVE] **—ef•fec′tive•ly,** *adv.* **—ef•fec′tive•ness, ef•fec•tiv′i•ty,** *n.*
—Syn. 1. capable, competent. EFFECTIVE, EFFECTUAL, EFFICACIOUS, EFFICIENT refer to that which is able to produce a (desired) effect. EFFECTIVE is applied to that which has the power to, or which actually does, produce an effect: *an effective action, remedy, speech.* EFFECTUAL is used esp. of that which produces the effect desired or intended, or a decisive result: *An effectual bombardment silenced the enemy.* EFFICACIOUS suggests the capability of achieving a certain end: *an efficacious plan, medicine.* EFFICIENT (applied also to persons) implies the skillful use of energy or industry to accomplish desired results with little waste of effort: *efficient methods; an efficient manager.* **2.** operative. **3.** telling. **—Ant. 1.** futile, useless.

effec′tive cur′rent, *Elect.* the magnitude of an alternating current having the same heating effect as that of a given magnitude of direct current.

effec′tive dose′, the amount of a drug, or level of radiation exposure, that is sufficient to achieve the desired clinical improvement.

effec′tive resist′ance, *Elect.* the resistance to an alternating current, expressed as the ratio of the power dissipated to the square of the effective current.

effec′tive sound′ pres′sure, *Physics.* the square root of the mean of the squares of the sound pressures of a sound wave, measured at a given point over a certain time interval. Also called **sound pressure.**

ef•fec•tor (i fek′tər), *n.* **1.** Also, **effecter.** a person or thing that effects. **2.** *Physiol.* an organ or cell that carries out a response to a nerve impulse. **3.** *Biochem.* a substance, as a hormone, that increases or decreases the activity of an enzyme. [1595–1605; < L, equiv. to *effec-* var. s. of *efficere* (see EFFECT) + *-tor* -TOR]

ef•fects (i fekts′), *n.pl.* goods; movables; personal property. [pl. of EFFECT]

ef•fec•tu•al (i fek′cho͞o əl), *adj.* **1.** producing or capable of producing an intended effect; adequate. **2.** valid or binding, as an agreement or document. [1350–1400; ME *effectuel* (< AF), late ME *effectual* < ML *effectuālis,* equiv. to L *effectu-,* s. of *effectus* EFFECT + *-ālis* -AL[1]] **—ef•fec′tu•al•ly,** *adv.* **—ef•fec′tu•al•ness, ef•fec′tu•al′i•ty,** *n.*
—Syn. 1. See **effective.**

ef•fec•tu•ate (i fek′cho͞o āt′), *v.t.*, **-at•ed, -at•ing.** to bring about; effect. [1570–80; < ML *effectuātus* brought to pass (ptp. of *effectuāre*), equiv. to L *effectu-,* s. of *effectus* EFFECT (see EFFECT) + *-ātus* -ATE[1]] **—ef•fec′tu•a′tion,** *n.*

ef•fem•i•na•cy (i fem′ə nə sē), *n.* the state or quality of being effeminate. [1595–1605; EFFEMIN(ATE) + -ACY]

ef•fem•i•nate (*adj.* i fem′ə nit; *v.* i fem′ə nāt′), *adj., v.*, **-nat•ed, -nat•ing.** —*adj.* **1.** (of a man or boy) having traits, tastes, habits, etc., traditionally considered feminine, as softness or delicacy. **2.** characterized by excessive softness, delicacy, self-indulgence, etc.: *effeminate luxury.* —*v.t., v.i.* **3.** to make or become effeminate. [1350–1400; ME < L *effēminātus,* equiv. to *ef-* EF- + *fēmin(a)* woman + *-ātus* -ATE[1]] **—ef•fem′i•nate•ly,** *adv.* **—ef•fem′i•nate•ness,** *n.* **—ef•fem′i•na′tion,** *n.*
—Syn. 1. See **female.**

ef•fem•i•nize (i fem′ə nīz′), *v.t.*, **-nized, -niz•ing.** to make effeminate. [1605–15; EFFEMIN(ATE) + -IZE]

ef•fen•di (i fen′dē), *n., pl.* **-dis.** **1.** a former Turkish title of respect, esp. for government officials. **2.** (in eastern Mediterranean countries) a man who is a member of the aristocracy. [1605–15; < Turk *efendi* < ModGk, Gk *authéntēs* doer, master. See AUTHENTIC]

ef•fer•ent (ef′ər ənt), *Anat., Physiol.* —*adj.* **1.** conveying or conducting away from an organ or part (opposed to *afferent*). —*n.* **2.** an efferent part, as a nerve or blood vessel. [1830–40; < L *efferent-* (s. of *efferēns* carrying off, prp. of *efferre*), equiv. to *ef-* EF- + *ferent-* carrying (*fer-* carry + *-ent-* -ENT)] **—ef′fer•ence,** *n.* **—ef′fer•ent•ly,** *adv.*

ef•fer•vesce (ef′ər ves′), *v.i.*, **-vesced, -vesc•ing.** **1.** to give off bubbles of gas, as fermenting liquors. **2.** to issue forth in bubbles. **3.** to show enthusiasm, excitement, liveliness, etc.: *The parents effervesced with pride over their new baby.* [1695–1705; < L *effervēscere,* equiv. to *ef-* EF- + *ferv-* hot (see FERVENT) + *-ēscere* -ESCE] **—ef′fer•ves′cence,** *n.*

ef•fer•ves•cent (ef′ər ves′ənt), *adj.* **1.** effervescing; bubbling. **2.** vivacious; gay; lively; sparkling. [1675–85; < L *effervēscent-* (s. of *effervēscēns*), prp. of *effervēscere* to EFFERVESCE; see -ENT] **—ef′fer•ves′cent•ly,** *adv.*

ef•fete (i fēt′), *adj.* **1.** lacking in wholesome vigor; degenerate; decadent: *an effete, overrefined society.* **2.** exhausted of vigor or energy; worn out: *an effete political force.* **3.** unable to produce; sterile. [1615–25; < L *effēta* exhausted from bearing, equiv. to *ef-* EF- + *fēta* having brought forth, fem. ptp. of lost v.; see FETUS] **—ef•fete′ly,** *adv.* **—ef•fete′ness,** *n.*
—Syn. 2. enervated, debilitated.

ef•fi•ca•cious (ef′i kā′shəs), *adj.* capable of having the desired result or effect; effective as a means, measure, remedy, etc.: *The medicine is efficacious in stopping a cough.* [1520–30; < L *efficāci-* (s. of *efficāx*) effectual. See EFFICIENT, -ACIOUS] **—ef′fi•ca′cious•ly,** *adv.* **—ef′fi•ca′cious•ness,** *n.*

ef•fi•cac•i•ty (ef′i kas′i tē), *n., pl.* **-ties.** efficacy.

ef•fi•ca•cy (ef′i kə sē), *n., pl.* **-cies.** capacity for producing a desired result or effect; effectiveness: *a remedy of great efficacy.* [1520–30; < L *efficācia,* equiv. to *efficāc-* (see EFFICACIOUS) + *-ia* -Y[3]]

ef•fi•cien•cy (i fish′ən sē), *n., pl.* **-cies.** **1.** the state or quality of being efficient; competency in performance. **2.** accomplishment of or ability to accomplish a job with a minimum expenditure of time and effort: *The assembly line increased industry's efficiency.* **3.** the ratio of the work done or energy developed by a machine, engine, etc., to the energy supplied to it, usually expressed as a percentage. **4.** See **efficiency apartment.** [1585–95; < L *efficientia,* equiv. to *efficient-* (see EFFICIENT) + *-ia* -Y[3]]

effi′ciency apart′ment, a small apartment consisting typically of a combined living room and bedroom area, a bathroom, and a kitchenette. Also called **efficiency.** [1925–30]

effi′ciency ex′pert, a person who studies the methods, procedures, and job characteristics of a business or factory with the object of devising ways to increase the efficiency of equipment and personnel. Also called **effi′ciency engineer′.** Cf. **time and motion study.** [1910–15, *Amer.*]

ef•fi•cient (i fish′ənt), *adj.* **1.** performing or functioning in the best possible manner with the least waste of time and effort; having and using requisite knowledge, skill, and industry; competent; capable: *a reliable, efficient secretary.* **2.** satisfactory and economical to use: *Our new air conditioner is more efficient than our old one.* **3.** producing an effect, as a cause; causative. **4.** utilizing a particular commodity or product with maximum efficiency (usually used in combination): *a fuel-efficient engine.* [1350–1400; ME (< MF) < L *efficient-* (s. of *efficiēns*), equiv. to *ef-* EF- + *fic-,* comb. form of *facere* to make, DO[1] + *-ent-* -ENT] **—ef•fi′cient•ly,** *adv.*
—Syn. 1. effectual. See **effective.**

effi′cient cause′, *Aristotelianism.* See under **cause** (def. 8b).

Ef•fie (ef′ē), *n.* a female given name.

ef•fi•gy (ef′i jē), *n., pl.* **-gies.** **1.** a representation or image, esp. sculptured, as on a monument. **2.** a crude representation of someone disliked, used for purposes of ridicule. **3. in effigy,** in public view in the form of an effigy: *a leader hanged in effigy by the mob.* [1530–40; (< MF) < L *effigia,* equiv. to *effig-* (*ef-* EF- + *fig-* shape, form; see FIGURE) + *-ia* -Y[3]] **—ef•fig•i•al** (i fij′ē əl), *adj.*

eff•ing (ef′ing), *adj., adv. Slang.* (used as an intensifier). [1940–45; euphemism for *fucking,* with *ef* as spelled form of the name of the initial letter]

Ef•fing•ham (ef′ing ham′), *n.* a town in central Illinois. 11,270.

ef•fleu•rage (ef′lə räzh′), *n.* a delicate stroking motion in massage. [1885–90; < F, equiv. to *effleur(er)* (to) stroke as one would a flower (i.e., lightly; see EF-, FLOWER) + *-age* -AGE]

ef•flo•resce (ef′lə res′), *v.i.*, **-resced, -resc•ing.** **1.** to burst into bloom; blossom. **2.** *Chem.* **a.** to change either throughout or on the surface to a mealy or powdery substance upon exposure to air, as a crystalline substance through loss of water of crystallization. **b.** to become incrusted or covered with crystals of salt or the like through evaporation or chemical change. [1765–75; < L *efflōrēscere* to blossom out, equiv. to *ef-* EF- + *flōrēscere* to begin to bloom (*flōr(i)-,* s. of *flōs* flower + *-ēscere* -ESCE)]

ef•flo•res•cence (ef′lə res′əns), *n.* **1.** the state or a period of flowering. **2.** an example or result of growth and development: *These works are the efflorescence of his genius.* **3.** *Chem.* **a.** the act or process of efflorescing. **b.** the resulting powdery substance or incrustation. **4.** *Pathol.* a rash or eruption of the skin. [1620–30; < F < ML *efflōrēscentia.* See EFFLORESCE, -ENCE]

ef•flo•res•cent (ef′lə res′ənt), *adj.* **1.** efflorescing; blossoming. **2.** *Chem.* **a.** subject to efflorescence. **b.** covered with or forming an efflorescence. [1810–20; < L *efflōrēscent-* (s. of *efflōrēscēns*), prp. of *efflōrēscere* to EFFLORESCE; see -ENT]

ef•flu•ence (ef′lo͞o əns), *n.* **1.** the action or process of flowing out; efflux. **2.** something that flows out; emanation. [1595–1605; < L *efflu-* outflow (*ef-* EF- + *flu-* flow) + -ENCE]

ef•fluent (ef′lo͞o ənt), *adj.* **1.** flowing out or forth. —*n.* **2.** something that flows out or forth; outflow; effluence. **3.** a stream flowing out of a lake, reservoir, etc. **4.** sewage that has been treated in a septic tank or sewage treatment plant. **5.** sewage or other liquid waste that is discharged into a body of water, etc. [1720–30; < L *effluent-* (s. of *effluēns* flowing out, prp. of *effluere*), equiv. to *ef-* EF- + *flu-* flow + *-ent-* -ENT]

ef•flu•vi•um (i flo͞o′vē əm), *n., pl.* **-vi•a** (-vē ə), **-vi•ums.** a slight or invisible exhalation or vapor, esp. one that is disagreeable or noxious. [1640–50; < L, equiv. to *ef-* EF- + *fluv-,* base of *fluere* to flow (see EFFLUENT) + *-ium* -IUM] **—ef•flu′vi•al,** *adj.*

ef•flux (ef′luks), *n.* **1.** outward flow, as of water. **2.** something that flows out; effluence. **3.** a passing or lapse of time. **4.** a passing away; expiration; ending. Also, **ef•flux•ion** (i fluk′shən) (for defs. 3, 4). [1635–45; < ML *effluxus,* equiv. to L *ef-* EF- + *fluc-,* var. s. of *fluere* to flow + *-sus,* for *-tus* suffix of v. action]

ef•fort (ef′ərt), *n.* **1.** exertion of physical or mental power: *It will take great effort to achieve victory.* **2.** an earnest or strenuous attempt: *an effort to keep to the schedule.* **3.** something done by exertion or hard work: *I thought it would be easy, but it was an effort.* **4.** an achievement, as in literature or art: *The painting is one of his finest efforts.* **5.** the amount of exertion expended for a specified purpose: *the war effort.* **6.** *Chiefly Brit.* **a.** an organized community drive or achievement. **b.** a fund-raising drive. **7.** *Mech.* the force or energy that is applied to a machine for the accomplishment of useful work. [1480–90; < MF; OF *esfort, esforz,* deriv. of *esforcier* to force (*es-* EX-[1] + *forcier* to FORCE)]
—Syn. 1. struggle, striving. EFFORT, APPLICATION, ENDEAVOR, EXERTION imply actions directed or force expended toward a definite end. EFFORT is an expenditure of energy to accomplish some objective: *He made an effort to control himself.* APPLICATION is continuous effort plus careful attention: *constant application to duties.* ENDEAVOR means a continued and sustained series of efforts to achieve some, often worthy and difficult, end: *a constant endeavor to be useful.* EXERTION is the vigorous and often strenuous expenditure of energy, frequently without an end: *out of breath from exertion.*

ef•fort•ful (ef′ərt fəl), *adj.* marked by effort or exertion; labored. [1895–1900; EFFORT + -FUL] **—ef′fort•ful•ly,** *adv.*

ef•fort•less (ef′ərt lis), *adj.* requiring or involving no effort; displaying no signs of effort; easy: *an effortless writing style.* [1795–1805; EFFORT + -LESS] **—ef′fort•less•ly,** *adv.* **—ef′fort•less•ness,** *n.*

ef′fort syn′drome, *Pathol.* See **cardiac neurosis.**

ef•frac•tion (i frak′shən), *n. Law.* a breaking into a house, store, etc., by force; forcible entry. [1830–40; < F: lit., a breaking open < L *ef-* EF- + *frāction-* FRACTION] **—ef•frac′tor,** *n.*

ef•fron•ter•y (i frun′tə rē), *n., pl.* **-ter•ies.** **1.** shameless or impudent boldness; barefaced audacity: *She had the effrontery to ask for two free samples.* **2.** an act or instance of this. [1705–15; < F *effronterie,* equiv. to OF *esfront* shameless (*es-* EX-[1] + *front* brow; see FRONT) + *-erie* -ERY]
—Syn. 1. impertinence, impudence, cheek.

ef•ful•gent (i ful′jənt, i fo͝ol′-), *adj.* shining forth brilliantly; radiant. [1730–40; < L *effulgent-* (s. of *effulgēns,* prp. of *effulgēre*), equiv. to *ef-* EF- + *fulg(ēre)* to shine + *-ent-* -ENT] **—ef•ful′gence,** *n.* **—ef•ful′gent•ly,** *adv.*

ef•fuse (*v.* i fyo͞oz′; *adj.* i fyo͞os′), *v.*, **-fused, -fus•ing,** *adj.* —*v.t.* **1.** to pour out or forth; shed; disseminate: *The town effuses warmth and hospitality.* —*v.i.* **2.** to exude; flow out. **3.** *Physics.* (of a gas) to flow through a very small orifice. —*adj.* **4.** scattered; profuse. **5.** *Bot.* spread out loosely. **6.** (of certain shells) having the lips separated by a gap or groove. [1350–1400; ME < L *effūs(us)* (ptp. of *effundere*) poured out, equiv. to *ef-* EF- + *fūsus* poured (see FUSE[2])]

CONCISE ETYMOLOGY KEY: <, descended or borrowed from; >, whence; b., blend of, blended; c., cognate with; cf., compare; deriv., derivative; equiv., equivalent; imit., imitative; obl., oblique; r., replacing; s., stem; sp., spelling, spelled; resp., respelling, respelled; trans., translation; ?, origin unknown; *, unattested; ‡, probably earlier than. See the full key inside the front cover.

ef•fu•sion (i fyōō′zhən), *n.* **1.** the act of effusing or pouring forth. **2.** something that is effused. **3.** an unrestrained expression, as of feelings: *poetic effusions.* **4.** *Pathol.* **a.** the escape of a fluid from its natural vessels into a body cavity. **b.** the fluid that escapes. **5.** *Physics.* the flow of a gas through a small orifice at such density that the mean distance between the molecules is large compared with the diameter of the orifice. [1350–1400; ME (< AF) < L *effūsiōn-* (s. of *effūsiō*), equiv. to *ef-* EF- + *fūsion-* FUSION]

ef•fu•sive (i fyōō′siv), *adj.* **1.** unduly demonstrative; lacking reserve: *effusive greetings; an effusive person.* **2.** pouring out; overflowing. **3.** *Geol.* extrusive (def. 3). [1655–65; EFFUSE + -IVE] **—ef•fu′sive•ly,** *adv.* **—ef•fu′sive•ness,** *n.*

Ef•fy (ef′ē), *n.* a female given name.

Ef•ik (ef′ik), *n., pl.* **Ef•iks,** (*esp. collectively*) **Ef•ik** for 1. **1.** a member of a people of southeastern Nigeria near the mouth of the Calabar River, closely related to the Ibibio. **2.** the Benue-Congo language of these people.

EFL, English as a foreign language: the study of English by nonnative speakers living in a non-English-speaking environment. Cf. **ESL**

EFM, See **electronic fetal monitor.**

efph, equivalent full-power hour.

eft[1] (eft), *n.* **1.** a newt, esp. the eastern newt, *Notophthalmus viridescens* (**red eft**), in its immature terrestrial stage. **2.** *Obs.* a lizard. [bef. 1000; ME *evet(e)*, OE *efete;* cf. NEWT]

eft[2] (eft), *adv. Archaic.* **1.** again. **2.** afterward. [bef. 900; ME, OE; akin to AFT, AFTER]

EFT, See **electronic funds transfer.** Also, **EFTS**

EFTA, See **European Free Trade Association.**

EFTS, electronic funds transfer system.

eft•soon (eft sōōn′), *adv. Archaic.* soon afterward. [bef. 950; ME *eftsone*, OE *eftsōna.* See EFT[2], SOON]

Eg., **1.** Egypt. **2.** Egyptian.

e.g., for example; for the sake of example; such as. [< L *exempli grātiā*]

e•gad (i gad′, ē gad′), *interj.* (used as an expletive or mild oath): *Egad, I never thought of that!* Also, **e•gads** (i gadz′, ē gadz′). [1665–75; euphemistic alter. of *oh God!*]

E•ga•di (eg′ə dē; *It.,* e′gä dē), *n.* a group of islands in the Mediterranean Sea off the coast of W Sicily. 15 sq. mi. (39 sq. km). Also called **Aegadian Islands, Aegadean Islands.** Ancient, **Aegates.**

egads′ but′ton, *Rocketry Slang.* a switch that triggers the destruction in flight of a malfunctioning missile. Also called **chicken switch.**

e•gal (ē′gal), *adj. Archaic.* equal. [1350–1400; ME *egall* < AF, OF *egal* < L *aequālis*]

E galaxy. See **elliptical galaxy.**

e•gal•i•tar•i•an (i gal′i târ′ē ən), *adj.* **1.** asserting, resulting from, or characterized by belief in the equality of all people, esp. in political, economic, or social life. *—n.* **2.** a person who adheres to egalitarian beliefs. [1880–85; alter. of EQUALITARIAN with F *égal* r. EQUAL] **—e•gal′i•tar′i•an•ism,** *n.*

é•ga•li•té (ā ga lē tā′), *n. French.* equality.

Eg•bert (eg′bərt), *n.* **1.** A.D. 775?–839, king of the West Saxons 802–839; 1st king of the English 828–839. **2.** a male given name: from an Old English word meaning "bright sword."

E•ger (ā′gər), *n.* German name of **Ohře.**

e•gest (ē jest′, i jest′), *v.t.* to discharge, as from the body; void (opposed to *ingest*). [1600–10; < L *ēgest(us)* (ptp. of *ēgerere*) carried out, equiv. to *ē-* E- + *ges-* (var. of *ger-*) carry + *-tus* ptp. suffix] **—e•ges′tive,** *adj.*

e•ges•ta (ē jes′tə, i jes′-), *n.* (*used with a singular or plural v.*) matter egested from the body, as excrement. [1780–90; neut. pl. of L *ēgestus* carried out. See EGEST]

e•ges•tion (i jes′chən), *n.* the process of egesting; the voiding of the refuse of digestion. [1375–1425; ME < L *ēgestiōn-* (s. of *ēgestiō*), equiv. to *ēgest-* (see EGEST) + *-iōn-* -ION]

egg[1] (eg), *n.* **1.** the roundish reproductive body produced by the female of certain animals, as birds and most reptiles, consisting of an ovum and its envelope of albumen, jelly, membranes, egg case, or shell, according to species. **2.** such a body produced by a domestic bird, esp. the hen. **3.** the contents of an egg or eggs: *raw egg; fried eggs.* **4.** anything resembling a hen's egg. **5.** Also called **egg cell.** the female gamete; ovum. **6.** *Informal.* person: *He's a good egg.* **7.** *Slang.* an aerial bomb. **8.** **egg on one's face,** *Informal.* humiliation or embarrassment resulting from having said or done something foolish or unwise: *They were afraid to back the losing candidate and wind up with egg on their faces.* **9.** **lay an egg,** *Informal.* to fail wretchedly, esp. to be unsuccessful in front of an audience: *He laid an egg as the romantic hero.* **10.** **put all one's eggs in one basket,** to venture all of something that one possesses in a single enterprise. **11.** **walk on eggs,** to walk or act very cautiously. *—v.t.* **12.** to prepare (food) by dipping in beaten egg. [bef. 900; ME < ON; r. ME *ey*, OE *ǣg*, G *Ei* egg; akin to L *ōvum*, Gk *ōión* egg] **—egg′less,** *adj.* **—egg′y,** *adj.*

—Pronunciation. EGG, like *beg, leg,* and other words where "short e" precedes a "hard g" sound, is pronounced with the vowel (e) of *bet* and *let*, except in parts of New England and the South Midland and southern U.S., where these words are frequently said with (-āg), to rhyme with *vague* and *plague*, especially in the speech of the less educated. This raising of (e) to a higher vowel (ā), articulated with the upper surface of the tongue closer to the palate, also occurs before (zh), as in *measure, pleasure,* and *treasure.*

egg[2] (eg), *v.t.* to incite or urge; encourage (usually fol. by *on*). [1150–1200; ME < ON *eggja* to incite, deriv. of *egg* EDGE]

egg′ and dart′, *Archit.* a design for enriching an ovolo or echinus, consisting of a closely set, alternating series of oval and pointed forms. [1870–75]

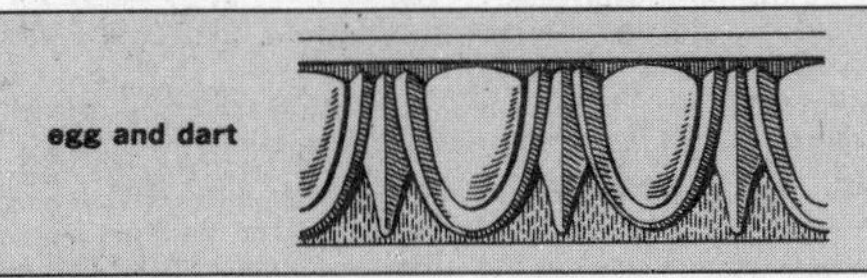
egg and dart

egg′ and spoon′ race′, a novelty race in which contestants each carry an egg in a spoon to the finish line, the winner being the first to finish without dropping or breaking the egg. [1890–95]

egg•beat•er (eg′bē′tər), *n.* **1.** a small rotary beater for beating eggs, whipping cream, etc. **2.** *Slang.* a helicopter. [1820–30, *Amer.;* EGG[1] + BEATER]

egg′ case′, *Entomol.* ootheca. [1840–50]

egg′ cell′, egg (def. 5). [1875–80]

egg′ coal′, **1.** anthracite in sizes ranging from 3¼ to 2$\frac{7}{16}$ in. (8 to 6 cm), intermediate between broken coal and stove coal. **2.** bituminous coal in sizes ranging from 4 to 1½ in. (10 to 4 cm). [1850–55, *Amer.*]

egg•crate (eg′krāt′), *adj.* of or resembling a horizontal construction divided by vertical partitions into cell-like areas, used esp. for directing downward rays of overhead light: *eggcrate ceiling fixtures.* Also, **egg′-crate′.** [EGG[1] + CRATE]

egg′ cream′, a cold beverage made with milk, flavoring syrup, and soda water. [‡1950–55]

egg•cup (eg′kup′), *n.* a small cup or bowl for serving a boiled egg. [1825–35; EGG[1] + CUP]

egg′drop soup′ (eg′drop′), a soup made by stirring beaten eggs into a simmering broth. [EGG[1] + DROP]

egg•er (eg′ər), *n.* See **tent caterpillar.** [1695–1705; EGG[1] + -ER[1]; the cocoon is egg-shaped]

egg′ foo′ yung′ (fōō′ yung′), *Chinese-American Cookery.* a dish of a pancake-shaped omelet containing a mixture of chopped foods. Also, **egg′ fu′ yung′.** [< dial. Chin (Guangdong) *fùh yùhng*, equiv. to Chin *fúrong* egg white, lit., the name of a kind of hibiscus]

egg•head (eg′hed′), *n. Informal* (*often disparaging*). an intellectual. [1915–20; EGG[1] + HEAD]

egg•head•ed (eg′hed′id), *adj. Informal* (*often disparaging*). of or befitting an egghead. [1915–20; EGGHEAD + -ED[3]] **—egg′head′ed•ness,** *n.*

Eg•gle•ston (eg′əl stən), *n.* **Edward,** 1837–1902, U.S. author, editor, and clergyman.

egg•nog (eg′nog′), *n.* a drink made of eggs, milk or cream, sugar, and, usually, rum or wine. [1765–75, *Amer.;* EGG[1] + NOG[1]]

egg•plant (eg′plant′, -plänt′), *n.* **1.** a plant, *Solanum melongena esculentum*, of the nightshade family, cultivated for its edible, dark-purple or occasionally white or yellow fruit. **2.** the fruit of this plant used as a table vegetable. **3.** a blackish purple color; aubergine. [1760–70; EGG[1] + PLANT]

egg′ roll′, *Chinese-American Cookery.* a cylindrical casing of egg dough filled with a minced mixture of meat or shrimp, bamboo shoots, onions, etc., and fried in deep fat. [1940–45]

egg′ roll′ing, a contest or race in which eggs are rolled over a lawn, using a spoon or paddle, most commonly held as a children's entertainment during the Easter season.

eggs′ Ben′edict, (*sometimes l.c.*) a dish consisting of toast or toasted halves of English muffin covered with a thin slice of fried or broiled ham, poached eggs, and a topping of hollandaise sauce. [1925–30; allegedly after a patron of the Waldorf-Astoria Hotel in New York City, for whom the dish was first made (in some accounts, by Oscar Tschirky (1866–1950), the hotel's maitre d')]

egg-shaped (eg′shāpt′), *adj.* having an oval form, usually with one end larger than the other. [1760–70]

egg•shell (eg′shel′), *n.* **1.** the shell of a bird's egg, consisting of keratin fibers and calcite crystals. **2.** a pale yellowish-white color. **3.** rather bulky paper having a slightly rough finish. *—adj.* **4.** like an eggshell, as in thinness and delicacy; very brittle; fragile. **5.** being pale yellowish-white in color. **6.** having little or no gloss: *eggshell white paint.* [1250–1300; ME *ayschelle.* See EGG[1], SHELL]

egg′ stone′, oolite. [1815–25]

egg′ tim′er, a small hourglass or clock device running about three to five minutes, used to time the boiling of an egg. [1880–85]

egg′ tooth′, a calcareous prominence at the tip of the beak or upper jaw of an embryonic bird or reptile, used to break through the eggshell at hatching. [1890–95]

egg′ white′, the white of an egg, esp. a hen's egg, used in cooking; albumen. [1895–1900]

e•gis (ē′jis), *n.* aegis.

eg•lan•tine (eg′lən tīn′, -tēn′), *n.* the sweetbrier. [1350–1400; ME < MF; OF *aiglent* (< VL **aculentum*, neut. of **aculentus* prickly, equiv. to L *acu(s)* needle + *-lentus* adj. suffix) + *-ine* -INE[1]]

Eg•lev•sky (i glef′skē, eg′ləf skē), *n.* **An•dré** (än′drā, än drā′), 1917–77, U.S. ballet dancer, born in Russia.

EGmc, East Germanic.

e•go (ē′gō, eg′ō), *n., pl.* **e•gos.** **1.** the "I" or self of any person; a person as thinking, feeling, and willing, and distinguishing itself from the selves of others and from objects of its thought. **2.** *Psychoanal.* the part of the psychic apparatus that experiences and reacts to the outside world and thus mediates between the primitive drives of the id and the demands of the social and physical environment. **3.** egotism; conceit; self-importance: *Her ego becomes more unbearable each day.* **4.** self-esteem or self-image; feelings: *Your criticism wounded his ego.* **5.** (*often cap.*) *Philos.* **a.** the enduring and conscious element that knows experience. **b.** *Scholasticism.* the complete person comprising both body and soul. **6.** *Ethnol.* a person who serves as the central reference point in the study of organizational and kinship relationships. [1780–90; < L: I; psychoanalytic term is trans. of G (*das*) *Ich* (the) I]

e•go-al•ien (ē′gō āl′yən, -ā′lē ən, eg′ō-), *adj.* ego-dystonic.

e′go anal′ysis, psychoanalytic study of the ways in which the ego resolves internal conflicts and develops a mature capacity for rational thought and action.

e•go•cen•tric (ē′gō sen′trik, eg′ō-), *adj.* **1.** having or regarding the self or the individual as the center of all things: *an egocentric philosophy that ignores social causes.* **2.** having little or no regard for interests, beliefs, or attitudes other than one's own; self-centered: *an egocentric person; egocentric demands upon the time and patience of others.* *—n.* **3.** an egocentric person. [1895–1900; EGO + -CENTRIC] **—e•go•cen•tric•i•ty** (ē′gō sen tris′i tē, eg′ō-), *n.* **—e′go•cen′trism,** *n.*

—Syn. 2. self-absorbed, self-obsessed. **—Ant. 2.** altruistic, unselfish.

e′gocen′tric speech′, *Psycholinguistics.* speech typically observed in young children that is not addressed to other people.

e•go-dys•ton•ic (ē′gō dis ton′ik, eg′ō-), *adj. Psychiatry.* of or pertaining to aspects of one's behavior or attitudes viewed as inconsistent with one's fundamental beliefs and personality (contrasted with *ego-syntonic*). Also, **ego-alien.**

e′go ide′al, *Psychoanal.* a more or less conscious ideal of personal excellence derived from a composite image of the characteristics of persons, initially those of the parents, with whom the individual identifies. [1920–25]

e•go•ism (ē′gō iz′əm, eg′ō-), *n.* **1.** the habit of valuing everything only in reference to one's personal interest; selfishness (opposed to *altruism*). **2.** egotism or conceit. **3.** *Ethics.* the view that morality ultimately rests on self-interest. [1775–85; < F *égoïsme.* See EGO, -ISM]

—Syn. 1. See **egotism.**

e•go•ist (ē′gō ist, eg′ō-), *n.* **1.** a self-centered or selfish person (opposed to *altruist*). **2.** an arrogantly conceited person; egotist. **3.** an adherent of the metaphysical principle of the ego, or self; solipsist. [1775–85; < F *égoïste.* See EGO, -IST]

e•go•is•tic (ē′gō is′tik, eg′ō-), *adj.* **1.** pertaining to or of the nature of egoism. **2.** being centered in or preoccupied with oneself and the gratification of one's own desires; self-centered (opposed to *altruistic*). Also, **e′go•is′ti•cal.** [1825–35; EGOIST + -IC] **—e′go•is′ti•cal•ly,** *adv.*

e•go•ma•ni•a (ē′gō mā′nē ə, -mān′yə, eg′ō-), *n.* psychologically abnormal egotism. [1815–25; EGO + -MANIA; modeled on *monomania*] **—e′go•ma′ni•ac′,** *n.* **—e•go•ma•ni•a•cal** (ē′gō mə nī′i kəl, eg′ō-), *adj.*

e•goph•o•ny (ē gof′ə nē), *n.* a vocal sound heard through a stethoscope and resembling the bleating of a goat, often occurring in cases of pleurisy with effusion. **—e•go•phon•ic** (ē′gə fon′ik), *adj.* [1850–55; < NL *egophonia* < Gk *aigo-* comb. form of *aix* goat (s. *aig-;* cf. AEGIS) + -PHONY]

e′go psychol′ogy, a school of neo-Freudian psychology holding that the ego has autonomous energy and functions independently.

e•go-syn•ton•ic (ē′gō sin ton′ik, eg′ō-), *adj. Psychiatry.* of or pertaining to aspects of one's behavior or attitudes viewed as acceptable and consistent with one's fundamental personality and beliefs (contrasted with *ego-dystonic*).

e•go•tism (ē′gə tiz′əm, eg′ə-), *n.* **1.** excessive and objectionable reference to oneself in conversation or writing; conceit; boastfulness. **2.** selfishness; self-centeredness; egoism. [1705–15; < L *ego* EGO + -ISM; *-t-* perh. after DESPOTISM, IDIOTISM[2]]

—Syn. 1. EGOTISM, EGOISM refer to preoccupation with one's ego or self. EGOTISM is the common word for obtrusive and excessive reference to and emphasis upon oneself and one's own importance: *His egotism alienated all his friends.* EGOISM, a less common word, is used especially in philosophy, ethics, or metaphysics, where it emphasizes the importance of or preoccupation with self in relation to other things: *sufficient egoism to understand one's central place in the universe.* See also **pride.**

—Ant. 1. humility, modesty, altruism.

e•go•tist (ē′gə tist, eg′ə-), *n.* **1.** a conceited, boastful person. **2.** a selfish person; egoist. [1705–15; EGOT(ISM) + -IST]

e•go•tis•tic (ē′gə tis′tik, eg′ə-), *adj.* **1.** pertaining to or characterized by egotism. **2.** given to talking about oneself; vain; boastful; opinionated. **3.** indifferent to the well-being of others; selfish. Also, **e′go•tis′ti•cal.** [1855–60; EGOTIST + -IC] **—e′go•tis′ti•cal•ly,** *adv.*

e′go trip′, *Informal.* an act or course of action undertaken primarily to satisfy one's vanity or for self-gratification: *Her charitable activity was one long ego trip.* [1965–70]

e•go-trip (ē′gō trip′, eg′ō-), *v.i.,* **-tripped, -trip•ping.** *Informal.* to behave in a self-serving manner. [1965–70] **—e′go-trip′per,** *n.*

CONCISE PRONUNCIATION KEY: *act, cāpe, dâre, pärt; set, ēqual; if, īce; ox, ōver, ôrder, oil, bŏŏk, bōōt, out; up, ûrge; child; sing; shoe; thin, that;* zh as in *treasure.* ə = *a* as in *alone, e* as in *system, i* as in *easily, o* as in *gallop, u* as in *circus;* ə as in *fire* (fīər), *hour* (ouər). l and n can serve as syllabic consonants, as in *cradle* (krād′l), and *button* (but′n). See the full key inside the front cover.

EGR, *Auto.* See **exhaust-gas recirculation.**

e•gre•gious (i grē′jəs, -jē əs), *adj.* **1.** extraordinary in some bad way; glaring; flagrant: *an egregious mistake; an egregious liar.* **2.** *Archaic.* distinguished or eminent. [1525–35; < L *ēgregius* preeminent, equiv. to *ē-* E- + *greg-*, s. of *grex* flock + *-ius* adj. suffix; see -OUS] —**e•gre′gious•ly,** *adv.* —**e•gre′gious•ness,** *n.* —**Syn. 1.** gross, outrageous, notorious.

e•gress (*n.* ē′gres; *v.* i gres′), *n.* **1.** the act or an instance of going, esp. from an enclosed place. **2.** a means or place of going out; an exit. **3.** the right or permission to go out. **4.** *Astron.* emersion (def. 1). —*v.i.* **5.** to go out; emerge. [1530–40; < L *ēgressus* going out, escape, equiv. to *ēgred(ī)* to go out (*ē-* E- + *-gredī*, comb. form of *gradī* to go, step; cf. GRADE) + *-tus* suffix of v. action]

e•gres•sion (i gresh′ən), *n.* a going out; egress. [1500–10; < L *ēgressiōn-* (s. of *ēgressiō*) a going out, equiv. to *ēgress(us)*, ptp. of *ēgredī* (see EGRESS) + *-iōn-* -ION]

e•gres•sive (i gres′iv), *adj.* **1.** of or pertaining to egress. **2.** *Phonet.* produced with an outward flow of air from the lungs, as most speech sounds (opposed to *ingressive*). [1685–95; < L *ēgress(us)* (see EGRESSION) + -IVE]

egret, *Casmerodius albus,* length 3½ ft. (1.1 m)

e•gret (ē′grit, eg′rit, ē gret′, ē′gret), *n.* **1.** any of several usually white herons that grow long, graceful plumes during the breeding season, as *Egretta garzetta* **(little egret),** of the Old World. **2.** aigrette. [1400–50; late ME *egret(e)* < AF *egret* (cf. MF *égreste,* AIGRETTE), alter. (with *-on* exchanged for *-et* -ET) of dial. OF *aigron* < Gmc; see HERON]

EGR valve, *Auto.* See under **exhaust-gas recirculation.**

E•gypt (ē′jipt), *n.* **1. Arab Republic of.** a republic in NE Africa. 39,600,000; 386,198 sq. mi. (1,000,252 sq. km). *Cap.:* Cairo. Arabic, **Misr.** Formerly (1958–71), **United Arab Republic. 2.** an ancient kingdom in NE Africa: divided into the Nile Delta **(Lower Egypt)** and the area from Cairo S to the Sudan **(Upper Egypt).**

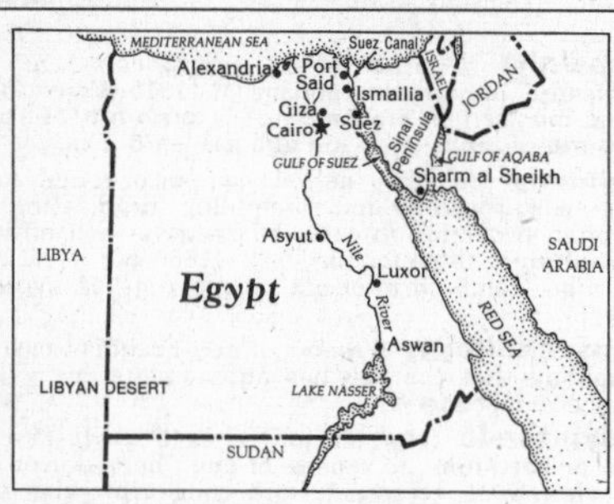

Egypt., Egyptian (def. 4). Also, **Egypt**

E•gyp•ti•ac (i jip′tē ak′), *adj.* of or pertaining to ancient Egypt. [1630–40; < L *Aegyptiacus* < Gk *aigyptiakós*, equiv. to *aigýpti(os)* Egyptian, deriv. of *Aígyptos* the Nile, Egypt + *-akos* -AC]

E•gyp•tian (i jip′shən), *adj.* **1.** of or pertaining to Egypt or its people: *Egyptian architecture.* **2.** *Obs.* of or pertaining to the Gypsies. —*n.* **3.** a native or inhabitant of Egypt. **4.** the extinct Afroasiatic language of the ancient Egyptians. *Abbr.:* Egypt. **5.** a printing type having square serifs. [1350–1400; ME (see EGYPT, -IAN); r. *Egiptish*, OE *Egiptisc*, equiv. to *Egipt-* + *-isc* -ISH[1]] —**E•gyp′tian•ism, E•gyp•tic•i•ty** (ē′jip tis′i tē), *n.*

Egyp′tian cal′endar, the calendar of ancient Egypt, having a year consisting of twelve 30-day months, with five additional days at the end, leap year not being considered.

Egyp′tian clo′ver, berseem. [1895–1900]

Egyp′tian co′bra, a highly venomous cobra, *Naja haje*, inhabiting northern and central Africa and Jordan, growing to a length of 8 ft. (2.4 m) or more. [1905–10]

Egyp′tian cot′ton, a variety of Sea Island cotton, having silky, strong fibers, grown chiefly in northern Africa. [1875–80]

E•gyp•tian•ize (i jip′shə nīz′), *v.*, **-ized, -iz•ing.** —*v.t.* **1.** to make Egyptian; assign Egyptian origin or characteristics to. —*v.i.* **2.** to become Egyptian; adopt Egyptian manners or characteristics. Also, *esp. Brit.,* **E•gyp′tian•ise′.** [1655–65; EGYPTIAN + -IZE] —**E•gyp′tian•i•za′tion,** *n.*

CONCISE ETYMOLOGY KEY: <, descended or borrowed from; >, whence; b., blend of, blended; c., cognate with; cf., compare; deriv., derivative; equiv., equivalent; imit., imitative; obl., oblique; r., replacing; s., stem; sp., spelling, spelled; resp., respelling, respelled; trans., translation; ?, origin unknown; *, unattested; ‡, probably earlier than. See the full key inside the front cover.

Egyp′tian lo′tus, 1. either of two Egyptian water lilies of the genus *Nymphaea,* as *N. caerulea* **(blue lotus),** having light blue flowers, or *N. lotus* **(white lotus),** having white flowers. **2.** See **Indian lotus.**

E•gyp•tol•o•gy (ē′jip tol′ə jē), *n.* the scientific study of Egyptian antiquities. [1855–60; EGYPT + -O- + -LOGY] —**E•gyp•to•log•i•cal** (i jip′tə loj′i kəl), *adj.* —**E′gyp•tol′o•gist,** *n.*

eh (ā, e), *interj.* (an interrogative utterance, usually expressing surprise or doubt or seeking confirmation).

EHF, See **extremely high frequency.** Also, **ehf**

Eh′lers-Dan′los syn′drome (ā′lərz dan′los, -ləs), *Pathol.* a rare hereditary disease of connective tissue, characterized by joint hypermotility and abnormally stretchable skin. [after Edvard *Ehlers* (1863–1937), Danish dermatologist, and Henri Alexandre *Danlos* (1844–1912), French dermatologist, who separately reported it in 1901 and 1908]

Eh•ren•breit•stein (ā′rən brīt′shtīn), *n.* a fortress in Coblenz, West Germany, built in the 12th century.

Eh•ren•burg (er′ən bûrg′, -bo͝org′; *Russ.* e ryinbo͞ork′), *n.* **Il•ya Gri•gor•ie•vich** (ē lyä′ gryi gô′ryi-vyich), 1891–1967, Russian novelist and journalist.

Ehr•lich (âr′likh), *n.* **Paul** (poul), 1854–1915, German physician, bacteriologist, and chemist: Nobel prize for medicine 1908.

EHS, Environmental Health Services.

EHV, extra high voltage.

E.I., 1. East Indian. **2.** East Indies.

Eich•mann (ik′mən, īkh′-; *Ger.* īkh′män′), *n.* **Adolf,** 1906–62, German Nazi official: executed for war crimes.

ei′co•sa•pen•ta•e•no′ic ac′id (ī′kō sə pen′tə i-nō′ik, ī′kō-), *Biochem.* See **EPA.** [< Gk *eikosa-*, comb. form of *eikosi* twenty + PENTA- + -ENE + -O- + -IC]

ei•der (ī′dər), *n.* **1.** See **eider duck. 2.** eiderdown. [1735–45; < Icel *æthar* (in 18th century spelled *ædar*), gen. sing. of *æthur* eider duck, in phrase *ædar dūnn* down of the eider duck; sp. *eider* < G or Sw]

ei•der•down (ī′dər doun′), *n.* **1.** down, or soft feathers, from the breast of the female eider duck. **2.** a heavy quilt or comforter, esp. one filled with eiderdown. **3.** a warm, lightweight knitted or woven fabric of wool, cotton, or man-made fibers, napped on one or both sides, used for sleepwear, infants' clothing, etc. [1765–75; EIDER + DOWN[2]]

eider duck, *Soamateria mollissima,* length 2 ft. (0.6 m)

ei′der duck′, any of several large sea ducks of the genus *Soamateria* and allied genera of the Northern Hemisphere, the females of which yield eiderdown. [1850–55]

ei•det•ic (ī det′ik), *adj.* **1.** of, pertaining to, or constituting visual imagery vividly experienced and readily reproducible with great accuracy and in great detail. **2.** of or pertaining to eidos. [1920–25; < Gk *eidētikós*, equiv. to *eîd(os)* EIDOS + *-ētikos* -ETIC]

ei•do•lon (ī dō′lən), *n., pl.* **-la** (-lə), **-lons. 1.** a phantom; apparition. **2.** an ideal. [1820–30; see IDOL]

ei•dos (ī′dos, ā′-), *n., pl.* **ei•de** (ī′dē, ā′dā). the formal content of a culture, encompassing its system of ideas, criteria for interpreting experience, etc. [< Gk *eîdos* something seen, form; akin to Gk *ideîn*, L *vidēre* to see; see WIT[2]]

Eif•fel (ī′fəl; *Fr.* e fel′), *n.* **A•le•xan•dre Gus•tave** (a lek sän′dr[ə] gys tav′), 1832–1923, French civil engineer and pioneer aerodynamic researcher.

Eif′fel Tow′er, a tower of skeletal iron construction in Paris, France: built for the exposition of 1889. 984 ft. (300 m) high. [named after A. G. EIFFEL, its engineer and principal designer]

Ei•gen (ī′gən), *n.* **Man•fred** (män′frāt), born 1927, German chemist: Nobel prize 1967.

ei•gen•func•tion (ī′gən fungk′shən), *n. Math.* a characteristic vector in a vector space in which the elements are functions. Also called **proper function.** [1925–30; < G *Eigenfunktion*, equiv. to *eigen-* characteristic, particular + *Funktion* FUNCTION]

ei•gen•val•ue (ī′gən val′yo͞o), *n. Math.* See **characteristic root.** [1925–30; partial trans. of G *Eigenwert*, equiv. to *eigen-* characteristic, particular + *Wert* VALUE]

ei•gen•vec•tor (ī′gən vek′tər), *n. Math.* See **characteristic vector.** [1955–60; < G *Eigenvektor*]

eight (āt), *n.* **1.** a cardinal number, seven plus one. **2.** a symbol for this number, as 8 or VIII. **3.** a set of this many persons or things, as the crew of an eight-oared racing shell. **4.** a playing card the face of which bears eight pips. **5.** *Informal.* **a.** an automobile powered by an eight-cylinder engine. **b.** an eight-cylinder engine. —*adj.* **6.** amounting to eight in number. [bef. 1000; ME *eighte*, OE *(e)ahta*; c. D *acht*, OS, OHG *ahto* (G *acht*), ON *ātta*, Goth *ahtau*, L *octō*, Gk *oktṓ*, OIr *ocht*, Welsh *wyth*, Breton *eiz*, Tocharian B *okt*, Lith *aštuoni*, Albanian *tetë*, Armenian *uth*, Pers *hasht*, Skt *aṣṭáu*; appar. an old dual in form, but not clear of what]

eight•ball (āt′bôl′), *n.* **1.** *Pool.* **a.** a black ball bearing the number eight. **b.** a game in which one player or side must pocket all of either the solid-color balls or the striped ones before being permitted to attempt the pocketing of the eightball, which wins. **2.** *Slang.* an inept person. **3. behind the eightball,** *Informal.* in a difficult, disadvantageous, or uncomfortable situation: *He hasn't studied all term, and now he's behind the eightball.* [1930–35, *Amer.*; EIGHT + BALL[1]]

eight′ cut′, *Jewelry.* See **single cut.**

8d, *Symbol.* eightpenny.

eight•een (ā′tēn′), *n.* **1.** a cardinal number, ten plus eight. **2.** a symbol for this number, as 18 or XVIII. **3.** a set of this many persons or things. —*adj.* **4.** amounting to 18 in number. [bef. 1000; ME *ehtetene*, OE *eahtatēne*; c. ON *āttjān*, G *achtzehn*. See EIGHT, -TEEN]

eight•een•mo (ā′tēn′mō), *n., pl.* **-mos,** *adj. Bookbinding.* octodecimo. [EIGHTEEN + -MO]

eight•eenth (ā′tēnth′), *adj.* **1.** next after the seventeenth; being the ordinal number for 18. **2.** being one of 18 equal parts. —*n.* **3.** an eighteenth part, esp. of one (1/18). **4.** the eighteenth member of a series. [bef. 900; ME *eightenthe*, *eightethe*, OE *eahtatēotha*. See EIGHTEEN + -TH[2]]

Eight′eenth Amend′ment, an amendment to the U.S. Constitution, ratified in 1918, prohibiting the manufacture, sale, or transportation of alcoholic beverages for consumption: repealed in 1933.

eight•een-wheel•er (ā′tēn hwē′lər, -wē′-), *n.* a large tractor-trailer, usually having ten wheels on the cab and eight on the trailer.

eight•fold (āt′fōld′), *adj.* **1.** comprising eight parts or members. **2.** eight times as great or as much. —*adv.* **3.** in eightfold measure. [1550–60; EIGHT + -FOLD]

Eight′fold Path′, *Buddhism.* the eight pursuits of one seeking enlightenment, comprising right understanding, motives, speech, action, means of livelihood, effort, intellectual activity, and contemplation.

Eight′fold Way′, *Physics.* a scheme for classifying hadrons according to a symmetry principle based on strangeness and isotopic spin: a forerunner of the quark model. [1925–30; so named because hadrons with low mass and spin form groups of eight; with jocular allusion to the *Eightfold Way* of Buddhism (see EIGHTFOLD PATH)]

eighth (ātth, āth), *adj.* **1.** next after the seventh. **2.** being one of eight equal parts. —*n.* **3.** an eighth part, esp. of one (1/8). **4.** the eighth member of a series. **5.** *Music.* octave. —*adv.* **6.** in the eighth place; eighthly. [bef. 1000; ME *eightethe*, OE *eahtotha*; c. OHG *ahtoda*, ON *āttandi*, Goth *ahtud-*. See EIGHT, -TH[2]]

Eighth′ Amend′ment, an amendment to the U.S. Constitution, ratified in 1791 as part of the Bill of Rights, guaranteeing reasonable bail, fines, and punishment.

Eighth′ Command′ment, "Thou shalt not steal": eighth of the Ten Commandments. Cf. **Ten Commandments.**

eighth•ly (ātth′lē āth′-), *adv.* in the eighth place; eighth.

eighth′ note′, *Music.* a note having one eighth of the time value of a whole note; quaver. See illus. under **note.** [1885–90, *Amer.*]

eighth′ rest′, *Music.* a rest equal in time value to an eighth note. See illus. under **rest.** [1885–90]

800 number, any toll-free telephone number, usually with a 3-digit code of 800, established, as by a business, so that people from widespread areas can call for merchandise, information, or services.

eight•i•eth (ā′tē ith), *adj.* **1.** next after the seventy-ninth; being the ordinal number for 80. **2.** being one of 80 equal parts. —*n.* **3.** an eightieth part, esp. of one (1/80). **4.** the eightieth member of a series. [1350–1400; ME *eightetithe*, OE *(hund)eahtatigotha* eightieth. See EIGHTY, -TH[2]]

eight•pen•ny (āt′pen′ē), *adj.* **1.** noting a nail 2½ in. (64 mm) long. **2.** costing or amounting to the sum of eight pennies. *Symbol:* 8d [1490–1500; EIGHT + -PENNY]

eights (āts), *n.* (*used with a singular v.*). See **crazy eights.**

eight-spot (āt′spot′), *n. Slang.* a playing card the face of which bears eight pips.

eight′-track tape′ (āt′trak′), a magnetic-tape cartridge, esp. one carrying four pairs of stereo tracks of prerecorded sound or music. Also, **8-track tape.**

eight•y (ā′tē), *n., pl.* **eight•ies,** *adj.* —*n.* **1.** a cardinal number, ten times eight. **2.** a symbol for this number, as 80 or LXXX. **3.** a set of this many persons or things. **4. eighties,** the numbers, years, degrees, or the like, from 80 through 89, as in referring to numbered streets, indicating the years of a lifetime or of a century, or degrees of temperature. —*adj.* **5.** amounting to 80 in number. [bef. 850; ME *eighteti*, OE *eahtatig*. See EIGHT, -TY[1]]

eight•y-eight (ā′tē āt′), *n.* **1.** a cardinal number, 80 plus 8. **2.** a symbol for this number, as 88 or LXXXVIII. **3.** a set of this many persons or things. **4.** *Slang.* the keys of a piano or the piano itself: *tickle the old eighty-eight.* —*adj.* **5.** amounting to 88 in number.

eight•y-eighth (ā′tē ātth′, -āth′), *adj.* **1.** next after the eighty-seventh; being the ordinal number for 88. **2.** being one of 88 equal parts. —*n.* **3.** an eighty-eighth part, esp. of one (1/88). **4.** the eighty-eighth member of a series.

eight•y-fifth (ā′tē fifth′), *adj.* **1.** next after the eighty-fourth; being the ordinal number for 85. **2.** being one of 85 equal parts. —*n.* **3.** an eighty-fifth part, esp. of one (1/85). **4.** the eighty-fifth member of a series.

eight•y-first (ā′tē fûrst′), *adj.* **1.** next after the eightieth; being the ordinal number for 81. **2.** being one of 81 equal parts. —*n.* **3.** an eighty-first part, esp. of one (1/81). **4.** the eighty-first member of a series.

eight·y-five (ā′tē fīv′), *n.* **1.** a cardinal number, 80 plus 5. **2.** a symbol for this number, as 85 or LXXXV. **3.** a set of this many persons or things. —*adj.* **4.** amounting to 85 in number.

eight·y-four (ā′tē fôr′, -fōr′), *n.* **1.** a cardinal number, 80 plus 4. **2.** a symbol for this number, as 84 or LXXXIV. **3.** a set of this many persons or things. —*adj.* **4.** amounting to 84 in number.

eight·y-fourth (ā′tē fôrth′, -fōrth′), *adj.* **1.** next after the eighty-third; being the ordinal number for 84. **2.** being one of 84 equal parts. —*n.* **3.** an eighty-fourth part, esp. of one (1/84). **4.** the eighty-fourth member of a series.

eight·y-nine (ā′tē nīn′), *n.* **1.** a cardinal number, 80 plus 9. **2.** a symbol for this number, as 89 or LXXXIX. **3.** a set of this many persons or things. —*adj.* **4.** amounting to 89 in number.

eight·y-nin·er (ā′tē nī′nər), *n.* a person who began homesteading in Oklahoma in 1889. [1900–05, *Amer.*]

eight·y-ninth (ā′tē nīnth′), *adj.* **1.** next after the eighty-eighth; being the ordinal number for 89. **2.** being one of 89 equal parts. —*n.* **3.** an eighty-ninth part, esp. of one (1/89). **4.** the eighty-ninth member of a series.

eight·y-one (ā′tē wun′), *n.* **1.** a cardinal number, 80 plus 1. **2.** a symbol for this number, as 81 or LXXXI. **3.** a set of this many persons or things. —*adj.* **4.** amounting to 81 in number.

eight·y-sec·ond (ā′tē sek′ənd), *adj.* **1.** next after the eighty-first; being the ordinal number for 82. **2.** being one of 82 equal parts. —*n.* **3.** an eighty-second part, esp. of one (1/82). **4.** the eighty-second member of a series.

eight·y-sev·en (ā′tē sev′ən), *n.* **1.** a cardinal number, 80 plus 7. **2.** a symbol for this number, as 87 or LXXXVII. **3.** a set of this many persons or things. —*adj.* **4.** amounting to 87 in number.

eight·y-sev·enth (ā′tē sev′ənth), *adj.* **1.** next after the eighty-sixth; being the ordinal number for 87. **2.** being one of 87 equal parts. —*n.* **3.** an eighty-seventh part, esp. of one (1/87). **4.** the eighty-seventh member of a series.

eight·y-six (ā′tē siks′), *n.* **1.** a cardinal number, 80 plus 6. **2.** a symbol for this number, as 86 or LXXXVI. **3.** a set of this many persons or things. **4.** *Slang.* a customer considered undesirable or unwelcome and refused service at a bar or restaurant. —*adj.* **5.** amounting to 86 in number. **6.** *Slang.* sold out; out of stock. —*v.t.* *Slang.* **7.** to refuse to serve (an undesirable or unwelcome customer) at a bar or restaurant. **8.** to reject; discard. [1960–65, for def. 7; sense "refuse" perh. as rhyming slang for NIX[1]]

eight·y-sixth (ā′tē siksth′), *adj.* **1.** next after the eighty-fifth; being the ordinal number for 86. **2.** being one of 86 equal parts. —*n.* **3.** an eighty-sixth part, esp. of one (1/86). **4.** the eighty-sixth member of a series.

eight·y-third (ā′tē thûrd′), *adj.* **1.** next after the eighty-second; being the ordinal number for 83. **2.** being one of 83 equal parts. —*n.* **3.** an eighty-third part, esp. of one (1/83). **4.** the eighty-third member of a series.

eight·y-three (ā′tē thrē′), *n.* **1.** a cardinal number, 80 plus 3. **2.** a symbol for this number, as 83 or LXXXIII. **3.** a set of this many persons or things. —*adj.* **4.** amounting to 83 in number.

eight·y-two (ā′tē to͞o′), *n.* **1.** a cardinal number, 80 plus 2. **2.** a symbol for this number, as 82 or LXXXII. **3.** a set of this many persons or things. —*adj.* **4.** amounting to 82 in number.

Eijk·man (īk′män), *n.* **Chris·ti·aan** (kʀis′tē än′), 1858–1930, Dutch physician: Nobel prize 1929.

ei·kon (ī′kon), *n.* icon (defs. 1, 2).

Ei·lat (ā lät′), *n.* a seaport at the N tip of the Gulf of Aqaba, in S Israel. 19,400. Also, **Elath.**

Ei·leen (ī lēn′, ā lēn′), *n.* a female given name, form of **Helen.**

E. Ind., East Indian.

Eind·ho·ven (īnt′hō′vən), *n.* a city in S Netherlands. 195,669.

ein·kan·ter (īn′kän tər), *n.* a pebble or boulder having a single facet formed by the action of windblown sand. [< G, equiv. to *ein* ONE + *Kante* edge + *-er* -ER[1]]

ein·korn (īn′kôrn), *n.* a wheat, *Triticum monococcum,* having a one-grained spikelet, grown as a forage crop in Europe and Asia. [1900–05; < G, equiv. to *ein* ONE + *Korn* grain]

Ein·stein (īn′stīn; *Ger.* īn′shtīn′), *n.* **1. Al·bert** (al′bərt; *Ger.* äl′beʀt), 1879–1955, German physicist, U.S. citizen from 1940: formulator of the theory of relativity; Nobel prize 1921. **2. Al·fred** (al′frid; *Ger.* äl′fʀet), 1880–1952, German musicologist in U.S. **3.** (*l.c.*) *Physics, Chem.* a unit of radiant energy, equal to the energy of radiation that is capable of photochemically changing one mol of a photosensitive substance.

Ein′stein equa′tion, *Physics.* any of several equations formulated by Albert Einstein, esp. the mass-energy equation, $E=mc^2$. [1920–25]

Ein·stein·i·an (īn stī′nē ən), *adj.* pertaining to Albert Einstein or his theories, esp. the theory of relativity. [1920–25; EINSTEIN + -IAN]

ein·stein·i·um (īn stī′nē əm), *n. Chem., Physics.* a transuranic element. *Symbol:* Es; *at. no.:* 99. [1950–55; named after Albert EINSTEIN; see -IUM]

Ein′stein mod′el, *Astron.* Einstein's solution of the equations of general relativity with the cosmological constant. The solution describes an isotropic, homogeneous, static universe with no cosmological redshift. Also called **Ein′stein u′niverse.**

Ein′stein's equiv′alency prin′ciple, *Physics.* See **equivalence principle.**

Ein′stein shift′, *Physics, Astron.* formerly, gravitational redshift. [1930–35]

Ein′stein's photoelec′tric equa′tion, *Physics.* the equation that relates the energy of a photoelectron to the difference between the product of the frequency of the incident radiation times Planck's constant and the energy needed to remove the photoelectron from the substance. [named after Albert EINSTEIN]

Ein′stein the′ory, *Physics.* relativity (def. 2). Also called **Ein′stein's the′ory of relativ′ity.** [1920–25; named after Albert EINSTEIN]

Eint·ho·ven (īnt′hō′vən), *n.* **Wil·lem** (vil′əm), 1860–1927, Dutch physiologist: Nobel prize for medicine 1924.

EIR, Environmental Impact Report.

Eir·e (âr′ə, ī′rə, âr′ē, ī′rē), *n.* **1.** the Irish name of **Ireland.** **2.** a former name (1937–49) of the Republic of **Ireland.**

ei·ren·ic (ī ren′ik, ī rē′nik), *adj.* irenic.

EIS, Environmental Impact Statement.

eis·e·ge·sis (ī′si jē′sis), *n., pl.* **-ses** (-sēz). an interpretation, esp. of Scripture, that expresses the interpreter's own ideas, bias, or the like, rather than the meaning of the text. [1890–95; < Gk *eiségesis,* equiv. to *eis-* into + (*h*)*ēge-* (s. of *hēgeîsthai* to lead) + *-sis* -SIS] —**ei·se·get·ic** (ī′si jet′ik), **ei′se·get′i·cal,** *adj.*

Ei·se·nach (ī′zə näкн′), *n.* a city in SW East Germany. 50,026.

Ei·sen·how·er (ī′zən hou′ər), *n.* **Dwight David,** 1890–1969, U.S. general and statesman: Chief of Staff 1945–48; 34th president of the U.S. 1953–61.

Ei′senhower jack′et. See **battle jacket.**

Ei·sen·staedt (ī′zən stat′), *n.* **Alfred,** born 1898, U.S. news photographer, born in Germany.

Ei·sen·stein (ī′zən stīn′; *for 1 also Ger.* ī′zən shtīn′; *for 2 also Russ.* ā zyin shtyān′), *n.* **1. Fer·di·nand Gott·hold Max** (feʀ′di nänt′ gôt′hôlt mäks), 1823–52, German mathematician. **2. Ser·gei Mi·khai·lo·vich** (syiʀ gyā′ myi кнī′lə vyich), 1898–1948, Russian theatrical and motion-picture director.

Eisk (*Russ.* yāsk), *n.* Yeisk.

eis·tedd·fod (ī steth′vod, ā steth′-), *n., pl.* **eis·tedd·fods, eis·tedd·fod·au** (ā′steth vod′ī, ī′steth-). (in Wales) an annual festival, with competitions among poets and musicians. [1815–25; < Welsh: lit., session, equiv. to *eistedd* sitting + *fod,* var. (by lenition) of *bod* being] —**eis′tedd·fod′ic,** *adj.*

ei·ther (ē′thər, ī′thər), *adj.* **1.** one or the other of two: *You may sit at either end of the table.* **2.** each of two; the one and the other: *There are trees on either side of the river.* —*pron.* **3.** one or the other: *There are two roads into the town, and you can take either. Either will do.* —*conj.* **4.** (a coordinating conjunction that, when preceding a word or statement followed by the disjunctive *or,* serves to emphasize the possibility of choice): *Either come or write.* —*adv.* **5.** also; too; as well; to the same degree (used after negative clauses coordinated by *and, or,* or *nor,* or after negative subordinate clauses): *He's not fond of parties, and I'm not either. If you don't come, she won't come either.* [bef. 900; ME; OE *ǣgther,* contr. of *ǣghwæther* each of two, both]

—Usage. When the pronoun EITHER is the subject and comes immediately before the verb, the verb is singular: *Either is good enough. Either grows well in this soil.* When EITHER is followed by a prepositional phrase with a plural object, there is a tendency to use a plural verb, but a singular verb is more common: *Either of them is* (or *are*) *good enough. Either of the shrubs grows* (or *grow*) *well in this soil.*

As an adjective EITHER refers only to two of anything: *either side of the river; using either hand.* As a pronoun EITHER sometimes occurs in reference to more than two (*either of the three children*), but ANY is more common in this construction (*any of the three children*). As a conjunction, EITHER often introduces a series of more than two: *The houses were finished with either cedar siding or stucco or brick. The pizza is topped with either anchovies, green peppers, or mushrooms.*

Usage guides commonly say that the verb used with subjects joined by the correlative conjunctions EITHER . . . OR (or NEITHER . . . NOR) is singular or plural depending on the number of the noun or pronoun nearer the verb: *Either the parents or the school determines the program. Either the school or the parents determine the program.* Practice in this matter varies, however, and often the presence of one plural, no matter what its position, results in a plural verb: *Either the parents or the school determine the program.*

In carefully edited writing, these correlative conjunctions are usually placed so that what follows the first correlative is parallel to what follows the second: *The damage was done by either the wind or vandals or either by the wind or by vandals* (not *done either by the wind or vandals*). See also **neither.**

—Pronunciation. The pronunciations (ē′thər) and (nē′thər), with the vowel (ē) of *see,* are the usual ones in American English for the words EITHER and NEITHER. The pronunciations (ī′thər) and (nī′thər), with the (ī) vowel of *bite,* occur occasionally for these words, chiefly in the speech of the educated and in the network standard English of radio and television. Both the (ē) and (ī) pronunciations existed in British English, and in the 19th century the (ī) came to predominate in standard British speech. In American English, therefore, it reflects a recent borrowing from British speech rather than a survival from the time of early settlement, influenced as well by the *ei* spelling, which is pronounced as (ī) in such words as *height* and *stein.*

ei·ther-or (ē′thər ôr′, ī′thər-), *adj.* allowing no equivocation; being limited in choice to two options: *It's an either-or situation—you pay the bill or you lose the company's services.* [1925–30]

EJ (ē′jā′), *Informal.* **1.** electronic journalism. **2.** electronic journalist.

e·jac·u·late (*v.* i jak′yə lāt′; *n.* i jak′yə lit), *v.,* **-lat·ed, -lat·ing,** *n.* —*v.t.* **1.** to utter suddenly and briefly; exclaim. **2.** to eject (semen). **3.** to eject suddenly and swiftly; discharge. —*v.i.* **4.** to eject semen. —*n.* **5.** the semen emitted in an ejaculation. [1570–80; < L *ējaculātus* (ptp. of *ējaculārī*) shot out, equiv. to *ē-* E- + *jacul(um)* javelin (*jac(ere)* to throw + *-ulum* -ULE) + *-ātus* -ATE[1]]

e·jac·u·la·tion (i jak′yə lā′shən), *n.* **1.** an abrupt, exclamatory utterance. **2.** the act or process of ejaculating, esp. the discharge of semen by the male reproductive organs. [1595–1605; EJACULATE + -ION]

e·jac·u·la·tor (i jak′yə lā′tər), *n.* **1.** a person or thing that ejaculates. **2.** *Animal Husb.* a device used to obtain semen from a male animal by electrical stimulation of the reproductive organs. [1720–30; EJACULATE + -OR[2]]

e·jac·u·la·to·ry (i jak′yə lə tôr′ē, -tōr′ē), *adj.* **1.** pertaining to or of the nature of an exclamatory utterance. **2.** *Physiol.* pertaining to ejaculation. Also, **e·jac·u·la·tive** (i jak′yə lā′tiv, -lə tiv). [1635–45]

ejac′ulatory duct′, *Anat.* a canal through which semen is ejaculated: in human males, the canal that passes from the seminal vesicle and vas deferens, conveying semen to the urethra. [1745–55]

ejac′ulatory incom′petence, inability of a male to achieve orgasm and to ejaculate during sexual intercourse despite adequacy of erection.

e·ject (i jekt′), *v.t.* **1.** to drive or force out; expel, as from a place or position: *The police ejected the hecklers from the meeting.* **2.** to dismiss, as from office or occupancy. **3.** to evict, as from property. **4.** to throw out, as from within; throw off. —*v.i.* **5.** to propel oneself from a damaged or malfunctioning airplane, as by an ejection seat: *When the plane caught fire, the pilot ejected.* [1545–55; < L *ējectus* (ptp. of *ējicere*) thrown out, equiv. to *ē-* E- + *jec-* (comb. form of *jacere*) throw + *-tus* ptp. suffix] —**Syn. 1–3.** oust.

e·jec·ta (i jek′tə), *n.* (*used with a singular or plural v.*) matter ejected, as from a volcano in eruption. [1885–90; neut. pl. of L *ējectus.* See EJECT]

e·jec·tion (i jek′shən), *n.* **1.** an act or instance of ejecting. **2.** the state of being ejected. **3.** something ejected, as lava. [1560–70; < L *ējectiōn-* (s. of *ējectiō*) a throwing out, equiv. to *eject-* (see EJECT) + *-iōn-* -ION]

ejec′tion cap′sule, a cockpit designed to be ejected from an aircraft in an emergency and usually fitted with survival equipment.

ejec′tion seat′, an airplane seat that can be ejected with the pilot in an emergency. Also called **ejec′tor seat′.** [1940–45]

e·jec·tive (i jek′tiv), *adj.* **1.** serving to eject. **2.** *Phonet.* (of a voiceless stop, affricate, or fricative) produced with air compressed above the closed glottis. —*n.* **3.** *Phonet.* an ejective stop, affricate, or fricative. [1650–60; EJECT + -IVE] —**e·jec′tive·ly,** *adv.*

e·ject·ment (i jekt′mənt), *n.* **1.** the act of ejecting. **2.** *Law.* a possessory action wherein the title to real property may be tried and the possession recovered. [1560–70; EJECT + -MENT]

e·jec·tor (i jek′tər), *n.* **1.** a person or thing that ejects. **2.** (in a firearm or gun) the mechanism that after firing throws out the empty cartridge or shell. **3.** Also called **eductor.** a device for inducing a flow of a fluid from a chamber or vessel by using the pressure of a jet of water, air, steam, etc., to create a partial vacuum in such a way as to entrain the fluid to be removed. **4.** any of various devices for removing work from a machine or die. [1630–40; EJECT + -OR[2]]

e·ji·da·ta·rio (*Sp.* e hē′thä tä′ʀyô), *n., pl.* **-rios** (*Sp.* -ʀyôs). a member of an ejido. [< MexSp, equiv. to *ejid(o)* EJIDO + Sp *-atario* (learned) < L; see -ATE[1], -ARY]

e·ji·do (*Sp.* e hē′thô), *n., pl.* **-dos** (*Sp.* -thôs). a Mexican farm communally owned and operated by the inhabitants of a village on an individual or cooperative basis. [1885–90; < MexSp; Sp: common fields (immediately outside a village) < L *exitus* EXIT]

ejusd., (in prescriptions) of the same. [< L *ējusdem*]

eka-, *Chem.* a prefix used to designate the first element of the same family in the periodic table beyond the one to whose name it is prefixed, as ekaselenium for technetium. [< Skt *eka* one]

E·ka·te·rin·burg (i kat′ər in bûrg′; *Russ.* yi kə tyiʀyin bo͝oʀk′), *n.* a city in the Russian Federation in Asia, in the Ural Mountains. 1,367,000. Formerly (1924–91), **Sverdlovsk.**

E·ka·te·ri·no·dar (i kat′ə rē′nə där′; *Russ.* yi kə tyiʀyi nu där′), *n.* a former name of **Krasnodar.**

E·ka·te·ri·no·slav (i kat′ə rē′nə släf′, -släv′; *Russ.* yi kə tyi ʀyi nu släf′), *n.* a former name of **Dnepropetrovsk.**

eke[1] (ēk), *v.t.,* **eked, ek·ing.** **1.** to increase; enlarge; lengthen. **2. eke out, a.** to make (a living) or support (existence) laboriously: *They managed to eke out a living by farming a small piece of land.* **b.** to supplement; add to; stretch: *to eke out an income with odd jobs.* [bef. 1000; ME *eken,* OE *ēac(i)an* (intrans.), deriv. of *ēaca* (n.) increase; ME *echen,* OE *ēcan,* var. of *īecan* (transit.) < WGmc **aukjan;* both akin to ON *auka,* Goth *aukan,* L *augēre,* Gk *auxánein* to increase, amplify]

eke[2] (ēk), *adv. Archaic.* also. [bef. 900; ME *eek,* OE *ēc, ēac;* c. G *auch,* ON, Goth *auk*]

EKG, **1.** electrocardiogram. **2.** electrocardiograph. [< G *E(lectro)k(ardio)g(ramme)*]

e·kis·tic (i kis′tik), *adj.* of or pertaining to ekistics. Also, **e·kis′ti·cal.** [1965–70; see EKISTICS]

e·kis·ti·cian (i ki stish′ən, ē′ki-), *n.* a person who specializes in ekistics. [1965–70; see EKISTICS, -IAN]

e·kis·tics (i kis′tiks), *n.* (*used with a singular v.*) the scientific study of human settlements, drawing on diverse disciplines, including architecture, city planning, and behavioral science. [1955–60; coined by Constantine A. Doxiadus (1913–1975), Greek urbanologist, ult. < Gk *oikistikós,* deriv. of *oikisía* settlement, deriv. of *oîkos* house; see ICS]

e·kue·le (e kwā′lē, -lā), *n.* a paper money, brass coin, and monetary unit of Equatorial Guinea, equal to 100 centimos: replaced the peseta in 1973. Also, **ek·pwe·le** (ek pwā′lē, -lā).

el[1] (el), *n. Informal.* See **elevated railroad.** [by shortening]

el[2] (el), *n.* ell[1].

el[3] (el), *n.* the letter *l.*

el., elevation.

El Aa·iún (el′ ä yōōn′), a city in and the capital of Western Sahara. 28,010.

e·lab·o·rate (*adj.* i lab′ər it; *v.* i lab′ə rāt′), *adj., v.,* **-rat·ed, -rat·ing.** —*adj.* **1.** worked out with great care and nicety of detail; executed with great minuteness: *elaborate preparations; elaborate care.* **2.** marked by intricate and often excessive detail; complicated. —*v.t.* **3.** to work out carefully or minutely; develop to perfection. **4.** to add details to; expand. **5.** to produce or develop by labor. **6.** *Physiol.* to convert (food, plasma, etc.) by means of chemical processes into a substance more suitable for use within the body. —*v.i.* **7.** to add details in writing, speaking, etc.; give additional or fuller treatment (usually fol. by *on* or *upon*): *to elaborate upon a theme or an idea.* [1575–85; < L *ēlabōrātus* (ptp. of *ēlabōrāre*) worked out, equiv. to *ē-* E- + *labōr-* work + *-ātus* -ATE[1]] —**e·lab′o·rate·ly,** *adv.* —**e·lab′o·rate·ness,** *n.* —**e·lab′o·ra′tive,** *adj.* —**e·lab′o·ra′tor,** *n.*
—**Syn. 1.** perfected, painstaking. **2.** ornate. ELABORATE, LABORED, STUDIED apply to that which is worked out in great detail. That which is ELABORATE is characterized by great, sometimes even excessive, minuteness of detail: *elaborate preparations for a banquet.* That which is LABORED is marked by excessive, often forced or uninspired, effort: *a labored style of writing.* That which is STUDIED is accomplished with care and deliberation, and is done purposely, sometimes even having been rehearsed: *a studied pose.* **3, 7.** refine, improve. —**Ant. 1.** simple.

elab′orated code′, *Sociolinguistics.* a style of language use associated with formal situations and characterized by explicitness, lack of dependence on the external context, syntactic complexity, and individuality of expression. Cf. **code** (def. 11b), **restricted code.**

e·lab·o·ra·tion (i lab′ə rā′shən), *n.* **1.** an act or instance of elaborating. **2.** the state of being elaborated; elaborateness. **3.** something that is elaborated. **4.** *Psychiatry.* an unconscious process of expanding and embellishing a detail, esp. while recalling and describing a representation in a dream so that latent content of the dream is brought into a logical and comprehensible order. [1570–80; < L *ēlabōrātiōn-* (s. of *ēlabōrātiō*), equiv. to *ēlabōrāt-* (see ELABORATE) + *-iōn-* -ION]

e·lae·ni·a (i lē′nē ə), *n.* any of numerous tropical American flycatchers of the genus *Elaenia,* having short crests and small bills. [< NL (1835), orig. *Elaïnia* < Gk *elainéa,* fem. of *elaíneos* pertaining to the olive, deriv. of *elaía* OLIVE; so named from the birds' color]

el·ae·op·tene (el′ē op′tēn), *n. Chem.* eleoptene.

el·ae·o·the·si·um (el′ē ō thē′shē əm, -sē əm, ē′lē-), *n., pl.* **-si·a** (-shē ə, -sē ə). alipterion. [< Gk *elaiothésion* oiling-room, equiv. to *élaio(n)* OIL + *-thesion* suffix indicating place (deriv. of *thésis* placing, setting; see THESIS)]

El·a·gab·a·lus (el′ə gab′ə ləs, ē′lə-), *n.* Heliogabalus.

E·laine (i lān′), *n.* **1.** any of several women in Arthurian romance, as the daughter of King Pelles and the mother, by Lancelot, of Sir Galahad. **2.** a female given name, form of **Helen.**

El A·la·mein (el ä′lä mān′, -ä′lə-), a town on the N coast of Egypt, ab. 70 mi. (113 km) W of Alexandria: decisive British victory October 1942. Also called **Alamein.**

E·lam (ē′ləm), *n.* an ancient kingdom E of Babylonia and N of the Persian Gulf. *Cap.:* Susa. Also called **Susiana.**

E·lam·ite (ē′lə mīt′), *n.* **1.** a native or inhabitant of ancient Elam. **2.** Also, **Elamitic.** a language of unknown affinities, spoken by the Elamites as late as the 1st century B.C., written c3500–c2500 B.C. in a linear script and thereafter in a cuneiform script. —*adj.* **3.** of or pertaining to Elam, its people, or their language. [ELAM + -ITE[1]]

E·lam·it·ic (ē′lə mit′ik), *n.* **1.** Elamite (def. 2). —*adj.* **2.** Elamite. [ELAMITE + -IC]

é·lan (ā län′, ā lan′; *Fr.* ā län′), *n.* dash; impetuous ardor: *to dance with great élan.* [1875–80; F, MF *eslan* a dash, rush, n. deriv. of *eslancer* to dart, equiv. to *es-* EX-[1] + *lancer* to LANCE[1]]

é·lan·cé (ā län′sā; *Fr.* ā län sā′), *n., pl.* **-cés** (-sāz; *Fr.* -sā′). *Ballet.* a quick darting movement. [< F, n. use of ptp. of *élancer* to dart. See ÉLAN]

e·land (ē′lənd), *n., pl.* **e·lands,** (*esp. collectively*) **e·land.** either of two large African antelopes of the genus *Taurotragus,* having long, spirally twisted horns: now rare. [1780–90; < Afrik < D *eland* elk (MD *elen, elant*) < early modern G *Elen(d),* prob. < Lith *élnis* (now *élnis;* akin to OCS *jelenĭ* stag) or an OPruss equivalent; akin to ELK]

CONCISE ETYMOLOGY KEY: <, descended or borrowed from; >, whence; b., blend of, blended; c., cognate with; cf., compare; deriv., derivative; equiv., equivalent; imit., imitative; obl., oblique; r., replacing; s., stem; sp., spelling, spelled; resp., respelling, respelled; trans., translation; ?, origin unknown; *, unattested; ‡, probably earlier than. See the full key inside the front cover.

eland, *Taurotragus oryx,* 5½ ft. (1.7 m) high at shoulder; horns to 3½ ft. (1.1 m); length to 11 ft. (3.4 m)

é·lan vi·tal (*Fr.* ā län vē tal′), (esp. in Bergsonian philosophy) the creative force within an organism that is responsible for growth, change, and necessary or desirable adaptations. [1905–10; < F: lit., vital ardor]

el·a·pid (el′ə pid), *n.* **1.** any of numerous cosmopolitan snakes of the family Elapidae, having permanently erect fangs in the front of the upper jaw and including the New World coral snakes, the cobras, and most Australian snakes. —*adj.* **2.** belonging or pertaining to the Elapidae. [1880–85; < NL *Elapidae,* equiv. to *Elap-* (s. of *Elaps* name of genus << Gk *éllops* a sea-fish) + *-idae* -ID[2]]

e·lapse (i laps′), *v.,* **e·lapsed, e·laps·ing,** *n.* —*v.i.* **1.** (of time) to slip or pass by: *Thirty minutes elapsed before the performance began.* —*n.* **2.** the passage or termination of a period of time; lapse. [1635–45; < L *ēlapsus* (ptp. of *ēlābī* to slip away), equiv. to *e-* E- + *lab-* slip + *-sus* for *-tus* ptp. suffix]

E·la·ra (ē′lər ə), *n. Astron.* a small moon of the planet Jupiter.

E.L.A.S., Hellenic People's Army of Liberation, the military organization of the EAM: Greek resistance force in World War II. [< ModGk *E(thnikòs) L(aikòs) A(peleutherōtikòs) S(tratós)*]

e·las·mo·branch (i las′mə brangk′, i laz′-), *adj.* **1.** belonging or pertaining to the Elasmobranchii, the subclass of cartilaginous fishes comprising the sharks and rays. —*n.* **2.** an elasmobranch fish. [1870–75; < NL *Elasmobranchii,* equiv. to Gk *elasm(ós)* beaten metal (deriv. of *elaúnein;* see ELASTIC) + *-o-* -O- + *-branchii,* pl. of *-branchius,* NL coinage based on Gk *bránchia* BRANCHIA]

e·las·tance (i las′təns), *n. Elect.* the reciprocal of capacitance. [1880–85; ELAST(IC) + -ANCE]

e·las·tase (i las′tās, -taz), *n. Biochem.* a pancreatic protease that catalyzes the hydrolysis of elastin and other related proteins to polypeptides and amino acids. [1945–50; ELAST(IN) + -ASE]

e·las·tic (i las′tik), *adj.* **1.** capable of returning to its original length, shape, etc., after being stretched, deformed, compressed, or expanded: *an elastic waistband; elastic fiber.* **2.** spontaneously expansive, as gases. **3.** flexible; accommodating; adaptable; tolerant: *elastic rules and regulations.* **4.** springing back or rebounding; springy: *He walks with an elastic step.* **5.** readily recovering from depression or exhaustion; buoyant: *an elastic temperament.* **6.** *Econ.* relatively responsive to change, as to a proportionate increase in demand as the result of a decrease in price. Cf. **inelastic** (def. 2). **7.** *Physics.* of, pertaining to, or noting a body having the property of elasticity. —*n.* **8.** webbing, or material in the form of a band, made elastic, as with strips of rubber. **9.** something made from this material, as a garter. **10.** See **rubber band.** [1645–55; < NL *elasticus* expanding spontaneously, equiv. to Gk *elast(ós)* (late var. of *elatós* ductile, beaten (of metal), deriv. of *elaúnein, elân* beat out, forge) + *-icus* -IC] —**e·las′ti·cal·ly,** *adv.*
—**Syn. 3.** resilient, pliant. —**Ant. 3.** rigid, inflexible, intolerant, unyielding.

elas′tic clause′, a statement in the U.S. Constitution (Article I, Section 8) granting Congress the power to pass all laws necessary and proper for carrying out the enumerated list of powers.

elas′tic colli′sion, *Mech.* a collision in which the total kinetic energy of the colliding bodies or particles is the same after the collision as it was before (opposed to *inelastic collision*). [1925–30]

elas′tic deforma′tion, *Physics.* the temporary change in length, volume, or shape produced in an elastic substance by a stress that is less than the elastic limit of the substance.

e·las·tic·i·ty (i la stis′i tē, ē′la stis′-), *n.* **1.** the state or quality of being elastic. **2.** flexibility; resilience; adaptability: *a statement with a great elasticity of meaning.* **3.** buoyancy; ability to resist or overcome depression. **4.** *Physics.* the property of a substance that enables it to change its length, volume, or shape in direct response to a force effecting such a change and to recover its original form upon the removal of the force. [1655–65; ELASTIC + -ITY]

e·las·ti·cize (i las′tə sīz′), *v.t.,* **-cized, -ciz·ing.** to make elastic, as by furnishing with elastic bands: *to elasticize the waistband of a dress.* Also, *esp. Brit.,* **e·las′ti·cise′.** [ELASTIC + -IZE]

elas′tic lim′it, *Physics.* the greatest stress that can be applied to an elastic body without causing permanent deformation. Also called **limit of proportionality, proportional limit.** [1860–65]

elas′tic mod′ulus, *Physics.* See **modulus of elasticity.** [1935–40]

elas′tic scat′tering, *Physics.* the scattering of particles due to an elastic collision. [1930–35]

elas′tic tis′sue, *Anat.* connective tissue consisting chiefly of yellow, elastic fibers and composing certain ligaments and the walls of the arteries. [1860–65]

elas′tic wave′, *Physics.* a wave propagated by the elastic deformation of a medium. [1930–35]

e·las·tin (i las′tin), *n. Biochem.* a protein constituting the basic substance of elastic tissue. [1870–75; ELAST(IC) + -IN[2]]

e·las·to·mer (i las′tə mər), *n. Chem.* an elastic substance occurring naturally, as natural rubber, or produced synthetically, as butyl rubber or neoprene. [1935–40; ELAST(IC) + -O- + Gk *méros* a part] —**e·las·to·mer·ic** (i las′tə mer′ik), *adj.*

e·late (i lāt′), *v.,* **e·lat·ed, e·lat·ing,** *adj.* —*v.t.* **1.** to make very happy or proud: *news to elate the hearer.* —*adj.* **2.** elated. [1350–1400; ME *elat* proud, exalted < L *ēlātus* carried away, lifted up (ptp. of *efferre*), equiv. to *ē-* E- + *lā-* carry, lift (see TRANSLATE) + *-tus* ptp. suffix]

e·lat·ed (i lā′tid), *adj.* very happy or proud; jubilant; in high spirits: *an elated winner of a contest.* [1605–15; ELATE + -ED[2]] —**e·lat′ed·ly,** *adv.* —**e·lat′ed·ness,** *n.*
—**Syn.** overjoyed, ecstatic. —**Ant.** dejected.

el·a·ter (el′ə tər), *n.* **1.** *Bot.* an elastic filament serving to disperse spores. **2.** *Zool.* elaterid. **3.** *Obs.* elasticity. [1645–55; < NL < Gk *elatḗr* driver, equiv. to *ela-* (s. of *elaúnein* to drive; see ELASTIC) + *-tēr* n. suffix]

e·lat·er·id (i lat′ər id), *n.* **1.** any beetle of the family Elateridae, comprising the click beetles. —*adj.* **2.** belonging or pertaining to the family Elateridae. [< NL *Elateridae,* equiv. to *Elater* the type genus (< Gk; see ELATER) + *-idae* -ID[2]]

e·lat·er·ite (i lat′ə rīt′), *n.* an elastic, rubbery, brownish natural asphalt. [1820–30; ELATER + -ITE[1]]

E·lath (ā lät′), *n.* Eilat.

e·la·tion (i lā′shən), *n.* a feeling or state of great joy or pride; exultant gladness; high spirits. [1350–1400; ME *elacioun* (< AF) < L *ēlātiōn-* (s. of *ēlātiō*), equiv. to *ēlāt(us)* (see ELATE) + *-iōn-* -ION]

e·la·tive (ē′lə tiv, el′ə-), *Gram.* —*adj.* **1.** noting a case, as in Finnish, whose function is to indicate motion out of or away from. —*n.* **2.** an elative case. **3.** an adjectival form, as in Arabic, denoting intensity or superiority, approximately equivalent to the comparative and superlative of other languages. [1585–95; < L *ēlāt(us)* (see ELATE) + -IVE]

E layer, the radio-reflective ionospheric layer of maximum electron density, normally found at an altitude between 60 and 75 mi. (100 and 120 km). Also called **Heaviside layer, Kennelly-Heaviside layer.** [1930–35]

E·la·zig (e lä zi′), *n.* a city in central Turkey. 131,116.

El·ba (el′bə), *n.* an Italian island in the Mediterranean, between Corsica and Italy: the scene of Napoleon's first exile 1814–15. 26,830; 94 sq. mi. (243 sq. km).

El·ba·san (el′bä sän′), *n.* a city in central Albania. 50,700.

El·be (*Ger.* el′bə; *Eng.* elb), *n.* a river in central Europe, flowing from the W Czech Republic NW through Germany to the North Sea. 725 mi. (1165 km) long. Czech, **Labe.**

El·ber·feld (el′bər felt′), *n.* a former city in W West Germany, now incorporated into Wuppertal.

El·bert (el′bərt), *n.* **1. Mount,** a mountain in central Colorado, in the Sawatch range: second highest peak of the Rocky Mountains in the U.S. 14,431 ft. (4399 m). **2.** a male given name.

El·ber·ta (el bûr′tə), *n.* a freestone peach having reddish-yellow skin. [1925–30, *Amer.;* said to be after *Elberta* Rumph, wife of a 19th-cent. Georgia grower]

El·bląg (el′blôngk), *n.* a seaport in N Poland: formerly in Germany. 89,800. German, **El·bing** (el′bing).

el·bow (el′bō), *n.* **1.** the bend or joint of the human arm between upper arm and forearm. **2.** the corresponding joint in the forelimb of a quadruped. See diag. under **horse. 3.** something bent like an elbow, as a sharp turn in a road or river, or a piece of pipe bent at an angle. **4.** *Archit.* crossette. **5.** Also called **ell, el.** a plumbing pipe or pipe connection having a right-angled bend. **6. at one's elbow,** within easy reach; nearby: *A virtue of the cottage is that the ocean is at your elbow.* **7. bend, lift,** or **crook an elbow,** *Informal.* to drink alcoholic beverages. **8. give the elbow,** shove aside, get rid of, or reject. **9. out at the elbows, a.** poorly dressed; shabby. **b.** impoverished. Also, **out at elbows. 10. rub elbows with,** to mingle socially with; associate with: *a resort where royalty rubs elbows with the merely rich.* **11. up to one's elbows,** very busy; engrossed: *I am up to my elbows in answering mail.* Also, **up to the elbows.** —*v.t.* **12.** to push with or as if with the elbow; jostle. **13.** to make (one's way) by so pushing. —*v.i.* **14.** to elbow one's way: *He elbowed through the crowd.* [bef. 1000; ME *elbowe,* OE *el(n)boga;* c. MD *elle(n)bōghe,* OHG *el(l)inbogo* (G *Ellenbogen*), ON *ǫl(n)bogi;* lit., "forearm-bend." See ELL[2], BOW[1]]

el·bow-bend·er (el′bō ben′dər), *n. Slang.* a person fond of drinking alcoholic beverages. —**el′bow-bend′ing,** *n., adj.*

el′bow catch′, an L-shaped catch, as for a door, having a piece for the thumb on one arm and a hooked end for engaging a hooked plate on the other.

el′bow grease′, strenuous physical exertion: *a job requiring elbow grease.* [1630–40]

el•bow•room (el′bō ro͞om′, -ro͝om′), *n.* **1.** ample room; space in which to move freely. **2.** scope; opportunity: *a job with elbowroom.* [1530–40; ELBOW + ROOM]

El•brus (el bro͞os′), *n.* a mountain in the S Russian Federation, in the Caucasus range: the highest peak in Europe, 18,465 ft. (5628 m). Also, **El•bruz′.**

El•burz′ Moun′tains (el bo͝orz′), a mountain range in N Iran, along the S coast of the Caspian Sea. Highest peak, Mt. Demavend, 18,606 ft. (5671 m).

El Ca•jon (el′ kə hōn′), a city in SW California. 73,892.

El Cam•po (el kam′pō), a town in S Texas. 10,462.

El Cap•i•tan (el kap′i tan′), a mountain in E California, in the Sierra Nevada Mountains: precipice that rises over 3300 ft. (1000 m) above Yosemite Valley.

El Cen•tro (el sen′trō), a city in S California. 23,996.

El Cer•ri•to (el′ sə rē′tō), a city in W California, on San Francisco Bay. 22,731.

El•che (el′che), *n.* a city in E Spain. 122,663.

el cheap•o (el′ chē′pō), *Slang.* cheapo.

El Cid Cam•pe•a•dor (*Sp.* el thēd′ käm′pe ä thôr′, sēd′). See **Cid, The.**

El Cor•do•bés (el kôr′thô ves′), (*Manuel Benítez Pérez*), born 1936, Spanish bullfighter.

eld (eld), *n. Archaic.* **1.** age. **2.** old age. **3.** antiquity. [bef. 1000; ME *elde,* OE *eldo, ieldo,* deriv. of *(e)ald* OLD; see WORLD]

eld•er[1] (el′dər), *adj. a compar. of* **old** *with* **eldest** *as superl.* **1.** of greater age; older. **2.** of higher rank; senior: *an elder officer.* **3.** of or pertaining to former times; earlier: *Much that was forbidden by elder custom is accepted today.* —*n.* **4.** a person who is older or higher in rank than oneself. **5.** an aged person. **6.** an influential member of a tribe or community, often a chief or ruler; a superior. **7.** a presbyter. **8.** (in certain Protestant churches) a lay member who is a governing officer, often assisting the pastor in services. **9.** *Mormon Ch.* a member of the Melchizedek priesthood. [bef. 900; ME; OE *eldra,* comp. of *eald* OLD]
—**Syn. 1.** See **older.** —**Ant. 1.** younger.

el•der[2] (el′dər), *n.* any tree or shrub belonging to the genus *Sambucus,* of the honeysuckle family, having pinnate leaves, clusters of white flowers, and red or black, berrylike fruit. [bef. 900; ME *eldre, elrene, ellerne,* OE *ellærn;* c. MLG *ellern*]

el•der•ber•ry (el′dər ber′ē, -bə rē), *n., pl.* **-ries. 1.** the berrylike fruit of the elder, used in making wine and jelly. **2.** elder[2]. [1400–50; late ME *eldirbery.* See ELDER[2], BERRY]

Eld′er Ed′da. See under ***Edda.***

eld′er hand′. See **eldest hand.** [1580–90]

El•der•hos•tel (el′dər hos′tl), *Trademark.* an international nonprofit organization that offers older adults short-term, low-cost courses, housing, and meals, usually on college campuses.

eld•er•ly (el′dər lē), *adj.* **1.** somewhat old; near old age: *a resort for elderly people.* **2.** of or pertaining to persons in later life. [1605–15; ELDER[1] + -LY] —**eld′er•li•ness,** *n.*
—**Syn. 1.** See **old.**

eld′er states′man, 1. an influential citizen, often a retired high official, whose advice is sought by government leaders. **2.** any influential member of a company, group, etc., whose advice is respected. **3.** *Japanese Hist.* any of the political leaders who retired from official office but continued to exert a strong influence in the government and who controlled the emperor's privy council, esp. in the period 1898–1914. [1900–05]

eld•est (el′dist), *adj. a superl. of* **old** *with* **elder** *as compar.* oldest; first-born; of greatest age: *eldest brother; eldest sister; eldest born.* [bef. 900; ME; OE *eldesta,* superl. of *(e)ald* OLD]

eld′est hand′, *Cards.* the player on the dealer's left. Also, **elder hand.** Also called **age, edge.** Cf. **pone**[2] (def. 1). [1590–1600]

El Do•ra•do (el′ də rä′dō, -rā′- *or, Sp.,* el dô rä′thô *for 1, 2;* el′ də rā′dō *for 3, 4*), **1.** a legendary treasure city of South America, sought by the early Spanish explorers. **2.** any place offering great wealth. **3.** a city in S Arkansas. 26,685. **4.** a town in S Kansas. 10,510.

El•dred (el′drid), *n.* a male given name: from Old English words meaning "old" and "counsel."

el•dress (el′dris), *n.* a laywoman who is a governing officer in certain Protestant churches. [1630–40; ELDER[1] + -ESS]
—**Usage.** See **-ess.**

El•dridge (el′drij), *n.* **1. (David) Roy,** born 1911, U.S. jazz trumpeter. **2.** a male given name.

el•dritch (el′drich), *adj.* eerie; weird; spooky. Also, **el′drich, elritch.** [1500–10; earlier *elrich,* equiv. to OE *el-* foreign, strange, uncanny (see ELSE) + *rice* kingdom (see RICH); hence "of a strange country, pertaining to the Otherworld"; cf. OE *ellende* in a foreign LAND, exiled (c. G *Elend* penury, distress), Runic Norse *alja-markiR* foreigner]

E•le•a (ē′lē ə), *n.* an ancient Greek city in SW Italy, on the coast of Lucania.

El•ea•nor (el′ə nər, -nôr′), *n.* a female given name, form of **Helen.** Also, **El•e•a•no•ra** (el′ē ə nôr′ə, -nōr′ə).

El′eanor of Aq′uitaine, 1122?–1204, queen of Louis VII of France 1137–52; queen of Henry II of England 1154–89.

El•e•at•ic (el′ē at′ik), *adj.* **1.** of or pertaining to Elea. **2.** noting or pertaining to a school of philosophy, founded by Parmenides, that investigated the phenomenal world, especially with reference to the phenomena of change. —*n.* **3.** a philosopher of the Eleatic school. [1685–95; < L *Eleāticus* < Gk *Eleātikós.* See ELEA, -TIC] —**El′e•at′i•cism,** *n.*

El•e•a•zar (el′ē ā′zər), *n.* a son of Aaron and his successor in the priesthood. Num. 20:28.

el•e•cam•pane (el′i kam pān′), *n.* a composite weed, *Inula helenium,* naturalized in North America, having large yellow flowers and aromatic leaves and root. [1350–1400; ME, equiv. to OE *ele(ne), eolone* (metathetic alter. of ML *enula,* L *inula* elecampane) + ME *campane* < ML *campāna,* equiv. to *camp(us)* field + *-āna,* fem. of *-ānus* -ANE, -AN]

e•lect (i lekt′), *v.t.* **1.** to choose or select by vote, as for an office: *to elect a mayor.* **2.** to determine in favor of (a method, course of action, etc.). **3.** to pick out; choose: *First-year students may elect French, Spanish, or German.* **4.** *Theol.* (of God) to select for divine mercy or favor, esp. for salvation. —*v.i.* **5.** to choose or select someone or something, as by voting. —*adj.* **6.** selected, as for an office, but not yet inducted (usually used in combination following a noun): *the governor-elect.* **7.** select or choice: *an elect circle of artists.* **8.** *Theol.* chosen by God, esp. for eternal life. —*n.* **the elect, 9.** a person or the persons chosen or worthy to be chosen. **10.** *Theol.* a person or persons chosen by God, esp. for favor or salvation. [1250–1300; ME < L *ēlēctus* chosen (ptp. of *ēligere*), equiv. to *ē-* E- + *leg-* choose + *-tus* ptp. suffix; see ELITE] —**e•lec•tee** (i lek tē′), *n.*
—**Syn. 3.** See **choose.** —**Ant. 1, 2.** reject.

elect., 1. electric. **2.** electrical. **3.** electrician. **4.** electricity. Also, **elec.**

e•lect•a•ble (i lek′tə bəl), *adj.* capable of, or having a reasonable chance of, being elected, as to public office. [1875–80; ELECT + -ABLE] —**e•lect′a•bil′i•ty,** *n.*

e•lect•ed (i lek′tid), *adj.* **1.** chosen by vote, as for an office (contrasted with *appointed*): *an elected official.* —*n.* **2.** elect (def. 10). [1550–60; ELECT + -ED[2]]

e•lec•tion (i lek′shən), *n.* **1.** the selection of a person or persons for office by vote. **2.** a public vote upon a proposition submitted. **3.** the act of electing. **4.** *Theol.* the choice by God of individuals, as for a particular work or for favor or salvation. [1225–75; < L *ēlēctiōn-* (s. of *ēlēctiō*), equiv. to *ēlēct(us)* (see ELECT) + *-iōn-* -ION; r. ME *eleccioun* < AF]

elec′tion board′. See **board of elections.**

elec′tion cake′, *New England Cookery.* a spicy fruitcake baked in loaves: formerly served on town meeting days after the voting. [1795–1805, *Amer.*]

Elec′tion Day′, 1. (in the U.S.) the first Tuesday after the first Monday in November on which national elections are held for electors of the President and Vice President in those years evenly divisible by four. On even years constituents elect members of the House of Representatives for two-year terms and one third of the Senate for six-year terms. **2.** (*often l.c.*) any day designated for the election of public officials. [1640–50]

elec′tion dis′trict, precinct (def. 3). [1790–1800, *Amer.*]

e•lec•tion•eer (i lek′shə nēr′), *v.i.* to work for the success of a particular candidate, party, ticket, etc., in an election. [1780–90; ELECTION + -EER] —**e•lec′tion•eer′er,** *n.*

e•lec•tive (i lek′tiv), *adj.* **1.** pertaining to the principle of electing to an office, position, etc. **2.** chosen by election, as an official. **3.** bestowed by or derived from election, as an office. **4.** having the power or right of electing to office, as a body of persons. **5.** open to choice; optional; not required: *an elective subject in college; elective surgery.* **6.** *Chem.* selecting for combination or action; tending to combine with certain substances in preference to others: *elective attraction.* —*n.* **7.** an optional study; a course that a student may select from among alternatives. [1520–30; < ML *ēlēctīvus,* equiv. to L *ēlēct(us)* (see ELECT) + *-īvus* -IVE] —**e•lec′tive•ly,** *adv.* —**e•lec′tive•ness,** *n.*
—**Syn. 5.** voluntary, discretionary. —**Ant. 5.** required, obligatory, necessary.

e•lec•tor (i lek′tər), *n.* **1.** a person who elects or may elect, esp. a qualified voter. **2.** a member of the electoral college of the U.S. **3.** (*usually cap.*) one of the German princes entitled to elect the emperor of the Holy Roman Empire. [1425–75; late ME *electo(u)r* < LL *ēlēctor* chooser, equiv. to *eleg-,* var. s. of *ēligere* (see ELECT) + *-tor* -TOR]

e•lec•tor•al (i lek′tər əl), *adj.* **1.** pertaining to electors or election. **2.** consisting of electors. [1665–75; ELECTOR + -AL[1]] —**e•lec′tor•al•ly,** *adv.*

elec′toral col′lege, (*often caps.*) a body of electors chosen by the voters in each state to elect the President and Vice President of the U.S. [1790–1800, *Amer.*]

elec′toral vote′, the vote cast in the electoral college of the U.S. by the representatives of each state in a presidential election. [1815–25, *Amer.*]

e•lec•tor•ate (i lek′tər it), *n.* **1.** the body of persons entitled to vote in an election. **2.** the dignity or territory of an Elector of the Holy Roman Empire. [1665–75; ELECTOR + -ATE[3]]

electr-, var. of **electro-** before a vowel: *electrode.*

E•lec•tra (i lek′trə), *n.* **1.** Also, **Elektra.** *Class. Myth.* the daughter of Agamemnon and Clytemnestra who incited her brother Orestes to kill Clytemnestra and her lover Aegisthus. **2.** *Astron.* one of the six visible stars in the Pleiades.

Elec′tra com′plex, *Psychoanal.* the unresolved, unconscious libidinous desire of a daughter for her father: designation based on the Greek myth of Electra and Agamemnon. Cf. **Oedipus complex.** [1910–15]

e•lec•tress (i lek′tris), *n.* the wife or widow of an Elector of the Holy Roman Empire. [1610–20; ELECT(O)R + -ESS]

e•lec•tret (i lek′trit), *n. Elect.* a dielectric that possesses a permanent or semipermanent electric polarity, analogous to a permanent magnet. [1880–85; ELECTR(ICITY) + (MAGN)ET]

e•lec•tric (i lek′trik), *adj.* **1.** pertaining to, derived from, produced by, or involving electricity: *an electric shock.* **2.** producing, transmitting, or operated by electric currents: *an electric bell; electric cord.* **3.** electrifying; thrilling; exciting; stirring: *The atmosphere was electric with excitement.* **4.** (of a musical instrument) **a.** producing sound by electrical or electronic means: *an electric piano.* **b.** equipped with connections to an amplifier-loudspeaker system: *an electric violin.* —*n.* **5.** *Railroads.* **a.** an electric locomotive. **b.** *Informal.* a railroad operated by electricity. **6.** electricity: *residential users of gas and electric.* **7.** something, as an appliance, vehicle, or toy, operated by electricity. **8.** *Archaic.* a substance that is a nonconductor of electricity, as glass or amber, used to store or to excite an electric charge. [1640–50; < NL *electricus,* equiv. to L *ēlectr(um)* amber (see ELECTRUM) + *-icus* -IC]
—**Syn. 3.** spirited, rousing, dynamic. —**Ant. 3.** dull, uninspired, prosaic.

e•lec•tri•cal (i lek′tri kəl), *adj.* **1.** electric. **2.** concerned with electricity: *an electrical consultant.* [ELECTRIC + -AL[1]] —**e•lec′tri•cal•ly,** *adv.*

elec′trical degree′, *Elect.* the 360th part of a cycle of alternating current.

elec′trical engineer′ing, the branch of engineering that deals with the practical application of the theory of electricity to the construction of machinery, power supplies, etc. [1880–85] —**elec′trical engineer′.**

elec′trical scan′ning, 1. *Electronics.* a technique for varying the sector covered by a transmitting or receiving antenna by electrical means without moving the antenna. **2.** Also called **electronic scanning.** *Television.* the technique used in scanning a surface to reproduce or transmit a picture.

elec′trical storm′, thunderstorm. Also, **electric storm.** [1940–45, *Amer.*]

elec′trical transcrip′tion, 1. a radio broadcast from a phonograph record. **2.** the phonograph record itself.

elec′tric arc′, arc (def. 2). [1880–85]

elec′tric arc′ weld′ing. See **arc welding.** [1890–95]

elec′tric blue′, a vivid, light-to-moderate blue color. [1890–95]

elec′tric cat′fish, a freshwater fish, *Malapterurus electricus,* of the Nile and tropical central Africa, that discharges electric shocks to immobilize prey and defend itself.

elec′tric cell′, cell[1] (def. 7a).

elec′tric chair′, 1. a chair used to electrocute criminals sentenced to death. **2.** the penalty of legal electrocution. [1870–75, *Amer.*]

elec′tric charge′, *Physics.* one of the basic properties of the elementary particles of matter giving rise to all electric and magnetic forces and interactions. The two kinds of charge are given negative and positive algebraic signs: measured in coulombs. Also called **charge, electricity.**

elec′tric cir′cuit, circuit (def. 9a). [1760–70]

elec′tric cur′rent, *Elect.* the time rate of flow of electric charge, in the direction that a positive moving charge would take and having magnitude equal to the quantity of charge per unit time: measured in amperes. Also called **current, electricity.** [1830–40]

elec′tric di′pole mo′ment, *Elect.* a vector quantity associated with two equal charges of opposite sign separated by a specified distance, having magnitude equal to the product of the charge and the distance between the charges and having direction from the negative to the positive charge along the line between the charges.

elec′tric displace′ment, *Elect.* the part of the electric field that is determined solely by free charges, without reference to the dielectric properties of the surrounding medium: measured in coulombs per square meter. *Symbol:* D Also called **displacement.** [1880–85]

elec′tric eel′, an eellike, freshwater fish, *Electrophorus electricus,* found in the Amazon and Orinoco rivers and tributaries, sometimes over 6 ft. (1.8 m) long, capable of emitting strong electric discharges. [1785–95]

elec′tric eye′, 1. photocell. **2.** See **electron-ray tube.** [1925–30]

elec′tric field′, *Elect.* a vector quantity from which is determined the magnitude and direction of the force (**elec′tric force′**) on a charged particle due to the presence of other charged particles, accelerated charged particles, or time-varying currents. *Symbol:* E [1895–1900]

elec′tric field′ inten′sity, *Physics.* See **electric intensity.** Also called **elec′tric field′ strength′.** [1960–65]

elec′tric flux′, the lines of force that make up an electric field. [1900–05]

elec′tric fur′nace, a furnace in which the heat required is produced through electricity. [1880–85]

elec′tric glow′, *Elect.* See **corona discharge.**

elec′tric guitar′, a guitar equipped with electric or magnetic pickups that permit its sound to be amplified and fed to a loudspeaker. [1935–40]

e•lec•tri•cian (i lek trish′ən, ē′lek-), *n.* a person who installs, operates, maintains, or repairs electric devices or electrical wiring. [1745–55, *Amer.;* ELECTRIC + -IAN]

elec′tric inten′sity, *Physics.* the magnitude of an electric field at a point in the field, equal to the force that would be exerted on a small unit charge placed at the point. Also called **electric field intensity, electric field strength.**

e•lec•tric•i•ty (i lek tris′i tē, ē′lek-), *n.* **1.** See **electric charge. 2.** See **electric current. 3.** the science dealing with electric charges and currents. **4.** a state or feeling of excitement, anticipation, tension, etc. [1640–50; ELECTRIC + -ITY]

elec′tric light′, 1. an incandescent lamp. **2.** the light produced by such a lamp.

elec′tric mo′tor, motor (def. 4). [1885–90]

elec′tric nee′dle, *Surg.* acusector.

elec′tric or′gan, (in certain fishes) an organ composed of electroplaques. [1865–70]

elec′tric poten′tial, 1. Also called **potential.** *Elect.* (at any point in an electric field) the work done per unit charge in moving an infinitesimal point charge from a common reference point to the given point. *Symbol: V* **2.** *Physiol.* See **action potential.** [1870–75]

elec′tric ray′, any ray of the family Torpedinidae, capable of emitting strong electric discharges. [1765–75]

elec′tric shock′, shock[1] (def. 6). [1940–45]

elec′tric storm′, thunderstorm. [1870–75, *Amer.*]

elec′tric susceptibil′ity, *Elect.* (when the components of electrical polarization are linear combinations of the components of the electric field) the coefficient or set of coefficients that multiply the components of the electric field. Also called **susceptibility.** Cf. **polarization** (def. 3b).

elec′tric torch′, *Brit.* torch[1] (def. 4). [1870–75]

elec′tric wave′. See **electromagnetic wave.** [1870–75]

E•lec•tri•des (i lek′tri dēz′), *n.pl. Class. Myth.* the Amber Islands.

e•lec•tri•fy (i lek′trə fī′), *v.t.,* **-fied, -fy•ing. 1.** to charge with or subject to electricity; apply electricity to. **2.** to supply (a region, community, etc.) with electric power: *The valley wasn't electrified until 1936.* **3.** to equip for the use of electric power, as a railroad. **4.** to excite greatly; thrill: *to electrify an audience.* [1735–45; ELECTR- + -IFY] **—e•lec′tri•fi•ca′tion,** *n.* **—e•lec′tri•fi′er,** *n.*
—Syn. 4. stir, rouse, dazzle.

e•lec•tro (i lek′trō), *n., pl.* **-tros.** electrotype. [by shortening]

electro-, a combining form representing **electric** or **electricity** in compound words: *electromagnetic.* Also, *esp. before a vowel,* **electr-.** [ELECTR(IC) + -O-]

e•lec•tro•a•cous•tic (i lek′trō ə ko͞o′stik), *adj.* of or pertaining to electroacoustics. Also, **e•lec′tro•a•cous′ti•cal.** [1930–35; ELECTRO- + ACOUSTIC] **—e•lec′tro•a•cous′ti•cal•ly,** *adv.*

e•lec•tro•a•cous•tics (i lek′trō ə ko͞o′stiks), *n.* (*used with a singular v.*) the branch of electronics that deals with the conversion of electricity into acoustical energy and vice versa. [1925–30; ELECTRO- + ACOUSTICS]

e•lec•tro•a•nal•y•sis (i lek′trō ə nal′ə sis), *n.* chemical analysis by electrochemical methods. [1900–05; ELECTRO- + ANALYSIS] **—e•lec•tro•an•a•lyt•ic** (i lek′trō an′-l it′ik), **e•lec′tro•an′a•lyt′i•cal,** *adj.*

e•lec•tro•bi•ol•o•gy (i lek′trō bī ol′ə jē), *n.* the branch of biology dealing with electric phenomena in plants and animals. [1840–50; ELECTRO- + BIOLOGY] **—e•lec•tro•bi•o•log•i•cal** (i lek′trō bī′ə loj′i kəl), *adj.* **—e•lec′tro•bi′o•log′i•cal•ly,** *adv.* **—e•lec′tro•bi•ol′o•gist,** *n.*

e•lec•tro•ca•lor′ic effect′ (i lek′trō kə lôr′ik, -lor′-), *Thermodynamics.* the temperature change accompanying a change in the electric intensity of a thermally isolated system. [ELECTRO- + CALORIC]

e•lec•tro•car•di•o•gram (i lek′trō kär′dē ə gram′), *n. Med.* the graphic record produced by an electrocardiograph. *Abbr.:* EKG, ECG Also called **cardiogram.** [1900–05; ELECTRO- + CARDIOGRAM]

e•lec•tro•car•di•o•graph (i lek′trō kär′dē ə graf′, -gräf′), *n. Med.* a galvanometric device that detects and records the minute differences in electric potential caused by heart action and occurring between different parts of the body: used in the diagnosis of heart disease. Also called **cardiograph.** [1910–15; ELECTRO- + CARDIOGRAPH] **—e•lec•tro•car•di•o•graph•ic** (i lek′trō kär′dē ə graf′ik), *adj.* **—e•lec′tro•car′di•o•graph′i•cal•ly,** *adv.* **—e•lec•tro•car•di•og•ra•phy** (i lek′trō kär′dē og′rə fē), *n.*

e•lec•tro•cau•ter•y (i lek′trō kô′tə rē), *n., pl.* **-ter•ies.** *Med.* **1.** a hand-held, needlelike cautery heated by an electric current. **2.** Also, **e•lec′tro•cau′ter•i•za′tion.** the process of cutting and cauterizing skin simultaneously, or coagulating blood from vessels around a surgical incision, by means of an electrocautery. [1880–85; ELECTRO- + CAUTERY]

e•lec•tro•chem′i•cal equiv′alent (i lek′trə kem′i-kəl), *Physical Chem.* the mass, in grams, of a substance deposited on the electrode of a voltameter by 1 coulomb of electricity. [1880–85]

elec′trochem′ical se′ries, *Chem.* See **electromotive series.** [1940–45]

e•lec•tro•chem•is•try (i lek′trō kem′ə strē), *n.* the branch of chemistry that deals with the chemical changes produced by electricity and the production of electricity by chemical changes. [1820–30; ELECTRO- + CHEMISTRY] **—e•lec•tro•chem•i•cal** (i lek′trō kem′i-kəl), *adj.* **—e•lec′tro•chem′i•cal•ly,** *adv.* **—e•lec′tro•chem′ist,** *n.*

CONCISE ETYMOLOGY KEY: <, descended or borrowed from; >, whence; b., blend of, blended; c., cognate with; cf., compare; deriv., derivative; equiv., equivalent; imit., imitative; obl., oblique; r., replacing; s., stem; sp., spelling, spelled; resp., respelling, respelled; trans., translation; ?, origin unknown; *, unattested; ‡, probably earlier than. See the full key inside the front cover.

e•lec•tro•co•ag•u•la•tion (i lek′trō kō ag′yə lā′-shən), *n. Med., Surg.* the coagulation of a tumor or other diseased tissue by means of diathermy. [1910–15; ELECTRO- + COAGULATION]

e•lec•tro•con•duc•tive (i lek′trō kən duk′tiv), *adj. Elect.* having the property or capability of conducting electricity. [ELECTRO- + CONDUCTIVE]

e•lec′tro•con•vul′sive ther′apy (i lek′trō kən-vul′siv, i lek′-), *Psychiatry.* a treatment for serious mental illnesses, as severe depressive disorders, involving the application to the head of electric current in order to induce a seizure: usually administered after sedatives and muscle relaxants. *Abbr.:* ECT Also called **electroshock.** Cf. **shock therapy.** [1945–50; ELECTRO- + CONVULSIVE]

e•lec•tro•cor•ti•co•gram (i lek′trō kôr′ti kə gram′), *n. Med.* a record of the electrical activity of the cerebral cortex. Cf. **electrocorticography.** [1935–40; ELECTRO- + CORTICO- + -GRAM[1]]

e•lec•tro•cor•ti•cog•ra•phy (i lek′trō kôr′ti kog′rə-fē), *n. Med.* a technique for surveying the electrical activity of the cerebral cortex by means of an electroencephalograph and electrodes attached to the brain. [ELECTRO- + CORTICO- + -GRAPHY]

e•lec•tro•crat•ic (i lek′trə krat′ik), *adj. Physical Chem.* noting a colloid that owes its stability to the electric charge of the particles on its surface. Cf. **lyocratic.** [ELECTRO- + -CRAT + -IC]

e•lec•tro•cute (i lek′trə kyo͞ot′). *v.t.,* **-cut•ed, -cut•ing. 1.** to kill by electricity. **2.** to execute (a criminal) by electricity, as in an electric chair. [1885–90, *Amer.*; ELECTRO- + (EXE)CUTE] **—e•lec′tro•cu′tion,** *n.*

e•lec•trode (i lek′trōd), *n. Elect.* a conductor, not necessarily metallic, through which a current enters or leaves a nonmetallic medium, as an electrolytic cell, arc generator, vacuum tube, or gaseous discharge tube. [1825–35; ELECTR- + -ODE[2]]

e•lec•tro•de•pos•it (i lek′trō di poz′it), *Physical Chem.* **—n. 1.** a deposit, usually of metal, produced by electrolysis. **—v.t. 2.** to deposit by electrolysis. [1860–65; ELECTRO- + DEPOSIT] **—e•lec•tro•dep•o•si•tion** (i lek′trō dep′ə zish′ən, -dē′pə-), *n.*

e•lec•tro•der•mal (i lek′trō dûr′məl), *adj.* of or pertaining to electrical properties or electrical activity of the skin, esp. with reference to changes in resistance. [1945–50; ELECTRO- + DERMAL]

e•lec•tro•di•ag•no•sis (i lek′trō dī′əg nō′sis), *n., pl.* **-ses** (-sēz). *Med.* diagnosis by the observation of the changes in electric irritability that occur as a result of a disease, as recorded by an electroencephalogram or the like. [ELECTRO- + DIAGNOSIS] **—e•lec•tro•di•ag•nos•tic** (i lek′trō dī′əg nos′tik), *adj.* **—e•lec′tro•di′ag•nos′ti•cal•ly,** *adv.*

e•lec•tro•di•al•y•sis (i lek′trō dī al′ə sis), *n., pl.* **-ses** (sēz′). *Physical Chem.* dialysis in which electrodes of opposite charge are placed on either side of a membrane to accelerate diffusion. [1920–25; ELECTRO- + DIALYSIS] **—e•lec•tro•di•a•lit•ic** (i lek′trō dī′ə lit′ik), *adj.* **—e•lec′tro•di′a•lit′i•cal•ly,** *adv.*

elec′tro•dis′charge machin′ing (i lek′trō dis′-chärj), *Metall.* a technique for shaping the surfaces of a metal object by immersing in a dielectric liquid the object and a tool that emits an electric discharge of high current density and short duration.

e•lec•tro•dis•so•lu•tion (i lek′trō dis′ə lo͞o′shən), *n. Physical Chem.* the dissolving of a substance from an electrode by electrolysis. [ELECTRO- + DISSOLUTION]

e•lec•tro•dy•nam•ic (i lek′trō dī nam′ik), *adj.* **1.** pertaining to the force of electricity in motion. **2.** pertaining to electrodynamics. Also, **e•lec′tro•dy•nam′i•cal.** [1820–30; ELECTRO- + DYNAMIC]

e•lec•tro•dy•nam•ics (i lek′trō dī nam′iks), *n.* (*used with a singular v.*) the branch of physics that deals with the interactions of electric, magnetic, and mechanical phenomena. [1820–30; ELECTRO- + DYNAMICS]

e•lec•tro•dy•na•mom•e•ter (i lek′trō dī′nə mom′-i tər), *n. Elect.* an instrument that uses the interaction between the magnetic fields produced by the currents in two coils or sets of coils to measure current, voltage, or power. [1875–80; ELECTRO- + DYNAMOMETER]

e•lec•tro•en•ceph•a•lo•gram (i lek′trō en sef′ə lə-gram′), *n. Med.* a graphic record produced by an electroencephalograph. *Abbr.:* **EEG** [1930–35; ELECTRO- + ENCEPHALOGRAM]

e•lec•tro•en•ceph•a•lo•graph (i lek′trō en sef′ə lə-graf′, -gräf′), *n. Med.* an instrument for measuring and recording the electric activity of the brain. [1935–40; ELECTRO- + ENCEPHALOGRAPH] **—e•lec•tro•en•ceph•a•lo•graph•ic** (i lek′trō en sef′ə lə graf′ik), **e•lec′tro•en•ceph′a•lo•graph′i•cal,** *adj.* **—e•lec′tro•en•ceph′a•lo•graph′i•cal•ly,** *adv.* **—e•lec•tro•en•ceph•a•log•ra•phy** (i lek′trō en sef′ə log′rə fē), *n.*

e•lec•tro•end•os•mo•sis (i lek′trō en′doz mō′sis, -dos-), *n. Physical Chem.* electro-osmosis. [ELECTRO- + ENDOSMOSIS]

e•lec•tro•ex•trac•tion (i lek′trō ik strak′shən), *n. Physical Chem.* the recovery of metal from metallic salts by means of electrolysis. Also called **electrowinning.** [ELECTRO- + EXTRACTION]

e•lec•tro•form (i lek′trə fôrm′), *v.t. Metall.* to form (an object) by the electrodeposition of a metal upon a mold, often a wax mold. [1950–55; ELECTRO- + FORM]

e•lec•tro•form•ing (i lek′trə fôr′ming), *n. Metall.* the act or process of forming a metallic object by electroplating a removable mandrel or matrix. [1950–55; ELECTRO- + FORMING]

e•lec•tro•gen•e•sis (i lek′trə jen′ə sis), *n. Physiol.* the generation of electricity in living organisms or tissue. [1885–90; ELECTRO- + -GENESIS] **—e•lec′tro•gen′ic,** *adj.*

e•lec•tro•graph (i lek′trə graf′, -gräf′), *n.* **1.** a curve or plot automatically traced by the action of an electric device, as an electrometer or an electrically controlled pen. **2.** *Print.* an apparatus for engraving metal plates on cylinders used in printing. **3.** *Telecommunications.* **a.** an apparatus for electrically transmitting pictures. **b.** a picture produced by such a device. [1830–40; ELECTRO- + -GRAPH] **—e•lec•tro•graph•ic** (i lek′trə graf′ik), *adj.* **—e•lec•trog•ra•phy** (i lek trog′rə fē, ē′lek-), *n.*

e•lec•tro•he•mos•ta•sis (i lek′trō hi mos′tə sis, -hē′mə stā′sis, -hem′ə-), *n. Med.* hemostasis by means of an electric device, as an electrocautery. [ELECTRO- + HEMOSTASIS]

e•lec•tro•hy•drau•lic (i lek′trō hī drô′lik, -drol′ik), *adj. Mach.* (of a mechanism) combining electrical and hydraulic components. [1920–25; ELECTRO- + HYDRAULIC]

e•lec•tro•jet (i lek′trə jet′), *n. Geophysics.* a current of ions existing in the upper atmosphere, moving with respect to the surface of the earth, and causing various auroral phenomena. [1950–55; ELECTRO- + JET[1]]

e•lec•tro•ki•net•ics (i lek′trō ki net′iks, -kī-), *n.* (*used with a singular v.*) the branch of physics that deals with electricity in motion. [1880–85; ELECTRO- + KINETICS] **—e•lec′tro•ki•net′ic,** *adj.*

e•lec′tro•less plat′ing (i lek′trō lis), a technique of plating metal by chemical rather than electrical means, in which the piece to be plated is immersed in a reducing agent that, when catalyzed by certain materials, changes metal ions to metal that forms a deposit on the piece. [ELECTRO- + -LESS]

e•lec•trol•o•gist (i lek trol′ə jist), *n.* a person skilled in the use of electrolysis for removing moles, warts, or unwanted hair. [1900–05; ELECTRO(LYSIS) + -LOG(Y) + -IST]

e•lec•tro•lu•mi•nes•cence (i lek′trō lo͞o′mə nes′-əns), *n.* luminescence produced by the activation of a dielectric phosphor by an alternating current. [1900–05; ELECTRO- + LUMINESCENCE] **—e•lec′tro•lu′mi•nes′•cent,** *adj.*

e•lec•trol•y•sis (i lek trol′ə sis, ē′lek-), *n.* **1.** *Physical Chem.* the passage of an electric current through an electrolyte with subsequent migration of positively and negatively charged ions to the negative and positive electrodes. **2.** the destruction of hair roots, tumors, etc., by an electric current. [1830–40; ELECTRO- + -LYSIS]

e•lec•tro•lyte (i lek′trə līt′), *n.* **1.** *Physical Chem.* **a.** Also called **elec′trolyt′ic conduc′tor.** a conducting medium in which the flow of current is accompanied by the movement of matter in the form of ions. **b.** any substance that dissociates into ions when dissolved in a suitable medium or melted and thus forms a conductor of electricity. **2.** *Physiol.* any of certain inorganic compounds, mainly sodium, potassium, magnesium, calcium, chloride, and bicarbonate, that dissociate in biological fluids into ions capable of conducting electrical currents and constituting a major force in controlling fluid balance within the body. [1825–35; ELECTRO- + -LYTE]

e•lec•tro•lyt•ic (i lek′trə lit′ik), *adj.* **1.** pertaining to or derived by electrolysis. **2.** pertaining to an electrolyte. Also, **e•lec′tro•lyt′i•cal.** [1835–45; ELECTRO- + -LYTIC] **—e•lec′tro•lyt′i•cal•ly,** *adv.*

elec′trolyt′ic cell′, cell[1] (def. 8). [1935–40]

electrolyt′ic dissocia′tion, *Physical Chem.* the separation of the molecule of an electrolyte into its constituent atoms. [1905–10]

electrolyt′ic interrupt′er, *Elect.* a current interrupter consisting of a cell with two electrodes that is immersed in an electrolyte such that the passage of current through the cell causes bubbles to form in the electrolyte, the bubbles breaking the circuit.

electrolyt′ic machin′ing, *Metall.* removal of metal from a piece by electrolysis.

electrolyt′ic protec′tion. See **cathodic protection.**

e•lec•tro•lyze (i lek′trə līz′), *v.t.,* **-lyzed, -lyz•ing.** *Physical Chem.* to decompose by electrolysis. Also, *esp. Brit.,* **e•lec′tro•lyse′.** [1825–35; ELECTRO- + -LYZE] **—e•lec′tro•ly•za′tion,** *n.* **—e•lec′tro•lyz′er,** *n.*

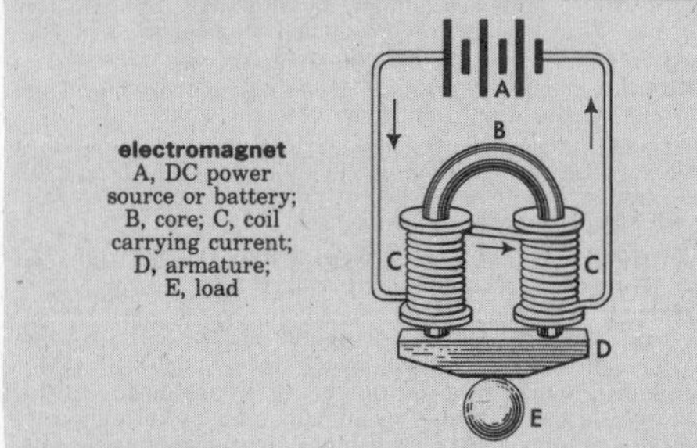

electromagnet
A, DC power source or battery; B, core; C, coil carrying current; D, armature; E, load

e•lec•tro•mag•net (i lek′trō mag′nit), *n.* a device consisting of an iron or steel core that is magnetized by electric current in a coil that surrounds it. [1815–25; ELECTRO- + MAGNET]

e•lec•tro•mag•net•ic (i lek′trō mag net′ik), *adj.* of or pertaining to electromagnetism or electromagnetic fields. [1815–25; ELECTRO- + MAGNETIC] **—e•lec′tro•mag•net′i•cal•ly,** *adv.*

elec′tromagnet′ic field′, *Elect.* the coupled electric and magnetic fields that are generated by time-varying currents and accelerated charges. Cf. **Maxwell's field equations.**

elec′tromagnet′ic induc′tion, *Elect.* the induction of an electromotive force by the motion of a conductor across a magnetic field or by a change in magnetic flux in a magnetic field.

elec′tromagnet′ic pulse′. See **EMP.**

elec′tromagnet′ic pump′, a device that causes an electrically conducting fluid to flow by means of electromagnetic induction.

electromagnet′ic radia′tion, *Physics.* radiation consisting of electromagnetic waves, including radio waves, infrared, visible light, ultraviolet, x-rays, and gamma rays. [1950–55]

e•lec•tro•mag•net•ics (i lek′trō mag net′iks), *n.* (*used with a singular v.*) electromagnetism (def. 2). [ELECTROMAGNET + -ICS]

elec′tromagnet′ic spec′trum, the entire spectrum, considered as a continuum, of all kinds of electric, magnetic, and visible radiation, from gamma rays having a wavelength of 0.001 angstrom to long waves having a wavelength of more than 1 million km. [1935–40]

elec′tromagnet′ic tape′. See **magnetic tape.**

elec′tromagnet′ic u′nit, a unit, as an abampere, in the system of units derived from the magnetic effects of an electric current. *Abbr.:* emu, EMU [1910–15]

elec′tromagnet′ic wave′, *Physics.* a wave produced by the acceleration of an electric charge and propagated by the periodic variation of intensities of, usually, perpendicular electric and magnetic fields. Also called **electric wave.** [1905–10]

e•lec•tro•mag•net•ism (i lek′trō mag′ni tiz′əm), *n.* **1.** the phenomena associated with electric and magnetic fields and their interactions with each other and with electric charges and currents. **2.** Also, **electromagnetics.** the science that deals with these phenomena. [1820–30; ELECTRO- + MAGNETISM]

e•lec•tro•me•chan•i•cal (i lek′trō mə kan′i kəl), *adj.* of or pertaining to mechanical devices or systems electrically actuated, as by a solenoid. [1885–90; ELECTRO- + MECHANICAL]

e•lec•tro•met•al•lur•gy (i lek′trō met′l ûr′jē, -mətal′ər jē), *n.* the branch of metallurgy dealing with the processing of metals by means of electricity. [1830–40; ELECTRO- + METALLURGY] **—e•lec′tro•met′al•lur′gi•cal,** *adj.* **—e•lec′tro•met′al•lur′gist,** *n.*

e•lec•tro•me•te•or (i lek′trō mē′tē ər), *n.* any visible or audible manifestation of atmospheric electricity, as lightning or thunder. [ELECTRO- + METEOR]

e•lec•trom•e•ter (i lek trom′i tər, ē′lek-), *n.* a calibrated device used for measuring extremely low voltages. [1945–50; ELECTRO- + -METER] **—e•lec•tro•met•ric** (i lek′trō me′trik), **e•lec′tro•met′ri•cal,** *adj.* **—e•lec′tro•met′ri•cal•ly,** *adv.* **—e•lec•trom′e•try,** *n.*

e•lec•tro•mo•tive (i lek′trə mō′tiv), *adj.* pertaining to, producing, or tending to produce a flow of electricity. [1800–10; ELECTRO- + MOTIVE]

elec′tromo′tive force′, *Elect.* the energy available for conversion from nonelectric to electric form, or vice versa, per unit of charge passing through the source of the energy; the potential difference between the terminals of a source of electrical energy: expressed in volts. *Abbr.:* emf Also called **pressure.** [1825–35]

elec′tromo′tive se′ries, *Chem.* the classification of metals in the order of their electrode potentials. Also called **electrochemical series.**

e•lec•tro•my•o•gram (i lek′trə mī′ə gram′), *n. Med.* a graphic record of the electric currents associated with muscular action. *Abbr.:* EMG [1915–20; ELECTRO- + MYOGRAM]

e•lec•tro•my•o•graph (i lek′trō mī′ə graf′, -gräf′), *n.* a device for recording electric currents from an active muscle to produce an electromyogram. *Abbr.:* EMG [1945–50; ELECTRO- + MYOGRAPH] **—e•lec•tro•my•o•graph•ic** (i lek′trō mī′ə graf′ik), *adj.* **—e•lec′tro•my′•o•graph′i•cal•ly,** *adv.* **—e•lec•tro•my•og•ra•phy** (i lek′trō mī og′rə fē), *n.*

e•lec•tron (i lek′tron), *n.* **1.** Also called **negatron.** *Physics, Chem.* an elementary particle that is a fundamental constituent of matter, having a negative charge of 1.602×10^{-19} coulombs, a mass of 9.108×10^{-31} kilograms, and spin of ½, and existing independently or as the component outside the nucleus of an atom. **2.** *Elect.* a unit of charge equal to the charge on one electron. [term first suggested in 1891 by Irish physicist G. J. Stoney (1826–1911); ELECTR(IC) + *-on* (from the names of charged particles, as ION, CATION, ANION) with perh. accidental allusion to Gk *ēlektron* amber (see ELECTRIC)]

elec′tron affin′ity, *Physics, Chem.* the quantitative measure, usually given in electron-volts, of the tendency of an atom or molecule to capture an electron and to form a negative ion.

elec′tron cam′era, *Electronics.* an apparatus that converts an optical image into a corresponding electric current by electronic means without the intervention of mechanical scanning. [1935–40]

elec′tron diffrac′tion, *Physics.* the phenomenon whereby electron waves scattered by the regularly spaced atoms of a crystal produce diffraction patterns characteristic of the crystal structure and the wavelength. [1925–30]

e•lec•tro•neg•a•tive (i lek′trō neg′ə tiv), *adj. Physical Chem.* **1.** containing negative electricity; tending to migrate to the positive pole in electrolysis. **2.** assuming negative potential when in contact with a dissimilar substance. **3.** nonmetallic. [1800–10; ELECTRO- + NEGATIVE] **—e•lec′tro•neg′a•tiv′i•ty,** *n.*

e•lec•tro•neu•tral (i lek′trō nōō′tral, -nyōō′-), *adj. Elect.* neutral (def. 9b). [ELECTRO- + NEUTRAL] **—e•lec′tro•neu•tral′i•ty,** *n.*

elec′tron gun′, *Electronics, Television.* a device consisting of the cathode ray tube, which emits electrons, and a surrounding electrostatic or electromagnetic apparatus, which controls, focuses, and accelerates the stream of electrons (**elec′tron beam′**). Also called **gun.** [1920–25]

e•lec•tron•ic (i lek tron′ik, ē′lek-), *adj.* **1.** of or pertaining to electronics or to devices, circuits, or systems developed through electronics. **2.** of or pertaining to electrons or to an electron. **3.** (of a musical instrument) using electric or electronic means to produce or modify the sound. **4.** of, pertaining to, or controlled by computers, or computer products and services. [1900–05; ELECTRON + -IC] **—e•lec•tron′i•cal•ly,** *adv.*

electron′ic bank′ing, banking transactions conducted through computerized systems, as electronic funds transfer by automated-teller machines, intended to speed operations, reduce costs, etc. [1975–80]

electron′ic Bohr′ mag′neton, *Physics.* See **Bohr magneton.**

electron′ic brain′, an electronic computer. [1940–45]

electron′ic bul′letin board′. See **BBS.**

electron′ic cinematog′raphy, *Motion Pictures, Television.* cinematography using an electronic video camera to create a videotape that can be viewed on a monitor, edited electronically, and transferred to film for motion-picture projectors.

electron′ic coun′termeasures, the use of electronic technology to jam and deceive enemy radars, esp. those used for air defense and interception. *Abbr.:* ECM [1965–70]

electron′ic crime′, any criminal activity involving the use of computers, as the illegal transfer of funds from one account to another or the stealing, changing, or erasing of data in an electronic data bank.

electron′ic da′ta proc′essing. See **EDP.** [1960–65]

electron′ic ed′iting, **1.** *Television.* the editing of videotape by electronic operations without cutting and splicing the tape. **2.** *Motion Pictures.* the editing of film assisted by a duplicate of the action on videotape.

electron′ic engineer′ing, a branch of engineering that deals with the design, fabrication, and operation of circuits, electronic devices, and systems. **—electron′ic engineer′.**

electron′ic fe′tal mon′itor, a device used to monitor the fetal heartbeat and the strength of the mother's uterine contractions during labor. *Abbr:* EFM

electron′ic flash′, *Photog.* a flash lamp, usually attached to a camera or housed within the camera body, that produces brilliant flashes of light by the discharge of current through a gas-filled tube. Also called **flashtube.** [1945–50]

electron′ic funds′ trans′fer, the use of telecommunications networks to transfer funds from one financial institution, as a bank, to another, or to withdraw funds from one's own account to deposit in a creditor's. *Abbr.:* EFT [1970–75]

electron′ic game′. See **video game.** [1975–80]

electron′ic igni′tion, an automotive ignition in which electrical pulses are generated electronically, usually by transistors controlled by sensing devices, without the use of mechanically actuated breaker points. Also called **breakerless ignition.**

electron′ic im′aging, a system of photography using a sensor placed behind a camera lens to translate an image into an electronic signal, which can be stored on a disk or magnetic tape for playback on a VCR or videodisc player and viewing on a television screen.

electron′ic intel′ligence. See **elint.**

electron′ic jour′nalism, television news reportage. *Abbr.:* EJ [1970–75] **—electron′ic jour′nalist.**

electron′ic mail′, a system for sending messages from one individual to another via telecommunications links between computers or terminals. Also called **e-mail.** [1975–80]

electron′ic mu′sic, electronically produced sounds recorded on tape and arranged by the composer to form a musical composition. [1930–35]

electron′ic neutri′no, *Physics.* electron-neutrino.

electron′ic news′ gath′ering, *Television.* See **ENG.**

e•lec•tron•ics (i lek tron′iks, ē′lek-), *n.* (*used with a singular v.*) the science dealing with the development and application of devices and systems involving the flow of electrons in a vacuum, in gaseous media, and in semiconductors. [1905–10; see ELECTRONIC, -ICS]

electron′ic scan′ning. See **electrical scanning** (def. 2).

electron′ic spread′sheet, a type of software for microcomputers that offers the user a visual display of a simulated worksheet and the means of using it for financial plans, budgets, etc.

electron′ic surveil′lance, surveillance or the gathering of information by surreptitious use of electronic devices, as in crime detection or espionage. [1970–75]

electron′ic tube′. See **electron tube.**

elec′tron lens′, a combination of static or varying electric and magnetic fields, used to focus streams of electrons in a manner similar to that of an optical lens. [1930–35]

elec′tron mi′croscope, a microscope of extremely high power that uses beams of electrons focused by magnetic lenses instead of rays of light, the magnified image being formed on a fluorescent screen or recorded on a photographic plate: its magnification is substantially greater than that of any optical microscope. [1930–35]

elec′tron mul′tiplier, *Electronics.* a vacuum tube containing a number of dynodes that serve to amplify the flow of electrons from the cathode by means of secondary emission. [1935–40]

e•lec•tron-neu•tri•no (i lek′tron nōō trē′nō, -nyōō-), *n., pl.* **-nos.** *Physics.* a type of neutrino that obeys a conservation law together with the electron, with the total number of electrons and electron-neutrinos minus the total number of their antiparticles remaining constant. Also called **electronic neutrino, e-neutrino.** Cf. **lepton.**

elec′tron op′tics, the study and use of the physical and optical properties of beams of electrons under the influence of electric or magnetic fields. [1915–20]

e•lec′tron-ray tube′ (i lek′tron rā′), *Electronics.* a small cathode-ray tube having a fluorescent screen on which the pattern varies with the voltage applied to the grid: used chiefly in radio receivers to indicate accuracy of tuning. Also called **electric eye.**

elec′tron spin′ res′onance, *Physics.* the flipping back and forth between two spin directions of electrons in a magnetic field when electromagnetic radiation of the proper frequency is applied. *Abbr.:* ESR Also called **elec′tron paramagnet′ic res′onance, spin resonance.** [1950–55]

elec′tron tel′escope, a telescope in which an infrared image of a distant object is focused on the photosensitive cathode of an image tube. [1945–50]

elec′tron trans′port, *Biochem.* the stepwise transfer of electrons from one carrier molecule, as a flavoprotein or a cytochrome, to another along the respiratory chain and ultimately to oxygen during the aerobic production of ATP. [1950–55]

elec′tron tube′, an electronic device that consists, typically, of a sealed glass bulb containing two or more electrodes: used to generate, amplify, and rectify electric oscillations and alternating currents. Also called **electronic tube.** Cf. **gas tube, vacuum tube.** [1920–25]

e•lec•tron-volt (i lek′tron vōlt′), *n. Physics.* a unit of energy, equal to the energy acquired by an electron accelerating through a potential difference of one volt and equivalent to 1.602×10^{-19} joules. *Abbr.:* eV, ev Also, **elec′tron volt′.** [1925–30]

e•lec•tro•oc•u•lo•gram (i lek′trō ok′yə lə gram′), *n. Ophthalm.* a record of the changes in electrical potential that occur between the front and back of the eyeball as the eyes move between two fixed points: used to detect retinal dysfunction. *Abbr.:* EOG [1945–50; ELECTRO- + OCULO- + -GRAM[1]]

e•lec•tro•op•tics (i lek′trō op′tiks), *n.* (*used with a singular v.*) the branch of physics dealing with the effects of electrical fields on optical phenomena, as in the Kerr effect. Also, **e•lec′tro•op′tics.** [1890–95] **—e•lec′•tro•op′ti•cal,** *adj.* **—e•lec′tro•op′ti•cal•ly,** *adv.*

e•lec•tro•or•gan′ic chem′istry (i lek′trō ôr gan′ik), the branch of chemistry dealing with the electrochemistry of organic compounds. Also, **electroorgan′ic chem′istry.**

e•lec•tro•os•mo•sis (i lek′trō oz mō′sis, -os-), *n. Physical Chem.* the motion of a liquid through a membrane under the influence of an applied electric field. Also, **e•lec′tro•os•mo′sis, electrosmosis.** Also called **electroendosmosis.** [1905–10] **—e•lec•tro•os•mot•ic** (i lek′trō oz mot′ik, -os-), *adj.* **—e•lec′tro•os•mot′i•cal•ly,** *adv.*

e•lec•tro•phil•ic (i lek′trə fil′ik), *adj. Chem.* of or pertaining to electron acceptance in covalent bonding (opposed to *nucleophilic*). [1940–45; ELECTR(ON) + -O- + -PHILIC] **—e•lec′tro•phil′i•cal•ly,** *adv.*

e•lec•tro•pho•rese (i lek′trō fə rēs′), *v.t.* **-resed, -res•ing.** *Physical Chem.* to subject (a colloidal solution) to electrophoresis. [1965–70; back formation from ELECTROPHORESIS]

e•lec•tro•pho•re•sis (i lek′trō fə rē′sis), *n.* **1.** Also called **cataphoresis.** *Physical Chem.* the motion of colloidal particles suspended in a fluid medium, due to the influence of an electric field on the medium. **2.** *Biol.* this technique, applied to sorting proteins according to their responses to an electric field. Cf. **gel electrophoresis.** [1910–15; ELECTRO- + Gk *phórēsis* a being borne; see -PHORE, -SIS] **—e•lec•tro•pho•ret•ic** (i lek′trō fə ret′ik), *adj.*

e•lec•troph•o•rus (i lek trof′ər əs, ē′lek-), *n., pl.* **-o•ri** (-ə rī′). an instrument for generating static electricity by means of induction. [1770–80; ELECTRO- + *-phorus,* Latinization of -PHORE]

e•lec•tro•pho•tog•ra•phy (i lek′trō fə tog′rə fē), *n.* photography using electric rather than chemical processes to transfer an image onto paper, as in xerography. [1890–95; ELECTRO- + PHOTOGRAPHY] **—e•lec•tro•pho•to•graph•ic** (i lek′trə fō′tə graf′ik), *adj.*

e•lec•tro•phys•i•ol•o•gy (i lek′trō fiz′ē ol′ə jē), *n.* the branch of physiology dealing with the electric phenomena associated with the body and its functions. [1880–85; ELECTRO- + PHYSIOLOGY] **—e•lec•tro•phys•i•o•log•i•cal** (i lek′trō fiz′ē ə loj′i kəl), **e•lec′tro•phys′i•o•log′ic,** *adj.* **—e•lec′tro•phys′i•o•log′i•cal•ly,** *adv.* **—e•lec′tro•phys′i•ol′o•gist,** *n.*

e•lec•tro•plaque (i lek′trə plak′), *n.* (in certain fishes) one of a number of plates forming an electric organ, consisting of modified muscle tissue having an electric charge. Also, **e•lec•tro•plax** (i lek′trə plaks′). [ELECTRO- + PLAQUE]

e•lec•tro•plate (i lek′trə plāt′), *v.,* **-plat•ed, -plat•ing,** *n.* —*v.t.* **1.** to plate or coat with a metal by electrolysis. —*n.* **2.** electroplated articles or ware. [1860–65; ELECTRO- + PLATE[1]] **—e•lec′tro•plat′er,** *n.*

e•lec•tro•pol•ish (i lek′trō pol′ish), *v.t.* to give a smooth surface to (metal) by dissolving projecting ir-

CONCISE PRONUNCIATION KEY: act, cāpe, dâre, pärt; set, ēqual; *if,* ice; ox, ōver, ôrder, oil, bŏŏk, bōōt, out; up, ûrge; child; sing; shoe; thin, *that;* zh as in *treasure.* ə = *a* as in *alone, e* as in *system, i* as in *easily, o* as in *gallop, u* as in *circus;* ᵊ as in *fire* (fīᵊr), *hour* (ouᵊr). l and n can serve as syllabic consonants, as in *cradle* (krād′l), and *button* (but′n). See the full key inside the front cover.

regularities at the anode of an electrolytic cell. [1955–60; ELECTRO- + POLISH]

e•lec•tro•pos•i•tive (i lek′trō poz′i tiv), *adj. Physical Chem.* **1.** containing positive electricity; tending to migrate to the negative pole in electrolysis. **2.** assuming positive potential when in contact with a dissimilar substance. **3.** basic, as an element or group. [1840–50; ELECTRO- + POSITIVE]

e•lec•tro•re•cep•tor (i lek′trō ri sep′tər), *n. Zool.* any of an array of tiny, electrically sensitive ampullar organs present in sharks, electric eels, catfish, and certain other fishes, each organ being composed of a bundle of nerve fibers and sensory cells within a gel-filled conducting duct that can pick up weak electrical currents emitted by creatures moving in the water. [ELECTRO- + RECEPTOR]

e•lec•tro•re•duc•tion (i lek′trō ri duk′shən), *n.* the process in which electrons are added to a substance near the cathode of an electrolytic cell. [1925–30; ELECTRO- + REDUCTION]

e•lec•tro•re•fin•ing (i lek′trō ri fī′ning), *n.* the process for refining a metal in an electrolytic cell, in which the impure metal is used as the anode and the refined metal is deposited on the cathode. [ELECTRO- + REFINING]

e•lec•tro•ret•i•no•gram (i lek′trō ret′n ə gram′), *n. Ophthalm.* the graphic record obtained by electroretinography. *Abbr.:* ERG [1935–40; ELECTRO- + RETINO- + -GRAM[1]]

e•lec•tro•ret•i•no•graph (i lek′trō ret′n ə graf′, -gräf′), *n. Ophthalm.* an instrument that measures the electrical response of the retina to light stimulation. [1960–65; ELECTRO- + RETINO- + -GRAPH] **—e•lec•tro•ret•i•no•graph•ic** (i lek′trō ret′n ə graf′ik), *adj.* **—e•lec′tro•ret′i•no•graph′i•cal•ly,** *adv.* **—e•lec•tro•ret•i•nog•ra•phy** (i lek′trō ret′n og′rə fē), *n.*

e•lec•tro•scope (i lek′trə skōp′), *n.* a device for detecting the presence and determining the sign of electric charges by means of electrostatic attraction and repulsion, often between two pieces of gold leaf enclosed in a glass-walled chamber. [1815–25; ELECTRO- + -SCOPE] **—e•lec•tro•scop•ic** (i lek′trə skop′ik), *adj.*

e•lec•tro•sen•si•tive (i lek′trə sen′si tiv), *adj.* sensitive to electric current. [ELECTRO- + SENSITIVE]

e•lec•tro•shock (i lek′trə shok′), *n.* **1.** See **electroconvulsive therapy. 2.** shock[1] (def. 6). —*v.t.* **3.** *Psychiatry.* to administer electroconvulsive therapy to. **4.** to pass an electric current through. [1940–45; ELECTRO- + SHOCK[1]]

e•lec•tros•mo•sis (i lek′troz mō′sis, -tros-), *n. Physical Chem.* electro-osmosis.

e•lec•tro•stat•ic (i lek′trə stat′ik), *adj. Elect.* of or pertaining to static electricity. [1865–70; ELECTRO- + STATIC] **—e•lec′tro•stat′i•cal•ly,** *adv.*

elec′trostat′ic gen′erator, *Physics, Elect.* See **Van de Graaff generator.** [1930–35]

electrostat′ic induc′tion, *Elect.* the electrification of a conductor when placed near a charged body. [1875–80]

elec′trostat′ic lens′, an electron lens that focuses an electron beam by passing it through a series of electrodes kept at different voltages. [1950–55]

electrostat′ic precip′itator, a device for removing small particles of smoke, dust, oil, etc., from air by passing the air first through an electrically charged screen that gives a charge to the particles, then between two charged plates where the particles are attracted to one surface.

elec′trostat′ic print′ing, a printing or dry photocopying process, as xerography, in which images are reproduced using electrostatic charges and toner instead of ink and pressure.

e•lec•tro•stat•ics (i lek′trə stat′iks), *n.* (*used with a singular v.*) the branch of physics dealing with electric phenomena not associated with electricity in motion. [1820–30; ELECTRO- + STATICS]

elec′trostat′ic u′nit, *Elect.* a unit, as a statampere, in the system of electric units derived from the force of repulsion between two static charges. *Abbr.:* esu, ESU [1855–60]

e•lec•tro•stric•tion (i lek′trə strik′shən), *n. Physics.* elastic deformation produced by an electric field, independent of the polarity of the field. [ELECTRO- + STRICTION] **—e•lec′tro•stric′tive,** *adj.*

e•lec•tro•sur•ger•y (i lek′trō sûr′jə rē), *n.* the use in surgery of an electric instrument, as an acusector, or of an electric current, as in electrocoagulation; surgical diathermy. [1905–10; ELECTRO- + SURGERY] **—e•lec•tro•sur•gi•cal** (i lek′trō sûr′ji kəl), *adj.*

e•lec•tro•syn•the•sis (i lek′trō sin′thə sis), *n. Chem.* synthesis effected by electrolytic oxidation or reduction. [1835–45; ELECTRO- + SYNTHESIS] **—e•lec•tro•syn•thet•ic** (i lek′trō sin thet′ik), *adj.*

e•lec•tro•tax•is (i lek′trō tak′sis), *n. Biol.* galvanotaxis. [ELECTRO- + -TAXIS] **—e•lec•tro•tac•tic** (i lek′trō tak′tik), *adj.*

e•lec•tro•tech•nics (i lek′trō tek′niks), *n.* (*used with a singular v.*) the study or science of practical and industrial applications of electricity. Also, **e•lec•tro•tech•nol•o•gy** (i lek′trō tek nol′ə jē). [1880–85; ELECTRO- + TECHNICS] **—e•lec′tro•tech′nic, e•lec′tro•tech′ni•cal,** *adj.* **—e•lec•tro•tech•ni•cian** (i lek′trō tek nish′ən), *n.*

e•lec•tro•ther•a•peu•tics (i lek′trō ther′ə pyōō′tiks), *n.* (*used with a singular v.*) therapeutics based on the curative effects of electricity. [1885–90; ELECTRO- + THERAPEUTICS] **—e•lec′tro•ther′a•peu′tic, e•lec′tro•ther′a•peu′ti•cal,** *adj.*

e•lec•tro•ther•a•pist (i lek′trō ther′ə pist), *n.* a person who specializes in electrotherapeutics. [1925–30; ELECTROTHERAP(Y) + -IST]

e•lec•tro•ther•a•py (i lek′trō ther′ə pē), *n.* treatment of diseases by means of electricity; electrotherapeutics. [1880–85; ELECTRO- + THERAPY]

e•lec•tro•ther•mal (i lek′trō thûr′məl), *adj.* pertaining to both electricity and heat, esp. to the production of heat by electric current. Also, **e•lec′tro•ther′mic.** [1880–85; ELECTRO- + THERMAL] **—e•lec′tro•ther′mal•ly,** *adv.*

e•lec•tro•tin (i lek′trō tin′), *v.t.,* **-tinned, -tin•ning.** to plate or coat (a base metal) with tin by electrolysis. [1885–90; ELECTRO- + TIN]

e•lec•trot•o•nus (i lek trot′n əs, ē′lek-), *n. Physiol.* the altered state of a nerve during the passage of an electric current through it. [1855–60; < NL; see ELECTRO-, TONUS] **—e•lec•tro•ton•ic** (i lek′trə ton′ik), *adj.*

e•lec•tro•type (i lek′trə tīp′), *n., v.,* **-typed, -typ•ing.** —*n.* **1.** a facsimile, for use in printing, of a block of type, an engraving, or the like, consisting of a thin copper or nickel shell deposited by electrolytic action in a wax, lead, or plastic mold of the original and backed with lead alloy. **2.** electrotypy. —*v.t.* **3.** to make an electrotype of. [1830–40; ELECTRO- + TYPE] **—e•lec′tro•typ′er,** *n.*

e•lec•tro•typ•y (i lek′trə tī′pē), *n.* the process of making electrotypes. [ELECTROTYPE + -Y[3]] **—e•lec•tro•typ•ic** (i lek′trō tip′ik), *adj.* **—e•lec•tro•typ•ist** (i lek′trō tī′pist), *n.*

e•lec•tro•va•lence (i lek′trō vā′ləns), *n. Chem.* **1.** Also called **polar valence.** the valence of an ion, equal to the number of positive or negative charges acquired by an atom through a loss or gain of electrons. **2.** Also called **elec′trova′lent bond′.** See **ionic bond.** Also, **e•lec′tro•va′len•cy.** [1920–25; ELECTRO(N) + VALENCE] **—e•lec′tro•va′lent,** *adj.* **—e•lec′tro•va′lent•ly,** *adv.*

e•lec′tro•weak the′ory (i lek′trō wēk′), *Physics.* a gauge theory that unifies quantum electrodynamics with the theory of weak interactions. Also called **Salam-Weinberg theory, Weinberg-Salam theory.** Cf. **intermediate vector boson.** [1975–80; ELECTRO- + WEAK; alternate name after U.S. physicist Steven *Weinberg* (born 1933) and Pakistani physicist Abdus *Salam* (born 1926)]

e•lec•tro•win•ning (i lek′trō win′ing), *n.* electroextraction. [1935–40; ELECTRO- + WINNING]

e•lec•trum (i lek′trəm), *n.* **1.** an amber-colored alloy of gold and silver used in ancient times. **2.** an alloy composed of about 50 percent copper, 30 percent nickel, and 20 percent zinc. **3.** German silver; nickel silver. [1350–1400; ME < L < Gk *ēlektron* amber, alloy of gold and silver]

e•lec•tu•ar•y (i lek′chōō er′ē), *n., pl.* **-ar•ies.** *Pharm., Vet. Med.* a pasty mass composed of a medicine, usually in powder form, mixed in a palatable medium, as syrup, honey, or other sweet substance: used esp. for animals and administered by application to the teeth, tongue, or gums. [1350–1400; ME *electuarie* < LL *elect(u)ārium* a medicinal lozenge, alter. (by confusion with L *ēlēctus* (adj.) choice, good quality, *ēlēctus* (n.) choice) of Gk *ekleiktón* lozenge (neut. verbal adj. of *ekleíchein* to lick up; *ek-* EC- + *leíchein* to LICK); see -ARY]

el•ee•mos•y•nar•y (el′ə mos′ə ner′ē, -moz′-, el′ē ə-), *adj.* **1.** of or pertaining to alms, charity, or charitable donations; charitable. **2.** derived from or provided by charity. **3.** dependent on or supported by charity: *an eleemosynary educational institution.* [1610–20; < ML *eleēmosynārius,* equiv. to LL *eleēmosyn(a)* (see ALMS) + L *-ārius* -ARY]

el•e•gance (el′i gəns), *n.* **1.** elegant quality: *elegance of dress.* **2.** something elegant; a refinement. [1500–10; < MF < L *ēlegantia* choiceness. See ELEGANT, -ANCE]

el•e•gan•cy (el′i gən sē), *n., pl.* **-cies.** elegance. [1525–35; < L *ēlegantia.* See ELEGANT, -ANCY]

el•e•gant (el′i gənt), *adj.* **1.** tastefully fine or luxurious in dress, style, design, etc.: *elegant furnishings.* **2.** gracefully refined and dignified, as in tastes, habits, or literary style: *an elegant young gentleman; an elegant prosodist.* **3.** graceful in form or movement: *an elegant wave of the hand.* **4.** appropriate to refined taste: *a man devoted to elegant pursuits.* **5.** excellent; fine; superior: *an absolutely elegant wine.* **6.** (of scientific, technical, or mathematical theories, solutions, etc.) gracefully concise and simple; admirably succinct. [1400–50; late ME (< MF) < L *ēlegant-* (s. of *ēlegāns*) tasteful, choice, equiv. to *ēleg-* (akin to *ēlig-* select; see ELECT) + *-ant-* -ANT; orig. prp. of lost v.] **—el′e•gant•ly,** *adv.*
—Syn. 1. See **fine. 2.** polished, courtly.

el•e•gi•ac (el′i jī′ək, -ak, i lē′jē ak′), *adj.* Also, **el′e•gi′a•cal. 1.** used in, suitable for, or resembling an elegy. **2.** expressing sorrow or lamentation: *elegiac strains.* **3.** *Class. Pros.* noting a distich the first line of which is a dactylic hexameter and the second a pentameter, or a verse differing from the hexameter by suppression of the arsis or metrically unaccented part of the third and the sixth foot. —*n.* **4.** an elegiac or distich verse. **5.** a poem in such distichs or verses. [1575–85; (< MF) < L *elegīacus* < Gk *elegeiakós.* See ELEGY, -AC]

elegi′ac pentam′eter, *Class. Pros.* pentameter (def. 2).

elegi′ac quat′rain. See **heroic quatrain.**

elegi′ac stan′za, a four-line iambic pentameter stanza rhyming alternately. Also called **heroic stanza.**

el•e•gist (el′i jist), *n.* the author of an elegy. [1765–75; ELEG(Y) + -IST]

e•le•git (i lē′jit), *n. Law.* a writ of execution against a judgment debtor's goods, property, or land, held by the judgment creditor until payment of the debt, as from rents on the land. [1495–1505; < L: he has chosen, perf. 3rd pers. sing. ind. of *ēligere;* so called from wording of writ]

el•e•gize (el′i jīz′), *v.,* **-gized, -giz•ing.** —*v.t.* **1.** to lament in or as if in an elegy. —*v.i.* **2.** to compose an elegy. Also, *esp. Brit.,* **el′e•gise′.** [1695–1705; ELEG(Y) + -IZE]

el•e•gy (el′i jē), *n., pl.* **-gies. 1.** a mournful, melancholy, or plaintive poem, esp. a funeral song or a lament for the dead. **2.** a poem written in elegiac meter. **3.** a sad or mournful musical composition. [1505–15; (< MF) < L *elegīa* < Gk *elegeía,* orig. neut. pl. of *elegeîos* elegiac, equiv. to *éleg(os)* a lament + *-eios* adj. suffix]

El′egy Writ′ten in a Coun′try Church′yard, a poem (1750) by Thomas Gray.

e•lek•tra (i lek′trə), *n.* an electronic navigational system establishing approximate position through coincidence in amplitude of two radio signals. [special use of Gk *ēlektra,* pl. of *ēlektron.* See ELECTRON]

E•lek•tra (i lek′trə), *n.* Electra (def. 1).

E•lek•tro•stal (i lek′trə stäl′; *Russ.* i lyik tru stäl′), *n.* a city in the Russian Federation, in Europe, E of Moscow. 147,000. Formerly, **Zatishye.**

elem., 1. element; elements. **2.** elementary.

el•e•ment (el′ə mənt), *n.* **1.** a component or constituent of a whole or one of the parts into which a whole may be resolved by analysis: *Bricks and mortar are elements of every masonry wall.* **2.** *Chem.* one of a class of substances that cannot be separated into simpler substances by chemical means. See table on next page. See also chart under **periodic table. 3.** a natural habitat, sphere of activity, environment, etc.: *to be in one's element; Water is the element of fish.* **4. elements, a.** atmospheric agencies or forces; weather: *a ruddy complexion from exposure to the elements.* **b.** the rudimentary principles of an art, science, etc.: *the elements of grammar.* **c.** the bread and wine of the Eucharistic service. **5.** any group of people singled out within a larger group by identifiable behavior patterns, common interests, ethnic similarities, etc.: *He worried that the protest rally would attract the radical element.* **6.** one of the substances, usually earth, water, air, and fire, formerly regarded as constituting the material universe. **7.** *Math.* **a.** an infinitesimal part of a given quantity, similar in nature to it. **b.** an entity that satisfies all the conditions of belonging to a given set. **8.** *Geom.* one of the points, lines, planes, or other geometrical forms, of which a figure is composed. **9.** *Astron.* any of the data required to define the precise nature of an orbit and to determine the position of a planet in the orbit at any given time. **10.** *Elect.* an electric device with terminals for connection to other electrical devices. **11.** *Radio.* one of the electrodes in a vacuum tube. **12.** *Astrol.* any of the four triplicity groupings of signs: fire, earth, air, or water. **13.** *Optics.* any of the lenses or other components constituting an optical system. **14.** *Gram.* any word, part of a word, or group of words that recurs in various contexts in a language with relatively constant meaning. [1250–1300; ME (< AF) < L *elementum* one of the four elements, letter of the alphabet, first principle, rudiment]
—Syn. ELEMENT, COMPONENT, CONSTITUENT, INGREDIENT refer to units that are parts of whole or complete substances, systems, compounds, or mixtures. ELEMENT denotes a fundamental, ultimate part: *the basic elements of matter; resolve the problem into its elements.* COMPONENT and CONSTITUENT refer to a part that goes into the making of a complete system or compound. COMPONENT often refers to one of a number of parts: *a new component for the stereo system.* CONSTITUENT suggests a necessary part of the whole: *The constituents of a molecule of water are two atoms of hydrogen and one of oxygen.* INGREDIENT is most frequently used in nonscientific contexts: *the ingredients of a cake; the ingredients of a successful marriage.*

element 104, *Chem., Physics.* unnilquadium. [1975–80]

element 105, *Chem., Physics.* unnilpentium. [1975–80]

element 106, *Chem., Physics.* unnilhexium. [1975–80]

element 107, *Chem., Physics.* unnilseptium. [1975–80]

el•e•men•tal (el′ə men′tl), *adj.* **1.** of the nature of an ultimate constituent; simple; uncompounded. **2.** pertaining to rudiments or first principles. **3.** starkly simple, primitive, or basic: *a spare, elemental prose style; hate, lust, and other elemental emotions.* **4.** pertaining to the agencies, forces, or phenomena of physical nature: *elemental gods.* **5.** comparable to the great forces of nature, as in power or magnitude: *elemental grandeur.* **6.** of, pertaining to, or of the nature of the four elements, earth, water, air, and fire, or of any one of them. **7.** pertaining to chemical elements. [1485–95; < ML *elementālis.* See ELEMENT, -AL[1]] **—el′e•men′tal•ly,** *adv.*

el•e•men•ta•ry (el′ə men′tə rē, -trē), *adj.* **1.** pertaining to or dealing with elements, rudiments, or first principles: *an elementary grammar.* **2.** of or pertaining to an elementary school: *elementary teachers.* **3.** of the nature of an ultimate constituent; simple or uncompounded. **4.** pertaining to the four elements, earth, water, air, and fire, or to the great forces of nature; elemental. **5.** *Chem.* of or noting one or more elements. [1400–50; late ME *elementare* (< MF *elementaire*) < L *elementārius.* See ELEMENT, -ARY] **—el•e•men•tar•i•ly** (el′ə men ter′ə lē), *adv.* **—el′e•men′ta•ri•ness,** *n.*
—Syn. 1. ELEMENTARY, PRIMARY, RUDIMENTARY refer to what is basic and fundamental. ELEMENTARY refers to the introductory, simple, easy facts or parts of a subject that must necessarily be learned first in order to understand succeeding ones: *elementary arithmetic.* PRIMARY may mean much the same as ELEMENTARY; however, it usually emphasizes the idea of what comes first even more than that of simplicity: *primary steps.* RUDIMENTARY applies to what is undeveloped or imperfect: *a rudimentary form of government.*

el′emen′tary charge′, *Physics.* the unit of electric charge of which all free charges found in nature are in-

CONCISE ETYMOLOGY KEY: <, descended or borrowed from; >, whence; b., blend of, blended; c., cognate with; cf., compare; deriv., derivative; equiv., equivalent; imit., imitative; obl., oblique; r., replacing; s., stem; sp., spelling, spelled; resp., respelling, respelled; trans., translation; ?, origin unknown; *, unattested; ‡, probably earlier than. See the full key inside the front cover.

CHEMICAL ELEMENTS

Name	Symbol	Atomic No.	Atomic Mass*	Name	Symbol	Atomic No.	Atomic Mass*
Actinium	**Ac**	89	(227)	Neodymium	**Nd**	60	144.24
Aluminum	**Al**	13	26.98154	Neon	**Ne**	10	20.18
Americium	**Am**	95	(243)	Neptunium	**Np**	93	(237)
Antimony	**Sb**	51	121.75	Nickel	**Ni**	28	58.71
Argon	**Ar**	18	39.948	Niobium	**Nb**	41	92.9064
Arsenic	**As**	33	74.9216	Nitrogen	**N**	7	14.0067
Astatine	**At**	85	(210)	Nobelium	**No**	102	(256)
Barium	**Ba**	56	137.34	Osmium	**Os**	76	190.2
Berkelium	**Bk**	97	(247)	Oxygen	**O**	8	15.999
Beryllium	**Be**	4	9.01218	Palladium	**Pd**	46	106.4
Bismuth	**Bi**	83	208.9808	Phosphorus	**P**	15	30.97376
Boron	**B**	5	10.81	Platinum	**Pt**	78	195.09
Bromine	**Br**	35	79.904	Plutonium	**Pu**	94	(242)
Cadmium	**Cd**	48	112.41	Polonium	**Po**	84	(210)
Calcium	**Ca**	20	40.08	Potassium	**K**	19	39.098
Californium	**Cf**	98	(249)	Praseodymium	**Pr**	59	140.907
Carbon	**C**	6	12.011	Promethium	**Pm**	61	(147)
Cerium	**Ce**	58	140.12	Protactinium	**Pa**	91	(231)
Cesium	**Cs**	55	132.9054	Radium	**Ra**	88	(226)
Chlorine	**Cl**	17	35.453	Radon	**Rn**	86	(222)
Chromium	**Cr**	24	51.996	Rhenium	**Re**	75	186.2
Cobalt	**Co**	27	58.9332	Rhodium	**Rh**	45	102.9055
Copper	**Cu**	29	63.546	Rubidium	**Rb**	37	85.468
Curium	**Cm**	96	(247)	Ruthenium	**Ru**	44	101.07
Dysprosium	**Dy**	66	162.50	Samarium	**Sm**	62	150.4
Einsteinium	**Es**	99	(254)	Scandium	**Sc**	21	44.9559
Erbium	**Er**	68	167.26	Selenium	**Se**	34	78.96
Europium	**Eu**	63	151.96	Silicon	**Si**	14	28.086
Fermium	**Fm**	100	(253)	Silver	**Ag**	47	107.87
Fluorine	**F**	9	18.99840	Sodium	**Na**	11	22.9898
Francium	**Fr**	87	(223)	Strontium	**Sr**	38	87.62
Gadolinium	**Gd**	64	157.25	Sulfur	**S**	16	32.06
Gallium	**Ga**	31	69.72	Tantalum	**Ta**	73	180.948
Germanium	**Ge**	32	72.59	Technetium	**Tc**	43	(99)
Gold	**Au**	79	196.967	Tellurium	**Te**	52	127.60
Hafnium	**Hf**	72	178.49	Terbium	**Tb**	65	158.9254
Helium	**He**	2	4.00260	Thallium	**Tl**	81	204.37
Holmium	**Ho**	67	164.9304	Thorium	**Th**	90	232.0381
Hydrogen	**H**	1	1.0079	Thulium	**Tm**	69	168.9342
Indium	**In**	49	114.82	Tin	**Sn**	50	118.69
Iodine	**I**	53	126.9045	Titanium	**Ti**	22	47.9
Iridium	**Ir**	77	192.2	Tungsten	**W**	74	183.85
Iron	**Fe**	26	55.847	Unnilhexium	**Unh**	106	(263)
Krypton	**Kr**	36	83.80	Unnilpentium	**Unp**	105	(260)
Lanthanum	**La**	57	138.91	Unnilquadium	**Unq**	104	(257)
Lawrencium	**Lr**	103	(257)	Unnilseptium	**Uns**	107	(262)
Lead	**Pb**	82	207.2	Uranium	**U**	92	238.03
Lithium	**Li**	3	6.94	Vanadium	**V**	23	50.941
Lutetium	**Lu**	71	174.97	Xenon	**Xe**	54	131.30
Magnesium	**Mg**	12	24.305	Ytterbium	**Yb**	70	173.04
Manganese	**Mn**	25	54.9380	Yttrium	**Y**	39	88.9059
Mendelevium	**Md**	101	(256)	Zinc	**Zn**	30	65.38
Mercury	**Hg**	80	200.59	Zirconium	**Zr**	40	91.22
Molybdenum	**Mo**	42	95.94				

*Approx. values for radioactive elements given in parentheses.

tegral multiples, equal to 1.602×10^{-19} coulombs, the charge of the proton.

el′emen′tary func′tion, *Math.* one of a class of functions that is generally taken to include power, exponential, and trigonometric functions, their inverses, and finite combinations of them.

el′emen′tary par′ticle, *Physics.* any lepton, hadron, photon, or graviton, the particles once thought to be the indivisible components of all matter or radiation. Also called **fundamental particle, particle.** [1930–35]

el′emen′tary proc′ess, *Physical Chem.* a chemical process complete in one step, characterized by the simultaneous interaction of all the atoms of two or more molecules.

elemen′tary school′, the lowest school giving formal instruction, teaching the rudiments of learning, and extending usually from six to eight years. Also called **primary school.** [1835–45]

el•e•mi (el′ə mē), *n., pl.* **-mis.** any of various fragrant resins from certain trees, esp. *Canarium commune,* used chiefly in the manufacture of varnishes, lacquers, ointments, and in perfumery. Also called **gum elemi.** [1535–45; short for *gum elemi* < NL *gummi elimī;* cf. Ar *allāmī* the elemi]

El•e•na (el′ə nə, ə lā′nə; *It.* e le′nä), *n.* a female given name, form of **Helen.**

e•len•chus (i leng′kəs), *n., pl.* **-chi** (-kī, -kē). a logical refutation; an argument that refutes another argument by proving the contrary of its conclusion. [1655–65; < L < Gk *élenchos* refutation]

El•e•nore (el′ə nər, -nôr′), *n.* a female given name, form of **Helen.** Also, **El′e•nor, El•e•o•no•ra** (el′ē ə nôr′ə, -nōr′ə), **El•e•o•nore** (el′ē ə nôr′, -nōr′).

el•e•op•tene (el′ē op′tēn), *n. Chem.* the liquid part of a volatile oil (opposed to *stearoptene*). Also, **elaeoptene.** [< Gk *élaio(n)* oil + *ptēn(ós)* winged (akin to *pétesthai* to fly); see -ENE]

el•e•pai•o (el′ə pī′ō), *n., pl.* **-pai•os.** a small brown-backed or gray-backed Hawaiian flycatcher, *Chasiempis sandwichensis,* having white wing bars, a white rump, and a blackish cocked tail. [< Hawaiian *ʻelepaio*]

el•e•phant (el′ə fənt), *n., pl.* **-phants,** (*esp. collectively*) **-phant** for 1. **1.** either of two large, five-toed pachyderms of the family Elephantidae, characterized by a long, prehensile trunk formed of the nose and upper lip, including *Loxodonta africana* **(African elephant),** with enormous flapping ears, two fingerlike projections at the end of the trunk, and ivory tusks, and *Elephas maximus* **(Indian elephant),** with smaller ears, one projection at the end of the trunk, and ivory tusks almost exclusively in males: *L. africana* is threatened; *E. maximus* is endangered. **2.** a representation of this animal, used in the U.S. since 1874 as the emblem of the Republican party. **3.** See **white elephant. 4.** *Chiefly Brit.* a size of drawing or writing paper, 23 × 28 in. (58 × 71 cm). Cf. **double elephant.** [1250–1300; ME (< AF) < L *elephantus* < Gk *elephant-* (s. of *eléphās*) elephant; r. ME *olifaunt* < AF < VL **olifantus,* for L *elephantus* (with regular L *o* from *e* before dark *l*)] **—el′e•phan•toid′,** *adj.*

el′ephant bird′, any of several huge, extinct, flightless birds of the genus *Aepyornis,* of Madagascar, reaching a height of about 9 ft. (2.7 m). [1885–90]

El′ephant Butte′, a dam and irrigation reservoir in SW New Mexico, on the Rio Grande. Dam, 309 ft. (94 m) high.

el′ephant ear′, a large, flat, sugared pastry somewhat resembling an elephant's ear in shape. [1905–10, for an earlier sense]

el′ephant fish′, any of several long-snouted fishes belonging to the genus *Callorhynchus,* of the family Callorhynchidae (Chimaeridae), inhabiting deep waters of the Southern Hemisphere. [1765–75]

el′ephant fo′lio, *Print.* **1.** a very large folio. **2.** an American book size with a height measurement between 24 and 25 in. (61 and 63.5 cm). [1875–80]

el′ephant grass′, 1. See **napier grass. 2.** a cattail, *Typha elephantina,* of southern Asia, used for making rope and baskets. [1825–35]

el′ephant gun′, a gun of very large caliber, as .410 or greater, used in killing elephants or other big game.

African elephant, *Loxodonta africana,* 11 ft. (3.4 m) high at shoulder; tusks 6 to 8 ft. (1.8 m to 2.4 m)

Indian elephant, *Elephas maximus,* 9 ft. (2.7 m) high at shoulder; tusks 4 to 5 ft. (1.2 m to 1.5 m)

el•e•phan•ti•a•sis (el′ə fən tī′ə sis, -fan-), *n.* **1.** *Pathol.* a chronic filarial disease resulting in lymphatic obstruction, characterized by marked enlargement of the parts affected, esp. of the legs and scrotum, transmitted by mosquitoes. **2.** untoward growth or development: *bureaucratic elephantiasis.* [1575–85; < L < Gk *elephantíāsis,* equiv. to *elephant-* ELEPHANT + *-iāsis* -IASIS]

el•e•phan•tine (el′ə fan′tēn, -tīn, -tin, el′ə fən tēn′, -tīn′), *adj.* **1.** pertaining to or resembling an elephant. **2.** huge, ponderous, or clumsy: *elephantine movements; elephantine humor.* [1620–30; < L *elephantinus* < Gk *elephántinos.* See ELEPHANT, -INE[1]]

el′ephant man's′ disease′, neurofibromatosis. [from the name given to Englishman John Merrick (1862 or 63–90), who suffered from an extreme form of the disorder and was exhibited as a freak]

el′ephant seal′, either of two seals of the genus *Mirounga,* of the Pacific coast of North America and the Antarctic Ocean, having a curved proboscis resembling an elephant's trunk. Also called **sea elephant.** [1835–45]

el•e•phant's-ear (el′ə fənts ēr′), *n.* the taro. [1865–70, *Amer.*]

el•e•phant's-foot (el′ə fənts fo͝ot′), *n., pl.* **-foots.** a climbing vine, *Dioscorea elephantipes,* of southern Africa, having a massive, edible, yamlike tuber. Also called **Hottentot's bread, tortoise plant.** [1810–20]

el′ephant shrew′, any of several African insectivores of the family Macroscelididae, having long hind legs and a long, sensitive snout. [1865–70]

el′e•phant's-trunk snake′ (el′ə fənts trungk′), a wart snake, *Acrochordus javanicus,* having a stout body that resembles the trunk of an elephant.

E•lets (yə lets′; *Russ.* yi lyets′), *n.* Yelets.

El•eu•sin•i•an (el′yo͝o sin′ē ən), *adj.* **1.** of or pertaining to Eleusis or to the Eleusinian mysteries. **—***n.* **2.** a native or inhabitant of Eleusis. [1635–45; < L *Eleusini(us)* < Gk *Eleusínios* of Eleusis + -AN]

Eleusin′ian mys′teries, the mysteries, celebrated annually at Eleusis and Athens in ancient times, in memory of the abduction and return of Persephone and in honor of Demeter and Bacchus. [1635–45]

E•leu•sis (i lo͞o′sis), *n.* a city in ancient Greece, in Attica.

E•leu•ther•a (i lo͞o′thər ə), *n.* an island in the N Bahamas. 6247; 164 sq. mi. (425 sq. km).

El•eu•the•ri•us (el′yo͝o thēr′ē əs), *n.* **Saint,** pope A.D. 175–189.

elev., elevation.

el•e•vate (*v.* el′ə vāt′; *adj.* el′ə vāt′, -vit), *v.,* **-vat•ed, -vat•ing,** *adj.* **—***v.t.* **1.** to move or raise to a higher place or position; lift up. **2.** to raise to a higher state, rank, or office; exalt; promote: *to elevate an archbishop to cardinal.* **3.** to raise to a higher intellectual or spiritual level: *Good poetry may elevate the mind.* **4.** to raise the spirits; put in high spirits. **5.** to raise (the voice) in pitch or volume. **—***adj.* **6.** *Archaic.* raised; elevated. [1490–1500; < L *ēlevātus* lightened, lifted up (ptp. of *ēlevāre*), equiv. to *ē-* E- + *lev-* light + *-ātus* -ATE[1]]
—Syn. 1. lift, hoist. **2.** advance, upgrade, dignify. ELEVATE, ENHANCE, EXALT, HEIGHTEN mean to raise or make higher in some respect. To ELEVATE is to raise something up to a higher level, position, or state: *to elevate the living standards of a group.* To ENHANCE is to add to the attractions or desirability of something: *Landscaping enhances the beauty of the grounds.* To EXALT is to raise very high in rank, character, estimation, mood, etc.: *A king is exalted above his subjects.* To HEIGHTEN is to increase the strength or intensity: *to heighten one's powers of concentration.*

el•e•vat•ed (el′ə vā′tid), *adj.* **1.** raised up, esp. above the ground or above the normal level: *an elevated platform; an elevated pulse.* **2.** exalted or noble; lofty: *elevated thoughts.* **3.** elated; joyful. **—***n.* **4.** an elevated railroad. [1545–55; ELEVATE + -ED[2]]

el′evated rail′road, a railroad system operating on an elevated structure, as over streets. Also called **el.** [1865–70, *Amer.*]

el•e•va•tion (el′ə vā′shən), *n.* **1.** the height to which something is elevated or to which it rises: *The elevation of the tower is 80 feet.* **2.** the altitude of a place above sea level or ground level. **3.** an elevated place, thing, or part; an eminence. **4.** loftiness; grandeur or dignity; nobleness: *elevation of mind.* **5.** the act of elevating. **6.** the state of being elevated. **7.** *Archit.* a drawing or design that represents an object or structure as being projected geometrically on a vertical plane parallel to one of its sides. **8.** *Survey.* **a.** Also called **angle of elevation.** the angle between the line from an observer or instrument to an object above the observer or instrument and a horizontal line. **b.** the distance above a datum level. **9.** the ability of a dancer to stay in the air while executing a step or the height thus attained. **10. the Elevation,** *Rom. Cath. Ch.* the lifting by the celebrant of the Eucharistic elements immediately after consecration, for adoration by the communicants. [1350–1400; ME < AF < L *ēlevātiōn-* (s. of *ēlevātiō*), equiv. to *ēlevāt(us)* (see ELEVATE) + *-iōn-* -ION]
—Syn. 1. See **height. 3.** height; hill; mountain; plateau. **4.** exaltation, nobility. **—Ant. 1.** depth.

el•e•va•tor (el′ə vā′tər), *n.* **1.** a person or thing that elevates or raises. **2.** a moving platform or cage for carrying passengers or freight from one level to another, as in a building. **3.** any of various mechanical devices for raising objects or materials. **4.** a building in which grain is stored and handled by means of mechanical elevator and conveyor devices. **5.** *Aeron.* a hinged horizontal surface on an airplane or the like, used to control the longitudinal inclination and usually placed at the tail end of the fuselage. **6.** See **elevator shoe.** [1640–50; < LL *ēlevātor,* equiv. to *ēlevā(re)* (see ELEVATE) + *-tor* -TOR]

el′evator shoe′, a shoe with a thick insole designed to increase the wearer's height. [named after a former trademark, *Elevators*]

e•lev•en (i lev′ən), *n.* **1.** a cardinal number, ten plus one. **2.** a symbol for this number, as 11 or XI. **3.** a set of this many persons or things, as a football team. —*adj.* **4.** amounting to eleven in number. [bef. 900; ME *eleven(e),* OE *ellefne, endleofan;* c. OHG *einlif* (G *elf*), ON *ellifu,* Goth *ainlib-,* lit., one remaining (after counting 10). See ONE, LEAVE[1]]

e•lev•ens•es (i lev′ən ziz), *n. Brit.* **1.** (*usually used with a plural v.*) a midmorning break for refreshments. **2.** the refreshments taken. [1860–65; orig. dial.; doubly pluralized form of ELEVEN, perh. as ellipsis of *eleven hours* eleven o'clock]

e•lev•enth (i lev′ənth), *adj.* **1.** next after the tenth; being the ordinal number for 11. **2.** being one of 11 equal parts. —*n.* **3.** an eleventh part, esp. of one (1/11). **4.** the eleventh member of a series. [bef. 1000; ME *enleventh, enlefte,* OE *endlyfta* (akin to OFris *andlofta,* OS *ellifto*). See ELEVEN, -TH[2]]

Elev′enth Amend′ment, an amendment to the U.S. Constitution, ratified in 1795, that prohibited an individual from suing a state government in the federal courts.

elev′enth hour′, the last possible moment for doing something: *to change plans at the eleventh hour.* [1820–30]

el•e•von (el′ə von′), *n. Aeron.* a control surface functioning both as an elevator and as an aileron. [1940–45; ELEV(ATOR) + (AILER)ON]

elf (elf), *n., pl.* **elves** (elvz). **1.** (in folklore) one of a class of preternatural beings, esp. from mountainous regions, with magical powers, given to capricious and often mischievous interference in human affairs, and usually imagined to be a diminutive being in human form; sprite; fairy. **2.** a diminutive person, esp. a child. **3.** a mischievous person, esp. a child. [bef. 1000; ME, back formation from *elven,* OE *elfen* nymph (i.e., female elf), var. of *ælfen; see* ELFIN] —**elf′like′,** *adj.*
—**Syn. 1.** See **fairy.**

ELF, See **extremely low frequency.** Also, **elf**

El Fai•yum (el′ fī yōōm′, fā-), Faiyum (def. 2). Also, **El′ Fa•yum′.**

El Fa•sher (el fash′ər), a city in W Sudan. 46,380.

El Fer•rol (el feʀ rôl′), a seaport in NW Spain: naval arsenal and dockyard. 87,736. Also called **Ferrol.**

elf•in (el′fin), *adj.* **1.** of or like an elf. **2.** small and charmingly sprightly, merry, or mischievous. —*n.* **3.** an elf. [1560–70; alter. of ME *elven* elf, OE *elfen, ælfen* nymph, equiv. to *ælf* elf + *-en* fem. suffix (c. G *-in*); *ælf* c. G *Alp* nightmare, puck, ON *alfr* elf]

elf•in•wood (el′fin wŏŏd′), *n.* krummholz. [1900–05; ELFIN + WOOD[1]]

elf•ish (el′fish), *adj.* elflike; elfin; small and mischievous. Also, **elvish.** [1535–45; alter. of ELVISH] —**elf′ish•ly,** *adv.* —**elf′ish•ness,** *n.*
—**Syn.** prankish, impish.

elf•land (elf′land′), *n.* the realm or world of elves; fairyland. [1475–85; ELF + LAND]

elf•lock (elf′lok′), *n.* a tangled lock of hair. [1585–95; ELF + LOCK[2]]

El Fos•tat (el′ fōō stät′), al-Fustat. Also, **el′-Fus•tat′.**

elf′ owl′, a small, insectivorous owl, *Micrathene whitneyi,* of the southwestern U.S. and Mexico. [1885–90, *Amer.*]

El•gar (el′gər, -gär), *n.* **Sir Edward,** 1857–1934, English composer.

El•gin (el′jin *for 1;* el′gin *for 2*), *n.* **1.** a city in NE Illinois. 63,798. **2.** former name of **Moray.**

El′gin mar′bles (el′gin, -jin), a group of Greek sculptures of the 5th century B.C., originally on the Parthenon in Athens, and supposedly sculptured under the direction of Phidias: presently in the British Museum in London. [after Thomas Bruce, 7th Earl of *Elgin* (1766–1841), who arranged for their removal from Athens]

El Gi•za (el gē′zə), Giza. Also, **El Gi′zeh.**

El•gon (el′gon), *n.* an extinct volcano in E Africa, on the boundary between Uganda and Kenya. 14,176 ft. (4321 m).

El Gre•co (el grek′ō; *Sp.* el gʀe′kô), (*Domenikos Theotocopoulos*), 1541–1614, Spanish painter, born in Crete.

El Ha•sa (el hä′sə), Hasa.

el•hi (el′hī), *adj.* elementary and high-school: *the elhi textbook market.* [1945–50; EL(EMENTARY) + HI(GH SCHOOL)]

E•li (ē′lī), *n.* **1.** a Hebrew judge and priest. I Sam. 1–4. **2.** Also, **El•ie** (el′ē). a male given name: from a Hebrew word meaning "height."

E•li•a (ē′lē ə), *n.* the pen name of Charles Lamb.

E•li•as (i lī′əs), *n.* **1.** *Douay Bible.* Elijah (def. 1). **2.** a male given name, Greek form of **Elijah.**

e•lic•it (i lis′it), *v.t.* to draw or bring out or forth; educe; evoke: *to elicit the truth; to elicit a response with a question.* [1635–45; < L *ēlicitus* drawn out (ptp. of *ēlicere*), equiv. to *ē-* E- + *lici-* draw, lure + *-tus* ptp. suffix] —**e•lic′i•ta′tion,** *n.* —**e•lic′i•tor,** *n.*

e•lide (i līd′), *v.t.,* **e•lid•ed, e•lid•ing. 1.** to omit (a vowel, consonant, or syllable) in pronunciation. **2.** to suppress; omit; ignore; pass over. **3.** *Law.* to annul or quash. [1585–95; < L *ēlīdere* to strike out, equiv. to *ē-* E- + *-līdere,* comb. form of *laedere* to wound]

el•i•gi•ble (el′i jə bəl), *adj.* **1.** fit or proper to be chosen; worthy of choice; desirable: *to marry an eligible bachelor.* **2.** meeting the stipulated requirements, as to participate, compete, or work; qualified. **3.** legally qualified to be elected or appointed to office: *eligible for the presidency.* —*n.* **4.** a person or thing that is eligible: *Among the eligibles, only a few are running for office.* [1555–65; (< MF) < LL *ēligibilis,* equiv. to L *ē-* E- + *ligi-* select + *-bilis;* see -IBLE] —**el′i•gi•bil′i•ty, el′i•gi•ble•ness,** *n.* —**el′i•gi•bly,** *adv.*
—**Syn. 1.** suitable, fitting. —**Ant. 1.** ineligible, unsuitable, unacceptable.

el′igible pa′per, *Banking.* notes, bills, and acceptances qualifying for rediscount by a Federal Reserve Bank.

El•i•hu (el′ə hyōō′, i lī′hyōō), *n.* **1.** a young man who entered into discourse with Job. Job. 32–37. **2.** a male given name. [< Heb *ĕlīhū* lit., my God is he]

E•li•jah (i lī′jə), *n.* **1.** a Hebrew prophet of the 9th century B.C. I Kings 17; II Kings 2. **2.** a male given name. [< Heb *ēliyyāh* lit., my God is Yahweh]

Eli′jah Muham′mad, (*Elijah Poole*) 1897–1975, U.S. religious leader of the Black Muslims 1934–75.

Eli′jah's chair′, a chair customarily set apart in honor of the prophet Elijah at the Jewish rite of circumcision.

Eli′jah's cup′, a cup of wine customarily set apart in honor of the prophet Elijah at the Jewish Passover Seder.

e•lim•i•nate (i lim′ə nāt′), *v.t.,* **-nat•ed, -nat•ing. 1.** to remove or get rid of, esp. as being in some way undesirable: *to eliminate risks; to eliminate hunger.* **2.** to omit, esp. as being unimportant or irrelevant; leave out: *I have eliminated all statistical tables, which are of interest only to the specialist.* **3.** to remove from further consideration or competition, esp. by defeating in a contest. **4.** to eradicate or kill: *to eliminate the enemy.* **5.** *Physiol.* to void or expel from an organism. **6.** *Math.* to remove (a quantity) from an equation by elimination. [1560–70; 1915–20 for def. 4; < L *ēlīminātus* turned out of doors (ptp. of *ēlīmināre*), equiv. to *ē-* E- + *līmin-,* s. of *līmen* threshold + *-ātus* -ATE[1]] —**e•lim′i•na•bil′i•ty** (i lim′ə nə bil′i tē), *n.* —**e•lim′i•na′tive,** *adj.*
—**Syn. 1, 2.** reject. —**Ant. 2.** include.

e•lim•i•na•tion (i lim′ə nā′shən), *n.* **1.** the act of eliminating. **2.** the state of being eliminated. **3.** *Math.* the process of solving a system of simultaneous equations by using various techniques to remove the variables successively. **4.** *Sports.* a game, bout, or match in a tournament in which an individual or team is eliminated from the competition after one defeat. [1595–1605; ELIMINATE + -ION]

e•lim•i•na•tor (i lim′ə nā′tər), *n.* **1.** a person or thing that eliminates. **2.** Also called **battery eliminator.** a device that operates from a power line to supply current and voltage to a circuit designed to be operated by a battery. [1880–85; ELIMINATE + -OR[2]] —**e•lim•i•na•to•ry** (i lim′ə nə tôr′ē, -tōr′ē), *adj.*

El•i•nor (el′ə nər, -nôr′), *n.* a female given name, form of **Helen.**

el•int (el′int, i lint′), *n.* **1.** the gathering of military or other intelligence through the monitoring of electronic signals other than voice communications, as satellite transmissions, rocket telemetry, and radar. **2.** sigint. Also **El′int, ELINT** Cf. **comint, humint, sigint.** [1965–70; *el(ectronic) int(elligence)*]

El•in•var (el′in vär′), *Trademark.* an alloy of iron, nickel, chromium, and other constituents, resistant to rust and magnetization and having a low rate of thermal expansion.

El•i•ot (el′ē ət, el′yət), *n.* **1. Charles William,** 1834–1926, U.S. educator: president of Harvard University 1869–1909. **2. George** (*Mary Ann Evans*), 1819–80, English novelist. **3. John** (*"the Apostle of the Indians"*), 1604–90, American colonial missionary. **4. Sir John,** 1592–1632, English statesman. **5. T(homas) S(tearns)** (stûrnz), 1888–1965, British poet and critic, born in the U.S.: Nobel prize 1948. **6.** a male given name, form of **Elias.**

El•i•phaz (el′ə faz′), *n.* **1.** a son of Esau and Adah. Gen. 36:2–4. **2.** a friend of Job. Job 2:11.

E•lis (ē′lis), *n.* **1.** an ancient country in W Greece, in the Peloponnesus: site of the ancient Olympic Games. **2.** the capital of this country.

E•li•sa (i lis′ə, e lē′sə), *n.* a female given name, form of **Elizabeth.** Also, **E•li•sia** (i lish′ə).

ELISA (i lī′zə, -sə), *n.* **1.** *Med.* a sensitive diagnostic test for past or current exposure to an infectious agent, as the AIDS virus: a sample of blood is added to proteins from the agent, and any antibodies that combine with the proteins, indicating a history of infection, are detected by adding a test antibody linked to an enzyme that causes a color change. **2.** *Biol., Med.* any similar test using proteins as a probe for the identification of antibodies or antigens. [*e(nzyme-)l(inked) i(mmuno)s(orbent) a(ssay)*]

E•lis•a•beth (i liz′ə bəth), *n.* **1.** the mother of John the Baptist. Luke 1:5–25. **2.** a female given name.

E•lis•a•beth•ville (i liz′ə bəth vil′), *n.* former name of **Lubumbashi.**

E•li•sa•vet•grad (i liz′ə vet′grad; *Russ.* yi lyi sə vyit-gʀät′), *n.* a former name of **Kirovograd.**

E•li•sa•vet•pol (i liz′ə vet′pōl; *Russ.* yi lyi sə vyit-pôl′), *n.* a former name of **Kirovabad.**

E•lise (i lēs′), *n.* a female given name, form of **Elizabeth.**

E•li•sha (i lī′shə), *n.* **1.** Also, *Douay Bible,* **El•i•se•us** (el′i sē′əs). a Hebrew prophet of the 9th century B.C., the successor of Elijah. II Kings 3–9. **2.** a male given name. [< Heb *ĕlīshūa'* lit., God has saved]

e•li•sion (i lizh′ən), *n.* **1.** the omission of a vowel, consonant, or syllable in pronunciation. **2.** (in verse) the omission of a vowel at the end of one word when the next word begins with a vowel, as *th'orient.* **3.** an act or instance of eliding or omitting anything. [1575–85; < L *ēlīsiōn-* (s. of *ēlīsiō*) a striking out, equiv. to *ēlīs(us)* (ptp. of *ēlīdere;* see ELIDE) + *-iōn-* -ION]

e•lis•or (i lī′zər), *n. Law.* a person appointed by a court to perform the duties of a sheriff or coroner who is disqualified from acting in a certain case. Also, **eslisor.** [1400–50; late ME *elisour* < AF, equiv. to *elis-* (var. s. of *elire* to choose < L *ēligere*) + *-our* -OR[2]]

E•lis•sa (i lis′ə), *n.* **1.** Phoenician name of **Dido. 2.** a female given name, form of **Elizabeth.**

e•lite (i lēt′, ā lēt′), *n.* **1.** (*often used with a plural v.*) the choice or best of anything considered collectively, as of a group or class of persons. **2.** (*used with a plural v.*) persons of the highest class: *Only the elite were there.* **3.** a group of persons exercising the major share of authority or influence within a larger group: *the power elite of a major political party.* **4.** a type, approximately 10-point in printing-type size, widely used in typewriters and having 12 characters to the inch. Cf. **pica[1].** —*adj.* **5.** representing the most choice or select; best: *an elite group of authors.* Also, **é•lite′.** [1350–1400; ME *elit* a person elected to office < MF *e(s)lit* ptp. of *e(s)lire* to choose; see ELECT]

e•lit•ism (i lē′tiz əm, ā lē′-), *n.* **1.** practice of or belief in rule by an elite. **2.** consciousness of or pride in belonging to a select or favored group. [1950–55; ELITE + -ISM] —**e•lit′ist,** *n., adj.*

elix., (in prescriptions) elixir.

e•lix•ir (i lik′sər), *n.* **1.** *Pharm.* a sweetened, aromatic solution of alcohol and water containing, or used as a vehicle for, medicinal substances. **2.** Also called **elix′ir of life′.** an alchemic preparation formerly believed to be capable of prolonging life. **3.** an alchemic preparation formerly believed to be capable of transmuting base metals into gold. **4.** the quintessence or absolute embodiment of anything. **5.** a panacea; cure-all; sovereign remedy. [1350–1400; ME < ML < Ar *al iksīr* alchemical preparation < LGk *xḗrion* drying powder (for wounds), equiv. to Gk *xēr(ós)* dry + *-ion,* neut. of *-ios* adj. suffix]

Eliz., Elizabethan.

E•li•za (i lī′zə), *n.* a female given name, form of **Elizabeth.**

E•liz•a•beth (i liz′ə bəth), **1.** *Douay Bible.* Elisabeth. **2.** (*Elizaveta Petrovna*) 1709–62, empress of Russia 1741–62 (daughter of Peter the Great). **3.** (*Pauline Elizabeth Ottilie Luise, Princess of Wied*) (*"Carmen Sylva"*) 1843–1916, queen of Rumania 1881–1914 and author. **4.** (*Elizabeth Angela Marguerite Bowes-Lyon*) born 1900, queen consort of George VI of Great Britain (mother of Elizabeth II). **5. Saint,** 1207–31, Hungarian princess and religious mystic. **6.** a city in NE New Jersey. 106,201. **7.** a female given name: from a Hebrew word meaning "oath of God."

Elizabeth I, (*Elizabeth Tudor*) 1533–1603, queen of England 1558–1603 (successor of Mary I; daughter of Henry VIII and Anne Boleyn).

Elizabeth II, (*Elizabeth Alexandra Mary Windsor*) born 1926, queen of Great Britain since 1952 (daughter of George VI).

E•liz•a•be•than (i liz′ə bē′thən, -beth′ən), *adj.* **1.** of or pertaining to the reign of Elizabeth I, queen of England, or to her times: *Elizabethan diplomacy; Elizabethan music.* **2.** noting or pertaining to an English Renaissance style of architecture of the reign of Elizabeth I characterized by fantastic sculptured or molded ornament of German or Flemish origin, symmetrical layouts, and an emphasis on domestic architecture. Cf. **Jacobean** (def. 2). —*n.* **3.** an English person who lived during the Elizabethan period, esp. a poet or dramatist. [1810–20; ELIZABETH + -AN]

Elizabethan court cupboard

Elizabe′than son′net. See **Shakespearean sonnet.**

Eliz′abeth Cit′y, a city in NE North Carolina. 13,784.

E•liz•a•beth•ton (i liz′ə beth′tən), *n.* a city in NE Tennessee. 12,431.

E•liz•a•beth•town (i liz′ə bəth toun′), *n.* a town in central Kentucky. 15,380.

El Ja•di•da (el′ zhə dē′də), a city on the W central coast of Morocco. 102,000.

elk (elk), *n., pl.* **elks,** (*esp. collectively*) **elk** for 1, 2. **1.** Also called **European elk.** the moose, *Alces alces.* **2.** Also called **American elk, wapiti.** a large North American deer, *Cervus canadensis,* the male of which has large, spreading antlers. See illus. on next page. **3.** a pliable leather used for sport shoes, made originally of elk hide but now of calfskin or cowhide tanned and smoked to resemble elk hide. **4.** (*cap.*) a member of a fraternal organization **(Benevolent and Protective Order of Elks)** that supports or contributes to various charitable causes. [bef. 900; ME; OE *eolc, eolh;* c. G *Elch* (OHG *el(a)ho*), L *alcēs,* Gk *álkē*]

CONCISE ETYMOLOGY KEY: <, descended or borrowed from; >, whence; b., blend of, blended; c., cognate with; cf., compare; deriv., derivative; equiv., equivalent; imit., imitative; obl., oblique; r., replacing; s., stem; sp., spelling, spelled; resp., respelling, respelled; trans., translation; ?, origin unknown; *, unattested; ‡, probably earlier than. See the full key inside the front cover.

elk (def. 2), *Cervus canadensis,* 5 ft. (1.5 m) high at shoulder; antlers 5 ft. (1.5 m); length 8 ft. (2.4 m)

elk′ clo′ver, a plant, *Aralia californica,* of the ginseng family, native to the west coast of North America, having umbels of greenish or whitish flowers and berrylike fruit, grown as an ornamental.

El Ke·rak (el ker′äk, ke räk′), Kerak.

elk′ grass′. See **bear grass.**

Elk′ Grove′ Vil′lage, a town in NE Illinois. 28,907.

El Kha·lil (el′ kä lēl′), Arabic name of **Hebron** (def. 1).

Elk·hart (elk′härt, el′kärt), *n.* a city in N Indiana. 41,305.

elk·hound (elk′hound′), *n.* See **Norwegian elkhound.** [1885–90; ELK + HOUND[1]]

ell[1] (el), *n.* **1.** an extension usually at right angles to one end of a building. **2.** elbow (def. 5). **3.** something that is L-shaped. Also, **el.** [1765–75; a sp. of the letter name, or by shortening of ELBOW]

ell[2] (el), *n.* a former measure of length, varying in different countries: in England equal to 45 in. (114 cm). [bef. 950; ME, OE *eln;* c. ON *eln,* OHG *elina,* Goth *aleina,* L *ulna,* Gk *ōlénē.* See ELBOW]

El·la (el′ə), *n.* a female given name: from a Germanic word meaning "all."

-ella a suffix used as a formative in taxonomic names, esp. genus names of bacteria: *chorella; pasteurella; salmonella.* [< NL, L, fem. of *-ellus;* see -ELLE]

el·lag′ic ac′id (ə laj′ik), *Pharm.* a yellow crystalline substance, $C_{14}H_6O_8$, isolated from oak galls and tannins and used as a hemostatic. [1800–10; < F *ellagique,* equiv. to *ellag-* anagram of *galle* GALL[3] + *-ique* -IC]

El·las (e läs′), *n.* Modern Greek name of **Greece.**

-elle a noun suffix occurring in loanwords from French, where it originally formed diminutives, now often with a derivative sense in which the diminutive force is lost (*bagatelle; prunelle; rondelle*); also in Anglicized forms of Latin words ending in *-ella* (*organelle*). [< F < L *-ella,* fem. of *-ellus,* forming diminutives corresponding to stems ending in *-ul-* -ULE, *-r-* (see CASTELLUM), *-n-* (see PATELLA)]

El·len (el′ən), *n.* a female given name, form of **Helen.** Also, **El′lin.**

El·lens·burg (el′ənz bûrg′), *n.* a town in central Washington. 11,752.

El·ler·y (el′ə rē), *n.* a male given name.

Elles′mere Is′land (elz′mēr), an island in the Arctic Ocean, NW of Greenland: a part of Canada. 76,600 sq. mi. (198,400 sq. km).

El·let (el′it), *n.* **Charles, Jr.,** 1810–62, U.S. civil engineer: builder of suspension bridges.

El·li (el′ē), *n. Scand. Myth.* an old woman, a personification of old age, who defeated Thor in a wrestling match. [< Icel *elli,* lit., old age. Cf. ELD]

El′lice Is′lands (el′is), a former name of **Tuvalu.**

El′li·cott Cit′y (el′i kət), a city in N central Maryland, near Baltimore. 21,784.

El·ling·ton (el′ing tən), *n.* **Edward Kennedy** (*"Duke"*), 1899–1974, U.S. jazz pianist, composer, arranger, and conductor.

El·li·ott (el′ē ət, el′yət), *n.* **1. Herb(ert James),** born 1938, Australian track-and-field athlete. **2.** Also, **El′li·ot.** a male given name, form of **Elias.**

el·lipse (i lips′), *n. Geom.* a plane curve such that the sums of the distances of each point in its periphery from two fixed points, the foci, are equal. It is a conic section formed by the intersection of a right circular cone by a plane that cuts the axis and the surface of the cone. Typical equation: $(x^2/a^2) + (y^2/b^2) = 1$. If $a = b$ the ellipse is a circle. See diag. under **conic section.** [1745–55; < F < L *ellipsis* ELLIPSIS; or by back formation from the pl. ELLIPSES]

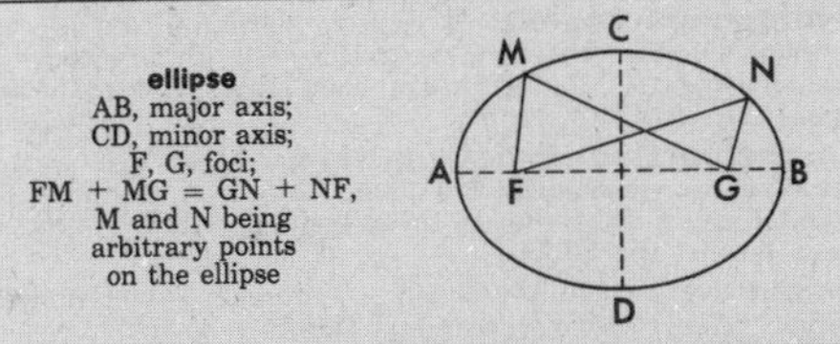

ellipse
AB, major axis; CD, minor axis; F, G, foci; FM + MG = GN + NF, M and N being arbitrary points on the ellipse

el·lip·sis (i lip′sis), *n., pl.* **-ses** (-sēz). **1.** *Gram.* **a.** the omission from a sentence or other construction of one or more words that would complete or clarify the construction, as the omission of *who are, while I am,* or *while we are* from *I like to interview people sitting down.* **b.** the omission of one or more items from a construction in order to avoid repeating the identical or equivalent items that are in a preceding or following construction, as the omission of *been to Paris* from the second clause of *I've been to Paris, but they haven't.* **2.** *Print.* a mark or marks as ——, . . . , or * * *, to indicate an omission or suppression of letters or words. [1560–70; < L *ellipsis* < Gk *élleipsis* an omission, equiv. to *el-* (var. of *en-* EN-[2]) + *leip-* (s. of *leipein* to leave) + *-sis* -SIS]

el·lip·so·graph (i lip′sə graf′, -gräf′), *n.* an instrument for drawing ellipses, as a trammel. Also, **elliptograph.** [ELLIPSE + -O- + -GRAPH]

el·lip·soid (i lip′soid), *n.* **1.** *Geom.* a solid figure all plane sections of which are ellipses or circles. Typical equation: $(x^2/a^2) + (y^2/b^2) + (z^2/c^2) = 1$. —*adj.* **2.** ellipsoidal. [1715–25; < F *ellipsoïde.* See ELLIPSE, -OID]

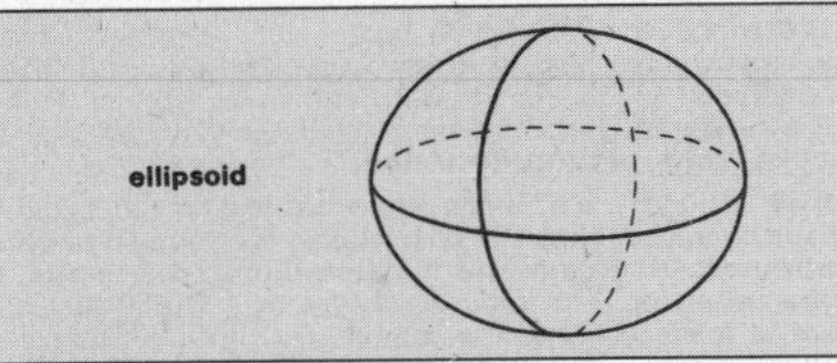
ellipsoid

el·lip·soi·dal (i lip soid′l, el′ip-, ē′lip-), *adj.* pertaining to or having the form of an ellipsoid. [1825–35; ELLIPSOID + -AL[1]]

el·lip·som·e·ter (i lip som′i tər, el′ip-, ē′lip-), *n. Optics.* an instrument that measures the ellipticity of polarized light, used for determining the thickness of thin films. [ELLIPSE + -O- + -METER]

el·lipt (i lipt′), *v.t. Gram.* to delete by ellipsis. [by back formation from ELLIPTICAL]

el·lip·ti·cal (i lip′ti kəl), *adj.* Also, **el·lip′tic. 1.** pertaining to or having the form of an ellipse. **2.** pertaining to or marked by grammatical ellipsis. **3.** (of speech or writing) expressed with extreme or excessive economy; relieved of irrelevant matter: *to converse in elliptical sentences.* **4.** (of a style of speaking or writing) tending to be ambiguous, cryptic, or obscure: *an elliptical prose that is difficult to translate.* —*n.* **5.** *Astron.* See **elliptical galaxy.** [1650–60; < Gk *elleiptik(ós)* defective (see ELLIPSIS, -TIC) + -AL[1]] —**el·lip′ti·cal·ness,** *n.*

ellip′tical gal′axy, *Astron.* a type of galaxy having the shape of a spheroid or ellipsoid, rather than a disk. Also called **elliptical, E galaxy.**

ellip′tical light′, *Optics.* light that has been elliptically polarized.

el·lip·ti·cal·ly (i lip′tik lē), *adv.* **1.** in the form of an ellipse. **2.** in an elliptical manner; by an ellipse. **3.** with great economy of words or expression; concisely: *to speak elliptically.* **4.** without sufficient transition or a logical connection between thoughts, ideas, or expressions; ambiguously or cryptically: *to jump elliptically from generalities to specifics.* [1810–20; ELLIPTICAL + -LY]

ellip′tical polariza′tion, *Physics.* polarization of an electromagnetic wave in which the vector representing the instantaneous intensity of the electric field describes an elliptical helix in the direction of propagation. Cf. **circular polarization.**

ellip′tic func′tion, *Math.* one of a class of transcendental functions related to elliptic integrals and analogous to trigonometric functions. [1835–45]

ellip′tic geom′etry. See **Riemannian geometry** (def. 1).

ellip′tic in′tegral, *Math.* a certain kind of definite integral that is not expressible by means of elementary functions. [1880–85]

el·lip·tic·i·ty (i lip tis′i tē, el′ip-, ē′lip-), *n.* the degree of divergence of an ellipse from a circle. [1745–55; *elliptic-* (see ELLIPTICAL) + -ITY]

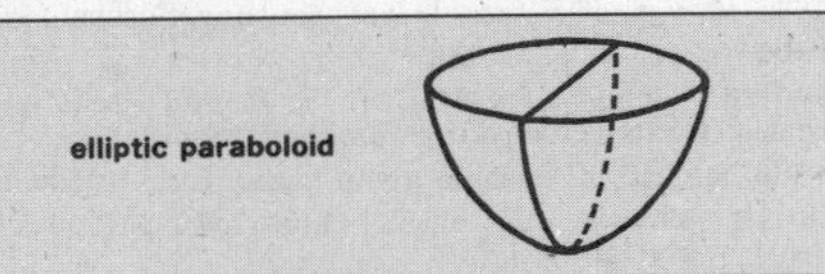
elliptic paraboloid

ellip′tic parab′oloid, *Geom.* a paraboloid that can be put into a position such that its sections parallel to one coordinate plane are ellipses, while its sections parallel to the other two coordinate planes are parabolas. Cf. **hyperbolic paraboloid.**

ellip′tic spring′, a spring formed from two leaf springs having their convex sides outward.

el·lip·to·graph (i lip′tə graf′, -gräf′), *n.* ellipsograph. [1850–55]

El·lis (el′is), *n.* **1. Alexander John** (*Alexander John Sharpe*), 1814–90, English phonetician and mathematician. **2. (Henry) Have·lock** (hav′lok), 1859–1939, English psychologist and writer.

El′lis Is′land, an island in upper New York Bay: a former U.S. immigrant examination station.

El·li·son (el′ə sən), *n.* **Ralph (Wal·do),** (wôl′dō, wol′-), born 1914, U.S. novelist, essayist, and lecturer.

El·lo·ra (e lôr′ə, e lōr′ə), *n.* a village in S central India: important Hindu archaeological site. Also, **Elura.**

Ells·worth (elz′wûrth), *n.* **1. Lincoln,** 1880–1951, U.S. polar explorer. **2. Oliver,** 1745–1807, U.S. jurist and statesman: Chief Justice of the U.S. 1796–1800. **3.** a male given name.

Ells′worth Land′, a region in Antarctica, bordered by the Weddell Sea on the E, Byrd Land on the SW, and Palmer Land on the N: discovered 1935.

elm (elm), *n.* **1.** any tree of the genus *Ulmus,* as *U. procera* **(English elm),** characterized by the gradually spreading columnar manner of growth of its branches. Cf. **American elm, elm family. 2.** the wood of such a tree. [bef. 1000; ME, OE; c. OHG *elm;* akin to ON *almr,* L *ulmus*]

El·man (el′mən), *n.* **Mi·scha** (mē′shə), 1891–1967, U.S. violinist, born in Russia.

El Man·su·ra (el′ man so͝or′ə), a city in NE Egypt, in the Nile delta: scene of the defeat of the Crusaders 1250 and the capture of Louis IX by the Mamelukes. 215,000. Also called **Mansura.**

elm′ bark′ bee′tle, 1. Also called **smaller European elm bark beetle.** a shiny, dark reddish-brown bark beetle, *Scolytus multistriatus,* originating in Europe and now widespread in the U.S.: the primary vector of Dutch elm disease. **2.** Also called **native elm bark beetle.** a bark beetle, *Hylurgopinus opaculus,* of eastern North America, that also transmits Dutch elm disease. [1905–10]

elm′ blight′. See **Dutch elm disease.**

El·mer (el′mər), *n.* a male given name: from Old English words meaning "noble" and "famous."

elm′ fam′ily, the plant family Ulmaceae, typified by deciduous trees having simple and often toothed leaves, small petalless flowers, winged fleshy or nutlike fruit, and watery sap, and including the elm, hackberry, and planer tree.

Elm·hurst (elm′hûrst), *n.* a city in NE Illinois, W of Chicago. 44,251.

El·mi·ra (el mī′rə), *n.* a city in S central New York. 35,327.

El Mis·ti (el mēs′tē), a volcano in S Peru, in the Andes. 19,200 ft. (5880 m). Also called **Misti.**

elm′ leaf′ bee′tle, a chrysomelid beetle, *Galerucella luteola,* of eastern North America, that feeds on the foliage of elm. [1880–85, *Amer.*]

El·mont (el′mont), *n.* a town on W Long Island, in SE New York. 27,592.

El Mon·te (el mon′tē), a city in SW California, near Los Angeles. 79,494.

Elm′wood Park′ (elm′wo͝od′), **1.** a city in NE Illinois. 24,016. **2.** a city in NE New Jersey. 18,377.

El Ni·ño (el nēn′yō; *Sp.* el nē′nyô), a warm ocean current of variable intensity that develops after late December along the coast of Ecuador and Peru and sometimes causes catastrophic weather conditions. [< Sp: lit., the child, i.e., the Christ child, alluding to the appearance of the current near Christmas]

El O·beid (el′ ō bād′), a city in the central Sudan: Egyptian army defeated by Mahdist forces 1883. 66,000. Also, **Obeid, Al-Obeid.** Arabic, **Al-Ubayyid.**

el·o·cu·tion (el′ə kyo͞o′shən), *n.* **1.** a person's manner of speaking or reading aloud in public: *The actor's elocution is faultless.* **2.** the study and practice of oral delivery, including the control of both voice and gesture. [1500–10; < L *ēlocūtiōn-* (s. of *ēlocūtiō*) a speaking out, equiv. to *ē-* E- + *locūtiōn-* LOCUTION] —**el·o·cu·tion·ar·y** (el′ə kyo͞o′shə ner′ē), *adj.* —**el′o·cu′tion·ist,** *n.*

e·lo·de·a (i lō′dē ə), *n.* any of several New World submersed aquatic plants of the genus *Elodea,* having numerous, usually whorled leaves. Also called **anacharis, ditchmoss, waterweed.** [< NL (1803), equiv. to Gk *(h)elṓd(ēs)* marshy (deriv. of *hélos* marsh; see -ODE[1]) + NL *-ea* -EA]

E·lo·him (e lō′him; *Seph. Heb.* e lô hēm′; *Ashk. Heb.* e′lō him′; *in nonliturgical use by Orthodox Jews* e lô-kēm′, e′lō kim′), *n.* God, esp. as used in the Hebrew text of the Old Testament. [< Heb *ĕlōhīm,* pl. of *ĕlōah* God] —**El·o·him·ic** (el′ō him′ik), *adj.*

E·lo·hism (e lō′hiz əm, el′ō hiz′əm), *n.* the worship of Elohim or the religious system based on such worship. [ELOH(IM) + -ISM]

E·lo·hist (e lō′hist, el′ō-), *n.* a writer of one of the major sources of the Hexateuch, in which God is characteristically referred to as *Elohim* rather than *Yahweh.* Cf. **Yahwist.** [1860–65; < Heb *ĕlōah* God + -IST] —**El′o·his′tic,** *adj.*

e·loign (i loin′), *v.t.* to remove to a distance, esp. to take beyond the jurisdiction of a law court. Also, **e·loin′.** [1490–1500; < AF, OF *e(s)loigner* to go or take far < VL **exlongiāre,* for L *ēlongāre;* see ELONGATE]

El·o·ise (el′ō ēz′, el′ō ēz′), *n.* a female given name.

e·lon·gate (i lông′gāt, i long′-, ē′lông gāt′, ē′long-), *v.,* **-gat·ed, -gat·ing,** *adj.* —*v.t.* **1.** to draw out to greater length; lengthen; extend. —*v.i.* **2.** to increase in length. —*adj.* Also, **e·lon′gat·ed. 3.** extended; lengthened. **4.** long and thin. [1530–40; < LL *ēlongātus* lengthened out, ptp. of *ēlongāre* to make longer, make distant, remove, equiv. to L *ē-* E- + *-longāre,* deriv. of *longus* LONG, *longē* far off] —**e·lon·ga·tive** (ē′lông gā′tiv, ē′long-), *adj.*

e·lon·ga·tion (i lông gā′shən, i long-, ē′lông-, ē′long-), *n.* **1.** the act of elongating or the state of being elongated. **2.** something that is elongated. **3.** *Astron.* the angular distance, measured from the earth, between a planet or the moon and the sun or between a satellite and the planet about which it revolves. [1350–1400; ME < LL *ēlongātiōn-* (s. of *ēlongātiō*), equiv. to *ēlongāt(us)* (see ELONGATE) + *-iōn-* -ION]

e·lope (i lōp′), *v.i.,* **e·loped, e·lop·ing. 1.** to run off secretly to be married, usually without the consent or knowledge of one's parents. **2.** to run away with a lover. **3.** to leave without permission or notification; escape. [1590–1600; ME **alopen* to run away (whence

AF *aloper*). See A-[3], LOPE] **—e•lope′ment,** *n.* **—e•lop′•er,** *n.*

el•o•quence (el′ə kwəns), *n.* **1.** the practice or art of using language with fluency and aptness. **2.** eloquent language or discourse: *a flow of eloquence.* [1350–1400; ME < AF < L *ēloquentia.* See ELOQUENT, -ENCE]

el•o•quent (el′ə kwənt), *adj.* **1.** having or exercising the power of fluent, forceful, and appropriate speech: *an eloquent orator.* **2.** characterized by forceful and appropriate expression: *an eloquent speech.* **3.** movingly expressive: *looks eloquent of disgust.* [1350–1400; ME (< AF) < L *ēloquent-* (s. of *ēloquēns,* prp. of *ēloquī*) speaking out, eloquent, equiv. to *ē-* E- + *loqu-* speak + *-ent-* -ENT] **—el′o•quent•ly,** *adv.* **—el′o•quent•ness,** *n.*
—Syn. ELOQUENT, FLUENT, ARTICULATE, EXPRESSIVE are adjectives that characterize speech or speakers notable for their effectiveness. ELOQUENT suggests clarity and power: *an eloquent plea for disarmament.* FLUENT, with a root sense of flowing, refers to easy, smooth, facile speech: *fluent in three languages.* ARTICULATE characterizes a clear and effective speaker or speech: *an articulate spokesman for tax reform.* EXPRESSIVE focuses on rendering intelligible or meaningful the ideas or feelings of a speaker or writer and implies an especially effective, vivid use of language: *a deeply moving, powerfully expressive evocation of a city childhood.* See also **fluent.**

El Oued (el wed′), a city in E Algeria. 11,429. Also, **Al-Oued.**

El Pas•o (el pas′ō), a city in W Texas, on the Rio Grande. 425,259.

El•pe•nor (el pē′nôr), *n.* (in the *Odyssey*) a companion of Odysseus who was killed when he fell off the roof of Circe's palace.

El Pen•sa•dor Me•xi•ca•no (*Sp.* el pen′sä t͟hôr′ me hē kä′nô), pen name of José Joaquín Fernández de Lizardi.

El Re•no (el rē′nō), a city in central Oklahoma. 15,486.

el•ritch (el′rich), *adj.* eldritch.

El•roy (el′roi), *n.* a male given name.

El•sa (el′sə), *n.* a female given name, form of **Elizabeth.**

El Sal•va•dor (el sal′və dôr′; *Sp.* el säl′vä t͟hôr′), a republic in NW Central America. 4,200,000; 13,176 sq. mi. (34,125 sq. km). *Cap.:* San Salvador. Also called **Salvador.**

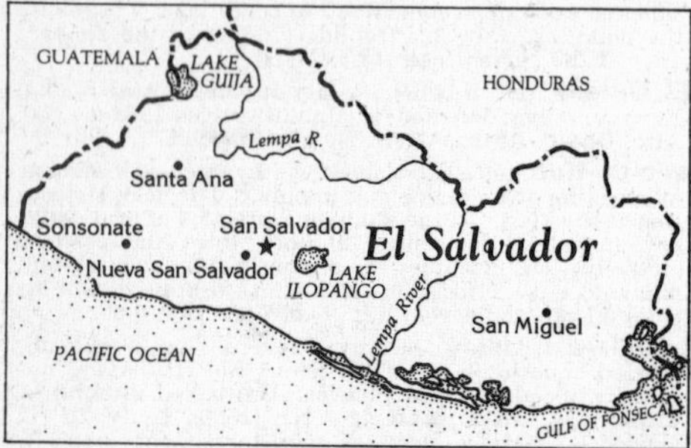

else (els), *adj.* **1.** other than the persons or things mentioned or implied: *What else could I have done?* **2.** in addition to the persons or things mentioned or implied: *Who else was there?* **3.** other or in addition (used in the possessive following an indefinite pronoun): *someone else's money.* **—***adv.* **4.** if not (usually prec. by *or*): *It's a macaw, or else I don't know birds.* **5.** in some other way; otherwise: *How else could I have acted?* **6.** at some other place or time: *Where else might I find this book?* **7. or else,** or suffer the consequences: *Do what I say, or else.* [bef. 1000; ME, OE *elles* (c. OHG *elles*), equiv. to *ell-* other (c. Goth *aljis,* L *alius,* OIr *aile* Gk *állos,* Armenian *ayl* other; cf. ELDRITCH) + *-es* -S[1]]
—Usage. The possessive forms of SOMEBODY ELSE, EVERYBODY ELSE, etc., are *somebody else's, everybody else's,* the forms *somebody's else, everybody's else* being considered nonstandard in present-day English. One exception is the possessive for WHO ELSE, which is occasionally formed as *whose else* when a noun does not immediately follow: *Is this book yours? Whose else could it be? No, it's somebody else's.*

El Se•gun•do (el sə gun′dō, -go͝on′-), a city in SW California, near Los Angeles. 13,752.

El•se•ne (el′sə nə), *n.* Dutch name of **Ixelles.**

El•se•vier (el′zə vēr′, -vər, -sə-), *n., adj.* Elzevir.

else•where (els′hwâr′, -wâr′), *adv.* somewhere else; in or to some other place: *You will have to look elsewhere for an answer.* [bef. 900; ME *elleswher,* OE *elles hwǣr.* See ELSE, WHERE]

else•whith•er (els′hwit͟h′ər, -wit͟h′-, els hwit͟h′-, -wit͟h′-), *adv. Archaic.* in another direction; toward a different place or goal. [bef. 1000; ME *elleswhider,* OE *elleshwider.* See ELSE, WHITHER]

El•sie (el′sē), *n.* a female given name, form of **Elizabeth.**

El•si•nore (el′sə nôr′, -nōr′), *n.* Helsingør.

El•speth (el′speth, -spəth), *n.* a female given name, form of **Elizabeth.**

El•ton (el′tn), *n.* a male given name.

CONCISE ETYMOLOGY KEY: <, descended or borrowed from; >, whence; b., blend of, blended; c., cognate with; cf., compare; deriv., derivative; equiv., equivalent; imit., imitative; obl., oblique; r., replacing; s., stem; sp., spelling, spelled; resp., respelling, respelled; trans., translation; ?, origin unknown; *, unattested; ‡, probably earlier than. See the full key inside the front cover.

El Tor•o (el tôr′ō), a city in SW California. 38,153.

el•u•ant (el′yo͞o ənt), *n.* a liquid used for elution. [1940–45; < L *ēlu(ere)* to wash out (see ELUTE) + -ANT]

É•lu•ard (ā ly ar′), *n.* **Paul** (pôl), (*Eugène Grindel*), 1895–1952, French poet.

el•u•ate (el′yo͞o it, -āt′), *n.* a liquid solution resulting from eluting. [1930–35; < L *ēlu(ere)* to wash out (see ELUTE) + -ATE[1]]

e•lu•ci•date (i lo͞o′si dāt′), *v.,* **-dat•ed, -dat•ing.** **—***v.t.* **1.** to make lucid or clear; throw light upon; explain: *an explanation that elucidated his recent strange behavior.* **—***v.i.* **2.** to provide clarification; explain. [1560–70; < LL *ēlūcidātus* (ptp. of *ēlūcidāre*) enlightened, equiv. to *ē-* E- + *lūcid(us)* LUCID + *-ātus* -ATE[1]] **—e•lu′ci•da′tion,** *n.* **—e•lu′ci•da′tive,** *adj.* **—e•lu′ci•da′tor,** *n.*
—Syn. clarify. See **explain.**

e•lu•cu•brate (i lo͞o′kyo͝o brāt′), *v.t.,* **-brat•ed, -brat•ing.** to produce (esp. literary work) by long and intensive effort. [1615–25; < L *ēlūcubrātus,* ptp. of *ēlūcubrāre* to spend the night over (a literary work). See E-, LUCUBRATE] **—e•lu′cu•bra′tion,** *n.*

e•lude (i lo͞od′), *v.t.,* **e•lud•ed, e•lud•ing.** **1.** to avoid or escape by speed, cleverness, trickery, etc.; evade: *to elude capture.* **2.** to escape the understanding, perception, or appreciation of: *The answer eludes me.* [1530–40; < L *ēlūdere* to deceive, evade, equiv. to *ē-* E- + *lūdere* to play, deceive] **—e•lud′er,** *n.*
—Syn. 1. shun, dodge. See **escape.**

E•lul (el′o͝ol; *Seph. Heb.* e lo͞ol′; *Ashk. Heb.* e′ləl), *n.* the twelfth month of the Jewish calendar. Cf. **Jewish calendar.** [< Heb *ĕlūl*]

E•lu•ra (e lo͝or′ə), *n.* Ellora.

e•lu•sion (i lo͞o′zhən), *n.* the act of eluding; evasion. [1540–50; < LL *ēlūsiōn-* (s. of *ēlūsiō*) deception, evasion, equiv. to *ēlūs(us),* ptp. of *ēlūdere* to ELUDE (*ē-* E- + *lūd-* play + *-tus* ptp. suffix) + *-iōn-* -ION]

e•lu•sive (i lo͞o′siv), *adj.* **1.** eluding clear perception or complete mental grasp; hard to express or define: *an elusive concept.* **2.** cleverly or skillfully evasive: *a fish too elusive to catch.* Also, **e•lu•so•ry** (i lo͞o′sə rē, -zə-). [1710–20; ELUS(ION) + -IVE] **—e•lu′sive•ly,** *adv.* **—e•lu′sive•ness,** *n.*
—Syn. 2. tricky, slippery, shifty; puzzling, baffling.

e•lute (ē lo͞ot′, i lo͞ot′), *v.t.,* **e•lut•ed, e•lut•ing.** *Physical Chem.* to remove by dissolving, as absorbed material from an adsorbent. [1725–35; < L *ēlūtus,* ptp. of *ēluere* to wash out, equiv. to *ē-* E- + *-luere,* comb. form of *lavere* to wash (see LAVE)] **—e•lu′tion,** *n.*

e•lu•tri•ate (i lo͞o′trē āt′), *v.t.,* **-at•ed, -at•ing.** **1.** to purify by washing and straining or decanting. **2.** to separate the light and heavy particles of by washing. [1725–35; < L *ēlutriāt(us)* (ptp. of *ēlutriāre*) washed out, equiv. to *ē-* E- + *lutri-* wash + *-ātus* -ATE[1]] **—e•lu′tri•a′tion,** *n.*

e•lu•tri•a•tor (i lo͞o′trē ā′tər), *n.* a machine for separating particles of mineral by elutriation. [1900–05; ELUTRIATE + -OR[2]]

e•lu•vi•al (i lo͞o′vē əl), *adj.* of or pertaining to eluviation or eluvium. [1860–65; ELUVI(UM) + -AL[1]]

e•lu•vi•ate (i lo͞o′vē āt′), *v.i.,* **-at•ed, -at•ing.** to undergo eluviation. [1925–30; ELUVI(UM) + -ATE[1]]

e•lu•vi•a•tion (i lo͞o′vē ā′shən), *n.* the movement through the soil of materials brought into suspension or dissolved by the action of water. [1925–30; ELUVIATE + -ION]

e•lu•vi•um (i lo͞o′vē əm), *n., pl.* **-vi•a** (-vē ə). *Geol.* a deposit of soil, dust, etc., formed from the decomposition of rock and found in its place of origin. [1880–85; formed on the model of ALLUVIUM from L *ēluere* (of water) to wash out (soil, etc.); see ELUTE]

El•va (el′və), *n.* a female given name: from an Old English word meaning "elf."

el•ver (el′vər), *n.* a young eel, esp. one that is migrating up a stream from the ocean. Also called **glass eel.** [1630–40; var. of *ellfare,* lit., eel-journey. See EEL, FARE]

elves (elvz), *n.* pl. of **elf.**

El•vi•ra (el vī′rə, -vēr′ə), *n.* a female given name: from a Germanic word meaning "elf counsel."

El•vis (el′vis), *n.* a male given name, form of **Elwin.**

elv•ish (el′vish), *adj.* elfish. [1150–1200; ME; see ELF, -ISH[1]] **—elv′ish•ly,** *adv.*

El•win (el′win), *n.* a male given name. Also, **El•vin** (el′vin), **El′wyn.**

El•wood (el′wo͝od′), *n.* a city in central Indiana. 10,867.

E•ly (ē′lē *for 1, 2;* ē′lī *for 3*), *n.* **1. Isle of,** a former administrative county in E England: now part of Cambridgeshire. **2.** a town on this island: medieval cathedral. 9969. **3.** a male given name.

El•y•ot (el′ē ət, el′yət), *n.* **Sir Thomas,** c1490–1546, English scholar and diplomat.

E•lyr•i•a (i lēr′ē ə), *n.* a city in N Ohio. 52,474.

E•lyse (i lēs′), *n.* a female given name, form of **Elizabeth.**

E•ly•sée (ā lē zā′), *n.* **1.** a palace in Paris: the official residence of the president of France. **2.** the French government (usually prec. by *the*).

E•ly•sian (i lizh′ən, i lē′zhən), *adj.* **1.** of, pertaining to, or resembling Elysium. **2.** blissful; delightful. [1570–80; ELYSI(UM) + -AN]

E•ly•si•um (i lizh′ē əm, i lē′zhē-, i liz′-, i lē′zē-, i lizh′əm), *n.* **1.** Also called **Ely′sian Fields′.** *Class. Myth.* the abode of the blessed after death. **2.** any similarly conceived abode or state of the dead. **3.** any place or state of perfect happiness; paradise. **4.** an area in the northern hemisphere of Mars, appearing as a light region when viewed telescopically from the earth. [1590–1600; < L < Gk *Ēlýsion* (*pedíon*) the Elysian (plain)]

el•y•tra (el′i trə), *n.* pl. of **elytron.**

el•y•troid (el′i troid′), *adj.* resembling an elytron. [1860–65; ELYTR(ON) + -OID]

el•y•tron (el′i tron′), *n., pl.* **-tra** (-trə). one of the pair of hardened forewings of certain insects, as beetles, forming a protective covering for the posterior or flight wings. Also called **wing case, wing cover.** See diag. under **beetle.** [1745–55; < NL < Gk *élytron* a covering] **—el•y•trous** (el′i trəs), *adj.*

el•y•trum (el′i trəm), *n., pl.* **-tra** (-trə). *Obs.* elytron. [Latinized var. of ELYTRON]

El•ze•vir (el′zə vēr′, -vər, -sə-), *n.* **1. Louis,** c1540–1617, Dutch printer: founder of a printing firm at Leyden (1591?) that was operated by his descendants through the 18th century. **2.** a book produced by this printing house. **3.** a style of printing type with firm hairlines and stubby serifs. **—***adj.* **4.** of or pertaining to the Elzevir family or the books it published. **5.** indicating the type originated by this family. Also, **Elsevier, El′ze•vier′.** **—El′ze•vir′i•an,** *adj.*

em (em), *n., pl.* **ems,** *adj.* **—***n.* **1.** the letter *M, m.* **2.** Also called **mut, mutton.** *Print.* **a.** the square of any size of type used as the unit of measurement for matter printed in that type size. **b.** (originally) the portion of a line of type occupied by the letter *M* in type of the same size. **3.** See **em pica.** **—***adj.* **4.** *Print.* having the area of an em quad or the length of an em dash. [1860–65]

EM, 1. electromagnetic. **2.** electromotive. **3.** electronic mail. **4.** electron microscope; electron microscopy. **5.** end matched. **6.** Engineer of Mines. **7.** enlisted man; enlisted men.

Em, *Symbol, Physical Chem.* emanation (def. 3).

'em (əm), *pron. Informal.* them: *Put 'em down there.* [1350–1400; ME *hem,* OE *heom,* dat. and acc. pl. of HE[1]]

em-[1], var. of **en-[1]** before *b, p,* and sometimes *m: embalm.* Cf. **im-[1].**

em-[2], var. of **en-[2]** before *b, m, p, ph: embolism, emphasis.*

E.M., 1. Earl Marshal. **2.** Engineer of Mines.

e•ma•ci•ate (i mā′shē āt′), *v.t.,* **-at•ed, -at•ing.** to make abnormally lean or thin by a gradual wasting away of flesh. [1640–50; < L *ēmaciātus,* wasted away, equiv. to *ē-* E- + *maciātus,* ptp. of *maciāre* to produce leanness (*maci(ēs)* leanness + *-ātus* -ATE[1])]

e•ma•ci•at•ed (i mā′shē ā′tid), *adj.* marked by emaciation. [1655–65; EMACIATE + -ED[2]]
—Syn. thin, wasted, puny, gaunt, haggard, scrawny.

e•ma•ci•a•tion (i mā′shē ā′shən, -sē-), *n.* **1.** abnormal thinness caused by lack of nutrition or by disease. **2.** the process of emaciating. [1655–65; < L *ēmaciāt(us)* (see EMACIATE) + -ION]

em•a•gram (em′ə gram′), *n. Meteorol.* a thermodynamic chart indicating temperature as the abscissa on a linear scale and pressure as the ordinate on a logarithmic scale. [EM + (DI)AGRAM]

e-mail. See **electronic mail.** Also, **E-mail.**

em•a•lan•gen•i (em′ə läng gen′ē), *n.* pl. of **lilangeni.**

em•a•nant (em′ə nənt), *adj.* emanating or issuing from or as if from a source. [1605–15; (< F) < L *ēmānant-* (s. of *ēmānāns* outflowing, prp. of *ēmānāre*), equiv. to *ē-* E- + *mān-* flow + *-ant-* -ANT]

em•a•nate (em′ə nāt′), *v.,* **-nat•ed, -nat•ing.** **—***v.i.* **1.** to flow out, issue, or proceed, as from a source or origin; come forth; originate. **—***v.t.* **2.** to send forth; emit. [1780–90; < L *ēmānātus* having flowed out (ptp. of *ēmānāre*), equiv. to *ē-* E- + *mān-* flow + *-ātus* -ATE[1]] **—em′a•na′tive,** *adj.* **—em′a•na′tor,** *n.* **—em•a•na•to•ry** (em′ə nə tôr′ē, -tōr′ē), *adj.*
—Syn. 1. arise, spring, flow. See **emerge.**

em•a•na•tion (em′ə nā′shən), *n.* **1.** an act or instance of emanating. **2.** something that emanates or is emanated. **3.** *Physical Chem.* a gaseous product of radioactive disintegration, including radon, thoron, and actinon. *Symbol:* Em [1560–70; < LL *ēmānātiōn-* (s. of *ēmānātiō*), equiv. to *ēmānāt(us)* (see EMANATE) + *-iōn-* -ION] **—em′a•na′tion•al,** *adj.*

e•man•ci•pate (i man′sə pāt′), *v.t.,* **-pat•ed, -pat•ing.** **1.** to free from restraint, influence, or the like. **2.** to free (a slave) from bondage. **3.** *Roman and Civil Law.* to terminate paternal control over. [1615–25; < L *ēmancipātus* (ptp. of *ēmancipāre*) freed from control, equiv. to *ē-* E- + *man(us)* hand + *-cip-* (comb. form of *capere* to seize) + *-ātus* -ATE[1]] **—e•man′ci•pa′tive,** *adj.* **—e•man′ci•pa′tor,** *n.*
—Syn. 1, 2. See **release.**

e•man•ci•pat•ed (i man′sə pā′tid), *adj.* **1.** not constrained or restricted by custom, tradition, superstition, etc.: *a modern, emancipated woman.* **2.** freed, as from slavery or bondage. [1720–30; EMANCIPATE + -ED[2]]

e•man•ci•pa•tion (i man′sə pā′shən), *n.* **1.** the act of emancipating. **2.** the state or fact of being emancipated. [1625–35; < L *ēmancipātiōn-* (s. of *ēmancipātiō*), equiv. to *ēmancipāt(us)* (see EMANCIPATE) + *-iōn-* -ION]

e•man•ci•pa•tion•ist (i man′sə pā′shə nist), *n.* a person who advocates emancipation, esp. an advocate of the freeing of human beings from slavery. [1815–25; EMANCIPATION + -IST]

Emancipa′tion Proclama′tion, *U.S. Hist.* the proclamation issued by President Lincoln on January 1, 1863, freeing the slaves in those territories still in rebellion against the Union.

E•man•u•el (i man′yo͞o əl), *n.* a male given name: from a Hebrew word meaning "God is with us."

e•mar•gi•nate (i mär′jə nāt′, -nit), *adj.* **1.** notched at the margin. **2.** *Bot.* notched at the apex, as a petal or leaf. See illus. on next page. Also, **e•mar′gi•nat′ed.** [1785–95; < L *ēmarginātus* deprived of its edge, equiv. to *ē-* E- + *margin-* (see MARGIN) + *ātus* -ATE[1]] **—e•mar′gi•nate′ly,** *adv.* **—e•mar′gi•na′tion,** *n.*

emarginate leaves

e•mas•cu•late (*v.* i mas′kyə lāt′; *adj.* i mas′kyə lit, -lāt′), *v.,* **-lat•ed, -lat•ing,** *adj.* —*v.t.* **1.** to castrate. **2.** to deprive of strength or vigor; weaken. —*adj.* **3.** deprived of or lacking strength or vigor; effeminate. [1600–10; < L *ēmasculātus* (ptp. of *ēmasculāre*), equiv. to *ē-* E- + *mascul(us)* MALE + *-ātus* -ATE[1]] —**e•mas′cu•la′tion,** *n.* —**e•mas′cu•la′tive,** *adj.* —**e•mas′cu•la′tor,** *n.* —**e•mas•cu•la•to•ry** (i mas′kyə lə tôr′ē, -tōr′ē), *adj.*
—**Syn. 2.** debilitate, undermine, devitalize, soften.

em•ba•cle (em bä′kəl, -bak′əl), *n.* an accumulation of broken ice in a river. Cf. **debacle** (def. 2). [< F, equiv. to *em-* EM-[1] + *(dé)bâcle* DEBACLE]

em•balm (em bäm′), *v.t.* **1.** to treat (a dead body) so as to preserve it, as with chemicals, drugs, or balsams. **2.** to preserve from oblivion; keep in memory: *his deeds embalmed in the hearts of his disciples.* **3.** to cause to remain unchanged; prevent the development of. **4.** to impart a balmy fragrance to. [1300–50; ME *embalmen, embaumen* < OF *emba(u)smer,* equiv. to *em-* EM-[1] + *-ba(u)smer,* v. deriv. of *ba(u)sme* BALM] —**em•balm′er,** *n.* —**em•balm′ment,** *n.*

em•bank (em bangk′), *v.t.* to enclose or protect with an embankment. [1640–50; EM-[1] + BANK[1]]

em•bank•ment (em bangk′mənt), *n.* **1.** a bank, mound, dike, or the like, raised to hold back water, carry a roadway, etc. **2.** the action of embanking. [1780–90; EMBANK + -MENT]

em•bar (em bär′), *v.t.,* **-barred, -bar•ring. 1.** to stop or hinder, as by a bar. **2.** to enclose within bars; imprison. [1425–75; late ME *embarren* < AF, MF *embarrer,* equiv. to *em-* EM-[1] + *barrer* to BAR[1]]

em•bar•ca•de•ro (em bär′kə dâr′ō), *n., pl.* **-ros. 1.** a pier, wharf, or landing place. **2.** (*sometimes cap.*) a waterfront section in San Francisco: piers and seafood restaurants. [1840–50, *Amer.*; < AmerSp, Sp: pier, docking place, equiv. to *embarcad(o)* ptp. of *embarcar* to EMBARK, launch + *-ero* < L *-ārium* -ARIUM]

em•bar•ca•tion (em′bär kā′shən), *n.* embarkation.

em•bar•go (em bär′gō), *n., pl.* **-goes,** *v.,* **-goed, -go•ing.** —*n.* **1.** an order of a government prohibiting the movement of merchant ships into or out of its ports. **2.** an injunction from a government commerce agency to refuse freight for shipment, as in case of congestion or insufficient facilities. **3.** any restriction imposed upon commerce by edict. **4.** a restraint or hindrance; prohibition. —*v.t.* **5.** to impose an embargo on. [1595–1605; < Sp, deriv. of *embargar* to hinder, embarrass < VL **imbarricāre,* equiv. to *im-* IM-[1] + *-barricāre* (**barr(a)* BAR[1] + *-icāre* causative suffix)]
—**Syn. 4.** ban, restriction, interdiction, postscription.

em•bark (em bärk′), *v.i.* **1.** to board a ship, aircraft, or other vehicle, as for a journey. **2.** to start an enterprise, business, etc. —*v.t.* **3.** to put or receive on board a ship, aircraft, or other vehicle. **4.** to involve (someone) in an enterprise. **5.** to venture or invest (something) in an enterprise. [1540–50; < MF *embarquer* < Sp *embarcar,* equiv. to *em-* EM-[1] + *-barcar,* v. deriv. of *barca* BARK[3]]

em•bar•ka•tion (em′bär kā′shən), *n.* the act, process, or an instance of embarking. Also, **embarcation.** [1635–45; < F *embarcation* < Sp *embarcación.* See EMBARK, -ATION]

em•bark•ment (em bärk′mənt), *n.* an embarkation. [1590–1600; EMBARK + -MENT]

em•bar•ras de ri•chesses (äN bA Räd[ə] Rē shes′), *French.* embarrassment of riches; confusing overabundance.

em•bar•rass (em bar′əs), *v.t.* **1.** to cause confusion and shame to; make uncomfortably self-conscious; disconcert; abash: *His bad table manners embarrassed her.* **2.** to make difficult or intricate, as a question or problem; complicate. **3.** to put obstacles or difficulties in the way of; impede: *The motion was advanced in order to embarrass the progress of the bill.* **4.** to beset with financial difficulties; burden with debt: *The decline in sales embarrassed the company.* —*v.i.* **5.** to become disconcerted, abashed, or confused. [1665–75; < F *embarrasser* < Sp *embarazar* < Pg *embaraçar,* equiv. to *em-* EM-[1] + *-baraçar,* v. deriv. of *baraço, baraça* cord, strap, noose (of obscure orig.)] —**em•bar•rassed•ly** (em bar′əst lē, -ə sid lē), *adv.* —**em•bar′rass•ing•ly,** *adv.*
—**Syn. 1.** discompose, discomfit, chagrin. See **confuse. 3.** hamper, hinder.

em•bar•rass•ment (em bar′əs mənt), *n.* **1.** the state of being embarrassed; disconcertment; abashment. **2.** an act or instance of embarrassing. **3.** something that embarrasses. **4.** an overwhelmingly excessive amount; overabundance: *an embarrassment of riches.* **5.** the state of being in financial difficulties. **6.** *Med.* impairment of functioning associated with disease: *respiratory embarrassment.* [1670–80; < F *embarrassement.* See EMBARRASS, -MENT]
—**Syn. 1.** discomposure. See **shame.**

em•bas•sa•dor (em bas′ə dər), *n. Archaic.* ambassador.

em•bas•sage (em′bə sij), *n. Archaic.* embassy. [var. of *ambassage* < OF *ambasse* (< ML *ambactia* office; see EMBASSY) + -AGE]

em•bas•sy (em′bə sē), *n., pl.* **-sies. 1.** a body of persons entrusted with a mission to a sovereign or government, esp. an ambassador and his or her staff. **2.** the official headquarters of an ambassador. **3.** the function or office of an ambassador. **4.** a mission headed by an ambassador. [1570–80; var. of *ambassy* < MF *ambassee,* OF *ambasce, ambaxee* << OPr *ambaissada,* deriv. of *embayssar* to send a delegate < ML *ambasciāre,* deriv. of *ambascia* service, office, deriv., by a Gmc intermediary (cf. Goth *andbahti,* OHG *ambahti*) of Gallo-L *ambactus* retainer, servant (< Gaulish, equiv. to *amb-* around, AMBI- + *-act-* verbal adj. of **ag-* drive, lead; cf. ACT, Welsh *amaeth* husbandman); cf. AMBASSADOR]

em•bat•tle[1] (em bat′l), *v.t.,* **-tled, -tling. 1.** to arrange in order of battle; prepare for battle; arm. **2.** to fortify (a town, camp, etc.). [1350–1400; ME *embatailen* < MF *embataillier.* See EM-[1], BATTLE[1]]

em•bat•tle[2] (em bat′l), *v.t.,* **-tled, -tling.** to furnish with battlements. [1350–1400; ME *embatailen.* See EM-[1], BATTLE[2]]

em•bat•tled (em bat′ld), *adj.* **1.** disposed or prepared for battle. **2.** engaged in or beset by conflict or struggle. [1350–1400; ME; see EMBATTLE[1], -ED[2]; def. 2 prob. by assoc. with the general sense "restrict, enclose" of many verbs formed with EM-[1], EN-[1]]

em•bat•tle•ment (em bat′l mənt), *n.* battlement. [1400–1450; late ME *embatailment.* See EMBATTLE[2], -MENT]

em•bay (em bā′), *v.t.* **1.** to enclose in or as if in a bay; surround or envelop. **2.** to form into a bay. [1575–85; EM-[1] + BAY[1]]

em•bay•ment (em bā′mənt), *n.* **1.** a bay. **2.** *Physical Geog.* the process by which a bay is formed. [1805–15; EMBAY + -MENT]

Em•den (em′dən), *n.* one of a breed of large, white domestic geese having orange shanks, toes, and bill. Also, **Emden.**

em•bed (em bed′), *v.,* **-bed•ded, -bed•ding.** —*v.t.* **1.** to fix into a surrounding mass: *to embed stones in cement.* **2.** to surround tightly or firmly; envelop or enclose: *Thick cotton padding embedded the precious vase in its box.* **3.** to incorporate or contain as an essential part or characteristic: *A love of color is embedded in all of her paintings.* **4.** *Histol.* to infiltrate (a biological tissue) with molten paraffin or other plastic material that later solidifies, enabling the preparation to be sliced very thin for viewing under a microscope. **5.** *Math.* to map a set into another set. **6.** *Gram.* to insert (a construction, as a phrase or clause) into a larger construction, as a clause or sentence. —*v.i.* **7.** to be or become fixed or incorporated, as into a surrounding mass: *Glass embeds in the soft tar of the road.* Also, **imbed.** [1770–80; EM-[1] + BED] —**em•bed′ment,** *n.*

em•bed•ding (em bed′ing), *n. Math.* the mapping of one set into another. Also, **imbedding.** [EMBED + -ING[1]]

em•bel•lish (em bel′ish), *v.t.* **1.** to beautify by or as if by ornamentation; ornament; adorn. **2.** to enhance (a statement or narrative) with fictitious additions. [1300–50; ME *embelisshen* < AF, MF *embeliss-* (s. of *embelir*), equiv. to *em-* EM-[1] + *bel-* (< L *bellus* pretty) + *-iss-* -ISH[2]] —**em•bel′lish•er,** *n.*
—**Syn. 1.** decorate, garnish, bedeck, embroider.

em•bel•lish•ment (em bel′ish mənt), *n.* **1.** an ornament or decoration. **2.** a fictitious addition, as to a factual statement. **3.** *Music.* **a.** ornament (def. 8). **b.** See **auxiliary tone. 4.** the act of embellishing. **5.** state of being embellished. [1615–25; EMBELLISH + -MENT]

em•ber (em′bər), *n.* **1.** a small live piece of coal, wood, etc., as in a dying fire. **2. embers,** the smoldering remains of a fire. [bef. 1000; ME *eemer, emeri,* OE *ǣmerge, ǣmyrie* (c. ON *eimyrja,* OHG *eimuria*), equiv. to *ǣm-* (c. ON *eimr* steam) + *-erge, -yrie,* akin to OE *ys(e)le* ember, L *ūrere* to burn]

Em′ber day′, any of the days in the quarterly three-day period of prayer and fasting (the Wednesday, Friday, and Saturday after the first Sunday in Lent, after Whitsunday, after Sept. 14, and after Dec. 13) observed in the Roman Catholic Church and other Western churches. [bef. 1050; ME *ymber day,* OE *ymbrendæg,* pl. *-dagas,* equiv. to *ymbryne* recurrence (*ymb(e)* around + *ryne* a running) + *dæg* DAY]

em•ber•i•zine (em′bə rī′zin, -zīn), *Ornith.* —*adj.* **1.** belonging or pertaining to the subfamily Emberizinae, comprising the buntings, New World sparrows, and related birds. —*n.* **2.** an emberizine bird. [< NL *Emberizinae,* equiv. to *Emberiz(a)* the bunting genus (< dial. G; cf. Swiss G *Ämerzen, Imbrütze*; OHG *amarzo, amirzo,* hypocoristic forms of *amaro* (>G *Ammer* bunting), short for **amarofogal* lit., emmer-bird; see EMMER, YELLOWHAMMER) + *-inae* -INAE]

em•bez•zle (em bez′əl), *v.t.,* **-zled, -zling.** to appropriate fraudulently to one's own use, as money or property entrusted to one's care. [1375–1425; late ME *embesilen* < AF *embeseiller* to destroy, make away with, equiv. to *em-* EM-[1] + *beseiller,* OF *beseiller* to destroy < ?] —**em•bez′zle•ment,** *n.* —**em•bez′zler,** *n.*
—**Syn.** misappropriate.

em•bi•id (em′bē id), *n.* See **web spinner.** [< NL *Embiidae* the web spinner family, equiv. to *Embi(a)* a genus (< Gk, fem. of *émbios* having life) + *-idae* -ID[2]]

em•bi•ot•o•cid (em′bē ot′ə sid -ə tos′id, -tō′sid), *adj.* **1.** belonging or pertaining to the family Embiotocidae, comprising the surfperches. —*n.* **2.** an embiotocid fish. [< NL *Embiotocidae,* equiv. to *Embiotoc(a)* name of genus (< Gk *émbio(s)* having life + *-tokē,* fem. of *-tokos* bearing offspring) + *-idae* -ID[2]]

em•bit•ter (em bit′ər), *v.t.* **1.** to make bitter; cause to feel bitterness: *Failure has embittered him.* **2.** to make bitter or more bitter in taste. Also, **imbitter.** [1595–1605; EM-[1] + BITTER] —**em•bit′ter•er,** *n.* —**em•bit′ter•ment,** *n.*
—**Syn. 1.** sour, rankle, envenom.

Em•bla (em′blä), *n. Scand. Myth.* the first woman, made by the gods from a tree. Cf. **Ask.** [< ON, prob. akin to *almr* ELM]

em•blaze[1] (em blāz′), *v.t.,* **-blazed, -blaz•ing. 1.** to illuminate, as by a blaze. **2.** to kindle. [1515–25; EM-[1] + BLAZE[1]] —**em•blaz′er,** *n.*

em•blaze[2] (em blāz′), *v.t.,* **-blazed, -blaz•ing.** *Archaic.* to emblazon. [1625–35] —**em•blaz′er,** *n.*

em•bla•zon (em blā′zən), *v.t.* **1.** to depict, as on an escutcheon in heraldry. **2.** to decorate with brilliant colors. **3.** to proclaim; celebrate or extol. [1585–95; EM-[1] + BLAZON] —**em•bla′zon•er,** *n.*

em•bla•zon•ment (em blā′zən mənt), *n.* **1.** the act of emblazoning. **2.** something that is emblazoned. [1790–1800; EMBLAZON + -MENT]

em•bla•zon•ry (em blā′zən rē), *n.* **1.** the act or art of emblazoning; heraldic decoration. **2.** brilliant representation or embellishment. [1660–70; EM-[1] + BLAZONRY]

em•blem (em′bləm), *n.* **1.** an object or its representation, symbolizing a quality, state, class of persons, etc.; symbol: *The olive branch is an emblem of peace.* **2.** a sign, design, or figure that identifies or represents something: *the emblem of a school.* **3.** an allegorical picture, often inscribed with a motto supplemental to the visual image with which it forms a single unit of meaning. **4.** *Obs.* an inlaid or tessellated ornament. —*v.t.* **5.** to represent with an emblem. [1400–50; late ME < L *emblēma* inlaid or mosaic work < Gk *émblēma* something put on, equiv. to *em-* EM-[2] + *blêma* something thrown or put; cf. *embállein* to throw in or on]
—**Syn. 1.** token, sign, figure, image, device, badge.

em•blem•at•ic (em′blə mat′ik), *adj.* pertaining to, of the nature of, or serving as an emblem; symbolic. Also, **em′blem•at′i•cal.** [1635–45; < Gk *emblēmat-,* s. of *emblēma* (see EMBLEM) + -IC] —**em′blem•at′i•cal•ly,** *adv.* —**em′blem•at′i•cal•ness,** *n.*

em•blem•a•tist (em blem′ə tist), *n.* a designer, maker, or user of emblems. [1640–50; *emblemat-* (see EMBLEMATIC) + -IST]

em•blem•a•tize (em blem′ə tīz′), *v.t.,* **-tized, -tiz•ing.** to serve as an emblem of; represent by an emblem. Also, *esp. Brit.,* **em•blem′a•tise′.** [1605–15; *emblemat-* (see EMBLEMATIC) + -IZE]

em•ble•ments (em′blə mənts), *n.pl. Law.* the products or profits of land that has been sown or planted. [1485–95; pl. of *emblement* < AF, MF *emblaement,* equiv. to *emblae(r)* (< ML *imblādāre* to sow with grain, equiv. to *im-* IM-[1] + *blād(um)* grain (> F *blé*) < Gmc (cf. MD *blaad,* OE *blǣd*) + *-āre* inf. suffix) + *-ment* -MENT]

em•bod•i•ment (em bod′ē mənt), *n.* **1.** the act of embodying. **2.** the state or fact of being embodied. **3.** a person, being, or thing embodying a spirit, principle, abstraction, etc; incarnation. **4.** something embodied. [1820–30; EMBODY + -MENT]

em•bod•y (em bod′ē), *v.t.,* **-bod•ied, -bod•y•ing. 1.** to give a concrete form to; express, personify, or exemplify in concrete form: *to embody an idea in an allegorical painting.* **2.** to provide with a body; incarnate; make corporeal: *to embody a spirit.* **3.** to collect into or include in a body; organize; incorporate. **4.** to embrace or comprise. Also, **imbody.** [1540–50; EM-[1] + BODY] —**em•bod′i•er,** *n.*

em•boî•té (*Fr.* äN bwA tā′), *n., pl.* **-tés** (-tā′). *Ballet.* a step, performed in series, in which the dancer stands on the toes with legs together and then springs up, swinging one foot out and around to the front of the other. Cf. **déboîté.** [< F: lit., boxed in, ptp. of *emboîter;* see EM-[1], BOÎTE]

em•bold•en (em bōl′dən), *v.t.* to make bold or bolder; hearten; encourage. Also, **imbolden.** [1495–1505; EM-[1] + BOLD + -EN[1]]

em•bol•ic (em bol′ik), *adj.* **1.** *Pathol.* pertaining to an embolus or to embolism. **2.** *Embryol.* of, pertaining to, or resulting from emboly. [1865–70; EMBOL(US) + -IC]

em•bo•lism (em′bə liz′əm), *n.* **1.** *Pathol.* the occlusion of a blood vessel by an embolus. **2.** intercalation, as of a day in a year. **3.** a period of time intercalated. **4.** (in a Eucharistic service) the prayer following the final petitions of the Lord's Prayer. [1350–1400; ME < ML *embolismus* intercalation < LGk *embolismós,* equiv. to *embol-* (see EMBOLUS) + *-ismos* -ISM] —**em′bo•lis′mic,** *adj.*

em•bo•lite (em′bə līt′), *n.* a mineral, chloride and bromide of silver, used as a minor source of silver. [1840–50; < Gk *emból(ion)* insertion (see EMBOLUS) + -ITE[1]]

em•bo•li•za•tion (em′bə lə zā′shən), *n.* obstruction of a blood vessel or organ by an embolus. [1945–50; EMBOL(US) + -IZATION]

em•bo•lus (em′bə ləs), *n., pl.* **-li** (-lī′). *Pathol.* undissolved material carried by the blood and impacted in some part of the vascular system, as thrombi or fragments of thrombi, tissue fragments, clumps of bacteria, protozoan parasites, fat globules, or gas bubbles. [1660–70; < L: piston < Gk *émbolos* stopper, equiv. to *em-* EM-[2] + *bólos* a throw, akin to *bállein* to throw]

em•bo•ly (em′bə lē), *n., pl.* **-lies.** *Embryol.* the pushing or growth of one part into another, as in the formation of certain gastrulas. [1875–80; < Gk *embolḗ* a putting into place, akin to *embállein* to throw in]

em•bon•point (*Fr.* äN bôN pwaN′), *n.* excessive plumpness; stoutness. [1655–65; < F, lit., in good condition]

em•bosk (em bosk′), *v.t.* to hide or conceal (something, oneself, etc.) with or as if with foliage, greenery, or the like: *to embosk oneself within a grape arbor.* [EM-[1] + BOSK]

em•bos•om (em bo͝oz′əm, -bo͞o′zəm), *v.t.* **1.** to enfold, envelop, or enclose. **2.** to take into or hold in the bosom; embrace. **3.** to cherish; foster. Also, **imbosom.** [1580–90; EM-[1] + BOSOM]

CONCISE PRONUNCIATION KEY: act, cāpe, dâre, pärt; set, ēqual; *if,* īce; ox, ōver, ôrder, oil, bo͝ok, bo͞ot, out; up, ûrge; child; sing; shoe; thin, *th*at; zh as in *treasure.* ə = *a* as in *alone, e* as in *system, i* as in *easily,* o as in *gallop, u* as in *circus;* [ə] as in *fire* (fī[ə]r), *hour* (ou[ə]r). l and n can serve as syllabic consonants, as in *cradle* (krād′l), and *button* (but′n). See the full key inside the front cover.

em·boss (em bôs′, -bos′), *v.t.* **1.** to raise or represent (surface designs) in relief. **2.** to decorate (a surface) with raised ornament. **3.** *Metalworking.* to raise a design on (a blank) with dies of similar pattern, one the negative of the other. Cf. **coin** (def. 12). **4.** to cause to bulge out; make protuberant. [1350–1400; ME *embosen* < MF *embocer,* equiv. to *em-* EM-[1] + *boce* BOSS[2]] —**em·boss′a·ble,** *adj.* —**em·boss′er,** *n.* —**em·boss′ment,** *n.*

em·bou·chure (äm′bo͞o sho͝or′, äm′bo͞o sho͝or′; *Fr.* äɴ bo͞o shʏʀ′), *n., pl.* **-chures** (-sho͝orz′; *Fr.* -shʏʀ′). **1.** the mouth of a river. **2.** the opening out of a valley into a plain. **3.** *Music.* **a.** the mouthpiece of a wind instrument. **b.** the adjustment of a player's mouth to such a mouthpiece. [1750–60; < F, equiv. to *embouch(er)* to put (an instrument) to one's mouth (*em-* EM- + *bouche* mouth < L *bucca* puffed cheek) + *-ure* -URE]

em·bour·geoise·ment (em bo͝or′zhwäz mənt, -mänt′, äm-; *Fr.* äɴ bo͞oʀ zhwaz mäɴ′), *n.* the acquisition or adoption of middle-class values and manners. [< F, equiv. to *s'embourgeois(er)* to become bourgeois (see EM-[1], BOURGEOIS[1]) + *-ment* -MENT]

em·bowed (em bōd′), *adj.* bent; vaulted; arched. [1475–85; EMBOW + -ED[2]]

em·bow·el (em bou′əl, -boul′), *v.t.,* **-eled, -el·ing** or (*esp. Brit.*) **-elled, -el·ling. 1.** to disembowel. **2.** *Obs.* to enclose. [1515–25; EM-[1] + BOWEL]

em·bow·er (em bou′ər), *v.t., v.i.* to shelter in or as in a bower; cover or surround with foliage. Also, **imbower.** [1570–80; EM-[1] + BOWER[1]]

em·brace[1] (em brās′), *v.,* **-braced, -brac·ing,** *n.* —*v.t.* **1.** to take or clasp in the arms; press to the bosom; hug. **2.** to take or receive gladly or eagerly; accept willingly: *to embrace an idea.* **3.** to avail oneself of: *to embrace an opportunity.* **4.** to adopt (a profession, a religion, etc.): *to embrace Buddhism.* **5.** to take in with the eye or the mind. **6.** to encircle; surround; enclose. **7.** to include or contain: *An encyclopedia embraces a great number of subjects.* —*v.i.* **8.** to join in an embrace. —*n.* **9.** an act or instance of embracing. [1300–50; ME < AF, OF *embracier,* equiv. to *em-* EM-[1] + *bracier* to embrace, deriv. of *brace* the two arms; see BRACE] —**em·brace′a·ble,** *adj.* —**em·brace′ment,** *n.* —**em·brac′er,** *n.*
—**Syn. 2.** adopt, espouse, welcome. **3.** seize. **7.** comprise, cover, embody. See **include.** —**Ant. 7.** exclude.

em·brace[2] (em brās′), *v.t.,* **-braced, -brac·ing.** *Law.* to attempt to influence (a judge or jury) through corrupt means. [1400–1450; late ME: to influence, prejudice, bribe (a jury), perh. the same word as EMBRACE[1], influenced by *embrasen* to set on fire (< MF *embraser;* see EM-[1], BRAISE)] —**em·brac′er,** *n.*

em·brace·or (em brā′sər), *n. Law.* a person guilty of embracery. [1400–50; late ME < AF; MF *embraseor* instigator, equiv. to *embras(er)* (see EMBRACE[2]) + *-eor* < L *-ātor-* -ATOR]

em·brac·er·y (em brā′sə rē), *n., pl.* **-er·ies.** *Law.* an attempt to influence a judge or jury by corrupt means, as by bribery, threats, or promises. Also, **imbracery.** [1400–50; late ME *embracerie.* See EMBRACE[2], -ERY]

em·brac·ive (em brā′siv), *adj.* **1.** thoroughly embracing or encompassing. **2.** given to embracing or caressing. [1850–55; EMBRACE[1] + -IVE] —**em·brac′ive·ly,** *adv.*

em·branch·ment (em branch′mənt, -bränch′-), *n.,* **1.** a branching or ramification. **2.** a branch. [1820–30; < F *embranchement,* equiv. to *em-* EM-[1] + *branche* BRANCH + *-ment* -MENT]

em·bran·gle (em brang′gəl), *v.t.,* **-gled, -gling.** to embroil. Also, **imbrangle.** [1655–65; EM-[1] + *brangle* (b. BRAWL and WRANGLE)] —**em·bran′gle·ment,** *n.*

em·bra·sure (em brā′zhər), *n.* **1.** (in fortification) an opening, as a loophole or crenel, through which missiles may be discharged. **2.** *Archit.* a splayed enlargement of a door or window toward the inner face of a wall. **3.** *Dentistry.* the space between adjacent teeth. [1695–1705; < F, equiv. to *embras(er)* to enlarge a window or door opening, make an embrasure (appar. the same v. as *embraser* to set on fire (see EMBRACE[2]), though sense shift unclear) + *-ure* -URE] —**em·bra′sured,** *adj.*

em·brit·tle (em brit′l), *v.t., v.i.,* **-tled, -tling.** to make or become brittle. [1900–05; EM-[1] + BRITTLE]

em·brit·tle·ment (em brit′l mənt), *n.* the act or process of becoming brittle, as steel from exposure to certain environments or heat treatment or because of the presence of impurities. [1915–20; EMBRITTLE + -MENT]

em·bro·cate (em′brō kāt′, -brə-), *v.t.,* **-cat·ed, -cat·ing.** to moisten and rub with a liniment or lotion. [1605–15; < ML *embrocātus* (ptp. of *embrocāre*), equiv. to LL *embroch(a)* (< Gk *embrochḗ* infusion, equiv. to *em-* EM-[2] + *brochḗ* a making wet) + *-ātus* -ATE[1]]

em·bro·ca·tion (em′brō kā′shən, -brə-), *n.* **1.** the act of embrocating a bruised or diseased part of the body. **2.** the liquid used for this; a liniment or lotion. [1400–50; late ME. See EMBROCATE, -ION]

em·bro·glio (em brōl′yō), *n., pl.* **-glios.** imbroglio. [confused with EMBROIL]

em·broi·der (em broi′dər), *v.t.* **1.** to decorate with ornamental needlework. **2.** to produce or form in needlework. **3.** to adorn or embellish rhetorically, esp. with ornate language or fictitious details: *He embroidered the account of the shipwreck to hold his listeners' interest.* —*v.i.* **4.** to do embroidery. **5.** to add embellishments; exaggerate (often fol. by *on* or *upon*). [1350–1400; EM-[1] + BROIDER; r. ME *embroderen,* freq. of *embroden* < MF *embro(u)der,* equiv. to *em-* EM-[1] + OF *brosder,* deriv. of *brosd* < Gmc (see BRAD)] —**em·broi′der·er,** *n.*
—**Syn. 3.** elaborate, exaggerate, color, fancify.

CONCISE ETYMOLOGY KEY: <, descended or borrowed from; >, whence; b., blend of, blended; c., cognate with; cf., compare; deriv., derivative; equiv., equivalent; imit., imitative; obl., oblique; r., replacing; s., stem; sp., spelling, spelled; resp., respelling, respelled; trans., translation; ?, origin unknown; *, unattested; ‡, probably earlier than. See the full key inside the front cover.

em·broi·der·ess (em broi′dər is), *n.* a woman who embroiders. [1715–25; EMBROIDER + -ESS]
—**Usage.** See **-ess.**

em·broi·der·y (em broi′də rē, -drē), *n., pl.* **-der·ies. 1.** the art of working raised and ornamental designs in threads of silk, cotton, gold, silver, or other material, upon any woven fabric, leather, paper, etc., with a needle. **2.** embroidered work or ornamentation. **3.** elaboration or embellishment, as in telling a story. [1350–1400; ME *embrouderie* needlework on cloth < MF *embroud(er)* + ME *-erie* -ERY; *oi* from EMBROIDER]

embroi′dery nee′dle, a needle with a long eye, used for embroidery and fine darning. [1885–90]

em·broil (em broil′), *v.t.* **1.** to bring into discord or conflict; involve in contention or strife. **2.** to throw into confusion; complicate. [1595–1605; < MF *embrouiller,* equiv. to *em-* EM-[1] + *brouiller* to BROIL[2]] —**em·broil′er,** *n.* —**em·broil′ment,** *n.*

em·brown (em broun′), *v.t., v.i.* to make or become brown or dark. [1660–70; EM-[1] + BROWN]

em·brue (em bro͞o′), *v.t.,* **-brued, -bru·ing.** imbrue.

em·brute (em bro͞ot′), *v.t., v.i.,* **-brut·ed, -brut·ing.** imbrute.

embry-, var. of **embryo-** before a vowel.

em·bry·ec·to·my (em′brē ek′tə mē), *n., pl.* **-mies.** *Surg.* removal of an embryo. [EMBRY- + -ECTOMY]

em·bry·o (em′brē ō′), *n., pl.* **-os,** *adj.* —*n.* **1.** the young of a viviparous animal, esp. of a mammal, in the early stages of development within the womb, in humans up to the end of the second month. Cf. **fetus. 2.** *Bot.* the rudimentary plant usually contained in the seed. **3.** any multicellular animal in a developmental stage preceding birth or hatching. **4.** the beginning or rudimentary stage of anything: *He charged that the party policy was socialism in embryo.* —*adj.* **5.** embryonic. [1580–90; < ML *embryon-, embryo* < Gk *émbryon,* n. use of neut. of *émbryos* ingrowing, equiv. to *em-* EM-[2] + *bry-* (s. of *brýein* to swell) + *-os* adj. suffix]

embryo-, a combining form representing **embryo** in compound words: *embryology.* Also, *esp. before a vowel,* **embry-.**

em·bry·og·e·ny (em′brē oj′ə nē), *n.* the formation and development of the embryo, as a subject of scientific study. Also, **em·bry·o·gen·e·sis** (em′brē ō jen′ə sis). [1825–35; EMBRYO- + -GENY] —**em·bry·o·gen·ic** (em′brē ō jen′ik), **em·bry·o·ge·net·ic** (em′brē ō jə net′ik), *adj.*

embryol., embryology.

em·bry·ol·o·gist (em′brē ol′ə jist), *n.* a specialist in embryology. [1840–50; EMBRYOLOG(Y) + -IST]

em·bry·ol·o·gy (em′brē ol′ə jē), *n., pl.* **-gies. 1.** the science dealing with the formation, development, structure, and functional activities of embryos. **2.** the origin, growth, and development of an embryo: *the embryology of the chick.* [1840–50; EMBRYO- + -LOGY] —**em·bry·o·log·i·cal** (em′brē ə loj′i kəl), **em′bry·o·log′ic,** *adj.* —**em′bry·o·log′i·cal·ly,** *adv.*

em·bry·on·ic (em′brē on′ik), *adj.* **1.** pertaining to or in the state of an embryo. **2.** rudimentary; undeveloped. Also, **em·bry·o·nal** (em′brē ə nl, em′brē ōn′l). [1840–50; *embryon-* (see EMBRYO) + -IC] —**em′bry·on′i·cal·ly,** *adv.*
—**Syn. 2.** underdeveloped, immature, unfinished.

em′bryon′ic disk′, *Embryol.* **1.** Also called **em′bryon′ic shield′.** in the early embryo of mammals, the flattened inner cell mass that arises at the end of the blastocyst stage and from which the embryo begins to differentiate. **2.** the blastodisk of yolky eggs. [1935–40]

em′bryon′ic mem′brane. See **extraembryonic membrane.** [1945–50]

em′bryo sac′, *Bot.* the megaspore of a seed-bearing plant, situated within the ovule, giving rise to the endosperm and forming the egg cell or nucleus from which the embryo plant develops after fertilization. [1870–75]

em·bry·ot·o·my (em′brē ot′ə mē), *n., pl.* **-mies.** *Surg.* dismemberment of a fetus, when natural delivery is impossible, in order to effect its removal. [1715–25; < F *embryotomie.* See EMBRYO-, -TOMY]

em·bry·o·tox·ic (em′brē ō tok′sik), *adj.* poisonous to embryos. [EMBRYO- + TOXIC]

em′bryo trans′fer, the transfer of a developing embryo to or from the uterus of a surrogate mother. Also called **em′bryo trans′plant.** [1970–75]

em·bry·o·troph (em′brē ə trof′, -trôf′), *n. Embryol.* the nutrient material, composed chiefly of secretions from the uterine glands, degenerating uterine tissue, and substances in the maternal blood, that nourishes a mammalian embryo prior to the formation of the placenta. Cf. **hemotroph.** [< F; see EMBRYO-, HEMOTROPH] —**em·bry·o·troph·ic** (em′brē ə trof′ik, -trō′fik), *adj.* —**em·bry·o·tro·phy** (em′brē o′trə fē), *n.*

em·bus (im bus′, em-), *v.i., v.t.,* **-bussed, -bus·sing.** to get or put on a bus. [1925–30; EM-[1] + BUS]

em·cee (em′sē′), *n., v.,* **-ceed, -cee·ing.** —*n.* **1.** master of ceremonies. —*v.t.* **2.** to act as master of ceremonies for. —*v.i.* **3.** to act as master of ceremonies. [1935–35, *Amer.*; sp. form of M.C.]

em′ dash′, *Print.* a dash one em long.

Em·den (em′dən), *n.* a seaport in NW West Germany. 53,400.

Em·den (em′dən), *n.* Embden.

eme (ēm), *n. Chiefly Scot.* **1.** friend. **2.** uncle. [bef. 1000; ME *eem(e),* OE *ēam;* c. D *oom,* G (arch.) *Ohm, Oheim;* akin to UNCLE]

-eme, a suffix used principally in linguistics to form nouns with the sense "significant contrastive unit," at the level of language specified by the stem: *morpheme; tagmeme.* [extracted from PHONEME]

e·meer (ə mēr′, ā mēr′, ā′mēr), *n.* emir.

e·meer·ate (ə mēr′it, -āt, ā mēr′-), *n.* emirate (defs. 1, 2).

E·mel·ia (i mēl′yə), *n.* a female given name.

Em·e·line (em′ə lēn′, -lin′), *n.* a female given name. Also, **Em·e·lin** (em′ə lin′), **Em·e·li·na** (em′ə lē′nə, -lī′nə).

e·mend (i mend′), *v.t.* **1.** to edit or change (a text). **2.** to free from faults or errors; correct. [1375–1425; late ME (< MF *emender*) < L *ēmendāre* to correct, equiv. to *ē-* E- + *mend(um)* fault + *-āre* inf. suffix] —**e·mend′a·ble,** *adj.*
—**Syn. 1, 2.** See **amend.**

e·men·date (ē′mən dāt′, em′ən-, i men′dāt), *v.t.,* **-dat·ed, -dat·ing.** to emend (a text). [1875–80; < L *ēmendātus,* ptp. of *ēmendāre.* See EMEND, -ATE[1]] —**e′men·da′tor,** *n.*

e·men·da·tion (ē′mən dā′shən, em′ən-), *n.* **1.** a correction or change, as of a text. **2.** the act of emending. [1530–40; < L *ēmendātiōn-* (s. of *ēmendātiō*), equiv. to *ēmendāt(us)* (see EMENDATE) + *-iōn-* -ION] —**e·men·da·to·ry** (i men′də tôr′ē, -tōr′ē), *adj.*

em·er·ald (em′ər əld, em′rəld), *n.* **1.** a rare variety of beryl that is colored green by chromium and valued as a gem. **2.** See **emerald green. 3.** *Print.* (in Britain) a 6½-point type of a size between nonpareil and minion. **4.** *Ornith.* any of numerous small bright green hummingbirds of the genus *Chlorostilbon.* —*adj.* **5.** having a clear, deep-green color. [1250–1300; ME *emeraude, emeralde* < AF, OF *esmeraude, esmeralde, esmeragde* < L *smaragdus* < Gk *smáragdos;* prob. ult. < Sem *b-r-q* shine (> > Skt *marāk(a)la* emerald)]

em′erald cut′, *Jewelry.* a type of step cut, used esp. on emeralds and diamonds, in which the girdle has the form of a square or rectangle with truncated corners.

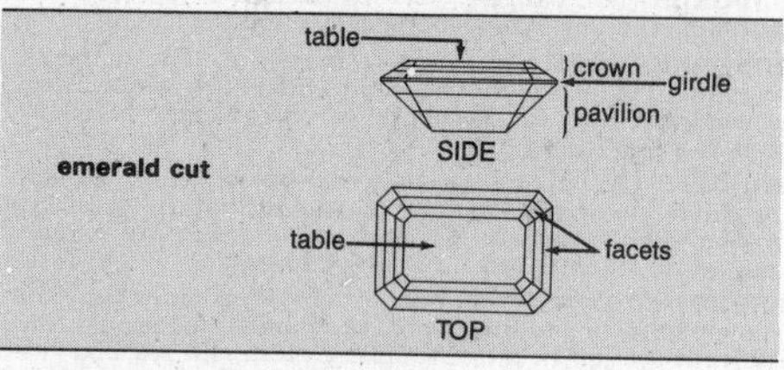

em′erald green′, a clear, deep-green color. [1875–80] —**em′er·ald-green′,** *adj.*

Em′erald Isle′, Ireland (def. 2).

e·merge (i mûrj′), *v.i.,* **e·merged, e·merg·ing. 1.** to come forth into view or notice, as from concealment or obscurity: *a ghost emerging from the grave; a ship emerging from the fog.* **2.** to rise or come forth from or as if from water or other liquid. **3.** to come up or arise, as a question or difficulty. **4.** to come into existence; develop. **5.** to rise, as from an inferior or unfortunate state or condition. [1630–40; < L *ēmergere* to arise out of, equiv. to *ē-* E- + *mergere* to dive, sink]
—**Syn. 1.** EMERGE, EMANATE, ISSUE mean to come forth. EMERGE is used of coming forth from a place shut off from view, or from concealment, or the like, into sight and notice: *The sun emerges from behind the clouds.* EMANATE is used of intangible things, as light or ideas, spreading from a source: *Rumors often emanate from irresponsible persons.* ISSUE is often used of a number of persons, a mass of matter, or a volume of smoke, sound, or the like, coming forth through any outlet or outlets: *The crowd issued from the building.*

e·mer·gence (i mûr′jəns), *n.* **1.** the act or process of emerging. **2.** an outgrowth, as a prickle, on the surface of a plant. **3.** *Evolution.* the appearance of new properties or species in the course of development or evolution. [1640–50; < F < ML; see EMERGENCY]

e·mer·gen·cy (i mûr′jən sē), *n., pl.* **-cies,** *adj.* —*n.* **1.** a sudden, urgent, usually unexpected occurrence or occasion requiring immediate action. **2.** a state, esp. of need for help or relief, created by some unexpected event: *a weather emergency; a financial emergency.* —*adj.* **3.** granted, used, or for use in an emergency: *an emergency leave; emergency lights.* [1625–35; < ML *ēmergentia,* equiv. to *ēmerg-* (see EMERGE) + *-entia* -ENCY. See EMERGENT]
—**Syn. 1.** exigency, extremity, pinch, quandary, plight. EMERGENCY, CRISIS, STRAITS refer to dangerous situations. An EMERGENCY is a situation demanding immediate action: *A power failure created an emergency in transportation.* A CRISIS is a vital or decisive turning point in a condition or state of affairs, and everything depends on the outcome of it: *Help arrived when affairs had reached a crisis.* STRAIT (usually STRAITS) suggests a pressing situation, often one of need or want: *The family was in desperate straits for food and clothing.*

emer′gency boat′, *Naut.* See **accident boat.**

emer′gency brake′, 1. Also called **parking brake.** a special brake used to prevent a motor vehicle from rolling after it has stopped or been parked. Cf. **brake**[1] (def. 1). **2.** any brake meant to stop a vehicle in an emergency. [1895–1900]

emer′gency room′, a hospital area equipped and staffed for the prompt treatment of acute illness, trauma, or other medical emergencies. *Abbr.:* ER

e·mer·gent (i mûr′jənt), *adj.* **1.** coming into view or notice; issuing. **2.** emerging; rising from a liquid or other surrounding medium. **3.** coming into existence, esp. with political independence: *the emergent nations of Africa.* **4.** arising casually or unexpectedly. **5.** calling for immediate action; urgent. **6.** *Evolution.* displaying emergence. —*n.* **7.** *Ecol.* an aquatic plant having its stem, leaves, etc., extending above the surface of the water. [1350–1400; ME (< MF) < L *ēmergent-* (s. of *ēmergēns*) arising out of, prp. of *ēmergere* to EMERGE] —**e·mer′gent·ly,** *adv.* —**e·mer′gent·ness,** *n.*

emer′gent evolu′tion, the origin of entirely new

properties at certain critical stages or levels in the course of evolution, as multicellular organisms, sexual reproduction, or nervous systems. [1920–25]

emer′gent norms′, *Sociol.* new norms that define appropriate behavior in ambiguous situations, as those developed by members of a crowd.

e·mer·gi·cen·ter (i mûr′jə sen′tər), *n.* a walk-in facility for treatment of minor medical emergencies. [1980–85; EMERG(ENCY) + -I- + CENTER]

e·merg·ing (i mûr′jing), *adj.* emergent (def. 3): *emerging nations.* [1640–50; EMERGE + -ING²]

e·mer·i·ta (i mer′i tə), *adj., n., pl.* **-tae** (-tē′). *—adj.* **1.** (of a woman) retired or honorably discharged from active professional duty, but retaining the title of one's office or position. *—n.* **2.** a woman with such status. [< L, fem. of *ēmeritus* EMERITUS]

e·mer·i·tus (i mer′i təs), *adj., n., pl.* **-ti** (-tī′, -tē′). *—adj.* **1.** retired or honorably discharged from active professional duty, but retaining the title of one's office or position: *dean emeritus of the graduate school; editor in chief emeritus.* *—n.* **2.** an emeritus professor, minister, etc. [1785–95; < L *ēmeritus* having fully earned (ptp. of *ēmerēre*), equiv. to *ē-* E- + *meri-* earn + *-tus* ptp. suffix]

em·er·ize (em′ə rīz′), *v.t.,* **-ized, -iz·ing.** to finish (fabric) with a cylinder covered with emery in order to make the raised nap even and give luster to the fabric. Also, *esp. Brit.,* **em′er·ise′.** [EMER(Y) + -IZE]

e·mersed (i mûrst′), *adj. Bot.* risen or standing out of water, surrounding leaves, etc. [1680–90; < L *ēmersus* (ptp. of *ēmergere* to EMERGE) + -ED²]

e·mer·sion (i mûr′zhən, -shən), *n.* **1.** Also called **egress.** *Astron.* the emergence of a heavenly body from an eclipse, an occultation, or a transit. Cf. **immersion** (def. 5). **2.** *Archaic.* the act of emerging. [1625–35; < L *ēmers(us)* (ptp. of *ēmergere* to EMERGE) + -ION]

Em·er·son (em′ər sən), *n.* **Ralph Wal·do,** (wôl′dō, wol′-), 1803–82, U.S. essayist and poet. **—Em·er·so·ni·an** (em′ər sō′nē ən), *adj.*

em·er·y (em′ə rē, em′rē), *n.* a granular mineral substance consisting typically of corundum mixed with magnetite or hematite, used powdered, crushed, or consolidated for grinding and polishing. [1475–85; < MF *emeri,* OF *esmeril* < VL **smēriculum,* equiv. to MGk *smêri* (for Gk *smýris* rubbing powder; akin to SMEAR) + L *-culum* -CULE²]

Em·er·y (em′ə rē, em′rē), *n.* a male or female given name.

em′ery board′, a small, stiff strip of paper or cardboard, coated with powdered emery, used in manicuring.

em′ery cloth′, emery-coated cloth used as an abrasive.

em′ery wheel′. See **grinding wheel.** [1850–55]

em·e·sis (em′ə sis), *n. Pathol.* vomitus. [1870–75; < NL < Gk *émesis* a vomiting, equiv. to *eme-* (s. of *emeîn* to vomit) + *-sis* -SIS]

E.Met., Engineer of Metallurgy.

e·met·ic (ə met′ik), *adj.* **1.** causing vomiting, as a medicinal substance. *—n.* **2.** an emetic medicine or agent. [1650–60; < L *emeticus* < Gk *emetikós,* equiv. to *éme-t(os)* vomiting + *-ikos* -IC] **—e·met′i·cal·ly,** *adv.*

em·e·tine (em′i tēn′, -tin), *n. Pharm.* a crystalline or white powdery substance, $C_{29}H_{40}N_2O_4$, the active principle of ipecac: used chiefly in the treatment of amebic dysentery and as an emetic and expectorant. [1810–20; < Gk *émet(os)* vomiting + -INE²; cf. F *émétine*]

emf, See **electromotive force.** Also, **EMF, E.M.F., e.m.f.**

EMG, 1. electromyogram. **2.** electromyograph. **3.** electromyography.

-emia, a combining form occurring in compound words that denote a condition of the blood, as specified by the initial element: *hyperemia.* Also, **-aemia, -haemia, -hemia.** [< NL < Gk *-(h)aimia* (as in *anaimía* want of blood), equiv. to *haim-* (s. of *haîma*) blood + *-ia* -IA]

e·mic (ē′mik), *adj. Ling.* pertaining to or being a significant unit that functions in contrast with other units in a language or other system of behavior. Cf. **etic.** [1950–55; extracted from PHONEMIC; coined by U.S. linguist Kenneth L. Pike (born 1912)]

e·mic·tion (i mik′shən), *n.* urination. [1660–70; < LL *ēmict(us)* (ptp. of *ēmingere* to make water) (equiv. to *ē-* E- + *mig-* urinate (c. OE *migan,* ON *miga*) + *-tus* ptp. suffix) + -ION]

em·i·grant (em′i grənt), *n.* **1.** a person who emigrates, as from his or her native country or region: *They welcomed the emigrants from Italy.* *—adj.* **2.** emigrating. [1745–55, *Amer.;* < L *ēmigrant-* (s. of *ēmigrāns*) moving away (prp. of *ēmigrāre*), equiv. to *ē-* E- + *migrant-* (*migr-* remove + *-ant-* -ANT)]
—Syn. 1. émigré, expatriate.

em·i·grate (em′i grāt′), *v.i.,* **-grat·ed, -grat·ing.** to leave one country or region to settle in another; migrate: *to emigrate from Ireland to Australia.* [1770–80; < L *ēmigrātus* moved away (ptp. of *ēmigrāre*), equiv. to *ē-* E- + *migrātus* (*migr-* remove + *ātus* -ATE¹)] **—em′i·gra′·tive,** *adj.* **—Syn.** See **migrate.**

em·i·gra·tion (em′i grā′shən), *n.* **1.** an act or instance of emigrating. **2.** a body of emigrants; emigrants collectively. **3.** *Physiol.* diapedesis. [1640–50; < LL *ēmigrātiōn-* (s. of *ēmigrātiō*) removal. See EMIGRATE, -ION] **—em′i·gra′tion·al,** *adj.*

em·i·gra·to·ry (em′i grə tôr′ē, -tōr′ē), *adj.* migratory. [1830–40; EMIGRATE + -ORY¹]

é·mi·gré (em′i grā′; *Fr.* ā mē grā′), *n., pl.* **-grés** (-grāz′; *Fr.* -grā′). **1.** an emigrant, esp. a person who flees from his or her native land because of political conditions. **2.** a person who fled from France because of opposition to or fear of the revolution that began in 1789. [1785–95; < F: n. use of ptp. of *émigrer* < L *ēmigrāre* to EMIGRATE]

E·mil (ā′məl, ē′məl; *Ger.* ā′mēl), *n.* a male given name: from Latin *Aemilius,* a family name. Also, **É·mile** (ā mēl′).

É·mile (*Fr.* ā mēl′), *n.* a didactic novel (1762) by J. J. Rousseau, dealing principally with the author's theories of education.

E·mi·lia-Ro·ma·gna (e mē′lyä rô mä′nyä), *n.* a region in N Italy. 3,948,135; 8547 sq. mi. (22,135 sq. km).

Em·i·ly (em′ə lē), *n.* a female given name: from a Latin word meaning "industrious." Also, **Em′i·lie.**

é·min·cé (*Fr.* ā maN sā′), *n.* a dish of leftover meat, sliced thin and warmed in a sauce. [1905–10; < F: lit., chopped up, ptp. of *émincer,* equiv. to *é-* EX-¹ + *mincer,* MF *mincier;* see MINCE]

em·i·nence (em′ə nəns), *n.* **1.** high station, rank, or repute: *philosophers of eminence.* **2.** a high place or part; a hill or elevation; height. **3.** (*cap.*) *Rom. Cath. Ch.* a title of honor, applied to cardinals (usually prec. by *His* or *Your*). **4.** *Anat.* an elevation or projection, esp. on a bone. [1375–1425; late ME < AF < L *ēminentia,* equiv. to *ēmin-* (base of *ēminēre* to stand out; see EMINENT) + *-entia* -ENCE]
—Syn. 1. conspicuousness, note, fame. **2.** prominence.

é·mi·nence grise (*Fr.* ā mē näNs grēz′), *pl.* **é·mi·nences grises** (*Fr.* ā mē näNs grēz′). See **gray eminence.** [< F]

em·i·nen·cy (em′ə nən sē), *n., pl.* **-cies.** eminence.

em·i·nent (em′ə nənt), *adj.* **1.** high in station, rank, or repute; prominent; distinguished: *eminent statesmen.* **2.** conspicuous, signal, or noteworthy: *eminent fairness.* **3.** lofty; high: *eminent peaks.* **4.** prominent; projecting; protruding: *an eminent nose.* [1375–1425; late ME (< AF) < L *ēminent-* (s. of *ēminēns*) outstanding (prp. of *ēminēre* to stick out, project), equiv. to *ē-* E- + *min-* (see IMMINENT) + *-ent-* -ENT] **—em′i·nent·ly,** *adv.*
—Syn. 1. celebrated, renowned, illustrious, outstanding. See **famous. 2.** noted; notable.

em′inent domain′, *Law.* the power of the state to take private property for public use with payment of compensation to the owner. [1730–40]

E·mi·ne·scu (ye′mē ne′sko͞o), *n.* **Mi·ha·il** (mē′hä ēl′), (*Mihail Iminovici*), 1850–89, Rumanian poet.

e·mir (ə mēr′, ā mēr′, ā′mēr), *n.* **1.** a chieftain, prince, commander, or head of state in some Islamic countries. **2.** a title of honor of the descendants of Muhammad. **3.** (*cap.*) the former title of the ruler of Afghanistan. **4.** a title of certain Turkish officials. Also, **emeer, amir, ameer.** [1615–25; < Ar *amīr* commander]

e·mir·ate (ə mēr′it, -āt, ā mēr′-, em′ər it), *n.* **1.** the office or rank of an emir. **2.** the state or territory under the jurisdiction of an emir. **3. the Emirates.** See **United Arab Emirates.** Also, **emeerate** (for defs. 1, 2). [1860–65; EMIR + -ATE³]

em·is·sar·y (em′ə ser′ē), *n., pl.* **-sar·ies,** *adj.* *—n.* **1.** a representative sent on a mission or errand: *emissaries to negotiate a peace.* **2.** an agent sent on a mission of a secret nature, as a spy. **3.** *Anat.* sending or coming out, as certain veins that pass through the skull and connect the venous sinuses inside with the veins outside. **4.** pertaining to an emissary. *—adj.* **5.** *Archaic.* sent forth, as on a mission. [1595–1605; < L *ēmissārius* one sent out, equiv. to *ēmiss-* (see EMISSION) + *-ārius* -ARY]
—Syn. 1. delegate, ambassador, envoy, legate.

e·mis·sion (i mish′ən), *n.* **1.** an act or instance of emitting: *the emission of poisonous fumes.* **2.** something that is emitted; discharge; emanation. **3.** an act or instance of issuing, as paper money. **4.** *Electronics.* a measure of the number of electrons emitted by the heated filament or cathode of a vacuum tube. **5.** an ejection or discharge of semen or other fluid from the body. **6.** the fluid ejected or discharged. [1600–10; (< MF) < L *ēmissiōn-* (s. of *ēmissiō*), equiv. to *ēmiss(us),* ptp. of *ēmittere* to EMIT (*ē-* E- + *mit-* send + *-tus* ptp. suffix) + *-iōn-* -ION]
—Syn. 5. ejaculation. **6.** ejaculate.

emis′sion neb′ula, *Astron.* a bright diffuse nebula that emits light as a result of ionization of its gas atoms by ultraviolet radiation, as the Orion Nebula, planetary nebulae, and supernova remnants, as the Crab Nebula.

emis′sion spec′trum, *Physics.* the spectrum formed by electromagnetic radiations emitted by a given source, characteristic of the source and the type of excitation inducing the radiations. [1885–90]

e·mis·sive (i mis′iv), *adj.* **1.** serving to emit. **2.** pertaining to emission. [1730–40; EMISS(ION) + -IVE]

em·is·siv·i·ty (em′ə siv′i tē, ē′mə-), *n. Thermodynamics.* the ability of a surface to emit radiant energy compared to that of a black body at the same temperature and with the same area. [1875–80; EMISSIVE + -ITY]

e·mit (i mit′), *v.t.,* **e·mit·ted, e·mit·ting. 1.** to send forth (liquid, light, heat, sound, particles, etc.); discharge. **2.** to give forth or release (a sound): *He emitted one shrill cry and then was silent.* **3.** to utter or voice, as opinions. **4.** to issue, as an order or a decree. **5.** to issue formally for circulation, as paper money. [1620–30; < L *ēmittere* to send forth, equiv. to *ē-* E- + *mittere* to send]

e·mit·tance (i mit′ns), *n. Optics.* the total flux emitted per unit area. Cf. **luminous emittance, radiant emittance.** [1935–40; EMIT + -ANCE]

e·mit·ter (i mit′ər), *n.* **1.** a person or thing that emits. **2.** *Electronics.* an electrode on a transistor from which a flow of electrons or holes enters the region between the electrodes. [1880–85; EMIT + -ER¹]

Em·lyn (em′lin), *n.* **1.** a female given name, form of **Emily. 2.** a male given name.

Em·ma (em′ə), *n.* a female given name, form of **Erma.**

Em·ma (em′ə), *n.* a novel (1815) by Jane Austen.

Em·man·u·el (i man′yo͞o əl, *for 1, 2; Fr.* e ma ny el′ *for 3*), *n.* **1.** Jesus Christ, esp. as the Messiah. Matt. 1:23. **2.** Immanuel. **3. Pierre** (pyer), born 1916, French poet.

em·mar·ble (i mär′bəl), *v.t.,* **-bled, -bling.** to represent in or adorn with marble; make like marble. Also, **enmarble.** [1590–1600; EM-¹ + MARBLE]

Em·ma·us (ə mā′əs), *n.* a city in E Pennsylvania. 11,001.

Em·me·line (em′ə lēn′, -līn′), *n.* a female given name, form of **Amelia.**

Em·men (em′ən), *n.* a city in NE Netherlands. 90,450.

em·men·a·gogue (ə men′ə gôg′, -gog′, ə mē′nə-), *Med.* *—n.* **1.** a medicine or procedure that promotes menstrual discharge. *—adj.* **2.** Also, **em·men·a·gog·ic** (ə men′ə goj′ik, -gog′-, ə mē′nə-). stimulating the menstrual flow. [1695–1705; < Gk *émmēn(a)* menses (see EMMENIA) + -AGOGUE]

em·men·i·a (ə men′ē ə, ə mē′nē ə), *n.* (*used with a singular or plural v.*), *Physiol.* menses. [< Gk *emmēnia,* neut. pl. of *emmēnios* monthly, equiv. to *em-* EM-² + *mēn* month (akin to L *mēnsis* MONTH)]

Em·men·tha·ler (em′ən tä′lər), *n.* a Swiss cheese made from cow's milk and containing small holes. Also, **Em·men·tal** (em′ən täl′), **Em′men·ta′ler, Em′men·thal′, Em′menthaler cheese′.** [< G, after *Emmental* a valley in Switzerland; see -ER¹]

em·mer (em′ər), *n.* a wheat, *Triticum turgidum dicoccon,* having a two-grained spikelet, grown as a forage crop in Europe, Asia, and the western U.S. [1905–10; < G; MHG *emer,* OHG *amari,* by-form of *amar(o)* (> G *Amelkorn* emmer); cf. YELLOWHAMMER]

em·met (em′it), *n. Chiefly Dial.* an ant. [bef. 900; ME *emete,* OE *ǣmette* ANT]

Em·met (em′it), *n.* **1. Robert,** 1778–1803, Irish patriot. **2.** a male given name.

em·me·tro·pi·a (em′i trō′pē ə), *n. Ophthalm.* the normal refractive condition of the eye, in which the rays of light are accurately focused on the retina. [1860–65; < NL, equiv. to *emmetr-* (s. of Gk *émmetros* in measure, equiv. to *em-* EM-² + *métr(on)* measure + *-os* adj. suffix) + *-opia* -OPIA] **—em′me·trope′,** *n.* **—em·me·trop·ic** (em′i trop′ik, -trō′pik), *adj.*

Em·mett (em′it), *n.* **1. Daniel Decatur,** 1815–1904, U.S. songwriter and minstrel-show performer and producer: composer of "Dixie." **2.** a male given name.

Em·my (em′ē), *n., pl.* **-mys. 1.** (*sometimes l.c.*) any of several statuettes awarded annually by the National Academy of Television Arts and Sciences for excellence in television programming, production, or performance. **2.** Also, **Em′mie.** a female given name, form of **Emma.**

Em·my·lou (em′ē lo͞o′, em′ē lo͞o′), *n.* a female given name.

e·mol·lient (i mol′yənt), *adj.* **1.** having the power of softening or relaxing, as a medicinal substance; soothing, esp. to the skin: *emollient lotions for the face.* *—n.* **2.** an emollient medicine, lotion, salve, etc. [1635–45; < L *ēmollient-* (s. of *ēmolliēns*) softening up (prp. of *ēmollīre*), equiv. to *ē-* E- + *molli(s)* soft + *-ent-* -ENT] **—e·mol′lience,** *n.*
—Syn. 1. relieving, palliative, healing, assuasive.

e·mol·u·ment (i mol′yə mənt), *n.* profit, salary, or fees from office or employment; compensation for services: *Tips are an emolument in addition to wages.* [1470–80; < L *ēmolumentum* advantage, benefit, equiv. to *ēmol(ere)* to grind out, produce by grinding (*ē-* E- + *molere* to grind; see MILL¹) + *-u-,* var. before labials of *-i-* -I- + *-mentum* -MENT]
—Syn. earnings, pay, recompense, stipend, honorarium.

Em·o·ry (em′ə rē), *n.* a male or female given name.

Em′ory oak′, a shrubby oak, *Quercus emoryi,* of the southwestern U.S. and Mexico, yielding a hard, heavy wood. [1880–85, *Amer.;* named after W.H. *Emory* (d. 1887), American engineer]

e·mote (i mōt′), *v.i.,* **e·mot·ed, e·mot·ing. 1.** to show or pretend emotion: *to emote over the beauties of nature.* **2.** to portray emotion in acting, esp. exaggeratedly or ineptly; behave theatrically: *The actress emoted for all she was worth.* [1915–20, *Amer.;* back formation from EMOTION] **—e·mot′er,** *n.*

e·mot·i·con (i mō′ti kon′), *n. Computers.* an abbreviation or icon used on a network, as *IMHO* for "in my humble opinion" or *:-),* a sideways smile face, to indicate amusement. [1980–85; b. EMOTION and ICON]

e·mo·tion (i mō′shən), *n.* **1.** an affective state of consciousness in which joy, sorrow, fear, hate, or the like, is experienced, as distinguished from cognitive and volitional states of consciousness. **2.** any of the feelings of joy, sorrow, fear, hate, love, etc. **3.** any strong agitation of the feelings actuated by experiencing love, hate, fear, etc., and usually accompanied by certain physiological changes, as increased heartbeat or respiration, and often overt manifestation, as crying or shaking. **4.** an instance of this. **5.** something that causes such a reaction: *the powerful emotion of a great symphony.* [1570–80; appar. < MF *esmotion,* derived on the model of *movoir: motion,* from *esmovoir* to set in motion, move the feelings < VL **exmovēre,* for L *ēmovēre;* see E-, MOVE, MOTION] **—e·mo′tion·a·ble,** *adj.* **—e·mo′tion·less,** *adj.*
—Syn. 1. See **feeling.**

e·mo·tion·al (i mō′shə nl), *adj.* **1.** pertaining to or involving emotion or the emotions. **2.** subject to or easily affected by emotion: *We are an emotional family, given to demonstrations of affection.* **3.** appealing to the emotions: *an emotional request for contributions.* **4.** showing or revealing very strong emotions: *an emotional scene in a play.* **5.** actuated, effected, or determined by emotion rather than reason: *An emotional decision is often a wrong decision.* **6.** governed by emotion: *He is in a highly emotional state of mind.* [1840–50; EMOTION + -AL¹] **—e·mo′tion·al·ly,** *adv.*

CONCISE PRONUNCIATION KEY: act, cāpe, dâre, pärt; set, ēqual; *if,* īce; ox, ōver, ôrder, oil, bo͝ok, bo͞ot, out; up, ûrge; child; sing; shoe; thin, *th*at; zh as in *treasure.* ə = *a* as in *alone, e* as in *system, i* as in *easily, o* as in *gallop, u* as in *circus;* ᵊ as in *fire* (fīᵊr), *hour* (ouᵊr). l and n can serve as syllabic consonants, as in *cradle* (krād′l), and *button* (but′n). See the full key inside the front cover.

—**Syn.** 2. temperamental, effusive, demonstrative, sentimental. —**Ant.** 2. undemonstrative, unsentimental, inexpressive.

emo′tional depriva′tion, a lack of adequate psychological nurturance, usually occurring in the early developmental years.

e•mo•tion•al•ism (i mō′shə nl iz′əm), *n.* **1.** excessively emotional character: *the emotionalism of sentimental fiction.* **2.** strong or excessive appeal to the emotions: *the emotionalism of patriotic propaganda.* **3.** a tendency to display or respond with undue emotion, esp. morbid emotion. **4.** unwarranted expression or display of emotion. [1860–65; EMOTIONAL + -ISM]
—**Syn.** sentimentality, mawkishness.

e•mo•tion•al•ist (i mō′shə nl ist), *n.* **1.** a person who appeals to the emotions, esp. unduly. **2.** a person easily affected by emotion. **3.** a person who bases conduct, or the theory of conduct, upon feelings rather than reason: *a romantic emotionalist.* [1865–70; EMOTIONAL + -IST] —**e•mo′tion•al•is′tic,** *adj.*

e•mo•tion•al•i•ty (i mō′shə nal′i tē), *n.* emotional state or quality: *the emotionality of the artistic temperament.* [1860–65; EMOTIONAL + -ITY]

e•mo•tion•al•ize (i mō′shə nl īz′), *v.t.,* **-ized, -iz•ing.** to make emotional; treat as a matter of emotion. Also, *esp. Brit.,* **e•mo′tion•al•ise′.** [1875–80; EMOTIONAL + -IZE]

e•mo•tive (i mō′tiv), *adj.* **1.** characterized by or pertaining to emotion: *the emotive and rational capacities of humankind.* **2.** productive of or directed toward the emotions: *Artistic distortion is often an emotive use of form.* [1725–35; EMOT(ION) + -IVE] —**e•mo′tive•ly,** *adv.* —**e•mo′tive•ness, e•mo•tiv•i•ty** (ē′mō tiv′i tē, i mō-), *n.*

emo′tive mean′ing, the emotional connotation of a word or expression that is used instead of one having a similar meaning but less affective quality, as the connotation of "murder" when used instead of "homicide" or "drunk" instead of "inebriated." [1940–45]

EMP, electromagnetic pulse: a burst of electromagnetic energy produced by a nuclear explosion in the atmosphere, considered capable of widespread damage to power lines, telecommunications, and electronic equipment.

Emp., 1. Emperor. 2. Empire. 3. Empress.

emp., (in prescriptions) a plaster. [< L *emplastrum*]

e.m.p., (in prescriptions) after the manner prescribed; as directed. [< L *ex mōdō praescriptō*]

em•pale (em pāl′), *v.t.,* **-paled, -pal•ing.** impale (defs. 1–5). —**em•pale′ment,** *n.* —**em•pal′er,** *n.*

em•pa•na•da (em′pə nä′də; *Sp.* em′pä nä′thä), *n. Latin-American Cookery.* a turnover or mold of pastry filled with chopped or ground meat, vegetables, fruit, etc., and usually baked or fried. [1920–25; < AmerSp, equiv. to *em-* EM-[1] + *pan* bread + *-ada,* fem. of *-ado* -ATE[1]]

em•pan•el (em pan′l), *v.t.,* **-eled, -el•ing** or (*esp. Brit.*) **-elled, -el•ling.** impanel.

em•pa•thet•ic (em′pə thet′ik), *adj.* of, pertaining to, or characterized by empathy: *a sensitive, empathetic school counselor.* Also, **em•path•ic** (em path′ik). [1930–35; EMPATH(Y) + -ETIC] —**em′pa•thet′i•cal•ly, em•path′i•cal•ly,** *adv.*

em•pa•thize (em′pə thīz′), *v.i.,* **-thized, -thiz•ing.** to experience empathy (often fol. by *with*): *His ability to empathize with people made him an excellent marriage counselor.* Also, *esp. Brit.,* **em′pa•thise′.** [1920–25; EMPATH(Y) + -IZE]

em•pa•thy (em′pə thē), *n.* **1.** the intellectual identification with or vicarious experiencing of the feelings, thoughts, or attitudes of another. **2.** the imaginative ascribing to an object, as a natural object or work of art, feelings or attitudes present in oneself: *By means of empathy, a great painting becomes a mirror of the self.* [1900–05; < Gk *empátheia* affection, equiv. to *em-* EM-[2] + *path-* (base of *páschein* to suffer) + *-eia* -IA; present meaning translates G *Einfühlung*]
—**Syn. 1.** See **sympathy.**

Em•ped•o•cles (em ped′ə klēz′), *n.* c490–c430 B.C., Greek philosopher and statesman.

em•pen•nage (äm′pə näzh′, em′-; *Fr.* än pe nazh′), *n., pl.* **-nag•es** (-nä′zhiz; *Fr.* -nazh′). the rear part of an airplane or airship, usually comprising the stabilizer, elevator, vertical fin, and rudder. [1905–10; < F: lit., feathering, equiv. to *empenn(er)* to feather an arrow (*em-* EM-[1] + *-penner,* deriv. of *penne* feather; see PEN[1]) + *-age* -AGE]

em•per•or (em′pər ər), *n.* **1.** the male sovereign or supreme ruler of an empire: *the emperors of Rome.* **2.** *Chiefly Brit.* a size of drawing or writing paper, 48 × 72 in. (122 × 183 cm). [1175–1225; ME *empero(u)r* < AF; OF *empereor* < L *imperātor* orig., one who gives orders, ruler, equiv. to *imperā(re)* to order, command (*im-* IM-[1] + *-perāre,* comb. form of *parāre* to provide, PREPARE) + *-tor* -TOR] —**em′per•or•ship′,** *n.*

em′peror but′terfly, any of several brush-footed butterflies of the family Nymphalidae, usually having brilliantly colored wings.

Em′peror Jones′, The, a play (1920) by Eugene O'-Neill.

em′peror moth′, any of several large saturniid moths, esp. *Saturnia pavonia* of temperate forests in Europe and Asia, characterized by heavily scaled wings with large, transparent eyespots. [1865–70]

CONCISE ETYMOLOGY KEY: <, descended or borrowed from; >, whence; b., blend of, blended; c., cognate with; cf., compare; deriv., derivative; equiv., equivalent; imit., imitative; obl., oblique; r., replacing; s., stem; sp., spelling, spelled; resp., respelling, respelled; trans., translation; ?, origin unknown; *, unattested; ‡, probably earlier than. See the full key inside the front cover.

em′peror pen′guin, the largest of the penguins, *Aptenodytes forsteri,* of the coasts of Antarctica, having bluish-gray and black plumage on the back, head, and wings, a white chest, and a patch of orange on each side of the neck. See illus. under **penguin.** [1880–85]

em•per•y (em′pə rē), *n., pl.* **-per•ies.** absolute dominion; sovereignty. [1250–1300; ME *emperie* < AF < L *imperium* mastery, sovereignty, empire, equiv. to *impe-r(āre)* to rule (see EMPEROR) + *-ium* -IUM]

em•pha•sis (em′fə sis), *n., pl.* **-ses** (-sēz′). **1.** special stress laid upon, or importance attached to, anything: *The president's statement gave emphasis to the budgetary crisis.* **2.** something that is given great stress or importance: *Morality was the emphasis of his speech.* **3.** *Rhet.* **a.** special and significant stress of voice laid on particular words or syllables. **b.** stress laid on particular words, by means of position, repetition, or other indication. **4.** intensity or force of expression, action, etc.: *Determination lent emphasis to his proposals.* **5.** prominence, as of form or outline: *The background detracts from the emphasis of the figure.* **6.** *Electronics.* preemphasis. [1565–75; < L < Gk *émphasis* indication, equiv. to *em-* EM-[2] + *phásis* PHASIS]

em•pha•size (em′fə sīz′), *v.t.,* **-sized, -siz•ing.** to give emphasis to; lay stress upon; stress: *to emphasize a point; to emphasize the eyes with mascara.* Also, *esp. Brit.,* **em′pha•sise′.** [1820–30; EMPHAS(IS) + -IZE]
—**Syn.** accent, accentuate, highlight.

em•phat•ic (em fat′ik), *adj.* **1.** uttered, or to be uttered, with emphasis; strongly expressive. **2.** using emphasis in speech or action. **3.** forceful; insistent: *a big, emphatic man; I must be emphatic about this particular.* **4.** very impressive or significant; strongly marked; striking: *the emphatic beauty of sunset.* **5.** clearly or boldly outlined: *It stands, like a great, stone dagger, emphatic against the sky.* **6.** *Gram.* of or pertaining to a form used to add emphasis, esp., in English, stressed auxiliary *do* in affirmative sentences, as in *He did call you* or *I do like it.* **7.** *Phonet.* having a secondary velar articulation, as certain dental consonants in Arabic. —*n.* **8.** an emphatic consonant. [1700–10; < Gk *emphatikós* indicative, forceful, equiv. to **emphat(ós)* (*em-* EM-[2] + *phatós,* var. of *phantós* visible, equiv. to *phan-,* s. of *phaínesthai* to appear + *-tos* adj. suffix) + *-ikos* -IC] —**em•phat′i•cal•ly,** *adv.* —**em•phat′i•cal•ness,** *n.*
—**Syn. 3.** positive, energetic, forcible, pronounced, decided, unequivocal, definite. —**Ant. 3.** weak.

em•phy•se•ma (em′fə sē′mə, -zē′-), *n. Pathol.* **1.** a chronic, irreversible disease of the lungs characterized by abnormal enlargement of air spaces in the lungs accompanied by destruction of the tissue lining the walls of the air spaces. **2.** any abnormal distention of an organ, or part of the body, with air or other gas. [1655–65; < NL < Gk *emphýsēma* inflation, equiv. to *em-* EM-[2] + *phȳsē-* (var. s. of *phȳsân* to blow) + *-ma* n. suffix denoting result of action] —**em•phy•sem•a•tous** (em′fə-sem′ə təs, -sē′mə-, -zem′ə-, -zē′mə-), *adj.* —**em′phy•se′mic,** *adj.*

em′ pi′ca, *Print.* a unit of measurement equal to about one-sixth of an inch (4 mm). Also called **em.**

Empire méridienne

em•pire (em′pīər; *for 8–10 also* om pēr′), *n.* **1.** a group of nations or peoples ruled over by an emperor, empress, or other powerful sovereign or government: usually a territory of greater extent than a kingdom, as the former British Empire, French Empire, Russian Empire, Byzantine Empire, or Roman Empire. **2.** a government under an emperor or empress. **3.** (*often cap.*) the historical period during which a nation is under such a government: *a history of the second French empire.* **4.** supreme power in governing; imperial power; sovereignty: *Austria's failure of empire in central Europe.* **5.** supreme control; absolute sway: *passion's empire over the mind.* **6.** a powerful and important enterprise or holding of large scope that is controlled by a single person, family, or group of associates: *The family's shipping empire was founded 50 years ago.* **7.** (*cap.*) a variety of apple somewhat resembling the McIntosh. —*adj.* **8.** (*cap.*) characteristic of or developed during the first French Empire, 1804–15. **9.** (*usually cap.*) (of women's attire and coiffures) of the style that prevailed during the first French Empire, in clothing being characterized esp. by décolletage and a high waistline, coming just below the bust, from which the skirt hangs straight and loose. **10.** (*often cap.*) noting or pertaining to the style of architecture, furnishings, and decoration prevailing in France and imitated to a greater or lesser extent in various other countries, c1800–30: characterized by the use of delicate but elaborate ornamentation imitated from Greek and Roman examples or containing classical allusions, as animal forms for the legs of furniture, bas-reliefs of classical figures, motifs of wreaths, torches, caryatids, lyres, and urns and by the occasional use of military and Egyptian motifs and, under the Napoleonic Empire itself, of symbols alluding to Napoleon I, as bees or the letter *N.* [1250–1300; ME < AF, OF < L *imperium;* see EMPERY]
—**Syn. 4.** dominion, rule, supremacy.

em′pire build′er, a person who plans or works to extend dominion or control, as over territory, political organizations, or business enterprises. [1890–95]

em′pire build′ing, the plans, activities, achievements, etc., of an empire builder. [1895–1900]

Em′pire Day′, **1.** (in Canada) the last school day before Victoria Day, observed with patriotic activities in the schools. **2.** former name of **Commonwealth Day.**

Em′pire State′, the state of New York (used as a nickname).

Em′pire State′ of the South′, Georgia (used as a nickname).

em•pir•ic (em pir′ik), *n.* **1.** a person who follows an empirical method. **2.** a quack; charlatan. —*adj.* **3.** empirical. [1520–30; < L *empiricus* < Gk *empeirikós* experienced, equiv. to *em-* EM-[2] + *peir-* (s. of *peirân* to attempt) + *-ikos* -IC]

em•pir•i•cal (em pir′i kəl), *adj.* **1.** derived from or guided by experience or experiment. **2.** depending upon experience or observation alone, without using scientific method or theory, esp. as in medicine. **3.** provable or verifiable by experience or experiment. [1560–70; EMPIRIC + -AL[1]] —**em•pir′i•cal•ly,** *adv.* —**em•pir′i•cal•ness,** *n.*
—**Syn. 1, 2.** practical, firsthand, pragmatic. —**Ant. 1, 2.** secondhand, theoretical.

empir′ical for′mula, *Chem.* a chemical formula indicating the elements of a compound and their relative proportions, as $(CH_2O)_n$. Cf. **molecular formula, structural formula.** [1820–30]

em•pir•i•cism (em pir′ə siz′əm), *n.* **1.** empirical method or practice. **2.** *Philos.* the doctrine that all knowledge is derived from sense experience. Cf. **rationalism** (def. 2). **3.** undue reliance upon experience, as in medicine; quackery. **4.** an empirical conclusion. [1650–60; EMPIRIC + -ISM] —**em•pir′i•cist,** *n., adj.*

Em•pi•rin (em′pə rin, -prin), *Trademark.* a brand of aspirin.

em•pi•rism (em′pə riz′əm), *n. Philos.* empiricism (def. 2). [1710–20; EMPIR(IC) + -ISM] —**em•pi•ris•tic** (em′pə-ris′tik), *adj.*

em•place (em plās′), *v.t.,* **-placed, -plac•ing.** to put in place or position: *A statue was emplaced in the square.* [1860–65; back formation from EMPLACEMENT]

em•place•ment (em plās′mənt), *n.* **1.** *Fort.* the space, platform, or the like, for a gun or battery and its accessories. **2.** a putting in place or position; location: *the emplacement of a wall.* **3.** *Geol.* **a.** the intrusion of igneous rocks into a particular position. **b.** the development of an ore deposit in a particular place. [1795–1805; < F, equiv. to obs. *emplac(er)* to place (*em-* EM-[1] + *placer* to PLACE) + *-ment* -MENT]

em•plane (em plān′), *v.i., v.t.,* **-planed, -plan•ing.** enplane. [EM-[1] + (AIR)PLANE]

em•plec•tite (em plek′tit), *n.* a mineral, copper and bismuth sulfide, occurring in the form of thin gray prisms, found with quartz. [1855–60; < Gk *émplekt(os)* inwoven (*em-* EM-[2] + *plek-,* s. of *plékein* to plait + *-tos* adj. suffix) + -ITE[1]]

em•ploy (em ploi′), *v.t.* **1.** to hire or engage the services of (a person or persons); provide employment for; have or keep in one's service: *This factory employs thousands of people.* **2.** to keep busy or at work; engage the attentions of: *He employs himself by reading after work.* **3.** to make use of (an instrument, means, etc.); use; apply: *to employ a hammer to drive a nail.* **4.** to occupy or devote (time, energies, etc.): *I employ my spare time in reading. I employ all my energies in writing.* —*n.* **5.** employment; service: *to be in someone's employ.* [1425–75; late ME *employen* < AF, MF *emploier* << L *implicāre* to enfold (LL: to engage); see IMPLICATE]

em•ploy•a•ble (em ploi′ə bəl), *adj.* **1.** able to be employed; usable. **2.** capable of holding a job and available for hire. —*n.* **3.** a person who is able to work and is available to be hired. [1685–95; EMPLOY + -ABLE] —**em•ploy′a•bil′i•ty,** *n.*

em•ploy•ee (em ploi′ē, em ploi ē′, em′ploi ē′), *n.* a person working for another person or a business firm for pay. Also, **em•ploy′e, em•ploy′é.** [1825–35; < F *employé* employed, ptp. of *employer* to EMPLOY; see -EE]

em•ploy•er (em ploi′ər), *n.* **1.** a person or business that employs one or more people, esp. for wages or salary: *a fair employer.* **2.** a person or thing that makes use of or occupies someone or something: *an inadequate employer of one's time.* [1590–1600; EMPLOY + -ER[1]]

em•ploy•ment (em ploi′mənt), *n.* **1.** an act or instance of employing someone or something. **2.** the state of being employed; employ; service: *to begin or terminate employment.* **3.** an occupation by which a person earns a living; work; business. **4.** the total number of people gainfully employed or working. **5.** an activity or the like that occupies a person's time: *She found knitting a comforting employment for her idle hours.* [1585–95; EMPLOY + -MENT]
—**Syn. 3.** vocation, calling; job, trade, profession.

employ′ment a′gency, an agency that helps find jobs for persons seeking employment or assists employers in finding persons to fill positions that are open. Also called **employ′ment bu′reau.** [1885–90, *Amer.*]

em•poi•son (em poi′zən), *v.t.* **1.** to corrupt: *to empoison the minds of the young.* **2.** to embitter: *His own failure has empoisoned him.* **3.** *Archaic.* to poison. [1275–1325; ME *empoysonen* < OF *empoisoner.* See EM-[1], POISON] —**em•poi′son•ment,** *n.*

Em•po•ri•a (em pôr′ē ə, -pōr′-), *n.* a city in E Kansas. 25,287.

em•po•ri•um (em pôr′ē əm, -pōr′-), *n., pl.* **-po•ri•ums, -po•ri•a** (-pôr′ē ə, -pōr′-). **1.** a large retail store, esp. one selling a great variety of articles. **2.** a place, town, or city of important commerce, esp. a principal center of trade: *New York is one of the world's great emporiums.* [1580–90; < L < Gk *empórion* market, emporium, equiv. to *émporos* merchant, orig. traveler, passenger (*em-* EM-[2] + *póros* passage, voyage; cf. *en pórōi* on a voyage, en route) + *-ion* n. suffix of place]
—**Syn. 1.** market, marketplace, bazaar.

em•pov•er•ish (em pov′ər ish, -pov′rish), *v.t. Obs.* impoverish.

em•pow•er (em pou′ər), *v.t.* **1.** to give power or au-

thority to; authorize, esp. by legal or official means: *I empowered my agent to make the deal for me. The local ordinance empowers the board of health to close unsanitary restaurants.* **2.** to enable or permit: *Wealth empowered him to live a comfortable life.* [1645–55; EM-[1] + POWER] **—em•pow′er•ment,** *n.*
—Syn. 1. warrant, commission, license, qualify.

em•press (em′pris), *n.* **1.** a female ruler of an empire. **2.** the consort of an emperor. [1125–75; ME *emperice, emperesse* < AF; OF *emperesse, empereriz* < L *imperātricem,* acc. of *imperātrix,* fem. of *imperātor.* See EMPEROR, -TRIX]
—Usage. See **-ess.**

em•presse•ment (äɴ pres mäɴ′), *n., pl.* ***-ments*** (-mäɴ′). *French.* display of cordiality.

em′press tree′. See **princess tree.**

em•prise (em prīz′), *n.* **1.** an adventurous enterprise. **2.** knightly daring or prowess. Also, **em•prize′.** [1250–1300; ME < AF, OF, n. use of fem. of *empris* (ptp. of *emprendre* to undertake), equiv. to *em-* EM-[1] + *pris* taken (see PRIZE[1])]

Emp•son (emp′sən), *n.* **William,** 1906–84, English critic and poet.

emp•tor (emp′tər, -tôr), *n.* (esp. in legal usage) a person who purchases or contracts to purchase; buyer. [1870–75; < L: buyer, equiv. to *em(ere)* to buy + *-tor* -TOR, with intrusive *-p-*]

emp•ty (emp′tē), *adj.,* **-ti•er, -ti•est,** *v.,* **-tied, -ty•ing,** *n., pl.* **-ties.** *—adj.* **1.** containing nothing; having none of the usual or appropriate contents: *an empty bottle.* **2.** vacant; unoccupied: *an empty house.* **3.** without cargo or load: *an empty wagon.* **4.** destitute of people or human activity: *We walked along the empty streets of the city at night.* **5.** destitute of some quality or qualities; devoid (usually fol. by *of*): *Theirs is a life now empty of happiness.* **6.** without force, effect, or significance; hollow; meaningless: *empty compliments; empty pleasures.* **7.** not employed in useful activity or work; idle: *empty summer days.* **8.** *Math.* (of a set) containing no elements; null; void. **9.** hungry: *I'm feeling rather empty—let's have lunch.* **10.** without knowledge or sense; frivolous; foolish: *an empty head.* **11.** completely spent of emotion: *The experience had left him with an empty heart.* *—v.t.* **12.** to make empty; deprive of contents; discharge the contents of: *to empty a bucket.* **13.** to discharge (contents): *to empty the water out of a bucket.* *—v.i.* **14.** to become empty: *The room emptied rapidly after the lecture.* **15.** to discharge contents, as a river: *The river empties into the sea.* *—n.* **16.** *Informal.* something that is empty, as a box, bottle, or can: *Throw the empties into the waste bin.* [bef. 900; ME (with intrusive *-p-*); OE *ǣmettig* vacant (*ǣmett(a)* leisure (*ǣ-* A-[3] + Gmc **mōtithō* accommodation; cf. MUST[1], MEET[1]) + *-ig* -Y[1])] **—emp′ti•a•ble,** *adj.* **—emp′ti•er,** *n.* **—emp′ti•ly,** *adv.* **—emp′ti•ness,** *n.*
—Syn. 1. vacuous. EMPTY, VACANT, BLANK, VOID denote absence of content or contents. EMPTY means without appropriate or accustomed contents: *an empty refrigerator.* VACANT is usually applied to that which is temporarily unoccupied: *a vacant chair; three vacant apartments.* BLANK applies to surfaces free from any marks or lacking appropriate markings, openings, etc.: *blank paper; a blank wall.* VOID emphasizes completely unfilled space with vague, unspecified, or no boundaries: *void and without form.* **6.** delusive, vain. **12.** unload, unburden. **—Ant. 1.** full.

emp′ty cal′orie, a calorie whose source has little or no nutritional value: *Junk food has only empty calories.* [1965–70, *Amer.*]

emp•ty-hand•ed (emp′tē han′did), *adj.* **1.** having nothing in the hands, as in doing no work: *While we were carrying out the luggage, he stood by empty-handed.* **2.** having gained nothing: *to return from a quest empty-handed.* **3.** bringing no gift, donation, etc.: *They came to the birthday party empty-handed.* [1605–15]

emp•ty-head•ed (emp′tē hed′id), *adj.* lacking intelligence or knowledge; foolish; brainless. [1640–50] **—emp′ty-head′ed•ness,** *n.*

emp′ty morph′, a morph, as the first *o* in *psychology,* which is considered to have no meaning and is not assigned to any morpheme.

emp′ty nest′er, a parent whose child or children have reached adulthood and moved away from home. [*empty nest* + -ER[1]]

emp′ty nest′ syn′drome, a depressed state felt by some parents after their children have left home. [1970–75]

Emp′ty Quar′ter. See **Rub′ al Khali.**

emp′ty word′, (esp. in Chinese grammar) a word or morpheme that has no lexical meaning and that functions as a grammatical link or marker, rather than as a contentive. Cf. **full word, function word.** [1890–95]

em•pur•ple (em pûr′pəl), *v.t., v.i.,* **-pled, -pling.** **1.** to color or become purple or purplish. **2.** to darken or redden; flush. [1580–90; EM-[1] + PURPLE]

em•py•e•ma (em′pē ē′mə, -pi-), *n. Pathol.* a collection of pus in a body cavity, esp. the pleural cavity. Also called **pyothorax.** [1605–15; < LL < Gk *empýēma* abscess, equiv. to *em-* EM-[2] + *pyē-* (var. s. of *pyeîn* to suppurate, akin to *pýon, pýos* pus) + *-ma* n. suffix denoting result of action] **—em′py•e′mic,** *adj.*

em•pyr•e•al (em pir′ē əl, -pī rē-, em′pə rē′əl, -pī-), *adj.* **1.** pertaining to the highest heaven in the cosmology of the ancients. **2.** pertaining to the sky; celestial: *empyreal blue.* **3.** formed of pure fire or light: *empyreal radiance.* Also, **empyrean.** [1475–85; < LL *empyre(us),* var. of *empyrius* (< Gk *empýrios* fiery, equiv. to *em-* EM-[2] + *pŷr* fire + *-ios* adj. suffix) + -AL[1]]

em•py•re•an (em′pə rē′ən, -pi-, em pir′ē ən, -pī′rē-), *n.* **1.** the highest heaven, supposed by the ancients to contain the pure element of fire. **2.** the visible heavens; the firmament. *—adj.* **3.** empyreal. [1605–15; < LL *empyre(us)* EMPYREAL + -AN]

em′ quad′, **1.** a square unit of area, one em on each side. **2.** a quad having such an area. Cf. **quad**[2] (def. 1). [1870–75]

EMS, **1.** emergency medical service. **2.** European Monetary System.

EMT, emergency medical technician.

e•mu (ē′myo͞o), *n.* a large, flightless, ratite bird, *Emu (Dromaius) novaehollandiae,* of Australia, resembling the ostrich but smaller and having a feathered head and neck and rudimentary wings. [1605–15; earlier *emeu* (in earliest E source *emia, eme*), ult. < Pg *ema,* attested in 1541 as a name for the cassowary (further orig. obscure); the replacement of *-a* by *-eu,* etc., is unexplained]

emu,
Emu novaehollandiae,
standing height 5 ft. (1.5 m);
length 6 ft. (1.8 m)

EMU, **1.** Also, **emu** See **electromagnetic unit.** **2.** *Aerospace.* See **extravehicular mobility unit.**

em•u•late (*v.* em′yə lāt′; *adj.* em′yə lit), *v.,* **-lat•ed, -lat•ing,** *adj.* *—v.t.* **1.** to try to equal or excel; imitate with effort to equal or surpass: *to emulate one's father as a concert violinist.* **2.** to rival with some degree of success: *Some smaller cities now emulate the major capitals in their cultural offerings.* **3.** *Computers.* **a.** to imitate (a particular computer system) by using a software system, often including a microprogram or another computer that enables it to do the same work, run the same programs, etc., as the first. **b.** to replace (software) with hardware to perform the same task. *—adj.* **4.** *Obs.* emulous. [1580–90; < L *aemulātus,* ptp. of *aemulārī* to rival. See EMULOUS, -ATE[1]] **—em′u•la′tive,** *adj.* **—em′u•la′tive•ly,** *adv.* **—em′u•la′tor,** *n.*
—Syn. 1. follow, copy.

em•u•la•tion (em′yə lā′shən), *n.* **1.** effort or desire to equal or excel others. **2.** *Obs.* jealous rivalry. [1545–55; < L *aemulātiōn-* (s. of *aemulātiō*). See EMULATE, -ION]
—Syn. 1. imitation, competition.

e•mul•gens (i mul′jənz), *n.* (in prescriptions) an emulsifying agent. [< L, prp. of *ēmulgēre;* see EMULSION]

em•u•lous (em′yə ləs), *adj.* **1.** desirous of equaling or excelling; filled with emulation: *boys emulous of their fathers.* **2.** arising from or of the nature of emulation, as actions or attitudes. **3.** *Obs.* jealous; envious. [1350–1400; ME < L *aemulus* vying with; see -ULOUS] **—em′u•lous•ly,** *adv.* **—em′u•lous•ness,** *n.*

emuls., (in prescriptions) an emulsion. [< L *ēmulsiō*]

e•mul•si•fy (i mul′sə fī′), *v.t., v.i.,* **-fied, -fy•ing.** to make into or form an emulsion. [1855–60; < L *ēmuls(us)* (see EMULSION) + -IFY] **—e•mul′si•fi′a•ble, e•mul′si•ble,** *adj.* **—e•mul′si•fi′a•bil′i•ty, e•mul′si•bil′i•ty,** *n.* **—e•mul′si•fi•ca′tion,** *n.* **—e•mul′si•fi′er,** *n.*

e•mul•sion (i mul′shən), *n.* **1.** *Physical Chem.* any colloidal suspension of a liquid in another liquid. **2.** such a suspension used in cosmetics. **3.** *Pharm.* a liquid preparation consisting of two completely immiscible liquids, one of which, as minute globules coated by a gum or other mucilaginous substance, is dispersed throughout the other: used as a means of making a medicine palatable. **4.** *Photog.* a composition sensitive to some or all of the actinic rays of light, consisting of one or more of the silver halides suspended in gelatin, applied in a thin layer to one surface of a film or the like. [1605–15; < NL *ēmulsiōn-* (s. of *ēmulsiō*), equiv. to L *ēmuls(us)* milked out (*ē-* E- + *mulsus,* ptp. of *mulgēre* to milk) + *-iōn-* -ION] **—e•mul′sive,** *adj.*

e•mul•soid (i mul′soid), *n. Physical Chem.* a sol having a liquid disperse phase. Cf. **suspensoid.** [1905–10; < L *ēmuls(us)* (see EMULSION) + -OID] **—e•mul•soi•dal** (i mul soid′l, ē′mul-), *adj.*

e•munc•to•ry (i mungk′tə rē), *n., pl.* **-ries,** *adj. Physiol.* *—n.* **1.** a part or organ of the body, as the skin or a kidney, that functions in carrying off waste products. *—adj.* **2.** excretory. [1535–45; < NL *ēmunctōrium* (n.), *ēmunctōrius* (adj.), equiv. to L *ēmung(ere)* to wipe one's nose (*ē-* E- + *-mungere,* akin to *mūcus* MUCUS) + *-tōrium* -TORY[2], *-tōrius* -TORY[1]]

en (en), *n.* **1.** the letter *N, n.* **2.** Also called **nut.** *Print.* half of the width of an em. *—adj.* **3.** *Print.* having the area of an en quad or the length of an en: *en quad; en dash.* [1785–95]

en-[1], a prefix occurring originally in loanwords from French and productive in English on this model, forming verbs with the general sense "to cause (a person or thing) to be in" the place, condition, or state named by the stem; more specifically, "to confine in or place on" (*enshrine; enthrone; entomb*); "to cause to be in" (*enslave; entrust; enrich; encourage; endear*); "to restrict" in the manner named by the stem, typically with the additional sense "on all sides, completely" (*enwind; encircle; enclose; entwine*). This prefix is also attached to verbs in order to make them transitive, or to give them a transitive marker if they are already transitive (*enkindle; enliven; enshield; enface*). Also, *before labial consonants,* **em-**[1]. Cf. **be-, in-**[2]. [ME < OF < L *in-* IN-[2]]

en-[2], a prefix meaning "within, in," occurring in loanwords from Greek: *energy; enthusiasm.* Also, *before labial consonants,* **em-**[2]. [< Gk (often through L); c. IN-[1], IN-[2]]

-en[1], a suffix formerly used to form transitive and intransitive verbs from adjectives (*fasten; harden; sweeten*), or from nouns (*heighten; lengthen; strengthen*). [ME, OE *-n-* (as in ME *fast-n-en,* OE *fæst-n-ian* to make fast, fasten); c. *-n-* of like verbs in other Gmc languages (ON *fastna*)]

-en[2], a suffix used to form adjectives of source or material from nouns: *ashen; golden; oaken.* [ME, OE; c. OHG *-īn,* Goth *-eins,* L *-inus;* see -INE[1]]

-en[3], a suffix used to mark the past participle in many strong and some weak verbs: *taken; proven.* [ME, OE; c. G *-en,* ON *-inn*]

-en[4], a suffix used in forming the plural of some nouns: *brethren; children; oxen.* [ME; OE *-an,* case ending of n-stem nouns, as in *naman* obl. sing., and nom. and acc. pl. of *nama* name; akin to n-stem forms in other IE languages, as in L *nōmen, nōmin-* name]

-en[5], a diminutive suffix: *kitten; maiden.* [ME, OE, from neut. of -EN[2]]

en•a•ble (en ā′bəl), *v.t.,* **-bled, -bling.** **1.** to make able; give power, means, competence, or ability to; authorize: *This document will enable him to pass through the enemy lines unmolested.* **2.** to make possible or easy: *Aeronautics enables us to overcome great distances.* [1375–1425; ME; see EN-[1], ABLE] **—en•a′bler,** *n.*
—Syn. 1. empower, qualify, allow, permit.

en•a•bling (en ā′bling), *adj. Law.* conferring new legal powers or capacities, esp. by removing a disability; having the right to license or regulate: *an enabling act; enabling power.* [1670–80; ENABLE + -ING[2]]

en•act (en akt′), *v.t.* **1.** to make into an act or statute: *Congress has enacted a new tax law.* **2.** to represent on or as on the stage; act the part of: *to enact Hamlet.* [1375–1425; late ME *enacten.* See EN-[1], ACT] **—en•act′a•ble,** *adj.* **—en•ac′tor,** *n.*

en•ac•tive (en ak′tiv), *adj.* having power to enact or establish, as a law. [1650–60; ENACT + -IVE]

en•act•ment (en akt′mənt), *n.* **1.** the act of enacting. **2.** the state or fact of being enacted. **3.** something that is enacted; a law or statute. **4.** a single provision of a law. [1810–20; ENACT + -MENT]

en•ac•to•ry (en ak′tə rē), *adj. Law.* of or pertaining to an enactment that creates new rights and obligations. [1835–45; ENACT + -ORY[1]]

en•al•la•ge (en al′ə jē), *n. Rhet.* the use of one grammatical form in place of another, as the plural for the singular in the editorial use of *we.* [1575–85; < LL < Gk *enallagḗ* an interchange, deriv. from base of *enallássein* to give in exchange; cf. EN-[2], AGIO]

e•nam•el (i nam′əl), *n., v.,* **-eled, -el•ing** or (*esp. Brit.*) **-elled, -el•ling.** *—n.* **1.** a glassy substance, usually opaque, applied by fusion to the surface of metal, pottery, etc., as an ornament or for protection. **2.** enamelware. **3.** any of various varnishes, paints, coatings, etc., drying to a hard, glossy finish. **4.** any enamellike surface with a bright luster. **5.** an artistic work executed in enamel. **6.** *Dentistry.* the hard, glossy, calcareous covering of the crown of a tooth, containing only a slight amount of organic substance. See diag. under **tooth.** *—v.t.* **7.** to inlay or overlay with enamel. **8.** to form an enamellike surface upon: *to enamel cardboard.* **9.** to decorate as with enamel; variegate with colors. [1275–1325; ME *enamelen* < AF *enameler, enamailler,* equiv. to *en-* EN-[1] + *-amaler,* deriv. of *asmal, esmal* enamel, OF *esmail* (*-al* taken as the suffix *-ail*) < Old Low Franconian **smalt-* something melted, c. G *Schmalz* fat; akin to SMELT[1]; cf. SMALTO] **—e•nam′el•er;** *esp. Brit.,* **e•nam′el•ler,** *n.* **—e•nam′el•ist;** *esp. Brit.,* **e•nam′el•list,** *n.* **—e•nam′el•work′,** *n.*

e•nam•el•ing (i nam′ə ling), *n.* **1.** the art, act, or work of a person who enamels. **2.** a decoration or coating of enamel. Also, *esp. Brit.,* **e•nam′el•ling.** [1400–50; late ME; see ENAMEL, -ING[1]]

e•nam•el•ware (i nam′əl wâr′), *n.* metalware, as cooking utensils, covered with an enamel surface. [1900–05; ENAMEL + WARE[1]]

en a•mi (ä nᴀ mē′), *French.* as a friend: *to confide in someone en ami.*

en•am•or (i nam′ər), *v.t.* **1.** to fill or inflame with love (usually used in the passive and fol. by *of* or sometimes *with*): *to be enamored of a certain lady; a brilliant woman with whom he became enamored.* **2.** to charm or captivate. Also, *esp. Brit.,* **en•am′our.** [1350–1400; ME *enamouren* < OF *enamourer.* See EN-[1], AMOUR] **—en•am′ored•ness;** *esp. Brit.,* **en•am′oured•ness,** *n.*
—Syn. 2. fascinate, bewitch, enchant, enrapture.

enantio-, a combining form meaning "opposite," "opposing," used in the formation of compound words: *enantiomorph.* [< Gk, comb. form of *enantíos.* See EN-[2], ANTI-]

en•an•ti•o•mer (i nan′tē ə mər), *n. Chem.* either of a pair of optical isomers that are mirror images of each other. Cf. **diastereoisomer.** [ENANTIO- + -MER]

en•an•ti•o•morph (i nan′tē ə môrf′), *n. Crystall.* either of two crystals exhibiting enantiomorphism. [< G (1856); see ENANTIO-, -MORPH]

en•an•ti•o•mor•phism (i nan′tē ə môr′fiz əm), *n. Crystall.* the existence of two chemically identical crystal forms as mirror images of each other. [1895–1900; ENANTIOMORPH + -ISM] **—en•an′ti•o•mor′phic, en•an′ti•o•mor′phous,** *adj.*

en•an•ti•o•sis (i nan′tē ō′sis), *n., pl.* **-ses** (-sēz). *Rhet.* a figure of speech in which what is meant is the opposite of what is said; irony. [1650–60; < Gk *enantíōsis.* See ENANTIO-, -OSIS]

en•an•ti•ot•ro•py (i nan′tē o′trə pē), *n. Crystall.* polymorphism in which one of the polymorphs may revert to the state of the other at a critical temperature and pressure. Cf. **monotropy.** [< G *Enantiotropie* (1888) < Gk *enantiotropía* contrariety of character. See ENANTIO-, -TROPY] —**en·an·ti·o·trop·ic** (i nan′tē ə-trop′ik, -trō′pik), *adj.*

en·ar·gite (en är′jīt, en′ər jīt′), *n.* a mineral, copper arsenic and sulfide, Cu_3AsS_4, occurring in the form of black orthorhombic crystals having perfect cleavage: an important source of copper. [1850–55; < Gk *enarg(és)* brilliant (*en-* EN-[2] + *-argēs*, akin to *argós* bright, *árgyros* silver) + -ITE[1]]

en·ar·thro·sis (en′är thrō′sis), *n., pl.* **-ses** (-sēz). *Anat., Zool.* See **ball-and-socket joint.** [1625–35; < NL < Gk *enárthrōsis;* see EN-[2], ARTHROSIS[1]] —**en·ar·thro·di·al** (en′är thrō′dē əl), *adj.*

e·nate (ē′nāt), *n.* **1.** a person related on one's mother's side. Cf. **agnate, cognate.** —*adj.* **2.** Also, **e·nat·ic** (ē nat′ik). related on one's mother's side. [< L *ēnātus,* ptp. of *ēnāscī* to issue forth, be born]

e·na·tion (ē nā′shən), *n. Bot.* a small outgrowth of plant tissue, usually on a leaf, caused by virus infection. [1835–45; < L *ēnāt(us)* sprouted, sprung forth (see ENATE) + -ION]

en bloc (äɴ blôk′; *Eng.* en blok′), *French.* as a whole.

en brosse (äɴ brôs′), *French.* (of hair) cut to stand straight in an even row on top, often as a crew cut.

enc., **1.** enclosed. **2.** enclosure. **3.** encyclopedia. [1900–05]

en·cae·nia (en sēn′yə, -sē′nē ə), *n.* **1.** (*used with a plural v.*) festive ceremonies commemorating the founding of a city or the consecration of a church. **2.** (*often cap.*) (*often used with a singular v.*) ceremonies at Oxford University in honor of founders and benefactors. [1350–1400; ME < LL < Gk *enkaínia* (neut. pl.), equiv. to *en-* EN-[2] + *-kainia,* deriv. of *kainós* new]

en·cage (en kāj′), *v.t.,* **-caged, -cag·ing.** to confine in or as in a cage; coop up. Also, **incage.** [1585–95; EN-[1] + CAGE]

en·camp (en kamp′), *v.i.* **1.** to settle or lodge in a camp. —*v.t.* **2.** to make into a camp. **3.** to lodge or place in a camp. [1540–50; EN-[1] + CAMP[1]]

en·camp·ment (en kamp′mənt), *n.* **1.** an act or instance of encamping; lodgment in a camp. **2.** the place or quarters occupied in camping; camp. [1590–1600; ENCAMP + -MENT]

en·cap·su·late (en kap′sə lāt′, -syŏŏ-), *v.,* **-lat·ed, -lat·ing.** —*v.t.* **1.** to place in or as if in a capsule. **2.** to summarize or condense. —*v.i.* **3.** to become enclosed in or as if in a capsule. [1860–65; EN-[1] + CAPSULATE] —**en·cap′su·la′tion,** *n.*

en·cap·sule (en kap′səl, -syōōl), *v.t., v.i.,* **-suled, -sul·ing.** encapsulate. [1875–80; EN-[1] + CAPSULE]

En·car·na·ción (eng′kär nä syôn′), *n.* a city in SE Paraguay, on the Paraná River. 24,211.

en·car·nal·ize (en kär′nl īz′), *v.t.,* **-ized, -iz·ing.** to invest with a worldly or sensual nature or form; make carnal: *the soul encarnalized by the gross body.* Also, **incarnalize.** Also, *esp. Brit.,* **en·car′nal·ise′.** [1840–50; EN-[1] + CARNAL + -IZE]

en·car·pus (en kär′pəs), *n., pl.* **-pi** (-pī). an ornament having draperies, weapons, etc., arranged in the manner of a festoon. [< Gk *énkarpos* containing fruit (see EN-[2], -CARPOUS); r. *encarpe* < Gk *énkarpa,* neut. pl. of *énkarpos*]

en car·ré (äɴ kä ʀā′), *French.* (of a bet in roulette) placed at the intersection of four numbers so as to share in any that wins. [lit., squared]

en·case (en kās′), *v.t.,* **-cased, -cas·ing.** to enclose in or as in a case: *We encased the ancient vase in glass to preserve it.* Also, **incase.** [1625–35; EN-[1] + CASE[2]]

en·case·ment (en kās′mənt), *n.* **1.** the act of encasing. **2.** the state of being encased. **3.** something that encases; case. Also, **incasement.** [1735–45; ENCASE + -MENT]

en·caus·tic (en kô′stik), *adj.* **1.** painted with wax colors fixed with heat, or with any process in which colors are burned in. —*n.* **2.** a work of art produced by an encaustic process. [1650–60; < L *encausticus* < Gk *enkaustikós* for burning in. See EN-[2], CAUSTIC] —**en·caus′ti·cal·ly,** *adv.*

-ence, a noun suffix equivalent to **-ance,** corresponding to the suffix **-ent** in adjectives: *abstinence; continence; dependence; difference.* [ME < OF < L *-entia,* equiv. to *-ent-* -ENT + *-ia* -Y[3]]

en·ceinte[1] (en sānt′, än sant′; *Fr.* äɴ saɴt′), *adj.* pregnant; with child. [1590–1600; < MF < LL *incincta,* perh. lit. "ungirded," equiv. to L *in-* IN-[3] + *cincta,* fem. of *cinctus,* ptp. of *cingere* to belt, gird, surround]

en·ceinte[2] (en sānt′, än sant′; *Fr.* äɴ saɴt′), *n., pl.* **-ceintes** (-sānts′, -sants′; *Fr.* -saɴt′). **1.** a wall or enclosure, as of a fortified place. **2.** the place enclosed. [1700–10; < F: enclosure, also girding fence or rampart < L *incincta,* n. use of fem. of *incinctus* girded in (ptp. of *incingere*), equiv. to *in-* IN-[2] + *cing-* gird + *-tus* ptp. suffix]

En·cel·a·dus (en sel′ə dəs), *n.* **1.** *Class. Myth.* a giant with a hundred arms buried under Mount Etna, in Sicily. **2.** *Astron.* a natural satellite of the planet Saturn.

encephal-, var. of **encephalo-** before a vowel: *encephalic.*

en·ceph·a·lal·gi·a (en sef′ə lal′jē ə), *n. Med.* headache (def. 1). [ENCEPHAL- + -ALGIA]

en·ceph·a·las·the·ni·a (en sef′ə ləs thē′nē ə), *n. Pathol.* mental fatigue caused by emotional stress. [ENCEPHAL- + ASTHENIA]

en·ce·phal·ic (en′sə fal′ik), *adj.* of or pertaining to the encephalon or brain. [1825–35; ENCEPHAL- + -IC]

en·ceph·a·li·tis (en sef′ə lī′tis), *n. Pathol.* **1.** inflammation of the substance of the brain. **2.** Also called **encephali′tis le·thar′gi·ca** (li thär′ji kə). a form of this condition, caused by a filterable virus and characterized by apathy and abnormal sleepiness; sleeping sickness. [1835–45; ENCEPHAL- + -ITIS] —**en·ceph·a·lit·ic** (en-sef′ə lit′ik), *adj.*

encephalo-, a combining form meaning "brain," used in the formation of compound words: *encephalograph.* Also, *esp. before a vowel,* **encephal-.** [< Gk *enképhalos.* See ENCEPHALON]

en·ceph·a·lo·gram (en sef′ə lə gram′), *n. Med.* an x-ray of the brain, usually involving replacement of some cerebrospinal fluid by air or other gas that circulates to the brain's ventricular spaces and acts as a contrast medium. [1925–30; ENCEPHALO- + -GRAM[1]]

en·ceph·a·lo·graph (en sef′ə lə graf′, -gräf′), *n. Med.* **1.** an encephalogram. **2.** an electroencephalograph. [1930–35; ENCEPHALO- + -GRAPH] —**en·ceph·a·lo·graph·ic** (en sef′ə lə graf′ik), *adj.* —**en·ceph′a·lo·graph′i·cal·ly,** *adv.* —**en·ceph·a·log·ra·phy** (en sef′ə log′rə fē), *n.*

en·ceph·a·lo·ma (en sef′ə lō′mə), *n., pl.* **-mas, -ma·ta** (-mə tə). *Pathol.* **1.** a brain tumor. **2.** hernia of the brain. [ENCEPHAL- + -OMA]

en·ceph·a·lo·ma·la·cia (en sef′ə lō mə lā′shə, -shē ə), *n. Pathol.* a softness or degeneration of brain tissue, as caused by impairment of the blood supply; softening of the brain. [1835–45; < NL; see ENCEPHALO-, MALACIA]

en·ceph·a·lo·my·e·li·tis (en sef′ə lō mī′ə lī′tis), *n. Pathol.* inflammation of the brain and spinal cord. [1905–10; ENCEPHALO- + MYELITIS] —**en·ceph·a·lo·my·e·lit·ic** (en sef′ə lō mī′ə lit′ik), *adj.*

en·ceph·a·lo·my·o·car·di·tis (en sef′ə lō mī′ō kär-dī′tis), *n. Pathol.* a viral infection of the central nervous system and skeletal and heart muscle causing degeneration of tissue. [1945–50; ENCEPHALO- + MYOCARDITIS]

en·ceph·a·lon (en sef′ə lon′, -lən), *n., pl.* **-la** (-lə). *Anat.* the brain. [1735–45; < NL, alter. (*-on* for *-os*) of Gk *enképhalos* (adj.) within the head, as masc. n., brain; see EN-[2], -CEPHALOUS]

en·ceph·a·lop·a·thy (en sef′ə lop′ə thē), *n. Psychiatry.* any brain disease. [1865–70; ENCEPHALO- + -PATHY]

en·ceph·a·lo·sis (en sef′ə lō′sis), *n. Pathol.* organic disease of the brain. [ENCEPHAL- + -OSIS]

en·ceph·a·lot·o·my (en sef′ə lot′ə mē), *n., pl.* **-mies.** surgical incision or dissection of the brain. [ENCEPHALO- + -TOMY]

en·chain (en chān′), *v.t.* **1.** to bind in or as in chain or chains; fetter; restrain: *to be enchained by ignorance and superstition.* **2.** to hold fast, as the attention. [1350–1400; ME < AF, OF *enchainer, enchaener.* See EN-[1], CHAIN] —**en·chain′ment,** *n.*

en·chaîne·ment (*Fr.* äɴ shen mäɴ′), *n., pl.* **-ments** (*Fr.* -mäɴ′). *Ballet.* a series of steps constituting a phrase. [1820–30; < F; see ENCHAIN, -MENT]

en·chant (en chant′, -chänt′), *v.t.* **1.** to subject to magical influence; bewitch: *fairytales about witches who enchant handsome princes and beautiful maidens.* **2.** to delight to a high degree: *Her gaiety and wit have enchanted us all.* **3.** to impart a magic quality or effect to. [1325–75; ME < AF, MF *enchanter* < L *incantāre* to put a spell on; see INCANTATION]
—**Syn. 2.** fascinate, attract; captivate, enrapture.

en·chant·er (en chan′tər, -chän′-), *n.* **1.** a person who enchants or delights. **2.** a magician; sorcerer. [1250–1300; ENCHANT + -ER[1]; r. ME *enchantour* < AF; OF *enchanteor* < LL *incantātor,* equiv. to L *incantā(re)* (see INCANTATION) + *-tor* -TOR]

enchant′er's night′shade, any of several plants belonging to the genus *Circaea,* of the evening primrose family, of cool and temperate regions of the Northern Hemisphere, having white flowers. [1590–1600]

en·chant·ing (en chan′ting, -chän′-), *adj.* charming; captivating: *an enchanting smile.* [1545–55; ENCHANT + -ING[2]] —**en·chant′ing·ly,** *adv.*

en·chant·ment (en chant′mənt, -chänt′-), *n.* **1.** the art, act, or an instance of enchanting. **2.** the state of being enchanted. **3.** something that enchants: *Music is an enchantment that never fails.* [1250–1300; ME *enchantement* < AF, OF < L *incantāmentum.* See ENCHANT, -MENT]
—**Syn. 1.** magic, sorcery, fascination, witchery. **3.** spell, charm.

en·chant·ress (en chan′tris, -chän′-), *n.* **1.** a woman who practices magic; sorceress. **2.** an irresistibly charming or fascinating woman: *an enchantress who breaks men's hearts.* [1325–75; ME *enchanteresse* < AF, MF. See ENCHANTER, -ESS]
—**Syn. 1.** witch, siren. **2.** seductress, temptress, vamp, charmer.
—**Usage.** See **-ess.**

en·chase (en chās′), *v.t.,* **-chased, -chas·ing. 1.** to place (gems) in an ornamental setting. **2.** to decorate with inlay, embossing, or engraving. [1425–75; late ME < MF *enchasser* to case in, equiv. to *en-* EN-[1] + *-chasser,* deriv. of *chasse* CASE[2]] —**en·chas′er,** *n.*

en·chi·la·da (en′chə lä′də, -lad′ə), *n. Mexican Cookery.* **1.** a tortilla rolled and filled with a seasoned mixture, usually containing meat, and covered with a sauce flavored with chili. **2. big** or **top enchilada,** *Slang.* someone regarded as the most important, influential, or dominant person in an organization: *The police are hoping to catch the syndicate's big enchilada in the next raid.* **3. whole enchilada,** *Slang.* the entirety of something, esp. something impressive or outstanding: *She has a job with money, prestige, and satisfaction—the whole enchilada.* [1885–90; < AmerSp, fem. of Sp *enchilado* spiced with chili (ptp. of *enchilar*), equiv. to *en-* EN-[1] + *chil(e)* CHILI + *-ado* -ATE[1]]

en·chi·rid·i·on (en′kī rid′ē ən, -ki-), *n., pl.* **-rid·i·ons, -rid·i·a** (-rid′ē ə). a handbook; manual. [1535–45; < LL < Gk *encheirídion* handbook, equiv. to *en-* EN-[2] + *cheír* hand + *-idion* dim. suffix]

en·chon·dro·ma (en′kən drō′mə), *n., pl.* **-mas, -ma·ta** (-mə tə). *Pathol.* a growth of cartilage within the shaft or substance of a bone. [1840–50; < NL < Gk *en-* EN-[2] + *chóndr(os)* cartilage + *-ōma* -OMA] —**en·chon·drom·a·tous** (en′kən drom′ə təs, -drō′mə-), *adj.*

en·cho·ri·al (en kôr′ē əl, -kōr′-), *adj.* (esp. of demotic writing) belonging to or used in a particular country. Also, **en·chor·ic** (en kôr′ik, -kor′-). [1815–25; < LL *enchōri(us)* (< Gk *enchṓrios* native, equiv. to *en-* EN-[2] + *chṓr(ā)* country + *-ios* adj. suffix) + -AL[1]]

en·ci·na (en sē′nə), *n.* **1.** the live oak, *Quercus virginiana.* **2.** See **California live oak.** [1905–10, *Amer.;* < AmerSp, Sp: holm oak, by syncope, shortening, and assimilation < LL *īlicīna* holm oak, orig. fem. of *īlicīnus* pertaining to holm oak, equiv. to L *īlic-* (s. of *īlex*) ILEX + *-inus* -INE[1]] —**en·ci′nal,** *adj.*

En·ci·na (en thē′nä, -sē′), *n.* **Juan del** (hwän del), 1468?–1529?, Spanish poet, composer, and playwright.

en·cinc·ture (en singk′chər), *v.,* **-tured, -tur·ing,** *v.t.* to gird or encompass with or as with a belt or girdle: *A ring of hills encinctures the town.* [1805–15; EN-[1] + CINCTURE]

en·ci·pher (en sī′fər), *v.t.* to convert (a message, communication, etc.) into cipher. [1570–80; EN-[1] + CIPHER] —**en·ci′pher·er,** *n.* —**en·ci′pher·ment,** *n.*

en·cir·cle (en sûr′kəl), *v.t.,* **-cled, -cling. 1.** to form a circle around; surround; encompass: *to encircle an enemy.* **2.** to make a circling movement around; make the circuit of. [1350–1400; ME; see EN-[1], CIRCLE] —**en·cir′cle·ment,** *n.*

En′cke's com′et (eng′kəz, -kēz), a comet, discovered by J.L. Pons, with a period of 3.3 years, the shortest period known. [named after Johann F. *Encke* (1791–1865), German astronomer]

En′cke's divi′sion, *Astron.* a dark region within the outer major ring of Saturn. [see ENCKE'S COMET]

encl., **1.** enclosed. **2.** enclosure.

en clair (äɴ kler′), *French.* (esp. of diplomatic messages) in ordinary language; not written or sent in code or cipher. [lit., in clear]

en·clasp (en klasp′, -kläsp′), *v.t.* to hold in or as in a clasp or embrace. Also, **inclasp.** [1590–1600; EN-[1] + CLASP]

en·clave (en′klāv, än′-), *n., v.,* **-claved, -clav·ing.** —*n.* **1.** a country, or esp., an outlying portion of a country, entirely or mostly surrounded by the territory of another country. **2.** any small, distinct area or group enclosed or isolated within a larger one: *a Chinese-speaking enclave in London.* —*v.t.* **3.** to isolate or enclose (esp. territory) within a foreign or uncongenial environment; make an enclave of: *The desert enclaved the little settlement.* [1865–70; < F, MF, n. deriv. of *enclaver* < VL **inclāvāre* to lock in, equiv. to L *in-* IN-[2] + *clāv(is)* key + *-āre* inf. suffix]

en·clit·ic (en klit′ik), *adj.* **1.** (of a word) closely connected in pronunciation with the preceding word and not having an independent accent or phonological status. —*n.* **2.** an enclitic word, as Latin *que* "and" in *arma virumque,* "arms and the man." [1650–60; < LL *encliticus* < Gk *enklitikós,* equiv. to *en-* EN-[2] + *klít(os)* slope + *-ikos* -IC] —**en·clit′i·cal·ly,** *adv.*

en·close (en klōz′), *v.t.,* **-closed, -clos·ing. 1.** to shut or hem in; close in on all sides: *a valley enclosed by tall mountains.* **2.** to surround, as with a fence or wall: *to enclose land.* **3.** to insert in the same envelope, package, or the like: *He enclosed a check. A book was sent with the bill enclosed.* **4.** to hold or contain: *His letter enclosed a check.* **5.** *Rom. Cath. Ch.* **a.** to restrict to the enclosure of a monastery or convent. **b.** (of a monastery, convent, church, etc.) to establish or fix the boundary of an enclosure. Also, **inclose.** [1275–1325; ME *en-, inclosen.* See IN-[1], CLOSE] —**en·clos′a·ble,** *adj.* —**en·clos′er,** *n.*
—**Syn. 1, 2.** encircle, encompass, ring, girdle.

en·clo·sure (en klō′zhər), *n.* **1.** something that encloses, as a fence or wall. **2.** something that is enclosed, as a paper sent in a letter. **3.** the separation and appropriation of land by means of a fence. **4.** a tract of land surrounded by a fence. **5.** an act or instance of enclosing. **6.** the state of being enclosed. **7.** *Rom. Cath. Ch.* the part of a monastery or convent canonically separated or restricted as the living quarters of the religious, from which a person may leave only with special permission or gain entrance to by special dispensation. Also, **inclosure.** [1530–40; ENCLOSE + -URE; cf. AF *enclosure*]

enclo′sure act′, *Eng. Hist.* any of the acts of Parliament passed from 1709 to 1869, requiring that private lands be fenced off from common lands. [1880–85]

en·clothe (en klōth′), *v.t.,* **-clothed, -cloth·ing.** clothe (def. 3). [1825–35; EN-[1] + CLOTHE]

en·code (en kōd′), *v.t.,* **-cod·ed, -cod·ing.** to convert (a message, information, etc.) into code. [1930–35; EN-[1] + CODE] —**en·cod′a·ble,** *adj.* —**en·code′ment,** *n.* —**en·cod′er,** *n.*

en·coi·gnure (en kon′yər, -koin′-, än-; *Fr.* äɴ kô-nyʏʀ′), *n., pl.* **-coi·gnures** (-kon′yərz, -koin′-; *Fr.* -kô-nyʏʀ′). *Fr. Furniture.* a low corner cabinet. [1840–50; < F; see EN-[1], COIGN, -URE]

en·col·pi·on (en kōl′pē ən, en kol′pē on′), *n., pl.* **-pi·a** (-pē ə). *Eastern Ch.* a pectoral medallion bearing the image of Christ or the Virgin Mary, worn by bishops. Also, **enkolpion.** [< MGk *enkólpion;* Gk, n. use of neut. of *enkólpios* of the bosom, equiv. to *en-* EN-[2] + *kólp(os)* bosom, lap + *-ios* adj. suffix]

en·co·mi·ast (en kō′mē ast′, -əst), *n.* a person who utters or writes an encomium; eulogist. [1600–10; < Gk

CONCISE ETYMOLOGY KEY: <, descended or borrowed from; >, whence; b., blend of, blended; c., cognate with; cf., compare; deriv., derivative; equiv., equivalent; imit., imitative; obl., oblique; r., replacing; s., stem; sp., spelling, spelled; resp., respelling, respelled; trans., translation; ?, origin unknown; *, unattested; ‡, probably earlier than. See the full key inside the front cover.

enkōmiast(ḗs), equiv. to *enkōmi(on)* ENCOMIUM + *-astēs* agent n. suffix] **—en·co′mi·as′tic,** *adj.* **—en·co′mi·as′ti·cal·ly,** *adv.*

en·co·mi·en·da (en kō′mē en′də, -kom′ē-; *Sp.* eng′-kô myen′dä), *n., pl.* **-das** (-dəz; *Sp.* -däs). (formerly in Spanish America) **1.** the system, instituted in 1503, under which a Spanish soldier or colonist was granted a tract of land or a village together with its Indian inhabitants. **2.** the land or village together with its inhabitants. [1800–10; < Sp: charge, commission, recommendation. See EN-[1], COMMEND]

en·co·mi·um (en kō′mē əm), *n., pl.* **-mi·ums, -mi·a** (-mē ə). a formal expression of high praise; eulogy: *An encomium by the President greeted the returning hero.* [1580–90; < L < Gk *enkṓmion,* equiv. to *en-* EN-[2] + *kōm(os)* a revel + *-ion* n. suffix]

en·com·pass (en kum′pəs), *v.t.* **1.** to form a circle about; encircle; surround: *He built a moat to encompass the castle.* **2.** to enclose; envelop: *The folds of a great cloak encompassed her person.* **3.** to include comprehensively: *a work that encompasses the entire range of the world's religious beliefs.* **4.** *Obs.* to outwit. [1545–55; EN-[1] + COMPASS] **—en·com′pass·ment,** *n.*

en·co·pre·sis (en′kə prē′sis), *n., pl.* **-ses** (-sēz). *Psychiatry.* involuntary defecation. [< NL < Gk *en-* EN-[2] + *kópr(os)* dung + *-esis,* as in ENURESIS] **—en·co·pret·ic** (en′kə pret′ik), *adj.*

en·core (äng′kôr, -kōr, än′-), *interj., n., v.,* **-cored, -cor·ing.** *—interj.* **1.** again; once more (used by an audience in calling for an additional number or piece). *—n.* **2.** a demand, as by applause, for a repetition of a song, act, etc., or for a performance of a number or piece additional to those on a program, or for a reappearance by the performers, as at the end of a concert, recital, etc. **3.** the performance or reappearance in response to such a demand: *He chose a Chopin nocturne for his encore.* **4.** any repeated or additional performance or appearance, as a rerun of a telecast or a rematch in sports. *—v.t.* **5.** to call for a repetition of. **6.** to call for an encore from (a performer). [1705–15; < F: still, yet, besides < L *hinc hā hōrā* or *hinc ad hōram* until this hour]

en·coun·ter (en koun′tər), *v.t.* **1.** to come upon or meet with, esp. unexpectedly: *to encounter a new situation.* **2.** to meet with or contend against (difficulties, opposition, etc.): *We encounter so many problems in our work.* **3.** to meet (a person, military force, etc.) in conflict: *We will encounter the enemy at dawn.* *—v.i.* **4.** to meet, esp. unexpectedly or in conflict: *We were angry when we encountered, but we parted with smiles.* *—n.* **5.** a meeting with a person or thing, esp. a casual, unexpected, or brief meeting: *Our running into each other was merely a chance encounter.* **6.** a meeting of persons or groups that are in conflict or opposition; combat; battle: *Another such encounter and we may lose the war.* **7.** *Psychol.* a meeting of two or more people, as the members of an encounter group or a number of married couples **(marriage encounter),** conducted to promote direct emotional confrontations among the participants, esp. as a form of therapy **(encoun′ter ther′apy).** [1250–1300; ME *encountren* < AF *enco(u)ntrer;* OF < VL **incontrāre,* equiv. to *in-* IN-[2] + *-contrāre,* deriv. of *contrā* against; see COUNTER[3]] **—en·coun′ter·er,** *n.*

encoun′ter group′, *Psychol.* a group of people who meet, usually with a trained leader, to increase self-awareness and social sensitivity, and to change behavior through interpersonal confrontation, self-disclosure, and strong emotional expression. [1965–70]

encoun′ter ses′sion, *Psychol.* a meeting of an encounter group.

en·cour·age (en kûr′ij, -kur′-), *v.t.,* **-aged, -ag·ing.** **1.** to inspire with courage, spirit, or confidence: *His coach encouraged him throughout the marathon race to keep on running.* **2.** to stimulate by assistance, approval, etc.: *One of the chief duties of a teacher is to encourage students.* **3.** to promote, advance, or foster: *Poverty often encourages crime.* [1400–50; late ME *encoragen* < AF, MF *encorag(i)er.* See EN-[1], COURAGE] **—en·cour′ag·er,** *n.* **—en·cour′ag·ing·ly,** *adv.*
—Syn. 1. embolden, hearten, reassure. **2.** urge; support, aid, help. **—Ant. 1.** discourage, dishearten.

en·cour·age·ment (en kûr′ij mənt, -kur′-), *n.* **1.** the act of encouraging. **2.** the state of being encouraged. **3.** something that encourages: *Praise is the greatest encouragement.* [1560–70; ENCOURAGE + -MENT]
—Syn. 3. praise, support, boost, lift, endorsement.

en·crim·son (en krim′zən, -sən), *v.t.* to make crimson. [1765–75; EN-[1] + CRIMSON]

en·cri·nite (en′krə nīt′), *n.* a fossil crinoid. [1800–10; < NL *encrin(us)* (< Gk *en-* EN-[2] + *krínon* lily) + -ITE[1]]

en·croach (en krōch′), *v.i.* **1.** to advance beyond proper, established, or usual limits; make gradual inroads: *A dictatorship of the majority is encroaching on the rights of the individual.* **2.** to trespass upon the property, domain, or rights of another, esp. stealthily or by gradual advances. [1275–1325; ME *encrochen* < AF *encrocher,* OF *encrochier* to catch hold of, seize, equiv. to *en-* EN-[1] + *-crochier,* v. deriv. of *croc* hook < Gmc; see CROOKED, CROOK] **—en·croach′er,** *n.*
—Syn. 1, 2. See **trespass.**

en·croach·ment (en krōch′mənt), *n.* **1.** an act or instance of encroaching. **2.** anything taken by encroaching. [1425–75; late ME *encrochement* < AF. See ENCROACH, -MENT]

en croûte (äɴ kroot′), *French Cookery.* baked in a pastry crust. [< F: lit., in (a) crust]

en·crust (en krust′), *v.t., v.i.* incrust.

en·crus·ta·tion (en′kru stā′shən), *n.* incrustation.

en·crypt (en kript′), *v.t.* to encipher or encode. [1940–45; EN-[1] + *-crypt* (abstracted from *cryptic, cryptography,* etc.), modeled on *encode*] **—en·cryp′tion, en′·cryp·ta′tion,** *n.*

en·cul·tu·rate (en kul′chə rāt′), *v.t.,* **-rat·ed, -rat·ing.** to change, modify, or adapt (behavior, ideas, etc.) by enculturation. [back formation from ENCULTURATION] **—en·cul·tu·ra·tive** (en kul′chə rā′tiv, -chər ə tiv), *adj.*

en·cul·tu·ra·tion (en kul′chə rā′shən), *n.* the process whereby individuals learn their group's culture, through experience, observation, and instruction. [1945–50; EN-[1] + (AC)CULTURATION]

en·cum·ber (en kum′bər), *v.t.* **1.** to impede or hinder; hamper; retard: *Red tape encumbers all our attempts at action.* **2.** to block up or fill with what is obstructive or superfluous: *a mind encumbered with trivial and useless information.* **3.** to burden or weigh down: *She was encumbered with a suitcase and several packages.* **4.** to burden with obligations, debt, etc. Also, **incumber.** [1300–50; ME *encombren* < AF, MF *encombrer,* equiv. to *en-* EN-[1] + *-combrer,* v. deriv. of *combre* dam, weir < early ML *combrus* < Gaulish **comberos* confluence, bringing together (cf. *Quimper,* in Brittany < Breton *Kemper*); see COM-, BEAR[1]] **—en·cum′ber·ing·ly,** *adv.*

en·cum·brance (en kum′brəns), *n.* **1.** something that encumbers; something burdensome, useless, or superfluous; burden; hindrance: *Poverty was a lifelong encumbrance.* **2.** a dependent person, esp. a child. **3.** *Law.* a burden or claim on property, as a mortgage. Also, **incumbrance.** [1275–1325; ME *encombraunce* < MF *encombrance.* See ENCUMBER, -ANCE]

en·cum·branc·er (en kum′brən sər), *n. Law.* a person who holds an encumbrance. [1855–60; ENCUMBRANCE + -ER[1]]

-ency, a noun suffix, equivalent to **-ence:** *consistency; dependency; exigency.* [-ENCE + -Y[3]]

ency., encyclopedia. Also, **encyc., encycl.**

en·cyc·li·cal (en sik′li kəl, -sī′kli-), *n.* **1.** *Rom. Cath. Ch.* a letter addressed by the pope to all the bishops of the church. *—adj.* **2.** (of a letter) intended for wide or general circulation; general. Also, **en·cyc′lic.** [1610–20; < LL *encyclicus* (< Gk *enkýklios,* with *-icus* -IC for *-ios,* equiv. to *en-* EN-[2] + *kýkl(os)* circle, CYCLE + *-ios* adj. suffix) + -AL[1]]

en·cy·clo·pe·di·a (en sī′klə pē′dē ə), *n.* **1.** a book or set of books containing articles on various topics, usually in alphabetical arrangement, covering all branches of knowledge or, less commonly, all aspects of one subject. **2.** (*cap.*) the French work edited by Diderot and D'Alembert, published in the 18th century, distinguished by its representation of the views of the Enlightenment. Also, **en·cy′clo·pae′di·a.** [1525–35; < NL *encyclopaedia* < Gk *enkyklopaidía,* a misreading of *enkýklios paideía* circular (i.e., well-rounded) education. See ENCYCLICAL, PEDI-[2]]

en·cy·clo·pe·dic (en sī′klə pē′dik), *adj.* **1.** pertaining to or of the nature of an encyclopedia; relating to all branches of knowledge. **2.** comprehending a wide variety of information; comprehensive: *an encyclopedic memory.* Also, **en·cy′clo·pae′dic, en·cy′clo·pe′di·cal, en·cy′clo·pae′di·cal.** [1815–25; ENCYCLOPED(IA) + -IC] **—en·cy′clo·pe′di·cal·ly, en·cy′clo·pae′di·cal·ly,** *adv.*
—Syn. 2. all-embracing, all-inclusive, exhaustive, wide-ranging.

en·cy·clo·pe·dism (en sī′klə pē′diz əm), *n.* **1.** encyclopedic learning. **2.** (*often cap.*) the doctrines and influence of the Encyclopedists. Also, **en·cy′clo·pae′dism.** [1825–35; ENCYCLOPED(IA) + -ISM]

en·cy·clo·pe·dist (en sī′klə pē′dist), *n.* **1.** a compiler of or contributor to an encyclopedia. **2.** (*often cap.*) one of the collaborators on the French Encyclopedia. Also, **en·cy′clo·pae′dist.** [1645–55; ENCYCLOPED(IA) + -IST]

en·cyst (en sist′), *v.t., v.i. Biol.* to enclose or become enclosed in a cyst. [1835–45; EN-[1] + CYST] **—en·cyst′·ment, en′cys·ta′tion,** *n.*

end[1] (end), *n.* **1.** the last part or extremity, lengthwise, of anything that is longer than it is wide or broad: *the end of a street; the end of a rope.* **2.** a point, line, or limitation that indicates the full extent, degree, etc., of something; limit; bounds: *kindness without end; to walk from end to end of a city.* **3.** a part or place at or adjacent to an extremity: *at the end of the table; the west end of town.* **4.** the furthermost imaginable place or point: *an island at the very end of the world.* **5.** termination; conclusion: *The journey was coming to an end.* **6.** the concluding part: *The end of her speech had to be cut short because of time.* **7.** an intention or aim: *to gain one's ends.* **8.** the object for which a thing exists; purpose: *The happiness of the people is the end of government.* **9.** an outcome or result: *What is to be the end of all this bickering?* **10.** termination of existence; death: *He met a horrible end.* **11.** a cause of death, destruction, or ruin: *Another war would be the end of civilization.* **12.** a remnant or fragment: *mill end; ends and trimmings.* **13.** a share or part in something: *He does his end of the job very well.* **14.** *Textiles.* a warp thread running vertically and interlaced with the filling yarn in the woven fabric. **15.** *Football.* **a.** either of the linemen stationed farthest from the center. **b.** the position played by this lineman. **16.** *Archery.* the number of arrows to be shot by a competitor during one turn in a match. **17.** *Cricket.* a wicket, esp. the one where the batsman is taking a turn. **18.** a unit of a game, as in curling or lawn bowling. **19.** *Kantianism.* any rational being, regarded as worthy to exist for its own sake. **20.** either half of a domino. **21.** *Knots.* the part of a rope, beyond a knot or the like, that is not used. **22. at loose ends,** without an occupation or plans; unsettled; uncertain: *He spent two years wandering about the country at loose ends.* **23. at one's wit's end,** at the end of one's ideas or mental resources; perplexed: *I'm at my wit's end with this problem.* Also, **at one's wits' end. 24. end for end,** in reverse position; inverted: *The cartons were turned end for end.* **25. end on,** with the end next to or facing: *He backed the truck until it was end on with the loading platform.* **26. end to end,** in a row with ends touching: *The pipes were placed end to end on the ground.* **27. go off the deep end,** *Informal.* to act in a reckless or agitated manner; lose emotional control: *She went off the deep end when she lost her job.* **28. in the end,** finally; after all: *In the end they shook hands and made up.* **29. keep** or **hold one's end up,** to perform one's part or share adequately: *The work is demanding, but he's holding his end up.* **30. make an end of,** to conclude; stop: *Let's make an end of this foolishness and get down to work.* **31. make ends meet,** to live within one's means: *Despite her meager income, she tried to make ends meet.* Also, **make both ends meet. 32. no end,** *Informal.* very much or many: *They were pleased no end by the warm reception.* **33. on end, a.** having the end down; upright: *to stand a box on end.* **b.** continuously; successively: *They talked for hours on end.* **34. put an end to,** to cause to stop; terminate; finish: *The advent of sound in motion pictures put an end to many a silent star's career.* **35. the end,** *Slang.* the ultimate; the utmost of good or bad: *His stupidity is the end.*
—v.t. **36.** to bring to an end or conclusion: *We ended the discussion on a note of optimism.* **37.** to put an end to; terminate: *This was the battle that ended the war.* **38.** to form the end of: *This passage ends the novel.* **39.** to cause the demise of; kill: *A bullet through the heart ended him.* **40.** to constitute the most outstanding or greatest possible example or instance of (usually used in the infinitive): *You just committed the blunder to end all blunders.*
—v.i. **41.** to come to an end; terminate; cease: *The road ends at Rome.* **42.** to issue or result: *Extravagance ends in want.* **43.** to reach or arrive at a final condition, circumstance, or goal (often fol. by *up*): *to end up in the army; to end as a happy person.*
—adj. **44.** final or ultimate: *the end result.* [bef. 900; ME, OE *ende;* c. OFris *enda,* MD *e(i)nde,* OS *endi,* OHG *anti,* G *Ende,* ON *endi(r),* Goth *andeis* end < Gmc **anthja-;* akin to Skt *ánta-* end] **—end′er,** *n.*
—Syn. 4. tip, bound, limit, terminus. **5.** END, CLOSE, CONCLUSION, FINISH, OUTCOME refer to the termination of something. END implies a natural termination or completion, or an attainment of purpose: *the end of a day, of a race; to some good end.* CLOSE often implies a planned rounding off of something in process: *the close of a conference.* CONCLUSION suggests a decision or arrangement: *All evidence leads to this conclusion; the conclusion of peace terms.* FINISH emphasizes completion of something begun: *a fight to the finish.* OUTCOME suggests the issue of something that was in doubt: *the outcome of a game.* **7.** See **aim.**

end[2] (end), *v.t. Brit. Dial.* to put wheat, hay, or other grain into a stack or barn. [1600–10; perh. var. of dial. *in* to harvest (OE *innian* to lodge, put up). See INN]

end-, var. of **endo-** before a vowel: *endameba.*

end., endorsed.

end-all (end′ôl′), *n.* **1.** the ultimate purpose, object, or conclusion: *Money is the be-all and end-all of his existence.* **2.** something that brings things to such an end or conclusion. [1595–1605]

en·dam·age (en dam′ij), *v.t.,* **-aged, -ag·ing.** to damage. [1325–75; ME < AF; see EN-[1], DAMAGE]

end·a·me·ba (en′də mē′bə), *n., pl.* **-bae** (-bē), **-bas.** *Biol.* any protozoan of the genus *Endamoeba,* members of which are parasitic in the digestive tracts of various invertebrates, including cockroaches and termites. Also, **end′a·moe′ba.** [< NL (1879); see END-, AMEBA] **—end′a·me′bic, end′a·moe′bic,** *adj.*

end·an·ge·i·tis (en′dan jē ī′tis), *n. Pathol.* an inflammation of the innermost lining of a blood vessel. Also, **end·an·gi·tis** (en′dan jī′tis), **end′an·gi·i′tis.** [END- + *angeitis;* see ANGI-, -ITIS]

en·dan·ger (en dān′jər), *v.t.* to expose to danger; imperil: *It was foolish to endanger your life in that way.* [1400–50; late ME; see EN-[1], DANGER] **—en·dan′ger·ment,** *n.*
—Syn. threaten, jeopardize, hazard, risk.

en·dan·gered (en dān′jərd), *adj.* **1.** threatened with a danger: *endangered lives of trapped coal miners.* **2.** threatened with extinction: *The bald eagle may be endangered.* [1590–1600; ENDANGER + -ED[2]]

endan′gered spe′cies, a species at risk of extinction because of human activity, changes in climate, changes in predator-prey ratios, etc., esp. when officially designated as such by a governmental agency such as the U.S. Fish and Wildlife Service. [1965–70]

end·a·or·ti·tis (en′dā ôr tī′tis), *n. Pathol.* an inflammation of the innermost lining of the aorta. [END- + AORT(A) + -ITIS]

end·arch (en′därk), *adj. Bot.* (of a primary xylem or root) developing from the periphery; having the oldest cells closest to the core. [1895–1900; END- + *-arch* having a point of origin (as specified)] **—end′ar·chy,** *n.*

end′ around′, *Football.* a play on offense in which an end, after running into the backfield, takes a handoff and attempts to run around the opposite end of the line. [1925–30]

end·ar·ter·ec·to·my (en där′tə rek′tə mē), *n., pl.* **-mies.** the surgical stripping of a fat-encrusted, thickened arterial lining so as to open or widen the artery for improved blood circulation. [1955–60; ENDARTER(IUM) + -ECTOMY]

end·ar·te·ri·um (en′där tēr′ē əm), *n., pl.* **-te·ri·a** (-tēr′ē ə). *Anat.* the innermost lining of an artery. [< NL; see END-, ARTERY] **—end′ar·te′ri·al,** *adj.*

en′ dash′, *Print.* a dash one en long.

end-blown (end′blōn′), *adj.* (of a flute) having a mouthpiece at the end of the tube so that the player blows into the instrument. Cf. **transverse** (def. 2).

end·brain (end′brān′), *n.* the telencephalon. [1925–30; trans. of TELENCEPHALON]

end′ brush′, *Cell Biol.* an abundant, tuftlike branching at the axon ending of certain nerve cells. [1880–85]

end′ bulb′, *Anat.* any of various types of oval or

CONCISE PRONUNCIATION KEY: act, cāpe, dâre, pärt; set, ēqual; if, ice; ox, ōver, ôrder, oil, bo͝ok, bo͞ot, out; up, ûrge; child; sing; shoe; thin, *th*at; zh as in *treasure.* ə = *a* as in *alone, e* as in *system, i* as in *easily, o* as in *gallop, u* as in *circus;* ᵊ as in *fire* (fīᵊr), *hour* (ouᵊr). l and n can serve as syllabic consonants, as in *cradle* (krād′l), and *button* (but′n). See the full key inside the front cover.

rounded structures occurring at the ends of nerve fibers, ranging from slight enlargements to complex corpuscles that act as sensory receptors for pain, touch, cold, etc.

end-con·sum·er (end′kən so͞o′mər), *n.* an end user. [1965–70]

en·dear (en dēr′), *v.t.* **1.** to make dear, esteemed, or beloved: *He endeared himself to his friends with his gentle ways.* **2.** *Obs.* to make costly. [1570–80; EN-[1] + DEAR]

en·dear·ing (en dēr′ing), *adj.* **1.** tending to make dear or beloved. **2.** manifesting or evoking affection: *an endearing smile.* [1615–25; ENDEAR + -ING[2]] —**en·dear′ing·ly,** *adv.*

en·dear·ment (en dēr′mənt), *n.* **1.** the act of endearing. **2.** the state of being endeared. **3.** something that endears; an action or utterance showing affection: *to murmur endearments.* [1605–15; ENDEAR + -MENT]

en·deav·or (en dev′ər), *v.i.* **1.** to exert oneself to do or effect something; make an effort; strive: *We must constantly endeavor if we are to succeed.* —*v.t.* **2.** to attempt; try: *He endeavors to keep things neat in his apartment.* **3.** *Archaic.* to attempt to achieve or gain. —*n.* **4.** a strenuous effort; attempt. Also, *esp. Brit.,* **en·deav′our.** [1350–1400; ME *endeveren,* from the phrase *putten in devoir* to make an effort, assume responsibility; cf. AF *se mettre en deveir.* See EN-[1], DEVOIR] —**en·deav′or·er;** *esp. Brit.,* **en·deav′our·er,** *n.*
—**Syn. 1, 2.** See **try. 4.** See **effort.**

En·de·cott (en′di kət, -kot′), *n.* **John,** 1588?–1665, colonial governor of Massachusetts 1644–65, born in England. Also, **Endicott.**

en·dem·ic (en dem′ik), *adj.* Also, **en·dem′i·cal. 1.** natural to or characteristic of a specific people or place; native; indigenous: *endemic folkways; countries where high unemployment is endemic.* **2.** belonging exclusively or confined to a particular place: *a fever endemic to the tropics.* —*n.* **3.** an endemic disease. [1655–65; < NL *endēmicus,* equiv. to Gk *éndēm*(os) endemic (*en-* EN-[2] + *dêm*(os) people + *-os* adj. suffix) + L *-icus* -IC] —**en·dem′i·cal·ly,** *adv.* —**en·de·mism** (en′də miz′əm), **en·de·mic·i·ty** (en′də mis′i tē), *n.*

En·der (en′dər), *n.* **Kor·ne·li·a** (kôr nāl′yə, -nā′lē ə), born 1958, East German swimmer.

En′der·by Land′ (en′dər bē), a part of the coast of Antarctica, E of Queen Maud Land: discovered 1831.

end·er·gon·ic (en′dər gon′ik), *adj. Biochem.* (of a biochemical reaction) requiring energy. Cf. **exergonic.** [1935–40; END- + Gk *érgon* work + -IC]

en·der·mic (en dûr′mik), *adj.* acting through the skin, as a medicine, by absorption. [1825–35; EN-[1] + -DERM + -IC] —**en·der′mi·cal·ly,** *adv.*

En·ders (en′dərz), *n.* **John Franklin,** 1897–1985, U.S. bacteriologist: Nobel prize for medicine 1954.

en dés·ha·bil·lé (äN dā zA bē yā′), *French.* in dishabille; not fully or carefully dressed.

end′ game′, *Chess.* the final stage of a game, usually following the exchange of queens and the serious reduction of forces. Also, **end′game′.** [1880–85]

end·gate (end′gāt′), *n.* tailboard. [1870–75; END[1] + GATE[1]]

end′ grain′, wood grain, as at the end of a board, resulting from a cut across the grain. [1880–85] —**end′-grain′,** *adj.*

end·hand (end′hand′), *n. Cards.* the dealer in a game with three players. Cf. **forehand** (def. 7), **middlehand.** [1670–80; END[1] + HAND]

En·di·cott (en′di kət, -kot′), *n.* **1. John.** See **Endecott, John. 2.** a city in S New York, on the Susquehanna River. 14,457.

end·ing (en′ding), *n.* **1.** a bringing or coming to an end; termination; close: *Putting away the Christmas ornaments marked the ending of the season.* **2.** the final or concluding part; conclusion: *a story with a happy ending.* **3.** death; destruction. **4.** *Gram.* a morpheme, esp. an inflection, at the end of a word, as *-s* in *cuts.* **5.** (not in technical use) any final word part, as the *-ow* of *widow.* [bef. 1000; ME *endyng,* OE *endung.* See END[1], -ING[1]]

en·dive (en′dīv, än′dēv; *Fr.* äN dēv′), *n., pl.* **-dives** (-dīvz, -dēvz; *Fr.* -dēv′). **1.** a composite plant, *Cichorium endivia,* having a rosette of often curly-edged leaves used in salads. Cf. **escarole. 2.** Also called **Belgian endive, French endive, witloof.** a young chicory plant, deprived of light to form a narrow head of whitish leaves that are eaten as a cooked vegetable or used raw in salads. **3.** *Furniture.* an ornamental motif having the form of an arrangement of acanthus or endive leaves. [1325–75; ME < MF << MGk *entýbia,* pl. of *entýbion,* deriv. of earlier *éntybon* < L *intubum, intibum,* earlier *intubus* chicory, endive, perh. < Sem]

end′ leaf′, *Bookbinding.* See **end paper.** [1885–90]

end·less (end′lis), *adj.* **1.** having or seeming to have no end, limit, or conclusion; boundless; infinite; interminable; incessant: *an endless series of complaints; Time is endless.* **2.** made continuous, as by joining the two ends of a single length: *an endless chain or belt.* [bef. 900; ME *endelees,* OE *endelēas.* See END[1], -LESS] —**end′less·ly,** *adv.* —**end′less·ness,** *n.*
—**Syn. 1.** limitless, illimitable, unending, unceasing, continuous, perpetual. See **eternal.**

end′ line′, *Sports.* **1.** a line at each end of a court or playing field at right angles to the sidelines that defines one of the lengthwise boundaries of the playing area. **2.** a line at each end of a football field parallel to and 10 yds. (9 m) behind the goal line. [1915–20, *Amer.*]

CONCISE ETYMOLOGY KEY: <, descended or borrowed from; >, whence; b., blend of, blended; c., cognate with; cf., compare; deriv., derivative; equiv., equivalent; imit., imitative; obl., oblique; r., replacing; s., stem; sp., spelling, spelled; resp., respelling, respelled; trans., translation; ?, origin unknown; *, unattested; ‡, probably earlier than. See the full key inside the front cover.

end·long (end′lông′, -long′), *adv. Archaic.* lengthwise. [1175–1225; ME *endelong;* r. OE *andlong* ALONG]

end′ man′, 1. a man at one end of a row or line. **2.** a man at either end of the line of performers of a minstrel troupe, who plays on the bones or tambourine and carries on humorous dialogue with the interlocutor. [1860–65, *Amer.*]

end′ mat′ter, *Print.* See **back matter.**

end′ mem′ber, *Mineral.* either of two pure compounds occurring in various proportions in a series of solid solutions that comprises a mineral group.

end′ mill′, (in a milling machine) a rotating cutting tool having a cylindrical shank with teeth at the end, used for machining the faces and sides of metal pieces and other objects.

end·most (end′mōst′), *adj.* farthest; most distant; last: *the endmost lands of the earth.* [1765–75; END[1] + -MOST]

end·note (end′nōt′), *n.* a note, as of explanation, emendation, or the like, added at the end of an article, chapter, etc. [END[1] + NOTE]

endo-, a combining form meaning "within," used in the formation of compound words: *endocardial.* Also, *esp. before a vowel,* **end-.** [< Gk, comb. form of *éndon* within; c. OIr *ind-,* OL *endo-* in, on]

en·do·bi·ot·ic (en′dō bī ot′ik), *Biol.* —*adj.* **1.** of or pertaining to an organism that exists as a parasite or symbiont entirely within the tissues of a host organism. —*n.* **2.** any such parasitic or symbiotic organism. [1895–1900; ENDO- + BIOTIC]

en·do·blast (en′də blast′), *n. Embryol.* **1.** endoderm (def. 1). **2.** hypoblast (def. 2). [1890–95; ENDO- + -BLAST] —**en′do·blas′tic,** *adj.*

en·do·car·di·al (en′dō kär′dē əl), *adj. Anat.* **1.** situated within the heart; intracardiac. **2.** Also, **en·do·car·di·ac** (en′dō kär′dē ak′). of or pertaining to the endocardium. [1840–50; ENDO- + Gk *kardí(a)* heart + -AL[1]; or ENDOCARDI(UM) + -AL[1]]

en·do·car·di·tis (en′dō kär dī′tis), *n. Pathol.* inflammation of the endocardium. [1830–40; < NL; see ENDO-, CARDITIS] —**en·do·car·dit·ic** (en′dō kär dit′ik), *adj.*

en·do·car·di·um (en′dō kär′dē əm), *n., pl.* **-di·a** (-dē ə). *Anat.* the serous membrane that lines the cavities of the heart. [1870–75; ENDO- + -CARDIUM]

en·do·carp (en′də kärp′), *n. Bot.* the inner layer of a pericarp, as the stone of certain fruits. See diag. under **pericarp.** [1820–30; ENDO- + -CARP]

en·do·car·poid (en′dō kär′poid), *adj.* (of a lichen) having the fruiting body embedded in the thallus. [< NL *Endocarp(on)* a genus of lichens (see ENDO-, -CARP) + -OID]

en·do·cast (en′də kast′, -käst′), *n. Archaeol.* **1.** See **endocranial cast. 2.** steinkern. [1945–50; ENDO(CRANIAL) + CAST[1]]

en·do·cen·tric (en′dō sen′trik), *adj. Gram.* (of a construction or compound) having the same syntactic function in the sentence as one of its immediate constituents. *Cold water* is an endocentric construction, since it functions as would the noun *water. Greenhouse* is an endocentric compound, since it is a noun as is its head *house.* Cf. **exocentric.** [1930–35; ENDO- + -CENTRIC]

en′docra′nial cast′, *Archaeol.* a cast of the inside of the cranium, as of a fossil skull, used to determine brain size and shape. Also called **endocast.** [1920–25]

en·do·cra·ni·um (en′dō krā′nē əm), *n., pl.* **-ni·a** (-nē ə). *Anat.* **1.** the inner lining membrane of the skull; the dura mater. **2.** the inside surface of the skull. [1875–80; < NL; see ENDO-, CRANIUM] —**en′do·cra′ni·al,** *adj.*

en·do·crine (en′də krin, -krīn′, -krēn′), *Anat., Physiol.* —*adj.* Also, **en·do·cri·nal** (en′də krīn′l, -krēn′l), **en·do·crin·ic** (en′də krin′ik), **endocrinous. 1.** secreting internally into the blood or lymph. **2.** of or pertaining to an endocrine gland or its secretion. —*n.* **3.** an internal secretion; hormone. **4.** See **endocrine gland.** Cf. **exocrine.** [1910–15; ENDO- + *-crine* < Gk *krī́nein* to separate]

en′docrine gland′, any of various glands, as the thyroid, adrenal, and pituitary glands, that secrete certain substances or hormones directly into the blood or lymph; ductless gland. [1910–15]

en·do·cri·nol·o·gy (en′dō krə nol′ə jē, -krī-), *n.* the branch of biology dealing with the endocrine glands and their secretions, esp. in relation to their processes or functions. [1915–20; ENDOCRINE + -O- + -LOGY] —**en·do·crin·o·log·ic** (en′dō krin′l oj′ik, -krīn′-, -krēn′-), **en′do·crin′o·log′i·cal,** *adj.* —**en′do·cri·nol′o·gist,** *n.*

en·doc·ri·nous (en dok′rə nəs), *adj.* endocrine. [1910–15; ENDOCRINE + -OUS]

en·do·cy·to·bi·ol·o·gy (en′dō sī′tō bī ol′ə jē), *n.* the branch of biology that deals with the anatomy and function of the organelles and other structures within the cell. [1980–85; ENDO- + CYTO- + BIOLOGY]

en·do·cy·tose (en′dō sī tōs′, -tōz′), *v.i.,* **-tosed, -tos·ing.** *Physiol.* (of a cell) to take within by the process of endocytosis. [1970–75; back formation from ENDOCYTOSIS]

en·do·cy·to·sis (en′dō sī tō′sis), *n. Physiol.* the transport of solid matter or liquid into a cell by means of a coated vacuole or vesicle (distinguished from *exocytosis*). Cf. **phagocytosis, pinocytosis.** [1960–65; ENDO- + -CYTE + -OSIS, perh. on the model of PHAGOCYTOSIS] —**en·do·cyt·ic** (en′dō sit′ik), **en·do·cy·tot·ic** (en′dō sī tot′ik), *adj.*

en·do·derm (en′də dûrm′), *n.* **1.** Also called **endoblast.** *Embryol.* the innermost cell layer of the embryo in its gastrula stage. **2.** *Anat.* the innermost body tissue that derives from this layer, as the gut lining. Also, **entoderm.** [1825–35; < F *endoderme;* see ENDO-, -DERM] —**en′do·der′mal, en′do·der′mic,** *adj.*

en·do·der·mis (en′dō dûr′mis), *n. Bot.* a specialized tissue in the roots and stems of vascular plants, composed of a single layer of modified parenchyma cells forming the inner boundary of the cortex. [1880–85; ENDO- + -DERMIS]

en·do·don·tics (en′dō don′tiks), *n.* (*used with a singular v.*) the branch of dentistry dealing with the cause, diagnosis, prevention, and treatment of diseases of the dental pulp, usually by removal of the nerve and other tissue of the pulp cavity and its replacement with suitable filling material; pulp canal therapy; root canal therapy. Also, **en·do·don·tia** (en′dō don′shə, -shē ə), **en·do·don·tol·o·gy** (en′dō don tol′ə jē). [1945–50; < NL *endodont(ia)* in same sense (see END-, -ODONT, -IA) + -ICS] —**en′do·don′tic,** *adj.*

en·do·don·tist (en′dō don′tist), *n.* a specialist in endodontics. Also, **en·do·don·tol·o·gist** (en′dō don tol′ə jist). [1945–50; ENDODONT(ICS) + -IST]

en·do·don·ti·um (en′dō don′shē əm), *n. Dentistry.* pulp (def. 4). [< NL; see END-, -ODONT, -IUM]

en·do·en·zyme (en′dō en′zīm), *n. Biochem.* an enzyme that functions within a cell. Cf. **exoenzyme.** [ENDO- + ENZYME]

en·do·er·gic (en′dō ûr′jik), *adj. Chem.* endothermic (opposed to *exoergic*). [1935–40; ENDO- + -ERGIC]

end-of-file (end′əv fīl′), *n. Computers.* See **EOF**

en·dog·a·my (en dog′ə mē), *n.* marriage within a specific tribe or similar social unit. Cf. **exogamy** (def. 1). [1860–65; ENDO- + -GAMY] —**en·dog′a·mous, en·do·gam·ic** (en′dō gam′ik), *adj.*

en·do·ge·net·ic (en′dō jə net′ik), *adj. Geol.* arising from or relating to the interior of the earth (opposed to *exogenetic*). Also, **en·do·gen·ic** (en′dō jen′ik), **endogenous.** [ENDO- + -GENETIC]

en·dog·e·nous (en doj′ə nəs), *adj.* **1.** proceeding from within; derived internally. **2.** *Biol.* growing or developing from within; originating within. **3.** *Pathol.* (of a disease) resulting from conditions within the organism rather than externally caused. **4.** *Biochem.* pertaining to the metabolism of nitrogenous elements of cells and tissues. **5.** *Geol.* endogenetic. [1825–35; ENDO- + -GENOUS] —**en·do·ge·nic·i·ty** (en′dō jə nis′i tē), *n.* —**en·dog′e·nous·ly,** *adv.*

endog′enous depres′sion, *Psychiatry.* a severe form of depression usually characterized by insomnia, weight loss, and inability to experience pleasure, thought to be of internal origin and not influenced by external events. Also called **melancholia.** [1960–65]

en·dog·e·ny (en doj′ə nē), *n. Biol.* development or growth from within. Also, **en·do·gen·e·sis** (en′dō jen′ə sis). [1880–85; ENDO- + -GENY]

en·do·lith·ic (en′dō lith′ik), *adj.* living embedded in the surface of rocks, as certain lichens. [1885–90; ENDO- + -LITHIC]

en·do·lymph (en′də limf′), *n. Anat.* the fluid contained within the membranous labyrinth of the ear. [1830–40; ENDO- + LYMPH] —**en·do·lym·phat·ic** (en′dō lim fat′ik), *adj.*

en·do·mem·brane (en′dō mem′brān), *n. Cell. Biol.* the outer membrane of any of the organelles within the cell. [ENDO- + MEMBRANE]

endome′trial aspira′tion. See under **menstrual extraction.**

en·do·me·tri·o·sis (en′dō mē′trē ō′sis), *n. Pathol.* the presence of uterine lining in other pelvic organs, esp. the ovaries, characterized by cyst formation, adhesions, and menstrual pains. [1920–25; < NL; see ENDOMETRIUM, -OSIS]

en·do·me·tri·tis (en′dō mi trī′tis), *n. Pathol.* inflammation of the lining of the uterus. [1870–75; < NL; see ENDOMETRIUM, -ITIS]

en·do·me·tri·um (en′dō mē′trē əm), *n., pl.* **-tri·a** (-trē ə). *Anat.* the mucous membrane lining the uterus. [1880–85; ENDO- + NL *-metrium* < Gk *mḗtr(a)* womb + *-ion* dim. suffix] —**en′do·me′tri·al,** *adj.*

en·do·mi·to·sis (en′dō mī tō′sis), *n. Genetics.* replication of the chromosomes without nuclear division of the cell. [1940–45; ENDO- + MITOSIS]

en·do·mix·is (en′dō mik′sis), *n. Biol.* a periodic reorganization of the cell nucleus observed in certain ciliated protozoans. [1914; ENDO- + Gk *míxis* mixing]

en·do·morph (en′də môrf′), *n.* **1.** a mineral enclosed within another mineral. Cf. **perimorph. 2.** a person of the endomorphic type. [1880–85; ENDO- + -MORPH]

en·do·mor·phic (en′də môr′fik), *adj.* **1.** *Mineral.* **a.** occurring in the form of an endomorph. **b.** of or pertaining to endomorphs. **c.** taking place within a rock mass. **2.** having a heavy body build roughly characterized by the relative prominence of structures developed from the embryonic endoderm (contrasted with *ectomorphic, mesomorphic*). [1885–90; < F *endomorphique;* see ENDO-, -MORPHIC] —**en′do·mor′phy,** *n.*

en·do·mor·phism (en′dō môr′fiz əm, -də), *n.* **1.** *Petrol.* a change brought about within the mass of an intrusive igneous rock. **2.** *Math.* a homomorphism of a set into itself. [1950–55; ENDOMORPH(IC) + -ISM]

en·do·my·o·car·di·tis (en′dō mī′ō kär dī′tis), *n. Pathol.* inflammation of the heart muscle and the inner lining of the heart. [1940–45; ENDO- + MYOCARDITIS]

en·do·nu·cle·ase (en′dō no͞o′klē ās′, -āz′, -nyo͞o′-), *n. Biochem.* any of a group of enzymes that degrade DNA or RNA molecules by breaking linkages within the polynucleotide chains. [1960–65; ENDO- + NUCLEASE]

en·do·par·a·site (en′dō par′ə sīt′), *n.* an internal parasite (opposed to *ectoparasite*). [1880–85; ENDO- + PARASITE] —**en·do·par·a·sit·ic** (en′dō par′ə sit′ik), *adj.*

en·do·pep·ti·dase (en′dō pep′ti dās′, -dāz′), *n. Biochem.* an enzyme that catalyzes the cleavage of a polypeptide or protein at interior positions of the amino acid chain. [1935–40; ENDO- + PEPTIDASE]

en·do·pe·rid·i·um (en′dō pə rid′ē əm), *n., pl.* **-rid·i·a** (-rid′ē ə). *Bot.* the inner of the two layers into which the peridium is divided. [< NL; see ENDO-, PERIDIUM] **—en′do·pe·rid′i·al,** *adj.*

en·doph·a·gous (en dof′ə gəs), *adj.* (of certain parasitic insects) feeding from within a host organism. [ENDO- + -PHAGOUS]

en·do·pha·sia (en′dō fā′zhə, -zhē ə, -zē ā), *n.* internal speech with no audible vocalization. Cf. **exophasia.** [< It *endofasia.* See ENDO-, -PHASIA]

en·doph·o·ra (en dof′ər ə), *n. Gram.* the use of a word or phrase to refer to something either preceding it or following it within a text or discourse; anaphora or cataphora. Cf. **exophora.** [ENDO- + (ANA)PHORA] **—en·do·phor·ic** (en′də fôr′ik, -for′-), *adj.*

en·doph·thal·mi·tis (en dof′thal mī′tis, -dop′-), *n. Pathol.* inflammation of the ocular cavities, caused by infection, trauma, or allergic reaction. [END- + OPHTHALMITIS]

en·do·phyte (en′də fīt′), *n. Bot.* a plant living within another plant, usually as a parasite. [1825–35; ENDO- + -PHYTE] **—en·do·phyt·ic** (en′də fit′ik), *adj.* **—en′do·phyt′i·cal·ly,** *adv.* **—en·doph·y·tous** (en dof′i təs), *adj.*

en·do·plasm (en′də plaz′əm), *n. Cell Biol.* the inner portion of the cytoplasm of a cell. Cf. **ectoplasm** (def. 1). [1880–85; ENDO- + -PLASM] **—en′do·plas′mic,** *adj.*

endoplas′mic retic′ulum, *Cell Biol.* a network of tubular membranes within the cytoplasm of the cell, occurring either with a smooth surface **(smooth endoplasmic reticulum)** or studded with ribosomes **(rough endoplasmic reticulum),** involved in the transport of materials. See illus. under **cell.** [1945–50]

en·dop·o·dite (en dop′ə dīt′), *n. Zool.* the inner or medial branch of a two-branched crustacean leg or appendage. Also, **en·do·pod** (en′də pod′). Cf. **exopodite, protopodite.** [1865–70; ENDO- + *-podite* < Gk *pod-* (s. of *poús*) FOOT + -ITE[1]] **—en·dop·o·dit·ic** (en dop′ə dit′ik), *adj.*

en·do·proct (en′də prokt′), *n.* entoproct.

En·do·proc·ta (en′də prok′tə), *n.* Entoprocta.

en·do·pter·y·gote (en′dō ter′i gōt′), *adj.* **1.** belonging or pertaining to the superorder Endopterygota, comprising the insects that undergo complete metamorphosis. **—***n.* **2.** an endopterygote insect. [1925–30; < NL *Endopterygota* a group of insects. See ENDO-, PTERYGOTE]

end′ or′gan, *Cell Biol.* one of several specialized structures at the peripheral end of sensory or motor nerve fibers. [1875–80]

en·do·rhe·ic (en′də rē′ik), *adj.* of or pertaining to interior drainage basins. [1925–30; *endorhe(ism)* (< F *endor(rh)éisme* interior drainage; see ENDO-, RHEO-, -ISM) + -IC] **—en′do·rhe′ism,** *n.*

en·dor·phin (en dôr′fin), *n.* any of a group of peptides occurring in the brain and other tissues of vertebrates, and resembling opiates, that react with the brain's opiate receptors to raise the pain threshold. [1970–75; *end(ogenous) (m)orphine,* with *-ine* resp. as -IN[2]]

en·dor·sa·tion (en′dôr sā′shən), *n. Canadian.* endorsement. [1865–70; ENDORSE + -ATION]

en·dorse (en dôrs′), *v.,* **-dorsed, -dors·ing,** *n.* **—***v.t.* **1.** to approve, support, or sustain: *to endorse a political candidate.* **2.** to designate oneself as payee of (a check) by signing, usually on the reverse side of the instrument. **3.** to sign one's name on (a commercial document or other instrument). **4.** to make over (a stated amount) to another as payee by one's endorsement. **5.** to write (something) on the back of a document, paper, etc.: *to endorse instructions; to endorse one's signature.* **6.** to acknowledge (payment) by placing one's signature on a bill, draft, etc. **—***n.* **7.** *Heraldry.* a narrow pale, about one quarter the usual width and usually repeated several times. Also, **indorse** (for defs. 1–6). [1350–1400; var. (with *en-* for *in-*) of earlier *indorse* < ML *indorsāre* to endorse, equiv. to L *in-* IN-[2] + *-dorsāre,* deriv. of *dorsum* back; r. *endoss,* ME *endossen* < OF *endosser,* equiv. to *en-* EN-[1] + *-dosser,* deriv. of *dos* < L *dorsum*] **—en·dors′a·ble,** *adj.* **—en·dors′er, en·dor′sor,** *n.* **—en·dors′ing·ly,** *adv.* **—en·dor′sive,** *adj.*
—Syn. 1. sanction, ratify, uphold, sustain, back, second.

en·dor·see (en dôr sē′, en′dôr-, en dôr′sē), *n.* **1.** a person to whom a negotiable document is endorsed. **2.** a candidate or applicant who is endorsed by a person or group. Also, **indorsee.** [1760–70; ENDORSE + -EE]

en·dorse·ment (en dôrs′mənt), *n.* **1.** approval or sanction: *The program for supporting the arts won the government's endorsement.* **2.** the placing of one's signature, instructions, etc., on a document. **3.** the signature, instructions, etc., placed on the reverse of a commercial document, for the purpose of assigning the interest therein to another. **4.** a clause under which the stated coverage of an insurance policy may be altered. Also, **indorsement.** [1540–50; ENDORSE + -MENT; cf. AF *endorsement*]

endorse′ment in blank′. See **blank endorsement.**

en·do·sarc (en′də särk′), *n. Biol.* the endoplasm of a protozoan (opposed to *ectosarc*). [1865–70; ENDO- + -SARC] **—en′do·sar′cous,** *adj.*

en·do·scope (en′də skōp′), *n. Med.* a slender, tubular optical instrument used as a viewing system for examining an inner part of the body and, with an attached instrument, for biopsy or surgery. [1860–65; ENDO- + -SCOPE] **—en·do·scop·ic** (en′də skop′ik), *adj.* **—en·dos·co·pist** (en dos′kə pist), *n.*

en·dos·co·py (en dos′kə pē), *n., pl.* **-pies.** an examination by means of an endoscope. [ENDO- + -SCOPY]

en·do·skel·e·ton (en′dō skel′i tn), *n. Zool.* the internal skeleton or framework of the body of an animal (opposed to *exoskeleton*). [1830–40; ENDO- + SKELETON] **—en′do·skel′e·tal,** *adj.*

en·dos·mo·sis (en′doz mō′sis, -dos-), *n.* **1.** *Biol.* osmosis toward the inside of a cell or vessel. **2.** *Physical Chem.* the flow of a substance from an area of lesser concentration to one of greater concentration (opposed to *exosmosis*). [1830–40; Latinization of now obs. *endosmose* < F; see END-, OSMOSIS] **—en·dos·mot·ic** (en′doz mot′ik, -dos-), *adj.* **—en′dos·mot′i·cal·ly,** *adv.*

en·do·some (en′də sōm′), *n. Cell Biol.* a smooth sac within the cell, formed by or fused with coated vesicles that shed their clathrin, in which ligands are separated from their receptors and from which the receptors are returned to the cell surface. [ENDO- + -SOME[3]]

en·do·sperm (en′də spûrm′), *n. Bot.* nutritive matter in seed-plant ovules, derived from the embryo sac. [1840–50; < F *endosperme;* see ENDO-, SPERM]

en·do·spore (en′də spôr′, -spōr′), *n.* **1.** *Bot., Mycol.* the inner coat of a spore. Cf. **intine. 2.** *Bacteriol.* a spore formed within a cell of a rod-shaped organism. [1870–75; ENDO- + SPORE] **—en·dos·por·ous** (en dos′pər əs, en′dō spôr′-, -spōr′-), *adj.* **—en·dos′por·ous·ly,** *adv.*

en·do·spo·ri·um (en′də spôr′ē əm, -spōr′-), *n., pl.* **-spo·ri·a** (-spôr′ē ə, -spōr′-). *Bot., Mycol.* intine. [ENDO- + NL *-sporium* < Gk *spor(á)* seed + *-ion* dim. suffix]

en·dos·te·um (en dos′tē əm), *n., pl.* **-te·a** (-tē ə). *Anat.* the membrane lining the medullary cavity of a bone. [1880–85; END- + NL *osteum* < Gk *ostéon* bone] **—en·dos′te·al,** *adj.*

en·dos·to·sis (en′do stō′sis, -də-), *n. Anat.* bone formation beginning in the substance of cartilage. [1865–70; END- + OSTOSIS]

en·do·style (en′də stīl′), *n. Anat.* a ciliated groove or pair of grooves in the pharynx of various lower chordates, such as tunicates, cephalochordates, and larval cyclostomes, serving to accumulate food particles and pass them along the digestive tract. [1850–55; ENDO- + -STYLE[1]; so called because the groove is said to resemble a hollow rod from certain viewing angles]

en·do·sul·fan (en′dō sul′fan), *n. Chem.* a chlorinated hydrocarbon insecticide and miticide, $C_9H_6Cl_6O_3S$, in widespread use on food and forage crops. [1960–65; END(RIN) + -O- + SULF- + *-an,* for -ANE]

en·do·sym·bi·ont (en′dō sim′bē ont′, -bī-), *n.* a symbiont that lives within the body of the host. Also, **en·do·sym·bi·ote** (en′dō sim′bē ōt′, -bī-). [ENDO- + SYMBIONT]

en·do·sym·bi·o·sis (en′dō sim′bē ō′sis, -bī-), *n. Biol.* symbiosis in which one symbiont lives within the body of the other. [1935–40; ENDO- + SYMBIOSIS] **—en·do·sym·bi·ot·ic** (en′dō sim′bē ot′ik, -bī-), *adj.*

en·do·the·ci·um (en′dō thē′shē əm, -sē əm), *n., pl.* **-ci·a** (-shē ə, -sē ə). *Bot.* **1.** the lining of the cavity of an anther. **2.** (in mosses) the central mass of cells in the rudimentary capsule, from which the archespore is generally developed. **3.** (in bryophytes) the central mass of cells in the capsule, including the spores and columella. [1825–35; ENDO- + THECIUM] **—en·do·the·ci·al** (en′dō thē′shē əl, -shəl, -sē əl), *adj.*

en·do·the·li·oid (en′dō thē′lē oid′), *adj.* resembling endothelium. [1865–70; ENDOTHELI(UM) + -OID]

en·do·the·li·o·ma (en′dō thē′lē ō′mə), *n., pl.* **-mas, -ma·ta** (-mə tə). *Pathol.* a tumor originating from the endothelium. [< G *Endotheliom* (1875); see ENDOTHELIUM, -OMA]

en·do·the·li·um (en′dō thē′lē əm), *n., pl.* **-li·a** (-lē ə). a type of epithelium composed of a single layer of smooth, thin cells that lines the heart, blood vessels, lymphatics, and serous cavities. [1870–75; ENDO- + NL *-thelium;* cf. EPITHELIUM] **—en′do·the′li·al,** *adj.*

en·do·therm (en′də thûrm′), *n.* a warm-blooded animal. [1945–50; ENDO- + -THERM]

en·do·ther·mic (en′dō thûr′mik), *adj.* **1.** *Chem.* noting or pertaining to a chemical change that is accompanied by an absorption of heat (opposed to *exothermic*). **2.** *Zool.* warm-blooded. Also, **en·do·ther·mal** (en′dō thûr′məl). [< F *endothermique* (1879); see ENDO-, -THERM, -IC] **—en′do·ther′mi·cal·ly,** *adv.* **—en′do·ther′my, en′do·ther′mism,** *n.*

en·do·tox·in (en′dō tok′sin), *n. Biochem.* the toxic protoplasm liberated when a microorganism dies and disintegrates, as in *Eberthella typhi,* the causative agent of typhoid fever. Cf. **exotoxin.** [1900–05; ENDO- + TOXIN] **—en′do·tox′ic,** *adj.*

en·do·tra·che·al (en′dō trā′kē əl), *adj.* placed or passing within the trachea: *an endotracheal tube.* [1905–10; ENDO- + TRACHEAL]

en·do·troph·ic (en′dō trof′ik, -trō′fik), *adj.* (of a mycorrhiza) growing inside the cells of the root. [< G *endotrophisch* (1887); see ENDO-, -TROPHIC]

en·dow (en dou′), *v.t.* **1.** to provide with a permanent fund or source of income: *to endow a college.* **2.** to furnish, as with some talent, faculty, or quality; equip: *Nature has endowed her with great ability.* **3.** *Obs.* to provide with a dower. **—***v.i.* **4.** (of a life-insurance policy) to become payable; yield its conditions. [1350–1400; ME *endowen* < OF *endouer,* equiv. to *en-* EN-[1] + *douer* < L *dōtāre* to dower, equiv. to *dōt-* (s. of *dōs*) dowry + *-āre* inf. suffix] **—en·dow′er,** *n.*
—Syn. 2. invest, clothe, endue.

en·dow·ment (en dou′mənt), *n.* **1.** the act of endowing. **2.** the property, funds, etc., with which an institution or person is endowed. **3.** Usually, **endowments.** an attribute of mind or body; a gift of nature. [1425–75; late ME < AF *endowement;* see ENDOW, -MENT]
—Syn. 2. gift, grant, bequest. **3.** capacity, talent, faculties, ability, capability.

endow′ment insur′ance, life insurance providing for the payment of a stated sum to the insured if he or she lives beyond the maturity date of the policy, or to a beneficiary if the insured dies before that date. [1860–65, *Amer.*]

end′ pa′per, *Bookbinding.* a sheet of paper, often distinctively colored or ornamented, folded vertically once to form two leaves, one of which is pasted flat to the inside of the front or back cover of a book, with the other pasted to the inside edge of the first or last page to form a flyleaf. Also called **end leaf, end sheet.** [1810–20]

end′ plate′, 1. *Mining.* one of the shorter members of a set. Cf. **wall plate** (def. 3). **2.** *Cell Biol.* a specialized area on the surface of a muscle fiber where a motor neuron makes contact with the muscle, consisting of an irregularly shaped trough into which the terminal portion of the axon fits. [1875–80]

end·play (end′plā′), *Bridge.* **—***n.* **1.** any play, usually near the end of a contract, that puts one of the opposing players in the lead and forces the opponents to lose one or more tricks that they would have won if their side had not been leading. **—***v.t.* **2.** to put into the lead by an endplay. [1930–35; END[1] + PLAY]

end′ point′, 1. a final goal or finishing point; terminus. **2.** *Chem.* the point in a titration usually noting the completion of a reaction and marked by a change of some kind, as of the color of an indicator. **3.** *Math.* endpoint. [1895–1900]

end·point (end′point′), *n. Math.* the point on each side of an interval marking its extremity on that side. Also, **end point.** [1895–1900; END[1] + POINT]

end′ prod′uct, the final or resulting product, as of an industry, process of growth, etc.: *Cloth is one of the end products of cotton manufacture.* [1935–40]

end′ rhyme′, *Pros.* rhyme of the terminal syllables of lines of poetry.

end′ run′, 1. *Football.* Also called **end′ sweep′, sweep.** a running play in which the ball-carrier attempts to outflank the defensive end. **2.** *Informal.* **a.** an evasive or diversionary maneuver. **b.** an attempt to surmount a difficulty without confronting it directly. [1900–05, *Amer.*]

end·shake (end′shāk′), *n. Horol.* the free longitudinal movement of arbors or the like between bearings. [1880–85; END[1] + SHAKE]

end′ sheet′, *Bookbinding.* See **end paper.**

end-stopped (end′stopt′), *adj. Pros.* (of a line of verse) ending at the end of a syntactic unit that is usually followed by a pause in speaking and a punctuation mark in writing. [1875–80]

Ends·ville (endz′vil), *adj.* (*sometimes l.c.*) *Slang.* **1.** most wonderful or exciting: *a rock band that was regarded as Endsville in the late fifties.* **2.** (of a location, circumstance, etc.) most isolated or undesirable. [see END[1], DRAGSVILLE]

end′ ta′ble, a small table placed beside a chair or at the end of a sofa. [1850–55, *Amer.*]

en·due (en do͞o′, -dyo͞o′), *v.t.,* **-dued, -du·ing. 1.** to invest or endow with some gift, quality, or faculty. **2.** to put on; assume: *Hamlet endued the character of a madman.* **3.** to clothe. Also, **indue.** [1350–1400; ME *endewen* to induct, initiate < AF, OF *enduire* < L *indūcere* to lead in, cover, INDUCE]

en·dur·a·ble (en do͝or′ə bəl, -dyo͝or′-), *adj.* capable of being endured; bearable; tolerable. [1600–10; ENDURE + -ABLE] **—en·dur′a·bil′i·ty, en·dur′a·ble·ness,** *n.* **—en·dur′a·bly,** *adv.*

en·dur·ance (en do͝or′əns, -dyo͝or′-), *n.* **1.** the fact or power of enduring or bearing pain, hardships, etc. **2.** the ability or strength to continue or last, esp. despite fatigue, stress, or other adverse conditions; stamina: *He has amazing physical endurance.* **3.** lasting quality; duration: *His friendships have little endurance.* **4.** something endured, as a hardship; trial. [1485–95; ENDURE + -ANCE]
—Syn. 1. See **patience.**

endur′ance race′, an auto race over a closed course designed to test the endurance of both driver and vehicle and won by the car that covers the longest distance in an arbitrarily allotted time or by the car that is first to cover a predetermined long distance.

endur′ance ra′tio. See **fatigue ratio.**

en·dur·ant (en do͝or′ənt, -dyo͝or′-), *adj.* capable of enduring hardship, misfortune, or the like. [1865–70; ENDURE + -ANT]

en·dure (en do͝or′, -dyo͝or′), *v.,* **-dured, -dur·ing.** **—***v.t.* **1.** to hold out against; sustain without impairment or yielding; undergo: *to endure great financial pressures with equanimity.* **2.** to bear without resistance or with patience; tolerate: *I cannot endure your insults any longer.* **3.** to admit of; allow; bear: *His poetry is such that it will not endure a superficial reading.* **—***v.i.* **4.** to continue to exist; last: *These words will endure as long as people live who love freedom.* **5.** to support adverse force or influence of any kind; suffer without yielding; suffer patiently: *Even in the darkest ages humanity has endured.* **6.** to have or gain continued or lasting acknowledgment or recognition, as of worth, merit or greatness: *His plays have endured for more than three centuries.* [1275–1325; ME *enduren* < AF, OF *endurer* < L *indūrāre* to harden, make lasting, equiv. to *in-* IN-[2] + *dūrāre* to last, be or become hard, deriv. of *dūrus* hard] **—en·dur′er,** *n.*
—Syn. 2. stand, support, suffer, brook. See **bear**[1]. **4.** abide. See **continue. —Ant. 4.** fail, die.

en·dur·ing (en do͝or′ing, -dyo͝or′-), *adj.* **1.** lasting; permanent: *a poet of enduring greatness.* **2.** patient; long-suffering. [1525–35; ENDURE + -ING[2]] **—en·dur′ing·ly,** *adv.* **—en·dur′ing·ness,** *n.*

en·dur·o (en do͝or′ō, -dyo͝or′ō), *n., pl.* **-dur·os.** an endurance race for automobiles or sometimes motorcycles. [appar. a pseudo It or Sp deriv. of ENDURANCE]

end′ use′ (yo͞os), the ultimate use for which something is intended or to which it is put. [1950–55] **—end′-use′,** *adj.*

end′ us′er, the ultimate user for whom a machine, as a computer, or product, as a computer program, is designed. Also, **end′-us′er.** [1960–65]

end•ways (end′wāz′), *adv.* **1.** on end: *We set the table endways in order to fix the legs.* **2.** with the end upward or forward. **3.** toward the ends or end; lengthwise. **4.** with ends touching; end to end. Also, **end•wise** (end′-wīz′). [1565–75; END[1] + -WAYS]

En•dym•i•on (en dim′ē ən), *n.* **1.** *Class. Myth.* a young man kept forever youthful through eternal sleep and loved by Selene. **2.** (*italics*) a narrative poem (1818) by John Keats.

end′ zone′, **1.** *Football.* an area at each end of the field between the goal line and the end line. **2.** *Ice Hockey.* an area at each end of the rink between the goal line and the closer of the two blue lines. Cf. **neutral zone.** [1910–15]

ENE, east-northeast. Also, **E.N.E.**

-ene, *Chem.* a suffix used to form names of unsaturated hydrocarbons (*anthracene; benzene*), esp. those of the alkene series (*butylene*). [< Gk *-ēnē,* fem. of *-ēnos,* adj. suffix denoting origin or source]

en•e•ma (en′ə mə), *n. Med.* **1.** the injection of a fluid into the rectum to cause a bowel movement. **2.** the fluid injected. **3.** Also called **en′ema bag′.** a rubber bag or other device for administering an enema. [1675–85; < LL < Gk: injection, equiv. to *en-* EN-[2] + *(h)e-* (s. of *hiénai* to throw) + *-ma* n. suffix]

en•e•my (en′ə mē), *n., pl.* **-mies,** *adj.* **—*n.*** **1.** a person who feels hatred for, fosters harmful designs against, or engages in antagonistic activities against another; an adversary or opponent. **2.** an armed foe; an opposing military force: *The army attacked the enemy at dawn.* **3.** a hostile nation or state. **4.** a citizen of such a state. **5.** **enemies,** persons, nations, etc., that are hostile to one another: *Let's make up and stop being enemies.* **6.** something harmful or prejudicial: *His unbridled ambition is his worst enemy.* **7. the Enemy,** the Devil; Satan. **—*adj.*** **8.** belonging to a hostile power or to any of its nationals: *enemy property.* **9.** *Obs.* inimical; ill-disposed. [1250–1300; ME *enemi* < AF, OF < L *inimīcus* unfriendly, equiv. to *in-* IN-[3] + *amīcus* friendly, friend; see AMICABLE]
—Usage. See **collective noun.**
—Syn. 1. antagonist. ENEMY, FOE refer to a dangerous public or personal adversary. ENEMY emphasizes the idea of hostility: *to overcome the enemy; a bitter enemy.* FOE, a more literary word, may be used interchangeably with ENEMY, but emphasizes somewhat more the danger to be feared from such a one: *deadly foe; arch foe of humankind (the Devil).* **—Ant. 1.** friend. **2.** ally.

en′emy al′ien, an alien residing in a country at war with the one of which he or she is a citizen. [1945–50]

E•ne•o•lith•ic (ē′nē ō lith′ik), *adj.* Chalcolithic. Also, **Aenolithic.** [1910–15]

en•er•get•ic (en′ər jet′ik), *adj.* **1.** possessing or exhibiting energy, esp. in abundance; vigorous: *an energetic leader.* **2.** powerful in action or effect; effective: *to take energetic measures against crime.* Also, **en′er•get′i•cal.** [1645–55; < Gk *energētikós,* equiv. to *energē-* (*en-* EN-[2] + *ergē-,* var. s. of *ergein* to be active; see ENERGY) + *-tikos* -TIC] **—en′er•get′i•cal•ly,** *adv.*
—Syn. 1. See **active. 2.** effectual, strong, potent.

en•er•get•ics (en′ər jet′iks), *n.* (*used with a singular v.*) the branch of physics that deals with energy. [1850–55; see ENERGETIC, -ICS] **—en′er•get′i•cist,** *n.* **—en•er•ge•tis•tic** (en′ər ji tis′tik), *adj.*

en•er•gism (en′ər jiz′əm), *n. Ethics.* the theory that self-realization is the highest good. [1890–95; < G *Energismus.* See ENERGY, -ISM] **—en′er•gist,** *n., adj.* **—en′•er•gis′tic,** *adj.*

en•er•gize (en′ər jīz′), *v.,* **-gized, -giz•ing.** **—*v.t.*** **1.** to give energy to; rouse into activity: *to energize the spirit with brave words.* **2.** to supply electrical current to or store electrical energy in. **—*v.i.*** **3.** to be in operation; put forth energy. Also, *esp. Brit.,* **en′er•gise′.** [1745–55; ENERG(Y) + -IZE]

en•er•giz•er (en′ər jī′zər), *n.* **1.** a person or thing that energizes. **2.** *Pharm.* antidepressant (def. 2). [1740–50; ENERGIZE + -ER[1]]

en•er•gy (en′ər jē), *n., pl.* **-gies.** **1.** the capacity for vigorous activity; available power: *I eat chocolate to get quick energy.* **2.** an adequate or abundant amount of such power: *I seem to have no energy these days.* **3.** Often, **energies.** a feeling of tension caused or seeming to be caused by an excess of such power: *to work off one's energies at tennis.* **4.** an exertion of such power: *She plays tennis with great energy.* **5.** the habit of vigorous activity; vigor as a characteristic: *Foreigners both admire and laugh at American energy.* **6.** the ability to act, lead others, effect, etc., forcefully. **7.** forcefulness of expression: *a writing style abounding with energy.* **8.** *Physics.* the capacity to do work; the property of a system that diminishes when the system does work on any other system, by an amount equal to the work so done; potential energy. *Symbol:* E **9.** any source of usable power, as fossil fuel, electricity, or solar radiation. [1575–85; < LL *energīa* < Gk *enérgeia* activity, equiv. to *energe-* (s. of *energeîn* to be active; see EN-[2], WORK) + *-ia* -Y[3]]
—Syn. 1. vigor, force, potency. **5.** zeal, push.

en′ergy au′dit, a technical check of energy use, as in a home or factory, to monitor and evaluate consumption. [1975–80]

en′ergy band′, *Physics.* band (def. 10).

CONCISE ETYMOLOGY KEY: <, descended or borrowed from; >, whence; b., blend of, blended; c., cognate with; cf., compare; deriv., derivative; equiv., equivalent; imit., imitative; obl., oblique; r., replacing; s., stem; sp., spelling, spelled; resp., respelling, respelled; trans., translation; ?, origin unknown; *, unattested; ‡, probably earlier than. See the full key inside the front cover.

en′ergy effi′ciency ra′tio, a measure of the efficiency of a heating or cooling system, as a heat pump or air conditioner, equal to the output in B.T.U./hour to the input in watts: *A high-efficiency home window air conditioner has an energy efficiency ratio of 7.5 or more. Abbr.:* EER

en′ergy lev′el, **1.** a comparative level of capacity for vigorous activity: *The child has a high energy level.* **2.** Also called **en′ergy state′.** *Physics.* one of a quantized series of states in which matter may exist, each having constant energy and separated from others in the series by finite quantities of energy. [1905–10]

en•er•vate (*v.* en′ər vāt′; *adj.* i nûr′vit), *v.,* **-vat•ed, -vat•ing,** *adj.* **—*v.t.*** **1.** to deprive of force or strength; destroy the vigor of; weaken. **—*adj.*** **2.** enervated. [1595–1605; < L *ēnervātus* weakened (ptp. of *ēnervāre*) equiv. to *ē-* E- + *nerv(us)* sinew (see NERVE) + *-ātus* -ATE[1]; cf. AF *enervir,* F *énerver*] **—en′er•va′tion,** *n.* **—en′er•va′tive,** *adj.* **—en′er•va′tor,** *n.*
—Syn. 1. enfeeble, debilitate, sap, exhaust.

en•er•vat•ed (en′ər vā′tid), *adj.* without vigor, force, or strength; languid. [1650–60; ENERVATE + -ED[2]]

E•nes•co (e nes′kō), *n.* **Georges** (zhôrzh), 1881–1955, Rumanian violinist, composer, and conductor: teacher of Yehudi Menuhin. Also, **E•nes•cu** (e nes′ko͞o).

e-neu•tri•no (ē′no͞o trē′nō, ē′nyo͞o-), *n., pl.* **-nos.** *Physics.* electron-neutrino.

en•face (en fās′), *v.t.,* **-faced, -fac•ing.** **1.** to write, print, or stamp something on the face of (a note, draft, etc.). **2.** to write, print, or stamp (something) on the face of a note, draft, etc. [1860–65; EN-[1] + FACE] **—en•face′ment,** *n.*

en fa•mille (äɴ fa mē′yᵊ), *French.* in or with the family; at home: *to dine* en famille.

en•fants per•dus (äɴ fäɴ per dy′), *French.* soldiers assigned to a dangerous post. [lit., lost children]

en•fant ter•ri•ble (äɴ fäɴ te rē′blᵊ), *pl.* ***en•fants ter•ri•bles*** (äɴ fäɴ te rē′blᵊ). *French.* **1.** an incorrigible child, as one whose behavior is embarrassing. **2.** an outrageously outspoken or bold person who says and does indiscreet or irresponsible things. **3.** a person whose work, thought, or lifestyle is so unconventional or avant-garde as to appear revolutionary or shocking.

en•fee•ble (en fē′bəl), *v.t.,* **-bled, -bling.** to make feeble; weaken: *That bout of pneumonia enfeebled him.* [1300–50; ME *enfeblen* < OF *enfeblir.* See EN-[1], FEEBLE] **—en•fee′ble•ment,** *n.* **—en′fee′bler,** *n.*
—Syn. enervate, debilitate.

en•feoff (en fef′, -fēf′), *v.t.* **1.** to invest with a freehold estate in land. **2.** to give as a fief. [1350–1400; ME *enfe(o)ffen* < AF *enfe(o)ffer,* equiv. to *en-* -EN-[1] + OF *fiefer, fiever,* deriv. of *fief* FIEF] **—en•feoff′ment,** *n.*

en•fet•ter (en fet′ər), *v.t.* to bind with or as with fetters. [1595–1605; EN-[1] + FETTER]

en•fe•ver (en fē′vər), *v.t.* to cause or excite fever in. [1640–50; EN[1]- + FEVER]

En•field (en′fēld′), *n.* **1.** a borough of Greater London, England. 261,900. **2.** a town in N Connecticut. 42,695. **3.** See **Enfield rifle.**

En′field ri′fle, **1.** a single-shot, muzzleloading rifle, of .577 caliber, used by the British army in the Crimean War and in limited numbers by both sides in the American Civil War. **2.** a bolt-action, breech-loading, .303-caliber magazine rifle introduced in Britain in 1902. **3.** an American .30-caliber rifle used in World War I by U.S. troops, patterned after the British Enfield rifle. Also called **Enfield.** [named after ENFIELD, England, where it was first made]

en•fi•lade (en′fə lād′, -läd′, en′fə lād′, -läd′), *n., v.,* **-lad•ed, -lad•ing.** **—*n.*** **1.** *Mil.* **a.** a position of works, troops, etc., making them subject to a sweeping fire from along the length of a line of troops, a trench, a battery, etc. **b.** the fire thus directed. **2.** *Archit.* **a.** an axial arrangement of doorways connecting a suite of rooms with a vista down the whole length of the suite. **b.** an axial arrangement of mirrors on opposite sides of a room so as to give an effect of an infinitely long vista. **—*v.t.*** **3.** *Mil.* to attack with an enfilade. [1695–1705; < F, equiv. to *enfil(er)* to thread, string (*en-* EN-[1] + *-filer,* deriv. of *fil* < L *filum* thread) + *-ade* -ADE[1]]

en•fin (äɴ faɴ′), *adv. French.* in conclusion; finally. [lit., in (the) end]

en•flame (en flām′), *v.t., v.i.,* **-flamed, -flam•ing.** inflame.

en•fleu•rage (äɴ′flə räzh′; *Fr.* äɴ flœ RAZH′), *n.* a process of extracting perfumes by exposing inodorous oils or fats to the exhalations of flowers. [1850–55; < F, equiv. to *enfleur(er)* to impregnate with scent of flowers (*en-* EN-[1] + *-fleurer,* deriv. of *fleur* FLOWER) + *-age* -AGE]

en•flu•rane (en′flo͝o rān′), *n. Pharm.* a volatile liquid, $C_3H_2ClF_5O$, used as a general anesthetic in surgery. [*en-* unclearly derived + *(tri)flu(o)r(oeth)ane*]

en•fold (en fōld′), *v.t.* **1.** to wrap up; envelop: *to enfold someone in a cloak.* **2.** to surround as if with folds: *He wished to enfold her in the warmth of his love. What happened is enfolded in mystery.* **3.** to hug or clasp; embrace: *She enfolded him in her arms.* **4.** to form into a fold or folds: *The material of the skirt had been enfolded to form a loose, graceful drape.* Also, **infold.** [1585–95; EN-[1] + FOLD[1]] **—en•fold′er,** *n.* **—en•fold′ment,** *n.*

en•force (en fôrs′, -fōrs′), *v.t.,* **-forced, -forc•ing.** **1.** to put or keep in force; compel obedience to: *to enforce a rule; Traffic laws will be strictly enforced.* **2.** to obtain (payment, obedience, etc.) by force or compulsion. **3.** to impose (a course of action) upon a person: *The doctor enforced a strict dietary regimen.* **4.** to support (a demand, claim, etc.) by force: *to enforce one's rights as a citizen.* **5.** to impress or urge (an argument, contention, etc.) forcibly; lay stress upon: *He enforced his argument by adding details.* [1275–1325; ME *enforcen* < AF *enforcer,* OF *enforcier, enforc(ir),* equiv. to *en-* EN-[1] + *forci(e)r* to FORCE] **—en•force′a•ble,** *adj.* **—en•force′a•bil′i•ty,** *n.* **—en•forc•ed•ly** (en fôr′sid lē, -fōr′-), *adv.* **—en•forc′•er,** *n.* **—en•forc′ive,** *adj.*
—Syn. 1. administer, impose, execute, apply.

en•force•ment (en fôrs′mənt, -fōrs′-), *n.* **1.** the act or process of enforcing. **2.** something that enforces. [1425–75; late ME < AF, OF. See ENFORCE, -MENT]

en•forc•er (en fôr′sər, -fōr′-), *n.* **1.** a person or thing that enforces. **2.** the member of a group, esp. of a gang, charged with keeping dissident members obedient. **3.** a person, esp. a public official, who enforces laws, regulations, rules, or the like. **4.** Also called **policeman.** *Ice Hockey.* a physically intimidating or willingly belligerent player who is counted on to retaliate when rough tactics are used by the opposing team. [1570–80; ENFORCE + -ER[1]]

en•fran•chise (en fran′chīz), *v.t.,* **-chised, -chis•ing.** **1.** to grant a franchise to; admit to citizenship, esp. to the right of voting. **2.** to endow (a city, constituency, etc.) with municipal or parliamentary rights. **3.** to set free; liberate, as from slavery. Also, **franchise.** [1505–15; < MF, OF *enfranchiss-* (long s. of *enfranchir* to free), equiv. to *en-* EN-[1] + *franch-* free (see FRANK[1]) + *-iss-* -ISH[2]] **—en•fran•chise•ment** (en fran′chiz mənt, -chīz-), *n.* **—en•fran′chis•er,** *n.*

eng (eng), *n.* the symbol, ŋ, that, in the International Phonetic Alphabet and in the pronunciation alphabets of some dictionaries, represents the voiced velar nasal consonant indicated in this dictionary by (ng), as in the pronunciations of *cling* (kling) and *clink* (klingk). Also called **agma, angma.** [1955–60; by analogy with the names of *m* and *n*]

ENG, *Television.* electronic news gathering: a system of news reporting that uses portable television cameras to videotape pictures and sound, esp. when combined with the transmission of the signal to a television station for immediate broadcast.

Eng., **1.** England. **2.** English.

eng., **1.** engine. **2.** engineer. **3.** engineering. **4.** engraved. **5.** engraver. **6.** engraving.

En•ga•dine (eng′gə dēn′, eng′gə dēn′), *n.* the valley of the Inn River in E Switzerland: resorts. 60 mi. (97 km) long.

en•gage (en gāj′), *v.,* **-gaged, -gag•ing.** **—*v.t.*** **1.** to occupy the attention or efforts of (a person or persons): *He engaged her in conversation.* **2.** to secure for aid, employment, use, etc.; hire: *to engage a worker; to engage a room.* **3.** to attract and hold fast: *The novel engaged her attention and interest.* **4.** to attract or please: *His good nature engages everyone.* **5.** to bind, as by pledge, promise, contract, or oath; make liable: *He engaged himself to repay his debt within a month.* **6.** to betroth (usually used in the passive): *They were engaged last week.* **7.** to bring (troops) into conflict; enter into conflict with: *Our army engaged the enemy.* **8.** *Mech.* to cause (gears or the like) to become interlocked; interlock with. **9.** to attach or secure. **10.** *Obs.* to entangle or involve. **—*v.i.*** **11.** to occupy oneself; become involved: *to engage in business or politics.* **12.** to take employment: *She engaged in her mother's business.* **13.** to pledge one's word; assume an obligation: *I was unwilling to engage on such terms.* **14.** to cross weapons; enter into conflict: *The armies engaged early in the morning.* **15.** *Mech.* (of gears or the like) to interlock. [1515–25; < MF *engager,* OF *engagier.* See EN-[1], GAGE[1]] **—en•gag′er,** *n.*
—Syn. 1. absorb, engross, interest, involve. **—Ant. 2.** discharge. **8.** release.

en•ga•gé (*Fr.* äɴ ga zhā′), *adj.* choosing to involve oneself in or commit oneself to something: *Some of the political activists grew less engagé as the years passed.* [1950–55; < F: lit., engaged]

en•gaged (en gājd′), *adj.* **1.** busy or occupied; involved: *deeply engaged in conversation.* **2.** pledged to be married; betrothed: *an engaged couple.* **3.** under engagement; pledged: *an engaged contractor.* **4.** entered into conflict with: *desperately engaged armies.* **5.** *Mech.* **a.** interlocked. **b.** (of wheels) in gear with each other. **6.** *Archit.* (of a distinct member) built so as to be truly or seemingly attached in part to the structure before which it stands: *an engaged column.* [1605–15; ENGAGE + -ED[2]] **—en•gag•ed•ly** (en gā′jid lē, -gājd′-), *adv.* **—en•gag′•ed•ness,** *n.*

en•gage•ment (en gāj′mənt), *n.* **1.** the act of engaging or the state of being engaged. **2.** an appointment or arrangement: *a business engagement.* **3.** betrothal: *They announced their engagement.* **4.** a pledge; an obligation or agreement: *All his time seems to be taken up with social engagements.* **5.** employment, or a period or post of employment, esp. in the performing arts: *Her engagement at the nightclub will last five weeks.* **6.** an encounter, conflict, or battle: *We have had two very costly engagements with the enemy this week alone.* **7.** *Mech.* the act or state of interlocking. **8. engagements,** *Com.* financial obligations. [1615–25; ENGAGE + -MENT]
—Syn. 4. contract, promise.

engage′ment cal′endar, an appointment book for the daily recording of social engagements and other appointments.

engage′ment ring′, a ring, often a diamond, given by a man to his fiancée at the time of their engagement as a token of their betrothal. [1860–65]

en•gag•ing (en gā′jing), *adj.* winning; attractive; pleasing: *an engaging smile.* [1665–75; ENGAGE + -ING[2]] **—en•gag′ing•ly,** *adv.* **—en•gag′ing•ness,** *n.*
—Syn. charming, agreeable.

en garde (än gärd′; *Fr.* äɴ GARD′), *Fencing.* (used as the call to the fencers by the director of a match to assume the prescribed position preparatory to action.) [< F: on guard]

en•gar•land (en gär′lənd), *v.t.* to encircle with or as with a garland. [1575–85; EN-[1] + GARLAND]

en•ga•wa (eng gä′wä), *n.* a floor extension at one side of a Japanese-style house, usually facing a yard or garden and serving as passageway and sitting space. [< Japn, equiv. to *en* edge, veranda (< MChin, equiv. to

Chin *yuán*) + *-gawa* comb. form of *kawa* (earlier *kafa*) side]

Eng. D., Doctor of Engineering.

En·gel (eng′gəl), *n.* **Leh·man** (lā′mən), born 1910, U.S. conductor and composer.

En′gel·mann spruce′ (eng′gəl mən), **1.** a narrow, conical spruce, *Picea engelmannii,* of western North America, having short, dense branches and yielding a soft, pale-yellow wood. **2.** the soft, light wood of this tree, used in the construction of buildings and in the manufacture of paper, boxes, etc. [1865–70; named after G. *Engelmann* (1809–84), German-American botanist]

En·gels (eng′gəlz; *for 1 also Ger.* eng′əls; *for 2 also Russ.* en′gyils), *n.* **1. Frie·drich** (frē′drikh), 1820–95, German socialist in England: collaborated with Karl Marx in systematizing Marxism. **2.** a city in the Russian Federation in Europe, on the Volga River opposite Saratov. 182,000.

En′gel's law′, the assertion that the percentage of a family's income spent on food decreases as its income increases. [named after Ernst *Engel* (1821–96), German economist]

en·gen·der (en jen′dər), *v.t.* **1.** to produce, cause, or give rise to: *Hatred engenders violence.* **2.** to beget; procreate. —*v.i.* **3.** to be produced or caused; come into existence: *Conditions for a war were engendering in Europe.* [1275–1325; ME < OF *engendrer* < L *ingenerāre,* equiv. to *in-* EN-[1] + *generāre* to beget; see GENERATE] —**en·gen′der·er,** *n.* —**en·gen′der·ment,** *n.*
—**Syn. 1.** beget, occasion, excite, stir up. **1, 2.** create.

En·ghien, d′ (dän gan′), *n.* **Duc** (dyk) (*Louis Antoine Henry de Bourbon-Condé*), 1772–1804, French prince: executed by Napoleon I.

en·gild (en gild′), *v.t.* to brighten with or as with golden light: *rays of the sun engilding the city's towers.* [1350–1400; ME; see EN-[1], GILD[1]]

engin., engineering.

en·gine (en′jən), *n.* **1.** a machine for converting thermal energy into mechanical energy or power to produce force and motion. **2.** a railroad locomotive. **3.** a fire engine. **4.** any mechanical contrivance. **5.** a machine or instrument used in warfare, as a battering ram, catapult, or piece of artillery. **6.** *Obs.* an instrument of torture, esp. the rack. [1250–1300; ME *engin* < AF, OF < L *ingenium* nature, innate quality, esp. mental power, hence a clever invention, equiv. to *in-* IN-[2] + *-genium,* equiv. to *gen-* begetting (see KIN) + *-ium* -IUM] —**en′gine·less,** *adj.*

en′gine block′, *Auto.* See **cylinder block.**

en′gine com′pany, a unit of a city's fire department in command of one or more fire-fighting vehicles. [1810–20, *Amer.*]

en·gi·neer (en′jə nēr′), *n.* **1.** a person trained and skilled in the design, construction, and use of engines or machines, or in any of various branches of engineering: *a mechanical engineer; a civil engineer.* **2.** a person who operates or is in charge of an engine. **3.** Also called **locomotive engineer.** *Railroads.* a person who operates or is in charge of a locomotive. **4.** a member of an army, navy, or air force specially trained in engineering work. **5.** a skillful manager: *a political engineer.* —*v.t.* **6.** to plan, construct, or manage as an engineer: *He's engineered several big industrial projects.* **7.** to design or create using the techniques or methods of engineering: *The motor has been engineered to run noiselessly.* **8.** to arrange, manage, or carry through by skillful or artful contrivance: *He certainly engineered the election campaign beautifully.* [1350–1400; ENGINE + -EER; r. ME *engin(e)our* < AF *engineor* OF *engigneor* < ML *ingeniātor,* equiv. to *ingeniā(re)* to design, devise (v. deriv. of *ingenium;* see ENGINE) + L *-tor* -TOR]

en·gi·neer·ing (en′jə nēr′ing), *n.* **1.** the art or science of making practical application of the knowledge of pure sciences, as physics or chemistry, as in the construction of engines, bridges, buildings, mines, ships, and chemical plants. **2.** the action, work, or profession of an engineer. **3.** skillful or artful contrivance; maneuvering. [1710–20; ENGINEER + -ING[1]]

engineer′ing geol′ogy, the application of geologic principles, techniques, and data to mining, construction, petroleum engineering, and ground-water utilization. [1860–65]

engineer's′ chain′. See under **chain** (def. 8a).

en′gine house′, a building in which a fire engine is stationed. [1725–35]

en·gine·man (en′jən man′, -mən), *n., pl.* **-men** (-men′, -mən). a person who operates or helps to operate an engine or locomotive. [1715–25; ENGINE + MAN[1]]

en·gine·ry (en′jən rē), *n., pl.* **-ries. 1.** engines collectively; machinery. **2.** engines of war collectively. **3.** skillful or artful contrivance. [1595–1605; ENGINE + -RY]

en′gine turn′ing, ornamentation having the form of a pattern of circular arcs, engraved by a rose engine. [1880–85]

en·gird (en gûrd′), *v.t.,* **-girt** or **-gird·ed, -gird·ing.** to encircle; encompass: *The equator engirds the earth.* [1560–70; EN-[1] + GIRD[1]]

en·gir·dle (en gûr′dl), *v.t.,* **-dled, -dling.** to engird. [1595–1605; EN-[1] + GIRDLE]

en·gla·cial (en glā′shəl), *adj. Geol.* **1.** within the ice of a glacier. **2.** believed to have been formerly within the ice of a glacier: *englacial debris.* [1890–95; EN-[1] + GLACIAL] —**en·gla′cial·ly,** *adv.*

Eng·land (ing′glənd *or, often,* -lənd), *n.* the largest division of the United Kingdom, constituting, with Scotland and Wales, the island of Great Britain. 45,870,062; 50,327 sq. mi. (130,347 sq. km) *Cap.:* London.

En·gle (eng′gəl), *n.* **Paul (Hamilton),** 1908–91, U.S. poet and educator.

En·gle·wood (eng′gəl wo͝od′), *n.* **1.** a city in central Colorado, 30,021. **2.** a city in NE New Jersey. 23,701. **3.** a town in SW Ohio. 11,329. **4.** a town in W Florida. 10,229.

Eng·lish (ing′glish *or, often,* -lish), *adj.* **1.** of, pertaining to, or characteristic of England or its inhabitants, institutions, etc. **2.** belonging or pertaining to, or spoken or written in, the English language. —*n.* **3.** the people of England collectively, esp. as distinguished from the Scots, Welsh, and Irish. **4.** the Germanic language of the British Isles, widespread and standard also in the U.S. and most of the British Commonwealth, historically termed Old English (c450–c1150), Middle English (c1150–c1475), and Modern English (after c1475). *Abbr.:* E **5.** English language, composition, and literature as offered as a course of study in school. **6.** a specific variety of this language, as that of a particular time, place, or person: *American English; Shakespearean English.* **7.** simple, straightforward language: *What does all that jargon mean in English?* **8.** *Sports.* (*sometimes l.c.*) **a.** a spinning motion imparted to a ball, esp. in billiards. **b.** See **body English. 9.** *Print.* a 14-point type of a size between pica and Columbian. **10.** a grade of calendered paper having a smooth matte finish. —*v.t.* **11.** to translate into English: *to English Euripides.* **12.** to adopt (a foreign word) into English; Anglicize. **13.** (*sometimes l.c.*) *Sports.* to impart English to (a ball). [bef. 900; ME; OE *Englisc,* equiv. to *Engle* (pl.) the English (cf. L *Angli;* see ANGLE) + *-isc* -ISH[1]] —**Eng′lish·ness,** *n.*

Eng′lish bond′, *Masonry.* a brickwork bond having alternate courses of headers and stretchers in which the headers are centered on stretchers and the joints between stretchers line up vertically in all courses. See illus. under **bond.** [1815–25]

Eng′lish break′fast, a hearty breakfast typically including eggs, bacon or ham, toast, and tea or coffee. Cf. **continental breakfast.** [1800–10]

Eng′lish Cana′dian, an English-speaking Canadian. [1810–20]

Eng′lish Chan′nel, an arm of the Atlantic between S England and N France, connected with the North Sea by the Strait of Dover. 350 mi. (565 km) long; 20–100 mi. (32–160 km) wide.

Eng′lish Civ′il War′, the war (1642–46) between the Parliamentarians and the Royalists, sometimes extended to include the events of the period 1646–48.

Eng′lish cock′er span′iel, one of an English breed of compact medium-sized sporting dogs having a medium-length coat of various solid colors or parti-colored, low-set, droopy ears, fairly short legs, and a docked tail, originally raised as a hunting dog. [1945–50]

Eng′lish cross′ bond′, *Masonry.* a brickwork bond in which the vertical joints of the stretchers in any course are in line with the centers of the first stretchers above and below. See illus. under **bond.** Also called **Dutch bond.** [1885–90]

Eng′lish dai′sy, the common European daisy, *Bellis perennis.* [1885–90]

Eng′lish elm′. See under **elm** (def. 1).

Eng·lish·er (ing′gli shər *or, often,* -li-), *n.* a person who translates from a foreign language into English. [1790–1800; ENGLISH + -ER[1]]

Eng′lish fin′ish, *Print.* a smooth, unglossed finish on paper, obtained by calendering paper that has short fibers and a high mineral content. Cf. **English** (def. 10). [1930–35]

Eng′lish fox′hound, one of an English breed of medium-sized hunting dogs, slightly larger than the American foxhound, having a short, dense, glossy coat, in combinations of black, tan, or white, with low-set ears, and very straight legs, originally used for hunting foxes in packs. [1935–40]

Eng′lish goose′berry, a spiny Eurasian and northern African shrub, *Ribes uva-crispa,* of the saxifrage family, having green flowers in sparse clusters and acid, bristly green, red, or yellow fruit.

Eng′lish hol′ly. See under **holly** (def. 1).

Eng′lish horn′, a large oboe, a fifth lower in pitch than the ordinary oboe, having a pear-shaped bell and producing a mellow tone. Also called **cor anglais.** [1830–40]

English horn

Eng′lish i′ris, an iris, *Iris xiphiodes,* native to the Pyrenees, having two or three deep purple-blue flowers with golden patches.

Eng·lish·ism (ing′gli shiz′əm *or, often,* -li-), *n.* **1.** a Briticism. **2.** attachment to what is English. [1850–55; ENGLISH + -ISM]

Eng′lish i′vy, ivy (def. 1). [1810–20, *Amer.*]

Eng′lish lau′rel. See **cherry laurel** (def. 1).

Eng·lish·ly (ing′glish lē *or, often,* -lish-), *adv.* in the manner or style of the English people. [1520–30; ENGLISH + -LY]

Eng·lish·man (ing′glish mən *or, often,* -lish-), *n., pl.* **-men. 1.** a native or a naturalized citizen of England. **2.** an English ship. [bef. 950; ME; OE *Engliscman.* See ENGLISH, MAN[1]]

Eng′lish muf′fin, a rather flat muffin made from yeast dough, typically baked on a griddle, and then split and toasted before being eaten. [1925–30]

Eng′lish Pale′, pale[2] (def. 6).

Eng′lish pea′, *Southern and South Midland U.S.* pea[1] (defs. 1, 2).

Eng′lish plan′tain, a common plantain weed, *Plantago lanceolata,* having narrow basal leaves and a dense head of small, whitish flowers. Also called **ribgrass, ribwort.** [1835–45, *Amer.*]

Eng′lish prim′rose. See under **primrose** (def. 1).

Eng′lish red′, a Venetian red pigment and color.

Eng′lish Revolu′tion, the events of 1688–89 by which James II was expelled and the sovereignty conferred on William and Mary. Also called **Bloodless Revolution, Glorious Revolution.**

Eng·lish·ry (ing′glish rē *or, often,* -lish-), *n.* **1.** the fact of being English, esp. by birth. **2.** a population that is English or of English descent: *the Englishry of Ireland.* [1250–1300; late ME *Englisherie* < AF *Englescherie,* equiv. to ME *Englisch* ENGLISH + AF *-erie* -ERY]

Eng′lish sad′dle, a saddle having a steel cantle and pommel, no horn, full side flaps usually set forward, a well-padded leather seat, and a saddletree or frame designed to conform to the line of the rider's back. See diag. under **saddle.** [1930–35]

Eng′lish sen′nit. See **flat sennit.** [‡1960–65]

Eng′lish set′ter, one of a breed of medium-sized, long-haired bird dogs having a flat, usually black-and-white or tan-and-white coat. [1855–60]

English setter, 2 ft. (0.6 m) high at shoulder

Eng′lish sheep′dog. See **Old English sheepdog.**

Eng′lish sole′. See under **lemon sole.**

Eng′lish son′net. See **Shakespearean sonnet.** [1900–05]

Eng′lish spar′row. See **house sparrow.** [1875–80, *Amer.*]

Eng′lish spring′er span′iel, one of an English breed of springer spaniels having a medium-length, usually black-and-white or liver-and-white coat. [1915–20]

Eng′lish sys′tem. See **Bradford spinning.** [1925–30]

Eng′lish toy′ span′iel, one of a British breed of toy spaniels having a long, silky coat, a rounded head, and a short, upturned muzzle. [1930–35]

Eng′lish wal′nut, 1. a walnut tree, *Juglans regia.* **2.** the nut of this tree, widely used in cookery. [1765–75, *Amer.*]

Eng·lish·wom·an (ing′glish wo͝om′ən *or, often,* -lish-), *n., pl.* **-wom·en.** a woman who is a native or citizen of England. [1520–30; ENGLISH + WOMAN]

Eng′lish yew′, a yew, *Taxus baccata,* of Eurasia and northern Africa, grown as an ornamental. [1925–30]

en·glut (en glut′), *v.t.,* **-glut·ted, -glut·ting. 1.** to gulp down. **2.** *Archaic.* to fill to satisfaction; satiate. [1485–95; < MF *englotir* AF *englutir* < LL *inglūttīre* to swallow, equiv. to L *in-* IN-[2] + *glūttīre* to swallow; see GLUTTON]

en·gorge (en gôrj′), *v.t., v.i.,* **-gorged, -gorg·ing. 1.** to swallow greedily; glut or gorge. **2.** *Pathol.* to congest with blood. [1505–15; < MF *engorger.* See EN-[1], GORGE] —**en·gorge′ment,** *n.*

engr., 1. engineer. **2.** engraved. **3.** engraver. **4.** engraving.

en·graft (en graft′, -gräft′), *v.t.* **1.** *Hort.* to insert, as a scion of one tree or plant into another, for propagation: *to engraft a peach on a plum.* —*v.i.* **2.** *Surg.* (of living tissue) to become grafted. Also, **ingraft.** [1575–85; EN-[1] + GRAFT[1]] —**en′graf·ta′tion, en·graft′ment,** *n.*

en·grail (en grāl′), *v.t.* **1.** to ornament the edge of with curved indentations. **2.** *Minting.* to make dots or curves on the cylindrical edge of (a coin, medal, etc.) so as to form a pattern. [1375–1425; late ME *engrelen* < AF, MF *engresler,* equiv. to *en-* EN-[1] + *gresler* to make slender << L *gracilis* GRACILE; cf. F *grêle* kind of file, deriv. of *grêler*] —**en·grail′ment,** *n.*

en·grailed (en grāld′), *adj. Heraldry.* having an edge of a charge consisting of a number of concave curves. Cf. **invected.** [1350–1400; ME *engrelede.* See ENGRAIL, -ED[2]]

en·grain (en grān′), *v.t., adj.* ingrain (defs. 1, 2).

en·grained (en grānd′, en′grānd′), *adj.* ingrained. —**en·grain·ed·ly** (en grā′nid lē, -grānd′-), *adv.*

en·gram (en′gram), *n.* a presumed encoding in neural tissue that provides a physical basis for the persistence

CONCISE PRONUNCIATION KEY: act, cāpe, dâre, pärt; set, ēqual; *if,* ice; ox, ōver, ôrder, oil, bo͝ok, bo͞ot, out; up, ûrge; child; sing; shoe; thin, *that;* zh as in *treasure.* ə = *a* as in *alone, e* as in *system, i* as in *easily, o* as in *gallop, u* as in *circus;* ᵊ as in *fire* (fīᵊr), *hour* (ouᵊr). l and n can serve as syllabic consonants, as in *cradle* (krād′l), and *button* (but′n). See the full key inside the front cover.

of memory; a memory trace. Also called **trace.** [1905–10; EN-[2] + -GRAM[1]] —**en·gram′mic,** *adj.*

en·grave (en grāv′), *v.t.,* **-graved, -grav·ing. 1.** to chase (letters, designs, etc.) on a hard surface, as of metal, stone, or the end grain of wood: *She had the jeweler engrave her name on the back of the watch.* **2.** to print from such a surface. **3.** to mark or ornament with incised letters, designs, etc.: *He engraved the ring in a floral pattern.* **4.** to impress deeply; infix: *That image is engraved on my mind.* [1500–10; < MF *engraver;* see EN-[1], GRAVE[3]] —**en·grav′a·ble,** *adj.* —**en·grav′er,** *n.*

engrav′er bee′tle. See **bark beetle.** [1895–1900; so called because its boring resembles engraving]

engrav′er's trick′, *Heraldry.* a conventional method of indicating a tincture, as by printing or carving without color. Also called **herald's trick.**

en·grav·ing (en grā′ving), *n.* **1.** the act or art of a person who or thing that engraves. **2.** the art of forming designs by cutting, corrosion by acids, a photographic process, etc., on the surface of a metal plate, block of wood, or the like, for or as for the purpose of taking off impressions or prints of the design so formed. **3.** the design engraved. **4.** an engraved plate or block. **5.** an impression or print from this. [1595–1605; ENGRAVE + -ING[1]]

en·gross (en grōs′), *v.t.* **1.** to occupy completely, as the mind or attention; absorb: *Their discussion engrossed his attention. She is engrossed in her work.* **2.** to write or copy in a clear, attractive, large script or in a formal manner, as a public document or record: *to engross a deed.* **3.** to acquire the whole of (a commodity), in order to control the market; monopolize. [1275–1325; ME *engros(s)en* to gather in large quantities, draft (a will, etc.) in final form < AF *engrosser,* partly < ML *ingrossāre* to thicken, write large and thick (L *in-* IN-[2] + *gross(us)* thick + *-āre* inf. suffix); partly < AF, MF *en gros* in quantity, wholesale < L *in* + *grossus;* see GROSS] —**en·gross·ed·ly** (en grō′sid lē, -grōst′-), *adv.* —**en·gross′er,** *n.*
—**Syn. 1.** involve, immerse, engage.

engrossed′ bill′, *U.S. Govt.* a bill that has been passed in one house of Congress. Cf. **enrolled bill.**

en·gross·ing (en grō′sing), *adj.* fully occupying the mind or attention; absorbing: *I'm reading the most engrossing book.* [1475–85; ENGROSS + -ING[2]] —**en·gross′ing·ly,** *adv.*

en·gross·ment (en grōs′mənt), *n.* **1.** the act of engrossing. **2.** the state of being engrossed or absorbed: *to read with engrossment.* **3.** an engrossed copy of a document. [1520–30; ENGROSS + -MENT]

en·gulf (en gulf′), *v.t.* **1.** to swallow up in or as in a gulf; submerge: *The overflowing river has engulfed many small towns along its banks.* **2.** to plunge or immerse, as into a gulf: *He engulfed himself in his studies.* Also, **ingulf.** [1545–55; EN-[1] + GULF] —**en·gulf′ment,** *n.*
—**Syn. 1.** envelop, bury, inundate, deluge, swamp.

en·ha·lo (en hā′lō), *v.t.,* **-loed, -lo·ing.** to surround with or as with a halo. [1835–45; EN-[1] + HALO]

en·hance (en hans′, -häns′), *v.t.,* **-hanced, -hanc·ing. 1.** to raise to a higher degree; intensify; magnify: *The candlelight enhanced her beauty.* **2.** to raise the value or price of: *Rarity enhances the worth of old coins.* [1325–75; ME *enhauncen* < AF *enhauncer,* appar. for OF *enhaucer,* equiv. to *en-* EN-[1] + *haucer* to raise (F *hausser*) < VL **altiāre* (deriv. of L *altus* high, with *h-* < Gmc; see HAUGHTY), though *-n-* is unexplained] —**en·hance′ment,** *n.* —**en·hanc′ive,** *adj.*
—**Syn. 2.** See **elevate.** —**Ant. 1.** diminish. **2.** reduce.

enhanced′ radia′tion weap′on. See **neutron bomb.** [1976]

en·hanc·er (en han′sər, -hän′-), *n.* **1.** a person or thing that enhances. **2.** *Genetics.* a gene or gene fragment that activates other genes. [ENHANCE + -ER[1]]

en·har·mon·ic (en′här mon′ik), *adj. Music.* having the same pitch in the tempered scale but written in different notation, as G sharp and A flat. [1590–1600; < LL *enharmonicus* < Gk *enarmónios* (*-icus* r. *-ios*), equiv. to *en-* EN-[2] + *harmoni(a)* HARMONY + *-os* adj. suffix] —**en′har·mon′i·cal·ly,** *adv.*

en·heart·en (en här′tn), *v.t.* to hearten. [1600–10; EN-[1] + HEARTEN]

E·nid (ē′nid), *n.* **1.** a city in N Oklahoma. 50,363. **2.** *Arthurian Romance.* the constant and patient wife of Sir Geraint in *The Mabinogion* and in Tennyson's *Idylls of the King.* **3.** a female given name.

e·nig·ma (ə nig′mə), *n., pl.* **-mas, -ma·ta** (-mə tə). **1.** a puzzling or inexplicable occurrence or situation: *His disappearance is an enigma that has given rise to much speculation.* **2.** a person of puzzling or contradictory character: *To me he has always been an enigma, one minute completely insensitive, the next moved to tears.* **3.** a saying, question, picture, etc., containing a hidden meaning; riddle. **4.** (*cap.*) a German-built enciphering machine developed for commercial use in the early 1920's and later adapted and appropriated by German and other Axis powers for military use through World War II. [1530–40; < L *aenigma* < Gk *aínigma,* equiv. to *ainik-* (s. of *ainíssesthai* to speak in riddles, deriv. of *aînos* fable) + *-ma* n. suffix of result]
—**Syn. 1.** problem. See **puzzle.**

en·ig·mat·ic (en′ig mat′ik, ē′nig-), *adj.* resembling an enigma; perplexing; mysterious. Also, **en′ig·mat′i·cal.** [1620–30; < LL *aenigmaticus* < Gk *ainigmatikós,* equiv. to *ainigmat-* (s. of *aínigma*) ENIGMA + *-ikos* -IC] —**en′ig·mat′i·cal·ly,** *adv.*
—**Syn.** puzzling, baffling, cryptic. See **ambiguous.**

en·isle (en īl′), *v.t.,* **-isled, -isl·ing. 1.** to make an island of. **2.** to place on an island. **3.** to isolate. [1605–15; EN-[1] + ISLE]

En·i·we·tok (en′ə wē′tok, ə nē′wi tok′), *n.* an atoll in the NW Marshall Islands: atomic and hydrogen bomb tests 1947–52.

en·jamb·ment (en jam′mənt, -jamb′-), *n., pl.* **-ments** (-mənts). *Pros.* the running on of the thought from one line, couplet, or stanza to the next without a syntactical break. [1830–40; < F *enjambement,* equiv. to *enjamb(er)* to stride over, project, encroach (*en-* EN-[1] + *-jamber,* deriv. of *jambe* leg; see JAMB[1]) + *-ment* -MENT] —**en·jambed′,** *adj.*

en·join (en join′), *v.t.* **1.** to prescribe (a course of action) with authority or emphasis: *The doctor enjoined a strict diet.* **2.** to direct or order to do something: *He was enjoined to live more frugally.* **3.** *Law.* to prohibit or restrain by an injunction. [1175–1225; ME *enjoi(g)nen* < OF *enjoindre* < L *injungere* to fasten to, bring upon. See IN-[2], JOIN] —**en·join′er,** *n.* —**en·join′ment,** *n.*
—**Syn. 2.** charge, bid, command, require. **3.** proscribe, interdict, ban.

en·join·der (en join′dər), *n.* **1.** a prohibition by injunction. **2.** an emphatic directive or order. [1890–95; from ENJOIN, after REJOINDER]

en·joy (en joi′), *v.t.* **1.** to experience with joy; take pleasure in: *He enjoys Chinese food.* **2.** to have and use with satisfaction; have the benefit of: *He enjoys an excellent income from his trust funds.* **3.** to find or experience pleasure for (oneself): *She seems to enjoy herself at everything she does.* **4.** to undergo (an improvement): *Automobile manufacturers have enjoyed a six-percent rise in sales over the past month.* **5.** to have intercourse with. [1350–1400; ME *enjoyen* to make joyful < OF *enjoier* to give joy to. See EN-[1], JOY] —**en·joy′er,** *n.* —**en·joy′ing·ly,** *adv.*
—**Syn. 1.** appreciate, fancy, relish, savor. **2.** possess, own.

en·joy·a·ble (en joi′ə bəl), *adj.* giving or capable of giving joy or pleasure: *a very enjoyable film.* [1635–45; ENJOY + -ABLE] —**en·joy′a·ble·ness,** *n.* —**en·joy′a·bly,** *adv.*
—**Syn.** pleasant, agreeable, delightful, satisfying. —**Ant.** boring, unpleasant; hateful, detestable, loathsome.

en·joy·ment (en joi′mənt), *n.* **1.** the act of enjoying. **2.** the possession, use, or occupancy of anything with satisfaction or pleasure: *to have the enjoyment of a large income.* **3.** a particular form or source of pleasure: *Hunting is his greatest enjoyment.* **4.** *Law.* the exercise of a right: *the enjoyment of an estate.* [1545–55; ENJOY + -MENT]
—**Syn. 2.** delight, gratification. See **pleasure.**

en·keph·al·in (en kef′ə lin), *n. Biochem.* either of two pentapeptides that bind to morphine receptors in the central nervous system and have opioid properties of relatively short duration; one pentapeptide **(Met enkephalin)** has the amino acid sequence Tyr-Gly-Gly-Phe-Met and the other **(Leu enkephalin)** has the sequence Tyr-Gly-Gly-Phe-Leu. [1970–75; < Gk *enképhal(os)* ENCEPHALON + -IN[2]]

En·ki (en′kē), *n.* a Sumerian water god and god of wisdom: the counterpart of the Akkadian Ea.

En·ki·du (en′kē do͞o), *n.* the servant and friend of Gilgamesh.

en·kin·dle (en kin′dl), *v.t., v.i.,* **-dled, -dling.** to kindle into flame, ardor, activity, etc. [1540–50; EN-[1] + KINDLE] —**en·kin′dler,** *n.*

en·kol·pi·on (en kōl′pē ən, en kol′pē on′), *n., pl.* **-pi·a** (-pē ə). encolpion.

enl., 1. enlarge. **2.** enlarged. **3.** enlisted.

en·lace (en lās′), *v.t.,* **-laced, -lac·ing. 1.** to interlace; intertwine: *to enlace strands of rope.* **2.** to bind or encircle with or as with a lace or cord: *Vines enlaced the tree.* Also, **inlace.** [1325–75; ME *enlacen* < OF *enlacier.* See EN-[1], LACE] —**en·lace′ment,** *n.*

en·large (en lärj′), *v.,* **-larged, -larg·ing.** —*v.t.* **1.** to make larger; increase in extent, bulk, or quantity; add to: *They enlarged the house by adding an east wing.* **2.** to increase the capacity or scope of; expand: *We've decided to enlarge the company.* **3.** to make (a photographic print) larger than the negative by projecting the negative's image through a lens onto photographic printing paper. —*v.i.* **4.** to grow larger; increase; expand. **5.** to speak or write at large; expatiate: *to enlarge upon a point.* [1350–1400; ME *enlargen* < OF *enlargir, enlarger.* See EN-[1], LARGE] —**en·large′a·ble,** *adj.* —**en·larg·ed·ly** (en lär′jid lē, -lärjd′-), *adv.* —**en·larg′ed·ness,** *n.* —**en·larg′ing·ly,** *adv.*
—**Syn. 1.** extend, magnify, amplify, dilate. See **increase.** —**Ant. 1.** diminish. **2.** contract.

en·large·ment (en lärj′mənt), *n.* **1.** an act of enlarging; increase, expansion, or amplification. **2.** anything, as a photograph, that is an enlarged form of something. **3.** anything that enlarges something else; addition: *The new wing formed a considerable enlargement to the building.* [1530–40; ENLARGE + -MENT]

en·larg·er (en lär′jər), *n. Photog.* an apparatus used for making projection prints, having a head for holding, illuminating, and projecting a film negative and a bed for holding a sheet of sensitized printing paper. Also called **projection printer.** Cf. **contact printer.** [1535–45, for an earlier sense; ENLARGE + -ER[1]]

en·light·en (en līt′n), *v.t.* **1.** to give intellectual or spiritual light to; instruct; impart knowledge to: *We hope the results of our research will enlighten our colleagues.* **2.** *Archaic.* to shed light upon. [1350–1400; ME *enli(g)htenen.* See EN-[1], LIGHTEN[1]] —**en·light′ened·ly,** *adv.* —**en·light′ened·ness,** *n.* —**en·light′en·er,** *n.* —**en·light′en·ing·ly,** *adv.*
—**Syn. 1.** illumine, edify, teach, inform. —**Ant. 1.** mystify, confuse, perplex, puzzle.

en·light·en·ment (en līt′n mənt), *n.* **1.** the act of enlightening. **2.** the state of being enlightened: *to live in spiritual enlightenment.* **3.** (*usually cap.*) *Buddhism, Hinduism.* prajna. **4. the Enlightenment,** a philosophical movement of the 18th century, characterized by belief in the power of human reason and by innovations in political, religious, and educational doctrine. [1660–70; ENLIGHTEN + -MENT]

En·lil (en′lil), *n.* the king of the Sumerian gods and the god of the air.

en·list (en list′), *v.i.* **1.** to enroll, usually voluntarily, for military service: *He decided to enlist in the Marines.* **2.** to enter into some cause, enterprise, etc. —*v.t.* **3.** to engage for military service: *to enlist men for the army.* **4.** to secure (a person, services, etc.) for some cause, enterprise, etc.: *They enlisted us to serve as ushers at the meeting.* [1690–1700; EN-[1] + LIST[1]] —**en·list′er,** *n.*
—**Syn. 2.** volunteer, join.

enlist′ed man′, any member of the U.S. armed services who is not a commissioned officer or a warrant officer, esp. one ranking below a noncommissioned officer or a petty officer. [1715–25]

enlist′ed wom′an, any female member of the U.S. armed services who is not a commissioned officer or a warrant officer, esp. one ranking below a noncommissioned officer or a petty officer.

en·list·ee (en lis tē′), *n.* **1.** a person who enlists for military service. Cf. **draftee. 2.** an enlisted man or woman. [ENLIST + -EE]

en·list·ment (en list′mənt), *n.* **1.** the period of time for which one is committed to military service. **2.** an act of enlisting. [1740–50; ENLIST + -MENT]

en·liv·en (en lī′vən), *v.t.* **1.** to make vigorous or active; invigorate: *The wit of Mencken enlivened his age.* **2.** to make sprightly or cheerful; brighten: *Flowers enliven any room.* [1625–35; obs. *enlive* to give life to (EN-[1] + LIFE) + -EN[1]] —**en·liv′en·er,** *n.* —**en·liv′en·ing·ly,** *adv.* —**en·liv′en·ment,** *n.*
—**Syn. 1.** animate, inspirit, vivify, stimulate, quicken. **2.** gladden. See **cheer.** —**Ant. 2.** depress.

en·mar·ble (en mär′bəl), *v.t.,* **-bled, -bling.** emmarble.

en masse (än mas′, en; *Fr.* äN MAS′), in a mass; all together; as a group: *The people rushed to the gate en masse.* [1795–1805; < F]

en·mesh (en mesh′), *v.t.* to catch, as in a net; entangle: *He was enmeshed by financial difficulties.* Also, **immesh, inmesh.** [1595–1605; EN-[1] + MESH] —**en·mesh′ment,** *n.*

en·mi·ty (en′mi tē), *n., pl.* **-ties.** a feeling or condition of hostility; hatred; ill will; animosity; antagonism. [1250–1300; ME *enemite* < MF; OF *enemistie* < VL **inimicitāt-* (s. of **inimicitās*), equiv. to L *inimic(us)* ENEMY + *-itāt-* -ITY]
—**Syn.** malice, acrimony, rancor.

En·na (en′ə; *It.* en′nä), *n.* a city in SW Italy, on central Sicily. 27,705.

-enne a personal noun suffix occurring in loanwords from French, where it forms feminine nouns corresponding to masculine nouns ending in *-en* (*comedienne, doyenne*); on this model, of very limited productivity in English, forming distinctively feminine nouns from words ending in *-an: equestrienne.*
—**Usage.** The few English words that end in -ENNE, indicating the feminine counterpart of a traditionally masculine term ending in *-en* or *-an,* usually carry little implication of inferiority. Many women, however, prefer that no distinction be made and that, as with other gender-specific words, the terms once reserved for males be applied to males and females alike. English is quite inconsistent in adopting such feminine nouns. *Equestrian* has the form *equestrienne; pedestrian* has no corresponding feminine term. Although we have both *comedienne* and *tragedienne,* there is no feminine variant for *thespian.* See also **-ess, -ette, -trix.**

ennea-, a combining form meaning "nine," used in the formation of compound words: *enneahedron.* [< Gk, comb. form of *ennéa* NINE]

en·ne·ad (en′ē ad′), *n.* **1.** a group of nine persons or things. **2.** *Egyptian Religion.* **a.** (*cap.*) a group of nine related deities, including Osiris, Isis, and Set, whose lineage and functions were arranged and explained by the theologians of Heliopolis. **b.** any group of deities arranged in a similar way, often more or less than nine in number. [1645–55; < Gk *enneád-* (s. of *enneás*), equiv. to *enné(a)* NINE + *-ad-* -AD[1]] —**en′ne·ad′ic,** *adj.*

en·ne·a·gon (en′ē ə gon′), *n.* nonagon. [1650–60; < Gk *enneágōnos;* see ENNEA-, -GON]

en·ne·a·he·dron (en′ē ə hē′drən), *n., pl.* **-dra** (-drə). a solid figure having nine faces. [ENNEA- + -HEDRON] —**en′ne·a·he′dral,** *adj.*

en·ne·a·style (en′ē ə stīl′), *adj.* **1.** *Archit.* having nine columns. **2.** (of a classical temple) having nine columns on one front or on each. Also, **en′ne·a·styl′ar.** [1870–75; ENNEA- + -STYLE[2]]

en·ne·a·sty·los (en′ē ə stī′los), *n.* an enneastyle building, as a classical temple. [ENNEA- + Gk *-stylos* -STYLE[2]]

en·ne·a·syl·lab·ic (en′ē ə si lab′ik), *adj.* consisting of or pertaining to nine syllables. [< Gk *enneasýllab(os)* nine-syllable (see ENNEA-, SYLLABLE) + -IC]

En·nis (en′is), *n.* **1.** a town in N Texas. 12,110. **2.** a male given name.

En·ni·us (en′ē əs), *n.* **Quin·tus** (kwin′təs), 239–169? B.C., Roman poet.

en·no·ble (en nō′bəl), *v.t.,* **-bled, -bling. 1.** to elevate in degree, excellence, or respect; dignify; exalt: *a personality ennobled by true generosity.* **2.** to confer a title of nobility on. [1425–75; late ME *ennobelen* < MF, OF *en-*

CONCISE ETYMOLOGY KEY: <, descended or borrowed from; >, whence; b., blend of, blended; c., cognate with; cf., compare; deriv., derivative; equiv., equivalent; imit., imitative; obl., oblique; r., replacing; s., stem; sp., spelling, spelled; resp., respelling, respelled; trans., translation; ?, origin unknown; *, unattested; ‡, probably earlier than. See the full key inside the front cover.

noblir. See EN-¹, NOBLE] —**en·no′ble·ment,** *n.* —**en·no′bler,** *n.* —**en·no′bling·ly,** *adv.*

En·no·sig·ae·us (en′ə sig′ē əs), *n. Class. Myth.* an epithet of Poseidon, meaning "earth-shaker."

en·nui (än wē′, än′wē; *Fr.* äɴ nwē′), *n.* a feeling of utter weariness and discontent resulting from satiety or lack of interest; boredom: *The endless lecture produced an unbearable ennui.* [1660–70; < F: boredom; OF *enui* displeasure; see ANNOY]
—**Syn.** listlessness, tedium, lassitude, languor.

E·noch (ē′nək), *n.* **1.** the father of Methuselah. Gen. 5:22. **2.** a son of Cain. Gen. 4:17. **3.** a male given name: from a Hebrew word meaning "teacher."

E′noch Ar′den (är′dn), **1.** (*italics*) a narrative poem (1864) by Tennyson. **2.** its hero. **3.** a missing person who is presumed dead but is later found to be alive.

e·no·ki (e nok′ē), *n.* a thin, long-stemmed and tiny-capped white mushroom, *Flamma velutipes,* native to the northern mountain ranges of Japan and prized as a food. [< Japn *enoki(-take),* equiv. to *enoki* hackberry, Chinese nettle tree (< **ey no kiy;* **ai* hackberry + *no* particle + **koy* tree) + *take* mushroom]

e·nol (ē′nôl, ē′nol), *n. Chem.* an organic compound containing a hydroxyl group attached to a doubly linked carbon atom, as in >C=C(OH)−. [1935–40; appar. < Gk (*h*)*én* one (neut.) + -OL¹] —**e·nol·ic** (ē nol′ik), *adj.*

E·no·la (i nō′lə), *n.* a female given name.

E·no′la Gay′, the name of the American B-29 bomber, piloted by Col. Paul Tibbets, Jr., that dropped the atomic bomb on Hiroshima, Japan, on Aug. 6, 1945.

e·no·late (ēn′l āt′), *n. Chem.* any metallic derivative of an enol. [1960–65; ENOL + -ATE²]

e·no·lize (ēn′l īz′), *v.t., v.i.,* **-lized, -liz·ing.** *Chem.* to convert into an enol or enolate. Also, *esp. Brit.,* **e′no·lise′.** [1935–40; ENOL + -IZE] —**e′no·liz′a·ble,** *adj.* —**e′no·li·za′tion,** *n.*

e·nol·o·gy (ē nol′ə jē), *n.* oenology. —**e·no·log·i·cal** (ē′nl oj′i kəl), *adj.* —**e·nol′o·gist,** *n.*

e·norm (ē nôrm′), *adj. Archaic.* enormous; huge; vast. [1425–75; late ME *enorme* < MF < L *ēnormis,* equiv. to *ē-* E- + *norm(a)* NORM + *-is* adj. suffix]

e·nor·mi·ty (i nôr′mi tē), *n., pl.* **-ties 1.** outrageous or heinous character; atrociousness: *the enormity of war crimes.* **2.** something outrageous or heinous, as an offense: *The bombing of the defenseless population was an enormity beyond belief.* **3.** greatness of size, scope, extent, or influence; immensity: *The enormity of such an act of generosity is staggering.* [1425–75; late ME *enormite* < MF < L *ēnormitās.* See ENORM, -TY²]
—**Syn. 1.** monstrousness, heinousness. **3.** hugeness, vastness.
—**Usage. 3.** ENORMITY has been in frequent and continuous use in the sense "immensity" since the 18th century: *The enormity of the task was overwhelming.* Some hold that ENORMOUSNESS is the correct word in that sense and that ENORMITY can only mean "outrageousness" or "atrociousness": *The enormity of his offenses appalled the public.* ENORMITY occurs regularly in edited writing with the meanings both of great size and of outrageous or horrifying character, behavior, etc. Many people, however, continue to regard ENORMITY in the sense of great size as nonstandard.

e·nor·mous (i nôr′məs), *adj.* **1.** greatly exceeding the common size, extent, etc.; huge; immense: *an enormous fortune.* **2.** outrageous or atrocious: *enormous wickedness; enormous crimes.* [1525–35; ENORM + -OUS] —**e·nor′mous·ly,** *adv.*
—**Syn. 1.** vast, colossal, gigantic, mammoth, prodigious, stupendous. See **huge.**

e·nor·mous·ness (i nôr′məs nis), *n.* very great or abnormal size, bulk, degree, etc.; immensity; hugeness. [1795–1805; ENORMOUS + -NESS]
—**Usage.** See **enormity.**

E·nos (ē′nəs), *n.* **1.** the son of Seth. Gen. 5:6. **2.** a male given name.

e·no·sis (i nō′sis, ē nō′-; *Gk.* e′nô sēs), *n.* (*sometimes cap.*) a movement for securing the political union of Greece and Cyprus. [1935–40; < ModGk *énōsis,* Gk *hénōsis* union, equiv. to *henō-,* var. s. of *henoûn* to unify (deriv. of *hén,* neut. of *heîs* one) + *-sis* -SIS] —**e·no′sist,** *n.*

e·nough (i nuf′), *adj.* **1.** adequate for the want or need; sufficient for the purpose or to satisfy desire: *enough water; noise enough to wake the dead.* —*pron.* **2.** an adequate quantity or number; sufficiency. —*adv.* **3.** in a quantity or degree that answers a purpose or satisfies a need or desire; sufficiently. **4.** fully or quite: *ready enough.* —*interj.* **5.** (used to express impatience or exasperation): *Enough! I heard you the first time.* [bef. 900; ME *enogh,* OE *genōh;* c. G *genug,* Goth *ganohs,* ON *nōgr;* akin to OE *geneah* it suffices, Skt *naśati* (he) reaches]
—**Syn. 1.** ample. **3.** adequately, amply, reasonably.

e·nounce (i nouns′), *v.t.,* **e·nounced, e·nounc·ing. 1.** to utter or pronounce, as words; enunciate. **2.** to announce, declare, or proclaim. **3.** to state definitely, as a proposition. [1795–1805; E- + (AN)NOUNCE, modeled on F *énoncer* < L *ēnuntiāre* to tell; see ENUNCIATE] —**e·nounce′ment,** *n.*

En·o·vid (en ov′id), *Trademark.* a brand name for a hormonal compound used in medicine in varying doses for ovulation control, adjustment of the menses, severe uterine bleeding, or threatened habitual abortion.

e·now (i nou′; *formerly* i nō′), *adj., adv. Archaic.* enough. [bef. 1050; ME *inow,* OE *genōg* (var. of *genōh* ENOUGH), conflated with ME *inowe,* OE *genōge,* pl. of *genōg* ENOUGH]

en pa·pil·lote (äɴ pa pē yôt′), *French.* (of meat or fish) cooked and served in a wrapping of foil or oiled paper.

en pas·sant (än′ pa sänt′; *Fr.* äɴ pä säɴ′), **1.** (*italics*) *French.* in passing; by the way. **2.** *Chess.* a method by which a pawn that is moved two squares can be captured by an opponent's pawn commanding the square that was passed. [1655–65]

en·phy·tot·ic (en′fī tot′ik), *adj.* **1.** (of a plant disease) regularly affecting but not destroying the plants in a given area. —*n.* **2.** any enphytotic disease. [EN-² + Gk *phyt(ón)* plant + -OTIC]

en·plane (en plān′), *v.,* **-planed, -plan·ing.** —*v.i.* **1.** to board an airplane: *We enplaned in New York at noon and arrived in Washington an hour later.* —*v.t.* **2.** to allow to board or put on board an airplane: *We will be enplaning passengers shortly.* Also, **emplane.** [1940–45; EN-¹ + PLANE¹] —**en·plane′ment,** *n.*

en plein air (äɴ ple neʀ′), *French.* in the open air.

en prise (än′ prēz′; *Fr.* äɴ pʀēz′), *Chess.* in line for capture; likely to be captured. [1815–25; < F; see PRIZE¹]

en′ quad′, *Print.* **1.** a square unit of an area, one en on each side. **2.** a quad having such an area. Cf. **quad²** (def. 1). [1900–05]

en·quire (en kwīᵊr′), *v.i., v.t.,* **-quired, -quir·ing.** inquire.

en·quir·y (en kwīᵊr′ē, en′kwə rē), *n., pl.* **-quir·ies.** inquiry.

en·rage (en rāj′), *v.t.,* **-raged, -rag·ing.** to make extremely angry; put into a rage; infuriate: *His supercilious attitude enraged me.* [1490–1500; < MF *enrager.* See EN-¹, RAGE] —**en·rag·ed·ly** (en rā′jid lē, -rājd′-), *adv.* —**en·rage′ment,** *n.*
—**Syn.** anger, inflame, madden. ENRAGE, INCENSE, INFURIATE imply stirring to violent anger. To ENRAGE or TO INFURIATE is to provoke wrath: *They enrage (infuriate) him by their deliberate and continual injustice.* To INCENSE is to inflame with indignation or anger: *to incense a person by making insulting remarks.* —**Ant.** appease, pacify.

en rap·port (än′ ra pôr′, -pōr′, rə-; *Fr.* äɴ ʀa pôʀ′), in sympathy or accord; in agreement; congenial. [< F]

en·rapt (en rapt′), *adj.* rapt; transported; enraptured: *a violinist's enrapt audience.* [1600–10; EN-¹ + RAPT]

en·rap·ture (en rap′chər), *v.t.,* **-tured, -tur·ing.** to move to rapture; delight beyond measure: *We were enraptured by her singing.* [1730–40; EN-¹ + RAPTURE] —**en·rap′tured·ly,** *adv.*
—**Syn.** enthrall, transport, entrance, enchant.

en·rav·ish (en rav′ish), *v.t.* to enrapture. [1590–1600; EN-¹ + RAVISH]

en·reg·is·ter (en rej′ə stər), *v.t.* to register; record. [1515–25; < MF *enregistrer.* See EN-¹, REGISTER] —**en·reg′is·tra′tion,** *n.*

en rè·gle (äɴ ʀe′glᵊ), *French.* in order; according to the rules; correct.

en·rich (en rich′), *v.t.* **1.** to supply with riches, wealth, abundant or valuable possessions, etc.: *Commerce enriches a nation.* **2.** to supply with abundance of anything desirable: *to enrich the mind with knowledge.* **3.** to add greater value or significance to: *Art enriches life.* **4.** to adorn or decorate: *a picture frame enriched with gold.* **5.** to make finer in quality, as by supplying desirable elements or ingredients: *to enrich soil.* **6.** to increase the proportion of a valuable mineral or isotope in (a substance or material): *The fuel was enriched with uranium 235 for the nuclear reactor.* **7.** *Nutrition.* **a.** to restore to (a food) a nutrient that has been lost during an early stage of processing: *to enrich flour with thiamine, iron, niacin, and riboflavin.* **b.** to add vitamins and minerals to (food) to enhance its nutritive value. [1350–1400; ME *enrichen* < OF *enrichir.* See EN-¹, RICH] —**en·rich′er,** *n.* —**en·rich′ing·ly,** *adv.*
—**Syn. 3.** elevate, improve, enhance, endow.

en·rich·ment (en rich′mənt), *n.* **1.** an act of enriching. **2.** the state of being enriched. **3.** something that enriches: *the enrichments of education and travel.* [1620–30; ENRICH + -MENT]

En·ri·co (en rē′kō; *It.* en ʀē′kô), *n.* a male given name: Italian form of **Henry.**

En·ri·qui·llo (en′ri kē′ō; *Sp.* en′ʀē kē′yô), *n.* **Lake,** a saltwater lake, below sea level, in the SW Dominican Republic.

en·robe (en rōb′), *v.t.,* **-robed, -rob·ing.** to dress; attire: *The king was enrobed in velvet.* [1585–95; EN-¹ + ROBE] —**en·rob′er,** *n.*

en·rol (en rōl′), *v.t., v.i.,* **-rolled, -rol·ling.** enroll.

en·roll (en rōl′), *v.t.* **1.** to write the name of (a person) in a roll or register; place upon a list; register: *It took two days to enroll the new students.* **2.** to enlist (oneself). **3.** to put in a record; record: *to enroll the minutes of a meeting; to enroll the great events of history.* **4.** to roll or wrap up: *fruit enrolled in tissue paper.* **5.** *Naut.* to document (a U.S. vessel) by issuing a certificate of enrollment. —*v.i.* **6.** to enroll oneself: *He enrolled in college last week.* [1300–50; ME *enrollen* < OF *enroller.* See EN-¹, ROLL] —**en·roll′er,** *n.*

enrolled′ bill′, *U.S. Govt.* a copy of a bill passed by both houses of Congress, signed by their presiding officers, and sent to the President for signature. Cf. **engrossed bill.** [1780–90, *Amer.*]

en·roll·ee (en rō lē′, -rō′lē), *n.* a person enrolled, in a class, school, course of study, etc. [ENROLL + -EE]

en·roll·ment (en rōl′mənt), *n.* **1.** the act or process of enrolling. **2.** the state of being enrolled. **3.** the number of persons enrolled, as for a course or in a school. Also, **en·rol′ment.** [1525–35; ENROLL + -MENT]

en·root (en ro͞ot′, -ro͝ot′), *v.t.* **1.** to fix by the root. **2.** to attach or place securely; implant deeply. [1480–90; EN-¹ + ROOT¹]

en route (än ro͞ot′, en; *Fr.* äɴ ʀo͞ot′), on the way: *The plane crashed en route from Cairo to Athens.* [1770–80; < F]

ens (enz, ens), *n., pl.* **en·ti·a** (en′shē ə, -tē ə), *Metaphys.* an existing or real thing; an entity. [< L *ēns,* prp. of *esse* to be]

Ens., Ensign.

en·sam·ple (en sam′pəl), *n. Archaic.* example. [1200–50; ME < OF, var. (*en-* EN- r. *es-*) of *essample* < OF < L *exemplum* EXAMPLE]

en·san·guine (en sang′gwin), *v.t.,* **-guined, -guin·ing.** to stain or cover with or as with blood: *a flag ensanguined with the blood of battle.* [1660–70; EN-¹ + SANGUINE]

En·sche·de (en′sᴋʜə dā′), *n.* a city in E Netherlands. 144,346.

en·sconce (en skons′), *v.t.,* **-sconced, -sconc·ing. 1.** to settle securely or snugly: *I found her in the library, ensconced in an armchair.* **2.** to cover or shelter; hide securely: *He ensconced himself in the closet in order to eavesdrop.* [1580–90; EN-¹ + SCONCE²]

en·scroll (en skrōl′), *v.t.* **1.** to commemorate or record in a permanent manner, by or as if by inscribing on parchment. **2.** to write or inscribe on a scroll. Also, **inscroll.** [1905–10; EN-¹ + SCROLL]

en·sem·ble (än säm′bəl, -sämb′; *Fr.* äɴ säɴ′blᵊ), *n., pl.* **-sem·bles** (-säm′bəlz, -sämbz′; *Fr.* -säɴ′blᵊ). **1.** all the parts of a thing taken together, so that each part is considered only in relation to the whole. **2.** the entire costume of an individual, esp. when all the parts are in harmony: *She was wearing a beautiful ensemble by one of the French designers.* **3.** a set of furniture. **4.** *Music.* **a.** the united performance of an entire group of singers, musicians, etc. **b.** the group so performing: *a string ensemble.* **5.** a group of supporting entertainers, as actors, dancers, and singers, in a theatrical production. [1740–50; < F: together < L *insimul,* equiv. to *in-* IN-² + *simul* together; see SIMULTANEOUS]
—**Syn. 1.** totality, entirety, aggregate.

ensem′ble act′ing, an approach to acting that aims for a unified effect achieved by all members of a cast working together on behalf of the play, rather than emphasizing individual performances. [1925–30]

En·se·na·da (en′se nä′thä; *Eng.* en′sə nä′də), *n.* a seaport in N Lower California, in NW Mexico. 113,320.

en·se pe·tit pla·ci·dam sub li·ber·ta·te qui·e·tem (en′se pe′tit plä′ki däm′ so͝ob lē′beʀ tä′te kwē-ā′tem; *Eng.* en′sē pē′tit plas′i dam′ sub lib′ər tā′tē kwī ē′tem), *Latin.* by the sword she seeks quiet peace under liberty: motto of Massachusetts.

en·sep·ul·cher (en sep′əl kər), *v.t.* to place in a sepulcher; entomb. [1810–20; EN-¹ + SEPULCHER]

en·serf (en sûrf′), *v.t.* to make a serf of; place in bondage. [1880–85; EN-¹ + SERF]

en·sheathe (en shēth′), *v.t.,* **-sheathed, -sheath·ing.** to enclose in or as in a sheath; sheathe. Also, **en·sheath′,** (en shēth′), **insheathe, insheath.** [1585–95; EN-¹ + SHEATHE]

en·shrine (en shrīn′), *v.t.,* **-shrined, -shrin·ing. 1.** to enclose in or as in a shrine: *His love for her is enshrined forever in his poetry.* **2.** to cherish as sacred: *The memory of our friendship will be enshrined in my heart.* Also, **inshrine.** [1575–85; EN-¹ + SHRINE] —**en·shrine′·ment,** *n.*

en·shroud (en shroud′), *v.t.* to shroud; conceal. [1575–85; EN-¹ + SHROUD]

en·si·form (en′sə fôrm′), *adj.* sword-shaped; xiphoid. [1535–45; < L *ēnsi(s)* sword + -FORM]

en·sign (en′sīn; *Mil.* en′sən), *n.* **1.** a flag or banner, as a military or naval standard used to indicate nationality. **2.** a badge of office or authority, as heraldic arms. **3.** a sign, token, or emblem: *the dove, an ensign of peace.* **4.** *U.S. Navy and Coast Guard.* the lowest commissioned officer, ranking next below a lieutenant, junior grade, and equal to a second lieutenant in the Army. **5.** *Archaic.* standard-bearer (def. 1). [1325–75; ME *ensigne* < OF *enseigne* < L *insignia;* see INSIGNIA] —**en′sign·ship′, en′sign·cy,** *n.*
—**Syn. 1.** pennant, streamer.

en′sign staff′, a staff at the stern of a vessel at which the ensign is flown. Also called **poop staff.** [1700–10]

en·si·lage (en′sə lij), *n., v.,* **-laged, -lag·ing.** —*n.* **1.** the preservation of green fodder in a silo or pit. **2.** fodder preserved. —*v.t.* **3.** ensile. [1875–80; < F; see ENSILE, -AGE]

en·sile (en sīl′, en′sīl), *v.t.,* **-siled, -sil·ing. 1.** to preserve (green fodder) in a silo. **2.** to make into ensilage. [1880–85; < F *ensiler* < Sp *ensilar,* equiv. to *en-* EN-¹ + *-silar,* v. deriv. of *silo* SILO] —**en·si′la·bil′i·ty,** *n.*

-ensis a Latin adjectival suffix meaning "pertaining to," "originating in," used in modern Latin scientific coinages, esp. derivatives of placenames: *canadensis; carolinensis.* [< L *-ēnsis;* cf. -ESE]

en·sky (en skī′), *v.t.,* **-skied** or **-skyed, -sky·ing.** to place in or as if in the heavens; exalt. [1595–1605; EN-¹ + SKY]

en·slave (en slāv′), *v.t.,* **-slaved, -slav·ing.** to make a slave of; reduce to slavery: *His drug addiction has completely enslaved him.* [1635–45; EN-¹ + SLAVE] —**en·slave′ment,** *n.* —**en·slav′er,** *n.*
—**Syn.** enchain, shackle; control, dominate. —**Ant.** free, liberate, release.

en·snare (en snâr′), *v.t.,* **-snared, -snar·ing.** to capture in, or involve as in, a snare: *to be ensnared by lies; to ensnare birds.* Also, **insnare.** [1585–95; EN-¹ + SNARE¹] —**en·snare′ment,** *n.* —**en·snar′er,** *n.* —**en·snar′ing·ly,** *adv.*
—**Syn.** entrap, entangle, enmesh. —**Ant.** release.

en·snarl (en snärl′), *v.t.* to entangle in or as in a snarl. [1585–95; EN-¹ + SNARL²]

CONCISE PRONUNCIATION KEY: act, cāpe, dâre, pärt; set, ēqual; if, īce; ox, ōver, ôrder, oil, bo͝ok, bo͞ot, out; up, ûrge; child; sing; shoe; thin, *th*at; zh as in *treasure.* ə = *a* as in *alone, e* as in *system, i* as in *easily, o* as in *gallop, u* as in *circus;* ᵊ as in *fire* (fīᵊr), *hour* (ouᵊr). l and n can serve as syllabic consonants, as in *cradle* (krād′l), and *button* (but′n). See the full key inside the front cover.

en so·leil (än sô lā′), *Heraldry.* (of a charge) surrounded by rays, as of the sun: *a white rose en soleil.* [< F: lit., in (the form of the) sun]

En·sor (en′sôr), *n.* **James,** 1860–1949, Belgian painter.

en·sor·cell (en sôr′səl), *v.t.* to bewitch: *The beauty of the moon ensorcelled them.* Also, **en·sor′cel.** [1535–45; < MF *ensorceler* to bewitch, dissimilated var. of *ensorcerer.* See EN-[1], SORCERER] **—en·sor′cell·ment,** *n.*

en·soul (en sōl′), *v.t.* **1.** to endow with a soul. **2.** to place or cherish in the soul: *lines of Shakespeare ensouled by all.* Also, **insoul.** [1625–35; EN-[1] + SOUL]

en·spell (en spel′), *v.t.* to cast a spell on. [1880–85; EN-[1] + SPELL[2]]

en·sphere (en sfēr′), *v.t.,* **-sphered, -spher·ing. 1.** to enclose in or as if in a sphere. **2.** to form into a sphere. Also, **insphere.** [1605–15; EN-[1] + SPHERE]

en·spir·it (en spir′it), *v.t.* inspirit.

en·sta·tite (en′stə tīt′), *n. Mineral.* a yellow-green fibrous magnesium silicate, an orthorhombic pyroxene found in norites containing less than five percent ferrous oxide. [1855–60; < Gk *enstát(ēs)* adversary + -ITE[1]] **—en·sta·tit·ic** (en′stə tit′ik), *adj.*

en·sue (en sōō′), *v.i.,* **-sued, -su·ing. 1.** to follow in order; come afterward, esp. in immediate succession: *As the days ensued, he recovered his strength.* **2.** to follow as a consequence; result: *When those two friends meet, a battle of wits ensues.* [1350–1400; ME *ensuen* < AF *ensuer* (c. OF *ensui(v)re*). See EN-[1], SUE] **—en·su′ing·ly,** *adv.*
—Syn. 1, 2. See **follow. 2.** issue, arise, flow.

en suite (än swēt′), *French.* in succession; in a series or set.

en·sure (en shŏŏr′, -shûr′), *v.t.,* **-sured, -sur·ing. 1.** to secure or guarantee: *This letter will ensure you a hearing.* **2.** to make sure or certain: *measures to ensure the success of an undertaking.* **3.** to make secure or safe, as from harm. **4.** insure (defs. 1–3). [1350–1400; ME *ensuren* < AF *enseurer.* See EN-[1], SURE] **—en·sur′er,** *n.*
—Syn. 3. protect, guard, safeguard.

en·swathe (en swoth′, -swāth), *v.t.,* **-swathed, -swath·ing.** to swathe. [1590–1600; EN-[1] + SWATHE] **—en·swathe′ment,** *n.*

ENT, *Med.* ear, nose, and throat.

-ent, a suffix, equivalent to **-ant,** appearing in nouns and adjectives of Latin origin: *accident; different.* [< L *-ent-* (s. of *-ēns*), prp. suffix of conjugations 2, 3, 4]

en·tab·la·ture (en tab′lə chər, -chŏŏr′), *n. Archit.* the entire construction of a classical temple or the like between the columns and the eaves, usually composed of an architrave, a frieze, and a cornice. See diag. under **column.** [1605–15; < MF < It *intavolatura;* see IN-[2], TABLE, -ATE[1], -URE]

en·ta·ble·ment (en tā′bəl mənt), *n.* the platform above the dado on a pedestal. [1655–65; < F, equiv. to *entable(r)* to table (see EN-[1], TABLE) + *-ment* -MENT]

en·tail (*v.* en tāl′; *n.* en tāl′, en′tāl), *v.t.* **1.** to cause or involve by necessity or as a consequence: *a loss entailing no regret.* **2.** to impose as a burden: *Success entails hard work.* **3.** to limit the passage of (a landed estate) to a specified line of heirs, so that it cannot be alienated, devised, or bequeathed. **4.** to cause (anything) to descend to a fixed series of possessors. *—n.* **5.** the act of entailing. **6.** the state of being entailed. **7.** any predetermined order of succession, as to an office. **8.** something that is entailed, as an estate. **9.** the rule of descent settled for an estate. [1350–1400; ME *entailen* (v.), *entail* (n.). See EN-[1], TAIL[2]] **—en·tail′er,** *n.* **—en·tail′ment,** *n.*

ent·a·me·ba (en′tə mē′bə), *n., pl.* **-bae** (-bē), **-bas.** *Biol.* any protozoan of the genus *Entamoeba,* members of which are parasitic in vertebrates, including the human pathogens *E. gingivalis,* found in dental plaque, and *E. histolytica,* the cause of amebic dysentery. Also, **ent′a·moe′ba.** Cf. **endameba.** [< NL; see ENTO-, AMEBA]

en·tan·gle (en tang′gəl), *v.t.,* **-gled, -gling. 1.** to make tangled; ensnarl; intertwine. **2.** to involve in or as in a tangle; ensnare; enmesh: *to be entangled by intrigue.* **3.** to involve in difficulties. **4.** to confuse or perplex. [1530–40; EN-[1] + TANGLE] **—en·tan′gle·a·ble,** *adj.* **—en·tan′gled·ly,** *adv.* **—en·tan′gled·ness,** *n.* **—en·tan′gler,** *n.* **—en·tan′gling·ly,** *adv.*
—Syn. 3. See **involve. 4.** bewilder.

en·tan·gle·ment (en tang′gəl mənt), *n.* **1.** the act of entangling. **2.** the state of being entangled. **3.** something that entangles; snare; involvement; complication. [1630–40; ENTANGLE + -MENT]

en·ta·sis (en′tə sis), *n. Archit.* a slight convexity given to a column or tower, as to correct an optical illusion. [1745–55; < Gk, equiv. to *enta-* (var. s. of *enteínein* to stretch tight, equiv. to *en-* EN-[2] + *teínein* to stretch) + *-sis* -SIS]

En·teb·be (en teb′ə, -teb′ē), *n.* a town in S Uganda, on Lake Victoria: international airport. 21,096.

en·tel·e·chy (en tel′ə kē), *n., pl.* **-chies. 1.** a realization or actuality as opposed to a potentiality. **2.** (in vitalist philosophy) a vital agent or force directing growth and life. [1595–1605; < LL *entelechia* < Gk *entelécheia,* equiv. to *en-* EN-[2] + *tél(os)* goal + *éch(ein)* to have + *-eia* -Y[3]] **—en·te·lech·i·al** (en′tə lek′ē əl), *adj.*

en·tel·lus (en tel′əs), *n., pl.* **-lus·es.** hanuman (def. 1). [1835–45; < NL, a specific epithet]

en·tente (än tänt′; *Fr.* äN täNt′), *n., pl.* **-tentes** (-tänts′; *Fr.* -täNt′). **1.** an arrangement or understanding between two or more nations agreeing to follow a particular policy with regard to affairs of international concern. **2.** an alliance of parties to such an understanding. [1830–45; < F: understanding, OF: intention, n. use of fem. of *entent,* ptp. of *entendre* to INTEND]
—Syn. 1. agreement, accord, rapprochement.

en·tente cor·diale (än tänt′ kôr dyäl′; *Fr.* äN täNt′ kôR dyAl′), a friendly understanding, esp. between two or more nations. [1835–45; < F]

en·ter (en′tər), *v.i.* **1.** to come or go in: *Knock before you enter.* **2.** to be admitted into a school, competition, etc.: *Some contestants enter as late as a day before the race.* **3.** to make a beginning (often fol. by *on* or *upon*): *We have entered upon a new phase in history.* **4.** *Theat.* to come upon the stage (used in stage directions as the 3rd person imperative sing. or pl.): *Enter Othello, and Iago at a distance.* *—v.t.* **5.** to come or go into: *He just entered the building. The thought never entered my mind.* **6.** to penetrate or pierce: *The bullet entered the flesh.* **7.** to put in or insert. **8.** to become a member of; join: *to enter a club.* **9.** to cause to be admitted, as into a school, competition, etc.: *to enter a horse in a race.* **10.** to make a beginning of or in, or begin upon; engage or become involved in: *He entered the medical profession.* **11.** to share in; have an intuitive understanding of: *In order to appreciate the novel, one must be able to enter the spirit of the work.* **12.** to make a record of; record or register: *to enter a new word in a dictionary.* **13.** *Law.* **a.** to make a formal record of (a fact). **b.** to occupy or to take possession of (lands); make an entrance, entry, ingress in, under claim of a right to possession. **c.** to file an application for (public lands). **14.** *Computers.* to put (a document, program, data, etc.) into a computer system: *Enter your new document into the word-processing system.* **15.** to put forward, submit, or register formally: *to enter an objection to a proposed action; to enter a bid for a contract.* **16.** to report (a ship, cargo, etc.) at the custom house. **17. enter into, a.** to participate in; engage in. **b.** to investigate; consider: *We will enter into the question of inherited characteristics at a future time.* **c.** to sympathize with; share in. **d.** to form a constituent part or ingredient of: *There is another factor that enters into the situation.* **e.** to go into a particular state: *to enter into a state of suspended animation.* [1200–50; ME *entren* < OF *entrer* < L *intrāre* to enter, deriv. of *intrā* within] **—en′ter·a·ble,** *adj.* **—en′ter·er,** *n.*
—Ant. 1. leave. **7.** remove.

enter-, var. of **entero-** before a vowel: *enteritis.*

en·ter·al (en′tər əl), *adj.* enteric. [1900–05; ENTER- + -AL[1]] **—en′ter·al·ly,** *adv.*

en·ter·al·gia (en′tə ral′jə, -jē ə), *n. Pathol.* pain in the intestine; colic. [< NL; see ENTER-, -ALGIA]

en·ter·ec·to·my (en′tə rek′tə mē), *n., pl.* **-mies.** *Surg.* excision of part of the intestine. [1875–80; ENTER- + -ECTOMY]

en′tered hound′, *Fox Hunting.* a foxhound that has hunted regularly for one or more seasons.

en·ter·ic (en ter′ik), *adj.* **1.** of or pertaining to the enteron; intestinal. *—n.* **2. enterics,** *Bacteriol.* enterobacteria. [1865–70; < Gk *enterikós.* See ENTER-, -IC]

enter′ic fe′ver, *Pathol.* typhoid (def. 1). [1865–70]

en·ter·i·tis (en′tə rī′tis), *n.* **1.** *Pathol.* inflammation of the intestines, esp. the small intestine. **2.** *Vet. Pathol.* distemper[1] (def. 1c). [1800–10; < NL; see ENTER-, -ITIS]

entero-, a combining form meaning "intestine," used in the formation of compound words: *enterology.* Also, *esp. before a vowel,* **enter-.** [< Gk, comb. form of *énteron* intestine]

en·ter·o·bac·te·ri·a (en′tə rō bak tēr′ē ə), *n.pl., sing.* **-te·ri·um** (-tēr′ē əm). rod-shaped Gram-negative bacteria of the family Enterobacteriaceae, as those of the genera *Escherichia, Salmonella,* and *Shigella,* occurring normally or pathogenically in the intestines of humans and other animals, and the genus *Erwinia,* occurring in plants. Also called **enterics.** [1950–55; ENTERO- + BACTERIA] **—en′ter·o·bac·te′ri·al,** *adj.*

en·ter·o·bi·a·sis (en′tə rō bī′ə sis), *n. Pathol.* infestation with pinworms. [1925–30; < NL, equiv. to *enterob(ius)* an intestinal worm (ENTERO- + Gk *bíos* life) + *-iasis* -IASIS]

en·ter·o·coele (en′tər ə sēl′), *n. Anat.* the body cavity formed from an outpocketing of the archenteron, typical of echinoderms and chordates. Also, **en′ter·o·coel′.** [1875–80; ENTERO- + -COELE]

en·ter·o·co·li·tis (en′tə rō kō lī′tis, -kə-), *n. Pathol.* inflammation of the small intestine and the colon. [1855–60; < NL; see ENTERO-, COLITIS]

en·ter·o·hep·a·ti·tis (en′tə rō hep′ə tī′tis), *n.* **1.** *Pathol.* inflammation of the intestines and liver. **2.** *Vet. Pathol.* blackhead (def. 3). [1890–95; ENTERO- + HEPATITIS]

en·ter·ol·o·gy (en′tə rol′ə jē), *n.* the branch of medicine dealing with the intestines. [1715–25; ENTERO- + -LOGY] **—en·ter·o·log·ic** (en′tər ə loj′ik), **en′ter·o·log′i·cal,** *adj.* **—en′te·rol′o·gist,** *n.*

en·ter·on (en′tə ron′, -tər ən), *n., pl.* **-ter·a** (-tər ə). *Anat., Zool.* the alimentary canal; the digestive tract. [1835–45; < NL < Gk *énteron* intestine]

en·ter·op·a·thy (en′tə rop′ə thē), *n. Pathol.* any abnormality of the intestinal tract. [1890–95; ENTERO- + PATHY]

en·ter·op·neust (en′tər əp nōōst′, -nyōōst′), *n.* any of various invertebrate animals of the class Enteropneusta, comprising the acorn worms. [< NL *Enteropneusta,* equiv. to Gk *entero-* ENTERO- + *-pneusta,* neut. pl. of *pneustós* breathed, verbal of *pneîn* to breathe]

en·ter·os·to·my (en′tə ros′tə mē), *n., pl.* **-mies.** *Surg.* the making of an artificial opening into the intestine, which opens onto the abdominal wall, for feeding or drainage. [1875–80; ENTERO- + -STOMY] **—en′ter·os′to·mal,** *adj.*

en·ter·o·tox·e·mi·a (en′tə rō tok sē′mē ə), *n.* **1.** *Vet. Pathol.* a systemic disease of livestock, caused by intestinal toxins of the bacterium *Clostridium perfringens,* characterized by diarrhea and convulsions, and usually rapidly fatal. **2.** (not in technical use) diarrhea in domestic rabbits. [1930–35; ENTERO- + TOXEMIA]

en·ter·o·tox·in (en′tə rō tok′sin), *n. Pathol.* a toxic substance produced by certain bacteria that on ingestion causes violent vomiting and diarrhea. [1935–40; ENTERO- + TOXIN]

en·ter·o·vi·rus (en′tə rō vī′rəs), *n., pl.* **-rus·es.** *Pathol.* any of several picornaviruses of the genus *Enterovirus,* including poliovirus, that infect the human gastrointestinal tract and cause diseases of the nervous system. [1955–60; ENTERO- + VIRUS] **—en′ter·o·vi′ral,** *adj.*

en·ter·o·zo·a (en′tər ə zō′ə), *n. pl., sing.* **-zo·on** (-zō′on). (*often cap.*) *Biol.* entozoa. [< NL; see ENTERO-, -ZOA] **—en′ter·o·zo′an,** *adj., n.*

en·ter·prise (en′tər prīz′), *n.* **1.** a project undertaken or to be undertaken, esp. one that is important or difficult or that requires boldness or energy: *To keep the peace is a difficult enterprise.* **2.** a plan for such a project. **3.** participation or engagement in such projects: *Our country was formed by the enterprise of resolute men and women.* **4.** boldness or readiness in undertaking; adventurous spirit; ingenuity. **5.** a company organized for commercial purposes; business firm. **6.** (*cap.*) *Mil.* the first nuclear-powered U.S. aircraft carrier, commissioned in 1961, with a displacement of 89,000 tons (80,723 m ton) and eight reactors. **7.** (*cap., italics*) *U.S. Aerospace.* the first space shuttle, used for atmospheric flight and landing tests. [1400–50; late ME < MF, n. use of fem. of *entrepris* (ptp. of *entreprendre* to undertake) < L *inter-* INTER- + *prēnsus* grasped, seized, contr. of *prehēnsus,* equiv. to *pre-* PRE- + *hend-* take hold of + *-tus* ptp. suffix] **—en′ter·prise′less,** *adj.*
—Syn. 1. plan, undertaking, venture. **4.** drive, aggressiveness, push, ambition.

En·ter·prise (en′tər prīz′), *n.* a city in S Alabama. 18,033.

en·ter·pris·er (en′tər prī′zər), *n.* a person who undertakes or engages in some enterprise; entrepreneur. [1515–25; ENTERPRISE + -ER[1]]

en′terprise zone′, an area or locality in which businesses are allowed certain tax advantages and are subject to fewer government regulations in order to stimulate its economy.

en·ter·pris·ing (en′tər prī′zing), *adj.* **1.** ready to undertake projects of importance or difficulty, or untried schemes; energetic in carrying out any undertaking: *Business is in need of enterprising young people.* **2.** characterized by great imagination or initiative: *an enterprising foreign policy.* [1565–75; ENTERPRISE + -ING[2]] **—en′ter·pris′ing·ly,** *adv.*
—Syn. 1. venturous, venturesome, resourceful, adventurous. See **ambitious. —Ant. 1.** timid, cautious.

en·ter·tain (en′tər tān′), *v.t.* **1.** to hold the attention of pleasantly or agreeably; divert; amuse. **2.** to have as a guest; provide food, lodging, etc., for; show hospitality to. **3.** to admit into the mind; consider: *He never entertained such ideas.* **4.** to hold in the mind; harbor; cherish: *They secretly entertained thoughts of revenge.* **5.** *Archaic.* to maintain or keep up. **6.** *Obs.* to give admittance or reception to; receive. *—v.i.* **7.** to exercise hospitality; entertain company; provide entertainment for guests: *They loved to talk, dance, and entertain.* [1425–75; late ME *entertenen* to hold mutually < MF *entretenir* << VL **intertenēre,* equiv. to L *inter-* INTER- + *tenēre* to hold]
—Syn. 1. beguile, regale. See **amuse. —Ant. 1.** bore. **3.** reject.

en·ter·tain·er (en′tər tā′nər), *n.* **1.** a singer, comedian, dancer, reciter, or the like, esp. a professional one. **2.** a person who entertains; host: *She was one of the capital's great entertainers.* [1525–35; ENTERTAIN + -ER[1]]

en·ter·tain·ing (en′tər tā′ning), *adj.* affording entertainment; amusing; diverting: *We spent an entertaining evening at the theater.* [1615–25; ENTERTAIN + -ING[2]] **—en′ter·tain′ing·ly,** *adv.*

en·ter·tain·ment (en′tər tān′mənt), *n.* **1.** the act of entertaining; agreeable occupation for the mind; diversion; amusement: *Solving the daily crossword puzzle is an entertainment for many.* **2.** something affording pleasure, diversion, or amusement, esp. a performance of some kind: *The highlight of the ball was an elaborate entertainment.* **3.** hospitable provision for the needs and wants of guests. **4.** a divertingly adventurous, comic, or picaresque novel. **5.** *Obs.* maintenance in service. [1525–35; ENTERTAIN + -MENT]

en·thal·py (en′thal pē, en thal′-), *n., pl.* **-pies.** *Thermodynamics.* a quantity associated with a thermodynamic system, expressed as the internal energy of a system plus the product of the pressure and volume of the system, having the property that during an isobaric process, the change in the quantity is equal to the heat transferred during the process. *Symbol:* H Also called **heat content, total heat.** [1925–30; < Gk *enthálp(ein)* to warm in (*en-* EN-[2] + *thálpein* to warm) + -Y[3]]

en·thet·ic (en thet′ik), *adj.* introduced from without, as diseases propagated by inoculation. [1865–70; < Gk *enthetikós,* equiv. to *énthet(os)* (verbid of *entithénai* to put in, equiv. to *en-* EN-[2] + *tithénai* to put) + *-ikos* -IC]

en·thral (en thrôl′), *v.t.,* **-thralled, -thral·ling.** enthrall. **—en·thral′ment,** *n.*

en·thrall (en thrôl′), *v.t.* **1.** to captivate or charm: *a performer whose grace, skill, and virtuosity enthrall her audiences.* **2.** to put or hold in slavery; subjugate: *to be enthralled by illusions and superstitions.* Also, **inthral, inthrall.** [1570–80; EN-[1] + THRALL] **—en·thrall′er,** *n.* **—en·thrall′ing·ly,** *adv.* **—en·thrall′ment,** *n.*
—Syn. 1. spellbind, enchant, transport, enrapture.

en·throne (en thrōn′), *v.t.,* **-throned, -thron·ing. 1.** to place on or as on a throne. **2.** to invest with sovereign or episcopal authority. **3.** to exalt. Also, **inthrone.** [1600–10; EN-[1] + THRONE]

en·throne·ment (en thrōn′mənt), *n.* **1.** the act of enthroning. **2.** the state or occasion of being enthroned.

CONCISE ETYMOLOGY KEY: <, descended or borrowed from; >, whence; b., blend of, blended; c., cognate with; cf., compare; deriv., derivative; equiv., equivalent; imit., imitative; obl., oblique; r., replacing; s., stem; sp., spelling, spelled; resp., respelling, respelled; trans., translation; ?, origin unknown; *, unattested; ‡, probably earlier than. See the full key inside the front cover.

Also, **en·thron·i·za·tion** (en thrō′nə zā′shən). [1675–85; ENTHRONE + -MENT]

en·thuse (en tho͞oz′), *v.*, **-thused, -thus·ing.** —*v.i.* **1.** to be or become enthusiastic; show enthusiasm: *All the neighbors enthused over the new baby.* —*v.t.* **2.** to cause to become enthusiastic. [1820–30, *Amer.*; back formation from ENTHUSIASM]
—**Usage.** The verb ENTHUSE is a 19th-century back formation from the noun *enthusiasm.* Originally an Americanism, ENTHUSE is now standard and well established in the speech and all but the most formal writing of educated persons, in both Britain and the United States. It is used as a transitive verb meaning "to cause to become enthusiastic" (*The liveliness of the dance enthused the audience*) and as an intransitive verb meaning "to show enthusiasm" (*She enthused warmly over his performance*). Despite its long history and frequent occurrence, however, ENTHUSE is still strongly disapproved of by many.

en·thu·si·asm (en tho͞o′zē az′əm), *n.* **1.** absorbing or controlling possession of the mind by any interest or pursuit; lively interest: *He shows marked enthusiasm for his studies.* **2.** an occupation, activity, or pursuit in which such interest is shown: *Hunting is his latest enthusiasm.* **3.** any of various forms of extreme religious devotion, usually associated with intense emotionalism and a break with orthodoxy. [1570–80; < LL *enthūsiasmus* < Gk *enthousiasmós,* equiv. to *enthousí(a)* possession by a god (*énthous,* var. of *éntheos* having a god within, equiv. to *en-* EN-[2] + *-thous, -theos* god-possessing + *-ia* Y[3]) + *-asmos,* var., after vowel stems, of *-ismos* -ISM]
—**Syn. 1.** eagerness, warmth, fervor, zeal, ardor, passion, devotion. —**Ant. 1.** indifference.

en·thu·si·ast (en tho͞o′zē ast′, -ist), *n.* **1.** a person who is filled with enthusiasm for some principle, pursuit, etc.; a person of ardent zeal: *a sports enthusiast.* **2.** a religious visionary or fanatic. [1600–10; < Gk *enthousiastḗs* one inspired, equiv. to *enthousi-* (see ENTHUSIASM) + *-astēs,* var. of *-istēs* -IST after *i*]
—**Syn. 1.** zealot, devotee, fan.

en·thu·si·as·tic (en tho͞o′zē as′tik), *adj.* full of or characterized by enthusiasm; ardent: *He seems very enthusiastic about his role in the play.* [1595–1605; < Gk *enthousiastikós.* See ENTHUSIAST, -IC] —**en·thu′si·as′ti·cal·ly,** *adv.*
—**Syn.** eager, fervent, zealous, passionate, vehement, fervid, impassioned.

en·thy·meme (en′thə mēm′), *n. Logic.* a syllogism or other argument in which a premise or the conclusion is unexpressed. [1580–90; < L *enthȳmēma* < Gk *enthȳ́mēma* thought, argument, equiv. to *enthȳmē-,* var. s. of *enthȳmeîsthai* to ponder (*en-* EN-[2] + *-thȳmeîsthai* v. deriv. of *thȳmós* spirit, thought) + *-ma* n. suffix of result] —**en·thy·me·mat·ic** (en′thə mē mat′ik), *adj.*

en·ti·a (en′shē ə, -tē ə), *n.* pl. of **ens.**

en·tice (en tīs′), *v.t.*, **-ticed, -tic·ing.** to lead on by exciting hope or desire; allure; inveigle: *They were enticed westward by dreams of gold.* [1250–1300; ME *enticen* < OF *enticier* to incite < VL **intitiāre,* equiv. to L *in-* IN-[2] + *-titiāre,* v. deriv. of **titius,* for *titiō* piece of burning wood] —**en·tic′ing·ly,** *adv.* —**en·tic′ing·ness,** *n.*
—**Syn.** lure, attract, decoy, tempt. —**Ant.** repel.

en·tice·ment (en tīs′mənt), *n.* **1.** the act or practice of enticing, esp. to evil. **2.** the state of being enticed. **3.** something that entices; allurement. [1275–1325; ME < OF; see ENTICE, -MENT]

en·tire (en tīər′), *adj.* **1.** having all the parts or elements; whole; complete: *He wrote the entire novel in only six weeks.* **2.** full or thorough: *He has been given entire freedom of choice in this matter.* **3.** not broken, mutilated, or decayed; intact: *We were fortunate to find this relic entire.* **4.** unimpaired or undiminished: *His entire energies have gone into making the enterprise a success.* **5.** being wholly of one piece; undivided; continuous: *The entire mood of the symphony was joyful.* **6.** *Bot.* without notches or indentations, as leaves. **7.** not gelded: *an entire horse.* **8.** *Obs.* wholly of one kind; unmixed or pure. —*n.* **9.** *Archaic.* the whole; entirety. **10.** an ungelded animal, esp. a stallion. [1350–1400; ME *entere* < MF *entier* < L *integrum,* acc. of *integer* whole; see INTEGER] —**en·tire′ness,** *n.*
—**Syn. 1.** See **complete.** —**Ant. 1.** partial. **3.** defective.

en tire-bou·chon (*Fr.* äN tēʀ bo͞o shôN′), *Ballet.* a position in which the thigh of one leg is raised up high to the side and the point of the toe touches the knee of the supporting leg. [< F; lit., like a corkscrew]

entire′ func′tion, *Math.* a function of a complex variable that has a derivative for all finite values of the variable.

en·tire·ly (en tīər′lē), *adv.* **1.** wholly or fully; completely or unreservedly: *I am not entirely satisfied with the architect's design.* **2.** solely or exclusively. [1300–50; ME; see ENTIRE, -LY]
—**Syn. 1.** totally, thoroughly.

en·tire·ty (en tīər′tē -tī′ri-), *n., pl.* **-ties.** **1.** the state of being entire; completeness: *Homer's* Iliad *is rarely read in its entirety.* **2.** something that is entire; the whole: *He devoted the entirety of his life to medical research.* [1300–50; ME *enter(e)te* < MF *entierete* < L *integritāt-* (s. of *integritās*). See INTEGER, -ITY]

en·ti·sol (en′ti sôl′, -sol′), *n.* a fertile soil of recent origin that is distinguished by a lack of horizons and is found worldwide in all climates. [1970–75; *ent-* (according to the U.S. Soil Conservation Service, initiator of the term, a "meaningless syllable") + -I- + -SOL]

en·ti·tle (en tīt′l), *v.t.*, **-tled, -tling.** **1.** to give (a person or thing) a title, right, or claim to something; furnish with grounds for laying claim: *His executive position entitled him to certain courtesies rarely accorded others.* **2.** to call by a particular title or name: *What was the book entitled?* **3.** to designate (a person) by an honorary title. Also, **intitle.** [1350–1400; ME *entitlen* < AF *entitler,* var. of MF *entituler* < LL *intitulāre.* See EN-[1], TITLE]
—**Syn.** authorize, qualify.

en·ti·tle·ment (en tīt′l mənt), *n.* **1.** the act of entitling. **2.** the state of being entitled. **3.** the right to guaranteed benefits under a government program, as Social Security or unemployment compensation. [1825–35; ENTITLE + -MENT]

en·ti·ty (en′ti tē), *n., pl.* **-ties.** **1.** something that has a real existence; thing: *corporeal entities.* **2.** being or existence, esp. when considered as distinct, independent, or self-contained: *He conceived of society as composed of particular entities requiring special treatment.* **3.** essential nature: *The entity of justice is universality.* [1590–1600; < ML *entitās,* equiv. to *enti-* (s. of *ēns*), prp. of *esse* to be + *-tās* -TY[2]] —**en·ti·ta·tive** (en′ti tā′tiv), *adj.* —**en′ti·ta′tive·ly,** *adv.*

ento-, a combining form meaning "within," used in the formation of compound words: *entoderm.* [comb. form repr. Gk *entós*]

en·to·blast (en′tə blast′), *n. Embryol.* **1.** endoderm. **2.** hypoblast (def. 2). [1860–65; ENTO- + -BLAST] —**en·to·blas·tic** (en′tə blas′tik), *adj.*

en·to·derm (en′tə dûrm′), *n. Embryol.* endoderm. [1875–80; ENTO- + -DERM] —**en·to·der·mal** (en′tə dûr′məl), **en′to·der′mic,** *adj.*

en·toil (en toil′), *v.t.* to take in toils; ensnare; enmesh. [1575–85; EN-[1] + TOIL[2]]

en·tomb (en to͞om′), *v.t.* **1.** to place in a tomb; bury; inter. **2.** to serve as a tomb for: *Florentine churches entomb many great men.* Also, **intomb.** [1425–75; late ME *entoumben* < MF *entomber.* See EN-[1], TOMB] —**en·tomb′ment,** *n.*

entomo-, a combining form meaning "insect," used in the formation of compound words: *entomology.* [comb. form of Gk *éntomos* notched, *éntoma* (n. use of neut. pl.) insects, verbid of *entémnein* to cut in or up, equiv. to *en-* EN-[2] + *tómos* cut; see -TOMY]

en·to·mo·fau·na (en′tə mō fô′nə), *n., pl.* **-nas, -nae** (-nē). (*used with a singular or plural v.*) the insect life of a region or habitat. [1950–55; ENTOMO- + FAUNA]

entomol., **1.** entomological. **2.** entomology. Also, **entom.**

en·to·mol·o·gy (en′tə mol′ə jē), *n.* the branch of zoology dealing with insects. [1760–70; ENTOMO- + -LOGY] —**en·to·mo·log·i·cal** (en′tə mə loj′i kəl), **en′to·mo·log′ic,** *adj.* —**en′to·mo·log′i·cal·ly,** *adv.* —**en′to·mol′o·gist,** *n.*

en·to·moph·a·gous (en′tə mof′ə gəs), *adj.* feeding on insects; insectivorous. [1830–40; ENTOMO- + -PHAGOUS]

en·to·moph·i·lous (en′tə mof′ə ləs), *adj.* pollinated by or having spores distributed by insects. [1875–80; ENTOMO- + -PHILOUS] —**en′to·moph′i·ly,** *n.*

en·top·ic (en top′ik), *adj. Anat.* being or occurring in the usual place. [< Gk *éntop(os)* in place (see EN-[2], TOPO-) + -IC]

en·to·proct (en′tə prokt′), *n. Zool.* **1.** any of various sessile, chiefly marine, mosslike animals of the phylum Entoprocta (formerly a subphylum of Bryophyta), occasionally solitary polyps but usually forming branching colonies, each individual polyp having an almost closed ring of tentacles within which lie the mouth and anus. —*adj.* **2.** belonging or pertaining to the phylum Entoprocta. Also called **endoproct.** Cf. **ectoproct.** [1935–40; see ENTOPROCTA]

En·to·proc·ta (en′tə prok′tə), *n.* a small phylum of invertebrates comprising the entoprocts: considered a subphylum of Bryozoa, from which it is distinguished by having the anus of the polyp near the mouth within the crown of tentacles. Also called **Endoprocta.** Cf. **Ectoprocta.** [< NL, equiv. to *ento-* ENTO- + *-procta* < Gk *-prōkta,* neut. pl. of *-prōktos,* adj. deriv. of *prōktós* anus, rectum]

en·tou·rage (än′to͞o räzh′), *n.* **1.** a group of attendants or associates, as of a person of rank or importance: *The opera singer traveled with an entourage of 20 people.* **2.** surroundings; environment: *a house with a charming entourage of trees and flowers.* **3.** *Archit.* the landscaping and other nearby environmental features shown on a rendering of a building. [1825–35; < F, equiv. to *entour(er)* to surround (deriv. of *entour* around, equiv. to *en* in + *tour* circuit; see TOUR) + *-age* -AGE]
—**Syn. 1.** retinue, following, cortege, escort.

en·to·zo·an (en′tə zō′ən), *n. Biol.* **1.** entozoon. —*adj.* **2.** of or pertaining to an entozoon. [ENTOZO(ON) + -AN]

en·to·zo·ic (en′tə zō′ik), *adj.* (of a parasitic animal) living within the body of its host. [1860–65; ENTOZO(A) + -IC]

en·to·zo·on (en′tə zō′on), *n., pl.* **-zo·a** (-zō′ə). any animal parasite, as an intestinal worm, that lives within the body of its host (opposed to *ectozoon*). Also, **entozoan.** [1825–35; ENTO- + -ZOON]

en·tr'acte (än trakt′, än′trakt; *Fr.* äN tʀakt′), *n., pl.* **-tr'actes** (-trakts′, -trakts; *Fr.* -tʀakt′). **1.** the interval between two consecutive acts of a theatrical or operatic performance. **2.** a performance, as of music or dancing, given during such an interval. **3.** a piece of music or the like for such performance. [1740–50; < F, equiv. to *entre* between (< L *inter*) + *acte* ACT]

en·trails (en′trālz, -trəlz), *n.pl.* **1.** the internal parts of the trunk of an animal body. **2.** the intestines. **3.** the internal parts of anything: *the entrails of a machine.* [1250–1300; ME *entrailles* < AF, MF < VL **intrālia* (cf. early ML *intrālia*), alter., by suffix change (see -AL[1]), of L *interānea* guts, neut. pl. of *interāneus;* see *inter-,* -AN, -EOUS]
—**Syn.** viscera, intestines, insides, innards, guts.

en·train[1] (en trān′), *v.i.* **1.** to go aboard a train. —*v.t.* **2.** to put aboard a train. [1880–85; EN-[1] + TRAIN] —**en·train′er,** *n.*

en·train[2] (en trān′), *v.t.* **1.** *Chem.* (of a substance, as a vapor) to carry along (a dissimilar substance, as drops of liquid) during a given process, as evaporation or distillation. **2.** (of a liquid) to trap (bubbles). **3.** *Meteorol.* to transfer (air) into an organized air current from the surrounding atmosphere (opposed to *detrain*). [1560–70; < MF *entrainer,* equiv. to *en-* EN-[1] + *trainer* to drag, trail; see TRAIN] —**en·train′ment,** *n.*

en·trance[1] (en′trəns), *n.* **1.** an act of entering, as into a place or upon new duties. **2.** a point or place of entering; an opening or passage for entering, as a doorway. **3.** the right, privilege, or permission to enter; admission: *People improperly dressed will be refused entrance to the theater.* **4.** *Theat.* the moment or place in the script at which an actor comes on the stage. **5.** *Music.* **a.** the point in a musical score at which a particular voice or instrument joins the ensemble. **b.** the way in which this is done: *a sloppy entrance.* **6.** a manner, means, or style of entering a room, group, etc.; way of coming into view: *She mimicked Joan's entrance.* **7.** *Naut.* the immersed portion of a hull forward of the middle body (opposed to *run*). [1425–75; late ME *entraunce* < MF *entrance.* See ENTER, -ANCE]
—**Syn. 1, 2.** entry, ingress. **3.** ENTRANCE, ADMITTANCE, ADMISSION refer to the possibility of entering a place or a group. ENTRANCE may refer to either possibility: *Entrance is by way of the side door; entrance into a card game.* ADMITTANCE refers more to place and suggests entrance that may be permitted or denied: *to gain admittance to a building; no admittance.* ADMISSION refers more to special groups and suggests entrance by payment, by formal or special permission, privilege, and the like: *admission to a concert, a game, to candidacy, the bar, to society.* —**Ant. 1, 2.** exit.

en·trance[2] (en trans′, -träns′), *v.t.*, **-tranced, -tranc·ing.** **1.** to fill with delight or wonder; enrapture. **2.** to put into a trance: *to be hypnotically entranced.* [1585–95; EN-[1] + TRANCE[1]] —**en·trance′ment,** *n.*
—**Syn. 1.** enthrall, spellbind, fascinate, transport.

en′trance pu′pil, *Optics.* the image of the aperture viewed from the objective of an optical system limiting the rays that enter the system. Cf. **exit pupil.**

en·trance·way (en′trəns wā′), *n.* an entryway. [1860–65, *Amer.*; ENTRANCE[1] + WAY]

en·tranc·ing (en tran′sing, -trän′-), *adj.* delightful; enchanting. [1835–45; ENTRANCE[2] + -ING[2]] —**en·tranc′ing·ly,** *adv.*

en·trant (en′trənt), *n.* **1.** a competitor in a contest. **2.** a new member, as of an association or school. **3.** a person who enters. [1625–35; < F, n. use of *entrant,* prp. of *entrer* to ENTER]

en·trap (en trap′), *v.t.*, **-trapped, -trap·ping.** **1.** to catch in or as in a trap; ensnare: *The hunters used nets to entrap the lion.* **2.** to bring unawares into difficulty or danger: *He entrapped himself in the web of his own lies.* **3.** to lure into performing an act or making a statement that is compromising or illegal. **4.** to draw into contradiction or damaging admission: *The questioner entrapped her into an admission of guilt.* **5.** *Law.* to catch by entrapment. [1525–35; < MF *entraper.* See EN-[1], TRAP[1]] —**en·trap′per,** *n.* —**en·trap′ping·ly,** *adv.*
—**Syn. 1.** capture, snare, trap.

en·trap·ment (en trap′mənt), *n.* **1.** the luring by a law-enforcement agent of a person into committing a crime. **2.** an act or process of entrapping. **3.** a state of being entrapped. [1590–1600; ENTRAP + -MENT]

en·treas·ure (en trezh′ər), *v.t.*, **-ured, -ur·ing.** to lay up in or as in a treasury. [1590–1600; EN-[1] + TREASURE]

en·treat (en trēt′), *v.t.* **1.** to ask (a person) earnestly; beseech; implore; beg: *to entreat the judge for mercy.* **2.** to ask earnestly for (something): *He entreated help in his work.* —*v.i.* **3.** to make an earnest request or petition. [1300–50; ME *entreten* < MF *entrait(i)er.* See EN-[1], TREAT] —**en·treat′ing·ly,** *adv.* —**en·treat′ment,** *n.*
—**Syn. 1.** pray, importune, sue, solicit. See **appeal.**

en·treat·y (en trē′tē), *n., pl.* **-treat·ies.** earnest request or petition; supplication. [1515–25; ENTREAT + -Y[3]]
—**Syn.** appeal, suit, plea, solicitation.

en·tre·chat (*Fr.* äN tʀə shä′), *n., pl.* **-chats** (*Fr.* -shä′). *Ballet.* a jump in which the dancer crosses the feet a number of times while in the air. [1765–75; < F, alter. of It (*capriola*) *intrecciata* intwined (caper), equiv. to *in-* IN-[2] + *trecci-* TRESS + *-ata* -ATE[1]]

en·tre·côte (*Fr.* äN tʀə kōt′), *n., pl.* **-côtes** (*Fr.* -kōt′). a steak sliced from between the ribs of a rib roast cut. [1835–45; < F < L *inter-* INTER- + *costa* rib]

en·trée (än′trā), *n.* **1.** a dish served as the main course of a meal. **2.** *Older Use.* a dish served at dinner between the principal courses. **3.** the privilege of entering; access. **4.** a means of obtaining entry: *His friendship with an actor's son was his entrée into the theatrical world.* **5.** the act of entering; entrance. Also, **en′tree.** [1775–85; < F, n. use of fem. ptp. of *entrer* to enter; see ENTRY]
—**Syn. 3, 4.** admission, entry.

en·tre·lac (en′trə lak′), *n. Print.* a decorative border of interlaced garlands and leaves. [< F; akin to *entrelacer* to INTERLACE]

en·tre·mets (än′trə mā′; *Fr.* äN tʀə me′), *n., pl.* **-mets** (-māz′; *Fr.* -me′). (*used with a singular or plural v.*) **1.** a dish or dishes served at dinner between the principal courses or with the roast or other main course; side dish. **2.** the sweet dishes or dessert course served after a cheese course. [1425–75; late ME < MF; OF *entremes.* See INTER-, MESS]

en·trench (en trench′), *v.t.* **1.** to place in a position of strength; establish firmly or solidly: *safely entrenched behind undeniable facts.* **2.** to dig trenches for defensive purposes around (oneself, a military position, etc.). —*v.i.* **3.** to encroach; trespass; infringe (usually fol. by

CONCISE PRONUNCIATION KEY: act, cāpe, dâre, pärt; set, ēqual; *if,* īce; ox, ōver, ôrder, oil, bo͝ok, bo͞ot, out; up, ûrge; child; sing; shoe; thin, *th*at; zh as in *treasure.* ə = *a* as in *alone, e* as in *system, i* as in *easily, o* as in *gallop, u* as in *circus;* ə as in *fire* (fīər), *hour* (ouər). l and n can serve as syllabic consonants, as in *cradle* (krād′l), and *button* (but′n). See the full key inside the front cover.

on or upon): *to entrench on the domain or rights of another.* Also, **intrench.** [1545–55; EN-[1] + TRENCH]
—Syn. 1. settle, ensconce, set, implant, embed.

entrench′ing tool′. See **intrenching tool.** [1765–75]

en•trench•ment (en trench′mənt), *n.* **1.** the act of entrenching. **2.** an entrenched position. **3.** Usually, **entrenchments.** an earth breastwork or ditch for protection against enemy fire. [1580–90; ENTRENCH + -MENT]

en•tre nous (än′trə nōō′; *Fr.* äN trə nōō′), between ourselves; confidentially. [1680–90; < F]

en•tre•pôt (än′trə pō′; *Fr.* äN trə pō′), *n., pl.* **-pôts** (-pōz′; *Fr.* -pō′). **1.** a warehouse. **2.** a commercial center where goods are received for distribution, transshipment, or repackaging. Also, **en′tre•pot′.** [1715–25; < F, equiv. to *entre* INTER- + *pôt* < L *positum,* n. use of neut. ptp. of *pōnere* to put, place (modeled on *dépôt* DEPOT)]

en•tre•pre•neur (än′trə prə nûr′, -nŏŏr′; *Fr.* äN trə prə nœr′), *n., pl.* **-neurs** (-nûrz′, -nŏŏrz′; *Fr.* -nœr′), *v.* —*n.* **1.** a person who organizes and manages any enterprise, esp. a business, usually with considerable initiative and risk. **2.** an employer of productive labor; contractor. —*v.t.* **3.** to deal with or initiate as an entrepreneur. —*v.i.* **4.** to act as an entrepreneur. [1875–80; < F: lit., one who undertakes (some task), equiv. to *entrepren(dre)* to undertake (< L *inter-* INTER- + *prendere* to take, var. of *prehendere*) + *-eur* -EUR. See ENTERPRISE] **—en′tre•pre•neur′i•al,** *adj.* **—en′tre•pre•neur′i•al•ly,** *adv.* **—en′tre•pre•neur′i•al•ism, en′tre•pre•neur′ism,** *n.* **—en′tre•pre•neur′ship,** *n.*

en•tre•sol (en′tər sol′, än′trə-, en′-; *Fr.* äN trə sôl′), *n., pl.* **-sols** (-solz′; *Fr.* -sôl′). *Archit.* a low floor between two higher floors, the lower one usually being a ground floor; mezzanine. [1765–75; < F: lit., between-floor, equiv. to *entre-* INTER- + *sol* floor < L *solum* ground]

en•tro•py (en′trə pē), *n.* **1.** *Thermodynam.* **a.** (on a macroscopic scale) a function of thermodynamic variables, as temperature, pressure, or composition, that is a measure of the energy that is not available for work during a thermodynamic process. A closed system evolves toward a state of maximum entropy. **b.** (in statistical mechanics) a measure of the randomness of the microscopic constituents of a thermodynamic system. *Symbol:* S **2.** (in data transmission and information theory) a measure of the loss of information in a transmitted signal or message. **3.** (in cosmology) a hypothetical tendency for the universe to attain a state of maximum homogeneity in which all matter is at a uniform temperature **(heat death). 4.** a doctrine of inevitable social decline and degeneration. [< G *Entropie* (1865); see EN-[2], -TROPY] **—en•tro•pic** (en trō′pik, -trop′ik), *adj.* **—en•tro′pi•cal•ly,** *adv.*

en•trust (en trust′), *v.t.* **1.** to charge or invest with a trust or responsibility; charge with a specified office or duty involving trust: *We entrusted him with our lives.* **2.** to commit (something) in trust to; confide, as for care, use, or performance: *to entrust a secret, money, powers, or work to another.* Also, **intrust.** [1595–1605; EN-[1] + TRUST] **—en•trust′ment,** *n.*

en•try (en′trē), *n., pl.* **-tries. 1.** an act of entering; entrance. **2.** a place of ingress or entrance, esp. an entrance hall or vestibule. **3.** permission or right to enter; access. **4.** the act of entering or recording something in a book, register, list, etc. **5.** the statement, item, etc., so entered or recorded. **6.** a person or thing entered in a contest or competition. **7.** See **vocabulary entry. 8.** *Law.* act of taking possession of lands or tenements by entering or setting foot on them. **9.** the giving of an account of a ship's cargo at a custom house, to obtain permission to land the goods. **10.** *Accounting.* the record of any transaction found in a bookkeeper's journal. **11.** *Bookkeeping.* **a.** See **double entry. b.** See **single entry. 12.** *Mining.* adit (def. 2). **13.** Also called **en′try card′.** *Bridge.* a winning card in one's hand or the hand of one's partner that gives the lead to one hand or the other. [1250–1300; ME *entre(e)* < OF *entree* < L *intrāta* (n. use of fem. of *intrātus,* ptp. of *intrāre* to ENTER), equiv. to *intr-* enter + *-āta* -ATE[1]]
—Syn. 5. record, note, memo, jotting.

en′try blank′, a printed form to be filled out, as by an entrant in a contest.

en•try-lev•el (en′trē lev′əl), *adj.* **1.** of, pertaining to, or filling a low-level job in which an employee may gain experience or skills: *This year's college graduates have a limited choice of entry-level jobs.* **2.** suitable for or affordable by people buying or entering the market for the first time: *These less expensive entry-level homes sell quite well.* **3.** relatively simple in design, limited in capability, and low in cost: *entry-level home computers and word processors.*

en•try•way (en′trē wā′), *n.* a passage for affording entrance. [1740–50, *Amer.*; ENTRY + WAY]

en•twine (en twīn′), *v.t., v.i.,* **-twined, -twin•ing.** to twine with, about, around, or together. Also, **intwine.** [1590–1600; EN-[1] + TWINE[1]] **—en•twine′ment,** *n.*

en•twist (en twist′), *v.t.* to twist together or about. Also, **intwist.** [1580–90; EN-[1] + TWIST]

e•nu•cle•ate (*v.* i nōō′klē āt′, i nyōō′-; *adj.* i nōō′klē-it, -āt′, i nyōō′-), *v.,* **-at•ed, -at•ing,** *adj.* —*v.t.* **1.** *Biol.* to deprive of the nucleus. **2.** to remove (a kernel, tumor, eyeball, etc.) from its enveloping cover. **3.** *Archaic.* to bring out; disclose; explain. —*adj.* **4.** having no nucleus. [1540–50; < L *ēnucleātus* (ptp. of *ēnucleāre* to remove the pit from (fruit)), equiv. to *ē-* E- + *nucle(us)* NUCLEUS + *-ātus* -ATE[1]] **—e•nu′cle•a′tion,** *n.*

e•nuf (i nuf′), *adj., pron., adv., interj. Eye Dialect.* enough.

CONCISE ETYMOLOGY KEY: <, descended or borrowed from; >, whence; b., blend of, blended; c., cognate with; cf., compare; deriv., derivative; equiv., equivalent; imit., imitative; obl., oblique; r., replacing; s., stem; sp., spelling, spelled; resp., respelling, respelled; trans., translation; ?, origin unknown; *, unattested; ‡, probably earlier than. See the full key inside the front cover.

E•nu•gu (ā nōō′gōō), *n.* a city in SE Nigeria. 172,000.

e•nu•mer•a•ble (i nōō′mər ə bəl, i nyōō′-), *adj.* countable (def. 2b). [1885–90; ENUMER(ATE) + -ABLE] **—e•nu′mer•a•bly,** *adv.*

e•nu•mer•ate (i nōō′mə rāt′, i nyōō′-), *v.t.,* **-at•ed, -at•ing. 1.** to mention separately as if in counting; name one by one; specify, as in a list: *Let me enumerate the many flaws in your hypothesis.* **2.** to ascertain the number of; count. [1640–50; < L *ēnumerātus* (ptp. of *ēnumerāre*), equiv. to *ē-* -E + *numer(us)* NUMBER + *-ātus* -ATE[1]] **—e•nu•mer•a•tive** (i nōō′mə rā′tiv, -mər ə-, i nyōō′-), *adj.* **—e•nu′mer•a′tor,** *n.*
—Syn. 1. recapitulate, recount.

e•nu•mer•a•tion (i nōō′mə rā′shən, i nyōō′-), *n.* **1.** an act of enumerating. **2.** a catalog or list. [1545–55; < L *ēnumerātiōn-* (s. of *ēnumerātiō*). See ENUMERATE, -ION]

e•nun•ci•ate (i nun′sē āt′), *v.,* **-at•ed, -at•ing.** —*v.t.* **1.** to utter or pronounce (words, sentences, etc.), esp. in an articulate or a particular manner: *He enunciates his words distinctly.* **2.** to state or declare definitely, as a theory. **3.** to announce or proclaim: *to enunciate one's intentions.* —*v.i.* **4.** to pronounce words, esp. in an articulate or a particular manner. [1615–25; < L *ēnūntiātus* (ptp. of *ēnūntiāre*), equiv. to *ē-* E- + *nūnti(us)* messenger, message + *-ātus* -ATE[1]] **—e•nun′ci•a•ble,** *adj.* **—e•nun′ci•a•bil′i•ty,** *n.* **—e•nun′ci•a′tive, e•nun′ci•a•to′ry,** *adj.* **—e•nun′ci•a′tive•ly,** *adv.* **—e•nun′ci•a′tor,** *n.*

e•nun•ci•a•tion (i nun′sē ā′shən), *n.* **1.** an act or manner of enunciating. **2.** utterance or pronunciation. **3.** a formal announcement or statement: *the enunciation of a doctrine.* [1545–55; < L *ēnūntiātiōn-* (s. of *ēnūntiātiō*). See ENUNCIATE, -ION]

en•ure (en yŏŏr′, -ŏŏr′), *v.t., v.i.,* **-ured, -ur•ing.** inure.

en•u•re•sis (en′yə rē′sis), *n. Med.* lack of control of urination, esp. during sleep; bed-wetting; urinary incontinence. [1790–1800; < NL < Gk *en-* EN-[2] + *ourē-* (var. s. of *oureîn* to urinate) + *-sis* -SIS] **—en•u•ret•ic** (en′yə-ret′ik), *adj.*

env., envelope.

en•vel•op (*v.* en vel′əp; *n.* en vel′əp, en′və ləp, än′-), *v.,* **-oped, -op•ing.** *n.* —*v.t.* **1.** to wrap up in or as in a covering: *The long cloak she was wearing enveloped her completely.* **2.** to serve as a wrapping or covering for, as a membrane of an organ or a sheath. **3.** to surround entirely. **4.** *Mil.* to attack (an enemy's flank). —*n.* **5.** envelope. [1350–1400; ME *envolupen* < OF *envoluper,* equiv. to *en-* EN-[1] + *voloper* to envelop, of obscure orig.; cf. OPr *(en)volopar,* It *inviluppare* to envelop, It *viluppo* tuft, bundle, confusion, referred to ML *faluppa* chaff, wisp of straw, perh. influenced by the descendants of L *volvere* to roll] **—en•vel′op•er,** *n.*
—Syn. 1. enfold, cover, hide, conceal. **3.** encompass, enclose.

en•ve•lope (en′və lōp′, än′-), *n.* **1.** a flat paper container, as for a letter or thin package, usually having a gummed flap or other means of closure. **2.** something that envelops; a wrapper, integument, or surrounding cover. **3.** *Biol.* a surrounding or enclosing structure, as a corolla or an outer membrane. **4.** *Geom.* a curve or surface tangent to each member of a set of curves or surfaces. **5.** *Radio.* (of a modulated carrier wave) a curve connecting the peaks of a graph of the instantaneous value of the electric or magnetic component of the carrier wave as a function of time. **6.** the fabric structure enclosing the gasbag of an aerostat. **7.** the gasbag itself. **8.** *Electronics.* the airtight glass or metal housing of a vacuum tube. Also, **envelop.** [1700–10; < F *enveloppe,* deriv. of *envelopper* to ENVELOP]

en′velope chemise′, teddy.

en•vel•op•ment (en vel′əp mənt), *n.* **1.** an act of enveloping. **2.** the state of being enveloped. **3.** a wrapping or covering. **4.** *Mil.* an attack on an enemy's flank. [1755–65; ENVELOP + -MENT]

en•ven•om (en ven′əm), *v.t.* **1.** to impregnate with venom; make poisonous. **2.** to embitter. [1250–1300; ME *envenimen* < OF *envenimer.* See EN-[1], VENOM]

En•ver Pa•sha (en ver′ pä shä′), 1881–1922, Turkish soldier and statesman.

en•vi•a•ble (en′vē ə bəl), *adj.* worthy of envy; very desirable: *an enviable position.* [1595–1605; ENVY + -ABLE] **—en′vi•a•ble•ness,** *n.* **—en′vi•a•bly,** *adv.*
—Syn. advantageous, fortunate, lucky.

en•vi•er (en′vē ər), *n.* a person who feels envy. [1500–10; ENVY + -ER[1]]

en•vi•ous (en′vē əs), *adj.* **1.** full of, feeling, or expressing envy: *envious of a person's success; an envious attack.* **2.** *Archaic.* **a.** emulous. **b.** enviable. [1250–1300; ME < AF; OF *envieus* < L *invidiōsus* INVIDIOUS] **—en′vi•ous•ly,** *adv.* **—en′vi•ous•ness,** *n.*
—Syn. 1. resentful, jealous, covetous.

en•vi•ron (en vī′rən, -vī′ərn), *v.t.* to form a circle or ring round; surround; envelop: *a house environed by pleasant grounds; to be environed by bad influences.* [1300–50; ME *envirounen* < OF *environner,* deriv. of *environ* around (*en* EN-[1] + *viron* a circle; *vir(er)* to turn, VEER + *-on* n. suffix)]

environ., **1.** environment. **2.** environmental. **3.** environmentalism. **4.** environmentalist.

en•vi•ron•ment (en vī′rən mənt, -vī′ərn-), *n.* **1.** the aggregate of surrounding things, conditions, or influences; surroundings; milieu. **2.** *Ecol.* the air, water, minerals, organisms, and all other external factors surrounding and affecting a given organism at any time. **3.** the social and cultural forces that shape the life of a person or a population. **4.** *Computers.* the hardware or software configuration, or the mode of operation, of a computer system: *In a time-sharing environment, transactions are processed as they occur.* **5.** an indoor or outdoor setting that is characterized by the presence of environmental art that is itself designed to be site-specific. [1595–1605; ENVIRON + -MENT] **—en•vi′ron•men′tal,** *adj.* **—en•vi′ron•men′tal•ly,** *adv.*
—Syn. 1. locale, environs. ENVIRONMENT, MILIEU, AMBIANCE, SETTING, SURROUNDINGS all refer to what makes up the atmosphere or background against which someone or something is seen. ENVIRONMENT may refer either to actual physical surroundings or to social or cultural background factors: *an environment of crime and grinding poverty.* MILIEU, encountered most often in literary writing, refers to intangible aspects of the environment: *an exhilarating milieu of artistic ferment and innovation.* AMBIANCE applies to the atmosphere of the surroundings, their mood or tone: *an ambiance of ease and elegance.* SETTING suggests a background that sets something off: *a perfect setting for the emerald.* SURROUNDINGS alludes specifically to the physical aspects of the environment: *awoke in strange surroundings; blend in with her surroundings.*

envi′ronmen′tal art′, artistic works that are planned, often on a grand scale, to surround or to involve the participation of the spectator. [1965–70] **—envi′ronmen′tal art′ist.**

environmen′tal design′, **1.** the ordering of the large-scale aspects of the environment by means of architecture, engineering, landscape architecture, urban planning, regional planning, etc., usually in combination. **2.** the study or practice of this.

en•vi•ron•men•tal•ist (en vī′rən men′tl ist, -vī′ərn-), *n.* **1.** an expert on environmental problems. **2.** any person who advocates or works to protect the air, water, animals, plants, and other natural resources from pollution or its effects. **3.** a person who believes that differences between individuals or groups, esp. in moral and intellectual attributes, are predominantly determined by environmental factors, as surroundings, upbringing, or experience (opposed to *hereditarian*). [1915–20; ENVIRONMENTAL + -IST] **—en•vi′ron•men′tal•ism,** *n.*

Environmen′tal Protec′tion A′gency. See **EPA.**

environmen′tal resist′ance, the limiting effect of environmental conditions on the numerical growth of a population. [1925–30]

envi′ronmen′tal sci′ence, the branch of science concerned with the physical, chemical, and biological conditions of the environment and their effect on organisms. [1965–70]

en•vi•rons (en vī′rənz, -vī′ərnz, en′vər ənz, -vī ərnz), *n.pl.* **1.** the surrounding parts or districts, as of a city; outskirts; suburbs. **2.** surrounding objects; surroundings; environment. **3.** an area or space close by; vicinity. [1655–65; < F (pl.); r. ME *environ* < OF, n. use of *environ* around; see ENVIRON]

en•vis•age (en viz′ij), *v.t.,* **-aged, -ag•ing. 1.** to contemplate; visualize: *He envisages an era of great scientific discoveries.* **2.** *Archaic.* to look in the face of; face. [1810–20; < F *envisager.* See EN-[1], VISAGE] **—en•vis′age•ment,** *n.*
—Syn. 1. picture, imagine, conceive, envision.

en•vi•sion (en vizh′ən), *v.t.* to picture mentally, esp. some future event or events: *to envision a bright future.* [1920–25; EN-[1] + VISION]

en•voy[1] (en′voi, än′-), *n.* **1.** a diplomatic agent. **2.** any accredited messenger or representative. **3.** Also called **en′voy extraor′dinary, minister plenipotentiary.** a diplomatic agent of the second rank, next in status after an ambassador. [1635–45; < F *envoyé* envoy, n. use of ptp. of *envoyer* to send < VL **inviāre,* presumably orig. to be on a journey, v. deriv. of L *in viā* on one's way, en route]
—Syn. 1, 2. delegate, emissary, deputy.

en•voy[2] (en′voi, än′-), *n.* a short stanza concluding a poem in certain archaic metrical forms, as a ballade, and serving as a dedication, or a similar postscript to a prose composition. Also, **en′voi.** [1350–1400; ME *envoye* < OF, deriv. of *envoyer* to send; see ENVOY[1]]

en•vy (en′vē), *n., pl.* **-vies,** *v.,* **-vied, -vy•ing.** —*n.* **1.** a feeling of discontent or covetousness with regard to another's advantages, success, possessions, etc. **2.** an object of envious feeling: *Her intelligence made her the envy of her classmates.* **3.** *Obs.* ill will. —*v.t.* **4.** to regard with envy; be envious of: *He envies her the position she has achieved in her profession.* —*v.i.* **5.** *Obs.* to be affected with envy. [1250–1300; (n.) ME *envie* < OF < L *invidia,* equiv. to *invid(us)* envious (deriv. of *invidēre* to envy; see INVIDIOUS) + *-ia* -Y[3]; (v.) ME *envien* < OF *envier* < ML *invidiāre,* deriv. of L *invidia*] **—en′vy•ing•ly,** *adv.*
—Syn. 1. enviousness. ENVY and JEALOUSY are very close in meaning. ENVY denotes a longing to possess something awarded to or achieved by another: *to feel envy when a friend inherits a fortune.* JEALOUSY, on the other hand, denotes a feeling of resentment that another has gained something that one more rightfully deserves: *to feel jealousy when a coworker receives a promotion.* JEALOUSY also refers to anguish caused by fear of unfaithfulness. **4.** resent. ENVY, BEGRUDGE, COVET refer to one's attitude toward the possessions or attainments of others. To ENVY is to feel resentful and unhappy because someone else possesses, or has achieved, what one wishes oneself to possess, or to have achieved: *to envy the wealthy, a woman's beauty, an honest man's reputation.* To BEGRUDGE is to be unwilling that another should have the possessions, honors, or credit that person deserves: *to begrudge a man a reward for heroism.* To COVET is to long jealously to possess what someone else possesses: *I covet your silverware.*

en•weave (en wēv′), *v.t.,* **-wove** or **-weaved, -wo•ven** or **-wove** or **-weaved, -weav•ing.** inweave.

en•wheel (en hwēl′, -wēl′), *v.t. Obs.* to encircle. [1595–1605; EN[1]- + WHEEL]

en•wind (en wīnd′), *v.t.,* **-wound, -wind•ing.** to wind or coil about; encircle. Also, **inwind.** [1590–1600; EN-[1] + WIND[2]]

en•womb (en wōōm′), *v.t.* to enclose in or as if in the womb. [1580–90; EN-[1] + WOMB]

en•wrap (en rap′), *v.t.,* **-wrapped, -wrap•ping. 1.** to wrap or envelop in something. **2.** to surround or envelop, as in slumber, longing, etc. **3.** to absorb or engross, as in thought. Also, **inwrap.** [1350–1400; ME *enwrappen;* see EN-[1], WRAP]

en•wreathe (en rēth′), *v.t.,* **-wreathed, -wreath•ing.** to surround or encircle with or as with a wreath. Also, **inwreathe.** [1610–20; EN-[1] + WREATHE]

en•wrought (en rôt′), *adj.* inwrought.

E•ny•o (i nī′ō), *n.* an ancient Greek war goddess.

en•zo•ot•ic (en′zō ot′ik), *adj. Vet. Med.* **1.** (of diseases) prevailing among or afflicting animals in a particular locality. Cf. **endemic.** —*n.* **2.** an enzootic disease. [1875–80; EN-[2] + ZO- + -OTIC, modeled on EPIZOOTIC] —**en′zo•ot′i•cal•ly,** *adv.*

en•zy•got•ic (en′zī got′ik, -zi-), *adj. Embryol.* monozygotic. [EN-[1] + ZYGOTIC] —**en•zy•gos•i•ty** (en′zī gos′i tē, -zi-), *n.*

en•zy•mat•ic (en′zī mat′ik, -zi-), *adj.* of or pertaining to an enzyme. Also, **en•zy•mic** (en zī′mik, -zim′ik). [1895–1900; ENZYME + -ATIC] —**en′zy•mat′i•cal•ly, en•zy′mi•cal•ly,** *adv.*

en•zyme (en′zīm), *n. Biochem.* any of various proteins, as pepsin, originating from living cells and capable of producing certain chemical changes in organic substances by catalytic action, as in digestion. Cf. **-ase.** [1880–85; < MGk *énzymos* leavened (Gk *en-* EN-[2] + *zým(ē)* leaven + *-os* adj. suffix)]

en•zy•mol•o•gy (en′zī mol′ə jē, -zi-), *n.* the branch of biology that deals with the chemistry, biochemistry, and effects of enzymes. [1895–1900; ENZYME + -O- + -LOGY] —**en′zy•mol′o•gist,** *n.*

en•zy•mol•y•sis (en′zī mol′ə sis, -zi-), *n. Biochem.* the decomposition of a chemical compound catalyzed by the presence of an enzyme. [ENZYME + -O- + -LYSIS] —**en•zy•mo•lyt•ic** (en′zə mə lit′ik), *adj.*

EO, executive order.

eo-, a combining form meaning "early," "primeval," used in the formation of compound words: *Eocene; eohippus.* [< Gk, comb. form of *ēṓs* (Attic *héōs*) dawn; akin to EAST, AURORA]

e.o., ex officio.

E•o•an•thro•pus (ē′ō an′thrə pəs, -ən thrō′pəs), *n.* the genus to which the now-discredited Piltdown man was assigned. [< NL (1913) < Gk *ēo-* EO- + *ánthrōpos* man]

EOB, Executive Office Building.

E•o•cene (ē′ə sēn′), *Geol.* —*adj.* **1.** noting or pertaining to an epoch of the Tertiary Period, occurring from 55 to 40 million years ago and characterized by the advent of the modern mammalian orders. See table under **geologic time.** —*n.* **2.** the Eocene Epoch or Series. [1825–35; EO- + -CENE]

EOE, 1. equal-opportunity employer: one pledged not to discriminate on the basis of race, sex, age, religion, national origin, etc., in hiring or promoting. **2.** *Informal (disparaging).* an employee who is considered to have been hired only to satisfy equal-opportunity regulations.

EOF, *Computers.* end-of-file: a code, marker, or signal used to indicate the end of a file of data.

EOG, electrooculogram.

E•o•gene (ē′ə jēn′), *adj., n. Geol.* (formerly) Paleogene.

e•o•hip•pus (ē′ō hip′əs), *n.* the earliest known horse, a member of the extinct genus *Hyracotherium* (*Eohippus*), from the early Eocene Epoch of the Northern Hemisphere; a terrier-sized herbivore having four hoofed toes on each forefoot and three on each hind foot, and low-crowned teeth. Also called **dawn horse, hyracotherium.** [1875–80; < NL, equiv. to *eo-* EO- + Gk *híppos* horse]

eohippus,
Hyracotherium,
9 in. (23 cm) high
at shoulder;
length 18 in. (46 cm)

e•o ip•so (ā′ō ip′sō; *Eng.* ē′ō ip′sō), *Latin.* by that very fact.

E•o•li•an (ē ō′lē ən), *adj.* **1.** (*l.c.*) *Geol.* noting or pertaining to sand or rock material carried or arranged by the wind. **2.** Aeolian. —*n.* **3.** Aeolian (def. 3). [1920–25]

E•ol•ic (ē ol′ik), *n., adj.* Aeolian. Also, **Aeolic.**

e•ol•i•pile (ē ol′ə pīl′), *n.* aeolipile.

e•o•lith (ē′ə lith), *n.* a chipped stone of the late Tertiary Period in Europe once thought to have been flaked by humans but now known to be the product of natural, nonhuman agencies. [1890–95; EO- + -LITH] —**e′o•lith′ic,** *adj.*

e.o.m., *Chiefly Com.* end of the month. Also, **E.O.M.**

e•on (ē′ən, ē′on), *n.* **1.** an indefinitely long period of time; age. **2.** the largest division of geologic time, comprising two or more eras. **3.** *Astron.* one billion years. Also, **aeon.** [see AEON]

e•o•ni•an (ē ō′nē ən), *adj.* aeonian.

e•on•ism (ē′ə niz′əm), *n. Psychiatry.* the adoption of feminine mannerisms, clothing, etc., by a male. [1925–30; after the Chevalier d'*Éon* (d. 1810), Frenchman who posed as a woman]

e•o no•mi•ne (ā′ō nō′mi ne′; *Eng.* ē′ō nom′i nē), *Latin.* by that name.

EOP, Executive Office of the President.

E•os (ē′os), *n.* the ancient Greek goddess of the dawn, identified by the Romans with Aurora.

e•o•sin (ē′ə sin), *n. Chem.* **1.** Also called **bromeosin, tetrabromofluorescein.** a red, crystalline, water-insoluble solid, $C_{20}H_8Br_4O_5$, derived from fluorescein by bromination: used chiefly as an acid dye for dyeing silk a rose red color and as a histological stain. **2.** any of a variety of eosinlike dyes. Also, **e•o•sine** (ē′ə sin, -sēn′). [1865–70; < Gk *ēṓs* dawn (see EO-) + -IN[2]] —**e′o•sin′ic,** *adj.* —**e′o•sin•like′,** *adj.*

e•o•sin•o•phil (ē′ə sin′ə fil), *Biol.* —*n.* **1.** *Histol.* any cell, tissue, organism, or substance that has an affinity for eosin and other acid stains. **2.** *Cell Biol.* a leukocyte having eosinophilic granules in the cytoplasm and usually a bilobate nucleus. —*adj.* **3.** eosinophilic. Also, **e•o•sin•o•phile** (ē′ə sin′ə fīl′). [1885–90; EOSIN + -O- + -PHIL(E)]

e•o•sin•o•phil•i•a (ē′ə sin′ə fil′ē ə, -fēl′yə), *n. Med.* the presence of an abnormally increased number of eosinophils in the blood. [1895–1900; < NL; see EOSINOPHIL, -IA]

e•o•sin•o•phil•ic (ē′ə sin′ə fil′ik), *adj. Histol.* having an affinity for eosin and other acid dyes; acidophilic. Also, **e•o•si•noph•i•lous** (ē′ə si nof′ə ləs), **eosinophil.** [1895–1900; EOSINOPHIL + -IC]

Eöt′vös exper′iment (ut′vush, et′-; *Hung.* œt′vœsh), *Physics.* an experiment to confirm that all materials respond equally to gravity and that gravitational mass and inertial mass are equivalent. Cf. **equivalence principle.** [named after Roland *Eötvös* (1848–1919), Hungarian physicist, who first performed the experiment]

Eöt′vös tor′sion bal′ance, a torsion balance for measuring horizontal gradients of gravity, used in geophysical explorations. [1915–20; see EÖTVÖS EXPERIMENT]

Eöt′vös u′nit, a unit of measure of horizontal gradients of gravity, equal to one billionth of a gal per horizontal centimeter. [1960–65; see EÖTVÖS EXPERIMENT]

-eous, an adjectival suffix with the meanings "composed of," "resembling, having the nature of," occurring in loanwords from Latin (*igneous; ligneous; vitreous*); also, as a semantically neutral suffix, found on adjectives of diverse origin, sometimes with corresponding nouns ending in **-ty**[2] (*beauteous; courteous; hideous; homogeneous; plenteous; righteous*). [< L *-eus;* see -OUS]

E•o•zo•ic (ē′ə zō′ik), *adj. Geol.* (formerly) noting or pertaining to the Precambrian Era, esp. the period including the beginnings of animal life. [1875–80; EO- + ZO- + -IC]

EP, 1. See **European plan. 2.** See **extended play.**

ep-, var. of **epi-** before a vowel or *h: epaxial.*

Ep., Epistle.

EPA, 1. *U.S. Govt.* Environmental Protection Agency: an independent federal agency, created in 1970, that sets and enforces rules and standards that protect the environment and control pollution. **2.** eicosapentaenoic acid: an omega-3 fatty acid present in fish oils.

e•pact (ē′pakt), *n.* **1.** the difference in days between a solar year and a lunar year. **2.** the number of days since the new moon at the beginning of the calendar year, January 1. [1545–55; < LL *epacta* < Gk *epaktḗ,* n. use of fem. of *epaktós* added, equiv. to *ep-* EP- + *ag(ein)* to lead + *-tos* verbid suffix]

ep•a•go•ge (ep′ə gō′jē), *n. Logic.* induction of a general proposition from particular propositions. [< Gk *epagōgḗ* a bringing to, argument by induction, equiv. to *ep-* EP- + *agōgḗ* guide, method (deriv. of *ágein* to lead)] —**ep•a•gog•ic** (ep′ə goj′ik), *adj.*

E•pam•i•non•das (i pam′ə non′dəs), *n.* 418?–362 B.C., Theban general and statesman.

ep•a•na•lep•sis (ep′ə nə lep′sis), *n. Rhet.* a repetition of a word or a phrase with intervening words setting off the repetition, sometimes occurring with a phrase used both at the beginning and end of a sentence, as in *Only the poor really know what it is to suffer; only the poor.* [1575–85; < Gk *epanálēpsis* lit., resumption, taking up again, equiv. to *ep-* EP- + *ana-* ANA- + *lêpsis* taking hold (*lēp-,* var. s. of *lambánein* to take + *-sis* -SIS)]

ep•a•naph•o•ra (ep′ə naf′ər ə), *n. Rhet.* anaphora (def. 1). [1670–80; < Gk *epanaphorá* referring, reference. See EP-, ANAPHORA]

e•pan•o•dos (i pan′ə dos′), *n. Rhet.* **1.** the repetition of a group of words in reverse order. **2.** the recapitulation of the main ideas of a speech, esp. in the reverse order. **3.** the resumption of the main thread of a speech after a digression. [1580–90; < Gk *epánodos* recapitulation, rising, return, equiv. to *ep-* EP- + *an(a)-* ANA- + *(h)odós* way, road, path]

ep•a•nor•tho•sis (ep′ə nôr thō′sis), *n., pl.* **-ses** (-sēz). *Rhet.* the rephrasing of an immediately preceding word or statement for the purpose of intensification, emphasis, or justification, as in "Seems, madam! Nay, it is; I know not 'seems.'" [1570–80; < Gk *epanórthōsis* correcting, revision. See EP-, ANA-, ORTHOSIS]

ep•arch (ep′ärk), *n.* **1.** the prefect or governor of an eparchy. **2.** *Eastern Ch.* a bishop or metropolitan of an eparchy. [1650–60; < Gk *éparchos* commander, governor, prefect. See EP-, -ARCH]

ep•ar•chy (ep′är kē), *n., pl.* **-chies. 1.** (in modern Greece) one of the administrative subdivisions of a province. **2.** (in ancient Greece) a province. [1790–1800; < Gk *eparchía* prefecture, province. See EPARCH, -Y[3]] —**ep•ar′chi•al,** *adj.*

é•paule•ment (*Fr.* ā pōl mäN′), *n., pl.* **-ments** (*Fr.* -mäN′). *Ballet.* a position in which the shoulders are at right angles to the direction of the supporting leg, with one shoulder thrust forward and one back. [1680–90; < F, equiv. to *épaule* (see EPAULET) + *-ment* -MENT]

ep•au•let (ep′ə let′, -lit, ep′ə let′), *n.* an ornamental shoulder piece worn on uniforms, chiefly by military officers. Also, **ep′au•lette′.** [1775–85; < F *épaulette,* equiv. to *épaule* shoulder (< L *spatula* blade; see SPATULA) + *-ette* -ETTE]

ep′aulette tree′, an Asian tree, *Pterostyrax hispida,* of the storax family, having fragrant, white, hanging clusters of flowers from 7 to 10 in. (18 to 25 cm) long.

é•pau•lière (ā′pōl yâr′; *Fr.* ā pō lyer′), *n., pl.* **é•pau•lières** (ā′pōl yârz′; *Fr.* ā pō lyer′). *Armor.* pauldron. [< F, equiv. to *épaule* (see EPAULET) + *-ière,* fem. form of *-ier* -IER[2]; cf. BRASSIERE]

ep•ax•i•al (ep ak′sē əl), *adj. Anat.* above or posterior to an axis. [1870–75; EP- + AXIAL] —**ep•ax′i•al•ly,** *adv.*

ep•a•zote (ep′ə zōt′), *n.* See **Mexican tea.** [1970–75; < MexSp < Nahuatl *epazōtl*]

é•pée (ā pā′, ep′ā), *n. Fencing.* **1.** a rapier with a three-sided blade and a guard over the tip. **2.** the art or sport of fencing with an épée, points being made by touching any part of the opponent's body with the tip of the weapon. Also, **e•pee′.** [1885–90; < F: sword < L *spatha* sword < Gk *spáthē* blade. See SPADE[1]]

É•pée (ā pā′), *n.* **Charles Michel, Abbé de l',** 1712–89, French priest and teacher of the deaf: pioneer in the development of sign language.

é•pée•ist (ā pā′ist, ep′ā-), *n.* a person who fences with an épée. [1905–10; < F *épéiste.* See ÉPÉE, -IST]

e•pei•ric (i pī′rik), *adj.* extending inland from a continental margin: *an epeiric sea.* [1920–25; < Gk *épeir(os)* mainland, continent + -IC]

ep•ei•rog•e•ny (ep′ī roj′ə nē), *n. Geol.* vertical or tilting movement of the earth's crust, generally affecting broad areas of a continent. Also, **e•pei•ro•gen•e•sis** (i pī′rō jen′ə sis), **epirogeny.** [1885–90; < Gk *épeiro(s)* mainland, continent + -GENY] —**e•pei′ro•gen′ic, e•pei•ro•ge•net•ic** (i pī′rō jə net′ik), *adj.*

ep•ei•so•di•on (ep′ī sō′dē on′), *n., pl.* **-di•a** (-dē ə). (in ancient Greek drama) an interlude or section alternating with the stasimon, esp. in tragedy, varying in number from three to six and containing the main action of the drama. Also, **episode.** [< Gk *epeisódion;* see EPISODE]

ep•en•ceph•a•lon (ep′ən sef′ə lon′, -lən), *n., pl.* **-lons, -la** (-lə). *Anat.* the hindbrain. [1850–55; EP- + ENCEPHALON] —**ep•en•ce•phal•ic** (ep′ən sə fal′ik), *adj.*

ep•en•dy•ma (ə pen′də mə), *n. Anat.* a membrane lining the canal of the spinal cord and the ventricles of the brain. [1870–75; < Gk *epéndyma* a covering, garment, equiv. to *ependý(ein)* to put on, over (*ep-* EP- + *en-* EN-[2] + *dýein* to put on) + *-ma* suffix of result] —**ep•en′dy•mal, e•pen′dy•mar•y** (ə pen′də mer′ē), *adj.*

ep•en•the•sis (ə pen′thə sis), *n., pl.* **-ses** (-sēz′). the insertion of one or more sounds in the middle of a word, as the schwa in the nonstandard pronunciation (el′əm) of *elm.* [1650–60; < LL: insertion of a letter < Gk *epénthesis* equiv. to *ep-* EP- + *en-* EN-[2] + *thésis* placing; see THESIS] —**ep•en•thet•ic** (ep′ən thet′ik), *adj.*

ep•en•the•size (ə pen′thə sīz′), *v.t.,* **-sized, -siz•ing.** to insert as an epenthetic sound. Also, *esp. Brit.,* **ep•en′•the•sise′.** [1875–80; EPENTHES(IS) + -IZE]

e•pergne (i pûrn′, ā pârn′), *n.* an ornamental piece for the center of a table, for holding fruit, flowers, etc. [1755–65; perh. < F *épargne* treasury, saving, n. deriv. of *épargner* to save < Gmc; cf. G *sparen* to save, SPARE]

ep•ex•e•ge•sis (ep ek′si jē′sis), *n., pl.* **-ses** (-sēz). *Rhet.* **1.** the addition of a word or words to explain a preceding word or sentence. **2.** the word or words so added. [1615–25; < Gk *epexḗgēsis* explanation. See EP-, EXEGESIS]

ep•ex•e•get•ic (ep ek′si jet′ik), *adj.* of, serving as, or like an epexegesis. Also, **ep•ex′e•get′i•cal.** [1885–90; < Gk *epexēgētikós.* See EPEXEGESIS, -TIC] —**ep•ex′e•get′i•cal•ly,** *adv.*

eph-, var. of **epi-** before an aspirate: *ephedrine.*

Eph., Ephesians.

e•phah (ē′fə, ef′ä), *n.* a Hebrew unit of dry measure, equal to about a bushel (35 l). Also, **e′pha.** [1350–1400; ME < Heb *ēphāh*]

e•phebe (i fēb′, ef′ēb), *n.* a young man, esp. an ephebus. [1690–1700; < L *ephēbus* < Gk *éphēbos,* equiv. to *ep-* EP- + *-hēbos,* deriv. of *hḗbē* manhood] —**e•phe′bic,** *adj.*

e•phe•bus (i fē′bəs), *n., pl.* **-bi** (-bī). a youth of ancient Greece just entering manhood or commencing training for full Athenian citizenship. [< L; see EPHEBE]

e•phed•ra (i fed′rə, ef′i drə), *n.* any of various plants of the genus *Ephedra,* growing in dry regions and having branching stems with dry scalelike leaves. [< NL (Linnaeus) < Gk *ephédra* the horsetail plant, lit., sitting (upon a place), equiv. to *ep-* EP- + *hédra* seat, sitting (see CATHEDRA)]

e•phed•rine (i fed′rin, ef′i drēn′, -drin), *n. Pharm.* a white, crystalline alkaloid, $C_{10}H_{15}N$, obtained from a species of *Ephedra* or synthesized: used in medicine chiefly for the treatment of asthma, hay fever, and colds. [1885–90; < NL *Ephedr(a)* EPHEDRA + -INE[2]]

e•phem•er•a (i fem′ər ə), *n., pl.* **-er•as, -er•ae** (-ə rē′) for 2. **1.** a pl. of **ephemeron. 2.** an ephemerid. [1670–80; < Gk *ephḗmera,* neut. pl. of *ephḗmeros,* taken as sing.; see EPHEMERAL]

e•phem•er•al (i fem′ər əl), *adj.* **1.** lasting a very short time; short-lived; transitory: *the ephemeral joys of childhood.* **2.** lasting but one day: *an ephemeral flower.* —*n.* **3.** anything short-lived, as certain insects. [1570–80; < Gk *ephḗmer(os)* short-lived, lasting but a day (*ep-* EP- + *hēmér(a)* day + *-os* adj. suffix) + -AL[1]] —**e•phem′er•al•ly,** *adv.* —**e•phem′er•al•ness,** *n.*

—**Syn. 1.** fleeting, evanescent, transient, momentary, brief. —**Ant. 1.** permanent.

e·phem·er·al·i·ty (i fem′ə ral′i tē), *n., pl.* **-ties** for 2. **1.** the quality or condition of being ephemeral. **2.** something transitory. [1815–25; EPHEMERAL + -ITY]

e·phem·er·id (i fem′ər id), *n.* an insect of the order Ephemeroptera, comprising the mayflies. Also called **ephemeropteran.** [1870–75; < NL *Ephemeridae.* See EPHEMERAL, -ID[2]]

e·phem·er·is (i fem′ər is), *n., pl.* **e·phe·mer·i·des** (ef′ə mer′i dēz′). **1.** a table showing the positions of a heavenly body on a number of dates in a regular sequence. **2.** an astronomical almanac containing such tables. **3.** *Archaic.* an almanac or calendar. [1545–55; < L *ephēmeris* day book, diary < Gk *ephēmerís* diary, account book, deriv. of *ephḗmeros;* see EPHEMERAL]

ephem′eris sec′ond, *Astron.* the unit of ephemeris time, defined as a precise fraction of the length of the tropical year 1900. [1965–70]

ephem′eris time′, *Astron.* time measured by the orbital movements of the earth, the moon, and the planets. [1945–50]

e·phem·er·on (i fem′ə ron′, -ər ən), *n., pl.* **-er·a** (-ər ə), **-er·ons. 1.** anything short-lived or ephemeral. **2. ephemera,** items designed to be useful or important for only a short time, esp. pamphlets, notices, tickets, etc. [1570–80; < Gk *ephḗmeron* short-lived insect, n. use of neut. of *ephḗmeros;* see EPHEMERAL]

e·phem·er·op·ter·an (i fem′ə rop′tər ən), *adj.* **1.** belonging or pertaining to the insect order Ephemeroptera, comprising the mayflies. —*n.* **2.** ephemerid. [< NL *Ephemeropter(a)* (equiv. to Gk *ephḗmer(on)* EPHEMERON + -o- -O- + *-ptera,* neut. pl. of *-pteros* -PTEROUS) + -AN]

e·phem·er·ous (i fem′ər əs), *adj.* ephemeral. [see EPHEMERAL, -OUS]

Ephes., Ephesians.

E·phe·sian (i fē′zhən), *adj.* **1.** of or pertaining to Ephesus. —*n.* **2.** a native or inhabitant of Ephesus. [1350–1400; ME *Effesian* < L *Ephesi(us)* (< Gk *Ephésios*) + -AN]

E·phe·sians (i fē′zhənz), *n.* (*used with a singular v.*) a book of the New Testament, written by Paul. *Abbr.:* Eph., Ephes., Ephs.

Eph·e·sus (ef′ə səs), *n.* an ancient city in W Asia Minor, S of Smyrna (Izmir): famous temple of Artemis, or Diana; early Christian community.

e·phip·pi·um (i fip′ē əm), *n., pl.* **e·phip·pi·a** (i fip′ē ə). *Zool.* a thick shell, consisting of two chitinous plates, that encloses and protects the winter eggs of a cladoceran. [1835–45; < NL < Gk *ephíppion,* n. use of neut. of *ephíppios* for putting on a horse, equiv. to *ep-* EP- + *hipp(os)* horse + *-ios* adj. suffix] —**e·phip′pi·al,** *adj.*

eph·od (ef′od, ē′fod), *n. Judaism.* a richly embroidered, apronlike vestment having two shoulder straps and ornamental attachments for securing the breastplate, worn with a waistband by the high priest. Ex. 28:6, 7, 25–28. [1350–1400; ME < ML < Heb *ēphōd,* appar. meaning "idol" in some passages]

eph·or (ef′ôr, ef′ər), *n., pl.* **-ors, -or·i** (-ə rī′). one of a body of magistrates in various ancient Dorian states, esp. at Sparta, where a body of five was elected annually by the people. [1580–90; < L *ephorus* < Gk *éphoros* overseer, guardian, ruler (cf. *ephorân* to look over, equiv. to *ep-* EP- + *horân* to see, look)] —**eph′or·al,** *adj.* —**eph·or·ate** (ef′ə rāt′, -ər it), **eph·or·al·ty** (ef′ər-əl tē), *n.*

E·phra·im (ē′frē əm, ē′frəm; *for 4 also* ef′rəm), *n.* **1.** the younger son of Joseph. Gen. 41:52. **2.** the tribe of Israel traditionally descended from him. Gen. 48:1. **3.** the Biblical kingdom of the Hebrews in N Palestine, including ten of the twelve tribes. Cf. **Judah** (def. 3). **4.** a male given name.

E·phra·im·ite (ē′frē ə mīt′, ē′frə mīt), *n.* **1.** a member of the tribe of Ephraim. **2.** an inhabitant of the northern kingdom of Israel. —*adj.* **3.** Also, **E·phra·i·mit·ic** (ē′frē ə mit′ik, ē′frə mit′-). of or pertaining to the tribe of Ephraim or the Ephraimites. [1605–15; EPHRAIM + -ITE[1]]

Eph·ra·ta (ef′rə tə), *n.* a town in SE Pennsylvania. 11,095.

Ephs., Ephesians.

epi-, a prefix occurring in loanwords from Greek, where it meant "upon," "on," "over," "near," "at," "before," "after" (*epicedium; epidermis; epigene; epitome*); on this model, used in the formation of new compound words (*epicardium; epinephrine*). Also, **ep-, eph-.** [< Gk, prefixal use of *epí,* prep. and adv.]

ep·i·ben·thos (ep′ə ben′thos), *n. Biol.* the aggregate of organisms living on the sea bottom between low tide and 100 fathoms (180 m). [EPI- + BENTHOS]

ep·i·bi·ot·ic (ep′ə bī ot′ik), *Biol.* —*adj.* **1.** of or pertaining to an organism that lives, usually parasitically, both on the surface and within the body of its host. —*n.* **2.** any such organism, as certain fungi. [1925–30; EPI- + BIOTIC]

ep·i·blast (ep′ə blast′), *n. Embryol.* the primordial outer layer of a young embryo before the segregation of the germ layers, capable of becoming the ectoderm and containing cells capable of becoming the mesoderm and endoderm. [1865–70; EPI- + -BLAST] —**ep′i·blas′tic,** *adj.*

e·pib·o·ly (i pib′ə lē), *n., pl.* **-lies.** *Embryol.* the movement and spreading out of cells into sheets of tissue that overlie or surround other groups of cells, esp. as in the formation of certain gastrulas. [1870–75; < Gk *epibolḗ* a throwing on, equiv. to *epi-* EPI- + *bol-* (var. s. of *bállein* to throw) + *-ē* n. suffix] —**ep·i·bol·ic** (ep′ə bol′ik), *adj.*

CONCISE ETYMOLOGY KEY: <, descended or borrowed from; >, whence; b., blend of, blended; c., cognate with; cf., compare; deriv., derivative; equiv., equivalent; imit., imitative; obl., oblique; r., replacing; s., stem; sp., spelling, spelled; resp., respelling, respelled; trans., translation; ?, origin unknown; *, unattested; ‡, probably earlier than. See the full key inside the front cover.

ep·ic (ep′ik), *adj.* Also, **ep′i·cal. 1.** noting or pertaining to a long poetic composition, usually centered upon a hero, in which a series of great achievements or events is narrated in elevated style: *Homer's* Iliad *is an epic poem.* **2.** resembling or suggesting such poetry: *an epic novel on the founding of the country.* **3.** heroic; majestic; impressively great: *the epic events of the war.* **4.** of unusually great size or extent: *a crime wave of epic proportions.* —*n.* **5.** an epic poem. **6.** epic poetry. **7.** any composition resembling an epic. **8.** something worthy to form the subject of an epic: *The defense of the Alamo is an American epic.* **9.** (*cap.*) Also called **Old Ionic.** the Greek dialect represented in the *Iliad* and the *Odyssey,* apparently Aeolic modified by Ionic. [1580–90; < L *epicus* < Gk *epikós.* See EPOS, -IC] —**ep′i·cal·ly,** *adv.* —**ep′ic·like′,** *adj.*

ep·i·ca·lyx (ep′i kā′liks, -kal′iks), *n., pl.* **-ca·lyx·es, -ca·ly·ces** (-kā′lə sēz′, -kal′ə-). *Bot.* an involucre resembling an outer calyx, as in the mallow. [1865–70; EPI- + CALYX]

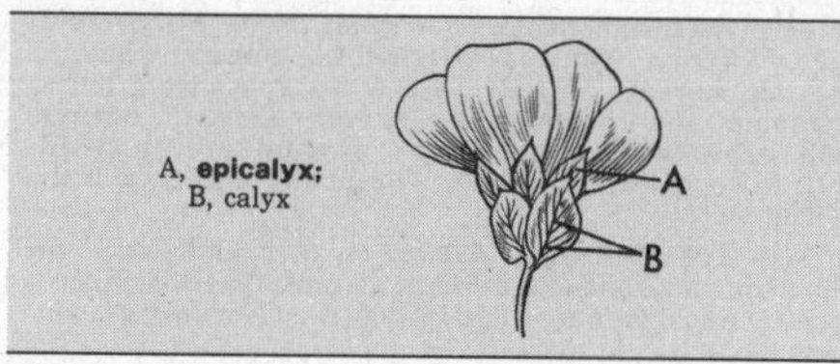

A, **epicalyx;**
B, calyx

ep·i·can·thus (ep′i kan′thəs), *n., pl.* **-thi** (-thī, -thē). *Anat.* a fold of skin extending from the eyelid over the inner canthus of the eye, common among Mongoloid peoples. Also called **ep′ican′thic fold′, eyefold.** [1860–65; < NL; see EPI-, CANTHUS] —**ep′i·can′thic,** *adj.*

ep·i·car·di·um (ep′i kär′dē əm), *n., pl.* **-di·a** (-dē ə). *Anat.* the inner serous layer of the pericardium, lying directly upon the heart. [1860–65; < NL; see EPI-, -CARDIUM] —**ep′i·car′di·al, ep′i·car′di·ac′,** *adj.*

ep·i·carp (ep′i kärp′), *n. Bot.* the outermost layer of a pericarp, as the rind or peel of certain fruits. See diag. under **pericarp.** [1825–35; EPI- + -CARP]

Ep·i·cas·te (ep′i kas′tē), *n.* Jocasta.

ep·i·ce·di·um (ep′ə sē′dē əm, -si dī′əm), *n., pl.* **-ce·di·a** (-sē′dē ə, -si dī′ə). a funeral song; dirge. [1580–90; < NL < Gk *epikḗdeion,* n. use of neut. of *epikḗdeios* of a funeral, equiv. to *epi-* EPI- + *kēde-* (s. of *kêdos* care, sorrow) + *-ios* adj. suffix] —**ep′i·ce′di·al, ep′i·ce′di·an,** *adj.*

ep·i·cene (ep′i sēn′), *adj.* **1.** belonging to, or partaking of the characteristics of, both sexes: *Fashions in clothing are becoming increasingly epicene.* **2.** flaccid; feeble; weak: *an epicene style of writing.* **3.** effeminate; unmasculine. **4.** (of Greek and Latin nouns) of the same gender class regardless of the sex of the being referred to, as Latin *vulpēs* "fox or vixen" is always grammatically feminine. **5.** *Gram.* (of a noun or pronoun) capable of referring to either sex, as *attendant, chairperson, Kim, one,* or *they;* having common gender. —*n.* **6.** a person or thing that is epicene. [1400–50; late ME < L *epicoenus* of both genders < Gk *epíkoinos* common to many, equiv. to *epi-* EPI- + *koinós* common] —**ep′i·cen′ism,** *n.*

ep·i·cen·ter (ep′ə sen′tər), *n.* **1.** Also **epicentrum.** *Geol.* a point, directly above the true center of disturbance, from which the shock waves of an earthquake apparently radiate. **2.** a focal point, as of activity: *Manhattan's Chinatown is the epicenter of the city's Chinese community.* Also, *esp. Brit.,* **ep′i·cen′tre.** [1885–90; < NL *epicentrum* < Gk *epíkentros* on the center. See EPI-, CENTER] —**ep′i·cen′tral,** *adj.*

ep·i·cen·trum (ep′ə sen′trəm, ep′ə sen′-), *n., pl.* **-trums, -tra** (-trə). *Geol.* epicenter.

ep·i·chlo·ro·hy·drin (ep′i klôr′ə hī′drin, -klōr′-), *n. Chem.* a highly volatile liquid with a chloroformlike odor, C_3H_5ClO: used as a solvent for resins and in the production of epoxy and phenoxy resins. [EPI- + CHLOROHYDRIN]

ep·i·cist (ep′ə sist), *n.* a writer of epic poetry. [1850–55; EPIC + -IST]

ep′ic machin′ery. See under **machinery** (def. 5).

ep·i·con·dyle (ep′i kon′dīl, -dl), *n. Anat.* a rounded protuberance at the end of a bone, serving as a place of attachment for ligaments, tendons, and muscles. [1830–40; EPI- + CONDYLE] —**ep·i·con·dyl·i·an** (ep′i kon dil′ē ən), **ep′i·con·dyl′ic, ep·i·con·dyl·ar** (ep′i kon′dl ər), *adj.*

ep·i·con·dy·li·tis (ep′i kon′dl ī′tis, -dl ī′-), *n. Pathol.* irritation or inflammation of the epicondyle or surrounding tissue, esp. at the elbow. Cf. **tennis elbow.** [EPICONDYLE + -ITIS]

ep·i·con·ti·nen·tal (ep′i kon′tn en′tl), *adj.* found or located in or on a continent: *epicontinental minerals; an epicontinental sea.* [1900–05; EPI- + CONTINENTAL]

ep·i·cot·yl (ep′i kot′l, ep′i kot′l), *n. Bot.* (in the embryo of a plant) that part of the stem above the cotyledons. See diag. under **cotyledon.** [1875–80; EPI- + Gk *kotýlē* cup]

ep·i·cra·ni·um (ep′i krā′nē əm), *n., pl.* **-ni·a** (-nē ə). **1.** *Anat.* the layer of scalp formed by muscle and flattened tendon. **2.** *Entomol.* the top of the head in insects, usually including the frons, genae, and vertex. [1885–90; EPI- + CRANIUM]

e·pic·ri·sis[1] (i pik′rə sis), *n.* a critical study or evaluation. [< Gk *epíkrisis* a judgment (cf. *epikrínein* to judge, equiv. to *epi-* EPI- + *krínein* to judge); see CRISIS]

ep·i·cri·sis[2] (ep′i krī′sis, ep′ē-), *n. Med.* something that follows a crisis; a secondary crisis. [EPI- + CRISIS]

ep·i·crit·ic (ep′i krit′ik), *adj. Physiol.* noting or pertaining to a discriminating responsiveness to small variations in pain or temperature stimuli (opposed to *protopathic*). [1900–05; < Gk *epikritikós* determinative. See EPICRISIS[1], -TIC]

ep′ic sim′ile, a simile developed over several lines of verse, esp. one used in an epic poem. Also called **Homeric simile.** [1940–45]

Ep·ic·te·tus (ep′ik tē′təs), *n.* A.D. c60–c120, Greek Stoic philosopher and teacher, mainly in Rome. —**Ep·ic·te·tian** (ep′ik tē′shən), *adj.*

ep·i·cure (ep′i kyŏŏr′), *n.* **1.** a person who cultivates a refined taste, esp. in food and wine; connoisseur. **2.** *Archaic.* a person dedicated to sensual enjoyment. [1350–1400 for earlier sense; 1555–65 for def. 2; ME *Epicures, Epicureis* Epicureans (pl.) < L *Epicūrēus* (sing.) (see EPICUREAN)]

—**Syn. 1.** gastronome, gourmet, epicurean. **2.** voluptuary, sensualist, gourmand. —**Ant. 1.** ascetic.

ep·i·cu·re·an (ep′i kyŏŏ rē′ən, -kyŏŏr′ē-), *adj.* **1.** fond of or adapted to luxury or indulgence in sensual pleasures; having luxurious tastes or habits, esp. in eating and drinking. **2.** fit for an epicure: *epicurean delicacies.* **3.** (*cap.*) of, pertaining to, or characteristic of Epicurus or Epicureanism. —*n.* **4.** an epicure. **5.** (*cap.*) a disciple of Epicurus. [1350–1400; ME *Epicurien* < L *Epicūrē(us)* of Epicurus (< Gk *Epikoúreios*) + -AN]

—**Syn. 2.** gourmet, luxury, lavish, deluxe, rich. —**Ant. 2.** austere, simple, plain, modest, frugal.

Ep·i·cu·re·an·ism (ep′i kyŏŏ rē′ə niz′əm, -kyŏŏr′ē-), *n.* **1.** the philosophical system or doctrine of Epicurus, holding that the external world is a series of fortuitous combinations of atoms and that the highest good is pleasure, interpreted as freedom from disturbance or pain. **2.** (*l.c.*) epicurean indulgence or habits. Also, **Ep·i·cur·ism** (ep′i kyŏŏ riz′əm, ep′i kyŏŏr′iz əm). [1745–55; EPICUREAN + -ISM]

Ep·i·cu·rus (ep′i kyŏŏr′əs), *n.* 342?–270 B.C., Greek philosopher.

ep·i·cu·ti·cle (ep′i kyōō′ti kəl), *n.* the thin, waxy outer layer of the insect exoskeleton. [1925–30; EPI- + CUTICLE]

ep·i·cy·cle (ep′ə sī′kəl), *n.* **1.** *Astron.* a small circle the center of which moves around in the circumference of a larger circle: used in Ptolemaic astronomy to account for observed periodic irregularities in planetary motions. **2.** *Math.* a circle that rolls, externally or internally, without slipping, on another circle, generating an epicycloid or hypocycloid. [1350–1400; ME < MF < LL *epicyclus* < Gk *epíkyklos.* See EPI-, CYCLE] —**ep·i·cy·clic** (ep′ə sī′klik, -sik′lik), *adj.*

ep′icy′clic train′, *Mach.* a train of gears or pulleys in which one or more of the axes revolve about a central axis. [1885–90]

ep·i·cy·cloid (ep′ə sī′kloid), *n. Geom.* a curve generated by the motion of a point on the circumference of a circle that rolls externally, without slipping, on a fixed circle. Equation: $x = (a + b) \cos \theta - b \cos [(a + b)\theta/b]$ and $y = (a + b) \sin \theta - b \sin [(a + b)\theta/b]$. Cf. **epitrochoid.** [1780–90; EPICYCLE + -OID] —**ep′i·cy·cloi′dal,** *adj.*

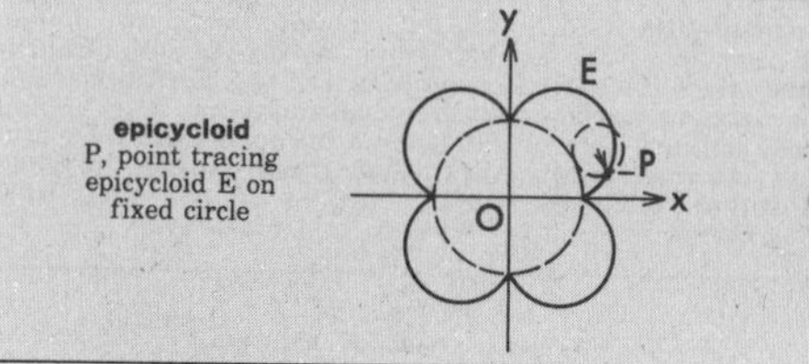

epicycloid
P, point tracing
epicycloid E on
fixed circle

ep′icycloi′dal gear′, one of the gears of an epicyclic train.

Ep·i·dau·rus (ep′i dôr′əs), *n.* an ancient town in S Greece, in Argolis: sanctuary of Asclepius; outdoor theater still in use.

ep·i·dem·ic (ep′i dem′ik), *adj.* **1.** Also, **ep′i·dem′i·cal.** (of a disease) affecting many persons at the same time, and spreading from person to person in a locality where the disease is not permanently prevalent. **2.** extremely prevalent; widespread. —*n.* **3.** a temporary prevalence of a disease. **4.** a rapid spread or increase in the occurrence of something: *an epidemic of riots.* [1595–1605; obs. *epidem(y)* (< LL *epidēmia* < Gk *epidēmía* staying in one place, among the people, equiv. to *epi-* EPI- + *dêm(os)* people of a district + *-ia* -Y[3]) + -IC] —**ep′i·dem′i·cal·ly,** *adv.* —**ep·i·de·mic·i·ty** (ep′i də mis′i tē), *n.*

epidem′ic encephali′tis, *Pathol.* See **sleeping sickness** (def. 2).

epidem′ic pleurodyn′ia, *Pathol.* pleurodynia (def. 2).

ep·i·de·mi·ol·o·gy (ep′i dē′mē ol′ə jē, -dem′ē-), *n.* the branch of medicine dealing with the incidence and prevalence of disease in large populations and with detection of the source and cause of epidemics of infectious disease. [1870–75; EPIDEMI(C) + -O- + -LOGY] —**ep·i·de·mi·o·log·i·cal** (ep′i dē′mē ə loj′i kəl, -dem′ē-), *adj.* —**ep′i·de′mi·o·log′i·cal·ly,** *adv.* —**ep′i·de′mi·ol′o·gist,** *n.*

ep·i·den·drum (ep′i den′drəm), *n.* any of numerous tropical American orchids of the genus *Epidendrum,* having variously colored, often showy flowers. [1785–95; < NL; see EPI-, -DENDRON]

ep·i·der·mis (ep′i dûr′mis), *n.* **1.** *Anat.* the outer, nonvascular, nonsensitive layer of the skin, covering the true skin or corium. **2.** *Zool.* the outermost living layer of an animal, usually composed of one or more layers of cells. **3.** *Bot.* a thin layer of cells forming the outer integument of seed plants and ferns. [1620–30; < LL: surface skin < Gk *epidermis* upper skin. See EPI-, DERMA] **—ep′i·der′mal, ep′i·der′mic,** *adj.* **—ep′i·der′mi·cal·ly,** *adv.*

ep·i·di·a·scope (ep′i dī′ə skōp′), *n. Optics.* a type of magic lantern that projects the image of an opaque object onto a screen. Also called **episcope.** [1900–05; EPI- + DIA- + -SCOPE]

ep·i·did·y·mis (ep′i did′ə mis), *n., pl.* **-di·dym·i·des** (-di dim′i dēz′, -did′ə mi-). *Anat.* an elongated organ on the posterior surface of a testis that constitutes the convoluted beginning of the vas deferens. [1600–10; < Gk *epididymis;* see EPI-, DIDYMOUS] **—ep′i·did′y·mal,** *adj.*

ep·i·di·o·rite (ep′i dī′ə rīt′), *n. Petrog.* a schistose metamorphic rock resulting from the alteration of augite to hornblende in a gabbro or dolerite. [1885–90; EPI- + DIORITE]

ep·i·dote (ep′i dōt′), *n.* a mineral, calcium aluminum iron silicate, $Ca_2(Al, Fe)_3Si_3O_{12}(OH)$, occurring in green prismatic crystals. [1800–10; < F *épidote* < Gk **epidotós* given besides, increased (verbid of *epididónai*), equiv. to *epi-* EPI- + *dotós* given (verbid of *didónai*)] **—ep·i·dot·ic** (ep′i dot′ik), *adj.*

ep·i·du·ral (ep′i do͝or′əl, -dyo͝or′-), *adj.* **1.** *Anat.* situated on or outside the dura mater. **—***n.* **2.** *Pharm.* See **epidural anesthesia.** [1880–85; < EPI- + DUR(A MATER) + -AL[1]]

epidu′ral anesthe′sia, anesthesia produced by the injection of an anesthetic into the lumbar area of the spine in the space between the spinal cord and the dura, which eliminates sensation from the point of insertion downward, used esp. in childbirth. Also called **epidural.**

ep·i·fo·cal (ep′ə fō′kəl), *adj. Geol.* epicentral. [1895–1900; EPI- + FOCAL]

ep·i·gam·ic (ep′i gam′ik), *adj. Zool.* attracting the opposite sex, as the colors of certain birds. [1885–90; < Gk *epígam(os)* marriageable (see EPI-, -GAMOUS) + -IC]

ep·i·gas·tric (ep′i gas′trik), *adj.* lying upon, distributed over, or pertaining to the epigastrium. [1650–60; EPIGASTR(IUM) + -IC]

ep·i·gas·tri·um (ep′i gas′trē əm), *n., pl.* **-tri·a** (-trē ə). *Anat.* the upper and median part of the abdomen, lying over the stomach. [1675–85; < NL < Gk *epigástrion,* n. use of neut. of *epigástrios* over the stomach. See EPI-, GASTR-, IUM]

ep·i·ge·al (ep′i jē′əl), *adj.* **1.** *Entomol.* living near the surface of the ground, as on low herbs or other surface vegetation. **2.** *Bot.* epigeous. Also, **ep′i·ge′an.** [1860–65; EPIGE(OUS) + -AL[1]]

ep·i·gene (ep′i jēn′), *adj. Geol.* formed or originating on the earth's surface (opposed to *hypogene*). [1815–25; < F *épigène* < Gk *epigenḗs* born after, growing after. See EPI-, -GEN]

ep·i·gen·e·sis (ep′i jen′ə sis), *n.* **1.** *Biol.* **a.** the theory that an embryo develops from the successive differentiation of an originally undifferentiated structure (opposed to *preformation*). **b.** the approximately stepwise process by which genetic information, as modified by environmental influences, is translated into the substance and behavior of an organism. **2.** *Geol.* ore deposition subsequent to the original formation of the enclosing country rock. [1800–10; EPI- + -GENESIS] **—ep′i·gen′e·sist, e·pig·e·nist** (i pij′ə nist), *n.* **—ep·i·ge·net·ic** (ep′i jə net′ik), *adj.* **—ep′i·ge·net′i·cal·ly,** *adv.*

e·pig·e·nous (i pij′ə nəs), *adj. Bot.* growing on the surface, esp. the upper surface, as fungi on leaves. [1865–70; EPI- + -GENOUS]

ep·i·ge·ous (ep′i jē′əs), *adj. Bot.* **1.** growing on or close to the ground. **2.** (of cotyledons) lifted above ground in germination. [1825–35; < Gk *epígeios* on, of the world, equiv. to *epi-* EPI- + *-geios* (*ge-,* s. of *gê* earth + *-ios* adj. suffix); see -OUS]

ep·i·glot·tis (ep′i glot′is), *n., pl.* **-glot·tis·es, -glot·ti·des** (-glot′i dēz′). *Anat.* a thin, valvelike, cartilaginous structure that covers the glottis during swallowing, preventing the entrance of food and drink into the larynx. See diag. under **larynx.** [1605–15; < Gk *epiglōttís;* see EPI-, GLOTTIS] **—ep′i·glot′tal, ep′i·glot′tic, ep·i·glot·tid·e·an** (ep′i glo tid′ē ən), *adj.*

ep·i·gone (ep′i gōn′), *n.* an undistinguished imitator, follower, or successor of an important writer, painter, etc. Also, **ep·i·gon** (ep′i gon′). [1860–65; < L *epigonus* < Gk *epígonos* (one) born afterward, equiv. to *epi-* EPI- + *-gonos,* akin to *gígnesthai* to be born] **—ep·i·gon·ic** (ep′i gon′ik), *adj.* **—e·pig·o·nism** (i pig′ə niz′əm, e pig′-, ep′ə gō′niz im, -gon′iz-), *n.*

e·pig·o·nus (i pig′ə nəs), *n., pl.* **-ni** (-nī′). epigone.

ep·i·gram (ep′i gram′), *n.* **1.** any witty, ingenious, or pointed saying tersely expressed. **2.** epigrammatic expression: *Oscar Wilde had a genius for epigram.* **3.** a short, often satirical poem dealing concisely with a single subject and usually ending with a witty or ingenious turn of thought. [1400–50; late ME < L *epigramma* < Gk *epígramma* inscription, epigram. See EPI-, -GRAM[1]] **—Syn. 1.** witticism, quip, bon mot.

ep·i·gram·mat·ic (ep′i grə mat′ik), *adj.* **1.** of or like an epigram; terse and ingenious in expression. **2.** containing or favoring the use of epigrams. Also, **ep′i·gram·mat′i·cal.** [1695–1705; < L *epigrammaticus* < Gk *epigrammatikós,* equiv. to *epigrammat-* (s. of *epígramma*) EPIGRAM + *-ikos* -IC] **—ep′i·gram·mat′i·cal·ly,** *adv.* **—ep·i·gram·ma·tism** (ep′i gram′ə tiz′əm), *n.*

ep·i·gram·ma·tize (ep′i gram′ə tīz′), *v.,* **-tized, -tiz·ing.** **—***v.t.* **1.** to express in epigrams. **2.** to make epigrams about (a person or thing). **—***v.i.* **3.** to make epigrams. Also, *esp. Brit.,* **ep′i·gram′ma·tise′.** [1685–95; < Gk *epigrammatízein;* see EPIGRAMMATIC + -IZE] **—ep′i·gram′ma·tist,** *n.*

ep·i·graph (ep′i graf′, -gräf′), *n.* **1.** an inscription, esp. on a building, statue, or the like. **2.** an apposite quotation at the beginning of a book, chapter, etc. [1615–25; < Gk *epigraphḗ* inscription. See EPI-, -GRAPH]

ep·i·graph·ic (ep′i graf′ik), *adj.* **1.** of or pertaining to epigraphs or epigraphy. **2.** of the style characteristic of epigraphs. Also, **ep′i·graph′i·cal.** [1855–60; EPIGRAPH + -IC] **—ep′i·graph′i·cal·ly,** *adv.*

e·pig·ra·phy (i pig′rə fē), *n.* **1.** the study or science of epigraphs or inscriptions, esp. of ancient inscriptions. **2.** inscriptions collectively. [1850–55; EPIGRAPH + -Y[3]] **—e·pig′ra·phist, e·pig′ra·pher,** *n.*

e·pig·y·nous (i pij′ə nəs), *adj. Bot.* **1.** (of flowers) having all floral parts conjoint and generally divergent from the ovary at or near its summit. **2.** (of stamens, petals, etc.) having the parts so arranged. [1820–30; EPI- + -GYNOUS] **—e·pig′y·ny,** *n.*

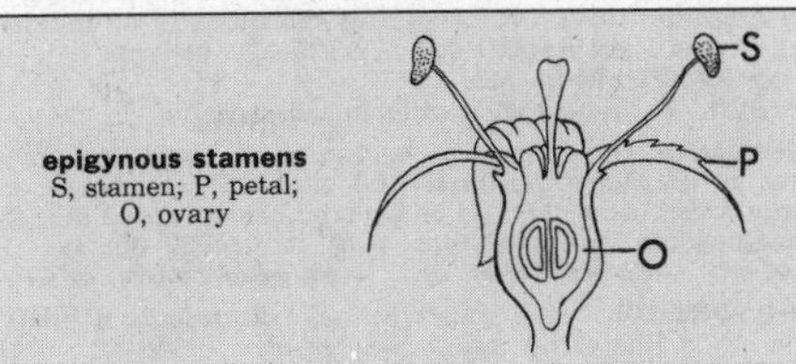

epigynous stamens
S, stamen; P, petal;
O, ovary

e·pig·y·num (i pij′ə nəm), *n. Zool.* the chitinous plate in arachnids that covers the opening to the female genital tract. Also, **ep·i·gyne** (ep′i jin′). [1890–95; < NL, equiv. to *epi-* EPI- + *-gynum* < Gk *-gynon,* neut. of *-gynos;* see -GYNOUS]

ep·i·late (ep′ə lāt′), *v.t.,* **-lat·ed, -lat·ing.** to remove (hair) from by means of physical, chemical, or radiological agents; depilate. [1885–90; < F *épil(er)* (< L *ē-* E- + *pil(us)* hair + *-er* inf. suffix) + -ATE[1]] **—ep′i·la′tion,** *n.* **—ep′i·la′tor,** *n.*

ep·i·lep·sy (ep′ə lep′sē), *n. Pathol.* a disorder of the nervous system, characterized either by mild, episodic loss of attention or sleepiness **(petit mal)** or by severe convulsions with loss of consciousness **(grand mal).** [1570–80; < LL *epilēpsia* < Gk *epilēpsía* epileptic seizure, equiv. to *epilēpt(os)* suffering from epilepsy (verbid of *epilambánein* to get hold of, attack; *epi-* EPI- + *lambánein* to seize) + *-ia* -Y[3], with *ti* > *si*]

ep·i·lep·tic (ep′ə lep′tik), *Pathol.* **—***adj.* **1.** pertaining to or symptomatic of epilepsy. **—***n.* **2.** a person affected by epilepsy. [1600–10; < LL *epilēpticus* < Gk *epilēptikós,* equiv. to *epílēpt(os)* (see EPILEPSY) + *-ikos* -IC] **—ep′i·lep′ti·cal·ly,** *adv.*

ep·i·lim·ni·on (ep′ə lim′nē on′, -ən), *n., pl.* **-ni·a** (-nē ə). (in certain lakes) the layer of water above the thermocline. [1905–10; EPI- + Gk *límnion* small pond, dim. of *límnē* pool, lake] **—ep·i·lim·net·ic** (ep′ə lim net′ik), **ep′i·lim′ni·al,** *adj.*

ep·i·lith·ic (ep′ə lith′ik), *adj.* (of plants) growing on stones. [EPI- + -LITHIC]

ep·i·logue (ep′ə lôg′, -log′), *n.* **1.** a concluding part added to a literary work, as a novel. **2.** a speech, usually in verse, delivered by one of the actors after the conclusion of a play. **3.** the person speaking this. Also, **ep′i·log′.** [1375–1425; late ME *epiloge* < L *epilogus* < Gk *epílogos* peroration of a speech, equiv. to *epi-* EPI- + *lógos* word]

ep·i·me·di·um (ep′ə mē′dē əm), *n., pl.* **-ums.** any of various Old World plants belonging to the genus *Epimedium,* of the barberry family, having small, pinnate leaves and spurred white, yellow, or reddish flowers. [< NL (Linnaeus), L *epimēdion* < Gk *epimḗdion* a plant of uncert. identity, equiv. to *epi-* EPI- + *mḗdion* plant of the genus *Campanula*]

ep·i·mer (ep′ə mər), *n. Chem.* either of a pair of isomeric aldose compounds, esp. of certain sugars, that differ from each other in the positions of the H and OH at the second atom from the end of the carbon chain, as d-glucose and d-mannose. Also, **e·pim·er·ide** (ə pim′ə rīd′). [1910–15; EPI- + -MER] **—ep·i·mer·ic** (ep′ə mer′ik), *adj.*

ep·i·mer·ize (ep′ə mə rīz′), *v.t.* **-ized, -iz·ing.** to convert into an epimer. Also, *esp. Brit.,* **ep′i·mer·ise′.** [1925–30; EPIMER + -IZE]

ep·i·mor·phism (ep′ə môr′fiz əm), *n. Math.* a homomorphism that maps from one set onto a second set. [EPI- + -MORPHISM]

ep·i·mor·pho·sis (ep′ə môr′fə sis, -môr fō′-), *n. Zool.* a form of development in segmented animals in which body segmentation is completed before hatching. [EPI- + MORPHOSIS] **—ep′i·mor′phic,** *adj.*

ep·i·my·o·car·di·um (ep′ə mī′ə kär′dē əm), *n., pl.* **-di·a** (-dē ə). *Embryol.* the outer, mesodermal layer of the embryonic heart, which develops into the epicardium and the myocardium. [EPI- + MYOCARDIUM] **—ep′i·my′o·car′di·al,** *adj.*

ep·i·my·si·um (ep′ə miz′ē əm, -mizh′-), *n., pl.* **-my·si·a** (-miz′ē ə, -mizh′-). *Anat.* the sheath of connective tissue around a muscle. [1895–1900; NL, irreg. from EPI- + Gk *mŷs* mouse, muscle (cf. MYO-) + -IUM]

É·pi·nal (ā pē nal′), *n.* a city in and the capital of Vosges, in NE France. 42,810.

ep·i·na·os (ep′ə nā′os), *n., pl.* **-na·oi** (-nā′oi). a rear vestibule, as of a classical temple. Also called **opisthodomos, posticum.** Cf. **pronaos.** [EPI- + NAOS]

ep·i·nas·ty (ep′ə nas′tē), *n. Bot.* (esp. of leaves) increased growth on the upper surface of an organ or part, causing it to bend downward. [1875–80; EPI- + Gk *nast(ós)* pressed close + -Y[3]] **—ep′i·nas′tic,** *adj.*

ep·i·neph·rine (ep′ə nef′rin, -rēn), *n.* **1.** *Biochem.* a hormone secreted by the adrenal medulla upon stimulation by the central nervous system in response to stress, as anger or fear, and acting to increase heart rate, blood pressure, cardiac output, and carbohydrate metabolism. **2.** *Pharm.* a commercial form of this substance, extracted from the adrenal glands of sheep and cattle, or synthesized: used chiefly as a heart stimulant, to constrict the blood vessels, and to relax the bronchi in asthma. Also, **ep′i·neph′rin.** Also called **adrenaline.** [1895–1900; EPI- + Gk *nephr(ós)* kidney + -INE[2]]

ep·i·neu·ri·um (ep′ə no͝or′ē əm, -nyo͝or′-), *n., pl.* **-neu·ri·a** (-no͝or′ē ə, -nyo͝or′-). *Anat.* the dense sheath of connective tissue that surrounds the trunk of a nerve. [1880–85; < NL, equiv. to *epi-* EPI- + Gk *neûron* sinew, tendon + NL *-ium* -IUM] **—ep′i·neu′ri·al,** *adj.*

é·pin·glé (ā pang′glā, ā′pang glā′), *n.* a ribbed fabric constructed in plain weave, used in the manufacture of women's dress goods. [< F, special use of *épingle* pin]

ep·i·o·nych·i·um (ep′ē ō nik′ē əm), *n., pl.* **-nych·i·a** (-nik′ē ə). eponychium.

Ep·i·pa·le·o·lith·ic (ep′ə pā′lē ə lith′ik, -pal′ē-), *adj.* of, pertaining to, or characteristic of the human cultures existing at the end of the Paleolithic and the beginnings of the Mesolithic periods of the Stone Age. [1920–25; EPI- + PALEOLITHIC]

ep·i·pas·tic (ep′ə pas′tik), *Med.* **—***adj.* **1.** suitable for use as a dusting powder. **—***n.* **2.** an epipastic substance or preparation. [1700–10; < Gk *epípast(os)* sprinkled over (verbid of *epipássein,* equiv. to *epi-* EPI- + *pássein* to sprinkle) + -IC]

ep·i·pe·lag·ic (ep′ē pə laj′ik), *adj.* of or pertaining to the stratum of the oceanic zone where enough light is present for photosynthesis to occur. [1935–40; EPI- + PELAGIC]

ep·i·pet·a·lous (ep′ə pet′l əs), *adj.* (of a flower) having the stamens attached to the petals. [1835–45; EPI- + PETALOUS]

Epiph., Epiphany.

Ep·i·pha·ni·a (ep′ə fə nī′ə), *n.* ancient name of the city **Hama.**

e·piph·a·nize (i pif′ə nīz′), *v.t.,* **-nized, -niz·ing.** *Literature.* to describe or represent in an epiphany. Also, *esp. Brit.,* **e·piph′a·nise′.** [EPIPHANY + -IZE]

e·piph·a·ny (i pif′ə nē), *n., pl.* **-nies.** **1.** (*cap.*) a Christian festival, observed on January 6, commemorating the manifestation of Christ to the gentiles in the persons of the Magi; Twelfth-day. **2.** an appearance or manifestation, esp. of a deity. **3.** a sudden, intuitive perception of or insight into the reality or essential meaning of something, usually initiated by some simple, homely, or commonplace occurrence or experience. **4.** a literary work or section of a work presenting, usually symbolically, such a moment of revelation and insight. [1275–1325; ME *epiphanie* < LL *epiphania* < LGk *epipháneia,* Gk: apparition, equiv. to *epi-* EPI- + *phan-* (s. of *phaínein* to appear) + *-eia* -Y[3]] **—ep·i·phan·ic** (ep′ə fan′ik), **e·piph′a·nous,** *adj.*

ep·i·phe·nom·e·nal·ism (ep′ə fə nom′ə nl iz′əm), *n.* the doctrine that consciousness is merely an epiphenomenon of physiological processes, and that it has no power to affect these processes. [1895–1900; EPI- + PHENOMENALISM] **—ep′i·phe·nom′e·nal·ist,** *n.*

ep·i·phe·nom·e·non (ep′ə fə nom′ə non′, -nən), *n., pl.* **-na** (-nə), **-nons.** **1.** *Pathol.* a secondary or additional symptom or complication arising during the course of a disease. **2.** any secondary phenomenon. [1700–10; EPI- + PHENOMENON] **—ep′i·phe·nom′e·nal,** *adj.* **—ep′i·phe·nom′e·nal·ly,** *adv.*

ep·i·phloe·dal (ep′ə flēd′l), *adj. Mycol.* growing on bark, as a lichen. Also, **ep′i·phloe′dic.** [EPI- + Gk *phloi(ós)* bark of trees + hiatus-filling *-d-* + -AL[1]]

ep·i·pho·ne·ma (ep′ə fō nē′mə), *n., pl.* **-mas, -mae** (-mē). *Rhet.* a sentence that is an exclamation, a general or striking comment, or a succinct summary of what has previously been said. [1570–80; < L *epiphōnēma* exclamation < Gk *epiphṓnēma.* See EPI-, PHONEME]

e·piph·o·ra (i pif′ər ə), *n.* **1.** *Pathol.* an overflow of tears due to excessive secretion of the lacrimal glands or obstruction of the lacrimal ducts. **2.** *Rhet.* epistrophe (def. 1). [1650–60; < L *epiphora* an afflux, repetition < Gk *epiphorá* a bringing upon. See EPI-, -PHORE]

ep·i·phragm (ep′ə fram′), *n.* **1.** a calcified or membranous septum produced by certain land snails during hibernation and functioning to cover the shell opening and prevent desiccation. **2.** *Bot.* a membrane enclosing the capsule in certain mosses. [1820–30; < Gk *epíphragma* covering, lid, equiv. to *epi-* EPI- + *phrágma* fence] **—ep·i·phrag·mal** (ep′ə frag′məl), *adj.*

ep·i·phy·lax·is (ep′ə fī lak′sis, -fi-), *n. Med.* reinforcement of the defenses of the body against disease. [< NL < Gk *epi-* EPI- + *phýlaxis* a watching, guarding]

ep·i·phyll (ep′ə fil), *n. Bot.* an epiphyte that grows on the surface, esp. the upper surface, of leaves, as a lichen. [EPI- + -PHYLL] **—ep′i·phyl′lous, ep·i·phyl·line** (ep′ə-fil′ēn, -in), *adj.*

ep·i·phyl·lum (ep′ə fil′əm), *n.* any of several mostly epiphytic cacti of the genus *Epiphyllum,* native to tropical America, having large, fragrant white flowers. Also called **orchid cactus.** [< NL, equiv. to Gk *epi-* EPI- + Gk *phýllon* leaf; so called from the leaflike branches on which the flower grows]

e·piph·y·sis (i pif′ə sis), *n., pl.* **-ses** (-sēz′). *Anat.* **1.** a part or process of a bone separated from the main body of the bone by a layer of cartilage and subsequently uniting with the bone through further ossification. **2.** See **pineal gland.** [1625–35; < NL < Gk *epíphysis* a growth upon, equiv. to *epi-* EPI- + *phýsis* growth (*phý(ein)* to make grow, bring forth, produce + *-sis* -SIS)] **—ep·i·phys·e·al** (ep′ə fiz′ē əl, i pif′ə sē′əl, -zē′-), **ep′i·phys′i·al,** *adj.*

ep·i·phyte (ep′ə fīt′), *n. Bot.* a plant that grows

CONCISE PRONUNCIATION KEY: act, cāpe, dâre, pärt; set, ēqual; if, ice; ox, ōver, ôrder, oil, bo͝ok, bo͞ot, out; up, ûrge; child; sing; shoe; thin, *th*at; zh as in *treasure.* ə = a as in *alone,* e as in *system,* i as in *easily,* o as in *gallop,* u as in *circus;* ə as in *fire* (fīər), *hour* (ouər). l and n can serve as syllabic consonants, as in *cradle* (krād′l), and *button* (but′n). See the full key inside the front cover.

above the ground, supported nonparasitically by another plant or object, and deriving its nutrients and water from rain, the air, dust, etc.; air plant; aerophyte. [1840–50; EPI- + -PHYTE] —**ep′i·phyt·ic** (ep′ə fit′ik), **ep′i·phyt′i·cal,** *adj.* —**ep′i·phyt′i·cal·ly,** *adv.*

ep·i·phy·tot·ic (ep′ə fī tot′ik), *adj.* **1.** (of a disease) destroying a large number of plants in an area at the same time. —*n.* **2.** the widespread, destructive outbreak of a plant disease. [1895–1900; EPI- + -PHYTE + -OTIC]

ep·i·pu·bis (ep′ə pyo͞o′bis), *n., pl.* **-bes** (-bēz). *Zool.* either of a pair of bones in front of the pubis of marsupials. Also called **marsupial bones.** [1895–1900; EPI- + PUBIS] —**ep′i·pu′bic,** *adj.*

ep·i·rog·e·ny (ep′i roj′ə nē), *n. Geol.* epeirogeny. —**e·pi·ro·gen·ic** (i pī′rə jen′ik), **e·pi·ro·ge·net·ic** (i pī′rō jə net′ik), *adj.*

E·pi·rus (i pī′rəs), *n.* **1.** an ancient district in NW Greece and S Albania. **2.** a modern region in NW Greece. 310,344; 3573 sq. mi. (9255 sq. km). —**E·pi·rote** (i pī′rōt), **E·pei·rot** (i pī′rət), *n.*

Epis., **1.** Episcopal. **2.** Episcopalian. **3.** Epistle.

Episc., **1.** Episcopal. **2.** Episcopalian.

e·pis·ci·a (i pish′ē ə, i pish′ə), *n.* any of several tropical American plants of the genus *Episcia,* often cultivated as houseplants for their textured, variegated foliage and showy flowers. [1865–70; < NL < Gk *episkiá* fem. of *episkiós* shaded, equiv. to *epi-* EPI- + *-skios,* adj. deriv. of *skiá* shade, shadow]

e·pis·co·pa·cy (i pis′kə pə sē), *n., pl.* **-cies. 1.** government of the church by bishops; church government in which there are three distinct orders of ministers, namely bishops, priests or presbyters, and deacons. **2.** episcopate. [1640–50; EPISCOP(ATE) + -ACY]

e·pis·co·pal (i pis′kə pəl), *adj.* **1.** of or pertaining to a bishop: *episcopal authority.* **2.** based on or recognizing a governing order of bishops: *an episcopal hierarchy.* **3.** (*cap.*) designating the Anglican Church or some branch of it, as the Episcopal Church in America. —*n.* **4.** (*cap.*) *Informal.* an Episcopalian. [1425–75; late ME < LL *episcopālis.* See BISHOP, -AL[1]] —**e·pis′co·pal·ly,** *adv.*

Epis′copal Church′ in Amer′ica, the church in the U.S. that inherited the doctrine, discipline, and forms of worship of the Church of England, from which it became an independent body within the Anglican communion: known before 1976 as the Protestant Episcopal Church.

E·pis·co·pa·lian (i pis′kə pāl′yən, -pā′lē ən), *adj.* **1.** pertaining or adhering to the Episcopal Church in America. **2.** (*l.c.*) pertaining or adhering to the episcopal form of church government. —*n.* **3.** a member of the Episcopal Church in America. **4.** (*l.c.*) an adherent of the episcopal system of church government. [1680–90; EPISCOPAL + -IAN] —**E·pis′co·pa′lian·ism,** *n.*

e·pis·co·pal·ism (i pis′kə pə liz′əm), *n.* the theory of church polity according to which the supreme ecclesiastical authority is vested in the episcopal order as a whole, and not in any individual except by delegation. [EPISCOPAL + -ISM]

Epis′copal vic′ar, vicar (def. 2).

e·pis·co·pate (i pis′kə pit, -pāt′), *n.* **1.** the office and dignity of a bishop; bishopric. **2.** the order or body of bishops. **3.** the incumbency of a bishop. **4.** the diocese of a bishop. [1635–45; < LL *episcopātus* the office of a bishop. See BISHOP, -ATE[3]]

ep·i·scope (ep′ə skōp′), *n. Optics.* epidiascope.

e·pis·co·pize (i pis′kə pīz′), *v.,* **-pized, -piz·ing.** —*v.t.* **1.** to make a bishop of. **2.** to convert to Episcopalianism. —*v.i.* **3.** to function as a bishop. Also, *esp. Brit.,* **e·pis′co·pise′.** [1640–50; EPISCOP(AL) + -IZE]

e·pis·co·tist·er (ə pis′kə tis′tər, ep′i skə tis′tər), *n.* a disk with a sector removed that when rotated in front of a light source allows the periodic passage of flashes of light: used in studying the motion of a body. Also, **e·pis′ko·tist′er.** [1900–05; < Gk *episkot(ízein)* to overshadow (see EPI-, SCOTIA, -IZE) + -IST + -ER[1]]

ep·i·se·meme (ep′ə sē′mēm), *n.* the meaning of a tagmeme. [EPI- + SEMEME]

ep·i·sep·a·lous (ep′ə sep′ə ləs), *adj.* (of a flower) having the stamens attached to the sepals. [1880–85; EPI- + -SEPALOUS]

e·pi·si·ot·o·my (ə pē′zē ot′ə mē, ep′ə sī-), *n., pl.* **-mies.** *Obstet., Surg.* an incision into the perineum and vagina to allow sufficient clearance for birth. [1875–80; < Gk *episío(n)* pubic region + -TOMY]

ep·i·sode (ep′ə sōd′, -zōd′), *n.* **1.** an incident in the course of a series of events, in a person's life or experience, etc. **2.** an incident, scene, etc., within a narrative, usually fully developed and either integrated within the main story or digressing from it. **3.** one of a number of loosely connected, but usually thematically related, scenes or stories constituting a literary work. **4.** epeisodion. **5.** *Music.* an intermediate or digressive passage, esp. in a contrapuntal composition. **6.** *Motion Pictures, Radio, and Television.* any one of the separate productions that constitute a serial. [1670–80; < Gk *epeisódion* addition, episode, n. use of neut. of *epeisódios* coming in addition, equiv. to *ep-* EP- + *eísod(os)* entrance (*eis-* into + (*h*)*odós* road, way) + *-ios* adj. suffix]
—**Syn. 1.** happening. See **event.**

ep·i·sod·ic (ep′ə sod′ik, -zod′-), *adj.* **1.** pertaining to or of the nature of an episode. **2.** divided into separate or tenuously related parts or sections; loosely connected: *an episodic novel.* **3.** occurring sporadically or incidentally. Also, **ep′i·sod′i·cal.** [1705–15; EPISODE + -IC] —**ep′i·sod′i·cal·ly,** *adv.*
—**Syn. 2.** rambling, wandering, digressive.

ep·i·some (ep′ə sōm′), *n. Genetics.* bacterial DNA that is extrachromosomal and that may replicate autonomously as a plasmid or become incorporated into the chromosome and replicate with it. [1930–35; EPI- + -SOME[3]] —**ep′i·so′mal,** *adj.* —**ep′i·so′mal·ly,** *adv.*

ep·i·spas·tic (ep′ə spas′tik), *adj.* **1.** raising a blister. —*n.* **2.** a blistering agent; vesicatory. [1650–60; < Gk *epispastikós* adapted, drawing to one's self. See EPI-, SPASTIC]

ep·i·spore (ep′i spôr′, -spōr′), *n. Bot., Mycol.* the principal outer covering of a spore. [1825–35; EPI- + SPORE]

Epist., Epistle.

e·pis·ta·sis (i pis′tə sis), *n., pl.* **-ses** (-sēz′). **1.** *Genetics.* a form of interaction between nonallelic genes in which one combination of such genes has a dominant effect over other combinations. **2.** *Med.* **a.** the stoppage of a secretion or discharge. **b.** a scum that forms on a urine specimen upon standing. [1915–20; < Gk *epístasis* stopping, stoppage. See EPI-, STASIS] —**ep·i·stat·ic** (ep′ə stat′ik), *adj.*

ep·i·stax·is (ep′ə stak′sis), *n. Pathol.* nosebleed. [1785–95; < Gk *epístaxis* a dripping, equiv. to *epi-* EPI- + *stag-,* s. of *stázein* to drip, drop + *-sis* -SIS]

ep·i·ste·mic (ep′ə stē′mik, -stem′ik), *adj.* of or pertaining to knowledge or the conditions for acquiring it. [1920–25; < Gk *epistēmikós,* equiv. to *epistḗm(ē)* knowledge + *-ikos* -IC] —**ep′i·ste′mi·cal·ly,** *adv.*

e·pis·te·mol·o·gy (i pis′tə mol′ə jē), *n.* a branch of philosophy that investigates the origin, nature, methods, and limits of human knowledge. [1855–60; < Gk *epistḗm(ē)* knowledge + -O- + -LOGY] —**e·pis·te·mo·log·i·cal** (i pis′tə mə loj′i kəl), *adj.* —**e·pis′te·mo·log′i·cal·ly,** *adv.* —**e·pis′te·mol′o·gist,** *n.*

ep·i·ster·num (ep′ə stûr′nəm), *n., pl.* **-na** (-nə). **1.** *Anat.* manubrium. **2.** *Entomol.* the anterior portion of a pleuron. [1850–55; EPI- + STERNUM]

e·pis·tle (i pis′əl), *n.* **1.** a letter, esp. a formal or didactic one; written communication. **2.** (*usually cap.*) one of the apostolic letters in the New Testament. **3.** (*often cap.*) an extract, usually from one of the Epistles of the New Testament, forming part of the Eucharistic service in certain churches. [bef. 900; ME; OE *epistol* < L *epistula, epistola* < Gk *epistolḗ* message, letter, equiv. to *epi-* EPI- + *stol-* (var. s. of *stéllein* to send) + *-ē* n. suffix]

epis′tle side′, the right side of a church, facing the altar. Cf. **gospel side.** [1880–85]

Epis′tle to the Gala′tians, a New Testament letter written by St. Paul the Apostle to the Christian churches of Galatia.

e·pis·to·lar·y (i pis′tl er′ē), *adj.* **1.** contained in or carried on by letters: *an epistolary friendship.* **2.** of, pertaining to, or consisting of letters. [1650–60; < L *epistolāris* of, belonging to a letter. See EPISTLE, -AR[1]]

epis′tolary nov′el, a novel written in the form of a series of letters.

e·pis·to·ler (i pis′tl ər), *n.* **1.** Also, **e·pis′to·list.** a writer of an epistle. **2.** the person who reads or chants the epistle in the Eucharistic service. Also, **e·pis·tler** (i pis′lər, i pist′-). [1520–30; < L *epistol(a)* EPISTLE + -ER[1]]

ep·i·stol·ic (ep′ə stol′ik), *adj.* epistolary. Also, **ep′i·stol′i·cal.** [1735–45; < L *epistolicus* < Gk *epistolikós* suited to a letter. See EPISTLE, -IC]

e·pis·to·lize (i pis′tl īz′), *v.,* **-lized, -liz·ing.** —*v.i.* **1.** to write a letter. —*v.t.* **2.** to write a letter to. Also, *esp. Brit.,* **e·pis′to·lise′.** [1625–35; < L *epistol(a)* EPISTLE + -IZE]

e·pis·to·log·ra·phy (i pis′tl og′rə fē), *n.* the practices and principles of letter writing; art of epistolary composition. [1885–90; < L *epistol(a)* EPISTLE + -O- + -GRAPHY]

e·pis·tro·phe (i pis′trə fē), *n.* **1.** Also called **epiphora.** *Rhet.* the repetition of a word or words at the end of two or more successive verses, clauses, or sentences, as in "I should do Brutus wrong, and Cassius wrong. . . ." Cf. **anaphora** (def. 1). **2.** *Neoplatonism.* the realization by an intellect of its remoteness from the One. [1640–50; < NL < Gk *epistrophḗ;* see EPI-, STROPHE]

ep·i·style (ep′ə stīl′), *n.* the architrave of a classical building. [1555–65; < L *epistȳlium* the crossbeam resting on the column < Gk *epistȳ́lion* crossbeam of architrave (*epi-* EPI- + *stŷl(os)* a column, pillar, post + *-ion* dim. suffix)] —**ep′i·sty′lar,** *adj.*

ep·i·syl·lo·gism (ep′ə sil′ə jiz′əm), *n. Logic.* a syllogism one of the premises of which is the conclusion of a preceding syllogism; any of the syllogisms included in a polysyllogism except the first one. Cf. **polysyllogism.** [1855–60; < NL *episyllogismus.* See EPI-, SYLLOGISM]

epit., **1.** epitaph. **2.** epitome.

ep·i·taph (ep′i taf′, -täf′), *n.* **1.** a commemorative inscription on a tomb or mortuary monument about the person buried at that site. **2.** a brief poem or other writing in praise of a deceased person. —*v.t.* **3.** to commemorate in or with an epitaph. [1350–1400; ME *epitaphe* < L *epitaphium* < Gk *epitáphion* over or at a tomb, equiv. to *epi-* EPI- + *táph(os)* tomb + *-ion* n., adj. suffix] —**ep′i·taph′ic** (ep′i taf′ik), *adj.* —**ep′i·taph′ist,** *n.* —**ep′i·taph′less,** *adj.*

e·pit·a·sis (i pit′ə sis), *n., pl.* **-ses** (-sēz′). the part of an ancient drama, following the protasis, in which the main action is developed. Cf. **catastasis, catastrophe** (def. 4), **protasis.** [1580–90; < Gk *epítasis* emphasis, increase of intensity, stretching, equiv. to *epi-* EPI- + *ta-* (var. s. of *teínein* to stretch) + *-sis* -SIS]

ep·i·tax·is (ep′i tak′sis), *n., pl.* **-tax·es** (-tak′sēz). *Crystall.* an oriented overgrowth of crystalline material upon the surface of another crystal of different chemical composition but similar structure. [1950–55; < NL; see EPI-, -TAXIS] —**ep′i·tax′i·al, ep′i·tax′ic,** *adj.*

ep·i·tax·y (ep′i tak′sē), *n., pl.* **-tax·ies.** *Crystall.* epitaxis.

ep·i·tha·la·mi·on (ep′ə thə lā′mē on′, -ən), *n., pl.* **-mi·a** (-mē ə). a song or poem in honor of a bride and bridegroom. [1580–90; < Gk: nuptial, n. use of neut. of *epithalámios* nuptial. See EPI-, THALAMUS]

ep·i·tha·la·mi·um (ep′ə thə lā′mē əm), *n., pl.* **-mi·ums, -mi·a** (-mē ə). epithalamion. —**ep·i·tha·lam·ic** (ep′ə thə lam′ik), *adj.*

ep·i·thal·a·mus (ep′ə thal′ə məs), *n., pl.* **-mi** (-mī′). *Anat.* the dorsal area of the diencephalon containing a habenula and the pineal gland. [1900–05; < NL; see EPI-, THALAMUS]

ep·i·the·ci·um (ep′ə thē′shē əm, -sē əm), *n., pl.* **-ci·a** (-shē ə, -sē ə). *Mycol.* the surface layer of tissue of the fruiting body of lichens and fungi, formed by the union of the tips of the paraphyses over the spore sacs. [1875–80; < NL; see EPI-, THECIUM] —**ep·i·the·ci·al** (ep′ə thē′shē əl, -shəl), *adj.*

ep·i·the·li·al·ize (ep′ə thē′lē ə līz′), *v.t., v.i.,* **-ized, -iz·ing.** to form a covering of epithelial cells over, as a wound. Also, *esp. Brit.,* **ep′i·the′li·al·ise′.** [EPITHELIAL + -IZE] —**ep′i·the′li·al·i·za′tion,** *n.*

ep′ithe′lial pearl′, *Pathol.* pearl[1] (def. 8).

ep·i·the·li·oid (ep′ə thē′lē oid′), *adj.* resembling epithelium. [1875–80; EPITHELI(UM) + -OID]

ep·i·the·li·o·ma (ep′ə thē′lē ō′mə), *n., pl.* **-mas, -ma·ta** (-mə tə). *Pathol.* a growth or tumor consisting chiefly of epithelial cells. [1870–75; EPITHELI(UM) + -OMA] —**ep·i·the·li·om·a·tous** (ep′ə thē′lē om′ə təs, -ō′mə-), *adj.*

ep·i·the·li·o·mus·cu·lar (ep′ə thē′lē ō mus′kyə lər), *adj. Zool.* of or pertaining to an epithelial cell of a coelenterate that contains contractile fibrils and acts as a muscle. [EPITHELI(UM) + -O- + MUSCULAR]

ep·i·the·li·um (ep′ə thē′lē əm), *n., pl.* **-li·ums, -li·a** (-lē ə). *Biol.* any animal tissue that covers a surface, or lines a cavity or the like, and that, in addition, performs any of various secretory, transporting, or regulatory functions. [1740–50; < NL < Gk *epi-* EPI- + *thēl(ḗ)* teat + NL *-ium* -IUM] —**ep′i·the′li·al,** *adj.*

ep·i·thet (ep′ə thet′), *n.* **1.** any word or phrase applied to a person or thing to describe an actual or attributed quality: *"Richard the Lion-Hearted" is an epithet of Richard I.* **2.** a characterizing word or phrase firmly associated with a person or thing and often used in place of an actual name, title, or the like, as "man's best friend" for "dog." **3.** a word, phrase, or expression used invectively as a term of abuse or contempt, to express hostility, etc. [1570–80; < L *epitheton* epithet, adjective < Gk *epítheton* epithet, something added, equiv. to *epi-* EPI- + *the-* (var. s. of *tithénai* to put) + *-ton* neut. verbal suffix] —**ep′i·thet′ic, ep′i·thet′i·cal,** *adj.*
—**Syn. 1, 2.** nickname, sobriquet, designation, appellation. **3.** curse, insult, abuse, expletive, obscenity.

e·pit·o·me (i pit′ə mē), *n.* **1.** a person or thing that is typical of or possesses to a high degree the features of a whole class: *He is the epitome of goodness.* **2.** a condensed account, esp. of a literary work; abstract. [1520–30; < L *epitomē* abridgment < Gk *epitomḗ* abridgment, surface incision. See EPI-, -TOME] —**ep·i·tom·i·cal** (ep′i tom′i kəl), **ep′i·tom′ic,** *adj.*
—**Syn. 1.** embodiment, exemplification, model, typification, quintessence.

e·pit·o·mist (i pit′ə mist), *n.* a person who writes an epitome. [1605–15; EPITOM(E) + -IST]

e·pit·o·mize (i pit′ə mīz′), *v.t.,* **-mized, -miz·ing. 1.** to contain or represent in small compass; serve as a typical example of; typify: *This meadow epitomizes the beauty of the whole area.* **2.** to make an epitome of: *to epitomize an argument.* Also, *esp. Brit.,* **e·pit′o·mise′.** [1590–1600; EPITOM(E) + -IZE] —**e·pit′o·mi·za′tion,** *n.* —**e·pit′o·miz′er,** *n.*

ep·i·tope (ep′i tōp′), *n. Immunol.* determinant (def. 3). [EPI- + *-tope* < Gk *tópos* place; cf. TOPO-]

ep·i·tra·che·li·on (e′pē trä khē′lē ôn; *Eng.* ep′i trə kē′lē on′, -kēl′yən), *n., pl.* **-che·li·a** (-khē′lē ä; *Eng.* -kē′lē ə, -kēl′yə). *Gk. Orth. Ch.* a silk stole worn by clergy. [< Gk, equiv. to *epi-* EPI- + *tráchēl(os)* neck + *-ion,* neut. of *-ios* adj. suffix]

ep·i·trich·i·um (ep′i trik′ē əm), *n., pl.* **-ums.** *Embryol.* the outermost layer of the epidermis in most mammalian fetuses, usually disappearing before birth. Also called **periderm.** [1880–85; < NL EPI- + *-trichium* < Gk *tríchion,* dim. of *thríx* hair (see TRICHION); so called because hair develops under it in human embryos] —**ep′i·trich′i·al,** *adj.*

ep·i·tro·choid (ep′i trō′koid), *Geom.* a plane curve generated by the motion of a fixed point on the radius or extension of the radius of a circle that rolls externally, without slipping, on a fixed circle. The epitrochoid is a

CONCISE ETYMOLOGY KEY: <, descended or borrowed from; >, whence; b., blend of, blended; c., cognate with; cf., compare; deriv., derivative; equiv., equivalent; imit., imitative; obl., oblique; r., replacing; s., stem; sp., spelling, spelled; resp., respelling, respelled; trans., translation; ?, origin unknown; *, unattested; ‡, probably earlier than. See the full key inside the front cover.

generalization of the epicycloid. [1835–45; EPI- + TROCHOID]

ep•i•xy•lous (ep′ə zī′ləs), *adj. Mycol.* growing on wood, as certain fungi. [EPI- + XYL- + -OUS]

ep•i•zo•ic (ep′ə zō′ik), *adj. Biol.* externally parasitic. [1855–60; EPIZO(ON) + -IC] **—ep′i•zo′ism,** *n.*

ep•i•zo•on (ep′ə zō′on, -ən), *n., pl.* **-zo•a** (-zō′ə). *Biol.* an external parasite or commensal on the body of an animal; ectozoon. Also, **ep′i•zo′ite.** [1830–40; < NL; see EPI-, -ZOON]

ep•i•zo•ot•ic (ep′ə zō ot′ik), *Vet. Med.* —*adj.* **1.** (of diseases) spreading quickly among animals. —*n.* **2.** an epizootic disease. [1740–50; EPI- + ZO(O)- + -OTIC] **—ep′i•zo•ot′i•cal•ly,** *adv.*

epizoot′ic lymphangi′tis, *Vet. Pathol.* a chronic, contagious fungal disease of horses and certain other ungulates, caused by *Histoplasma farciminosum* and characterized by inflammation and ulceration of lymph glands, mucous membranes, and skin.

ep•i•zo•o•ty (ep′ə zō′ə tē), *n., pl.* **-ties.** epizootic. [1775–85; EPIZOOT(IC) + -Y[3]]

e plu•ri•bus u•num (e plōō′ri bŏŏs′ ōō′nŏŏm; *Eng.* ē′ plŏŏr′ə bəs yōō′nəm), *Latin.* out of many, one (motto of the U.S.).

ep•och (ep′ək *or, esp. Brit.,* ē′pok), *n.* **1.** a particular period of time marked by distinctive features, events, etc.: *The treaty ushered in an epoch of peace and good will.* **2.** the beginning of a distinctive period in the history of anything: *The splitting of the atom marked an epoch in scientific discovery.* **3.** a point of time distinguished by a particular event or state of affairs; a memorable date: *His coming of age was an epoch in his life.* **4.** *Geol.* any of several divisions of a geologic period during which a geologic series is formed. Cf. **age** (def. 12). See table under **geologic time.** **5.** *Astron.* **a.** an arbitrarily fixed instant of time or date, usually the beginning of a century or half century, used as a reference in giving the elements of a planetary orbit or the like. **b.** the mean longitude of a planet as seen from the sun at such an instant or date. **6.** *Physics.* the displacement from zero at zero time of a body undergoing simple harmonic motion. [1605–15; < NL *epocha* < Gk *epochḗ* pause, check, fixed time, equiv. to *ep-* EP- + *och-* (var. s. of *échein* to have) + *-ē* n. suffix]
—Syn. 1. date, era, time. See **age.**

ep•och•al (ep′ə kəl *or, esp. Brit.,* ē′po-), *adj.* **1.** of, pertaining to, or of the nature of an epoch. **2.** extremely important, significant, or influential. [1675–85; EPOCH + -AL[1]] **—ep′och•al•ly,** *adv.*

ep•och-mak•ing (ep′ək mā′king *or, esp. Brit.,* ē′pok-), *adj.* opening a new era, as in human history, thought, or knowledge; epochal: *an epoch-making discovery.* [1870–75]

ep•ode (ep′ōd), *n.* **1.** *Class. Pros.* a kind of lyric poem, invented by Archilochus, in which a long verse is followed by a short one. **2.** the part of a lyric ode following the strophe and antistrophe and composing with them a triadic unit. [1590–1600; < L *epōdos* < Gk *epōidós* an aftersong, singing after. See EP-, ODE]

ep•o•nych•i•um (ep′ə nik′ē əm), *n., pl.* **-nych•i•a** (-nik′ē ə), **1.** *Embryol.* the modified outer layer of the epidermis that partially covers the fetal fingernails and toenails and that persists after birth as the cuticle. **2.** *Anat.* a thin, cuticular fold extending over the lunula of a nail. Also, **eponychium.** [1880–85; < NL, equiv. to *ep-* EP- + *onych-* (see ONYX) + *-ium* -IUM]

ep•o•nym (ep′ə nim), *n.* **1.** a person, real or imaginary, from whom something, as a tribe, nation, or place, takes or is said to take its name: *Brut, the supposed grandson of Aeneas, is the eponym of the Britons.* **2.** any ancient official whose name was used to designate his year of office. [1840–50; back formation from EPONYMOUS] **—ep′o•nym′ic,** *adj.*

ep•on•y•mous (ə pon′ə məs), *adj.* giving one's name to a tribe, place, etc.: *Romulus, the eponymous founder of Rome.* [1840–50; < Gk *epṓnymos* giving name. See EP-, -ONYM, -OUS]

ep•on•y•my (ə pon′ə mē), *n.* the derivation of names from eponyms. [1860–65; < Gk *epōnymía* surname, derived name. See EPONYMOUS, -Y[3]]

ep•o•pee (ep′ə pē′, ep′ə pē′), *n.* **1.** an epic. **2.** epic poetry. Also, **ep•o•poe•ia** (ep′ə pē′ə). [1690–1700; < F *épopée* < Gk *epopoiía*, equiv. to *épo(s)* EPOS + *poi(eîn)* to make + *-ia* -IA]

ep•os (ep′os), *n.* **1.** an epic. **2.** epic poetry. **3.** a group of poems, transmitted orally, concerned with parts of a common epic theme. **4.** a series of events suitable for treatment in epic poetry. [1825–35; < L < Gk *épos* speech, tale, song; akin to L *vōx* VOICE, Skt *vácas* word, hymn]

ep•ox•i•da•tion (e pok′si dā′shən, i pok′-), *n. Chem.* a reaction that yields an epoxide. [1940–45; EPOXIDE + -ATION]

ep•ox•ide (e pok′sīd, i pok′-), *n. Chem.* an organic chemical that contains a group consisting of an oxygen atom bound to two already connected atoms, usually carbon **(epox′y group′).** Cf. **epoxy** (def. 2). [EP- + OXIDE]

p•ox•i•dize (e pok′si dīz′, i pok′-), *v.t.,* **-dized, -dizng.** *Chem.* to change (a chemical compound) into an poxide. Also, *esp. Brit.,* **e•pox′i•dise′.** [EPOXIDE + -IZE, n the model of OXIDIZE]

p•ox•y (i pok′sē, i pok′-), *adj., n., pl.* **-ox•ies.,** *v.,* **-oxed, -ox•y•ing.** *Chem.* —*adj.* **1.** having the structure of an epoxide. —*n.* **2.** Also called **epox′y res′in.** any of a class of resins derived by polymerization from epoxides: used chiefly in adhesives, coatings, electrical insulation, solder mix, and castings. —*v.t.* **3.** to bond (two materials) by means of an epoxy resin. [1915–20; EP- + OXY-[2]]

Ep′ping For′est (ep′ing), a park in E England, NE of London: formerly a royal forest.

EPROM (ē′prom), *n. Computers.* a memory chip whose contents can be erased by a mechanism using ultraviolet light and reprogrammed for other purposes. Cf. **PROM** [*e(rasable) p(rogrammable) r(ead)-o(nly) m(emory)*]

EPS, earnings per share.

ep•si•lon (ep′sə lon′, -lən *or, esp. Brit.,* ep sī′lən), *n.* **1.** the fifth letter of the Greek alphabet (E, ϵ). **2.** the vowel sound represented by this letter. **3.** *Math.* an arbitrarily small quantity, used to indicate that a given quantity is small, or close to zero. [< Gk *è psilón* bare, simple *e* (as opposed to diphthongal spellings which in later Gk represented the same sound)]

ep•si•lon-del•ta (ep′sə lon′del′tə, -lən- *or, esp. Brit.,* ep sī′lən-), *adj. Math.* of or pertaining to a method or proof in calculus involving arbitrarily small numbers.

ep•si•lon-neigh•bor•hood (ep′sə lon′nā′bər hŏŏd′, -lən- *or, esp. Brit.,* ep sī′lən-), *n. Math.* the set of all points whose distance from a given point is less than some specified number *epsilon.*

Ep•som (ep′səm), *n.* a town in Surrey, SE England, S of London: site of a famous racetrack **(Ep′som Downs′)** where the annual Derby is held. 71,100. Official name, **Ep′som and Ew′ell.**

ep•som•ite (ep′sə mīt′), *n. Mineral.* the natural form of Epsom salt, $Mg_2SO_4 \cdot 7H_2O$, found as a crust in caves and lake deposits. [1805–15; named after EPSOM; see -ITE[1]]

Ep′som salt′, Often, **Epsom salts.** *Chem., Pharm.* hydrated magnesium sulfate, $MgSO_4 \cdot 7H_2O$, occurring as small colorless crystals: used in fertilizers, the dyeing of fabrics, leather tanning, etc., and in medicine chiefly as a cathartic. [1760–70; after EPSOM; so called from its presence in the local mineral water]

Ep•stein (ep′stīn), *n.* **Sir Jacob,** 1880–1959, English sculptor, born in the U.S.

Ep′stein-Barr′ vi′rus (ep′stīn bär′), a type of herpes virus that causes infectious mononucleosis. *Abbr.:* EBV [after M. A. *Epstein* (b. 1921), British pathologist, and Y. M. *Barr,* British virologist, who isolated the virus in 1964]

EPT, excess-profits tax.

ep•u•lo (ep′yə lō′; *Lat.* ep′ŏŏ lō′), *n., pl.* **ep•u•lo•nes** (ep′yə lō′nēz; *Lat.* ep′ŏŏ lō′nes). (in ancient Rome) a member of a body of priests who performed sacred rites during sacrificial banquets in honor of the gods. [< L *epulō* orig., banqueter, diner]

ep•u•ra•tion (ep′yə rā′shən), *n.* a purification or purge, as of government officials considered disloyal or treacherous. [1790–1800; < F, equiv. to *épur(er)* to purify (see E-, PURE) + *-ation* -ATION]

Ep′worth League′ (ep′wərth), the Methodist youth organization, founded in 1889 to promote fellowship, worship, Christian service, and the study of the Scriptures.

EQ, educational quotient.

eq., **1.** equal. **2.** equation. **3.** equivalent.

eqpt., equipment.

eq•ua•ble (ek′wə bəl, ē′kwə-), *adj.* **1.** free from many changes or variations; uniform: *an equable climate; an equable temperament.* **2.** uniform in operation or effect, as laws. [1635–45; < L *aequābilis* that can be made equal, similar, equiv. to *aequ(us)* equal, even + *-ābilis* -ABLE] **—eq′ua•bil′i•ty, eq′ua•ble•ness,** *n.* **—eq′ua•bly,** *adv.*
—Syn. 1. steady, even, temperate. **—Ant. 1.** variable.

e•qual (ē′kwəl), *adj., n., v.,* **e•qualed, e•qual•ing** or (*esp. Brit.*) **e•qualled, e•qual•ling.** —*adj.* **1.** as great as; the same as (often fol. by *to* or *with*): *The velocity of sound is not equal to that of light.* **2.** like or alike in quantity, degree, value, etc.; of the same rank, ability, merit, etc.: *two students of equal brilliance.* **3.** evenly proportioned or balanced: *an equal contest.* **4.** uniform in operation or effect: *equal laws.* **5.** adequate or sufficient in quantity or degree: *The supply is equal to the demand.* **6.** having adequate powers, ability, or means: *He was equal to the task.* **7.** level, as a plain. **8.** tranquil or undisturbed: *to confront death with an equal mind.* **9.** impartial or equitable. —*n.* **10.** a person or thing that is equal. —*v.t.* **11.** to be or become equal to; meet or match: *So far the rate of production doesn't equal the demand. If A equals B and B equals C, then A equals C.* **12.** to make or do something equal to: *No matter how he tries, he can't equal his brother's achievements.* **13.** *Archaic.* to make equal; equalize. **14.** *Obs.* to recompense fully. [1350–1400; ME (adj.) < L *aequālis* equal, like, equiv. to *aequ(us)* even, plain, just + *-ālis* -AL[1]]
—Syn. 2. proportionate, commensurate, coordinate, correspondent. EQUAL, EQUIVALENT, TANTAMOUNT imply a correspondence between two or more things. EQUAL indicates a correspondence in all respects or in a particular respect: *A dime is equal to 10 cents* (that is, in purchasing power). EQUIVALENT indicates a correspondence in one or more respects, but not in all: *An egg is said to be the equivalent of a pound of meat in nutritive value.* TANTAMOUNT, a word of limited application, is used of immaterial things that are equivalent: *The prisoner's refusal to answer was tantamount to an admission of guilt.* **4.** even, uniform, regular, unvarying, invariant. **6.** suited, fitted. **10.** peer, compeer, match, mate, fellow. **—Ant. 2.** different. **6.** inadequate.
—Usage. See **unique.**

e′qual-ar′e•a projec′tion (ē′kwəl âr′ē ə), *Cartog.* a projection in which regions on the earth's surface that are of equal area are represented as equal.

E′qual Employ′ment Opportu′nity Commis′•sion, *U.S. Govt.* an independent federal agency created under the Civil Rights Act of 1964, as amended, to police a program **(E′qual Employ′ment Opportu′nity)** to eliminate discrimination in employment based on race, color, age, sex, national origin, religion, or mental or physical handicap. *Abbr.:* EEOC

e•qual•i•tar•i•an (i kwol′i târ′ē ən), *adj.* **1.** pertaining or adhering to the doctrine of equality among all people; egalitarian. —*n.* **2.** a person who adheres to the doctrine of equality among all people. [1790–1800; EQUALIT(Y) + -ARIAN] **—e•qual′i•tar′i•an•ism,** *n.*

e•qual•i•ty (i kwol′i tē), *n., pl.* **-ties.** **1.** the state or quality of being equal; correspondence in quantity, degree, value, rank, or ability. **2.** uniform character, as of motion or surface. **3.** *Math.* a statement that two quantities are equal; equation. [1350–1400; ME < L *aequālitāt-* (s. of *aequālitās*). See EQUAL, -ITY]
—Syn. 1. equivalency, parity, correspondence, sameness; justice, fairness, impartiality.

Equal′ity State′, Wyoming (used as a nickname).

equaliza′tion fund′. See **stabilization fund.**

e•qual•ize (ē′kwə līz′), *v.t.,* **-ized, -iz•ing.** **1.** to make equal: *to equalize tax burdens.* **2.** to make uniform: *to equalize a rate of production.* Also, *esp. Brit.,* **e′qual•ise′.** [1580–90; EQUAL + -IZE] **—e′qual•i•za′tion,** *n.*

e•qual•iz•er (ē′kwə lī′zər), *n.* **1.** a person or thing that equalizes. **2.** any of various devices or appliances for equalizing strains, pressures, etc. **3.** *Elect.* an electric network of inductance, capacitance, or resistance established between two points in a given network to secure some constant relation, as even attenuation, between the two points. **4.** *Slang.* a weapon, as a pistol, blackjack, or switchblade knife. [1785–95; EQUALIZE + -ER[1]]

e•qual•ly (ē′kwə lē), *adv.* **1.** in an equal or identical manner: *to treat rich and poor equally.* **2.** to an equal degree or extent: *You are equally matched.* [1350–1400; ME; see EQUAL, -LY]

e′qual opportu′nity, policies and practices in employment and other areas that do not discriminate against persons on the basis of race, color, religion, sex, age, mental or physical handicap, or national origin. **—e′qual-op′por•tu′ni•ty,** *adj.*

E′qual Rights′ Amend′ment. See **ERA** (def. 3).

e′qual sign′, *Math.* the symbol (=), used in a mathematical expression to indicate that the terms it separates are equal. Also, **e′quals sign′.** [1905–10]

e′qual tem′perament, *Music.* the division of an octave into 12 equal semitones, as in the tuning of a piano.

e′qual time′, an equal amount of time on the air, which radio and television licensees are required to offer to opposing candidates for public office and to those voicing diverging views on public referendums. [1960–65]

E•qua•nil (ē′kwə nil), *Pharm., Trademark.* a brand of meprobamate.

e•qua•nim•i•ty (ē′kwə nim′i tē, ek′wə-), *n.* mental or emotional stability or composure, esp. under tension or strain; calmness; equilibrium. [1600–10; < L *aequanimitās*, equiv. to *aequ(us)* even, plain, equal + *animus* mind, spirit, feelings + *-itās* -ITY]
—Syn. serenity, self-possession, aplomb. **—Ant.** panic, disquiet, discomposure, agitation.

e•quan•i•mous (i kwan′ə məs), *adj.* having or showing equanimity; even-tempered: *It was difficult to remain equanimous in the face of such impertinence.* [1645–55; < L *aequanim(us)* (see EQUANIMITY) + -OUS] **—e•quan′i•mous•ly,** *adv.* **—e•quan′i•mous•ness,** *n.*

e•quant (ē′kwənt, ē′kwant), *adj.* (of a crystal) having all axes of the same length (opposed to *anisometric*). [< L *aequant-*, s. of *aequāns*, prp. of *aequāre*; see EQUATE]

e•quate (i kwāt′), *v.t.,* **e•quat•ed, e•quat•ing.** **1.** to regard, treat, or represent as equivalent: *We cannot equate the possession of wealth with goodness.* **2.** to state the equality of or between; put in the form of an equation: *to equate growing prosperity with the physical health of a nation.* **3.** to reduce to an average; make such correction or allowance in as will reduce to a common standard of comparison. [1375–1425; late ME < L *aequātus* (ptp. of *aequāre* to make equal), equiv. to *aequ(us)* EQUAL + *-ātus* -ATE[1]] **—e•quat′a•bil′i•ty,** *n.* **—e•quat′a•ble,** *adj.*

e•qua•tion (i kwā′zhən, -shən), *n.* **1.** the act of equating or making equal; equalization: *the symbolic equation of darkness with death.* **2.** equally balanced state; equilibrium. **3.** *Math.* an expression or a proposition, often algebraic, asserting the equality of two quantities. **4.** *Chem.* a symbolic representation showing the kind and amount of the starting materials and products of a reaction. [1350–1400; ME < L *aequātiōn-* (s. of *aequātiō*) an equalizing. See EQUATE, -ION]

e•qua•tion•al (i kwā′zhə nl, -shə-), *adj.* **1.** of, using, or involving equations. **2.** *Biol.* pertaining to the second or nonreductional cell division in meiosis, in which each chromosome divides into two equal parts. **3.** *Gram.* (of a sentence or predication) consisting of a subject and a complement with or without a copula: *"Very interesting, those books" is an equational sentence.* [1860–65; EQUATION + -AL[1]] **—e•qua′tion•al•ly,** *adv.*

equa′tional verb′, copula (def. 2). [1960–65]

equa′tion move′ment, *Horol.* a movement in certain clocks **(equa′tion clock′)** for driving a hand **(equa′tion hand′)** that shows the relation of the mean day of 24 hours to the length of the current solar day.

equa′tion of mo′tion, an equation describing the rate of change with time of the velocity of a body, a collection of particles, or a fluid. [1850–55]

equa′tion of state′, *Physics.* an equation relating the temperature, pressure, and volume of a given ther-

CONCISE PRONUNCIATION KEY: act, cāpe, dâre, pärt; set, ēqual; *if,* īce; ox, ōver, ôrder, oil, bŏŏk, bōōt, out; up, ûrge; child; sing; shoe; thin, *that;* zh as in *treasure.* ə = *a* as in *alone, e* as in *system, i* as in *easily, o* as in *gallop, u* as in *circus;* ᵊ as in *fire* (fīᵊr), *hour* (ouᵊr). l and n can serve as syllabic consonants, as in *cradle* (krād′l), and *button* (but′n). See the full key inside the front cover.

modynamic system. Also called **characteristic equation.**

equa′tion of time′, *Astron.* apparent time minus mean solar time, ranging from minus 14 minutes in February to over 16 minutes in November. [1720–30]

e•qua•tor (i kwā′tər), *n.* **1.** the great circle on a sphere or heavenly body whose plane is perpendicular to the axis, equidistant everywhere from the two poles of the sphere or heavenly body. **2.** the great circle of the earth that is equidistant from the North Pole and South Pole. **3.** a circle separating a surface into two congruent parts. **4.** See **celestial equator.** [1350–1400; ME < ML *aequātor,* L: equalizer (of day and night, as when the sun crosses the equator). See EQUATE, -TOR]

e•qua•to•ri•al (ē′kwə tôr′ē əl, -tōr′-, ek′wə-), *adj.* **1.** of, pertaining to, or near an equator, esp. the equator of the earth. **2.** of, like, or typical of the regions at the earth's equator: *equatorial temperatures.* —*n.* **3.** a telescope mounting having two axes of motion, one parallel to the earth's axis and one at right angles to it. [1655–65; EQUATOR + -IAL] —**e′qua•to′ri•al•ly,** *adv.*

E′quato′rial Coun′tercurrent, an ocean current that flows E between the west-flowing equatorial currents. Also called **Cromwell Current.**

E′quato′rial Cur′rent, 1. See **North Equatorial Current. 2.** See **South Equatorial Current.**

E′quato′rial Guin′ea, a republic in W equatorial Africa, comprising the mainland province of Río Muni and the island province of Bioko: formerly a Spanish colony. 400,000; 10,824 sq. mi. (28,034 sq. km). *Cap.:* Malabo. Formerly, **Spanish Guinea. —E′quato′rial Guin′ean.**

e′quato′rial plane′, *Astron.* the plane passing through the equator of the earth or another celestial body. [1890–95]

e′quato′rial plate′, *Cell Biol.* the central plane of the spindle in a dividing cell, to which chromosomes migrate during the metaphase of mitosis or meiosis. [1885–90]

e′quato′rial tide′, a semimonthly tide that appears when the moon is over the equator.

e′quato′rial trough′, the quasi-continuous belt of low atmospheric pressure that lies between the subtropical high-pressure belts of the Northern and Southern hemispheres.

e•qua•tor•ward (i kwā′tər wərd), *adv.* **1.** toward the equator: *a ship sailing equatorward.* —*adj.* **2.** facing or tending toward the equator. [1870–75; EQUATOR + -WARD] Also, **e•qua′tor•wards.**

eq•uer•ry (ek′wə rē, i kwer′ē), *n., pl.* **-ries. 1.** an officer of a royal or similar household, charged with the care of the horses. **2.** an officer of the British royal household who attends the sovereign or other member of the royal family. [1520–30; alter. (influenced by L *equus* horse) of earlier *esquiry, escuirie* < MF *escuirie* stable, squires collectively, deriv. of *escuyer* SQUIRE; see -Y[3]]

e•ques•tri•an (i kwes′trē ən), *adj.* **1.** of or pertaining to horseback riding or horseback riders: *equestrian skill.* **2.** mounted on horseback: *equestrian knights.* **3.** representing a person mounted on a horse: *an equestrian statue.* **4.** pertaining to or composed of knights or mounted warriors: *an equestrian code of honor.* **5.** of or pertaining to the ancient Roman equites. —*n.* **6.** a person who rides horses. [1650–60; < L *equestri(s)* (cf. *eques* horseman) + -AN] —**e•ques′tri•an•ism,** *n.*

e•ques•tri•enne (i kwes′trē en′), *n.* a woman who rides horses. [1860–65; EQUESTRI(AN) + -ENNE]
—Usage. See **-enne.**

e•qui (ē′kwē, ek′wē), *n. Ling.* See **equi NP deletion.**

equi-, a combining form meaning "equal," used in the formation of compound words: *equimolecular.* [ME < L *aequi-,* comb. form repr. *aequus* equal]

e•qui•an•gu•lar (ē′kwē ang′gyə lər, ek′wē-), *adj.* having all the angles equal. [1650–60; EQUI- + ANGULAR] —**e′qui•an′gu•lar′i•ty,** *n.*

equian′gular hyper′bola. See **rectangular hyperbola.**

e•qui•ca•lor•ic (ē′kwi kə lôr′ik, -lor′-, ek′wi-), *adj. Physiol.* yielding equal amounts of energy in metabolism. [1935–40; EQUI- + CALORIC]

e•qui•dis•tance (ē′kwi dis′təns, ek′wi-), *n.* equal distance. [1620–30; EQUI- + DISTANCE]

e•qui•dis•tant (ē′kwi dis′tənt, ek′wi-), *adj.* equally distant. [1560–70; < MF < LL *aequidistant-* (s. of *aequidistāns*). See EQUI-, DISTANT] —**e′qui•dis′tant•ly,** *adv.*

e•qui•form (ē′kwə fôrm′, ek′wə-), *adj.* having the same shape or serving the same purpose. Also, **e′qui•for′mal.** [< LL *aequiformis.* See EQUI-, -FORM]

e•qui•lat•er•al (ē′kwə lat′ər əl, ek′wə-), *adj.* **1.** having all the sides equal: *an equilateral triangle.* —*n.* **2.** a figure having all its sides equal. **3.** a side equivalent, or equal, to others. [1560–70; < LL *aequilaterālis.* See EQUI-, LATERAL] —**e′qui•lat′er•al•ly,** *adv.*

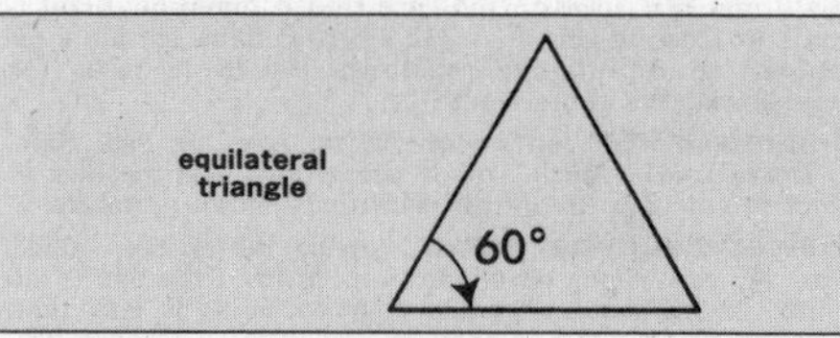

equilat′eral hyper′bola. See **rectangular hyperbola.** [1875–80]

e•quil•i•brant (i kwil′ə brənt), *n. Physics.* a counterbalancing force or system of forces. [1880–85; < F *équilibrant.* See EQUILIBRIUM, -ANT]

e•quil•i•brate (i kwil′ə brāt′, ē′kwə li′brāt, ek′wə-), *v.,* **-brat•ed, -brat•ing.** —*v.t.* **1.** to balance equally; keep in equipoise or equilibrium. **2.** to be in equilibrium with; counterpoise. —*v.i.* **3.** to be in equilibrium; balance. [1625–35; < LL *aequilibrātus,* ptp. of *aequilibrāre* to be in EQUILIBRIUM; see -ATE[1]] —**e•quil′i•bra′tion,** *n.* —**e•quil′i•bra′tor,** *n.*

e•quil•i•brist (i kwil′ə brist, ē′kwə lib′rist, ek′wə-), *n.* a performer who is skilled at balancing in unusual positions and hazardous movements, as a tightrope walker in a circus. [1750–60; < F *équilibriste.* See EQUILIBRIUM, -IST] —**e•quil′i•bris′tic,** *adj.*

e•qui•lib•ri•um (ē′kwə lib′rē əm, ek′wə-), *n., pl.* **-ri•ums, -ri•a** (-rē ə). **1.** a state of rest or balance due to the equal action of opposing forces. **2.** equal balance between any powers, influences, etc.; equality of effect. **3.** mental or emotional balance; equanimity: *The pressures of the situation caused her to lose her equilibrium.* **4.** *Chem.* the condition existing when a chemical reaction and its reverse reaction proceed at equal rates. [1600–10; < L *aequilībrium,* equiv. to *aequi-* EQUI- + *libr(a)* balance + *-ium* -IUM] —**e•quil•i•bra•to•ry** (i kwil′ə-brə tôr′ē, -tōr′ē, ē′kwə lib′rə-, ek′wə-), *adj.*
—Syn. 1. equipoise, steadiness, stability.

equilib′rium price′, the price at which the quantity of a product offered is equal to the quantity of the product in demand.

equilib′rium valve′, (in a reciprocating engine) a valve opening a passage from one end of a cylinder to the other to equalize pressure upon both faces of the piston. [1870–75]

e•qui•mo•lec•u•lar (ē′kwə mə lek′yə lər, ek′wə-), *adj. Physics, Chem.* containing equal numbers of molecules. [1905–10; EQUI- + MOLECULAR]

e•quine (ē′kwīn, ek′wīn), *adj.* **1.** of, pertaining to, or resembling a horse: *a bold, equine face.* —*n.* **2.** a horse. [1770–80; < L *equinus,* equiv. to *equ(us)* horse + *-inus* -INE[1]] —**e′quine•ly,** *adv.* —**e•quin′i•ty,** *n.*

e′quine distem′per, *Vet. Pathol.* distemper[1] (def. 1b).

e′quine encephali′tis, *Pathol., Vet. Pathol.* a viral disease of horses and mules that is communicable to humans, marked by inflammation of the brain and spinal cord.

e′quine infec′tious ane′mia, *Pathol., Vet. Pathol.* See **swamp fever** (def. 2).

e′quine metri′tis, *Vet. Pathol.* a highly contagious inflammation of the uterus affecting mostly thoroughbred mares.

e•qui•noc•tial (ē′kwə nok′shəl, ek′wə-), *adj.* **1.** pertaining to an equinox or the equinoxes, or to the equality of day and night. **2.** pertaining to the celestial equator. **3.** occurring at or about the time of an equinox. **4.** *Bot.* (of a flower) opening regularly at a certain hour. —*n.* **5.** See **celestial equator. 6.** See **equinoctial storm.** [1350–1400; ME < L *aequinoctiālis* pertaining to the equinox. See EQUINOX, -AL[1]]

e′quinoc′tial cir′cle, *Astron.* See **celestial equator.** [1350–1400; ME]

e′quinoc′tial line′. See **celestial equator.** [1350–1400; ME]

e′quinoc′tial point′, either of the two points at which the celestial equator and the ecliptic intersect each other; the position of the sun's center at the equinoxes. [1720–30]

e′quinoc′tial rains′, rainy seasons that occur, in numerous regions near the equator, near or soon after the times of the equinoxes.

e′quinoc′tial storm′, a storm of violent winds and rain occurring at or near the time of an equinox and popularly, but erroneously, believed to be physically associated with it. Also called **equinoctial, line gale, line storm.**

e′quinoc′tial year′, year (def. 4b).

e•qui•nox (ē′kwə noks′, ek′wə-), *n.* **1.** the time when the sun crosses the plane of the earth's equator, making night and day of approximately equal length all over the earth and occurring about March 21 **(vernal equinox** or **spring equinox)** and September 22 **(autumnal equinox). 2.** either of the equinoctial points. [1350–1400; ME < ML *equinoxium,* for L *aequinoctium* the time of equal days and nights (*aequi-* EQUI- + *noct-* (s. of *nox*) NIGHT + *-ium* -IUM)]

equi NP deletion, *Ling.* a rule of transformational grammar that deletes the underlying subject of a complement clause if it is coreferential with the subject or object of the main clause, as in *John promised to return the money,* where the underlying subject (*John*) of *return* has been deleted. Also called **equi.** [appar. short for *equivalent NP*]

e•quip (i kwip′), *v.t.,* **e•quipped, e•quip•ping. 1.** to furnish or provide with whatever is needed for use or for any undertaking; fit out, as a ship or army: *They spent several thousand dollars to equip their boat.* **2.** to dress; array: *He equipped himself in all his finery.* **3.** to furnish with intellectual or emotional resources; prepare: *Education and travel have equipped her to deal with all sorts of people.* [1515–25; < MF *equiper,* OF *esquiper* to fit out, equip, prob. < ON *skipa* to put in order, arrange, man (a ship)] —**e•quip′per,** *n.*
—Syn. 1. outfit, rig. See **furnish.**

equip., equipment.

eq•ui•page (ek′wə pij), *n.* **1.** a carriage. **2.** a carriage drawn by horses and attended by servants. **3.** outfit, as of a ship, an army, or a soldier; equipment. **4.** *Archaic.* **a.** a set of small household articles, as of china. **b.** a collection of articles for personal ornament or use. [1570–80; < MF; see EQUIP, -AGE]

e′qui•par•ti′tion of en′ergy (ē′kwə pär tish′ən, ek′wə-, ē′kwə-, ek′wə), *Thermodynamics.* the theorem that the kinetic energy is the same for each degree of freedom in a system in thermal equilibrium. [1900–05; EQUI- + PARTITION]

e•quip•ment (i kwip′mənt), *n.* **1.** anything kept, furnished, or provided for a specific purpose. **2.** the act of equipping a person or thing. **3.** the state of being equipped. **4.** the personal knowledge and skill required for a task, occupation, etc.: *He has the necessary equipment for law.* **5.** the rolling stock of a railroad. [1710–20; EQUIP + -MENT]
—Syn. 1. apparatus, paraphernalia, accouterment.

e•qui•poise (ē′kwə poiz′, ek′wə-), *n., v.,* **-poised, -pois•ing.** —*n.* **1.** an equal distribution of weight; even balance; equilibrium. **2.** a counterpoise. —*v.t.* **3.** to equal or offset in weight; balance. [1625–35; EQUI- + POISE[1]]

e•qui•pol•lent (ē′kwə pol′ənt, ek′wə-), *adj.* **1.** equal in power, effect, etc.; equivalent. **2.** *Logic.* (of propositions, propositional forms, etc.) logically equivalent in any of various specified ways. —*n.* **3.** an equivalent. [1375–1425; late ME < L *aequipollent-* (s. of *aequipollēns*) of equal value, equiv. to *aequi-* EQUI- + *pollent-* (s. of *pollēns*) able, prp. of *pollēre* to be strong] —**e′qui•pol′lence, e′qui•pol′len•cy,** *n.* —**e′qui•pol′lent•ly,** *adv.*

e•qui•pon•der•ance (ē′kwə pon′dər əns, ek′wə-), *n.* equality of weight; equipoise. Also, **e′qui•pon′der•an•cy.** [1765–75; *equiponder(ant)* (< ML *aequiponderant-,* s. of *aequiponderāns,* prp. of *aequiponderāre;* see EQUI-, PONDER, -ANT) + -ANCE] —**e′qui•pon′der•ant,** *adj.*

e•qui•pon•der•ate (ē′kwə pon′də rāt′, ek′wə-), *v.t.,* **-at•ed, -at•ing.** to equal or offset in weight, force, importance, etc.; counterbalance. [1635–45; < ML *aequiponderātus,* ptp. of *aequiponderāre.* See EQUI-, PONDER, -ATE[1]] —**e′qui•pon′der•a′tion,** *n.*

e•qui•po•tent (ē′kwə pōt′nt, ek′wə-), *adj.* equal in power, ability, or effect. [1870–75; EQUI- + POTENT[1]]

e•qui•po•ten•tial (ē′kwə pə ten′shəl, ek′wə-), *adj. Physics.* of the same or exhibiting uniform potential at every point: *an equipotential surface.* [1670–80; EQUI- + POTENTIAL] —**e′qui•po•ten′ti•al′i•ty,** *n.*

e•qui•prob•a•bi•lism (ē′kwə prob′ə bə liz′əm, ek′-wə-), *n. Rom. Cath. Theol.* a theory that in cases of doubt as to the lawfulness or unlawfulness of an action, it is permissible to follow either argument. Cf. **probabilism** (def. 2). [1885–90; EQUI- + PROBABILISM]

e•qui•prob•a•ble (ē′kwə prob′ə bəl, ek′wə-), *adj.* equal in probability. [1920–25; EQUI- + PROBABLE] —**e′qui•prob′a•bil′i•ty,** *n.* —**e′qui•prob′a•bly,** *adv.*

e•qui•ro•tal (ē′kwə rōt′l, ek′wə-), *adj.* having wheels all of the same size or diameter, as a vehicle. [1830–40; EQUI- + L *rot(a)* wheel + -AL[1]]

eq•ui•se•toid (ek′wə sē′toid), *n.* any plant of the phylum or division Equisetophyta (or Sphenopsida), including the horsetails and many extinct species of the Carboniferous Period. Also called **sphenopsid.** [< NL *Equiset(um)* EQUISETUM + -OID]

eq•ui•se•tum (ek′wə sē′təm), *n., pl.* **-tums, -ta** (-tə). any plant of the genus *Equisetum,* comprising the horsetails. [1820–30; < NL; L *equisaetum,* equiv. to *equi-,* comb. form of *equus* horse + *saet(a)* bristle + *-um* neut. n. suffix] —**eq′ui•se′tic,** *adj.*

eq•ui•ta•ble (ek′wi tə bəl), *adj.* **1.** characterized by equity or fairness; just and right; fair; reasonable: *equitable treatment of all citizens.* **2.** *Law.* **a.** pertaining to or valid in equity. **b.** pertaining to the system of equity, as distinguished from the common law. [1640–50; EQUIT(Y) + -ABLE] —**eq′ui•ta•ble•ness,** *n.* —**eq′ui•ta•bly,** *adv.*
—Syn. impartial, proper, unbiased. **—Ant.** unfair, unjust, unequitable, biased, prejudiced.

eq•ui•tant (ek′wi tənt), *adj. Bot.* straddling or overlapping, as leaves whose bases overlap the leaves above or within them. [1820–30; < L *equitant-* (s. of *equitāns*) (prp. of *equitāre* to ride), equiv. to *equit-* (s. of *eques;* see EQUITES) + *-ant-* -ANT]

eq•ui•ta•tion (ek′wi tā′shən), *n.* the act or art of riding on horseback. [1555–65; < L *equitātiōn-* (s. of *equitātiō*), equiv. to *equitāt(us)* (ptp. of *equitāre* to ride) + *-iōn-* -ION]

eq•ui•tes (ek′wi tēz′), *n.pl. Rom. Hist.* **1.** mounted military units; cavalry. **2.** members of a specially privileged class derived from the ancient Roman cavalry and having status intermediate between those of senatorial rank and the common people. [< L, pl. of *eques* horseman, deriv. of *equus* horse]

eq•ui•ty (ek′wi tē), *n., pl.* **-ties. 1.** the quality of being fair or impartial; fairness; impartiality: *the equity of Sol-*

CONCISE ETYMOLOGY KEY: <, descended or borrowed from; >, whence; b., blend of, blended; c., cognate with; cf., compare; deriv., derivative; equiv., equivalent; imit., imitative; obl., oblique; r., replacing; s., stem; sp., spelling, spelled; resp., respelling, respelled; trans., translation; ?, origin unknown; *, unattested; ‡, probably earlier than. See the full key inside the front cover.

omon. **2.** something that is fair and just. **3.** *Law.* **a.** the application of the dictates of conscience or the principles of natural justice to the settlement of controversies. **b.** a system of jurisprudence or a body of doctrines and rules developed in England and followed in the U.S., serving to supplement and remedy the limitations and the inflexibility of the common law. **c.** an equitable right or claim. **d.** an equity of redemption. **4.** the monetary value of a property or business beyond any amounts owed on it in mortgages, claims, liens, etc. **5.** *Informal.* ownership, esp. when considered as the right to share in future profits or appreciation in value. **6.** the interest of the owner of common stock in a corporation. **7.** (in a margin account) the excess of the market value of the securities over any indebtedness. **8.** (*cap.*) See **Actors' Equity Association.** [1275–1325; ME *equite* < L *aequitās.* See EQUI-, -TY[2]]

eq′uity cap′ital, that portion of the capital of a business provided by the sale of stock. [1960–65]

eq′uity conver′sion. See **reverse-annuity mortgage.**

eq′uity of redemp′tion, **1.** the right of a mortgagor to redeem the property by paying the debt, even after default in payment of the sum owed. **2.** the interest of an owner of land subject to a mortgage. [1705–15]

eq′uity secu′rity, a security, esp. a common stock, representing an ownership rather than a debt claim. [1925–30]

eq′uity stock′, capital stock, either common or preferred.

equiv., equivalent.

e•quiv•a•lence (i kwiv′ə ləns *or, for 3,* ē′kwə vā′ləns), *n.* **1.** the state or fact of being equivalent; equality in value, force, significance, etc. **2.** an instance of this; an equivalent. **3.** *Chem.* the quality of having equal valence. **4.** *Logic, Math.* **a.** Also called **material implication.** the relation between two propositions such that the second is not false when the first is true. **b.** Also called **material equivalence.** the relation between two propositions such that they are either both true or both false. **c.** the relation between two propositions such that each logically implies the other. —*adj.* **5.** (of a logical or mathematical relationship) reflexive, symmetrical, and transitive. Also, **equivalency** (for defs. 1, 2). [1535–45; < MF < ML *aequivalentia,* equiv. to L *aequivalent-* EQUIVALENT + *-ia* -IA; see -ENCE]

equiv′alence class′, *Math.* the set of elements associated by an equivalence relation with a given element of a set. [1950–55]

equiv′alence prin′ciple, *Physics.* (in relativity) the principle that, in any small region of space-time, the effects of a gravitational field are indistinguishable from those of an appropriate acceleration of the frame of reference. Also called **Einstein's equivalency principle, principle of equivalence.** [1915–20]

equiv′alence rela′tion, *Math.* a relation that is reflexive, symmetrical, and transitive, as equality. [1945–50]

e•quiv•a•len•cy (i kwiv′ə lən sē), *n., pl.* **-cies.** equivalence (defs. 1, 2). [1525–35; < ML *aequivalentia.* See EQUIVALENT, -ENCY]

e•quiv•a•lent (i kwiv′ə lənt *or, for 5,* ē′kwə vā′lənt), *adj.* **1.** equal in value, measure, force, effect, significance, etc.: *His silence is equivalent to an admission of guilt.* **2.** corresponding in position, function, etc.: *In some ways their prime minister is equivalent to our president.* **3.** *Geom.* having the same extent, as a triangle and a square of equal area. **4.** *Math.* (of two sets) able to be placed in one-to-one correspondence. **5.** *Chem.* having the same capacity to combine or react chemically. —*n.* **6.** something that is equivalent. [1425–75; late ME < LL *aequivalent-* (s. of *aequivalēns*), prp. of *aequivalēre.* See EQUI-, -VALENT] —**e•quiv′a•lent•ly,** *adv.*
—**Syn. 1.** See **equal.**

equiv′alent weight′, *Chem.* the combining power, esp. in grams **(gram equivalent),** of an element or compound, equivalent to hydrogen as a standard of 1.00797 or oxygen as a standard of 8; the atomic weight divided by the valence. [1925–30]

e•qui•valve (ē′kwə valv′), *adj.* (of a bivalve mollusk) having the valves of the shell equal in shape and size. [1860–65; EQUI- + VALVE]

e•quiv•o•cal (i kwiv′ə kəl), *adj.* **1.** allowing the possibility of several different meanings, as a word or phrase, esp. with intent to deceive or misguide; susceptible of double interpretation; deliberately ambiguous: *an equivocal answer.* **2.** of doubtful nature or character; questionable; dubious; suspicious: *aliens of equivocal loyalty.* **3.** of uncertain significance; not determined: *an equivocal attitude.* [1375–1425; late ME *equivoc* (< LL *aequivocus* ambiguous, equiv. to L *aequi-* EQUI- + *vōc-,* s. of *vōx* vox + *-us* adj. suffix) + -AL[1]] —**e•quiv′o•cal′•i•ty, e•quiv•o•ca•cy** (i kwiv′ə kə sē), *n.* —**e•quiv′o•cal•ly,** *adv.* —**e•quiv′o•cal•ness,** *n.*
—**Syn. 1.** See **ambiguous.**

e•quiv•o•cate (i kwiv′ə kāt′), *v.i.,* **-cat•ed, -cat•ing.** to use ambiguous or unclear expressions, usually to avoid commitment or in order to mislead; prevaricate or hedge: *When asked directly for his position on disarmament, the candidate only equivocated.* [1375–1425; late ME < ML *aequivocātus,* ptp. of *aequivocāre;* see EQUIVOCAL, -ATE[1]] —**e•quiv′o•cat′ing•ly,** *adv.* —**e•quiv′o•ca′tor,** *n.*
—**Syn.** evade, stall, dodge.

e•quiv•o•ca•tion (i kwiv′ə kā′shən), *n.* **1.** the use of equivocal or ambiguous expressions, esp. in order to mislead or hedge; prevarication. **2.** an equivocal, ambiguous expression; equivoque: *The speech was marked by elaborate equivocations.* **3.** *Logic.* a fallacy caused by the double meaning of a word. [1350–1400; ME *equivocacion* < LL *aequivocātiōn-* (s. of *aequivocātiō*). See EQUIVOCATE, -ION]

eq•ui•voque (ek′wə vōk′, ē′kwə-), *n.* **1.** an equivocal term; an ambiguous expression. **2.** a play on words; pun. **3.** double meaning; ambiguity. Also, **eq′ui•voke′.** [1350–1400; ME *equivoc* adj.; see EQUIVOCAL]

E•quu•le•us (i kwōō′lē əs), *n., gen.* **-le•i** (-lē ī′). *Astron.* the Little Horse, a small northern constellation between Delphinus and Aquarius.

er (ə, ər), *interj.* (used to express or represent a pause, hesitation, uncertainty, etc.).

ER, **1.** efficiency report. **2.** See **emergency room.**

Er, *Symbol, Chem.* erbium.

-er[1], **1.** a suffix used in forming nouns designating persons from the object of their occupation or labor (*hatter; tiler; tinner; moonshiner*), or from their place of origin or abode (*Icelander; southerner; villager*), or designating either persons or things from some special characteristic or circumstance (*six-footer; three-master; teetotaler; fiver; tenner*). **2.** a suffix serving as the regular English formative of agent nouns, being attached to verbs of any origin (*bearer; creeper; employer; harvester; teacher; theorizer*). Cf. **-ier[1], -yer.** [ME *-er(e),* a coalescence of OE *-ere* agentive suffix (c. OHG *-āri,* Goth *-areis* < Gmc **-arjaz* (> Slav **-arĭ*) < L *-ārius* -ARY) and OE *-ware* forming nouns of ethnic or residential orig. (as *Rōmware* Romans), c. OHG *-āri* < Gmc **-warioz* people]

-er[2], a noun suffix occurring in loanwords from French in the Middle English period, most often names of occupations (*archer; butcher; butler; carpenter; grocer; mariner; officer*), but also other nouns (*corner; danger; primer*). Some historical instances of this suffix, as in *banker* or *gardener,* where the base is a recognizable modern English word, are now indistinguishable from denominal formations with **-er[1],** as *miller* or *potter.* [ME < AF *-er,* equiv. to OF *-er, -ier* < L *-ārius, -ārium.* Cf. -ARY, -EER, -IER[2]]

-er[3], a termination of nouns denoting action or process: *dinner; rejoinder; remainder; trover.* [< F, orig. inf. suffix *-er, -re*]

-er[4], a suffix regularly used in forming the comparative degree of adjectives: *harder; smaller.* [ME *-er(e), -re,* OE *-ra, -re;* c. G *-er*]

-er[5], a suffix regularly used in forming the comparative degree of adverbs: *faster.* [ME *-er(e), -re,* OE *-or;* c. OHG *-or,* G *-er*]

-er[6], a formal element appearing in verbs having frequentative meaning: *flicker; flutter; shiver; shudder.* [ME; OE *-r-;* c. G *-(e)r-*]

-er[7], a suffix that creates informal or jocular mutations of more neutral words, which are typically clipped to a single syllable if polysyllabic, before application of the suffix, and which sometimes undergo other phonetic alterations: *bed-sitter; footer; fresher; rugger.* Most words formed thus have been limited to English public-school and university slang; few, if any, have become current in North America, with the exception of *soccer,* which has also lost its earlier informal character. Cf. **-ers.** [prob. modeled on nonagentive uses of -ER[1]; said to have first become current in University College, Oxford, 1875–80]

E.R., **1.** East Riding (Yorkshire). **2.** East River (New York City). **3.** King Edward. [< NL *Edwardus Rex*] **4.** Queen Elizabeth. [< NL *Elizabeth Regina*] **5.** See **emergency room.**

e•ra (ēr′ə, er′ə), *n.* **1.** a period of time marked by distinctive character, events, etc.: *The use of steam for power marked the beginning of an era.* **2.** the period of time to which anything belongs or is to be assigned: *She was born in the era of hansoms and gaslight.* **3.** a system of chronologic notation reckoned from a given date: *The era of the Romans was based upon the time the city of Rome was founded.* **4.** a point of time from which succeeding years are numbered, as at the beginning of a system of chronology: *Caesar died many years before our era.* **5.** a date or an event forming the beginning of any distinctive period: *The year 1492 marks an era in world history.* **6.** *Geol.* a major division of geologic time composed of a number of periods. See table under **geologic time.** [1605–15; < LL *aera* fixed date, era, epoch (from which time is reckoned), prob. special use of L *aera* counters (pl. of *aes* piece of metal, money, brass); c. Goth *aiz,* OE *ār* ORE, Skt *ayas* metal]
—**Syn. 1.** See **age.**

ERA, **1.** Also, **era** *Baseball.* See **earned run average.** **2.** Emergency Relief Administration. **3.** Equal Rights Amendment: proposed 27th amendment to the U.S. Constitution that would prohibit discrimination on the basis of sex.

e•ra•di•ate (i rā′dē āt′), *v.i., v.t.,* **-at•ed, -at•ing.** to radiate. [1640–50; E- + RADIATE] —**e•ra′di•a′tion,** *n.*

e•rad•i•ca•ble (i rad′i kə bəl), *adj.* capable of being eradicated. [1840–50; < LL *ērādīcābilis,* equiv. to L *ērādīc(āre)* to ERADICATE + *-ābilis* -ABLE] —**e•rad′i•ca•bly,** *adv.*

e•rad•i•cate (i rad′i kāt′), *v.t.,* **-cat•ed, -cat•ing.** **1.** to remove or destroy utterly; extirpate: *to eradicate smallpox throughout the world.* **2.** to erase by rubbing or by means of a chemical solvent: *to eradicate a spot.* **3.** to pull up by the roots: *to eradicate weeds.* [1555–65; < L *ērādīcātus* rooted out (ptp. of *ērādīcāre*), equiv. to *ē-* E- + *rādīc-* (s. of *rādīx*) ROOT[1] + *-ātus* -ATE[1]] —**e•rad•i•cant** (i rad′i kənt), *adj., n.* —**e•rad′i•ca′tion,** *n.* —**e•rad′i•ca′tive,** *adj.* —**e•rad′i•ca′tor,** *n.*
—**Syn. 1.** obliterate, uproot, exterminate, annihilate. See **abolish.**

e•rase (i rās′), *v.,* **e•rased, e•ras•ing.** —*v.t.* **1.** to rub or scrape out, as letters or characters written, engraved, etc.; efface. **2.** to eliminate completely: *She couldn't erase the tragic scene from her memory.* **3.** to obliterate (material recorded on magnetic tape or a magnetic disk): *She erased the message.* **4.** to obliterate recorded material from (a magnetic tape or disk): *He accidentally erased the tape.* **5.** *Computers.* to remove (data) from computer storage. **6.** *Slang.* to murder: *The gang had to erase him before he informed on them.* —*v.i.* **7.** to give way to effacement readily or easily. **8.** to obliterate characters, letters, markings, etc., from something. [1595–1605; < L *ērāsus* (ptp. of *ērādere*), equiv. to *ē-* E- + *rāsus* scraped; see RAZE] —**e•ras′a•bil′i•ty,** *n.* —**e•ras′a•ble,** *adj.*
—**Syn. 1.** expunge, obliterate. See **cancel.** —**Ant. 1, 3.** restore.

e•ras•er (i rā′sər), *n.* **1.** a device, as a piece of rubber or cloth, for erasing marks made with pen, pencil, chalk, etc. **2.** a person or thing that erases. [1780–90; ERASE + -ER[1]]

eras′ing head′, the part of a tape recorder that erases material previously recorded on magnetic tape. Also, **erase′ head′.** [1955–60]

e•ra•sion (i rā′zhən, -shən), *n.* **1.** the act of erasing. **2.** *Surg.* **a.** the scraping away of tissue, esp. of bone. **b.** Also called **arthrectomy.** excision of a joint. [1780–90; ERASE + -ION]

Er•a•sis•tra•tus (er′ə sis′trə təs), *n.* c300–250 B.C., Greek physician and physiologist.

E•ras•mi•an (i raz′mē ən), *adj.* **1.** of, pertaining to, or like Erasmus. —*n.* **2.** a follower of Erasmus. [1750–60; ERASM(US) + -IAN] —**E•ras′mi•an•ism,** *n.*

E•ras•mus (i raz′məs), *n.* **1. Des•i•de•ri•us** (des′i-dēr′ē əs), 1466?–1536, Dutch humanist, scholar, theologian, and writer. **2.** a male given name: from a Greek word meaning "beloved."

E•ras•tian (i ras′chən, -tē ən), *adj.* **1.** of or pertaining to Thomas Erastus or Erastianism. —*n.* **2.** an advocate of Erastianism. [1645–55; ERAST(US) + -IAN]

E•ras•tian•ism (i ras′chə niz′əm, -tē ə niz′-), *n.* the doctrine, advocated by Thomas Erastus, of the supremacy of the state over the church in ecclesiastical matters. [1675–85; ERASTIAN + -ISM]

E•ras•tus (i ras′təs; *Ger.* ā räs′tōōs), *n.* **1. Thom•as** (tom′əs; *Ger.* tō′mäs), 1524–83, Swiss-German theologian. **2.** a male given name: from a Greek word meaning "lovable."

e•ra•sure (i rā′shər), *n.* **1.** an act or instance of erasing. **2.** a place where something has been erased; a spot or mark left after erasing: *You can't sign a contract with so many erasures in it.* [1725–35; ERASE + -URE]

Er•a•to (er′ə tō′), *n. Class. Myth.* the Muse of love poetry.

Er•a•tos•the•nes (er′ə tos′thə nēz′), *n.* 276?–195? B.C., Greek mathematician and astronomer at Alexandria.

Er•bil (ēr′bil, âr′-), *n.* a town in N Iraq: built on the site of ancient Arbela. 90,320. Also, **Arbil, Irbil.**

er•bi•um (ûr′bē əm), *n. Chem.* a rare-earth metallic element, having pink salts. *Symbol:* Er; *at. wt.:* 167.26; *at. no.:* 68. [1835–45; < NL, named after *Ytterby,* Sweden, where first found; see -IUM]

Er•cel•doune (ûr′səl dōōn′), *n.* **Thomas of.** See **Thomas of Erceldoune.**

Er•ci•lla (ER thē′lyä, -sē′yä), *n.* **A•lon•so de** (ä lôn′sô the), 1533–94, Spanish epic poet; soldier in the conquest of Chile.

Erck•mann-Cha•tri•an (ERK mAn shA trē äN′), *n.* joint pen name of **É•mile Erckmann** (ā mēl′), 1822–99, and **A•le•xan•dre Chatrian** (A lek säN′drᵊ), 1826–90, collaborating French novelists and dramatists.

ere (âr), *prep., conj.* before. [bef. 900; ME; OE *ǣr, ēr* (c. G *ehr*), comp. of *ār* soon, early; c. Goth *air.* See ERST, EARLY]

Er•e•bus (er′ə bəs), *n.* **1.** *Class. Myth.* the darkness under the earth, imagined either as the abode of sinners after death or of all the dead. **2. Mount,** a volcano in Antarctica, on Ross Island. 13,202 ft. (4024 m). [< L < Gk *Érebos;* c. Armenian *erek* evening, Skt *rájas* darkness, Goth *riquis* darkness]

E•rech (ē′rek, er′ek), *n.* Biblical name of **Uruk.**

E•re•chim (*Port.* i Ri shēm′), *n.* a city in S Brazil. 32,426.

E•rech•the•um (i rek′thē əm, er′ik thē′əm), *n.* a temple at Athens on the Acropolis, begun c420 B.C., having two Ionic porches and a porch of caryatids: regarded as one of the finest examples of classical architecture. Also, **E•rech•thei•on** (i rek′thī ən, -on′, er′ik thī′ən).

e•rect (i rekt′), *adj.* **1.** upright in position or posture: *to stand or sit erect.* **2.** raised or directed upward: *a dog with ears erect.* **3.** *Bot.* vertical throughout; not spreading or declined: *an erect stem; an erect leaf or ovule.* **4.** *Heraldry.* **a.** (of a charge) represented palewise: *a sword erect.* **b.** (of an animal or part of an animal) represented upright: *a boar's head erect.* **5.** *Optics.* (of an image) having the same position as the object; not inverted. —*v.t.* **6.** to build; construct; raise: *to erect a house.* **7.** to raise and set in an upright or vertical position: *to erect a telegraph pole.* **8.** to set up or establish, as an institution; found. **9.** to bring about; cause to come into existence: *to erect barriers to progress.* **10.** *Geom.* to draw or construct (a line or figure) upon a given line, base, or the like. **11.** to form or create legally (usually fol. by *into*): *to erect a territory into a state.* **12.** *Optics.* to change (an inverted image) to the normal position. **13.** *Mach.* to assemble; make ready for use. —*v.i.* **14.** to become erect; stand up or out. [1350–1400; ME < L *ērēctus* raised up (ptp. of *ērigere*), equiv. to *ē-* E- + *reg-* guide, direct (see ROYAL) + *-tus* ptp. suffix] —**e•rect′a•ble,** *adj.* —**e•rect′ly,** *adv.* —**e•rect′ness,** *n.*

—**Syn.** 1. standing, vertical. See **upright.** 6. upraise. —**Ant.** 1. reclining.

e•rec•tile (i rek′tl, -til, -tīl), *adj.* **1.** capable of being erected or set upright. **2.** *Anat.* capable of being distended with blood and becoming rigid, as tissue. [1820–30; < F *érectile.* See ERECT, -ILE] —**e•rec•til•i•ty** (i rek-til′i tē, ē′rek-), *n.*

erect′ing prism′, *Optics.* See **Dove prism.** [1870–75]

e•rec•tion (i rek′shən), *n.* **1.** the act of erecting. **2.** the state of being erected. **3.** something erected, as a building or other structure. **4.** *Physiol.* a distended and rigid state of an organ or part containing erectile tissue, esp. of the penis or the clitoris. [1495–1505; < LL *ērēctiōn-* (s. of *ērēctiō*). See ERECT, -ION]

e•rec•tive (i rek′tiv), *adj.* tending to erect. [1605–15; ERECT + -IVE]

e•rec•tor (i rek′tər), *n.* **1.** Also, **e•rect′er.** a person or thing that erects. **2.** *Anat.* a muscle that erects the body or one of its parts. [1530–40; ERECT + -OR²]

Erec′tor Set′, *Trademark.* a brand of children's building game.

E region, the region of the ionosphere in which the E layer forms. [1935–40]

-erel, var. of **-rel.**

ere•long (âr lông′, -long′), *adv.* before long; soon. [1570–80; ERE + LONG¹]

er•e•mite (er′ə mīt′), *n.* a hermit or recluse, esp. one under a religious vow. [1150–1200; ME < LL *erēmīta* HERMIT] —**er•e•mit•ic** (er′ə mit′ik), **er′e•mit′i•cal, er•e•mit•ish** (er′ə mī′tish), *adj.* —**er′e•mit′ism,** *n.*

er•e•moph•i•lous (er′ə mof′ə ləs), *adj. Ecol.* requiring a desert habitat. [< NL *eremo-* (see EREMOPHYTE) + -PHILOUS]

er•e•mo•phyte (er′ə mō fīt′, i rē′mə-), *n. Bot:* a plant that grows in desert conditions. [< NL *eremo-* (comb. form repr. Gk *érēmos* solitary, empty; see HERMIT) + -PHYTE]

ere•now (âr nou′), *adv.* before this time. [1300–50; ME *ar now.* See ERE, NOW]

E•resh•ki•gal (ä resh′kē′gäl, er′esh kig′əl), *n.* the Sumerian and Akkadian goddess of death; consort of Nergal. Also, **E•resh•ki•gel** (ä resh′kē′gel, er′esh kig′-əl).

er•e•thism (er′ə thiz′əm), *n. Physiol.* an unusual or excessive degree of irritability or stimulation in an organ or tissue. [1790–1800; < F *éréthisme* < Gk *erethismós* irritation, equiv. to *ereth(ízein)* to irritate + *-ismos* -ISM] —**er′e•this′mic, er•e•this•tic** (er′ə this′tik), **er•e•thit•ic** (er′ə thit′ik), **e•reth•ic** (ə reth′ik, e reth′-), *adj.*

Er′etz Is′rael, (er′its), the land of Israel. Also, **Er′•etz Yis•ra•el′** (*Seph. Heb.* eʀ′ets yis rä el′; *Ashk. Heb.* eʀ′its yis ʀoil′). [< Heb *ereṣ yiśrāʾēl*]

er•ev (eʀ′ev; *Eng.* er′əv), *n. Hebrew.* the day before a Jewish holiday or the Jewish Sabbath: Erev *Yom Kippur.* [ʿ*erebh* lit., eve, evening]

E•re•van (yer′ə vän′; *Russ.* yi ʀyi vän′), *n.* Yerevan.

ere•while (âr hwīl′, -wīl′), *adv. Archaic.* a while before; formerly. [1250–1300; ME; see ERE, WHILE]

Er•e•whon (er′ə hwon′, -hwən, -won′, -wən), *n.* a satirical novel (1872) by Samuel Butler.

Er•furt (eʀ′fo͝oʀt), *n.* a city in and the capital of Thuringia, in central Germany. 220,016.

erg¹ (ûrg), *n. Physics.* the centimeter-gram-second unit of work or energy, equal to the work done by a force of one dyne when its point of application moves through a distance of one centimeter in the direction of the force; 10^{-7} joule. [1870–75; < Gk *érgon* WORK]

erg² (erg), *n. Geol.* any vast area covered with sand, as parts of the Sahara Desert. [1870–75; < F < Ar *ʿirq*]

ERG, electroretinogram.

erg-, var. of **ergo-¹** before a vowel: *ergodic.*

er•gate (ûr′gāt), *n.* a worker ant. [1905–10; < Gk *ergátēs* worker, doer, producer, equiv. to *érgon* WORK + *-atēs* agent suffix]

er•ga•tive (ûr′gə tiv), *adj.* **1.** *Gram.* **a.** (in certain languages, as Basque, Eskimo, and some Caucasian languages) noting a case that indicates the subject of a transitive verb and is distinct from the case indicating the subject of an intransitive verb. **b.** similar to such a case in function or meaning, esp. in indicating an agent, as the subject *She* in *She opened the door,* in contrast to the subject *The door* in *The door opened.* **2.** *Ling.* pertaining to a type of language that has an ergative case or in which the direct object of a transitive verb has the same form as the subject of an intransitive verb. Cf. **accusative** (def. 2). —*n. Gram.* **3.** the ergative case. **4.** a word in the ergative case. **5.** a form or construction of similar function or meaning. [1945–50; < Gk *ergát(ēs)* worker (see ERGATE) + -IVE] —**er′ga•tiv′i•ty,** *n.*

-ergic, a combining form with the meanings "activated by," "sensitive to," "releasing," "resembling the effect produced by" the substance or phenomenon specified by the initial element: *dopaminergic.* [appar. orig. in ADRENERGIC and CHOLINERGIC, prob. on the model of ALLERGIC]

er•go (ûr′gō, er′gō), *conj., adv.* therefore. [1350–1400; < L]

ergo-¹, a combining form meaning "work": *ergograph.* Also, *esp. before a vowel,* **erg-.** [comb. form repr. Gk *érgon*]

CONCISE ETYMOLOGY KEY: <, descended or borrowed from; >, whence; b., blend of, blended; c., cognate with; cf., compare; deriv., derivative; equiv., equivalent; imit., imitative; obl., oblique; r., replacing; s., stem; sp., spelling, spelled; resp., respelling, respelled; trans., translation; ?, origin unknown; *, unattested; ‡, probably earlier than. See the full key inside the front cover.

ergo-², a combining form of **ergot:** *ergotoxine.* [< F]

er•god•ic (ûr god′ik), *adj. Math., Statistics.* of or pertaining to the condition that, in an interval of sufficient duration, a system will return to states that are closely similar to previous ones: the assumption of such a condition underlies statistical methods used in modern dynamics and atomic theory. [1925–30; ERG- + Gk *(h)od(ós)* way, road + -IC] —**er•go•dic•i•ty** (ûr′gə dis′i tē), *n.*

er•go•graph (ûr′gə graf′, -gräf′), *n.* an instrument that records the amount of work done when a muscle contracts. [1890–95; ERGO-¹ + -GRAPH] —**er′go•graph′ic** (ûr′gə graf′ik), *adj.*

er•gom•e•ter (ûr gom′i tər), *n.* a device designed to measure muscle power. [1875–80; ERGO-¹ + -METER] —**er•go•met•ric** (ûr′gə me′trik), *adj.*

er•go•nom•ics (ûr′gə nom′iks), *n.* (*used with a singular or plural v.*) See **human engineering.** [1945–50; ERGO- + *-nomics* (see -NOMY, -ICS) on the model of AGRONOMICS, BIONOMICS, etc.] —**er′go•nom′ic, er•go•no•met•ric** (ûr′gə nə me′trik), *adj.* —**er′go•nom′i•cal•ly,** *adv.* —**er•gon•o•mist** (ûr gon′ə mist), *n.* —**Usage.** See **-ics.**

er•go•no•vine (ûr′gə nō′vēn, -vin), *n. Pharm.* an alkaloid, $C_{19}H_{23}N_3O_2$, obtained from ergot or produced synthetically, used chiefly in obstetrics to induce uterine contractions or control uterine bleeding. [1935–40; ERGO-² + *nov-* (< L *novus* NEW) + -INE²]

er•gos•ter•ol (ûr gos′tə rōl′, -rôl), *n. Biochem.* a colorless, crystalline, water-insoluble sterol, $C_{28}H_{43}OH$, that occurs in ergot and yeast and that, when irradiated with ultraviolet light, is converted to vitamin D. [1885–90; ERGO-² + STEROL]

er•got (ûr′gət, -got), *n.* **1.** *Plant Pathol.* **a.** a disease of rye and other cereal grasses, caused by a fungus of the genus *Claviceps,* esp. *C. purpurea,* which replaces the affected grain with a long, hard, blackish sclerotial body. **b.** the sclerotial body itself. **2.** *Pharm.* the dried sclerotium of *C. purpurea,* developed on rye plants: used in the production of ergotamine and ergotoxine. [1675–85; < F: lit., a rooster's spur; OF *argos, argoz, argot* spur(s)]

er•got•a•mine (ûr got′ə mēn′, -min), *n. Pharm.* a crystalline, water-soluble polypeptide, $C_{33}H_{35}N_5O_5$, obtained from ergot, used to stimulate uterine contractions during labor and in the treatment of migraine. [1920–25; ERGOT + -AMINE]

er•got•in (ûr′gə tin), *n. Pharm.* any of various extracts of ergot used in medicine. Also, **er′got•ine.** [ERGOT + -IN²]

er•got•ism (ûr′gə tiz′əm), *n. Pathol.* a condition caused by eating rye or some other grain that is infected with ergot fungus or by taking an overdose of a medicine containing ergot, characterized by cramps, spasms, and a form of gangrene. [1850–55; ERGOT + -ISM]

er•go•tox•ine (ûr′gə tok′sēn, -sin), *n. Pharm.* a white, crystalline, water-insoluble alkaloid, $C_{35}H_{41}N_5O_6$, obtained from ergot, used chiefly in obstetrics as a uterine stimulant. [1905–10; ERGO-² + TOXINE]

Er•go•trate (ûr′gə trāt′), *Pharm., Trademark.* a brand of ergonovine.

Er•gun He (*Chin.* œʀ′gʏn′ hœ′), *Pinyin.* Argun.

Er•hard (âr′härt; *Ger.* eʀ′häʀt), *n.* **Ludwig,** 1897–1977, West German economist and government official: chancellor 1963–66.

Er•hardt (âr′härt; *Ger.* eʀ′häʀt), *n.* a male given name.

Er•ic (er′ik), *n.* **1.** See **Eric the Red. 2.** a male given name: ultimately from Germanic words meaning "one" and "ruler."

er•i•ca (er′i kə), *n.* any of numerous low-growing evergreen shrubs or small trees belonging to the genus *Erica,* of the heath family, including several species of heather. [1820–30; < NL *Erica,* L < Gk *ereíkē* heath (plant), akin to OIr *froech,* Russ *véres(k)*]

Er•i•ca (er′i kə), *n.* a female given name: derived from *Eric.*

er•i•ca•ceous (er′i kā′shəs), *adj.* belonging to the Ericaceae, the heath family of plants. Cf. **heath family.** [1880–85; < NL *Ericace(ae)* (see ERICA, -ACEAE) + -OUS]

er•i•ce•tic•o•lous (er′ə si tik′ə ləs), *adj.* requiring a heath or heathlike habitat. [< L **ericēt(um)* place where heath grows (deriv. of *erica* heath; see ERICA) + -I- + -COLOUS]

Er•ic•son (er′ik sən), *n.* **Leif** (lēf; *Icel.* lāv), fl. A.D. c1000, Norse mariner: according to Icelandic saga, discoverer of Vinland (son of Eric the Red). Old Norse, **Eiríkson.** Also, **Ericsson.**

Er•ics•son (er′ik sən), *n.* **1. John,** 1803–89, Swedish engineer and inventor; in the U.S. after 1839. **2.** See **Ericson, Leif.**

Er′ic the Red′, born A.D. c950, Norse mariner: explorer and colonizer of Greenland c985. Also called **Eric.**

E•rid•a•nus (i rid′n əs), *n., gen.* **-a•ni** (-n ī′). *Astron.* the River, a large southern constellation between Cetus and Orion, containing the bright star Achernar.

Er•i•du (er′i do͞o′), *n.* an ancient Sumerian and Babylonian city near the Euphrates in S Iraq: center for the worship of Ea; partially excavated.

E•rie (ēr′ē), *n., pl.* **E•ries,** (*esp. collectively*) **E•rie** for 3. **1. Lake,** a lake between the NE central United States and SE central Canada: the southernmost lake of the Great Lakes; Commodore Perry's defeat of the British in 1813. 239 mi. (385 km) long; 9940 sq. mi. (25,745 sq. km). **2.** a port in NW Pennsylvania, on Lake Erie. 119,123. **3.** a member of a tribe of American Indians formerly living along the southern shore of Lake Erie.

E′rie Canal′, a canal in New York between Albany and Buffalo, connecting the Hudson River with Lake Erie: completed in 1825. See illus. in next column. Cf. **New York State Barge Canal** (def. 2).

E•rig•e•na (i rij′ə nə), *n.* **Jo•han•nes Sco•tus** (jō han′-ēz skō′təs, -han′is), A.D. c810–c877, Irish philosopher and theologian.

e•rig•er•on (i rij′ə ron′, -ər ən), *n.* any composite plant of the genus *Erigeron,* having flower heads resembling those of the asters but with narrower and usually more numerous white or purple rays. [1595–1605; < L *ērigeron* the plant groundsel < Gk *ērigérōn,* equiv. to *êri* early (c. ERE) + *gérōn* (see GERONTO-)]

E•rig•o•ne (i rig′ə nē′), *n. Class. Myth.* a daughter of Clytemnestra and Aegisthus who hanged herself when Orestes was acquitted of the murder of her parents.

Er•ik (er′ik), *n.* a male given name.

Er•i•ka (er′i kə), *n.* a female given name.

Er•ik•son (er′ik sən), *n.* **Erik (Hom•burg•er)** (hom′-bûr gər), 1902–94, U.S. psychoanalyst, born in Germany.

Er•i•man•thus (er′ə man′thəs), *n.* Erymanthus.

Er•in (er′in), *n.* **1.** *Literary.* Ireland. **2.** a female given name.

er•i•na•ceous (er′ə nā′shəs), *adj. Zool.* of the hedgehog kind or family. [< L *ērināce(us)* hedgehog + -OUS]

E•rin•ys (i rin′is, i rī′nis), *n., pl.* **E•rin•y•es** (i rin′ē-ēz′). *Gk. Myth.* any of the Furies.

er•i•og•o•num (er′ē og′ə nəm, -ē ə gō′nəm), *n.* any of various plants belonging to the genus *Eriogonum,* of the buckwheat family, native to southern and western North America. Cf. **umbrella plant** (def. 2). [< NL *Eriogonum* genus name, equiv. to Gk *erio-* (comb. form of *érion* wool) + *-gonum* < Gk *-gonon,* neut. of *-gonos,* -kneed, -jointed, adj. deriv. of *gónu* knee; so called because the jointed stems are covered with hair]

er•i•o•phyl•lous (er′ē ō fil′əs), *adj. Bot.* having leaves covered with a woolly pubescence. [< Gk *erio-* (comb. form of *érion* wool) + -PHYLLOUS]

E•ris (ēr′is, er′is), *n.* the ancient Greek goddess of discord and the sister of Ares: identified with the Roman goddess Discordia.

ERISA (ə ris′ə), *n.* Employee Retirement Income Security Act.

er•is•tic (e ris′tik), *adj.* **1.** Also, **er•is′ti•cal.** pertaining to controversy or disputation; controversial. —*n.* **2.** a person who engages in disputation; controversialist. **3.** the art of disputation. [1630–40; < Gk *eristikós,* equiv. to *erist(ós)* (verbal of *erízein,* deriv. of *éris* discord) + *-ikos* -IC] —**er•is′ti•cal•ly,** *adv.*

Er•i•tre•a (er′i trē′ə; *It.* e′ʀe tʀe′ä), *n.* a province of Ethiopia, on the Red Sea: formerly an Italian colony. 1,947,600; 47,076 sq. mi. (121,927 sq. km). *Cap.:* Asmara. —**Er′i•tre′an,** *adj., n.*

E•ri•van (yer′ə vän′; *Russ.* yi ʀyi vän′), *n.* Yerevan.

erk (ûrk), *n. Brit. Slang.* **1.** an aircraftsman of the lowest rank in the Royal Air Force. **2.** a worthless, stupid person; jerk. [1920–25; earlier naval slang for any noncommissioned rank; of uncert. orig.]

Er•lan•der (eʀ′län dəʀ), *n.* **Ta•ge (Fri•tiof)** (tä′gə fʀē′chəf), 1901–85, Swedish statesman: prime minister 1946–69.

Er•lan•ger (ûr′lang ər), *n.* **1. Joseph,** 1874–1965, U.S. physiologist: Nobel prize for medicine 1944. **2.** a city in N Kentucky. 14,433.

Er′len•mey•er flask′ (ûr′lən mī′ər, er′-), a flask having a wide base, narrow neck, and conical form, convenient in laboratory experimentation for swirling liquids by hand. [1885–90; named after E. *Erlenmeyer* (d. 1909), German chemist]

erl•king (ûrl′king′), *n.* (in German and Scandinavian mythology) a spirit or personified natural power that works mischief, esp. to children. [1790–1800; < G *Erlkönig* alder (tree) king, J. G. von Herder's mistrans. of Dan *ellerkonge,* var. of *elverkonge* king of the elves]

Er•ma (ûr′mə), *n.* a female given name.

Er•man•a•ric (er man′ə rik), *n.* a fourth-century ruler in the Black Sea area: probably identical with Jormunrek.

er•mine (ûr′min), *n., pl.* **-mines,** (*esp. collectively*) **-mine,** *adj.* —*n.* **1.** an Old World weasel, *Mustela erminea,* having in its winter color phase a white coat with black at the tip of the tail. See illus. on next page. Cf. **stoat. 2.** any of various weasels having a white winter coat. **3.** the lustrous, white, winter fur of the ermine, often having fur from the animal's black tail tip inserted at intervals for contrast. **4.** the rank, position, or status of a king, peer, or judge, esp. one in certain European countries who wears, or formerly wore, a robe trimmed with ermine, as on official or state occasions. **5.** *Heraldry.* a fur, consisting of a conventional representation of tails, often with a pattern of dots, sable on argent. —*adj.* **6.** made of, covered, or adorned with ermine. [1150–1200; ME < OF (*h*)*ermine*, n. use of fem. of (*h*)*ermin* (masc. adj.) < L *Armenius*, short for *Armenius* (*mūs*) Armenian (rat)] —**er′mined,** *adj.*

ermine, *Mustela erminea,* head and body 7½ in. (19.1 cm); tail 4½ in. (11.4 cm)

-ern, an adjective suffix occurring with names of directions: *northern; southern.* [ME, OE *-erne;* c.OHG *-rōni* (as in *nordrōni* northern)]

Er·na (ûr′nə), *n.* a female given name: from an Old English word meaning "eagle."

Er·na·ku·lam (er nä′kə ləm), *n.* a city in S Kerala, in SW India, on the Malabar Coast. 213,811.

erne (ûrn), *n.* See **sea eagle.** Also, **ern.** [bef. 1000; ME *ern, arn,* OE *earn;* c. OHG *arn* (G *Aar*), MLG *arn*(*e*); akin to Lith *erēlis* eagle, Gk *órnis* bird]

Er·nest (ûr′nist), *n.* a male given name: from an Old English word meaning "vigor, intent."

Er·nes·tine (ûr′nə stēn′), *n.* a female given name: derived from *Ernest.*

Er·nie (ûr′nē), *n.* **1.** a male given name, form of **Ernest. 2.** a female given name, form of **Ernestine.**

Ernst (ûrnst; *Ger.* ernst), *n.* **1. Max** (maks; *Ger.* mäks), 1891–1976, German painter, in the U.S. 1941–49, in France 1949–76. **2.** a male given name, form of **Ernest.**

e·rode (i rōd′), *v.,* **e·rod·ed, e·rod·ing.** —*v.t.* **1.** to eat into or away; destroy by slow consumption or disintegration: *Battery acid had eroded the engine. Inflation erodes the value of our money.* **2.** to form (a gully, butte, or the like) by erosion. —*v.i.* **3.** to become eroded. [1605–15; < L *ērōdere,* equiv. to *ē-* E- + *rōdere* to gnaw] —**e·rod′i·ble, e·rod′a·ble, e·ro·si·ble** (i rō′zə bəl, -sə-), *adj.* —**e·rod′i·bil′i·ty, e·rod′a·bil′i·ty,** *n.*
—**Syn. 1.** corrode, waste, ravage, spoil. —**Ant. 1.** strengthen, reinforce.

e·rod·ent (i rōd′nt), *adj.* eroding; erosive: *the erodent power of wind.* [< L *ērōdent-* (s. of *ērōdēns*). See ERODE, -ENT]

e·rog·e·nous (i roj′ə nəs), *adj.* **1.** especially sensitive to sexual stimulation, as certain areas of the body: *erogenous zones.* **2.** arousing or tending to arouse sexual desire; sexually stimulating. Also, **er·o·gen·ic** (er′ə jen′ik). [1885–90; < Gk *érō*(*s*) EROS + -GENOUS] —**e·rog·e·ne·i·ty** (i roj′ə nē′i tē), *n.*

E·ro′i·ca Sym′phony (e rō′i kə), the third symphony (1804) in E♭, opus 55, by Beethoven.

-eroo a suffix that creates familiar, usually jocular variations of semantically more neutral nouns; normally added to monosyllabic bases, or merged with bases ending in *-er: flopperoo; smackeroo; switcheroo.* [of unclear orig.; perh. extracted from BUCKAROO, though this word appears to have been conformed to a preexisting suffix (or word), the stress and final tense vowel being otherwise unaccounted for]

E·ros (ēr′os, er′os), *n., pl.* **E·ro·tes** (ə rō′tēz) for 2, 3. **1.** the ancient Greek god of love, identified by the Romans with Cupid. **2.** a representation of this god. **3.** a winged figure of a child representing love or the power of love. **4.** (*sometimes l.c.*) physical love; sexual desire. Cf. **agape**[2] (def. 2). **5.** *Astron.* an asteroid that approaches to within 14 million miles (22½ million km) of the earth once every 44 years. **6.** *Psychiatry.* **a.** the libido. **b.** instincts for self-preservation collectively.

e·rose (i rōs′), *adj.* **1.** uneven, as if gnawed away. **2.** *Bot.* having the margin irregularly incised as if gnawed, as a leaf. [1785–95; < L *ērōsus,* ptp. of *ērōdere.* See ERODE] —**e·rose′ly,** *adv.*

e·ro·sion (i rō′zhən), *n.* **1.** the act or state of eroding; state of being eroded. **2.** the process by which the surface of the earth is worn away by the action of water, glaciers, winds, waves, etc. [1535–45; < L *ērōsiōn-* (s. of *ērōsiō*). See EROSE, -ION] —**e·ro′sion·al,** *adj.*

ero′sion sur′face, *Geol.* an eroded land surface, esp. one that is nearly flat and featureless.

e·ro·sive (i rō′siv), *adj.* serving to erode; causing erosion. [1820–30; < L *ērōs*(*us*) (see EROSE) + -IVE] —**e·ro′sive·ness, e·ro·siv′i·ty,** *n.*

e·rot·ic (i rot′ik), *adj.* Also, **e·rot′i·cal. 1.** arousing or satisfying sexual desire: *an erotic dance.* **2.** of, pertaining to, or treating of sexual love; amatory: *an erotic novel.* **3.** subject to or marked by strong sexual desire. —*n.* **4.** an erotic poem. **5.** an erotic person. [1615–25; < Gk *erōtikós* of love, caused by love, given to love, equiv. to *erōt-* (s. of *érōs*) EROS + *-ikos* -IC] —**e·rot′i·cal·ly,** *adv.*
—**Syn. 1.** sensuous, sexy, aphrodisiac, erogenous.

e·rot·i·ca (i rot′i kə), *n.* (*used with a singular or plural v.*) literature or art dealing with sexual love. [1850–55; < Gk, neut. pl. of *erōtikós* EROTIC]

e·rot·i·cism (i rot′ə siz′əm), *n.* **1.** the sexual or erotic quality or character of something. **2.** the use of sexually arousing or suggestive symbolism, settings, allusions, situations, etc., in art, literature, drama, or the like. **3.** the condition of being sexually aroused or excited. **4.** sexual drive or tendency. **5.** an abnormally persistent sexual drive. Also, **er·o·tism** (er′ə tiz′əm). [1880–85; EROTIC + -ISM] —**e·rot′i·cist,** *n.*

e·rot·i·cize (i rot′ə sīz′), *v.t.,* **-cized, -ciz·ing.** to render or make erotic: *a painting eroticized with voluptuous figures and symbols.* Also, *esp. Brit.,* **e·rot′i·cise′.** [1910–15; EROTIC + -IZE] —**e·rot′i·ci·za′tion,** *n.*

eroto-, a combining form with the meaning "sexual desire," used in the formation of compound words: *erotomania.* [< Gk, comb. form, equiv. to *erōt-* (s. of *érōs*) EROS + -o- -O-]

e·ro·to·gen·e·sis (i rō′tə jen′ə sis, i rot′ə-), *n.* the arousal of erotic impulses. [< NL; see EROTO-, -GENESIS]

e·ro·to·gen·ic (i rō′tə jen′ik, i rot′ə-), *adj.* erogenous. [1905–10; EROTO- + -GENIC]

e·ro·to·ma·ni·a (i rō′tə mā′nē ə, -mān′yə, i rot′ə-), *n. Psychiatry.* abnormally strong or persistent sexual desire. [1870–75; EROTO- + -MANIA] —**e·ro·to·ma·ni·ac** (i rō′tə mā′nē ak′, i rot′ə-), *n.* —**e·ro·to·man·ic** (i rō′tə man′ik, i rot′ə-), *adj.*

ERP, See **European Recovery Program.** Also, **E.R.P.**

err (ûr, er), *v.i.* **1.** to go astray in thought or belief; be mistaken; be incorrect. **2.** to go astray morally; sin: *To err is human.* **3.** *Archaic.* to deviate from the true course, aim, or purpose. [1275–1325; ME *erren* < OF *errer* < L *errāre;* akin to Goth *airzjan,* OHG *irrôn,* G *irren*] —**err′a·bil′i·ty,** *n.* —**err′a·ble,** *adj.*
—**Syn. 2.** transgress, lapse.

er·ran·cy (er′ən sē, ûr′-), *n., pl.* **-cies. 1.** the state or an instance of erring. **2.** tendency to err. [1615–25; < L *errantia* a wandering. See ERRANT, -CY]

er·rand (er′ənd), *n.* **1.** a short and quick trip to accomplish a specific purpose, as to buy something, deliver a package, or convey a message, often for someone else. **2.** the purpose of such a trip: *He finished his errands.* **3.** a special mission or function entrusted to a messenger; commission. [bef. 900; ME *erande,* OE *ǣrende;* c. OHG *ārunti;* cf. OE *ār* messenger, Goth *airus*]
—**Syn. 1, 2.** mission, task, assignment, chore.

er·rant (er′ənt), *adj.* **1.** deviating from the regular or proper course; erring; straying. **2.** journeying or traveling, as a medieval knight in quest of adventure; roving adventurously. **3.** moving in an aimless or lightly changing manner: *an errant breeze.* [1300–50; ME *erraunt* < MF, OF *errant,* prp. of *errer, edrer* to travel < VL **iterāre* to journey, for LL *itinerārī,* deriv. of *iter,* s. *itiner-* journey (see ITINERARY); confused with MF *errant,* prp. of *errer* to ERR] —**er′rant·ly,** *adv.*

er·rant·ry (er′ən trē), *n., pl.* **-ries.** conduct or performance like that of a knight-errant. [1645–55; ERRANT + -RY]

er·ra·re hu·ma·num est (er rä′re hōō mä′nōōm est′; *Eng.* e râr′ē hyōō mā′nəm est′), *Latin.* to err is human.

er·ra·ta (i rä′tə, i rā′-, i rat′ə), *n.* **1.** pl. of **erratum. 2.** a list of errors and their corrections inserted, usually on a separate page or slip of paper, in a book or other publication; corrigenda. [1625–35]
—**Usage.** ERRATA is originally the plural of the singular Latin noun *erratum.* Like many such borrowed nouns (*agenda; candelabra*), it came by the mid-17th century to be used as a singular noun, meaning "a list of errors or corrections to be made (in a book)." Despite objections by some to this singular use, it is common in standard English: *The errata begins on page 237.* When ERRATA clearly means "errors," it takes plural verbs and pronouns: *Although errata were frequent in the first printing, most of them were corrected in subsequent printings.* As a singular noun, ERRATA has developed an English plural form ERRATAS, which is rarely used.

er·rat·ic (i rat′ik), *adj.* **1.** deviating from the usual or proper course in conduct or opinion; eccentric; queer: *erratic behavior.* **2.** having no certain or definite course; wandering; not fixed: *erratic winds.* **3.** *Geol.* noting or pertaining to a boulder or the like carried by glacial ice and deposited some distance from its place of origin. **4.** (of a lichen) having no attachment to the surface on which it grows. —*n.* **5.** an erratic or eccentric person. **6.** *Geol.* an erratic boulder or the like. [1325–75; ME < L *errāticus,* equiv. to *errāt*(*us*) (ptp. of *errāre* to ERR) + *-icus* -IC] —**er·rat′i·cal·ly,** *adv.* —**er·rat′i·cism,** *n.*
—**Syn. 1.** unpredictable, unstable, capricious. —**Ant. 1.** consistent, regular, stable.

er·ra·tum (i rä′təm, i rā′-, i rat′əm), *n., pl.* **-ta** (-tə). **1.** an error in writing or printing. **2.** a statement of an error and its correction inserted, usually on a separate page or slip of paper, in a book or other publication; corrigendum. [1580–90; < L, n. use of *errātum* wandered, erred, strayed (neut. ptp. of *errāre*). See ERR, -ATE[1]]
—**Usage.** See **errata.**

er·rhine (er′īn, er′in), *Med.* —*adj.* **1.** designed to be snuffed into the nose. **2.** occasioning discharges from the nose. —*n.* **3.** a medicine to be snuffed up the nostrils to promote sneezing and increased discharges. [1595–1605; < NL *errhinum* < Gk *érrinon*]

err·ing (ûr′ing, er′-), *adj.* **1.** going astray; in error; wrong. **2.** sinning. [1300–50; ME; r. ME *errand.* See ERR, -ING[2]] —**err′ing·ly,** *adv.*

Er·rol (er′əl), *n.* a male given name.

erron., **1.** erroneous. **2.** erroneously.

er·ro·ne·ous (ə rō′nē əs, e rō′-), *adj.* **1.** containing error; mistaken; incorrect; wrong: *an erroneous answer.* **2.** straying from what is moral, decent, proper, etc. [1350–1400; ME < L *errōneus* straying, equiv. to *errōn-* (s. of *errō*) wanderer (deriv. of *err-;* see ERR) + *-eus* -EOUS] —**er·ro′ne·ous·ly,** *adv.* —**er·ro′ne·ous·ness,** *n.*
—**Syn. 1.** inaccurate, untrue, false. —**Ant. 1.** accurate.

er·ror (er′ər), *n.* **1.** a deviation from accuracy or correctness; a mistake, as in action or speech: *His speech contained several factual errors.* **2.** belief in something untrue; the holding of mistaken opinions. **3.** the condition of believing what is not true: *in error about the date.* **4.** a moral offense; wrongdoing; sin. **5.** *Baseball.* a misplay that enables a base runner to reach base safely or advance a base, or a batter to have a turn at bat prolonged, as the dropping of a ball batted in the air, the fumbling of a batted or thrown ball, or the throwing of a wild ball, but not including a passed ball or wild pitch. **6.** *Math.* the difference between the observed or approximately determined value and the true value of a quantity. **7.** *Law.* **a.** a mistake in a matter of fact or law in a case tried in a court of record. **b.** See **writ of error. 8.** *Philately.* a stamp distinguished by an error or errors in design, engraving, selection of inks, or setting up of the printing apparatus. Cf. **freak**[1] (def. 5), **variety** (def. 8). [1250–1300; ME *errour* < L *errōr-* (s. of *error*), equiv. to *err-* ERR + *-or* -OR[1]] —**er′ror·less,** *adj.* —**er′ror·less·ly,** *adv.*
—**Syn. 1.** blunder, slip, oversight. See **mistake. 4.** fault, transgression, trespass, misdeed.

er′ror anal′ysis, *Ling.* the systematic study of deviations from target-language norms in the course of second-language acquisition, esp. in terms of the learner's developing interlanguage. [1960–65]

er′ror coin′, *Numis.* a coin showing evidence of a mistake in its manufacture.

er′ror of clo′sure, *Survey.* **1.** the amount by which a closed traverse fails to satisfy the requirements of a true mathematical figure, as the length of line joining the true and computed position of the same point. **2.** the ratio of this linear error to the perimeter of the traverse. **3.** (for angles) the amount by which the sum of the observed angles fails to equal the true sum. **4.** (in leveling) the amount by which an elevation determined by a series of levels fails to agree with an established elevation. Also called **closing error.**

ers (ûrs, ärs), *n.* ervil. [MF < OPr < LL *ervus,* var. of L *ervum.* See ERVIL]

ERS, Emergency Radio Service. Also, **E.R.S.**

-ers, a semantically empty suffix that creates informal variations of more neutral nouns and adjectives by processes of truncation identical to those of **-er**[7] (*champers; preggers; starkers*); unlike that suffix, however, **-ers** is apparently productive, and words formed with it do not appear to belong to a restricted linguistic register, as university slang. [perh. a conflation of -ER[7] with the final element of BONKERS and CRACKERS (unless these words themselves contain this suffix); cf. -S[3]]

er·satz (er′zäts, -säts, er zäts′, -säts′), *adj.* **1.** serving as a substitute; synthetic; artificial: *an ersatz coffee made from grain.* —*n.* **2.** an artificial substance or article used to replace something natural or genuine; a substitute. [1870–75; < G *Ersatz* a substitute (deriv. of *ersetzen* to replace)]

Erse (ûrs), *n.* **1.** Gaelic, esp. Scots Gaelic. —*adj.* **2.** of or pertaining to Gaelic, esp. Scots Gaelic.

Er·skine (ûr′skin), *n.* **1. John** (*Erskine of Carnock*), 1695–1768, Scottish writer on law. **2. John,** 1879–1951, U.S. novelist, poet, and essayist. **3.** a male given name.

erst (ûrst), *adv. Archaic.* before the present time; formerly. [bef. 1000; ME *erest,* OE *ǣrest* (c. OHG *ērist,* G *erst*), equiv. to *ǣr* ERE + *-est* -EST[1]]

erst·while (ûrst′hwīl′, -wīl′), *adj.* **1.** former; of times past: *erstwhile friends.* —*adv.* **2.** *Archaic.* formerly; erst. [1560–70; ERST + WHILE]
—**Syn. 1.** past, bygone, previous. —**Ant. 1.** current, present.

ERT, estrogen replacement therapy.

Er·te·bøl·le (er′tə bol′ə, -bul′ə), *adj.* of, pertaining to, or characteristic of a late Mesolithic culture of the western Baltic coast associated with kitchen middens and having pottery in its later phases. [1925–30; after the type site, on the Jutland coast]

ERTS, Earth Resources Technology Satellite.

er·ub (âr′ōōv, er′-; *Seph. Heb.* e rōōv′; *Ashk. Heb.* ā′rōōv), *n., pl.* **er·u·bin** (âr′ōō vin′, er′-; *Seph. Heb.* e rōō vēn′; *Ashk. Heb.* ā rōō′vin), **er·ubs.** *Judaism.* eruv.

er·u·bes·cent (er′ōō bes′ənt), *adj.* becoming red or reddish; blushing. [1730–40; < L *ērubēscent-* (s. of *ērubēscēns*), prp. of *ērubēscere.* See E-, RUBESCENT] —**er′u·bes′cence,** *n.*

e·ru′cic ac′id (i rōō′sik), *Chem.* a solid fatty acid, a homologue of oleic acid, derived from oils of mustard seed and rapeseed. [1865–70; < NL *Eruc*(*a*) the rocket genus (L *ērūca;* cf. ROCKET[2]) + -IC]

e·ru·ci·form (i rōō′sə fôrm′), *adj.* caterpillarlike. [1870–75; < L *ērūc*(*a*) caterpillar + -I- + -FORM]

e·ruct (i rukt′), *v.t., v.i.* **1.** to belch forth, as gas from the stomach. **2.** to emit or issue violently, as matter from a volcano. [1660–70; < L *ēructāre* to vomit, discharge violently, freq. of *ērūgere*]

e·ruc·tate (i ruk′tāt), *v.t., v.i.,* **-tat·ed, -tat·ing.** to eruct. [1630–40; < L *ēructātus* discharged, sent forth. See ERUCT, -ATE[1]] —**e·ruc·ta·tion** (i ruk tā′shən, ē′ruk-), *n.* —**e·ruc·ta·tive** (i ruk′tə tiv), *adj.*

er·u·dite (er′yōō dīt′, er′ōō-), *adj.* characterized by great knowledge; learned or scholarly: *an erudite professor; an erudite commentary.* [1375–1425; late ME < L *ērudītus,* equiv. to *ērud-* (*ē-* E- + *rud-* unformed, rough, RUDE) + *-ītus* -ITE[2]] —**er′u·dite′ly,** *adv.* —**er′u·dite′ness,** *n.* —**Syn.** educated, knowledgeable; wise, sapient.

er·u·di·tion (er′yōō dish′ən, er′ōō-), *n.* knowledge acquired by study, research, etc.; learning; scholarship. [1350–1400; ME < L *ērudītiōn-* (s. of *ērudītiō*) an instruction. See ERUDITE, -ION] —**er′u·di′tion·al,** *adj.*
—**Syn.** See **learning.**

e·rum·pent (i rum′pənt), *adj.* **1.** bursting forth. **2.** (of fungi or algae) prominent; projecting from or bursting through host tissue. [1640–50; < L *ērumpent-* (s. of

CONCISE PRONUNCIATION KEY: *act, cāpe, dâre, pärt; set, ēqual; if, īce; ox, ōver, ôrder, oil, bo͝ok, bo͞ot, out; up, ûrge; child; sing; shoe; thin, that;* zh as in *treasure.* ə = *a* as in *alone, e* as in *system, i* as in *easily, o* as in *gallop, u* as in *circus;* ᵊ as in *fire* (fīᵊr), *hour* (ouᵊr). l and n can serve as syllabic consonants, as in *cradle* (krād′l), and *button* (but′n). See the full key inside the front cover.

ērumpēns), prp. of *ērumpere,* equiv. to *ē-* E- + *rumpere* to break; see -ENT]

e•rupt (i rupt′), *v.i.* 1. to burst forth: *Molten lava erupted from the top of the volcano.* 2. (of a volcano, geyser, etc.) to eject matter. 3. to break out of a pent-up state, usually in a sudden and violent manner: *Words of anger erupted from her.* 4. to break out in a skin rash: *Hives erupted all over his face and hands.* 5. (of teeth) to grow through surrounding hard and soft tissues and become visible in the mouth. —*v.t.* 6. to release violently; burst forth with: *She erupted angry words.* 7. (of a volcano, geyser, etc.) to eject (matter). [1650–60; < L *ēruptus* burst forth, broken out (ptp. of *ērumpere*), equiv. to *ē-* E- + *ruptus,* ptp. of *rumpere* to break, RUPTURE] —**e•rupt′i•ble,** *adj.*
—**Syn. 1, 6.** vent.

e•rup•tion (i rup′shən), *n.* 1. an issuing forth suddenly and violently; outburst; outbreak. 2. *Geol.* the ejection of molten rock, steam, etc., as from a volcano or geyser. 3. something that is erupted or ejected, as molten rock, volcanic ash, or steam. 4. *Pathol.* a. the breaking out of a rash or the like. b. a rash or exanthem. [1375–1425; late ME < L *ēruptiōn-* (s. of *ēruptiō*). See ERUPT, -ION] —**e•rup′tion•al,** *adj.*

e•rup•tive (i rup′tiv), *adj.* 1. bursting forth, or tending to burst forth. 2. pertaining to or of the nature of an eruption. 3. *Geol.* noting a rock formed by the eruption of molten material. 4. *Pathol.* causing or accompanied by an eruption or rash. —*n.* 5. *Geol.* an eruptive rock. [1640–50; < F *éruptif.* See ERUPT, -IVE] —**e•rup′tive•ly,** *adv.* —**e•rup•tiv′i•ty, e•rup′tive•ness,** *n.*

er•uv (âr′o͝ov, er′-; *Seph. Heb.* e′ʀo͞ov; *Ashk. Heb.* ā′ʀo͝ov), *n., pl.* **er•u•vin** (âr′o͞o vin′, er′-; *Seph. Heb.* e ʀo͞o vēn′; *Ashk. Heb.* ā ʀo͞o′vin), **er•uvs.** *Judaism.* 1. any of three rabbinical enactments that ease certain Sabbath restrictions. 2. a line delineating an area in which Orthodox Jews may carry on certain activities normally forbidden on the Sabbath. Also, **erub.** [< Heb *'ērūbh* lit., mixture, mixing]

E.R.V., English Revised Version.

er•vil (ûr′vil), *n.* a vetch, *Vicia ervilia,* grown in Europe for forage. Also called **ers.** [1545–55; < L *ervilia,* akin to *ervum* bitter vetch; prob. of non-IE orig.]

Er•vin (ûr′vin), *n.* 1. **Samuel James, Jr.** (*Sam*), 1896–1985, U.S. jurist and politician: senator 1954–74. 2. a male given name.

Er•vine (ûr′vin), *n.* **St. John Greer** (grēr), 1883–1971, Irish dramatist and novelist.

Er•ving (ûr′ving), *n.* **Julius Winfield** (*"Dr. J"*), born 1950, U.S. basketball player.

Er•win (ûr′win), *n.* a male given name: from Old English words meaning "boar" and "friend."

Er•win•i•a (ûr win′ē ə), *n. Bacteriol.* a genus of rod-shaped bacteria that are pathogenic for plants. [< NL; named after *Erwin* F. Smith (1854–1927), American pathologist; see -IA]

-ery, a suffix of nouns denoting occupation, business, calling or condition, place or establishment, goods or products, things collectively, qualities, actions, etc.: *archery; bakery; cutlery; fishery; trickery; witchery.* [ME < OF *-erie,* equiv. to *-ier* -ER[2] + *-ie* -Y[3]]

Er•y•man′thi•an boar′ (er′ə man′thē ən), *Class. Myth.* a savage boar that plagued Arcadia and was captured by Hercules.

Er•y•man•thus (er′ə man′thəs), *n.* a mountain in S Greece, in the NW Peloponnesus. 7295 ft. (2225 m). Also, **Erimanthus, Er•y•man•thos** (er′ə man′thəs, -thos; *Gk.* e ʀē′män thôs). Also called **Olonos.**

er•y•sip•e•las (er′ə sip′ə ləs, ēr′ə-), *n.* 1. *Pathol.* an acute, febrile infectious disease, caused by a specific streptococcus, characterized by diffusely spreading deep-red inflammation of the skin or mucous membranes. 2. Also called **swine erysipelas.** *Vet. Pathol.* a disease of swine, caused by the organism *Erysipelothrix rhusiopathiae,* characterized by urticaria, vegetative endocarditis, arthritis, and sometimes septicemia. [1350–1400; ME *erisipila* < L *erysipelas* < Gk, equiv. to *erysi-* (prob. akin to *erythrós* red) + *-pelas* prob. skin (akin to *pélma* sole of the foot; cf. L *pellis* skin)] —**er•y•si•pel•a•tous** (er′ə si pel′ə təs, ēr′-), *adj.*

er•y•sip•e•loid (er′ə sip′ə loid′, ēr′ə-), *n. Pathol.* a disease of humans contracted by contact with the bacillus *Erysipelothrix rhusiopathiae,* which causes erysipelas in swine, characterized by a painful local ulcer, generally on one of the hands. [1885–90; ERISIPEL(AS) + -OID]

er•y•sip•e•lo•thrix (er′ə sip′ə lō thriks′, ēr′ə-), *n. Bacteriol.* any of several rod-shaped, facultatively anaerobic bacteria of the genus *Erysipelothrix,* often forming long filaments and occurring as parasites on mammals, birds, and fish. [< NL, irreg. < Gk *erysipel(as)* ERYSIPELAS, + *-o-* -O- + *thrix* a hair]

er•y•the•ma (er′ə thē′mə), *n. Pathol.* abnormal redness of the skin due to local congestion, as in inflammation. [1760–70; < NL < Gk, equiv. to *eryth(rós)* red + *-ēma* n. suffix] —**er•y•the•mat•ic** (er′ə thi mat′ik), **er•y•them•a•tous** (er′ə them′ə təs, -thē′mə-), **er′y•the′mic, er′y•the′mal,** *adj.*

er•y•thor•bate (er′ə thôr′bāt), *n. Chem.* a salt of erythorbic acid. [1960–65; ERYTHRORB(IC ACID) + -ATE[2]]

er′y•thor′bic ac′id (er′ə thôr′bik, er′-), *Chem.* a crystalline compound, $C_6H_8O_6$, soluble in water: used as an antioxidant for food and as a reducing agent in photography. [1960–65; ERYTH(R)- + (ASC)ORBIC]

e•ryth•rism (i rith′riz əm, er′ə thriz′əm), *n.* abnormal redness, as of plumage or hair. [1885–90; ERYTHR- + -ISM] —**er•y•thris•mal** (er′ə thriz′məl), **er•y•thris•tic** (er′ə thris′tik), *adj.*

e•ryth•rite (i rith′rīt, er′ə thrīt′), *n.* 1. a mineral, hydrous cobalt arsenate, $Co_3As_2O_8 \cdot 8H_2O$, occurring as a powdery, usually red incrustation on cobalt minerals; cobalt bloom. 2. erythritol. [1835–45; ERYTHR- + -ITE[1]]

e•ryth•ri•tol (i rith′ri tôl′, -tol′), *n. Chem., Pharm.* a white, crystalline, water-soluble, sweet-tasting, tetrahydroxyl compound, $C_4H_{10}O_4$, related to the carbohydrates, obtained from certain lichens and used for coronary vasodilation and in the treatment of hypertension. [1890–95; ERYTHRITE + -OL[1]]

erythro-, a combining form meaning "red," used in the formation of compound words: *erythrocyte.* Also, *esp. before a vowel,* **erythr-.** [< Gk *erythrós* red, reddish]

e•ryth•ro•blast (i rith′rə blast′), *n. Anat.* a nucleated cell in the bone marrow from which red blood cells develop. [1885–90; ERYTHRO- + -BLAST] —**e•ryth′ro•blas′tic,** *adj.*

e•ryth•ro•blas•to•sis (i rith′rō bla stō′sis), *n. Pathol.* 1. the presence of erythroblasts in the blood. 2. Also called **eryth′roblasto′sis fe•ta′lis** (fi tal′is), **erythroblasto′sis ne•o•na•to′rum** (nē′ə nə tôr′əm, -tōr′-). this condition in the fetus or newborn, usually caused by an Rh incompatibility between mother and baby. [1930–35; ERYTHROBLAST + -OSIS] —**e•ryth•ro•blas•tot•ic** (i rith′rō bla stot′ik), *adj.*

E•ryth•ro•cin (i rith′rə sin), *Pharm., Trademark.* a brand of erythromycin.

e•ryth•ro•cyte (i rith′rə sīt′), *n. Physiol.* See **red blood cell.** [1890–95; ERYTHRO- + -CYTE] —**e•ryth•ro•cyt•ic** (i rith′rə sit′ik), *adj.*

e•ryth•ro•cy•tom•e•ter (i rith′rō sī tom′i tər), *n.* an apparatus used for counting red blood cells. [ERYTHROCYTE + -O- + -METER] —**e•ryth′ro•cy•tom′e•try,** *n.*

e•ryth•ro•my•cin (i rith′rə mī′sin), *n. Pharm.* an antibiotic, $C_{37}H_{67}NO_{13}$, produced by an actinomycete, *Streptomyces erythraeus,* used chiefly in the treatment of diseases caused by many Gram-positive and some Gram-negative organisms. [1950–55; ERYTHRO- + -MYCIN]

e•ryth•ro•pho•bi•a (i rith′rə fō′bē ə), *n. Psychiatry.* 1. an abnormal fear of the color red. 2. extreme fear of blushing. [1890–95; < NL; see ERYTHRO-, -PHOBIA]

e•ryth•ro•poi•e•sis (i rith′rō poi ē′sis), *n.* the production of red blood cells. [1915–20; ERYTHRO(CYTE) + -POIESIS] —**e•ryth•ro•poi•et•ic** (i rith′rō poi et′ik), *adj.*

e•ryth•ro•poi•e•tin (i rith′rō poi′i tn, -poi ēt′n), *n. Biochem.* a hormone that stimulates production of red blood cells and hemoglobin in the bone marrow, synthesized in response to low levels of oxygen in the tissues. [1945–50; ERYTHROPOIET(IC) + -IN[2]]

er•y•throp•sin (er′ə throp′sin), *n. Biochem.* rhodopsin. [ERYTHRO- + (RHODO)PSIN]

Erz′ Moun′tains (ârts), a mountain range in central Europe, on the boundary between Germany and the Czech Republic. Highest peak, Keilberg, 4080 ft. (1245 m). German, **Erz•ge•bir•ge** (eʀts′gə bēʀ′gə).

Er•zu•rum (eʀ′zə ʀo͞om′), *n.* a city in NE Turkey in Asia. 162,925. Also, **Er′ze•rum′.**

Es, *Symbol, Chem.* einsteinium.

-es[1], a plural suffix occurring in loanwords from Greek: *Hyades.* [< Gk *-es*]

-es[2], var. of **-s[2]** in verbs ending in *s, z, ch, sh,* or post-consonantal *y: passes; buzzes; pitches; dashes; studies.*

-es[3], var. of **-s[3]** in nouns ending in *s, z, ch, sh,* or post-consonantal *y,* and in nouns in *f* with *v* in the plural: *losses; fuzzes; riches; ashes; babies; sheaves.*

E.S., Education Specialist.

ESA, See **European Space Agency.**

E•sa•ki (i sä′kē), *n.* **Leo,** born 1925, Japanese physicist, in the U.S. since 1960: Nobel prize 1973.

E•sar•had•don (ē′sär had′n), *n.* (*Assur-akh-iddin*), died 669 B.C., king of Assyria 681–669 B.C.

E•sau (ē′sô), *n.* a son of Isaac and Rebekah, twin brother of Jacob, to whom he sold his birthright. Gen. 25:21–25.

es•bat (es′bat), *n.* a convocation of witches. [1965–70; appar. a contemporary borrowing of OF *esbat* amusement, diversion (F *ébat*), deriv. of *esbattre* frolic, equiv. to *es-* EX- + *battre* < L *battuere* pound, beat; cf. obs. E *esbatement* amusement]

Es•bjerg (es′byeʀ), *n.* a seaport in SW Denmark. 68,097.

Es•bo (es′bo͞o), *n.* Swedish name of **Espoo.**

Esc., escudo; escudos.

esc., escrow.

es•ca•drille (es′kə dril′, es′kə dril′; *Fr.* es kA dʀē′yᵊ), *n., pl.* **-drilles** (-drilz′, -drilz′; *Fr.* -dʀē′yᵊ). 1. a squadron or divisional unit of airplanes: *the Lafayette Escadrille of World War I.* 2. *Obs.* a small naval squadron. [1910–15; < F: flotilla, MF < Sp *escuadrilla,* dim. of *escuadra* SQUADRON]

Es•ca•drille A•mér•i•caine (es′kə dril′ ə mer′i-kān′; *Fr.* es kA dʀē′yᵊ A mā ʀē ken′). See under **Lafayette Escadrille.**

es•ca•lade (es′kə lād′, -läd′, es′kə lād′, -läd′), *n., v.,* **-lad•ed, -lad•ing.** —*n.* 1. a scaling or mounting by means of ladders, esp. in an assault upon a fortified place. —*v.t.* 2. to mount, pass, or enter by means of ladders. [1590–1600; < MF < OPr *escalada, equiv. to *escal(ar)* to SCALE[3] + *-ada* -ADE[1]] —**es′ca•lad′er,** *n.*

es•ca•late (es′kə lāt′), *v.t., v.i.,* **-lat•ed, -lat•ing.** 1. to increase in intensity, magnitude, etc.: *to escalate a war; a time when prices escalate.* 2. to raise, lower, rise, or descend on or as if on an escalator. [1920–25; back formation from ESCALATOR] —**es′ca•la′tion,** *n.* —**es•ca•la•to•ry** (es′kə lə tôr′ē, -tōr′ē), *adj.*
—**Syn.** 1. advance, mount, swell. —**Ant.** 1. lower, decrease, fall.
—**Pronunciation.** See **percolate.**

es•ca•la•tor (es′kə lā′tər), *n.* 1. Also called **moving staircase, moving stairway.** a continuously moving stairway on an endless loop for carrying passengers up or down. 2. a means of rising or descending, increasing or decreasing, etc., esp. by stages: *the social escalator.* 3. See **escalator clause.** —*adj.* 4. of, pertaining to, or included in an escalator clause: *The union demands escalator protection of wages.* [1895–1900, *Amer.*; formerly a trademark; perh. ESCAL(ADE) + (ELEV)ATOR]

es′calator clause′, a provision in a contract calling for adjustments, usually increases, in charges, wages, or other payments, based on fluctuations in production costs, the cost of living, or other variables. Also called, *esp. Brit.,* **escala′tion clause′.** [1925–30, *Amer.*]

es•cal•lop (e skol′əp, e skal′-), *v.t.* 1. to bake (food cut into pieces) in a sauce or other liquid, often with crumbs on top; scallop. 2. to bake (fish, potatoes, etc.) in scallop shells. —*n.* 3. scallop. 4. *Heraldry.* a representation of a scallop shell, traditionally associated with pilgrimages and crusades. Also, **es•cal′op** (for defs. 1–3). [1425–75; late ME < MF, OF *escalope, escalipe* shell (of a nut, snail, etc.), perh. < MD *scelpe, scolpe* mollusk shell (D *schelp;* perh. akin to SCALP)]

es•ca•lope (es′kə lōp′; *Fr.* es kA lôp′), *n., pl.* **-lopes** (-lōps′; *Fr.* -lôp′). *French Cookery.* 1. scallop (def. 5). 2. a dish of thinly sliced meat, fish, potatoes, etc., baked in a sauce and often topped with bread crumbs. [1600–10; < F; see ESCALLOP; relation of the sense "thin slice" to the OF meaning "shell (of a nut, snail, etc.)" is uncert.]

Es•ca•na•ba (es′kə nä′bə), *n.* a city in NW Michigan, in the Upper Peninsula. 14,355.

es•ca•pade (es′kə pād′, es′kə pād′), *n.* 1. a reckless adventure or wild prank. 2. an escape from confinement or restraint. [1645–55; < F < Sp *escapada,* equiv. to *escap(ar)* to ESCAPE + *-ada* -ADE[1]]
—**Syn.** caper, antic, caprice.

es•cape (i skāp′), *v.,* **-caped, -cap•ing,** *n., adj.* —*v.i.* 1. to slip or get away, as from confinement or restraint; gain or regain liberty: *to escape from jail.* 2. to slip away from pursuit or peril; avoid capture, punishment, or any threatened evil. 3. to issue from a confining enclosure, as a fluid. 4. to slip away; fade: *The words escaped from memory.* 5. *Bot.* (of an originally cultivated plant) to grow wild. 6. (of a rocket, molecule, etc.) to achieve escape velocity. —*v.t.* 7. to slip away from or elude (pursuers, captors, etc.): *He escaped the police.* 8. to succeed in avoiding (any threatened or possible danger or evil): *She escaped capture.* 9. to elude (one's memory, notice, search, etc.). 10. to fail to be noticed or recollected by (a person): *Her reply escapes me.* 11. (of a sound or utterance) to slip from or be expressed by (a person, one's lips, etc.) inadvertently. —*n.* 12. an act or instance of escaping. 13. the fact of having escaped. 14. a means of escaping: *We used the tunnel as an escape.* 15. avoidance of reality: *She reads mystery stories as an escape.* 16. leakage, as of water or gas, from a pipe or storage container. 17. *Bot.* a plant that originated in cultivated stock and is now growing wild. 18. *Physics, Rocketry.* the act of achieving escape velocity. 19. *Computers.* a key (frequently labeled ESC) found on microcomputer keyboards and used for any of various functions, as to interrupt a command or move from one part of a program to another. —*adj.* 20. for or providing an escape: *an escape route.* [1250–1300; ME *escapen, ascapen* < ONF *escaper* (F *échapper*) < VL *excappāre, v. deriv. (with *ex-* EX-[1]) of LL *cappa* hooded cloak (see CAP[1])] —**es•cap′a•ble,** *adj.* —**es•cape′less,** *adj.* —**es•cap′er,** *n.* —**es•cap′ing•ly,** *adv.*
—**Syn.** 1. flee, abscond, decamp. 7. dodge, flee, avoid. ESCAPE, ELUDE, EVADE mean to keep free of something. To ESCAPE is to succeed in keeping away from danger, pursuit, observation, etc.: *to escape punishment.* To ELUDE implies baffling pursuers or slipping through an apparently tight net: *The fox eluded the hounds.* To EVADE is to turn aside from or go out of reach of a person or thing: *to evade the police.* See also **avoid.** 12. flight.

escape′ art′ist, 1. an entertainer expert in getting out of handcuffs, ropes, chains, trunks, or other confining devices. 2. an inmate of a prison who has a reputation for being able to escape confinement. [1940–45]

escape′ clause′, a provision in a contract that enables a party to terminate contractual obligations in specified circumstances. [1940–45]

es•cap•ee (i skā pē′, es′kā-), *n.* a person who escapes, esp. from a prison or other place of detention. [1860–65; ESCAPE + -EE]

escape′ hatch′, 1. a hatch used for emergency escape, as from a submarine or aircraft. 2. a means of avoiding a troublesome situation; a ready or handy way out. [1920–25]

escape′ mech′anism, *Psychol.* a means of avoiding an unpleasant life situation, as daydreaming. [1930–35]

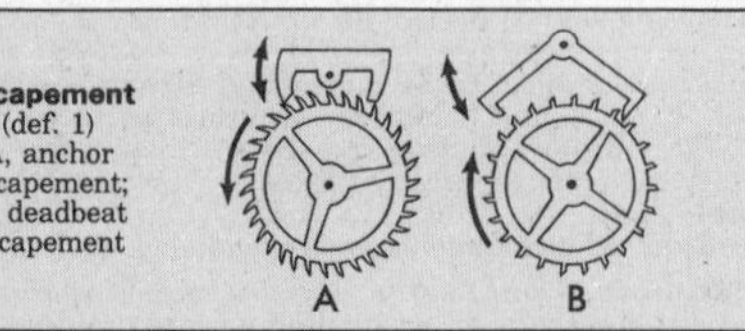

escapement (def. 1) A, anchor escapement; B, deadbeat escapement

es•cape•ment (i skāp′mənt), *n.* 1. *Horol.* the portion of a watch or clock that measures beats and controls the speed of the going train. Cf. **anchor escapement, deadbeat** (def. 1), **lever escapement.** 2. a mechanism for regulating the motion of a typewriter carriage, consisting of pawls and a toothed wheel or rack. 3. a mechanism in a piano that causes a hammer to fall back into rest position immediately after striking a string. 4. an act of escaping. 5. *Archaic.* a way of escape; outlet. [1730–40; ESCAPE + -MENT (calque of F *échappement*)]

CONCISE ETYMOLOGY KEY: <, descended or borrowed from; >, whence; b., blend of, blended; c., cognate with; cf., compare; deriv., derivative; equiv., equivalent; imit., imitative; obl., oblique; r., replacing; s., stem; sp., spelling, spelled; resp., respelling, respelled; trans., translation; ?, origin unknown; *, unattested; ‡, probably earlier than. See the full key inside the front cover.

escape′ment er′ror, *Horol.* loss of isochronism in the movement of a pendulum as a result of its relation to the escapement.

escape′ veloc′ity, *Physics, Rocketry.* the minimum speed that an object at a given distance from a gravitating body must have so that it will continue to move away from the body instead of orbiting about it. [1950–55]

es•cape•way (i skāp′wā′), *n.* **1.** a passage designed for the purpose of escape or through which escape is possible. **2.** See **fire escape.** [ESCAPE + WAY]

escape′ wheel′, *Horol.* a toothed wheel for regulating a going train to which it is geared, engaging intermittently with the pallets of a pendulum or balance mechanism in such a way as to cause the mechanism to oscillate rhythmically, and in so doing free the going train for part of each oscillation. Also called **scape wheel.** See diag. under **lever escapement.** [1880–85]

es•cap•ism (i skā′piz əm), *n.* the avoidance of reality by absorption of the mind in entertainment or in an imaginative situation, activity, etc. [1930–35; ESCAPE + -ISM] —**es•cap′ist,** *adj., n.*

es•cap•ol•o•gy (i skā pol′ə jē, es′kā-), *n. Chiefly Brit.* the method or skill of extricating oneself from handcuffs, chains, etc., as of a magician or other performer. [1935–40; ESCAPE + -O- + -LOGY] —**es•cap•ol′o•gist,** *n.*

es•car•got (es KAR gō′; *Eng.* es′kär gō′), *n., pl.* ***-gots*** (-gō′; *Eng.* -gōz′). *French.* an edible snail.

es•ca•role (es′kə rōl′), *n.* a broad-leaved form of *Cichorium endivia,* used in salads. Cf. **endive** (def. 1). [1895–1900; < F < It *scar(i)ola* < LL *ēscāriola* chicory, equiv. to L *ēscār(us)* fit for eating (L *ēsc(a)* food + *-ārius* -ARY) + *-ola* -OLE[1]]

es•carp (i skärp′), *n.* **1.** *Fort.* the inner slope or wall of the ditch surrounding a rampart. See diag. under **bastion. 2.** any similar steep slope. —*v.t.* **3.** to make into an escarp; give a steep slope to; furnish with escarps. [1680–90; < F, MF *escarpe* < It *scarpa* < Gmc; see SCARP[1]]

es•carp•ment (i skärp′mənt), *n.* **1.** *Geol.* a long, precipitous, clifflike ridge of land, rock, or the like, commonly formed by faulting or fracturing of the earth's crust. Cf. **scarp**[1] (def. 1). **2.** ground cut into an escarp around a fortification or defensive position. [1795–1805; < F *escarpement.* See ESCARP, -MENT]

Es•caut (es kō′), *n.* French name of **Scheldt.**

-esce, a suffix appearing in verbs borrowed from Latin, where it had an inchoative meaning: *convalesce; putresce.* [< L *-ēscere*]

-escence, a suffix of nouns denoting action or process, change, state or condition, etc., and corresponding to verbs ending in *-esce* or adjectives ending in *-escent: convalescence; luminescence.* [< L *-ēscentia.* See -ESCE, -ENCE]

-escent, a suffix of adjectives borrowed from Latin, where it had an inchoative force; often corresponding to verbs in *-esce* and nouns in *-escence: convalescent; recrudescent.* [< L, s. of *-ēscēns,* prp. ending]

esch•a•lot (esh′ə lot′, esh′ə lot′), *n.* shallot. [1695–1705; < F, MF *eschalotte,* dim. of *eschaloigne* SCALLION]

es•char (es′kär, -kər), *n. Pathol.* a hard crust or scab, as from a burn. [1375–1425; late ME *escare* < LL *eschara* < Gk *eschára* hearth, brazier, coals and therefore indication of burning; cf. SCAR[1]]

es•cha•rot•ic (es′kə rot′ik), *Med.* —*adj.* **1.** producing an eschar, as a medicinal substance; caustic. —*n.* **2.** an escharotic agent. [1605–15; < LL *escharōticus* < Gk *escharōtikós.* See ESCHAR, -OTIC]

es•cha•tol•o•gy (es′kə tol′ə jē), *n. Theol.* **1.** any system of doctrines concerning last, or final, matters, as death, the Judgment, the future state, etc. **2.** the branch of theology dealing with such matters. [1835–45; < Gk *éschato(s)* last + -LOGY] —**es•cha•to•log•i•cal** (es′kə tl-oj′i kəl, e skat′l-), *adj.* —**es′cha•to•log′i•cal•ly,** *adv.* —**es′cha•tol′o•gist,** *n.*

es•cheat (es chēt′), *Law.* —*n.* **1.** the reverting of property to the state or some agency of the state, or, as in England, to the lord of the fee or to the crown, when there is a failure of persons legally qualified to inherit or to claim. **2.** the right to take property subject to escheat. —*v.i.* **3.** to revert by escheat, as to the crown or the state. —*v.t.* **4.** to make an escheat of; confiscate. [1250–1300; ME *eschete* < OF *eschete, escheoite,* fem. ptp. of *escheoir* < VL **excadēre* to fall to a person's share, equiv. to L *ex-* EX-[1] + *cadere* to fall (VL *cadēre*)] —**es•cheat′a•ble,** *adj.*

es•cheat•age (es chē′tij), *n.* the right of succeeding to an escheat. [1605–15; ESCHEAT + -AGE]

es•cheat•or (es chē′tər), *n.* an officer in charge of escheats. [1250–1300; ME *eschetour* < AF. See ESCHEAT, -OR[2]]

Esch•e•rich•i•a co•li (esh′ə rik′ē ə kō′lī), *n. Bacteriol.* a species of rod-shaped, facultatively anaerobic bacteria in the large intestine of humans and other animals, sometimes pathogenic. [< NL, named after T. *Escherich* (d. 1911), German physician; see -IA]

es•chew (es chōō′), *v.t.* to abstain or keep away from; shun; avoid: *to eschew evil.* [1300–50; ME *eschewen* < OF *eschiver, eschever* < Gmc; cf. OHG *sciuhen,* G *scheuchen,* SHY[2]] —**es•chew′al,** *n.* —**es•chew′er,** *n.*
—**Syn.** circumvent, boycott; forgo.

Es•cof•fier (es kô fyā′), *n.* **Georges Au•guste** (zhôrzh′ ō gyst′), 1846–1935, French chef and author of cookbooks.

es•co•lar (es′kə lär′), *n., pl.* (*esp. collectively*) **-lar,** (*esp. referring to two or more kinds or species*) **-lars.** a snake mackerel, esp. *Lepidocybium flavobrunneum.* [1885–90; < Sp: lit., scholar; so called from the spectaclelike rings around the eyes]

Es•con•di•do (es′kən dē′dō), *n.* a city in SW California. 62,480.

es•con•son (i skon′sən), *n.* sconcheon.

Es•co•ri•al (e skôr′ē əl, -skōr′-; *Sp.* es′kô RYÄL′), *n.* a building in central Spain, 27 miles (43 km) NW of Madrid, containing a monastery, palace, church, and mausoleum of the Spanish sovereigns: erected 1563–84. Also, **Escurial.**

es•cort (*n.* es′kôrt; *v.* i skôrt′), *n.* **1.** a group of persons, or a single person, accompanying another or others for protection, guidance, or courtesy: *An escort of sailors accompanied the queen.* **2.** an armed guard, as a body of soldiers or ships: *The president traveled with a large escort of motorcycle police.* **3.** a man or boy who accompanies a woman or girl in public, as to a social event. **4.** protection, safeguard, or guidance on a journey: *to travel without escort.* —*v.t.* **5.** to attend or accompany as an escort. [1570–80; < F < It *scorta,* deriv. of *scorgere* to conduct < VL **excorrigere.* See EX-[1], CORRECT]
—**Syn. 4.** convoy. **5.** conduct, usher, squire, chaperon, take, guide. See **accompany.**

es′cort car′rier, *Navy.* a small aircraft carrier used chiefly as an antisubmarine escort for a convoy or task force. [1940–45]

es′cort fight′er, a fighter plane equipped to accompany other planes, esp. bombers, on missions as a protection against air attack. [1945–50]

e•scribe (i skrīb′), *v.t.,* **e•scribed, e•scrib•ing.** *Geom.* to draw a circle outside of a triangle tangent to one side of the triangle and to the extensions of the other two sides. [1550–60; E- + L *scribere* to write; see SCRIBE[1]]

es•cri•toire (es′kri twär′), *n.* See **writing desk** (def. 1). [1605–15; < F, MF < L *scrīptōrium.* See SCRIBE[1], -TORY[2]]

es•crow (*n.* es′krō, i skrō′; *v.* i skrō′, es′krō), *Law.* —*n.* **1.** a contract, deed, bond, or other written agreement deposited with a third person, by whom it is to be delivered to the grantee or promisee on the fulfillment of some condition. **2. in escrow,** in the keeping of a third person for delivery to a given party upon the fulfillment of some condition. —*v.t.* **3.** to place in escrow: *The home seller agrees to escrow the sum of $1000 with his attorney.* [1590–1600; < AF *escro(u)we,* OF *escro(u)e.* See SCROLL]

es•cu•age (es′kyōō ij), *n.* scutage. [1505–15; < AF, OF, equiv. to *escu* (< L *scūtum* shield) + *-age* -AGE]

Es•cu•de•ro (es′kōō thě′RÔ), *n.* **Vi•cen•te** (bē then′-te), 1892?–1980, Spanish dancer.

es•cu•do (e skōō′dō; *Port.* es kōō′dōō; *Sp.* es kōō′thô), *n., pl.* **-dos** (-dōz; *Port.* -dōōs; *Sp.* -thôs). **1.** a coin and monetary unit of Portugal and Cape Verde, equal to 100 centavos. **2.** a former coin and monetary unit of Angola, Guinea-Bissau, and Mozambique. **3.** a former paper money and monetary unit of Chile, equal to 100 condors or 1000 pesos, replaced by the new peso in 1975. **4.** any of various former gold coins of Spain, Spanish America, and Portugal. **5.** a former silver coin of Spain, discontinued in 1868. [1815–25; < Sp: shield < L *scūtum*]

Es•cuin•tla (es kwēn′tlä), *n.* a city in S central Guatemala. 33,205.

Es•cu•la•pi•an (es′kyōō lā′pē ən), *n., adj.* Aesculapian.

es•cu•lent (es′kyə lənt), *adj.* **1.** suitable for use as food; edible. —*n.* **2.** something edible, esp. a vegetable. [1615–25; < L *ēsculentus* edible, full of food, equiv. to *ēsc(a)* food (cf. ESCAROLE) + *-ulentus* -ULENT]

es•cu•lin (es′kyə lin), *n. Chem.* a white, crystalline, slightly water-soluble glucoside, $C_{15}H_{16}O_9$, obtained from the bark of the common horse chestnut and used chiefly in skin preparations as a protective against sunburn. Also, **aesculin.** [< It *esculina* < NL *Aescul(us)* (first part of genus name of species that produces it) + It *-ina* -IN[2]]

Es•cu•ri•al (e skyŏŏr′ē əl), *n.* Escorial.

es•cutch•eon (i skuch′ən), *n.* **1.** a shield or shieldlike surface on which a coat of arms is depicted. See illus. under **coat of arms. 2.** an ornamental or protective plate around a keyhole, door handle, drawer pull, light switch, etc. **3.** *Naut.* a panel on the stern of a vessel bearing its name and port of registry. **4. blot on one's escutcheon,** a stain on one's reputation; disgrace. [1470–80; < ONF *escuchon* << L *scūtum* shield] —**es•cutch′eoned,** *adj.*

Esd., Esdras.

Es•dra•e•lon (es′drā ē′lon, -drə-, ez′-), *n.* a plain in N Israel, extending from the Mediterranean near Mt. Carmel to the Jordan River: scene of ancient battles. Also called **Plain of Jezreel.** Cf. **Megiddo.**

Es•dras (ez′drəs), *n.* **1.** either of the first two books of the Apocrypha, I Esdras or II Esdras. **2.** *Douay Bible.* **a.** Ezra (def. 1). **b.** either of two books, I Esdras or II Esdras, corresponding to the books of Ezra and Nehemiah, respectively, in the Authorized Version.

Es•dud (is dōōd′), *n.* Ashdod.

ESE, east-southeast. Also, **E.S.E.**

-ese, a suffix forming adjectival derivatives of place names, esp. countries or cities; frequently used nominally to denote the inhabitants of the place or their language: *Faroese; Japanese; Vietnamese; Viennese.* By analogy with such language names, **-ese** occurs in coinages denoting in a disparaging, often facetious way a characteristic jargon, style, or accent: *Brooklynese; bureaucratese; journalese; computerese.* [prob. orig. < It *-ese,* later repr. Sp, Pg *-es,* F *-ais, -ois,* all < L *-ēnsem* -ENSIS]

es•em•plas•tic (es′em plas′tik, -əm-), *adj.* having the ability to shape diverse elements or concepts into a unified whole: *the esemplastic power of a great mind to simplify the difficult.* [1810–20; < Gk *es-,* dial. var. of *eis-* into + *(h)én,* neut. of *heîs* one + PLASTIC; irreg. coinage by S.T. Coleridge; cf. G *Ineinsbildung,* term used by Schelling]

E•se•nin (yə sä′nin; *Russ.* yi sye′nyin), *n.* **Ser•gey A•le•ksan•dro•vich** (*Russ.* syiR gyā′ u lyi ksän′dRə-vyich). See **Yesenin, Sergey Aleksandrovich.**

es•er•ine (es′ə rēn′, -rin), *n. Chem.* physostigmine. [1875–80; *eser-* (name for the Calabar bean) + -INE[2]]

Esh•kol (esh′kôl, esh kôl′), *n.* **Le•vi** (lē′vē, lā′vē), (*Levi Shkolnik*), 1895–1969, Israeli statesman, born in Russia: prime minister 1963–69.

Es•i•drix (es′i driks), *Pharm., Trademark.* a brand of hydrochlorothiazide.

-esis, a suffix of Greek origin used to form nouns of action or process: *ecesis.* [< Gk *-ē-* v. formative + *-sis* -SIS]

Esk., Eskimo.

es•ker (es′kər), *n. Geol.* a serpentine ridge of gravelly and sandy drift, believed to have been formed by streams under or in glacial ice. [1850–55; < Ir *eiscir* ridge of mountains]

E•skil•stu•na (es′kil stōō′nə, -styōō′-), *n.* a city in SE Sweden, W of Stockholm. 90,354.

Es•ki•mo (es′kə mō′), *n., pl.* **-mos,** (*esp. collectively*) **-mo** for 1. **1.** a member of an indigenous people of Greenland, northern Canada, Alaska, and northeastern Siberia, characterized by short, stocky build and light-brown complexion. **2.** either of two related languages spoken by the Eskimos, one in Greenland, Canada, and northern Alaska, the other in southern Alaska and Siberia. Cf. **Inuit, Yupik.** [1575–85; < earlier *Esqimawe(s),* appar. via F (of 16th-century Basque fishermen) < Sp *esquimao(s)* < Montagnais (F sp.) *aiachkimeou-* a name for the Micmac, extended or transferred to the Labrador Eskimo among the eastern Montagnais; perh. lit., snowshoe-netter (cf. Ojibwa *aškime·* to net snowshoes); cf. HUSKY] —**Es′ki•mo′an,** *adj.* —**Es•ki•moid** (es′kə-moid′), *adj.*
—**Usage.** The name INUIT, by which the native people of the Arctic from northern Alaska to western Greenland call themselves, has largely supplanted ESKIMO in Canada and is used officially by the Canadian government. Many Inuit consider ESKIMO derogatory, in part because the word was, erroneously, long thought to mean literally "eater of raw meat." INUIT has also come to be used in a wider sense, to name all people traditionally called ESKIMO, regardless of local self-designations. Nonetheless, ESKIMO continues in use in all parts of the world, especially in historical and archaeological contexts and in reference to the people as a cultural and linguistic unity. The term *Native American* is sometimes used to include Eskimo and Aleut peoples. See also **Indian.**

Es•ki•mo-Al•eut (es′kə mō′ə lōōt′, -al′ē ōōt′), *n.* **1.** a stock of languages, consisting of Eskimo and Aleut. —*adj.* **2.** of or belonging to Eskimo-Aleut.

Es′kimo cur′lew, a New World curlew, *Numenius borealis,* that breeds in northern North America: now nearly extinct. [1805–15, *Amer.*]

Es′kimo dog′, 1. one of a breed of strong, medium-sized dogs having a dense, coarse coat, used in arctic regions for hunting and pulling sleds. **2.** any dog of the arctic regions of North America used for pulling sleds. Also called **husky.** [1865–75]

Eskimo dog, 2 ft. (0.6 m) high at shoulder

Es•ki•mol•o•gy (es′kə mol′ə jē), *n.* the study of Eskimo civilization, language, culture, etc. [ESKIMO + -LOGY] —**Es′ki•mol′o•gist,** *n.*

Es′kimo Pie′, *Trademark.* a small bar of ice cream coated with chocolate and skewered on a narrow, thin stick, by which it is held in the hand for eating.

Es•ki•şe•hir (es kē′she hēr′), *n.* a city in W Turkey in Asia. 258,266. Also, **Es•ki′she•hir′.**

ESL, English as a second language: the study of English by nonnative speakers in an English-speaking environment. Cf. **EFL.**

es•li•sor (ā lē′zôr, -zər), *n. Law.* elisor.

Es•me•ral•da (ez′mə ral′də; *Sp.* es′me RÄL′dä), *n.* a female given name: from a Greek word meaning "emerald."

Es•me•ral•das (es′me RÄL′däs), *n.* a seaport in NW Ecuador. 60,364.

Es•mond (ez′mənd), *n.* a male given name.

es•ne (ez′nē, -ne), *n.* (in Anglo-Saxon England) a member of the lowest class; laborer. [bef. 950; < OE; c. OHG *asni,* Goth *asneis* day laborer, harvester, akin to *asans* harvest]

es•ne•cy (es′nə sē), *n. Obs.* (in English law) the right of the oldest member of a coparcenary to have first choice of share upon division of the inheritance. [1600–10; < ML *aesnecia,* Latinization of OF *ainsneece, ainsnesse* position of an older brother or sister, deriv. of *ainsne* elder (cf. L *antenātus* (one) born before another)]

eso-, a combining form meaning "inner," used in the formation of compound words: *esonarthex.* [< Gk, comb. form repr. *ésō* within]

ESOL (ē′sôl, es′əl), *n.* English for speakers of other languages: a field of language training including EFL and ESL. Cf. **TESOL**

es•o•nar•thex (es′ō när′theks), *n.* an inner narthex. [1840–50; ESO- + NARTHEX]

ESOP (ē′sop), *n.* a plan under which a company's capital stock is acquired by its employees or workers. [1970–75; *e(mployee) s(tock) o(wnership) p(lan)*]

e•soph•a•ge•al (i sof′ə jē′əl, ē′sə faj′ē əl), *adj.* pertaining to the esophagus. [1800–10; ESOPHAG(US) + *-eal*, var. of -IAL]

esoph′age′al speech′, *Speech Pathol.* a technique for producing speech sounds without using the larynx, for people whose larynges are lacking or disabled, by expelling swallowed air that is modified by the tongue, lips, and palate as in normal speech.

e•soph•a•gus (i sof′ə gəs, ē sof′-), *n., pl.* **-gi** (-jī′, gī′). *Anat., Zool.* a muscular passage connecting the mouth or pharynx with the stomach in invertebrate and vertebrate animals; gullet. [1350–1400; < NL *oesophagus* < Gk *oisophágos* gullet, lit., channel for eating (*oiso-*, akin to *oísein*, fut. inf. of *phérein* to carry + *-phagos* eating); r. ME *ysophagus* < ML]

es•o•ter•ic (es′ə ter′ik), *adj.* **1.** understood by or meant for only the select few who have special knowledge or interest; recondite: *poetry full of esoteric allusions.* **2.** belonging to the select few. **3.** private; secret; confidential. **4.** (of a philosophical doctrine or the like) intended to be revealed only to the initiates of a group: *the esoteric doctrines of Pythagoras.* [1645–55; < Gk *esōterikós* inner, equiv. to *esṓter(os)* inner + *-ikos* -IC] **—es′o•ter′i•cal•ly,** *adv.*
—Syn. 1. abstruse, arcane, cryptic, enigmatic.

es•o•ter•i•ca (es′ə ter′i kə), *n.pl.* **1.** things understood by or meant for a select few; recondite matters or items. **2.** curiosa (def. 1). [1925–30; < NL, n. use of neut. pl. of Gk *esōterikós* ESOTERIC]

es•o•ter•i•cism (es′ə ter′ə siz′əm), *n.* **1.** the state or quality of being esoteric. **2.** esoteric principles or writings. [1840–50; ESOTERIC + -ISM] **—es′o•ter′i•cist,** *n.*

es•o•ter•ism (es′ə tə riz′əm, es′ə ter′iz-), *n.* esotericism. [1825–35; < Gk *esṓter(os)* inner + -ISM] **—es′o•ter•ist,** *n.*

es•o•ter•y (es′ə ter′ē), *n.* esotericism. [1755–65; < Gk *esṓter(os)* inner + -Y³]

es•o•tro•pi•a (es′ə trō′pē ə), *n. Ophthalm.* strabismus in which one eye deviates inward. [< NL; see ESO-, -TROPE, -IA] **—es•o•trop•ic** (es′ə trop′ik), *adj.*

ESP, extrasensory perception: perception or communication outside of normal sensory capability, as in telepathy and clairvoyance.

esp., especially.

es•pa•drille (es′pə dril′), *n.* **1.** a flat shoe with a cloth upper, a rope sole, and sometimes lacing that ties around the ankle. **2.** a casual shoe resembling this, often with a wedge heel instead of a flat sole. [1860–65; < F < Pr *espardilho*, dim. of *espart* ESPARTO]

es•pa•gnole (es′pən yōl′, -pan-; *Fr.* e spA nyôl′), *n.* See **brown sauce.** Also called **espagnole′ sauce′.** [1835–45; < F: lit., Spanish]

es•pa•gno•lette (i span′yə let′, i span′yə let′), *n.* **1.** (on a French window or the like) one of a pair of rods, controlled by a knob mechanism, having hooked ends that engage catches in the head and sill of the frame. **2.** *Furniture.* a feature, often a bronze mount, set at the top of a leg and having the form of a female breast. [1865–70; < F < Pr *espagnouleto*, dim. of *espanhol* Spanish]

es•pal•ier (i spal′yər, -yā), *n.* **1.** a trellis or framework on which the trunk and branches of fruit trees or shrubs are trained to grow in one plane. **2.** a plant so trained. —*v.t.* **3.** to train on an espalier. **4.** to furnish with an espalier. [1655–65; < F, MF: trellis < It *spalliera* back rest, espalier, equiv. to *spall(a)* shoulder, support + *-iera* -IER²]

espalier (def. 1)

Es•pa•ña (es pä′nyä), *n.* Spanish name of **Spain.**

es•pa•ñol (es pä nyôl′), *n., pl.* **-ño•les** (-nyô′les) for 2, *adj. Spanish.* —*n.* **1.** the Spanish language. **2.** a native or inhabitant of Spain. —*adj.* **3.** of or pertaining to Spain, the Spanish people, or the Spanish language.

Es•par•te•ro (es′pär te′rô), *n.* **Bal•do•me•ro** (bäl′dô me′rô), **Count of Lu•cha•na** (lo͞o chä′nä), 1792–1879, Spanish general and statesman.

es•par•to (i spär′tō), *n., pl.* **-tos.** any of several grasses, esp. *Stipa tenacissima*, of southern Europe and northern Africa, used for making paper, cordage, etc. Also, **espar′to grass′.** [1585–95; < Sp < L *spartum* < Gk *spárton* rope made of *spártos* kind of rush]

espec., especially.

es•pe•cial (i spesh′əl), *adj.* **1.** special; exceptional; outstanding: *of no especial importance; an especial friend.* **2.** of a particular kind, or peculiar to a particular one; particular: *your especial case.* [1350–1400; ME < MF < L *speciālis* pertaining to a particular kind. See SPECIAL] **—es•pe′cial•ness,** *n.*
—Usage. See **special.**

es•pe•cial•ly (i spesh′ə lē), *adv.* particularly; exceptionally; markedly: *Be especially watchful.* [1350–1400; ME; see ESPECIAL, -LY]
—Syn. signally, notably; mainly. ESPECIALLY, CHIEFLY, PARTICULARLY, PRINCIPALLY refer to those cases that seem to be significant. ESPECIALLY and PARTICULARLY single out the most prominent case or example (often in order to particularize a general statement): *Winter is especially severe on old people. Corn grows well in the Middle West, particularly in Iowa.* CHIEFLY and PRINCIPALLY imply that the general statement applies to a majority of the cases in question, and have a somewhat comparative force: *Owls fly chiefly at night. Crime occurs principally in large cities.*
—Usage. See **special.**

es•per•ance (es′pər əns), *n. Obs.* hope. [1400–50; late ME *esperaunce* < MF *esperance* < VL **spērantia*, equiv. to L *spērant-* (s. of *spērāns*) hoping (prp. of *spērāre*, deriv. of *spēs* hope) + *-ia* -IA]

Es•pe•ran•to (es′pə rän′tō, -ran′-), *n.* an artificial language invented in 1887 by L. L. Zamenhof (1859–1917), a Polish physician and philologist, and intended for international use. It is based on word roots common to the major European languages. [1890–95; orig. pseudonym of inventor; lit., the hoping one. See ESPERANCE] **—Es′pe•ran′tism,** *n.* **—Es′pe•ran′tist,** *n.*

es•pi•al (i spī′əl), *n.* **1.** the act of spying. **2.** the act of keeping watch; observation. [1350–1400; ME *espiaille* < MF. See ESPY, -AL²]

es•pi•o•nage (es′pē ə näzh′, -nij, es′pē ə näzh′), *n.* **1.** the act or practice of spying. **2.** the use of spies by a government to discover the military and political secrets of other nations. **3.** the use of spies by a corporation or the like to acquire the plans, technical knowledge, etc., of a competitor: *industrial espionage.* [1785–95; < F *espionnage*, MF *espionage*, equiv. to *espionn(er)* to spy (deriv. of *espion* spy < It *spione* < Gmc; akin to G *spähen* to look out) + *-age* -AGE]

Es•pí•ri•to San•to (es pē′RE to͞o sän′to͞o), a state in E Brazil. 2,063,610; 15,196 sq. mi. (39,360 sq. km). *Cap.:* Vitória.

es•pla•nade (es′plə näd′, -nād′, es′plə näd′, -nād′), *n.* any open, level space, esp. one serving for public walks or drives. [1675–85; < F < It *spianata*, n. use of fem. ptp. of *spianare* < L *explānāre* to level; see -ADE]

es•plees (i splēz′), *n.* (*used with a plural v.*) *Law.* the yield from land, as produce or rents. [1590–1600; < AF *esple(t)z* < ML *explēta*, pl. of *explētum* revenue, r. L *explicitum* something unfolded. See EXPLOIT¹]

Es•poo (es′pô), *n.* a city in S Finland, W of Helsinki. 133,556. Swedish, **Esbo.**

Es•po•si•to (es′pə zē′tō), *n.* **Phil(ip Anthony),** born 1942, Canadian ice-hockey player, in the U.S. since 1962.

es•pous•al (i spou′zəl, -səl), *n.* **1.** adoption or advocacy, as of a cause or principle. **2.** Sometimes, **espousals. a.** a marriage ceremony. **b.** an engagement or betrothal celebration. [1275–1325; ME *espousaille* < MF, OF *espousailles* < L *spōnsālia* (n. use of neut. pl. of *spōnsālis*), equiv. to *spōns(us)* SPOUSE + *-ālia* -AL²]

es•pouse (i spouz′, i spous′), *v.t.,* **-poused, -pous•ing. 1.** to make one's own; adopt or embrace, as a cause. **2.** to marry. **3.** to give (a woman) in marriage. [1425–75; late ME < MF *espouser* < L *spōnsāre* to betroth, espouse] **—es•pous′er,** *n.*
—Syn. 1. support, champion, advocate.

es•pres•si•vo (es′pre sē′vō; *It.* es′pRes sē′vô), *Music.* —*adj.* **1.** expressive. —*adv.* **2.** expressively.

es•pres•so (e spres′ō), *n., pl.* **-sos. 1.** a strong coffee prepared by forcing live steam under pressure, or boiling water, through ground dark-roast coffee beans. **2.** a cup of this coffee. [1940–45; < It (*caffè*) *espresso* pressed (coffee)]

es•prit (e sprē′), *n.* sprightliness of spirit or wit; lively intelligence. [1585–95; < F < L *spīritus* SPIRIT]

es•prit de corps (e sprē′ də kôr′), a sense of unity and of common interests and responsibilities, as developed among a group of persons closely associated in a task, cause, enterprise, etc. [1770–80; < F]
—Syn. camaraderie, bonding, solidarity, fellowship.

Es•pron•ce•da (es′prôn the′thä, -se′-), *n.* **Jo•sé de** (hô se′ the), 1808–42, Spanish poet.

es•py (i spī′), *v.t.,* **-pied, -py•ing.** to see at a distance; catch sight of. [1175–1225; ME *espyen* < OF *espier* << Gmc; cf. G *spähen* to spy]
—Syn. discern, descry, discover, perceive, make out.

Es•py (es′pē), *n.* **James Pol•lard** (pol′ərd), 1785–1860, U.S. meteorologist.

Esq., Esquire. Also, **Esqr.**

e•squa•mate (ē skwā′māt), *adj.* having no squamae, or scales; not scaly. [E- + SQUAMATE]

esque, an adjective suffix indicating style, manner, resemblance, or distinctive character: *arabesque; Romanesque; picturesque.* [< F < It *-esco* << Gmc; see -ISH¹]

Es•qui•line (es′kwə lin′), *n.* one of the seven hills on which ancient Rome was built.

Es•qui•malt (i skwī′môlt), *n.* a naval base and seaport on the SE end of Vancouver Island, in SW British Columbia, in SW Canada: suburb of Victoria.

Es•qui•mau (es′kə mō′), *n., pl.* **-maux** (-mō′, -mōz′), (*esp. collectively*) **-mau,** *adj.* a former spelling of **Eskimo. —Es′qui•mau′an,** *adj.*

es•quire (es′kwīᵊr, eskwīᵊr′), *n., v.,* **-quired, -quir•ing.** —*n.* **1.** (*cap.*) an unofficial title of respect, having no precise significance, sometimes placed, esp. in its abbreviated form, after a man's surname in formal written address: in the U.S., usually applied to lawyers, women as well as men; in Britain, applied to a commoner considered to have gained the social position of a gentleman. *Abbr.:* Esq. **2.** squire (def. 2). **3.** a man belonging to the order of English gentry ranking next below a knight. **4.** *Archaic.* squire (def. 1). —*v.t.* **5.** to raise to the rank of esquire. **6.** to address as "Esquire." **7.** to escort or attend in public. [1425–75; late ME *esquier* < MF *escuier* < L *scūtārius* shield bearer, equiv. to *scūt(um)* (see SCUTAGE) + *-ārius* -ARY]

ESR, 1. erythrocyte sedimentation rate: the rate at which red blood cells settle in a column of blood, serving as a diagnostic test. **2.** electron spin resonance.

es•rog (es′rōg, -rəg), *n., pl.* **es•ro•gim** (es rō′gim), **es•rogs.** *Judaism.* etrog.

ess (es), *n.* **1.** the letter *S, s.* **2.** something shaped like an S: *The road wound among the mountains in great esses.* [1530–40]

-ess, a suffix forming distinctively feminine nouns: *countess; goddess; lioness.* [ME *-esse* < OF < LL *-issa* < Gk]
—Usage. Since at least the 14th century, English has both borrowed feminine nouns in -ESS from French (*-esse* in French and in some early English forms) and applied the French ending to native or naturalized words, most frequently agent nouns in *-er* or *-or.* Some of the earliest borrowings—titles for the nobility and church dignitaries—are still in use, among them *countess, princess, duchess, empress, abbess,* and *prioress.* Of the scores of new nouns that were created from the 14th century on, many have long ago disappeared entirely from use: *devouress; dwelleress.* But many have survived, although their use has declined sharply in the latter half of the 20th century.
Nouns in -ESS denoting occupation or profession are rapidly disappearing from American English. The fourth edition of the *Dictionary of Occupational Titles* (DOT), published by the U.S. Department of Labor in 1977, specifies genderless titles for thousands of occupations. Airlines now refer to cabin personnel as *flight attendants,* not *stewards* and *stewardesses.* In the arts, *authoress, editress, poetess, sculptress,* and similar terms are considered offensive by many and are almost always replaced by *author, editor, poet, sculptor.* Nouns in -ESS designating the holder of public office are hardly ever encountered in modern American usage. Women holding the office of ambassador, mayor, or governor are referred to by those titles rather than by the older, sex-marked *ambassadress, mayoress,* or *governess.* (*Governess* has developed a special sense in relation to childcare; this use is less common in the U.S. than in Britain.) Among other terms almost never used in modern American English are *ancestress, directress, instructress, manageress, oratress,* and *proprietress.* If the sex of the performer is not relevant to performance of the task or function, the neutral term in *-er* or *-or* is now widely used.
Some nouns in -ESS are still current: *actress* (but some women in the acting profession prefer to be called *actors*); *adventuress; enchantress; heiress* (largely in journalistic writing); *hostess* (but women who conduct radio and television programs are referred to as *hosts*); *millionairess; murderess; postmistress* (but not in official U.S. government use); *seamstress; seductress; sorceress; temptress;* and *waitress* (the DOT substitute *server* has not been widely adopted).
Jewess and *Negress* are generally considered offensive today. *Mistress* has given way to *master* in the sense of one who has acquired expertise in something: *She is a master at interpreting financial reports.* See also **-enne, -ette, -trix.**

Es•sa•oui•ra (es′ə wēr′ə), *n.* a seaport in W Morocco. 30,061. Formerly, **Mogador.**

es•say (*n.* es′ā *for 1, 2;* es′ā, e sā′ *for 3–5; v.* e sā′), *n.* **1.** a short literary composition on a particular theme or subject, usually in prose and generally analytic, speculative, or interpretative. **2.** anything resembling such a composition: *a picture essay.* **3.** an effort to perform or accomplish something; attempt. **4.** *Philately.* a design for a proposed stamp differing in any way from the design of the stamp as issued. **5.** *Obs.* a tentative effort; trial; assay. —*v.t.* **6.** to try; attempt. **7.** to put to the test; make trial of. [1475–85; < MF *essayer*, c. AF *assayer* to ASSAY < LL *exagium* a weighing, equiv. to **exag(ere)*, for L *exigere* to examine, test, lit., to drive out (see EXACT) + *-ium* -IUM] **—es•say′er,** *n.*

es•say•ist (es′ā ist), *n.* a writer of essays. [1600–10; ESSAY + -IST]

es•say•is•tic (es′ā is′tik), *adj.* **1.** of, pertaining to, or like an essay, esp. in style, format, or organization and often in reflecting a more personal approach than a treatise, thesis, or the like. **2.** resembling formal exposition. **3.** expository; discursive; explanatory. [1860–65; ESSAY + -ISTIC]

es′say ques′tion, a question on a test or examination on a given topic requiring a written analysis or explanation, usually of a specified length. [1945–50]

es•se (es′se; *Eng.* es′ē), *n. Latin.* being; existence.

Es•sen (es′ən), *n.* a city in W Germany: the chief city of the Ruhr River valley. 623,000.

es•sence (es′əns), *n.* **1.** the basic, real, and invariable nature of a thing or its significant individual feature or features: *Freedom is the very essence of our democracy.* **2.** a substance obtained from a plant, drug, or the like, by distillation, infusion, etc., and containing its characteristic properties in concentrated form. **3.** an alcoholic solution of an essential oil; spirit. **4.** a perfume; scent. **5.** *Philos.* the inward nature, true substance, or constitution of anything, as opposed to what is accidental, phenomenal, illusory, etc. **6.** something that exists, esp. a spiritual or immaterial entity. **7. in essence,** essentially; at bottom, often despite appearances: *For all his bluster, he is in essence a shy person.* **8. of the essence,** absolutely essential; critical; crucial: *In chess, cool nerves are of the essence.* [1350–1400; ME *essencia* < ML, for L *essentia.* See ESSE, -ENCE]
—Syn. 1. substance, spirit, lifeblood, heart, principle, soul, core.

es•sence d'o•ri•ent (es′əns dôr′ē ənt, -ent′, dōr′-; *Fr.* e säns dô ryän′), *Jewelry.* a preparation for coating glass beads to make imitation pearls, derived from

CONCISE ETYMOLOGY KEY: <, descended or borrowed from; >, whence; b., blend of, blended; c., cognate with; cf., compare; deriv., derivative; equiv., equivalent; imit., imitative; obl., oblique; r., replacing; s., stem; sp., spelling, spelled; resp., respelling, respelled; trans., translation; ?, origin unknown; *, unattested; ‡, probably earlier than. See the full key inside the front cover.

the scales of fish, esp. of the bleak. [< F: lit., essence of the Orient]

es′sence of ber′gamot, bergamot (def. 2).

Es·sene (es′ēn, e sēn′), *n. Judaism.* a member of a Palestinian sect, characterized by asceticism, celibacy, and joint holding of property, that flourished from the 2nd century B.C. to the 2nd century A.D. —**Es·se·ni·an** (e sē′nē ən), **Es·sen·ic** (e sen′ik), *adj.*

es·sen·tial (ə sen′shəl), *adj.* **1.** absolutely necessary; indispensable: *Discipline is essential in an army.* **2.** pertaining to or constituting the essence of a thing. **3.** noting or containing an essence of a plant, drug, etc. **4.** being such by its very nature or in the highest sense; natural; spontaneous: *essential happiness.* **5.** *Math.* **a.** (of a singularity of a function of a complex variable) noting that the Laurent series at the point has an infinite number of terms with negative powers. **b.** (of a discontinuity) noting that the function is discontinuous and has no limit at the point. Cf. **removable** (def. 2). —*n.* **6.** a basic, indispensable, or necessary element; chief point: *Concentrate on essentials rather than details.* [1300–50; ME *essencial* < ML *essenciālis* for LL *essentiālis.* See ESSENCE, -AL[1]] —**es·sen′tial·ly,** *adv.* —**es·sen′tial·ness,** *n.*
—**Syn. 1.** fundamental, basic, inherent, intrinsic, vital. See **necessary. 2.** ESSENTIAL, INHERENT, INTRINSIC refer to that which is in the natural composition of a thing. ESSENTIAL suggests that which is in the very essence or constitution of a thing: *Oxygen and hydrogen are essential in water.* INHERENT means inborn or fixed from the beginning as a permanent quality or constituent of a thing: *properties inherent in iron.* INTRINSIC implies belonging to the nature of a thing itself, and comprised within it, without regard to external considerations or accidentally added properties: *the intrinsic value of diamonds.* —**Ant. 2.** incidental, extraneous, extrinsic; accidental.

essen′tial ami′no ac′id, *Biochem.* any amino acid that is required by an animal for growth but that cannot be synthesized by the animal's cells and must be supplied in the diet. [1935–40]

essen′tial hyperten′sion, *Pathol.* persistent high blood pressure of no known cause.

es·sen·tial·ism (ə sen′shə liz′əm), *n. Educ.* a doctrine that certain traditional concepts, ideals, and skills are essential to society and should be taught methodically to all students, regardless of individual ability, need, etc. Cf. **progressivism.** [1935–40; ESSENTIAL + -ISM] —**es·sen′tial·ist,** *n., adj.*

es·sen·ti·al·i·ty (ə sen′shē al′i tē), *n., pl.* **-ties** for 2. **1.** the quality of being essential; essential character. **2.** an essential feature, element, or point. [1610–20; ESSENTIAL + -ITY]

es·sen·tial·ize (ə sen′shə līz′), *v.t.,* **-ized, -iz·ing.** to extract the essence from; express the essence of. Also, *esp. Brit.,* **es·sen′tial·ise′.** [1660–70; ESSENTIAL + -IZE]

essen′tial oil′, any of a class of volatile oils obtained from plants, possessing the odor and other characteristic properties of the plant, used chiefly in the manufacture of perfumes, flavors, and pharmaceuticals. [1665–75]

es·se quam vi·de·ri (es′se kwäm wi′de rē; *Eng.* es′ē kwam vi dâr′ī), *Latin.* to be rather than to seem: motto of North Carolina.

Es·se·qui·bo (es′i kwē′bō), *n.* a river flowing from S Guyana N to the Atlantic. ab. 550 mi. (885 km) long.

Es·sex (es′iks), *n.* **1. 2nd Earl of.** See **Devereux, Robert. 2.** a county in SE England. 1,410,900; 1418 sq. mi. (3670 sq. km). **3.** a town in N Maryland, near Baltimore. 39,614. **4.** a town in W Vermont. 14,392.

Es′sex Jun′to (jun′tō), *U.S. Hist.* **1.** a group of extreme Federalist party members from Essex county, Massachusetts. **2.** any Federalist. [1795–1805, *Amer.*]

Es′sex ta′ble, *Carpentry.* a chart tabulating the number of board feet, to the nearest twelfth, contained in pieces of wood one inch thick and of varying standard sizes.

es·sive (es′iv), *Gram.* —*adj.* **1.** noting a case, as in Finnish, whose distinctive function is to indicate a state of being. —*n.* **2.** the essive case. [1900–05; < Finnish *essivi* < L *ess(e)* to be + *-īvus* -IVE]

es·soin (i soin′), *n.* (in England) an excuse for nonappearance in a court of law at the prescribed time. [1300–50; ME *essoine* < AF, OF *essoigne, essoine,* n. deriv. of *essoinier* to put forward such an excuse, v. deriv. (with *es-* EX-) of *sogne,* ult. < Old Low Franconian **sunnja* legal excuse, care (cf. OS *sunnea,* ON *syn* denial, Goth *sunja* truth)]

es·so·nite (es′ə nīt′), *n. Mineral.* a variety of grossularite garnet. Also called **cinnamon stone, hessonite.** [1810–20; < F < Gk *hḗssōn* less, inferior + *-ītēs* -ITE[1]]

Es·sonne (e sôn′), *n.* a department in N France. 923,061; 699 sq. mi. (1810 sq. km). *Cap.:* Évry.

EST, Eastern Standard Time. Also, **E.S.T., e.s.t.**

-est[1], a suffix forming the superlative degree of adjectives and adverbs: *warmest; fastest; soonest.* [ME; OE *-est, -ost.* Cf. Gk *-isto-*]

-est[2], a native English suffix formerly used to form the second person singular indicative of verbs: *knowest; sayest; goest.* Also, **-st.** [ME; OE *-est, -ast, -st,* 2nd pers. sing. pres. indic. endings of some verbs (*-s* earlier verbal ending + *-t,* by assimilation from *thū* THOU[1]) and 2nd pers. sing. past endings of weak verbs (earlier *-es* + *-t*)]

est., **1.** established. **2.** estate. **3.** estimate. **4.** estimated. **5.** estuary.

estab., established.

es·tab·lish (i stab′lish), *v.t.* **1.** to found, institute, build, or bring into being on a firm or stable basis: *to establish a university; to establish a medical practice.* **2.** to install or settle in a position, place, business, etc.: *to establish one's child in business.* **3.** to show to be valid or true; prove: *to establish the facts of the matter.* **4.** to cause to be accepted or recognized: *to establish a custom; She established herself as a leading surgeon.* **5.** to bring about permanently: *to establish order.* **6.** to enact, appoint, or ordain for permanence, as a law; fix unalterably. **7.** to make (a church) a national or state institution. **8.** *Cards.* to obtain control of (a suit) so that one can win all the subsequent tricks in it. [1325–75; ME *establissen* < MF *establiss-,* extended s. of *establir* < L *stabilire,* akin to *stabilis* STABLE[2]] —**es·tab′lish·a·ble,** *adj.* —**es·tab′lish·er,** *n.*
—**Syn. 1.** form, organize. See **fix. 3.** verify, substantiate. **6.** decree. —**Ant. 1.** abolish. **3.** disprove.

estab′lished church′, a church that is recognized by law, and sometimes financially supported, as the official church of a nation. Also called **state church.** Cf. **national church.** [1650–60]

es·tab·lish·ment (i stab′lish mənt), *n.* **1.** the act or an instance of establishing. **2.** the state or fact of being established. **3.** something established; a constituted order or system. **4.** (*often cap.*) the existing power structure in society; the dominant groups in society and their customs or institutions; institutional authority (usually prec. by *the*): *The Establishment believes exploring outer space is worth any tax money spent.* **5.** (*often cap.*) the dominant group in a field of endeavor, organization, etc. (usually prec. by *the*): *the literary Establishment.* **6.** a household; place of residence including its furnishings, grounds, etc. **7.** a place of business together with its employees, merchandise, equipment, etc. **8.** a permanent civil, military, or other force or organization. **9.** an institution, as a school, hospital, etc. **10.** the recognition by a state of a church as the state church. **11.** the church so recognized, esp. the Church of England. **12.** *Archaic.* a fixed or settled income. [1475–85; 1920–25 for def. 4; ESTABLISH + -MENT]

es·tab·lish·men·tar·i·an (i stab′lish mən târ′ē ən), *adj.* **1.** of or pertaining to an established church, esp. the Church of England, or the principle of state religion. **2.** (*often cap.*) of, pertaining to, or favoring a political or social establishment. —*n.* **3.** a supporter or adherent of the principle of the establishment of a church by state law; an advocate of state religion. **4.** (*often cap.*) a person who belongs to or favors a political or social establishment. [1840–50; ESTABLISHMENT + -ARIAN] —**es·tab′lish·men·tar′i·an·ism,** *n.*

es·ta·fette (es′tə fet′), *n.* a mounted courier. [1785–95; < F < It *staffetta,* dim. of *staffa* stirrup < Gmc (cf. STAPES); see -ETTE]

Es·taing, d′ (des taN′), **Charles Hec·tor** (sHARl ek tôR′), 1729–94, French admiral.

es·ta·min (es′tə min), *n.* a worsted fabric constructed in twill weave with a rough surface. Also, **es·ta·mene** (es′tə mēn′). [1695–1705; < F *estamine* << L *stāminea,* fem. of *stāmineus* made of threads. See STAMEN, -EOUS]

es·ta·mi·net (es tA mē ne′), *n., pl.* **-nets** (-ne′). *French.* a bistro or small café. [1805–15]

es·tam·pie (e stäm pē′), *n.* a medieval dance and instrumental form, in several repeated sections, associated chiefly with the trouvères. [< F, OF, deriv. of *estampir* to roar, resound < Gmc; see STAMP]

es·tan·cia (e stän′sē ə; *Sp.* es tän′syä), *n., pl.* **-cias** (-sē əz; *Sp.* -syäs). (in Spanish America) a landed estate or a cattle ranch. [1695–1705; < AmerSp, Sp: dwelling]

es·tate (i stāt′), *n., v.,* **-tat·ed, -tat·ing.** —*n.* **1.** a piece of landed property, esp. one of large extent with an elaborate house on it: *to have an estate in the country.* **2.** *Law.* **a.** property or possessions. **b.** the legal position or status of an owner, considered with respect to property owned in land or other things. **c.** the degree or quantity of interest that a person has in land with respect to the nature of the right, its duration, or its relation to the rights of others. **d.** interest, ownership, or property in land or other things. **e.** the property of a deceased person, a bankrupt, etc., viewed as an aggregate. **3.** *Brit.* a housing development. **4.** a period or condition of life: *to attain to man's estate.* **5.** a major political or social group or class, esp. one once having specific political powers, as the clergy, nobles, and commons in France or the lords spiritual, lords temporal, and commons in England. **6.** condition or circumstances with reference to worldly prosperity, estimation, etc.; social status or rank. **7.** *Obs.* pomp or state. **8.** *Obs.* high social status or rank. —*v.t.* **9.** *Obs.* to establish in or as in an estate. [1175–1225; ME *estat* < MF; c. Pr *estat.* See STATE]
—**Syn. 1.** See **property.**

estate′ a′gent, *Brit.* **1.** the steward or manager of a landed estate. **2.** a real-estate agent; realtor. [1875–80]

es·tate-bot·tling (i stāt′bot′l ing, -bot′ling), *n.* a practice whereby a vineyard bottles its own wine. —**es·tate′-bot′tled,** *adj.*

estate′ car′, *Brit.* See **station wagon.** [1945–50]

Estates′ Gen′eral, *French Hist.* the States-General.

estate′ tax′, a tax imposed on a decedent's property, assessed on the gross estate prior to distribution to the heirs. Also called **death tax.** [1905–10]

Es·te (es′tā), *n.* a city in NE Italy: medieval fortress; ancient Roman ruins. 17,060. Ancient, **Ateste.**

es·teem (i stēm′), *v.t.* **1.** to regard highly or favorably; regard with respect or admiration: *I esteem him for his honesty.* **2.** to consider as of a certain value or of a certain type; regard: *I esteem it worthless.* **3.** *Obs.* to set a value on; appraise. —*n.* **4.** favorable opinion or judgment; respect or regard: *to hold a person in esteem.* **5.** *Archaic.* opinion or judgment; estimation; valuation. [1400–50; late ME *estemen,* < MF *estimer* < L *aestimāre* to fix the value of]
—**Syn. 1.** honor, revere, respect. See **appreciate. 4.** favor, admiration, honor, reverence, veneration. See **respect.** —**Ant. 1.** disdain.

Es·telle (i stel′), *n.* a female given name: from a Latin word meaning "star." Also, **Es·tel·la** (i stel′ə).

Es·te·po·na (es′te pô′nä; *Eng.* es′tə pō′nə), *n.* a seaport in S Spain, on the Mediterranean: resort center. 21,163.

es·ter (es′tər), *n. Chem.* a compound produced by the reaction between an acid and an alcohol with the elimination of a molecule of water, as ethyl acetate, $C_4H_8O_2$, or dimethyl sulfate, $C_2H_6SO_4$. [1850–55; coined by L. Gmelin (1788–1853), German chemist]

es·ter·ase (es′tə rās′, -rāz′), *n. Biochem.* any enzyme that hydrolyzes an ester into an alcohol and an acid. [1915–20; ESTER + -ASE]

es′ter gum′, *Chem.* any of several hard resins produced by the esterification of a natural resin, esp. rosin, with a polyhydric alcohol, chiefly glycerol: used in the manufacture of paints, varnishes, and lacquers. [1935–40]

Es·ter·ha·zy (es′tər hä′zē; *Fr.* e steR A zē′), *n.* **Ma·rie Charles Fer·di·nand Wal·sin** (mA Rē′ sHARl feR dē nän′ vAl saN′), 1847–1923, French army officer who confessed forging evidence that convicted Alfred Dreyfus.

Es·ter·há·zy (es′tər hä′zē; *Hung.* es′teR hä′zi), *n.* **Prince Mi·klós Jó·zsef** (mi′klōsh yō′zhef), 1714–90, Hungarian patron of the arts. Also, **Es′ter·ha′zy.**

es·ter·i·fy (e ster′ə fī′), *v.t., v.i.,* **-fied, -fy·ing.** *Chem.* to convert into an ester. [1900–05; ESTER + -IFY] —**es·ter′i·fi′a·ble,** *adj.* —**es·ter′i·fi·ca′tion,** *n.*

Es·tes (es′tēz, -tis), *n.* a male given name.

Es′tes Park′, a summer resort in N Colorado. 2703.

Esth., **1.** *Bible.* Esther. **2.** Esthonia.

Es·ther (es′tər), *n.* **1.** the wife of Ahasuerus. **2.** a book of the Bible bearing her name. *Abbr.:* Esth. **3.** a number of prayers, visions, interpretations of dreams, etc., that are included in the Douay Bible as chapters 10–16. **4.** a female given name.

es·the·sia (es thē′zhə, -zhē ə, -zē ə), *n.* capacity for sensation or feeling; sensitivity. Also, **aesthesia.** [1875–80; < Gk *aisthēs(is)* (see ESTHESIS) + -IA]

es·the·si·om·e·ter (es thē′zē om′i tər), *n. Med.* an instrument for measuring the degree of tactile sensibility. [ESTHES(IS) + -O- + -METER] —**es·the′si·om′e·try,** *n.*

es·the·sis (es thē′sis), *n.* sensation; feeling. Also, **aesthesis.** [1850–55; < Gk *aísthēsis* sensation, perception]

es·thete (es′thēt), *n.* aesthete.

es·thet·ic (es thet′ik), *adj., n.* aesthetic.

es·thet·i·cal (es thet′i kəl), *adj.* aesthetical. —**es·thet′i·cal·ly,** *adv.*

es·the·ti·cian (es′thi tish′ən), *n.* **1.** aesthetician. **2.** a person trained to administer facials, advise customers on makeup and the care of skin and hair, etc. Cf. **beautician** (def. 1).

es·thet·i·cism (es thet′ə siz′əm), *n.* aestheticism.

es·thet·ics (es thet′iks), *n.* (*used with a singular v.*) aesthetics.

Es·tho·ni·a (e stō′nē ə, e stōn′yə, es thō′nē ə, -thōn′yə), *n.* Estonia.

Es·tho·ni·an (e stō′nē ən, es thō′-), *adj., n.* Estonian.

Es·tienne (es tyen′), *n.* **1.** Also, **Étienne.** a family of French printers, book dealers, and scholars, including esp. **Hen·ri** (äN Rē′), died 1520; his son, **Ro·bert** (Rô beR′), 1503?–59; **Henri** (son of Robert), 1531?–98. **2.** a French printing firm founded by this family.

es·ti·ma·ble (es′tə mə bəl), *adj.* **1.** worthy of esteem; deserving respect or admiration. **2.** capable of being estimated. [1425–75; late ME < MF < L *aestimābilis,* equiv. to *aestim(āre)* to ESTEEM + *-ābilis* -ABLE] —**es′ti·ma·ble·ness,** *n.* —**es′ti·ma·bly,** *adv.*
—**Syn. 1.** reputable, respectable, admirable, laudable, meritorious, excellent, good. —**Ant. 1.** contemptible.

es·ti·mate (*v.* es′tə māt′; *n.* es′tə mit, -māt′), *v.,* **-mat·ed, -mat·ing,** *n.* —*v.t.* **1.** to form an approximate judgment or opinion regarding the worth, amount, size, weight, etc., of; calculate approximately: *to estimate the cost of a college education.* **2.** to form an opinion of; judge. —*v.i.* **3.** to make an estimate. —*n.* **4.** an approximate judgment or calculation, as of the value, amount, time, size, or weight of something. **5.** a judgment or opinion, as of the qualities of a person or thing. **6.** a statement of the approximate charge for work to be done, submitted by a person or business firm ready to undertake the work. [1525–35; < L *aestimātus,* ptp. of *aestimāre* to value, estimate; see -ATE[1]] —**es′ti·mat′ing·ly,** *adv.* —**es′ti·ma′tor,** *n.*
—**Syn. 1.** compute, count, reckon, gauge, assess, value, evaluate, appraise. **4.** valuation, calculation, appraisal.

es·ti·ma·tion (es′tə mā′shən), *n.* **1.** judgment or opinion: *In my estimation the boy is guilty.* **2.** esteem; respect. **3.** approximate calculation; estimate: *to make an estimation of one's expenditures.* [1325–75; ME *estimacioun* < MF < L *aestimātiōn-* (s. of *aestimātiō*). See ESTIMATE, -ION]
—**Syn. 2.** appreciation, regard, honor, veneration.

es·ti·ma·tive (es′tə mā′tiv), *adj.* **1.** capable of estimating. **2.** pertaining to or based upon estimation; estimated. [1350–1400; ME < ML *aestimātīvus.* See ESTIMATE, -IVE]

e·stip·u·late (ē stip′yə lit, -lāt′), *adj. Bot.* exstipulate.

es·ti·val (es′tə vəl, e stī′vəl), *adj.* pertaining or appropriate to summer. [1350–1400; ME < LL *aestīvālis,* equiv. to L *aestīv(us)* of or relating to summer + *-ālis* -AL[1]]

es·ti·vate (es′tə vāt′), *v.i.,* **-vat·ed, -vat·ing. 1.** to spend the summer, as at a specific place or in a certain activity. **2.** *Zool.* to pass the summer in a torpid condition. [1620–30; < L *aestīvātus,* ptp. of *aestīvāre* to reside

CONCISE PRONUNCIATION KEY: act, cāpe, dâre, pärt; set, ēqual; if, īce; ox, ōver, ôrder, oil, bo͝ok, bo͞ot, out; up, ûrge; child; sing; shoe; thin, *that;* zh as in *treasure.* ə = *a* as in *alone, e* as in *system, i* as in *easily, o* as in *gallop, u* as in *circus;* ə as in *fire* (fīər), *hour* (ouər). l and n can serve as syllabic consonants, as in *cradle* (krād′l), and *button* (but′n). See the full key inside the front cover.

during the summer (akin to *aestivus* of or relating to summer); see -ATE[1]] **—es′ti·va′tor,** *n.*

es·ti·va·tion (es′tə vā′shən), *n.* **1.** *Zool.* the act of estivating. **2.** *Bot.* the arrangement of the parts of a flower in the bud. [1615–25; ESTIVATE + -ION]

es·toc (e stok′; *Fr.* e stôk′), *n., pl.* **es·tocs** (e stoks′; *Fr.* e stôk′). a thrusting sword of the 13th–17th centuries having a long, narrow blade of rectangular section. [1820–30; < OF: lit., point (of a sword). See STOCK]

es·to·ca·da (es′tə kä′də; *Sp.* es′tô kä′thä), *n.* the thrust of the sword by the matador into the bull in the final stage of a bullfight, designed to kill the bull. [1570–80; < Sp < MF *estoqu(ier)* to give sword thrusts (see ESTOC) + Sp *-ada* -ADE[1]]

Es·to·ni·a (e stō′nē ə, e stōn′yə), *n.* a republic in N Europe, on the Baltic, S of the Gulf of Finland: an independent republic 1918–40; annexed by the Soviet Union 1940; regained independence 1991. 1,573,000; 17,413 sq. mi. (45,100 sq. km). *Cap.:* Tallinn. Also, **Esthonia.**

Es·to·ni·an (e stō′nē ən), *adj.* **1.** of or pertaining to Estonia or its people. **—***n.* **2.** a member of a Finnish people inhabiting Estonia, Livonia, and other districts of Russia. **3.** the Uralic language of Estonia, very closely related to Finnish. Also, **Esthonian.** [1785–95; ESTONI(A) + -AN]

es·top (e stop′), *v.t.,* **-topped, -top·ping. 1.** *Law.* to hinder or prevent by estoppel. **2.** *Archaic.* to stop. [1250–1300; ME < AF *estopper,* OF *estoper* to stop up, deriv. of *estoupe* < L *stuppa* tow. Cf. STUFF]

es·to per·pe·tu·a (es′tō pɛr pet′o͞o ä′; *Eng.* es′tō pər pech′o͞o ə), *Latin.* may she live forever: motto of Idaho.

es·top·page (e stop′ij), *n.* the condition of being estopped. [1695–1705; < F; see ESTOP, -AGE]

es·top·pel (e stop′əl), *n. Law.* a bar or impediment preventing a party from asserting a fact or a claim inconsistent with a position that party previously took, either by conduct or words, esp. where a representation has been relied or acted upon by others. [1575–85; < MF *estoupail* stopper. See ESTOP, -AL[2]]

Es·to·ril (esh′to͞o rēl′), *n.* a town in W Portugal, W of Lisbon: seaside resort. 15,740.

Es·tour·nelles de Con·stant, d′ (de sto͞or nel də kôn stän′), **Paul Hen·ri Ben·ja·min Bal·luat** (pôl än rē′ ban zha man′ ba lwa′), **Baron Constant de Re·becque** (də rə bek′), 1852–1924, French diplomat: Nobel peace prize 1909.

es·to·vers (e stō′vərz), *n.pl. Law.* necessaries allowed by law, as wood and timber to a tenant or alimony to a spouse. [1250–1300; ME << AF, n. use of OF *estovoir, estover* to be necessary << L *est opus* there is need]

Es·tra·da Ca·bre·ra (es trä′thä kä vre′rä), **Manuel** (mä nwel′), 1857–1924, Guatemalan politician: president 1898–1920.

es·trade (e sträd′), *n.* **1.** a slightly raised platform in a room or hall. **2.** a platform, as for a throne or bed of state. [1690–1700; < F < Sp *estrado* part of a room in which a carpet is spread < L *strātum;* see STRATUM]

es·tra·di·ol (es′trə dī′ôl, -ol), *n.* **1.** *Biochem.* an estrogenic hormone, $C_{18}H_{24}O_2$, produced by the maturing Graafian follicle, that causes proliferation and thickening of the tissues and blood vessels of the endometrium. **2.** *Pharm.* a commercial form of this compound, obtained from the urine of pregnant humans and mares or synthesized, used in the treatment of estrogen deficiency and certain menopausal and postmenopausal conditions. [1930–35; *estra-* (comb. form repr. ESTRIN) + DI-[1] + -OL[1]]

es·tra·gon (es′trə gon′), *n.* tarragon.

es·tral (es′trəl), *adj.* estrous. [ESTR(US) + -AL[1]]

es·trange (i strānj′), *v.t.,* **-tranged, -trang·ing. 1.** to turn away in feeling or affection; make unfriendly or hostile; alienate the affections of: *Their quarrel estranged the two friends.* **2.** to remove from accustomed surroundings or keep at a distance: *The necessity for traveling on business has estranged him from his family.* **3.** to divert from the original use or possessor. [1475–85; < MF, OF *estranger;* c. Pg *estranhar,* Sp *estrañar,* It *straniare* < ML *extrāneāre* to treat as a stranger. See STRANGE] **—es·trange′ment,** *n.* **—es·trang′er,** *n.*

—Syn. ESTRANGE, ALIENATE, DISAFFECT share the sense of causing (someone) to turn away from a previously held state of affection, comradeship, or allegiance. ESTRANGE often implies replacement of love or belonging by apathy or hostility: *erstwhile lovers estranged by a misunderstanding.* ALIENATE often calls attention to the cause of antagonism or separation: *His inconsiderate behavior alienated both friends and family.* DISAFFECT usually refers to relationships involving allegiance or loyalty rather than love or affection: *disaffected workers, demoralized by ill-considered management policies.*

es·tranged (i strānjd′), *adj.* displaying or evincing a feeling of alienation; alienated. [1545–55; ESTRANGE + -ED[2]] **—es·trang·ed·ness** (i strān′jid nis, -strānjd′-), *n.*

es·tray (i strā′), *n.* **1.** a person or animal that has strayed. **2.** *Law.* a domestic animal, as a horse or a sheep, found wandering or without an owner. **—***v.i.* **3.** *Archaic.* to stray. [1250–1300; ME *astrai* < AF *estray,* deriv. of OF *estraier* to STRAY]

es·treat (e strēt′), *Eng. Law.* **—***n.* **1.** a true copy or extract of an original writing or record, as of a fine. **—***v.t.* **2.** to make an estreat of (a fine, levy, etc.) for prosecution. **3.** to levy (fines) under an estreat or exact (something) by way of fine or levy. [1250–1300; ME *estrete* < AF, c. OF *estraite* (ptp. of *extraire*) < L *extracta* (fem. ptp. of *extrahere*); see EXTRACT]

Es·tre·ma·du·ra (es′trə mä tho͞o′rä), *n.* a region in W Spain, formerly a province. Also, **Extremadura.**

es·tril·did (es′tril did), *Ornith.* **—***adj.* **1.** of or pertaining to the family Estrildidae, comprising the grass finches, waxbills, mannikins, and other small finches. **—***n.* **2.** a bird of the family Estrildidae. Also, **es·tril·dine** (es′tril dīn′, -din). [< NL *Estrildidae,* equiv. to *Estrild(a)* the type genus (from the Linnaean specific name *Astrild* < Sw: the god of love, literary coinage based on ON *ástareldr* lit., love-fire; the bird was appar. so named from its red bill) + *-idae* -ID[2]]

es·trin (es′trin), *n. Biochem., Pharm.* estrone. [< NL; see ESTRUS, -IN[2]]

es·tri·ol (es′trē ôl′, -ol′, -trī-), *n.* **1.** *Biochem.* an estrogenic hormone, $C_{18}H_{21}(OH)_3$, occurring in urine during pregnancy. **2.** *Pharm.* a commercial form of this compound, obtained from human placentas or the urine of pregnant women, used in conditions involving estrogen deficiency. [1930–35; ES(TRIN) + TRI- + -OL[1]]

es·tro·gen (es′trə jən), *n. Biochem.* any of several major female sex hormones produced primarily by the ovarian follicles of female mammals, capable of inducing estrus, developing and maintaining secondary female sex characteristics, and preparing the uterus for the reception of a fertilized egg: used, esp. in synthetic form, as a component of oral contraceptives, in certain cancer treatments, and in other therapies. [1925–30; ESTR(US) + -O- + -GEN]

es·tro·gen·ic (es′trə jen′ik), *adj.* **1.** *Biochem.* promoting or producing estrus. **2.** of, pertaining to, or caused by estrogen. [1925–30; (def. 1) ESTR(US) + -O- + -GENIC; (def. 2) ESTROGEN + -IC] **—es′tro·gen′i·cal·ly,** *adv.*

es′trogen replace′ment ther′apy, the administration of estrogen, esp. in postmenopausal women, to reduce the chance of osteoporosis and sometimes to lower cholesterol levels. *Abbr.:* ERT [1980–85]

es·trone (es′trōn), *n.* **1.** *Biochem.* an estrogenic hormone, $C_{18}H_{22}O_2$, produced by the ovarian follicles and found during pregnancy in urine and placental tissue. **2.** *Pharm.* a commercial form of this compound, obtained from the urine of pregnant women or synthesized from ergosterol, used in the treatment of estrogen deficiency and certain menopausal and postmenopausal conditions. Also, **estrin.** [1930–35; ESTR(IN) + -ONE]

es·trous (es′trəs), *adj.* pertaining to or involving the estrus. Also, **estral, oestrous.** [1895–1900; see OESTROUS]

es′trous cy′cle, a series of physiological changes in sexual and other organs in female mammals, extending from one period of heat to the next, accompanied by behavioral changes indicating interest in mating.

es·trus (es′trəs), *n. Zool.* **1.** Also, **es·trum** (es′trəm), **oestrus.** the period of heat or rut; the period of maximum sexual receptivity of the female. **2.** See **estrous cycle.** [1885–90; < L *oestrus* OESTRUS] **—es·tru·al** (es′tro͞o əl), *adj.*

es·tu·a·rine (es′cho͞o ə rīn′, -ər in), *adj.* **1.** formed in an estuary. **2.** found in estuaries. [1840–50; ESTUAR(Y) + -INE[1]]

es·tu·ar·y (es′cho͞o er′ē), *n., pl.* **-ar·ies. 1.** that part of the mouth or lower course of a river in which the river's current meets the sea's tide. **2.** an arm or inlet of the sea at the lower end of a river. [1530–40; < L *aestuārium* channel, creek, inlet, equiv. to *aestu(s)* tide + *-ārium* -ARY] **—es·tu·ar·i·al** (es′cho͞o âr′ē əl), *adj.*

esu, *Elect.* See **electrostatic unit.** Also, **ESU**

e·su·ri·ent (i so͝or′ē ənt), *adj.* hungry; greedy. [1665–75; < L *ēsurient-* (s. of *ēsuriēns,* prp. of *ēsurīre*) hungering, equiv. to *ēsur-* hunger + *-ent-* -ENT] **—e·su′ri·ence, e·su′ri·en·cy,** *n.* **—e·su′ri·ent·ly,** *adv.*

et (et), *v. Chiefly North Atlantic, South Midland, and Southern U.S. Nonstandard.* a pt. of **eat.**

et (et), *conj. Latin.* and.

-et, a noun suffix having properly a diminutive force (now lost in many words): *islet; tablet; midget; plummet.* Cf. **-ette.** [ME < OF *-et* (masc.), *-ette* (fem.)]

Et, *Symbol, Chem.* ethyl.

E.T., 1. Eastern time. **2.** extraterrestrial (def. 2). Also, **ET**

e.t., electrical transcription.

e·ta (ā′tə, ē′tə), *n.* **1.** the seventh letter of the Greek alphabet (H, η). **2.** the vowel sound represented by this letter. [< Gk *êta;* cf. Heb *ḥeth* HETH]

E.T.A., estimated time of arrival. Also, **ETA**

E′ta Aq′uarids (ā′tə, ē′tə), *Astron.* See under **Aquarids.**

E′ta Cari′nae, a star and its surrounding nebula in the constellation Carina. [NL: Eta (seventh) of CARINA]

é·ta·gère (ā′tä zhâr′, ā′tə-; *Fr.* ā ta zhɛr′), *n., pl.* **-gères** (-zhârz′; *Fr.* -zhɛr′). a stand with a series of open shelves for small objects, bric-a-brac, etc. Also, **e·ta·gere** (ā′tä zhâr′, ā′tə-). [1850–55; < F]

étagère

et al. (et al′, äl′, ôl′), **1.** and elsewhere. [< L *et alibi*] **2.** and others. [< L *et aliī* (masc. pl.), *et alia* (neut. pl.)]

e·ta·lon (āt′l on′), *n. Optics.* an interferometer consisting of two glass plates that reflect approximately half of each ray of light incident upon them and that are separated by a small, fixed distance: used to compare wavelengths and to study atomic spectra. [1900–05; < F; MF *estalon* standard, deriv. of OF *estal* place < Gmc; see STALL[1]]

e′ta me′son, *Physics.* a neutral meson with strangeness 0 that is its own antiparticle. *Symbol:* η [1960–65]

et·a·mine (et′ə mēn′), *n.* a lightweight cotton or worsted fabric constructed in plain weave and loosely woven. [1750–60; < F; see ESTAMIN]

et·a·oin shrd·lu (et′ē oin′ shûrd′lo͞o, -ō′in, ē′tē-), the letters produced by running the finger down the first two vertical rows of keys at the left of the keyboard of a Linotype machine: used as a temporary marking slug or to indicate that an earlier mistake in the line necessitates resetting, but sometimes inadvertently cast and printed. [1955–60]

é·tape (ā tap′; *Fr.* ā tap′), *n., pl.* **é·tapes** (ā taps′; *Fr.* ā tap′). *Mil.* **1.** a place where troops camp after a day's march. **2.** a day's march. **3.** *Archaic.* supplies issued to troops during a march. [< F; MF *estaple* < MD *stapel* warehouse; see STAPLE[2]]

e·tat·ism (ā tä′tiz əm), *n.* See **state socialism.** [1920–25; < F *étatisme,* equiv. to *état* state (OF *estat* < L *status* STATUS) + *-isme* -ISM] **—e·tat′ist,** *adj.*

etc., See **et cetera.**

et cet·er·a (et set′ər ə, se′trə), and others; and so forth; and so on (used to indicate that more of the same sort or class might have been mentioned, but for brevity have been omitted): *He had dogs, cats, guinea pigs, frogs, et cetera, as pets. Abbr.:* etc. [1100–50; late OE < L]

—Usage. ET CETERA, a Latin phrase, appears in English writing most frequently in its abbreviated form, ETC. This phrase is used frequently in technical and business writing, somewhat less frequently in general informal writing, and sometimes in literary or formal writing. Expressions such as *and so forth* and *and so on* are useful substitutes. Because "and" is included in the meaning of ET CETERA, the expression *and et cetera* is redundant.

—Pronunciation. Pronunciations with (k) substituted for the first (t): (ek set′ər ə) or (ek se′trə), although occasionally used by educated speakers, are usually considered nonstandard.

et·cet·er·a (et set′ər ə, -se′trə), *n., pl.* **-er·as. 1.** a number of other things or persons unspecified. **2. etceteras,** extras or sundries. [1375–1425; n. use of ET CETERA]

etch (ech), *v.t.* **1.** to cut, bite, or corrode with an acid or the like; engrave with an acid or the like, as to form a design in furrows that when charged with ink will give an impression on paper. **2.** to produce (a design, image, etc.) by this method, as on copper or glass. **3.** to outline clearly or sharply; delineate, as a person's features or character. **4.** to fix permanently in or implant firmly on the mind; root in the memory: *Our last conversation is etched in my memory.* **5.** *Geol.* to cut (a feature) into the surface of the earth by means of erosion: *A deep canyon was etched into the land by the river's rushing waters.* **—***v.i.* **6.** to practice the art of etching. **—***n.* **7.** *Print.* an acid used for etching. [1625–35; < D *etsen* < G *ätzen* to etch, orig. cause to eat; c. OE *ettan* to graze; akin to EAT] **—etch′er,** *n.*

etch·ant (ech′ənt), *n.* a chemical used to etch designs into metal, glass, or other material. [1925–30; ETCH + -ANT]

etch·ing (ech′ing), *n.* **1.** the act or process of making designs or pictures on a metal plate, glass, etc., by the corrosive action of an acid instead of by a burin. **2.** an impression, as on paper, taken from an etched plate. **3.** the design so produced. **4.** a metal plate bearing such a design. [1625–35; ETCH + -ING[1]]

etch′ing ground′, ground[1] (def. 11). [1780–90]

E.T.D., estimated time of departure. Also, **ETD**

E·te·o·cles (i tē′ə klēz′), *n. Class. Myth.* a son of Oedipus and the brother of Polynices, by whom he was slain. Cf. **Seven against Thebes** (def. 1).

E·te·o·clus (i tē′ə kləs), *n. Class. Myth.* one of the Seven against Thebes.

Et·e·o·cre·tan (et′ē ō krēt′n, ē′tē-), *adj.* noting or pertaining to certain inscriptions found on Crete, written in an early form of the Greek alphabet. [1890–95; < Gk *Eteókrēt(es)* true Cretans (*ete(ós)* true, genuine + *-o-* -O- + *Krēt-,* s. of *Krēs* Cretan + *-es,* pl. of *-ēs* adj. suffix) + -AN, after CRETAN]

e·ter·nal (i tûr′nl), *adj.* **1.** without beginning or end; lasting forever; always existing (opposed to *temporal*): *eternal life.* **2.** perpetual; ceaseless; endless: *eternal quarreling; eternal chatter.* **3.** enduring; immutable: *eternal principles.* **4.** *Metaphys.* existing outside all relations of time; not subject to change. **—***n.* **5.** something that is eternal. **6. the Eternal,** God. [1350–1400; ME

CONCISE ETYMOLOGY KEY: <, descended or borrowed from; >, whence; b., blend of, blended; c., cognate with; cf., compare; deriv., derivative; equiv., equivalent; imit., imitative; obl., oblique; r., replacing; s., stem; sp., spelling, spelled; resp., respelling, respelled; trans., translation; ?, origin unknown; *, unattested; ‡, probably earlier than. See the full key inside the front cover.

< LL *aeternālis,* equiv. to *aetern(us)* (see ETERNE) + *-ālis* -AL[1]] **—e·ter·nal·i·ty** (ē′tûr nal′i tē), **e·ter′nal·ness,** *n.* **—e·ter′nal·ly,** *adv.*
—Syn. 1. permanent, unending. ETERNAL, ENDLESS, EVERLASTING, PERPETUAL imply lasting or going on without ceasing. That which is ETERNAL is, by its nature, without beginning or end: *God, the eternal Father.* That which is ENDLESS never stops but goes on continuously as if in a circle: *an endless succession of years.* That which is EVERLASTING will endure through all future time: *a promise of everlasting life.* PERPETUAL implies continuous renewal as far into the future as one can foresee: *perpetual strife between nations.* **3.** timeless, immortal, deathless, undying, imperishable, indestructible. **—Ant. 1.** transitory. **3.** mutable.

Eter′nal Cit′y, The, the city of Rome, Italy.

e·ter·nal·ize (i tûr′nl īz′), *v.t.,* **-ized, -iz·ing.** to eternize. Also, *esp. Brit.,* **e·ter′nal·ise′.** [1610–20; ETERNAL + -IZE]

e·terne (i tûrn′), *adj. Archaic.* eternal. [1325–75; ME < L *aeternus,* contr. of *aeviternus,* equiv. to *aev(um)* age + *-i-* -I- + *-ternus,* extended form of *-ernus* suffix of temporal adjectives]

e·ter·ni·ty (i tûr′ni tē), *n., pl.* **-ties. 1.** infinite time; duration without beginning or end. **2.** eternal existence, esp. as contrasted with mortal life: *the eternity of God.* **3.** *Theol.* the timeless state into which the soul passes at a person's death. **4.** an endless or seemingly endless period of time: *We had to wait an eternity for the check to arrive.* **5. eternities,** the truths or realities of life and thought that are regarded as timeless or eternal. [1325–75; ME *eternite* < L *aeternitās.* See ETERNE, -ITY]

e·ter·nize (i tûr′nīz), *v.t.,* **-nized, -niz·ing. 1.** to make eternal; perpetuate. **2.** to immortalize. Also, *esp. Brit.,* **e·ter′nise.** [1560–70; < ML *ēternizāre.* See ETERNE, -IZE] **—e·ter′ni·za′tion,** *n.*

e·te·sian (i tē′zhən), *adj.* (of certain Mediterranean winds) occurring annually. [1595–1605; < L *etēsi(ae)* < Gk *etēsiai (ánemoi)* periodic (winds) + -AN]

ete′sian cli′mate. See **Mediterranean climate.**

eth (eth), *n.* a letter in the form of a crossed *d,* written đ or ð, used in Old English writing to represent both voiced and unvoiced *th* and in modern Icelandic and in phonetic alphabets to represent voiced *th.* Also, **edh.**

-eth[1], an ending of the third person singular present indicative of verbs, now occurring only in archaic forms or used in solemn or poetic language: *doeth* or *doth; hopeth; sitteth.* Also, **-th.** [OE *-eth, -ath, -oth, -th;* akin to L *-t*]

-eth[2], var. of **-th**[2], the ordinal suffix, used when the cardinal number ends in *-y: twentieth; thirtieth.*

Eth., Ethiopia.

eth′a·cryn′ic ac′id (eth′ə krin′ik, eth′-), *Pharm.* a whitish crystalline powder, $C_{13}H_{12}Cl_2O_4$, that is a potent diuretic used in the treatment of acute pulmonary edema and other edemas associated with such diseases as congestive heart failure, cirrhosis of the liver, and renal disease. [1960–65; appar. (M)ETH(YLENE) + AC(ETIC) + (BUTY)RY(L) + *(phe)n(oxy)* + -IC]

eth·al (eth′al, ē′thal), *n. Chem.* See **cetyl alcohol.** [1830–40; ETH(ER) + -AL[3]]

eth·am·bu·tol (e tham′byə tôl′, -tol′), *n. Pharm.* an antimicrobial substance, $C_{10}H_{24}N_2O_2$, active against susceptible bacteria of the genus *Mycobacterium,* in the treatment, in combination with other drugs, of tuberculosis. [1960–65; ETH(YLENE) + AM(INE) + BUT(AN)OL]

E·than (ē′thən), *n.* a male given name: from a Hebrew word meaning "strength."

eth·a·nal (eth′ə nal′, -nl), *n. Chem.* acetaldehyde. [ETHANE + -AL[3]]

eth·ane (eth′ān), *n. Chem.* a colorless, odorless, flammable gas, C_2H_6, of the methane series, present in natural gas, illuminating gas, and crude petroleum: used chiefly in organic synthesis and as a fuel gas. Also called **dimethyl.** [1870–75; ETH(YL) + -ANE]

Eth·a·nim (eth′ə nim; *Seph. Heb.* e tä nēm′), *n. Chiefly Biblical.* a month equivalent to Tishri in the modern Jewish calendar. I Kings 8:2. [< Heb *ēthānīm*]

eth·a·nol (eth′ə nôl′, -nol′), *n. Chem.* alcohol (def. 1). [1895–1900; ETHANE + -OL[1]]

eth·a·nol·a·mine (eth′ə nol′ə mēn′, -nō′lə-, -nə lam′in), *n. Chem.* a viscous liquid with an odor of ammonia, C_2H_7NO, used to remove carbon dioxide and hydrogen sulfide from natural gas, and in the manufacture of antibiotics. Also called **colamine.** [1895–1900; ETHANOL + AMINE]

eth·chlor·vy·nol (eth′klôr vīn′l, -klōr-), *n. Pharm.* a colorless to yellow, pungent, aromatic liquid, C_7H_9ClO, used as a hypnotic and sedative, esp. in the short-term management of insomnia. [ETH(YL) + CHLOR(O)- + V(IN)Y(L) + (CARBIN)OL]

Eth·el (eth′əl), *n.* a female given name: from a Germanic word meaning "noble."

Eth·el·bert (eth′əl bûrt′), *n.* **1.** A.D. 552?–616, king of Kent 560–616. **2.** a male given name: from Old English words meaning "noble" and "bright."

Eth·el·red II (eth′əl red′), *("the Unready")* A.D. 968?–1016, king of the English 978–1016.

Eth·el·stan (eth′əl stan′), *n.* Athelstan.

eth·ene (eth′ēn), *n. Chem.* ethylene (def. 2). [1870–75; ETH(YL) + -ENE]

eth·e·phon (eth′ə fon′), *n. Chem.* a solid compound, $C_2H_6ClO_3P$, used as a growth regulator to accelerate the ripening of tomatoes, citrus fruit, apples, and other crops. [1970–75; as shortening of the chemical name *2-chloroethanephosphonic acid;* see CHLORO-, ETHANE, PHOSPHO-, -ONIC]

e·ther (ē′thər), *n.* **1.** Also called **diethyl ether, diethyl oxide, ethyl ether, ethyl oxide, sulfuric ether.** *Chem., Pharm.* a colorless, highly volatile, flammable liquid, $C_4H_{10}O$, having an aromatic odor and sweet, burning taste, derived from ethyl alcohol by the action of sulfuric acid: used as a solvent and, formerly, as an inhalant anesthetic. **2.** *Chem.* (formerly) one of a class of compounds in which two organic groups are attached directly to an oxygen atom, having the general formula ROR. **3.** the upper regions of space; the clear sky; the heavens. **4.** the medium supposed by the ancients to fill the upper regions of space. **5.** *Physics.* a hypothetical substance supposed to occupy all space, postulated to account for the propagation of electromagnetic radiation through space. Cf. **Michelson-Morley experiment.** Also, **aether** (for defs. 3–5). [1350–1400; ME < L *aethēr* the upper air, pure air, ether < Gk *aithḗr,* akin to *aíthein* to glow, burn, OE *ād* funeral pyre, L *aestus* heat] **—e·ther·ic** (i ther′ik, i thēr′-), *adj.*

e·the·re·al (i thēr′ē əl), *adj.* **1.** light, airy, or tenuous: *an ethereal world created through the poetic imagination.* **2.** extremely delicate or refined: *ethereal beauty.* **3.** heavenly or celestial: *gone to his ethereal home.* **4.** of or pertaining to the upper regions of space. **5.** *Chem.* pertaining to, containing, or resembling ethyl ether. Also, **aethereal** (for defs. 1–4). [1505–15; < L *aethere(us)* (< Gk *aithérios*), equiv. to *aether-* ETHER + *-eus* adj. suffix + -AL[1]] **—e·the′re·al′i·ty, e·the′re·al·ness,** *n.* **—e·the′re·al·ly,** *adv.* **—e·the′re·ous,** *adj.*

e·the·re·al·ize (i thēr′ē ə līz′), *v.t.,* **-ized, -iz·ing.** to make ethereal. Also, *esp. Brit.,* **e·the′re·al·ise′.** [1820–30; ETHEREAL + -IZE] **—e·the′re·al·i·za′tion,** *n.*

Eth·er·ege (eth′ər ij, eth′rij), *n.* **Sir George,** 1635?–91, English dramatist.

e·ther·i·fy (i ther′ə fī′, ē′thər-), *v.t.,* **-fied, -fy·ing.** *Chem.* to convert into an ether. [1855–60; ETHER + -IFY] **—e·ther′i·fi·ca′tion,** *n.*

e·ther·ize (ē′thə rīz′), *v.t.,* **-ized, -iz·ing. 1.** *Med.* to put under the influence of ether; anesthetize. **2.** to render groggy or numb, as if by an anesthetic. Also, *esp. Brit.,* **e′ther·ise′.** [1740–50; ETHER + -IZE] **—e′ther·i·za′tion,** *n.* **—e′ther·iz′er,** *n.*

E·ther·net (ē′thər net′), *Trademark.* a local-area network protocol featuring a bus topology and a 10 megabit per second data transfer rate.

eth·ic (eth′ik), *n.* **1.** the body of moral principles or values governing a particular culture or group: *the Christian ethic.* **2.** a complex of moral precepts held or rules of conduct followed by an individual: *a personal ethic.* [1350–1400; ME *etik, etic* < L *ēthicus* < Gk *ēthikós,* equiv. to *ēth(os)* ETHOS + *-ikos* -IC]

eth·i·cal (eth′i kəl), *adj.* **1.** pertaining to or dealing with morals or the principles of morality; pertaining to right and wrong in conduct. **2.** being in accordance with the rules or standards for right conduct or practice, esp. the standards of a profession: *It was not considered ethical for physicians to advertise.* **3.** (of drugs) sold only upon medical prescription. [1600–10; ETHIC + -AL[1]] **—eth′i·cal·ly,** *adv.* **—eth′i·cal·ness, eth′i·cal′i·ty,** *n.*
—Syn. 2. moral, upright, honest, righteous, virtuous.

Eth′ical Cul′ture, a movement founded by Felix Adler in 1876 that stresses the importance of ethical behavior independent of religious beliefs.

eth·i·cist (eth′ə sist), *n.* a person who specializes in or writes on ethics or who is devoted to ethical principles. Also, **eth·i·cian** (e thish′ən). [1890–95; ETHIC + -IST]

eth·i·cize (eth′ə sīz′), *v.t.,* **-cized, -ciz·ing.** to make ethical; treat or regard as ethical. [1810–20; ETHIC + -IZE]

eth·ics (eth′iks), *n.pl.* **1.** (*used with a singular or plural v.*) a system of moral principles. **2.** the rules of conduct recognized in respect to a particular class of human actions or a particular group, culture, etc.: *medical ethics; Christian ethics.* **3.** moral principles, as of an individual. **4.** (*used with a singular v.*) that branch of philosophy dealing with values relating to human conduct, with respect to the rightness and wrongness of certain actions and to the goodness and badness of the motives and ends of such actions. Cf. **axiological ethics, deontological ethics.** [1400–50; late ME ETHIC + -S[3], modeled on Gk *tà ēthiká,* neut. pl.]
—Syn. 2. See **moral.**

Eth′ics of the Fa′thers. See ***Pirke Avoth.***

e·thin·a·mate (i thin′ə māt′), *n. Pharm.* a crystalline, slightly water-soluble powder, $C_9H_{13}NO_2$, used as a hypnotic. [formerly a trademark]

eth·ine (eth′īn, e thīn′), *n. Chem.* acetylene. [1875–80; ETH(YL) + -INE[1]]

eth·i·on·a·mide (eth′ē on′ə mīd′), *n. Pharm.* an antimicrobial substance, $C_8H_{10}N_2S$, used against susceptible *Mycobacterium tuberculosis* in combination with other drugs in the treatment of any active form of tuberculosis. [1960–65; E(THYL) + THION(IC) + AMIDE]

E·thi·op (ē′thē op′), *adj., n.* Ethiopian. Also, **E·thi·ope** (ē′thē ōp′). [1350–1400; ME < L *Aethiops* < Gk *Aithíops*]

E·thi·o·pi·a (ē′thē ō′pē ə), *n.* **1.** Formerly, **Abyssinia.** a republic in E Africa: formerly a monarchy. 30,200,000; 409,266 sq. mi. (1,060,000 sq. km). Present boundaries include Eritrea. *Cap.:* Addis Ababa. **2.** Also called **Abyssinia.** an ancient region in NE Africa, bordering on Egypt and the Red Sea.

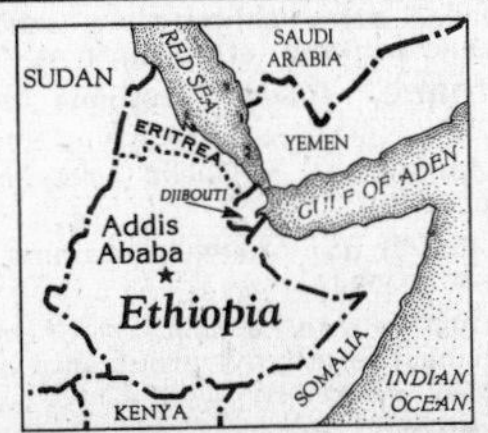

E·thi·o·pi·an (ē′thē ō′pē ən), *adj.* **1.** of or pertaining to Ethiopia or to its inhabitants. **2.** belonging to the part of Africa south of the equator. **3.** *Zoogeog.* belonging to a geographical division comprising Africa south of the tropic of Cancer, the southern part of the Arabian Peninsula, and Madagascar. **4.** *Archaic.* black African. **—n. 5.** a native of Ethiopia. **6.** a member of any of various supposedly dark-skinned peoples regarded by the ancients as coming from a country lying south of Egypt. **7.** *Archaic.* a black African. [1545–55]

Ethio′pian Church′, the Monophysitic church founded by Frumentius in the 4th century A.D., and resembling the Coptic Church in doctrine, practice, and discipline, but using Ethiopic in its liturgy. Also called **Abyssinian Church.** [1900–05]

E·thi·op·ic (ē′thē op′ik, -ō′pik), *adj.* **1.** Ethiopian. **—n. 2.** a subdivision of Semitic languages that includes Amharic, Tigré, Tigrinya, and Geez, all of Ethiopia. **3.** Geez. [1650–60; < L *Aethiopicus.* See ETHIOP, -IC]

eth·moid (eth′moid), *Anat.* **—adj. 1.** Also, **eth·moi′dal.** of or pertaining to a bone at the base of the cranium and the root of the nose, containing numerous perforations for the filaments of the olfactory nerve. **—n. 2.** the ethmoid bone. [1735–45; < Gk *ēthmoeidḗs* sievelike; see -OID]

eth·narch (eth′närk), *n.* the ruler of a people, tribe, or nation. [1635–45; < Gk *ethnárchēs.* See ETHNO-, -ARCH]

eth·nar·chy (eth′när kē), *n., pl.* **-chies.** the government, office, or jurisdiction of an ethnarch. [1605–15; < Gk *ethnarchía.* See ETHNARCH, -Y[3]]

eth·nic (eth′nik), *adj.* **1.** pertaining to or characteristic of a people, esp. a group **(eth′nic group′)** sharing a common and distinctive culture, religion, language, or the like. **2.** referring to the origin, classification, characteristics, etc., of such groups. **3.** being a member of an ethnic group, esp. of a group that is a minority within a larger society: *ethnic Chinese in San Francisco.* **4.** of, pertaining to, or characteristic of members of such a group. **5.** belonging to or deriving from the cultural, racial, religious, or linguistic traditions of a people or country: *ethnic dances.* **6.** *Obsolete.* pagan; heathen. **—n. 7.** a member of an ethnic group. [1325–75; ME *ethnik* heathen < LL *ethnicus* < Gk *ethnikós.* See ETHNO-, -IC] **—eth′ni·cal·ly,** *adv.*
—Syn. 1. native, national, indigenous; cultural, racial.

eth·ni·cal (eth′ni kəl), *adj.* **1.** ethnic. **2.** of, pertaining to, or concerned with ethnology. [1540–50; ETHNIC + -AL[1]]

eth′nic cleans′ing, the elimination of an unwanted ethnic group from a society, as by genocide or forced migration.

eth·nic·i·ty (eth nis′i tē), *n.* ethnic traits, background, allegiance, or association. [1765–75, for earlier sense; ETHNIC + -ITY]

ethno-, a combining form meaning "race," "culture," "people," used in the formation of compound words: *ethnography.* [< Gk, comb. form of *éthnos*]

eth·no·ar·chae·ol·o·gy (eth′nō är′kē ol′ə jē), *n.* the branch of archaeology that studies contemporary primitive cultures and technologies as a way of providing analogies and thereby patterns for prehistoric cultures. Also, **eth′no·ar′che·ol′o·gy.** [1970–75; ETHNO- + ARCHAEOLOGY] **—eth′no·ar′chae·ol′o·gist,** *n.*

eth·no·bi·ol·o·gy (eth′nō bī ol′ə jē), *n. Anthropol.* **1.** the scientific study of the way plants and animals are treated or used by different human cultures. **2.** the doctrine that cultural behavior is determined biologically, as by race: no longer in technical use. [ETHNO- + BIOLOGY] **—eth·no·bi·o·log·i·cal** (eth′nō bī′ə loj′i kəl), *adj.* **—eth′no·bi·ol′o·gist,** *n.*

eth·no·bot·a·ny (eth′nō bot′n ē), *n.* **1.** the plant lore and agricultural customs of a people. **2.** *Anthropol.* the systematic study of such lore and customs. [1885–90, *Amer.*] **—eth·no·bo·tan·ic** (eth′nō bə tan′ik), **eth′no·bo·tan′i·cal,** *adj.* **—eth′no·bot′a·nist,** *n.*

eth·no·cen·trism (eth′nō sen′triz əm), *n.* **1.** *Sociol.* the belief in the inherent superiority of one's own ethnic group or culture. **2.** a tendency to view alien groups or cultures from the perspective of one's own. [1905–10; ETHNO- + CENT(E)R + -ISM] **—eth′no·cen′tric,** *adj.* **—eth′no·cen′tri·cal·ly,** *adv.* **—eth·no·cen·tric·i·ty** (eth′nō sen tris′i tē), *n.*

ethnog., ethnography.

eth·nog·ra·phy (eth nog′rə fē), *n.* a branch of anthropology dealing with the scientific description of individual cultures. [1825–35; ETHNO- + -GRAPHY] **—eth·nog′ra·pher,** *n.* **—eth·no·graph·ic** (eth′nə graf′ik), **eth′no·graph′i·cal,** *adj.* **—eth′no·graph′i·cal·ly,** *adv.*

ethnog′raphy of speak′ing, *Anthropol. Ling.* the scientific description of the varieties and characteristics of language use within a culture. Also called **ethnog′raphy of communica′tion.**

eth·no·his·to·ry (eth′nō his′tə rē), *n.* a branch of anthropology dealing with the development of cultures, as through the analysis of archaeological findings. [1950–55; ETHNO- + HISTORY] **—eth·no·his·to·ri·an** (eth′nō hi stôr′ē ən, -stor′-), *n.* **—eth·no·his·tor·i·cal** (eth′nō hi stôr′i kəl, -stor′-), **eth′no·his·tor′ic,** *adj.* **—eth′no·his·tor′i·cal·ly,** *adv.*

ethnol., 1. ethnological. **2.** ethnology.

eth·no·lin·guis·tics (eth′nō ling gwis′tiks), *n.* (*used with a singular v.*) the study of language as an aspect or part of culture, esp. the study of the influence of language on culture and of culture on language. [1945–50; ETHNO- + LINGUISTICS] **—eth′no·lin′guist,** *n.* **—eth′no·lin·guis′tic,** *adj.*

eth·nol·o·gy (eth nol′ə jē), *n.* **1.** a branch of anthropology that analyzes cultures, esp. in regard to their historical development and the similarities and dissimilarities between them. **2.** (formerly) a branch of anthropology dealing with the origin, distribution, and distinguishing characteristics of the races of humankind. [1835–45; ETHNO- + -LOGY] —**eth·no·log·i·cal** (eth′nə loj′i kəl), **eth′no·log′ic,** *adj.* —**eth′no·log′i·cal·ly,** *adv.* —**eth·nol′o·gist,** *n.*

eth·no·meth·od·ol·o·gy (eth′nō meth′ə dol′ə jē), *n.* the sociological study of the rules and rituals underlying ordinary social activities and interactions. [1960–65; ETHNO- + METHODOLOGY] —**eth′no·meth′od·ol′o·gist,** *n.*

eth·no·mu·si·col·o·gy (eth′nō myo͞o′zi kol′ə jē), *n.* the study of folk and primitive music and of their relationship to the peoples and cultures to which they belong. [1945–50; ETHNO- + MUSICOLOGY] —**eth·no·mu·si·co·log·i·cal** (eth′nō myo͞o′zi kə loj′i kəl), *adj.* —**eth′no·mu′si·co·log′i·cal·ly,** *adv.* —**eth′no·mu′si·col′o·gist,** *n.*

eth·no·phar·ma·col·o·gy (eth′nō fär′mə kol′ə jē), *n.* the scientific study of substances used medicinally, esp. folk remedies, by different ethnic or cultural groups. [1975–80; ETHNO- + PHARMACOLOGY] —**eth·no·phar·ma·co·log·i·cal** (eth′nō fär′mə kə loj′i kəl), **eth′no·phar′ma·co·log′ic,** *adj.*

eth·nos (eth′nos), *n.* an ethnic group. [< Gk *ethnós;* cf. ETHNO-]

eth·no·sci·ence (eth′nō sī′əns), *n.* the study of the systems of knowledge and classification of material objects and concepts by primitive and non-Western peoples. [1960–65; ETHNO- + SCIENCE]

eth·no·ther·a·py (eth′nō ther′ə pē), *n. Psychol.* a type of group therapy that focuses on the special needs and concerns of a particular ethnic minority. [ETHNO- + THERAPY]

et hoc ge·nus om·ne (et hōk′ ge′no͝os ōm′ne; *Eng.* et hok′ jē′nəs om′nē), *Latin.* and all this (or that) sort of thing. Also, **et id genus omne.**

e·tho·gram (ē′thə gram′), *n. Ethology.* a pictorial inventory of the repertoire of behavior patterns shown by the members of a species. [1965–70; *etho-* (as comb. form repr. ETHOLOGY) + -GRAM[1]]

ethol., ethology.

e·thol·o·gy (ē thol′ə jē, i thol′-), *n.* the study of animal behavior with emphasis on the behavioral patterns that occur in natural environments. [1895–1900; earlier, as the study of relations between an organism and its environment < F *éthologie,* coined by French zoologist I. Geoffroy Saint-Hilaire (1805–61); see ETHOS, -LOGY] —**e·tho·log·i·cal** (ē′thə loj′i kəl, eth′ə-), *adj.* —**e′tho·log′i·cal·ly,** *adv.* —**e·thol′o·gist,** *n.*

e·thos (ē′thos, ē′thōs, eth′os, -ōs), *n.* **1.** *Sociol.* the fundamental character or spirit of a culture; the underlying sentiment that informs the beliefs, customs, or practices of a group or society; dominant assumptions of a people or period: *In the Greek ethos the individual was highly valued.* **2.** the character or disposition of a community, group, person, etc. **3.** the moral element in dramatic literature that determines a character's action rather than his or her thought or emotion. [1850–55; < Gk: custom, habit, character]

eth·o·sux·i·mide (eth′ō suk′sə mīd′), *n. Pharm.* an anticonvulsant, $C_7H_{11}NO_2$, used in medicine to treat certain kinds of epilepsy, esp. petit mal. [ETH(YL) + -O- + *suximide* appar. shortening of *succinimide* (SUCCIN(IC) + IMIDE)]

eth·ox·ide (eth ok′sīd), *n. Chem.* ethylate. [ETH(YL) + OXIDE]

eth·ox·y (e thok′sē), *n. Chem.* the radical C_2H_5O–. Also called **eth·ox·yl** (e thok′sil). [ETH(YL) + OXY-[2] (+ -(Y)L)]

eth·rog (es′rōg, -rəg, et′-; *Seph. Heb.* et RÔG′; *Ashk. Heb.* es RŌG′), *n., pl.* **eth·rogs, eth·ro·gim** (*Seph. Heb.* et RÔ gēm′; *Ashk. Heb.* es RŌ′gim). *Judaism.* etrog.

eth·yl (eth′əl), *adj.* **1.** *Chem.* containing the ethyl group, as ethyl ether, $C_4H_{10}O$. —*n.* **2.** a type of antiknock fluid, containing tetraethyl lead and other ingredients for a more even combustion. [< G *Ethyl,* coined by J. von Liebig in 1834; see ETHER, -YL]

eth′yl ac′etate, *Chem.* a colorless, volatile, flammable liquid, $C_4H_8O_2$, having a fragrant, fruitlike odor: used chiefly as a scent in the manufacture of perfumes, flavorings, and confections, and as a solvent for paints, varnishes, and lacquers. Also called **acetic ether.** [1870–75]

eth′yl al′cohol, *Chem.* alcohol (def. 1). [1865–70]

eth·yl·a·mine (eth′əl ə mēn′, -min, -am′in), *n. Chem.* a flammable liquid with an odor of ammonia, C_2H_7N, used as a stabilizer for rubber latex, as a dye intermediate, and in organic synthesis. [1840–50; ETHYL + AMINE]

eth′yl a·mi·no·ben′zo·ate (ə mē′nō ben′zō āt′, -it, am′ə nō-), *Pharm.* benzocaine. [AMINO- + BENZOATE]

eth·yl·ate (eth′ə lāt′), *v.,* **-at·ed, -at·ing,** *n. Chem.* —*v.t.* **1.** to introduce one or more ethyl groups into (a compound). —*n.* **2.** Also called **ethoxide.** a metallic derivative of ethyl alcohol, as potassium ethylate, KOC_2H_5. [1860–65; ETHYL + -ATE[1]] —**eth′yl·a′tion,** *n.*

eth·yl·ben·zene (eth′əl ben′zēn, -ben zēn′), *n. Chem.* a colorless liquid, C_8H_{10}, used chiefly as an intermediate in the manufacture of styrene and as a solvent and diluent for paints and varnishes. [1870–75; ETHYL + BENZENE]

CONCISE ETYMOLOGY KEY: <, descended or borrowed from; >, whence; b., blend of, blended; c., cognate with; cf., compare; deriv., derivative; equiv., equivalent; imit., imitative; obl., oblique; r., replacing; s., stem; sp., spelling, spelled; resp., respelling, respelled; trans., translation; ?, origin unknown; *, unattested; ‡, probably earlier than. See the full key inside the front cover.

eth′yl bu′tyrate, *Chem.* a colorless, volatile, nontoxic liquid having the odor of pineapple, $C_6H_{12}O_2$, used chiefly in flavoring extracts, and in the manufacture of perfumes and sprays. Also called **eth′yl bu′tan·o·ate** (byo͞o′tan ō āt′, byo͞o tan′).

eth′yl cap′ro·ate (kap′rō āt′), *Chem.* a colorless to yellow liquid, soluble in alcohol or ether, $C_8H_{16}O_2$, used chiefly in artificial fruit essences and organic synthesis. Also, **eth′yl cap′ro·nate** (kap′rō nāt′). Also called **ethyl hexoate.** [CAPRO(IC) + -ATE[2]]

eth′yl car′ba·mate (kär′bə māt′, kär bam′āt), *Chem.* urethane (def. 2).

eth′yl cel′lulose, *Chem.* an ethyl ether of cellulose, in the form of white granules obtained from the treatment of wood pulp with alkali: used in plastics and lacquers.

eth′yl chlo′ride, *Chem.* a flammable gas, C_2H_5Cl, used as a refrigerant, solvent, and anesthetic. Also called **chloroethane.**

eth·yl·di·chlo·ro·ar·sine (eth′əl dī klôr′ō är′sēn, -klōr′-), *n. Chem.* a colorless, volatile, poisonous liquid, $C_2H_5AsCl_2$, having an irritating, fruitlike odor: formerly used as a blister gas. [ETHYL + DI-[1] + CHLORO-[2] + ARSINE]

eth′yl e·nan′thate (i nan′thāt), *Chem.* See **ethyl oenanthate.**

eth·yl·e·na·tion (eth′ə lə nā′shən), *n. Chem.* the process of introducing an ethylene group into a compound. [ETHYLENE + -ATION]

eth·yl·ene (eth′ə lēn′), *Chem.* —*adj.* **1.** containing the ethylene group. —*n.* **2.** Also called **ethene, olefiant gas.** a colorless, flammable gas, C_2H_4, having a sweet, unpleasant odor and taste, the first member of the ethylene series, usually obtained from petroleum and natural gas: used as an agent to improve the color of citrus fruits, in the synthesis of polyethylene, ethylene dibromide, ethylene oxide, and other organic compounds, and in medicine chiefly as an inhalation anesthetic. [1850–55; ETHYL + -ENE] —**eth·yl·e·nic** (eth′ə lē′nik, -len′ik), *adj.*

eth′ylene al′cohol, glycol (def. 1).

eth′yl·ene·di′a·mine·tet′ra·a·ce′tic ac′id (eth′-ə lēn dī′ə mēn te′trə ə sē′tik, -set′ik, -min-; eth′ə lēn-dī′ə mēn te′trə ə sē′tik, -set′ik, -min-), *Chem., Pharm.* See **EDTA.** [1940–45; ETHYLENE + DIAMINE + TETRA- + ACETIC ACID]

eth′ylene dibro′mide, *Chem.* See **EDB.** Also called **eth′ylene bro′mide.**

eth′ylene dichlo′ride, *Chem.* a colorless, heavy, oily, toxic liquid, $C_2H_4Cl_2$, having a chloroformlike odor: used in the synthesis of vinyl chloride, and as a solvent for fats, waxes, resins, etc. Also called **dichloroethane, eth′ylene chlo′ride.**

eth′ylene gly′col, *Chem.* glycol (def. 1). [1900–05]

eth′ylene group′, *Chem.* the bivalent group, $-C_2H_4-$, derived from ethylene or ethane. Also called **eth′ylene rad′ical.**

eth′ylene ox′ide, *Chem.* a colorless, odorless, gaseous, toxic, ring compound, C_2H_4O, usually obtained by the oxidation of ethylene: used chiefly in the synthesis of ethylene glycol. [1895–1900]

eth′ylene se′ries, *Chem.* See **alkene series.**

eth′yl e′ther, *Chem.* ether (def. 1). [1875–80]

eth′yl group′, *Chem.* the univalent group, C_2H_5–, derived from ethane. Also called **eth′yl rad′ical.**

eth′yl hex′o·ate (hek′sō āt′), *Chem.* See **ethyl caproate.** [*hexo(ic acid)* (from HEXANE) + -ATE[2]]

e·thyl·ic (e thil′ik), *adj.* of, pertaining to, or characteristic of the ethyl group. [1865–70; ETHYL + -IC]

eth′yl mal′onate, *Chem.* a colorless, water-insoluble liquid, $C_7H_{12}O_4$, having a pleasant, aromatic odor: used chiefly as an intermediate in the synthesis of barbiturates.

eth′yl mercap′tan, *Chem.* mercaptan.

eth′yl ni′trate, *Chem.* a colorless, sweet, water-insoluble, extremely explosive liquid, $C_2H_5NO_3$, used chiefly in organic synthesis. Also called **nitric ether.**

eth′yl ni′trite, *Chem.* a colorless or yellowish, very volatile, highly aromatic, flammable liquid, $C_2H_5NO_2$, used chiefly in the preparation of organic substances. Also called **nitrous ether.** [1865–70]

eth′yl ni′trite spir′it, *Pharm.* a four percent solution of ethyl nitrite in alcohol, formerly used in medicine as a diaphoretic, diuretic, and antispasmodic. Also called **spirit of nitrous ether, sweet spirit of nitre.**

eth′yl oe·nan′thate (i nan′thāt), *Chem.* a colorless to yellowish, oily, water-insoluble liquid, $C_9H_{18}O_2$, having a fruitlike odor, found naturally in the alcohols of cognac and other wines: synthesized for use chiefly as artificial flavoring in various alcoholic beverages. Also, **ethyl enanthate.** [OENANTH(IC) + -ATE[2]]

eth′yl ox′ide, *Chem.* ether (def. 1).

eth′yl sul′fide, *Chem.* a colorless, oily, slightly water-soluble liquid, $C_4H_{10}S$, having a garliclike odor: used chiefly as a solvent for certain salts and in organic synthesis. Also called **eth′yl·thi·o·e·ther** (eth′əl thī′ō ē′-thər), **eth·yl·thi·o·eth·ane** (eth′əl thī′ō eth′ān).

eth′yl u′rethane, *Chem.* urethane (def. 2). Also, **eth′yl u′rethan.**

eth·yne (eth′īn, e thīn′), *n. Chem.* acetylene. [ETH(YL) + *-yne* (var. of -INE[2])]

e·thy·nyl (e thīn′l), *adj. Chem.* containing the ethynyl group. [ETHYNE + -YL]

e·thy·nyl·a·tion (e thīn′l ā′shən), *n. Chem.* the process of introducing the ethynyl group into a compound. [ETHYNYL (GROUP) + -ATION]

ethy′nyl group′, *Chem.* the univalent group HC≡C–, derived from acetylene. Also called **ethy′nyl rad′ical.**

ETI, extraterrestrial intelligence.

et·ic (et′ik), *adj. Ling.* pertaining to or being the raw data of a language or other area of behavior, without considering the data as significant units functioning within a system. Cf. **emic.** [1950–55; extracted from PHONETIC; see EMIC]

-etic, a suffix used in the formation of adjectives: *eidetic.* [< L *-eticus,* Gk *-etikos,* equiv. to *-et-,* a formative occurring in some nouns + *-ikos* -IC]

et id ge·nus om·ne (et id′ ge′no͝os ōm′ne; *Eng.* et id′ jē′nəs om′nē), *Latin.* See **et hoc genus omne.**

É·tienne (*Fr.* ā tyen′), *n.* Estienne (def. 1).

e·ti·o·late (ē′tē ə lāt′), *v.,* **-lat·ed, -lat·ing.** —*v.t.* **1.** to cause (a plant) to whiten or grow pale by excluding light: *to etiolate celery.* **2.** to cause to become weakened or sickly; drain of color or vigor. —*v.i.* **3.** (of plants) to whiten or grow pale through lack of light. [1785–95; < F *étioler* to make pale, etiolate (plants), prob. deriv., based on N French dial. forms, of standard F *éteule,* OF *estoble, estuble* STUBBLE; see -ATE[1]] —**e′ti·o·la′tion,** *n.*

e·ti·o·log·ic (ē′tē ə loj′ik), *adj.* **1.** of or pertaining to causes or origins. **2.** *Pathol.* originating from; causal: *etiologic agent.* **3.** of or pertaining to etiology. Also, **e′ti·o·log′i·cal.** [1900–05; ETIOLOG(Y) + -IC] —**e′ti·o·log′i·cal·ly,** *adv.*

e·ti·ol·o·gy (ē′tē ol′ə jē), *n., pl.* **-gies. 1.** *Pathol.* **a.** the study of the causes of diseases. **b.** the cause or origin of a disease. **2.** the study of causation. **3.** any study of causes, causation, or causality, as in philosophy, biology, or physics. Also, **aetiology.** [1545–55; < L *aetiologia* < Gk *aitiología* determining the cause of something, equiv. to *aití(a)* cause + -o- -o- + *-logia* -LOGY] —**e′ti·ol′o·gist,** *n.*

et·i·quette (et′i kit, -ket′), *n.* **1.** conventional requirements as to social behavior; proprieties of conduct as established in any class or community or for any occasion. **2.** a prescribed or accepted code of usage in matters of ceremony, as at a court or in official or other formal observances. **3.** the code of ethical behavior regarding professional practice or action among the members of a profession in their dealings with each other: *medical etiquette.* [1740–50; < F *étiquette,* MF *estiquette* ticket, memorandum, deriv. of *estiqu(i)er* to attach, stick < Gmc. See STICK[2], -ETTE]
—**Syn. 1.** ETIQUETTE, DECORUM, PROPRIETY imply observance of the formal requirements governing behavior in polite society. ETIQUETTE refers to conventional forms and usages: *the rules of etiquette.* DECORUM suggests dignity and a sense of what is becoming or appropriate for a person of good breeding: *a fine sense of decorum.* PROPRIETY (usually plural) implies established conventions of morals and good taste: *She never fails to observe the proprieties.*

Et·na (et′nə), *n.* **Mount,** Also, **Aetna.** an active volcano in E Sicily. 10,758 ft. (3280 m).

ETO, (in World War II) European Theater of Operations. Also, **E.T.O.**

é·toile (ā twal′), *n., pl.* ***é·toiles*** (ā twal′). *French.* **1.** a star or something shaped like a star. **2.** See **prima ballerina.**

E·ton (ēt′n), *n.* a town in Berkshire, in S England, on the Thames River, W of London: the site of Eton College. 3954.

E′ton col′lar, a broad, stiff collar, originally of linen, as that worn folded outside an Eton jacket. [1890–95]

E′ton Col′lege, a preparatory school for boys in Eton, England, founded in 1440 by Henry VI.

E·to·ni·an (ē tō′nē ən), *n.* **1.** a person who is or has been a pupil at Eton College. —*adj.* **2.** of or pertaining to Eton College. [1740–50; ETON + -IAN]

E′ton jack′et, **1.** a boy's black waist-length jacket with wide lapels and an open front, as worn by students at Eton College. **2.** a similar short jacket worn by women. [1880–85]

Eton jacket (def. 1)

e·tor·phine (i tôr′fēn, i tōr′-), *n. Pharm.* a narcotic analgesic, $C_{25}H_{33}NO_4$, used for immobilizing large animals. [1970–75; prob. *et(henom)orphine* a chemical component; see ETHENE, -O-, MORPHINE]

é·touf·fée (ā′to͞o fā′), *n., pl.* **-fées** (-fāz′; *Fr.* -fā′). *New Orleans Cookery.* a stew of crayfish, vegetables and seasonings, served over white rice. [< LaF; F (*à l'*)*étouffée* cooked in a closed vessel with little liquid, braised; n. use of fem. ptp. of *étouffer* lit., to smother, suffocate, OF *estofer,* appar. b. *estoper* to obstruct (< VL **stuppāre;* see ESTOP) and *estofer* to STUFF]

Etr., Etruscan (def. 3).

et·rog (es′rōg, -rəg, et′-; *Seph. Heb.* et RÔG′; *Ashk. Heb.* es RŌG′), *n., pl.* **et·rogs, et·ro·gim** (*Seph. Heb.* et-RÔ gēm′; *Ashk. Heb.* es RŌ′gim). *Judaism.* a citron for use with the lulav during the Sukkoth festival service. Also, **ethrog, esrog.** [< Heb *ethrōgh*]

E•tru•ri•a (i trŏŏr′ē ə), *n.* an ancient country located between the Arno and Tiber rivers, roughly corresponding to modern Tuscany in W Italy.

E•trus•can (i trus′kən), *adj.* **1.** pertaining to Etruria, its inhabitants, civilization, art, or language. —*n.* **2.** an inhabitant of ancient Etruria. **3.** the extinct language of Etruria, not known to be related to any other language. *Abbr.:* Etr. Also, **E•tru•ri•an** (i trŏŏr′ē ən). [1700–10; < L *Etrusc(us)* of Etruria + -AN]

Etrus′can ware′, a black ceramic ware ornamented in encaustic colors, developed by Josiah Wedgwood. [1955–60]

E•trus•col•o•gy (ē′tru skol′ə jē), *n.* the study of Etruscan antiquities. [1885–90; ETRUSC(AN) + -O- + -LOGY] —**E′trus•col′o•gist,** *n.*

ETS, *Trademark.* Educational Testing Service.

et seq., *pl.* **et seqq., et sqq.** and the following. [< L *et sequēns*]

et seqq., and those following. Also, **et sqq.** [< L *et sequentēs, et sequentia*]

Et•ta (et′ə), *n.* a female given name, form of **Henrietta.**

Et•tarre (i tär′, e tär′ə), *n. Arthurian Romance.* the vain and heartless lady beloved by Sir Pelleas.

-ette, a noun suffix occurring originally in loanwords from French, where it has been used in a variety of diminutive and hypocoristic formations (*brunette; cigarette; coquette; etiquette; rosette*); as an English suffix, **-ette** forms diminutives (*kitchenette; novelette; sermonette*), distinctively feminine nouns (*majorette; usherette*), and names of imitation products (*leatherette*). Cf. **-et.** [< F, fem. of *-et* -ET]

—Usage. English nouns in which the suffix -ETTE designates a feminine role or identity have been perceived by many people as implying inferiority or insignificance: *bachelorette; drum majorette; farmerette; suffragette; usherette.* Of these terms, only *drum majorette*—or sometimes just *majorette*—is still widely used, usually applied to one of a group of young women who perform baton twirling with a marching band. A woman or man who actually leads a band is a *drum major. Baton twirler* is often used instead of (*drum*) *majorette. Farmer, suffragist,* and *usher* are applied to both men and women, thus avoiding any trivializing effect of the -ETTE ending. See also **-enne, -ess, -trix.**

et tu, Bru•te (et tōō′ brōō′tā), *Latin.* and thou, Brutus!: alleged dying words of Julius Caesar uttered as his friend Brutus stabbed him.

é•tude (ā′tōōd, ā′tyōōd, ā tōōd′, ā tyōōd′; *Fr.* ā tyd′), *n., pl.* **é•tudes** (ā′tōōdz, ā′tyōōdz, ā tōōdz′, ā tyōōdz′; *Fr.* ā tyd′). **1.** a musical composition, usually instrumental, intended mainly for the practice of some point of technique. **2.** study[1] (def. 12). [1830–40; < F; see STUDY[1]]

e•tui (ā twē′, et′wē), *n., pl.* **e•tuis.** a small, often decorative case, esp. one for needles, toilet articles, or the like. Also, **e•twee′.** [1605–15; < F *étui,* OF *estui* holder, n. deriv. of *estuier* to keep < VL **studiāre* to treat with care]

et ux., *Chiefly Law.* See ***et uxor.***

et ux•or (et uk′sôr, -sōr, ug′zôr, -zōr), *Latin.* and wife (used chiefly in its abbreviated form, in legal abstracts of title). *Abbr.:* et ux.

ETV, See **educational television.**

et vir (et vēr′), *Latin.* and husband (used chiefly in legal abstracts of title).

ety., etymology.

etym., **1.** etymological. **2.** etymology. Also, **etymol.**

et•y•mol•o•gize (et′ə mol′ə jīz′), *v.,* **-gized, -giz•ing.** —*v.t.* **1.** to trace the history of (a word). —*v.i.* **2.** to study etymology. **3.** to give or suggest the etymology of words. Also, *esp. Brit.,* **et′y•mol′o•gise′.** [1520–30; < LL *etymologizāre.* See ETYMOLOGY, -IZE] —**et′y•mol′o•giz′a•ble,** *adj.*

et•y•mol•o•gy (et′ə mol′ə jē), *n., pl.* **-gies. 1.** the derivation of a word. **2.** an account of the history of a particular word or element of a word. **3.** the study of historical linguistic change, esp. as manifested in individual words. [1350–1400; ME < L *etymologia* < Gk *etymología,* equiv. to *etymológ(os)* studying the true meanings and values of words (*étymo(s)* true (see ETYMON) + *lógos* word, reason) + *-ia* -Y[3]] —**et•y•mo•log•i•cal** (et′ə mə loj′i kəl), **et′y•mo•log′ic,** *adj.* —**et′y•mo•log′i•cal•ly,** *adv.* —**et′y•mol′o•gist,** *n.*

et•y•mon (et′ə mon′), *n., pl.* **-mons, -ma** (-mə). the linguistic form from which another form is historically derived, as the Latin *cor* "heart," which is the etymon of English *cordial,* or the Indo-European **k̑(e)rd-,* which is the etymon of Latin *cor,* Greek *kardía,* Russian *serdtse,* and English *heart.* [1560–70; < L: the origin of a word < Gk *étymon* the essential meaning of a word seen in its origin or traced to its grammatical parts (neut. of *étymos* true, actual, real)]

Et•zel (et′səl), *n. Germanic Legend.* Attila: represented in the *Nibelungenlied* as the second husband of Kriemhild after the death of Siegfried. Cf. **Atli.**

Eu, *Symbol, Chem.* europium.

eu-, a combining form meaning "good," "well," occurring chiefly in words of Greek origin (*eupepsia*); in scientific coinages, esp. taxonomic names, it often has the sense "true, genuine" (*eukaryote*) [< Gk, comb. form of *eús* good (adj.) or *eú, eû* (neut., used as adv.) well]

eu•bac•te•ri•a (yōō′bak tēr′ē ə), *n.pl., sing.* **-te•ri•um** (-tēr′ē əm). *Bacteriol.* spherical or rod-shaped bacteria of the order Eubacteriales, characterized by simple, undifferentiated cells with rigid walls; true bacteria. [1935–40; < NL; see EU-, BACTERIA]

Eu•boe•a (yōō bē′ə), *n.* a Greek island in the W Aegean Sea. 165,369; 1586 sq. mi. (4110 sq. km). *Cap.:* Chalcis. Also called **Negropont.** Modern Greek, **Evvoia.** —**Eu•boe′an,** *adj., n.* —**Eu•bo•ic** (yōō bō′ik), *adj.*

eu•caine (yōō kān′, yōō′kān), *n. Pharm.* a white, crystalline solid, $C_{15}H_{21}NO_2$, formerly a local anesthetic, used in veterinary medicine as a substitute for cocaine. Also called **benzamine.** [1895–1900; EU- + *-caine* (as in COCAINE)]

eu•ca•lyp•tol (yōō′kə lip′tôl, -tōl), *n. Chem.* cineole. Also, **eu•ca•lyp•tole** (yōō′kə lip′tōl). [1875–80; EUCALYPT(US) + -OL[2]]

eu•ca•lyp•tus (yōō′kə lip′təs), *n., pl.* **-ti** (-tī), **-tus•es.** any of numerous often tall trees belonging to the genus *Eucalyptus,* of the myrtle family, native to Australia and adjacent islands, having aromatic evergreen leaves that are the source of medicinal oils and heavy wood used as timber. Also, **eu•ca•lypt** (yōō′kə lipt′). [1800–10; < NL < Gk eu- EU- + *kalyptós* covered, wrapped, akin to *kalýptein* to cover] —**eu′ca•lyp′tic,** *adj.*

eu•car•pic (yōō kär′pik), *adj.* (of a fungus) having only part of the thallus converted into fruiting bodies. Also, **eu•car′pous.** Cf. **holocarpic.** [EU- + -CARPIC]

eu•car•y•ote (yōō kar′ē ōt′, -ē ət), *n.* eukaryote. —**eu•car•y•ot•ic** (yōō kar′ē ot′ik), *adj.*

Eu•cha•rist (yōō′kə rist), *n.* **1.** the sacrament of Holy Communion; the sacrifice of the Mass; the Lord's Supper. **2.** the consecrated elements of the Holy Communion, esp. the bread. **3.** (*l.c.*) the giving of thanks; thanksgiving. **4.** *Christian Science.* spiritual communion with God. [1350–1400; ME *eukarist* < LL *eucharistia* < Gk *eucharistía* gratefulness, thanksgiving. See EU-, CHARISMA, -IA] —**Eu′cha•ris′tic, Eu′cha•ris′ti•cal,** *adj.* —**Eu′cha•ris′ti•cal•ly,** *adv.*

Eu•chite (yōō′kīt), *n.* a member of a mendicant, ascetic sect living chiefly in Syria and Mesopotamia in the 4th–7th centuries A.D., and holding a belief that the demon in each person can be expelled only by ceaseless prayer. Also called **Messalian.** [1575–85]

eu•cho•lo•gi•on (*Gk.* ef′KHô lô′yē ôn; *Eng.* yōō′kə lō′jē on′, -ən), *n., pl.* **-gi•a** (*Gk.* -yē ä; *Eng.* -jē ə). *Eastern Ch.* a service book containing liturgies, prayers, and other rites. Also, **euchology.** [1645–55; < eccl. Gk *euchológion* prayer book, equiv. to *euch(é)* prayer + *-o-* -O- + *-log-* word + *-ion* n. suffix]

eu•chol•o•gy (yōō kol′ə jē), *n., pl.* **-gies.** euchologion. [1650–60]

eu•chre (yōō′kər), *n., v.,* **-chred, -chring.** —*n.* **1.** *Cards.* a game played by two, three, or four persons, usually with the 32, but sometimes with the 28 or 24, highest cards in the pack. **2.** an instance of euchring or being euchred. —*v.t.* **3.** to get the better of (an opponent) in a hand at euchre by the opponent's failure to win three tricks after having made the trump. **4.** *Slang.* to cheat; swindle. [1835–45, *Amer.*; orig. uncert.]

eu•chred (yōō′kərd), *adj. Australian Informal.* utterly done in or at the end of one's tether; exhausted. [1865–70; EUCHRE + -ED[2]]

eu•chro•ma•tin (yōō krō′mə tin), *n. Genetics.* the part of a chromosome that condenses maximally during metaphase and contains most of the genetically active material. [1930–35; EU- + CHROMATIN] —**eu•chro•mat•ic** (yōō′krə mat′ik), *adj.*

eu•chro•mo•some (yōō krō′mə sōm′), *n. Genetics.* autosome. [1910–15; EU- + CHROMOSOME]

Euck•en (oi′kən), *n.* **Ru•dolph Chris•toph** (rōō′dôlf kris′tôf), 1846–1926, German philosopher: Nobel prize for literature 1908.

eu•clase (yōō′klās, -klāz), *n.* a rare green or blue mineral, beryllium aluminum silicate, $BeAlSiO_4(OH)$, occurring in prismatic crystals. [1795–1805; < F; see EU-, -CLASE]

Eu•clid (yōō′klid), *n.* **1.** fl. c300 B.C., Greek geometrician and educator at Alexandria. **2.** a city in NE Ohio, near Cleveland. 59,999.

Eu•clid•e•an (yōō klid′ē ən), *adj.* of or pertaining to Euclid, or adopting his postulates. Also, **Eu•clid′i•an.** [1650–60; < L *Euclīdē(us)* of Euclid (< Gk *Eukleídeios*) + -AN]

Euclid′ean al′gorithm, *Algebra.* a method based on the division algorithm for finding the greatest common divisor of two given integers. [1950–55]

Euclid′ean geom′etry, geometry based upon the postulates of Euclid, esp. the postulate that only one line may be drawn through a given point parallel to a given line. [1860–65]

Euclid′ean group′, *Math.* the set of rigid motions that are also affine transformations.

Euclid′ean space′, *Math.* **1.** ordinary two- or three-dimensional space. **2.** any vector space on which a real-valued inner product is defined. Also called **Cartesian space.** [1880–85]

eu•crite (yōō′krīt), *n. Petrog.* a basic gabbro consisting mainly of bytownite and augite. [1895–1900; < G *Eukrit* < Gk *eúkritos* readily chosen, equiv. to *eu-* EU- + *kritós* separated (verbid of *krínein*)]

eu•cryp•tite (yōō krip′tīt), *n.* a mineral, lithium aluminum silicate, $LiAlSiO_4$, occurring in colorless to white hexagonal crystals: used as a source of lithium. [EU- + CRYPT(O)- + -ITE[1]]

eu•de•mon (yōō dē′mən), *n.* a good or benevolent demon or spirit. Also, **eu•dae′mon.** [1620–30; < Gk *eudaímōn* blessed with a good genius, fortunate, happy, equiv. to *eu-* EU- + *daímōn* destiny, fortune, lot; see DEMON]

eu•de•mo•ni•a (yōō′di mō′nē ə), *n.* **1.** happiness; well-being. **2.** *Aristotelianism.* happiness as the result of an active life governed by reason. Also, **eu′dae•mo′•ni•a.** [< Gk *eudaimonía.* See EUDEMON, -IA]

eu•de•mon•ic (yōō′di mon′ik), *adj.* **1.** pertaining or conducive to happiness. **2.** pertaining to eudemonics or eudemonism. Also, **eu′dae•mon′ic.** [1825–35; < Gk *eudaimonikós.* See EUDEMON, -IC]

eu•de•mon•ics (yōō′di mon′iks), *n.* (*usually used with a singular v.*) **1.** the theory or art of happiness. **2.** the practice of eudemonism. Also, **eu′dae•mon′ics.** [1825–35; see EUDEMONIC, -ICS]

eu•de•mon•ism (yōō dē′mə niz′əm), *n. Ethics.* the doctrine that the basis of moral obligations is to be found in the tendency of right actions to produce happiness. Also, **eu•dae′mon•ism.** [1820–30; EUDEMON + -ISM] —**eu•de′mon•ist,** *n.* —**eu•de′mon•is′tic,** *adj.* —**eu•de′mon•is′ti•cal•ly,** *adv.*

eu•di•om•e•ter (yōō′dē om′i tər), *n. Chem.* a graduated glass measuring tube for gas analysis. [1770–80; < Gk *eúdio(s)* clear, mild (lit., well skied, equiv. to *eu-* EU- + *di-,* s. of *Zeus* god of the sky + *-os* adj. suffix) + -METER] —**eu•di•o•met•ric** (yōō′dē ə me′trik), **eu′di•o•met′ri•cal,** *adj.* —**eu′di•o•met′ri•cal•ly,** *adv.*

eu•di•om•e•try (yōō′dē om′i trē), *n. Chem.* the measurement and analysis of gases with the eudiometer. [1790–1800; EUDIOMET(E)R + -Y[3]]

Eu•do•ra (yōō dôr′ə, -dōr′ə), *n.* a female given name.

Eu•dox•us (yōō dok′səs), *n.* a crater in the first quadrant of the face of the moon: about 40 miles (64 km) in diameter.

Eu•e•mer•us (yōō ē′mər əs, -em′ər-), *n.* Euhemerus.

Eu•fau•la (yōō fô′lə), *n.* a town in SE Alabama. 12,097.

eu•fla•vine (yōō flā′vēn, -vin), *n. Chem.* acriflavine. [EU- + FLAVINE]

Eu•gene (yōō jēn′ *or, for 2,* yōō′jēn), *n.* **1.** a city in W Oregon. 105,624. **2.** a male given name: from a Greek word meaning "wellborn."

Eu•gène (œ zhen′), *n.* **Prince** (*François Eugène de Savoie-Carignan*), 1663–1736, Austrian general, born in France.

Eugene I. See **Eugenius I.**

Eugene II. See **Eugenius II.**

Eugene III. See **Eugenius III.**

Eugene IV. See **Eugenius IV.**

Eu•ge•ni•a (yōō jē′nē ə, -jēn′yə), *n.* a female given name: from a Greek word meaning "nobility." Also, **Eu•ge•nie** (yōō jē′nē).

eu•gen•ic (yōō jen′ik), *adj.* **1.** of or bringing about improvement in the type of offspring produced. **2.** having good inherited characteristics. Also, **eu•gen′i•cal.** Cf. **dysgenic.** [1880–85; < Gk *eugen(ḗs)* wellborn (see EU-, -GEN) + -IC] —**eu•gen′i•cal•ly,** *adv.*

eu•gen•i•cist (yōō jen′ə sist), *n.* **1.** a specialist in eugenics. **2.** an advocate of eugenic measures. Also, **eu•ge•nist** (yōō′jə nist, yōō jen′ist). [1905–10; EUGENIC + -IST]

eu•gen•ics (yōō jen′iks), *n.* (*used with a singular v.*) the study of or belief in the possibility of improving the qualities of the human species or a human population, esp. by such means as discouraging reproduction by persons having genetic defects or presumed to have inheritable undesirable traits **(negative eugenics)** or encouraging reproduction by persons presumed to have inheritable desirable traits **(positive eugenics).** [1880–85; see EUGENIC, -ICS]

Eu•gé•nie (œ zhā nē′), *n.* **Comtesse de Te•ba** (de te′bä), (*Marie Eugénie de Montijo de Guzmán*), 1826–1920, wife of Napoleon III, born in Spain: Empress of France 1853–71.

Eu•ge•ni•us I (yōō jē′nē əs, -jēn′yəs), **Saint,** died A.D. 657, pope 654–657. Also, **Eugene I.**

Eugenius II, died A.D. 827, Italian ecclesiastic: pope 824–827. Also, **Eugene II.**

Eugenius III, (*Bernardo Pignatelli* or *Paganelli*) died 1153, Italian ecclesiastic: pope 1145–53. Also, **Eugene III.**

Eugenius IV, (*Gabriele* or *Gabriel Condolmieri* or *Condulmer*) 1383–1447, Italian ecclesiastic: pope 1431–47. Also, **Eugene IV.**

eu•ge•nol (yōō′jə nôl′, -nōl′), *n. Chem., Pharm.* a colorless, oily, spicy, aromatic, very slightly water-soluble liquid, $C_{10}H_{12}O_2$, extracted from certain essential oils, as oil of cloves: used chiefly in perfumery and in dentistry as an antiseptic. Also called **eugen′ic ac′id.** [1885–90; < NL *Eugen(ia)* name of genus of trees (after Prince EUGÈNE of Savoy; see -IA) + -OL[2]]

eu•ge•o•syn•cline (yōō jē′ō sing′klīn, -sin′-), *n. Geol.* a former marine zone, bordering an ocean basin, marked by very thick deposits of sediment in which the products of volcanic activity are associated with clastic sediments. [1940–45; EU- + GEOSYNCLINE] —**eu•ge′o•syn•cli′nal,** *adj.*

CONCISE PRONUNCIATION KEY: act, cāpe, dâre, pärt; set, ēqual; *if,* īce; ox, ōver, ôrder, oil, bŏŏk, bōōt, out; up, ûrge; child; sing; shoe; thin, *th*at; zh as in *treasure.* ə = *a* as in *alone, e* as in *system, i* as in *easily, o* as in *gallop, u* as in *circus;* ᵊ as in *fire* (fīᵊr), *hour* (ouᵊr). l and n can serve as syllabic consonants, as in *cradle* (krād′l), and *button* (but′n). See the full key inside the front cover.

Eu·gle·na (yōō glē′nə), *n.* a genus of green freshwater protozoans having a reddish eyespot and a single flagellum, found esp. in stagnant waters. [1895–1900; < NL < Gk *eu-* EU- + *glḗnē* the pupil, eyeball, socket of a joint]

eu·gle·no·phyte (yōō glē′nə fīt′), *n. Biol.* any member of the protist phylum Euglenophyta, comprising unicellular organisms, either green and photosynthetic or colorless and nonphotosynthetic, characterized by one or two anterior flagella and, in photosynthetic forms, an eyespot at the base of the flagella: in some classification schemes, an order of the animal phylum Mastigophora or the plant division Chlorophyta. Also called **eu·gle·nid** (yōō glē′nid), **eu·gle·noid** (yōō glē′noid). [< NL *Euglenophyta;* see EUGLENA, -O-, -PHYTE]

eu·gon·ic (yōō gon′ik), *adj. Bacteriol.* thriving on artificial media, as certain bacteria (opposed to *dysgonic*). [EU- + GON(O)- + -IC]

eu·he·dral (yōō hē′drəl), *adj. Petrog.* idiomorphic (def. 1). [1905–10; EU- + -HEDRAL]

eu·he·mer·ism (yōō hē′mə riz′əm, -hem′ə-), *n.* **1.** (*often cap.*) the theory of Euhemerus that the mythologies of various gods arose out of the deification of dead heroes. **2.** the theory that mythology is derived from history. [1840–50; EUHEMER(US) + -ISM] **—eu·he′mer·ist,** *n.* **—eu·he′mer·is′tic,** *adj.* **—eu·he′mer·is′ti·cal·ly,** *adv.*

eu·he·mer·ize (yōō hē′mə rīz′, -hem′ə-), *v.t., v.i.,* **-ized, -iz·ing.** to treat or explain (myths) by euhemerism. Also, *esp. Brit.,* **eu·he′mer·ise′.** [1840–50; EUHEMER(US) + -IZE]

Eu·he·mer·us (yōō hē′mər əs, -hem′ər-), *n.* fl. c300 B.C., Greek mythographer. Also, **Euemerus, Evemerus.** Cf. **euhemerism.**

eu·kar·y·ote (yōō kar′ē ōt′, -ē ət), *n. Biol.* any organism having as its fundamental structural unit a cell type that contains specialized organelles in the cytoplasm, a membrane-bound nucleus enclosing genetic material organized into chromosomes, and an elaborate system of division by mitosis or meiosis, characteristic of all life forms except bacteria, blue-green algae, and other primitive microorganisms. Also, **eucaryote.** Cf. **prokaryote.** [< NL *Eukaryota,* earlier *Eucaryotes* (1925) "those having a true nucleus," equiv. to *eu-* EU- + Gk *káry(on)* nut, kernel (see KARYO-) + NL *-ota, -otes;* see -OTE] **—eu·kar·y·ot·ic** (yōō kar′ē ot′ik), *adj.*

eu·ki·net·ics (yōō′ki net′iks), *n.* (*used with a singular v.*) *Dance.* an applied system of controlled body movement, developed by Kurt Jooss and designed to enlarge a dancer's potential for expressiveness. [EU- + KINETICS]

eu·la·chon (yōō′lə kon′), *n.* candlefish. [1800–10, *Amer.;* < Chinook Jargon, prob. < Clatsop (a division of the Lower Chinook once resident on the south bank of the Columbia and the adjacent coast) *u-ƛalxʷó(n),* said to mean "brook trout"]

Eu·ler (oi′lər; *Ger., Swed.* oi′lər), *n.* **1. Le·on·hard** (*Ger.* lā′ôn härt′), 1707–83, Swiss mathematician. **2. Ulf Svan·te von** (o͝olf svän′tə fôn), 1905–83, Swedish physiologist: Nobel prize for medicine 1970.

Eu·ler-Chel·pin (oi′lər kel′pin), *n.* **Hans Karl Au·gust Si·mon von** (häns kärl ou′go͝ost zē′mōn fən), 1873–1964, German chemist in Sweden: Nobel prize 1929.

Eu′ler's di′agram, *Logic.* one of a number of graphic representations of the logical relations among classes by means of relations among circles or other geometric figures. [named after L. EULER]

Eu′ler's for′mula, 1. *Math.* the theorem that $e^{ix} = \cos x + i \sin x$. **2.** *Mech.* a formula for determining the maximum load that can be applied to a given column without causing it to buckle. [1945–50; named after L. EULER]

Eu′ler's phi′-func·tion, *Math.* the function that assigns to each integer the number of positive integers less than the given integer and relatively prime to the given integer. Also called **phi-function.** [named after L. EULER]

Eu·less (yōō′lis), *n.* a city in N Texas. 24,002.

eu·lo·gi·a (yōō lō′jē ə; *for 2 also Gk.* ev′lô yē′ä), *n.* **1.** Also called **antidoron, holy bread.** *Eastern Ch.* blessed bread given to the congregation during vespers or at the end of the liturgy. **2.** *Gk. Orth. Ch.* a blessing. [1745–55; < LL < Gk *eulogía* praise, blessing. See EU-, -LOGY, -IA]

eu·lo·gist (yōō′lə jist), *n.* a person who eulogizes. [1800–10; EULOG(Y) + -IST]

eu·lo·gis·tic (yōō′lə jis′tik), *adj.* pertaining to or containing eulogy; laudatory. Also, **eu′lo·gis′ti·cal.** [1815–25; EULOGIST + -IC] **—eu′lo·gis′ti·cal·ly,** *adv.*

eu·lo·gi·um (yōō lō′jē əm), *n., pl.* **-gi·ums, -gi·a** (-jē ə). **1.** a eulogy. **2.** eulogistic language. [1700–10; < ML, equiv. to L *eu-* EU- + (*ē*)*logium* inscription on a tombstone]

eu·lo·gize (yōō′lə jīz′), *v.t.,* **-gized, -giz·ing. 1.** to praise highly. **2.** to speak or write a eulogy about. Also, *esp. Brit.,* **eu′lo·gise′.** [1800–10; EULOG(Y) + -IZE] **—eu′lo·gi·za′tion,** *n.* **—eu′lo·giz′er,** *n.*
—Syn. 1. extol, laud, commend, panegyrize.

eu·lo·gy (yōō′lə jē), *n., pl.* **-gies. 1.** a speech or writing in praise of a person or thing, esp. a set oration in honor of a deceased person. **2.** high praise or commendation. [1585–95; < LL *eulogia* EULOGIA and ML *eulogium* EULOGIUM]

-eum, a suffix occurring in some Latin scientific names (*peritoneum*), and in the corresponding loanwords in English (*petroleum*).

CONCISE ETYMOLOGY KEY: <, descended or borrowed from; >, whence; b., blend of, blended; c., cognate with; cf., compare; deriv., derivative; equiv., equivalent; imit., imitative; obl., oblique; r., replacing; s., stem; sp., spelling, spelled; resp., respelling, respelled; trans., translation; ?, origin unknown; *, unattested; ‡, probably earlier than. See the full key inside the front cover.

Eu·mae·us (yōō mē′əs), *n.* (in the *Odyssey*) the faithful swineherd of Odysseus.

eu·mel·a·nin (yōō mel′ə nin), *n. Biochem.* a pigment containing melanin, found in bird feathers. [EU- + MELANIN]

Eu·men·es I (yōō men′ēz), king of Pergamum. 263–241 B.C.

Eumenes II, king of Pergamum. 197–c159 B.C.

Eu·men·i·des (yōō men′i dēz′), *n.* **1.** (*used with a plural v.*) *Class. Myth.* a euphemistic name for the Furies, meaning "the Kindly Ones." **2.** (*italics*) (*used with a singular v.*) a tragedy (485 B.C.) by Aeschylus. Cf. ***Oresteia.***

Eu·met·a·zo·a (yōō met′ə zō′ə), *n.* the major division, or subkingdom, of Animalia comprising the eumetazoans. [< NL; see EU-, METAZOA]

eu·met·a·zo·an (yōō met′ə zō′ən), *n.* **1.** any of a major division, or subkingdom, of multicellular animals with a digestive tract, including all animals except the sponges. —*adj.* **2.** of or pertaining to the Eumetazoa. [EUMETAZO(A) + -AN]

Eu·my·co·ta (yōō′mī kō′tə), *n. Biol.* a phylum of true fungi, distinguished from the funguslike slime molds, Myxomycota, and similar organisms by having a mycelial thallus: in some classification systems, the class Eumycetes. [< NL; see EU-, MYCO-, -OTA]

Eu·nice (yōō′nis), *n.* **1.** a city in S central Louisiana. 12,479. **2.** a female given name: from a Greek word meaning "good victory."

Eu·no·mi·a (yōō nō′mē ə), *n. Class. Myth.* one of the Horae: the personification of order.

eu·nuch (yōō′nək), *n.* a castrated man, esp. one formerly employed by Oriental rulers as a harem guard or palace official. [1350–1400; ME *eunuk* < L *eunūchus* < Gk *eunoûchos* eunuch, chamberlain, equiv. to *eune-,* s. of *eunḗ* bed, place of sleeping + *-ochos* keeping (akin to *échein* to hold)]

eu·nuch·ism (yōō′nə kiz′əm), *n.* the state of being a eunuch. Also, **eu·nuch·ry** (yōō′nək rē). [1610–20; EUNUCH + -ISM]

eu·nuch·ize (yōō′nə kīz′), *v.t.,* **-ized, -iz·ing.** to castrate; emasculate. Also, *esp. Brit.,* **eu′nuch·ise′.** [1625–35; EUNUCH + -IZE]

eu·nuch·oid (yōō′nə koid′), *adj.* **1.** affected with eunuchoidism. —*n.* **2.** a person affected with eunuchoidism. [1905–10; EUNUCH + -OID]

eu·nuch·oid·ism (yōō′nə koi diz′əm), *n. Pathol.* an abnormal condition in males, characterized by lack of fully developed reproductive organs and the manifestation of certain female sex characteristics, as high voice or lack of facial and body hair, resulting from the absence of a normal production of male sex hormones. [1920–25; EUNUCHOID + -ISM]

eu·on·y·mus (yōō on′ə məs), *n.* any of several shrubs or small trees of the genus *Euonymus,* of northern temperate regions, having opposite leaves, branching clusters of small, greenish or purplish flowers, and crimson or rose-colored capsules that on opening disclose the seed. Also, **evonymus.** [1760–70; < NL; L, n. use of Gk *euṓnymos* of good name. See EU-, -ONYM, -OUS]

eu·pa·to·ri·um (yōō′pə tôr′ē əm, -tōr′-), *n.* any of numerous composite plants of the genus *Eupatorium,* having flat-topped clusters of flowers and comprising the bonesets or thoroughworts. [1570–80; < NL < Gk *eupatórion* hemp agrimony, after *Eupátōr* surname of Mithridates, said to have first used it]

eu·pat·rid (yōō pa′trid, yōō′pə-), *n., pl.* **eu·pat·ri·dae** (yōō pa′tri dē′). one of the hereditary aristocrats of ancient Athens and other states of Greece, who at one time formed the ruling class. [1825–35; < Gk *eupatrídēs,* lit., of a good father, of noble descent, equiv. to *eu-* EU- + *patr-* (s. of *patḗr*) FATHER + *-idēs* -ID²]

Eu·pen and Mal·mé·dy (*Fr.* œ pen′; mAl mā dē′), a district on the Belgian-German border: ceded to Belgium 1919; reannexed to Germany 1940; now part of Belgium.

eu·pep·sia (yōō pep′shə, -sē ə), *n.* good digestion (opposed to *dyspepsia*). Also, **eu·pep·sy** (yōō′pep sē). [1700–10; < NL < Gk *eupepsía* good digestion, equiv. to *eu-* EU- + *péps(is)* digestion + *-ia* -IA] **—eu·pep·tic** (yōō pep′tik), *adj.*

eu·phe·mism (yōō′fə miz′əm), *n.* **1.** the substitution of a mild, indirect, or vague expression for one thought to be offensive, harsh, or blunt. **2.** the expression so substituted: *"To pass away" is a euphemism for "to die."* [1650–60; < Gk *euphēmismós* the use of words of good omen, equiv. to *eu-* EU- + *phḗm(ē)* speaking, fame + *-ismos* -ISM] **—eu′phe·mist,** *n.* **—eu′phe·mis′tic, eu′phe·mis′ti·cal, eu·phe·mi·ous** (yōō fē′mē əs), *adj.* **—eu′phe·mis′ti·cal·ly, eu·phe′mi·ous·ly,** *adv.*

eu·phe·mize (yōō′fə mīz′), *v.,* **-mized, -miz·ing.** —*v.t.* **1.** to refer to by means of euphemism. —*v.i.* **2.** to employ euphemism. Also, *esp. Brit.,* **eu′phe·mise′.** [1855–60; < Gk *euphēmízein* to use words of good omen. See EUPHEMISM, -IZE] **—eu′phe·mi·za′tion,** *n.* **—eu′phe·miz′er,** *n.*

eu·pho·ni·a (yōō fō′nē ə, -fōn′yə), *n.* any of several small tanagers of the genus *Euphonia,* having a melodious song, most species of which have yellow and glossy black plumage. [1585–95; < NL; see EUPHONY]

eu·phon·ic (yōō fon′ik), *adj.* pertaining to or characterized by euphony. Also, **eu·phon′i·cal.** [1805–15; EUPHON(Y) + -IC] **—eu·phon′i·cal·ly,** *adv.* **—eu·phon′i·cal·ness,** *n.*

eu·pho·ni·ous (yōō fō′nē əs), *adj.* pleasant in sound; agreeable to the ear; characterized by euphony: *a sweet, euphonious voice.* [1765–75; EUPHONY + -OUS] **—eu·pho′ni·ous·ly,** *adv.* **—eu·pho′ni·ous·ness,** *n.*

eu·pho·ni·um (yōō fō′nē əm), *n.* a brass musical instrument similar to the baritone tuba but somewhat smaller, with a wider bore and mellower tone, and often having a second bell. [1860–65; EUPH(ONY) + (HARM)ONIUM]

euphonium

eu·pho·nize (yōō′fə nīz′), *v.t.,* **-nized, -niz·ing.** to make euphonious. Also, *esp. Brit.* **eu′pho·nise′.** [1765–75; EUPHON(Y) + -IZE]

eu·pho·ny (yōō′fə nē), *n., pl.* **-nies.** agreeableness of sound; pleasing effect to the ear, esp. a pleasant sounding or harmonious combination or succession of words: *the majestic euphony of Milton's poetry.* [1615–25; < LL *euphōnia* < Gk *euphōnía.* See EU-, -PHONY]

eu·phor·bi·a (yōō fôr′bē ə), *n.* any plant of the genus *Euphorbia,* comprising the spurges. [1350–1400; ME *euforbia* for L *euphorbea,* an African plant named after *Euphorbos,* a Greek physician]

eu·phor·bi·a·ceous (yōō fôr′bē ā′shəs), *adj.* belonging to the Euphorbiaceae, the spurge family of plants. Cf. **spurge family.** [1850–55; < NL *Euphorbiace(ae)* name of family (see EUPHORBIA, -ACEAE) + -OUS]

eu·pho·ri·a (yōō fôr′ē ə, -fōr′-), *n. Psychol.* a feeling of happiness, confidence, or well-being sometimes exaggerated in pathological states as mania. [1880–85; < NL < Gk *euphoría* state of well-being. See EU-, -PHORE, -IA] **—eu·phor·ic** (yōō fôr′ik, -for′-), *adj.*

eu·pho·ri·ant (yōō fôr′ē ənt, -fōr′-), *adj.* **1.** tending to induce euphoria. —*n.* **2.** a euphoriant substance. [EUPHORI(A) + -ANT]

eu·pho·ri·gen·ic (yōō fôr′i jen′ik, -fōr′-), *adj.* giving rise to a feeling of well-being. [EUPHOR(IA) + -I- + -GENIC]

eu·pho′tic zone′ (yōō fō′tik), *Oceanog.* the layer of sea water that receives enough sunlight for photosynthesis to occur: it varies greatly with season and latitude, from 0 to 1200 ft. (0–360 m). [1960–65; EU- + PHOTIC]

eu·phra·sy (yōō′frə sē), *n., pl.* **-sies.** *Bot.* eyebright. [1425–75; late ME *eufrasie* < ML *eufrasia* < Gk *euphrasía* cheerfulness, gladness (cf. *euphraínein* to cheer, be glad)]

Eu·phra·tes (yōō frā′tēz), *n.* a river in SW Asia, flowing from E Turkey through Syria and Iraq, joining the Tigris to form the Shatt-al-Arab near the Persian Gulf. 1700 mi. (2735 km) long. **—Eu·phra′te·an,** *adj.*

eu·phroe (yōō′frō, -vrō), *n. Naut.* a suspended batten or plate of wood or brass pierced with holes through which the cords of a crowfoot are rove to suspend an awning. [1805–15; pseudolearned English spelling of D *juffrouw* euphroe, lit., *jong* young + *vrouw* woman; c. G *Jungfrau*]

Eu·phros·y·ne (yōō fros′ə nē′), *n. Class. Myth.* one of the Graces. [< Gk, personification of *euphrosýnē* mirth, merriment]

Eu·phu·es (yōō′fyōō ēz′), *n.* the main character in John Lyly's works *Euphues, the Anatomy of Wit* (1579), and *Euphues and His England* (1580). Cf. **euphuism.**

eu·phu·ism (yōō′fyōō iz′əm), *n.* **1.** an affected style in imitation of that of Lyly, fashionable in England about the end of the 16th century, characterized chiefly by long series of antitheses and frequent similes relating to mythological natural history, and alliteration. Cf. **Euphues. 2.** any similar ornate style of writing or speaking; high-flown, periphrastic language. [1590–1600; EUPHU(ES) + -ISM] **—eu′phu·ist,** *n.* **—eu′phu·is′tic, eu′phu·is′ti·cal,** *adj.* **—eu′phu·is′ti·cal·ly,** *adv.*

eu·plas·tic (yōō plas′tik), *adj. Physiol.* capable of being transformed into organized tissue. [1840–50; < Gk *eúplast(os)* malleable + -IC. See EU-, PLASTIC]

Eur-, var. of **Euro-** before a vowel.

-eur a suffix occurring in loanwords from French, usually agent nouns formed from verbs (*entrepreneur; voyeur*), less commonly adjectives (*agent provocateur*). [< F; OF *-o(u)r* < L *-ōr-* -OR² and *-eo(u)r* < L *-ātōr-* -ATOR; see -TOR]

Eur., 1. Europe. **2.** European.

Eur·af·ri·can (yo͝o raf′ri kən, yə-), *adj.* **1.** of mixed European and African descent. —*n.* **2.** a person of European and African descent. [1885–90; EUR- + AFRICAN]

Eu·rail·pass (yo͝o rāl′pas′, -päs′, yə-, yo͝or′āl-, yûr′-), *n.* a pass allowing unlimited railroad travel during a specified time period and for a fixed price in participating European countries. [1970–75; *Eur(opean) rail(road) pass*]

Eur·a·mer·i·can (yo͝or′ə mer′i kən, yûr′-), *adj.* Euro-American. [1940–45; EUR- + AMERICAN]

Eur·a·sia (yo͝o rā′zhə, -shə, yə-), *n.* Europe and Asia considered together as one continent. [EUR- + ASIA]

Eur·a·sian (yo͝o rā′zhən, -shən, yə-), *adj.* **1.** of or pertaining to Eurasia. **2.** of mixed European and Asian descent. —*n.* **3.** the offspring of a European and an Asian. [1835–45; EURASI(A) + -AN]

Eura′sian Plate′, a major tectonic division of the earth's crust, comprising the continents of Europe and Asia as well as several suboceanic basins (the West European, Norwegian, Lofoten, Aleutian, and South China Basins), separated from the North American Plate by the subsea Reykjanes Ridge, bounded on the south by the African and Indo-Australian Plates, and on the east by the Philippine and Pacific Plates.

Eur·at·om (yo͝o rat′əm, yə-, yo͝or′at′-, yûr′-), *n.* an organization formed in 1957, comprising France, the Netherlands, Belgium, Luxembourg, Italy, and West Germany, for coordinated action in developing and marketing their nuclear resources. Also, **EURATOM** [*Eur*(*opean*) *Atom*(*ic Energy Community*)]

Eure (œr), *n.* a department in NW France. 422,952; 2331 sq. mi. (6035 sq. km). *Cap.:* Evreux.

Eure-et-Loir (œr ā lwar′), *n.* a department in central France. 335,151; 2293 sq. mi. (5940 sq. km). *Cap.:* Chartres.

eu·re·ka (yo͝o rē′kə, yə-), *interj.* **1.** (*cap.*) I have found (it): the reputed exclamation of Archimedes when, after long study, he discovered a method of detecting the amount of alloy mixed with the gold in the crown of the king of Syracuse. **2.** (used as an exclamation of triumph at a discovery.) [1560–70; < Gk *heúrēka,* 1st person sing. perf. indic. of *heurískein* to find, discover]

Eu·re·ka (yo͝o rē′kə, yə-), *n.* a city in NW California. 24,153.

eu·rhyth·mic (yo͝o rith′mik, yə-), *adj.* **1.** characterized by a pleasing rhythm; harmoniously ordered or proportioned. **2.** of or pertaining to eurhythmics. Also, **eurythmic, eu·rhyth′mi·cal, eurythmical.** [1825–35; EURHYTHM(Y) + -IC] —**eu·rhyth′mi·cal·ly,** *adv.*

eu·rhyth·mics (yo͝o rith′miks, yə-), *n.* (*used with a singular or plural v.*) the art of interpreting in bodily movements the rhythm of musical compositions: applied to a method invented by Emile Jaques-Dalcroze, a Swiss composer, aiming to develop the sense of rhythm and symmetry. Also, **eurythmics.** [1910–15; see EURHYTHMIC, -ICS]

eu·rhyth·my (yo͝o rith′mē, yə-), *n.* rhythmical movement or order; harmonious motion or proportion. Also, **eurythmy.** [1615–25; < L *eurythmia* < Gk *eurythmía* good proportion, gracefulness. See EU-, RHYTHM, -Y[3]]

Eu·rip·i·des (yo͝o rip′i dēz′, yə-), *n.* c480–406? B.C., Greek dramatist. —**Eu·rip′i·de′an,** *adj.*

eu·ri·pus (yo͝o rī′pəs, yə-), *n., pl.* **-pi** (-pī). a strait, esp. one in which the flow of water is violent. [1595–1605; < L *eurīpus* < Gk *eúrīpos* (applied esp. to the strait between Euboea and Boeotia, equiv. to *eu-* EU- + *-rīpos* rusher, akin to *rhipḗ* rush]

eu·ro (yo͝or′ō, yûr′-), *n., pl.* **-ros,** (*esp. collectively*) **-ro.** wallaroo. [< Ngajuri (Australian Aboriginal language spoken around Jamestown and Peterborough, South Australia) *yuru*]

Eu·ro (yo͝or′ō, yûr′ō), *adj. Informal.* European: *a Euro expert.* [independent use of EURO-]

Euro-, a shortening of **European** used as a combining form, esp. with the meaning "western European," particularly in reference to the European financial market or the European Economic Community: *Eurodollar; Eurofarmers.* Also, *esp. before a vowel,* **Eur-.**

Eu·ro-A·mer·i·can (yo͝or′ō ə mer′i kən, yûr′-), *adj.* common to Europe and to America. Also, **Euramerican.** [1925–30]

Eu·ro·bank (yo͝or′ə bangk′, yûr′-), *n.* a western European bank that deals in Eurocurrency. [1965–70; EURO- + BANK[2]] —**Eu′ro·bank′er,** *n.* —**Eur′o·bank′·ing,** *n.*

Eu·ro·bond (yo͝or′ə bond′), *n.* a bond issued by a non-European corporation and offered for sale in the European market, to be repaid in the currency of issue, esp. a U.S. corporate bond denominated and yielding interest in U.S. dollars. [EURO- + BOND[1]]

Eu·ro·cen·tric (yo͝or′ə sen′trik, yûr′-), *adj.* **1.** centered on Europe and Europeans. **2.** considering Europe and Europeans as focal to world culture, history, economics, etc. [1960–65; EURO- + -CENTRIC] —**Eu′ro·cen′trism,** *n.*

Eu·roc·ly·don (yo͝o rok′li don′, yə-), *n.* gregale. [1605–15; < Gk *euroklýdōn,* equiv. to *Eûro*(*s*) EURUS + *klýdōn* wave, surge; cf. *klýzein* to dash against, wash]

Eu·ro·com·mu·nism (yo͝or′ə kom′yə niz′əm, yûr′-), *n.* a form of Communism in some western European nations that claims to be independent of the Soviet Union. [1970–75; EURO- + COMMUNISM] —**Eu′ro·com′mu·nist,** *n., adj.*

Eu·ro·crat (yo͝or′ə krat′, yûr′-), *n.* a member of the executive and technical staff at the headquarters of the European Common Market. [1960–65; EURO- + -CRAT] —**Eu′ro·crat′ic,** *adj.*

Eu·ro·cur·ren·cy (yo͝or′ō kûr′ən sē, -kur′-, yûr′-), *n., pl.* **-cies.** funds deposited in the bank of a European country in the currency of another country. Also called **Eu·ro·mon·ey** (yo͝or′ə mun′ē, yûr′-). [EURO- + CURRENCY]

Eu·ro·dol·lar (yo͝or′ə dol′ər, yûr′-), *n.* a U.S. dollar deposited in or credited to a European bank. Cf. **Asiadollar.** [1955–60; EURO- + DOLLAR]

Eu·ro·mar·ket (yo͝or′ō mär′kit, yûr′-, yo͝or′ə mär′-, yûr′-), *n.* **1.** Also, **Eu·ro·mart** (yo͝or′ə märt′, yûr′-). See **Common Market** (def. 1). **2.** *Finance.* the money market in Eurocurrency or Eurobonds. [EURO- + MARKET]

Eu·ro·pa (yo͝o rō′pə, yə-), *n.* **1.** Also, **Europe.** *Class. Myth.* a sister of Cadmus who was abducted by Zeus in the form of a bull and taken to Crete, where she bore him Rhadamanthus, Minos, and Sarpedon. **2.** *Astron.* a large natural satellite of the planet Jupiter.

Eu·ro·pat·ent (yo͝or′ō pat′nt, yûr′-), *n.* a patent on inventions that is granted by a central authority under a unified European convention and is valid in participating European countries. [1970–75; EURO- + PATENT]

Eu·rope (yo͝or′əp, yûr′- *for 1;* yo͝o rō′pē, yə- *for 2*), *n.* **1.** a continent in the W part of the landmass lying between the Atlantic and Pacific oceans, separated from Asia by the Ural Mountains on the E and the Caucasus Mountains and the Black and Caspian seas on the SE. In British usage, *Europe* sometimes contrasts with *England.* 702,300,000 including the Russian Federation; ab. 4,017,000 sq. mi. (10,404,000 sq. km). See map at top of page. **2.** *Class. Myth.* Europa (def. 1).

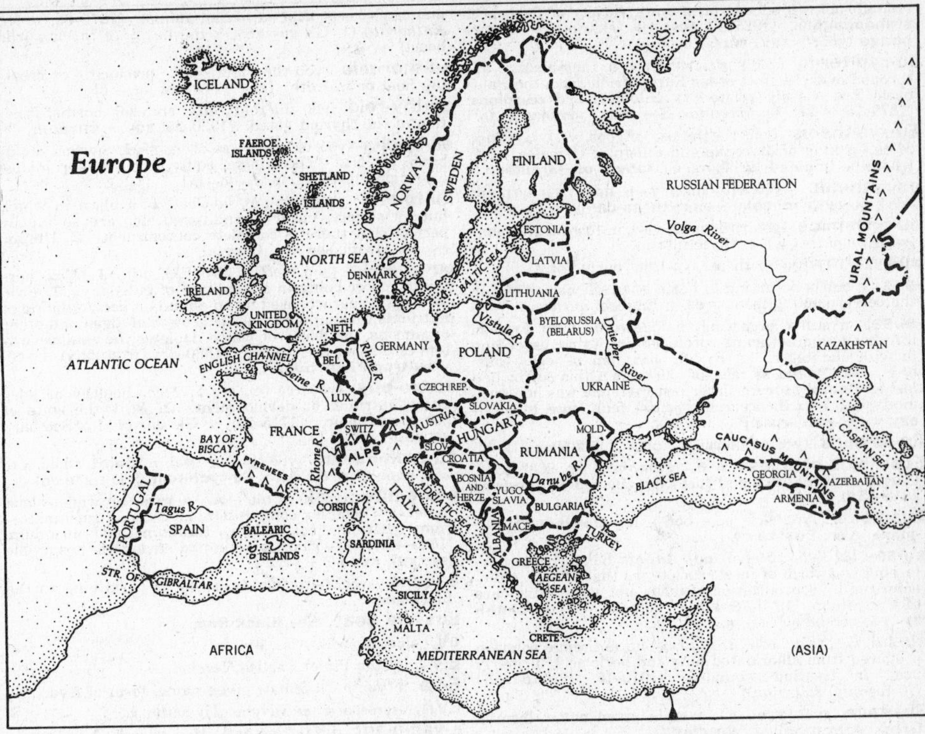

Eu·ro·pe·an (yo͝or′ə pē′ən, yûr′-), *adj.* **1.** of or pertaining to Europe or its inhabitants. **2.** native to or derived from Europe: *traditional European customs; European languages.* —*n.* **3.** a native or inhabitant of Europe. **4.** a person of European descent. **5.** (in East Africa and Asia) a white person; Caucasian. [1595–1605; < L *Eurōpae*(*us*) (see EUROPE, -EOUS) + -AN] —**Eu′ro·pe′an·ly,** *adv.*

Europe′an Atom′ic En′ergy Commu′nity. See **Euratom.**

Eu′rope′an beech′, a beech, *Fagus sylvatica,* of Europe, cultivated in North America in many ornamental varieties. [1860–65, *Amer.*]

Eu′rope′an bird′ cher′ry. See under **bird cherry** (def. 1).

Europe′an blastomyco′sis, *Pathol.* cryptococcosis.

Eu′rope′an chaf′er, a scarab beetle, *Amphimallon majalis.* [1945–50]

Eu′rope′an chest′nut. See under **chestnut** (def. 1).

Europe′an Coal′ and Steel′ Commu′nity, an economic union created in 1952 and providing for the pooling of coal, iron, and steel production in Belgium, France, Italy, Luxembourg, the Netherlands, and West Germany. [1950–55]

Europe′an Com′mon Mar′ket. See **Common Market** (def. 1). *Abbr.:* ECM

Eu′rope′an corn′ bor′er. See under **corn borer.** [1915–20, *Amer.*]

Eu′rope′an cran′berry. See under **cranberry** (def. 1).

Europe′an Econom′ic Commu′nity, official name of the **Common Market** (def. 1). *Abbr.:* EEC [1955–60]

Eu′rope′an el′der, an elder, *Sambucus nigra,* of Europe and Asia, bearing black fruit. Also called **bourtree.**

Eu′rope′an elk′, the moose, *Alces alces.*

Eu′rope′an finch′, greenfinch. [1945–50]

Europe′an Free′ Trade′ Associa′tion, an economic association established in 1960 and originally composed of Austria, Denmark, Britain, Norway, Portugal, Sweden, and Switzerland, that maintains free trade in industrial products among member countries. *Abbr.:* EFTA

Eu·ro·pe·an·ism (yo͝or′ə pē′ə niz′əm, yûr′-), *n.* **1.** European characteristics, ideas, methods, sympathies, etc. **2.** a European trait or practice. **3.** belief in or advocacy of the unification of Europe. [1820–30; EUROPEAN + -ISM]

Eu·ro·pe·an·ist (yo͝or′ə pē′ə nist, yûr′-), *n.* a person who advocates Europeanism, esp. the unification of Europe. [1965–70; EUROPEAN + -IST]

Eu·ro·pe·an·ize (yo͝or′ə pē′ə nīz′, yûr′-), *v.t.,* **-ized, -iz·ing.** to make European. Also, *esp. Brit.,* **Eu′ro·pe′an·ise′.** [1840–50; EUROPEAN + -IZE] —**Eu′ro·pe′an·i·za′tion,** *n.*

Eu′rope′an larch′, a pine tree, *Larix decidua,* of northern and central Europe, having slender, yellow-gray branchlets and oval cones with downy scales, grown for timber and as an ornamental. [1860–65, *Amer.*]

Eu′rope′an lin′den. See under **linden** (def. 1).

Eu′rope′an Mon′etary Sys′tem, a Common Market program designed to narrow the fluctuation of western European currencies against one another. *Abbr.:* EMS

Eu′rope′an Par′liament, a deliberative and legislative assembly of the European Community that advises member nations on policy matters.

Europe′an plan′, (in hotels) a system of paying a fixed rate that covers lodging and service but not meals. *Abbr.:* EP Cf. **American plan.** [1825–35, *Amer.*]

Eu′rope′an rasp′berry, an erect, shrubby plant, *Rubus idaeus,* of Eurasia, having conical or thimble-shaped red fruit.

Europe′an Recov′ery Pro′gram, a plan for aiding the European nations in economic recovery after World War II, proposed by U.S. Secretary of State George C. Marshall in 1947 and implemented in 1948 under the Economic Cooperation Administration. *Abbr.:* ERP, E.R.P. Also called **Marshall Plan.**

Europe′an red′ mite′, a red to red-brown mite, *Panonychus ulmi,* with white spots and dorsal spines: a widely distributed pest of fruit trees as well as other trees and shrubs. [1965–70]

Eu′rope′an red′start. See under **redstart** (def. 1).

Eu′rope′an Space′ A′gency, a multinational organization that provides for and promotes cooperation among its member European countries in space research and technology. *Abbr.:* ESA

Europe′an spruce′ saw′fly. See under **spruce sawfly.**

Europe′an white′ hel′lebore. See under **hellebore** (def. 2).

eu·ro·pi·um (yo͝o rō′pē əm, yə-), *n. Chem.* a rare-earth metallic element whose salts are light pink. *Symbol:* Eu; *at. wt.:* 151.96; *at. no.:* 63. [1900–05; EUROPE + -IUM]

Eu·ro·po·cen·tric (yo͝o rō′pə sen′trik, yo͝or′ə pə-), *adj.* Eurocentric. [1925–30; EUROPE + -O- + -CENTRIC, on the model of ETHNOCENTRIC, etc.] —**Eu·ro′po·cen′trism,** *n.*

Eu·rus (yo͝or′əs, yûr′-), *n.* the ancient Greek personification of the east wind. Cf. **Volturnus.**

eury-, a combining form meaning "broad," "wide," used in the formation of compound words: *eurypterid.* [< Gk, comb. form of *eurýs* wide]

Eu·ry·ba·tes (yo͝o rib′ə tēz′, yə-), *n.* (in the *Odyssey*) a companion of Odysseus.

eu·ry·bath (yo͝or′ə bath′, yûr′-), *n.* a eurybathic organism. [by back formation from EURYBATHIC]

eu·ry·bath·ic (yo͝or′ə bath′ik, yûr′-), *adj. Ecol.* of or pertaining to marine or freshwater life that can tolerate a wide range of depths (opposed to *stenobathic*). [1900–05; EURY- + Gk *báth*(*os*) depth + -IC]

Eu·ryb·i·a (yo͝o rib′ē ə), *n. Class. Myth.* a Titan, daughter of Pontus and Gaea.

Eu·ry·cle·a (yo͝or′i klē′ə, yûr′-), *n.* (in the *Odyssey*) the nurse of Telemachus who recognized the disguised Odysseus by a scar on his leg. Also, **Eu·ry·cli·a** (yo͝or′i klī′ə, yûr′-).

Eu·ryd·i·ce (yo͝o rid′ə sē′, yə-), *n. Class. Myth.* **1.** Also called **Agriope.** the wife of Orpheus. **2.** the wife of Creon of Thebes. Also, **Eu·ryd·i·ke** (yo͝o rid′i kē′, yə-).

Eu·rym·a·chus (yo͝o rim′ə kəs, yə-), *n.* (in the *Odyssey*) a deceitful suitor of Penelope.

eu·ryph·a·gous (yo͝o rif′ə gəs, yə-), *adj. Ecol.* (of an

CONCISE PRONUNCIATION KEY: act, cāpe, dâre, pärt; set, ēqual; *if,* ice; ox, ōver, ôrder, oil, bo͝ok, bo͞ot, out; up, ûrge; child; sing; shoe; thin, *that;* zh as in *treasure.* ə = *a* as in *alone, e* as in *system, i* as in *easily, o* as in *gallop, u* as in *circus;* ᵊ as in *fire* (fīᵊr), *hour* (ouᵊr). l and n can serve as syllabic consonants, as in *cradle* (krād′l), and *button* (but′n). See the full key inside the front cover.

animal) able to subsist on a wide variety of foods. Cf. **stenophagous.** [1925–30; EURY- + -PHAGOUS] **—eu·ry·phage** (yŏŏr′ə fāj′, yûr′-), *n.*

eu·ryp·ter·id (yŏŏ rip′tə rid, yə-), *n.* any aquatic arthropod of the extinct order Eurypterida, from the Paleozoic Era, closely related to trilobites and scorpions. [1870–75; < NL *Eurypteridae.* See EURY-, -PTEROUS, -ID[2]]

Eu·rys·the·us (yŏŏ ris′thē əs, -thyōōs, yə-), *n. Class. Myth.* a king of Mycenae and cousin of Hercules, upon whom he imposed 12 labors. Cf. **labors of Hercules.**

eu·ryth·mic (yŏŏ rith′mik, yə-), *adj.* eurhythmic. Also, **eu·ryth′mi·cal.** **—eu·ryth′mi·cal·ly,** *adv.*

eu·ryth·mics (yŏŏ rith′miks, yə-), *n.* (*used with a singular or plural v.*) eurhythmics.

eu·ryth·my (yŏŏ rith′mē, yə-), *n.* eurhythmy.

-eus, a suffix occurring in Latin scientific names and in the corresponding loanwords in English: *nucleus.*

-euse, a suffix occurring in loanwords from French, forming feminine nouns corresponding to nouns ending in *-eur: chanteuse.* [< F < L *-ōsa,* fem. of *-ōsus* -OSE[1] (>F *-eux*); taken as fem. of *-eur* when this suffix had lost its final consonant (later restored) and was homonymous with *-eux* (hence, masc. *-eu(r),* fem. *-euse,* by analogy with *-eux, -euse*)]

Eu·se·bi·us (yŏŏ sē′bē əs), *n.* pope A.D. 309 or 310.

Euse′bius of Caesare′a, (*Pamphili*) A.D. 263?–c340, Christian theologian and historian: Bishop of Caesarea c315–c340.

Eus·ke·ra (yōō′skər ə, e ōō′-), *n.* the Basque language. Also, **Eus′ka·ra.**

eu·so·cial (yōō sō′shəl), *adj. Animal Behav.* of or pertaining to a form of insect society, as that of ants, characterized by specialization of tasks and cooperative care of the young. [1970–75; EU- + SOCIAL] **—eu·so·ci·al·i·ty** (yōō sō′shē al′i tē), *n.*

eu·sol (yōō′sôl, -sol), *n. Pharm.* an antiseptic solution prepared from chlorinated lime and boric acid, formerly used in treating wounds. [1910–15; *E(dinburgh) U(niversity) sol(ution)*]

Eus·tace (yōō′stəs), *n.* a male given name: from a Greek word meaning "steadfast."

Eu·sta′chian tube′ (yōō stā′shən, -stā′kē ən), *Anat.* a canal extending from the middle ear to the pharynx; auditory canal. See diag. under **ear**[1]. [1735–45; named after EUSTACHIO; see -AN]

E·u·sta·chio (e′ōō stä′kyô), *n.* **Bar·to·lom·me·o** (bär′tô lôm me′ô), 1524?–1574, Italian anatomist. Latin, **Eu·sta·chi·us** (yōō stā′kē əs).

Eu·sta·cia (yōō stā′shə), *n.* a female given name.

eu·sta·sy (yōō′stə sē), *n., pl.* **-sies.** *Geol.* any uniformly global change of sea level that may reflect a change in the quantity of water in the ocean, or a change in the shape and capacity of the ocean basins. Also, **eu′·sta·cy.** [1945–50; nominalization of *eustatic* caused by eustasy (< G *eustatisch,* coined by Austrian geologist Edward Suess (1831–1914); see EU-, STATIC), with *-stasy* for *-stasis* STASIS, prob. on the model of ECSTASY] **—eu·stat·ic** (yōō stat′ik), *adj.* **—eu·stat′i·cal·ly,** *adv.*

eu·stele (yōō′stēl, yōō stē′lē), *n., pl.* **-steles.** *Bot.* an arrangement of the xylem and phloem in discrete strands, separated by areas of parenchymatous tissue. [1915–20; EU- + STELE]

eu·style (yōō′stīl), *adj.* having an intercolumniation of 2¼ diameters. See illus. under **intercolumniation.** [1555–65; < Gk *eústȳlos* well columned (i.e., with the columns well spaced); see EU-, -STYLE[2]]

eu·tax·y (yōō′tak sē, yōō tak′sē), *n.* good order or management. [1605–15; < Gk *eutaxía,* equiv. to *eútakt(os)* well arranged (see EU-, TACTIC) + *-ia* -Y[3]]

eu·tec·tic (yōō tek′tik), *Physical Chem.* —*adj.* **1.** of greatest fusibility: said of an alloy or mixture whose melting point is lower than that of any other alloy or mixture of the same ingredients. **2.** noting or pertaining to such a mixture or its properties: *a eutectic melting point.* —*n.* **3.** a eutectic substance. [1880–85; < Gk *eútēkt(os)* easily melted, dissolved (*eu-* EU- + *tēktós* melted) + -IC]

eu·tec·toid (yōō tek′toid), *adj.* **1.** resembling a eutectic. —*n.* **2.** a eutectoid alloy. [1900–05; EUTECT(IC) + -OID]

Eu·ter·pe (yōō tûr′pē), *n. Class. Myth.* the Muse of music and lyric poetry. **—Eu·ter′pe·an,** *adj.*

eu·tha·na·sia (yōō′thə nā′zhə, -zhē ə, -zē ə), *n.* **1.** Also called **mercy killing.** the act of putting to death painlessly or allowing to die, as by withholding extreme medical measures, a person or animal suffering from an incurable, esp. a painful, disease or condition. **2.** painless death. [1640–50; < NL < Gk *euthanasía* an easy death, equiv. to *eu-* EU- + *thánat(os)* death + *-ia* -Y[3]] **—eu·tha·na·si·ast** (yōō′thə nā′zē ast′), *n.* **—eu·tha·na·sic** (yōō′thə nā′zik), *adj.*

eu·tha·nize (yōō′thə nīz′), *v.t.,* **-nized, -niz·ing.** to subject to euthanasia: *to euthanize injured animals.* Also, **eu·than·a·tize** (yōō than′ə tīz′); *esp. Brit.,* **eu′tha·nise′, eu·than′a·tise′.** [1960–65; EUTHAN(ASIA) + -IZE]

eu·then·ics (yōō then′iks), *n.* (*used with a singular v.*) a science concerned with bettering the condition of human beings through the improvement of their environment. [1900–05; < Gk *euthēn(eîn)* to be well off, prosper + -ICS] **—eu·then·ist** (yōō then′ist, yōō′thə-nist), *n.*

eu·the·ri·an (yōō thēr′ē ən), *adj.* **1.** belonging or pertaining to the group Eutheria, comprising the placental mammals. —*n.* **2.** a eutherian animal. [1875–80; < NL *Eutheri(a)* (< Gk *eu-* EU- + *thēría,* pl. of *thērion* wild beast) + -AN]

eu·ther·mic (yōō thûr′mik), *adj.* producing or creating heat or warmth. [EU- + THERM- + -IC]

eu·thy·roid (yōō thī′roid), *adj.* showing normal function of the thyroid gland. [1920–25; EU- + THYROID]

eu·to·ci·a (yōō tō′shē ə, -sē ə), *n. Med.* normal childbirth. [< NL < Gk *eutokía,* equiv. to *eu-* EU- + *tók(os)* a bringing forth, birth + *-ia* -IA]

Eu·to·pi·a (yōō tō′pē ə), *n. Obs.* **1.** a place in which human society, natural conditions, etc., are so ideally perfect that there is complete contentment. **2.** Utopia. [< NL (1516); see EU-, UTOPIA]

eu·troph·ic (yōō trof′ik, -trō′fik), *adj.* **1.** *Med.* pertaining to or being in a condition of eutrophy. **2.** *Ecol.* (of a lake) characterized by an abundant accumulation of nutrients that support a dense growth of algae and other organisms, the decay of which depletes the shallow waters of oxygen in summer. [1880–85; EUTROPH(Y) + -IC] **—eu·troph′i·ca′tion,** *n.*

eu·tro·phy (yōō′trə fē), *n.* **1.** *Med.* healthy or adequate nutrition or development. **2.** *Ecol.* the state of being eutrophic. [1715–25; < Gk *eutrophía.* See EU-, TROPHO-, -Y[3]]

Eu·tych·i·a·nus (yōō tik′ē ā′nəs), *n.* **Saint,** died A.D. 283, pope 275–283. Also, **Eu·tych·i·an** (yōō tik′ē ən).

eux·e·nite (yōōk′sə nīt′), *n.* a rare, brownish-black mineral of complex composition, an oxide of calcium, cerium, yttrium, columbium, titanium, and uranium. [1840–45; < Gk *eúxen(os)* kind to strangers, hospitable (see EU-, XENO-) + -ITE[1]]

Eux·ine (yōōk′sin, -sīn), *adj.* of or pertaining to the Black Sea.

Eux′ine Sea′. See **Black Sea.**

eV, electron-volt. Also, **ev**

E.V., (of the Bible) English Version.

E·va (ē′və), *n.* a female given name, form of **Eve.**

EVA, *Aerospace.* extravehicular activity.

e·vac·u·ant (i vak′yōō ənt), *Med.* —*adj.* **1.** evacuating; promoting thorough evacuation, esp. from the bowels; cathartic; purgative. —*n.* **2.** an evacuant medicine or agent; cathartic; purgative. [1720–30; < L *ēvacuant-* (s. of *ēvacuāns,* prp. of *ēvacuāre*). See EVACUATE, -ANT]

e·vac·u·ate (i vak′yōō āt′), *v.,* **-at·ed, -at·ing.** —*v.t.* **1.** to leave empty; vacate. **2.** to remove (persons or things) from a place, as a dangerous place or disaster area, for reasons of safety or protection: *to evacuate the inhabitants of towns in the path of a flood.* **3.** to remove persons from (a city, town, building, area, etc.) for reasons of safety: *to evacuate the embassy after a bomb threat.* **4.** *Mil.* **a.** to remove (troops, wounded soldiers, civilians, etc.) from a war zone, combat area, etc. **b.** to withdraw from or quit (a town, fort, etc., that has been occupied). **5.** *Physiol.* to discharge or eject as through the excretory passages, esp. from the bowels. **6.** to deprive: *Fear evacuated their minds of reason.* **7.** to produce a vacuum in. —*v.i.* **8.** to leave a place because of military or other threats. **9.** to void; defecate. [1350–1400; ME < L *ēvacuātus* (ptp. of *ēvacuāre* to empty out, equiv. to *ē-* E- + *vacuāre* to empty); see VACUUM, -ATE[1]] **—Syn. 1.** empty, void, drain.

e·vac·u·a·tion (i vak′yōō ā′shən), *n.* **1.** the act or process of evacuating, or the condition of being evacuated; discharge or expulsion, as of contents. **2.** *Physiol.* discharge, as of waste matter through the excretory passages, esp. from the bowels. **3.** something evacuated or discharged. **4.** the removal of persons or things from an endangered area. **5.** clearance by removal of troops, equipment, etc. **6.** the withdrawal or removal of troops, civilians, etc. [1350–1400; ME *evacuacioun* < LL *ēvacuātiōn-* (s. of *ēvacuātiō*). See EVACUATE, -ION] **—e·vac·u·a·tive** (i vak′yōō ā′tiv), *adj.*

e·vac·u·a·tor (i vak′yōō ā′tər), *n.* **1.** a person or thing that evacuates. **2.** *Med.* an instrument for removing impacted feces from the rectum. [1605–15; EVACUATE + -OR[2]]

e·vac·u·ee (i vak′yōō ē′, i vak′yōō ē′), *n.* a person who is withdrawn or removed from a place of danger, a disaster area, etc. [1935–40; < F *évacué,* ptp. of *évacuer* to EVACUATE; see -EE]

e·vade (i vād′), *v.,* **e·vad·ed, e·vad·ing.** —*v.t.* **1.** to escape from by trickery or cleverness: *to evade one's pursuers.* **2.** to get around by trickery: *to evade rules.* **3.** to avoid doing or fulfilling: *to evade an obligation.* **4.** to avoid answering directly: *to evade a question.* **5.** to elude; escape: *The solution evaded him.* —*v.i.* **6.** to practice evasion. **7.** to elude or get away from someone or something by craft or slyness; escape. [1505–15; < L *ēvādere* to pass over, go out, equiv. to *ē-* E- + *vādere* to go, walk] **—e·vad′a·ble, e·vad′i·ble,** *adj.* **—e·vad′er,** *n.* **—e·vad′ing·ly,** *adv.*
—Syn. 1. avoid, dodge. See **escape. 6.** prevaricate, equivocate, fence. **—Ant. 1.** face, confront.

E·vad·ne (i vad′nē), *n. Class. Myth.* **1.** the wife of Capaneus who threw herself on his funeral pyre. **2.** a daughter of Pelias, king of Iolcus. Cf. **Amphinome.**

e·vag·i·nate (i vaj′ə nāt′), *v.t.,* **-nat·ed, -nat·ing.** to turn inside out, or cause to protrude by eversion, as a tubular organ. [1650–60; < LL *ēvāginātus* (ptp. of *ēvāgināre*) unsheathed, equiv. to *ē-* E- + *vāgin(a)* scabbard, sheath (see VAGINA) + *-ātus* -ATE[1]] **—e·vag·i·na·ble** (i vaj′ə nə bəl), *adj.* **—e·vag′i·na′tion,** *n.*

e·val·u·ate (i val′yōō āt′), *v.t.,* **-at·ed, -at·ing. 1.** to determine or set the value or amount of; appraise: *to evaluate property.* **2.** to judge or determine the significance, worth, or quality of; assess: *to evaluate the results of an experiment.* **3.** *Math.* to ascertain the numerical value of (a function, relation, etc.). [1835–45; back formation from EVALUATION] **—e·val·u·a·ble** (i val′yōō ə-bəl), *adj.* **—e·val′u·a′tive,** *adj.* **—e·val′u·a′tor,** *n.*
—Syn. 1, 2. weigh, estimate, gauge, value.

e·val·u·a·tion (i val′yōō ā′shən), *n.* **1.** an act or instance of evaluating or appraising. **2.** (esp. in medicine) a diagnosis or diagnostic study of a physical or mental condition. [1745–55; < F *évaluation.* See E-, VALUATION]

Ev·an (ev′ən), *n.* a male given name, Welsh form of **John.**

ev·a·nesce (ev′ə nes′, ev′ə nes′), *v.i.,* **-nesced, -nesc·ing.** to disappear gradually; vanish; fade away. [1815–25; < L *ēvānēscere* to VANISH] **—ev′a·nes′cence,** *n.* **—ev′a·nes′ci·ble,** *adj.*

ev·a·nes·cent (ev′ə nes′ənt), *adj.* **1.** vanishing; fading away; fleeting. **2.** tending to become imperceptible; scarcely perceptible. [1745–55; < L *ēvānēscent-* (s. of *ēvānēscēns*) vanishing, disappearing. See EVANESCE, -ENT] **—ev′a·nes′cent·ly,** *adv.*

Evang., Evangelical.

e·van·gel[1] (i van′jəl), *n.* **1.** the good tidings of the redemption of the world through Jesus Christ; the gospel. **2.** (*usually cap.*) any of the four Gospels. **3.** doctrine taken as a guide or regarded as of prime importance. **4.** good news or tidings. [1300–50; ME < LL *evangelium* < Gk *euangélion* good news (see EU-, ANGEL); r. ME *evangile* < MF]

e·van·gel[2] (i van′jəl), *n.* an evangelist. [1585–95; < LL *evangelus* < Gk *euángelos* (adj.) bringing good news. See EVANGEL[1]]

e·van·gel·i·ar·y (ē′van jel′ē er′ē, -ē ə rē, ev′ən-), *n., pl.* **-ar·ies.** evangelistary. [< ML *evangelārium;* see EVANGEL, -ARY]

e·van·gel·i·cal (ē′van jel′i kəl, ev′ən-), *adj.* Also, **e′van·gel′ic. 1.** pertaining to or in keeping with the gospel and its teachings. **2.** belonging to or designating the Christian churches that emphasize the teachings and authority of the Scriptures, esp. of the New Testament, in opposition to the institutional authority of the church itself, and that stress as paramount the tenet that salvation is achieved by personal conversion to faith in the atonement of Christ. **3.** designating Christians, esp. of the late 1970's, eschewing the designation of fundamentalist but holding to a conservative interpretation of the Bible. **4.** pertaining to certain movements in the Protestant churches in the 18th and 19th centuries that stressed the importance of personal experience of guilt for sin, and of reconciliation to God through Christ. **5.** marked by ardent or zealous enthusiasm for a cause. —*n.* **6.** an adherent of evangelical doctrines or a person who belongs to an evangelical church or party. [1525–35; < LL *evangelicus* (< LGk *euangelikós;* see EVANGEL[1], -IC) + -AL[1]] **—e′van·gel′i·cal·ly,** *adv.* **—e′van·gel′i·cal·ness, e′van·gel′i·cal′i·ty,** *n.*

e·van·gel·i·cal·ism (ē′van jel′i kə liz′əm, ev′ən-), *n.* **1.** evangelical doctrines or principles. **2.** adherence to evangelical principles or doctrines or to an evangelical church or party. [1825–35; EVANGELICAL + -ISM]

E·van·ge·line (i van′jə lēn′, -līn′, -lin), *n.* a female given name, invented by H.W. Longfellow. Also, **E·van·ge·li·na** (i van′jə lē′nə).

E·van·ge·line (i van′jə lin), *n.* a narrative poem (1847) by Longfellow.

e·van·ge·lism (i van′jə liz′əm), *n.* **1.** the preaching or promulgation of the gospel; the work of an evangelist. **2.** evangelicalism. **3.** missionary zeal, purpose, or activity. [1620–30; EVANGEL[2] + -ISM]

e·van·ge·list (i van′jə list), *n.* **1.** a Protestant minister or layperson who serves as an itinerant or special preacher, esp. a revivalist. **2.** a preacher of the gospel. **3.** (*cap.*) any of the writers (Matthew, Mark, Luke, and John) of the four Gospels. **4.** (in the primitive church) a person who first brought the gospel to a city or region. **5.** (*cap.*) *Mormon Ch.* a patriarch. **6.** a person marked by evangelical enthusiasm for or support of any cause. [1125–75; ME *evangeliste* < L *evangelista* < Gk *euangelistés.* See EVANGEL[1], -IST]

e·van·ge·lis·ta·ry (i van′jə lis′tə rē), *n., pl.* **-ries.** a book containing passages from the four Gospels to be read at a divine service. Also, **evangeliary.** [1640–50; < ML *ēvangelistārium.* See EVANGELIST, -ARY]

e·van·ge·lis·tic (i van′jə lis′tik), *adj.* **1.** pertaining to evangelists or to preachers of the gospel. **2.** evangelical. **3.** seeking to evangelize; striving to convert sinners. **4.** designed or fitted to evangelize. **5.** (*often cap.*) of or pertaining to the four Evangelists. [1835–45; EVANGELIST + -IC] **—e·van′ge·lis′ti·cal·ly,** *adv.*

e·van·ge·lize (i van′jə līz′), *v.,* **-lized, -liz·ing.** —*v.t.* **1.** to preach the gospel to. **2.** to convert to Christianity. —*v.i.* **3.** to preach the gospel; act as an evangelist. Also, *esp. Brit.,* **e·van′ge·lise′.** [1350–1400; ME *evangelisen* < LL *evangelizāre* < LGk *euangelízein.* See EVANGEL[1], -IZE] **—e·van′ge·li·za′tion,** *n.* **—e·van′ge·liz′er,** *n.*

e·van·ish (i van′ish), *v.i.* **1.** to vanish; disappear. **2.** to cease to be. [1300–50; ME *evanisshen* < MF *esvaniss-,* extended s. of *esvanir.* See E-, EVANESCE, VANISH]

Ev·ans (ev′ənz), *n.* **1. Sir Arthur John,** 1851–1941, English archaeologist. **2. Dame Edith,** 1888–1976, English actress. **3. Herbert Mc·Lean** (mə klān′), 1882–1971, U.S. embryologist and anatomist. **4. Mary Ann.** See **Eliot, George. 5. Maurice,** born 1901, U.S. actor and producer, born in England. **6. Oliver,** 1755–1819, U.S. inventor: constructed the first high-pressure steam engine in the U.S. 1801?. **7. Rob·ley Dun·gli·son** (rob′lē dung′glə sən), ("*Fighting Bob*"), 1846–1912, U.S. admiral. **8. Ru·dulph** (rōō′dulf), 1878–1960, U.S. sculptor.

Ev·ans·ton (ev′ən stən), *n.* a city in NE Illinois, on Lake Michigan, near Chicago. 73,706.

Ev·ans·ville (ev′ənz vil′), *n.* a city in SW Indiana, on the Ohio River. 130,496.

evap., 1. evaporate. **2.** evaporation.

e·vap·o·ra·ble (i vap′ər ə bəl), *adj.* capable of being evaporated. [1535–45; EVAPOR(ATE) + -ABLE] **—e·vap′·o·ra·bil′i·ty,** *n.*

e·vap·o·rate (i vap′ə rāt′), *v.,* **-rat·ed, -rat·ing.** —*v.i.* **1.** to change from a liquid or solid state into vapor; pass off in vapor. **2.** to give off moisture. **3.** to disappear;

vanish; fade: *His hopes evaporated.* —*v.t.* **4.** to convert into a gaseous state or vapor; drive off or extract in the form of vapor: *The warm sun evaporated the dew.* **5.** to extract moisture or liquid from, as by heat, so as to make dry or to reduce to a denser state: *to evaporate fruit.* **6.** to cause to disappear or fade; dissipate: *His involvement in the scandal evaporated any hope he had for a political career.* [1375–1425; late ME *evaporaten* < L *ēvapōrātus* (ptp. of *ēvapōrāre* to disperse in vapor); see E-, VAPOR, -ATE[1]]
—**Syn.** **1.** vaporize. **3.** evanesce. **5.** EVAPORATE, DEHYDRATE, DRY mean to abstract moisture from. To EVAPORATE is to remove moisture by means of heat, forced ventilation, or the like, and thus to produce condensation or shriveling: *to evaporate milk, sliced apples.* To DEHYDRATE is to remove moisture from a vegetable, fruit, or body tissue: *to dehydrate fruit; dehydrated from running.* To DRY may mean to wipe moisture off the surface or to withdraw moisture by natural means, such as exposure to air or heat: *to dry a dish, clothes.*

evap′orated milk′, unsweetened milk thickened and concentrated by evaporation of water content to approximately half the original weight and then sterilized and canned. [1865–70]

e•vap•o•ra•tion (i vap′ə rā′shən), *n.* **1.** the act or process of evaporating. **2.** the state of being evaporated. **3.** *Archaic.* matter or the quantity of matter evaporated or passed off in vapor. [1350–1400; ME *evaporacioun* < L *ēvapōrātiōn-* (s. of *ēvapōrātiō*). See EVAPORATE, -ION] —**e•vap•o•ra•tive** (i vap′ə rā′tiv, -ər ə tiv), *adj.* —**e•vap′•o•ra′tive•ly,** *adv.*

evapora′tion pan′, an atmometer consisting of a pan about 4 ft. (1.2 m) in diameter and 10 in. (25.4 cm) in depth.

e•vap•o•ra•tor (i vap′ə rā′tər), *n.* **1.** a device in which evaporation takes place, as for thickening syrup. **2.** the part of a refrigeration system in which the refrigerant absorbs heat and changes from a liquid to a gas. [1820–30; EVAPORATE + -OR[2]]

e•vap•o•rim•e•ter (i vap′ə rim′i tər), *n.* atmometer. [1820–30; EVAPOR(ATION) + -I- + -METER]

e•vap•o•rite (i vap′ə rīt′), *n. Geol.* any sedimentary rock, as gypsum or rock salt, formed by precipitation from evaporating seawater. [1920–25; EVAPOR(ATION) + -ITE[1]]

e•vap•o•tran•spi•ra•tion (i vap′ō tran′spə rā′shən), *n. Meteorol.* **1.** the process of transferring moisture from the earth to the atmosphere by evaporation of water and transpiration from plants. **2.** Also called **flyoff, water loss.** the total volume transferred by this process. [1945–50; EVAPO(RATION) + TRANSPIRATION]

Ev•a•ris•tus (ev′ə ris′təs), *n.* **Saint,** died A.D. 105, pope 97–105.

Ev•arts (ev′ərts), *n.* **William Maxwell,** 1818–1901, U.S. lawyer and statesman.

é•va•sé (ā′vä zā′), *adj.* widened at the top, as a vase or chimney flue. [< F, adj. use of ptp. of *évaser* to widen the mouth of, equiv. to *e-* E- + *vas* VASE + *-é* ptp. suffix]

e•va•sion (i vā′zhən), *n.* **1.** an act or instance of escaping, avoiding, or shirking something: *evasion of one's duty.* **2.** the avoiding of an argument, accusation, question, or the like, as by a subterfuge: *The old political boss was notorious for his practice of evasion.* **3.** a means of evading; subterfuge; an excuse or trick to avoid or get around something: *Her polite agreement was an evasion concealing what she really felt.* **4.** physical or mental escape. **5.** an act or instance of violating the tax laws by failing or refusing to pay all or part of one's taxes. [1375–1425; late ME < L *ēvāsiōn-* (s. of *ēvāsiō*), equiv. to *ēvās(us)* (ptp. of *ēvādere* to go out; see EVADE) + *-iōn-* -ION] —**e•va′sion•al,** *adj.*
—**Syn.** **1.** avoidance, dodging. **2.** prevarication, equivocation, quibbling.

e•va•sive (i vā′siv), *adj.* **1.** tending or seeking to evade; characterized by evasion: *an evasive answer.* **2.** elusive or evanescent. [1715–25; EVAS(ION) + -IVE] —**e•va′sive•ly,** *adv.* —**e•va′sive•ness,** *n.*

Ev•att (ev′ət), *n.* **Herbert Vere** (vēr), 1894–1966, Australian lawyer and statesman: president of the General Assembly of the United Nations 1948–49.

eve (ēv), *n.* **1.** (*sometimes cap.*) the evening or the day before a holiday, church festival, or any date or event: *Christmas Eve; the eve of an execution.* **2.** the period preceding or leading up to any event, crisis, etc.: *on the eve of the American Revolution.* **3.** the evening. [1200–50; ME; var. of EVEN[2]]

Eve (ēv), *n.* **1.** name of the first woman: wife of Adam and progenitor of the human race. Gen. 3:20. **2.** a female given name: from a Hebrew word meaning "life."

e•vec•tion (i vek′shən), *n. Astron.* a periodic irregularity in the moon's motion, caused by the attraction of the sun. [1650–60; < L *ēvectiōn-* (s. of *ēvectiō*) a going upwards, flight, equiv. to *ēvect(us)* (ptp. of *ēvehere* to carry forth, move forth) + *-iōn-* -ION] —**e•vec′tion•al,** *adj.*

Eve•lyn (ēv′lin *for 1, 3;* ev′ə lin *for 2, or, esp. Brit.,* ēv′lin, ē′və lin), *n.* **1. John,** 1620–1706, English diarist. **2.** Also, **Ev′e•lynne.** a female given name, form of **Eve. 3.** *Chiefly Brit.* a male given name.

E•ve•mer•us (i vē′mər əs, i vem′ər-), *n.* Euhemerus.

e•ven[1] (ē′vən), *adj.* **1.** level; flat; without surface irregularities; smooth: *an even road.* **2.** on the same level; in the same plane or line; parallel: *even with the ground.* **3.** free from variations or fluctuations; regular: *even motion.* **4.** uniform in action, character, or quality: *to hold an even course.* **5.** equal in measure or quantity: *Add even amounts of oil and vinegar.* **6.** divisible by two, as a number (opposed to *odd*). **7.** denoted by such a number: *the even pages of a book.* **8.** exactly expressible in integers, or in tens, hundreds, etc., without fractional parts: *an even seven miles.* **9.** *Math.* (of a function) having a sign that remains the same when the sign of each independent variable is changed at the same time. **10.** equally balanced or divided; equal: *Check to see if the scales are even.* **11.** leaving no balance of debt on either side; square: *We will not be even until I can repay him for saving my life.* **12.** calm; placid; not easily excited or angered: *an even temper.* **13.** equitable, impartial, or fair: *an even bargain.* —*adv.* **14.** evenly: *The road ran even over the fields.* **15.** still; yet (used to emphasize a comparative): *even more suitable.* **16.** (used to suggest that something mentioned as a possibility constitutes an extreme case or an unlikely instance): *Even the slightest noise disturbs him. Even if he attends, he may not participate.* **17.** just (used to emphasize occurrence, coincidence, or simultaneousness of occurrences): *Even as he lay dying, they argued over his estate.* **18.** fully or quite: *even to death.* **19.** indeed (used as an intensive for stressing the identity or truth of something): *He is willing, even eager, to do it.* **20.** exactly or precisely: *It was even so.* **21. break even,** to have one's profits equal one's losses; neither gain nor lose: *The company barely broke even last year.* **22. get even,** to be revenged; retaliate: *He vowed to get even for the insult.* —*v.t.* **23.** to make even; level; smooth (sometimes fol. by *out*): *to even a board with a plane.* **24.** to place in an even state as to claim or obligation; balance (often fol. by *up*): *to even up accounts.* —*v.i.* **25.** to become even: *The odds evened before the race.* **26. even out, a.** to make or become even, smooth, or flat: *The wrinkles will even out when the suit dries.* **b.** to become equal, balanced, stable, etc.: *optimistic that the situation would even out eventually.* [bef. 900; (adj.) ME; OE *efen;* c. Goth *ibns,* OHG *eban,* ON *jafn* even, equal; (adv.) ME *even(e),* OE *efne,* deriv. of the adj.; (v.) ME *evenen,* OE *efnan* to lower, deriv. of the adj.] —**e′ven•er,** *n.* —**e′ven•ly,** *adv.* —**e′ven•ness,** *n.*
—**Syn.** **1.** plane. See **level. 12.** tranquil, temperate, composed, peaceful. **13.** just. —**Ant. 1.** irregular. **12.** mercurial. **13.** biased.

e•ven[2] (ē′vən), *n. Archaic.* evening; eve. [bef. 950; ME; OE *ǣfen;* akin to G *Abend,* OFris *ēvend.* See EVENING]

E•ven (ā′wən, ev′ən), *n., pl.* **E•vens,** (*esp. collectively*) **E•ven** for 1. **1.** a member of a Siberian people living mainly in the Yakut ASSR in the Soviet Union. **2.** the Tungusic language spoken by the Even. Also called **Lamut.** [< Russ *évén* < Evenki *əwən*]

e•ven•fall (ē′vən fôl′), *n.* the beginning of evening; twilight; dusk. [1805–15; EVEN[2] + FALL]

e•ven•hand•ed (ē′vən han′did), *adj.* impartial; equitable: *evenhanded justice.* [1595–1605; EVEN + HANDED] —**e′ven•hand′ed•ly,** *adv.* —**e′ven•hand′ed•ness,** *n.*

eve•ning (ēv′ning), *n.* **1.** the latter part of the day and early part of the night. **2.** the period from sunset to bedtime: *He spent the evenings reading.* **3.** *Chiefly Midland and Southern U.S.* the time between noon and sunset, including the afternoon and twilight. **4.** any concluding or declining period: *the evening of life.* **5.** an evening's reception or entertainment: *Their evenings at home were attended by the socially prominent.* —*adj.* **6.** of or pertaining to evening: *The evening sky shone with stars.* **7.** occurring or seen in the evening: *the evening mist.* [bef. 1000; ME; OE *ǣfnung,* equiv. to *ǣfn(ian)* draw toward evening + *-ung* n. suffix]
—**Syn. 1.** eventide, dusk, twilight, gloaming, nightfall.

eve′ning bag′, a small handbag made of rich fabric or beaded, ornamented, etc., and carried by women on formal or dressy occasions, usually in the evening.

eve′ning cam′pion, a sticky, hairy European weed, *Silene alba,* of the pink family, having night-blooming, fragrant flowers, the male and female of which grow on separate plants. Also called **white campion.**

eve′ning dress′, formal or semiformal attire for evening wear. Also called **eve′ning clothes′.** Cf. **morning dress.** [1790–1800]

eve′ning em′erald, peridot: not a true emerald.

eve′ning gown′, a woman's formal dress, usually having a floor-length skirt. Also called **gown.**

eve′ning gros′beak, a North American grosbeak, *Coccothraustes vespertina,* having yellowish, black, and white plumage. [1820–30, *Amer.*]

eve′ning prayer′, *Anglican Ch.* evensong (def. 1). [1590–1600]

eve′ning prim′rose, **1.** a plant, *Oenothera biennis,* having yellow flowers that open at nightfall. **2.** any of various plants of the same or related genera. [1800–10]

eve′ning prim′rose fam′ily, the plant family Onagraceae, characterized by herbaceous plants having simple leaves, showy flowers with four sepals and four petals, and fruit in the form of a berry or a capsule, and including the clarkia, evening primrose, fuchsia, and willow herb.

eve•nings (ēv′ningz), *adv.* in or during the evening regularly: *She worked days and studied evenings.* [1865–80]

eve′ning school′. See **night school.** [1815–25]

eve′ning star′, **1.** a bright planet seen in the western sky at or soon after sunset, esp. Venus. **2.** any planet that rises before midnight. [1525–35]

eve′ning watch′, *Naut.* the watch from 4 P.M. until 8 P.M., often adopted in place of the two dogwatches.

E•ven•ki (i weng′kē, i veng′-), *n., pl.* **-kis,** (*esp. collectively*) **-ki** for 1. **1.** a member of a Siberian people living mainly in the Yakut ASSR, Khabarovsk territory, and Evenki National District in the Soviet Union. **2.** the Tungusic language spoken by the Evenki. [< Russ *èvénki* < Evenki *əwənki* self-designation used by various local groups of Evenki]

e•ven-mind•ed (ē′vən mīn′did), *adj.* not easily ruffled, disturbed, prejudiced, etc.; calm; equable. —**e′ven-mind′ed•ness,** *n.*

e′ven mon′ey, **1.** the equal sum staked by each bettor. **2.** equal odds in a wager: *It's even money that the home team will win.* [1890–95] —**e′ven-mon′ey,** *adj.*

e′ven permuta′tion, *Math.* a permutation of a set of n elements, $x_1, x_2, \ldots x_n$, that leaves unchanged the product of all differences of the form $(x_i - x_j)$, where i is less than j. Cf. **odd permutation.** [1930–35]

e•ven•song (ē′vən sông′, -song′), *n.* **1.** (*usually cap.*) Also called **evening prayer.** *Anglican Ch.* a form of worship said or sung in the evening. **2.** vesper (def. 3c). [bef. 1000; ME; OE *ǣfensang.* See EVEN[2], SONG]

e•ven-ste•ven (ē′vən stē′vən), *adj. Informal.* **1.** having no balance of debt on either side; even in the setting of accounts. **2.** having an equal chance or score; tied. Also, **e′ven-Ste′ven.** [1865–70; rhyming compound based on EVEN[1]]

e•vent (i vent′), *n.* **1.** something that happens or is regarded as happening; an occurrence, esp. one of some importance. **2.** the outcome, issue, or result of anything: *The venture had no successful event.* **3.** something that occurs in a certain place during a particular interval of time. **4.** *Physics.* in relativity, an occurrence that is sharply localized at a single point in space and instant of time. Cf. **world point. 5.** *Sports.* any of the contests in a program made up of one sport or of a number of sports: *The broad jump event followed the pole vault.* **6. in any event,** regardless of what happens; in any case. Also, **at all events. 7. in the event of,** if there should be: *In the event of rain, the party will be held indoors.* **8. in the event that,** if it should happen that; in case: *In the event that I can't come back by seven, you can eat without me.* [1560–70; < L *ēventus* occurrence, outcome, equiv. to *ēven(īre)* to occur, come out + *-tus* suffix of v. action] —**e•vent′less,** *adj.*
—**Syn. 1.** happening, affair, case, circumstance. EVENT, EPISODE, INCIDENT, OCCURRENCE are terms for a happening. An EVENT is usually an important happening: *historical events.* An EPISODE is one of a series of happenings in a person's life or in a narrative: *an episode in one's life.* An INCIDENT is an event of usually minor importance: *an amusing incident in a play.* An OCCURRENCE is something that happens, often by surprise: *His arrival was an unexpected occurrence.* **2.** consequence.

e•ven-tem•pered (ē′vən tem′pərd), *adj.* not easily ruffled, annoyed, or disturbed; calm. [1870–75]

e•vent•ful (i vent′fəl), *adj.* **1.** full of events or incidents, esp. of a striking character: *an exciting account of an eventful life.* **2.** having important issues or results; momentous. [1590–1600; EVENT + -FUL] —**e•vent′ful•ly,** *adv.* —**e•vent′ful•ness,** *n.*
—**Syn. 1.** noteworthy, memorable, unforgettable.

event′ hori′zon, *Astron.* the boundary around a black hole on and within which no matter or radiation can escape. [1970–75]

e•ven•tide (ē′vən tīd′), *n.* evening. [bef. 950; ME; OE *ǣfentīd.* See EVEN[2], TIDE[2]]

e•ven•tra•tion (ē′ven trā′shən), *n. Med.* **1.** protrusion of the abdominal viscera through an opening in the abdominal wall. **2.** disembowelment. [1830–40; < F, equiv. to *éventr(er)* to disembowel (see E-, VENTRAL) + *-ation* -ATION]

e•ven•tu•al (i ven′cho͞o əl), *adj.* **1.** happening at some indefinite future time or after a series of occurrences; ultimate: *His mistakes led to his eventual dismissal.* **2.** depending upon uncertain events; contingent. [1605–15; < L *ēventu(s)* EVENT + -AL[1], modeled of F *éventuel*]
—**Syn. 1.** subsequent, consequent, later, resulting.

e•ven•tu•al•i•ty (i ven′cho͞o al′i tē), *n., pl.* **-ties. 1.** a contingent event; a possible occurrence or circumstance: *Rain is an eventuality to be reckoned with in planning the picnic.* **2.** the state or fact of being eventual; contingent character. [1750–60; EVENTUAL + -ITY]

e•ven•tu•al•ly (i ven′cho͞o ə lē), *adv.* finally; ultimately; at some later time: *Eventually we will own the house free and clear.* [1650–60; EVENTUAL + -LY]

e•ven•tu•ate (i ven′cho͞o āt′), *v.i.,* **-at•ed, -at•ing. 1.** to have issue; result. **2.** to be the issue or outcome; come about. [1780–90; *Amer.;* < L *ēventu(s)* EVENT + -ATE[1]] —**e•ven′tu•a′tion,** *n.*

E•ven•tus (i ven′təs), *n. Rom. Religion.* See **Bonus Eventus.**

ev•er (ev′ər), *adv.* **1.** at all times; always: *an ever-present danger; He is ever ready to find fault.* **2.** continuously: *ever since then.* **3.** at any time: *Have you ever seen anything like it?* **4.** in any possible case; by any chance; at all (often used to intensify or emphasize a phrase or an emotional reaction as surprise or impatience): *How did you ever manage to do it? If the band ever plays again, we will dance.* **5. ever and again,** now and then; from time to time. Also, *Literary,* **ever and anon. 6. ever so,** to a great extent or degree; exceedingly: *They were ever so kind to me.* —*adj.* **7.** *South Midland and Southern U.S.* every: *She rises early ever morning.* [bef. 1000; ME; OE *ǣfre*]
—**Syn. 1.** eternally, perpetually, constantly. See **always.** —**Ant. 1.** never.

ev•er•bear•ing (ev′ər bâr′ing), *adj.* continuously producing or bringing forth, as a tree or shrub. [1925–30; EVER + BEARING]

ev•er•bloom•ing (ev′ər blo͞o′ming), *adj.* in bloom throughout most of the growing months of the year. [1890–95; EVER + BLOOMING]

Ev•er•dur (ev′ər do͝or′), *Trademark.* a brand name for any of several alloys of copper and silicon with other constituents, esp. manganese, having high resistance to corrosion.

Ev•er•est (ev′ər ist, ev′rist), *n.* **1. Mount,** a mountain in S Asia, on the boundary between Nepal and Tibet, in the Himalayas: the highest mountain in the world. 29,028 ft. (8848 m). **2.** high point; summit: *The book is an Everest in the field of historical scholarship.* **3.** a male given name.

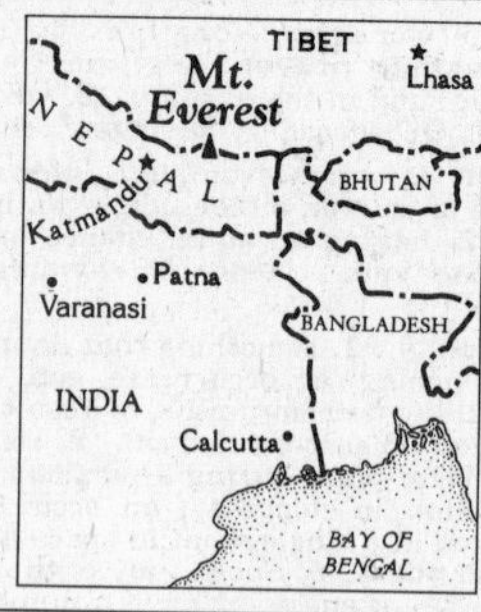

Ev•er•ett (ev′ər it, ev′rit), *n.* **1. Edward,** 1794–1865, U.S. statesman, orator, and writer. **2.** a seaport in NW Washington on Puget Sound. 54,413. **3.** a city in E Massachusetts, near Boston. 37,195. **4.** a male given name.

ev•er•glade (ev′ər glād′), *n.* a tract of low, swampy land, esp. in southern Florida, characterized by clumps of tall grass and numerous branching waterways. [1815–25, *Amer.*; EVER + GLADE]

Ev•er•glades (ev′ər glādz′), *n.* (*used with a plural v.*) a swampy and partly forested region in S Florida, mostly S of Lake Okeechobee. Over 5000 sq. mi. (12,950 sq. km).

Ev′erglades Na′tional Park′, a national park in the Everglades region of S Florida. 423 sq. mi. (1095 sq. km).

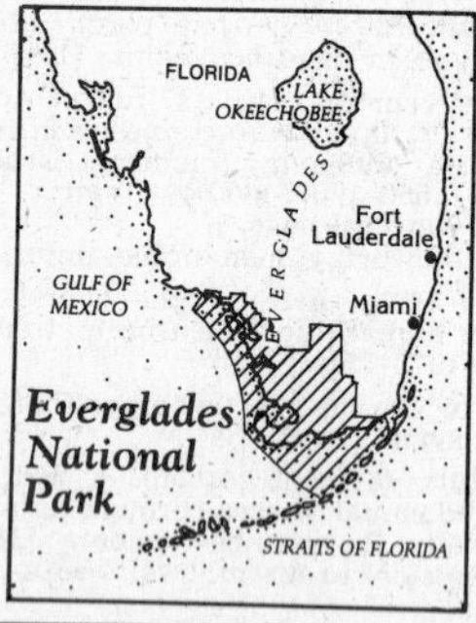

Ev•er•good (ev′ər go͝od′), *n.* **Philip** (*Philip Blashki*), 1901–73, U.S. painter.

ev•er•green (ev′ər grēn′), *adj.* **1.** (of trees, shrubs, etc.) having green leaves throughout the entire year, the leaves of the past season not being shed until after the new foliage has been completely formed. —*n.* **2.** an evergreen plant. **3. evergreens,** evergreen twigs or branches used for decoration. [1545–55; EVER + GREEN]

ev′ergreen magno′lia, a magnolia, *Magnolia grandiflora,* of the southern U.S., having evergreen foliage and large, fragrant, white flowers, grown as a shade and ornamental tree in the warmer parts of the U.S.: the state tree of Mississippi. Also called **bull bay, southern magnolia.** [1880–85]

ev′ergreen oak′, any of several oaks, as the holm oak, having evergreen foliage. [1675–85]

Ev′ergreen Park′, a city in NE Illinois, near Chicago. 22,260.

Ev′ergreen State′, the state of Washington (used as a nickname).

ev•er•last•ing (ev′ər las′ting, -lä′sting), *adj.* **1.** lasting forever; eternal: *everlasting future life.* **2.** lasting or continuing for an indefinitely long time: *the everlasting hills.* **3.** incessant; constantly recurring: *He is plagued by everlasting attacks of influenza.* **4.** wearisome; tedious: *She tired of his everlasting puns.* —*n.* **5.** eternal duration; eternity: *What is the span of one life compared with the everlasting?* **6. the Everlasting,** God. **7.** any of various plants that retain their shape or color when dried, as certain composite plants of the genera *Helichrysum, Gnaphalium,* and *Helipterum.* [1300–50; ME; see EVER, LASTING] —**ev′er•last′ing•ly,** *adv.* —**ev′er•last′ing•ness,** *n.*
—**Syn. 1.** See **eternal.** —**Ant. 1.** transitory.

ev′erlast′ing pea′, a fast-growing vinelike plant, *Lathyrus latifolius,* of Europe, having rose-pink flowers. Also called **perennial pea.** [1695–1705]

ev•er•more (ev′ər môr′, -mōr′), *adv.* **1.** always; continually; forever. **2.** at all future times; henceforth. [1175–1225; ME *evermor.* See EVER, MORE]

Ev•ers (ev′ərz), *n.* **1. (James) Charles,** born 1922, U.S. civil-rights leader. **2.** his brother **Med•gar (Wiley)** (med′gər), 1925–63, U.S. civil-rights leader.

e•ver•si•ble (i vûr′sə bəl), *adj.* capable of being everted. [1875–80; < L *ēversus* (ptp. of *ēvertere* to overturn, EVERT) + -IBLE]

e•ver•sion (i vûr′zhən, -shən), *n.* a turning or being turned outward or inside out. [1425–75; late ME < L *ēversiōn-* (s. of *ēversiō*), equiv. to *ēvers(us)* (see EVERSIBLE) + *-iōn-* -ION]

e•vert (i vûrt′), *v.t.* to turn outward or inside out. [1375–1425 for earlier ptp. sense; 1795–1805 for current sense; late ME < L *ēvertere* to overturn, equiv. to *ē-* E- + *vertere* to turn]

Ev•ert (ev′ərt), *n.* **Chris(tine Marie),** born 1954, U.S. tennis player.

e•ver•tor (i vûr′tər), *n. Anat.* a muscle that turns a part toward the outside. [1900–05; EVERT + -OR²]

ev•er•y (ev′rē), *adj.* **1.** being one of a group or series taken collectively; each: *We go there every day.* **2.** all possible; the greatest possible degree of: *every prospect of success.* **3. every bit,** in every respect; completely: *This is every bit as good as she says it is.* **4. every now and then,** on occasion; from time to time: *She bakes her own bread every now and then.* Also, **every once in a while, every so often. 5. every other,** every second; every alternate: *milk deliveries every other day.* **6. every which way,** in all directions; in disorganized fashion: *I brushed against the table, and the cards fell every which way.* [1125–75; ME *every, everich,* OE *ǣfre ǣlc* EVER EACH]
—**Syn. 1.** See **each.**

ev•er•y•bod•y (ev′rē bod′ē, -bud′ē), *pron.* every person. [1520–30; EVERY + BODY]
—**Usage.** See **each, else.**

ev•er•y•day (*adj.* ev′rē dā′; *n.* ev′rē dā′), *adj.* **1.** of or pertaining to every day; daily: *an everyday occurrence.* **2.** of or for ordinary days, as contrasted with Sundays, holidays, or special occasions: *everyday clothes.* **3.** such as is met with every day; ordinary; commonplace: *a placid, everyday scene.* —*n.* **4.** the routine or ordinary day or occasion: *We use inexpensive plates for everyday.* [1325–75; ME *everydayes.* See EVERY, DAY] —**eve′ry•day′ness,** *n.*
—**Syn. 2, 3.** workday, common, usual.

ev•er•y•how (ev′rē hou′), *adv. Archaic.* in all ways; in every manner. [1830–40; EVERY + HOW]

Ev•er•y•man (ev′rē man′), *n.* **1.** (*italics*) a 15th-century English morality play. **2.** (*usually l.c.*) an ordinary person; the typical or average person. —*pron.* **3.** everybody; everyone. [EVERY + MAN¹]

ev•er•y•one (ev′rē wun′, -wən), *pron.* every person; everybody. [1175–1225; ME *everichon.* See EVERY, ONE]
—**Usage.** See **each.**

ev•er•y•place (ev′rē plās′), *adv.* everywhere. [1915–20; EVERY + PLACE]
—**Usage.** See **anyplace.**

ev•er•y•thing (ev′rē thing′), *pron.* **1.** every thing or particular of an aggregate or total; all. **2.** something extremely important: *This news means everything to us.* —*n.* **3.** something that is extremely or most important: *Money is his everything.* [1350–1400; ME; see EVERY, THING¹]

ev•er•y•way (ev′rē wā′), *adv.* in every way; in every direction, manner, or respect: *They tried everyway to find the information.* [1560–70; EVERY + WAY]

ev•er•y•when (ev′rē hwen′, -wen′), *adv.* all the time; always. [1835–45; EVERY + WHEN]

ev•er•y•where (ev′rē hwâr′, -wâr′), *adv.* in every place or part; in all places. [1175–1225; ME *everihwer,* repr. 2 formations: *every* EVERY + *hwer* WHERE, and *ever* EVER + *ihwer* anywhere, everywhere (OE *gehwǣr;* see Y-, WHERE)]
—**Usage.** See **anyplace.**

ev•er•y•where-dense (ev′rē hwâr′dens′, -wâr′-), *adj. Math.* (of a set in a topological space) dense.

ev•er•y•wheres (ev′rē hwârz′, -wârz′), *adv. Nonstandard.* everywhere.

ev•er•y•wom•an (ev′rē wo͝om′ən), *n., pl.* **-wom•en.** an ordinary woman; a typical or average woman. [1965–70; EVERY + WOMAN, on the model of EVERYMAN]

Eve•sham (ēv′shəm, ē′shəm, ē′səm), *n.* a town in Hereford and Worcester county, in W England: battle 1265. 13,847.

E•vet•ta (i vet′ə), *n.* a female given name: from an African word meaning "a hunt."

evg., evening.

e•vict (i vikt′), *v.t.* **1.** to expel (a person, esp. a tenant) from land, a building, etc., by legal process, as for nonpayment of rent. **2.** to recover (property, titles, etc.) by virtue of superior legal title. [1400–50; late ME *evicten* < LL *ēvictus* having recovered one's property by law, L: ptp. of *ēvincere* to overcome, conquer, EVINCE), equiv. to *ē-* E- + *vic-* (ptp. s. of *vincere;* see VICTOR) + *-tus* ptp. suffix] —**e•vic′tion,** *n.* —**e•vic′tor,** *n.*
—**Syn. 1.** eject, remove, dispossess, dislodge.

e•vict•ee (i vik tē′, i vik′tē), *n.* a person who has been evicted. [1875–80; EVICT + -EE]

evic′tion clause′. See **stop clause.**

ev•i•dence (ev′i dəns), *n., v.,* **-denced, -denc•ing.** —*n.* **1.** that which tends to prove or disprove something; ground for belief; proof. **2.** something that makes plain or clear; an indication or sign: *His flushed look was visible evidence of his fever.* **3.** *Law.* data presented to a court or jury in proof of the facts in issue and which may include the testimony of witnesses, records, documents, or objects. **4. in evidence,** plainly visible; conspicuous: *The first signs of spring are in evidence.* —*v.t.* **5.** to make evident or clear; show clearly; manifest: *He evidenced his approval by promising his full support.* **6.** to support by evidence: *He evidenced his accusation with incriminating letters.* [1250–1300; ME (n.) < MF < L *ēvidentia.* See EVIDENT, -ENCE]
—**Syn. 3.** information, deposition, affidavit. EVIDENCE, EXHIBIT, TESTIMONY, PROOF refer to information furnished in a legal investigation to support a contention. EVIDENCE is any information so given, whether furnished by witnesses or derived from documents or from any other source: *Hearsay evidence is not admitted in a trial.* An EXHIBIT in law is a document or article that is presented in court as evidence: *The signed contract is Exhibit A.* TESTIMONY is usually evidence given by witnesses under oath: *The jury listened carefully to the testimony.* PROOF is evidence that is so complete and convincing as to put a conclusion beyond reasonable doubt: *proof of the innocence of the accused.* **5.** demonstrate.

ev•i•dent (ev′i dənt), *adj.* plain or clear to the sight or understanding: *His frown made it evident to all that he was displeased. It was evident that the project was a total failure.* [1350–1400; ME < L *ēvident-* (s. of *ēvidēns*), equiv. to *ē-* E- + *vident-* (s. of *vidēns*) prp. of *vidēre* to see; see VIDEO, -ENT] —**ev′i•dent•ness,** *n.*
—**Syn.** obvious, manifest, palpable, patent, unmistakable. See **apparent.** —**Ant.** concealed.

ev•i•den•tial (ev′i den′shəl), *adj.* noting, pertaining to, serving as, or based on evidence. [1600–10; < L *ēvidenti(a)* (see EVIDENCE) + -AL¹] —**ev′i•den′tial•ly,** *adv.*

ev•i•den•tia•ry (ev′i den′shə rē), *adj.* **1.** evidential. **2.** *Law.* pertaining to or constituting evidence. [1800–10; < L *ēvidenti(a)* EVIDENCE + -ARY]

ev•i•dent•ly (ev′i dənt lē, -dent′-; *for emphasis* ev′i-dent′lē), *adv.* obviously; apparently. [1325–75; ME; see EVIDENT, -LY]
—**Syn.** See **clearly.**

e•vil (ē′vəl), *adj.* **1.** morally wrong or bad; immoral; wicked: *evil deeds; an evil life.* **2.** harmful; injurious: *evil laws.* **3.** characterized or accompanied by misfortune or suffering; unfortunate; disastrous: *to be fallen on evil days.* **4.** due to actual or imputed bad conduct or character: *an evil reputation.* **5.** marked by anger, irritability, irascibility, etc.: *He is known for his evil disposition.* **6. the evil one,** the devil; Satan. —*n.* **7.** that which is evil; evil quality, intention, or conduct: *to choose the lesser of two evils.* **8.** the force in nature that governs and gives rise to wickedness and sin. **9.** the wicked or immoral part of someone or something: *The evil in his nature has destroyed the good.* **10.** harm; mischief; misfortune: *to wish one evil.* **11.** anything causing injury or harm: *Tobacco is considered by some to be an evil.* **12.** a harmful aspect, effect, or consequence: *the evils of alcohol.* **13.** a disease, as king's evil. —*adv.* **14.** in an evil manner; badly; ill: *It went evil with him.* [bef. 900; ME *evel, evil,* OE *yfel;* c. Goth *ubils,* OHG *ubil,* G *übel,* OFris, MD *evel*] —**e′vil•ly,** *adv.* —**e′vil•ness,** *n.*
—**Syn. 1.** sinful, iniquitous, depraved, vicious, corrupt, base, vile, nefarious. See **bad¹. 2.** pernicious, destructive. **7.** wickedness, depravity, iniquity, unrighteousness, corruption, baseness. **10.** disaster, calamity, woe, misery, suffering, sorrow. —**Ant. 1.** righteous.

e•vil•do•er (ē′vəl do͞o′ər, ē′vəl do͞o′ər), *n.* a person who does evil or wrong. [1350–1400; ME; see EVIL, DOER] —**e′vil•do′ing,** *n.*

e′vil eye′, **1.** a look thought capable of inflicting injury or bad luck on the person at whom it is directed. **2.** the power, superstitiously attributed to certain persons, of inflicting injury or bad luck by such a look. [bef. 1000; ME, OE] —**e′vil-eyed′,** *adj.*

e•vil-mind•ed (ē′vəl mīn′did), *adj.* **1.** having an evil disposition or harmful, malicious intentions. **2.** disposed to construe words, phrases, etc., in a lascivious, lewd manner; salacious. [1525–35] —**e′vil-mind′ed•ly,** *adv.* —**e′vil-mind′ed•ness,** *n.*

e•vince (i vins′), *v.t.,* **e•vinced, e•vinc•ing. 1.** to show clearly; make evident or manifest; prove. **2.** to reveal the possession of (a quality, trait, etc.). [1600–10; < L *ēvincere* to conquer, overcome, carry one's point, equiv. to *ē-* E- + *vincere* to conquer] —**e•vin′ci•ble,** *adj.*
—**Syn. 1.** See **display.**

e•vin•cive (i vin′siv), *adj.* serving to evince; indicative. [1800–10; EVINCE + -IVE]

e•vis•cer•ate (*v.* i vis′ə rāt′; *adj.* i vis′ər it, -ə rāt′), *v.,* **-at•ed, -at•ing,** *adj.* —*v.t.* **1.** to remove the entrails from; disembowel: *to eviscerate a chicken.* **2.** to deprive of vital or essential parts: *The censors eviscerated the book to make it inoffensive to the leaders of the party.* **3.** *Surg.* to remove the contents of (a body organ). [1600–10; < L *ēviscerātus,* ptp. of *ēviscerāre* to deprive of entrails, tear to pieces, equiv. to *ē-* E- + *viscer(a)* VISCERA + *-ātus* -ATE¹] —**e•vis′cer•a′tion,** *n.* —**e•vis′cer•a′tor,** *n.*

E•vi•ta (e vē′tə, -tä), *n.* a female given name, Spanish form of **Eva.**

ev•i•ta•ble (ev′i tə bəl), *adj.* capable of being avoided; avoidable. [1495–1505; < L *ēvitābilis.* See EVITE, -ABLE]

e•vite (i vīt′), *v.t.,* **e•vit•ed, e•vit•ing.** *Archaic.* to avoid; shun. [1495–1505; < L *ēvitāre,* equiv. to *ē-* E- + *vitāre* to avoid]

ev•o•ca•ble (ev′ə kə bəl, i vō′kə-), *adj.* capable of being evoked. [1885–90; EVOC(ATION) + -ABLE]

ev•o•ca•tion (ev′ə kā′shən, ē′vō kā′-), *n.* **1.** an act or instance of evoking; a calling forth: *the evocation of old memories.* **2.** *Law.* (formerly) an action of a court in summoning a case from another, usually lower, court for purposes of complete review and decision, as on an appeal in which the issue is incidental or procedural and the court of first instance has not yet rendered a decision on its merits; the removal of a case from one court to another. [1400–50; late ME *evocacioun* < L *ēvocātiōn-* (s. of *ēvocātiō*) calling forth, out, equiv. to *ēvocāt(us)* (ptp. of *ēvocāre* to EVOKE) + *-iōn-* -ION]

e•voc•a•tive (i vok′ə tiv, i vō′kə-), *adj.* tending to evoke: *The perfume was evocative of spring.* [1650–60; < L *ēvocātīvus,* equiv. to *ēvocāt(us)* (see EVOKE, -ATE¹) + *-īvus* -IVE] —**e•voc′a•tive•ly,** *adv.* —**e•voc′a•tive•ness,** *n.*

ev•o•ca•tor (ev′ə kā′tər, ē′vō-), *n.* a person who evokes, esp. one who calls up spirits. [1785–95; < L *ēvocātor* one who calls to arms, equiv. to *ēvocā(re)* to EVOKE + *-tor* -TOR]

CONCISE ETYMOLOGY KEY: <, descended or borrowed from; >, whence; b., blend of, blended; c., cognate with; cf., compare; deriv., derivative; equiv., equivalent; imit., imitative; obl., oblique; r., replacing; s., stem; sp., spelling, spelled; resp., respelling, respelled; trans., translation; ?, origin unknown; *, unattested; ‡, probably earlier than. See the full key inside the front cover.

e•voke (i vōk′), *v.t.*, **e•voked, e•vok•ing.** **1.** to call up or produce (memories, feelings, etc.): *to evoke a memory.* **2.** to elicit or draw forth: *His comment evoked protests from the shocked listeners.* **3.** to call up; cause to appear; summon: *to evoke a spirit from the dead.* **4.** to produce or suggest through artistry and imagination a vivid impression of reality: *a short passage that manages to evoke the smells, colors, sounds, and shapes of that metropolis.* [1615–25; < L *ēvocāre,* equiv. to *ē-* E- + *vocāre* to call (akin to *vōx* VOICE)] **—e•vok′er,** *n.*

evoked′ poten′tial, an electrical response of a nerve cell or group of nerve cells to externally induced stimulation, esp. to determine whether or not an area of the brain receives sensory information from a particular stimulus. [1965–70]

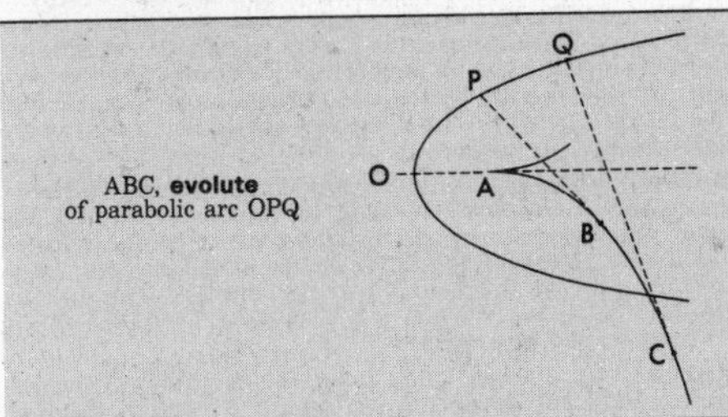

ABC, **evolute** of parabolic arc OPQ

ev•o•lute (ev′ə lo͞ot′ *or, esp. Brit.,* ē′və-), *n. Geom.* the locus of the centers of curvature of, or the envelope of the normals to, another curve. Cf. **involute** (def. 5). [1720–30; < L *ēvolūtus* (ptp. of *ēvolvere* to roll out, unfold, EVOLVE)]

ev•o•lu•tion (ev′ə lo͞o′shən *or, esp. Brit.,* ē′və-), *n.* **1.** any process of formation or growth; development: *the evolution of a language; the evolution of the airplane.* **2.** a product of such development; something evolved: *The exploration of space is the evolution of decades of research.* **3.** *Biol.* change in the gene pool of a population from generation to generation by such processes as mutation, natural selection, and genetic drift. **4.** a process of gradual, peaceful, progressive change or development, as in social or economic structure or institutions. **5.** a motion incomplete in itself, but combining with coordinated motions to produce a single action, as in a machine. **6.** a pattern formed by or as if by a series of movements: *the evolutions of a figure skater.* **7.** an evolving or giving off of gas, heat, etc. **8.** *Math.* the extraction of a root from a quantity. Cf. **involution** (def. 8). **9.** a movement or one of a series of movements of troops, ships, etc., as for disposition in order of battle or in line on parade. **10.** any similar movement, esp. in close order drill. [1615–25; < L *ēvolūtiōn-* (s. of *ēvolūtiō*) an unrolling, opening, equiv. to *ēvolūt(us)* (see EVOLUTE) + *-iōn-* -ION] **—ev′o•lu′tion•al,** *adj.* **—ev′o•lu′tion•al•ly,** *adv.*
—Syn. 1. unfolding, change, progression, metamorphosis. **—Ant. 1.** stasis, inactivity, changelessness.

ev•o•lu•tion•ar•y (ev′ə lo͞o′shə ner′ē *or, esp. Brit.,* ē′və-), *adj.* **1.** pertaining to evolution or development; developmental: *the evolutionary origin of species.* **2.** of, pertaining to, or in accordance with a theory of evolution, esp. in biology. **3.** pertaining to or performing evolutions. [1840–50; EVOLUTION + -ARY] **—ev′o•lu′tion•ar′i•ly,** *adv.*

evolu′tionary biol′ogy, the branches of biology that deal with the processes of change in populations of organisms, esp. taxonomy, paleontology, ethology, population genetics, and ecology.

ev•o•lu•tion•ist (ev′ə lo͞o′shə nist *or, esp. Brit.,* ē′və-), *n.* **1.** a person who believes in or supports a theory of evolution, esp. in biology. **2.** a person who supports a policy of gradual growth or development rather than sudden change or expansion. *—adj.* Also, **ev′o•lu′tion•is′tic. 3.** of or pertaining to evolution or evolutionists. **4.** believing in or supporting a theory of evolution, esp. in biology. [1855–60; EVOLUTION + -IST] **—ev′o•lu′tion•ism,** *n.* **—ev′o•lu′tion•is′ti•cal•ly,** *adv.*

ev•o•lu•tive (ev′ə lo͞o′tiv *or, esp. Brit.,* ē′və-), *adj.* **1.** of, pertaining to, or promoting evolution; evolutionary: *an evolutive process.* **2.** tending to evolve, or toward evolution. [1870–75; EVOLUT(ION) + -IVE]

e•volve (i volv′), *v.,* **e•volved, e•volv•ing.** *—v.t.* **1.** to develop gradually: *to evolve a scheme.* **2.** to give off or emit, as odors or vapors. *—v.i.* **3.** to come forth gradually into being; develop; undergo evolution: *The whole idea evolved from a casual remark.* **4.** *Biol.* to develop by a process of evolution to a different adaptive state or condition: *The human species evolved from an ancestor that was probably arboreal.* [1635–45; < L *ēvolvere* to unroll, open, unfold, equiv. to *ē-* E- + *volvere* to roll, turn] **—e•volv′a•ble,** *adj.* **—e•volve′ment,** *n.* **—e•volv′er,** *n.*

e•von•y•mus (e von′ə məs), *n.* euonymus.

É•vo•ra (ev′ər ə; *Port.* e′vo͝o Rə), *n.* a city in central Portugal: Roman ruins; cathedral. 23,665.

Ev•tu•shen•ko (yev′to͞o sheng′kō; *Russ.* yif to͞o-shen′kə), *n.* **Ev•ge•nii A•le•xan•dro•vich** (*Russ.* yivgye′nyē u lyi ksän′dRə vyich). See **Yevtushenko, Yevgeny Alexandrovich.**

e•vulse (i vuls′), *v.t.,* **e•vulsed, e•vuls•ing.** to extract forcibly: *to evulse an infected molar.* Cf. **avulse.**

e•vul•sion (i vul′shən), *n.* the act of plucking or pulling out; forcible extraction. [1605–15; < L *ēvulsiōn-* (s. of *ēvulsiō*), equiv. to *ēvuls(us)* plucked out (ptp. of *ēvellere,* equiv. to *ē-* E- + *vellere* to pluck) + *-iōn-* -ION]

Ev•voi•a (e′vē ä), *n.* Modern Greek name of **Euboea.**

ev•zone (ev′zōn), *n.* a member of an elite infantry corps in the Greek army. [1895–1900; < ModGk *eúzōnos,* Gk: well girt (i.e., well equipped). See EU-, ZONE]

EW, enlisted woman; enlisted women.

E′wa Beach′, (ā′wä, ā wä′), a town on S Oahu, in central Hawaii. 14,369.

E•wald (yo͞o′əld; *Ger.* ā′vält), *n.* a male given name.

Ew•an (yo͞o′ən), *n.* a male given name, Welsh form of **John.**

ewe (yo͞o; *Dial.* yō), *n.* a female sheep, esp. when fully mature. [bef. 1000; ME; OE *ēowu, ēwe;* c. OHG *ou, ouwi,* D *ooi,* L *ovis,* Gk *óïs, oîs,* Skt *ávi*]

E•we (ā′vā, ā′wā), *n.* **1.** a member of a people of Togo and Ghana, in western Africa. **2.** the Kwa language spoken by the Ewe people.

ewe′ lamb′, a young female sheep. [1350–1400; ME]

Ew•ell (yo͞o′el), *n.* **1. Richard Stod•dert** (stod′ərt), 1817–72, Confederate lieutenant general in the U.S. Civil War. **2.** a male given name.

ewe-neck (yo͞o′nek′), *n.* a thin hollow neck, low in front of the shoulder, as of a horse or other animal. [1695–1705] **—ewe′-necked′,** *adj.*

ew•er (yo͞o′ər), *n.* **1.** a pitcher with a wide spout. **2.** *Decorative Art.* a vessel having a spout and a handle, esp. a tall, slender vessel with a base. [1275–1325; ME < AF; OF *evier* < L *aquārius* vessel for water, equiv. to *aqu(a)* water + *-ārius* -ARY]

ewer (def. 2)

ew•er•y (yo͞o′ə rē), *n., pl.* **-er•ies.** *Archaic.* a room for storing ewers, towels, napkins, etc. [1350–1400; ME; see EWER, -Y^{3}]

E•wig-weib•li•che (ā′vikH vip′li KHə), *n. German.* the eternal feminine.

Ew•ing (yo͞o′ing), *n.* a township in W New Jersey. 34,842.

Ew′ing's sarco′ma, *Pathol.* a malignant stem-cell bone tumor, usually occurring in the leg or pelvis of children and young adults, characterized by pain, fever, and swelling. [named after James *Ewing* (1866–1943), U.S. pathologist, who described it]

ex^{1} (eks), *prep.* **1.** *Finance.* without, not including, or without the right to have: *ex interest; ex rights.* **2.** *Com.* free of charges to the purchaser until the time of removal from a specified place or thing: *ex ship; ex warehouse; ex elevator.* **3.** (in U.S. colleges and universities) from, but not graduated with, the class of: *ex '47.* [1835–45; < L. See EX-^{1}]

ex^{2} (eks), *n.* the letter X, *x.*

ex^{3} (eks), *n. Informal.* a former spouse; ex-wife or ex-husband. [1820–30; by shortening]

ex^{4} (eks), *adj. Slang.* excellent (def. 1). [by shortening]

ex-^{1}, a prefix meaning "out of," "from," and hence "utterly," "thoroughly," and sometimes imparting a privative or negative force or indicating a former title, status, etc.; freely used as an English formative: *exstipulate; exterritorial; ex-president* (former president); *ex-member; ex-wife.* Also, **e-, ef-.** [< L, comb. form of *ex, ē* (prep.) out (of), from, beyond]

ex-^{2}, var. of **exo-.**

ex-^{3}, a prefix identical in meaning with **ex-^{1},** occurring before vowels in words of Greek origin: *exarch; exegesis.* Also, **ec-.** [< Gk comb. form of *ex, ek,* out (of), from, beyond; see EC-, EX-^{1}]

Ex., Exodus.

ex., **1.** examination. **2.** examined. **3.** example. **4.** except. **5.** exception. **6.** exchange. **7.** excursion. **8.** executed. **9.** executive. **10.** express. **11.** extra.

ex•ac•er•bate (ig zas′ər bāt′, ek sas′-), *v.t.,* **-bat•ed, -bat•ing. 1.** to increase the severity, bitterness, or violence of (disease, ill feeling, etc.); aggravate. **2.** to embitter the feelings of (a person); irritate; exasperate. [1650–60; < L *exacerbātus* (ptp. of *exacerbāre* to exasperate, provoke), equiv. to *ex-* EX-^{1} + *acerbātus* ACERBATE] **—ex•ac′er•bat′ing•ly,** *adv.* **—ex•ac′er•ba′tion,** *n.*
—Syn. 1. intensify, inflame, worsen. **—Ant. 1.** relieve, soothe, alleviate.

ex•act (ig zakt′), *adj.* **1.** strictly accurate or correct: *an exact likeness; an exact description.* **2.** precise, as opposed to approximate: *the exact sum; the exact date.* **3.** admitting of no deviation, as laws or discipline; strict or rigorous. **4.** capable of the greatest precision: *exact instruments.* **5.** characterized by or using strict accuracy: *an exact thinker.* **6.** *Math.* (of a differential equation) noting that the collection of all terms, equated to zero, is an exact differential. *—v.t.* **7.** to call for, demand, or require: *to exact respect from one's children.* **8.** to force or compel the payment, yielding, or performance of: *to exact money; to exact tribute from a conquered people.* [1400–50; late ME *exacten* (v.) < L *exāctus* (ptp. of *exigere* drive out, thrust out), equiv. to *ex-* EX-^{1} + *ag(ere)* to drive + *-tus* ptp. suffix] **—ex•act′a•ble,** *adj.* **—ex•act′er, ex•ac′tor,** *n.* **—ex•act′ness,** *n.*
—Syn. 3. rigid, severe, unbending. **5.** methodical, careful, punctilious, demanding, scrupulous. **8.** wring. See **extract. —Ant. 1, 2.** imprecise.

ex•act•a (ig zak′tə), *n.* **1.** a type of bet, esp. on horse races, in which the bettor must select the first- and second-place finishers in exact order. **2.** a race in which such bets are made. Cf. **quinella.** Also called **perfecta.** [1960–65; ellipsis of AmerSp *quiniela exacta* exact quinella]

exact′ differen′tial, *Math.* an expression that is the total differential of some function. [1815–25]

ex•act•ing (ig zak′ting), *adj.* **1.** rigid or severe in demands or requirements: *an exacting teacher.* **2.** requiring close application or attention: *an exacting task.* **3.** given to or characterized by exaction; extortionate. [1575–85; EXACT + -ING^{2}] **—ex•act′ing•ly,** *adv.* **—ex•act′ing•ness,** *n.*

ex•ac•tion (ig zak′shən), *n.* **1.** the act of exacting; extortion: *the exactions of usury.* **2.** an amount or sum exacted. [1350–1400; ME *exactioun* < L *exāctiōn-* (s. of *exāctiō*) a demanding. See EXACT, -ION]

ex•ac•ti•tude (ig zak′ti to͞od′, -tyo͞od′), *n.* the quality of being exact; exactness; preciseness; accuracy. [1725–35; < F; see EXACT, -I-, -TUDE]

ex•act•ly (ig zakt′lē), *adv.* **1.** in an exact manner; precisely; accurately. **2.** in every respect; just: *He will do exactly what he wants.* **3.** quite so; that's right. [1525–35; EXACT + -LY]

exact′ sci′ence, a science, as chemistry or physics, that deals with quantitatively measurable phenomena of the material universe. [1860–65]

ex•ag•ger•ate (ig zaj′ə rāt′), *v.,* **-at•ed, -at•ing.** *—v.t.* **1.** to magnify beyond the limits of truth; overstate; represent disproportionately: *to exaggerate the difficulties of a situation.* **2.** to increase or enlarge abnormally: *Those shoes exaggerate the size of my feet.* *—v.i.* **3.** to employ exaggeration, as in speech or writing: *a person who is always exaggerating.* [1525–35; < L *exaggerātus* (ptp. of *exaggerāre* heap up), equiv. to *ex-* EX-^{1} + *agger* heap + *-ātus* -ATE^{1}] **—ex•ag′ger•at′ing•ly,** *adv.* **—ex•ag′ger•a′tor,** *n.*
—Syn. 1. embellish, amplify, embroider. **2.** inflate. **—Ant. 1.** minimize.

ex•ag•ger•at•ed (ig zaj′ə rā′tid), *adj.* **1.** unduly or unrealistically magnified: *to have an exaggerated opinion of oneself.* **2.** abnormally increased or enlarged. [1545–55; EXAGGERATE + -ED^{2}] **—ex•ag′ger•at′ed•ly,** *adv.*

ex•ag•ger•a•tion (ig zaj′ə rā′shən), *n.* **1.** the act of exaggerating or overstating. **2.** an instance of exaggerating; an overstatement: *His statement concerning the size of his income is a gross exaggeration.* [1555–65; < L *exaggerātiō-* (s. of *exaggerātiō*), equiv. to *exaggerāt(us)* (see EXAGGERATE) + *-iōn-* -ION]

ex•ag•ger•a•tive (ig zaj′ə rā′tiv, -ər ə tiv), *adj.* tending to exaggerate; involving or characterized by exaggeration. Also, **ex•ag•ger•a•to•ry** (ig zaj′ər ə tôr′ē, -tōr′ē). [1790–1800; EXAGGERATE + -IVE] **—ex•ag′ger•a′tive•ly,** *adv.*

ex•alt (ig zôlt′), *v.t.* **1.** to raise in rank, honor, power, character, quality, etc.; elevate: *He was exalted to the position of president.* **2.** to praise; extol: *to exalt someone to the skies.* **3.** to stimulate, as the imagination: *The lyrics of Shakespeare exalted the audience.* **4.** to intensify, as a color: *complementary colors exalt each other.* **5.** *Obs.* to elate, as with pride or joy. [1375–1425; late ME *exalten* < L *exaltāre* to lift up, equiv. to *ex-* EX-^{1} + *alt(us)* high + *-āre* inf. ending] **—ex•alt′er,** *n.*
—Syn. 1. promote, dignify, raise, ennoble. See **elevate. 2.** glorify. **—Ant. 1.** humble. **2.** depreciate.

ex•al•ta•tion (eg′zôl tā′shən, ek′sôl-), *n.* **1.** the act of exalting. **2.** the state of being exalted. **3.** elation of mind or feeling, sometimes abnormal or morbid in character; rapture: *mystical exaltation; euphoric exaltation.* **4.** *Chiefly Brit.* a flight of larks. **5.** *Astrol.* the sign of the zodiac in which the most positive influence of a planet is expressed (opposed to *fall*). **6.** *Chem.* (formerly) the process of subliming. [1350–1400; ME *exaltacioun* < L *exaltātiōn-* (s. of *exaltātiō*). See EXALT, -ATION]
—Syn. 3. exultation, transport, euphoria. See **ecstasy.**

ex•alt•ed (ig zôl′tid), *adj.* **1.** raised or elevated, as in rank or character; of high station: *an exalted personage.* **2.** noble or elevated; lofty: *an exalted style of writing.* **3.** rapturously excited. [1585–95; EXALT + -ED^{2}] **—ex•alt′ed•ly,** *adv.* **—ex•alt′ed•ness,** *n.*
—Syn. 1. sublime, grand.

ex•am (ig zam′), *n. Informal.* an examination, as in school. [1875–80; short form]

exam., **1.** examination. **2.** examined. **3.** examinee. **4.** examiner.

ex•a•men (ig zā′mən), *n. Eccles.* an examination, as of conscience. [1600–10; < L *exāmen* swarm of bees, device for weighing, balance < *exag-s-men, equiv. to *exag- base of *exigere* to drive out, inquire into, examine (see EXACT) + *-s-men* resultative n. suffix; cf. CONTAMINATE]

ex•am•i•nant (ig zam′ə nənt), *n.* an examiner. [1580–90; < L *exāminant-* (s. of *exāmināns,* prp. of *exāmināre*) weighing, trying, examining. See EXAMINE, -ANT]

ex•am•i•na•tion (ig zam′ə nā′shən), *n.* **1.** the act of examining; inspection; inquiry; investigation. **2.** the state of being examined. **3.** the act or process of testing pupils, candidates, etc., as by questions. **4.** the test itself; the list of questions asked. **5.** the answers, statements, etc., made by one examined. **6.** *Law.* formal interrogation. [1350–1400; ME *examinacioun* < L *exāminātiōn-* (s. of *exāminātiō*). See EXAMINE, -ATION] **—ex•am′i•na′tion•al,** *adj.*
—Syn. 1. observation. EXAMINATION, INSPECTION, SCRUTINY refer to a looking at something. An EXAMINATION usually means a careful noting of details: *A thorough examination of the plumbing revealed a defective pipe.* An INSPECTION is a formal and official examination:

CONCISE PRONUNCIATION KEY: act, cāpe, dâre, pärt; set, ēqual; if, īce; ox, ōver, ôrder, oil, bo͝ok, bo͞ot, out; up, ûrge; child; sing; shoe; thin, *th*at; zh as in *treasure.* ə = a as in *alone,* e as in *system,* i as in *easily,* o as in *gallop,* u as in *circus;* ᵊ as in *fire* (fīᵊr), *hour* (ouᵊr). l and n can serve as syllabic consonants, as in *cradle* (krād′l), and *button* (but′n). See the full key inside the front cover.

an inspection of records, a military inspection. SCRUTINY implies a critical and minutely detailed examination: *The papers seemed to be in good order, but they would not stand close scrutiny.* See also **investigation.**

ex·am·ine (ig zam′in), *v.t.*, **-ined, -in·ing. 1.** to inspect or scrutinize carefully: *to examine a prospective purchase.* **2.** to observe, test, or investigate (a person's body or any part of it), esp. in order to evaluate general health or determine the cause of illness. **3.** to inquire into or investigate: *to examine one's motives.* **4.** to test the knowledge, reactions, or qualifications of (a pupil, candidate, etc.), as by questions or assigning tasks. **5.** to subject to legal inquisition; put to question in regard to conduct or to knowledge of facts; interrogate: *to examine a witness; to examine a suspect.* [1275–1325; ME < MF *examiner* < L *exāmināre* to weigh, examine, test, equiv. to *exāmin-* (s. of *exāmen* EXAMEN) + *-āre* inf. ending] —**ex·am′in·a·ble,** *adj.* —**ex·am·i·na·to·ri·al** (ig zam′ə nə tôr′ē əl, -tōr′-), *adj.* —**ex·am′in·er,** *n.* —**ex·am′·in·ing·ly,** *adv.*
—**Syn. 1.** search, probe, explore, study. **3.** quiz.

ex·am·i·nee (ig zam′ə nē′), *n.* a person who is examined. [1780–90; EXAMINE + -EE]

ex·am·plar (ig zam′plər, -zäm′-), *n. Archaic.* exemplar.

ex·am·ple (ig zam′pəl, -zäm′-), *n., v.,* **-pled, -pling.** —*n.* **1.** one of a number of things, or a part of something, taken to show the character of the whole: *This painting is an example of his early work.* **2.** a pattern or model, as of something to be imitated or avoided: *to set a good example.* **3.** an instance serving for illustration; specimen: *The case histories gave carefully detailed examples of this disease.* **4.** an instance illustrating a rule or method, as a mathematical problem proposed for solution. **5.** an instance, esp. of punishment, serving as a warning to others: *Public executions were meant to be examples to the populace.* **6.** a precedent; parallel case: *an action without example.* —*v.t.* **7.** *Rare.* to give or be an example of; exemplify (used in the passive). [1350–1400; ME *exa(u)mple* < MF *example* < L *exemplum*, akin to *eximere* to take out (*ex-* EX-[1] + *emere* to buy, orig. take); r. ME *exemple* < L, as above]
—**Syn. 1.** EXAMPLE, SAMPLE, SPECIMEN refer to an individual phenomenon taken as representative of a type, or to a part representative of the whole. EXAMPLE is used of an object, condition, etc., that is assumed to illustrate a certain principle or standard: *a good example of baroque architecture.* SAMPLE refers to a small portion of a substance or to a single representative of a group or type that is intended to show what the rest of the substance or the group is like: *a sample of yarn.* SPECIMEN usually suggests that the "sample" chosen is intended to serve a scientific or technical purpose: *a blood specimen; zoological specimens.* **2.** See **ideal. 3.** See **case**[1].

ex·an·i·mate (eg zan′ə mit, -māt′, ek san′-), *adj.* **1.** inanimate or lifeless. **2.** spiritless; disheartened. [1525–35; < L *exanimātus* (ptp. of *exanimāre* to deprive of life), equiv. to *ex-* EX-[1] + *anim(a)* life, spirit + *-ātus* -ATE[1]] —**ex·an′i·ma′tion,** *n.*

ex a·ni·mo (eks ä′ni mō′; *Eng.* eks an′ə mō′), *Latin.* from the heart; sincerely.

ex an·te (eks′ an′tē), based on anticipated changes or activity in an economy (opposed to *ex post*). [< L: lit., from (what might lie) ahead; according to (what lies) ahead]

ex·an·them (eg zan′thəm, ig-, ek san′-), *n. Pathol.* an eruptive disease, esp. one attended with fever, as smallpox or measles. [1650–60; < LL *exanthēma* < Gk *exánthēma* skin eruption, breaking forth, lit., a bursting into flower, equiv. to *ex-* EX-[3] + *anthē-* (verbid s. of *antheîn* to blossom; see ANTHO-) + *-ma* n. suffix] —**ex·an·the·mat·ic** (eg zan′thə mat′ik, ek san′-), **ex·an·them·a·tous** (eg′zan them′ə təs, ek′san-), *adj.*

ex·an·the·ma (eg′zan thē′mə, ek′san-), *n., pl.* **-the·ma·ta** (-them′ə tə, -thē′mə-), **-the·mas.** exanthem. [1650–60]

ex·a·rate (ek′sə rāt′), *adj.* (of a pupa) having the antennae, legs, and wings free. Cf. **obtect.** [1865–70; < L *exarātus* (ptp. of *exarāre* to plow up). See EX-[1], ARABLE, -ATE[1]]

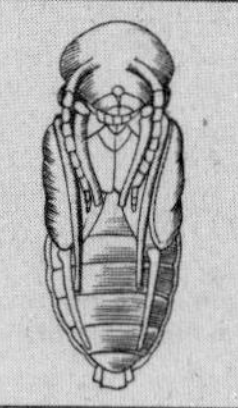

exarate pupa of clover seed chalcid fly, *Bruchophagus gibbus*

ex·arch[1] (ek′särk), *n.* **1.** *Eastern Ch.* **a.** a patriarch's deputy. **b.** a title originally applied to a patriarch but later applied only to a bishop ranking below a patriarch and above a metropolitan. **2.** the ruler of a province in the Byzantine Empire. [1580–90; < LL *exarchus* superintendent < Gk *éxarchos* overseer, leader, equiv. to *ex-* EX-[3] + *-archos* -ARCH] —**ex·arch′al,** *adj.*

ex·arch[2] (ek′särk), *adj. Bot.* (of a primary xylem or root) developing from the center; having the youngest cells closest to the core. [1890–95; EX-[2] + Gk *archḗ* beginning]

ex·ar·chate (ek′sär kāt′, -kit, ek sär′kāt), *n.* the office, jurisdiction, or province of an exarch. Also, **ex·ar·chy** (ek′sär kē). [1555–65; < ML *exarchātus* domain of an exarch. See EXARCH[1], -ATE[3]]

CONCISE ETYMOLOGY KEY: <, descended or borrowed from; >, whence; b., blend of, blended; c., cognate with; cf., compare; deriv., derivative; equiv., equivalent; imit., imitative; obl., oblique; r., replacing; s., stem; sp., spelling, spelled; resp., respelling, respelled; trans., translation; ?, origin unknown; *, unattested; ‡, probably earlier than. See the full key inside the front cover.

ex·as·per·ate (*v.* ig zas′pə rāt′; *adj.* ig zas′pər it), *v.,* **-at·ed, -at·ing,** *adj.* —*v.t.* **1.** to irritate or provoke to a high degree; annoy extremely: *He was exasperated by the senseless delays.* **2.** *Archaic.* to increase the intensity or violence of (disease, pain, feelings, etc.). —*adj.* **3.** *Bot.* rough; covered with hard, projecting points, as a leaf. [1525–35; < L *exasperātus* (ptp. of *exasperāre* to make rough, provoke), equiv. to *ex-* EX-[1] + *asper* harsh, rough + *-ātus* -ATE[1]] —**ex·as′per·at′ed·ly,** *adv.* —**ex·as′·per·at′er,** *n.* —**ex·as′per·at′ing·ly,** *adv.*
—**Syn. 1.** incense, anger, vex, inflame, infuriate. See **irritate. 2.** exacerbate.

ex·as·per·a·tion (ig zas′pə rā′shən), *n.* **1.** an act or instance of exasperating; provocation. **2.** the state of being exasperated; irritation; extreme annoyance: *Her exasperation at being interrupted was understandable.* [1540–50; < L *exasperātiōn-* (s. of *exasperātiō*) roughness, bitterness. See EXASPERATE, -ION]

Exc., Excellency.

exc., 1. excellent. **2.** except. **3.** exception. **4.** excudit. **5.** excursion.

Ex·cal·i·bur (ek skal′ə bər), *n. Arthurian Romance.* the magic sword of King Arthur.

ex·car·di·na·tion (eks kär′dn ā′shən), *n.* the transfer of a cleric from the jurisdiction of one bishop to that of another. [EX-[1] + (IN)CARDINATION]

ex ca·the·dra (eks′ kə thē′drə, kath′i drə), from the seat of authority; with authority: used esp. of those pronouncements of the pope that are considered infallible. [1810–20; < L *ex cathedrā* lit., from the chair]

ex·cau·date (eks kô′dāt), *adj. Zool.* tailless; lacking a tail or taillike process. [EX-[1] + CAUDATE]

ex·ca·vate (eks′kə vāt′), *v.t.,* **-vat·ed, -vat·ing. 1.** to make hollow by removing the inner part; make a hole or cavity in; form into a hollow, as by digging: *The ground was excavated for a foundation.* **2.** to make (a hole, tunnel, etc.) by removing material. **3.** to dig or scoop out (earth, sand, etc.). **4.** to expose or lay bare by or as if by digging; unearth: *to excavate an ancient city.* [1590–1600; < L *excavātus* (ptp. of *excavāre* to hollow out), equiv. to *ex-* EX-[1] + *cav(um)* hollow, CAVE + *-ātus* -ATE[1]]

ex·ca·va·tion (eks′kə vā′shən), *n.* **1.** a hole or cavity made by excavating. **2.** the act of excavating. **3.** an area in which excavating has been done or is in progress, as an archaeological site. [1605–15; < L *excavātiōn-* (s. of *excavātiō*) a hollowing. See EXCAVATE, -ION] —**ex′ca·va′tion·al,** *adj.*
—**Syn. 1.** See **hole.**

ex·ca·va·tor (eks′kə vā′tər), *n.* **1.** a person or thing that excavates. **2.** a power-driven machine for digging, moving, or transporting loose gravel, sand, or soil. **3.** a sharp, spoonlike instrument used for scraping out diseased tissue, as in dentistry. [1805–15; EXCAVATE + -OR[2]]

ex·ceed (ik sēd′), *v.t.* **1.** to go beyond in quantity, degree, rate, etc.: *to exceed the speed limit.* **2.** to go beyond the bounds or limits of: *to exceed one's understanding.* **3.** to surpass; be superior to; excel: *Her performance exceeded all the others.* —*v.i.* **4.** to be greater, as in quantity or degree. **5.** to surpass others; excel or be superior. [1325–75; ME *exceden* < L *excēdere* to go out or beyond. See EX-[1], CEDE] —**ex·ceed′a·ble,** *adj.* —**ex·ceed′er,** *n.*
—**Syn. 2.** overstep, transcend. **3.** outdo, outstrip, beat, cap, top.

ex·ceed·ing (ik sē′ding), *adj.* **1.** extraordinary; exceptional. —*adv.* **2.** *Archaic.* exceedingly. [1485–95; EXCEED + -ING[2]]

ex·ceed·ing·ly (ik sē′ding lē), *adv.* to an unusual degree; very; extremely: *The children were doing exceedingly well in school.* [1425–75; late ME. See EXCEEDING, -LY]

ex·cel (ik sel′), *v.,* **-celled, -cel·ling.** —*v.i.* **1.** to surpass others or be superior in some respect or area; do extremely well: *to excel in math.* —*v.t.* **2.** to surpass; be superior to; outdo: *He excels all other poets of his day.* [1400–50; late ME *excellen* < L *excellere*, equiv. to *ex-* EX-[1] + *-cellere* to rise high, tower (akin to *celsus* high)]
—**Syn. 2.** outstrip, eclipse, transcend, exceed, top, beat. EXCEL, OUTDO, SURPASS imply being better than others or being superior in achievement. To EXCEL is to be superior in some quality, attainment, or performance: *to excel opponents at playing chess.* To OUTDO is to make more successful effort than others: *to outdo competitors in the high jump.* To SURPASS is to go beyond others, esp. in a contest as to quality or ability: *to surpass one's classmates in knowledge of corporation law.*

ex·cel·lence (ek′sə ləns), *n.* **1.** the fact or state of excelling; superiority; eminence: *his excellence in mathematics.* **2.** an excellent quality or feature: *Use of herbs is one of the excellences of French cuisine.* **3.** (*usually cap.*) excellency (def. 1). [1350–1400; ME < MF < L *excellentia.* See EXCEL, -ENCE]
—**Syn. 1.** preeminence, transcendence, distinction. **2.** merit, virtue. —**Ant. 2.** inferiority.

ex·cel·len·cy (ek′sə lən sē), *n., pl.* **-cies. 1.** (*usually cap.*) Also, **Excellence.** a title of honor given to certain high officials, as governors, ambassadors, and Roman Catholic bishops and archbishops (prec. by *his, your,* etc.). **2.** (*usually cap.*) a person so entitled. **3.** (*usually cap.*) the title of the Governor General of Canada while in office. **4.** Usually, **excellencies.** excellent qualities or features. [1275–1325; ME *excellencie* < L *excellentia.* See EXCELLENT, -ENCY]

ex·cel·lent (ek′sə lənt), *adj.* **1.** possessing outstanding quality or superior merit; remarkably good. **2.** *Archaic.* extraordinary; superior. [1350–1400; ME < L *excellent-* (s. of *excellēns*), prp. of *excellere* to EXCEL; see -ENT] —**ex′cel·lent·ly,** *adv.*
—**Syn. 1.** worthy, estimable, choice, fine, first-rate, prime, admirable. —**Ant. 1.** inferior.

ex·cel·si·or (ik sel′sē ər, ek-), *n.* **1.** fine wood shavings, used for stuffing, packing, etc. **2.** *Print.* a 3-point type: a size smaller than brilliant. [1770–80, *Amer.*; formerly a trademark]

ex·cel·si·or (ek sel′si ōr′; *Eng.* ik sel′sē ôr′, ek-), *adj. Latin.* ever upward: motto of New York State.

Excel′sior Springs′, a town in W Missouri. 10,424.

ex·cept[1] (ik sept′), *prep.* **1.** with the exclusion of; excluding; save; but: *They were all there except me.* **2. except for,** if it were not for: *She would travel more except for lack of money.* —*conj.* **3.** only; with the exception (usually fol. by *that*): *parallel cases except that one is younger than the other.* **4.** otherwise than; but (fol. by an adv., phrase, or clause): *well fortified except here.* **5.** *Archaic.* unless. [1350–1400; ME: orig., ptp. adj. < L *exceptus* (ptp. of *excipere* to take out), equiv. to *ex-* EX-[1] + *-ceptus* (comb. form of *captus*, ptp. of *capere* to take)]
—**Syn. 1.** EXCEPT (more rarely EXCEPTING), BUT, SAVE point out something excluded from a general statement. EXCEPT emphasizes the excluding: *Take any number except 12.* BUT merely states the exclusion: *We ate all but one.* SAVE is now mainly found in poetic use: *nothing in sight save sky and sea.*

ex·cept[2] (ik sept′), *v.t.* **1.** to exclude; leave out: *present company excepted.* —*v.i.* **2.** to object (usually fol. by *to* or *against*): *to except to a statement; to except against a witness.* [1350–1400; ME *excepten* < MF *excepter* < L *exceptāre*, deriv. of *exceptus* (see EXCEPT[1])] —**ex·cept′a·ble,** *adj.*
—**Usage.** See **accept.**

ex·cept·ing (ik sep′ting), *prep.* **1.** excluding; barring; saving; with the exception of; except: *Excepting the last chapter, the book is finished.* —*conj.* **2.** *Archaic.* except; unless; save. [1540–50; EXCEPT[2] + -ING[2]]
—**Syn. 1.** See **except**[1].

ex·cep·tion (ik sep′shən), *n.* **1.** the act of excepting or the fact of being excepted. **2.** something excepted; an instance or case not conforming to the general rule. **3.** an adverse criticism, esp. on a particular point; opposition of opinion; objection; demurral: *a statement liable to exception.* **4.** *Law.* **a.** an objection, as to a ruling of the court in the course of a trial. **b.** a notation that an objection is preserved for purposes of appeal: *saving an exception.* **5. take exception, a.** to make an objection; demur: *They took exception to several points in the contract.* **b.** to take offense: *She took exception to what I said about her brother.* [1350–1400; ME *excepcioun* < L *exceptiōn-* (s. of *exceptiō*), equiv. to *except(us)* (see EXCEPT[1]) + *-iōn-* -ION] —**ex·cep′tion·less,** *adj.*

ex·cep·tion·a·ble (ik sep′shə nə bəl), *adj.* liable to exception or objection; objectionable. [1655–65; EXCEPTION + -ABLE] —**ex·cep′tion·a·ble·ness,** *n.* —**ex·cep′tion·a·bly,** *adv.*

ex·cep·tion·al (ik sep′shə nl), *adj.* **1.** forming an exception or rare instance; unusual; extraordinary: *The warm weather was exceptional for January.* **2.** unusually excellent; superior: *an exceptional violinist.* **3.** *Educ.* (of a child) **a.** being intellectually gifted. **b.** being physically or esp. mentally handicapped to an extent that special schooling is required. [1840–50; EXCEPTION + -AL[1]] —**ex·cep′tion·al′i·ty,** *n.* —**ex·cep′tion·al·ly,** *adv.* —**ex·cep′tion·al·ness,** *n.*
—**Syn. 1.** uncommon, singular, strange, unnatural, aberrant, anomalous. See **irregular.** —**Ant. 2.** average.

ex·cep·tive (ik sep′tiv), *adj.* **1.** being or making an exception. **2.** disposed to take exception; objecting. [1555–65; < LL *exceptīvus.* See EXCEPT[2], -IVE] —**ex·cep′tive·ly,** *adv.*

ex·cerpt (*n.* ek′sûrpt; *v.* ik sûrpt′, ek′sûrpt), *n.* **1.** a passage or quotation taken or selected from a book, document, film, or the like; extract. —*v.t.* **2.** to take or select (a passage) from a book, film, or the like; extract. **3.** to take or select passages from (a book, film, or the like); abridge by choosing representative sections. [1375–1425; late ME < L *excerptus* (ptp. of *excerpere* to pick out, pluck out), equiv. to *ex-* EX-[1] + *-cerp-* (comb. form of *carpere* to pluck) + *-tus* ptp. suffix] —**ex·cerpt′er, ex·cerp′tor,** *n.* —**ex·cerpt′i·ble,** *adj.* —**ex·cerp′tion,** *n.*
—**Syn. 1.** selection, portion, section, part.

ex·cerp·ta (ik sûrp′tə), *n.pl.* short selections or pieces of writing, esp. summary statements or parts of a longer work. [1630–40; < L, n. use of neut. pl. ptp. of *excerpere.* See EXCERPT]

ex·cess (*n.* ik ses′, ek′ses; *adj., v.* ek′ses, ik ses′), *n.* **1.** the fact of exceeding something else in amount or degree: *His strength is in excess of yours.* **2.** the amount or degree by which one thing exceeds another: *The bill showed an excess of several hundred dollars over the estimate.* **3.** an extreme or excessive amount or degree; superabundance: *to have an excess of energy.* **4.** a going beyond what is regarded as customary or proper: *to talk to excess.* **5.** immoderate indulgence; intemperance in eating, drinking, etc. —*adj.* **6.** more than or above what is necessary, usual, or specified; extra: *a charge for excess baggage; excess profits.* —*v.t.* **7.** to dismiss, demote, transfer, or furlough (an employee), esp. as part of a mass layoff. [1350–1400; ME (n. and adj.) < L *excessus* departure, digression, equiv. to *exced-*, var. s. of *excēdere* to EXCEED + *-tus* suffix of v. action]
—**Syn. 3.** surplus. —**Ant. 3.** lack, deficiency.

ex′cess bag′gage 1. passenger baggage weighing in excess of the allowed amount. **2.** *Informal.* an unnecessary burden.

ex′cess insur′ance, insurance covering a policyholder only for that portion of losses that exceeds a stated amount.

ex·ces·sive (ik ses′iv), *adj.* going beyond the usual, necessary, or proper limit or degree; characterized by excess: *excessive charges; excessive criticism.* [1350–1400; ME (see EXCESS, -IVE); r. ME *excessif* < MF] —**ex·ces′·sive·ly,** *adv.* —**ex·ces′sive·ness,** *n.*
—**Syn.** immoderate, extravagant, inordinate, exorbitant, unreasonable. —**Ant.** reasonable.

ex′cess-prof′its tax′ (ek′ses prof′its), a tax on the profits of a business enterprise in excess of the average profits for a number of base years, or of a specified rate of return on capital. [1910–15]

ex′cess sound′ pres′sure, *Physics.* See **sound pressure** (def. 1).

exch., **1.** exchange. **2.** exchequer.

ex•change (iks chānj′), *v.,* **-changed, -chang•ing,** *n.* —*v.t.* **1.** to give up (something) for something else; part with for some equivalent; change for another. **2.** to replace (returned merchandise) with an equivalent or something else: *Most stores will allow the purchaser to exchange goods.* **3.** to give and receive reciprocally; interchange: *to exchange blows; to exchange gifts.* **4.** to part with in return for some equivalent; transfer for a recompense; barter: *to exchange goods with foreign countries.* **5.** *Chess.* to capture (an enemy piece) in return for a capture by the opponent generally of pieces of equal value. —*v.i.* **6.** to make an exchange; engage in bartering, replacing, or substituting one thing for another. **7.** to pass or be taken in exchange or as an equivalent. —*n.* **8.** the act, process, or an instance of exchanging: *The contesting nations arranged for an exchange of prisoners; money in exchange for services.* **9.** something that is given or received in exchange or substitution for something else: *The car was a fair exchange.* **10.** a place for buying and selling commodities, securities, etc., typically open only to members. **11.** a central office or central station: *a telephone exchange.* **12.** the method or system by which debits and credits in different places are settled without the actual transfer of money, by means of bills of exchange representing money values. **13.** the discharge of obligations in different places by the transfer of credits. **14.** the amount or percentage charged for exchanging money, collecting a draft, etc. **15.** the reciprocal transfer of equivalent sums of money, as in the currencies of two different countries. **16.** the giving or receiving of a sum of money in one place for a bill ordering the payment of an equivalent sum in another. **17.** See **exchange rate.** **18.** the amount of the difference in value between two or more currencies, or between the values of the same currency at two or more places. **19.** the checks, drafts, etc., exchanged at a clearinghouse. **20.** *Chess.* a reciprocal capture of pieces of equivalent value by opponents in a single series of moves. [1250–1300; (v.) ME *eschaungen* < AF *eschaungier* < VL **excambiāre* (see EX-, CHANGE); (n.) ME *eschaunge* < AF (OF *eschange*), deriv. of *eschaungier*; modern sp. with *ex-* on the model of EX-[1]] —**ex•chang′er,** *n.*
—**Syn. 1.** interchange, commute, barter, trade, swap. **8.** interchange, trade, traffic, business, commerce, barter. **10.** market.

ex•change•a•ble (iks chān′jə bəl), *adj.* capable of being exchanged. [1565–75; EXCHANGE + -ABLE] —**ex•change′a•bil′i•ty,** *n.* —**ex•change′a•bly,** *adv.*
—**Syn.** EXCHANGEABLE, INTERCHANGEABLE apply to something that may replace something else. That which is EXCHANGEABLE may be exchanged for money, credit, or other purchases to the amount of the original purchase: *These dishes are exchangeable if you find they are not satisfactory.* INTERCHANGEABLE applies to those things capable of being reciprocally put in each other's place: *Standard parts are interchangeable.*

ex•chang•ee (iks chān jē′, -chān′jē, eks′chān jē′), *n.* a person who takes or has taken part in an exchange, as of students or prisoners. [EXCHANGE + -EE]

exchange′ equaliza′tion fund′. See **stabilization fund.**

exchange′ rate′, the ratio at which a unit of the currency of one country can be exchanged for that of another country. Also called **rate of exchange.** [1895–1900]

exchange′ stabiliza′tion fund′. See **stabilization fund.**

exchange′ stu′dent, a secondary-school or college student who studies for a period, usually one year, at a foreign institution as part of a reciprocal program between two institutions or countries.

ex•cheq•uer (eks′chek ər, iks chek′ər), *n.* **1.** a treasury, as of a state or nation. **2.** (in Great Britain) **a.** (*often cap.*) the governmental department in charge of the public revenues. **b.** (formerly) an office administering the royal revenues and determining all cases affecting them. **c.** (*cap.*) Also called **Court of Exchequer.** an ancient common-law court of civil jurisdiction in which cases affecting the revenues of the crown were tried, now merged in the King's Bench Division of the High Court. **3.** *Informal.* one's financial resources; funds: *I'd love to go, but the exchequer is a bit low.* [1250–1300; ME *escheker, eschequier* < AF *escheker, eschekier* (OF *eschequier*) chessboard, counting table. See CHECKER[1]]

ex•cide (ik sīd′), *v.t.,* **-cid•ed, -cid•ing.** to cut out; excise. [1750–60; < L *excīdere* to cut out, equiv. to *ex-* EX-[1] + *-cīdere* (comb. form of *caedere* to cut)]

ex•ci•mer (ek′sə mər), *n. Chem.* a molecular complex of two, usually identical, molecules that is stable only when one of them is in an excited state. [1960–65; EX-CI(TED) + (DI)MER]

ex•cip•i•ent (ik sip′ē ənt), *n. Pharm.* a pharmacologically inert, adhesive substance, as honey, syrup, or gum arabic, used to bind the contents of a pill or tablet. [1720–30; < L *excipient-* (s. of *excipiēns*), prp. of *excipere* to take out, except, take up, equiv. to *ex-* EX-[1] + *-cipi-* (s. of comb. form of *capere* to take) + *-ent-* -ENT]

ex•ci•ple (ek′sə pəl), *n. Mycol.* (in certain lichens) the rim or outer covering of the apothecium. Also, **ex•ci•pule** (ek′sə pyo͞ol′), **excipulum.** [1865–70; see EXCIPULUM]

ex•cip•u•lum (ek sip′yə ləm), *n., pl.* **-la** (-lə). *Mycol.* exciple. [1855–60; < NL, special use of ML *excipulum* device for catching fish. See EXCIPIENT, -ULE]

ex•cir•cle (eks′sûr′kəl), *n. Geom.* an escribed circle. [EX-[1] + CIRCLE]

ex•cis•a•ble (ek′sī zə bəl, ik sī′-), *adj.* subject to excise duty. [1680–90; EXCISE[1] + -ABLE]

ex•cise[1] (*n.* ek′sīz, -sīs; *v.* ek′sīz, ik sīz′), *n., v.,* **-cised, -cis•ing.** —*n.* **1.** an internal tax or duty on certain commodities, as liquor or tobacco, levied on their manufacture, sale, or consumption within the country. **2.** a tax levied for a license to carry on certain employments, pursue certain sports, etc. **3.** *Brit.* the branch of the civil service that collects excise taxes. —*v.t.* **4.** to impose an excise on. [1485–95; appar. < MD *excijs,* var. of *accijs* < ML *accīsa* tax, lit., a cut, n. use of fem. ptp. of L *accīdere* to cut into, equiv. to *ac-* AC- + *cīd-,* var. s. of *caedere* to cut + *-ta* fem. ptp. suffix, with *dt* > *s*]

ex•cise[2] (ik sīz′), *v.t.,* **-cised, -cis•ing. 1.** to expunge, as a passage or sentence, from a text. **2.** to cut out or off, as a tumor. [1570–80; < L *excīsus* cut out, hewn down, ptp. of *excīdere* to EXCIDE] —**ex•cis′a•ble,** *adj.*

ex•cise•man (ek′sīz mən, -sīs-), *n., pl.* **-men.** *Brit.* an officer who collects excise taxes and enforces excise laws. [1640–50; EXCISE[1] + MAN[1]]

ex•ci•sion (ek sizh′ən, ik-), *n.* **1.** the act of removal; an excising. **2.** *Surg.* the surgical removal of a foreign body or of tissue. **3.** excommunication. [1480–90; < L *excīsiōn-* (s. of *excīsiō*) a cutting out. See EXCISE[2], -ION] —**ex•ci′sion•al,** *adj.*

ex•cit•a•bil•i•ty (ik sī′tə bil′i tē), *n.* **1.** the quality of being excitable. **2.** *Physiol.* irritability. [1780–90; EXCITABLE + -ITY]

ex•cit•a•ble (ik sī′tə bəl), *adj.* **1.** easily excited: *Prima donnas had the reputation of being excitable and temperamental.* **2.** capable of being excited. [1600–10; < LL *excitābilis.* See EXCITE, -ABLE] —**ex•cit′a•ble•ness,** *n.* —**ex•cit′a•bly,** *adv.*
—**Syn. 1.** emotional, passionate, fiery. —**Ant. 1.** placid.

ex•cit•ant (ik sīt′nt, ek′si tənt), *adj.* **1.** exciting; stimulating. —*n.* **2.** *Physiol.* something that excites; a stimulant. [1600–10; < L *excitant-* (s. of *excitāns*), prp. of *excitāre.* See EXCITE, -ANT]

ex•ci•ta•tion (ek′sī tā′shən, -si-), *n.* **1.** the act of exciting. **2.** the state of being excited. **3.** *Elect.* **a.** the application of voltage to an electric device, as an electron-tube circuit, an antenna, or a dynamotor, often for producing a magnetic field in the device. **b.** the voltage applied. **4.** *Physics.* a process in which a molecule, atom, nucleus, or particle is excited. **5.** Also called **drive.** *Electronics.* the varying voltage applied to the control electrode of a vacuum tube. [1350–1400; ME *excitacioun* < LL *excitātiōn-* (s. of *excitātiō*), equiv. to L *excitāt(us)* (ptp. of *excitāre;* see EXCITE) + *-iōn-* -ION]

ex•cit•a•tive (ik sī′tə tiv), *adj.* tending to excite. Also, **ex•cit•a•to•ry** (ik sī′tə tôr′ē, -tōr′ē). [1480–90; < MF *excitatif* < L *excitāt-* (see EXCITATION) + *-īvus* -IVE]

ex•cite (ik sīt′), *v.t.,* **-cit•ed, -cit•ing. 1.** to arouse or stir up the emotions or feelings of: *to excite a person to anger; actions that excited his father's wrath.* **2.** to arouse or stir up (emotions or feelings): *to excite jealousy or hatred.* **3.** to cause; awaken: *to excite interest or curiosity.* **4.** to stir to action; provoke or stir up: *to excite a dog by baiting him.* **5.** *Physiol.* to stimulate: *to excite a nerve.* **6.** *Elect.* to supply with electricity for producing electric activity or a magnetic field: *to excite a dynamo.* **7.** *Physics.* to raise (an atom, molecule, etc.) to an excited state. [1300–50; ME < L *excitāre,* equiv. to *ex-* EX-[1] + *citāre,* freq. of *ciēre* to set in motion]
—**Syn. 1.** stir, awaken, stimulate, animate, kindle, inflame. **2.** evoke. **4.** disturb, agitate, ruffle.

ex•cit•ed (ik sī′tid), *adj.* **1.** stirred emotionally; agitated: *An excited crowd awaited the arrival of the famed rock group.* **2.** stimulated to activity; brisk: *an excited buying and selling of stocks.* [1650–60; EXCITE + -ED[2]] —**ex•cit′ed•ly,** *adv.* —**ex•cit′ed•ness,** *n.*
—**Syn. 1.** ruffled, discomposed, stormy, perturbed, impassioned. **2.** eager, active, enthusiastic.

excit′ed state′, *Physics.* any of the energy levels of a physical system, esp. an atom, molecule, etc., that has higher energy than the lowest energy level. [1925–30]

ex•cite•ment (ik sīt′mənt), *n.* **1.** an excited state or condition. **2.** something that excites. [1375–1425; late ME *excitament* encouragement < ML *excitāmentum.* See EXCITE, -MENT]
—**Syn. 1.** perturbation, commotion, ado. See **agitation.** —**Ant. 1.** serenity.

ex•cit•er (ik sī′tər), *n.* **1.** a person or thing that excites. **2.** *Elect.* an auxiliary generator that supplies energy for the excitation of another electric machine. [1350–1400; ME; see EXCITE, -ER[1]]

excit′er lamp′, a lamp that produces a light that passes through a film soundtrack and impinges on a photoelective cell causing current fluctuations that actuate a loudspeaker. [1935–40]

ex•cit•ing (ik sī′ting), *adj.* producing excitement; stirring; thrilling: *an exciting account of his trip to Tibet.* [1805–15; EXCITE + -ING[2]] —**ex•cit′ing•ly,** *adv.*

excit′ing cur′rent, *Elect.* See **field current.**

excito-, a combining form of **excitor** or **exciting:** *excitomotor.*

ex•ci•to•mo•tor (ik sī′tə mō′tər), *adj. Physiol.* causing an increase of motor activity: *excitomotor nerves.* Also, **ex•ci•to•mo•to•ry** (ik sī′tə mō′tə rē). [1830–40; EXCITO- + MOTOR]

ex•ci•ton (ik sī′ton, ek′si ton′), *n. Physics.* a localized, mobile excited state of a crystal, consisting of an electron and a hole bound together. [1935–40; EXCIT(ED) or EXCIT(ATION) + -ON[1]]

ex•ci•tor (ik sī′tər, -tôr), *n.* **1.** *Physiol.* a nerve whose stimulation excites greater action. **2.** *Archaic.* an exciter. [1810–20; EXCITE + -OR[2]]

excl., **1.** exclamation. **2.** excluding. **3.** exclusive.

ex•claim (ik sklām′), *v.i.* **1.** to cry out or speak suddenly and vehemently, as in surprise, strong emotion, or protest. —*v.t.* **2.** to cry out; say loudly or vehemently. [1560–70; earlier *exclame* < L *exclāmāre* to cry out. See EX-[1], CLAIM] —**ex•claim′er,** *n.*
—**Syn. 1, 2.** shout, proclaim, vociferate; yell, shriek, scream, holler, howl.

exclam., **1.** exclamation. **2.** exclamatory.

ex•cla•ma•tion (ek′sklə mā′shən), *n.* **1.** the act of exclaiming; outcry; loud complaint or protest: *The speech was continually interrupted by rude exclamations.* **2.** an interjection. **3.** *Rhet.* ecphonesis. [1350–1400; ME *exclamacio(u)n* < L *exclāmātiōn-* (s. of *exclāmātiō*) a calling out, equiv. to *exclāmāt(us)* (ptp. of *exclāmāre;* see EXCLAIM) + *-iōn-* -ION] —**ex′cla•ma′tion•al,** *adj.*
—**Syn. 1.** cry, ejaculation, vociferation.

exclama′tion point′, **1.** the sign (!) used in writing after an exclamation. **2.** this mark sometimes used in writing two or more times in succession to indicate intensity of emotion, loudness, etc.: *Long live the Queen!!* **3.** this mark sometimes used without accompanying words in writing direct discourse to indicate a speaker's dumbfounded astonishment: *"His wife just gave birth to quintuplets."* (!) Also called **exclama′tion mark′.** [1860–65]

ex•clam•a•to•ry (ik sklam′ə tôr′ē, -tōr′ē), *adj.* **1.** using, containing, or expressing exclamation: *an exclamatory sentence.* **2.** pertaining to exclamation. [1585–95; < L *exclāmāt(us)* called out (see EXCLAMATION) + -ORY[1]] —**ex•clam′a•to′ri•ly,** *adv.*

ex•clave (eks′klāv), *n.* a portion of a country geographically separated from the main part by surrounding alien territory: *West Berlin is an exclave of West Germany.* [1885–90; EX-[1] + *-clave,* modeled on ENCLAVE]

ex•clo•sure (ik sklō′zhər), *n.* an area protected against intruders, as by fences. [1915–20; EX-[1] + *-closure,* modeled on ENCLOSURE]

ex•clud•a•ble (ik sklo͞o′də bəl), *adj.* **1.** capable of being excluded. —*n.* **2.** something that is excluded or exempted. **3.** (in U.S. immigration statutes) an undesirable alien who is not legally eligible to enter the country: *Excludables include convicts and drug addicts.* Also, **ex•clud′i•ble.** [1915–20; EXCLUDE + -ABLE] —**ex•clud′a•bil′i•ty,** *n.*

ex•clude (ik sklo͞od′), *v.t.,* **-clud•ed, -clud•ing. 1.** to shut or keep out; prevent the entrance of. **2.** to shut out from consideration, privilege, etc.: *Employees and their relatives were excluded from participation in the contest.* **3.** to expel and keep out; thrust out; eject: *He was excluded from the club for infractions of the rules.* [1350–1400; ME < L *exclūdere* to shut out, cut off, equiv. to *ex-* EX-[1] + *-clūdere* (comb. form of *claudere* to close)] —**ex•clud′er,** *n.* —**ex•clu•so•ry** (ik sklo͞o′sə rē, -zə rē), *adj.*
—**Syn. 1.** bar, prohibit, except, omit, preclude. **3.** reject. —**Ant. 1.** include.

ex•clu•sion (ik sklo͞o′zhən), *n.* **1.** an act or instance of excluding. **2.** the state of being excluded. **3.** *Physiol.* a keeping apart; blocking of an entrance. [1375–1425; late ME < L *exclūsiōn-* (s. of *exclūsiō*), equiv. to *exclūs(us)* (ptp. of *exclūdere* to shut out; see EXCLUDE) + *-iōn-* -ION] —**ex•clu′sion•ar′y,** *adj.*

exclu′sionary rule′, a rule that forbids the introduction of illegally obtained evidence in a criminal trial. [1955–60]

exclu′sion clause′, *Insurance.* a clause in a policy stipulating risks not covered in the policy.

ex•clu•sion•ism (ik sklo͞o′zhə niz′əm), *n.* the principle, policy, or practice of exclusion, as from rights or privileges. [1840–50; EXCLUSION + -ISM] —**ex•clu′sion•ist, ex•clu′sion•er,** *n.*

exclu′sion prin′ciple, *Physics.* the principle that in any system described by quantum mechanics no two identical particles having spin equal to half an odd integer can be in the same quantum state: first postulated for the electrons in atoms. Also called **Pauli exclusion principle.** Cf. **fermion.** [1925–30]

ex•clu•sive (ik sklo͞o′siv, -ziv), *adj.* **1.** not admitting of something else; incompatible: *mutually exclusive plans of action.* **2.** omitting from consideration or account (often fol. by *of*): *a profit of ten percent, exclusive of taxes.* **3.** limited to the object or objects designated: *exclusive attention to business.* **4.** shutting out all others from a part or share: *an exclusive right to film the novel.* **5.** fashionable; stylish: *to patronize only the most exclusive designers.* **6.** charging comparatively high prices; expensive: *exclusive shops.* **7.** noting that in which no others have a share: *exclusive information.* **8.** single or sole: *the exclusive means of communication between two places.* **9.** disposed to resist the admission of outsiders to association, intimacy, etc.: *an exclusive circle of intimate friends.* **10.** admitting only members of a socially restricted or very carefully selected group: *an exclusive club.* **11.** excluding or tending to exclude, as from use or possession: *exclusive laws.* **12.** *Gram.* (of the first person plural) excluding the person or persons spoken to, as *we* in *We'll see you later.* Cf. **inclusive** (def. 4). —*n.* **13.** *Journalism.* a piece of news, or the reporting of a piece of news, obtained by a newspaper or other news organization, along with the privilege of using it first. **14.** an exclusive right or privilege: *to have an exclusive on providing fuel oil to the area.* [1400–50; 1900–05 for def. 13; late ME (adj.) < ML *exclūsīvus.* See EXCLUSION, -IVE] —**ex•clu′sive•ly,** *adv.* —**ex•clu′sive•ness, ex•clu•siv•i•ty,** (eks′klo͞o siv′i tē), *n.*
—**Syn. 9.** select, narrow, clannish, snobbish, restrictive, cliquish, illiberal. —**Ant. 2.** inclusive.

exclu′sive disjunc′tion, *Logic.* See under **disjunction** (def. 2b). [1940–45]

exclu′sive representa′tion, *Labor.* the right of a union, chosen by a majority of the employees in a plant, craft, industry, or department of a shop or business, to represent all the employees in the unit, regardless of whether they are members of the union or not.

ex•clu•siv•ism (ik sklo͞o′sə viz′əm, -zə-), *n.* the practice of being exclusive. [1825–35; EXCLUSIVE + -ISM] —**ex•clu′siv•ist,** *n.* —**ex•clu′siv•is′tic,** *adj.*

ex•cog•i•tate (eks koj′i tāt′), *v.t.*, **-tat•ed, -tat•ing. 1.** to think out; devise; invent. **2.** to study intently and carefully in order to grasp or comprehend fully. [1520–30; < L *excōgitātus* ptp. of *excōgitāre.* to devise, invent, think out. See EX-[1], COGITATE] **—ex•cog•i•ta•ble** (eks-koj′i tə bəl), *adj.* **—ex•cog′i•ta′tion,** *n.* **—ex•cog′i•ta′tive,** *adj.* **—ex•cog′i•ta′tor,** *n.*

ex•com•mu•ni•ca•ble (eks′kə myōō′ni kə bəl), *adj.* **1.** liable or deserving to be excommunicated, as a person. **2.** punishable by excommunication, as an offense. [1585–95; EXCOMMUNIC(ATE) + -ABLE]

ex•com•mu•ni•cate (*v.* eks′kə myōō′ni kāt′; *n., adj.* eks′kə myōō′ni kit, -kāt′), *v.,* **-cat•ed, -cat•ing,** *n., adj.* *—v.t.* **1.** to cut off from communion with a church or exclude from the sacraments of a church by ecclesiastical sentence. **2.** to exclude or expel from membership or participation in any group, association, etc.: *an advertiser excommunicated from a newspaper.* *—n.* **3.** an excommunicated person. *—adj.* **4.** cut off from communion with a church; excommunicated. [1375–1425; late ME *excommunicaten* (v.) < LL *excommūnicātus* lit., put out of the community (ptp. of *excommūnicāre*), equiv. to *ex-* EX-[1] + *commūn(is)* COMMON, public + *-ic-* (by analogy with *commūnicāre* to COMMUNICATE) + *-ātus* -ATE[1]] **—ex′com•mu′ni•ca′tor,** *n.*

ex•com•mu•ni•ca•tion (eks′kə myōō′ni kā′shən), *n.* **1.** the act of excommunicating. **2.** the state of being excommunicated. **3.** the ecclesiastical sentence by which a person is excommunicated. [1425–75; late ME < LL *excommūnicātiōn-* (s. of *excommūnicātiō*). See EXCOMMUNICATE, -ION]

ex•com•mu•ni•ca•tive (eks′kə myōō′ni kā′tiv, -kə tiv), *adj.* disposed or serving to excommunicate. [1815–25; EXCOMMUNICATE + -IVE]

ex•com•mu•ni•ca•to•ry (eks′kə myōō′ni kə tôr′ē, -tōr′ē), *adj.* relating to or causing excommunication. [1675–85; EXCOMMUNICATE + -ORY[1]]

ex•co•ri•ate (ik skôr′ē āt′, -skōr′-), *v.t.*, **-at•ed, -at•ing. 1.** to denounce or berate severely; flay verbally: *He was excoriated for his mistakes.* **2.** to strip off or remove the skin from: *Her palms were excoriated by the hard labor of shoveling.* [1375–1425; late ME < LL *excoriātus* (ptp. of *excoriāre* to strip, skin). See EX-[1], CORIUM, -ATE[1]]

ex•co•ri•a•tion (ik skôr′ē ā′shən, -skōr′-), *n.* **1.** the act of excoriating. **2.** the state of being excoriated. **3.** an excoriated place on the body. [1375–1425; late ME *excoriacioun* < ML *excoriātiōn-* (s. of *excoriātiō*). See EXCORIATE, -ION]

ex•cor•ti•cate (eks kôr′ti kāt′), *v.t.*, **-cat•ed, -cat•ing.** decorticate. [1375–1425 for earlier adj. sense; 1650–60 for current sense; late ME *excorticat* hulled < LL *excorticātus*, ptp. of *excorticāre* to peel. See EX-[1], CORTEX, -ATE]

ex•cre•ment (ek′skrə mənt), *n.* waste matter discharged from the body, esp. feces. [1525–35; < L *excrēmentum*, equiv. to *excrē-* (perf. s. of *excernere* to EXCRETE) + *-mentum* -MENT] **—ex•cre•men•tous** (ek′skrə men′təs), *adj.*

ex•cre•men•ti•tious (ek′skrə men tish′əs), *adj.* of or like excrement. Also, **ex•cre•men•tal** (ek′skrə men′tl). [1580–90; EXCREMENT + -ITIOUS] **—ex′cre•men•ti′tious•ly, ex′cre•men′tal•ly,** *adv.*

ex•cres•cence (ik skres′əns), *n.* **1.** an abnormal outgrowth, usually harmless, on an animal or vegetable body. **2.** a normal outgrowth, as hair or horns. **3.** any disfiguring addition. **4.** abnormal growth or increase. [1375–1425; late ME < L *excrēscentia.* See EXCRESCENT, -ENCE]

ex•cres•cen•cy (ik skres′ən sē), *n.* **1.** something that is excrescent; excrescence. **2.** a state of being excrescent. [1535–45; var. of EXCRESCENCE; see -ENCY]

ex•cres•cent (ik skres′ənt), *adj.* **1.** growing abnormally out of something else; superfluous. **2.** *Phonet.* (of a speech sound) inserted or added as a result of articulatory interaction or impetus, as the *t*-sound in *sense* (sents) or *against* (from Middle English *ageynes*), without grammatical or historical justification; intrusive; parasitic. [1600–10; < L *excrēscent-* (s. of *excrēscēns*), prp. of *excrēscere* to grow out. See EX-[1], CRESCENT] **—ex•cres′cent•ly,** *adv.*

ex•cre•ta (ik skrē′tə), *n.* (*usually used with a plural v.*) excreted matter, as urine, feces, or sweat. [1855–60; < L *excrēta* things sifted out or separated, neut. pl. of *excrētus*; see EXCRETE] **—ex•cre′tal,** *adj.*

ex•crete (ik skrēt′), *v.t.*, **-cret•ed, -cret•ing.** to separate and eliminate from an organic body; separate and expel from the blood or tissues, as waste or harmful matter. [1610–20; < L *excrētus* (ptp. of *excernere* to sift out, separate), equiv. to *ex-* EX-[1] + *crē-* (perf. s. of *cernere* to sift) + *-tus* ptp. suffix] **—ex•cret′er,** *n.* **—ex•cre′tive,** *adj.*

ex•cre•tion[1] (ik skrē′shən), *n.* **1.** the act of excreting. **2.** the substance excreted, as urine or sweat, or certain plant products. [1595–1605; < LL *excrētiōn-* (s. of *excrētiō*) that which is sifted out. See EXCRETE, -ION]

ex•cre•tion[2] (ik skrē′shən), *n.* **1.** the state of being excrescent. **2.** an excrescence. [1605–15; < LL *excrētiōn-* (s. of *excrētiō*), equiv. to L *excrēt(us)* (ptp. of *excrēscere*; see EX-[1], CRESCENT) + *iōn-* -ION[1]]

ex•cre•to•ry (ek′skri tôr′ē, -tōr′ē, ik skrē′tə rē), *adj.* pertaining to or concerned in excretion; having the function of excreting: *excretory organs.* [1675–85; EXCRETE + -ORY[1]]

ex•cru•ci•ate (ik skrōō′shē āt′), *v.t.*, **-at•ed, -at•ing. 1.** to inflict severe pain upon; torture: *The headache excruciated him.* **2.** to cause mental anguish to; irritate greatly. [1560–70; < L *excruciātus*, ptp. of *excruciāre* to torment, torture, equiv. to *ex-* EX-[1] + *cruciāre* to torment, crucify (deriv. of *crux* cross); see ATE[1]]

ex•cru•ci•at•ing (ik skrōō′shē ā′ting), *adj.* **1.** extremely painful; causing intense suffering; unbearably distressing; torturing: *an excruciating noise; excruciating pain.* **2.** exceedingly elaborate or intense; extreme: *done with excruciating care.* [1655–65; EXCRUCIATE + -ING[2]] **—ex•cru′ci•at′ing•ly,** *adv.*

—Syn. 1. unbearable, insufferable, unendurable, agonizing, racking.

ex•cru•ci•a•tion (ik skrōō′shē ā′shən), *n.* **1.** the act of excruciating. **2.** the state of being excruciated. **3.** an instance of this; torture. [1610–20; < LL *excruciātiōn-* (s. of *excruciātiō*)]

ex•cu•bi•to•ri•um (ek skyōō′bi tôr′ē əm, -tōr′-), *n., pl.* **-to•ri•a** (-tôr′ē ə, -tōr′-). (in an ancient Roman city) a night watchman's post or sentry box. [< L *excubitōrium*, equiv. to *excubi(tus)* (ptp. of *excubāre* to watch, lit., lie out; see EX-[1], INCUBUS) + *-tōrium* -TORY[2]]

excud., excudit.

ex•cu•dit (eks kōō′dit), *Latin.* he printed or engraved (this); she printed or engraved (this). *Abbr.:* exc., excud.

ex•cul•pate (ek′skul pāt′, ik skul′pāt), *v.t.*, **-pat•ed, -pat•ing.** to clear from a charge of guilt or fault; free from blame; vindicate. [1650–60; < L *exculpātus* freed from blame, equiv. to *ex-* EX-[1] + *culpātus* blamed (ptp. of *culpāre*; see CULPABLE)] **—ex•cul•pa•ble** (ik skul′pə-bəl), *adj.* **—ex′cul•pa′tion,** *n.*

ex•cul•pa•to•ry (ik skul′pə tôr′ē, -tōr′ē), *adj.* tending to clear from a charge of fault or guilt. [1770–80; EXCULPATE + -ORY[1]]

ex cu•ri•a (eks kyŏŏr′ē ə), out of court; without litigation. [< L *ex curiā*]

ex•cur•rent (ik skûr′ənt, -skur′-), *adj.* **1.** running out or forth. **2.** *Zool.* giving passage outward; affording exit: *the excurrent canal of certain sponges.* **3.** *Bot.* **a.** having the axis prolonged so as to form an undivided main stem or trunk, as the stem of the spruce. **b.** projecting beyond the apex, as the midrib in certain leaves. [1595–1605; < L *excurrent-* (s. of *excurrēns*) prp. of *excurrere* to run forth. See EX-[1], CURRENT]

ex•cur•sion (ik skûr′zhən, -shən), *n.* **1.** a short trip or outing to some place, usually for a special purpose and with the intention of a prompt return: *a pleasure excursion; a scientific excursion.* **2.** a trip on a train, ship, etc., at a reduced rate: *weekend excursions to mountain resorts.* **3.** the group of persons making such a journey: *an excursion of tourists.* **4.** a deviation or digression: *excursions into futile philosophizing.* **5.** *Physics.* the displacement of a body or a point from a mean position or neutral value, as in an oscillation. **6.** an accidental increase in the power level of a reactor, usually forcing its emergency shutdown. **7.** *Mach.* **a.** the range of stroke of any moving part. **b.** the stroke itself. **8.** *Obs.* a sally or raid. *—v.i.* **9.** to go on or take an excursion. *—adj.* **10.** of, pertaining to, or intended for use on excursions: *an excursion fare; an excursion bus.* [1565–75; < L *excursiōn-* (s. of *excursiō*). See EXCURSUS, -ION] **—ex•cur′sion•al, ex•cur′sion•ar′y,** *adj.*

ex•cur•sion•ist (ik skûr′zhə nist, -shə-), *n.* a person who goes on an excursion. [1820–30; EXCURSION + -IST]

excur′sion tick′et, a round-trip ticket at a reduced fare, often for use within a limited period of time. [1870–75]

ex•cur•sive (ik skûr′siv), *adj.* **1.** given to making excursions in speech, thought, etc.; wandering; digressive. **2.** of the nature of such excursions; rambling; desultory: *excursive conversation.* [1665–75; < L *excurs(us)* (see EXCURSUS) + -IVE] **—ex•cur′sive•ly,** *adv.* **—ex•cur′sive•ness,** *n.*

ex•cur•sus (ek skûr′səs), *n., pl.* **-sus•es, -sus. 1.** a detailed discussion of some point in a book, esp. one added as an appendix. **2.** a digression or incidental excursion, as in a narrative. [1795–1805; < L: a running out, sally, digression, deriv. of *excurrere* to run out. See EX-[1], COURSE]

ex•cur•va•ture (eks kûr′və chər), *n.* the condition of being curved outward or away from the center. Also, **ex•cur•va•tion** (ek′skər vā′shən). [EX-[1] + CURVATURE]

ex•curved (ek′skûrvd), *adj.* curving or curved outward. Also, **ex•cur•vate** (eks′kûr vāt′, ik skûr′vit). [1880–85; EX-[1] + CURVE + -ED[3]]

ex•cus•a•to•ry (ik skyōō′zə tôr′ē, -tōr′ē), *adj.* serving or intended to excuse. [1400–50; late ME < ML *excūsātōrius*, equiv. to LL *excūsā(re)* to EXCUSE + *-tōrius* -TORY[1]]

ex•cuse (*v.* ik skyōōz′; *n.* ik skyōōs′), *v.,* **-cused, -cus•ing,** *n.* *—v.t.* **1.** to regard or judge with forgiveness or indulgence; pardon or forgive; overlook (a fault, error, etc.): *Excuse his bad manners.* **2.** to offer an apology for; seek to remove the blame of: *He excused his absence by saying that he was ill.* **3.** to serve as an apology or justification for; justify: *Ignorance of the law excuses no one.* **4.** to release from an obligation or duty: *to be excused from jury duty.* **5.** to seek or obtain exemption or release for (oneself): *to excuse oneself from a meeting.* **6.** to refrain from exacting; remit; dispense with: *to excuse a debt.* **7.** to allow (someone) to leave: *If you'll excuse me, I have to make a telephone call.* **8. Excuse me,** (used as a polite expression, as when addressing a stranger, when interrupting or disagreeing with someone, or to request repetition of what has just been said.) *—n.* **9.** an explanation offered as a reason for being excused; a plea offered in extenuation of a fault or for release from an obligation, promise, etc.: *His excuse for being late was unacceptable.* **10.** a ground or reason for excusing or being excused: *Ignorance is no excuse.* **11.** the act of excusing someone or something. **12.** a pretext or subterfuge: *He uses his poor health as an excuse for evading all responsibility.* **13.** an inferior or inadequate specimen of something specified: *That coward is barely an excuse for a man. Her latest effort is a poor excuse for a novel.* [1175–1225; (v.) ME *escusen* < OF *escuser* < L *excūsāre* to put outside, exonerate, equiv. to *ex-* EX-[1] + *-cūsāre*, deriv. of *causa* CAUSE; (n.) ME *escuse* < OF, deriv. of *escuser;* modern sp. with *ex-* on the model of EX-[1]] **—ex•cus′a•ble,** *adj.* **—ex•cus′a•ble•ness,** *n.* **—ex•cus′a•bly,** *adv.* **—ex•cus′al,** *n.* **—ex•cuse′less,** *adj.* **—ex•cus′er,** *n.* **—ex•cus′ing•ly,** *adv.* **—ex•cus′ive,** *adj.* **—ex•cus′ive•ly,** *adv.*

—Syn. 1. EXCUSE, FORGIVE, PARDON imply being lenient or giving up the wish to punish. EXCUSE means to overlook some (usually) slight offense: *to excuse bad manners.* FORGIVE is applied to excusing more serious offenses: *to forgive and forget.* PARDON usually applies to a specific act of lenience or mercy by an official or superior: *The governor was asked to pardon the condemned criminal.* **3.** extenuate, palliate. **4.** free. **9.** justification. EXCUSE, APOLOGY both imply an explanation of some failure or failing. EXCUSE implies a desire to avoid punishment or rebuke. APOLOGY usually implies acknowledgment that one has been in the wrong. **12.** pretense, evasion, makeshift.

ex•cuss (ik skus′), *v.t. Law.* to take possession of (goods) by legal authority. [1560–70; < L *excussus*, ptp. of *excutere* to shake out, drive out, send forth, equiv. to *ex-* EX-[1] + *-cussus*, comb. form of *quassus*, ptp. of *quatere* to shake; disturb] **—ex•cus′sion,** *n.*

ex•cus•si•o (ek skush′ē ō′), *n. Civil Law.* the exhausting of every remedy against a principal debtor before proceeding against a surety. [< LL *excussiō*. See EXCUSS, -ION]

ex•di•rec•to•ry (eks′di rek′tə rē, -trē, -dī-), *adj. Brit.* (of a telephone number) unlisted in a telephone directory. [1935–40]

ex′ div′idend, exclusive of dividend: applied to a stock traded when payment of a dividend is pending, indicating that the price of the security does not include any dividend declared (distinguished from *cum dividend*). [1835–45]

Ex. Doc., executive document.

ex•e•at (ek′sē at′), *n.* **1.** permission granted by a bishop to a priest to leave the diocese. **2.** *Brit.* official permission for a student to be absent from a college or university. [1475–85; n. use of L *exeat* let (him) go out, 3rd pers. sing. pres. subj. of *exīre* to go out]

ex•ec (ig zek′), *n. Informal.* an executive, esp. in business. [1895–1900; by final shortening]

exec., 1. executive. **2.** executor.

ex•e•cra•ble (ek′si krə bəl), *adj.* **1.** utterly detestable; abominable; abhorrent. **2.** very bad: *an execrable stage performance.* [1350–1400 for earlier sense "expressing a curse"; 1480–90 for def. 1; ME < L *ex(s)ecrābilis* accursed, detestable. See EXECRATE, -ABLE] **—ex′e•cra•ble•ness,** *n.* **—ex′e•cra•bly,** *adv.*

ex•e•crate (ek′si krāt′), *v.,* **-crat•ed, -crat•ing.** *—v.t.* **1.** to detest utterly; abhor; abominate. **2.** to curse; imprecate evil upon; damn; denounce: *He execrated all who opposed him.* *—v.i.* **3.** to utter curses. [1555–65; < L *ex(s)ecrātus* (ptp. of *ex(s)ecrārī* to curse), equiv. to *ex-* EX-[1] + *secr-* (comb. form of *sacrāre* to consecrate; see SACRAMENT) + *-ātus* -ATE[1]] **—ex′e•cra′tor,** *n.*

ex•e•cra•tion (ek′si krā′shən), *n.* **1.** the act of execrating. **2.** a curse or imprecation. **3.** the object execrated; a thing held in abomination. [1350–1400; ME *execracioun* < L *ex(s)ecrātiōn-* (s. of *ex(s)ecrātiō*). See EXECRATE, -ION]

ex•e•cra•tive (ek′si krā′tiv, -krə-), *adj.* **1.** pertaining to or characterized by execration. **2.** prone to execrate. [1820–30; EXECRATE + -IVE] **—ex′e•cra′tive•ly,** *adv.*

ex•e•cra•to•ry (ek′si krə tôr′ē, -tōr′ē, -krā′tə rē), *adj.* **1.** pertaining to execration. **2.** having the nature of or containing an execration. [1605–15; EXECRATE + -ORY[1]]

ex•ec•u•tant (ig zek′yə tənt), *n.* **1.** a person who executes or performs, esp. musically. *—adj.* **2.** of or pertaining to a performer, esp. a musician. **3.** performing, esp. in public. [1855–60; < F *exécutant.* See EXECUTE, -ANT]

ex•e•cute (ek′si kyōōt′), *v.,* **-cut•ed, -cut•ing.** *—v.t.* **1.** to carry out; accomplish: *to execute a plan or order.* **2.** to perform or do: *to execute a maneuver; to execute a gymnastic feat.* **3.** to inflict capital punishment on; put to death according to law. **4.** to murder; assassinate. **5.** to produce in accordance with a plan or design: *a painting executed by an unknown artist.* **6.** to perform or play (a piece of music). **7.** *Law.* **a.** to give effect or force to (a law, decree, judicial sentence, etc.). **b.** to carry out the terms of (a will). **c.** to transact or carry through (a contract, mortgage, etc.) in the manner prescribed by law; complete and give validity to (a legal instrument) by fulfilling the legal requirements, as by signing or sealing. **8.** *Computers.* to run (a program or routine) or to carry out (an instruction in a program). *—v.i.* **9.** to perform or accomplish something, as an assigned task. **10.** *Sports.* to perform properly the fundamental moves or mechanics of a sport, game, position, or particular play; show smoothness in necessary skills: *We just didn't execute defensively.* [1350–1400; ME *executen* < OF *executer* < ML *execūtāre*, deriv. of L *execūtus*, ptp. of *ex(s)equī* to follow up, carry out (punishment), execute; see EX-[1], SEQUENCE] **—ex′e•cut′a•ble,** *adj.* **—ex′e•cut′er,** *n.*

—Syn. 1. achieve, complete, finish, consummate. **2.** See **perform. 3.** See **kill**[1]. **7a.** enforce, administer.

ex•e•cu•tion (ek′si kyōō′shən), *n.* **1.** the act or process of executing. **2.** the state or fact of being executed. **3.** the infliction of capital punishment or, formerly, of any legal punishment. **4.** the process of performing a judgment or sentence of a court: *The judge stayed execution of the sentence pending appeal.* **5.** a mode or style of performance; technical skill, as in music: *The pianist's execution of the sonata was consummate.* **6.** effective, usually destructive action, or the result attained by it (usually prec. by *do*): *The grenades did rapid execution.* **7.** *Law.* a judicial writ directing the enforcement of a judgment. **8.** *Computers.* the act of running, or the results of having run, a program or routine, or the performance of an instruction. [1250–1300; ME *execucioun* <

CONCISE ETYMOLOGY KEY: <, descended or borrowed from; >, whence; b., blend of, blended; c., cognate with; cf., compare; deriv., derivative; equiv., equivalent; imit., imitative; obl., oblique; r., replacing; s., stem; sp., spelling, spelled; resp., respelling, respelled; trans., translation; ?, origin unknown; *, unattested; ‡, probably earlier than. See the full key inside the front cover.

L *execūtiōn-* (s. of *execūtiō*). See EXECUTIVE, -ION] **—ex′•e•cu′tion•al,** *adj.*

ex•e•cu•tion•er (ek′si kyo͞o′shə nər), *n.* **1.** an official who inflicts capital punishment in pursuance of a legal warrant. **2.** a person who executes an act, will, judgment, etc. [1555–65; EXECUTION + -ER[1]]

ex•ec•u•tive (ig zek′yə tiv), *n.* **1.** a person or group of persons having administrative or supervisory authority in an organization. **2.** the person or persons in whom the supreme executive power of a government is vested. **3.** the executive branch of a government. *—adj.* **4.** of, pertaining to, or suited for carrying out plans, duties, etc.: *executive ability.* **5.** pertaining to or charged with the execution of laws and policies or the administration of public affairs: *executive appointments; executive committees.* **6.** designed for, used by, or suitable for executives: *an executive suite.* [1400–50; late ME < ML *execūtīvus,* equiv. to L *execūt(us)* (ptp. of *ex(s)equī;* see EXECUTE) + *-īvus* -IVE] **—ex•ec′u•tive•ly,** *adv.* **—ex•ec′u•tive•ness,** *n.*

exec′utive agree′ment, *U.S. Govt.* an agreement, usually pertaining to administrative matters and less formal than an international treaty, made between chiefs of state without senatorial approval. [1940–45]

exec′utive class′. See **business class.** [1960–65] **—exec′utive-class′,** *adj.*

exec′utive coun′cil, 1. a council having the highest executive authority. **2.** a council appointed to give advice to the head of a government. [1770–80, *Amer.*]

Exec′utive Man′sion, 1. the official residence of the governor of a U.S. state. **2.** See **White House** (def. 1). [1830–40, *Amer.*]

Exec′utive Of′fice of the Pres′ident, *U.S. Govt.* a group of federal agencies supervised by directors or staffs that work directly with the president or a presidential assistant.

exec′utive of′ficer, 1. the officer second in command of a military or naval organization. **2.** an officer charged with executive duties, as in a corporation. [1780–90]

exec′utive or′der, (*often caps.*) an order having the force of law issued by the president of the U.S. to the army, navy, or other part of the executive branch of the government. [1880–85, *Amer.*]

exec′utive park′. See **office park.**

exec′utive priv′ilege, the discretionary right claimed by certain U.S. presidents to withhold information from Congress or the judiciary. [1940–45]

exec′utive sec′retary, 1. a secretary with independent administrative responsibilities who assists an executive in a business firm. **2.** an official who directs the business operations of an organization, esp. a nonprofit one. [1945–50]

exec′utive ses′sion, *Govt.* a session, generally closed to the public, of a legislative body or its leaders. [1830–40, *Amer.*]

ex•ec•u•tor (ig zek′yə tər *or, for 1,* ek′si kyo͞o′tər), *n.* **1.** a person who executes, carries out, or performs some duty, job, assignment, artistic work, etc. **2.** *Law.* a person named in a decedent's will to carry out the provisions of that will. [1250–1300; ME *executour* < L *execūtor,* equiv. to *execū(tus)* (see EXECUTE) + *-tor,* -TOR; r. ME *esecutor* < AF *essecutour* < L, as above] **—ex•ec•u•to•ri•al** (ig zek′yə tôr′ē əl, -tōr′-), *adj.* **—ex•ec′u•tor•ship′,** *n.*

ex•ec•u•to•ry (ig zek′yə tôr′ē, -tōr′ē), *adj.* **1.** executive. **2.** *Law.* to be performed or executed. [1400–50; late ME *executorie* operative, being in effect < LL *ex(s)ecūtōrius* executive. See EXECUTE, -TORY[1]]

ex•ec•u•trix (ig zek′yə triks), *n., pl.* **ex•ec•u•tri•ces** (ig zek′yə trī′sēz), **ex•ec•u•trix•es.** *Law.* a woman named in a decedent's will to carry out the provisions of that will. [1350–1400; ME < LL *execūtrīx;* see EXECUTOR, -TRIX] **—Usage.** See **-trix.**

ex•e•dra (ek′si drə, ek sē′-), *n., pl.* **ex•e•drae** (ek′si drē′, ek sē′drē). **1.** (in ancient Greece and Rome) a room or covered area open on one side, used as a meeting place. **2.** a permanent outdoor bench, semicircular in plan and having a high back. Also, **exhedra.** [1700–10; < L: hall furnished with seats < Gk *exédra* (covered) walk with seats, equiv. to *ex-* EX-[3] + *(h)édra* seat, bench] **—ex′e•dral,** *adj.*

ex•e•ge•sis (ek′si jē′sis), *n., pl.* **-ses** (-sēz). critical explanation or interpretation of a text or portion of a text, esp. of the Bible. [1610–20; < Gk *exḗgēsis* an interpretation, explanation, equiv. to *ex-* EX-[3] + *(h)ēgē-* (verbid s. of *hēgeîsthai* to guide) + *-sis* -SIS]

ex•e•gete (ek′si jēt′), *n.* a person skilled in exegesis. Also, **ex•e•get•ist** (ek′si jet′ist). [1720–30; < Gk *exēgētḗs* guide, director, interpreter, equiv. to *exēgē-* (see EXEGESIS) + *-tēs* agent suffix]

ex•e•get•ic (ek′si jet′ik), *adj.* of or pertaining to exegesis; explanatory; interpretative. Also, **ex′e•get′i•cal.** [1645–55; < Gk *exēgētikós,* equiv. to *exēgēt(ḗs)* EXEGETE + *-ikos* -IC] **—ex′e•get′i•cal•ly,** *adv.*

ex•e•get•ics (ek′si jet′iks), *n.* (*used with a singular v.*) the science of exegesis; exegetic theology. [1850–55; see EXEGETIC, -ICS]

ex•em•pla (ig zem′plə), *n.* pl. of **exemplum.**

ex•em•plar (ig zem′plər, -plär), *n.* **1.** a model or pattern to be copied or imitated: *Washington is the exemplar of patriotic virtue.* **2.** a typical example or instance. **3.** an original or archetype: *Plato thought nature but a copy of ideal exemplars.* **4.** a copy of a book or text. [1350–1400; ME < L, var. of *exemplāre,* n. use of neut. of *exemplāris* EXEMPLARY; r. ME *exaumplere* < MF *examplaire* < L *exemplāris*]

ex•em•plar•ism (ig zem′plə riz′əm), *n. Theol.* **1.** the doctrine that all knowledge is based on the perception of the exemplars of reality that exist in the mind of God. **2.** the doctrine that the death of Christ is of service to humanity solely as an exemplar of perfect love and self-surrender. [1890–95; EXEMPLAR + -ISM]

ex•em•pla•ry (ig zem′plə rē, eg′zəm pler′ē), *adj.* **1.** worthy of imitation; commendable: *exemplary conduct.* **2.** serving as a warning: *an exemplary penalty.* **3.** serving as an illustration or specimen; illustrative; typical: *The sentences read are exemplary of the style of the essay as a whole.* **4.** serving as a model or pattern: *The authoritative and exemplary text of the work is in the Bodleian Library at Oxford University.* **5.** of, pertaining to, or composed of exempla: *the exemplary literature of the medieval period.* [1400–50 for earlier sense "model, exemplar"; 1580–90 for def. 1; late ME (n.) < L *exemplāris.* See EXEMPLUM, -ARY] **—ex•em′pla•ri•ly,** *adv.* **—ex•em′pla•ri•ness, ex′em•plar′i•ty,** *n.*
—Syn. 1. laudable, noteworthy, praiseworthy.

exem′plary dam′ages, *Law.* See **punitive damages.**

ex•em•pli cau•sa (ek sem′plē kou′sä; *Eng.* ig zem′plī kô′zə, -zem′plē), *Latin.* See **e.c.**

ex•em•pli•fi•ca•tion (ig zem′plə fi kā′shən), *n.* **1.** the act of exemplifying. **2.** something that exemplifies; an illustration or example. **3.** *Law.* an attested copy of a document, under official seal. [1400–50; late ME < ML *exemplificātiōn-* (s. of *exemplificātiō*) a setting forth, equiv. to *exemplificāt(us)* (ptp. of *exemplificāre* to EXEMPLIFY) + *-iōn-* -ION]

ex•em•pli•fi•ca•tive (ig zem′plə fi kā′tiv), *adj.* serving to exemplify. [1820–30; EXEMPLIFICAT(ION) + -IVE]

ex•em•pli•fy (ig zem′plə fī′), *v.t.,* **-fied, -fy•ing. 1.** to show or illustrate by example. **2.** to furnish or serve as an example of: *The plays of Wilde exemplify the comedy of manners.* **3.** *Law.* to transcribe or copy; make an attested copy of (a document) under seal. [1375–1425; late ME *exemplifien* < MF *exemplifier* < ML *exemplificāre* to copy. See EXEMPLUM, -IFY] **—ex•em′pli•fi′a•ble,** *adj.* **—ex•em′pli•fi′er,** *n.*
—Syn. 2. typify, epitomize, depict, embody.

ex•em•pli gra•ti•a (ek sem′plē grä′tē ä′; *Eng.* ig zem′plī grā′shē ə, -zem′plē), *Latin.* See **e.g.**

ex•em•plum (ig zem′pləm), *n., pl.* **-pla** (-plə). **1.** an example or model. **2.** an anecdote that illustrates or supports a moral point, as in a medieval sermon. [1885–90; < LL, L: lit., a pattern, model, copy]

ex•empt (ig zempt′), *v.t.* **1.** to free from an obligation or liability to which others are subject; release: *to exempt a student from an examination.* *—adj.* **2.** released from, or not subject to, an obligation, liability, etc.: *organizations exempt from taxes.* *—n.* **3.** a person who is exempt from an obligation, duty, etc. **4.** (in Britain) exon. [1325–75; (adj.) ME < OF < L *exemptus,* ptp. of *eximere* to take out, free, release, equiv. to *ex-* EX-[1] + *emptus* (ptp. of *emere* to buy, obtain); (v.) late ME *exempten* < OF *exempter,* deriv. of *exempt*] **—ex•empt′i•ble,** *adj.*
—Syn. 1. except, excuse, relieve.

exempt′ car′rier, a company operating vehicles performing services or carrying goods, as taxicabs or cargo trucks, that are not subject to the regulatory laws of the Interstate Commerce Act.

ex•emp•tion (ig zemp′shən), *n.* **1.** the circumstances of a taxpayer, as age or number of dependents, that allow him or her to make certain deductions from taxable income. **2.** the act of exempting. **3.** the state of being exempted; immunity. [1400–50; late ME < L *exemptiōn-* (s. of *exemptiō*) removal. See EXEMPT, -ION] **—ex•emp′tive,** *adj.*
—Syn. 3. exception. EXEMPTION, IMMUNITY, IMPUNITY imply special privilege or freedom from imposed requirements. EXEMPTION implies release or privileged freedom from some duty, tax, etc.: *exemption from military service.* IMMUNITY implies freedom from a penalty or from some liability, esp. one that is disagreeable or threatening: *immunity from disease.* IMPUNITY (limited mainly to the fixed expression *with impunity*) primarily suggests freedom from punishment: *The police force was so inadequate that crimes could be committed with impunity.* **—Ant. 3.** liability.

ex•en•ter•ate (*v.* ek sen′tə rāt′; *adj.* ek sen′tər it), *v.,* **-at•ed, -at•ing,** *adj.* *—v.t.* **1.** to remove the contents of; disembowel; eviscerate. *—adj.* **2.** *Surg.* eviscerate. [1600–10; < L *exenterātus* (ptp. of *exenterāre* to disembowel), equiv. to *ex-* EX-[1] + *enter-* (< Gk *éntera* entrails) + *-ātus* -ATE[1]] **—ex•en′ter•a′tion,** *n.*

ex•e•qua•tur (ek′si kwā′tər, -kwot′ər), *n.* **1.** a written recognition of a consul by the government of the state in which he or she is stationed giving authorization to exercise appropriate powers. **2.** an authorization granted by a secular ruler for the publication of papal bulls or other ecclesiastical enactments to give them binding force. [1780–90; < L: lit., he may perform, 3rd pers. sing. pres. subj. of *exequī.* See EXEQUY]

ex•e•quy (ek′si kwē), *n., pl.* **-quies. 1.** Usually, **exequies.** funeral rites or ceremonies; obsequies. **2.** a funeral procession. [1350–1400; ME *exequies* (pl.) < ML, L *exequiae* lit., train of followers, equiv. to *ex-* EX-[1] + *sequ(i)* to follow) + *-iae,* fem. pl. n. suffix] **—ex•e•qui•al** (ek sē′kwē əl), *adj.*

ex•er•cise (ek′sər sīz′), *n., v.,* **-cised, -cis•ing.** *—n.* **1.** bodily or mental exertion, esp. for the sake of training or improvement of health: *Walking is good exercise.* **2.** something done or performed as a means of practice or training: *exercises for the piano.* **3.** a putting into action, use, operation, or effect: *the exercise of caution.* **4.** a written composition, musical piece, or artistic work executed for practice or to illustrate a particular aspect of technique. **5.** Often, **exercises.** a traditional ceremony: *graduation exercises.* **6.** a religious observance or service. *—v.t.* **7.** to put through exercises, or forms of practice or exertion, designed to train, develop, condition, or the like: *to exercise a horse.* **8.** to put (faculties, rights, etc.) into action, practice, or use: *to exercise freedom of speech.* **9.** to use or display in one's action or procedure: *to exercise judgment.* **10.** to make use of (one's privileges, powers, etc.): *to exercise one's constitutional rights.* **11.** to discharge (a function); perform: *to exercise the duties of one's office.* **12.** to have as an effect: *to exercise an influence on someone.* **13.** to worry; make uneasy; annoy: *to be much exercised about one's health.* *—v.i.* **14.** to go through exercises; take bodily exercise. [1300–50; ME (n.) < MF *exercice* < L *exercitium,* equiv. to *exercit(us)* ptp. of *exercēre* to train (*ex-* EX-[1] + *-ercit-,* s. of comb. form of *arcēre* to restrain) + *-ium* n. suffix] **—ex′er•cis′a•ble,** *adj.*
—Syn. 1. activity; calisthenics, gymnastics. **2.** EXERCISE, DRILL, PRACTICE refer to activities undertaken for training in some skill. EXERCISE is the most general term and may be either physical or mental: *an exercise in arithmetic.* DRILL is disciplined repetition of set exercises, often performed in a group, directed by a leader: *military drill.* PRACTICE is repeated or methodical exercise: *Even great musicians require constant practice.* **3.** employment, application, practice, performance. **6.** ritual. **7.** discipline, drill, school. **9.** employ, apply, exert, practice. **13.** try, trouble. **—Ant. 1.** inaction.

ex′ercise bi′cycle, any of various stationary exercise apparatuses that resemble a bicycle, usually having handlebars, a seat, pedals, a device for adjusting tension or resistance in the pedaling mechanism, and sometimes a single front wheel: used esp. to improve the cardiovascular system. Also called **stationary bicycle.**

ex′ercise price′. See **striking price.**

ex•er•cis•er (ek′sər sī′zər), *n.* **1.** a person or thing that exercises. **2.** an athletic device or machine employed in exercising. **3.** a groom in a stable responsible for exercising horses. [1545–55; EXERCISE + -ER[1]]

ex•er•ci•ta•tion (ig zûr′si tā′shən), *n.* **1.** exercise or exertion, as of the faculties or powers of the body or mind: *an exercitation of the imagination.* **2.** practice or training: *exercitations in logical thinking.* **3.** the performance of a religious observance; an act of worship. **4.** a disquisition or discourse performed as a display of skill. [1325–75; ME *exercitacioun* < L *exercitātiōn-* (s. of *exercitātiō*) exercise, practice, equiv. to *exercitāt(us)* (ptp. of *exercitāre,* to exercise, freq. of *exercēre;* see EXERCISE) + *-iōn-* -ION]

Ex•er•cy•cle (ek′sər sī′kəl), *Trademark.* a brand of exercise bicycle.

ex•er•gon•ic (ek′sər gon′ik), *adj. Biochem.* (of a biochemical reaction) liberating energy. Cf. **endergonic.** [1935–40; EX-[3] + Gk *érgon* WORK + -IC]

ex•ergue (ig zûrg′, ek′sûrg, eg′zûrg), *n.* the space below the device on a coin or medal, sometimes separated from the field by a line. [1690–1700; < F, appar. < Gk *ex-* EX-[3] + *érgon* work] **—ex•ergu•al** (ig zûr′gəl, ek sûr′-), *adj.*

ex•ert (ig zûrt′), *v.t.* **1.** to put forth or into use, as power; exercise, as ability or influence; put into vigorous action: *to exert every effort.* **2.** to put (oneself) into strenuous, vigorous action or effort. [1650–60; < L *ex(s)ertus,* ptp. of *exserere* to thrust out, equiv. to *ex-* EX-[1] + *ser(ere)* to bind together + *-tus* ptp. suffix] **—ex•er′tive,** *adj.*

ex•er•tion (ig zûr′shən), *n.* **1.** vigorous action or effort: *physical and mental exertion.* **2.** an effort: *a great exertion to help others.* **3.** exercise, as of power or faculties. **4.** an instance of this. [1660–70; EXERT + -ION]
—Syn. 1. endeavor, struggle, attempt, activity, strain. See **effort.**

Ex•e•ter (ek′si tər), *n.* **1.** a city in Devonshire, in SW England: cathedral. 94,100. **2.** a town in SE New Hampshire. 11,024.

ex•e•unt (ek′sē ənt, -o͝ont′), *v.i.* (they) go offstage (used formerly as a stage direction, usually preceding the names of the characters): *Exeunt soldiers and townspeople.* [1475–85; < L, 3rd pers. pl. pres. indic. of *exīre* to EXIT[1]]

ex•e•unt om•nes (ek′sē ənt om′nēz, ek′sē o͝ont′ ōm′nās), they all go out (used formerly as a stage direction). [< L *exeunt omnēs*]

ex fa•ci•e (eks fā′shē ē′, eks fä′kē ā′), *Law.* (of a document) considered on the basis of its face; apparently: *The contract was ex facie satisfactory.* [1860–65; < L *ex faciē* on the face, from the face]

ex fac•to (eks fäk′tō; *Eng.* eks fak′tō), *Latin.* according to fact; actually.

ex•fil•trate (eks fil′trāt, eks′fil trāt′), *v.,* **-trat•ed, -trat•ing.** *—v.i.* **1.** to escape furtively from an area under enemy control. *—v.t.* **2.** to smuggle (military personnel) out of an area under enemy control. [1965–70; EX-[1] + (IN)FILTRATE] **—ex′fil•tra′tion,** *n.*

ex•fo•li•ate (eks fō′lē āt′), *v.,* **-at•ed, -at•ing.** *—v.t.* **1.** to throw off in scales, splinters, etc. **2.** to remove the surface of (a bone, the skin, etc.) in scales or laminae. *—v.i.* **3.** to throw off scales or flakes; peel off in thin fragments: *The bark of some trees exfoliates.* **4.** *Geol.* **a.** to split or swell into a scaly aggregate, as certain minerals when heated. **b.** to separate into rudely concentric layers or sheets, as certain rocks during weathering. **5.** *Med.* to separate and come off in scales, as scaling skin or any structure separating in flakes. [1605–15; < LL *exfoliātus* ptp. of *exfoliāre* to strip off leaves. See EX-[1], FOLIATE] **—ex•fo•li•a•tive** (eks fō′lē ā′tiv, -ə tiv), *adj.*

ex•fo•li•a•tion (eks fō′lē ā′shən), *n.* **1.** the act, state, or process of exfoliating. **2.** the state of being exfoliated. **3.** something that is exfoliated or scaled off. [1670–80; NL *exfoliātiōn-* (s. of *exfoliātiō*). See EXFOLIATE, -ION]

ex gra•ti•a (eks grā′shē ə), as a favor rather than as a matter of right: *ex gratia payments made to nonstriking workers.* [1760–70; < L *ex gratiā* out of goodwill]

ex•hal•ant (eks hā′lənt, ek sā′-), *adj.* **1.** exhaling; emitting. *—n.* **2.** something that exhales, as the ducts of certain mollusks. Also, **ex•hal′ent.** [1765–75; < L *exhālant-* (s. of *exhālāns*), prp. of *exhālāre* to EXHALE; see -ANT]

ex•ha•la•tion (eks′hə lā′shən, ek′sə-), *n.* **1.** the act of exhaling. **2.** something that is exhaled; vapor; emanation. [1350–1400; ME *exalacion* < L *exhālātiōn-* (s. of *exhālātiō*). See EXHALE, -ATION]

ex•hale (eks hāl′, ek sāl′), *v.,* **-haled, -hal•ing.** —*v.i.* **1.** to emit breath or vapor; breathe out. **2.** to pass off as vapor; pass off as an effluence. —*v.t.* **3.** to breathe out; emit (air, vapor, sound, etc.): *to exhale a sigh.* **4.** to give off as vapor: *The engine exhaled steam.* **5.** to draw out as a vapor or effluence; evaporate. [1350–1400; ME *exalen* < L *exhālāre,* equiv. to *ex-* EX-[1] + *hālāre* to breathe]

ex•haust (ig zôst′), *v.t.* **1.** to drain of strength or energy, wear out, or fatigue greatly, as a person: *I have exhausted myself working.* **2.** to use up or consume completely; expend the whole of: *He exhausted a fortune in stock-market speculation.* **3.** to draw out all that is essential in (a subject, topic, etc.); treat or study thoroughly. **4.** to empty by drawing out the contents: *to exhaust a tank of fuel oil.* **5.** to create a vacuum in. **6.** to draw out or drain off completely. **7.** to deprive wholly of useful or essential properties, possessions, resources, etc. **8.** *Chem., Pharm.* to deprive of ingredients by the use of solvents, as a drug. **9.** to destroy the fertility of (soil), as by intensive cultivation. —*v.i.* **10.** to pass out or escape, as spent steam from the cylinder of an engine. —*n. Mach.* **11.** the escape of steam or gases from the cylinder of an engine. **12.** the steam or gases ejected. **13.** Also called **exhaust system.** the parts of an engine through which the exhaust is ejected. [1515–25; 1895–1900 for def. 11; < L *exhaustus* emptied out, drained out, ptp. of *exhaurīre*] —**ex•haust′er,** *n.* —**ex•haust′i•ble,** *adj.* —**ex•haust′i•bil′i•ty,** *n.*
—**Syn. 1.** tire, enervate, prostrate, debilitate. **2.** waste, squander, dissipate. **4.** void. **12.** fumes, smoke, vapor. —**Ant. 1.** strengthen, invigorate. **4.** fill.

exhaust′ fan′, a fan for ventilating an interior by drawing air from the interior and expelling it outside. [1870–75]

exhaust′-gas recircula′tion (ig zôst′gas′), *Auto.* a method of returning part of the exhaust gases to an engine by means of a valve (**EGR valve**) in order to reduce the combustion temperature, which leads to a reduction in the formation of pollutants. *Abbr.:* EGR

ex•haust•ing (ig zô′sting), *adj.* producing or tending to produce fatigue, weariness, or the like: *an exhausting day; an exhausting child.* [1530–40; EXHAUST + -ING[2]] —**ex•haust′ing•ly,** *adv.*

ex•haus•tion (ig zôs′chən), *n.* **1.** the act or process of exhausting. **2.** the state of being exhausted. **3.** extreme weakness or fatigue. **4.** the total consumption of something: *the exhaustion of your vacation benefits for the year.* [1640–50; < NL *exhaustiōn-* (s. of *exhaustiō*). See EXHAUST, -ION]
—**Syn. 3.** weariness, lassitude.

ex•haus•tive (ig zôs′tiv), *adj.* **1.** exhausting a subject, topic, etc.; comprehensive; thorough: *He published an exhaustive study of Greek vases.* **2.** tending to exhaust or drain, as resources or strength: *a protracted, exhaustive siege of illness.* [1780–90; EXHAUST + -IVE] —**ex•haus′tive•ly,** *adv.* —**ex•haus′tive•ness,** *n.*

ex•haust•less (ig zôst′lis), *adj.* inexhaustible. [1705–15; EXHAUST + -LESS] —**ex•haust′less•ly,** *adv.* —**ex•haust′less•ness,** *n.*

exhaust′ man′ifold, *Auto.* a component of the exhaust system consisting of a collection of tubes, usually of cast iron, that channel the exhaust gases from the cylinders of an engine to the rest of the exhaust system. [1915–20]

exhaust′ sys′tem, exhaust (def. 13).

exhaust′ veloc′ity, *Rocketry.* the velocity, relative to a rocket, at which exhaust gases leave the nozzle of the rocket's engine.

ex•he•dra (ek sē′drə, eks hē′-), *n., pl.* **-drae** (-drē). exedra.

ex•hib•it (ig zib′it), *v.t.* **1.** to offer or expose to view; present for inspection: *to exhibit the latest models of cars.* **2.** to manifest or display: *to exhibit anger; to exhibit interest.* **3.** to place on show: *to exhibit paintings.* **4.** to make manifest; explain. **5.** *Law.* to submit (a document, object, etc.) in evidence in a court of law. **6.** *Med. Obs.* to administer (something) as a remedy. —*v.i.* **7.** to make or give an exhibition; present something to public view. —*n.* **8.** an act or instance of exhibiting; exhibition. **9.** something that is exhibited. **10.** an object or a collection of objects shown in an exhibition, fair, etc. **11.** *Law.* a document or object exhibited in court and referred to and identified in written evidence. [1400–50; late ME *exhibiten* to show < L *exhibitus* (ptp. of *exhibēre*), equiv. to *ex-* EX-[1] + *-hib-* (comb. form of *habēre* to have) + *-itus* -ITE[2]] —**ex•hib′it•a•ble,** *adj.* —**ex•hib′i•tor, ex•hib′it•er, ex•hib′it•ant,** *n.*
—**Syn. 1.** show, demonstrate. See **display. 2.** evince, disclose, betray, show, reveal. **8.** showing, show, display. **9, 11.** See **evidence. 10.** display. —**Ant. 2.** conceal.

ex•hi•bi•tion (ek′sə bish′ən), *n.* **1.** an exhibiting, showing, or presenting to view. **2.** a public display, as of the work of artists or artisans, the products of farms or factories, the skills of performers, or objects of general interest. **3.** an exposition or large fair of extended duration, as a world's fair. **4.** *Brit.* an allowance given to a student in a college, university, or school, usually upon the result of a competitive examination. **5.** *Med. Obs.* administration, as of a remedy. [1275–1325; ME *exhibicion* < LL *exhibitiōn-* (s. of *exhibitiō*) a presenting. See EXHIBIT, -ION]

ex•hi•bi•tion•er (ek′sə bish′ə nər), *n. Brit.* a student who receives an exhibition. [1565–75; EXHIBITION + -ER[1]]

exhibi′tion game′, an unofficial game played under regular game conditions between professional teams, usually as a part of preseason training or as a fund-raising event.

ex•hi•bi•tion•ism (ek′sə bish′ə niz′əm), *n.* **1.** a tendency to display one's abilities or to behave in such a way as to attract attention. **2.** *Psychiatry.* a disorder characterized esp. by a compulsion to exhibit the genitals in public. [1890–95; EXHIBITION + -ISM]

ex•hi•bi•tion•ist (ek′sə bish′ə nist), *n.* **1.** a person who behaves in ways intended to attract attention or display his or her powers, personality, etc. **2.** *Psychiatry.* a person afflicted with the compulsions of exhibitionism. [1815–25; EXHIBITION + -IST] —**ex′hi•bi′tion•is′tic,** *adj.* —**ex′hi•bi′tion•is′ti•cal•ly,** *adv.*

ex•hib•i•tive (ig zib′i tiv), *adj.* serving for exhibition; tending to exhibit. [1590–1600; < NL *exhibitīvus.* See EXHIBIT, -IVE] —**ex•hib′i•tive•ly,** *adv.*

ex•hib•i•to•ry (ig zib′i tôr′ē, -tōr′ē), *adj.* pertaining to or intended for exhibition or display. [1600–10; < LL *exhibitōrius* relating to showing, displaying. See EXHIBIT, -TORY[1]]

ex•hil•a•rant (ig zil′ər ənt), *adj.* **1.** exhilarating. —*n.* **2.** something that exhilarates. [1795–1805; < L *exhilarant-* (s. of *exhilarāns*), prp. of *exhilarāre* to gladden. See EXHILARATE, -ANT]

ex•hil•a•rate (ig zil′ə rāt′), *v.t.,* **-rat•ed, -rat•ing. 1.** to enliven; invigorate; stimulate: *The cold weather exhilarated the walkers.* **2.** to make cheerful or merry. [1530–40; < L *exhilarātus* ptp. of *exhilarāre* to gladden, equiv. to *ex-* EX-[1] + *hilarāre* to cheer (see HILARITY); see -ATE[1]] —**ex•hil′a•rat′ing•ly,** *adv.* —**ex•hil′a•ra′tor,** *n.*
—**Syn. 1.** animate, inspirit, elate. **2.** cheer, gladden. —**Ant. 1, 2.** depress.

ex•hil•a•ra•tion (ig zil′ə rā′shən), *n.* **1.** exhilarated condition or feeling. **2.** the act of exhilarating. [1615–25; < LL *exhilarātiōn-* (s. of *exhilarātiō*). See EXHILARATE, -ION]
—**Syn. 1.** animation, joyousness, jollity, hilarity.

ex•hil•a•ra•tive (ig zil′ə rā′tiv, -ər ə tiv), *adj.* tending to exhilarate. Also, **ex•hil•a•ra•to•ry** (ig zil′ər ə tôr′ē, -tōr′ē). [1860–65; EXHILARATE + -IVE]

ex•hort (ig zôrt′), *v.t.* **1.** to urge, advise, or caution earnestly; admonish urgently. —*v.i.* **2.** to give urgent advice, recommendations, or warnings. [1375–1425; late ME *ex(h)orte* < L *exhortārī* to encourage greatly, equiv. to *ex-* EX-[1] + *hortārī* to urge] —**ex•hort′er,** *n.* —**ex•hort′ing•ly,** *adv.*
—**Syn. 1, 2.** encourage, spur, press, goad.

ex•hor•ta•tion (eg′zôr tā′shən, ek′sôr-), *n.* **1.** the act or process of exhorting. **2.** an utterance, discourse, or address conveying urgent advice or recommendations. [1350–1400; ME *exhortacioun* < L *exhortātiōn-* (s. of *exhortātiō*) a pleading, urging. See EXHORTATIVE, -ION]
—**Syn. 1, 2.** See **advice.**

ex•hort•a•tive (ig zôr′tə tiv), *adj.* **1.** serving or intended to exhort. **2.** pertaining to exhortation. Also, **ex•hort•a•to•ry** (ig zôr′tə tôr′ē, -tōr′ē). [1400–50; late ME < L *exhortātīvus,* equiv. to *exhortāt(us)* (ptp. of *exhortārī* to EXHORT) + *-īvus* -IVE] —**ex•hort′a•tive•ly,** *adv.*

ex•hume (ig zo͞om′, -zyo͞om′, eks hyo͞om′), *v.t.,* **-humed, -hum•ing. 1.** to dig (something buried, esp. a dead body) out of the earth; disinter. **2.** to revive or restore after neglect or a period of forgetting; bring to light: *to exhume a literary reputation; to exhume old letters.* [1400–50; late ME < ML *exhumāre,* equiv. to L *ex-* EX-[1] + *humāre* to inter] —**ex•hu•ma•tion** (eks′hyo͞o mā′shən), *n.* —**ex•hum′er,** *n.*

ex•i•geant (ek′si jənt; *Fr.* eg zē zhäN′), *adj.* exigent. [< F]

ex•i•gen•cy (ek′si jən sē, ig zij′ən-), *n., pl.* **-cies. 1.** exigent state or character; urgency. **2.** Usually, **exigencies.** the need, demand, or requirement intrinsic to a circumstance, condition, etc.: *the exigencies of city life.* **3.** a case or situation that demands prompt action or remedy; emergency: *He promised help in any exigency.* Also, **ex′i•gence.** [1575–85; < ML *exigentia.* See EXIGENT, -ENCY]
—**Syn. 3.** crisis, contingency, plight, strait; predicament, fix, pinch.

ex•i•gent (ek′si jənt), *adj.* **1.** requiring immediate action or aid; urgent; pressing. **2.** requiring a great deal, or more than is reasonable. Also, **exigeant.** [1400–50; late ME < L *exigent-* (s. of *exigēns*) (prp. of *exigere* to drive out, demand), equiv. to *ex-* EX-[1] + *-ig-* (comb. form of *agere* to drive) + *-ent-* -ENT] —**ex′i•gent•ly,** *adv.*

ex•i•gi•ble (ek′si jə bəl), *adj.* liable to be exacted; requirable. [1600–10; < F; see EXIGENT, -IBLE]

ex•ig•u•ous (ig zig′yo͞o əs, ik sig′-), *adj.* scanty; meager; small; slender: *exiguous income.* [1645–55; < L *exiguus* scanty in measure or number, small, equiv. to *exig(ere)* (see EXIGENT) + *-uus* deverbal adj. suffix] —**ex•i•gu•i•ty** (ek′si gyo͞o′i tē), **ex•ig′u•ous•ness,** *n.* —**ex•ig′u•ous•ly,** *adv.*

ex•i•larch (eg′zə lärk′, ek′sə-), *n.* one of a line of hereditary rulers of the Jewish community in Babylonia from about the 2nd century A.D. to the beginning of the 11th century. [1890–95; EXILE + -ARCH]

ex•ile (eg′zil, ek′sil), *n., v.,* **-iled, -il•ing.** —*n.* **1.** expulsion from one's native land by authoritative decree. **2.** the fact or state of such expulsion: *to live in exile.* **3.** a person banished from his or her native land. **4.** prolonged separation from one's country or home, as by force of circumstances: *wartime exile.* **5.** anyone separated from his or her country or home voluntarily or by force of circumstances. **6. the Exile,** the Babylonian captivity of the Jews, 597–538 B.C. —*v.t.* **7.** to expel or banish (a person) from his or her country; expatriate. **8.** to separate from country, home, etc.: *Disagreements exiled him from his family.* [1250–1300; ME *exil* banishment < L *ex(s)ilium,* equiv. to *exsul* banished person + *-ium* -IUM] —**ex′il•a•ble,** *adj.* —**ex′il•er,** *n.*
—**Syn. 7, 8.** evict, drive out, cast out, eject, deport.

ex•il•ic (eg zil′ik, ek sil′-), *adj.* pertaining to exile, esp. that of the Jews in Babylon. Also, **ex•il′i•an.** [1870–75; EXILE + -IC]

Ex-Im (eks′im′), *n. Informal.* See **Export-Import Bank.** Also, **Ex′im′, Ex•im•bank** (ek′sim bangk′). [by shortening]

ex•im•i•ous (eg zim′ē əs), *adj. Obs.* distinguished; eminent; excellent. [1540–50; < L *eximius* select, distinguished, excellent (deriv. of *eximere* to take out, remove), equiv. to *ex-* EX-[1] + *-im-* (comb. form of *emere* to take) + *-ius* -IOUS] —**ex•im′i•ous•ly,** *adv.*

ex•ine (ek′sēn, -sin), *n. Bot.* the outer coat of a spore, esp. a pollen grain. Also, **extine.** [1880–85; EX-[1] + -INE[1]]

ex int., *Stock Exchange.* ex interest.

ex′ in′terest, *Stock Exchange.* without accrued interest. Also, **ex′-in′ter•est.**

ex•ist (ig zist′), *v.i.* **1.** to have actual being; be: *The world exists, whether you like it or not.* **2.** to have life or animation; live. **3.** to continue to be or live: *Belief in magic still exists.* **4.** to have being in a specified place or under certain conditions; be found; occur: *Hunger exists in many parts of the world.* **5.** to achieve the basic needs of existence, as food and shelter: *He's not living, he's merely existing.* [1595–1605; < L *ex(s)istere* to exist, appear, emerge, equiv. to *ex-* EX-[1] + *sistere* to stand] —**ex•ist′er,** *n.*
—**Syn. 3.** survive, persist, last, endure, stay, remain.

ex•ist•ence (ig zis′təns), *n.* **1.** the state or fact of existing; being. **2.** continuance in being or life; life: *a struggle for existence.* **3.** mode of existing: *They were working for a better existence.* **4.** all that exists: *Existence shows a universal order.* **5.** something that exists; entity; being. [1350–1400; ME < LL *ex(s)istentia.* See EXIST, -ENCE]

exist′ence the′orem, *Math.* any theorem that asserts the existence of some specified mathematical object. [1895–1900]

ex•ist•ent (ig zis′tənt), *adj.* **1.** existing; having existence. **2.** now existing. —*n.* **3.** a person or thing that exists. [1555–65; < L *existent-* (s. of *existēns*), prp. of *existere* to EXIST; see -ENT]

ex•is•ten•tial (eg′zi sten′shəl, ek′si-), *adj.* **1.** pertaining to existence. **2.** of, pertaining to, or characteristic of existentialism: *an existential hero.* [1685–95; < LL *existentiālis* relating to existing. See EXISTENCE, -AL[1]] —**ex′is•ten′tial•ly,** *adv.*

ex•is•ten•tial•ism (eg′zi sten′shə liz′əm, ek′si-), *n. Philos.* a philosophical attitude associated esp. with Heidegger, Jaspers, Marcel, and Sartre, and opposed to rationalism and empiricism, that stresses the individual's unique position as a self-determining agent responsible for the authenticity of his or her choices. [1940–45; < G *Existentialismus* (1919); see EXISTENTIAL, -ISM] —**ex′is•ten′tial•ist,** *adj., n.* —**ex′is•ten′tial•is′tic,** *adj.* —**ex′is•ten′tial•is′ti•cal•ly,** *adv.*

existen′tial psychol′ogy, 1. psychology limited to the observation and description of existent data as the content of experience. **2.** the psychological theories or doctrines of existentialism, esp. those dealing with the situation of humankind in a universe seen as purposeless or irrational.

ex′isten′tial quan′tifier, *Logic.* a quantifier indicating that the sentential function within its scope is true for at least one value of the variable included in the quantifier. Also called **particular quantifier.** Cf. **universal quantifier.** [1935–40]

ex•it[1] (eg′zit, ek′sit), *n.* **1.** a way or passage out: *Please leave the theater by the nearest exit.* **2.** any of the marked ramps or spurs providing egress from a highway: *Take the second exit after the bridge for the downtown shopping district.* **3.** a going out or away; departure: *to make one's exit.* **4.** a departure of an actor from the stage as part of the action of a play. **5.** Also called **ex′it card′.** *Bridge.* a card that enables a player to relinquish the lead when having it is a disadvantage. —*v.i.* **6.** to go out; leave. **7.** *Bridge.* to play an exit card. —*v.t.* **8.** to leave; depart from: *Sign out before you exit the building.* [1580–90; partly < L *exitus* act or means of going out, equiv. to *exi-,* var. s. of *exire* to go out (EX-[1] + *ire* to go) + *-tus* suffix of v. action; partly n., v. use of EXIT[2]]

ex•it[2] (eg′zit, ek′sit), *v.i.* (he or she) goes offstage (used as a stage direction, often preceding the name of the character): *Exit Falstaff.* [1530–40; < L *ex(i)it* lit., (he) goes out, 3rd sing. pres. of *exire;* see EXIT[1]]

ex′it poll′, a poll taken of a small percentage of voters as they leave the polls, used to forecast the outcome of an election or determine the reasons for voting decisions. —**ex′it poll′ing.**

ex′it pu′pil, *Optics.* the ridge of the entrance pupil of an optical system, indicating the place where the pupil of the eye should be placed to view the object. Also called **eye point.**

ex′it tax′, a tax formerly imposed on certain Soviet citizens who had been educated at government expense in the Soviet Union and wished to emigrate. [1970–75]

ex le•ge (eks le′ge; *Eng.* eks lē′jē), *Latin.* by virtue of law.

ex lib., ex libris.

ex li•bris (eks lē′bris, lī′-), *pl.* **-bris** for 2. **1.** from the library of (a phrase inscribed in or on a book before the name of the owner): *Ex libris Jane Doe.* **2.** an inscription in or on a book, to indicate the owner; bookplate. [1875–80; < L *ex libris* out of the books (of), from the books (of)]

Ex•moor (eks′mo͝or, -môr, -mōr), *n.* a moorland in SW

England, in Somersetshire and Devonshire: the scene of Blackmore's novel, *Lorna Doone.*

ex mo·re (eks mō′re; *Eng.* eks môr′ē, mōr′ē, môr′ā, mōr′ā), *Latin.* according to custom.

ex ni·hi·lo ni·hil fit (eks ni′hi lō′ ni′hil fit′; *Eng.* eks nī′hi lō′ nī′hil fit′, nē′hi lō′ nē′hil), *Latin.* nothing is created from nothing.

exo-, a combining form meaning "outside," "outer," "external," used in the formation of compound words: *exocentric.* Also, **ex-.** [< Gk, comb. form of *éxō* outside]

ex·o·bi·ol·o·gy (ek′sō bī ol′ə jē), *n.* the study of life beyond the earth's atmosphere, as on other planets. Also called **astrobiology, space biology.** [1955–60; EXO- + BIOLOGY] —**ex·o·bi·o·log·i·cal** (ek′sō bī′ə loj′i kəl), *adj.* —**ex′o·bi·ol′o·gist,** *n.*

ex·o·bi·o·ta (ek′sō bī ō′tə), *n.* extraterrestrial life. [EXO- + BIOTA]

ex·o·carp (ek′sō kärp′), *n. Bot.* epicarp. [1835–45; EXO- + -CARP]

ex·o·cen·tric (ek′sō sen′trik), *adj. Gram.* not having the same syntactic function in the sentence as any one of its immediate constituents. *In the garden* is an exocentric construction, since it does not function in the same way as the noun *garden.* The noun *bittersweet* is an exocentric compound, since it is a noun but its elements are both adjectives. Cf. **endocentric.** [1910–15; EXO- + -CENTRIC]

Ex·o·cet (ek′sō set′), *Trademark.* a winged, radar-guided French anti-ship missile, launched from the surface or an aircraft, that skims the waves at close to the speed of sound.

ex·o·crine (ek′sə krin, -krīn′, -krēn′), *Anat., Physiol.* —*adj.* **1.** secreting to an epithelial surface. **2.** of or pertaining to an exocrine gland or its secretion. —*n.* **3.** an external secretion. **4.** See **exocrine gland.** Cf. **endocrine.** [1910–15; EXO- + *-crine* < Gk *krínein* to separate]

ex′ocrine gland′, any of several glands, as the salivary glands, that secrete externally through a duct. [1925–30]

ex·o·cri·nol·o·gy (ek′sō krə nol′ə jē, -krī-), *n.* the study of the exocrine glands and their secretions. [EXOCRINE + -O- + -LOGY]

ex·o·cy·tose (ek′sō sī tōs′, -tōz′), *v.i.,* **-tosed, -tos·ing.** *Physiol.* (of a cell) to extrude by means of exocytosis. [back formation from EXOCYTOSIS]

ex·o·cy·to·sis (ek′sō sī tō′sis), *n. Physiol.* the transport of material out of a cell by means of a sac or vesicle that first engulfs the material and then is extruded through an opening in the cell membrane (distinguished from *endocytosis*). [1960–65; EXO- + -CYTE + -OSIS; cf. ENDOCYTOSIS] —**ex·o·cy·tot·ic** (ek′sō sī tot′ik), *adj.*

Exod., Exodus.

ex·o·der·mis (ek′sə dûr′mis), *n. Bot.* a temporary, protective layer of cells in some roots, as in certain orchids. [1895–1900; EXO- + -DERMIS] —**ex′o·der′mal,** *adj.*

ex·o·don·tics (ek′sə don′tiks), *n.* (*used with a singular v.*) the branch of dentistry dealing with the extraction of teeth. Also, **ex·o·don·tia** (ek′sə don′shə, -shē ə). [EX-[3] + -ODONT- + -ICS]

ex·o·don·tist (ek′sə don′tist), *n.* a specialist in exodontics. [1910–15; EXODONT(ICS) + -IST]

ex·o·dos (ek′sə dos′), *n., pl.* **-doi** (-doi′). (in ancient Greek drama) the final scene or departure, esp. in tragedy and usually Old Comedy: usually following the last *stasimon.* [< Gk *éxodos;* see EXODUS]

ex·o·dus (ek′sə dəs), *n.* **1.** a going out; a departure or emigration, usually of a large number of people: *the summer exodus to the country and shore.* **2. the Exodus,** the departure of the Israelites from Egypt under Moses. **3.** (*cap.*) the second book of the Bible, containing an account of the Exodus. *Abbr.:* Ex. [< L: a going out < Gk *éxodos* a marching out, going out, equiv. to *ex-* EX-[3] + (*h*)*odós* way]

ex·o·en·zyme (ek′sō en′zīm), *n. Biochem.* an enzyme, as pepsin, that functions outside the cell producing it. Also called **ectoenzyme.** Cf. **endoenzyme.** [1920–25; EXO- + ENZYME]

ex·o·er·gic (ek′sō ûr′jik), *adj. Chem.* exothermic (opposed to *endoergic*). [1940–45; EXO- + (SYN)ERGIC]

ex·o·e·ryth·ro·cyt·ic (ek′sō ə rith′rə sit′ik), *adj. Pathol.* outside of erythrocytes, as in the development of several malarial parasites in the liver. [1940–45; EXO- + ERYTHROCYTIC]

ex off., ex officio.

ex of·fi·ci·o (eks′ ə fish′ē ō′), by virtue of office or official position. [1525–35; < L] —**ex′-of·fi′ci·o′,** *adj.*

ex·og·a·my (ek sog′ə mē), *n.* **1.** marriage outside a specific tribe or similar social unit. Cf. **endogamy. 2.** *Biol.* the union of gametes of unrelated parents. [1860–65; EXO- + -GAMY] —**ex·og·a·mous** (ek sog′ə məs), **ex·o·gam·ic** (ek′sə gam′ik), *adj.*

ex·o·ge·net·ic (ek′sō jə net′ik), *adj.* **1.** Also, **ex·o·gen·ic** (ek′sə jen′ik), **exogenous.** *Geol.* arising from or relating to the surface of the earth (opposed to *endogenetic*). **2.** exogenous (defs. 2–4). [1870–75; EXO- + -GENETIC]

ex·og·e·nous (ek soj′ə nəs), *adj.* **1.** originating from outside; derived externally. **2.** *Bot.* **a.** (of plants, as the dicotyledons) having stems that grow by the addition of an annual layer of wood to the outside beneath the bark. **b.** pertaining to plants having such stems. **c.** belonging to the exogens. **3.** *Path.* (of a disease) externally caused rather than resulting from conditions within the organism. **4.** *Biochem.* of or noting the metabolic assimilation of proteins or other metabolites, the elimination of nitrogenous catabolites being in direct proportion to the amount of metabolites taken in. **5.** *Geol.* exogenetic (def. 1). Also, **exogenetic** (for defs. 2–4). [1820–30; EXO- + -GEN + -OUS] —**ex·og′e·nism,** *n.* —**ex·og′e·nous·ly,** *adv.*

ex·on[1] (ek′son), *n.* (in Britain) one of four yeomen of the guard who act as commanding officers in the absence of higher authority. Also called **exempt.** [1645–55; earlier *exant,* for F *exempt* (sp. altered to show F pronunciation)]

ex·on[2] (ek′son), *n. Genetics.* any portion of an interrupted gene that is represented in the RNA product and is translated into protein. Cf. **intron.** [1975–80; *ex(pressed sequence)* + -ON[1]]

ex·o·nar·thex (ek′sō när′theks), *n.* a covered walk, vestibule, or narthex situated before a narthex; an outer narthex. [1840–50; EXO- + NARTHEX]

ex·on·er·ate (ig zon′ə rāt′), *v.t.,* **-at·ed, -at·ing. 1.** to clear, as of an accusation; free from guilt or blame; exculpate: *He was exonerated from the accusation of cheating.* **2.** to relieve, as from an obligation, duty, or task. [1515–25; late ME < L *exonerātus* (ptp. of *exonerāre* to unburden, discharge), equiv. to *ex-* EX-[1] + *oner-* (s. of *onus*) a burden + *-ātus* -ATE[1]] —**ex·on′er·a′tion,** *n.* —**ex·on′er·a′tive,** *adj.* —**ex·on′er·a′tor,** *n.*
—**Syn. 1.** vindicate. See **absolve. 2.** release, discharge, free. —**Ant. 1.** blame.

ex·o·nu·mi·a (ek′sə nōō′mē ə, -nyōō′-), *n.pl.* items, as tokens or medals, that resemble money but are not intended to circulate as money. [1965–70; EXO- + NUM(ISMATIC) + -IA]

ex·o·nu·mist (ek′sə nōō′mist, -nyōō′-, ek′sə nōō′-, -nyōō′-), *n.* a person who collects exonumia. [EXONUM(IA) + -IST]

ex·o·path·ic (ek′sə path′ik), *adj. Pathol.* noting or pertaining to a disease whose cause is outside the body. [1880–85; EXO- + -PATHIC]

ex·o·pep·ti·dase (ek′sō pep′ti dās′, -dāz′), *n. Biochem.* any enzyme that catalyzes the removal of an amino acid from the end of a polypeptide chain. Cf. **endopeptidase.** [1935–40; EXO- + PEPTIDASE]

ex·o·pe·rid·i·um (ek′sō pə rid′ē əm), *n., pl.* **-rid·i·a** (-rid′ē ə). *Mycol.* the outer of the two layers into which the peridium is divided. [EXO- + PERIDIUM]

ex·o·pha·sia (ek′sō fā′zhə, -zhē ə), *n.* ordinary, vocalized, audible speech. Cf. **endophasia.** [< NL; see EXO-, -PHASIA]

ex·oph·o·ra (ek sof′ər ə), *n. Gram.* the use of a word or phrase to refer to something in the extralinguistic environment, as *that* in *Look at that,* said by someone pointing to a sunset. Cf. **endophora.** [EXO- + (ANA)PHORA] —**ex·o·phor·ic** (ek′sə fôr′ik, -for′-), *adj.*

ex′ophthal′mic goi′ter, *Pathol.* enlargement of the thyroid gland accompanied by exophthalmos, usually due to hyperthyroidism. [1875–80]

ex·oph·thal·mos (ek′sof thal′məs, -mos), *n. Pathol.* protrusion of the eyeball from the orbit, caused by disease, esp. hyperthyroidism, or injury. Also, **ex·oph·thal·mus** (ek′sof thal′məs), **ex·oph·thal·mi·a** (ek′sof thal′mē ə). [1870–75; < NL < Gk *exóphthalmos* with prominent eyes, equiv. to *ex-* EX-[3] + *ophthalmós* eye; see OPHTHALMIC] —**ex′oph·thal′mic,** *adj.*

ex·op·o·dite (ek sop′ə dīt′), *n. Zool.* the outer or lateral branch of a two-branched crustacean leg or appendage. Cf. **endopodite, protopodite.** Also, **ex·o·pod** (ek′sə pod′). [1865–70; EXO- + -POD + -ITE[1]] —**ex·op·o·dit·ic** (ek sop′ə dit′ik), *adj.*

ex·o·pter·y·gote (ek′sō ter′i gōt′), *adj.* **1.** belonging or pertaining to the class Exopterygota, comprising the insects that undergo incomplete metamorphosis. —*n.* **2.** an exopterygote insect. [< NL *Exopterygota,* equiv. to *exo-* EXO- + Gk *pterygōtá,* neut. pl. of *pterygōtós* winged]

exor., executor.

ex·o·ra·ble (ek′sər ə bəl), *adj.* susceptible of being persuaded or moved by entreaty. [1555–65; < L *exōrābilis,* equiv. to *exōrā(re)* to prevail upon, move by entreaty (*ex-* EX-[1] + *ōrāre* to pray, beg) + *-bilis* -BLE] —**ex′o·ra·bil′i·ty,** *n.*

ex·or·bi·tance (ig zôr′bi təns), *n.* the quality of being exorbitant; excessiveness. Also, **ex·or′bi·tan·cy.** [1400–50; late ME *exorbitaunce;* see EXORBITANT, -ANCE]

ex·or·bi·tant (ig zôr′bi tənt), *adj.* exceeding the bounds of custom, propriety, or reason, esp. in amount or extent; highly excessive: *to charge an exorbitant price; exorbitant luxury.* [1425–75; late ME < LL *exorbitant-* (s. of *exorbitāns,* prp. of *exorbitāre* to go out of the track), equiv. to *ex-* EX-[1] + *orbit(a)* wheel track (see ORBIT) + *-ant-* -ANT] —**ex·or′bi·tant·ly,** *adv.*
—**Syn.** inordinate, outrageous, extreme, extravagant, unreasonable, unconscionable. —**Ant.** fair, reasonable.

ex·or·cise (ek′sôr sīz′, -sər-), *v.t.,* **-cised, -cis·ing. 1.** to seek to expel (an evil spirit) by adjuration or religious or solemn ceremonies: *to exorcise a demon.* **2.** to free (a person, place, etc.) of evil spirits or malignant influences. Also, **ex′or·cize′.** [1350–1400; ME < LL *exorcizāre* < Gk *exorkízein,* equiv. to *ex-* EX-[3] + (*h*)*orkízein* to cause (someone) to swear an oath] —**ex′or·cise′ment,** *n.* —**ex′or·cis′er,** *n.*

ex·or·cism (ek′sôr siz′əm, -sər-), *n.* **1.** the act or process of exorcising. **2.** the ceremony or the formula used in exorcising: *An elaborate exorcism was pronounced over the sick man.* [1350–1400; ME *exorcisme* (< OF) < ML < Gk *exorkismós* administration of an oath. See EXORCISE, -ISM] —**ex·or·cis·mal** (ek′sôr siz′məl, -sər-), **ex·or·ci·so·ry** (ek′sôr sī′zə rē, -sər-), **ex′or·cis′ti·cal, ex′or·cis′tic,** *adj.*

ex·or·cist (ek′sôr sist, -sər-), *n.* **1.** a person who practices exorcism. **2.** *Rom. Cath. Ch.* **a.** a member of the second-ranking of the four minor orders. **b.** the order itself. Cf. **acolyte** (def. 2), **lector** (def. 2), **ostiary** (def. 1). [1350–1400; ME < LL *exorcista* < Gk *exorkistés.* See EXORCISM, -IST]

ex·or·di·um (ig zôr′dē əm, ik sôr′-), *n., pl.* **-di·ums, -di·a** (-dē ə). **1.** the beginning of anything. **2.** the introductory part of an oration, treatise, etc. [1525–35; < L *exōrdium,* equiv. to *ex-* EX-[1] + *ōrd(īrī)* to begin + *-ium* -IUM] —**ex·or′di·al,** *adj.*

ex·o·skel·e·ton (ek′sō skel′i tn), *n. Zool.* an external covering or integument, esp. when hard, as the shells of crustaceans (opposed to *endoskeleton*). [1840–50; EXO- + SKELETON] —**ex′o·skel′e·tal,** *adj.*

ex·os·mo·sis (ek′sos mō′sis, ek′soz-), *n.* **1.** *Biol.* osmosis toward the outside of a cell or vessel. **2.** *Physical Chem.* the flow of a substance from an area of greater concentration to one of lower concentration (opposed to *endosmosis*). [1830–40; Latinization of now obs. *exosmose* < F; see EX-[2], OSMOSIS] —**ex·os·mot·ic** (ek′sos mot′ik, -soz-), *adj.* —**ex′os·mot′i·cal·ly,** *adv.*

ex·o·sphere (ek′sō sfēr′), *n.* the highest region of the atmosphere, where the air density is so low that a fast-moving air molecule is more than 50 percent likely to escape from the atmosphere instead of hitting other molecules. [1950–55; EXO- + -SPHERE] —**ex·o·spher·i·cal** (ek′sə sfer′i kəl, -sfēr′-), **ex′o·spher′ic,** *adj.*

ex·o·spore (ek′sə spôr′, -spōr′), *n. Bot., Mycol.* the outer coat of a spore. [1855–60; EXO- + SPORE] —**ex·o·spor·al** (ek′sə spôr′əl, -spōr′-, ek sos′pər-), **ex′o·spor′·ous,** *adj.*

ex·os·to·sis (ek′so stō′sis, -sə-), *n., pl.* **-ses** (-sēz). *Pathol.* the abnormal formation of a bony growth on a bone or tooth. [1730–40; < NL < Gk *exóstōsis* an outgrowth. See EX-[3], OSTOSIS] —**ex′os·tosed′,** *adj.* —**ex·os·tot·ic** (ek′so stot′ik, -sə-), *adj.*

ex·o·ter·ic (ek′sə ter′ik), *adj.* **1.** suitable for or communicated to the general public. **2.** not belonging, limited, or pertaining to the inner or select circle, as of disciples or intimates. **3.** popular; simple; commonplace. **4.** pertaining to the outside; exterior; external. [1645–55; < LL *exōtericus* external < Gk *exōterikós,* equiv. to *exṓter(os)* inclined outward (*exō-* EXO- + *-teros* comp. suffix) + *-ikos* -IC] —**ex′o·ter′i·cal·ly,** *adv.* —**ex′o·ter′i·cism,** *n.*

ex·o·ter·i·ca (ek′sə ter′i kə), *n.pl.* ideas, principles, writings, or the like, of an exoteric nature. [< LL, neut. pl. of *exotericus* EXOTERIC]

ex·o·ther·mic (ek′sō thûr′mik), *adj. Chem.* noting or pertaining to a chemical change that is accompanied by a liberation of heat (opposed to *endothermic*). Also, **ex′o·ther′mal.** [1880–85; EXO- + THERMIC] —**ex′o·ther′mi·cal·ly, ex′o·ther′mal·ly,** *adv.* —**ex·o·ther·mic·i·ty** (ek′sō thər mis′i tē), *n.*

ex·ot·ic (ig zot′ik), *adj.* **1.** of foreign origin or character; not native; introduced from abroad, but not fully naturalized or acclimatized: *exotic foods; exotic plants.* **2.** strikingly unusual or strange in effect or appearance: *an exotic hairstyle.* **3.** of a uniquely new or experimental nature: *exotic weapons.* **4.** of, pertaining to, or involving stripteasing: *the exotic clubs where strippers are featured.* —*n.* **5.** something that is exotic: *The flower show included several tropical exotics with showy blooms.* **6.** an exotic dancer; stripper. [1590–1600; < L *exōticus* < Gk *exōtikós* foreign. See EXO-, -TIC] —**ex·ot′·i·cal·ly,** *adv.* —**ex·ot′ic·ness,** *n.*

ex·ot·i·ca (ig zot′i kə), *n.pl.* exotic things or objects. [1875–80; < L, neut. pl. of *exōticus* EXOTIC]

exot′ic danc′er, stripper (def. 3). [1950–55]

ex·ot·i·cism (ig zot′ə siz′əm), *n.* **1.** tendency to adopt what is exotic. **2.** exotic quality or character. **3.** anything exotic, as a foreign word or idiom. Also, **ex·o·tism** (eg′zə tiz′əm, ek′sə-). [1820–30; EXOTIC + -ISM] —**ex·ot′i·cist,** *n.*

ex·o·tox·in (ek′sō tok′sin), *n. Biochem.* a soluble toxin excreted by a microorganism. Cf. **endotoxin.** [1915–20; EXO- + TOXIN] —**ex′o·tox′ic,** *adj.*

ex·o·tro·pi·a (ek′sə trō′pē ə), *n. Ophthalm.* strabismus in which one or both eyes turn outward. [1895–1900; EXO- + Gk *-tropia* a turning; see TROPE, -IA]

exp., 1. expenses. **2.** expired. **3.** exponential. **4.** export. **5.** exported. **6.** exporter. **7.** express.

ex·pand (ik spand′), *v.t.* **1.** to increase in extent, size, volume, scope, etc.: *Heat expands most metals. He hopes to expand his company.* **2.** to spread or stretch out; unfold: *A bird expands its wings.* **3.** to express in fuller form or greater detail; develop: *to expand a short story into a novel.* **4.** *Math.* **a.** to write (a mathematical expression) so as to show the products of its factors. Cf. **factor** (def. 10). **b.** to rewrite (a mathematical expression) as a sum, product, etc., of terms of a particular kind: *to expand a function in a power series.* —*v.i.* **5.** to increase or grow in extent, bulk, scope, etc.: *Most metals expand with heat. The mind expands with experience.* **6.** to spread out; unfold; develop: *The buds had not yet expanded.* **7.** to express something more fully or in greater detail (usually fol. by *on* or *upon*): *to expand on a statement.* [1400–50; late ME *expanden* < L *expandere* to spread out, equiv. to *ex-* EX-[1] + *pandere* to extend, stretch] —**ex·pand′a·ble, ex·pand′i·ble,** *adj.* —**ex·pand′a·bil′i·ty, ex·pand′i·bil′i·ty,** *n.*
—**Syn. 1.** extend, swell, enlarge. See **increase.** EXPAND, DILATE, DISTEND, INFLATE imply becoming larger and filling more space. To EXPAND is to spread out, usually in every direction: *to expand one's chest.* To DILATE is esp. to increase the width or circumference, and applies to space enclosed within confines or to hollow bodies: *to dilate the pupils of the eyes.* To DISTEND is to stretch, often beyond the point of natural expansion: *to distend an artery.* To INFLATE is to blow out or swell a hollow body with air or gas: *to inflate a balloon.*

ex·pand·ed (ik span′did), *adj.* **1.** increased in area, bulk, or volume; enlarged: *an expanded version of a* story. **2.** spread out; extended: *the expanded frontiers of the Roman Empire.* **3.** Also, **extended.** *Print.* (of type) wider in proportion to its height. Cf. **condensed** (def. 4). [1400–50; late ME; see EXPAND, -ED[2]] —**ex·pand′ed·ness,** *n.*

expand′ed code′. See under **zip code.**

expand′ed met′al, sheet metal slotted and stretched to make a stiff network with openings of various patterns, used for lathing, wastebaskets, and various decorative and semistructural applications. [1885–90]

expand′ed plas′tic, plastic that is made light and spongy by the introduction of pockets of gas or air. Also called **foamed plastic, plastic foam.** [1940–45]

ex·pand·er (ik span′dər), *n.* **1.** a person or thing that expands. **2.** *Electronics.* a transducer that produces an output with a range of voltages greater than that of the input signal. Cf. **compressor** (def. 5). [1860–65; EXPAND + -ER[1]]

expand′ing u′niverse, *Astron.* a representation of the universe, based on the observed redshifts of distant galaxies, in which the galaxies are assumed to be receding from each other at a speed proportional to their separation as a result of the expansion of the universe. Cf. **Hubble's constant, cosmological redshift.** [1930–35]

ex·panse (ik spans′), *n.* **1.** an uninterrupted space or area; a wide extent of anything: *an expanse of water.* **2.** something that is spread out, esp. over a relatively large area: *that great expanse, the sky.* **3.** expansion; extension: *the wide expanse of scientific knowledge.* [1660–70; < NL *expānsum,* n. use of neut. of L *expānsus,* ptp. of *expandere* to EXPAND]
—**Syn. 1.** sweep, reach, range, stretch.

ex·pan·si·ble (ik span′sə bəl), *adj.* capable of being expanded: *Most metals are expansible.* [1685–95; < L *expāns(us)* (see EXPANSE) + -IBLE] —**ex·pan′si·bil′i·ty,** *n.*

ex·pan·sile (ik span′sil, -sīl), *adj.* **1.** capable of expanding; such as to expand. **2.** pertaining to expansion. [1720–30; EXPANS(ION) + -ILE]

ex·pan·sion (ik span′shən), *n.* **1.** the act or process of expanding. **2.** the state or quality of being expanded. **3.** the amount or degree of expanding. **4.** an expanded, dilated, or enlarged portion or form of a thing: *The present article is an expansion of one he wrote last year.* **5.** anything spread out; expanse. **6.** *Math.* **a.** the development at length of an expression indicated in a contracted form, as $a^2 + 2ab + b^2$ for the expression $(a + b)^2$. **b.** any mathematical series that converges to a function for specified values in the domain of the function, as $1 + x + x^2 + \ldots$ for $1/(1 - x)$ when $x < 1$. **7.** *Mach.* that part of the operation of an engine in which the volume of the working medium increases and its pressure decreases. **8.** an increase in economic and industrial activity (opposed to *contraction*). [1605–15; < LL *expānsiōn-* (s. of *expānsiō*) a spreading out. See EXPANSE, -ION] —**ex·pan′sion·al,** *adj.*

ex·pan·sion·ar·y (ik span′shə ner′ē), *adj.* tending toward expansion: *an expansionary economy.* [1935–40; EXPANSION + -ARY]

expan′sion at′tic, an attic space designed or suitable to be finished as a living space.

expan′sion bit′. See **expansive bit.**

expan′sion bolt′, *Building Trades.* a bolt inserted into a hole drilled in masonry and mechanically expanded to serve as an anchor for shelves, timbers, etc.

expan′sion card′, *Computers.* a card in a computer on which additional chips can be mounted to expand the computer's capabilities.

expan′sion cham′ber, *Physics.* See **cloud chamber.** [1930–35]

ex·pan·sion·ism (ik span′shə niz′əm), *n.* a policy of expansion, as of territory or currency: *the colonial expansionism of Europe in the 19th century.* [1895–1900; EXPANSION + -ISM] —**ex·pan′sion·ist,** *n., adj.* —**ex·pan′sion·is′tic,** *adj.*

expan′sion joint′, a joint between two parts of a structure, machine, etc., permitting expansion, as from heat, without structural damage. [1840–50]

expan′sion slot′, *Computers.* a connection in a computer, esp. a microcomputer, to which a new board can be added to expand the computer's capabilities. [1980–85]

expan′sion team′, *Sports.* a new team in a league, composed largely of players from established league teams and formed when the league expands its membership. [1965–70]

expan′sion wave′, a shock wave that expands the medium through which it is transmitted. Cf. **compression wave.**

ex·pan·sive (ik span′siv), *adj.* **1.** having a wide range or extent; comprehensive; extensive: *expansive mountain scenery.* **2.** (of a person's character or speech) effusive, unrestrained, free, or open: *Our expansive host welcomed us warmly.* **3.** tending to expand or capable of expanding. **4.** causing expansion: *the expansive force of heat.* **5.** working by expansion, as an engine. **6.** *Psychiatry.* marked by an abnormal euphoric state and by delusions of grandeur. [1645–55; EXPANS(ION) + -IVE] —**ex·pan′·sive·ly,** *adv.* —**ex·pan′sive·ness,** *n.*
—**Syn. 2.** sociable, extroverted, outgoing, genial, unreserved; gushy, gushing.

expan′sive bit′, *Carpentry.* an adjustable bit for drilling holes of different sizes. Also, **expansion bit.**

expan′sive classifica′tion, *Library Science.* a system of classifying books and other materials consisting of seven classification schemes, each after the first being progressively further subdivided.

ex·pan·siv·i·ty (ek′span siv′i tē), *n.* **1.** the quality or state of being expansive; expansiveness. **2.** *Physics.* See **coefficient of expansion.** [1830–40; EXPANSIVE + -ITY]

ex par·te (eks pär′tē), from or on one side only of a dispute, as a divorce suit; without notice to or the presence of the other party. [1665–75; < L]

ex·pat (eks pāt′), *n. Informal.* an expatriate: *a favorite hangout for expats.* [1960–65; by shortening]

ex·pa·ti·ate (ik spā′shē āt′), *v.i.,* **-at·ed, -at·ing. 1.** to enlarge in discourse or writing; be copious in description or discussion: *to expatiate upon a theme.* **2.** *Archaic.* to move or wander about intellectually, imaginatively, etc., without restraint. [1530–40; < L *expatiātus* ptp. of *ex(s)patiārī* to wander, digress, equiv. to *ex-* EX-[1] + *spatiārī* to walk about, deriv. of *spatium* SPACE; see -ATE[1]] —**ex·pa′ti·a′tion,** *n.* —**ex·pa′ti·a′tor,** *n.*

ex·pa·tri·ate (*v.* eks pā′trē āt′ *or, esp. Brit.,* -pa′trē-; *adj., n.* eks pā′trē it, -āt′ *or, esp. Brit.,* -pa′trē-), *v.,* **-at·ed, -at·ing,** *adj., n.* —*v.t.* **1.** to banish (a person) from his or her native country. **2.** to withdraw (oneself) from residence in one's native country. **3.** to withdraw (oneself) from allegiance to one's country. —*v.i.* **4.** to become an expatriate: *He expatriated from his homeland.* —*adj.* **5.** expatriated; exiled. —*n.* **6.** an expatriated person: *Many American writers were living as expatriates in Paris.* [1760–70; < ML *expatriātus* (ptp. of *expatriāre* to banish), equiv. to *ex-* EX-[1] + *patri(a)* native land + *-ātus* -ATE[1]] —**ex·pa′tri·a′tion,** *n.*

ex·pect (ik spekt′), *v.t.* **1.** to look forward to; regard as likely to happen; anticipate the occurrence or the coming of: *I expect to read it. I expect him later. She expects that they will come.* **2.** to look for with reason or justification: *We expect obedience.* **3.** *Informal.* to suppose or surmise; guess: *I expect that you are tired from the trip.* **4.** to anticipate the birth of (one's child): *Paul and Sylvia expect their second very soon.* —*v.i.* **5. be expecting,** to be pregnant: *The cat is expecting again.* [1550–60; < L *ex(s)pectāre* to look out for, await, equiv. to *ex-* EX-[1] + *spectāre* to look at, freq. of *specere;* see SPECTACLE] —**ex·pect′a·ble,** *adj.* —**ex·pect′a·bly,** *adv.* —**ex·pect′ed·ly,** *adv.* —**ex·pect′ed·ness,** *n.* —**ex·pect′er,** *n.* —**ex·pect′ing·ly,** *adv.*
—**Syn. 1.** EXPECT, ANTICIPATE, HOPE, AWAIT all imply looking to some future event. EXPECT implies confidently believing, usually for good reasons, that an event will occur: *to expect a visit from a friend.* ANTICIPATE is to look forward to an event and even to picture it: *Do you anticipate trouble?* HOPE implies a wish that an event may take place and an expectation that it will: *to hope for the best.* AWAIT (WAIT FOR) implies being alert and ready, whether for good or evil: *to await news after a cyclone.*
—**Usage. 3.** This sense of EXPECT (*I expect you went with them. I expect you want to leave now.*) is encountered in the speech of educated people but seldom in their writing.

ex·pect·an·cy (ik spek′tən sē), *n., pl.* **-cies. 1.** the quality or state of expecting; expectation; anticipatory belief or desire. **2.** the state of being expected. **3.** an object of expectation; something expected. Also, **ex·pect′ance.** [1590–1600; < ML *ex(s)pectantia.* See EXPECTANT, -ANCY]

ex·pect·ant (ik spek′tənt), *adj.* **1.** having expectations; expecting: *an excited, expectant audience.* **2.** pregnant; expecting: *an expectant mother.* **3.** characterized by expectations: *an expectant attitude.* **4.** in expectation; expected; prospective: *an expectant fortune.* —*n.* **5.** a person who expects or who waits in expectation. [1350–1400; ME < L *expectant-* (s. of *expectāns*), prp. of *expectāre* to EXPECT; see -ANT] —**ex·pect′ant·ly,** *adv.*

ex·pec·ta·tion (ek′spek tā′shən), *n.* **1.** the act or the state of expecting: *to wait in expectation.* **2.** the act or state of looking forward or anticipating. **3.** an expectant mental attitude: *a high pitch of expectation.* **4.** something expected; a thing looked forward to. **5.** Often, **expectations.** a prospect of future good or profit: *to have great expectations.* **6.** the degree of probability that something will occur: *There is little expectation that he will come.* **7.** *Statistics.* See **mathematical expectation. 8.** the state of being expected: *a large sum of money in expectation.* [1530–40; < L *expectātiōn-* (s. of *expectātiō*) an awaiting, equiv. to *expectāt(us)* (ptp. of *expectāre* to EXPECT) + *-iōn-* -ION] —**ex′pec·ta′tion·al,** *adj.* —**ex′pec·ta′tion·ist,** *n.*
—**Syn. 2.** expectancy, anticipation; hope, trust.

expecta′tion of life′. See **life expectancy.** [1715–25]

Ex′pecta′tion Sun′day, the Sunday before Whitsunday.

Expecta′tion Week′, the ten days between Ascension Day and Whitsunday. [1615–25]

ex·pect·a·tive (ik spek′tə tiv), *adj.* **1.** of or pertaining to expectation. **2.** characterized by expectation. [1480–90; < ML *expectātīvus.* See EXPECTATION, -IVE]

expect′ed val′ue, *Statistics, Math.* See **mathematical expectation.** [1945–50]

ex·pec·to·rant (ik spek′tər ənt), *Med., Pharm.* —*adj.* **1.** promoting the discharge of phlegm or other fluid from the respiratory tract. —*n.* **2.** an expectorant medicine. [1775–85; < L *expectorant-* (s. of *expectorāns*), prp. of *expectorāre* to EXPECTORATE; see -ANT]

ex·pec·to·rate (ik spek′tə rāt′), *v.,* **-rat·ed, -rat·ing.** —*v.i.* **1.** to eject or expel matter, as phlegm, from the throat or lungs by coughing or hawking and spitting; spit. —*v.t.* **2.** to eject or expel (matter) in this way. [1595–1605; < L *expectorātus* (ptp. of *expectorāre* to expel from the breast), equiv. to *ex-* EX-[1] + *pector-* (s. of *pectus*) breast + *-ātus* -ATE[1]] —**ex·pec′to·ra′tor,** *n.*

ex·pec·to·ra·tion (ik spek′tə rā′shən), *n.* **1.** the act of expectorating. **2.** matter that is expectorated. [1665–75; EXPECTORATE + -ION]

ex·pe·di·en·cy (ik spē′dē ən sē), *n., pl.* **-cies. 1.** the quality of being expedient; advantageousness; advisability. **2.** a regard for what is politic or advantageous rather than for what is right or just; a sense of self-interest. **3.** something expedient. Also, **ex·pe′di·ence.** [1605–15; < LL *expedientia.* See EXPEDIENT, -ENCY]

ex·pe·di·ent (ik spē′dē ənt), *adj.* **1.** tending to promote some proposed or desired object; fit or suitable for the purpose; proper under the circumstances: *It is expedient that you go.* **2.** conducive to advantage or interest, as opposed to right. **3.** acting in accordance with expediency. —*n.* **4.** a means to an end: *The ladder was a useful expedient for getting to the second floor.* **5.** a means devised or employed in an exigency; resource; shift: *Use any expedients you think necessary to get over the obstacles in your way.* [1350–1400; ME < L *expedient-* (s. of *expediēns*), prp. of *expedīre.* See EXPEDITE, -ENT] —**ex·pe′di·ent·ly,** *adv.*
—**Syn. 1.** advisable, appropriate, desirable; advantageous, profitable. **5.** device, contrivance, resort.
—**Ant. 1.** disadvantageous.

ex·pe·di·en·tial (ik spē′dē en′shəl), *adj.* pertaining to or regulated by expediency. [1840–50; EXPEDIENT + -IAL]

ex·ped·i·tate (ek sped′i tāt′), *v.t.,* **-tat·ed, -tat·ing.** to cut off the pads or claws of (an animal, esp. a dog) in order to inhibit deer chasing. [1495–1505; < ML *expeditātus* (ptp. of *expeditāre*), equiv. to L *ex-* EX-[1] + *pedit-* (s. of *pedes*) one who goes on foot + *-ātus* -ATE[1]] —**ex·ped′i·ta′tion,** *n.*

ex·pe·dite (ek′spi dīt′), *v.,* **-dit·ed, -dit·ing,** *adj.* —*v.t.* **1.** to speed up the progress of; hasten: *to expedite shipments.* **2.** to accomplish promptly, as a piece of business; dispatch: *to expedite one's duties.* **3.** to issue or dispatch, as an official document or letter. —*adj.* **4.** *Obs.* ready for action; alert. [1425–75; late ME < L *expedītus* (ptp. of *expedīre* to disengage, set the feet free), equiv. to *ex-* EX-[1] + *ped-* (s. of *pēs*) FOOT + *-ītus* -ITE[2]]
—**Syn. 1.** quicken, push, accelerate, hurry. —**Ant. 1.** delay.

ex·pe·dit·er (ek′spi dī′tər), *n.* a person or thing that expedites something, esp. one employed to move shipments on schedule, as for a railroad. Also, **ex′pe·di′tor.** [1890–95; EXPEDITE + -ER[1]]

ex·pe·di·tion (ek′spi dish′ən), *n.* **1.** an excursion, journey, or voyage made for some specific purpose, as of war or exploration. **2.** the group of persons, ships, etc., engaged in such an activity: *a large expedition of scientists and military personnel.* **3.** promptness or speed in accomplishing something: *He worked with great expedition.* [1400–50; late ME < L *expedītiōn-* (s. of *expedītiō*) a (military) traveling. See EXPEDITE, -ION]
—**Syn. 1.** See **trip. 3.** quickness, dispatch, alacrity.

ex·pe·di·tion·ar·y (ek′spi dish′ə ner′ē), *adj.* pertaining to or composing an expedition: *an expeditionary force.* [1700–10; EXPEDITION + -ARY]

ex·pe·di·tious (ek′spi dish′əs), *adj.* characterized by promptness; quick: *an expeditious answer to an inquiry.* [1590–1600; EXPED(ITION) + -ITIOUS] —**ex′pe·di′tious·ly,** *adv.* —**ex′pe·di′tious·ness,** *n.*
—**Syn.** prompt, swift, speedy, fast, rapid. —**Ant.** slow, leisurely, deliberate.

ex·pel (ik spel′), *v.t.,* **-pelled, -pel·ling. 1.** to drive or force out or away; discharge or eject: *to expel air from the lungs; to expel an invader from a country.* **2.** to cut off from membership or relations: *to expel a student from a college.* [1350–1400; ME *expellen* < L *expellere* to drive out, drive away, equiv. to *ex-* EX-[1] + *pellere* to push, drive] —**ex·pel′la·ble,** *adj.*
—**Syn. 2.** oust, dismiss, exile, excommunicate.

ex·pel·lant (ik spel′ənt), *adj.* expelling, or having the power to expel. Also, **ex·pel′lent.** [1815–25; var. of *expellent* (see -ANT) < L *expellent-* (s. of *expellēns*), prp. of *expellere* to EXPEL; see -ENT]

ex·pel·lee (ek′spe lē′, -spə-, ik spel′ē), *n.* a person who has been expelled, esp. one deported from a native or adopted country and resettled in another. [1885–90; EXPEL + -EE]

ex·pel·ler (ik spel′ər), *n.* **1.** a person or thing that expels. **2.** a press used to extract oil from corn, soybeans, etc. [1570–80; EXPEL + -ER[1]]

ex·pend (ik spend′), *v.t.* **1.** to use up: *She expended energy, time, and care on her work.* **2.** to pay out; disburse; spend. [1400–50; late ME < L *expendere* to weigh out, lay out, pay] —**ex·pend′er,** *n.*
—**Syn. 1.** consume, empty. See **spend.**

ex·pend·a·ble (ik spen′də bəl), *adj.* **1.** capable of being expended. **2.** (of an item of equipment or supply) consumed in use or not reusable. **3.** considered to be not worth keeping or maintaining. **4.** *Mil.* (of personnel, equipment, or supplies) capable of being sacrificed in order to accomplish a military objective. —*n.* **5.** Usually, **expendables.** an expendable person or thing. [1795–1805; EXPEND + -ABLE] —**ex·pend′a·bil′i·ty,** *n.*

ex·pend·i·ture (ik spen′di chər), *n.* **1.** the act of expending something, esp. funds; disbursement; consumption. **2.** something that is expended; expense: *Unnecessary expenditures include those for luxury items.* [1760–70; < ML *expendit(us)* laid out, paid (var. of *expēnsus,* ptp. of *expendere;* see EXPEND) + -URE]

ex·pense (ik spens′), *n., v.,* **-pensed, -pens·ing.** —*n.* **1.** cost or charge: *the expense of a good meal.* **2.** a cause or occasion of spending: *A car can be a great expense.* **3.** the act of expending; expenditure. **4. expenses, a.** charges incurred during a business assignment or trip. **b.** money paid as reimbursement for such charges: *to receive a salary and expenses.* **5. at the expense of,** at the sacrifice of; to the detriment of: *quantity at the expense of quality.* —*v.t.* **6.** to charge or write off as an expense. —*v.i.* **7.** to be expensed. [1350–1400; ME < LL *expēnsa,* n. use of fem. of *expēnsus,* ptp. of *expendere* to EXPEND] —**ex·pense′less,** *adj.*
—**Syn. 1.** outlay, expenditure. See **price.**

expense′ account′, an account of business expenditures, as travel, hotel room, meals, and entertainment connected with work, for which an employee will be reimbursed by an employer. [1870–75]

CONCISE ETYMOLOGY KEY: <, descended or borrowed from; >, whence; b., blend of, blended; c., cognate with; cf., compare; deriv., derivative; equiv., equivalent; imit., imitative; obl., oblique; r., replacing; s., stem; sp., spelling, spelled; resp., respelling, respelled; trans., translation; ?, origin unknown; *, unattested; ‡, probably earlier than. See the full key inside the front cover.

ex•pen•sive (ik spen′siv), *adj.* entailing great expense; very high-priced; costly: *an expensive party.* [1620–30; EXPENSE + -IVE] —**ex•pen′sive•ly,** *adv.* —**ex•pen′sive•ness,** *n.*
—**Syn.** EXPENSIVE, COSTLY, DEAR, HIGH-PRICED apply to something that is high in price. EXPENSIVE is applied to whatever entails considerable expense; it suggests a price more than the average person would normally be able to pay or a price paid only for something special: *an expensive automobile.* COSTLY implies that the price is a large sum, usually because of the fineness, preciousness, etc., of the object: *a costly jewel.* DEAR is commonly applied in England to something that is selling beyond its usual or just price. In the U.S., HIGH-PRICED is the usual equivalent. —**Ant.** cheap, low-priced.

ex•pe•ri•ence (ik spēr′ē əns), *n., v.,* **-enced, -enc•ing.** —*n.* **1.** a particular instance of personally encountering or undergoing something: *My encounter with the bear in the woods was a frightening experience.* **2.** the process or fact of personally observing, encountering, or undergoing something: *business experience.* **3.** the observing, encountering, or undergoing of things generally as they occur in the course of time: *to learn from experience; the range of human experience.* **4.** knowledge or practical wisdom gained from what one has observed, encountered, or undergone: *a man of experience.* **5.** *Philos.* the totality of the cognitions given by perception; all that is perceived, understood, and remembered. —*v.t.* **6.** to have experience of; meet with; undergo; feel: *to experience nausea.* **7.** to learn by experience. **8. experience religion,** to undergo a spiritual conversion by which one gains or regains faith in God. [1350–1400; ME < L *experientia,* equiv. to *experient-* (s. of *experiēns,* ptp. of *experīrī* to try, test; see EX-[1], PERIL) + *-ia* n. suffix; see -ENCE] —**ex•pe′ri•ence•a•ble,** *adj.* —**ex•pe′ri•ence•less,** *adj.*
—**Syn. 6.** encounter, know, endure, suffer. EXPERIENCE, UNDERGO refer to encountering situations, conditions, etc., in life, or to having certain sensations or feelings. EXPERIENCE implies being affected by what one meets with: *to experience a change of heart, bitter disappointment.* UNDERGO usually refers to the bearing or enduring of something hard, difficult, disagreeable, or dangerous: *to undergo severe hardships, an operation.*

ex•pe•ri•enced (ik spēr′ē ənst), *adj.* **1.** wise or skillful in a particular field through experience: *an experienced teacher.* **2.** having learned through experience; taught by experience: *experienced through adversity.* **3.** endured; undergone; suffered through: *experienced misfortunes.* [1560–70; EXPERIENCE + -ED[2]]
—**Syn. 1.** skilled, expert, practiced, veteran, accomplished, versed, adept, qualified.

expe′rience meet′ing. See **testimony meeting.** [1865–70, *Amer.*]

ex•pe•ri•enc•er (ik spēr′ē ən sər), *n.* **1.** a person or thing that experiences. **2.** (in case grammar) the semantic role of a noun phrase that indicates the perceiver of the action or state of affairs specified by the verb, as *the boy* in *The boy was warm* or in *The fly annoyed the boy.* [1860–65; EXPERIENCE + -ER[1]]

expe′rience ta′ble, *Insurance.* See **mortality table.** [1875–80]

ex•pe•ri•en•tial (ik spēr′ē en′shəl), *adj.* pertaining to or derived from experience. [1640–50; < ML *experientiālis.* See EXPERIENCE, -AL[1]] —**ex•pe′ri•en′tial•ly,** *adv.*

ex•pe•ri•en•tial•ism (ik spēr′ē en′shə liz′əm), *n.* *Epistemology.* any doctrine or theory that maintains that personal experience is the only or the principal basis of knowledge. [1860–65; EXPERIENTIAL + -ISM] —**ex•pe′ri•en′tial•ist,** *n.* —**ex•pe′ri•en′tial•is′tic,** *adj.*

ex•per•i•ment (*n.* ik sper′ə mənt; *v.* ek sper′ə ment′), *n.* **1.** a test, trial, or tentative procedure; an act or operation for the purpose of discovering something unknown or of testing a principle, supposition, etc.: *a chemical experiment; a teaching experiment; an experiment in living.* **2.** the conducting of such operations; experimentation: *a product that is the result of long experiment.* **3.** *Obs.* experience. —*v.i.* **4.** to try or test, esp. in order to discover or prove something: *to experiment with a new procedure.* [1325–75; ME: proof < L *experīmentum.* See EXPERIENCE, -MENT] —**ex•per′i•ment′er, ex•per′i•men′tor, ex•per′i•men•ta′tor,** *n.*
—**Syn. 1.** See **trial. 2.** research, investigation.

ex•per•i•men•tal (ik sper′ə men′tl), *adj.* **1.** pertaining to, derived from, or founded on experiment: *an experimental science.* **2.** of the nature of an experiment; tentative: *The new program is still in an experimental stage.* **3.** functioning as an experiment or used for experimentation: *an experimental airplane.* **4.** based on or derived from experience; empirical: *experimental knowledge.* —*n.* **5.** something that is experimental. [1400–50; late ME < ML *experīmentālis.* See EXPERIMENT, -AL[1]] —**ex•per′i•men′tal•ly,** *adv.*

ex•per•i•men•tal•ism (ik sper′ə men′tl iz′əm), *n.* **1.** doctrine or practice of relying on experimentation; empiricism. **2.** fondness for experimenting or innovating: *The psychologists' children were raised in an atmosphere of vigorous experimentalism.* [1825–35; EXPERIMENTAL + -ISM] —**ex•per′i•men′tal•ist,** *n.*

experimen′tal psychol′ogy, the branch of psychology dealing with the study of emotional and mental activity, as learning, in humans and other animals by means of experimental methods. [1875–80]

exper′imen′tal the′ater, the presentation of innovative works and the development of new concepts and techniques in stage production. [1925–30]

ex•per•i•men•ta•tion (ik sper′ə men tā′shən, -mən-), *n.* the act, process, practice, or an instance of making experiments. [1665–75; EXPERIMENT + -ATION] —**ex•per•i•men•ta•tive** (ik sper′ə men′tə tiv), *adj.*

exper′iment sta′tion, an establishment in which experiments in a particular line of research or activity, as agriculture or mining, are systematically carried on. [1870–75, *Amer.*]

ex•pert (*n., v.* ek′spûrt; *adj.* ek′spûrt, ik spûrt′), *n.* **1.** a person who has special skill or knowledge in some particular field; specialist; authority: *a language expert.* **2.** *Mil.* **a.** the highest rating in rifle marksmanship, above that of marksman and sharpshooter. **b.** a person who has achieved such a rating. —*adj.* **3.** possessing special skill or knowledge; trained by practice; skillful or skilled (often fol. by *in* or *at*): *an expert driver; to be expert at driving a car.* **4.** pertaining to, coming from, or characteristic of an expert: *expert work; expert advice.* —*v.t.* **5.** to act as an expert for. [1325–75; ME (adj.) < L *expertus,* ptp. of *experīrī* to try, EXPERIENCE] —**ex•pert′ly,** *adv.* —**ex•pert′ness,** *n.*
—**Syn. 1.** connoisseur, master. **3.** experienced, proficient, dexterous. See **skillful.** —**Ant. 3.** unskillful.

ex•per•tise[1] (ek′spər tēz′), *n.* **1.** expert skill or knowledge; expertness; know-how: *business expertise.* **2.** a written opinion by an expert, as concerning the authenticity or value of a work of art, manuscript, etc. [1865–70; < F: survey, report (made by experts); *-ise* taken as an abstract n. suffix. See EXPERT, -ISE[2]]

ex•pert•ise[2] (ek′spər tīz′), *v.t., v.i.,* **-ised, -ising.** *Chiefly Brit.* expertize.

ex•pert•ism (ek′spər tiz′əm), *n.* expertness or skill, esp. in a specific field. [1885–90; EXPERT + -ISM]

ex•pert•ize (ek′spər tīz′), *v.t., v.i.,* **-ized, -iz•ing.** to study or investigate as an expert. Also, *esp. Brit.,* **expertise.** [1885–90; EXPERT + -IZE]

ex′pert sys′tem, *Computers.* a program that gives answers, solutions, or diagnoses, based on available information, by following procedures that attempt to duplicate the thought processes and apply the knowledge of an expert in some particular field. [1975–80]

ex′pert wit′ness, a person, as a physician, who provides testimony at a legal proceeding in the form of professional opinions.

ex•pi•a•ble (ek′spē ə bəl), *adj.* capable of being expiated: *an expiable crime.* [1560–70; < LL *expiābilis,* equiv. to *expiā(re)* to EXPIATE + *-bilis* -BLE]

ex•pi•ate (ek′spē āt′), *v.t.,* **-at•ed, -at•ing.** to atone for; make amends or reparation for: *to expiate one's crimes.* [1585–95; < L *expiātus* (ptp. of *expiāre* to atone for, make good), equiv. to *ex-* EX-[1] + *piā(re)* to propitiate (see PIOUS) + *-tus* ptp. suffix] —**ex′pi•a′tor,** *n.*

ex•pi•a•tion (ek′spē ā′shən), *n.* **1.** the act of expiating. **2.** the means by which atonement or reparation is made. [1375–1425; late ME *expiacioun* < L *expiātiōn-* (s. of *expiātiō*) atonement, satisfaction. See EXPIATE, -ION] —**ex′pi•a′tion•al,** *adj.*

ex•pi•a•to•ry (ek′spē ə tôr′ē, -tōr′ē), *adj.* able to make atonement or expiation; offered by way of expiation: *expiatory sacrifices.* [1540–50; < LL *expiātōrius,* equiv. to *expiā(re)* (see EXPIATE) + *-tōrius* -TORY[1]]

ex•pi•ra•tion (ek′spə rā′shən), *n.* **1.** a coming to an end; termination; close: *the expiration of a contract.* **2.** the act of expiring, or breathing out; emission of air from the lungs. **3.** *Archaic.* death. [1375–1425; late ME *expiracioun* < L *expīrātiōn-* (s. of *expīrātiō*), equiv. to *expīrāt(us)* (ptp. of *ex(s)pīrāre* to EXPIRE) + *-iōn-* -ION]

expira′tion date′, the last date that a product, as food, should be used before it is considered spoiled or ineffective, usually specified on the label or package.

ex•pir•a•to•ry (ik spīr′ə tôr′ē, -tōr′ē), *adj.* pertaining to the expiration of air from the lungs. [1840–50; EXPIRAT(ION) + -ORY[1]]

ex•pire (ik spīr′), *v.,* **-pired, -pir•ing.** —*v.i.* **1.** to come to an end; terminate, as a contract, guarantee, or offer. **2.** to emit the last breath; die. **3.** to breathe out. **4.** to die out, as a fire. —*v.t.* **5.** to breathe out; emit (air) from the lungs. **6.** *Archaic.* to give off, emit, or eject. [1375–1425; late ME < L *ex(s)pīrāre* to breathe out, equiv. to *ex-* EX-[1] + *spīrāre* to breathe] —**ex•pir′er,** *n.* —**ex•pir′ing•ly,** *adv.*

ex•pi•ry (ik spīᵊr′ē, ek′spə rē), *n., pl.* **-ries. 1.** expiration of breath. **2.** an end or termination, as of life or a contract. [1745–55; EXPIRE + -Y[3]]

ex•pis•cate (ek′spə skāt′, ek spis′kāt), *v.t.,* **-cat•ed, -cat•ing.** *Chiefly Scot.* to find out by thorough and detailed investigation; discover through scrupulous examination. [1605–15; < L *expiscātus,* ptp. of *expiscārī* to fish out. See EX-, PISCI-, -ATE[1]] —**ex′pis•ca′tion,** *n.* —**ex•pis•ca•to•ry** (ek spis′kə tôr′ē, -tōr′ē), *adj.*

ex•plain (ik splān′), *v.t.* **1.** to make plain or clear; render understandable or intelligible: *to explain an obscure point.* **2.** to make known in detail: *to explain how to do something.* **3.** to assign a meaning to; interpret: *How can you explain such a silly remark?* **4.** to make clear the cause or reason of; account for: *I cannot explain his strange behavior.* —*v.i.* **5.** to give an explanation. **6. explain away, a.** to diminish or nullify the significance of by explanation: *He couldn't explain away his absence from home at the time the robbery was committed.* **b.** to dispel (doubts, difficulties, etc.) by explanation: *She explained away the child's fears.* [1375–1425; late ME *explanen* < L *explānāre* to smooth out, make intelligible, spread out on flat surface. See EX-[1], PLANE[1]] —**ex•plain′a•ble,** *adj.* —**ex•plain′er, ex•pla•na•tor** (ek′splə nā′tər), *n.*
—**Syn. 1.** explicate. EXPLAIN, ELUCIDATE, EXPOUND, INTERPRET imply making the meaning of something clear or understandable. To EXPLAIN is to make plain, clear, or intelligible something that is not known or understood: *to explain a theory or a problem.* To ELUCIDATE is to throw light on what before was dark and obscure, usually by illustration and commentary and sometimes by elaborate explanation: *They asked him to elucidate his statement.* To EXPOUND is to give a methodical, detailed, scholarly explanation of something, usually Scriptures, doctrines, or philosophy: *to expound the doctrine of free will.* To INTERPRET is to give the meaning of something by paraphrase, by translation, or by an explanation based on personal opinion: *to interpret a poem or a symbol.* **4.** justify. —**Ant. 1.** confuse.

ex•pla•nate (eks′plə nāt′, eks plā′nāt), *adj. Bot., Zool.* flattened; spread out. [1840–50; < L *explānātus,* ptp. of *explānāre* to EXPLAIN; see -ATE[1]]

ex•pla•na•tion (ek′splə nā′shən), *n.* **1.** the act or process of explaining. **2.** something that explains; a statement made to clarify something and make it understandable; exposition: *an explanation of a poem.* **3.** a meaning or interpretation: *to find an explanation for a mystery.* **4.** a mutual declaration of the meaning of words spoken, actions, motives, etc., with a view to adjusting a misunderstanding or reconciling differences: *After a long and emotional explanation they were friends again.* [1350–1400; ME *explanacioun* < L *explānātiōn-* (s. of *explānātiō*), equiv. to *explānāt(us)* (see EXPLANATE) + *-iōn-* -ION]
—**Syn. 1.** elucidation, explication, exposition, interpretation, description. **3.** solution, key, answer.

ex•plan•a•to•ry (ik splan′ə tôr′ē, -tōr′ē), *adj.* serving to explain: *an explanatory footnote.* Also, **ex•plan′a•tive.** [1610–20; < LL *explānātōrius.* See EXPLAIN, -TORY[1]] —**ex•plan′a•to′ri•ly, ex•plan′a•tive•ly,** *adv.*

ex•plant (*v.* eks plant′, -plänt′; *n.* eks′plant′, -plänt′), *v.t.* **1.** to take living material from an animal or plant and place it in a culture medium. —*n.* **2.** a piece of explanted tissue. [1570–80; < NL *explantāre.* See EX-[1], PLANT] —**ex′plan•ta′tion,** *n.*

ex•ple•ment (ek′splə mənt), *n. Math.* the quantity by which an angle or an arc falls short of 360° or a circle. [1585–95; < L *explēmentum* that which fills up, equiv. to *explē(re)* to fill (*ex-* EX-[1] + *plēre* to fill) + *-mentum* -MENT] —**ex•ple•men•tal** (ek′splə men′tl), **ex•ple•men•ta•ry** (ek′splə men′tə rē, -trē), *adj.*

ex′plemen′tary an′gle, *Math.* either of two angles that added together produce an angle of 360°.

ex•ple•tive (ek′spli tiv), *n.* **1.** an interjectory word or expression, frequently profane; an exclamatory oath. **2.** a syllable, word, or phrase serving to fill out. **3.** *Gram.* a word considered as regularly filling the syntactic position of another, as *it* in *It is his duty to go,* or *there* in *There is nothing here.* —*adj.* **4.** Also, **ex•ple•to•ry** (ek′spli tôr′ē, -tōr′ē). added merely to fill out a sentence or line, give emphasis, etc.: *Expletive remarks padded the speech.* [1600–10; < LL *explētīvus* serving to fill out, equiv. to L *explēt(us)* filled, filled up (ptp. of *explēre;* see EXPLEMENT) + *-īvus* -IVE] —**ex′ple•tive•ly,** *adv.*

ex•pli•ca•ble (ek′spli kə bəl, ik splik′ə bəl), *adj.* capable of being explained. [1550–60; < L *explicābilis,* equiv. to *explicā(re)* to EXPLICATE + *-bilis* -BLE]

ex•pli•can•dum (ek′spli kan′dəm), *n., pl.* **-da** (-də). a term or statement that is to be explained, as in a philosophical discussion. [1865–70; < L, neut. of ger. of *explicāre* to EXPLICATE]

ex•pli•cans (ek′spli kanz′), *n., pl.* **-can•ti•a** (-kan′shē ə). the meaning of a term or statement, as in a philosophical discussion. [1880–85; < L, prp. of *explicāre* to EXPLICATE]

ex•pli•cate (ek′spli kāt′), *v.t.,* **-cat•ed, -cat•ing. 1.** to make plain or clear; explain; interpret. **2.** to develop (a principle, theory, etc.). [1525–35; < L *explicātus* unfolded, set forth, ptp. of *explicāre,* equiv. to *ex-* EX-[1] + *plicāre* to fold; see -ATE[1]] —**ex′pli•ca′tor,** *n.*

ex•pli•ca•tion (ek′spli kā′shən), *n.* **1.** the act of explicating. **2.** an explanation; interpretation: *He gave a brilliant explication of James Joyce's book.* [1520–30; < MF < L *explicātiōn-* (s. of *explicātiō*). See EXPLICATE, -ION]

ex•pli•ca•tion de texte (ek splē kä syôɴ də tekst′), *pl.* ***ex•pli•ca•tions de texte*** (ek splē kä syôɴ də tekst′). *French.* an approach to literary criticism involving close examination, analysis, and exposition of the text of a work, and concentrating on language, style, content, and the interrelationships of the parts to the whole in regard to meaning and symbolism. [lit., explanation of text]

ex•pli•ca•tive (ek′spli kā′tiv, ik splik′ə tiv), *adj.* explanatory; interpretive. Also, **ex•pli•ca•to•ry** (ek′spli kə tôr′ē, -tōr′ē, ik splik′ə-). [1620–30; < L *explicātīvus.* See EXPLICATE, -IVE] —**ex′pli•ca′tive•ly,** *adv.*

ex•plic•it (ik splis′it), *adj.* **1.** fully and clearly expressed or demonstrated; leaving nothing merely implied; unequivocal: *explicit instructions; an explicit act of violence; explicit language.* **2.** clearly developed or formulated: *explicit knowledge; explicit belief.* **3.** definite and unreserved in expression; outspoken: *He was quite explicit as to what he expected us to do for him.* **4.** described or shown in realistic detail: *explicit sexual scenes.* **5.** *Math.* (of a function) having the dependent variable expressed directly in terms of the independent variables, as $y = 3x + 4$. Cf. **implicit** (def. 4). [1605–15; < L *explicitus* unfolded, set forth, var. ptp. of *explicāre.* See EXPLICATE] —**ex•plic′it•ly,** *adv.* —**ex•plic′it•ness,** *n.*
—**Syn. 1.** express, definite, precise, exact, unambiguous. **3.** open, forthright, unabashed. —**Ant. 1.** indefinite, ambiguous.

ex•plode (ik splōd′), *v.,* **-plod•ed, -plod•ing.** —*v.i.* **1.** to expand with force and noise because of rapid chemical change or decomposition, as gunpowder or nitroglycerine (opposed to *implode*). **2.** to burst, fly into pieces, or break up violently with a loud report, as a boiler from excessive pressure of steam. **3.** to burst forth violently or emotionally, esp. with noise, laughter, violent speech, etc.: *He exploded with rage when contradicted.* **4.** *Phonet.* (of plosives) to terminate the occlusive phase with a plosion. Cf. **implode** (def. 2). **5.** *Golf.* to play an explosion shot on a golf ball. —*v.t.* **6.** to cause (gunpowder, a boiler, etc.) to explode. **7.** to cause to be rejected; destroy the repute of; discredit or disprove: *to explode a theory.* **8.** *Phonet.* to end with plosion. **9.** *Golf.* to play an explosion shot on (a golf ball). **10.** *Obs.* to drive (a player, play, etc.) from the stage by loud expressions of disapprobation. [1530–40; < L *explōdere* to drive off by

CONCISE PRONUNCIATION KEY: act, cāpe, dâre, pärt; set, ēqual; *if,* ice; ox, ōver, ôrder, oil, bŏŏk, bōōt, out; up, ûrge; child; sing; shoe; thin, that; zh as in *treasure.* ə = *a* as in *alone,* e as in *system,* i as in *easily,* o as in *gallop,* u as in *circus;* ᵊ as in *fire* (fīᵊr), *hour* (ouᵊr). l and n can serve as syllabic consonants, as in *cradle* (krād′l), and *button* (but′n). See the full key inside the front cover.

clapping, drive away, equiv. to *ex-* EX-[1] + *plod-* var. s. of *plaudere* to clap, beat] —**ex·plod′er,** *n.*

explod′ed view′, a drawing, photograph, or the like, that shows the individual parts of a mechanism separately but indicates their proper relationship. [1960–65]

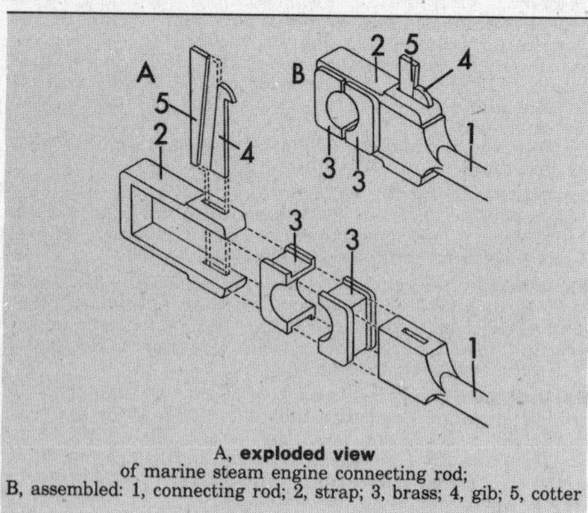

A, **exploded view** of marine steam engine connecting rod; B, assembled: 1, connecting rod; 2, strap; 3, brass; 4, gib; 5, cotter

ex·plod·ent (ik splōd′nt), *n.* an explosive. [1860–65; < L *explōdent-* (s. of *explōdēns*), prp. of *explōdere* to EXPLODE; see -ENT]

ex·ploit[1] (ek′sploit, ik sploit′), *n.* a striking or notable deed; feat; spirited or heroic act: *the exploits of Alexander the Great.* [1350–1400; ME *exploit, espleit* < OF *exploit,* AF *espleit* < L *explicitum,* neut. of *explicitus* (ptp.). See EXPLICIT]
—**Syn.** accomplishment. See **achievement.**

ex·ploit[2] (ik sploit′), *v.t.* **1.** to utilize, esp. for profit; turn to practical account: *to exploit a business opportunity.* **2.** to use selfishly for one's own ends: *employers who exploit their workers.* **3.** to advance or further through exploitation; promote: *He exploited his new movie through a series of guest appearances.* [1375–1425; < F *exploiter,* deriv. of *exploit* (n.); r. late ME *expleiten* to achieve < AF *espleiter,* deriv. of *espleit* (n.). See EXPLOIT[1]] —**ex·ploit′a·ble,** *adj.* —**ex·ploit′a·bil′i·ty,** *n.* —**ex·ploit′a·tive, ex·ploit·a·to·ry** (ik sploi′tə tôr′ē, -tōr′ē), **ex·ploit′ive,** *adj.* —**ex·ploit′er,** *n.*

ex·ploi·ta·tion (ek′sploi tā′shən), *n.* **1.** use or utilization, esp. for profit: *the exploitation of newly discovered oil fields.* **2.** selfish utilization: *He got ahead through the exploitation of his friends.* **3.** the combined, often varied, use of public-relations and advertising techniques to promote a person, movie, product, etc. [1795–1805; < F; see EXPLOIT, -ATION] —**ex′ploi·ta′tion·al,** *adj.* —**ex′ploi·ta′tion·al·ly,** *adv.*

ex·plo·ra·tion (ek′splə rā′shən), *n.* **1.** an act or instance of exploring or investigating; examination. **2.** the investigation of unknown regions. [1535–45; < L *explōrātiōn-* (s. of *explōrātiō*) an examination, equiv. to *explōrāt(us)* searched out, examined (ptp. of *explōrāre* to EXPLORE) + *-iōn-* -ION]

ex·plo·ra·tion·ist (ek′splə rā′shə nist), *n.* a person who searches for new sources of oil, natural gas, etc. [EXPLORATION + -IST]

ex·plor·a·to·ry (ik splôr′ə tôr′ē, -splōr′ə tōr′ē), *adj.* **1.** pertaining to or concerned with exploration: *an exploratory operation.* **2.** inclined to make explorations. Also, **ex·plor′a·tive.** [1425–75; late ME < L *explōrātōrius.* See EXPLORATION, -ORY[1]] —**ex·plor′a·tive·ly,** *adv.*

ex·plore (ik splôr′, -splōr′), *v.,* **-plored, -plor·ing.** —*v.t.* **1.** to traverse or range over (a region, area, etc.) for the purpose of discovery: *to explore the island.* **2.** to look into closely; scrutinize; examine: *Let us explore the possibilities for improvement.* **3.** *Surg.* to investigate into, esp. mechanically, as with a probe. **4.** *Obs.* to search for; search out. —*v.i.* **5.** to engage in exploration. [1575–85; < L *explōrāre* to search out, examine, equiv. to *ex-* EX-[1] + *plōrāre* to cry out, prob. orig. with reference to hunting cries] —**ex·plor′a·ble,** *adj.* —**ex·plor′a·bil′i·ty,** *n.* —**ex·plor′ing·ly,** *adv.*
—**Syn. 2.** probe, study, research, investigate, survey.

ex·plor·er (ik splôr′ər, -splōr′-), *n.* **1.** a person or thing that explores. **2.** a person who investigates unknown regions: *the great explorers of the Renaissance.* **3.** any instrument used in exploring or sounding a wound, a cavity in a tooth, or the like. **4.** (*cap.*) Also called **Explor′er Scout′.** a person between the ages 14 and 20 who is an active participant in the exploring program sponsored by the Boy Scouts of America. **5.** (*cap.*) *Aerospace.* one of a long series of U.S. scientific satellites: *Explorer 1* (1958) was the first U.S. artificial satellite. [1675–85; EXPLORE + -ER[1]]

explor′er tent′, a low, wide tent having a ridgepole and affording considerable sleeping space but very little headroom.

ex·plo·si·ble (ik splō′zə bəl, -sə-), *adj.* **1.** capable of being exploded. **2.** liable to explode. [1790–1800; EXPLOS(ION) + -IBLE] —**ex·plo′si·bil′i·ty,** *n.*

ex·plo·sim·e·ter (ek′splō zim′i tər, -sim′-), *n.* a device for measuring the concentration of potentially explosive fumes. [EXPLOSI(BILITY) + -METER]

ex·plo·sion (ik splō′zhən), *n.* **1.** an act or instance of exploding; a violent expansion or bursting with noise, as of gunpowder or a boiler (opposed to *implosion*). **2.** the noise itself: *The loud explosion woke them.* **3.** a violent outburst, as of laughter or anger. **4.** a sudden, rapid, or great increase: *a population explosion.* **5.** the burning of the mixture of fuel and air in an internal-combustion engine. **6.** *Phonet.* plosion. [1615–25; < L *explōsiōn-* (s. of *explōsiō*), equiv. to *explōs(us)* driven off by clapping (ptp. of *explōdere* to EXPLODE) + *-iōn-* -ION]

explo′sion shot′, *Golf.* a shot for playing a golf ball out of a sand trap in which the club is swung down into the sand just under and behind the ball. [1925–30]

ex·plo·sive (ik splō′siv), *adj.* **1.** tending or serving to explode: *an explosive temper; Nitroglycerin is an explosive substance.* **2.** pertaining to or of the nature of an explosion: *explosive violence.* **3.** likely to lead to violence or hostility: *an explosive issue.* **4.** *Phonet.* plosive. —*n.* **5.** an explosive agent or substance, as dynamite. **6.** *Phonet.* plosive. [1660–70; EXPLOS(ION) + -IVE] —**ex·plo′sive·ly,** *adv.* —**ex·plo′sive·ness,** *n.*

explosive D, dunnite.

explo′sive form′ing, the formation of objects from sheet metal in dies by the force of an explosive charge.

explo′sive riv′et, a rivet for driving into an inaccessible area, containing an explosive charge detonated after driving to expand the shank on the far side of the hole. [1945–50]

explo′sive weld′ing, welding by means of a controlled explosion that rapidly forces two pieces of metal together.

ex·po (ek′spō) *n., pl.* **-pos.** (*often cap.*) **1.** a world's fair or international exposition: *Expo '67 in Montreal.* **2.** any exhibition or show: *an annual computer expo.* [1960–65; by shortening]

ex·po·nent (ik spō′nənt *or, esp. for 3,* ek′spō nənt), *n.* **1.** a person or thing that expounds, explains, or interprets: *an exponent of modern theory in the arts.* **2.** a person or thing that is a representative, advocate, type, or symbol of something: *Lincoln is an exponent of American democracy.* **3.** *Math.* a symbol or number placed above and after another symbol or number to denote the power to which the latter is to be raised: *The exponents of the quantities* x^n, 2^m, y^4, *and* 3^5 *are, respectively, n, m, 4, and 5.* [1575–85; < L *expōnent-* (s. of *expōnēns*), prp. of *expōnere* to EXPOUND; see -ENT]
—**Syn. 1.** supporter, champion, proponent, promoter. **2.** embodiment, personification.

ex·po·nen·tial (ek′spō nen′shəl, -spə-), *adj.* **1.** of or pertaining to an exponent or exponents. **2.** *Math.* **a.** of or pertaining to the constant *e.* **b.** (of an equation) having one or more unknown variables in one or more exponents. —*n.* **3.** *Math.* **a.** the constant *e* raised to the power equal to a given expression, as e^{3x}, which is the exponential of $3x$. **b.** any positive constant raised to a power. [1695–1705; EXPONENT + -IAL] —**ex′po·nen′tial·ly,** *adv.*

ex′ponen′tial curve′, the graph of an equation of the form $y = ba^x$, where *a* and *b* are positive constants. [1695–1705]

ex′ponen′tial func′tion, *Math.* **1.** the function $y = e^x$. **2.** any function of the form $y = ba^x$, where *a* and *b* are positive constants. **3.** any function in which a variable appears as an exponent and may also appear as a base, as $y = x^{2x}$. [1890–95]

ex′ponen′tial horn′, a loudspeaker horn with a cross-sectional area varying as a constant raised to an exponent proportional to the distance from the vertex. [1925–30]

ex·po·nen·ti·a·tion (ek′spō nen′shē ā′shən, -spə-), *n.* *Math.* the raising of a number to any given power. [1900–05; EXPONENTI(AL) + -ATION, on model of SUBSTANTIATION, DIFFERENTIATION, etc.]

ex·po·ni·ble (ik spō′nə bəl), *Logic.* —*adj.* **1.** (of a proposition) requiring an expanded and revised statement to remove some obscurity. —*n.* **2.** an exponible proposition. [1560–70; < ML *expōnibilis.* See EXPOUND, -IBLE]

ex·port (*v.* ik spôrt′, -spōrt′, ek′spôrt, -spōrt; *n., adj.* ek′spôrt, -spōrt), *v.t.* **1.** to ship (commodities) to other countries or places for sale, exchange, etc. **2.** to send or transmit (ideas, institutions, etc.) to another place, esp. to another country. —*v.i.* **3.** to ship commodities to another country for sale, exchange, etc. —*n.* **4.** the act of exporting; exportation: *the export of coffee.* **5.** something that is exported; an article exported: *Coffee is a major export of Colombia.* —*adj.* **6.** of or pertaining to the exportation of goods or to exportable goods: *export duties.* **7.** produced for export: *an export beer.* [1475–85; < L *exportāre* to carry out, bear away, equiv. to *ex-* EX-[1] + *portāre* to carry, bear] —**ex·port′a·ble,** *adj.* —**ex·port′a·bil′i·ty,** *n.* —**ex·port′er,** *n.*

ex·por·ta·tion (ek′spôr tā′shən, -spōr-), *n.* **1.** the act of exporting; the sending of commodities out of a country, typically in trade. **2.** something exported. [1600–10; < L *exportātiōn-* (s. of *exportātiō*), equiv. to *exportāt(us)* (ptp. of *exportāre* to EXPORT) + *-iōn-* -ION]

Ex′port-Im′port Bank′ (ek′spôrt im′pôrt, ek′spōrt im′pōrt), a U.S. federal bank, established in 1934, that is authorized, in the interest of promoting foreign trade, to make loans to foreign governments and commercial enterprises, with the provision that such funds be used only to purchase U.S. goods.

ex·pos·al (ik spō′zəl), *n.* exposure. [1645–55; EXPOSE + -AL[2]]

ex·pose (ik spōz′), *v.t.,* **-posed, -pos·ing.** **1.** to lay open to danger, attack, harm, etc.: *to expose soldiers to gunfire; to expose one's character to attack.* **2.** to lay open to something specified: *to expose oneself to the influence of bad companions.* **3.** to uncover or bare to the air, cold, etc.: *to expose one's head to the rain.* **4.** to present to view; exhibit; display: *The storekeeper exposed his wares.* **5.** to make known, disclose, or reveal (intentions, secrets, etc.). **6.** to reveal or unmask (a crime, fraud, impostor, etc.): *to expose a swindler.* **7.** to hold up to public reprehension or ridicule (fault, folly, a foolish act or person, etc.). **8.** to desert in an unsheltered or open place; abandon, as a child. **9.** to subject, as to the action of something: *to expose a photographic plate to light.* **10. expose oneself,** to exhibit one's body, esp. one's genitals, publicly in an immodest or exhibitionistic manner. [1425–75; late ME *exposen* < OF *exposer,* equiv. to *ex-* EX-[1] + *poser* to put (see POSE[1]), rendering L *expōnere* to put out, expose, set forth in words; see EXPOUND] —**ex·pos′a·ble,** *adj.* —**ex·pos′a·bil′i·ty,** *n.* —**ex·pos′er,** *n.*
—**Syn. 1.** subject, endanger, imperil, jeopardize. **5.** uncover, unveil, betray. —**Ant. 2.** protect, shield. **5.** conceal, hide, cover up.

ex·po·sé (ek′spō zā′), *n.* a public exposure or revelation, as of something discreditable: *Certain cheap magazines make a fortune out of sensational exposés.* [1795–1805; < F, n. use of ptp. of *exposer* to EXPOSE]

ex·posed (ik spōzd′), *adj.* **1.** left or being without shelter or protection: *The house stood on a windy, exposed cliff.* **2.** laid open to view; unconcealed: *an exposed king of spades.* **3.** susceptible to attack; vulnerable. [1620–30; EXPOSE + -ED[2]] —**ex·pos·ed·ness** (ik spō′zid nis), *n.*

ex·pos·it (ik spoz′it), *v.t.* to expound, as a theory, cause, or the like. [1880–85; < L *expositus,* ptp. of *expōnere;* see EXPOSE, EXPOUND]

ex·po·si·tion (ek′spə zish′ən), *n.* **1.** a large-scale public exhibition or show, as of art or manufactured products: *an exposition of 19th-century paintings; an automobile exposition.* **2.** the act of expounding, setting forth, or explaining: *the exposition of a point of view.* **3.** writing or speech primarily intended to convey information or to explain; a detailed statement or explanation; explanatory treatise: *The students prepared expositions on familiar essay topics.* **4.** the act of presenting to view; display: *The singer gave a splendid exposition of vocal talent.* **5.** exposure (def. 10). **6.** the state of being exposed; exposure. **7.** *Music.* the first section of a fugue or a sonata form, in which the principal themes normally are introduced. **8.** (in a play, novel, etc.) dialogue, description, etc., that gives the audience or reader the background of the characters and the present situation. [1300–50; ME *exposicioun* < L *expositiōn-* (s. of *expositiō*), equiv. to *exposit(us)* (see EXPOSE) + *-iōn-* -ION] —**ex′po·si′tion·al,** *adj.*
—**Syn. 1.** exhibit, demonstration, display, presentation. **3.** elucidation, commentary; critique, interpretation, exegesis, explication.

ex·pos·i·tor (ik spoz′i tər), *n.* a person who expounds or gives an exposition. [1300–50; ME (< AF) < LL *expositor* exegete (L: one who exposes a child), equiv. to *exposi-,* var. s. of *expōnere* (see EXPOSE) + *-tor* -TOR] —**ex·pos·i·to·ri·al** (ik spoz′i tôr′ē əl, -tōr′-), *adj.* —**ex·pos′i·to′ri·al·ly,** *adv.*

ex·pos·i·to·ry (ik spoz′i tôr′ē, -tōr′ē), *adj.* of the nature of exposition; serving to expound, set forth, or explain: *an expository essay; expository writing.* Also, **ex·pos′i·tive.** [1590–1600; < ML *expositōrius.* See EXPOSITOR, -TORY[1]] —**ex·pos′i·to′ri·ly, ex·pos′i·tive·ly,** *adv.*

ex post (eks pōst′), based on analysis of past performance (opposed to *ex ante*). [1635–45; < L: from (what lies) behind, according to (what lies) behind]

ex post fac·to (eks′ pōst′ fak′tō), **1.** from or by subsequent action; subsequently; retrospectively; retroactively. **2.** having retroactive force; made or done subsequently: *an ex post facto law.* [1625–35; < L: from a thing done afterward, from what is done afterward]

ex·pos·tu·late (ik spos′chə lāt′), *v.i.,* **-lat·ed, -lat·ing.** to reason earnestly with someone against something that person intends to do or has done; remonstrate: *His father expostulated with him about the evils of gambling.* [1525–35; < L *expostulātus* demanded urgently, required (ptp. of *expostulāre*). See EX-[1], POSTULATE] —**ex·pos′tu·lat′ing·ly,** *adv.* —**ex·pos′tu·la′tor,** *n.*
—**Syn.** dispute, argue, protest; exhort, counsel.

ex·pos·tu·la·tion (ik spos′chə lā′shən), *n.* **1.** the act of expostulating; remonstrance; earnest and kindly protest: *In spite of my expostulations, he insisted on driving me home.* **2.** an expostulatory remark or address. [1580–90; < L *expostulātiōn-* (s. of *expostulātiō*) complaint. See EXPOSTULATE, -ION]

ex·pos·tu·la·to·ry (ik spos′chə lə tôr′ē, -tōr′ē), *adj.* expostulating; conveying expostulation. Also, **ex·pos·tu·la·tive** (ik spos′chə lā′tiv). [1580–90; EXPOSTULATE + -ORY[1]]

ex·po·sure (ik spō′zhər), *n.* **1.** the act of exposing. **2.** the fact or state of being exposed. **3.** disclosure, as of something private or secret: *the exposure of their invasion plans.* **4.** an act or instance of revealing or unmasking, as an impostor, crime, or fraud: *the exposure of graft and corruption.* **5.** presentation to view, esp. in an open or public manner: *His exposure of his anger shocked the company.* **6.** a laying open or subjecting to the action or influence of something: *exposure to the measles; The exposure of his theories to ridicule destroyed his self-confidence.* **7.** the condition of being exposed without protection to the effects of harsh weather, esp. the cold: *to suffer from exposure.* **8.** *Photog.* **a.** the act of presenting a photosensitive surface to rays of light. **b.** the total amount of light received by a photosensitive surface or an area of such a surface, expressed as the product of the degree of illumination and the period of illumination. **c.** the image resulting from the effects of light rays on a photosensitive surface. **9.** situation with regard to sunlight or wind; aspect: *a southern exposure.* **10.** a putting out or deserting, esp. of a child, without shelter or protection; abandonment. **11.** something exposed, as to view; an exposed surface: *exposures of rock.* **12.** public appearance, esp. on the mass media. **13.** a prominent, often overextended position or commitment, as in investment, that is considered precarious and risky: *The bank was nervous about its exposure in Iran.* [1595–1605; EXPOSE + -URE]
—**Syn. 3.** divulgement, revelation, exposé. **5.** display.
—**Ant. 1.** concealment.

expo′sure dose′, *Physics.* a measure of radiation based on the ability to produce ionization: expressed in roentgens. Also called **dose.**

CONCISE ETYMOLOGY KEY: <, descended or borrowed from; >, whence; b., blend of, blended; c., cognate with; cf., compare; deriv., derivative; equiv., equivalent; imit., imitative; obl., oblique; r., replacing; s., stem; sp., spelling, spelled; resp., respelling, respelled; trans., translation; ?, origin unknown; *, unattested; ‡, probably earlier than. See the full key inside the front cover.

expo′sure in′dex, *Photog.* a figure indicating the proper exposure for a film of a certain speed in a certain light.

expo′sure me′ter, *Photog.* an instrument for measuring the intensity of light in a certain place or upon a certain object, having an adjustable scale for determining the optimum relations of shutter speeds and stops at each intensity. Also called **light meter.** [1890–95]

ex•pound (ik spound′), *v.t.* **1.** to set forth or state in detail: *to expound theories.* **2.** to explain; interpret. —*v.i.* **3.** to make a detailed statement (often fol. by *on*). [1250–1300; ME *expounen, expounden* < OF *espondre* < L *expōnere* to put out, set forth, explain, equiv. to *ex-* EX-[1] + *pōnere* to put] —**ex•pound′er,** *n.*
—**Syn. 2.** See **explain.**

ex-pres•i•dent (eks′prez′i dənt), *n.* a former president: *ex-president of the company.* [1790–1800, *Amer.*]

ex•press (ik spres′), *v.t.* **1.** to put (thought) into words; utter or state: *to express an idea clearly.* **2.** to show, manifest, or reveal: *to express one's anger.* **3.** to set forth the opinions, feelings, etc., of (oneself), as in speaking, writing, or painting: *He can express himself eloquently.* **4.** to represent by a symbol, character, figure, or formula: *to express water as H_2O; to express unknown quantities algebraically.* **5.** to send by express: *to express a package or merchandise.* **6.** to press or squeeze out: *to express the juice of grapes.* **7.** to exude or emit (a liquid, odor, etc.), as if under pressure: *The roses expressed a sweet perfume.* **8.** *Genetics.* (of a gene) to be active in the production of (a protein or a phenotype). —*adj.* **9.** clearly indicated; distinctly stated; definite; explicit; plain: *He defied my express command.* **10.** special; definite: *We have an express purpose in being here.* **11.** direct or fast, esp. making few or no intermediate stops: *an express train; an express elevator.* **12.** used for direct or high-speed travel: *an express highway.* **13.** duly or exactly formed or represented: *an express image.* **14.** pertaining to an express: *an express agency.* —*n.* **15.** an express train, bus, elevator, etc. **16.** a system or method of sending freight, parcels, money, etc., that is faster and safer, but more expensive, than ordinary freight service: *We agree to send the package by express.* **17.** a company engaged in this business. **18.** *Brit.* a messenger or a message specially sent. **19.** something sent by express. —*adv.* **20.** by express: *to travel express.* **21.** *Obs.* expressly. [1275–1325; ME *expressen* < L *expressus* (ptp. of *exprimere*). See EX-[1], PRESS[1]] —**ex•press′er, ex•pres′sor,** *n.* —**ex•press′i•ble,** *adj.* —**ex•press′less,** *adj.*
—**Syn. 1.** declare, word, formulate. **2.** indicate. **4.** designate, signify, denote. **9.** obvious, unambiguous. **10.** particular, singular. **11.** swift, rapid, nonstop. **13.** accurate, precise. **16.** courier. —**Ant. 2.** conceal.

ex•press•age (ik spres′ij), *n.* **1.** the business of transmitting parcels, money, etc., by express. **2.** the charge for such transmission. [1855–60, *Amer.;* EXPRESS + -AGE]

express′ deliv′ery, *Brit.* See **special delivery.** [1890–1895]

expressed′ al′mond oil′. See **almond oil** (def. 1).

ex•pres•sion (ik spresh′ən), *n.* **1.** the act of expressing or setting forth in words: *the free expression of political opinions.* **2.** a particular word, phrase, or form of words: *old-fashioned expressions.* **3.** the manner or form in which a thing is expressed in words; wording; phrasing: *delicacy of expression.* **4.** the power of expressing in words: *joy beyond expression.* **5.** indication of feeling, spirit, character, etc., as on the face, in the voice, or in artistic execution: *the lyric expression embodied in his poetry.* **6.** a look or intonation expressing personal reaction, feeling, etc.: *a shocked expression.* **7.** the quality or power of expressing an attitude, emotion, etc.: *a face that lacks expression; to read with expression.* **8.** the act of expressing or representing, as by symbols. **9.** *Math.* a symbol or a combination of symbols representing a value, relation, or the like. **10.** *Ling.* the stylistic characteristics of an utterance (opposed to *meaning*). **11.** *Ling.* the system of verbal utterances specific to a language (opposed to *content*). **12.** the act of expressing or pressing out. **13.** *Computers.* a combination of variables, constants, and functions linked by operation symbols and any required punctuation that describe a rule for calculating a value. **14.** *Genetics.* **a.** the action of a gene in the production of a protein or a phenotype. **b.** expressivity (def. 2). [1425–75; late ME < L *expressiōn-* (s. of *expressiō*) a pressing out. See EXPRESS, -ION] —**ex•pres′sion•al,** *adj.* —**ex•pres′sion•less,** *adj.* —**ex•pres′sion•less•ly,** *adv.*
—**Syn. 1.** utterance, declaration, assertion, statement. **2.** term, idiom. See **phrase. 3.** language, diction, phraseology. **5.** manifestation, sign. **6.** aspect, air.

Ex•pres•sion•ism (ik spresh′ə niz′əm), *n.* **1.** *Fine Arts.* **a.** (*usually l.c.*) a manner of painting, drawing, sculpting, etc., in which forms derived from nature are distorted or exaggerated and colors are intensified for emotive or expressive purposes. **b.** a style of art developed in the 20th century, characterized chiefly by heavy, often black lines that define forms, sharply contrasting, often vivid colors, and subjective or symbolic treatment of thematic material. **c.** *German,* ***Ex•pres•si•o•nis•mus*** (eks pres′ē ō nis′mo͝os). modern art, esp. the experimental or nonacademic styles of contemporary art. **2.** (*often l.c.*) *Theat.* a style of playwriting and stage presentation stressing the emotional content of a play, the subjective reactions of the characters, symbolic or abstract representations of reality, and nonnaturalistic techniques of scenic design. **3.** *Literature.* a technique of distorting objects and events in order to represent them as they are perceived by a character in a literary work. **4.** (*usually l.c.*) a phase in the development of early 20th-century music marked by the use of atonality and complex, unconventional rhythm, melody, and form, intended to express the composer's psychological and emotional life. [1905–10; < G *Expressionismus.* See EXPRESSION, -ISM] —**Ex•pres′sion•ist,** *n., adj.* —**Ex•pres′sion•is′tic,** *adj.* —**Ex•pres′sion•is′ti•cal•ly,** *adv.*

ex•pres•sive (ik spres′iv), *adj.* **1.** full of expression; meaningful: *an expressive shrug.* **2.** serving to express; indicative of power to express: *a look expressive of gratitude.* **3.** of, pertaining to, or concerned with expression: *Dance is a highly expressive art.* **4.** *Sociol.* (of a crowd or group) engaging in nonpurposeful activity of an expressive and often rhythmic nature, as weeping, dancing, or shouting. Cf. **active** (def. 15), **orgiastic** (def. 2). **5.** *Ling.* of or pertaining to forms in which sounds denote a semantic field directly and nonarbitrarily, through sound symbolism based, to some degree, on synesthesia, as observable in onomatopoeia, rhyming and gradational compounds, and emotionally charged words such as hypocoristics and pejoratives. [1350–1400; ME < MF; see EXPRESS, -IVE] —**ex•pres′sive•ly,** *adv.* —**ex•pres′sive•ness,** *n.*
—**Syn. 1, 2.** EXPRESSIVE, MEANINGFUL, SIGNIFICANT, SUGGESTIVE imply the conveying of a thought, indicating an attitude of mind, or the like, by words or otherwise. EXPRESSIVE suggests conveying, or being capable of conveying, a thought, intention, emotion, etc., in an effective or vivid manner: *an expressive gesture.* MEANINGFUL and SIGNIFICANT imply an underlying and unexpressed thought whose existence is plainly shown although its precise nature is left to conjecture. MEANINGFUL implies a secret and intimate understanding between the persons involved: *Meaningful looks passed between them.* SIGNIFICANT suggests conveying important or hidden meaning: *On hearing this statement, he gave the officers a significant glance.* SUGGESTIVE implies an indirect or covert conveying of a meaning, sometimes mentally stimulating, sometimes verging on impropriety or indecency: *a suggestive story or remark.* See also **eloquent.**

ex•pres•siv•i•ty (ek′spre siv′i tē), *n.* **1.** the quality or state of being expressive. **2.** *Genetics.* the degree to which a particular gene produces its effect in an organism. Cf. **penetrance.** [1930–35; < G *Expressivität.* See EXPRESSIVE, -ITY]

express′ lane′. See **fast lane** (def. 1).

ex•press•ly (ik spres′lē), *adv.* **1.** for the particular or specific purpose; specially: *I came expressly to see you.* **2.** in an express manner; explicitly: *I asked him expressly to stop talking.* [1350–1400; ME; see EXPRESS, -LY]

Express′ Mail′, *Trademark.* an expedited domestic mailing service of the U.S. Postal Service, usually guaranteeing delivery overnight or within 24 hours. —**ex•press′-mail′,** *adj.*

ex•press•man (ik spres′mən, -man′), *n., pl.* **-men** (-mən, -men′). a person who makes collections or deliveries for an express company. [1830–40, *Amer.;* EXPRESS + MAN[1]]

ex•pres•so (ik spres′ō), *n., pl.* **-sos.** espresso. [by assoc. with EXPRESS]

express′ ri′fle, a rifle designed for firing at game at short range. [1880–85]

express′ war′ranty, a warranty stated explicitly in writing by the seller of merchandise or real property who is legally liable for its defects (distinguished from *implied warranty*).

ex•press•way (ik spres′wā′), *n.* a highway especially planned for high-speed traffic, usually having few if any intersections, limited points of access or exit, and a divider between lanes for traffic moving in opposite directions. Also called **limited access highway.** Cf. **superhighway.** [1940–45; EXPRESS + WAY]

ex•pro•pri•ate (eks prō′prē āt′), *v.t.,* **-at•ed, -at•ing. 1.** to take possession of, esp. for public use by the right of eminent domain, thus divesting the title of the private owner: *The government expropriated the land for a recreation area.* **2.** to dispossess (a person) of ownership: *The revolutionary government expropriated the landowners from their estates.* **3.** to take (something) from another's possession for one's own use: *He expropriated my ideas for his own article.* [1605–15; < ML *expropriātus* separated from one's own (ptp. of *expropriāre*), equiv. to *ex-* EX-[1] + *propri(āre)* to appropriate (deriv. of *proprius* PROPER) + *-ātus* -ATE[1]] —**ex•pro•pri•a•ble** (eks prō′prē ə bəl), *adj.* —**ex•pro′pri•a′tion,** *n.* —**ex•pro′pri•a′tion•ist,** *adj., n.* —**ex•pro′pri•a′tor,** *n.*

expt., experiment.

exptl., experimental.

ex•pugn•a•ble (ek spyo͞o′nə bəl, -spug′nə-), *adj.* able to be overcome, conquered, defeated, etc. [1560–70; < L *expugnābilis,* equiv. to *expugnā(re)* to take by storm (*ex-* EX-[1] + *pugnāre* to fight) + *-bilis* -BLE]

ex•pulse (ik spuls′), *v.t.,* **-pulsed, -puls•ing.** *Obs.* to expel. [< L *expulsus;* see EXPULSION]

ex•pul•sion (ik spul′shən), *n.* **1.** the act of driving out or expelling: *expulsion of air.* **2.** the state of being expelled: *The prisoner's expulsion from society embittered him.* [1350–1400; ME < L *expulsiōn-* (s. of *expulsiō*), equiv. to *expuls(us)* driven out (ptp. of *expellere* to EXPEL) + *-iōn-* -ION]

ex•pul•sive (ik spul′siv), *adj.* tending or serving to expel. [1350–1400; ME < MF *expulsive* (fem.) < ML *expulsīvus.* See EXPULSION, -IVE]

ex•punc•tion (ik spungk′shən), *n.* the act of expunging; erasure. [1600–10; < LL *expūnctiōn-* (s. of *expūnctiō*) a blotting out, equiv. to L *expūnct(us)* blotted out (ptp. of *expungere* to EXPUNGE) + *-iōn-* -ION]

ex•punge (ik spunj′), *v.t.,* **-punged, -pung•ing. 1.** to strike or blot out; erase; obliterate. **2.** to efface; wipe out or destroy. [1595–1605; < L *expungere* to blot out, erase, equiv. to *ex-* EX-[1] + *pungere* to prick] —**ex•pung′er,** *n.*

ex•pur•gate (ek′spər gāt′), *v.t.,* **-gat•ed, -gat•ing. 1.** to amend by removing words, passages, etc., deemed offensive or objectionable: *Most children read an expurgated version of Grimms' fairy tales.* **2.** to purge or cleanse of moral offensiveness. [1615–25; < L *expurgātus,* ptp. of *expurgāre* to clean out. See EX-[1], PURGE, -ATE[1]] —**ex′pur•ga′tion,** *n.* —**ex′pur•ga′tor,** *n.*
—**Syn. 1.** delete, excise, censor, purge, bowdlerize.

ex•pur•ga•to•ri•al (ik spûr′gə tôr′ē əl, -tōr′-), *adj.* pertaining to an expurgator or to expurgation. [1800–10; EXPURGATOR(Y) + -IAL]

ex•pur•ga•to•ry (ik spûr′gə tôr′ē, -tōr′ē), *adj.* **1.** serving to expurgate. **2.** of or pertaining to expurgation. [1615–25; EXPURGATE + -ORY[1]]

ex•quis•ite (ik skwiz′it, ek′skwi zit), *adj.* **1.** of special beauty or charm, or rare and appealing excellence, as a face, a flower, coloring, music, or poetry. **2.** extraordinarily fine or admirable; consummate: *exquisite weather.* **3.** intense, acute, or keen, as pleasure or pain. **4.** of rare excellence of production or execution, as works of art or workmanship: *the exquisite statues of the Renaissance.* **5.** keenly or delicately sensitive or responsive: *an exquisite ear for music; an exquisite sensibility.* **6.** of particular refinement or elegance, as taste, manners, etc., or persons. **7.** carefully sought out, chosen, ascertained, devised, etc. —*n.* **8.** *Archaic.* a person, esp. a man, who is excessively concerned about clothes, grooming, etc.; dandy; coxcomb. [1400–50; late ME < L *exquīsītus* sought after (ptp. of *exquīrere*). See EX-[1], QUEST, -ITE[2]] —**ex•quis′ite•ly,** *adv.* —**ex•quis′ite•ness,** *n.*
—**Syn. 1.** dainty, beautiful, elegant, rare. See **delicate. 2.** perfect, matchless. See **fine**[1]. **3.** poignant. **4.** select, choice, precious. **6.** discriminating. —**Ant. 1.** gross. **2.** ordinary. **3.** dull.
—**Pronunciation.** The pronunciation of EXQUISITE has undergone a rapid change from (ek′skwi zit) to (ik skwiz′it), with stress shifting to the second syllable. The newer pronunciation is still criticized by some, but is now more common in both the U.S. and England, and many younger educated speakers are not even aware of the older one. See **harass.**

exr., executor.

ex′ rights′, *Stock Exchange.* without having the right to subscribe to new issues of stock, the rights being retained by the seller of the stock. *Abbr.:* xr Also, **ex′-rights′.**

ex•san•gui•nate (eks sang′gwə nāt′), *v.,* **-nat•ed, -nat•ing.** —*v.t.* **1.** to drain of blood; make bloodless. —*v.i.* **2.** to bleed to death. [1790–1800; < LL *exsanguinātus* bloodless, deprived of blood (ptp. of *exsanguināre*), equiv. to L *ex-* EX-[1] + *sanguin-* (s. of *sanguis* blood; see SANGUINE) + *-ātus* -ATE[1]] —**ex•san′gui•na′tion,** *n.*

ex•san•guine (eks sang′gwin), *adj.* anemic; bloodless. [1640–50; < L *exsangu(is)* bloodless (see EX-[1], SANGUINE) + -INE[1]] —**ex′san•guin′i•ty,** *n.*

ex•scind (ek sind′), *v.t.* to cut out or off. [1655–65; < L *exscindere* to destroy, tear away, equiv. to *ex-* EX-[1] + *scindere* to cut, tear; see SCISSION]

ex•sect (ek sekt′), *v.t.* to cut out. [1635–45; < L *exsectus* cut out, cut away, ptp. of *ex(s)ecāre,* equiv. to *ex-* EX-[1] + *secāre* to cut; see SECT] —**ex•sec•tile** (ek sek′tl, -til, -tīl), *adj.* —**ex•sec′tion,** *n.*

ex•sert (ek sûrt′), *v.t.* **1.** to thrust out. —*adj.* **2.** thrust out; exserted. [1655–65; < L *exsertus* stretched out, put forth, var. of *exertus;* see EXERT] —**ex•ser′tion,** *n.*

ex•sert•ed (ek sûr′tid), *adj. Biol.* projecting beyond the surrounding parts, as a stamen. [1810–20; EXSERT + -ED[2]]

ex•ser•tile (ek sûr′tl, -til, -tīl), *adj. Biol.* capable of being exserted or protruded. [1820–30; < F *exertile.* See EXSERT, -ILE]

ex•sic•cate (ek′si kāt′), *v.,* **-cat•ed, -cat•ing.** —*v.t.* **1.** to dry or remove the moisture from, as a substance. **2.** to dry up, as moisture. —*v.i.* **3.** to dry up. [1375–1425; late ME < L *exsiccātus* dried up, ptp. of *exsiccāre,* equiv. to *ex-* EX-[1] + *siccāre* to dry, make dry; see -ATE[1]] —**ex′sic•ca′tion,** *n.* —**ex′sic•ca′tive,** *adj.* —**ex′sic•ca′tor,** *n.*

ex•sic•ca•tum (ek′si kā′təm), *n., pl.* **-tums, -ta** (-tə). *Bot., Mycol.* a specimen intentionally dried, esp. for herbarium display. [< NL, L *exsiccātum* something dried, neut. of *exsiccātus;* see EXSICCATE]

ex•so•lu•tion (eks′sə lo͞o′shən), *n. Mineral.* the process of exsolving. [< L *exsolūtiōn-* (s. of *exsolūtiō*). See EX-[1], SOLUTION]

ex•solve (eks solv′), *v.i.,* **-solved, -solv•ing.** *Mineral.* (of two minerals in solid solution) to separate from one another at a critical point in temperature. [< L *exsolvere.* See EX-[1], SOLVE]

ex•stip•u•late (eks stip′yə lit, -lāt′), *adj. Bot.* having no stipules. Also, **estipulate.** [1785–95; EX-[1] + STIPULE + -ATE[1]]

ex′ store′, *Com.* with shipping costs from the store or warehouse to be paid by the buyer or consignee.

ex•stro•phy (ek′strə fē), *n., pl.* **-phies.** *Pathol.* a birth defect resulting in the eversion of an organ: *exstrophy of the bladder.* [1830–40; < Gk *ekstroph(ḗ)* inversion of the uterus, lit., a turning inside out (see EC-, STROPHE) + -Y[3]]

ext., **1.** extension. **2.** exterior. **3.** external. **4.** extinct. **5.** extra. **6.** extract.

ex•tant (ek′stənt, ik stant′), *adj.* **1.** in existence; still existing; not destroyed or lost: *There are only three extant copies of the document.* **2.** *Archaic.* standing out; protruding. [1535–45; < L *ex(s)tant-* (s. of *ex(s)tāns*) standing out, prp. of *exstāre,* equiv. to *ex-* EX-[1] + *stāre* to STAND]

extd., extended.

ex•tem•po•ral (ik stem′pər əl), *adj. Archaic.* extemporaneous; extempore. [1560–70; < L *extemporālis* on the spur of the moment. See EXTEMPORE, -AL[1]] —**ex•tem′po•ral•ly,** *adv.*

ex•tem•po•ra•ne•ous (ik stem′pə rā′nē əs), *adj.* **1.**

CONCISE PRONUNCIATION KEY: act, cāpe, dâre, pärt; set, ēqual; *if,* īce; ox, ōver, ôrder, oil, bo͝ok, bo͞ot, out; up, ûrge; child; sing; shoe; thin, *th*at; zh as in *treasure.* ə = a as in *alone,* e as in *system,* i as in *easily,* o as in *gallop,* u as in *circus;* ᵊ as in *fire* (fīᵊr), *hour* (ouᵊr). l and n can serve as syllabic consonants, as in *cradle* (krād′l), and *button* (but′n). See the full key inside the front cover.

done, spoken, performed, etc., without special advance preparation; impromptu: *an extemporaneous speech.* **2.** previously planned but delivered with the help of few or no notes: *extemporaneous lectures.* **3.** speaking or performing with little or no advance preparation: *extemporaneous actors.* **4.** made for the occasion, as a shelter. [1650–60; < LL *extemporāneus* on the spur of the moment. See EXTEMPORE, -AN, -EOUS] —**ex·tem′po·ra′ne·ous·ly,** *adv.* —**ex·tem′po·ra′ne·ous·ness, ex·tem·po·ra·ne·i·ty** (ik stem′pə rə nē′i tē), *n.*
—**Syn. 1. 2.** EXTEMPORANEOUS (EXTEMPORE), IMPROMPTU, IMPROVISED are used of expression given without preparation or only partial preparation. EXTEMPORANEOUS and IMPROMPTU may both refer to speeches given without any preparation: *an extemporaneous* (*impromptu*) *speech.* EXTEMPORANEOUS may also refer to a speech given from notes or an outline: *extemporaneous lectures.* IMPROMPTU also refers to poems, songs, etc., delivered without preparation and at a moment's notice. IMPROVISED is applied to something composed (recited, sung, acted), at least in part, as one goes along: *an improvised piano accompaniment.* —**Ant. 1.** memorized.

ex·tem·po·rar·y (ik stem′pə rer′ē), *adj.* **1.** extemporaneous; extempore. **2.** *Obs.* sudden; unexpected. [1600–10; EXTEMPORE + -ARY] —**ex·tem·po·rar·i·ly** (ik stem′pə râr′ə lē, -rer′-), *adv.* —**ex·tem′po·rar′i·ness,** *n.*

ex·tem·po·re (ik stem′pə rē), *adv.* **1.** on the spur of the moment; without premeditation or preparation; offhand: *Questions were asked extempore from the floor.* **2.** without notes: *to speak extempore.* **3.** (of musical performance) by improvisation. —*adj.* **4.** extemporaneous; impromptu. [1545–55; < L: lit., out of the time, at the moment, equiv. to *ex* out of (see EX-[1]) + *tempore* the time (abl. sing. of *tempus*)]
—**Syn. 4.** See **extemporaneous.**

ex·tem·po·rize (ik stem′pə rīz′), *v.,* **-rized, -riz·ing.** —*v.i.* **1.** to speak extemporaneously: *He can extemporize on any of a number of subjects.* **2.** to sing, or play on an instrument, composing the music as one proceeds; improvise. **3.** to do or manage something in a makeshift way. —*v.t.* **4.** to make or devise extempore. **5.** *Music.* to compose offhand; improvise. Also, *esp. Brit.,* **ex·tem′·po·rise′.** [1635–45; EXTEMPORE + -IZE] —**ex·tem′po·ri·za′tion,** *n.* —**ex·tem′po·riz′er,** *n.*

ex·tend (ik stend′), *v.t.* **1.** to stretch out; draw out to the full length: *He extended the measuring tape as far as it would go.* **2.** to stretch, draw, or arrange in a given direction, or so as to reach a particular point, as a cord, wall, or line of troops. **3.** to stretch forth or hold out, as the arm or hand: *to extend one's hand in greeting.* **4.** to place at full length, esp. horizontally, as the body or limbs. **5.** to increase the length or duration of; lengthen; prolong: *to extend a visit.* **6.** to stretch out in various or all directions; expand; spread out in area: *A huge tent was extended over the field.* **7.** to enlarge the scope of, or make more comprehensive, as operations, influence, or meaning: *The European powers extended their authority in Asia.* **8.** to provide as an offer or grant; offer; grant; give: *to extend aid to needy scholars.* **9.** *Finance.* to postpone (the payment of a debt) beyond the time originally agreed upon. **10.** to increase the bulk or volume of, esp. by adding an inexpensive or plentiful substance. **11.** *Bookkeeping.* to transfer (figures) from one column to another. **12.** *Law.* **a.** *Brit.* to assess or value. **b.** to make a seizure or levy upon, as land, by a writ of extent. **13.** *Manège.* to bring (a horse) into an extended attitude. **14.** to exert (oneself) to an unusual degree. **15.** *Archaic.* to exaggerate. **16.** *Obs.* to take by seizure. —*v.i.* **17.** to be or become extended; stretch out in length, duration, or in various or all directions. **18.** to reach, as to a particular point. **19.** to increase in length, area, scope, etc. **20.** *Manège.* (of a horse) to come into an extended attitude. [1250–1300; ME *extenden* < L *extendere* to stretch out. See EX-[1], TEND[1]] —**ex·tend′i·ble, ex·tend′a·ble,** *adj.* —**ex·tend′i·bil′i·ty, ex·tend′a·bil′i·ty,** *n.*
—**Syn. 5.** continue. See **lengthen. 6.** enlarge; widen, dilate. **8.** bestow, impart. —**Ant. 1.** shorten, contract.

ex·tend·ed (ik sten′did), *adj.* **1.** stretched out: *extended wires.* **2.** continued or prolonged: *extended efforts.* **3.** spread out: *extended flags.* **4.** widespread or extensive; having extension or spatial magnitude: *extended treatment of a subject.* **5.** outstretched: *extended arms.* **6.** *Print.* expanded (def. 3). **7.** of or pertaining to a meaning of a word other than its original or primary meaning: *an extended sense.* **8.** *Manège.* **a.** (of a moving horse) noting an elongated pose in which the legs reach out from the body, the chin is out from the chest, etc. Cf. **collected** (def. 3a). **b.** (of the gait of a horse) characterized by long, low, usually fast strides. Cf. **collected** (def. 3b). [1400–50; late ME; see EXTEND, -ED[2]] —**ex·tend′·ed·ly,** *adv.* —**ex·tend′ed·ness,** *n.*

extend′ed care′, generalized health or nursing care for convalescents or the disabled, when hospitalization is not required.

extend′ed com′plex plane′, *Math.* the complex plane with a point at infinity added.

extend′ed cov′erage, *Insurance.* an extension of a casualty-insurance policy to provide insurance against risks not covered under the basic policy.

extend′ed fam′ily, 1. a kinship group consisting of a family nucleus and various relatives, as grandparents, usually living in one household and functioning as a larger unit. Cf. **nuclear family. 2.** (loosely) one's family conceived of as including aunts, uncles, cousins, in-laws, and sometimes close friends and colleagues. [1940–45]

extend′ed fore′cast, *Meteorol.* a forecast of weather conditions beyond the normal two-day forecast period.

CONCISE ETYMOLOGY KEY: <, descended or borrowed from; >, whence; b., blend of, blended; c., cognate with; cf., compare; deriv., derivative; equiv., equivalent; imit., imitative; obl., oblique; r., replacing; s., stem; sp., spelling, spelled; resp., respelling, respelled; trans., translation; ?, origin unknown; *, unattested; ‡, probably earlier than. See the full key inside the front cover.

extend′ed or′der, 1. an irregular formation of troops to suit the tactical requirements and the terrain. **2.** See **open order.**

extend′ed play′, a phonograph record of 45 r.p.m. that plays a longer time than the standard 45 r.p.m. record. *Abbr.:* EP [1950–55] —**extend′ed-play′,** *adj.*

extend′ed real′ num′ber sys′tem, *Math.* the set of all real numbers with the points plus infinity and minus infinity added.

extend′ed term′ insur′ance, life insurance in which a policyholder ceases to pay the premiums but keeps the full amount of the policy in force for whatever term the cash value permits.

ex·tend·er (ik sten′dər), *n.* **1.** a substance added to another substance, as to paint or food, to increase its volume or bulk: *to add cereal and soy protein to hamburger as extenders.* **2.** *Photog.* See under **converter** (def. 8). [1605–15; EXTEND + -ER[1]]

ex·ten·si·ble (ik sten′sə bəl), *adj.* capable of being extended. [1605–15; EXTENS(ION) + -IBLE] —**ex·ten′si·bil′i·ty, ex·ten′si·ble·ness,** *n.*

ex·ten·sile (ik sten′səl, -sīl), *adj. Chiefly Zool., Anat.* capable of being extended; adapted for stretching out; extensible; protrusible. [1735–45; EXTENS(ION) + -ILE]

ex·ten·sim·e·ter (ek′sten sim′i tər), *n.* extensometer.

ex·ten·sion (ik sten′shən), *n.* **1.** an act or instance of extending. **2.** the state of being extended. **3.** that by which something is extended; an addition: *a four-room extension to a house.* **4.** an additional period of time given one to meet an obligation: *My term paper wasn't finished so I asked for an extension.* **5.** something that can be extended; an extended object: *a table with drop-leaf extensions.* **6.** range of extending; degree of extensiveness; extent: *the extension of our knowledge.* **7.** an additional telephone that operates on the principal line. **8.** *Com.* a written engagement on the part of a creditor, allowing a debtor further time to pay a debt. **9.** *Physics.* that property of a body by which it occupies space. **10.** *Anat.* **a.** the act of straightening a limb. **b.** the position that a limb assumes when it is straightened. **11.** *Surg.* the act of pulling the broken or dislocated part of a limb in a direction from the trunk, in order to bring the ends of the bone into their natural situation. **12.** Also called **extent.** *Logic.* the class of things to which a term is applicable, as "the class of such beings as Plato and Alexander" to which the term "man" is applicable. Cf. **intension** (def. 5). **13.** *Math.* a function having a domain that includes the domain of a given function and that has the same value as the given function at each point in the domain of the given function. **14.** *Manège.* the act of bringing or coming into an extended attitude. —*adj.* **15.** of or pertaining to extension courses. [1350–1400; ME < L *extēnsiōn-* (s. of *extēnsiō*). See EXTENSIVE, -ION] —**ex·ten′sion·al′i·ty, ex·ten′sion·al·ism,** *n.* —**ex·ten′sion·al,** *adj.* —**ex·ten′sion·al·ly,** *adv.* —**ex·ten′·sion·less,** *adj.*
—**Syn. 1.** stretching, expansion, enlargement, increase, dilation. **3.** lengthening, protraction, continuation. **4.** delay. **6.** limit. —**Ant. 1.** contraction.

exten′sion a′gent, an agent employed by the county government to work with farmers to increase crop yields, prevent erosion, eliminate blights or pests, and the like. Cf. **county agent.**

exten′sion bolt′, a bolt fitted into a mortise in a door or the like, sliding into a socket in the head or the sill and having a head projecting from the surface of the door.

exten′sion cord′, *Elect.* an electric cord having a standard plug at one end and a standard electric jack at the other. [1945–50]

exten′sion cours′es, (in many universities and colleges) a program for persons not regularly enrolled as students, frequently provided through evening classes or classes in off-campus centers, or by correspondence. Cf. **university extension.** [1880–85]

exten′sion field′, *Math.* a field that contains a given field as a subfield.

exten′sion lad′der, a ladder having two or more sections joined by a sliding mechanism that allows the ladder to be extended to the total length. [1870–75]

exten′sion li′brary ser′vice, the provision of library materials and services outside the library's regular service center or outlet.

exten′sion rule′, a folding rule having a sliding part equal in length to one section so as to permit exact measurement of internal dimensions.

exten′sion tube′, *Photog.* any of a series of tubes of varying lengths placed between the lens and a camera body to facilitate closeup focusing. [1955–60]

ex·ten·si·ty (ik sten′si tē), *n.* **1.** the quality of having extension. **2.** *Psychol.* the attribute of sensation from which the perception of spatial extension is developed. [1825–35; < L *extēns(us)* (see EXTENSIVE) + -ITY]

ex·ten·sive (ik sten′siv), *adj.* **1.** of great extent; wide; broad: *an extensive area.* **2.** covering or extending over a great area: *extensive travels.* **3.** far-reaching; comprehensive; thorough: *extensive knowledge.* **4.** lengthy: *an extensive journey.* **5.** great in amount, number, or degree: *an extensive fortune; extensive political influence.* **6.** of or having extension: *Space is extensive, time durational.* **7.** noting or pertaining to a system of agriculture involving the use or cultivation of large areas of land with a minimum of labor and expense (opposed to *intensive*). [1375–1425; late ME < LL *extēnsīvus,* equiv. to L *extēns(us)* (ptp. of *extendere* to EXTEND) + *-īvus* -IVE] —**ex·ten′sive·ly,** *adv.* —**ex·ten′sive·ness, ex·ten·siv·i·ty** (ek′sten siv′i tē, ik-), *n.*
—**Syn. 1.** extended, large, spacious, ample, vast. —**Ant. 1, 3.** limited, narrow, confined. **3.** parochial.

ex·ten·som·e·ter (ek′sten som′i tər), *n.* an instrument for measuring minute degrees of expansion, contraction, or deformation. Also, **extensimeter.** [1885–90; EXTENS(ION) + -O- + -METER]

ex·ten·sor (ik sten′sər, -sôr), *n. Anat.* a muscle that serves to extend or straighten a part of the body. [1700–10; < NL, equiv. to L *extend(ere)* to EXTEND + *-tor* -TOR, with *-dt-* > *-s-*]

ex·tent (ik stent′), *n.* **1.** the space or degree to which a thing extends; length, area, volume, or scope: *the extent of his lands; to be right to a certain extent.* **2.** something extended, as a space; a particular length, area, or volume; something having extension: *the limitless extent of the skies.* **3.** *U.S. Law.* a writ, or a levy, by which a debtor's lands are valued and transferred to the creditor, absolutely or for a term of years. **4.** *Eng. Law.* **a.** Also called **writ of extent.** a writ to recover debts of a record due to the crown, under which land, property, etc., may be seized. **b.** a seizure made under such a writ. **5.** *Logic.* extension (def. 12). **6.** *Archaic.* assessment or valuation, as of land. [1250–1300; ME *extente* assessment < ML *extenta,* n. use of fem. of L *extentus,* ptp. of *extendere* to EXTEND]
—**Syn. 1.** magnitude, measure, amount, compass, range, expanse, stretch, reach, length.

ex·ten·u·ate (ik sten′yōō āt′), *v.t.,* **-at·ed, -at·ing. 1.** to represent (a fault, offense, etc.) as less serious: *to extenuate a crime.* **2.** to serve to make (a fault, offense, etc.) seem less serious. **3.** to underestimate, underrate, or make light of: *Do not extenuate the difficulties we are in.* **4.** *Archaic.* **a.** to make thin, lean, or emaciated. **b.** to reduce the consistency or density of. [1375–1425; late ME (adj.) < L *extenuātus,* ptp. of *extenuāre,* equiv. to *ex-* EX-[1] + *tenuāre* to make thin or small; see -ATE[1]] —**ex·ten′u·at′ing,** *adj.* —**ex·ten′u·at′ing·ly,** *adv.* —**ex·ten′u·a′tive,** *adj.* —**ex·ten′u·a′tor,** *n.*

exten′uating cir′cumstances, *Law.* circumstances that render conduct less serious and thereby serve to reduce the damages to be awarded or the punishment to be imposed. [1830–40]

ex·ten·u·a·tion (ik sten′yōō ā′shən), *n.* **1.** the act of extenuating. **2.** the state of being extenuated. **3.** something that extenuates; a partial excuse: *The youth of the defendant served as an extenuation.* [1375–1425; late ME *extenuacioun* < L *extenuātiōn-* (s. of *extenuātiō*). See EXTENUATE, -ION]

ex·ten·u·a·to·ry (ik sten′yōō ə tôr′ē, -tōr′ē), *adj.* tending to extenuate; characterized by extenuation; extenuating. [1800–10; < LL *extenuātōrius.* See EXTENUATE, -TORY[1]]

ex·te·ri·or (ik stēr′ē ər), *adj.* **1.** outer; being on the outer side: *the exterior surface; exterior decorations.* **2.** intended or suitable for outdoor use: *exterior paint.* **3.** situated or being outside; pertaining to or connected with what is outside: *the exterior territories of a country.* —*n.* **4.** the outer surface or part; outside. **5.** outward form or appearance: *She has a placid exterior, but inside she is tormented.* **6.** *Math.* the collection of points not contained in the closure of a given set. [1525–35; < L, comp. of *exter* or *exterus* on the outside, outward. See EX-[1]] —**ex·te′ri·or·ly,** *adv.*
—**Syn. 1.** outward, outside, external, superficial. **3.** outlying, extraneous, foreign; extrinsic. **4.** face. **5.** mien, aspect. —**Ant. 1, 4.** interior.

exte′rior an′gle, *Geom.* **1.** an angle formed outside parallel lines by a third line that intersects them. See diag. under **interior angle. 2.** an angle formed outside a polygon by one side and an extension of an adjacent side; the supplement of an interior angle of the polygon. [1885–90]

ex·te·ri·or·i·ty (ik stēr′ē ôr′i tē, -or′-), *n., pl.* **-ties. 1.** the state or fact of being exterior. **2.** something exterior. [1605–15; EXTERIOR + -ITY]

ex·te·ri·or·ize (ik stēr′ē ə rīz′), *v.t.,* **-ized, -iz·ing. 1.** to make exterior; externalize. **2.** *Surg.* to expose (an internal structure) temporarily outside the body, for observation, surgery, or experimentation. Also, *esp. Brit.,* **ex·te′ri·or·ise′.** [1875–80; EXTERIOR + -IZE] —**ex·te′ri·or·i·za′tion,** *n.*

ex·ter·mi·nate (ik stûr′mə nāt′), *v.t.,* **-nat·ed, -nat·ing.** to get rid of by destroying; destroy totally; extirpate: *to exterminate an enemy; to exterminate insects.* [1535–45; < L *exterminātus,* ptp. of *extermināre* to EXTERMINE; see -ATE[1]] —**ex·ter·mi·na·ble** (ik stûr′mə nə bəl), *adj.* —**ex·ter′mi·na′tion,** *n.*
—**Syn.** eradicate, abolish, annihilate, eliminate.

ex·ter·mi·na·tor (ik stûr′mə nā′tər), *n.* **1.** a person or thing that exterminates. **2.** a person or business establishment specializing in the elimination of vermin, insects, etc., from a building, apartment, etc., esp. by the controlled application of toxic chemicals. [1605–15; < LL *exterminātor.* See EXTERMINE, -ATOR]

ex·ter·mi·na·to·ry (ik stûr′mə nə tôr′ē, -tōr′ē), *adj.* serving or tending to exterminate. Also, **ex·ter·mi·na·tive** (ik stûr′mə nā′tiv). [1780–90; EXTERMINATE + -ORY[1]]

ex·ter·mine (ik stûr′min), *v.t.,* **-mined, -min·ing.** *Obs.* to exterminate. [1425–75; late ME < L *extermināre* to drive beyond the boundaries. See EX-[1], TERMINATE]

ex·tern (ek′stûrn; *for 3 also* ik stûrn′), *n.* **1.** a person connected with an institution but not residing in it, as a doctor or medical student at a hospital. **2.** a nun of a strictly enclosed order, as the Carmelites, who resides inside the convent but outside its enclosure and who chiefly goes on outside errands. —*adj.* **3.** *Archaic.* external; outer. [1525–35; < L *externus,* deriv. of *exter, exterus.* See EXTERIOR]

ex·ter·nal (ik stûr′nl), *adj.* **1.** of or pertaining to the outside or outer part; outer: *an external surface.* **2.** *Med.* to be applied to the outside of a body, as a remedy: *for external use only.* **3.** situated or being outside something; acting or coming from without: *external influences.* **4.** pertaining to the outward or visible appearance or show: *external acts of worship.* **5.** pertaining to or concerned with foreign countries: *external affairs; external commerce.* **6.** *Zool., Anat.* on the side farthest from the body, the median line, or the center of a radially symmetrical form. **7.** *Metaphys.* of or pertaining to the world of things, considered as independent of the perceiving mind: *external world.* —*n.* **8.** the outside;

outer surface; exterior. **9.** something that is external. **10. externals,** external features, circumstances, etc.; outward appearance; superficialities. [1375–1425; late ME; see EXTERN, -AL[1]] **—ex·ter′nal·ly,** *adv.*
—Syn. 1. outermost, exterior.

exter′nal au′ditory mea′tus, *Anat.* the canal extending from the opening in the external ear to the tympanic membrane.

ex·ter·nal-com·bus·tion (ik stûr′nl kəm bus′chən), *adj.* noting or pertaining to an engine, as a steam engine, in which fuel ignition takes place outside the cylinder, turbine, or the like, in which heat energy is transformed into mechanical force.

exter′nal degree′, a college degree granted a person for work and study done off campus. [1925–30]

exter′nal ear′, the outer portion of the ear, consisting of the auricle and the canal extending to the tympanic membrane. See diag. under **ear**[1].

exter′nal gal′axy, *Astron.* any galaxy other than the Milky Way.

exter′nal hem′orrhoid, *Pathol.* See under **hemorrhoid.**

exter′nal il′iac ar′tery, *Anat.* See **iliac artery** (def. 2).

ex·ter·nal·ism (ik stûr′nl iz′əm), *n.* attention to externals, esp. excessive attention to externals, as in religion. [1855–60; EXTERNAL + -ISM] **—ex·ter′nal·ist,** *n.*

ex·ter·nal·i·ty (ek′stər nal′i tē), *n., pl.* **-ties. 1.** the state or quality of being external. **2.** something external; an outward feature. **3.** excessive attention to externals. **4.** an external effect, often unforeseen or unintended, accompanying a process or activity: *to eliminate externalities such as air pollution through government regulation.* [1665–75; EXTERNAL + -ITY]

ex·ter·nal·i·za·tion (ik stûr′nl ə zā′shən), *n.* **1.** the act or process of externalizing. **2.** the quality or state of being externalized. **3.** something that is externalized. [1795–1805; EXTERNALIZE + -ATION]

ex·ter·nal·ize (ik stûr′nl īz′), *v.t.,* **-ized, -iz·ing. 1.** to make external; embody in an outward form. **2.** to regard as consisting of externals. **3.** to regard or treat as being caused by externals; attribute to external causes: *to externalize one's difficulties.* **4.** to direct (the personality) outward in social relationships. Also, *esp. Brit.,* **ex·ter′nal·ise′.** [1850–55; EXTERNAL + -IZE]

ex·ter·nal·iz·er (ik stûr′nl ī′zər), *n. Psychol.* a person who draws a locus of control from the external world, depending on others as a source of values, ideas, and security. [EXTERNALIZE + -ER[1]]

exter′nal jug′ular vein′. See under **jugular** (def. 1b).

exter′nal rela′tion, *Philos.* a relation between any two entities such that if they had not been in this relation to each other, the nature of each would not necessarily have been different. Cf. **internal relation.**

exter′nal stor′age, *Computers.* See **secondary storage.**

ex·tern·ship (ek′stûrn ship′), *n.* a required period of supervised practice done off campus or away from one's affiliated institution: *The young doctor served six months of externship at a nearby clinic.* [1940–45; EXTERN + -SHIP]

ex·ter·o·cep·tive (ek′stər ə sep′tiv), *adj. Physiol.* pertaining to exteroceptors, the stimuli acting upon them, or the nerve impulses initiated by them. [1905–10; *extero-* (comb. form of L *exterus* EXTERIOR) + (RE)CEPTIVE]

ex·ter·o·cep·tor (ek′stər ə sep′tər), *n. Physiol.* a receptor responding to stimuli originating outside the body. [1905–10; *extero-* (see EXTEROCEPTIVE) + (RE)CEPTOR]

ex·ter·ri·to·ri·al (eks′ter i tôr′ē əl, -tōr′-), *adj.* extraterritorial. [1850–55; EX-[1] + TERRITORIAL] **—ex·ter′·ri·to′ri·al′i·ty,** *n.* **—ex′ter·ri·to′ri·al·ly,** *adv.*

ex·tinct (ik stingkt′), *adj.* **1.** no longer in existence; that has ended or died out: *an extinct species of fish.* **2.** no longer in use; obsolete: *an extinct custom.* **3.** extinguished; quenched; not burning. **4.** having ceased eruption; no longer active: *an extinct volcano.* [1400–50; late ME < L *ex(s)tinctus* put out, quenched, ptp. of *ex(s)tinguere* to EXTINGUISH]
—Syn. 1. defunct, gone, vanished. See **dead. 2.** archaic. **3.** out.

ex·tinc·tion (ik stingk′shən), *n.* **1.** the act of extinguishing. **2.** the fact or condition of being extinguished or extinct. **3.** suppression; abolition; annihilation: *the extinction of an army.* **4.** *Biol.* the act or process of becoming extinct; a coming to an end or dying out: *the extinction of a species.* **5.** *Psychol.* the reduction or loss of a conditioned response as a result of the absence or withdrawal of reinforcement. **6.** *Astron.* the diminution in the intensity of starlight caused by absorption as it passes through the earth's atmosphere or through interstellar dust. **7.** *Crystall., Optics.* the darkness that results from rotation of a thin section to an angle **(extinc′·tion an′gle)** at which plane-polarized light is absorbed by the polarizer. [1375–1425; late ME *extinccio(u)n* < L *ex(s)tinctiōn-* (s. of *ex(s)tinctiō*). See EXTINCT, -ION]

ex·tinc·tive (ik stingk′tiv), *adj.* tending or serving to extinguish. [1590–1600; EXTINCT + -IVE]

ex·tine (ek′stēn, -stīn), *n. Bot.* exine. [1825–35; < L *ext(imus)* most outward + -INE[1]]

ex·tin·guish (ik sting′gwish), *v.t.* **1.** to put out (a fire, light, etc.); put out the flame of (something burning or lighted): *to extinguish a candle.* **2.** to put an end to or bring to an end; wipe out of existence; annihilate: *to extinguish hope.* **3.** to obscure or eclipse, as by superior brilliance. **4.** *Law.* to discharge (a debt), as by payment. [1535–45; < L *ex(s)tingu(ere)* (*ex-* EX-[1] + *stinguere* to quench) + -ISH[2]] **—ex·tin′guish·a·ble,** *adj.* **—ex·tin′·guish·ment,** *n.*
—Syn. 1. quench, smother, snuff out, blow out. **—Ant. 1.** light, ignite.

ex·tin·guish·ant (ik sting′gwi shənt), *n.* a substance used in extinguishing fires. [EXTINGUISH + -ANT]

ex·tin·guish·er (ik sting′gwi shər), *n.* **1.** a person or thing that extinguishes. **2.** See **fire extinguisher. 3.** an instrument consisting of a cone-shaped cup attached to a handle or the end of a pole, for extinguishing a candle by momentarily closing off the burning wick from the air. Cf. **candlesnuffer.** [1550–60; EXTINGUISH + -ER[1]]

extinguisher (def. 3)

ex·tir·pate (ek′stər pāt′, ik stûr′pāt), *v.t.,* **-pat·ed, -pat·ing. 1.** to remove or destroy totally; do away with; exterminate. **2.** to pull up by or as if by the roots; root up: *to extirpate an unwanted hair.* [1530–40; < L *ex(s)tirpātus* plucked up by the stem (ptp. of *ex(s)tirpāre*), equiv. to *ex-* EX-[1] + *stirp-* (s. of *stirps*) stem + *-ātus* -ATE[1]] **—ex′tir·pa′tion,** *n.* **—ex′tir·pa′tive,** *adj.* **—ex′tir·pa′tor,** *n.*

extn., extension.

ex·tol (ik stōl′, -stol′), *v.t.,* **-tolled, -tol·ling.** to praise highly; laud; eulogize: *to extol the beauty of Naples.* Also, **ex·toll′.** [1350–1400; ME *extollen* < L *extollere* to lift up, raise, equiv. to *ex-* EX-[1] + *tollere* to lift, raise up] **—ex·tol′ler,** *n.* **—ex·tol′ling·ly,** *adv.* **—ex·tol′ment, ex·toll′ment,** *n.*
—Syn. glorify, exalt, celebrate. **—Ant.** disparage.

ex·tor·sive (ik stôr′siv), *adj. Law.* serving or tending to extort: *extorsive measures.* [1660–70; < L *extors(us)* (ptp. of *extorquēre;* see EXTORT) + -IVE] **—ex·tor′sive·ly,** *adv.*

ex·tort (ik stôrt′), *v.t.* **1.** *Law.* **a.** to wrest or wring (money, information, etc.) from a person by violence, intimidation, or abuse of authority; obtain by force, torture, threat, or the like. **b.** to take illegally by reason of one's office. **2.** to compel (something) of a person or thing: *Her wit and intelligence extorted their admiration.* [1375–1425; late ME (adj.) < L *extortus,* ptp. of *extorquēre,* equiv. to *ex-* EX-[1] + *torquēre* to twist] **—ex·tort′er,** *n.* **—ex·tor′tive,** *adj.*
—Syn. 1. See **extract.**

ex·tor·tion (ik stôr′shən), *n.* **1.** an act or instance of extorting. **2.** *Law.* the crime of obtaining money or some other thing of value by the abuse of one's office or authority. **3.** oppressive or illegal exaction, as of excessive price or interest: *the extortions of usurers.* **4.** anything extorted. [1250–1300; ME *extorcion* < LL *extortiōn-* (s. of *extortiō*). See EXTORT, -ION]
—Syn. 1, 4. blackmail.

ex·tor·tion·ar·y (ik stôr′shə ner′ē), *adj.* characterized by or given to extortion. [1795–1805; EXTORTION + -ARY]

ex·tor·tion·ate (ik stôr′shə nit), *adj.* **1.** grossly excessive; exorbitant: *extortionate prices.* **2.** characterized by extortion, as persons: *extortionate moneylenders.* [1780–90; EXTORTION + -ATE[1]] **—ex·tor′tion·ate·ly,** *adv.*

ex·tor·tion·ist (ik stôr′shə nist), *n.* a person who engages in extortion. Also, **ex·tor′tion·er.** [1880–85; EXTORTION + -IST]

extr., extract.

ex·tra (ek′strə), *adj.* **1.** beyond or more than what is usual, expected, or necessary; additional: *an extra copy of a newspaper; an extra charge.* **2.** larger or better than what is usual: *an extra binding.* —*n.* **3.** something extra or additional: *the little amenities and extras that make life pleasant.* **4.** an additional expense. **5.** a special edition of a newspaper, other than a regular edition. **6.** something of superior quality. **7.** *Motion Pictures, Television.* a person hired by the day to play a minor part, as a member of a mob or crowd. **8.** an additional worker. **9.** Usually, **extras.** *Cricket.* a score or run not made from the bat, as a bye or a wide. —*adv.* **10.** in excess of the usual or specified amount: *an extra high price.* **11.** beyond the ordinary degree; unusually; uncommonly: *done extra well; extra large.* [1770–80; by shortening of EXTRAORDINARY]

extra-, a prefix meaning "outside," "beyond," freely used as an English formative: *extrajudicial; extraterritorial; extra-atmospheric.* Also, **extro-.** [< L, comb. form of *extrā* (adv. and prep.) outside (of), without]

ex·tra-at·mos·pher·ic (ek′strə at′məs fer′ik, -fēr′-), *adj.* outside the earth's atmosphere. [1870–75]

ex′tra-base′ hit′ (ek′strə bās′), *Baseball.* a base hit that enables a batter to reach more than one base safely, as a two-base hit, three-base hit, or home run. [1945–50]

ex·tra·bold (ek′strə bōld′), *Print.* —*n.* **1.** unusually heavy boldface type. —*adj.* **2.** in extrabold. [EXTRA- + BOLD]

ex·tra·budg·et·ar·y (ek′strə buj′i ter′ē), *adj.* not included in a budget: *to acquire extrabudgetary funds.* [EXTRA- + BUDGETARY]

ex·tra·ca·non·i·cal (ek′strə kə non′i kəl), *adj. Eccles.* not included in the canon of Scripture. [1825–35; EXTRA- + CANONICAL]

ex·tra·cap·su·lar (ek′strə kap′sə lər, -kaps′yŏŏ-), *adj.* outside a capsule or capsular thing. [1880–85; EXTRA- + CAPSULAR]

ex·tra·cel·lu·lar (ek′strə sel′yə lər), *adj. Biol.* outside a cell or cells. [1865–70; EXTRA- + CELLULAR] **—ex′tra·cel′lu·lar·ly,** *adv.*

ex·tra·chro·mo·so·mal (ek′strə krō′mə sō′məl), *adj. Genetics.* of or pertaining to DNA that exists outside the main chromosome and acts independently. [1935–40; EXTRA- + CHROMOSOMAL]

ex·tra·con·densed (ek′strə kən denst′), *adj. Print.* (of type) narrower than condensed type in proportion to its height.

ex·tra·cor·po·re·al (ek′strə kôr pôr′ē əl, -pōr′-), *adj.* occurring or situated outside the body, as a heart-lung machine used to oxygenate the blood during surgery. [1860–65; EXTRA- + CORPOREAL] **—ex′tra·cor·po′re·al·ly,** *adv.*

ex′tra cov′er, *Cricket.* **1.** the position of a fielder between mid off and cover point. **2.** the fielder occupying this position. Also, **ex′tra cov′er point′.** [1865–70]

ex·tract (*v.* ik strakt′ *or, esp. for 5,* ek′strakt; *n.* ek′strakt), *v.t.* **1.** to get, pull, or draw out, usually with special effort, skill, or force: *to extract a tooth.* **2.** to deduce (a doctrine, principle, interpretation, etc.): *He extracted a completely personal meaning from what was said.* **3.** to derive or obtain (pleasure, comfort, etc.) from a particular source: *He extracted satisfaction from the success of his sons.* **4.** to take or copy out (matter), as from a book. **5.** to make excerpts from (a book, pamphlet, etc.). **6.** to extort (information, money, etc.): *to extract a secret from someone.* **7.** to separate or obtain (a juice, ingredient, etc.) from a mixture by pressure, distillation, treatment with solvents, or the like. **8.** *Math.* **a.** to determine (the root of a quantity that has a single root). **b.** to determine (a root of a quantity that has multiple roots). —*n.* **9.** something extracted. **10.** a passage taken from a book, article, etc.; excerpt; quotation. **11.** a solution or preparation containing the active principles of a drug, plant juice, or the like; concentrated solution: *vanilla extract.* **12.** a solid, viscid, or liquid substance extracted from a plant, drug, or the like, containing its essence in concentrated form: *beef extract.* [1375–1425; late ME < L *extractus* (ptp. of *extrahere*). See EX-[1], TRACT[1]] **—ex·tract′a·ble, ex·tract′i·ble,** *adj.* **—ex·tract′a·bil′i·ty, ex·tract′i·bil′i·ty,** *n.*
—Syn. 1. pry out. **6.** evoke, educe, draw out, elicit. EXTRACT, EXACT, EXTORT, WREST imply using force to remove something. To EXTRACT is to draw forth something as by pulling, importuning, or the like: *to extract a confession by torture.* To EXACT is to impose a penalty, or to obtain by force or authority, something to which one lays claim: *to exact payment.* To EXTORT is to wring something by intimidation or threats from an unwilling person: *to extort money by threats of blackmail.* To WREST is to take by force or violence in spite of active resistance: *The courageous minority wrested power from their oppressors.* **7.** withdraw, distill. **10.** citation, selection. **11.** decoction, distillation.

ex·tract·ant (ik strak′tənt), *n. Chem.* a liquid used to remove a solute from a solution. [EXTRACT + -ANT]

ex·trac·tion (ik strak′shən), *n.* **1.** an act or instance of extracting: *the extraction of a molar.* **2.** the state or fact of being extracted. **3.** descent or lineage: *to be of foreign extraction.* **4.** something extracted; extract. [1375–1425; late ME *extraccioun* < LL *extractiōn-* (s. of *extractiō*). See EXTRACT, -ION]

ex·trac·tive (ik strak′tiv), *adj.* **1.** tending or serving to extract, or based upon extraction: *coal, oil, copper, and other extractive industries.* **2.** capable of being extracted, as from the earth: *extractive fuels.* **3.** of, pertaining to, or involving extraction: *extractive surgery.* **4.** of or of the nature of an extract. —*n.* **5.** something extracted. [1590–1600; EXTRACT + -IVE]

extrac′tive met′allurgy, the technology of extracting metal from ore.

ex·trac·tor (ik strak′tər), *n.* **1.** a person or thing that extracts. **2.** (in a firearm or cannon) the mechanism that, after firing, pulls an empty or unfired cartridge or shell case out of the chamber and brings it into place for action by the ejector. **3.** a centrifuge for spinning wet laundry so as to remove excess water. **4.** *Med., Dentistry.* an instrument for drawing out, extracting, or pulling. [1605–15; EXTRACT + -OR[2]]

ex′tract print′ing. See **discharge printing.**

ex·tra·cur·ric·u·lar (ek′strə kə rik′yə lər), *adj.* **1.** outside the regular curriculum or program of courses: *football, orchestra, and other extracurricular activities.* **2.** outside one's regular work, responsibilities, or routine. **3.** *Informal.* outside the conventional bounds of propriety or ethics: *Does his wife know he has an extracurricular girlfriend?* [1920–25; EXTRA- + CURRICULAR]

ex·tra·dit·a·ble (ek′strə dī′tə bəl, ek′strə dī′-), *adj.* **1.** capable of being extradited; subject to extradition: *an extraditable person.* **2.** capable of incurring extradition: *an extraditable offense.* [1880–85; EXTRADITE + -ABLE]

ex·tra·dite (ek′strə dīt′), *v.t.,* **-dit·ed, -dit·ing. 1.** to give up (an alleged fugitive or criminal) to another state, nation, or authority. **2.** to obtain the extradition of. [1860–65; back formation from EXTRADITION]

ex·tra·di·tion (ek′strə dish′ən), *n.* the surrender of an alleged fugitive from justice or criminal by one state, nation, or authority to another. [1830–40; < F; see EX-[1], TRADITION]

ex′tra div′idend. See **special dividend.**

ex·tra·dos (ek′strə dos′, -dōs′, ek strā′dos, -dōs), *n., pl.* **-dos** (-dōz′, -dōz), **-dos·es.** *Archit.* the exterior curve or surface of an arch or vault. Also called **back.** Cf. **intrados.** See diag. under **arch.** [1765–75; < F, equiv. to *extra-* EXTRA- + *dos* back (< L *dorsum* DORSUM)]

ex·tra·dosed (ek strā′dost), *adj.* (of an arch) having a curved intrados, the form of which is repeated by the extrados. [EXTRADOS + -ED[3]]

ex·tra·em·bry·on·ic (ek′strə em′brē on′ik), *adj.* **1.** situated outside the embryo. **2.** pertaining to structures outside the embryo. [EXTRA- + EMBRYONIC]

ex′traembryon′ic mem′brane, *Embryol.* any of

CONCISE PRONUNCIATION KEY: act, cāpe, dâre, pärt; set, ēqual; *if,* īce; ox, ōver, ôrder, oil, bŏŏk, bōōt, out; up, ûrge; child; sing; shoe; thin, *that;* zh as in *treasure.* ə = *a* as in *alone, e* as in *system, i* as in *easily, o* as in *gallop, u* as in *circus;* ᵊ as in *fire* (fīᵊr), *hour* (ouᵊr). l and n can serve as syllabic consonants, as in *cradle* (krād′l), and *button* (but′n). See the full key inside the front cover.

the tissues, derived from the fertilized egg, that enclose or otherwise contribute to the support of the developing embryo, as the yolk sac, allantois, amnion, and chorion. Also called **embryonic membrane.**

ex•tra•flo•ral (ek′strə flôr′əl, -flōr′-), *adj. Bot.* situated outside the flower, as a nectary. [EXTRA- + FLORAL]

ex•tra•ga•lac•tic (ek′strə gə lak′tik), *adj.* outside the Milky Way system. [1850–55; EXTRA- + GALACTIC]

extragalac′tic neb′ula, (formerly) galaxy (def. 1a).

ex•tra•ju•di•cial (ek′strə jo͞o dish′əl), *adj.* **1.** outside of judicial proceedings; beyond the action or authority of a court. **2.** beyond, outside, or against the usual procedure of justice; legally unwarranted: *an extrajudicial penalty.* [1620–30; EXTRA- + JUDICIAL] **—ex′tra•ju•di′•cial•ly,** *adv.*

ex•tra•lat•er•al (ek′strə lat′ər əl), *adj.* of or pertaining to the right of a mine owner to the vein or lode of an ore when it extends under an adjacent mining property. [EXTRA- + LATERAL]

ex•tra•le•gal (ek′strə lē′gəl), *adj.* being beyond the province or authority of law: *There were only extralegal recourses for their grievances.* [1635–45; EXTRA- + LEGAL] **—ex′tra•le′gal•ly,** *adv.*

ex•tra•lim•it•al (ek′strə lim′i tl), *adj.* not found within a given geographical area: *an extralimital species of bird.* [1870–75; EXTRA- + LIMIT + -AL]

ex•tra•lin•guis•tic (ek′strə ling gwis′tik), *adj.* not included within the realm of language or linguistics. [1925–30; EXTRA- + LINGUISTIC] **—ex′tra•lin•guis′ti•cal•ly,** *adv.*

ex•tral•i•ty (ik stral′i tē), *n.* extraterritoriality. [1920–25; by syncope]

ex•tra•mar•i•tal (ek′strə mar′i tl), *adj.* pertaining to sexual relations with someone other than one's spouse: *extramarital affairs.* [1925–30; EXTRA- + MARITAL]

ex•tra•met•ri•cal (ek′strə me′tri kəl), *adj. Pros.* containing one or more syllables in addition to those required by the meter: *an extrametrical line.* [1860–65; EXTRA- + METRICAL]

ex•tra•mun•dane (ek′strə mun dān′, -mun′dān), *adj.* beyond our world or the material universe. [1655–65; < LL *extrāmundānus* beyond the world. See EXTRA-, MUNDANE]

ex•tra•mu•ral (ek′strə myo͝or′əl), *adj.* **1.** involving representatives of more than one school: *extramural athletics.* **2.** outside the walls or boundaries, as of a city or town or a university: *extramural teaching; an extramural church.* Cf. **intramural** (defs. 1, 2). [1850–55; EXTRA- + MURAL. Cf. LL *extramūrānus,* in same sense] **—ex′tra•mu′ral•ly,** *adv.*

ex•tra•ne•ous (ik strā′nē əs), *adj.* **1.** introduced or coming from without; not belonging or proper to a thing; external; foreign: *extraneous substances in our water.* **2.** not pertinent; irrelevant: *an extraneous remark; extraneous decoration.* [1630–40; < L *extrāneus* external, foreign, equiv. to *extr(a)-* EXTRA- + *-ān(us)* -AN + *-eus* -EOUS] **—ex•tra′ne•ous•ly,** *adv.* **—ex•tra′ne•ous•ness,** *n.*
—Syn. 1. extrinsic, adventitious, alien. **2.** inappropriate, nonessential, superfluous. **—Ant. 1.** intrinsic. **2.** pertinent, relevant.

ex•tra•nu•cle•ar (ek′strə no͞o′klē ər, -nyo͞o′- *or, by metathesis,* -kyə lər), *adj. Cell Biol.* pertaining to or affecting the parts of a cell outside the nucleus. [1885–90; EXTRA- + NUCLEAR]
—Pronunciation. See **nuclear.**

ex′tra•oc′u•lar mus′cle (ek′strə ok′yə lər, ek′-strə-), *Anat.* See **extrinsic eye muscle.** [1935–40; EXTRA- + OCULAR]

ex•tra•or•di•naire (eks tʀa ôʀ dē neʀ′), *adj. French.* extraordinary; uncommon; remarkable.

ex•traor•di•nar•y (ik strôr′dn er′ē, ek′strə ôr′-), *adj.* **1.** beyond what is usual, ordinary, regular, or established: *extraordinary costs.* **2.** exceptional in character, amount, extent, degree, etc.; noteworthy; remarkable: *extraordinary speed; an extraordinary man.* **3.** (of an official, employee, etc.) outside of or additional to the ordinary staff; having a special, often temporary task or responsibility: *minister extraordinary and plenipotentiary.* [1425–75; late ME *extraordinarie* < L *extrāordinārius* beyond what is ordinary. See EXTRA-, ORDINARY] **—ex•traor•di•nar•i•ly** (ik strôr′dn âr′ə lē, ek′strə ôr′-), *adv.* **—ex•traor′di•nar′i•ness,** *n.*
—Syn. 1. inordinate. **2.** uncommon, singular, rare, phenomenal, special, signal. **—Ant. 1, 2.** common, usual.

extraor′dinary ju′bilee. See under **jubilee** (def. 5b).

extraor′dinary ray′, *Optics, Crystall.* the part of a doubly refracted ray that has changed speed and vibrations in the principal plane of the crystal. [1870–75]

extraor′dinary wave′, *Radio.* (of the two waves into which a radio wave is divided in the ionosphere under the influence of the earth's magnetic field) the wave with characteristics different from those that the undivided wave would have exhibited in the absence of the magnetic field. Also called **X-wave.** Cf. **ordinary wave.** [1880–85]

ex•tra•phys•i•cal (ek′strə fiz′i kəl), *adj.* outside the physical; not subject to physical laws. [1815–25; EXTRA- + PHYSICAL]

ex•tra•plan•e•tar•y (ek′strə plan′i ter′ē), *adj.* existing or occurring in outer space beyond a planet, esp. away from Earth. [1865–70; EXTRA- + PLANETARY]

CONCISE ETYMOLOGY KEY: <, descended or borrowed from; >, whence; b., blend of, blended; c., cognate with; cf., compare; deriv., derivative; equiv., equivalent; imit., imitative; obl., oblique; r., replacing; s., stem; sp., spelling, spelled; resp., respelling, respelled; trans., translation; ?, origin unknown; *, unattested; ‡, probably earlier than. See the full key inside the front cover.

ex′tra point′, *Football.* conversion (def. 13).

ex•trap•o•late (ik strap′ə lāt′), *v.,* **-lat•ed, -lat•ing.** *—v.t.* **1.** to infer (an unknown) from something that is known; conjecture. **2.** *Statistics.* to estimate (the value of a variable) outside the tabulated or observed range. **3.** *Math.* to estimate (a function that is known over a range of values of its independent variable) to values outside the known range. *—v.i.* **4.** to perform extrapolation. [1825–35; EXTRA- + (INTER)POLATE] **—ex•trap′o•la′tion,** *n.* **—ex•trap′o•la′tive, ex•trap•o•la•to•ry** (ik-strap′ə lə tôr′ē, -tōr′ē), *adj.* **—ex•trap′o•la′tor,** *n.*

ex•tra•pose (ek′strə pōz′), *v.t.,* **-posed, -pos•ing.** *Ling.* to shift (a syntactic construction) to the end of a sentence. [back formation from EXTRAPOSITION]

ex•tra•po•si•tion (ek′strə pə zish′ən), *n. Ling.* a rule of transformational grammar that shifts a subordinate or modifying clause to the end of a sentence, as in changing *That you sign the paper is necessary* to *It is necessary that you sign the paper.* [1925–30; EXTRA- + POSITION; appar. coined by Otto Jespersen]

ex•tra•pro•fes•sion•al (ek′strə prə fesh′ə nl), *adj.* outside ordinary limits of professional interest or duty. [1790–1800; EXTRA- + PROFESSIONAL]

ex•tra•py•ram•i•dal (ek′strə pi ram′i dl), *adj.* **1.** pertaining to or involving nerve tracts other than the pyramidal tracts, esp. the corpus striatum and its associated structures. **2.** located outside the pyramidal tracts. [EXTRA- + PYRAMIDAL]

extrapyram′idal sys′tem, *Anat.* the part of the central nervous system, including the descending motor fibers other than those of the pyramidal tract, that regulates muscle tone, posture, and other aspects of body movement. [1960–65]

ex•tra•sen•so•ri•al (ek′strə sen sôr′ē əl, -sōr′-), *adj.* extrasensory. [EXTRA- + SENSORIAL]

ex•tra•sen•so•ry (ek′strə sen′sə rē), *adj.* outside one's normal sense perception. [1930–35; EXTRA- + SENSORY]

ex′trasen′sory percep′tion. See **ESP.** [1930–35]

ex•tra•so•lar (ek′strə sō′lər), *adj.* outside, or originating outside, the sun or the solar system. [1885–90; EXTRA- + SOLAR[1]]

ex•tra•sys•to•le (ek′strə sis′tə lē), *n. Pathol.* a premature contraction of the heart, resulting in momentary interruption of the normal heartbeat. Also called **premature beat, premature contraction.** [1895–1900; < NL; see EXTRA-, SYSTOLE] **—ex•tra•sys•tol•ic** (ek′strə sis-tol′ik), *adj.*

ex•tra•ter•res•tri•al (ek′strə tə res′trē əl), *adj.* **1.** outside, or originating outside, the limits of the earth. *—n.* **2.** an extraterrestrial being: *a science fiction novel about extraterrestrials conquering the earth.* [1865–70; EXTRA- + TERRESTRIAL] **—ex′tra•ter•res′tri•al•ly,** *adv.*

ex•tra•ter•ri•to•ri•al (ek′strə ter′i tôr′ē əl, -tōr′-), *adj.* **1.** beyond local territorial jurisdiction, as the status of persons resident in a country but not subject to its laws. **2.** pertaining to such persons. Also, **exterritorial.** [1865–70; EXTRA- + TERRITORIAL] **—ex′tra•ter′ri•to′ri•al•ly,** *adv.*

ex•tra•ter•ri•to•ri•al•i•ty (ek′strə ter′i tôr′ē al′i tē, -tōr′-), *n.* **1.** immunity from the jurisdiction of a nation, granted to foreign diplomatic officials, foreign warships, etc. **2.** the applicability or exercise of a sovereign's laws outside its territory. Also, **exterritoriality.** [1830–40; EXTRA- + TERRITORIALITY]

ex′tra•trop′i•cal cy′clone (ek′strə trop′i kəl, ek′-), any large-scale, cyclonic storm that is not a tropical cyclone, esp. the common frontal cyclone of the middle and high latitudes. [1920–25; EXTRA- + TROPICAL]

ex•tra•u•ter•ine (ek′strə yo͞o′tər in, -tə rīn′), *adj.* being or developing outside the uterus. [1700–10; EXTRA- + UTERINE]

ex′trau′terine preg′nancy, *Med.* See **ectopic pregnancy.**

ex•trav•a•gance (ik strav′ə gəns), *n.* **1.** excessive or unnecessary expenditure or outlay of money. **2.** an instance of this: *That sports car is an inexcusable extravagance.* **3.** unrestrained or fantastic excess, as of actions or opinions. **4.** an extravagant action, notion, etc.: *the extravagances one commits in moments of stress.* [1635–45; < F, MF; see EXTRAVAGANT, -ANCE]
—Syn. 3. lavishness, profusion. **—Ant. 1.** frugality.

ex•trav•a•gan•cy (ik strav′ə gən sē), *n., pl.* **-cies.** extravagance. [1615–25; EXTRAVAG(ANT) + -ANCY]

ex•trav•a•gant (ik strav′ə gənt), *adj.* **1.** spending much more than is necessary or wise; wasteful: *an extravagant shopper.* **2.** excessively high: *extravagant expenses; extravagant prices.* **3.** exceeding the bounds of reason, as actions, demands, opinions, or passions. **4.** going beyond what is deserved or justifiable: *extravagant praise.* **5.** *Obs.* wandering beyond bounds. [1350–1400; ME < ML *extrāvagant-* (s. of *extrāvagāns*), prp. of *extrāvagārī,* equiv. to *extrā-* EXTRA- + *vagārī* to wander] **—ex•trav′a•gant•ly,** *adv.* **—ex•trav′a•gant•ness,** *n.*
—Syn. 1. imprudent, spendthrift, prodigal. **2.** immoderate, excessive, inordinate. **3.** unreasonable, unrestrained, fantastic, wild, absurd, preposterous. **—Ant. 1.** prudent, thrifty. **2.** moderate. **3.** reasonable.

ex•trav•a•gan•za (ik strav′ə gan′zə), *n.* **1.** a musical or dramatic composition or production, as comic opera or musical comedy, marked by a loose structure, a frivolous theme, and elaborate costuming and staging. **2.** any lavish or opulent show, event, assemblage, etc.: *an extravaganza of new housewares on the twelfth floor.* [1745–55; alter. of It *(e)stravaganza* extravagance]

ex•trav•a•gate (ik strav′ə gāt′), *v.i.,* **-gat•ed, -gat•ing.** *Archaic.* **1.** to wander beyond bounds; roam at will; stray. **2.** to go beyond the bounds of propriety or reason. [1590–1600; < ML *extrāvagātus* strayed, wandered away from, ptp. of *extrāvagārī.* See EXTRAVAGANT, -ATE[1]]

ex•tra•vag•i•nal (ek′strə vaj′ə nl), *adj.* **1.** *Bot.* developing outside the sheath, as the young shoots of certain grasses. **2.** *Anat.* located outside the vagina. [EXTRA- + VAGINAL]

ex•trav•a•sate (ik strav′ə sāt′), *v.,* **-sat•ed, -sat•ing,** *n.* *—v.t.* **1.** *Pathol.* to force out from the proper vessels, as blood, esp. so as to diffuse through the surrounding tissues. **2.** *Geol.* to pour forth, as lava, from a subterranean source in a molten state. *—v.i.* **3.** *Pathol.* to be extravasated, as blood. **4.** *Geol.* to pour forth lava or the like. *—n.* **5.** *Pathol.* the extravasated material; extravasation. [1655–65; EXTRA- + VAS + -ATE[1]]

ex•trav•a•sa•tion (ik strav′ə sā′shən), *n.* **1.** the act of extravasating. **2.** the matter extravasated. [1670–80; EXTRAVASATE + -ION]

ex•tra•vas•cu•lar (ek′strə vas′kyə lər), *adj. Anat.* situated outside a blood vessel or vessels. [1795–1805; EXTRA- + VASCULAR]

ex•tra•ve•hic•u•lar (ek′strə vē hik′yə lər), *adj. Aerospace.* of, pertaining to, or being an activity performed by an astronaut outside a space vehicle while in orbit: *an extravehicular activity.* [1960–65; EXTRA- + VEHICULAR]

ex′travehic′ular mobil′ity u′nit, a spacesuit worn by a space-shuttle astronaut during an extravehicular activity. *Abbr.:* EMU

ex•tra•ver•sion (ek′strə vûr′zhən, -shən; ek′strə-vûr′-), *n. Psychol.* extroversion (def. 1). [1685–95] **—ex′tra•ver′sive, ex′tra•ver′tive,** *adj.* **—ex′tra•ver′sive•ly, ex′tra•ver′tive•ly,** *adv.*

ex•tra•vert (ek′strə vûrt′), *n., adj., v.t.* extrovert.

ex•tra•vir•gin (ek′strə vûr′jin), *adj.* (of olive oil) made from the first pressing of highest-quality olives.

ex•tre•ma (ik strē′mə), *n. Math.* pl. of **extremum.**

Ex•tre•ma•du•ra (*Sp.* es′tʀe mä tho͞o′ʀä), *n.* Estremadura.

ex•tre•mal (ik strē′məl), *adj. Math.* of or pertaining to an extremum or the calculation of extrema: *an extremal problem.* [1400–50; late ME. See EXTREM(UM), -AL[1]]

ex•treme (ik strēm′), *adj.,* **-trem•er, -trem•est,** *n.* *—adj.* **1.** of a character or kind farthest removed from the ordinary or average: *extreme measures.* **2.** utmost or exceedingly great in degree: *extreme joy.* **3.** farthest from the center or middle; outermost; endmost: *the extreme limits of a town.* **4.** farthest, utmost, or very far in any direction: *an object at the extreme point of vision.* **5.** exceeding the bounds of moderation: *extreme fashions.* **6.** going to the utmost or very great lengths in action, habit, opinion, etc.: *an extreme conservative.* **7.** last or final: *extreme hopes.* *—n.* **8.** the utmost or highest degree, or a very high degree: *cautious to an extreme.* **9.** one of two things as remote or different from each other as possible: *the extremes of joy and grief.* **10.** the furthest or utmost length; an excessive length, beyond the ordinary or average: *extremes in dress.* **11.** an extreme act, measure, condition, etc.: *the extreme of poverty.* **12.** *Math.* **a.** the first or the last term, as of a proportion or series. **b.** a relative maximum or relative minimum value of a function in a given region. **13.** *Logic.* the subject or the predicate of the conclusion of a syllogism; either of two terms that are separated in the premises and brought together in the conclusion. **14.** *Archaic.* the utmost point, or extremity, of something. [1425–75; late ME < L *extrēmus,* superl. of *exterus* outward. See EXTERIOR] **—ex•treme′ness,** *n.*
—Syn. 2. greatest, highest; superlative. **3.** ultimate, last, uttermost, remotest. **6.** extravagant, immoderate, excessive, fanatical, uncompromising, unreasonable. See **radical.** **—Ant. 6.** moderate.

ex•treme•ly (ik strēm′lē), *adv.* in an extreme degree; exceedingly: *extremely cold.* [1525–35; EXTREME + -LY]

extreme′ly high′ fre′quency, *Radio.* any frequency between 30 and 300 gigahertz. *Abbr.:* EHF, ehf [1950–55]

extreme′ly low′ fre′quency, *Radio.* any frequency between 30 and 300 hertz. *Abbr.:* ELF, elf [1965–70]

ex′treme unc′tion (ek′strēm, ik strēm′), *Rom. Cath. Ch.* See **anointing of the sick.** [1570–80]

ex•trem•ism (ik strē′miz əm), *n.* a tendency or disposition to go to extremes or an instance of going to extremes, esp. in political matters: *leftist extremism; the extremism of the Nazis.* [1860–65; EXTREME + -ISM]

ex•trem•ist (ik strē′mist), *n.* **1.** a person who goes to extremes, esp. in political matters. **2.** a supporter or advocate of extreme doctrines or practices. *—adj.* **3.** belonging or pertaining to extremists. [1840–50; EXTREME + -IST]

ex•trem•i•ty (ik strem′i tē), *n., pl.* **-ties. 1.** the extreme or terminal point, limit, or part of something. **2.** a limb of the body. **3.** Usually, **extremities.** the end part of a limb, as a hand or foot: *to experience cold in one's extremities.* **4.** Often, **extremities.** a condition or circumstance of extreme need, distress, etc.: *to suffer the extremities of being poor.* **5.** the utmost or any extreme degree: *the extremity of joy.* **6.** an extreme or extraordinary measure, act, etc.: *to go to any extremity to feed the children.* **7.** extreme nature or character: *the extremity of his views on foreign trade.* **8.** *Archaic.* a person's last moment before death. [1325–75; ME < L *extrēmitās.* See EXTREME, -ITY]
—Syn. 1. end, termination; verge; border, boundary.

ex•tre•mum (ik strē′məm), *n., pl.* **-ma** (-mə). *Math.* a maximum or minimum value of a function in a specified neighborhood. [1900–05; < NL, n. use of neut. of L *extrēmus* EXTREME]

ex•tri•ca•ble (ek′stri kə bəl, ik strik′ə bəl), *adj.* capable of being extricated. [1615–25; < L *extric(āre)* (see EXTRICATE) + -ABLE]

ex•tri•cate (ek′stri kāt′), *v.t.,* **-cat•ed, -cat•ing. 1.** to free or release from entanglement; disengage: *to extricate someone from a dangerous situation.* **2.** to liberate

(gas) from combination, as in a chemical process. [1605–15; < L *extricātus* (ptp. of *extricāre*), equiv. to *ex-* EX-[1] + *tric(ae)* perplexities + *-ātus* -ATE[1]] **—ex′tri·ca′tion,** *n.*
—Syn. 1. loose, rescue, deliver, save, recover.

ex·trin·sic (ik strin′sik, -zik), *adj.* **1.** not essential or inherent; not a basic part or quality; extraneous: *facts that are extrinsic to the matter under discussion.* **2.** being outside a thing; outward or external; operating or coming from without: *extrinsic influences.* **3.** *Anat.* (of certain muscles, nerves, etc.) originating outside the anatomical limits of a part. Also, **ex·trin′si·cal.** [1535–45; < LL *extrinsecus* outward, adj. use of L *extrinsecus* (adv.) on the outward side, equiv. to *extrim-* (*ext(e)r* outer (see EXTERIOR) + *-im* adv. suffix) + *secus* beside (deriv. of *sequī* to follow)] **—ex·trin′si·cal·ly,** *adv.*

extrin′sic eye′ mus′cle, *Anat.* any of six small muscles that control the horizontal, vertical, and rotating movements of the eyeball. Also called **extraocular muscle.**

extrin′sic fac′tor, *Biochem.* See **vitamin B_{12}.** [1925–30]

extro-, var. of **extra-** (used to contrast with **intro-**): *extrovert.*

ex·trorse (ek strôrs′, ek′strôrs), *adj. Bot.* turned or facing outward, as anthers that open toward the perianth. [1855–60; < LL *extrorsus* in outward direction, equiv. to *extr(a)-* EXTRA- + *(v)orsus* (adv.) turned] **—ex·trorse′ly,** *adv.*

ex·tro·spec·tion (ek′strə spek′shən), *n.* the consideration and observation of things external to the self; examination and study of externals. [EXTRO- + (IN-TRO)SPECTION)] **—ex′tro·spec′tive,** *adj.*

ex·tro·ver·sion (ek′strə vûr′zhən, -shən, ek′strə-vûr′-, -strō-), *n.* **1.** Also, **extraversion.** *Psychol.* **a.** the act of directing one's interest outward or to things outside the self. **b.** the state of being concerned primarily with things outside the self, with the external environment rather than with one's own thoughts and feelings. Cf. **introversion** (def. 3). **2.** *Pathol.* a turning inside out, as of the eyelids or of the bladder. [1650–60; 1915–20 for def. 1; EXTRO- + L *versiōn-* (s. of *versiō*) a turning] **—ex′tro·ver′sive, ex′tro·ver′tive,** *adj.* **—ex′tro·ver′sive·ly, ex′tro·ver′tive·ly,** *adv.*

ex·tro·vert (ek′strə vûrt′, -strō-),*n.* **1.** an outgoing, gregarious person. **2.** *Psychol.* a person characterized by extroversion; a person concerned primarily with the physical and social environment (opposed to *introvert*). *—adj.* **3.** Also, **ex′tro·vert′ed.** *Psychol.* marked by extroversion. *—v.t.* **4.** *Psychol.* to direct (the mind, one's interest, etc.) outward or to things outside the self. Also, **extravert.** [1665–75; EXTRO- + L *vertere* to turn]

ex·trude (ik strōōd′), *v.,* **-trud·ed, -trud·ing.** *—v.t.* **1.** to thrust out; force or press out; expel: *to extrude molten rock.* **2.** to form (metal, plastic, etc.) with a desired cross section by forcing it through a die. *—v.i.* **3.** to protrude. **4.** to be extruded: *This metal extrudes easily.* [1560–70; < L *extrūdere* to thrust out, drive out, equiv. to *ex-* EX-[1] + *trūdere* to thrust, push] **—ex·trud′er,** *n.* **—ex·tru·si·ble** (ik strōō′sə bəl, -zə-), **ex·trud′a·ble,** *adj.*

ex·tru·sile (ik strōō′sil, -zil, -sīl, -zīl), *adj.* able to be thrust out or extruded. [1840–50; EXTRUS(ION) + -ILE]

ex·tru·sion (ik strōō′zhən), *n.* **1.** the act of extruding or the state of being extruded. **2.** something that is extruded. [1530–40; < ML *extrūsiōn-* (s. of *extrūsiō*), equiv. to L *extrūs(us)* (ptp. of *extrūdere* to EXTRUDE) + *-iōn-* -ION]

extru′sion press′, a machine that shapes semisoft metals or plastics by forcing them through dies. [1935–40]

ex·tru·sive (ik strōō′siv, -ziv), *adj.* **1.** tending to extrude. **2.** pertaining to extrusion. **3.** Also, **effusive.** *Geol.* noting or pertaining to a class of igneous rocks that have been forced out in a molten or plastic condition upon the surface of the earth. [1810–20; EXTRUS(ION) + -IVE]

ex·u·ber·ance (ig zōō′bər əns), *n.* **1.** Also, **ex·u′ber·an·cy.** the state of being exuberant. **2.** an instance of this: *His pranks are youthful exuberances.* [1630–40; < L *exūberantia.* See EXUBERANT, -ANCE]

ex·u·ber·ant (ig zōō′bər ənt), *adj.* **1.** effusively and almost uninhibitedly enthusiastic; lavishly abundant: *an exuberant welcome for the hero.* **2.** abounding in vitality; extremely joyful and vigorous. **3.** extremely good; overflowing; plentiful: *exuberant health.* **4.** profuse in growth or production; luxuriant; superabundant: *exuberant vegetation.* [1425–75; late ME < L *exūberant-* (s. of *exūberāns*), prp. of *exūberāre*, equiv. to *ex-* EX-[1] + *ūberāre* to be fruitful (deriv. of *ūber* fertile); see -ANT] **—ex·u′ber·ant·ly,** *adv.*

ex·u·ber·ate (ig zōō′bə rāt′), *v.i.,* **-at·ed, -at·ing.** to be exuberant; superabound; overflow. [1425–75; late ME < L *exūberātus.* See EXUBERANT, -ATE[1]]

ex·u·date (eks′yŏŏ dāt′, ek′sə-, eg′zə-), *n.* a substance exuded; exudation. [1875–80; EXUDE + -ATE[1]]

ex·u·da·tion (eks′yŏŏ dā′shən, ek′sə-, eg′zə-), *n.* **1.** the act of exuding. **2.** something that is exuded. **3.** a discharge of certain elements of the blood into the tissues. [1605–15; < LL *ex(s)ūdātiōn-* (s. of *ex(s)ūdātiō*), equiv. to *ex(s)ūdāt(us)* (ptp. of *ex(s)ūdāre* to EXUDE) + *-iōn-* -ION] **—ex·u·da·tive** (ig zōō′də tiv, ik sōō′-), *adj.*

ex·ude (ig zōōd′, ik sōōd′), *v.,* **-ud·ed, -ud·ing.** *—v.i.* **1.** to come out gradually in drops, as sweat, through pores or small openings; ooze out. *—v.t.* **2.** to send out, as sweat; emit through pores or small openings. **3.** to project or display conspicuously or abundantly; radiate: *to exude cheerfulness.* [1565–75; < L *ex(s)ūdāre*, equiv. to *ex-* EX-[1] + *sūdāre* to sweat]

ex·ult (ig zult′), *v.i.* **1.** to show or feel a lively or triumphant joy; rejoice exceedingly; be highly elated or jubilant: *They exulted over their victory.* **2.** *Obs.* to leap, esp. for joy. [1560–70; < L *ex(s)ultāre* to leap up, equiv. to *ex-* EX-[1] + *-sultāre* (comb. form of *saltāre* to leap)] **—ex·ult′ing·ly,** *adv.*
—Syn. 1. delight, glory, revel.

ex·ult·ant (ig zul′tnt), *adj.* exulting; highly elated; jubilant; triumphant. [1645–55; < L *ex(s)ultant-* (s. of *ex(s)ultāns*), prp. of *exultāre* to EXULT; see -ANT] **—ex·ult′ant·ly,** *adv.*

ex·ul·ta·tion (eg′zul tā′shən, ek′sul-), *n.* the act of exulting; lively or triumphant joy, as over success or victory. Also, **ex·ult·an·cy** (ig zul′tn sē), **ex·ult′ance.** [1375–1425; late ME < L *ex(s)ultātiōn-* (s. of *ex(s)ultātiō*), equiv. to *ex(s)ultāt(us)* (ptp. of *ex(s)ultāre* to EXULT) + *-iōn-* -ION]

ex·urb (ek′sərb, eg′zərb), *n.* a small, usually prosperous, community situated beyond the suburbs of a city. [1950–55, *Amer.*; EX-[1] + (SUB)URB]

ex·ur·ban (ek sûr′bən, eg zûr′-), *adj.* of, pertaining to, or characteristic of exurbs and exurbanites. [1900–05; EX-[1] + (SUB)URBAN]

ex·ur·ban·ite (ek sûr′bə nīt′, eg zûr′-), *n.* a person who lives in an exurb, esp. one who has moved there from a city. [1950–55; EX-[1] + (SUB)URBANITE]

ex·ur·bi·a (ek sûr′bē ə, eg zûr′-), *n.* a generalized area comprising the exurbs. [1950–55, *Amer.*; EX-[1] + (SUB)URBIA]

ex·u·vi·ae (ig zōō′vē ē′, ik sōō′-), *n.pl.* the cast skins, shells, or other coverings of animals. [1645–55; < L, deriv. of *exuere* to remove, strip off, divest oneself of, equiv. to *ex-* EX-[1] + *-uere* to put on] **—ex·u′vi·al,** *adj.*

ex·u·vi·ate (ig zōō′vē āt′, ik sōō′-), *v.i., v.t.,* **-at·ed, -at·ing.** to cast off or shed (exuviae); molt. [1850–55; EXUVI(AE) + -ATE[1]] **—ex·u′vi·a′tion,** *n.*

ex vo·to (eks wō′tō; *Eng.* eks vō′tō), *Latin.* from, or in pursuance of, a vow. [1815–25]

ex-vo·to (eks vō′tō), *n., pl.* **-tos.** *n.* a painting or other object left as an offering in fulfillment of a vow or in gratitude, as for recovery from an illness or injury. [1815–25; < L *ex vōtō* lit., out of a vow]

ex-works (eks′wûrks′), *adj. Brit.* direct from the factory, excluding delivery costs, distribution costs, retail commission, etc.: *the ex-works price.* [1965–70]

-ey[1], var. of **-y**[1], esp. after *y: clayey.*

-ey[2], var. of **-y**[2], esp. after *y.*

E·yak (ē′yak), *n., pl.* **E·yaks,** (*esp. collectively*) **E·yak** for 1. **1.** a member of a small tribe of Indians formerly inhabiting the southeastern coast of Alaska. **2.** the language of the Eyak, related to the Athabaskan languages.

e·ya·let (ä′yä let′), *n.* vilayet. [1850–55; < Turk *eyalet* < Ar *iyālat*]

ey·as (ī′əs), *n.* **1.** a nestling. **2.** *Falconry.* a young falcon taken from the nest for training. Also, *esp. Brit.,* **ey′ass.** [1480–90; var. of *nyas, nias* (*a nyas* taken as *an eyas*) < MF *niais* nestling, deriv. of L *nidus* NEST]

Eyck (ik), *n.* **Hu·bert van** (hyōō′bərt van; *Du.* hʏ′bɛʀt vän), or **Huy·brecht van** (*Du.* hoi′bʀɛкнт vän), 1366–1426, and his brother **Jan van** (*Du.* yän vän) (*Jan van Brugge*), 1385?–1440: Flemish painters.

eye (ī), *n., pl.* **eyes,** (*Archaic*) **ey·en** or **eyne;** *v.,* **eyed, ey·ing** or **eye·ing.** *—n.* **1.** the organ of sight, in vertebrates typically one of a pair of spherical bodies contained in an orbit of the skull and in humans appearing externally as a dense, white, curved membrane, or sclera, surrounding a circular, colored portion, or iris, that is covered by a clear, curved membrane, or cornea, and in the center of which is an opening, or pupil, through which light passes to the retina. **2.** the aggregate of structures situated within or near the orbit that assist, support, or protect the eye. **3.** this organ with respect to the color of the iris: *blue eyes.* **4.** the region surrounding the eye: *a black eye; puffy eyes.* **5.** sight; vision: *a sharp eye.* **6.** the power of seeing; appreciative or discriminating visual perception: *the eye of an artist.* **7.** a look, glance, or gaze: *to cast one's eye at a beautiful necklace.* **8.** an attentive look, close observation, or watch: *to be under the eye of a guard.* **9.** regard, view, aim, or intention: *to have an eye to one's own advantage.* **10.** a manner or way of looking at a thing; estimation; opinion: *in the eyes of the law.* **11.** a center of light, intelligence, influence, etc. **12.** something resembling or suggesting the eye in appearance, shape, etc., as the opening in the lens of a camera, a peephole, or a buttonhole. **13.** *Bot.* **a.** the bud of a potato, Jerusalem artichoke, etc. **b.** a small, contrastingly colored part at the center of a flower. **14.** the central spot of a target; bull's-eye. **15.** a choice center cut of meat: *an eye of round; the eye of the rib.* **16.** one of the round spots on the tail feathers of a peacock. **17.** the hole in a needle. **18.** a hole made in a thing for the insertion of some object, as the handle of a tool: *the eye of an ax.* **19.** a metal or other ring through which something, as a rope or rod, is passed. **20.** the loop into which a hook is inserted. **21.** *Electronics.* a photoelectric cell or similar device used to perform a function analogous to visual inspection. **22.** *Building Trades.* a ring on the end of a tension member, as an eye bar or eye bolt, for connection with another member. **23.** a hole formed during the maturation of cheese, esp. Emmenthaler or Gruyère. **24.** a loop worked at the end of a rope. **25.** *Meteorol.* the approximately circular region of relatively light winds and fair weather found at the center of a severe tropical cyclone. **26. eyes,** *Naut.* the extreme forward part of the upper deck at the bow of a vessel. **27.** *Naut.* the precise direction from which a wind is blowing. **28. an eye for an eye,** repayment in kind, as revenge for an injustice. **29. be all eyes,** to give all one's attention to something; look intently. **30. catch someone's eye,** to draw or attract someone's attention: *to catch the waiter's eye.* **31. give (someone) the eye,** *Informal.* to look fixedly at (another person), esp. with obvious admiration; ogle: *She ignored the men who were giving her the eye.* **32. have an eye for,** to have the ability to appreciate distinctions in; be discerning or perceptive about: *She has an eye for antique furniture.* **33. have eyes only for, a.** to want no other person or thing but: *She was always surrounded by admirers, but she had eyes only for Harry.* **b.** to see, or view, or desire to see only. Also, **only have eyes for.** **34. in a pig's eye,** *Slang.* absolutely not; never: *In a pig's eye I will!* **35. keep an eye on,** to watch over attentively: *Please keep an eye on my plants while I'm away.* **36. keep an eye out for,** to be vigilant in looking or watching for: *The announcer told his listeners to keep an eye out for the escaped criminal.* **37. keep one's eyes open,** to be especially alert or observant. **38. lay, clap,** or **set eyes on,** *Informal.* to catch sight of; see: *They had never laid eyes on such a big car before.* **39. make eyes at,** to gaze flirtatiously or amorously at. **40. my eye!** *Informal.* (a mild exclamation of contradiction or surprise): *He says he wasn't told about this? My eye!* **41. open one's eyes,** to bring someone to a realization of the truth or of something previously unknown: *A trip through Asia opened his eyes to the conditions under which millions had to live.* **42. pick the eyes out,** *Australia and New Zealand.* to select the best parts or items. **43. run one's eye over,** to glance briefly at; examine hastily. **44. see eye to eye,** to have exactly the same opinion; agree: *They have never been able to see eye to eye on politics.* **45. see with half an eye,** to see or realize immediately or with ease: *Anyone can see with half an eye that the plan is doomed to fail.* **46. shut one's eyes to,** to refuse to see or consider; disregard: *We can no longer shut our eyes to the gravity of the situation.* **47. sight for sore eyes,** a welcome sight; a pleasant surprise: *After our many days in the desert, the wretched village was a sight for sore eyes.* **48. with an eye to,** with a plan or purpose of: *with an eye to one's future.* **49. with one's eyes open,** aware of the inherent or potential risks: *She signed the papers with her eyes open.* *—v.t.* **50.** to fix the eyes upon; view: *to eye the wonders of nature.* **51.** to observe or watch narrowly: *She eyed the two strangers with suspicion.* **52.** to make an eye in: *to eye a needle.* *—v.i.* **53.** *Obs.* to appear to the eye. [bef. 900; ME *eie, ie,* OE *ēge,* var. of *ēage;* c. G *Auge;* akin to L *oculus,* Gk *ṓps,* Skt *akṣi*] **—eye′a·ble,** *adj.* **—eye′like′,** *adj.* **—ey′er,** *n.*

eye (human)
A, ciliary muscle; B, ciliary processes; C, suspensory ligament; D, iris; E, conjunctiva; F, cornea; G, pupil; H, crystalline lens; I, anterior chamber; J, posterior chamber; K, ocular muscles; L, sclera; M, choroid coat; N, retina; O, vitreous humor; P, blind spot; Q, optic nerve; R, retinal artery

eye′ appeal′, the quality of appealing to the eye; attractiveness; beauty. [1925–30, *Amer.*]

eye·ball (ī′bôl′), *n.* **1.** the ball or globe of the eye. *—v.t.* **2.** *Informal.* to look at, check, or observe closely: *two opponents eyeballing each other.* [1580–90; 1900–05 for def. 2; EYE + BALL[1]] **—eye′ball′er,** *n.*

eye·ball-to-eye·ball (ī′bôl′tə ī′bôl′, -tōō-), *adj., adv.* close or direct and often hostile; face-to-face: *an eyeball-to-eyeball confrontation.* [1960–65]

eye′ bank′, a place for the storage of corneas that have been removed from the eyes of people recently deceased, used for transplanting to the eyes of persons having corneal defects. [1940–45, *Amer.*]

eye·bar (ī′bär′), *n. Civ. Engin.* a tension member, used esp. in bridge and roof trusses, having the form of a metal bar enlarged at each end to include an eye. [1885–90; EYE + BAR[1]]

eye′ bath′, eyecup. [1820–30]

eye·beam (ī′bēm′), *n.* a beam or glance of the eye. [1580–90; EYE + BEAM]

eye·bolt (ī′bōlt′), *n.* a bolt having a ring-shaped head. [1760–70; EYE + BOLT[1]]

eye·bright (ī′brīt′), *n.* **1.** any of various plants belonging to the genus *Euphrasia,* of the figwort family, as *E. officinalis* of Europe, formerly used for treating diseases of the eye. **2.** the scarlet pimpernel. See under **pimpernel.** [1525–35; EYE + BRIGHT]

eye·brow (ī′brou′), *n.* **1.** the arch or ridge forming the upper part of the orbit of the eye. **2.** the fringe of hair growing on this arch or ridge. **3.** a dormer having a roof that is an upwardly curved continuation of the main roof plane. **4.** *Print., Journ.* kicker (def. 9). **5.** *Naut.* a curved molding protecting a port from falling or dripping water. [1575–85; EYE + BROW]

eyebrow, (def. 3)

eye′brow pen′cil, a pencil for outlining and shading eyebrows. [1880–85]

eye-catch·er (ī′kach′ər), *n.* a person or thing that attracts the attention. [1920–25] **—eye′-catch′ing,** *adj.*

eye′ chart′, *Ophthalm.* a chart for testing vision,

CONCISE PRONUNCIATION KEY: act, cāpe, dâre, pärt; set, ēqual; *if,* īce; ox, ōver, ôrder, oil, bŏŏk, bōōt, out; up, ûrge; child; sing; shoe; thin, *that;* zh as in *treasure.* ə = *a* as in *alone, e* as in *system, i* as in *easily, o* as in *gallop, u* as in *circus;* ə as in *fire* (fīər), *hour* (ouər). l and n can serve as syllabic consonants, as in *cradle* (krād′l), and *button* (but′n). See the full key inside the front cover.

typically containing letters, symbols, or pictures in rows of decreasing size that are to be read or identified at a fixed distance. [1940–45]

eye′ con′tact, **1.** the act of looking directly into another's eyes: *We never made eye contact at any time during the interview.* **2.** *Psychol.* a meeting of the eyes of two persons, regarded as a meaningful nonverbal form of communication. [1960–65]

eye•cup (ī′kup′), *n.* a device for applying eyewash to the eye, consisting of a cup or glass with a rim shaped to fit snugly around the orbit of the eye. Also called **eye bath.** [1870–75, *Amer.*; EYE + CUP]

eyed (īd), *adj.* **1.** having an eye or eyes: *an eyed needle; an eyed potato.* **2.** having eyes of a specified kind (usually used in combination): *a blue-eyed baby.* **3.** having eyelike spots. [1325–75; ME; see EYE, -ED[3]]

eye′ di′alect, the literary use of misspellings that are intended to convey a speaker's lack of education or use of humorously dialectal pronunciations but that are actually no more than respellings of standard pronunciations, as *wimmin* for "women," *wuz* for "was," and *peepul* for "people." [1920–25]

eye′ doc′tor, **1.** an ophthalmologist. **2.** an optometrist. [1880–85]

—**Syn.** The term EYE DOCTOR refers generally to an ophthalmologist, but is also used informally (and imprecisely) in referring to an optometrist. An OPHTHALMOLOGIST is a physician who specializes in the diagnosis and treatment of diseases of the eye. Ophthalmologists may prescribe and fit eyeglasses and contact lenses and also treat eye diseases with drugs and surgery. An OPTOMETRIST is not a physician. Optometrists are professionally licensed to test a person for vision defects, prescribe and fit glasses and contact lenses, and prescribe therapeutic exercises, but they do not perform surgery and in most U.S. states may not prescribe drugs. An OPTICIAN is licensed to make, sell, and fit glasses and, in most U.S. states, contact lenses prescribed by an ophthalmologist or optometrist. The term OCULIST, which formerly referred to an ophthalmologist, is no longer used.

eye•drop•per (ī′drop′ər), *n.* a dropper, esp. one for applying eye drops. [1935–40; EYE + DROPPER]

eye′ drops′, *Med.* drops for use in the eyes, as to relieve discomfort or to dilate the pupils before an eye examination. Also, **eye′drops′.** [1935–40]

eye-fill•ing (ī′fil′ing), *adj.* attractive to the eye; providing an eyeful. [1895–1900]

eye•fold (ī′fōld′), *n.* epicanthus. Also, **eye′ fold′.** [EYE + FOLD[1]]

eye•ful (ī′fo͝ol), *n., pl.* **-fuls.** **1.** an amount of foreign matter thrown, blown, etc., into the eye: *an eyeful of dust.* **2.** as much as one can or wants to see: *The tourists got an eyeful of slum life.* **3.** *Informal.* a very attractive person, esp. a beautiful woman. [1825–35; EYE + -FUL]

eye•glass (ī′glas′, ī′gläs′), *n.* **1.** **eyeglasses,** glass (def. 5). **2.** a single lens used to aid vision, esp. one worn or carried on the person; monocle. **3.** an eyepiece. **4.** an eyecup. [1605–15; EYE + GLASS]

eye•ground (ī′ground′), *n.* the fundus of the eye as seen through an ophthalmoscope, examined chiefly to determine changes in the blood vessels. [1895–1900; EYE + GROUND[1]]

eye•hole (ī′hōl′), *n.* **1.** a hole to look through, as in a mask or a curtain. **2.** a circular opening for the insertion of a pin, hook, rope, etc.; eye. **3.** See **eye socket.** [1630–40; EYE + HOLE]

eye•hook (ī′ho͝ok′), *n.* See **hook and eye** (def. 3). [EYE + HOOK]

eye•lash (ī′lash′), *n.* **1.** one of the short, thick, curved hairs growing as a fringe on the edge of an eyelid. **2.** the fringe of hairs itself. [1745–55; EYE + LASH[1]]

eye′ lens′, *Optics.* the lens of an eyepiece closest to the eye. [1870–75]

eye•less (ī′lis), *adj.* **1.** lacking eyes: *eyeless fish that evolved in dark caves.* **2.** lacking sight; blind. [1560–70; EYE + LESS]

CONCISE ETYMOLOGY KEY: <, descended or borrowed from; >, whence; b., blend of, blended; c., cognate with; cf., compare; deriv., derivative; equiv., equivalent; imit., imitative; obl., oblique; r., replacing; s., stem; sp., spelling, spelled; resp., respelling, respelled; trans., translation; ?, origin unknown; *, unattested; ‡, probably earlier than. See the full key inside the front cover.

eye•let (ī′lit), *n., v.,* **-let•ed** or **-let•ted, -let•ing** or **-let•ting.** —*n.* **1.** a small hole, usually round and finished along the edge, as in cloth or leather for the passage of a lace or cord or as in embroidery for ornamental effect. **2.** a lightweight fabric pierced by small holes finished with stitching and often laid out in flowerlike designs. **3.** a metal ring for lining a small hole; grommet. **4.** an eyehole in a wall, mask, etc. **5.** Also, **oillet, oyelet, oylet.** (in medieval architecture) a small aperture in a wall used as a window or loophole. **6.** a small eye. —*v.t.* **7.** to make an eyelet in. **8.** to insert metal eyelets in. [1350–1400; ME *oillet* < OF *oillet,* equiv. to *oill* eye (< L *oculus;* see OCULAR) + *-et* -ET; influenced by EYE]

eye•let•eer (ī′li tēr′), *n.* a small, pointed instrument for making eyelet holes. [1870–75; EYELET + -EER]

eye•lid (ī′lid′), *n.* the movable lid of skin that serves to cover and uncover the eyeball. [1200–50; ME; see EYE, LID]

eye•lift (ī′lift′), *n.* cosmetic blepharoplasty. Also called **eye tuck.** [EYE + LIFT, on the model of FACE-LIFT]

eye•lin•er (ī′lī′nər), *n.* a cosmetic for the eyelids, usually applied in a thin line close to the lashes to accentuate the eyes. [1955–60; EYE + LINER[1]]

eye-mind•ed (ī′mīn′did), *adj.* disposed to perceive one's environment in visual terms and to recall sights more vividly than sounds, smells, etc. Cf. **ear-minded, motor-minded.** [1885–90] —**eye′-mind′ed•ness,** *n.*

ey•en (ī′ən), *n. Archaic.* pl. of **eye.**

eye•o•pen•er (ī′ō′pə nər), *n.* **1.** an experience or disclosure that gives one a sudden realization or understanding: *Her disclosures about her childhood were a real eyeopener.* **2.** a drink of liquor taken early in the day and intended to wake a person up fully. [1810–20, *Amer.*; EYE + OPENER]

eye-o•pen•ing (ī′ō′pə ning), *adj.* serving as an eye-opener; enlightening: *an eye-opening investigation of government corruption.*

eye•piece (ī′pēs′), *n.* the lens or combination of lenses in an optical instrument through which the eye views the image formed by the objective lens or lenses; ocular. See diag. under **microscope.** [1780–90; EYE + PIECE]

eye•pit (ī′pit′), *n.* See **eye socket.** [1225–75; ME; see EYE, PIT[1]]

eye′ point′, *Optics.* See **exit pupil.** [1855–60]

eye-pop•per (ī′pop′ər), *n. Informal.* something that causes astonishment or excitement. [1940–45]

eye-pop•ping (ī′pop′ing), *adj. Informal.* astonishing or thrilling.

eye′ rhyme′. See **sight rhyme.** [1870–75]

eye•serv•ice (ī′sûr′vis), *n.* work or service done only when the employer is watching. [1520–30; EYE + SERVICE] —**eye′serv′ant, eye′serv′er,** *n.*

eye•shade (ī′shād′), *n.* a visor worn on the head or forehead to shield the eyes from overhead light. [1835–45; EYE + SHADE]

eye′ shad′ow, a cosmetic coloring material applied to the eyelids. Also, **eye′shad′ow.** [1925–30]

eye•shot (ī′shot′), *n.* **1.** range of vision; view: *The ship passed within eyeshot.* **2.** *Archaic.* a glance. [1590–1600; EYE + SHOT[1]]

eye•sight (ī′sīt′), *n.* **1.** the power or faculty of seeing. **2.** the act or fact of seeing. **3.** the range of the eye: *to come within eyesight.* [1150–1200; ME; see EYE, SIGHT]

eyes′ left′, *Mil.* (at ceremonies) the command to turn the head and eyes to the left in salute.

eye′ sock′et, the socket or orbit of the eye. [1835–45]

eye•some (ī′səm), *adj. Archaic.* pleasant to look at. [1575–85; EYE + -SOME[1]]

eyes-on•ly (īz′ōn′lē), *adj.* (of a communication) secret or confidential and meant to be seen only by the person to whom it is directed: *an eyes-only report.* [1970–75]

eye•sore (ī′sôr′, ī′sōr′), *n.* something unpleasant to look at: *The run-down house was an eyesore to the neighbors.* [1250–1300; ME; see EYE, SORE]

eye′ splice′, a splice made in a rope by turning back one end and interweaving it with the main body of the rope so as to form a loop. See illus. under **splice.** [1760–70]

eye•spot (ī′spot′), *n.* **1.** a sensory organ of lower animals, having a light-perceiving function. **2.** an eyelike spot, as on the tail of a peacock; eye. **3.** *Plant Pathol.* a disease of plants, characterized by elliptical lesions on the leaves and stems, stunting of growth, and rotting, caused by any of several fungi. [1580–90; EYE + SPOT]

eyes′ right′, *Mil.* (at ceremonies) the command to turn the head and eyes to the right in salute.

eye•stalk (ī′stôk′), *n. Zool.* the stalk or peduncle upon which the eye is borne in lobsters, shrimps, etc. [1850–55; EYE + STALK[1]]

eye•stone (ī′stōn′), *n.* a small calcareous body, flat on one side and convex on the other, passed between the eye and the eyelid to bring out cinders or other foreign matter. [1670–80; EYE + STONE]

eye•strain (ī′strān′), *n.* a sensation of discomfort produced in the eyes by their excessive or improper use: *to have eyestrain from reading fine print in poor light.* [1870–75; EYE + STRAIN]

eye•strings (ī′stringz′), *n.pl. Obs.* the muscles, nerves, or tendons of the eye. [1595–1605; EYE + STRING + -S[3]]

eye•tooth (ī′to͞oth′), *n., pl.* **-teeth** (-tēth′). **1.** *Dentistry.* a canine tooth of the upper jaw: so named from its position under the eye. **2.** **cut one's eyeteeth, a.** to gain sophistication or experience; become worldly-wise. **b.** Also, **cut one's eyeteeth on.** to be initiated or gain one's first experience in (a career, hobby, skill, etc.). **3.** **give one's eyeteeth,** to give something one considers very precious, usually in exchange for an object or situation one desires: *She would give her eyeteeth for that job.* [1570–80; EYE + TOOTH]

eye′ tuck′, eyelift.

eye•wash (ī′wosh′, ī′wôsh′), *n.* **1.** Also called **collyrium.** *Pharm.* a solution applied locally to the eye for irrigation or administering medication. **2.** *Informal.* nonsense; bunk. [1865–70; EYE + WASH]

eye•wa•ter (ī′wô′tər, ī′wot′ər), *n. Archaic.* **1.** natural tears or a watery discharge from the eye. **2.** a lotion for the eyes. [1580–90; EYE + WATER]

eye•wear (ī′wâr′), *n.* any of various devices, as spectacles, contact lenses, or goggles, for aiding the vision or protecting the eyes. [1925–30; EYE + WEAR]

eye•wink (ī′wingk′), *n.* **1.** a wink of the eye. **2.** *Obs.* a look or glance. [1590–1600; EYE + WINK]

eye•wink•er (ī′wing′kər), *n.* **1.** an eyelash. **2.** anything that enters or irritates the eye and causes blinking. [1800–10; EYEWINK + -ER[1]]

eye•wit•ness (*n.* ī′wit′nis, ī′wit′nis; *v.* ī′wit′nis), *n.* **1.** a person who actually sees some act, occurrence, or thing and can give a firsthand account of it: *There were two eyewitnesses to the murder.* —*v.t.* **2.** to view with one's own eyes: *to eyewitness a murder.* [1530–40; EYE + WITNESS]

eye′ worm′, a filarial worm, *Loa loa,* of western and central Africa, that is parasitic in the skin, or subcutaneous tissue, of human beings, often migrating into the eye region. [1585–95]

eyne (īn), *n. Archaic.* pl. of **eye.**

ey•ot (ī′ət, āt), *n. Brit. Dial.* ait.

ey•ra (âr′ə, ī′rə), *n.* a jaguarundi. [1855–60; < AmerSp < Tupi *eira(ra)*]

eyre (âr), *n. Old Eng. Law.* **1.** a circuit made by an itinerant judge **(justice in eyre)** in medieval England. **2.** a county court held by a justice in eyre. [1250–1300; ME *eyre* < AF; OF *erre,* deriv. of *errer* to journey; see ERR]

Eyre (âr), *n.* **Lake,** a shallow salt lake in S South Australia. 3430 sq. mi. (8885 sq. km).

Eyre′ Penin′sula, a peninsula in S Australia, E of the Great Australian Bight. Also, **Eyre's′ Penin′sula** (ârz).

ey•rie (âr′ē, ēr′ē), *n.* aerie. Also, **ey′ry.**

ey•rir (ā′rēr), *n., pl.* **au•rar** (oi′rär). an aluminum bronze coin of Iceland, the 100th part of a króna. [1925–30; < Icel; ON: ounce, unit of money (c. Sw *öre*) < L *aureus* golden]

Ey•senck (ī′sengk), *n.* **Hans J(urgen)** (yûr′gən), born 1916, British psychologist, born in Germany.

Eysk (äsk), *n.* Yeisk.

EZ, easy: used as an abbreviation. [rebus sp.]

Ez., Ezra. Also, **Ezr.**

Ez•e•chi•as (ez′i kī′əs), *n. Douay Bible.* Hezekiah.

Ezek., Ezekiel.

E•ze•ki•el (i zē′kē əl), *n.* **1.** a Major Prophet of the 6th century B.C. **2.** a book of the Bible bearing his name. *Abbr.:* Ezek. **3.** **Moses Jacob,** 1844–1917, U.S. sculptor, in Rome. **4.** a male given name: from a Hebrew word meaning "God strengthens." Also, *Douay Bible,* **E•ze•chi•el** (i zē′kē əl) (for defs. 1, 2).

Ezr., Ezra.

Ez•ra (ez′rə), *n.* **1.** a Jewish scribe and prophet of the 5th century B.C., who with Nehemiah led the revival of Judaism in Palestine. **2.** a book of the Bible bearing his name. *Abbr.:* Ezr. **3.** a male given name: from a Hebrew word meaning "help."

DEVELOPMENT OF MAJUSCULE								
NORTH SEMITIC	GREEK		ETR	LATIN		MODERN		
						GOTHIC	ITALIC	ROMAN
ϒ	˥	—	ꟻ	ꟻ	F	𝔉	*F*	F

DEVELOPMENT OF MINUSCULE					
ROMAN CURSIVE	ROMAN UNCIAL	CAROL MIN.	MODERN		
			GOTHIC	ITALIC	ROMAN
F	F	ſ	𝔣	*f*	f

The sixth letter of the English alphabet developed from North Semitic *waw*, denoted by a symbol resembling Y. A variant (see **U**) was adopted by the Greeks as *digamma* (**Ϝ**), which had a *w*-like sound, but later dropped out of use as an alphabetic character, surviving only as a numeral. In early Latin, the *f*-sound was represented by *wh*; but the *h* was soon discontinued. The minuscule (f) is a scribal variant of the capital.

F, f (ef), *n., pl.* **F's** or **Fs, f's** or **fs. 1.** the sixth letter of the English alphabet, a consonant. **2.** any spoken sound represented by the letter *F* or *f*, as in *fat, differ,* or *huff.* **3.** something having the shape of an F. **4.** a written or printed representation of the letter *F* or *f.* **5.** a device, as a printer's type, for reproducing the letter *F* or *f.*

F, 1. Fahrenheit. **2.** female. **3.** *Genetics.* filial. **4.** firm. **5.** franc; francs. **6.** French.

F, *Symbol.* **1.** the sixth in order or in a series. **2.** (*sometimes l.c.*) (in some grading systems) a grade or mark that indicates academic work of the lowest quality; failure. **3.** *Music.* **a.** the fourth tone in the scale of C major or the sixth tone in the relative minor scale, A minor. **b.** a string, key, or pipe tuned to this tone. **c.** a written or printed note representing this tone. **d.** (in the fixed system of solmization) the fourth tone of the scale of C major, called *fa.* **e.** the tonality having F as the tonic note. **4.** (*sometimes l.c.*) the medieval Roman numeral for 40. Cf. **Roman numerals. 5.** *Math* **a.** field. **b.** function (of). **6.** (*sometimes l.c.*) *Elect.* farad. **7.** *Chem.* fluorine. **8.** (*sometimes l.c.*) *Physics.* **a.** force. **b.** frequency. **c.** fermi. **9.** *Biochem.* phenylalanine.

f, 1. firm. **2.** *Photog.* See **f-number. 3.** *Music.* forte.

f, *Symbol, Optics.* See **focal length.**

F-, *Mil.* (in designations of aircraft) fighter: *F-105.*

F., 1. Fahrenheit. **2.** February. **3.** Fellow. **4.** forint. **5.** franc; francs. **6.** France. **7.** French. **8.** Friday.

f., 1. (in prescriptions) make. [< L *fac*] **2.** *Elect.* farad. **3.** farthing. **4.** father. **5.** fathom. **6.** feet. **7.** female. **8.** feminine. **9.** (in prescriptions) let them be made. [< L *fīant*] **10.** (in prescriptions) fiat. **11.** filly. **12.** fine. **13.** fluid (ounce). **14.** folio. **15.** following. **16.** foot. **17.** form. **18.** formed of. **19.** franc. **20.** from. **21.** *Math.* function (of). **22.** (in the Netherlands) guilder; guilders. [< D *florijn* FLORIN, now replaced by *gulden* GUILDER, but still abbr. f(l).]

f/, *Photog.* See **f-number.** Also, **f/, f:**

F_1 layer (ef′ wun′). See under **F layer.**

F_2 layer (ef′ to͞o′). See under **F layer.**

fa (fä), *n. Music.* **1.** the syllable used for the fourth tone of a diatonic scale. **2.** (in the fixed system of solmization) the tone F. Cf. **sol-fa** (def. 1). [1275–1325; ME; see GAMUT]

fā (fä), *n.* the twentieth letter of the Arabic alphabet. [< Ar]

FAA, *U.S. Govt.* Federal Aviation Administration: the division of the Department of Transportation that inspects and rates civilian aircraft and pilots, enforces the rules of air safety, and installs and maintains air-navigation and traffic-control facilities.

F.A.A.A.S., 1. Fellow of the American Academy of Arts and Sciences. **2.** Fellow of the American Association for the Advancement of Science.

fab (fab), *adj. Slang.* fabulous (def. 2). [1960–65; by shortening]

fa·ba·ceous (fə bā′shəs), *adj.* belonging to the Fabaceae, an alternative name for the plant family Leguminosae. Cf. **legume family.** [1720–30; < NL *Fabace(ae)* (*Fab(a)* the type genus (L: bean) + *-aceae* -ACEAE) + -OUS]

fa·ba·da (fə bä′də; *Sp.* fä vä′thä), *n., pl.* **-das** (-dəz; *Sp.* -thäs). *Spanish Cookery.* a stew of broad beans usually cooked with pork, sausage, and bacon. [< dial. Sp. (Asturias), equiv. to *fab(a)* bean (< L) + *-ada* -ADE[1]]

Fa·ber·gé (fab′ər zhā′ *for 1;* fab′ər jā′, -zhā′ *or, Fr.,* fA beR zhā′ *for 2*), *n.* **1. (Peter) Carl Gus·ta·vo·vich** (kärl gə stä′və vich), 1846–1920, Russian goldsmith and jeweler. **2.** fine gold and enamel ware made in St. Petersburg, Russia, in the late 19th and early 20th centuries, much of it for the Russian court.

Fa·bi·an (fā′bē ən), *adj.* **1.** seeking victory by delay and harassment rather than by a decisive battle as in the manner of Fabius Maximus: *Fabian policy.* **2.** of or pertaining to the Fabian Society. —*n.* **3.** a member of or sympathizer with the Fabian Society. [1590–1600; < L *Fabiānus*]

Fa·bi·an (fā′bē ən), *n.* **1. Saint,** died A.D. 250, pope 236–250. **2.** a male given name.

Fa·bi·an·ism (fā′bē ə niz′əm), *n.* the theories of economic and social reform advocated by the Fabian Society. [1885–90; FABIAN + -ISM]

Fa′bian Soci′ety, a socialist organization founded in England in 1884, favoring the gradual spread of socialism by peaceful means.

Fa·bi·us Max·i·mus (fā′bē əs mak′sə məs), (*Quintus Fabius Maximus Verrucosus*) ("*Cunctator*") 275–203 B.C., Roman statesman and general: defeated Hannibal's army by harassment without risking a pitched battle.

fa·ble (fā′bəl), *n., v.,* **-bled, -bling.** —*n.* **1.** a short tale to teach a moral lesson, often with animals or inanimate objects as characters; apologue: *the fable of the tortoise and the hare; Aesop's fables.* **2.** a story not founded on fact: *This biography is largely a self-laudatory fable.* **3.** a story about supernatural or extraordinary persons or incidents; legend: *the fables of gods and heroes.* **4.** legends or myths collectively: *the heroes of Greek fable.* **5.** an untruth; falsehood: *This boast of a cure is a medical fable.* **6.** the plot of an epic, a dramatic poem, or a play. **7.** idle talk: *old wives' fables.* —*v.i.* **8.** to tell or write fables. **9.** to speak falsely; lie: *to fable about one's past.* —*v.t.* **10.** to describe as if actually so; talk about as if true: *She is fabled to be the natural daughter of a king.* [1250–1300; ME *fable, fabel, fabul* < AF, OF < L *fābula* a story, tale, equiv. to *fā(ri)* to speak + *-bula* suffix of instrument] —**fa′bler,** *n.*
—**Syn. 1.** See **legend.**

fa·bled (fā′bəld), *adj.* **1.** celebrated in fables: *a fabled goddess of the wood.* **2.** having no real existence; fictitious: *a fabled chest of gold.* [1730–40; FABLE + -ED[3]]

fab·li·au (fab′lē ō′; *Fr.* fA blē ō′), *n., pl.* **fab·li·aux** (fab′lē ōz′; *Fr.* fA blē ō′). a short metrical tale, usually ribald and humorous, popular in medieval France. [1795–1805; < F; ONF form of OF *fablel, fableau,* equiv. to *fable* FABLE + *-el* dim. suffix; see -ELLE]

Fa·bre (fä′bər; *Fr.* fA′bR[ə]), *n.* **Jean Hen·ri** (zhän äN-Rē′), 1823–1915, French entomologist and popular writer on insect life.

fab·ric (fab′rik), *n.* **1.** a cloth made by weaving, knitting, or felting fibers: *woolen fabrics.* **2.** the texture of the woven, knitted, or felted material: *cloth of a soft, pliant fabric.* **3.** framework; structure: *the fabric of society.* **4.** a building; edifice. **5.** the method of construction. **6.** the act of constructing, esp. of a church building. **7.** the maintenance of such a building. **8.** *Petrog.* the spatial arrangement and orientation of the constituents of a rock. [1475–85; (< MF *fabrique*) < L *fabrica* craft, esp. metalworking or building, workshop. See FORGE[1]]

fab·ri·cant (fab′ri kənt), *n.* a maker or manufacturer. [1750–60; < L *fabricant-* (s. of *fabricāns*) making, prp. of *fabricāre.* See FABRIC, -ANT]

fab·ri·cate (fab′ri kāt′), *v.t.,* **-cat·ed, -cat·ing. 1.** to make by art or skill and labor; construct: *The finest craftspeople fabricated this clock.* **2.** to make by assembling parts or sections. **3.** to devise or invent (a legend, lie, etc.). **4.** to fake; forge (a document, signature, etc.). [1400–50; late ME < L *fabricātus* made, ptp. of *fabricāre.* See FABRIC, -ATE[1]] —**fab′ri·ca′tive,** *adj.* —**fab′ri·ca′tor,** *n.*
—**Syn. 1.** See **manufacture.**

fab·ri·ca·tion (fab′ri kā′shən), *n.* **1.** the act or process of fabricating; manufacture. **2.** something fabricated, esp. an untruthful statement: *His account of the robbery is a complete fabrication.* [1475–1500; < L *fabricātiōn-* (s. of *fabricātiō*). See FABRICATE, -ION]
—**Syn. 2.** See **fiction.**

Fa·bri·ci·us (fə brish′ē əs, -brish′əs; *Dan.* fä bRē′-syo͞os), *n.* **Jo·han Chris·tian** (yō′hän kris′chən; *Dan.* yō hän′ kris′tyän), 1743–1808, Danish entomologist.

Fab·ri·koid (fab′ri koid′), *Trademark.* a brand of waterproof fabric having a cloth foundation and a pyroxylin surface, used esp. as a substitute for leather in bookbindings, upholstery, etc.

Fa·bri·ti·us (fä bRē′tsē o͞os), *n.* **Ca·rel** (kä′Rəl), 1622–54: Dutch painter: pupil of Rembrandt.

fab·u·lar (fab′yə lər), *adj.* of or pertaining to a story, novel, or the like written in the form of a fable. [1675–85; < L *fābulāris,* equiv. to *fābul(a)* FABLE + *-āris* -AR[1]]

fab·u·list (fab′yə list), *n.* **1.** a person who invents or relates fables. **2.** a liar. [1585–95; < MF *fabuliste,* equiv. to < *fābul(a)* FABLE + *-iste* -IST]

fab·u·lous (fab′yə ləs), *adj.* **1.** almost impossible to believe; incredible. **2.** *Informal.* exceptionally good or unusual; marvelous; superb: *a fabulous bargain; a fabulous new house.* **3.** told about in fables; purely imaginary: *the fabulous exploits of Hercules.* **4.** known about only through myths or legends. [1540–50; < L *fābulōsus,* equiv. to *fābul(a)* FABLE + *-ōsus* -OUS] —**fab′u·lous·ly,** *adv.* —**fab′u·lous·ness,** *n.*
—**Syn. 3.** fabled, fictitious, invented, fictional.

fac., 1. facsimile. **2.** factor. **3.** factory. **4.** faculty.

fa·cade (fə säd′, fa-), *n.* **1.** *Archit.* **a.** the front of a building, esp. an imposing or decorative one. **b.** any side of a building facing a public way or space and finished accordingly. **2.** a superficial appearance or illusion of something: *They managed somehow to maintain a facade of wealth.* Also, **fa·çade′.** [1650–60; < F < Upper It *faciada,* It *facciata,* equiv. to *facci(a)* FACE + *-ata* -ADE[1]]

facade (def. 1)

face (fās), *n., v.,* **faced, fac·ing.** —*n.* **1.** the front part of the head, from the forehead to the chin. **2.** a look or expression on this part: *a sad face.* **3.** an expression or look that indicates ridicule, disgust, etc.; grimace: *The child put on a face when told to go to bed.* **4.** cosmetics; makeup: *Excuse me while I go to the powder room to put on my face.* **5.** impudence; boldness: *to have the face to ask such a rude question.* **6.** outward appearance: *These are just old problems with new faces. The future presented a fair face to the fortunate youth.* **7.** outward show or pretense, esp. as a means of preserving one's dignity or of concealing a detrimental fact, condition, etc.: *Though shamed beyond words, he managed to show a bold face.* **8.** good reputation; dignity; prestige: *They hushed up the family scandal to preserve face.* **9.** the amount specified in a bill or note, exclusive of interest. **10.** the manifest sense or express terms, as of a document. **11.** the geographic characteristics or general appearance of a land surface. **12.** the surface: *the face of the earth.* **13.** the side, or part of a side, upon which the use of a thing depends: *the clock's face; the face of a playing card.* **14.** the most important or most frequently seen side; front: *the face of a building.* **15.** the

outer or upper side of a fabric; right side. **16.** the acting, striking, or working surface of an implement, tool, etc. **17.** *Geom.* any of the bounding surfaces of a solid figure: *a cube has six faces.* **18.** Also called **working face.** *Mining.* the front or end of a drift or excavation, where the material is being or was last mined. **19.** *Print.* **a.** the working surface of a type, of a plate, etc. See diag. under **type. b.** Also called **typeface.** any design of type, including a full range of characters, as letters, numbers, and marks of punctuation, in all sizes: *Caslon is one of the most popular faces.* See table under **typeface. c.** Also called **typeface.** the general style or appearance of type: *broad or narrow face.* **20.** *Naut., Aeron.* the rear or after side of a propeller blade (opposed to *back*). **21.** *Fort.* either of the two outer sides that form the salient angle of a bastion or the like. See diag. under **bastion. 22.** *Crystall.* any of the plane surfaces of a crystal. **23.** *Electronics.* faceplate (def. 3). **24.** *Archaic.* sight; presence: *to flee from the face of the enemy.* **25. face to face, a.** facing or opposite one another: *We sat face to face at the table.* **b.** in an open, personal meeting or confrontation: *The leaders spoke face to face about a reduction in nuclear arms.* **26. face to face with,** in close proximity to; narrowly escaping; confronting: *face to face with death.* **27. fly in the face of.** See **fly**[1] (def. 21). **28. get out of someone's face** (usually used imperatively) **a.** *Southern U.S.* go away!; leave. **b.** *Slang.* to stop bothering or annoying someone. **29. in the face of, a.** in spite of; notwithstanding: *She persevered in the face of many obstacles.* **b.** when confronted with: *They were steadfast in the face of disaster.* **30. lose face,** to suffer disgrace, humiliation, or embarrassment: *It was impossible to apologize publicly without losing face.* **31. make a face,** to grimace, as in distaste or contempt; contort one's face in order to convey a feeling or to amuse another: *She made a face when she was told the work wasn't finished. The children made me laugh by making faces.* **32. on the face of it,** to outward appearances; superficially; seemingly: *On the face of it, there was no hope for a comeback.* **33. put on a bold face,** to give the appearance of confidence or assurance: *Everyone knew that he had been fired, even though he put on a bold face.* Also, **put a bold face on. 34. save face,** to avoid disgrace, humiliation, or embarrassment: *She tried to save face by saying that the bill had never arrived.* **35. set one's face against,** to disapprove strongly of; oppose: *My parents have set their face against my becoming an actress.* **36. show one's face,** to make an appearance; be seen: *I would be ashamed to show my face in such an outlandish outfit. Just show your face at the party and then you can leave.* **37. to one's face,** in one's presence; brazenly; directly: *Tell him to his face that he's a liar!*
—*v.t.* **38.** to look toward or in the direction of: *to face the light.* **39.** to have the front toward or permit a view of: *The building faces Fifth Avenue. The bedroom faces the park.* **40.** to confront directly: *to be faced with a problem; to face the future confidently.* **41.** to confront courageously, boldly, or impudently (usually fol. by *down* or *out*): *He could always face down his detractors.* **42.** to oppose or to meet defiantly: *to face fearful odds; Army faces Navy in today's football game.* **43.** to cover or partly cover with a different material in front: *They faced the old wooden house with brick.* **44.** to finish the edge of a garment with facing. **45.** to turn the face of (a playing card) upwards. **46.** to dress or smooth the surface of (a stone or the like). **47.** to cause (soldiers) to turn to the right, left, or in the opposite direction. **48.** *Ice Hockey.* (of a referee) to put (the puck) in play by dropping it between two opposing players each having his or her stick on the ice and facing the goal of the opponent.
—*v.i.* **49.** to turn or be turned (often fol. by *to* or *toward*): *She faced toward the sea.* **50.** to be placed with the front in a certain direction (often fol. by *on, to,* or *toward*): *The house faces on the street. The barn faces south.* **51.** to turn to the right, left, or in the opposite direction: *Left face!* **52.** *Ice Hockey.* to face the puck (often fol. by *off*). **53. face down,** to confront boldly or intimidate (an opponent, critic, etc.). **54. face off,** *Ice Hockey.* to start a game or period with a face-off. **55. face the music.** See **music** (def. 9). **56. face up to, a.** to acknowledge; admit: *to face up to the facts.* **b.** to meet courageously; confront: *He refused to face up to his problems.* [1250–1300; (n.) ME < AF, OF < VL **facia,* for L *faciēs* FACIES; (v.) late ME *facen,* deriv. of the n.] —**face′a·ble,** *adj.*
—**Syn. 1.** FACE, COUNTENANCE, VISAGE refer to the front of the (usually human) head. The FACE is the combination of the features: *a face with broad cheekbones.* COUNTENANCE, a more formal word, denotes the face as it is affected by or reveals the state of mind, and hence often signifies the look or expression on the face: *a thoughtful countenance.* VISAGE, still more formal, refers to the face as seen in a certain aspect, esp. as revealing seriousness or severity: *a stern visage.* **2.** appearance, aspect, mien. **7.** exterior. **14.** façade. **43.** veneer.

face′ an′gle, *Geom.* the angle formed by two successive edges of a polyhedron. [1910–15]

face′ bow′ (bō), *Dentistry.* a device for determining the relationship of the maxillae to the mandibular joint. Also, **face′bow′.** [1935–40]

face′ card′, the king, queen, or jack of playing cards. [1665–75]

face-cen·tered (fās′sen′tərd), *adj. Crystall.* (of a crystal structure) having lattice points on the faces of the unit cells. Cf. **body-centered.** [1910–15]

face·cloth (fās′klôth′, -kloth′), *n., pl.* **-cloths** (-klôthz′, -klothz′, -klôths′, -kloths′). washcloth. Also called, *Brit.,* **face′ flan′nel.** [1595–1605; FACE + CLOTH]

faced (fāst), *adj.* having a specified kind of face or number of faces (usually used in combination): *a sweet-faced child; the two-faced god.* [1490–1500; FACE + -ED[3]]

face·down (*adv.* fās′doun′; *n.* fās′doun′), *adv.* **1.** with the face or the front or upper surface downward: *He was lying facedown on the floor. Deal the cards face-down on the table.* —*n.* **2.** Also, **face′-down′.** *Informal.* a direct confrontation; showdown. [1930–35; (def. 1) FACE + DOWN[1]; (def. 2) n. use of v. phrase *face down*]

face′ gear′, *Mach.* a disklike gear having teeth cut on the face more or less radially and engaging with a spur or helical pinion, the axis of which is at right angles to it.

face-hard·en (fās′här′dn), *v.t.* to harden the surface of (metal), as by chilling or casehardening. [1895–1900]

face·less (fās′lis), *adj.* **1.** without a face: *a faceless apparition.* **2.** lacking personal distinction or identity: *a faceless mob.* **3.** unidentified or unidentifiable; concealing one's identity: *a faceless kidnapper.* [1560–70; FACE + -LESS] —**face′less·ness,** *n.*

face-lift (fās′lift′), *n.* **1.** Also, **face′ lift′ing, face′-lift′ing.** plastic surgery on the face for elevating sagging tissues and eliminating wrinkles and other signs of age; rhytidectomy. **2.** a renovation or restyling, as of a room or building, intended to give an attractive, more up-to-date appearance. —*v.t.* **3.** to perform a face-lift upon. **4.** to renovate or restyle in order to give a fresher, more modern appearance: *Our old offices have been face-lifted with new furniture.* Also, **face′lift′.** [1920–25, *Amer.*]

face′ mask′, 1. *Sports.* the protective equipment, usually made of steel or plastic, that guards the face, as the steel cage worn by a baseball catcher or the molded plastic covering worn by a hockey goalkeeper. **2.** any of various similar devices to shield the face, sometimes attached to or forming part of a helmet, as that worn by workers engaged in a hazardous activity. Also, **face′·mask′.** [1905–10; FACE + MASK]

face-nail (fās′nāl′), *v.t.* to secure with nails driven perpendicular to the surface. Cf. **toenail** (def. 4).

face-off (fās′ôf′, -of′), *n. Ice Hockey.* **1.** the act of facing the puck, as at the start of a game. **2.** an open confrontation. [1895–1900; n. use of v. phrase *face off*]

face·plate (fās′plāt′), *n.* **1.** (on a lathe) a perforated plate, mounted on the live spindle, to which the work is attached. **2.** the part of a protective headpiece, as a diver's or astronaut's helmet, that covers the upper portion of the face, often of transparent material and sometimes movable. **3.** Also called **face.** *Electronics.* the glass front of a cathode ray tube upon which the image is displayed. **4.** a protective plate, as one surrounding an electric outlet or light switch. Cf. **switch plate.** [1835–45; FACE + PLATE[1]]

face′ pow′der, a cosmetic powder used to give a mat finish to the face. [1855–60]

fac·er (fā′sər), *n.* **1.** a person or thing that faces. **2.** *Informal.* a blow in the face. **3.** *Brit. Informal.* an unexpected major difficulty, dilemma, or defeat. [1505–15; FACE + -ER[1]]

face-sav·er (fās′sā′vər), *n.* something that saves one's prestige or dignity: *Allow him the face-saver of resigning instead of being fired.* [1940–45] —**face′-sav′·ing,** *n., adj.*

fac·et (fas′it), *n., v.,* **-et·ed, -et·ing** or (*esp. Brit.*) **-et·ted, -et·ting.** —*n.* **1.** one of the small, polished plane surfaces of a cut gem. **2.** a similar surface cut on a fragment of rock by the action of water, windblown sand, etc. **3.** aspect; phase: *They carefully examined every facet of the argument.* **4.** *Archit.* any of the faces of a column cut in a polygonal form. **5.** *Zool.* one of the corneal lenses of a compound arthropod eye. **6.** *Anat.* a small, smooth, flat area on a hard surface, esp. on a bone. **7.** *Dentistry.* a small, highly burnished area, usually on the enamel surface of a tooth, produced by abrasion between opposing teeth in chewing. —*v.t.* **8.** to cut facets on. [1615–25; < F *facette* little face. See FACE, -ET]

fa·cete (fə sēt′), *adj. Archaic.* facetious. [1595–1605; < L *facētus* clever, witty] —**fa·cete′ly,** *adv.* —**fa·cete′ness,** *n.*

fa·ce·ti·ae (fə sē′shē ē′), *n.pl.* amusing or witty remarks or writings. [1520–30; < L, pl. of *facētia* something witty. See FACETE, -IA]

face′ time′, 1. a brief appearance on television. **2.** a brief face-to-face meeting, esp. with someone important. [1975–80]

fa·ce·tious (fə sē′shəs), *adj.* **1.** not meant to be taken seriously or literally: *a facetious remark.* **2.** amusing; humorous. **3.** lacking serious intent; concerned with something nonessential, amusing, or frivolous: *a facetious person.* [1585–95; FACETE + -IOUS; see FACETIAE] —**fa·ce′tious·ly,** *adv.* —**fa·ce′tious·ness,** *n.*
—**Syn. 2.** See **humorous.**

fac′et joint′, *Anat.* any of the four projections that link one vertebra of the spine to an adjacent vertebra.

face-to-face (fās′tə fās′), *adj.* **1.** with the fronts or faces toward each other. **2.** involving close contact or direct opposition: *a face-to-face confrontation.* [1300–50; ME]

face′ tow′el, a small towel for the face. [1920–25]

face·up (fās′up′), *adv.* with the face or the front or upper surface upward: *Place the cards faceup on the table.* [1960–65; FACE + UP]

face val·ue (fās′ val′yōō *for 1;* fās′ val′yōō *for 2*), **1.** the value printed on the face of a stock, bond, or other financial instrument or document. **2.** apparent value: *Do not accept promises at face value.* [1875–80]

fa·cia (fā′shə), *n. Chiefly Brit.* dashboard (def. 1). Also, **fascia.** Also called **fa′cia board′.** [1880–85; sp. var. of FASCIA, perh. through confusion with L *faciēs,* E FACE, FACIAL, etc.]

fa·cial (fā′shəl), *adj.* **1.** of the face: *facial expression.* **2.** for the face: *a facial cream.* —*n.* **3.** a treatment to beautify the face. [1600–10; 1910–15 for def. 3; < ML *faciālis.* See FACE, -AL[1]] —**fa′cial·ly,** *adv.*

fa′cial an′gle, *Craniom.* the angle formed by a line from nasion to prosthion at its intersection with the plane of the Frankfurt horizontal. [1815–25]

fac′ial in′dex, *Craniom.* the ratio of the breadth of a face to its height. [1885–90]

fa′cial nerve′, *Anat.* either one of the seventh pair of cranial nerves composed of motor fibers that control muscles of the face except those used in chewing. [1810–20]

fa′cial neural′gia, *Pathol.* See **tic douloureux.**

fa′cial tis′sue, a soft, disposable paper tissue esp. for cleansing the face or for use as a handkerchief. [1925–30]

fa·ci·es (fā′shē ēz′, -shēz), *n., pl.* **fa·ci·es. 1.** general appearance, as of an animal or vegetable group. **2.** *Geol.* the appearance and characteristics of a sedimentary deposit, esp. as they reflect the conditions and environment of deposition and serve to distinguish the deposit from contiguous deposits. Cf. **metamorphic facies. 3.** *Med.* a facial expression characteristic of a disease or pathological condition. **4.** *Archaeol.* a distinctive phase of a prehistoric cultural tradition. [1350–1400, for an earlier sense; ME < L: form, figure, appearance, face, akin to *facere* to make]

fac·ile (fas′il *or, esp. Brit.,* -īl), *adj.* **1.** moving, acting, working, proceeding, etc., with ease, sometimes with superficiality: *facile fingers; a facile mind.* **2.** easily done, performed, used, etc.: *a facile victory; a facile method.* **3.** easy or unconstrained, as manners or persons. **4.** affable, agreeable, or complaisant; easily influenced: *a facile temperament; facile people.* [1475–85; < L *facilis* that can be done, easy, equiv. to *fac(ere)* to do, make + *-ilis* -ILE] —**fac′ile·ly,** *adv.* —**fac′ile·ness,** *n.*
—**Syn. 1.** smooth, flowing, fluent; glib. **2.** superficial. **3.** bland, suave; urbane.

fa·ci·le prin·ceps (fä′ki le′ prıng′keps; *Eng.* fas′ə-lē prin′seps), *Latin.* easily the first or best.

fa·ci·lis de·scen·sus A·ver·no (fä′ki lis des ken′-sōōs ä wer′nō; *Eng.* fas′ə lis di sen′səs ə vûr′nō), *Latin.* (the) descent to hell is easy; it is easy to take the downward path. Vergil, *Aeneid,* 6:126.

fa·cil·i·tate (fə sil′i tāt′), *v.t.,* **-tat·ed, -tat·ing. 1.** to make easier or less difficult; help forward (an action, a process, etc.): *Careful planning facilitates any kind of work.* **2.** to assist the progress of (a person). [1605–15; FACILIT(Y) + -ATE[1]] —**fa·cil′i·ta′tive,** *adj.*

fa·cil·i·ta·tion (fə sil′i tā′shən), *n.* **1.** the act or process of facilitating. **2.** *Physiol.* the lowering of resistance in a neural pathway to an impulse, resulting from previous or simultaneous stimulation. [1610–20; FACILITATE + -ION]

fa·cil·i·ta·tor (fə sil′i tā′tər), *n.* **1.** a person or thing that facilitates. **2.** a person responsible for leading or coordinating the work of a group, as one who leads a group discussion: *Each committee will meet with its facilitator.* [1815–25; FACILITATE + -OR[2]]

fa·cil·i·ty (fə sil′i tē), *n., pl.* **-ties. 1.** Often, **facilities. a.** something designed, built, installed, etc., to serve a specific function affording a convenience or service: *transportation facilities; educational facilities; a new research facility.* **b.** something that permits the easier performance of an action, course of conduct, etc.: *to provide someone with every facility for accomplishing a task; to lack facilities for handling bulk mail.* **2.** readiness or ease due to skill, aptitude, or practice; dexterity: *to compose with great facility.* **3.** ready compliance: *Her facility in organizing and directing made her an excellent supervisor.* **4.** an easy-flowing manner: *facility of style.* **5.** the quality of being easily or conveniently done or performed. **6.** Often, **facilities.** *Informal.* a rest room, esp. one for use by the public, as in a theater or restaurant. **7.** freedom from difficulty, controversy, misunderstanding, etc.: *facility of understanding.* [1375–1425; late ME *facilite* (< MF) < L *facilitās.* See FACILE, -ITY]

fac·ing (fā′sing), *n.* **1.** a covering in front, for ornament, protection, etc., as an outer layer of stone on a brick wall. **2.** a lining applied to the edge of a garment for ornament or strengthening. **3.** material turned outward or inward, as a cuff or hem. **4. facings,** coverings of a different color applied on the collar, cuffs, or other parts of a military coat. [1350–1400; ME; see FACE, -ING[1]]

fac′ing tool′, *Metalworking.* a lathe tool for smoothing a plane surface at right angles to the axis of rotation. [1880–85]

fa·çon (fA sôN′), *n., pl.* **-çons** (-sôN′). *French.* **1.** a fashion; manner; style. **2.** workmanship; make. [1795–1805]

fa·con·ne (fas′ə nā′, fas′ə nā′), *adj.* **1.** (of a fabric) having a small and elaborate pattern. —*n.* **2.** a fabric having a faconne pattern or motif. **3.** the small and elaborate pattern on a faconne fabric. [1890–95; < F *façonné,* ptp. of *façonner* to work, FASHION; see -EE]

F.A.C.P., Fellow of the American College of Physicians. Also, **FACP**

FACS, 1. *Biol.* fluorescence-activated cell sorter: a machine that sorts cells according to whether or not they have been tagged with antibodies carrying a fluorescent dye, separating the cells mechanically in a vibrating nozzle, imparting a positive or negative charge to cells that fluoresce, and then passing the cells through an electric field to deflect them into appropriate containers. **2.** Also, **F.A.C.S.** Fellow of the American College of Surgeons.

facsim., facsimile.

fac·sim·i·le (fak sim′ə lē), *n., v.,* **-led, -le·ing,** *adj.* —*n.* **1.** an exact copy, as of a book, painting, or manuscript. **2.** Also called **fax.** *Telecommunications.* **a.** a method or device for transmitting documents, drawings, photographs, or the like, by means of radio or telephone for exact reproduction elsewhere. **b.** an image transmitted by such a method. **3.** dropout (def. 5). —*v.t.* **4.** to reproduce in facsimile; make a facsimile of. —*adj.* **5.** Also, **fax.** *Telecommunications.* **a.** (of an image) copied by means of facsimile: *facsimile mail.* **b.** (of a method or

CONCISE ETYMOLOGY KEY: <, descended or borrowed from; >, whence; b., blend of, blended; c., cognate with; cf., compare; deriv., derivative; equiv., equivalent; imit., imitative; obl., oblique; r., replacing; s., stem; sp., spelling, spelled; resp., respelling, respelled; trans., translation; ?, origin unknown; *, unattested; ‡, probably earlier than. See the full key inside the front cover.

device) used to produce a facsimile: *facsimile transmission.* [1655–65; earlier *fac simile* make the like, equiv. to L *fac* (impv. of *facere*) + *simile,* n. use of neut. of *similis* like; see SIMILE]
—Syn. 1. replica, likeness. **1, 4.** duplicate.

facsim′ile cat′alog, *Library Science.* a catalog that includes small reproductions of the items listed, as paintings, slides, designs, or the like.

fact (fakt), *n.* **1.** something that actually exists; reality; truth: *Your fears have no basis in fact.* **2.** something known to exist or to have happened: *Space travel is now a fact.* **3.** a truth known by actual experience or observation; something known to be true: *Scientists gather facts about plant growth.* **4.** something said to be true or supposed to have happened: *The facts given by the witness are highly questionable.* **5.** *Law.* Often, **facts.** an actual or alleged event or circumstance, as distinguished from its legal effect or consequence. Cf. **question of fact, question of law. 6. after the fact,** *Law.* after the commission of a crime: *an accessory after the fact.* **7. before the fact,** *Law.* prior to the commission of a crime: *an accessory before the fact.* **8. in fact,** actually; really; indeed: *In fact, it was a wonder that anyone survived.* [1530–40; < L *factum* something done, deed, n. use of neut. of *factus* done, ptp. of *facere* to DO[1]] **—fact′ful,** *adj.*

fact′ find′er, *n.* a person who searches impartially for the facts or actualities of a subject or situation, esp. one appointed to conduct an official investigation, as in a labor-management conflict. Also, **fact′-find′er.** [1925–30] **—fact′-find′ing,** *n., adj.*

fac·tic·i·ty (fak tis′i tē), *n.* the condition or quality of being a fact; factuality. [1940–45; FACT + *-icity* (-IC + -ITY), perh. after AUTHENTICITY]

fac·tion[1] (fak′shən), *n.* **1.** a group or clique within a larger group, party, government, organization, or the like: *a faction in favor of big business.* **2.** party strife and intrigue; dissension: *an era of faction and treason.* [1500–10; < L *factiōn-* (s. of *factiō*) a doing, company, equiv. to *fact(us)* done (see FACT) + *-iōn-* -ION]
—Syn. 2. discord, disagreement, schism, split, friction.

fac·tion[2] (fak′shən), *n. Informal.* **1.** a form of writing or filmmaking that treats real people or events as if they were fictional or uses them as an integral part of a fictional account. **2.** a novel, film, play, or other presentation in this form. [1965–70; b. FACT and FICTION]

fac·tion·al (fak′shə nl), *adj.* **1.** of a faction or factions. **2.** self-interested; partisan: *Factional interests had obstructed justice.* [1640–50; FACTION[1] + -AL[1]] **—fac′·tion·al·ism,** *n.* **—fac′tion·al·ist,** *n.*

fac·tious (fak′shəs), *adj.* **1.** given to faction; dissentious: *A factious group was trying to undermine the government.* **2.** pertaining to or proceeding from faction: *factious quarrels.* [1525–35; < L *factiōsus* fond of doing, busy, of a company or party, equiv. to *facti-* (see FACTION[1]) + *-ōsus* -OUS] **—fac′tious·ly,** *adv.* **—fac′tious·ness,** *n.*
—Syn. 1. divisive, disputatious, mutinous, contentious.

fac·ti·tious (fak tish′əs), *adj.* **1.** not spontaneous or natural; artificial; contrived: *factitious laughter; factitious enthusiasm.* **2.** made; manufactured: *a decoration of factitious flowers and leaves.* [1640–50; < L *facticius* made by art, artificial. See FACT, -ITIOUS] **—fac·ti′tious·ly,** *adv.* **—fac·ti′tious·ness,** *n.*

facti′tious disor′der, *Psychiatry.* any of various syndromes, as Münchausen syndrome, characterized by physical or psychological symptoms intentionally produced by a person and under voluntary control.

fac·ti·tive (fak′ti tiv), *adj. Gram.* noting or pertaining to verbs that express the idea of making or rendering in a certain way and that take a direct object and an additional word or group of words indicating the result of the process, as *made* in *They made him king.* [1840–50; < NL *factitivus,* equiv. to *factit-* (s. of L *factitāre* to do often, practice, declare (someone) to be) + *-īvus* -IVE] **—fac′ti·tive·ly,** *adv.*

fac·tive (fak′tiv), *Ling.* **—adj. 1.** (of a verb, adjective, or noun phrase) presupposing the truth of an embedded sentence that serves as complement, as *realize* in *I didn't realize that he had left,* which presupposes that it is true that he had left. **—n. 2.** a factive expression. [1605–15; FACT + -IVE] **—fac·tiv′i·ty,** *n.*

fact′ of life′, **1.** any aspect of human existence that must be acknowledged or regarded as unalterable: *Old age is a fact of life.* **2. facts of life,** the facts concerning sex, reproduction, and birth: *to teach children the facts of life.* [1850–55]

fac·toid (fak′toid), *n.* something fictitious or unsubstantiated that is presented as fact, devised esp. to gain publicity and accepted because of constant repetition. [FACT + -OID] **—fac·toi′dal,** *adj.*

fac·tor (fak′tər), *n.* **1.** one of the elements contributing to a particular result or situation: *Poverty is only one of the factors in crime.* **2.** *Math.* one of two or more numbers, algebraic expressions, or the like, that when multiplied together produce a given product; a divisor: *6 and 3 are factors of 18.* **3.** *Biochem.* any of certain substances necessary to a biochemical or physiological process, esp. those whose exact nature and function are unknown. **4.** a business organization that lends money on accounts receivable or buys and collects accounts receivable. **5.** a person who acts or transacts business for another; an agent. **6.** an agent entrusted with the possession of goods to be sold in the agent's name; a merchant earning a commission by selling goods belonging to others. **7.** a person or business organization that provides money for another's new business venture; one who finances another's business. **8.** See **factor of production. 9.** *Scot.* the steward or bailiff of an estate. **—v.t. 10.** *Math.* to express (a mathematical quantity) as a product of two or more quantities of like kind, as $30 = 2 \cdot 3 \cdot 5$, or $x^2 - y^2 = (x + y)(x - y)$. Cf. **expand** (def. 4a). **11.** to act as a factor for. **—v.i. 12.** to act as a factor. **13. factor in** or **into,** to include as an essential element, esp. in forecasting or planning: *You must factor insurance payments into the cost of maintaining a car.* [1400–50; late ME *facto(u)r* < L *factor* maker, perpetrator, equiv. to *fac(ere)* to make, do + *-tor* -TOR] **—fac′tor·a·ble,** *adj.* **—fac′tor·a·bil′i·ty,** *n.* **—fac′tor·ship′,** *n.*

factor VIII. See **antihemophilic factor.** [1960–65]

factor IX. See **Christmas factor.**

fac·tor·age (fak′tər ij), *n.* **1.** the action or business of a factor. **2.** the allowance or commission paid to a factor. [1605–15; FACTOR + -AGE]

fac′tor anal′ysis, *Statistics.* the use of one of several methods for reducing a set of variables to a lesser number of new variables, each of which is a function of one or more of the original variables. [1930–35]

fac′tor group′, *Math.* See **quotient group.** [1895–1900]

fac·to·ri·al (fak tôr′ē əl, -tōr′-), *n.* **1.** *Math.* the product of a given positive integer multiplied by all lesser positive integers: The quantity four factorial (4!) = 4 · 3 · 2 · 1 = 24. *Symbol: n!,* where *n* is the given integer. **—adj. 2.** *Math.* of or pertaining to factors or factorials. **3.** of or pertaining to a factor or a factory. [1810–20; FACTOR + -IAL] **—fac·to′ri·al·ly,** *adv.*

fac·tor·ing (fak′tər ing), *n.* **1.** *Com.* the business of purchasing and collecting accounts receivable or of advancing cash on the basis of accounts receivable. **2.** the act or process of separating an equation, formula, cryptogram, etc., into its component parts. [FACTOR + -ING[1]]

fac·tor·ize (fak′tə rīz′), *v.t.,* **-ized, -iz·ing. 1.** *Math.* to resolve into factors. **2.** *Law.* garnishee (def. 1). Also, *esp. Brit.,* **fac′tor·ise′.** [1855–60; FACTOR + -IZE] **—fac′tor·i·za′tion,** *n.*

fac′tor of adhe′sion, *Railroads.* the ratio of the force that can be exerted on driving wheels with full traction to the weight on the driving wheels, usually expressed as a percentage. Also called **adhesion, adhesive factor.**

fac′tor of produc′tion, any instrument, agent, etc., employed in the production of goods and services.

fac′tor of safe′ty, the ratio of the maximum stress that a structural part or other piece of material can withstand to the maximum stress estimated for it in the use for which it is designed. Also called **safety factor.** [1855–60]

fac·to·ry (fak′tə rē, -trē), *n., pl.* **-ries. 1.** a building or group of buildings with facilities for the manufacture of goods. **2.** any place producing a uniform product, without concern for individuality: *They call it a law school, but it's just a degree factory.* **3.** (formerly) an establishment for factors and merchants carrying on business in a foreign country. [1550–60; < ML *factōria.* See FACTOR, -Y[3]] **—fac′to·ry·like′,** *adj.*

fac′tory out′let, a store that sells factory-made goods directly to consumers for less than current retail prices.

fac′tory price′, *Com.* the price quoted for manufactured goods for pickup at the gate of a factory, before certain handling, shipping, and similar costs.

fac′tory ship′, 1. a whaling ship equipped to process killed whales and to transport the oil and by-products. **2.** Also called **fac′tory trawl′er.** a large fishing vessel, usually a stern trawler, equipped for processing and freezing fish at sea. [1925–30]

fac·to·tum (fak tō′təm), *n.* **1.** a person, as a handyman or servant, employed to do all kinds of work around the house. **2.** any employee or official having many different responsibilities. [1560–70; < ML, equiv. to L *fac* make, do (impv. of *facere*) + *tōtum,* neut. of *tōtus* all]

fac·tu·al (fak′cho͞o əl), *adj.* **1.** of or pertaining to facts; concerning facts: *factual accuracy.* **2.** based on or restricted to facts: *a factual report.* [1825–35; FACT + *-ual,* after EFFECTUAL or ACTUAL] **—fac′tu·al·ly,** *adv.* **—fac′tu·al′i·ty, fac′tu·al·ness,** *n.*

fac·tu·al·ism (fak′cho͞o ə liz′əm), *n.* emphasis on, devotion to, or extensive reliance upon facts: *the factualism of scientific experiment.* [1945–50; FACTUAL + -ISM] **—fac′tu·al·ist,** *n.* **—fac′tu·al·is′tic,** *adj.*

fac·tum (fak′təm), *n., pl.* **-ta** (-tə). a statement of the facts in a controversy or legal case. [1740–50; < L; see FACT]

fac·ture (fak′chər), *n.* **1.** the act, process, or manner of making anything; construction. **2.** the thing made. [1375–1425; late ME < L *factūra* the making (of something). See FACT, -URE]

fac·u·la (fak′yə lə), *n., pl.* **-lae** (-lē′). *Astron.* an irregular, unusually bright patch on the sun's surface. [1700–10; < L: little torch, equiv. to *fac-* (s. of *fax*) torch + *-ula* -ULE] **—fac′u·lar,** *adj.*

fac·ul·ta·tive (fak′əl tā′tiv), *adj.* **1.** conferring a faculty, privilege, permission, or the power of doing or not doing something: *a facultative enactment.* **2.** left to one's option or choice; optional: *The last questions in the examination were facultative.* **3.** that may or may not take place; that may or may not assume a specified character. **4.** *Biol.* having the capacity to live under more than one specific set of environmental conditions, as a plant that can lead either a parasitic or a nonparasitic life or a bacterium that can live with or without air (opposed to *obligate*). **5.** of or pertaining to the faculties. [1810–20; < NL *facultātivus.* See FACULTY, -IVE] **—fac′·ul·ta′tive·ly,** *adv.*

fac·ul·ty (fak′əl tē), *n., pl.* **-ties. 1.** an ability, natural or acquired, for a particular kind of action: *a faculty for making friends easily.* **2.** one of the powers of the mind, as memory, reason, or speech: *Though very sick, he is in full possession of all his faculties.* **3.** an inherent capability of the body: *the faculties of sight and hearing.* **4.** exceptional ability or aptitude: *a president with a faculty for management.* **5.** *Educ.* **a.** the entire teaching and administrative force of a university, college, or school. **b.** one of the departments of learning, as theology, medicine, or law, in a university. **c.** the teaching body, sometimes with the students, in any of these departments. **6.** the members of a learned profession: *the medical faculty.* **7.** a power or privilege conferred by the state, a superior, etc.: *The police were given the faculty to search the building.* **8.** *Eccles.* a dispensation, license, or authorization. [1350–1400; ME *faculte* < AF, MF < L *facultāt-* (s. of *facultās*) ability, power, equiv. to *facil(is)* easy (see FACILE) + *-tāt-* -TY[2]; cf. FACILITY]
—Syn. 1. capacity, aptitude, knack, potential, skill. See **ability.**

fad (fad), *n.* a temporary fashion, notion, manner of conduct, etc., esp. one followed enthusiastically by a group. [1825–35; n. use of dial. *fad* to look after things, busy oneself with trifles, back formation from obs. *faddle* to play with, fondle. See FIDDLE] **—fad′like′,** *adj.*
—Syn. craze, vogue, rage.

fad·dish (fad′ish), *adj.* **1.** like a fad. **2.** given to fads: *a faddish, sophisticated crowd.* [1850–55; FAD + -ISH[1]] **—fad′dish·ness,** *n.*

fad·dist (fad′ist), *n.* a person following a fad or given to fads, as one who seeks and adheres briefly to a passing variety of unusual diets, beliefs, etc. [1880–85; FAD + -IST] **—fad′dism,** *n.*

fad·dy (fad′ē), *adj.,* **-di·er, -di·est,** *n.* faddish. [1815–25; FAD + -Y[1]]

fade (fād), *v.,* **fad·ed, fad·ing,** *n.* **—v.i. 1.** to lose brightness or vividness of color. **2.** to become dim, as light, or lose brightness of illumination. **3.** to lose freshness, vigor, strength, or health: *The tulips have faded.* **4.** to disappear or die gradually (often fol. by *away* or *out*): *His anger faded away.* **5.** *Motion Pictures, Television.* **a.** to appear gradually, esp. by becoming lighter (usually fol. by *in*). **b.** to disappear gradually, esp. by becoming darker (usually fol. by *out*). **6.** *Broadcasting, Recording.* **a.** to increase gradually in volume of sound, as in recording or broadcasting music, dialogue, etc. (usually fol. by *in*). **b.** to decrease gradually in volume of sound (usually fol. by *out*). **7.** *Football.* (of an offensive back, esp. a quarterback) to move back toward one's own goal line, usually with the intent to pass, after receiving the snapback from center or a hand-off or lateral pass behind the line of scrimmage (usually fol. by *back*): *The quarterback was tackled while fading back for a pass.* **8.** (of an automotive brake) to undergo brake fade. **—v.t. 9.** to cause to fade: *Sunshine faded the drapes.* **10.** (in dice throwing) to make a wager against (the caster). **11.** *Motion Pictures, Television.* **a.** to cause (a scene) to appear gradually (usually fol. by *in*). **b.** to cause (a scene) to disappear gradually (usually fol. by *out*). **12.** *Broadcasting, Recording.* to cause (the volume of sound) to increase or decrease gradually (usually fol. by *in* or *out*). **—n. 13.** an act or instance of fading. **14.** *Motion Pictures, Television Informal.* a fade-out. **15.** *Auto.* See **brake fade.** [1275–1325; 1915–20 for def. 5; ME *faden,* deriv. of *fade* pale, dull < AF, OF < VL **fatidus,* for L *fatuus* FATUOUS] **—fad′a·ble,** *adj.* **—fad′ed·ly,** *adv.* **—fad′ed·ness,** *n.*
—Syn. 4. See **disappear.**

fade·a·way (fād′ə wā′), *n.* **1.** an act or instance of fading away. **2.** *Baseball.* screwball (def. 2). **3.** *Baseball.* a slide made by a base runner to one side of the base, with one leg bent and stretched back to catch hold of the base. **4.** *Basketball.* a jump shot made while the player is falling away from the basket. [1905–10, *Amer.*; n. use of v. phrase *fade away*]

fade-in (fād′in′), *n.* **1.** *Motion Pictures, Television.* a gradual increase in the visibility of a scene. **2.** *Broadcasting, Recording.* a gradual increase in the volume of sound, esp. of recorded or broadcast music, dialogue, or the like, usually starting from complete inaudibility. [1915–20; n. use of v. phrase *fade in*]

fade·less (fād′lis), *adj.* not fading or diminishing; unfading. [1645–55; FADE + -LESS]

fade-out (fād′out′), *n.* **1.** *Motion Pictures, Television.* a gradual decrease in the visibility of a scene. **2.** *Broadcasting, Recording.* a gradual decrease in the volume of sound, esp. of recorded or broadcast music, dialogue, or the like, usually ending in complete inaudibility. **3.** a gradual disappearance or reduction: *the fade-out of a brilliant career.* [1915–20; n. use of v. phrase *fade out*]

fad·er (fā′dər), *n.* **1.** a person or thing that fades. **2.** *Motion Pictures, Broadcasting, Recording.* a multiple-unit volume control used in changing gradually from one signal source to another, decreasing the volume from the first audio or visual source while increasing the volume from the second. [1930–35; FADE + -ER[1]]

Fa·de·yev (fə dā′ef, -ev; *Russ.* fu dye′yif), *n.* **A·le·ksandr A·le·ksan·dro·vich** (al′ig zan′dər al′ig zan′drə vich, -zän′-; *Russ.* u lyi ksändr′ u lyi ksän′drə vyich), 1901–56, Russian novelist. Also, **Fa·de′ev.**

FAdm, Fleet Admiral.

fa·do (fä′do͝o; *Eng.* fä′dō), *n.* **1.** a Portuguese folk song typically of doleful or fatalistic character and usually accompanied on the guitar. **2.** a dance to the music of such a song. [1900–05; < Pg < L *fātum* FATE]

fae·ces (fē′sēz), *n.* (*used with a plural v.*) *Chiefly Brit.* feces. **—fae·cal** (fē′kəl), *adj.*

fa·e·na (fä ā′nə), *n.* the final third of a bullfight in which the matador uses a muleta and the sword in making the final series of passes preparatory to the kill. [1925–30; < Sp: lit., task < Catalan < L *facienda,* neut. pl. (taken as fem. sing.) of *faciendum* what is to be done, ger. of *facere* to do, make; cf. HACIENDA]

Fa·en·za (fä en′zə; *It.* fä en′tsä), *n.* a city in N Italy, SE of Bologna. 55,612.

CONCISE PRONUNCIATION KEY: *act, cāpe, dâre, pärt; set, ēqual; if, īce; ox, ōver, ôrder, oil, bo͝ok, bo͞ot, out; up, ûrge; child; sing; shoe; thin, that;* zh as in *treasure.* ə = *a* as in *alone, e* as in *system, i* as in *easily, o* as in *gallop, u* as in *circus;* ˈ as in *fire* (fīˈr), *hour* (ouˈr). l and n can serve as syllabic consonants, as in *cradle* (krād′l), and *button* (but′n). See the full key inside the front cover.

fa·er·ie (fā′ə rē, fâr′ē), *n.* **1.** the imaginary land of the fairies; fairyland. **2.** *Archaic.* a fairy. —*adj.* **3.** fairy. Also, **faery.** [1580–90; sp. var. of FAIRY]

Fa′erie Queene′, The (kwēn), a chivalric romance in verse (1590–96) by Edmund Spenser.

Faer′oe Is′lands (fâr′ō), a group of 21 islands in the N Atlantic between Great Britain and Iceland, belonging to Denmark but having extensive home rule. 41,211; 540 sq. mi. (1400 sq. km). *Cap.:* Torshavn. Also, **Faroe Islands.** Also called **Faer′oes, Faroes.** Danish, **Faer·ö·er·ne** (fɛʀ œ′ʀ nə).

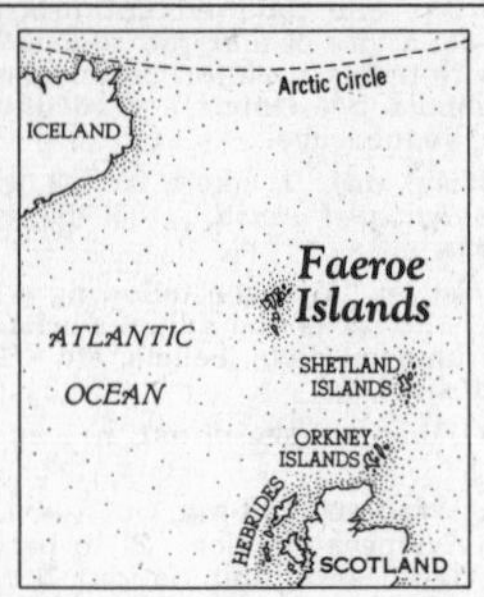

Faer·o·ese (fâr′ō ēz′, -ēs′), *n., pl.* **-ese,** *adj.* —*n.* **1.** a native or inhabitant of the Faeroe Islands. **2.** the Scandinavian language spoken there. —*adj.* **3.** of or pertaining to the Faeroe Islands, its people, or their language. Also, **Faroese.** [1850–55]

fa·er·y (fā′ə rē, fâr′ē), *n., pl.* **fa·er·ies,** *adj.* faerie. Also, **fa′ër·y.**

Faf·nir (fäv′nir, fôv′-), *n. Scand. Myth.* a dragon, a son of Hreidmar and the brother of Otter and Regin: he killed Hreidmar for the cursed treasure of Andvari and was killed in turn by Sigurd at the instigation of Regin.

fag[1] (fag), *v.,* **fagged, fag·ging,** *n.* —*v.t.* **1.** to tire or weary by labor; exhaust (often fol. by *out*): *The long climb fagged us out.* **2.** *Brit.* to require (a younger public-school pupil) to do menial chores. **3.** *Naut.* to fray or unlay the end of (a rope). —*v.i.* **4.** *Chiefly Brit.* to work until wearied; work hard: *to fag away at French.* **5.** *Brit. Informal.* to do menial chores for an older public-school pupil. —*n.* **6.** *Slang.* a cigarette. **7.** a fag end, as of cloth. **8.** a rough or defective spot in a woven fabric; blemish; flaw. **9.** *Chiefly Brit.* drudgery; toil. **10.** *Brit. Informal.* a younger pupil in a British public school required to perform certain menial tasks for, and submit to the hazing of, an older pupil. **11.** a drudge. [1425–75; late ME *fagge* broken thread in cloth, loose end (of obscure orig.); sense development appar.: drooping end > to droop, tire > to make weary > drudgery, drudge (cf. relationship of FLAG[1] to FLAG[3]); (def. 6) a shortening of FAG END (a butt, hence a cigarette)]

fag[2] (fag), *n. Slang (disparaging and offensive).* faggot[2]. [1920–25, *Amer.*; by shortening] —**fag′gish,** *adj.*

fa·ga·ceous (fə gā′shəs), *adj.* belonging to the Fagaceae, the beech family of plants. Cf. **beech family.** [< NL *Fagace(ae)* name of the family (*Fag(us)* the type genus (L *fāgus* BEECH) + *-aceae* -ACEAE) + -OUS]

fag′ end′, **1.** the last part or very end of something: *the fag end of a rope.* **2.** the unfinished end of a piece of cloth; remnant. [1605–15]

Fag·gi (fä′jē; *It.* fäd′jē), *n.* **Al·fe·o** (al fā′ō; *It.* äl fe′ô), 1885–1966, U.S. sculptor, born in Italy.

fag·got[1] (fag′ət), *n. Brit.* fagot.

fag·got[2] (fag′ət), *n. Slang (disparaging and offensive).* a male homosexual. [1910–15, *Amer.*; cf. *faggot* a contemptuous term for a woman (from ca. 1590), perh. the same word as FAGOT] —**fag′got·y, fag′got·ty,** *adj.*

fag·got·ry (fag′ə trē), *n. Slang (disparaging and offensive).* male homosexuality. [1965–70; FAGGOT[2] + -RY]

fag·gy (fag′ē), *adj.,* **-gi·er, -gi·est.** *Slang (disparaging and offensive).* **1.** of or resembling a male homosexual. **2.** coyly affected. [1965–70; FAG[2] + -Y[1]] —**fag′gi·ness,** *n.*

fag′ hag′, *Slang (disparaging and offensive).* a heterosexual female who seeks out or particularly enjoys the company of male homosexuals. [1965–70]

Fa·gin (fā′gin), *n.* **1.** (in Dickens' *Oliver Twist*) a villainous old man who trains and uses young boys as thieves. **2.** Also, **fa′gin.** a person who teaches crime to others.

fa·gio·lo (fä jô′lô), *n., pl.* ***-li*** (-lē). *Italian.* a kidney bean.

fag·ot (fag′ət), *n.* **1.** a bundle of sticks, twigs, or branches bound together and used as fuel, a fascine, a torch, etc. **2.** a bundle; bunch. **3.** a bundle of pieces of iron or steel to be welded, hammered, or rolled together at high temperature. **4.** See **bouquet garni.** —*v.t.* **5.** to bind or make into a fagot. **6.** to ornament with fagoting. Also, *Brit.,* **faggot.** [1250–1300; ME < AF, OF; of obscure orig.] —**fag′ot·er,** *n.*

fag·ot·ing (fag′ə ting), *n.* an openwork decoration of fabric in which thread is drawn in crisscross stitches across an open seam. Also, *Brit.,* **fag′got·ing.** [1880–85; FAGOT + -ING[1]]

CONCISE ETYMOLOGY KEY: <, descended or borrowed from; >, whence; b., blend of, blended; c., cognate with; cf., compare; deriv., derivative; equiv., equivalent; imit., imitative; obl., oblique; r., replacing; s., stem; sp., spelling, spelled; resp., respelling, respelled; trans., translation; ?, origin unknown; *, unattested; ‡, probably earlier than. See the full key inside the front cover.

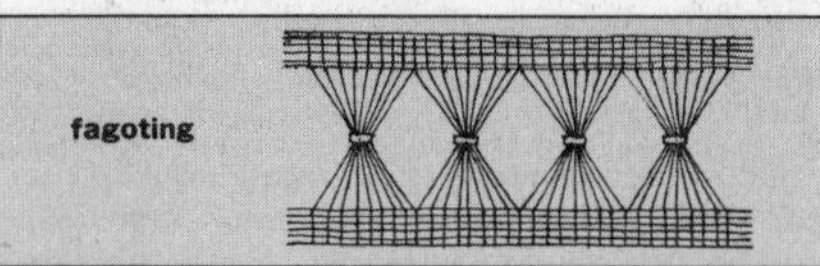

Fahd (fäd), *n.* (*Fahd ibn Abdul-Aziz al Saud*) born 1922, king of Saudi Arabia since 1982 (son of ibn-Saud and brother of Khalid).

Fahne′stock clip′ (fän′stok′, fôn′-), *Elect.* a type of terminal using a spring that clamps readily onto a connecting wire. [after James D. *Fahnestock,* U.S. electrical engineer]

Fahr., Fahrenheit (thermometer). Also, **Fah.**

Fahr·en·heit (far′ən hīt′; *Ger.* fäʀ′ən hīt′), *n.* **1. Ga·bri·el Da·ni·el** (*Ger.* gä′bʀē el′ dä′nē el′), 1686–1736, German physicist: devised a temperature scale and introduced the use of mercury in thermometers. —*adj.* **2.** noting, pertaining to, or measured according to a temperature scale **(Fahr′enheit scale′)** in which 32° represents the ice point and 212° the steam point. *Symbol:* F See illus. under **thermometer.**

Fa·ial (fä yäl′), *n.* an island in the Azores, in the N Atlantic. 20,343; 66 sq. mi. (171 sq. km). Also, **Fayal.**

fa·ïence (fī äns′, fā-; *Fr.* fa yäɴs′), *n.* glazed earthenware or pottery, esp. a fine variety with highly colored designs. Also, **fa·ïence′.** [1705–15; < F, orig. pottery of *Faenza,* city in northern Italy]

fail (fāl), *v.i.* **1.** to fall short of success or achievement in something expected, attempted, desired, or approved: *The experiment failed because of poor planning.* **2.** to receive less than the passing grade or mark in an examination, class, or course of study: *He failed in history.* **3.** to be or become deficient or lacking; be insufficient or absent; fall short: *Our supplies failed.* **4.** to dwindle, pass, or die away: *The flowers failed for lack of rain.* **5.** to lose strength or vigor; become weak: *His health failed after the operation.* **6.** to become unable to meet or pay debts or business obligations; become insolvent or bankrupt. **7.** (of a building member, structure, machine part, etc.) to break, bend, crush, or be otherwise destroyed or made useless because of an excessive load. **8.** to stop functioning or operating: *The electricity failed during the storm.* —*v.t.* **9.** to be unsuccessful in the performance or completion of: *He failed to do his duty.* **10.** (of some expected or usual resource) to prove of no use or help to: *His friends failed him. Words failed her.* **11.** to receive less than a passing grade or mark in: *He failed history.* **12.** to declare (a person) unsuccessful in a test, course of study, etc.; give less than a passing grade to: *The professor failed him in history.* —*n.* **13.** *Stock Exchange.* **a.** a stockbroker's inability to deliver or receive security within the required time after sale or purchase. **b.** such an undelivered security. **14.** *Obs.* failure as to performance, occurrence, etc. **15. without fail,** with certainty; positively: *I will visit you tomorrow without fail.* [1175–1225; ME *failen* < AF, OF *faillir* < VL **fallire,* for L *fallere* to disappoint, deceive]

fail·ing (fā′ling), *n.* **1.** an act or instance of failing; failure: *His failing is due to general incompetence.* **2.** a defect or fault; shortcoming; weakness: *His lack of knowledge is a grave failing.* —*prep.* **3.** in the absence or default of: *Failing payment, we shall sue.* [1250–1300; ME; see FAIL, -ING[1]] —**fail′ing·ly,** *adv.* —**fail′ing·ness,** *n.*
—**Syn. 2.** See **fault.**

faille (fīl, fāl; *Fr.* fa′yᵊ), *n.* a soft, transversely ribbed fabric of silk, rayon, or lightweight taffeta. [1520–30; < MF, OF; of obscure orig.]

fail-safe (fāl′sāf′), *adj., n., v.,* **-safed, -saf·ing.** —*adj.* **1.** *Electronics.* pertaining to or noting a mechanism built into a system, as in an early warning system or a nuclear reactor, for insuring safety should the system fail to operate properly. **2.** equipped with a secondary system that insures continued operation even if the primary system fails. **3.** (*sometimes cap.*) of, pertaining to, or designating a system of coded military controls in which bombers dispatched to a prearranged point as part of a standard operating procedure cannot advance farther without direct orders from a designated authority and cannot have the nuclear warheads they carry armed until they have passed their prearranged point. **4.** guaranteed to work; totally reliable: *a fail-safe recipe for a cheese soufflé.* —*n.* **5.** (*sometimes cap.*) the point beyond which the bombers cannot go without specific instruction; the fail-safe point. **6.** something designed to work or function automatically to prevent breakdown of a mechanism, system, or the like. —*v.t.* **7.** to make fail-safe. [1945–50; appar. from v. phrase *to fail safe(ly)*]

fail-soft (fāl′sôft′, -soft′), *adj.* pertaining to or noting facilities built into a system, as in an automobile or a computer, for continuing operations on an interim basis and probably with reduced efficiency, if parts of the system fail. [play on FAIL-SAFE]

fail·ure (fāl′yər), *n.* **1.** an act or instance of failing or proving unsuccessful; lack of success: *His effort ended in failure. The campaign was a failure.* **2.** nonperformance of something due, required, or expected: *a failure to do what one has promised; a failure to appear.* **3.** a subnormal quantity or quality; an insufficiency: *the failure of crops.* **4.** deterioration or decay, esp. of vigor, strength, etc.: *The failure of her health made retirement necessary.* **5.** a condition of being bankrupt by reason of insolvency. **6.** a becoming insolvent or bankrupt: *the failure of a bank.* **7.** a person or thing that proves unsuccessful: *He is a failure in his career. The cake is a failure.* [1635–45; FAIL + -URE; r. *failer* a (de)fault < AF (n. use of inf.), for OF *faillir*]

fain (fān), *adv.* **1.** gladly; willingly: *He fain would accept.* —*adj.* **2.** content; willing: *They were fain to go.* **3.** *Archaic.* constrained; obliged: *He was fain to obey his Lord.* **4.** *Archaic.* glad; pleased. **5.** *Archaic.* desirous; eager. [bef. 900; ME; OE *fæg(e)n;* c. ON *feginn* happy; akin to FAIR[1]]

fai·naigue (fə nāg′), *v.i.,* **-naigued, -nai·guing. 1.** *Brit. Dial.* to shirk; evade work or responsibility. **2.** to renege at cards. [of uncert. orig.] —**fai·nai′guer,** *n.*

fai·né·ant (fā′nē ənt; *Fr.* fe nā äɴ′), *adj., n., pl.* **-ants** (-ənts; *Fr.* -äɴ′). —*adj.* **1.** Also, **fai·ne·ant** (fā′nē ənt). idle; indolent. —*n.* **2.** an idler. [1610–20; < F, earlier *fait-nient,* lit., he does nothing, pseudo-etymological alter. of OF *faignant* idler, n. use of prp. of *se faindre* to shirk. See FEIGN, FAINT] —**fai·ne·ance** (fā′nē əns), *n.*

faint (fānt), *adj.,* **-er, -est,** *v., n.* —*adj.* **1.** lacking brightness, vividness, clearness, loudness, strength, etc.: *a faint light; a faint color; a faint sound.* **2.** feeble or slight: *faint resistance; faint praise; a faint resemblance.* **3.** feeling weak, dizzy, or exhausted; about to lose consciousness: *faint with hunger.* **4.** lacking courage; cowardly; timorous: *Faint heart never won fair maid.* **5.** *Law.* unfounded: *a faint action.* —*v.i.* **6.** to lose consciousness temporarily. **7.** to lose brightness. **8.** *Archaic.* to grow weak; lose spirit or courage. —*n.* **9.** a temporary loss of consciousness resulting from a decreased flow of blood to the brain; a swoon: *to fall into a faint.* [1250–1300; ME < AF, OF, ptp. of *faindre,* var. of *feindre* to FEIGN] —**faint′er,** *n.* —**faint′ing·ly,** *adv.* —**faint′ish,** *adj.* —**faint′ish·ness,** *n.* —**faint′ly,** *adv.* —**faint′ness,** *n.*
—**Syn. 1.** indistinct, ill-defined, dim, faded, dull. **2.** faltering, irresolute, weak. **3.** languid. **4.** pusillanimous, fearful, timid, dastardly. **6.** pass out, black out.

faint·heart (fānt′härt′), *n.* person who lacks courage; coward. [1570–80; back formation from FAINTHEARTED]

faint·heart·ed (fānt′här′tid), *adj.* lacking courage; cowardly; timorous. [1400–50; late ME *feynt hertyd.* See FAINT, HEARTED] —**faint′heart′ed·ly,** *adv.*

faints (fānts), *n.* (*used with a plural v.*) the impure spirit produced in the first and last stages of the distillation of whiskey. Also, **feints.** Cf. **foreshots.** [1735–45; n. use (in pl.) of FAINT (adj.)]

faint·y (fān′tē), *adj.,* **faint·i·er, faint·i·est.** *Southern U.S.* feeling faint; about to lose consciousness. Also, **faint·i·fied** (fān′tə fīd′). [1520–30; FAINT + -Y[1]]

fair[1] (fâr), *adj.,* **-er, -est,** *adv.,* **-er, -est,** *n., v.* —*adj.* **1.** free from bias, dishonesty, or injustice: *a fair decision; a fair judge.* **2.** legitimately sought, pursued, done, given, etc.; proper under the rules: *a fair fight.* **3.** moderately large; ample: *a fair income.* **4.** neither excellent nor poor; moderately or tolerably good: *fair health.* **5.** marked by favoring conditions; likely; promising: *in a fair way to succeed.* **6.** *Meteorol.* **a.** (of the sky) bright; sunny; cloudless to half-cloudy. **b.** (of the weather) fine; with no prospect of rain, snow, or hail; not stormy. **7.** *Naut.* (of a wind or tide) tending to aid the progress of a vessel. **8.** unobstructed; not blocked up: *The way was fair for our advance.* **9.** without irregularity or unevenness: *a fair surface.* **10.** free from blemish, imperfection, or anything that impairs the appearance, quality, or character: *Her fair reputation was ruined by gossip.* **11.** easy to read; clear: *fair handwriting.* **12.** of a light hue; not dark: *fair skin.* **13.** pleasing in appearance; attractive: *a fair young maiden.* **14.** seemingly good or sincere but not really so: *The suitor beguiled his mistress with fair speeches.* **15.** courteous; civil: *fair words.* **16.** *Med.* (of a patient's condition) having stable and normal vital signs and other favorable indicators, as appetite and mobility, but being in some discomfort and having the possibility of a worsening state. **17.** *Dial.* scarcely; barely: *It was just fair daylight when we started working.* **18. fair to middling,** *Informal.* only tolerably good; so-so. —*adv.* **19.** in a fair manner: *He doesn't play fair.* **20.** straight; directly, as in aiming or hitting: *He threw the ball fair to the goal.* **21.** favorably; auspiciously. **22.** *Brit., Australian.* entirely; completely; quite: *It happened so quickly that it fair took my breath away.* **23. bid fair,** to seem likely: *This entry bids fair to win first prize.* **24. fair and square, a.** honestly; justly; straightforwardly: *He won the race fair and square.* **b.** honest; just; straightforward: *He was admired for being fair and square in all his dealings.* —*n.* **25.** *Archaic.* something that is fair. **26.** *Archaic.* **a.** a woman. **b.** a beloved woman. —*v.t.* **27.** to make the connection or junction of (surfaces) smooth and even. **28.** *Shipbuilding.* **a.** to draw and adjust (the lines of a hull being designed) to produce regular surfaces of the correct form. **b.** to adjust the form of (a frame or templet) in accordance with a design, or cause it to conform to the general form of a hull. **c.** to restore (a bent plate or structural member) to its original form. **d.** to align (the frames of a vessel under construction) in proper position. **29.** to bring (rivet holes in connecting structural members) into perfect alignment. **30.** *Obs.* to make fair. —*v.i.* **31. fair off** or **up,** *South Midland and Southern U.S.* (of the weather) to clear: *It's supposed to fair off toward evening.* [bef. 900; ME; OE *fæger;* c. OS, OHG *fagar,* ON *fagr,* Goth *fagrs*] —**fair′ness,** *n.*
—**Syn. 1.** FAIR, IMPARTIAL, DISINTERESTED, UNPREJUDICED refer to lack of bias in opinions, judgments, etc. FAIR implies the treating of all sides alike, justly and equitably: *a fair compromise.* IMPARTIAL, like FAIR, implies showing no more favor to one side than another, but suggests particularly a judicial consideration of a case: *an impartial judge.* DISINTERESTED implies a fairness arising particularly from lack of desire to obtain a selfish advantage: *The motives of her guardian were entirely disinterested.* UNPREJUDICED means not influenced or swayed by bias, or by prejudice caused by irrelevant considerations: *an unprejudiced decision.* **4.** passable, tolerable, average, middling. **8.** open, clear, unencumbered. **10.** clean, spotless, pure, untarnished, unsullied, unstained. **11.** legible, distinct. **12.** blond, pale. **13.** pretty, comely, lovely. **15.** polite, gracious.

fair[2] (fâr), *n.* **1.** an exhibition, usually competitive, of farm products, livestock, etc., often combined in the U.S. with entertainment and held annually by a county or state. **2.** a periodic gathering of buyers and sellers in an appointed place. **3.** an exposition in which different exhibitors participate, sometimes with the purpose of buying or selling: *a science fair.* **4.** an exhibition and sale of articles to raise money, often for some charitable purpose. [1300–50; ME *feire* < AF, OF < LL *fēria* religious festival, holiday (ML: market), in L only pl.; akin to FEAST]

fair′ ball′, *Baseball.* a batted ball that both lands and settles within the foul lines in the infield, or that is within the foul lines when bounding to the outfield past first or third base, or that first lands within the foul lines of the outfield or would if it were not caught or deflected. [1855–60]

Fair•banks (fâr′bangks′), *n.* **1. Charles Warren,** 1852–1918, political leader: vice president of the U.S. 1905–09. **2. Douglas,** 1883–1939, U.S. film actor. **3.** a city in central Alaska, on the Tanana River. 22,645.

Fair•born (fâr′bôrn′), *n.* a city in W Ohio, near Dayton. 39,702.

fair′ catch′, *Football.* a catch of a kicked ball in which the receiver signals that he or she will not advance the ball and therefore may not be interfered with or tackled. [1855–60]

fair′ cop′y, 1. a copy of a document made after final correction. **2.** the condition of such a copy. **3.** an exact copy. [1810–20]

Fair′ Deal′, the principles of the liberal wing of the Democratic party under the leadership of President Harry S Truman, consisting largely of a continuation and development of the principles of the New Deal. Cf. **Great Society, New Deal, New Frontier.** [1945–50] —**Fair′ Deal′er.**

fair′ din′kum, *Australian.* dinkum.

fair′ employ′ment, the policy or practice of employing people on the basis of their capabilities only, without regard to race, sex, national origin, or religion.

Fair•fax (fâr′faks), *n.* **1. Thomas** (*3rd Baron Fairfax of Cameron*), 1612–71, British general: commander in chief of the parliamentary army 1645–50. **2. Thomas** (*6th Baron Fairfax of Cameron*), 1692–1782, English colonist in Virginia. **3.** a town in NE Virginia. 19,390. **4.** a male given name.

Fair•field (fâr′fēld′), *n.* **1.** a city in central California. 58,099. **2.** a town in SW Connecticut. 54,849. **3.** a town in central Ohio. 30,777. **4.** a city in central Alabama. 13,040.

fair′ game′, a legitimate or likely object of attack, mockery, etc.: *With his fat, round face, the politician was fair game for the cartoonists.* [1795–1805]

fair•ground (fâr′ground′), *n.* Often, **fairgrounds.** a place where fairs, horse races, etc., are held; in the U.S. usually an area set aside by a city, county, or state for an annual fair and often containing exhibition buildings. [1735–45; FAIR[2] + GROUND[1]]

fair-haired (fâr′hârd′), *adj.* **1.** having light-colored hair. **2. fair-haired boy,** *Informal.* a person, esp. a young one, considered especially promising by a superior or the members of a group: *the fair-haired boy of the literary set.* [1620–30; FAIR[1] + HAIR + -ED[3]]

Fair•ha•ven (fâr′hā′vən), *n.* a city in SE Massachusetts. 15,759.

fair′ hous′ing. See **open housing.**

fair•i•ly (fâr′ə lē), *adv.* in a manner suggestive of fairies; delicately. [1860–65; FAIRY + -LY]

fair•ing (fâr′ing), *n.* **1.** a structure on the exterior of an aircraft or boat, for reducing drag. **2.** a structure, as a rigid, transparent, plastic sheet, at the front of a motorcycle, bicycle, etc., for deflecting wind and rain. [1910–15; FAIR[1] + -ING[1]]

fair•ish (fâr′ish), *adj.* **1.** moderately good, large, or well: *a fairish income.* **2.** moderately light in color: *a fairish complexion.* [1605–15; FAIR[1] + -ISH[1]]

Fair′ Lawn′, a city in NE New Jersey. 32,229.

fair•lead (fâr′lēd′), *n.* **1.** a pulley, thimble, etc., used to guide a rope forming part of the rigging of a ship, crane, etc., in such a way as to prevent chafing. **2.** *Mach.* (on power shovels or cranes) a swiveling mounting for sheaves, over which cables pass. Also, **fair′lead′•er.** [1855–60; FAIR[1] + LEAD[1]]

fair′ list′. See **white list.**

fair•ly (fâr′lē), *adv.* **1.** in a fair manner; justly or honestly; impartially. **2.** moderately; tolerably: *a fairly heavy rain.* **3.** properly; legitimately: *a claim fairly made.* **4.** clearly; distinctly: *fairly seen.* **5.** *Chiefly Southern U.S.* **a.** actually; completely: *The wheels fairly spun.* **b.** almost; practically: *He slipped off the roof and fairly broke his neck.* **6.** *Obs.* softly. **7.** *Obs.* courteously. [1350–1400; ME; see FAIR[1], -LY]

fair′ mar′ket price′, the price of something at which both a seller and a buyer are willing to strike a deal. [1925–30]

fair-mind•ed (fâr′mīn′did), *adj.* characterized by fair judgment; impartial; unprejudiced: *a wise and fair-minded judge.* [1870–75] —**fair′-mind′ed•ness,** *n.*

Fair•mont (fâr′mont), *n.* **1.** a city in W West Virginia. 23,863. **2.** a town in S Minnesota. 11,506.

fair′ness doc′trine (fâr′nis), a policy mandated by the Federal Communications Commission, requiring radio and television stations to grant equal time to a political candidate, group, etc., to present an opposing viewpoint to one already aired. [1965–70]

Fair′ Oaks′, 1. Also called **Seven Pines.** a locality in E Virginia, near Richmond: battle 1862. **2.** a town in central California, near Sacramento. 22,602.

fair′ play′, just and honorable treatment, action, or conduct: *The political campaign was notably lacking in fair play.* [1585–95]

fair′ sex′, women collectively. [1680–90]

fair′ shake′, *Informal.* an equitable opportunity or treatment: *The judges promised that every entrant in the contest would get a fair shake.* [1820–30, *Amer.*]

fair-spo•ken (fâr′spō′kən), *adj.* speaking or spoken in a courteous, civil, or plausible manner; smooth-spoken. [1425–75; late ME] —**fair′-spo′ken•ness,** *n.*

fair′ ter′ritory, *Baseball.* the area beginning with and including home plate and extending between and including foul lines into which a batter must bat the ball as a prerequisite for a safe hit.

fair′ trade′, trade carried on under a fair-trade agreement. [1715–25]

fair-trade (fâr′trād′), *v.,* **-trad•ed, -trad•ing,** *adj.* (formerly) —*v.t.* **1.** to sell (a commodity) under a fair-trade agreement. —*v.i.* **2.** to sell a commodity under a fair-trade agreement. —*adj.* **3.** subject to or resulting from a fair-trade agreement: *fair-trade items; fair-trade prices.* [1940–45] —**fair′-trad′er,** *n.*

fair′-trade′ agree′ment, an agreement or contract between a manufacturer and a retailer to sell a branded or trademarked product at no less than a specific price: legally prohibited after 1975. [1935–40]

fair′-trade′ law′, a state or federal law authorizing fair-trade agreements: repealed 1975.

Fair•view (fâr′vyo͞o′), *n.* a town in NE New Jersey. 10,519.

Fair′view Heights′, a city in SW Illinois. 12,414.

Fair′view Park′, a city in N Ohio. 19,311.

fair•way (fâr′wā′), *n.* **1.** an unobstructed passage, way, or area. **2.** *Golf.* **a.** the part of the course where the grass is cut short between the tees and the putting greens, exclusive of the rough, trees, and hazards. **b.** the mowed part of any hole between the tee and the green: *The foursome is now on the tenth fairway.* **3.** *Naut.* **a.** the navigable portion of a river, harbor, or other partly enclosed body of water. **b.** the channel customarily navigated by vessels in such a body of water. [1515–25; 1905–10 for def. 2; FAIR[1] + WAY]

fair-weath•er (fâr′weth′ər), *adj.* **1.** used in or intended for fair weather only. **2.** weakening or failing in time of trouble: *His fair-weather friends left him when he lost his money.* [1730–40]

Fair•weath•er (fâr′weth′ər), *n.* **Mount,** a mountain in SE Alaska. 15,292 ft. (4660 m).

fair•y (fâr′ē), *n., pl.* **fair•ies,** *adj.* —*n.* **1.** (in folklore) one of a class of supernatural beings, generally conceived as having a diminutive human form and possessing magical powers with which they intervene in human affairs. **2.** *Slang* (*disparaging and offensive*). a male homosexual. —*adj.* **3.** of or pertaining to fairies: *fairy magic.* **4.** of the nature of a fairy; fairylike. **5.** See **fairy green.** [1250–1300; ME *faierie* < OF: enchantment, fairyland. See FAY[1], -ERY]
—**Syn. 1.** pixy, leprechaun. FAIRY, BROWNIE, ELF, SPRITE are terms for imaginary beings, thought to be helpful or harmful to people. FAIRY is the most general name for such beings: *a good fairy as a godmother.* A BROWNIE is a good-natured tiny being who appears usually at night to do household tasks: *Perhaps the brownies will come and mow the lawn tonight.* ELF suggests a young, mischievous fairy: *That child is a perfect little elf.* SPRITE suggests a fairy of pleasing appearance, older than an elf; it may, however, be impish or even hostile: *a dainty sprite.*

fair′y blue′bird, any fruit-eating passerine bird of the genus *Irena,* of the East Indies, the males of the several species being characteristically black below and purple-blue above.

fair′y glove′. See **purple foxglove.** [1865–70]

fair′y green′, a medium yellow-green color. Also called **fairy.**

fair•y•hood (fâr′ē ho͝od′), *n.* **1.** a fairy nature or state: *the fairyhood of Puck.* **2.** fairies collectively. [1825–35; FAIRY + -HOOD]

fair•y•ism (fâr′ē iz′əm), *n.* **1.** fairylike quality. **2.** belief in fairies. [1705–15; FAIRY + -ISM]

fair′y lamp′, a lamp using a candle as the source of illumination, usually constructed of glass or ceramic material, set on a metal base, and having a fabric shade. [1890–95]

fair•y•land (fâr′ē land′), *n.* **1.** the imaginary realm of fairies. **2.** any enchantingly beautiful region. [1580–90; FAIRY + LAND]

fair′y lil′y, 1. a Texan bulbous plant, *Zephyranthes drummondii,* of the amaryllis family, having a fragrant white flower, with a reddish outer surface, that blooms at night. **2.** See **atamasco lily. 3.** zephyranthes.

fair′y prim′rose, a tender primrose, *Primula malacoides,* of China, having hairy leaves and small, pink or lilac-colored flowers.

fair′y ring′, any of numerous mushrooms of meadows and open woods, esp. the well-known *Marasmius oreades,* that spread in rings originating from mycelial growth: formerly supposed to mark the paths laid by dancing fairies. [1590–1600]

fair′y shrimp′, any member of the crustacean order Anostraca, characterized by an elongate trunk with more than 20 segments and the absence of a carapace, typically found swimming ventral side up in fresh water. [1855–60]

fair•y-slip•per (fâr′ē slip′ər), *n.* Calypso (def. 2).

fair′y stone′, 1. a fossil or other oddly shaped stone or crystal. **2.** a stone arrowhead. **3.** a megalith or other stone monument of ancient origin. [1785–95]

fair′y tale′, 1. a story, usually for children, about elves, hobgoblins, dragons, fairies, or other magical creatures. **2.** an incredible or misleading statement, account, or belief. Also called **fair′y sto′ry.** [1740–50]

fair′y wand′, devil's-bit.

Fai•sal (fī′səl), *n.* (*Faisal Abdul-Aziz al Saud al Faisal*) 1904–75, king of Saudi Arabia 1964–75 (son of ibn-Saud and brother of Saud).

Faisal I, 1885–1933, king of Syria 1920; king of Iraq 1921–33. Also, **Feisal I, Feisul I.**

Faisal II, 1935–58, king of Iraq 1939–58 (grandson of Faisal I). Also, **Feisal II, Faisul II.**

fais-do-do (fā′dō dō′), *n., pl.* **-dos.** *Louisiana.* a country dance party. [< LaF; F: go to sleep! (*fais* 2d sing. impv. of *faire* to do, make; *dodo* nursery word for "sleep," prob. based on *dod(el)iner* to nod, dandle (a child), influenced by *dormir* to sleep]

fait ac•com•pli (fe tᴀ kôn plē′), *pl.* ***faits ac•com•plis*** (fe zᴀ kôn plē′). *French.* an accomplished fact; a thing already done: *The enemy's defeat was a* fait accompli *long before the formal surrender.* [1835–45]

faites vos jeux (fet′ vō zhœ′), *French.* (esp. in roulette) place your bets.

faith (fāth), *n.* **1.** confidence or trust in a person or thing: *faith in another's ability.* **2.** belief that is not based on proof: *He had faith that the hypothesis would be substantiated by fact.* **3.** belief in God or in the doctrines or teachings of religion: *the firm faith of the Pilgrims.* **4.** belief in anything, as a code of ethics, standards of merit, etc.: *to be of the same faith with someone concerning honesty.* **5.** a system of religious belief: *the Christian faith; the Jewish faith.* **6.** the obligation of loyalty or fidelity to a person, promise, engagement, etc.: *Failure to appear would be breaking faith.* **7.** the observance of this obligation; fidelity to one's promise, oath, allegiance, etc.: *He was the only one who proved his faith during our recent troubles.* **8.** *Christian Theol.* the trust in God and in His promises as made through Christ and the Scriptures by which humans are justified or saved. **9. in faith,** in truth; indeed: *In faith, he is a fine lad.* [1200–50; ME *feith* < AF *fed,* OF *feid, feit* < L *fidem,* acc. of *fidēs* trust, akin to *fidere* to trust. See CONFIDE]

Faith (fāth), *n.* a female given name.

faith′ cure′, 1. a method of attempting to cure disease by prayer and religious faith. **2.** a cure thus effected. [1880–85]

faith•ful (fāth′fəl), *adj.* **1.** strict or thorough in the performance of duty: *a faithful worker.* **2.** true to one's word, promises, vows, etc. **3.** steady in allegiance or affection; loyal; constant: *faithful friends.* **4.** reliable, trusted, or believed. **5.** adhering or true to fact, a standard, or an original; accurate: *a faithful account; a faithful copy.* **6.** *Obs.* full of faith; believing. —*n.* **7. the faithful, a.** the believers, esp. members of a Christian church or adherents of Islam. **b.** the body of loyal members of any party or group. [1250–1300; ME *feithful.* See FAITH, -FUL] —**faith′ful•ly,** *adv.* —**faith′ful•ness,** *n.*
—**Syn. 1, 3.** true, devoted, staunch. **3.** FAITHFUL, CONSTANT, LOYAL imply qualities of stability, dependability, and devotion. FAITHFUL implies long-continued and steadfast fidelity to whatever one is bound to by a pledge, duty, or obligation: *a faithful friend.* CONSTANT suggests firmness and steadfastness in attachment: *a constant affection.* LOYAL implies unswerving allegiance to a person, organization, cause, or idea: *loyal to one's associates, one's country.* **5.** precise, exact.

faith′ heal′ing, 1. healing effected through prayer or religious faith; divine healing. **2.** a method employing faith or prayer in the hope of receiving such healing. [1880–85] —**faith′ heal′er.**

faith•less (fāth′lis), *adj.* **1.** not adhering to allegiance, promises, vows, or duty: *the faithless behavior of Benedict Arnold.* **2.** not trustworthy; unreliable. **3.** without trust or belief. **4.** being without religious faith. **5.** (among Christians) bereft of Christian faith. [1250–1300; ME *faithles.* See FAITH, -LESS] —**faith′less•ly,** *adv.*

fai•tour (fā′tər), *n. Archaic.* impostor; fake. [1300–50; ME < AF: impostor, OF *faitor* perpetrator, lit., doer, maker < L *factor.* See FACTOR]

Fai•yum (fī yo͞om′), *n.* **1.** a province in N central Egypt: many archaeological remains. 691 sq. mi. (1790 sq. km). **2.** Also called **El Faiyum, El Fayum.** a city in and the capital of this province, SW of Cairo. 167,700. —*adj.* **3.** pertaining to or designating a style of portrait painting developed in Egypt under Roman rule, examples of which have been found principally in Faiyum dating from the 2nd and 3rd centuries A.D., characterized chiefly by the frontality of the head, the modeling of form, and emphasis on the eyes. Also, **Fayum.**

fa•ja (fä′hä), *n.* a broad, brightly colored sash traditionally worn by Spanish and Latin American men. [1835–45; < Sp: belt, strip, band; orig. dial. or < Catalan < L *fascia* FASCIA]

Fa•jar•do (fä här′thô), *n.* a city in NE Puerto Rico. 26,928.

fa•ji•tas (fä hē′təz, fə-), *n.* (*used with a singular or plural v.*) a Tex-Mex dish of thin strips of marinated and grilled meat, served with tortillas, salsa, etc. [1975–80; < AmerSp, pl. of *fajita* lit., little sash, dim. of Sp *faja* belt, strip, band (orig. dial. or < Catalan < L *fascia* FASCIA]

fake[1] (fāk), *v.,* **faked, fak•ing,** *n., adj.* —*v.t.* **1.** prepare or make (something specious, deceptive, or fraudulent): *to fake a report showing nonexistent profits.* **2.** to conceal the defects of or make appear more attractive, interesting, valuable, etc., usually in order to deceive: *The story was faked a bit to make it more sensational.* **3.** to pretend; simulate: *to fake illness.* **4.** to accomplish by trial and error or by improvising: *I don't know the job, but I can fake it.* **5.** to trick or deceive (an opponent) by making a fake (often fol. by *out*): *The running back faked out the defender with a deft move and scored.* **6.** *Jazz.* **a.** to improvise: *to fake an accompaniment.* **b.** to play (music) without reading from a score. —*v.i.* **7.** to fake something; pretend. **8.** to give a fake to an opponent. **9. fake out,** *Slang.* **a.** to trick; deceive: *She faked me out by acting friendly and then stole my job.* **b.** to surprise, as by a sudden reversal: *They thought we weren't coming back, but we faked them out by showing up during dinner.* —*n.* **10.** anything made to appear otherwise than it actually is; counterfeit: *This diamond necklace is a fake.* **11.** a person who fakes; faker: *The doctor with the reputed cure for cancer proved to be a fake.* **12.** a spurious report or story. **13.** *Sports.* a simulated play or move intended to deceive an opponent. —*adj.* **14.** designed to deceive or cheat; not real; counterfeit. [1805–15; orig. vagrants' slang: to do for, rob, kill (someone), shape (something); perh. var. of obs. *feak, feague* to beat, akin to D *veeg* a slap, *vegen* to sweep, wipe]

—**Syn. 3.** feign, affect, dissemble, sham, fabricate. **11.** fraud, impostor, quack, charlatan, deceiver.

fake[2] (fāk), *v.,* **faked, fak•ing,** *n. Naut.* —*v.t.* **1.** to lay (a rope) in a coil or series of long loops so as to allow to run freely without fouling or kinking (often fol. by *down*). —*n.* **2.** any complete turn of a rope that has been faked down. **3.** any of the various ways in which a rope may be faked down. Also, **flake.** [1350–1400; ME *faken* to coil (a rope), of obscure orig.]

fake′ book′, a collection of lead sheets for musicians, esp. a songbook of standards for use by jazz instrumentalists. Cf. **lead sheet.** [1955–60]

fak•er (fā′kər), *n.* **1.** a person who fakes. **2.** a petty swindler. **3.** a peddler or street vendor of articles of dubious value. [1840–50; FAKE[1] + -ER[1]]

fak•er•y (fā′kə rē), *n., pl.* **-er•ies.** the practice or result of faking. [1885–90; FAKE[1] + -ERY]

fa•kir (fə kēr′, fā′kər), *n.* **1.** a Muslim or Hindu religious ascetic or mendicant monk commonly considered a wonder-worker. **2.** a member of any Islamic religious order; dervish. Also, **fa•keer** (fə kēr′). [1600–10; < Ar *faqīr* poor]

fa-la (fä lä′), *n.* **1.** a text or refrain in old songs. **2.** a type of part song or madrigal popular in the 16th and 17th centuries. Also, **fal la.** [1585–95; special use of *fa la,* meaningless sound sequence found in old popular refrains]

fa•la•fel (fə lä′fəl), *n. Middle Eastern Cookery.* an appetizer or snack consisting of a small croquette made with fava-bean flour or ground chick peas, seasoned with toasted sesame seeds and salt, often served in pita bread. Also, **fa•la′fil, felafel.** [1950–55; < Ar *falāfil,* deriv. of *filfil* pepper]

Fa•lange (fā′lanj; *Sp.* fä län′he), *n.* the official state political party in Spain from 1936 until disbandment in 1977. [< Sp, short for *Falange Española Tradicionalista* Traditionalist Spanish Phalanx]

Fa•lan•gist (fə lan′jist), *n.* a member of the Falange. [1935–40; < Sp *falangista;* see FALANGE, -IST]

Fa•la•sha (fä lä′shə, fə-), *n., pl.* **-shas,** (*esp. collectively*) **-sha.** a member of an Ethiopian people who speak a Hamitic language and who practice a form of Judaism.

fal•ba•la (fal′bə lə), *n.* a furbelow or puckered flounce for decorating dresses in the 17th century. Also, **fal•be•lo** (fal′bə lō′). [1695–1705; < F < It. See FURBELOW]

fal•cate (fal′kāt), *adj.* curved like a scythe or sickle; hooked; falciform. Also, **fal′cat•ed.** [1820–30; < L *falcātus* sickle-shaped, equiv. to *falc-* (s. of *falx*) sickle + *-ātus* -ATE[1]]

fal•chion (fôl′chən, -shən), *n.* **1.** a broad, short sword having a convex edge curving sharply to the point. **2.** *Archaic.* any sword. [1275–1325; ME *fauchoun* (with *l* restored in 16th cent.) < OF *fauchon* < VL **falciōn-,* s. of *falciō,* deriv. of L *falx,* s. *falc-* sickle]

fal•cial (fal′shəl, -chəl, fôl′-), *adj. Anat.* of or pertaining to a falx. [< NL; see FALX, -IAL]

fal•ci•form (fal′sə fôrm′), *adj.* sickle-shaped; falcate. [1760–70; < L *falci-* (s. of *falx*) sickle + -FORM]

fal•con (fôl′kən, fal′-, fô′kən), *n.* **1.** any of several birds of prey of the family Falconidae, esp. of the genus *Falco,* usually distinguished by long, pointed wings, a hooked beak with a toothlike notch on each side of the upper bill, and swift, agile flight, typically diving to seize prey: some falcon species are close to extinction. **2.** *Falconry.* **a.** the female gyrfalcon. **b.** falcon-gentle. **c.** any bird of prey trained for use in falconry. Cf. **tercel. 3.** a small, light cannon in use from the 15th to the 17th century. **4.** (*cap.*) *Mil.* a family of air-to-air guided missiles, some of them capable of carrying nuclear warheads. [1200–50; ME *fauco(u)n, falcon* < AF, OF *faucon* < LL *falcōn-* (s. of *falcō*) hawk (said to be deriv. of *falx,* s. *falc-* sickle, referring to the sicklelike talons)] —**fal•co•nine** (fôl′kə nīn′, -nin, fal′-, fô′kə-), *adj.* —**fal′co•noid′,** *adj.*

peregrine falcon,
Falco peregrinus,
length 18 in. (46 cm)

fal•con•er (fôl′kə nər, fal′-, fô′kə-), *n.* **1.** a person who hunts with falcons or follows the sport of hawking. **2.** a person who trains hawks for hunting. [1350–1400; ME *falkenar* (< ML *falcōnārius*), *fauconer* < AF; OF *fauconier* < ML; see FALCON, -ER[2]]

fal•co•net (fôl′kə net′, fal′-, fô′kə-), *n.* any of several small Asian falcons, esp. of the genus *Microhierax.* [1850–55; FALCON + -ET]

fal•con-gen•tle (fôl′kən jen′tl, fal′-, fô′kən-), *n.* **1.** the female peregrine falcon. **2.** any female falcon. [1350–1400; trans. of F *faucon gentil;* r. ME *gentil fauco(u)n, facon jent,* etc.]

fal•con•i•form (fôl kō′nə fôrm′, fal-, fô kō′-, fôl′kə-nə-, fal′-, fô′kə-), *adj.* of, pertaining to, or belonging to the order Falconiformes, comprising the vultures, hawks, eagles, ospreys, falcons, caracaras, etc. [< NL *falconiformes;* see FALCON, -IFORMES]

fal•con•ry (fôl′kən rē, fal′-, fô′kən-), *n.* **1.** the sport of hunting with falcons, hawks, eagles, etc.; hawking. **2.** the art of training hawks to hunt. [1565–75; FALCON + -RY, modeled on F *fauconnerie*]

fal•da (fol′də), *n.* a white silk vestment extending from the waist to the ground, worn over the cassock by the pope on solemn occasions. [< It < Gmc; see FOLD[1]]

fal•de•ral (fal′də ral′), *n.* **1.** mere nonsense; foolish talk or ideas. **2.** a trifle; gimcrack; gew-gaw. Also, **fal•de•rol** (fal′də rol′), **folderol.** [1695–1705; orig. as a nonsense refrain in songs; of obscure orig.]

fald•stool (fôld′sto͞ol′), *n.* **1.** a chair or seat, originally one capable of being folded, used by a bishop or other prelate when officiating in his own church away from his throne or in a church not his own. **2.** a movable folding stool or desk at which worshipers kneel during certain acts of devotion. **3.** such a stool placed at the south side of the altar, at which the kings or queens of England kneel at their coronation. **4.** a desk at which the litany is said or sung. [1595–1605; < ML *faldistolium* < WGmc **faldistōl* (cf. OHG *faltistuol,* late OE *fældestōl, fyldestōl*); see FOLD[1], STOOL; cf. FAUTEUIL]

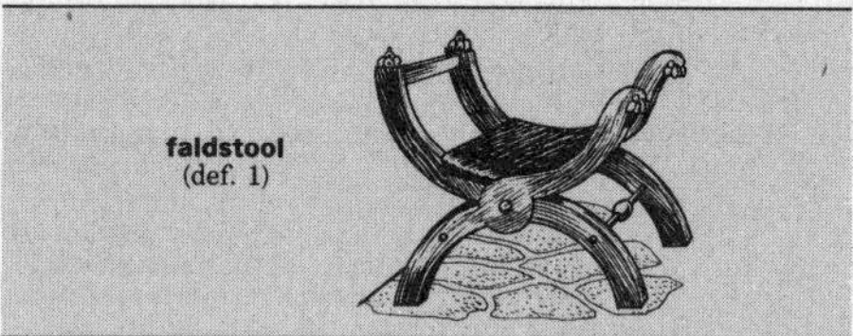
faldstool
(def. 1)

Fa•ler•ni•an (fə lûr′nē ən), *adj.* (esp. of a wine celebrated by Horace) of, coming from, or made in a district of Campania, Italy. [1720–30; < L (*ager*) *Falern(us)* Falernian (field) + -IAN]

Fa•lie•ri (*It.* fä lye′rē), *n.* **Ma•ri•no** (*It.* mä rē′nô), 1278?–1355, Venetian army commander: doge of Venice 1354–55. Also, **Fa•lie′ro** (*It.* fä lye′rô).

Fa•lis•can (fə lis′kən), *n., pl.* **-cans,** (*esp. collectively*) **-can** for 1. **1.** a member of an ancient people who inhabited southern Etruria. **2.** the Italic language spoken by this people, closely related to Latin. —*adj.* **3.** of or pertaining to the Faliscans or their language. [1590–1600; < L *Falisc(us)* of Falerii, major city of the Faliscans + -AN]

Fal•ken•hayn (fäl′kən hīn′), *n.* **E•rich von** (ā′rikh fən), 1861–1922, German general of World War I.

Fal•kirk (fôl′kûrk), *n.* **1.** an administrative district in the Central region, in S central Scotland. 143,167; 110 sq. mi. (285 sq. km). **2.** a city in this district, W of Edinburgh: Scots under Wallace defeated by the English 1298. 37,489.

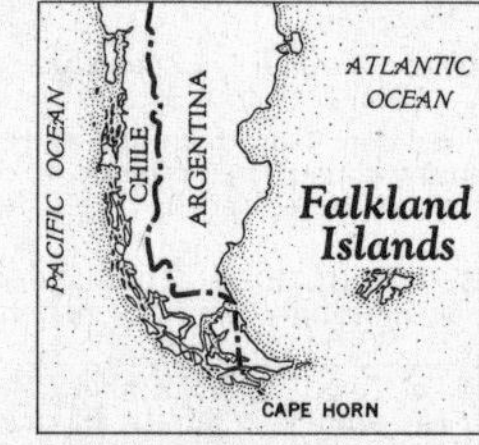

Falk′land Is′lands (fôk′lənd), a self-governing British colony also claimed by Argentina: site of a war between the two nations in 1982. 2000; 4618 sq. mi. (11,961 sq. km). Also called **Falk′lands.** Spanish, **Islas Malvinas.**

Falk•ner (fôk′nər), *n.* **William.** See **Faulkner, William.**

fall (fôl), *v.,* **fell, fall•en, fall•ing,** *n.* —*v.i.* **1.** to drop or descend under the force of gravity, as to a lower place through loss or lack of support. **2.** to come or drop down suddenly to a lower position, esp. to leave a standing or erect position suddenly, whether voluntarily or not: *to fall on one's knees.* **3.** to become less or lower; become of a lower level, degree, amount, quality, value, number, etc.; decline: *The temperature fell ten degrees. Stock prices fell to a new low for the year.* **4.** to subside or abate. **5.** extend downward; hang down: *Her hair falls to her shoulders.* **6.** to become lowered or directed downward, as the eyes: *My eyes fell before his steady gaze.* **7.** to become lower in pitch or volume: *Her voice fell, and she looked about in confusion.* **8.** to succumb to temptation or sin, esp. to become unchaste or to lose one's innocence. **9.** to lose status, dignity, position, character, etc. **10.** to succumb to attack: *The city fell to the enemy.* **11.** to be overthrown, as a government. **12.** to drop down wounded or dead, esp. to be slain: *to fall in battle.* **13.** to pass into some physical, mental, or emotional condition: *to fall asleep; to fall in love.* **14.** to envelop or come as if by dropping, as stillness or night. **15.** to issue forth: *Witty remarks fall easily from his lips.* **16.** to come by lot or chance: *The chore fell to him.* **17.** to come by chance into a particular position: *to fall among thieves.* **18.** to come to pass, occur, or become at a certain time: *Christmas falls on a Monday this year. The rent falls due the first of every month.* **19.** to have its proper place: *The accent falls on the last syllable.* **20.** to come by right: *The inheritance fell to the only living relative.* **21.** to be naturally divisible (usually fol. by *into*): *The story fell into two distinct parts.* **22.** to lose animation; appear disappointed, as the face: *His face fell when he heard the bad news.* **23.** to slope or extend in a downward direction: *The field falls gently to the river.* **24.** to be directed, as light, sight, etc., on something: *His eyes fell upon the note on the desk.* **25.** to collapse, as through weakness, damage, poor construction, or the like; topple or sink: *The old tower fell under its own weight. The cake fell when he slammed the oven door.* **26.** (of an animal, esp. a lamb) to be born: *Two lambs fell yesterday.* —*v.t.* **27.** to fell (a tree, animal, etc.). **28. fall all over oneself,** to show unusual or excessive enthusiasm or eagerness, esp. in the hope of being favored or rewarded: *The young trainees fell all over themselves to praise the boss's speech.* Also, **fall over oneself. 29. fall away, a.** to withdraw support or allegiance: *The candidate's supporters fell away when he advocated racial discrimination.* **b.** to become lean or thin; diminish; decline. **c.** to forsake one's faith, cause, or principles: *Many fell away because they were afraid of reprisals.* **30. fall back,** to give way; recede; retreat: *The relentless shelling forced the enemy to fall back.* **31. fall back on** or **upon, a.** Also, **fall back to.** to retreat to: *They fell back on their entrenchments. The troops fell back to their original position.* **b.** to have recourse to; rely on: *They had no savings to fall back on.* **32. fall behind, a.** to lag, in pace or progress: *We are falling behind in our work. Fatigued, some of the marchers fell behind.* **b.** to fail to pay (a debt, obligation, etc.) at the appointed time: *She fell behind in her tax payments, and the property was confiscated.* **33. fall down,** *Informal.* to perform disappointingly; to disappoint; fail: *He was doing well on the exam until he fell down on the last essay question.* **34. fall for,** *Slang.* **a.** to be deceived by: *Imagine falling for such an old trick.* **b.** to fall in love with: *He's not at all the type you would expect her to fall for.* **35. fall foul** or **afoul of.** See **foul** (def. 20). **36. fall in, a.** to fall to pieces toward the interior; sink inward. **b.** to take one's place in the ranks, as a soldier. **c.** Also, **fall in with.** to become acquainted with, esp. by chance: *We fell in with an interesting couple from Paris.* **37. fall off, a.** to separate from; withdraw. **b.** to decrease in number, amount, or intensity; diminish: *Tourism falls off when the summer is over.* **c.** *Naut.* to deviate from the heading; fall to leeward. **d.** *South Midland and Southern U.S.* to lose weight, usually due to illness: *She was sick all winter and fell off till she was just skin and bones.* **38. fall off the roof,** *Slang* (*older use*). to menstruate. **39. fall on** or **upon, a.** to assault; attack: *The enemy fell on them suddenly from the rear.* **b.** to be the obligation of: *It has fallen on me to support the family.* **c.** to experience; encounter: *Once well-to-do, they had fallen on hard times.* **d.** to chance upon; come upon: *I fell upon the idea while looking through a magazine.* **40. fall on one's feet.** See **land** (def. 25). **41. fall out, a.** to quarrel; disagree: *We fell out over who was to wash the dishes.* **b.** to happen; occur: *It fell out that we met by chance weeks later.* **c.** to leave one's place in the ranks, as a soldier: *They were ordered to fall out when the parade ended.* **d.** *Slang.* to burst out laughing. **e.** *South Midland and Southern U.S.* to become unconscious; pass out. **42. fall out of bed,** to get out of bed quickly. **43. fall over backward(s). a.** See **bend** (def. 15). **b.** to exhibit great eagerness, esp. in pursuit of one's own advantage: *The candidate fell over backward in support of the issues that would win votes.* **44. fall or come short.** See **short** (def. 30). **45. fall through,** to come to nothing; fail of realization: *Despite all his efforts, the deal fell through.* **46. fall to, a.** to apply oneself; begin: *to fall to work.* **b.** to begin to eat: *They fell to and soon finished off the entire turkey.* **47. fall under, a.** to be the concern or responsibility of. **b.** to be classified as; be included within: *That case falls under the heading of errors of judgment.*

—*n.* **48.** an act or instance of falling or dropping from a higher to a lower place or position. **49.** that which falls or drops: *a heavy fall of rain.* **50.** the season of the year that comes after summer and before winter; autumn. **51.** a becoming less; a lowering or decline; a sinking to a lower level: *the fall of the Roman Empire.* **52.** the distance through which anything falls: *It is a long fall to the ground from this height.* **53.** Usually, **falls.** a cataract or waterfall. **54.** downward slope or declivity: *the gentle rise and fall of the meadow.* **55.** a falling from an erect position, as to the ground: *to have a bad fall.* **56.** a hanging down: *a fall of long hair.* **57.** a succumbing to temptation; lapse into sin. **58. the Fall,** (*sometimes l.c.*) *Theol.* the lapse of human beings into a state of natural or innate sinfulness through the sin of Adam and Eve. **59.** *Slang.* an arrest by the police. **60.** surrender or capture, as of a city. **61.** proper place: *the fall of an accent on a syllable.* **62.** *Wrestling.* **a.** an act or instance of holding or forcing an opponent's shoulders against the mat for a specified length of time. **b.** a match or division of a match. **63.** a hairpiece consisting of long hair that is attached to one's own hair at the crown and usually allowed to hang freely down the back of the head so as to cover or blend with the natural hair. **64.** an opaque veil hanging loose from the back of a hat. **65.** See **falling band. 66.** a decorative cascade of lace, ruffles, or the like. **67.** *Mach., Naut.* the part of the rope of a tackle to which the power is applied in hoisting. **68.** *Hunting.* a deadfall. **69.** the long soft hair that hangs over the forehead and eyes of certain terriers. **70.** *Armor.* a pivoted peak projecting over the face opening of a burgonet. **71.** *Astrol.* the sign of the zodiac in which the most negative influence of a planet is expressed (as opposed to *exaltation*). **72.** *Mining.* rock or ore that has collapsed from a roof, hanging wall, or the sides of a passage. [bef. 900; ME *fallen,* OE *feallan;* c. G *fallen,* ON *falla;* akin to Lith *pùlti* to fall]

Fall (fôl), *n.* **Albert Bacon,** 1861–1944, U.S. politician: senator 1912–21; secretary of the Interior 1921–23; convicted in Teapot Dome scandal.

Fall, The, (French, *La Chute*), a novel (1957) by Albert Camus.

fal la (fäl lä′), fa-la.

CONCISE ETYMOLOGY KEY: <, descended or borrowed from; >, whence; b., blend of, blended; c., cognate with; cf., compare; deriv., derivative; equiv., equivalent; imit., imitative; obl., oblique; r., replacing; s., stem; sp., spelling, spelled; resp., respelling, respelled; trans., translation; ?, origin unknown; *, unattested; ‡, probably earlier than. See the full key inside the front cover.

Fal·la (fä′yə; *Sp.* fä′lyä), *n.* **Ma·nuel de** (mä nwel′ de), 1876–1946, Spanish composer.

fal·la·cious (fə lā′shəs), *adj.* **1.** containing a fallacy; logically unsound: *fallacious arguments.* **2.** deceptive; misleading: *fallacious testimony.* **3.** disappointing; delusive: *a fallacious peace.* [1500–10; < L *fallāciōsus* deceitful, deceptive. See FALLACY, -OUS] —**fal·la′cious·ly,** *adv.* —**fal·la′cious·ness,** *n.*

fal·la·cy (fal′ə sē), *n., pl.* **-cies. 1.** a deceptive, misleading, or false notion, belief, etc.: *That the world is flat was at one time a popular fallacy.* **2.** a misleading or unsound argument. **3.** deceptive, misleading, or false nature; erroneousness. **4.** *Logic.* any of various types of erroneous reasoning that render arguments logically unsound. **5.** *Obs.* deception. [1350–1400; < L *fallācia* a trick, deceit, equiv. to *fallāc-* (s. of *fallāx*) deceitful, fallacious + *-ia* -Y³; r. ME *fallace* < MF]
—**Syn. 1.** misconception, delusion, misapprehension.

fal·lal (fal lal′), *n.* a bit of finery; a showy article of dress. Also, **fal-lal′.** [1700–10; perh. syncopated var. of FALDERAL] —**fal·lal′er·y,** *n.*

fall·back (fôl′bak′), *n.* **1.** an act or instance of falling back. **2.** something or someone to turn or return to, esp. for help or as an alternative: *His teaching experience would be a fallback if the business failed.* —*adj.* **3.** Also, **fall′-back′.** of or designating something kept in reserve or as an alternative: *The negotiators agreed on a fallback position.* [1750–60, *Amer.*; n., adj. use of v. phrase *fall back*]

fall′ can′kerworm. See under **cankerworm.** See illus. under **geometrid.**

fall·en (fô′lən), *v.* **1.** pp. of **fall.** —*adj.* **2.** having dropped or come down from a higher place, from an upright position, or from a higher level, degree, amount, quality, value, number, etc. **3.** on the ground; prostrate; down flat: *Exhausted, the racers lay fallen by the road.* **4.** degraded or immoral. **5.** (of a woman) having lost her chastity. **6.** overthrown, destroyed, or conquered: *a fallen city.* **7.** dead: *fallen troops.*

Fall′en Tim′bers, a battle site on the Maumee River, near present-day Maumee, Ohio, where a confederation of Indian tribes (**Northwest Indian Confederation**) was defeated by Gen. Anthony Wayne (1794): state park.

fall·er (fô′lər), *n.* **1.** a person or thing that falls. **2.** any of various devices that operate by falling. **3.** *Textiles.* a device for cleaning, straightening, and separating fibers during combing of worsted stock, consisting of a series of metal pins set into a rectangular bar or rod. **4.** a logger hired to cut down trees; feller. [1400–50; late ME; see FALL, -ER¹]

fall·fish (fôl′fish′), *n., pl.* **-fish·es,** (*esp. collectively*) **-fish.** a large minnow, *Semotilus corporalis,* of eastern North America. [1805–15, *Amer.*; FALL + FISH]

fall′ front′, a part of a desk front, hinged at the lower end and opening out to provide a writing surface. Also called **drop front.** [1900–05]

fall′ guy′, *Slang.* **1.** an easy victim. **2.** a scapegoat. [1905–10, *Amer.*]

fal·li·ble (fal′ə bəl), *adj.* **1.** (of persons) liable to err, esp. in being deceived or mistaken. **2.** liable to be erroneous or false; not accurate: *fallible information.* [1375–1425; late ME < ML *fallibilis,* equiv. to L *fall(i)* (pass. of *fallere* to deceive) + *-ibilis* -IBLE] —**fal′li·bil′i·ty, fal′li·ble·ness,** *n.* —**fal′li·bly,** *adv.*

fall′ing ac′tion, the part of a literary plot that occurs after the climax has been reached and the conflict has been resolved. Cf. **rising action.**

fall′ing band′, a large, flat collar, usually trimmed with lace, worn by men in the 17th century. Also called **fall.** [1590–1600]

fall′ing diph′thong, *Phonet.* a diphthong in which the first of the two apparent vocalic elements is of greater stress or sonority and the second is of lesser stress or sonority, as in (ī), (ou), (oi), etc. Cf. **rising diphthong.** [1885–90]

fall′ing door′. See **flap door** (def. 1). [1745–55]

fall·ing-out (fô′ling out′), *n., pl.* **fall·ings-out, fall·ing-outs.** a quarrel or estrangement between persons formerly in close association with one another. [1560–70; nominalization of v. phrase *fall out;* see -ING¹]

fall′ing rhythm′, *Pros.* a rhythmic pattern created by the succession of metrical feet each of which is composed of one accented syllable followed by one or more unaccented syllables. Also called **descending rhythm.** [1915–20]

fall′ing sick′ness, epilepsy. [1520–30]

fall′ing star′, an incandescent meteor; a shooting star. [1555–65]

fall′ing weath′er, *Chiefly Midland U.S.* wet weather, as rain or snow.

fall′ line′, 1. an imaginary line, marked by waterfalls and rapids, where rivers descend abruptly from an upland to a lowland. **2.** (*caps.*) *Eastern U.S.* the imaginary line between the Piedmont and the Atlantic coastal plain. **3.** *Skiing.* the path of natural descent from one point on a slope to another. [1880–85, *Amer.*]

fall·off (fôl′ôf′, -of′), *n.* a decline in quantity, vigor, etc. [1595–1605; n. use of v. phrase *fall off*]

fal·lo′pi·an tube′ (fə lō′pē ən), one of a pair of long, slender ducts in the female abdomen that transport ova from the ovary to the uterus and, in fertilization, transport sperm cells from the uterus to the released ova; the oviduct of higher mammals. Also, **Fallo′pian tube′.** [1700–10; named after Gabriello *Fallopio* (d. 1562), Italian anatomist; see -IAN]

fall·out (fôl′out′), *n.* **1.** the settling to the ground of airborne particles ejected into the atmosphere from the earth by explosions, eruptions, forest fires, etc., esp. such settling from nuclear explosions (**radioactive fallout**). Cf. **rainout. 2.** the particles themselves. Cf. **rainout. 3.** an unexpected or incidental effect, outcome, or product: *the psychological fallout of being obese.* **4.** effects; results: *emotional fallout from a divorce.* Also, **fall′-out′.** [1945–50; n. use of v. phrase *fall out*]

fal·low¹ (fal′ō), *adj.* **1.** (of land) plowed and left unseeded for a season or more; uncultivated. **2.** not in use; inactive: *My creative energies have lain fallow this year.* —*n.* **3.** land that has undergone plowing and harrowing and has been left unseeded for one or more growing seasons. —*v.t.* **4.** to make (land) fallow for agricultural purposes. [1275–1325; ME *falwe;* cf. OE *fealga,* pl. of **fealh,* as gloss of ML *occas* harrows] —**fal′low·ness,** *n.*

fal·low² (fal′ō), *adj.* pale-yellow; light-brown; dun. [bef. 1000; ME *fal(o)we,* OE *fealu;* c. G *falb*]

fal′low deer′, a Eurasian deer, *Dama dama,* with a fallow or yellowish coat. [1540–50]

fallow deer (male), *Dama dama,* 3 ft. (0.9 m) high at shoulder; antlers to 2½ ft. (0.8 m); length 5 ft. (1.5 m)

Fall′ Riv′er, a seaport in SE Massachusetts, on an arm of Narragansett Bay. 92,574.

Falls (fôlz), *n.* a town in NE Pennsylvania, on the Susquehanna River. 36,083.

fall′ web′worm. See under **webworm.** [1860–65, *Amer.*]

fall′ wind′ (wind), *Meteorol.* a strong, cold, downhill wind. Cf. **gravity wind, foehn.** [1865–70]

Fal·mouth (fal′məth), *n.* **1.** a seaport in S Cornwall, in SW England. 17,883. **2.** a town in SE Massachusetts. 23,640.

F.A.L.N., Armed Forces of National Liberation: a militant underground organization whose objective is independence for Puerto Rico. Also, **FALN** [< Sp *F(uerzas) A(rmadas de) L(iberación) N(acional)*]

false (fôls), *adj.,* **fals·er, fals·est,** *adv.* —*adj.* **1.** not true or correct; erroneous: *a false statement.* **2.** uttering or declaring what is untrue: *a false witness.* **3.** not faithful or loyal; treacherous: *a false friend.* **4.** tending to deceive or mislead; deceptive: *a false impression.* **5.** not genuine; counterfeit. **6.** based on mistaken, erroneous, or inconsistent impressions, ideas, or facts: *false pride.* **7.** used as a substitute or supplement, esp. temporarily: *false supports for a bridge.* **8.** *Biol.* having a superficial resemblance to something that properly bears the name: *the false acacia.* **9.** not properly, accurately, or honestly made, done, or adjusted: *a false balance.* **10.** inaccurate in pitch, as a musical note. —*adv.* **11.** dishonestly; faithlessly; treacherously: *Did he speak false against me?* **12. play someone false,** to betray someone; be treacherous or faithless. [bef. 1000; ME, OE *fals* < L *falsus* feigned, false, orig. ptp. of *fallere* to deceive; reinforced by or reborrowed from AF, OF *fals,* fem. *false* < L] —**false′ly,** *adv.* —**false′ness,** *n.*
—**Syn. 1.** mistaken, incorrect, wrong, untrue. **2.** untruthful, lying, mendacious. **3.** insincere, hypocritical, disingenuous, disloyal, unfaithful, inconstant, perfidious, traitorous. **4.** misleading, fallacious. **5.** artificial, spurious, bogus, forged. FALSE, SHAM, COUNTERFEIT agree in referring to something that is not genuine. FALSE is used mainly of imitations of concrete objects; it sometimes implies an intent to deceive: *false teeth; false hair.* SHAM is rarely used of concrete objects and usually has the suggestion of intent to deceive: *sham title; sham tears.* COUNTERFEIT always has the implication of cheating; it is used particularly of spurious imitation of coins, paper money, etc.

false′ aca′cia. See **black locust.**

false′ alarm′, 1. a false report of a fire in progress to a fire department. **2.** something that excites unfounded alarm or expectation: *Rumors of an impending transit strike proved to be a false alarm.* [1570–80]

false′ al′oe, any of several plants of the genus *Manfreda,* esp. *M. virginica,* of the southeastern U.S., having spikes of fragrant, greenish-yellow flowers.

false′ ara′lia, any of several Polynesian shrubs or small trees belonging to the genus *Dizygotheca,* of the ginseng family, having palmately compound, mottled leaves and often grown as a houseplant.

false′ arrest′, *Law.* arrest or detention of a person contrary to or unauthorized by law. [1925–30]

false′ beech′drops. See under **pinesap.** [1855–60, *Amer.*]

false′ bot′tom, a horizontal partition above the actual bottom of a box, trunk, etc., esp. one forming a secret compartment. [1790–1800]

false′ bread′-fruit (bred′fro͞ot′), ceriman.

false′ buck′thorn, a spiny shrub or small tree, *Bumelia lanuginosa,* of the sapodilla family, native to the southern U.S., having gummy, milky sap and white, bell-shaped flowers and yielding a hard, light-brown wood.

false′ card′, *Chiefly Bridge.* a card played to give an opponent a mistaken idea of the quality or length of one's holding in the suit led. [1875–80]

false-card (fôls′kärd′), *v.i. Chiefly Bridge.* to play a false card.

false′ cast′, *Angling.* a throw of the line in fly casting in which the line, leader, and fly are prevented from hitting the water.

false′ col′or, photography using infrared-sensitive film that produces images in which heat-emitting areas or objects appear red. [1965–70] —**false′-col′or,** *adj.*

false′ col′ors, 1. the flag of a country other than one's own, esp. when used deceptively. **2.** false or deceptive actions or statements; misrepresentation. [1565–75, for literal sense]

false′ dawn′, zodiacal light occurring before sunrise. [1825–35]

False′ Decre′tals, the Pseudo-Isidorian documents.

false′ drag′onhead, a North American plant, *Physostegia virginiana,* of the mint family, having a spike of tubular, two-lipped, pink or white flowers. Also called **obedient plant.**

false′ face′, a mask covering the face. [1810–20]

false′ front′, 1. a façade falsifying the size, finish, or importance of a building, esp. one having a humble purpose or cheap construction. **2.** any deceptive appearance: *He hid his great shyness behind a false front of aggressiveness.* [1885–90, *Amer.*]

false′ fruit′, *Bot.* See **accessory fruit.**

false-heart·ed (fôls′här′tid), *adj.* having a false or treacherous heart; deceitful; perfidious. [1565–75] —**false′-heart′ed·ly,** *adv.* —**false′-heart′ed·ness,** *n.*

false′ hel′lebore, any of various plants belonging to the genus *Veratrum,* of the lily family, esp. a North American species, *V. viride,* which has clusters of yellowish-green flowers and is the source of substances used in certain medicines and insecticides. Also called **Indian poke, white hellebore.**

false·hood (fôls′ho͝od), *n.* **1.** a false statement; lie. **2.** something false; an untrue idea, belief, etc.: *The Nazis propagated the falsehood of racial superiority.* **3.** the act of lying or making false statements. **4.** lack of conformity to truth or fact. **5.** *Obs.* deception. [1250–1300; ME *falshede.* See FALSE, -HOOD]
—**Syn. 1.** FALSEHOOD, FIB, LIE, UNTRUTH refer to something untrue or incorrect. A FALSEHOOD is a statement that distorts or suppresses the truth, in order to deceive: *to tell a falsehood about one's ancestry in order to gain acceptance.* A FIB denotes a trivial falsehood, and is often used to characterize that which is not strictly true: *a polite fib.* A LIE is a vicious falsehood: *to tell a lie about one's neighbor.* An UNTRUTH is an incorrect statement, either intentionally misleading (less harsh, however, than falsehood or lie) or arising from misunderstanding or ignorance: *I'm afraid you are telling an untruth.* **3.** untruthfulness, inveracity, mendacity.

false′ hori′zon, a line or plane that simulates the horizon, used in altitude-measuring devices or the like. [1805–15]

false′ impris′onment, *Law.* the unlawful restraint of a person from exercising the right to freedom of movement. [1760–70]

false′ in′digo, 1. any of several North American shrubs belonging to the genus *Amorpha,* of the legume family, esp. *A. fruticosa,* having compound leaves with pinnate leaflets and long, dense clusters of purplish flowers. **2.** any of various plants belonging to the genus *Baptisia,* of the legume family, native to North America, as *B. australis,* having trifoliate leaves and long clusters of purplish-blue flowers.

false′ ip′ecac. See **bowman's root.**

false′ la′bor, *Obstet.* irregular contractions of the uterus prior to actual labor and without accompanying dilation of the cervix.

false′ lil′y of the val′ley. See **wild lily of the valley.**

false′ mil′dew. See **downy mildew** (def. 1).

false′ mi′terwort, foamflower. [1865–70]

false′ move′, 1. a movement that may be interpreted as threatening. **2.** an act or action that can cause trouble or damage; mistake: *If the bus driver had made one false move, we would have skidded off the icy road.*

false′ pond′, *Western U.S.* a mirage.

false′ preg′nancy, *Pathol., Vet. Pathol.* physiological signs of pregnancy without conception; pseudocyesis. Also called **pseudopregnancy.** [1880–85]

false′ pretens′es, 1. a deliberate misrepresentation of facts, as to obtain title to money or property. **2.** the use of such misrepresentation. [1750–60]

false′ rib′, *Anat.* any of the lower five ribs on either side of the body, which are not directly attached to the sternum. [1490–1500]

false′ Sol′omon's-seal, any of several plants belonging to the genus *Smilacina,* of the lily family, having long, arching clusters of greenish-white flowers. Also called **false′ spike′nard.** [1895–1900]

false′ start′, 1. *Sports.* a premature start by one or more of the contestants, as in a swimming or track event, necessitating calling the field back to start again. **2.** a failure to begin an undertaking successfully. [1805–15]

false-start (fôls′stärt′), *v.i. Sports.* to leave the starting line or position too early and thereby necessitate repeating the signal to begin a race. [1805–15]

false′ step′, 1. a stumble. **2.** an unwise or blundering act.

false′ teeth′, a denture, esp. a pair of removable full dentures of both jaws. [1785–95]

false′ to′paz, citrine (def. 2).

fal·set·to (fôl set′ō), *n., pl.* **-tos,** *adj., adv.* —*n.* **1.** an unnaturally or artificially high-pitched voice or register, esp. in a man. **2.** a person, esp. a man, who sings with such a voice. —*adj.* **3.** of, noting, or having the quality and compass of such a voice. —*adv.* **4.** in a falsetto. [1765–75; < It, equiv. to *fals(o)* (< L *falsus* FALSE) + *-etto* -ET]

false′ vam′pire, any large, carnivorous bat of the families Megadermatidae and Phyllostomatidae, of Africa, Asia, and Australia, erroneously reputed to suck the blood of animals and humans.

false′ vo′cal cords′, *Anat.* the upper pair of vocal cords, not concerned with vocal production. Cf. **true vocal cords, vocal cords.**

false•work (fôls′wûrk′), *n.* framework for supporting a structure under construction that is not yet capable of supporting itself. [1870–75; FALSE + WORK]

fals•ie (fôl′sē), *n. Informal.* either of a pair of shaped pads, made of rubber, fabric, or the like, for wearing inside a brassiere to give the breasts a larger or more shapely appearance. [1940–45, *Amer.*; FALSE + -IE]

fal•si•fy (fôl′sə fī), *v.*, **-fied, -fy•ing.** —*v.t.* **1.** to make false or incorrect, esp. so as to deceive: *to falsify income-tax reports.* **2.** to alter fraudulently. **3.** to represent falsely: *He falsified the history of his family to conceal his humble origins.* **4.** to show or prove to be false; disprove: *to falsify a theory.* —*v.i.* **5.** to make false statements. [1400–50; late ME *falsifien* < MF *falsifier* < LL *falsificāre.* See FALSE, -IFY] —**fal′si•fi′a•ble,** *adj.* —**fal′si•fi′a•bil′i•ty,** *n.* —**fal•si•fi•ca•tion** (fôl′sə fi-kā′shən), *n.* —**fal′si•fi′er,** *n.*
—**Syn. 1, 3.** See **misrepresent. 4.** rebut, discredit, refute, confute, controvert.

fal•si•ty (fôl′si tē), *n., pl.* **-ties. 1.** the quality or condition of being false; incorrectness; untruthfulness; treachery. **2.** something false; falsehood. [1225–75; ME *falsete* < AF < LL *falsitās.* See FALSE, -ITY]

Fal•staff (fôl′staf, -stäf), *n.* **1. Sir John,** the jovial, fat knight of brazen assurance and few scruples in Shakespeare's *Henry IV,* Parts 1 and 2, and *The Merry Wives of Windsor.* **2.** (*italics*) an opera (1893) by Giuseppe Verdi, with a libretto by Arrigo Boito based on the Shakespearean character.

Fal•staff•i•an (fôl staf′ē ən), *adj.* of, pertaining to, or having the qualities of Falstaff, esp. his robust, bawdy humor, good-natured rascality, and brazen braggadocio: *Falstaffian wit.* [1800–10; FALSTAFF + -IAN]

Fal•ster (fäl′stər), *n.* an island in SE Denmark. 45,906; 198 sq. mi. (513 sq. km).

falt•boat (fält′bōt′), *n.* a small boat having a collapsible wooden frame covered with waterproof cloth or plastic. Also, **foldboat.** [1925–30; < G *Faltboot* folding boat. See FOLD[1], BOAT]

fal•ter (fôl′tər), *v.i.* **1.** to hesitate or waver in action, purpose, intent, etc.; give way: *Her courage did not falter at the prospect of hardship.* **2.** to speak hesitatingly or brokenly. **3.** to move unsteadily; stumble. —*v.t.* **4.** to utter hesitatingly or brokenly: *to falter an apology.* —*n.* **5.** the act of faltering; an unsteadiness of gait, voice, action, etc. **6.** a faltering sound. [1300–50; ME *falteren,* of obscure orig.; perh. akin to ON *faltrast* to bother with, be troubled with] —**fal′ter•er,** *n.* —**fal′ter•ing•ly,** *adv.*

Fal•well (fôl′wel), *n.* **Jerry L.,** born 1933, U.S. evangelist and political activist.

falx (falks, fôlks), *n., pl.* **fal•ces** (fal′sēz, fôl′-). *Anat.* a structure shaped like a sickle, as a fold of dura mater separating the cerebral hemispheres. [1700–10; < NL, L: sickle] —**fal•cial** (fal′shəl, fôl′-), *adj.*

fam., 1. familiar. **2.** family.

F.A.M., Free and Accepted Masons. Also, **F. & A.M.**

fa•ma•cide (fā′mə sīd′), *n. Law.* a person who destroys another's reputation; a defamer or slanderer. [< L *fāma* FAME + -CIDE]

Fa•ma•gu•sta (fä mə gōō′stə), *n.* a seaport on the E coast of Cyprus, on an inlet of the Mediterranean: castle; large cathedral (now a mosque). 38,960.

fame (fām), *n., v.,* **famed, fam•ing.** —*n.* **1.** widespread reputation, esp. of a favorable character; renown; public eminence: *to seek fame as an opera singer.* **2.** common estimation or opinion generally held of a person or thing; reputation. —*v.t.* **3.** *Archaic.* to have or spread the renown of; to make famous. [1175–1225; ME < AF, OF < L *fāma* talk, public opinion, repute, akin to *fārī* to speak] —**fame′less,** *adj.*

famed (fāmd), *adj.* very well known and, often, highly regarded; famous. [1525–35; FAME + -ED[3]]

Fa•meuse (fə myōōz′), *n.* an American variety of red apple that ripens in early winter. Also called **snow apple.** [1800–10; < F, fem. of *fameux* FAMOUS]

fa•mil•ial (fə mil′yəl, -mil′ē əl), *adj.* **1.** of, pertaining to, or characteristic of a family: *familial ties.* **2.** appearing in individuals by heredity: *a familial disease.* [1895–1900; < F; see FAMILY, -AL[1]]

famil′ial hy′percholes′terole′mia, *Pathol.* an inherited metabolic disorder caused by a lack or malfunction of receptors for the low-density lipoproteins that activate removal of cholesterol from the blood. *Abbr.:* FH.

fa•mil•iar (fə mil′yər), *adj.* **1.** commonly or generally known or seen: *a familiar sight.* **2.** well-acquainted; thoroughly conversant: *to be familiar with a subject.* **3.** informal; easygoing; unceremonious; unconstrained: *to write in a familiar style.* **4.** closely intimate or personal: *a familiar friend; to be on familiar terms.* **5.** unduly intimate; too personal; taking liberties; presuming: *The duchess disliked familiar servants.* **6.** domesticated; tame. **7.** of or pertaining to a family or household. —*n.* **8.** a familiar friend or associate. **9.** *Witchcraft and Demonology.* **a.** an animal, as a cat, that embodies a supernatural spirit and aids a witch in performing magic. **b.** See **familiar spirit. 10.** *Rom. Cath. Ch.* **a.** an officer of the Inquisition, employed to arrest accused or suspected persons. **b.** a person who belongs to the household of the pope or of a bishop, rendering domestic though not menial service. [1300–50; ME < L *familiāris* of a household (see FAMILY, -AR[1]); r. ME *famulier* < MF < L, as above] —**fa•mil′iar•ly,** *adv.* —**fa•mil′iar•ness,** *n.*
—**Syn. 4.** FAMILIAR, CONFIDENTIAL, INTIMATE suggest a long association between persons. FAMILIAR means well-acquainted with another person: *a familiar friend.* CONFIDENTIAL suggests a sense of mutual trust that extends to the sharing of confidences and secrets: *a confidential adviser.* INTIMATE suggests close acquaintance or connection, often based on interest, sympathy, or affection: *intimate and affectionate letters.* **5.** forward, bold.

fa•mil•i•ar•i•ty (fə mil′ē ar′i tē, -mil yar′-), *n., pl.* **-ties. 1.** thorough knowledge or mastery of a thing, subject, etc. **2.** the state of being familiar; friendly relationship; close acquaintance; intimacy. **3.** an absence of ceremony and formality; informality. **4.** freedom of behavior justified only by the closest relationship; undue intimacy. **5.** Often, **familiarities.** an instance of such freedom, as in action or speech. **6.** a sexual liberty or impropriety. [1350–1400; ME *familiarite* (< AF) < L *familiāritās* intimacy. See FAMILIAR, -ITY]
—**Syn. 3.** unconstraint. **4.** liberty, freedom, license.

fa•mil•iar•ize (fə mil′yə rīz′), *v.*, **-ized, -iz•ing.** —*v.t.* **1.** to make (oneself or another) well-acquainted or conversant with something. **2.** to make (something) well-known; bring into common knowledge or use. **3.** *Archaic.* to make familiar; establish (a person) in friendly intimacy. —*v.i.* **4.** *Archaic.* to associate in a familiar way. Also, *esp. Brit.,* **fa•mil′iar•ise′.** [1600–10; FAMILIAR + -IZE] —**fa•mil′iar•i•za′tion,** *n.* —**fa•mil′iar•iz′er,** *n.*
—**Syn. 1.** accustom, acquaint.

famil′iar spir′it, a supernatural spirit or demon supposed to attend on or serve a person. Also called **familiar.** [1555–65]

fam•i•lism (fam′ə liz′əm), *n. Sociol.* the subordination of the personal interests and prerogatives of an individual to the values and demands of the family: *Familism characterized the patriarchal family.* [1635–45; FAMIL(Y) + -ISM] —**fam′i•list,** *n.* —**fam′i•lis′tic,** *adj.*

fam•i•ly (fam′ə lē, fam′lē), *n., pl.* **-lies,** *adj.* —*n.* **1.** parents and their children, considered as a group, whether dwelling together or not. **2.** the children of one person or one couple collectively: *We want a large family.* **3.** the spouse and children of one person: *We're taking the family on vacation next week.* **4.** any group of persons closely related by blood, as parents, children, uncles, aunts, and cousins: *to marry into a socially prominent family.* **5.** all those persons considered as descendants of a common progenitor. **6.** *Chiefly Brit.* approved lineage, esp. noble, titled, famous, or wealthy ancestry: *young men of family.* **7.** a group of persons who form a household under one head, including parents, children, and servants. **8.** the staff, or body of assistants, of an official: *the office family.* **9.** a group of related things or people: *the family of romantic poets; the halogen family of elements.* **10.** a group of people who are generally not blood relations but who share common attitudes, interests, or goals and, frequently, live together: *Many hippie communes of the sixties regarded themselves as families.* **11.** a group of products or product models made by the same manufacturer or producer. **12.** *Biol.* the usual major subdivision of an order or suborder in the classification of plants, animals, fungi, etc., usually consisting of several genera. **13.** *Slang.* a unit of the Mafia or Cosa Nostra operating in one area under a local leader. **14.** *Ling.* the largest category into which languages related by common origin can be classified with certainty: *Indo-European, Sino-Tibetan, and Austronesian are the most widely spoken families of languages.* Cf. **stock** (def. 12), **subfamily** (def. 2). **15.** *Math.* **a.** a given class of solutions of the same basic equation, differing from one another only by the different values assigned to the constants in the equation. **b.** a class of functions or the like defined by an expression containing a parameter. **c.** a set. —*adj.* **16.** of, pertaining to, or characteristic of a family: *a family trait.* **17.** belonging to or used by a family: *a family automobile; a family room.* **18. in a** or **the family way,** pregnant. [1350–1400; ME *familie* < L *familia* a household, the slaves of a household, equiv. to *famul(us)* servant, slave + *-ia* -Y[3]]
—**Usage.** See **collective noun.**

fam′ily Bi′ble, a large Bible usually having pages at the front for recording the marriages, births, and deaths in a family. [1775–85]

fam′ily cir′cle, 1. the closely related members of a family as a group. **2.** a section in a theater containing less expensive seats, as the topmost gallery. [1800–10]

fam′ily court′. See **court of domestic relations.** [1930–35]

fam′ily doc′tor, a general practitioner. Also called **fam′ily physi′cian.** [1840–50]

fam′ily hour′, *Television Informal.* any broadcast period from 6 P.M. to 9 P.M. when programs of general interest to the family are broadcast. Also called **family time.** [1970–75]

fam′ily jew′els, *Slang.* the male genitals.

fam′ily man′, 1. a man who has a wife and one or more children. **2.** a man devoted to his family and home. [1780–90]

fam′ily name′, 1. the hereditary surname of a family. **2.** a given name frequently used in a family. [1690–1700]

fam′ily of curves′, *Math.* a collection of curves whose equations differ only by values assigned a parameter or parameters.

fam′ily plan′, a special rate, esp. of air passenger carriers, under which the head of a household purchasing a full-fare ticket may take other family members at reduced fares on certain days. Also called **fam′ily fare′, fam′ily-fare′ plan′.**

fam′ily plan′ning, 1. the concept or a program of limiting the size of families through the spacing or prevention of pregnancies, esp. for economic reasons. **2.** (loosely) birth control. [1935–40]

fam′ily prac′tice, medical specialization in general practice, requiring training beyond that of general practice and leading to board certification. Also called **fam′ily med′icine.** —**fam′ily practi′tioner.**

fam′ily room′, a room in a house used as a center for family activities. [1850–55]

fam′ily style′, (of a meal) with the serving platters on the table so that all present can serve themselves. [1930–35, *Amer.*]

fam′ily ther′apy, the psychotherapeutic treatment of more than one member of a family simultaneously at the same session, based on the assumption that problems can best be understood and corrected by observing the interaction of family members and identifying methods for improving their interrelationships. [1975–80]

fam′ily time′, *Television Informal.* See **family hour.**

fam′ily tree′, a genealogical chart showing the ancestry, descent, and relationship of all members of a family or other genealogical group. Also called **genealogical tree.** [1800–10]

fam′i•ly-tree′ the′ory (fam′ə lē trē′, fam′lē-), *Historical Ling.* a theory that describes language change in terms of genetically related languages developing in successive splits from a common parent language, such as Indo-European, as depicted by a family tree diagram. Cf. **wave theory.** [1930–35]

fam′ily way′. See **family** (def. 18). [1790–1800]

fam•ine (fam′in), *n.* **1.** extreme and general scarcity of food, as in a country or a large geographical area. **2.** any extreme and general scarcity. **3.** extreme hunger; starvation. [1325–75; ME < MF, deriv. of *faim* hunger (< L *famēs*); see -INE[2]]
—**Syn. 2.** dearth, paucity, poverty, meagerness, scantness.

fam•ish (fam′ish), *v.t., v.i. Archaic.* **1.** to suffer or cause to suffer extreme hunger; starve. **2.** to starve to death. [1350–1400; ME *famisshe,* equiv. to *famen* to starve (< AF, MF *afamer* < VL **affamāre,* equiv. to L *af-* AF- + *famāre,* deriv. of *famēs* hunger) + *-isshe* -ISH[2]]

fam•ished (fam′isht), *adj.* extremely hungry: *to be famished after a hike; famished, homeless multitudes.* [1375–1425; late ME; see FAMISH, -ED[2]]
—**Syn.** See **hungry.**

fa•mous (fā′məs), *adj.* **1.** having a widespread reputation, usually of a favorable nature; renowned; celebrated: *a famous writer.* **2.** *Informal.* first-rate; excellent: *The singer gave a famous performance.* **3.** notorious (used pejoratively). [1350–1400; ME < AF < L *fāmōsus.* See FAME, -OUS] —**fa′mous•ly,** *adv.* —**fa′mous•ness,** *n.*
—**Syn. 1.** famed, notable, illustrious. FAMOUS, CELEBRATED, EMINENT, DISTINGUISHED refer to someone or something widely and favorably known. FAMOUS is the general word: *a famous lighthouse.* CELEBRATED originally referred to something commemorated, but now usually refers to someone or something widely known for conspicuous merit, services, etc.: *a celebrated writer.* EMINENT implies high standing among one's contemporaries, esp. in one's own profession or craft: *an eminent physician.* DISTINGUISHED adds to EMINENT the idea of honors conferred more or less publicly: *a distinguished scientist.* —**Ant. 1.** unknown, obscure.

fam•u•lus (fam′yə ləs), *n., pl.* **-li** (-lī′). a servant or attendant, esp. of a scholar or a magician. [1830–40; < L: servant, slave; cf. FAMILY]

fan[1] (fan), *n., v.,* **fanned, fan•ning.** —*n.* **1.** any device for producing a current of air by the movement of a broad surface or a number of such surfaces. **2.** an implement of feathers, leaves, paper, cloth, etc., often in the shape of a long triangle or of a semicircle, for waving lightly in the hand to create a cooling current of air about a person: *We sat on the veranda, cooling ourselves with palm-leaf fans.* **3.** anything resembling such an implement, as the tail of a bird. **4.** any of various devices consisting essentially of a series of radiating vanes or blades attached to and revolving with a central hub-like portion to produce a current of air: *ceiling fan; wall fan.* **5.** a series of revolving blades supplying air for winnowing or cleaning grain. **6.** *Horol.* fly[1] (def. 34). **7.** a semicircular decoration of bunting. **8.** *Physical Geog.* an alluvial fan. **9. hit the fan,** *Slang.* to become suddenly more awkward, embarrassing, or troublesome: *When news of the incident was leaked to the press, everything hit the fan at once.* —*v.t.* **10.** to move or agitate (the air) with or as if with a fan. **11.** to cause air to blow upon, as from a fan; cool or refresh with or as if with a fan: *He fanned his face with a newspaper.* **12.** to stir to activity with or as if with a fan: *to fan a flame; to fan emotions.* **13.** (of a breeze, current of air, etc.) to blow upon, as if driven by a fan: *A cool breeze fanned the shore.* **14.** to spread out like a fan: *The dealer fanned the cards.* **15.** *Informal.* to move (oneself) quickly: *You'll fan your tail out of here if you know what's good for you.* **16.** *Agric.* to winnow, esp. by an artificial current of air. **17.** *Baseball.* (of a pitcher) to strike out (a batter). **18.** *Chiefly South Midland and Southern U.S.* to punish by spanking; spank: *Your mother will fan you good if you break that dish.* —*v.i.* **19.** to strike, swing, or brush lightly at something. **20.** *Western U.S.* (*chiefly cowboy use*). to slap the flanks of (a horse or other animal) repeatedly with a hat to get it to move or move faster. **21.** to spread out like a fan (often fol. by *out*): *The forest fire fanned out in all directions.* **22.** *Baseball.* (of a batter) to strike out, usually by swinging at and missing the pitch charged as the third strike. [bef. 900; ME, OE *fann* < L *vannus* winnowing basket] —**fan′like′,** *adj.* —**fan′ner,** *n.*

fan[2] (fan), *n.* an enthusiastic devotee, follower, or admirer of a sport, pastime, celebrity, etc.: *a baseball fan; a*

great fan of Charlie Chaplin. [1885–90, *Amer.*; short for FANATIC]
—**Syn.** supporter, enthusiast, partisan, booster, addict.

Fan (fan, fän), *n., pl.* **Fans,** (*esp. collectively*) **Fan.** Fang.

fa·na (fə nä′), *n. Islam.* the ecstatic union of the Sufi with the Divine. [1865–70; < Ar *fanāʼ* annihilation]

Fa·na·ka·lo (fä′nə kə lō′, fä′nə kə lō′), *n.* a lingua franca based on English, Afrikaans, Xhosa, and Zulu, used esp. in the mines of South Africa. Also, **Fa·na·ga·lo** (fä′nə gə lō′, fä′nə gə lō′). [1945–50; < Fanakalo (*kuluma*) *fana ga lo* (to speak) like this < Zulu]

fa·nat·ic (fə nat′ik), *n.* **1.** a person with an extreme and uncritical enthusiasm or zeal, as in religion or politics. —*adj.* **2.** fanatical. [1515–25; < L *fānāticus* pertaining to a temple, inspired by orgiastic rites, frantic, equiv. to *fān(um)* temple + *-āticus*, equiv. to *-āt(us)* -ATE[1] + *-icus* -IC]
—**Syn. 1.** enthusiast, zealot, bigot, hothead, militant. FANATIC, ZEALOT, MILITANT, DEVOTEE refer to persons showing more than ordinary support for, adherence to, or interest in a cause, point of view, or activity. FANATIC and ZEALOT both suggest excessive or overweening devotion to a cause or belief. FANATIC further implies unbalanced or obsessive behavior: *a wild-eyed fanatic.* ZEALOT, only slightly less unfavorable in implication than FANATIC, implies single-minded partisanship: *a tireless zealot for tax reform.* MILITANT stresses vigorous, aggressive support for or opposition to a plan or ideal and suggests a combative stance. DEVOTEE is a milder term than any of the foregoing, suggesting enthusiasm but not to the exclusion of other interests or possible points of view: *a jazz devotee.*

fa·nat·i·cal (fə nat′i kəl), *adj.* motivated or characterized by an extreme, uncritical enthusiasm or zeal, as in religion or politics. Also, **fanatic.** [1540–50; FANATIC + -AL[1]] —**fa·nat′i·cal·ly,** *adv.* —**fa·nat′i·cal·ness,** *n.*
—**Syn.** enthusiastic, zealous, frenzied, rabid. See **intolerant, radical.**

fa·nat·i·cism (fə nat′ə siz′əm), *n.* fanatical character, spirit, or conduct. [1705–15; FANATIC + -ISM]

fa·nat·i·cize (fə nat′ə sīz′), *v.,* **-cized, -ciz·ing.** —*v.t.* **1.** to make fanatical. —*v.i.* **2.** to act with or show fanaticism. Also, *esp. Brit.,* **fa·nat′i·cise′.** [1705–15; FANATIC + -IZE]

fan·back (fan′bak′), *adj.* **1.** (of a chair) having a fan-shaped back. **2.** (of a Windsor chair or the like) having a back of vertical spindles fanning out from seat to upper rail. [FAN[1] + BACK[1]]

fan′ belt′, (in automotive vehicles) a belt, driven by the crankshaft of an engine, that turns a fan for drawing cooling air through the radiator. [1920–25]

fan·cied (fan′sēd), *adj.* unreal; imaginary: *to be upset by fancied grievances.* [1560–70; FANCY + -ED[2]]

fan·ci·er (fan′sē ər), *n.* **1.** a person having a liking for or interest in something; enthusiast: *a fancier of sports cars.* **2.** a person who breeds animals, plants, etc., esp. in order to improve the strain: *a horse fancier.* [1755–65; FANCY + -ER[1]]

fan·ci·ful (fan′si fəl), *adj.* **1.** characterized by or showing fancy; capricious or whimsical in appearance: *a fanciful design of butterflies and flowers.* **2.** suggested by fancy; imaginary; unreal: *fanciful lands of romance.* **3.** led by fancy rather than by reason and experience; whimsical: *a fanciful mind.* [1620–30; FANCY + -FUL] —**fan′ci·ful·ly,** *adv.* —**fan′ci·ful·ness,** *n.*
—**Syn. 2.** visionary, baseless, illusory.

fan·ci·fy (fan′si fī′), *v.t.,* **-fied, -fy·ing.** to make fancy or fanciful; dress up; embellish. [1650–60; FANCY + -FY]

fan′ club′, a club enthusiastically devoted to a movie star or other celebrity or to a sports team. [1925–30]

fan·cy (fan′sē), *n., pl.* **-cies,** *adj.,* **-ci·er, -ci·est,** *v.,* **-cied, -cy·ing,** *interj.* —*n.* **1.** imagination or fantasy, esp. as exercised in a capricious manner. **2.** the artistic ability of creating unreal or whimsical imagery, decorative detail, etc., as in poetry or drawing. **3.** a mental image or conception: *He had happy fancies of being a famous actor.* **4.** an idea or opinion with little foundation; illusion: *Her belief that she can sing is a mere fancy.* **5.** a caprice; whim; vagary: *It was his fancy to fly to Paris occasionally for dinner.* **6.** capricious preference; inclination; a liking: *to take a fancy to walking barefoot in the streets.* **7.** critical judgment; taste. **8.** the breeding of animals to develop points of beauty or excellence. **9.** love. **10. the fancy,** *Archaic.* people deeply interested in a sport, art, etc. —*adj.* **11.** made, designed, grown, adapted, etc., to please the taste or fancy; of superfine quality or exceptional appeal: *fancy goods; fancy fruits.* **12.** ornamental; decorative; not plain: *a cake with a fancy icing.* **13.** depending on imagination or caprice; whimsical; irregular: *a fancy conception of time.* **14.** bred to develop points of beauty or excellence, as an animal. **15.** much too costly; exorbitant or extravagant: *a consultant who charges fancy fees.* —*v.t.* **16.** to form a conception of; picture to oneself: *Fancy living with that egotist all your life!* **17.** to believe without being absolutely sure or certain: *I fancy you are my new neighbor.* **18.** to take a liking to; like. **19.** to breed to develop a special type of animal. **20. fancy up,** to make superficially showy by way of improvement: *an old car fancied up with a bright new paint job.* —*interj.* **21.** (used as an exclamation of mild surprise): *They invited you, too? Fancy!* [1350–1400; ME *fan(t)sy,* syncopated var. of *fantasie* FANTASY] —**fan′ci·ness,** *n.*
—**Syn. 2.** FANCY, FANTASY, IMAGINATION refer to qualities in literature or other artistic composition. The creations of FANCY are casual, whimsical, and often amusing, being at once less profound and less moving or inspiring than those of imagination: *letting one's fancy play freely on a subject; an impish fancy.* FANTASY now usually suggests an unrestrained or extravagant fancy, often resulting in caprice: *The use of fantasy in art creates interesting results.* The term and concept of creative IMAGINATION are less than two hundred years old; previously only the *reproductive* aspect had been recognized, hardly to be distinguished from memory. "Creative imagination" suggests that the memories of actual sights and experiences may so blend in the mind of the writer or artist as to produce something that has never existed before—often a hitherto unperceived vision of reality: *to use imagination in portraying character and action.* **3.** thought, notion, impression, idea; phantasm. **5.** quirk, humor, crotchet. **11.** fine, elegant, choice. **12.** decorated, ornate. **16.** envision, conceive, imagine.

fan′cy dive′, any of the series of specified dives executed in fancy diving, as the jackknife or gainer.

fan′cy div′ing, diving competition from a springboard into water, the contestants being judged chiefly by their grace and control in executing a specified series of dives in a prescribed manner. —**fan′cy div′er.**

fan′cy dress′, a costume for a ball, masquerade, etc., chosen to please the fancy, usually a costume characteristic of a particular period or place, class of persons, or historical or fictitious character. [1760–70]

fan′cy fern′, a common fern, *Dryopteris austriaca spinulosa,* having delicate, lacy leaves and used extensively in floral arrangements.

fan·cy-free (fan′sē frē′), *adj.* free from any emotional tie or influence, esp. that of love. [1580–90]

fan′cy gera′nium. See **show geranium.**

fan′cy man′, 1. a woman's lover. **2.** a pimp. [1805–15]

fan′cy wom′an, 1. an immoral woman, esp. a man's mistress. **2.** a prostitute. Also, **fan′cy la′dy.** [1805–15]

fan·cy·work (fan′sē wûrk′), *n.* ornamental needlework. [1800–10; FANCY + WORK]

fan′ dance′, a solo dance performed by a nude or nearly nude woman using fans for covering. [1875–80] —**fan′ danc′er.**

fan·dan·go (fan dang′gō), *n., pl.* **-gos. 1.** a lively Spanish or Spanish-American dance in triple time, performed by a man and woman playing castanets. **2.** a piece of music for such a dance or one having its rhythm. **3.** (esp. in the southwest U.S.) a ball or dance. [1740–50; < Sp, of uncert. orig.]

fan′ del′ta, a partially submerged alluvial fan that has merged with a delta. [1915–20]

F and Gs, *Bookbinding.* folded and gathered pages: unbound printed sheets folded into signatures and gathered into the proper sequence for binding. Also, **F&Gs**

fan·dom (fan′dəm), *n.* fans collectively, as of a motion-picture star or a professional game or sport. [1900–05, *Amer.*; FAN[2] + -DOM]

F. & T., *Insurance.* fire and theft.

fane (fān), *n.* **1.** a temple. **2.** *Archaic.* a church. [1350–1400; ME < L *fānum* temple, sanctuary]

fa·ne·ga (fə nā′gə; *Sp.* fä ne′gä), *n., pl.* **-gas** (-gəz; *Sp.* -gäs). **1.** a unit of dry measure in Spanish-speaking countries, equal in Spain to 1.58 U.S. bushels (55.7 liters). **2.** a Mexican unit of land measure, equal to 8.81 acres (3.57 hectares). [1495–1505; < Sp < Ar *faniqah* big bag]

fa·ne·ga·da (fä′ne gä′thä), *n., pl.* **-das** (-thäs). a unit of land measure in Spanish-speaking countries varying from 1¼ to 1¾ acres (0.5 to 0.7 hectare). [< Sp; see FANEGA, -ADE[1]]

Fan·euil (fan′l, -yəl; *formerly* fun′l; *spelling pron.* fan′yo͞o əl), *n.* **Peter,** 1700–43, American merchant: builder of Faneuil Hall.

Fan′euil Hall′, a market house and public hall in Boston, Massachusetts, called "the Cradle of Liberty" because it was used as a meeting place by American patriots immediately before the Revolutionary War.

Fan·fa·ni (fän fä′nē), *n.* **A·min·to·re** (ä′mēn tô′Re), born 1908, Italian statesman: premier 1954, 1958–59, and 1960–63.

fan·fare (fan′fâr), *n.* **1.** a flourish or short air played on trumpets or the like. **2.** an ostentatious display or flourish. **3.** publicity or advertising. [1760–70; < F, expressive word akin to *fanfaron* FANFARON.]

fan·fa·ron (fan′fə ron′), *n.* **1.** a braggart. **2.** a fanfare. [1615–25; < F < Sp *fanfarrón* braggart, said to be of expressive orig.]

fan·fa·ron·ade (fan′fər ə nād′), *n.* bragging; bravado; bluster. [1645–55; < F *fanfaronnade* < Sp *fanfarronada.* See FANFARON, -ADE[1]]

fan·fish (fan′fish′), *n., pl.* **-fish·es,** (*esp. collectively*) **-fish.** a pelagic fish, *Pteraclis velifera,* having greatly expanded dorsal and anal fins. [FAN[1] + FISH]

fan·fold (fan′fōld′), *n.* **1.** a pad or tablet of invoices, bills, blank sheets, etc., interleaved with carbon paper for making a copy or copies of the writing or typing on the uppermost leaf. —*adj.* **2.** (of a pad or tablet of invoices, bills, blank sheets, etc.) made up in such a form. **3.** pertaining to continuous-form paper, folded like a fan or accordion so that it will stack. [1940–45; FAN[1] + FOLD[1]]

fang[1] (fang), *n.* **1.** one of the long, sharp, hollow or grooved teeth of a venomous snake by which poison is injected. **2.** a canine tooth. **3.** a tooth resembling a dog's. **4.** the root of a tooth. **5.** one of the chelicerae of a spider. **6.** a pointed, tapering part of a thing. **7.** *Mach.* the tang of a tool. [bef. 1050; ME, OE: something caught; c. G *Fang* capture, booty, ON *fang* a grasp, hold. See FANG[2]] —**fanged** (fangd), *adj.* —**fang′less,** *adj.* —**fang′like′,** *adj.*

F

F, **fangs**
(of rattlesnake)

fang[2] (fang), *v.t. Brit. Dial.* to seize; grab. [bef. 900; ME *fangen* to seize, catch; c. OS *fangan,* G *fangen,* var. of proto-Gmc **fanhan-,* whence OE *fōn,* c. OS, OHG, Goth *fāhan,* ON *fā;* akin to OE *gefangian* to fasten]

Fang (fang, fäng, fäN), *n., pl.* **Fangs,** (*esp. collectively*) **Fang** for 1. **1.** Also called **Pahouin, Pangwe.** a member of an indigenous people of Gabon, Cameroon, and adjacent areas. **2.** the Bantu language spoken by this people. Also, **Fan.**

Fan·gio (fän′jē ō′; *Sp.* fäng′hyô), *n.* **Juan Ma·nuel** (wän′ man wel′; *Sp.* hwän′ mä nwel′), born 1911, Argentine racing-car driver.

fan·go (fang′gō), *n.* clay or mud, esp. a clay obtained from certain hot springs in Battaglio, Italy, used as a hot application in the treatment of certain diseases. [1895–1900; < It: mud < Gmc; cf. OE *fūht* damp, Skt *pañkas* mire. See FEN[1]]

fan·ion (fan′yən), *n.* a small flag, originally carried by military brigades, used by soldiers and surveyors as a positional marker. [1700–10; < F, dim. of *fanon* FANON]

fan·jet (fan′jet′), *n.* **1.** Also called **turbofan.** a jet engine having a large impeller that takes in air, which is used partly for the combustion of fuel and partly as exhaust. **2.** an airplane having one or more such engines. Also, **fan′ jet′.** [1880–85, in earlier sense; FAN[1] + JET[1]]

fan·leaf (fan′lēf′), *n.* a disease of grapevines, characterized by the deformation of leaves into a fanlike shape and caused by a virus transmitted in grafting. [FAN[1] + LEAF]

fan′ let′ter, a letter sent by an admiring fan, as to a celebrity. [1930–35]

fan·light (fan′līt′), *n.* a window over a door or another window, esp. one having the form of a semicircle or of half an ellipse. [1835–45; FAN[1] + LIGHT[1]]

fan′ magazine′, a magazine containing information and gossip about celebrities. Cf. **fanzine.** [1925–30]

fan′ mail′, fan letters collectively. [1920–25]

Fan·nie (fan′ē), *n.* a female given name, form of **Frances.** Also, **Fan′ny.**

Fan′nie Mae′, 1. See **Federal National Mortgage Association. 2.** any of the publicly traded securities collateralized by a pool of mortgages backed by the Federal National Mortgage Association. Also, **Fan′ny Mae′.** Cf. **Freddie Mac, Ginnie Mae.** [altered from *FNMA,* the association's initials]

fan′ning mill′, *Agric.* a machine for winnowing grain by the action of riddles and sieves and an air blast. [1740–50]

fan·ny (fan′ē), *n., pl.* **-nies.** *Informal.* the buttocks. [1925–30; of obscure orig; relation, if any, to Brit. *fanny* "vulva" (vulgar) is unclear]

fan′ny pack′, a small zippered pouch suspended from a belt around the waist. [1970–75]

Fa·no (fä′nô), *n.* a town in central Italy, on the Adriatic Sea: cathedral; Roman ruins. 52,139. Ancient, **Fanum Fortunae.**

fan·on (fan′ən), *n. Eccles.* **1.** a maniple. **2.** Also called **orale.** a striped scarflike vestment worn by the pope over the alb when celebrating solemn Pontifical Mass. [1350–1400; ME *fano(u)n* < AF; OF *fanum* < Old Low Franconian **fano* piece of fabric; cf. OHG, OS *fano* in same sense (G *Fahne* flag), early ML *fano* maniple; see VANE, GONFALON]

Fa·non (fan′ən; *Fr.* fȧ nôN′), *n.* **Frantz (O·mar)** (frants ō′mär; *Fr.* fRäNts ô MAR′), 1925–61, West Indian psychiatrist and political theorist, born in Martinique.

fan′ palm′, 1. a palm having fan-shaped leaves, as the talipot. **2.** See **Chinese fan palm.** [1810–20, *Amer.*]

fan′ roof′, a vaulted roof having fan tracery.

fan·tab·u·lous (fan tab′yə ləs), *adj. Slang.* extremely good; wonderful. [1955–60; b. FANTASTIC and FABULOUS]

fantail
(def. 2)

fan·tail (fan′tāl′), *n.* **1.** a tail, end, or part shaped like a fan. **2.** one of a breed of domestic pigeons, having a fan-shaped tail. **3.** any of various small birds having fanlike tails, as the Old World flycatchers of the genus *Rhipidura* and the American wood warblers of the genus *Euthlypis.* **4.** See **fantail goldfish. 5.** *Building Trades, Archit.* a structure or structural member having a number of radiating parts, as an arch centering. **6.** *Naut.* **a.** the part of a rounded stern extending abaft the aftermost perpendicular; rounded counter. **b.** the area within this. **7.** *Western U.S.* a mustang. —*adj.* **8.** *Cookery.* (of shrimp) shelled, split almost through, and flattened slightly before cooking. [1720–30; FAN[1] + TAIL[1]] —**fan′-tailed′,** *adj.*

CONCISE PRONUNCIATION KEY: act, cāpe, dâre, pärt; set, ēqual; *if,* ice; ox, ōver, ôrder, oil, bo͝ok, bo͞ot, out; up, ûrge; child; sing; shoe; thin, t͟hat; zh as in *treasure.* ə = *a* as in *alone,* e as in *system,* i as in *easily,* o as in *gallop,* u as in *circus;* ᵊ as in *fire* (fīᵊr), *hour* (ouᵊr). l and n can serve as syllabic consonants, as in *cradle* (krād′l), and *button* (but′n). See the full key inside the front cover.

fan′tail dart′er, a North American freshwater fish, *Etheostoma flabellare,* of the perch family.

fan′tail gold′fish, an artificially bred, hardy variety of goldfish, usually oval-shaped and deep orange or calico, with a deeply cleft, four-lobed tail held in line with the body. Also called **fantail.** Cf. **veiltail goldfish.**

fan-tan (fan′tan′), *n.* **1.** Also, **fan′ tan′.** Also called **parliament, sevens.** *Cards.* a game in which the players play their sevens and other cards forming sequences in the same suits as their sevens, the winner being the player who first runs out of cards. **2.** a Chinese gambling game in which a pile of coins, counters, or objects is placed under a bowl and bets are made on what the remainder will be after they have been counted off in fours. [1875–80; < Chin *fān tān* lit., repeated divisions, or < cognate dial. forms]

fan·ta·sia (fan tā′zhə, -zhē ə, fan′tə zē′ə), *n.* **1.** *Music.* **a.** a composition in fanciful or irregular form or style. **b.** a potpourri of well-known airs arranged with interludes and florid embellishments. **2.** fantasy (def. 9). **3.** something considered to be unreal, weird, exotic, or grotesque. [1715–25; < It; see FANTASY]

fan·ta·sied (fan′tə sēd), *adj.* **1.** conceived of in or as a fantasy; imagined; storied. **2.** dreamt of or hoped for; longingly imagined; fancied: *a fantasied career as a fashion model.* **3.** *Obs.* filled with fantasy or fancy; imaginative or whimsical. [1555–65; FANTASY + -ED[2], -ED[3]]

fan·ta·sist (fan′tə sist, -zist; fan tā′zhist), *n.* a person who writes or composes fantasies or fantasias in music, poetry, or the like. [1920–25; FANTAS(Y) + -IST]

fan·ta·size (fan′tə sīz′), *v.,* **-sized, -siz·ing.** —*v.i.* **1.** to conceive fanciful or extravagant notions, ideas, suppositions, or the like (often fol. by *about*): *to fantasize about the ideal job.* —*v.t.* **2.** to create in one's fancy, daydreams, or the like; imagine: *to fantasize a trip through space.* Also, **phantasize.** Also, *esp. Brit.,* **fan′ta·sise′.** [1925–30; FANTAS(Y) + -IZE] **—fan′ta·siz′er,** *n.*

fan·tasm (fan′taz əm), *n.* phantasm.

fan·tas·ma·go·ri·a (fan taz′mə gôr′ē ə, -gōr′-), *n.* phantasmagoria. **—fan·tas′ma·go′ric,** *adj.* **—fan·tas′ma·go′ri·cal·ly,** *adv.*

fan·tast (fan′tast), *n.* a visionary or dreamer. Also, **phantast.** [1580–90; < G, var. of *Phantast* < Gk *phantastḗs* boaster; mod. sense by assoc. with FANTASTIC]

fan·tas·tic (fan tas′tik), *adj.* **1.** conceived or appearing as if conceived by an unrestrained imagination; odd and remarkable; bizarre; grotesque: *fantastic rock formations; fantastic designs.* **2.** fanciful or capricious, as persons or their ideas or actions: *We never know what that fantastic creature will say next.* **3.** imaginary or groundless in not being based on reality; foolish or irrational: *fantastic fears.* **4.** extravagantly fanciful; marvelous. **5.** incredibly great or extreme; exorbitant: *to spend fantastic sums of money.* **6.** highly unrealistic or impractical; outlandish: *a fantastic scheme to make a million dollars betting on horse races.* **7.** *Informal.* extraordinarily good: *a fantastic musical.* Also, **fan·tas′ti·cal.** [1350–1400; ME *fantastik* pertaining to the imaginative faculty < ML *fantasticus,* var. of LL *phantasticus* < Gk *phantastikós* able to present or show (to the mind), equiv. to **phantad-,* base of *phantázein* to make visible (akin to *phānós* light, bright, *phaínein* to make appear) + *-tikos* -TIC] **—fan·tas′ti·cal·ly,** *adv.* **—fan·tas′ti·cal·ness, fan·tas′ti·cal′i·ty,** *n.*
—Syn. 1. FANTASTIC, BIZARRE, GROTESQUE share a sense of deviation from what is normal or expected. FANTASTIC suggests a wild lack of restraint, a fancifulness so extreme as to lose touch with reality: *a fantastic scheme for a series of space cities.* In informal use, FANTASTIC often means simply "exceptionally good": *a fantastic meal.* BIZARRE means markedly unusual or extraordinarily strange, sometimes whimsically so: *bizarre costumes for Mardi Gras; bizarre behavior.* GROTESQUE implies shocking distortion or incongruity, sometimes ludicrous, more often pitiful or tragic: *a grotesque mixture of human and animal features; grotesque contrast between the forced smile and sad eyes: a gnarled tree suggesting the figure of a grotesque human being.*

fan·tas·ti·cate (fan tas′ti kāt′), *v.t.,* **-cat·ed, -cat·ing.** to make or render fantastic. [1590–1600; FANTASTIC + -ATE[1]]

fan·ta·sy (fan′tə sē, -zē), *n., pl.* **-sies,** *v.,* **-sied, -sy·ing.** —*n.* **1.** imagination, esp. when extravagant and unrestrained. **2.** the forming of mental images, esp. wondrous or strange fancies; imaginative conceptualizing. **3.** a mental image, esp. when unreal or fantastic; vision: *a nightmare fantasy.* **4.** *Psychol.* an imagined or conjured up sequence fulfilling a psychological need; daydream. **5.** a hallucination. **6.** a supposition based on no solid foundation; visionary idea; illusion: *dreams of Utopias and similar fantasies.* **7.** caprice; whim. **8.** an ingenious or fanciful thought, design, or invention. **9.** Also, **fantasia.** *Literature.* an imaginative or fanciful work, esp. one dealing with supernatural or unnatural events or characters: *The stories of Poe are fantasies of horror.* **10.** *Music.* fantasia (def. 1). —*v.t., v.i.* **11.** to form mental images; imagine; fantasize. **12.** *Rare.* to write or play fantasias. Also, **phantasy.** [1275–1325; ME *fantasie* imaginative faculty, mental image (< AF, OF) < L *phantasia* < Gk *phantasía* an idea, notion, image, lit., a making visible; see FANTASTIC, -Y[3]]
—Syn. 1. See **fancy.**

fan·ta·sy·land (fan′tə sē land′, -zē-), *n.* **1.** a place or circumstance existing only in the imagination or as an ideal; dream world. **2.** an amusement park whose attractions are based on a theme, as fairy tales or exotic locales; theme park. [1965–70; FANTASY + LAND]

Fan·ti (fan′tē, fän′-), *n.* a Kwa language spoken in Ghana that is mutually intelligible with Twi.

CONCISE ETYMOLOGY KEY: <, descended or borrowed from; >, whence; b., blend of, blended; c., cognate with; cf., compare; deriv., derivative; equiv., equivalent; imit., imitative; obl., oblique; r., replacing; s., stem; sp., spelling, spelled; resp., respelling, respelled; trans., translation; ?, origin unknown; *, unattested; ‡, probably earlier than. See the full key inside the front cover.

Fan·tin-La·tour (fäɴ taɴ lä to͞or′), *n.* **(Ig·nace) Hen·ri (Jo·seph Thé·o·dore)** (ē nyas′ äɴ rē′ zhô zef′ tā ô-dôr′), 1836–1904, French painter.

fan·tod (fan′tod), *n.* **1.** Usually, **fantods.** a state of extreme nervousness or restlessness; the willies; the fidgets (usually prec. by *the*): *We all developed the fantods when the plane was late in arriving.* **2.** Sometimes, **fantods.** a sudden outpouring of anger, outrage, or a similar intense emotion. [1835–40; appar. *fant(igue)* (earlier *fantique,* perh. b. FANTASY and FRANTIC; *-igue* prob. by assoc. with FATIGUE) + *-od(s),* of obscure orig.; see -S[3]]

fan·tom (fan′təm), *n., adj.* phantom.

Fa·num For·tu·nae (fā′nəm fôr to͞o′nē, -tyo͞o′-), ancient name of **Fano.**

fan′ vault′, a vault composed of a number of concave conoidal surfaces, usually four, springing from the corners of the vaulting compartment and touching or intersecting at the top, often decorated with ribs. See illus. under **vault[1].**

fan′ vault′ing, a system of fan vaults. [1795–1805]

fan·weed (fan′wēd′), *n.* the pennycress, *Thlaspi arvense.* [FAN[1] + WEED[1]]

fan′ win′dow, *Archit.* a window having a fanlike form with radiating sash bars, used esp. as a fanlight. [1870–75]

fan·wise (fan′wīz′), *adv.* spread out like an open fan: *to hold cards fanwise.* [1880–85; FAN[1] + -WISE]

fan′ worm′. See **feather-duster worm.** [1850–55]

fan·wort (fan′wûrt′, -wôrt′), *n.* any aquatic plant belonging to the genus *Cabomba,* of the water lily family, having very small flowers and submerged and floating leaves. See illus. under **dimorphism.** [FAN[1] + WORT[2]]

fan·zine (fan zēn′, fan′zēn), *n.* a magazine or other periodical produced inexpensively by and for fans of science fiction and fantasy writing, comic books, popular music, or other specialized popular interests. [1945–50; *Amer.*; FAN[2] + (MAGA)ZINE]

FAO, See **Food and Agriculture Organization.**

F.A.Q., *Australian.* fair average quality. Also, **f.a.q.**

fa·qih (fä kē′), *n., pl.* **fa·qihs, fu·qa·ha** (fo͞o kä′hä). *Islam.* an Islamic religious lawyer. [< Ar *faqīh*]

fa·qir (fə kēr′, fä′kər), *n.* fakir. Also, **fa·quir′.**

far (fär), *adv., adj.,* **far·ther** or **fur·ther, far·thest** or **fur·thest.** —*adv.* **1.** at or to a great distance; a long way off; at or to a remote point: *We sailed far ahead of the fleet.* **2.** at or to a remote or advanced time: *We talked far into the night.* **3.** at or to a great, advanced, or definite point of progress, or degree: *Having come this far, we might as well continue.* **4.** much or many: *I need far more time. We gained far more advantages.* **5. as far as.** See **as[1]** (def. 16). **6. by far, a.** by a great deal; very much: *too expensive by far.* **b.** plainly; obviously: *This melon is by far the ripest of the lot.* **7. far and away,** by far; undoubtedly: *She is far and away the smartest one in the class.* **8. far and wide,** to great lengths; over great distances: *He traveled far and wide in search of his missing son.* Also, **far and near, near and far. 9. far be it from me,** I do not wish or dare (to interrupt, criticize, etc.): *Far be it from me to complain, but it's getting stuffy in here.* **10. far out,** *Slang.* **a.** unconventional; offbeat: *His sense of humor is far out.* **b.** radical; extreme: *political opinions that are far out.* **c.** recondite or esoteric: *an interest in art that was considered far out.* **11. go far, a.** to attain success: *With so much talent he should go far.* **b.** to have a great effect toward; help: *The new evidence will go far toward proving the defendant's guilt.* **12. how far,** to what distance, extent, or degree: *She didn't know how far they had gone in the mathematics text. How far do you think they can be trusted?* **13. so far, a.** up to now: *So far, I've had no reply to my request.* **b.** up to a certain point or extent: *We were able to plan only so far because of various factors beyond our control.* **14. so far so good,** succeeding or managing adequately to this point; doing well thus far: *The work is difficult, but so far so good.* **15. thus far, a.** up to the present; up to now: *We have met no resistance to our plan thus far.* **b.** to a particular degree, point, or extent: *When you get thus far in the experiment, consult with the professor.* —*adj.* **16.** being at a great distance; remote in time or place: *a far country; the far future.* **17.** extending to a great distance: *the far frontiers of empire.* **18.** more distant of the two: *the far side.* **19. a far cry from.** See **cry** (def. 30). **20. few and far between.** See **few** (def. 2). **21. on the far side of.** See **side** (def. 21). **22. the far side.** See **side** (def. 24). [bef. 900; ME *far, fer,* OE *feorr;* c. OHG *ferr,* ON *fjar,* Goth *fairra;* akin to G *fern* far, L *porrō* forward, further] **—far′ness,** *n.*
—Usage. See **as, farther.**

far·ad (far′əd, -ad), *n. Elect.* the SI unit of capacitance, formally defined to be the capacitance of a capacitor between the plates of which there appears a potential difference of one volt when it is charged by a quantity of electricity equal to one coulomb. *Symbol:* F [1860–65; named after M. FARADAY]

Far·a·day (far′ə dē, -dā′), *n.* **1. Michael,** 1791–1867, English physicist and chemist: discoverer of electromagnetic induction. **2.** a unit of electricity used in electrolysis, equal to 96,500 coulombs.

Far′aday cage′, *Physics.* an enclosure constructed of grounded wire mesh or parallel wires that shields sensitive electrical instruments from electrostatic interference. Also called **Far′aday shield′.** [1915–20; named after M. FARADAY]

Far′aday dark′ space′, *Physics.* the dark region between the negative glow and the positive column in a vacuum tube occurring when the pressure is low. [1890–95; named after M. FARADAY]

Far′aday effect′, the rotation of the plane of polarization of plane-polarized light as the light passes through certain isotropic media in the direction of a strong magnetic field in which the medium is placed. Also called **magnetic rotation.** [1885–90; named after M. FARADAY]

fa·rad·ic (fə rad′ik), *adj. Elect.* of or pertaining to a discontinuous, asymmetric, alternating current from the secondary winding of an induction coil. [1875–80; < F *faradique.* See FARAD, -IC]

far·a·dize (far′ə dīz′), *v.t.,* **-dized, -diz·ing.** *Med.* to stimulate or treat (muscles or nerves) with induced alternating electric current (distinguished from *galvanize*). [1860–65; < F *faradiser.* See FARAD, -IZE] **—far′a·di·za′tion,** *n.* **—far′a·diz′er,** *n.* **—far′a·dism,** *n.*

far·an·dole (far′ən dōl′; *Fr.* FA RÄN dôl′), *n., pl.* **-doles** (-dōlz′; *Fr.* -dôl′). **1.** a lively dance, of Provençal origin, in which all the dancers join hands and execute various figures. **2.** the music for this dance. [1860–65; < F < Pr *farandoulo,* perh. a conflation of *b(a)randello* with same sense, deriv. of *brandà* to move, rock (< Gmc; see BRANDISH) and *flandrinà* to dawdle, ult. deriv. of *Flandres* FLANDERS]

far·a·way (fär′ə wā′), *adj.* **1.** distant; remote: *faraway lands.* **2.** dreamy, preoccupied: *a faraway look.* [1810–20; FAR + AWAY]

farce (färs), *n., v.,* **farced, farc·ing.** —*n.* **1.** a light, humorous play in which the plot depends upon a skillfully exploited situation rather than upon the development of character. **2.** humor of the type displayed in such works. **3.** foolish show; mockery; a ridiculous sham. **4.** *Cookery.* forcemeat. —*v.t.* **5.** to season (a speech or composition), esp. with witty material. **6.** *Obs.* to stuff; cram. [1300–50; (n.) ME *fars* stuffing < MF *farce* < VL **farsa,* n. use of fem. of L *farsus,* earlier *fartus* stuffed, ptp. of *farcīre* to stuff; (v.) ME *farsen* < OF *farcir* < L *farcīre*]
—Syn. 3. burlesque, travesty.

farce·meat (färs′mēt′), *n. Cookery.* forcemeat.

far·ceur (fär sûr′; *Fr.* FAR SŒR′), *n., pl.* **-ceurs** (-sûrz′; *Fr.* -SŒR′). **1.** a writer or director of or actor in farce. **2.** a joker; wag. [1775–85; < F, MF, equiv. to *farc(er)* to joke, banter (deriv. of *farce* FARCE) + *-eur* -EUR]

far·ceuse (*Fr.* FAR SŒZ′), *n., pl.* **-ceus·es** (*Fr.* -SŒZ′). a woman skilled in farce. [< F; see FARCEUR, -EUSE]

far·ci (fär sē′; *Fr.* FAR SĒ′), *adj. Cookery.* stuffed. [1900–05; < F, ptp. of *farcir* to stuff < L *farcīre*]

far·ci·cal (fär′si kəl), *adj.* **1.** pertaining to or of the nature of farce. **2.** resembling farce; ludicrous; absurd. [1710–20; FARCE + -ICAL] **—far′ci·cal′i·ty, far′ci·cal·ness,** *n.* **—far′ci·cal·ly,** *adv.*

far·cy (fär′sē), *n., pl.* **-cies.** *Vet. Pathol.* a form of glanders chiefly affecting the skin and superficial lymphatic vessels of horses and mules. [1375–1425; late ME *farsy(n)* < AF, MF *farcin* < LL *farcīminum* glandular disease (L *farcī(re)* to stuff + LL *-minum* for L *-men* n. suffix)]

far′cy bud′, *Vet. Pathol.* an ulcerated swelling, produced in farcy. Also called **far′cy but′ton.** [1835–45]

fard (färd), *Archaic.* —*n.* **1.** facial cosmetics. —*v.t.* **2.** to apply cosmetics to (the face). [1400–50; late ME < MF, OF: n. deriv. of *farder* to apply makeup, prob. < Old Low Franconian **farwidōn* to dye, color (cf. OHG *farwjan,* G *färben*)]

far·del (fär′dl), *n. Archaic.* a bundle; burden. [1375–1425; late ME < AF, OF < OPr, equiv. to *fard(a)* bundle (<< Ar *fardah* load) + *-el* < L *-ellus;* see -ELLE]

far·del-bound (fär′dl bound′), *adj. Vet. Pathol.* (of ruminants) having the food impacted in the third compartment of the stomach; costive; constipated. [1815–25]

fare (fâr), *n., v.,* **fared, far·ing.** —*n.* **1.** the price of conveyance or passage in a bus, train, airplane, or other vehicle. **2.** a person or persons who pay to be conveyed in a vehicle; paying passenger. **3.** a person who hires a public vehicle and its driver. **4.** food; diet: *hearty fare.* **5.** something offered to the public, for entertainment, enjoyment, consumption, etc.: *literary fare.* **6.** *Archaic.* state of things. —*v.i.* **7.** to experience good or bad fortune, treatment, etc.; get on: *He fared well in his profession.* **8.** to go; turn out; happen (used impersonally): *It fared ill with him.* **9.** to go; travel. **10.** to eat and drink: *They fared sumptuously.* [bef. 1000; ME *faren,* OE *faran;* c. G *fahren,* ON *fara,* Goth *faran;* akin to EMPORIUM, PORT[5], PRAM[2]] **—far′er,** *n.*
—Syn. 4. See **food.**

Far′ East′, the countries of E Asia, including China, Japan, Korea, and sometimes adjacent areas. [1840–50, *Amer.*] **—Far′ East′ern.**

Far′ East′ern Re′gion, former name of **Khabarovsk.**

fare-beat·er (fâr′bē′tər), *n.* a person who illegally avoids paying a fare, as by entering a public bus through the exit door. **—fare′-beat′ing,** *n.*

fare·box (fâr′boks′), *n.* a metal box for passenger fares, as on a bus or streetcar. [FARE + BOX[1]]

fare-thee-well (fâr′thē wel′), *n.* **1.** a state of perfection: *The meal was done to a fare-thee-well.* **2.** the maximum effect; fullest measure or extent: *an actress who plays each scene to a fare-thee-well.* Also, **fare-you-well** (fâr′yo͞o wel′).

fare·well (fâr′wel′), *interj.* **1.** goodby; may you fare well: *Farewell, and may we meet again in happier times.* —*n.* **2.** an expression of good wishes at parting: *They made their farewells and left.* **3.** leave-taking; departure: *a fond farewell.* **4.** a party given to a person who is about to embark on a long journey, retire, leave an organization, etc. —*adj.* **5.** parting; valedictory; final: *a farewell performance.* [1325–75; ME *farwel.* See FARE, WELL[1]]

Fare·well (fâr′wel′), *n.* **Cape,** a cape in S Greenland: most southerly point of Greenland.

farewell′ address′, **1.** (*caps.*) *U.S. Hist.* a statement that President George Washington published in a Philadelphia newspaper in 1796 to announce that he would not run for a third term and to give his views on foreign and domestic policy. **2.** a speech delivered by someone upon leaving a job, post, etc.

Farewell′ to Arms′, A, a novel (1929) by Ernest Hemingway.

fare·well-to-spring (fâr wel′tə spring′), *n.* a slender, showy plant, *Clarkia amoena,* of the evening primrose family, native to western North America, having satiny, cup-shaped, lilac-crimson or reddish-pink flowers and roundish fruit. [1900–05, *Amer.*]

Fa′rey se′quence (fâr′ē), *Math.* the increasing sequence of fractions in which numerator and denominator have no common divisor other than one and in which the denominator is less than or equal to a given positive integer *p.* For $p = 4$, the Farey sequence of order 4 is $^0/_1$, $^1/_4$, $^1/_3$, $^1/_2$, $^2/_3$, $^3/_4$, $^1/_1$. [after English mathematician John *Farey* (1766–1826), who proposed the terms of the sequence in 1816]

far-famed (fär′fāmd′), *adj.* widely known; famous. [1615–25]

far·fel (fär′fəl), *n., pl.* **-fel.** *Jewish Cookery.* a solid foodstuff broken into small pieces: *matzo farfel; noodle farfel.* [1890–95; < Yiddish *farfl;* cf. MHG *varveln* noodles]

far-fetched (fär′fecht′), *adj.* improbable; not naturally pertinent; being only remotely connected; forced; strained: *He brought in a far-fetched example in an effort to prove his point.* Also, **far′fetched′.** [1575–85] **—far′-fetched′ness, far′fetched′ness,** *n.*

far-flung (fär′flung′), *adj.* **1.** extending over a great distance. **2.** widely disbursed or distributed. [1890–95]

Far·go (fär′gō), *n.* **1. William George,** 1818–81, U.S. businessman: pioneered in express shipping and banking. **2.** a city in SE North Dakota. 61,308.

far-gone (fär′gôn′, -gon′), *adj.* **1.** remote. **2.** approaching the end, as of life, duration, usefulness, etc.: *The sleeve is too far-gone to mend.* [1770–80]

Far·i·bault (fâr′ə bō′), *n.* a city in SE Minnesota. 16,241.

fa·ri·na (fə rē′nə), *n.* **1.** flour or meal made from cereal grains and cooked as cereal, used in puddings, soups, etc. **2.** *Chiefly Brit.* starch, esp. potato starch. [1350–1400; ME < L *farīna* meal, flour, equiv. to *far* emmer + *-īna,* fem. of *-īnus* -INE¹]

far·i·na·ceous (far′ə nā′shəs), *adj.* **1.** consisting or made of flour or meal, as food. **2.** containing or yielding starch, as seeds; starchy. **3.** mealy in appearance or nature. [1640–50; < L *farīnāceus.* See FARINA, -ACEOUS]

Fa·ri·nel·li (far′ə nel′ē; *It.* fä′rē nel′lē), *n.* **Car·lo** (kär′lō; *It.* kär′lô), (*Carlo Broschi*), 1705–82, Italian operatic male soprano.

far·i·nose (far′ə nōs′), *adj.* **1.** yielding farina. **2.** resembling farina; farinaceous. **3.** covered with a mealy powder. [1720–30; < LL *farīnōsus* mealy. See FARINA, -OSE¹] **—far′i·nose′ly,** *adv.*

far·kle·ber·ry (fär′kəl ber′ē), *n., pl.* **-ries.** a shrub or small tree, *Vaccinium arboreum,* of the heath family, native to the southern U.S., bearing small, waxy, white flowers and black, many-seeded berries. [1755–65, *Amer.*; *farkle* (of obscure orig.) + BERRY]

farl (färl), *n. Scot.* a thin, circular cake of flour or oatmeal. Also, **farle.** [1715–25; contr. of *fardel* a three-cornered cake, orig., the 4th part of a round cake (ME *ferdell,* repr. OE *fēortha dǣl* fourth part)]

Far·ley (fär′lē), *n.* **1. James A(loysius),** 1888–1976, U.S. political leader. **2.** a male given name.

farm (färm), *n.* **1.** a tract of land, usually with a house, barn, silo, etc., on which crops and often livestock are raised for livelihood. **2.** land or water devoted to the raising of animals, fish, plants, etc.: *a pig farm; an oyster farm; a tree farm.* **3.** a similar, usually commercial, site where a product is manufactured or cultivated: *a cheese farm; a honey farm.* **4.** the system, method, or act of collecting revenue by leasing a territory in districts. **5.** a country or district leased for the collection of revenue. **6.** a fixed yearly amount accepted from a person in view of local or district taxes that he or she is authorized to collect. **7.** a tract of land on which an industrial function is carried out, as the drilling or storage of oil or the generation of electricity by solar power. **8.** *Eng. Hist.* **a.** the rent or income from leased property. **b.** the condition of being leased at a fixed rent; possession under lease; a lease. **9.** Also called **farm team, farm′ club′.** *Chiefly Baseball.* a team in a minor league that is owned by or affiliated with a major-league team, for training or keeping players until ready or needed. **10.** *Obs.* a fixed yearly amount payable in the form of rent, taxes, or the like. **11. buy the farm,** *Slang.* to die or be killed. *—v.t.* **12.** to cultivate (land). **13.** to take the proceeds or profits of (a tax, undertaking, etc.) on paying a fixed sum. **14.** to let or lease (taxes, revenues, an enterprise, etc.) to another for a fixed sum or a percentage (often fol. by *out*). **15.** to let or lease the labor or services of (a person) for hire. **16.** to contract for the maintenance of (a person, institution, etc.): *a county that farms its poor.* *—v.i.* **17.** to cultivate the soil; operate a farm. **18. farm out, a.** to assign (work, privileges, or the like) to another by financial agreement; subcontract; lease: *The busy shipyard farmed out two construction jobs to a smaller yard.* **b.** to assign the care of (a child or dependent person) to another: *She farms her elderly aunt out to a retired nurse during the workweek.* **c.** *Chiefly Baseball.* to assign (a player) to a farm. **d.** to exhaust (farmland) by overcropping. **e.** to drill (oil or gas wells), esp. by subcontract on land owned or leased by another. [1250–1300; ME *ferme* lease, rented land, rent < AF, OF < VL **ferma,* deriv. of **fermāre,* for L *firmāre* to make firm, confirm. See FIRM¹] **—farm′a·ble,** *adj.*

farm′ belt′, 1. an area or region noted principally for farming. **2.** (*caps.*) the central states of the midwestern U.S., in which agriculture is significant.

Farm′ Bu′reau. See **American Farm Bureau Federation.**

farm·er (fär′mər), *n.* **1.** a person who farms; person who operates a farm or cultivates land. **2.** an unsophisticated person from a rural area; yokel. **3.** a person who undertakes some service, as the care of children or the poor, at a fixed price. **4.** a person who undertakes the collection of taxes, duties, etc., paying a fixed sum for the privilege of retaining them. **5.** *Cards.* **a.** a variety of twenty-one played with a 45-card pack, the object being to obtain cards having a total worth of 16. **b.** the dealer in this game. [1350–1400; ME *fermer* < AF; OF *fermier* collector of revenue. See FARM, -ER²] **—farm′er·like′,** *adj.*

Far·mer (fär′mər), *n.* **1. Fannie (Mer·ritt)** (mer′it), 1857–1915, U.S. authority on cooking. **2. James (Leonard),** born 1920, U.S. civil-rights leader.

farm′er cheese′, a cheese made by pressing together the soft white curds of whole milk or partly skimmed milk, similar in texture to dry cottage cheese. Also, **farm′er's cheese′.** [1945–50]
—Regional Variation. See **cottage cheese.**

farm·er·ette (fär′mə ret′), *n. Older Use.* a girl or woman working on a farm. [1915–20, *Amer.*; FARMER + -ETTE]
—Usage. See **-ette.**

farm·er-gen·er·al (fär′mər jen′ər əl), *n., pl.* **farmers-gen·er·al.** (in France, under the old monarchy) a member of a company of capitalists that farmed certain taxes. [1705–15; trans. of F *fermier-général*] **—far′·mer-gen′er·al·ship′,** *n.*

farm′er in the dell′, a game, accompanied by a song with several verses, in which one person, designated as the farmer, occupies the center of a circle of persons and is joined in the circle by other players designated as wife, child, nurse, cat, rat, and cheese, these then leaving the circle in order except for the one designated as cheese, who is left standing alone in the circle at the end.

Farm′er-La′bor par′ty (fär′mər lā′bər), **1.** a political party in Minnesota, founded in 1920 and merged with the Democratic party in 1944. **2.** a political party founded in Chicago in 1919 and dissolved in 1924.

Farm′ers' Alli′ance, *U.S. Hist.* an informal name for various regional political organizations that farmers established in the 1880's and that led to the formation of the Peoples' party in 1891–92.

Farm′ers Branch′, a city in NE Texas. 24,863.

farm′ers coop′erative, an organization of farmers for marketing their products or buying supplies.

farm′er's lung′, a lung disorder caused by inhalation of moldy hay dust, marked by shortness of breath, dry cough, and weight loss. [1940–45]

farm′ers' mar′ket, 1. a market or group of stalls and booths where farmers and sometimes other vendors sell their products directly to consumers. **2.** the gathering of those who sell and buy farmers' products.

Far′mer's reduc′er (fär′mərz), *Photog.* a solution of ferricyanide and hypo for reducing density and increasing contrast in a negative. [named after E. H. *Farmer* (d. 1944), English photographer]

farm·er·y (fär′mə rē), *n., pl.* **-er·ies.** *Chiefly Brit.* the buildings, yards, etc., of a farm. [1650–60; FARM + -ERY]

farm′ hand′, a person who works on a farm, esp. a hired worker; hired hand. [1835–45]

farm·house (färm′hous′), *n., pl.* **-hous·es** (-hou′ziz). a house on a farm, esp. the one used by the farmer and farmer's family. [1590–1600; FARM + HOUSE]

farm·ing (fär′ming), *n.* **1.** the business of operating a farm. **2.** the practice of letting or leasing taxes, revenue, etc., for collection. [1545–55; FARM + -ING¹]

Farm·ing·ton (fär′ming tən), *n.* **1.** a city in NW New Mexico. 30,729. **2.** a town in N Connecticut. 16,407. **3.** a town in SE Michigan. 11,022.

Farm′ington Hills′, a city in SE Michigan. 58,056.

farm·land (färm′land′), *n.* land under cultivation or capable of being cultivated: *to protect valuable farmland from erosion.* [1630–40; FARM + LAND]

farm·out (färm′out′), *n.* **1.** an act or instance of farming out or leasing, as land for oil exploration. **2.** something farmed out. [n. use of v. phrase *farm out*]

farm·sit·ter (färm′sit′ər), *n. Canadian.* a person who takes temporary charge of a farm during the absence or incapacity of the owner.

farm·stead (färm′sted′), *n.* a farm together with its buildings. [1800–10; FARM + STEAD]

farm′ sys′tem, any small-scale or localized network or industry that provides experience and exposure for beginners, similar to that of a baseball farm. [1925–30]

farm′ team′, *Chiefly Baseball.* farm (def. 9).

farm·work·er (färm′wûr′kər), *n.* See **farm hand.** [FARM + WORKER]

farm·yard (färm′yärd′), *n.* a yard or enclosure surrounded by or connected with farm buildings. [1740–50; FARM + YARD²]

Far·ne·se (fär ne′ze), *n.* **A·les·san·dro** (ä′les sän′-drô), **Duke of Parma,** 1545–92, Italian general, statesman, and diplomat.

far·ne·sol (fär′nə sôl′, -sol′), *n. Chem.* a colorless, unsaturated, liquid alcohol, $C_{15}H_{26}O$, having a slight floral odor, extracted from the flowers of the acacia, cassia oil, or the like: used in perfumery. [1900–05; < NL (*Acacia*) *farnes*(*iana*) Farnese acacia (named after Cardinal O. *Farnese,* 17th-century Italian) + -OL¹]

Farns·worth (färnz′wûrth′), *n.* **Phi·lo Taylor** (fī′lō), 1906–71, U.S. physicist and inventor: pioneer in the field of television.

far·o (fâr′ō), *n. Cards.* a gambling game in which players place bets on a special board or layout, betting on each series of two cards as they are drawn from a box containing the dealer's or banker's pack. [1725–35; sp. var. of *Pharaoh* (cf. It *faraone,* F *pharaon*), alleged to be orig. a designation for the king of hearts in the game. See PHARAOH]

Fa·ro (fä′rōō), *n.* a seaport in S Portugal. 20,470.

Far′oe Is′lands (fâr′ō). See **Faeroe Islands.** Also, **Far′oes.**

Far·o·ese (fâr′ō ēz′, -ēs′), *n., pl.* **-ese,** *adj.* Faeroese. [1850–55; FAEROE (ISLANDS) + -ESE]

far-off (fär′ôf′, -of′), *adj.* distant; remote. [1580–90]

fa·rouche (fa rōōsh′), *adj. French.* **1.** fierce. **2.** sullenly unsociable or shy.

Fa·rouk I (fä rōōk′, fə-). See **Faruk I.**

far-out (fär′out′), *adj. Slang.* **1.** unconventional; offbeat; avant-garde. **2.** radical; extreme. **3.** recondite or esoteric. [1950–55] **—far′-out′ness,** *n.*

far′ piece′, *Chiefly Midland and Southern U.S.* a considerable distance: *They moved a far piece from here.*

far-point (fär′point′), *n. Ophthalm.* the point farthest from the eye at which an object is clearly focused on the retina when accommodation of the eye is completely relaxed. Cf. **near-point.** [1875–80]

Far·quhar (fär′kwər, -kwär, -kər), *n.* **George,** 1678–1707, English playwright, born in Ireland.

far·rag·i·nous (fə raj′ə nəs), *adj.* heterogeneous; mixed: *a farraginous collection of random ideas.* [1605–15; < L *farrāgin-* (s. of *farrāgō*) mixed grains (see FARRAGO) + -OUS]

far·ra·go (fə rä′gō, -rā′-), *n., pl.* **-goes.** a confused mixture; hodgepodge; medley: *a farrago of doubts, fears, hopes, and wishes.* [1625–35; < L: lit., mixed crop of feed grains, equiv. to *farr-* (s. of *far*) emmer + *-āgō* suffix noting kind or nature]

Far·ra·gut (far′ə gət), *n.* **David Glasgow,** 1801–70, U.S. admiral: won the battles of New Orleans and Mobile Bay for the Union in the U.S. Civil War.

Far·rar (fə rär′), *n.* **Geraldine** (*Mrs. Lou Tellegen*), 1882–1967, U.S. operatic soprano.

far-reach·ing (fär′rē′ching), *adj.* extending far in influence, effect, etc.: *the far-reaching effect of his speech.* [1815–25] **—far′-reach′ing·ly,** *adv.* **—far′-reach′ing·ness,** *n.*

Far·rell (far′əl), *n.* **1. Eileen,** born 1920, U.S. soprano. **2. James T(homas),** 1904–79, U.S. novelist.

far·rest (fär′ist), *adj. Chiefly Midland U.S. Nonstandard.* farthest.

far·ri·er (far′ē ər), *n. Chiefly Brit.* a blacksmith. [1375–1425; var. of *ferrier* < MF, OF < L *ferrārius* smith (see FERRUM, -ARY); r. late ME *fer(r)our* < AF, OF *ferreor* < L **ferrātor*]

far·row¹ (far′ō), *n.* **1.** a litter of pigs. *—v.t.* **2.** (of swine) to bring forth (young). *—v.i.* **3.** to produce a litter of pigs. [bef. 900; ME *farwen* to give birth to a litter of pigs, deriv. of OE *fearh* pig (c. L *porcus*); akin to G *Ferkel* young pig]

far·row² (far′ō), *adj.* (of a cow) not pregnant. [1485–95; akin to D dial. *verwe-* (in *verwekoe* barren cow), OE *fearr* ox]

far·ru·ca (fə rōō′kə; *Sp.* fär rōō′kä), *n., pl.* **-cas** (-kəz; *Sp.* -käs). a Spanish flamenco dance. [1930–35; < Sp; cf. *farruco* defiant, bold, arrogant, allegedly after *farruco* a Galician or Asturian who has recently emigrated, hypocoristic form of *Francisco* Francis]

Fars (färs), *n.* a province in SW Iran. 2,806,000; 51,466 sq. mi. (133,297 sq. km).

far·see·ing (fär′sē′ing), *adj.* **1.** having foresight; sagacious; discerning. **2.** able to see objects distinctly at a great distance: *Hawks are farseeing birds.* [1840–50; FAR + SEE¹ + -ING²] **—far′see′ing·ness,** *n.* **—far′·se′er,** *n.*

Far·si (fär′sē), *n.* the modern Iranian language of Iran and western Afghanistan, written in the Arabic alphabet; modern Persian.

far·sight·ed (fär′sī′tid, -sī′tid), *adj.* **1.** seeing objects at a distance more clearly than those near at hand; hyperopic. **2.** seeing to a great distance. **3.** wise, as in foreseeing future developments: *a farsighted statesman.* [1635–45; FAR + SIGHT + -ED³] **—far′sight′ed·ly,** *adv.* **—far′sight′ed·ness,** *n.*
—Syn. 3. foresighted, farseeing, prescient, discerning, prudent, perspicacious.

fart (färt), *Vulgar.* *—n.* **1.** a flatus expelled through the anus. **2.** an irritating or foolish person. *—v.i.* **3.** to expel a flatus through the anus; break wind. **4. fart around,** to spend time foolishly or aimlessly. [1350–1400; ME *ferten, farten* (v.), *fert, fart* (n.); c. Gk *pérdein* (v.), *pordḗ* (n.)]

far·ther (fär′thər), *adv., compar. of* **far** *with* **farthest** *as superl.* **1.** at or to a greater distance: *He went farther down the road.* **2.** at or to a more advanced point: *They are going no farther in their studies.* **3.** at or to a greater degree or extent: *The application of the law was extended farther.* *—adj., compar. of* **far** *with* **farthest** *as superl.* **4.** more distant or remote than something or some place nearer: *the farther side of the mountain.* **5.** extending or tending to a greater distance: *He made a still farther trip.* **6.** *Nonstandard.* further (defs. 5, 6). [1300–50; ME *ferther;* orig. var. of FURTHER]
—Usage. Although some usage guides insist that only FARTHER should be used for physical distance (*We walked farther than we planned*), FARTHER and FURTHER have been used interchangeably throughout much of their histories. However, only FURTHER is used in the adverbial sense "moreover" (*Further, you hurt my feelings*) and in the adjectival senses "more extended" (*no further comment*) and "additional" (*Further bulletins came in*). The expression ALL THE FARTHER (or FURTHER) in place

CONCISE PRONUNCIATION KEY: *act, cāpe, dâre, pärt; set, ēqual; if, ice; ox, ōver, ôrder, oil, bo͝ok, bo͞ot, out; up, ûrge; child; sing; shoe; thin, that;* zh *as in treasure.* ə = *a* as in *alone, e* as in *system, i* as in *easily, o* as in *gallop, u* as in *circus;* ᵊ as in *fire* (fīᵊr), *hour* (ouᵊr). l and n can serve as syllabic consonants, as in *cradle* (krād′l), and *button* (but′n). See the full key inside the front cover.

of *as far as* occurs chiefly in informal speech: *This is all the farther the train goes.* See also **all.**

Far′ther In′dia, Indochina.

far·ther·most (fär′thər mōst′, -məst), *adj.* most distant or remote; farthest. [1610–20; FARTHER + -MOST]

far·thest (fär′thist), *adj., superl. of* **far** *with* **farther** *as compar.* **1.** most distant or remote. **2.** most extended; longest. —*adv., superl. of* **far** *with* **farther** *as compar.* **3.** at or to the greatest distance. **4.** at or to the most advanced point. **5.** at or to the greatest degree or extent. [1350–1400; ME *ferthest;* orig. var. of FURTHEST]

far·thing (fär′thing), *n.* **1.** a former bronze coin of Great Britain, equal to one-fourth of a British penny: withdrawn in 1961. **2.** something of very small value: *I don't care a farthing for your opinion.* [bef. 950; ME *ferthing,* OE *fēorthing.* See FOURTH, -ING[3]]

far·thin·gale (fär′thing gāl′), *n.* a hoop skirt or framework for expanding a woman's skirt, worn in the 16th and 17th centuries. [1545–55; earlier *verdynggale* < MF *verdugale,* alter. of OSp *verdugado,* equiv. to *verdug(o)* tree-shoot, rod (*verd(e)* green (< L *viridis*) + *-ugo* n. suffix) + *-ado* -ADE[1]; so called from rod used to extend skirt]

farthingale (Elizabethan period)

far′thingale chair′, an English chair of c1600 having no arms, a straight and low back, and a high seat. [1900–05]

Fa·ruk I (fə ro͞ok′, fä-), 1920–65, king of Egypt from 1936 until his abdication in 1952. Also, **Farouk.**

Far′ West′, the area of the U.S. west of the Great Plains. —**Far′ West′ern.**

FAS, **1.** See **fetal alcohol syndrome. 2.** Foreign Agricultural Service.

F.A.S., *Com.* free alongside ship: without charge to the buyer for goods delivered alongside ship. Also, **f.a.s.**

FASB, See **Financial Accounting Standards Board.**

fas·ces (fas′ēz), *n.* (*usually used with a singular v.*) a bundle of rods containing an ax with the blade projecting, borne before Roman magistrates as an emblem of official power. [1590–1600; < L, pl. of *fascis* bundle, pack]

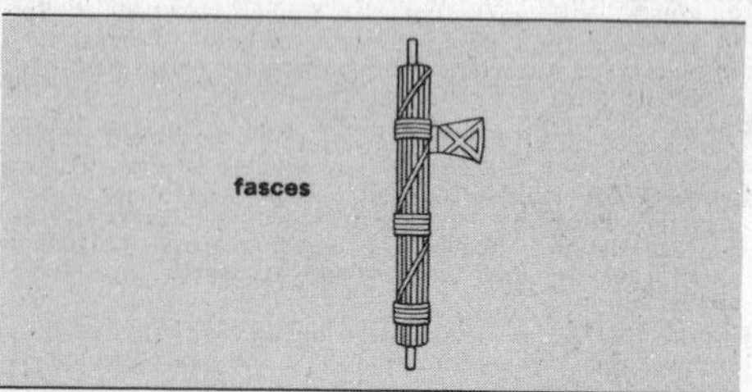
fasces

Fa·sching (fä′shing), *n.* a carnival celebration that precedes Lent in German-speaking countries and communities; Shrovetide. [1910–15; < G, orig. Bavarian and Austrian dial.; MHG *vaschanc, vastschang,* perh. equiv. to *vast-* Lent (G *Fasten;* see FAST[2]) + *schanc* distribution or pouring of drinks, referring to the dispensing of liquor prohibited during Lent]

fas·ci·a (fash′ē ə *for 1, 3–5;* fä′shə *for 2*), *n., pl.* **fas·ci·ae** (fash′ē ē′) *for 1, 3–5;* **fas·cias** (fä′shəz) *for 2.* **1.** a band or fillet, as for binding the hair. **2.** Also called **fas′cia board′.** facia. **3.** *Archit.* **a.** any relatively broad, flat, horizontal surface, as the outer edge of a cornice, a stringcourse, etc. **b.** any of a number of horizontal bands, usually three in number, each projecting beyond the one below to form the architrave in the Ionic, Corinthian, and Composite orders. **4.** *Anat., Zool.* **a.** a band or sheath of connective tissue investing, supporting, or binding together internal organs or parts of the body. **b.** tissue of this kind. **5.** *Zool., Bot.* a distinctly marked band of color. [1555–65; < L: band, bandage; akin to FASCES] —**fas′ci·al,** *adj.*

fas·ci·ate (fash′ē āt′ -ē it), *adj.* **1.** bound with a band, fillet, or bandage. **2.** *Bot.* abnormally compressed into a band or bundle, as stems grown together. **3.** *Zool.* **a.** composed of bundles. **b.** bound together in a bundle. **c.** marked with a band or bands. Also, **fas′ci·at′ed.** [1650–60; FASCI(A) + -ATE[1]] —**fas′ci·ate′ly,** *adv.*

fas·ci·a·tion (fash′ē ā′shən), *n.* **1.** the act of binding up or bandaging. **2.** the process of becoming fasciate. **3.** the resulting state. **4.** an abnormality in a plant, in which a stem enlarges into a flat, ribbonlike shape resembling several stems fused together. [1640–50; FASCIATE + -ION]

CONCISE ETYMOLOGY KEY: <, descended or borrowed from; >, whence; b., blend of, blended; c., cognate with; cf., compare; deriv., derivative; equiv., equivalent; imit., imitative; obl., oblique; r., replacing; s., stem; sp., spelling, spelled; resp., respelling, respelled; trans., translation; ?, origin unknown; *, unattested; ‡, probably earlier than. See the full key inside the front cover.

fas·ci·cle (fas′i kəl), *n.* **1.** a section of a book or set of books being published in installments as separate pamphlets or volumes. **2.** a small bundle, tight cluster, or the like. **3.** *Bot.* a close cluster, as of flowers or leaves. **4.** *Anat.* a small bundle of nerve or muscle fibers. [1490–1500; < L *fasciculus,* dim. of *fascis.* See FASCES, -CLE[1]]

fas·cic·u·lar (fə sik′yə lər), *adj.* pertaining to or forming a fascicle; fasciculate. [1650–60; FASCICUL(US) + -AR[1]]

fas·cic·u·late (fə sik′yə lit, -lāt′), *adj.* arranged in a fascicle or fascicles. Also, **fas·cic′u·lat′ed.** [1785–95; FASCICUL(US) + -ATE[1]]

fas·cic·u·la·tion (fə sik′yə lā′shən), *n.* a fascicular condition. [1935–40; FASCICULATE + -ION]

fas·ci·cule (fas′i kyo͞ol′), *n.* a fascicle, esp. of a book. [1690–1700; var. of FASCICULUS and FASCICLE; see -CULE]

fas·cic·u·lus (fə sik′yə ləs), *n., pl.* **-li** (-lī′). **1.** a fascicle, as of nerve or muscle fibers. **2.** a fascicle of a book. [1705–15; < L; see FASCICLE]

fas·ci·i·tis (fash′ē ī′tis, fas′-), *n. Pathol.* inflammation of the fascia. [1890–95; FASCI(A) + -ITIS]

fas·ci·nate (fas′ə nāt′), *v.,* **-nat·ed, -nat·ing.** —*v.t.* **1.** to attract and hold attentively by a unique power, personal charm, unusual nature, or some other special quality; enthrall: *a vivacity that fascinated the audience.* **2.** to arouse the interest or curiosity of; allure. **3.** to transfix or deprive of the power of resistance, as through terror: *The sight of the snake fascinated the rabbit.* **4.** *Obs.* to bewitch. **5.** *Obs.* to cast under a spell by a look. —*v.i.* **6.** to capture the interest or hold the attention. [1590–1600; < L *fascinātus,* ptp. of *fascināre* to bewitch, cast a spell on, v. deriv. of *fascinum* evil spell, bewitchment] —**fas′ci·nat′ed·ly,** *adv.* —**fas′ci·na′tive,** *adj.*
—**Syn. 1.** bewitch, enchant, spellbind, charm.

fas·ci·nat·ing (fas′ə nā′ting), *adj.* of great interest or attraction; enchanting; charming; captivating: *a fascinating story; fascinating jewelry.* [1640–50; FASCINATE + -ING[2]] —**fas′ci·nat′ing·ly,** *adv.*

fas·ci·na·tion (fas′ə nā′shən), *n.* **1.** the power or action of fascinating. **2.** the state or an instance of being fascinated: *They watched in fascination.* **3.** a fascinating quality; powerful attraction; charm: *the fascination of foreign travel.* **4.** *Cards.* a form of solitaire. [1595–1605; < L *fascinātiōn-* (s. of *fascinātiō*) a bewitching. See FASCINATE, -ION]

fas·ci·na·tor (fas′ə nā′tər), *n.* **1.** a person or thing that fascinates. **2.** a scarf of crochet work, lace, or the like, narrowing toward the ends, worn as a head covering by women. [1740–50; < LL; see FASCINATE, -TOR]

fas·cine (fa sēn′, fə-), *n. Fort.* a long bundle of sticks bound together, used in building earthworks and batteries and in strengthening ramparts. [1680–90; < F < L *fascina* bundle of sticks. See FASCES, -INE[1]]

fas·ci·o·li·a·sis (fə sē′ə lī′ə sis, -sī′-), *n. Vet. Pathol.* liver-rot. [1885–90; < NL *Fasciol(a)* name of genus of liver flukes (L: small bandage) + -IASIS]

fas·ci·o·lop·si·a·sis (fas′ē ō lop sī′ə sis, fə sē′ə-, -sī′-), *n.* a parasitic disease caused by flukes of the genus *Fasciolopsis* and characterized by abdominal pain and diarrhea: common in the Far East. [1885–90; < NL *Fasciolops(is)* genus name (equiv. to L *fasciol(a)* band, ribbon (dim. of *fascia* bandage) + *-opsis* -OPSIS) + -IASIS]

fas·cism (fash′iz əm), *n.* **1.** (*sometimes cap.*) a governmental system led by a dictator having complete power, forcibly suppressing opposition and criticism, regimenting all industry, commerce, etc., and emphasizing an aggressive nationalism and often racism. **2.** (*sometimes cap.*) the philosophy, principles, or methods of fascism. **3.** (*cap.*) a fascist movement, esp. the one established by Mussolini in Italy 1922–43. [1915–20; < It *fascismo,* equiv. to *fasc(io)* bundle, political group (see FASCES) + *-ismo* -ISM]

fas·cist (fash′ist), *n.* **1.** a person who believes in or sympathizes with fascism. **2.** (*often cap.*) a member of a fascist movement or party. **3.** a person who is dictatorial or has extreme right-wing views. —*adj.* **4.** Also, **fa·scis·tic** (fə shis′tik). of or like fascism or fascists. [1915–20; < It *fascista,* equiv. to *fasc(io)* (see FASCISM) + *-ista* -IST] —**fa·scis′ti·cal·ly,** *adv.*

Fa·scis·ta (fə shis′tə; *It.* fä shē′stä), *n., pl.* **Fa·scis·ti** (fə shis′tē; *It.* fä shē′stē). a member of the Fascist movement in Italy. [1920–25; < It: FASCIST]

fas·cist·ize (fash′is tīz′), *v.t.,* **-ized, -iz·ing.** to make fascist; convert to fascism or a fascist philosophy or methods. Also, *esp. Brit.,* **fas′cist·ise′.** [1935–40; FASCIST + -IZE] —**fas′cist·i·za′tion,** *n.*

fash·ion (fash′ən), *n.* **1.** a prevailing custom or style of dress, etiquette, socializing, etc.: *the latest fashion in dresses.* **2.** conventional usage in dress, manners, etc., esp. of polite society, or conformity to it: *the dictates of fashion; to be out of fashion.* **3.** manner; way; mode: *in a warlike fashion.* **4.** the make or form of anything: *He liked the fashion of the simple, sturdy furniture.* **5.** a kind; sort: *All fashions of people make up the world.* **6.** *Obs.* workmanship. **7.** *Obs.* act or process of making. **8. after** or **in a fashion,** in some manner or other or to some extent; in a makeshift, unskillful, or unsatisfactory way: *He's an artist after a fashion.* —*v.t.* **9.** to give a particular shape or form to; make: *The cavemen fashioned tools from stones.* **10.** to accommodate; adjust; adapt: *doctrines fashioned to the varying hour.* **11.** *Shipbuilding.* to bend (a plate) without preheating. **12.** *Obs.* to contrive; manage. [1250–1300; ME *facioun* shape, manner < AF *faço(u)n, façun,* OF *faceon* < L *factiōn-* (s. of *factiō*) a doing, company. See FACTION] —**fash′ion·less,** *adj.*
—**Syn. 1.** mode; fad, rage, craze. FASHION, STYLE, VOGUE imply popularity or widespread acceptance of manners, customs, dress, etc. FASHION is that which characterizes or distinguishes the habits, manners, dress, etc., of a period or group: *the fashions of the 18th century.* STYLE is sometimes the equivalent of FASHION, but also denotes conformance to a prevalent standard: *to be in style; a chair in the Queen Anne style.* VOGUE suggests the temporary popularity of certain fashions: *this year's vogue in popular music.* **4.** shape, cut, pattern, figure. **9.** frame, construct, mold. **10.** suit, fit.

fash·ion·a·ble (fash′ə nə bəl), *adj.* **1.** observant of or conforming to the fashion; stylish: *a fashionable young woman.* **2.** of, characteristic of, used, or patronized by the world of fashion: *a fashionable shop.* **3.** current; popular: *a fashionable topic of conversation.* —*n.* **4.** a fashionable person. [1600–10; FASHION + -ABLE] —**fash′ion·a·ble·ness, fash′ion·a·bil′i·ty,** *n.* —**fash′·ion·a·bly,** *adv.*
—**Syn. 1.** chic, smart, modish, voguish, elegant. —**Ant.** out-of-date; passé.

fash′ion coor′dinator, a person in a department store or other establishment who coordinates activities centered upon or related to fashion, as fashion themes, shows, displays, and promotion.

fash·ion·er (fash′ə nər), *n.* **1.** a person who fashions, forms, or gives shape to anything. **2.** a tailor or modiste. [1540–50; FASHION + -ER[1]]

fash′ion plate′, **1.** a person who consistently wears the latest style in dress. **2.** an illustration showing the prevailing or new fashion in clothes. [1850–55]

Fa·sho·da (fə shō′də), *n.* a village in the SE Sudan, on the White Nile: conflict of British and French colonial interests 1898 (**Fasho′da In′cident**). Modern name, **Kodok.**

fas·nacht (fôs′näk′, -näkt′), *n. Chiefly Pennsylvania.* a deep-fried raised doughnut; originally served on Shrove Tuesday as the last sweet treat before Lent. Also, **fast·nacht** (fôst′näk′, -näkt′). [< PaG; G *Fastnacht;* see FAST[2], NIGHT]

fast[1] (fast, fäst), *adj.,* **-er, -est,** *adv.,* **-er, -est,** *n.* —*adj.* **1.** moving or able to move, operate, function, or take effect quickly; quick; swift; rapid: *a fast horse; a fast pain reliever; a fast thinker.* **2.** done in comparatively little time; taking a comparatively short time: *a fast race; fast work.* **3.** (of time) **a.** indicating a time in advance of the correct time, as of a clock. **b.** noting or according to daylight-saving time. **4.** adapted to, allowing, productive of, or imparting rapid movement: *a hull with fast lines; one of the fastest pitchers in baseball.* **5.** characterized by unrestrained conduct or lack of moral conventions, esp. in sexual relations; wanton; loose: *Some young people in that era were considered fast, if not downright promiscuous.* **6.** characterized by hectic activity: *leading a fast life.* **7.** resistant: *acid-fast.* **8.** firmly fixed in place; not easily moved; securely attached. **9.** held or caught firmly, so as to be unable to escape or be extricated: *an animal fast in a trap.* **10.** firmly tied, as a knot. **11.** closed and made secure, as a door, gate, or shutter. **12.** such as to hold securely: *to lay fast hold on a thing.* **13.** firm in adherence; loyal; devoted: *fast friends.* **14.** permanent, lasting, or unchangeable: *a fast color; a hard and fast rule.* **15.** *Informal.* **a.** (of money, profits, etc.) made quickly or easily and sometimes deviously: *He earned some fast change helping the woman with her luggage.* **b.** cleverly quick and manipulative in making money: *a fast operator when it comes to closing a business deal.* **16.** *Photog.* **a.** (of a lens) able to transmit a relatively large amount of light in a relatively short time. **b.** (of a film) requiring a relatively short exposure time to attain a given density. **17.** *Horse Racing.* **a.** (of a track condition) completely dry. **b.** (of a track surface) very hard. **18. pull a fast one,** *Informal.* to play an unfair trick; practice deceit: *He tried to pull a fast one on us by switching the cards.* —*adv.* **19.** quickly, swiftly, or rapidly. **20.** in quick succession: *Events followed fast upon one another to the crisis.* **21.** tightly; firmly: *to hold fast.* **22.** soundly: *fast asleep.* **23.** in a wild or dissipated way. **24.** ahead of the correct or announced time. **25.** *Archaic.* close; near: *fast by.* **26. play fast and loose.** See **play** (def. 76). —*n.* **27.** a fastening for a door, window, or the like. [bef. 900; ME; OE *fæst* firm; c. D *vast,* ON *fastr* firm, G *fest;* akin to FAST[2]]
—**Syn. 1, 2.** fleet, speedy. See **quick. 5.** dissipated, dissolute, profligate, immoral; wild, prodigal. **8.** secure, tight, immovable, firm. **9.** inextricable. **13.** faithful, steadfast. **14.** enduring. **21.** securely, fixedly, tenaciously. **23.** recklessly, wildly, prodigally. —**Ant. 1, 2.** slow. **5, 6.** restrained. **8.** loose.

fast[2] (fast, fäst), *v.i.* **1.** to abstain from all food. **2.** to eat only sparingly or of certain kinds of food, esp. as a religious observance. —*v.t.* **3.** to cause to abstain entirely from or limit food; put on a fast: *to fast a patient for a day before surgery.* —*n.* **4.** an abstinence from food, or a limiting of one's food, esp. when voluntary and as a religious observance; fasting. **5.** a day or period of fasting. [bef. 1000; ME *fasten,* OE *fæstan;* c. G *fasten,* Goth *fastan,* ON *fasta*]

fast[3] (fast, fäst), *n.* a chain or rope for mooring a vessel. [1670–80; alter., by assoc. with FAST[1], of late ME *fest,* perh. n. use of *fest,* ptp. of *festen* to FASTEN, or < ON *festr* mooring rope]

fast·back (fast′bak′, fäst′-), *n.* **1.** a form of back for an automobile body consisting of a single, unbroken convex curve from the top to the rear bumper. **2.** a car having such a back. Cf. **notchback.** [1960–65 *Amer.*; FAST[1] + BACK[1]]

fast·ball (fast′bôl′, fäst′-), *n. Baseball.* a pitch thrown at or near a pitcher's maximum velocity. [1910–15; FAST[1] + BALL[1]]

fast′ break′, *Basketball.* a play or method of play that brings the ball from one end of the court to the other quickly, usually by one or two quick passes in an attempt by the offensive team to score before the defensive team can get into position. [1945–50]

fast-break (fast′brāk′, fäst′-), *v.i.,* **-broke, -bro·ken, -break·ing.** *Basketball.* to execute or play in the style of a fast break.

fast-break·ing (fast′brā′king, fäst′-), *adj.* (of a news story) occurring suddenly, and often portending a series of events or further developments in rapid succession.

fast′-breed′er reac′tor (fast′brē′dər, fäst′-),

Physics. a breeder reactor in which there is no moderator and fission is caused by high-energy neutrons. Also, **fast′ breed′er reac′tor.**

fast′ buck′, *Slang.* money made easily or quickly and sometimes unscrupulously: *He speculated briefly in the commodities market in the hope of making a fast buck.* Also called **fast′ dol′lar.** [1945–50, *Amer.*] **—fast′-buck′,** *adj.*

fast-count (fast′kount′, fäst′-), *v.t.* to short-change.

fast-cut (fast′kut′, fäst′-), *v.i.,* **-cut, -cut·ting.** *Television.* to go abruptly from one brief scene to another.

fast′ day′, a day on which fasting is observed, esp. such a day appointed by some ecclesiastical or civil authority. [1300–50; ME]

fas·ten (fas′ən, fä′sən), *v.t.* **1.** to attach firmly or securely in place; fix securely to something else. **2.** to make secure, as an article of dress with buttons, clasps, etc., or a door with a lock, bolt, etc. **3.** to enclose securely, as a person or an animal (usually fol. by *in*): *to fasten a monkey in a cage.* **4.** to attach, associate, or connect: *to fasten a nickname on someone.* **5.** to direct (the eyes, thoughts, etc.) intently: *to fasten one's eyes on a speaker.* —*v.i.* **6.** to become fast, fixed, or firm. **7.** to close firmly or securely; lock: *This clasp won't fasten.* **8.** to take a firm hold; seize (usually fol. by *on* or *upon*): *to fasten on an idea.* **9.** to focus attention; concentrate (usually fol. by *on* or *upon*): *His gaze fastened on the jewels.* [bef. 900; ME *fastenen,* OE *fæstnian;* c. ON *fastna* to betroth; akin to FAST[1]]
—Syn. 1. connect, link, hook, clasp, clinch, rivet, clamp, bind, tie, tether.

fas·ten·er (fas′ə nər, fä′sə-), *n.* **1.** any of various devices for fastening. **2.** any of various devices, as a snap or hook and eye, for holding together two objects or parts sometimes required to be separate, as two edges or flaps of a piece of clothing. **3.** a worker who fastens things together. [1620–30; FASTEN + -ER[1]]

fas·ten·ing (fas′ə ning, fä′sə-), *n.* something that fastens, as a lock or clasp. [1125–75; ME; see FASTEN, -ING[1]]

fast′ food′, food, as hamburgers, pizza, or fried chicken, that is prepared in quantity by a standardized method and can be dispensed quickly at inexpensive restaurants for eating there or elsewhere. [1965–70, *Amer.*]

fast-food (fast′fo͞od′, fäst′-), *adj.* of or specializing in fast food. [1965–70, *Amer.*]

fast-food·er (fast′fo͞o′dər, fäst′-), *n. Informal.* **1.** Also, **fast-food·er·y** (fast′fo͞o′də rē, fäst′-). a restaurant that sells fast food. **2.** a person or company that operates a fast-food business. [FAST FOOD + -ER[1]]

fast′ for′ward, 1. a function of an electronic recording device, as a tape recorder or cassette deck, that allows the tape to be advanced rapidly. **2.** the button or switch that activates this function.

fast-for·ward (fast′fôr′wərd, fäst′-), *v.i.* (on a recording device or projector) to advance a tape or film rapidly, using the fast forward.

fast′ ice′, ice that is frozen to, grounded on, or attached to the bottom of an area covered by shallow water. Cf. **ice foot.** [1930–35]

fas·tid·i·ous (fa stid′ē əs, fə-), *adj.* **1.** excessively particular, critical, or demanding; hard to please: *a fastidious eater.* **2.** requiring or characterized by excessive care or delicacy; painstaking. [1375–1425; late ME < L *fastīdiōsus* squeamish, equiv. to *fastīdi(um)* lack of appetite, disgust, perh. by syncope of **fastutīdium* (*fastu-,* comb. form of *fastus* pride, conceit + *-tīdium* comb. form of *taedium* TEDIUM) + *-ōsus* -OUS] **—fas·tid′i·ous·ly,** *adv.* **—fas·tid′i·ous·ness,** *n.*
—Syn. 1. See **particular.**

fas·tig·i·ate (fa stij′ē it, -āt′), *adj.* **1.** rising to a pointed top. **2.** *Zool.* joined together in a tapering adhering group. **3.** *Bot.* **a.** erect and parallel, as branches. **b.** having such branches. Also, **fas·tig′i·at′ed.** [1655–65; < L *fastīgi(um)* height, highest point + -ATE[1]]

fas·tig·i·um (fa stij′ē əm), *n., pl.* **-i·ums, -i·a** (-ē ə). *Med.* the highest point of a fever or disease; the period of greatest development of an infection. [1670–80; < L]

fast′ lane′, 1. Also called **express lane.** the lane of a multilane roadway that is used by fast-moving vehicles, as when passing slower traffic. **2.** *Informal.* any scene, activity, or pursuit that is exciting, high-pressured, competitive, swift-moving, and sometimes dissipated or dangerous: *Alcoholism and stress are often the price for living life in the fast lane.* Cf. **fast track.** [1965–70]

fast′ mo′tion, *Cinematog.* action that appears to move faster than normal on the screen, accomplished by filming the action at less than normal speed in the camera and then projecting it at normal speed. Cf. **time-lapse photography.** [1910–15]

fast-mov·ing (fast′mo͞o′ving, fäst′-), *adj.* **1.** moving or capable of moving at high speed. **2.** (of a novel, play, or the like) having sustained action and interest with events following one another rapidly; lively in plot. [1930–35]

fast·ness (fast′nis, fäst′-), *n.* **1.** a secure or fortified place; stronghold: *a mountain fastness.* **2.** the state of being fixed or firm: *the fastness of democratic institutions.* **3.** the state of being rapid. [bef. 900; ME; OE *fæstnes.* See FAST[1], -NESS]

Fast′ of Es′ther, *Judaism.* See **Taanith Esther.**

Fast′ of Ged·a·li′ah (ged′ə lī′ə, gi dal′yə), *Judaism.* See **Tzom Gedaliah.**

fast′ one′, *Informal.* a shrewd action, esp. when unscrupulous or dishonest; an unfair trick, deceitful practice, dishonest dealing, etc.: *He pulled a fast one on me by paying me with a worthless check.* [1920–25, *Amer.*]

fast-talk (fast′tôk′, fäst′-), *v.t.* to persuade with facile argument, usually with the intention to deceive or to overwhelm rational objections: *The salesperson tried to fast-talk me into buying a suit I didn't want.* [1945–50, *Amer.*]

fast′ tel′egram, 1. a type of domestic telegram sent at full rate with a minimum charge for 10 words or less and accepted for immediate delivery. **2.** the service offering such a telegram. Cf. **overnight telegram, personal-opinion telegram.**

fast′ time′, *Informal.* See **daylight-saving time.** [1930–35, *Amer.*]

fast′ track′, 1. a racetrack dry and hard enough for optimum speed. **2.** a railroad track for express trains. **3.** *Informal.* a situation or course of action that is intensely pressured or competitive, esp. one in which a person advances rapidly to a higher level in a business or profession: *With two promotions in six months, he seems to have chosen the fast track.* **4. on a** or **the fast track,** *Informal.* **a.** advancing or being promoted more rapidly than usual, esp. in business or other organizational positions: *an executive on the fast track.* **b.** expanding or being developed or handled rapidly and often innovatively: *a company on the fast track in computer technology.* Cf. **fast lane.**

fast-track (fast′trak′, fäst′-), *v.i., v.t.* **1.** to advance or develop rapidly. —*adj.* **2.** of or pertaining to the fast track. **—fast′-track′er,** *n.*

fast-twitch (fast′twich′, fäst′-), *adj. Physiol.* of or pertaining to muscle fiber that contracts relatively rapidly, utilized esp. in actions requiring maximum effort of short duration, as sprinting (distinguished from *slow-twitch*). Also, **fast′twitch′.**

fas·tu·ous (fas′cho͞o əs), *adj.* **1.** haughty; arrogant. **2.** showy; ostentatious. [1630–40; < L *fastuōsus,* equiv. to *fastu(s)* haughtiness, arrogance (cf. FASTIDIOUS) + *-ōsus* -OUS] **—fas′tu·ous·ly,** *adv.*

fast′ work′er, *Informal.* **1.** a person who is quick and shrewd in gaining personal advantage: *A fast worker, he soon knew everyone who had any pull.* **2.** a person who charms or fast-talks members of the opposite sex easily. [1920–25]

fat (fat), *adj.,* **fat·ter, fat·test,** *n., v.,* **fat·ted, fat·ting.** —*adj.* **1.** having too much flabby tissue; corpulent; obese: *a fat person.* **2.** plump; well-fed: *a good, fat chicken.* **3.** consisting of or containing fat; greasy; oily: *fat gravy; fat meat.* **4.** profitable, as an office: *a fat job on the city commission.* **5.** affording good opportunities, esp. for gain: *a fat business contract.* **6.** wealthy; prosperous; rich: *He grew fat on dishonest profits.* **7.** big, broad, or extended; thick: *a fat sheaf of bills.* **8.** plentiful; abundant: *a fat supply of food.* **9.** plentifully supplied: *a fat larder; a fat feast.* **10.** dull; stupid: *fat clumsiness of manner.* **11.** abounding in a particular element: *Fat pine is rich in resin.* **12.** (of paint) having more oil than pigment. Cf. **lean**[2] (def. 6). **13.** (of coal) highly bituminous; rich in volatile hydrocarbons. **14.** *Ceram.* long[1] (def. 25). **15.** fertile, as land: *Everything grows in this fat soil.* **16. a fat chance,** *Slang.* a very slight chance; small probability: *A fat chance he has of winning the title!* **17. a fat lot,** *Slang.* little or not at all: *A fat lot they care about anyone else's troubles!* —*n.* **18.** any of several white or yellowish greasy substances, forming the chief part of adipose tissue of animals and also occurring in plants, that when pure are colorless, odorless, and tasteless and are either solid or liquid esters of glycerol with fatty acids; fats are insoluble in water or cold alcohol but soluble in ether, chloroform, or benzene: used in the manufacture of soap, paints, and other protective coatings and in cooking. **19.** animal tissue containing much of this substance; loose flesh; flabbiness: *to have rolls of fat around one's waist.* **20.** the richest or best part of anything. **21.** obesity; corpulence: *In his later years, he inclined to fat.* **22.** *Slang.* especially profitable or advantageous work. **23.** an overabundance or excess; superfluity. **24.** action or lines in a dramatic part that permit an actor to display abilities. **25.** Also, **phat.** Also called **lift.** *Typesetting.* matter that can be composed easily and profitably, esp. from standing type, illustrations, or the like: *fat work.* Cf. **lean**[2] (def. 11). **26. chew the fat.** See **chew** (def. 9). **27. the fat is in the fire, a.** an irrevocable action or chain of events has been started; the die is cast: *Now that they have been given an ultimatum, the fat is in the fire.* **b.** the decision, whether good or bad, has been made. **c.** the crisis is imminent. **28. the fat of the land,** the best or richest of anything obtainable: *to live on the fat of the land.* —*v.t., v.i.* **29.** to make or become fat. [bef. 1000; ME; OE *fǣtt,* orig. ptp. of *fǣtan* to cram, load, adorn; c. Goth *fētjan* to adorn; akin to VAT] **—fat′less,** *adj.* **—fat′like′,** *adj.*
—Syn. 1. portly, adipose, pudgy. See **stout. 3.** unctuous, fatty. **4.** lucrative, remunerative. **8.** copious. **10.** sluggish. **15.** rich, fruitful, productive. **—Ant. 1.** thin. **3.** lean. **10.** clever. **15.** sterile, barren.

fa·tal (fāt′l), *adj.* **1.** causing or capable of causing death; mortal; deadly: *a fatal accident; a fatal dose of poison.* **2.** causing destruction, misfortune, ruin, or failure: *The withdrawal of funds was fatal to the project.* **3.** decisively important; fateful: *The fatal day finally arrived.* **4.** proceeding from or decreed by fate; inevitable: *a fatal series of events.* **5.** influencing or concerned with fate; fatalistic. **6.** *Obs.* doomed. **7.** *Obs.* prophetic. [1350–1400; ME (< OF) < L *fātālis* of fate. See FATE, -AL[1]] **—fa′tal·ness,** *n.*
—Syn. 1. FATAL, DEADLY, LETHAL, MORTAL apply to something that has caused or is capable of causing death. FATAL may refer to either the future or the past; in either case, it emphasizes inevitability and the inescapable—the disastrous, whether death or dire misfortune: *The accident was fatal. Such a mistake would be fatal.* DEADLY looks to the future, and suggests that which is likely to cause death (though not inevitably so): *a deadly poison, disease.* Like DEADLY, LETHAL looks to the future but, like many other words of Latin origin, suggests a more technical usage: *a lethal dose; a gas that is lethal.* MORTAL looks to the past and refers to death that has actually occurred: *He received a mortal wound. The disease proved to be mortal.* **2.** ruinous, disastrous, calamitous, catastrophic, devastating. **4.** predestined, foreordained. **—Ant. 1.** life-giving.

fa·tal·ism (fāt′l iz′əm), *n.* **1.** the acceptance of all things and events as inevitable; submission to fate: *Her fatalism helped her to face death with stoic calm.* **2.** *Philos.* the doctrine that all events are subject to fate or inevitable predetermination. [1670–80; FATAL + -ISM] **—fa′tal·ist,** *n.* **—fa′tal·is′tic,** *adj.* **—fa′tal·is′ti·cal·ly,** *adv.*

fa·tal·i·ty (fā tal′i tē, fə-), *n., pl.* **-ties. 1.** a disaster resulting in death. **2.** a death resulting from such an occurrence: *a rise in highway fatalities.* **3.** the quality of causing death or disaster; a fatal influence; deadliness. **4.** predetermined liability to disaster, misfortune, etc.: *a fatality for saying the wrong thing.* **5.** the quality of being predetermined by or subject to fate: *There is a fatality in human affairs that leads to destruction.* **6.** the fate or destiny of a person or thing: *Death is the ultimate fatality of all human beings.* **7.** a fixed, unalterably predetermined course of things; inevitability: *to resign oneself to the fatality of life.* [1480–90; < LL *fātālitās.* See FATAL, -ITY]

fa·tal·ly (fāt′l ē), *adv.* **1.** in a manner leading to death or disaster: *He was injured fatally in the accident.* **2.** by a decree of fate or destiny; by inevitable predetermination. [1375–1425; late ME; see FATAL, -LY]

Fa·ta Mor·ga·na (*It.* fä′tä môr gä′nä), *Meteorol.* a mirage consisting of multiple images, as of cliffs and buildings, that are distorted and magnified to resemble elaborate castles, often seen near the Straits of Messina. [1810–20; < It, trans. of MORGAN LE FAY, associated in literature with magical castles]

fat·back (fat′bak′), *n.* **1.** *Chiefly South Midland and Southern U.S.* the fat and fat meat from the upper part of a side of pork, usually cured by salt. **2.** a menhaden. **3.** the bluefish, *Pomatomus saltatrix.* **4.** a mullet. [1700–10, *Amer.;* FAT + BACK[1]]

fat·bod·y (fat′bod′ē), *n., pl.* **-bod·ies.** *Entomol.* a diffuse tissue of insects, having numerous functions including food storage, metabolism, and storage of wastes and in some insects modified as a light-producing organ. Also, **fat′ body′, fat′-bod′y.** [1865–70; FAT + BODY]

fat′ cat′, *Slang.* **1.** a wealthy person from whom large political campaign contributions are expected. **2.** any wealthy person, esp. one who has become rich quickly through questionable dealings. **3.** an important, influential, or famous person. **4.** a person who has become lazy or self-satisfied as the result of privilege or advantage. [1925–30, *Amer.*]

fat′ cell′, *Biol.* a cell in loose connective tissue that is specialized for the synthesis and storage of fat. Also called **adipocyte.** [1910–15]

Fat′ Cit′y, *Slang.* an easy and prosperous condition or circumstance: *With a new house and a better-paying job, she's in Fat City.* Also, **fat′ cit′y.** [1960–65]

fat′ de′pot. See **adipose tissue.** [1945–50]

fate (fāt), *n., v.,* **fat·ed, fat·ing.** —*n.* **1.** something that unavoidably befalls a person; fortune; lot: *It is always his fate to be left behind.* **2.** the universal principle or ultimate agency by which the order of things is presumably prescribed; the decreed cause of events; time: *Fate decreed that they would never meet again.* **3.** that which is inevitably predetermined; destiny: *Death is our ineluctable fate.* **4.** a prophetic declaration of what must be: *The oracle pronounced their fate.* **5.** death, destruction, or ruin. **6. the Fates,** *Class. Myth.* the three goddesses of destiny, known to the Greeks as the Moerae and to the Romans as the Parcae. —*v.t.* **7.** to predetermine, as by the decree of fate; destine (used in the passive): *a person who was fated to be the savior of the country.* [1325–75; ME < L *fātum* utterance, decree of fate, destiny, orig. neut. of *fātus,* ptp. of *fārī* to speak]
—Syn. 1. karma, kismet; chance, luck. FATE, DESTINY, DOOM refer to the idea of a fortune, usually adverse, that is predetermined and inescapable. The three words are frequently interchangeable. FATE stresses the irrationality and impersonal character of events: *It was Napoleon's fate to be exiled.* The word is often lightly used, however: *It was my fate to meet her that very afternoon.* DESTINY emphasizes the idea of an unalterable course of events, and is often used of a propitious fortune: *It was his destiny to save his nation.* DOOM esp. applies to the final ending, always unhappy or terrible, brought about by destiny or fate: *He met his doom bravely.* **7.** foreordain, preordain.

fat·ed (fā′tid), *adj.* subject to, guided by, or predetermined by fate; destined. [1595–1605; FATE + -ED[3]]

fate·ful (fāt′fəl), *adj.* **1.** having momentous significance or consequences; decisively important; portentous: *a fateful meeting between the leaders of the two countries.* **2.** fatal, deadly, or disastrous. **3.** controlled or determined by destiny; inexorable. **4.** prophetic; ominous. [1705–15; FATE + -FUL] **—fate′ful·ly,** *adv.* **—fate′ful·ness,** *n.*
—Syn. 1, 4. See **ominous.**

fate′ map′, *Embryol.* a diagram or series of diagrams indicating the later structures or adult parts that develop from specific regions of an embryo or egg cortex.

fat′ farm′, *Informal.* a sanitarium or a resort that specializes in helping people lose weight. [1965–70]

fath, fathom (def. 1).

fat·head (fat′hed′), *n.* **1.** *Slang.* a stupid person; fool. **2.** sheephead. **3.** See **fathead minnow.** [1830–40; FAT + HEAD]

fat·head·ed (fat′hed′id), *adj.* foolish; fatuous; witless. [1500–10, for literal sense; FATHEAD + -ED[3]] **—fat′·head′ed·ly,** *adv.* **—fat′head′ed·ness,** *n.*

fat′head min′now, a North American cyprinid fish,

Pimephales promelas, having an enlarged, soft head. Also called **fathead.**

fa•ther (fä′thər), *n.* **1.** a male parent. **2.** a father-in-law, stepfather, or adoptive father. **3.** any male ancestor, esp. the founder of a race, family, or line; progenitor. **4.** a man who exercises paternal care over other persons; paternal protector or provider: *a father to the poor.* **5.** a person who has originated or established something: *the father of modern psychology; the founding fathers.* **6.** a precursor, prototype, or early form: *The horseless carriage was the father of the modern automobile.* **7.** one of the leading men in a city, town, etc.: *a scandal involving several of the city fathers.* **8.** *Chiefly Brit.* the oldest member of a society, profession, etc. Cf. **dean**[1] (def. 3). **9.** a priest. **10.** (*cap.*) *Theol.* the Supreme Being and Creator; God. **11.** a title of respect for an elderly man. **12. the Father,** *Theol.* the first person of the Trinity. **13.** Also called **church father.** *Ch. Hist.* any of the chief early Christian writers, whose works are the main sources for the history, doctrines, and observances of the church in the early ages. **14.** *Eccles.* **a.** (*often cap.*) a title of reverence, as for church dignitaries, officers of monasteries, monks, confessors, and esp. priests. **b.** a person bearing this title. **15. fathers,** *Rom. Hist.* See **conscript fathers.** —*v.t.* **16.** to beget. **17.** to be the creator, founder, or author of; originate. **18.** to act as a father toward. **19.** to acknowledge oneself the father of. **20.** to assume as one's own; take the responsibility of. **21.** to charge with the begetting of. —*v.i.* **22.** to perform the tasks or duties of a male parent; act paternally: *Somehow he was able to write a book while fathering.* [bef. 900; ME *fader,* OE *fæder;* c. G *Vater,* L *pater,* Gk *patḗr,* Skt *pitar,* OIr *athir,* Armenian *hayr*] —**fa′ther•like′,** *adj.*

Fa′ther Christ′mas, *Brit.* See **Santa Claus.** [1650–60]

fa′ther confes′sor, *Eccles.* confessor (def. 2).

fa′ther fig′ure, a man embodying or seeming to embody the qualities of an idealized conception of the male parent, eliciting from others the emotional responses that a child typically has toward its father. Also called **fa′ther im′age.** [1930–35]

fa•ther•hood (fä′thər ho͝od′), *n.* **1.** the state of being a father. **2.** fathers collectively. **3.** the qualities or spirit of a father. [1350–1400; late ME *faderhode;* r. ME *faderheed.* See FATHER, -HOOD]

fa•ther-in-law (fä′thər in lô′), *n., pl.* **fa•thers-in-law.** the father of one's husband or wife. [1350–1400; ME; see FATHER, IN, LAW[1]]

fa•ther•land (fä′thər land′), *n.* **1.** one's native country. **2.** the land of one's ancestors. [1615–25; FATHER + LAND]

fa•ther•less (fä′thər lis), *adj.* **1.** not having a living father: *a fatherless boy.* **2.** not having a known or legally responsible father. [bef. 1000; ME *faderles,* OE *fæderlēas.* See FATHER, -LESS]

fa•ther•ly (fä′thər lē), *adj.* **1.** of, like, or befitting a father. —*adv.* **2.** *Obs.* in the manner of a father. [bef. 1000; ME *faderly,* OE *fæderlic.* See FATHER, -LY] —**fa′•ther•li•ness,** *n.*
—**Syn. 1.** FATHERLY, PATERNAL refer to the relationship of a male parent to his children. FATHERLY has emotional connotations; it always suggests a kind, protective, tender, or forbearing attitude: *fatherly advice.* PATERNAL may suggest a kindly, proprietary attitude: *paternal interest;* but it may also be used objectively, as a legal and official term: *his paternal grandmother; paternal estate.*

Fa′ther's Day′, a day, usually the third Sunday in June, set aside in honor of fathers.

fa′ther sub′stitute, *Psychol.* a male who replaces an absent father and becomes an object of attachment. Also called **fa′ther sur′rogate.** [1935–40]

Fa′ther Time′, the personification of time as an old man, usually in a white robe, having a white beard, and carrying a scythe.

fath•o•gram (fath′ə gram′), *n.* the record made by a sonic depth finder. [1945–50; FATHO(METER) + -GRAM[1]]

fath•om (fath′əm), *n., pl.* **fath•oms,** (*esp. collectively*) **fath•om,** *v.* —*n.* **1.** a unit of length equal to six feet (1.8 meters): used chiefly in nautical measurements. *Abbr.:* fath —*v.t.* **2.** to measure the depth of by means of a sounding line; sound. **3.** to penetrate to the truth of; comprehend; understand: *to fathom someone's motives.* [bef. 900; ME *fathme,* OE *fæthm* span of outstretched arms; c. G *Faden* six-foot measure, ON *fathmr;* akin to PATENT] —**fath′om•a•ble,** *adj.* —**fath′om•er,** *n.*

Fa•thom•e•ter (fa thom′i tər), *Trademark.* a brand of sonic depth finder.

fath•om•less (fath′əm lis), *adj.* **1.** impossible to measure the depth of; bottomless. **2.** impossible to understand; incomprehensible: *fathomless motives.* [1600–10; FATHOM + -LESS] —**fath′om•less•ly,** *adv.*

fa•tid•ic (fā tid′ik, fə-), *adj.* prophetic. Also, **fa•tid′i•cal.** [1665–75; < L *fātidicus,* equiv. to *fāti-* (comb. form of *fātum* FATE) + *-dicus* one who utters, deriv. of *dīcere* to say] —**fa•tid′i•cal•ly,** *adv.*

fat•i•ga•ble (fat′i gə bəl), *adj.* susceptible to fatigue. [1600–10; < L *fatīgābilis,* equiv. to *fatīgā(re)* to tire + *-bilis* -BLE] —**fat′i•ga•ble•ness, fat′i•ga•bil′i•ty,** *n.*

fa•tigue (fə tēg′), *n., adj., v.,* **-tigued, -ti•guing.** —*n.* **1.** weariness from bodily or mental exertion. **2.** a cause of weariness; slow ordeal; exertion: *the fatigue of driving for many hours.* **3.** *Physiol.* temporary diminution of the irritability or functioning of organs, tissues, or cells after excessive exertion or stimulation. **4.** *Civ. Engin.* the weakening or breakdown of material subjected to stress, esp. a repeated series of stresses. **5.** Also called **fatigue′ du′ty.** *Mil.* **a.** labor of a generally nonmilitary kind done by soldiers, such as cleaning up an area, digging drainage ditches, or raking leaves. **b.** the state of being engaged in such labor: *on fatigue.* **6. fatigues,** *Mil.* See **fatigue clothes.** —*adj.* **7.** of or pertaining to fatigues or any clothing made to resemble them: *The guerrilla band wore fatigue pants and field jackets. She brought fatigue shorts to wear on the hike.* —*v.t.* **8.** to weary with bodily or mental exertion; exhaust the strength of: *Endless chatter fatigues me.* **9.** *Civ. Engin.* to subject (a material) to fatigue. —*v.i.* **10.** to become fatigued. **11.** *Civ. Engin.* (of a material) to undergo fatigue. [1685–95; < F *fatigue* (n.), *fatiguer* (v.) < L *fatīgāre* to tire] —**fa•tigue′less,** *adj.* —**fa•ti′guing•ly,** *adv.*
—**Syn. 8.** tire, debilitate, enervate.

fatigue′ clothes′, a soldier's uniform for fatigue duty. Also called **fatigues.** [1830–40]

fa•tigued (fə tēgd′), *adj.* tired; wearied. [1785–95; FATIGUE + -ED[2]]
—**Syn.** See **tired**[1].

fatigue′ life′, the number of applications of a given stress to which a sample of metal can be subjected before failing.

fatigue′ lim′it, the maximum stress to which a material can be subjected without failing. [1910–15]

fatigue′ ra′tio, the ratio between the fatigue limit and the tensile strength of a material. Also called **endurance ratio.**

Fa•ti•ha (fä′tē hä′), *n. Islam.* the first chapter of the Koran, recited at the beginning of every rak'ah. [< Ar *fātihah* exordium]

Fat•i•ma (fat′ə mə, fä′tē mä′), *n.* **1.** A.D. 606?–632, daughter of Muhammad and wife of Ali. **2.** the seventh and last wife of Bluebeard, popularly a symbol for feminine curiosity. **3.** a female given name.

Fá•ti•ma (fä′ti mə), *n.* a village in central Portugal, N of Lisbon: Roman Catholic shrine.

Fat•i•mid (fat′ə mid), *n.* **1.** any caliph of the North African dynasty, 909–1171, claiming descent from Fatima and Ali. **2.** any descendant of Fatima and Ali. Also, **Fat•i•mite** (fat′ə mīt′). [1720–30]

fat•ling (fat′ling), *n.* a young animal, as a calf or a lamb, fattened for slaughter. [1520–30; FAT + -LING[1]]

fat′ lip′, a swollen mouth or lip, as from a blow: *He said if I didn't shut up he'd give me a fat lip.*

fat•ly (fat′lē), *adv.* **1.** in the manner of a fat person; ponderously. **2.** richly: *a fatly endowed foundation.* **3.** with self-satisfaction; smugly. [1505–15; FAT + -LY]

Fat′ Man′, the code name for the plutonium-core, implosion-type atom bomb the U.S. first tested and then dropped on Nagasaki in 1945. Cf. **Little Boy.**

fat′ meat′, *Chiefly Southern U.S.* fatback (def. 1).

fat•ness (fat′nis), *n.* **1.** the state or condition of being fat; obesity; corpulence. **2.** richness; fertility; abundance: *the fatness of the land.* [bef. 1000; ME *fatnesse,* OE *fǣtnes.* See FAT, -NESS]

fat′ pine′, *Midland and Southern U.S.* lightwood. [1665–75, *Amer.*]

fats (fats), *n.* (*used with a plural v.*) cattle fattened and ready for market. [pl. of FAT]

Fat•shan (fät′shän′), *n. Older Spelling.* Foshan.

fat•si•a (fat′sē ə), *n.* a shrub or small tree, *Fatsia japonica,* of the ginseng family, having large, glossy, palmately compound leaves and often grown as a houseplant. [< NL, perh. irreg. < Japn *yatsude* the name of the plant]

fat•so (fat′sō), *n., pl.* **-sos, -soes.** *Slang.* a fat person (often used as a disparaging and offensive term of address). [1940–45; perh. *Fats* a nickname for a fat person (see FAT, -S[4]) + -O; also compared with *fat sow,* G *Fettsau*]

fat-sol•u•ble (fat′sol′yə bəl), *adj. Chem.* soluble in oils or fats. [1920–25]

fat•stock (fat′stok′), *n. Chiefly Brit.* livestock that has been fattened for market. [1875–80; FAT + STOCK]

fat′-tailed sheep′ (fat′tāld′), one of a class of sheep with much fat along the sides of the tail bones, raised for their meat and widely distributed in southeast Europe, northern Africa, and Asia. [1835–45]

fat•ten (fat′n), *v.t.* **1.** to make fat. **2.** to feed (animals) abundantly before slaughter. **3.** to enrich: *to fatten the soil; to fatten one's pocketbook.* **4.** *Cards.* **a.** *Poker.* to increase the number of chips in (a pot). **b.** *Pinochle.* to play a card that scores high on (a trick) expected to be taken by a partner. —*v.i.* **5.** to grow fat. [1545–55; FAT + -EN[1]] —**fat′ten•a•ble,** *adj.* —**fat′ten•er,** *n.*

fat•tish (fat′ish), *adj.* somewhat fat. [1325–75; ME; see FAT, -ISH[1]] —**fat′tish•ness,** *n.*

fat•ty[1] (fat′ē), *adj.,* **-ti•er, -ti•est.** —*adj.* **1.** consisting of, containing, or resembling fat: *fatty tissue.* **2.** *Pathol.* characterized by overproduction or excessive accumulation of fat. [1350–1400; ME; see FAT, -Y[1]] —**fat′ti•ly,** *adv.* —**fat′ti•ness,** *n.*

fat•ty[2] (fat′ē), *n., pl.* **-ties.** *Informal (often disparaging and offensive).* a person who is overweight or obese. [1790–1800; FAT + -Y[2]]

fat′ty ac′id, *Biochem.* any of a class of aliphatic acids, esp. palmitic, stearic, or oleic acid, consisting of a long hydrocarbon chain ending in a carboxyl group that bonds to glycerol to form a fat. [1860–65]

fat′ty degenera′tion, *Pathol.* deterioration of the cells of the body, accompanied by the formation of fat globules within the diseased cells. [1875–80]

fat′ty oil′. *Chem.* See **fixed oil.** [1825–35]

fat′ty tu′mor, *Pathol.* lipoma. [1795–1805]

fa•tu•i•tous (fə to͞o′i təs, -tyo͞o′-), *adj.* complacently stupid; foolish. [1725–35; FATUIT(Y) + -OUS] —**fa•tu′i•tous•ness,** *n.*

fa•tu•i•ty (fə to͞o′i tē, -tyo͞o′-), *n., pl.* **-ties.** **1.** complacent stupidity; foolishness. **2.** something foolish; bêtise. [1530–40; < L *fatuitās.* See FATUOUS, -ITY]

fat•u•ous (fach′o͞o əs), *adj.* **1.** foolish or inane, esp. in an unconscious, complacent manner; silly. **2.** unreal; illusory. [1625–35; < L *fatuus* silly, foolish, idiotic; see -OUS] —**fat′u•ous•ly,** *adv.* —**fat′u•ous•ness,** *n.*
—**Syn. 1.** dense, dull, dim-witted. See **foolish.**

fat•wa (fät′wä), *n.* an Islamic religious decree issued by the 'ulama. [1985–90; < Ar *fatwā*]

fat-wit•ted (fat′wit′id), *adj.* stupid; dull-witted. [1590–1600]

fat•wood (fat′wo͝od′), *n. South Atlantic States.* kindling; lightwood. [1905–10; FAT + WOOD[1]]

fau•bourg (fō′bo͝or, -bo͞org; *Fr.* fō bo͞or′), *n., pl.* **-bourgs** (-bo͝orz, -bo͞orgz; *Fr.* -bo͞or′). a suburb or a quarter just outside a French city. [1425–75; late ME *faubourgh* < MF *fau(x)bourg,* alter., by assoc. with *faux* FALSE, of OF *forsborc,* equiv. to *fors-* outside of (< L *foris* outside; cf. FOREIGN) + *borc* city < < Gmc (see BOROUGH)]

fau•cal (fô′kəl), *adj.* **1.** pertaining to the fauces or opening of the throat. **2.** *Phonet.* **a.** pharyngeal. **b.** exploded into the pharynx, as the release of the *t*-sound of *catnip* or the *d*-sound of *madness.* [1860–65; FAUC(ES) + -AL[1]]

fau•car•i•a (fô kâr′ē ə), *n.* any succulent plant of the genus *Faucaria,* comprising several species native to southern Africa and having solitary yellow or white flowers. [< NL (1926), perh. equiv. to L *fauc(ēs)* throat, narrow passage + *-āria* -ARIA]

fau•ces (fô′sēz), *n., pl.* **-ces.** **1.** *Anat.* the cavity at the back of the mouth, leading into the pharynx. **2.** a vestibule of an ancient Roman house. [1375–1425; late ME < L] —**fau•cial** (fô′shəl), *adj.*

fau•cet (fô′sit), *n.* any device for controlling the flow of liquid from a pipe or the like by opening or closing an orifice; tap; cock. [1350–1400; ME < MF *fausset* peg for a vent, perh. equiv. to *fauss(er)* to force in, damage, warp, lit., to falsify (< LL *falsāre;* see FALSE) + *-et* -ET]
—**Regional Variation.** SPIGOT is a common variant for FAUCET and is widely used in the Midland U.S. In the Northern U.S., FAUCET is more commonly used.

fau•chard (fō shär′; *Fr.* fō SHAR′), *n., pl.* **-chards** (-shärz′; *Fr.* -SHAR′). a shafted weapon having a knifelike blade with a convex cutting edge and a beak on the back for catching the blade of an aggressor's weapon. [< F; OF *fauchart,* equiv. to *fauch(er)* to cut with a scythe (< VL **falcāre,* deriv. of L *falx,* s. *falc-* sickle) + *-art* -ART]

faugh (pf; *spelling pron.* fô), *interj.* (used to express contempt or disgust.) [1535–45]

fauld (fôld), *n. Armor.* a piece below the breastplate, composed of lames and corresponding to the culet in back. See diag. under **armor.** [var. of FOLD[1]]

Faulk•ner (fôk′nər), *n.* **William,** 1897–1962, U.S. novelist and short-story writer. Nobel prize 1949.

Faulk•ner•i•an (fôk nēr′ē ən), *adj.* of, pertaining to, characteristic of, or resembling the literary style of William Faulkner. [1950–55, *Amer.;* FAULKNER + -IAN]

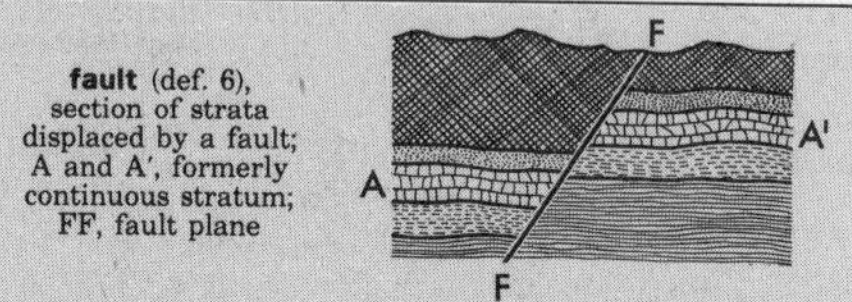

fault (def. 6), section of strata displaced by a fault; A and A′, formerly continuous stratum; FF, fault plane

fault (fôlt), *n.* **1.** a defect or imperfection; flaw; failing: *a fault in the brakes; a fault in one's character.* **2.** responsibility for failure or a wrongful act: *It is my fault that we have not finished.* **3.** an error or mistake: *a fault in addition.* **4.** a misdeed or transgression: *to confess one's faults.* **5.** *Sports.* (in tennis, handball, etc.) **a.** a ball that when served does not land in the proper section of an opponent's court. **b.** a failure to serve the ball according to the rules, as from within a certain area. **6.** *Geol., Mining.* a break in the continuity of a body of rock or of a vein, with dislocation along the plane of the fracture (**fault plane**). **7.** *Manège.* (of a horse jumping in a show) any of a number of improper executions in negotiating a jump, as a tick, knockdown, refusal, or run-out. **8.** *Elect.* a partial or total local failure in the insulation or continuity of a conductor or in the functioning of an electric system. **9.** *Hunting.* a break in the line of scent; a losing of the scent; check. **10.** *Obs.* lack; want. **11. at fault, a.** open to censure; blameworthy: *to be at fault for a mistake.* **b.** in a dilemma; puzzled: *to be at fault as to where to go.* **c.** (of hounds) unable to find the scent. **12. find fault,** to seek and make known defects or flaws; complain; criticize: *He constantly found fault with my behavior.* **13. to a fault,** to an extreme degree; excessively: *She was generous to a fault.* —*v.i.* **14.** to commit a fault; blunder; err. **15.** *Geol.* to undergo faulting. —*v.t.* **16.** *Geol.* to cause a fault in. **17.** to find fault with, blame, or censure. [1250–1300; ME *faute* < AF, MF < VL **fallita,* n. use of fem. of **fallitus,* for L *falsus,* ptp. of *fallere* to be wrong]
—**Syn. 1.** blemish; frailty, shortcoming. FAULT, FAILING, FOIBLE, WEAKNESS, VICE imply shortcomings or imperfections in a person. FAULT is the common word used to refer to any of the average shortcomings of a person; when it is used, condemnation is not necessarily implied: *Of his many faults the greatest is vanity.* FOIBLE, FAILING, WEAKNESS all tend to excuse the person referred to. Of these FOIBLE is the mildest, suggesting a weak point

that is slight and often amusing, manifesting itself in eccentricity rather than in wrongdoing: *the foibles of artists.* WEAKNESS suggests that the person in question is unable to control a particular impulse, and gives way to self-indulgence: *a weakness for pretty women.* FAILING is closely akin to FAULT, except that it is particularly applied to humanity at large, suggesting common, often venial, shortcomings: *Procrastination and making excuses are common failings.* VICE (which may also apply to a sin in itself, apart from a person: *the vice of gambling*) is the strongest term, and designates a habit that is truly detrimental or evil. **—Ant. 1.** virtue, strength, merit.

fault′ block′, *Geol.* a mass of rock bounded on at least two opposite sides by faults. Cf. **block faulting.** [1895–1900]

fault′ brec′cia, *Geol.* angular rock fragments produced by fracture and grinding during faulting and distributed within or adjacent to the fault plane. [1890–95]

fault·find·er (fôlt′fīn′dər), *n.* a person who habitually finds fault, complains, or objects, esp. in a petty way. [1555–65; FAULT + FINDER]

fault·find·ing (fôlt′fīn′ding), *n.* **1.** the act of pointing out faults, esp. faults of a petty nature; carping. *—adj.* **2.** tending to find fault; disposed to complain or object; captious. [1620–30; FAULT + FINDING] **—Syn. 2.** critical, censorious.

fault·less (fôlt′lis), *adj.* without fault, flaw, or defect; perfect. [1300–50; ME *fautles.* See FAULT, -LESS] **—fault′less·ly,** *adv.* **—fault′less·ness,** *n.* **—Syn.** flawless, impeccable, exemplary, irreproachable.

fault′ line′, *Geol.* the intersection of a fault with the surface of the earth or other plane of reference. [1865–70]

fault′ plane′, *Geol.* See under **fault** (def. 6). [1885–90]

fault′ scarp′, *Geol.* scarp[1] (def. 1). [1895–1900]

fault·y (fôl′tē), *adj.,* **fault·i·er, fault·i·est.** having faults or defects; imperfect. [1300–50; ME *fauty.* See FAULT, -Y[1]] **—fault′i·ly,** *adv.* **—fault′i·ness,** *n.*

fault′ zone′, *Geol.* a network of interconnected fractures representing the surficial expression of a fault. [1930–35]

faun (fôn), *n. Class. Myth.* one of a class of rural deities represented as men with the ears, horns, tail, and later also the hind legs of a goat. [1325–75; ME (< OF *faune*) < L *faunus;* cf. FAUNUS] **—faun′like′,** *adj.*

fau·na (fô′nə), *n., pl.* **-nas, -nae** (-nē). **1.** the animals of a given region or period considered as a whole. **2.** a treatise on the animals of a given region or period. **3.** (*cap.*) *Rom. Relig.* See **Bona Dea.** [1765–75; < NL, special use of L *Fauna,* a feminine counterpart to FAUNUS; cf. FLORA] **—fau′nal,** *adj.* **—fau′nal·ly,** *adv.*

Faun′tleroy suit′, a formal outfit for a boy composed of a hip-length jacket and knee-length pants, often in black velvet, and a wide, lacy collar and cuffs, usually worn with a broad sash at the waist and sometimes a large, loose bow at the neck, popular in the late 19th century. Also called **Lord Fauntleroy suit, Little Lord Fauntleroy suit.** [after the title character of the novel *Little Lord Fauntleroy* (1886) by F. H. Burnett]

Fau·nus (fô′nəs), *n.* an ancient Italian woodland deity, later identified with Pan.

Fau·ré (fō rā′), *n.* **Ga·bri·el Ur·bain** (ga brē el′ o͞or-ban′), 1845–1924, French composer.

Faust (foust), *n.* **1. Jo·hann** (yō′hän), c1480–c1538, German magician, alchemist, and astrologer. **2.** the chief character of a medieval legend, represented as selling his soul to the devil in exchange for knowledge and power. **3.** (*italics*) a tragedy by Goethe (Part 1, 1808; Part 2, 1832). **4.** (*italics*) an opera (1859) by Charles Gounod.

Faus·ti·an (fou′stē ən), *adj.* **1.** of, pertaining to, or characteristic of Faust: *a Faustian novel.* **2.** sacrificing spiritual values for power, knowledge, or material gain: *a Faustian pact with the Devil.* **3.** characterized by spiritual dissatisfaction or torment. **4.** possessed with a hunger for knowledge or mastery. [1875–80; FAUST + -IAN]

Faus·tus (fou′stəs, fô′-), *n.* See **Doctor Faustus.**

faute de mieux (fōt də myœ′), *French.* for lack of something better. [1760–70]

fau·teuil (fō′til; *Fr.* fō tœ′yᵊ), *n., pl.* **-teuils** (-tilz; *Fr.* -tœ′yᵊ). *Fr. Furniture.* an upholstered armchair, esp. one with open sides. Cf. **bergère.** [1735–45; < F; OF *faldestoel, faudestueil* < Old Low Franconian **faldistôl;* see FALDSTOOL]

Fauve (fōv), *n.* (*sometimes l.c.*) any of a group of French artists of the early 20th century whose works are characterized chiefly by the use of vivid colors in immediate juxtaposition and contours usually in marked contrast to the color of the area defined. [1910–15; < F: wild beast, n. use of *fauve* wild, lit., tawny < Gmc; see FALLOW[2]] **—Fauv′ism,** *n.* **—Fauv′ist,** *n.*

faux (fō), *adj.* artificial or imitation; fake: *a brooch with faux pearls.* [1670–80; < F; OF *fals* < L *falsus* FALSE]

faux·bour·don (fō′bər don′; *Fr.* fō bo͞or dôn′), *n.* **1.** *Music.* a 15th-century compositional technique employing three voices, the upper and lower voices progressing an octave or a sixth apart while the middle voice extemporaneously doubles the upper part at a fourth below. **2.** the use of progressions of parallel sixth chords. [1875–80; < F: lit., false bourdon]

faux-na·ïf (fō′nä ēf′), *adj.* **1.** marked by a pretense of simplicity or innocence; disingenuous. *—n.* **2.** a person who shrewdly affects an attitude or pose of simplicity or innocence. [1940–45; < F; see FAUX, NAIVE]

faux pas (fō pä′), *pl.* **faux pas** (fō päz′; *Fr.* fō pä′). a slip or blunder in etiquette, manners, or conduct; an embarrassing social blunder or indiscretion. [1670–80; < F: lit., false step] **—Syn.** error; impropriety.

fa′va bean′ (fä′və), **1.** a plant, *Vicia faba,* native to the Old World, bearing large pods containing edible seeds. **2.** the seed or pod of this plant. Also called **broad bean, horse bean.** [1940–45; < It < L *faba* bean]

fave (fāv), *n., adj. Slang.* favorite. [by shortening]

fa·ve·la (fə vel′ə; *Port.* fä ve′lä), *n.* a shantytown in or near a city, esp. in Brazil; slum area. [1945–50; < Brazilian Pg: alleged to be a name given to a hill in the vicinity of Rio de Janeiro, where such towns were built ca. 1900; lit., a shrub of the family Euphorbiaceae, deriv. of Pg *fava* bean < L *faba*]

fa·ve·la·do (fä′və lä′dō, fə vel ä′-; *Port.* fä′ve lä′-do͞o), *n., pl.* **-dos** (-dōz; *Port.* -do͞os). a person who lives in a favela. [1960–65; < Brazilian Pg, equiv. to *favel(a)* FAVELA + *-ado* << L *-ātus* -ATE[1]]

fa·vel·la (fə vel′ə), *n., pl.* **-vel·lae** (-vel′ē). (in certain red algae) a cystocarp covered by a gelatinous envelope. [1855–60; < NL, equiv. to L *fav(us)* honeycomb + *-ella* -ELLE]

fav·el·lid·i·um (fav′ə lid′ē əm), *n., pl.* **-lid·i·a** (-lid′ē ə). (in certain red algae) a cystocarp wholly or partly immersed in a frond. [1855–60; < NL; see FAVELLA, -IDIUM]

fa·ve·o·late (fə vē′ə lāt′, -lit), *adj.* honeycombed; alveolate; pitted. [1865–70; FAVEOL(US) + -ATE[1]]

fa·ve·o·lus (fə vē′ə ləs), *n., pl.* **-li** (-lī′). a small pit or cavity resembling a cell of a honeycomb; alveola. [1880–85; < NL, equiv. to L *fav(us)* honeycomb + *(alv)eolus* little cavity; see ALVEOLAR]

fa·vism (fä′viz əm), *n. Pathol.* acute hemolytic anemia caused by ingestion or inhalation of fava bean pollen. [1900–05; < It *favismo,* equiv. to *fav(a)* bean + *-ismo* -ISM]

fa·vo·ni·an (fə vō′nē ən), *adj.* **1.** of or pertaining to the west wind. **2.** mild or favorable; propitious. [1650–60; < L *Favōniānus.* See FAVONIUS, -AN. Cf. FOEHN]

Fa·vo·ni·us (fə vō′nē əs), *n.* the ancient Roman personification of the west wind. Cf. **Zephyrus.**

fa·vor (fā′vər), *n.* **1.** something done or granted out of goodwill, rather than from justice or for remuneration; a kind act: *to ask a favor.* **2.** friendly or well-disposed regard; goodwill: *to win the favor of the king.* **3.** the state of being approved or held in regard: *to be in favor at court; styles that are now in favor.* **4.** excessive kindness or unfair partiality; preferential treatment: *to treat some people with favor and others with neglect.* **5.** a gift bestowed as a token of goodwill, kind regard, love, etc., as formerly upon a knight by his lady. **6.** a ribbon, badge, etc., worn in evidence of goodwill or loyalty, as by an adherent of a political party. **7.** a small gift or decorative or festive item, as a noisemaker or paper hat, often distributed to guests at a party. **8.** Usually, **favors.** sexual intimacy, esp. as permitted by a woman. **9.** *Archaic.* a letter, esp. a commercial one. **10. find favor with,** to gain the favor of; be liked by: *The play found favor with the opening-night audience.* **11. in favor of, a.** on the side of; in support of: *to be in favor of reduced taxation.* **b.** to the advantage of. **c.** (of a check, draft, etc.) payable to: *Make out your checks in favor of the corporation.* **12. in one's favor,** to one's credit or advantage: *All the comments were in your favor.* **13. out of favor,** no longer liked or approved; no longer popular or fashionable: *He's out of favor with the president and may soon be fired.* *—v.t.* **14.** to regard with favor: *to favor an enterprise.* **15.** to prefer; treat with partiality: *The father favored his younger son.* **16.** to show favor to; oblige: *The king favored him with an audience.* **17.** to be favorable to; facilitate: *The wind favored their journey.* **18.** to deal with, treat, or use gently: *to favor a lame leg.* **19.** to aid or support: *He favored his party's cause with ample funds.* **20.** to bear a physical resemblance to; resemble: *to favor one's father's side of the family.* Also, *esp. Brit.,* **favour.** [1250–1300; ME *favo(u)r* < AF, OF < L *favōr-* (s. of *favor*) goodwill, equiv. to *fav(ēre)* to be favorably inclined + *-ōr-* -OR[1]] **—fa′vor·er,** *n.*
—Syn. 2. FAVOR, GOODWILL imply a kindly regard or friendly disposition shown by an individual or group. FAVOR may be merely an attitude of mind: *to look with favor on a proposal.* GOODWILL is more active and leads often to outward manifestations of friendly approval: *By frequent applause the audience showed its goodwill toward the speaker.* **5.** present. **14.** approve, countenance, sanction. **16.** encourage, patronize. **19.** help, assist. **—Ant. 2.** animosity, malice. **14.** disapprove.

fa·vor·a·ble (fā′vər ə bəl, fāv′rə-), *adj.* **1.** characterized by approval or support; positive: *a favorable report.* **2.** creating or winning favor; pleasing: *to make a favorable impression.* **3.** affording advantage, opportunity, or convenience; advantageous: *a favorable position.* **4.** (of an answer) granting what is desired. **5.** boding well; propitious: *The signs are favorable for a new start.* [1300–50; ME < AF, MF < L *favōrābilis.* See FAVOR, -ABLE] **—fa′vor·a·ble·ness,** *n.* **—fa′vor·a·bly,** *adv.*

fa·vor·ance (fā′vər əns, fāv′rəns), *n. Chiefly South Midland and Southern U.S.* **1.** a liking or preference: *My family always had a favorance for farming.* **2.** family resemblance: *There's a lot of favorance between him and his brothers.* [FAVOR + -ANCE]

fa·vored (fā′vərd), *adj.* **1.** regarded or treated with preference or partiality: *Her beauty made her the favored child.* **2.** enjoying special advantages; privileged: *to be born into the favored classes.* **3.** of specified appearance (usually used in combination): *ill-favored.* [1350–1400; ME *favo(u)red.* See FAVOR, -ED[2]] **—fa′vored·ly,** *adv.* **—fa′vored·ness,** *n.*

fa·vor·ite (fā′vər it, fāv′rit), *n.* **1.** a person or thing regarded with special favor or preference: *That song is an old favorite of mine.* **2.** *Sports.* a competitor considered likely to win. **3.** a person or thing popular with the public. **4.** a person treated with special or undue favor by a king, official, etc.: *favorites at the court.* *—adj.* **5.** regarded with particular favor or preference: *a favorite child.* [1575–85; < MF < It *favorito,* ptp. of *favorire* to favor. See FAVOR, -ITE[2]]

fa′vorite son′, *U.S. Politics.* (at a national political convention) a candidate nominated for office by delegates from his or her own state. [1780–90, *Amer.*]

fa·vor·it·ism (fā′vər i tiz′əm, fāv′ri-), *n.* **1.** the favoring of one person or group over others with equal claims; partiality: *to show favoritism toward the youngest child.* **2.** the state of being a favorite. [1755–65; FAVORITE + -ISM]

fav·o·site (fav′ə sīt′), *n.* any of numerous corals of the extinct genus *Favosites,* most common during the Silurian and Devonian periods, having polygonal cells with rows of pores in the walls. [1825–35; < NL *Favosites,* equiv. to L *fav(us)* honeycomb + *-ōs(us)* -OSE[1] + Gk *-ītēs* -ITE[1]]

fa·vour (fā′vər), *n., v.t. Chiefly Brit.* favor. **—Usage.** See **-or**[1].

Fa·vrile′ Glass′ (fəv rēl′), *Trademark.* a brand of iridescent art glass, introduced by L. C. Tiffany c1890 and used by him for blown vases, flower holders, etc.

fa·vus (fā′vəs), *n., pl.* **fa·vus·es** for 1, **fa·vi** (fā′vī) for 2. **1.** *Pathol.* a skin disease, esp. of the scalp, characterized by dry yellow encrustations that have an unpleasant odor, usually caused by the fungus *Trichophyton schoenleinii.* **2.** a hexagonal paving tile or stone. [1705–10; < NL, special use of L *favus* honeycomb]

Fawkes (fôks), *n.* **Guy,** 1570–1606, English conspirator and leader in the Gunpowder plot of 1605: Guy Fawkes Day is observed on November 5 by the building of effigies and bonfires.

fawn[1] (fôn), *n.* **1.** a young deer, esp. an unweaned one. **2.** a light yellowish-brown color. *—adj.* **3.** light yellowish-brown. *—v.i.* **4.** (of a doe) to bring forth young. [1225–75; ME *fawn, foun* < MF *faon, foun, feon* << VL **fētōn-,* s. of **fētō* offspring, deriv. of L *fētus* FETUS] **—fawn′like′,** *adj.*

fawn[1] of white-tailed deer, *Odocoileus virginianus*

fawn[2] (fôn), *v.i.* **1.** to seek notice or favor by servile demeanor: *The courtiers fawned over the king.* **2.** (of a dog) to behave affectionately. [bef. 1000; ME *fawnen,* OE *fagnian,* var. of *fægnian* to rejoice, make glad, deriv. of *fægen* happy; see FAIN] **—fawn′er,** *n.* **—fawn′ing·ly,** *adv.* **—fawn′ing·ness,** *n.* **—Syn. 1.** toady, truckle, flatter, kowtow.

fawn′ lil′y, any of several lilies of the genus *Erythronium,* of western North America, as *E. californicum,* having mottled leaves and cream-white flowers. [1890–95]

fawn·y (fô′nē), *adj.,* **fawn·i·er, fawn·i·est,** of a color like fawn. [1840–50; FAWN[1] + -Y[1]]

fax (faks), *Telecommunications.* *—n.* **1.** facsimile (def. 2). *—adj.* **2.** facsimile (def. 5). *—v.t.* **3.** to transmit a facsimile of (printed matter, photographs, or the like) electronically: *Fax the information to all our branch offices.* [by shortening and resp.]

Fax′a Bay′ (fäk′sə), an inlet of the Atlantic Ocean on the SW coast of Iceland.

fay[1] (fā), *n.* a fairy. [1350–1400; ME *faie, fei* < MF *feie, fee* << L *Fāta* FATE]

fay[2] (fā), *n. Obs.* faith. [1250–1300; ME *fai, fei* < AF, var. of *feid* FAITH]

fay[3] (fā), *n. Slang.* ofay. [1925–30; by shortening]

Fay (fā), *n.* a female given name, form of **Faith.** Also, **Faye.**

Fa·yal (fä yäl′), *n.* Faial.

fay·al·ite (fā′ə līt′, fī ä′līt), *n. Mineral.* the iron end member of the olivine group, Fe_2SiO_4. [1835–45; named after FAYAL; see -ITE[1]]

Fay·ette·ville (fā′it vil′), *n.* **1.** a city in S North Carolina. 59,507. **2.** a city in NW Arkansas. 36,604.

Fa·yum (fī yo͞om′), *n., adj.* Faiyum.

faze (fāz), *v.t.,* **fazed, faz·ing.** to cause to be disturbed or disconcerted; daunt: *The worst insults cannot faze him.* [1820–30, *Amer.;* dial form. of FEEZE] **—Syn.** disconcert, discomfit, perturb, fluster, confound.

f.b., 1. freight bill. **2.** *Sports.* fullback.

F.B.A., Fellow of the British Academy.

FBI, *U.S. Govt.* Federal Bureau of Investigation: the federal agency charged with investigations for the Attorney General and with safeguarding national security.

FBO, for the benefit of. Also, **F/B/O**

FC, foot-candle. Also, **fc**

f.c., 1. *Baseball.* fielder's choice. **2.** *Print.* follow copy.

FCA, Farm Credit Administration.

FCC, *U.S. Govt.* Federal Communications Commission: a board charged with regulating broadcasting and interstate communication by wire, radio, and television.

FCIA, Foreign Credit Insurance Association.

CONCISE PRONUNCIATION KEY: act, cāpe, dâre, pärt; set, ēqual; if, īce; ox, ōver, ôrder, oil, bo͝ok, bo͞ot, out; up, ûrge; child; sing; shoe; thin, *th*at; zh as in *treasure.* ə = *a* as in *alone, e* as in *system, i* as in *easily, o* as in *gallop, u* as in *circus;* ᵊ as in *fire* (fīᵊr), *hour* (ouᵊr). l and n can serve as syllabic consonants, as in *cradle* (krād′l), and *button* (but′n). See the full key inside the front cover.

FCIC, Federal Crop Insurance Corporation.

F clef, *Music.* See **bass clef.**

fcp., foolscap.

fcs., francs.

fcy., fancy.

F.D., **1.** Fidei Defensor. **2.** fire department. **3.** focal distance.

FDA, See **Food and Drug Administration.**

FD&C color, any of the synthetic pigments and dyes that are approved by the FDA for use in foods, drugs, and cosmetics.

Fdg, *Banking.* funding.

FDIC, See **Federal Deposit Insurance Corporation.**

FDR, Franklin Delano Roosevelt.

Fe, *Symbol, Chem.* iron. [< L *ferrum*]

fe., fecit.

fe·al·ty (fē′əl tē), *n., pl.* **-ties. 1.** *Hist.* **a.** fidelity to a lord. **b.** the obligation or the engagement to be faithful to a lord, usually sworn to by a vassal. **2.** fidelity; faithfulness. [1275–1325; ME *feute, feaute, fealtye* < AF, OF *feauté, fealté* < L *fidēlitāt-* (s. of *fidēlitās*) FIDELITY; internal *-au-, -al-* from *feal,* reshaping (by substitution of *-al-* -AL[1]) of *fe(d)eil* < L *fidēlis*]
—Syn. 2. loyalty, devotion.

fear (fēr), *n.* **1.** a distressing emotion aroused by impending danger, evil, pain, etc., whether the threat is real or imagined; the feeling or condition of being afraid. **2.** a specific instance of or propensity for such a feeling: *an abnormal fear of heights.* **3.** concern or anxiety; solicitude: *a fear for someone's safety.* **4.** reverential awe, esp. toward God. **5.** that which causes a feeling of being afraid; that of which a person is afraid: *Cancer is a common fear.* —*v.t.* **6.** to regard with fear; be afraid of. **7.** to have reverential awe of. **8.** *Archaic.* to experience fear in (oneself). —*v.i.* **9.** to have fear; be afraid. [bef. 900; ME *fere,* OE *fǣr* sudden attack or danger; c. OS *fār* ambush, D *gevaar,* G *Gefahr* danger, ON *fār* disaster]
—Syn. 1. apprehension, consternation, dismay, terror, fright, panic, horror, trepidation. FEAR, ALARM, DREAD all imply a painful emotion experienced when one is confronted by threatening danger or evil. ALARM implies an agitation of the feelings caused by awakening to imminent danger; it names a feeling of fright or panic: *He started up in alarm.* FEAR and DREAD usually refer more to a condition or state than to an event. FEAR is often applied to an attitude toward something, which, when experienced, will cause the sensation of fright: *fear of falling.* DREAD suggests anticipation of something, usually a particular event, which, when experienced, will be disagreeable rather than frightening: *She lives in dread of losing her money.* The same is often true of FEAR, when used in a negative statement: *She has no fear she'll lose her money.* **6.** apprehend, dread.

Fear (fēr), *n.* **1.** a river in SE North Carolina. 202 mi. (325 km) long. **2. Cape,** a cape at its mouth.

feared (fērd), *adj. Dial.* afraid; afeard. [aph. form of AFEARD]

fear·ful (fēr′fəl), *adj.* **1.** causing or apt to cause fear; frightening: *a fearful apparition.* **2.** feeling fear, dread, apprehension, or solicitude: *fearful for his life; fearful lest he commit suicide.* **3.** full of awe or reverence: *fearful of the Lord.* **4.** showing or caused by fear: *fearful behavior.* **5.** extreme in size, intensity, or badness: *a fearful head cold; fearful poverty.* [1300–50; ME *ferful.* See FEAR, -FUL] **—fear′ful·ly,** *adv.* **—fear′ful·ness,** *n.*
—Syn. 2. afraid, timid, timorous, apprehensive, uneasy, distrustful; solicitous, anxious, concerned, worried.

fear·less (fēr′lis), *adj.* without fear; bold or brave; intrepid. [1350–1400; ME *fereles.* See FEAR, -LESS] **—fear′less·ly,** *adv.* **—fear′less·ness,** *n.*
—Syn. See **brave. —Ant.** cowardly.

fear·nought (fēr′nôt′), *n.* **1.** a stout woolen cloth for overcoats. **2.** an outer garment of this cloth. Also, **fear′naught′.** [1765–75; FEAR + NOUGHT]

fear·some (fēr′səm), *adj.* **1.** causing fear: *a fearsome noise.* **2.** causing awe or respect: *a fearsome self-confidence.* **3.** afraid; timid. [1760–70; FEAR + -SOME[1]] **—fear′some·ly,** *adv.* **—fear′some·ness,** *n.*

fea·sance (fē′zəns), *n. Law.* the doing or performing of an act, as of a condition or duty. [1530–40; < AF *fesa(u)nce,* OF *faisance,* equiv. to *fais-* (var. s. of *faire* << L *facere* to do) + *-ance* -ANCE]

fea·si·ble (fē′zə bəl), *adj.* **1.** capable of being done, effected, or accomplished: *a feasible plan.* **2.** probable; likely: *a feasible theory.* **3.** suitable: *a road feasible for travel.* [1425–75; late ME *feseable, faisible* < AF, OF, equiv. to *fes-, fais-* (var. s. of *faire* < L *facere* to do) + *-ible* -IBLE] **—fea′si·bil′i·ty, fea′si·ble·ness,** *n.* **—fea′si·bly,** *adv.*
—Syn. 1. See **possible.**

feast (fēst), *n.* **1.** any rich or abundant meal: *The steak dinner was a feast.* **2.** a sumptuous entertainment or meal for many guests: *a wedding feast.* **3.** something highly agreeable: *The Rembrandt exhibition was a feast for the eyes.* **4.** a periodical celebration or time of celebration, usually of a religious nature, commemorating an event, person, etc.: *Every year, in September, the townspeople have a feast in honor of their patron saint.* —*v.i.* **5.** to have or partake of a feast; eat sumptuously. **6.** to dwell with gratification or delight, as on a picture or view. —*v.t.* **7.** to provide or entertain with a feast. **8. feast one's eyes,** to gaze with great joy, admiration, or relish: *to feast one's eyes on the Grand Canyon.* [1150–1200; ME *feste* < OF < L *fēsta,* neut. pl. (taken as fem. sing. n.) of *fēstus* festal, festive, equiv. to *fēs-* (akin to FAIR[2]) + *-tus* adj. suffix] **—feast′er,** *n.* **—feast′less,** *adj.*
—Syn. 2. FEAST, BANQUET imply large social events, with an abundance of food. A FEAST is a meal with a plenteous supply of food and drink for a large company: *to provide a feast for all company employees.* A BANQUET is an elaborate feast for a formal and ceremonious occasion: *the main speaker at a banquet.*

feast′ day′, a day, esp. a church holiday, for feasting and rejoicing. [1250–1300; ME]

Feast′ of Booths′, Sukkoth.

Feast′ of Dedica′tion, Hanukkah. Also called **Feast′ of Lights′.**

Feast′ of Fools′, (esp. in France) a mock-religious celebration in the Middle Ages, held on or about January 1. Also called **Festival of Fools.**

Feast′ of Lan′terns, Bon.

Feast′ of Lots′, Purim.

Feast′ of Or′thodoxy, *Eastern Ch.* a solemn festival held on the first Sunday of Lent **(Orthodoxy Sunday)** commemorating the restoration of the use of icons in the church (A.D. 842) and the triumph over all heresies.

Feast of St. Peter's Chains. See under **Lammas** (def. 2).

Feast′ of Tab′ernacles, Sukkoth. [1350–1400; ME]

Feast′ of Weeks′, Shavuoth.

feast-or-fam·ine (fēst′ər fam′in), *adj.* characterized by alternating, extremely high and low degrees of prosperity, success, volume of business, etc.: *artists who lead a feast-or-famine life.*

feat[1] (fēt), *n.* **1.** a noteworthy or extraordinary act or achievement, usually displaying boldness, skill, etc.: *Arranging the treaty was a diplomatic feat.* **2.** *Obs.* a specialized skill; profession. [1300–50; ME *fet, fait* < AF, OF < L *factum* FACT]
—Syn. 1. accomplishment. See **achievement.**

feat[2] (fēt), *adj.* **-er, -est.** *Archaic.* **1.** apt; skillful; dexterous. **2.** suitable. **3.** neat. [1400–50; late ME < MF *fait* made (to fit) < L *factus,* ptp. of *facere* to make, do]

feath·er (feth′ər), *n.* **1.** one of the horny structures forming the principal covering of birds, consisting typically of a hard, tubular portion attached to the body and tapering into a thinner, stemlike portion bearing a series of slender, barbed processes that interlock to form a flat structure on each side. **2.** kind; character; nature: *two boys of the same feather.* **3.** something like a feather, as a tuft or fringe of hair. **4.** something very light, small, or trivial: *Your worry is a mere feather.* **5.** *Archery.* one of the vanes at the tail of an arrow or dart. **6.** *Carpentry.* a spline for joining the grooved edges of two boards. **7.** *Masonry.* See under **plug and feathers. 8.** a featherlike flaw, esp. in a precious stone. **9.** *Mach.* See **feather key. 10.** *Archaic.* attire. **11.** *Obs.* plumage. **12. a feather in one's cap,** a praiseworthy accomplishment; distinction; honor: *Being chosen class president is a feather in her cap.* **13. birds of a feather.** See **bird** (def. 12). **14. in fine** or **high feather,** in good form, humor, or health: *feeling in fine feather.* **15. ruffle someone's feathers,** to anger, upset, or annoy (another person). **16. smooth one's ruffled** or **rumpled feathers,** to regain one's composure; become calm: *After the argument, we each retired to our own rooms to smooth our ruffled feathers.* —*v.t.* **17.** to provide with feathers, as an arrow. **18.** to clothe or cover with or as with feathers. **19.** *Rowing.* to turn (an oar) after a stroke so that the blade becomes nearly horizontal, and hold it thus as it is moved back into position for the next stroke. **20.** *Aeron.* **a.** to change the blade angle of (a propeller) so that the chords of the blades are approximately parallel to the line of flight. **b.** to turn off (an engine) while in flight. —*v.i.* **21.** to grow feathers. **22.** to be or become feathery in appearance. **23.** to move like feathers. **24.** *Rowing.* to feather an oar. **25. feather into,** *South Midland U.S.* to attack (a person, task, or problem) vigorously. **26. feather one's nest,** to take advantage of the opportunities to enrich oneself: *The mayor had used his term of office to feather his nest.* [bef. 900; ME, OE *fether;* c. D *veder,* G *Feder,* ON *fjǫthr;* akin to Gk *pterón,* Skt *pátram* wing, feather] **—feath′er·less,** *adj.* **—feath′er·less·ness,** *n.* **—feath′er·like′,** *adj.*

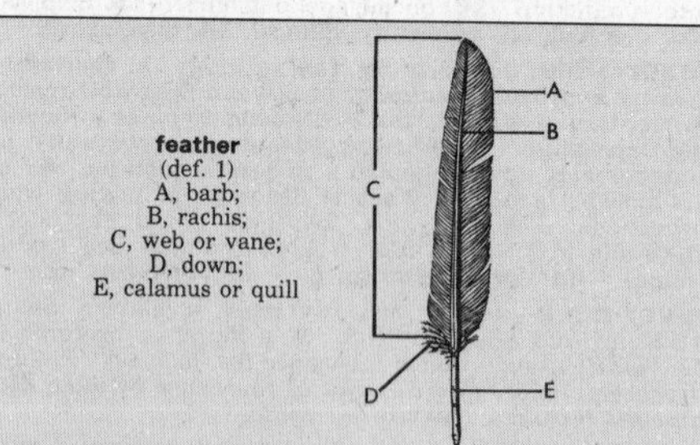

feather
(def. 1)
A, barb;
B, rachis;
C, web or vane;
D, down;
E, calamus or quill

feath·er·back (feth′ər bak′), *n.* any freshwater fish of the family Notopteridae, of Asia and western Africa, having a small, feathery dorsal fin and a very long anal fin extending from close behind the head to the tip of the tail. [FEATHER + BACK[1]]

feath′er band′ing, *Furniture.* decorative banding of veneer or inlay having the grain laid diagonally to the grain of the principal surface.

feath′er bed′, a mattress or a bed cover, as a quilt, stuffed with soft feathers. [bef. 1000; ME, OE]

feath·er·bed (feth′ər bed′), *v.t., v.i.,* **-bed·ded, -bed·ding.** to subject to or engage in featherbedding. [1945–50; back formation from FEATHERBEDDING]

feath·er·bed·ding (feth′ər bed′ing), *n.* the practice of requiring an employer to hire unnecessary employees, to assign unnecessary work, or to limit production according to a union rule or safety statute: *Featherbedding forced the railroads to employ firemen on diesel locomotives.* [1920–25; FEATHER + BEDDING]

feath·er·bone (feth′ər bōn′), *n.* a substitute for whalebone, made from the quills of domestic fowls. [1885–90, *Amer.;* FEATHER + BONE]

feath·er·brain (feth′ər brān′), *n.* a foolish or giddy person; scatterbrain. Also, **featherhead.** [1830–40; FEATHER + BRAIN] **—feath′er·brained′,** *adj.*

feath·er·cut (feth′ər kut′), *n.* a woman's hair style in which the hair is cut in short and uneven lengths and formed into small curls with featherlike tips. [1935–40; FEATHER + CUT]

feath′er dust′er, a brush for dusting, made of a bundle of large feathers attached to a short handle. [1855–60]

feath′er-dust·er worm′ (feth′ər dus′tər), any tube-dwelling polychaete worm of the families Sabellidae and Serpulidae, the numerous species having a crown of feathery tentacles used in feeding and respiration. Also called **fan worm, feather worm.**

feath·ered (feth′ərd), *adj.* **1.** clothed, covered, or provided with feathers, as a bird or an arrow. **2.** quick; rapid; speedy; swift: *feathered feet.* **3.** (of a veneer) cut to show a figure resembling a plume. [bef. 1000; ME *fethered,* OE *gefetherede,* see FEATHER, -ED[3]]

feath·er·edge (feth′ər ej′), *n.* **1.** an edge that thins out like a feather. **2.** the thinner edge of a wedge-shaped board or plank. **3.** a tool for giving a smooth, even finish to plasterwork at corners. **4.** (in silver work) a band of closely spaced oblique lines engraved along an edge of a piece. [1610–20; FEATHER + EDGE] **—feath′er·edged′,** *adj.*

feath′er gera′nium, a Eurasian weed, *Chenopodium botrys,* of the goosefoot family, having clusters of inconspicuous flowers and unpleasant smelling, lobed leaves. Also called **Jerusalem oak.** [1855–60, *Amer.*]

feath′er grass′, any American grass of the genus *Stipa,* having a feathery appendage. [1770–80]

feath·er·head (feth′ər hed′), *n.* featherbrain. [1825–35; FEATHER + HEAD] **—feath′er·head′ed,** *adj.*

feath·er·ing (feth′ər ing), *n.* **1.** a covering of feathers; plumage. **2.** the arrangement of feathers on an arrow. **3.** *Music.* a very light and delicate use of the violin bow. [1520–30; FEATHER + -ING[1]]

feath′er key′, *Mach.* a rectangular key connecting the keyways of a shaft and a hub of a gear, pulley, etc., fastened in one keyway and free to slide in the other so that the hub can drive or be driven by the shaft at various positions along it. Also called **feather, spline.**

feath·er-leg·ged (feth′ər leg′id, -legd′), *adj. Southern U.S.* cowardly. [1870–75]

feath·er·light (feth′ər līt′), *adj.* extremely light; light as a feather. [1830–40; FEATHER + LIGHT[2]]

feath′er mer′chant, *Older Slang.* a person who avoids responsibility and effort; loafer. [1775–85]

feath′er palm′, any palm having large pinnate or bipinnate leaves, as the date palm or royal palm.

feath′er shot′, *Metall.* fine bean shot.

feath′er star′, a free-swimming crinoid. [1860–65]

feath·er·stitch (feth′ər stich′), *n.* **1.** an embroidery stitch producing work in which a succession of branches extend alternately on each side of a central stem. —*v.t.* **2.** to ornament by featherstitch. [1825–35; FEATHER + STITCH[1]]

feath′er-tail glid′er (feth′ər tāl′). See **pygmy glider.**

feath′er tract′, pteryla. [1875–80]

feath·er-veined (feth′ər vānd′), *adj. Bot.* (of a leaf) having a series of veins branching from each side of the midrib toward the margin; pinnately veined. [1860–65]

feath·er·weight (feth′ər wāt′), *n.* **1.** a boxer or other contestant intermediate in weight between a bantamweight and a lightweight, esp. a professional boxer weighing up to 126 lb. (57 kg). **2.** an insignificant person or thing: *He thinks he's a major composer, but he's just a featherweight.* —*adj.* **3.** belonging to the class of featherweights, esp. in boxing. **4.** extremely light in weight: *a featherweight quilt.* **5.** unimportant; trifling; slight. [1805–15; FEATHER + WEIGHT]

feath′er worm′. See **feather-duster worm.**

feath·er·y (feth′ə rē), *adj.* **1.** clothed or covered with feathers; feathered. **2.** resembling feathers; light; airy; unsubstantial: *feathery clouds.* [1570–80; FEATHER + -Y[1]] **—feath′er·i·ness,** *n.*

feat·ly (fēt′lē), *adv.* **1.** suitably; appropriately. **2.** skillfully. **3.** neatly; elegantly. —*adj.* **4.** graceful; elegant. [1300–50; ME *fetly.* See FEAT[2], -LY] **—feat′li·ness,** *n.*

fea·ture (fē′chər), *n., v.,* **-tured, -tur·ing.** —*n.* **1.** a prominent or conspicuous part or characteristic: *Tall buildings were a new feature on the skyline.* **2.** something offered as a special attraction: *This model has several added features.* **3.** Also called **fea′ture film′.** the main motion picture in a movie program: *What time is the feature?* **4.** any part of the face, as the nose, chin, or eyes: *prominent features.* **5. features,** the face; countenance: *to compose one's features for the photographers.* **6.** the form or cast of the face: *delicate of feature.* **7.** a column, cartoon, etc., appearing regularly in a newspaper or magazine. **8.** See **feature story. 9.** *Archaic.* make, form, or shape. —*v.t.* **10.** to be a feature or distinctive mark of: *It was industrial expansion that featured the last century.* **11.** to make a feature of; give prominence to: *to feature a story or picture in a newspaper.* **12.** to delineate the main characteristics of; depict; outline. **13.** *Informal.* to conceive of; imagine; fancy: *He couldn't quite feature himself as a bank president.* **14.** *Older Use.* to resemble in features; favor. —*v.i.* **15.** to play a major part. [1350–1400; 1905–10 for def. 3; ME *feture* < AF, MF *faiture* < L *factūra* a making. See FACT, -URE]

—Syn. 1. FEATURE, CHARACTERISTIC, PECULIARITY refer to a distinctive trait of an individual or of a class. FEATURE suggests an outstanding or marked property that attracts attention: *Complete harmony was a feature of the convention.* CHARACTERISTIC means a distinguishing mark or quality (or one of such) always associated in one's mind with a particular person or thing: *Defiance is one of his characteristics.* PECULIARITY means that distinct or unusual characteristic that marks off an individual in the class to which he, she, or it belongs: *A blue-black tongue is a peculiarity of the chow chow.*

fea·tured (fē′chərd), *adj.* **1.** made a feature or highlight; given prominence: *a featured article; a featured actor.* **2.** having features or a certain kind of features (usually used in combination): *a well-featured face.* **3.** *Obs.* formed; fashioned. [1375–1425; late ME *fetured.* See FEATURE, -ED[3]]

fea·ture-length (fē′chər length′), *adj.* long enough to be made a feature; of full length: *a feature-length story; a feature-length film.* [1935–40]

fea·ture·less (fē′chər lis), *adj.* without distinctive features; uninteresting, plain, or drab: *a featureless landscape.* [1590–1600; FEATURE + -LESS]

fea′ture sto′ry, 1. a newspaper or magazine article or report of a person, event, an aspect of a major event, or the like, often having a personal slant and written in an individual style. Cf. **follow-up** (def. 3b), **hard news, news story. 2.** the main or most prominent story in a magazine. Also called **feature.** [1910–15]

feaze[1] (fēz), *v.t.,* **feazed, feaz·ing.** *Naut.* to untwist (the end of a rope). [1560–70; akin to D *vezelen* to fray, MD *veze* frayed edge, OE *fæs* fringe]

feaze[2] (fēz, fāz), *n.* feeze.

feaz·ing (fē′zing), *n. Naut.* Often, **feazings.** an unraveled portion at the end of a rope. [1815–25; FEAZE[1] + -ING[1]]

FEB, Fair Employment Board.

Feb., February.

febri-, a combining form meaning "fever," used in the formation of compound words: *febriferous.* [comb. form repr. L *febris* FEVER]

fe·bric·i·ty (fi bris′i tē), *n.* the state of being feverish. [1870–75; < ML *febricitās,* equiv. to L **febric(us)* feverish (see FEBRI-, -IC) + *-itās* -ITY]

fe·bric·u·la (fi brik′yə lə), *n.* a slight and short fever, esp. when of obscure causation. [1740–50; < L; see FEBRI-, -CULE[1]]

feb·ri·fa·cient (feb′rə fā′shənt), *adj.* **1.** producing fever. *—n.* **2.** something that produces fever. [1795–1805; FEBRI- + -FACIENT]

fe·brif·er·ous (fi brif′ər əs), *adj.* producing fever. [1870–75; FEBRI- + -FEROUS]

fe·brif·ic (fi brif′ik), *adj.* producing or marked by fever. [1700–10; FEBRI- + -FIC]

fe·brif·u·gal (fi brif′yə gəl, feb′rə fyōō′gəl), *adj.* of or acting as a febrifuge. [1655–65; see FEBRIFUGE, -AL[1]]

feb·ri·fuge (feb′rə fyōōj′), *adj.* **1.** serving to dispel or reduce fever, as a medicine. *—n.* **2.** such a medicine or agent. **3.** a cooling drink. [1680–90; < F < LL *febrifugia* plant good for curing fever. See FEBRI-, -FUGE]

fe·brile (fē′brəl, feb′rəl *or, esp. Brit.,* fē′bril), *adj.* pertaining to or marked by fever; feverish. [1645–55; < NL, ML *febrīlis.* See FEVER, -ILE] **—fe·bril·i·ty** (fi bril′i tē), *n.*

feb·ris (feb′ris), *n., pl.* **-res** (-rēz). (in prescriptions) fever. [< L]

Feb·ru·ar·y (feb′rōō er′ē, feb′yōō-), *n., pl.* **-ar·ies.** the second month of the year, ordinarily containing 28 days, but containing 29 days in leap years. *Abbr.:* Feb. [bef. 1000; ME; OE *Februarius* < L, short for *Februārius mēnsis* expiatory month, after *februa* (pl.) expiatory offerings; see -ARY]

—Pronunciation. Many people try to pronounce FEBRUARY with both (r) sounds, as shown above. The common pronunciation (feb′yōō er′ē), with the first (r) replaced by (y), is the result of dissimilation, the tendency of like sounds to become unlike when they follow each other closely. An additional influence is analogy with *January.* Although sometimes criticized, the dissimilated pronunciation of FEBRUARY is used by educated speakers and is considered standard.

Feb′ruary Revolu′tion. See **Russian Revolution** (def. 1).

FEC, Federal Election Commission.

fec., fecit.

fe·cal (fē′kəl), *adj.* of, pertaining to, or being feces. [1535–45; FEC(ES) + -AL[1]]

fe·cal·oid (fē′kə loid′), *adj.* like or resembling feces. [1880–85; FECAL + -OID]

fe·ces (fē′sēz), *n.* (*used with a plural v.*) **1.** waste matter discharged from the intestines through the anus; excrement. **2.** dregs; sediment. Also, *esp. Brit.,* **faeces.** [1425–75; late ME < L *faecēs* grounds, dregs, sediment (pl. of *faex*)]

Fech·ner (fekн′nər), *n.* **Gus·tav The·o·dor** (gŏŏs′täf tā′ô dōr′), 1801–87, German physicist, psychologist, and philosopher.

fe·cit (fā′kit; *Eng.* fē′sit), *v. Latin.* he made (it); she made (it): formerly used on works of art after the name of the artist. *Abbr.:* fe., fec.

feck·less (fek′lis), *adj.* **1.** ineffective; incompetent; futile: *feckless attempts to repair the plumbing.* **2.** having no sense of responsibility; indifferent; lazy. [1590–1600; orig. Scots, equiv. to *feck,* late ME (Scots) *fek,* aph. form of *effeck* (Scots form of EFFECT) + -LESS] **—feck′less·ly,** *adv.* **—feck′less·ness,** *n.*

fec·u·la (fek′yə lə), *n., pl.* **-lae** (-lē′). **1.** fecal matter, esp. of insects. **2.** foul or muddy matter; dregs. [< L *faecula* burnt tartar, dried lees of wine, equiv. to *faec-* (s. of *faex;* see FECES) + *-ula* -ULE]

fec·u·lent (fek′yə lənt), *adj.* full of dregs or fecal matter; foul, turbid, or muddy. [1425–75; late ME < L *faeculentus* full of dregs. See FECES, -ULENT] **—fec′u·lence,** *n.*

fe·cund (fē′kund, -kənd, fek′und, -ənd), *adj.* **1.** producing or capable of producing offspring, fruit, vegetation, etc., in abundance; prolific; fruitful: *fecund parents; fecund farmland.* **2.** very productive or creative intellectually: *the fecund years of the Italian Renaissance.* [1375–1425; late ME < L *fēcundus,* equiv. to *fē-* (see FETUS) + *-cundus* adj. suffix; r. late ME *fecounde* < AF]

fe·cun·date (fē′kən dāt′, fek′ən-), *v.t.,* **-dat·ed, -dat·ing. 1.** to make prolific or fruitful. **2.** *Biol.* to impregnate or fertilize. [1625–35; < L *fēcundātus* made fruitful, fertilized (ptp. of *fēcundāre*). See FECUND, -ATE[1]] **—fe′cun·da′tion,** *n.* **—fe′cun·da′tor,** *n.* **—fe·cun·da·to·ry** (fi kun′də tôr′ē, -tōr′ē), *adj.*

fe·cun·di·ty (fi kun′di tē), *n.* **1.** the quality of being fecund; capacity, esp. in female animals, of producing young in great numbers. **2.** fruitfulness or fertility, as of the earth. **3.** the capacity of abundant production: *fecundity of imagination.* [1375–1425; late ME < L *fēcunditās* fruitfulness, fertility. See FECUND, -ITY]

fed[1] (fed), *v.* **1.** pt. and pp. of **feed. 2. fed up,** impatient; disgusted; bored: *They were fed up with the same old routine.*

fed[2] (fed), *n.* (*sometimes cap.*) *Slang.* a federal official or law-enforcement officer. [1915–20; by shortening]

Fed (fed), *n.* **the Fed,** *Informal.* **1.** the Federal Reserve System. **2.** the Federal Reserve Board.

Fed., Federal.

fed., **1.** federal. **2.** federated. **3.** federation.

fe·da·yee (fe dä yē′), *n., pl.* **-yeen** (-yēn′). a member of an Arab commando group operating esp. against Israel. [1950–55; < dial. Ar *fidā'ī* (pl. *fidā'iyīn*) one who sacrifices himself (esp. for his country)]

fed·dan (fə dän′, -dan′), *n., pl.* **-dan, -dans.** an Egyptian unit of area equivalent to 1.038 acres (0.42 ha). [< Ar *faddān* lit., yoke of oxen]

fed·e·li·ni (fed′l ē′nē), *n.* an extremely fine, strandlike pasta, thinner than vermicelli. [< It, var. of *fidel(l)ini,* dim. of *fidelli,* Upper It form of *filelli,* pl. of *filello,* equiv. to *filo* thread (< L *fīlum*) + *-ello* dim. suffix; see -ELLE]

fed·er·a·cy (fed′ər ə sē), *n., pl.* **-cies.** a confederacy. [1640–50; by aphesis]

fed·er·al (fed′ər əl), *adj.* **1.** pertaining to or of the nature of a union of states under a central government distinct from the individual governments of the separate states: *the federal government of the U.S.* **2.** of, pertaining to, or noting such a central government: *federal offices.* **3.** (*cap.*) *U.S. Hist.* **a.** of or pertaining to the Federalists or to the Federalist party. **b.** supporting the principles of the Federalist party. **c.** (in the Civil War) pertaining to or supporting the Union government. **d.** relating to or adhering to the support of the Constitution. **4.** (*cap.*) pertaining to or designating the styles of the decorative arts and architecture current in the U.S. from c1780 to c1830. **5.** of or pertaining to a compact or a league, esp. a league between nations or states. *—n.* **6.** an advocate of federation or federalism. **7.** (*cap.*) *U.S. Hist.* **a.** a Federalist. **b.** an adherent of the Union government during the Civil War; Unionist. **c.** a soldier in the Federal army. [1635–45; earlier *foederal* < L *foeder-* (s. of *foedus*) league + -AL[1]] **—fed′er·al·ly,** *adv.* **—fed′er·al·ness,** *n.*

Fed′eral Avia′tion Administra′tion. See **FAA.**

Fed′eral Bu′reau of Investiga′tion. See **FBI.**

Fed′eral Cap′ital Ter′ritory, former name of **Australian Capital Territory.**

fed′eral case′, 1. a matter that falls within the jurisdiction of a federal court or a federal law-enforcement agency. **2. make a federal case of** or **out of,** *Informal.* to exaggerate the importance of or make an issue out of (something trivial). [1950–55]

Fed′eral Communica′tions Commis′sion. See **FCC.**

Fed′eral Constitu′tion. See **Constitution of the United States.**

fed′eral court′, a court of a federal government, esp. one established under the Constitution of the United States. [1780–90, *Amer.*]

Fed′eral Depos′it Insur′ance Corpora′tion, a public corporation, established in 1933, that insures, up to a specified amount, all demand deposits of member banks. *Abbr.:* FDIC

Fed′eral Dis′trict, a district in which the national government of a country is located, esp. one in Latin America. Spanish, Portuguese, ***Distrito Federal.***

fed′eral dis′trict court′. See **district court** (def. 2). [1930–35]

Fed′eral En′ergy Reg′ulatory Commis′sion, an independent agency of the U.S. federal government, created in 1978 and originally within the Department of Energy, charged with setting rates for transportation and sale of electricity, transportation of oil by pipeline, and the licensing of hydroelectric power projects. *Abbr.:* FERC

fed·er·al·ese (fed′ər ə lēz′, -lēs′), *n.* (*often cap.*) awkward, evasive, or pretentious prose said to characterize the publications and correspondence of U.S. federal bureaus. [FEDERAL + -ESE]

Fed′eral Home′ Loan′ Mort′gage Corpora′tion, a private corporation authorized by the U.S. Congress whose chief function is to buy federally insured home mortgages and help develop nonfederally insured mortgages. *Abbr.:* FHLMC

Fed′eral Hous′ing Administra′tion, a governmental agency created in 1934 to help homeowners finance the purchase and repair of their homes and to stimulate housing construction. *Abbr.:* FHA

fed·er·al·ism (fed′ər ə liz′əm), *n.* **1.** the federal principle of government. **2.** *U.S. Hist.* **a.** advocacy of the federal system of government. **b.** (*cap.*) the principles of the Federalist party. [1780–90, *Amer.;* FEDERAL + -ISM]

fed·er·al·ist (fed′ər ə list), *n.* **1.** an advocate of federalism. **2.** (*cap.*) *U.S. Hist.* a member or supporter of the Federalist party. *—adj.* **3.** Also, **fed′er·al·is′tic.** of federalism or the Federalists. [1780–90, *Amer.;* FEDERAL + -IST]

Fed′eralist, The, a series of 85 essays (1787–88) by Alexander Hamilton, James Madison, and John Jay, written in support of the Constitution.

Fed′eralist par′ty, 1. a political group that favored the adoption by the states of the Constitution. **2.** a political party in early U.S. history advocating a strong central government. Also, **Fed′eral par′ty.**

fed·er·al·ize (fed′ər ə līz′), *v.t.,* **-ized, -iz·ing. 1.** to bring under the control of a federal government: *to federalize the National Guard.* **2.** to bring together in a federal union. Also, *esp. Brit.,* **fed′er·al·ise′.** [1795–1805; FEDERAL + -IZE] **—fed′er·al·i·za′tion,** *n.*

Fed′eral Land′ Bank′, a U.S. federal bank for making long-term loans to farmers.

Fed′eral Na′tional Mort′gage Associa′tion, a U.S. government-sponsored private corporation whose chief function is to supply funds for home mortgages through continuous purchases of mortgages from lending institutions. *Abbr.:* FNMA

Fed′eral Pow′er Commis′sion. See **FPC.**

Fed′eral Reg′ister, a bulletin, published daily by the U.S. federal government, containing the schedule of hearings before Congressional and federal agency committees, together with orders, proclamations, etc., released by the executive branch of the government.

Fed′eral Repub′lic of Cameroon′, official name of **Cameroon.**

Fed′eral Repub′lic of Ger′many, 1. official name of **Germany. 2.** (formerly) official name of **West Germany.**

Fed′eral Reserve′ Bank′. See under **Federal Reserve System.**

Fed′eral Reserve′ Board′. See under **Federal Reserve System.**

Fed′eral Reserve′ dis′trict, the district served by a certain Federal Reserve Bank.

Fed′eral Reserve′ note′, a form of paper money issued by a Federal Reserve Bank.

Fed′eral Reserve′ Sys′tem, a U.S. federal banking system that is under the control of a central board of governors **(Federal Reserve Board)** with a central bank **(Federal Reserve Bank)** in each of 12 districts and that has wide powers in controlling credit and the flow of money as well as in performing other functions, as regulating and supervising its member banks.

Fed′eral Sav′ings and Loan′ Insur′ance Corpora′tion, a public corporation, established in 1934, that insures, up to a specified amount, all deposits in member savings and loan associations. *Abbr.:* FSLIC

Fed′eral Trade′ Commis′sion. See **FTC.**

fed·er·ate (*v.* fed′ə rāt′; *adj.* fed′ər it), *v.,* **-at·ed, -at·ing,** *adj.* *—v.t., v.i.* **1.** to unite in a federation. **2.** to organize on a federal basis. *—adj.* **3.** federated; allied. [1665–75; < L *foederātus* leagued together, allied, equiv. to *foeder-* (nom. s. *foedus*) league + *-ātus* -ATE[1]] **—fed′er·a′tor,** *n.*

fed′erated church′, a church whose membership includes two or more congregations of different denominational affiliation. [1925–30]

Fed′erated Ma′lay States′, a former federation of four native states in British Malaya: Negri Sembilan, Pahang, Perak, and Selangor.

fed·er·a·tion (fed′ə rā′shən), *n.* **1.** the act of federating or uniting in a league. **2.** the formation of a political unity, with a central government, by a number of separate states, each of which retains control of its own internal affairs. **3.** a league or confederacy. **4.** a federated body formed by a number of nations, states, societies, unions, etc., each retaining control of its own internal affairs. [1715–25; < LL *foederātiōn-* (s. of *foederātiō*) a leaguing. See FEDERATE, -ION]

Federa′tion of Rhode′sia and Nya′saland. See **Rhodesia and Nyasaland, Federation of.**

Federa′tion of the West′ In′dies. See **West Indies** (def. 2).

fed·er·a·tive (fed′ə rā′tiv, -ər ə tiv), *adj.* **1.** pertaining to or of the nature of a federation. **2.** inclined to federate. [1680–90; FEDERATE + -IVE] **—fed·er·a·tive·ly** (fed′ə rā′tiv lē, -ər ə tiv-), *adv.*

Fe·din (fye′dyin), *n.* **Kon·stan·tin A·le·ksan·dro·vich** (kən stun tyēn′ u lyi ksän′drə vyich), 1892–1977, Russian novelist and short-story writer.

fedn., federation.

fe·do·ra (fi dôr′ə, -dōr′ə), *n.* a soft felt hat with a curled brim, worn with the crown creased lengthwise. [1885–90, *Amer.;* said to be named after *Fédora,* play by Victorien Sardou (1831–1908)]

Fed. Res. Bd., Federal Reserve Board.

Fed. Res. Bk., Federal Reserve Bank.

fee (fē), *n., v.,* **feed, fee·ing.** *—n.* **1.** a charge or pay-

ment for professional services: *a doctor's fee.* **2.** a sum paid or charged for a privilege: *an admission fee.* **3.** a charge allowed by law for the service of a public officer. **4.** *Law.* **a.** an estate of inheritance in land, either absolute and without limitation to any particular class of heirs **(fee simple)** or limited to a particular class of heirs **(fee tail).** **b.** an inheritable estate in land held of a feudal lord on condition of the performing of certain services. **c.** a territory held in fee. **5.** a gratuity; tip. —*v.t.* **6.** to give a fee to. **7.** *Chiefly Scot.* to hire; employ. [1250–1300; ME < AF; OF *fie,* var. of *fief* FIEF. See FEUDAL] —**fee/less,** *adj.*
—**Syn. 1.** stipend, salary, emolument; honorarium.

feeb (fēb), *n. Slang (disparaging and offensive).* a feeble-minded person. [1910–15; by shortening]

fee·ble (fē/bəl), *adj.,* **-bler, -blest. 1.** physically weak, as from age or sickness; frail. **2.** weak intellectually or morally: *a feeble mind.* **3.** lacking in volume, loudness, brightness, distinctness, etc.: *a feeble voice; feeble light.* **4.** lacking in force, strength, or effectiveness: *feeble resistance; feeble arguments.* [1125–75; ME *feble* < OF, var. of *fleible* (by dissimilation) < L *flēbilis* lamentable, equiv. to *flē(re)* to weep + *-bilis* -BLE] —**fee/ble·ness,** *n.* —**fee/blish,** *adj.* —**fee/bly,** *adv.*
—**Syn. 1.** See **weak.**

fee·ble-mind·ed (fē/bəl mīn/did), *adj.* **1.** lacking the normal mental powers. **2.** *Med.* (formerly) mentally retarded. Cf. **idiot, imbecile, moron. 3.** stupid; unintelligent: *feeble-minded remarks.* **4.** *Archaic.* lacking firmness of mind; indecisive. [1525–35] —**fee/·ble-mind/ed·ly,** *adv.* —**fee/ble-mind/ed·ness,** *n.*

feed (fēd), *v.,* **fed, feed·ing,** *n.* —*v.t.* **1.** to give food to; supply with nourishment: *to feed a child.* **2.** to yield or serve as food for: *This land has fed 10 generations.* **3.** to provide as food. **4.** to furnish for consumption. **5.** to satisfy; minister to; gratify: *Poetry feeds the imagination.* **6.** to supply for maintenance or operation, as to a machine: *to feed paper into a photocopier.* **7.** to provide with the necessary materials for development, maintenance, or operation: *to feed a printing press with paper.* **8.** to use (land) as pasture. **9.** *Theat. Informal.* **a.** to supply (an actor, esp. a comedian) with lines or action, the responses to which are expected to elicit laughter. **b.** to provide cues to (an actor). **c.** *Chiefly Brit.* to prompt: *Stand in the wings and feed them their lines.* **10.** *Radio and Television.* to distribute (a local broadcast) via satellite or network. —*v.i.* **11.** (esp. of animals) to take food; eat: *cows feeding in a meadow; to feed well.* **12.** to be nourished or gratified; subsist: *to feed on grass; to feed on thoughts of revenge.* **13. chain feed,** to pass (work) successively into a machine in such a manner that each new piece is held in place by or connected to the one before. —*n.* **14.** food, esp. for farm animals, as cattle, horses or chickens. **15.** an allowance, portion, or supply of such food. **16.** *Informal.* a meal, esp. a lavish one. **17.** the act of feeding. **18.** the act or process of feeding a furnace, machine, etc. **19.** the material, or the amount of it, so fed or supplied. **20.** a feeding mechanism. **21.** *Elect.* feeder (def. 10). **22.** *Theat. Informal.* **a.** a line spoken by one actor, the response to which by another actor is expected to cause laughter. **b.** an actor, esp. a straight man, who provides such lines. **23.** a local television broadcast distributed by satellite or network to a much wider audience, esp. nationwide or international. **24. off one's feed,** *Slang.* **a.** reluctant to eat; without appetite. **b.** dejected; sad. **c.** not well; ill. [bef. 950; ME *feden,* OE *fēdan;* c. Goth *fodjan,* OS *fōdian.* See FOOD] —**feed/a·ble,** *adj.*
—**Syn. 1, 2.** nourish, sustain. **5.** nurture, support, encourage, bolster. **14.** FEED, FODDER, FORAGE, PROVENDER mean food for animals. FEED is the general word: *pig feed; chicken feed.* FODDER is esp. applied to dry or green feed, as opposed to pasturage, fed to horses, cattle, etc.: *fodder for winter feeding; Cornstalks are good fodder.* FORAGE is food that an animal obtains (usually grass, leaves, etc.) by searching about for it: *Lost cattle can usually live on forage.* PROVENDER denotes dry feed, such as hay, oats, or corn: *a supply of provender in the haymow and corn cribs.* —**Ant. 1, 2.** starve.

feed·back (fēd/bak/), *n.* **1.** *Electronics.* **a.** the process of returning part of the output of a circuit, system, or device to the input, either to oppose the input **(negative feedback)** or to aid the input **(positive feedback). b.** See **acoustic feedback. 2.** the furnishing of data concerning the operation or output of a machine to an automatic control device or to the machine itself, so that subsequent or ongoing operations of the machine can be altered or corrected. **3.** a reaction or response to a particular process or activity: *He got very little feedback from his speech.* **4.** evaluative information derived from such a reaction or response: *to study the feedback from an audience survey.* **5.** *Psychol.* knowledge of the results of any behavior, considered as influencing or modifying further performance. Cf. **biofeedback. 6.** *Biol.* a self-regulatory biological system, as in the synthesis of some hormones, in which the output or response affects the input, either positively or negatively. [1915–20; n. use of v. phrase *feed back*]

feed/back loop/, *Computers, Electronics.* the path by which some of the output of a circuit, system, or device is returned to the input. Cf. **closed loop.** [1980–85]

feed/ bag/, 1. Also called **nose bag.** a bag for feeding horses, placed before the mouth and fastened around the head with straps. **2. put on the feed bag,** *Slang.* to have a meal; eat. Also, **feed/bag/.** [1830–40, *Amer.*]

feed·box (fēd/boks/), *n.* **1.** a box for animal feed. **2.** a casing for the feeding mechanism of a machine. [1830–40, *Amer.;* FEED + BOX[1]]

feed·er (fē/dər), *n.* **1.** a person or thing that supplies food or feeds something. **2.** a bin or boxlike device from which farm animals may eat, esp. such a device designed to allow a number of chickens to feed simultaneously or to release a specific amount of feed at regular intervals. **3.** a person or thing that takes food or nourishment. **4.** a livestock animal that is fed an enriched diet to fatten it for market. Cf. **stocker** (def. 2). **5.** a person or device that feeds a machine, printing press, etc. **6.** a tributary stream. **7.** bird feeder. **8.** See **feeder line. 9.** See **feeder road. 10.** Also, **feed.** *Elect.* a conductor, or group of conductors, connecting primary equipment in an electric power system. **11.** *Brit.* a baby's bib. **12.** *Theat. Slang.* See **straight man.** —*adj.* **13.** being, functioning as, or serving as a feeder. **14.** pertaining to livestock to be fattened for market. [1350–1400; ME; see FEED, -ER[1]]

feed/er line/, a branch of a main transportation line, as of an airline or railroad. [1890–95]

feed/er road/, a secondary road used to bring traffic to a major road. [1955–60]

feed·grain (fēd/grān/), *n.* **1.** any cereal grain used as a feed for livestock, poultry, or other animals. **2.** a preparation of feed composed of grain or containing grain, esp. any commercially processed feed used principally for finishing cattle or poultry for market. Also, **feed/ grain/.** [FEED + GRAIN]

feed·ing (fē/ding), *n.* **1.** the act of a person or thing that feeds. **2.** an instance of eating or of taking or being given nourishment. **3.** grazing land. [bef. 900; ME *feding,* OE *fēding.* See FEED, -ING[1]]

feed/ing cup/. See **spout cup.** [1880–85]

feed/ing fren/zy, *Slang.* a ruthless attack on or exploitation of someone esp. by the media. [1985–90]

feed·lot (fēd/lot/), *n.* **1.** a plot of ground, often near a stockyard, where livestock are gathered to be fattened for market. **2.** a commercial establishment that operates a feedlot. Also, **feed/ lot/.** Also called **feed·yard** (fēd/yärd/). [1885–90; FEED + LOT]

feed·stock (fēd/stok/), *n.* raw material for processing or manufacturing industry. Also, **feed/ stock/.** [1930–35; FEED + STOCK]

feed·stuff (fēd/stuf/), *n.* feed (def. 14). [1855–60, *Amer.;* FEED + STUFF]

feed·through (fēd/thrōō/), *n. Electronics.* a connector used to pass a conductor through a circuit board or enclosure. [n. use of v. phrase *feed through*]

feed·wa·ter (fēd/wô/tər, -wot/ər), *n.* water to be supplied to a boiler from a tank or condenser for conversion into steam. Also, **feed/ wa/ter.** [1860–65; FEED + WATER]

fee-for-serv·ice (fē/fər sûr/vis), *adj.* pertaining to the charging of fees for specific services rendered in health care, as distinguished from participating in a prepaid medical practice: *fee-for-service medicine.*

feel (fēl), *v.,* **felt, feel·ing,** *n.* —*v.t.* **1.** to perceive or examine by touch. **2.** to have a sensation of (something), other than by sight, hearing, taste, or smell: *to feel a toothache.* **3.** to find or pursue (one's way) by touching, groping, or cautious moves. **4.** to be or become conscious of. **5.** to be emotionally affected by: *to feel one's disgrace keenly.* **6.** to experience the effects of: *The whole region felt the storm.* **7.** to have a particular sensation or impression of (often used reflexively and usually fol. by an adjunct or complement): *to feel oneself slighted.* **8.** to have a general or thorough conviction of; think; believe: *I feel he's guilty.* —*v.i.* **9.** to have perception by touch or by any nerves of sensation other than those of sight, hearing, taste, and smell. **10.** to make examination by touch; grope. **11.** to perceive a state of mind or a condition of body: *to feel happy; to feel well.* **12.** to have a sensation of being: *to feel warm.* **13.** to make itself perceived or apparent; seem: *How does it feel to be rich?* **14. feel for, a.** to feel sympathy for or compassion toward; empathize with: *I know you're disappointed and upset, and I feel for you.* **b.** *Southeastern Pennsylvania and Maryland.* to have a liking or desire for: *If you feel for more pie, just help yourself.* **15. feel like,** *Informal.* to have a desire for; be favorably disposed to: *I don't feel like going out tonight. Do you feel like a movie?* **16. feel like oneself,** to be in one's usual frame of mind or state of health: *She hasn't been feeling like herself since the accident.* Also, **feel oneself. 17. feel no pain.** See **pain** (def. 5). **18. feel out,** to attempt to ascertain (the nature of a situation, someone's attitude, etc.) by indirect or subtle means: *Why not feel out the other neighbors' opinions before you make a complaint.* **19. feel up,** *Slang (vulgar).* to fondle or touch (someone) in a sexual manner. **20. feel up to,** *Informal.* to feel or be able to; be capable of: *He didn't feel up to going to the theater so soon after his recent illness.* —*n.* **21.** a quality of an object that is perceived by feeling or touching: *the soft feel of cotton.* **22.** a sensation of something felt; a vague mental impression or feeling: *a feel of winter; a feel of sadness in the air.* **23.** the sense of touch: *soft to the feel.* **24.** native ability or acquired sensitivity: *to have a feel for what is right.* **25.** *Informal.* an act or instance of touching with the hand or fingers. **26.** *Slang (vulgar).* an act or instance of feeling up. **27. cop a feel,** *Slang (vulgar).* to touch another person's body sexually, often in a quick and surreptitious way. [bef. 900; ME *felen,* OE *fēlan;* c. OS *fōlian,* G *fühlen;* akin to ON *falma* to grope. See FUMBLE]

feel·er (fē/lər), *n.* **1.** a person or thing that feels. **2.** a proposal, remark, hint, etc., designed to bring out the opinions or purposes of others: *Interested in an accord, both labor and management were putting out feelers.* **3.** *Zool.* an organ of touch, as an antenna or a tentacle. **4.** Also called **feel/er gauge/.** *Engin.* a gauge having several blades of known thickness, used for measuring clearances. **5.** *Naut.* a device for indicating that the lead of a mechanical sounding device has come to the bottom. [1520–30; FEEL + -ER[1]]

feel-good (fēl/gŏŏd/), *adj. Informal.* intended to make one happy or satisfied: *a feel-good movie; feel-good politics.* [1975–80; *Amer.*]

feel·ing (fē/ling), *n.* **1.** the function or the power of perceiving by touch. **2.** physical sensation not connected with sight, hearing, taste, or smell. **3.** a particular sensation of this kind: *a feeling of warmth; a feeling of pain.* **4.** the general state of consciousness considered independently of particular sensations, thoughts, etc. **5.** a consciousness or vague awareness: *a feeling of inferiority.* **6.** an emotion or emotional perception or attitude: *a feeling of joy; a feeling of sorrow.* **7.** capacity for emotion, esp. compassion: *to have great feeling for the sufferings of others.* **8.** a sentiment; attitude; opinion: *The general feeling was in favor of the proposal.* **9. feelings,** sensibilities; susceptibilities: *to hurt one's feelings.* **10.** fine emotional endowment. **11.** (in music, art, etc.) **a.** emotion or sympathetic perception revealed by an artist in his or her work: *a poem without feeling.* **b.** the general impression conveyed by a work: *a landscape painting with a spacious feeling.* **c.** sympathetic appreciation, as of music: *to play with feeling.* —*adj.* **12.** sensitive; sentient. **13.** readily affected by emotion; sympathetic: *a feeling heart.* **14.** indicating or characterized by emotion: *a feeling reply.* [1125–75; ME; see FEEL, -ING[1], -ING[2]] —**feel/ing·ly,** *adv.* —**feel/ing·ness,** *n.*
—**Syn. 5.** FEELING, EMOTION, PASSION, SENTIMENT refer to pleasurable or painful sensations experienced when one is stirred to sympathy, anger, fear, love, grief, etc. FEELING is a general term for a subjective point of view as well as for specific sensations: *to be guided by feeling rather than by facts; a feeling of sadness, of rejoicing.* EMOTION is applied to an intensified feeling: *agitated by emotion.* PASSION is strong or violent emotion, often so overpowering that it masters the mind or judgment: *stirred to a passion of anger.* SENTIMENT is a mixture of thought and feeling, esp. refined or tender feeling: *Recollections are often colored by sentiment.* **6.** sympathy, empathy, tenderness, sensitivity, sentiment. **12.** emotional, tender. **13.** impassioned, passionate.

fee/ sim/ple. See under **fee** (def. 4a). [1425–75; late ME < AF]

fee-split·ting (fē/split/ing), *n.* the practice of dividing a fee for professional services between two professional persons, as between a referring doctor and a specialist, without the knowledge of the client. [1940–45] —**fee/-split/ter,** *n.*

feet (fēt), *n.* **1.** a pl. of **foot. 2. drag one's feet,** to act or proceed slowly or without enthusiasm; to be reluctant to act, comply, etc.: *We can't begin the project until the steering committee stops dragging its feet.* **3. on one's feet, a.** in a standing position. **b.** in an independent or secure position: *The loan helped him get on his feet again.* **c.** in a restored or recovered state; able to continue: *Psychotherapy helped her get back on her feet after her breakdown.* **4. sit at the feet of,** to attend upon as a disciple or follower: *American writers and painters no longer sit at the feet of Europeans.* **5. stand on one's own feet, a.** to be financially self-supporting. **b.** to be independent: *Overprotective parents do not prepare their children to stand on their own feet.* Also, **stand on one's own two feet. 6. sweep one off one's feet,** to impress or overwhelm by ability, enthusiasm, or charm: *The gaiety of the occasion swept them off their feet.*

fee/ tail/. See under **fee** (def. 4a). [1250–1300; ME < AF]

feet·first (fēt/fûrst/), *adv.* **1.** with the feet foremost. **2.** *Slang.* on a stretcher or in a coffin; dead. [1945–50; FEET + FIRST]

feet/ of clay/, 1. a weakness or hidden flaw in the character of a greatly admired or respected person: *He was disillusioned to find that even Lincoln had feet of clay.* **2.** any unexpected or critical fault. [1855–60]

feeze (fēz, fāz), *n. Dial.* **1.** a state of vexation or worry. **2.** a violent rush or impact. Also, **feaze.** [1350–1400; ME *fese* blast, rush, *fesen* to drive, chase, frighten; cf. OE (Anglian) *fēsan,* (West Saxon) *fӯsan*]

feign (fān), *v.t.* **1.** to represent fictitiously; put on an appearance of: *to feign sickness.* **2.** to invent fictitiously or deceptively, as a story or an excuse. **3.** to imitate deceptively: *to feign another's voice.* —*v.i.* **4.** to make believe; pretend: *She's only feigning, she isn't really ill.* [1250–1300; ME *fei(g)nen* < OF *feign-,* present s. of *feindre* < L *fingere* to shape, invent, feign] —**feign/er,** *n.* —**feign/ing·ly,** *adv.*
—**Syn. 4.** See **pretend.**

feigned (fānd), *adj.* **1.** pretended; sham; counterfeit: *feigned enthusiasm.* **2.** assumed; fictitious: *a feigned name.* **3.** disguised: *a feigned voice.* [1325–75; ME; see FEIGN, -ED[2]] —**feign·ed·ly** (fā/nid lē), *adv.* —**feign/·ed·ness,** *n.*

fei·jo·a (fā yō/ə, -hō/ə), *n.* **1.** a shrub, *Feijoa sellowiana,* of the myrtle family, native to South America, bearing edible, greenish, plumlike fruit. **2.** the fruit of this shrub. Also called **pineapple guava.** [< NL (1858), after João da Silva *Feijó* (1760–1824), Brazilian soldier and naturalist; see -A[2]]

fei·jo·a·da (*Port.* fā zhŏŏ ä/dä; *Eng.* fā jwä/də), *n. Brazilian Cookery.* a dish of rice and black beans baked with various kinds of meat and sausage. [< Brazilian Pg, deriv. of Pg *feijão* bean, earlier *feijoes* (pl.) < L *faseolus,* dim. of *fasēlus* a legume, perh. the cowpea < Gk *phásēlos;* see -ADE[1]]

Fein·ing·er (fī/ning ər), *n.* **1. An·dre·as (Bernhard Lyonel)** (an drā/əs, än-), born 1906, U.S. photographer, born in France. **2.** his father, **Lyonel (Charles Adrian),** 1871–1956, U.S. painter.

fein·schmeck·er (fīn/shmek/ər), *n., pl.* ***-schmeck·er.*** *German.* gourmet.

feint (fānt), *n.* **1.** a movement made in order to deceive an adversary; an attack aimed at one place or point merely as a distraction from the real place or point of attack: *the feints of a skilled fencer.* **2.** a feigned or assumed appearance: *His air of approval was a feint to conceal his real motives.* —*v.i.* **3.** to make a feint. —*v.t.* **4.** to deceive with a feint. **5.** to make a false show of; simulate. [1275–1325; ME < OF *feinte,* n. use of fem. of *feint* pretended, ptp. of *feindre* to FEIGN]

feints (fānts), *n.pl.* faints.

feir·ie (fēr′ē), *adj. Scot.* healthy; strong. [1375–1425; late ME (Scots) *fery,* equiv. to *fer* (OE *fēre* able-bodied, fit, deriv. of *fōr* journey; see FARE) + -Y[1]]

Fei·sal I (fī′səl). See **Faisal I.** Also, **Feisul I.**

Feisal II. See **Faisal II.** Also, **Feisul II.**

feist (fīst), *n.* **1.** *Chiefly South Midland and Southern U.S.* a small mongrel dog, esp. one that is ill-tempered; cur; mutt. —*v.i.* **2.** *South Midland U.S.* to prance or strut about: *Look at him feist around in his new clothes.* Also, **fice, fist.** [1760–70; cf. (from 16th cent.) *fisting hound, fisting cur,* as contemptuous epithets for any kind of dog (prp. of *fist* to break wind, late ME; cf. OE *fisting* breaking wind, MLG *vīst,* G *Fist* fart); (def. 2) perh. back formation from FEISTY]

feist·y (fī′stē), *adj.,* **feist·i·er, feist·i·est. 1.** full of animation, energy, or courage; spirited; spunky; plucky: *The champion is faced with a feisty challenger.* **2.** ill-tempered; pugnacious. **3.** troublesome; difficult: *feisty legal problems.* [1895–1900, *Amer.*; FEIST + -Y[1]] —**feist′i·ly,** *adv.* —**feist′i·ness,** *n.*

fe·la·fel (fə lä′fəl), *n.* falafel.

Fel·dene (fel′dēn), *Pharm., Trademark.* a brand of piroxicam.

feld·spar (feld′spär′, fel′-), *n.* any of a group of minerals, principally aluminosilicates of potassium, sodium, and calcium, characterized by two cleavages at nearly right angles: one of the most important constituents of igneous rocks. Also, **felspar.** [1750–60; *feld-* (< G: field) + SPAR[3]; r. *feldspath* < G (*Feld* field + *Spath* spar)]

feld·spath·ic (feld spath′ik, fel-, feld′spath-, fel′-), *adj. Mineral.* of, pertaining to, or containing feldspar. Also, **felspathic, feld′spath·ose′, felspathose.** [1825–35; < G *Feldspath* (see FELDSPAR) + -IC]

feld·spath·oid (feld′spa thoid′, fel′-), *Mineral.* —*adj.* **1.** Also, **feld′spath·oi′dal.** of or pertaining to a group of minerals similar in chemical composition to certain feldspars except for a lower silica content. —*n.* **2.** a mineral of this group, as nepheline. [1895–1900; < G *Feldspath* (see FELDSPAR) + -OID]

Fe·lice (fə lēs′), *n.* a female given name, form of **Felicia.**

Fe·li·cia (fə lish′ə, -lish′ē ə, -lē′shə, -lis′ē ə), *n.* a female given name: from a Latin word meaning "happy."

fe·li·cif·ic (fē′lə sif′ik), *adj.* causing or tending to cause happiness. [1860–65; < L *fēlīci-* (s. of *fēlīx*) happy + -FIC]

fe·lic·i·tate (fi lis′i tāt′), *v.,* **-tat·ed, -tat·ing,** *adj.* —*v.t.* **1.** to compliment upon a happy event; congratulate. **2.** *Archaic.* to make happy. —*adj.* **3.** *Obs.* made happy. [1595–1605; < LL *fēlīcitātus* made happy (ptp. of *fēlīcitāre*). See FELICITY, -ATE[1]] —**fe·lic′i·ta′tor,** *n.*

fe·lic·i·ta·tion (fi lis′i tā′shən), *n.* an expression of good wishes; congratulation. [1700–10; FELICITATE + -ION]

fe·lic·i·tous (fi lis′i təs), *adj.* **1.** well-suited for the occasion, as an action, manner, or expression; apt; appropriate: *The chairman's felicitous anecdote set everyone at ease.* **2.** having a special ability for suitable manner or expression, as a person. [1725–35; FELICIT(Y) + -OUS] —**fe·lic′i·tous·ly,** *adv.* —**fe·lic′i·tous·ness,** *n.*

fe·lic·i·ty (fi lis′i tē), *n., pl.* **-ties. 1.** the state of being happy, esp. in a high degree; bliss: *marital felicity.* **2.** an instance of this. **3.** a source of happiness. **4.** a skillful faculty: *felicity of expression.* **5.** an instance or display of this: *the many felicities of the poem.* **6.** *Archaic.* good fortune. [1350–1400; ME *felicite* (< AF) < L *fēlīcitās,* equiv. to *fēlīci-* (s. of *fēlīx*) happy + *-tās* -TY[2]]
—**Syn. 1.** See **happiness.**

Fe·lic·i·ty (fi lis′i tē), *n.* a female given name, form of **Felicia.** Also, **Fe·lic·i·ta** (fi lis′i tə).

fe·lid (fē′lid), *n.* any animal of the family Felidae, comprising the cats. [1890–95; < NL *Felidae;* see FELIS, -ID[2]]

fe·line (fē′līn), *adj.* **1.** belonging or pertaining to the cat family, Felidae. **2.** catlike; characteristic of animals of the cat family: *a feline tread.* **3.** sly, stealthy, or treacherous. —*n.* **4.** an animal of the cat family. [1675–85; < L *fēl(ēs)* (see FELIS) + -INE[1]; cf. LL *fēlīneus* of a wild cat] —**fe′line·ly,** *adv.* —**fe′line·ness, fe·lin·i·ty** (fi lin′i tē), *n.*

fe′line distem′per, distemper[1] (def. 1c). Also called **fe′line agranulocyto′sis, fe′line infec′tious enteri′tis, fe′line panleukope′nia.** [1940–45]

fe′line leuke′mia vi′rus, a retrovirus, mainly affecting cats, that depresses the immune system and leads to opportunistic infections, lymphosarcoma, and other disorders. *Abbr.:* FeLV, FLV [1975–80]

Fe·li·pe (fe lē′pe), *n.* **Le·ón (Ca·mi·no)** (le ôn′ kä mē′nô), 1884–1968, Spanish poet, in South America after 1939.

Fe·lis (fē′lis), *n.* a genus of mostly small cats, including the domestic cat, margay, puma, and ocelot, sharing with certain cats of related genera an inability to roar due to ossification of the hyoid bone in the larynx. Cf. ***Panthera.*** [< NL (Linnaeus); L *fēlis, fēlēs* any of several small carnivores, including the wild cat]

Fe·lix (fē′liks), *n.* a male given name: from a Latin word meaning "happy, lucky."

Felix I, Saint, died A.D. 274, pope 269–274.

Felix III, Saint, died A.D. 492, pope 483–492.

Felix IV, Saint, died A.D. 530, pope 526–530.

fell[1] (fel), *v.* pt. of **fall.**

fell[2] (fel), *v.t.* **1.** to knock, strike, shoot, or cut down; cause to fall: *to fell a moose; to fell a tree.* **2.** *Sewing.* to finish (a seam) by sewing the edge down flat. —*n.* **3.** *Lumbering.* the amount of timber cut down in one season. **4.** *Sewing.* a seam finished by felling. [bef. 900; ME *fellen,* OE *fellan,* causative of *feallan* to FALL; c. Goth *falljan* to cause to fall]

fell[3] (fel), *adj.* **1.** fierce; cruel; dreadful; savage. **2.** destructive; deadly: *fell poison; fell disease.* **3. at** or **in one fell swoop.** See **swoop** (def. 5). [1250–1300; ME *fel* < OF, nom. of *felon* wicked. See FELON] —**fell′ness,** *n.*

fell[4] (fel), *n.* the skin or hide of an animal; pelt. [bef. 900; ME, OE; c. D *vel,* G *Fell,* ON *-fjall* (in *berfjall* bearskin), Goth *-fill* (in *thrutsfill* scab-skin, leprosy); akin to L *pellis* skin, hide]

fell[5] (fel), *n. Scot. and North Eng.* an upland pasture, moor, or thicket; a highland plateau. [1300–50; ME < ON *fell, fjall* hill, mountain, akin to G *Felsen* rock, cliff]

fel·la (fel′ə), *n. Informal.* fellow. [cf. FELLER[1]]

fell·a·ble (fel′ə bəl), *adj.* capable of being or fit to be felled. [1575–85; FELL[2] + -ABLE]

fel·lah (fel′ə), *n., pl.* **fel·lahs,** *Arab.* **fel·la·hin, fel·la·heen** (fel′ə hēn′). a native peasant or laborer in Egypt, Syria, etc. [1735–45; < Ar *fallāḥ* peasant]

fel·late (fə lāt′), *v.,* **-lat·ed, -lat·ing.** —*v.t.* **1.** to perform fellatio on. —*v.i.* **2.** to engage in fellatio. [1965–70; by back formation from FELLATIO] —**fel·la′tor,** *n.*

fel·la·ti·o (fə lā′shē ō′, -lä′tē ō′, fe-), *n.* oral stimulation of the penis, esp. to orgasm. Also, **fel·la·tion** (fə lā′shən, fe-). [1885–90; < NL *fellātiō,* equiv. to L *fel(l)ā-t(us)* (ptp. of *fel(l)āre* to suck) + *-iō* -ION]

fell·er[1] (fel′ər), *n. Informal.* fellow. [1815–25; orig. dial.; by reduction of (ō) to (ə) and merger with words ending in *-er*]

fell·er[2] (fel′ər), *n.* **1.** a person or thing that fells. **2.** *Sewing.* a person or thing that fells a seam. [1350–1400; ME *fellere.* See FELL[2], -ER[1]]

Fel·ler (fel′ər), *n.* **Robert William Andrew** (*Bob*), born 1918, U.S. baseball player.

Fel·li·ni (fə lē′nē; *It.* fel lē′nē), *n.* **Fe·de·ri·co** (*It.* fe′de rē′kô), born 1920, Italian film director and writer.

fell·mon·ger (fel′mung′gər, -mong′-), *n. Chiefly Brit.* a preparer of skins or hides of animals, esp. sheepskins, prior to leather making. [1520–30; FELL[4] + MONGER] —**fell′mon′ger·ing, fell′mon′ger·y,** *n.*

fel·loe (fel′ō), *n.* the circular rim, or a part of the rim of a wheel, into which the outer ends of the spokes are inserted. Also, **felly.** [bef. 900; ME *felwe,* OE *felg(e);* c. G *Felge*]

fel·low (fel′ō), *n.* **1.** a man or boy: *a fine old fellow; a nice little fellow.* **2.** *Informal.* beau; suitor: *Mary had her fellow over to meet her folks.* **3.** *Informal.* person; one: *They don't treat a fellow very well here.* **4.** a person of small worth or no esteem. **5.** a companion; comrade; associate: *They have been fellows since childhood.* **6.** a person belonging to the same rank or class; equal; peer: *The doctor conferred with his fellows.* **7.** one of a pair; mate; match: *a shoe without its fellow.* **8.** *Educ.* **a.** a graduate student of a university or college to whom an allowance is granted for special study. **b.** *Brit.* an incorporated member of a college, entitled to certain privileges. **c.** a member of the corporation or board of trustees of certain universities or colleges. **9.** a member of any of certain learned societies: *a fellow of the British Academy.* **10.** *Obs.* a partner. —*v.t.* **11.** to make or represent as equal with another. **12.** *Archaic.* to produce a fellow to; match. —*adj.* **13.** belonging to the same class or group; united by the same occupation, interests, etc.; being in the same condition: *fellow students; fellow sufferers.* [bef. 1050; ME *felowe, felawe,* late OE *fēolaga* < ON *fēlagi* partner in a joint undertaking, equiv. to *fē* money, property (c. OE *feoh,* G *Vieh*) + *-lagi* bedfellow, comrade; akin to LAIR[1], LIE[2]]

fel′low crea′ture, a kindred creature, esp. a fellow human being. [1640–50]

fel′low feel′ing, 1. sympathetic feeling; sympathy: *to have fellow feeling for the unfortunate.* **2.** a sense of joint interest: *to act out of fellow feeling to support one's country.* [1605–15]

fel·low·ly (fel′ō lē), *adj.* **1.** sociable or friendly. —*adv.* **2.** in a sociable or friendly manner. [1175–1225; ME *feolahlich, felawely;* see FELLOW, -LY]

fel·low·man (fel′ō man′), *n., pl.* **-men.** another member of the human race, esp. a kindred human being: *Don't deny full recognition to your fellowmen.* Also, **fel′low man′.** [1750–60]

fel′low serv′ant, (under the fellow-servant rule) an employee working with another employee for the same employer. [1525–35]

fel′low-serv′ant rule′ (fel′ō sûr′vənt), the common-law rule that the employer is not liable to an employee for injuries resulting from the negligence of a fellow employee.

fel·low·ship (fel′ō ship′), *n., v.,* **-shipped** or **-shiped, -ship·ping** or **-ship·ing.** —*n.* **1.** the condition or relation of being a fellow: *the fellowship of mankind.* **2.** friendly relationship; companionship: *the fellowship of father and son.* **3.** community of interest, feeling, etc. **4.** communion, as between members of the same church. **5.** friendliness. **6.** an association of persons having similar tastes, interests, etc. **7.** a company, guild, or corporation. **8.** *Educ.* **a.** the body of fellows in a college or university. **b.** the position or emoluments of a fellow of a college or university, or the sum of money he or she receives. **c.** a foundation for the maintenance of a fellow in a college or university. —*v.t.* **9.** to admit to fellowship, esp. religious fellowship. —*v.i.* **10.** to join in fellowship, esp. religious fellowship. [1150–1200; ME *felaweshipe.* See FELLOW, -SHIP]
—**Syn. 2.** comradeship, camaraderie, friendship, society, intimacy.

fel′low trav′eler, 1. a person who supports or sympathizes with a political party, esp. the Communist party, but is not an enrolled member. **2.** anyone who, although not a member, supports or sympathizes with some organization, movement, or the like. —**fel·low-trav·el·ing** (fel′ō trav′ə ling, -trav′ling), *adj.* [1605–15, for literal sense]

fel·ly[1] (fel′ē), *n., pl.* **-lies.** felloe. [ME *felien* (pl.), var. of *felwe* FELLOE]

fel·ly[2] (fel′ē), *adv.* in a fell manner; fiercely; ruthlessly. [1250–1300; ME *felliche.* See FELL[3], -LY]

fe·lo-de-se (fel′ō di sē′, -sā′), *n., pl.* **fe·lo·nes-de-se** (fel′ə nēz′di sē′, -sā′, fə lō′nēz-), **fe·los-de-se** (fel′ōz-di sē′, -sā′). **1.** a person who commits suicide or commits an unlawful malicious act resulting in his or her own death. **2.** the act of suicide. [1645–55; < AL, equiv. to *felō* a felon + *dē* in respect to, of + *sē* oneself]

fel·on[1] (fel′ən), *n.* **1.** *Law.* a person who has committed a felony. **2.** *Archaic.* a wicked person. —*adj.* **3.** *Archaic.* wicked; malicious; treacherous. [1250–1300; ME *fel(o)un* wicked < AF; OF *fel* (nom.), *felun* (obl.) wicked person, traitor, perh. < Old Low Franconian **fillo,* n. corresponding to OS *fillian* to ill-treat, whip, MD *villen* to flay, OHG *fillen* to beat, whip; cf. FELL[3]]

fel·on[2] (fel′ən), *n.* an acute and painful inflammation of the deeper tissues of a finger or toe, usually near the nail: a form of whitlow. [1375–1425; late ME *felo(u)n* < ML *fellōn-* (s. of *fellō*) scrofulous tumor, of uncert. orig.]

fe·lo·ni·ous (fə lō′nē əs), *adj.* **1.** *Law.* pertaining to, of the nature of, or involving a felony: *felonious homicide; felonious intent.* **2.** wicked; base; villainous. [1375–1425; FELONY + -OUS; r. late ME *felonous* < AF, OF] —**fe·lo′ni·ous·ly,** *adv.* —**fe·lo′ni·ous·ness,** *n.*

fel·on·ry (fel′ən rē), *n.* **1.** the whole body or class of felons. **2.** the convict population of a penal colony. [1830–40; FELON + -RY]

fel·o·ny (fel′ə nē), *n., pl.* **-nies.** *Law.* **1.** an offense, as murder or burglary, of graver character than those called misdemeanors, esp. those commonly punished in the U.S. by imprisonment for more than a year. **2.** *Early Eng. Law.* any crime punishable by death or mutilation and forfeiture of lands and goods. [1250–1300; ME *felonie* < AF, OF: villainy, a felony. See FELON[1], -Y[3]]

fel′ony mur′der, a killing treated as a murder because, though unintended, it occurred during the commission or attempted commission of a felony, as robbery.

fel·sic (fel′sik), *adj. Geol.* (of rocks) consisting chiefly of feldspars, feldspathoids, quartz, and other light-colored minerals. Cf. **mafic.** [1910–15; FEL(DSPAR) + S(ILICA) + -IC]

fel·site (fel′sīt), *n.* a dense, fine-grained, igneous rock consisting typically of feldspar and quartz, both of which may appear as phenocrysts. [1785–95; FELS(PAR) + -ITE[1]] —**fel·sit·ic** (fel sit′ik), *adj.*

fel·spar (fel′spär′), *n.* feldspar. [< G *Fels* rock + SPAR[3], by false etymological analysis]

fel·spath·ic (fel spath′ik), *adj.* feldspathic. Also, **fel′·spath·ose′.**

felt[1] (felt), *v.* pt. and pp. of **feel.**

felt[2] (felt), *n.* **1.** a nonwoven fabric of wool, fur, or hair, matted together by heat, moisture, and great pressure. **2.** any article made of this material, as a hat. **3.** any matted fabric or material, as a mat of asbestos fibers, rags, or old paper, used for insulation and in construction. —*adj.* **4.** pertaining to or made of felt. —*v.t.* **5.** to make into felt; mat or press together. **6.** to cover with or as with felt. —*v.i.* **7.** to become matted together. [bef. 1000; ME, OE; c. G *Filz;* see FILTER]

felt·ing (fel′ting), *n.* **1.** felted material, either woven or felt fabric. **2.** the act or process of making felt. **3.** the materials of which felt is made. [1680–90; FELT[2] + -ING[1]]

felt′ mark′er, a felt pen with a wide nib for making identifying marks, as on clothing.

felt′ side′, the top side of a sheet of paper, the side against the felt rollers during manufacture, normally preferred for printing. Cf. **wire side.** [1955–60]

felt′-tip pen′ (felt′tip′), a pen that holds quick-drying ink conveyed to a writing surface by means of a felt nib. Also called **felt′ pen′.** [1955–60]

fe·luc·ca (fə luk′ə, -lo͞o′kə), *n.* **1.** a sailing vessel, lateen-rigged on two masts, used in the Mediterranean Sea and along the Spanish and Portuguese coasts. **2.** a small fishing boat formerly used in the San Francisco Bay area. [1620–30; earlier *falluca* < Sp *faluca,* earlier var. of *falūa,* perh. < Catalan *faluga* < Ar *falūwah* small cargo ship]

felucca (def. 1)

FeLV, feline leukemia virus.

fem (fem), *Slang.* —*adj.* **1.** feminine. —*n.* **2.** a woman. **3.** femme. [by shortening]

fem., 1. female. **2.** feminine.

FEMA, Federal Emergency Management Agency.

fe·male (fē′māl), *n.* **1.** a person bearing two X chromosomes in the cell nuclei and normally having a

CONCISE PRONUNCIATION KEY: *act, cāpe, dâre, pärt; set, ēqual; if, īce; ox, ōver, ôrder, oil, bo͝ok, bo͞ot, out; up, ûrge; child; sing; shoe; thin, that;* zh as in *treasure.* ə = *a* as in *alone, e* as in *system, i* as in *easily, o* as in *gallop, u* as in *circus;* ° as in *fire* (fī°r), *hour* (ou°r). l and n can serve as syllabic consonants, as in *cradle* (krād′l), and *button* (but′n). See the full key inside the front cover.

vagina, a uterus and ovaries, and developing at puberty a relatively rounded body and enlarged breasts, and retaining a beardless face; a girl or woman. **2.** an organism of the sex or sexual phase that normally produces egg cells. **3.** *Bot.* a pistillate plant. —*adj.* **4.** of, pertaining to, or being a female animal or plant. **5.** of, pertaining to, or characteristic of a female person; feminine: *female suffrage; female charm.* **6.** composed of females: *a female readership.* **7.** *Bot.* **a.** designating or pertaining to a plant or its reproductive structure that produces or contains elements requiring fertilization. **b.** (of seed plants) pistillate. **8.** *Mach.* being or having a recessed part into which a corresponding part fits: *a female plug.* Cf. **male** (def. 5). [1275–1325; ME, var. (by assoc. with MALE) of *femelle* < AF, OF *femel(l)e* < L *fēmella,* dim. of *fēmina* woman (see -ELLE); in VL developing the sense "female of an animal"] —**fe′male·ness,** *n.*

—**Syn. 1.** See **woman. 4–7.** FEMALE, FEMININE, EFFEMINATE are adjectives that describe women and girls or attributes and conduct culturally ascribed to them. FEMALE, which is applied to plants and animals as well as to human beings, is a biological or physiological descriptor, classifying individuals on the basis of their potential or actual ability to produce offspring in bisexual reproduction. It contrasts with MALE in all uses: *her oldest female relative; the female parts of the flower.* FEMININE refers essentially to qualities or behaviors deemed by a culture or society to be especially appropriate to or ideally associated with women and girls. In American and Western European culture, these have traditionally included features such as delicacy, gentleness, gracefulness, and patience: *to dance with feminine grace; a feminine sensitivity to moods.* FEMININE is also, less frequently, used to refer to physical features: *a lovely feminine figure; small, feminine hands.* EFFEMINATE is most often applied derogatorily to men or boys, suggesting that they have character or behavior traits culturally believed to be appropriate to women and girls rather than to men: *an effeminate horror of rough play; an effeminate speaking style.* See also **womanly.**

fe′male circumci′sion, clitoridectomy.

fe′male imper′sonator, a male performer who dresses as and impersonates women. [1905–10]

fe′male rhyme′. See **feminine rhyme.** [1660–70]

fe′male suf′frage. See **woman suffrage.** [1865–70]

feme (fem), *n. Law.* a woman or wife. [1585–95; < AF, OF *fem(m)e* < L *fēmina* woman; akin to FETUS, FECUND]

feme′ cov′ert (kuv′ərt), *pl.* **femes covert.** *Law.* a married woman. [1520–30; < AF: covered (protected) woman]

feme′ sole′ (sōl), *pl.* **femes sole.** *Law.* **1.** an unmarried woman, whether never married, widowed, or divorced. **2.** a married woman who is independent of her husband with respect to property. [1520–30; < AF]

feme′-sole′ trad′er (fem′sōl′), *Law.* a married woman who is entitled to carry on business on her own account and responsibility, independently of her husband. Also called **feme′-sole′ mer′chant.**

fem·ic (fem′ik), *adj. Petrol.* of or pertaining to a group of rock-forming minerals in which iron and magnesium are essential components. Cf. **mafic.** [1900–05; < L *fe(r-rum)* iron + M(AGNESIUM) + -IC]

fem·i·cide (fem′ə sīd′), *n.* **1.** the act of killing a woman. **2.** a person who kills a woman. [1820–30; FEME + -I- + -CIDE]

fem·i·na·cy (fem′ə nə sē), *n., pl.* **-cies.** feminine nature. [1840–50; < L *fēmin(a)* + -ACY]

fem·i·ne·i·ty (fem′ə nē′i tē), *n.* feminine nature; womanliness. [1810–20; < L *fēmine(us)* of a woman (*fēmin(a)* woman + *-eus* -EOUS) + -ITY]

fem·i·nine (fem′ə nin), *adj.* **1.** pertaining to a woman or girl: *feminine beauty; feminine dress.* **2.** having qualities traditionally ascribed to women, as sensitivity or gentleness. **3.** effeminate; womanish: *a man with a feminine walk.* **4.** belonging to the female sex; female: *feminine staff members.* **5.** *Gram.* noting or pertaining to that one of the three genders of Latin, Greek, German, etc., or one of the two genders of French, Spanish, Hebrew, etc., having among its members most nouns referring to females, as well as other nouns, as Latin *stella* "star," or German *Zeit* "time." —*n. Gram.* **6.** the feminine gender. **7.** a noun or other element in or marking that gender. [1350–1400; ME < AF, OF: fem. of *feminin* < L of *fēminīnus,* equiv. to *fēmin(a)* woman (see FETUS) + *-inus* -INE[1]] —**fem′i·nine·ly,** *adv.* —**fem′i·nine·ness,** *n.*

—**Syn. 2.** See **female.**

fem′inine caesu′ra, *Pros.* a caesura occurring immediately after an unstressed or short syllable.

fem′inine end′ing, 1. *Pros.* an unaccented syllable at the close of a line of poetry, often one that is added to the metrical pattern as an extra syllable. **2.** *Gram.* a termination or final syllable marking a feminine word: In Latin *-ā* is a feminine ending for the ablative case in the singular. [1890–95]

fem′inine rhyme′, *Pros.* a rhyme either of two syllables of which the second is unstressed **(double rhyme),** as in *motion, notion,* or of three syllables of which the second and third are unstressed **(triple rhyme),** as in *fortunate, importunate.* Also called **female rhyme.** [1865–70]

fem·i·nin·i·ty (fem′ə nin′i tē), *n.* **1.** the quality of being feminine; womanliness. **2.** women collectively. **3.** effeminacy. Also, **fe·min·i·ty** (fi min′i tē). [1350–1400; ME *femininite.* See FEMININE, -ITY]

CONCISE ETYMOLOGY KEY: <, descended or borrowed from; >, whence; b., blend of, blended; c., cognate with; cf., compare; deriv., derivative; equiv., equivalent; imit., imitative; obl., oblique; r., replacing; s., stem; sp., spelling, spelled; resp., respelling, respelled; trans., translation; ?, origin unknown; *, unattested; ‡, probably earlier than. See the full key inside the front cover.

fem·i·nism (fem′ə niz′əm), *n.* **1.** the doctrine advocating social, political, and all other rights of women equal to those of men. **2.** (*sometimes cap.*) an organized movement for the attainment of such rights for women. **3.** feminine character. [1890–95; < F *féminisme;* see FEMININE, -ISM] —**fem′i·nist,** *n., adj.* —**fem′i·nis′tic,** *adj.*

fem·i·nize (fem′ə nīz′), *v.t., v.i.,* **-nized, -niz·ing.** to make or become feminine. Also, *esp. Brit.,* **fem′i·nise′.** [1645–55; < L *fēmin(a)* woman + -IZE] —**fem′i·ni·za′·tion,** *n.*

Fem′ Lib′, *Informal* (*sometimes disparaging*). See **women's liberation.** Also, **Fem′lib′.** [*Fem(inine) Lib(eration)*] —**fem′ lib′ber.**

femme (fem), *n. Slang.* a lesbian who is notably feminine in appearance. Also, **fem.** [< F: woman; see FEME]

femme fa·tale (fem′ fə tal′, -täl′, fā-; *Fr.* fam fa-tal′), *pl.* **femmes fa·tales** (fem′ fə talz′, -tälz′, fā-; *Fr.* fam fa tal′). an irresistibly attractive woman, esp. one who leads men into difficult, dangerous, or disastrous situations; siren. [< F: lit., fatal woman]

fem·o·ral (fem′ər əl), *adj.* of, pertaining to, or situated at, in, or near the thigh or femur. [1775–85; < L *femor-* (s. of *femur*) thigh + -AL[1]]

fem′oral ar′tery, *Anat.* the main artery of the thigh, supplying blood to the leg. [1775–85]

femto-, a combining form used in the names of units of measurement which are 10^{-15} (one quadrillionth) smaller than the unit denoted by the base word. [< Dan, Norw *femt(en)* fifteen + -o-]

fem·to·me·ter (fem′tə mē′tər), *n. Physics.* fermi. *Symbol:* fm [1970–75; FEMTO- + METER[1]]

fe·mur (fē′mər), *n., pl.* **fe·murs, fem·o·ra** (fem′ər ə). **1.** *Anat.* a bone in the human leg extending from the pelvis to the knee, that is the longest, largest, and strongest in the body; thighbone. See diag. under **skeleton. 2.** *Zool.* a corresponding bone of the leg or hind limb of an animal. **3.** *Entomol.* the third segment of the leg of an insect (counting from the base), situated between the trochanter and the tibia. See diag. under **coxa.** [1555–65; < L: thigh]

fen[1] (fen), *n.* **1.** low land covered wholly or partially with water; boggy land; a marsh. **2. the Fens,** a marshy region W and S of The Wash, in E England. [bef. 900; ME, OE; c. ON *fen* quagmire, Goth *fani* mud, D *ven,* G *Fenn* fen, bog]

fen[2] (fen), *n., pl.* **fen.** an aluminum coin and monetary unit of the People's Republic of China, the hundredth part of a yuan or the tenth part of a jiao. [1905–10; < Chin *fēn*]

fe·na·gle (fi nā′gəl), *v.t., v.i.,* **-gled, -gling.** finagle.

fence (fens), *n., v.,* **fenced, fenc·ing.** —*n.* **1.** a barrier enclosing or bordering a field, yard, etc., usually made of posts and wire or wood, used to prevent entrance, to confine, or to mark a boundary. **2.** *Informal.* a person who receives and disposes of stolen goods. **3.** the place of business of such a person. **4.** the act, practice, art, or sport of fencing. **5.** skill in argument, repartee, etc. **6.** *Mach.* a guard or guide, as for regulating the movements of a tool or work. **7.** *Carpentry.* a slotted guide used esp. with a framing square to lay out cuts on rafters and staircase strings. **8.** *Archaic.* a means of defense; a bulwark. **9. mend one's fences,** to strengthen or reestablish one's position by conciliation or negotiation: *One could tell by his superficially deferential manner that he was trying to mend his fences.* **10. on the fence,** uncommitted; neutral; undecided: *The party leaders are still on the fence.* —*v.t.* **11.** to enclose by some barrier, establishing exclusive right to possession: *to fence a farm.* **12.** to separate by or as by a fence or fences (often fol. by *in, off, out,* etc.): *to fence off a corner of one's yard; to fence out unwholesome influences.* **13.** to defend; protect; guard: *The president was fenced by bodyguards wherever he went.* **14.** to ward off; keep out. **15.** *Informal.* to sell (stolen goods) to a fence. **16.** *Naut.* to reinforce (an opening in a sail or the like) by sewing on a grommet or other device. —*v.i.* **17.** to practice the art or sport of fencing. **18.** to parry arguments; strive to avoid giving direct answers; hedge: *The mayor fenced when asked if he would run again.* **19.** (of a horse) to leap over a fence. **20.** *Obs.* to raise a defense. [1300–50; ME *fens,* aph. for *defens* DEFENSE] —**fence′like′,** *adj.*

fence′ liz′ard, either of two spiny lizards, *Sceloporus undulatus* and *S. occidentalis,* of the U.S. and northern Mexico, often seen on fences. [1865–70, *Amer.*]

fence-mend·ing (fens′men′ding), *Informal.* —*n.* **1.** the practice of reestablishing or strengthening personal, business, or political contacts and relationships by conciliation or negotiation, as after a dispute, disagreement, or period of inactivity. —*adj.* **2.** of, pertaining to, or promoting fence-mending. [1940–45; *Amer.*]

fence-off (fens′ôf′, -of′), *n. Fencing.* a match between individual contestants or teams for settling a tie. [n. use of v. phrase *fence off*]

fenc·er (fen′sər), *n.* **1.** a person who practices the art of fencing with a sword, foil, etc. **2.** a person who fences. **3.** a horse trained to jump barriers, as for show or sport. **4.** *Australian.* a person who builds or repairs fences. [1565–75; FENCE + -ER[1]]

fence-sit·ter (fens′sit′ər), *n.* a person who remains neutral or undecided in a controversy. [1900–05] —**fence′-sit′ting,** *n.*

fenc·ing (fen′sing), *n.* **1.** the art, practice, or sport in which an épée, foil, or saber is used for defense and attack. **2.** a parrying of arguments; avoidance of direct answers: *political fencing on important issues.* **3.** an enclosure or railing. **4.** fences collectively. **5.** material for fences. [1425–75; late ME *fensing* safeguarding, maintenance. See FENCE, -ING[1]]

fend (fend), *v.t.* **1.** to ward off (often fol. by *off*): *to fend off blows.* **2.** to defend. —*v.i.* **3.** to resist or make defense: *to fend against poverty.* **4.** to parry; fence. **5.** to shift; provide: *to fend for oneself.* [1250–1300; ME *fenden,* aph. var. of *defenden* to DEFEND]

—**Syn. 5.** manage, make out, get along.

fend·er (fen′dər), *n.* **1.** the pressed and formed sheet-metal part mounted over the road wheels of an automobile, bicycle, etc., to reduce the splashing of mud, water, and the like. **2.** a device on the front of a locomotive, streetcar, or the like, for clearing the track of obstructions. **3.** a mudguard or splashboard on a horse-drawn vehicle. **4.** *Naut.* a piece of timber, bundle of rope, or the like, hung over the side of a vessel to lessen shock or prevent chafing, as between the vessel and a dock or another vessel. **5.** a low metal guard before an open fireplace, to keep back falling coals. **6.** a person or thing that wards something off. [1350–1400; ME *fendour,* aph. var. of *defendour* DEFENDER]

fend′er bend′er, *Informal.* a collision between motor vehicles in which there is only minor damage. Also, **fend′er-bend′er.** [1960–65]

fend·ered (fen′dərd), *adj.* provided or protected with fenders or a fender. [1785–95; FENDER + -ED[3]]

fend′er pile′, a pile, usually one of a group, set beside ferry slips, wharves, etc., to guide approaching vessels and driven so as to yield slightly when struck in order to lessen the shock of contact. Also called **pile fender.** [1730–40]

Fé·ne·lon (fānᵊ lôN′), *n.* **Fran·çois de Sa·li·gnac de La Mothe** (fräN swa′ də sa lē nyak′ də la môt′), 1651–1715, French theologian and writer.

fen·er·a·tion (fen′ə rā′shən), *n. Law.* the lending of money on interest. [1590–1600; < L *faenerātiōn-* (s. of *faenerātiō*), equiv. to *faenerāt(us)* (ptp. of *faenerārī* to lend on interest) + *-iōn-* -ION]

fe·nes·tra (fi nes′trə), *n., pl.* **-trae** (-trē). **1.** *Anat., Zool.* a small opening or perforation, as in a bone, esp. between the middle and inner ear. **2.** *Entomol.* a transparent spot in an otherwise opaque surface, as in the wings of certain butterflies and moths. **3.** *Archit.* a windowlike opening. [1820–30; < NL, special use of L *fenestra* window, hole (in a wall)] —**fe·nes′tral,** *adj.*

fe·nes·trat·ed (fen′ə strā′tid, fi nes′trā-), *adj. Archit.* having windows; windowed; characterized by windows. Also, **fe·nes′trate.** [1820–30; < L *fenestrātus* furnished with windows (see FENESTRA, -ATE[1]) + -ED[2]]

fen·es·tra·tion (fen′ə strā′shən), *n.* **1.** the design and disposition of windows and other exterior openings of a building. **2.** *Furniture.* an ornamental motif having the form of a blind arcade or arch, as in medieval cabinetwork. **3.** *Med., Surg.* **a.** a perforation in a structure. **b.** an operation to effect such an opening. **c.** Also called **fenestra′tion opera′tion, Lempert operation.** the creation of an artificial opening into the labyrinth of the ear to restore hearing loss from otosclerosis. [1840–50; < L *fenestrāt(us)* (see FENESTRATED) + -ION]

fen·flu·ra·mine (fen flŏŏr′ə mēn′), *n. Pharm.* a sympathomimetic substance, $C_{12}H_{16}F_3N$, used mainly as an anorectic in the treatment of obesity. [1965–70; by contr., resp. and rearrangement of (*trifluoromethyl*)-*phenethylamine*]

Feng·jie (fœng′jyœ′), *n. Pinyin.* a city in E Sichuan province, in S central China, on the Chang Jiang. 250,000. Also, *Wade-Giles,* **Feng·chieh** (fung′jyu′); *Older Spelling,* **Feng·kieh** (fung′gyu′, -jyu′). Formerly, **Guizhou.**

Feng·tien (fung′tyen′), *n. Wade-Giles.* **1.** a former name of **Shenyang. 2.** former name of **Liaoning.**

Feng Yu-hsiang (fung′ yōō′shyäng′), ("*Christian General*") 1880–1948, Chinese general. Also, *Pinyin,* **Feng′ Yu′xiang′.**

Fe·ni·an (fē′nē ən, fēn′yən), *n.* **1.** a member of an Irish revolutionary organization founded in New York in 1858, which worked for the establishment of an independent Irish republic. **2.** (in late Irish legends) a member of a group of warriors always ready to defend Ireland against its enemies. [1810–20; < Ir *féinne* (gen. of *fiann* band of Fenians) + -IAN; influenced by OIr *féne* ancient inhabitant of Ireland] —**Fe′ni·an·ism,** *n.*

Fe′nian cy′cle, the cycle of legends describing and glorifying the bravery, battles, and wandering life of the Irish Fenians, esp. under the leadership of Finn.

fen·land (fen′land′, -lənd), *n.* a low area of marshy ground. [FEN[1] + LAND]

fen·man (fen′mən), *n., pl.* **-men.** *Brit.* a dweller in the Fens of England. [1600–10; FEN[1] + -MAN]

fen·nec (fen′ek), *n.* a small, pale yellowish-brown fox, *Fennecus zerda,* of northern Africa, having large, pointed ears. [1780–90; < Ar *fanak* < Pers]

fen·nel (fen′l), *n.* **1.** a plant, *Foeniculum vulgare,* of the parsley family, having feathery leaves and umbels of small, yellow flowers. **2.** Also, **fen′nel seed′.** the aromatic fruits of this plant, used in cookery and medicine. **3.** any of various more or less similar plants, as *Ferula communis* **(giant fennel),** a tall, ornamental plant. [bef. 900; ME *fenel,* OE *fenol,* var. of *finu(g)l* < VL **fenuclum,* for L *fēniculum, faeniculum,* equiv. to *faeni-* (comb. form of *faenum* hay) + *-culum* -CLE[1]]

fen·nel·flow·er (fen′l flou′ər), *n.* **1.** any of various plants belonging to the genus *Nigella,* of the buttercup family, esp. *N. sativa,* the seeds of which are used, esp. in the East, as a condiment and medicine. **2.** the flower of this plant. [1855–60; FENNEL + FLOWER]

fen·ny (fen′ē), *adj.* **1.** marshy. **2.** inhabiting or growing in fens. [bef. 1000; ME; OE *fennig.* See FEN[1], -Y[1]]

fen·o·pro·fen (fen′ō prō′fən), *n. Pharm.* a white crystalline powder, $C_{30}H_{26}CaO_6$, used as an antipyretic, analgesic, and anti-inflammatory in the treatment of rheumatoid arthritis. [contr., resp. and rearrangement of *phenoxyphenyl* and *propionic acid*]

Fen·rir (fen′rir), *n. Scand. Myth.* a wolflike monster, a son of Loki and Angerboda, chained by Gleipnir but destined to be released at Ragnarok to eat Odin and to be killed by Vidar. Also called **Fen·ris-wolf** (fen′ris wŏŏlf′).

fen·ster (fen′stər), *n. Geol.* an erosional break in an overthrust rock sheet, exposing the rocks that underlie the sheet. Also called **window.** [1920–25; < G: lit., window; OHG *fënster* < L *fenestra*]

fen·ta·nyl (fen′tə nil), *n. Pharm.* a synthetic, short-acting narcotic analgesic and sedative, $C_{28}H_{36}N_2O_8$, used in combination with other drugs in anesthesia and in neuroleptanalgesia. [contr. and resp. of the chemical name]

fen·u·greek (fen′yo͝o grēk′, fen′o͝o-), *n.* a plant, *Trigonella foenum-graecum,* of the legume family, indigenous to western Asia, but extensively cultivated elsewhere, chiefly for forage and for its mucilaginous seeds, which are used in medicine. [bef. 1000; ME *fenugrek,* OE *fēnogrēcum* < L *fēnum Graecum* lit., Greek hay. See FENNEL]

feo·da·ry (fyo͞o′də rē), *n., pl.* **-ries. 1.** a feudal vassal. **2.** *Obs.* a confederate or accomplice. [1350–1400; ME *feodarie* < ML *feodārius.* See FEUD², -ARY]

feoff (fef, fēf), *v.t.* to invest with a fief or fee; enfeoff. [1250–1300; ME *feoffen* < AF *fe(o)ffer,* OF *fiefer,* deriv. of *fief* FIEF] **—feof′for, feoff′er,** *n.*

feoff·ee (fef′ē, fē fē′), *n.* a person invested with a fief. [1275–1325; ME *feoffe* < AF, ptp. of *feoffer* to FEOFF; see -EE] **—feoff·ee′ship,** *n.*

Fe·o·sol (fē′ə sôl′, -sol′), *Pharm., Trademark.* a brand of ferrous sulfate.

FEPA, Fair Employment Practices Act.

FEPC, Fair Employment Practices Committee.

fer (fûr; *unstressed* fər), *prep., conj. Informal.* for.

-fer, a combining form meaning "that which carries" the thing specified by the initial element, used in the formation of compound words: *aquifer; conifer; foraminifer.* [< L, deriv. of *ferre* to BEAR¹, in L generally forming adjs.; the corresponding E adjs. add -OUS; see -FEROUS]

FERA, Federal Emergency Relief Administration.

fe·rae na·tu·rae (fē′rē nə to͝or′ē, -tyo͝or′ē), *Law.* (of animals) wild or undomesticated (distinguished from *domitae naturae*). [1655–65; < L: lit., of a wild nature]

fe·ral¹ (fēr′əl, fer′-), *adj.* **1.** existing in a natural state, as animals or plants; not domesticated or cultivated; wild. **2.** having reverted to the wild state, as from domestication: *a pack of feral dogs roaming the woods.* **3.** of or characteristic of wild animals; ferocious; brutal. [1595–1605; < ML, LL *ferālis* bestial, wild, equiv. to L *fer(a)* wild beast + *-ālis* -AL¹]

fe·ral² (fēr′əl, fer′-), *adj.* **1.** causing death; fatal. **2.** funereal; gloomy. [1615–25; < L *fērālis* of the dead, funerary, fatal]

fer·bam (fûr′bam), *n. Chem.* an iron carbamate, $C_9H_{18}FeN_3S_6$, used chiefly as a fungicide for protecting certain farm crops. [1945–50; *fer(ric dimethyl dithiocar)bam(ate)*]

Fer·ber (fûr′bər), *n.* **Edna,** 1887–1968, U.S. novelist, short-story writer, and playwright.

fer·ber·ite (fûr′bə rīt′), *n.* a mineral, ferrous tungstate, $FeWO_4$, in the wolframite group: a source of tungsten. [1805–15; named after R. *Ferber,* 19th-century German mineralogist; see -ITE¹]

FERC, See **Federal Energy Regulatory Commission.**

fer-de-lance (fer′dl ans′, -äns′), *n.* a large pit viper, *Bothrops atrox,* of tropical America. [1875–80; < F: lit., spearhead]

Fer·di·nand (fûr′dn and′), *n.* a male given name: from Germanic words meaning "bold" and "peace."

Fer·di·nand I (fûr′dn and′; *Ger.* feʀ′di nänt′), **1.** Spanish, **Fernando I.** (*"Ferdinand the Great"*) died 1065, king of Castile 1033–65, king of Navarre and Leon 1037–65; emperor of Spain 1056–65. **2.** 1503–64, king of Bohemia and Hungary 1526–64; emperor of the Holy Roman Empire 1558–64 (brother of Emperor Charles V). **3.** (*Maximilian Karl Leopold Maria*) 1861–1948, king of Bulgaria 1908–18.

Ferdinand II, 1. (*"the Catholic"*) 1452–1516, founder of the Spanish monarchy 1506: king of Sicily 1468–1516, king of Aragon 1479–1516; as Ferdinand III, king of Naples 1504–16; as King Ferdinand V, joint sovereign (with Isabella I) of Castile 1474–1504. **2.** 1578–1637, king of Bohemia 1617–19, 1620–37; king of Hungary 1619?–37; emperor of the Holy Roman Empire 1620–37.

Ferdinand III, 1. See **Ferdinand II** (def. 1). **2.** 1608–57, king of Hungary 1625–57, king of Bohemia 1627–57, king of Germany 1636–57; emperor of the Holy Roman Empire 1637–57 (son of Ferdinand II).

Ferdinand V. See **Ferdinand II** (def. 1).

Ferdinand VI, 1713–59, king of Spain 1746–59 (son of Philip V).

Ferdinand VII, 1784–1833, king of Spain 1808, 1814–33.

Fer·dus (fer′dəs), *n.* Firdausi.

fer·dutzt (fər dutst′), *adj. Chiefly Pennsylvania German Area.* confused; bewildered. [< PaG, G *verdutzt* bewildered, nonplussed < MD, ptp. of *verdotten* to confuse; akin to DOTE]

fere (fēr), *n. Archaic.* a companion; mate. [bef. 1000; ME; OE *gefēra,* deriv. of *fēran* to go; akin to FARE, FEIRIE]

Fer·ga·na (fer gä′nə, fər-; *Russ.* fyiʀ gu nä′), *n.* a city in E Uzbekistan, in the SW Soviet Union in Asia, SE of Tashkent. 176,000. Formerly, **Skobelev.**

Fer·gus (fûr′gəs), *n.* **1.** *Irish Legend.* one of the great warrior kings of Ulster. **2.** a male given name.

Fer′gus Falls′, a city in W central Minnesota. 12,519.

Fer·gu·son (fûr′gə sən), *n.* a city in E Missouri, near St. Louis. 24,740.

fer·gu·son·ite (fûr′gə sə nīt′), *n.* a rare-earth mineral, yttrium columbate and tantalate, found in pegmatites. [1820–30; named after R. *Ferguson,* 19th-century Scottish physician; see -ITE¹]

fer·hoo·dle (fər ho͞od′l), *v.t.,* **-dled, -dling.** *Chiefly Pennsylvania German Area.* to confuse or mix up: *Don't ferhoodle the things in that drawer.* [< PaG *verhuddle* to tangle, confuse; cf. G *verhudeln* to bungle, botch]

fe·ri·a (fēr′ē ə), *n., pl.* **fe·ri·ae** (fēr′ē ē′), **fe·ri·as.** *Eccles.* a weekday on which no feast is celebrated. [1850–55; < LL: day of the week (e.g. *secunda fēria* second day, Monday); in L only pl. *fēriae* holidays; see FAIR²] **—fe′·ri·al,** *adj.*

fe·ria (fe′ʀyä; *Eng.* fer′ē ə), *n., pl.* **fe·rias** (fe′ʀyäs; *Eng.* fer′ē əz). *Spanish.* a local festival or fair in Spain or Spanish America, usually held in honor of a patron saint.

fe·rine (fēr′īn, -in), *adj.* feral¹. [1530–40; < L *ferīnus,* equiv. to *fer(a)* a wild animal (n. use of fem. of *ferus* wild) + *-inus* -INE¹]

fer·i·ty (fer′i tē), *n.* **1.** a wild, untamed, or uncultivated state. **2.** savagery; ferocity. [1525–35; < L *feritās,* equiv. to *fer(us)* wild, untamed + *-itās* -ITY]

Fer·lin·ghet·ti (fûr′ling get′ē), *n.* **Lawrence,** born 1920?, U.S. poet associated with the Beat Generation.

fer·ly (fer′lē), *n., pl.* **-lies,** *adj. Scot.* **—n. 1.** something unusual, strange, or causing wonder or terror. **2.** astonishment; wonder. **—adj. 3.** unexpected; strange; unusual. Also, **fer′lie.** [bef. 900; ME; OE *fǣrlic,* equiv. to *fǣr* FEAR + *-lic* -LY; c. G *gefährlich* dangerous, D *gevaarlijk*]

Fer·man·agh (fər man′ə), *n.* **1.** a county in SW Northern Ireland. 50,255; 653 sq. mi. (1691 sq. km). *Co. seat:* Enniskillen. **2.** an administrative district including this county. 50,979; 715 sq. mi. (1851 sq. km).

Fer·mat (feʀ mA′; *Eng.* fer mä′), *n.* **Pierre de** (pyeʀ də), 1601–65, French mathematician.

fer·ma·ta (fer mä′tə; *It.* feʀ mä′tä), *n., pl.* **-tas,** *It.* **-te** (-te). *Music.* **1.** the sustaining of a note, chord, or rest for a duration longer than the indicated time value, with the length of the extension at the performer's discretion. **2.** a symbol 𝄐 placed over a note, chord, or rest indicating a fermata. [1875–80; < It: stop, pause, n. use of fem. of ptp. of *fermare* to stop < L *firmāre* to make firm. See FIRM¹, -ATE¹]

Fer·mat's′ last′ the′orem (fer mäz′), *Math.* the unproved theorem that the equation $x^n + y^n = z^n$ has no solution for x, y, z nonzero integers when n is greater than 2. [1860–65; named after P. de FERMAT]

Fermat's′ prin′ciple, *Optics.* the law that the path taken by a ray of light in going from one point to another point will be the path that requires the least time. [1885–90; named after P. de FERMAT]

Fermat's′ the′orem, *Math.* the theorem that an integer raised to a prime power leaves the same remainder as the integer itself when divided by the prime. [1805–15; named after P. de FERMAT]

fer·ment (*n.* fûr′ment; *v.* fər ment′), *n.* **1.** Also called **organized ferment.** any of a group of living organisms, as yeasts, molds, and certain bacteria, that cause fermentation. **2.** Also called **unorganized ferment.** an enzyme. **3.** fermentation. **4.** agitation; unrest; excitement; commotion; tumult: *The new painters worked in a creative ferment. The capital lived in a political ferment.* **—v.t. 5.** to act upon as a ferment. **6.** to cause to undergo fermentation. **7.** to inflame; foment: *to ferment prejudiced crowds to riot.* **8.** to cause agitation or excitement in: *Reading fermented his active imagination.* **—v.i. 9.** to be fermented; undergo fermentation. **10.** to seethe with agitation or excitement. [1350–1400; ME < L *fermentum* yeast (n.), *fermentāre* to cause to rise (v.); akin to BARM, L *fervēre* to boil] **—fer·ment′a·ble,** *adj.* **—fer·ment′a·bil′i·ty,** *n.*

fer·men·ta·tion (fûr′men tā′shən), *n.* **1.** the act or process of fermenting. **2.** a change brought about by a ferment, as yeast enzymes, which convert grape sugar into ethyl alcohol. **3.** agitation; excitement. [1350–1400; ME *fermentacioun* < LL *fermentātiōn-* (s. of *fermentātiō*), equiv. to L *fermentāt(us)* fermented (see FERMENT, -ATE¹) + *-iōn-* -ION]

fermenta′tion al′cohol, alcohol (def. 1).

fer·ment·a·tive (fər men′tə tiv), *adj.* **1.** tending to produce or undergo fermentation. **2.** pertaining to or of the nature of fermentation. [1655–65; obs. *fermentate* to cause to ferment (< L *fermentātus;* see FERMENT, -ATE¹) + -IVE] **—fer·ment′a·tive·ly,** *adv.* **—fer·ment′a·tive·ness** *n.*

fer·mi (fûr′mē; *It.* feʀ′mē), *n. Physics.* a unit of length, 10^{-15} m, used in measuring nuclear distances. *Symbol:* F Also called **femtometer.** [named after E. FERMI]

Fer·mi (fûr′mē; *It.* feʀ′mē), *n.* **En·ri·co** (en rē′kō; *It.* en ʀē′kô), 1901–54, Italian physicist, in the U.S. after 1939: Nobel prize 1938.

Fer′mi-Di·rac′ statis′tics (fûr′mē də rak′), *Physics.* quantum statistics defining the possible arrangements of particles in a given system in terms of the exclusion principle. Also, **Fer′mi statis′tics.** Cf. **fermion.** [1925–30; named after E. FERMI and A. M. DIRAC]

fer·mi·on (fûr′mē on′), *n. Physics.* any particle that obeys the exclusion principle and Fermi-Dirac statistics; fermions have spins that are half an odd integer: $^1/_2$, $^3/_2$, $^5/_2$, ... [1945–50; FERMI + (MES)ON]

fer·mi·um (fûr′mē əm), *n. Chem., Physics.* a transuranic element. *Symbol:* Fm; *at. no.:* 100. [1950–55; named after E. FERMI; see -IUM]

fern (fûrn), *n.* any seedless, nonflowering vascular plant of the class Filicinae, of tropical to temperate regions, characterized by true roots produced from a rhizome, triangular fronds that uncoil upward and have a branching vein system, and reproduction by spores contained in sporangia that appear as brown dots on the underside of the fronds. [bef. 900; ME *ferne,* OE *fearn;* c. G *Farn* fern, Skt *parṇá* feather] **—fern′less,** *adj.* **—fern′like′,** *adj.*

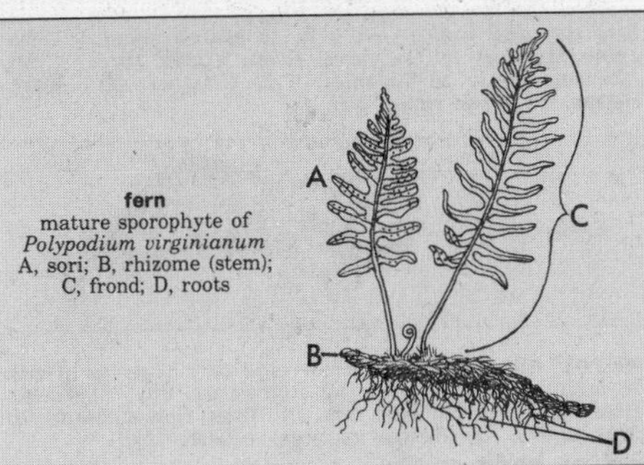

fern
mature sporophyte of *Polypodium virginianum*
A, sori; B, rhizome (stem); C, frond; D, roots

Fern (fûrn), *n.* a female given name.

Fer·nan·dez (fer nan′dez, fər-; *Sp.* feʀ nän′deth, -des), *n.* **Juan** (hwän, wän; *Span.* hwän), 1536?–1602?, Spanish navigator: explorer in South America and the Pacific.

Fer·nán·dez de Li·zar·di (feʀ nän′des the lē säʀ′thē), **Jo·sé Joa·quín** (hô se′ hwä kēn′), (*"El Pensador Mexicano"*), 1776–1827, Mexican journalist and novelist.

Fer·nan·do I (*Sp.* feʀ nän′dô). See **Ferdinand I** (def. 1).

Fer·nan·do de No·ro·nha (feʀ nänn′do͞o də nô ʀô′nyə), an island in the S Atlantic, ab. 125 mi. (200 km) E of easternmost tip of Brazil: a Brazilian penal colony. 10 sq. mi. (26 sq. km).

Fer·nan·do Po (fər nan′dō pō′), a former name of **Bioko.** Also, **Fernan′do Po′o** (pō′ō).

fern′ aspar′agus. See **asparagus fern.**

fern′ bar′, a stylish bar or tavern conspicuously decorated with ferns and other greenery.

fern·brake (fûrn′brāk′), *n.* a thicket or dense growth of ferns. [1605–15; FERN + BRAKE²]

Fern·dale (fûrn′dāl′), *n.* a city in SE Michigan, near Detroit. 26,227.

fern·er·y (fûr′nə rē), *n., pl.* **-er·ies. 1.** a collection of ferns in a garden or a potted display. **2.** a place or a glass case in which ferns are grown for ornament. [1830–40; FERN + -ERY]

fern′ seed′, the spores of ferns, formerly supposed to have the power to make persons invisible. [1590–1600]

fern·y (fûr′nē), *adj.,* **fern·i·er, fern·i·est. 1.** pertaining to, consisting of, or like ferns: *ferny leaves.* **2.** abounding in or overgrown with ferns: *ferny undergrowth.* [1515–25; FERN + -Y¹]

fe·ro·cious (fə rō′shəs), *adj.* **1.** savagely fierce, as a wild beast, person, action, or aspect; violently cruel: *a ferocious beating.* **2.** extreme or intense: *a ferocious thirst.* [1640–50; < L *ferōc-,* s. of *ferōx* savage, fierce (*fer(us)* wild (see FERAL¹, FIERCE) + *-ōx* having such an appearance; akin to -OPSIS) + -IOUS] **—fe·ro′cious·ly,** *adv.* **—fe·ro′cious·ness,** *n.*
—Syn. 1. rapacious. See **fierce.**

fe·roc·i·ty (fə ros′i tē), *n.* a ferocious quality or state; savage fierceness. [1600–10; < L *ferōcitās,* equiv. to *ferōc-,* s. of *ferōx* FEROCIOUS + *-itās* -ITY]

-ferous, a combining form meaning "bearing," "producing," "yielding," "containing," "conveying," used in the formation of compound words: *coniferous; pestiferous.* Cf. **-fer.** [ME; see -FER, -OUS]

Fer·ra·ra (fə rär′ə; *It.* feʀ ʀä′ʀä), *n.* a city in N Italy, near the Po River: medieval university and cathedral. 154,876.

Fer·ra·ro (fə rär′ō), *n.* **Geraldine Anne** ("Gerry"), born 1935, U.S. politician: congresswoman 1978–84; first woman chosen as the vice-presidential nominee of a major political party 1984.

fer·rate (fer′āt), *n. Chem.* a salt of the hypothetical ferric acid, H_2FeO_4. [1850–55; < L *ferr(um)* iron + -ATE²]

fer·re·dox·in (fer′ə dok′sin), *n. Biochem.* any of a group of red-brown proteins containing iron and sulfur and acting as an electron carrier during photosynthesis, nitrogen fixation, or oxidation-reduction reactions. [1962; < L *fer(rum)* iron + REDOX + -IN²]

Fer′rel's law′ (fer′əlz), the law that wind is deflected to the right in the Northern Hemisphere and to the left in the Southern Hemisphere, derived from the application of the Coriolis effect to air masses. [named after W. *Ferrel* (d. 1891), American meteorologist]

fer·re·ous (fer′ē əs), *adj.* of, resembling, or containing iron: *a ferreous alloy.* [1640–50; < L *ferreus,* equiv. to *ferr(um)* iron + *-eus* -EOUS]

Fer·re·ro (feʀ ʀe′ʀô), *n.* **Gu·gliel·mo** (go͞o lyel′mô), 1871–1942, Italian historian and sociologist.

fer·ret¹ (fer′it), *n.* **1.** a domesticated, usually redeyed, and albinic variety of the polecat, used in Europe for driving rabbits and rats from their burrows. See illus. on next page. **2.** See **black-footed ferret.** **—v.t. 3.** to drive out by using or as if using a ferret (often fol. by *out*): *to ferret rabbits from their burrows; to ferret out enemies.* **4.** to hunt with ferrets. **5.** to hunt over with ferrets: *to ferret a field.* **6.** to search out, discover, or bring to light (often fol. by *out*): *to ferret out the facts.* **7.** to harry, worry, or torment: *His problems ferreted*

CONCISE PRONUNCIATION KEY: *act, cāpe, dâre, pärt; set, ēqual; if, īce; ox, ōver, ôrder, oil, bo͝ok, bo͞ot, out; up, ûrge; child; sing; shoe; thin, that;* zh as in *treasure.* ə = *a* as in *alone, e* as in *system, i* as in *easily, o* as in *gallop, u* as in *circus;* ᵊ as in *fire* (fīᵊr), *hour* (ouᵊr). l and n can serve as syllabic consonants, as in *cradle* (krād′l), and *button* (but′n). See the full key inside the front cover.

him day and night. —*v.i.* **8.** to search about. [1350–1400; ME *fer(r)et(te), fyret, furet* < MF *furet* < VL **furittus,* equiv. to *fūr* thief (< L) + *-ittus* -ET] —**fer′ret·er,** *n.* —**fer′ret·y,** *adj.*

ferret (def. 1)

fer·ret[2] (fer′it), *n.* a narrow tape or ribbon, as of silk or cotton, used for binding, trimming, etc. [1570–80; alter. of It *fioretto* floss silk, lit., little flower, equiv. to *fior(e)* (< L *flōrem;* see FLOWER) + *-etto* -ET]

fer′ret badg′er, any of several small omnivores of the genus *Melogale,* of southern and eastern Asia, having a bushy tail and distinctive white or yellow markings on a black face.

ferri-, a combining form with the meanings "iron," "ferric," used in the formation of compound words: *ferriferous; ferricyanide.* Also, **ferro-.** [< L, comb. form of *ferrum* iron]

fer·ri·age (fer′ē ij), *n.* **1.** conveyance or transportation by a ferryboat. **2.** the fare charged for ferrying. [1400–50; late ME; see FERRY, -AGE]

fer·ric (fer′ik), *adj. Chem.* of or containing iron, esp. in the trivalent state. [1790–1800; < L *ferr(um)* iron + -IC]

fer′ric ammo′nium ox′alate, *Chem.* a green, crystalline, water-soluble, synthetically produced powder, $(NH_4)_3Fe(C_2O_4)_3 \cdot 3H_2O$, used chiefly in the manufacture of blueprint paper. Also called **ammonioferric oxalate, iron ammonium oxalate.**

fer′ric chlo′ride, *Chem.* a compound that in its anhydrous form, $FeCl_3$, occurs as a black-brown, water-soluble solid; in its hydrated form, $FeCl_3 \cdot xH_2O$, it occurs in orange-yellow, deliquescent crystals: used chiefly in engraving, for deodorizing sewage, as a mordant, and in medicine as an astringent and styptic. Also called **iron trichloride, iron perchloride.** [1890–95]

fer′ric ox′ide, *Chem.* a dark-red, crystalline, water-insoluble solid, Fe_2O_3, occurring naturally, as hematite and rust, or synthesized: used chiefly as a pigment, as a mordant, as a coating for magnetic recording tape, and in the manufacture of polishing compounds. Also called **iron oxide.** [1880–85]

fer′ric so′dium ox′alate, *Chem.* an emerald-green, crystalline, extremely water-soluble salt, used in photography and blueprinting. Also called **iron sodium oxalate.**

fer′ri·cy·an′ic ac′id (fer′ī sī an′ik, fer′ē-), *Chem.* a brown, crystalline, unstable, water-soluble solid, $H_3Fe(CN)_6$, obtained by the interaction of a ferricyanide and an acid. [1850–55; FERRI- + CYANIC]

fer·ri·cy·a·nide (fer′ī sī′ə nīd′, fer′ē-), *n. Chem.* a salt of ferricyanic acid, as potassium ferricyanide, $K_3Fe(CN)_6$. [1865–70; FERRI- + CYANIDE]

fer·rif·er·ous (fə rif′ər əs), *adj.* producing or yielding iron: *ferriferous rock.* [1805–15; FERRI- + -FEROUS]

fer·ri·he·mo·glo·bin (fer′ī hē′mə glō′bin, -hem′ə-, fer′ē-), *n. Biochem.* methemoglobin. [FERRI- + HEMOGLOBIN]

fer·ri·mag·net·ic (fer′ī mag net′ik, fer′ē-), *adj. Physics.* noting or pertaining to a substance, as a ferrite, in which the magnetic moments of some neighboring atoms point in opposite directions, with a net magnetization still resulting because of differences in magnitudes of the opposite moments. Cf. **antiferromagnetic, diamagnetic, ferromagnetic.** [1950–55; FERRI- + MAGNETIC; cf. F *ferrimagnétisme*]

Ferris wheel

Fer′ris wheel′ (fer′is), an amusement ride consisting of a large upright wheel rotating on a fixed stand and having seats around its rim suspended freely so that they remain right side up as they revolve. [1890–95; named after G. W. G. *Ferris* (d. 1896), American engineer]

fer·rite (fer′īt), *n.* **1.** *Chem.* a compound, as $NaFeO_2$, formed when ferric oxide is combined with a more basic metallic oxide. **2.** *Metall.* the pure iron constituent of ferrous metals, as distinguished from the iron carbides. [1875–80; < L *ferr(um)* iron + -ITE[1]]

CONCISE ETYMOLOGY KEY: <, descended or borrowed from; >, whence; b., blend of, blended; c., cognate with; cf., compare; deriv., derivative; equiv., equivalent; imit., imitative; obl., oblique; r., replacing; s., stem; sp., spelling, spelled; resp., respelling, respelled; trans., translation; ?, origin unknown; *, unattested; ‡, probably earlier than. See the full key inside the front cover.

fer·ri·tin (fer′i tn), *n. Biochem.* an amber-colored, crystalline protein, found in the liver, spleen, and bone marrow, that consists of apoferritin combined with a ferric hydroxide-ferric phosphate complex and that stores iron for use in metabolism. [1935–40; FERRITE + -IN[2]]

ferro-, var. of **ferri-:** *ferroconcrete.* In chemical terminology, the meanings of **ferri-** and **ferro-** are specialized to correspond to *ferric* and *ferrous.* [< L *ferr(um)* iron + -O-]

fer·ro·al·loy (fer′ō al′oi, -ə loi′), *n.* an alloy of iron with some element other than carbon, used to introduce the element in the manufacture of steel. [1900–05; FERRO- + ALLOY]

fer·ro·a·lu·mi·num (fer′ō ə lo͞o′mə nəm), *n.* a ferroalloy containing up to 80 percent aluminum. [1885–90; FERRO- + ALUMINUM]

fer·ro·ce·ment (fer′ō si ment′), *adj.* **1.** (of a boat hull) constructed of mortar troweled over a wire mesh that has been preshaped over a mold. **2.** (of a boat) having such a hull. [FERRO- + CEMENT]

fer·ro·cene (fer′ə sēn′), *n. Chem.* **1.** Also called **dicyclopentadienyliron.** an orange, crystalline, water-insoluble coordination compound, $(C_5H_5)_2Fe$, having a camphorlike odor: used chiefly as an antiknock agent for gasoline and as a catalyst. Cf. **metallocene. 2.** Also called **dicyclopentadienyl metal.** any of a class of analogous compounds containing a metal other than iron, as nickel or osmium. [1950–55; FERRO- + C(YCLOPENTADI)ENE]

fer·ro·ce·ri·um (fer′ō sēr′ē əm), *n.* an alloy of 65 percent misch metal and 35 percent iron, used in flints for cigarette lighters. [< NL; see FERRO-, CERIUM]

fer·ro·chro·mi·um (fer′ō krō′mē əm), *n.* a ferroalloy containing up to 70 percent chromium. Also, **fer·ro·chrome** (fer′ə krōm′). [1875–80; FERRO- + CHROMIUM]

fer·ro·con·crete (fer′ō kon′krēt, -kong′-, -kon krēt′, -kong-), *n.* See **reinforced concrete.** [1895–1900; FERRO- + CONCRETE]

fer′ro·cy·an′ic ac′id (fer′ō sī an′ik, fer′-), *Chem.* a white, crystalline, unstable, water-soluble solid, $H_4Fe(CN)_6$, obtained by the interaction of a ferrocyanide and an acid. [1810–20; FERRO- + CYANIC]

fer·ro·cy·a·nide (fer′ō sī′ə nīd′, -nid), *n. Chem.* a salt of ferrocyanic acid, as potassium ferrocyanide, $K_4Fe(CN)_6$. [1835–45; FERRO- + CYANIDE]

fer·ro·e·lec·tric (fer′ō i lek′trik), *Physics.* —*adj.* **1.** pertaining to a substance that possesses spontaneous electric polarization such that the polarization can be reversed by an electric field. —*n.* **2.** a ferroelectric substance. [1930–35; FERRO- + ELECTRIC; by analogy with FERROMAGNETIC] —**fer′ro·e·lec′tri·cal·ly,** *adv.* —**fer·ro·e·lec·tric·i·ty** (fer′ō i lek tris′i tē, -ē′lek-), *n.*

Fer·rol (*Sp.* fer rôl′), *n.* See **El Ferrol.**

fer·ro·mag·ne·sian (fer′ō mag nē′zhən, -shən), *adj. Mineral.* (of minerals and rocks) containing iron and magnesium. [1900–05; FERRO- + MAGNESIAN]

fer·ro·mag·net (fer′ō mag′nit), *n. Physics.* a ferromagnetic substance. [1940–45; FERRO- + MAGNET]

fer·ro·mag·net·ic (fer′ō mag net′ik), *adj. Physics.* noting or pertaining to a substance, as iron, that below a certain temperature, the Curie point, can possess magnetization in the absence of an external magnetic field; noting or pertaining to a substance in which the magnetic moments of the atoms are aligned. Cf. **antiferromagnetic, diamagnetic, ferrimagnetic, paramagnetic.** [1840–50; FERRO- + MAGNETIC] —**fer·ro·mag·ne·tism** (fer′ō mag′ni tiz′əm), *n.*

fer·ro·man·ga·nese (fer′ō mang′gə nēs′, -nēz′), *n.* a ferroalloy containing up to 90 percent manganese. [1880–85; FERRO- + MANGANESE]

fer·ro·mo·lyb·de·num (fer′ō mə lib′də nəm, -mol′ib dē′-), *n.* a ferroalloy containing up to 60 percent molybdenum. [1900–05; FERRO- + MOLYBDENUM]

fer·ro·nick·el (fer′ō nik′əl), *n.* a ferroalloy containing up to 45 percent nickel. [FERRO- + NICKEL]

fer·ro·sil·i·con (fer′ō sil′i kən, -kon′), *n.* a ferroalloy containing up to 95 percent silicon. [1880–85; FERRO- + SILICON]

fer·ro·ti·ta·ni·um (fer′ō tī tā′nē əm, -ti-), *n.* a ferroalloy containing up to 45 percent titanium. [1890–95; FERRO- + TITANIUM]

fer·ro·tung·sten (fer′ō tung′stən), *n.* a ferroalloy containing up to 80 percent tungsten. [1880–85; FERRO- + TUNGSTEN]

fer·ro·type (fer′ə tīp′), *v.,* **-typed, -typ·ing,** *n. Photog.* —*v.t.* **1.** to put a glossy surface on (a print) by pressing, while wet, on a metal sheet **(fer′rotype tin′).** —*n.* **2.** Also called **tintype.** a positive photograph made on a sensitized sheet of enameled iron or tin. **3.** the process of making such photographs. [1835–45; FERRO- + -TYPE]

fer·rous (fer′əs), *adj. Chem.* of or containing iron, esp. in the bivalent state. [1860–65; < L *ferr(um)* iron + -OUS]

fer′rous ox′ide, *Chem.* a black powder, FeO, insoluble in water, soluble in acid. Also called **iron monoxide.** [1870–75]

fer′rous sul′fate, *Chem., Pharm.* a bluish-green, crystalline, saline-tasting, water-soluble heptahydrated solid, $FeSO_4 \cdot 7H_2O$, used chiefly in the manufacture of other iron salts, in water purification, fertilizer, inks, pigments, tanning, photography, and in medicine in the treatment of anemia. Also called **copperas, green vitriol, iron vitriol, iron sulfate.** [1860–65]

fer′rous sul′fide, *Chem.* a dark or black metallic crystalline compound, FeS, insoluble in water, soluble in acids, used in ceramics and to generate hydrogen sulfide.

fer·ro·va·na·di·um (fer′ō və nā′dē əm), *n.* a ferroalloy containing up to 55 percent vanadium. [1900–05; FERRO- + VANADIUM]

fer·ro·zir·co·ni·um (fer′ō zər kō′nē əm), *n.* a ferroalloy containing up to 40 percent zirconium. [FERRO- + ZIRCONIUM]

fer·ru·gi·nous (fə ro͞o′jə nəs), *adj.* **1.** *Geol.* iron-bearing: *ferruginous clays.* **2.** of the color of iron rust. [1655–65; < L *ferrūginus* rust-colored, deriv. of *ferrūgin-,* s. of *ferrūgō* iron-rust, deriv. of *ferrum* iron; see -OUS]

fer·rule (fer′əl, -o͞ol), *n., v.,* **-ruled, -rul·ing.** —*n.* **1.** a ring or cap, usually of metal, put around the end of a post, cane, or the like, to prevent splitting. **2.** a short metal sleeve for strengthening a tool handle at the end holding the tool. **3.** a bushing or adapter holding the end of a tube and inserted into a hole in a plate in order to make a tight fit, used in boilers, condensers, etc. **4.** a short ring for reinforcing or decreasing the interior diameter of the end of a tube. **5.** a short plumbing fitting, covered at its outer end and caulked or otherwise fixed to a branch from a pipe so that it can be removed to give access to the interior of the pipe. **6.** *Angling.* **a.** either of two fittings on the end of a section of a sectional fishing rod, one fitting serving as a plug and the other as a socket for fastening the sections together. **b.** one of two or more small rings spaced along the top of a casting rod to hold and guide the line. —*v.t.* **7.** to furnish with a ferrule. Also, **ferule.** [1605–15; alter. (appar. conformed to L *ferrum* iron, -ULE) of *verrel, verril,* late ME *virole* < MF (c. ML *virola*) < L *viriola,* equiv. to *viri(a)* bracelet + *-ola* -OLE[1]]

fer·ry (fer′ē), *n., pl.* **-ries,** *v.,* **-ried, -ry·ing.** —*n.* **1.** a commercial service with terminals and boats for transporting persons, automobiles, etc., across a river or other comparatively small body of water. **2.** a ferryboat. **3.** a service for flying airplanes over a particular route, esp. the delivery of airplanes to an overseas purchaser or base of operations. **4.** the legal right to ferry passengers, cargo, etc., and to charge for the service. —*v.t.* **5.** to carry or convey back and forth over a fixed route in a boat or plane. **6.** to fly (an airplane) over a particular route, esp. for delivery. —*v.i.* **7.** to go in a ferry. [bef. 1150; ME *ferien,* OE *ferian* to carry; c. ON *ferja,* Goth *farjan;* akin to FARE]

fer·ry·boat (fer′ē bōt′), *n.* a boat used to transport passengers, vehicles, etc., across a river or the like. [1400–50; late ME *feryboot.* See FERRY, BOAT]

fer′ry bridge′, *Civ. Engin.* See **transporter bridge.** [1870–75]

fer·ry·man (fer′ē mən), *n., pl.* **-men.** a person who owns or operates a ferry. [1425–75; late ME *feryman.* See FERRY, MAN[1]]

fer·tile (fûr′tl or, *esp. Brit.,* -tīl), *adj.* **1.** bearing, producing, or capable of producing vegetation, crops, etc., abundantly; prolific: *fertile soil.* **2.** bearing or capable of bearing offspring. **3.** abundantly productive: *a fertile imagination.* **4.** producing an abundance (usually fol. by *of* or *in*): *a land fertile of wheat.* **5.** conducive to productiveness: *fertile showers.* **6.** *Biol.* **a.** fertilized, as an egg or ovum; fecundated. **b.** capable of growth or development, as seeds or eggs. **7.** *Bot.* **a.** capable of producing sexual reproductive structures. **b.** capable of causing fertilization, as an anther with fully developed pollen. **c.** having spore-bearing organs, as a frond. **8.** *Physics.* (of a nuclide) capable of being transmuted into a fissile nuclide by irradiation with neutrons: *Uranium 238 and thorium 232 are fertile nuclides.* Cf. **fissile** (def. 2). **9.** produced in abundance. [1425–75; late ME (< MF) < L *fertilis* fruitful, akin to *ferre* to BEAR[1]; see -ILE] —**fer′tile·ly,** *adv.* —**fer′tile·ness,** *n.*
—**Syn. 1–3.** fecund, teeming. See **productive.**
—**Ant. 1–3.** sterile, barren.

Fer′tile Cres′cent, 1. an agricultural region extending from the Levant to Iraq. **2.** an area in the Middle and Near East: formerly fertile, now partly desert.

fer·til·i·ty (fər til′i tē), *n.* **1.** the state or quality of being fertile. **2.** *Biol.* the ability to produce offspring; power of reproduction: *the amazing fertility of rabbits.* **3.** the birthrate of a population. **4.** (of soil) the capacity to supply nutrients in proper amounts for plant growth when other factors are favorable. [1375–1425; late ME *fertilite* (< MF) < L *fertilitās.* See FERTILE, -ITY]

fertil′ity cult′, 1. a religious cult devoted to the enhancement of the fertility of persons, plants, or animals, by means of rituals often associated with a particular deity. **2.** the body of members of such a cult. [1930–35]

fertil′ity drug′, *Pharm.* a substance that enhances the ability to produce young. Also called **fertil′ity pill′.** [1965–70]

fer·ti·li·za·tion (fûr′tl ə zā′shən), *n.* **1.** an act, process, or instance of fertilizing. **2.** the state of being fertilized. **3.** *Biol.* **a.** the union of male and female gametic nuclei. **b.** fecundation or impregnation of animals or plants. **4.** the enrichment of soil, as for the production of crops. [1855–60; FERTILIZE + -ATION] —**fer′ti·li·za′tion·al,** *adj.*

fer·ti·lize (fûr′tl īz′), *v.t.,* **-lized, -liz·ing. 1.** *Biol.* **a.** to render (the female gamete) capable of development by uniting it with the male gamete. **b.** to fecundate or impregnate (an animal or plant). **2.** to make fertile; enrich: *to fertilize farmland.* **3.** to make productive. Also, *esp. Brit.,* **fer′ti·lise′.** [1640–50; FERTILE + -IZE] —**fer′ti·liz′a·ble,** *adj.* —**fer′ti·liz′a·bil′i·ty,** *n.*

fer·ti·liz·er (fûr′tl ī′zər), *n.* **1.** any substance used to fertilize the soil, esp. a commercial or chemical manure. **2.** a person, insect, etc., that fertilizes an animal or plant: *Bees are fertilizers of flowers.* [1655–65; FERTILIZE + -ER[1]]

fer·til·i·zin (fər til′ə zin), *n. Biochem.* See **jelly coat.** [1919; FERTILIZE + -IN[2]]

fer·u·la (fer′o͝o lə, fer′yo͝o-), *n., pl.* **-las, -lae** (-lē′). **1.** *Bot.* any of various plants belonging to the genus *Ferula,* of the parsley family, chiefly of the Mediterranean region and central Asia, generally tall and coarse with dissected leaves, many of the Asian species yielding strongly scented, medicinal gum resins. **2.** ferule[1] (def. 1). [1350–1400; ME < NL, L; see FERULE[1]]

fer·ule[1] (fer′əl, -o͞ol), *n., v.,* **-ruled, -ul·ing.** —*n.* **1.**

Also, **ferula.** a rod, cane, or flat piece of wood for punishing children, esp. by striking them on the hand. —*v.t.* **2.** to punish with a ferule. [1375–1425; late ME *ferula, ferul(e)* giant fennel < L *ferula* schoolmaster's rod (lit., stalk of giant fennel); r. OE *ferele* < L]

fer·ule[2] (fer′əl, -o͞ol), *n., v.t.,* **-uled, -ul·ing.** ferrule.

fe·ru′lic ac′id (fə ro͞o′lik), *Chem.* a compound, $C_{10}H_{10}O_4$, found in small amounts in plants, that occurs in two isomers, one a yellow oily liquid and the other crystalline. [1875–80; FERUL(A) + -IC]

ferv., (in prescriptions) boiling. [< L *fervēns*]

fer·ven·cy (fûr′vən sē), *n.* warmth or intensity of feeling; ardor; zeal; fervor. [1375–1425; late ME < LL *ferventia* (see FERVENT, -ENCY); r. *fervence* < MF < L *ferventia*]

fer·vent (fûr′vənt), *adj.* **1.** having or showing great warmth or intensity of spirit, feeling, enthusiasm, etc.; ardent: *a fervent admirer; a fervent plea.* **2.** hot; burning; glowing. [1350–1400; ME (< AF) < L *fervent-* (s. of *fervēns*) prp. of *fervēre* to boil; see -ENT] —**fer′vent·ly,** *adv.* —**fer′vent·ness,** *n.*
—**Syn. 1.** fervid, impassioned, passionate.

fer·vid (fûr′vid), *adj.* **1.** heated or vehement in spirit, enthusiasm, etc.: *a fervid orator.* **2.** burning; glowing; intensely hot. [1590–1600; < L *fervidus* boiling. See FERVENT, -ID[4]] —**fer·vid′i·ty,** *n.* —**fer′vid·ly,** *adv.*

Fer·vi·dor (fûr′vi dôr′; *Fr.* fer vē dôr′), *n.* Thermidor. [< F, appar. b. *ferv(eur)* FERVOR and *(therm)idor* THERMIDOR]

fer·vor (fûr′vər), *n.* **1.** great warmth and earnestness of feeling: *to speak with great fervor.* **2.** intense heat. Also, *esp. Brit.,* **fer′vour.** [1350–1400; ME *fervo(u)r* < AF < L *fervor* heat (see FERVENT, -OR[1])]
—**Syn. 1.** ardor, passion, zeal.

fes·cen·nine (fes′ə nīn′, -nin), *adj.* scurrilous; licentious; obscene: *fescennine mockery.* [1595–1605; < L *Fescennīnus* of, belonging to Fescennia, a town in Etruria noted for jesting and scurrilous verse; see -INE[1]]

fes·cue (fes′kyo͞o), *n.* **1.** Also called **fes′cue grass′.** any grass of the genus *Festuca,* some species of which are cultivated for pasture or lawns. **2.** a pointer, as a straw or slender stick, used to point out the letters in teaching children to read. [1350–1400; earlier *festue,* ME *festu* < MF < VL **festūcum,* for L *festūca* stalk, straw]

fes′cue foot′, *Vet. Pathol.* a disease of the feet of cattle associated with feeding on certain fungus-infested fescue grasses, characterized by lameness and sometimes leading to gangrene. [1945–50]

fess[1] (fes), *n. Heraldry.* an ordinary in the form of a broad horizontal band across the middle of an escutcheon. Also, **fesse.** [1350–1400; ME *fesse* < AF << L *fascia* FASCIA]

fess[2] (fes), *v.t., v.i. Informal.* **fess up,** to admit or concede, esp. freely. [1830–40; aph. shortening of CONFESS]

fess[3] (fes), *n. Chiefly South Midland and Southern U.S.* a teacher. Also, **fes′sor.** [shortening of PROFESSOR]

Fes·sen·den (fes′ən dən), *n.* **William Pitt,** 1806–69, U.S. statesman.

fess′ point′, *Heraldry.* the central point of an escutcheon. Also called **heart point.** [1555–65]

-fest, a combining form occurring in compound words that have the general sense "an assembly of people engaged in a common activity"; the first element of the compound usually specifies the activity: *gabfest; lovefest; slugfest; songfest.* [< G *Fest* festival, holiday (see FEAST), as in *Sängerfest* choral festival]

fes·ta (fes′tə), *n.* a feast, festival, or holiday. [1810–20; < It < L: holiday, pl. of *fēstum.* See -FEST]

fes·tal (fes′tl), *adj.* pertaining to or befitting a feast, festival, holiday, or gala occasion. [1470–80; < L *fēst(um)* FEAST + -AL[1]] —**fes′tal·ly,** *adv.*

fes·ter (fes′tər), *v.i.* **1.** to form pus; generate purulent matter; suppurate. **2.** to cause ulceration, as a foreign body in the flesh. **3.** to putrefy or rot. **4.** to rankle, as a feeling of resentment. —*v.t.* **5.** to cause to rankle: *Malice festered his spirit.* —*n.* **6.** an ulcer; a rankling sore. **7.** a small, purulent, superficial sore. [1350–1400; (n.) ME *festir, festre* < AF, OF *festre* < L *fistula* FISTULA (for *-l-* > *-r-* cf. CHAPTER); (v.) ME *festryn,* deriv. of the n. or < OF *festrir*]

fes·ti·na len·te (fes tē′nä len′te; *Eng.* fe stī′nə len′tē, fe stē′nə len′tā), *Latin.* make haste slowly.

fes·ti·nate (*v.* fes′tə nāt′; *adj.* fes′tə nāt′, -nit), *v.,* **-nat·ed, -nat·ing,** *adj.* —*v.t., v.i.* **1.** to hurry; hasten. —*adj.* **2.** hurried. [1595–1605; < L *festīnātus* hurried, ptp. of *festīnāre;* see -ATE[1]] —**fes′ti·nate′ly,** *adv.*

fes·ti·na·tion (fes′tə nā′shən), *n. Pathol.* a gait marked by an involuntary hurrying in walking, observed in certain nerve diseases. [1530–40; < L *festīnātiōn-* (s. of *festīnātiō*) a hastening. See FESTINATE, -ION]

fes·ti·val (fes′tə vəl), *n.* **1.** a day or time of religious or other celebration, marked by feasting, ceremonies, or other observances: *the festival of Christmas; a Roman festival.* **2.** a periodic commemoration, anniversary, or celebration: *an annual strawberry festival.* **3.** a period or program of festive activities, cultural events, or entertainment: *a music festival.* **4.** gaiety; revelry; merrymaking. —*adj.* **5.** festal: *a festival atmosphere of unrestrained joy.* [1300–50; ME < ML *fēstivālis* (*diēs*) holy (day). See FESTIVE, -AL[1]]

Fes′tival of Fools′. See **Feast of Fools.**

fes·tive (fes′tiv), *adj.* **1.** pertaining to or suitable for a feast or festival: *festive decorations; a festive meal.* **2.** joyous; merry: *a festive mood.* [1645–55; < L *fēstīvus* merry, equiv. to *fēst(us)* festal + *-īvus* -IVE] —**fes′tive·ly,** *adv.* —**fes′tive·ness,** *n.*

fes·tiv·i·ty (fe stiv′i tē), *n., pl.* **-ties. 1.** a festive celebration or occasion. **2. festivities,** festive events or activities: *the festivities of Christmas.* **3.** festive character or quality; gaiety; merriment. [1350–1400; ME *festivite* (< OF) < L *fēstīvitās.* See FESTIVE, -ITY]

fes·toon (fe sto͞on′), *n.* **1.** a string or chain of flowers, foliage, ribbon, etc., suspended in a curve between two points. **2.** a decorative representation of this, as in architectural work or on pottery. **3.** a fabric suspended, draped, and bound at intervals to form graceful loops or scalloped folds. **4.** *Dentistry.* the garlandlike area of the gums surrounding the necks of the teeth. —*v.t.* **5.** to adorn with or as with festoons: *to festoon a hall.* **6.** to form into festoons: *to festoon flowers and leaves.* **7.** *Dentistry.* to reproduce natural gum patterns around the teeth or a denture. **8.** to connect by festoons. [1670–80; < F *feston* < It *festone* decoration for a feast, deriv. of *festa* FESTA]

festoon (def. 2)

fes·toon·er·y (fe sto͞o′nə rē), *n.* **1.** a decoration of festoons. **2.** festoons collectively. [1830–40; FESTOON + -ERY]

fest·schrift (fest′shrift′), *n., pl.* **-schrift·en** (-shrif′tən), **-schrifts.** (*often cap.*) a volume of articles, essays, etc., contributed by many authors in honor of a colleague, usually published on the occasion of retirement, an important anniversary, or the like. [1900–05; < G, equiv. to *Fest* feast, festival + *Schrift* writing]

fes·tu·ca (fes to͞o′kə, -styo͞o′-), *n.* any grass of the genus *Festuca,* chiefly characterized by tufted blades and spikelets, comprising the fescues. [< NL (Linnaeus), L; see FESCUE]

FET, 1. *Banking.* federal estate tax. **2.** *Electronics.* field-effect transistor.

F.E.T., Federal Excise Tax.

fet·a (fet′ə), *n.* a soft, white, brine-cured Greek cheese made from sheep's milk or goat's milk. [1935–40; < ModGk, short for *tyrì phéta,* equiv. to *tyrí* cheese (Gk *tyrós*) + *phéta* slice < It *fetta* (see FETTUCCINE)]

fe·tal (fēt′l), *adj. Embryol.* of, pertaining to, or having the character of a fetus. Also, **foetal.** [1805–15; FET(US) + -AL[1]]

fe′tal al′cohol syn′drome, a variable cluster of birth defects that may include facial abnormalities, growth deficiency, mental retardation, and other impairments, caused by the mother's consumption of alcohol during pregnancy. *Abbr.:* FAS [1975–80]

fe′tal posi′tion, a bodily posture resembling that of the fetus in the uterus, in which the body is curled with head and limbs drawn in, sometimes assumed in states of fear or emotional withdrawal. [1960–65]

fetch[1] (fech), *v.t.* **1.** to go and bring back; return with; get: *to go up a hill to fetch a pail of water.* **2.** to cause to come; bring: *to fetch a doctor.* **3.** to sell for or bring (a price, financial return, etc.): *The horse fetched $50 more than it cost.* **4.** *Informal.* to charm; captivate: *Her beauty fetched the coldest hearts.* **5.** to take (a breath). **6.** to utter (a sigh, groan, etc.). **7.** to deal or deliver (a stroke, blow, etc.). **8.** to perform or execute (a movement, step, leap, etc.). **9.** *Chiefly Naut. and Brit. Dial.* to reach; arrive at: *to fetch port.* **10.** *Hunting.* (of a dog) to retrieve (game). —*v.i.* **11.** to go and bring things. **12.** *Chiefly Naut.* to move or maneuver. **13.** *Hunting.* to retrieve game (often used as a command to a dog). **14.** to go by an indirect route; circle (often fol. by *around* or *about*): *We fetched around through the outer suburbs.* **15. fetch about,** *Naut.* (of a sailing vessel) to come onto a new tack. **16. fetch and carry,** to perform menial tasks. **17. fetch up, a.** *Informal.* to arrive or stop. **b.** *Older Use.* to raise (children); bring up: *She had to fetch up her younger sisters.* **c.** *Naut.* (of a vessel) to come to a halt, as by lowering an anchor or running aground; bring up. —*n.* **18.** the act of fetching. **19.** the distance of fetching: *a long fetch.* **20.** *Oceanog.* **a.** an area where ocean waves are being generated by the wind. **b.** the length of such an area. **21.** the reach or stretch of a thing. **22.** a trick; dodge. [bef. 1000; ME *fecchen,* OE *fecc(e)an,* var. of *fetian* to fetch (cf. ME *feten, fetten,* Brit. dial. *fet;* akin to OE *-fat* in *sīthfat* journey, G *fassen* to grasp)] —**fetch′er,** *n.*
—**Syn. 1.** See **bring.**

fetch[2] (fech), *n.* wraith (def. 1). [1780–90; perh. short for *fetch-life* one sent to fetch the soul of a dying person]

fetch·ed (fech′id, fetcht), *adj. South Midland U.S.* damned: *Jim beat up every fetched one of them.* [1850–55, *Amer.*; appar. FETCH + -ED[2]]

fetch·ing (fech′ing), *adj.* charming; captivating. [1875–80; FETCH + -ING[2]] —**fetch′ing·ly,** *adv.*

fete (fāt, fet), *n., pl.* **fetes,** *v.,* **fet·ed, fet·ing.** —*n.* **1.** a day of celebration; holiday: *The Fourth of July is a great American fete.* **2.** a festive celebration or entertainment: *The ball was the greatest fete of the season.* **3.** a religious feast or festival: *a fete lasting several days in honor of a saint.* —*v.t.* **4.** to entertain at or honor with a fete: *to fete a visiting celebrity.* Also, **fête** (fāt, fet; *Fr.* fet). [1745–55; < F *fête,* earlier *feste* FEAST]

fête cham·pê·tre (fet shäN pe′trᵊ), *pl.* ***fêtes cham·pê·tres*** (fet shäN pe′trᵊ). *French.* an outdoor festival or a garden party.

fete′ day′, a festival day. [1810–20]

fête ga·lante (fet gA läNt′), *pl.* ***fêtes ga·lantes*** (fet gA läNt′). *French.* **1.** See ***fête champêtre.*** **2.** a representation, in art, of elegantly dressed groups at play in a rural or parklike setting.

fet·e·ri·ta (fet′ə rē′tə), *n.* a grain sorghum cultivated for grain and forage. [1910–15; < Sudanese Ar *feterīta*]

fe·tial (fē′shəl), *adj.* concerned with declarations of war and treaties of peace: *fetial law.* [1525–35; < L *fētiālis* pertaining to a *fētiālis,* a member of the Roman college of priests who acted as representatives in disputes with foreign nations]

fe·ti·cide (fē′tə sīd′), *n.* the act of destroying a fetus or causing an abortion. Also, **foeticide.** [1835–45; FET(US) + -I- + -CIDE] —**fe′ti·cid′al,** *adj.*

fet·id (fet′id, fē′tid), *adj.* having an offensive odor; stinking. Also, **foetid.** [1590–1600; < L *fētidus,* equiv. to *fēt-* (s. of *fētēre* to stink) + *-idus* -ID[4]] —**fet′id·ly,** *adv.* —**fet′id·ness, fe·tid′i·ty,** *n.*
—**Syn.** malodorous, smelly, noisome.

fe·tip·a·rous (fē tip′ər əs), *adj.* (of a marsupial) bearing young before they are fully developed. Also, **foetiparous.** [FET(US) + -I- + -PAROUS]

fet·ish (fet′ish, fē′tish), *n.* **1.** an object regarded with awe as being the embodiment or habitation of a potent spirit or as having magical potency. **2.** any object, idea, etc., eliciting unquestioning reverence, respect, or devotion: *to make a fetish of high grades.* **3.** *Psychol.* any object or nongenital part of the body that causes a habitual erotic response or fixation. Also, **fet′ich.** [1605–15; earlier *fateish* < Pg *feitiço* charm, sorcery (n.), artificial (adj.) < L *factīcius* FACTITIOUS; r. *fatisso, fetisso* < Pg, as above] —**fet′ish·like′,** *adj.*
—**Syn. 1.** talisman, amulet.

fet·ish·ism (fet′i shiz′əm, fē′ti-), *n.* **1.** belief in or use of fetishes. **2.** *Psychiatry.* the compulsive use of some object, or part of the body, as a stimulus in the course of attaining sexual gratification, as a shoe, a lock of hair, or underclothes. **3.** blind devotion: *a fetishism of sacrifice to one's children.* Also, **fet′ich·ism.** [1795–1805; FETISH + -ISM] —**fet′ish·ist,** *n.* —**fet′ish·is′tic,** *adj.* —**fet′·ish·is′ti·cal·ly,** *adv.*

fet·ish·ize (fet′i shīz′), *v.t.,* **-ized, -iz·ing.** to make a fetish of. Also, *esp. Brit.,* **fet′ish·ise′.** [FETISH + -IZE]

fet·lock (fet′lok′), *n.* **1.** the projection of the leg of a horse behind the joint between the cannon bone and great pastern bone, bearing a tuft of hair. See diag. under **horse. 2.** the tuft of hair itself. **3.** Also called **fet′lock joint′.** the joint at this point. [1275–1325; ME *fitlok,* akin to MHG *viz(ze)loch,* ult. deriv. of Gmc **fet-,* a gradational var. of **fōt-* FOOT]

fe·tol·o·gy (fē tol′ə jē), *n.* a field of medicine involving the study, diagnosis, and treatment of the fetus. [1960–65; FET(US) + -O- + -LOGY] —**fe·tol′o·gist,** *n.*

fe·tor (fē′tər), *n.* a strong, offensive smell; stench. Also, **foetor.** [1475–1500; < L, equiv. to *fēt-* (s. of *fētēre* to stink) + *-or* -OR[1]; r. earlier *fetour* < MF < L *fētōr-,* s. of *fētor*]

fe·to·scope (fē′tə skōp′), *n.* a tubular fiberoptic instrument used for diagnostic examination of the fetus and interior of the uterus. [1970–75; FET(US) + -O- + -SCOPE] —**fe·to·scop·ic** (fē′tə skop′ik), *adj.* —**fe·tos·co·pist** (fē tos′kə pist), *n.*

fe·tos·co·py (fē tos′kə pē), *n., pl.* **-pies.** examination by means of a fetoscope. [1970–75; FET(US) + -O- + -SCOPY]

fet·ter (fet′ər), *n.* **1.** a chain or shackle placed on the feet. **2.** Usually, **fetters.** anything that confines or restrains: *Boredom puts fetters upon the imagination.* —*v.t.* **3.** to put fetters upon. **4.** to confine; restrain. [bef. 900; ME, OE *feter;* c. OHG *fezzera,* ON *fjoturr;* akin to FOOT] —**fet′ter·er,** *n.* —**fet′ter·less,** *adj.*

fet′ter bone′, the great pastern bone of a horse. See under **pastern** (def. 2).

fet·ter·bush (fet′ər bo͝osh′), *n.* **1.** an evergreen shrub, *Lyonia lucida,* of the heath family, native to the southern U.S., having clusters of fragrant, white flowers. **2.** a similar shrub, *Pieris floribunda,* having long upright clusters of small white flowers. **3.** any of several heathlike shrubs of the southern U.S. [1855–60, *Amer.*; FETTER + BUSH[1]; so called because it impedes walkers]

fet·tle (fet′l), *n., v.,* **-tled, -tling.** —*n.* **1.** state; condition: *in fine fettle.* —*v.t.* **2.** *Ceram.* to remove mold marks from (a cast piece). **3.** *Metall.* **a.** to remove sand from (a casting). **b.** to repair the hearth of (an open-hearth furnace). [1300–50; ME *fetle* to shape, prepare, back formation from *fetled,* OE **fetelede* girded up, equiv. to *fetel* belt + *-ede* -ED[2]]

fet·tling (fet′ling), *n. Metall.* the material with which the hearth of a puddling furnace is lined, usually a dolomite or refractory mixture. [1860–65; FETTLE + -ING[1]]

fet·tuc·ci·ne (fet′ə chē′nē; *It.* fet′to͞ot chē′ne), *n.* (*used with a singular or plural v.*) pasta cut in flat narrow strips. Also, **fet·tuc·ci·ni** (fet′ə chē′nē). [1910–15; < It, pl. of *fettuccina,* dim. of *fettuccia,* dim. of *fetta* slice, ribbon < **offetta* < L *off(a)* flour cake, lump of food + It *-etta* dim. suffix (see -ETTE)]

fet·tuc·ci·ne Al·fre·do (fet′ə chē′nē al frā′dō; *It.* fet′to͞ot chē′ne äl fre′dō), *Italian Cookery.* fettuccine in cream sauce with grated Parmesan cheese. [1960–65; said to be after *Alfredo* all'Augusteo, a restaurant in Rome where it was first served]

fe·tus (fē′təs), *n., pl.* **-tus·es.** *Embryol.* (used chiefly of viviparous mammals) the young of an animal in the womb or egg, esp. in the later stages of development when the body structures are in the recognizable form of its kind, in humans after the end of the second month of gestation. Also, *esp. Brit.,* **foetus.** Cf. **embryo** (def. 2).

CONCISE PRONUNCIATION KEY: act, cāpe, dâre, pärt; set, ēqual; if, īce; ox, ōver, ôrder, oil, bo͝ok, bo͞ot, out; up, ûrge; child; sing; shoe; thin, *th*at; zh as in *treasure.* ə = *a* as in *alone, e* as in *system, i* as in *easily, o* as in *gallop, u* as in *circus;* ᵊ as in *fire* (fīᵊr), *hour* (ouᵊr). l and n can serve as syllabic consonants, as in *cradle* (krād′l), and *button* (but′n). See the full key inside the front cover.

[1350–1400; ME < L *fētus* bringing forth of young, hence that which is born, offspring, young still in the womb, equiv. to *fē-* (v. base attested in L only in n. derivatives, as *fēmina* woman, *fēcundus* FECUND, etc.; cf. Gk *thḗsthai* to suck, milk, OHG *tāan* to suck, OIr *denid* (he) sucks) + *-tus* suffix of v. action]

Feucht•wang•er (foiKHT′väng′əʀ), *n.* **Li•on** (lē′ôn), 1884–1958, German novelist and dramatist.

feud[1] (fyo͞od), *n.* **1.** Also called **blood feud.** a bitter, continuous hostility, esp. between two families, clans, etc., often lasting for many years or generations. **2.** a bitter quarrel or contention: *a feud between labor and management.* —*v.i.* **3.** to engage in a feud. [1300–50; var. of *fead* (*a* misread as *u*), ME *fede* < MF *fe(i)de* < OHG *fēhida;* c. OE *fǣhth* enmity. See FOE, -TH[1]]
—Syn. 2. argument, difference.

feud[2] (fyo͞od), *n.* fee (def. 4). [1605–15; < ML *feudum,* var. of *feodum.* See FEE]

feu•dal (fyo͞od′l), *adj.* **1.** of, pertaining to, or like the feudal system, or its political, military, social, and economic structure. **2.** of or pertaining to the Middle Ages. **3.** of, pertaining to, or of the nature of a fief or fee: *a feudal estate.* **4.** of or pertaining to the holding of land in a fief or fee. [1605–15; < ML *feudālis.* See FEUD[2], -AL[1]] **—feu′dal•ly,** *adv.*

feu•dal•ism (fyo͞od′l iz′əm), *n.* the feudal system, or its principles and practices. [1830–40; FEUDAL[1] + -ISM] **—feu′dal•ist,** *n.* **—feu′dal•is′tic,** *adj.*

feu•dal•i•ty (fyo͞o dal′i tē), *n., pl.* **-ties. 1.** the state or quality of being feudal. **2.** the principles and practices of feudalism. **3.** a fief or fee. [1695–1705; FEUDAL + -ITY; r. *feodality* < F *féodalité*]

feu•dal•ize (fyo͞od′l īz′), *v.t.,* **-ized, -iz•ing.** to make feudal; bring under the feudal system. Also, *esp. Brit.,* **feu′dal•ise′.** [1820–30; FEUDAL + -IZE] **—feu′dal•i•za′tion,** *n.*

feu′dal sys′tem, the political, military, and social system in the Middle Ages, based on the holding of lands in fief or fee and on the resulting relations between lord and vassal. [1770–80]

feu•da•to•ry (fyo͞o′də tôr′ē, -tōr′ē), *n., pl.* **-ries,** *adj.* —*n.* **1.** a person who holds lands by feudal tenure; a feudal vassal. **2.** a fief or fee. —*adj.* **3.** (of a kingdom or state) under the overlordship of another sovereign or state. **4.** (of a feudal estate) holding or held by feudal tenure. [1585–95; < ML *feudā(tor)* fief-holder (see FEUD[2], -ATOR) + -TORY[1], -TORY[2]]

feud•ist[1] (fyo͞o′dist), *n.* a person who participates in a feud. [1900–05, *Amer.;* FEUD[1] + -IST]

feud•ist[2] (fyo͞o′dist), *n.* a writer or authority on feudal law. [1600–10; FEUD[2] + -IST]

Feu•er•bach (foi′ər bäKH′, -bäk′; *Ger.* foi′əʀ bäKH′), *n.* **Ludwig An•dre•as** (än drā′əs, an-; *Ger.* än dʀā′äs), 1804–72, German philosopher.

feuil•le•ton (foi′i tn; *Fr.* fœyə tôɴ′), *n., pl.* **-tons** (-tnz; *Fr.* -tôɴ′). **1.** a part of a European newspaper devoted to light literature, fiction, criticism, etc. **2.** an item printed in the feuilleton. [1835–45; < F, equiv. to *feuillet* little leaf (*feuille* (< L *folium* leaf) + *-et* -ET) + *-on* n. suffix] **—feuil•le•ton•ism** (foi′i tn iz′əm, fœ′yi-), *n.* **—feuil′le•ton•ist,** *n.* **—feuil′le•ton•is′tic,** *adj.*

fe•ver (fē′vər), *n.* **1.** an abnormal condition of the body, characterized by undue rise in temperature, quickening of the pulse, and disturbance of various body functions. **2.** an abnormally high body temperature. **3.** the number of degrees of such a temperature above the normal. **4.** any of a group of diseases in which high temperature is a prominent symptom: *scarlet fever.* **5.** intense nervous excitement: *The audience was in a fever of anticipation.* —*v.t.* **6.** to affect with or as with fever: *The excitement fevered him.* [bef. 1000; ME; OE *fefer* < L *febr-* (s. of *febris*) fever; reinforced by AF *fevre,* OF *fievre* < L, as above] **—fe′ver•less,** *adj.*

fe′ver blis′ter. See **cold sore.** [1880–85]

fe•ver•few (fē′vər fyo͞o′), *n.* a bushy composite plant, *Chrysanthemum parthenium,* bearing small white flowers, formerly used as a remedy for fever and headache. [1400–50; late ME < AF **feverfue* (r. early ME *fever fugie,* OE *feferfuge*) < LL *febrifugia.* See FEBRIFUGE]

fe′ver heat′, 1. the heat of fever; body heat exceeding 98.6°F (37°C). **2.** feverish excitement. [1830–40]

fe•ver•ish (fē′vər ish), *adj.* **1.** having fever. **2.** pertaining to, of the nature of, or resembling fever: *a feverish excitement.* **3.** excited, restless, or uncontrolled, as if from fever. **4.** having a tendency to produce fever. [1350–1400; ME *feverisch.* See FEVER, -ISH[1]] **—fe′ver•ish•ly,** *adv.* **—fe′ver•ish•ness,** *n.*
—Syn. 3. frenzied, impatient, fervent, wrought-up.

fe•ver•ous (fē′vər əs), *adj.* feverish. [1350–1400; ME; see FEVER, -OUS] **—fe′ver•ous•ly,** *adv.*

fe′ver pitch′, a high degree of excitement, as of a gathering of people: *The announcement of victory brought the crowd to fever pitch.* [1910–15]

fe•ver•root (fē′vər ro͞ot′, -ro͝ot′), *n.* See **horse gentian.** [1735–45, *Amer.;* FEVER + ROOT[1]]

fe′ver ther′apy, *Med.* therapy by means of an artificially induced fever. [1920–25]

fe′ver tree′, 1. any of several trees that produce or are believed to produce a febrifuge, as the blue gum, which is believed to prevent malaria. **2.** a small tree, *Pinckneya pubens,* of the madder family, native to the southeastern U.S., having a bark used as a tonic and febrifuge. [1865–70, *Amer.*]

fe′ver twig′, the bittersweet, *Celastrus scandens.* [1880–85]

CONCISE ETYMOLOGY KEY: <, descended or borrowed from; >, whence; b., blend of, blended; c., cognate with; cf., compare; deriv., derivative; equiv., equivalent; imit., imitative; obl., oblique; r., replacing; s., stem; sp., spelling, spelled; resp., respelling, respelled; trans., translation; ?, origin unknown; *, unattested; ‡, probably earlier than. See the full key inside the front cover.

fe•ver•weed (fē′vər wēd′), *n.* **1.** any plant belonging to the genus *Eryngium,* of the parsley family, esp. *E. foetidum,* of the West Indies, or *E. campestre,* of Europe. **2.** any of various plants believed to reduce fever. [1835–45, *Amer.;* FEVER + WEED[1]]

fe•ver•wort (fē′vər wûrt′, -wôrt′), *n.* **1.** See **horse gentian. 2.** the thoroughwort or boneset. [1605–15; FEVER + WORT[2]]

few (fyo͞o), *adj.,* **-er, -est,** *n., pron.* —*adj.* **1.** not many but more than one: *Few artists live luxuriously.* **2. few and far between,** at widely separated intervals; infrequent: *In Nevada the towns are few and far between.* —*n.* **3.** (*used with a plural v.*) a small number or amount: *Send me a few.* **4. quite a few,** a fairly large number; many: *There were quite a few interesting things to do.* **5. the few,** a special, limited number; the minority: *That music appeals to the few.* —*pron.* **6.** (*used with a plural v.*) a small number of persons or things: *A dozen people volunteered, but few have shown up.* [bef. 900; ME *fewe,* OE *fēawe;* c. Goth *fawai;* akin to L *paucus* few, *paulus* little, *pauper* poor, Gk *paûros* little, few]

few•er (fyo͞o′ər), *adj.* **1.** of a smaller number: *fewer words and more action.* —*pron.* **2.** (*used with a plural v.*) a smaller number: *Fewer have come than we hoped.* [ME *fewere,* OE **fēawran.* See FEW, -ER[4]]
—Usage. See **less.**

few•ness (fyo͞o′nis), *n.* the state of being few or small in quantity; paucity. [bef. 900; ME *fewenesse,* OE *fēawnes.* See FEW, -NESS]

-fex, a combining form meaning "maker," used in the formation of compound words: *spinifex.* [< L, equiv. to *-fec-* (comb. form of *facere* to make) + *-s* nom. sing. ending. See -FIC]

fey (fā), *adj.* **1.** *Brit. Dial.* doomed; fated to die. **2.** *Chiefly Scot.* appearing to be under a spell; marked by an apprehension of death, calamity, or evil. **3.** supernatural; unreal; enchanted: *elves, fairies, and other fey creatures.* **4.** being in unnaturally high spirits, as were formerly thought to precede death. **5.** whimsical; strange; otherworldly: *a strange child with a mysterious smile and a fey manner.* [bef. 900; ME; OE *fǣge* doomed to die; c. ON *feigr* doomed, G *feig* cowardly]

Feyn•man (fīn′mən), *n.* **Richard Phillips,** born 1918, U.S. physicist: Nobel prize 1965.

Feyn′man di′agram, *Physics.* a network of lines that represents a series of emissions and absorptions of elementary particles by other elementary particles, from which the probability of the series can be calculated. Also called **Feyn′man graph′.** [1965–70; named after R. P. FEYNMAN, who devised it]

fez (fez), *n., pl.* **fez•zes.** a felt cap, usually of a red color, having the shape of a truncated cone, and ornamented with a long black tassel, worn by men in Egypt and North Africa: formerly the national headdress of the Turks. [1795–1805; < Turk *fes,* after *Fes* FEZ] **—fez′zy,** *adj.*

fez

Fez (fez), *n.* a city in N Morocco: formerly one of the traditional capitals of the sultanate in the former French zone. 1,137,800.

Fez•zan (fez zän′), *n.* a former province in SW Libya: part of the Sahara with numerous oases. 220,000 sq. mi. (570,000 sq. km).

ff, 1. folios. **2.** (and the) following (pages, verses, etc.). **3.** *Music.* fortissimo.

FFA, See **Future Farmers of America.**

F.F.A., *Com.* free from alongside (ship). Also, **f.f.a.**

FFC, 1. Foreign Funds Control. **2.** free from chlorine.

F.F.I., free from infection.

F.F.V., First Families of Virginia.

f.g., *Basketball, Football.* field goal; field goals.

fgn., foreign.

FGP, Foster Grandparent Program.

FGT, federal gift tax.

FH, *Pathol.* familial hypercholesterolemia.

FHA, 1. Farmers' Home Administration. **2.** Federal Housing Administration. **3.** Future Homemakers of America.

FHLB, Federal Home Loan Bank.

FHLBA, Federal Home Loan Bank Administration.

FHLBB, Federal Home Loan Bank Board.

FHLBS, Federal Home Loan Bank System.

FHLMC, Federal Home Loan Mortgage Corporation.

f-hole (ef′hōl′), *n.* either of two *f*-shaped holes in the body of a violin, cello, or similar stringed instrument.

FHWA, Federal Highway Administration.

fi (fē), *n. Music.* the solmization syllable used for the semitone between the fourth and fifth degrees of a scale.

F.I., Falkland Islands.

FIA, Federal Insurance Administration.

fi•a•cre (fē ä′kər, -äk′; *Fr.* fyA′kʀə), *n., pl.* **fi•a•cres** (fē ä′kərz, -äks′; *Fr.* fyA′kʀə). a small horse-drawn carriage. [1690–1700; < F; after the Hotel de St. *Fiacre* in Paris, where such carriages were first for hire]

Fia•na•ran•tso•a (fyə när′ənt sō′ə, -so͞o′ə), *n.* a city in E central Madagascar. 55,500.

fi•an•cé (fē′än sā′, fē än′sā), *n.* a man engaged to be married; a man to whom a woman is engaged. [1850–55; < F: betrothed, ptp. of *fiancer,* OF *fiancier,* v. deriv. of *fiance* a promise, equiv. to *fi(er)* to trust (< VL **fīdāre,* L *fīdere*) + *-ance* -ANCE; see -EE]

fi•an•cée (fē′än sā′, fē än′sā), *n.* a woman engaged to be married; a woman to whom a man is engaged. [1850–55; < F; fem. of FIANCÉ]

fi•an•chet•to (fē′ən ket′ō, -chet′ō), *n., pl.* **-chet•ti** (-ket′ē, -chet′ē), *v. Chess.* —*n.* **1.** the development of a bishop, in an opening move, by advancing one or two pawns so as to permit movement along the bishop's diagonal. —*v.i., v.t.* **2.** to set up or develop as a fianchetto. [1840–50; < It; see FLANK, -ET]

Fi•an•na (fē′ə nə), *n.pl. Irish Hist.* the Fenians.

Fi′anna Fáil′ (foil, fīl), a political party in Ireland, organized in 1927 by Eamon De Valera, that was one of the leading parties in the establishment of the Irish republic. [< Ir: Fenians of Ireland]

fi•as•co (fē as′kō *or, esp. for 2,* -äs′kō), *n., pl.* **-cos, -coes. 1.** a complete and ignominious failure. **2.** a round-bottomed glass flask for wine, esp. Chianti, fitted with a woven, protective raffia basket that also enables the bottle to stand upright. [1850–55; < It: lit., bottle < Gmc (see FLASK[1]); sense "failure" from It phrase *far fiasco* to fail, lit., to make a bottle, idiom of uncert. orig.]
—Syn. 1. disaster, catastrophe, debacle, flop, bomb.

fi•at (fē′ät, -at; fī′ət, -at), *n.* **1.** an authoritative decree, sanction, or order: *a royal fiat.* **2.** a formula containing the word *fiat,* by which a person in authority gives sanction. **3.** an arbitrary decree or pronouncement, esp. by a person or group of persons having absolute authority to enforce it: *The king ruled by fiat.* [1625–35; < L: let it be done, 3rd sing. pres. subj. of *fierī* to become]

fi•at jus•ti•ti•a, ru•at cae•lum (fē′ät yo͞os tē′tē ä′ ro͞o′ät kī′lo͝om; *Eng.* fē′ät jus tish′ē ə ro͞o′at sē′ləm, fī′ət), *Latin.* let there be justice though the heavens fall.

fi•at lux (fē′ät lo͝oks′; *Eng.* fē′ät luks′, fī′ət), *Latin.* let there be light.

fi′at mon′ey, paper currency made legal tender by a fiat of the government, but not based on or convertible into coin. [1870–75, *Amer.*]

fib (fib), *n., v.,* **fibbed, fib•bing.** —*n.* **1.** a small or trivial lie; minor falsehood. —*v.i.* **2.** to tell a fib. [1560–70; short for *fibble-fable* nonsense, gradational compound based on FABLE] **—fib′ber, fib′ster,** *n.*
—Syn. 1. See **falsehood.**

fi•ber (fī′bər), *n.* **1.** a fine, threadlike piece, as of cotton, jute, or asbestos. **2.** a slender filament: *a fiber of platinum.* **3.** filaments collectively. **4.** matter or material composed of filaments: *a plastic fiber.* **5.** something resembling a filament. **6.** an essential character, quality, or strength: *people of strong moral fiber.* **7.** *Bot.* **a.** filamentous matter from the bast tissue or other parts of plants, used for industrial purposes. **b.** a slender, threadlike root of a plant. **c.** a slender, tapered cell which, with like cells, serves to strengthen tissue. **8.** *Anat., Zool.* a slender, threadlike element or cell, as of nerve, muscle, or connective tissue. **9.** *Nutrition.* Also called **bulk, dietary fiber, roughage. a.** the structural part of plants and plant products that consists of carbohydrates, as cellulose and pectin, that are wholly or partially indigestible and when eaten stimulate peristalsis in the intestine. **b.** food containing a high amount of such carbohydrates, as whole grains, fruits, and vegetables. **10.** *Chem.* See **vulcanized fiber. 11.** *Optics.* See **optical fiber.** Also, *esp. Brit.,* **fibre.** [1350–1400; 1970–75 for def. 9; ME *fibre* (< MF) < L *fībra* filament] **—fi′ber•less,** *adj.*

fi•ber•board (fī′bər bôrd′, -bōrd′), *n.* **1.** a building material made of wood or other plant fibers compressed and cemented into rigid sheets. **2.** a sheet of this. [1895–1900; FIBER + BOARD]

fi′ber bun′dle, *Optics.* a flexible bundle of optical glass that transmits images.

fi•bered (fī′bərd), *adj.* (of plaster) having an admixture of hair or fiber. [1770–80; FIBER + -ED[3]]

fi•ber•fill (fī′bər fil′), *n.* synthetic fibers, as polyester, used as a filling or insulating material for pillows, cushions, comforters, winter garments, etc. [1960–65, *Amer.;* FIBER + FILL]

Fi•ber•glas (fī′bər glas′, -gläs′), *Trademark.* a brand of fiberglass.

fi•ber•glass (fī′bər glas′, -gläs′), *n.* **1.** a material consisting of extremely fine filaments of glass that are combined in yarn and woven into fabrics, used in masses as a thermal and acoustical insulator, or embedded in various resins to make boat hulls, fishing rods, and the like. —*v.t.* **2.** to cover or form with fiberglass. —*v.i.* **3.** to use or work with fiberglass. Also, **fi′ber glass′.** [1935–40, *Amer.;* FIBER + GLASS]

fi•ber•ize (fī′bə rīz′), *v.t.,* **-ized, -iz•ing.** to break or crack into fibers. Also, *esp. Brit.,* **fi′ber•ise′.** [1930–35; FIBER + -IZE, after PULVERIZE] **—fi′ber•iz′er,** *n.* **—fi′ber•i•za′tion,** *n.*

fi•ber•op•tic (fī′bər op′tik), *adj.* of or pertaining to instruments utilizing fiber optics. [1960–65; FIBER + OPTIC]

fi′ber op′tics, the branch of optics that deals with the transmission of light through transparent fibers, as in the form of pulses for the transmission of data or communications, or through fiber bundles for the transmission of images. Cf. **optical fiber.** [1960–65]

fi′ber pen′. See **felt-tip pen.**

fi•ber•scope (fī′bər skōp′), *n. Optics.* an optical instrument consisting of a fiber bundle with an objective lens at one end and an eyepiece at the other, for viewing objects not accessible to direct viewing. [1950–55; FIBER + -SCOPE]

Fi•bi•ger (fē′bə gər; *Dan.* fē′bē gəʀ), *n.* **Jo•han•nes**

An·dre·as Grib (yō hä′nis än drĕ′äs grēb), 1867–1928, Danish pathologist: Nobel prize for medicine 1926.

Fi·bo·nac′ci num′bers (fē′bō nä′chē), *Math.* the unending sequence 1, 1, 2, 3, 5, 8, 13, 21, 34, . . . where each term is defined as the sum of its two predecessors. Also called **Fibonac′ci se′quence.** [1890–95; after Leonardo *Fibonacci,* 13th-century Italian mathematician]

fibr-, var. of **fibro-** before a vowel: *fibrin.*

fi·bra·tus (fī brā′təs), *adj. Meteorol.* (of a cloud) hairlike or striated in composition. Also, **filosus.** [< L: fibered, hairlike, equiv. to *fibr(a)* FIBER + *-ātus* -ATE[1]]

fi·bre (fī′bər), *n. Chiefly Brit.* fiber.

fi·bri·form (fī′brə fôrm′, fib′rə-), *adj.* of the form of a fiber or fibers. [1840–50; FIBR- + -I- + -FORM]

fi·bril (fī′brəl, fib′rəl), *n.* **1.** a small or fine fiber or filament. **2.** *Bot.* any of the delicate hairs on the young roots of some plants. **3.** *Cell Biol.* any threadlike structure or filament. [1655–65; < NL *fibrilla,* equiv. to L *fibr(a)* fiber + *-illa* dim. suffix] **—fi′bril·lar,** *adj.* **—fi′bril·lose′,** *adj.*

fi·bril·la (fī bril′ə, fi-), *n., pl.* **-bril·lae** (-bril′ē). a fibril.

fi·bril·late (fī′brə lāt′, fib′rə-), *v.,* **-lat·ed, -lat·ing.** —*v.t.* **1.** to cause to undergo fibrillation. —*v.i.* **2.** to undergo fibrillation. [1830–40; FIBRILL(A) + -ATE[1]] **—fi′bril·la′tive,** *adj.*

fi·bril·la·tion (fī′brə lā′shən, *or, esp. for 2,* fib′rə-), *n.* **1.** the formation of fibrils. **2.** *Pathol.* uncontrolled twitching or quivering of muscular fibrils. [1830–40; FIBRILLATE + -ION]

fi·bril·li·form (fī bril′ə fôrm′, fi-), *adj.* of the form of a fibril. [1840–50; FIBRILL(A) + -I- + -FORM]

fi·brin (fī′brin), *n.* **1.** the insoluble protein end product of blood coagulation, formed from fibrinogen by the action of thrombin in the presence of calcium ions. **2.** *Bot.* a fibrinlike substance found in some plants; gluten. [1790–1800; FIBR- + -IN[2]] **—fi′brin·ous,** *adj.*

fibrino-, a combining form representing **fibrin** in compound words: *fibrinolysis.*

fi·brin·o·gen (fī brin′ə jən), *n. Biochem.* a globulin occurring in blood and yielding fibrin in blood coagulation. [1870–75; FIBRINO- + -GEN]

fi·brin·o·gen·ic (fī′brə nō jen′ik), *adj. Physiol.* producing fibrin. Also, **fi·brin·og·e·nous** (fī′brə noj′ə nəs). [1875–80; FIBRINO- + -GENIC] **—fi′brin·o·gen′i·cal·ly,** *adv.*

fi·bri·noid (fī′brə noid′, fib′rə-), *adj.* **1.** having the characteristics of fibrin. —*n.* **2.** an acellular homogenous protein resembling fibrin, present in the maturing placenta and in certain diseased blood vessels and connective tissues. [1905–10; FIBRIN + -OID]

fi·bri·nol·y·sin (fī′brə nol′ə sin), *n. Biochem.* a proteolytic enzyme, formed in the blood from plasminogen, that causes the breakdown of the fibrin in blood clots. Also called **plasmin.** [1910–15; FIBRINO- + LYSIN]

fi·bri·nol·y·sis (fī′brə nol′ə sis), *n., pl.* **-ses** (-sēz′). *Biochem.* the disintegration or dissolution of fibrin, esp. by enzymatic action. [1905–10; FIBRINO- + -LYSIS] **—fi·bri·no·lyt·ic** (fī′brə nō lit′ik, fī brin′l it′-), *adj.*

fibro-, a combining form meaning "fiber," used in the formation of compound words: *fibrolite.* Also, *esp. before a vowel,* **fibr-.** [comb. form repr. L *fibra* FIBER]

fi·bro·ad·e·no·ma (fī′brō ad′n ō′mə), *n., pl.* **-mas, -ma·ta** (-mə tə). a benign tumor originating from glandular tissue, as in the female breast. [1890–95; FIBRO- + ADENOMA]

fi·bro·blast (fī′brə blast′), *n. Cell Biol.* a cell that contributes to the formation of connective tissue fibers. [1875–80; FIBRO- + -BLAST] **—fi′bro·blas′tic,** *adj.*

fi·bro·car·ti·lage (fī′brō kär′tl ij, -kärt′lij), *n. Anat., Zool.* **1.** a type of cartilage having a large number of fibers. **2.** a part or structure composed of such cartilage. [1825–35; FIBRO- + CARTILAGE] **—fi·bro·car·ti·lag·i·nous** (fī′brō kär′tl aj′ə nəs), *adj.*

fi·bro·cys·tic (fī′brō sis′tik), *adj.* showing or having the increased fibrosis associated with dilated glandular structure, as in the breast nodules of fibrocystic disease. [1850–55; FIBRO- + CYSTIC]

fibrocys′tic disease′, *Pathol.* a common condition, occurring esp. among middle-aged women, characterized by the presence of one or more benign breast cysts, which may become swollen and painful. Also called **cystic mastitis.**

fi·broid (fī′broid), *adj.* **1.** resembling fiber or fibrous tissue. **2.** composed of fibers, as a tumor. —*n.* **3.** fibroma. **4.** leiomyoma. [1850–55; FIBR- + -OID]

fi·bro·in (fī′brō in), *n. Biochem.* an indigestible protein that is a principal component of spider webs and silk. [1860–65; < F *fibroïne;* see FIBRO-, -IN[2]]

fi·bro·lite (fī′brə līt′), *n. Mineral.* sillimanite. [1795–1805; FIBRO- + -LITE]

fi·bro·ma (fī brō′mə), *n., pl.* **-mas, -ma·ta** (-mə tə). *Pathol.* a tumor consisting essentially of fibrous tissue. [1840–50; FIBR- + -OMA] **—fi·brom·a·tous** (fī brom′ə təs), *adj.*

fi·bro·nec·tin (fī′brə nek′tin), *n. Cell Biol.* a fibrous protein that binds to collagen, fibrin, and other proteins and also to the cell membranes, functioning as an anchor and connector. [1975–80; FIBRO- + L *nect(ere)* to bind, join together (see CONNECT, NEXUS) + -IN[2]]

fi·bro·pla·sia (fī′brə plā′zhə, -zhē ə, -zē ə), *n. Med.* the formation of fibrous tissue. [1925–30; < NL; see FIBRO-, -PLASIA] **—fi·bro·plas·tic** (fī′brə plas′tik), *adj.*

fi·bro·sar·co·ma (fī′brō sär kō′mə), *n., pl.* **-mas, -ma·ta** (-mə tə). *Pathol.* a sarcoma derived from fibroblast cells, often able to generate collagen. [1875–80; FIBRO- + SARCOMA]

fi·bro·sis (fī brō′sis), *n. Pathol.* the development in an organ of excess fibrous connective tissue. [1870–75; FIBR- + -OSIS] **—fi·brot·ic** (fī brot′ik), *adj.*

fi·brous (fī′brəs), *adj.* containing, consisting of, or resembling fibers. [1620–30; FIBR- + -OUS] **—fi′brous·ly,** *adv.* **—fi′brous·ness,** *n.*

fi·bro·vas·cu·lar (fī′brō vas′kyə lər), *adj. Bot.* composed of fibrous and conductive tissue, as in the vascular systems of higher plants: *a fibrovascular bundle.* [1835–45; FIBRO- + VASCULAR]

fib·u·la (fib′yə lə), *n., pl.* **-lae** (-lē′), **-las.** **1.** *Anat.* the outer and thinner of the two bones of the human leg, extending from the knee to the ankle. See diag. under **skeleton.** **2.** *Zool.* a corresponding bone, often rudimentary or ankylosed with the tibia, of the leg or hind limb of an animal. **3.** a clasp or brooch, often ornamented, used by the ancient Greeks and Romans. [1665–75; < NL; L *fībula* bolt, pin, clasp, prob. < **fīvibula,* equiv. to *fīv(ere),* early form of *fīgere* to fasten, FIX + *-i-* -I- + *-bula* suffix denoting instrument; the bone so called from its resemblance to the tongue of a clasp] **—fib′u·lar,** *adj.*

-fic, a combining form meaning "making," "producing," "causing," appearing in adjectives borrowed from Latin: *frigorific; honorific; pacific; prolific.* [< L *-ficus* making, producing, equiv. to *-fic-* (comb. form of *facere* to make) + *-us* adj. suffix; in some words r. *-fique* < MF < L *-ficus*]

FICA (fī′kə, fē′-), Federal Insurance Contributions Act: U.S. government legislation under which taxes are levied for the support of Social Security. Also, **F.I.C.A.**

-fication, a combining form of nouns of action or state corresponding to verbs ending in *-fy: deification; pacification.* [< L *-ficātiōn-* (s. of *-ficātiō*) a making, equiv. to *-ficā(re)* -FY + *-tiōn-* -TION; in some words r. ME *-ficacioun* < AF]

fice (fīs), *n.* feist.

fiche (fēsh), *n.* microfiche. [by shortening]

Fich·te (fiкн′tə), *n.* **Jo·hann Gott·lieb** (yō′hän gôt′lēp), 1762–1814, German philosopher.

Fich·te·an (fik′tē ən, fiкн′-), *adj.* **1.** of, pertaining to, or resembling the philosophy of Johann Fichte. —*n.* **2.** an adherent or advocate of this philosophy. [1810–20; FICHTE + -AN] **—Fich′te·an·ism,** *n.*

fi·chu (fish′o͞o; *Fr.* fē shʏ′), *n., pl.* **fich·us** (fish′o͞oz; *Fr.* fē shʏ′). a woman's kerchief or shawl, generally triangular in shape, worn draped over the shoulders or around the neck with the ends drawn together on the breast. [1795–1805; < F: n. use of *fichu,* ptp. of *ficher* to drive in, fix (informally, to throw, fling; hence, something put on hastily, loosely attached) < VL **fīgicāre,* for L *fīgere;* cf. FINCA]

fick·le (fik′əl), *adj.* **1.** likely to change, esp. due to caprice, irresolution, or instability; casually changeable: *fickle weather.* **2.** not constant or loyal in affections: *a fickle lover.* [bef. 1000; ME *fikel,* OE *ficol* deceitful, akin to *fǣcen* treachery, *fician* to deceive, *gefic* deception] **—fick′le·ness,** *n.*

—Syn. **1.** unstable, unsteady, variable, capricious, fitful. **2.** inconstant. **1, 2.** FICKLE, INCONSTANT, CAPRICIOUS, VACILLATING describe persons or things that are not firm or steady in affection, behavior, opinion, or loyalty. FICKLE implies an underlying perversity as a cause for the lack of stability: *the fickle seasons, disappointing as often as they delight; once lionized, now rejected by a fickle public.* INCONSTANT suggests an innate disposition to change: *an inconstant lover, flitting from affair to affair.* CAPRICIOUS implies unpredictable changeability arising from sudden whim: *a capricious administration constantly and inexplicably changing its signals; a capricious and astounding reversal of position.* VACILLATING means changeable due to lack of resolution or firmness: *an indecisive, vacillating leader, apparently incapable of a sustained course of action.*

fick·le-mind·ed (fik′əl mīn′did), *adj.* (of a person) prone to casual change; inconstant. [1590–1600]

fi·co (fē′kō), *n., pl.* **-coes.** fig[1] (def. 4). [1570–80; < It *fico, fica* FIG[1]]

fict., fiction.

fic·tile (fik′tl; *Brit.* fik′tīl), *adj.* **1.** capable of being molded. **2.** made of earth, clay, etc., by a potter. **3.** of or pertaining to pottery. [1620–30; < L *fictilis* earthen (lit., moldable), equiv. to *fict(us)* shaped (ptp. of *fingere*) + *-ilis* -ILE]

fic·tion (fik′shən), *n.* **1.** the class of literature comprising works of imaginative narration, esp. in prose form. **2.** works of this class, as novels or short stories: *detective fiction.* **3.** something feigned, invented, or imagined; a made-up story: *We've all heard the fiction of her being in delicate health.* **4.** the act of feigning, inventing, or imagining. **5.** an imaginary thing or event, postulated for the purposes of argument or explanation. **6.** *Law.* an allegation that a fact exists that is known not to exist, made by authority of law to bring a case within the operation of a rule of law. [1375–1425; late ME < L *fictiōn-* (s. of *fictiō*) a shaping, hence a feigning, fiction, equiv. to *fict(us)* molded (ptp. of *fingere*) + *-iōn-* -ION] **—fic′tion·al,** *adj.* **—fic′tion·al·ly,** *adv.*

—Syn. **3.** fable, fantasy. FICTION, FABRICATION, FIGMENT suggest a story that is without basis in reality. FICTION suggests a story invented and fashioned either to entertain or to deceive: *clever fiction; pure fiction.* FABRICATION applies particularly to a false but carefully invented statement or series of statements, in which some truth is sometimes interwoven, the whole usually intended to deceive: *fabrications to lure speculators.* FIGMENT applies to a tale, idea, or statement often made up to explain, justify, or glorify oneself: *His rich uncle was a figment of his imagination.* **—Ant.** **3.** fact.

fic·tion·al·ize (fik′shə nl īz′), *v.t.,* **-ized, -iz·ing.** to make into fiction; give a somewhat imaginative or fictional version of: *to fictionalize a biography.* Also, **fictionize.** Also, *esp. Brit.,* **fic′tion·al·ise′.** [1920–25; FICTIONAL + -IZE] **—fic′tion·al·i·za′tion,** *n.* **—fic′·tion·al·iz′er,** *n.*

fic·tion·eer (fik′shə nēr′), *n.* a writer of fiction, esp. a prolific one whose works are of mediocre quality. [1920–25; FICTION + -EER] **—fic′tion·eer′ing,** *n.*

fic·tion·ist (fik′shə nist), *n.* a writer of fiction; a novelist or short-story writer. Also, **fic′tion·er.** [1820–30; FICTION + -IST]

fic·tion·ize (fik′shə nīz′), *v.t.,* **-ized, -iz·ing.** fictionalize. Also, *esp. Brit.,* **fic′tion·ise′.** [1825–35; FICTION + -IZE] **—fic′tion·i·za′tion,** *n.*

fic·ti·tious (fik tish′əs), *adj.* **1.** created, taken, or assumed for the sake of concealment; not genuine; false: *fictitious names.* **2.** of, pertaining to, or consisting of fiction; imaginatively produced or set forth; created by the imagination: *a fictitious hero.* [1605–15; < L *ficticius* artificial, equiv. to *fict(us)* shaped, feigned (see FICTION) + *-icius* -ITIOUS] **—fic·ti′tious·ly,** *adv.* **—fic·ti′tious·ness,** *n.*

—Syn. **1.** spurious, fake. **2.** fictional.

ficti′tious force′, *Physics.* any force that is postulated to account for apparent deviations from Newton's laws of motion appearing in an accelerated reference system.

ficti′tious per′son, *Law.* a legal entity or artificial person, as a corporation.

fic·tive (fik′tiv), *adj.* **1.** fictitious; imaginary. **2.** pertaining to the creation of fiction: *fictive inventiveness.* [1485–95; FICT(ION) + -IVE] **—fic′tive·ly,** *adv.*

fi·cus (fī′kəs), *n., pl.* **fi·cus, fi·cus·es.** any of numerous chiefly tropical trees, shrubs, and vines belonging to the genus *Ficus,* of the mulberry family, having milky sap and large, thick or stiff leaves, including the edible fig, the banyan, and many species grown as ornamentals. [< NL (Linnaeus); L *fīcus* FIG]

fid (fid), *n. Naut.* **1.** a stout bar of wood or metal placed across a lower spar so as to support a higher one. **2.** a stout bar used to hold a running bowsprit in its extended position. **3.** a wooden or metal pin for parting strands of a rope. **4.** a bar or pin used as a key or toggle. [1605–15; orig. uncert.]

-fid, a combining form meaning "divided," "lobed," occurring in adjectives borrowed from Latin (*bifid*); on this model, used in the formation of compound words (*pinnatifid*). [< L *-fidus* divided, equiv. to *-fid-* (var. s. of *findere* to split) + *-us* adj. suffix]

fid., fiduciary.

fid·dle (fid′l), *n., v.,* **-dled, -dling.** —*n.* **1.** a musical instrument of the viol family. **2.** violin: *Her aunt plays first fiddle with the state symphony orchestra.* **3.** *Naut.* a small ledge or barrier raised in heavy weather to keep dishes, pots, utensils, etc., from sliding off tables and stoves. **4.** *Brit. Informal.* swindle; fraud. **5. fine as a fiddle,** *South Midland and Southern U.S.* See **fiddle** (def. 6). **6. fit as a fiddle,** in perfect health; very fit: *The doctor told him he was fit as a fiddle.* Also, **as fit as a fiddle.** **7. play second fiddle.** See **second fiddle.** —*v.i.* **8.** to play on the fiddle. **9.** to make trifling or fussing movements with the hands (often fol. by *with*): *fiddling with his cuffs.* **10.** to touch or manipulate something, as to operate or adjust it; tinker (often fol. by *with*): *You may have to fiddle with the antenna to get a clear picture on the TV.* **11.** to waste time; trifle; dally (often fol. by *around*): *Stop fiddling around and get to work.* **12.** *Brit. Informal.* to cheat. —*v.t.* **13.** to play (a tune) on a fiddle. **14.** to trifle or waste (usually used with *away*): *to fiddle time away.* **15.** *Bookbinding.* to bind together (sections or leaves of a book) by threading a cord through holes cut lengthwise into the back. **16.** *Brit. Informal.* **a.** to falsify: *to fiddle the account books.* **b.** to cheat: *to fiddle the company out of expense money.* [bef. 1000; ME; OE *fithele* (c. G *Fiedel,* D *vedel,* OHG *fidula*) prob. < VL **vītula* (cf. VIOL, VIOLA[1]), perh. deriv. of L *vītulārī* to rejoice]

fid′dle back′, a chair back having a solid splat similar in form to that of a fiddle.

fid·dle·back (fid′l bak′), *n.* **1.** something shaped like a fiddle. —*adj.* **2.** resembling the back or outline of a violin. **3.** (of a veneer figure) having close, fine, dark stripes. [1885–90; FIDDLE + BACK[1]]

fid′dleback spi′der. See **brown recluse spider.** [so called from its violin-shaped marking]

fid′dle bow′ (bō *for 1, 2;* bou *for 3*), **1.** a bow with which the strings of the violin or a similar instrument are set in vibration. **2.** a bow for driving the arbor of a small lathe, as one used by watchmakers. **3.** *Naut.* See **clipper bow.** [1820–30]

fid·dle-de-dee (fid′l di dē′), *interj.* (used to express irritation, dismissive indifference, or scorn.) Also, **fid′·dle·de·dee′, fid′dle·dee·dee′.** [1775–85; FIDDLE + *-de-* (redupl. prefix) + (TWEEDLE)DEE in obs. sense of fiddler]

fid·dle-fad·dle (fid′l fad′l), *n., v.,* **-dled, -dling,** *interj.* —*n.* **1.** nonsense. **2.** something trivial. —*v.i.* **3.** to fuss with trifles. —*interj.* **4.** (used to express irritation, impatience, etc.) [1570–80; gradational compound based on FIDDLE] **—fid′dle-fad′dler,** *n.*

fid·dle-foot·ed (fid′l fo͝ot′id), *adj. Informal.* restlessly wandering. [1945–50]

fid·dle·head (fid′l hed′), *n.* **1.** *Naut.* a billethead having a form similar to the volute carved at the upper end of a violin. **2.** the young, coiled frond of various species of ferns, eaten as a vegetable. [1790–1800; FIDDLE + HEAD]

fid′dle pat′tern, a pattern of spoon or fork having a handle that narrows abruptly from a broad, flat upper part and terminates with a pronounced shoulder above the bowl or tines. [1835–45]

fid·dler (fid′lər), *n.* **1.** a person who plays a fiddle. **2.** a person who dawdles or trifles. [bef. 1100; ME, OE *fithelere;* c. D *vedelaar,* G *Fiedler.* See FIDDLE, -ER[1]]

fid′dler bee′tle, a black scarab beetle, *Eupoecila australasiae,* having markings resembling a violin. [1915–20]

fid′dler crab′, any small, burrowing crab of the genus *Uca,* characterized by one greatly enlarged claw in the male. [1700–10, *Amer.*]

fiddler crab, *Uca pugilator,* shell width about 1 in. (2.5 cm)

fid·dler·fish (fid′lər fish′), *n., pl.* (*esp. collectively*) **-fish,** (*esp. referring to two or more kinds or species*) **-fish·es.** any of several guitarfishes, esp. *Trygonorhina fasciata,* of Australia. [FIDDLER + FISH]

fid·dle·stick (fid′l stik′), *n.* anything; a bit: *I don't care a fiddlestick for what they say.* [1400–50; late ME *fidillstyk.* See FIDDLE, STICK[1]]

fid·dle·sticks (fid′l stiks′), *interj.* (used to express impatience, dismissal, etc.)

fid·dle·wood (fid′l wŏŏd′), *n.* **1.** the heavy, hard, durable wood of various West Indian and other trees. **2.** any of these trees, esp. species of the genera *Citharexylum* and *Vitex.* [1705–15; FIDDLE + WOOD[1]]

fid·dling (fid′ling), *adj.* trifling; trivial: *a fiddling sum of money.* [1425–75; late ME; see FIDDLE, -ING[2]]

fi·de·i·com·mis·sar·y (fī′dē ī kom′i ser′ē), *n., pl.* **-sar·ies,** *adj. Civil Law.* —*n.* **1.** the recipient of a fideicommissum. —*adj.* **2.** of, pertaining to, or resembling a fideicommissum. [1875–80; < LL *fideī commissārius,* equiv. to *fideī commiss(um)* a FIDEICOMMISSUM + *-ārius* -ARY]

fi·de·i·com·mis·sum (fī′dē ī kə mis′əm), *n., pl.* **-mis·sa** (-mis′ə). *Civil Law.* a request by a decedent that the heir or legatee to the estate convey a specified part of the estate to another person, or permit another person to enjoy such a part. [1720–30; < LL *fideī commissum* entrusted to faith, equiv. to *fideī,* dat. sing. of *fidēs* FAITH + *commissum,* ptp. of *committere* to COMMIT]

Fi·de·i De·fen·sor (fē′de ē′ de fen′sōr; *Eng.* fī′dē ī′ di fen′sôr), *Latin.* Defender of the Faith: one of the titles of English sovereigns.

fi·de·ism (fē′dā iz′əm, fī′dē-), *n.* exclusive reliance in religious matters upon faith, with consequent rejection of appeals to science or philosophy. [1880–85; < L *fidē-*s. of *fidēs* FAITH + -ISM; prob. first coined in F (*fidéisme*)] —**fi′de·ist,** *n.* —**fi′de·is′tic,** *adj.*

Fi·del (fi del′; *Sp.* fē thel′), *n.* a male given name.

Fi·de·lio (fi dāl′yō), *n.* an opera (1805) by Ludwig van Beethoven.

Fi·del·ism (fi del′iz əm), *n.* Castroism. Also called **Fi·de·lis·mo** (fē′de lēz′mō, -liz′-; *Sp.* fe′the lēz′mô). [1955–60; *Fidel* (CASTRO) + -ISM] —**Fi·del′ist,** *n.*

Fi·de·lis·ta (fē′de lē′stə; *Sp.* fe′the lēs′tä), *n., pl.* **-lis·tas** (-lē′stəz; *Sp.* -lēs′täs). Fidelist. [1955–60; < Sp *fidelista,* equiv. to *Fidel* (CASTRO) + *-ista* -IST]

fi·del·i·ty (fi del′i tē, fī-), *n., pl.* **-ties.** **1.** strict observance of promises, duties, etc.: *a servant's fidelity.* **2.** loyalty: *fidelity to one's country.* **3.** conjugal faithfulness. **4.** adherence to fact or detail. **5.** accuracy; exactness: *The speech was transcribed with great fidelity.* **6.** *Audio, Video.* the degree of accuracy with which sound or images are recorded or reproduced. [1375–1425; late ME *fidelite* (< MF) < L *fidēlitās,* equiv. to *fidēli-* (s. of *fidēlis* loyal, equiv. to *fidē(s)* FAITH + *-lis* adj. suffix) + *-tās* -TY[2]]
—**Syn.** **2.** See **loyalty.** **5.** precision, faithfulness, rigor, meticulousness. —**Ant.** **2.** disloyalty.

fidg·et (fij′it), *v.i.* **1.** to move about restlessly, nervously, or impatiently. —*v.t.* **2.** to cause to fidget; make uneasy. —*n.* **3.** Often, **fidgets.** the condition or an instance of being nervously restless, uneasy, or impatient. **4.** Also, **fidg′et·er.** a person who fidgets. [1665–75; cf. dial. *fidge* to fidget, akin to the synonymous expressive words *fitch, fig, fike;* cf. ON *fikjast* to be eager, OSw *fikja* to be restless] —**fidg′et·ing·ly,** *adv.*

fidg·et·y (fij′i tē), *adj.* **1.** restless; impatient; uneasy. **2.** nervously and excessively fussy. [FIDGET + -Y[1]]

FIDO (fī′dō), *n. Aeron.* a system for evaporating the fog above airfield runways by the heat from burners. [1940–45; *f(og) i(nvestigation) d(ispersal) o(perations)*]

fi·du·cial (fi dōō′shəl, -dyōō′-), *adj.* **1.** accepted as a fixed basis of reference or comparison: *a fiducial point; a fiducial temperature.* **2.** based on or having trust: *fiducial dependence upon God.* [1565–75; < LL *fīdūciālis,* equiv. to *fīdūci(a)* trust (akin to *fīdere* to trust) + *-ālis* -AL[1]] —**fi·du′cial·ly,** *adv.*

fi·du·ci·ar·y (fi dōō′shē er′ē, -dyōō′-), *n., pl.* **-ar·ies,** *adj.* —*n.* **1.** *Law.* a person to whom property or power is entrusted for the benefit of another. —*adj.* **2.** *Law.* of or pertaining to the relation between a fiduciary and his or her principal: *a fiduciary capacity; a fiduciary duty.* **3.** of, based on, or in the nature of trust and confidence, as in public affairs: *a fiduciary obligation of government employees.* **4.** depending on public confidence for value or currency, as fiat money. [1585–95; < L *fīdūciārius* of something held in trust, equiv. to *fīdūci(a)* trust + *-ārius* -ARY] —**fi·du′ci·ar′i·ly,** *adv.*

fidu′ciary bond′, a bond filed by a fiduciary administering an estate as surety.

fie (fī), *interj.* **1.** (used to express mild disgust, disapprobation, annoyance, etc.) **2.** (used to express the humorous pretense of being shocked.) [1250–1300; ME *fi* < MF < L; cf. ON *fȳ,* L *phy*]

Fied·ler (fēd′lər), *n.* **Arthur,** 1894–1979, U.S. symphony conductor.

fief (fēf), *n.* **1.** a fee or feud held of a feudal lord; a tenure of land subject to feudal obligations. **2.** a territory held in fee. **3.** fiefdom. [1605–15; < F, var. of OF *fieu, fie,* c. AF *fe* FEE < Gmc; cf. OHG *fihu,* OE *feoh* cattle, property; akin to L *pecū* flock of sheep, *pecus* cattle, *pecūnia* wealth]

fief·dom (fēf′dəm), *n.* **1.** the estate or domain of a feudal lord. **2.** *Informal.* anything, as an organization or real estate, owned or controlled by one dominant person or group. [1805–15; FIEF + -DOM]

field (fēld), *n.* **1.** an expanse of open or cleared ground, esp. a piece of land suitable or used for pasture or tillage. **2.** *Sports.* **a.** a piece of ground devoted to sports or contests; playing field. **b.** (in betting) all the contestants or numbers that are grouped together as one: *to bet on the field in a horse race.* **c.** (in football) the players on the playing ground. **d.** the area in which field events are held. **3.** *Baseball.* **a.** the team in the field, as opposed to the one at bat. **b.** the outfield. **4.** a sphere of activity, interest, etc., esp. within a particular business or profession: *the field of teaching; the field of Shakespearean scholarship.* **5.** the area or region drawn on or serviced by a business or profession; outlying areas where business activities or operations are carried on, as opposed to a home or branch office: *our representatives in the field.* **6.** a job location remote from regular workshop facilities, offices, or the like. **7.** *Mil.* **a.** the scene or area of active military operations. **b.** a battleground. **c.** a battle. **d.** *Informal.* an area located away from the headquarters of a commander. **8.** an expanse of anything: *a field of ice.* **9.** any region characterized by a particular feature, resource, activity, etc.: *a gold field.* **10.** the surface of a canvas, shield, etc., on which something is portrayed: *a gold star on a field of blue.* **11.** (in a flag) the ground of each division. **12.** *Physics.* the influence of some agent, as electricity or gravitation, considered as existing at all points in space and defined by the force it would exert on an object placed at any point in space. Cf. **electric field, gravitational field, magnetic field.** **13.** Also called **field of view.** *Optics.* the entire angular expanse visible through an optical instrument at a given time. **14.** *Elect.* the structure in a generator or motor that produces a magnetic field around a rotating armature. **15.** *Math.* a number system that has the same properties relative to the operations of addition, subtraction, multiplication, and division as the number system of all real numbers; a commutative division ring. **16.** *Photog.* the area of a subject that is taken in by a lens at a particular diaphragm opening. **17.** *Psychol.* the total complex of interdependent factors within which a psychological event occurs and is perceived as occurring. **18.** *Computers.* **a.** one or more related characters treated as a unit and constituting part of a record, for purposes of input, processing, output, or storage by a computer: *If the hours-worked field is blank or zero, the program does not write a check for that employee.* **b.** (in a punch card) any number of columns regularly used for recording the same information. **19.** *Television.* one half of the scanning lines required to form a complete television frame. In the U.S., two fields are displayed in 1/30 second: all the odd-numbered lines in one field and all the even lines in the next field. Cf. **frame** (def. 9). **20.** *Numis.* the blank area of a coin, other than that of the exergue. **21.** *Fox Hunting.* the group of participants in a hunt, exclusive of the master of foxhounds and his staff. **22.** *Heraldry.* the whole area or background of an escutcheon. **23. in the field, a.** in actual use or in a situation simulating actual use or application; away from a laboratory, workshop, or the like: *The machine was tested for six months in the field.* **b.** in contact with a prime source of basic data: *The anthropologist is working in the field in Nigeria.* **c.** within a given profession: *The public knows little of him, but in the field he's known as a fine mathematician.* **24. keep the field,** to remain in competition or in battle; continue to contend: *The troops kept the field under heavy fire.* **25. out in left field.** See **left field** (def. 3). **26. play the field,** *Informal.* **a.** to vary one's activities. **b.** to date a number of persons rather than only one: *He wanted to play the field for a few years before settling down.* **27. take the field, a.** to begin to play, as in football or baseball; go into action. **b.** to go into battle: *They took the field at dawn.*
—*v.t.* **28.** *Baseball, Cricket.* **a.** to catch or pick up (the ball) in play: *The shortstop fielded the grounder and threw to first for the out.* **b.** to place (a player, group of players, or a team) in the field to play. **29.** to place in competition: *to field a candidate for governor.* **30.** to answer or reply skillfully: *to field a difficult question.* **31.** to put into action or on duty: *to field police cars to patrol an area.* **32.** *Informal.* field-test.
—*v.i. Baseball, Cricket.* **33.** to act as a fielder; field the ball. **34.** to take to the field.
—*adj.* **35.** *Sports.* **a.** of, taking place, or competed for on the field and not on the track, as the discus throw or shot put. **b.** of or pertaining to field events. **36.** *Mil.* of or pertaining to campaign and active combat service as distinguished from service in rear areas or at headquarters: *a field soldier.* **37.** of or pertaining to a field. **38.** grown or cultivated in a field. **39.** working in the fields of a farm: *field laborers.* **40.** working as a salesperson, engineer, representative, etc., in the field: *an insurance company's field agents.* [bef. 1000; ME, OE *feld;* c. G *Feld*]

Field (fēld), *n.* **1. Cyrus West,** 1819–92, U.S. financier: projector of the first Atlantic cable. **2. David Dudley, Jr.,** 1805–94, U.S. jurist (brother of Cyrus West and Stephen Johnson Field). **3. Erastus Salisbury,** 1805–1900, U.S. painter. **4. Eugene,** 1850–95, U.S. poet and journalist. **5. Marshall,** 1834–1906, U.S. merchant and philanthropist. **6. Stephen Johnson,** 1816–99, U.S. jurist: associate justice of the U.S. Supreme Court 1863–97 (brother of Cyrus West and David Dudley Field).

field′ ar′my, army (def. 2).

field′ artil′lery, artillery mobile enough to accompany troops in the field. [1635–45]

field′ bed′, a small bed having an arched canopy on short posts. [1820–30, *Amer.*]

field′ cap′tain, *Sports.* a member of a team taking active part in a game who is authorized to make decisions for the team, esp. in regard to planning plays, deciding whether to accept penalties called by an official against the opponents, etc.

field′ chick′weed. See **starry grasswort.** [1830–40]

field′ coil′, *Elect.* a coil that generates a magnetic field when an electric current is passed through it: used in various electrical devices, as motors, generators, or electromagnets.

field′ corn′, feed corn grown for stock. [1855–60, *Amer.*]

field′ crick′et. See under **cricket**[1] (def. 1). [1590–1600]

field′ crop′, any of the herbaceous plants grown on a large scale in cultivated fields: primarily a grain, forage, sugar, oil, or fiber crop. [1855–60]

field′ cur′rent, *Elect.* the current in a field winding. Also called **exciting current.**

field′ day′, **1.** a day devoted to outdoor sports or athletic contests, as at a school. **2.** an outdoor gathering; outing; picnic. **3.** a day for military exercises and display. **4.** an occasion or opportunity for unrestricted activity, amusement, etc.: *The children had a field day with their new skateboards.* [1740–50]

field′ depend′ence, a psychological trait associated with having an external locus of orientation (contrasted with *field independence*). —**field′-de·pend′ent,** *adj.*

field′-ef·fect transis′tor (fēld′i fekt′), *Electronics.* a transistor in which the output current is varied by varying the value of an electric field within a region of the device. *Abbr.:* FET [1950–55]

field′ emis′sion, *Physics.* the removal of electrons from a metallic conductor by a strong electric field. [1925–30]

field′-e·mis·sion mi′croscope (fēld′i mish′ən), a device in which electrons liberated by field emission are accelerated toward a fluorescent screen to form a magnified image of the emitting surface. Cf. **field-ion microscope.** [1950–55]

field·er (fēl′dər), *n.* **1.** *Baseball, Cricket.* a player who fields the ball. **2.** *Baseball.* any of the players of the infield or the outfield, esp. an outfielder. [1275–1325 for an earlier sense; ME. See FIELD, -ER[1]]

field′er's choice′, *Baseball.* a fielder's attempt to put out a base runner rather than the batter when a play at first base would put out the batter. [1900–05, *Amer.*]

field′ event′, an event in a track meet that involves throwing something, as a discus or javelin, or jumping and is not performed on the running track. [1895–1900]

field′ ex′ercise, a military exercise in which mock warfare is staged between two forces. [1850–55]

field·fare (fēld′fâr′), *n.* a European thrush, *Turdus pilaris,* having reddish-brown plumage with an ashy head and a blackish tail. [bef. 1100; ME *feldefare* (with two *f*'s by alliterative assimilation), OE *feldeware* perh., field dweller]

field·gate (fēld′gāt′), *n.* the site in an oil field where natural gas is separated from crude oil after the latter reaches the surface, for movement through pipelines. [1890–95; FIELD + GATE[1]]

field′ glass′, Usually, **field glasses.** binoculars for use out of doors. [1885–90]

field′ goal′, **1.** *Football.* a three-point goal made by place-kicking or drop-kicking the ball between the opponent's goalposts above the crossbar. **2.** *Basketball.* a goal made while the ball is in play. [1890–95]

field′ grade′, military rank applying to mid-level army officers, as majors, lieutenant colonels, and colonels. Cf. **company grade.** [1945–50]

field′ guide′, a portable illustrated book to help identify birds, plants, rocks, etc., as on a nature walk.

field′ hand′, a person who works in the fields of a farm or plantation. [1820–30, *Amer.*]

field′ hock′ey, a game played on a rectangular field having a netted goal at each end, in which two teams of 11 players each compete in driving a small leather-covered ball into the other's goal, each player being equipped with a stick having a curved end or blade that is flat on one side and rounded on the other. [1900–05]

field′ hos′pital, *Mil.* an organization of medical personnel with medical equipment for establishing a temporary hospital at isolated posts or in the field to support ground troops in combat. [1695–1705]

field′ house′, **1.** a building housing the dressing facilities, storage spaces, etc., used in connection with an athletic field. **2.** a building used for indoor athletic events, as track events or basketball. [1890–95, *Amer.*]

field′ independ′ence, a psychological trait associated with having an internal locus of orientation (contrasted with *field dependence*).

Field·ing (fēl′ding), *n.* **Henry,** 1707–54, English novelist, dramatist, and essayist.

field′ing av′erage, *Baseball.* a measure of the fielding ability of a player, obtained by dividing the number of put-outs and assists by the number of put-outs, assists, and errors and carrying out the result to

CONCISE ETYMOLOGY KEY: <, descended or borrowed from; >, whence; b., blend of, blended; c., cognate with; cf., compare; deriv., derivative; equiv., equivalent; imit., imitative; obl., oblique; r., replacing; s., stem; sp., spelling, spelled; resp., respelling, respelled; trans., translation; ?, origin unknown; *, unattested; ‡, probably earlier than. See the full key inside the front cover.

three decimal places. A player with ten errors in 600 chances has a fielding average of .984. [1945–50]

field′ inten′sity, *Physics.* See **field strength.**

field′-i·on mi′croscope (fēld′ī′ən, -ī′on), a device in which the atomic structure of the surface of a conductor is made visible by introducing helium gas into the device and applying a high voltage to ionize and accelerate the gas toward a fluorescent screen. Cf. **field-emission microscope.** [1950–55]

field′ jack′et, a close-fitting jacket for wear by soldiers in the field.

field′ lark′, *South Midland and Southern U.S.* meadowlark. [1670–80]

field′ lark′spur, a European plant, *Consolida regalis,* of the buttercup family, having sparse clusters of blue or violet-colored flowers and smooth fruit.

field′ lens′, *Optics.* the lens in an eyepiece that is farthest from the eye and that deviates rays toward the center of the eye lens. [1830–40]

field′ line′, *Physics.* See **line of force.**

field′ mag′net, a magnet for producing a magnetic field, as in a particle accelerator or an electric motor. [1880–85]

field′ mar′shal, an officer of the highest military rank in the British and certain other armies, and of the second highest rank in the French army. [1570–80]

field′ mint′, an herb, *Mentha arvensis,* of North America, having downy leaves and small flowers that grow in circles in the leaf axils.

field′ mouse′, any of various short-tailed mice or voles inhabiting fields and meadows. [1570–80]

field′ mush′room. See under **mushroom** (def. 2). [1825–35]

field′ of′ficer, *Mil.* an officer holding a field grade. [1650–60]

field′ of fire′, the area covered by a weapon or group of weapons firing from a given position.

field′ of hon′or, the scene of a battle or duel. [1815–25]

field′ of quo′tients, *Math.* a field whose elements are pairs of elements of a given commutative integral domain such that the second element of each pair is not zero. The field of rational numbers is the field of quotients of the integral domain of integers. Also called **field′ of frac′tions.**

field′ of view′, *Optics.* field (def. 13). [1805–15]

field′ of vi′sion, the entire view encompassed by the eye when it is trained in any particular direction. Also called **visual field.** [1930–35]

field′ pea′, a variety of the common pea, *Pisum sativum arvense,* grown for forage and silage. [1700–10]

field′ pen′ny-cress, the common penny-cress, *Thlaspi arvense.*

field′ pop′py. See **corn poppy.**

field′ ra′tion, *U.S. Army.* ration issued and authorized for troops in the field.

Fields (fēldz), *n.* **W. C.** (*William Claude Dukenfield*), 1880–1946, U.S. vaudeville and motion-picture comedian.

fields·man (fēldz′mən), *n., pl.* **-men.** *Brit.* a fielder in cricket. [1760–70; FIELD + 's[1] + MAN[1]]

field′ span′iel, one of a British breed of spaniels having a flat or slightly waved, usually black coat, used for hunting and retrieving game. [1865–70]

field′ spar′row, a common North American finch, *Spizella pusilla,* found in brushy pasturelands. [1800–10, *Amer.*]

field·stone (fēld′stōn′), *n.* unfinished stone as found in fields, esp. when used for building purposes. [1790–1800; FIELD + STONE]

field′ stop′, *Optics.* the aperture that limits the field of view of a lens or system of lenses.

field′ strength′, *Physics.* the vector sum of all forces exerted by a field on a unit mass, unit charge, unit magnetic pole, etc., at a given point within the field. Also called **field intensity.** [1895–1900]

field-strip (fēld′strip′), *v.t.,* **-stripped** or (*Rare*) **-stript, -strip·ping.** *Mil.* **1.** to take apart (a weapon) for cleaning, lubrication, and repair or for inspection. **2.** to roll up the paper and scatter the tobacco of (a cigarette butt). [1945–50]

field-test (fēld′test′), *v.t.* to test (a device or product) under various conditions of actual use. [1915–20, *Amer.*]

field′ the′ory, *Physics.* a detailed mathematical description of the distribution and movement of matter under the influence of one or more fields. [1900–05]

field′ tri′al, **1.** a competition among sporting dogs under natural conditions in the field, in which the animals are judged on the basis of excellence of performance in hunting. **2.** a trial of a new product or procedure to determine its efficiency or usefulness in actual performance. [1840–50]

field′ trip′, **1.** a trip by students to gain firsthand knowledge away from the classroom, as to a museum, factory, geological area, or environment of certain plants and animals. **2.** a trip by a scholar or researcher to gather data firsthand, as to a geological, archaeological, anthropological, or other site. [1955–60]

field′ wind′ing (wīn′ding), *Elect.* the electrically conducting circuit, usually a number of coils wound on individual poles and connected in series, that produces the magnetic field in a motor or generator. [1890–95]

field·work (fēld′wûrk′), *n.* **1.** Also, **field′ work′.** work done in the field, as research, exploration, surveying, or interviewing: *archaeological fieldwork.* **2.** *Fort.* a temporary fortification constructed in the field. [1735–45; FIELD + WORK] —**field′work′er, field′-work′er,** *n.*

fiend (fēnd), *n.* **1.** Satan; the devil. **2.** any evil spirit; demon. **3.** a diabolically cruel or wicked person. **4.** a person or thing that causes mischief or annoyance: *Those children are little fiends.* **5.** *Informal.* a person who is extremely addicted to some pernicious habit: *an opium fiend.* **6.** *Informal.* a person who is excessively interested in some game, sport, etc.; fan; buff: *a bridge fiend.* **7.** a person who is highly skilled or gifted in something: *a fiend at languages.* [bef. 900; ME *feend,* OE *fēond;* c. G *Feind,* ON *fjandr,* Goth *fijands* foe, orig. prp. of *fijan* to hate] —**fiend′like′,** *adj.*
—**Syn. 3.** monster, savage, brute, beast, devil.

fiend·ish (fēn′dish), *adj.* diabolically cruel and wicked. [1520–30; FIEND + -ISH[1]] —**fiend′ish·ly,** *adv.* —**fiend′ish·ness,** *n.*

fierce (fērs), *adj.,* **fierc·er, fierc·est. 1.** menacingly wild, savage, or hostile: *fierce animals; a fierce look.* **2.** violent in force, intensity, etc.: *fierce winds.* **3.** furiously eager or intense: *fierce competition.* **4.** *Informal.* extremely bad or severe: *a fierce cold.* [1250–1300; ME *fiers* < AF *fers,* OF *fiers* (nom.) < L *ferus* wild, fierce; cf. FERAL[1], FEROCIOUS] —**fierce′ly,** *adv.* —**fierce′ness,** *n.*
—**Syn. 1.** untamed; cruel, fell, brutal; barbarous, bloodthirsty, murderous. FIERCE, FEROCIOUS, TRUCULENT suggest vehemence and violence of temper, manner, or action: *fierce in repelling a foe.* FEROCIOUS implies fierceness or cruelty, esp. of a bloodthirsty kind, in disposition or action: *a ferocious glare; ferocious brutality toward helpless refugees.* TRUCULENT suggests an intimidating or bullying fierceness of manner or conduct: *His truculent attitude kept them terrified and submissive.* **2, 3.** furious, passionate, turbulent.

fi·e·ri fa·ci·as (fī′ə rī′ fā′shē as′), *Law.* a writ commanding a sheriff to levy and sell as much of a debtor's property as is necessary to satisfy a creditor's claim against the debtor. *Abbr.:* FI. FA., fi. fa. [1425–75; late ME < L: lit., have it made, equiv. to *fierī* to be made + *faciās* cause, 2nd sing. pres. subj. of *facere* to bring about]

fier·y (fīər′ē, fī′ə rē), *adj.,* **fier·i·er, fier·i·est. 1.** consisting of, attended with, characterized by, or containing fire: *a volcano's fiery discharge.* **2.** intensely hot: *fiery desert sands.* **3.** like or suggestive of fire: *a fiery red; angry, fiery eyes.* **4.** intensely ardent, impetuous, or passionate: *fiery courage; a fiery speech.* **5.** easily angered or provoked: *a fiery temper.* **6.** causing a burning sensation, as certain liquors or condiments. **7.** inflamed, as a tumor or sore. **8.** *Mining Older Use.* **a.** highly flammable. **b.** containing highly flammable gas. [1225–75; ME *fi(e)ry.* See FIRE, -Y[1]] —**fier′i·ly,** *adv.* —**fier′i·ness,** *n.*
—**Syn. 3.** flaming, flashing, glowing, burning. **4.** fervent, vehement, spirited, impassioned.

fier′y cross′, a burning cross, the rallying symbol of ancient Scotland and later of the Highlanders in case of war; later adopted by other organizations, including the Ku Klux Klan. Also called **fire cross.**

Fie·so·le (*It.* fye′zô le), *n.* **1. Gio·van·ni da** (*It.* jô-vän′nē dä). See **Angelico, Fra. 2.** a town in central Italy, near Florence: Etruscan and ancient Roman ruins; cathedral. 14,138.

fi·es·ta (fē es′tə; *Sp.* fyes′tä), *n., pl.* **-tas** (-təz; *Sp.* -täs). **1.** any festival or festive celebration. **2.** (in Spain and Latin America) a festive celebration of a religious holiday. [1835–45, *Amer.;* < Sp < L *fēsta;* see FEAST]

fies·ta de to·ros (fyes′tä the tô′rôs; *Eng.* fē es′tə dā tôr′ōs, tōr′-), *pl.* ***fies·tas de to·ros*** (fyes′täs the tô′rôs; *Eng.* fē es′təz dā tôr′ōs, tōr′-). *Spanish.* bullfight; corrida. Also called ***fiesta taurina.***

fies·ta tau·ri·na (fyes′tä tou rē′nä), *pl.* ***fies·tas tau·ri·nas*** (fyes′täs tou rē′näs). *Spanish.* See ***fiesta de toros.***

Fies′ta ware′, molded, opaque-glazed earthenware produced in a wide range of colors from 1936 to 1969.

FI. FA. (fī′ fā′), *Law.* See **fieri facias.** Also, **fi. fa.**

fife (fīf), *n., v.,* **fifed, fif·ing.** —*n.* **1.** a high-pitched transverse flute used commonly in military and marching musical groups. —*v.i., v.t.* **2.** to play on a fife. [1540–50; < G *Pfeife* PIPE[1]] —**fif′er,** *n.*

fife (def. 1)

Fife (fīf), *n.* **1.** Also called **Fife·shire** (fīf′shēr, -shər). a historic county in E Scotland. **2.** a region in E Scotland. 336,339; 504 sq. mi. (1305 sq. km).

fife′ rail′, *Naut.* a rail surrounding or next to the mast of a sailing vessel for use in holding the pins to which some of the running rigging is belayed. Cf. **pin rail.** [1715–25]

FIFO (fī′fō), *n.* **1.** See **first-in, first-out. 2.** *Computers.* a storage and retrieval technique, used mainly for data, in which the first item stored is also the first item retrieved.

fif·teen (fif′tēn′), *n.* **1.** a cardinal number, ten plus five. **2.** a symbol for this number, as 15 or XV. **3.** a set of this many persons or things. —*adj.* **4.** amounting to 15 in number. [bef. 900; ME, OE *fiftēne.* See FIVE, -TEEN]

fif·teenth (fif′tēnth′), *adj.* **1.** next after the fourteenth; being the ordinal number for 15. **2.** being one of 15 equal parts. —*n.* **3.** a fifteenth part, esp. of one (1/15). **4.** the fifteenth member of a series. **5.** *Music.* the interval of two octaves. [bef. 900; ME *fiftenthe* (see FIFTEEN, -TH[2]); r. ME *fiftethe,* OE *fīftēotha*]

Fif′teenth Amend′ment, an amendment to the U.S. Constitution, ratified in 1870, prohibiting the restriction of voting rights "on account of race, color, or previous condition of servitude."

fifth (fifth *or, often,* fith), *adj.* **1.** next after the fourth; being the ordinal number for five. **2.** being one of five equal parts. **3.** *Auto.* of, pertaining to, or operating at the gear transmission ratio at which the drive shaft speed is greater than that of fourth gear for a given engine crankshaft speed: *fifth gear.* —*adv.* **4.** in the fifth place; fifthly. —*n.* **5.** a fifth part, esp. of one (1/5). **6.** the fifth member of a series. **7.** a fifth part of a gallon of liquor or spirits; 4/5 of a quart (about 750 milliliters). **8.** *Auto.* fifth gear. **9.** *Music.* **a.** a tone on the fifth degree from another tone (counted as the first). **b.** the interval between such tones. **c.** the harmonic combination of such tones. **10. take the Fifth,** *Informal.* to decline on the basis of the Fifth Amendment to the U.S. Constitution to answer a question when testifying. [bef. 1000; earlier *fift,* ME *fifte,* OE *fīfta; -th* by analogy with FOURTH, etc.]

Fifth′ Amend′ment, an amendment to the U.S. Constitution, ratified in 1791 as part of the Bill of Rights, providing chiefly that no person be required to testify against himself or herself in a criminal case and that no person be subjected to a second trial for an offense for which he or she has been duly tried previously.

fifth′ col′umn, 1. a group of people who act traitorously and subversively out of a secret sympathy with an enemy of their country. **2.** (originally) Franco sympathizers in Madrid during the Spanish Civil War: so called in allusion to a statement in 1936 that the insurgents had four columns marching on Madrid and a fifth column of sympathizers in the city ready to rise and betray it. —**fifth′ col′umnist.**

Fifth′ Command′ment, "Honor thy father and thy mother, that thy days may be long upon the land which the Lord thy God giveth thee": fifth of the Ten Commandments. Cf. **Ten Commandments.**

fifth′ dimen′sion, *Math., Physics.* a theoretical dimension beyond or in addition to a fourth dimension.

fifth′ estate′, any class or group in society other than the nobility, the clergy, the middle class, and the press. [1965–70]

fifth′ force′, a theoretical force in nature in addition to the strong and weak forces, gravitation, and the electromagnetic force. [1975–80]

fifth·ly (fifth′lē), *adv.* in the fifth place; fifth.

fifth′ mon′archy, the fifth and final monarchy following the Assyrian, Persian, Greek (under Alexander the Great), and Roman monarchies, supposed to have been prophesied in Dan. 2.

Fifth′ Mon′archy Men′, *Eng. Hist.* (during the Commonwealth in the 17th century) a militant sect of Puritans who identified the fifth monarchy with the millennial reign of Christ and who believed they should help to inaugurate that reign by force.

fifth′ posi′tion, *Ballet.* a position similar to the first position, but with one foot in front, the heel and toe of the front foot adjacent to the toe and heel of the back foot. See illus. under **first position.**

Fifth′ Repub′lic, the republic established in France in 1958, the successor to the Fourth Republic.

fifth′ wheel′, 1. a horizontal ring or segment of a ring, consisting of two bands that slide on each other, placed above the front axle of a carriage and designed to support the forepart of the body while allowing it to turn freely in a horizontal plane. **2.** a similar device used as a coupling to connect a semitrailer to a tractor. **3.** a similar coupling between a heavy-duty pickup truck and a camping trailer **(fifth-wheel trailer)** that extends over the bed of the truck. **4.** an extra wheel for a four-wheeled vehicle. **5.** a superfluous, unneeded, or unwanted person or thing: *They enjoy making any outsider feel like a fifth wheel.* [1870–75]

fifth′-wheel trail′er (fifth′hwēl′, -wēl′ *or, often,* fith′-). See under **fifth wheel.** (def. 3).

fif·ti·eth (fif′tē ith), *adj.* **1.** next after the forty-ninth; being the ordinal number for 50. **2.** being one of 50 equal parts. —*n.* **3.** a fiftieth part, esp. of one (1/50). **4.** the fiftieth member of a series. [bef. 1000; ME *fiftithe,* OE *fīftigotha.* See FIFTY, -TH[2]]

fif·ty (fif′tē), *n., pl.* **-ties,** *adj.* —*n.* **1.** a cardinal number, ten times five. **2.** a symbol for this number, as 50 or L. **3.** a set of this many persons or things. **4. fifties,** the numbers, years, degrees, or the like, from 50 through 59, as in referring to numbered streets, indicating the years of a lifetime or of a century, or degrees of temperature: *She lives in the East Fifties. He's in his late fifties.* **5.** *Informal.* a fifty-dollar bill: *He had a fifty and two tens in his wallet.* —*adj.* **6.** amounting to 50 in number. [bef. 900; ME; OE *fīftig.* See FIVE, -TY[1]]

fif·ty-eight (fif′tē āt′), *n.* **1.** a cardinal number, 50 plus 8. **2.** a symbol for this number, as 58 or LVIII. **3.** a set of this many persons or things. —*adj.* **4.** amounting to 58 in number.

fif·ty-eighth (fif′tē ātth′, -āth′), *adj.* **1.** next after the fifty-seventh; being the ordinal number for 58. **2.** being one of 58 equal parts. —*n.* **3.** a fifty-eighth part, esp. of one (1/58). **4.** the fifty-eighth member of a series.

fif·ty-fifth (fif′tē fifth′ *or, often,* -fith′), *adj.* **1.** next after the fifty-fourth; being the ordinal number for 55. **2.** being one of 55 equal parts. —*n.* **3.** a fifty-fifth part, esp. of one (1/55). **4.** the fifty-fifth member of a series.

fif·ty-fif·ty (fif′tē fif′tē), *adj.* **1.** equally good and bad, likely and unlikely, favorable and unfavorable, etc.: *a fifty-fifty chance of winning.* —*adv.* **2.** in an evenly or equally divided way: *The board voted fifty-fifty on the* merger. **3. go fifty-fifty (on),** to share equally in the cost, responsibility, or profits (of): *We went fifty-fifty on the dinner check.* Also, **50-50.** [1910–15, *Amer.*]

fif·ty-first (fif′tē fûrst′), *adj.* **1.** next after the fiftieth; being the ordinal number for 51. **2.** being one of 51 equal parts. —*n.* **3.** a fifty-first part, esp. of one (1/51). **4.** the fifty-first member of a series.

fif·ty-five (fif′tē fīv′), *n.* **1.** a cardinal number, 50 plus 5. **2.** a symbol for this number, as 55 or LV. **3.** a set of this many persons or things. —*adj.* **4.** amounting to 55 in number.

fif·ty-four (fif′tē fôr′, -fōr′), *n.* **1.** a cardinal number, 50 plus 4. **2.** a symbol for this number, as 54 or LIV. **3.** a set of this many persons or things. —*adj.* **4.** amounting to 54 in number.

Fif′ty-four-for′ty or Fight′ (fif′tē fôr′fôr′tē, -fōr′-), *U.S. Hist.* a slogan popular in 1846, esp. among Democrats, who asserted U.S. ownership of the entire Oregon country, including the part that Great Britain claimed between 49° and 54° 40′ N latitude.

fif·ty-fourth (fif′tē fôrth′, -fōrth′), *adj.* **1.** next after the fifty-third; being the ordinal number for 54. **2.** being one of 54 equal parts. —*n.* **3.** a fifty-fourth part, esp. of one (1/54). **4.** the fifty-fourth member of a series.

fif·ty-nine (fif′tē nīn′), *n.* **1.** a cardinal number, 50 plus 9. **2.** a symbol for this number, as 59 or LIX. **3.** a set of this many persons or things. —*adj.* **4.** amounting to 59 in number.

fif·ty-ninth (fif′tē nīnth′), *adj.* **1.** next after the fifty-eighth; being the ordinal number for 59. **2.** being one of 59 equal parts. —*n.* **3.** a fifty-ninth part, esp. of one (1/59). **4.** the fifty-ninth member of a series.

fif·ty-one (fif′tē wun′), *n.* **1.** a cardinal number, 50 plus 1. **2.** a symbol for this number, as 51 or LI. **3.** a set of this many persons or things. —*adj.* **4.** amounting to 51 in number.

fif·ty·pen·ny (fif′tē pen′ē), *adj.* noting a nail 5½ in. (14 cm) long. *Abbr.:* 50d [FIFTY + -PENNY]

fif·ty-sec·ond (fif′tē sek′ənd), *adj.* **1.** next after the fifty-first; being the ordinal number for 52. **2.** being one of 52 equal parts. —*n.* **3.** a fifty-second part, esp. of one (1/52). **4.** the fifty-second member of a series.

fif·ty-sev·en (fif′tē sev′ən), *n.* **1.** a cardinal number, 50 plus 7. **2.** a symbol for this number, as 57 or LVII. **3.** a set of this many persons or things. —*adj.* **4.** amounting to 57 in number.

fif·ty-sev·enth (fif′tē sev′ənth), *adj.* **1.** next after the fifty-sixth; being the ordinal number for 57. **2.** being one of 57 equal parts. —*n.* **3.** a fifty-seventh part, esp. of one (1/57). **4.** the fifty-seventh member of a series.

fif·ty-six (fif′tē siks′), *n.* **1.** a cardinal number, 50 plus 6. **2.** a symbol for this number, as 56 or LVI. **3.** a set of this many persons or things. —*adj.* **4.** amounting to 56 in number.

fif·ty-sixth (fif′tē siksth′), *adj.* **1.** next after the fifty-fifth; being the ordinal number for 56. **2.** being one of 56 equal parts. —*n.* **3.** a fifty-sixth part, esp. of one (1/56). **4.** the fifty-sixth member of a series.

fif·ty-third (fif′tē thûrd′), *adj.* **1.** next after the fifty-second; being the ordinal number for 53. **2.** being one of 53 equal parts. —*n.* **3.** a fifty-third part, esp. of one (1/53). **4.** the fifty-third member of a series.

fif·ty-three (fif′tē thrē′), *n.* **1.** a cardinal number, 50 plus 3. **2.** a symbol for this number, as 53 or LIII. **3.** a set of this many persons or things. —*adj.* **4.** amounting to 53 in number.

fif·ty-two (fif′tē to͞o′), *n.* **1.** a cardinal number, 50 plus 2. **2.** a symbol for this number, as 52 or LII. **3.** a set of this many persons or things. —*adj.* **4.** amounting to 52 in number.

fig[1] (fig), *n.* **1.** any tree or shrub belonging to the genus *Ficus,* of the mulberry family, esp. a small tree, *F. carica,* native to southwestern Asia, bearing a turbinate or pear-shaped fruit that is eaten fresh, preserved, or dried. **2.** the fruit of such a tree or shrub, or of any related species. **3.** any of various plants having a fruit somewhat resembling this. **4.** a contemptibly trifling or worthless amount; the least bit: *His help wasn't worth a fig.* **5.** a gesture of contempt. [1175–1225; ME *fige* < OF < OPr *figa* < VL **fica,* for L *ficus*]

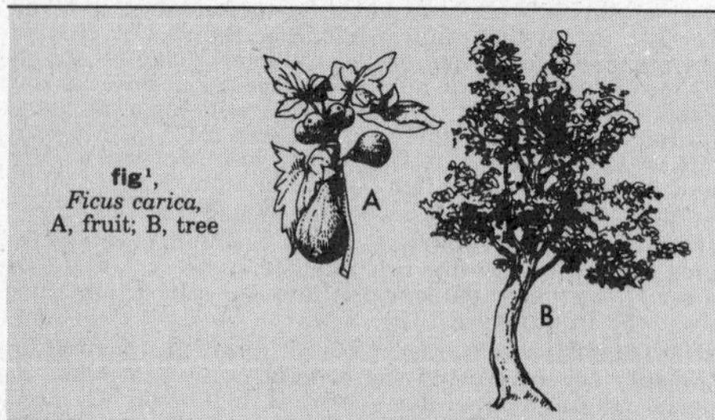

fig[1], *Ficus carica,* A, fruit; B, tree

fig[2] (fig), *n.* **1.** dress or array: *to appear at a party in full fig.* **2.** condition: *to feel in fine fig.* [1685–95; earlier *feague* to liven, whip up < G *fegen* to furbish, sweep, clean; akin to FAIR[1]]

fig., **1.** figurative. **2.** figuratively. **3.** figure; figures.

fig·eat·er (fig′ē′tər), *n.* See **green June beetle.** [1865–70, *Amer.*; FIG[1] + EATER]

CONCISE ETYMOLOGY KEY: <, descended or borrowed from; >, whence; b., blend of, blended; c., cognate with; cf., compare; deriv., derivative; equiv., equivalent; imit., imitative; obl., oblique; r., replacing; s., stem; sp., spelling, spelled; resp., respelling, respelled; trans., translation; ?, origin unknown; *, unattested; ‡, probably earlier than. See the full key inside the front cover.

fig·ger (fig′ər), *v.i. Pron. Spelling.* figure.

fig·gy (fig′ē), *adj.,* **-gi·er, -gi·est.** containing figs: *a figgy cake.* [1540–50; FIG[1] + -Y[1]]

fight (fīt), *n., v.,* **fought, fight·ing.** —*n.* **1.** a battle or combat. **2.** any contest or struggle: *a fight for recovery from an illness.* **3.** an angry argument or disagreement: *Whenever we discuss politics, we end up in a fight.* **4.** *Boxing.* a bout or contest. **5.** a game or diversion in which the participants hit or pelt each other with something harmless: *a pillow fight; a water fight.* **6.** ability, will, or inclination to fight: *There was no fight left in him.* —*v.i.* **7.** to engage in battle or in single combat; attempt to defend oneself against or to subdue, defeat, or destroy an adversary. **8.** to contend in any manner; strive vigorously for or against something: *He fought bravely against despair.* —*v.t.* **9.** to contend with in battle or combat; war against: *England fought Germany.* **10.** to contend with or against in any manner: *to fight despair; to fight the passage of a bill.* **11.** to carry on (a battle, duel, etc.). **12.** to maintain (a cause, quarrel, etc.) by fighting or contending. **13.** to make (one's way) by fighting or striving. **14.** to cause or set (a boxer, animal, etc.) to fight. **15.** to manage or maneuver (troops, ships, guns, planes, etc.) in battle. **16. fight it out,** to fight until a decision is reached: *Let them fight it out among themselves.* **17. fight shy of.** See **shy**[1] (def. 9). **18. fight with windmills.** See **tilt**[1] (def. 10). [bef. 900; (v.) ME *fi(g)hten,* OE *fe(o)htan* (c. G *fechten*); (n.) ME *fi(g)ht,* OE *feohte, (ge)feoht,* deriv. of the v. base] —**fight′a·ble,** *adj.* —**fight′a·bil′i·ty,** *n.* —**fight′ing·ly,** *adv.*

—**Syn. 1, 2.** encounter, engagement, affray, fray, action, skirmish, melee; scuffle, tussle, row, riot. FIGHT, COMBAT, CONFLICT, CONTEST denote a struggle of some kind. FIGHT connotes a hand-to-hand struggle for supremacy, literally or in a figurative sense. COMBAT suggests an armed encounter, to settle a dispute. CONFLICT implies a bodily, mental, or moral struggle caused by opposing views, beliefs, etc. CONTEST applies to either a friendly or a hostile struggle for a definite prize or aim.

fight·er (fī′tər), *n.* **1.** a boxer; pugilist. **2.** *Mil.* an aircraft designed to seek out and destroy enemy aircraft in the air and to protect bomber aircraft. **3.** a person who fights, struggles, resists, etc. **4.** a person with the will, courage, determination, ability, or disposition to fight, struggle, resist, etc. **5.** an animal, as a dog, trained to fight or having the disposition to fight. [bef. 1000; ME; OE *fēohtere.* See FIGHT, -ER[1]]

fight·er-bomb·er (fī′tər bom′ər), *n. Mil.* an aircraft that combines the functions of a fighter and a bomber. [1935–40]

fight·er-in·ter·cep·tor (fī′tər in′tər sep′tər), *n. Mil.* a fighter plane used for the defense of a region against air attack, esp. by attacking bombers.

fight·ing (fī′ting), *adj.* **1.** fit to fight: *a boxer who's no longer in fighting shape.* **2.** tending or meant to stir up a fight or hostility: *fighting words.* [1300–50; ME; see FIGHT, -ING[2]]

fight′ing chair′, a chair fastened to the deck at the stern of a seagoing fishing boat for use by an angler in landing a large fish. [1945–50, *Amer.*]

fight′ing chance′, a possibility of success following a struggle. [1885–90]

fight′ing cock′, a gamecock.

Siamese fighting fish, *Betta splendens,* length 2½ in. (6.4 cm)

fight′ing fish′, any of several brightly colored labyrinth fishes of the genus *Betta,* found in Southeast Asia. Also called **betta.** Cf. **Siamese fighting fish.**

Fight′ing French′. See **Free French.**

fight′-or-flight′ reac′tion (fīt′ôr flīt′), *Physiol., Psychol.* the response of the sympathetic nervous system to a stressful event, preparing the body to fight or flee, associated with the adrenal secretion of epinephrine and characterized by increased heart rate, increased blood flow to the brain and muscles, raised sugar levels, sweaty palms and soles, dilated pupils, and erect hairs. Also called **fight′-or-flight′ response′.**

fig′ leaf′, **1.** the leaf of a fig tree. **2.** a representation of a fig leaf, used as an ornament in architecture, as a cover for the genitalia on a statue or in a painting, etc. **3.** something intended to conceal what may be considered indecorous or indecent: *to approach the facts of life with the fig leaves of roundabout expressions.* [1525–35]

fig′ mar′igold, any of various plants of the genus *Mesembryanthemum,* having showy flowers of white, yellow, or pink. [1725–35]

fig·ment (fig′mənt), *n.* **1.** a mere product of mental invention; a fantastic notion: *The noises in the attic were just a figment of his imagination.* **2.** a feigned, invented, or imagined story, theory, etc.: *biographical and historical figments.* [1400–50; late ME < L *figmentum* something made or feigned, equiv. to *fig-* (base of *fingere* to mold, feign) + *-mentum* -MENT]

—**Syn. 2.** See **fiction.**

Fi·gue·res (fē ge′RES), *n.* **Jo·sé** (hô se′), born 1906, Costa Rican businessman and political leader: president 1953–58, 1970–74.

fig·ur·al (fig′yər əl), *adj.* consisting of figures, esp. human or animal figures: *the figural representations contained in ancient wall paintings.* [1400–50; late ME < LL *figūrālis,* equiv. to L *figūra* FIGURE + *-ālis* -AL[1]] —**fig′ur·al·ly,** *adv.*

fig′u·rate num′ber (fig′yər it), *Math.* a number having the property that the same number of equally spaced dots can be arranged in the shape of a regular geometrical figure. [1605–15]

fig·u·ra·tion (fig′yə rā′shən), *n.* **1.** the act of shaping into a particular figure. **2.** the resulting figure or shape: *emblematic figurations of the sun and the moon.* **3.** the act of representing figuratively. **4.** a figurative representation: *allegorical figurations.* **5.** the act of marking or adorning with a design. **6.** *Music.* **a.** the employment of passing notes or other embellishments. **b.** the figuring of a bass part. [1400–50; late ME *figuracioun* < L *figūrātiōn-* (s. of *figūrātiō*) a shaping. See FIGURATE, -ION]

fig·ur·a·tive (fig′yər ə tiv), *adj.* **1.** of the nature of or involving a figure of speech, esp. a metaphor; metaphorical; not literal: *a figurative expression.* **2.** metaphorically so called: *His remark was a figurative boomerang.* **3.** abounding in or fond of figures of speech: *Elizabethan poetry is highly figurative.* **4.** representing by means of a figure or likeness, as in drawing or sculpture. **5.** representing by a figure or emblem; emblematic. [1350–1400; ME < LL *figūrātīvus* (see FIGURATE, -IVE); r. ME *figuratif* < MF] —**fig′ur·a·tive·ly,** *adv.* —**fig′ur·a·tive·ness,** *n.*

—**Syn. 3.** ornate, ornamental, flowery, elaborate, florid, grandiloquent.

fig·ure (fig′yər; *esp. Brit.* fig′ər), *n., v.,* **-ured, -ur·ing.** —*n.* **1.** a numerical symbol, esp. an Arabic numeral. **2.** an amount or value expressed in numbers. **3. figures,** the use of numbers in calculating; arithmetic: *to be poor at figures.* **4.** a written symbol other than a letter. **5.** form or shape, as determined by outlines or exterior surfaces: *to be round, square, or cubical in figure.* **6.** the bodily form or frame: *a slender or graceful figure.* **7.** an individual bodily form or a person with reference to form or appearance: *A tall figure stood in the doorway.* **8.** a character or personage, esp. one of distinction: *a well-known figure in society.* **9.** a person's public image or presence: *a controversial political figure.* **10.** the appearance or impression made by a person or sometimes a thing: *to make quite a figure in financial circles; to present a wretched figure of poverty.* **11.** a representation, pictorial or sculptured, esp. of the human form: *The frieze was bordered with the figures of men and animals.* **12.** an emblem, type, or symbol: *The dove is a figure of peace.* **13.** *Rhet.* a figure of speech. **14.** a textural pattern, as in cloth or wood: *draperies with an embossed silk figure.* **15.** a distinct movement or division of a dance. **16.** a movement, pattern, or series of movements in skating. **17.** *Music.* a short succession of musical notes, as either a melody or a group of chords, that produces a single complete and distinct impression. **18.** *Geom.* a combination of geometric elements disposed in a particular form or shape: *The circle, square, and polygon are plane figures. The sphere, cube, and polyhedron are solid figures.* **19.** *Logic.* the form of a categorical syllogism with respect to the relative position of the middle term. **20.** *Optics.* the precise curve required on the surface of an optical element, esp. the mirror or correcting plate of a reflecting telescope. **21.** the natural pattern on a sawed wood surface produced by the intersection of knots, burls, growth rings, etc. **22.** a phantasm or illusion. **23. cut a figure.** See **cut** (defs. 42, 44b). —*v.t.* **24.** to compute or calculate (often fol. by *up*): *to figure up a total.* **25.** to express in figures. **26.** to mark or adorn with a design or pattern. **27.** to portray by speech or action. **28.** to represent or express by a figure of speech. **29.** to represent by a pictorial or sculptured figure, a diagram, or the like; picture or depict; trace (an outline, silhouette, etc.). **30.** *Informal.* to conclude, judge, reason, or think about: *I figured that you wanted me to stay.* **31.** *Music.* **a.** to embellish with passing notes or other decorations. **b.** to write figures above or below (a bass part) to indicate accompanying chords. —*v.i.* **32.** to compute or work with numerical figures. **33.** to be or appear, esp. in a conspicuous or prominent way: *His name figures importantly in my report.* **34.** *Informal.* (of a situation, act, request, etc.) to be logical, expected, or reasonable: *He quit the job when he didn't get a raise—it figured.* **35. figure in,** to add in: *Figure in rent and utilities as overhead.* **36. figure on,** *Informal.* **a.** to count or rely on. **b.** to take into consideration; plan on: *You had better figure on running into heavy traffic leaving the city.* **37. figure out,** *Informal.* **a.** to understand; solve: *We couldn't figure out where all the money had gone.* **b.** to calculate; compute. **38. figure up,** *Informal.* to total: *The bill figures up to exactly $1000.* [1175–1225; ME < OF < L *figūra* shape, trope, equiv. to *fig-* (base of *fingere* to shape) + *-ūra* -URE] —**fig′ur·a·ble,** *adj.* —**fig′ure·less,** *adj.* —**fig′·ur·er,** *n.*

—**Syn. 1.** number. **2.** sum, total; price. **5.** See **form. 8.** personality. **24.** reckon.

fig·ured (fig′yərd), *adj.* **1.** ornamented with a device or pattern: *figured silk; figured wallpaper.* **2.** formed or shaped: *figured stones.* **3.** represented by a pictorial or sculptured figure: *The god is figured as part man, part beast.* **4.** *Music.* **a.** florid. **b.** having the accompanying chords indicated by figures. **5.** figurative, as language. [1350–1400; ME, ptp. of *figuren* to FIGURE; see -ED[2]] —**fig·ured·ly** (fig′yərd lē, -yər id-), *adv.*

fig′ured bass′ (bās), *Music.* a bass part in which the notes have numbers under them indicating the chords to be played. [1795–1805]

fig′ured glass′, plate or sheet glass having a pattern rolled onto one side of the surface.

fig′ure eight′, a figure or form composed of two loops formed by a continuous line crossing itself, as in the figure 8, esp. as traced on ice in figure skating. Also called **figure of eight.** [1595–1605]

fig·ure-ground (fig′yər ground′), *n. Psychol.* a property of perception in which there is a tendency to see parts of a visual field as solid, well-defined objects standing out against a less distinct background.

fig·ure·head (fig′yər hed′), *n.* **1.** a person who is head of a group, company, etc., in title but actually has no real authority or responsibility: *Most modern kings and queens are figureheads.* **2.** *Naut.* a carved full-length figure or bust built into the bow of a sailing ship. [1755–65; FIGURE + HEAD]

fig′ure of eight′, **1.** See **figure eight. 2.** a knot resembling the figure 8. See illus. under **knot.** [1595–1605]

fig′ure of speech′, *Rhet.* any expressive use of language, as a metaphor, simile, personification, or antithesis, in which words are used in other than their literal sense, or in other than their ordinary locutions, in order to suggest a picture or image or for other special effect. Cf. **trope** (def. 1). [1815–25]

fig′ure skate′, a shoe skate used in figure skating, esp. one having a blade shorter than that of a racing skate, usually not extending beyond the toe or heel, and with notches or sawteeth on the curved forward edge. Cf. **racing skate.**

fig′ure skat′ing, **1.** ice skating in which the skater traces intricate patterns on the ice. **2.** a type of ice skating developed from this, emphasizing jumps, spins, and other movements that combine athletic skills and dance techniques. **3.** a competitive sport in which the skater is required to execute school figures and to perform one or more original programs of difficult jumps, spins, etc., to a musical setting. [1865–70] —**fig′ure skat′er.**

fig•ur•ine (fig′yə rēn′), *n.* a small ornamental figure of pottery, metal, plastic, etc.; statuette. [1850–55; < F < It *figurina,* equiv. to *figur(a)* FIGURE + *-ina* -INE[1] (here dim.)]

fig′ wasp′, a chalcid wasp, *Blastophaga psenes,* introduced into the U.S. from Europe, that pollinates figs, usually of the Smyrna variety. [1880–85]

fig•wort (fig′wûrt′, -wôrt′), *n.* any of numerous tall, usually coarse woodland plants of the genus *Scrophularia,* having a terminal cluster of small greenish-brown to purplish-brown flowers. [1540–50; FIG[1] + WORT[2]]

fig′wort fam′ily, the plant family Scrophulariaceae, characterized by herbaceous plants and shrubs having alternate or opposite leaves, often showy two-lipped or irregular flowers, fruit in the form of a capsule or berry, and including the figwort, foxglove, Indian paintbrush, mullein, speedwell, and snapdragon.

Fi•ji (fē′jē), *n.* **1.** an independent archipelago of some 800 islands in the S Pacific, N of New Zealand, composed of the Fiji Islands and a smaller group to the NW: formerly a British colony, now a member of the Commonwealth of Nations. 585,000; 7040 sq. mi. (18,235 sq. km). *Cap.:* Suva. **2.** Fijian (def. 2).

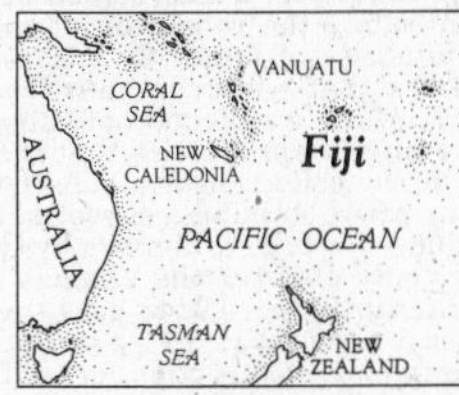

Fi•ji•an (fē′jē ən, fi jē′ən), *adj.* **1.** of or pertaining to Fiji, its people, or their language. —*n.* **2.** a native of the Fiji Islands. **3.** the Austronesian language spoken by the Fijians.

Fi′ji Is′lands, a group of islands in the S Pacific constituting most of the country of Fiji.

fikh (fik), *n. Islam.* fiqh.

fil (fil), *n.* fils.

fil•a•gree (fil′ə grē′), *n., adj., v.t.,* **-greed, -gree•ing.** filigree.

fil•a•ment (fil′ə mənt), *n.* **1.** a very fine thread or threadlike structure; a fiber or fibril: *filaments of gold.* **2.** a single fibril of natural or synthetic textile fiber, of indefinite length, sometimes several miles long. **3.** a long slender cell or series of attached cells, as in some algae and fungi. **4.** *Bot.* the stalklike portion of a stamen, supporting the anther. See diag. under **flower. 5.** *Ornith.* the barb of a down feather. **6.** (in a light bulb or other incandescent lamp) the threadlike conductor, often of tungsten, in the bulb that is heated to incandescence by the passage of current. **7.** *Electronics.* the heating element (sometimes also acting as a cathode) of a vacuum tube, resembling the filament in an incandescent bulb. **8.** *Astron.* a solar prominence, as viewed within the sun's limb. [1585–95; < NL *filāmentum,* equiv. to LL *filā(re)* to wind thread, spin (see FILE[1]) + L *-mentum* -MENT] —**fil′a•ment•ed,** *adj.*

fil•a•men•ta•ry (fil′ə men′tə rē), *adj.* pertaining to or of the nature of a filament. [1835–45; FILAMENT + -ARY]

fil•a•men•tous (fil′ə men′təs), *adj.* **1.** composed of or containing filaments. **2.** pertaining to or resembling a filament. **3.** bearing filaments. [1665–75; FILAMENT + -OUS]

fi•lar (fī′lər), *adj.* **1.** of or pertaining to a thread or threads. **2.** having threads or the like. [1870–75; < L *fīl(um)* a thread + -AR[1]]

fi•lar•i•a (fi lâr′ē ə), *n., pl.* **-lar•i•ae** (-lâr′ē ē′). any small, threadlike roundworm of the family Filariidae and related families, carried as a larva by mosquitoes and parasitic when adult in the blood or tissues of vertebrates. [< NL (1787), equiv. to L *fīl(um)* thread + *-āria* -ARIA]

fi•lar•i•al (fi lâr′ē əl), *adj.* **1.** belonging to the genus *Filaria* and allied genera of the family Filariidae. **2.** *Pathol.* pertaining to or noting infection by filariae: *filarial disease.* [1880–85; FILARI(A) + -AL[1]]

fil•a•ri•a•sis (fil′ə rī′ə sis), *n.* infection by filarial worms in the blood and lymph channels, lymph glands, and other tissues, the various species causing skin swellings, blindness, or elephantiasis if untreated. [1875–80; FILAR(IA) + -IASIS]

fi•lar•i•id (fi lâr′ē id), *adj.* **1.** of or pertaining to filariae. —*n.* **2.** a filaria. [1925–30; FILARI(A) + -ID[2]]

fi•lasse (fi las′), *n.* any of various vegetable fibers, other than cotton, processed for manufacture into yarn. [1855–60; < F; OF *filace* < VL **filācea,* equiv. to L *fīl(um)* thread + *-ācea,* fem. of *-āceus;* see -ACEOUS]

fi•late (fī′lāt), *adj. Zool.* threadlike. [1820–30; < L *fīl(um)* a thread + -ATE[1]]

fil•a•ture (fil′ə chər, -chŏŏr′), *n.* **1.** the act of forming into threads. **2.** a reel for drawing off silk from cocoons. **3.** the reeling of silk from cocoons. **4.** an establishment for reeling silk. [1750–60; < F < ML *fīlātūra* the spinning art, equiv. to *fīlāt(us)* spun (ptp. of *fīlāre;* see FILAMENT) + *-ūra* -URE]

fil•bert (fil′bərt), *n.* **1.** the thick-shelled, edible nut of certain cultivated varieties of hazel, esp. of *Corylus avellana,* of Europe. **2.** a tree or shrub bearing such nuts. [1250–1300; ME, short for *filbert nut,* so called because ripe by Aug. 22 (St. Philbert's day)]

filch (filch), *v.t.* to steal (esp. something of small value); pilfer: *to filch ashtrays from fancy restaurants.* [1250–1300; ME *filchen* to attack (in a body), take as booty, OE *fylcian* to marshal (troops), draw (soldiers) up in battle array, deriv. of *gefylce* band of men; akin to FOLK] —**filch′er,** *n.* —**filch′ing•ly,** *adv.*
—**Syn.** purloin, take, swipe, lift, snaffle, pinch.

Filch′ner Ice′ Shelf′ (filk′nər, filкн′-), an ice barrier in Antarctica, in the SE Weddell Sea, bordered on the W by Berkner Island.

file[1] (fīl), *n., v.,* **filed, fil•ing.** —*n.* **1.** a folder, cabinet, or other container in which papers, letters, etc., are arranged in convenient order for storage or reference. **2.** a collection of papers, records, etc., arranged in convenient order: *to make a file for a new account.* **3.** *Computers.* a collection of related data or program records stored on some input/output or auxiliary storage medium: *This program's main purpose is to update the customer master file.* **4.** a line of persons or things arranged one behind another (distinguished from *rank*). **5.** *Mil.* **a.** a person in front of or behind another in a military formation. **b.** one step on a promotion list. **6.** one of the vertical lines of squares on a chessboard. **7.** a list or roll. **8.** a string or wire on which papers are strung for preservation and reference. **9. on file,** arranged in order for convenient reference; in a file: *The names are on file in the office.* —*v.t.* **10.** to place in a file. **11.** to arrange (papers, records, etc.) in convenient order for storage or reference. **12.** *Journalism.* **a.** to arrange (copy) in the proper order for transmittal by wire. **b.** to transmit (copy), as by wire or telephone: *He filed copy from Madrid all through the war.* —*v.i.* **13.** to march in a file or line, one after another, as soldiers: *The parade filed past endlessly.* **14.** to make application: *to file for a civil-service job.* [1425–75; late ME *filen* < MF *filer* to string documents on a thread or wire, OF: to wind or spin thread < LL *fīlāre,* v. deriv. of L *fīlum* thread, string] —**file′a•ble,** *adj.* —**fil′er,** *n.*
—**Syn. 11.** classify, label, catalog, index, list, categorize.

file[2] (fīl), *n., v.,* **filed, fil•ing.** —*n.* **1.** a long, narrow tool of steel or other metal having a series of ridges or points on its surfaces for reducing or smoothing surfaces of metal, wood, etc. **2.** a small, similar tool for trimming and cleaning fingernails; nail file. **3.** *Brit. Slang.* a cunning, shrewd, or artful person. —*v.t.* **4.** to reduce, smooth, or remove with or as if with a file. [bef. 900; ME; OE *fīl, fēol;* c. G *Feile;* akin to Gk *pikrós* sharp] —**file′a•ble,** *adj.* —**fil′er,** *n.*

file[3] (fīl), *v.t.,* **filed, fil•ing.** *Archaic.* to defile; corrupt. [bef. 1000; ME; OE *fӯlan* to befoul, defile, deriv. of *fūl* FOUL]

fi•lé (fi lā′, fē′lā), *n. New Orleans Cookery.* a powder made from the ground leaves of the sassafras tree, used as a thickener and to impart a pungent taste to soups, gumbos, and other dishes. Also called **filé′ pow′der.** [1800–10, *Amer.*; < LaF; lit., twisted, ropy, stringy (perh. orig. applied to dishes thickened with the powder), ptp. of F *filer;* see FILE[1]]

file′ band′, an endless steel band to which straight lengths of steel files are attached, used on a band mill or band saw.

file′ card′, a card of a size suitable for filing, typically 3 × 5 in. (7.62 × 12.7 cm) or 4 × 6 in. (10.16 × 15.24 cm). [1965–70]

file′ clerk′, an office employee whose principal work is to file and retrieve papers, records, etc. [1915–20]

file•fish (fīl′fish′), *n., pl.* (*esp. collectively*) **-fish,** (*esp. referring to two or more kinds or species*) **-fish•es. 1.** any of several flattened marine fishes of the family Monacanthidae, having an elongated head with a small mouth and small, spiny scales. **2.** a triggerfish. [1765–75; FILE[2] + FISH]

file′ fol′der, a thin cardboard folder of a size to be stored in the drawer of a file cabinet and for containing correspondence and other files.

file′ foot′age, *Television.* film footage already on file; stock footage of crowds, cityscapes, football games, etc.

Fi•lene (fi lēn′, fī-), *n.* **Edward Albert,** 1860–1937, U.S. retail merchant.

fi•let (fi lā′, fil′ā; *Fr.* fē le′), *n., pl.* **fi•lets** (fi lāz′, fil′az; *Fr.* fē le′), *v.t.* fillet (defs. 1, 10).

filet′ lace′, a square mesh net or lace, originally knotted by hand but now copied by machine. [1905–10; < F *filet* net (OF *file* something spun, ptp. of *filer;* see FILE[1]) + *-et* -ET]

fi•let mi•gnon (fi lā′ min yon′, min′yon; *Fr.* fē le mē nyôɴ′), *pl.* **fi•lets mi•gnons** (fi lā′ min yonz′, min′yonz; *Fr.* fē le mē nyôɴ′). a small, tender round of steak cut from the thick end of a beef tenderloin. [1905–10; < F: dainty fillet]

fil•i•al (fil′ē əl), *adj.* **1.** of, pertaining to, or befitting a son or daughter: *filial obedience.* **2.** noting or having the relation of a child to a parent. **3.** *Genetics.* pertaining to the sequence of generations following the parental generation, each generation being designated by an *F* followed by a subscript number indicating its place in the sequence. [1350–1400; ME < LL *fīliālis,* equiv. to L *fīli(us)* son + *-ālis* -AL[1]] —**fil′i•al•ly,** *adv.* —**fil′i•al•ness,** *n.*

fil•i•ate (fil′ē āt′), *v.t.,* **-at•ed, -at•ing.** *Law.* to determine judicially the paternity of, as a child born out of wedlock. Cf. **affiliate** (def. 5). [1785–95; < ML *fīliātus* like the father (said of a son), equiv. to L *fīli(us)* son + *-ātus* -ATE[1]]

fil•i•a•tion (fil′ē ā′shən), *n.* **1.** the fact of being the child of a certain parent. **2.** descent as if from a parent; derivation. **3.** *Law.* the judicial determination of the paternity of a child, esp. of one born out of wedlock. **4.** the relation of one thing to another from which it is derived. **5.** the act of filiating. **6.** the state of being filiated. **7.** an affiliated branch, as of a society. [1425–75; late ME *filiacion* < ML *fīliātiōn-* (s. of *fīliātiō*). See FILIATE, -ION]

fil•i•beg (fil′ə beg′), *n.* the kilt or pleated skirt worn by Scottish Highlanders. Also, **philibeg.** [1740–50; < ScotGael, equiv. to *feile* kilt + *beag* little]

fil•i•bus•ter (fil′ə bus′tər), *n.* **1.** *U.S. Politics.* **a.** the use of irregular or obstructive tactics by a member of a legislative assembly to prevent the adoption of a measure generally favored or to force a decision against the will of the majority. **b.** an exceptionally long speech, as one lasting for a day or days, or a series of such speeches to accomplish this purpose. **c.** a member of a legislature who makes such a speech. **2.** an irregular military adventurer, esp. one who engages in an unauthorized military expedition into a foreign country to foment or support a revolution. —*v.i.* **3.** *U.S. Politics.* to impede legislation by irregular or obstructive tactics, esp. by making long speeches. **4.** to act as an irregular military adventurer, esp. for revolutionary purposes. —*v.t.* **5.** *U.S. Politics.* to impede (legislation) by irregular or obstructive tactics, esp. by making long speeches. [1580–90; < Sp *filibustero* < MF *flibustier,* var. of *fribustier;* see FREEBOOTER] —**fil′i•bus′ter•er,** *n.* —**fil′i•bus′ter•ism,** *n.* —**fil′i•bus′ter•ous,** *adj.*

fil•i•cide (fil′ə sīd′), *n.* **1.** a person who kills his or her son or daughter. **2.** the act of killing one's son or daughter: *Ancient myth contains numerous examples of filicide.* [1655–65; < L *fīli(us)* son (*fīli(a)* daughter) + -CIDE] —**fil′i•cid′al,** *adj.*

fil•i•form (fil′ə fôrm′, fī′lə-), *adj.* threadlike; filamentous. [1750–60; < L *fīl(um)* a thread + -I- + -FORM]

fil•i•grain (fil′i grān′), *n.* filigree. Also, **fil′i•grane′.** [1660–70; < F *filigrane* watermark, filigree < It *filigrana* < L *fīli-,* comb. form of *fīlum* thread + *grāna,* pl. of *grānum* GRAIN]

fil•i•gree (fil′i grē′), *n., adj., v.,* **-greed, -gree•ing.** —*n.* **1.** delicate ornamental work of fine silver, gold, or other metal wires, esp. lacy jewelers' work of scrolls and arabesques. **2.** anything very delicate or fanciful: *a filigree of frost.* —*adj.* **3.** composed of or resembling filigree. —*v.t.* **4.** to adorn with or form into filigree. Also, **filagree, fillagree.** [1685–95; earlier *filigreen,* var. of FILIGRAIN]

fil•ings (fī′lingz), *n.pl.* particles removed by a file. [1350–1400; ME; see FILE[2], -ING[1], -S[3]]

fil•i•o•pi•e•tis•tic (fil′ē ō pī′i tis′tik), *adj. Anthropol.* of or pertaining to reverence of forebears or tradition, esp. if carried to excess. [1890–95; < L *fīli(us)* son (cf. FILIAL) + -O- + PIETISTIC]

Fil•i•pi•no (fil′ə pē′nō), *n., pl.* **-nos,** *adj.* —*n.* **1.** a native or inhabitant of the Philippines. **2.** Pilipino. —*adj.* **3.** Philippine. [1895–1900; < Sp, derived from (*las Islas*) *Filipinas* PHILIPPINE (Islands)]

fil•is•ter (fil′ə stər), *n. Carpentry.* fillister.

fill (fil), *v.t.* **1.** to make full; put as much as can be held into: *to fill a jar with water.* **2.** to occupy to the full capacity: *Water filled the basin. The crowd filled the hall.* **3.** to supply to an extreme degree or plentifully: *to fill a house with furniture; to fill the heart with joy.* **4.** to satisfy fully the hunger of; satiate: *The roast beef filled the diners.* **5.** to put into a receptacle: *to fill sand into a pail.* **6.** to be plentiful throughout: *Fish filled the rivers.* **7.** to extend throughout; pervade completely: *The odor filled the room.* **8.** to furnish with an occupant: *The landlord filled the vacancy yesterday.* **9.** to provide (an office or opening) with an incumbent: *The company is eager to fill the controllership.* **10.** to occupy and perform the duties of (a vacancy, position, post, etc.). **11.** to supply the requirements or contents of (an order), as for goods; execute. **12.** to supply (a blank space) with written matter, decorative work, etc. **13.** to meet satisfactorily, as requirements: *This book fills a great need.* **14.** to make up, compound, or otherwise provide the contents of (a medical prescription). **15.** to stop up or close (a cavity, hole, etc.): *to fill a tooth.* **16.** *Cookery.* to insert a filling into: *to fill cupcakes with custard.* **17.** *Naut.* **a.** to distend (a sail) by pressure of the wind so as to impart headway to a vessel. **b.** to brace (a yard) so that the sail will catch the wind on its after side. **18.** to adulterate: *to fill soaps with water.* **19.** *Civ. Engin., Building Trades.* to build up the level of (an area) with earth, stones, etc. —*v.i.* **20.** to become full: *The hall filled rapidly. Our eyes filled with tears.* **21.** to increase in atmospheric pressure: *a filling cyclone.* **22.** to become distended, as sails with the wind. **23. fill and stand on,** *Naut.* (of a sailing vessel) to proceed on a tack after being hove to or halted facing the wind; fill away. **24. fill away,** *Naut.* **a.** to fall off the wind and proceed on a board. **b.** to brace the yards, so that sails that have been aback will stand full. **25. fill in, a.** to supply miss-

ing or desired information: *Fill in the facts of your business experience.* **b.** to complete by adding detail, as a design or drawing: *to fill in a sketch with shadow.* **c.** to substitute for: *to fill in for a colleague who is ill.* **d.** to fill with some material: *to fill in a crack with putty.* **e.** *Informal.* to supply (someone) with information: *Please fill me in on the morning news.* **26. fill out, a.** to complete (a document, list, etc.) by supplying missing or desired information. **b.** to become larger, fuller, or rounder, as the figure: *The children have begun to fill out since I saw them last.* **27. fill the bill.** See **bill**[1] (def. 12). **28. fill up, a.** to fill completely: *to fill up a glass; to fill up a fuel tank.* **b.** to become completely filled: *The riverbed filled up as a result of the steady rains.* —*n.* **29.** a full supply; enough to satisfy want or desire: *to eat one's fill.* **30.** an amount of something sufficient for filling; charge. **31.** *Civ. Engin., Building Trades.* a quantity of earth, stones, etc., for building up the level of an area of ground: *These houses were built on fill.* Cf. **backfill. 32.** the feed and water in the digestive tract of a livestock animal, esp. that consumed before marketing. [bef. 900; ME *fillen,* OE *fyllan;* c. G *füllen,* Goth *fulljan* to make full; see FULL[1]] —**fill′a•ble,** *adj.*
—**Syn. 2.** crowd, pack, jam, cram. **13.** satisfy, answer.

fil•la•gree (fil′ə grē′), *n., adj., v.t.,* **-greed, -greeing.** filigree.

fille de joie (fē′yᵊ də zhwä′), *pl.* ***filles de joie*** (fē′yᵊ də zhwä′). *French.* a prostitute. [lit., pleasure girl]

filled′ gold′, a composition consisting of gold-plating welded to and rolled with a backing of brass or other base metal, at least 1/20 of the total weight being that of the gold. Also called **rolled gold.** Cf. **gold-filled.**

filled′ milk′, milk containing a substitute for the butterfat. [1930–35]

fill•er (fil′ər), *n.* **1.** a person or thing that fills: *a filler for pies; a filler of orders.* **2.** a thing or substance used to fill a gap, cavity, or the like. **3.** a substance used to fill cracks, pores, etc., in a surface before painting or varnishing. **4.** a liquid, paste, or the like used to coat a surface or to give solidity, bulk, etc., to a substance, as paper or a chemical powder. **5.** *Journalism.* material, considered of secondary importance, used to fill out a column or page. **6.** an implement used in filling, as a funnel. **7.** cotton, down, or other material used to stuff or pad an object, as a quilt or cloth toy. **8.** material placed between the insole and the exterior sole of a shoe. **9.** *Ling.* (esp. in tagmemics) one of a class of items that can fit into a given slot in a construction. **10.** *Building Trades.* a plate, slab, block, etc., inserted between two parallel members to connect them. **11.** the tobacco forming the body of a cigar. **12.** metal in the form of a rod or wire, used in brazing, welding, and soldering. [1490–1500; FILL + -ER[1]]

fil•lér (fē′lâr, fil′âr), *n., pl.* **-lér.** an aluminum coin of Hungary, the 100th part of a forint. Also, **fil′ler.** [1900–05; < Hungarian < MHG *vierer* type of coin, equiv. to *vier* FOUR + *-er* -ER[1]]

fil′let (fil′it; *usually* fi lā′ *for 1, 10*), *n.* **1.** *Cookery.* **a.** a boneless cut or slice of meat or fish, esp. the beef tenderloin. **b.** a piece of veal or other meat boned, rolled, and tied for roasting. **2.** a narrow band of ribbon or the like worn around the head, usually as an ornament; headband. **3.** any narrow strip, as wood or metal. **4.** a strip of any material used for binding. **5.** *Bookbinding.* **a.** a decorative line impressed on a book cover, usually at the top and bottom of the back. **b.** a rolling tool for impressing such lines. **6.** *Archit.* **a.** Also called **list.** a narrow flat molding or area, raised or sunk between larger moldings or areas. See diag. under **molding. b.** a narrow portion of the surface of a column left between adjoining flutes. **7.** *Anat.* lemniscus. **8.** a raised rim or ridge, as a ring on the muzzle of a gun. **9.** *Metall.* a concave strip forming a rounded interior angle in a foundry pattern. —*v.t.* **10.** *Cookery.* **a.** to cut or prepare (meat or fish) as a fillet. **b.** to cut fillets from. **11.** to bind or adorn with or as if with a fillet. **12.** *Mach.* to round off (an interior angle) with a fillet. Also, **filet** (for defs. 1, 10). [1300–50; ME *filet* < AF, MF, equiv. to *fil* thread + *-et* -ET]

fil•let•ing (fil′i ting), *n. Building Trades.* material, as mortar, used as a substitute for flashing. [1590–1600; FILLET + -ING[1]]

fil′let weld′ (fil′it), *Metalworking.* a weld with a triangular cross section joining two surfaces that meet in an interior right angle. [1925–30]

fill-in (fil′in′), *n.* **1.** a person or thing that fills in, as a substitute, replacement, or insertion: *She's a fill-in for workers on vacation.* **2.** a brief, informative summary; a rundown. [1915–20; n. use of v. phrase *fill in*]

fill•ing (fil′ing), *n.* **1.** an act or instance of filling. **2.** something that is put in to fill something else: *They used sand as filling for the depression.* **3.** *Dentistry.* a substance such as cement, amalgam, gold, or the like, used to fill a cavity caused by decay in a tooth. **4.** a food mixture that goes into something, as if to fill it: *sandwich filling; pie filling.* **5.** Also called **pick, weft, woof.** *Textiles.* yarn carried by the shuttle and interlacing at right angles with the warp in woven cloth. See diag. under **weave.** [1350–1400; ME; see FILL, -ING[1]]

fill′ing knit′ting. See **weft knitting.**

fill′ing sta′tion. See **service station** (def. 1).

fil•lip (fil′əp), *v.t.* **1.** to strike with the nail of a finger snapped from the end of the thumb. **2.** to tap or strike smartly. **3.** to drive by or as by a fillip: *Anticipation filliped his passion.* —*v.i.* **4.** to make a fillip with the fingers. —*n.* **5.** an act or instance of filliping; a smart tap or stroke. **6.** anything that tends to rouse, excite, or revive; a stimulus: *Praise is an excellent fillip for waning ambition.* [1425–75; late ME *philippe* to make a signal or sound with thumb and right forefinger; expressive word of uncert. orig; cf. FLIP]

fil•li•peen (fil′ə pēn′), *n.* philopena.

fil•lis•ter (fil′ə stər), *n. Carpentry.* **1.** a rabbet or groove, as one on a window sash to hold the glass and putty. **2.** Also called **fil′lister plane′.** a plane for cutting rabbets or grooves. Also, **filister.** [1810–20; orig. uncert.]

fil′lister head′, a cylindrical screw head. See illus. under **screw.**

fill′ light′, *Photog.* a light used to eliminate or soften shadows caused by the main source of illumination.

Fill•more (fil′môr, -mōr), *n.* **Mil•lard** (mil′ərd), 1800–74, 13th president of the United States 1850–53.

fill-up (fil′up′), *n.* an act or instance of filling up, as a tank with fuel. [1850–55; n. use of v. phrase *fill up*]

fil•ly (fil′ē), *n., pl.* **-lies. 1.** a young female horse. **2.** *Informal.* a girl or young woman. [1400–50; late ME *fyly* < ON *fyla* female FOAL]

film (film), *n.* **1.** a thin layer or coating: *a film of grease on a plate.* **2.** a thin sheet of any material: *a film of ice.* **3.** a thin skin or membrane. **4.** a delicate web of filaments or fine threads. **5.** a thin haze, blur, or mist. **6.** *Photog.* **a.** a cellulose nitrate or cellulose acetate composition made in thin sheets or strips and coated with a sensitive emulsion for taking photographs. **b.** a strip or roll of this. **c.** the coating of emulsion on such a sheet or strip or on a photographic plate. **7.** *Motion Pictures.* **a.** a strip of transparent material, usually cellulose triacetate, covered with a photographic emulsion and perforated along one or both edges, intended for the recording and reproduction of images. **b.** a similar perforated strip covered with an iron oxide emulsion **(magfilm),** intended for the recording and reproduction of both images and sound. **c.** See **motion picture. 8.** Often, **films, a.** motion pictures collectively. **b.** the motion-picture industry, or its productions, operations, etc. **c.** motion pictures, as a genre of art or entertainment: *experimental film.* —*v.t.* **9.** to cover with a film, thin skin, or pellicle: *filmed eyes.* **10.** *Motion Pictures.* **a.** to photograph with a motion-picture camera. **b.** to reproduce in the form of motion pictures: *to film a novel.* —*v.i.* **11.** to become covered by a film: *The water filmed over with ice.* **12.** *Motion Pictures.* **a.** to be reproduced in a motion picture, esp. in a specified manner: *This story films easily.* **b.** to direct, make, or otherwise engage in the production of motion pictures. [bef. 1000; 1890–95 for def. 6; 1900–05 for def. 7; ME *filme,* OE *filmen* membrane; akin to FELL[4]] —**film′like′,** *adj.*
—**Syn. 11.** mist, haze, cloud, veil.

film•a•ble (fil′mə bəl), *adj.* noting or pertaining to a story or to a literary work readily adaptable to motion picture form. [1915–20; FILM + -ABLE]

film′ badge′, a badgelike device that indicates whether a dose of radiation has been received: worn by workers subject to radiation exposure. [1940–45]

film•card (film′kärd′), *n.* microfiche. [1960–65; FILM + CARD[1]]

film′ clip′, a strip of motion-picture film, esp. an excerpt from a longer film or one inserted as part of another presentation, as of a telecast or full-length motion picture. [1955–60]

film•dom (film′dəm), *n.* the motion-picture industry. Also called **moviedom, screenland.** [1910–15; FILM + -DOM]

film′ gate′, (in motion-picture cameras and projectors) a mechanism that holds the film flat in the focal plane of the lens during exposure or projection.

film•go•er (film′gō′ər), *n.* a person who attends motion-picture showings. [1915–20; FILM + GOER]

fil•mi (fil′mē), *n.* a style of Indian popular vocal music accompanied by sitar and tabla and used in Indian films. [1985–90; ult. der. of E FILM]

film•ic (fil′mik), *adj.* **1.** of, pertaining to, or characteristic of motion pictures: *a filmic adaptation of a novel.* **2.** containing characteristics resembling those of motion pictures. [1925–30; FILM + -IC] —**film′i•cal•ly,** *adv.*

film•ing (fil′ming), *n.* the act or period of photographing, esp. of a motion picture. [1885–90; FILM + -ING[1]]

film•i•za•tion (fil′mə zā′shən), *n.* an adaptation of a novel, play, etc., for a motion picture. [1915–20, *Amer.;* FILM + -IZATION]

film•land (film′land′), *n.* filmdom. [1910–15; FILM + LAND]

film′ li′brary, a collection of films, motion pictures, videodiscs, videocassettes, and any other materials stored on film.

film•mak′er (film′mā′kər), *n.* **1.** Also called **moviemaker.** a producer or director of motion pictures, esp. one working in all phases of production: *the leading young filmmakers of France.* **2.** a person who makes film, esp. for use in photography. [1905–10; FILM + MAKER] —**film′mak′ing,** *n.*

film′ noir′ (nwär), a motion picture with an often grim urban setting, photographed in somber tones and permeated by a feeling of disillusionment, pessimism, and despair. [1955–60; < F: lit., black film]

film•og•ra•phy (fil mog′rə fē), *n., pl.* **-phies. 1.** a collection of writings about motion pictures, esp. detailed essays dealing with specific films. **2.** a listing of motion pictures by actor, director, genre, etc., and usually including pertinent facts about the production of each film. [1960–65; FILM + (BIBLI)OGRAPHY]

film′ pack′, *Photog.* a number of sheets of film arranged one over the other and connected so that they can be exposed successively. [1960–65]

film′ record′er, a photographic device for producing a sound strip on a motion-picture film.

film•set (film′set′), *v.,* **-set, -set•ting,** *adj. Print.* —*v.t.* **1.** to photocompose. —*adj.* **2.** (of type) set on a photocomposer. [1950–55; FILM + SET] —**film′set′ter,** *n.*

film•set•ting (film′set′ing), *n. Print.* photocomposition. [1950–55; FILM + SET + -ING[1]]

film′ speed′, *Photog.* speed (def. 5a). [1910–15]

film•strip (film′strip′), *n.* a length of film containing a series of related transparencies for projection on a screen. [1925–30; FILM + STRIP[2]]

film•y (fil′mē), *adj.,* **film•i•er, film•i•est. 1.** thin and light; fine and gauzy: *a gown of a filmy material.* **2.** hazy or misty; glazed: *filmy eyes.* [1595–1605; FILM + -Y[1]] —**film′i•ly,** *adv.* —**film′i•ness,** *n.*

fi•lo (fē′lō), *n.* phyllo.

Fi•lo•fax (fī′lə faks′), *Trademark.* a datebook also containing space for addresses, a calendar, and specialized inserts, as maps and checklists.

fi•lo•plume (fil′ə plo͞om′, fī′lə-), *n. Ornith.* a specialized, hairlike feather having a slender shaft with few or no barbs. [1880–85; < NL *filopluma,* equiv. to L *fīl(um)* a thread + -o- -o- + *plūma* PLUME]

fi•lo•po•di•um (fil′ə pō′dē əm, fī′lə-), *n., pl.* **-di•a** (-dē ə). *Cell Biol.* a long, hairlike pseudopod composed of ectoplasm. [see FILUM, -O-, -PODIUM]

fi•lose (fī′lōs), *adj.* **1.** threadlike. **2.** ending in a threadlike process. [1815–25; < L *fīl(um)* a thread + -OSE[1]]

fi•lo•sus (fi lō′səs), *adj. Meteorol.* fibratus. [< NL, equiv. to L *fīl(um)* thread + *-ōsus* -OSE[1]]

fils (fils), *n., pl.* **fils. 1.** a coin and monetary unit of Bahrain, Iraq, Jordan, and Kuwait, the 100th part of a dinar. **2.** a bronze coin of the United Arab Emirates, the 100th part of a dirham. **3.** (formerly) an aluminum coin and monetary unit of the Yemen Arab Republic, the 100th part of a riyal. Also, **fil.** [1885–90; < Ar, prob. < Gk *phóllis* a kind of coin]

fils (fēs), *n., pl.* ***fils.*** *French.* son: used after a name with the meaning of *Jr.,* as in *Dumas fils.* Cf. **père.**

filt., (in prescriptions) filter. [< NL *filtrā*]

fil•ter (fil′tər), *n.* **1.** any substance, as cloth, paper, porous porcelain, or a layer of charcoal or sand, through which liquid or gas is passed to remove suspended impurities or to recover solids. **2.** any device, as a tank or tube, containing such a substance for filtering. **3.** any of various analogous devices, as for removing dust from air or impurities from tobacco smoke, or for eliminating certain kinds of light rays. **4.** *Informal.* a filter-tipped cigarette or cigar. **5.** *Photog.* a lens screen of dyed gelatin or glass for controlling the rendering of color or for diminishing the intensity of light. **6.** *Electronics, Physics.* a circuit or device that passes certain frequencies and blocks others. **7.** *Math.* a collection of subsets of a topological space, having the properties that the intersection of two subsets in the collection is a subset in the collection and that any set containing a subset in the collection is in the collection. —*v.t.* **8.** to remove by the action of a filter. **9.** to partially obstruct the passage of: *The thick leaves filtered the sunlight.* **10.** to pass through or as if through a filter. —*v.i.* **11.** to pass or slip through slowly, as through an obstruction or a filter: *Enemy agents filtered into the embattled country.* [1375–1425; late ME *filtre* < ML *filtrum* felt, piece of felt used to strain liquids < Gmc; see FELT[2]] —**fil′ter•er,** *n.*
—**Syn. 11.** penetrate, sift, seep, trickle, leak.

fil•ter•a•ble (fil′tər ə bəl), *adj.* **1.** capable of being filtered. **2.** *Microbiol.* capable of passing through bacteria-retaining filters. Also, **filtrable.** [1905–10; FILTER + -ABLE] —**fil′ter•a•bil′i•ty, fil′ter•a•ble•ness,** *n.*

fil′terable vi′rus, a virus particle small enough to pass through a filter of diatomaceous earth or porcelain, which will not pass bacteria: chiefly historical or an informal indicator of size, as synthetic membrane filters now permit passage of the smallest virus. [1910–15]

fil′ter bed′, a pond or tank having a false bottom covered with sand and serving to filter river or pond waters. [1870–75]

fil′ter fac′tor, *Photog.* a number indicating the increased exposure that a particular film should receive when a photograph is taken using a particular filter. [1920–25]

fil′ter feed′er, an aquatic animal that feeds on particles or small organisms strained out of water by circulating them through its system: includes most of the stationary feeders, as clams, oysters, barnacles, corals, sea squirts, and sponges. [1925–30]

fil′ter pa′per, porous paper used in filtering. [1890–95]

fil′ter tip′, 1. a mouthpiece for a cigarette or cigar having a means of filtering the smoke. **2.** a cigarette or cigar having such a mouthpiece. [1930–35] —**fil′ter-tipped′,** *adj.*

filth (filth), *n.* **1.** offensive or disgusting dirt or refuse; foul matter: *the filth dumped into our rivers.* **2.** foul condition: *to live in filth.* **3.** moral impurity, corruption, or obscenity. **4.** vulgar or obscene language or thought. [bef. 1000; ME; OE *fȳlth.* See FOUL, -TH[1]]

filth•y (fil′thē), *adj.,* **filth•i•er, filth•i•est,** *adv., v.,* **filth•ied, filth•y•ing.** —*adj.* **1.** foul with, characterized by, or having the nature of filth; disgustingly or completely dirty. **2.** vile; vulgar; obscene: *filthy language.* **3.** contemptibly vile or objectionable: *to treat one's friends in a filthy manner.* **4.** (of money) abundantly supplied (often fol. by *with*): *They're filthy with money.* —*adv.* **5.** (of money or wealth) very; extremely: *filthy rich.* —*v.t.* **6.** to make filthy; foul. [1350–1400; ME; see FILTH, -Y[1]] —**filth′i•ly,** *adv.* —**filth′i•ness,** *n.*
—**Syn. 1.** See **dirty.**

filth′y lu′cre, money: *to lose one's health for the sake of filthy lucre.* [1520–30]

fil•tra•ble (fil′trə bəl), *adj.* filterable. —**fil′tra•bil′i•ty,** *n.*

fil•trate (fil′trāt), *v.,* **-trat•ed, -trat•ing,** *n.* —*v.t., v.i.* **1.** to filter. —*n.* **2.** liquid that has been passed through a filter. [1605–15; < ML *filtrātus* filtered, ptp. of *filtrāre*. See FILTER, -ATE[1]] **—fil′trat·a·ble,** *adj.* **—fil·tra′tion,** *n.*

fi·lum (fī′ləm), *n., pl.* **-la** (-lə). a threadlike structure; filament. [1855–60; < L: a thread, filament, fiber]

fim·ble (fim′bəl), *n.* the male or staminate plant of hemp, which is harvested before the female or pistillate plant. [1400–50; late ME *femaille* (*hempe*) FEMALE (hemp)]

fim·bri·a (fim′brē ə), *n., pl.* **-bri·ae** (-brē ē′). Often, **fimbriae.** *Bot., Zool.* a fringe or fringed border. [1745–55; < NL; L *fimbriae* (pl.) border, fringe] **—fim′bri·al,** *adj.*

fim·bri·ate (*adj.* fim′brē it, -āt′; *v.* fim′brē āt′), *adj., v.,* **-at·ed, -at·ing.** —*adj.* **1.** Also, **fim′bri·at′ed.** *Bot., Zool.* having a border of hairs or filiform processes. —*v.t.* **2.** *Heraldry.* to line (an ordinary) with a thin border of a different tincture. [1480–90; < L *fimbriātus* fringed. See FIMBRIA, -ATE[1]]

fimbriate petals

fim·bri·a·tion (fim′brē ā′shən), *n. Bot., Zool.* **1.** fimbriate or fringed condition. **2.** a fringe or fringelike part. [1860–65; < ML *fimbriātiōn-* (s. of *fimbriātiō*). See FIMBRIATE, -ION]

fim·bril·late (fim bril′it, -āt), *adj. Bot., Zool.* bordered by or having a small or fine fringe. [< NL *fimbrill*(*a*) little fringe (see FIMBRIA) + -ATE[1]]

fi·mic·o·lous (fī mik′ə ləs, fə-), *adj. Ecol.* of or pertaining to an organism that lives on or in animal excrement. [1870–75; < L *fim*(*um*) dung + -I- + -COLOUS]

fin[1] (fin), *n., v.,* **finned, fin·ning.** —*n.* **1.** a membranous, winglike or paddlelike organ attached to any of various parts of the body of fishes and certain other aquatic animals, used for propulsion, steering, or balancing. **2.** *Naut.* **a.** a horizontal, often adjustable, winglike appendage to the underwater portion of a hull, as one for controlling the dive of a submarine or for damping the roll of a surface vessel. **b.** See **fin keel. 3.** Also called **vertical stabilizer.** *Aeron.* any of certain small, subsidiary structures on an aircraft, designed to increase directional stability. **4.** any of a number of standing ridges on an ordinarily hot object, as a radiator, a cylinder of an internal-combustion engine, etc., intended to maximize heat transfer to the surrounding air by exposing a large surface area. **5.** any part, as of a mechanism, resembling a fin. **6.** *Metall.* a ridge of metal squeezed through the opening between two rolls, dies, or halves of a mold in which a piece is being formed under pressure. Cf. **flash** (def. 11). **7.** *Auto.* an ornamental structure resembling an aeronautical fin that is attached to the body of an automobile, as on each rear fender **(tail fin). 8.** *Slang.* the arm or hand. **9.** Usually, **fins.** flipper (def. 2). —*v.t.* **10.** to cut off the fins from (a fish); carve or cut up, as a chub. **11.** to provide or equip with a fin or fins. —*v.i.* **12.** to move the fins; lash the water with the fins, as a whale when dying. [bef. 1000; ME, OE *finn;* c. D *vin,* LG *finne;* akin to Sw *fena*] **—fin′less,** *adj.* **—fin′like′,** *adj.*

fin[2] (fin), *n. Slang.* a five-dollar bill. [1865–70; earlier *finnip, finnup, fin*(*n*)*if*(*f*) a five-pound note < Yiddish *fin*(*e*)*f* five < MHG *vumf, vimf;* see FIVE]

Fin., 1. Finland. **2.** Finnish.

fin., 1. finance. **2.** financial. **3.** finish.

fin·a·ble (fī′nə bəl), *adj.* subject to a fine; punishable by a fine. Also, **fineable.** [1475–85; FINE[2] + -ABLE] **—fin′a·ble·ness,** *n.*

fi·na·gle (fi nā′gəl), *v.,* **-gled, -gling.** —*v.t.* **1.** to trick, swindle, or cheat (a person) (often fol. by *out of*): *He finagled the backers out of a fortune.* **2.** to get or achieve (something) by guile, trickery, or manipulation: *to finagle an assignment to the Membership Committee.* —*v.i.* **3.** to practice deception or fraud; scheme. Also, **fenagle.** [1925–30, *Amer.*; *finaig-* (var. of FAINAIGUE) + -LE] **—fi·na′gler,** *n.*

fi·nal (fīn′l), *adj.* **1.** pertaining to or coming at the end; last in place, order, or time: *the final meeting of the year.* **2.** ultimate: *The final goal is world peace.* **3.** conclusive or decisive: *a final decision.* **4.** constituting the end or purpose: *a final result.* **5.** pertaining to or expressing the end or purpose: *a final clause.* **6.** *Law.* **a.** precluding further controversy on the questions passed upon: *The judicial determination of the Supreme Court is final.* **b.** determining all issues presented, so that no further decision upon the merits of the issues is necessary: *a final judgment or decree.* **7.** *Phonet.* occurring at the end of a word or syllable, as the (t) sound in *bit* or *bite.* —*n.* **8.** that which is last; that which forms an end or termination. **9.** Often, **finals. a.** the last and decisive game, match, contest, or round in a series, as in sports. **b.** the last, usually comprehensive, examination in a course of study. **10.** the last edition of a newspaper published on any day. **11.** *Music.* the tonic note of a church mode. [1300–50; 1915–20 for def. 10; ME < L *fīnālis,* equiv. to *fīn*(*is*) end + *-ālis* -AL[1]]
—Syn. 1. See **last**[1]. **3.** definite, irrevocable, irreversible, unalterable. **—Ant. 1.** initial, first.

fi′nal cause′, *Aristotelianism.* See under **cause** (def. 8b). [1350–1400]

fi′nal cut′, *Motion Pictures.* the final edited version of a film, approved by the director and producer. Cf. **rough cut.**

fi·na·le (fi nal′ē, -nä′lē), *n.* **1.** the last piece, division, or movement of a concert, opera, or composition. **2.** the concluding part of any performance, course of proceedings, etc.; end. [1715–25; < It, n. use of *finale* (adj.) < L *fīnālis* FINAL]

fi·nal·ism (fīn′l iz′əm), *n.* the doctrine or belief that all events are determined by their purposes or goals. [1905–10; FINAL + -ISM]

fi·nal·ist (fīn′l ist), *n.* a person entitled to participate in the final or decisive contest in a series, as in musical or athletic competition. [1895–1900; FINAL + -IST]

fi·nal·i·ty (fī nal′i tē), *n., pl.* **-ties** for 2. **1.** the state, quality, or fact of being final; conclusiveness or decisiveness. **2.** something that is final; an ultimate act, utterance, belief, etc. [1535–45; FINAL + -ITY]

fi·na·lize (fīn′l īz′), *v.,* **-lized, -liz·ing.** —*v.t.* **1.** to put into final form; complete all the details of. —*v.i.* **2.** to complete an agreement; conclude negotiations: *We should finalize by the end of the week.* Also, *esp. Brit.,* **fi′na·lise′.** [1920–25; FINAL + -IZE] **—fi′na·li·za′tion,** *n.* **—fi′na·liz′er,** *n.*
—Usage. See **-ize.**

Fi′nal Judg′ment, judgment (def. 8).

fi·nal·ly (fīn′l ē), *adv.* **1.** at the final point or moment; in the end. **2.** in a final manner; conclusively or decisively. [1325–75; ME; see FINAL, -LY]

Fi′nal Solu′tion, the Nazi program of annihilating the Jews of Europe during the Third Reich. [1945–50; trans. of G *endgültige Lösung*]

fi·nance (fi nans′, fī′nans), *n., v.,* **-nanced, -nanc·ing.** —*n.* **1.** the management of revenues; the conduct or transaction of money matters generally, esp. those affecting the public, as in the fields of banking and investment. **2. finances,** the monetary resources, as of a government, company, organization, or individual; revenue. —*v.t.* **3.** to supply with money or capital; obtain money or credit for. —*v.i.* **4.** to raise money or capital needed for financial operations. [1350–1400; ME *finaunce* < AF, MF *finance,* equiv. to *fin*(*er*) to end, settle, pay (see FINE[2]) + *-ance* -ANCE] **—fi·nance′a·ble** *adj.*

fi′nance bill′, *Govt.* a bill or act of a legislature to obtain funds for the public treasury. [1900–05]

fi′nance charge′, interest or a fee charged for borrowing money or buying on credit.

fi′nance com′pany, an institution engaged in such specialized forms of financing as purchasing accounts receivable, extending credit to retailers and manufacturers, discounting installment contracts, and granting loans with goods as security. [1925–30]

fi·nan·cial (fi nan′shəl, fī-), *adj.* **1.** pertaining to monetary receipts and expenditures; pertaining or relating to money matters; pecuniary: *financial operations.* **2.** of or pertaining to those commonly engaged in dealing with money and credit. [1760–70; FINANCE + -IAL] **—fi·nan′cial·ly,** *adv.*
—Syn. 1. FINANCIAL, FISCAL, MONETARY, PECUNIARY refer to matters concerned with money. FINANCIAL usually refers to money matters or transactions of some size or importance: *a financial wizard.* FISCAL is used esp. in connection with government funds, or those of any organization: *the end of the fiscal year.* MONETARY relates esp. to money as such: *a monetary system or standard.* PECUNIARY refers to money as used in making ordinary payments: *a pecuniary obligation or reward.*

Finan′cial Account′ing Stand′ards Board′, an independent organization founded in 1973, responsible chiefly for establishing generally accepted accounting principles. *Abbr.:* FASB

finan′cial plan′ning, 1. the devising of a program for the allocation and management of finances and capital through budgeting, investment, etc. **2.** the business of devising such programs. **—finan′cial plan′ner.**

fin·an·cier (fin′ən sēr′, fī′nən-; *Brit.* fi nan′sē ər), *n.* **1.** a person skilled or engaged in managing large financial operations, whether public or corporate. —*v.t.* **2.** to finance. —*v.i.* **3.** to act as a financier. [1610–20; < F; see FINANCE, -IER[2]]

fi·nan·cière (*Fr.* fē nän syer′), *adj.* of or pertaining to a garnish or sauce prepared typically with truffles, mushrooms, quenelles, olives, Madeira, and sometimes sweetbreads and cockscombs: *vol-au-vent financière.* [< F, short for adv. phrase *à la financière* in the manner of a financier. Cf. À LA MODE]

fi·nanc·ing (fi nan′sing, fī′nan-), *n.* **1.** the act of obtaining or furnishing money or capital for a purchase or enterprise. **2.** the funds so obtained. [1820–30; FINANCE (v.) + -ING[1]]

fin·back (fin′bak′), *n.* any baleen whale of the genus *Balaenoptera,* having a prominent dorsal fin, esp. *B. physalus,* of the Atlantic and Pacific coasts; rorqual: an endangered species. Also called **fin′back whale′, fin whale.** [1715–25; FIN + BACK[1]]

finback, *Balaenoptera physalus,* length 60 to 70 ft. (18 to 21.3 m)

fin·ca (fing′kə; *Sp.* fēng′kä), *n., pl.* **-cas** (-kəz; *Sp.* -käs). a ranch or large farm in a Spanish-speaking country, esp. a plantation in tropical Spanish America. [1905–10; < Sp: property, real estate, farm (appar. orig., amount left over; hence, a sum of money > income from a property > the property itself), deriv. of OSp *fincar* to remain, stative deriv. of *fincar* (Sp *hincar*) to drive in, fix, sink (a nail), alter. of *ficar* (< VL **figicāre,* for L *figere;* cf. FICHU), with *-n-* perh. from dial. *finsar* to mark out (ult. < **fixāre;* see FIX)]

finch (finch), *n.* **1.** any of numerous small passerine birds of the family Fringillidae, including the buntings, sparrows, crossbills, purple finches, and grosbeaks, most of which have a short, conical bill adapted for eating seeds. **2.** any of various nonfringilline birds, esp. the weaverbirds of the family Ploceidae and the tropical members of the subfamily Emberizinae. [bef. 900; ME; OE *finc;* c. D *vink,* G *Fink;* akin to Gk *spingos* finch]

purple finch, *Carpodacus purpureus,* length 6 in. (15 cm)

find (fīnd), *v.,* **found, find·ing,** *n.* —*v.t.* **1.** to come upon by chance; meet with: *He found a nickel in the street.* **2.** to locate, attain, or obtain by search or effort: *to find an apartment; to find happiness.* **3.** to locate or recover (something lost or misplaced): *I can't find my blue socks.* **4.** to discover or perceive after consideration: *to find something to be true.* **5.** to gain or regain the use of: *His anger finally helped him find his tongue.* **6.** to ascertain by study or calculation: *to find the sum of several numbers.* **7.** to feel or perceive: *He finds it so.* **8.** to become aware of, or discover (oneself), as being in a condition or location: *After a long illness, he found himself well again. She woke to find herself at home.* **9.** to discover: *Columbus found America in 1492.* **10.** *Law.* **a.** to determine after judicial inquiry: *to find a person guilty.* **b.** to pronounce as an official act (an indictment, verdict, or judgment). **11.** to provide or furnish: *Bring blankets and we'll find the rest of the equipment for the trip.* **12.** *South Midland and Southern U.S.* (of farm animals) to give birth to: *The brown cow found a calf yesterday.* —*v.i.* **13.** to determine an issue after judicial inquiry: *The jury found for the plaintiff.* **14.** *Hunting Brit.* to come upon game. **15. find fault.** See **fault** (def. 12). **16. find oneself,** to discover where one's real interests or talents lie, and follow them: *After trying many occupations, he finally found himself and became an account executive.* **17. find out, a.** to discover or confirm the truth of (something). **b.** to detect or expose, as a crime or offense. **c.** to uncover the true nature, identity, or intentions of (someone): *They found him out before he could launch the rebellion.* —*n.* **18.** an act of finding or discovering. **19.** something found; a discovery, esp. a valuable or gratifying one: *Our cook was a find.* **20.** *Hunting.* a discovery of game, esp. foxes. [bef. 900; ME *finden,* OE *findan;* c. G *finden,* D *vinden,* ON *finna,* Goth *finthan*] **—find′a·ble,** *adj.*
—Syn. 2. achieve, win, earn, acquire.

find·er (fīn′dər), *n.* **1.** a person or thing that finds. **2.** *Photog.* **a.** a range finder. **b.** Also called **viewfinder.** a camera part or attachment enabling a photographer to determine what will be included in the picture. **3.** *Astron.* a small, wide-angled telescope attached to a larger one for locating objects to be studied. **4.** a person or firm that acts as agent in initiating a business transaction. [1250–1300; ME *findere.* See FIND, -ER[1]]

fin de siè·cle (faN də sye′klᵊ), *French.* **1.** the end of the 19th century. **2.** Sometimes, ***fin-de-siècle.*** of, pertaining to, or characterized by concepts of art, society, etc., associated with the end of the 19th century.

find·ing (fīn′ding), *n.* **1.** the act of a person or thing that finds; discovery. **2.** Often, **findings.** something that is found or ascertained. **3.** *Law.* a decision or verdict after judicial inquiry. **4. findings,** tools, materials, etc., used by artisans. [bef. 1000; ME, OE; see FIND, -ING[1]]

Find·lay (fin′lē, find′-), *n.* a city in NW Ohio. 35,594.

fine[1] (fīn), *adj.,* **fin·er, fin·est,** *adv., v.,* **fined, fin·ing,** *n.* —*adj.* **1.** of superior or best quality; of high or highest grade: *fine wine.* **2.** choice, excellent, or admirable: *a fine painting.* **3.** consisting of minute particles: *fine sand; a fine purée.* **4.** very thin or slender: *fine thread.* **5.** keen or sharp, as a tool: *Is the knife fine enough to carve well?* **6.** delicate in texture; filmy: *fine cotton fabric.* **7.** delicately fashioned: *fine tracery.* **8.** highly skilled or accomplished: *a fine musician.* **9.** trained to the maximum degree, as an athlete. **10.** characterized by or affecting refinement or elegance: *a fine lady.* **11.** polished or refined: *fine manners.* **12.** affectedly ornate or elegant: *A style so fine repels the average reader.* **13.** delicate or subtle: *a fine distinction.* **14.** bright and clear: *a fine day; fine skin.* **15.** healthy; well: *In spite of his recent illness, he looks fine.* **16.** showy or smart; elegant in appearance: *a bird of fine plumage.* **17.** good-looking or handsome: *a fine young man.* **18.** (of a precious metal or its alloy) free from impurities or containing a large amount of pure metal: *fine gold; Sterling silver is 92.5 percent fine.* —*adv.* **19.** *Informal.* in an excellent manner; very well: *He did fine on the exams. She sings fine.* **20.** very small: *She writes so fine I can hardly read it.* **21.** *Billiards, Pool.* in such a way that the driven ball barely touches the object ball in passing. **22.** *Naut.* as close as possible to the wind: *sailing fine.* **23. cut fine,** to calculate precisely, esp. without allowing for possible error or accident: *To finish in ten minutes is to cut it too fine.* —*v.i.* **24.** to become fine or finer, as by refining. **25.** to become less, as in size or proportions; reduce; diminish (often fol. by *down*): *The plumpness fines down with exercise.* —*v.t.* **26.** to make fine or finer, esp. by refining or pulverizing. **27.** to reduce the size or proportions of (often used with *down* or *away*): *to fine down the heavy features; to fine away superfluous matter in a design.* **28.** to clarify (wines or spirits) by filtration. —*n.* **29. fines, a.** *Min-*

CONCISE PRONUNCIATION KEY: *act, cāpe, dâre, pärt; set, ēqual; if, īce; ox, ōver, ôrder, oil, bŏŏk, bōōt, out; up, ûrge; child; sing; shoe; thin, that;* zh as in *treasure.* ə = *a* as in *alone, e* as in *system, i* as in *easily, o* as in *gallop, u* as in *circus;* ᵊ as in *fire* (fīᵊr), *hour* (ouᵊr). l and n can serve as syllabic consonants, as in *cradle* (krād′l), and *button* (but′n). See the full key inside the front cover.

ing. crushed ore sufficiently fine to pass through a given screen. Cf. **short** (def. 37a). **b.** *Agric.* the fine bits of corn kernel knocked off during handling of the grain. [1250–1300; ME *fin* < AF, OF < L *fīnis* end, utmost limit, highest point]
—**Syn. 1.** finished, consummate, perfect; select. FINE, CHOICE, ELEGANT, EXQUISITE are terms of praise with reference to quality. FINE is a general term: *a fine horse, person, book.* CHOICE implies a discriminating selection of the object in question: *a choice piece of steak.* ELEGANT suggests a refined and graceful superiority that is generally associated with luxury and a cultivated taste: *elegant furnishings.* EXQUISITE suggests an admirable delicacy, finish, or perfection: *an exquisite piece of lace.* **3.** powdered, pulverized. **5.** acute. —**Ant. 1.** inferior.

fine[2] (fīn), *n., v.,* **fined, fin•ing.** —*n.* **1.** a sum of money imposed as a penalty for an offense or dereliction: *a parking fine.* **2.** *Law.* a fee paid by a feudal tenant to the landlord, as on the renewal of tenure. **3.** *Eng. Law.* (formerly) a conveyance of land through decree of a court, based upon a simulated lawsuit. **4.** *Archaic.* a penalty of any kind. **5. in fine, a.** in short; briefly. **b.** in conclusion; finally: *It was, in fine, a fitting end to the story.* —*v.t.* **6.** to subject to a fine or pecuniary penalty; punish by a fine: *The judge fined him and released him on parole.* [1150–1200; ME *fin* < AF, OF < L *fīnis* end, ML: settlement, payment]

fi•ne[3] (fē′nā), *n. Music.* **1.** the end of a repeated section, whether *da capo* or *dal segno.* **2.** the end of a composition that comprises several movements. [1790–1800; < It < L *fīnis* end]

fine[4] (fēn), *n.* ordinary French brandy, usually with no indication of the maker's name or location. [1920–25; short for F *fine (champagne) de la maison* bar brandy. Cf. FINE CHAMPAGNE]

fine•a•ble (fī′nə bəl), *adj.* finable. —**fine′a•ble•ness,** *n.*

fine′ art′ (fīn), a visual art considered to have been created primarily for aesthetic purposes and judged for its beauty and meaningfulness, specifically, painting, sculpture, drawing, watercolor, graphics, and architecture. Cf. **commercial art.** [1760–70]

fine bouche (fēn bo͞osh′), *French.* refined taste; educated palate. [lit., sensitive mouth]

Fine Cham•pagne (*Fr.* fēn shäN pAN′yᵊ), a high-quality cognac distilled from grapes grown in the Grande Champagne or Petite Champagne vineyards of western France. [1865–70; < F]

fine′ comb′, a fine-tooth comb.

fine-comb (fīn′kōm′), *v.t.* **1.** to use a fine-tooth comb on. **2.** to search through thoroughly.

fine-cut (fīn′kut′), *adj.* cut into very thin strips (contrasted with *rough-cut*): *fine-cut tobacco.* [1830–40, *Amer.*]

fine-draw (fīn′drô′), *v.t.,* **-drew, -drawn, -draw•ing. 1.** *Sewing.* to sew together so finely that the joining is not noticeable. **2.** to draw out to extreme fineness, tenuity, or subtlety. [1725–35] —**fine′-draw′er,** *n.*

fine-drawn (fīn′drôn′), *adj.* drawn out to extreme fineness or thinness. [1830–40]

fine-grain (fīn′grān′), *adj. Photog.* **1.** (of an image) having an inconspicuous or invisible grain. **2.** (of a developer or emulsion) permitting the grain of an image to be inconspicuous or invisible. Also, **fine-grained.** [1925–30]

fine-grained (fīn′grānd′), *adj.* **1.** being of fine grain or texture, as certain types of wood, leather, etc. **2.** *Photog.* fine-grain. [1530–40]

fine•ly (fīn′lē), *adv.* **1.** in a fine manner; excellently; elegantly; delicately; minutely; nicely; subtly. **2.** in fine particles or pieces: *finely chopped onions.* [1275–1325; ME *fineliche.* See FINE[1], -LY]

fine′ nail′ (fīn), a short steel finishing nail from 1 to 1½ in. (2.5 to 3.8 cm) long.

fine•ness (fīn′nis), *n.* **1.** the state or quality of being fine. **2.** the proportion of pure precious metal in an alloy, often expressed in parts per thousand. [1400–50; late ME; see FINE[1], -NESS]

fine′ness ra′tio, 1. *Aeron.* the ratio of the length of a streamlined body, as a rocket or airplane hull, to its maximum diameter. **2.** *Rocketry.* See **aspect ratio** (def. 4a).

fine′ print′ (fīn), **1.** printed matter in small-sized type. **2.** the detailed wording of a contract, lease, insurance policy, or the like, often set in type smaller than the main body of the document and including general restrictions or qualifications that could be considered disadvantageous: *Make sure you read the fine print before signing.* Also called **small print.** [1955–60] —**fine′-print′,** *adj.*

fin•er (fī′nər), *adj. Math.* of or pertaining to a topology or a topological space whose open sets include all the open sets of a second specified topology on the space. Cf. **coarser.** [special use of comp. of FINE[1]]

fin•er•y[1] (fī′nə rē), *n.* fine or showy dress, ornaments, etc. [1670–80; FINE[1] + -ERY]

fin•er•y[2] (fī′nə rē), *n., pl.* **-er•ies.** *Metalworking.* a hearth for converting cast iron into wrought iron; refinery. [1600–10; < MF *finerie,* equiv. to *fin(er)* to refine (see FINE[1]) + *erie* -ERY]

fines herbes (fēn′ erb′, ûrb′; *Fr.* fēn zerb′), *Cookery.* a combination of finely chopped herbs, as parsley, chervil, and chives, used for flavoring soups, sauces, omelets, etc., or as a garnish. [1840–50; < F: fine herbs]

fine•spun (fīn′spun′), *adj.* **1.** spun or drawn out to a fine thread. **2.** highly or excessively refined or subtle. Also, **fine′-spun′.** [1640–50; FINE[1] + SPUN]

fi•nesse (fi ness′), *n., v.,* **-nessed, -ness•ing.** —*n.* **1.** extreme delicacy or subtlety in action, performance, skill, discrimination, taste, etc. **2.** skill in handling a difficult or highly sensitive situation; adroit and artful management: *exceptional diplomatic finesse.* **3.** a trick, artifice, or stratagem. **4.** *Bridge, Whist.* an attempt to win a trick with a card while holding a higher card not in sequence with it, in the hope that the card or cards between will not be played. —*v.i.* **5.** to use finesse or artifice. **6.** to make a finesse at cards. —*v.t.* **7.** to bring about by finesse or artifice. **8.** to make a finesse with (a card). **9.** to force the playing of (a card) by a finesse. [1400–50; late ME: degree of excellence or purity < MF < VL **fīnitia.* See FINE[1], -ICE]
—**Syn. 1, 2.** tact, diplomacy, savoir faire, circumspection, sensitivity, sensibility.

fin•est (fī′nist), *n.* (*used with a plural v.*) *Informal.* the police: *New York City's finest.* [1925–30, *Amer.*]

fi•nes•tra (fi nes′trə), *n.* an aperture, esp. a ventilator in the wall of a tomb. [< It: window < L *fenestra*]

fine′ struc′ture (fīn), *Physics.* a group of lines that are observed in the spectra of certain elements, as hydrogen, and that are caused by various couplings of the azimuthal quantum number and the angular momentum quantum number. Cf. **hyperfine structure.** [1915–20]

fine′-tooth comb′ (fīn′to͞oth′), **1.** a comb having narrow, closely set teeth. **2. go over** or **through with a fine-tooth comb,** to examine in close detail; search thoroughly; fine-comb: *The police went over the apartment with a fine-tooth comb.* Also, **fine′-toothed comb′** (fīn′to͞otht′, -to͞othd′). [1830–40]

fine-tune (fīn′to͞on′, -tyo͞on′), *v.t.,* **-tuned, -tun•ing. 1.** to tune (a radio or television receiver) to produce the optimum reception for the desired station or channel by adjusting a control knob or bar. **2.** tune (def. 16). **3.** to make minor adjustments in so as to produce stability, improvement, or the precise results desired: *to fine-tune the nation's economy.* [1920–25] —**fine′-tun′er,** *n.*

fin•fish (fin′fish′), *n., pl.* (*esp. collectively*) **-fish,** (*esp. referring to two or more kinds or species*) **-fish•es.** a true fish, as distinguished from a shellfish. Also, **fin′ fish′.** [1685–95; FIN[1] + FISH]

fin•foot (fin′fo͝ot′), *n., pl.* **-foots.** any of several aquatic birds of the family Heliornithidae, of South America, Asia, and Africa, related to the rails and coots and characterized by lobate toes. Also called **sun grebe.** [1885–90; FIN[1] + FOOT]

fin-foot•ed (fin′fo͝ot′id), *adj. Ornith.* **1.** web-footed. **2.** having feet with the toes separately furnished with flaps, as the finfoots and coots. [1640–50]

Fin′gal's Cave′ (fing′gəlz), **1.** a cave on the island of Staffa, in the Hebrides, Scotland. 227 ft. (69 m) long; 42 ft. (13 m) wide. **2.** (*italics*) an overture, op. 26, composed in 1832 by Felix Mendelssohn.

fin•ger (fing′gər), *n.* **1.** any of the terminal members of the hand, esp. one other than the thumb. **2.** a part of a glove made to receive a finger. **3.** the breadth of a finger as a unit of measurement; digit. **4.** the length of a finger: approximately 4½ in. (11 cm). **5.** *Slang.* an informer or spy. **6.** something like a finger in form or use, as a projection or pointer: *a finger of land leading out into the bay; the finger on the speedometer.* **7.** any of various projecting parts of machines. **8. burn one's fingers,** to suffer injury or loss by meddling or by acting rashly: *If you get involved in the controversy, you may burn your fingers.* **9. give (someone) the finger,** *Slang.* to express contempt for by or as by the obscene gesture of pointing the middle finger upward while folding the other fingers against the palm. **10. have a finger in the pie, a.** to have an interest or share in something. **b.** to meddle in something. **11. keep one's fingers crossed,** to wish for good luck or success, as in a specific endeavor: *Keep your fingers crossed that I get the job.* **12. lay** or **put one's finger on, a.** to indicate exactly; remember: *I know the name, but I can't put my finger on it.* **b.** to discover; locate: *I haven't been able to lay my finger on the book you requested.* **13. not lift a finger,** to make not even a small attempt; do nothing: *The house was falling into ruin, but he wouldn't lift a finger to repair it.* **14. put the finger on,** *Slang.* finger (def. 22). **15. slip through one's fingers, a.** to elude one, as an opportunity not taken; escape: *She let the chance of a lifetime slip through her fingers.* **b.** to pass or be consumed quickly: *Money just slips through his fingers.* **16. snap one's fingers (at),** to exhibit disdain or contempt (for): *She snaps her fingers at the local gossip.* **17. twist** or **wrap around one's little finger,** to exert one's influence easily or successfully upon: *He has a remarkable talent for twisting people around his little finger.* —*v.t.* **18.** to touch with the fingers; toy or meddle with; handle. **19.** to touch with the fingers so as to mar or spoil: *Please don't finger the vegetables.* **20.** to pilfer; filch. **21.** *Music.* **a.** to play on (an instrument) with the fingers. **b.** to perform or mark (a passage of music) with a certain fingering. **22.** *Slang.* **a.** to inform against or identify (a criminal) to the authorities: *He fingered the man who robbed the bank.* **b.** to designate as a victim, as of murder or other crime. —*v.i.* **23.** to touch or handle something with the fingers. **24.** to extend in or as in the shape of a finger: *Landing piers finger out into the river along the city's shoreline.* [bef. 900; ME, OE; c. G *Finger,* D *vinger,* ON *fingr,* Goth *figgrs*] —**fin′ger•er,** *n.* —**fin′ger•less,** *adj.*

fin•ger•board (fing′gər bôrd′, -bōrd′), *n.* **1.** (of a violin, cello, etc.) the strip of wood on the neck against which the strings are stopped by the fingers. **2.** keyboard. [1665–75; FINGER + BOARD]

fin′ger bowl′, a small bowl to hold water for rinsing the fingers at table. [1855–60]

fin•ger•breadth (fing′gər bredth′, -bretth′), *n.* the breadth of a finger: approximately ¾ in. (2 cm). [1585–95; FINGER + BREADTH]

fin•gered (fing′gərd), *adj.* **1.** having fingers, esp. of a specified kind or number (often used in combination): *a five-fingered glove.* **2.** spoiled or marred by handling, as merchandise. **3.** *Zool., Bot.* digitate. **4.** (of a musical score) marked to show which fingers should be used in playing the notes. [1520–30; FINGER + -ED[3]]

fin•ger•flow•er (fing′gər flou′ər), *n.* See **purple foxglove.** [1620–30; FINGER + FLOWER]

fin′ger food′, food intended to be picked up with the fingers and eaten.

fin•ger•fuck (fing′gər fuk′), *v.t., v.i. Slang* (*vulgar*). to stimulate the genitals of a girl or woman manually.

fin′ger gate′, *Metall.* any of a number of small runners radiating from a single gate to distribute metal in several parts of the mold cavity.

fin′ger grass′, any of various grasses of the genus *Chloris,* having several narrow spikes in a terminal cluster. Also called **windmill grass.** [1815–25, *Amer.*]

fin′ger hole′, 1. one of a set of holes for the finger on the rotating dial of a telephone. **2.** one of two holes or more on a bowling ball for holding the ball. **3.** one of a series of holes on a wind instrument for changing the pitch by being opened or closed. [1875–80]

fin•ger•ing (fing′gər ing), *n.* **1.** the act of a person who fingers. **2.** *Music.* **a.** the action or method of using the fingers in playing on an instrument. **b.** the indication of the way the fingers are to be used in performing a piece of music. [1350–1400; ME; see FINGER, -ING[1]]

Fin′ger Lakes′, a group of elongated glacial lakes in central and W New York: resort region.

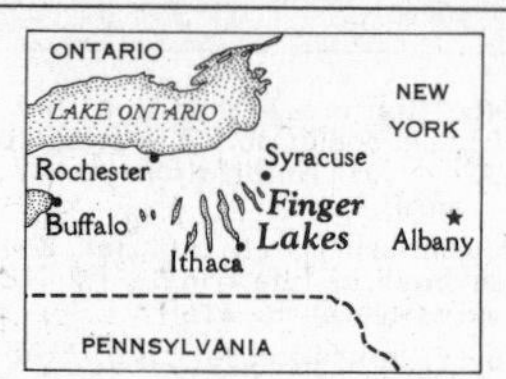

fin•ger•ling (fing′gər ling), *n.* **1.** a young or small fish, esp. a very small salmon or trout. **2.** something very small. [1400–50; late ME: fingerstall. See FINGER, -LING[1]]

fin′ger man′, *Slang.* a person who points out someone to be murdered, robbed, etc. [1925–30, *Amer.*]

fin′ger mark′, a mark, esp. a smudge or stain, made by a finger. Also, **fin′ger•mark′.** [1830–40] —**fin′ger-marked′,** *adj.*

fin•ger•nail (fing′gər nāl′), *n.* **1.** the nail at the end of a finger. **2.** *Print.* a parenthesis. [1200–50; ME; see FINGER, NAIL]

fin′ger paint′, a jellylike paint, used chiefly by children in painting, usually with their fingers. [1945–50] —**fin′ger paint′ing.**

fin•ger-paint (fing′gər pānt′), *v.t., v.i.* to paint by using finger paints. [1950–55]

fin′ger post′, a post with one or more directional signs, terminating in a pointed finger or hand. [1775–85]

fin•ger•print (fing′gər print′), *n.* **1.** an impression of the markings of the inner surface of the last joint of the thumb or other finger. **2.** such an impression made with ink for purposes of identification. **3.** any unique or distinctive pattern that presents unambiguous evidence of a specific person, substance, disease, etc. —*v.t.* **4.** to take or record the fingerprints of. [1855–60; FINGER + PRINT]

fin′ger pup′pet, a miniature puppet fitting over and manipulated by one finger.

fin′ger read′ing, the reading of Braille by means of the fingertips.

fin•ger•spell (fing′gər spel′), *v.t., v.i.* to communicate by fingerspelling. [FINGER + SPELL[1]]

fin•ger•spell•ing (fing′gər spel′ing), *n.* the communication in sign language of a word or other expression by rendering its written form letter by letter in a manual alphabet. [FINGER + SPELLING]

fin•ger•stall (fing′gər stôl′), *n.* a covering used to protect a finger. [1425–75; late ME *fyngyr stalle.* See FINGER, STALL[1]]

fin•ger•tip (fing′gər tip′), *n.* **1.** the tip or end of a finger. **2.** a covering used to protect the end joint of a finger. **3. at one's fingertips, a.** close at hand; easily or immediately available. **b.** at one's command or disposal, as recall of factual information: *He has the answer at his fingertips.* **4. to one's fingertips,** thoroughly; perfectly: *She was a politician to her fingertips.* —*adj.* **5.** extending to the fingertips, as a coat, veil, etc.: *a fingertip jacket.* [1835–45; FINGER + TIP[1]]

fin′ger wave′, *Hairdressing.* a wave set by impressing the fingers into hair dampened by lotion or water. [1930–35]

fi•ni (fē nē′), *adj. French.* finished; done.

fin•i•al (fin′ē əl, fī′nē-), *n.* **1.** *Archit.* a relatively small, ornamental, terminal feature at the top of a gable, pinnacle, etc. **2.** an ornamental termination to the top of a piece of furniture, or of one part of such a piece. **3.** *Typography.* a curve terminating the main stroke of the characters in some italic fonts. [1400–50; late ME, deriv. of L *fīnis* end; see -AL[1]] —**fin′i•aled,** *adj.*

fin•i•cal (fin′i kəl), *adj.* finicky. [1585–95; FINE[1] + -ICAL]

fin•ick (fin′ik), *v.i.* **1.** to affect extreme daintiness or refinement. **2.** to trifle or dawdle. [1700–10; back formation from FINICAL]

fin•ick•y (fin′i kē), *adj.,* **-ick•i•er, -ick•i•est.** excessively particular or fastidious; difficult to please; fussy.

CONCISE ETYMOLOGY KEY: <, descended or borrowed from; >, whence; b., blend of, blended; c., cognate with; cf., compare; deriv., derivative; equiv., equivalent; imit., imitative; obl., oblique; r., replacing; s., stem; sp., spelling, spelled; resp., respelling, respelled; trans., translation; ?, origin unknown; *, unattested; ‡, probably earlier than. See the full key inside the front cover.

Also, **finnicky, fin·i·king** (fin′i king). [1815–25; FINICK + -Y[1]] —**Syn.** exacting, demanding, meticulous; choosy, picky.

fin·ing (fī′ning), *n.* **1.** the process by which fused glass is freed of undissolved gases. **2.** the process of clarifying or filtering a wine or spirit. [1495–1505; FINE[1] + -ING[1]]

fin·is (fin′is, fē nē′, fī′nis), *n.* end; conclusion. [1425–75; late ME (< F) < L *finis;* see FINE[1]]

fi·nis co·ro·nat o·pus (fē′nis kō rō′nät ō′po͝os; *Eng.* fin′is kô rō′nat ō′pəs, kō-), *Latin.* the end crowns the work.

fin·ish (fin′ish), *v.t.* **1.** to bring (something) to an end or to completion; complete: *to finish a novel; to finish breakfast.* **2.** to come to the end of (a course, period of time, etc.): *to finish school.* **3.** to use completely (often fol. by *up* or *off*): *to finish up a can of paint; to finish off the rest of the milk.* **4.** to overcome completely; destroy or kill (often fol. by *off*): *This spray will finish off the cockroaches.* **5.** to complete and perfect in detail; put the final touches on (sometimes fol. by *up*): *He decided to finish his plan more carefully. She finished up a painting.* **6.** to put a finish on (wood, metal, etc.): *We finished the desk in antique red lacquer.* **7.** to perfect (a person) in education, accomplishments, social graces, etc. **8.** to ready (livestock) for market by feeding a diet calculated to produce the desired weight. —*v.i.* **9.** to come to an end: *The course finishes in January.* **10.** to complete a course, project, etc. (sometimes fol. by *up*): *I finished before he did. It was nine o'clock when we finished up.* **11.** (of livestock) to become fattened for market. **12.** **finish with, a.** to bring to completion: *She's finished with her latest novel.* **b.** to put aside, break all relations with, or reject finally: *He's finished with football and will play only baseball now. After the way they treated us, we're finished with them.* —*n.* **13.** the end or conclusion; the final part or last stage. **14.** the end of a hunt, race, etc.: *a close finish.* **15.** a decisive ending: *a fight to the finish.* **16.** the quality of being finished or completed with smoothness, elegance, etc.: *to admire the finish of one's writing.* **17.** educational or social polish. **18.** the manner in which an object is perfected or finished in its preparation, or an effect imparted in finishing. **19.** the surface coating or texture of wood, metal, etc. **20.** something used or serving to finish, complete, or perfect a thing. **21.** woodwork or the like, esp. in the interior of a building, not essential to the structure but used for purposes of ornament, neatness, etc.: *a finish of black walnut.* **22.** Also called **fin′ish coat′, fin′ishing coat′.** a final coat of plaster or paint. **23.** a material for application in finishing. **24.** *Animal Husb.* the fat tissue of livestock. **25.** the flavor remaining in the mouth after a wine has been swallowed. [1300–50; ME *finisshen* < AF, MF *finiss-,* long s. of *finir* < L *fīnīre* to end. See FINE[1]] —**fin′ish·er,** *n.* —**Syn. 1.** terminate, conclude, close. **14.** See **end[1].**

fin·ished (fin′isht), *adj.* **1.** ended or completed. **2.** completed or perfected in all details, as a product: *to pack and ship finished items.* **3.** polished to the highest degree of excellence: *a dazzling and finished piece of writing.* **4.** highly skilled or accomplished: *a finished violinist.* **5.** condemned, doomed, or in the process of extinction: *The aristocracy was finished after the revolution.* **6.** (of livestock) fattened and ready for market. [1575–85; FINISH + -ED[2]]

fin′isher card′, (in manufacturing fibers) the last card in the carding process, for converting stock into roving. Cf. **breaker card, intermediate card.**

fin′ishing nail′, a slender nail with a small globular head, used for finish work, being driven to slightly beneath the surface and covered with putty or the like. Cf. **casing nail.** See illus. under **nail.**

fin′ishing school′, a private school, usually at the high-school or junior-college level, that teaches young women social graces and prepares them for life in society. [1830–40]

fin′ish line′, a line marking the end of a race. [1895–1900]

Fin·is·tère (fin′ə stâr′; *Fr.* fē nē steʀ′), *n.* a department in W France. 804,088; 2714 sq. mi. (7030 sq. km). *Cap.:* Quimper.

Fin·is·terre (fin′ə stâr′; *Sp.* fē′nēs teʀ′ʀe), *n.* **Cape,** a headland in NW Spain: the westernmost point of Spain.

fi·nite (fī′nīt), *adj.* **1.** having bounds or limits; not infinite; measurable. **2.** *Math.* **a.** (of a set of elements) capable of being completely counted. **b.** not infinite or infinitesimal. **c.** not zero. **3.** subject to limitations or conditions, as of space, time, circumstances, or the laws of nature: *man's finite existence on earth.* —*n.* **4.** something that is finite. [1375–1425; late ME < L *fīnītus,* ptp. of *fīnīre* to stop, limit. See FINE[1], -ITE[2]] —**fi′nite·ly,** *adv.* —**fi′nite·ness,** *n.* —**Syn. 1.** bounded, limited, circumscribed, restricted.

fi′nite clause′, a clause with a finite verb in its predicate.

fi′nite dec′imal, *Math.* See **terminating decimal.**

fi′nite dif′ference, *Math.* difference (def. 9c). [1800–10]

fi·nite-di·men·sion·al (fī′nīt di men′shə nl, -dī-), *adj. Math.* (of a vector space) having a basis consisting of a finite number of elements.

fi′nite in′tersection prop′erty, *Math.* the property of a collection of nonempty sets in which the intersections of all possible finite numbers of the sets each contain at least one element.

fi′nitely ad′ditive func′tion, *Math.* a set function that upon operating on the union of a finite number of disjoint sets gives the same result as the sum of the functional values of each set. Cf. **countably additive function.**

fi′nite verb′, a verb form that distinguishes person, number, and tense, and also mood or aspect, as *opens* in *She opens the door.* [1785–95]

fi·ni·to (fi nē′tō), *adj. Informal.* finished; ended. [< It, ptp. of *finire* < L *fīnīre* to FINISH]

fin·i·tude (fin′i to͞od′, -tyo͞od′, fī′ni-), *n.* a finite state or quality. [1635–45; FINI(TE) + -TUDE]

fink (fingk), *Slang.* —*n.* **1.** a strikebreaker. **2.** a labor spy. **3.** an informer; stool pigeon. **4.** a contemptible or thoroughly unattractive person. —*v.i.* **5.** to inform to the police; squeal. **6.** to act as a strikebreaker; scab. **7.** **fink out, a.** to withdraw from or refuse to support a project, activity, scheme, etc.; renege: *He said he'd lend me his motorcycle, but he finked out.* **b.** to become untrustworthy. [1900–05, *Amer.;* compared with G *Fink* lit., FINCH, colloquial epithet for an undesirable person, esp. an untidy or loose-living one (often in compounds, as *Duckfink* sycophant, *Schmierfink* untidy writer); but the transmission of this word to E and the range of meanings of the E word have not been clarified fully]

fin′ keel′, *Naut.* a finlike projection extending downward from the keel of a sailboat, serving to prevent lateral motion and acting as additional ballast.

Fin·land (fin′lənd), *n.* **1.** Finnish, **Suomi.** a republic in N Europe: formerly a province of the Russian Empire. 4,700,000; 130,119 sq. mi. (337,010 sq. km). *Cap.:* Helsinki. **2.** **Gulf of,** an arm of the Baltic, S of Finland.

Fin·land·er (fin′lən dər), *n.* an inhabitant of Finland, esp. a native who customarily speaks Swedish. [1720–30; FINLAND + -ER[1]]

Fin·land·i·a (fin lan′dē ə), *n.* symphonic poem, op. 26, composed in 1899 by Jean Sibelius.

Fin·land·i·za·tion (fin′lən də zā′shən), *n.* **1.** the neutralization of a country in terms of its allegiance to the superpowers, in the way that the Soviet Union has rendered Finland neutral and friendly without making it a satellite state or requiring that it adopt Communism. **2.** such a neutral status pursued as a deliberate act of policy by a lesser power. [1965–70; FINLAND + -IZATION]

Fin·land·ize (fin′lən dīz′), *v.t.,* **-ized, -iz·ing.** to subject to Finlandization. Also, *esp. Brit.,* **Fin′land·ise′.** [1970–75; back formation from FINLANDIZATION]

Fin·lay (fin′lā, -lē, fin lī′), *n.* **Car·los Juan** (kär′lōs wän), 1833–1915, U.S. physician, born in Cuba: first to suggest mosquito as carrier of yellow fever.

fin·let (fin′lit), *n.* a small, detached ray of a fin in certain fishes, as mackerels. [1870–75; FIN + -LET]

Fin·let·ter (fin′let′ər), *n.* **Thomas Knight,** 1893–1980, U.S. lawyer and diplomat.

Fin·ley (fin′lē), *n.* a male given name.

fin·mark (fin′märk′), *n.* the markka of Finland. Also, **finnmark.** [< Sw; see FINN, MARK[2]]

Finn (fin), *n.* **1.** a native or inhabitant of Finland. **2.** any native speaker of Finnish. **3.** a native speaker of any Finnic language.

Finn (fin), *n. Irish Legend.* a leader of the Fenian warriors and the father of Ossian: the subject of many legends. Also, **Fionn.** Also called **Fionn MacCumal.**

Finn., Finnish. Also, **Finn**

fin·nan had·die (fin′ən had′ē), smoked haddock. Also, **fin′nan had′dock.** [1805–15; lit., haddock of *Findhorn,* fishing port in Scotland; see -IE]

Finn·bo·ga·dót·tir (fin′bō gə dô′tər; *Icel.* fin′bô gä-dô′tiʀ), *n.* **Vig·dís** (*Icel.* vig dēs′), born 1930, Icelandic political leader: president since 1980.

finned (find), *adj.* having fins. [1300–50; ME *finnede.* See FIN, -ED[3]]

Fin′ne·gans Wake′ (fin′i gənz), a novel (1922–39) by James Joyce.

Fin·ney (fin′ē), *n.* **Charles Gran·di·son** (gran′di sən), 1792–1875, U.S. clergyman and educator.

Finn·ic (fin′ik), *n.* **1.** a subdivision of the Finno-Ugric branch of the Uralic language family that includes Finnish, Estonian, Lapp, Mordvin, Udmurt, Mari, and Komi. —*adj.* **2.** of, pertaining to, or characteristic of Finnic. Also, **Finnish.** [1660–70; FINN + -IC]

fin·nick (fin′ik), *v.i.* finick.

fin·nick·y (fin′i kē), *adj.* **-nick·i·er, -nick·i·est.** finicky.

Finn·ish (fin′ish), *n.* **1.** the principal language of Finland, a Uralic language related closely to Estonian and remotely to Hungarian. *Abbr.:* Finn. **2.** Finnic. —*adj.* **3.** of or pertaining to Finland or its inhabitants. **4.** Finnic. [1780–90; FINN + -ISH[1]]

finn·mark (fin′märk′), *n.* finmark.

Finno-, a combining form representing **Finnish** or **Finnic** in compound words: *Finno-Ugric.* [FINN + -O-]

Fin′no-Rus′so War′ (fin′ō rus′ō), the war (1939–40) between Finland and the Soviet Union.

Fin·no-U·gri·an (fin′ō o͞o′grē ən, -yo͞o′-), *adj.* **1.** pertaining to the Finns and the Ugrians. **2.** Finno-Ugric. —*n.* **3.** Finno-Ugric. [1875–80]

Fin·no-U·gric (fin′ō o͞o′grik, -yo͞o′-), *n.* **1.** the major branch of the Uralic family of languages, subdivided into Finnic, which includes Finnish and Estonian, and Ugric, which includes Hungarian. —*adj.* **2.** of or pertaining to these languages. Also, **Finno-Ugrian.** [1875–80]

fin·ny (fin′ē), *adj.,* **-ni·er, -ni·est.** **1.** pertaining to or abounding in fish. **2.** having fins; finned. **3.** finlike. [1580–90; FIN + -Y[1]]

fi·no (fē′nō; *Sp.* fē′nô), *n.* a pale, very dry sherry of Spain. [1840–50; < Sp: lit., FINE[1]]

fi·no·cchi·o (fi nō′kē ō′), *n., pl.* **-cchi·os.** See **Florence fennel.** Also, **fi·no′chi·o′.** [1715–25; < It *finocchio* < VL **fenuculum,* for L *fēniculum, faeniculum* FENNEL]

fin′ ray′, ray[1] (def. 9b). [1860–65]

fin. sec., financial secretary.

Fin·sen (fin′sən), *n.* **Niels Ry·berg** (nēls ʀʏ′beʀ), 1860–1904, Danish physician: Nobel prize 1903.

fin·spot (fin′spot′), *n.* any clinid fish of the genus *Paraclinus,* having an eyelike spot on the dorsal fin, as *P. integripinnis,* of California. [FIN + SPOT]

Fin·ster·aar·horn (fin′stər är′hôrn), *n.* a mountain in S central Switzerland: highest peak of the Bernese Alps, 14,026 ft. (4275 m).

fin′ whale′, finback. [1880–85]

F.I.O., free in and out: a term of contract in which a ship charterer pays for loading and unloading.

Fi·o·na (fē ō′nə), *n.* a female given name.

Fionn (fyo͞on, fin), *n. Irish Legend.* Finn. Also called **Fionn′ Mac·Cumal′** (mə ko͞ol′).

fiord (fyôrd, fyōrd; *Norw.* fyōʀ, fyo͞oʀ), *n.* fjord.

fio·ri·tu·ra (fē ôr′i to͞or′ə, -ōr′-; *It.* fyô′ʀē to͞o′ʀä), *n., pl.* **-tu·re** (-to͞or′ā; *It.* -to͞o′ʀe). *Music.* the ornamentation of a melody, often extemporized by the performer, as in Italian opera during the 18th century. [1835–45; < It, equiv. to *fiorit(o)* flowery, orig. ptp. of *fiorire* to FLOWER + *-ura* -URE]

fip′pen·ny bit′ (fip′ə nē, fip′nē), the Spanish half real, the value of which was about six cents. Also called **fip′penny piece′.** [1795–1805, *Amer.;* assimilated var. of *five-penny bit*]

fip·ple (fip′əl), *n. Music.* a plug stopping the upper end of a pipe, as a recorder or a whistle, and having a narrow slit through which the player blows. [1620–30; perh. special use of dial. *fipple* loose lower lip, pouting lip; cf. ON *flipi* lower lip of a horse, Norw *flipe* flap, lappet. See FLIP[1], FLAP, FLABBY]

fip′ple flute′, *Music.* a recorder or other flutelike instrument equipped with a fipple. [1910–15]

fiqh (fik), *n. Islam.* the system of jurisprudence: the legal foundation of Islamic religious, political, and civil life. Also, **fikh.** [< Ar]

fir (fûr), *n.* **1.** any coniferous tree belonging to the genus *Abies,* of the pine family, characterized by its pyramidal style of growth, flat needles, and erect cones. **2.** the wood of such a tree. [1250–1300; ME *firre,* OE *fyrh;* c. OS *furie;* akin to OE *furh-* (in *fuhrwudu* pine), ON *fura* fir, L *quercus* oak (< **perkwu-*)]

Fir·bolg (fēr′bul əg), *n., pl.* **-bolgs,** (*esp. collectively*) **-bolg.** *Irish Legend.* any member of a pre-Celtic race from Greece who were first defeated by the Fomorians and ousted by the Tuatha De Danann.

Fir·dau·si (fēr dou′sē), *n.* (*Abul Qasim Mansu* or *Hasan*), 932–1020, Persian poet. Also, **Ferdus, Fir·dou·si, Fir·du·si** (fər do͞o′sē).

fire (fīᵊr), *n., v.,* **fired, fir·ing.** —*n.* **1.** a state, process, or instance of combustion in which fuel or other material is ignited and combined with oxygen, giving off light, heat, and flame. **2.** a burning mass of material, as on a hearth or in a furnace. **3.** the destructive burning of a building, town, forest, etc.; conflagration. **4.** heat used for cooking, esp. the lighted burner of a stove: *Put the kettle on the fire.* **5.** See **Greek fire.** **6.** flashing light; luminous appearance. **7.** brilliance, as of a gem. **8.** burning passion; excitement or enthusiasm; ardor. **9.** liveliness of imagination. **10.** fever or inflammation. **11.** severe trial or trouble; ordeal. **12.** exposure to fire as a means of torture or ordeal. **13.** strength, as of an alcoholic beverage. **14.** a spark or sparks. **15.** the discharge of firearms: *enemy fire.* **16.** the effect of firing military weapons: *to pour fire upon the enemy.* **17.** *Brit.* a gas or electric heater used for heating a room. **18.** *Literary.* a luminous object, as a star: *heavenly fires.* **19.** **between two fires,** under physical or verbal attack from two or more sides simultaneously: *The senator is between two fires because of his stand on the bill.* **20.** **build a fire under,** *Informal.* to cause or urge to take action, make a decision quickly, or work faster: *If somebody doesn't build a fire under that committee, it will never reach a decision.* **21.** **catch fire, a.** Also, **catch on fire.** to become ignited; burn: *The sofa caught fire from a lighted cigarette.* **b.** to create enthusiasm: *His new book did not catch fire among his followers.* **22.** **fight fire with fire,** to use the same tactics as one's opponent; return like for like. **23.** **go through fire and water,** to brave any danger or endure any trial: *He said he would go through fire and water to win her hand.*

CONCISE PRONUNCIATION KEY: act, cāpe, dâre, pärt; set, ēqual; *if,* īce; ox, ōver, ôrder, oil, bo͝ok, bo͞ot, out; up, ûrge; child; sing; shoe; thin, *that;* zh as in *treasure.* ə = a as in *alone,* e as in *system,* i as in *easily,* o as in *gallop,* u as in *circus;* ᵊ as in *fire* (fīᵊr), *hour* (ouᵊr). l and n can serve as syllabic consonants, as in *cradle* (krād′l), and *button* (but′n). See the full key inside the front cover.

24. hang fire, a. to be delayed in exploding, or fail to explode. **b.** to be undecided, postponed, or delayed: *The new housing project is hanging fire because of concerted opposition.* **25. miss fire, a.** to fail to explode or discharge, as a firearm. **b.** to fail to produce the desired effect; be unsuccessful: *He repeated the joke, but it missed fire the second time.* **26. on fire, a.** ignited; burning; afire. **b.** eager; ardent; zealous: *They were on fire to prove themselves in competition.* **27. play with fire,** to trifle with a serious or dangerous matter: *He didn't realize that insulting the border guards was playing with fire.* **28. set fire to, a.** to cause to burn; ignite. **b.** to excite; arouse; inflame: *The painting set fire to the composer's imagination.* Also, **set on fire. 29. take fire, a.** to become ignited; burn. **b.** to become inspired with enthusiasm or zeal: *Everyone who heard him speak immediately took fire.* **30. under fire, a.** under attack, esp. by military forces. **b.** under censure or criticism: *The school administration is under fire for its policies.*

—*v.t.* **31.** to set on fire. **32.** to supply with fuel; attend to the fire of: *They fired the boiler.* **33.** to expose to the action of fire; subject to heat. **34.** to apply heat to in a kiln for baking or glazing; burn. **35.** to heat very slowly for the purpose of drying, as tea. **36.** to inflame, as with passion; fill with ardor. **37.** to inspire. **38.** to light or cause to glow as if on fire. **39.** to discharge (a gun). **40.** to project (a bullet or the like) by or as if by discharging from a gun. **41.** to subject to explosion or explosive force, as a mine. **42.** to hurl; throw: *to fire a stone through a window.* **43.** to dismiss from a job. **44.** *Vet. Med.* to apply a heated iron to (the skin) in order to create a local inflammation of the superficial structures, with the intention of favorably affecting deeper inflammatory processes. **45.** to drive out or away by or as by fire.

—*v.i.* **46.** to take fire; be kindled. **47.** to glow as if on fire. **48.** to become inflamed with passion; become excited. **49.** to shoot, as a gun. **50.** to discharge a gun: *to fire at a fleeing enemy.* **51.** to hurl a projectile. **52.** *Music.* to ring the bells of a chime all at once. **53.** (of plant leaves) to turn yellow or brown before the plant matures. **54.** (of an internal-combustion engine) to cause ignition of the air-fuel mixture in a cylinder or cylinders. **55.** (of a nerve cell) to discharge an electric impulse. **56. fire away,** *Informal.* to begin to talk and continue without slackening, as to ask a series of questions: *The reporters fired away at the president.* **57. fire off, a.** to discharge (as weapons, ammunition, etc.): *Police fired off canisters of tear gas.* **b.** to write and send hurriedly: *She fired off an angry letter to her congressman.* [bef. 900; (n.) ME; OE *fȳr;* c. ON *fúrr,* G *Feuer,* Gk *pŷr* (see PYRO-); (v.) ME *firen* to kindle, inflame, deriv. of the n.] —**fir′er,** *n.*

fire′ alarm′, 1. a signal that warns that a fire has started. **2.** a bell, buzzer, siren, horn, etc., that provides such a signal. [1840–50, *Amer.*]

fire-and-brim·stone (fīər′ən brim′stōn′), *adj.* threatening punishment in the hereafter: *a fire-and-brimstone sermon.* [1795–1805]

fire′ ant′, any of several omnivorous ants, as the migrant *Solenopsis geminata* originating in tropical and subtropical South America, having a sting that produces a burning sensation. [1790–1800]

fire′ appara′tus, equipment for extinguishing destructive fires. [1900–05]

fire′ ar′ea, any area of a building that is enclosed by fire-resistant partitions.

fire·arm (fīər′ärm′), *n.* a small arms weapon, as a rifle or pistol, from which a projectile is fired by gunpowder. [1640–50; FIRE + ARM[2]] —**fire′armed′,** *adj.*

fire·back (fīər′bak′), *n.* **1.** a piece, lining the rear of a fireplace, usually of cast iron. **2.** the rear of a fireplace. [1870–75; FIRE + BACK[1]]

fire·ball (fīər′bôl′), *n.* **1.** a ball of fire, as the sun; a shooting star. **2.** a luminous meteor, sometimes exploding. **3.** lightning having the appearance of a globe of fire; ball lightning. **4.** the highly luminous central portion of a nuclear explosion. **5.** a ball filled with explosive or combustible material, used as a projectile to injure the enemy by explosion or to set fire to their works. **6.** *Informal.* an exceptionally energetic or ambitious person. [1545–55; FIRE + BALL[1]]

fire·ball·er (fīər′bô′lər), *n. Baseball Slang.* a hard-throwing fastball pitcher. [FIREBALL + -ER[1]]

fire′ balloon′, a montgolfier. [1815–25]

fire·base (fīər′bās′), *n. Mil.* an artillery base, esp. one set up quickly to support advancing troops or to forestall enemy advances. [1965–70; FIRE + BASE[1]]

fire′ bee′tle, any of numerous click beetles of the genus *Pyrophorus,* of tropical America, having luminous reddish or greenish spots on the body. [1835–45]

fire·bird (fīər′bûrd′), *n.* any of several small birds having bright red or orange plumage, esp. the Baltimore oriole. [1815–25; FIRE + BIRD]

Fire·bird, The (fīər′bûrd′), a ballet (1910) with music by Stravinsky.

fire′ blight′, *Plant Pathol.* a disease of pears, apples, quinces, etc., characterized by blossom, twig, and fruit blight and stem cankers, caused by a bacterium, *Erwinia amylovora.* [17[illegible]0; from the burnt look of the foliage]

fire·board (fīər′bôrd′, -bōrd′), *n.* **1.** a board used to close a fireplace. **2.** *Chiefly South Midland U.S.* a mantel; mantelpiece. [1820–30; FIRE + BOARD]

fire·boat (fīər′bōt′), *n.* a powered vessel equipped to fight fires on boats, docks, shores, etc. [1875–80; FIRE + BOAT]

CONCISE ETYMOLOGY KEY: <, descended or borrowed from; >, whence; b., blend of, blended; c., cognate with; cf., compare; deriv., derivative; equiv., equivalent; imit., imitative; obl., oblique; r., replacing; s., stem; sp., spelling, spelled; resp., respelling, respelled; trans., translation; ?, origin unknown; *, unattested; ‡, probably earlier than. See the full key inside the front cover.

fire·bomb (fīər′bom′), *n.* **1.** an explosive device with incendiary effects. —*v.t.* **2.** to attack with a firebomb or firebombs. [1895–1900; FIRE + BOMB]

fire′ boss′, *Mining.* a person who inspects a mine for the presence of noxious gases, dangerous roofs, and other hazards. Also called **gasman;** *Brit.,* **fireman.** Cf. **mine examiner.** [1880–85, *Amer.*]

fire·box (fīər′boks′), *n.* **1.** the box or chamber containing the fire of a steam boiler, furnace, etc. **2.** the furnace of a locomotive, where coal, oil, or other fuel is burned to generate steam. **3.** a box or panel with a device for notifying the fire station of an outbreak of fire. **4.** *Obs.* a tinderbox. [1545–55; FIRE + BOX[1]]

fire·brand (fīər′brand′), *n.* **1.** a piece of burning wood or other material. **2.** a person who kindles strife or encourages unrest; an agitator; troublemaker. [1175–1225; ME; see FIRE, BRAND]

fire·brat (fīər′brat′), *n.* a bristletail, *Thermobia domestica,* that lives in areas around furnaces, boilers, steampipes, etc. [1890–95; FIRE + BRAT]

fire·break (fīər′brāk′), *n.* a strip of plowed or cleared land made to check the spread of a prairie or forest fire. [1890–95; FIRE + BREAK]

fire·brick (fīər′brik′), *n.* a brick made of fire clay. [1785–95; FIRE + BRICK]

fire′ brigade′, 1. a group of firefighters, esp. as formed temporarily or called upon to assist a fire department in an emergency. **2.** a small fire department privately employed by an institution. [1825–35]

fire·bug (fīər′bug′), *n. Informal.* arsonist; incendiary; pyromaniac. [1870–75, *Amer.;* FIRE + BUG[1]]

fire·bush (fīər′bo͝osh′), *n.* any of several shrubs having bright red flowers or foliage, as the burning bush. [1880–85; FIRE + BUSH[1]]

fire′ cher′ry. See **pin cherry.** [1895–1900, *Amer.*]

fire′ chief′, the officer in charge of a municipality's fire department or departments. [1885–90]

fire′ clay′, a refractory clay used for making crucibles, firebricks, etc. [1810–20]

fire′ code′. See under **code** (def. 3).

fire′ com′pany, 1. a company of firefighters. **2.** a fire-insurance company. [1730–40, *Amer.*]

fire′ control′, *Mil.* technical and sometimes automatic supervision of artillery or naval gunfire on a target, as for range, elevation, etc. [1885–90] —**fire′-con·trol′,** *adj.*

fire·crack·er (fīər′krak′ər), *n.* a paper or cardboard cylinder filled with an explosive and having a fuse, for discharging to make a noise, as during a celebration. [1820–30, *Amer.;* FIRE + CRACKER]

fire′cracker flow′er, 1. a plant, *Dichelostemma ida-maia,* of the amaryllis family, native to California and Oregon, having clusters of tubular scarlet flowers. **2.** crossandra. [1905–10, *Amer.*]

fire·crest (fīər′krest′), *n.* a European kinglet, *Regulus ignicapillus,* having a bright, orange-red patch on the top of the head. [1835–45; FIRE + CREST]

fire′ cross′. See **fiery cross.**

fire-cure (fīər′kyo͝or′), *v.t.,* **-cured, -cur·ing.** to cure (tobacco) by means of open fires, the smoke and flame imparting a creosotic flavor. [1880–85, *Amer.*]

fire′ cur′tain. See **safety curtain.** [1910–15, *Amer.*]

fire·damp (fīər′damp′), *n. Mining.* **1.** a combustible gas consisting chiefly of methane, formed esp. in coal mines, and dangerously explosive when mixed with certain proportions of atmospheric air. **2.** the explosive mixture itself. [1670–80; FIRE + DAMP]

fire′ depart′ment, 1. the department of a municipal government charged with the prevention and extinguishing of fire. **2.** the personnel in such a department. [1815–25, *Amer.*]

fire·dog (fīər′dôg′, -dog′), *n. Chiefly South Midland and Southern U.S.* andiron. [1785–95; FIRE + DOG]

fire′ door′, 1. a door through which a boiler or furnace is fired or through which the fire is inspected. **2.** a fireproof or fire-resistant door in a building, intended to isolate an area from fire. [1830–40]

fire·drake (fīər′drāk′), *n.* a mythical fiery dragon. [bef. 900; ME *fyrdrake,* OE *fȳrdraca.* See FIRE, DRAKE[2]]

fire′ drill′, 1. a practice drill for a company of firefighters, the crew of a ship, etc., to train them in their duties in case of fire. **2.** a drill for pupils in a school, employees in a factory, etc., to train them in the manner of exit to be followed in case of fire. [1890–95]

fire-eat·er (fīər′ē′tər), *n.* **1.** an entertainer who pretends to eat fire. **2.** an easily provoked, belligerent person. **3.** *U.S. Hist.* an early and extreme Southern advocate of secession before the Civil War. [1665–75] —**fire′-eat′ing,** *adj., n.*

fire′ en′gine, a vehicle equipped for firefighting, now usually a motor truck having a motor-driven pump for shooting water or chemical solutions at high pressure. Also called **fire truck.** [1670–80]

fire′ escape′, an apparatus or structure used to escape from a burning building, as a metal stairway down an outside wall. [1670–80]

fire′ extin′guisher, a portable container, usually filled with special chemicals for putting out a fire. [1830–40]

fire·fight (fīər′fīt′), *n.* an exchange of gunfire between two opposing forces, esp. a skirmish between military forces. [1895–1900; FIRE + FIGHT]

fire·fight·er (fīər′fī′tər), *n.* a person who fights destructive fires. Also, **fire′ fight′er.** [1900–05; FIRE + FIGHTER] —**fire′fight′ing,** *n., adj.*

fire·fly (fīər′flī′), *n., pl.* **-flies.** any nocturnal beetle of the family Lampyridae, characterized by a soft body with a light-producing organ at the rear of the abdomen. Also called **glowfly, lightning bug.** Cf. **glowworm.** [1650–60; FIRE + FLY[2]]

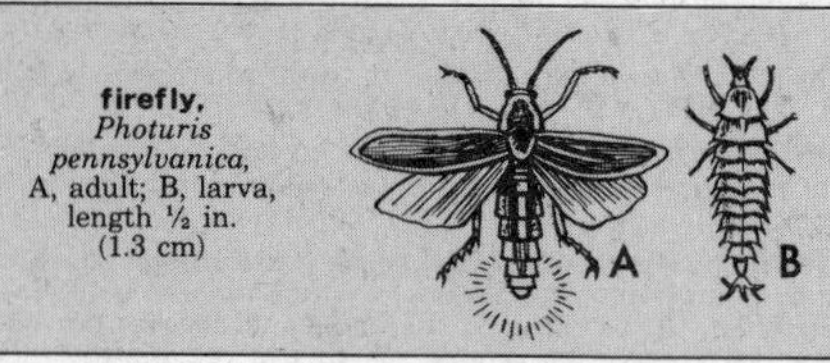

firefly, *Photuris pennsylvanica,* A, adult; B, larva, length ½ in. (1.3 cm)

fire′ gild′ing, a process of gilding metalwork in which the metal base is coated with an amalgam of gold and mercury, the latter subsequently being driven off by heat. Also called **amalgam gilding.** [1825–35]

fire·guard (fīər′gärd′), *n.* **1.** a protective framework of wire in front of a fireplace. **2.** *Western U.S.* a firebreak. [1825–35, *Amer.;* FIRE + GUARD]

fire′ hat′, a helmet worn by a firefighter as a defense against falling materials from burning structures. [1850–55, *Amer.*]

fire hat

fire·horse (fīər′hôrs′), *n.* a horse used to pull a horse-drawn fire engine. [1825–35, *Amer.;* FIRE + HORSE]

fire′ hose′, a special heavy-duty hose for use in fighting destructive fires.

fire·house (fīər′hous′), *n., pl.* **-hous·es** (-hou′ziz). See **fire station.** [1895–1900; FIRE + HOUSE]

fire′ hy′drant, a hydrant for use in extinguishing fires. Also called **fireplug.** [1940–45]

fire′ insur′ance, insurance covering any loss or damage caused by fire. [1790–1800]

fire′ i′rons, the implements used for tending a fireplace, as tongs and poker. [1250–1300; ME *fire-yren*]

Fire′ Is′land, a narrow sand spit off S Long Island, New York: summer resort and lighthouse station. ¼–½ mi. (0.4–0.8 km) wide; 30 mi. (48 km) long.

fire·less (fīər′lis), *adj.* **1.** lacking fire; without a fire. **2.** lacking spirit or enthusiasm. [1350–1400; ME *fuyrles.* See FIRE, -LESS]

fire′less cook′er, an insulated container that seals in heat to cook food. [1905–10, *Amer.*]

fire·light (fīər′līt′), *n.* the light from a fire, as on a hearth. [bef. 900; ME *firlight,* OE *fȳrlēoht.* See FIRE, LIGHT[1]]

fire′ line′, firebreak. [1900–05, *Amer.*]

fire·lock (fīər′lok′), *n.* a gun having a lock in which the priming is ignited by sparks struck from flint and steel, as the flintlock musket. [1540–50; FIRE + LOCK[1]]

fire·man (fīər′mən), *n., pl.* **-men. 1.** a person employed to extinguish or prevent fires; firefighter. **2.** a person employed to tend fires; stoker. **3.** *Railroads.* **a.** a person employed to fire and lubricate a steam locomotive. **b.** a person employed to assist the engineer of a diesel or electric locomotive. **4.** *U.S. Navy.* an enlisted person assigned to the care and operation of a ship's machinery. **5.** *Brit. Mining.* See **fire boss. 6.** *Baseball.* See **relief pitcher.** [1620–30 for sense "gunner"; FIRE + -MAN]

—**Usage.** See **-man.**

fire′ mar′shal, 1. an official heading a bureau for the prevention or investigation of fires. **2.** a person who has charge of the fire-prevention equipment and personnel of an industrial plant. [1860–65]

Fi·ren·ze (fē ren′dze), *n.* Italian name of **Florence.**

fire′ o′pal, a red Mexican opal, often with a color play. [1810–20]

fire·pan (fīər′pan′), *n.* a metal grate for holding hot coals. [bef. 1000; ME, OE; see FIRE, PAN[1]]

fire′ pink′, a plant, *Silene virginica,* of the pink family, having loose clusters of brilliant scarlet flowers. [1855–60, *Amer.*]

fire·pit (fīər′pit′), *n.* a pit dug into the ground or made from stones, masonry, etc., for keeping a fire used for cooking or warmth. [FIRE + PIT[1]]

fire·place (fīər′plās′), *n.* **1.** the part of a chimney that opens into a room and in which fuel is burned; hearth. **2.** any open structure, usually of masonry, for keeping a fire, as at a campsite. [1645–55; FIRE + PLACE]

fire-plow (fīər′plou′), *n.* a stick that is rubbed in a wooden groove to produce sparks for igniting a fire. [1890–95]

fire·plug (fīər′plug′), *n.* See **fire hydrant.** [1705–15; FIRE + PLUG]

fire′ point′, *Chem.* the lowest temperature at which a volatile liquid, after its vapors have been ignited, will give off vapors at a rate sufficient to sustain combustion.

fire-pol·ish (fīər′pol′ish), *v.t. Glassmaking.* to smooth (glass) by reheating to remove tool marks or other imperfections in the surface.

fire′ pot′, the part of a household furnace in which the fire is made. Also, **fire′pot′.** [1620–30]

fire•pow•er (fīər′pou′ər), *n.* **1.** the capability of a military force, unit, or weapons system as measured by the amount of gunfire, number of missiles, etc., deliverable to a target. **2.** the capability or potential, as of an organization, for action or achieving results. Also, **fire′ pow′er.** [1910–15; FIRE + POWER]

fire•proof (fīər′pro͞of′), *adj.* **1.** resistant to destruction by fire. **2.** totally or almost totally unburnable. —*v.t.* **3.** to make fireproof. [1630–40; FIRE + -PROOF]

fire•proof•ing (fīər′pro͞o′fing), *n.* **1.** the act or process of rendering fireproof. **2.** material for use in making anything fireproof. [1865–70; FIREPROOF + -ING[1]]

fire′ red′, **1.** a strong reddish-orange color. **2.** Also called **fire′ red′ ton′er.** a brilliant reddish-orange dye. [1350–1400; ME]

fire′ resist′ance, the amount of resistance of a material or construction to fire.

fire-re•sist•ant (fīər′ri zis′tənt), *adj.* **1.** totally or almost totally unburnable. **2.** fire-retardant. [1900–05]

fire-re•tard•ant (fīər′ri tär′dnt), *adj.* able to slow or check the spread of destructive fire. [1910–15]

fire•room (fīər′ro͞om′, -ro͝om′), *n. Naut.* a chamber in which the boilers of a steam vessel are fired. Also called **stokehold, stokehole.** [1830–40; *Amer.*]

fire•safe (fīər′sāf′), *adj.* being so constructed or protected as to be safe from destruction by fire. [FIRE + SAFE] —**fire′safe′ty,** *n., adj.*

fire′ sale′, **1.** a special sale of merchandise actually or supposedly damaged by fire. **2.** a sale, as of assets, at reduced prices, in order to raise money quickly. [1890–95, *Amer.*] —**fire′-sale′,** *adj.*

fire′ screen′, a screen placed in front of a fireplace for protection, esp. from sparks. [1750–60]

fire′ set′ting, *Mining.* an ancient method of shattering rock by building a fire against it so as to cause it to split as a result of uneven internal stresses.

fire′ ship′, a vessel loaded with combustibles and explosives, ignited, and set adrift to destroy an enemy's ships or constructions. [1580–90]

fire•side (fīər′sīd′), *n.* **1.** Also called **hearthside.** the space about a fire or hearth. **2.** home. **3.** home or family life. —*adj.* **4.** informal and friendly in manner: *The politician's fireside manner helped her win votes.* [1555–65; FIRE + SIDE[1]]

fire′side chat′, an informal address by a political leader over radio or television, esp. as given by President Franklin D. Roosevelt beginning in 1933.

fire′ sign′, any of the three astrological signs, Aries, Leo, or Sagittarius, that are grouped together because of the shared attributes of enthusiasm, vitality, and interest in spiritual things. Cf. **triplicity.**

fire′ sta′tion, a building in which firefighting apparatus and usually fire department personnel are housed; firehouse. [1895–1900]

fire•stone (fīər′stōn′), *n.* a fire-resisting stone, esp. a kind of sandstone used in fireplaces, furnaces, etc. [bef. 1000; late ME *fyyrstone,* OE *fȳrstān.* See FIRE, STONE]

Fire•stone (fīər′stōn′), *n.* **Harvey Samuel,** 1868–1938, U.S. industrialist and rubber manufacturer.

fire•stop (fīər′stop′), *n.* any object built into a building frame to block a concealed hollow space through which a fire might pass from one part of the building to another. [1895–1900; *Amer.*; FIRE + STOP]

fire•storm (fīər′stôrm′), *n.* **1.** an atmospheric phenomenon, caused by a large fire, in which the rising column of air above the fire draws in strong winds often accompanied by rain. **2.** a raging fire of great intensity, as one fueled by oil or gas, that spreads rapidly. Also, **fire′ storm′.** [1575–85; FIRE + STORM]

fire′ support′, support given by artillery and aircraft to infantry and armored vehicles.

fire′ tem′ple, a place of worship for Zoroastrians. [1735–45]

fire•thorn (fīər′thôrn′), *n.* any of several evergreen, thorny Asian shrubs belonging to the genus *Pyracantha,* of the rose family, many species of which are cultivated for their foliage and ornamental fruits. [1905–10, *Amer.*]

fire′ tow′er, **1.** a tower, as on a mountain, from which a watch for fires is kept. **2.** See **drill tower.** [1820–30]

fire•trap (fīər′trap′), *n.* **1.** a building that, because of its age, material, structure, or the like, is esp. dangerous in case of fire. **2.** (in a building) any arrangement of structural, flooring, and finish members creating concealed passages through which fire can spread to other parts of the building. [1880–85; FIRE + TRAP[1]]

fire′ truck′. See **fire engine.** [1930–35; FIRE + TRUCK[1]]

fire′-tube boil′er (fīər′to͞ob′, -tyo͞ob′), any boiler for generating steam by passing hot gases and other combustible products through tubes **(fire′ tubes′)** immersed in water to a chimney or uptake. Cf. **water-tube boiler.**

fire′ wall′, a partition made of fireproof material to prevent the spread of a fire from one part of a building or ship to another or to isolate an engine compartment, as on a plane, automobile, etc. Also, **fire′wall′.** [1750–60, *Amer.*]

fire•ward•en (fīər′wôr′dn), *n.* a person having authority in the prevention or extinguishing of fires, as in towns or camps. [1705–15; FIRE + WARDEN]

fire•wa•ter (fīər′wô′tər, -wot′ər), *n.* alcoholic drink; liquor. [1820–30; FIRE + WATER; prob. a trans. of an expression in an Algonquian language, as Ojibwa *iš-kote·wa·po·* whiskey (earlier, other distilled liquors), equiv. to *iškote·w-,* comb. form of *iškote·* fire + *-a·po·* liquid]

fire•weed (fīər′wēd′), *n.* any of various plants appearing in recently burned clearings, as the willow herb, *Epilobium angustifolium.* [1775–85, *Amer.*; FIRE + WEED[1]]

fire•wood (fīər′wo͝od′), *n.* wood suitable for fuel. [1350–1400; ME *ferwode.* See FIRE, WOOD[1]]

fire•work (fīər′wûrk′), *n.* **1.** Often, **fireworks.** a combustible or explosive device for producing a striking display of light or a loud noise, used for signaling or as part of a celebration. **2.** **fireworks, a.** a pyrotechnic display. **b.** a display of violent temper or fierce activity. **c.** any spectacular display, esp. of wit or of a technical feat by a musician or dancer. [1550–60; FIRE + WORK]

fire•worm (fīər′wûrm′), *n.* **1.** the larva of any of several moths, as *Rhopobota naevana* **(black-headed fireworm),** which feeds on the leaves of cranberries and causes them to wither. **2.** glowworm. [1560–70; FIRE + WORM]

fir•ing (fīər′ing), *n.* **1.** the act of a person or thing that fires. **2.** material for a fire; fuel. **3.** the act of baking ceramics or glass. [1375–1425; late ME; see FIRE, -ING[1]]

fir′ing glass′, a drinking glass of the 18th century having a conical, rounded body on a thick stem and a heavy spreading foot. Also called **hammering glass.** [1900–05]

fir′ing line′, **1.** *Mil.* **a.** the positions at which troops are stationed to fire upon the enemy or targets. **b.** the troops firing from this line. **2.** the forefront of any action or activity, esp. a controversy. [1880–85]

fir′ing pin′, *Ordn.* a plunger in the firing mechanism of a firearm or cannon that strikes the cartridge primer, igniting the propelling charge. [1870–75]

fir′ing range′, range (def. 5). [1880–85]

fir′ing squad′, **1.** a military detachment assigned to execute a condemned person by shooting. **2.** a military detachment assigned to fire a salute at the burial of a person being honored. [1900–05]

fir•kin (fûr′kin), *n.* **1.** a British unit of capacity usually equal to a quarter of a barrel. **2.** a small wooden vessel or tub for butter, lard, etc. [1400–50; late ME *ferdkyn, firdekyn,* equiv. to *ferde* (var. of *ferthe* FOURTH) + *-kin* -KIN]

firm[1] (fûrm), *adj.,* **-er, -est,** *v., adv.,* **-er, -est.** —*adj.* **1.** not soft or yielding when pressed; comparatively solid, hard, stiff, or rigid: *firm ground; firm texture.* **2.** securely fixed in place. **3.** not shaking or trembling; steady: *a firm voice.* **4.** not likely to change; fixed; settled; unalterable: *a firm belief.* **5.** steadfast or unwavering, as persons or principles: *firm friends.* **6.** indicating firmness or determination: *a firm expression.* **7.** not fluctuating much or falling, as prices, values, etc.: *The stock market was firm today.* —*v.t.* **8.** to make firm; tighten or strengthen (sometimes fol. by *up*): *to firm up one's hold on something.* **9.** to steady or fix (sometimes fol. by *up*): *to firm up prices.* —*v.i.* **10.** to become firm or fixed (sometimes fol. by *up*): *Butter firms by churning.* **11.** (of prices, markets, etc.) to recover; become stronger, as after a decline (sometimes fol. by *up*): *Stock prices firmed again today.* —*adv.* **12.** firmly: *He stood firm.* [1300–50; < L *firmus;* r. ME *ferm* < MF < L] —**firm′ly,** *adv.* —**firm′ness,** *n.*

—**Syn. 1.** FIRM, HARD, SOLID, STIFF are applied to substances that tend to retain their form unaltered in spite of pressure or force. FIRM often implies that something has been brought from a yielding state to a fixed or elastic one: *An increased amount of pectin makes jellies firm.* HARD is applied to substances so resistant that it is difficult to make any impression upon their surface or to penetrate their interior: *as hard as a stone.* SOLID is applied to substances that without external support retain their form and resist pressure: *Water in the form of ice is solid.* It sometimes denotes the opposite of hollow: *a solid block of marble.* STIFF implies rigidity that resists a bending force: *as stiff as a poker.* **2.** fast, stable, immovable. **4.** established, confirmed. **5.** determined, immovable, staunch, reliable. —**Ant. 1.** yielding, soft.

firm[2] (fûrm), *n.* **1.** a partnership or association for carrying on a business. **2.** the name or title under which associated parties transact business: *the firm of Smith & Jones.* [1565–75; < Sp *firma* signature (hence, legal name of a partnership, etc.), n. deriv. *firmar* to sign < L *firmāre* to strengthen, confirm, deriv. of *firmus* FIRM[1]] —**Syn. 1.** company, business, concern, house.

fir•ma•ment (fûr′mə mənt), *n.* the vault of heaven; sky. [1250–1300; ME < LL *firmāmentum* sky, L: support, prop, stay, equiv. to *firmā(re)* to strengthen, support (see FIRM[2]) + *-mentum* -MENT] —**fir•ma•men•tal** (fûr′mə men′tl), *adj.*

fir•man (fûr′mən, fər män′), *n., pl.* **-mans.** an edict or administrative order issued by or in the name of a Middle Eastern sovereign (formerly by an Ottoman Turkish sultan). [1610–20; < Turk *ferman* < Pers *farmān*]

fir′mer chis′el (fûr′mər), *Carpentry.* a narrow-bladed chisel for paring and mortising, driven by hand pressure or with a mallet. [1680–90; *firmer* < F *fermoir,* b. *formoir* that which forms (deriv. of *former* to FORM < L *fōrmāre*) and *fermer* to make firm (< L *firmāre*)]

fir′mer gouge′, *Carpentry.* a narrow-bladed gouge similar in manner of use to a firmer chisel. [1885–90]

firm•ware (fûrm′wâr′), *n. Computers.* a microprogram stored in ROM, designed to implement a function that had previously been provided in software. [1965–70; FIRM[1] + (SOFT)WARE]

firn (fērn), *n.* névé. [1850–55; < G (Swiss), n. use of *firn* last year's, old; c. OE *fyrn* former, ancient, Goth *fairneis;* akin to ON *forn* ancient. See BEFORE]

firn•i•fi•ca•tion (fēr′nə fi kā′shən), *n.* the process by which snow changes into névé. [1920–25; FIRN + -I- + -FICATION]

fir•ry (fûr′ē), *adj.,* **-ri•er, -ri•est.** **1.** of or pertaining to the fir. **2.** made of fir. **3.** abounding in firs. [1825–35; FIR + -Y[1]]

first (fûrst), *adj.* **1.** being before all others with respect to time, order, rank, importance, etc., used as the ordinal number of *one: the first edition; the first vice president.* **2.** *Music.* highest or chief among several voices or instruments of the same class: *first alto; first horn.* **3.** *Auto.* low (def. 31). **4.** **first thing,** before anything else; at once; promptly: *I'll call you first thing when I arrive.* —*adv.* **5.** before all others or anything else in time, order, rank, etc. **6.** before some other thing, event, etc.: *If you're going, phone first.* **7.** for the first time: *She first visited Atlanta in 1980.* **8.** in preference to something else; rather; sooner: *I'd die first.* **9.** in the first place; firstly. **10.** **first and last,** everything considered; above all else; altogether: *First and last, it is important to know oneself.* **11.** **first off,** *Informal.* at the outset; immediately: *He wanted to know first off why he hadn't been notified.* —*n.* **12.** the person or thing that is first in time, order, rank, etc. **13.** the beginning. **14.** the first part; first member of a series. **15.** *Music.* **a.** the voice or instrument that takes the highest or chief part in its class, esp. in an orchestra or chorus. **b.** a leader of a part or group of performers. **16.** *Auto.* low gear; first gear: *She shifted into first and drove off.* **17.** the winning position or rank in a race or other competition. **18.** *Baseball.* See **first base.** **19.** Usually, **firsts.** *Com.* **a.** a product or goods of the first or highest quality. **b.** goods produced according to specifications, without visible flaws. Cf. **second**[1] (def. 23), **third** (def. 12). **20.** *Brit. Univ.* **a.** first-class honors. Cf. **class** (def. 18). **b.** a person who has won such honors. [bef. 1000; ME; OE *fyr(e)st* (see FORE[1], -EST); c. G *Fürst* prince] —**first′ness,** *adj.*

first′ aid′, emergency aid or treatment given to someone injured, suddenly ill, etc., before regular medical services arrive or can be reached. [1880–85] —**first′-aid′,** *adj.* —**first′-aid′er,** *n.*

First′ Amend′ment, an amendment to the U.S. Constitution, ratified in 1791 as part of the Bill of Rights, prohibiting Congress from interfering with freedom of religion, speech, assembly, or petition.

first′ ax′iom of countabil′ity, *Math.* See under **axiom of countability.**

First′ Bal′kan War′. See **Balkan War** (def. 1).

first′ base′, **1.** *Baseball.* **a.** the first in counterclockwise order of the bases from home plate. **b.** the position of the player covering the area of the infield near first base. **2.** **get to first base,** *Informal.* **a.** to succeed in the initial phase of a plan or undertaking: *His suggestions for labor-saving techniques never got to first base.* **b.** to engage in petting that goes no further than kissing. [1835–45, *Amer.*]

first′ base′man, *Baseball.* the player whose position is first base. [1855–60, *Amer.*]

first•born (fûrst′bôrn′), *adj.* **1.** first in the order of birth; eldest. —*n.* **2.** a firstborn child. **3.** a first result or product. [1300–50; ME; see FIRST, BORN]

First′ Cause′, *Theol.* God. [1895–1900]

first′-cause′ ar′gument (fûrst′kôz′), *Philos.* an argument for the existence of God, asserting the necessity of an uncaused cause of all subsequent series of causes, on the assumption that an infinite regress is impossible. Cf. **cosmological argument.**

First′ Cham′ber. See under **States-General** (def. 1).

first′ class′, **1.** the best, finest, or highest class, grade, or rank. **2.** the most expensive and most luxurious class of accommodation on trains, ships, airplanes, etc. **3.** (in the U.S. Postal Service) the class of mail consisting of letters, postal cards, or the like, together with all mailable matter sealed against inspection. **4.** *Brit. Univ.* the group receiving the highest distinction in an honors course. [1740–50]

first-class (fûrst′klas′, -kläs′), *adj.* **1.** of the highest or best class or quality: *a first-class movie.* **2.** best-equipped and most expensive: *a first-class railroad car.* **3.** given or entitled to preferred treatment, handling, etc.: *first-class mail.* —*adv.* **4.** by first-class conveyance: *to travel first-class.* [1780–90]

first′ class′man (klas′mən, kläs′-), *pl.* **-men.** a fourth-year student at a U.S. military academy. [1885–90]

first-come (fûrst′kum′), *adj.* arranged, considered, or done in order of application or arrival, as for purposes of service: *orders filled on a first-come basis.*

first•com•er (fûrst′kum′ər), *n.* a person who arrives first or among the first. [1860–65, *Amer.*; FIRST + COMER]

First′ Command′ment, "Thou shalt have no other gods before me": first of the Ten Commandments. Cf. **Ten Commandments.**

first′ con′sonant shift′, the consonant shift described by Grimm's law, which distinguishes Germanic languages from other Indo-European languages. Cf. **consonant shift, second consonant shift.** [1930–35]

first′ cous′in, **1.** cousin (def. 1). **2.** anything or anyone closely related to or resembling another: *The film producer tried not to make the movie a first cousin to his last hit.* [1965–70]

first′ dark′, *Southern U.S.* twilight.

First′ day′, (among Quakers) Sunday. [1645–55]

first′-day cov′er (fûrst′dā′, -dā′), *Philately.* a cover marked so as to indicate that it was mailed on the first day of issue of the stamp it bears and from one of the cities at which the stamp was issued on that day. [1935–40]

first-de•gree (fûrst′di grē′), *adj.* **1.** of or pertaining to the lowest or first in a series. **2.** of or pertaining to the highest or most serious in a series.

first′-degree′ burn′, *Pathol.* See under **burn**[1] (def. 47). [1920–25]

CONCISE PRONUNCIATION KEY: act, cāpe, dâre, pärt; set, ēqual; *if,* ice; ox, ōver, ôrder, oil, bo͝ok, bo͞ot, out; up, ûrge; child; sing; shoe; thin, *that;* zh as in *treasure.* ə = *a* as in *alone,* e as in *system,* i as in *easily,* o as in *gallop,* u as in *circus;* ə as in *fire* (fīər), *hour* (ouər). l and n can serve as syllabic consonants, as in *cradle* (krād′l), and *button* (but′n). See the full key inside the front cover.

first′-degree′ mur′der, *Law.* See under **murder** (def. 1).

first′ deriv′ative, *Math.* the derivative of a function: *Velocity is the first derivative of distance with respect to time.* Cf. **second derivative.** [1825–35]

first′ divi′sion, *Sports.* the half of a league comprising the teams having the best records at a particular time (opposed to *second division*).

first′-dol′lar cov′erage (fûrst′dol′ər), *Insurance.* insurance that provides payment for the full loss up to the insured amount with no deductibles.

first′ edi′tion, 1. the whole number of copies of a literary work printed first, from the same type, and issued together. **2.** an individual copy from this number. **3.** the first printing of a newspaper for a given date. [1900–05]

First′ Em′pire, the empire (1804–14) established in France by Napoleon Bonaparte.

first′ estate′, the first of the three estates: the clergy in France; the Lords Spiritual in England. Cf. **estate** (def. 5). [1930–35]

first′ fam′ily, 1. a family having the highest or one of the highest social ranks in a given place. **2.** (*often caps.*) the family of the president of the U.S. or the family of the governor of a state. **3.** a family descended from a colonist or early settler in a country, region, etc.: *one of the first families of Virginia.* [1835–45, *Amer.*]

first′ floor′, 1. the ground floor of a building. **2.** the floor above the ground floor of a building. [1655–65]

first-foot (fûrst′fo͝ot′), *Scot.* —*n.* Also, **first′-foot′er. 1.** the first person to cross the threshold of a house on New Year's Day. **2.** the first person met after starting out on the day of an important occasion. —*v.t.* **3.** to enter (a house) first on New Year's Day. —*v.i.* **4.** to be the first to enter a house on New Year's Day. [1880–85]

first′ fruits′, 1. the earliest fruit of the season. **2.** the first product or result of anything. [1350–1400; ME]

first-gen•er•a•tion (fûrst′jen′ə rā′shən), *adj.* **1.** being the first generation of a family to be born in a particular country. **2.** being a naturalized citizen of a particular country; immigrant: *the child of first-generation Americans.*

first•hand (fûrst′hand′), *adv.* **1.** from the first or original source: *We heard the news of the accident firsthand from a witness.* —*adj.* **2.** of or pertaining to the first or original source. **3.** direct from the original source: *firsthand knowledge of the riot.* Also, **first′-hand′.** [1690–1700; FIRST + HAND]

first-in, first-out (fûrst′in′, fûrst′out′), **1.** an inventory plan that assumes that items purchased first will be sold first and that by valuing inventory items at the price of the most recent purchases, inventory values will be comparable to any rise in prices. *Abbr.:* FIFO Cf. **last-in, first-out. 2.** *Computers.* See **FIFO** (def. 2).

first′ inten′tion, *Logic.* See under **intention** (def. 5a).

First′ Interna′tional, a socialistic organization (1864–76) formed to unite and promote the interests of workers throughout the world. Cf. **international** (def. 6).

first′ la′dy, 1. (*often caps.*) the wife of the president of the U.S. or of the governor of a state. **2.** the wife of the head of any country: *the first lady of Brazil.* **3.** the foremost woman in any art, profession, or the like: *first lady of the American theater.* [1850–55]

first′ law′ of mo′tion, *Physics.* See under **law of motion.**

first′ law′ of thermodynam′ics. See under **law of thermodynamics** (def. 1).

first′ lien′. See **prior lien.**

first′ lieuten′ant, *Mil.* an officer ranking next above second lieutenant and next below a captain. [1775–85]

first′ light′, *Southern U.S.* dawn. [1945–50]

first-line (fûrst′līn′), *adj.* **1.** available for immediate service, esp. combat service: *first-line troops.* **2.** of prime importance or quality. [1895–1900]

first•ling (fûrst′ling), *n.* **1.** the first of its kind to be produced or to appear. **2.** first offspring. **3.** a first product or result. [1525–35; FIRST + -LING[1]]

First′ Lord′, *Brit.* the head of a board commissioned to perform the duties of a high office of state: *First Lord of the Admiralty.* [1805–15]

first•ly (fûrst′lē), *adv.* in the first place; first. [1525–35; FIRST + -LY]

first′ mate′, the officer of a merchant vessel next in command beneath the captain. Also called **chief mate, chief officer, first officer, mate.**

first′ mes′senger, *Biochem.* a hormone that triggers a biochemical reaction at a site removed from its release. Cf. **second messenger.** [1975–80]

first′ mort′gage, a mortgage having priority over other mortgages on property. [1850–55] —**first′-mort′gage,** *adj.*

first′ name′. See **given name.** [1200–50; ME]

first-name (*adj.* fûrst′nām′; *v.* fûrst′nām′), *adj., v.,* **-named, -nam•ing.** —*adj.* **1.** of or pertaining to one's first, or given, name; familiar; intimate: *They were on a first-name basis soon after meeting.* —*v.t.* **2.** to address (someone) by his or her first name, esp. as a sign of informality or familiarity: *The boss doesn't like the employees to first-name her.*

CONCISE ETYMOLOGY KEY: <, descended or borrowed from; >, whence; b., blend of, blended; c., cognate with; cf., compare; deriv., derivative; equiv., equivalent; imit., imitative; obl., oblique; r., replacing; s., stem; sp., spelling, spelled; resp., respelling, respelled; trans., translation; ?, origin unknown; *, unattested; ‡, probably earlier than. See the full key inside the front cover.

first′ night′. See **opening night.** [1705–15]

first-night•er (fûrst′nī′tər), *n.* a person who often or usually attends the theater, opera, etc., on opening night. Also, **first′-night′er.** [1880–85; FIRST NIGHT + -ER[1]]

first′ offend′er, a person convicted of an offense of law for the first time. [1840–50]

first′ of′ficer, 1. See **first mate. 2.** copilot.

first′ pa′pers, *Informal.* an official declaration of intention filed by a resident alien desiring to become a U.S. citizen: not required by law after 1952. Also, **first′ pa′per.** Cf. **second papers, citizenship papers.** [1910–15, *Amer.*]

first′ per′son, 1. the grammatical person used by a speaker in statements referring to himself or herself or to a group including himself or herself, as *I* and *we* in English. **2.** a form in the first person. [1935–40]

First′ Point′ of Ar′ies, the vernal equinox.

first′ posi′tion, *Ballet.* a position of the feet in which the heels are back to back and the toes point out to the sides. [1880–85]

A, **first position;** B, second position; C, third position; D, fourth position; E, fifth position

first′ post′. See under **post**[2] (def. 7).

first′ prin′ciple, any axiom, law, or abstraction assumed and regarded as representing the highest possible degree of generalization.

first′ quar′ter, *Astron.* the instant, approximately one week after a new moon, when one half of the moon's disk is illuminated by the sun. See diag. under **moon.** [1905–10]

first′ quar′tile, *Statistics.* (in a frequency distribution) the smallest quartile; the twenty-fifth percentile; the value of the variable below which one quarter of the elements are located.

first-rate (fûrst′rāt′), *adj.* **1.** excellent; superb. **2.** of the highest rank, rate, or class. —*adv.* **3.** very well. [1660–70]

First′ Read′er, *Christian Science.* the elected official of a church or society who conducts the services and meetings and reads from the writings of Mary Baker Eddy and the Scriptures. Cf. **Second Reader.** [1895–1900]

first′ read′ing, *Parl. Proc.* the reading of a bill when it is first introduced in a legislative body. [1695–1705]

First′ Reich′, the Holy Roman Empire until its dissolution in 1806. Cf. **Reich.**

First′ Repub′lic, the republic established in France in 1792 and replaced by the First Empire in 1804.

first′ run′, *Motion Pictures.* the initial exhibition period for a film. [1910–15] —**first′-run′,** *adj.*

first′ ser′geant, *U.S. Army.* the senior noncommissioned officer of a company, squadron, etc., responsible for personnel and administration. [1870–75]

First′ State′, Delaware (used as a nickname).

first′ strike′, the initial use of nuclear weapons in a conflict, in which the attacker tries to destroy the adversary's strategic nuclear forces. [1960–65]

first-string (fûrst′string′), *adj.* **1.** composed of regular members, participants, etc. (distinguished from *substitute*): *the first-string team.* **2.** foremost; main: *the first-string critics.* [1915–20] —**first′-string′er,** *n.*

first-term•er (fûrst′tûr′mər), *n.* a person serving his or her first term, as a member of the U.S. Congress. [1885–90, *Amer.; first term* + -ER[1]]

first-time (fûrst′tīm′), *adj.* used, appearing, contending, etc., for the first time: *a first-time candidate.*

first-tim•er (fûrst′tī′mər), *n.* a person who does, experiences, or attends something for the first time. [*first time* + -ER[1]]

first′ wa′ter, 1. (formerly) the highest degree of fineness in a diamond or other precious stone. Cf. **water** (def. 13). **2.** the finest quality; highest rank. [1745–55]

First′ World′, the major industrialized non-Communist nations, including those in Western Europe, the United States, Canada, and Japan. Cf. **Second World, Third World, Fourth World.** [1970–75]

First′ World′ War′. See **World War I.**

firth (fûrth), *n. Chiefly Scot.* a long, narrow indentation of the seacoast. Also, **frith.** [1400–50; late ME (Scots) < ON *firth-,* s. of *fjǫrthr* FJORD]

Firth (fûrth), *n.* **John Rupert,** 1890–1960, English linguist. —**Firth′i•an,** *adj.*

fisc (fisk), *n.* a royal or state treasury; exchequer. [1590–1600; < MF < L *fiscus* treasury, moneybag, lit., basket, bag]

fis•cal (fis′kəl), *adj.* **1.** of or pertaining to the public treasury or revenues: *fiscal policies.* **2.** of or pertaining to financial matters in general. —*n.* **3.** (in some countries) a prosecuting attorney. **4.** *Philately.* a revenue stamp. [1530–40; < L *fiscālis.* See FISC, -AL[1]] —**fis′cal•ly,** *adv.*
—**Syn. 1.** See **financial.**

fis′cal a′gent, a person or organization serving as another's financial agent. [1835–45]

fis′cal year′, any yearly period without regard to the calendar year, at the end of which a firm, government, etc., determines its financial condition. [1835–45, *Amer.*]

Fisch•er (fish′ər), *n.* **1. Edwin,** 1886–1960, Swiss pianist. **2. E•mil** (ā′mil), 1852–1919, German chemist: Nobel prize 1902. **3. Ernst Otto,** born 1918, German chemist: Nobel prize 1973. **4. Hans** (häns), 1881–1945, German chemist: Nobel prize 1930. **5. Robert James** (*"Bobby"*), born 1943, U.S. chess player.

Fisch•er-Dies•kau (fish′ər dē′skou; *Ger.* fish′ᴇʀ dēs′kou), *n.* **Die•trich** (dē′trik; *Ger.* dē′tʀɪᴋʜ), born 1925, German baritone.

Fisch′er-Tropsch′ proc′ess (fish′ər trōpsh′, -tropsh′), *Chem.* a catalytic hydrogenation method to produce liquid hydrocarbon fuels from carbon monoxide. [1930–35; named after F. *Fischer* (d. 1948), and H. *Tropsch* (d. 1935), German chemists]

Fisch•er von Er•lach (fish′ᴇʀ fən ᴇʀ′läᴋʜ), **Jo•hann Bern•hard** (yô′hän bᴇʀn′häʀt), 1656–1723, Austrian architect.

fish (fish), *n., pl.* (*esp. collectively*) **fish,** (*esp. referring to two or more kinds or species*) **fish•es,** *v.* —*n.* **1.** any of various cold-blooded, aquatic vertebrates, having gills, commonly fins, and typically an elongated body covered with scales. **2.** (loosely) any of various other aquatic animals. **3.** the flesh of fishes used as food. **4. Fishes,** *Astron., Astrol.* the constellation or sign of Pisces. **5.** *Informal.* a person: *an odd fish; a poor fish.* **6.** a long strip of wood, iron, etc., used to strengthen a mast, joint, etc. **7.** *Cards Slang.* an incompetent player whose incompetence can be exploited. **8.** *Slang.* a dollar: *He sold the car for 500 fish.* **9.** *Slang.* a new prison inmate. **10. drink like a fish,** to drink alcoholic beverages to excess: *Nobody invites him out because he drinks like a fish.* **11. fish out of water,** a person out of his or her proper or accustomed environment: *He felt like a fish out of water in an academic atmosphere.* **12. neither fish nor fowl,** having no specific character or conviction; neither one nor the other. **13. other fish to fry,** other matters requiring attention: *When it was time to act, they had other fish to fry.* —*v.t.* **14.** to catch or attempt to catch (any species of fish or the like). **15.** to try to catch fish in (a stream, lake, etc.): *Let's fish the creek.* **16.** to draw, as by fishing (often fol. by *up* or *out*): *He fished a coin out of his pocket for the boy.* **17.** to search through, as by fishing. **18.** *Naut.* **a.** to secure (an anchor) by raising the flukes. **b.** to reinforce (a mast or other spar) by fastening a spar, batten, metal bar, or the like, lengthwise over a weak place. —*v.i.* **19.** to catch or attempt to catch fish, as by angling or drawing a net. **20.** to search carefully: *He fished through all his pockets but his wallet was gone.* **21.** to seek to obtain something indirectly or by artifice: *to fish for compliments; to fish for information.* **22.** to search for or attempt to catch onto something under water, in mud, etc., by the use of a dredge, rake, hook, or the like. **23.** to attempt to recover detached tools or other loose objects from an oil or gas well. **24. fish in troubled waters,** to take advantage of troubled or uncertain conditions for personal profit. **25. fish or cut bait,** to choose a definite course of action, esp. to decide whether to participate in or retreat from an activity. **26. fish out,** to deplete (a lake, stream, etc.) of fish by fishing. [bef. 900; (n.) ME *fis(c)h, fyssh,* OE *fisc;* c. D *vis,* G *Fisch,* ON *fiskr,* Goth *fisks;* akin to L *piscis,* Ir *iasc;* (v.) ME *fishen,* OE *fiscian,* c. D *visschen,* G *fischen,* ON *fiska,* Goth *fiskôn*] —**fish′less,** *adj.*

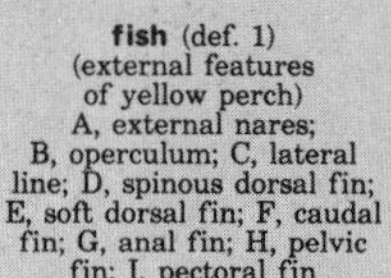
fish (def. 1) (external features of yellow perch) A, external nares; B, operculum; C, lateral line; D, spinous dorsal fin; E, soft dorsal fin; F, caudal fin; G, anal fin; H, pelvic fin; I, pectoral fin

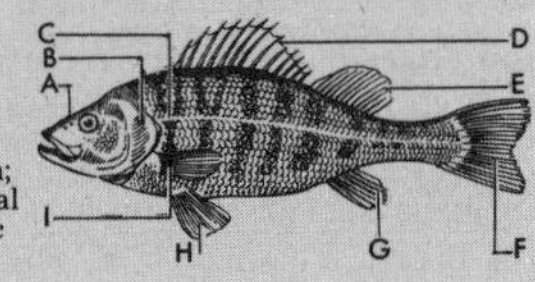

Fish (fish), *n.* **Hamilton,** 1808–93, U.S. statesman: secretary of state 1869–77.

fish•a•ble (fish′ə bəl), *adj.* **1.** that may be fished in: *nonpolluted, fishable streams.* **2.** lawful to be fished in: *a lake that is fishable only with a permit.* [1605–15; FISH + -ABLE] —**fish′a•bil′i•ty,** *n.*

fish′ and chips′, fried fish fillets and French fries. [1875–80]

fish-bel•lied (fish′bel′ēd), *adj. Building Trades, Mach.* (of a beam or rail) having a convex underside. [1825–35]

fish•bowl (fish′bōl′), *n.* **1.** a glass bowl for goldfish, snails, etc. **2.** a place, job, or condition in which one's activities are open to public view or scrutiny. Also, **fish′ bowl′.** [1905–10; FISH + BOWL[1]]

fish′ cake′, a fried ball or cake of shredded fish, esp. salt codfish, and mashed potato. Also called **fish′ ball′.** [1850–55]

fish′ crow′, a crow, *Corvus ossifragus,* of the Atlantic and Gulf coasts of North America, that feeds on fish, mollusks, etc. [1805–15, *Amer.*]

fish′ cul′ture, the artificial propagation and breeding of fish. [1860–65]

fish′ doc′tor, a scaleless, brightly colored eelpout, *Gymnelis viridis,* of Arctic waters.

fish′ duck′, *Informal.* merganser. [1855–60, *Amer.*]

fish•er (fish′ər), *n.* **1.** any animal that catches fish for food. **2.** a fisherman. **3.** a dark-brown or blackish marten, *Martes pennanti,* of northern North America. See illus. on next page. **4.** the fur of this animal. [bef. 900; ME *fisscher* fisherman, OE *fiscere.* See FISH, -ER[1]]

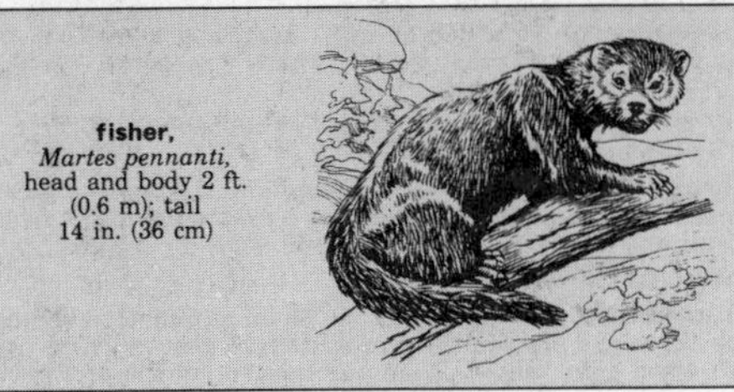
fisher, *Martes pennanti,* head and body 2 ft. (0.6 m); tail 14 in. (36 cm)

Fish•er (fish′ər), *n.* **1. Andrew,** 1862–1928, Australian statesman, born in Scotland: prime minister 1908–09, 1910–13, 1914–15. **2. Dorothy Can•field** (kan′fēld′), (*Dorothea Frances Canfield Fisher*), 1879–1958, U.S. novelist. **3. Irving,** 1867–1947, U.S. political economist. **4. Saint John** (*"John of Rochester"*), c1469–1535, English Roman Catholic prelate and humanist: executed for treason. **5. John Arbuthnot, 1st Baron Fisher of Kil•ver•stone** (kil′vər stən), 1841–1920, British admiral.

Fish′er King′, *Arthurian Romance.* (in the story of Percival) the custodian of the Grail.

fish•er•man (fish′ər mən), *n., pl.* **-men,** *adj.* —*n.* **1.** a person who fishes, whether for profit or pleasure. **2.** a ship used in fishing. —*adj.* **3.** Also, **fish′er•man's.** of, pertaining to, or designating a knitting pattern consisting primarily of cable-stitches executed in a characteristically thick, traditionally off-white yarn, or a garment made in this pattern and yarn: *a fisherman sweater.* [1400–50; late ME *fissherman;* see FISHER, -MAN]

fish′erman's bend′, a knot made by taking a round turn on the object to which the rope is to be fastened, passing the end of the rope around the standing part and under the round turn, and securing the end. See illus. under **knot.** Also called **anchor bend, anchor knot.** [1855–60]

fish′erman's ring′, *Rom. Cath. Ch.* the signet ring worn by the pope. [1720–30]

fish•er•y (fish′ə rē), *n., pl.* **-er•ies. 1.** a place where fish are bred; fish hatchery. **2.** a place where fish or shellfish are caught. **3.** the occupation or industry of catching, processing, or selling fish or shellfish. **4.** *Law.* the right to fish in certain waters or at certain times. [1520–30; FISH + ERY]

fish•eye (fish′ī′), *n., pl.* **-eyes. 1.** (in plasterwork) a surface defect having the form of a spot. **2.** an unfriendly or suspicious look. **3. fisheyes,** *Slang.* tapioca pudding. Also, **fish′ eye′** (for defs. 1, 2). [FISH + EYE]

fish′eye lens′, *Photog.* a hemispherical plano-convex lens for photographing in a full 180° in all directions in front of the camera, creating a circular image having an increasing amount of distortion from the center to the periphery. [1960–65]

fish′ farm′, a facility in which fish are bred for commercial purposes. [1860–65] —**fish′ farm′ing.**

fish′ flake′, a platform for drying fish. [1760–70, *Amer.*]

fish′ flour′, powdered fish, high in protein, used as an ingredient in other foods. [1875–80]

fish•fly (fish′flī′), *n., pl.* **-flies.** a neuropterous insect of the family Corydalidae that is similar to but smaller than a dobsonfly. [1865–70; FISH + FLY²]

fish′ fork′, a small fork having usually three tines, used for eating fish at table.

fish′ fry′, 1. a picnic or other gathering at which fish are fried and eaten. **2.** fried fish. [1815–25, *Amer.*]

fish′ gera′nium. See **zonal geranium.** [1860–65, *Amer.*]

fish•gig (fish′gig′), *n.* a spearlike implement with barbed prongs for spearing fish in the water. Also called **fizgig.** [1635–45; alter. (by assoc. with FISH) of FIZGIG, prob. by folk etym. < Sp *fisga* harpoon]

fish′ hatch′ery, a facility where fish eggs are hatched and the fry raised, esp. to stock lakes, streams, and ponds. [1880–85, *Amer.*]

fish′ hawk′, osprey (def. 1). [1700–10, *Amer.*]

fish•hook (fish′ho͝ok′), *n.* a hook used in fishing. [1350–1400; ME *fischhook.* See FISH, HOOK]

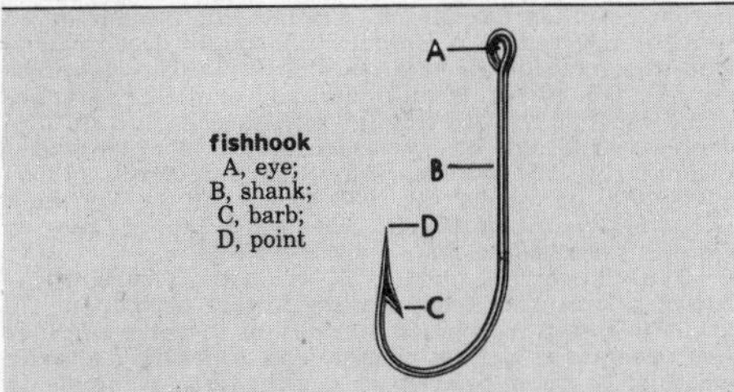

fishhook A, eye; B, shank; C, barb; D, point

fish′hook cac′tus, a large cactus, *Ferocactus wislizenii,* of the southwestern U.S. and Mexico, having hooked spines and red or yellow flowers. [1845–50, *Amer.*]

fish•ing (fish′ing), *n.* **1.** the act of catching fish. **2.** the technique, occupation, or diversion of catching fish. **3.** a place or facility for catching fish. [1250–1300; ME *fisshing.* See FISH, -ING¹]

fish′ing banks′, a relatively shallow area of the sea in which fish are usually abundant. [1755–65]

fish′ing expedi′tion, *Informal.* **1.** a legal proceeding mainly for the purpose of interrogating an adversary, or of examining his or her property and documents, in order to gain useful information. **2.** any inquiry carried on without any clearly defined plan or purpose in the hope of discovering useful information. Also called **fishing trip.** [1960–65]

fish′ing ground′, a part of a body of water where the fishing is usually good. [1635–45]

fish′ing line′, fishline.

fish′ing pole′, a long, slender rod of wood or other material with a line and hook fastened to one end for use in catching fish. Also called **fish pole.** [1785–95, *Amer.*]

fish′ing rod′, a long, slender, cylindrical, flexible rod usually made of bamboo, steel, or fiberglass, for use with a reel and line in catching fish. Cf. **fly rod.** [1545–55]

fish′ing smack′, any of various fore-and-aft-rigged fishing vessels of rather large size, often containing a well to keep the catch alive. [1775–85]

fish′ing trip′. See **fishing expedition.**

fish′ing worm′, *Midland and Southern U.S.* an earthworm.
—**Regional Variation.** See **earthworm.**

fish•kill (fish′kil′), *n.* the sudden destruction of large quantities of fish, as by pollution. Also, **fish′ kill′.** [1960–65; FISH + KILL¹]

fish′ knife′, a small knife with a spatulalike blade, used with a fork in cutting fish at table. [1375–1425; late ME *fishknif*]

fish′ lad′der, a series of ascending pools constructed to enable salmon or other fish to swim upstream around or over a dam. [1860–65, *Amer.*]

fish•line (fish′līn′), *n.* a line attached to a fishhook used in fishing. Also, **fishing line.** [1630–40, *Amer.*; FISH + LINE¹]

fish′ louse′, any of numerous small crustaceans, esp. certain copepods, parasitic on the skin and gills of fish.

fish′ meal′, dried fish ground for use as fertilizer, animal feed, or an ingredient in other foods. Also, **fish′•meal′.** [1850–55]

fish•mon•ger (fish′mung′gər, -mong′-), *n. Chiefly Brit.* a dealer in fish, esp. for eating. [1300–50; ME *fysshmongere.* See FISH, MONGER]

fish•net (fish′net′), *n.* **1.** a net for catching fish. **2.** a fabric having an open mesh resembling a fishnet. —*adj.* **3.** being of an open-mesh weave: *fishnet stockings.* [bef. 1000; ME; OE *fiscnett.* See FISH, NET¹]

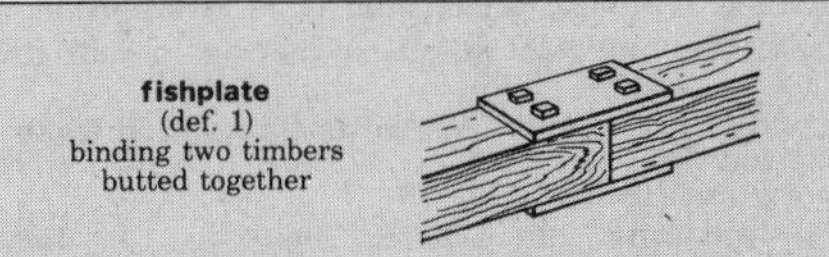
fishplate (def. 1) binding two timbers butted together

fish•plate (fish′plāt′), *n.* **1.** a metal or wooden plate or slab, bolted to each of two members that have been butted or lapped together. **2.** *Railroads Now Rare.* a joint bar. [1850–55; *fish,* alter. of F *fiche* fastening, deriv. of *ficher* to fasten, fix (see FICHU) + PLATE¹]

fish′ pole′. See **fishing pole.** [1825–35, *Amer.*]

fish•pond (fish′pond′), *n.* a small pond containing fish, often one in which edible fish are raised for commercial purposes, as for stocking lakes and streams or wholesaling. [1250–1300; ME; see FISH, POND]

fish•pound (fish′pound′), *n.* a submerged net used in commercial fishing for capturing fish. [1855–60, *Amer.*; FISH + POUND³]

fish′ pro′tein con′centrate, an odorless and tasteless high-protein food additive made from ground fish and suitable for human consumption. *Abbr.:* FPC [1960–65]

fish•skin (fish′skin′), *n. Slang.* **1.** a condom. **2.** a dollar bill. [1645–55, for literal sense; FISH + SKIN]

fish′ slice′, 1. a broad-bladed kitchen implement with a long handle, for turning fish in frying. **2.** *Chiefly Brit.* a broad-bladed implement for serving fish at table. [1885–90]

fish′ stick′, an oblong piece of fried fish, usually breaded. [1950–55]

fish′ sto′ry, *Informal.* an exaggerated or incredible story: *It was just another one of his fish stories.* [1810–20, *Amer.*]

fish′ tack′le, *Naut.* a tackle for fishing an anchor. [1680–90]

fish•tail (fish′tāl′), *v.i.* **1.** to swerve or skid from side to side, as the rear end of a car. **2.** to slow an airplane by causing its tail to move rapidly from side to side. —*n.* **3.** such a maneuver. **4.** a gas burner having two jets crossing each other so as to produce a flame resembling a fish's tail. **5.** a device having a long, narrow slot at the top, placed over a gas jet, as of a Bunsen burner, to give a thin, fanlike flame. **6.** *Jewelry.* a setting consisting of four prominent triangular corner prongs to hold the stone. [1400–50; late ME. See FISH, TAIL¹]

fish•tank (fish′tank′), *n.* a glass-sided tank for keeping, displaying, or observing live fish or other aquatic animals. [‡1935–40; FISH + TANK]

fish′ ward′en, a public official who enforces game laws relating to fish. [1780–90, *Amer.*]

fish′ wheel′. See **salmon wheel.**

fish•wife (fish′wīf′), *n., pl.* **-wives. 1.** a woman who sells fish. **2.** a coarse-mannered, vulgar-tongued woman. [1375–1425; late ME *fisshwyf.* See FISH, WIFE]

fish•worm (fish′wûrm′), *n. Chiefly New Eng. and Northern and Midland U.S.* an earthworm. [1850–55, *Amer.*; FISH + WORM]
—**Regional Variation.** See **earthworm.**

fish•y (fish′ē), *adj.,* **fish•i•er, fish•i•est. 1.** like a fish in shape, smell, taste, or the like. **2.** consisting of fish. **3.** abounding in fish. **4.** *Informal.* improbable, as a story; unlikely. **5.** *Informal.* of questionable character; suspicious: *The sudden knockout was fishy.* **6.** dull and expressionless: *fishy eyes.* [1540–50; FISH + -Y¹] —**fish′i•ly,** *adv.* —**fish′i•ness,** *n.*
—**Syn. 5.** peculiar, queer, strange, suspect, dubious.

Fisk (fisk), *n.* **James,** 1834–72, U.S. financier and stock speculator.

Fiske (fisk), *n.* **1. John** (*Edmund Fisk Green; John Fisk*), 1842–1901, U.S. philosopher and historian. **2. Minnie Mad•dern** (mad′ərn) (*Marie Augusta Davey*), 1865–1932, U.S. actress.

fissi-, a combining form meaning "cleft," used in the formation of compound words: *fissiparous.* [< L, comb. form of *fissus* cloven, *fissum* fissure, special uses of ptp. of *findere* to split]

fis•sile (fis′əl), *adj.* **1.** capable of being split or divided; cleavable. **2.** *Physics.* **a.** fissionable. **b.** (of a nuclide) capable of undergoing fission induced by low-energy neutrons, as uranium 233 and 235. [1655–65; < L *fissilis,* equiv. to *fiss(us)* (see FISSI-) + *-ilis* -ILE] —**fis•sil′i•ty,** *n.*

fis•sion (fish′ən), *n.* **1.** the act of cleaving or splitting into parts. **2.** Also called **nuclear fission.** *Physics.* the splitting of the nucleus of an atom into nuclei of lighter atoms, accompanied by the release of energy. Cf. **fusion** (def. 4). **3.** *Biol.* the division of an organism into new organisms as a process of reproduction. —*v.i.* **4.** *Physics.* to undergo fission. —*v.t.* **5.** *Physics.* to cause to undergo fission. [1835–45; < L *fissiōn-* (s. of *fissiō*) a splitting, dividing, equiv. to *fiss(us)* divided (see FISSI-) + *-iōn-* -ION]

fis•sion•a•ble (fish′ə nə bəl), *adj. Physics.* capable of or possessing a nucleus or nuclei capable of undergoing fission: *a fissionable nucleus; fissionable material.* Also, **fissile.** [1940–45; FISSION + -ABLE] —**fis′sion•a•bil′i•ty,** *n.*

fis′sion bomb′. See **atomic bomb.** [1940–45]

fis•si•pal•mate (fis′ə pal′māt), *adj. Anat.* (of birds) having the toes lobed or partially webbed. [FISSI- + PALMATE]

fis•sip•a•rous (fi sip′ər əs), *adj.* reproducing by fission. [1825–35; FISSI- + -PAROUS] —**fis•sip′a•rous•ly,** *adv.* —**fis•sip′a•rous•ness,** *n.*

fis•si•ped (fis′ə ped′), *n.* **1.** any member of the suborder Fissipedia, carnivorous mammals that have separate toes, as bears, badgers, dogs, cats, and raccoons. —*adj.* **2.** of or pertaining to the Fissipedia. **3.** cleft-footed or cloven-hoofed. [1640–50; < LL *fissiped-* s. of *fissipēs* cloven-footed (see FISSI-, -PED)]

fis•si•ros•tral (fis′ə ros′trəl), *adj. Ornith.* **1.** having a broad, deeply cleft beak or bill, as the swallows and goatsuckers. **2.** (of the bill) deeply cleft. [FISSI- + ROSTRAL]

fissirostral bill of nightjar, *Caprimulgus europaeus*

fis•sure (fish′ər), *n., v.,* **-sured, -sur•ing.** —*n.* **1.** a narrow opening produced by cleavage or separation of parts. **2.** cleavage (def. 1). **3.** *Anat.* a natural division or groove in an organ, as in the brain. —*v.t.* **4.** to make fissures in; cleave; split. —*v.i.* **5.** to open in fissures; become split. [1375–1425; late ME < L *fissūra* cleaving, cleft, fissure, equiv. to *fiss(us)* divided (see FISSI-) + *-ūra* -URE] —**fis′su•ral,** *adj.* —**fis′sure•less,** *adj.*

fis′sure of Ro•lan′do (rō lan′dō, -län′-). See **central sulcus.** [named after L. *Rolando* (d. 1831), Italian anatomist]

fis′sure of Syl′vi•us (sil′vē əs). See **lateral fissure.** [named after Franciscus *Sylvius* (Latinization of Franz de la Boë, d.1672), German anatomist]

fist¹ (fist), *n.* **1.** the hand closed tightly, with the fingers doubled into the palm. **2.** *Informal.* the hand. **3.** *Informal.* a person's handwriting. **4.** *Print.* index (def. 8). —*v.t.* **5.** to make (one's hand) into a fist. **6.** to grasp in the fist. [bef. 900; ME; OE *fȳst;* c. G *Faust* fist; perh. akin to FIVE]

fist² (fist), *n.* feist.

fist•fight (fist′fīt′), *n.* a fight using bare fists. [1595–1605; FIST¹ + FIGHT]

fist•ful (fist′fo͝ol), *n., pl.* **-fuls.** a handful: *a fistful of pennies.* [1605–15; FIST¹ + -FUL]
—**Usage.** See **-ful.**

fist•i•an•a (fis′tē an′ə, -ä′nə), *n. Informal.* the sport or world of boxing: *one of fistiana's most colorful characters.* [1830–40; FISTI(CUFF) + -ANA]

fist•ic (fis′tik), *adj.* of boxing; pugilistic: *fistic heroes.* [1800–10; FIST¹ + -IC]

fist•i•cuff (fis′ti kuf′), *n.* **1.** a cuff or blow with the fist. **2. fisticuffs,** combat with the fists. —*v.t., v.i.* **3.** to strike or fight with the fists. [1595–1605; earlier *fisty cuff.* See FIST¹, -Y¹, CUFF²] —**fist′i•cuff′er,** *n.*

fist•note (fist′nōt′), *n.* a printed note, as in a piece of text, distinguished by the figure of a fist with a pointing index finger. [1930–35; FIST¹ + NOTE]

fis·tu·la (fis′cho͝o lə), *n., pl.* **-las, -lae** (-lē′). **1.** *Pathol.* a narrow passage or duct formed by disease or injury, as one leading from an abscess to a free surface, or from one cavity to another. **2.** *Surg.* an opening made into a hollow organ, as the bladder or eyeball, for drainage. **3.** *Vet. Pathol.* any of various suppurative inflammations, as in the withers of a horse (**fis′tulous with′ers**), characterized by the formation of passages or sinuses through the tissues and to the surface of the skin. **4.** *Obs.* a pipe, as a flute. [1350–1400; ME < L: pipe, tube, fistula]

fis·tu·lize (fis′cho͝o līz′), *v.,* **-lized, -liz·ing.** —*v.i.* **1.** *Pathol.* to form a fistula. —*v.t.* **2.** *Surg.* to make a fistula. Also, *esp. Brit.,* **fis′tu·lise′.** [FISTUL(A) + -IZE] —**fis′tu·li·za′tion,** *n.*

fis·tu·lous (fis′cho͝o ləs), *adj.* **1.** *Pathol.* pertaining to or resembling a fistula. **2.** tubelike; tubular. **3.** containing tubes or tubelike parts. Also, **fis′tu·lar, fis·tu·late** (fis′cho͝o lit). [1570–80; < L *fistulōsus.* See FISTULA, -OUS]

fit^1 (fit), *adj.,* **fit·ter, fit·test,** *v.,* **fit·ted** or **fit, fit·ting,** *n.* —*adj.* **1.** adapted or suited; appropriate: *This water isn't fit for drinking. A long-necked giraffe is fit for browsing treetops.* **2.** proper or becoming: *fit behavior.* **3.** qualified or competent, as for an office or function: *a fit candidate.* **4.** prepared or ready: *crops fit for gathering.* **5.** in good physical condition; in good health: *He's fit for the race.* **6.** *Biol.* **a.** being adapted to the prevailing conditions and producing offspring that survive to reproductive age. **b.** contributing genetic information to the gene pool of the next generation. **c.** (of a population) maintaining or increasing the group's numbers in the environment. **7. fit to be tied,** *Informal.* extremely annoyed or angry: *He was fit to be tied when I told him I'd wrecked the car.* **8. fit to kill,** *Informal.* to the limit; exceedingly: *She was dressed up fit to kill.* —*v.t.* **9.** to be adapted to or suitable for (a purpose, object, occasion, etc.). **10.** to be proper or becoming for. **11.** to be of the right size or shape for: *The dress fitted her perfectly.* **12.** to adjust or make conform: *to fit a ring to the finger.* **13.** to make qualified or competent: *qualities that fit one for leadership.* **14.** to prepare: *This school fits students for college.* **15.** to put with precise placement or adjustment: *He fitted the picture into the frame.* **16.** to provide; furnish; equip: *to fit a door with a new handle.* —*v.i.* **17.** to be suitable or proper. **18.** to be of the right size or shape, as a garment for the wearer or any object or part for a thing to which it is applied: *The shoes fit.* **19. fit out** or **up,** to furnish with supplies, equipment, clothing, furniture, or other requisites; supply; equip: *to fit out an expedition.* —*n.* **20.** the manner in which a thing fits: *The fit was perfect.* **21.** something that fits: *The coat is a poor fit.* **22.** the process of fitting. [1325–75; ME *fitten;* akin to MD *vitten* to befit] —**fit′ta·ble,** *adj.*
—**Syn. 1.** suitable, apt, corresponding, meet, applicable, apropos. **2.** fitting, befitting. **5.** healthy, hale, hardy, strong, robust.
—**Usage.** Both FIT and FITTED are standard as past tense and past participle of FIT^1: *The new door fit* (or *fitted*) *the old frame perfectly. The suit had fitted* (or *fit*) *well last year.* FITTED is somewhat more common than FIT in the sense "to adjust, make conform": *The tailor fitted the suit with a minimum of fuss.* In the passive voice, FITTED is the more common past participle: *The door was fitted with a new handle.*

fit^2 (fit), *n.* **1.** a sudden, acute attack or manifestation of a disease, esp. one marked by convulsions or unconsciousness: *a fit of epilepsy.* **2.** an onset, spell, or period of emotion, feeling, inclination, activity, etc.: *a fit of anger; a fit of weeping.* **3. by** or **in fits and starts,** at irregular intervals; intermittently: *This radio works by fits and starts.* **4. throw a fit,** to become extremely excited or angry: *Your father will throw a fit when he hears what you have done.* [bef. 1000; ME; OE *fitt* round of fighting. See FIT^3]

fit^3 (fit), *n. Archaic.* **1.** a song, ballad, or story. **2.** a division of a song, ballad, or story. [bef. 900; ME; OE *fitt* round of singing, canto, song, speech]

fit^4 (fit), *v. Nonstandard (chiefly older use).* pt. of **fight.**

FIT, *Banking.* Federal Insurance Tax.

fitch (fich), *n.* **1.** the European polecat, *Mustela putorius.* **2.** its fur, often dyed to imitate other furs. Also, **fitch·et** (fich′it), **fitch·ew** (fich′o͞o). [1400–50; late ME *fiche, feche, fuche* polecat fur < MD *fisse, visse, vitsche* polecat]

Fitch (fich), *n.* **1. John,** 1743–98, U.S. inventor: pioneer in development of the steamboat. **2. (William) Clyde,** 1865–1909, U.S. playwright.

Fitch·burg (fich′bûrg), *n.* a city in N Massachusetts. 39,580.

fit·ful (fit′fəl), *adj.* coming, appearing, acting, etc., in fits or by spells; recurring irregularly. [1595–1605; FIT^2 + -FUL] —**fit′ful·ly,** *adv.* —**fit′ful·ness,** *n.*
—**Syn.** sporadic, intermittent, erratic, haphazard.

fit·ly (fit′lē), *adv.* **1.** in a proper or suitable manner. **2.** at a proper or suitable time. [1540–50; FIT^1 + -LY]

fit·ment (fit′mənt), *n.* **1.** equipment; furnishing. **2. fitments,** fittings: *the fitments of a ship.* [1600–10; FIT^1 + -MENT]

fit·ness (fit′nis), *n.* **1.** health. **2.** capability of the body of distributing inhaled oxygen to muscle tissue during increased physical effort. **3.** Also called **Darwinian fitness.** *Biol.* **a.** the genetic contribution of an individual to the next generation's gene pool relative to the average for the population, usually measured by the number of offspring or close kin that survive to reproductive age. **b.** the ability of a population to maintain or increase its numbers in succeeding generations. [1570–80; FIT^1 + -NESS]

fit·ted (fit′id), *adj.* made so as to follow closely the contours of a form or shape: *fitted clothes; fitted sheets.* [1730–40; FIT^1 + -ED^2] —**fit′ted·ness,** *n.*

fit·ten (fit′n), *adj. South Midland and Southern U.S.* **1.** suitable; appropriate. **2.** pleasing, attractive, or delicious: *That pie was mighty fitten.* [1635–45; FIT^1 + -EN^3]

fit·ter (fit′ər), *n.* **1.** a person or thing that fits. **2.** a person who fits garments. **3.** a worker who fits together or adjusts the parts of machinery. **4.** a person who supplies and fixes fittings or fixtures. **5.** a person who furnishes or equips with whatever is necessary for some purpose. [1650–60; FIT^1 + -ER^1]

fit·ting (fit′ing), *adj.* **1.** suitable or appropriate; proper or becoming. —*n.* **2.** the act of a person or thing that fits. **3.** an act or instance of trying on clothes that are being made or altered to determine proper fit. **4.** anything provided as equipment, parts, supply, etc. **5.** Usually, **fittings.** furniture, fixtures, etc., as of a building or apartment. [1525–35; FIT^1 + -ING^2, -ING^1] —**fit′ting·ly,** *adv.* —**fit′ting·ness,** *n.*
—**Syn. 1.** fit, meet, right, decorous, seemly.

fit′ting room′, a room, as in a clothing store, where garments are tried on and measurements taken for alterations or other changes.

fit·to·ni·a (fi tō′nē ə), *n.* either of two plants, *Fittonia gigantea* or *F. verschaffeltii,* of the acanthus family, native to South America, having conspicuously veined leaves and often cultivated as a houseplant. [< NL (1865), after Sarah Mary and Elizabeth *Fitton,* 19th-century Irish botanical writers; see -IA]

Fitz·ger·ald (fits jer′əld), *n.* **1. Ella,** 1918–96, U.S. jazz singer. **2. F(rancis) Scott (Key),** 1896–1940, U.S. novelist and short-story writer. **3.** a town in central Georgia. 10,187. **4.** a male given name.

Fitz·Ger·ald (fits jer′əld), *n.* **1. Edward,** 1809–83, English poet: translator of drama and poetry, esp. of Omar Khayyám. **2. George Francis,** 1851–1901, Irish physicist.

FitzGer′ald contrac′tion, *Physics.* the hypothesis that a moving body exhibits a contraction in the direction of motion when its velocity is close to the speed of light. Also called **Fitz·Ger′ald-Lo′rentz contrac′tion** (fits jer′əld lôr′ents, -lōr′-), **Lorentz-FitzGerald contraction.** [1915–20; named after G. F. FITZGERALD]

Fitz·hugh (fits hyo͞o′ *or, often,* -yo͞o′), *n.* a male given name.

Fitz·roy (fits roi′), *n.* **Augustus Henry, 3rd Duke of Graf·ton** (graf′tən, gräf′-), 1735–1811, British statesman: prime minister 1768–70.

Fitz·sim·mons (fit sim′ənz, fits-), *n.* **1. James** (*"Sunny Jim"*), 1874–1966, U.S. racehorse trainer. **2. Robert Prometheus** 1862–1917, English boxer: world heavyweight champion 1897–99.

Fiu·me (fyo͞o′me), *n.* Italian name of **Rijeka.**

five (fīv), *n.* **1.** a cardinal number, four plus one. **2.** a symbol for this number, as 5 or V. **3.** a set of this many persons or things. **4.** a playing card, die face, or half of a domino face with five pips. **5.** *Informal.* a five-dollar bill: *Can you give me two fives for a ten?* **6. take five,** *Informal.* to take a brief respite. —*adj.* **7.** amounting to five in number. [bef. 1000; 1925–30 for def. 6; ME; OE *fīf;* c. D *vijf,* G *fünf,* ON *fimm,* Goth *fimf,* L *quinque,* Gk *pénte,* Skt *pancha*]

five-and-ten (fīv′ən ten′), *n.* **1.** Also called **five′-and-ten′-cent store′** (fīv′ən ten′sent′), **five′-and-dime′** (fīv′ən dīm′), **dime store, ten-cent store.** a store offering a wide assortment of inexpensive items, formerly costing five or ten cents, for personal and household use. —*adj.* **2.** of, pertaining to, or characteristic of a five-and-ten. [1875–80]

five-by-five (fīv′bī fīv′), *adj. Slang (facetious).* short and fat. [1925–30]

Five′ Civ′ilized Na′tions, the collective name for the Cherokee, Creek, Choctaw, Chickasaw, and Seminole tribes of Indians who, in spite of their adaptation to European culture, were deported to the Indian Territory from 1830 to 1840. Also called **Five′ Civ′ilized Tribes′.**

Five′-El′ements School′ (fīv′el′ə mənts). See **Yin-Yang School.**

five-fin·ger (fīv′fing′gər), *n.* **1.** any of certain species of potentilla having leaves of five leaflets, as *Potentilla canadensis.* **2.** See **Virginia creeper.** [bef. 1000; ME; OE *fīffingre*]

five·fold (fīv′fōld′), *adj.* **1.** five times as great or as much. **2.** comprising five parts or members. —*adv.* **3.** in fivefold measure. [bef. 1000; ME *fiffold,* OE *fīffeald.* See FIVE, -FOLD]

five-gait·ed (fīv′gā′tid), *adj. Manège.* noting an American saddle horse that has been trained to execute the rack and slow gait in addition to the walk, trot, and canter, and that is used chiefly for showing. Cf. **three-gaited.**

five′ hun′dred, *Cards.* a variety of euchre in which a joker and widow are included, the object being to score 500 points first. [1915–20, *Amer.*]

five′ hun′dred rum′my, *Cards.* a variety of rummy in which the winner is the first player to score 500 points. Also called **pinochle rummy.**

five-leg·ged (fīv′leg′id, -legd′), *adj. Naut.* (of a schooner) having five masts.

Five′ Na′tions, a confederacy of Iroquoian Indians: the Mohawk, Oneida, Onondaga, Cayuga, and Seneca, and, after the 18th century, the Tuscarora.

five′ o'clock′ shad′ow, the rather dark stubble that appears on a man's face some hours after shaving, typically in the late afternoon if he shaved in the morning. Also, **five′-o'clock shad′ow.** [1935–40]

five·pen·ny (fīv′pen′ē), *adj.* **1.** noting a nail 1¾ in. (4.4 cm) long. *Symbol:* 5d **2.** worth five pence. [1790–1800; FIVE + -PENNY]

fiv·er (fī′vər), *n. Slang.* **1.** a five-dollar bill. **2.** *Brit.* a five-pound note. [1830–40; FIVE + -ER^1]

fives (fīvz), *n.* (*used with a singular v.*) *Brit.* a game resembling handball, played on a court having a front wall and two side walls. [1630–40; FIVE + -S^3]

five′ sens′es, sense (def. 1).

five-speed (fīv′spēd′), *n.* **1.** (in an automotive vehicle or bicycle) a transmission or system of gears having five forward gear ratios. **2.** an automotive vehicle or bicycle having such a transmission or system of gears. —*adj.* **3.** having five forward gear ratios.

five-spot (fīv′spot′), *n.* **1.** a playing card or the upward face of a die bearing five pips; a domino one half of which bears five pips. **2.** *Slang.* a five-dollar bill. **3.** a low plant, *Nemophila maculata,* of the waterleaf family, native to western and central California, having white flowers with a purple spot at the tip of each of its five petals. [1900–05, *Amer.*]

five-star (fīv′stär′), *adj.* **1.** having five stars to indicate rank or quality: *a five-star general; a five-star brandy.* **2.** of the highest quality. [1910–15]

Five′ Towns′. See **the Potteries.**

five W's, *Journalism.* who, what, when, where, and why: along with *how,* the essential questions about the subject of a news story that the lead is traditionally expected to answer.

Five′-Year Plan′ (fīv′yēr′), (*sometimes l.c.*) any plan for national economic or industrial development specifying goals to be reached within a period of five years, esp. as undertaken by the Soviet Union and China. [1925–30; orig. prob. as trans. of Russ *pyatilétka*]

fix (fiks), *v.,* **fixed** or **fixt, fix·ing,** *n.* —*v.t.* **1.** to repair; mend. **2.** to put in order or in good condition; adjust or arrrange: *She fixed her hair in a bun.* **3.** to make fast, firm, or stable. **4.** to place definitely and more or less permanently: *to fix a circus poster to a wall.* **5.** to settle definitely; determine: *to fix a price.* **6.** to direct (the eyes, the attention, etc.) steadily: *His eyes were fixed on the distant ship.* **7.** to attract and hold (the eye, the attention, etc.). **8.** to make set or rigid. **9.** to put into permanent form. **10.** to put or place (responsibility, blame, etc.) on a person. **11.** to assign or refer to a definite place, time, etc. **12.** to provide or supply with (something needed or wanted): *How are you fixed for money?* **13.** *Informal.* to arrange or influence the outcome or action of, esp. privately or dishonestly: *to fix a jury; to fix a game.* **14.** to get (a meal); prepare (food): *What time shall I fix supper?* **15.** *Informal.* to put in a condition or position to make no further trouble. **16.** *Informal.* to get even with; get revenge upon: *I'll fix him!* **17.** *Informal.* to castrate or spay (an animal, esp. a pet). **18.** *Chem.* **a.** to make stable in consistency or condition; reduce from fluidity or volatility to a more stable state. **b.** to convert atmospheric nitrogen into a useful compound, as a nitrate fertilizer. **19.** *Photog.* to render (an image) permanent by removing light-sensitive silver halides. **20.** *Microscopy.* to kill, make rigid, and preserve for microscopic study.
—*v.i.* **21.** to become fixed. **22.** to become set; assume a rigid or solid form. **23.** to become stable or permanent. **24.** to settle down. **25.** *Slang.* to inject oneself with a narcotic. **26.** *Chiefly Southern U.S.* to prepare; plan (usually fol. by an infinitive): *I was just fixing to call you. We're fixing to go to Colorado this summer.* **27. fix on** or **upon,** to decide on; determine: *We won't be able to fix on a location for the banquet until we know the number of guests.* **28. fix one's wagon,** *Informal.* to exact retribution for an offense; treat someone vengefully: *I'll dock his pay and that will fix his wagon.* **29. fix up,** *Informal.* **a.** to arrange for: *to fix up a date.* **b.** to provide with; furnish. **c.** to repair; renew. **d.** to smooth over; solve: *They weren't able to fix up their differences.*
—*n.* **30.** *Informal.* a position from which it is difficult to escape; predicament. **31.** *Informal.* a repair, adjustment, or solution, usually of an immediate nature: *Can you think of a fix for the problem?* **32.** *Navig.* **a.** a charted position of a vessel or aircraft, determined by two or more bearings taken on landmarks, heavenly bodies, etc. **b.** the determining of the position of a ship, plane, etc., by mathematical, electronic, or other means: *The navigator took a fix on the sun and steered the ship due north.* **33.** a clear determination: *Can you get a fix on what he really means?* **34.** *Slang.* **a.** an injection of heroin or other narcotic. **b.** the narcotic or amount of narcotic injected. **c.** a compulsively sought dose or infusion of something: *to need one's daily fix of soap operas on TV.* **35.** *Slang.* **a.** an underhand or illegal arrangement, esp. one secured through bribery or influence. **b.** a contest, situation, etc., whose outcome is prearranged dishonestly. **36. in a fix,** *Older Slang.* pregnant. [1350–1400; 1900–05 for def. 32; 1935–40 for def. 34; ME *fixen* (v.) < ML *fixāre,* deriv. of L *fixus* fixed, ptp. of *fīgere* to fasten] —**fix′a·ble,** *adj.* —**fix′a·bil′i·ty,** *n.*
—**Syn. 1.** correct, amend. **3, 4.** fasten, secure, stabilize. FIX, ESTABLISH imply making firm or permanent. To FIX is to fasten in position securely or to make more or less permanent against change, esp. something already existing: *to fix a bayonet on a gun; fix a principle in one's mind.* To ESTABLISH is to make firm or permanent something (usually newly) originated, created, or ordained: *to establish a business, a claim to property.* **5.** establish, define. **30.** dilemma, plight, quandary.
—**Usage.** FIX meaning "to repair" appears to have been used first in America, but it is long established and has been used in England since the early 19th century: *The engineer quickly fixed the faulty valve.* The verb use is fully standard in all varieties of speech and writing, and objections to it on the grounds of style merely reflect personal prejudice, not the practice of educated speakers and writers. The noun FIX meaning "repair, adjustment" is informal.
FIX (TO) meaning "to prepare, plan (to)" is another Americanism: *We're fixing to go to town.* It once occurred in all the eastern coastal states, but it is now

chiefly an informal spoken form in the South Midland and South.

fix•ate (fik′sāt), *v.*, **-at•ed, -at•ing.** —*v.t.* **1.** to fix; make stable or stationary. —*v.i.* **2.** to become fixed. **3.** *Psychoanal.* to develop a fixation; suffer an arrest in one's emotional or sexual development. [1880–85; < L *fix(us)* fixed, firm (see FIX) + -ATE[1]]

fix•a•tion (fik sā′shən), *n.* **1.** the act of fixing or the state of being fixed. **2.** *Chem.* **a.** reduction from a volatile or fluid to a stable or solid form. **b.** the process of converting atmospheric nitrogen into a useful compound, as a nitrate fertilizer. **3.** *Photog.* the process of rendering an image permanent by removal of light-sensitive silver halides. **4.** *Psychoanal.* a partial arrest of emotional and instinctual development at an early point in life, due to a severe traumatic experience or an overwhelming gratification. **5.** a preoccupation with one subject, issue, etc.; obsession: *All her life she had a fixation on stories of violent death.* [1350–1400; ME *fixacion* < ML *fixātiōn-* (s. of *fixātiō*) a reduction to a fixed state. See FIX, -ATION]

fix•a•tive (fik′sə tiv), *adj.* **1.** serving to fix; making fixed or permanent. —*n.* Also, **fix•a•tif** (fik′sə tiv, -tēf′). **2.** a fixative substance, as a gummy liquid sprayed on a drawing to prevent blurring, or a solution for killing, hardening, and preserving material for microscopic study. **3.** Also called **fixer.** *Photog.* a chemical substance, as sodium thiosulfate, used to promote fixation. **4.** a substance that retards evaporation, as in the manufacture of perfume. [1635–45; FIX + -ATIVE]

fix•a•tor (fik′sā tər), *n.* a device incorporating a metal bar and pins that is used in stabilizing difficult bone fractures. Also, **fix′at•er.** [1870–75; FIX + -ATOR]

fixed (fikst), *adj.* **1.** fastened, attached, or placed so as to be firm and not readily movable; firmly implanted; stationary; rigid. **2.** rendered stable or permanent, as color. **3.** set or intent upon something; steadily directed: *a fixed stare.* **4.** definitely and permanently placed: *a fixed buoy; a fixed line of defense.* **5.** not fluctuating or varying; definite: *a fixed purpose.* **6.** supplied with or having enough of something necessary or wanted, as money. **7.** coming each year on the same calendar date: *Christmas is a fixed holiday, but Easter is not.* **8.** put in order. **9.** *Informal.* arranged in advance privately or dishonestly: *a fixed horse race.* **10.** *Chem.* **a.** (of an element) taken into a compound from its free state. **b.** nonvolatile, or not easily volatilized: *a fixed oil.* **11.** *Math.* (of a point) mapped to itself by a given function. Cf. **Brouwer fixed-point theorem.** [1350–1400; ME; see FIX, -ED[2]] —**fix•ed•ly** (fik′sid lē, fikst′lē), *adv.* —**fix′•ed•ness,** *n.*
—**Syn. 3.** constant, steady, unvarying, unwavering, firm.

fixed′ ac′tion pat′tern, *Ethology.* a highly stereotyped pattern of behavior that is characteristic of a particular species. [said to be a trans. of G *Erbkoordination,* term used by Konrad Lorenz]

fixed′ as′set, any long-term asset, as a building, tract of land, or patent. Also called **capital asset.** [1895–1900]

fixed′ bridge′, *Dentistry.* a partial denture that is secured permanently in the mouth by being cemented to the adjacent teeth or roots.

fixed′ cap′ital, capital goods, as machinery and tools, that are relatively durable and can be used repeatedly in the production of goods. Cf. **circulating capital.** [1840–50]

fixed′ charge′, **1.** an expense that cannot be modified. **2.** a periodic obligation, as taxes, interest on bonds, etc. **3. fixed charges,** such charges as depreciation, rent, interest, etc., arising out of the maintenance of fixed assets. [1890–95, *Amer.*]

fixed′ cost′, a cost unvarying with a change in the volume of business (distinguished from *variable cost*).

fixed′-do′ sys′tem (fikst′dō′), *Music.* a system of solmization in which the syllable *do* is always C, regardless of the key. Cf. **movable-do system.**

fixed′-fo′cus cam′era (fikst′fō′kəs), a camera with an unadjustable focal length and with a relatively large depth of field. [1890–95]

fixed′ ide′a, a persistent or obsessing idea, often delusional, that can, in extreme form, be a symptom of psychosis. [1820–30]

fixed-in•come (fikst′in′kum), *adj.* gaining or yielding a more or less uniform rate of income. [1855–60]

fixed′ invest′ment trust′. See **unit trust** (def. 1).

fixed-length (fikst′lengkth′, -length′), *adj. Computers.* referring to a field, record, computer word, or other entity whose length does not vary.

fixed′ liabil′ity, a liability, as a mortgage or debenture, that will not mature for a relatively long time.

fixed′ oil′, *Chem.* a natural vegetable or animal oil that is nonvolatile, as lard oil, linseed oil, etc. Also called **fatty oil.** [1790–1800]

fixed′ price′, a price established by a seller, by agreement or by authority, as the price to be charged invariably. [1905–10] —**fixed′-price′,** *adj.*

fixed′-rate mort′gage (fikst′rāt′), a home mortgage for which equal monthly payments of interest and principal are paid over the life of the loan, usually for a term of 30 years.

fixed′ sign′, *Astrol.* any of the four astrological signs, Taurus, Leo, Scorpio, or Aquarius, that are grouped together because of their placement midway between solstices and equinoxes and characterized by identification of those born under the sign with the shared attribute of motivation through subjective values toward a well-defined goal. Cf. **quadruplicity.**

fixed′ star′, *Astron.* any of the stars which apparently always retain the same position in respect to one another. [1555–65]

fixed′ trust′. See **unit trust** (def. 1). [1925–30]

fixed-wing (fikst′wing′), *adj.* of or pertaining to aircraft that derive lift from the motion of air over aerodynamically designed surfaces that are rigidly and permanently attached to the fuselage.

fix•er (fik′sər), *n.* **1.** a person or thing that fixes. **2.** *Informal.* a person who arranges matters in advance through bribery or influence. **3.** *Photog.* fixative (def. 3). **4.** *Slang.* a person who sells narcotics to addicts. [1840–50; FIX + -ER[1]]

fix•er-up•per (fik′sər up′ər), *n. Informal.* **1.** a person who is handy at making repairs. **2.** a rundown dwelling offered at a bargain price and suitable for improvement by a new owner, often with the object of resale at a considerable profit. [*fix up* + -ER[1], pleonastically suffixed to both words]

fix•ing (fik′sing), *n.* **1.** the act of a person or thing that fixes. **2. fixings.** Also, **fix•in's** (fik′sinz). *Informal.* **a.** the necessary ingredients: *salad fixings.* **b.** the appropriate accompaniments; trimmings: *turkey with all the fixings.* **3.** See **gold fixing.** [1425–75; late ME; see FIX, -ING[1]]

fix-it (fiks′it′), *adj. Informal.* of, pertaining to, doing, or involving repairs, adjustments, or improvements: *a fix-it shop; a political fix-it man.* Also, **fix′it′.**

fix•i•ty (fik′si tē), *n., pl.* **-ties** for 2. **1.** the state or quality of being fixed; stability; permanence. **2.** something fixed, stable, or permanent. [1660–70; < NL *fixitās.* See FIX, -ITY]

fixt (fikst), *v.* a pt. and pp. of **fix.**

fix•ture (fiks′chər), *n.* **1.** something securely, and usually permanently, attached or appended, as to a house, apartment building, etc.: *a light fixture; kitchen fixtures.* **2.** a person or thing long established in the same place or position. **3.** *Mach.* **a.** any of various devices for holding work in a machine tool, esp. one for machining in a straight line, as in a planer or milling machine. **b.** any of various devices for holding parts in certain positions during welding, assembly, etc. **4.** *Law.* a movable chattel, as a machine or heating plant, that, by reason of annexation to real property and adaptation to continuing use in connection with the realty, is considered a part of the realty. **5.** *Fox Hunting.* one of a series of meets scheduled by a hunt to take place at a time and location listed on a card **(fix′ture card′)** that is sent, usually once a month, to each member of a hunt. **6.** the act of fixing. **7.** *Brit.* an event that takes place regularly. [1590–1600; var. of obs. *fixure* (< LL *fixūra;* see FIX, -URE), with *-t-* from MIXTURE] —**fix′ture•less,** *adj.*

fix-up (fiks′up′), *n.* repair; improvement: *fix-ups that will make the house more salable.* [1825–35, *Amer.*; n. use of v. phrase *fix up*]

Fi•zeau (fē zō′), *n.* **Ar•mande Hip•po•lyte Louis** (AR-män′ ē pô lēt′ lwē), 1819–96, French physicist.

fiz•gig (fiz′gig′), *n.* **1.** a type of firework that makes a loud hissing sound. **2.** a whirling toy that makes a whizzing noise. **3.** fishgig. **4.** *Australian.* a police informer. [1520–30; earlier *fisgig,* equiv. to *fis* (late ME *fise* term of abuse; akin to ON *fīsa* to break wind; cf. FIZZLE) + *gig* (ME *gigge* girl; see GIGGLE)]

fizz (fiz), *v.i.* **1.** to make a hissing or sputtering sound; effervesce. —*n.* **2.** a fizzing sound; effervescence. **3.** soda water or other effervescent water. **4.** an iced mixed drink made of liquor, lemon juice, sugar, and soda: *gin fizz.* **5.** *Brit. Informal.* champagne. [1655–65; back formation from FIZZLE] —**fizz′er,** *n.*

fiz•zle (fiz′əl), *v.,* **-zled, -zling,** *n.* —*v.i.* **1.** to make a hissing or sputtering sound, esp. one that dies out weakly. **2.** *Informal.* to fail ignominiously after a good start (often fol. by *out*): *The reform movement fizzled out because of poor leadership.* —*n.* **3.** a fizzling, hissing, or sputtering. **4.** *Informal.* a failure; fiasco. [1525–35; earlier *fysel* to break wind, freq. of **fise* < ON *fīsa* to break wind; akin to FEIST]
—**Syn. 2.** miscarry, collapse, founder.

fizz•wa•ter (fiz′wô′tər, -wot′ər), *n.* effervescent water; soda water. [FIZZ + WATER]

fizz•y (fiz′ē), *adj.,* **fizz•i•er, fizz•i•est.** bubbly; fizzing. [1850–55; FIZZ + -Y[1]]

fjeld (fyeld; *Norw.* fyel), *n.* a rocky, barren plateau of the Scandinavian peninsula. [1855–60; < Norw; see FELL[5]]

fjord (fyôrd, fyōrd; *Norw.* fyōr, fyŏŏr), *n.* **1.** a long, narrow arm of the sea bordered by steep cliffs: usually formed by glacial erosion. **2.** (in Scandinavia) a bay. Also, **fiord.** [< Norw; see FIRTH] —**fjord′ic,** *adj.*

FL, 1. Florida (approved esp. for use with zip code). **2.** foreign language.

fL, foot-lambert.

fl, *Sports.* flanker.

Fl., 1. Flanders. **2.** Flemish.

fl., 1. floor. **2.** florin. **3.** flourished. [< L *flōruit*] **4.** fluid. **5.** (in the Netherlands) guilder; guilders. [< D *florin*]

Fla., Florida.

flab (flab), *n.* **1.** flabby flesh; unwanted fat: *Daily exercise will get rid of the flab around your waist.* **2.** the condition of being flabby: *Most of the new recruits had run to flab in civilian life.* [1920–25; back formation from FLABBY]

flab•ber•gast (flab′ər gast′), *v.t.* to overcome with surprise and bewilderment; astound. [1765–75; var. of *flabagast* (perh. FLABB(Y) + AGHAST)] —**flab′ber•gast′•er,** *n.*
—**Syn.** amaze, astonish, stagger, nonplus, confound; perplex, confuse, mystify.

flab•by (flab′ē), *adj.,* **-bi•er, -bi•est. 1.** hanging loosely or limply, as flesh or muscles; flaccid. **2.** having such flesh. **3.** lacking strength or determination. [1690–1700; appar. expressive alter. of earlier *flappy,* with same sense; see FLAP, -Y[1]; cf. late ME *flabband* (attested once), evidently with sense "flapping"] —**flab′bi•ly,** *adv.* —**flab′bi•ness,** *n.*

fla•bel•late (flə bel′it, -āt), *adj. Bot., Zool.* fan-shaped. Also, **fla•bel•li•form** (flə bel′ə fôrm′). [1810–20; < L *flābell(um)* fan + -ATE[1]]

flabelli-, a combining form of **flabellum:** *flabelliform.*

fla•bel•lum (flə bel′əm), *n., pl.* **-bel•la** (-bel′ə). **1.** a fan, esp. one used in religious ceremonies. **2.** a fan-shaped part. [1865–70; < L *flābellum* fan, dim. of *flābra* breezes, equiv. to *flā(re)* to BLOW[2] + *-bra,* pl. of *-brum* n. suffix of means; see CASTELLUM for formation]

flac•cid (flak′sid, flas′id), *adj.* **1.** soft and limp; not firm; flabby: *flaccid biceps.* **2.** lacking force; weak: *flaccid prose.* [1610–20; < L *flaccidus* flabby, equiv. to *flacc(ēre)* to grow weak, languish + *-idus* -ID[4]] —**flac•cid′i•ty, flac′cid•ness,** *n.* —**flac′cid•ly,** *adv.*

flack[1] (flak), *n. Sometimes Disparaging.* **1.** See **press agent. 2.** publicity. —*v.i.* **3.** to serve as a press agent or publicist: *to flack for a new rock group.* —*v.t.* **4.** to promote; publicize: *to flack a new record.* [1935–40; said to be after Gene *Flack,* a movie publicity agent]

flack[2] (flak), *n.* flak.

flack•er•y (flak′ə rē), *n. Sometimes Disparaging.* publicity and promotion; press-agentry. [FLACK[1] + -ERY]

flac•on (flak′ən; *Fr.* fla kôn′), *n., pl.* **flac•ons** (flak′ənz; *Fr.* fla kôn′). a small bottle or flask with a stopper, esp. one used for perfume. [1815–25; < F; see FLAGON]

flag[1] (flag), *n., v.,* **flagged, flag•ging.** —*n.* **1.** a piece of cloth, varying in size, shape, color, and design, usually attached at one edge to a staff or cord, and used as the symbol of a nation, state, or organization, as a means of signaling, etc.; ensign; standard; banner; pennant. **2.** *Ornith.* the tuft of long feathers on the legs of falcons and most hawks; the lengthened feathers on the crus or tibia. **3.** *Hunting.* the tail of a deer or of a setter dog. **4.** *Journalism.* **a.** the nameplate of a newspaper. **b.** masthead (def. 1). **c.** the name of a newspaper as printed on the editorial page. **5.** a tab or tag attached to a page, file card, etc., to mark it for attention. **6.** *Music.* hook (def. 12a). **7.** *Motion Pictures, Television.* a small gobo. **8.** Usually, **flags.** the ends of the bristles of a brush, esp. a paintbrush, when split. **9.** *Computers.* a symbol, value, or other means of identifying data of interest, or of informing later parts of a program what conditions earlier parts have encountered. **10. strike the flag, a.** to relinquish command, as of a ship. **b.** to submit or surrender: *His financial situation is growing worse, but he's not ready to strike the flag.* Also, **strike one's flag.** —*v.t.* **11.** to place a flag or flags over or on; decorate with flags. **12.** to signal or warn (a person, automobile, etc.) with or as if with a flag (sometimes fol. by *down*): *to flag a taxi; to flag down a passing car.* **13.** to communicate (information) by or as if by a flag. **14.** to decoy, as game, by waving a flag or the like to excite attention or curiosity. **15.** to mark (a page in a book, file card, etc.) for attention, as by attaching protruding tabs. **16.** (of a brush) to split the ends of the bristles. [1475–85; perh. b. FLAP (n.) and FAG[1] (n.) in obs. sense "flap"] —**flag′ger,** *n.* —**flag′less,** *adj.*

flag[2] (flag), *n.* **1.** any of various plants with long, sword-shaped leaves, as the sweet flag. **2.** See **blue flag. 3.** the long, slender leaf of such a plant or of a cereal. [1350–1400; ME *flagge*]

flag[3] (flag), *v.i.,* **flagged, flag•ging. 1.** to fall off in vigor, energy, activity, interest, etc.: *Public enthusiasm flagged when the team kept losing.* **2.** to hang loosely or limply; droop. [1535–45; perh. b. of FLAP (v.) and FAG[1] (v.) in obs. sense "to droop". See FLAG[1]]
—**Syn. 1.** dwindle, wilt, slump, sag, wane.

flag[4] (flag), *n., v.,* **flagged, flag•ging.** —*n.* **1.** flagstone (def. 1). **2. flags,** flagstone (def. 2). —*v.t.* **3.** to pave with flagstones. [1400–50; late ME *flagge* piece of sod; akin to ON *flaga* slab] —**flag′ger,** *n.*

flag′ day′, (*sometimes caps.*) *Brit.* See **tag day.** [1910–15]

Flag′ Day′, June 14, the anniversary of the day (June 14, 1777) when Congress adopted the Stars and Stripes as the national flag of the United States.

fla•gel•la (flə jel′ə), *n.* a pl. of **flagellum.**

flag•el•lant (flaj′ə lənt, flə jel′ənt), *n.* **1.** a person who flagellates or scourges himself or herself for religious discipline. **2.** a person who derives sexual pleasure from whipping or being whipped by another person. **3.** (*often cap.*) one of a medieval European sect of fanatics who practiced scourging in public. —*adj.* **4.** flagellating. **5.** severely criticizing: *a flagellant attack on the opposition party.* [1555–65; < L *flagellant-* (s. of *flagellāns*) whipping, prp. of *flagellāre.* See FLAGELLUM, -ANT] —**flag′el•lant•ism,** *n.*

fla•gel•lar (flə jel′ər), *adj. Biol.* of or pertaining to a flagellum. [1885–90; FLAGELL(UM) + -AR[1]]

Flag•el•la•ta (flaj′ə lā′tə), *n.* Mastigophora. [< NL, neut. pl. of L *flagellātus* FLAGELLATE]

flag•el•late (*v.* flaj′ə lāt′; *adj., n.* flaj′ə lit, -lāt′), *v.,* **-lat•ed, -lat•ing,** *adj., n.* —*v.t.* **1.** to whip; scourge; flog; lash. —*adj.* **2.** Also, **flag′el•lat′ed.** *Biol.* having flagella. **3.** *Bot.* producing filiform runners or runnerlike branches, as the strawberry. **4.** pertaining to or caused by flagellates. —*n.* **5.** any protozoan of the phylum (or class) Mastigophora, having one or more flagella. See illus. on next page. [1615–25; < L *flagellātus,* ptp. of *flagellāre* to whip. See FLAGELLUM, -ATE[1]] —**flag′el•la′tor,** *n.* —**flag•el•la•to•ry** (flaj′ə lə tôr′ē, -tōr′ē), *adj.*

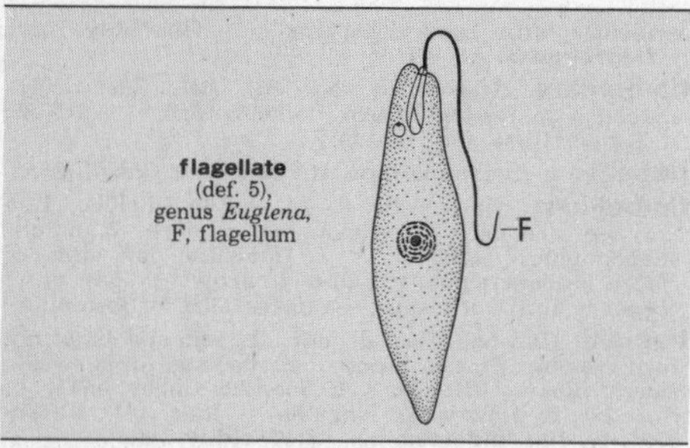

flagellate (def. 5), genus *Euglena,* F, flagellum

flag·el·la·tion (flaj′ə lā′shən), *n.* **1.** the act or process of flagellating. **2.** a masochistic or sadistic act in which the participants receive erotic stimulation from whipping or being whipped. [1400–50; late ME < LL *flagellātiōn-,* s. of *flagellātiō.* See FLAGELLATE, -ION]

fla·gel·li·form (flə jel′ə fôrm′), *adj. Biol.* long, slender, and flexible, like the lash of a whip. [1820–30; < L *flagell(um)* a whip, scourge + -I- + -FORM]

fla·gel·lum (flə jel′əm), *n., pl.* **-gel·la** (-jel′ə), **-gel·lums. 1.** *Biol.* a long, lashlike appendage serving as an organ of locomotion in protozoa, sperm cells, etc. **2.** *Bot.* a runner. **3.** Also called **clavola.** *Entomol.* (in an antenna) the whiplike portion above the basal joints. **4.** a whip or lash. [1800–10; < L: whip, lash, dim. of *flagrum* a whip, scourge]

flag·eo·let (flaj′ə let′, -lā′), *n.* **1.** a small end-blown flute with four finger holes in front and two in the rear. **2.** any fipple flute. [1650–60; < F, sp. var. of OF *flajolet,* equiv. to *flajol* flute (< VL **flabeolum,* deriv. of L *flāre* to BLOW²) + *-et* -ET]

flageolet (def. 1)

fla·geo·let (fla zhô le′), *n., pl.* ***-lets*** (-le′). *French.* a green baby lima bean.

flag·fish (flag′fish′), *n., pl. (esp. collectively)* **-fish,** *(esp. referring to two or more kinds of species)* **-fish·es. 1.** Also called **American flagfish.** a killifish, *Jordanella floridae,* inhabiting swamps and streams of Florida, having a blue-brown back and whitish sides with red stripes, often kept in aquariums. **2.** any of several other brightly colored fishes. [FLAG¹ + FISH]

flag′ foot′ball, a form of touch football in which the ball-carrier's progress is stopped when an opponent pulls a flag from the ball-carrier's pocket or belt. [1950–55]

Flagg (flag), *n.* **James Montgomery,** 1877–1960, U.S. painter and illustrator.

flag·ging[1] (flag′ing), *adj.* **1.** dwindling. **2.** weak, fatigued, or drooping. [1535–45; FLAG³ + -ING²] **—flag′·ging·ly,** *adv.*

flag·ging[2] (flag′ing), *n.* **1.** flagstones collectively. **2.** a pavement or walk of flagstones. [1615–25; FLAG⁴ + -ING¹]

flag·gy[1] (flag′ē), *adj.,* **-gi·er, -gi·est.** flagging; drooping; limp. [1555–65; FLAG³ + -Y¹]

flag·gy[2] (flag′ē), *adj.* consisting of or resembling flags or flagstone; laminate. [1840–50; FLAG⁴ + -Y¹]

flag·gy[3] (flag′ē), *adj.* abounding in, consisting of, or resembling flag plants. [1350–1400; ME *flaggi.* See FLAG², -Y¹]

fla·gi·tious (flə jish′əs), *adj.* **1.** shamefully wicked, as persons, actions, or times. **2.** heinous or flagrant, as a crime; infamous. [1350–1400; ME *flagicious* < L *flāgitiōsus,* equiv. to *flāgiti(um)* shame, scandal + *-ōsus* -OUS] **—fla·gi′tious·ly,** *adv.* **—fla·gi′tious·ness,** *n.*

flag·man (flag′mən), *n., pl.* **-men. 1.** a person who signals with a flag or lantern, as at a railroad crossing. **2.** a person who has charge of or carries a flag. [1660–70; FLAG¹ + -MAN]

flag′ of conven′ience, the foreign flag under which merchant ships register in order to save on taxes or wages, or to avoid government regulations. [1955–60]

flag′ of′ficer, 1. a naval officer above the rank of captain, as a fleet admiral, admiral, vice-admiral, rear admiral, or commodore, who is entitled to display a flag indicating his or her rank. **2.** (formerly) an officer in command of a fleet, squadron, or group of ships. [1655–65]

flag′ of truce′, *Mil.* a white flag displayed as an invitation to the enemy to confer, or carried as a sign of peaceful intention by one sent to deal with the enemy. [1620–30]

flag·on (flag′ən), *n.* **1.** a large bottle for wine, liquors, etc. **2.** a container for holding liquids, as for use at table, esp. one with a handle, a spout, and usually a cover. [1425–75; late ME, var. of *flakon* < MF *fla(s)con* < LL *flascōn-* (s. of *flascō*) FLASK]

CONCISE ETYMOLOGY KEY: <, descended or borrowed from; >, whence; b., blend of, blended; c., cognate with; cf., compare; deriv., derivative; equiv., equivalent; imit., imitative; obl., oblique; r., replacing; s., stem; sp., spelling, spelled; resp., respelling, respelled; trans., translation; ?, origin unknown; *, unattested; ‡, probably earlier than. See the full key inside the front cover.

flag·pole (flag′pōl′), *n.* a staff or pole on which a flag is or can be displayed. Also called **flagstaff.** [1880–85; FLAG¹ + POLE¹]

flag′ rank′, naval rank above that of captain. [1890–95]

fla·grant (flā′grənt), *adj.* **1.** shockingly noticeable or evident; obvious; glaring: *a flagrant error.* **2.** notorious; scandalous: *a flagrant crime; a flagrant offender.* **3.** *Archaic.* blazing, burning, or glowing. [1400–50; late ME < L *flagrant-* (s. of *flagrāns*), prp. of *flagrāre* to burn; see -ANT] **—fla′gran·cy, fla′grance, fla′grant·ness,** *n.* **—fla′grant·ly,** *adv.*

—Syn. 2. disgraceful, monstrous, egregious. FLAGRANT, GLARING, GROSS, OUTRAGEOUS, RANK are adjectives suggesting extreme offensiveness. FLAGRANT, with a root sense of flaming or flaring, suggests evil or immorality so evident that it cannot be ignored or overlooked: *a flagrant violation of the law.* GLARING, meaning "shining brightly," is similar to FLAGRANT in emphasizing conspicuousness but usually lacks the imputation of immorality: *a glaring error in computing the interest.* GROSS, which basically signifies excessive size, is even more negative in implication than the foregoing two terms, suggesting a mistake or impropriety of major proportions: *a gross miscarriage of justice.* OUTRAGEOUS describes acts so far beyond the limits of decent behavior or accepted standards as to be totally insupportable: *an outrageous abuse of the public trust.* RANK, with its suggestion of bad odor, describes open offensiveness of the most objectionable kind, inviting total and unalloyed disapprobation: *rank dishonesty, stinking to high heaven; Only rank stupidity would countenance such a step.*

fla·gran·te de·lic·to (flə gran′tē di lik′tō), *Law.* in the very act of committing the offense. [< L]

flag′ seat′, *Furniture.* a seat woven from reeds, rushes, or iris leaves.

flag·ship (flag′ship′), *n.* **1.** a ship carrying the flag officer or the commander of a fleet, squadron, or the like, and displaying the officer's flag. **2.** the main vessel of a shipping line. **3.** any of the best or largest ships or airplanes operated by a passenger line. **4.** the best or most important one of a group or system: *This store is the flagship of our retail chain.* —*adj.* **5.** being or constituting a flagship. [1665–75; FLAG¹ + SHIP]

flag′ smut′, *Plant Pathol.* a disease of cereals and other grasses, characterized by stripes of black spores on the affected leaves and stems, which later dry up and become shredded, caused by several smut fungi of the genus *Urocystis.*

Flag·stad (flag′stad; *Norw.* fläg′stä), *n.* **Kir·sten Ma·rie** (kûr′stən mə rē′; *Norw.* KHish′tən mä Rē′ə, KHiR′stən), 1895–1962, Norwegian operatic soprano.

flag·staff (flag′staf′, -stäf′), *n., pl.* **-staves, -staffs.** flagpole. [1605–15; FLAG¹ + STAFF¹]

Flag·staff (flag′staf′, -stäf′), *n.* a city in central Arizona. 34,641. ab. 6900 ft. (2100 m) high.

flag′ sta′tion, a railroad station where trains stop only when a flag or other signal is displayed or when passengers are to be discharged. Also called **flag′ stop′.** [1845–50, *Amer.*]

flag·stick (flag′stik′), *n. Golf.* pin (def. 12). [1925–30; FLAG¹ + STICK¹]

flag·stone (flag′stōn′), *n.* **1.** Also called **flag.** a flat stone slab used esp. for paving. **2. flagstones,** a walk, terrace, etc., paved with flagstones. **3.** rock, as sandstone or shale, suitable for splitting into flagstones. [1720–30; FLAG⁴ + STONE]

flag-wav·er (flag′wā′vər), *n.* **1.** a person who signals by waving a flag. **2.** an enthusiastic, demonstrative patriot. **3.** a song or musical number intended to arouse patriotic fervor. [1890–95]

flag-wav·ing (flag′wā′ving), *n.* an ostentatiously emotional display of patriotism or factionalism. [1890–95]

Fla·her·ty (fla′ər tē, flä′-), *n.* **Robert Joseph,** 1884–1951, U.S. pioneer in the production of documentary motion pictures.

flail (flāl), *n.* **1.** an instrument for threshing grain, consisting of a staff or handle to one end of which is attached a freely swinging stick or bar. **2.** a similar instrument used as a weapon of war. —*v.t., v.i.* **3.** to beat or swing with or as if with a flail. [bef. 1100; ME *fleil* (n.), OE *flighel* (prob. misspelling of **flegil*), c. D *vlegel,* G *Flegel* < WGmc **flagil-* < LL *flagellum* flail, L: whip, scourge. See FLAGELLUM]

flair (flâr), *n.* **1.** a natural talent, aptitude, or ability; bent; knack: *a flair for writing rhymes.* **2.** smartness of style, manner, etc.: *Their window display has absolutely no flair at all.* **3.** keen perception or discernment. **4.** *Hunting.* scent; sense of smell. [1350–1400; ME < F, OF: scent, n. deriv. of *flairier* to reek << VL **flāgrāre,* dissimilated var. of L *frāgrāre.* See FRAGRANT]

—Syn. 2. chic, dash, panache, verve; oomph, pizazz.

flak (flak), *n.* **1.** antiaircraft fire, esp. as experienced by the crews of combat airplanes at which the fire is directed. **2.** criticism; hostile reaction; abuse: *Such an unpopular decision is bound to draw a lot of flak from the press.* Also, **flack.** [1935–40; < G *Fl(ieger)a(bwehr) k(anone)* antiaircraft gun, equiv. to *Flieger* aircraft (lit., flyer) + *Abwehr* defense + *Kanone* gun, CANNON]

flake[1] (flāk), *n., v.,* **flaked, flak·ing.** —*n.* **1.** a small, flat, thin piece, esp. one that has been or become detached from a larger piece or mass: *flakes of old paint.* **2.** any small piece or mass: *a flake of snow.* **3.** a stratum or layer. **4.** *Slang.* an eccentric person; screwball. **5.** *Slang.* cocaine. **6.** a usually broad, often irregular piece of stone struck from a larger core and sometimes retouched to form a flake tool. —*v.i.* **7.** to peel off or separate in flakes. **8.** to fall in flakes, as snow. —*v.t.* **9.** to remove in flakes. **10.** to break flakes or chips from; break into flakes: *to flake fish for a casserole.* **11.** to cover with or as if with flakes. **12.** to form into flakes. [1350–1400; (n.) ME; akin to OE *flac-* in *flacox* flying (said of arrows), ON *flakka* to rove, wander, MD *vlacken* to flutter; (in def. 4) by back formation from FLAKY, in sense "eccentric, odd"; (v.) late ME: to fall in flakes, deriv. of the n.] **—flake′less,** *adj.* **—flak′er,** *n.*

flake[2] (flāk), *n.* a frame, as for drying fish. [1300–50; ME *flake, fleke* < ON *flaki, fleki* bridge, hurdle]

flake[3] (flāk), *n., v.,* **flaked, flak·ing.** *Naut.* —*n.* **1.** fake² (defs. 1, 2). —*v.t.* **2.** fake² (def. 3). **3.** to lower (a fore-and-aft sail) so as to drape the sail equally on both sides over its boom. [1620–30; appar. var. of FAKE²]

flake[4] (flāk), *v.,* **flaked, flak·ing. flake out,** *Slang.* to fall asleep; take a nap. [1935–40; perh. expressive var. of FLAG³; cf. Brit. dial. *flack* to hang loosely, flap]

flake·board (flāk′bôrd′, -bōrd′), *n.* a form of particle board. [FLAKE¹ + BOARD]

flake·let (flāk′lit), *n.* a small flake, as of snow. [1885–90; FLAKE¹ + -LET]

flake′ tool′, a Paleolithic or later stone tool made from a flake struck from a larger core. [1945–50]

flake′ white′. See **lead white.** [1650–60]

flak′ jack′et, 1. *U.S. Air Force.* an armored garment made of steel plates covered by a padded fabric, designed to protect vital parts of the body from shrapnel. **2.** a protective vest, esp. one that is bulletproof. Also called **flak′ vest′.** [1955–60]

flak′ suit′, *U.S. Air Force.* a suit of two or more padded armored garments designed to protect the body from shrapnel. [1955–60]

flak·y (flā′kē), *adj.,* **flak·i·er, flak·i·est. 1.** of or like flakes. **2.** lying or cleaving off in flakes or layers. **3.** *Slang.* eccentric; wacky; dizzy: *a flaky math professor.* Also, **flak′ey** [1570–80; 1965–70 for def. 3; FLAKE¹ + -Y¹; sense of def. 3 prob. FLAKE⁴ + -Y¹, though influenced by FLAKE¹] **—flak′i·ly,** *adv.* **—flak′i·ness,** *n.*

flam[1] (flam), *n., v.,* **flammed, flam·ming.** *Informal.* —*n.* **1.** a deception or trick. **2.** a falsehood; lie. —*v.t., v.i.* **3.** to deceive; delude; cheat. [1615–25; short for FLIM-FLAM]

flam[2] (flam), *n.* a drumbeat consisting of two notes in quick succession, with the accent on the second. [1790–1800; imit.]

flam·bé (fläm bā′; *Fr.* flän bā′), *adj., v.,* **-béed, -bé·ing.** —*adj.* **1.** Also, **flam·béed** (fläm bād′). (of food) served in flaming liquor, esp. brandy: *steak flambé.* **2.** *Ceram.* **a.** (of a glaze) dense and streaked with contrasting colors, usually red and blue. **b.** (of a ceramic object) covered with a flambé glaze. —*v.t.* **3.** to pour liquor over and ignite. [1885–90; < F, ptp. of *flamber* to flame. See FLAMBEAU]

flam·beau (flam′bō), *n., pl.* **-beaux** (-bōz), **-beaus. 1.** a flaming torch. **2.** a torch for use at night in illuminations, processions, etc. **3.** a large, decorated candlestick. **4.** an ornament having the form of a flaming torch. [1625–35; < F: torch, deriv. of OF *flambe* FLAME]

flam·boy·ant (flam boi′ənt), *adj.* **1.** strikingly bold or brilliant; showy: *flamboyant colors.* **2.** conspicuously dashing and colorful: *the flamboyant idol of international society.* **3.** florid; ornate; elaborately styled: *flamboyant speeches.* **4.** *Archit.* **a.** having the form of an ogee, as a bar of tracery. **b.** noting or pertaining to French Gothic architecture of the late 15th and early and middle 16th centuries, characterized by the use of flamboyant tracery, intricacy of detailing, virtuosity of workmanship, attenuation of parts, and frequent complication of interior space. —*n.* **5.** See **royal poinciana.** [1825–35; < F, prp. of *flamboyer* to flame, flair, deriv. of OF *flambe* FLAME; see -ANT] **—flam·boy′ance, flam·boy′an·cy,** *n.* **—flam·boy′ant·ly,** *adv.*

flame (flām), *n., v.,* **flamed, flam·ing.** —*n.* **1.** burning gas or vapor, as from wood or coal, that is undergoing combustion; a portion of ignited gas or vapor. **2.** Often, **flames.** the state or condition of blazing combustion: *to burst into flames.* **3.** any flamelike condition; glow; inflamed condition. **4.** brilliant light; scintillating luster. **5.** bright coloring; a streak or patch of color. **6.** See **flame color. 7.** intense ardor, zeal, or passion. **8.** *Informal.* an object of one's passionate love; sweetheart: *He's taking out his new flame tonight.* —*v.i.* **9.** to burn with a flame or flames; burst into flames; blaze. **10.** to glow like flame; shine brilliantly; flash. **11.** to burn or burst forth with strong emotion; break into open anger, indignation, etc. **12.** *Computer Jargon.* to enter on an electronic bulletin board text expressing opinions, gossip, etc., often in a ranting and unrestrained manner. —*v.t.* **13.** to subject to the action of flame or fire. **14.** to flambé. **15. flame out, a.** (of a jet engine) to cease to function due to an interruption of the fuel supply or to faulty combustion. **b.** to burst out in or as if in flames. [1300–50; (n.) ME *flaume* < AF, var. of *flaumbe;* OF *flambe,* earlier *flamble* < L *flammula,* dim. of *flamma* flame (see -ULE); (v.) ME *flaumen* < AF *flaum(b)er;* OF *flamber* < L *flammāre,* deriv. of *flamma*] **—flam′er,** *n.* **—flame′less,** *adj.* **—flame′like′,** *adj.*

—Syn. 1. fire. FLAME, BLAZE, CONFLAGRATION refer to the light and heat given off by combustion. FLAME is the common word, referring to a combustion of any size: *the light of a match flame.* BLAZE usually denotes a quick, hot, bright, and comparatively large flame: *The fire burst into a blaze.* CONFLAGRATION refers to destructive flames which spread over a considerable area: *A conflagration destroyed Chicago.*

flame′ azal′ea, an azalea, *Rhododendron calendulaceum,* of the eastern U.S., having yellow, orange, or scarlet flowers. [1840–50, *Amer.*]

flame′ cell′, *Zool.* one of the hollow cells terminating the branches of the excretory tubules of certain invertebrates, having a tuft of continuously moving cilia. [1885–90]

flame′ col′or, bright reddish-orange. Also called **flame.** [1600–10] **—flame′-col′ored,** *adj.*

flame′ cul′tivator, *Agric.* an implement that kills weeds by scorching them with a directed flow of flaming gas. Also called **flame thrower, weed burner.**

flame·fish (flām′fish′), *n., pl.* **-fish·es,** *(esp. collec-*

tively) **-fish.** a cardinalfish, *Apogon maculatus,* of Atlantic coastal waters from Florida to Brazil. [FLAME + FISH]

flame′-fu′sion proc′ess (flām′fyōō′zhən). See **Verneuil process.**

fla·men (flā′mən, -men), *n., pl.* **fla·mens, fla·mi·nes** (flam′ə nēz′). (in ancient Rome) a priest. [1300–50; < L *flamen* (perh. earlier **flādmen;* akin to OE *blōtan* to sacrifice); r. ME *flamin* < L *flāmin-* (s. of *flāmen*)]

fla·men·co (flä meng′kō, flə-), *n., pl.* **-cos,** *adj.* —*n.* **1.** a style of dancing, characteristic of the Andalusian Gypsies, that is strongly rhythmic and involves vigorous actions, as clapping the hands and stamping the feet. **2.** a style of instrumental or vocal music originating in southern Spain and typically of an intensely rhythmic, improvisatory character, performed by itself or as an accompaniment to flamenco dancing. —*adj.* **3.** Also, **fla·men′can.** of or like the music and dances of the Andalusian Gypsies: *flamenco rhythms.* [1895–1900; < Sp: pertaining to the Andalusian Gypsies, lit., FLEMING; the sense shift is variously explained]

flame-of-the-woods (flām′əv *th*ə wŏŏdz′), *n., pl.* **flames-of-the-woods.** an Indian evergreen shrub, *Ixora coccinea,* of the madder family, having red, tubular flowers in dense clusters. Also called **jungle geranium.**

flame-out (flām′out′), *n. Aeron.* the failure of a jet engine due to an interruption of the fuel supply or to faulty combustion. Also, **flame′out′.** Also called **blowout.** [1945–50; n. use of v. phrase *flame out*]

flame·proof (flām′prōōf′), *adj.* **1.** resisting the effect of flames; not readily ignited or burned by flames. —*v.t.* **2.** to make flameproof. [1885–90; FLAME + -PROOF]

flame′ retard′ant, a compound used in cloth and plastic material to raise the ignition point of the material, thus making it resistant to fire. [1945–50]

flame′ stitch′, an ornamental stitch, used on bedspreads, upholstery fabrics, and the like, producing rows of ogees in various colors. [1960–65]

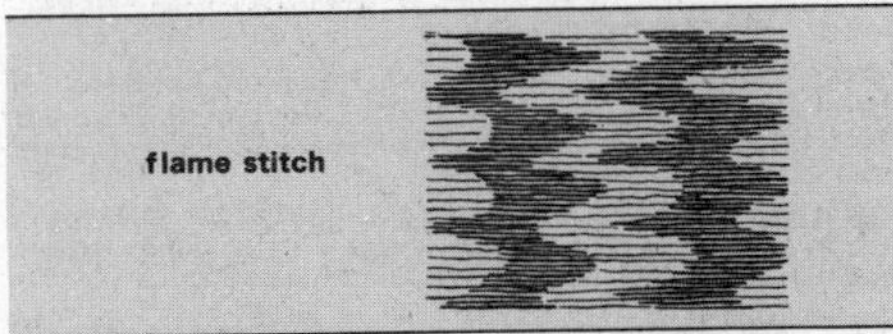
flame stitch

flame·throw·er (flām′thrō′ər), *n.* **1.** a weapon, either mounted or portable, that sprays ignited incendiary fuel for some distance. **2.** *Agric.* See **flame cultivator.** [1915–20; FLAME + THROWER]

flame′ tree′, **1.** either of two trees, *Brachychiton acerifolius* or *B. australis,* native to Australia, having clusters of bright scarlet flowers. **2.** See **royal poinciana.** [1865–70]

flam·ing (flā′ming), *adj.* **1.** emitting flames; blazing; burning; fiery. **2.** like a flame in brilliance, heat, or shape. **3.** intensely ardent or passionate: *flaming youth.* [1350–1400; ME *flammande.* See FLAME, -ING²] —**flam′ing·ly,** *adv.*

fla·min·go (flə ming′gō), *n., pl.* **-gos, -goes.** any of several aquatic birds of the family Phoenicopteridae, having very long legs and neck, webbed feet, a bill bent downward at the tip, and pinkish to scarlet plumage. [1555–65; cf. Pg. *flamengo,* Sp *flamenco* lit., FLEMING (cf. FLAMENCO); appar. orig. a jocular name, from the conventional Romance image of the Flemish as ruddy-complexioned]

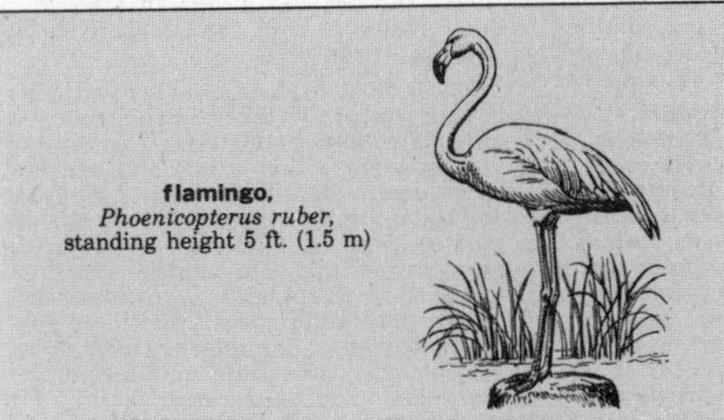
flamingo,
Phoenicopterus ruber,
standing height 5 ft. (1.5 m)

fla·min·go-flow·er (flə ming′gō flou′ər), *n.* a central American plant, *Anthurium scherzeranum,* of the arum family, having a red, coiled spadix and a bright red, shiny, heart-shaped spathe, grown as an ornamental. [1880–85]

Fla·min′i·an Way′ (flə min′ē ən), an ancient Roman road extending N from Rome to what is now Rimini. 215 mi. (345 km) long.

Fla·min·i·us (flə min′ē əs), *n.* **Ga·ius** (gā′əs), died 217 B.C., Roman statesman and general who was defeated by Hannibal.

flam·ma·ble (flam′ə bəl), *adj.* easily set on fire; combustible; inflammable. [1805–15; < L *flammā(re)* to set on fire + -BLE] —**flam′ma·bil′i·ty,** *n.*
—**Usage.** See **inflammable.**

Flam·ma·rion (flA mA RYÔN′), *n.* **(Ni·co·las) Ca·mille** (nē kô lä′ kA mē′yᵊ), 1842–1925, French astronomer and author.

Flam·steed (flam′stēd), *n.* **John,** 1646–1719, English astronomer.

flam·y (flā′mē), *adj.,* **flam·i·er, flam·i·est.** of or like flame. [1485–95; FLAME + -Y¹]

flan (flan, flän; *for 1 also Sp.* flän; *for 2 also Fr.* fläN), *n., pl.* **flans** (flanz, flänz; *for 2 also Fr.* fläN); *Sp.* **fla·nes** (flä′nes) for 1. **1.** *Spanish Cookery.* a dessert of sweetened egg custard with a caramel topping. **2.** an open, tartlike pastry, the shell of which is baked in a bottomless band of metal **(flan ring)** on a baking sheet, removed from the ring and filled with custard, cream, fruit, etc. **3.** a piece of metal shaped ready to form a coin, but not yet stamped by the die. **4.** the metal of which a coin is made, as distinct from its design. [1840–50; < F; OF *flaon* < LL *fladōn-,* s. of *fladō* < Gmc; cf. OHG *flado* (G *Fladen*) flat cake]

Flan·a·gan (flan′ə gən), *n.* **Edward Joseph** (*"Father Flanagan"*), 1886–1948, U.S. Roman Catholic priest, born in Ireland: founder of a farm village for wayward boys.

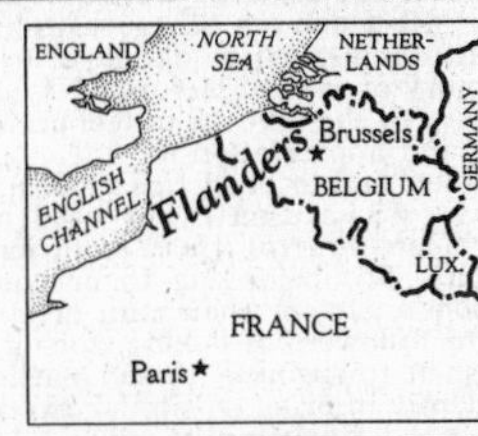

Flan·ders (flan′dərz), *n.* a medieval country in W Europe, extending along the North Sea from the Strait of Dover to the Scheldt River: the corresponding modern regions include the provinces of East Flanders and West Flanders in W Belgium, and the adjacent parts of N France and SW Netherlands.

Flan′ders pop′py. See **corn poppy.** [1920–25]

flâ·ne·rie (flänᵊ Rē′), *n. French.* idleness; dawdling.

flâ·neur (flä nœR′), *n., pl.* ***-neurs*** (-nœR′). *French.* idler; dawdler; loafer.

flange (flanj), *n., v.,* **flanged, flang·ing.** —*n.* **1.** a projecting rim, collar, or ring on a shaft, pipe, machine housing, etc., cast or formed to give additional strength, stiffness, or supporting area, or to provide a place for the attachment of other objects. **2.** a broad ridge or pair of ridges projecting from the edge of a rolled metal shape generally at right angles, in order to strengthen or stiffen it. **3.** a ring or collar, usually provided with holes for bolts, and screwed or welded over the end of a tube or pipe to permit other objects to be attached to it. **4.** (in plumbing) a plate or flat ring bolted to the flange at the end of a length of pipe to close the end or to connect it with the flange of another such length: *blind flange; spectacle flange.* —*v.i.* **5.** to project like, or take the form of, a flange. [1425–75; late ME *flaunche* side charge (on shield face) < MF *flanche,* fem. of *flanc* FLANK] —**flange′less,** *adj.* —**flang′er,** *n.*

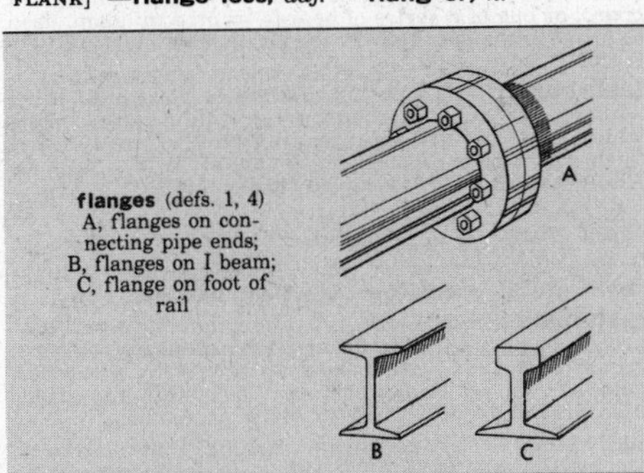

flanges (defs. 1, 4)
A, flanges on connecting pipe ends;
B, flanges on I beam;
C, flange on foot of rail

flange·way (flanj′wā), *n. Railroads.* an opening, parallel to a rail, made through platforms, pavements, track structures, etc., to permit passage of wheel flanges. [FLANGE + WAY]

flank (flangk), *n.* **1.** the side of an animal or a person between the ribs and hip. **2.** the thin piece of flesh constituting this part. **3.** a slice of meat from the flank of an animal. **4.** the side of anything, as of a building. **5.** *Mil., Navy.* the extreme right or left side of an army or fleet, or a subdivision of an army or fleet. **6.** *Fort.* **a.** the right or left side of a work or fortification. **b.** the part of a bastion that extends from the curtain to the face and protects the curtain and the opposite face. See diag. under **bastion. 7.** *Mach.* (on a screw thread or the like) either of the two vertical inclined surfaces between the crest and the root. —*v.t.* **8.** to stand or be placed or posted at the flank or side of. **9.** to defend or guard at the flank. **10.** *Mil.* to menace or attack the flank of. **11.** to pass around or turn the flank of. —*v.i.* **12.** to occupy a position at the flank or side. **13.** to present the flank or side. [bef. 1100; ME; late OE *flanc* < OF < Frankish; cf. OHG *hlanca* loin]
—**Syn. 8.** line, edge, skirt, border.

flan·ken (fläng′kən), *n.* **1.** a strip of meat from the front end of the short ribs of beef. **2.** *Jewish Cookery.* a dish of this meat boiled and often served with horseradish or a horseradish-flavored sauce. [1945–50; < Yiddish, pl. of *flank* (< G) < F or OF; see FLANK]

flank·er (flang′kər), *n.* **1.** a person or thing that flanks. **2.** *Mil.* one of a body of soldiers placed on the flank of an army to guard a line of march. **3.** *Fort.* a fortification projecting so as to defend another work or to command the flank of an assailing body. **4.** *Football.* **a.** Also called **flank′er back′.** an offensive back who lines up outside of an end. **b.** See **split end.** [1540–50; FLANK + -ER¹]

flank′ speed′, the maximum possible speed of a ship.

flan·nel (flan′l), *n., v.,* **-neled, -nel·ing** or (*esp. Brit.*), **-nelled, -nel·ling.** —*n.* **1.** a soft, slightly napped fabric of wool or wool and another fiber, used for trousers, jackets, shirts, etc. **2.** a soft, warm, light fabric of cotton or cotton and another fiber, thickly napped on one side and used for sleepwear, undergarments, sheets, etc. **3.** **flannels, a.** an outer garment, esp. trousers, made of flannel. **b.** woolen undergarments. **4.** *Brit.* **a.** a washcloth. **b.** *Informal.* nonsense; humbug; empty talk. **c.** *Informal.* flattery; insincere or overdone praise. —*v.t.* **5.** to cover or clothe with flannel. **6.** to rub with flannel. [1300–50; ME *flaunneol,* perh. dissimilated var. of *flanyn* sackcloth < Welsh; cf. Welsh *gwlanen* woolen article, equiv. to *gwlân* WOOL (akin to L *lāna*) + *-en* suffix denoting a single item (as a piece of a mass noun or sing. of a collective pl.)]

flan·nel·board (flan′l bôrd′, -bōrd′), *n.* a flannel-covered surface to which other flannel pieces, as letters of the alphabet, numbers, etc., adhere merely by contact, used mainly in schools as a visual aid. [FLANNEL + BOARD]

flan′nel cake′, *Chiefly North Midland U.S.* griddlecake; pancake. [1785–95]
—**Regional Variation.** See **pancake.**

flan·nel·et (flan′l et′), *n.* a warm, soft cotton fabric, plain or printed, napped on one side. Also, **flan′nel·ette′.** [1880–85; FLANNEL + -ET]

flan·nel-leaf (flan′l lēf′), *n.* the common mullein, *Verbascum thapsus.* Also called **flan′nel plant′.** [1815–25]

flan·nel·ly (flan′l ē), *adj.* **1.** made of or resembling flannel. **2.** thick or blurred, as speech. [1830–40; FLANNEL + -Y¹]

flan·nel·mouth (flan′l mouth′), *n., pl.* **-mouths** (-mou*th*z′). **1.** a person whose speech is thick, slow, or halting. **2.** a person whose speech is smoothly deceptive. [1880–85, *Amer.*; FLANNEL + MOUTH]

flan·nel·mouthed (flan′l mou*th*d′, -moutht′), *adj.* **1.** talking thickly, slowly, or haltingly. **2.** characterized by deceptive or shifty speech. [1880–85, *Amer.*; FLANNEL + MOUTH + -ED³]

flan′nelmouth suck′er, *Ichthyol.* a sucker, *Catostomus latipinnis,* of the Colorado River and its tributaries.

flan·ning (flan′ing), *n. Archit.* the splay of a sconcheon. [1840–50; dial. *flan* to splay + -ING¹]

flan′ ring′. See under **flan** (def. 2). [1905–10]

flap (flap), *v.,* **flapped, flap·ping,** *n.* —*v.i.* **1.** to swing or sway back and forth loosely, esp. with noise: *A loose shutter flapped outside the window.* **2.** to move up and down, as wings; flap the wings, or make similar movements. **3.** to strike a blow with something broad and flexible. **4.** *Slang.* to become excited or confused, esp. under stress: *a seasoned diplomat who doesn't flap easily.* —*v.t.* **5.** to move (wings, arms, etc.) up and down. **6.** to cause to swing or sway loosely, esp. with noise. **7.** to strike with something broad and flat. **8.** to toss, fold, shut, etc., smartly, roughly, or noisily. **9.** *Phonetics.* to pronounce (a sound) with articulation resembling that of a flap: *The British often flap their r's.* —*n.* **10.** something flat and broad that is attached at one side only and hangs loosely or covers an opening: *the flap of an envelope; the flap of a pocket.* **11.** either of the two segments of a book jacket folding under the book's front and back covers. **12.** one leaf of a folding door, shutter, or the like. **13.** a flapping motion. **14.** the noise produced by something that flaps. **15.** a blow given with something broad and flat. **16.** *Slang.* **a.** a state of nervous excitement, commotion, or disorganization. **b.** an emergency situation. **c.** scandal; trouble. **17.** *Surg.* a portion of skin or flesh that is partially separated from the body and may subsequently be transposed by grafting. **18.** *Aeron.* a movable surface used for increasing the lift or drag of an airplane. **19.** *Phonet.* **a.** a rapid flip of the tongue tip against the upper teeth or alveolar ridge, as in the *r*-sound in a common British pronunciation of *very,* or the *t*-sound in the common American pronunciation of *water.* **b.** a trill. **c.** a flipping out of the lower lip from a position of pressure against the upper teeth so as to produce an audible pop, as in emphatic utterances containing *f*-sounds or *v*-sounds. **20.** *Building Trades.* **a.** Also called **backflap hinge, flap′ hinge′.** a hinge having a strap or plate for screwing to the face of a door, shutter, or the like. See illus. under **hinge. b.** one leaf of a hinge. [1275–1325; ME *flappe* a blow, slap, *flappen* to hit, slap; cf. D *flap, flappen*] —**flap′less,** *adj.*

flap·doo·dle (flap′dōōd′l), *n. Informal.* nonsense; bosh. [1820–30; orig. uncert.]

flap′ door′, **1.** Also called **falling door.** a door hinged at the bottom so as to fall downward and outward. **2.** a door placed horizontally or on a shallow incline, as an exterior cellar door. [1835–45]

flap·drag·on (flap′drag′ən), *n.* **1.** an old game in which the players snatch raisins, plums, etc., out of burning brandy, and eat them. **2.** the object so caught and eaten. [1580–90; FLAP + DRAGON]

flap·er·on (flap′ə ron′), *n. Aeron.* a control surface functioning both as a flap and as an aileron. [FLAP + (AIL)ERON]

flap·jack (flap′jak′), *n.* **1.** a pancake or griddlecake. **2.** *Brit.* a small case for face powder; compact. [1590–1600; FLAP + JACK¹]
—**Regional Variation. 1.** See **pancake.**

flap·pa·ble (flap′ə bəl), *adj. Informal.* easily upset or confused, esp. under stress. [1965–70; back formation from UNFLAPPABLE]

flap·per (flap′ər), *n.* **1.** something broad and flat used

CONCISE PRONUNCIATION KEY: *act, cāpe, dâre, pärt; set, ēqual; if, ice; ox, ōver, ôrder, oil, bŏŏk, bōōt, out; up, ûrge; child; sing; shoe; thin, that;* zh *as in treasure.* ə = *a* as in *alone, e* as in *system, i* as in *easily, o* as in *gallop, u* as in *circus;* ᵊ as in *fire* (fīᵊr), *hour* (ouᵊr). l and n can serve as syllabic consonants, as in *cradle* (krād′l), and *button* (but′n). See the full key inside the front cover.

for striking or for making a noise by striking. **2.** a broad, flat, hinged or hanging piece; flap. **3.** a young woman, esp. one who, during the 1920's, behaved and dressed in a boldly unconventional manner. **4.** a young bird just learning to fly. **5.** *Slang.* the hand. [1560–70; FLAP + -ER[1]] —**flap′per·dom,** *n.* —**flap′per·ish,** *adj.* —**flap′per·ism,** *n.*

flap·py (flap′ē), *adj.,* **-pi·er, -pi·est.** slack or loose, so as to flap readily. [1900–05; FLAP + -Y[1]; prob. re-formation and not continuous with obs. *flappy* FLABBY]

flaps (flaps), *n.* (*used with a singular v.*) *Vet. Pathol.* swelling of the lips of a horse. [FLAP (n.) + -S[3]]

flap′ valve′. See **clack valve.** [1865–70]

flare (flâr), *v.,* **flared, flar·ing,** *n.* —*v.i.* **1.** to burn with an unsteady, swaying flame, as a torch or candle in the wind. **2.** to blaze with a sudden burst of flame (often fol. by *up*): *The fire flared up as the paper caught.* **3.** to start up or burst out in sudden, fierce activity, passion, etc. (often fol. by *up* or *out*): *Tempers flared at the meeting. Violence flared up in a new section of the city.* **4.** to shine or glow. **5.** to spread gradually outward, as the end of a trumpet, the bottom of a wide skirt, or the sides of a ship. —*v.t.* **6.** to cause (a candle, torch, etc.) to burn with a swaying flame. **7.** to display conspicuously or ostentatiously. **8.** to signal by flares of fire or light. **9.** to cause (something) to spread gradually outward in form. **10.** *Metall.* to heat (a high-zinc brass) to such a high temperature that the zinc vapors begin to burn. **11.** to discharge and burn (excess gas) at a well or refinery. **12. flare out** or **up,** to become suddenly enraged: *She flares up easily.* —*n.* **13.** a flaring or swaying flame or light, as of torches in the wind. **14.** a sudden blaze or burst of flame. **15.** a bright blaze of fire or light used as a signal, a means of illumination or guidance, etc. **16.** a device or substance used to produce such a blaze of fire or light. **17.** a sudden burst, as of zeal or of anger. **18.** a gradual spread outward in form; outward curvature: *the flare of a skirt.* **19.** something that spreads out. **20.** *Optics.* unwanted light reaching the image plane of an optical instrument, resulting from extraneous reflections, scattering by lenses, and the like. **21.** *Photog.* a fogged appearance given to an image by reflection within a camera lens or within the camera itself. **22.** Also called **solar flare.** *Astron.* a sudden and brief brightening of the solar atmosphere in the vicinity of a sunspot that results from an explosive release of particles and radiation. **23.** *Football.* a short pass thrown to a back who is running toward a sideline and is not beyond the line of scrimmage. **24.** *Television.* a dark area on a picture tube caused by variations in light intensity. [1540–50; orig. meaning: spread out, said of hair, a ship's sides, etc.; cf. OE *flǣre* either of the spreading sides at the end of the nose]
—**Syn. 1.** flame. **3.** erupt, explode, flash, blaze, flame. **14.** flash.

flare·back (flâr′bak′), *n.* **1.** a blast of flame that sometimes issues from the breech of a large gun or cannon when it is opened after firing. **2.** a brief, unexpected recurrence: *a flareback of winter in May.* [1900–05; n. use of v. phrase *flare back*]

flare′ star′, *Astron.* a dwarf star that exhibits sudden increases of magnitude similar to solar flares. Also called **UV Ceti star.** [1950–55]

flare-up (flâr′up′), *n.* **1.** a sudden flaring up of flame or light. **2.** a sudden outburst or intensification, as of anger or tensions. **3.** a sudden outbreak of violence, disease, or any other condition thought to be quelled, checked, or inactive. [1830–40; n. use of v. phrase *flare up*]

flar·ing (flâr′ing), *adj.* **1.** blazing; flaming. **2.** glaringly bright or showy. **3.** spreading gradually outward in form: *a flaring skirt.* [1585–95; FLARE + -ING[2]] —**flar′ing·ly,** *adv.*

flash (flash), *n.* **1.** a brief, sudden burst of bright light: *a flash of lightning.* **2.** a sudden, brief outburst or display of joy, wit, etc. **3.** a very brief moment; instant: *I'll be back in a flash.* **4.** *Informal.* flashlight (def. 1). **5.** superficial, meretricious, or vulgar showiness; ostentatious display. **6.** Also called **news flash.** *Journalism.* a brief dispatch sent by a wire service, usually transmitting preliminary news of an important story or development. Cf. **bulletin** (def. 2). **7.** *Photog.* **a.** bright artificial light thrown briefly upon a subject during an exposure. **b.** See **flash lamp. c.** flashbulb. **d.** flashtube. **8.** the sudden flame or intense heat produced by a bomb or other explosive device. **9.** a sudden thought, insight, inspiration, or vision. **10.** *Slang.* rush (def. 25). **11.** *Metall.* **a.** a ridge of metal left on a casting by a seam between parts of the mold. **b.** a ridge formed at the edge of a forging or weld where excess metal has been squeezed out. **12.** *Poker.* a hand containing all five suits in a game played with a five-suit pack. **13.** a device, as a lock or sluice, for confining and releasing water to send a boat down a shallow stream. **14.** the rush of water thus produced. **15.** See **hot flash. 16.** *Obs.* the cant or jargon of thieves, vagabonds, etc. **17. flash in the pan, a.** a brief, intense effort that produces no really significant result. **b.** a person who makes such an effort; one who enjoys short-lived success.
—*v.i.* **18.** to break forth into sudden flame or light, esp. transiently or intermittently: *a buoy flashing in the distance.* **19.** to gleam. **20.** to burst suddenly into view or perception: *The answer flashed into his mind.* **21.** to move like a flash. **22.** to speak or behave with sudden anger, outrage, or the like (often fol. by *out*): *to flash out at a stupid remark.* **23.** to break into sudden action. **24.** *Slang.* to open one's clothes and expose the genitals suddenly, and usually briefly, in public. **25.** *Slang.* to experience the intense effects of a narcotic or stimulant drug. **26.** to dash or splash, as the sea or waves. **27.** *Archaic.* to make a flash or sudden display.
—*v.t.* **28.** to emit or send forth (fire or light) in sudden flashes. **29.** to cause to flash, as powder by ignition or a sword by waving. **30.** to send forth like a flash. **31.** to communicate instantaneously, as by radio or telegraph. **32.** to make an ostentatious display of: *He's forever flashing a large roll of bills.* **33.** to display suddenly and briefly: *She flashed her ID card at the guard.* **34.** to change (water) instantly into steam by pouring or directing onto a hot surface. **35.** to increase the flow of water in (a river, channel, etc.). **36.** *Glassmaking and Ceram.* **a.** to coat (plain glass or a glass or ceramic object) with a layer of colored, opalescent, or white glass. **b.** to apply (such a layer). **c.** to color or make (glass) opaque by reheating. **37.** *Building Trades.* to protect from leakage with flashing. **38.** *Cards.* to expose (a card) in the process of dealing. **39.** *Archaic.* to dash or splash (water). **40. flash on,** *Slang.* **a.** to have a sudden thought, insight, or inspiration about. **b.** to have a sudden, vivid memory or mental picture of: *I just flashed on that day we spent at the lake.* **c.** to feel an instantaneous understanding and appreciation of.
—*adj.* **41.** sudden and brief: *a flash storm.* **42.** showy or ostentatious. **43.** caused by or used as protection against flash: *flash injuries; flash clothing.* **44.** counterfeit or sham. **45.** belonging to or connected with thieves, vagabonds, etc., or their cant or jargon. **46.** of or pertaining to followers of boxing, racing, etc. [1350–1400; ME *flasshen* to sprinkle, splash, earlier *flask(i)en;* prob. phonesthemic in orig.; cf. similar expressive words with *fl-* and *-sh*] —**flash′ing·ly,** *adv.*
—**Syn. 1.** flare, gleam, glare. **3.** twinkling, wink. **19.** scintillate. FLASH, GLANCE, GLINT, GLITTER mean to send forth a sudden gleam (or gleams) of bright light. To FLASH is to send forth light with a sudden, transient brilliancy: *A shooting star flashed briefly.* To GLANCE is to emit a brilliant flash of light as a reflection from a smooth surface: *Sunlight glanced from the glass windshield.* GLINT suggests a hard bright gleam of reflected light, as from something polished or burnished: *Light glints from silver or from burnished copper.* To GLITTER is to reflect intermittent flashes of light from a hard surface: *Ice glitters in the moonlight.* **42.** flashy, gaudy, tawdry; pretentious, superficial. **44.** false, fake.

FLASH (flash), *n.* a precedence code for handling messages about initial enemy contact or operational combat messages of extreme urgency within the U.S. military.

flash·back (flash′bak′), *n.* **1.** a device in the narrative of a motion picture, novel, etc., by which an event or scene taking place before the present time in the narrative is inserted into the chronological structure of the work. **2.** an event or scene so inserted. **3.** Also called **flash′back hallucino′sis.** *Psychiatry.* **a.** the spontaneous recurrence of visual hallucinations or other effects of a drug, as LSD, long after the use of the drug has been discontinued. **b.** recurrent and abnormally vivid recollection of a traumatic experience, as a battle, sometimes accompanied by hallucinations. [1910–15; 1965–70 for def. 3; n. use of v. phrase *flash back*]

flash·board (flash′bôrd′, -bōrd′), *n. Civ. Engin.* a board, or one of a series of boards, as on a milldam, used to increase the depth of the impounded water. [1760–70; FLASH + BOARD]

flash·bulb (flash′bulb′), *n. Photog.* a glass bulb, filled with oxygen and aluminum or zirconium wire or foil, which, when ignited electrically, burns with a brilliant flash to provide momentary illumination of a subject. Also, **flash′ bulb′.** Also called **flash.** [1930–35; FLASH + BULB]

flash′ burn′, a burn produced by brief exposure to intense, radiant heat, as from an explosion. [1945–50]

flash′ butt′ weld′ing. See **flash welding.**

flash·card (flash′kärd′), *n.* a card having words, numerals, or pictures on it, designed for gaining a rapid response from pupils when held up briefly by a teacher, used esp. in reading, arithmetic, or vocabulary drills. Also, **flash′ card′.** [1920–25; FLASH + CARD[1]]

flash·cube (flash′kyōōb′), *n.* a cube, for attaching to a camera, that contains a flashbulb in each vertical side and rotates automatically for taking four flash pictures in succession. [1960–65; FLASH + CUBE[1]]

flashed′ glass′, clear glass flashed with a thin layer of colored glass or a coating of metallic oxide. [1875–80]

flash·er (flash′ər), *n.* **1.** a person or thing that flashes. **2.** a flashing light operated by a switching device that automatically turns it on and off alternately. **3.** a signal light on an automotive vehicle that can be made to flash, as to indicate the intention of making a turn or to call attention to a vehicle that has slowed or stopped in a hazardous place. Cf. **turn signal. 4.** the switching device that operates such a light. **5.** *Slang.* a person, esp. a man, who exposes the genitals suddenly, and usually briefly, in public. [1605–15; FLASH + -ER[1]]

flash′ flood′, a sudden and destructive rush of water down a narrow gully or over a sloping surface, caused by heavy rainfall. [1935–40]
—**Syn.** See **flood.**

flash-for·ward (flash′fôr′wərd), *n.* **1.** a device in the narrative of a motion picture, novel, etc., by which a future event or scene is inserted into the chronological structure of the work. **2.** an event or scene so inserted. [1945–50; FLASH + FORWARD, on the model of FLASHBACK]

flash-freeze (flash′frēz′), *v.t.,* **-froze, -fro·zen, -freez·ing.** quick-freeze.

flash·gun (flash′gun′), *n. Photog.* a device that simultaneously discharges a flashbulb and operates a camera shutter. [1925–30; FLASH + GUN[1]]

flash·ing (flash′ing), *n.* **1.** *Building Trades.* pieces of sheet metal or the like used to cover and protect certain joints and angles, as where a roof comes in contact with a wall or chimney, esp. against leakage. **2.** the act of creating an artificial flood in a conduit or stream, as in a sewer for cleansing it. **3.** *Photog., Motion Pictures.* the process of increasing film speed by exposing undeveloped film briefly to a weak light source before using it or of exposing photographic printing paper to reduce contrast. [1775–85; FLASH + -ING[1]]

flash′ing point′, *Physical Chem.* See **flash point** (def. 1). [1875–80]

flash′ lamp′, *Photog.* a lamp for providing momentary illumination of the subject of a photograph. Also, **flash′lamp′.** Also called **flash.** [1885–90]

flash·light (flash′lit′), *n.* **1.** Also called, *esp. Brit.,* **torch.** a small, portable electric lamp powered by dry batteries or a tiny generator. **2.** a light that flashes, as a lighthouse beacon. **3.** any source of artificial light as used in flash photography. [1885–90; FLASH + LIGHT[1]]

flash′light fish′, any of several fishes, esp. *Photoblepharon palpebratus,* inhabiting deep, dark waters and having light organs that can be closed with a lid. [1970–75]

flash-lock (flash′lok′), *n.* stanch[1] (def. 5).

flash·o·ver (flash′ō′vər), *n.* **1.** *Elect.* a disruptive discharge around or over the surface of a solid or liquid insulator. **2.** the moment of conflagration or complete incineration caused by superheated air or combustibles. —*v.i.* **3.** *Elect.* to have or experience a flashover. [1890–95; orig. n. use of v. phrase *flash over*]

flash′ photog′raphy, photography using a momentary flash of artificial light as a source of illumination.

flash′ photol′ysis, *Chem.* the study of photochemical reaction mechanisms in gases by analyzing spectroscopically the reaction products in a gas mixture irradiated with a powerful light flash. [1945–50]

flash′ pic′ture, a photograph made using flash photography.

flash′ point′, **1.** Also, **flashing point.** *Physical Chem.* the lowest temperature at which a liquid in a specified apparatus will give off sufficient vapor to ignite momentarily on application of a flame. **2.** a critical point or stage at which something or someone suddenly causes or creates some significant action: *A 10 percent drop in mortgage rates will produce a flash point in the housing market.* **3.** a critical situation or area having the potential of erupting in sudden violence: *The Mideast has been the flash point for a series of conflicts.* Also, **flash′·point′.** [1875–80]

flash′ spec′trum, *Astron.* the emission spectrum of the chromosphere of the sun, which dominates the solar spectrum in the seconds just before and after a total solar eclipse. [1895–1900]

flash·tube (flash′tōōb′, -tyōōb′), *n. Photog.* See **electronic flash.** Also, **flash′ tube′.** Also called **flash.** [1940–45; FLASH + TUBE]

flash′ weld′ing, a method of welding metal edge-to-edge with a powerful electric flash followed by the application of pressure. Also called **flash butt welding.**

flash·y (flash′ē), *adj.,* **flash·i·er, flash·i·est. 1.** sparkling or brilliant, esp. in a superficial way or for the moment: *a flashy performance.* **2.** ostentatiously or vulgarly smart; showy; gaudy: *flashy clothes.* [1575–85; FLASH + -Y[1]] —**flash′i·ly,** *adv.* —**flash′i·ness,** *n.*
—**Syn. 2.** See **gaudy**[1].

flask[1] (flask, fläsk), *n.* **1.** a bottle, usually of glass, having a rounded body and a narrow neck, used esp. in laboratory experimentation. **2.** a flat metal or glass bottle for carrying in the pocket: *a flask of brandy.* **3.** an iron container for shipping mercury, holding a standard commercial unit of 76 lb. (34 kg). **4.** *Metall.* a container into which sand is rammed around a pattern to form a mold. [1375–1425; late ME: cask, keg < AF, OF *flaske* < LL *flasca,* earlier *flascō,* of uncert. orig.; cf. OE *flasce, flaxe,* OHG *flasca* (G *flasche*); cf. FLAGON]

flask[2] (flask, fläsk), *n. Ordn.* **1.** the armored plates making up the sides of a gun-carriage trail. **2.** *Obs.* the bed of a gun carriage. [1570–80; < dial. F *flasque* cheek of a gun carriage < LL *flasca* FLASK[1]]

flask·et (flas′kit, flä′skit), *n.* **1.** a small flask. **2.** a long, shallow basket. [1425–75; late ME *flaskett* < OF *flasquet,* dim. of *flasque* FLASK[1]]

flat[1] (flat), *adj.,* **flat·ter, flat·test,** *n., v.,* **flat·ted, flat·ting,** *adv.* —*adj.* **1.** horizontally level: *a flat roof.* **2.** level, even, or without unevenness of surface, as land or tabletops. **3.** having a surface that is without marked projections or depressions: *a broad, flat face.* **4.** lying horizontally and at full length, as a person; prostrate: *He was flat on the canvas after the knockdown.* **5.** lying wholly on or against something: *The banner was flat against the wall.* **6.** thrown down, laid low, or level with the ground, as fallen trees or buildings. **7.** having a generally level shape or appearance; not deep or thick: *a flat plate.* **8.** (of the heel of a shoe) low and broad. **9.** spread out, as an unrolled map or the open hand. **10.** deflated; collapsed: *a flat tire.* **11.** absolute, downright, or positive; without qualification: *a flat denial.* **12.** without modification or variation: *a flat rate.* **13.** *Informal.* lacking money; broke. **14.** without vitality or animation; lifeless; dull: *flat writing.* **15.** having lost its flavor, sharpness, or life, as wine or food; stale. **16.** (of a beverage) having lost its effervescence. **17.** without flavor; not spiced: *flat cooking.* **18.** prosaic, banal, or insipid: *a flat style.* **19.** pointless, as a remark or joke. **20.** commercially inactive: *a flat day in the stock market.* **21.** (of a painting) not having the illusion of volume or depth. **22.** (of a photograph or painting) lacking contrast or gradations of tone or color. **23.** (of paint) without gloss; not shiny; mat. **24.** not clear, sharp, or ringing, as sound or a voice. **25.** lacking resonance and variation in pitch; monotonous: *a flat delivery of the speech.* **26.** *Music.* **a.** (of a tone) lowered a half step in pitch: *B flat.* **b.** below an intended pitch, as a note; too low (opposed to *sharp*). **27.** *Gram.* derived without change in form, as English *to brush* from the noun *brush* and adverbs that do not add *-ly* to the adjective form as *fast, cheap,* and *slow.* **28.** *Phonet.* lenis; voiced. **29.** *Naut.* (of a sail) **a.** cut with little or no fullness. **b.** trimmed as nearly fore-and-aft as possible, for sailing to windward. **30. flat a,** the *a*-sound (a) of *glad, bat,* or *act.* **31. flat aft,** *Naut.* trimmed so that fore-and-aft sails present as flat a surface as possible, as in sailing close to the wind. **32. flat on one's back.** See **back** (def. 19).

CONCISE ETYMOLOGY KEY: <, descended or borrowed from; >, whence; b., blend of, blended; c., cognate with; cf., compare; deriv., derivative; equiv., equivalent; imit., imitative; obl., oblique; r., replacing; s., stem; sp., spelling, spelled; resp., respelling, respelled; trans., translation; ?, origin unknown; *, unattested; ‡, probably earlier than. See the full key inside the front cover.

—*n.* **33.** something flat. **34.** a shoe, esp. a woman's shoe, with a flat heel or no heel. **35.** a flat surface, side, or part of anything: *He struck me with the flat of his hand.* **36.** flat or level ground; a flat area: *salt flats.* **37.** a marsh, shoal, or shallow. **38.** *Music.* **a.** (in musical notation) the character ♭, which when attached to a note or to a staff degree lowers its significance one chromatic half step. **b.** a tone one chromatic half step below another: *The flat of B is B flat.* **c.** (on keyboard instruments, with reference to any given note) the key next below or to the left. **39.** *Theat.* a piece of scenery consisting of a wooden frame, usually rectangular, covered with lightweight board or fabric. **40.** a broad, thin book, chiefly for children: *a juvenile flat.* **41.** *Informal.* a deflated automobile tire. **42.** (in postal use) a large flat package, as in a manila envelope, for mailing. **43.** *Archit.* a flat roof or deck. **44.** *Naut.* **a.** Also called **platform.** a partial deck between two full decks. **b.** a low, flat barge or lighter. **45.** *Shipbuilding.* **a.** a broad, flat piece of iron or steel for overlapping and joining two plates at their edges. **b.** a straight timber in a frame or other assembly of generally curved timbers. **46.** an iron or steel bar of rectangular cross section. **47.** *Textiles.* one of a series of laths covered with card clothing, used in conjunction with the cylinder in carding. **48.** *Photog.* one or more negatives or positives in position to be reproduced. **49.** *Print.* a device for holding a negative or positive flat for reproduction by photoengraving. **50.** *Hort.* a shallow, lidless box or tray used for rooting seeds and cuttings and for growing young plants. **51.** a similar box used for shipping and selling fruits and vegetables. **52.** *Football.* the area of the field immediately inside of or outside of an offensive end, close behind or at the line of scrimmage. **53. flats,** *Informal.* flat races between horses. Cf. **flat race.**
—*v.t.* **54.** to make flat. **55.** *Music.* to lower (a pitch), esp. one half step. —*v.i.* **56.** to become flat. **57. flat in,** *Naut.* to pull the clew of (a fore-and-aft sail) as nearly amidships as possible. Also, **flatten in.**
—*adv.* **58.** in a flat position; horizontally; levelly. **59.** in a flat manner; positively; absolutely. **60.** completely; utterly: *flat broke.* **61.** exactly; precisely: *She ran around the track in two minutes flat.* **62.** *Music.* below the true pitch: *to sing flat.* **63.** *Finance.* without interest. **64. fall flat,** to fail to produce the desired effect; fail completely: *His attempts at humor fell flat.* **65. flat out,** *Informal.* **a.** without hesitation; directly or openly: *He told us flat out he'd been a double agent.* **b.** at full speed or with maximum effort. [1275–1325; ME < ON *flatr,* akin to OE *flet* (see FLAT[2]), Gk *platýs* (see PLATY-, PLATE[1])] —**flat′ly,** *adv.* —**flat′ness,** *n.*
—**Syn. 1.** plane. See **level. 4.** low, prone. **11.** outright, peremptory, categorical. **14.** boring, spiritless, prosaic. **17.** vapid, unsavory. —**Ant. 1, 4.** upright.

flat[2] (flat), *n. Chiefly Brit.* an apartment or suite of rooms on one floor forming a residence. [1795–1805; var. of obs. *flet,* OE: floor, house, hall; akin to FLAT[1]]

flat′ arch′, *Archit.* an arch having a more or less flat intrados and extrados with voussoirs radiating from a center below the arch. See illus. under **arch.** Also called **jack arch.** [1705–15]

flat′ back′, 1. a book spine presenting a completely flat surface. **2.** a book bound with such a spine. [1900–05]

flat•bed (flat′bed′), *n.* a truck or trailer having an open body in the form of a platform without sides or stakes. Also called **flat′bed trail′er, flat′bed truck′.** Cf. **stake truck.** [1870–75, for an earlier sense; FLAT[1] + BED]

flat′-bed plot′ter, a mechanized drafting device, usually computer driven, incorporating a moving pen whose horizontal and vertical range in two dimensions is limited only by the size of the bed of the device. Also, **flat′bed plot′ter.**

flat′-bed press′. See **cylinder press.**

flat•boat (flat′bōt′), *n.* a large, flat-bottomed boat for use in shallow water, esp. on rivers. [1650–60; FLAT[1] + BOAT]

flat′ bond′, a bond that is traded without accrued interest as part of the price.

flat-bot•tomed (flat′bot′əmd), *adj.* (of boats) having a flat bottom. [1575–85]

flat•bread (flat′bred′), *n.* **1.** Also, **flat•brod** (flat′-brōd). a thin, waferlike bread, usually rye, baked esp. in Scandinavian countries. **2.** Also, **flat′ bread′.** any of various often unleavened breads baked in round, flat loaves or cakes, as those eaten in India, the Middle East, and Italy. [1875–80; perh. orig. trans. of Norw *flatbröd*]

flat′ bug′, any of numerous flattened bugs of the family Aradidae, inhabiting the underside of bark and feeding on fungi. Also called **fungus bug.** [1890–95]

flat•car (flat′kär′), *n.* a railroad car consisting of a platform without sides or top. [1860–65, *Amer.;* FLAT[1] + CAR[1]]

flat′ char′acter, an easily recognized character type in fiction who may not be fully delineated but is useful in carrying out some narrative purpose of the author. Cf. **round character, stock character.**

flat′-coat•ed retriev′er (flat′kō′tid), one of an English breed of large sporting dogs having a flat, dense, shiny black or liver-colored coat, small ears, and long jaws, used for retrieving game from both water and land. [1945–50]

flat-earth•er (flat′ûr′thər), *n.* **1.** a person who adheres to the idea that the earth is flat. **2.** a person who clings to an idea or theory that has long been proved wrong. [1930–35; *flat earth* + -ER[1]]

flat′-felled seam′ (flat′feld′), a seam on the face of a garment, as on the outside of the legs of blue jeans, made by overlapping and interlocking one seam allowance with the other and top-stitching them together onto the garment with two parallel rows of stitches. [1935–40]

flat-file (flat′fīl′), *adj.* of or pertaining to a database system in which each database consists of a single file not linked to any other file. [1980–85]

flat•fish (flat′fish′), *n., pl.* (*esp. collectively*) **-fish,** (*esp. referring to two or more kinds or species*) **-fish•es.** any fish of the order Heterosomata (Pleuronectiformes), including the halibut, sole, flounder, etc., having a greatly compressed body and swimming on one side, with both eyes on the upper side in the adult. [1700–10; FLAT[1] + FISH]

flat•foot (flat′fo͝ot′ *or, for 1,* -fo͝ot′), *n., pl.* **-feet** for 1, **-foots** for 2, 3. **1.** *Pathol.* **a.** a condition in which the arch of the foot is flattened so that the entire sole rests upon the ground. **b.** Also, **flat foot.** a foot with such an arch. **2.** *Slang.* a police officer; cop. **3.** *Older Slang.* a sailor. [1865–70; FLAT[1] + FOOT]

flat•foot•ed (flat′fo͝ot′id), *adj.* **1.** having flatfeet. **2.** taking or showing an uncompromising stand in a matter; firm and explicit: *a flatfooted denial.* **3.** clumsy or plodding; maladroit: *flatfooted writing.* **4. catch one flatfooted,** to catch one unprepared; surprise: *The amount of the bill caught us flatfooted.* [1595–1605; FLATFOOT + -ED[3]] —**flat′foot′ed•ly,** *adv.* —**flat′foot′ed•ness,** *n.*

flat-grained (flat′grānd′), *adj.* (of sawed lumber) having the annual rings at an angle of less than 45° with the broader surfaces.

flat′ head′, a flat screw head. See illus. under **screw.**

flat•head (flat′hed′), *n., pl.* (*esp. collectively*) **-head,** (*esp. referring to two or more kinds or species*) **-heads.** any of several scorpaenoid fishes of the family Platycephalidae, chiefly inhabiting waters of the Indo-Pacific region and used for food. [1825–35; FLAT[1] + HEAD]

Flat•head (flat′hed′), *n.* **1.** a member of a tribe of Salishan Indians of northwest Montana. **2.** a Chinook Indian. [1530–40; so called from their supposed practice of flattening their children's heads]

flat′head cat′fish, a yellow and brown catfish, *Pylodictus olivaris,* common in the central U.S., having a flattened head and a projecting lower jaw. Also called **goujon, mudcat, shovelnose catfish, spoonbill catfish.** [1940–45]

flat′head•ed ap′ple tree′ bor′er (flat′hed′id). See **apple tree borer** (def. 1). [1880–85]

flat′headed bor′er, the larva of a metallic woodboring beetle, having an expanded and flattened anterior end. Also called **hammerhead.** [1880–85]

flat•i•ron (flat′ī′ərn), *n.* **1.** a nonelectric iron with a flat bottom, heated for use in pressing clothes, cloth, etc. **2.** *Geol.* (in the Western U.S.) a triangular hogback that resembles a flatiron resting on its base. [1735–45; FLAT[1] + IRON]

flat′-joint′ point′ing (flat′joint′), *Masonry.* pointing having flush joints of common mortar. [1815–25]

flat-knit (flat′nit′), *adj.* (of a fabric) made by flat knitting. Cf. **circular-knit.** [1955–60]

flat′ knit′ting, a knitting process in which the yarn is knitted horizontally on needles set in a straight line. Cf. **circular knitting.** [1935–40]

flat′ knot′, *Naut.* See **reef knot.** [1950–55]

flat•land (flat′land′), *n.* a region that lacks appreciable topographic relief. [1725–35, *Amer.;* FLAT[1] + -LAND] —**flat′land′er,** *n.*

flat•let (flat′lit), *n. Brit.* a residential apartment with only one or two rooms. [1920–25; FLAT[2] + -LET]

flat′ light′, *Photog.* even front lighting of a subject, producing little contrast, no shadows, and no modeling.

flat•ling (flat′ling), *adv.* Also, **flat′lings.** *Brit. Dial.* **1.** in a flat position; with the flat side, as of a sword. **2.** flatly or positively. —*adj.* **3.** *Obs.* dealt with the flat side. [1325–75; ME; see FLAT[1], -LING[2]]

flat-out (flat′out′), *adj. Informal.* **1.** moving or working at top speed or with maximum effort; all-out: *a flat-out effort by all contestants.* **2.** downright; thoroughgoing: *Many of the paintings were flat-out forgeries.* [1925–30]

flat′-plate collec′tor (flat′plāt′), a type of solar collector consisting of a series of flat glass or plastic plates with black metal surfaces that absorb solar energy. [1975–80]

flat′ race′, *Track, Horse Racing.* a race run on a level track having no hurdles, water jumps, hedges, or the like to hinder the speed of the entrants. [1840–50] —**flat′ rac′ing.**

flat-rolled (flat′rōld′), *adj.* (of steel or other metal) rolled into flat sheets, strips, etc. [1930–35]

flat-saw (flat′sô′), *v.t.,* **-sawed, -sawed** or **-sawn, -saw•ing.** plain-saw. [1880–85]

flat′ sen′nit, a rope made of three or more yarns or strands plaited together. Also called **common sennit, English sennit.**

flat′ sil′ver, silver table utensils, as knives, forks, and spoons. [1925–30, *Amer.*]

flat′ sour′, 1. fermentation occurring in canned foods after sealing. **2.** canned food so fermented. [1925–30]

flat•ten (flat′n), *v.t.* **1.** to make flat. **2.** to knock down: *The boxer flattened his opponent in the second round.* —*v.i.* **3.** to become flat. **4. flatten in,** *Naut.* See **flat[1]** (def. 57). **5. flatten out,** *Aeron.* to fly into a horizontal position, as after a dive. [1620–30; FLAT[1] + -EN[1]] —**flat′ten•er,** *n.*
—**Syn. 2.** ground, fell, prostrate, deck, floor.

flat•ter[1] (flat′ər), *v.t.* **1.** to try to please by complimentary remarks or attention. **2.** to praise or compliment insincerely, effusively, or excessively: *She flatters him by constantly praising his books.* **3.** to represent favorably; gratify by falsification: *The portrait flatters her.* **4.** to show to advantage: *a hairstyle that flatters the face.* **5.** to play upon the vanity or susceptibilities of; cajole, wheedle, or beguile. **6.** to please or gratify by compliments or attentions: *I was flattered by their invitation.* **7.** to feel satisfaction with (oneself), esp. with reference to an accomplishment, act, or occasion: *He flattered himself that the dinner had gone well.* **8.** to beguile with hope; encourage prematurely, falsely, etc. —*v.i.* **9.** to use flattery. [1175–1225; ME *flat(t)eren* to float, flutter, fawn upon, OE *floterian* to float, flutter; for sense development, cf. FLICKER[1], ON *flathra;* reinforced by OF *flatter* to flatter, lit., to stroke, caress (prob. < Frankish **flat-* FLAT[1])] —**flat′ter•a•ble,** *adj.* —**flat′ter•er,** *n.* —**flat′ter•ing•ly,** *adv.*

flat•ter[2] (flat′ər), *n.* **1.** a person or thing that makes something flat. **2.** a flat-faced blacksmith's tool, laid on a forging and struck with a hammer to smooth the surface of the forging. **3.** a drawplate with a flat orifice for drawing flat metal strips, as for watch springs. [1705–15; FLAT[1] + -ER[1]]

flat•ter•y (flat′ə rē), *n., pl.* **-ter•ies. 1.** the act of flattering. **2.** a flattering compliment or speech; excessive, insincere praise. [1275–1325; ME *flaterie* < MF, equiv. to *flat(er)* to flatter + *-erie* -ERY. Cf. FLATTER[1]]
—**Syn. 2.** sycophancy, toadying, fawning, pandering.

flat′ tire′, 1. a pneumatic tire that has lost all or most of its air through leakage, puncture, or the like. **2.** *Older Slang.* a dull or socially inept person. [1920–25]

flat•tish (flat′ish), *adj.* somewhat flat. [1605–15; FLAT[1] + -ISH[1]]

flat•top (flat′top′), *n. Informal.* **1.** an aircraft carrier. **2.** a type of crew cut in which the hair is cropped in a flat plane across the top. Also, **flat′-top′.** [1940–45; FLAT[1] + TOP[1]] —**flat′-topped′,** *adj.*

flat•u•lent (flach′ə lənt), *adj.* **1.** generating gas in the alimentary canal, as food. **2.** attended with, caused by, or suffering from such an accumulation of gas. **3.** having unsupported pretensions; inflated and empty; pompous; turgid: *a flatulent style.* [1590–1600; < NL *flātulentus;* see FLATUS, -ULENT] —**flat′u•lence, flat′u•len•cy,** *n.* —**flat′u•lent•ly,** *adv.*

fla•tus (flā′təs), *n., pl.* **-tus•es.** intestinal gas produced by bacterial action on waste matter in the intestines and composed primarily of hydrogen sulfide and varying amounts of methane. Also called **gas.** [1660–70; < NL; L: a blowing, breathing, breath, equiv. to *flā(re)* to blow + *-tus* suffix of v. action]

flat•ware (flat′wâr′), *n.* **1.** utensils, as knives, forks, and spoons, used at the table for serving and eating food. **2.** dishes or containers for the table that are more or less flat, as plates and saucers (distinguished from *hollowware*). [1850–55; FLAT[1] + WARE[1]]

flat•wise (flat′wīz′), *adv.* with the flat side, rather than the edge, foremost or in contact. Also, **flat•ways** (flat′wāz′). [1595–1605; FLAT[1] + -WISE]

flat•woods (flat′wo͝odz′), *n.* (*used with a plural v.*) a woodland in a low-lying region having little drainage. [1835–45, *Amer.;* FLAT[1] + WOODS]

flat•work (flat′wûrk′), *n.* sheets, tablecloths, etc., that are ordinarily ironed mechanically, as on a mangle, rather than by hand. Also called **flat′ wash′.** [1920–25; FLAT[1] + WORK]

flat•worm (flat′wûrm′), *n.* any worm of the phylum Platyhelminthes, having bilateral symmetry and a soft, solid, usually flattened body, including the planarians, tapeworms, and trematodes; platyhelminth. [1895–1900; FLAT[1] + WORM]

Flau•bert (flō bâr′; *Fr.* flō bεʀ′), *n.* **Gus•tave** (gys-tav′), 1821–80, French novelist.

flaunt (flônt), *v.i.* **1.** to parade or display oneself conspicuously, defiantly, or boldly. **2.** to wave conspicuously in the air. —*v.t.* **3.** to parade or display ostentatiously: *to flaunt one's wealth.* **4.** to ignore or treat with disdain: *He was expelled for flaunting military regulations.* —*n.* **5.** the act of flaunting. **6.** *Obs.* something flaunted. [1560–70; of obscure orig.; cf. Norw dial. *flanta* to show off] —**flaunt′er,** *n.* —**flaunt′ing•ly,** *adv.*
—**Syn. 3.** flourish, exhibit, vaunt, show off.
—**Usage. 4.** The use of FLAUNT TO mean "to ignore or treat with disdain" (*He flaunts community standards with his behavior*) is strongly objected to by many usage guides, which insist that only FLOUT can properly express this meaning. From its earliest appearance in English in the 16th century, FLAUNT has had the meanings "to display oneself conspicuously, defiantly, or boldly" in public and "to parade or display ostentatiously." These senses approach those of FLOUT, which dates from about the same period: "to treat with disdain, scorn, or contempt; scoff at; mock." A sentence like *Once secure in his new social position, he was able to flaunt his lower-class origins* can thus be ambiguous in current English. Considering the similarity in pronunciation of the two words, it is not surprising that FLAUNT has assumed the meanings of FLOUT and that this use has appeared in the speech and edited writing of even well-educated, literate persons. Nevertheless, many regard the senses of FLAUNT and FLOUT as entirely unrelated and concerned speakers and writers still continue to keep them separate.

flaunt•y (flôn′tē), *adj.,* **flaunt•i•er, flaunt•i•est. 1.** (of persons) given to display; inclined to be showy or vain. **2.** (of things) gaudy; flashy. [1790–1800; FLAUNT + -Y[1]] —**flaunt′i•ly,** *adv.* —**flaunt′i•ness,** *n.*

flau•tist (flô′tist, flou′-), *n.* flutist. [1855–60; < It *flautista,* equiv. to *flaut(o)* FLUTE + *-ista* -IST]

flav-, var. of **flavo-** before a vowel: *flavone.*

flav., (in prescriptions) yellow. [< L *flāvus*]

fla•ves•cent (flə ves′ənt), *adj.* turning yellow; yellowish. [1850–55; < L *flāvēscent-,* s. of *flāvēscēns,* prp. of *flāvēscere* to become yellow. See FLAV-, -ESCE, -ENT]

Fla•vi•a (flā′vē ə), *n.* a female given name.

fla•vin (flā′vin), *n. Biochem.* **1.** a complex heterocyclic ketone that is common to the nonprotein part of several important yellow enzymes, the flavoproteins. **2.** quercetin. Also, **flavine.** [1850–55; FLAV- + -IN[2]]

-flavin, a combining form occurring in compound words which denote natural derivatives of flavin: *riboflavin.*

fla•vine (flā′vin, -vēn), *n.* **1.** *Chem.* See **acriflavine hydrochloride.** **2.** *Biochem.* flavin.

flavo-, a combining form meaning "yellow," used in the formation of compound words (*flavopurpurin*); in some biochemical terms, specialized in meaning to indicate **flavin** (*flavoprotein*). Also, *esp. before a vowel,* **flav-.** [< L *flāv(us)* yellow, blonde + -o-]

fla•vo•bac•te•ri•um (flā′vō bak tēr′ē əm), *n., pl.* **-te•ri•a** (-tēr′ē ə). *Bacteriol.* any of several rod-shaped, aerobic to facultatively anaerobic bacteria of the genus *Flavobacterium,* inhabiting soil and water. [< NL; see FLAVO-, BACTERIUM]

fla•vone (flā′vōn), *n. Chem.* **1.** a colorless, crystalline, water-insoluble compound, $C_{15}H_{10}O_2$, the parent substance of a group of naturally occurring derivatives some of which have been used as yellow dyes. **2.** any derivative of this compound. [1895–1900; < G *Flavon*]

fla•vo•nol (flā′və nôl′, -nol′), *n. Chem.* **1.** the 3-hydroxy derivative of flavone, many of whose derivatives, as quercetin, are naturally occurring yellow dyes. **2.** any derivative of this compound. [1895–1900; FLAVONE + -OL[1]]

fla•vo•pro•tein (flā′vō prō′tēn, -tē ən), *n. Biochem.* an enzyme, containing riboflavin and linked chemically with a protein, active in the oxidation of foods in animal cells. [1930–35; FLAVO- + PROTEIN]

fla•vo•pur•pu•rin (flā′vō pûr′pyə rin), *n. Chem.* a yellow, crystalline anthraquinone dye, $C_{14}H_8O_5$, isomeric with purpurin. [FLAVO- + PURPURIN]

fla•vor (flā′vər), *n.* **1.** taste, esp. the distinctive taste of something as it is experienced in the mouth. **2.** a substance or extract that provides a particular taste; flavoring. **3.** the characteristic quality of a thing: *He captured the flavor of the experience in his book.* **4.** a particular quality noticeable in a thing: *language with a strong nautical flavor.* **5.** *Physics.* any of the six labels given to the distinct kinds of quark: up, down, strange, charm, bottom, and top. **6.** *Archaic.* smell, odor, or aroma. —*v.t.* **7.** to give flavor to (something). Also, *esp. Brit.,* **flavour.** [1300–50; ME < MF *fla(o)ur* < LL **flātor* stench, breath, alter. of L *flātus* a blowing, breathing, (see FLATUS), perh. with *-or* of *fētor* FETOR] —**fla′vor•less,** *adj.*
—**Syn. 1.** See **taste. 2.** seasoning. **3.** essence, spirit.

fla•vor•ful (flā′vər fəl), *adj.* full of flavor; tasty. [1925–30; FLAVOR + -FUL] —**fla′vor•ful•ly,** *adv.*

fla•vor•ing (flā′vər ing), *n.* something that gives flavor; a substance or preparation used to give a particular flavor to food or drink: *vanilla flavoring.* [1835–45]

fla′vor of the month′, *Informal.* the subject of intense, usually temporary interest; the current fashion. [1975–80]

fla•vor•ous (flā′vər əs), *adj.* **1.** full of flavor. **2.** pleasant to the taste or smell. [1690–1700; FLAVOR + -OUS]

fla•vor•some (flā′vər səm), *adj.* **1.** of a full, rich, pleasant flavor; tasty. **2.** having or giving a particular flavor. [1850–55; FLAVOR + -SOME[1]]

fla•vor•y (flā′və rē), *adj.* rich in flavor, as a tea. [1720–30; FLAVOR + -Y[1]]

fla•vour (flā′vər), *n. Chiefly Brit.* flavor.

flaw[1] (flô), *n.* **1.** a feature that mars the perfection of something; defect; fault: *beauty without flaw; the flaws in our plan.* **2.** a defect impairing legal soundness or validity. **3.** a crack, break, breach, or rent. —*v.t.* **4.** to produce a flaw in. —*v.i.* **5.** to contract a flaw; become cracked or defective. [1275–1325; ME *flaw(e), flage,* perh. < ON *flaga* sliver, flake] —**flaw′less,** *adj.* —**flaw′less•ly,** *adv.* —**flaw′less•ness,** *n.*
—**Syn. 1.** imperfection, blot, spot. See **defect. 3.** fissure, rift.

flaw[2] (flô), *n.* **1.** Also called **windflaw.** a sudden, usually brief windstorm or gust of wind. **2.** a short spell of rough weather. **3.** *Obs.* a burst of feeling, fury, etc. [1475–85; < ON *flaga* attack, squall] —**flaw′y,** *adj.*

flawed (flôd), *adj.* characterized by flaws; having imperfections: *a flawed gem; a seriously flawed piece of work.* [1595–1605; FLAW[1] + -ED[3]] —**flawed′ness,** *n.*

flax (flaks), *n.* **1.** any plant of the genus *Linum,* esp. *L. usitatissimum,* a slender, erect, annual plant having narrow, lance-shaped leaves and blue flowers, cultivated for its fiber and seeds. **2.** the fiber of this plant, manufactured into linen yarn for thread or woven fabrics. **3.** any of various plants resembling flax. [bef. 900; ME; OE *fleax;* c. D, LG *vlas,* G *Flachs*]

flax•en (flak′sən), *adj.* **1.** made of flax. **2.** pertaining to flax. **3.** resembling flax. **4.** of the pale yellowish color of dressed flax. Also, **flax′y.** [1510–20; FLAX + -EN[2]]

flax′ lil′y. See **New Zealand flax.**

Flax•man (flaks′mən), *n.* **John,** 1755–1826, English sculptor and draftsman.

flax•seed (flaks′sēd′), *n.* the seed of flax, yielding linseed oil; linseed. [1555–65; FLAX + SEED]

flay (flā), *v.t.* **1.** to strip off the skin or outer covering of. **2.** to criticize or scold with scathing severity. **3.** to deprive or strip of money or property. [bef. 900; ME *flen,* OE *flēan;* c. MD *vlaen,* ON *flā*] —**flay′er,** *n.*
—**Syn. 2.** castigate, excoriate, upbraid, chew out.

F layer, *Physics.* the highest of the radio-reflective ionospheric layers, beginning at an altitude of ab. 80 mi. (130 km) and consisting of two parts, the lower part (**F_1 layer**) being detectable in the daytime only, the higher (**F_2 layer** or **Appleton layer**) being constant and constituting the ionospheric layer most favorable for long-range radio communication. [1925–30]

F.L.B., Federal Land Bank.

fld., **1.** field. **2.** fluid.

fl dr, fluid dram; fluid drams.

fldxt, (in prescriptions) fluidextract. [< L *fluidextractum*]

flea (flē), *n.* **1.** any of numerous small, wingless bloodsucking insects of the order Siphonaptera, parasitic upon mammals and birds and noted for their ability to leap. **2.** either of two common fleas of the genus *Ctenocephalides,* the very small, black *C. felis* (**cat flea**) or the similar but larger *C. canis* (**dog flea**), both of which infest cats, dogs, and occasionally humans. **3.** any of various small beetles and crustaceans that leap like a flea or swim in a jumpy manner, as the water flea and beach flea. **4. flea in one's ear, a.** a disconcerting rebuke or rebuff: *The next time he shows his face around here he'll get a flea in his ear.* **b.** a broad hint. [bef. 900; ME *fle,* OE *flēah, flēa;* c. G *Floh;* akin to FLEE]

dog flea, *Ctenocephalides canis,* length 1/8 in. (0.3 cm)

flea•bag (flē′bag′), *n. Slang.* **1.** a cheap, run-down hotel or rooming house. **2.** any shabby or low-grade public establishment. **3.** a worthless racehorse. **4.** a dog, esp. one that is flea-ridden. **5.** a bed. **6.** a sleeping bag. [1825–35; FLEA + BAG]

flea•bane (flē′bān′), *n.* any of various composite plants, as *Pulicaria dysenterica,* of Europe, or *Erigeron philadelphicus,* of the U.S., reputed to destroy or drive away fleas. [1540–50; FLEA + BANE]

flea′ bee′tle, any leaf beetle of the genera *Haltica, Epitrix,* etc., the various species of which have the rear legs adapted for jumping. [1835–45]

flea•bite (flē′bīt′), *n.* **1.** the bite of a flea. **2.** the red spot caused by the bite of a flea. **3.** any petty annoyance or irritation, as a trifling wound. [1400–50; late ME *flee byte.* See FLEA, BITE]

flea-bit•ten (flē′bit′n), *adj.* **1.** bitten by a flea or fleas. **2.** infested with fleas. **3.** shabby; dilapidated; wretched. **4.** (of a horse) having a light-colored coat with small, dark spots or streaks. [1560–70]

flea′ col′lar, a dog or cat collar impregnated with a chemical for repelling or killing fleas. [1965–70]

fleam (flēm), *n.* **1.** *Surg.* a kind of lancet, as for opening veins. **2.** the beveled leading edge of a sawtooth. [1375–1425; late ME *fleme, fleom* < MF *flieme* << LL *phlebotomus,* < Gk *phlebotómon;* see PHLEBO-, TOME]

flea′ mar′ket, a market, often outdoors, consisting of a number of individual stalls selling old or used articles, curios and antiques, cut-rate merchandise, etc. [1920–25] —**flea′-mar′ket•er, flea′-mar•ket•eer′,** *n.*

flea•pit (flē′pit′), *n. Brit. Slang.* a shabby public place, esp. a run-down motion-picture theater. [1935–40; FLEA + PIT[1]]

flea•wort (flē′wûrt′, -wôrt′), *n.* a European plantain, *Plantago psyllium,* having seeds that are used in medicine. Also called **psyllium.** [bef. 1000; ME *flewort,* OE *flēawyrt.* See FLEA, WORT[2]]

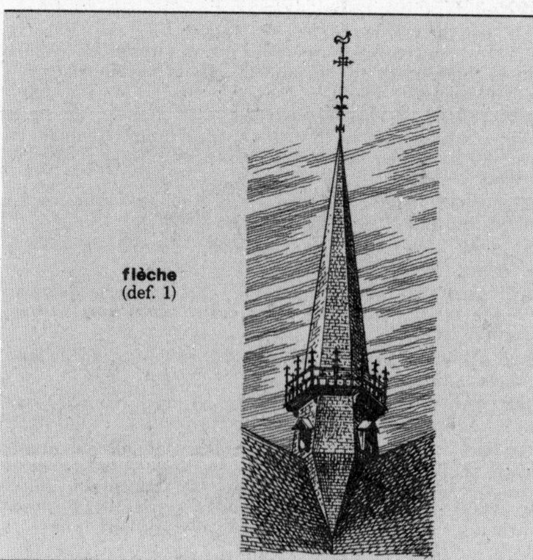

flèche (def. 1)

flèche (flāsh; *Fr.* flesh), *n., pl.* **flè•ches** (flā′shiz; *Fr.* flesh). **1.** *Archit.* a steeple or spire, esp. one in the Gothic style, emerging from the ridge of a roof. **2.** *Fort.* a fieldwork consisting of two faces forming a salient angle with an open gorge. **3.** *Fencing.* a method of attack with saber or épée in which the attacker leaves from the rear foot and advances rapidly toward the opponent. [1700–10; < F: lit., arrow, prob. < Gmc. Cf. FLY[1]]

flèches d'a•mour (flesh dᴀ mōōr′), *French.* See **love arrows.**

flé•chette (flā shet′), *n., pl.* **flé•chettes** (flā shets′; *Fr.* flā shet′). **1.** *Mil.* a small, dartlike metal projectile used as shrapnel in antipersonnel bombs and shells. **2.** a bullet with a thin, hard metal spine, designed to tumble on impact and thus cause an incapacitating wound. [1910–15; < F; see FLÈCHE, -ETTE]

fleck (flek), *n.* **1.** a speck; a small bit: *a fleck of dirt.* **2.** a spot or small patch of color, light, etc.: *the dapple mare with flecks of gray.* **3.** a spot or mark on the skin, as a freckle. —*v.t.* **4.** to mark with a fleck or flecks; spot; dapple. [1350–1400; ME *flekked* spotted; akin to ON *flekkr* spot, streak, OHG *flec* (G *Fleck*), MLG, MD *vlecken* to soil] —**fleck′less,** *adj.* —**fleck′less•ly,** *adv.* —**fleck′y,** *adj.*
—**Syn. 4.** bespeckle, spatter, dot, speck, daub.

flec•tion (flek′shən), *n.* **1.** the act of bending. **2.** the state of being bent. **3.** a bend; bent part. **4.** *Anat.* flexion. **5.** *Gram.* inflection (def. 2). Also, *esp. Brit.,* **flexion** (for defs. 1–3). [< L *flexiōn-* (s. of *flexiō*) a bending, turning, change. See FLEX, -ION] —**flec′tion•al,** *adj.* —**flec′tion•less,** *adj.*

fled (fled), *v.* pt. and pp. of **flee.**

Fle•der•maus, Die (*Ger.* dē flā′dəʀ mous′; *Eng.* dē flā′dər mous′), an opera (1874) by Johann Strauss, Jr.

fledge (flej), *v.,* **fledged, fledg•ing,** *adj.* —*v.t.* **1.** to bring up (a young bird) until it is able to fly. **2.** to furnish with or as if with feathers or plumage. **3.** to provide (an arrow) with feathers. —*v.i.* **4.** (of a young bird) to acquire the feathers necessary for flight. —*adj.* **5.** *Archaic.* (of young birds) able to fly. [1350–1400; ME *flegge* (fully-)fledged, OE **flecge,* as var. of *-flycge;* c. OHG *flucki,* MLG *vlügge* (>G *flügge*); akin to FLY[1]] —**fledge′less,** *adj.*

fledged (flejd), *adj.* **1.** having the plumage or feathers necessary for flight. **2.** having the characteristics of maturity. [1570–80; FLEDGE + -ED[2]]

fledg•ling (flej′ling), *n.* **1.** a young bird just fledged. **2.** an inexperienced person. —*adj.* **3.** young, new, or inexperienced: *a fledgling diver.* Also, *esp. Brit.,* **fledge′•ling.** [1820–30; FLEDGE + -LING[1]]
—**Syn. 2.** novice, tyro, beginner, freshman, greenhorn.

fledg•y (flej′ē), *adj.,* **fledg•i•er, fledg•i•est.** feathered or feathery. [1575–85; FLEDGE + -Y[1]]

flee (flē), *v.,* **fled, flee•ing.** —*v.i.* **1.** to run away, as from danger or pursuers; take flight. **2.** to move swiftly; fly; speed. —*v.t.* **3.** to run away from (a place, person, etc.). [bef. 900; ME *fleen,* OE *flēon;* c. OHG *flichan* (G *fliehen*), Goth *thliuhan;* cf. OE *fleogan* to FLY[1]]
—**Syn. 3.** evade, escape, avoid, shun, elude.

fleece (flēs), *n., v.,* **fleeced, fleec•ing.** —*n.* **1.** the coat of wool that covers a sheep or a similar animal. **2.** the wool shorn from a sheep at one shearing. **3.** something resembling a fleece: *a fleece of clouds in a blue sky.* **4.** a fabric with a soft, silky pile, used for warmth, as for lining garments. **5.** the soft nap or pile of such a fabric. —*v.t.* **6.** to deprive of money or belongings by fraud, hoax, or the like; swindle: *He fleeced the stranger of several dollars.* **7.** to remove the fleece of (a sheep). **8.** to overspread, as with a fleece; fleck with fleecelike masses: *a host of clouds fleecing the summer sky.* [bef. 1000; ME *flees,* OE *flēos, flȳs;* c. MD *vlies,* MHG *vlius,* G *Vlies*] —**fleece′a•ble,** *adj.* —**fleece′less,** *adj.* —**fleece′like′,** *adj.* —**fleec′er,** *n.*

fleeced (flēst), *adj.* **1.** having a fleece of a specified kind (usually used in combination): *a thick-fleeced animal.* **2.** covered with fleece or a fleecelike material. **3.** (of a fabric) having a softly napped surface. [1520–30; FLEECE + -ED[3]]

fleece-vine (flēs′vīn′), *n.* See **silver-lace vine.**

fleec•y (flē′sē), *adj.,* **fleec•i•er, fleec•i•est.** covered with, consisting of, or resembling a fleece or wool: *soft, fleecy clouds.* [1560–70; FLEECE + -Y[1]] —**fleec′i•ly,** *adv.* —**fleec′i•ness,** *n.*

fleer[1] (flēr), *v.i.* **1.** to grin or laugh coarsely or mockingly. —*v.t.* **2.** to mock or deride. —*n.* **3.** a fleering look; a jeer or gibe. [1350–1400; ME *flerien* (v.) < Scand; cf. Norw *flire* a grin] —**fleer′ing•ly,** *adv.*

fle•er[2] (flē′ər), *n.* a person who flees. [1325–75; ME; see FLEE, -ER[1]]

fleet[1] (flēt), *n.* **1.** the largest organized unit of naval ships grouped for tactical or other purposes. **2.** the largest organization of warships under the command of a single officer. **3.** a number of naval vessels or vessels carrying armed crew members. **4.** a large group of ships, airplanes, trucks, etc., operated by a single company or under the same ownership: *He owns a fleet of cabs.* **5.** a large group of airplanes, automobiles, etc., moving or operating together. [bef. 1000; ME *flete,* OE *flēot,* deriv. of *flēotan* to float; see FLEET[2]]

fleet[2] (flēt), *adj.,* **-er, est,** *v.* —*adj.* **1.** swift; rapid: *to be fleet of foot; a fleet horse.* —*v.i.* **2.** to move swiftly; fly. **3.** *Naut.* to change position; shift. **4.** *Archaic.* **a.** to glide along like a stream. **b.** to fade; vanish. **5.** *Obs.* to float; drift; swim. —*v.t.* **6.** to cause (time) to pass lightly or swiftly. **7.** *Naut.* **a.** to move or change the position of. **b.** to separate the blocks of (a tackle). **c.** to lay (a rope) along a deck. [bef. 900; ME *fleten* to be fleet, OE *flēotan* to float; see FLOAT] —**fleet′ly,** *adv.* —**fleet′•ness,** *n.*
—**Syn. 6.** speed, hasten; beguile.

fleet[3] (flēt), *n. Brit. Dial.* **1.** an arm of the sea; inlet. **2.** a creek; stream; watercourse. **3. the Fleet,** a former prison in London, long used for debtors. [bef. 900; ME *flete,* OE *flēot* flowing water; c. G *Fliess* brook; (def. 3) after *the Fleet* a stream, later covered and used as a sewer, near which the prison was located]

fleet′ ad′miral, *U.S. Navy.* the highest ranking naval officer, ranking next above admiral. [1945–50]

fleet′ ballis′tic mis′sile submarine′, a nuclear submarine fitted with launchers to fire ballistic missiles either underwater or from the surface. Cf. **SSBN**

fleet-foot•ed (flēt′fŏŏt′id), *adj.* able to run fast. [1585–95]

fleet•ing (flē′ting), *adj.* passing swiftly; vanishing quickly; transient; transitory: *fleeting beauty; a fleeting*

CONCISE ETYMOLOGY KEY: <, descended or borrowed from; >, whence; b., blend of, blended; c., cognate with; cf., compare; deriv., derivative; equiv., equivalent; imit., imitative; obl., oblique; r., replacing; s., stem; sp., spelling, spelled; resp., respelling, respelled; trans., translation; ?, origin unknown; *, unattested; ‡, probably earlier than. See the full key inside the front cover.

glance. [1325–75; ME; see FLEET[2], -ING[2]] —**fleet′ing·ly,** *adv.* —**fleet′ing·ness,** *n.*
—**Syn.** passing, flitting, flying, brief, fugitive.

Fleet′ Street′, a street in central London, England: location of many newspaper offices; often used figuratively to mean the entire British newspaper world. [1375–1425; late ME *Flete Strete,* after a nearby stream; see FLEET[3]]

Fle·gen·heim·er (flā′gən hī′mər), *n.* **Arthur** (*"Dutch Schultz"*), 1902–35, U.S. gangster.

fleh·men (flā′mən), *n. Animal Behav.* a behavioral response of many male mammals, esp. deer, antelope, and other artiodactyls, consisting of lip curling and head raising after sniffing a female's urine. [< G *Flehmen,* n. use of inf.: (of a domestic ungulate) to curl the lip; cf. dial. (Upper Saxony) *flemmen* to look spiteful; further relations unclear]

flei·shig (flā′shig, -shik), *adj. Judaism.* (in the dietary laws) consisting of, made from, or used only for meat or meat products: *a fleishig set of dishes; a fleishig meal.* Cf. **milchig, pareve.** [1940–45; < Yiddish *fleyshik;* cf. MHG *vleishic* pertaining to meat; see FLESH, -Y[1]]

Flem., Flemish. Also, **Flem**

Flem·ing (flem′ing), *n.* **1.** a native of Flanders. **2.** a Flemish-speaking Belgian. [1350–1400; ME < MD *Vlaeminc,* equiv. to *Vlaem-* (see FLEMISH) + *-ing* -ING[3]; late OE *Flæming* perh. < OFris]

Flem·ing (flem′ing), *n.* **1. Sir Alexander,** 1881–1955, Scottish bacteriologist and physician: discoverer of penicillin 1928; Nobel prize for medicine 1945. **2. Ian (Lancaster),** 1908–64, British writer of suspense novels. **3. Peggy (Gale),** born 1948, U.S. figure skater.

Flem′ing valve′, *Electronics.* (formerly) a diode. [named after Sir John Ambrose *Fleming* (1849–1945), English inventor and electrical engineer]

Flem·ish (flem′ish), *adj.* **1.** of or pertaining to Flanders, its people, or their language. **2.** pertaining to or designating the style of art, esp. painting, as developed principally in Flanders and northern France during the 15th century, chiefly characterized by sharply delineated forms, naturalistic proportions, clear, usually cool colors, and the use of perspective. —*n.* **3.** the people of Flanders collectively; the Flemings. **4.** the Dutch language as spoken in northern Belgium: one of the official languages of Belgium. *Abbr.:* Flem., Flem [1275–1325; ME < MD *Vlaemsch,* equiv. to *Vlaem-* (see FLEMING) + *-sch* -ISH[1]]

Flem′ish bond′, *Masonry.* a brickwork bond having alternate stretchers and headers in each course, each header being centered above and below a stretcher. See illus. under **bond.** [1765–75]

Flem′ish gi′ant, one of a breed of large domestic rabbits of Belgian origin, having a solid gray, white, or black coat, and raised for its meat and fur. [1895–1900]

Flem′ish scroll′, a scroll, as on a chair leg, having the form of two intersecting and oppositely curved C-scrolls.

Flemish scroll

Flem·ming (flem′ing), *n.* **Wal·ther** (väl′tər), 1843–1905, German cell biologist.

flense (flens), *v.t.,* **flensed, flens·ing. 1.** to strip the blubber or the skin from (a whale, seal, etc.). **2.** to strip off (blubber or skin). Also, **flench** (flench), **flinch.** [1805–15; < Dan *flense* or D *flensen*] —**flens′er,** *n.*

flesh (flesh), *n.* **1.** the soft substance of a human or other animal body, consisting of muscle and fat. **2.** muscular and fatty tissue. **3.** this substance or tissue in animals, viewed as an article of food, usually excluding fish and sometimes fowl; meat. **4.** fatness; weight. **5.** the body, esp. as distinguished from the spirit or soul: *The spirit is willing but the flesh is weak.* **6.** the physical or animal nature of humankind as distinguished from its moral or spiritual nature: *the needs of the flesh.* **7.** humankind. **8.** living creatures generally. **9.** a person's family or relatives. **10.** *Bot.* the soft, pulpy portion of a fruit, vegetable, etc., as distinguished from the core, skin, shell, etc. **11.** the surface of the human body; skin: *A person with tender flesh should not expose it to direct sunlight.* **12.** See **flesh color. 13. in the flesh,** present and alive before one's eyes; in person: *The movie star looked quite different in the flesh.* **14. pound of flesh,** something that strict justice demands is due, but can only be paid with great loss or suffering to the payer. **15. press the flesh,** *Informal.* to shake hands, as with voters while campaigning: *The senator is busy as ever pressing the flesh on the campaign trail.* —*v.t.* **16.** to plunge (a weapon) into the flesh. **17.** *Hunting.* to feed (a hound or hawk) with flesh in order to make it more eager for the chase. Cf. **blood** (def. 23). **18.** to incite and accustom (persons) to bloodshed or battle by an initial experience. **19.** to inflame the ardor or passions of by a foretaste. **20.** to overlay or cover (a skeleton or skeletal frame) with flesh or with a fleshlike substance. **21.** to give dimension, substance, or reality to (often fol. by *out*): *The playwright fleshed out the characters.* **22.** to remove adhering flesh from (hides), in leather manufacture. **23.** *Archaic.* to satiate with flesh or fleshly enjoyments; surfeit; glut. [bef. 900; ME *flesc,* OE *flǣsc;* c. OFris *flēsk,* OHG *fleisk* (G *Fleisch*), ON *flesk* bacon] —**flesh′less,** *adj.*

flesh′ and blood′, 1. offspring or relatives: *one's own flesh and blood.* **2.** the human body or nature: *more than flesh and blood can endure.* [1200–50; ME]

flesh′ col′or, the color of a white person's skin; yellowish pink; pinkish cream. [1605–15] —**flesh′-col′ored,** *adj.*

fleshed (flesht), *adj.* having flesh, esp. of a specified type (usually used in combination): *dark-fleshed game birds.* [1375–1425; late ME; see FLESH, -ED[3]]

flesh·er (flesh′ər), *n.* **1.** a person who fleshes hides. **2.** a tool for fleshing hides. [1325–75; ME *fleshour.* See FLESH, -ER[1]]

flesh′ fly′, any fly of the family Sarcophagidae, comprising species that deposit their eggs or larvae in carrion or in the flesh of living animals. [1275–1325; ME]

flesh·hook (flesh′ho͝ok′), *n.* **1.** a hook for use in lifting meat, as from a pot. **2.** a hook to hang meat on. [1275–1325; ME; see FLESH, HOOK]

flesh·ings (flesh′ingz), *n.* (*used with a plural v.*) flesh-colored tights. [1830–40; FLESH + (STOCK)INGS]

flesh·ly (flesh′lē), *adj.,* **-li·er, -li·est. 1.** of or pertaining to the flesh or body; bodily, corporeal, or physical. **2.** carnal; sensual: *fleshly pleasures.* **3.** worldly, rather than spiritual. **4.** having a sensuous quality: *the fleshly poetry of the 17th century.* **5.** *Obs.* having much flesh; fleshy. [bef. 900; ME; OE *flǣsclic.* See FLESH, -LY] —**flesh′li·ness,** *n.*
—**Syn. 2.** See **carnal.**

flesh·ment (flesh′mənt), *n. Obs.* the state of being stimulated, as by a successful first attempt at something. [1595–1605; FLESH (defs. 17, 18) + -MENT]

flesh′ ped′dler, *Slang.* **1.** an employment agent or agency, esp. one that recruits executives. **2.** a theatrical agent. **3.** a pimp. **4.** a prostitute. [1930–35]

flesh·pot (flesh′pot′), *n.* **1. fleshpots, a.** places offering luxurious and unrestrained pleasure or amusement: *the fleshpots of Las Vegas.* **b.** luxurious and unrestrained living. **2.** a pot or vessel containing flesh or meat. [1525–35; FLESH + POT[1]]

flesh′ wound′ (wo͞ond), a wound that does not penetrate beyond the flesh; a slight or superficial wound. [1665–75]

flesh·y (flesh′ē), *adj.,* **flesh·i·er, flesh·i·est. 1.** having much flesh; plump; fat. **2.** consisting of or resembling flesh. **3.** *Bot.* consisting of fleshlike substance; pulpy, as a fruit; thick and tender, as a succulent leaf. [1325–75; ME; see FLESH, -Y[1]] —**flesh′i·ly,** *adj.* —**flesh′i·ness,** *n.*

FLETC, Federal Law Enforcement Training Center.

fletch (flech), *v.t.* to provide (an arrow) with a feather. [1625–35; back formation from FLETCHER]

fletch·er (flech′ər), *n.* a person who makes arrows. [1350–1400; ME *flecher* < OF *flechier.* See FLÈCHE, -ER[2]]

Fletch·er (flech′ər), *n.* **1. John,** 1579–1625, English dramatist: collaborated with Francis Beaumont 1606?–16; with Philip Massinger 1613–25. **2. John Gould,** 1886–1950, U.S. poet. **3.** a male given name.

Fletch·er·ism (flech′ə riz′əm), *n.* the practice of chewing food until it is reduced to a finely divided, liquefied mass: advocated by Horace Fletcher, 1849–1919, U.S. nutritionist. [1905–10, *Amer.;* *Fletcher* + -ISM]

Fletch·er·ize (flech′ə rīz′), *v.i., v.t.,* **-ized, -iz·ing.** to chew (food) slowly and thoroughly. Also, *esp. Brit.,* **Fletch′er·ise′.** [1900–05, *Amer.;* see FLETCHERISM, -IZE]

Flett′ner control′ (flet′nər), *Aeron.* servocontrol (def. 3). [named after A. *Flettner* (1885–1961), German engineer and inventor]

Fleur (flûr, flo͝or; *Fr.* flœr), *n.* a female given name.

fleur-de-lis (flûr′dl ē′, -ēs′, flo͝or′-; *Fr.* flœr də lēs′), *n., pl.* **fleurs-de-lis** (flûr′dl ēz′, flo͝or′-; *Fr.* flœr də lēs′). **1.** a heraldic device somewhat resembling three petals or floral segments of an iris tied by an encircling band. **2.** the heraldic bearing of the royal family of France. **3.** the iris flower or plant. Also, **fleur-de-lys** (for defs. 1, 2). [1300–50; < F; r. ME *flourdelis* < AF *flour de lis,* lit., lily flower]

fleurs-de-lis as used on royal arms of France, before 1376

fleur-de-lys (flûr′dl ē′, -ēs′, flo͝or′-; *Fr.* flœr də lēs′), *n., pl.* **fleurs-de-lys** (flûr′dl ēz′, flo͝or′-; *Fr.* flœr də lēs′). fleur-de-lis (defs. 1, 2).

fleu·rette (flŏŏ ret′, flo͞o-), *n.* an ornament formed like a small conventionalized flower. [1805–15; < F: lit., little flower]

Fleu·rette (flŏŏ ret′, flo͞o-; *Fr.* flœ ret′), *n.* a female given name.

fleu·ron (flûr′on, flo͝or′-), *n.* **1.** a floral motif, as one used as a terminal point or in a decorative series on an object. **2.** *Print.* flower (def. 6). [1350–1400; < F; OF *floron,* equiv. to *flor* FLOWER + *-on* n. suffix; r. ME *flouroun* < OF]

fleu·ry (flûr′ē, flo͝or′ē), *adj. Heraldry.* **1.** terminating in fleurs-de-lis: *a cross fleury.* **2.** ornamented with fleurs-de-lis. Also, **flory.** [1375–1425; late ME *flourre* < MF *fleure,* deriv. of *fleur* FLOWER; see -EE]

Fleu·ry (flœ rē′), *n.* **1. An·dré Her·cule de** (äN drā′ er kyl′ də), 1653–1743, French cardinal and statesman. **2. Claude** (klōd), 1640–1723, French ecclesiastical historian.

flew[1] (flo͞o), *v.* a pt. of **fly**[1].

flew[2] (flo͞o), *n.* flue[3].

flews (flo͞oz), *n.pl.* the large, pendulous sides of the upper lip of certain dogs, as bloodhounds. See diag. under **dog.** [1565–75; orig. uncert.]

flex[1] (fleks), *v.t.* **1.** to bend, as a part of the body: *He flexed his arms to show off his muscles.* **2.** to tighten (a muscle) by contraction. —*v.i.* **3.** to bend. —*n.* **4.** the act of flexing. **5.** *Brit.* **a.** any flexible, insulated electric cord; an electric cord or extension cord. **b.** *Slang.* an elastic band, as a garter. **6.** *Math.* an inflection point. [1515–25; (adj.) < L *flexus,* ptp. of *flectere* to bend, turn; (n.) < L *flexus* act of bending, equiv. to *flect(ere)* + *-tus* suffix of v. action]

flex[2] (fleks), *adj. Informal.* flexible: *a flex program of workers' benefits.* [shortening of FLEXIBLE]

flex·a·gon (flek′sə gon′), *n.* a three-dimensional figure having polygonal faces that is constructed from a folded sheet of paper in such a way that different faces are exposed when the figure is flexed along its folds. [FLEX[1] + *-agon* (as in HEXAGON, PENTAGON, etc.)]

flexed (flekst), *adj. Heraldry.* (of a human leg) depicted as bent at the knee. [1515–25; FLEX[1] + -ED[2]]

flex·i·ble (flek′sə bəl), *adj.* **1.** capable of being bent, usually without breaking; easily bent: *a flexible ruler.* **2.** susceptible of modification or adaptation; adaptable: *a flexible schedule.* **3.** willing or disposed to yield; pliable: *a flexible personality.* —*n.* **4.** a flexible substance or material, as rubber or leather. [1375–1425; late ME < L *flexibilis* pliant, easily bent. See FLEX[1], -IBLE] —**flex′i·bil′i·ty, flex′i·ble·ness,** *n.* —**flex′i·bly,** *adv.*
—**Syn. 1.** pliable, elastic, supple. FLEXIBLE, LIMBER, PLIANT refer to that which bends easily. FLEXIBLE refers to that which is capable of being bent and adds sometimes the idea of compressibility or expansibility: *a flexible piece of rubber hose.* LIMBER is esp. applied to the body to refer to ease of movement; it resembles FLEXIBLE except that there is an idea of even greater ease in bending: *a limber dancer.* PLIANT stresses an inherent quality or tendency to bend that does not require force or pressure from the outside; it may mean merely adaptable or may have a derogatory sense: *a pliant character.* **2.** tractable, compliant. —**Ant. 1.** stiff. **2.** rigid.

flex′ible disk′, *Computers.* See **floppy disk.**

flex′i·ble-rate mort′gage (flek′sə bəl rāt′). See **adjustable-rate mortgage.**

flex·ile (flek′sil *or, esp. Brit.,* -sīl), *adj.* flexible; pliant; tractable; adaptable. [1625–35; < L *flexilis* pliant, pliable. See FLEX[1], -ILE] —**flex·il′i·ty,** *n.*

flex·ion (flek′shən), *n.* **1.** *Anat.* **a.** the act of bending a limb. **b.** the position that a limb assumes when it is bent. **2.** *Chiefly Brit.* flection (defs. 1–3). [1595–1605; < L *flexiōn-* (s. of *flexiō*) a bending, turning. See FLEX[1], -ION] —**flex′ion·al,** *adj.* —**flex′ion·less,** *adj.*

Flex·ner (fleks′nər), *n.* **1. Abraham,** 1866–1959, U.S. educator. **2.** his brother **Simon,** 1863–1946, U.S. pathologist and bacteriologist.

flex·og·ra·phy (flek sog′rə fē), *n. Print.* a relief printing technique similar to letterpress that employs rubber or soft plastic plates, a simple inking system, and fast-drying inks. Also called **flex′ograph′ic print′ing.** [1950–55; FLEX[1] or FLEX[2] + -O- + -GRAPHY] —**flex·o·graph·ic** (flek′sə graf′ik), *adj.*

flex·or (flek′sər), *n. Anat.* a muscle that serves to flex or bend a part of the body. [1605–15; < NL; see FLEX[1], -TOR]

flex′ point′, *Math.* See **inflection point.**

flex·time (fleks′tīm′), *n.* a system of working that allows an employee to choose, within limits, the hours for starting and leaving work each day. Also, **flex·i·time** (flek′si tīm′). [1970–75; FLEX[2] + TIME] —**flex′tim′er, flex′i·tim′er,** *n.*

flex·u·os·i·ty (flek′sho͞o os′i tē), *n.* the quality or condition of being flexuous. [1605–15; < LL *flexuōsitās.* See FLEXUOUS, -ITY]

flex·u·ous (flek′sho͞o əs), *adj.* full of bends or curves; sinuous. [1595–1605; < L *flexuōsus* full of turns, winding, crooked, equiv. to *flexu(s)* (see FLEX[1]) + *-ōsus* -OUS] —**flex′u·ous·ly,** *adv.* —**flex′u·ous·ness,** *n.*

flex·ure (flek′shər), *n.* **1.** the act of flexing or bending. **2.** the state of being flexed or bent. **3.** the part bent; bend; fold. [1585–95; < L *flexūra* a bending, turning, winding. See FLEX[1], -URE] —**flex′ur·al,** *adj.*

fley (flā), *v.,* **fleyed, fley·ing.** *Chiefly Scot.* to frighten; terrify. [1175–1225; ME *flaien, fleien,* OE *-flīgan* (in *āflygan*); c. ON *fleygia* to cause to fly. Cf. FLY[1]] —**fley·ed·ly** (flā′id lē), *adv.* —**fley′ed·ness,** *n.*

flib·ber·ti·gib·bet (flib′ər tē jib′it), *n.* **1.** a chattering or flighty, light-headed person. **2.** *Archaic.* a gossip. [1425–75; late ME *flepergebet, flipergebet;* reduplicative compound of obscure orig.]

flic (flik; *Fr.* flēk), *n., pl.* **flics** (fliks; *Fr.* flēk). *Slang.* a police officer; cop. [1895–1900; < F (slang), perh. < G; cf. *flick* boy, in early mod. G thieves' argot (of obscure orig.)]

flic·flac (flik′flak′), *n.* a step in dancing in which the feet strike rapidly together. [1850–55; < F; imit.]

CONCISE PRONUNCIATION KEY: act, cāpe, dâre, pärt; set, ēqual; *if,* ice; ox, ōver, ôrder, oil, bo͝ok, bo͞ot, out; up, ûrge; child; sing; shoe; thin, *that;* zh as in *treasure.* ə = *a* as in *alone, e* as in *system, i* as in *easily, o* as in *gallop, u* as in *circus;* ′ as in *fire* (fī′r), *hour* (ou′r). l and n can serve as syllabic consonants, as in *cradle* (krād′l), and *button* (but′n). See the full key inside the front cover.

flicht•er (fliKH′tər), *v.i. Scot.* **1.** (of birds) to fly feebly; flutter. **2.** to tremble; quiver. Also, **flighter.** [1505–15; *flicht* FLIGHT + -ER[6]]

flick[1] (flik), *n.* **1.** a sudden light blow or tap, as with a whip or the finger: *She gave the horse a flick with her riding crop.* **2.** the sound made by such a blow or tap. **3.** a light and rapid movement: *a flick of the wrist.* **4.** something thrown off with or as if with a jerk: *a flick of mud.* —*v.t.* **5.** to strike lightly with a whip, the finger, etc. **6.** to remove with such a stroke: *to flick away a crumb.* **7.** to move (something) with a sudden stroke or jerk. —*v.i.* **8.** to move with a jerk or jerks. **9.** to flutter. [1400–50; late ME *flykke;* appar. imit.]

flick[2] (flik), *n. Slang.* a motion picture. Also, **flicker.** [1925–30; shortening of FLICKER[1]]

flick•er[1] (flik′ər), *v.i.* **1.** to burn unsteadily; shine with a wavering light: *The candle flickered in the wind and went out.* **2.** to move to and fro; vibrate; quiver: *The long grasses flickered in the wind.* **3.** to flutter. —*v.t.* **4.** to cause to flicker. —*n.* **5.** an unsteady flame or light. **6.** a flickering movement. **7.** a brief occurrence or appearance: *a flicker of hope.* **8.** Often, **flickers.** *Slang.* flick[2]. **9.** *Ophthalm.* the visual sensation of flickering that occurs when the interval between intermittent flashes of light is too long to permit fusion. [bef. 1000; ME *flikeren* (v.) OE *flicorian* to flutter; c. D *flikkeren*] —**flick′er•ing•ly,** *adv.* —**flick′er•y,** *adj.*
—**Syn. 1.** flare, flash, gleam, shimmer.

flick•er[2] (flik′ər), *n.* any of several American woodpeckers of the genus *Colaptes,* having the underside of the wings and tail brightly marked with yellow or red and noted for taking insects from the ground as well as trees. [1800–10, *Amer.;* said to be imit. of the bird's note]

flick•er•tail (flik′ər tāl′), *n.* See **Richardson ground squirrel.** [1885–90, *Amer.;* FLICKER[1] + TAIL[1]]

Flick′ertail State′, North Dakota (used as a nickname).

flick-knife (flik′nīf′), *n. Chiefly Brit.* switchblade. Also, **flick′ knife′.** [1955–60]

flied (flīd), *v.* a pt. and pp. of **fly**[1].

fli•er (flī′ər), *n.* **1.** something that flies, as a bird or insect. **2.** an aviator or pilot. **3.** an airplane passenger, esp. one who travels regularly by air. **4.** a person or thing that moves with great speed. **5.** some part of a machine having a rapid motion. **6.** a small handbill; circular. **7.** *Informal.* a flying jump or leap: *He took a flier off the bridge.* **8.** *Informal.* a risky or speculative venture: *Our flier in uranium stocks was a disaster.* **9.** one of the steps in a straight flight of stairs. Cf. **winder** (def. 2). **10.** a trapeze artist; aerialist. **11.** a silvery-green sunfish, *Centrarchus macropterus,* found from Virginia to Florida and through the lower Mississippi valley. Also, **flyer.** [1400–50; late ME; see FLY[1], -ER[1]]

flight[1] (flīt), *n.* **1.** the act, manner, or power of flying. **2.** the distance covered or the course taken by a flying object: *a 500-mile flight; the flight of the ball.* **3.** a trip by an airplane, glider, etc. **4.** a scheduled trip on an airline: *a 5 o'clock flight.* **5.** a number of beings or things flying or passing through the air together: *a flight of geese.* **6.** the basic tactical unit of military air forces, consisting of two or more aircraft. **7.** the act, principles, or technique of flying an airplane: *flight training.* **8.** a journey into or through outer space: *a rocket flight.* **9.** swift movement, transition, or progression: *the flight of time.* **10.** a soaring above or transcending ordinary bounds: *a flight of fancy.* **11.** a series of steps between one floor or landing of a building and the next. **12.** *Archery.* **a.** See **flight arrow. b.** the distance such an arrow travels when shot. —*v.i.* **13.** (of wild fowls) to fly in coordinated flocks. [bef. 900; ME; OE *flyht;* c. D *vlucht;* akin to FLY[1]]
—**Syn. 5.** flock. **9.** rush, dash, fleetingness.

flight[2] (flīt), *n.* **1.** an act or instance of fleeing or running away; hasty departure. **2. put to flight,** to force to flee or run away; rout: *She succeeded in putting the intruder to flight.* **3. take flight,** to retreat; run away; flee: *The wild animals took flight before the onrushing fire.* Also, **take to flight.** [1150–1200; ME; c. G *Flucht;* akin to FLEE]

flight′ ar′row, *Archery.* **1.** an arrow having a conical or pyramidal head without barbs. **2.** any long and light arrow for long-distance shooting; a shaft or arrow for the longbow, as distinguished from the bolt. [1795–1805]

flight′ attend′ant, an airline employee who serves meals, attends to passengers' comfort, etc., during a flight. Also called **cabin attendant.** [1955–60]

flight′ bag′, a lightweight shoulder bag designed for carrying sundries aboard an aircraft. [1940–45]

flight′ cap′. See **overseas cap.**

flight′ control′, **1.** the direction of airplane movements, esp. takeoffs and landings, by messages from the ground. **2.** the system by which this direction is done. **3.** the office from which this direction is done. **4.** the system by which the pilot of an airplane controls the movement of the airplane. [1935–40]

flight′ deck′, **1.** *Navy.* the upper deck of an aircraft carrier, constructed and equipped for the landing and takeoff of aircraft. **2.** *Aeron.* (in certain aircraft) an elevated compartment containing the instruments and controls used by the pilot, copilot, and flight engineer to operate the aircraft. [1920–25]

flight′ engineer′, a member of an aircraft crew responsible for the mechanical systems, fueling, and servicing of the craft. [1935–40]

flight•er (fliKH′tər), *v.i. Scot.* flichter.

flight′ feath′er, *Ornith.* one of the large, stiff feathers of the wing and tail of a bird that are essential to flight. [1725–35]

flight′ forma′tion, an arrangement of two or more airplanes flying together in a group, usually in a predetermined pattern.

flight′ in′dicator, *Aeron.* See **artificial horizon** (def. 3).

flight′ in′strument, any instrument used to indicate the altitude, attitude, airspeed, drift, or direction of an aircraft.

flight′ lead′er, a pilot who commands a flight of military airplanes.

flight•less (flīt′lis), *adj.* incapable of flying: *flightless birds such as the moa, rhea, and dodo.* [1870–75; FLIGHT[1] + -LESS]

flight′ line′, an area for the servicing and maintenance of airplanes that includes parking ramps and hangars. [1940–45]

flight′ nurse′, a nurse in the U.S. Air Force who tends patients being transported by airplane.

flight′ of′ficer, an officer of the U.S. Army Air Force in World War II, having a rank equivalent to that of a warrant officer junior grade.

flight′ of ide′as, *Psychiatry.* a rapid flow of thought, manifested by accelerated speech with abrupt changes from topic to topic: a symptom of some mental illnesses, esp. manic disorder.

flight′ path′, the trajectory of a moving aircraft or spacecraft relative to a fixed reference. [1910–15]

flight′ pay′, a pay supplement allowed by the U.S. Air Force to certain crew members who attain a minimum flight time per month. [1925–30]

flight′ plan′, an oral or written report to an air traffic control facility describing the route of a projected flight. [1935–40]

flight′ record′er, an electronic device aboard an aircraft that automatically records some aspects of the aircraft's performance in flight. [1945–50]

flight′ shoot′ing, *Archery.* competitive shooting for distance only. [1795–1805]

flight′ sim′ulator, a device used in pilot and crew training that provides a cockpit environment and sensations of flight under actual conditions. [1945–50]

flight′ strip′, **1.** *Aeron.* **a.** a strip of cleared land used as an emergency runway for aircraft. **b.** runway. **2.** a series of continuous aerial reconnaissance photographs. [1935–40]

flight′ sur′geon, a medical officer in the U.S. Air Force who is trained in aviation medicine. [1920–25]

flight-test (flīt′test′), *v.t.* to test (an airplane or the like) in flight. [1930–35]

flight•wor•thy (flīt′wûr′thē), *adj.* being in proper physical or mechanical condition for safe flight; airworthy: *a flightworthy spacecraft.* [1965–70; FLIGHT[1] + -WORTHY] —**flight′wor′thi•ness,** *n.*

flight•y (flī′tē), *adj.,* **flight•i•er, flight•i•est. 1.** given to flights of fancy; capricious; frivolous. **2.** slightly delirious; light-headed; mildly crazy. **3.** irresponsible: *He said I was too flighty to be a good supervisor.* **4.** *Archaic.* swift or fleet. [1545–55; FLIGHT[1] + -Y[1]] —**flight′i•ly,** *adv.* —**flight′i•ness,** *n.*
—**Syn. 1.** mercurial, undependable, irresponsible.

flim•flam (flim′flam′), *n., v.,* **-flammed, -flam•ming.** *Informal.* —*n.* **1.** a trick or deception, esp. a swindle or confidence game involving skillful persuasion or clever manipulation of the victim. **2.** a piece of nonsense; twaddle; bosh. —*v.t.* **3.** to trick, deceive, swindle, or cheat: *A fortuneteller flimflammed her out of her savings.* [1530–40; gradational compound of expressive orig.] —**flim′flam′mer,** *n.* —**flim′flam′mer•y,** *n.*

flim•sy (flim′zē), *adj.,* **-si•er, -si•est,** *n., pl.* **-sies.** —*adj.* **1.** without material strength or solidity: *a flimsy fabric; a flimsy structure.* **2.** weak; inadequate; not effective or convincing: *a flimsy excuse.* —*n.* **3.** a thin kind of paper, esp. for use in making several copies at a time of an article, telegraphic dispatch, or the like, as in newspaper work. **4.** a copy of a report or dispatch on such paper. [1695–1705; *flim-* (perh. metathetic var. of FILM) + -SY] —**flim′si•ly,** *adv.* —**flim′si•ness,** *n.*
—**Syn. 1.** shoddy, weak, unstable, unsteady. **2.** unconvincing, lame, vague. —**Ant. 1.** sturdy.

flinch[1] (flinch), *v.i.* **1.** to draw back or shrink, as from what is dangerous, difficult, or unpleasant. **2.** to shrink under pain; wince. **3.** *Croquet.* to let the foot slip from the ball in the act of croqueting. —*v.t.* **4.** to draw back or withdraw from. —*n.* **5.** an act of flinching. [1555–65; perh. nasalized var. of dial. *flitch* to flit, shift one's position] —**flinch′er,** *n.* —**flinch′ing•ly,** *adv.*
—**Syn. 1.** recoil, withdraw, blench.

flinch[2] (flinch), *v.t.* flense.

flin•ders (flin′dərz), *n.pl.* splinters; small pieces or fragments. [1400–50; late ME *flendris,* perh. < Scand; cf. Norw *flindra* splinter; perh. akin to FLINT]

Flin•ders (flin′dərz), *n.* **Matthew,** 1774–1814, English navigator and explorer: surveyed coast of Australia.

Flin′ders bar′, *Navig.* a bar of soft iron, mounted vertically beneath a compass to compensate for vertical magnetic currents. See diag. under **binnacle.** [1880–85; named after M. FLINDERS]

Flin′ders grass′, a drought-resistant pasture grass, *Iseilema membranacea,* native to inland regions of Australia and used as fodder. Also, **flin′ders grass′.**

Flin′ders Range′, a mountain range in S Australia. Highest peak, St. Mary Peak, 3900 ft. (1190 m).

fling (fling), *v.,* **flung, fling•ing,** *n.* —*v.t.* **1.** to throw, cast, or hurl with force or violence: *to fling a stone.* **2.** to move (oneself) violently with impatience, contempt, or the like: *She flung herself angrily from the room.* **3.** to put suddenly or violently: *to fling a suspect into jail.* **4.** to project or speak sharply, curtly, or forcefully: *He flung his answer at the questioner.* **5.** to involve (oneself) vigorously in an undertaking. **6.** to move, do, or say (something) quickly: *to fling a greeting in passing.* **7.** to send suddenly and rapidly: *to fling fresh troops into a battle.* **8.** to throw aside or off. **9.** to throw to the ground, as in wrestling or horseback riding. —*v.i.* **10.** to move with haste or violence; rush; dash. **11.** to fly into violent and irregular motions, as a horse; to throw the body about, as a person. **12.** to speak harshly or abusively (usually fol. by *out*): *He flung out disgustedly against the whole human race.* —*n.* **13.** an act of flinging. **14.** a short period of unrestrained pursuit of one's wishes or desires: *The week of partying was my last fling before starting a new job.* **15.** an attempt at something: *He took a fling at playwriting.* **16.** a critical or contemptuous remark; gibe. **17.** Also called **Highland fling.** a lively Scottish dance characterized by flinging movements of the arms and legs. [1250–1300; ME; cf. Sw *flänga* to fly, race]

fling•er (fling′ər), *n.* **1.** a person or thing that flings. **2.** Also called **slinger, thrower.** a device, mounted on a rotating shaft, for throwing lubricant onto a bearing or for keeping grit out of a bearing by centrifugal force. [1490–1500; FLING + -ER[1]]

flint (flint), *n.* **1.** a hard stone, a form of silica resembling chalcedony but more opaque, less pure, and less lustrous. **2.** a piece of this, esp. as used for striking fire. **3.** a chunk of this used as a primitive tool or as the core from which such a tool was struck. **4.** something very hard or unyielding. **5.** a small piece of metal, usually an iron alloy, used to produce a spark to ignite the fuel in a cigarette lighter. —*v.t.* **6.** to furnish with flint. [bef. 900; ME, OE; c. MD *vlint,* Dan *flint;* cf. PLINTH] —**flint′like′,** *adj.*

Flint (flint), *n.* **1. Austin,** 1812–86, U.S. physician: founder of Bellevue and Buffalo medical colleges. **2.** his son **Austin,** 1836–1915, U.S. physiologist and physician. **3.** a city in SE Michigan. 159,611. **4.** Flintshire.

flint′ corn′, a variety of corn, *Zea mays indurata,* having very hard-skinned kernels not subject to shrinkage. [1695–1705, *Amer.*]

flint′ glass′, *Optics.* an optical glass of high dispersion and a relatively high index of refraction, composed of alkalis, lead oxide, and silica, with or without other bases, sometimes used as the diverging lens component of an achromatic lens. [1665–75]

flint•head (flint′hed′), *n.* the wood stork, *Mycteria americana.* [1790–1800, for an earlier sense; FLINT + HEAD]

flint•lock (flint′lok′), *n.* **1.** an outmoded gunlock in which a piece of flint striking against steel produces sparks that ignite the priming. **2.** a firearm with such a lock. [1675–85; FLINT + LOCK[1]]

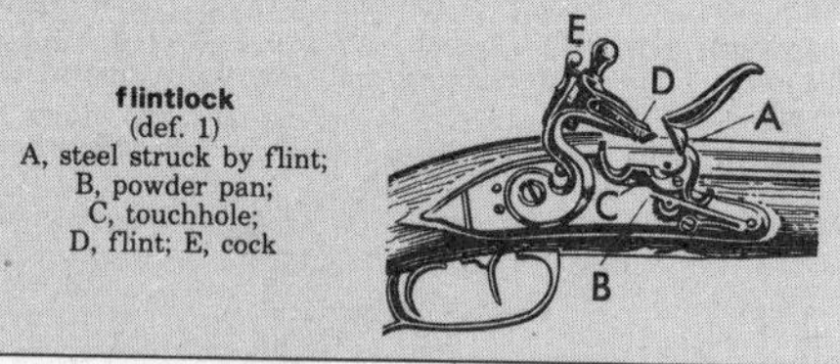

flintlock (def. 1)
A, steel struck by flint; B, powder pan; C, touchhole; D, flint; E, cock

Flint•shire (flint′shēr, -shər), *n.* a historic county in Clwyd, in NE Wales. Also called **Flint.**

flint•y (flin′tē), *adj.,* **flint•i•er, flint•i•est. 1.** composed of, containing, or resembling flint, esp. in hardness. **2.** unyielding; unmerciful; obdurate: *a flinty heart.* [1530–40; FLINT + -Y[1]] —**flint′i•ly,** *adv.* —**flint′i•ness,** *n.*

flip[1] (flip), *v.,* **flipped, flip•ping,** *n.* —*v.t.* **1.** to toss or put in motion with a sudden impulse, as with a snap of a finger and thumb, esp. so as to cause to turn over in the air: *to flip a coin.* **2.** to move (something) suddenly or jerkily. **3.** to turn over, esp. with a short rapid gesture: *to flip pancakes with a spatula.* **4.** *Slang.* to make (someone) insane, irrational, angry, or highly excited (usually fol. by *out*). **5.** *Finance.* to resell, esp. quickly, or to refinance, as a mortgage loan. —*v.i.* **6.** to make a flicking movement; strike at something smartly or sharply; snap. **7.** to move oneself with or as if with flippers: *The seals flipped along the beach.* **8.** to move with a jerk or jerks. **9.** to turn over or perform a somersault in the air. **10.** *Slang.* **a.** to react to something in an excited, astonished, or delighted manner: *He really flipped over his new girlfriend.* **b.** to become insane, irrational, angry, or highly excited (often fol. by *out*). **11. flip one's lid** or **wig,** *Slang.* See **lid** (def. 8). —*n.* **12.** an instance of flipping; a smart tap or strike. **13.** a sudden jerk. **14.** a somersault, esp. one performed in the air: *a back flip off the diving board.* **15.** *Cards.* a variety of seven-card stud in which each player receives the first four cards facedown and selects two of them to expose before receiving the next card. **16.** *Slang.* See **flip side.** [1585–95; 1955–60 for def. 10; see FILLIP]

flip[2] (flip), *n.* **1.** a mixed drink made with liquor or wine, sugar, and egg, topped with powdered nutmeg and served hot or cold. **2.** a drink, popular esp. in the 18th century, made with beer or ale mixed with rum or other liquor, sweetened and served hot. [1675–85; perh. n. use of FLIP[1], so called from tossing or flipping of ingredients in preparation]

flip[3] (flip), *adj.,* **flip•per, flip•pest.** *Informal.* flippant; pert. [1840–50; adj. use of FLIP[1]]

flip′ chart′, a set of sheets, as of cardboard or paper, hinged at the top so that they can be flipped over to show information or illustrations in sequence. [1960–65]

flip-flop (flip′flop′), *n., adv., v.,* **-flopped, -flop•ping.** —*n.* **1.** *Informal.* a sudden or unexpected reversal, as of direction, belief, attitude, or policy. **2.** a backward somersault. **3.** Also called **flip′-flop cir′cuit.** *Electronics.* an electronic circuit having two stable conditions, each

CONCISE ETYMOLOGY KEY: <, descended or borrowed from; >, whence; b., blend of, blended; c., cognate with; cf., compare; deriv., derivative; equiv., equivalent; imit., imitative; obl., oblique; r., replacing; s., stem; sp., spelling, spelled; resp., respelling, respelled; trans., translation; ?, origin unknown; *, unattested; ‡, probably earlier than. See the full key inside the front cover.

one corresponding to one of two alternative input signals. **4.** any of several similar devices having two alternative states, the change of state being caused by some input signal or by some change of input. **5.** the sound and motion of something flapping, as a wind-blown shutter; a banging to and fro. **6.** any backless, usually open-toed flat shoe or slipper. **7.** a flat, backless rubber sandal, usually secured on the foot by a thong between the first two toes, as for use at a beach, swimming pool, etc. Cf. **thong, zori. 8.** (in advertising) a display or presentation, usually on an easel, consisting of a series of pages hinged at the top and flipped over in sequence. —*adv.* **9.** with repeated sounds and motions, as of something flapping. —*v.i.* **10.** *Informal.* to make a sudden or unexpected reversal, as of direction, belief, attitude, or policy: *The opposition claimed that the President had flip-flopped on certain issues.* **11.** to execute a backward somersault. **12.** to flap; bang to and fro: *The door flip-flopped in the high wind.* Also, **flip-flap** (flip′flap′) (for defs. 2, 5, 9, 12), **flip′flop** (for defs. 6, 7). [1655–65]

flip·pant (flip′ənt), *adj.* **1.** frivolously disrespectful, shallow, or lacking in seriousness; characterized by levity: *The audience was shocked by his flippant remarks about patriotism.* **2.** *Chiefly Dial.* nimble, limber, or pliant. **3.** *Archaic.* glib; voluble. [1595–1605; appar. FLIP[1] + -ANT] —**flip′pan·cy, flip′pant·ness,** *n.* —**flip′pant·ly,** *adv.*
—**Syn. 1.** saucy, impertinent, impudent.

flip·per (flip′ər), *n.* **1.** a broad, flat limb, as of a seal or whale, especially adapted for swimming. **2.** Also called **fin.** one of a pair of paddlelike devices, usually of rubber, worn on the feet as an aid in scuba diving and swimming. **3.** *Theat.* a narrow flat hinged or attached at right angles to a larger flat. **4.** *Slang.* the hand. **5.** someone or something that flips. [1815–25; FLIP[1] + -ER[1]]

flip·ping (flip′ing), *adj., adv. Chiefly Brit. Slang.* (used as an intensifier): *I'm flipping tired of your excuses.* [1910–15; FLIP[1] + -ING[2]; perh. euphemistically echoing *fucking*]

flip′ side′, *Informal.* **1.** the reverse and usually less popular side of a phonograph record. **2.** an opposite, reverse, or sharply contrasted side or aspect of something or someone: *The flip side of their charitable activities is a desire for publicity.* [1945–50]

Flip-Top (flip′top′), *Trademark.* **1.** a brand name for a cigarette box having a hinged upper lid or cover. —*adj.* **2.** (*l.c.*) pop-top (def. 1). —*n.* **3.** (*l.c.*) pop-top (defs. 2, 3).

flip-up (flip′up′), *adj.* **1.** having a movable part hinged so as to be capable of being flipped upward when necessary: *a flip-up visor.* —*n.* **2.** a flip-up device. [adj., n. use of v. phrase *flip up*]

flirt (flûrt), *v.i.* **1.** to court triflingly or act amorously without serious intentions; play at love; coquet. **2.** to trifle or toy, as with an idea: *She flirted with the notion of buying a sports car.* **3.** to move with a jerk or jerks; dart about: *butterflies flirting from flower to flower.* —*v.t.* **4.** to give a sudden or brisk motion to; wave smartly, as a fan. **5.** to throw or propel with a toss or jerk; fling suddenly. —*n.* **6.** Also, **flirt′er.** a person who is given to flirting. **7.** a quick throw or toss; sudden jerk or darting motion. [1540–50; expressive word; cf. similar initial cluster in FLAP, FLICK[1], FLIP[1], and final elements of SQUIRT, SPURT, etc.] —**flirt′ing·ly,** *adv.*
—**Syn. 1.** tease. **1, 2.** dally. **6.** minx, coquette, tease.

flirt·a·ble (flûr′tə bəl), *adj.* ready or willing to flirt. [1855–60; FLIRT + -ABLE] —**flirt′a·bil′i·ty,** *n.*

flir·ta·tion (flûr tā′shən), *n.* **1.** the act or practice of flirting; coquetry. **2.** a love affair that is not serious. [1710–20; FLIRT + -ATION] —**flir·ta′tion·al,** *adj.* —**flir·ta′tion·less,** *adj.*

flir·ta·tious (flûr tā′shəs), *adj.* **1.** given or inclined to flirtation. **2.** pertaining to or suggesting flirtation. Also, **flirt′y.** [1825–35; FLIRTAT(ION) + -IOUS] —**flir·ta′tious·ly,** *adv.* —**flir·ta′tious·ness,** *n.*

flit (flit), *v.,* **flit·ted, flit·ting,** *n.* —*v.i.* **1.** to move lightly and swiftly; fly, dart, or skim along: *bees flitting from flower to flower.* **2.** to flutter, as a bird. **3.** to pass quickly, as time: *hours flitting by.* **4.** *Chiefly Scot. and North Eng.* **a.** to depart or die. **b.** to change one's residence. —*v.t.* **5.** *Chiefly Scot.* to remove; transfer; oust or dispossess. —*n.* **6.** a light, swift movement; flutter. **7.** *Scot. and North Eng.* a change of residence; instance of moving to a new address. **8.** *Slang* (*disparaging and offensive*). a male homosexual. [1150–1200; ME *flitten* < ON *flytja* to carry, convey, Sw *flytta.* See FLEET[2]] —**flit′ting·ly,** *adv.*
—**Syn. 1.** See **fly**[1].

flitch (flich), *n.* **1.** the side of a hog (or, formerly, some other animal) salted and cured: *a flitch of bacon.* **2.** a steak cut from a halibut. **3.** *Carpentry.* **a.** a piece, as a board, forming part of a flitch beam. **b.** a thin piece of wood, as a veneer. **c.** a bundle of veneers, arranged as cut from the log. **d.** a log about to be cut into veneers. **e.** cant[2] (def. 8). —*v.t.* **4.** to cut into flitches. **5.** *Carpentry.* to assemble (boards or the like) into a laminated construction. [bef. 900; ME *flicche,* OE *flicca;* c. MLG *vlicke,* ON *flikki*]

flitch′ beam′, *Carpentry.* a beam composed of planks bolted together side by side and often reinforced with a plate of iron or steel. Also called **flitch′ gird′er, sandwich beam, sandwich girder.** [1880–85]

flitch·plate (flich′plāt′), *n. Carpentry.* an iron or steel plate for reinforcing a flitch beam. [1885–90; FLITCH + PLATE[1]]

flite (flīt), *v.,* **flit·ed, flit·ing,** *n. Scot. and North Eng.* —*v.i.* **1.** to dispute; wrangle; scold; jeer. —*n.* **2.** a dispute or wrangle; scolding. Also, **flyte.** [bef. 900; (v.) ME *fliten,* OE *flītan* to strive, contend; akin to MHG *vlīzen* (G *Fleiss* industry), OS *flītan;* (n.) ME; OE *flīt* strife, abuse, deriv. of the v.]

flit′ gun′, a hand-held, pump action sprayer for liquid insecticide. [1925–30]

flit·ing (flī′ting), *n.* **1.** contention. **2.** a literary war of words, in versified dialogue. [1150–1200; ME; see FLITE, -ING[1]]

flit·ter[1] (flit′ər), *v.i., v.t.* to flutter. [1535–45; FLIT + -ER[6]]

flit·ter[2] (flit′ər), *n.* a person or thing that flits. [1535–45; FLIT + -ER[1]]

flit·ter[3] (flit′ər), *n.* fine metallic fragments, esp. as used for ornamentation. [1840–50; < G]

flit·ter[4] (flit′ər), *n. Southern U.S.* a fritter or pancake. [appar. by dissimilation from FRITTER[2]]

flit·ter·mouse (flit′ər mous′), *n., pl.* **-mice** (-mīs′). bat[2] (def. 1). [1540–50; FLITTER[1] + MOUSE; calque of G *Fledermaus*]

fliv·ver (fliv′ər), *n.* **1.** *Older Slang.* an automobile, esp. one that is small, inexpensive, and old. **2.** *Slang.* something of unsatisfactory quality or inferior grade. [1905–10, *Amer.;* orig. uncert.]

Flo (flō), *n.* a female given name, form of **Florence.**

float (flōt), *v.i.* **1.** to rest or remain on the surface of a liquid; be buoyant: *The hollow ball floated.* **2.** to move gently on the surface of a liquid; drift along: *The canoe floated downstream.* **3.** to rest or move in a liquid, the air, etc.: *a balloon floating on high.* **4.** to move lightly and gracefully: *She floated down the stairs.* **5.** to move or hover before the eyes or in the mind: *Romantic visions floated before his eyes.* **6.** to pass from one person to another: *A nasty rumor about his firm is floating around town.* **7.** to be free from attachment or involvement. **8.** to move or drift about: *to float from place to place.* **9.** to vacillate (often fol. by *between*). **10.** to be launched, as a company, scheme, etc. **11.** (of a currency) to be allowed to fluctuate freely in the foreign-exchange market instead of being exchanged at a fixed rate. **12.** (of an interest rate) to change periodically according to money-market conditions. **13.** *Com.* to be in circulation, as an acceptance; be awaiting maturity. —*v.t.* **14.** to cause to float. **15.** to cover with water or other liquid; flood; irrigate. **16.** to launch (a company, scheme, etc.); set going. **17.** to issue on the stock market in order to raise money, as stocks or bonds. **18.** to let (a currency or interest rate) fluctuate in the foreign-exchange or money market. **19.** to make smooth with a float, as the surface of plaster. **20.** *Theat.* to lay down (a flat), usually by bracing the bottom edge of the frame with the foot and allowing the rest to fall slowly to the floor. —*n.* **21.** something that floats, as a raft. **22.** something for buoying up. **23.** an inflated bag to sustain a person in water; life preserver. **24.** (in certain types of tanks, cisterns, etc.) a device, as a hollow ball, that through its buoyancy automatically regulates the level, supply, or outlet of a liquid. **25.** *Naut.* a floating platform attached to a wharf, bank, or the like, and used as a landing. **26.** *Aeron.* a hollow, boatlike structure under the wing or fuselage of a seaplane or flying boat, keeping it afloat in water. **27.** *Angling.* a piece of cork or other material for supporting a baited line in the water and indicating by its movements when a fish bites. **28.** *Zool.* an inflated organ that supports an animal in the water. **29.** a vehicle bearing a display, usually an elaborate tableau, in a parade or procession: *Each class prepared a float for the football pageant.* **30.** a glass of fruit juice or soft drink with one or more scoops of ice cream floating in it: *a root-beer float.* **31.** (esp. in the northeastern U.S.) a milk shake with one or more scoops of ice cream floating in it. **32.** paddle[1] (def. 6). **33.** *Banking.* uncollected checks and commercial paper in process of transfer from bank to bank. **34.** the total amount of any cost-of-living or other variable adjustments added to an employee's pay or a retiree's benefits: *a float of $6 per month on top of Social Security benefits.* **35.** an act or instance of floating, as a currency on the foreign-exchange market. **36.** *Building Trades.* **a.** a flat tool for spreading and smoothing plaster or stucco. **b.** a tool for polishing marble. **37.** a single-cut file of moderate smoothness. **38.** a loose-fitting, sometimes very full dress without a waistline. **39.** (in weaving and knitting) a length of yarn that extends over several rows or stitches without being interworked. **40.** *Brit.* a sum of money used by a storekeeper to provide change for the till at the start of a day's business. **41.** *Brit.* a small vehicle, usually battery powered, used to make deliveries, as of milk. **42.** a low-bodied dray for transporting heavy goods. **43.** *Geol., Mining.* **a.** loose fragments of rock, ore, etc., that have been moved from one place to another by the action of wind, water, etc. **b.** ore that has been washed downhill from an orebody and is found lying on the surface of the ground. **c.** any mineral in suspension in water. **44.** Usually, **floats.** *Brit. Theat.* footlights. [bef. 1000; ME *floten,* OE *flotian;* c. ON *flota,* MD *vloten;* akin to OE *flēotan* to FLEET[2]]
—**Syn. 3.** hover, waft, drift, suspend.

float·a·ble (flō′tə bəl), *adj.* **1.** capable of floating; that can be floated. **2.** that can be floated on, as a river. [1820–30; FLOAT + -ABLE] —**float′a·bil′i·ty,** *n.*

float·age (flō′tij), *n.* flotage. [1620–30]

float·a·tion (flō tā′shən), *n.* flotation. [1800–10]

float·board (flōt′bôrd′, -bōrd′), *n.* paddle[1] (def. 6). [1710–20; FLOAT + BOARD]

float′ bowl′, *Auto.* the bowl-shaped section of a carburetor in which a reserve of fuel is maintained, the fuel level being regulated by a float. Also called **float′ cham′ber.**

float′ bridge′, a bridge, as from a pier to a boat, floating at one end and hinged at the other to permit loading and unloading at any level of water. [1685–95]

float·el (flō tel′), *n.* a boat or ship that serves as a hotel, sometimes permanently moored to a dock. [b. FLOAT and HOTEL]

float·er (flō′tər), *n.* **1.** a person or thing that floats. **2.** *Informal.* a person who is continually changing his or her place of abode, employment, etc. **3.** *U.S. Politics.* a voter not attached to any party, esp. a person whose vote may be purchased. **4.** a person who fraudulently votes, usually for pay, in different places in the same election. **5.** *Animal Behav.* a territorial animal that has been unable to claim a territory and is forced into undefended, marginal areas with limited resources. **6.** a speck or string that appears to be drifting across the eye just outside the line of vision, caused by cells or cell fragments in the vitreous humor registering on the retina; musca volitans. **7.** Also called **floating policy.** *Insurance.* a policy that insures movable personal property. **8.** *Finance.* any security or note that has a floating rate. **9.** *Med. Slang.* a corpse found floating in a body of water. **10.** *Australian.* a meat pie served in a plate of gravy or pea soup. [1710–20; FLOAT + -ER[1]]

float-feed (flōt′fēd′), *adj. Mach.* equipped with a float to control the feed. [1900–05]

float′ glass′, extremely smooth, nearly distortion-free plate glass manufactured by pouring molten glass onto a surface of molten tin. [1955–60]

float·ing (flō′ting), *adj.* **1.** being buoyed up on water or other liquid. **2.** having little or no attachment to a particular place; moving from one place to another: *a floating work force.* **3.** *Pathol.* away from its proper position, esp. in a downward direction: *a floating kidney.* **4.** not fixed or settled in a definite place or state: *a floating population.* **5.** *Finance.* **a.** in circulation or use, or not permanently invested, as capital. **b.** composed of sums due within a short time: *a floating debt.* **6.** *Mach.* **a.** having a soft suspension greatly reducing vibrations between the suspended part and its support. **b.** working smoothly. [1555–65; FLOAT + -ING[2]] —**float′ing·ly,** *adv.*

Float′ing Cloud′, The. See ***Drifting Cloud, The.***

float′ing dock′, a submersible, floating structure used as a dry dock, having a floor that is submerged, slipped under a floating vessel, and then raised so as to raise the vessel entirely out of the water. Also called **float′ing dry′ dock′.** [1865–70]

float′ing founda′tion, a foundation used in yielding soil, having for its footing a raft tending to displace a weight greater than that of the building.

float′ing gang′, a group of railroad workers who service or repair the track but are not assigned to a particular section. Cf. **section gang.** [1860–65, *Amer.*]

float′ing heart′, 1. any of certain aquatic plants belonging to the genus *Nymphoides,* of the gentian family, esp. *N. aquatica,* having floating, more or less heart-shaped leaves and a cluster of small, white, five-petaled flowers. **2.** a related plant, *Nymphoides cordata,* of North America, having a cluster of white flowers and round or somewhat oval leaves that are purple beneath. [1855–60, *Amer.*]

float′ing is′land, 1. a dessert consisting of boiled custard with portions of meringue, whipped cream, or whipped egg whites and sometimes jelly floating upon it or around it. **2.** a floating mass of earth and partly decayed vegetation held together by interlacing roots, as on a lake: usually formed by the accumulation of plant litter; sometimes artificially built on wooden platforms, as in the Orient. [1630–40]

float′ing parti′tion, *Carpentry.* a partition running parallel to and between two joists and resting on blocking between them.

float′ing point′, a decimal point whose location is not fixed, used esp. in computer operations.

float′ing pol′icy, 1. (in marine insurance) a policy that provides protection of a broad nature for shipments of merchandise and that is valid continuously until canceled. **2.** floater (def. 7). [1830–40, *Amer.*]

float′ing rib′, *Anat.* one member of the two lowest pairs of ribs, which are attached neither to the sternum nor to the cartilages of other ribs. [1825–35]

float′ing screed′, *Building Trades.* screed (def. 3).

float′ing stock′, stock not held for permanent investment and hence available for speculation; stock held by brokers and speculators rather than investors.

float′ing supply′, the aggregate supply of ready-to-market goods or securities.

float′ing vote′, those voters collectively who are not permanently attached to any political party. [1840–50] —**float′ing vot′er.**

float·plane (flōt′plān′), *n. Aeron.* a seaplane having landing gear consisting of one or more floats. Also, **float′ plane′.** Cf. **flying boat.** [1920–25; FLOAT + PLANE[1]]

float·stone (flōt′stōn′), *n. Masonry.* a stone for rubbing bricks to be gauged. [1695–1705; FLOAT + STONE]

float′ switch′, an electric switch controlled by a conductor floating in a liquid.

float′ valve′, a valve admitting or discharging a liquid to or from a tank and regulated by a float on the surface of the liquid within the tank to maintain a nearly constant height of liquid. [1870–75]

float·y (flō′tē), *adj.,* **float·i·er, float·i·est. 1.** able to float; buoyant. **2.** (of a boat) requiring little water to float. [1300–50; ME *floty.* See FLOAT, -Y[1]]

floc (flok), *n., v.,* **flocced, floc·cing.** —*n.* **1.** Also, **flock.** a tuftlike mass, as in a chemical precipitate. —*v.t., v.i.* **2.** to amass or collect into flocs. [1920–25; < L *floccus* FLOCCUS]

floc·cil·la·tion (flok′sə lā′shən), *n. Pathol.* a delirious picking of the bedclothes by the patient, as in certain fevers. Also called **carphology.** [1835–45; < L *flocc(us)* FLOCCUS + *-ill(us)* dim. suffix + -ATION]

floc·ci·nau·ci·ni·hil·i·pil·i·fi·ca·tion (flok′sə nô′sə-nī′hil ə pil′ə fi kā′shən), *n. Rare.* the estimation of something as valueless (encountered mainly as an example of one of the longest words in the English language).

CONCISE PRONUNCIATION KEY: *act, cāpe, dâre, pärt; set, ēqual; if, īce; ox, ōver, ôrder, oil, bŏŏk, bōōt, out; up, ûrge; child; sing; shoe; thin, that;* zh as in *treasure.* ə = *a* as in *alone, e* as in *system, i* as in *easily, o* as in *gallop, u* as in *circus;* ᵊ as in *fire* (fīᵊr), *hour* (ouᵊr). l and n can serve as syllabic consonants, as in *cradle* (krād′l), and *button* (but′n). See the full key inside the front cover.

[1735–45; < L *flocci* + *nauci* + *nihili* + *pili* all meaning "of little or no value, trifling" + -FICATION]

floc•cose (flok′ōs), *adj.* **1.** *Bot.* consisting of or bearing woolly tufts or long soft hairs. **2.** flocculent. [1745–55; < LL *floccōsus* full of tufts of wool. See FLOCCUS, -OSE[1]]

floc•cu•lant (flok′yə lənt), *n.* a chemical for producing flocculation of suspended particles, as to improve the plasticity of clay for ceramic purposes. [FLOCCULE + -ANT]

floc•cu•late (flok′yə lāt′), *v.*, **-lat•ed, -lat•ing.** —*v.t.* **1.** to form into flocculent masses. —*v.i.* **2.** to form flocculent masses, as a cloud or a chemical precipitate; form aggregated or compound masses of particles. [1820–30; FLOCCUL(US) + -ATE[1]] —**floc•cu•la•ble** (flok′yə lə bəl), *adj.* —**floc′cu•la′tion,** *n.* —**floc′cu•la′tor,** *n.*

floc•cule (flok′yo͞ol), *n.* **1.** something resembling a small flock or tuft of wool. **2.** a bit of flocculent matter, as in a liquid. [1835–45; < NL *flocculus.* See FLOCCUS, -ULE]

floc•cu•lent (flok′yə lənt), *adj.* **1.** like a clump or tuft of wool. **2.** covered with a soft, woolly substance. **3.** consisting of or containing loose woolly masses. **4.** flocky. **5.** *Chem.* consisting of flocs and floccules. [1790–1800; FLOCC(US) + -ULENT] —**floc′cu•lence, floc′cu•len•cy,** *n.* —**floc′cu•lent•ly,** *adv.*

floc′culent precip′itate, *Chem.* a woolly-looking precipitate, as aluminum hydroxide formed by the addition of ammonia to an aluminum-salt solution. [1790–1800]

floc•cu•lus (flok′yə ləs), *n., pl.* **-li** (-lī′). **1.** floccule. **2.** *Astron.* one of the bright or dark patches on the sun's surface, visible in a spectroheliogram. [1790–1800; < NL; see FLOCCULE]

floc•cus (flok′əs), *n., pl.* **floc•ci** (flok′sī, -sē), *adj.* —*n.* **1.** a small tuft of woolly hairs. —*adj.* **2.** *Meteorol.* (of a cloud) having elements in the form of small, rounded tufts. [1835–45; < L: tuft of wool]

flock[1] (flok), *n.* **1.** a number of animals of one kind, esp. sheep, goats, or birds, that keep or feed together or are herded together. **2.** a large number of people; crowd. **3.** a large group of things: *a flock of letters to answer.* **4.** (in New Testament and ecclesiastical use) **a.** the Christian church in relation to Christ. **b.** a single congregation in relation to its pastor. **5.** *Archaic.* a band or company of persons. —*v.i.* **6.** to gather or go in a flock or crowd: *They flocked around the football hero.* [bef. 1000; (n.) ME; OE *floc;* c. ON *flokkr;* (v.) ME, deriv. of the n.] —**flock′less,** *adj.*
—**Syn. 1, 2.** bevy, covey, flight, gaggle; brood, hatch, litter; shoal, school, swarm, group, company. FLOCK, DROVE, HERD, PACK refer to a company of animals, often under the care or guidance of someone. FLOCK is the popular term, which applies to groups of animals, esp. of sheep or goats, and companies of birds: *This lamb is the choicest of the flock. A flock of wild geese flew overhead.* DROVE is esp. applied to a number of oxen, sheep, or swine when driven in a group: *A drove of oxen was taken to market. A large drove of swine filled the roadway.* HERD is usually applied to large animals such as cattle, originally meaning those under the charge of someone; but by extension, to other animals feeding or driven together: *a buffalo herd; a herd of elephants.* PACK applies to a number of animals kept together or keeping together for offense or defense: *a pack of hounds kept for hunting; a pack of wolves.* As applied to people, DROVE, HERD, and PACK carry a contemptuous implication.
—**Usage.** See **collective noun.**

flock[2] (flok), *n.* **1.** a lock or tuft of wool, hair, cotton, etc. **2.** (*sometimes used with a plural v.*) wool refuse, shearings of cloth, old cloth torn to pieces, or the like, for upholstering furniture, stuffing mattresses, etc. **3.** Also called **flocking.** (*sometimes used with a plural v.*) finely powdered wool, cloth, etc., used for producing a velvetlike pattern on wallpaper or cloth or for coating metal. **4.** floc (def. 1). —*v.t.* **5.** to stuff with flock, as a mattress. **6.** to decorate or coat with flock, as wallpaper, cloth, or metal. [1250–1300; ME *flok* < OF *floc* < L *floccus* FLOCCUS. Cf. OHG *floccho*]

flock•bed (flok′bed′), *n.* a bed with a mattress stuffed with wool refuse, shearings of cloth, or the like. [1300–50; ME; see FLOCK[2], BED]

flock′ dot′, a pattern of dots or figures that are not woven but attached to cloth with adhesive.

flock•ing (flok′ing), *n.* **1.** a velvetlike pattern produced on wallpaper or cloth decorated with flock. **2.** flock[2] (def. 3). [1870–75; FLOCK + -ING[1]]

flock′ pa′per, a wallpaper treated with flock to emphasize a design or effect. [1740–50]

flock•y (flok′ē), *adj.,* **flock•i•er, flock•i•est.** like or characterized by flocks or tufts; flocculent. [1590–1600; FLOCK[2] + -Y[1]]

Flod•den (flod′n), *n.* a hill in NE England, in Northumberland county: the invading Scots were disastrously defeated here by the English, 1513.

floe (flō), *n.* **1.** Also called **ice floe.** a sheet of floating ice, chiefly on the surface of the sea, smaller than an ice field. **2.** a detached floating portion of such a sheet. [1810–20; perh. < Norw *flo* layer (cf. ON *flō* layer, level); c. OE *flōh* piece, flagstone; cf. FLAW[1]]

floe•berg (flō′bûrg), *n.* a mass of ice floes resembling an iceberg. [1875–80; FLOE + BERG; modeled on *iceberg*]

flog (flog, flôg), *v.t.,* **flogged, flog•ging. 1.** to beat with a whip, stick, etc., esp. as punishment; whip; scourge. **2.** *Slang.* **a.** to sell, esp. aggressively or vigorously. **b.** to promote; publicize. [1670–80; perh. b. FLAY and *jog,* var. of JAG[1] to prick, slash; but cf. FLAGELLATE] —**flog′ga•ble,** *adj.* —**flog′ger,** *n.*
—**Syn. 1.** thrash, lash.

CONCISE ETYMOLOGY KEY: <, descended or borrowed from; >, whence; b., blend of, blended; c., cognate with; cf., compare; deriv., derivative; equiv., equivalent; imit., imitative; obl., oblique; r., replacing; s., stem; sp., spelling, spelled; resp., respelling, respelled; trans., translation; ?, origin unknown; *, unattested; ‡, probably earlier than. See the full key inside the front cover.

flo•ka•ti (flō kä′tē), *n., pl.* **-tis.** a thick, woolen rug with a shaggy pile, originally handwoven in Greece. [1965–70; < ModGk *phlokátē* a blanket or sleeveless cape of shaggy cloth < Balkan Rom; cf. Aromanian *flucat* shaggy, fleecy < VL; see FLOCCUS, -ATE[1]]

flong (flong, flông), *n.* *Print.* the material of which a stereotype mold is made. [1875–80; alter. of F *flan* FLAN]

flood (flud), *n.* **1.** a great flowing or overflowing of water, esp. over land not usually submerged. **2.** any great outpouring or stream: *a flood of tears.* **3. the Flood,** the universal deluge recorded as having occurred in the days of Noah. Gen. 7. **4.** the rise or flowing in of the tide (opposed to *ebb*). **5.** a floodlight. **6.** *Archaic.* a large body of water. —*v.t.* **7.** to overflow in or cover with a flood; fill to overflowing: *Don't flood the bathtub.* **8.** to cover or fill, as if with a flood: *The road was flooded with cars.* **9.** to overwhelm with an abundance of something: *to be flooded with mail.* **10.** *Auto.* to supply too much fuel to (the carburetor), so that the engine fails to start. **11.** to floodlight. —*v.i.* **12.** to flow or pour in or as if in a flood. **13.** to rise in a flood; overflow. **14.** *Pathol.* **a.** to suffer uterine hemorrhage, esp. in connection with childbirth. **b.** to have an excessive menstrual flow. [bef. 900; ME *flod* (n.), OE *flōd;* c. Goth *flōdus,* OHG *fluot* (G *Flut*)] —**flood′a•ble,** *adj.* —**flood′er,** *n.* —**flood′less,** *adj.* —**flood′like′,** *adj.*
—**Syn. 1.** FLOOD, FLASH FLOOD, DELUGE, FRESHET, INUNDATION refer to the overflowing of normally dry areas, often after heavy rains. FLOOD is usually applied to the overflow of a great body of water, as, for example, a river, although it may refer to any water that overflows an area: *a flood along the river; a flood in a basement.* A FLASH FLOOD is one that comes so suddenly that no preparation can be made against it; it is usually destructive, but begins almost at once to subside: *a flash flood caused by a downpour.* DELUGE suggests a great downpouring of water, sometimes with destruction: *The rain came down in a deluge.* FRESHET suggests a small, quick overflow such as that caused by heavy rains: *a freshet in an abandoned watercourse.* INUNDATION, a literary word, suggests the covering of a great area of land by water: *the inundation of thousands of acres.* **8, 9.** inundate, deluge.

flood′ control′, *Civ. Engin.* the act or technique of controlling river flow with dams, dikes, artificial channels, etc., so as to minimize the occurrence of floods. [1925–30, *Amer.*]

flood•ers (flud′ərz), *n.* (*used with a plural v.*) *Slang.* See **high waters.** [FLOOD + -ER[1] + -S[3]]

flood•gate (flud′gāt′), *n.* **1.** *Civ. Engin.* a gate designed to regulate the flow of water. **2.** anything serving to control the indiscriminate flow or passage of something. [1175–1225; ME; see FLOOD, GATE]

flood•ing (flud′ing), *n.* a form of psychotherapy in which the patient receives abrupt and intense, rather than gradual, exposure to a fear-producing situation. [1665–75, for sense "flood"; see FLOOD + -ING[1]]

flood′ insur′ance, insurance covering loss or damage to property arising from a flood, flood tide, or the like.

flood′ lamp′, a floodlight. [1915–20]

flood•light (flud′līt′), *n., v.,* **-light•ed** or **-lit, -light•ing.** —*n.* **1.** an artificial light so directed or diffused as to give a comparatively uniform illumination over a rather large given area. **2.** a lamp or projector that produces such a light. —*v.t.* **3.** to light up or illuminate with a floodlight. [1920–25; FLOOD + LIGHT[1]]

flood′light projec′tor, a powerful lamp having a reflector curved to produce a floodlight. [1920–25]

flood′ plain′, a nearly flat plain along the course of a stream or river that is naturally subject to flooding. Also, **flood′plain′.** [1870–75]

flood′ tide′, the inflow of the tide; rising tide. [1710–20]

flood′ wall′, *Civ. Engin.* a wall built along a shore or bank to prevent floods by giving a raised, uniform freeboard and by allowing unimpeded flow to water in a channel. [1950–55]

flood•wa•ter (flud′wô′tər, -wot′ər), *n.* the water that overflows as the result of a flood. [1785–95; FLOOD + WATER]

flood•way (flud′wā′), *n.* the channel and adjacent shore areas under water during a flood, esp. as determined for a flood of a given height. [1885–90; FLOOD + WAY]

floo•ey (flo͞o′ē), *adj. Slang.* amiss or awry. Also, **floo′ie.** [of obscure orig.; cf. BLOOEY]

floor (flôr, flōr), *n.* **1.** that part of a room, hallway, or the like, that forms its lower enclosing surface and upon which one walks. **2.** a continuous, supporting surface extending horizontally throughout a building, having a number of rooms, apartments, or the like, and constituting one level or stage in the structure; story. **3.** a level, supporting surface in any structure: *the elevator floor.* **4.** one of two or more layers of material composing a floor: *rough floor; finish floor.* **5.** a platform or prepared level area for a particular use: *a threshing floor.* **6.** the bottom of any more or less hollow place: *the floor of a tunnel.* **7.** a more or less flat extent of surface: *the floor of the ocean.* **8.** the part of a legislative chamber, meeting room, etc., where the members sit, and from which they speak. **9.** the right of one member to speak from such a place in preference to other members: *The senator from Alaska has the floor.* **10.** the area of a floor, as in a factory or retail store, where items are actually made or sold, as opposed to offices, supply areas, etc.: *There are only two salesclerks on the floor.* **11.** the main part of a stock or commodity exchange or the like, as distinguished from the galleries, platform, etc. **12.** the bottom, base, or minimum charged, demanded, or paid: *The government avoided establishing a price or wage floor.* **13.** *Mining.* an underlying stratum, as of ore, usually flat. **14.** *Naut.* **a.** the bottom of a hull. **b.** any of a number of deep, transverse framing members at the bottom of a steel or iron hull, generally interrupted by and joined to any vertical keel or keelsons. **c.** the lowermost member of a frame in a wooden vessel. **15. mop** or **wipe the floor with,** *Informal.* to overwhelm completely; defeat: *He expected to mop the floor with his opponents.* **16. take the floor,** to arise to address a meeting. —*v.t.* **17.** to cover or furnish with a floor. **18.** to bring down to the floor or ground; knock down: *He floored his opponent with one blow.* **19.** to overwhelm; defeat. **20.** to confound or puzzle; nonplus: *I was floored by the problem.* **21.** Also, **floorboard.** to push (a foot-operated accelerator pedal) all the way down to the floor of a vehicle, for maximum speed or power. [bef. 900; ME *flor,* OE *flōr;* c. ON *flōr,* MLG *vlōr,* MHG *vluor* (G *Flur*)] —**floor′less,** *adj.*

floor•age (flôr′ij, flōr′-), *n.* floor space. [1725–35; FLOOR + -AGE]

floor•board (flôr′bôrd′, flōr′bōrd′), *n.* **1.** any of the boards composing a floor. **2.** the floor of an automotive vehicle. —*v.t.* **3.** floor (def. 21). [1880–85; FLOOR + BOARD]

floor′ bro′ker, a member of a stock or commodity exchange who executes orders on the floor of the exchange for other brokers. Cf. **floor trader.** [1910–15]

floor•cloth (flôr′klôth′, -kloth′, flōr′-), *n., pl.* **-cloths** (-klôthz′, -klothz′, -klôths′, -kloths′). **1.** a cloth for washing or wiping floors. **2.** a piece of cloth or the like, as crash, drugget, or linoleum, used with or without a carpet for covering a floor. **3.** See **ground cloth.** [1740–50; FLOOR + CLOTH]

floor•cov•er (flôr′kuv′ər, flōr′-), *n.* material, esp. a nonfabric material, as linoleum, vinyl tile, or ceramic tile, used to cover a floor. Also called **floor′ cov′ering.** [FLOOR + COVER]

floor•er (flôr′ər, flōr′-), *n.* **1.** a person who lays floors. **2.** a person, blow, etc., that knocks someone or something to the floor. **3.** *Informal.* something that beats, overwhelms, or confounds. [1785–95; FLOOR + -ER[1]]

floor′ ex′ercise, *Gymnastics.* a competition in which each entrant performs a routine of acrobatic tumbling feats and balletic movements without any apparatus on a specifically designated floor space, usually 12 m (39 ft.) square and having a matlike covering. [1970–75]

floor′ fur′nace, a small self-contained furnace placed just below the floor of the space to be heated. [1950–55]

floor•ing (flôr′ing, flōr′-), *n.* **1.** a floor. **2.** floors collectively. **3.** materials for making floors. [1615–25; FLOOR + -ING[1]]

floor′ing brad′, a brad having a very small head, made in lengths from 2 to 4 in. (5 to 10 cm).

floor′ing saw′, *Carpentry.* a saw having a curved edge.

floor′ lamp′, a tall lamp designed to stand on the floor. [1890–95]

floor′ lead′er, *U.S. Govt.* the majority leader or minority leader in either the Senate or the House of Representatives. [1895–1900; *Amer.*]

floor-length (flôr′lengkth′, -length′, flōr′-), *adj.* extending to the floor: *a floor-length skirt.* Cf. **full-length.** [1935–40]

floor′ loom′, a loom in which the harnesses are moved by treadles, leaving the weaver's hands free to operate the shuttle. Also called **treadle loom.**

floor•man (flôr′mən, flōr′-), *n., pl.* **-men. 1.** a floor manager. **2.** any person who represents a management, as in assisting customers or maintaining a smooth business operation. **3.** a laborer, mechanic, or maintenance worker hired to do heavy work, as in a factory or oil field. [1910–15; FLOOR + -MAN]

floor-man•age (flôr′man′ij, flōr′-), *v.t.,* **-aged, -ag•ing.** to act as or in the manner of a floor manager.

floor′ man′ager, 1. a person assigned to direct the proceedings on the floor of an assembly, as at a political convention. **2.** the stage manager of a television program. [1885–90, *Amer.*]

floor′ mod′el, a radio, television set, or other furnishing or appliance intended to stand on the floor rather than on a table; console.

floor′ pan′, a solid bottom, found in some types of automobiles, that adds rigidity to the structure and serves as the base for the seats.

floor′ plan′, a diagram of one room, apartment, or entire floor of a building, usually drawn to scale. [1865–70]

floor′ plan′ning, a system of financing that permits a dealer to borrow money to buy goods, which become the security for the loan that is repaid when the merchandise is sold. Also called **floor′ plan′ financ′ing.**

floor′ pock′et, *Theat.* See under **stage pocket.**

floor′ price′, a minimum price required of an item being auctioned. Also called **reserve price.** [1950–55]

floor′ sam′ple, an appliance, piece of furniture, or other article of merchandise that has been used for display or demonstration and is usually offered at a reduced price. [1955–60]

floor•shift (flôr′shift′, flōr′-), *n.* a gearshift set into the floor of an automotive vehicle. [FLOOR + SHIFT]

floor′ show′, a nightclub entertainment typically consisting of a series of singing, dancing, and often comedy acts. [1925–30]

floor-through (flôr′thro͞o′, flōr′-), *adj.* **1.** occupying the entire depth of a building: *a floor-through apartment.* —*n.* **2.** a floor-through dwelling. [1965–70]

floor′ trad′er, a member of a stock or commodity exchange who executes orders on the floor of the exchange for his or her own account. Cf. **floor broker.**

floor•walk•er (flôr′wô′kər, flōr′-), *n.* a person employed in a store to direct customers and supervise salespeople. [1875–80, *Amer.*; FLOOR + WALKER]

floor-work (flôr′wûrk′, flōr′-), *n. Dance.* a sequence of exercises done at the beginning of a class or before a performance in sitting and supine positions on the floor in order to stretch and warm up the body.

floo·zy (flo͞o′zē), *n., pl.* **-zies.** *Slang.* a gaudily dressed, usually immoral woman, esp. a prostitute. Also, **floo′sie, floo′sy, floo′zie.** [1905–10; orig. uncert.]

flop (flop), *v.,* **flopped, flop·ping,** *n.* —*v.i.* **1.** to fall or plump down suddenly, esp. with noise; drop or turn with a sudden bump or thud (sometimes fol. by *down*): *The puppy flopped down on the couch.* **2.** to change suddenly, as from one side or party to another (often fol. by *over*). **3.** to be a complete failure; fail: *The play flopped dismally.* **4.** *Informal.* to sleep or be lodged: *to flop at a friend's house.* **5.** to swing loosely; bounce; flap: *His long hair flops in his eyes when he runs.* —*v.t.* **6.** to drop with a sudden bump or thud: *He flopped his books on a chair.* **7.** to dispose (oneself) in a heavily negligent manner: *to flop oneself in a chair.* **8.** to invert (the negative of a photograph) so that the right and left sides are transposed. —*n.* **9.** an act of flopping. **10.** the sound of flopping; a thud. **11.** a failure: *The new comedy was a flop.* **12.** *Informal.* a place to sleep; temporary lodging: *The mission offered a flop and a free breakfast.* [1595–1605; 1890–95 for def. 11; var. of FLAP] —**flop′per,** *n.* —**Syn. 11.** fiasco, disaster, debacle; bomb, dog.

flop-eared (flop′ērd′), *adj.* having long, drooping ears, as a hound. [1840–50]

flop′ forg′ing, *Metalworking.* forging of both sides of a piece from the same die, the sides being identical.

flop·house (flop′hous′), *n., pl.* **-hous·es** (-hou′ziz). a cheap, run-down hotel or rooming house. [1890–95]

flop·o·ver (flop′ō′vər), *n.* a continuous, vertical movement of a television image picture caused by interference in reception or by improper tuning. [1950–55; n. use of v. phrase *flop over*]

flop·pe·roo (flop′ə ro͞o′), *n., pl.* **-roos.** *Slang.* flop (def. 11). [1935–40; FLOP + -EROO]

flop·pers (flop′ərz), *n.* (*used with a singular or plural v.*) See **air plant** (def. 2). [FLOP + -ER[1] + -S[3]]

flop·py (flop′ē), *adj.,* **-pi·er, -pi·est,** *n.* —*adj.* **1.** tending to flop. —*n.* **2.** See **floppy disk.** [1855–60; FLOP + -Y[1]] —**flop′pi·ly,** *adv.* —**flop′pi·ness,** *n.*

flop′py disk′, *Computers.* a thin, flexible plastic disk coated with magnetic material, on which data and programs can be stored for later retrieval. Also, **flop′py·disk′.** Also called **floppy, diskette, flexible disk, magnetic disk.** [1970–75]

Flop′ti·cal disk′ (flop′ti kəl), *Trademark.* a small, high-capacity, removable disk for storing computer data that combines magnetic floppy disk and optical disc technologies.

flor-, var. of **flori-:** *florist.*

flor., flourished. [< L *flōruit*]

flo·ra (flôr′ə, flōr′ə), *n., pl.* **flo·ras, flo·rae** (flôr′ē, flōr′ē) for 2. **1.** the plants of a particular region or period, listed by species and considered as a whole. **2.** a work systematically describing such plants. **3.** plants, as distinguished from fauna. **4.** the aggregate of bacteria, fungi, and other microorganisms normally occurring on or in the bodies of humans and other animals: *intestinal flora.* [1655–65; < NL, L *Flōra* the Roman goddess of flowers (used from the 17th cent. in the titles of botanical works), deriv. of L *flōr-* (s. of *flōs*) FLOWER]

Flo·ra (flôr′ə, flōr′ə), *n.* a female given name.

flo·ral (flôr′əl, flōr′-), *adj.* **1.** pertaining to or consisting of flowers: *floral decoration.* **2.** of or pertaining to floras or a flora. —*n.* **3.** something, as a fabric, garment, wallpaper, or household item, having a floral pattern: *Let's replace these drapes with florals.* [1640–50; < L *Flōrālis* pertaining to *Flōra.* See FLORA, -AL[1]] —**flo′ral·ly,** *adv.*

flo′ral em′blem, a flower or plant serving as the emblem of a city, state, nation, etc.

flo′ral en′velope, *Bot.* the calyx and corolla of a flower. [1820–30]

flo′ral leaf′, *Bot.* one of the modified leaves forming the perianth of a flower, as a sepal or petal. [1745–55]

Flo′ral Park′, a city on W Long Island, in SE New York. 16,805.

Flo·ré·al (flô rä al′), *n.* (in the French Revolutionary calendar) the eighth month of the year, extending from April 20 to May 19. [1795–1805; < F < L *flōre(us)* of flowers (*flōr-,* s. of *flōs* flower + *-eus* adj. suffix) + F *-al* -AL[1]]

Flor·ence (flôr′əns, flor′-), *n.* **1.** Italian, **Firenze.** a city in central Italy, on the Arno River: capital of the former grand duchy of Tuscany. 464,425. **2.** a city in NW Alabama, on the Tennessee River. 37,029. **3.** a city in E South Carolina. 30,062. **4.** a town in N Kentucky. 15,586. **5.** a female given name: from a Latin word meaning "flowery."

Flor′ence fen′nel, a variety of fennel, *Foeniculum vulgare azoricum,* having enlarged leaf bases, which are blanched and used esp. as an ingredient in salads. Also called **finocchio.**

Flor′ence flask′, a round bottle having a flat bottom and long neck, for use in laboratories. [1735–45]

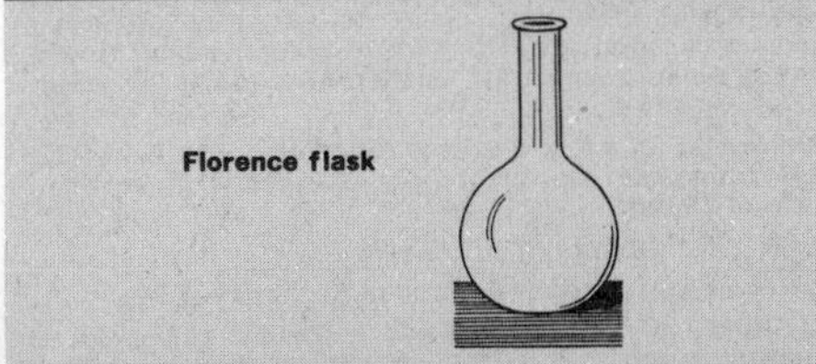

Flor·en·tine (flôr′ən tēn′, -tīn′, flor′-), *adj.* **1.** of or pertaining to Florence, Italy: *the Florentine poets of the 14th century.* **2.** pertaining to or designating the style of art developed in Florence during the late 13th to 15th centuries. **3.** (of food) prepared with spinach: *eggs Florentine.* —*n.* **4.** a native or inhabitant of Florence, Italy. **5.** (*often l.c.*) a chocolate-coated cookie made with orange peel and almonds. [1535–45; < L *Flōrentīnus* pertaining to *Flōrentia* FLORENCE; see -INE[1]]

Flor′entine stitch′. See under **bargello** (def. 2).

flo·res (flôr′ēz, flōr′-), *n.* (*used with a plural v.*) *Chem.* flower (def. 11). [1655–65; < L *flōrēs* pl. of *flōs* FLOWER]

Flo·res (*Sp.* flô′res *for 1;* flôr′is, -ēz, flōr′- *for 2; Port.* flô′rish *for 3*), *n.* **1. Juan Jo·sé** (hwän hô se′), 1800–64, Ecuadorian general and statesman: president 1830–35, 1839–45. **2.** one of the Lesser Sunda Islands in Indonesia, separated from Sulawesi by the Flores Sea. ab. 200,000 with adjacent islands; 7753 sq. mi. (20,080 sq. km). **3.** the westernmost island of the Azores, in the N Atlantic. 55 sq. mi. (142 sq. km).

flo·res·cence (flô res′əns, flō-, flə-), *n.* the act, state, or period of flowering; bloom. [1785–95; < L *flōrēsc(ēns)* (prp. of *flōrēscere* to begin blooming, inchoative deriv. of *flōrēre* to bloom, deriv. of *flōs* FLOWER) + -ENCE] —**flo·res′cent,** *adj.*

Flo′res Sea′ (flôr′is, -ēz, flōr′-), a sea between Sulawesi and the Lesser Sunda Islands in Indonesia. ab. 180 mi. (290 km) wide.

flo·ret (flôr′it, flōr′-), *n.* **1.** a small flower. **2.** *Bot.* one of the closely clustered small flowers that make up the flower head of a composite flower, as the daisy. **3.** one of the tightly clustered divisions of a head of broccoli or cauliflower. **4.** Also, **flo·rette** (flô ret′, flō-). spun silk obtained from floss. **5.** *Print.* flower (def. 6). [1350–1400; ME *flouret* < OF *florete,* dim. of *flor* FLOWER; see -ET]

Flo·rey (flôr′ē, flōr′ē), *n.* **Sir Howard Walter,** 1898–1968, Australian pathologist in England: Nobel prize for medicine 1945.

flori-, a combining form meaning "flower," used in the formation of compound words: *floriferous.* Also, **flor-.** [< L *flōri-,* equiv. to *flōr-* (s. of *flōs*) flower + *-i-* -I-]

Flo·ri·a·nóp·o·lis (flôr′ē ə nop′ə lis, flōr′-; *Port.* flô′ryə nô′po͝o lēs′), *n.* a seaport in and the capital of Santa Catarina state, on an island off the S coast of Brazil. 196,055. Formerly, **Desterro.**

flo·ri·at·ed (flôr′ē ā′tid, flōr′-), *adj.* made of or decorated with floral ornamentation: *floriated design; floriated china.* Also, **flo·ri·ate** (flôr′ē it, -āt′, flōr′-). [1835–45; FLORI- + -ATE[1] + -ED[2]]

flo·ri·bun·da (flôr′ə bun′də, flōr′-), *n.* any of a class of roses characterized by a long blooming period and the production of large flowers often in thick clusters. [1895–1900; < NL, n. use of fem. of *flōribundus* flowering freely, equiv. to *flōri-* FLORI- + *-bundus* adj. suffix]

flo·ri·can (flôr′i kən, flōr′-), *n.* any of various smaller species of bustards. [orig. uncert.]

flo·ri·cul·ture (flôr′i kul′chər, flōr′-), *n.* the cultivation of flowers or flowering plants, esp. for ornamental purposes. [1815–25; FLORI- + CULTURE] —**flo′ri·cul′tur·al,** *adj.* —**flo′ri·cul′tur·al·ly,** *adv.* —**flo′ri·cul′tur·ist,** *n.*

flor·id (flôr′id, flor′-), *adj.* **1.** reddish; ruddy; rosy: *a florid complexion.* **2.** flowery; excessively ornate; showy: *florid writing.* **3.** *Obs.* abounding in or consisting of flowers. [1635–45; < L *flōridus,* equiv. to *flōr(ēre)* to bloom (see FLORESCENCE) + *-idus* -ID[4]] —**flo·rid·i·ty** (flô rid′i tē, flə-), **flor′id·ness,** *n.* —**flor′id·ly,** *adv.* —**Syn. 2.** flamboyant, grandiloquent, rococo; flash.

Flor·i·da (flôr′i də, flor′-), *n.* a state in the SE United States between the Atlantic and the Gulf of Mexico. 9,739,992. 58,560 sq. mi. (151,670 sq. km). *Cap.:* Tallahassee. *Abbr.:* FL (for use with zip code), Fla. —**Flo·rid·i·an** (flə rid′ē ən), **Flor′i·dan,** *adj., n.*

Flor′ida Cur′rent, the part of the Gulf Stream which extends from the Florida Strait to Cape Hatteras.

Flor′ida Keys′, a chain of small islands and reefs off the coast of S Florida. ab. 225 mi. (362 km) long.

Flor′ida moss′. See **Spanish moss.** [1885–90, *Amer.*]

Flor′ida room′, a sunroom.

Flor′ida Strait′, a strait between Florida, Cuba, and the Bahamas, connecting the Gulf of Mexico and the Atlantic.

Flor′ida vel′vet bean′, a tropical vine, *Mucuna deeringiana,* of the legume family, having showy, purple flowers in drooping clusters and black, hairy pods: grown as an ornamental.

flo·rif·er·ous (flô rif′ər əs, flō-), *adj.* flower-bearing. [1650–60; < L *flōrifer* (see FLORI-, -FER) + -OUS] —**flo·rif′er·ous·ly,** *adv.* —**flo·rif′er·ous·ness,** *n.*

flo·ri·le·gi·um (flôr′ə lē′jē əm, flōr′-), *n., pl.* **-gi·a** (-jē ə). a collection of literary pieces; anthology. [1640–50; < NL *flōrilegium,* equiv. to L *flōri-* FLORI- + *leg(ere)* to gather + *-ium* -IUM, on the model of *spicilegium* gleaning; a calque of Gk *anthología* ANTHOLOGY]

flor·in (flôr′in, flor′-), *n.* **1.** a cupronickel coin of Great Britain, formerly equal to two shillings or the tenth part of a pound and retained in circulation equal to 10 new pence after decimalization in 1971: first issued in 1849 as a silver coin. **2.** the guilder of the Netherlands. **3.** a former gold coin of Florence, first issued in 1252 and widely imitated. **4.** a former gold coin of England, first issued under Edward III. **5.** a former gold coin of Austria, first issued in the middle of the 14th century. [1275–1325; ME < MF < OIt *fiorino* Florentine coin stamped with a lily, deriv. of *fiore* flower < L *flōrem,* acc. of *flōs* FLOWER]

Flor·in (flôr′in, flor′-), *n.* a town in central California, near Sacramento. 16,523.

Flo·ri·o (flôr′ē ō′, flōr′-), *n.* **John,** 1553?–1625, English lexicographer and translator.

Flor·is·sant (flôr′ə sənt), *n.* a city in E Missouri, near St. Louis. 55,372.

flo·rist (flôr′ist, flōr′-, flor′-), *n.* **1.** a retailer of flowers, ornamental plants, etc. **2.** a grower of flowers. [1615–25; FLOR- + -IST]

flo·ris·tic (flô ris′tik, flō-), *adj.* pertaining to flowers or a flora. [1895–1900; FLOR- + -ISTIC] —**flo·ris′ti·cal·ly,** *adv.*

flo′rists' foam′, a rigid, deformable, spongelike plastic used in floral arrangements to secure the stems of flowers.

-florous, a combining form meaning "-flowered," "having flowers," used in the formation of adjectives: *uniflorous.* [< L *-flōrus.* See FLORI-, -OUS]

flo·ru·it (flō′ro͞o it; *Eng.* flôr′yo͞o it, flōr′-, flor′-), *n. Latin.* he (or she) flourished: used to indicate the period during which a person flourished, esp. when the exact birth and death dates are unknown. *Abbr.:* fl., flor.

flo·ry (flôr′ē, flōr′ē), *adj. Heraldry.* fleury.

Flo·ry (flôr′ē, flōr′ē), *n.* **Paul John,** 1910–85, U.S. chemist: pioneer in research on polymers; Nobel prize 1974.

floss (flôs, flos), *n.* **1.** the cottony fiber yielded by the silk-cotton tree. **2.** silk filaments with little or no twist, used in weaving as brocade or in embroidery. **3.** any silky, filamentous matter, as the silk of corn. **4.** See **dental floss.** —*v.i.* **5.** to use dental floss on the teeth. —*v.t.* **6.** to clean (the teeth) with dental floss. Also called **floss′ silk′** (for defs. 1-3). [1750–60; prob. < F *floche,* as in *soie floche* floss silk, OF *flosche* down, velvet pile (of uncert. orig.)] —**floss′er,** *n.*

floss′ hole′, *Metall.* a hole in a puddling furnace for the removal of ash or slag. [1830–40; *floss* slag < G *Flosz* in same sense]

Flos·sie (flô′sē, flos′ē), *n.* a female given name, form of **Florence.**

floss·y (flô′sē, flos′ē), *adj.,* **floss·i·er, floss·i·est. 1.** made of or resembling floss; downy. **2.** showily stylish; excessively ornamented or fancy. [1830–40; FLOSS + -Y[1]] —**floss′i·ly,** *adv.* —**floss′i·ness,** *n.*

flo·tage (flō′tij), *n.* **1.** an act of floating. **2.** the state of floating. **3.** floating power; buoyancy. **4.** anything that floats; flotsam. **5.** the part of a ship above the water line. Also, **floatage.** [1620–30; FLOAT + -AGE; cf. F *flottage*]

flo·ta·tion (flō tā′shən), *n.* **1.** an act or state of floating. **2.** the launching of a commercial venture, bond issue, loan, etc. **3.** *Metall.* a process for separating the different minerals in a mass of powdered ore based on their tendency to sink in, or float on, a given liquid. **4.** the science of floating bodies. Also, **floatation.** [1800–10; FLOAT + -ATION; cf. F *flottaison* (see FLOTSAM)]

flo·til·la (flō til′ə), *n.* **1.** a group of small naval vessels, esp. a naval unit containing two or more squadrons. **2.** a group moving together: *The governor was followed by a whole flotilla of reporters.* [1705–15; < Sp, dim. of *flota* fleet < F *flotte* < OE *flota*]

Flo·tow (flō′tō), *n.* **Frie·drich von** (frē′drikh fən), 1812–83, German composer.

flot·sam (flot′səm), *n.* **1.** the part of the wreckage of a ship and its cargo found floating on the water. Cf. **jetsam, lagan. 2.** material or refuse floating on water. **3.** useless or unimportant items; odds and ends. **4.** a vagrant, penniless population: *the flotsam of the city slums in medieval Europe.* Also called **flot′sam and jet′sam** (for defs. 3, 4). [1600–10; < AF *floteson,* deriv. of *floter* to float < OE *flotian*]

flounce[1] (flouns), *v.,* **flounced, flounc·ing,** *n.* —*v.i.* **1.** to go with impatient or impetuous, exaggerated movements: *The star flounced out of the studio in a rage.* **2.** to throw the body about spasmodically; flounder. —*n.* **3.** an act or instance of flouncing; a flouncing movement. [1535–45; of obscure orig.; perh. akin to Norw *flunsa* to hurry] —**Syn. 1.** storm, bound, prance, bounce.

flounce[2] (flouns), *n., v.,* **flounced, flounc·ing.** —*n.* **1.** a strip of material gathered or pleated and attached at one edge, with the other edge left loose or hanging: used for trimming, as on the edge of a skirt or sleeve or on a

CONCISE PRONUNCIATION KEY: act, cāpe, dâre, pärt; set, ēqual; *if,* īce; ox, ōver, ôrder, oil, bo͝ok, bo͞ot, out; up, ûrge; child; sing; shoe; thin, *that;* zh as in *treasure.* ə = *a* as in *alone,* *e* as in *system,* *i* as in *easily,* *o* as in *gallop,* *u* as in *circus;* ᵊ as in *fire* (fīᵊr), *hour* (ouᵊr). l and n can serve as syllabic consonants, as in *cradle* (krād′l), and *button* (but′n). See the full key inside the front cover.

one edge, with the other edge left loose or hanging: used for trimming, as on the edge of a skirt or sleeve or on a curtain, slipcover, etc. —*v.t.* **2.** to trim with flounces. [1665–75; alter. of FROUNCE]

flounc·ing (floun′sing), *n.* **1.** material used in making flounces. **2.** trimming consisting of a flounce. [1760–70; FLOUNCE[2] + -ING[1]]

flounc·y[1] (floun′sē), *adj.*, **flounc·i·er, flounc·i·est.** marked by flouncing movement: *an affected, flouncy walk.* [FLOUNCE[1] + -Y[1]]

flounc·y[2] (floun′sē), *adj.*, **flounc·i·er, flounc·i·est.** decorated with flounces: *an elaborate flouncy blouse.* [FLOUNCE[2] + -Y[1]]

floun·der[1] (floun′dər), *v.i.* **1.** to struggle with stumbling or plunging movements (usually fol. by *about, along, on, through,* etc.): *He saw the child floundering about in the water.* **2.** to struggle clumsily or helplessly: *He floundered helplessly on the first day of his new job.* [1570–80; perh. b. FLOUNCE[1] and FOUNDER[2]] —**floun′der·ing·ly,** *adv.*
—**Syn. 2.** falter, waver, muddle.

floun·der[2] (floun′dər), *n., pl.* (*esp. collectively*) **-der,** (*esp. referring to two or more kinds or species*) **-ders. 1.** a European, marine flatfish, *Platichthys flesus,* used for food. **2.** any of numerous similar or closely related non-European flatfishes. **3.** any flatfish other than soles. [1400–50; late ME < AF *floundre* < Scand; cf. Norw *flundra*]

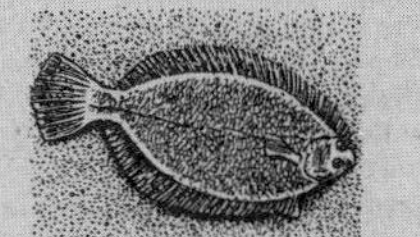

winter flounder, *Pseudopleuronectes americanus,* length 1½ ft. (0.5 m)

flour (flouᵊr, flou′ər), *n.* **1.** the finely ground meal of grain, esp. the finer meal separated by bolting. **2.** the finely ground and bolted meal of wheat, as that used in baking. **3.** a finely ground, powdery foodstuff, as of dehydrated potatoes, fish, or bananas. **4.** a fine, soft powder: *flour of emery.* —*v.t.* **5.** to make (grain or the like) into flour; grind and bolt. **6.** to sprinkle or dredge with flour: *Flour the chicken before frying.* —*v.i.* **7.** (of mercury) to refuse to amalgamate with another metal because of some impurity of the metal; lie on the surface of the metal in the form of minute globules. **8.** to disintegrate into minute particles. [1200–50; ME; special use of FLOWER. Cf. F *fleur de farine* the flower or finest part of the meal] —**flour′less,** *adj.*

flour′ bee′tle, any of several brown darkling beetles, esp. of the genus *Tribolium,* that infest, breed in, feed on, and often pollute flour, stored grain, and other stored produce. [1885–90]

flour·ish (flûr′ish, flur′-), *v.i.* **1.** to be in a vigorous state; thrive: *a period in which art flourished.* **2.** to be in its or in one's prime; be at the height of fame, excellence, influence, etc. **3.** to be successful; prosper. **4.** to grow luxuriantly, or thrive in growth, as a plant. **5.** to make dramatic, sweeping gestures: *Flourish more when you act out the king's great death scene.* **6.** to add embellishments and ornamental lines to writing, letters, etc. **7.** to sound a trumpet call or fanfare. —*v.t.* **8.** to brandish dramatically; gesticulate with: *a conductor flourishing his baton for the crescendo.* **9.** to decorate or embellish (writing, a page of script, etc.) with sweeping or fanciful curves or lines. —*n.* **10.** an act or instance of brandishing. **11.** an ostentatious display. **12.** a decoration or embellishment, esp. in writing: *He added a few flourishes to his signature.* **13.** *Rhet.* a parade of fine language; an expression used merely for effect. **14.** a trumpet call or fanfare. **15.** a condition or period of thriving: *in full flourish.* [1250–1300; ME *florisshen* < MF *floriss-*, long s. of *florir* << L *flōrēre* to bloom, deriv. of *flōs* FLOWER] —**flour′ish·er,** *n.*
—**Syn. 1.** grow, increase. See **succeed. 9.** ornament. **12.** ornament, adornment. —**Ant. 1.** fade, decline.

flour·ish·ing (flûr′i shing, flur′-), *adj.* growing vigorously; thriving; prosperous: *a flourishing little business.* [1250–1300; ME; see FLOURISH, -ING[2]] —**flour′ish·ing·ly,** *adv.*

flour′ mill′, a mill for grinding grain into flour. [1800–10]

flour·y (flouᵊr′ē, flou′ə rē), *adj.* **1.** of, pertaining to, or resembling flour. **2.** white with flour. [1585–95; FLOUR + -Y[1]]

flout (flout), *v.t.* **1.** to treat with disdain, scorn, or contempt; scoff at; mock: *to flout the rules of propriety.* —*v.i.* **2.** to show disdain, scorn, or contempt; scoff, mock, or gibe (often fol. by *at*). —*n.* **3.** a disdainful, scornful, or contemptuous remark or act; insult; gibe. [1350–1400; ME *flouten* to play the FLUTE; cf. D *fluiten* to play the flute, jeer] —**flout′er,** *n.* —**flout′ing·ly,** *adv.*
—**Usage.** See **flaunt.**

flow (flō), *v.i.* **1.** to move along in a stream: *The river flowed slowly to the sea.* **2.** to circulate: *blood flowing through one's veins.* **3.** to stream or well forth: *Warmth flows from the sun.* **4.** to issue or proceed from a source: *Orders flowed from the office.* **5.** to menstruate. **6.** to come or go as in a stream: *A constant stream of humanity flowed by.* **7.** to proceed continuously and smoothly: *Melody flowed from the violin.* **8.** to hang loosely at full length: *Her hair flowed over her shoulders.* **9.** to abound in something: *The tavern flowed with wine.* **10.** to rise and advance, as the tide (opposed to *ebb*). —*v.t.* **11.** to cause or permit to flow: *to flow paint on a wall before brushing.* **12.** to cover with water or other liquid; flood. —*n.* **13.** an act of flowing. **14.** movement in or as if in a stream. **15.** the rate of flowing. **16.** the volume of fluid that flows through a passage of any given section during a unit of time: *Oil flow of the well was 500 barrels a day.* **17.** something that flows; stream. **18.** an outpouring or discharge of something, as in a stream: *a flow of blood.* **19.** menstruation. **20.** an overflowing; flood. **21.** the rise of the tide (opposed to *ebb*). **22.** *Mach.* progressive distortion of a metal object under continuous service at high temperature. **23.** *Physics.* the transference of energy: *heat flow.* [bef. 900; (v.) ME *flowen,* OE *flōwan;* akin to MLG *vlōien,* ON *flōa;* (n.) late ME: surge of a wave, deriv. of the v.] —**flow′a·ble,** *adj.* —**flow′a·bil′i·ty,** *n.*
—**Syn. 1.** FLOW, GUSH, SPOUT, SPURT refer to certain of the movements characteristic of fluids. FLOW is the general term: *Water flows. A stream of blood flows.* To GUSH is to rush forth copiously from a cavity, in as large a volume as can issue therefrom, as the result of some strong impelling force: *The water will gush out if the main breaks.* SPOUT and SPURT both imply the ejecting of a liquid from a cavity by some internal impetus given to it. SPOUT implies a rather steady, possibly well-defined, jet or stream, not necessarily of long duration but always of considerable force: *A whale spouts.* SPURT implies a forcible, possibly sudden, spasmodic, or intermittent issue or jet: *The liquid spurted out suddenly when the bottle cap was pushed in.* SPOUT applies only to liquids; the other terms apply also to gases. **7.** run. **9.** teem.

flow·age (flō′ij), *n.* **1.** an act of flowing; flow. **2.** the state of being flooded. **3.** flowing or overflowing water, or other liquid. **4.** *Mech.* gradual internal motion or deformation. [1820–30, *Amer.*; FLOW + -AGE]

flow·back (flō′bak′), *n.* return or redistribution of something that has been received or acquired.

flow′ brec′cia, *Petrol.* a volcanic breccia that has solidified from a lava flow.

flow′ chart′, 1. Also called **flow sheet.** a detailed diagram or chart of the operations and equipment through which material passes, as in a manufacturing process. **2.** a graphic representation, using symbols interconnected with lines, of the successive steps in a procedure or system. Also, **flow′chart′.** Also called **flow′ di′agram.** [1915–20]

flow′ cleav′age, *Petrol.* cleavage resulting from the parallel alignment of the mineral constituents of a rock when in a plastic condition.

flow·er (flou′ər), *n.* **1.** the blossom of a plant. **2.** *Bot.* **a.** the part of a seed plant comprising the reproductive organs and their envelopes if any, esp. when such envelopes are more or less conspicuous in form and color. **b.** an analogous reproductive structure in other plants, as the mosses. **3.** a plant, considered with reference to its blossom or cultivated for its floral beauty. **4.** state of efflorescence or bloom: *Peonies were in flower.* **5.** an ornament representing a flower. **6.** Also called **fleuron, floret.** *Print.* an ornamental piece of type, esp. a stylized floral design, often used in a line to decorate chapter headings, page borders, or bindings. **7.** an ornament or adornment. **8.** the finest or most flourishing period: *Poetic drama was in flower in Elizabethan England.* **9.** the best or finest member or part of a number, body, or whole: *the flower of American youth.* **10.** the finest or choicest product or example. **11. flowers,** (*used with a singular v.*) *Chem.* a substance in the form of a fine powder, esp. as obtained by sublimation: *flowers of sulfur.* —*v.i.* **12.** to produce flowers; blossom; come to full bloom. **13.** to come out into full development; mature. —*v.t.* **14.** to cover or deck with flowers. **15.** to decorate with a floral design. [1150–1200; ME *flour* flower, best of anything < OF *flor, flour, flur* < L *flōr-* (s. of *flōs*). Cf. BLOSSOM]
—**Syn. 13.** develop, flourish, bloom, blossom, ripen.

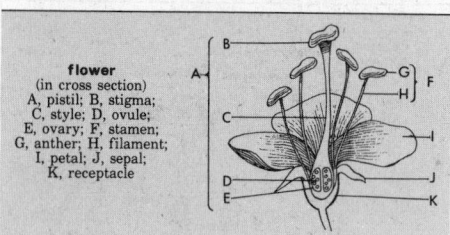

flower (in cross section) A, pistil; B, stigma; C, style; D, ovule; E, ovary; F, stamen; G, anther; H, filament; I, petal; J, sepal; K, receptacle

flow·er·age (flou′ər ij), *n.* the process or state of flowering. [1680–90; FLOWER + -AGE]

flow′er bee′tle, 1. any of numerous, usually brightly colored beetles, as of the families Malachiidae and Dasytidae, that live on flowers and are predaceous on other insects. **2.** any of certain scarabaeid beetles of the subfamily Cetoniinae that feed on pollen. [1835–45, *Amer.*]

flow′er box′, a box used for growing decorative plants in or around the home, often attached to a window ledge. [1875–80]

flow′er bud′. See under **bud**[1] (def. 1a). [1870–75]

flow′er bug′, any of several bugs of the family Anthocoridae that live on flowers and are predaceous on aphids and other small insects. [1885–90]

flow′er child′, (esp. in the 1960's) a young person, esp. a hippie, rejecting conventional society and advocating love, peace, and simple, idealistic values. [1965–70, *Amer.*; from the conventional image of such people as carrying and distributing flowers]

flow·er-de-luce (flou′ər də lo͞os′), *n.* the iris flower or plant. [1630–40; Anglicization of F *fleur de lis*]

flow·ered (flou′ərd), *adj.* **1.** having flowers. **2.** decorated with flowers or a floral pattern: *a flowered dress.* [1300–50; ME; see FLOWER, -ED[3]]

flow·er·er (flou′ər ər), *n.* a plant that flowers at a specific time or in a certain manner. [1850–55; FLOWER + -ER[1]]

flow·er·et (flou′ər it), *n.* a small flower; floret. [1350–1400; ME, var. of FLORET]

flow′er fly′. See **syrphid fly.** [1835–45]

flow′er girl′, 1. a young girl at a wedding ceremony who precedes the bride and carries or scatters flowers in her path. **2.** *Brit.* a woman who sells flowers in the street. [1780–90]

flow′er head′, *Bot.* an inflorescence consisting of a dense cluster of small, stalkless flowers; capitulum. [1835–45]

flow·er·ing (flou′ər ing), *adj.* bearing flowers. [1250–1300; ME; see FLOWER, -ING[2]]

flow′ering dog′wood, a North American dogwood tree, *Cornus florida,* having small greenish flowers in the spring, surrounded by white or pink bracts that resemble petals: the state flower and the state tree of Virginia. Also called **boxwood.** [1835–45]

flow′ering flax′, a plant, *Linum grandiflorum,* of northern Africa, having quickly fading, red or pink flowers.

flow′ering ma′ple, any of various shrubs belonging to the genus *Abutilon,* of the mallow family, having large, bright-colored flowers.

flow′ering moss′, pyxie. [1855–60]

flow′ering plant′, a plant that produces flowers, fruit, and seeds; angiosperm. [1860–65]

flow′ering quince′, any shrub belonging to the genus *Chaenomeles,* of the rose family, native to eastern Asia, having showy, waxy flowers and a quincelike fruit, grown widely as an ornamental.

flow′ering rasp′berry, a shrub, *Rubus ordoratus,* of eastern North America, having loose clusters of showy purplish or rose-purple flowers and inedible, dry, red fruit. [1805–15]

flow′ering tobac′co, any plant belonging to the genus *Nicotiana,* of the nightshade family, as *N. alata* and *N. sylvestris,* having clusters of fragrant flowers that usually bloom at night, grown as an ornamental.

flow′ering win′tergreen. See **fringed polygala.** [1810–20, *Amer.*]

flow·er·less (flou′ər lis), *adj.* **1.** having or producing no flowers. **2.** *Bot.* having no true seeds; cryptogamic. [1490–1500; FLOWER + -LESS] —**flow′er·less·ness,** *n.*

flow·er·let (flou′ər lit), *n.* a small flower; floret. [FLOWER + -LET]

flow·er·like (flou′ər līk′), *adj.* resembling or in the shape of a flower; delicate; graceful. [FLOWER + -LIKE]

flow·er-of-Jove (flou′ər əv jōv′), *n., pl.* **flow·ers-of-Jove.** a white, woolly plant, *Lychnis flos-jovis,* of the pink family, having red or purple flowers in dense clusters. [trans. of NL *Flōs-Jovis*]

flow·er·peck·er (flou′ər pek′ər), *n.* any of numerous small, arboreal, usually brightly colored oscine birds of the family Dicaeidae, of southeastern Asia and Australia. [1880–85; FLOWER + PECKER]

flow′er peo′ple, flower children. [1965–70]

flow·er·pot (flou′ər pot′), *n.* a container in which to grow and display plants. [1590–1600; FLOWER + POT[1]]

flow′ers of sul′fur, *Pharm.* sublimed sulfur in the form of a fine yellow powder, used in medicine chiefly to kill parasites and fungi and to treat certain skin diseases.

flow′ers of tan′, a common slime mold, *Fuligo septica,* of the central and eastern U.S., having large sporophores and yellowish, foamy plasmodia, that during a wet growing season may spread to cover large areas of lawns, woody debris, and growing plants. [1880–85]

flow′ers of zinc′. See **zinc oxide.**

flow·er·y (flou′ə rē), *adj.*, **-er·i·er, -er·i·est. 1.** covered with or having many flowers. **2.** decorated with floral designs. **3.** rhetorically ornate or precious: *flowery language.* **4.** resembling a flower in fragrance: *a Rhine wine with a flowery aroma.* [1300–50; ME; see FLOWER, -Y[1]] —**flow′er·i·ly,** *adv.* —**flow′er·i·ness,** *n.*
—**Syn. 3.** florid, showy, elaborate. See **bombastic.**

flow·ing (flō′ing), *adj.* **1.** moving in or as in a stream: *flowing water.* **2.** proceeding smoothly or easily; facile: *flowing language.* **3.** long, smooth, graceful, and without sudden interruption or change of direction: *flowing lines; flowing gestures.* **4.** hanging loosely at full length: *flowing hair.* **5.** abounding; having in excess: *a land flowing with milk and honey.* [bef. 950; ME *flowynge,* OE *flōwende.* See FLOW, -ING[2]] —**flow′ing·ly,** *adv.* —**flow′ing·ness,** *n.*

flow′ing trac′ery, *Archit.* See **curvilinear tracery.**

flow·me·ter (flō′mē′tər), *n.* an instrument for measuring the flow rate of a fluid in a pipe. [1915–20; FLOW + -METER]

flown[1] (flōn), *v.* a pp. of **fly**[1].

flown[2] (flōn), *adj.* **1.** decorated with colors that have been fluidly blended: *flown ceramic ware.* **2.** *Archaic.* filled to excess. [ME *flōwen;* ptp. of FLOW]

flow′ sheet′. See **flow chart** (def. 1). [1910–15]

flow·stone (flō′stōn′), *n. Petrol.* a layered deposit of calcium carbonate, $CaCO_3$, left by thin sheets of flowing water, as in a cave. Cf. **dripstone.** [1920–25, Amer.; FLOW + STONE]

Floyd (floid), *n.* **1. Carlisle (Sessions, Jr.),** born 1926, U.S. composer, esp. of operas. **2.** a male given name, form of **Lloyd.**

fl. oz., fluid ounce; fluid ounces.

FLRA, Federal Labor Relations Authority.

flu (flo͞o), *n.* **1.** influenza. **2.** a specific variety of influenza, usually named for its point of dissemination or its animal vector: *Hong Kong flu; swine flu.* [1830–40; shortened form]

flub (flub), *v.,* **flubbed, flub·bing,** *n.* —*v.t., v.i.* **1.** to perform poorly; blunder; bungle: *He flubbed the last shot and lost the match.* —*n.* **2.** a blunder. [1920–25, *Amer.*; orig. uncert.]

flub·dub (flub′dub′), *n.* pretentious nonsense or show; airs. [1885–90, *Amer.*; orig. uncert.]

fluc·tu·ant (fluk′cho͞o ənt), *adj.* **1.** fluctuating; varying; unstable. **2.** undulating; moving or seeming to move in waves. [1550–60; < L *fluctuant-* (s. of *fluctuāns*) (prp. of *fluctuāre* to undulate). See FLUCTUATE, -ANT]

fluc·tu·ate (fluk′cho͞o āt′), *v.,* **-at·ed, -at·ing.** —*v.i.* **1.** to change continually; shift back and forth; vary irregularly: *The price of gold fluctuated wildly last month.* **2.** to move back and forth in waves. —*v.t.* **3.** to cause to fluctuate. [1625–35; < L *fluctuātus* undulated, ptp. of *fluctuāre* to flow, equiv. to *fluctu(s)* a flowing (deriv. of *fluere* to flow) + *-ātus* -ATE[1]]
—**Syn. 1.** See **waver. 2.** oscillate.

fluc·tu·a·tion (fluk′cho͞o ā′shən), *n.* **1.** continual change from one point or condition to another. **2.** wavelike motion; undulation. **3.** *Genetics.* a body variation due to environmental factors and not inherited. [1400–50; late ME < L *fluctuātiōn-* (s. of *fluctuātiō*) a fluctuation, wavering. See FLUCTUATE, -ION]

flu·cy·to·sine (flo͞o sī′tə sēn′), *n. Pharm.* a synthetic whitish crystalline powder, $C_4H_4FN_3O$, with antifungal activity, used in the treatment of systemic and eye fungal infections caused by susceptible strains of *Candida* or *Cryptococcus.* [FLU(ORO)- + CYTOSINE]

flue[1] (flo͞o), *n.* **1.** a passage or duct for smoke in a chimney. **2.** any duct or passage for air, gas, or the like. **3.** a tube, esp. a large one, in a fire-tube boiler. **4.** *Music.* **a.** See **flue pipe. b.** Also called **windway.** a narrow slit in the upper end of an organ pipe through which the air current is directed. [1555–65; earlier *flew,* perh. repr. OE *flēwsa* a flowing, the form *flews* being taken as pl.]

flue[2] (flo͞o), *n.* downy matter; fluff. [1580–90; perh. to be identified with OE *flug-* (in *flugol* swift, fleeting); akin to FLY[1]. Cf. LG *flug*]

flue[3] (flo͞o), *n.* a fishing net. Also, **flew.** [1350–1400; ME *flowe;* cf. MD *vluwe* fishing net]

flue-cure (flo͞o′kyo͝or′), *v.t.,* **-cured, -cur·ing.** to dry or cure by warm air that has been passed through flues. [1905–10]

flu·ent (flo͞o′ənt), *adj.* **1.** spoken or written with ease: *fluent French.* **2.** able to speak or write smoothly, easily, or readily: *a fluent speaker; fluent in six languages.* **3.** easy; graceful: *fluent motion; fluent curves.* **4.** flowing, as a stream. **5.** capable of flowing; fluid, as liquids or gases. **6.** easily changed or adapted; pliant. [1580–90; < L *fluent-* (s. of *fluēns*) flowing, prp. of *fluere;* see -ENT] —**flu′en·cy, flu′ent·ness,** *n.* —**flu′ent·ly,** *adv.*
—**Syn. 1, 2.** FLUENT, GLIB, VOLUBLE may refer to a flow of words. FLUENT suggests the easy and ready flow of an accomplished speaker and is usually a term of commendation: *a fluent and interesting speech.* GLIB implies an excessive fluency divorced from sincerity or profundity; it often suggests talking smoothly and hurriedly to cover up or deceive, not giving the hearer a chance to stop and think; it may also imply a plausible, prepared, and well-rehearsed lie: *He had a glib answer for everything.* VOLUBLE implies the overcopious and often rapid flow of words characteristic of a person who loves to talk: *She overwhelmed him with her voluble answer.* See also **eloquent.**

flue′ pipe′, an organ pipe having a flue. [1850–55]

flu·er·ics (flo͞o er′iks), *n.* (*used with a singular v.*) *Engin.* fluidics. [appar. irreg. < L *fluer(e)* to flow + -ICS] —**flu·er′ic,** *adj.*

flue′ stop′, a rank of flue pipes in an organ. [1850–55]

fluff (fluf), *n.* **1.** light, downy particles, as of cotton. **2.** a soft, light, downy mass: *a fluff of summer clouds.* **3.** something of no consequence: *The book is pure fluff, but fun to read.* **4.** an error or blunder, esp. an actor's memory lapse in the delivery of lines. —*v.t.* **5.** to make into fluff; shake or puff out (feathers, hair, etc.) into a fluffy mass (often fol. by *up*): *to fluff up the sofa pillows.* **6.** to make a mistake in: *The leading man fluffed his lines.* —*v.i.* **7.** to become fluffy; move, float, or settle down like fluff. **8.** to make a mistake, esp. in the delivery of lines by a performer; blunder. [1780–90; perh. b. FLUE[2] and PUFF] —**fluff′er,** *n.*

fluff·y (fluf′ē), *adj.,* **fluff·i·er, fluff·i·est. 1.** of, resembling, or covered with fluff. **2.** light or airy: *a fluffy cake.* **3.** having little or no intellectual weight; superficial or frivolous: *fluffy thinking.* [1815–25; FLUFF + -Y[1]] —**fluff′i·ly,** *adv.* —**fluff′i·ness,** *n.*

flügelhorn

flü·gel·horn (flo͞o′gəl hôrn′; *Ger.* fly′gəl hôʀn′), *n.* a brass wind instrument with three valves, usually pitched in B flat and used esp. in military bands. Also, **flu′gel·horn′, flue′gel·horn′.** [1850–55; < G, equiv. to *Flügel* wing + *Horn* horn] —**flü′gel·horn′ist, flu′gel·horn′ist, flue′gel·horn′ist,** *n.*

flu·gel·man (flo͞o′gəl mən), *n., pl.* **-men.** fugleman.

flu·id (flo͞o′id), *n.* **1.** a substance, as a liquid or gas, that is capable of flowing and that changes its shape at a steady rate when acted upon by a force tending to change its shape. —*adj.* **2.** pertaining to a substance that easily changes its shape; capable of flowing. **3.** consisting of or pertaining to fluids. **4.** changing readily; shifting; not fixed, stable, or rigid: *fluid movements.* **5.** convertible into cash: *fluid assets.* [1595–1605; < L *fluidus,* equiv. to *flu(ere)* to flow + *-idus* -ID[4]] —**flu·id′al,** *adj.* —**flu′id·ly, flu′id·al·ly,** *adv.* —**flu′id·ness,** *n.*
—**Syn. 2.** See **liquid.**

flu′id cou′pling, *Mach.* an apparatus in which a fluid, usually oil, transmits torque from one shaft to another, producing an equal torque in the other shaft. Also called **hydraulic coupling.** Cf. **hydraulic torque converter.** [1935–40]

flu′id dram′, the eighth part of a fluid ounce. *Abbr.:* fl dr; *Symbol:* f ʒ Also, **fluid′ drachm′.**

flu′id drive′, *Auto.* a power coupling for permitting a smooth start in any gear, consisting of two vaned rotors in a sealed casing filled with oil, such that one rotor, driven by the engine, moves the oil to drive the other rotor, which in turn drives the transmission. [1940–45]

flu′id dynam′ics, the branch of fluid mechanics dealing with the properties of fluids in motion.

flu·id·ex·tract (flo͞o′id ek′strakt), *n. Pharm.* a liquid preparation, containing alcohol as a solvent or as a preservative, that contains in each cubic centimeter the medicinal activity of one gram of the crude drug in powdered form. [1850–55; FLUID + EXTRACT]

flu·id·ics (flo͞o id′iks), *n.* (*used with a singular v.*) the technology dealing with the use of a flowing liquid or gas in various devices, esp. controls, to perform functions usually performed by an electric current in electronic devices. Also called **fluerics.** [1960–65; FLUID + -ICS] —**flu·id′ic,** *adj.*

flu·id·i·ty (flo͞o id′i tē), *n.* **1.** the quality or state of being fluid. **2.** *Physics.* **a.** the ability of a substance to flow. **b.** a measure of this ability, the reciprocal of the coefficient of viscosity. Cf. **rhe.** [1595–1605; FLUID + -ITY]

flu·id·ize (flo͞o′i dīz′), *v.,* **-ized, -iz·ing.** —*v.t.* **1.** to make (something) fluid. **2.** *Chem.* to suspend or transport (finely divided particles) in a stream of gas or air. —*v.i.* **3.** to become fluid. Also, *esp. Brit.,* **flu′id·ise′.** [1850–55; FLUID + -IZE] —**flu′id·i·za′tion,** *n.* —**flu′id·iz′er,** *n.*

flu′id mechan′ics, an applied science dealing with the basic principles of gaseous and liquid matter. Cf. **fluid dynamics.** [1940–45]

flu′id ounce′, a measure of capacity equal to $\frac{1}{16}$ pint or 1.8047 cubic inches (29.573 milliliters) in the U.S., and equal to $\frac{1}{20}$ of an imperial pint, or 1.7339 cubic inches (28.413 milliliters) in Great Britain. *Abbr.:* fl. oz; *Symbol:* f ℥ [1880–85]

flu′id pres′sure, *Physics, Mech.* the pressure exerted by a fluid, directly proportional to the specific gravity at any point and to the height of the fluid above the point. [1835–45]

fluke[1] (flo͝ok), *n.* **1.** the part of an anchor that catches in the ground, esp. the flat triangular piece at the end of each arm. See diag. under **anchor. 2.** a barb, or the barbed head, of a harpoon, spear, arrow, or the like. **3.** either half of the triangular tail of a whale. [1555–65; perh. special use of FLUKE[3]]

fluke[2] (flo͝ok), *n.* **1.** an accidental advantage; stroke of good luck: *He got the job by a fluke.* **2.** an accident or chance happening. **3.** an accidentally successful stroke, as in billiards. [1855–60; of obscure orig.; cf. dial. *fluke* a guess]

fluke[3] (flo͝ok), *n.* **1.** any of several American flounders of the genus *Paralichthys,* esp. *P. dentatus,* found in the Atlantic Ocean. **2.** any of various other flatfishes. **3.** a trematode. [bef. 900; ME *flok(e), fluke,* OE *flōc;* c. ON *flōki;* cf. OHG *flah* flat (G *flach*)] —**fluke′less,** *adj.*

fluk·ey (flo͞o′kē), *adj.,* **fluk·i·er, fluk·i·est.** fluky.

fluk·y (flo͞o′kē), *adj.,* **fluk·i·er, fluk·i·est. 1.** obtained by chance rather than skill. **2.** uncertain, as a wind. [1865–70; FLUKE[2] + -Y[1]] —**fluk′i·ness,** *n.*

flum·a·did·dle (flum′ə did′l, flum′ə did′l), *n.* **1.** utter nonsense. **2.** worthless frills. Also, **fumadiddle.** [1840–50, *Amer.*; appar. FLUM(MERY) + *-a-* unstressed linking vowel + DIDDLE[2]]

flume (flo͞om), *n., v.,* **flumed, flum·ing.** —*n.* **1.** a deep narrow defile containing a mountain stream or torrent. **2.** an artificial channel or trough for conducting water, as one used to transport logs or provide water power. **3.** an amusement park ride in which passengers are carried in a boatlike or loglike conveyance through a narrow, water-filled chute or over a water slide. —*v.t.* **4.** to transport in a flume. **5.** to divert (a stream) by a flume. [1125–75; ME *flum* < OF << L *flūmen* stream]

flum·mer·y (flum′ə rē), *n., pl.* **-mer·ies. 1.** oatmeal or flour boiled with water until thick. **2.** fruit custard or blancmange usually thickened with cornstarch. **3.** any of various dishes made of flour, milk, eggs, sugar, etc. **4.** complete nonsense; foolish humbug. [1615–25; < Welsh *llymru,* with ending assimilated to -ERY]

flum·mox (flum′əks), *v.t. Informal.* to bewilder; confound; confuse. [1830–40; orig. uncert.]

flump (flump), *v.i., v.t.* **1.** to plump down suddenly or heavily; flop. —*n.* **2.** the act or sound of flumping. [1810–20; b. of FLOP + PLUMP]

flung (flung), *v.* pt. and pp. of **fling.**

flunk (flungk), *v.i.* **1.** to fail in a course or examination. **2. flunk out,** to fail and be unable to continue in: *He flunked out of flight school.* —*v.t.* **3.** to fail to get a passing mark in: *to flunk math.* **4.** to give a failing grade to; remove (a student) as unqualified from a school or course. —*n.* **5.** a failure, as in a course or examination. [1815–25, *Amer.*; perh. akin to FLINCH[1], FUNK[1]]

flun·key (flung′kē), *n., pl.* **-keys.** flunky. —**flun′key·ism,** *n.*

flunk·out (flungk′out′), *n.* a person who has flunked out of school or a course. [n. use of v. phrase *flunk out*]

flun·ky (flung′kē), *n., pl.* **-kies. 1.** a male servant in livery. **2.** an assistant who does menial work. **3.** a toady; yes-man. Also, **flunkey.** [1775–85; perh. alter. of FLANKER] —**flun′ky·ism,** *n.*

fluo-, var. of **fluoro-:** *fluoboric.*

flu·o·bo·rate (flo͞o′ə bôr′āt, -it, -bōr′-), *n. Chem.* a salt of fluoboric acid. [FLUO- + BORATE]

flu·o·bo·ric (flo͞o′ə bôr′ik, -bōr′-), *adj. Chem.* containing the univalent group BF_4^-. [1805–15; FLUO- + BORIC]

flu′obo′ric ac′id, *Chem.* a clear, colorless liquid, HBF_4, that ionizes abundantly in solution, used chiefly in the synthesis of fluoborates. [1810–20]

flu·o·phos·phate (flo͞o′ə fos′fāt), *n. Chem.* fluorophosphate.

flu′o·phos·phor′ic ac′id (flo͞o′ō fos fôr′ik, -for′-, flo͞o′-), *Chem.* See **fluorophosphoric acid.**

flu·or (flo͞o′ôr, -ər), *n. Mineral.* fluorite. [1615–25; < L *fluor* a flowing; so called from its use as a flux]

fluor-, var. of **fluoro-** before a vowel: *fluorene; fluoric.*

fluor·ap·a·tite (flo͝or ap′ə tīt′, flôr-, flōr-), *n.* a crystalline mineral, $Ca_5(PO_4)_3F$, formed from hydroxyapatite in the presence of fluoride, that has a hardening effect on bones and teeth. [1880–85; < G *Fluorapatit;* see FLUOR-, APATITE]

fluor·ene (flo͝or′ēn, -in, flôr′-, flōr′-), *n. Chem.* a white, crystalline, water-insoluble solid, $C_{13}H_{10}$, used chiefly in the manufacture of resins and dyes. [1880–85; < F; see FLUOR-, -ENE]

fluo·resce (flo͝o res′, flô-, flō-), *v.i.,* **-resced, -resc·ing.** to exhibit fluorescence. [1870–75; back formation from FLUORESCENCE] —**fluo·resc′er,** *n.*

fluo·res·ce·in (flo͝o res′ē in, flô-, flō-), *n. Chem.* an orange-red, crystalline, water-insoluble solid, $C_{20}H_{12}O_5$, that in alkaline solutions produces an orange color and an intense green fluorescence: used to trace subterranean waters and in dyes. Also, **flu′o·res′ce·ine.** Also called **resorcinolphthalein.** [1875–80; FLUORESCE + -IN[2]]

fluo·res·cence (flo͝o res′əns, flô-, flō-), *n. Physics, Chem.* **1.** the emission of radiation, esp. of visible light, by a substance during exposure to external radiation, as light or x-rays. Cf. **phosphorescence** (def. 1). **2.** the property possessed by a substance capable of such emission. **3.** the radiation so produced. [1852; FLUOR(SPAR) + -ESCENCE, on the model of OPALESCENCE, in reference to the mineral's newly discovered property]

fluo·res′cence-ac·ti·vat·ed cell′ sort′er (flo͝o-res′əns ak′ti vā′tid, flô-, flō-). See **FACS.**

fluo·res·cent (flo͝o res′ənt, flô-, flō-), *adj.* **1.** possessing the property of fluorescence; exhibiting fluorescence. **2.** strikingly bright, vivid, or glowing: *plastic toys in fluorescent colors.* —*n.* **3.** a lighting fixture that utilizes a fluorescent lamp. [1850–55; FLUOR- + -ESCENT]

fluores′cent lamp′, a tubular electric discharge lamp in which light is produced by the fluorescence of phosphors coating the inside of the tube. [1895–1900]

flu·or·ic (flo͞o ôr′ik, -or′-), *adj.* **1.** *Chem.* pertaining to or obtained from fluorine. **2.** *Mineral.* of, pertaining to, or derived from fluorite. [1780–90; < F *fluorique.* See FLUOR-, -IC]

fluor·i·date (flo͝or′i dāt′, flôr′-, flōr′-), *v.t.,* **-dat·ed, -dat·ing.** to introduce a fluoride into: *to fluoridate drinking water.* [1945–50; back formation from FLUORIDATION]

fluor·i·da·tion (flo͝or′i dā′shən, flôr′-, flōr′-), *n.* the addition of fluorides to the public water supply to reduce the incidence of tooth decay. [1900–05; FLUORIDE + -ATION]

fluor·ide (flo͝or′īd, flôr′-, flōr′-), *n. Chem.* **1.** a salt of hydrofluoric acid consisting of two elements, one of which is fluorine, as sodium fluoride, NaF. **2.** a compound containing fluorine, as methyl fluoride, CH_3F. [1820–30; FLUOR- + -IDE]

fluor·i·dize (flo͝or′i dīz′, flôr′-, flōr′-), *v.t.,* **-dized, -diz·ing.** to treat, impregnate, or affect with a fluoride. Also, *esp. Brit.,* **fluor′i·dise′.** [1935–40; FLUORIDE + -IZE] —**fluor′i·di·za′tion,** *n.*

fluo·rim·e·ter (flo͝o rim′i tər, flô-, flō-), *n.* fluorometer.

fluor·i·nate (flo͝or′ə nāt′, flôr′-, flōr′-), *v.t.,* **-nat·ed, -nat·ing.** *Chem.* to treat or combine with fluorine. [1930–35; FLUORINE + -ATE[1]] —**fluor′i·na′tion,** *n.*

fluor·ine (flo͝or′ēn, -in, flôr′-, flōr′-), *n. Chem.* the most reactive nonmetallic element, a pale-yellow, corrosive, toxic gas that occurs combined, esp. in fluorite, cryolite, phosphate rock, and other minerals. *Symbol:* F; *at. wt.:* 18.9984; *at. no.:* 9. [1805–15; FLUOR(IC) + -INE[2]]

fluor′ine dat′ing, a method of determining the relative age of fossil bones found in the same excavation by comparing their fluorine content. [1945–50]

fluo·rite (flo͝or′īt, flôr′-, flōr′-), *n.* a common mineral, calcium fluoride, CaF_2, occurring in green, blue, purple, yellow, or colorless crystals, usually in cubes: the principal source of fluorine, used also as a flux in metallurgy and for ornament. Also called **fluor, fluorspar, fluor spar.** [1865–70; < It; see FLUOR-, -ITE[1]]

fluoro-, 1. a combining form with the meanings "fluorine," "fluoride," used in the formation of compound words: *fluorocarbon.* **2.** a combining form with the meaning "fluorescence," used in the formation of compound words: *fluoroscopy.* Also, **fluo-;** *esp. before a vowel,* **fluor-.** [< NL; see FLUOR, -O-]

fluor•o•car•bon (flo͝or′ō kär′bən, flôr′-, flōr′-), *n. Chem.* any of a class of compounds produced by substituting fluorine for hydrogen in a hydrocarbon, and characterized by great chemical stability: used chiefly as a lubricant, refrigerant, fire extinguishing agent, and in industrial and other applications in which chemical, electrical, flame, and heat resistance is essential; banned as an aerosol propellant in the U.S. because of concern about ozone layer depletion. Cf. **chlorofluorocarbon, chlorofluoromethane.** [1935–40; FLUORO- + CARBON]

fluor•o•chrome (flo͝or′ə krōm′, flôr′-, flōr′-), *n. Histol.* any of a group of fluorescent dyes used to label biological material. [FLUORO- + -CHROME]

fluo•rog•ra•phy (flo͝o rog′rə fē, flô-, flō-), *n.* photofluorography. [1940–45; FLUORO- + -GRAPHY]

fluo•rom•e•ter (flo͝o rom′i tər, flô-, flō-), *n.* an instrument for measuring fluorescence, often as a means of determining the nature of the substance emitting the fluorescence. Also, **fluorimeter.** [1895–1900; FLUORO- + -METER] —**fluor•o•met•ric** (flo͝or′ə me′trik, flôr′ə-, flōr′ə-), *adj.* —**fluo•rom′e•try,** *n.*

fluor•o•phos•phate (flo͝or′ō fos′fāt, flôr′-, flōr′-), *n. Chem.* a salt or ester of a fluorophosphoric acid. Also, **fluophosphate.** [FLUORO- + PHOSPHATE]

fluor′o•phos•phor′ic ac′id (flo͝or′ō fos fôr′ik, -for′-, flôr′-, flōr′-, flo͝or′ō-, flôr′-, flōr′-), *Chem.* any of three acids containing fluorine and phosphorus, HPF_6, HPO_2F_2, or H_2PO_3F. Also, **fluophosphoric acid.** [FLUORO- + PHOSPHORIC]

fluor•o•plas•tic (flo͝or′ə plas′tik, flôr′-, flōr′-), *n. Chem.* any of the plastics, as Teflon, in which hydrogen atoms of the hydrocarbon chains are replaced by fluorine atoms. Also called **fluor•o•pol•y•mer** (flo͝or′ə pol′ə mər, flôr′-, flōr′-). [FLUORO- + PLASTIC]

fluor•o•scope (flo͝or′ə skōp′, flôr′-, flōr′-), *n.* a tube or box fitted with a screen coated with a fluorescent substance, used for viewing objects, esp. deep body structures, by means of x-ray or other radiation. [1895–1900, *Amer.;* FLUORO- + -SCOPE]

fluor•o•scop•ic (flo͝or′ə skop′ik, flôr′-, flōr′-), *adj.* of or pertaining to the fluoroscope or fluoroscopy. [1895–1900; FLUOROSCOPE + -IC] —**fluor′o•scop′i•cal•ly,** *adv.*

fluo•ros•co•py (flo͝o ros′kə pē, flô-, flō-), *n.* the use of or examination by means of a fluoroscope. [1895–1900; FLUORO- + -SCOPY] —**fluo•ros′co•pist,** *n.*

fluo•ro•sis (flo͝o rō′sis, flô-, flō-), *n. Pathol.* **1.** an abnormal condition caused by excessive intake of fluorides, characterized in children by discoloration and pitting of the teeth and in adults by pathological bone changes. **2.** Also called **mottled enamel.** *Dentistry.* the changes in tooth enamel symptomatic of fluorosis. [1925–30; FLUOR- + -OSIS]

fluor•o•u•ra•cil (flo͝or′ə yo͝or′ə sil, flôr′-, flōr′-), *n. Pharm.* a pyrimidine analog, $C_4H_3FN_2O_2$, used in the treatment of certain cancers. [FLUORO- + URACIL]

fluo•or•spar (flo͞o′ôr spär′, -ər-), *n. Mineral.* fluorite. Also, **flu′or spar′.** [1785–95; FLUOR- + SPAR[3]]

flu•o•sil•i•cate (flo͞o′ə sil′i kit, -kāt′), *n. Chem.* a salt of fluosilicic acid. [FLUO- + SILICATE]

flu′o•si•lic′ic ac′id (flo͞o′ō si lis′ik, flo͞o′-), *Chem.* an unstable acid, H_2SiF_6, known only in its colorless, poisonous, fuming aqueous solution or in the form of its salts: used chiefly as a wood preservative, a disinfectant, and as a hardening agent in the manufacture of ceramic ware, cement, and concrete. [FLUO- + SILICIC]

flu•phen•a•zine (flo͞o fen′ə zēn′), *n. Pharm.* a potent tranquilizer, $C_{22}H_{26}F_3N_3OS$, derived from phenothiazine and used in various forms for the management of certain neurological or psychotic disorders and for short-term treatment of acute anxiety. [1955–60; FLU(ORO)- + PHENAZINE]

flu•raz•e•pam (flo͞o raz′ə pam′), *n. Pharm.* a benzodiazepine, $C_{21}H_{23}ClFN_3O$, used in its hydrochloride form as a sedative and hypnotic in the management of insomnia and to alleviate anxiety states. [FLU(O)R- + (DI)AZEPAM]

flur•ried (flûr′ēd, flur′-), *adj.* marked by confusion or agitation. [FLURRY + -ED[2]]

flur•ry (flûr′ē, flur′ē), *n., pl.* **-ries,** *v.,* **-ried, -ry•ing.** —*n.* **1.** a light, brief shower of snow. **2.** sudden commotion, excitement, or confusion; nervous hurry: *There was a flurry of activity before the guests arrived.* **3.** *Stock Exchange.* **a.** a brief rise or fall in prices. **b.** a brief, unusually heavy period of trading. **4.** a sudden gust of wind. —*v.t.* **5.** to put (a person) into a flurry; confuse; fluster. —*v.i.* **6.** (of snow) to fall or be blown in a flurry. **7.** to move in an excited or agitated manner. [1680–90, *Amer.;* b. FLUTTER and HURRY] —**flur′ried•ly,** *adv.*
—**Syn. 2.** upset, pother, stir, to-do, fuss, fluster, ado.

flush[1] (flush), *n.* **1.** a blush; rosy glow: *a flush of embarrassment on his face.* **2.** a rushing or overspreading flow, as of water. **3.** a sudden rise of emotion or excitement: *a flush of anger.* **4.** glowing freshness or vigor: *the flush of youth.* **5. hot flush.** See **hot flash. 6.** a cleansing preparation that acts by flushing: *an oil flush for the car's engine.* —*v.t.* **7.** to redden; cause to blush or glow: *Winter air flushed the children's cheeks.* **8.** to flood or spray thoroughly with water, as for cleansing purposes: *They flushed the wall with water and then scrubbed it down.* **9.** to wash out (a sewer, toilet, etc.) by a sudden rush of water. **10.** *Metall.* **a.** to remove slag from (a blast furnace). **b.** to spray (a coke oven) to cool the gases generated and wash away the ammonia and tars distilled. **11.** to animate or excite; inflame: *flushed with success.* —*v.i.* **12.** to blush; redden. **13.** to flow with a rush; flow and spread suddenly. **14.** to operate by flushing; undergo flushing: *The toilet won't flush.* [1540–50; perh. extended senses of FLUSH[3]; cf. similar phonesthemic elements and meanings of BLUSH, GUSH, FLASH] —**flush′a•ble,** *adj.* —**flush′er,** *n.* —**flush′ing•ly,** *adv.* —**flush′ness,** *n.*
—**Syn. 3.** access, rush, flood, impulse, thrill.

flush[2] (flush), *adj.* **1.** even or level, as with a surface; forming the same plane: *The bottom of the window is flush with the floor.* **2.** having direct contact; being right next to; immediately adjacent; contiguous: *The table was flush against the wall.* **3.** well-supplied, as with money; affluent; prosperous: *He was feeling flush on payday.* **4.** abundant or plentiful, as money. **5.** having a ruddy or reddish color; blushing. **6.** full of vigor; lusty. **7.** full to overflowing. **8.** *Print.* even or level with the right margin **(flush right)** or the left margin **(flush left)** of the type page; without an indention. —*adv.* **9.** on the same level; in a straight line; without a change of plane: *to be made flush with the top of the table.* **10.** in direct contact; squarely: *It was set flush against the edge.* —*v.t.* **11.** to make flush or even. **12.** to improve the nutrition of (a ewe) to bring on optimum physiological conditions for breeding. —*v.i.* **13.** to send out shoots, as plants in spring. —*n.* **14.** a fresh growth, as of shoots and leaves. [1540–50; perh. all sense developments of FLUSH[1]] —**flush′ness,** *n.*

flush[3] (flush), *Hunting.* —*v.t.* **1.** to rouse and cause to start up or fly off: *to flush a woodcock.* —*v.i.* **2.** to fly out or start up suddenly. —*n.* **3.** a flushed bird or flock of birds. [1250–1300; ME *flusshen,* first attested as ptp. *fluste, fliste;* of uncert. orig.]

flush[4] (flush), *Cards.* —*adj.* **1.** consisting entirely of cards of one suit: *a flush hand.* —*n.* **2.** a hand or set of cards all of one suit. Cf. **royal flush, straight flush. 3.** *Pinochle.* a meld of ace, king, queen, jack, and ten of the trump suit. Cf. **marriage** (def. 8), **royal marriage.** [1520–30; cf. F (obs.) *flus,* var. of *flux* flow, flush (cf. phrase *run* of cards) < L *fluxus* FLUX]

flush-decked (flush′dekt′), *adj. Naut.* having a weather deck flush with the hull. [1620–30]

flush′ girt′, *Carpentry.* a girt running parallel to joists and at the same level. Cf. **drop girt.**

Flush•ing (flush′ing), *n.* Dutch, **Vlissingen.** a seaport on Walcheren Island, in the SW Netherlands. 46,055.

flush′ left′. See under **flush**[2] (def. 8).

flush′ right′. See under **flush**[2] (def. 8).

flus•ter (flus′tər), *v.t.* **1.** to put into a state of agitated confusion: *His constant criticism flustered me.* **2.** to excite and confuse with drink. —*v.i.* **3.** to become agitatedly confused. —*n.* **4.** nervous excitement or confusion. [1375–1425; late ME *flostren;* cf. BLUSTER, ON *flaustra* to hurry]
—**Syn. 1.** upset, bewilder, disconcert, disturb. **4.** turmoil, agitation, upset, bewilderment, distraction.

flus•trat•ed (flus′trā tid) *adj.,* flustered; agitated. Also, **flus′ter•at′ed.** [*flustrate* (b. FLUSTER and FRUSTRATE) + -ED[2]]

flute (def. 1)

flute (flo͞ot), *n., v.,* **flut•ed, flut•ing.** —*n.* **1.** a musical wind instrument consisting of a tube with a series of fingerholes or keys, in which the wind is directed against a sharp edge, either directly, as in the modern transverse flute, or through a flue, as in the recorder. **2.** an organ stop with wide flue pipes, having a flutelike tone. **3.** *Archit., Furniture.* a channel, groove, or furrow, as on the shaft of a column. See diag. under **column. 4.** any groove or furrow, as in a ruffle of cloth or on a piecrust. **5.** one of the helical grooves of a twist drill. **6.** a slender, footed wineglass of the 17th century, having a tall, conical bowl. **7.** a similar stemmed glass, used esp. for champagne. —*v.i.* **8.** to produce flutelike sounds. **9.** to play on a flute. **10.** (of a metal strip or sheet) to kink or break in bending. —*v.t.* **11.** to utter in flutelike tones. **12.** to form longitudinal flutes or furrows in: *to flute a piecrust.* [1350–1400; ME *floute* < MF *flaüte, flahute, fleüte* < OPr *flaüt* (perh. alter. of *flaujol, flauja*) < VL **flabeolum.* See FLAGEOLET, LUTE] —**flute′like′,** *adj.*

flut•ed (flo͞o′tid), *adj.* **1.** fine, clear, and mellow; flutelike: *fluted notes.* **2.** having flutes, grooves, or the like: *a fluted column; fluted material; fluted stone tools.* [1605–15; FLUTE + -ED[3]]

flut•er (flo͞o′tər), *n.* **1.** a person who makes flutings. **2.** *Archaic.* a flutist. [1350–1400; ME *flouter, floutour* < OF *fleuteur, flauteor,* equiv. to *flaut(er)* to play the flute + *-eur, -eor* < L *-ōr-* -OR[2] or *-ātōr-* -ATOR]

flut•ey (flo͞o′tē), *adj.,* **flut•i•er, flut•i•est.** fluty.

flut•ing (flo͞o′ting), *n.* **1.** something having ornamental grooves, as a Greek column. **2.** a groove, furrow, or flute, or a series of these. [1475–85; FLUTE + -ING[1]]

flut•ist (flo͞o′tist), *n.* a flute player. Also, **flautist.** [1595–1605; FLUTE + -IST; see FLAUTIST]

flut•ter (flut′ər), *v.i.* **1.** to wave, flap, or toss about: *Banners fluttered in the breeze.* **2.** to flap the wings rapidly; fly with flapping movements. **3.** to move in quick, irregular motions; vibrate. **4.** to beat rapidly, as the heart. **5.** to be tremulous or agitated. **6.** to go with irregular motions or aimless course: *to flutter back and forth.* —*v.t.* **7.** to cause to flutter; vibrate; agitate. **8.** to throw into nervous or tremulous excitement; cause mental agitation; confuse. —*n.* **9.** a fluttering movement: *He made little nervous flutters with his hands.* **10.** a state of nervous excitement or mental agitation: *a flutter of anticipation.* **11.** See **flutter kick. 12.** *Audio.* a variation in pitch resulting from rapid fluctuations in the speed of a recording. Cf. **wow**[2] (def. 1). **13.** *Chiefly Brit.* a small wager or speculative investment. [bef. 1000; ME *floteren,* OE *floterian,* freq. of *flotian* to FLOAT] —**flut′ter•er,** *n.* —**flut′ter•ing•ly,** *adv.*
—**Syn. 2.** See **fly**[1]. **10.** flurry, twitter, stir, dither.

flut•ter•board (flut′ər bôrd′, -bōrd′), *n.* a kickboard. [1945–50; FLUTTER + BOARD]

flut′ter kick′, a swimming kick in which the legs make rapid alternate up-and-down movements while the knees remain rigid, as in the crawl. [1930–35]

flut′ter mill′, *Chiefly South Midland and Southern U.S.* a flutter wheel, esp. a small one designed as a child's plaything. [1865–70, *Amer.*]

flut′ter wheel′, a waterwheel at the bottom of a chute, turned by the falling water. [1810–20]

flut•ter•y (flut′ə rē), *adj.* fluttering; apt to flutter. [1350–1400; ME; see FLUTTER, -Y[1]]

flut•y (flo͞o′tē), *adj.,* **flut•i•er, flut•i•est.** having the tone and rather high pitch variation of a flute: *a person of fastidious manner and fluty voice.* Also, **flutey.** [1815–25; FLUTE + -Y[1]]

flu•vi•al (flo͞o′vē əl), *adj.* **1.** of or pertaining to a river: *a meandering fluvial contour.* **2.** produced by or found in a river: *fluvial plants.* [1350–1400; ME < L *fluviālis,* equiv. to *fluvi(us)* river (deriv. of *fluere* to flow) + *-ālis* -AL[1]]

flu•vi•a•tile (flo͞o′vē ə til, -tīl′), *adj.* pertaining or peculiar to rivers; found in or near rivers. [1590–1600; < L *fluviātilis,* equiv. to *fluvi-* (see FLUVIAL) + *-ātil(is)* assoc. suffix]

flu•vi•o•ma•rine (flo͞o′vē ō mə rēn′), *adj.* of or formed by the combined action of river and sea. [1840–50; < L *fluvi-* river (see FLUVIAL) + -O- + MARINE]

flux (fluks), *n.* **1.** a flowing or flow. **2.** the flowing in of the tide. **3.** continuous change, passage, or movement: *His political views are in a state of flux.* **4.** *Physics.* **a.** the rate of flow of fluid, particles, or energy. **b.** a quantity expressing the strength of a field of force in a given area. **5.** *Chem., Metall.* **a.** a substance used to refine metals by combining with impurities to form a molten mixture that can be readily removed. **b.** a substance used to remove oxides from and prevent further oxidation of fused metal, as in soldering or hot-dip coating. **c.** (in the refining of scrap or other metal) a salt or mixture of salts that combines with nonmetallic impurities, causing them to float or coagulate. **6.** fusion. —*v.t.* **7.** to melt; make fluid. **8.** to fuse by the use of flux. **9.** *Obs.* to purge. —*v.i.* **10.** to flow. [1350–1400; ME < L *fluxus* a flowing, equiv. to *fluc-,* var. s. of *fluere* to flow + *-tus* suffix of v. action, with *ct* > *x*]
—**Syn. 1.** course, current, flood, stream.

flux′ den′sity, *Physics.* the magnetic, radiant, or electric flux per unit of cross-sectional area. [1895–1900]

flux′ gate′, *Physics.* an instrument for indicating the field strength of an external magnetic field, as that of the earth: used in some gyrocompasses and magnetometers. Also called **flux′ valve′.** [1945–50]

flux•ion (fluk′shən), *n.* **1.** an act of flowing; a flow or flux. **2.** *Math.* the derivative relative to the time. [1535–45; < MF < LL *fluxiōn-* (s. of *fluxiō*) a flowing. See FLUX, -ION] —**flux′ion•al, flux′ion•ar•y,** *adj.* —**flux′ion•al•ly,** *adv.*

flux′ link′age, *Elect.* the product of the magnetic flux and the number of turns in a given coil.

flux•me•ter (fluks′mē′tər), *n. Physics.* an instrument for measuring magnetic flux, consisting essentially of a ballistic galvanometer. [1900–05; FLUX + -METER]

fly[1] (flī), *v.,* **flew** or, for 11, 19, **flied, flown, fly•ing,** *n., pl.* **flies.** —*v.i.* **1.** to move through the air using wings. **2.** to be carried through the air by the wind or any other force or agency: *bits of paper flying about.* **3.** to float or flutter in the air: *flags flying in the breeze.* **4.** to travel in an aircraft or spacecraft. **5.** to move suddenly and quickly; start unexpectedly: *He flew from the room.* **6.** to change rapidly and unexpectedly from one state or position to another: *The door flew open.* **7.** to flee; escape. **8.** to travel in space: *The probe will fly past the planet.* **9.** to move or pass swiftly: *How time flies!* **10.** to move with an aggressive surge: *A mother fox will fly at anyone approaching her kits.* **11.** *Baseball.* **a.** to bat a fly ball: *He flied into right field.* **b.** to fly out. **12.** *Informal.* to be acceptable, believable, or feasible: *It seemed like a good idea, but it just wouldn't fly.* —*v.t.* **13.** to make (something) float or move through the air: *to fly a kite.* **14.** to operate (an aircraft, spacecraft, or the like). **15.** to hoist aloft, as for display, signaling, etc.: *to fly a flag.* **16.** to operate an aircraft or spacecraft over: *to fly the Pacific.* **17.** to transport or convey by air: *We fly merchandise to Boston.* **18.** to escape from; flee: *to fly someone's wrath.* **19.** *Theat.* **a.** to hang (scenery) above a stage by means of rigging supported by the gridiron. **b.** to raise (scenery) from the stage or acting area into the flies. **20. fly blind.** See **blind** (def. 33). **21. fly in the face of,** to act in defiance of (authority, custom, etc.). Also, **fly in the teeth of. 22. fly off the handle.** See **handle** (def. 8). **23. fly out.** *Baseball, Softball.* to be put out by hitting a fly ball that is caught by a player of the opposing team. **24. go fly a kite,** *Slang.* **a.** to put up with or get used to matters as they stand. **b.** to confine oneself to one's own affairs. **c.** to cease being a nuisance: *If she gets mad enough she'll tell me to go fly a kite.* **25. let fly, a.** to hurl or propel (a weapon, missile, etc.). **b.** to give free rein to an emotion: *She let fly with a barrage of angry words.*
—*n.* **26.** a strip of material sewn along one edge of a garment opening for concealing buttons, zippers, or other fasteners. **27.** a flap forming the door of a tent. **28.** Also called **tent fly.** a piece of canvas extending

over the ridgepole of a tent and forming an outer roof. **29.** an act of flying; a flight. **30.** the course of a flying object, as a ball. **31.** *Baseball.* See **fly ball. 32.** *Brit.* a light, covered, public carriage drawn by one horse; hansom; hackney coach. **33.** *Mach.* a horizontal arm, weighted at each end, that pivots about the screw of a press so that when the screw is lowered the momentum of the fly will increase the force of the press. **34.** Also called **fan.** *Horol.* a regulating device for chime and striking mechanisms, consisting of an arrangement of vanes on a revolving axis. **35.** *Print.* **a.** (in some presses) the apparatus for removing the printed sheets to the delivery table. **b.** Also called **flyboy.** (formerly) a printer's devil employed to remove printed sheets from a press. **36.** (on a flag) **a.** the horizontal dimension of a flag as flown from a vertical staff. **b.** the end of the flag farther from the staff. Cf. **hoist** (def. 8). **37. flies.** Also called **fly loft.** *Theat.* the space above the stage used chiefly for storing scenery and equipment. **38.** *Naut.* a propellerlike device streamed to rotate and transfer information on speed to a mechanical log. **39. on the fly, a.** during flight; before falling to the ground: *to catch a baseball on the fly.* **b.** hurriedly; without pausing: *We had dinner on the fly.* [bef. 900; ME *flien,* OE *flēogan;* c. OHG *fliogan,* G *fliegen,* ON *fljuga*] **—fly′a·ble,** *adj.* **—fly′a·bil′i·ty,** *n.*

—Syn. 1. FLY, FLIT, FLUTTER, HOVER, SOAR refer to moving through the air as on wings. FLY is the general term: *Birds fly. Airplanes fly.* To FLIT is to make short rapid flights from place to place: *A bird flits from tree to tree.* To FLUTTER is to agitate the wings tremulously, either without flying or in flying only short distances: *A young bird flutters out of a nest and in again.* To HOVER is to linger in the air, or to move over or about something within a narrow area or space: *hovering clouds; a hummingbird hovering over a blossom.* To SOAR is to (start to) fly upward to a great height usually with little advance in any other direction, or else to (continue to) fly at a lofty height without visible movement of the wings: *Above our heads an eagle was soaring.*

fly[2] (flī), *n., pl.* **flies. 1.** Also called **true fly.** any of numerous two-winged insects of the order Diptera, esp. of the family Muscidae, as the common housefly. **2.** any of various winged insects, as the mayfly or firefly. **3.** *Angling.* a fishhook dressed with hair, feathers, silk, tinsel, etc., so as to resemble an insect or small fish, for use as a lure or bait. **4.** (*cap.*) *Astron.* the constellation Musca. **5. fly in the ointment,** a detrimental factor; detraction: *If there's one fly in the ointment, it's that there may not be the money to finish the job.* [bef. 950; ME *flie,* OE *flēoge, flȳge;* c. MD *vliege* (D *vlieg*), OHG *flioga* (G *Fliege*); akin to FLY[1]] **—fly′less,** *adj.*

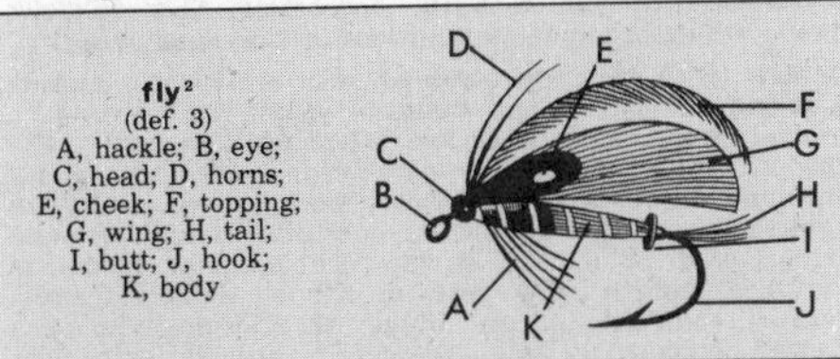

fly[2] (def. 3) A, hackle; B, eye; C, head; D, horns; E, cheek; F, topping; G, wing; H, tail; I, butt; J, hook; K, body

fly[3] (flī), *adj. Brit. Informal.* **1.** clever; keen; ingenious. **2.** agile; nimble. [1805–15; perh. special use of FLY[1]]

fly′ ag′aric, a very poisonous common woodland mushroom, *Amanita muscaria,* having a glossy red or orange cap with white spots, formerly a fly poison. [1780–90]

fly′ ash′, 1. fine particles of ash of a solid fuel carried out of the flue of a furnace with the waste gases produced during combustion. **2.** such ash recovered from the waste gases, used chiefly as a reinforcing agent in the manufacture of bricks, concrete, etc. [1930–35]

fly·a·way (flī′ə wā′), *adj.* **1.** fluttering or streaming in the wind; windblown: *flyaway hair.* **2.** flighty; frivolous; giddy. **3.** ready for flight: *flyaway aircraft.* [1765–75; adj. use of v. phrase *fly away*]

fly·back (flī′bak′), *n. Electronics.* the return to its starting point of the electron beam in a cathode ray tube, as after the completion of a line in a television picture or of a trace in an oscilloscope. [1930–35; n. use of v. phrase *fly back*]

fly′ ball′, *Baseball.* a ball that is batted up into the air. Also called **fly.** Cf. **ground ball.** [1860–65, *Amer.*]

fly·belt (flī′belt′), *n.* an area having a large number of tsetse flies. [1890–95; FLY[2] + BELT]

fly′ block′, *Mach., Naut.* **1.** (in a Spanish burton or the like) a block, supported by a runner, through which the hauling part of the fall is rove. **2.** any block that shifts with the movement of its tackle. [1835–45]

fly·blow (flī′blō′), *v.,* **-blew, -blown, -blow·ing,** *n.* **—***v.t.* **1.** to deposit eggs or larvae on (meat or other food). **—***n.* **2.** one of the eggs or young larvae of a blowfly, deposited on meat or other food. [1550–60; FLY[2] + BLOW[2]]

fly·blown (flī′blōn′), *adj.* **1.** covered with flyblows: *flyblown meat.* **2.** tainted or contaminated; spoiled. [1565–75; FLY[2] + BLOWN[1]]

fly·boat (flī′bōt′), *n.* a small, fast boat. [1570–80; < D *vlieboot,* equiv. to *Vlie* (name of a channel along the North Sea island of Vlieland) + *boot* BOOT; *vlie* later altered by assoc. with FLY[1]]

fly′ book′, *Angling.* a booklike case for artificial flies. [1840–50]

fly·boy (flī′boi′), *n.* **1.** *Print.* fly[1] (def. 35b). **2.** *Slang.* **a.** a member of an aircrew, esp. a pilot. **b.** any member of the U.S. Air Force. [1835–45; FLY[1] + BOY]

fly·bridge (flī′brij′), *n. Naut.* See **flying bridge.** Also, **fly′ bridge′.** [1605–15; FLY[1] + BRIDGE[1]]

fly·by (flī′bī′), *n., pl.* **-bys. 1.** the flight of a spacecraft close enough to a celestial object, as a planet, to gather scientific data. **2.** *Aeron.* **a.** Also called **flypast.** a low-altitude flight of an aircraft for the benefit of ground observers. **b.** flyover (def. 1). Also, **fly′-by′.** [1950–55, *Amer.*; n. use of v. phrase *fly by*]

fly-by-night (flī′bī nīt′), *adj.* **1.** not reliable or responsible, esp. in business; untrustworthy: *a fly-by-night operation.* **2.** not lasting; brief; impermanent; transitory: *a fly-by-night theater.* **—***n.* Also, **fly′-by-night′er. 3.** a person or thing that is unreliable, esp. a debtor who evades or attempts to evade creditors. **4.** a person regarded as a poor credit risk. [1790–1800]

fly-by-wire (flī′bī wīᵊr′), *adj.* (of aircraft or spacecraft) activated entirely by electronic controls.

fly-cast (flī′kast′, -käst′), *v.i.,* **-cast, -cast·ing.** *Angling.* to fish by fly casting.

fly′ cast′ing, *Angling.* the act or technique of casting with an artificial fly as the lure, the rod used being longer and more flexible than that used in bait casting. [1885–90]

fly·catch·er (flī′kach′ər), *n.* **1.** any of numerous Old World birds of the family Muscicapidae, that feed on insects captured in the air. **2.** Also called **tyrant flycatcher.** any of numerous similar American birds of the family Tyrannidae. [1590–1600; FLY[2] + CATCHER]

fly·er (flī′ər), *n.* **1.** *Textiles.* **a.** a rotating device that adds twist to the slubbing or roving and winds the stock onto a spindle or bobbin in a uniform manner. **b.** a similar device for adding twist to yarn. **2.** flier. [1400–50; late ME; see FLY[1], -ER[1]]

fly-fish (flī′fish′), *v.i. Angling.* to fish with artificial flies as bait. [1745–55]

fly-fish·ing (flī′fish′ing), *n. Angling.* a method of fishing in which fly casting is used. [1645–55]

fly′ front′, a flap of material down one side of the front opening of a garment to conceal buttons, fasteners, or the like, as on a coat or dress. [1890–95]

fly′ gal′lery, *Theat.* a narrow platform at the side of a stage from which ropes are manipulated to raise or lower scenery, battens, etc. Also called **fly′ floor′.** [1885–90]

fly′ hon′eysuckle, either of two honeysuckle shrubs, *Lonicera canadensis,* of eastern North America, or *L. xylosteum,* of Eurasia, having paired yellowish flowers tinged with red. [1810–20]

fly-in (flī′in′), *n.* **1.** a convention, entertainment, or other gathering at which participants arrive by air: *the annual fly-in of cattle breeders.* **—***adj.* **2.** of or for those who arrive and usually depart by air: *a fly-in safari.* **3.** accessible only by air: *a remote, fly-in fishing camp.* [1940–45; n., adj. use of v. phrase *fly in*]

fly·ing (flī′ing), *adj.* **1.** making flight or passing through the air; that flies: *a flying insect; an unidentified flying object.* **2.** floating, fluttering, waving, hanging, or moving freely in the air: *flying banners; flying hair.* **3.** extending through the air. **4.** moving swiftly. **5.** made while moving swiftly: *a flying leap.* **6.** very hasty or brief; fleeting or transitory: *a flying visit; a flying remark.* **7.** designed or organized for swift movement or action. **8.** fleeing, running away, or taking flight: *They pursued the flying enemy.* **9.** *Naut.* (of a sail) having none of its edges fastened to spars or stays. **—***n.* **10.** the act of moving through the air on wings; flight. **—***adv.* **11.** *Naut.* without being fastened to a yard, stay, or the like: *a sail set flying.* [bef. 1000; ME (n.); OE *flēogende* (adj.). See FLY[1], -ING[2], -ING[1]]

fly′ing boat′, a seaplane whose main body is a hull adapted for floating. Cf. **floatplane.** [1900–05]

fly′ing bomb′. See **robot bomb.** [1940–45]

fly′ing bond′, *Masonry.* a brickwork bond having random, widely spaced headers. Also called **Yorkshire bond.**

fly′ing box′car, *Informal.* a large airplane designed to carry cargo. [1930–35]

fly′ing bridge′, 1. Also called **flybridge, fly bridge, monkey bridge.** *Naut.* a small, often open deck or platform above the pilothouse or main cabin, having duplicate controls and navigational equipment. **2.** *Archit.* skybridge (def. 2). [1480–90]

fly′ing but′tress, *Archit.* a segmental arch transmitting an outward and downward thrust to a solid buttress that through its inertia transforms the thrust into a vertical one. See illus. under **buttress.** [1660–70]

fly′ing char′acin, hatchetfish (def. 2).

fly′ing cir′cus, 1. a squadron of airplanes operating together, esp. any of several squadrons of famous World War I aviators. **2.** a carnival troupe, or the like, offering exhibitions of stunt flying at fairs, circuses, etc.

fly′ing col′ors, overwhelming victory; triumph; success: *He passed the test with flying colors.* [1700–10]

fly′ing col′umn, *Mil.* (formerly) a force of troops equipped and organized to move swiftly and independently of a principal unit to which it is attached. [1865–70]

fly′ing doc′tor, *Australian.* a doctor listed with local authorities as willing to be flown to remote areas to give emergency medical care. [1925–30]

fly′ing drag′on, any of several arboreal lizards of the genus *Draco,* having an extensible membrane between the limbs along each side by means of which it makes long, gliding leaps. Also called **flying lizard.**

Fly′ing Dust′bin, petard (def. 3). [1940–45]

Fly′ing Dutch′man, 1. a legendary Dutch ghost ship supposed to be seen at sea, esp. near the Cape of Good Hope. **2.** the captain of this ship, supposed to have been condemned to sail the sea, beating against the wind, until the Day of Judgment.

fly′ing field′, *Aeron.* a small landing field with short runways and facilities for servicing airplanes on a lesser scale than an airport. [1925–30]

fly′ing fish′, 1. any fish of the family Exocoetidae, having stiff and greatly enlarged pectoral fins enabling it to glide considerable distances through the air after leaping from the water. **2.** (*caps.*) *Astron.* the constellation Volans. [1505–15]

flying fish, *Cypselurus californicus,* length to 1½ ft. (0.5 m)

Fly′ing For′tress, a heavy bomber, the B-17, with four radial piston engines, widely used over Europe and the Mediterranean by the U.S. Air Force in World War II.

fly′ing fox′, 1. any large fruit bat of the genus *Pteropus,* of Old World tropical regions, having a foxlike head. **2.** *Australian.* an aerial conveyor belt or suspended carrier operating on cables, often used to convey ore, dirt, or the like, over rivers and gorges in mining or construction operations. [1750–60]

fly′ing frog′, either of two East Indian frogs, *Rhacophorus nigrapalmatus* and *R. pardalis,* having broadly webbed feet permitting long, gliding leaps. [1680–90]

fly′ing gang′way, *Naut.* See **monkey bridge** (def. 2).

fly′ing gur′nard, any marine fish of the family Dactylopteridae, esp. *Dactylopterus volitans,* having greatly enlarged, colorful pectoral fins that enable it to glide short distances through the air. Also called **butterflyfish, flying robin.** [1880–85]

fly′ing jen′ny, *Chiefly Midland and Southern U.S.* a merry-go-round, esp. a relatively small or unadorned one. Also called **fly′ing fil′ly, flying mare.**

fly′ing jib′, *Naut.* the outer or outermost of two or more jibs, set well above the jib boom. See diag. under **ship.** [1825–35]

fly′ing jib′ boom′, *Naut.* an extension on a jib boom, to which a flying jib is fastened. [1825–35]

fly′ing kite′, *Naut.* **1.** any of various sails set above the royals or skysails in light weather; jolly jumper. **2.** any of various light upper staysails, studdingsails, or jibs. **3.** (in yachting) any of various racing sails, as spinnakers or balloon jibs. Also called **kite.** [1810–20]

fly′ing le′mur, either of two lemurlike mammals, *Cynocephalus variegatus,* of southeastern Asia and the East Indies, or *C. volans,* of the Philippines, having broad folds of skin on both sides of the body to aid in gliding from tree to tree: now rare. [1880–85]

fly′ing liz′ard. See **flying dragon.** [1850–55]

fly′ing machine′, a vehicle that sustains itself in and propels itself through the air; an airplane, helicopter, glider, or the like. [1730–40]

fly′ing mare′, 1. *Wrestling.* a method of attack in which a wrestler grasps the wrist of the opponent, turns in the opposite direction, and throws the opponent over the shoulder and down. **2.** See **flying jenny.** [1745–55]

fly′ing moor′, *Naut.* the act of mooring a vessel between two anchors, the first dropped while the vessel is under way.

fly′ing mouse′. See **pygmy glider.** [1930–35]

fly′ing phalan′ger, any of various small phalangers of Australia and New Guinea, having a parachutelike fold of skin on each side of the body to give gliding assistance in leaping.

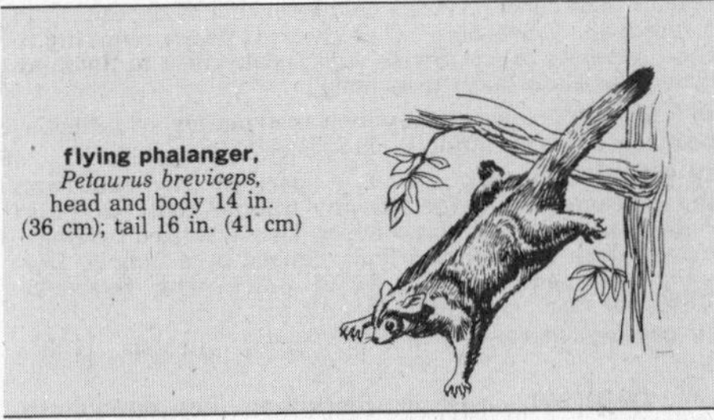
flying phalanger, *Petaurus breviceps,* head and body 14 in. (36 cm); tail 16 in. (41 cm)

fly′ing rob′in. See **flying gurnard.**

fly′ing sau′cer, any of various disk-shaped objects allegedly seen flying at high speeds and altitudes, often with extreme changes in speed and direction, and thought by some to be manned by intelligent beings from outer space. Cf. **UFO.** [1945–50]

fly′ing shear′, *Metalworking.* (in a continuous rolling mill) a shear that moves with the piece being cut. [1900–05]

fly′ing squad′, a trained, mobile group of police officers, business executives, labor officials, or the like, capable of performing specialized tasks whenever or wherever sent, often for use in emergencies. [1925–30]

fly′ing squir′rel, any of various nocturnal tree squirrels, as *Glaucomys volans,* of the eastern U.S., having folds of skin connecting the fore and hind legs, permitting long, gliding leaps. [1605–15]

flying squirrel, *Glaucomys volans,* head and body 8 in. (20 cm); tail 4 in. (10 cm)

fly′ing start′, **1.** a start, as in sailboat racing, in which the entrants begin moving before reaching the starting line. **2.** a start or beginning of anything, characterized by the participant's vigor and enthusiasm and sometimes by a certain advantage over competitors: *She's off to a flying start in her new job.* [1850–55]

fly′ing tack′le, *Football.* a tackle made by hurling one's body through the air at the player carrying the ball.

Fly′ing Ti′gers, the nickname of U.S. fighter pilots, the American Volunteer Group (AVG), who fought against the Japanese in China during World War II.

fly′ing wing′, *Aeron.* an airplane whose wings form almost all the airframe, with the fuselage almost or entirely within the wing structure. [1935–40]

fly•leaf (flī′lēf′), *n., pl.* **-leaves.** a blank leaf in the front or the back of a book. [1825–35; FLY[1] (n., in combination: something fastened by the edge) + LEAF]

fly′ line′, *Angling.* a line for use in fly-fishing.

fly′ loft′, *Theat.* fly[1] (def. 37).

fly•man (flī′mən), *n., pl.* **-men.** *Theat.* a stagehand, esp. one who operates the apparatus in the flies. [1835–45; FLY[1] + -MAN]

fly′ net′, a net or fringe to protect a horse from flies or other insects.

fly•off (flī′ôf′, -of′), *n.* **1.** *Meteorol.* evapotranspiration (def. 1). **2.** a competition between aircraft of various manufacturers to establish superior performance, esp. in order to gain a government contract. [1965–70; (def. 1) prob. FLY[1] + (RUN)OFF; (def. 2) FLY[1] + -OFF]

fly•o•ver (flī′ō′vər), *n.* **1.** a formation of aircraft in flight for observation from the ground, esp. a prearranged, low-altitude flight over a public gathering. **2.** a flight over a simulated target by a bomber or bombing planes. **3.** a flight over a specified area, as for viewing: *We booked a one-hour flyover of the Grand Canyon.* **4.** the action of passing or flying overhead: *rumors of another UFO flyover.* **5.** *Brit.* an overhead crossing, esp. a highway overpass. [1900–05; n. use of v. phrase *fly over*]

fly•pa•per (flī′pā′pər), *n.* paper designed to destroy flies by catching them on its sticky surface or poisoning them on contact. [1840–50; FLY[2] + PAPER]

fly•past (flī′past′, -päst′), *n.* flyby (def. 2a). [1910–15; n. use of v. phrase *fly past*]

fly′ rail′, **1.** *Furniture.* a horizontally swinging bracket for supporting a drop leaf. **2.** Also called **fly′-rail′, working rail.** *Theat.* the upper row of pins or cleats on a pin rail, used for tying off or fastening lines of scenery to be flied. [1850–55]

Fly′ Riv′er (flī), a river in New Guinea, flowing SE from the central part to the Gulf of Papua, ab. 800 mi. (1290 km) long.

fly′ rod′, *Angling.* a light, extremely flexible fishing rod specially designed for use in fly-fishing. [1675–85]

flysch (flish), *n. Geol.* an association of certain types of marine sedimentary rocks characteristic of deposition in a foredeep. [1845–55; < G < Swiss G *flisch* referring to such deposits in the Swiss Alps; perh. akin to Swabian dial. *flins* slate (akin to FLINT)]

fly′ sheet′, a sheet on which instructions or information are printed; handbill. [1825–35]

fly•speck (flī′spek′), *n.* **1.** a speck or tiny stain from the excrement of a fly. **2.** any minute spot. **3.** *Plant Pathol.* a disease of pome fruits, characterized by small, raised, dark spots on the fruit, caused by a fungus, *Leptothyrium pomi.* —*v.t.* **4.** to mark with flyspecks. [1850–55; FLY[2] + SPECK]

fly-strike (flī′strīk′), *n. Vet. Pathol.* myiasis. [1935–40]

fly′ swat′ter, a device for killing flies, mosquitoes, and other insects, usually a square sheet of wire mesh attached to a long handle. Also, **fly′-swat′ter, fly′swat′ter.** [1885–90]

flyte (flīt), *v.i.,* **flyt•ed, flyt•ing,** *n. Scot. and North Eng.* flite.

fly•ti•er (flī′tī′ər), *n. Angling.* a person who makes artificial lures for fly-fishing. [1880–85; FLY[2] + TIER[2]]

fly•trap (flī′trap′), *n.* **1.** any of various plants that entrap insects, esp. Venus's-flytrap. **2.** a trap for flies. [1765–75; FLY[2] + TRAP[1]]

fly-up (flī′up′), *n.* a formal ceremony at which a girl leaves her Brownie troop, receives a pair of embroidered wings for her uniform, and becomes a member of an intermediate Girl Scout troop. [n. use of v. phrase *fly up*]

CONCISE ETYMOLOGY KEY: <, descended or borrowed from; >, whence; b., blend of, blended; c., cognate with; cf., compare; deriv., derivative; equiv., equivalent; imit., imitative; obl., oblique; r., replacing; s., stem; sp., spelling, spelled; resp., respelling, respelled; trans., translation; ?, origin unknown; *, unattested; ‡, probably earlier than. See the full key inside the front cover.

fly•way (flī′wā′), *n.* a route between breeding and wintering areas taken by concentrations of migrating birds. [1890–95; FLY[1] + WAY]

fly•weight (flī′wāt′), *n.* a boxer or other contestant of the lightest competitive class, esp. a professional boxer weighing up to 112 lb. (51 kg). [1905–10; FLY[2] + WEIGHT]

fly•wheel (flī′hwēl′, -wēl′), *n. Mach.* a heavy disk or wheel rotating on a shaft so that its momentum gives almost uniform rotational speed to the shaft and to all connected machinery. [1775–85; FLY[1] + WHEEL]

FM, **1.** *Electronics.* frequency modulation: a method of impressing a signal on a radio carrier wave by varying the frequency of the carrier wave. **2.** *Radio.* a system of radio broadcasting by means of frequency modulation. **3.** of, pertaining to, or utilizing such a system. Cf. **AM.**

Fm, *Symbol, Chem.* fermium.

fm, *Symbol, Physics.* femtometer.

fm., **1.** fathom. **2.** from.

f.m., (in prescriptions) make a mixture. [< L *fiat mistūra*]

FMB, Federal Maritime Board.

FMC, Federal Maritime Commission.

FMCS, Federal Mediation and Conciliation Service.

FM cyclotron, *Physics.* synchrocyclotron.

F.Mk., finmark; Finnish markka. Also, **FMk**

fn, footnote.

FNMA, Federal National Mortgage Association.

f-number (ef′num′bər), *n. Optics, Photog.* a number corresponding to the ratio of the focal length to the diameter of a lens system, esp. a camera lens. In *f*/1.4, 1.4 is the f-number and signifies that the focal length of the lens is 1.4 times as great as the diameter. *Abbr.: f/, f/, f,* f: Also, **f number.** Also called **focal ratio, speed, stop number.** Cf. **relative aperture.** [1890–95]

Fo (fō), *n. Chinese.* Buddha (def. 1).

fo., folio.

F.O., **1.** field officer. **2.** foreign office. **3.** *Mil.* forward observer.

foal (fōl), *n.* **1.** a young horse, mule, or related animal, esp. one that is not yet one year of age. —*v.t., v.i.* **2.** to give birth to (a colt or filly). [bef. 950; (n.) ME *fole,* OE *fola;* c. OHG *folo* (G *Fohlen*); akin to L *pullus* young animal, Gk *pôlos* foal; (v.) ME, deriv. of the n.]

foam (fōm), *n.* **1.** a collection of minute bubbles formed on the surface of a liquid by agitation, fermentation, etc.: *foam on a glass of beer.* **2.** the froth of perspiration, caused by great exertion, formed on the skin of a horse or other animal. **3.** froth formed from saliva in the mouth, as in epilepsy and rabies. **4.** a thick frothy substance, as shaving cream. **5.** (in firefighting) **a.** a chemically produced substance that smothers the flames on a burning liquid by forming a layer of minute, stable, heat-resistant bubbles on the liquid's surface. **b.** the layer of bubbles so formed. **6.** a dispersion of gas bubbles in a solid, as foam glass, foam rubber, polyfoam, or foamed metal. **7.** *Literary.* the sea. —*v.i.* **8.** to form or gather foam; emit foam; froth. —*v.t.* **9.** to cause to foam. **10.** to cover with foam. **11.** to insulate with foam. **12.** to make (plastic, metal, etc.) into a foam. **13.** **foam at the mouth,** to be extremely or uncontrollably angry. [bef. 900; ME *fom,* OE *fām;* c. G *Feim*] —**foam′a•ble,** *adj.* —**foam′er,** *n.* —**foam′ing•ly,** *adv.* —**foam′less,** *adj.* —**foam′like′,** *adj.*
—**Syn. 1.** froth, spume, head, fizz; scum.

foamed′ met′al, *Chem., Metallurgy.* a uniform foamlike metal structure produced when hydrogen bubbles are evolved from metal hydrides uniformly dispersed throughout a host metal or metal alloy: used as a structural material because of its shock-absorbing properties and light weight. Also, **foam′ met′al.**

foamed′ plas′tic. See **expanded plastic.** [1935–40]

foam•flow•er (fōm′flou′ər), *n.* a North American plant, *Tiarella cordifolia,* having a cluster of small, usually white flowers. Also called **false miterwort.** [1890–95; FOAM + FLOWER]

foam′ glass′, cellular glass made by fusing powdered glass with carbon particles or other gas-generating material, used chiefly for industrial purposes. [1945–50]

foam′ rub′ber, a light, spongy rubber, used for mattresses, cushions, etc. [1940–45]

foam•y (fō′mē), *adj.,* **foam•i•er, foam•i•est.** **1.** covered with or full of foam. **2.** consisting of foam. **3.** resembling foam. **4.** pertaining to foam. [bef. 1000; ME *fomy,* OE *fāmig.* See FOAM, -Y[1]] —**foam′i•ly,** *adv.* —**foam′i•ness,** *n.*

fob[1] (fob), *n.* **1.** a small pocket just below the waistline in trousers for a watch, keys, change, etc. Cf. **watch pocket. 2.** a short chain or ribbon, usually with a medallion or similar ornament, attached to a watch and worn hanging from a pocket. **3.** the medallion or ornament itself. [1645–55; orig. uncert.; cf. G dial. *Fuppe* pocket]

fob[2] (fob), *v.t.,* **fobbed, fob•bing. 1.** *Archaic.* to cheat; deceive. **2. fob off, a.** to cheat someone by substituting something spurious or inferior; palm off (often fol. by *on*): *He tried to fob off an inferior brand on us.* **b.** to put (someone) off by deception or trickery. [1350–1400; ME *fobben;* c. G *foppen* to delude; cf. FOB[1]]

f.o.b., *Com.* free on board: without charge to the buyer for goods placed on board a carrier at the point of shipment: *automobiles shipped f.o.b. Detroit.* Also, **F.O.B.**

FOBS, See **fractional orbital bombardment system.** Also, **F.O.B.S.**

fo•cac•cia (fō kä′chə), *n., pl.* **-cias.** a large, round, flat Italian bread, sprinkled before baking with olive oil, salt, and often herbs. [1975–80; < It < LL *focacia* (neut. pl.), der. of L *focus* hearth, perh. with *-āceus* -ACEOUS]

fo•cal (fō′kəl), *adj.* of or pertaining to a focus. [1685–95; < NL *focālis.* See FOCUS, -AL[1]] —**fo′cal•ly,** *adv.*

fo′cal ar′ea, *Ling.* (in dialect geography) an area whose dialect has exerted influence on the dialects of surrounding areas, as reflected in a set of isoglosses more or less concentrically surrounding it. Cf. **relic area, transition area.**

fo′cal infec′tion, *Pathol., Dentistry.* an infection in which bacteria are localized in some region, as the tissue around a tooth, from which they may spread to some other organ or structure of the body. [1920–25]

fo•cal•ize (fō′kə līz′), *v.t., v.i.,* **-ized, -iz•ing. 1.** to bring or come to a focus. **2.** to localize. Also, *esp. Brit.,* **fo′cal•ise′.** [1835–45; FOCAL + -IZE] —**fo′cal•i•za′•tion,** *n.*

fo′cal length′, *Optics.* **1.** the distance from a focal point of a lens or mirror to the corresponding principal plane. *Symbol: f* **2.** the distance between an object lens and its corresponding focal plane in a telescope. Also called **fo′cal dis′tance.** [1745–55]

fo′cal plane′, *Optics.* **1.** a plane through a focal point and normal to the axis of a lens, mirror, or other optical system. Cf. **principal plane. 2.** the transverse plane in a telescope where the real image of a distant view is in focus. [1890–95]

fo′cal-plane shut′ter (fō′kəl plān′), *Photog.* a camera shutter situated directly in front of the film. Cf. **curtain shutter.** [1900–05]

fo′cal point′, **1.** Also called **principal focus.** *Optics.* either of two points on the axis of a mirror, lens, or other optical system, one point being such that rays diverging from it are deviated parallel to the axis upon refraction or reflection by the system and the other point being such that rays parallel to the axis of the system converge to the point upon refraction or reflection by the system. **2.** the point at which all elements or aspects converge; center of activity or attention. **3.** the central or principal point of focus. [1705–15]

fo′cal ra′tio, *Optics., Photog.* f-number. [1925–30]

fo′cal sei′zure, *Pathol.* an epileptic manifestation arising from a localized anomaly in the brain, as a small tumor or scar, and usually involving a single motor or sensory mechanism but occasionally spreading to other areas and causing convulsions and loss of consciousness.

Foch (fosh; *Fr.* fôsh), *n.* **Fer•di•nand** (fer dē näɴ′), 1851–1929, French marshal.

fo•ci (fō′sī, -kī), *n.* a pl. of **focus.**

fo•com•e•ter (fō kom′i tər), *n. Optics.* an instrument for measuring the focal length of a lens or other optical system. [1850–55; FOC(US) + -O- + -METER]

fo'c's'le (fōk′səl), *n. Naut.* forecastle. Also, **fo'c'sle.** [resp., reflecting syncope and loss of pre-consonantal *r*]

fo•cus (fō′kəs), *n., pl.* **-cus•es, -ci** (-sī, -kī), *v.,* **-cused, -cus•ing** or (*esp. Brit.*) **-cussed, -cus•sing.** —*n.* **1.** a central point, as of attraction, attention, or activity: *The need to prevent a nuclear war became the focus of all diplomatic efforts.* **2.** *Physics.* a point at which rays of light, heat, or other radiation, meet after being refracted or reflected. **3.** *Optics.* **a.** the focal point of a lens. **b.** the focal length of a lens. **c.** the clear and sharply defined condition of an image. **d.** the position of a viewed object or the adjustment of an optical device necessary to produce a clear image: *in focus; out of focus.* **4.** *Geom.* (of a conic section) a point having the property that the distances from any point on a curve to it and to a fixed line have a constant ratio for all points on the curve. See diag. under **ellipse, hyperbola, parabola. 5.** *Geol.* the point of origin of an earthquake. **6.** *Pathol.* the primary center from which a disease develops or in which it localizes. —*v.t.* **7.** to bring to a focus or into focus: *to focus the lens of a camera.* **8.** to concentrate: *to focus one's thoughts.* —*v.i.* **9.** to become focused. [1635–45; < L: fireplace, hearth] —**fo′cus•a•ble,** *adj.* —**fo′cus•er,** *n.* —**Syn. 1.** center, heart, core, nucleus.

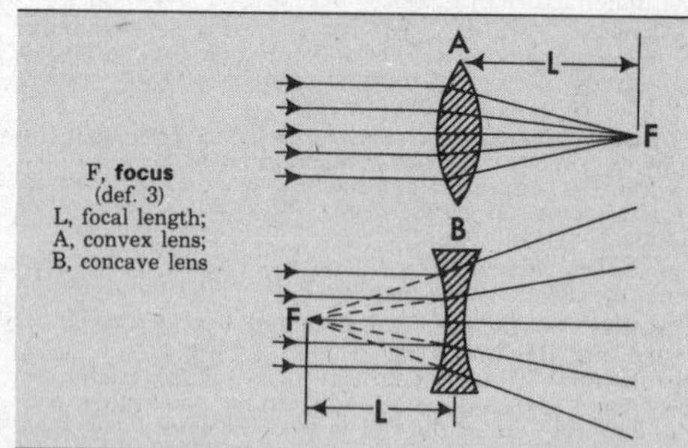

F, **focus** (def. 3)
L, focal length;
A, convex lens;
B, concave lens

fo′cusing cloth′, an opaque cloth surrounding the ground glass of a camera so as to shield the eyes of the photographer from light that would otherwise prevent seeing the image in the ground glass. [1850–55]

fo′cusing screen′, *Photog.* See under **reflex camera.** [1855–60]

fod•der (fod′ər), *n.* **1.** coarse food for livestock, composed of entire plants, including leaves, stalks, and grain, of such forages as corn and sorghum. **2.** people considered as readily available and of little value: *cannon fodder.* **3.** raw material: *fodder for a comedian's routine.* —*v.t.* **4.** to feed with or as if with fodder. [bef. 1000; ME; OE *fodder, fōdor;* c. G *Futter;* akin to FOOD]
—**Syn. 1.** See **feed.**

fod•der•beet (fod′ər bēt′), *n.* sugar beet used as fodder. Also, **fod′der beet′.** [FODDER + BEET[1]]

fodg•el (foj′əl), *adj. Scot.* fat; stout; plump. [1715–25; *fodge* (var. of FADGE) a short, fat person + *-el* adj. suffix]

foe (fō), *n.* **1.** a person who feels enmity, hatred, or malice toward another; enemy: *a bitter foe.* **2.** a military enemy; hostile army. **3.** a person belonging to a hostile

army or nation. **4.** an opponent in a game or contest; adversary: *a political foe.* **5.** a person who is opposed in feeling, principle, etc., to something: *a foe to progress in civil rights.* **6.** a thing that is harmful to or destructive of something: *Sloth is the foe of health.* [bef. 900; ME *foo,* OE *fāh* hostile, *gefāh* enemy; c. OHG *gifēh* at war. See FEUD[1]]
—**Syn. 1.** See **enemy. 1, 3–5.** opponent, antagonist.
—**Ant. 1–3.** friend.

F.O.E., Fraternal Order of Eagles.

foehn (fān; *Ger.* fœn),*n.* a warm, dry wind descending a mountain, as on the north side of the Alps. Also, **föhn.** [1860–65; < G *Föhn* (orig. in Alpine dialects), MHG *foenne,* OHG *phōnno* < VL **faōnius,* for L *Favōnius* FAVONIUS]

foe·man (fō′mən), *n., pl.* **-men.** *Literary.* an enemy in war. [bef. 1000; ME *foman,* OE *fāhman.* See FOE, MAN[1]]

Foerst′ner bit′ (fôrst′nər). *Carpentry.* See **Forstner bit.**

foe·ti·cide (fē′ti sīd′), *n.* feticide.

foet·id (fet′id, fē′tid), *adj.* fetid.

foe·tip·a·rous (fē tip′ər əs), *adj.* fetiparous.

foe·tol·o·gy (fē tol′ə jē), *n.* fetology.

foe·tor (fē′tər), *n.* fetor.

foe·tus (fē′təs), *n., pl.* **-tus·es.** fetus.

fog[1] (fog, fôg), *n., v.,* **fogged, fog·ging.** —*n.* **1.** a cloudlike mass or layer of minute water droplets or ice crystals near the surface of the earth, appreciably reducing visibility. Cf. **ice fog, mist, smog. 2.** any darkened state of the atmosphere, or the diffused substance that causes it. **3.** a state of mental confusion or unawareness; daze; stupor: *The survivors were in a fog for days after the catastrophe.* **4.** *Photog.* a hazy effect on a developed negative or positive, caused by light other than that forming the image, by improper handling during development, or by the use of excessively old film. **5.** *Physical Chem.* a mixture consisting of liquid particles dispersed in a gaseous medium. —*v.t.* **6.** to cover or envelop with or as if with fog: *The steam in the room fogged his glasses.* **7.** to confuse or obscure: *The debate did little else but fog the issue.* **8.** to bewilder or perplex: *to fog the mind.* **9.** *Photog.* to produce fog on (a negative or positive). —*v.i.* **10.** to become enveloped or obscured with or as if with fog. **11.** *Photog.* (of a negative or positive) to become affected by fog. [1535–45; perh. by back formation from FOGGY. See FOG[2]] —**fog′·less,** *adj.*
—**Syn. 3.** obfuscation. See **cloud. 7.** becloud, obfuscate, dim, blur, darken. **8.** daze, befuddle, muddle, mystify. —**Ant. 3.** clarity. **7.** clarify. **10.** clear.

fog[2] (fog, fôg), *n. U.S. and Brit. Dial.* **1.** a second growth of grass, as after mowing. **2.** long grass left standing in fields during the winter. [1300–50; ME *fogge, fog* < Scand; cf. Norw *fogg* long grass on damp ground, FOGGY]

Fo·gar·ty (fō′gər tē), *n.* **Anne,** 1919–80, U.S. fashion designer.

fog′ bank′, a stratum of fog as seen from a distance. [1650–60]

fog·bound (fog′bound′, fôg′-), *adj. Naut.* unable to sail or navigate because of heavy fog. [1850–55; FOG[1] + -BOUND[1]]

fog·bow (fog′bō′, fôg′-), *n.* a bow, arc, or circle of white or yellowish hue seen in or against a fog bank; a rainbow formed by fog droplets. Also called **mistbow, seadog, white rainbow.** [1825–35; FOG[1] + (RAIN)BOW]

fog·dog (fog′dôg′, -dog′, fôg′), *n.* a bright spot sometimes seen in a fog bank. [1865–70; see FOG[1], SUNDOG]

fog′ drip′, water falling to the ground from trees, esp. conifers, that have collected the moisture from fog.

fo·gey (fō′gē), *n., pl.* **-geys.** fogy.

fog′ for′est, the thick forest growth at fairly high elevations on tropical mountains, where there is a prevalence of clouds, high humidity, and mild temperature.

fog·gage (fog′ij, fô′gij), *n. Chiefly Scot.* fog[2]. [1490–1500; < AL *fogāgium.* See FOG[2], -AGE]

fog·ger (fog′ər, fô′gər), *n.* a device that spreads a chemical, as an insecticide, in the form of a fog. [FOG[1] + -ER[1]]

Fog·gia (fôd′jä),*n.* a city in SE Italy. 153,736.

fog′ gun′, a gun, fired at regular intervals, used as a warning signal in fog.

fog·gy (fog′ē, fô′gē), *adj.,* **-gi·er, -gi·est. 1.** thick with or having much fog; misty: *a foggy valley; a foggy spring day.* **2.** covered or enveloped as if with fog: *a foggy mirror.* **3.** blurred or obscured as if by fog; not clear; vague: *I haven't the foggiest notion of where she went.* **4.** bewildered; perplexed. **5.** *Photog.* affected by fog. [1520–30; FOG[2] + -Y[1]; orig. meaning marshy, thick, murky] —**fog′gi·ly,** *adv.* —**fog′gi·ness,** *n.*
—**Syn. 3.** fuzzy, hazy, dim, murky, muddled.

Fog′gy Bot′tom, 1. a low-lying area bordering the Potomac River in Washington, D.C. **2.** *Informal.* the U.S. Department of State, whose office building is located in this area.

fog·horn (fog′hôrn′, fôg′-), *n.* **1.** a deep, loud horn for sounding warning signals in foggy weather, as to ships. **2.** a deep, loud voice. [1855–60; FOG[1] + HORN]

fog′ light′, an automobile headlight throwing light of a color intended to diminish the effect of fog, dust, etc., in the air. [1960–65]

fo·gram (fō′grəm), *n.* an old-fashioned or overly conservative person; fogy. Also, **fo′grum.** [1765–75; orig. uncert.]

fog′ sig′nal, any of various types of signal used as a warning by vessels navigating in fog or mist. [1750–60]

fo·gy (fō′gē), *n., pl.* **-gies.** an excessively conservative or old-fashioned person, esp. one who is intellectually dull (usually prec. by *old*): *The board of directors were old fogies still living in the 19th century.* Also, **fogey.** [1770–80; orig. uncert.] —**fo′gy·ish,** *adj.* —**fo′·gy·ism,** *n.*

foh (fô), *interj.* faugh.

föhn (fān; *Ger.* fœn), *n. Meteorol.* foehn.

FOIA, See **Freedom of Information Act.**

foi·ble (foi′bəl), *n.* **1.** a minor weakness or failing of character; slight flaw or defect: *an all-too-human foible.* **2.** the weaker part of a sword blade, between the middle and the point (opposed to *forte*). [1640–50; < F, obs. form of *faible* FEEBLE]
—**Syn. 1.** frailty, quirk, crotchet, eccentricity, peculiarity. See **fault.** —**Ant. 1.** strength.

foie gras (fwä grä′; *Fr.* fwä gʀä′), the liver of specially fattened geese or ducks, used as a table delicacy, esp. in the form of a paste **(pâté de foie gras).** [1810–20; < F: lit., fat liver]

foil[1] (foil), *v.t.* **1.** to prevent the success of; frustrate; balk: *Loyal troops foiled his attempt to overthrow the government.* **2.** to keep (a person) from succeeding in an enterprise, plan, etc. —*n.* **3.** *Archaic.* a defeat; check; repulse. [1250–1300; ME *foilen,* < AF *foller,* OF *fuler* to trample, full (cloth). See FULL[2]] —**foil′a·ble,** *adj.*
—**Syn. 1.** thwart; impede, hamper.

foil[2] (foil), *n.* **1.** metal in the form of very thin sheets: *aluminum foil.* **2.** the metallic backing applied to glass to form a mirror. **3.** a thin layer of metal placed under a gem in a closed setting to improve its color or brilliancy. **4.** a person or thing that makes another seem better by contrast: *The straight man was an able foil to the comic.* **5.** *Archit.* an arc or a rounded space between cusps, as in the tracery of a window or other ornamentation. **6.** an airfoil or hydrofoil. —*v.t.* **7.** to cover or back with foil. **8.** to set off by contrast. [1350–1400; ME *foille, foil* < OF *fuelle, fueille, foille* (< L *folia* leaves), *fuel, fueil, foil* (< L *folium* leaf, blade)]
—**Syn. 4.** contrast, complement, counterpart.

foil[3] (foil), *n. Fencing.* **1.** a flexible four-sided rapier having a blunt point. **2. foils,** the art or practice of fencing with this weapon, points being made by touching the trunk of the opponent's body with the tip of the weapon. [1585–95; orig. uncert.]

foil·borne (foil′bôrn′, -bōrn′), *adj.* (of a vessel) moving on the water on hydrofoils, with the hull out of the water. [1960–65; FOIL[2] + BORNE[1]]

foiled (foild), *adj. Archit.* ornamented with foils, as a gable, spandrel, or balustrade. [1655–65; FOIL[2] + -ED[3]]

foils·man (foilz′mən), *n., pl.* **-men.** *Fencing.* a person who fences with a foil. [1925–30; FOIL[3] + -'S[1] + MAN[1]]

foin (foin), *Archaic.* —*n.* **1.** a thrust with a weapon. —*v.i.* **2.** to thrust with a weapon; lunge. [1325–75; ME (v.), appar. < OF *foine* fish spear < L *fuscina*]

Fo·ism (fō′iz əm), *n.* Chinese Buddhism. [Fo + -ISM] —**Fo′ist,** *n.*

foi·son (foi′zən), *n. Archaic.* **1.** abundance; plenty. **2.** abundant harvest. [1250–1300; ME *foisoun* < MF *foison* < L *fūsiōn-* (s. of *fūsiō*) an outpouring. See FUSION]

foist (foist), *v.t.* **1.** to force upon or impose fraudulently or unjustifiably (usually fol. by *on* or *upon*): *to foist inferior merchandise on a customer.* **2.** to bring, put, or introduce surreptitiously or fraudulently (usually fol. by *in* or *into*): *to foist political views into a news story.* [1535–45; < D dial. *vuisten,* deriv. of *vuist* FIST]

Fo·kine (fō kēn′), *n.* **Mi·chel Mi·khay·lo·vich** (mishel′ mi hī′lə vich), 1880–1942, Russian choreographer and ballet dancer, in the U.S. after 1925.

Fok·ker (fok′ər; *Du.* fok′əʀ), *n.* **1. An·tho·ny Her·man Ge·rard** (*Du.* än tō′nē hεʀ′män gā′ʀäʀt), 1890–1939, Dutch airplane designer and builder. **2.** an aircraft designed or built by Fokker, esp. as used by Germany in World War I.

fol., 1. folio. **2.** (in prescriptions) a leaf. [< L *folium*] **3.** followed. **4.** following.

fol·a·cin (fol′ə sin), *n. Biochem.* See **folic acid.** [1945–50; FOL(IC) AC(ID) + -IN[2]]

fold[1] (fōld), *v.t.* **1.** to bend (cloth, paper, etc.) over upon itself. **2.** to bring into a compact form by bending and laying parts together (often fol. by *up*): *to fold up a map; to fold one's legs under oneself.* **3.** to bring (the arms, hands, etc.) together in an intertwined or crossed manner; clasp; cross: *He folded his arms on his chest.* **4.** to bend or wind (usually fol. by *about, round,* etc.): *to fold one's arms about a person's neck.* **5.** to bring (the wings) close to the body, as a bird on alighting. **6.** to enclose; wrap; envelop: *to fold something in paper.* **7.** to embrace or clasp; enfold: *to fold someone in one's arms.* **8.** *Cards.* to place (one's cards) facedown so as to withdraw from the play. **9.** *Informal.* to bring to an end; close up: *The owner decided to fold the business and retire.* —*v.i.* **10.** to be folded or be capable of folding: *The doors fold back.* **11.** *Cards.* to place one's cards facedown so as to withdraw from the play. **12.** *Informal.* to fail in business; be forced to close: *The newspaper folded after 76 years.* **13.** *Informal.* to yield or give in: *Dad folded and said we could go after all.* **14. fold in,** *Cookery.* to mix in or add (an ingredient) by gently turning one part over another: *Fold in the egg whites.* **15. fold up,** *Informal.* **a.** to break down; collapse: *He folded up when the prosecutor discredited his story.* **b.** to fail, esp. to go out of business.
—*n.* **16.** a part that is folded; pleat; layer: *folds of cloth.* **17.** a crease made by folding: *He cut the paper along the fold.* **18.** a hollow made by folding: *to carry something in the fold of one's dress.* **19.** a hollow place in undulating ground: *a fold of the mountains.* **20.** *Geol.* a portion of strata that is folded or bent, as an anticline or syncline, or that connects two horizontal or parallel portions of strata of different levels (as a monocline). **21.** *Journalism.* **a.** the line formed along the horizontal center of a standard-sized newspaper when it is folded after printing. **b.** a rough-and-ready dividing line, esp. on the front page and other principal pages, between stories of primary and lesser importance. **22.** a coil of a serpent, string, etc. **23.** the act of folding or doubling over. **24.** *Anat.* a margin or ridge formed by the folding of a membrane or other flat body part; plica. [bef. 900; (v.) ME *folden, falden,* OE *faldan;* c. G. *falten;* (v.) ME *fald,* deriv. of the *n.;* akin to L *plicāre* to fold, *plectere* to PLAIT, twine, Gk *plékein;* cf. -FOLD] —**fold′a·ble,** *adj.*

fold[2] (fōld), *n.* **1.** an enclosure for sheep or, occasionally, other domestic animals. **2.** the sheep kept within it. **3.** a flock of sheep. **4.** a church. **5.** the members of a church; congregation: *He preached to the fold.* **6.** a group sharing common beliefs, values, etc.: *He rejoined the fold after his youthful escapade.* —*v.t.* **7.** to confine (sheep or other domestic animals) in a fold. [bef. 900; ME *fold, fald,* OE *fald, falod;* akin to OS *faled* pen, enclosure, MLG *vālt* pen, enclosure, manure heap, MD *vaelt, vaelde*]

-fold, a native English suffix meaning "of so many parts," or denoting multiplication by the number indicated by the stem or word to which the suffix is attached: *twofold; manifold.* [ME; OE *-fald, -feald,* c. OFris, OS *-fald,* G *-falt,* ON *-faldr,* Goth *-falths,* all repr. the Gmc base of FOLD[1]; akin to Gk *-ploos, -plous* (see HAPLO-, DIPLO-), L *-plus* (see SIMPLE, DOUBLE, etc.), *-plex* -PLEX]

fold·a·way (fōld′ə wā′), *adj.* **1.** designed to be folded out of the way when not in use: *a foldaway bed.* —*n.* **2.** an object, as a bed, that can be folded and stored away when not in use. [1955–60; FOLD[1] + (HIDE)AWAY]

fold·boat (fōld′bōt′), *n.* faltboat.

fold-down (fōld′doun′), *adj.* designed to be folded out for use and collapsed when not in use: *a fold-down tray on the back of an airplane seat; a fold-down trailer for camping.* [adj. use of v. phrase *fold down*]

fold·er (fōl′dər), *n.* **1.** a person or thing that folds. **2.** a printed sheet, as a circular or timetable, folded into a number of usually pagelike sections. **3.** a folded sheet of light cardboard used to cover or hold papers, letters, etc., as in a file. [1545–55; FOLD[1] + -ER[1]]

fol·de·rol (fol′də rol′), *n.* falderal.

fold′ing chair′, a chair that can be collapsed flat for easy storage or transport. [1670–80]

fold′ing door′, a door with hinged sections that can be folded flat against one another when opened. [1605–15]

fold′ing mon′ey, *Informal.* See **paper money.** [1925–30]

fold′ing rule′. See **zigzag rule.**

fold·out (fōld′out′), *n.* **1.** a page larger than the trim size of a magazine or book, folded one or more times so as not to extend beyond the pages; gatefold. —*adj.* **2.** that must be unfolded to be used, read, viewed, etc.: *a cabinet with a foldout table.* Also, **fold′-out′.** [1945–50; n., adj. use of v. phrase *fold out*]

fold·up (fōld′up′), *n.* **1.** something, as a chair or bed, that can be folded up and stored away when not in use. **2.** termination or closing: *the foldup of the town's newspaper.* **3.** a giving in; capitulation: *a foldup of management under union pressure.* Also, **fold′-up′.** [1890–95; n. use of v. phrase *fold up*]

Fo′ley cath′eter, an indwelling catheter used for draining urine from the bladder and having an inflatable part at the bladder end that allows the tube to be kept in place for variable time periods. [named after F.E.B. *Foley* (1891–1966), U.S. urologist]

fo·li·a[1] (fō′lē ə), *n.* pl. of **folium.**

fo·li·a[2] (fə lē′ə), *n.* a wild and noisy Portuguese carnival dance accompanied by tambourines, performed at a frantic pace by men dressed as women and often carrying masked boys on their shoulders. [see FOLÍA]

fo·lí·a (*Sp.* fô lē′ä), *n., pl.* **-lí·as** (*Sp.* -lē′äs). an early medieval Iberian dance accompanied by mime and songs, performed during celebrations of the solstice and New Year festivals. [1780–85; < Sp *folía* or Pg *folia* lit., madness, folly << OPr, equiv. to *fol* foolish, mad + *-ia* -Y[3]; see FOOL[1], FOLLY]

fo·li·a·ceous (fō′lē ā′shəs), *adj.* **1.** of, like, or of the nature of a plant leaf; leaflike. **2.** bearing leaves or leaflike parts. **3.** pertaining to or consisting of leaves. **4.** consisting of leaflike plates or laminae; foliated. [1650–60; < L *foliāceus* leafy, like a leaf. See FOLIUM, -ACEOUS] —**fo′li·a′ceous·ness,** *n.*

fo·li·age (fō′lē ij), *n.* **1.** the leaves of a plant, collectively; leafage. **2.** leaves in general. **3.** the representation of leaves, flowers, and branches in painting, architectural ornament, etc. [1400–50; late ME *folage* < MF *fueillage, foillage,* deriv. of *feuille* leaf; influenced by L *folium* FOLIUM. See FOIL[2], -AGE] —**fo′li·aged,** *adj.*

fo′liage plant′, any plant grown chiefly for its attractive leaves. [1860–65]

fo·li·ar (fō′lē ər), *adj.* of, pertaining to, or having the nature of a leaf or leaves. [1870–75; < NL *foliāris.* See FOLIUM, -AR[1]]

fo·li·ate (*adj.* fō′lē it, -āt′; *v.* fō′lē āt′), *adj., v.,* **-at·ed, -at·ing.** —*adj.* **1.** covered with or having leaves. **2.** like a leaf, as in shape. **3.** Also, **foliated.** *Archit.* **a.** ornamented with or composed of foils: *foliate tracery.* **b.** ornamented with representations of foliage: *a foliate capital.* **4.** *Petrol., Mineral.* foliated (def. 2). —*v.i.* **5.** to put forth leaves. **6.** to split into thin leaflike layers or laminae. —*v.t.* **7.** to shape like a leaf or leaves. **8.** to decorate with foils or foliage. **9.** to form into thin sheets. **10.** to spread over with a thin metallic backing. **11.** *Print.* to number the folios or leaves, as distinguished from pages, of (a manuscript or book). [1620–30; < L *foliātus* leafy. See FOLIUM, -ATE[1]]

CONCISE PRONUNCIATION KEY: *act, cāpe, dâre, pärt; set, ēqual; if, īce; ox, ōver, ôrder, oil, bo͝ok, bo͞ot, out; up, ûrge; child; sing; shoe; thin,* t͟h*at;* zh *as in treasure.* ə = *a as in alone, e as in system, i as in easily, o as in gallop, u as in circus;* ᵊ *as in fire* (fīᵊr), *hour* (ouᵊr). l *and* n *can serve as syllabic consonants, as in cradle* (krād′l), *and button* (but′n). See the full key inside the front cover.

fo•li•at•ed (fō′lē ā′tid), *adj.* **1.** shaped like a leaf or leaves: *foliated ornaments.* **2.** Also, **foliate.** *Petrol., Mineral.* consisting of thin and separable laminae. **3.** *Archit.* foliate (def. 3). [1640–50; FOLIATE + -ED[2]]

fo′liated joint′, a joint between the rabbeted and overlapping edges of two boards, forming a continuous surface on each side. [1870–75]

fo•li•a•tion (fō′lē ā′shən), *n.* **1.** the act or process of putting forth leaves. **2.** the state of being in leaf. **3.** *Bot.* **a.** the arrangement of leaves within a bud. **b.** the arrangement of leaves on a plant. **4.** leaves or foliage. **5.** *Print.* the consecutive numbering of the folios or leaves, as distinguished from pages, of a manuscript or book. **6.** the total number of such leaves. **7.** *Petrol.* a form of lamination produced in rocks by metamorphism. **8.** ornamentation with foliage, or an arrangement of foliage. **9.** *Archit.* **a.** ornamentation with foils. **b.** ornamentation with representations of foliage. **10.** formation into thin sheets. **11.** the application of foil to glass to make a mirror. [1615–25; FOLIATE + -ION]

fo•li•a•ture (fō′lē ə chər), *n.* a cluster of leaves; foliage. [1670–80; < LL *foliātūra* foliage. See FOLIATE, -URE]

fo•lic (fō′lik, fol′ik), *adj.* of or derived from folic acid. [< L *fol(ium)* FOLIUM + -IC]

fo′lic ac′id, *Biochem.* a water-soluble vitamin that is converted to a coenzyme essential to purine and thymine biosynthesis: deficiency causes a form of anemia. [1940–45]

fo•lie (fô lē′), *n., pl.* ***-lies*** (-lē′). *French.* madness; insanity. [1795–1805]

fo•lie à deux (fo lē′ ə do͞o′; *Fr.* fô lē A dœ′), *pl.* **fo•lies à deux** (fo lēz′ ə do͞o′; *Fr.* fô lē ZA dœ′). *Psychiatry.* the sharing of delusional ideas by two people who are closely associated. [1890–95; < F]

fo•lie de gran•deur (*Fr.* fô lēdᵊ GRÄN dœR′), *pl.* **fo•lies de gran•deur** (*Fr.* fô lēdᵊ GRÄN dœR′). *Psychiatry.* a delusion of grandeur; megalomania. Also, **folie des grandeurs** (*Fr.* fô lē dā GRÄN dœR′). [< F]

Fo•lies Ber•gère (*Fr.* fô lē beR zheR′), a Parisian music hall founded in 1869 and noted for the lavish spectacle and mildly risqué content of its entertainments. [< F: the Bergère Follies, after *rue Bergère,* a street near which it was originally located]

fo•li•ic•o•lous (fō′lē ik′ə ləs), *adj.* **1.** growing on leaves, as certain liverworts. **2.** parasitic on leaves, as certain fungi. [1870–75; FOL(IUM) + -I- + -COLOUS]

fo•li•if•er•ous (fō′lē if′ər əs), *adj. Bot.* bearing leaves or leaflike structures. [1820–30; FOL(IUM) + -I- + -FEROUS]

fo•lin′ic ac′id (fō lin′ik), *Biochem., Pharm.* a crystalline, slightly water-soluble solid, $C_{20}H_{23}N_7O_7$, produced by fermentation or derived from folic acid, used in medicine in the treatment of certain anemias. [1945–50; FOL(IC) + -IN[2] + -IC]

fo•li•o (fō′lē ō′), *n., pl.* **-li•os,** *adj., v.,* **-li•oed, -li•o•ing.** —*n.* **1.** a sheet of paper folded once to make two leaves, or four pages, of a book or manuscript. **2.** a volume having pages of the largest size, formerly made from such a sheet. **3.** a leaf of a manuscript or book numbered only on the front side. **4.** *Print.* **a.** (in a book) the number of each page. **b.** (in a newspaper) the number of each page together with the date and the name of the newspaper. **5.** *Bookkeeping.* a page of an account book or a left-hand page and a right-hand page facing each other and having the same serial number. **6.** *Law.* a certain number of words, in the U.S. generally 100, taken as a unit for computing the length of a document. —*adj.* **7.** pertaining to or having the format of a folio: *a folio volume.* —*v.t.* **8.** to number each leaf or page of. **9.** *Law.* to mark each folio in (a pleading or the like) with the proper number. [1525–35; < L *foliō* (orig. in phrase *in foliō* in a leaf, sheet), abl. of *folium* FOLIUM]

fo•li•o•late (fō′lē ə lāt′), *adj. Bot.* pertaining to or consisting of leaflets (often used in combination, as *bifoliolate*). [1865–70; < NL *foliolātus.* See FOLIOLE, -ATE[1]]

fo•li•ole (fō′lē ōl′), *n. Bot.* **1.** a leaflet, as of a compound leaf. **2.** a small leaflike organ or appendage. [1785–95; < F < LL *foliolum,* equiv. to L *foli(um)* leaf + *-olum* -OLE[1]]

fo•li•ose (fō′lē ōs′), *adj.* **1.** *Bot.* leafy. **2.** *Mycol.* having a leaflike thallus loosely attached to a surface, as certain lichens. Cf. **crustose, fruticose.** Also, **fo•li•ous** (fō′lē əs). [1720–30; < L *foliōsus.* See FOLIUM, -OSE[1]]

-folious, a combining form meaning "having leaves (of a specified number or type)": *unifolious.* [comb. form repr. L *foliōsus* FOLIOSE]

fo•li•o ver•so (fō′lē ō′ weR′sō; *Eng.* fō′lē ō′ vûr′sō), *Latin.* the back of the page.

fo•li•um (fō′lē əm), *n., pl.* **-li•a** (-lē ə). **1.** a thin leaflike stratum or layer; a lamella. **2.** *Geom.* a loop; part of a curve terminated at both ends by the same node. Equation: $x^3 + y^3 = 3axy$. [1840–50; < NL, L: lit., a leaf]

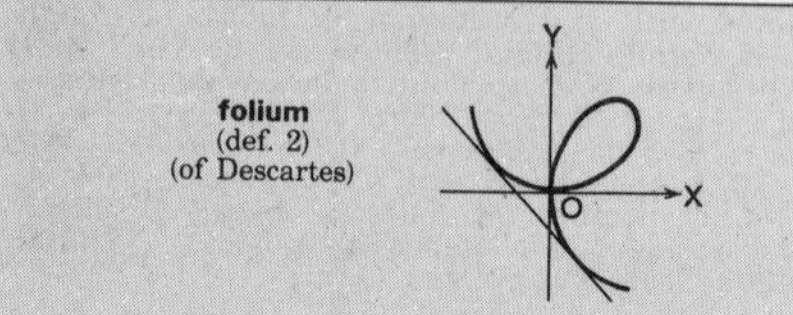

folium (def. 2) (of Descartes)

CONCISE ETYMOLOGY KEY: <, descended or borrowed from; >, whence; b., blend of, blended; c., cognate with; cf., compare; deriv., derivative; equiv., equivalent; imit., imitative; obl., oblique; r., replacing; s., stem; sp., spelling, spelled; resp., respelling, respelled; trans., translation; ?, origin unknown; *, unattested; ‡, probably earlier than. See the full key inside the front cover.

fo•li•vore (fō′lə vôr′, -vōr′), *n.* any chiefly leaf-eating animal or other organism, as the koala of Australia that subsists on eucalyptus. [1970–75; FOLI(UM) + -VORE] —**fo•liv•o•rous** (fō liv′ər əs), *adj.*

folk (fōk), *n.* **1.** Usually, **folks.** (*used with a plural v.*) people in general: *Folks say there wasn't much rain last summer.* **2.** Often, **folks.** (*used with a plural v.*) people of a specified class or group: *country folk; poor folks.* **3.** (*used with a plural v.*) people as the carriers of culture, esp. as representing the composite of social mores, customs, forms of behavior, etc., in a society: *The folk are the bearers of oral tradition.* **4. folks,** *Informal.* **a.** members of one's family; one's relatives: *All his folks come from France.* **b.** one's parents: *Will your folks let you go?* **5.** *Archaic.* a people or tribe. **6. just folks,** *Informal.* (of persons) simple, unaffected, unsophisticated, or open-hearted people: *He enjoyed visiting his grandparents because they were just folks.* —*adj.* **7.** of or originating among the common people: *folk beliefs; a folk hero.* **8.** having unknown origins and reflecting the traditional forms of a society: *folk culture; folk art.* [bef. 900; ME; OE *folc;* c. OS, ON *folk,* OHG *folk* (G *Volk*)] —**Syn. 4.** kinfolk, kin, relations, people; clan, tribe.

folk′ art′, artistic works, as paintings, sculpture, basketry, and utensils, produced typically in cultural isolation by untrained often anonymous artists or by artisans of varying degrees of skill and marked by such attributes as highly decorative design, bright bold colors, flattened perspective, strong forms in simple arrangements, and immediacy of meaning. [1920–25] —**folk′-art′,** *adj.* —**folk′ art′ist.**

folk′ dance′, **1.** a dance that originated among, and has been transmitted through, the common people. Cf. **court dance. 2.** a piece of music for such a dance. [1905–10] —**folk′ danc′er.** —**folk′ danc′ing.**

Folke•stone (fōk′stən), *n.* a seaport in E Kent, in SE England, on the Strait of Dover. 43,760.

Fol•ke•ting (fōl′kə ting′), *n.* **1.** the unicameral parliament of Denmark. **2.** *Hist.* the lower house of the Rigsdag. Also, **Fol•ke•thing** (fōl′kə ting′). [< Dan; see FOLK, THING[2]]

folk′ etymol′ogy, **1.** a modification of a linguistic form according either to a falsely assumed etymology, as *Welsh rarebit* from *Welsh rabbit,* or to a historically irrelevant analogy, as *bridegroom* from *bridegome.* **2.** a popular but false notion of the origin of a word. [1880–85]

folk•ie (fō′kē), *n., adj.,* **folk•i•er, folk•i•est.** *Informal.* —*n.* **1.** See **folk singer.** —*adj.* **2.** of or pertaining to folk singers or folk music. Also, **folky.** [1960–65; FOLK (SINGER) + -IE]

folk•ish (fō′kish), *adj.* **1.** of or resembling the common people: *folkish crafts.* **2.** resembling or based on folklore, folk music, or folk dances: *a violin concerto that is strongly folkish.* Also, **folk•like** (fōk′līk′). [1935–40; FOLK + -ISH[1]] —**folk′ish•ness,** *n.*

folk•life (fōk′līf′), *n.* the everyday life of the common people, esp. of a particular region, country, or period: *18th-century New England folklife.* [1920–25; FOLK + LIFE]

folk•lore (fōk′lôr′, -lōr′), *n.* **1.** the traditional beliefs, legends, customs, etc., of a people; lore of a people. **2.** the study of such lore. **3.** a body of widely held but false or unsubstantiated beliefs. [1846; FOLK + LORE; coined by English scholar and antiquary William John Thoms (1803–85)] —**folk′lor′ist,** *n.* —**folk′lor•is′tic,** *adj.*

folk•lor•ic (fōk′lôr′ik, -lōr′-), *adj.* based on or resembling folklore: *folkloric music.* [1880–85; FOLKLORE + -IC] —**folk•lor′i•cal•ly,** *adv.*

folk•lor•i•co (fōk lôr′i kō, -lōr′-), *n.* **1.** Mexican folk dancing, esp. a program or repertoire of such dances. —*adj.* **2.** containing, using, or performing folklorico: *a visiting folklorico dance troupe.* Also, **folk•lór′i•co.** [< Sp *folklórico* folkloristic, folk (adj.), equiv. to *folklor(e)* (< E) + *-ico* -IC]

folk′ mass′, a liturgical mass in which traditional music is replaced by folk music. [1960–65]

folk′ med′icine, health practices arising from superstition, cultural traditions, or empirical use of native remedies, esp. food substances. [1895–1900]

folk•moot (fōk′mo͞ot′), *n.* (formerly, in England) a general assembly of the people of a shire, town, etc. Also, **folk•mote, folk•mot** (fōk′mōt′). [bef. 1000; ME; OE *folcmōt* folk meeting. See FOLK, MOOT[1]]

folk′ mu′sic, **1.** music, usually of simple character and anonymous authorship, handed down among the common people by oral tradition. **2.** music by known composers that has become part of the folk tradition of a country or region. [1885–90]

folk•nik (fōk′nik), *n. Slang.* a devotee or performer of folk music. [1965–70, *Amer.;* FOLK (MUSIC) + -NIK]

folk•right (fōk′rīt′), *n.* a law or right of the people as opposed to that of the privileged classes. [bef. 1000; ME; OE *folcriht.* See FOLK, RIGHT]

folk′ rock′, a style of music combining characteristics of rock-'n'-roll and folk music, often exemplified by protest songs to a rock-'n'-roll beat, and at its height of popularity in the late 1960's. Also, **folk′-rock′.** [1965–70; FOLK + ROCK[2]] —**folk′-rock′er,** *n.*

folk-sing (fōk′sing′), *n.* an informal gathering for the singing of folk songs.

folk′ sing′er, a singer who specializes in folk songs, usually providing his or her own accompaniment on a guitar. [1895–1900]

folk′ sing′ing, the singing of folk songs, esp. by a group of people. [1905–10]

folk′ soci′ety, *Sociol.* an often small, homogeneous, and isolated community or society functioning chiefly through primary contacts and strongly attached to its traditional ways of living.

folk′ song′, **1.** a song originating among the people of a country or area, passed by oral tradition from one singer or generation to the next, often existing in several versions, and marked generally by simple, modal melody and stanzaic, narrative verse. **2.** a song of similar character written by a known composer. [1865–70]

folk•sy (fōk′sē), *adj.,* **-si•er, -si•est. 1.** friendly or neighborly; sociable. **2.** very informal; familiar; unceremonious: *The politician affected a folksy style.* **3.** belonging to the common people, esp. in regard to a conscious use of mannerisms, speech patterns, attitudes, etc.: *folksy humor.* [1850–55, *Amer.;* FOLKS + -Y[1], or FOLK + -SY] —**folk′si•ness,** *n.*

folk′ tale′, **1.** a tale or legend originating and traditional among a people or folk, esp. one forming part of the oral tradition of the common people. **2.** any belief or story passed on traditionally, esp. one considered to be false or based on superstition. Also, **folk′tale′.** Also called **folk′ sto′ry.** [1890–95]

folk•ways (fōk′wāz′), *n.pl. Sociol.* the ways of living, thinking, and acting in a human group, built up without conscious design but serving as compelling guides of conduct. [FOLK + WAYS; term introduced in a book of the same title (1907) by W. G. Sumner]

folk•y (fō′kē), *n., pl.* **folk•ies,** *adj.,* **folk•i•er, folk•i•est.** *Informal.* folkie. [1935–40; FOLK + -Y[2]]

foll., following.

fol•li•cle (fol′i kəl), *n.* **1.** *Anat.* **a.** a small cavity, sac, or gland. **b.** one of the small ovarian sacs containing an immature ovum; Graafian follicle. **2.** *Bot.* a dry seed vessel, or pod, consisting of a single carpel, splitting at maturity only along the front part of the suture. [1640–50; < L *folliculus* small bag, shell, pod. See FOLLIS, -CLE[1]]

follicle of milkweed

fol′licle mite′, any mite of the family Demodicidae, parasitic in hair follicles of various mammals, including humans. [1920–25]

fol′li•cle-stim•u•lat•ing hor′mone (fol′i kəl stim′yə lā′ting), *Biochem.* See **FSH** [1945–50]

fol•lic•u•lar (fə lik′yə lər), *adj.* **1.** pertaining to, consisting of, or resembling a follicle or follicles; provided with follicles. **2.** *Pathol.* affecting or originating in a follicle or follicles. Also, **fol•lic•u•late** (fə lik′yə lit, -lāt′), **fol•lic′u•lat′ed.** [1670–80; < L *follicul(us)* (see FOLLICLE) + -AR[1]]

follic′ular phase′, a stage of the menstrual cycle, from onset of menstruation to ovulation. Cf. **luteal phase.**

fol•lic•u•lin (fə lik′yə lin), *n. Biochem.* estrone. [1925–30; < L *follicul(us)* (see FOLLICLE) + -IN[2]]

fol•lic•u•li•tis (fə lik′yə lī′tis), *n. Pathol.* inflammation of hair follicles. [1855–60; < L *follicul(us)* (see FOLLICLE) + -ITIS]

fol•lis (fol′is), *n., pl.* **fol•les** (fol′ēz). **1.** a bag of copper or bronze coins with a fixed weight, used as money of account in the later Roman Empire. **2.** a silver-plated copper coin of ancient Rome, first issued by Diocletian. **3.** a copper coin of the Eastern Roman Empire, A.D. c500. [1880–85; < LL; cf. L *follis* bag, purse]

fol•low (fol′ō), *v.t.* **1.** to come after in sequence, order of time, etc.: *The speech follows the dinner.* **2.** to go or come after; move behind in the same direction: *Drive ahead, and I'll follow you.* **3.** to accept as a guide or leader; accept the authority of or give allegiance to: *Many Germans followed Hitler.* **4.** to conform to, comply with, or act in accordance with; obey: *to follow orders; to follow advice.* **5.** to imitate or copy; use as an exemplar: *They follow the latest fads.* **6.** to move forward along (a road, path, etc.): *Follow this road for a mile.* **7.** to come after as a result or consequence; result from: *Reprisals often follow victory.* **8.** to go after or along with (a person) as companion. **9.** to go in pursuit of: *to follow an enemy.* **10.** to try for or attain to: *to follow an ideal.* **11.** to engage in or be concerned with as a pursuit: *He followed the sea as his true calling.* **12.** to watch the movements, progress, or course of: *to follow a bird in flight.* **13.** to watch the development of or keep up with: *to follow the news.* **14.** to keep up with and understand (an argument, story, etc.): *Do you follow me?* —*v.i.* **15.** to come next after something else in sequence, order of time, etc. **16.** to happen or occur after something else; come next as an event: *After the defeat great disorder followed.* **17.** to attend or serve. **18.** to go or come after a person or thing in motion. **19.** to result as an effect; occur as a consequence: *It follows then that he must be innocent.* **20. follow out,** to carry to a conclusion; execute: *They followed out their orders to the letter.* **21. follow suit.** See **suit** (def. 13). **22. follow through, a.** to carry out fully, as a stroke of a club in golf, a racket in tennis, etc. **b.** to continue an effort, plan, proposal, policy, etc., to its completion. **23. follow up, a.** to pursue closely and tenaciously. **b.** to increase the effectiveness of by further action or repetition. **c.** to pursue to a solution or conclusion. —*n.* **24.** the act of following. **25.** *Billiards, Pool.* See **follow shot** (def. 2). **26.** follow-up (def. 3). [bef. 900; ME *folwen,* OE *folgian;* c. OS *folgon,* OHG *folgēn, folgōn* (G *folgen*)] —**fol′low•a•ble,** *adj.* —**Syn. 3.** obey. **4.** heed, observe. **8.** accompany, attend. **9.** pursue, chase; trail, track, trace. **19.** arise, proceed. FOLLOW, ENSUE, RESULT, SUCCEED imply coming after something else, in a natural sequence. FOLLOW is the general word: *We must wait to see what follows. A detailed account follows.* ENSUE implies a logical sequence, what might be expected normally to come after a given act, cause, etc.: *When the power lines were cut, a paralysis of transportation ensued.* RESULT emphasizes the connection between a cause or event and its effect, consequence, or outcome: *The accident resulted in injuries to those involved.* SUCCEED implies coming after in time, particularly coming into a title, office, etc.: *Formerly the oldest son succeeded to his father's title.* **—Ant. 1.** precede. **2, 3.** lead. **4.** disregard. **9.** flee.

fol·low·er (fol′ō ər), *n.* **1.** a person or thing that follows. **2.** a person who follows another in regard to his or her ideas or belief; disciple or adherent. **3.** a person who imitates, copies, or takes as a model or ideal: *He was little more than a follower of current modes.* **4.** an attendant, servant, or retainer. **5.** *Brit. Informal.* a boyfriend or suitor, esp. of a maidservant. **6.** *Mach.* a part receiving motion from or following the movements of another part, esp. a cam. **7.** *Engin., Building Trades.* a concrete form attached to the head of a timber pile to permit casting of a concrete cap or pier. [bef. 900; ME *folwer,* OE *folgere.* See FOLLOW, -ER[1]]
—Syn. 2. supporter. FOLLOWER, ADHERENT, PARTISAN refer to someone who demonstrates allegiance to a person, a doctrine, a cause, and the like. FOLLOWER often has an implication of personal relationship or of slavish acquiescence. ADHERENT, a more formal word, has implications of active championship of a person or a point of view. PARTISAN, ordinarily meaning a person prejudiced and unreasoning in adherence to a party, during World War II took on the meaning of a member of certain groups in occupied countries of Europe who carried on underground resistance to the Nazis. **—Ant. 2.** opponent, adversary, enemy, foe.

fol·low·er·ship (fol′ō ər ship′), *n.* **1.** the ability or willingness to follow a leader. **2.** a group of followers or supporters; following. [1925–30; FOLLOWER + -SHIP]

fol·low·ing (fol′ō ing), *n.* **1.** a body of followers, attendants, adherents, etc. **2.** the body of admirers, attendants, patrons, etc., of someone or something: *That television show has a large following.* **3. the following,** that which comes immediately after, as pages, lines, etc.: *See the following for a list of exceptions.* —*adj.* **4.** that follows or moves in the same direction: *a following wind.* **5.** that comes after or next in order or time; ensuing: *the following day.* **6.** that is now to follow; now to be mentioned, described, related, or the like: *Check the following report for details.* [1250–1300; ME *folwing.* See FOLLOW, -ING[1], -ING[2]]

fol·low-on (fol′ō on′, -ôn′), *adj.* following or evolving as the next logical step: *Aircraft manufacturers can expect follow-on sales for spare parts.* [1875–80; n. use of v. phrase *follow on (something)*]

fol′low shot′, 1. *Motion Pictures, Television.* a traveling shot made as the camera moves along with the subject: *a follow shot of the buffalo stampede, taken from a low-flying helicopter.* **2.** *Billiards, Pool.* a stroke that causes the cue ball to roll forward after striking the object ball. Cf. **draw shot.** [1905–10]

fol′low the lead′er, a child's game in which players, one behind the other, follow a leader and must repeat or follow everything he or she does. [1825–35]

fol·low-through (fol′ō thro͞o′, -thro͞o′), *n.* **1.** the completion of a motion, as in the stroke of a tennis racket. **2.** the portion of such a motion after the ball has been hit. **3.** the act of continuing a plan, project, scheme, or the like to its completion. [1895–1900; n. use of v. phrase *follow through*]

fol·low-up (fol′ō up′), *n.* **1.** the act of following up. **2.** an action or thing that serves to increase the effectiveness of a previous one, as a second or subsequent letter, phone call, or visit. **3.** Also called **follow.** *Journalism.* **a.** a news story providing additional information on a story or article previously published. **b.** Also called **sidebar, supplementary story.** a minor news story used to supplement a related story of major importance. Cf. **feature story** (def. 1), **human-interest story, shirttail.** —*adj.* **4.** designed or serving to follow up, esp. to increase the effectiveness of a previous action: *a follow-up interview; a follow-up offer.* **5.** of or pertaining to action that follows an initial treatment, course of study, etc.: *follow-up care for mental patients; a follow-up survey.* [1920–25; n., adj. use of v. phrase *follow up*]

fol·ly (fol′ē), *n., pl.* **-lies** for 2–6. **1.** the state or quality of being foolish; lack of understanding or sense. **2.** a foolish action, practice, idea, etc.; absurdity: *the folly of performing without a rehearsal.* **3.** a costly and foolish undertaking; unwise investment or expenditure. **4.** *Archit.* a whimsical or extravagant structure built to serve as a conversation piece, lend interest to a view, commemorate a person or event, etc.: found esp. in England in the 18th century. **5. follies,** a theatrical revue. **6.** *Obs.* wickedness; wantonness. [1175–1225; ME *folie* < OF, deriv. of *fol, fou* foolish, mad. See FOOL[1]]
—Syn. 2. imprudence, rashness, mistake, foolishness, indiscretion, injudiciousness; madness, lunacy.

Fol·som (fōl′səm), *n.* a town in central California. 11,003.

Fol·som (fōl′səm), *adj.* of, pertaining to, or characteristic of a prehistoric North American cultural tradition extensive in the Great Plains about 11,000 years ago and typified by the use of the Folsom point. [after *Folsom,* a village in NE New Mexico, near where remains typifying the culture were found in 1925]

Fol′som man′, 1. a Paleo-Indian of the Folsom tradition. **2.** a human skull found in Midland, Texas, that is believed to be contemporary with the Folsom tradition. [1930–35, *Amer.*]

Fol′som point′, a flint point characteristic of the Folsom tradition, typically leaf-shaped and fluted, with small basal extensions, and used on a projectile, as a spear, for hunting game. [1930–35]

Fo·mal·haut (fō′məl hôt′, -mə lō′), *n. Astron.* a star of the first magnitude and the brightest star in the constellation Piscis Austrinus. [1585–95; < SpAr *fam alḥawt* mouth of the fish; so called from its position in the constellation]

fo·ment (fō ment′), *v.t.* **1.** to instigate or foster (discord, rebellion, etc.); promote the growth or development of: *to foment trouble; to foment discontent.* **2.** to apply warm water or medicated liquid, ointments, etc., to (the surface of the body). [1350–1400; ME *fomenten* < LL *fōmentāre,* v. deriv. of L *fōmentum* soothing application, poultice, contr. of **fōvimentum,* equiv. to *fōv(ēre)* to keep warm + -i- -I- + *-mentum* -MENT] **—fo·ment′er,** *n.*
—Syn. 1. incite, provoke, arouse, inflame, excite, stir up; encourage, stimulate.

fo·men·ta·tion (fō′men tā′shən), *n.* **1.** encouragement of discord, rebellion, etc.; instigation. **2.** the application of warm liquid, ointments, etc., to the surface of the body. **3.** the liquid, ointments, etc., so applied. [1350–1400; ME < LL *fōmentātiōn-* (s. of *fōmentātiō*), equiv. to *fōmentāt(us)* (ptp. of *fōmentāre* to FOMENT) + *-iōn-* -ION]

fo·mes (fō′mēz), *n., pl.* **fom·i·tes** (fom′i tēz′, fō′mi-). Usually, **fomites.** *Med.* any agent, as clothing or bedding, that is capable of absorbing and transmitting the infecting organism of a disease. [1650–60; < L *fōmes* kindling wood, tinder, akin to *fovēre* to keep warm]

Fo·mor·i·an (fō môr′ē ən), *n. Irish Legend.* one of a race of pirates or sea demons who raided and pillaged Ireland but were finally defeated: sometimes associated with the hostile powers of nature. Also, **Fo·mor** (fō′môr).

Fon (fon), *n., pl.* **Fons,** (*esp. collectively*) **Fon** for 1. **1.** a member of a people living mainly in Benin. **2.** the Kwa language, very closely related to Ewe, spoken by the Fon people.

fond[1] (fond), *adj.,* **-er, -est. 1.** having a liking or affection for (usually fol. by *of*): *to be fond of animals.* **2.** loving; affectionate: *to give someone a fond look.* **3.** excessively tender or overindulgent; doting: *a fond parent.* **4.** cherished with strong or unreasoning feeling: *to nourish fond hopes of becoming president.* **5.** *Archaic.* foolish or silly. **6.** *Archaic.* foolishly credulous or trusting. [1300–50; ME *fond, fonned* (ptp. of *fonnen* to be foolish, orig., to lose flavor, sour)]
—Syn. 2. cherishing. **5.** infatuated. **6.** gullible.

fond[2] (fond; *Fr.* fôɴ), *n., pl.* **fonds** (fondz; *Fr.* fôɴ). **1.** a background or groundwork, esp. of lace. **2.** *Obs.* fund; stock. [1655–65; < F; see FUND]

fon·da (fôn′dä; *Eng.* fon′də), *n., pl.* **-das** (-däs; *Eng.* -dəz). *Spanish.* an inn or restaurant.

Fon·da (fon′də), *n.* **Henry,** 1905–82, U.S. actor.

fon·dant (fon′dənt; *Fr.* fôɴ däɴ′), *n.* **1.** a thick, creamy sugar paste, the basis of many candies. **2.** a candy made of this paste. [1875–80; < F: lit., melting, prp. of *fondre* to melt, FOUND[3]]

Fond du Lac (fon′ də lak′, jo͝o lak′), a city in E Wisconsin, on Lake Winnebago. 35,863.

fon·dle (fon′dl), *v.,* **-dled, -dling.** —*v.t.* **1.** to handle or touch lovingly, affectionately, or tenderly; caress: *to fondle a precious object; to fondle a child.* **2.** *Obs.* to treat with fond indulgence. —*v.i.* **3.** to show fondness, as by manner, words, or caresses. [1685–95; *fond* (v.) (deriv. of FOND[1]) + -LE] **—fon′dler,** *n.* **—fon′dling·ly,** *adv.*
—Syn. 1. cuddle, snuggle, pet, pat, stroke.

fond·ly (fond′lē), *adv.* **1.** in a fond manner; lovingly or affectionately: *He looked fondly at his child.* **2.** *Archaic.* with complacent credulity; foolishly. [1300–50; ME; see FOND[1], -LY]

fond·ness (fond′nis), *n.* **1.** the state or quality of being fond. **2.** tenderness or affection. **3.** doting affection. **4.** a liking or weakness for something: *He has a fondness for sweets.* **5.** *Archaic.* complacent credulity; foolishness. [1350–1400; ME; see FOND[1], -NESS]
—Syn. 4. predilection, partiality, preference.

fon·du (fon do͞o′, -dyo͞o′, fon′do͞o, -dyo͞o *for 1; Fr.* fôɴ dʏ′ *for 1, 2*), *adj., n., pl.* **-dus** (*Fr.* -dʏ′) for 2. —*adj.* **1.** fondue (def. 4). —*n.* **2.** *Ballet.* a slow bending of the supporting leg. [1840–50; < F, ptp. of *fondre* to melt, FOUND[3]]

fon·due (fon do͞o′, -dyo͞o′, fon′do͞o, -dyo͞o; *Fr.* fôɴ dʏ′), *n., pl.* **-dues** (-do͞oz′, -dyo͞oz′, -do͞oz, -dyo͞oz; *Fr.* -dʏ′), *adj. Cookery.* —*n.* **1.** a saucelike dish of Swiss origin made with melted cheese and seasonings together with dry white wine, usually flavored with kirsch: served as a hot dip for pieces of bread. **2.** a dish of hot liquid in which small pieces of food are cooked or dipped: *beef fondue; chocolate fondue.* **3.** a baked soufflélike dish usually containing cheese and cracker crumbs or bread crumbs. —*adj.* **4.** Also, **fondu.** melted. [1875–80; < F; fem. of *fondu* FONDU]

Fong (fông, fong), *n.* **Hiram L(e·ong)** (lē ông′, -ong′), born 1907, U.S. lawyer and senator from Hawaii 1959–77.

Fon·se·ca (fon sā′kə; *Sp.* fôn se′kä), *n.* **Gulf of,** a bay of the Pacific Ocean in W Central America, bordered by El Salvador on the W, Honduras on the NE, and Nicaragua on the S. ab. 700 sq. mi. (1800 sq. km).

fons et o·ri·go (fôns′ et ō rē′gō; *Eng.* fonz′ et ō rī′gō, ō rē′-), *Latin.* source and origin.

font[1] (font), *n.* **1.** a receptacle, usually of stone, as in a baptistery or church, containing the water used in baptism. **2.** a receptacle for holy water; stoup. **3.** a productive source: *The book is a font of useful tips for travelers.* **4.** the reservoir for oil in a lamp. **5.** *Archaic.* a fountain. [bef. 1000; ME; OE *font, fant* < L *font-* (s. of *fōns*) baptismal font, spring, fountain]

font[2] (font), *n. Print.* a complete assortment of type of one style and size. Also, *Brit.,* **fount.** [1570–80; < MF *fonte* < VL **funditus* a pouring, molding, casting, verbal n. from L *fundere* to pour. See FOUND[3]]

Fon·taine·bleau (fon′tin blō′; *Fr.* fôɴ ten blō′), *n.* a town in N France, SE of Paris: famous palace, long a favorite residence of French kings; extensive forest. 19,595.

Fon′tainebleau School′, a group of artists, many of them Italian and Flemish, who worked on the decorations of the palace of Fontainebleau in the 16th century.

font·al (fon′tl), *adj.* **1.** pertaining to or coming from a fountain or spring. **2.** pertaining to or being the source of something: *fontal concepts.* **3.** of or pertaining to a font, as of baptism. [1650–60; < ML *fontālis.* See FONT[1], -AL[1]]

Fon·tan·a (fon tan′ə; *for 1 also It.* fôn tä′nä), *n.* **1. Do·me·ni·co** (də men′i kō′; *It.* dô me′nē kô′), 1543–1607, Italian architect. **2.** a city in S California. 37,109.

fon·ta·nel (fon′tn el′), *n. Anat.* one of the spaces, covered by membrane, between the bones of the fetal or young skull. Also, **fon′ta·nelle′.** [1375–1425; late ME *fontinel* < MF *fontanele* little spring, dim. of *fontaine* FOUNTAIN]

fon·tange (fôɴ tänzh′), *n., pl.* **-tanges** (-tänzh′). Often, **fontanges.** commode (def. 4). [1680–90; < F, named after Marie Angélique de Scorraille de Roussilles, Duchess of *Fontanges* (1661–81), mistress of Louis XIV]

Fon·tanne (fon tan′), *n.* **Lynn,** 1887–1983, U.S. actress, born in England (wife of Alfred Lunt).

Fon·teyn (fon tān′), *n.* **Dame Mar·got** (mär′gō), (*Margaret Hookham*), 1919–91, English ballerina.

fon·ti·na (fon tē′nə), *n.* a type of Italian cheese, semisoft to firm, made of cow's or sheep's milk. [1935–40; < It < Upper It dial. (Val d'Aosta), of uncert. orig.]

font′ name′, a Christian name; baptismal name; first name. [1655–65]

Foo·chow (fo͞o′chou′; *Chin.* fo͞o′jō′), *n.* **1.** *Older Spelling.* Fuzhou. **2.** Also called **Northern Min.** a dialect of Chinese spoken in and around Foochow. Cf. **Min.**

food (fo͞od), *n.* **1.** any nourishing substance that is eaten, drunk, or otherwise taken into the body to sustain life, provide energy, promote growth, etc. **2.** more or less solid nourishment, as distinguished from liquids. **3.** a particular kind of solid nourishment: *a breakfast food; dog food.* **4.** whatever supplies nourishment to organisms: *plant food.* **5.** anything serving for consumption or use: *food for thought.* [bef. 1000; ME *fode,* OE *fōda;* cf. OE *fēdan,* Goth *fōdjan* to FEED; cf. FODDER[1], FOSTER] **—food′less,** *adj.* **—food′less·ness,** *n.*
—Syn. 1. nutriment, aliment, bread, sustenance, victuals; meat, viands; diet, menu. FOOD, FARE, PROVISIONS, RATION(S) all refer to nutriment. FOOD is the general word: *Breakfast foods have become very popular. Many animals prefer grass as food.* FARE refers to the whole range of foods that may nourish a person or animal: *an extensive bill of fare; The fare of some animals is limited in range.* PROVISIONS is applied to a store or stock of necessary things, esp. food, prepared beforehand: *provisions for a journey.* RATION implies an allotment or allowance of provisions: *a daily ration for each man of a company.* RATIONS often means food in general: *to be on short rations.*

food′ ad′ditive, additive (def. 4).

food·a·hol·ic (fo͞o′də hô′lik, -hol′ik), *n.* a person having an excessive, often uncontrollable craving for food. [1960–65; FOOD + -AHOLIC]

Food′ and Ag′riculture Organiza′tion, the agency of the United Nations that institutes and administers programs, esp. in underdeveloped countries, for improving farming methods and increasing food production. *Abbr.:* FAO

Food′ and Drug′ Administra′tion, *U.S. Govt.* a division of the Department of Health and Human Services that protects the public against impure and unsafe foods, drugs, and cosmetics. *Abbr.:* FDA

food′ bank′, an agency, group, or center that collects food and distributes it to the needy.

food′ chain′, *Ecol.* a series of organisms interrelated in their feeding habits, the smallest being fed upon by a larger one, which in turn feeds a still larger one, etc. [1925–30]

food′ fish′, any fish used for food by human beings. [1860–65]

food-gath·er·ing (fo͞od′gath′ər ing), *adj.* procuring food by hunting or fishing or the gathering of seeds, berries, or roots, rather than by the cultivation of plants or the domestication of animals; foraging. [1925–30]

food′ grain′, any cereal grain produced for human consumption. [1875–80]

food·ie (fo͞o′dē), *n. Slang.* a person keenly interested in food, esp. in eating or cooking. [FOOD + -IE, perh. in part extracted from JUNKIE]

food′ mill′, a hand-operated kitchen device for puréeing fruits and vegetables.

food′ of the gods′, asafetida.

food′ poi′soning, an acute gastrointestinal condition characterized by such symptoms as headache, fever, chills, abdominal and muscular pain, nausea, diarrhea, and prostration, caused by foods that are naturally toxic, as poisonous mushrooms, by vegetable foods that are chemically contaminated, as by insecticides, or by bacteria or their toxins, esp. of the genus *Salmonella.* [1885–90]

food′ proc′essor, an electric appliance with interchangeable blades within a closed container into which food is inserted for slicing, shredding, mincing, chopping, puréeing, or otherwise processing at high speeds. Also called **processor.** [1970–75] **—food′ proc′essing.**

food′ pyr′amid, *Ecol.* (of a food chain) successive

levels of predation in a food chain represented schematically as a pyramid because upper levels normally consist of decreasing numbers of larger predators. [1945–50]

food′ sci′ence, the study of the nature of foods and the changes that occur in them naturally and as a result of handling and processing. [1965–70]

food′ serv′ice, the preparation, delivery, serving, etc., of ready-to-eat foods: *The cafeteria employs over 20 people in food service.*

food′ stamp′, any of the coupons sold under a federal program to eligible needy persons at less than face value, redeemable for food at designated grocery stores or markets. Also called **food′ cou′pon.** [1935–40]

food•stuff (fo͞od′stuf′), *n.* a substance used or capable of being used as nutriment. [1870–75; FOOD + STUFF]

food′ vac′uole, *Cell Biol.* a membrane-enclosed cell vacuole with a digestive function, containing material taken up in by the process of phagocytosis. See diag. under **ameba.** [1885–90]

food′ ves′sel, *Archaeol.* an early Bronze Age grave vessel, 1600–1300 B.C., found in Ireland and northern Britain and intended for the use of the deceased in the afterlife. [1870–75]

food′ web′, *Ecol.* a series of organisms related by predator-prey and consumer-resource interactions; the entirety of interrelated food chains in an ecological community. Also called **food′ cy′cle.** [1960–65]

foo•fa•raw (fo͞o′fə rô′), *n.* **1.** a great fuss or disturbance about something very insignificant. **2.** an excessive amount of decoration or ornamentation, as on a piece of clothing, a building, etc. [1930–35; orig. uncert.]

fool[1] (fo͞ol), *n.* **1.** a silly or stupid person; a person who lacks judgment or sense. **2.** a professional jester, formerly kept by a person of royal or noble rank for amusement: *the court fool.* **3.** a person who has been tricked or deceived into appearing or acting silly or stupid: *to make a fool of someone.* **4.** an ardent enthusiast who cannot resist an opportunity to indulge an enthusiasm (usually prec. by a present participle): *He's just a dancing fool.* **5.** a weak-minded or idiotic person. **6. be nobody's fool,** to be wise or shrewd. —*v.t.* **7.** to trick, deceive, or impose on: *They tried to fool him.* —*v.i.* **8.** to act like a fool; joke; play. **9.** to jest; pretend; make believe: *I was only fooling.* **10. fool around, a.** to putter aimlessly; waste time: *She fooled around all through school.* **b.** to philander or flirt. **c.** to be sexually promiscuous, esp. to engage in adultery. **11. fool away,** to spend foolishly, as time or money; squander: *to fool away the entire afternoon.* **12. fool with,** to handle or play with idly or carelessly: *to be hurt while fooling with a loaded gun; to fool with someone's affections.* [1225–75; ME *fol, fool* < OF *fol* < L *follis* bellows, bag; cf. FOLLIS]
—**Syn. 1.** simpleton, dolt, dunce, blockhead, numskull, ignoramus, dunderhead, ninny, nincompoop, booby, saphead, sap. **2.** zany, clown. **5.** moron, imbecile, idiot. **7.** delude, hoodwink, cheat, gull, hoax, cozen, dupe, gudgeon. —**Ant. 1.** genius.

fool[2] (fo͞ol), *n. British Cookery.* a dish made of fruit, scalded or stewed, crushed and mixed with cream or the like: *gooseberry fool.* [1590–1600; prob. special use of FOOL[1]]

fool•er•y (fo͞o′lə rē), *n., pl.* **-er•ies. 1.** foolish action or conduct. **2.** a foolish action, performance, or thing. [1545–55; FOOL[1] + -ERY]

fool•fish (fo͞ol′fish′), *n., pl.* **-fish•es,** (*esp. collectively*) **-fish.** filefish (def. 1). [1835–45, *Amer.*; FOOL[1] + FISH]

fool•har•dy (fo͞ol′här′dē), *adj.,* **-di•er, -di•est.** recklessly or thoughtlessly bold; foolishly rash or venturesome. [1175–1225; ME *folhardy* < OF *fol hardi.* See FOOL[1], HARDY] —**fool′har′di•ly,** *adv.* —**fool′har′di•ness,** *n.*
—**Syn.** impetuous, headlong, heedless, incautious.

fool′ hen′, any of various grouse, as the spruce grouse, that can be killed easily because of their relative tameness. [1750–60]

fool•ish (fo͞o′lish), *adj.* **1.** resulting from or showing a lack of sense; ill-considered; unwise: *a foolish action, a foolish speech.* **2.** lacking forethought or caution. **3** trifling, insignificant, or paltry. [1250–1300; ME *folish, foolish.* See FOOL[1], -ISH[1]] —**fool′ish•ly,** *adv.* —**fool′ish•ness,** *n.*
—**Syn. 1, 2.** senseless, vacant, vapid, simple, witless. FOOLISH, FATUOUS, SILLY, INANE, STUPID, ASININE imply weakness of intellect and lack of judgment. FOOLISH implies lack of common sense or good judgment or, sometimes, weakness of mind: *a foolish decision; The child seems foolish.* FATUOUS implies being not only foolish, dull, and vacant in mind, but complacent and highly self-satisfied as well: *fatuous and self-important; fatuous answers.* SILLY denotes extreme and conspicuous foolishness; it may also refer to pointlessness of jokes, remarks, etc.: *silly and senseless behavior; a perfectly silly statement.* INANE applies to silliness that is notably lacking in content, sense, or point: *inane questions that leave one no reply.* STUPID implies natural slowness or dullness of intellect, or, sometimes, a benumbed or dazed state of mind; it is also used to mean foolish or silly: *well-meaning but stupid; rendered stupid by a blow; It is stupid to do such a thing.* ASININE originally meant like an ass; it applies to witlessly stupid conversation or conduct and suggests a lack of social grace or perception: *He failed to notice the reaction to his asinine remarks.* **1.** imprudent, unreasonable, foolhardy, irrational; thoughtless, nonsensical, ridiculous, absurd, pointless, preposterous.

fool•proof (fo͞ol′pro͞of′), *adj.* **1.** involving no risk or harm, even when tampered with. **2.** never-failing: *a foolproof method.* [1900–05, *Amer.*; FOOL[1] + -PROOF]

CONCISE ETYMOLOGY KEY: <, descended or borrowed from; >, whence; b., blend of, blended; c., cognate with; cf., compare; deriv., derivative; equiv., equivalent; imit., imitative; obl., oblique; r., replacing; s., stem; sp., spelling, spelled; resp., respelling, respelled; trans., translation; ?, origin unknown; *, unattested; ‡, probably earlier than. See the full key inside the front cover.

fools•cap (fo͞olz′kap′), *n.* **1.** a type of inexpensive writing paper, esp. legal-size, lined, yellow sheets, bound in tablet form. **2.** *Chiefly Brit.* a size of drawing or printing paper, 13½ × 17 in. (34 × 43 cm). *Abbr.*: cap., fcp. **3.** Also called **fools′cap octa′vo.** a size of book, about 4¼ × 6¾ in. (11 × 17 cm), untrimmed. **4.** Also called **fools′cap quar′to.** *Chiefly Brit.* a size of book, about 6¾ × 8½ in. (17 × 22 cm) untrimmed. **5.** See **fool's cap** (def. 1). [1690–1700; so called from the watermark of a fool's cap formerly used on such paper]

fool's′ cap′, 1. a traditional jester's cap or hood, often multicolored and usually having several drooping peaks from which bells are hung. **2.** See **dunce cap.** [1625–35]

fool's′ er′rand, a completely absurd, pointless, or useless errand.

fool's′ gold′, iron or copper pyrites, sometimes mistaken for gold. [1870–75, *Amer.*]

fool's′ par′adise, a state of enjoyment based on false beliefs or hopes; a state of illusory happiness. [1425–75; late ME]

fool's-pars•ley (fo͞olz′pärs′lē), *n.* an Old World fetid, poisonous plant, *Aethusa cynapium,* resembling parsley. [1745–55]

foot (fo͝ot), *n., pl.* **feet** for 1–4, 8–11, 16, 19, 21; **foots** for 20; *v.* —*n.* **1.** (in vertebrates) the terminal part of the leg, below the ankle joint, on which the body stands and moves. **2.** (in invertebrates) any part similar in position or function. **3.** such a part considered as the organ of locomotion. **4.** a unit of length, originally derived from the length of the human foot. It is divided into 12 inches and equal to 30.48 centimeters. *Abbr.*: ft., f. **5.** foot soldiers; infantry. **6.** walking or running motion; pace: *swift of foot.* **7.** quality or character of movement or motion; tread; step. **8.** any part or thing resembling a foot, as in function, placement, shape, etc. **9.** *Furniture.* **a.** a shaped or ornamented feature terminating a leg at its lower part. **b.** any of several short legs supporting a central shaft, as of a pedestal table. **10.** a rim, flange, or flaring part, often distinctively treated, serving as a base for a table furnishing or utensil, as a glass, teapot, or candlestick. **11.** the part of a stocking, sock, etc., covering the foot. **12.** the lowest part, or bottom, of anything, as of a hill, ladder, page, etc. **13.** a supporting part; base. **14.** the part of anything opposite the top or head: *He waited patiently at the foot of the checkout line.* **15.** the end of a bed, grave, etc., toward which the feet are placed: *Put the blanket at the foot of the bed, please.* **16.** *Print.* the part of the type body that forms the sides of the groove, at the base. See diag. under **type. 17.** the last, as of a series. **18.** that which is written at the bottom, as the total of an account. **19.** *Pros.* a group of syllables constituting a metrical unit of a verse. **20.** Usually, **foots. a.** sediment or dregs. **b.** footlights. **21.** *Naut.* the lower edge of a sail. **22. get off on the right** or **wrong foot,** to begin favorably or unfavorably: *He got off on the wrong foot with a tactless remark about his audience.* **23. get** or **have a** or **one's foot in the door,** to succeed in achieving an initial stage or step. **24. have one foot in the grave.** See **grave**[1] (def. 5). **25. on foot,** by walking or running, rather than by riding. **26. put one's best foot forward, a.** to attempt to make as good an impression as possible. **b.** to proceed with all possible haste; hurry. **27. put one's foot down,** to take a firm stand; be decisive or determined. **28. put one's foot in it** or **into it,** *Informal.* to make an embarrassing blunder. Also, **put one's foot in** or **into one's mouth. 29. set foot on** or **in,** to go on or into; enter: *Don't set foot in this office again!* **30. under foot,** in the way: *That cat is always under foot when I'm getting dinner.*
—*v.i.* **31.** to walk; go on foot (often fol. by *it*): *We'll have to foot it.* **32.** to move the feet rhythmically, as to music or in dance (often fol. by *it*). **33.** (of vessels) to move forward; sail: *to foot briskly across the open water.* —*v.t.* **34.** to walk or dance on: *footing the cobblestones of the old city.* **35.** to perform (a dance): *cavaliers footing a galliard.* **36.** to traverse on or as if on foot. **37.** to make or attach a foot to: *to foot a stocking.* **38.** to pay or settle: *I always end up footing the bill.* **39.** to add (a column of figures) and set the sum at the foot (often fol. by *up*). **40.** to seize with talons, as a hawk. **41.** to establish. **42.** *Archaic.* to kick, esp. to kick away. **43.** *Obs.* to set foot on. [bef. 900; ME; OE *fōt*; c. G *Fuss*; akin to L *pēs* (s. *ped-*), Gk *poús* (s. *pod-*)]

foot•age (fo͝ot′ij), *n.* **1.** length or extent in feet: *the footage of lumber.* **2.** *Mining.* **a.** payment by the running foot of work done. **b.** the amount so paid. **3.** a motion-picture scene or scenes: *newsreel footage; jungle footage.* [1890–95; FOOT + -AGE]

foot′-and-mouth′ disease′ (fo͝ot′n mouth′), *Vet. Pathol.* an acute, contagious, febrile disease of cattle, hogs, sheep, and other hoofed animals, caused by any of various rhinoviruses and characterized by vesicular eruptions in the mouth and about the hoofs, teats, and udder. Also called **hoof-and-mouth disease, aphthous fever, aftosa.** [1860–65]

foot•ball (fo͝ot′bôl′), *n.* **1.** a game in which two opposing teams of 11 players each defend goals at opposite ends of a field having goal posts at each end, with points being scored chiefly by carrying the ball across the opponent's goal line and by place-kicking or drop-kicking the ball over the crossbar between the opponent's goal posts. Cf. **conversion** (def. 13), **field goal** (def. 1), **safety** (def. 6), **touchdown. 2.** the ball used in this game, an inflated oval with a bladder contained in a casing usually made of leather. **3.** *Chiefly Brit.* Rugby (def. 3). **4.** *Chiefly Brit.* soccer. **5.** something sold at a reduced or special price. **6.** any person or thing treated roughly or tossed about: *They're making a political football of this issue.* **7.** (*cap.*) *U.S. Govt. Slang.* a briefcase containing the codes and options the president would use to launch a nuclear attack, carried by a military aide and kept available to the president at all times. —*v.t.* **8.** *Informal.* to offer for sale at a reduced or special price. [1350–1400; ME *fut ball.* See FOOT, BALL[1]]

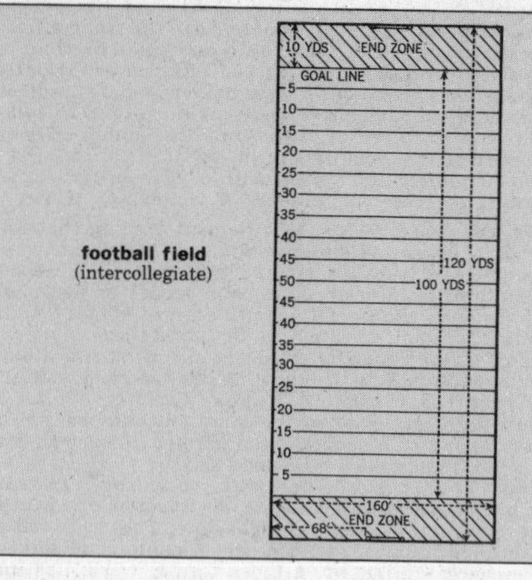

football field (intercollegiate)

foot•ball•er (fo͝ot′bô′lər), *n.* **1.** a football player, esp. a member of a college or professional team. **2.** *Chiefly Brit.* a soccer player. [1875–80; FOOTBALL + -ER[1]]

foot•bath (fo͝ot′bath′, -bäth′), *n., pl.* **-baths** (-bat͟hz′, -bät͟hz′, -baths′, -bäths′). **1.** a bath for soothing or cleaning the feet. **2.** a shallow receptacle containing chemically treated water for disinfecting the feet, as in a shower room or at the entrance to a swimming pool. [1590–1600; FOOT + BATH[1]]

foot•bind•ing (fo͝ot′bīn′ding), *n.* (formerly in China) the act or practice of tightly binding the feet of infant girls to keep the feet as small as possible.

foot•board (fo͝ot′bôrd′, -bōrd′), *n.* **1.** a board or small platform on which to support the foot or feet. **2.** an upright piece across the foot of a bedstead. **3.** a treadle. [1755–65, *Amer.*; FOOT + BOARD]

foot•boy (fo͝ot′boi′), *n.* a boy in livery employed as a servant; page. [1580–90; FOOT + BOY, modeled on *footman*]

foot′ brake′, a brake that is operated by pressure on a foot pedal, as in an automobile.

foot•bridge (fo͝ot′brij′), *n.* a bridge intended for pedestrians only. [1325–75; ME *fotbrigge.* See FOOT, BRIDGE[1]]

foot-can•dle (fo͝ot′kan′dl), *n. Optics.* a unit of illuminance or illumination, equivalent to the illumination produced by a source of one candle at a distance of one foot and equal to one lumen incident per square foot. *Abbr.*: FC Also, **foot′can′dle.** [1905–10]

foot•care (fo͝ot′kâr′), *adj.* of or pertaining to the care of one's feet: *a footcare specialist.* [FOOT + CARE]

foot•cloth (fo͝ot′klôth′, -kloth′), *n., pl.* **-cloths** (-klôt͟hz′, -klot͟hz′, -klôths′, -kloths′). **1.** a carpet or rug. **2.** a richly ornamented caparison for a horse, hanging to the ground. [1300–50; ME. See FOOT, CLOTH]

foot′ doc′tor, a podiatrist. [1865–70, *Amer.*]

foot-drag•ging (fo͝ot′drag′ing), *n.* reluctance or failure to proceed or act promptly. Also, **foot′drag′ging.** [1945–50; from the v. phrase *drag one's feet*]

foot′ drop′, *Pathol.* extension of the foot caused by paralysis of the flexor muscles of the leg. [1905–10]

Foote (fo͝ot), *n.* **1. Andrew Hull,** 1806–63, U.S. naval officer. **2. Arthur William,** 1853–1937, U.S. organist.

foot•ed (fo͝ot′id), *adj.* having a foot or feet (often used in combination): *a four-footed animal.* [1425–75; late ME; see FOOT, -ED[3]]

foot•er (fo͝ot′ər), *n.* **1.** *Brit. Informal.* **a.** Rugby (def. 3). **b.** soccer. **2.** *Archaic.* a person who walks; walker; pedestrian. **3.** *Computers.* a line of information placed at the end of a page for purposes of identification. [1600–10; FOOT + -ER[1]]

foot•fall (fo͝ot′fôl′), *n.* **1.** a footstep. **2.** the sound of footsteps: *She heard a footfall on the stairs.* [1600–10; FOOT + FALL]

foot′ fault′, *Tennis.* a fault consisting in the failure of the server to keep both feet behind the base line until the ball is hit or to keep at least one foot on the ground while hitting the ball. [1885–90]

foot•fault (fo͝ot′fôlt′), *v.i. Tennis.* to commit a foot fault. [v. use of FOOT FAULT]

foot•gear (fo͝ot′gēr′), *n.* covering for the feet, as shoes, boots, etc. [1830–40; FOOT + GEAR]

Foot′ Guards′, (in Britain) an infantry unit forming part of the ceremonial guard of the monarch. Cf. **Coldstream Guards, household troops.** [1665–75]

foot•hill (fo͝ot′hil′), *n.* a low hill at the base of a mountain or mountain range. [1840–50, *Amer.*; FOOT + HILL]

foot•hold (fo͝ot′hōld′), *n.* **1.** a place or support for the feet; a place where a person may stand or walk securely. **2.** a secure position, esp. a firm basis for further progress or development: *They gained a foothold in the New York market before beginning their national campaign.* [1615–25; FOOT + HOLD[1]]

foot•ie (fo͝ot′ē), *n. Informal.* footsie.

foot•ing (fo͝ot′ing), *n.* **1.** the basis or foundation on which anything is established. **2.** the act of one who moves on foot, as in walking or dancing. **3.** a secure and established position. **4.** a place or support for the feet; surface to stand on; foothold. **5.** a firm placing of the feet; stability: *He regained his footing.* **6.** *Building Trades, Civ. Engin.* the part of a foundation bearing directly upon the earth. **7.** position or status assigned to a person, group, etc., in estimation or treatment. **8.** mutual standing; reciprocal relation: *to be on a friendly footing with someone.* **9.** entrance into a new position or relationship: *to gain a footing in society.* **10.** a fee demanded from a person upon entrance into a trade, society, etc. **11.** the act of adding a foot to something, as to a stocking. **12.** that which is added as a foot. **13.** the act of adding up a column of figures. **14.** the total of such a column. [1350–1400; ME; see FOOT, -ING[1]]

foot′ing piece′, *Building Trades.* one of a series of horizontal transverse timbers supporting a platform or staging.

foot-in-mouth (fo͝ot′n mouth′), *adj.* (of a statement) inappropriate, insensitive, or imprudent. [1965–70; from idiomatic phrase *put one's foot in one's mouth*]

foot′-in-mouth′ disease′, *Informal (facetious).* the habit of making inappropriate, insensitive, or imprudent statements. [1965–70; pun on FOOT-AND-MOUTH DISEASE, with allusion to FOOT-IN-MOUTH]

foot-lam•bert (fo͝ot′lam′bərt), *n. Optics.* a unit of luminance or photometric brightness, equal to the luminance of a surface emitting a luminous flux of one lumen per square foot, the luminance of a perfectly reflecting surface receiving an illumination of one foot-candle. *Abbr.:* fL Also, **foot′lam′bert.** [1920–25]

foot•le (fo͝ot′l), *v.,* **-led, -ling,** *n. Informal.* —*v.i.* **1.** to act or talk in a foolish or silly way. —*n.* **2.** nonsense; foolishness; silliness. [1890–95; orig. uncert.; cf. FOOTY]

foot•less (fo͝ot′lis), *adj.* **1.** lacking a foot or feet. **2.** having no support or basis; unsubstantial: *footless dreams of glory.* **3.** awkward, helpless, or inefficient. [1350–1400; ME; see FOOT, -LESS]

foot•let (fo͝ot′lit), *n.* a low sock for women covering either the whole foot below the ankle or only the toes, worn for protection or warmth. [FOOT + -LET]

foot′ lev′el, a foot rule, hinged in the middle, having a spirit level in one section and a graduated arc from which the angle made by the two sections can be read. [1720–30]

foot•light (fo͝ot′līt′), *n.* **1.** Usually, **footlights.** *Theat.* the lights at the front of a stage that are nearly on a level with the feet of the performers. **2. the footlights,** the stage; acting profession. [1830–40; FOOT + LIGHT[1]]

foot′ line′, 1. *Print.* a line at the bottom of a page of type, esp. a black line or a line containing the folio. **2.** *Curling.* See **foot score.** [1670–80]

foot•ling (fo͝ot′ling), *adj. Informal.* **1.** foolish; silly: *ridiculous, footling remarks.* **2.** trifling or useless. [1895–1900; FOOTLE + -ING[2]]

foot•lock•er (fo͝ot′lok′ər), *n.* a small trunk designed to be kept at the foot of a bed, esp. to contain a soldier's personal effects. [1940–45, *Amer.*; FOOT + LOCKER]

foot•loose (fo͝ot′lo͞os′), *adj.* free to go or travel about; not confined by responsibilities. [1690–1700; FOOT + LOOSE]
—**Syn.** unencumbered, carefree, fancy-free, unattached.

foot•man (fo͝ot′mən), *n., pl.* **-men. 1.** a liveried servant who attends the door or carriage, waits on table, etc. **2.** a metal stand before a fire, to keep something hot. **3.** *Archaic.* an infantryman. [1250–1300; ME *fotman.* See FOOT, MAN[1]]

foot•mark (fo͝ot′märk′), *n.* a footprint. [1635–45; FOOT + MARK[1]]

foot′men's gal′lery, the rearmost section of seats in the balcony of an English theater, esp. in the late 17th and early 18th centuries.

foot•note (fo͝ot′nōt′), *n., v.,* **-not•ed, -not•ing.** —*n.* **1.** an explanatory or documenting note or comment at the bottom of a page, referring to a specific part of the text on the page. **2.** a minor or tangential comment or event added or subordinated to a main statement or more important event. —*v.t.* **3.** to add a footnote or footnotes to (a text, statement, etc.); annotate: *to footnote a dissertation.* [1835–45; FOOT + NOTE]

foot•pace (fo͝ot′pās′), *n.* **1.** walking pace. **2.** a raised portion of a floor; platform. **3.** a landing or resting place at the end of a short flight of steps. [1530–40; FOOT + PACE[1]]

foot•pad (fo͝ot′pad′), *n., v.,* **-pad•ded, -pad•ding.** —*n.* **1.** a highwayman or robber who goes on foot. —*v.i.* **2.** to proceed stealthily on foot. [1675–85; FOOT + PAD[2]]

foot•path (fo͝ot′path′, -päth′), *n., pl.* **-paths** (-paths′, -päths′, -paths′, -päths′). **1.** a path for people going on foot. **2.** *Brit.* footway (def. 2). [1520–30; FOOT + PATH]

foot•plate (fo͝ot′plāt′), *n.* **1.** *Carpentry.* a plate running beneath and supporting a row of studs; mudsill. **2.** a platform or special floor area on which workers stand to operate a machine. [1840–50; FOOT + PLATE[1]]

foot-pound (fo͝ot′pound′), *n. Physics.* a foot-pound-second unit of work or energy, equal to the work done by a force of one pound when its point of application moves through a distance of one foot in the direction of the force. *Abbr.:* ft-lb [1840–50]

foot-pound•al (fo͝ot′poun′dl), *n. Physics.* a foot-pound-second unit of work or energy equal to the work done by a force of one poundal when its point of application moves through a distance of one foot in the direction of the force. *Abbr.:* ft-pdl [1885–90]

foot-pound-sec•ond (fo͝ot′pound′sek′ənd), *adj. Physics.* of or pertaining to the system of units in which the foot, pound, and second are the principal units of length, mass, and time. *Abbr.:* fps, f.p.s. [1890–95]

foot•print (fo͝ot′print′), *n.* **1.** a mark left by the shod or unshod foot, as in earth or sand. **2.** an impression of the sole of a person's foot, esp. one taken for purposes of identification. **3.** *Informal.* the track of a tire, esp. on wet pavement. **4.** the area affected by an increase in the level of sound or noise, as that generated by an airplane. **5.** *Telecommunications.* the area of the earth's surface within which a communications satellite's signals can be received. **6.** *Aerospace.* the area within which it is predicted that a spacecraft or its debris will land. **7.** the surface space of a desk or tabletop occupied by a piece of equipment, esp. a microcomputer or related device. [1545–55; FOOT + PRINT]

foot•race (fo͝ot′rās′), *n.* a race run by contestants on foot. [1655–65; FOOT + RACE[1]]

foot′ rail′, *Furniture.* a stretcher connecting the legs of a piece of furniture, as a chair or table, upon which the feet may be rested. [1865–70]

foot′ reflexol′ogy, reflexology (def. 1).

foot•rest (fo͝ot′rest′), *n.* a support for a person's feet, as an attachment to a barber's chair or a dentist's chair. [1860–65; FOOT + REST[1]]

foot•rope (fo͝ot′rōp′), *n. Naut.* **1.** the portion of the boltrope to which the lower edge of a sail is sewn. **2.** a rope suspended a few feet beneath a yard, bowsprit, jib boom, or spanker boom to give a footing for a person handling sails. [1765–75; FOOT + ROPE]

foot′ rot′, 1. Also called **fouls, stinkyfoot.** *Vet. Pathol.* an infection of sheep, causing inflammatory changes in the area of the hoofs and lameness. **2.** *Plant Pathol.* a stem rot at ground level; crown rot. [1800–10; FOOT + ROT]

foot′ rule′, a ruler one foot (30.48 cm) in length. [1720–30]

foot′ score′, *Curling.* a line at each end of the rink that is at right angles to its length. Also called **foot line.**

foot•scrap•er (fo͝ot′skrā′pər), *n.* a metal bar, set in a small frame and attached to a doorstep, used in cleaning mud from the bottoms of the shoes before entering a house. [1870–75, *Amer.*; FOOT + SCRAPER]

foot•sie (fo͝ot′sē), *n. Informal.* **1.** Sometimes, **footsies.** the act of flirting or sharing a surreptitious intimacy. **2. play footsie** or **footsies with, a.** to flirt with, esp. by clandestinely touching someone's foot or leg; be slyly or furtively intimate with. **b.** to seek advantage from, esp. by discreet or stealthy means; curry favor with. Also, **footie.** [1930–35; FOOT + *-sie,* sp. var. of -SY]

foot•slog (fo͝ot′slog′), *v.i.,* **-slogged, -slog•ging.** to go on foot through or as if through mud. [1895–1900; FOOT + SLOG] —**foot′slog′ger,** *n.*

foot′ sol′dier, an infantryman. [1615–25]

foot•sore (fo͝ot′sôr′, -sōr′), *adj.* having sore or tender feet, as from much walking. [1710–20; FOOT + SORE] —**foot′sore′ness,** *n.*

foot•stalk (fo͝ot′stôk′), *n. Bot., Zool.* a pedicel; peduncle. [1555–65; FOOT + STALK[1]]

foot•stall (fo͝ot′stôl′), *n.* **1.** the stirrup of a woman's sidesaddle. **2.** *Archit.* a pedestal, plinth, or base, as of a statue, column, or pier. [1575–85; FOOT + STALL[1]]

foot•step (fo͝ot′step′), *n.* **1.** the setting down of a foot, or the sound so produced; footfall; tread. **2.** the distance covered by a step in walking; pace. **3.** a footprint. **4.** a step by which to ascend or descend. **5. follow in someone's footsteps,** to succeed or imitate another person. [1175–1225; ME *foote steppe.* See FOOT, STEP]

foot•stone (fo͝ot′stōn′), *n.* **1.** a stone placed at the foot of a grave. **2.** *Masonry.* a kneeler at the foot of a gable. [1875–80; FOOT + STONE. Cf. HEADSTONE]

foot•stool (fo͝ot′sto͞ol′), *n.* a low stool upon which to rest one's feet when seated. [1520–30; FOOT + STOOL]

foot-ton (fo͝ot′tun′), *n. Physics.* a foot-pound-second unit of work or energy, equivalent to 2240 foot-pounds and equal to the energy expended in raising a ton of 2240 pounds a distance of one foot against the force of gravity. [1865–70]

foot•wall (fo͝ot′wôl′), *n.* **1.** *Mining.* the top of the rock stratum underlying a vein or bed of ore. Cf. **hanging wall** (def. 1). **2.** *Geol.* a mass of rock lying beneath a fault plane. [1640–50; FOOT + WALL]

foot′ warm′er, any of various devices, as a small stove, for keeping one's feet warm. [1805–15]

foot•way (fo͝ot′wā′), *n.* **1.** a way or path for people going on foot. **2.** Also called **footpath.** *Brit.* a sidewalk. [1425–75; late ME *fotewey.* See FOOT, WAY]

foot•wear (fo͝ot′wâr′), *n.* articles to be worn on the feet, as shoes, slippers, or boots. [1880–85, *Amer.*; FOOT + WEAR]

foot•well (fo͝ot′wel′), *n.* a recessed compartment in front of the seats of a vehicle. [1970–75; FOOT + WELL[2]]

foot•work (fo͝ot′wûrk′), *n.* **1.** the use of the feet, as in tennis, boxing, or dancing. **2.** travel by foot from one place to another, as in gathering facts or fulfilling an assignment; legwork: *The project entailed a great deal of footwork.* **3.** the act or process of maneuvering, esp. in a skillful manner: *It took a bit of fancy footwork to avoid the issue.* [1560–70; FOOT + WORK]

foot•worn (fo͝ot′wôrn′, -wōrn′), *adj.* **1.** worn down by the feet: *a footworn pavement.* **2.** footsore. [1785–95; FOOT + WORN]

foo•ty (fo͞o′tē), *adj.,* **-ti•er, -ti•est.** *N. Brit. Dial.* poor; worthless; paltry. [1740–50; var. of *foughty* musty; cf. OE *fūht* moist, damp (c. G *feucht*); see -Y[1]]

foo•zle (fo͞o′zəl), *v.,* **-zled, -zling,** *n.* —*v.t., v.i.* **1.** to bungle; play clumsily: *to foozle a stroke in golf; to foozle on the last hole.* —*n.* **2.** act of foozling, esp. a bad stroke in golf. [1825–35; perh. < dial. G *fuseln* to work badly, clumsily, hurriedly]

fop (fop), *n.* a man who is excessively vain and concerned about his dress, appearance, and manners. [1400–50; late ME *foppe, fop;* akin to FOB[2]]
—**Syn.** dandy, coxcomb, popinjay, peacock, swell, dude.

fop•per•y (fop′ə rē), *n., pl.* **-per•ies. 1.** the clothes, manners, actions, etc., of a fop. **2.** something foppish. [1540–50; FOP + -ERY]

fop•pish (fop′ish), *adj.* resembling or befitting a fop; excessively refined and fastidious in taste and manner. [1595–1605; FOP + -ISH[1]] —**fop′pish•ly,** *adv.* —**fop′pish•ness,** *n.*

for (fôr; *unstressed* fər), *prep.* **1.** with the object or purpose of: *to run for exercise.* **2.** intended to belong to, or be used in connection with: *equipment for the army; a closet for dishes.* **3.** suiting the purposes or needs of: *medicine for the aged.* **4.** in order to obtain, gain, or acquire: *a suit for alimony; to work for wages.* **5.** (used to express a wish, as of something to be experienced or obtained): *O, for a cold drink!* **6.** sensitive or responsive to: *an eye for beauty.* **7.** desirous of: *a longing for something; a taste for fancy clothes.* **8.** in consideration or payment of; in return for: *three for a dollar; to be thanked for one's efforts.* **9.** appropriate or adapted to: *a subject for speculation; clothes for winter.* **10.** with regard or respect to: *pressed for time; too warm for April.* **11.** during the continuance of: *for a long time.* **12.** in favor of; on the side of: *to be for honest government.* **13.** in place of; instead of: *a substitute for butter.* **14.** in the interest of; on behalf of: *to act for a client.* **15.** in exchange for; as an offset to: *blow for blow; money for goods.* **16.** in punishment of: *payment for the crime.* **17.** in honor of: *to give a dinner for a person.* **18.** with the purpose of reaching: *to start for London.* **19.** contributive to: *for the advantage of everybody.* **20.** in order to save: *to flee for one's life.* **21.** in order to become: *to train recruits for soldiers.* **22.** in assignment or attribution to: *an appointment for the afternoon; That's for you to decide.* **23.** such as to allow of or to require: *too many for separate mention.* **24.** such as results in: *his reason for going.* **25.** as affecting the interests or circumstances of: *bad for one's health.* **26.** in proportion or with reference to: *He is tall for his age.* **27.** in the character of; as being: *to know a thing for a fact.* **28.** by reason of; because of: *to shout for joy; a city famed for its beauty.* **29.** in spite of: *He's a decent guy for all that.* **30.** to the extent or amount of: *to walk for a mile.* **31.** (used to introduce a subject in an infinitive phrase): *It's time for me to go.* **32. for it,** *Brit.* See **in** (def. 21). —*conj.* **33.** seeing that; since. **34.** because. [bef. 900; ME, OE; c. OS *for;* akin to FORE[1], L *per* through, Gk *pró* before, ahead]
—**Syn. 34.** See **because.**

for-, a prefix meaning "away," "off," "to the uttermost," "extremely," "wrongly," or imparting a negative or privative force, occurring in verbs and nouns formed from verbs of Old or Middle English origin, many of which are now obsolete or archaic: *forbid; forbear; forswear; forbearance.* [ME, OE; cf. G *ver-,* Gk *peri-,* L *per-*]

For., Forester.

for., 1. foreign. **2.** forester. **3.** forestry.

F.O.R., free on rails. Also, **f.o.r.**

fo•ra (fôr′ə, fōr′ə), *n.* a pl. of **forum.**

for•age (fôr′ij, for′-), *n., v.,* **-aged, -ag•ing.** —*n.* **1.** food for horses or cattle; fodder; provender. **2.** the seeking or obtaining of such food. **3.** the act of searching for provisions of any kind. **4.** a raid. —*v.i.* **5.** to wander or go in search of provisions. **6.** to search about; seek; rummage; hunt: *He went foraging in the attic for old mementos.* **7.** to make a raid. —*v.t.* **8.** to collect forage from; strip of supplies; plunder: *to forage the countryside.* **9.** to supply with forage. **10.** to obtain by foraging. [1275–1325; ME < OF *fourrage,* deriv. of *fuerre* FODDER (< Gmc)] —**for′ag•er,** *n.*
—**Syn. 1.** See **feed.**

for′age cap′, *Mil.* (formerly) a small, low, undress cap. [1820–30]

for•ag•ing (fôr′i jing, for′-), *n.* **1.** the acquisition of food by hunting, fishing, or the gathering of plant matter. —*adj.* **2.** characterized by or dependent upon the acquisition of food by such means; food-gathering: *a foraging people.*

for′aging ant′, any of several ants, as army ants, that forage as part of a large group.

For•a•ker (fôr′ə kər, for′-), *n.* **Mount,** a mountain in central Alaska, in the Alaska Range, near Mt. McKinley. 17,280 ft. (5267 m).

for•am (fôr′əm), *n.* foraminifer. [by shortening]

fo•ra•men (fə rā′mən), *n., pl.* **-ram•i•na** (-ram′ə nə). an opening, orifice, or short passage, as in a bone or in the integument of the ovule of a plant. [1665–75; < L *forāmen* hole, opening, equiv. to *forā(re)* to BORE, pierce + *-men* resultative n. suffix] —**fo•ram•i•nal** (fə ram′ə nl), *adj.*

fora′men mag′num (mag′nəm), *Anat.* the large opening in the base of the skull forming the passage from the cranial cavity to the spinal canal. [1880–85; < NL: lit., great hole]

fo•ram•i•nate (fə ram′ə nit), *adj.* full of holes or foramina. Also, **fo•ram′i•nous.** [1590–1600; < LL *forāminātus* bored, pierced, equiv. to *forāmin-* (s. of *forāmen*) FORAMEN + *-ātus* -ATE[1]] —**fo•ram′i•na′tion,** *n.*

for•a•min•i•fer (fôr′ə min′ə fər, for′-), *n., pl.* **for•a•min•i•fers, fo•ram•i•nif•er•a** (fə ram′ə nif′ər ə). any chiefly marine protozoan of the sarcodinian order Foraminifera, typically having a linear, spiral, or concentric shell perforated by small holes or pores through which pseudopodia extend. Also called **fo•ram•i•nif•er•an** (fə ram′ə nif′ər ən), **foram.** [1835–45; < NL *Foraminifera,* equiv. to L *forāmin-,* s. of *forāmen* FORAMEN + *-ifera;* see -I-, -FER] —**fo•ram′i•nif′er•al, fo•ram′i•nif′er•ous,** *adj.*

for•as•much as (fôr′əz much′ az′, əz, fər-), *Chiefly Law.* in view of the fact that; seeing that; since. [1250–1300; ME; see FOR, AS[1], MUCH]

for•ay (fôr′ā, for′ā), *n.* **1.** a quick raid, usually for the purpose of taking plunder: *Vikings made a foray on the port.* **2.** a quick, sudden attack: *The defenders made a foray outside the walls.* **3.** an initial venture: *a successful foray into politics.* —*v.i.* **4.** to make a raid; pillage; maraud. **5.** to invade or make one's way, as for profit or adventure: *foreign industries foraying into U.S. markets.* —*v.t.* **6.** to ravage in search of plunder; pillage. [1350–1400; ME *forraien,* appar. by back formation from *forrayour, forreour, forrier* < OF *forrier, fourrier,* equiv. to

CONCISE PRONUNCIATION KEY: act, cāpe, dâre, pärt; set, ēqual; if, īce; ox, ōver, ôrder, oil, bo͝ok, bo͞ot, out; up, ûrge; child; sing; shoe; thin, *th*at; zh as in *treasure.* ə = *a* as in *alone, e* as in *system, i* as in *easily, o* as in *gallop, u* as in *circus;* ′ as in *fire* (fī′r), *hour* (ou′r). l and n can serve as syllabic consonants, as in *cradle* (krād′l), and *button* (but′n). See the full key inside the front cover.

fo(u)rr(er), deriv. of *fuerre* provender (see FORAGE) + *-ier* -IER²] **—for′ay·er,** *n.*
—Syn. 1. attack, assault, invasion, incursion, sortie.

forb (fôrb), *n.* any herb that is not a grass or grasslike. [1920–25; < Gk *phorbḗ* food, fodder, deriv. of *phérbein* to feed; akin to OE *beorgan, birgan* to taste, eat, ON *bergja* to taste]

for·bade (fər bad′, -bād′, fôr-), *v.* a pt. of **forbid.** Also, **for·bad** (fər bad′, fôr-), **forbid.**

for·bear¹ (fôr bâr′), *v.,* **-bore, -borne, -bear·ing.** *—v.t.* **1.** to refrain or abstain from; desist from. **2.** to keep back; withhold. **3.** *Obs.* to endure. *—v.i.* **4.** to refrain; hold back. **5.** to be patient or self-controlled when subject to annoyance or provocation. [bef. 900; ME *forberen,* OE *forberan.* See FOR-, BEAR¹] **—for·bear′er,** *n.* **—for·bear′ing·ly,** *adv.*
—Syn. 1. forgo, sacrifice, renounce.

for·bear² (fôr′bâr′), *n.* forebear.

for·bear·ance (fôr bâr′əns), *n.* **1.** the act of forbearing; a refraining from something. **2.** forbearing conduct or quality; patient endurance; self-control. **3.** an abstaining from the enforcement of a right. **4.** a creditor's giving of indulgence after the day originally fixed for payment. [1570–80; FORBEAR¹ + -ANCE]
—Syn. 1. abstinence. **2.** tolerance, toleration, sufferance; indulgence.

Forbes (fôrbz), *n.* **1. Esther,** 1894?–1967, U.S. novelist. **2. George William,** 1869–1947, New Zealand statesman: prime minister 1930–35.

Forbes-Rob·ert·son (fôrbz′rob′ərt sən), *n.* **Sir Johnston,** 1853–1937, English actor and theatrical manager.

for·bid (fər bid′, fôr-), *v.t.,* **-bade** or **-bad** or **-bid, -bid·den** or **-bid, -bid·ding. 1.** to command (a person) not to do something, have something, etc., or not to enter some place: *to forbid him entry to the house.* **2.** to prohibit (something); make a rule or law against: *to forbid the use of lipstick; to forbid smoking.* **3.** to hinder or prevent; make impossible. **4.** to exclude; bar: *Burlesque is forbidden in many cities.* [bef. 1000; ME *forbeden,* OE *forbēodan.* See FOR-, BID¹] **—for·bid′der,** *n.*
—Syn. 1, 2. interdict. FORBID, INHIBIT, PROHIBIT, TABOO indicate a command to refrain from some action. FORBID, a common and familiar word, usually denotes a direct or personal command of this sort: *I forbid you to go. It was useless to forbid children to play in the park.* INHIBIT implies a checking or hindering of impulses by the mind, sometimes involuntarily: *to inhibit one's desires; His responsiveness was inhibited by extreme shyness.* PROHIBIT, a formal or legal word, means usually to forbid by official edict, enactment, or the like: *to prohibit the sale of liquor.* TABOO, primarily associated with primitive superstition, means to prohibit by common disapproval and by social custom: *to taboo a subject in polite conversation.* **3.** preclude, stop, obviate, deter.

for·bid·dance (fər bid′ns, fôr-), *n.* **1.** the act of forbidding. **2.** the state of being forbidden. [1600–10; FORBID + -ANCE]

for·bid·den (fər bid′n, fôr-), *v.* **1.** a pp. of **forbid.** *—adj.* **2.** not allowed; prohibited: *a forbidden food in his religion.* **3.** *Physics.* involving a change in quantum numbers that is not permitted by the selection rules: *forbidden transition.* **—for·bid′den·ly,** *adv.* **—for·bid′·den·ness,** *n.*

Forbid′den Cit′y, a walled section of Peking, built in the 15th century, containing the imperial palace and other buildings of the imperial government of China.

forbid′den fruit′, 1. the fruit of the tree of knowledge of good and evil, tasted by Adam and Eve against God's prohibition. Gen. 2:17; 3:3. **2.** any unlawful pleasure, esp. illicit sexual indulgence. **3.** pomelo (def. 1).

for·bid·ding (fər bid′ing, fôr-), *adj.* **1.** grim; unfriendly; hostile; sinister: *his forbidding countenance.* **2.** dangerous; threatening: *forbidding clouds; forbidding cliffs.* [1710–15; FORBID + -ING²] **—for·bid′ding·ly,** *adv.* **—for·bid′ding·ness,** *n.*

for·bore (fôr bôr′, -bōr′), *v.* pt. of **forbear¹.**

for·borne (fôr bôrn′, -bōrn′), *v.* pp. of **forbear¹.**

For′bush de′crease (fôr′bo͝osh), *Astron.* the sudden decrease in the intensity of cosmic rays after an increase in solar activity. Also called **For′bush effect′.** [after Scott E. Forbush (b. 1904), U.S. physicist]

for·by (fôr bī′), *prep., adv. Chiefly Scot.* **1.** close by; near. **2.** besides. Also, **for·bye′.** [1200–50; ME; see FOR-, BY]

force (fôrs, fōrs), *n., v.,* **forced, forc·ing.** *—n.* **1.** physical power or strength possessed by a living being: *He used all his force in opening the window.* **2.** strength or power exerted upon an object; physical coercion; violence: *to use force to open the window; to use force on a person.* **3.** strength; energy; power; intensity: *a personality of great force.* **4.** power to influence, affect, or control; efficacious power: *the force of circumstances; a force for law and order.* **5.** *Law.* unlawful violence threatened or committed against persons or property. **6.** persuasive power; power to convince: *They felt the force of his arguments.* **7.** mental or moral strength: *force of character.* **8.** might, as of a ruler or realm; strength for war. **9.** Often, **forces.** the military or fighting strength, esp. of a nation. **10.** any body of persons combined for joint action: *a sales force.* **11.** intensity or strength of effect: *the force of her acting.* **12.** *Physics.* **a.** an influence on a body or system, producing or tending to produce a change in movement or in shape or other effects. **b.** the intensity of such an influence. *Symbol:* F, f **13.** any influence or agency analogous to physical force: *social forces.* **14.** binding power, as of a contract. **15.** *Baseball.* See **force play. 16.** value; significance; meaning. **17.** *Billiards.* a stroke in which the cue ball is forcibly struck directly below the center in such a manner as to cause it to stop abruptly, bound back, or roll off to one side after hitting the object ball. **18. in force, a.** in operation; effective: *This ancient rule is no longer in force.* **b.** in large numbers; at full strength: *They attacked in force.*
—v.t. **19.** to compel, constrain, or oblige (oneself or someone) to do something: *to force a suspect to confess.* **20.** to drive or propel against resistance: *He forced his way through the crowd. They forced air into his lungs.* **21.** to bring about or effect by force. **22.** to bring about of necessity or as a necessary result: *to force a smile.* **23.** to put or impose (something or someone) forcibly on or upon a person: *to force one's opinions on others.* **24.** to compel by force; overcome the resistance of: *to force acceptance of something.* **25.** to obtain or draw forth by or as if by force; extort: *to force a confession.* **26.** to enter or take by force; overpower: *They forced the town after a long siege.* **27.** to break open (a door, lock, etc.). **28.** to cause (plants, fruits, etc.) to grow or mature at an increased rate by artificial means. **29.** to press, urge, or exert (an animal, person, etc.) to violent effort or to the utmost. **30.** to use force upon. **31.** to rape. **32.** *Baseball.* **a.** to cause (a base runner) to be put out by obliging the runner, as by a ground ball, to vacate a base and attempt to move to the next base in order to make room for another runner or the batter. **b.** to cause (a base runner or run) to score, as by walking a batter with the bases full (often fol. by *in*). **33.** *Cards.* **a.** to compel (a player) to trump by leading a suit of which the player has no cards. **b.** to compel a player to play (a particular card). **c.** to compel (a player) to play so as to make known the strength of the hand. **34.** *Photog.* **a.** to develop (a print or negative) for longer than usual in order to increase density or bring out details. **b.** to bring out underexposed parts of (a print or negative) by adding alkali to the developer. **35.** *Archaic.* to give force to; strengthen; reinforce.
—v.i. **36.** to make one's way by force. [1250–1300; (n.) ME < MF < VL **fortia,* deriv. of L *fortis* strong; (v.) ME *forcen* < AF, OF *forcer,* deriv. of the n.] **—force′a·ble,** *adj.* **—force′less,** *adj.* **—forc′er,** *n.* **—forc′ing·ly,** *adv.*
—Syn. 3. vigor. See **strength. 4.** compulsion, constraint. **6.** efficacy, effectiveness, cogency, potency, validity. **19.** coerce. **20.** impel. **26.** overcome; violate, ravish, rape. **—Ant. 3.** weakness. **6.** impotence.

force′ cup′, plunger (def. 3). [1905–10]

forced (fôrst, fōrst), *adj.* **1.** enforced or compulsory: *forced labor.* **2.** strained, unnatural, or affected: *a forced smile.* **3.** subjected to force. **4.** required by circumstances; emergency: *a forced landing of an airplane.* [1540–50; FORCE + -ED²] **—forc·ed·ly** (fôr′sid lē, fōr′-), *adv.* **—forc′ed·ness,** *n.*

forced′ cod′ing, *Computers.* See **minimum-access programming.**

forced-draft (fôrst′draft′, -dräft′, fōrst′-), *adj.* **1.** using a flow of air or air forced through a pipe or system of pipes by fans or blowers: *a forced-draft central heating system.* **2.** proceeding at full speed or intensity: *forced-draft production of the medicine.* [1860–65]

forced′ march′, *Mil.* any march that is longer than troops are accustomed to and maintained at a faster pace than usual, generally undertaken for a particular objective under emergency conditions. [1760–70]

force-draft (fôrs′draft′, -dräft′, fōrs′-), *v.t.* **1.** to draft (a law, proposal, or the like) quickly or under extreme pressure: *The committee must force-draft a code of ethics to present to the meeting tomorrow.* **2.** to cause to proceed at full speed or intensity.

forced′ sale′, *Law.* a sale held as a result of a judicial order. [1840–50, *Amer.*]

force′ feed′, lubrication under pressure, as from a pump, used esp. in internal-combustion engines. [1915–20]

force-feed (fôrs′fēd′, fōrs′-), *v.t.,* **-fed, -feed·ing. 1.** to compel to take food, esp. by means of a tube inserted into the throat: *They force-fed the prisoners in the hunger strike.* **2.** to compel to absorb or assimilate: *The recruits were force-fed a military attitude.* [1905–10]

force′ fit′, *Mach.* See **press fit.**

force·ful (fôrs′fəl, fōrs′-), *adj.* **1.** full of force; powerful; vigorous; effective: *a forceful plea for peace.* **2.** acting or driven with force. [1565–75; FORCE + -FUL] **—force′ful·ly,** *adv.* **—force′ful·ness,** *n.*
—Syn. 1. cogent, telling.

force ma·jeure (*Fr.* fôrs ma zhœr′), *pl.* **forces ma·jeures** (*Fr.* fôrs ma zhœr′). *Law.* an unexpected and disruptive event that may operate to excuse a party from a contract. [1880–85; < F: lit., superior force]

force·meat (fôrs′mēt′, fōrs′-), *n. Cookery.* a mixture of finely chopped and seasoned foods, usually containing egg white, meat or fish, etc., used as a stuffing or served alone. Also, **farcemeat.** [1680–90; *force,* var. of obs. *farce* stuffing + MEAT]

force′ of hab′it, behavior occurring without thought and by virtue of constant repetition; habit. [1920–25]

force-out (fôrs′out′, fōrs′-), *n. Baseball.* a put-out of a base runner on a force play. [1895–1900, *Amer.*; n. use of v. phrase *force out*]

force′ play′, *Baseball.* a situation in which a base runner is forced to advance to a base or to home plate as a result of the batter becoming a base runner or to make room for another base runner. [1895–1900, *Amer.*]

for·ceps (fôr′səps, -seps), *n., pl.* **-ceps, -ci·pes** (-sə pēz′). **1.** an instrument, as pincers or tongs, for seizing and holding objects, as in surgical operations. **2.** *Anat., Zool.* a part or feature resembling a forceps, esp. a pair of appendages at the posterior of certain insects. [1625–35; < L: pair of tongs, pincers, said to be a contr. of **formiceps,* equiv. to *form(us)* warm + *-i-* -I- + *-ceps* -taker, deriv. of *capere* to take (cf. PRINCE), i.e., that which takes hot things; cf., however, *forpex, forfex* tongs, shears, from which *forceps* may have been formed by folk etym.] **—for′ceps·like′,** *adj.* **—for·cip·i·al** (fôr sip′ē əl), *adj.*

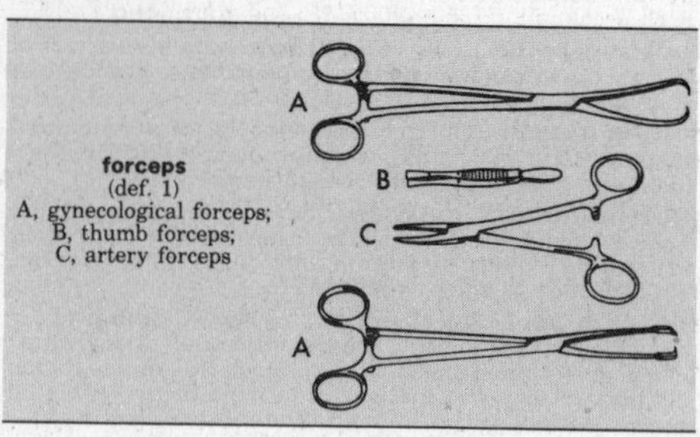

forceps
(def. 1)
A, gynecological forceps;
B, thumb forceps;
C, artery forceps

force′ pump′, a pump that delivers a liquid under pressure, so as to eject it forcibly. Cf. **lift pump.** [1650–60]

forc·er¹ (fôr′sər, fōr′-), *n.* a person or thing that forces. [1550–60; FORCE + -ER¹]

forc·er² (fôr′sər, fōr′-), *n. Archaic.* a coffer or chest. [1300–50; ME < OF]

for·ci·ble (fôr′sə bəl, fōr′-), *adj.* **1.** done or effected by force: *forcible entry into a house.* **2.** producing a powerful effect; having force; effective. **3.** convincing, as reasoning: *a forcible theory.* **4.** characterized by the use of force or violence. [1350–1400; ME < MF; see FORCE, -IBLE] **—for′ci·ble·ness, for′ci·bil′i·ty,** *n.* **—for′ci·bly,** *adv.*

for·ci·pate (fôr′sə pāt′, fōr′-), *adj.* having the shape of or resembling a forceps. [1660–70; < L *forcip-* (s. of *forceps*) FORCEPS + -ATE¹]

ford (fôrd, fōrd), *n.* **1.** a place where a river or other body of water is shallow enough to be crossed by wading. *—v.t.* **2.** to cross (a river, stream, etc.) at a ford. [bef. 900; ME (n.), OE; c. OFris *forda,* G *Furt;* akin to ON *fjǫrthr,* FARE, PORT¹] **—ford′a·ble,** *adj.*

Ford (fôrd, fōrd), *n.* **1. Ford Mad·ox** (mad′əks), (*Ford Madox Hueffer*), 1873–1939, English novelist, poet, critic, and editor. **2. Gerald R(udolph, Jr.)** (*Leslie Lynch King, Jr.*), born 1913, U.S. political leader: congressman 1948–73; vice president 1973–74; 38th president of the U.S. 1974–77. **3. Guy Stanton,** 1873–1963, U.S. historian, educator, and editor. **4. Henry,** 1863–1947, U.S. automobile manufacturer. **5. John,** 1586?–c1640, English playwright. **6. John** (*Sean O'Feeney*), 1895–1973, U.S. film director. **7.** a male given name.

ford·less (fôrd′lis, fōrd′-), *adj.* **1.** having no ford. **2.** that cannot be crossed on foot: *a fordless stream.* [1640–50; FORD + -LESS]

for·do (fôr do͞o′), *v.t.,* **-did, -done, -do·ing.** *Archaic.* **1.** to do away with; kill; destroy. **2.** to ruin; undo. Also, **foredo.** [bef. 900; ME *fordon,* OE *fordōn* (see FORE-, DO¹); c. D *verdoen,* OHG *fartuon*]

for·done (fôr dun′), *adj. Archaic.* exhausted with fatigue. Also, **foredone.** [1580–90; ptp. of FORDO]

fore¹ (fôr, fōr), *adj.* **1.** situated at or toward the front, as compared with something else. **2.** first in place, time, order, rank, etc.; forward; earlier. **3.** *Naut.* **a.** of or pertaining to a foremast. **b.** noting a sail, yard, boom, etc., or any rigging belonging to a fore lower mast or to some upper mast of a foremast. **c.** noting any stay running aft and upward to the head of a fore lower mast or to some specified upper mast of a foremast: *fore topmast stay.* **d.** situated at or toward the bow of a vessel; forward. *—adv.* **4.** *Naut.* at or toward the bow. **5.** forward. **6.** *Obs.* before. **7. fore and aft,** *Naut.* in, at, or to both ends of a ship. *—n.* **8.** the forepart of anything; front. **9. the fore,** *Naut.* the foremast. **10. to the fore, a.** into a conspicuous place or position; to or at the front. **b.** at hand; ready; available. **c.** still alive. *—prep., conj.* **11.** Also, **'fore.** *Informal.* before. [by construal of FORE- as an adj., hence nominalized; *fore and aft* perh. as trans. of D or LG; sense "before" (defs. 6, 11) perh. continuation of ME, OE *fore* in this sense, or as aph. form of AFORE]

fore² (fôr, fōr), *interj. Golf.* (used as a cry of warning to persons on a course who are in danger of being struck by the ball.) [1875–80; prob. aph. var. of BEFORE]

fore-, a prefix meaning "before" (in space, time, condition, etc.), "front," "superior," etc.: *forehead; forecastle; forecast; foretell; foreman.* [comb. form repr. ME, OE *for(e)*]

fore-and-aft (fôr′ənd aft′, -äft′, fōr′-), *Naut.* *—adj.* **1.** located along or parallel to a line from the stem to the stern. *—adv.* **2.** fore¹ (def. 7). [1610–20]

fore-and-af·ter (fôr′ənd af′tər, äf′-, fōr′-), *n.* **1.** *Naut.* **a.** a sailing vessel with a fore-and-aft rig. **b.** a beam running fore and aft across a hatchway to support hatch covers laid athwart the hatchway. **c.** a vessel having a sharp stern; a double ender. **2.** deerstalker (def. 2). [1815–25; FORE-AND-AFT + -ER¹]

fore′-and-aft′ rig′, *Naut.* a rig in which the principal sails are fore-and-aft. [1825–35] **—fore′-and-aft′-rigged′,** *adj.*

fore′-and-aft′ sail′, any of various sails, as jib-headed sails, gaff sails, lugsails, lateen sails, spritsails, staysails, and jibs, that do not set on yards and whose normal position, when not trimmed, is in a fore-and-aft direction amidships. [1810–20]

fore′-and-aft′ top′sail. See **gaff topsail** (def. 1).

fore·arm¹ (fôr′ärm′, fōr′-), *n.* **1.** *Anat.* the part of the arm between the elbow and the wrist. **2.** *Zool.* the corresponding part of the foreleg between the elbow and the knee in certain quadrupeds. See diag. under **horse.** [1735–45; FORE- + ARM¹]

fore·arm² (fôr ärm′, fōr-), *v.t.* to prepare in advance

CONCISE ETYMOLOGY KEY: <, descended or borrowed from; >, whence; b., blend of, blended; c., cognate with; cf., compare; deriv., derivative; equiv., equivalent; imit., imitative; obl., oblique; r., replacing; s., stem; sp., spelling, spelled; resp., respelling, respelled; trans., translation; ?, origin unknown; *, unattested; ‡, probably earlier than. See the full key inside the front cover.

or beforehand, esp. for difficulties. [1585–95; FORE- + ARM[2]]

fore•bear (fôr′bâr′, fōr′-), *n.* Usually, **forebears.** ancestors; forefathers. Also, **forbear.** [1425–75; ME (Scots), equiv. to *fore-* FORE- + *-bear* being, var. of *beer;* see BE, -ER[1]]

fore•bode (fôr bōd′, fōr-), *v.,* **-bod•ed, -bod•ing.** —*v.t.* **1.** to foretell or predict; be an omen of; indicate beforehand; portend: *clouds that forebode a storm.* **2.** to have a strong inner feeling or notion of (a future misfortune, evil, catastrophe, etc.); have a presentiment of. —*v.i.* **3.** to prophesy. **4.** to have a presentiment. [1595–1605; FORE- + BODE] —**fore•bod′er,** *n.*
—**Syn. 1.** foreshadow, presage, forecast, augur.

fore•bod•ing (fôr bō′ding, fōr-), *n.* **1.** a prediction; portent. **2.** a strong inner feeling or notion of a future misfortune, evil, etc.; presentiment. —*adj.* **3.** that forebodes, esp. evil. [1350–1400; ME *forbodyng* (n.); see FOREBODE, -ING[1], -ING[2]] —**fore•bod′ing•ly,** *adv.* —**fore•bod′ing•ness,** *n.*

fore•bod•y (fôr′bod′ē, fōr′-), *n., pl.* **-bod•ies.** *Naut.* the part of a ship's hull forward of the middle body. [1605–15; FORE- + BODY]

fore•brain (fôr′brān′, fōr′-), *n. Anat.* **1.** Also called **prosencephalon.** the anterior of the three primary divisions of the brain in the embryo of a vertebrate, or the part of the adult brain derived from this tissue including the diencephalon and telencephalon. **2.** the telencephalon. [1875–80; FORE- + BRAIN]

fore•cad•die (fôr′kad′ē, fōr′-), *n. Golf.* a caddie positioned on the course at a distance from the tee or a given lie, to locate balls after they are hit. [1785–95; FORE- + CADDIE]

fore•cast (fôr′kast′, -käst′, fōr′-), *v.,* **-cast** or **-cast•ed, -cast•ing,** *n.* —*v.t.* **1.** to predict (a future condition or occurrence); calculate in advance: *to forecast a heavy snowfall; to forecast lower interest rates.* **2.** to serve as a prediction of; foreshadow. **3.** to contrive or plan beforehand; prearrange. —*v.i.* **4.** to conjecture beforehand; make a prediction. **5.** to plan or arrange beforehand. —*n.* **6.** a prediction, esp. as to the weather. **7.** a conjecture as to something in the future. **8.** the act, practice, or faculty of forecasting. **9.** *Archaic.* foresight in planning. [1350–1400; ME (n.) plan. See FORE-, CAST[1]] —**fore′cast′a•ble,** *adj.* —**fore′cast′er,** *n.*
—**Syn. 1.** foretell, anticipate. See **predict. 3.** project. **4, 7.** guess, estimate. **9.** forethought, prescience.

fore•cas•tle (fōk′səl, fôr′kas′əl, -kä′səl, fōr′-), *n. Naut.* **1.** a superstructure at or immediately aft of the bow of a vessel, used as a shelter for stores, machinery, etc., or as quarters for sailors. **2.** any sailors' quarters located in the forward part of a vessel, as a deckhouse. **3.** the forward part of the weather deck of a vessel, esp. that part forward of the foremast. Also, **fo'c's'le, fo'c'sle.** [1300–50; ME *forcastel.* See FORE-, CASTLE]

F, forecastle (def. 1)

fore′castle deck′, *Naut.* a partial weather deck on top of a forecastle superstructure; topgallant forecastle. [1850–55]

fore′castle head′, *Naut.* **1.** the extreme fore part of a forecastle superstructure. **2.** the extreme fore part of the main weather deck of a vessel that has no forecastle superstructure.

fore-check (fôr′chek′, fōr′-), *v.i. Ice Hockey.* to obstruct or impede the movement or progress of an attacking opponent in the opponent's own defensive zone. Cf. **back-check, check**[1] (def. 15). [1950–55]

fore•choir (fôr′kwīᵊr′, fōr′-), *n.* antechoir. [FORE- + CHOIR]

fore•cit•ed (fôr′sī′tid, fōr′-), *adj.* previously cited. [1570–80; FORE- + CITED]

fore′ clip′ping, a word formed by omitting the first part of the form from which it is derived. Cf. **apheresis, back clipping, clipped form.**

fore•close (fôr klōz′, fōr-), *v.,* **-closed, -clos•ing.** —*v.t.* **1.** *Law.* **a.** to deprive (a mortgagor or pledgor) of the right to redeem his or her property, esp. on failure to make payment on a mortgage when due, ownership of property then passing to the mortgagee. **b.** to take away the right to redeem (a mortgage or pledge). **2.** to shut out; exclude; bar. **3.** to hinder or prevent, as from doing something. **4.** to establish an exclusive claim to. **5.** to close, settle, or answer beforehand. —*v.i.* **6.** to foreclose a mortgage or pledge. [1250–1300; ME *foreclosen* < OF *forclos,* ptp. of *forclore* to exclude, equiv. to *for-* out + *clore* to shut (< L *claudere*)] —**fore•clos′a•ble,** *adj.*

fore•clo•sure (fôr klō′zhər, fōr-), *n. Law.* the act of foreclosing a mortgage or pledge. [1720–30; FORECLOSE + -URE]

fore•con•scious (fôr′kon′shəs, fōr′-), *n. Psychol.* the preconscious. [1920–25; FORE- + CONSCIOUS]

fore•course (fôr′kôrs′, fōr′kōrs′), *n.* the lowermost sail on a square-rigged foremast; a square foresail. See diag. under **ship.** [1620–30; FORE- + COURSE]

fore•court (fôr′kôrt′, fōr′kōrt′), *n.* **1.** *Tennis.* the part of either half of a tennis court that lies between the net and the line that marks the inbounds limit of a service. Cf. **backcourt** (def. 1). **2.** a courtyard before the entrance to a building or group of buildings. [1525–35; FORE- + COURT]

fore•date (fôr dāt′, fōr-), *v.t.,* **-dat•ed, -dat•ing.** to antedate. [1855–60; FORE- + DATE[1]]

fore•deck (fôr′dek′, fōr′-), *n. Naut.* the fore part of a weather deck, esp. between a bridge house or superstructure and a forecastle superstructure. [1555–65; FORE- + DECK[1]]

fore•deep (fôr′dēp′, fōr′-), *n. Geol.* an elongate sediment-filled sea-floor depression bordering an island arc or other orogenic belt. [1905–10; FORE- + DEEP]

fore•do (fôr dōō′, fōr-), *v.t.,* **-did, -done, -do•ing.** fordo.

fore•done (fôr dun′, fōr-), *adj.* fordone.

fore•doom (*v.* fôr dōōm′, fōr-; *n.* fôr′dōōm′, fōr′-), *v.t.* **1.** to doom beforehand; destine. —*n.* **2.** *Archaic.* a doom ordained beforehand; destiny. [1555–65; FORE- + DOOM]

fore′ edge′, the front outer edge of a book, opposite the bound edge. [1655–65]

fore′-edge paint′ing (fôr′ej′, fōr′-), a technique of painting a picture on the fore edge of a book, often in such a manner that only when the pages are slightly fanned the picture is revealed. [1910–15]

fore•face (fôr′fās′, fōr′-), *n.* the area of the head that is in front of the eyes: applied esp. to four-legged mammals. [1535–45, for an earlier sense; FORE- + FACE]

fore•fa•ther (fôr′fä′thər, fōr′-), *n.* an ancestor. [1250–1300; ME *forefader.* See FORE-, FATHER] —**fore′•fa′ther•ly,** *adj.*
—**Syn.** forebear, progenitor, patriarch, forerunner.

Fore′fathers' Day′, the anniversary of the day (December 21, 1620, in Old Style December 11) on which the Pilgrims landed at Plymouth, Mass. Owing to an error in changing the date from the Old Style to the New, it is generally observed on December 22. [1820–30]

fore•feel (*v.* fôr fēl′, fōr-; *n.* fôr′fēl′, fōr′-), *v.,* **-felt, -feel•ing,** *n.* —*v.t.* **1.** to feel or perceive beforehand; have a presentiment of. —*n.* **2.** a feeling beforehand. [1570–80; FORE- + FEEL]

fore•fend (fôr fend′, fōr-), *v.t.* forfend.

fore•fin•ger (fôr′fing′gər, fōr′-), *n.* the first finger next to the thumb. Also called **index finger.** [1400–50; late ME *forefyngure.* See FORE-, FINGER]

fore•foot (fôr′fŏŏt′, fōr′-), *n., pl.* **-feet. 1.** *Zool.* one of the front feet of a quadruped, an insect, etc. **2.** *Naut.* **a.** the point at which the stem of a hull joins the keel; the forward end of a keel. **b.** a curved member at this point in a wooden hull. [1325–75; ME *forfot, forefote.* See FORE-, FOOT]

fore•front (fôr′frunt′, fōr′-), *n.* **1.** the foremost part or place. **2.** the position of greatest importance or prominence: *in the forefront of today's writers.* [1425–75; late ME *forfrount, forefrount.* See FORE-, FRONT]

fore•gath•er (fôr gath′ər, fōr-), *v.i.* forgather.

fore•gift (fôr′gift′, fōr′-), *n. Brit.* an advance payment or premium paid by a tenant on taking or renewing a lease. [1735–45; FORE- + GIFT]

fore•glimpse (fôr′glimps′, fōr′-), *n.* a revelation or glimpse of the future. [1890–95; FORE- + GLIMPSE]

fore•go[1] (fôr gō′, fōr-), *v.t., v.i.,* **-went, -gone, -go•ing.** to go before; precede. [bef. 900; ME *forgon, forgan,* OE *foregān.* See FORE-, GO[1]] —**fore•go′er,** *n.*

fore•go[2] (fôr gō′, fōr-), *v.t.,* **-went, -gone, -go•ing.** forgo. —**fore•go′er,** *n.*

fore•go•ing (fôr gō′ing, fōr-), *adj.* previously stated, written, or occurring; preceding: *The foregoing paragraph presents the problem.* [1400–50; late ME; see FOREGO[1], -ING[2]]
—**Syn.** precedent, previous, prior, earlier, former.

fore•gone (fôr gôn′, -gon′, fōr-; fôr′gôn′, -gon′, fōr′-), *adj.* **1.** that has gone before; previous; past. **2.** determined in advance; inevitable. [1590–1600; FORE- + GONE] —**fore•gone′ness,** *n.*

fore′gone′ conclu′sion, 1. an inevitable conclusion or result. **2.** a conclusion, opinion, or decision formed in advance of proper consideration of evidence, arguments, etc. [1595–1605]

fore•ground (fôr′ground′, fōr′-), *n.* **1.** the ground or parts situated, or represented as situated, in the front; the portion of a scene nearest to the viewer (opposed to *background*). **2.** a prominent or important position; forefront. [1685–95; FORE- + GROUND[1]]

fore•gut (fôr′gut′, fōr′-), *n.* **1.** *Zool.* **a.** the first portion of the vertebrate alimentary canal, extending from the pharynx and esophagus to the end of the stomach or gizzard and, in some animals, the anterior duodenum, functioning in the ingestion, temporary storage, and partial digestion of food. **b.** the first portion of the alimentary canal in arthropods and annelids, composed of ectodermal, chitin-lined tissue and usually comprising the pharynx, esophagus, crop, and gizzard. **2.** *Embryol.* (in mammals) the upper part of the embryonic alimentary canal from which the pharynx, esophagus, lung, stomach, liver, pancreas, and part of the duodenum develop. Cf. **midgut, hindgut.** [1885–90; FORE- + GUT]

fore•hand (fôr′hand′, fōr′-), *adj.* **1.** (in tennis, squash, etc.) of, pertaining to, or noting a stroke made from the same side of the body as that of the hand holding the racket, paddle, etc. Cf. **backhand** (def. 5). **2.** being in front or ahead. **3.** foremost or leading. **4.** done beforehand; given or made in advance, as a payment. —*n.* **5.** (in tennis, squash, etc.) a forehand stroke. **6.** the part of a horse that is in front of the rider. **7.** *Cards.* the player on the dealer's left, in a game with three players. Cf. **endhand, middlehand. 8.** *Archaic.* a superior or advantageous position. —*adv.* **9.** (in tennis, squash, etc.) with a forehand stroke. [1535–45; FORE- + HAND]

fore•hand•ed (fôr′han′did, fōr′-), *adj.* **1.** forehand (def. 1). **2.** capable of dealing or coping with unexpected problems. **3.** providing for the future; prudent; thrifty. **4.** in good financial circumstances; well-to-do. —*adv.* **5.** forehand (def. 9). [1585–95; FOREHAND + -ED[3]] —**fore′•hand′ed•ly,** *adv.* —**fore′hand′ed•ness,** *n.*

fore•head (fôr′id, for′-; fôr′hed′, fōr′-), *n.* **1.** the part of the face above the eyebrows; brow. **2.** the fore or front part of anything. [bef. 1000; ME *forehe(v)ed,* OE *forhēafod.* See FORE-, HEAD]

fore•hearth (fôr′härth′, fōr′-), *n.* (in a blast furnace or cupola) a reservoir for iron or slag, accessible through a door at hearth level. [1880–85; FORE- + HEARTH]

fore•hoof (fôr′hŏŏf′, -hōōf′, fōr′-), *n., pl.* **-hoofs, -hooves.** the hoof of a front leg. [1760–70; FORE- + HOOF]

for•eign (fôr′in, for′-), *adj.* **1.** of, pertaining to, or derived from another country or nation; not native: *foreign cars.* **2.** of or pertaining to contact or dealings with other countries; connected with foreign affairs. **3.** external to one's own country or nation: *a foreign country.* **4.** carried on abroad, or with other countries: *foreign trade.* **5.** belonging to or coming from another district, province, etc. **6.** located outside a specific district, province, etc. **7.** *Law.* **a.** of or pertaining to law outside of local jurisdiction. **b.** of or pertaining to another jurisdiction, as of another nation or state. **8.** belonging to or proceeding from other persons or things: *a statement supported by foreign testimony.* **9.** not belonging to the place or body where found: *foreign matter in a chemical mixture.* **10.** not related to or connected with the thing under consideration: *foreign to our discussion.* **11.** alien in character; irrelevant or inappropriate; remote. **12.** strange or unfamiliar. [1200–50; ME *forein* < OF *forain, forein* < VL **forānus,* deriv. of L *forās* outside] —**for′eign•ly,** *adv.* —**for′eign•ness,** *n.*
—**Syn. 1, 3.** alien. **4.** international. **11.** extraneous, outside.

for′eign affairs′, activities of a nation in its relationships with other nations; international relations. [1605–15]

for′eign aid′, economic, technical, or military aid given by one nation to another for purposes of relief and rehabilitation, for economic stabilization, or for mutual defense. Also called **aid.** [1955–60] —**for′eign-aid′,** *adj.*

for′eign bill′, a bill of exchange drawn on a payer in one country by a maker in another. Cf. **inland bill.** [1675–85]

for•eign-born (fôr′in bôrn′, for′-), *adj.* born in a country other than that in which one resides. [1855–60, *Amer.*]

for′eign com′merce. See under **commerce** (def. 1).

for′eign correspond′ent, a correspondent, as for a periodical, assigned to send back articles and news dispatches from a foreign country for publication.

for•eign•er (fôr′ə nər, for′-), *n.* **1.** a person not native to or naturalized in the country or jurisdiction under consideration; alien. **2.** a person from outside one's community. **3.** a thing produced in or brought from a foreign country. **4.** *Naut.* a foreign vessel. [1375–1425; late ME *foreiner.* See FOREIGN, -ER[1]]
—**Syn. 1.** outlander. See **stranger.**

for′eign exchange′, 1. commercial paper drawn on a person or corporation in a foreign nation. **2.** the process of balancing accounts in commercial transactions between business organizations of different nations. [1685–95]

for•eign-flag (fôr′in flag′, for′-), *adj.* **1.** (of a vessel or aircraft) having a registry under a nationality other than one's own: *rivalry between U.S.-flag freighters and foreign-flag ships.* **2.** (esp. of a ship) owned by a national of one country and registered under the maritime laws of another country: *Some foreign-flag vessels are actually owned by American shipping companies.*

for•eign•ism (fôr′ə niz′əm, for′-), *n.* **1.** a foreign custom, mannerism, etc. **2.** any trait, deviating from accepted speech standards, derived from a foreign language. **3.** imitation of anything foreign. **4.** a foreign quality. [1850–55; FOREIGN + -ISM]

for′eign le′gion, 1. a military unit consisting of foreign volunteers in the service of a state. **2.** (*caps.*) a specialized military unit of the French army, consisting of volunteers of all nationalities assigned to military operations and duties outside France. [1880–85, *Amer.*]

for′eign min′ister, (in countries other than the U.S.) a cabinet minister who conducts and supervises foreign and diplomatic relations with other states. Also called, *esp. Brit.,* **foreign secretary.** Cf. **secretary of state** (def. 1). [1700–10] —**for′eign min′istry.**

for′eign mis′sion, 1. mission (def. 6). **2.** mission (def. 3). [1800–10]

for′eign of′fice, the department of a government that handles foreign affairs. [1855–60]

for′eign pol′icy, a policy pursued by a nation in its dealings with other nations, designed to achieve national objectives. [1905–10]

for′eign rela′tions, 1. the dealings and relationships between nations. **2.** the field of foreign affairs: *an expert in foreign relations.* **3.** the quality or character of foreign affairs as a consequence of foreign policy: *a deterioration in their foreign relations.* [1800–10, *Amer.*]

for′eign sec′retary, *Chiefly Brit.* See **foreign minister.** [1650–60]

for′eign serv′ice, (*often caps.*) a division of the U.S. Department of State or of a foreign office that maintains diplomatic and consular posts and personnel in other countries. [1925–30]

for′eign-trade′ zone′ (fôr′in trād′, for′-). See **free port** (def. 1).

fore•judge[1] (fôr juj′, fōr-), *v.t.,* **-judged, -judg•ing.** to

CONCISE PRONUNCIATION KEY: act, cāpe, dâre, pärt; set, ēqual; if, īce; ox, ōver, ôrder, oil, bŏŏk, bōōt, out; up, ûrge; child; sing; shoe; thin, *th*at; zh as in *treasure.* ə = *a* as in *alone, e* as in *system, i* as in *easily, o* as in *gallop, u* as in *circus;* ᵊ as in *fire* (fīᵊr), *hour* (ouᵊr). l and n can serve as syllabic consonants, as in *cradle* (krād′l), and *button* (but′n). See the full key inside the front cover.

judge beforehand; prejudge. [1555–65; FORE- + JUDGE] —**fore·judg′er**, *n.*

fore·judge[2] (fôr juj′, fōr-), *v.t.*, **-judged, -judg·ing.** forjudge.

fore·know (fôr nō′, fōr-), *v.t.*, **-knew, -known, -know·ing.** to know beforehand. [1400–50; late ME *foreknowen.* See FORE-, KNOW] —**fore·know′a·ble**, *adj.* —**fore·know′er**, *n.* —**fore·know′ing·ly**, *adv.*
—**Syn.** foresee, divine, discern, anticipate.

fore·knowl·edge (fôr′nol′ij, fōr′-, fôr nol′ij, fōr-), *n.* knowledge of something before it exists or happens; prescience: *Did you have any foreknowledge of the scheme?* [1525–35; FORE- + KNOWLEDGE]
—**Syn.** presentiment, premonition; foresightedness.

for·el (fôr′əl, for′-), *n.* **1.** a slipcase for a book. **2.** parchment of poor quality, used in its natural color for making book covers. Also, **forrel.** [1250–1300; ME *forel* case, sheath < OF *forrel, fourrel,* dim. of *fuerre* sheath. See FUR]

fore·la·dy (fôr′lā′dē, fōr′-), *n., pl.* **-dies.** a forewoman. [1885–90, *Amer.*; FORE- + LADY]
—**Usage.** See **lady.**

fore·land (fôr′land′, fōr′-), *n.* **1.** a cape, headland, or promontory. **2.** land or territory lying in front. [1300–50; ME *forlonde.* See FORE-, LAND]

fore·leg (fôr′leg′, fōr′-), *n.* one of the front legs of a quadruped, an insect, etc. [1375–1425; late ME *forlegge.* See FORE-, LEG]

fore·limb (fôr′lim′, fōr′-), *n.* a front limb of an animal. [1785–95; FORE- + LIMB]

fore·lock[1] (fôr′lok′, fōr′-), *n.* **1.** the lock of hair that grows from the fore part of the head. **2.** (of a horse) a tuft of hair above or on the forehead. See diag. under **horse.** [1640–50; FORE- + LOCK[2]; prob. not continuous with OE *foreloccas* (pl.), attested once]

fore·lock[2] (fôr′lok′, fōr′-), *n.* **1.** a pin or flat wedge passed through a hole near the end of a threadless bolt to fasten parts together. —*v.t.* **2.** to fasten by means of a forelock. [1275–1325; ME *forelok.* See FORE-, LOCK[1]]

fore·man (fôr′mən, fōr′-), *n., pl.* **-men. 1.** a person in charge of a particular department, group of workers, etc., as in a factory or the like. **2.** the member of a jury selected to preside over and speak for all the jurors on the panel. [1175–1225; ME *forman* chief servant, steward. See FORE-, MAN[1]] —**fore′man·ship′**, *n.*
—**Usage.** See **-man.**

fore·mast (fôr′mast′, -mäst′, fōr′-; *Naut.* fôr′məst, fōr′-), *n. Naut.* the mast nearest the bow in all vessels having two or more masts. [1575–85; FORE- + MAST[1]]

fore·milk (fôr′milk′, fōr′-), *n.* colostrum. [1900–05; FORE- + MILK]

fore·most (fôr′mōst′, -məst, fōr′-), *adj., adv.* first in place, order, rank, etc.: *the foremost surgeons.* [bef. 1000; FORE[1] + -MOST; r. ME, OE *formest,* equiv. to *form(a)* first, var. of *fruma* (cf. L *prīmus*) + *-est* -EST]
—**Syn.** primary, prime, chief, principal, paramount.

fore·moth·er (fôr′muth′ər, fōr′-), *n.* a female ancestor. [1575–85; FORE- + MOTHER[1] on the model of FOREFATHER]

fore·name (fôr′nām′, fōr′-), *n.* a name that precedes the family name or surname; first name. [1525–35; FORE- + NAME]

fore·named (fôr′nāmd′, fōr′-), *adj.* named before; mentioned before in the same writing or speech; aforementioned. [1150–1200; ME. See FORE-, NAMED]

fore·noon (*n.* fôr′no͞on′, fōr′-; *adj.* fôr′no͞on′, fōr′-), *n.* **1.** the period of daylight before noon. **2.** the latter part of the morning. —*adj.* **3.** of or pertaining to the forenoon. [1375–1425; late ME. See FORE-, NOON]

fore′noon watch′, *Naut.* the watch from 8 A.M. until noon. [1825–35]

fo·ren·sic (fə ren′sik), *adj.* **1.** pertaining to, connected with, or used in courts of law or public discussion and debate. **2.** adapted or suited to argumentation; rhetorical. —*n.* **3. forensics,** (*used with a singular or plural v.*) the art or study of argumentation and formal debate. [1650–60; < L *forēns(is)* of, belonging to the forum, public (see FORUM, -ENSIS) + -IC] —**fo·ren·si·cal·i·ty** (fə ren′si kal′i tē), *n.* —**fo·ren′si·cal·ly**, *adv.*

foren′sic anthropol′ogy, the branch of physical anthropology in which anthropological data, criteria, and techniques are used to determine the sex, age, genetic population, or parentage of skeletal or biological materials in questions of civil or criminal law.

foren′sic chem′istry, the application of facts concerning chemistry to questions of civil and criminal law. Also called **legal chemistry.**

foren′sic med′icine, the application of medical knowledge to questions of civil and criminal law, esp. in court proceedings. Also called **foren′sic jurispru′dence, legal medicine, medical jurisprudence.** [1835–45]

foren′sic psychi′atry, the use of psychiatric knowledge and techniques in questions of law, as in determining legal insanity.

fore·or·dain (fôr′ôr dān′, fōr′-), *v.t.* **1.** to ordain or appoint beforehand. **2.** to predestine; predetermine. [1400–50; late ME *forordeinen.* See FORE-, ORDAIN] —**fore′or·dain′ment**, *n.*

fore·or·di·nate (fôr ôr′dn āt′, fōr-), *v.t.*, **-nat·ed, -nat·ing.** foreordain. [1855–60; back formation from FOREORDINATION]

fore·or·di·na·tion (fôr′ôr dn ā′shən, fōr′-), *n.* **1.** previous ordination or appointment. **2.** predestination. [1620–30; FORE- + ORDINATION]

fore·part (fôr′pärt′, fōr′-), *n.* the first, front, or early part. [1350–1400; ME *forpart.* See FORE-, PART]

fore·passed (fôr past′, -päst′, fōr-), *adj.* already in the past; bygone. Also, **fore·past′.** [1550–60; FORE- + PASSED]

fore·paw (fôr′pô′, fōr′-), *n.* the paw of a foreleg. [1815–25; FORE- + PAW]

fore·peak (fôr′pēk′, fōr′-), *n. Naut.* the extreme forward part of the interior of a hull (opposed to *afterpeak*). [1685–95; FORE- + PEAK[1]]

fore·per·son (fôr′pûr′sən, fōr′-), *n.* a foreman or forewoman. [FORE(MAN) + -PERSON]
—**Usage.** See **-person.**

fore′ plane′, *Carpentry.* a plane, intermediate in size between a jack plane and a jointer plane, used for preliminary smoothing. [1695–1705]

fore·play (fôr′plā′, fōr′-), *n.* sexual stimulation, usually as a prelude to sexual intercourse. [1925–30; FORE- + PLAY]

fore·pleas·ure (fôr′plezh′ər, fōr′-), *n.* the aggregate of pleasurable sensations that lead to a heightened physical or emotional response, as of those aroused in sexual intercourse that lead to an orgasm. [1905–10; FORE- + PLEASURE, as trans. of G *Vorlust*]

fore·pole (*n.* fôr′pōl′, fōr′-; *v.* fôr pōl′, fōr-), *n., v.*, **-poled, -pol·ing.** *Mining.* —*n.* **1.** Also called **spile, spill.** any of a number of boards or timbers driven forward on top of a set to protect miners lengthening a tunnel from falling debris. —*v.t.* **2.** to reinforce (the end of an excavated tunnel) with forepoles. [1870–75, *Amer.*; FORE- + POLE[1]]

fore·quar·ter (fôr′kwôr′tər, -kwô′-, fōr′-), *n.* the forward end of half of a carcass, as of beef or lamb. [1490–1500; FORE- + QUARTER]

fore·reach (fôr rēch′, fōr-), *v.i.* **1.** to gain, as one ship on another. **2.** to maintain headway, as when coming about or drifting after taking in sail or stopping engines. —*v.t.* **3.** to gain upon; catch up with. **4.** to pass. [1635–45; FORE- + REACH]

fore·run (fôr run′, fōr-), *v.t.*, **-ran, -run, -run·ning. 1.** to run in front of; come before; precede. **2.** to be the precursor or harbinger of; prefigure. **3.** to anticipate or foretell. **4.** to forestall. **5.** to outrun or outstrip. [1505–15; FORE- + RUN; prob. not continuous with ME *forerennen* (intrans.) to run ahead, OE *fōryrnan*]

fore·run·ner (fôr′run′ər, fōr′-, fôr run′ər, fōr-), *n.* **1.** predecessor; ancestor; forebear; precursor. **2.** an omen, sign, or indication of something to follow; portent: *The warm evenings were a forerunner of summer.* **3.** a person who goes or is sent in advance to announce the coming of someone or something that follows; herald; harbinger. **4. the Forerunner,** John the Baptist. [1250–1300; ME *forrenner.* See FORE-, RUNNER]

fore·sad·dle (fôr′sad′l, fōr′-), *n.* the forepart of a saddle of veal, mutton, lamb, or venison. [1920–25; FORE- + SADDLE]

fore·said (fôr′sed′, fōr′-), *adj.* aforementioned; aforesaid. [bef. 1000; ME *forsaid,* OE *foresǣd.* See FORE-, SAID]

fore·sail (fôr′sāl′, fōr′-; *Naut.* fôr′səl, fōr′-), *n. Naut.* **1.** the lowermost sail on a foremast. See diag. under **ship. 2.** the staysail or jib, set immediately forward of the mainmast of a sloop, cutter, knockabout, yawl, ketch, or dandy. [1475–85; FORE- + SAIL]

fore·see (fôr sē′, fōr-), *v.*, **-saw, -seen, -see·ing.** —*v.t.* **1.** to have prescience of; to know in advance; foreknow. **2.** to see beforehand. —*v.i.* **3.** to exercise foresight. [bef. 900; ME; OE *foresēon.* See FORE-, SEE[1]] —**fore·see′a·ble**, *adj.* —**fore·see′a·bil′i·ty**, *n.* —**fore·se′er**, *n.*
—**Syn. 1.** divine, discern. See **predict.**

fore·shad·ow (fôr shad′ō, fōr-), *v.t.* to show or indicate beforehand; prefigure: *Political upheavals foreshadowed war.* [1570–80; FORE- + SHADOW] —**fore·shad′ow·er**, *n.*

fore·shank (fôr′shangk′, fōr′-), *n.* **1.** shin[1] (def. 2). **2.** See under **shank** (def. 4). [1920–25; FORE- + SHANK]

fore·sheet (fôr′shēt′, fōr′-), *n. Naut.* **1.** the sheet of a headsail. **2. foresheets,** (*used with a plural v.*) the space, in an open boat, in front of the foremost rower's seat. Also called **headsheet.** [1660–70; FORE- + SHEET]

fore·shock (fôr′shok′, fōr′-), *n. Geol.* a relatively small earthquake that precedes a greater one by a few days or weeks and originates at or near the focus of the larger earthquake. [1900–05; FORE- + SHOCK[1]]

fore·shore (fôr′shôr′, fōr′shōr′), *n.* **1.** the ground between the water's edge and cultivated land; land along the edge of a body of water. **2.** the part of the shore between the high-water mark and low-water mark. [1755–65; FORE- + SHORE[1]]

fore·short·en (fôr shôr′tn, fōr-), *v.t.* **1.** *Fine Arts.* to reduce or distort (parts of a represented object that are not parallel to the picture plane) in order to convey the illusion of three-dimensional space as perceived by the human eye: often done according to the rules of perspective. **2.** to abridge, reduce, or contract; make shorter. [1600–10; FORE- + SHORTEN]

fore·shots (fôr′shots′, fōr′-), *n.pl.* the weak spirits that come over in the initial phase in distilling whiskey. Cf. **faints.** [1830–40; FORE- + SHOT[1] + -S[3]]

fore·show (fôr shō′, fōr-), *v.t.*, **-showed, -shown, -show·ing. 1.** to show beforehand. **2.** foretell; foreshadow. [bef. 1000; ME *forescewen,* OE *foresceāwian.* See FORE-, SHOW]

fore·side (fôr′sīd′, fōr′-), *n.* the front side or part. [1350–1400; ME; see FORE-, SIDE[1]]

fore·sight (fôr′sīt′, fōr′-), *n.* **1.** care or provision for the future; provident care; prudence. **2.** the act or power of foreseeing; prevision; prescience. **3.** an act of looking forward. **4.** knowledge or insight gained by or as by looking forward; a view of the future. **5.** *Survey.* **a.** a sight or reading taken on a forward point. **b.** (in leveling) a rod reading on a point the elevation of which is to be determined. [1250–1300; ME *forsight.* See FORE-, SIGHT] —**fore′sight′ed**, *adj.* —**fore′sight′ed·ly**, *adv.* —**fore′sight′ed·ness**, *n.* —**fore′sight′ful**, *adj.*
—**Syn. 1.** See **prudence. 4.** foreknowledge.

fore·skin (fôr′skin′, fōr′-), *n.* the prepuce of the penis. [1525–35; FORE- + SKIN; prob. on the model of G *Vorhaut* (Luther); cf. PREPUCE]

fore·sleeve (fôr′slēv′, fōr′-), *n.* **1.** the part of the sleeve covering the forearm. **2.** a detachable sleeve or part of a sleeve, often having an ornamental function. [1350–1400; ME; see FORE-, SLEEVE]

fore·speak (fôr spēk′, fōr-), *v.t.*, **-spoke** or (*Archaic*) **-spake; -spo·ken** or (*Archaic*) **-spoke; -speak·ing. 1.** to predict; foretell. **2.** to ask for or claim in advance. [1250–1300; ME *forespeken.* See FORE-, SPEAK]

fore·spent (fôr spent′, fōr-), *adj.* forspent.

for·est (fôr′ist, for′-), *n.* **1.** a large tract of land covered with trees and underbrush; woodland. **2.** the trees on such a tract: *to cut down a forest.* **3.** a tract of wooded grounds in England formerly belonging to the sovereign and set apart for game. **4.** a thick cluster of vertical objects: *a forest of church spires.* —*v.t.* **5.** to supply or cover with trees; convert into a forest. [1250–1300; ME < OF < LL *forestis* (*silva*) an unenclosed wood (as opposed to a park), deriv. of L *foris* outside. Cf. FOREIGN] —**for′est·al, fo·res·tial** (fə res′chəl), *adj.* —**for′est·ed**, *adj.* —**for′est·less**, *adj.* —**for′est·like′**, *adj.*
—**Syn. 1.** FOREST, GROVE, WOOD refer to an area covered with trees. A FOREST is an extensive area, preserving some or all of its primitive wildness and usually having game or wild animals in it: *Sherwood Forest; the Black Forest.* A GROVE is a group or cluster of trees, usually not very large in area and cleared of underbrush. It is usually tended or cultivated: *a shady grove; a grove of pines; an orange grove; a walnut grove.* WOODS (or a WOOD) resembles a forest but is a smaller tract of land, less wild in character, and generally closer to civilization: *lost in the woods; a wood covering several acres.*

fore·staff (fôr′staf′, -stäf′, fōr′-), *n., pl.* **-staves, -staffs.** cross-staff. [1660–70; FORE- + STAFF[1]]

fore·stage (fôr′stāj′, fōr′-), *n.* the part of a stage in front of the proscenium or the closed curtain, as the apron or an extension of the apron. [1920–25; FORE- + STAGE]

fore·stall (fôr stôl′, fōr-), *v.t.* **1.** to prevent, hinder, or thwart by action in advance: *to forestall a riot by deploying police.* **2.** to act beforehand with or get ahead of; anticipate. **3.** to buy up (goods) in advance in order to increase the price when resold. **4.** to prevent sales at (a fair, market, etc.) by buying up or diverting goods. [1350–1400; ME *forstallen,* v. deriv. of *forstalle,* OE *foresteall* intervention (to defeat justice), waylaying. See FORE-, STALL[2]] —**fore·stall′er**, *n.* —**fore·stall′ment, forestal′ment**, *n.*
—**Syn. 1.** preclude, obviate, intercept, obstruct. **2.** prevent, avert.

for·est·a·tion (fôr′ə stā′shən, for′-), *n.* the planting of forests. [1895–1900, *Amer.*; FOREST + -ATION]

fore·stay (fôr′stā′, fōr′-), *n.* **1.** a stay leading aft and upward from the stem or knightheads of a vessel to the head of the fore lower mast; the lowermost stay of a foremast. **2.** a stay leading aft and upwards toward the mainmast of a sloop, knockabout, cutter, ketch, yawl, or dandy. [1325–75; ME *forstay.* See FORE-, STAY[3]]

fore·stay·sail (fôr′stā′sāl′, fōr′-; *Naut.* fôr′stā′səl, fōr′-), *n.* a triangular sail set on a forestay; the innermost headsail of a vessel. See diag. under **ship.** [1735–45; FORESTAY + SAIL]

for·est·er (fôr′ə stər, for′-), *n.* **1.** a person who is expert in forestry. **2.** an officer having responsibility for the maintenance of a forest. **3.** See **forest ranger. 4.** *Zool.* an animal of the forest. **5.** a large, gray kangaroo, *Macropus canguru.* **6.** any moth of the family Agaristidae, typically black with two yellowish or whitish spots on each wing. [1250–1300; ME < OF *forestier.* See FOREST, -ER[2]]

For·est·er (fôr′ə stər, for′-), *n.* **C(ecil) S(cott),** 1899–1966, English novelist and journalist.

for′est green′. See **Lincoln green.** [1800–10] —**for′est-green′**, *adj.*

For′est Grove′, a town in NW Oregon. 11,499.

For′est Hill′, a town in N Texas. 11,684.

For′est Hills′, a residential area in New York City, on W Long Island, in SE New York: former site of international tennis tournament.

fore·stick (fôr′stik′, fōr′-), *n.* the front log in a wood fire, as in a fireplace. [1785–95, *Amer.*; FORE- + STICK[1]]

for·est·land (fôr′ist land′, for′-), *n.* land containing or covered with forests. [1640–50; FOREST + LAND]

For′est of Dean′, a royal forest in Gloucestershire, in W England. ab. 180 sq. mi. (475 sq. km).

For′est Park′, 1. a city in NW Georgia. 18,782. **2.** a town in SW Ohio. 18,675. **3.** a town in NE Illinois; a suburb of Chicago. 15,177.

for′est rang′er, any of the officers employed by the government to supervise the care and preservation of forests, esp. public forests. [1820–30]

for′est reserve′, an area of forest set aside and preserved by the government as a wilderness, national park, or the like. [1880–85, *Amer.*]

for·est·ry (fôr′ə strē, for′-), *n.* **1.** the science of planting and taking care of trees and forests. **2.** the process of establishing and managing forests; forestation. **3.** forestland. [1685–95; < MF *foresterie.* See FOREST, -RY]

For′est Serv′ice, a division of the U.S. Department

CONCISE ETYMOLOGY KEY: <, descended or borrowed from; >, whence; b., blend of, blended; c., cognate with; cf., compare; deriv., derivative; equiv., equivalent; imit., imitative; obl., oblique; r., replacing; s., stem; sp., spelling, spelled; resp., respelling, respelled; trans., translation; ?, origin unknown; *, unattested; ‡, probably earlier than. See the full key inside the front cover.

of Agriculture, created in 1905, that protects and develops the national forests and grasslands.

for′est tent′ cat′erpillar. See under **tent caterpillar.** [1850–55, *Amer.*]

For•est•ville (fôr′ist vil′, for′-), *n.* a city in central Maryland, near Washington, D.C. 16,401.

fore•swear (fôr swâr′, fōr-), *v.t., v.i.,* **-swore, -sworn, -swear•ing.** forswear.

fore•taste (*n.* fôr′tāst′, fōr′-; *v.* fôr tāst′, fōr-), *n., v.,* **-tast•ed, -tast•ing.** —*n.* **1.** a slight and partial experience, knowledge, or taste of something to come in the future; anticipation. —*v.t.* **2.** to have some advance experience or knowledge of (something to come). [1400–50; late ME *fortaste.* See FORE-, TASTE]

fore•tell (fôr tel′, fōr-), *v.,* **-told, -tell•ing.** —*v.t.* to tell of beforehand; predict; prophesy. [1250–1300; ME *fortell.* See FORE-, TELL[1]] —**fore•tell′er,** *n.*
—**Syn.** forecast, augur, presage, forebode.

fore•thought (fôr′thôt′, fōr′-), *n.* **1.** thoughtful provision beforehand; provident care; prudence. **2.** a thinking of something beforehand; previous consideration; anticipation. [1250–1300; ME *forthoght.* See FORE-, THOUGHT[1]]
—**Syn. 1.** See **prudence.**

fore•thought•ful (fôr thôt′fəl, fōr-), *adj.* full of or having forethought; provident. [1800–10; FORETHOUGHT + -FUL] —**fore•thought′ful•ly,** *adv.* —**fore•thought′•ful•ness,** *n.*

fore•time (fôr′tīm′, fōr′-), *n.* former or past time; the past. [1530–40; FORE- + TIME]

fore•to•ken (*n.* fôr′tō′kən, fōr′-; *v.* fôr tō′kən, fōr-), *n.* **1.** a sign of a future event; omen; forewarning. —*v.t.* **2.** to foreshadow. [bef. 900; ME *fortokne,* OE *foretācn.* See FORE-, TOKEN]

fore•tooth (fôr′tōōth′, fōr′-), *n., pl.* **-teeth** (-tēth′). a tooth in the front of the mouth; incisor. [bef. 1000; ME, OE *for teth* (pl.). See FORE-, TOOTH]

fore•top (fôr′top′, fōr′-; *for 1 also Naut.* fôr′təp, fōr′-), *n.* **1.** a platform at the head of a fore lower mast of a ship. **2.** the forelock of an animal, esp. a horse. [1250–1300; ME *fortop.* See FORE-, TOP[1]]

fore-top•gal•lant (fôr′top gal′ənt, fōr′-; *Naut.* fôr′tə gal′ənt, fōr′-), *adj.* being a sail, yard, or rigging belonging to a fore-topgallant mast. See diag. under **ship.** [1620–30]

fore′-top•gal′lant mast′, the spar or section of a spar forming the topgallant portion of a foremast on a ship. [1620–30]

fore•top•man (fôr′top′mən, fōr′-; *Naut.* fôr′təp mən, fōr′-), *n., pl.* **-men.** a member of a ship's crew stationed on the foretop. [1810–20; FORETOP + -MAN]

fore-top•mast (fôr′top′mast′, -mäst′, fōr′-; *Naut.* fôr′top′məst, fōr′-), *n.* the spar or section of a pole mast serving as the topmast of a foremast on a ship. [1620–30]

fore-top•sail (fōr′top′sāl′, fôr′-; *Naut.* fōr′top′səl, fôr′-), *n.* a topsail set on a foremast on a ship. See diag. under **ship.** [1575–85]

for•ev•er (fôr ev′ər, fər-), *adv.* **1.** without ever ending; eternally: *to last forever.* **2.** continually; incessantly; always: *He's forever complaining.* **3. forever and a day,** eternally; always: *They pledged to love each other forever and a day.* —*n.* **4.** an endless or seemingly endless period of time: *It took them forever to make up their minds.* [1660–70; orig. phrase *for ever*]

for•ev•er•more (fôr ev′ər môr′, -mōr′, fər-), *adv.* forever hereafter. [1830–40; FOR + EVERMORE]

for•ev•er•ness (fôr ev′ər nis, fər-), *n.* permanence; eternity. [1940–45; FOREVER + -NESS]

fore•warn (fôr wôrn′, fōr-), *v.t.* to warn in advance. [1300–50; ME *forwarnen.* See FORE-, WARN] —**fore•warn′er,** *n.* —**fore•warn′ing•ly,** *adv.*
—**Syn.** caution, admonish, alert, prewarn, tip off.

fore•went (fôr went′, fōr-), *v.* pt. of **forego.**

fore•wing (fôr′wing′, fōr′-), *n.* either of the anterior and usually smaller pair of wings of an insect having four wings. [1885–90; FORE- + WING]

fore•wom•an (fôr′wŏŏm′ən, fōr′-), *n., pl.* **-wom•en. 1.** a woman in charge of a particular department or group of workers. **2.** a woman on a jury selected to preside over and speak for all the jurors on the panel. [1700–10; FORE- + WOMAN]
—**Usage.** See **-woman.**

fore•word (fôr′wûrd′, -wərd, fōr′-), *n.* a short introductory statement in a published work, as a book, esp. when written by someone other than the author. Cf. **afterword.** [1835–45; FORE- + WORD]
—**Syn.** See **introduction.**

fore•worn (fôr wōrn′, fōr wôrn′), *adj. Archaic.* forworn.

fore•yard (fôr′yärd′, fōr′-), *n.* **1.** a yard on the lower mast of a square-rigged foremast of a ship used to support the foresail. **2.** a yard on the lowest spar of the foremast of a topsail schooner used to hold out the clews of the topsail or lower topsails. **3.** a yard forming the main lower mast of a ketch or yawl used to support a square course. [1620–30; FORE- + YARD[2]]

For•far (fôr′fər, -fär), *n.* **1.** a town in the Tayside region, in E Scotland. 10,500. **2.** former name of **Angus.**

for•feit (fôr′fit), *n.* **1.** a fine; penalty. **2.** an act of forfeiting; forfeiture. **3.** something to which the right is lost, as for commission of a crime or misdeed, neglect of duty, or violation of a contract. **4.** an article deposited in a game because of a mistake and redeemable by a fine or penalty. **5. forfeits,** (*used with a singular v.*) a game in which such articles are taken from the players. —*v.t.* **6.** to subject to seizure as a forfeit. **7.** to lose or become liable to lose, as in consequence of crime, fault, or breach of engagement. —*adj.* **8.** lost or subject to loss by forfeiture. [1250–1300; ME *forfet* < OF (ptp. of *forfaire* to commit crime, to lose possession or right through a criminal act) < ML *foris factum* penalty, ptp. of *foris facere* to transgress, equiv. to L *foris* outside, wrongly + *facere* to make, do] —**for′feit•a•ble,** *adj.* —**for′feit•er,** *n.*
—**Syn. 7.** surrender, yield, relinquish, forgo, waive.

for•fei•ture (fôr′fi chər), *n.* **1.** an act of forfeiting. **2.** something that is forfeited; fine; mulct. [1300–50; ME *forfeiture, forfeture* < OF. See FORFEIT, -URE]

for•fend (fôr fend′), *v.t.* **1.** to defend, secure, or protect. **2.** to fend off, avert, or prevent. **3.** *Archaic.* forbid. Also, **forefend.** [1350–1400; ME *forfenden.* See FOR-, FEND]

for•fi•cate (fôr′fi kit, -kāt′), *adj.* deeply forked, as the tail of a bird. [1810–20; < L *forfic-* (s. of *forfex*) pair of shears (cf. FORCEPS) + -ATE[1]]

for•gat (fər gat′), *v. Archaic.* a pt. of **forget.**

for•gath•er (fôr gath′ər), *v.i.* **1.** to gather together; convene; assemble. **2.** to encounter someone, esp. by chance. Also, **foregather.** [1505–15; FOR- + GATHER]

for•gave (fər gāv′), *v.* pt. of **forgive.**

forge[1] (fôrj, fōrj), *v.,* **forged, forg•ing.** *n.* —*v.t.* **1.** to form by heating and hammering; beat into shape. **2.** to form or make, esp. by concentrated effort: *to forge a friendship through mutual trust.* **3.** to imitate (handwriting, a signature, etc.) fraudulently; fabricate a forgery. —*v.i.* **4.** to commit forgery. **5.** to work at a forge. **6.** (of a horse at a trot) to strike the forefeet with the shoes of the hind feet. —*n.* **7.** a special fireplace, hearth, or furnace in which metal is heated before shaping. **8.** the workshop of a blacksmith; smithy. [1250–1300; ME *forgen* < OF *forgier* < L *fabricāre* to fabricate; see FABRIC] —**forge′a•ble,** *adj.* —**forg′er,** *n.*
—**Syn. 2.** shape, fabricate, manufacture, fashion, mold.

forge[2] (fôrj, fōrj), *v.i.,* **forged, forg•ing. 1.** to move ahead slowly; progress steadily: *to forge through dense underbrush.* **2.** to move ahead with increased speed and effectiveness (usually fol. by *ahead*): *to forge ahead and finish the work in a burst of energy.* [1605–15; orig. uncert.]

for•ger•y (fôr′jə rē, fōr′-), *n., pl.* **-ger•ies. 1.** the crime of falsely making or altering a writing by which the legal rights or obligations of another person are apparently affected; simulated signing of another person's name to any such writing whether or not it is also the forger's name. **2.** the production of a spurious work that is claimed to be genuine, as a coin, a painting, or the like. **3.** something, as a coin, a work of art, or a writing, produced by forgery. **4.** an act of producing something forged. **5.** *Archaic.* invention; artifice. [1565–75; FORGE[1] + -ERY]

for•get (fər get′), *v.,* **-got** or (*Archaic*) **-gat; -got•ten** or **-got; -get•ting.** —*v.t.* **1.** to cease or fail to remember; be unable to recall: *to forget someone's name.* **2.** to omit or neglect unintentionally: *I forgot to shut the window before leaving.* **3.** to leave behind unintentionally; neglect to take: *to forget one's keys.* **4.** to omit mentioning; leave unnoticed. **5.** to fail to think of; take no note of. **6.** to neglect willfully; disregard or slight. —*v.i.* **7.** to cease or omit to think of something. **8. forget oneself,** to say or do something improper or unbefitting one's rank, position, or character. [bef. 900; FOR- + GET; r. ME *foryeten,* OE *forg(i)etan;* c. OS *fargetan,* OHG *firgezzan*] —**for•get′ta•ble,** *adj.* —**for•get′ter,** *n.*
—**Usage.** Both FORGOT and FORGOTTEN are used as the past participle of FORGET: *Many have already forgot* (or *forgotten*) *the hard times of the Depression.* Only FORGOTTEN is used attributively: *half-forgotten memories.*

for•get•ful (fər get′fəl), *adj.* **1.** apt to forget; that forgets: *a forgetful person.* **2.** heedless or neglectful (often fol. by *of*): *to be forgetful of others.* **3.** bringing on oblivion: *forgetful slumber.* [1350–1400; ME; see FORGET, -FUL] —**for•get′ful•ly,** *adv.* —**for•get′ful•ness,** *n.*
—**Syn. 1.** absent-minded, inattentive, unmindful.

for•ge•tive (fôr′ji tiv, fōr′-), *adj. Archaic.* inventive; creative. [1590–1600; perh. b. FORGE[1] and CREATIVE]

for•get-me-not (fər get′mē not′), *n.* **1.** either of two small Old World plants, *Myosotis sylvatica* or *M. scorpioides,* of the borage family, having a light-blue flower commonly regarded as an emblem of constancy and friendship. **2.** any of several other plants of the genus *Myosotis.* **3.** any of various similar plants, esp. of the genus *Anchusa* or *Cynoglossum.* [1525–35; trans. of MF *ne m'oubliez mye*]

for•get•ter•y (fər get′ə rē), *n.* a faculty or facility for forgetting; faulty memory: *a witness with a very convenient forgettery.* [1860–65, *Amer.;* FORGET + -ERY]

forge′ weld′ing, the welding of pieces of hot metal with pressure or blows.

forg•ing (fôr′jing, fōr′-), *n.* **1.** an act or instance of forging. **2.** something forged; a piece of forged work in metal. [1350–1400; ME; see FORGE[1], -ING[1]]

for•give (fər giv′), *v.,* **-gave, -giv•en, -giv•ing.** —*v.t.* **1.** to grant pardon for or remission of (an offense, debt, etc.); absolve. **2.** to give up all claim on account of; remit (a debt, obligation, etc.). **3.** to grant pardon to (a person). **4.** to cease to feel resentment against: *to forgive one's enemies.* **5.** to cancel an indebtedness or liability of: *to forgive the interest owed on a loan.* —*v.i.* **6.** to pardon an offense or an offender. [bef. 900; FOR- + GIVE; r. ME *foryiven,* OE *forgiefan*] —**for•giv′a•ble,** *adj.* —**for•giv′er,** *n.*
—**Syn. 1.** See **excuse. 3.** absolve, acquit.

for•give•ness (fər giv′nis), *n.* **1.** act of forgiving; state of being forgiven. **2.** disposition or willingness to forgive. [bef. 900; ME *forgifenesse,* OE *forgifennys.* See FORGIVE, -NESS]

for•giv•ing (fər giv′ing), *adj.* **1.** disposed to forgive; indicating forgiveness: *a forgiving soul; a forgiving smile.* **2.** tolerant: *The mountain is not forgiving of inexperienced climbers.* [1680–90; FORGIVE + -ING[2]] —**for•giv′ing•ly,** *adv.* —**for•giv′ing•ness,** *n.*

for•go (fôr gō′), *v.t.,* **-went, -gone, -go•ing. 1.** to abstain or refrain from; do without. **2.** to give up, renounce, or resign. **3.** *Archaic.* to neglect or overlook. **4.** *Archaic.* to quit or leave. **5.** *Obs.* to go or pass by. Also, **forego.** [bef. 950; ME *forgon,* OE *forgān.* See FOR-, GO[1]] —**for•go′er,** *n.*
—**Syn. 1.** forbear, sacrifice, forsake.

for•got (fər got′), *v.* a pt. and pp. of **forget.**

for•got•ten (fər got′n), *v.* a pp. of **forget.**

forgot′ten man′, 1. a person no longer in the mind of the general public. **2.** *U.S. Politics.* the average wage earner, regarded as economically deprived and forgotten or ignored by the federal government during the Great Depression. [1920–25]

for-in•stance (fər in′stəns), *n.* an instance or example: *Give me a for-instance of what you mean.*

for•int (fôr′int), *n.* an aluminum coin and the monetary unit of Hungary, equal to 100 fillér. *Abbr.:* F., Ft. [1945–50; < Hungarian < It *fiorino.* See FLORIN]

for•judge (fôr juj′), *v.t.,* **-judged, -judg•ing.** *Law.* to exclude, expel, dispossess, or deprive by a judgment. Also, **forejudge.** [1250–1300; ME *forjugen* < OF *forjugier,* equiv. to *for-* out + *jugier* to JUDGE] —**for•judg′ment,** *n.*

fork (fôrk), *n.* **1.** an instrument having two or more prongs or tines, for holding, lifting, etc., as an implement for handling food or any of various agricultural tools. **2.** something resembling or suggesting this in form. **3.** See **tuning fork. 4.** *Mach.* yoke[1] (def. 9). **5.** a division into branches. **6.** the point or part at which a thing, as a river or a road, divides into branches: *Bear left at the fork in the road.* **7.** either of the branches into which a thing divides. **8.** *Horol.* (in a lever escapement) the forked end of the lever engaging with the ruby pin. See diag. under **lever escapement. 9.** a principal tributary of a river. **10.** the support of the front wheel axles of a bicycle or motorcycle, having the shape of a two-pronged fork. **11.** the barbed head of an arrow. —*v.t.* **12.** to pierce, raise, pitch, dig, etc., with a fork. **13.** to make into the form of a fork. **14.** *Chess.* to maneuver so as to place (two opponent's pieces) under simultaneous attack by the same piece. —*v.i.* **15.** to divide into branches: *Turn left where the road forks.* **16.** to turn as indicated at a fork in a road, path, etc.: *Fork left and continue to the top of the hill.* **17. fork over** or **out** or **up,** *Informal.* to hand over; deliver; pay: *Fork over the money you owe me!* [bef. 1000; ME *forke,* OE *forca* < L *furca* fork, gallows, yoke] —**fork′less,** *adj.* —**fork′like′,** *adj.*

fork•ball (fôrk′bôl′), *n. Baseball.* a pitch thrown with the ball inserted between the index and middle fingers, causing it to dip sharply near home plate. [FORK + BALL[1]]

forked (fôrkt, fôr′kid), *adj.* **1.** having a fork or forklike branches. **2.** zigzag, as lightning. **3. to speak with** or **have a forked tongue,** to speak deceitfully; attempt to deceive. Also, **forky.** [1250–1300; ME; see FORK, -ED[3]] —**fork•ed•ly** (fôr′kid lē), *adv.* —**fork′ed•ness,** *n.*

forked′ chain′, *Chem.* See **branched chain.**

fork•ful (fôrk′fōōl), *n., pl.* **-fuls.** the amount a fork can hold. [1635–45; FORK + -FUL, prob. on the model of SPOONFUL]
—**Usage.** See **-ful.**

fork•lift (fôrk′lift′), *n.* **1.** Also called **fork′lift truck′, fork′ truck′.** a small vehicle with two power-operated prongs at the front that can be slid under heavy loads and then raised for moving and stacking materials in warehouses, shipping depots, etc. —*v.t.* **2.** to move or stack by forklift. [1940–45; FORK + LIFT]

forklift (def. 1)

fork′ lunch′eon. See ***déjeuner à la fourchette.*** [1935–40]

fork•y (fôr′kē), *adj.,* **fork•i•er, fork•i•est.** forked. [1500–10; FORK + -Y[1]] —**fork′i•ness,** *n.*

For•lì (fôr lē′), *n.* a city in N Italy, SE of Bologna. 109,758.

for•lorn (fôr lôrn′), *adj.* **1.** desolate or dreary; unhappy or miserable, as in feeling, condition, or appearance. **2.** lonely and sad; forsaken. **3.** expressive of hopelessness; despairing: *forlorn glances.* **4.** bereft; destitute: *forlorn of comfort.* [bef. 1150; ME *foreloren* (ptp. of *forlesen* to lose completely), OE *forloren* (ptp. of *forlēosan*); c. OHG *firliosan* (G *verlieren*), Goth *fraliusan.* See FOR-, LORN] —**for•lorn′ly,** *adv.* —**for•lorn′•ness,** *n.*
—**Syn. 1.** pitiful, pitiable, helpless, woebegone, comfortless. **2.** alone, lost, solitary. See **desolate. 4.** deprived. —**Ant. 1.** happy. **2.** accompanied.

forlorn′ hope′, 1. a perilous or desperate enterprise. **2.** a vain hope. **3.** *Obs.* a group of soldiers assigned to perform some unusually dangerous service. [1530–40; folk-etymological alter. of D *verloren hoop* lit., lost troop]

form (fôrm), *n.* **1.** external appearance of a clearly defined area, as distinguished from color or material; configuration: *a triangular form.* **2.** the shape of a

thing or person. **3.** a body, esp. that of a human being. **4.** a dummy having the same measurements as a human body, used for fitting or displaying clothing: *a dressmaker's form.* **5.** something that gives or determines shape; a mold. **6.** a particular condition, character, or mode in which something appears: *water in the form of ice.* **7.** the manner or style of arranging and coordinating parts for a pleasing or effective result, as in literary or musical composition: *a unique form for the novel.* **8.** *Fine Arts.* **a.** the organization, placement, or relationship of basic elements, as lines and colors in a painting or volumes and voids in a sculpture, so as to produce a coherent image; the formal structure of a work of art. **b.** three-dimensional quality or volume, as of a represented object or anatomical part. **c.** an object, person, or part of the human body or the appearance of any of these, esp. as seen in nature: *His work is characterized by the radical distortion of the human form.* **9.** any assemblage of things of a similar kind constituting a component of a group, especially of a zoological group. **10.** *Crystall.* the combination of all the like faces possible on a crystal of given symmetry. **11.** due or proper shape; orderly arrangement of parts; good order. **12.** *Philos.* **a.** the structure, pattern, organization, or essential nature of anything. **b.** structure or pattern as distinguished from matter. **c.** (*cap.*) *Platonism.* idea (def. 7c). **d.** *Aristotelianism.* that which places a thing in its particular species or kind. **13.** *Logic.* the abstract relations of terms in a proposition, and of propositions to one another. **14.** a set, prescribed, or customary order or method of doing something. **15.** a set order of words, as for use in religious ritual or in a legal document: *a form for initiating new members.* **16.** a document with blank spaces to be filled in with particulars before it is executed: *a tax form.* **17.** a typical document to be used as a guide in framing others for like cases: *a form for a deed.* **18.** a conventional method of procedure or behavior: *society's forms.* **19.** a formality or ceremony, often with implication of absence of real meaning: *to go through the outward forms of a religious wedding.* **20.** procedure according to a set order or method. **21.** conformity to the usages of society; formality; ceremony: *the elaborate forms prevalent in the courts of renaissance kings.* **22.** procedure or conduct, as judged by social standards: *Such behavior is very bad form. Good form demands that we go.* **23.** manner or method of performing something; technique: *The violin soloist displayed tremendous form.* **24.** physical condition or fitness, as for performing: *a tennis player in peak form.* **25.** *Gram.* **a.** a word, part of a word, or group of words forming a construction that recurs in various contexts in a language with relatively constant meaning. Cf. **linguistic form. b.** a particular shape of such a form that occurs in more than one shape. In *I'm, 'm* is a form of *am.* **c.** a word with a particular inflectional ending or other modification. *Goes* is a form of *go.* **26.** *Ling.* the shape or pattern of a word or other construction (distinguished from *substance*). **27.** *Building Trades.* temporary boarding or sheeting of plywood or metal for giving a desired shape to poured concrete, rammed earth, etc. **28.** a grade or class of pupils in a British secondary school or in certain U.S. private schools: *boys in the fourth form.* **29.** *Brit.* a bench or long seat. **30.** Also, *Brit.,* **forme.** *Print.* an assemblage of types, leads, etc., secured in a chase to print from. —*v.t.* **31.** to construct or frame. **32.** to make or produce. **33.** to serve to make up; serve as; compose; constitute: *The remaining members will form the program committee.* **34.** to place in order; arrange; organize. **35.** to frame (ideas, opinions, etc.) in the mind. **36.** to contract or develop (habits, friendships, etc.). **37.** to give form or shape to; shape; fashion. **38.** to give a particular form or shape to; fashion in a particular manner: *Form the dough into squares.* **39.** to mold or develop by discipline or instructions: *The sergeant's job was to form boys into men.* **40.** *Gram.* **a.** to make (a derivation) by some grammatical change: *The suffix "-ly" forms adverbs from adjectives.* **b.** to have (a grammatical feature) represented in a particular shape: *English forms plurals in "-s".* **41.** *Mil.* to draw up in lines or in formation. —*v.i.* **42.** to take or assume form. **43.** to be formed or produced: *Ice began to form on the window.* **44.** to take a particular form or arrangement: *The ice formed in patches across the window.* [1175–1225; ME *forme* < OF < L *fōrma* form, figure, model, mold, sort, ML: seat] —**form′a•ble,** *adj.* —**form′a•bly,** *adv.*
—**Syn. 1.** mold, cast, cut. FORM, FIGURE, OUTLINE, SHAPE refer to an appearance that can be recognized. FORM, FIGURE, and SHAPE are often used to mean an area defined by contour without regard to other identifying qualities, as color or material. OUTLINE refers to the line that delimits a form, figure, or shape: *the outline of a hill.* FORM often includes a sense of mass or volume: *a solid form.* SHAPE may refer to an outline or a form: *an "S" shape; a woman's shape.* FIGURE often refers to a form or shape determined by its outline: *the figure eight.* FORM and SHAPE may also be applied to abstractions: *the shape or form of the future.* FORM is applied to physical objects, mental images, methods of procedure, etc.; it is a more inclusive term than either SHAPE or FIGURE: *the form of a cross, of a ceremony, of a poem.* **5.** model, pattern, jig. **9.** sort, kind, order, type. **14.** ceremony, ritual, formula, formality, rule. **16.** blank. **19, 20.** system, mode, practice, formula. **31.** model, fabricate, mold, forge, cast, outline. **32.** create. **34.** systematize, dispose. **39.** teach, educate, train. —**Ant. 1.** substance.

-form, a combining form meaning "having the form of": *cruciform.* [< L *-fōrmis*]

form•a•bil•i•ty (fôr′mə bil′i tē), *n.* the capacity of a material, as sheet steel, to be readily bent, stamped, shaped, etc. [1815–25; FORM + -ABILITY]

for•mal[1] (fôr′məl), *adj.* **1.** being in accordance with the usual requirements, customs, etc.; conventional: *to pay one's formal respects.* **2.** marked by form or ceremony: *a formal occasion.* **3.** designed for wear or use at occasions or events marked by elaborate ceremony or prescribed social observance: *The formal attire included tuxedos and full-length gowns.* **4.** requiring a type of dress suitable for such occasions: *a formal dance.* **5.** observant of conventional requirements of behavior, procedure, etc., as persons; ceremonious. **6.** excessively ceremonious: *a manner that was formal and austere.* **7.** being a matter of form only; perfunctory: *We expected more than just formal courtesy.* **8.** made or done in accordance with procedures that ensure validity: *a formal authorization.* **9.** of, pertaining to, or emphasizing the organization or composition of the constituent elements in a work of art perceived separately from its subject matter: *a formal approach to painting; the formal structure of a poem.* **10.** being in accordance with prescribed or customary forms: *a formal siege.* **11.** *Theat.* (of a stage setting) generalized and simplified in design, esp. of architectural elements, and serving as a permanent set for a play irrespective of changes in location. **12.** acquired in school; academic: *He had little formal training in economics.* **13.** symmetrical or highly organized: *a formal garden.* **14.** of, reflecting, or noting a usage of language in which syntax, pronunciation, etc., adhere to traditional standards of correctness and usage is characterized by the absence of casual, contracted, and colloquial forms: *The paper was written in formal English.* **15.** *Philos.* **a.** pertaining to form. **b.** *Aristotelianism.* not material; essential. **16.** *Logic.* See **formal logic. 17.** pertaining to the form, shape, or mode of a thing, esp. as distinguished from the substance: *formal writing, bereft of all personality.* **18.** being such merely in appearance or name; nominal: *a formal head of the government having no actual powers.* **19.** *Math.* **a.** (of a proof) in strict logical form with a justification for every step. **b.** (of a calculation) correct in form; made with strict justification for every step. **c.** (of a calculation, derivation, representation, or the like) of or pertaining to manipulation of symbols without regard to their meaning.
—*n.* **20.** a dance, ball, or other social occasion that requires formalwear. **21.** an evening gown.
—*adv.* **22.** in formal attire: *We're supposed to go formal.* [1350–1400; ME *formal, formel* < L *fōrmālis.* See FORM, -AL[1]] —**for′mal•ness,** n.
—**Syn. 2.** FORMAL, ACADEMIC, CONVENTIONAL may have either favorable or unfavorable implications. FORMAL may mean in proper form, or may imply excessive emphasis on empty form. In the favorable sense, ACADEMIC applies to scholars or higher institutions of learning; it may, however, imply slavish conformance to mere rules, or to belief in impractical theories. CONVENTIONAL, in a favorable sense, applies to desirable conformity with accepted conventions or customs; but it more often is applied to arbitrary, forced, or meaningless conformity. **5.** conforming, conformist. **6.** punctilious. **8.** official.

for•mal[2] (fôr′mal), *n. Chem.* methylal. [1895–1900; from FORMALDEHYDE]

for′mal cause′ (fôr′məl), *Aristotelianism.* See under **cause** (def. 8b). [1350–1400; ME]

form•al•de•hyde (fôr mal′də hīd′, fər-), *n. Chem.* a colorless, toxic, potentially carcinogenic, water-soluble gas, CH_2O, having a suffocating odor, usually derived from methyl alcohol by oxidation: used chiefly in aqueous solution, as a disinfectant and preservative, and in the manufacture of various resins and plastics. Also called **methanal.** Cf. **formalin.** [1870–75; FORM(IC) + ALDEHYDE; modeled on G *Formaldehyd*]

for•ma•lin (fôr′mə lin), *n. Chem.* a clear, colorless, aqueous solution of 40 percent formaldehyde. Also called **formol.** [1890–95; formerly a trademark]

for•mal•ism (fôr′mə liz′əm), *n.* **1.** strict adherence to, or observance of, prescribed or traditional forms, as in music, poetry, and art. **2.** *Relig.* strong attachment to external forms and observances. **3.** *Ethics.* a doctrine that acts are in themselves right or wrong regardless of consequences. **4.** *Logic, Math.* a doctrine, which evolved from a proposal of David Hilbert, that mathematics, including the logic used in proofs, can be based on the formal manipulation of symbols without regard to their meaning. [1830–40; FORMAL[1] + -ISM] —**for′mal•ist,** *n., adj.* —**for′mal•is′tic,** *adj.* —**for′mal•is′ti•cal•ly,** *adv.*

for•mal•i•ty (fôr mal′i tē), *n., pl.* **-ties. 1.** condition or quality of being formal; accordance with required or traditional rules, procedures, etc.; conventionality. **2.** rigorously methodical character. **3.** strict adherence to established rules and procedures; rigidity. **4.** observance of form or ceremony. **5.** marked or excessive ceremoniousness. **6.** an established order or method of proceeding: *the formalities of judicial process.* **7.** a formal act or observance. **8.** something done merely or mainly for form's sake; a requirement of custom or etiquette: *the formality of a thank-you note.* [1525–35; < L *fōrmālitās.* See FORMAL[1], -ITY]
—**Syn. 7.** rite, ritual, ceremony.

for•mal•ize (fôr′mə līz′), *v.t.,* **-ized, -iz•ing. 1.** to make formal, esp. for the sake of official or authorized acceptance: *to formalize an understanding by drawing up a legal contract.* **2.** to give a definite form or shape to. **3.** to state or restate (the rules or implied rules of a grammar or the like) in symbolic form. Also, *esp. Brit.,* **for′mal•ise′.** [1590–1600; FORMAL[1] + -IZE] —**for′mal•i•za′tion,** *n.* —**for′mal•iz′er,** *n.*

for′mal log′ic, the branch of logic concerned exclusively with the principles of deductive reasoning and with the form rather than the content of propositions. [1855–60]

for•mal•ly (fôr′mə lē), *adv.* **1.** in a formal manner: *The store was formally opened on Tuesday.* **2.** as regards form; in form: *It may be formally correct, but it is substantively wrong.* [1350–1400; ME. See FORMAL[1], -LY]

for•mal•wear (fôr′məl wâr′), *n.* clothing designed for or customarily worn on formal occasions, as tuxedos and evening gowns. Cf. **evening dress.** [FORMAL[1] + WEAR]

for•mant (fôr′mənt), *n.* **1.** *Music.* the range and number of partials present in a tone of a specific instrument, representing its timbre. **2.** *Acoustic Phonet.* one of the regions of concentration of energy, prominent on a sound spectrogram, that collectively constitute the frequency spectrum of a speech sound. The relative positioning of the first and second formants, whether periodic or aperiodic, as of the *o* of *hope* at approximately 500 and 900 cycles per second, is usually sufficient to distinguish a sound from all others. [1900–05; < L *formant-* (s. of *formāns*), prp. of *formāre* to FORM; see -ANT]

for•mat (fôr′mat), *n., v.,* **-mat•ted, -mat•ting.** —*n.* **1.** the shape and size of a book as determined by the number of times the original sheet has been folded to form the leaves. Cf. **duodecimo, folio** (def. 2), **octavo, quarto. 2.** the general physical appearance of a book, magazine, or newspaper, such as the typeface, binding, quality of paper, margins, etc. **3.** the organization, plan, style, or type of something: *The format of the show allowed for topical and controversial gags.* **4.** *Computers.* the arrangement of data for computer input or output, such as the number and size of fields in a record or the spacing and punctuation of information in a report. —*v.t.* **5.** to plan or provide a format for: *to format the annual telethon.* **6.** *Computers.* **a.** to set the format of (input or output): *Some word-processing programs format output in a variety of ways.* **b.** to prepare (a disk) for writing and reading. —*v.i.* **7.** to devise a format. [1830–40; < F < L (*liber*) *fōrmātus* (a book) formed (in a certain way)] —**for′mat•ter,** *n.*

for•mate (fôr′māt), *n. Chem.* a salt or ester of formic acid. [1800–10; FORM(IC) + -ATE[2]]

for•ma•tion (fôr mā′shən), *n.* **1.** the act or process of forming or the state of being formed: *the formation of ice.* **2.** the manner in which a thing is formed; disposition of parts; formal structure or arrangement. **3.** *Mil.* **a.** a particular disposition of troops, as in columns, squares, etc. **b.** any required assembling of the soldiers of a unit. **4.** *Geol.* **a.** a body of rocks classed as a stratigraphic unit for geologic mapping. Cf. **member** (def. 8). **b.** the process of depositing rock or mineral of a particular composition or origin. [1375–1425; late ME *formacioun* < L *fōrmātiōn-* (s. of *fōrmātiō*), equiv. to *fōrmāt(us)* (see FORM, -ATE[1]) + *-iōn-* -ION] —**for•ma′tion•al,** *adj.*
—**Syn. 1.** establishment, founding, organization.

form•a•tive (fôr′mə tiv), *adj.* **1.** giving form or shape; forming; shaping; fashioning; molding: *a formative process in manufacturing.* **2.** pertaining to formation or development: *a child's most formative years.* **3.** *Biol.* **a.** capable of developing new cells or tissue by cell division and differentiation: *formative tissue.* **b.** concerned with the formation of an embryo, organ, or the like. **4.** *Gram.* pertaining to a formative. —*n.* **5.** *Gram.* a derivational affix, particularly one that determines the part of speech of the derived word, as *-ness,* in *loudness, hardness,* etc. **6.** *Ling.* (in generative grammar) any element, as a word, affix, or inflectional ending, functioning as a minimal syntactic unit that can be used in forming larger constructions. [1480–90; < MF *formatif.* See FORMATION, -IVE] —**form′a•tive•ly,** *adv.* —**form′a•tive•ness,** *n.*
—**Syn. 2.** receptive, impressionable, susceptible.

form′ative el′ement, *Gram.* **1.** a morpheme that serves as an affix, not as a base, or root, in word formation. **2.** any noninflectional morpheme, whether base or affix. [1870–75]

form•board (fôrm′bôrd′, -bōrd′), *n.* a board or slab serving as a form for poured concrete. [1955–60; FORM + BOARD]

form′ class′, *Gram.* a class of words or forms in a given language that have one or more grammatical features in common, as, in Latin, all masculine nouns in the nominative singular, all masculine singular nouns, all masculine nouns, or all nouns. [1920–25]

form′ crit′icism, a method of textual analysis, applied especially to the Bible, in which the origin and history of certain passages are traced by isolating their literary forms, as miracle story, saying, or apothegm, on the assumption that they were fixed by oral tradition prior to compilation in written form. [1925–30] —**form-crit•i•cal** (fôrm′krit′i kəl), *adj.*

form′ drag′, *Physics.* the portion of the resisting force encountered by a body moving through a fluid that is due to the irregularity of shape of the body, reducible to a minimum by streamlining. [1930–35]

forme (fôrm), *n. Brit.* form (def. 30). [< F]

for•mée (fôr mā′), *adj.* paty. [1600–10; < F, fem. ptp. of *former* to FORM]

for•mer[1] (fôr′mər), *adj.* **1.** preceding in time; prior or earlier: *during a former stage in the proceedings.* **2.** past, long past, or ancient: *in former times.* **3.** preceding in order; being the first of two: *Our former manufacturing process was too costly.* **4.** being the first mentioned of two (distinguished from *latter*): *The former suggestion was preferred to the latter.* **5.** having once, or previously, been; erstwhile: *a former president.* [1125–75; ME, equiv. to *forme* (OE *forma* first) + *-er* -ER[4]. Cf. FOREMOST]
—**Syn. 3.** foregoing, antecedent. **5.** past, ex-.

form•er[2] (fôr′mər), *n.* **1.** a person or thing that forms or serves to form. **2.** a pupil in a particular form or grade, esp. in a British secondary school: *fifth formers.* [1300–50; ME *fourmer.* See FORM, -ER[1]]

for•mer•ly (fôr′mər lē), *adv.* **1.** in time past; in an earlier period or age; previously: *a custom formerly observed.* **2.** *Obs.* in time just past; just now. [1580–90; FORMER[1] + -LY]

form•fit•ting (fôrm′fit′ing), *adj.* designed to fit snugly around a given shape; close-fitting: *a formfitting blouse.* [1895–1900; FORM + FITTING]

form•ful (fôrm′fəl), *adj.* displaying excellent form, esp. in performing a sport. [1720–30; FORM + -FUL]

form′ ge′nus, *Biol.* an artificial taxonomic category including species, esp. of fossil forms, grouped together on the basis of morphological resemblance. [1870–75]

for•mic (fôr′mik), *adj.* **1.** of or pertaining to ants. **2.**

CONCISE ETYMOLOGY KEY: <, descended or borrowed from; >, whence; b., blend of, blended; c., cognate with; cf., compare; deriv., derivative; equiv., equivalent; imit., imitative; obl., oblique; r., replacing; s., stem; sp., spelling, spelled; resp., respelling, respelled; trans., translation; ?, origin unknown; *, unattested; ‡, probably earlier than. See the full key inside the front cover.

Chem. of or derived from formic acid. [1785–95; irreg. < L *formica* ant. Cf. F *formique*]

For•mi•ca (fôr mī′kə), *Trademark.* a brand of thermosetting plastic, usually used in transparent or printed sheets as a chemicalproof and heatproof covering for furniture, wall panels, etc.

for′mic ac′id, *Chem., Pharm.* a colorless, irritating, fuming, water-soluble liquid, CH_2O_2, originally obtained from ants and now manufactured synthetically, used in dyeing and tanning and in medicine chiefly as a counterirritant and astringent. [1785–95]

for•mi•car•i•um (fôr′mi kâr′ē əm), *n., pl.* **-car•i•a** (-kâr′ē ə). formicary. [1825–35]

for•mi•car•y (fôr′mi ker′ē), *n., pl.* **-car•ies.** an ant nest. [1810–20; < ML *formicārium* ant hill, n. use of neut. of **formicārius* of, pertaining to ants. See FORMIC, -ARIUM]

for•mi•ca•tion (fôr′mi kā′shən), *n.* a tactile hallucination involving the belief that something is crawling on the body or under the skin. [1700–10; < L (Pliny) *formicātiōn-*, s. of *formicātiō* a sensation that ants are crawling on one's skin, equiv. to *formicā(re)* to have such a sensation (v. deriv. of *formīca* ant) + *-tiōn-* -TION]

for•mi•da•ble (fôr′mi də bəl), *adj.* **1.** causing fear, apprehension, or dread: *a formidable opponent.* **2.** of discouraging or awesome strength, size, difficulty, etc.; intimidating: *a formidable problem.* **3.** arousing feelings of awe or admiration because of grandeur, strength, etc. **4.** of great strength; forceful; powerful: *formidable opposition to the proposal.* [1400–50; late ME < F < L *formidābilis* causing fear, equiv. to *formid-* (s. of *formīdāre* to fear) + *-ābilis* -ABLE] **—for′mi•da•ble•ness, for′mi•da•bil′i•ty,** *n.* **—for′mi•da•bly,** *adv.*
—Syn. 1. dreadful, appalling, threatening, menacing, fearful, frightful, horrible. **—Ant. 1.** pleasant.

form•less (fôrm′lis), *adj.* lacking a definite or regular form or shape; shapeless. [1585–95; FORM + -LESS] **—form′less•ly,** *adv.* **—form′less•ness,** *n.*

form′ let′ter, a standardized letter that can be sent to any number of persons, occasionally personalized by inserting the name of each recipient in the salutation. [1905–10, *Amer.*]

form′ nail′. See **scaffold nail.**

for•mol (fôr′môl, -mōl), *n. Chem.* formalin. [1890–95; formerly trademark]

For•mo•sa (fôr mō′sə), *n.* Taiwan.

Formo′sa Strait′. See **Taiwan Strait.**

For•mo•sus (fôr mō′səs), *n.* A.D. c816–896, Italian ecclesiastic: pope 891–896.

form′ stop′, (in poured-concrete construction) a board placed across a form to retain concrete until it sets.

for•mu•la (fôr′myə lə), *n., pl.* **-las, -lae** (-lē′). **1.** a set form of words, as for stating or declaring something definitely or authoritatively, for indicating procedure to be followed, or for prescribed use on some ceremonial occasion. **2.** any fixed or conventional method for doing something: *His mystery stories were written according to a popular formula.* **3.** *Math.* **a.** a rule or principle, frequently expressed in algebraic symbols. **b.** such a symbolic expression. **4.** *Chem.* an expression of the constituents of a compound by symbols and figures. Cf. **empirical formula, molecular formula, structural formula. 5.** a recipe or prescription: *a new formula for currant wine.* **6.** a special nutritive mixture, esp. of milk, sugar, and water, in prescribed proportions for feeding a baby. **7.** a formal statement of religious doctrine. **8.** (*cap.*) a set of specifications as to weight, engine displacement, fuel capacity, etc., for defining a class of racing cars (usually followed by a limiting numerical designation): *Some races are open to Formula One cars.* [1575–85; < L: register, form, rule. See FORM, -ULE]

for•mu•la•ic (fôr′myə lā′ik), *adj.* **1.** made according to a formula; composed of formulas: *a formulaic plot.* **2.** being or constituting a formula: *formulaic instructions.* [1880–85; FORMULA + -IC] **—for′mu•la′i•cal•ly,** *adv.*

for•mu•lar•ize (fôr′myə lə rīz′), *v.t.,* **-ized, -iz•ing.** formulate. Also, *esp. Brit.,* **for′mu•lar•ise′.** [1850–55; FORMULAR(Y) + -IZE] **—for′mu•lar•i•za′tion,** *n.* **—for′mu•lar•iz′er,** *n.*

for•mu•lar•y (fôr′myə ler′ē), *n., pl.* **-lar•ies,** *adj.* **—***n.* **1.** a collection or system of formulas. **2.** a set form of words; formula. **3.** *Pharm.* a book listing pharmaceutical substances and formulas for making medicinal preparations. **4.** *Eccles.* a book containing prescribed forms used in the service of a church. **—***adj.* **5.** of or pertaining to a formula or formulas: *the formulary aspect of a science.* **6.** of the nature of a formula: *He dispenses easy, formulary solutions to our problems.* [1535–45; < MF *formulaire*; see FORMULA, -ARY]

for•mu•late (fôr′myə lāt′), *v.t.,* **-lat•ed, -lat•ing. 1.** to express in precise form; state definitely or systematically: *He finds it extremely difficult to formulate his new theory.* **2.** to devise or develop, as a method, system, etc. **3.** to reduce to or express in a formula. [1855–60; FORMUL(A) + -ATE[1]] **—for•mu•la•ble** (fôr′myə lə bəl), *adj.* **—for′mu•la′tion,** *n.* **—for′mu•la′tor,** *n.*
—Syn. 1. articulate, frame, compose, define, specify.

for′mula u′nit, *Chem.* (of an ionic compound that does not form molecules, as most salts) the chemical formula with the least number of elements out of the set of empirical formulas having the same proportion of ions as elements: *NaCl is the formula unit for the ionic compound sodium chloride.*

for′mula weight′, *Chem.* **1.** (of a molecule) See **molecular weight. 2.** (of an ionic compound that does not form molecules) the sum of the atomic weights of the atoms of the formula unit.

for•mu•lism (fôr′myə liz′əm), *n.* adherence to or reliance on formulas. [1830–40; FORMUL(A) + -ISM] **—for′•mu•list,** *n.* **—for′mu•lis′tic,** *adj.*

for•mu•lize (fôr′myə līz′), *v.t.,* **-lized, -liz•ing.** formulate. Also, *esp. Brit.,* **for′mu•lise′.** [1850–55; FORMUL(A) + -IZE] **—for′mu•li•za′tion,** *n.* **—for′mu•liz′er,** *n.*

form′ word′. See **function word.** [1870–75]

form•work (fôrm′wûrk′), *n.* the structure of boards, bolts, etc., composing a form for poured-concrete or rammed-earth construction. [1915–20; FORM + WORK]

for•myl (fôr′mil), *adj. Chem.* containing the formyl group. [1875–80; FORM(IC) + -YL]

for•myl•ate (fôr′mə lāt′), *v.t.,* **-at•ed, -at•ing.** *Chem.* to introduce the formyl group into (an organic compound). [1930–35; FORMYL + -ATE[1]] **—for′myl•a′tion,** *n.*

for′myl group′, *Chem.* the univalent group HCO–, derived from formic acid. Also, **for′myl rad′ical.**

For•nax (fôr′naks), *n., gen.* **For•nac•is** (fôr nas′is, -nā′sis). *Astron.* the Furnace, a small southern constellation south of Cetus and Eridanus. [< L: lit., FURNACE, kiln, oven]

for•nent (fər nent′), *prep. Brit. dial.* **1.** in front of; facing. **2.** close to; next to. [1515–25; FORE[1] + (A)NENT]

For•ney (fôr′nē, fōr′-), *n., pl.* **-neys.** a steam locomotive having no front truck, four driving wheels, and a four-wheeled rear truck. See table under **Whyte classification.** [named after J. H. *Forney* (1829–1902), American engineer]

for•ni•cate[1] (fôr′ni kāt′), *v.i.,* **-cat•ed, -cat•ing.** to commit fornication. [1545–55; < LL *fornicātus* (ptp. of *fornicāri* to consort with prostitutes), equiv. to L *fornic-* (s. of *fornix*) arch, vault, basement, brothel + *-ātus* -ATE[1]] **—for′ni•ca′tor,** *n.*

for•ni•cate[2] (fôr′ni kit, -kāt′), *adj. Biol.* arched or vaulted in form. Also, **for′ni•cat′ed.** [1820–30; < L *fornicātus*, equiv. to *fornic-* (see FORNICATE[1]) + *-ātus* -ATE[1]]

for•ni•ca•tion (fôr′ni kā′shən), *n.* **1.** voluntary sexual intercourse between two unmarried persons or two persons not married to each other. **2.** *Bible.* idolatry. [1300–50; ME *fornicacioun* < LL *fornicātiōn-* (s. of *fornicātiō*). See FORNICATE[1], -ION] **—for•ni•ca•to•ry** (fôr′ni kə tôr′ē, -tōr′ē), *adj.*

for•ni•ca•trix (fôr′ni kā′triks), *n., pl.* **-ca•tri•ces** (-kə trī′sēz). a woman who commits fornication. [1580–90; < LL: prostitute; see FORNICATE, -TRIX]
—Usage. See **-trix.**

for•nic•i•form (fôr nis′ə fôrm′), *adj.* having the form of a vault. [1855–60; < L *fornic-* (s. of *fornix*) vault + -I- + -FORM]

for•nix (fôr′niks), *n., pl.* **-ni•ces** (-nə sēz′). *Anat.* any of various arched or vaulted structures, as an arching fibrous formation in the brain. [1675–85; < L: vault, arch] **—for′ni•cal,** *adj.*

for-prof•it (fər prof′it), *adj.* (of a business or institution) initiated or operated for the purpose of making a profit: *for-profit hospitals.*

for•rel (fôr′əl, for′-), *n. Bookbinding.* forel.

For•rest (fôr′ist, for′-), *n.* **1. Edwin,** 1806–72, U.S. actor. **2. John, 1st Baron,** 1847–1918, Australian explorer and statesman. **3. Nathan Bedford,** 1821–77, Confederate cavalry general in the U.S. Civil War.

For•res•tal (fôr′ə stl, -stôl′, for′-), *n.* **James Vincent,** 1892–1949, U.S. financier, secretary of Defense 1947–49.

For′rest Cit′y, a city in E Arkansas. 13,803.

for•sake (fôr sāk′), *v.t.,* **-sook, -sak•en, -sak•ing. 1.** to quit or leave entirely; abandon; desert: *She has forsaken her country for an island in the South Pacific.* **2.** to give up or renounce (a habit, way of life, etc.). [bef. 900; ME *forsaken* to deny, reject, OE *forsacan*, equiv. to *for-* FOR- + *sacan* to dispute] **—for•sak′er,** *n.*
—Syn. 1. See **desert**[2]. **2.** forswear, relinquish, forgo.

for•sak•en (fôr sā′kən), *v.* **1.** pp. of **forsake. —***adj.* **2.** deserted; abandoned; forlorn: *an old, forsaken farmhouse.* **—for•sak′en•ly,** *adv.* **—for•sak′en•ness,** *n.*

For•se•ti (fôr′set ē), *n. Scand. Myth.* the god of justice, the son of Balder and Nanna. [< ON: lit., one who presides; cf. Fris *Fositesland* name for Helgoland]

for•sook (fôr so͝ok′), *v.* a pt. of **forsake.**

for•sooth (fôr so͞oth′), *adv. Archaic.* (now used in derision or to express disbelief) in truth; in fact; indeed. [bef. 900; ME *forsothe*, OE *forsōth.* See FOR, SOOTH]

for•spent (fôr spent′), *adj. Archaic.* worn out; exhausted. Also, **forespent.** [ptp. of ME *forspenden*, OE *forspendan.* See FOR-, SPEND]

Forss•mann (fôrs′män, -mən, fōrs′-; *Ger.* fôʀs′män), *n.* **Wer•ner** (*Ger.* veʀ′nəʀ), 1904–79, German surgeon: Nobel prize for medicine 1956.

For•ster (fôr′stər), *n.* **E(dward) M(organ),** 1879–1970, English novelist.

for•ster•ite (fôr′stə rīt′), *n. Mineral.* the magnesium end member, Mg_2SiO_4, of the olivine group. [1815–25; named after J. R. *Forster* (1729–98), German naturalist; see -ITE[1]]

Forst′ner bit′ (fôrst′nər), *Carpentry.* a bit for drilling blind holes, guided from the rim rather than from the center to permit it to enter the wood at an oblique angle. Also, **Foerstner bit.** [1900–05; after Benjamin Forstner, its inventor]

for•swear (fôr swâr′), *v.,* **-swore, -sworn, -swear•ing. —***v.t.* **1.** to reject or renounce under oath: *to forswear an injurious habit.* **2.** to deny vehemently or under oath. **3.** to perjure (oneself). **—***v.i.* **4.** to swear falsely; commit perjury. [bef. 900; ME *forsweren*, OE *forswerian.* See FOR-, SWEAR] **—for•swear′er,** *n.*
—Syn. 1. abjure, relinquish, forgo, forsake, abandon.

for•sworn (fôr swôrn′, -swōrn′), *v.* **1.** pp. of **forswear. —***adj.* **2.** perjured. **—for•sworn′ness,** *n.*

for•syth•i•a (fôr sith′ē ə, -sī′thē ə, fər-), *n.* a shrub belonging to the genus *Forsythia*, of the olive family, native to China and southeastern Europe, species of which are cultivated for their showy yellow flowers, which blossom on the bare branches in early spring. [< NL, after William *Forsyth* (1737–1804), English horticulturist; see -IA]

fort (fôrt, fōrt), *n.* **1.** a strong or fortified place occupied by troops and usually surrounded by walls, ditches, and other defensive works; a fortress; fortification. **2.** any permanent army post. **3.** (formerly) a trading post. **4. hold the fort, a.** to defend one's position against attack or criticism. **b.** to maintain the existing state of affairs. [1550–60; < MF, n. use of adj. *fort* strong < L *fortis*]

fort., 1. fortification. **2.** fortified.

For•ta•le•za (fôr′tl ā′zə; *Port.* fôʀ′tə le′zə), *n.* a seaport in NE Brazil. 1,338,733. Also called **Ceará.**

for•ta•lice (fôr′tl is), *n.* **1.** a small fort; an outwork. **2.** *Archaic.* a fortress. [1375–1425; late ME < ML *fortalitia, fortalitium*, deriv. of L *fortis* strong. See FORTRESS]

For•tas (fôr′təs), *n.* **Abe,** 1910–1982, U.S. lawyer, government official, and jurist: associate justice of the U.S. Supreme Court 1965–69.

Fort′ Bel′voir (bel′vôr), a military reservation and U.S. Army training center in NE Virginia on the Potomac.

Fort′ Ben′jamin Har′rison, a military reservation and U.S. Army training center in central Indiana, NE of Indianapolis.

Fort′ Ben′ning (ben′ing), a military reservation and U.S. Army training center in W Georgia, S of Columbus; the largest infantry post in the U.S.

Fort′ Bliss′, a military reservation and U.S. Army training center NE of El Paso in W Texas.

Fort′ Boi′se, a fort formerly near Boise, in SW Idaho: an important post on the Oregon Trail.

Fort′ Bragg′, a military reservation and U.S. Army training center in S central North Carolina NW of Fayetteville.

Fort′ Camp′bell, a military reservation in SW Kentucky and NW Tennessee, NW of Clarksville, Tenn., and SW of Hopkinsville, Ky.

Fort′ Car′son, a military reservation in E central Colorado, S of Colorado Springs.

Fort′ Cas′per, a fort in central Wyoming, near Casper: an important post on the Oregon Trail.

Fort′ Col′lins, a city in N Colorado. 64,632.

Fort′ Dear′born, a former U.S. fort on the site of Chicago, 1803–37.

Fort-de-France (fôʀ də fräɴs′), *n.* a seaport on and the capital of Martinique, in the French West Indies. 97,000.

Fort′ De′trick (dē′trik), a military reservation in N Maryland, NW of Frederick.

Fort′ Dev′ens (dev′ənz), a military reservation and U.S. Army training center in NE Massachusetts, SW of Ayer.

Fort′ Dix′, a military reservation and U.S. Army training center in S central New Jersey, NNE of Mount Holly.

Fort′ Dodge′, a city in central Iowa, on the Des Moines River. 29,423.

Fort′ Don′elson, a Confederate fort in NW Tennessee, on the Cumberland River: captured by Union forces in 1862.

Fort′ Drum′, a military reservation in Watertown in N New York, approximately 10 mi. (16 km) E of Lake Ontario.

Fort′ Duquesne′, a French fort that stood on the site of Pittsburgh, Pa.: captured in 1758 by the British in the French and Indian War.

forte[1] (fôrt, fōrt *or, for 1,* fôr′tā), *n.* **1.** a strong point, as of a person; that in which one excels: *I don't know what her forte is, but it's not music.* **2.** the stronger part of a sword blade, between the middle and the hilt (opposed to *foible*). [1640–50; earlier *fort* < MF (see FORT); disyllabic pron. by assoc. with FORTE[2]]
—Syn. 1. talent, skill, excellence, strength, specialty; knack, bent.
—Pronunciation. In the sense of a person's strong point (*He draws well, but sculpture is his forte*), the older and historical pronunciation of FORTE is the one-syllable (fôrt) or (fōrt). The word is derived from the French word *fort* 'strong.' A two-syllable pronunciation (fôr′tā) is increasingly heard, especially from younger educated speakers, perhaps owing to confusion with the musical term *forte*, pronounced in English as (fôr′tā) and in Italian as (fôʀ′te). Both the one- and two-syllable pronunciations of FORTE are now considered standard.

for•te[2] (fôr′tā; *It.* fôʀ′te), *Music.* **—***adj.* **1.** (a direction) loud; with force (opposed to *piano*). **—***adv.* **2.** (a direction) loudly. **—***n.* **3.** a passage that is loud and forcible, or is intended to be so. [1715–25; < It < L *fortis* strong]

for•te-pi•a•no (fôr′tā pē ä′nō; *It.* fôʀ′te pyä′nô), *adj., adv. Music.* loud and immediately soft. [1760–70]

for•te•piano (fôr′tə pyä′nō), *n.* a piano of the late 18th and early 19th centuries with greater clarity but less volume, resonance, and dynamic range than a modern grand, revived in the late 20th century for the performance of the music of its period. [1760–70; early var. of PIANOFORTE]

Fort′ E′rie, a town in SE Ontario, in S Canada, on Lake Erie, at the beginning of the Niagara River, next to Buffalo, N.Y. 24,096.

Fort′ Eus′tis, a military reservation and U.S. Army

training center in SE Virginia near the James River, NW of Newport News.

Fort George G. Meade, a military reservation in central Maryland, SW of Baltimore.

Fort′ Gor′don, a military reservation and U.S. Army training center in N central Georgia, SW of Augusta.

forth (fôrth, fōrth), *adv.* **1.** onward or outward in place or space; forward: *to come forth; go forth.* **2.** onward in time, in order, or in a series: *from that day forth.* **3.** out, as from concealment or inaction; into view or consideration: *The author's true point comes forth midway through the book.* **4.** away, as from a place or country: *to journey forth.* —*prep.* **5.** *Archaic.* out of; forth from. [bef. 900; ME, OE; c. G *fort;* akin to FURTHER]

Forth (fôrth, fōrth), *n.* **1. Firth of,** an arm of the North Sea, in SE Scotland: estuary of Forth River. 48 mi. (77 km) long. **2.** a river in S central Scotland, flowing E into the Firth of Forth. 116 mi. (187 km) long.

forth•com•ing (fôrth′kum′ing, fōrth′-), *adj.* **1.** coming forth, or about to come forth; about to appear; approaching in time: *the forthcoming concert.* **2.** ready or available when required or expected: *He assured us that payment would be forthcoming.* **3.** frank and cooperative; candid: *In his testimony, the senator could have been more forthcoming.* **4.** friendly and outgoing; sociable. —*n.* **5.** a coming forth; appearance. [1515–25; FORTH + COMING] —**forth′com′ing•ness,** *n.*

Fort′ Hen′ry, a Confederate fort in NW Tennessee, on the Tennessee River: captured by Union forces in 1862.

Fort′ Hood′, a military reservation in central Texas, N of Austin.

forth•right (*adj., n.* fôrth′rīt′, fōrth′-; *adv.* fôrth′rīt′, fōrth′-, fôrth′rīt′, fōrth′-), *adj.* **1.** going straight to the point; frank; direct; outspoken: *It's sometimes difficult to be forthright and not give offense.* **2.** proceeding in a straight course; direct; straightforward: *a forthright glance.* —*adv.* Also, **forth′right′ly. 3.** straight or directly forward; in a direct or straightforward manner: *He told us forthright just what his objections were.* **4.** straightaway; at once; immediately: *He saw forthright that such an action was folly.* —*n.* **5.** *Archaic.* a straight course or path. [bef. 1000; ME; OE *forthrihte.* See FORTH, RIGHT] —**forth′right′ness,** *n.*

Fort′ Hua•chu′ca (wə cho͞o′kə, wä-), a military reservation and U.S. Army training center in SE Arizona, SE of Tucson.

forth•with (fôrth′with′, -wiŧħ′, fōrth′-), *adv.* immediately; at once; without delay: *Any official accused of dishonesty should be suspended forthwith.* [1250–1300; ME; see FORTH, WITH]

for•ti•eth (fôr′tē ith), *adj.* **1.** next after the thirty-ninth; being the ordinal number for 40. **2.** being one of 40 equal parts. —*n.* **3.** a fortieth part, esp. of one (1/40). **4.** the fortieth member of a series. [bef. 1100; ME *fourtithe,* OE *fēowertigotha.* See FORTY, -ETH]

for•ti•fi•ca•tion (fôr′tə fi kā′shən), *n.* **1.** the act of fortifying or strengthening. **2.** something that fortifies or protects. **3.** the art or science of constructing defensive military works. **4.** Often, **fortifications.** military works constructed for the purpose of strengthening a position; a fort: *Supposedly impregnable, the fortifications were quickly overrun.* **5.** a strengthening or improvement, as by addition of or intensification with another ingredient: *the fortification of milk with vitamin D; the fortification of wine with alcohol.* [1400–50; late ME < LL *fortificātiōn-* (s. of *fortificātiō*), equiv. to *fortificāt(us)* fortified (see FORTIFY, -ATE[1]) + *-iōn-* -ION]
—**Syn. 4.** fortress, citadel, stronghold, bulwark.

fortifica′tion ag′ate, an agate, used as a gem, having polygonal banding such that it suggests the plan of a bastion. [1880–85]

for′tified wine′, a wine, as port or sherry, to which brandy has been added in order to arrest fermentation or to increase the alcoholic content. [1905–10]

for•ti•fy (fôr′tə fī′), *v.,* **-fied, -fy•ing.** —*v.t.* **1.** to protect or strengthen against attack; surround or provide with defensive military works. **2.** to furnish with a means of resisting force or standing strain or wear: *to fortify cotton with nylon.* **3.** to make strong; impart strength or vigor to: *to fortify oneself with a good breakfast.* **4.** to increase the effectiveness of, as by additional ingredients: *to fortify a diet with vitamins; to fortify a lotion with lanolin.* **5.** to strengthen mentally or morally: *to be fortified by religious faith.* **6.** to confirm or corroborate: *to fortify an accusation with facts.* **7.** *Nutrition.* to add one or more ingredients to (a food) to increase its nutritional content. **8.** to add alcohol to (wine or the like). —*v.i.* **9.** to set up defensive works; erect fortifications. [1400–50; late ME *fortifien* < MF *fortifier* < LL *fortificāre,* equiv. to L *forti(s)* strong + *-ficāre* -FY] —**for′ti•fi′a•ble,** *adj.* —**for′ti•fi′er,** *n.* —**for′ti•fy′ing•ly,** *adv.*
—**Syn. 3.** strengthen, reinforce. **5.** hearten, embolden.

For′tin barom′eter (fôr′tan; *Fr.* fôʀ taɴ′), an adjustable cistern barometer, the most common of those employing mercury. [1870–75; named after J. *Fortin* (1750–1831), French physicist who invented it]

Fort′ Ir′win, a military reservation in SW California, NE of Barstow.

for•tis (fôr′tis), *adj., n., pl.* **-tes** (-tēz). *Phonet.* —*adj.* **1.** pronounced with considerable muscular tension and breath pressure, resulting in a strong fricative or explosive sound. In stressed position (p, t, k, ch, f, th, s, sh) and sometimes (h) are fortis in English as compared with (b, d, g, j, v, ŧħ, z, and zh), which are lenis. Cf. **lenis.** —*n.* **2.** a fortis consonant. [1905–10; < L: strong, powerful, firm]

CONCISE ETYMOLOGY KEY: <, descended or borrowed from; >, whence; b., blend of, blended; c., cognate with; cf., compare; deriv., derivative; equiv., equivalent; imit., imitative; obl., oblique; r., replacing; s., stem; sp., spelling, spelled; resp., respelling, respelled; trans., translation; ?, origin unknown; *, unattested; ‡, probably earlier than. See the full key inside the front cover.

for•tis•si•mo (fôr tis′ə mō′; *It.* fôʀ tēs′sē mô′), *Music.* —*adj.* **1.** (a direction) very loud. —*adv.* **2.** (a direction) very loudly. [1715–25; < It; superl. of *forte* FORTE[2]]

for•ti•tion (fôr tish′ən), *n.* **1.** *Phonet.* a phonological process that strengthens consonant articulation at the beginnings of syllables, causing devoicing or the formation of stops. **2.** *Ling.* a type of Celtic mutation that derives historically from phonological fortition. [FORT(IS) + -ITION, on the model of LENITION]

for•ti•tude (fôr′ti to͞od′, -tyo͞od′), *n.* mental and emotional strength in facing difficulty, adversity, danger, or temptation courageously: *Never once did her fortitude waver during that long illness.* [1350–1400; ME < L *fortitūdō* strength, firmness, courage, equiv. to *forti(s)* strong + *-tūdō* -TUDE]
—**Syn.** See **patience.**

for•ti•tu•di•nous (fôr′ti to͞od′n əs, -tyo͞od′-), *adj.* having or showing fortitude; marked by bravery or courage. [1745–55; < L *fortitūdin-* (s. of *fortitūdō*) FORTITUDE + -OUS]

Fort′ Jack′son, a military reservation and U.S. Army training center in N central South Carolina, NE of Columbia.

Fort′ Jef′ferson, a national monument in Dry Tortugas, Fla.: a federal prison 1863–73; now a marine museum.

Fort′ Kear′ney, a former fort in S Nebraska, near Kearney: an important post on the Oregon Trail.

Fort′ Knox′, a military reservation in N Kentucky, SSW of Louisville: location of U.S. federal gold depository since 1936.

Fort-La•my (*Fr.* fôʀ lᴀ mē′), *n.* former name of **N'Djamena.**

Fort′ Lar′amie, a former U.S. fort in SE Wyoming: important post on the Oregon Trail.

Fort′ Lau′der•dale (lô′dər dāl′), a city in SE Florida: seashore resort. 153,256.

Fort′ Leav′enworth, a military reservation and U.S. Army training center in E Kansas adjoining Leavenworth, one of the oldest (1827) military posts W of the Mississippi and site of federal penitentiary.

Fort′ Lee′, 1. a city in NE New Jersey. 32,449. **2.** a military reservation and U.S. Army training center in SE Virginia, NE of Petersburg.

Fort′ Leon′ard Wood′, a military reservation and U.S. Army training center in SW Missouri, SW of Rolla.

Fort Lesley J. McNair, a military reservation in SW Washington, D.C., on the Potomac River, SW of the Capitol.

Fort′ Lew′is, a military reservation in W central Washington State, SW of Tacoma.

Fort′ Mad′ison, a city in SE Iowa, on the Mississippi. 13,520.

Fort′ McClel′lan, a military reservation and U.S. Army training center in NE Alabama, NE of Anniston.

Fort′ McHen′ry, a fort in N Maryland, at the entrance to Baltimore harbor: during its bombardment by the British in 1814, Francis Scott Key wrote *The Star-Spangled Banner.*

Fort′ Mc•Mur′ray (mək mûr′ē, -mur′ē), a town in NE Alberta, in W Canada, on the Athabaska River. 31,000.

Fort′ Meigs′, a former fort in NW Ohio: unsuccessfully attacked by the British in 1813.

Fort′ Mims′, a stockade in SW Alabama, near the junction of the Alabama and Tombigbee rivers: Indian massacre 1813.

Fort′ Mon′mouth, a military reservation and U.S. Army training center in E central New Jersey, SE of Red Bank; site of signal school.

Fort′ Monroe′, 1. a fort at the entrance to Hampton Roads, in SE Virginia. **2.** a military reservation in SE Virginia, SE of Hampton at Old Point Comfort.

Fort′ Moul′trie (mo͞ol′trē), a fort in the harbor of Charleston, S.C.: defended against British in the American Revolution by Col. William Moultrie (1730–1805); in the Civil War, played an important role in the bombardment of Fort Sumter and in Confederate defense.

Fort′ My′er (mī′ər), a military reservation in N Virginia, N of Alexandria.

Fort′ My′ers (mī′ərz), a city on the W coast of Florida. 36,638.

fort•night (fôrt′nīt′, -nit), *n.* the space of fourteen nights and days; two weeks. [bef. 1000; ME *fourtenight,* contr. of OE *fēowertēne niht.* See FOURTEEN, NIGHT]

fort•night•ly (fôrt′nīt′lē), *adj., adv., n., pl.* **-lies.** —*adj.* **1.** occurring or appearing once a fortnight. —*adv.* **2.** once a fortnight. —*n.* **3.** a periodical issued every two weeks. [1790–1800; FORTNIGHT + -LY]

Fort′ Or′ange, a former Dutch fort on the site of Albany, N.Y.

Fort′ Payne′, a town in NE Alabama. 11,485.

Fort′ Peck′ (pek), a dam on the Missouri River in NE Montana.

Fort′ Pick′ens, a fort in NW Florida, at the entrance to Pensacola Bay: occupied by Union forces throughout the Civil War.

Fort′ Pierce′, a city on the E coast of Florida. 33,802.

Fort′ Polk′, a military reservation and U.S. Army training center in W central Louisiana, SW of Alexandria.

Fort′ Pulas′ki, a fort in E Georgia, at the mouth of the Savannah River: captured by Union forces in 1862; now a national monument.

FORTRAN (fôr′tran), *n. Computers.* a high-level programming language used mainly for solving problems in science and engineering. [1955–60; *for(mula) tran(slation)*]

for•tress (fôr′tris), *n.* **1.** a large fortified place; a fort or group of forts, often including a town; citadel. **2.** any place of exceptional security; stronghold. [1300–50; ME *forteresse* < OF < VL **fortaricia* (cf. ML *fortalitia*), equiv. to L *fort(is)* strong + *-ar-,* formative of uncertain meaning + *-icia* -ICE]

Fort′ Ri′ley, a military reservation in NE Kansas, NE of Junction City.

Fort′ Ruck′er (ruk′ər), a military reservation and U.S. Army training center in SE Alabama, NW of Dothan.

Fort′ Sam′ Hous′ton, a military reservation and U.S. Army training center in San Antonio, Tex.

Fort′ Sher′idan, a military reservation in NE Illinois, on W shore of Lake Michigan S of Lake Forest.

Fort′ Sill′, a military reservation and U.S. Army training center in SW Oklahoma, N of Lawton; field artillery school.

Fort′ Smith′, a city in W Arkansas, on the Arkansas River. 71,384.

Fort′ Stew′art, a military reservation in SE Georgia, SW of Savannah.

Fort′ Sum′ter, a fort in SE South Carolina, in the harbor of Charleston: its bombardment by the Confederates opened the Civil War on April 12, 1861.

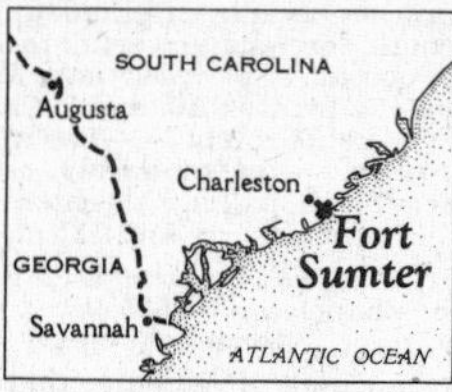

Fort′ Thom′as (tom′əs), a city in N Kentucky. 16,012.

for•tu•i•tous (fôr to͞o′i təs, -tyo͞o′-), *adj.* **1.** happening or produced by chance; accidental: *a fortuitous encounter.* **2.** lucky; fortunate: *a series of fortuitous events that advanced her career.* [1645–55; < L *fortuitus, fortuĭtus,* equiv. to *fortu-* (u-stem base, otherwise unattested, akin to *fors,* gen. *fortis* chance, luck) + *-itus, -ītus* adj. suffix (for formation cf. GRATUITOUS); see -OUS] —**for•tu′i•tous•ly,** *adv.* —**for•tu′i•tous•ness,** *n.*
—**Syn. 1.** incidental. See **accidental.**
—**Usage.** FORTUITOUS has developed in sense from "happening by chance" to "happening by lucky chance" to simply "lucky, fortunate." This development was probably influenced by the similarity of FORTUITOUS to FORTUNATE and perhaps to FELICITOUS: *A fortuitous late-night snowfall made for a day of great skiing.*
Many object to the use of FORTUITOUS to mean simply "fortunate" and insist that it should be limited to its original sense of "accidental." In modern standard use, however, FORTUITOUS almost always carries the senses both of accident or chance and luck or fortune. It is infrequently used in its sense of "accidental" without the suggestion of good luck, and even less frequently in the sense "lucky" without at least a suggestion of accident or chance: *A fortuitous encounter with a former schoolmate led to a new and successful career for the artist.*

for•tu•i•ty (fôr to͞o′i tē, -tyo͞o′-), *n., pl.* **-ties** for 2, 3. **1.** the state or quality of being fortuitous; fortuitous character. **2.** an accidental occurrence. **3.** an instance of great luck or good fortune. [1740–50; FORTUIT(OUS) + -Y[3]]

For•tu•na (fôr to͞o′nə, -tyo͞o′-), *n.* the ancient Roman goddess of fortune, identified with the Greek goddess Tyche.

for•tu•nate (fôr′chə nit), *adj.* **1.** having good fortune; receiving good from uncertain or unexpected sources; lucky: *a fortunate young actor who got the lead in the play.* **2.** bringing or indicating good fortune; resulting favorably; auspicious: *She made a fortunate decision to go on to medical school.* [1350–1400; ME *fortunat* < L *fortūnātus* made prosperous or happy (ptp. of *fortūnāre*). See FORTUNE, -ATE[1]] —**for′tu•nate•ly,** *adv.* —**for′tu•nate•ness,** *n.*
—**Syn. 1.** advantageous, successful, prosperous. FORTUNATE, HAPPY, LUCKY refer to persons who enjoy, or events that produce, good fortune. FORTUNATE implies that the success is obtained by the operation of favorable circumstances more than by direct effort; it is usually applied to grave or large matters (esp. those happening in the ordinary course of things): *fortunate in one's choice of a wife; a fortunate investment.* HAPPY emphasizes a pleasant ending or something that happens at just the right moment: *By a happy accident I received the package on time.* LUCKY, a more colloquial word, is applied to situations that turn out well by chance: *lucky at cards; my lucky day.*

for•tune (fôr′chən), *n., v.,* **-tuned, -tun•ing.** —*n.* **1.** position in life as determined by wealth: *to make one's fortune.* **2.** wealth or riches: *to lose a small fortune in bad investments.* **3.** great wealth; ample stock of money, property, and the like: *to be worth a fortune.* **4.** chance; luck: *They each had the bad fortune to marry the wrong person.* **5. fortunes.** things that happen or are to happen to a person in his or her life. **6.** fate; lot; destiny: *whatever my fortune may be.* **7.** (*cap.*) chance personified, commonly regarded as a mythical being distributing arbitrarily or capriciously the lots of life: *Perhaps Fortune will smile on our venture.* **8.** good luck; success; prosperity: *a family blessed by fortune.* **9.** *Archaic.* a wealthy woman; an heiress. **10. tell someone's fortune,** to profess to inform someone of future events in his or her own life; foretell. —*v.t.* **11.** *Archaic.* to endow (someone or something) with a fortune. —*v.i.* **12.** *Archaic.* to chance or happen; come by chance. [1250–1300; ME < OF < L *fortūna* chance, luck, fortune, deriv. of *fort-* (s. of *fors*) chance] —**for′tune•less,** *adj.*

—Syn. 4. fate, destiny, providence; kismet, karma. **7.** Moira; Lady Luck.

for′tune cook′ie, a thin folded wafer containing a prediction or maxim printed on a slip of paper: often served as a dessert in Chinese restaurants. [1960–65]

for′tune hunt′er, a person who hopes to prosper, esp. through marriage to someone of wealth. [1680–90] **—for′tune-hunt′ing,** *adj., n.*

for•tune•tell•er (fôr′chən tel′ər), *n.* a person who claims the ability to predict the future. Also, **for′•tune-tell′er.** [1580–90; FORTUNE + TELLER[1]]

for•tune•tell•ing (fôr′chən tel′ing), *n.* **1.** the act or practice of predicting the future. *—adj.* **2.** engaged in or used for fortunetelling. Also, **for′tune-tell′ing.** [1550–60; FORTUNE + TELL + -ING[1]]

Fort′ Victo′ria, a former name of **Masvingo.**

Fort′ Wal′ton Beach′, a city in NW Florida. 20,829.

Fort′ Wayne′, a city in NE Indiana. 172,196.

Fort′ Wil′liam. See under **Thunder Bay.**

Fort′ Worth′, a city in N Texas. 385,141.

for•ty (fôr′tē), *n., pl.* **-ties,** *adj.* *—n.* **1.** a cardinal number, ten times four. **2.** a symbol for this number, as 40 or XL or XXXX. **3.** a set of this many persons or things. **4. forties,** the numbers, years, degrees, or the like, from 40 through 49, as in referring to numbered streets, indicating the years of a lifetime or of a century, or degrees of temperature: *His office is in the West Forties. Her parents are in their forties. The temperature will be in the forties.* *—adj.* **5.** amounting to 40 in number. [bef. 950; ME *fourti,* OE *fēowertig* (c. OFris *fiuwertich,* OHG *fiorzug,* G *vierzig*). See FOUR, -TY[1]]

for•ty-eight (fôr′tē āt′), *n.* **1.** a cardinal number, 40 plus 8. **2.** a symbol for this number, as 48 or XLVIII. **3.** a set of this many persons or things. **4. the forty-eight,** the 48 contiguous states of the U.S. *—adj.* **5.** amounting to 48 in number.

for•ty-eighth (fôr′tē ātth′, -āth′), *adj.* **1.** next after the forty-seventh; being the ordinal number for 48. **2.** being one of 48 equal parts. *—n.* **3.** a forty-eighth part, esp. of one (1/48). **4.** the forty-eighth member of a series.

for•ty-eight•mo (fôr′tē āt′mō), *n., pl.* **-mos** for 2, *adj.* *—n.* **1.** a book size of about 2½ × 4 in. (6 × 10 cm), determined by printing on sheets folded to form 48 leaves or 96 pages. *Abbr.:* 48mo, 48° **2.** a book of this size. *—adj.* **3.** in forty-eightmo. [1885–90; FORTY-EIGHT + -MO]

for•ty-fifth (fôr′tē fifth′ *or, often,* -fith′), *adj.* **1.** next after the forty-fourth; being the ordinal number for 45. **2.** being one of 45 equal parts. *—n.* **3.** a forty-fifth part, esp. of one (1/45). **4.** the forty-fifth member of a series.

for•ty-first (fôr′tē fûrst′), *adj.* **1.** next after the fortieth; being the ordinal number for 41. **2.** being one of 41 equal parts. *—n.* **3.** a forty-first part, esp. of one (1/41). **4.** the forty-first member of a series.

for•ty-five (fôr′tē fīv′), *n.* **1.** a cardinal number, 40 plus 5. **2.** a symbol for this number, as 45 or XLV. **3.** a set of this many persons or things. *—adj.* **4.** amounting to 45 in number.

45, *n., pl.* **45s, 45's.** a seven-inch phonograph record played at 45 r.p.m., esp. a popular-music single. [1945–50]

.45, *n., pl.* **.45s, .45's.** a pistol, revolver, or cartridge of .45-caliber, or having a diameter of .45 inch. Also, **forty-five.**

for•ty-four (fôr′tē fôr′, -fōr′), *n.* **1.** a cardinal number, 40 plus 4. **2.** a symbol for this number, as 44 or XLIV. **3.** a set of this many persons or things. *—adj.* **4.** amounting to 44 in number.

for•ty-fourth (fôr′tē fôrth′, -fōrth′), *adj.* **1.** next after the forty-third; being the ordinal number for 44. **2.** being one of 44 equal parts. *—n.* **3.** a forty-fourth part, esp. of one (1/44). **4.** the forty-fourth member of a series.

For′ty Hours′, a Roman Catholic devotion in which the Blessed Sacrament is exposed for veneration for 40 hours by the churches of a diocese sequentially for two-day periods.

for•ty•ish (fôr′tē ish), *adj.* **1.** approaching or around the age of 40 years. **2.** around the number 40 or a quantity of 40. [1815–25; FORTY + -ISH[1]]

for•ty-nine (fôr′tē nīn′), *n.* **1.** a cardinal number, 40 plus 9. **2.** a symbol for this number, as 49 or XLIX. **3.** a set of this many persons or things. *—adj.* **4.** amounting to 49 in number.

for•ty-nin•er (fôr′tē nī′nər), *n.* a person, esp. a prospector, who went to California in 1849 during the gold rush. [1850–55, *Amer.*]

for•ty-ninth (fôr′tē nīnth′), *adj.* **1.** next after the forty-eighth; being the ordinal number for 49. **2.** being one of 49 equal parts. *—n.* **3.** a forty-ninth part, esp. of one (1/49). **4.** the forty-ninth member of a series.

for•ty-one (fôr′tē wun′), *n.* **1.** a cardinal number, 40 plus 1. **2.** a symbol for this number, as 41 or XLI. **3.** a set of this many persons or things. *—adj.* **4.** amounting to 41 in number.

for•ty•pen•ny (fôr′tē pen′ē), *adj.* being 5 in. (13 cm) long: *a fortypenny nail. Symbol:* 40d [1760–70; FORTY + -PENNY]

for•ty-sec•ond (fôr′tē sek′ənd), *adj.* **1.** next after the forty-first; being the ordinal number for 42. **2.** being one of 42 equal parts. *—n.* **3.** a forty-second part, esp. of one (1/42). **4.** the forty-second member of a series.

for•ty-sev•en (fôr′tē sev′ən), *n.* **1.** a cardinal number, 40 plus 7. **2.** a symbol for this number, as 47 or XLVII. **3.** a set of this many persons or things. *—adj.* **4.** amounting to 47 in number.

for•ty-sev•enth (fôr′tē sev′ənth), *adj.* **1.** next after the forty-sixth; being the ordinal number for 47. **2.** being one of 47 equal parts. *—n.* **3.** a forty-seventh part, esp. of one (1/47). **4.** the forty-seventh member of a series.

for•ty-six (fôr′tē siks′), *n.* **1.** a cardinal number, 40 plus 6. **2.** a symbol for this number, as 46 or XLVI. **3.** a set of this many persons or things. *—adj.* **4.** amounting to 46 in number.

for•ty-sixth (fôr′tē siksth′), *adj.* **1.** next after the forty-fifth; being the ordinal number for 46. **2.** being one of 46 equal parts. *—n.* **3.** a forty-sixth part, esp. of one (1/46). **4.** the forty-sixth member of a series.

for•ty-third (fôr′tē thûrd′), *adj.* **1.** next after the forty-second; being the ordinal number for 43. **2.** being one of 43 equal parts. *—n.* **3.** a forty-third part, esp. of one (1/43). **4.** the forty-third member of a series.

for•ty-three (fôr′tē thrē′), *n.* **1.** a cardinal number, 40 plus 3. **2.** a symbol for this number, as 43 or XLIII. **3.** a set of this many persons or things. *—adj.* **4.** amounting to 43 in number.

for•ty-two (fôr′tē to͞o′), *n.* **1.** a cardinal number, 40 plus 2. **2.** a symbol for this number, as 42 or XLII. **3.** a set of this many persons or things. **4.** a game for two persons or two partnerships played with dominoes but based upon the rules for all fours. *—adj.* **5.** amounting to 42 in number.

for′ty winks′, *Informal.* a short nap. [1815–25]

fo•rum (fôr′əm, fōr′əm), *n., pl.* **fo•rums, fo•ra** (fôr′ə, fōr′ə). **1.** the marketplace or public square of an ancient Roman city, the center of judicial and business affairs and a place of assembly for the people. **2.** a court or tribunal: *the forum of public opinion.* **3.** an assembly, meeting place, television program, etc., for the discussion of questions of public interest. **4. the Forum,** the forum in the ancient city of Rome. [1425–75; late ME < L: marketplace, public place, akin to *foris, forās* outside, *foris* DOOR]

for•ward (fôr′wərd), *adv.* Also, **forwards. 1.** toward or at a place, point, or time in advance; onward; ahead: *to move forward; from this day forward; to look forward.* **2.** toward the front: *Let's move forward so we can hear better.* **3.** into view or consideration; out; forth: *He brought forward several good suggestions.* **4.** toward the bow or front of a vessel or aircraft. **5.** ahead (defs. 4, 5). *—adj.* **6.** directed toward a point in advance; moving ahead; onward: *a forward motion.* **7.** being in a condition of advancement; well-advanced: *It was quite forward in the season when we finished our planting.* **8.** ready, prompt, or eager. **9.** presumptuous, impertinent, or bold: *a rude, forward child.* **10.** situated in the front or forepart: *the forward part of the ship.* **11.** of or pertaining to the future; for the future or forward delivery: *forward buying; a forward price.* **12.** lying ahead or to the front: *Take the forward path.* **13.** radical or extreme, as persons or opinions: *the forward trend in certain liberal thought.* *—n.* **14.** *Sports.* **a.** a player stationed in advance of others on a team. **b.** *Football.* a lineman. **c.** *Basketball.* either of two players stationed in the forecourt. **15.** *Finance.* something bought, as a security, for future delivery. *—v.t.* **16.** to send forward; transmit, esp. to a new address: *to forward a letter.* **17.** to advance or help onward; promote: *The training will help to forward your career.* *—v.i.* **18.** to advance or play a mechanism, recording tape, cassette, etc., in the forward direction: *to find a musical selection without forwarding through the whole cassette.* [bef. 900; ME; OE *for(e)weard.* See FORE[1], -WARD] **—for′ward•a•ble,** *adj.* **—for′ward•ly,** *adv.*

—Syn. 1. FORWARD, ONWARD both indicate a direction toward the front or a movement in a frontward direction. FORWARD applies to any movement toward what is or is conceived to be the front or a goal: *to face forward; to move forward in the aisles.* ONWARD applies to any movement in continuance of a course: *to march onward toward a goal.* **8.** willing, earnest, zealous. **9.** assuming, impudent. See **bold. 11.** early, preliminary, future, premature. **13.** unconventional, progressive. **17.** further, foster. **—Ant. 6.** backward.

for′ward deliv′ery, *Com.* delivery at a future date. [1925–30]

for′ward dive′. See **front dive.**

for′ward ech′elon, (in a military operation) the troops and officers in a combat zone or in a position to engage the enemy. Cf. **rear echelon.**

for•ward•er (fôr′wər dər), *n.* **1.** a person who forwards. **2.** See **freight forwarder.** [1540–50; FORWARD + -ER[1]]

for′ward exchange′, a foreign bill purchased at a stipulated price and payable at a future date. [1925–30]

for•ward•ing (fôr′wər ding), *n.* **1.** *Bookbinding.* a stage in which sections of a book are stitched, fitted with a back, pasted, etc., before being placed in the completed cover. **2.** *Engraving.* the process of starting a copper plate by etching and of finishing with a graver. [1625–35; FORWARD + -ING[1]]

for′warding a′gent. See **freight forwarder.** [1890–95]

for•ward-look•ing (fôr′wərd lo͝ok′ing), *adj.* planning for or anticipating possible future events, conditions, etc.; progressive. [1790–1800]

for•ward•ness (fôr′wərd nis), *n.* **1.** overreadiness to push oneself forward; lack of appropriate modesty; presumption; boldness. **2.** cheerful readiness; promptness; eagerness. **3.** condition of being in advance. [1515–25; FORWARD + -NESS]

for′ward pass′, *Football.* a pass in which the ball is thrown in the direction of advance toward the opponent's goal. [1900–05]

for′ward quota′tion, the price quoted on a forward delivery.

for•wards (fôr′wərdz), *adv.* forward. [1350–1400; FORWARD + -S[1]]

for•ward-think•ing (fôr′wərd thing′king), *adj.* planning or tending to plan for the future; forward-looking.

for•went (fôr went′), *v.* pt. of **forgo.**

For Whom′ the Bell′ Tolls′, a novel (1940) by Ernest Hemingway.

for•why (fôr hwī′, -wī′), *Archaic.* *—adv.* **1.** why; wherefore. *—conj.* **2.** because. [bef. 1000; ME; OE *for hwī.* See FOR, WHY]

for•worn (fôr wôrn′, -wōrn′), *adj. Archaic.* worn-out; exhausted. Also, **foreworn.** [1500–10; ptp. of obs. *forwear,* ME *forweren.* See FOR-, WEAR]

for•zan•do (fôrt sän′dō; *It.* fôʀ tsän′dô), *adj., adv. Music.* sforzando. [1820–30]

F.O.S., 1. free on station. **2.** free on steamer. Also, **f.o.s.**

Fos•dick (foz′dik), *n.* **Harry Emerson,** 1878–1969, U.S. preacher and author.

Fosh•an (fush′än′), *n. Pinyin, Wade-Giles.* a city in S central Guangdong province, in SE China, near Canton. 100,000. Also, **Fatshan.** Formerly, **Nanhai.**

Foss (fos), *n.* **Lu•kas** (lo͞o′kəs), born 1922, U.S. pianist, conductor, and composer; born in Germany.

fos•sa[1] (fos′ə), *n., pl.* **fos•sae** (fos′ē). *Anat.* a pit, cavity, or depression, as in a bone. [1820–30; < L: ditch, trench, fosse, short for *fossa (terra)* dug or dug out (earth), n. use of fem. of *fossus,* ptp. of *fodere* to dig]

fos•sa[2] (fos′ə), *n.* a forest-dwelling genetlike mammal, *Cryptoprocta ferox,* of the civet family, native to Madagascar, with a short coat of white, black, gray, or brown: now rare. Also called **fos′sa cat′.** [1830–40; < Malagasy; cf. earlier *fossane* (< F < Malagasy)]

fos•sar•i•an (fo sâr′ē ən, fô-), *n.* fossor. [< LL *fossāri(us)* (see FOSSA[1], -ARY) + -AN]

fosse (fos, fôs), *n.* **1.** a moat or defensive ditch in a fortification, usually filled with water. **2.** any ditch, trench, or canal. Also, **foss.** [1350–1400; ME < MF < L *fossa* FOSSA]

fos•sette (fo set′, fô-), *n.* **1.** a small hollow or depression, as in a bivalve shell; dimple. **2.** *Pathol.* a small, deep corneal ulcer. [1840–50; < F: dimple, small cavity. See FOSSE, -ETTE]

fos•sick (fos′ik), *Chiefly Australian.* *—v.i.* **1.** *Mining.* to undermine another's digging; search for waste gold in relinquished workings, washing places, etc. **2.** to search for any object by which to make gain: *to fossick for clients.* *—v.t.* **3.** to hunt; seek; ferret out. [1850–55; cf. dial. *fossick* troublesome person, *fussick* to bustle about, appar. FUSS + *-ick,* var. of -OCK] **—fos′sick•er,** *n.*

fos•sil (fos′əl), *n.* **1.** any remains, impression, or trace of a living thing of a former geologic age, as a skeleton, footprint, etc. **2.** a markedly outdated or old-fashioned person or thing. **3.** a linguistic form that is archaic except in certain restricted contexts, as *nonce* in *for the nonce,* or that follows a rule or pattern that is no longer productive, as the sentence *So be it.* *—adj.* **4.** of the nature of a fossil: *fossil insects.* **5.** belonging to a past epoch or discarded system; antiquated: *a fossil approach to economics.* [1555–65; < L *fossilis* dug up (cf. *fodere* to dig); r. earlier *fossile* < F] **—fos′sil•like′,** *adj.*

fos′sil fu′el, *Energy.* any combustible organic material, as oil, coal, or natural gas, derived from the remains of former life.

fos′sil gum′, any gum, found chiefly in the earth, that was yielded by a now fossilized tree. Cf. **amber.**

fos•sil•if•er•ous (fos′ə lif′ər əs), *adj.* bearing or containing fossils, as rocks or strata. [1840–50; FOSSIL + -I- + -FEROUS]

fos•sil•ize (fos′ə līz′), *v.,* **-ized, -iz•ing.** *—v.t.* **1.** *Geol.* to convert into a fossil; replace organic with mineral substances in the remains of an organism. **2.** to change as if into mere lifeless remains or traces of the past. **3.** to make rigidly antiquated: *Time has fossilized such methods.* *—v.i.* **4.** to become a fossil or fossillike: *The plant fossilized in comparatively recent geologic time.* **5.** *Ling.* (of a linguistic form, feature, rule, etc.) to become permanently established in the interlanguage of a second-language learner in a form that is deviant from the target-language norm and that continues to appear in performance regardless of further exposure to the target language. Also, *esp. Brit.,* **fos′sil•ise′.** [1785–95; FOSSIL + -IZE] **—fos′sil•iz′a•ble,** *adj.* **—fos′sil•i•za′tion,** *n.*

fos′sil tur′quoise. See **bone turquoise.**

fos•sor (fos′ər), *n.* (in the early Christian church) a minor clergyman employed as a gravedigger. Also called **fossarian.** [1850–55; < L: digger (LL: gravedigger), equiv. to *fod(ere)* to dig + *-tor* -TOR, with *dt* > *ss*]

fos•so•ri•al (fo sôr′ē əl, -sōr′-), *adj. Zool.* **1.** digging or burrowing. **2.** adapted for digging, as the hands, feet, and bone structure of moles, armadillos, and aardvarks. [1830–40; < LL *fossōri(us)* adapted to digging (equiv. to L *fod(ere)* to dig + *-tōrius* -TORY[1], with *dt* > *ss*) + -AL[1]]

fos•su•la (fos′yə lə), *n., pl.* **-lae** (-lē′). *Anat.* a small fossa. [1835–45; < L: a little ditch. See FOSSA, -ULE]

fos•ter (fô′stər, fos′tər), *v.t.* **1.** to promote the growth or development of; further; encourage: *to foster new ideas.* **2.** to bring up, raise, or rear, as a foster child. **3.** to care for or cherish. **4.** *Brit.* to place (a child) in a foster home. **5.** *Obs.* to feed or nourish. [bef. 1000; ME; OE *fōstor* nourishment, *fōstrian* to nourish; c. ON *fōstr;* akin to FOOD] **—fos′ter•er,** *n.* **—fos′ter•ing•ly,** *adv.*

—Syn. 1. favor, forward, advance; foment, instigate. **2.** nurse, nourish, sustain, support, maintain. **3.** See **cherish. —Ant. 1.** discourage.

Fos•ter (fô′stər, fos′tər), *n.* **1. Stephen (Collins),** 1826–64, U.S. songwriter. **2. William Z(eb•u•lon)** (zeb′yə lən), 1881–1961, U.S. labor organizer: leader in the Communist party. **3.** a male given name.

CONCISE PRONUNCIATION KEY: act, cāpe, dâre, pärt; set, ēqual; *if,* ice; ox, ōver, ôrder, oil, bo͝ok, bo͞ot, out; up, ûrge; child; sing; shoe; thin, *th*at; zh as in *treasure.* ə = *a* as in *alone, e* as in *system, i* as in *easily, o* as in *gallop, u* as in *circus;* ᵊ as in *fire* (fīᵊr), *hour* (ouᵊr). l and n can serve as syllabic consonants, as in *cradle* (krād′l), and *button* (but′n). See the full key inside the front cover.

fos·ter·age (fô′stər ij, fos′tər-), *n.* **1.** the act of fostering or rearing another's child as one's own. **2.** the condition of being a foster child. **3.** an act of promoting or encouraging: *The board will undertake the fosterage of our new project.* [1605–15; FOSTER + -AGE]

fos′ter broth′er, a boy brought up with another child of different parents. [bef. 1000; ME; OE *fōster brōthor*]

fos′ter care′, the raising or supervision of foster children, as orphans or delinquents, in an institution, group home, or private home, usually arranged through a government or social-service agency that provides remuneration for expenses.

fos′ter child′, **1.** a child raised by someone who is not its natural or adoptive parent. **2.** a needy child, as one living in an impoverished country, supported or aided by contribution to a specific charity. [1150–1200; ME *fostercild*]

Fos′ter Cit′y, a city in W California. 23,287.

fos′ter daugh′ter, a girl raised like one's own daughter, though not such by birth or adoption.

fos′ter fa′ther, a man who takes the place of a father in raising a child. [bef. 900; ME; OE]

fos′ter home′, a household in which a child is raised by someone other than its natural or adoptive parent.

fos·ter·ling (fô′stər ling, fos′tər-), *n.* See **foster child.** [bef. 1000; ME; OE *fōstorling.* See FOSTER, -LING[1]]

fos′ter moth′er, **1.** a woman who takes the place of a mother in raising a child. **2.** a nurse. [bef. 1000; ME; OE]

fos′ter par′ent, a foster father or foster mother.

fos′ter sis′ter, a girl brought up with another child of different parents. [1640–50]

fos′ter son′, a boy raised like one's own son, though not such by birth or adoption. [1400–50; late ME]

Fos·to·ri·a (fô stôr′ē ə, -stōr′-, fo-), *n.* a city in N Ohio. 15,743.

F.O.T., *Com.* free on truck. Also, **f.o.t.**

Foth·er·in·ghay (foth′ə ring gā′), *n.* a village in NE Northamptonshire, in E England, near Peterborough: Mary, Queen of Scots, imprisoned here and executed 1587.

fou (fo͞o), *adj. Scot.* drunk. [1525–35; Scots form of FULL]

fou (fo͞o), *adj. French.* crazy; foolish.

Fou·cault (fo͞o kō′), *n.* **Jean Ber·nard Lé·on** (zhäN beʀ naʀ′ lā ôN′), 1819–68, French physicist.

Foucault′ pen′dulum, *Physics.* a pendulum that demonstrates the rotation of the earth by exhibiting an apparent change in its plane of oscillation. [1850–55; named after J.B.L. FOUCAULT]

Fouc·quet (*Fr.* fo͞o ke′), *n.* Fouquet.

fou·dre (fo͞o′dʀᵉ), *n., pl.* ***fou·dres*** (fo͞o′dʀᵉ). *French.* a large cask for maturing, storing, and transporting wine.

fou·droy·ant (fo͞o droi′ənt; *Fr.* fo͞o dʀwa yäN′), *adj.* **1.** striking as with lightning; sudden and overwhelming in effect; stunning; dazzling. **2.** *Pathol.* (of disease) beginning in a sudden and severe form. [1830–40; < F, prp. of *foudroyer* to strike with lightning, deriv. of *foudre* lightning < L *fulgur*]

fouet·té (fwe tā′), *n., pl.* **-tés** (-tāz′; *Fr.* -tā′). *Ballet.* a whipping movement of the free leg, often executed during a turn. [1820–30; < F, ptp. of *fouetter* to whip]

fought (fôt), *v.* pt. and pp. of **fight.**

Fou·ji·ta (fo͞o′jē tä′), *n.* **Tsu·gou·ha·ru** (tso͞o′go͞o hä′ro͞o), 1886–1968, Japanese painter in France.

foul (foul), *adj.,* **-er, -est,** *adv., n., v.* —*adj.* **1.** grossly offensive to the senses; disgustingly loathsome; noisome: *a foul smell.* **2.** containing or characterized by offensive or noisome matter: *foul air; foul stagnant water.* **3.** filthy or dirty, as places, receptacles, clothes, etc. **4.** muddy, as a road. **5.** clogged or obstructed with foreign matter: *a foul gas jet.* **6.** unfavorable or stormy: *foul weather.* **7.** contrary, violent, or unfavorable, as the wind. **8.** grossly offensive in a moral sense. **9.** abominable, wicked, or vile, as deeds, crime, slander, etc. **10.** scurrilous, profane, or obscene; offensive: *foul language.* **11.** contrary to the rules or established usages, as of a sport or game; unfair: *a foul blow.* **12.** *Baseball.* pertaining to a foul ball or a foul line. **13.** limited in freedom of movement by obstruction, entanglement, etc.: *a foul anchor.* **14.** abounding in errors or in marks of correction, as a printer's proof, manuscript, or the like. **15.** *Naut.* **a.** (of the underwater portion of a hull) encrusted and impeded with barnacles, seaweed, etc. **b.** (of a mooring place) involving inconveniences and dangers, as of colliding with vessels or other objects when swinging with the tide. **c.** (of the bottom of a body of water) affording a poor hold for an anchor (opposed to *clean*). **16.** *North Eng. and Scot.* not fair; ugly or unattractive. **17.** *Obs.* disfigured.
—*adv.* **18.** in a foul manner; vilely; unfairly. **19.** *Baseball.* into foul territory; so as to be foul: *It looked like a homer when he hit it, but it went foul.* **20. fall foul** or **afoul of, a.** to collide with, as ships. **b.** to come into conflict with; quarrel. **c.** to make an attack; assault. **21. run foul** or **afoul of,** to come into collision or controversy with: *to run foul of the press.*
—*n.* **22.** something that is foul. **23.** a collision or entanglement: *a foul between two racing sculls.* **24.** a violation of the rules of a sport or game: *The referee called it a foul.* **25.** *Baseball.* See **foul ball.**
—*v.t.* **26.** to make foul; defile; soil. **27.** to clog or obstruct, as a chimney or the bore of a gun. **28.** to collide with. **29.** to cause to become entangled or caught, as a rope. **30.** to defile; dishonor; disgrace: *His reputation had been fouled by unfounded accusations.* **31.** *Naut.* (of barnacles, seaweed, etc.) to cling to (a hull) so as to encumber. **32.** *Baseball.* to hit (a pitched ball) foul (often fol. by *off* or *away*): *He fouled off two curves before being struck out on a fastball.*
—*v.i.* **33.** to become foul. **34.** *Naut.* to come into collision, as two boats. **35.** to become entangled or clogged: *The rope fouled.* **36.** *Sports.* to make a foul play; give a foul blow. **37.** *Baseball.* to hit a foul ball. **38. foul one's nest.** to dishonor one's own home, family, or the like. **39. foul out, a.** *Baseball.* to be put out by hitting a foul ball caught on the fly by a player on the opposing team. **b.** *Basketball.* to be expelled from a game for having committed more fouls than is allowed. **40. foul up,** *Informal.* to cause confusion or disorder; bungle; spoil. [bef. 900; (adj. and n.) ME *ful, foul,* OE *fūl;* c. Goth *fuls,* ON *fūll,* OHG *fūl;* akin to L *pūs* PUS, *pūtēre* to stink, Gk *pýon* pus; (adv.) ME *fule, foule,* deriv. of the adj.; (v.) ME *fulen,* deriv. of the adj.] —**foul′ly,** *adv.*
—**Syn. 1.** repulsive, repellent. **2.** fetid, putrid, stinking. **3.** unclean, polluted, sullied, soiled, stained, tainted, impure. See **dirty. 6.** rainy, tempestuous. **7.** adverse. **9.** base, shameful, infamous. **10.** smutty, vulgar, coarse, low. **26.** sully, stain, dirty, besmirch, taint, pollute. **30.** shame. —**Ant. 1.** pleasant. **3, 26.** clean. **5, 6.** clear.

fou·lard (fo͞o lärd′, fə-), *n.* a soft, lightweight silk, rayon, or cotton of plain or twill weave with printed design, for neckties, scarves, trimmings, etc. [1820–30; < F, of uncert. orig.]

foul′ ball′, *Baseball.* **1.** a batted ground ball that is hit and played outside the foul lines, or that passes outside the foul lines at first or third base, or that is played outside the foul line between home and first or third base regardless of where hit. **2.** a batted fly ball played or landing outside the foul lines. **3.** *Slang.* an incompetent, unlucky, or eccentric person. [1855–60, *Amer.*]

foul·brood (foul′bro͝od′), *n.* any of several bacterial diseases of honeybee larvae, characterized by the putrefying of body tissues. [1860–65; FOUL + BROOD]

fouled-up (fould′up′), *adj. Informal.* confused, chaotic, or disorganized. [1945–50]

foul·ing (fou′ling), *n.* an encrusted deposit, esp. on a submerged object, as the hull of a ship. [1350–1400; ME *fulinge;* see FOUL, -ING[1]]

foul′ line′, **1.** *Baseball.* either of the two lines connecting home plate with first and third base respectively, or their continuations to the end of the outfield. **2.** Also called **free throw line.** *Basketball.* a line on the court 15 ft. (4.6 m) from the backboard, from which foul shots are taken. **3.** *Bowling.* a line on an alley at right angles to the gutters and 60 ft. (18.3 m) from the center of the spot for the headpin, across which a bowler may not step for fair delivery of the ball. [1875–80, *Amer.*]

foul·mart (fo͞o′mərt, -märt′), *n.* foumart.

foul′ mat′ter, *Printing.* materials, as manuscript, galleys, or proofs, that have been superseded by revised proofs or galleys or by the bound book, and have been returned to the publisher by the printer. Also called **dead matter.**

foul·mouthed (foul′mouthd′, -moutht′), *adj.* using obscene, profane, or scurrilous language; given to filthy or abusive speech. [1590–1600; FOUL + MOUTH + -ED[3]]

foul·ness (foul′nis), *n.* **1.** the state or quality of being foul: *The foulness of the accusation incensed us all.* **2.** something that is foul; foul matter; filth. **3.** wickedness. [bef. 1150; ME; OE *fūlnes.* See FOUL, -NESS]

foul′ play′, **1.** any treacherous or unfair dealing, esp. involving murder: *We feared that he had met with foul play.* **2.** unfair conduct in a game. [1600–10]

foul′ pole′, *Baseball.* either of two poles, one on each foul line, being the vertical continuation of the outfield fence or wall, used by the umpire as a sight line in determining whether a fly ball hit near the foul line is a fair or foul ball.

fouls (foulz), *n.* (*used with a singular v.*) *Vet. Pathol.* See **foot rot.** [FOUL + -S[3]]

foul′ shot′, *Basketball.* **1.** a throw from the foul line, given a player after a foul has been called against an opponent. **2.** a score of one point made on this throw. Also called **free throw.** [1900–05]

foul′ tip′, *Baseball.* a pitched ball that glances off the bat into foul territory, usually near the catcher, ruled a strike if the catcher catches it before it hits the ground, otherwise ruled an ordinary foul ball. [1865–70, *Amer.*]

foul-up (foul′up′), *n. Informal.* **1.** a condition of difficulty or disorder brought on by inefficiency, stupidity, etc. **2.** failure of a mechanical part to operate correctly. **3.** a person who habitually makes mistakes; bungler. [1950–55, *Amer.;* n. use of v. phrase *foul up*]

fou·mart (fo͞o′mərt, -märt′), *n.* the European polecat, *Mustela putorius.* Also, **foulmart.** [1300–50; ME *fulmard, folmarde.* See FOUL, MARTEN]

found[1] (found), *v.* **1.** pt. and pp. of **find. 2.** equipped, outfitted, or furnished: *He bought a new boat, fully found.* —*adj.* **3.** *Brit.* provided or furnished without additional charge, as to a tenant; included within the price, rent, etc. (often used postpositively): *Room to let, laundry found.* —*n.* **4.** something that is provided or furnished without charge, esp. meals given a domestic: *Maid wanted, good salary and found.*

found[2] (found), *v.t.* **1.** to set up or establish on a firm basis or for enduring existence: *to found a new publishing company.* **2.** to lay the lowest part of (a structure) on a firm base or ground: *a house founded on solid rock.* **3.** to base or ground (usually fol. by *on* or *upon*): *a story founded on fact.* **4.** to provide a basis or ground for. [1250–1300; ME *founden* < OF *fonder* < L *fundāre,* deriv. of *fundus* bottom, foundation]
—**Syn. 1.** organize, inaugurate, institute, originate.

found[3] (found), *v.t.* **1.** to melt and pour (metal, glass, etc.) into a mold. **2.** to form or make (an article) of molten material in a mold; cast. [1350–1400; ME *fonden* < MF *fondre* to melt, cast < L *fundere* to pour, melt, cast]

found′ art′, art comprised of found objects.

foun·da·tion (foun dā′shən), *n.* **1.** the basis or groundwork of anything: *the moral foundation of both society and religion.* **2.** the natural or prepared ground or base on which some structure rests. **3.** the lowest division of a building, wall, or the like, usually of masonry and partly or wholly below the surface of the ground. **4.** the act of founding, setting up, establishing, etc.: *a policy in effect since the foundation.* **5.** the state of being founded. **6.** an institution financed by a donation or legacy to aid research, education, the arts, etc.: *the Ford Foundation.* **7.** an endowment for such an institution. **8.** a cosmetic, as a cream or liquid, used as a base for facial makeup. **9.** See **foundation garment. 10.** *Solitaire.* a card of given denomination on which other cards are to be added according to denomination or suit. [1350–1400; ME *foundacioun* < L *fundātiōn-* (s. of *fundātiō*), equiv. to *fundāt(us)* (ptp. of *fundāre;* see FOUND[2]) + *-iōn-* -ION] —**foun·da′tion·al,** *adj.* —**foun·da′tion·al·ly,** *adv.* —**foun·da′tion·ar′y,** *adj.*
—**Syn. 2.** See **base**[1]. **2, 3.** footing. **4, 5.** establishment, settlement. —**Ant. 2, 3.** superstructure.

Founda′tion Day′, former name of **Australia Day.**

founda′tion gar′ment, an undergarment, as a girdle or corset, worn by women to support or give shape to the contours of the body. Also called **foundation.** [1925–30]

founda′tion stone′, **1.** any of the stones composing the foundation of a building. **2.** a cornerstone. [1645–55]

found·er[1] (foun′dər), *n.* a person who founds or establishes. [1275–1325; ME; see FOUND[2], -ER[1]]

found·er[2] (foun′dər), *v.i.* **1.** (of a ship, boat, etc.) to fill with water and sink. **2.** to fall or sink down, as buildings, ground, etc.: *Built on a former lake bed, the building has foundered nearly ten feet.* **3.** to become wrecked; fail utterly: *The project foundered because public support was lacking.* **4.** to stumble, break down, or go lame, as a horse: *His mount foundered on the rocky path.* **5.** to become ill from overeating. **6.** *Vet. Pathol.* (of a horse) to suffer from laminitis. —*v.t.* **7.** to cause to fill with water and sink: *Rough seas had foundered the ship in mid-ocean.* **8.** *Vet. Pathol.* to cause (a horse) to break down, go lame, or suffer from laminitis. —*n.* **9.** *Vet. Pathol.* laminitis. [1300–50; ME *foundren* < MF *fondrer* to plunge to the bottom, submerge < VL **fundorāre,* deriv. of **fundor-,* taken as s. of L *fundus* bottom]
—**Syn. 3.** collapse, perish, succumb, topple, sink; flop.

found·er[3] (foun′dər), *n.* a person who founds or casts metal, glass, etc. [1175–1225; ME; see FOUND[3], -ER[1]]

found′er effect′, *Biol.* the accumulation of random genetic changes in an isolated population as a result of its proliferation from only a few parent colonizers.

foun·der·ous (foun′dər əs), *adj.* likely to cause foundering; miry; swampy. [1760–70; FOUNDER[2] + -OUS]

found′ers' shares′, *Finance.* shares of stock given, at least nominally, for consideration to the organizers or original subscribers of a corporation, sometimes carrying special voting privileges, but likely to receive dividends after other classes of stock. [1885–90]

found′ers' type′, *Brit. Print.* See **foundry type.**

Found′ing Fa′thers, **1.** the delegates to the Constitutional Convention in Philadelphia in 1787. **2.** (*often l.c.*) any group of founders: *the town's founding fathers.*

found·ling (found′ling), *n.* an infant or small child found abandoned; a child without a known parent or guardian. [1250–1300; ME *found(e)ling.* See FOUND[1], -LING[1]]

found′ling hos′pital, an institutional home for foundlings. [1750–60]

found′ ob′ject, a natural or manufactured object that is perceived as being aesthetically satisfying and exhibited as such. [1955–60; trans. of F *objet trouvé*]

found′ po′em, a composition made by combining fragments of such printed material as newspapers, signs, or menus, and rearranging them into the form of a poem. [1965–70; by analogy with FOUND OBJECT]

found·ress (foun′dris), *n.* a woman who establishes something, as an institution or religious order; founder. [1400–50; late ME *founderesse;* see FOUNDER[1], -ESS]
—**Usage.** See **-ess.**

foun′drous (foun′drəs), *adj.* founderous.

found·ry (foun′drē), *n., pl.* **-ries. 1.** an establishment for producing castings in molten metal. **2.** the act or process of founding or casting metal. **3.** the category of metal objects made by founding; castings. [1595–1605; < F *fonderie.* See FOUND[3], -ERY]

found′ry proof′, *Print.* a proof pulled for a final checking before printing plates are made.

found′ry type′, *Print.* type cast in individual characters for setting by hand. Also, *Brit.,* **founders' type.**

fount[1] (fount), *n.* **1.** a spring of water; fountain. **2.** a source or origin: *a fount of inspiration to his congregation.* [1585–95; short for FOUNTAIN]

fount[2] (fount, font), *n. Print. Brit.* font[2].

foun·tain (foun′tn), *n.* **1.** a spring or source of water; the source or head of a stream. **2.** the source or origin of anything. **3.** a jet or stream of water (or other liquid) made by mechanical means to spout or rise from an opening or structure, as to afford water for use, to cool the air, or to serve for ornament. **4.** a structure for discharging such a jet or a number of jets, often an elaborate or artistic work with basins, sculptures, etc. **5.** See **drinking fountain. 6.** See **soda fountain. 7.** a reservoir for a liquid to be supplied gradually or continuously, as in a fountain pen. **8.** *Heraldry.* a roundel barry-wavy, argent and azure. [1375–1425; late ME *fontayne* < OF *fontaine* < LL *fontāna,* n. use of fem. of L *fontānus* of a spring, equiv. to *font-* (s. of *fons*) spring +

-ānus -AN] —**foun′tained,** *adj.* —**foun′tain•less,** *adj.* —**foun′tain•like′,** *adj.*
—**Syn. 2.** birthplace, cradle, genesis, wellspring.

foun′tain grass′, a perennial grass, *Pennisetum setaceum,* of Ethiopia, having bristly spikes, often rose-purple, grown as an ornamental.

foun•tain•head (foun′tn hed′), *n.* **1.** a fountain or spring from which a stream flows; the head or source of a stream. **2.** a chief source of anything: *a fountainhead of information.* [1575–85; FOUNTAIN + HEAD]

Foun′tain of Youth′, a fabled spring whose waters were supposed to restore health and youth, sought in the Bahamas and Florida by Ponce de León, Narváez, De Soto, and others.

foun′tain pen′, a pen with a refillable reservoir that provides a continuous supply of usually fluid ink to its point. [1700–10]

foun′tain plant′, Joseph's-coat. [1890–95, *Amer.*]

Foun′tain Val′ley, a city in SW California. 55,080.

Fou•qué (fōō kā′), *n.* **Frie•drich Hein•rich Karl, Baron de la Motte-** (frē′drikh hīn′rikh kärl, də lä mōt′), 1777–1843, German romanticist: poet and novelist.

Fou•quet (*Fr.* fōō ke′), *n.* **1. Jean** or **Je•han** (*both Fr.* zhän), c1420–c80, French painter. **2. Ni•co•las** (nē kô-lä′), (*Marquis de Belle-Isle*), 1615–80, French statesman. Also, **Foucquet.**

Fou•quier-Tin•ville (fōō kyā tan vēl′), *n.* **An•toine Quen•tin** (än twan′ kän tan′), 1747?–95, French revolutionist: prosecutor during the Reign of Terror.

four (fôr, fōr), *n.* **1.** a cardinal number, three plus one. **2.** a symbol of this number, 4 or IV or IIII. **3.** a set of this many persons or things. **4.** a playing card, die face, or half of a domino face with four pips. **5. fours,** *Jazz.* alternate four-bar passages, as played in sequence by different soloists: *with guitar and piano trading fours.* **6.** *Auto.* **a.** an automobile powered by a four-cylinder engine. **b.** the engine itself. **7. on all fours.** See **all fours** (def. 3). —*adj.* **8.** amounting to four in number. [bef. 1000; ME *four, fower,* OE *fēower;* c. OHG *fior* (G *vier*), Goth *fidwor;* akin to L *quattuor,* Gk *tésseres* (Attic *téttares*)]

four-a-cat (fôr′ə kat′, fōr′-), *n.* See **four old cat.**

four•bag•ger (fôr′bag′ər, fōr′-), *n. Baseball.* See **home run.** [1925–30; FOUR + BAGGER]

four′-ball′ match′ (fôr′bôl′, -bôl′, fōr′-), *Golf.* a match, scored by holes, between two pairs of players, in which the four players tee off and the partners alternate in hitting the pair's ball having the better lie off the tee. [1900–05]

four-bang•er (fôr′bang′ər, fōr′-), *n. Auto. Slang.* a four-cylinder engine.

four′ bits′, *Slang.* 50 cents. [1830–40, *Amer.*] —**four′-bit′,** *adj.*

4 × 4 (fôr′ bī fôr′, fōr′ bī fōr′, bə), a four-wheeled automotive vehicle having four-wheel drive.

four-chan•nel (fôr′chan′l, fōr′-), *adj. Audio.* quadraphonic. [1965–70]

four•ché (fōōr shā′), *adj. Heraldry.* forked or divided into two at the extremity or in extremities: *a lion's tail fourché; a cross fourché.* Also, **four•chée′.** [1350–1400; ME < F; see FORK, -EE]

four•chette (fōōr shet′), *n.* **1.** *Anat.* the fold of skin that forms the posterior margin of the vulva. **2.** *Ornith.* furcula; wishbone. **3.** *Zool.* the frog of an animal's foot. **4.** a strip of leather or fabric joining the front and back sections of a glove finger. **5.** *Chiefly Bridge.* a tenace. [1745–55; < F, dim. of *fourche;* see FORK -ETTE]

four′-col′or prob′lem (fôr′kul′ər, fōr′-), *Math.* the problem, solved in 1976, of proving the theorem that any geographic map can be colored using only four colors so that no connected countries with a common boundary are colored the same color. Also called **four′-col′or the′orem.** [1875–80]

four′-col′or proc′ess, *Print.* a process for reproducing colored illustrations in a close approximation to their original hues by photographing the artwork successively through magenta, cyan, and yellow color-absorbing filters to produce four plates that are printed successively with yellow, red, blue, and black inks. [1895–1900]

Four′ Cor′ners, a point in the SW U.S., at the intersection of 37° N lat. and 109° W long., where the boundaries of four states—Arizona, Utah, Colorado, and New Mexico—meet: the only such point in the U.S.

four-cor•ners (fôr′kôr′nərz, fōr′-), *n.* (*used with a singular or plural v.*) *Northern and Western U.S.* a place where roads cross at right angles; a crossroads. Also, **four′ cor′ners.**

four-cy•cle (fôr′sī′kəl, fōr′-), *adj.* noting or pertaining to an internal-combustion engine in which a complete cycle in each cylinder requires four strokes, one to draw in air or an air-fuel mixture, one to compress it, one to ignite it and do work, and one to scavenge the cylinder. Also, **four-stroke.** Cf. **two-cycle.** [1905–10]

four-di•men•sion•al (fôr′di men′shə nl, fōr′-), *adj. Math.* of a space having points, or a set having elements, which require four coordinates for their unique determination. [1875–80]

Four•drin•i•er (fōōr drin′ē ər), *n.* a machine for manufacturing paper. [1830–40; named after Henry and Sealy *Fourdrinier,* 19th-century English papermakers]

four-eyed (fôr′īd′, fōr′-), *adj.* **1.** having or seeming to have four eyes. **2.** *Facetious or Disparaging.* wearing eyeglasses. [1880–85]

four′-eyed fish′, a small, surface-swimming fish, *Anableps anableps,* inhabiting shallow, muddy streams of Mexico and Central America, having each eye divided, with the upper half adapted for seeing in air and the lower half for seeing in water. Also, **four′eye fish′** (fôr′ī′, fōr′ī′). Also called **anableps, four-eyes.**

four′-eyed opos′sum, a small opossum, *Metachirops* (*Philander*) *opossum,* ranging from Mexico to Brazil, having a white spot above each eye.

four-eyes (fôr′īz′, fōr′-), *n., pl.* **-eyes. 1.** *Facetious or Disparaging.* a person who wears eyeglasses. **2.** See **four-eyed fish.** [1870–75]

4-F (fôr′ef′, fōr′-), *n.* **1.** a U.S. Selective Service classification designating a person considered physically, psychologically, or morally unfit for military duty. **2.** a person so classified.

four′ flush′, *Poker.* a hand having four cards of one suit and one card of another suit; an imperfect flush. [1885–90, *Amer.*]

four-flush (fôr′flush′, fōr′-), *v.i.* **1.** to bluff. **2.** *Poker.* to bluff on the basis of a four flush. [1895–1900, *Amer.*]

four•flush•er (fôr′flush′ər, fōr′-), *n.* a person who makes false or pretentious claims; bluffer. [1900–05, *Amer.;* FOUR FLUSH + -ER[1]]

four•fold (fôr′fōld′, fōr′-), *adj.* **1.** comprising four parts or members. **2.** four times as great or as much. —*adv.* **3.** in fourfold measure. [bef. 1000; ME *foure fald,* OE *feowerfealdum.* See FOUR, -FOLD]

four′fold block′, *Mach.* a block having four pulleys or sheaves. Cf. **block** (def. 11).

four′fold pur′chase, a tackle that is composed of a rope passed through two fourfold blocks in such a way as to provide mechanical power in the ratio of 1 to 5 or 1 to 4, depending on whether hauling is done on the running or the standing block and without considering friction. Cf. **tackle** (def. 2).

four-foot•ed (fôr′fōōt′id, fōr′-), *adj.* having four feet: *He considers his dog to be his four-footed friend.* [1125–75; ME *four foted*]

four′-footed but′terfly. See **brush-footed butterfly.**

four′ free′doms, freedom of speech, freedom of worship, freedom from want, and freedom from fear: stated as goals of U.S. policy by President Franklin D. Roosevelt on January 6, 1941.

four•gon (fōōr gôn′), *n., pl.* **-gons** (-gôn′). *French.* a long covered wagon for carrying baggage, goods, military supplies, etc.; a van or tumbril.

four-hand•ed (fôr′han′did, fōr′-), *adj.* **1.** involving four hands or players, as a game at cards: *Bridge is usually a four-handed game.* **2.** intended for four hands, as a piece of music for the piano. **3.** having four hands, or four feet adapted for use as hands; quadrumanous. Also, **four-hand** (fôr′hand′, fōr′-) (for defs. 1, 2). [1765–75]

Four′-H′ Club′ (fôr′āch′, fōr′-), an organization sponsored by the U.S. Department of Agriculture to instruct young people, originally in rural areas, in modern farming methods and other useful skills, as carpentry and home economics. Also, **4-H Club.** [so called from its aim to improve head, heart, hands, and health] —**4-H,** *adj.* —**4-H′er,** *n.*

Four′ Horse′men of the Apoc′alypse, four riders on white, red, black, and pale horses symbolizing pestilence, war, famine, and death, respectively. Rev. 6:2–8. Also called **Four′ Horse′men.**

Four′ Hun′dred, the exclusive social set of a city or area. Also, **400.** [1885–90, *Amer.;* allegedly after the capacity of the ballroom in the mansion of Mrs. William Astor, New York hostess of the late 19th century]

four′-hun•dred-day′ clock′ (fôr′hun′drəd dā′, fōr′-), a clock that needs to be wound once a year, having the works exposed under a glass dome and utilizing a torsion pendulum.

401(k) (fôr′ō′wun′kā′, fōr′-), *n.* a savings plan that allows employees to contribute a fixed amount of income to a retirement account and to defer taxes until withdrawal.

Fou•rier (fōōr′ē ā′, -ē ər; *for 1, 2 also Fr.* fōō ryā′), *n.* **1. Fran•çois Ma•rie Charles** (frän swa′ ma rē′ sharl), 1772–1837, French socialist, writer, and reformer. **2. Jean Bap•tiste Jo•seph** (zhän ba tēst′ zhō zef′), 1768–1830, French mathematician and physicist. **3.** a crater in the third quadrant of the face of the moon: about 36 miles (58 km) in diameter.

Fou′rier anal′ysis, *Physics, Math.* **1.** the expression of any periodic function as a sum of sine and cosine functions, as in an electromagnetic wave function. Cf. **Fourier series. 2.** See **harmonic analysis.** [1925–30; named after J.B.J. FOURIER]

Fou•ri•er•ism (fōōr′ē ə riz′əm), *n.* the social system proposed by François Marie Charles Fourier, under which society was to be organized into phalanxes or associations, each large enough for all industrial and social requirements. [1835–45; < F *fouriérisme.* See FOURIER, -ISM] —**Fou′ri•er•ist, Fou•ri•er•ite** (fōōr′ē ə rīt′), *n.* —**Fou′ri•er•is′tic,** *adj.*

Fou′rier se′ries, *Math.* an infinite series that involves linear combinations of sines and cosines and approximates a given function on a specified domain. [1875–80; see FOURIER ANALYSIS]

Fou′rier trans′form, *Math.* a mapping of a function, as a signal, that is defined in one domain, as space or time, into another domain, as wavelength or frequency, where the function is represented in terms of sines and cosines. [1920–25; see FOURIER ANALYSIS]

four-in-hand (fôr′in hand′, fōr′-), *n.* **1.** a long necktie to be tied in a slipknot with the ends left hanging. **2.** a vehicle drawn by four horses and driven by one person. **3.** a team of four horses. —*adj.* **4.** of or pertaining to a four-in-hand. [1785–95]

four-lane (fôr′lān′, fōr′-), *adj.* **1.** (of a highway) having two lanes for traffic in each direction: *a four-lane thruway.* —*n.* **2.** Also, **four-lan•er** (fôr′lā′nər, fōr′-). a four-lane highway.

four′-leaf clo′ver (fôr′lēf′, fōr′-), a clover leaf having four leaflets instead of the usual three, purported to bring good luck. [1840–50]

four-leg•ged (fôr′leg′id, -legd′, fōr′-), *adj.* **1.** having four legs. **2.** *Naut.* (of a schooner) having four masts. [1655–65]

four′-let•ter word′ (fôr′let′ər, fōr′-), **1.** any of a number of short words, usually of four letters, considered offensive or vulgar because of their reference to excrement or sex. **2.** any word, typically of four letters, that represents something forbidden, disliked, or regarded with extreme distaste: *In the dieter's vocabulary, "cake" is a four-letter word.* [1925–30]

four-mast•ed (fôr′mas′tid, -mä′stid, fōr′-), *adj. Naut.* carrying four masts.

four′-masted brig′, *Naut.* See **jackass bark** (def. 2).

Four′ Moderniza′tions, goals of the political leadership in China after the death of Mao Zedong: modernization of agriculture, industry, national defense, and science and technology. [trans. of Chin *sìge xiàndài-huà*]

Four′ No′ble Truths′, the doctrines of Buddha: all life is suffering, the cause of suffering is ignorant desire, this desire can be destroyed, the means to this is the Eightfold Path.

four-o'clock (fôr′ə klok′, fōr′-), *n.* **1.** a common garden plant, *Mirabilis jalapa,* of the four-o'clock family, having tubular red, white, yellow, or variegated flowers that open late in the afternoon. **2.** any plant of the same genus. [1750–60]

four′-o'clock fam′ily, the plant family Nyctaginaceae, characterized by chiefly tropical herbaceous plants and shrubs having colored, petallike bracts beneath petalless flowers and winged or grooved dry fruit, and including the bougainvillea and four-o'clock.

four′ of a kind′, *Poker.* a set of four cards of the same denominations. [1930–35]

four old cat (fôr′ ə kat′, fōr′), *Games.* three old cat played with four batters. Also, **four′ o'cat′, four-a-cat.** [1850–55]

four-on-the-floor (fôr′on thə flôr′, fōr′on thə flōr′, -ôn-), *Auto. n.* **1.** a four-speed manual transmission having the gearshift set into the floor. —*adj.* **2.** of or pertaining to such a transmission.

four′-part har′mony (fôr′pärt′, fōr′-), harmony in which each chord has four tones, creating, in sum, four melodic lines.

four•pence (fôr′pəns, fōr′-), *n. Brit.* a sum of money worth four English pennies. [1715–25; FOUR + PENCE]

four•pen•ny (fôr′pen′ē, -pə nē, fōr′-), *adj.* **1.** *Carpentry.* **a.** noting a nail $1\frac{1}{2}$ in. (3.8 cm) long. **b.** noting certain fine nails $1\frac{3}{8}$ in. (3.5 cm) long. *Symbol:* 4d **2.** *Brit.* of the amount or value of fourpence. [1375–1425; late ME. See FOUR, -PENNY]

four•plex (fôr′pleks, fōr′-), *n. Archit.* quadplex. [1970–75; FOUR + *-plex,* abstracted from DUPLEX (APARTMENT), in place of QUADRUPLEX]

four•post•er (fôr′pō′stər, fōr′-), *n.* **1.** a bed with four corner posts, as for supporting a canopy, curtains, etc. **2.** a four-masted sailing vessel. [1815–25; FOUR + POST[1] + -ER[1]]

four′ ques′tions, *Judaism.* the four questions about the significance of the Seder service, traditionally asked at the Passover Seder by the youngest person and answered by the reading of the Haggadah.

four•ra•gère (fōōr′ə zhâr′; *Fr.* fōō ra zher′), *n., pl.* **-gères** (-zhârz′; *Fr.* -zher′). (in French and U.S. military use) **1.** an ornament of cord worn on the shoulder. **2.** such a cord awarded as an honorary decoration, as to members of a regiment. [1915–20; < F]

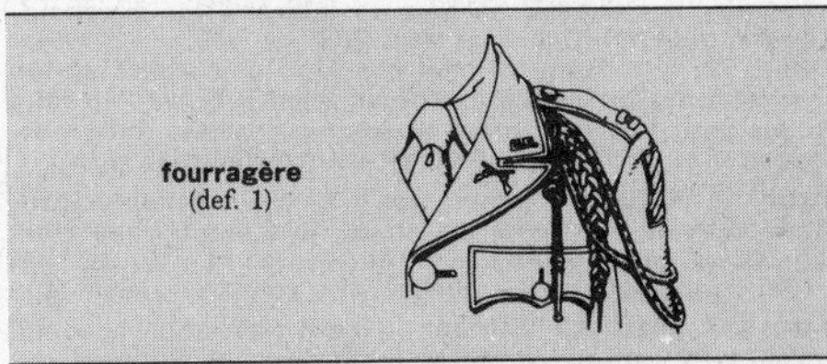
fourragère (def. 1)

four′-rowed bar′ley (fôr′rōd′, fōr′-), a class of barley having, in each spike, six rows of grain, with two pairs of rows overlapping. [1880–85]

four•score (fôr′skôr′, fōr′skōr′), *adj.* four times twenty; eighty. [1200–50; ME; see FOUR, SCORE]

four•some (fôr′səm, fōr′-), *n.* **1.** a company or set of four; two couples; a quartet: *to make up a foursome for bridge.* **2.** *Golf.* **a.** a match between two pairs of players, each of whom plays his or her own ball. **b.** Also called **Scotch foursome.** a match between two pairs of players, in which each pair plays one ball and partners stroke alternately. —*adj.* **3.** consisting of four persons, things, etc.; performed by or requiring four persons. [1540–50; FOUR + -SOME[2]]

four-spot (fôr′spot′, fōr′-), *n.* a playing card or the upward face of a die bearing four pips; a domino, one half of which bears four pips. [1875–80]

four•square (fôr′skwâr′, fōr′-), *adj.* **1.** consisting of four corners and four right angles; square: *a solid, foursquare building.* **2.** firm; steady; unswerving: *He maintained a foursquare position in the controversy.* **3.** forthright; frank; blunt: *a foursquare presentation of the*

CONCISE PRONUNCIATION KEY: act, cāpe, dâre, pärt; set, ēqual; if, īce; ox, ōver, ôrder, oil, bŏŏk, bōōt, out; up, ûrge; child; sing; shoe; thin, that; zh as in treasure. ə = a as in alone, e as in system, i as in easily, o as in gallop, u as in circus; ᵊ as in fire (fīᵊr), hour (ouᵊr). l and n can serve as syllabic consonants, as in cradle (krād′l), and button (but′n). See the full key inside the front cover.

company's financial condition. —*adv.* **4.** without equivocation; frankly; forthrightly. —*n.* **5.** a square. [1250–1300; ME *fouresquare.* See FOUR, SQUARE] —**four′square′ly,** *adv.* —**four′square′ness,** *n.*

four-star (fôr′stär′, fōr′-), *adj.* **1.** of or being a full general or admiral, as indicated by four stars on an insignia. **2.** rated or considered as being of the highest quality, esp. as indicated by four printed stars assigned in some rating systems: *a four-star restaurant.* [1920–25]

four-strip•er (fôr′strī′pər, fōr′-), *n.* a captain in the U.S. Navy.

four-stroke (fôr′strōk′, fōr′-), *adj. Mach.* four-cycle. [1895–1900]

four•teen (fôr′tēn′, fōr′-), *n.* **1.** a cardinal number, ten plus four. **2.** a symbol for this number, as 14 or XIV. **3.** a set of this many persons or things. —*adj.* **4.** amounting to 14 in number. [bef. 950; ME *fourtene,* OE *fēowertēne.* See FOUR, -TEEN]

four•teen•er (fôr′tē′nər, fōr′-), *n. Pros.* a line, esp. an iambic line, consisting of 14 syllables. [1820–30; FOURTEEN + -ER[1]]

Four′teen Points′, The, a statement of the war aims of the Allies, made by President Wilson on January 8, 1918.

four•teenth (fôr′tēnth′, fōr′-), *adj.* **1.** next after the thirteenth; being the ordinal number for 14. **2.** being one of 14 equal parts. —*n.* **3.** a fourteenth part, esp. of one (1/14). **4.** the fourteenth member of a series. [bef. 900; ME *fourtenthe,* OE *fēowertēotha.* See FOURTEEN, -TH[2]]

Four′teenth Amend′ment, an amendment to the U.S. Constitution, ratified in 1868, defining national citizenship and forbidding the states to restrict the basic rights of citizens or other persons.

fourth (fôrth, fōrth), *adj.* **1.** next after the third; being the ordinal number for four. **2.** being one of four equal parts. **3.** *Auto.* of, pertaining to, or operating at the gear transmission ratio at which the drive shaft speed is greater than that of third gear for a given engine crankshaft speed, but not so great as that of fifth gear, if such exists: *fourth gear.* —*n.* **4.** a fourth part, esp. of one (1/4). **5.** the fourth member of a series. **6.** *Music.* **a.** a tone on the fourth degree from a given tone (counted as the first). **b.** the interval between such tones. **c.** the harmonic combination of such tones. **7.** *Auto.* fourth gear: *She downshifted from fifth to fourth as we started up the hill.* **8.** (*cap.*) Independence Day; the Fourth of July (usually prec. by *the*). —*adv.* **9.** in the fourth place; fourthly. [bef. 950; ME *fourthe,* OE *fēowertha.* See FOUR, -TH[2]]

Fourth′ Amend′ment, an amendment to the U.S. Constitution, ratified in 1791 as part of the Bill of Rights, prohibiting unlawful search and seizure of personal property.

fourth′ class′, (in the U.S. Postal Service) the class of mail consisting of merchandise weighing one pound or more, including parcel post and all first-, second-, or third-class matter weighing 8 oz. (227 g) or more and not sealed against inspection. [1860–65, *Amer.*]

fourth-class (fôrth′klas′, -kläs′, fōrth′-), *adj.* **1.** of, pertaining to, or designated as a class next below third, as for mailing, shipping, etc. —*adv.* **2.** as fourth-class matter; by fourth-class mail: *Send it fourth-class.*

Fourth′ Command′ment, "Remember the sabbath day, to keep it holy": fourth of the Ten Commandments. Cf. **Ten Commandments.**

fourth′ dimen′sion, 1. *Physics, Math.* a dimension in addition to length, width, and depth, used so as to be able to employ geometrical language in discussing phenomena that depend on four variables: *Time is considered a fourth dimension for locating points in spacetime.* **2.** something beyond the kind of normal human experience that can be explained scientifically: *The story deals with ESP and other excursions into the fourth dimension.* [1870–75] —**fourth′-di•men′sion•al,** *adj.*

fourth′ estate′, (*often caps.*) **1.** the journalistic profession or its members; the press. **2.** a group other than the usual powers, as the three estates of France, that wields influence in the politics of a country. [1830–40]

Fourth′ Interna′tional, a loose federation of small groups of radical socialists formed in 1936 under the leadership of Leon Trotsky and hostile to the Soviet Union. Cf. **international** (def. 6).

fourth•ly (fôrth′lē, fōrth′-), *adv.* in the fourth place; fourth. [1520–30; FOURTH + -LY]

Fourth′ of July′. See **Independence Day.** [1770–80, *Amer.*]

fourth′ posi′tion, *Ballet.* a position in which the feet are at right angles to the direction of the body, the toes pointing out, with one foot forward and the other foot back. See illus. under **first position.** [1880–85]

Fourth′ Repub′lic, the republic established in France in 1945 and replaced by the Fifth Republic in 1958.

fourth′ wall′, *Theat.* the imaginary wall of a box set, separating the actors from the audience. [1800–10]

Fourth′ World′, the world's most poverty-stricken nations, esp. in Africa and Asia, marked by very low GNP per capita and great dependence upon foreign economic aid. Cf. **First World, Second World, Third World.** [1970–75]

four-way (fôr′wā′, fōr′-), *adj.* **1.** providing access or passage in four directions: *a four-way entrance.* **2.** applying to all four directions of traffic at an intersection: *a four-way stop sign.* **3.** exerting influence or benefit in four different ways: *a four-way blessing.* **4.** made up of four participants: *a four-way discussion.* [1815–25]

4WD, four-wheel drive.

four-wheel (fôr′hwēl′, -wēl′, fōr′-), *adj.* **1.** having four wheels. **2.** functioning on or driven by four wheels. Also, **four′-wheeled′.** [1730–40]

four′-wheel drive′, *Auto.* **1.** a drive system in which engine power is transmitted to all four wheels for improved traction. **2.** a vehicle having such a system. *Abbr.:* 4WD [1925–30] —**four′-wheel′-drive′,** *adj.*

four-wheel•er (fôr′hwē′lər, -wē′-, fōr′-), *n.* **1.** a four-wheel vehicle, esp. a hackney carriage. **2.** *CB and Auto. Slang.* a four-wheel automotive vehicle, as a car or small truck, esp. as distinguished from a vehicle having more than four wheels, as a tractor-trailer, or fewer than four wheels, as a motorcycle. [1840–50]

four-wheel•ing (fôr′hwē′ling, -wē′-, fōr′-), *n. Informal.* traveling in a vehicle using four-wheel drive. [FOUR-WHEEL + -ING[1]]

fou•ter (fo͞o′tər), *n. Archaic.* something that has no value (used in expressions of contempt): *A fouter for the world, say I!* Also, **fou•tra** (fo͞o′trə), **fou′tre.** [1585–95; < MF *foutre* to copulate with, copulate < L *futuere*]

fo•ve•a (fō′vē ə), *n., pl.* **-ve•ae** (-vē ē′). *Biol.* a small pit or depression in a bone or other structure. [1840–50; < L: pit] —**fo′ve•al,** *adj.*

fo′vea cen•tra′lis (sen trā′lis), *Ophthalm.* a small pit or depression at the back of the retina forming the point of sharpest vision. [1855–60; < NL: central fovea]

fo•ve•ate (fō′vē it, -āt′), *adj. Biol.* having foveae; pitted. Also, **fo′ve•at′ed.** [1850–55; FOVE(A) + -ATE[1]]

fo•ve•o•la (fō vē′ə lə), *n., pl.* **-lae** (-lē′). *Biol.* a small fovea; a very small pit or depression. [1840–50; < NL; dim. of FOVEA; see -OLE[1]] —**fo•ve′o•lar,** *adj.*

fo•ve•o•late (fō′vē ə lit, -lāt′), *adj. Biol.* having foveolae, or very small pits. Also, **fo′ve•o•lat′ed.** [1840–50; FOVEOL(A) + -ATE[1]]

fo•ve•ole (fō′vē ōl′), *n.* a foveola. Also, **fo•ve•o•let** (fō′vē ə let′, fō vē′ə lit).

fowl (foul), *n., pl.* **fowls,** (*esp. collectively*) **fowl,** *v.* —*n.* **1.** the domestic or barnyard hen or rooster; chicken. Cf. **domestic fowl. 2.** any of several other, usually gallinaceous, birds that are barnyard, domesticated, or wild, as the duck, turkey, or pheasant. **3.** (in market and household use) a full-grown domestic fowl for food purposes, as distinguished from a chicken or young fowl. **4.** the flesh or meat of a domestic fowl. **5.** any bird (used chiefly in combination): *waterfowl; wildfowl.* —*v.i.* **6.** to hunt or take wildfowl. [bef. 900; ME *foul,* OE *fugol, fugel;* c. OS *fugal,* Goth *fugls,* OHG *fogal* (G *Vogel*)]

fowl′ chol′era, *Vet. Pathol.* a specific, acute, diarrheal disease of fowls, esp. chickens, caused by a bacterium, *Pasteurella multocida.* Cf. **hemorrhagic septicemia.** [1880–85]

fowl•er (fou′lər), *n.* a hunter of birds. [bef. 900; ME *foweler,* OE *fughelere.* See FOWL, -ER[1]]

Fow•ler (fou′lər), *n.* **1. Henry H(am•ill)** (ham′əl), born 1908, U.S. lawyer and government official: secretary of the Treasury 1965–68. **2. Henry Watson,** 1858–1933, English lexicographer.

Fow′ler flap′, *Aeron.* a flap normally forming a part of the trailing edge of an airplane wing, capable of being moved backward and rotated downward in order to increase lift through increased camber and wing area. [named after Harlan D. *Fowler,* 20th-century American aeronautical engineer]

Fow′ler's toad′, an eastern U.S. toad, *Bufo woodhousii fowleri,* having an almost patternless white belly. [named after S. P. *Fowler* (d. 1888), American naturalist]

Fow•liang (fo͞o′lyäng′, fō′-), *n. Older Spelling.* former name of **Jingdezhen.**

fowl•ing (fou′ling), *n.* the practice or sport of shooting or snaring birds. [1350–1400; late ME *foulynge.* See FOWL, -ING[1]]

fowl′ing piece′, a shotgun for shooting wildfowl. [1590–1600]

fowl′ paral′ysis. See **Marek's disease.** [1930–35]

fowl′ plague′. See **avian influenza.**

fowl′ pox′, *Vet. Pathol.* a virus disease of chickens and other birds characterized by warty excrescences on the comb and wattles, and often by diphtherialike changes in the mucous membranes of the head. Also called **avian diphtheria, avian pox.** [1905–10]

fowl′ ty′phoid, *Vet. Pathol.* a septicemic disease of fowl, esp. chickens, caused by the bacterium *Salmonella gallinarum* and marked by fever, loss of appetite, thirst, anemic pallor of the skin of the head, and prostration.

red fox, *Vulpes vulpes,* 16 in. (41 cm) high at shoulder; head and body 2½ ft. (0.8 m); tail 1½ ft. (0.5 m)

fox (foks), *n., pl.* **fox•es,** (*esp. collectively*) **fox,** *v.* —*n.* **1.** any of several carnivores of the dog family, esp. those of the genus *Vulpes,* smaller than wolves, having a pointed, slightly upturned muzzle, erect ears, and a long, bushy tail. **2.** the fur of this animal. **3.** a cunning or crafty person. **4.** (*cap.*) a member of a tribe of North American Algonquian Indians, formerly in Wisconsin, later merged with the Sauk tribe. **5.** (*cap.*) the Algonquian language of the Fox, Sauk, and Kickapoo Indians. **6.** *Bible.* a scavenger, perhaps the jackal. Psalms 63:10; Lam. 5:18. **7.** a word formerly used in communications to represent the letter *F:* replaced by Foxtrot. **8.** *Slang.* an attractive young woman or young man. —*v.t.* **9.** to deceive or trick. **10.** to repair or make (a shoe) with leather or other material applied so as to cover or form part of the upper front. **11.** *Obs.* to intoxicate or befuddle. —*v.i.* **12.** to act cunningly or craftily. **13.** (of book leaves, prints, etc.) to become foxed. [bef. 900; 1960–65 for def. 9; ME, OE; c. OS *vohs,* MLG *vos,* OHG *fuhs* (G *Fuchs*). Cf. VIXEN] —**fox′like′,** *adj.*

Fox (foks), *n.* **1. Charles James,** 1749–1806, British orator and statesman. **2. George,** 1624–91, English religious leader and writer: founder of the Society of Friends. **3. John.** See **Foxe, John. 4. John William, Jr.,** 1863–1919, U.S. novelist. **5. Margaret,** 1833–93, and her sister **Katherine** (*"Kate"*), 1839–92, U.S. spiritualist mediums, born in Canada. **6. Sir William,** 1812–93, New Zealand statesman, born in England: prime minister 1856, 1861–62, 1869–72, 1873.

fox•ber•ry (foks′ber′ē, -bə rē), *n., pl.* **-ries.** the cowberry, *Vaccinium vitis-idaea.* [1775–85, *Amer.;* FOX + BERRY]

fox′ bolt′, an anchor bolt secured by a foxtail wedge forced into its end as it is screwed into a blind hole. [1870–75]

Fox•bor•ough (foks′bûr′ō, -bur′ō), *n.* a town in E Massachusetts. 14,148.

fox′ brush′, the tail of a fox. [1890–95]

Foxe (foks), *n.* **John,** 1516–87, English martyrologist.

foxed (fokst), *adj.* **1.** deceived; tricked. **2.** stained or spotted a yellowish brown, as by age: *a dog-eared and foxed volume of poetry.* **3.** (of museum specimens of birds and mammals) having melanin pigments that have oxidized with age to a reddish-brown color. [1605–15; FOX + -ED[2]]

fox•fire (foks′fīr′), *n. Chiefly Midland and Southern U.S.* **1.** organic luminescence, esp. from certain fungi on decaying wood. **2.** any of various fungi causing luminescence in decaying wood. Also, **fox′-fire′.** [1425–75; late ME; see FOX, FIRE]

foxglove, *Digitalis purpurea*

fox•glove (foks′gluv′), *n.* any Eurasian plant belonging to the genus *Digitalis,* of the figwort family, esp. *D. purpurea,* having drooping, tubular, purple or white flowers on tall spikes, and leaves that are the source of digitalis in medicine. [bef. 1000; ME *foxes glove,* OE *foxes glōfa.* See FOX, GLOVE]

fox′ grape′, 1. a vine, *Vitis labrusca,* chiefly of the northeastern U.S., from which numerous cultivated grape varieties have been developed. **2.** the usually purplish-black, thick-skinned, sweet, musky fruit of this vine. [1630–40, *Amer.*]

fox•hole (foks′hōl′), *n.* a small pit, usually for one or two soldiers, dug as a shelter in a battle area. [1915–20; FOX + HOLE]

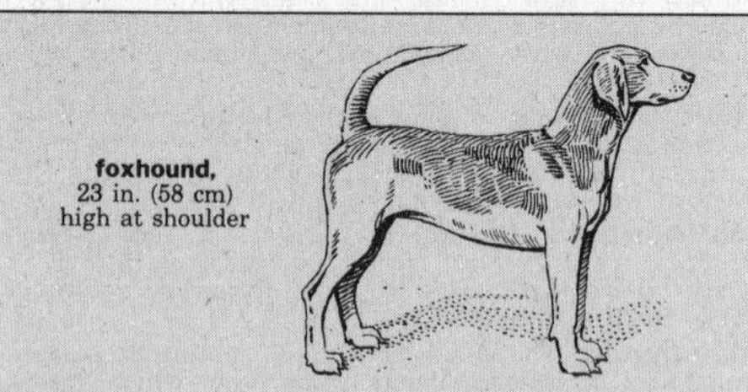

foxhound, 23 in. (58 cm) high at shoulder

fox•hound (foks′hound′), *n.* any of several breeds of medium-sized hounds trained to hunt foxes and having a glossy coat in combinations of black, tan, and white. Cf. **American foxhound, English foxhound.** [1755–65; FOX + HOUND[1]]

fox′ hunt′ing, a sport in which mounted hunters follow hounds in pursuit of a fox. [1665–75] —**fox′ hunt′er.**

fox•ing (fok′sing), *n.* **1.** material used to cover the upper portion of a shoe. **2.** discoloration, as of book leaves or prints. [FOX + -ING[1]]

fox′ snake′, a brown-blotched nonvenomous snake, *Elaphe vulpina,* of north-central U.S., that vibrates its tail and emits a pungent odor when disturbed. [1855–60; appar. so called from its reddish color]

fox′ spar′row, a North American sparrow, *Passerella iliaca,* having a bright rufous tail and streaked breast. [1860–65, *Amer.*]

CONCISE ETYMOLOGY KEY: <, descended or borrowed from; >, whence; b., blend of, blended; c., cognate with; cf., compare; deriv., derivative; equiv., equivalent; imit., imitative; obl., oblique; r., replacing; s., stem; sp., spelling, spelled; resp., respelling, respelled; trans., translation; ?, origin unknown; *, unattested; ‡, probably earlier than. See the full key inside the front cover.

fox′ squir′rel, any of several North American arboreal squirrels varying in color and of an exceptionally large size. [1675–85, *Amer.*]

fox·tail (foks′tāl′), *n.* **1.** the tail of a fox. **2.** any of various grasses having soft, brushlike spikes of flowers. [1375–1425; late ME; see FOX, TAIL[1]]

fox′tail mil′let, a grass, *Setaria italica,* of numerous varieties, introduced into the U.S. from Europe and Asia, and grown chiefly for use as hay. [1895–1900]

fox′tail wedge′, a wedge in the split end of a tenon, bolt, or the like, for spreading and securing it when driven into a blind mortise or hole. Also called **fox′ wedge′.** [1815–25]

fox′ ter′rier, either of two English breeds of small terriers having either a long, wiry coat or a short, flat coat, formerly used for driving foxes from their holes. [1815–25]

fox terrier, 15 in. (38 cm) high at shoulder

fox′ trot′, **1.** a social dance, in quadruple meter, performed by couples, characterized by various combinations of slow and quick steps. **2.** a pace, as of a horse, consisting of a series of short steps, as in slackening from a trot to a walk. [1870–75, *Amer.*]

fox-trot (foks′trot′), *v.i.,* **-trot·ted, -trot·ting.** to dance a fox trot. [1915–20]

Fox·trot (foks′trot′), *n.* a word used in communications to represent the letter *F.*

fox·y (fok′sē), *adj.,* **fox·i·er, fox·i·est. 1.** foxlike; cunning or crafty; slyly clever. **2.** yellowish or reddish brown, as of the color of the common red fox. **3.** *Slang.* **a.** sexually appealing; attractive. **b.** stylish; modish: *a foxy outfit.* **c.** exciting and appealing, as a place, entertainment, or the like. **4.** discolored or foxed: *pages of a book that had become foxy.* **5.** (of a wine) having the pronounced flavor natural to native American grape varieties, as that of fox grapes or of Concord or Catawba grapes. **6.** (esp. of a painting) having excessively warm tones; containing too much red. [1520–30; 1960–65 for def. 3; FOX + -Y[1]] **—fox′i·ly,** *adv.* **—fox′i·ness,** *n.*
—Syn. 1. wily, tricky, sly, artful.

foy·er (foi′ər, foi′ā; *Fr.* fwa yā′), *n., pl.* **-ers** (-ərz, -āz; *Fr.* -yā′). **1.** the lobby of a theater, hotel, or apartment house. **2.** a vestibule or entrance hall in a house or apartment. [1855–60; < F: fireplace, hearth (orig. a room to which theater audiences went for warmth between the acts) < Gallo-L **focārium,* equiv. to L *foc(us)* hearth (cf. FOCUS) + *-ārium* -ARIUM]

Foyt (foit), *n.* **A(nthony) J(oseph, Jr.),** born 1935, U.S. racing-car driver.

fo·zy (fō′zē, foz′ē), *adj.,* **-zi·er, -zi·est.** *Chiefly Scot.* **1.** spongy; loose-textured. **2.** (of a vegetable or fruit) overripe. **3.** (of a person) fat; flabby. **4.** *Informal.* dull-witted; stupid; fatheaded. [1815–25; cf. D *voos* spongy, LG *fussig*] **—fo′zi·ness,** *n.*

fp, 1. *Music.* forte-piano. **2.** *Sports.* forward pass.

F.P., foot-pound.

f.p., 1. fireplug. **2.** foolscap. **3.** foot-pound; foot-pounds. **4.** *Music.* forte-piano. **5.** freezing point. **6.** fully paid.

FPC, 1. Federal Power Commission: a board of five members established chiefly to regulate the natural gas and electric power industries engaged in interstate commerce: replaced by the Federal Energy Regulatory Commission. **2.** See **fish protein concentrate.**

FPHA, Federal Public Housing Authority.

Fpl, *Real Estate.* fireplace.

fpm, feet per minute. Also, **ft/min**

FPO, 1. field post office. **2.** fleet post office.

fps, 1. Also, **ft/sec** feet per second. **2.** foot-pound-second.

f.p.s., 1. feet per second. **2.** foot-pound-second. **3.** frames per second.

fpsps, feet per second per second. Also, **ft/s²**

FPT, freight pass-through.

FR, 1. *Real Estate.* family room. **2.** freight release.

Fr, *Symbol, Chem.* francium.

Fr., 1. Father. **2.** *pl.* **Fr., Frs.** franc. **3.** France. **4.** frater[1]. **5.** French. **6.** Friar. **7.** Friday.

fr., 1. fragment. **2.** *pl.* **fr., frs.** franc. **3.** from.

Fra (frä), *n. Rom. Cath. Ch.* a title of address for a friar or brother. [1885–90; < It, shortened form of *frate* brother, monk]

frab·jous (frab′jəs), *adj. Informal.* wonderful, elegant, superb, or delicious. [1872; coined by Lewis Carroll in *Through the Looking-Glass;* perh. meant to suggest FABULOUS or JOYOUS]

fra·cas (frā′kəs; *Brit.* frak′ä), *n.* a noisy, disorderly disturbance or fight; riotous brawl; uproar. [1720–30; < F < It *fracasso,* deriv. of *fracassare* to smash, equiv. to *fra-* (< L *infrā* among) completely + *cassare* to break; see CASSATION]

Fra·cas·to·ri·us (frā′ka stôr′ē əs, -stōr′-), *n.* a walled plain in the fourth quadrant of the face of the moon: about 60 mi. (97 km) in diameter.

frac·ta·ble (frak′tə bəl), *n. Archit.* (on a gable wall) a coping concealing the slopes of the roof, esp. one having an ornamental silhouette. [1680–90; obs. *fract* broken, cracked (see FRACTURE) + -ABLE]

frac·tal (frak′tl), *n. Math., Physics.* a geometrical or physical structure having an irregular or fragmented shape at all scales of measurement between a greatest and smallest scale such that certain mathematical or physical properties of the structure, as the perimeter of a curve or the flow rate in a porous medium, behave as if the dimensions of the structure **(frac′tal dimen′sions)** are greater than the spatial dimensions. [< F *fractale,* equiv. to L *frāct(us)* broken, uneven (see FRACTUS) + *-ale* -AL[2]; term introduced by French mathematician Benoit Mandelbrot (born 1924) in 1975]

frac·tion (frak′shən), *n.* **1.** *Math.* **a.** a number usually expressed in the form *a/b.* **b.** a ratio of algebraic quantities similarly expressed. **2.** *Chem.* (in a volatile mixture) a component whose range of boiling point temperatures allows it to be separated from other components by fractionation. **3.** a part as distinct from the whole of anything; portion or section: *The meeting started with a fraction of us present.* **4.** a very small part or segment of anything; minute portion: *Only a fraction of the work was completed on time.* **5.** a very small amount; a little bit: *It was only a fraction away from completion.* **6.** a piece broken off; fragment or bit. **7.** the act of breaking. **8.** *Eccles.* (in a Eucharistic service) the breaking of the Host. *—v.t., v.i.* **9.** to divide or break into fractions, sections, factions, etc.: *Dissension threatens to fraction the powerful union.* [1350–1400; ME *fraccioun* < LL *frāctiōn-* (s. of *frāctiō*) a breaking (in pieces), equiv. to L *frāct(us)* (ptp. of *frangere* to BREAK) + *-iōn-* -ION]
—Syn. 3, 6. See **part.**

frac·tion·al (frak′shə nl), *adj.* **1.** pertaining to fractions; comprising a part or the parts of a unit; constituting a fraction: *fractional numbers.* **2.** comparatively small; inconsiderable or insignificant: *The profit on the deal was fractional.* **3.** *Chem.* of or noting a process, as distillation, crystallization, or oxidation, by which the component substances of a mixture are separated according to differences in certain of their properties, as boiling point, critical temperature, or solubility. Also, **frac·tion·ar·y** (frak′shə ner′ē). [1665–75; FRACTION + -AL[1]] **—frac′tion·al·ly,** *adv.*

frac′tional cur′rency, coins or paper money of a smaller denomination than the basic monetary unit. [1860–65, *Amer.*]

frac′tional distilla′tion, *Chem.* the separation of volatile components of different boiling points in a mixture by the gradual increase of temperature and the separate collection of each component. [1855–60]

frac·tion·al·ize (frak′shə nl īz′), *v.t., v.i.,* **-ized, -iz·ing.** to divide or splinter into fractions, sections, factions, etc. Also, *esp. Brit.,* **frac′tion·al·ise′.** [1930–35; FRACTIONAL + -IZE] **—frac′tion·al·i·za′tion,** *n.*

frac′tional or′bital bombard′ment sys′tem, a missile or satellite with a nuclear warhead sent into a low orbit so that it can suddenly be directed at a target. *Abbr.:* FOBS, F.O.B.S.

frac·tion·ate (frak′shə nāt′), *v.t.,* **-at·ed, -at·ing. 1.** to separate or divide into component parts, fragments, divisions, etc. **2.** to separate (a mixture) into ingredients or into portions having different properties, as by distillation or crystallization; cause to undergo fractional distillation, crystallization, or the like. **3.** to obtain by such a process. [1865–70; FRACTION + -ATE[1]]

frac·tion·a·tion (frak′shə nā′shən), *n.* **1.** the act or process of fractionating. **2.** the state of being fractionated. **3.** *Mil.* the division of a missile's payload into several warheads. [1925–30; FRACTIONATE + -ION]

frac·tion·a·tor (frak′shə nā′tər), *n.* **1.** *Chem.* an apparatus for fractional distillation. Cf. **cracker. 2.** any apparatus capable of separating complex liquid substances, as blood, into their component parts. [FRACTIONATE + -OR[2]]

frac·tion·ize (frak′shə nīz′), *v.t., v.i.,* **-ized, -iz·ing.** to divide into fractions. Also, *esp. Brit.,* **frac′tion·ise′.** [1665–75; FRACTION + -IZE] **—frac′tion·i·za′tion,** *n.*

frac·tious (frak′shəs), *adj.* **1.** refractory or unruly: *a fractious animal that would not submit to the harness.* **2.** readily angered; peevish; irritable; quarrelsome: *an incorrigibly fractious young man.* [1715–25; FRACTI(ON) + -OUS] **—frac′tious·ly,** *adv.* **—frac′tious·ness,** *n.*
—Syn. 1. stubborn, difficult. **2.** testy, captious, petulant, snappish, pettish, waspish, touchy.

frac·tur (*Ger.* fʀäk to͞or′), *n.* Fraktur (def. 2).

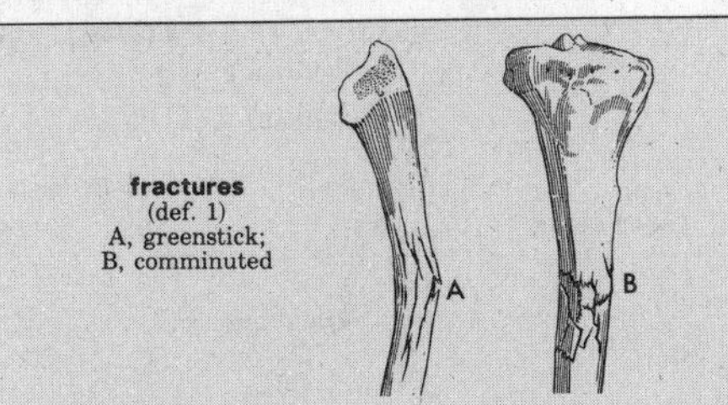

fractures (def. 1) A, greenstick; B, comminuted

frac·ture (frak′chər), *n., v.,* **-tured, -tur·ing.** *—n.* **1.** the breaking of a bone, cartilage, or the like, or the resulting condition. Cf. **comminuted fracture, complete fracture, compound fracture, greenstick fracture, simple fracture. 2.** the act of breaking; state of being broken. **3.** a break, breach, or split. **4.** the characteristic manner of breaking: *a material of unpredictable fracture.* **5.** the characteristic appearance of a broken surface, as of a mineral. *—v.t.* **6.** to cause or to suffer a fracture in (a bone, etc.). **7.** to break or crack. **8.** *Slang.* to amuse highly or cause to laugh heartily; delight: *The new comic really fractured the audience.* *—v.i.* **9.** to become fractured; break: *a mineral that does not fracture easily.* [1375–1425; late ME < MF < L *frāctūra* a breach, cleft, fracture, equiv. to *frāct(us)* (ptp. of *frangere* to BREAK) + *-ūra* -URE] **—frac′tur·a·ble,** *adj.* **—frac′tur·al,** *adj.* **—frac′tur·er,** *n.*
—Syn. 7. smash, shatter, splinter, rupture, split.

frac′ture zone′, *Oceanog.* a long, narrow rift on the ocean floor, separating areas of differing depth: where such a zone crosses a mid-ocean ridge, it displaces the ridge by faulting. Cf. **transform fault.** [1960–65]

frac·tus (frak′təs), *adj. Meteorol.* (of a cloud) containing small, individual elements that have a ragged appearance. [< L *frāctus* ptp. of *frangere* to BREAK]

frae (frā), *prep., adv. Scot.* from. [1175–1225; ME (north) *fra, frae* < ON *frā* FROM]

frae·nu·lum (frē′nyə ləm), *n., pl.* **-la** (-lə). frenulum.

frae·num (frē′nəm), *n., pl.* **-na** (-nə). frenum.

Fra Fi·lip·po Lip·pi (frä fi lip′ō lip′ē; *It.* fʀä fē lēp′pô lēp′pē). See **Lippi, Fra Filippo.**

frag (frag), *v.,* **fragged, frag·ging,** *n. U.S. Army and Marine Corps Slang.* *—v.t.* **1.** to kill, wound, or assault (esp. an unpopular or overzealous superior) with a fragmentation grenade. *—n.* **2.** See **fragmentation grenade.** [1965–70, *Amer.;* by shortening] **—frag′ger,** *n.*

frag·ile (fraj′əl; *Brit.* fraj′īl), *adj.* **1.** easily broken, shattered, or damaged; delicate; brittle; frail: *a fragile ceramic container; a very fragile alliance.* **2.** vulnerably delicate, as in appearance: *She has a fragile beauty.* **3.** lacking in substance or force; flimsy: *a fragile excuse.* [1505–15; < L *fragilis,* equiv. to *frag-* (var. s. of *frangere* to BREAK) + *-ilis* -ILE] **—frag′ile·ly,** *adv.* **—fra·gil·i·ty** (frə jil′i tē), **frag′ile·ness,** *n.*
—Syn. 1. See **frail[1].**

fragile X syndrome, a widespread form of mental retardation caused by a faulty gene on the X chromosome. [1980–85]

frag·ment (*n.* frag′mənt; *v.* frag′mənt, -ment, frag ment′), *n.* **1.** a part broken off or detached: *scattered fragments of the broken vase.* **2.** an isolated, unfinished, or incomplete part: *She played a fragment of her latest composition.* **3.** an odd piece, bit, or scrap. *—v.i.* **4.** to collapse or break into fragments; disintegrate: *The chair fragmented under his weight.* *—v.t.* **5.** to break (something) into pieces or fragments; cause to disintegrate: *Outside influences soon fragmented the Mayan culture.* **6.** to divide into fragments; disunify. [1375–1425; late ME < L *fragmentum* a broken piece, remnant, equiv. to *frag-* (s. of *frangere* to BREAK) + *-mentum* -MENT]
—Syn. 1–3. See **part.**

frag·men·tal (frag men′tl), *adj.* **1.** fragmentary. **2.** *Geol.* clastic (def. 3). [1790–1800; FRAGMENT + -AL[1]] **—frag·men′tal·ly,** *adv.*

frag·men·tar·y (frag′mən ter′ē), *adj.* consisting of or reduced to fragments; broken; disconnected; incomplete: *fragmentary evidence; fragmentary remains.* [1605–15; FRAGMENT + -ARY] **—frag′men·tar′i·ly,** *adv.* **—frag′men·tar′i·ness,** *n.*

frag·men·tate (frag′mən tāt′), *v.t., v.i.,* **-tat·ed, -tat·ing.** fragmentize. [1940–45; back formation from FRAGMENTATION]

frag·men·ta·tion (frag′mən tā′shən), *n.* **1.** the act or process of fragmenting; state of being fragmented. **2.** the disintegration, collapse, or breakdown of norms of thought, behavior, or social relationship. **3.** the pieces of an exploded fragmentation bomb or grenade. [1880–85; FRAGMENT + -ATION]

fragmenta′tion bomb′, a bomb designed to break into many small, high-velocity fragments when detonated. [1915–20]

fragmenta′tion grenade′, a grenade with a heavy metal casing that shatters, on exploding, into fragments that travel at high speed and with great force. [1955–60]

frag·ment·ed (frag′mən tid, -men-, frag men′-), *adj.* **1.** reduced to fragments. **2.** existing or functioning as though broken into separate parts; disorganized; disunified: *a fragmented personality; a fragmented society.* [1810–20; FRAGMENT + -ED[3]]

frag·ment·ize (frag′mən tīz′), *v.,* **-ized, -iz·ing.** *—v.t.* **1.** to break (something) into fragments; break (something) apart. *—v.i.* **2.** to fall into fragments. Also, *esp. Brit.,* **frag′ment·ise′.** [1805–15; FRAGMENT + -IZE] **—frag′ment·i·za′tion,** *n.* **—frag′ment·iz′er,** *n.*

frag·men·tized (frag′mən tīzd′), *adj.* fragmented.

Fra·go·nard (fʀa gô naʀ′), *n.* **Jean Ho·no·ré** (zhäɴ ô nô ʀā′), 1732–1806, French painter.

fra·grance (frā′grəns), *n.* **1.** the quality of being fragrant; a sweet or pleasing scent. **2.** perfume, cologne, toilet water, or the like. [1660–70; < F < LL *frāgrantia.* See FRAGRANT, -ANCE] **—Syn.** See **perfume.**

fra·gran·cy (frā′grən sē), *n., pl.* **-cies.** fragrance (def. 1). [1570–80]

fra·grant (frā′grənt), *adj.* **1.** having a pleasant scent or aroma; sweet-smelling; sweet-scented: *a fragrant rose.* **2.** delightful; pleasant: *fragrant memories.* [1400–50; late ME < L *frāgrant-* (s. of *frāgrāns*), prp. of *frāgrāre* to smell sweet] **—fra′grant·ly,** *adv.* **—fra′grant·ness,** *n.*
—Syn. 1. perfumed, odorous, redolent, aromatic.

fra′grant su′mac, a sprawling shrub, *Rhus aromatica,* of the cashew family, native to eastern North America, having aromatic foliage and greenish-yellow flowers in small spikes.

fraid·y-cat (frā′dē kat′), *n. Informal.* a timid, easily frightened person: often used by children. Also called **scaredy-cat.** [1905–10; *fraid* (aph. form of AFRAID) + -Y[1]]

CONCISE PRONUNCIATION KEY: act, cāpe, dâre, pärt; set, ēqual; *if,* ice; ox, ōver, ôrder, oil, bo͝ok, bo͞ot, out; up, ûrge; child; sing; shoe; thin, *th*at; zh as in *treasure.* ə = *a* as in *alone, e* as in *system, i* as in *easily, o* as in *gallop, u* as in *circus;* ᵊ as in *fire* (fīᵊr), *hour* (ouᵊr). l and n can serve as syllabic consonants, as in *cradle* (krād′l), and *button* (but′n). See the full key inside the front cover.

frail[1] (frāl), *adj.*, **-er, est. 1.** having delicate health; not robust; weak: *My grandfather is rather frail now.* **2.** easily broken or destroyed; fragile. **3.** morally weak; easily tempted. —*n.* **4.** *Older Slang (sometimes offensive).* a girl or woman. [1300–50; ME *frail(e), frel(e)* < OF < L *fragilis* FRAGILE] —**frail′ly,** *adv.* —**frail′ness,** *n.*

—**Syn. 1, 2.** feeble; breakable, frangible. FRAIL, BRITTLE, FRAGILE imply a delicacy or weakness of substance or construction. FRAIL applies particularly to health and immaterial things: *a frail constitution; frail hopes.* BRITTLE implies a hard material that snaps or breaks to pieces easily: *brittle as glass.* FRAGILE implies that the object must be handled carefully to avoid breakage or damage: *fragile bric-a-brac.* —**Ant. 1, 2.** sturdy.

frail[2] (frāl), *n.* **1.** a flexible basket made of rushes, used esp. for dried fruits, as dates, figs, or raisins. **2.** a certain quantity of raisins, about 75 lb. (34 kg), contained in such a basket. [1300–50; ME *frayel, fraelle* < OF *frayel* < ?]

frai•le•ro (frī lâr′ō; *Sp.* frī le′rô), *n., pl.* **-le•ros** (-lâr′ōz; *Sp.* -le′rôs). *Sp. Furniture.* an armchair of the Renaissance, having a leather seat and a leather back stretched between plain wooden members and having a broad front stretcher. Also called **friar's chair.** [< Sp: lit., of, belonging to a friar, deriv. of *fraile* friar]

frail•ty (frāl′tē, frā′əl-), *n., pl.* **-ties** for 3. **1.** the quality or state of being frail. **2.** moral weakness; liability to yield to temptation. **3.** a fault resulting from moral weakness: *frailties of the human flesh.* [1300–50; ME *frailte, frelete* < OF *frailete* < L *fragilitāt-* (s. of *fragilitās*). See FRAIL[1], -ITY]

—**Syn. 1.** delicacy, weakness, fragility. **2.** susceptibility, suggestibility. **3.** flaw, defect.

fraise (frāz), *n.* **1.** *Fort.* a defense consisting of pointed stakes projecting from the ramparts in a horizontal or an inclined position. **2.** a ruff worn around the neck in the 16th century. **3.** a woman's embroidered scarf worn with ends crossed on the chest and pinned with a brooch or the like, popular in the early 19th century. **4.** *Horol.* a cutting tool for correcting inaccuracies in the teeth of a timepiece wheel. [1765–75; < F, deriv. of *fraiser* to frizzle, curl < Pr *frezar* << Gmc; cf. OE *frīs* curled]

fraise (frez), *n., pl.* ***fraises*** (frez). *French.* **1.** strawberry. **2.** See **crème de fraise. 3.** a brandy distilled from strawberries.

fraise du bois (frez dʏ bwä′), *pl.* ***fraises du bois*** (frez dʏ bwä′). *French.* wild strawberry.

Frak•tur (fräk to͝or′), *n.* **1.** *Print.* German black-letter text, a style of type. **2.** (*usually l.c.*) Also, **fractur. a.** a stylized, highly decorative watercolor or watercolor-and-ink painting in the Pennsylvania-German tradition, often bearing elaborate calligraphy and standardized motifs, as birds, tulips, mermaids, and unicorns, and typically appearing on a book page, baptismal certificate or other family record, or merchant's advertisement. **b.** the elaborate calligraphy used in frakturs. [1900–05, *Amer.*; < G < L *frāctūra* action of breaking (in reference to the curlicues that broke up the continuous line of a word). See FRACTURE]

Fra Mau•ro (frä′ mär′ō, mô′rō), a walled plain in the third quadrant of the face of the moon: about 50 miles (80 km) in diameter.

fram•be•sia (fram bē′zhə), *n. Pathol.* yaws. Also, **fram•boe′sia.** [1760–70; < NL, Latinization of F *framboise.* See FRAMBOISE]

fram•boise (fräN bwaz′), *n., pl.* ***fram•boises*** (fräN-bwaz′). *French.* **1.** raspberry. **2.** See **crème de framboise. 3.** a brandy distilled from raspberries.

frame (frām), *n., v.,* **framed, fram•ing.** —*n.* **1.** a border or case for enclosing a picture, mirror, etc. **2.** a rigid structure formed of relatively slender pieces, joined so as to surround sizable empty spaces or nonstructural panels, and generally used as a major support in building or engineering works, machinery, furniture, etc. **3.** a body, esp. a human body, with reference to its size or build; physique: *He has a large frame.* **4.** a structure for admitting or enclosing something: *a window frame.* **5.** Usually, **frames.** (*used with a plural v.*) the framework for a pair of eyeglasses. **6.** form, constitution, or structure in general; system; order. **7.** a particular state, as of the mind: *an unhappy frame of mind.* **8.** *Motion Pictures.* one of the successive pictures on a strip of film. **9.** *Television.* a single traversal by the electron beam of all the scanning lines on a television screen. In the U.S. this is a total of 525 lines traversed in 1/30 second. Cf. **field** (def. 19). **10.** *Computers.* the information or image on a screen or monitor at any one time. **11.** *Bowling.* **a.** one of the ten divisions of a game. **b.** one of the squares on the scorecard, in which the score for a given frame is recorded. **12.** *Pool.* rack[1] (def. 3). **13.** *Baseball.* an inning. **14.** *Slang.* a frame-up. **15.** enclosing lines, usually forming a square or rectangle, to set off printed matter in a newspaper, magazine, or the like; a box. **16.** the structural unit that supports the chassis of an automobile. **17.** *Naut.* **a.** any of a number of transverse, riblike members for supporting and stiffening the shell of each side of a hull. **b.** any of a number of longitudinal members running between web frames to support and stiffen the shell plating of a metal hull. **18.** a machine or part of a machine supported by a framework, esp. as used in textile production: *drawing frame; spinning frame.* **19.** *Print.* the workbench of a compositor, consisting of a cabinet, cupboards, bins, and drawers, and having flat and sloping work surfaces on top. **20.** *Bookbinding.* an ornamental border, similar to a picture frame, stamped on the front cover of some books. **21. in frame,** *Shipbuilding.* (of a hull) with all frames erected and ready for planking or plating. —*v.t.* **22.** to form or make, as by fitting and uniting parts together; construct. **23.** to contrive, devise, or compose, as a plan, law, or poem: *to frame a new constitution.* **24.** to conceive or imagine, as an idea. **25.** *Informal.* to incriminate (an innocent person) through the use of false evidence, information, etc. **26.** to provide with or put into a frame, as a picture. **27.** to give utterance to: *Astonished, I attempted to frame adequate words of protest.* **28.** to form or seem to form (speech) with the lips, as if enunciating carefully. **29.** to fashion or shape: *to frame a bust from marble.* **30.** to shape or adapt to a particular purpose: *to frame a reading list for ninth graders.* **31.** *Informal.* to contrive or prearrange fraudulently or falsely, as in a scheme or contest. **32.** to adjust (film) in a motion-picture projector so as to secure exact correspondence of the outlines of the frame and aperture. **33.** to line up visually in a viewfinder or sight. **34.** *Archaic.* to direct, as one's steps. —*v.i.* **35.** *Archaic.* to betake oneself; resort. **36.** *Archaic.* to prepare, attempt, give promise, or manage to do something. [bef. 1000; 1910–15 for def. 8; 1920–25 for def. 25; (v.) ME *framen* to prepare (timber), OE *framian* to avail, profit; c. ON *frama* to further, OHG *(gi)framōn* to do; (n.) ME, deriv. of the v.] —**fram′a•ble, frame′a•ble,** *adj.* —**fram′a•ble•ness, frame′a•ble•ness,** *n.* —**frame′less,** *adj.* —**fram′er,** *n.*

frame′ house′, a house constructed with a skeleton framework of timber, as the ordinary wooden house. [1545–55]

frame′ line′, *Motion Pictures.* a horizontal line separating consecutive frames on a strip of film.

frame′ of ref′erence, *pl.* **frames of reference. 1.** a structure of concepts, values, customs, views, etc., by means of which an individual or group perceives or evaluates data, communicates ideas, and regulates behavior. **2.** Also called **reference frame.** *Physics.* a framework that is used for the observation and mathematical description of physical phenomena and the formulation of physical laws, usually consisting of an observer, a coordinate system, and a clock or clocks assigning times at positions with respect to the coordinate system. [1895–1900]

frame•pack (frām′pak′), *n.* a backpack attached to a supporting frame of usually lightweight metal. [FRAME + PACK[1]]

frame•shift (frām′shift′), *n. Genetics.* the addition or deletion of one or more nucleotides in a strand of DNA, which shifts the codon triplets of the genetic code of messenger RNA and causes a misreading during translation, resulting in an aberrant protein and therefore a mutation. [FRAME + SHIFT]

frame-up (frām′up′), *n. Informal.* a fraudulent incrimination of an innocent person. [1895–1900, *Amer.*; FRAME + UP, modeled on nominalizations of phrasal verbs, with *up* as perfective particle]

frame•work (frām′wûrk′), *n.* **1.** a skeletal structure designed to support or enclose something. **2.** a frame or structure composed of parts fitted and joined together. **3.** the construction or sale of frames. **4.** work done in, on, or with a frame. [1635–45; FRAME + WORK]

fram•ing (frā′ming), *n.* **1.** the act, process, or manner of constructing anything. **2.** the act of providing with a frame. **3.** a frame or a system of frames; framework. [1400–50; late ME; see FRAME, -ING[1]]

fram′ing chis′el, a woodworking chisel for heavy work and deep cuts, often having a handle reinforced to withstand blows from a metal hammer head. Also called **mortise chisel.** [1870–75]

Fram•ing•ham (frā′ming ham′), *n.* a town in E Massachusetts. 65,113.

fram′ing square′, a steel square usually having on its faces various tables and scales useful to the carpenter. Also called **steel square.**

Fran (fran), *n.* **1.** a male given name, form of **Francis. 2.** a female given name, form of **Frances.**

franc (frangk; *Fr.* fräN), *n., pl.* **francs** (frangks; *Fr.* fräN). **1.** an aluminum or nickel coin and monetary unit of France, equal to 100 centimes. *Abbr.:* F., f., Fr, fr. **2.** any of the monetary units of various other nations and territories, as Belgium, Liechtenstein, Luxembourg, Martinique, Senegal, Switzerland, and Tahiti, equal to 100 centimes. **3.** a former silver coin of France, first issued under Henry III. **4.** a former monetary unit of Algeria, Guinea, and Morocco. [1350–1400; ME *frank* < OF *franc,* so called because the coin was first inscribed with the name of the king as ML *Rēx Francōrum* King of the Franks]

Fran•çaix (fräN se′), *n.* **Jean** (zhäN), born 1912, French composer.

France (frans, fräns; *Fr.* fräNs), *n.* **1. A•na•tole** (A nA-tôl′), (*Jacques Anatole Thibault*), 1844–1924, French novelist and essayist: Nobel prize 1921. **2.** a republic in W Europe. 53,000,000; 212,736 sq. mi. (550,985 sq. km). *Cap.:* Paris. See map at bottom of page. **3.** *Heraldry.* fleurs-de-lis or upon azure: *a bordure of France.*

France′ An′cient, *Heraldry.* an escutcheon blazoned as follows: Azure, semé-de-lys or.

France′ Mod′ern, *Heraldry.* an escutcheon blazoned as follows: Azure, three fleurs-de-lis or.

Fran•ces (fran′sis), *n.* a female given name: derived from *Francis.*

Fran•ces•ca (fran ches′kə, frän-; *It.* fRän che′skä), *n.* **1. Pie•ro del•la** (pē âr′ō del′ə; *It.* pye′Rô del′lä), (*Piero dei Franceschi*), c1420–92, Italian painter. **2.** Also, **Fran•cis•ca** (fran sis′kə). a female given name, form of **Frances.**

Fran•ces•ca da Rim•i•ni (fran ches′kə də rim′ə nē, frän-; *It.* fRän che′skä dä Re′mē nē), died 1285?, Italian noblewoman: immortalized by Dante in the *Divine Comedy.*

Fran•ces•cat•ti (frän′chi skä′tē), *n.* **Zi•no** (zē′nō), born 1905, French violinist.

Franche-Com•té (fräNsh kôN tā′), *n.* a former province in E France: once a part of Burgundy.

fran•chise (fran′chīz), *n., v.,* **-chised, -chis•ing.** —*n.* **1.** a privilege of a public nature conferred on an individual, group, or company by a government: *a franchise to operate a bus system.* **2.** the right or license granted by a company to an individual or group to market its products or services in a specific territory. **3.** a store, restaurant, or other business operating under such a license. **4.** the territory over which such a license extends. **5.** the right to vote: *to guarantee the franchise of every citizen.* **6.** a privilege arising from the grant of a sovereign or government, or from prescription, which presupposes a grant. **7.** *Sports Slang.* a player of great talent or popular appeal, considered vitally important to a team's success or future. **8.** a legal immunity or exemption from a particular burden, exaction, or the like. **9.** *Obs.* freedom, esp. from imprisonment, servitude, or moral restraint. —*v.t.* **10.** to grant (an individual, company, etc.) a franchise: *The corporation has just franchised our local dealer.* **11.** enfranchise. [1250–1300; ME < OF, deriv. of *franc* free. See FRANK[1]] —**fran′chis•a•ble,** *adj.*

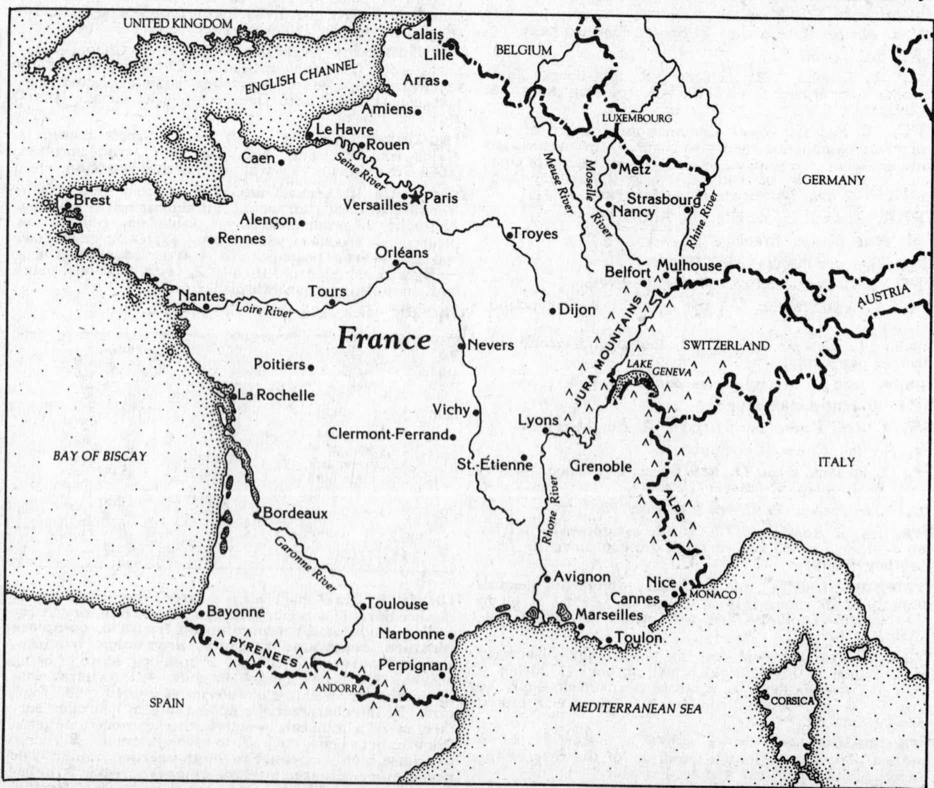

CONCISE ETYMOLOGY KEY: <, descended or borrowed from; >, whence; b., blend of, blended; c., cognate with; cf., compare; deriv., derivative; equiv., equivalent; imit., imitative; obl., oblique; r., replacing; s., stem; sp., spelling, spelled; resp., respelling, respelled; trans., translation; ?, origin unknown; *, unattested; ‡, probably earlier than. See the full key inside the front cover.

—**fran′chis•a•bil′i•ty,** *n.* —**fran•chise•ment** (fran′-chīz mənt, -chiz-), *n.*

fran′chise clause′, (esp. in marine-insurance policy) a clause stipulating that the insured will be responsible for any loss not in excess of a stated amount, and the insurance company will be liable for full payment of the loss equaling or exceeding the amount up to the insured amount. Cf. **deductible clause.**

fran•chi•see (fran′chī zē′), *n.* a person or company to whom a franchise is granted. [1960–65; FRANCHISE + -EE]

fran•chis•er (fran′chī zər), *n.* **1.** Also, **fran•chi•sor** (fran′chī zər, fran′chə zôr′). a person or company that grants a franchise. **2.** franchisee. [1835–45; FRANCHISE + -ER[1]]

Fran•chot (fran′chət), *n.* a male given name, form of **Francis.**

Fran•cia (frän′sē ə; *Sp.* fʀän′syä), *n.* **Jo•sé Gas•par Ro•drí•guez de** (hô se′ gäs pär′ ʀô thʀē′ges the), ("*El Supremo*"), 1766–1840, Paraguayan political leader: dictator 1814–40.

Fran•cie (fran′sē), *n.* a female given name, form of **Frances.**

Fran•cine (fran sēn′), *n.* a female given name, form of **Frances.**

Fran•cis (fran′sis), *n.* a male given name: from an Old French word meaning "Frenchman."

Francis I, 1. 1494–1547, king of France 1515–47. **2.** 1768–1835, first emperor of Austria 1804–35; as Francis II, last emperor of the Holy Roman Empire 1792–1806.

Francis II. See **Francis I** (def. 2).

Fran•cis•can (fran sis′kən), *adj.* **1.** of or pertaining to St. Francis or the Franciscans. —*n.* **2.** a member of the mendicant order founded by St. Francis in the 13th century. [1585–95; < ML *Francisc(us)* St. Francis of Assisi + -AN]

Fran•cis•co (fran sis′kō; *Sp.* fʀän sēs′kô, -thēs′-), *n.* a male given name, Spanish form of **Francis.**

Fran′cis Fer′dinand, 1863–1914, archduke of Austria: heir apparent to the thrones of Austria and Hungary whose assassination precipitated the outbreak of World War I (nephew of Francis Joseph I). German, **Franz Ferdinand.**

Francis Joseph I, 1830–1916, emperor of Austria 1848–1916; king of Hungary 1867–1916. German, **Franz Josef.**

Fran′cis of Assi′si, Saint (*Giovanni Francesco Bernardone*), 1182?–1226, Italian friar: founder of the Franciscan order.

Fran′cis of Pau′la (pou′lə; *It.* pä′o͞o lä), **Saint,** 1416–1507, Italian monk: founder of the order of Minims.

Fran′cis of Sales′ (sälz; *Fr.* sal), **Saint,** 1567–1622, French ecclesiastic and writer on theology: bishop of Geneva 1602–22.

Fran′cis Xa′vier, Saint. See **Xavier, Saint Francis.**

fran•ci•um (fran′sē əm), *n. Chem.* a radioactive element of the alkali metal group. *Symbol:* Fr; *at. no.:* 87. [1945–50; after FRANCE where first identified; see -IUM]

fran•cize (fran′sīz), *v.t.,* **-cized, -ciz•ing.** *Canadian.* to force to adopt French customs and the French language. Also, *esp. Brit.,* **fran′cise.** [FRANCE + -IZE] —**fran′ci•za′tion,** *n.* —**fran′ciz•er,** *n.*

Franck (frängk; *Fr.* fʀäɴk), *n.* **1. Cé•sar (Au•guste)** (sā zar′ ō gyst′), 1822–90, French composer, born in Belgium. **2. James,** 1882–1964, U.S. physicist, born in Germany: Nobel prize 1925.

Fran•co (frang′kō; *Sp.* fʀäng′kô), *n.* **Francisco,** (*Francisco Paulino Hermenegildo Teódulo Franco-Bahamonde*) ("*El Caudillo*"), 1892–1975, Spanish military leader and dictator: chief of state 1939–47; regent of the kingdom of Spain 1947–75. —**Fran′co•ism,** *n.* —**Fran′co•ist,** *n.*

Franco-, a combining form representing **French** or **France:** *Francophile; Franco-Prussian.* [< ML *Franc(us)* a Frank, a Frenchman + -O-]

Fran•co-A•mer•i•can (frang′kō ə mer′i kən), —*n.* **1.** an American of French or French-Canadian descent. —*adj.* **2.** of or pertaining to both France and America. [1855–60, *Amer.*]

Fran′co-Bel′gian sys′tem (frang′kō bel′jən). See **French system.**

fran•co•lin (frang′kə lin), *n.* any of numerous Eurasian and African partridges of the genus *Francolinus,* having sharply spurred legs. [1585–95; < F < It *francolino* < ?]

Fran•co•ni•a (frang kō′nē ə, -kōn′yə, fran-), *n.* a medieval duchy in Germany, largely in the valley of the Main River.

Fran•co•ni•an (frang kō′nē ən, -kōn′yən, fran-), *n.* **1.** a group of West Germanic dialects or languages, consisting of Frankish and the dialects descended from Frankish. —*adj.* **2.** of, pertaining to, or characteristic of Franconia. **3.** of or pertaining to Franconian. [1795–1805; FRANCONI(A) + -AN]

Fran•co•phile (frang′kə fīl′), *adj.* **1.** friendly to or having a strong liking for France or the French. —*n.* **2.** a person who is friendly to or has a strong admiration of France or the French. Also, **Fran•co•phil** (frang′kə fil). [1885–90; FRANCO- + -PHILE] —**Fran•co•phil•i•a** (frang′kə fil′ē ə, -fēl′yə), *n.*

Fran•co•phobe (frang′kə fōb′), *adj.* **1.** Also, **Fran′•co•pho′bic.** fearing or hating France, the French people, and French culture, products, etc. —*n.* **2.** a person who fears or hates France, the French people, French culture, products, etc. [1890–95; FRANCO- + -PHOBE] —**Fran′•co•pho′bi•a,** *n.*

Fran•co•phone (frang′kə fōn′), *adj.* **1.** Also, **Fran•co•phon•ic** (frang′kə fon′ik). speaking French, esp. as a member of a French-speaking population. —*n.* **2.** a person who speaks French, esp. a native speaker. [1895–1900; FRANCO- + -PHONE]

Fran•co-Pro•ven•çal (frang′kō prō′vən säl′, -prov′-ən-), *n.* a Romance dialect group of western Switzerland and neighboring parts of France: closely related to both Provençal and northern French.

Fran′co-Prus′sian War′ (frang′kō prush′ən), the war between France and Prussia, 1870–71.

franc-ti•reur (fʀäɴ tē ʀœʀ′), *n., pl.* ***francs-ti•reurs*** (fʀäɴ tē ʀœʀ′). *French.* a sharpshooter in the French army. [1800–10]

fran•gi•ble (fran′jə bəl), *adj.* easily broken; breakable: *Most frangible toys are not suitable for young children.* [1375–1425; late ME < OF, deriv. of L *frangere* to BREAK; see -IBLE] —**fran′gi•bil′i•ty, fran′gi•ble•ness,** *n.* —**Syn.** fragile, frail.

fran•gi•pane (fran′jə pān′), *n.* **1.** a kind of pastry cake, filled with cream, almonds, and sugar. **2.** the filling used in such a pastry. **3.** frangipani. [1670–80; < F < It. See FRANGIPANI]

fran•gi•pan•i (fran′jə pan′ē, -pä′nē), *n., pl.* **-pan•is, -pan•i. 1.** a perfume prepared from or imitating the odor of the flower of a tropical American tree or shrub, *Plumeria rubra,* of the dogbane family. **2.** the tree or shrub itself. [1860–65; < F *frangipane,* after Marquis Muzio *Frangipane* or *Frangipani* a 16th-century Italian nobleman, the supposed inventor of the perfume]

Fran•glais (fräng glā′; *Fr.* fʀäɴ gle′), *n.* (*sometimes l.c.*) French spoken or written with a large admixture of English words, esp. those of American origin. [1960–65; b. F *français* French and *anglais* English]

frank[1] (frangk), *adj.,* **-er, -est,** *n., v.* —*adj.* **1.** direct and unreserved in speech; straightforward; sincere: *Her criticism of my work was frank but absolutely fair.* **2.** without inhibition or subterfuge; direct; undisguised: *a frank appeal for financial aid.* **3.** *Pathol.* unmistakable; clinically evident: *frank blood.* **4.** *Archaic.* liberal or generous. **5.** *Obs.* free. —*n.* **6.** a signature or mark affixed by special privilege to a letter, package, or the like to ensure its transmission free of charge, as by mail. **7.** the privilege of franking letters, packages, etc. **8.** a franked letter, package, etc. —*v.t.* **9.** to mark (a letter, package, etc.) for transmission free of the usual charge, by virtue of official or special privilege; send free of charge, as mail. **10.** to convey (a person) free of charge. **11.** to enable to pass or go freely: *to frank a visitor through customs.* **12.** to facilitate the comings and goings of (a person), esp. in society: *A sizable inheritance will frank you faster than anything else.* **13.** to secure exemption for. **14.** *Carpentry.* to assemble (millwork, as sash bars) with a miter joint through the moldings and a butt joint or mortise-and-tenon joint for the rest. [1250–1300; ME < OF *franc* < LL *francus* free, orig. FRANK] —**frank′a•ble,** *adj.* —**frank′er,** *n.*
—**Syn. 1.** unrestrained, free, bold, uninhibited. FRANK, CANDID, OPEN, OUTSPOKEN imply a freedom and boldness in speaking. FRANK is applied to one unreserved in expressing the truth and to one's real opinions and sentiments: *a frank analysis of a personal problem.* CANDID suggests that one is sincere and truthful or impartial and fair in judgment, sometimes unpleasantly so: *a candid expression of opinion.* OPEN implies a lack of reserve or of concealment: *open antagonism.* OUTSPOKEN applies to a person who expresses himself or herself freely, even when this is inappropriate: *an outspoken and unnecessary show of disapproval.* —**Ant. 1.** restrained.

frank[2] (frangk), *n. Informal.* frankfurter. [1900–05, *Amer.*; by shortening]

Frank (frangk), *n.* **1.** a member of a group of ancient Germanic peoples dwelling in the regions of the Rhine, one division of whom, the Salians, conquered Gaul about A.D. 500, founded an extensive kingdom, and gave origin to the name *France.* **2.** (in the Levant) any native of western Europe. [bef. 900; ME *Franke,* OE *Franca* (c. OHG *Franko*), perh. from the Gmc base of OE *franka* spear, javelin, a weapon allegedly favored by the Franks]

Frank (frangk, frängk; *Russ.,* fʀänk; Ger. fʀängk), *n.* **1. Anne,** 1929–45, German Jewish girl who died in Belsen concentration camp in Germany: her diaries about her family hiding from Nazis in Amsterdam (1942–44) published in 1947. **2. Il•ya Mi•khai•lo•vich** (ē lyä′ myi-khī′ lə vyich), 1908–90, Russian physicist: Nobel prize 1958. **3. Le•on•hard** (lā′ôn härt), 1882–1961, German novelist. **4.** a male given name, form of **Francis** or **Franklin.**

Frank., Frankish.

franked mail′, official mail sent by members of Congress, the vice president, and other authorized officials. Cf. **frank**[1] (defs. 6–9). [1925–30]

Frank•en•stein (frang′kən stīn′), *n.* **1.** a person who creates a monster or a destructive agency that cannot be controlled or that brings about the creator's ruin. **2.** Also called **Frank′enstein mon′ster.** the monster or destructive agency itself. [1830–40; after a character in Mary Shelley's novel of the same name (1818)] —**Frank′en•stein′i•an,** *adj.*

Frank•en•tha•ler (frang′kən thô′lər, -thä′-), *n.* **Helen,** born 1928, U.S. painter.

Frank•fort (frangk′fərt), *n.* **1.** a city in and the capital of Kentucky, in the N part. 25,973. **2.** a city in central Indiana. 15,168. **3.** See **Frankfort on the Main.**

Frank′fort on the Main′ (mān), a city in W central Germany, on the Main River. 618,500. Also called **Frankfort.** German, **Frank•furt am Main** (fʀängk′fo͝ort äm min′), **Frank′furt.**

Frank′fort on the O′der (ō′dər), a city in NE Germany, on the Oder River. 85,158. German, **Frank•furt an der O•der** (fʀängk′fo͝ort än dər ō′dəʀ), **Frank′furt.**

frank•furt•er (frangk′fər tər), *n.* a small, cooked and smoked sausage of beef or beef and pork, with or without casing; hot dog; wiener. Also, **frank′fort, frank′•fort•er, frank′furt.** [1890–95, *Amer.*; < G: Frankfort sausage; see -ER[1]]

Frank•furt•er (frangk′fər tər), *n.* **Felix,** 1882–1965, U.S. jurist, born in Austria: associate justice of the U.S. Supreme Court 1939–62.

Frank′furt horizon′tal, *Craniom.* the plane established when right and left poria and left orbitale are in the same horizontal plane.

Frank•ie (frang′kē), *n.* a male given name, form of **Frank.**

frank•in•cense (frang′kin sens′), *n.* an aromatic gum resin from various Asian and African trees of the genus *Boswellia,* esp. *B. carteri,* used chiefly for burning as incense in religious or ceremonial practices, in perfumery, and in pharmaceutical and fumigating preparations. Also called **olibanum.** [1350–1400; ME *fraunk encense.* See FRANK[1], INCENSE[1]]

Frank•ish (frang′kish), *adj.* **1.** of or pertaining to the Franks. —*n.* **2.** the West Germanic language of the ancient Franks; Old Franconian. Cf. **Frank** (def. 1). [1585–95; FRANK + ISH[1]]

Frank•land (frangk′lənd), *n.* **Sir Edward,** 1825–99, English chemist: developed theory of valence.

frank•lin (frangk′lin), *n. Eng. Hist.* (in the 14th and 15th centuries) a freeholder who was not of noble birth. [1250–1300; ME *fra(u)nkelin* < AF *fraunclein,* equiv. to *fraunc* free, FRANK[1] + *-lein* -LING[1]; formed on the model of OF *chamberlain* CHAMBERLAIN]

Frank•lin (frangk′lin), *n.* **1. Benjamin,** 1706–90, American statesman, diplomat, author, scientist, and inventor. **2. Sir John,** 1786–1847, English Arctic explorer. **3. John Hope,** born 1915, U.S. historian and educator. **4.** a district in extreme N Canada, in the Northwest Territories, including the Boothia and Melville peninsulas, Baffin Island, and other Arctic islands. 549,253 sq. mi. (1,422,565 sq. km). **5.** a town in S Massachusetts. 18,217. **6.** a city in SE Wisconsin. 16,871. **7.** a town in central Tennessee. 12,407. **8.** a town in central Indiana. 11,563. **9.** a town in SW Ohio. 10,711. **10.** a male given name: from a Germanic word meaning "freeholder."

frank•lin•i•a (frangk lin′ē ə), *n.* a shrub or small tree, *Franklinia alatamaha,* of the tea family, originally native to the SE U.S. and now found only in cultivation, having glossy leaves and large, solitary white flowers. [< NL; named in honor of B. FRANKLIN; see -IA]

frank•lin•ite (frangk′li nīt′), *n.* a mineral of the spinel group, an oxide of zinc, manganese, and iron, occurring in black octahedral crystals or in masses: formerly mined for zinc. [1810–20, *Amer.*; named after Franklin, New Jersey, where it is found; see -ITE[1]]

Frank′lin Park′, a city in NE Illinois, near Chicago. 17,507.

Frank′lin's gull′, a black-headed North American gull, *Larus pipixcan,* feeding chiefly on insects. [1855–60, *Amer.*; named after Sir John FRANKLIN]

Frank′lin Square′, a town on W Long Island, in SE New York. 29,051.

Frank′lin stove′, 1. a cast-iron stove having the general form of a fireplace with enclosed top, bottom, side, and back, the front being completely open or able to be closed by doors. **2.** any of various fireplaces having a cast-iron top, back, and sides, with some provision for circulating air behind them in order to provide heat. [1780–90, *Amer.*; named after Benjamin FRANKLIN, who designed it]

Franklin stove
(def. 1)

frank•ly (frangk′lē), *adv.* in a frank manner; freely; candidly; openly; plainly: *He presented his arguments frankly and objectively.* [1530–40; FRANK[1] + -LY]

frank•ness (frangk′nis), *n.* plainness of speech; candor; openness. [1545–55; FRANK[1] + -NESS]

Fran•ko (fʀän kô′), *n.* **I•van** (ē vän′), 1856–1916, Ukrainian writer.

frank•pledge (frangk′plej′), *n. Old Eng. Law.* **1.** a system of dividing a community into tithings or groups of ten men, each member of which was responsible for the conduct of the other members of his group and for the assurance that a member charged with a breach of the law would be produced at court. **2.** a member of a tithing. **3.** the tithing itself. [1250–1300; ME *fra(u)nkplegge* < AF *frauncplege.* See FRANK[1], PLEDGE]

Frank•y (frang′kē), *n.* a male given name, form of **Frank.**

Fran•nie (fran′ē), *n.* a female given name, form of **Frances.** Also, **Fran′ny.**

CONCISE PRONUNCIATION KEY: act, cāpe, dâre, pärt; set, ēqual; *if,* īce; ox, ōver, ôrder, oil, bo͝ok, bo͞ot, out; up, ûrge; child; sing; shoe; thin, *th*at; zh as in *treasure.* ə = a as in *alone,* e as in *system,* i as in *easily,* o as in *gallop,* u as in *circus;* ə as in *fire* (fīər), *hour* (ouər). l and n can serve as syllabic consonants, as in *cradle* (krād′l), and *button* (but′n). See the full key inside the front cover.

fran·tic (fran′tik), *adj.* **1.** desperate or wild with excitement, passion, fear, pain, etc.; frenzied. **2.** *Archaic.* insane; mad. [1325–75; ME *frantik, frenetik* < OF *frenetique* < L *phrenēticus* delirious < Gk *phrenētikós.* See FRENZY, -TIC] —**fran′ti·cal·ly, fran′tic·ly,** *adv.* —**fran′tic·ness,** *n.*
—**Syn. 1.** overwrought, agitated, frenzied, distraught.

Franz (franz, frants; *Ger.* fʀänts), *n.* a male given name, German form of **Frank.**

Franz′ Fer′di·nand (fûr′dn and′; *Ger.* feʀ′di nänt′). See **Francis Ferdinand.**

Franz′ Jo′sef (jō′zəf, -səf; *Ger.* yō′zef). See **Francis Joseph I.**

Franz′ Jo′sef Land′ (land; *Ger.* länt), an archipelago in the Arctic Ocean, E of Spitzbergen and N of Novaya Zemlya: belongs to the Russian Federation. Also called **Fridtjof Nansen Land.**

Franz Jo·seph II (jō′zəf, -səf; *Ger.* yō′zef), born 1906, prince of Liechtenstein since 1938.

frap (frap), *v.t.,* **frapped, frap·ping.** *Naut.* to bind or wrap tightly with ropes or chains. [1300–50; ME *frappen* < OF *fraper* to strike, beat, prob. < Gmc (cf. ON *hrapa* to hurl, hurry)]

frappe (frap), *n. Northeastern U.S.* (*chiefly eastern New Eng.*). a milkshake made with ice cream. Also, **frappé.** [see FRAPPÉ]

frap·pé (fra pā′; *Fr.* fʀa pā′), *n., pl.* **-pés** (-pāz′; *Fr.* -pā′), *adj., v.,* **-péed, -pé·ing.** —*n.* **1.** a fruit juice mixture frozen to a mush, to be served as a dessert, appetizer, or relish. **2.** an after-dinner drink consisting of a liqueur, as crème de menthe, poured over cracked or shaved ice. **3.** frappe. **4.** *Ballet.* a beating of the toe of the working foot against the ankle of the supporting foot. —*adj.* **5.** chilled; iced; frozen. —*v.t.* **6.** to make a frappé of: *to frappé rum, fruit juice, and cracked ice.* [1840–50; < F: ptp. of *frapper* to ice, strike]

F.R.A.S., Fellow of the Royal Astronomical Society.

Fras·cat·i (fʀä skä′tē), *n.* a fruity white wine from Rome. [1930–35; after *Frascati,* city in central Italy]

Frasch′ proc′ess (fräsh), a method of mining sulfur by pumping superheated water down into the deposit, thereby melting it so that it can be pumped to the surface. [after Hermann *Frasch,* German-born U.S. chemical engineer, who developed it]

Fra·ser (frā′zər), *n.* **1. James Earle,** 1876–1953, U.S. sculptor. **2. (John) Malcolm,** born 1930, Australian political leader: prime minister 1975–83. **3. Peter,** 1884–1950, New Zealand statesman, born in Scotland: prime minister 1940–49. **4. Simon,** 1776–1862, Canadian explorer and fur trader, born in the U.S. **5.** a river in SW Canada, flowing S through British Columbia to the Pacific. 695 mi. (1119 km) long. **6.** a town in SE Michigan. 14,560. **7.** a male given name.

frass (fras), *n.* insect excrement. [1850–55; orig., the refuse and excrement of boring or leaf-eating insects < G *Frass* insect damage, corrosion, n. from base of *fressen* to eat (of animals); see FRESS, FRET[1]]

frat (frat), *n. Informal.* fraternity (def. 1). [1890–95, *Amer.*; by shortening]

fratch (frach), *Brit. Dial.* —*v.t.* **1.** to disagree; quarrel. —*n.* **2.** a quarrel; argument; dispute. [1400–50; late ME *fracchen* to creak, of uncert. orig.] —**fratch′er,** *n.*

fratch·ing (frach′ing), *n. Brit. Dial.* a quarrel; disagreement; argument. [1755–65; FRATCH + -ING[1]]

fra·ter[1] (frā′tər), *n.* **1.** a brother, as in a religious or fraternal order; comrade. **2.** a member of a college or university fraternity. [1555–65; < L *frāter* BROTHER]

fra·ter[2] (frā′tər), *n. Eccles. Hist. Obs.* the refectory of a religious house. Also, **fratry.** [1250–1300; ME *frater, freitour* < OF *fraitur,* short for *refreitor* < LL *rēfectōrium* REFECTORY]

fra·ter·nal (frə tûr′nl), *adj.* **1.** of or befitting a brother or brothers; brotherly. **2.** of or being a society of men associated in brotherly union, as for mutual aid or benefit: *a fraternal order; a fraternal association.* [1375–1425; late ME < L *frātern(us)* fraternal (deriv. of *frāter* BROTHER) + -AL[1]] —**fra·ter′nal·ism,** *n.* —**fra·ter′nal·ly,** *adv.*

frater′nal insur′ance, insurance underwritten by a fraternal society, under either a legal reserve plan or an assessment plan.

frater′nal soci′ety, a club or other association, usually of men, having a limited membership and devoted to professional, religious, charitable, or social activities.

frater′nal twin′, one of a pair of twins, not necessarily resembling each other, or of the same sex, that develop from two separately fertilized ova. Cf. **identical twin.** [1900–05]

fra·ter·ni·ty (frə tûr′ni tē), *n., pl.* **-ties. 1.** a local or national organization of male students, primarily for social purposes, usually with secret initiation and rites and a name composed of two or three Greek letters. **2.** a group of persons associated by or as if by ties of brotherhood. **3.** any group or class of persons having common purposes, interests, etc.: *the medical fraternity.* **4.** an organization of laymen for religious or charitable purposes; sodality. **5.** the quality of being brotherly; brotherhood: *liberty, equality, and fraternity.* **6.** the relation of a brother or between brothers. [1300–50; ME *fraternite* < L *frāternitās.* See FRATERNAL, -ITY]

frater′nity house′, a house occupied by a college or university fraternity. [1900–05]

frat·er·nize (frat′ər nīz′), *v.,* **-nized, -niz·ing.** —*v.i.* **1.** to associate in a fraternal or friendly way. **2.** to associate cordially or intimately with natives of a conquered country, enemy troops, etc. —*v.t.* **3.** *Archaic.* to bring into fraternal association or sympathy. Also, *esp. Brit.,* **frat′er·nise′.** [1605–15; < F *fraterniser* < ML *frāternizāre.* See FRATERNAL, -IZE] —**frat′er·ni·za′tion,** *n.* —**frat′er·niz′er,** *n.*
—**Syn. 1.** socialize, mingle, mix, consort, hobnob.

frat·ri·cide (fra′tri sīd′, frā′-), *n.* **1.** a person who kills his or her brother. **2.** the act of killing one's brother. [1490–1500; (def. 1) < MF < *frātricīda,* equiv. to *frātri-* (comb. form of *frāter*) BROTHER + *-cīda* -CIDE; (def. 2) < MF < LL *frātricīdium,* equiv. to *frātricīd(a)* + *-ium* n. suffix] —**frat′ri·cid′al,** *adj.*

fra·try (frā′trē), *n., pl.* **-tries.** frater[2]. [1530–40]

Frau (fʀou; *Eng.* frou), *n., pl.* ***Frau·en*** (fʀou′ən), *Eng.* **Fraus** (frouz). *German.* **1.** a married woman; a wife. **2.** the conventional German title of respect and term of address for a married woman, corresponding to *Mrs.*

fraud (frôd), *n.* **1.** deceit, trickery, sharp practice, or breach of confidence, perpetrated for profit or to gain some unfair or dishonest advantage. **2.** a particular instance of such deceit or trickery: *mail fraud; election frauds.* **3.** any deception, trickery, or humbug: *That diet book is a fraud and a waste of time.* **4.** a person who makes deceitful pretenses; sham; poseur. [1300–50; ME *fraude* < OF < ML *fraud-* (s. of *fraus*) deceit, injury] —**fraud′ful,** *adj.* —**fraud′ful·ly,** *adv.*
—**Syn. 1.** See **deceit. 3.** wile, hoax.

fraud·u·lent (frô′jə lənt), *adj.* **1.** characterized by, involving, or proceeding from fraud, as actions, enterprise, methods, or gains: *a fraudulent scheme to evade taxes.* **2.** given to or using fraud, as a person; cheating; dishonest. [1375–1425; late ME < L *fraudulentus.* See FRAUD, -ULENT] —**fraud′u·lence, fraud′u·len·cy,** *n.* —**fraud′·u·lent·ly,** *adv.*
—**Syn. 1, 2.** deceitful, deceptive, crooked, underhanded.

Frau·en·feld (*Ger.* fʀou′ən felt′), *n.* a town in and the capital of Thurgau, in N Switzerland. 18,400.

fraught (frôt), *adj.* **1. fraught with,** full of; accompanied by; involving: *a task fraught with danger.* **2.** *Archaic.* filled or laden (with): *ships fraught with precious wares.* —*n.* **3.** *Scot.* a load; cargo; freight (of a ship). [1300–50; ME < MD or MLG *vracht* freight money, FREIGHT; cf. OHG *frēht* earnings, OE *ǣht* possession]

Fräu·lein (fʀoi′līn; *Eng.* froi′lin *or, often,* frô′-, frou′-), *n., pl.* ***Fräu·lein.*** *Eng.* **Fräu·leins.** *German.* **1.** an unmarried woman. **2.** the conventional German title of respect and term of address for an unmarried woman, corresponding to *Miss.*

Fraun·ho·fer (froun′hō′fər, frou′ən hof′ər; *for 1 also Ger.* fʀoun′hō′fəʀ), *n.* **Jo·seph von** (jō′zəf von, -səf; *Ger.* yō′zef fən), 1787–1826, German optician and physicist.

Fraun′hofer lines′, *Astron.* the dark lines of the solar spectrum. [1830–40; named after J. von FRAUNHOFER]

Fra·va·shi (frə vä′shē), *n. Zoroastrianism.* the soul of a dead ancestor. [< Avestan]

frax·i·nel·la (frak′sə nel′ə), *n.* See **gas plant.** [1655–65; < NL, equiv. to L *frāxin(us)* ash tree + *-ella* fem. dim. suffix]

fray[1] (frā), *n.* **1.** a fight, battle, or skirmish. **2.** a competition or contest, esp. in sports. **3.** a noisy quarrel or brawl. **4.** *Archaic.* fright. —*v.t.* **5.** *Archaic.* to frighten. —*v.i.* **6.** *Archaic.* to fight or brawl. [1250–1300; ME *frai;* aph. var. of AFFRAY]

fray[2] (frā), *v.t.* **1.** to wear (cloth, rope, etc.) to loose, raveled threads or fibers at the edge or end; cause to ravel out. **2.** to wear by rubbing (sometimes fol. by *through*). **3.** to cause strain on (something); upset; discompose: *The argument frayed their nerves.* **4.** to rub. —*v.i.* **5.** to become frayed, as cloth; ravel out: *My sweater frayed at the elbows.* **6.** to rub against something: *tall grass fraying against my knees.* —*n.* **7.** a frayed part, as in cloth: *frays at the toes of well-worn sneakers.* [1375–1425; late ME *fraien* < OF *frayer, freier* to rub < L *fricāre.* See FRICTION]

Fra·zer (frā′zər), *n.* **1. Sir James George,** 1854–1941, Scottish anthropologist: writer of socio-anthropological studies. **2.** a male given name.

Fra·zier (frā′zhər), *n.* **E(dward) Franklin,** 1894–1962, U.S. sociologist.

fra·zil (frā′zəl, fraz′əl, frə zēl′, -zil′), *n.* ice crystals formed in turbulent water, as in swift streams or rough seas. [1885–90, *Amer.*; < CanF *frasil, frazil, fraisil,* F *fraisil* coal cinders, OF *faisil*]

fraz·zle (fraz′əl), *v.,* **-zled, -zling,** *n. Informal.* —*v.i., v.t.* **1.** to wear to threads or shreds; fray. **2.** to weary; tire out: *Those six eight-year-olds frazzled me.* —*n.* **3.** the state of being frazzled or worn-out. **4.** a remnant; shred. [1815–25; b. FRAY[2] and *fazzle,* ME *faselin* to unravel, c. G *faseln*]

fraz·zled (fraz′əld), *adj. Informal.* worn-out; fatigued: *a party that left us frazzled.* [1870–75; FRAZZLE + -ED[2]]

FRB, 1. Federal Reserve Bank. **2.** Federal Reserve Board. Also, **F.R.B.**

FRC, Federal Radio Commission.

FRCD, *Finance.* floating-rate certificate of deposit.

F.R.C.P., Fellow of the Royal College of Physicians.

F.R.C.S., Fellow of the Royal College of Surgeons.

freak[1] (frēk), *n.* **1.** any abnormal phenomenon or product or unusual object; anomaly; aberration. **2.** a person or animal on exhibition as an example of a strange deviation from nature; monster. **3.** a sudden and apparently causeless change or turn of events, the mind, etc.; an apparently capricious notion, occurrence, etc.: *That kind of sudden storm is a freak.* **4.** *Numis.* an imperfect coin, undetected at the mint and put into circulation. **5.** *Philately.* a stamp differing from others of the same printing because of creases, dirty engraving plates, etc. Cf. **error** (def. 8), **variety** (def. 8). **6.** *Slang.* **a.** a person who has withdrawn from normal, rational behavior and activities to pursue one interest or obsession: *a drug freak.* **b.** a devoted fan or follower; enthusiast: *a baseball freak.* **c.** a hippie. **7.** *Archaic.* capriciousness; whimsicality. —*adj.* **8.** unusual; odd; irregular: *a freak epidemic.* —*v.i., v.t.* **9.** to become or make frightened, nervous, or wildly excited: *The loud noise caused the horse to freak.* **10. freak out,** *Slang.* **a.** to enter into or cause a period of irrational behavior or emotional instability, as under the influence of a drug: *to be freaked out on LSD.* **b.** to lose or cause to lose emotional control from extreme excitement, shock, fear, joy, despair, etc.: *Seeing the dead body freaked him out.* [1555–65; 1965–70 for def. 6; perh. akin to OE *frician* to dance]
—**Syn. 3.** vagary, quirk, crotchet.

freak[2] (frēk), *v.t.* **1.** to fleck, streak, or variegate: *great splashes of color freaking the sky.* —*n.* **2.** a fleck or streak of color. [appar. introduced by Milton in *Lycidas* (1637), perh. as b. *freck* to mark with spots (perh. back formation from FRECKLE) and STREAK]

freak·ing (frē′king), *adj., adv. Slang.* (used as an intensifier). [1965–70; FREAK[1] + -ING[2]; euphemistically echoing *frigging* and *fucking*]

freak·ish (frē′kish), *adj.* **1.** queer; odd; unusual; grotesque: *a freakish appearance.* **2.** whimsical; capricious: *freakish behavior.* [1645–55; FREAK[1] + -ISH[1]] —**freak′·ish·ly,** *adv.* —**freak′ish·ness,** *n.*

freak′ of na′ture, 1. a person or animal that is born or grows with abnormal physical features. **2.** an unusual, unexpected natural phenomenon. [1840–50]

freak-out (frēk′out′), *n. Slang.* **1.** an act or instance of freaking out. **2.** a person who freaks out. Also, **freak′out′.** [1965–70; n. use of v. phrase *freak out*]

freak′ show′, 1. a display of people or animals with unusual or grotesque physical features, as at a circus or carnival sideshow. **2.** any ludicrous, bizarre, or dehumanizing occasion, function, performance, etc.; grotesque, circuslike event: *endless interviews and auditions that became a ridiculous freak show.* [1885–90]

freak·y (frē′kē), *adj.,* **freak·i·er, freak·i·est. 1.** freakish. **2.** *Slang.* **a.** frightening. **b.** weird; strange. **c.** of or pertaining to freaks. [1815–25; FREAK[1] + -Y[1]] —**freak′i·ly,** *adv.* —**freak′i·ness,** *n.*

Fré·chet (fʀā she′), *n.* **Re·né Mau·rice** (ʀə nā′ mô-ʀēs′), 1878–1973, French mathematician.

Fré·chette (*Fr.* fʀā shet′), *n.* **Louis Ho·no·ré** (*Fr.* lwē ô nô ʀā′), 1839–1908, Canadian poet and journalist.

freck·le (frek′əl), *n., v.,* **-led, -ling.** —*n.* **1.** one of the small, brownish spots on the skin that are caused by deposition of pigment and that increase in number and darken on exposure to sunlight; lentigo. **2.** any small spot or discoloration: *freckles of paint spattered on the floor.* —*v.t.* **3.** to cover with freckles; produce freckles on. —*v.i.* **4.** to become freckled. [1350–1400; b. obs. *frecken* freckle (ME *frekne* < ON **frekna*; cf. *freknōttr* speckled, Norw, Icel *frekna,* Sw *fräkna* freckle) and SPECKLE (n.)]

freck·le-faced (frek′əl fāst′), *adj.* having a face conspicuously covered with freckles. [1680–90]

freck·ly (frek′lē), *adj.,* **-li·er, -li·est.** full of freckles. [1695–1705; FRECKLE + -Y[1]]

Fred (fred), *n.* a male given name, form of **Frederick.**

Fre·da (frē′də, fred′ə), *n.* a female given name.

Fred·die (fred′ē), *n.* **1.** a male given name, form of **Fred. 2.** a female given name, form of **Freda.** Also, **Fred′dy.**

Fred′die Mac′, 1. See **Federal Home Loan Mortgage Corporation. 2.** a publicly traded security that represents participation in a pool of mortgages guaranteed by the Federal Home Loan Mortgage Corporation. Cf. **Fannie Mae, Ginnie Mae.** [1970–75; from the initials *FHLMC,* on the model of FANNIE MAE]

Fred·e·ri·ca (fred′ə rē′kə, fre drē′-), *n.* a female given name: derived from *Frederick.*

Fred·er·ick (fred′rik, -ər ik), *n.* **1.** a city in central Maryland. 27,557. **2.** Also, **Fred′er·ic.** a male given name: from Germanic words meaning "peace" and "ruler."

Frederick I, 1. (*"Frederick Barbarossa"*) 1123?–90, king of Germany 1152–90; king of Italy 1152–90: emperor of the Holy Roman Empire 1152–90. **2.** 1194–1250, king of Sicily 1198–1212: as Frederick II, king of Germany and emperor of the Holy Roman Empire 1215–50. **3.** 1657–1713, king of Prussia 1701–13 (son of Frederick William the Great Elector).

Frederick II, 1. See **Frederick I** (def. 2). **2.** (*"Frederick the Great"*) 1712–86, king of Prussia 1740–86 (son of Frederick William I).

Frederick III, 1. 1415–93, emperor of the Holy Roman Empire 1452–93; as Frederick IV, king of Germany 1440–93. **2.** (*"the Wise"*) 1463–1525, elector of Saxony 1486–1525: protector of Martin Luther.

Frederick IV. See **Frederick III** (def. 1).

Fred′erick Barbaros′sa. See **Frederick I** (def. 1).

Fred·er·icks·burg (fred′riks bûrg′, fred′ər iks-), *n.* a city in NE Virginia, on the Rappahannock River: scene of a Confederate victory 1862. 15,322.

Fred′erick the Great′. See **Frederick II** (def. 2).

Fred′erick Wil′liam, 1. (*"the Great Elector"*) 1620–88, elector of Brandenburg who increased the power and importance of Prussia. **2.** 1882–1951, German general: crown prince of Germany 1888–1918 (son of William II of Germany).

Frederick William I, 1688–1740, king of Prussia 1713–40.

Frederick William II, 1744–97, king of Prussia 1786–97.

CONCISE ETYMOLOGY KEY: <, descended or borrowed from; >, whence; b., blend of, blended; c., cognate with; cf., compare; deriv., derivative; equiv., equivalent; imit., imitative; obl., oblique; r., replacing; s., stem; sp., spelling, spelled; resp., respelling, respelled; trans., translation; ?, origin unknown; *, unattested; ‡, probably earlier than. See the full key inside the front cover.

Frederick William III, 1770–1840, king of Prussia 1797–1840.

Frederick William IV, 1795–1861, king of Prussia 1840–61 (brother of William I of Prussia).

Fred•er•ic•ton (fred′rik tən, fred′ər ik-), *n.* a city in and the capital of New Brunswick, in SE Canada, on the St. John River. 45,248.

Fre•de•rik IX (fʀe′thə ʀēk), 1899–1972, king of Denmark 1947–72 (son of Christian X).

Fred•e•ri•ka (fred′ə rē′kə, fre drē′-), *n.* a female given name.

Fre•de•riks•berg (fred′riks bûrg′, fred′ər iks-; *Dan.* fʀe′thə ʀeks baʀkн′), *n.* a city in E Denmark: a part of Copenhagen. 93,692.

Fre•do•nia (fri dōn′yə, -dō′nē ə), *n.* a town in W New York. 11,126.

Fred•ric (fred′rik), *n.* a male given name. Also, **Fred′•rich.**

free (frē), *adj.,* **fre•er, fre•est,** *adv., v.,* **freed, free•ing.** —*adj.* **1.** enjoying personal rights or liberty, as a person who is not in slavery: *a land of free people.* **2.** pertaining to or reserved for those who enjoy personal liberty: *They were thankful to be living on free soil.* **3.** existing under, characterized by, or possessing civil and political liberties that are, as a rule, constitutionally guaranteed by representative government: *the free nations of the world.* **4.** enjoying political autonomy, as a people or country not under foreign rule; independent. **5.** exempt from external authority, interference, restriction, etc., as a person or one's will, thought, choice, action, etc.; independent; unrestricted. **6.** able to do something at will; at liberty: *free to choose.* **7.** clear of obstructions or obstacles, as a road or corridor: *The highway is now free of fallen rock.* **8.** not occupied or in use: *I'll try to phone her again if the line is free.* **9.** exempt or released from something specified that controls, restrains, burdens, etc. (usually fol. by *from* or *of*): *free from worry; free of taxes.* **10.** having immunity or being safe (usually fol. by *from*): *free from danger.* **11.** provided without, or not subject to, a charge or payment: *free parking; a free sample.* **12.** given without consideration of a return or reward: *a free offer of legal advice.* **13.** unimpeded, as motion or movement; easy, firm, or swift. **14.** not held fast; loose; unattached: *to get one's arm free.* **15.** not joined to or in contact with something else: *The free end of the cantilever sagged.* **16.** acting without self-restraint or reserve: *to be too free with one's tongue.* **17.** ready or generous in giving; liberal; lavish: *to be free with one's advice.* **18.** given readily or in profusion; unstinted. **19.** frank and open; unconstrained, unceremonious, or familiar. **20.** unrestrained by decency; loose or licentious: *free behavior.* **21.** not subject to special regulations, restrictions, duties, etc.: *The ship was given free passage.* **22.** of, pertaining to, or characterized by free enterprise: *a free economy.* **23.** that may be used by or is open to all: *a free market.* **24.** engaged in by all present; general: *a free fight.* **25.** not literal, as a translation, adaptation, or the like; loose. **26.** uncombined chemically: *free oxygen.* **27.** traveling without power; under no force except that of gravity or inertia: *free flight.* **28.** *Phonet.* (of a vowel) situated in an open syllable (opposed to *checked*). **29.** at liberty to enter and enjoy at will (usually fol. by *of*): *to be free of a friend's house.* **30.** not subject to rules, set forms, etc.: *The young students had an hour of free play between classes.* **31.** easily worked, as stone, land, etc. **32.** *Math.* (of a vector) having specified magnitude and direction but no specified initial point. Cf. **bound**[1] (def. 9). **33.** Also, **large.** *Naut.* (of a wind) nearly on the quarter, so that a sailing vessel may sail free. **34.** not containing a specified substance (often used in combination): *a sugar-free soft drink.* **35.** (of a linguistic form) occurring as an independent construction, without necessary combination with other forms, as most words. Cf. **bound**[1] (def. 11). **36. for free,** *Informal.* without charge: *The tailor mended my jacket for free.* **37. free and clear,** *Law.* without any encumbrance, as a lien or mortgage: *They owned their house free and clear.* **38. free and easy, a.** unrestrained; casual; informal. **b.** excessively or inappropriately casual; presumptuous. **39. set free,** to release; liberate; free: *The prisoners were set free.* **40. with a free hand,** generously; freely; openhandedly: *He entertains visitors with a free hand.* **41.** without cost, payment, or charge. —*adv.* **42.** in a free manner; freely. **43.** *Naut.* away from the wind, so that a sailing vessel need not be close-hauled: *running free.* **44. make free with, a.** to use as one's own; help oneself to: *If you make free with their liquor, you won't be invited again.* **b.** to treat with too much familiarity; take liberties with. —*v.t.* **45.** to make free; set at liberty; release from bondage, imprisonment, or restraint. **46.** to exempt or deliver (usually fol. by *from*). **47.** to relieve or rid (usually fol. by *of*): *to free oneself of responsibility.* **48.** to disengage; clear (usually fol. by *from* or *of*). **49. free up, a.** to release, as from restrictions: *Congress voted to free up funds for the new highway system.* **b.** to disentangle: *It took an hour to free up the traffic jam.* [bef. 900; ME *fre,* OE *frēo;* c. Goth *freis,* OHG *frī* (G *frei*), D *vrij,* Skt *priyá-* dear. Cf. FRIEND, FRIDAY] —**free′ness,** *n.*
—**Syn. 44.** See **release.**

free′ a′gent, 1. a person who is self-determining and is not responsible for his or her actions to any authority. **2.** a professional athlete who is not under contract and is free to auction off his or her services and sign a contract with the team that offers the most money. [1840–50] —**free′ a′gency, free′ a′gentry.**

free′ air′, 1. See **free atmosphere. 2.** air not affected by local conditions. [1930–35]

free′ along′side ship′. See **F.A.S.** Also called **free′ along′side ves′sel.** [1900–05]

Free′ and Accept′ed Ma′sons. See under **Freemason** (def. 1).

free′ and com′mon soc′age. See **free socage.**

free′ ascent′, *Rocketry.* the upward traveling or path of a rocket carried by its own inertia after its engine has stopped operating.

free-as•so•ci•ate (frē′ə sō′shē āt′, -sē-), *v.i.,* **-at•ed, -at•ing.** to engage in free association. [1940–45]

free′ associa′tion, *Psychoanal.* the uncensored expression of the ideas, impressions, etc., passing through the mind of the analysand, a technique used to facilitate access to the unconscious. [1895–1900]

free′ at′mosphere, the part of the atmosphere that lies above the frictional influence of the earth's surface. Also called **free air.**

free′ balloon′, a balloon, often equipped to carry passengers, that drifts with air currents and whose ascent and descent are controlled by the release of ballast and buoyant gas. —**free′ balloon′ing.**

free•base (frē′bās′), *v.,* **-based, -bas•ing,** *n. Slang.* —*v.t.* **1.** to purify (cocaine) by dissolving in ether, sodium hydroxide, etc., and filtering off the precipitate. **2.** to ingest (freebased cocaine). —*v.i.* **3.** to freebase cocaine. —*n.* **4.** freebased cocaine. Also, **free′-base′.** [1975–80; FREE + BASE[1]] —**free′bas′er,** *n.*

free′ beach′, a beach that permits nude bathing. [1970–75]

free′ bid′, *Bridge.* a bid made in response to a partner's bid when responding is not required by convention or is not necessary to keep the auction open, as after an opponent's overcall.

free•bie (frē′bē), *n. Informal.* something given without charge or cost, as a ticket to a performance or sporting event or a free sample at a store. Also, **free′bee.** [1940–45, *Amer.;* FREE + *-bie,* of uncert. orig.; perh. orig. a n. phrase *free bee,* with BEE[2] as in *put the bee on* to borrow money with no intention of repaying it]

free-blown (frē′blōn′), *adj.* (of glass) blown and shaped manually and without the use of a mold. Cf. **blown-molded, offhand** (def. 5).

free•board (frē′bôrd′, -bōrd′), *n.* **1.** *Naut.* **a.** the distance between the level of the water and the upper surface of the freeboard deck amidships at the side of a hull: regulated by the agencies of various countries according to the construction of the hull, the type of cargo carried, the area of the world in which it sails, the type of water, and the season of the year. Cf. **load line. b.** (on a cargo vessel) the distance between the uppermost deck considered fully watertight and the official load line. **c.** the portion of the side of a hull that is above the water. **2.** *Civ. Engin.* the height of the watertight portion of a building or other construction above a given level of water in a river, lake, etc. [1670–80; FREE + BOARD; trans. of F *franc bord*]

free′board deck′, *Naut.* (on a cargo vessel) the uppermost deck officially considered to be watertight: used as the level from which the Plimsoll marks are measured. [1950–55]

free′board length′, *Naut.* the length of a vessel, measured on the summer load line from the fore side of the stem to some part of the stern, usually the after side of the rudderpost.

free•boot (frē′bo͞ot′), *v.i.* to act as a freebooter; plunder; loot. [1585–95; back formation from FREEBOOTER]

free•boot•er (frē′bo͞o′tər), *n.* a person who goes about in search of plunder; pirate; buccaneer. [1560–70; Anglicization of D *vrijbuiter,* equiv. to *vrij* free + *buit* BOOTY + *-er* -ER[1]]

free•boot•y (frē′bo͞o′tē), *n. Obs.* plunder; loot; spoils. [1615–25; FREEBOOT(ER) + (BOOT)Y]

free-bored (frē′bôrd′, -bōrd′), *adj.* (of a rifle) having a bore that is not rifled within a short distance of the breech, so that a fired cartridge travels about ½ in. (1.3 cm) before being engaged by the lands, thus reducing initial high pressures.

free•born (frē′bôrn′), *adj.* **1.** born free, rather than in slavery, bondage, or vassalage. **2.** pertaining to or befitting persons born free. [1300–50; ME *freborn, freeborn.* See FREE, BORN]

free′ charge′, any electric charge that can be placed on a conductor or on or within a dielectric or that moves freely in space (opposed to *polarization charge*).

free′ church′, 1. (*sometimes caps.*) a church free from state control. Cf. **established church. 2.** (*sometimes caps.*) a dissenting or nonconforming church. **3.** (*caps.*) Also, **Free Kirk.** (in Scotland) the church established by those who left the Church of Scotland in 1843. [1825–35, *Amer.*]

free′ church′man, 1. (*sometimes caps.*) a member of a free church. **2.** (*caps.*) a member of the Free Church of Scotland. [1840–50]

free′ cit′y, a city having an independent government and forming a sovereign state by itself. [1610–20]

free′ coin′age, the unrestricted coinage of bullion or of a specified metal, as silver, into money for any person bringing it to the mint, either with or without charge for minting. [1885–90, *Amer.*]

free′ compan′ion, a member of a band of mercenary soldiers during the Middle Ages. [1810–20]

free′ com′pany, a band of free companions. [1870–75]

free-cut•ting (frē′kut′ing), *adj.* (of a metal alloy) having good machinability: *free-cutting steel.* [1925–30]

free′ deliv′ery, the delivery of mail directly to the recipient's address without charge to the recipient: *Before free delivery people had to pick up their mail at the post office or pay a letter carrier to deliver it.* [1860–65]

free′ div′ing, *Chiefly Brit.* See **skin diving.** [1950–55] —**free′ div′er.**

freed•man (frēd′mən), *n., pl.* **-men.** a man who has been freed from slavery. [1595–1605; FREED + MAN[1]]

Freed′men's Bu′reau, *U.S. Hist.* an agency of the War Department set up in 1865 to assist freed slaves in obtaining relief, land, jobs, fair treatment, and education.

free•dom (frē′dəm), *n.* **1.** the state of being free or at liberty rather than in confinement or under physical restraint: *He won his freedom after a retrial.* **2.** exemption from external control, interference, regulation, etc. **3.** the power to determine action without restraint. **4.** political or national independence. **5.** personal liberty, as opposed to bondage or slavery: *a slave who bought his freedom.* **6.** exemption from the presence of anything specified (usually fol. by *from*): *freedom from fear.* **7.** the absence of or release from ties, obligations, etc. **8.** ease or facility of movement or action: *to enjoy the freedom of living in the country.* **9.** frankness of manner or speech. **10.** general exemption or immunity: *freedom from taxation.* **11.** the absence of ceremony or reserve. **12.** a liberty taken. **13.** a particular immunity or privilege enjoyed, as by a city or corporation: *freedom to levy taxes.* **14.** civil liberty, as opposed to subjection to an arbitrary or despotic government. **15.** the right to enjoy all the privileges or special rights of citizenship, membership, etc., in a community or the like. **16.** the right to frequent, enjoy, or use at will: *to have the freedom of a friend's library.* **17.** *Philos.* the power to exercise choice and make decisions without constraint from within or without; autonomy; self-determination. Cf. **necessity** (def. 7). [bef. 900; ME *fredom,* OE *frēodōm.* See FREE, -DOM]
—**Syn. 1.** FREEDOM, INDEPENDENCE, LIBERTY refer to an absence of undue restrictions and an opportunity to exercise one's rights and powers. FREEDOM emphasizes the opportunity given for the exercise of one's rights, powers, desires, or the like: *freedom of speech or conscience; freedom of movement.* INDEPENDENCE implies not only lack of restrictions but also the ability to stand alone, unsustained by anything else: *Independence of thought promotes invention and discovery.* LIBERTY, though most often interchanged with FREEDOM, is also used to imply undue exercise of freedom: *He took liberties with the text.* **9.** openness, ingenuousness. **12.** license. **16.** run.

free′dom fight′er, a fighter for freedom, esp. a person who battles against established forces of tyranny and dictatorship. [1940–45]

free′dom march′, an organized march protesting a government's restriction of or lack of support for civil rights, esp. such a march in support of racial integration in the U.S. in the 1960's. Also, **Free′dom March′.** [1960–65] —**free′dom march′er.**

Free′dom of Informa′tion Act′, *U.S. Govt.* a law enacted in 1966 requiring that government records except those relating to national security, confidential financial data, and law enforcement be made available to the public on request. *Abbr.:* FOIA

free′dom of speech′, the right of people to express their opinions publicly without governmental interference, subject to the laws against libel, incitement to violence or rebellion, etc. Also called **free speech.** [1940–45]

free′dom of the cit′y, 1. nominal citizenship in a city, conferred as an honor upon important visitors. **2.** (formerly) official citizenship in a city, conferred upon distinguished nonresidents. [1765–75]

free′dom of the press′, the right to publish newspapers, magazines, and other printed matter without governmental restriction and subject only to the laws of libel, obscenity, sedition, etc.

free′dom of the seas′, *Internat. Law.* the doctrine that ships of neutral countries may sail anywhere on the high seas without interference by warring powers. [1915–20]

free′dom ride′, (esp. in the 1960's) a bus trip made to parts of the southern U.S. by persons engaging in efforts to integrate racially segregated public facilities. Also, **Free′dom Ride′.** [1960–65, *Amer.*] —**free′dom rid′er.**

freed•wom•an (frēd′wo͝om′ən), *n., pl.* **-wom•en.** a woman who has been freed from slavery. [1865–70, *Amer.;* FREED + WOMAN]

free′ elec′tron, *Physics.* an electron that is not attached to an atom or molecule and is free to respond to outside forces. [1905–10]

free′ en′ergy, *Thermodynamics.* **1.** See **Gibbs function. 2.** See **Helmholtz function.**

free′ en′terprise, 1. an economic and political doctrine holding that a capitalist economy can regulate itself in a freely competitive market through the relationship of supply and demand with a minimum of governmental intervention and regulation. **2.** the practice of free enterprise in an economy, or the right to practice it. Also called **private enterprise.** [1885–90] —**free′-en′terpris′ing,** *adj.*

free′ en′terpriser, a person who practices or advocates free enterprise. [1940–45; FREE ENTERPRISE + -ER[1]]

free′ expan′sion, *Thermodynamics.* the expansion of a gas into an evacuated space without the transfer of heat or the performance of work.

free′ fall′, 1. the hypothetical fall of a body such that the only force acting upon it is that of gravity. **2.** the part of a parachute jump that precedes the opening of the parachute. **3.** a decline, esp. a sudden or rapid decline, as in value or prestige, that appears to be endless or bottomless: *The economy was in a free fall all winter.* Also, **free-fall** (for defs. 1, 2). [1915–20]

free-fall (frē′fôl′), *v.,* **-fell, -fall•en, -fall•ing,** *adj., n.* —*v.i.* **1.** (of parachutists) to descend initially, as for a designated interval, in a free fall: *The jumpers were required to free-fall for eight seconds.* —*adj.* **2.** denoting or suggesting a free fall: *a free-fall recession.* —*n.* **3.** free fall (defs. 1, 2).

free′-fire′ zone′ (frē′fīᵊr′), an area in which mili-

CONCISE PRONUNCIATION KEY: act, cāpe, dâre, pärt; set, ēqual; if, īce; ox, ōver, ôrder, oil, bo͝ok, bo͞ot, out; up, ûrge; child; sing; shoe; thin, *that;* zh as in *treasure.* ə = *a* as in *alone, e* as in *system, i* as in *easily, o* as in *gallop, u* as in *circus;* ᵊ as in *fire* (fīᵊr), *hour* (ouᵊr). l and n can serve as syllabic consonants, as in *cradle* (krād′l), and *button* (but′n). See the full key inside the front cover.

tary units have prior clearance to fire at will on any person or object encountered. [1965–70]

free′ flight′, unassisted or unconstrained flight, as the flight of a rocket or missile without guidance or after fuel exhaustion or motor cutoff. [1920–25]

free-float·ing (frē′flō′ting), *adj.* **1.** (of an emotional state) lacking an apparent cause, focus, or object; generalized: *free-floating hostility.* **2.** (of people) uncommitted, as to a doctrine, political party, etc.; independent: *free-floating opportunists.* **3.** capable of relatively free movement. [1920–25]

free-for-all (frē′fər ôl′), *n.* **1.** a fight, argument, contest, etc., open to everyone and usually without rules. **2.** any competition or contested situation that is disordered, impulsive, or out of control: *a free-for-all at the buffet table.* **3.** *Informal.* any enterprise or field of endeavor in which various companies, countries, participants, etc., compete without restriction: *a price-cutting free-for-all among local stores.* —*adj.* **4.** open to everyone. [1880–85, *Amer.*]
—**Syn. 1.** brawl, fracas, scrap, melee, donnybrook.

free′ form′, **1.** a shape having an irregular contour, chiefly used in nonrepresentational art and industrial design. **2.** *Ling.* a linguistic form that can occur by itself, as *fire, book,* or *run.* Cf. **bound form.** [1945–50]

free-form (*adj.* frē′fôrm′; *adv.* frē′fôrm′), *adj.* **1.** characterized by free form: *free-form sculpture.* **2.** not organized or planned in a conventional way: *a free-form international conglomerate.* **3.** encouraged to function or evolve without advance planning; spontaneous: *free-form management.* —*adv.* **4.** without restrictions or preconceptions: *The children were allowed to paint free-form.* Also, **free′form′.** [1950–55]

Free′ French′, (in World War II) the French movement, organized in London under the leadership of General Charles de Gaulle, that repudiated the 1940 armistice with the Nazis and the government established at Vichy and fought for the liberation of France and the restoration of the republic.

free′ gold′, **1.** treasury gold, including the legal reserve, not restricted to the redemption of gold certificates or other specific uses. **2.** *Mining.* gold found in loose particles or nuggets, as in a placer mine. [1895–1900]

free′ goods′, **1.** imported goods that are not subject to duty. **2.** goods having utilitarian value, as air and water, but available in such great quantities as to have no cost. [1770–80]

free′ hand′, unrestricted freedom or authority: *They gave the decorator a free hand.* [1925–30]

free·hand (frē′hand′), *adj.* **1.** drawn or executed by hand without guiding instruments, measurements, or other aids: *a freehand map.* —*adv.* **2.** in a freehand manner: *to draw freehand.* [1860–65; FREE + HAND]

free-hand·ed (frē′han′did), *adj.* **1.** generous; liberal. **2.** freehand. —*adv.* **3.** freehand. [1650–60] —**free′-hand′ed·ly,** *adv.* —**free′-hand′ed·ness,** *n.*

free-heart·ed (frē′här′tid), *adj.* light-hearted; spontaneous; frank; generous. [1350–1400; ME *free herted.* See FREE, HEARTED] —**free′-heart′ed·ly,** *adv.* —**free′-heart′ed·ness,** *n.*

free·hold (frē′hōld′), *Law.* **1.** an estate in land, inherited or held for life. —*n.* **2.** a form of tenure by which an estate is held in fee simple, fee tail, or for life. —*adj.* **3.** pertaining to, of the nature of, or held by freehold. [1375–1425; late ME *frehold* (see FREE, HOLD[1]); trans. of AF *franc tenement* (see FRANK[1], TENEMENT)]

Free·hold (frē′hōld′), *n.* a town in E New Jersey: battle of Monmouth courthouse 1778. 10,020. Formerly, **Monmouth.**

free·hold·er (frē′hōl′dər), *n.* **1.** the owner of a freehold. **2.** (in some U.S. counties) a registered voter who owns local property and has been a local resident for a specified length of time. [1325–75; ME *freholder* (see FREE, HOLDER); trans. of AF *fraunc tenaunt* (see FRANK[1], TENANT)]

free′ house′, *Brit.* a tavern that, having no affiliation or contract with a particular brewery, serves several brands of beer, ale, etc. [1855–60]

free′ing port′, *Naut.* an opening in the bottom of a bulwark, for rapid drainage of a weather deck in heavy seas; scupper. [1875–80]

free′ jazz′, spontaneously experimental, free-form jazz, popularized as an avant-garde phenomenon in the 1960's by various soloists and characterized by random expression and disregard for traditional structures, tonalities, and rhythms. Also called **new thing.**

free′ kick′, *Soccer.* an unhindered kick of a stationary ball, usually awarded to a player as the result of a foul committed by a player from the opposing team. Cf. **direct free kick, indirect free kick.** [1870–75]

Free′ Kirk′. See **free church** (def. 3). —**Free′ Kirk′·er.**

free′ lance′, **1.** a mercenary soldier or military adventurer of the Middle Ages, often of knightly rank, who offered his services to any state, party, or cause. **2.** freelance (defs. 1, 2).

free·lance (frē′lans′, -läns′, -lans′, -läns′), *n., v.,* **-lanced, -lanc·ing,** *adj., adv.* —*n.* Also, **free lance. 1.** Also, **freelancer.** a person who works as a writer, designer, performer, or the like, selling work or services by the hour, day, job, etc., rather than working on a regular salary basis for one employer. **2.** a person who contends in a cause or in a succession of various causes, as he or she chooses, without personal attachment or allegiance. —*v.i.* **3.** to act or work as a freelance: *The illustrator used to be employed by us but is freelancing now.* —*v.t.* **4.** to produce, sell, or accomplish as a freelance: *to freelance a magazine article.* —*adj.* **5.** of or pertaining to a freelance or the work of a freelance: *a freelance writer; freelance copyediting.* —*adv.* **6.** in the manner of a freelance: *She works freelance.* Also, **free′-lance′.** [FREE + LANCE[1]]

free·lanc·er (frē′lan′sər, -län′-), *n.* freelance (def. 1). Also, **free′-lanc′er.**

free′ list′, a list or register of articles that may be brought into a country duty-free. [1800–10]

free′ liv′er, a person who follows a way of life that freely indulges the appetites, desires, etc. [1705–15]

free-liv·ing (frē′liv′ing), *adj.* **1.** following a way of life in which one freely indulges the appetites, desires, etc. **2.** *Biol.* noting an organism that is neither parasitic, symbiotic, nor sessile. [1810–20]

free·load (frē′lōd′, -lōd′), *v.i. Informal.* **1.** to take advantage of others for free food, entertainment, etc. —*v.t.* **2.** to get by freeloading: *He freeloaded several meals a week.* [1950–55, *Amer;* back formation from *freeloader* (FREE + LOAD + -ER[1])] —**free′load′er,** *n.*

free′ love′, the doctrine or practice of having sexual relations or living together without legal marriage or continuing obligation. [1815–25]

free′ lunch′, **1.** food provided without charge in some bars and saloons to attract customers. **2.** *Informal.* something given with no expectation of repayment, service, responsibility, etc.: *In politics there's no free lunch—everyone expects favors to be repaid.* [1835–45]

free·ly (frē′lē), *adv.* in a free manner. [bef. 900; ME *freliche,* OE *frēolīce.* See FREE, -LY]

free-ma·chin·ing (frē′mə shē′ning), *adj.* **1.** (of certain metals) readily machinable at high speeds with low force. **2.** noting a class of steels having certain additives, as sulfur or lead, to make them readily machinable.

free·man (frē′mən), *n., pl.* **-men. 1.** a person who is free; a person who enjoys personal, civil, or political liberty. **2.** a person who enjoys or is entitled to citizenship, franchise, or other special privilege: *a freeman of a city.* [bef. 1000; ME *freman,* OE *frēoman.* See FREE, MAN[1]]

Free·man (frē′mən), *n.* **1. Douglas Sou·thall** (sou′thôl), 1886–1953, U.S. journalist and biographer. **2. Edward Augustus,** 1823–92, English historian. **3. Mary E(leanor Wilkins),** 1862–1930, U.S. novelist and short-story writer. **4.** a male given name.

free·mar·tin (frē′mär′tn), *n.* a female calf that is born as a twin with a male and is sterile as a result of exposure to masculinizing hormones produced by the male. [1675–85; orig. uncert.]

Free·ma·son (frē′mā′sən, frē′mā′-), *n.* **1.** a member of a widely distributed secret order **(Free and Accepted Masons),** having for its object mutual assistance and the promotion of brotherly love among its members. **2.** (*l.c.*) *Hist.* **a.** one of a class of skilled stoneworkers of the Middle Ages, possessing secret signs and passwords. **b.** a member of a society composed of such workers, which also included honorary members **(accepted masons)** not connected with the building trades. [1350–1400; ME *fremason.* See FREE, MASON] —**free·ma·son·ic** (frē′mə-son′ik), *adj.*

free·ma·son·ry (frē′mā′sən rē), *n.* **1.** secret or tacit brotherhood; fellowship; fundamental bond or rapport: *the freemasonry of those who hunger for knowledge.* **2.** (*cap.*) the principles, practices, and institutions of Freemasons. [1400–50; late ME *fremasonry.* See FREEMASON, -RY]

free′ on board′. See **f.o.b.** [1920–25]

free′ perspec′tive, exaggeration of perspectival devices to increase the illusion of depth, used esp. in stage-set painting and construction.

free′ port′, **1.** a port or special section of a port where goods may be unloaded, stored, and shipped without payment of customs duties. **2.** a port open under equal conditions to all traders. [1705–15]

Free·port (frē′pôrt′, -pōrt′), *n.* **1.** a village on SW Long Island, in SE New York. 38,272. **2.** a city in NW Illinois. 26,406. **3.** a city in SE Texas. 13,444.

free′ press′, a body of book publishers, news media, etc., not controlled or restricted by government censorship in political or ideological matters. [1760–70]

fre·er[1] (frē′ər), *n.* a person or thing that frees. [1600–10; FREE + -ER[1]]

fre·er[2] (frē′ər), *adj.* comparative of **free.**

free′ rad′ical, *Chem., Biochem.* an atom or molecule that bears an unpaired electron and is extremely reactive, capable of engaging in rapid chain reactions that destabilize other molecules and generate many more free radicals: in the body, deactivated by antioxidants, uric acid, and certain enzyme activities. Cf. **diradical.** [1895–1900]

free-range (frē′rānj′), *adj.* (of livestock and domestic poultry) permitted to graze or forage for grain, etc., rather than being confined to a feedlot or a small enclosure: *a free-range pig.* [1910–15]

free′ reach′, *Naut.* a course sailed by a sailing vessel having the wind on the quarter.

free′ reach′ing, *Naut.* sailing on a free reach.

free′ rein′, unhampered freedom of movement, choice, or action: *Students have free rein to choose their own class schedules.* [1950–55]

free′ ride′, **1.** *Informal.* something obtained without effort or cost: *The fact that you're the general's son doesn't mean you'll get a free ride in the army.* **2.** *Stud Poker.* a round of betting in which each player checks and therefore receives another card without having to contribute any chips to the pot. [1895–1900]

free′ rid′er, **1.** *Informal.* a person who obtains something without effort or cost. **2.** a nonunion worker who enjoys the benefits of union activities. Also, **free′-rid′er.** —**free′-rid′ing,** *n.*

free′ safe′ty, *Football.* a member of a secondary, usually the deepest-playing defender, with no specific assignment at the snap of the ball, but often covering the area of the field across from the weak side of the opponent's offensive line against runs and long pass plays. Also called **weak safety.**

free′ school′, a privately run school organized as an alternative to the traditional public or private school, usually following a highly flexible approach to the curriculum and teaching methods.

free′ sheet′, *Print.* paper made entirely from chemical pulp and therefore free of groundwood.

free·si·a (frē′zhē ə, -zē ə, -zhə), *n.* any of several plants belonging to the genus *Freesia,* of the iris family, native to southern Africa, having fragrant white, yellow, or sometimes rose-colored, tubular flowers. [1880–85; < NL; named after E. M. *Fries* (1794–1878), Swedish botanist; see -IA]

free′ sil′ver, *Econ.* the free coinage of silver, esp. at a fixed ratio with gold. [1875–80, *Amer.*] —**free′-sil′·ver,** *adj.*

free′ soc′age, *Medieval Hist.* land held by a tenant who rendered certain honorable and nonservile duties to his lord. Also called **free and common socage.** Cf. **villein socage.**

free′ soil′, *U.S. Hist.* a region, esp. a U.S. territory, prohibiting slavery prior to the Civil War. [1840–50, *Amer.*]

free-soil (frē′soil′), *adj. U.S. Hist.* **1.** pertaining to or opposing the extension of slavery in the Territories. **2.** pertaining to or characteristic of the Free Soil party. [1840–50, *Amer.*] —**free′-soil′ism,** *n.*

Free-Soil·er (frē′soi′lər), *n.* a member of the Free Soil party or a supporter of its principles. [1840–50, *Amer.;* FREE SOIL (PARTY) + -ER[1]]

Free′ Soil′ par′ty, a former U.S. political party (1848–56) that opposed the extension of slavery in the Territories not yet admitted to statehood.

free′ speech′. See **freedom of speech.** [1840–50, *Amer.*]

free-spend·ing (frē′spen′ding), *adj.* spending or tending to spend freely: *If you don't mend your free-spending ways, you'll go bankrupt.*

free′ spir′it, a person with a highly individual or unique attitude, lifestyle, or imagination; nonconformist.

free-spo·ken (frē′spō′kən), *adj.* given to speaking freely or without reserve; frank; outspoken. [1615–25] —**free′-spo′ken·ly,** *adv.* —**free′-spo′ken·ness,** *n.*

fre·est (frē′ist), *adj.* superlative of **free.**

free·stand·ing (frē′stan′ding), *adj.* **1.** (of sculpture or architectural elements) unattached to a supporting unit or background; standing alone. **2.** not affiliated with others of its kind; independent; autonomous: *a free-standing clinic, not connected with any hospital.* Also, **free′-stand′ing.** [1875–80; FREE + STANDING]

Free′ State′, **1.** *U.S. Hist.* (before the Civil War) a state in which slavery was prohibited. **2.** See **Irish Free State.** [1640–50]

Free′ Stat′er (stā′tər), **1.** a native or inhabitant of a Free State. **2.** a person of European descent who is a native or resident of the Orange Free State. [1895–1900; FREE STATE + -ER[1]]

free·stone (frē′stōn′), *n.* **1.** a fruit having a stone to which the flesh does not cling, as certain peaches and plums. **2.** the stone itself. **3.** any stone, as sandstone, that can be freely worked or quarried, esp. one that cuts well in all directions without splitting. —*adj.* **4.** having a stone from which the flesh is easily separated. [1250–1300; ME *freston* (see FREE, STONE); trans. of OF *franche piere;* see FRANK[1]]

Free′stone State′ (frē′stōn′), Connecticut (used as a nickname). [1840–50, *Amer.*]

free·style (frē′stīl′), *n.* **1.** *Swimming.* **a.** competition in which any of the standard strokes may be used, according to the swimmer's choice. **b.** the crawl. **2.** *Wrestling.* catch-as-catch-can. **3.** (in other sports) a performance or routine featuring relatively free, unrestricted movement or intended to demonstrate an individual's special skills or style, as in figure skating, gymnastics, or surfing. [1930–35; FREE + STYLE] —**free′styl′er,** *n.*

free-swim·mer (frē′swim′ər), *n. Zool.* an animal, as a fish, that swims about freely.

free-swim·ming (frē′swim′ing), *adj. Zool.* (of aquatic organisms) not attached to a base nor joined in a colony; capable of swimming about freely. [1890–95]

free-swing·ing (frē′swing′ing), *adj.* recklessly daring in action or style: *free-swinging stock market speculators.* [1945–50; FREE(WHEELING) + SWINGING] —**free′-swing′er,** *n.*

free·tail (frē′tāl′), *n.* a free-tailed bat. [FREE + TAIL[1]]

free′-tailed bat′ (frē′tāld′), any of various small, swift, insect-eating bats of the family Molossidae, common in warm climates, having thick, leathery ears and a tail that projects well beyond the tail membrane.

Free′ Ter′ritory of Trieste′. See **Trieste, Free Territory of.**

free·think·er (frē′thing′kər), *n.* a person who forms opinions on the basis of reason, independent of authority or tradition, esp. a person whose religious opinions differ from established belief. [1685–95; FREE + THINKER] —**free′think′ing,** *adj., n.*
—**Syn.** skeptic, agnostic; atheist.

free′ thought′, thought unrestrained by deference to authority, tradition, or established belief, esp. in matters of religion. [1705–15]

free′ throw′, *Basketball.* See **foul shot.** [1890–95]

free′ throw′ lane′, *Basketball.* the rectangular area, 19 ft. (5.7 m) long and usually 12 or 16 ft. (3.6 m or 4.8 m) wide, extending from the end line behind each backboard to the foul line and along the sides of which players line up during a foul shot. [1925–30]

free′ throw′ line′, *Basketball.* See **foul line** (def. 2). [1890–95]

Free•town (frē′toun′), *n.* a seaport in and the capital of Sierra Leone, in W Africa. 214,000.

free′ trade′, **1.** trade between countries, free from governmental restrictions or duties. **2.** international trade free from protective duties and subject only to such tariffs as are needed for revenue. **3.** the system, principles, or maintenance of such trade. **4.** *Chiefly Scot.* smuggling. [1600–10] —**free′-trade′,** *adj.*

free′ trad′er, a person who advocates free trade. Also, **free′-trad′er.** [1690–1700; FREE TRADE + -ER[1]]

free′-trade′ zone′, foreign-trade zone. See **free port** (def. 1). *Abbr.:* FTZ

free′ univer′sity, a school run informally by and for college students, organized to offer courses and approaches not usually offered in a college curriculum.

free′ var′iable, *Logic.* (in functional calculus) a variable occurring in a sentential function and not within the scope of any quantifier containing it. Cf. **bound variable.**

free′ varia′tion, *Ling.* a relation between the members of a pair of phones, phonemes, morphs, or other linguistic entities such that either of the two may occur in the same position with no change in the meaning of the utterance: in the first syllable of "economics," "e" and "ē" are in free variation. Cf. **complementary distribution.**

free′ verse′, *Prosody.* verse that does not follow a fixed metrical pattern. [1905–10] —**free-ver•si•fi•er** (frē′vûr′sə fī′ər), *n.*

free•way (frē′wā′), *n.* **1.** an express highway with no intersections, usually having traffic routed on and off by means of a cloverleaf. **2.** a toll-free highway. [1925–30, *Amer.*; FREE + WAY]

free•wheel (frē′hwēl′, -wēl′), *n.* **1.** a device in the transmission of a motor vehicle that automatically disengages the drive shaft whenever it begins to turn more rapidly than the engine. **2.** a form of rear bicycle wheel that has a device freeing it from the driving mechanism, as when the pedals are stopped in coasting. —*v.i.* **3.** (of a vehicle or its operator) to coast with the wheels disengaged from the driving mechanism. **4.** to move or function freely, independently, unconcernedly, or the like (often fol. by *about, through, around,* etc.): *The two friends freewheeled around the country after graduation.* [1895–1900; FREE + WHEEL]

free•wheel•er (frē′hwē′lər, -wē′-), *n.* **1.** a vehicle that can freewheel. **2.** a person who works or lives in an independent, often daring, way. **3.** a person who is primarily concerned with having a good time. [FREEWHEEL + -ER[1]]

free•wheel•ing (frē′hwē′ling, -wē′-), *adj.* **1.** operating in the manner of a freewheel. **2.** (of a person) moving about freely, independently, or irresponsibly. **3.** (of words, remarks, actions, etc.) unrestrained; irresponsible: *Loose, freewheeling charges were traded during the argument.* [1900–05; FREEWHEEL + -ING[2]]

free′ will′, **1.** free and independent choice; voluntary decision: *You took on the responsibility of your own free will.* **2.** *Philos.* the doctrine that the conduct of human beings expresses personal choice and is not simply determined by physical or divine forces.

free•will (frē′wil′), *adj.* **1.** made or done freely or of one's own accord; voluntary: *a freewill contribution to a political fund.* **2.** of or pertaining to the metaphysical doctrine of the freedom of the will: *the freewill controversy.* [1525–35; FREE + WILL[2]]

free′will′ of′fering, a voluntary religious contribution made in addition to what may be expected or required. [1525–35]

free′ world′, (*often caps.*) the nations of the world that function chiefly under democratic and capitalistic systems rather than under totalitarianism or Communism. [1945–50] —**free′-world′,** *adj.*

freeze (frēz), *v.,* **froze, fro•zen, freez•ing,** *n.* —*v.i.* **1.** to become hardened into ice or into a solid body; change from the liquid to the solid state by loss of heat. **2.** to become hard or stiffened because of loss of heat, as objects containing moisture: *Meat will freeze in a few hours.* **3.** to suffer the effects of intense cold; have the sensation of extreme cold: *We sat there freezing until the heat came on.* **4.** to be of the degree of cold at which water freezes: *It may freeze tonight.* **5.** to lose warmth of feeling; be stunned or chilled with fear, shock, etc.: *My heart froze when she told me the news.* **6.** to become immobilized through fear, shock, etc.: *When he got in front of the audience he froze.* **7.** to stop suddenly and remain motionless; halt: *I froze in my tracks.* **8.** to become obstructed by the formation of ice, as pipes: *Our basement water pipes often freeze in winter.* **9.** to die or be injured because of frost or cold. **10.** (of a screw, nail, or the like) to become rigidly fixed in place, as from rust or dirt. **11.** to become fixed to something by or as if by the action of frost. **12.** to become unfriendly, secretive, or aloof (often fol. by *up*): *He froze at such a personal question.* —*v.t.* **13.** to harden into ice; change from a fluid to a solid form by loss of heat; congeal. **14.** to form ice on the surface of (a river, pond, etc.). **15.** to harden or stiffen (an object containing moisture) by cold. **16.** to quick-freeze. **17.** to subject to freezing temperature; place in a freezer or in the freezing compartment of a refrigerator. **18.** to cause to suffer the effects of intense cold; produce the sensation of extreme cold in. **19.** to cause to lose warmth as if by cold; chill with fear; dampen the enthusiasm of. **20.** to cause (a person or animal) to become fixed through fright, alarm, shock, etc.: *Terror froze him to the steering wheel.* **21.** to kill by frost or cold: *A late snow froze the buds.* **22.** to fix fast with ice: *a sled frozen to a sidewalk.* **23.** to obstruct or close (a pipe or the like) by the formation of ice: *The storm had frozen the hydrant.* **24.** to fix (rents, prices, etc.) at a specific amount, usually by government order. **25.** to stop or limit production, use, or development of: *an agreement to freeze nuclear weapons.* **26.** *Finance.* to render impossible of liquidation or collection: *Bank loans are frozen in business depressions.* **27.** *Surg.* to render part of the body insensitive to pain or slower in its function by artificial means. **28.** *Cards.* **a.** *Canasta.* to play a wild card on (the discard pile) so as to make it frozen. **b.** *Poker.* to eliminate (other players) in a game of freezeout. **29.** to photograph (a moving subject) at a shutter speed fast enough to produce an unblurred, seemingly motionless image. **30.** *Motion Pictures.* to stop by means of a freeze-frame mechanism: *You can freeze the action at any point.* **31.** *Sports.* to maintain possession of (a ball or puck) for as long as possible, usually without trying to score, thereby reducing the opponent's opportunities for scoring. **32.** *Ice Hockey.* to hold (a puck) against the boards with the skates or stick, causing play to stop and forcing a face-off. **33. freeze on** or **onto,** *Informal.* to adhere closely to; hold on; seize. **34. freeze out,** to exclude or compel (somebody) to withdraw from membership, acceptance, a position of influence or advantage, etc., by cold treatment or severe competition. **35. freeze over,** to coat or become coated with ice: *The lake freezes over for several months each year.* —*n.* **36.** the act of freezing; state of being frozen. **37.** Also called **ice-up.** *Meteorol.* a widespread occurrence of temperatures below 32°F (0°C) persisting for at least several days: *A freeze is expected in the coastal areas.* **38.** a frost. **39.** a legislative action, esp. in time of national emergency, to control prices, rents, production, etc.: *The government put a freeze on new construction.* **40.** a decision by one or more nations to stop or limit production or development of weapons, esp. nuclear weapons. [bef. 1000; (v.) ME *fresen,* OE *frēosan;* c. MLG *vrēsen,* ON *frjósa,* OHG *friosan* (G *frieren*); (n.) late ME *frese,* deriv. of the v.] —**freez′a•ble,** *adj.* —**freez′a•bil′i•ty,** *n.*

freeze-dried (frēz′drīd′), *adj.* (of foods and beverages) preserved by means of freeze-drying: *freeze-dried coffee.* [1945–50]

freeze-dry (frēz′drī′), *v.t.,* **-dried, -dry•ing.** to subject to freeze-drying. [1945–50]

freeze-dry•ing (frēz′drī′ing), *n.* a process for drying heat-sensitive substances, as foods, blood plasma, antibiotics, and the like, by freezing the substance and then subliming the ice or other frozen solvent in a high vacuum. [1940–45]

freeze-etch (frēz′ech′), *v.t.* to prepare (material) for the electron microscope by freeze etching.

freeze′ etch′ing, *Biol.* the preparation of material for electron microscopic study by freeze fracturing and then subliming a layer of ice crystals from the fractured plane to expose the natural surfaces. Also, **freeze′-etch′ing.** [1965–70]

freeze-frac•ture (frēz′frak′chər), *v.t.,* **-tured, -tur•ing.** to prepare (material) for the electron microscope by freeze fracturing. [1965–70]

freeze′ frac′turing, *Biol.* a method of preparing a biological specimen for electron microscopic study by rapid freezing, cleaving with a sharp knife or razor, and then covering with a thin layer of metal to make the internal structural planes visible. Also, **freeze′-frac′tur•ing.** [1975–80]

freeze′ frame′, *Television, Motion Pictures.* **1.** Also called **stop motion.** an optical effect or technique in which a single frame of film is reprinted in a continuous series, which when shown gives the effect of a still photograph. **2.** a button or other mechanism on a projector, videocassette system, etc., allowing one to stop the projected picture at any point. Also, **freeze′-frame′.** [1955–60] —**freeze′-frame′,** *adj.*

freeze•out (frēz′out′), *n. Poker.* a game in which each player begins with a predetermined amount of money and must withdraw from the game once that amount is lost, until one player is left with all the winnings. Also, **freeze′-out′.** [1850–55, *Amer.*; n. use of v. phrase *freeze out*]

freez•er (frē′zər), *n.* **1.** a refrigerator, refrigerator compartment, cabinet, or room held at or below 32°F (0°C), used esp. for preserving and storing food. **2.** a machine containing cold brine, ice, etc., for making ice cream, sherbet, or the like. **3.** a person or thing that freezes or chills. [1835–45; FREEZE + -ER[1]]

freez′er burn′, light-colored spots that appear on frozen food, caused by loss of surface moisture due to faulty packaging or improper freezing methods.

freeze-up (frēz′up′), *n. Informal.* **1.** a freezing over of a body of water in an area. **2.** a period of below-freezing temperatures. **3.** the condition of being immobilized or inoperative through freezing: *car engine freeze-up in winter.* [1875–80, *Amer.*; n. use of v. phrase *freeze up*]

freez•ing (frē′zing), *adj.* **1.** (of temperatures) approaching, at, or below the freezing point. **2.** extremely or uncomfortably cold; chilled: *We were both freezing and welcomed the hot cocoa.* **3.** beginning to freeze or partially frozen; in the process of being or becoming frozen. [1605–15; FREEZE + -ING[2]] —**freez′ing•ly,** *adv.*

freez′ing driz′zle, drizzle that falls as a liquid but freezes into glaze or rime upon contact with the ground. [1955–60]

freez′ing point′, *Physical Chem.* the temperature at which a liquid freezes: *The freezing point of water is 32°F, 0°C.* [1740–50]

freez′ing rain′, rain that falls as a liquid but freezes into glaze upon contact with the ground. [1790–1800]

free′ zone′, a free-port area. [1900–05]

Fre•ge (frā′gə), *n.* **(Friedrich Ludwig) Gott•lob** (gôt′lōp), 1848–1925, German mathematician and logician.

F region, the ionospheric region in which the F layer forms. [1925–30]

Frei (frā), *n.* **E•duar•do** (e dwär′thô), born 1911, Chilean statesman: president 1964–70.

Frei•burg (frī′bŏŏrk′), *n.* **1.** a city in SW Baden-Württemberg, in SW West Germany. 174,000. **2.** German name of **Fribourg.**

freight (frāt), *n.* **1.** goods, cargo, or lading transported for pay, whether by water, land, or air. **2.** the ordinary conveyance or means of transport of goods provided by common carriers (distinguished from *express*): *Shipping by freight is less expensive.* **3.** the charges, fee, or compensation paid for such transportation: *We pay the freight.* **4.** (esp. in Britain) the cargo, or any part of the cargo, of a vessel; merchandise transported by water. **5.** *Chiefly Brit.* transportation of goods by water. **6.** See **freight train. 7.** *Slang.* cost or price, esp. when high: *I'd like a larger house, but can't afford the freight.* —*v.t.* **8.** to load; burden: *a story heavily freighted with private meaning.* **9.** to load with goods or merchandise for transportation: *It took all night to freight the ship.* **10.** to transport as freight; send by freight. [1350–1400; ME *freyght* (n.) < MD or MLG *vrecht,* var. of *vracht.* See FRAUGHT] —**freight′less,** *adj.*

—**Syn. 1.** FREIGHT, CARGO, SHIPMENT refer to goods being transported from place to place. FREIGHT is the general term for goods transported from one place to another by any means: *to send freight from New York to New Orleans.* CARGO is the term generally used for goods carried by ship or plane: *to send a cargo to Europe.* SHIPMENT is a quantity of goods destined for a particular place, no matter how sent: *a shipment of potatoes.* **3.** freightage, haulage. **8.** charge.

freight•age (frā′tij), *n.* **1.** the transportation of goods. **2.** the price for this. **3.** freight, cargo, or lading. [1685–95; FREIGHT + -AGE]

freight′ a′gent, a representative of a common carrier who manages the freight business in a local district. [1835–45, *Amer.*]

freight′ car′, any car for carrying freight. [1825–35]

freight′ en′gine, a locomotive for pulling freight trains, designed for high drawbar pull rather than high speed. [1860–65, *Amer.*]

freight•er (frā′tər), *n.* **1.** a vessel used mainly for carrying cargo. **2.** a large aircraft or spacecraft used primarily for transporting cargo and equipment: *The space station of the future will be supplied by robot freighters.* **3.** a person whose occupation it is to receive and forward freight. **4.** a person for whom freight is transported; shipper. [1615–25; FREIGHT + -ER[1]]

freight′ for′warder, a person or firm that arranges to pick up or deliver goods on instructions of a shipper or a consignee from or to a point by various necessary conveyances and common carriers. Also called **forwarder, forwarding agent.** [1920–25]

freight′ house′, a depot or storage place for freight. [1840–50, *Amer.*]

freight•lin•er (frāt′lī′nər), *n. Chiefly Brit.* a train for transporting containerized freight. [1960–65; FREIGHT + LINER[1]]

freight′ pass′-through, *Com.* a special allowance or discounted price given a bookseller or bookstore by a publishing house for paying the freight charge on a shipment of books ordered: so called because the shipping charge is passed on to the consumer by an increase in the suggested retail price for each book. *Abbr.:* FPT

freight′ ton′, ton[1] (def. 2).

freight′ train′, a train of freight cars. [1835–45]

Fre•ling•huy•sen (frē′ling hī′zən), *n.* **Frederick Theodore,** 1817–85, U.S. statesman.

Fre•man•tle (frē′man′tl), *n.* a seaport in SW Australia, near Perth. 25,990.

frem•i•tus (frem′i təs), *n., pl.* **-tus.** *Med.* palpable vibration, as of the walls of the chest. [1810–20; < NL, L: a roaring, murmuring, equiv. to *fremi-,* var. stem of *fremere* to roar, murmur + *-tus* suffix of v. action]

Fre•mont (frē′mont), *n.* **1.** a city in W California, near San Francisco Bay. 131,945. **2.** a city in E Nebraska, on the Platte River, near Omaha. 23,979. **3.** a city in N Ohio. 17,834.

Fré•mont (frē′mont), *n.* **John Charles,** 1813–90, U.S. general and explorer: first Republican presidential candidate, 1856.

fre•nate (frē′nāt), *adj.* having a frenum or frenulum. [< NL *frēnātus,* special use of L *frēnātus* furnished with a bridle. See FRENUM, -ATE[1]]

French (french), *adj.* **1.** of, pertaining to, or characteristic of France, its inhabitants, or their language, culture, etc.: *French cooking.* —*n.* **2.** the people of France and their direct descendants. **3.** a Romance language spoken in France, parts of Belgium and Switzerland, and in areas colonized after 1500 by France. *Abbr.:* F —*v.t.* **4.** (*often l.c.*) to prepare (food) according to a French method. **5.** (*often l.c.*) to cut (snap beans) into slivers or thin strips before cooking. **6.** (*often l.c.*) to trim the meat from the end of (a rib chop). **7.** (*often l.c.*) to prepare (meat) for cooking by slicing it into strips and pounding. **8.** *Slang.* to short-sheet (a bed). **9.** (*often l.c.*) *Slang (vulgar).* to give oral stimulation of the penis or vulva. [bef. 1150; ME *Frensh, French,* OE *Frenc(i)sc.* See FRANK, -ISH[1]] —**French′ness,** *n.*

French (french), *n.* **1. Alice** (*"Octave Thanet"*), 1850–1934, U.S. novelist and short-story writer. **2. Daniel Chester,** 1850–1931, U.S. sculptor. **3. Sir John Den•ton Pink•stone** (den′tn pingk′stōn, -stən), **1st Earl of Ypres,** 1852–1925, English field marshal in World War I.

French′ Acad′emy, an association of 40 scholars and men and women of letters, established in 1635 by Cardinal Richelieu and devoted chiefly to preserving the purity of the French language and establishing standards of proper usage. French, **Académie Française.**

French′ and In′dian War′, the war in America in which France and its Indian allies opposed England 1754–60: ended by Treaty of Paris in 1763.

French′ arch′, an arch similar to a flat arch, but having voussoirs inclined to the same angle on each side of the center.

French′ bean′, *Brit.* the pod of a green bean or wax bean, eaten as a vegetable. [1545–55]

French′ bed′, a bed without posts, terminating in identical outward-curving rolls at the head and the foot. [1815–25]

French′ bread′, a yeast-raised bread made of dough containing water and distinguished by its thick, well-browned crust, usually made in long, slender, tapered loaves. Cf. **baguette** (def. 3). [1680–90]

French′ bull′dog, one of a French breed of small, bat-eared dogs having a large, square head, a short tail, and a short, sleek coat. [1870–75, *Amer.*]

French′ Cameroons′, Cameroun (def. 2).

French′ Cana′dian, 1. a descendant of the early French colonists of Canada. **2.** the language of the French Canadians. **3.** one of a Canadian breed of small, dark-brown dairy cattle, raised chiefly in Quebec. [1750–60]

French′ chalk′, a talc for marking lines on fabrics. [1720–30]

French′ chop′, a rib chop, usually of lamb, with the meat trimmed from the end of the bone. [1920–25]

French′ col′ombard, colombard.

French′ Commu′nity, a cultural and economic association of France, its overseas departments and territories, and former French territories that chose to maintain association after becoming independent republics: formed 1958.

French′ Con′go, former name of the People's Republic of the Congo.

French′ crul′ler, cruller (def. 2).

French′ cuff′, a double cuff formed by folding back a wide band at the end of a sleeve, usually fastened by a cuff link. Cf. **barrel cuff.** [1915–20]

French′ curve′, a flat drafting instrument, usually consisting of a sheet of clear plastic, the edges of which are cut into several scroll-like curves enabling a draftsperson to draw lines of varying curvature. Also, **french′ curve′.** [1880–85]

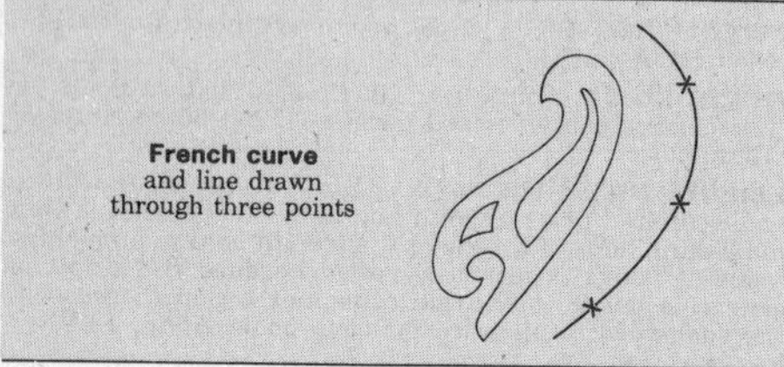
French curve and line drawn through three points

French-cut (french′kut′), *adj.* (esp. of string beans) sliced lengthwise into long, thin strips. Also, **French-style.**

French′ dip′, a hot sandwich of roast beef, pork, or lamb, served on a crusty roll over which seasoned pan juices are poured. Also called **French′-dip sand′wich.**

French′ door′, a door having glass panes throughout or nearly throughout its length. Also called **casement door.** [1920–25]

French′ drain′, a drainage trench filled to ground level with fragments of brick, rock, etc. [1770–80]

French′ dress′ing, (*often l.c.*) **1.** salad dressing prepared chiefly from oil, vinegar, and seasonings. **2.** a creamy and often sweet dressing, usually orange in color. [1880–85, *Amer.*]

French′ en′dive, endive (def. 2).

French′ Equato′rial Af′rica, a former federation of French territories in central Africa, including Chad, Gabon, Middle Congo (now People's Republic of the Congo), and Ubangi-Shari (now Central African Republic): each became independent in 1960.

French′ flat′, *Brit. Theat.* a flat that can be raised to or hung from the flies, and that contains practicable doors, windows, etc. [1875–80, *Amer.*]

French′ foot′, *Furniture.* **1.** Also called **knurl toe, scroll foot, whorl foot.** a foot of the mid-18th century having the form of a scroll, continuing the leg downward and outward, supported by a shoe. **2.** a bracket foot comprising a downward and outward continuation of the adjoining surfaces of the piece, the corner of the foot being a concave outward curve and the inner edges being a pair of ogee curves continuing the lines of the bottom rails downward.

French′ fries′, thin strips of potato that have been deep-fried. Also called **French′-fried pota′toes.** [1915–20]

French-fry (french′frī′), *v.t.,* **-fried, -fry·ing.** to fry in deep fat: *to French-fry onion rings.* Also, **french′-fry′.** [1925–30, *Amer.*]

French′ Gui·an′a (gē an′ə, gē ä′nə), an overseas department of France, on the NE coast of South America: formerly a French colony. 49,200; 35,135 sq. mi. (91,000 sq. km). *Cap.:* Cayenne. —**French′ Guianese′, French′ Guian′an.**

French′ Guin′ea, former name of **Guinea.**

French′ harp′, *Chiefly South Midland U.S.* harmonica (def. 1). [1880–85, *Amer.*]

French′ heel′, a high, curved heel, characterized by a heel breast curving into a shank, used on women's shoes. Cf. **Spanish heel.** [1655–65] —**French′-heeled′,** *adj.*

French′ horn′, a musical brass wind instrument with a long, coiled tube having a conical bore and a flaring bell. See illus. under **horn.** [1735–45]

French′ ice′ cream′, a type of ice cream in which an egg and cream mixture is cooked to a light custard before being frozen.

French·i·fy (fren′chə fī′), *v.t.,* **-fied, -fy·ing.** (*often l.c.*) to make (something or someone) resemble the French, as in manners, customs, or dress: *to Frenchify the spelling of one's name.* [1585–95; FRENCH + -IFY] —**French′i·fi·ca′tion,** *n.*

French′ In′dia, the five small former French territories in India, including Chandernagor, Karikal, Pondicherry, and Yanaon on the E coast, and Mahé on the W coast.

French′ Indochi′na, an area in SE Asia, formerly a French colonial federation including Cochin-China, the protectorates of Annam, Cambodia, Tonkin, and Laos, and the leased territory of Kwangchowan: now comprising the three independent states of Vietnam, Cambodia, and Laos. *Cap.:* Hanoi. Cf. **Indochina.**

French′ kid′, kidskin tanned by an alum or vegetable process and finished in a manner originally employed by the French.

French′ kiss′. See **soul kiss.** [1920–25]

French-kiss (french′kis′), *v.t., v.i.* to soul-kiss. [1925–30]

French′ leave′, a departure without ceremony, permission, or notice: *Taking French leave, he evaded his creditors.* [1765–75]

French′ let′ter, *Older Slang.* a condom. [1855–60]

French·man (french′mən), *n., pl.* **-men. 1.** a native or inhabitant of the French nation. **2.** a French ship. [bef. 1150; ME *Frenshman,* OE *Frencisc man.* See FRENCH, MAN[1]]

French′ mar′igold, a composite plant, *Tagetes patula,* of Mexico, having yellow flowers with red markings. [1540–50]

French′ Moroc′co. See under **Morocco** (def. 1).

French′ mul′berry, a shrub, *Callicarpa americana,* of the verbena family, of the south-central U.S. and the West Indies, having violet-colored fruit and bluish flowers.

French′ Ocean′ia, former name of **French Polynesia.**

French′ pan′cake, a thin, light pancake, usually served with a sweet or savory filling.

French′ pas′try, fine, rich, or fancy dessert pastry, esp. made from puff paste and filled with cream or fruit preparations. [1920–25]

French′ pitch′, *Music.* See **diapason normal pitch.**

French′ pol′ish, a furniture finish, consisting of shellac dissolved in spirits. [1810–20]

French-pol·ish (french′pol′ish), *v.t.* to finish or treat (a piece of furniture) with French polish. [1830–40]

French′ Polyne′sia, a French overseas territory in the S Pacific, including the Society Islands, Marquesas Islands, and other scattered island groups. 119,168; 1544 sq. mi. (4000 sq. km). *Cap.:* Papeete. Formerly, **French Oceania.**

French′ pox′, *Older Use* (*sometimes offensive*). syphilis. [1495–1505]

French′ Provin′cial, noting, pertaining to, or resembling a style of furnishings and decoration originating in the provinces of France in the 18th century, derived from but less ornate than styles then current in Paris and featuring simply carved wood furniture, often with decorative curved moldings. Also, **French′ provin′cial.** [1940–45]

French′ Revolu′tion, *Fr. Hist.* the revolution that began in 1789, overthrew the absolute monarchy of the Bourbons and the system of aristocratic privileges, and ended with Napoleon's overthrow of the Directory and seizure of power in 1799.

French′ Revolu′tionary cal′endar. See **Revolutionary calendar.**

French′ roll′, 1. a circular or oval bread roll having a hard or crispy crust. **2.** Also called **French twist.** a coiffure for women in which the hair is combed back from the face and arranged in a vertical roll on the back of the head. [1940–45]

French′ roof′, a mansard roof the sides of which are nearly perpendicular. [1660–70]

French′ rose′. See **Provence rose.** [1545–55]

French′ seam′, *Sewing.* a seam in which the raw edges of the cloth are completely covered by sewing them together, first on the right side, then on the wrong. [1885–90]

French′ Shore′, *Canadian.* either of two stretches of coastline inhabited mainly by Francophone Canadians: the W coast of Newfoundland and the SW coast of Nova Scotia between Yarmouth and Digby.

French′ Soma′liland, a former name of **Djibouti** (def. 1).

French-style (french′stīl′), *adj.* French-cut.

French′ Sudan′, former name of **Mali.**

French′ sys′tem, a method of spinning in which fibers of extremely short-staple wool are not twisted before being spun. Also called **continental system, Franco-Belgian system.** Cf. **Bradford spinning.**

French′ tam′arisk. See **salt cedar.**

French′ tel′ephone, handset (def. 1). [1930–35]

French′ tick′ler, *Slang.* a condom designed with knobs, projections, etc.

French′ toast′, bread dipped in a batter of egg and milk and sautéed until brown, usually served with syrup or sprinkled with sugar and cinnamon. [1650–60]

French′ twist′. See **French roll.** [1875–80]

French′ Un′ion, a former association of France and its overseas territories, colonies, and protectorates as constituted in 1946: superseded by the French Community in 1958.

French′ way′, *Slang.* cunnilingus or fellatio.

French·weed (french′wēd′), *n.* the penny-cress, *Thlaspi arvense.* [FRENCH + WEED[1]]

French′ West′ Af′rica, a former French federation in W Africa, including Dahomey (now Benin), French Guinea, French Sudan (now Mali), Ivory Coast, Mauritania, Niger, Senegal, and Upper Volta (now Burkina Fasso).

French′ West′ In′dies, the French islands in the Lesser Antilles of the West Indies, including Martinique and Guadeloupe and the five dependencies of Guadeloupe: administered as two overseas departments. 676,900; 1114 sq. mi. (2885 sq. km).

French′ win′dow, a pair of casement windows extending to the floor and serving as portals, esp. from a room to an outside porch or terrace. [1795–1805]

French·wom·an (french′wo͝om′ən), *n., pl.* **-wom·en.** a woman who is a native or inhabitant of the French nation. [1585–95; FRENCH + WOMAN]

French·y (fren′chē), *n., pl.* **French·ies,** *adj.* **French·i·er, French·i·est.** —*n.* **1.** *Informal.* a native or inhabitant of France or a person of French descent. —*adj.* **2.** characteristic or suggestive of the French people, French culture, etc. [1820–30; FRENCH + -Y[1], -Y[2]] —**French′i·ly,** *adv.* —**French′i·ness,** *n.*

Fre·neau (fri nō′), *n.* **Philip,** 1752–1832, U.S. poet and editor.

Fre·net′ for′mula (fre nā′), *Math.* one of a set of formulas for finding the curvature and torsion of a plane or space curve in terms of vectors tangent or normal to the curve. [named after their discoverer, Jean (or Frédéric) *Frenet* (1816–1900), French mathematician]

fre·net·ic (frə net′ik), *adj.* frantic; frenzied. Also, **fre·net′i·cal, phrenetic, phrenetical.** [1350–1400; ME; see FRANTIC] —**fre·net′i·cal·ly,** *adv.*

fren·u·lum (fren′yə ləm), *n., pl.* **-la** (-lə). **1.** *Anat., Zool.* a small frenum. **2.** *Entomol.* a strong spine or group of bristles on the hind wing of many butterflies and moths, projecting beneath the forewing and serving to hold the two wings together in flight. Also, **fraenulum.** [1890–95; < NL; see FRENUM, -ULE] —**fren′u·lar,** *adj.*

fre·num (frē′nəm), *n., pl.* **-na** (-nə). *Anat., Zool.* a fold of membrane that checks or restrains the motion of a part, as the fold on the underside of the tongue. Also, **fraenum.** [< NL; L *frēnum* bridle]

fren·zied (fren′zēd), *adj.* **1.** wildly excited or enthusiastic: *frenzied applause.* **2.** violently agitated; frantic; wild: *a frenzied mob.* Also, **phrensied.** [1790–1800; FRENZY + -ED[3]] —**fren′zied·ly,** *adv.*

fren·zy (fren′zē), *n., pl.* **-zies,** *v.,* **-zied, -zy·ing.** —*n.* **1.** extreme mental agitation; wild excitement or derangement. **2.** a fit or spell of violent mental excitement; a paroxysm characteristic of or resulting from a mania: *He is subject to these frenzies several times a year.* —*v.t.* **3.** to drive to frenzy; make frantic: *She was frenzied by fear when she smelled the smoke.* [1300–50; ME *frenesie* < OF < LL *phrenēsis* < LGk, for Gk *phrenitis;* see PHRENITIS] —**fren′zi·ly,** *adv.*
—**Syn. 2.** madness, insanity, lunacy, aberration; rage, fury, raving. —**Ant. 1.** calm. **2.** sanity.

Fre·on (frē′on), *Trademark.* a brand name for any of a class of liquid or gaseous fluorocarbon or chlorofluorocarbon products, used chiefly as refrigerants.

freq., 1. frequency. **2.** frequent. **3.** frequentative. **4.** frequently.

fre·quen·cy (frē′kwən sē), *n., pl.* **-cies. 1.** Also, **fre′·quence.** the state or fact of being frequent; frequent occurrence: *We are alarmed by the frequency of fires in the neighborhood.* **2.** rate of occurrence: *The doctor has increased the frequency of his visits.* **3.** *Physics.* **a.** the number of periods or regularly occurring events of any given kind in unit of time, usually in one second. **b.** the number of cycles or completed alternations per unit time of a wave or oscillation. *Symbol:* F; *Abbr.:* freq. **4.** *Math.* the number of times a value recurs in a unit change of the independent variable of a given function. **5.** *Statistics.* the number of items occurring in a given category. Cf. **relative frequency.** [1545–55; < L *frequentia* assembly, multitude, crowd. See FREQUENT, -CY]
—**Syn. 1.** regularity, repetition, recurrence.

fre′quency band′, *Radio and Television.* band[2] (def. 9). [1920–25]

fre′quency curve′, *Statistics.* a curve representing the frequency with which a variable assumes its values. [1890–95]

fre′quency distribu′tion, *Statistics.* the correspondence of a set of frequencies with the set of categories, intervals, or values into which a population is classified. [1890–95]

fre′quency func′tion, *Statistics.* See **probability density function** (def. 2).

fre′quency modula′tion, *Electronics, Radio.* See **FM.** [1920–25]

CONCISE ETYMOLOGY KEY: <, descended or borrowed from; >, whence; b., blend of, blended; c., cognate with; cf., compare; deriv., derivative; equiv., equivalent; imit., imitative; obl., oblique; r., replacing; s., stem; sp., spelling, spelled; resp., respelling, respelled; trans., translation; ?, origin unknown; *, unattested; ‡, probably earlier than. See the full key inside the front cover.

fre′quency pol′ygon, *Statistics.* a frequency curve consisting of connected line segments formed by joining the midpoints of the upper edges of the rectangles in a histogram whose class intervals are of uniform length. [1895–1900]

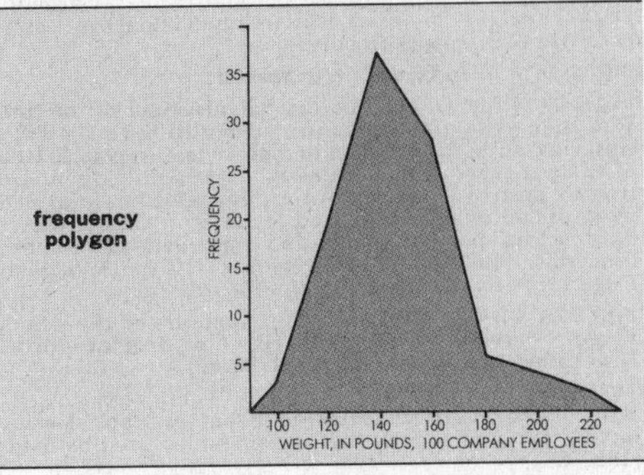

frequency polygon

fre′quency response′, *Electronics.* **1.** the effectiveness with which a circuit, device, or system processes and transmits signals fed into it, as a function of the signal frequency. **2.** Also called **fre′quency-response curve′.** a graph of frequency response, with signal amplitude or gain plotted against frequency. [1925–30]

fre·quent (*adj.* frē′kwənt; *v.* fri kwent′, frē′kwənt), *adj.* **1.** happening or occurring at short intervals: *to make frequent trips to Tokyo.* **2.** constant, habitual, or regular: *a frequent guest.* **3.** located at short distances apart: *frequent towns along the shore.* —*v.t.* **4.** to visit often; go often to; be often in: *to frequent the art galleries.* [1400–50; late ME: ample, profuse < L *frequent-* (s. of *frequēns*) crowded; (v.) (< MF *fréquenter*) < L *frequentāre,* deriv. of *frequēns*] —**fre·quent′a·ble,** *adj.* —**fre·quent′er,** *n.* —**fre′quent·ness,** *n.*

fre·quen·ta·tion (frē′kwən tā′shən), *n.* the practice of frequenting; habit of visiting often. [1400–50; late ME < MF *fréquentation* < L *frequentātiōn-* (s. of *frequentātiō*). See FREQUENT, -ATION]

fre·quen·ta·tive (fri kwen′tə tiv), *Gram.* —*adj.* **1.** noting or pertaining to a verb aspect expressing repetition of an action. —*n.* **2.** the frequentative aspect. **3.** a verb in the frequentative aspect, as *wrestle* from *wrest.* [1520–30; < L *frequentātīvus* denoting repetition of an act. See FREQUENT, -ATE[1], -IVE]

fre·quent·ly (frē′kwənt lē), *adv.* often; many times; at short intervals. [1525–35; FREQUENT + -LY]
—**Syn.** repeatedly. See **often.**

frère (frer), *n., pl.* ***frères*** (frer). *French.* **1.** brother. **2.** a fellow member of an organization. **3.** friar; monk.

fres·co (fres′kō), *n., pl.* **-coes, -cos,** *v.,* **-coed, -co·ing.** —*n.* **1.** Also called **buon fresco, true fresco.** the art or technique of painting on a moist, plaster surface with colors ground up in water or a limewater mixture. Cf. **fresco secco. 2.** a picture or design so painted. —*v.t.* **3.** to paint in fresco. [1590–1600; < It: cool, FRESH (< Gmc)] —**fres′co·er, fres′co·ist,** *n.*

Fres·co·bal·di (fres kô bäl′dē), *n.* **Gi·ro·la·mo** (jē-rô′lä mô), 1583–1643, Italian organist and composer.

fres′co sec′co, the technique of painting in watercolors on dry plaster. Also called **dry fresco, secco.** Cf. **fresco** (def. 1). [1835–45; < It: lit., dry fresco]

fresh (fresh), *adj.,* **-er, -est,** *n., v., adv.* —*adj.* **1.** newly made or obtained: *fresh footprints.* **2.** recently arrived; just come: *fresh from school.* **3.** new; not previously known, met with, etc.; novel: *to uncover fresh facts; to seek fresh experiences.* **4.** additional or further: *fresh supplies.* **5.** not salty, as water. **6.** retaining the original properties unimpaired; not stale or spoiled: *Is the milk still fresh?* **7.** not preserved by freezing, canning, pickling, salting, drying, etc.: *fresh vegetables.* **8.** not tired or fatigued; brisk; vigorous: *She was still fresh after that long walk.* **9.** not faded, worn, obliterated, etc.: *fresh paint; a fresh appearance.* **10.** looking youthful and healthy: *a fresh beauty that we all admired.* **11.** pure, cool, or refreshing, as air. **12.** denoting a young wine, esp. a white or rosé, that is clean, crisp, and uncomplicated. **13.** *Meteorol.* (of wind) moderately strong or brisk. **14.** inexperienced; green; callow: *Two hundred fresh recruits arrived at the training camp.* **15.** *Informal.* forward or presumptuous. **16.** (of a cow) having recently given birth to a calf. **17.** *Slang.* **a.** great; marvelous. **b.** informed; up-to-date. —*n.* **18.** the fresh part or time. **19.** a freshet. —*v.t., v.i.* **20.** to make or become fresh. —*adv.* **21.** newly; recently; just now: *He is fresh out of ideas. The eggs are fresh laid.* [bef. 900; ME; OE *fersc;* c. OFris *fersk,* OHG *frisc* (G *frisch*), ON *ferskr*] —**fresh′ly,** *adv.* —**fresh′ness,** *n.*
—**Syn. 1.** recent. See **new. 11.** invigorating, sweet, unadulterated. **14.** artless, untrained, raw, uncultivated, unskilled. —**Ant. 1.** old. **14.** skilled.

fresh′ breeze′, *Meteorol.* a wind of 19–24 mph (9–11 m/sec). Cf. **breeze**[1] (def. 2). [1795–1805]

fresh·en (fresh′ən), *v.t.* **1.** to make fresh; refresh, revive, or renew: *We need a good rain to freshen the flowers.* **2.** to remove saltiness from. **3.** *Naut.* to preserve (a rope in use) from prolonged friction or concentrated stress on any one part. —*v.i.* **4.** to become or grow fresh. **5.** (of a cow) **a.** to commence giving milk after calving. **b.** to give birth. **6. freshen up,** to make oneself feel freshly clean or neat, as by washing, changing clothes, etc.: *to freshen up after a long trip.* [1690–1700; FRESH + -EN[1]]

fresh·en·er (fresh′ə nər), *n.* **1.** something that freshens or refreshens: *An air freshener cleared the room of stale odors.* **2.** a soothing skin lotion. **3.** a beverage that makes the drinker feel refreshed. [1880–85; FRESHEN + -ER[1]]

fresh·er (fresh′ər), *n. Brit. Slang.* freshman. [1880–85; FRESH(MAN) + -ER[1]]

fresh·et (fresh′it), *n.* **1.** a freshwater stream flowing into the sea. **2.** a sudden rise in the level of a stream, or a flood, caused by heavy rains or the rapid melting of snow and ice. [1590–1600; FRESH (n.) + -ET]
—**Syn. 2.** See **flood.**

fresh′ gale′, *Meteorol.* a wind of 39–46 mph (17–33 m/sec). Cf. **gale**[1] (def. 2). [1575–85]

fresh·man (fresh′mən), *n., pl.* **-men,** *adj.* —*n.* **1.** a student in the first year of the course at a university, college, or high school. **2.** a novice; beginner. —*adj.* **3.** of, pertaining to, or characteristic of a freshman: *to outgrow one's freshman attitudes.* **4.** lacking seniority or experience; junior: *a freshman senator.* **5.** required of or suitable for freshmen: *freshman courses.* **6.** initial; first: *This is my freshman year with the company.* [1540–50; FRESH + -MAN] —**fresh′man·ship′,** *n.*
—**Usage.** See **-man.**

fresh·man·ic (fresh man′ik), *adj.* of, pertaining to, or characteristic of a freshman: *freshmanic enthusiasm.* [1830–40, *Amer.*; FRESHMAN + -IC]

fresh′man week′, a week at the beginning of the school year with a program planned to orient entering students, esp. at a college.

fresh′ness date′, the last date, usually specified on the label or packaging, that a food, as bread, is considered fresh, although it may be sold, ordinarily at reduced prices, or eaten after that date.

fresh′ wa′ter, **1.** water that does not contain a large amount of salt. **2.** inland water, as ponds, lakes, or streams, that is not salt. [bef. 900; ME; OE]

fresh·wa·ter (fresh′wô′tər, -wot′ər), *adj.* **1.** of or living in water that is fresh or not salt: *freshwater fish.* **2.** accustomed to fresh water only, and not to the sea: *a freshwater sailor.* **3.** small, provincial, or little known: *a freshwater college.* **4.** *Obs.* untrained or of little experience. Also, **fresh′-wa′ter.** [1520–30; FRESH + WATER]

fresh′water drum′, *Ichthyol.* an edible drum, *Aplodinotus grunniens,* of the fresh waters of North and Central America, sometimes reaching a weight of 60 lb. (27 kg). [1940–45]

fres·nel (frə nel′, *Fr.* frā nel′), *n.* a unit of frequency, equal to 10^{12} cycles per second. [1935–40; named after Augustin Jean *Fresnel* (1788–1827), French physicist]

Fresnel′ bi′prism, *Optics.* biprism. [1935–40; see FRESNEL]

Fresnel′ lens′, *Optics.* a large lens with a surface of concentric grooves of prismatic profile, used in automobile headlights, searchlights, spotlights, etc. [1840–50; see FRESNEL]

Fresnel′ mir′rors, *Optics.* two plane mirrors joined together in a way that makes them useful for studying interference patterns. [1965–70; see FRESNEL]

Fres·no (frez′nō), *n.* a city in central California. 218,202.

fress (fres), *v.i. Slang.* to eat or snack, esp. often or in large quantities. [< Yiddish *fresn* or G *fressen* (of animals) to eat, eat ravenously; see FRET[1]] —**fress′er,** *n.*

fret[1] (fret), *v.,* **fret·ted, fret·ting,** *n.* —*v.i.* **1.** to feel or express worry, annoyance, discontent, or the like: *Fretting about the lost ring isn't going to help.* **2.** to cause corrosion; gnaw into something: *acids that fret at the strongest metals.* **3.** to make a way by gnawing, corrosion, wearing away, etc.: *The river frets at its banks until a new channel is formed.* **4.** to become eaten, worn, or corroded (often fol. by *away*): *Limestone slowly frets away under pounding by the wind and rain.* **5.** to move in agitation or commotion, as water: *water fretting over the stones of a brook.* —*v.t.* **6.** to torment; irritate, annoy, or vex: *You mustn't fret yourself about that.* **7.** to wear away or consume by gnawing, friction, rust, corrosives, etc.: *the ocean fretting its shores.* **8.** to form or make by wearing away a substance: *The river had fretted an underground passage.* **9.** to agitate (water): *Strong winds were fretting the channel.* —*n.* **10.** an irritated state of mind; annoyance; vexation. **11.** erosion; corrosion; gnawing. **12.** a worn or eroded place. [bef. 900; ME *freten,* OE *fretan* to eat up, consume; c. OS *fretan,* Goth *fraitan,* OHG *frezzan* (G *fressen*)] —**fret′ter,** *n.*
—**Syn. 1.** fume, rage. **6.** worry, harass, goad, tease. **7.** erode, gnaw, corrode, abrade, grind, rub, rust. **10.** harassment, agitation, worry.

fret[2] (fret), *n., v.,* **fret·ted, fret·ting.** —*n.* **1.** an interlaced, angular design; fretwork. **2.** an angular design of bands within a border. **3.** *Heraldry.* a charge composed of two diagonal strips interlacing with and crossing at the center of a mascle. **4.** a piece of decoratively pierced work placed in a clock case to deaden the sound of the mechanism. —*v.t.* **5.** to ornament with a fret or fretwork. [1350–1400; ME *frette* < ?; cf. MF *frete* trelliswork, OE *fretwian,* var. of *frætwian* to adorn] —**fret′less,** *adj.*

fret[2] (def. 2)

fret[3] (fret), *n., v.,* **fret·ted, fret·ting.** —*n.* **1.** any of the ridges of wood, metal, or string, set across the fingerboard of a guitar, lute, or similar instrument, which help the fingers to stop the strings at the correct points. —*v.t.* **2.** to provide with frets. [1490–1500; orig. uncert.] —**fret′less,** *adj.*

fret·ful (fret′fəl), *adj.* disposed or quick to fret; irritable or peevish. Also, **fret·some** (fret′səm). [1585–95; FRET[1] + -FUL] —**fret′ful·ly,** *adv.* —**fret′ful·ness,** *n.*
—**Syn.** petulant, querulous, impatient, testy.

fret′ saw′, a long, narrow-bladed saw used to cut ornamental work from thin wood. Cf. **coping saw.** See illus. in next column. [1860–65]

fret saw

fret·ted (fret′id), *adj.* ornamented or provided with frets: *a fretted molding.* [1375–1425; late ME; see FRET[2], -ED[2]]

fret·ty[1] (fret′ē), *adj.,* **-ti·er, -ti·est.** fretful; irritable; peevish. [1835–45; FRET[1] + -Y[1]]

fret·ty[2] (fret′ē), *adj. Heraldry.* covered with crisscrossed and interlacing diagonal strips: *argent, fretty sable.* [1555–65; < MF *frette,* deriv. of *frete* trelliswork. See FRET[2], -EE]

fret·work (fret′wûrk′), *n.* **1.** ornamental work consisting of interlacing parts, esp. work in which the design is formed by perforation. **2.** any pattern of dark and light, such as that of perforated fretwork. [1595–1605; FRET[2] + WORK]

Freud (froid; *Ger.* froit), *n.* **1. Anna,** 1895–1982, British psychoanalyst, born in Austria (daughter of Sigmund Freud). **2. Sig·mund** (sig′mənd; *Ger.* zēkh′mo͝ont), 1856–1939, Austrian neurologist: founder of psychoanalysis.

Freud·i·an (froi′dē ən), *adj.* **1.** of or pertaining to Sigmund Freud or his doctrines, esp. with respect to the causes and treatment of neurotic and psychopathic states, the interpretation of dreams, etc. —*n.* **2.** a person, esp. a psychoanalyst, who adheres to the basic doctrines of Freud. [1905–10; FREUD + -IAN] —**Freud′i·an·ism,** *n.*

Freud′ian slip′, (in Freudian psychology) an inadvertent mistake in speech or writing that is thought to reveal a person's unconscious motives, wishes, or attitudes. Cf. **parapraxis.** [1950–55]

Freund's′ ad′juvant (froindz), *Immunol.* a water-in-oil emulsion injected with immunogen **(Freund's′ in′complete ad′juvant)** or with immunogen and killed mycobacteria **(Freund's′ complete′ ad′juvant)** to enhance the immune response to the immunogen. [1945–50; after Jules *Freund* (1891–1960), Hungarian-born U.S. immunologist]

Frey (frā), *n. Scand. Myth.* the god of peace, prosperity, and marriage: one of the Vanir, originally brought to Asgard as a hostage. [< ON *Freyr* orig., lord, master]

Frey·a (frā′ə), *n. Scand. Myth.* the goddess of love and fertility, sister of Frey, daughter of Njord; one of the Vanir. [< ON *Freyja* orig., lady, mistress, fem. of FREY; cf. G *Frau*]

Frey·re (frā′rə), *n.* **Gil·ber·to** (zhil ber′to͞o), 1900–87, Brazilian sociologist and anthropologist.

Frey·tag (frī′täk), *n.* **Gus·tav** (go͞os′täf), 1816–95, German novelist, playwright, and journalist.

F.R.G., Federal Republic of Germany.

F.R.G.S., Fellow of the Royal Geographical Society.

Fri., Friday.

fri·a·ble (frī′ə bəl), *adj.* easily crumbled or reduced to powder; crumbly: *friable rock.* [1555–65; < L *friābilis,* equiv. to *friā(re)* to rub, crumble + *-ābilis* -ABLE] —**fri′a·bil′i·ty, fri′a·ble·ness,** *n.*
—**Syn.** fragile, frangible.

fri·ar (frī′ər), *n.* **1.** *Rom. Cath. Ch.* a member of a religious order, esp. the mendicant orders of Franciscans, Dominicans, Carmelites, and Augustinians. **2.** *Print.* a blank or light area on a printed page caused by uneven inking of the plate or type. Cf. **monk** (def. 3). [1250–1300; ME *frier, frere* brother < OF *frere* < L *frāter* BROTHER]
—**Syn. 1.** See **monk.**

fri·ar·bird (frī′ər bûrd′), *n.* any of various Australasian honeyeaters, esp. of the genus *Philemon.* [1840–50; FRIAR + BIRD; so called from its tonsured head]

fri·ar·ly (frī′ər lē), *adj.* **1.** of or pertaining to friars. **2.** like a friar. [1540–50; FRIAR + -LY]

Fri′ar Mi′nor, *pl.* **Friars Minor.** *Rom. Cath. Ch.* a friar belonging to the branch of the Franciscan order that observes the strict rule of St. Francis. Cf. **capuchin** (def. 4), **Friar Minor Conventual.** [1520–30]

Fri′ar Mi′nor Cap′uchin, *pl.* **Friars Minor Capuchin.** *Rom. Cath. Ch.* capuchin (def. 4).

Fri′ar Mi′nor Conven′tual, *pl.* **Friars Minor Conventual.** *Rom. Cath. Ch.* a friar belonging to a branch of the Franciscan order that separated from the Observants in the 15th century, and that observes a modification of the rule of St. Francis. Also called **Conventual.** Cf. **Friar Minor, capuchin** (def. 4).

Fri′ar Preach′er, *pl.* **Friars Preachers.** a Dominican friar. [1150–1200; ME *frer prechour*]

fri′ar's chair′, frailero.

fri′ar's lan′tern. See **ignis fatuus.** (def. 1). [1625–35]

Fri′ar Tuck′ (tuk), the jolly, pugnacious friar who was a member of Robin Hood's band.

fri·ar·y (frī′ə rē), *n., pl.* **-ar·ies.** **1.** a monastery of friars, esp. those of a mendicant order. **2.** a brotherhood of friars. [1300–50; late ME *freyry, frayry,* ME *frari* < AF, OF *frairie, frarie;* see FRIAR, -Y[3]]

CONCISE PRONUNCIATION KEY: *act, cāpe, dâre, pärt; set, ēqual; if, īce; ox, ōver, ôrder, oil, bo͝ok, bo͞ot, out; up, ûrge; child; sing; shoe; thin, that;* zh as in *treasure.* ə = *a* as in *alone, e* as in *system, i* as in *easily, o* as in *gallop, u* as in *circus;* ' as in *fire* (fī'r), *hour* (ou'r). l and n can serve as syllabic consonants, as in *cradle* (krād′l), and *button* (but′n). See the full key inside the front cover.

frib•ble (frib′əl), *v.,* **-bled, -bling,** *n., adj.* —*v.i.* **1.** to act in a foolish or frivolous manner; trifle. —*v.t.* **2.** to waste foolishly (often fol. by *away*): *He fribbled away one opportunity after another.* —*n.* **3.** a foolish or frivolous person; trifler. **4.** anything trifling or frivolous. **5.** frivolousness. —*adj.* **6.** frivolous; foolish; trifling. [1620–30; perh. alter. of FRIVOL] —**frib′bler,** *n.*

Fri•bourg (*Fr.* frē bo͞or′), *n.* **1.** a canton in W Switzerland. 181,800; 644 sq. mi. (1668 sq. km). **2.** a town in and the capital of this canton. 40,500. German, **Freiburg.**

fric•an•deau (frik′ən dō′, frik′ən dō′), *n., pl.* **-deaus, -deaux** (-dōz′, -dōz′). a loin of veal, larded and braised, or roasted. Also, **fricando.** [1700–10; < F, MF, equiv. to *fric(asser)* to FRICASSEE (with *-asser* taken as a suffix) + *-ande* n. suffix (see VIAND) + *-eau* dim. suffix (<< L *-ellus;* see -ELLE)]

fric•an•do (frik′ən dō′, frik′ən dō′), *n., pl.* **-does.** fricandeau.

fric•as•see (frik′ə sē′), *n., v.,* **-seed, -see•ing.** —*n.* **1.** meat, esp. chicken or veal, browned lightly, stewed, and served in a sauce made with its own stock. —*v.t.* **2.** to prepare as a fricassee. [1560–70; < MF, n. use of fem. ptp. of *fricasser* to cook chopped food in its own juice, prob. equiv. to *fri(re)* to FRY + *casser* to break, crack (< L *quassāre* to shake, damage, batter); cf., however, dial. *fricâssié,* perh. with a reflex of VL *coāctiāre,* v. deriv. of L *coāctus* compressed, condensed, ptp. of *cōgere;* see COGENT]

fri•ca•tion (fri kā′shən), *n. Phonet.* an audible, constrained rush of air accompanying and characteristic of fricatives. [1525–35; < L *fricātiōn-* (s. of *fricātiō*), equiv. to *fricāt(us)* rubbed (ptp. of *fricāre;* see FRICTION) + *-iōn-* -ION]

fric•a•tive (frik′ə tiv), *Phonet.* —*adj.* **1.** (of a speech sound) characterized by audible friction produced by forcing the breath through a constricted or partially obstructed passage in the vocal tract; spirantal; spirant. —*n.* **2.** Also called **spirant.** a fricative consonant, as (th), (v), or (h). [1855–60; FRICAT(ION) + -IVE]

Frick (frik), *n.* **Henry Clay,** 1849–1919, U.S. industrialist, art patron, and philanthropist.

fric•tion (frik′shən), *n.* **1.** surface resistance to relative motion, as of a body sliding or rolling. **2.** the rubbing of the surface of one body against that of another. **3.** dissension or conflict between persons, nations, etc., because of differing ideas, wishes, etc. [1575–85; < L *frictiōn-* (s. of *frictiō*) a rubbing, equiv. to *frict(us)* (ptp. of *fricāre*) + *-iōn-* -ION] —**fric′tion•less,** *adj.* —**fric′tion•less•ly,** *adv.*
—**Syn. 3.** discord, dissidence, clash, antagonism, contention, wrangling.

fric•tion•al (frik′shə nl), *adj.* **1.** of, pertaining to, or of the nature of friction. **2.** moved, worked, or produced by friction. [1840–50; FRICTION + -AL[1]] —**fric′tion•al•ly,** *adv.*

fric′tion clutch′, *Mach.* a clutch in which one part turns another by friction between them. [1835–45]

fric′tion drive′, *Auto.* a power transmission system utilizing a set of friction gears so arranged that varying their positions relative to one another gives a wide range of speed ratios. [1905–10]

fric′tion gear′ing, wheels or disks transmitting power by means of frictional contact. [1885–90]

fric′tion head′, (in a hydraulic system) the part of a head of water or of another liquid that represents the energy that the system dissipates through friction with the sides of conduits or channels and through heating from turbulent flow. [1885–90]

fric′tion lay′er. See **surface boundary layer.**

fric′tion match′, a kind of match tipped with a compound that ignites by friction. [1830–40, *Amer.*]

fric′tion pile′, *Engin., Building Trades.* a pile depending on the friction of surrounding earth for support. Cf. **point-bearing pile.**

fric′tion saw′, a high-speed circular saw, usually toothless, that is used for cutting metals by using frictional heat to melt the material adjacent to it.

fric′tion tape′, a cloth or plastic adhesive tape, containing a moisture-resistant substance, used esp. to insulate and protect electrical wires and conductors. [1915–20]

fric′tion weld′ing, a method of welding thermoplastics or metals by the heat generated by rubbing the members to be joined against each other under pressure. [1945–50]

Fri•day (frī′dā, -dē), *n.* the sixth day of the week, following Thursday. [bef. 1000; ME; OE *Frīgedæg* Freya's day, equiv. to *Frīge* (gen. sing. of *Frēo*) + *dæg* day; *Frēo* is identical with OE adj. *frēo* free]

Fri•days (frī′dāz, -dēz), *adv.* on Fridays: *We're paid Fridays.*

fridge (frij), *n. Informal.* a refrigerator. [1925–30; by shortening of REFRIGERATOR or FRIGIDAIRE]

Frid•ley (frid′lē), *n.* a city in SE Minnesota, near Minneapolis. 30,228.

Fridt′jof Nan′sen Land′ (frit′yôf nän′sən, nan′-). See **Franz Josef Land.**

fried (frīd), *adj.* **1.** cooked in a pan or on a griddle over direct heat, usually in fat or oil. **2.** *Slang.* **a.** drunk; inebriated. **b.** intoxicated from drugs; high. **c.** exhausted or incapacitated through intemperance; burned-out. —*v.* **3.** pt. and pp. of **fry**[1].

Fried (frēd; *Ger.* frēt), *n.* **Al•fred Her•mann** (al′frid hûr′mən; *Ger.* äl′frāt her′män), 1864–1921, Austrian writer and journalist: Nobel peace prize 1911.

Frie•da (frē′də), *n.* a female given name.

Frie•dan (fri dan′), *n.* **Betty (Naomi Gold•stein)** (gōld′stēn), born 1921, U.S. women's-rights leader and writer.

fried•cake (frīd′kāk′), *n. Chiefly Inland North.* a doughnut or other small cake cooked in deep fat. [1855–60, *Amer.;* FRIED + CAKE]

Frie•del′-Crafts′ reac′tion (frē del′krafts′, -kräfts′), a reaction for the synthesis of hydrocarbons and ketones by the alkylation or acylation of an aromatic compound in the presence of a catalyst, typically anhydrous aluminum chloride. [1895–1900; after French chemist Charles *Friedel* (1832–99) and U.S. chemist J. M. *Crafts* (1832–1917), its discoverers]

Fried•man (frēd′mən), *n.* **Milton,** born 1912, U.S. economist: Nobel prize 1976.

Fried′mann mod′el (frēd′mən), *Astron.* any model of the universe deduced from a homogeneous, isotropic solution of Einstein's field equations without a cosmological constant. Such models form the mathematical basis for many modern cosmologies and provide for expansion or contraction of the universe. Also called **Fried′mann u′niverse.** [named after Alexander *Friedmann,* (1885–1925), Russian mathematician, who made the necessary calculations in 1922]

Frie•drich (frē′drik; *Ger.* frē′drikh), *n.* a male given name.

friend (frend), *n.* **1.** a person attached to another by feelings of affection or personal regard. **2.** a person who gives assistance; patron; supporter: *friends of the Boston Symphony.* **3.** a person who is on good terms with another; a person who is not hostile: *Who goes there? Friend or foe?* **4.** a member of the same nation, party, etc. **5.** (*cap.*) a member of the Religious Society of Friends; a Quaker. **6. make friends with,** to enter into friendly relations with; become a friend to. —*v.t.* **7.** *Rare.* to befriend. [bef. 900; ME *friend, frend,* OE *frēond* friend, lover, relative (c. OS *friund,* OHG *friunt* (G *Freund*), Goth *frijōnds*), orig. prp. of *frēogan,* c. Goth *frijōn* to love] —**friend′less,** *adj.* —**friend′less•ness,** *n.*
—**Syn. 1.** comrade, chum, crony, confidant. See **acquaintance. 2.** backer, advocate. **4.** ally, associate, confrere, compatriot. —**Ant. 1, 4.** enemy, foe.

friend′ at court′, a friend in a position of influence or power who may advance one's interests, esp. a helpful person who is close to someone in authority. [1645–55]

friend•ed (fren′did), *adj. Archaic.* provided with or accompanied by friends. [1350–1400; ME *frended.* See FRIEND, -ED[2]]

friend•ly (frend′lē), *adj.,* **-li•er, -li•est,** *adv., n., pl.* **-lies.** —*adj.* **1.** characteristic of or befitting a friend; showing friendship: *a friendly greeting.* **2.** like a friend; kind; helpful: *a little friendly advice.* **3.** favorably disposed; inclined to approve, help, or support: *a friendly bank.* **4.** not hostile or at variance; amicable: *a friendly warship; friendly natives.* **5.** *Computers.* user-friendly. —*adv.* **6.** Also, **friend′li•ly.** in a friendly manner; like a friend. —*n.* **7.** a person who is in sympathetic relationship to oneself or one's side; one who shows no hostility. [bef. 900; ME *frendly,* OE *frēondlīc.* See FRIEND, -LY] —**friend′li•ness,** *n.*
—**Syn. 1.** companionable, neighborly. **2.** kindly, amiable, cordial, genial, affectionate, kind-hearted. **3.** benevolent, well-disposed, helpful, favorable; advantageous, propitious. —**Ant. 3.** antagonistic.

friend′ly fire′, **1.** *Insurance.* a fire deliberately set and remaining contained, as in a fireplace or boiler, from which any resulting loss cannot be claimed as an insurance liability (opposed to *hostile fire*). **2.** (in military combat) fire, as by artillery, by one's own forces, esp. when causing damage near or casualties to one's own troops.

Friend′ly Is′lands, Tonga.

friend′ of the court′, *Law.* See **amicus curiae.** [1940–45]

friend•ship (frend′ship), *n.* **1.** the state of being a friend; association as friends: *to value a person's friendship.* **2.** a friendly relation or intimacy. **3.** friendly feeling or disposition. [bef. 900; ME; OE *frēondscipe.* See FRIEND, -SHIP]
—**Syn. 2.** harmony, accord, understanding, rapport.

Friends•wood (frendz′wo͝od′), *n.* a city in SE Texas. 10,719.

fri•er (frī′ər), *n.* fryer.

fries (frīz), *n.* **1.** pl. of **fry**[1]. **2.** *Informal.* fried potatoes. —*v.* **3.** 3rd pers. sing. pres. indic. of **fry**[1].

Fries (frēz), *n.* **Charles Carpenter,** 1887–1967, U.S. linguist.

Frie•sian (frē′zhən), *adj., n.* **1.** Frisian. **2.** *Chiefly Brit.* Holstein (def. 1).

Fries•land (frēz′lənd; *Du.* frēs′länt′), *n.* a province in the N Netherlands. 592,061; 1431 sq. mi. (3705 sq. km). *Cap.:* Leeuwarden. Also, *esp. Brit.,* **Frisian.**

frieze[1] (frēz), *n.* **1.** *Archit.* **a.** the part of a classical entablature between the architrave and the cornice, usually decorated with sculpture in low relief. See diag. under **column. b.** any decorative band on an outside wall, broader than a stringcourse and bearing lettering, sculpture, etc. **2.** any decorative band at the top or beneath the cornice of an interior wall, a piece of furniture, etc. **3.** *Furniture.* skirt (def. 6b). [1555–65; < MF *frise,* perh. < ML *phrygium, frigium, frisium* embroidered cloth, embroidery, L *Phrygium,* neut. of *Phrygius* Phrygian]

frieze[2] (frēz), *n.* a heavy, napped woolen cloth for coats. [1350–1400; ME *frise* < OF; see FRIEZE[1]]

friez•ing (frē′zing), *n.* carved or painted work formerly decorating the upper parts of the hulls of vessels, esp. in the 16th and 17th centuries. [1760–70; FRIEZE[1] + -ING[1]]

frig[1] (frig), *v.t., v.i.,* **frigged, frig•ging.** *Slang* (*vulgar*). —*v.t.* **1.** to copulate with. **2.** to take advantage of; victimize. **3.** to masturbate. —*v.i.* **4.** to copulate. **5.** to masturbate. **6. frig around** or **about,** to fool around; waste time. [1425–75; earlier, to move about restlessly, rub; late ME *friggen* to quiver]

frig[2] (frij), *n. Informal.* refrigerator.

frig•ate (frig′it), *n.* **1.** a fast naval vessel of the late 18th and early 19th centuries, generally having a lofty ship rig and heavily armed on one or two decks. **2.** any of various types of modern naval vessels ranging in size from a destroyer escort to a cruiser, frequently armed with guided missiles and used for aircraft carrier escort duty, shore bombardment, and miscellaneous combat functions. [1575–85; < MF *frégate* < It *fregata,* Sicilian *fragata* (> Sp, Catalan, Pg); of obscure orig.]

frig′ate bird′, any predacious seabirds of the genus *Fregata,* having fully webbed feet. Also, **frig′ate•bird′.** Also called **man-o'-war bird.** [1730–40]

frig′ate mack′erel, a small, blue-green, black-striped fish, *Auxis thazard,* abundant in tropical seas, having dark, oily flesh that is sometimes used as food. [1880–85]

Frigg (frig), *n. Scand. Myth.* wife of Odin and chief of the goddesses. [< ON, c. OS *fri,* OE *freo* wife; cf. G *Frau*]

frig•ging (frig′in, -ing), *adj., adv. Slang.* (used as an intensifier). [1700–10 for earlier ger. sense; 1920–25 for current sense; FRIG[1] + -ING[2]]

fright (frīt), *n.* **1.** sudden and extreme fear; a sudden terror. **2.** a person or thing of shocking, grotesque, or ridiculous appearance. —*v.t.* **3.** to frighten. [bef 900; ME; OE *frytu, fyrhto;* akin to G *Furcht*]
—**Syn. 1.** dismay, consternation, alarm. See **terror.**

fright•en (frīt′n), *v.t.* **1.** to make afraid or fearful; throw into a fright; terrify; scare. **2.** to drive (usually fol. by *away, off,* etc.) by scaring: *to frighten away pigeons from the roof.* —*v.i.* **3.** to become frightened: *a timid child who frightens easily.* [1660–70; FRIGHT + -EN[1]] —**fright′en•a•ble,** *adj.* —**fright′en•er,** *n.* —**fright′en•ing•ly,** *adv.*
—**Syn. 1.** shock, startle, dismay, intimidate. FRIGHTEN, ALARM, SCARE, TERRIFY, TERRORIZE, APPALL all mean to arouse fear in people or animals. To FRIGHTEN is to shock with sudden, startling, but usually short-lived fear, esp. that arising from the apprehension of physical harm: *to frighten someone by a sudden noise.* To ALARM is to arouse the feelings through the realization of some imminent or unexpected danger: *to alarm someone by a scream.* To SCARE is to frighten, often without the presence of real danger: *Horror movies really scare me.* To TERRIFY is to strike with violent, overwhelming, or paralyzing fear: *to terrify a city by lawless acts.* To TERRORIZE is to terrify in a general, continued, systematic manner, either wantonly or in order to gain control: *His marauding armies terrorized the countryside.* To APPALL is to overcome or confound by dread, dismay, shock, or horror: *The suffering caused by the earthquake appalled him.*

fright•ened (frīt′nd), *adj.* **1.** thrown into a fright; afraid; scared; terrified: *a frightened child cowering in the corner.* **2.** afraid; fearful (usually fol. by *of*): *He has always been frightened of heights.* [1715–25; FRIGHTEN + -ED[2]] —**fright′ened•ly,** *adv.*
—**Syn. 2.** See **afraid.**

fright•ful (frīt′fəl), *adj.* **1.** such as to cause fright; dreadful, terrible, or alarming: *A frightful howl woke us.* **2.** horrible, shocking, or revolting: *The storm did frightful damage.* **3.** *Informal.* unpleasant; disagreeable: *We had a frightful time.* **4.** *Informal.* very great; extreme: *That actor is very talented but a frightful ham.* [1200–50; ME; see FRIGHT, -FUL] —**fright′ful•ly,** *adv.* —**fright′ful•ness,** *n.*
—**Syn. 1.** fearful, awful. **2.** hideous, dread, horrid, ghastly; gruesome. —**Ant. 1, 2.** delightful.

fright′ wig′, a wig of wild, unruly hair, esp. hair projecting outward in all directions, as worn by some clowns and comedians to give a comic effect of extreme fright or excitement. [1925–30]

frig•id (frij′id), *adj.* **1.** very cold in temperature: *a frigid climate.* **2.** without warmth of feeling; without ardor or enthusiasm: *a frigid reaction to the suggested law.* **3.** stiff or formal: *a welcome that was polite but frigid.* **4.** (of a woman) **a.** inhibited in the ability to experience sexual excitement during sexual activity. **b.** unresponsive to sexual advances or stimuli. **5.** unemotional or unimaginative; lacking passion, sympathy, or sensitivity: *a correct, but frigid presentation.* [1590–1600; < L *frīgidus,* equiv. to *frīg(us)* coldness (akin to Gk *rhîgos;* see RIGID) + *-idus* -ID[4]] —**frig′id•ness,** *n.* —**frig′id•ly,** *adv.*
—**Syn. 3.** aloof, standoffish, distant, frosty, chilly, cool.

Frig•id•aire (frij′i dâr′), *Trademark.* a brand of electric refrigerator.

frig•i•dar•i•um (frij′i dâr′ē əm), *n., pl.* **-dar•i•a** (-dâr′ē ə). (in an ancient Roman bath) a room having a bath of unheated water. [< L; see FRIGID, -ARIUM]

fri•gid•i•ty (fri jid′i tē), *n.* **1.** the state or condition of being frigid. **2.** (in women) inhibition, not caused by a physical disorder or medication, of sexual excitement during sexual activity. [1400–50; late ME *frigidite* coldness (< MF *frigidité*) < LL *frīgiditās;* see FRIGID, -ITY]

frig•i•do•re•cep•tor (frij′i dō rē sep′tər), *n. Physiol., Biol.* a receptor stimulated by cold. [FRIGID + -O- + RECEPTOR]

Frig′id Zone′, either of two regions, one between the Arctic Circle and the North Pole, or one between the Antarctic Circle and the South Pole. [1590–1600]

frig•o•rif•ic (frig′ə rif′ik), *adj.* causing or producing cold. [1660–70; < L *frīgorificus* cooling, equiv. to *frīgor-* (s. of *frīgus*) cold + *-i-* -I- + *-ficus* -FIC]

fri•jol (frē′hōl, frē hōl′; *Sp.* frē hôl′), *n., pl.* **fri•jo•les**

CONCISE ETYMOLOGY KEY: <, descended or borrowed from; >, whence; b., blend of, blended; c., cognate with; cf., compare; deriv., derivative; equiv., equivalent; imit., imitative; obl., oblique; r., replacing; s., stem; sp., spelling, spelled; resp., respelling, respelled; trans., translation; ?, origin unknown; *, unattested; ‡, probably earlier than. See the full key inside the front cover.

(frē′hōlz, frē hō′lēz; *Sp.* fʀē hô′les). any bean of the genus *Phaseolus,* esp. the kidney bean, the seeds of which are used for food in Mexico, the southwestern U.S., etc. Also, **fri·jo·le** (frē hō′lē). [1570–80; < Sp, earlier *fresol, fesol* < a dial. source, akin to Galician *freixó, feixoo,* earlier *feijoo* < L *faseolus;* see FEIJOADO]

fri·jo·les re·fri·tos (fʀē hô′les ʀe fʀē′tôs), *Mexican Cookery.* See **refried beans.** [< MexSp, Sp]

frill (fril), *n.* **1.** a trimming, as a strip of cloth or lace, gathered at one edge and left loose at the other; ruffle. **2.** something resembling such a trimming, as the fringe of hair on the chest of some dogs. **3.** affectation of manner, style, etc. **4.** something superfluous. **5.** *Photog.* wrinkling or loosening of an emulsion at the edges, usually due to excessively high temperature during developing. —*v.t.* **6.** to trim or ornament with a frill or frills. **7.** to form into a frill. —*v.i.* **8.** *Photog.* (of an emulsion) to become wrinkled or loose. [1585–95; orig. uncert.] —**frill′er,** *n.*

frilled′ liz′ard, a medium-sized Australian lizard, *Chlamydosaurus kingi,* having a large, cloaklike flap of skin on the neck that stiffens during courtship or threat displays, forming a wide ruff. [1860–65; FRILL + -ED[3]]

frilled lizard, *Chlamydosaurus kingi,* length 2½ to 3 ft. (80 to 90 cm) including tail

frill·ing (fril′ing), *n.* frilled edging. [1805–15; FRILL + -ING[1]]

frill·y (fril′ē), *adj.,* **frill·i·er, frill·i·est. 1.** covered with or marked by frills: *Some of the more elaborate dress shirts have frilly fronts.* **2.** frivolous; inconsequential: *After a day of intense concentration and serious business, they feel like doing something frilly and amusing.* [1835–45; FRILL + -Y[1]] —**frill′i·ness,** *n.*

Fri·maire (fʀē mer′), *n.* (in the French Revolutionary calendar) the third month of the year, extending from November 21 to December 20. [1830–40; < F, equiv. to *frim(as)* hoarfrost, deriv. of OF *frim* (< Gmc; cf. OE *hrim* RIME[2]) + *-aire* -ARY]

Friml (frim′əl), *n.* **Rudolf,** 1881–1972, U.S. composer and pianist, born in Czechoslovakia.

fringe (frinj), *n., v.,* **fringed, fring·ing.** —*n.* **1.** a decorative border of thread, cord, or the like, usually hanging loosely from a raveled edge or separate strip. **2.** anything resembling or suggesting this: *a fringe of grass around a swimming pool.* **3.** an outer edge; margin; periphery: *on the fringe of the art world.* **4.** something regarded as peripheral, marginal, secondary, or extreme in relation to something else: *the lunatic fringe of a strong political party.* **5.** *Optics.* one of the alternate light and dark bands produced by diffraction or interference. **6.** See **fringe benefit.** —*v.t.* **7.** to furnish with or as if with a fringe. **8.** to serve as a fringe for, or to be arranged around or along so as to suggest a fringe: *armed guards fringing the building.* [1325–75; ME *frenge* < OF (F *frange*) < VL *frimbia, metathetic var. of LL *fimbria,* L *fimbriae* fringe] —**fringe′less,** *adj.* —**fringe′like′,** *adj.* —**fring′y,** *adj.*
—**Syn. 2.** edge, border, skirt, rim.

fringe′ ar′ea, *Radio and Television.* an area just beyond the outer limits of satisfactory reception, characterized by a weak and possibly unstable signal. [1945–50]

fringe′ ben′efit, any of various benefits, as free life or health insurance, paid holidays, a pension, etc., received by an employee in addition to regular pay. [1945–50]

fringed′ gen′tian, a plant of the genus *Gentianopsis* (or *Gentiana*), esp. *G. crinita,* having a tubular blue corolla with four fringed petals. [1805–15, *Amer.*]

fringed′ or′chis, any of several American orchids of the genus *Habenaria,* having a cut, fringed lip. Also called **fringed′ or′chid.**

fringed′ polyg′ala, a North American milkwort, *Polygala paucifolia,* having flowers with purplish-pink, winglike petals and a fringed tube. Also called **flowering wintergreen, gaywings.**

fringe·head (frinj′hed′), *n.* any fish of the genus *Neoclinus,* characterized by a row of fleshy processes on the head, as *N. blanchardi* **(sarcastic fringehead),** of California coastal waters. [FRINGE + HEAD]

fringe′-toed liz′ard (frinj′tōd′), an iguanid lizard, *Uma notata,* of sandy deserts of the western U.S. and Mexico, having a wedge-shaped snout and toes fringed with long, pointed scales.

fringe′ tree′, a shrub or small tree, *Chionanthus virginicus,* of the olive family, native to the southern U.S., bearing open clusters of white flowers with long, narrow petals. Also called **old-man's-beard.** [1720–30, *Amer.*]

frin·gil·lid (frin jil′id), *adj.* **1.** Also, **frin·gil·line** (frin jil′in, -in) belonging or pertaining to the family Fringillidae, comprising the finches and related birds. —*n.* **2.** a fringillid bird. [1850–55; < NL *Fringillidae* name of family, equiv. to L *fringill(a)* chaffinch + *-idae* -ID[2]]

fring′ing for′est. See **gallery forest.** [1900–05]

fring′ing reef′, a coral reef close to and along the land. [1835–45]

frip·per·y (frip′ə rē), *n., pl.* **-per·ies. 1.** finery in dress, esp. when showy, gaudy, or the like. **2.** empty display; ostentation. **3.** gewgaws; trifles. [1560–70; < F *friperie,* OF *freperie,* equiv. to *frepe* rag + *-erie* -ERY]

frip·pet (frip′it), *n. Brit. Slang.* a pretty, frivolous young woman. [1905–10; perh. FRIPP(ERY) + -ET]

Fris., Frisian. Also, **Fris**

Fris·bee (friz′bē), *Trademark.* a brand of plastic concave disk, used for various catching games by sailing it between two or more players and thrown by making it spin as it is released with a flick of the wrist. [trademark resp. of *frisbie,* from the *Frisbie* Pie Company of Bridgeport, Connecticut; throwable metal pie tins such as those produced by the company are alleged to have been the inspiration for the plastic disk]

Frisch (frish; *Ger., Norw.* fʀish), *n.* **1. Karl von** (kärl von; *Ger.* kärl fən), born 1886, Austrian zoologist: Nobel prize for physiology 1973. **2. Max (Ru·dolf)** (maks ro͞o′dolf; *Ger.* mäks ʀo͞o′dôlf), 1911–91, Swiss novelist and playwright. **3. Ot·to Ro·bert** (ot′ō rob′ərt; *Ger.* ôt′ō ʀō′bəʀt), born 1904, Austrian physicist. **4. Rag·nar** (ʀäng′när), 1895–1973, Norwegian economist: Nobel prize 1969.

Frisch·es Haff (frish′is häf′), a lagoon in N Poland. 52 mi. (84 km) long; 4–12 mi. (6–19 km) wide.

Fris·co (fris′kō), *n. Informal.* San Francisco. [1850–55, *Amer.*; by shortening]

fri·sé (fri zā′), *n.* a rug or upholstery fabric having the pile in uncut loops or in a combination of cut and uncut loops. [1880–85; < F: n. use of ptp. of *friser* to curl, prob. deriv. of *fris-,* s. of *frire* to FRY, some foods taking on a curllike form when fried]

Frise′ ai′leron (frēz), *Aeron.* an aircraft wing control surface designed with its leading edge extending forward of its axis of rotation so that when the aileron's trailing edge is raised the leading edge extends below the bottom surface of the wing. [1930–35; named after Leslie G. *Frise* (born 1897), British engineer]

fri·sette (fri zet′), *n.* a fringe of curled or frizzed hair, usually artificial, worn on the forehead by women. Also, **frizette.** [1810–20; < F; see FRISÉ, -ETTE]

fri·seur (fʀē zœʀ′), *n., pl.* **-seurs** (-zœʀ′). *French.* a hairdresser.

Fri·sian (frizh′ən, frē′zhən), *adj.* **1.** of or pertaining to Friesland, its inhabitants, or their language. —*n.* **2.** a native or inhabitant of Friesland or the Frisian Islands. **3.** the Germanic language most closely related to English, spoken in Friesland and nearby islands. *Abbr.:* Fris., Fris **4.** *Chiefly Brit.* **a.** Friesland. **b.** Holstein (def. 1). Also, **Friesian.** [1590–1600; < L *Frisi(i)* the people of a Germanic tribe + -AN]

Fri′sian carv′ing, (in Pennsylvania Dutch furniture) geometrical incised carving.

Fri′sian Is′lands, a chain of islands in the North Sea, extending along the coasts of the Netherlands, Germany, and Denmark: includes groups belonging to the Netherlands **(West Frisian Islands)** and to Germany **(East Frisian Islands)** and a group divided between Germany and Denmark **(North Frisian Islands).**

frisk (frisk), *v.i.* **1.** to dance, leap, skip, or gambol; frolic: *The dogs and children frisked about on the lawn.* —*v.t.* **2.** to search (a person) for concealed weapons, contraband goods, etc., by feeling the person's clothing: *The police frisked both of the suspects.* —*n.* **3.** a leap, skip, or caper. **4.** a frolic or gambol. **5.** the act of frisking a person. [1425–75; late ME, as adj. < MF *frisque,* perh. a sp. var. (with mute s) of *fri(c)que* lively, smart < Gmc (cf. MD *vrec,* OHG *freh* avaricious, MHG *vrech* brave, G *frech* insolent); or < MF (Flanders) *frisque* < MD *frisc* FRESH] —**frisk′er,** *n.* —**frisk′ing·ly,** *adv.*

fris·ket (fris′kit), *n.* **1.** a mask of thin paper laid over an illustration to shield certain areas when using an airbrush. **2.** *Print.* a mask of strong paper set in a rectangular frame attached to the tympan of certain presses and cut up so as to prevent accidental soiling or printing by furniture or the chase. [1675–85; < F *frisquette.* See FRISK, -ET]

frisk·y (fris′kē), *adj.,* **frisk·i·er, frisk·i·est.** lively; frolicsome; playful. [1515–25; FRISK + -Y[1]] —**frisk′i·ly,** *adv.* —**frisk′i·ness,** *n.*

fris·son (frē sōN′; *Fr.* fʀē sôN′), *n., pl.* **-sons** (-sōNz′; *Fr.* -sôN′). a sudden, passing sensation of excitement; a shudder of emotion; thrill: *The movie offers the viewer the occasional frisson of seeing a character in mortal danger.* [1770–80; < F: shiver, shudder, OF *friçons* (pl.) < LL *frictiōnem,* acc. of *frictiō* shiver (taken as deriv. of *frīgēre* to be cold), L: massage, FRICTION]

frit (frit), *n., v.,* **frit·ted, frit·ting.** —*n.* **1.** *Ceram.* **a.** a fused or partially fused material used as a basis for glazes or enamels. **b.** the composition from which artificial soft porcelain is made. **2.** fused or calcined material prepared as part of the batch in glassmaking. —*v.t.* **3.** to fuse (materials) in making frit. Also, **fritt.** [1655–65; < It *fritta,* fem. ptp. of *friggere* to fry < L *frīgere* to roast]

frites (fʀet), *n.pl. French.* French fries.

frit′ fly′, a minute European fly, *Oscinella frit,* the larvae of which are serious pests of wheat and other cereals. [1880–85; of obscure orig.]

frith (frith), *n.* firth.

frith·stool (frith′sto͞ol′), *n.* (in Anglo-Saxon England) a seat in a church, placed near the altar, for persons who claimed the right of sanctuary. [bef. 1000; OE *frithstōl,* equiv. to *frith* peace, security (akin to ON *frithr,* Goth *Frithareiks* Frederick; see FRIEND) + *stōl* STOOL]

frit·il·lar·i·a (frit′l âr′ē ə), *n.* any liliaceous plant of the genus *Fritillaria,* comprising bulbous herbs having drooping, bell-shaped flowers. [1570–80; < NL, name of genus, equiv. to L *fritill(us)* dice box + *-āria* -ARY]

frit·il·lar·y (frit′l er′ē), *n., pl.* **-lar·ies.** any of several orange-brown nymphalid butterflies, usually marked with black lines and dots and with silvery spots on the undersides of the wings. [1625–35; < NL; see FRITILLARIA]

frit·ta·ta (fri tä′tə; *It.* fʀēt tä′tä), *n., pl.* **-tas,** *It.* **-te** (-te). *Italian Cookery.* an omelet resembling a large pancake and containing vegetables, seasonings, and often ricotta, Parmesan, or other cheese. [1930–35; < It: omelet, equiv. to *fritt(o)* fried (see FRIT) + *-ata* -ADE[1]]

frit·ter[1] (frit′ər), *v.t.* **1.** to squander or disperse piecemeal; waste little by little (usually fol. by *away*): *to fritter away one's money; to fritter away an afternoon.* **2.** to break or tear into small pieces or shreds. —*v.i.* **3.** to dwindle, shrink, degenerate, etc. (often fol. by *away*): *to watch one's fortune fritter away.* **4.** to separate or break into fragments: *a plastic material having a tendency to fritter.* —*n.* **5.** a small piece, fragment, or shred. [1720–30; earlier *fitter,* deriv. of *fit* (OE *fitt*) a part] —**frit′ter·er,** *n.*
—**Syn. 1.** dissipate, frivol away, idle away.

frit·ter[2] (frit′ər), *n.* a small cake of batter, sometimes containing corn, fruit, clams, or some other ingredient, fried in deep fat or sautéed. [1350–1400; ME *friture, frytour* < OF *friture* < LL *frictūra* a frying, equiv. to L *frict(us),* ptp. of *frīgere* to FRY + *-ūra* -URE]

frit·to mi·sto (frē′tō mē′stō; *It.* fʀēt′tô mē′stô), *Italian Cookery.* small pieces of meat, fish, or vegetables dipped in batter and deep-fried. [1900–05; < It: lit., mixed fried (food)]

fritz (frits), *Informal.* —*n.* **1. on the fritz,** not in working order: *Our TV went on the fritz last night.* —*v.i.* **2. fritz out,** to become inoperable. [1900–05; of obscure orig.]

Fritz (frits), *n.* **1.** *Older Slang (sometimes offensive).* a German, esp. a German soldier. **2.** a male given name. [1910–15; < G; common nickname for *Friedrich*]

Fri·u·li·an (frē o͞o′lē ən), *n.* a Rhaeto-Romanic dialect spoken by about half a million people of the plains of extreme NE Italy. [1875–80; *Friuli* region of Italy + -AN]

Fri·u·li–Ve·ne·zia Giu·lia (fʀē o͞o′lē ve ne′tsyä jo͞o′lyä), a region in NE Italy: formerly part of Venezia Giulia, most of which was ceded to Yugoslavia in 1947. 1,242,987; 2947 sq. mi. (7630 sq. km).

friv·ol (friv′əl), *v.,* **-oled, -ol·ing** or (*esp. Brit.*) **-olled, -ol·ling.** *Informal.* —*v.i.* **1.** to behave frivolously; trifle. —*v.t.* **2.** to spend frivolously (usually fol. by *away*): *to frivol away one's time.* [1865–70; back formation from FRIVOLOUS] —**friv′ol·er;** *esp. Brit.,* **friv′ol·ler,** *n.*

fri·vol·i·ty (fri vol′i tē), *n., pl.* **-ties** for 2. **1.** the quality or state of being frivolous: *the frivolity of Mardi Gras.* **2.** a frivolous act or thing: *It was a frivolity he had a hard time living down.* [1790–1800; < F *frivolité.* See FRIVOLOUS, -ITY]
—**Syn. 1.** self-indulgence, irresponsibility, triviality, abandon, levity, foolishness.

friv·o·lous (friv′ə ləs), *adj.* **1.** characterized by lack of seriousness or sense: *frivolous conduct.* **2.** self-indulgently carefree; unconcerned about or lacking any serious purpose. **3.** (of a person) given to trifling or undue levity: *a frivolous, empty-headed person.* **4.** of little or no weight, worth, or importance; not worthy of serious notice: *a frivolous suggestion.* [1425–75; late ME *frivolus* worthless, trifling; see -OUS] —**friv′o·lous·ly,** *adv.* —**friv′o·lous·ness,** *n.*
—**Syn. 3.** idle, silly, foolish, childish, puerile. **4.** light, trifling, petty, paltry, trivial, flimsy. —**Ant. 3.** serious. **4.** weighty.

friz (friz), *v.i., v.t.,* **frizzed, friz·zing,** *n., pl.* **friz·zes.** frizz[1]. —**friz′er,** *n.*

fri·zette (fri zet′), *n.* frisette.

frizz[1] (friz), —*v.i., v.t.* **1.** to form into small, crisp curls or little tufts. —*n.* **2.** the state of being frizzed. **3.** something frizzed; frizzed hair. Also, **friz.** [1650–60; back formation from FRIZZLE[1]] —**frizz′er,** *n.*

frizz[2] (friz), *v.i., v.t.* frizzle[2]. —**frizz′er,** *n.*

friz·zle[1] (friz′əl), *v.,* **-zled, -zling,** *n.* —*v.t., v.i.* **1.** to form into small, crisp curls; frizz. —*n.* **2.** a short, crisp curl. [1555–65; orig. uncert.; cf. OE *fris* curled, OFris *frēsle* lock of hair] —**friz′zler,** *n.*

friz·zle[2] (friz′əl), *v.,* **-zled, -zling.** —*v.i.* **1.** to make a sizzling or sputtering noise in frying or the like: *the sound of bacon frizzling on the stove.* —*v.t.* **2.** to make (food) crisp by frying. [1830–40; FR(Y) + (S)IZZLE]

friz·zly (friz′lē), *adj.,* **-zli·er, -zli·est.** frizzy. [1700–10; FRIZZLE[1] + -Y[1]]

friz·zy (friz′ē), *adj.,* **-zi·er, -zi·est.** formed into small, tight curls, as hair; frizzed. Also, **frizzly.** [1865–70; FRIZZ[1] + -Y[1]] —**friz′zi·ly,** *adv.* —**friz′zi·ness,** *n.*

Frl., Fräulein.

FRN, *Finance.* floating-rate note.

fro (frō), *adv.* **1.** *Obs.* from; back. **2. to and fro,** alternating from one place to another; back and forth: *The trees were swaying to and fro in the wind.* [1150–1200; ME *frō, frā* < ON *frā* from; akin to OE *fram* FROM]

CONCISE PRONUNCIATION KEY: act, cāpe, dâre, pärt; set, ēqual; if, īce; ox, ōver, ôrder, oil, bo͝ok, bo͞ot, out; up, ûrge; child; sing; shoe; thin, that; zh as in *treasure.* ə = *a* as in *alone, e* as in *system, i* as in *easily, o* as in *gallop, u* as in *circus;* ᵊ as in *fire* (fīᵊr), *hour* (ouᵊr). l and n can serve as syllabic consonants, as in *cradle* (krād′l), and *button* (but′n). See the full key inside the front cover.

'fro (frō), *adj., n., pl.* **'fros.** *Informal.* Afro. Also, **fro.** [1970–75; by shortening]

Fro·bish·er (frō′bi shər, frob′i-), *n.* **Sir Martin,** 1535?–94, English navigator and explorer.

Fro′bisher Bay′, an arm of the Atlantic Ocean extending NW into SE Baffin Island, Northwest Territories, Canada.

frock (frok), *n.* **1.** a gown or dress worn by a girl or woman. **2.** a loose outer garment worn by peasants and workers; smock. **3.** a coarse outer garment with large sleeves, worn by monks. **4.** See **frock coat.** —*v.t.* **5.** to provide with, or clothe in, a frock. **6.** to invest with priestly or clerical office. [1300–50; ME *froke* < OF *froc* < Frankish; cf. OS, OHG *hroc* coat] —**frock′less,** *adj.*

frock′ coat′, a man's close-fitting, knee-length coat, single-breasted or double-breasted and with a vent in the back. [1735–45]

froe (frō), *n.* frow.

Froe·bel (fʀœ′bəl), *n.* **Frie·drich** (frē′dʀɪkʜ), 1782–1852, German educational reformer: founder of the kindergarten system. —**Froe·bel·i·an** (frə bē′lē ən, -bēl′yən, frā-), *adj.*

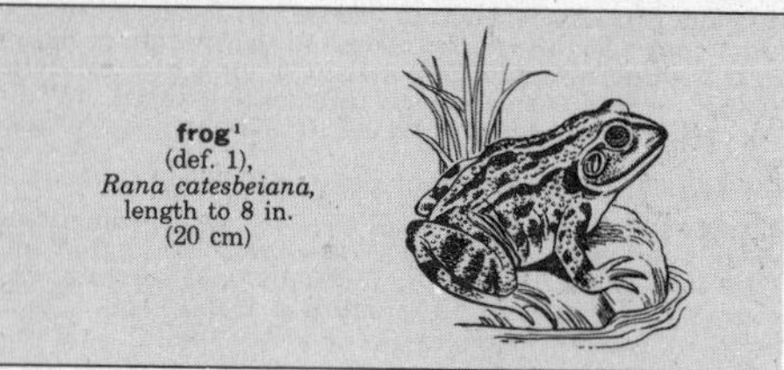

frog[1] (def. 1), *Rana catesbeiana,* length to 8 in. (20 cm)

frog[1] (frog, frôg), *n., v.,* **frogged, frog·ging,** *adj.* —*n.* **1.** any tailless, stout-bodied amphibian of the order Anura, including the smooth, moist-skinned frog species that live in a damp or semiaquatic habitat and the warty, drier-skinned toad species that are mostly terrestrial as adults. **2.** Also called **true frog, ranid.** any frog of the widespread family Ranidae, most members of which are semiaquatic and have smooth, moist skin and relatively long hind legs used for leaping. Cf. **toad** (def. 2). **3.** a slight hoarseness, usually caused by mucus on the vocal cords: *a frog in the throat.* **4.** (*often cap.*) *Slang* (*disparaging and offensive*). a French person or a person of French descent. **5.** a small holder made of heavy material, placed in a bowl or vase to hold flower stems in position. **6.** a recessed panel on one of the larger faces of a brick or the like. **7.** *Music.* nut (def. 11b). —*v.i.* **8.** to hunt and catch frogs. —*adj.* **9.** (*often cap.*) *Slang* (*disparaging and offensive*). French or Frenchlike. [bef. 1000; ME *frogge,* OE *frogga, frocga;* cf. dial., ME *frosh,* ON *froskr,* OHG *frosk* (G *Frosch*); (defs. 4, 9) because Frenchmen were stereotypically thought of as eating frogs; (defs. 5, 6) of unclear derivation and perh. of distinct orig.] —**frog′like′,** *adj.*

frog[2] (frog, frôg), *n.* **1.** an ornamental fastening for the front of a coat, consisting of a button and a loop through which it passes. **2.** a sheath suspended from a belt and supporting a scabbard. [1710–20; perh. < Pg *froco* < L *floccus* FLOCK[2]]

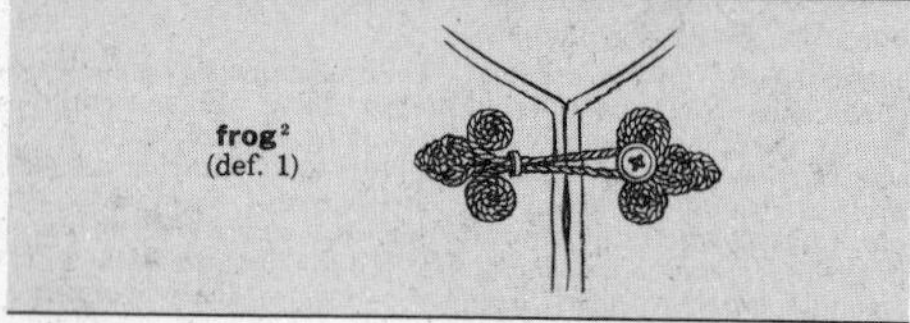

frog[2] (def. 1)

frog[3] (frog, frôg), *n.* *Railroads.* a device at the intersection of two tracks to permit the wheels and flanges on one track to cross or branch from the other. [1840–50, *Amer.;* of uncert. orig.]

frog[4] (frog, frôg), *n.* *Zool.* a triangular mass of elastic, horny substance in the middle of the sole of the foot of a horse or related animal. [1600–10; cf. earlier *frush* in same sense (prob. < F *fourchette* FOURCHETTE); presumably identified with dial. *frosh* frog, hence with FROG[1]]

frog·bit (frog′bit′, frôg′-), *n.* frog's-bit. [1570–80]

frog·eye (frog′ī′, frôg′ī′), *n., pl.* **-eyes** for 1. **1.** a small, whitish leaf spot with a narrow darker border, produced by certain fungi. **2.** a plant disease so characterized. [1910–15; FROG[1] + EYE] —**frog′eyed′,** *adj.*

frog·fish (frog′fish′, frôg′-), *n., pl.,* (*esp. collectively*) **-fish,** (*esp. referring to two or more kinds or species*) **-fish·es.** **1.** any tropical marine fish of the family Antennariidae, having a wide, froglike mouth and broad, limblike pectoral fins. **2.** angler (def. 3). [1640–50; FROG[1] + FISH]

frog·gy (frog′ē, frô′gē), *adj.,* **-gi·er, -gi·est.** **1.** of or characteristic of a frog. **2.** abounding in frogs. **3.** marked by a slight hoarseness, resembling a frog's croak: *the old prospector's froggy voice.* [1605–15; FROG[1] + -Y[1]]

frog·hop·per (frog′hop′ər, frôg′-), *n.* any of numerous leaping, homopterous insects of the family Cercopidae, which in the immature stages live in a spittlelike secretion on plants. Also called **spittle insect, spittlebug.** [1705–15; FROG[1] + HOPPER]

frog′ kick′, *Swimming.* a type of kick in which the legs are bent at the knees, extended outward, and then brought together forcefully. [1935–40]

frog′ lil′y, a yellow water lily. [1865–70, *Amer.*]

frog·man (frog′man′, -mən, frôg′-), *n., pl.* **-men** (-men′, -mən). a swimmer specially equipped with air tanks, wet suit, diving mask, etc., for underwater demolition, salvage, military operations, scientific exploration, etc. [1940–45; FROG[1] + MAN[1]]

frog·march (frog′märch′, frôg′-), *v.t.* to force (a person) to march with the arms pinioned firmly behind the back. [1930–35; FROG[1] + MARCH[1]]

frog·mouth (frog′mouth′, frôg′-), *n., pl.* **-mouths** (-mouthz′, -mouths′). any Australian and Oriental bird of the family Podargidae, related to the goatsuckers, having a broad, flattened, froglike mouth. [1850–55; FROG[1] + MOUTH]

frog's-bit (frogz′bit′, frôgz′-), *n.* **1.** an aquatic, floating plant, *Hydrocharis morsus-ranae,* of Eurasia, having thick, roundish, spongy leaves. **2.** an aquatic, floating plant, *Limnobium spongia,* of tropical America, having reddish-brown spotted, oblong, heart-shaped, or ovate leaves. Also, **frogbit.** [1570–80]

frog′ spit′, **1.** Also, **frog′ spit′tle.** any of several filamentous freshwater green algae forming floating masses. **2.** cuckoo-spit (def. 1). [1815–25]

frog′ stick′er, **1.** *Slang.* a knife, esp. one carried as a weapon. **2.** *Chiefly South Midland and Southern U.S.* a pocketknife. [1830–40]

frog·stool (frog′stōōl′, frôg′-), *n.* *Midland and Southern U.S.* (*sometimes facetious*). a toadstool. [FROG[1] + STOOL]

Froh·man (frō′mən), *n.* **Charles,** 1860–1915, U.S. theatrical producer.

froi·deur (fʀwa dœʀ′), *n.* *French.* an attitude of haughty aloofness; cold superiority.

Frois·sart (froi′särt; *Fr.* fʀwa saʀ′), *n.* **Jean** (zhäɴ), 1333?–c1400, French chronicler.

frol·ic (frol′ik), *n., v.,* **-icked, -ick·ing,** *adj.* —*n.* **1.** merry play; merriment; gaiety; fun. **2.** a merrymaking or party. **3.** playful behavior or action; prank. —*v.i.* **4.** to gambol merrily; to play in a frisky, light-spirited manner; romp: *The children were frolicking in the snow.* **5.** to have fun; engage in merrymaking; play merry pranks. —*adj.* **6.** merry; full of fun. [1530–40; < D *vrolijk* joyful (c. G *fröhlich*), equiv. to *vro* glad + *-lijk* -LY] —**frol′ick·er,** *n.*
—**Syn. 4.** sport, revel.

frol·ic·some (frol′ik səm), *adj.* merrily playful; full of fun. [1690–1700; FROLIC + -SOME[1]] —**frol′ic·some·ly,** *adv.* —**frol′ic·some·ness,** *n.*

from (frum, from; *unstressed* frəm), *prep.* **1.** (used to specify a starting point in spatial movement): *a train running west from Chicago.* **2.** (used to specify a starting point in an expression of limits): *The number of stores will be increased from 25 to 30.* **3.** (used to express removal or separation, as in space, time, or order): *two miles from shore; 30 minutes from now; from one page to the next.* **4.** (used to express discrimination or distinction): *to be excluded from membership; to differ from one's father.* **5.** (used to indicate source or origin): *to come from the Midwest; to take a pencil from one's pocket.* **6.** (used to indicate agent or instrumentality): *death from starvation.* **7.** (used to indicate cause or reason): *From the evidence, he must be guilty.* [bef. 950; ME; OE, var. of *fram* from (prep.), forward (adv.); c. Goth *fram,* ON *frā* (see FRO), *fram* (adv.)]

fro·mage (frô mazh′), *n.* *French.* cheese.

Fro·men·tin (frô män taɴ′), *n.* **Eu·gène** (œ zhen′), 1820–76, French painter, critic, and author.

Fromm (from), *n.* **Er·ich** (er′ik), 1900–80, U.S. psychoanalyst and author, born in Germany.

frond (frond), *n.* *Bot.* **1.** an often large, finely divided leaf, esp. as applied to the ferns and certain palms. **2.** a leaflike expansion not differentiated into stem and foliage, as in lichens. [1745–55; < L *frond-* (s. of *frōns*) branch, bough, foliage] —**frond′ed,** *adj.*

fron·des·cence (fron des′əns), *n.* **1.** the process or period of putting forth leaves, as a tree, plant, or the like. **2.** leafage; foliage. [1835–45; < NL *frondēscentia,* deriv. of L *frondēscent-* (s. of *frondēscēns*) becoming leafy (prp. of *frondēscere,* deriv. of *frondēre* to have leaves); see FROND, -ESCENSE] —**fron·des′cent,** *adj.*

fron·deur (fron dûr′; *Fr.* fʀôɴ dœʀ′), *n., pl.* **-deurs** (-dûrz′; *Fr.* -dœʀ′). a rebel; rioter. [1790–1800; < F: lit., a participant in the Fronde (the rebellion against royal authority during the minority of Louis XIV), equiv. to *Fronde* + *-eur* -EUR]

Fron·di·zi (fron dē′zē; *Sp.* frôn dē′sē), *n.* **Ar·tu·ro** (är-tŏŏr′ō; *Sp.* är tōō′rô), born 1908, Argentine lawyer and political leader; president of Argentina 1958–62.

fron·dose (fron′dōs), *adj.* **1.** bearing fronds. **2.** resembling a frond. [1715–25; < L *frondōsus* abounding in foliage, equiv. to *frond-* FROND + *-ōsus* -OSE[1]]

frons (fronz), *n., pl.* **fron·tes** (fron′tēz). the upper anterior portion of the head of an insect, above or behind the clypeus. [1855–60; < NL, L *frōns* forehead, FRONT]

front (frunt), *n.* **1.** the foremost part or surface of anything. **2.** the part or side of anything that faces forward: *the front of a jacket.* **3.** the part or side of anything, as a building, that seems to look out or to be directed forward: *He sat in the front of the restaurant.* **4.** any side or face, as of a building. **5.** a façade, considered with respect to its architectural treatment or material: *a cast-iron front.* **6.** a property line along a street or the like: *a fifty-foot front.* **7.** a place or position directly before anything: *We decided to plant trees in the front.* **8.** a position of leadership in a particular endeavor or field: *She rose to the front of her profession.* **9.** *Mil.* **a.** the foremost line or part of an army. **b.** a line of battle. **c.** the place where combat operations are carried on. **10.** an area of activity, conflict, or competition: *news from the business front.* **11.** land facing a road, river, etc. **12.** *Brit.* a promenade along a seashore. **13.** *Informal.* a distinguished person listed as an official of an organization, for the sake of prestige, and who is usually inactive. **14.** a person or thing that serves as a cover or disguise for some other activity, esp. one of a secret, disreputable, or illegal nature; a blind: *The store was a front for foreign agents.* **15.** outward impression of rank, position, or wealth. **16.** bearing or demeanor in confronting anything: *a calm front.* **17.** haughtiness; self-importance: *That clerk has the most outrageous front.* **18.** the forehead, or the entire face: *the statue's gracefully chiseled front.* **19.** a coalition or movement to achieve a particular end, usually political: *the people's front.* **20.** something attached or worn at the breast, as a shirt front or a dickey: *to spill gravy down one's front.* **21.** *Meteorol.* an interface or zone of transition between two dissimilar air masses. **22.** *Theat.* **a.** the auditorium. **b.** the business offices of a theater. **c.** the front of the stage; downstage. **23. in front,** in a forward place or position: *Sit down, you in front!* **24. in front of, a.** ahead of: *to walk in front of a moving crowd.* **b.** outside the entrance of: *to wait in front of a house.* **c.** in the presence of: *to behave badly in front of company.* **25. out front, a.** outside the entrance: *He's waiting out front.* **b.** ahead of competitors: *This advertising campaign ought to put our business way out front.* **c.** *Theat.* in the audience or auditorium. **d.** *Informal.* candidly; frankly: *Say what you mean out front.* **26. up front,** *Informal.* **a.** in advance; before anything else: *You'll have to make a payment of $5,000 up front.* **b.** frank; open; direct: *I want you to be up front with me.*
—*adj.* **27.** of or pertaining to the front. **28.** situated in or at the front: *front seats.* **29.** *Phonet.* (of a speech sound) articulated with the tongue blade relatively far forward in the mouth, as the sounds of *lay.*
—*v.t.* **30.** to have the front toward; face: *Our house fronts the lake.* **31.** to meet face to face; confront. **32.** to face in opposition, hostility, or defiance. **33.** to furnish or supply a front to: *to front a building with sandstone.* **34.** to serve as a front to: *A long, sloping lawn fronted their house.* **35.** *Informal.* to provide an introduction to; introduce: *a recorded message that is fronted with a singing commercial.* **36.** to lead (a jazz or dance band). **37.** *Phonet.* to articulate (a speech sound) at a position farther front in the mouth. **38.** *Ling.* to move (a constituent) to the beginning of a clause or sentence.
—*v.i.* **39.** to have or turn the front in some specified direction: *Our house fronts on the lake.* **40.** to serve as a cover or disguise for another activity, esp. something of a disreputable or illegal nature: *The shop fronts for a narcotics ring.*
—*interj.* **41.** (used to call or command someone to come, look, etc., to the front, as in an order to troops on parade or in calling a hotel bellboy to the front desk): *Front and center, on the double!* [1250–1300; ME *frount, front* < AF, OF < L *front-* (s. of *frōns*) forehead, brow, front]

front., frontispiece.

front·ad (frun′tad), *adv.* *Anat., Zool.* toward the front. [FRONT + -AD[3]]

front·age (frun′tij), *n.* **1.** the front of a building or lot. **2.** the lineal extent of this front: *a frontage of 200 feet.* **3.** the direction it faces: *The house has an ocean frontage.* **4.** land abutting on a river, street, etc.: *He was willing to pay the higher cost of a lake frontage.* **5.** the land between a building and the street, a body of water, etc.: *He complained that the new sidewalk would decrease his frontage.* [1615–25; FRONT + -AGE]

front′age road′, a local road that runs parallel to an expressway, providing access to roadside stores and businesses; a service road. [1945–50]

fron·tal (frun′tl), *adj.* **1.** of, in, or at the front: *a frontal view; frontal attack.* **2.** *Anat.* **a.** of, pertaining to, or situated near the forehead or the frontal bone. **b.** coronal (def. 4c). **3.** *Meteorol.* of or pertaining to the division between dissimilar air masses: *frontal zone; frontal surface.* **4.** *Fine Arts.* **a.** exhibiting frontality. **b.** parallel to the surface in the pictorial arts or seen from the front view in sculpture: *the frontal plane.* —*n.* **5.** *Eccles.* a movable cover or hanging for the front of an altar. **6.** frontlet (def. 1). **7.** *Anat.* any of several parts in the frontal region, esp. the frontal bone. [1275–1325; < LL *frontālis* (NL, in anatomy sense); r. ME *frountel* < OF *frontel.* See FRONT, -AL[1]] —**front′al·ly,** *adv.*

fron′tal bone′, *Anat.* a broad membrane bone of the skull, forming the forehead and the upper portion of each orbit. See diag. under **skull.** [1735–45]

fron′tal cy′clone, any extratropical cyclone associated with a front: the most common cyclonic storm.

fron′tal gy′rus, *Anat.* any of several convolutions on the outer surface of the frontal lobe of the cerebrum. Also, **fron′tal convolu′tion.**

fron·tal·i·ty (frun tal′i tē, fron-), *n.* *Fine Arts.* **1.** the representation of the front view of figures or objects in a work of art. **2.** the organization of planes parallel to the picture plane in the pictorial arts, or the composition of volumes entirely from the front view in sculpture. [1900–05; FRONTAL + -ITY]

fron′tal lobe′, *Anat.* the anterior part of each cerebral hemisphere, in front of the central sulcus. [1875–80]

fron′tal lobot′omy, See **prefrontal lobotomy.**

front′ bench′, *Brit.* **1.** (in the House of Commons) either of two seats near the Speaker, on which the leaders of the major parties sit. **2.** the leaders who occupy a front bench. Cf. **back bench.** [1890–95] —**front′ bench′er.**

front′ burn′er, *Informal.* a condition or position of top priority: *Put the project on the front burner and finish it as soon as possible.* Cf. **back burner.** [1965–70; by analogy with BACK BURNER] —**front′-burn′er,** *adj.*

front′ court′, **1.** the section of the court nearest the front wall in certain games, as squash or handball. **2.** *Basketball.* **a.** a team's offensive half of the court. **b.** the players who play offensively in the front court, including the center and the two forwards. [1945–50]

front′ desk′. See **reception desk.**

front′ dive′, a dive from a position facing the water in which the diver jumps up from the springboard, rotating the body forward, and enters the water either headfirst or feetfirst. Also called **forward dive.** [1930–35]

front′ door′, 1. the main entrance to a house or other building, usually facing a street. 2. *Informal.* anything offering the best, most direct, or most straightforward approach to a place, situation, objective, etc. [1740–50]

front-drive (frunt′drīv′), *adj.* 1. (of an automotive vehicle) having front-wheel drive. —*n.* 2. See **front-wheel drive.**

Fron·te·nac (fron′tn ak′; *Fr.* frôNtᵊ nAk′), *n.* **Louis de Bu·ade de** (lwē də bY Ad′ də), c1620–98, French governor of Canada 1672–82, 1689–98.

front′-end load′ (frunt′end′), the sales commission and other fees taken out of the first year's payment under a contractual plan for purchasing shares of a mutual fund (**front′-end load′ fund′**) over a period of years. Also called **front′ load′.** [1960–65]

front′-end load′er, a loader having a shovel or bucket at the end of an articulated arm located at the front of the vehicle. Also called **front-loader.** [1955–60]

front′-end′ proc′essor, *Computers.* a small computer or other dedicated device that performs preliminary processing of data for a host computer. [1970–75]

fron·ten·is (frun ten′is, fron-), *n.* a Latin American game, resembling squash, played with rackets and a hard rubber ball on a three-walled court similar to a jai alai court. [1940–45; < Amer Sp, b. Sp *frontón* FRONTON and *tenis* TENNIS]

front·er (frun′tər), *n.* a person who belongs to a group or organization, esp. a political one, that is or is presumed to be a cover or disguise for another activity: *a Communist fronter.* [FRONT + -ER[1]]

front′ foot′, a foot measured along the front of a lot. [1805–15, *Amer.*]

front′ four′, *Football.* the four defensive players positioned on the line of scrimmage in a common defensive alignment to guard against the run and to rush the passer. Also called **front line.**

fron·tier (frun tēr′, fron-; *also, esp. Brit.,* frun′tēr), *n.* 1. the part of a country that borders another country; boundary; border. 2. the land or territory that forms the furthest extent of a country's settled or inhabited regions. 3. Often, **frontiers. a.** the limit of knowledge or the most advanced achievement in a particular field: *the frontiers of physics.* **b.** an outer limit in a field of endeavor, esp. one in which the opportunities for research and development have not been exploited: *the frontiers of space exploration.* 4. *Math.* boundary (def. 2). —*adj.* 5. of, pertaining to, or located on the frontier: *a frontier town.* [1350–1400; ME *frounter* < OF *frontier,* equiv. to *front* (in the sense of opposite side; see FRONT) + *-ier* -IER[2]] —**fron·tier′less,** *adj.* —**fron·tier′like′,** *adj.*
—**Syn. 1.** See **boundary.**

fron·tiers·man (frun tērz′mən, fron- *or, esp. Brit.,* frun′tērz-), *n., pl.* **-men.** a person, esp. a man, who lives on the frontier, esp. in sparsely settled regions. [1775–85, *Amer.*; FRONTIERS + -MAN]

fron·tis (frun′tis), *n.* the front wall of a cancha or jai alai court. Cf. **rebote** (def. 1). [< Sp, appar. alter. of *frente* front]

fron·tis·piece (frun′tis pēs′, fron′-), *n.* 1. an illustrated leaf preceding the title page of a book. 2. *Archit.* a façade, or a part or feature of a façade, often highlighted by ornamentation. [1590–1600; alter. (conformed to PIECE) of earlier *frontispice* < F < ML *frontispicium,* equiv. to L *fronti-* FRONT + *-spicium* (comb. form repr. *specere* to look at)]

front·lash (frunt′lash′), *n.* an action or opinion that is in reaction to a backlash. [1965–70; FRONT + LASH, modeled on *backlash*]

front·less (frunt′lis), *adj. Archaic.* shameless; unblushing. [1595–1605; FRONT + -LESS] —**front′less·ly,** *adv.* —**front′less·ness,** *n.*

front·let (frunt′lit), *n.* 1. Also, **frontal.** a decorative band, ribbon, or the like, worn across the forehead: *The princess wore a richly bejeweled frontlet.* 2. the forehead of an animal. 3. *Ornith.* the forehead when marked by a different color or texture of the plumage. 4. *Judaism.* the phylactery worn on the forehead. [1425–75; late ME *frontlet* < OF, dim. of *frontel* FRONTAL]

front′ line′, 1. front (def. 9). 2. the visible forefront in any action, activity, or field: *TV reporters are constantly involved in the front line of events.* 3. *Football.* See **front four.** 4. *Basketball.* See **front court** (def. 2b). [1915–20]

front-line (frunt′līn′), *adj.* 1. located or designed to be used at a military front line: *a front-line ambulance helicopter.* 2. of, pertaining to, or involving the forefront in any action, activity, or field: *a front-line TV reporter.* 3. highly experienced or proficient in the performance of one's duties. [1910–15]

front·list (frunt′list′), *n.* a publisher's sales list of newly or recently published books, esp. those of popular or ephemeral appeal. Cf. **backlist.** [FRONT + LIST[1]]

front′ load′. See **front-end load.** [1975–80]

front-load (*adj.* frunt′lōd′; *v.* frunt′lōd′), *adj.* 1. Also, **front′-load′ed.** front-loading (def. 1). —*v.t.* 2. to load or fill from the front: *to front-load a washing machine; to front-load a video recorder.* 3. to put in from the front; insert: *to front-load eight pounds of clothing; to front-load a cassette.* 4. to make fees, costs, commissions, etc., applicable at the beginning of (a contract, designated period, or the like): *The striking teachers prefer to front-load their fringe benefits.* Cf. **back-load.** 5. to concentrate maximum effort on (an activity) at the outset: *The politician front-loaded his campaigning.* [1975–80]

front′ load′er, a machine or appliance, as a washing machine, loaded and unloaded through an opening in the front (as distinguished from a *top loader*). Also, **front-loader.** [1955–60]

front-load·er (frunt′lō′dər), *n.* 1. See **front-end loader.** 2. See **front loader.**

front-loading (frunt′lō′ding), *adj.* 1. designed to be loaded, supplied, or tended from the front: *a front-loading washer; a front-loading VCR.* —*n.* 2. the practice of expending maximum effort, collecting a fee, interest, or commissions, etc., as early as possible: *the front-loading of commissions on insurance premiums.*

front·man (frunt′man′), *n., pl.* **-men** (-men′). 1. a performer, as a singer, who leads a musical group. 2. a person who serves as the nominal head of an organization and who represents it publicly. Also, *esp. for* 2, **front′ man′.** [1935–40, *Amer.*; FRONT + MAN[1]]

front′ mat′ter, *Print.* all material in a book that precedes the text proper, as the title page, copyright page, table of contents, dedication, and preface. Also called **preliminaries.** Cf. **back matter.** [1905–10, *Amer.*]

front′ mon′ey, 1. money paid in advance, as for goods or services, to a commission agent or the like. 2. capital necessary to begin a business enterprise. 3. Also called **advance fee.** money furnished by a company to a financier under a promise to procure funds for it. [1925–30]

front′ nine′, *Golf.* the first nine holes on an eighteen-hole course.

fronto-, a combining form used in compound words referring to the frontal bone or lobe (*frontoparietal*) or, in meteorological terms, to a frontal zone (*frontogenesis*). [L *front-* (s. of *frōns*) forehead, front + -o-]

front′ of′fice, the executive or administrative office of a company, organization, etc. [1895–1900, *Amer.*] —**front′-of′fice,** *adj.*

fron·to·gen·e·sis (frun′tə jen′ə sis), *n. Meteorol.* the formation or increase of a front or frontal zone. Cf. **frontolysis.** [1930–35; FRONTO- + -GENESIS]

fron·tol·y·sis (frun tol′ə sis), *n. Meteorol.* the dissipation or decrease of a front or frontal zone. Cf. **frontogenesis.** [1935–40; FRONTO- + -LYSIS]

fron·ton (fron′ton, fron ton′), *n.* 1. a building in which jai alai is played, containing the cancha or court and sometimes having facilities for betting. 2. *Informal.* jai alai. [1690–1700; < Sp *frontón,* irreg. aug. of *frente* forehead, FRONT]

fron·to·pa·ri·e·tal (frun′tō pə rī′i tl), *adj. Anat.* 1. of or pertaining to the frontal and parietal bones of the cranium. 2. of or pertaining to the frontal and parietal lobes of a cerebral hemisphere. [1870–75; FRONTO- + PARIETAL]

front-page (frunt′pāj′), *adj., v.,* **-paged, -pag·ing.** —*adj.* 1. of major importance; worth putting on the first page of a newspaper. —*v.t.* 2. to run (copy) on the front page, esp. of a newspaper. [1900–05, *Amer.*]

front′ projec′tion, *Television.* a display system that projects an enlarged television picture on the front surface of a reflective screen.

Front′ Range′, a mountain range extending from central Colorado to S Wyoming: part of the Rocky Mountains. Highest peak, Grays Peak, 14,274 ft. (4350 m).

front-rank (frunt′rangk′), *adj.* among the best or most important; foremost; topnotch. [1590–1600]

front′ room′, a room at the front of a house, esp. a parlor. [1670–80]

Front′ Roy′al, a town in N Virginia. 11,126.

front′ run′ner, 1. a person who leads in any competition. 2. an entrant in a race who breaks to the front immediately and establishes the pace for the field. 3. an entrant in a race who performs well only when ahead of the field. Also, **front′-run′ner, front′run′ner.** [1935–40, *Amer.*]

front·stall (frunt′stôl′), *n. Armor.* chanfron. [1595–1605; FRONT + STALL[1]]

front′ walk′over, *Gymnastics.* See under **walkover** (def. 4).

front·ward (frunt′wərd), *adv.* in a direction toward the front. Also, **front′wards.** [1545–55; FRONT + -WARD]

front′-wheel drive′ (frunt′ hwēl′, -wēl′), *Auto.* a drive system in which engine power is transmitted through the front wheels only. [1925–30]

front′ win′dow. See **cottage window.**

frore (frôr, frōr), *adj. Archaic.* frozen; frosty. [1200–50; ME *froren;* ptp. of FREEZE]

frosh (frosh), *n., pl.* **frosh.** *Informal.* a college or high-school freshman. [1910–15; by alter. and shortening]

frost (frôst, frost), *n.* 1. a degree or state of coldness sufficient to cause the freezing of water. 2. Also called **hoarfrost.** a covering of minute ice needles, formed from the atmosphere at night upon the ground and exposed objects when they have cooled by radiation below the dew point, and when the dew point is below the freezing point. 3. the act or process of freezing. 4. coldness of manner or temperament: *We noticed a definite frost in his greeting.* 5. *Informal.* a coolness between persons. 6. *Informal.* something that meets with lack of enthusiasm, as a theatrical performance or party; failure; flop. 7. a milk shake, frappe, or similar drink: *a chocolate frost.* 8. **degree of frost,** *Brit.* the degree of temperature Fahrenheit below the freezing point: *10 degrees of frost is equivalent to 22°F.* —*v.t.* 9. to cover with frost. 10. to give a frostlike surface to (glass, metal, etc.). 11. to ice (a cake, cookies, etc.). 12. to bleach selected strands of (a person's hair) in order to create highlights. 13. to kill or injure by frost: *a freezing rain that badly frosted the tomato plants.* 14. to make angry: *I was frosted by his critical comment.* —*v.i.* 15. to become covered with frost or freeze (often fol. by *up* or *over*): *The windshield has frosted over.* 16. (of varnish, paint, etc.) to dry with a film resembling frost. [bef. 900; ME, OE *frost, forst;* c. OS, OHG, ON *frost;* akin to FREEZE] —**frost′less,** *adj.* —**frost′like′,** *adj.*
—**Syn. 4.** aloofness, coolness, distance, remoteness.

Frost (frôst, frost), *n.* **Robert (Lee),** 1874–1963, U.S. poet.

Frost·belt (frôst′belt′, frost′-), *n.* (*often l.c.*) Snowbelt. Also, **Frost′ Belt′.** [1975–80; FROST + BELT]

frost·bite (frôst′bīt′, frost′-), *n., v.,* **-bit, -bit·ten, -bit·ing.** —*n.* 1. injury to any part of the body after excessive exposure to extreme cold, sometimes progressing from initial redness and tingling to gangrene. —*v.t.* 2. to injure by frost or extreme cold. [1605–15; FROST + BITE]

frost′bite sail′ing, the sport of sailing in temperate latitudes during the winter despite cold weather. Also called **frost′bite boat′ing.**

frost·bit·ten (frôst′bit′n, frost′-), *adj.* 1. injured by frost or extreme cold. —*v.t.* 2. pp. of **frostbite.** [1585–95]

frost·ed (frô′stid, fros′tid), *adj.* 1. covered with or having frost. 2. made frostlike in appearance, as certain translucent glass: *a frosted window; a frosted light bulb.* 3. coated or decorated with frosting or icing, as a cake. 4. (of hair) highlighted, esp. by bleaching selected strands. 5. made with ice cream: *frosted malted.* 6. quick-frozen. —*n.* 7. a thick beverage, usually made with milk, flavoring syrup, and ice cream whipped together. [1635–45; FROST + -ED[2]]

frost′ feath′ers. See **ice feathers.**

frost·fish (frôst′fish′, frost′-), *n., pl.* (*esp. collectively*) **-fish,** (*esp. referring to two or more kinds or species*) **-fish·es.** 1. either of two North American fishes, the tomcod of the Atlantic Ocean or the round whitefish, that appear when frost sets in. 2. cutlassfish. [1625–35, *Amer.*; FROST + FISH]

frost·flow·er (frôst′flou′ər, frost′-), *n.* 1. a plant, *Milla biflora,* of the amaryllis family, native to the southwestern U.S. and Mexico. 2. its waxy-white, starlike flower. 3. any aster. Also called **Mexican star** (for defs. 1, 2). [1825–35, *Amer.*; FROST + FLOWER]

frost′ flow′ers. See **ice flowers** (def. 2). [1840–50]

frost′ grape′. See **riverbank grape.** [1780–90, *Amer.*]

frost′ heave′, *Geol.* an uplift in soil caused by the freezing of internal moisture. [1945–50]

frost·ing (frô′sting, fros′ting), *n.* 1. a sweet mixture, cooked or uncooked, for coating or filling cakes, cookies, and the like; icing. 2. a dull or lusterless finish, as on metal or glass. 3. a process of highlighting the hair by bleaching selected strands. 4. a material used for decorative work, as signs, displays, etc., made from coarse flakes of powdered glass. 5. **the frosting on the cake,** something added to make a thing better or more desirable. Also, **icing on the cake.** [1610–20; FROST + -ING[1]]

frost·line (frôst′līn′, frost′-), *n.* 1. the maximum depth at which soil is frozen. 2. the lower limit of permafrost. Cf. **permafrost table.** [1860–65, *Amer.*; FROST + LINE[1]]

frost′ point′, the temperature of the air at which hoarfrost begins to form.

frost′ smoke′, *Meteorol.* an ice fog caused by extremely cold air flowing over a body of comparatively warm water, esp. in polar regions. Also called **barber.** [1740–50]

frost·weed (frôst′wēd′, frost′-), *n.* a plant, *Helianthemum canadense,* of the rockrose family, native to eastern North America, having narrow leaves and a solitary yellow flower. [1830–40, *Amer.*; FROST + WEED[1]; so called from the ice crystals which form on it during the first frosts]

frost·work (frôst′wûrk′, frost′-), *n.* 1. the delicate tracery formed by frost, esp. on glass. 2. similar ornamentation, as on metal. [1640–50; FROST + WORK]

frost·y (frô′stē, fros′tē), *adj.,* **frost·i·er, frost·i·est.** 1. characterized by or producing frost; freezing; very cold: *frosty weather.* 2. consisting of or covered with a frost: *frosty designs on the windows; an avenue of frosty trees.* 3. lacking warmth of feeling; unfriendly: *Their frosty greeting puzzled us.* 4. resembling frost; white or gray: *a wedding dress of frosty satin.* 5. of or characteristic of old age: *a frosty brow.* [1350–1400; ME; see FROST, -Y[1]] —**frost′i·ly,** *adv.* —**frost′i·ness,** *n.* —**frost′less,** *adj.*

froth (frôth, froth), *n.* 1. an aggregation of bubbles, as on an agitated liquid or at the mouth of a hard-driven horse; foam; spume. 2. a foam of saliva or fluid resulting from disease. 3. something unsubstantial, trivial, or evanescent: *The play was a charming bit of froth.* —*v.t.* 4. to cover with froth: *giant waves frothing the sand.* 5. to cause to foam: *to froth egg whites with a whisk.* 6. to emit like froth: *a demagogue frothing his hate.* —*v.i.* 7. to give out froth; foam: *frothing at the mouth.* [1350–1400; ME *frothe* < ON *frotha* froth, scum] —**froth′er,** *n.*
—**Syn. 3.** triviality, frivolity, fluff, nonsense.

froth·y (frô′thē, froth′ē), *adj.,* **froth·i·er, froth·i·est.** 1. of, like, or having froth; foamy. 2. unsubstantial; trifling; shallow; empty. [1525–35; FROTH + -Y[1]] —**froth′i·ly,** *adv.* —**froth′i·ness,** *n.*

frot·tage (frô täzh′), *n.* 1. a technique in the visual arts of obtaining textural effects or images by rubbing lead, chalk, charcoal, etc., over paper laid on a granular or relieflike surface. Cf. **rubbing** (def. 2). 2. a work of art containing shapes and textures produced by frottage. 3. the practice of getting sexual stimulation and satisfaction by rubbing against something, esp. another person. [1930–35; < F, equiv. to *frott(er)* to rub (of uncert. orig.) + *-age* -AGE]

frot·teur (frô tûr′), *n.* a person who practices frottage. [< F; see FROTTAGE, -EUR]

Froude (fro͞od), *n.* **James Anthony,** 1818–94, English historian.

frou·frou (fro͞o′fro͞o′), *n.* **1.** elaborate decoration, as frills, ribbons, or ruffles, esp. on women's clothing. **2.** a rustling, particularly the rustling of silk, as in a woman's dress. [1865–70; < F; imit.]

frous·y (frou′zē), *adj.,* **frous·i·er, frous·i·est.** frowsy.

frouz·y (frou′zē), *adj.,* **frouz·i·er, frouz·i·est.** frowzy.

frow (frō), *n.* a cleaving tool having a wedge-shaped blade, with a handle set at right angles to it. Also, **froe.** [1615–25; earlier *frower,* perh. n. use of FROWARD in literal sense "turned away"]

fro·ward (frō′wərd, frō′ərd), *adj.* willfully contrary; not easily managed: *to be worried about one's froward, intractable child.* [1150–1200; ME *froward, fraward.* See FRO, -WARD] **—fro′ward·ly,** *adv.* **—fro′ward·ness,** *n.*
—Syn. obstinate, willful, disobedient, fractious, wayward, unmanageable, difficult. **—Ant.** docile, tractable.

frown (froun), *v.i.* **1.** to contract the brow, as in displeasure or deep thought; scowl. **2.** to look displeased; have an angry look. **3.** to view with disapproval; look disapprovingly (usually fol. by *on* or *upon*): *to frown upon a scheme.* —*v.t.* **4.** to express by a frown: *to frown one's displeasure.* **5.** to force or shame with a disapproving frown: *to frown someone into silence.* —*n.* **6.** a frowning look; scowl. **7.** any expression or show of disapproval: *a tax bill that received Congressional frowns.* [1350–1400; ME *frounen* < OF *froignier,* deriv. of *froigne* surly expression, prob. < Gaulish **frognā;* cf. Welsh *ffroen,* OBreton *fron* nostril, OIr *srón* nose < Celtic **srognā* or **sroknā*] **—frown′er,** *n.* **—frown′·ing·ly,** *adv.*
—Syn. 1. glower, lower, gloom.

frowst·y (frou′stē), *adj.,* **frowst·i·er, frowst·i·est.** *Brit. Informal.* musty; ill-smelling. [1860–65; perh. dial. var. of FROWZY] **—frowst′i·ly,** *adv.* **—frowst′i·ness,** *n.*

frows·y (frou′zē), *adj.,* **frows·i·er, frows·i·est.** frowzy. Also, **frousy.** **—frows′i·ly,** *adv.* **—frows′i·ness,** *n.*

frowz·y (frou′zē), *adj.,* **frowz·i·er, frowz·i·est. 1.** dirty and untidy; slovenly. **2.** ill-smelling; musty. Also, **frouzy.** [1675–85; orig. uncert.] **—frowz′i·ly,** *adv.* **—frowz′i·ness,** *n.*

froze (frōz), *v.* **1.** pt. of **freeze. 2.** *Nonstandard.* a pp. of **freeze.**

fro·zen (frō′zən), *v.* **1.** pp. of **freeze.** —*adj.* **2.** congealed by cold; turned into ice. **3.** covered with ice, as a stream. **4.** frigid; very cold. **5.** injured or killed by frost or cold. **6.** obstructed by ice, as pipes. **7.** chilly or cold in manner; unfeeling: *a frozen stare.* **8.** rigid; immobilized: *The child was frozen with fear.* **9.** quick-frozen: *frozen foods.* **10.** (of food) chilled or refrigerated. **11.** (esp. of a drink) mixed with ice and frappéed in an electric blender. **12.** in a form that is not readily convertible into cash; not liquid: *frozen assets.* **13.** not permitted to be changed or incapable of being altered; fixed: *frozen rents; frozen salaries.* **14.** *Canasta.* (of the discard pile) unable to be picked up by a player unless the player's hand contains a natural pair to match the top card of the pile. Cf. **freeze** (def. 26). **—fro′zen·ly,** *adv.* **—fro′zen·ness,** *n.*

fro′zen cus′tard, a smooth-textured, soft, frozen-food product of whole milk, and sometimes cream, egg yolk, etc., sweetened and variously flavored, often served in an ice-cream cone.

fro′zen dai′quiri, a cocktail consisting of rum, lemon or lime juice, and sugar, vigorously beaten together with finely crushed ice and served with a straw.

fro′zen fog′. See **ice fog.**

fro′zen pud′ding, a frozen or chilled dessert mixture of rich custard, nuts or candied fruit, and sometimes liquor.

frpl, *Real Estate.* fireplace.

FRS, Federal Reserve System.

Frs., Frisian.

frs., francs.

F.R.S., Fellow of the Royal Society.

F.R.S.L., Fellow of the Royal Society of Literature.

F.R.S.S., Fellow of the Royal Statistical Society.

frt., freight.

fruct-, var. of **fructi-** before a vowel: *fructose.*

fruct·ed (fruk′tid, fro͝ok′-, fro͞ok′-), *adj. Heraldry.* (of a tree or other plant) represented as bearing fruit, seeds, or the like: *an apple tree vert fructed gules.* [1600–10; < L *frūct(us)* (see FRUCTI-) + -ED[3]]

fructi-, a combining form meaning "fruit," used in the formation of compound words: *fructiferous.* Also, *esp. before a vowel,* **fruct-.** [< L, comb. form of *frūctus* FRUIT]

Fruc·ti·dor (fʀʏk tē dôʀ′), *n.* (in the French Revolutionary calendar) the twelfth month of the year, extending from August 18 to September 16. [1785–95; < F < L *frūcti-* FRUCTI- + Gk *dôron* gift]

fruc·tif·er·ous (fruk tif′ər əs, fro͝ok,- fro͞ok-), *adj.* fruit-bearing; producing fruit. [1625–35; < L *frūctiferus.* See FRUCTI-, -FER, -OUS] **—fruc·tif′er·ous·ly,** *adv.*

fruc·ti·fi·ca·tion (fruk′tə fi kā′shən, fro͝ok′-, fro͞ok′-), *n.* **1.** act of fructifying; the fruiting of a plant, fungus, etc. **2.** the fruit itself. **3.** the organs of fruiting; fruiting body. [1605–15; < LL *frūctificātiō-* (s. of *frūctificātiō*) a bearing of fruit, equiv. to L *frūctificāt(us)* (ptp. of *frūctificāre;* see FRUCTIFY) + *-iōn-* -ION]

fruc·ti·fi·ca·tive (fruk′tə fi kā′tiv, fro͝ok′-, fro͞ok′-), *adj.* having the ability to yield or produce fruit. [1885–90; FRUCTIFICAT(ION) + -IVE]

fruc·ti·fi·er (fruk′tə fī′ər, fro͝ok′-, fro͞ok′-), *n.* a person or thing that fructifies: *Fructifiers were added to enrich the dirt.* [1825–35; FRUCTIFY + -ER[1]]

fruc·ti·fy (fruk′tə fī′, fro͝ok′-, fro͞ok′-), *v.,* **-fied, -fy·ing.** —*v.i.* **1.** to bear fruit; become fruitful: *With careful tending the plant will fructify.* —*v.t.* **2.** to make fruitful or productive; fertilize: *warm spring rains fructifying the earth.* [1275–1325; ME *fructifien* < OF *fructifier* < L *frūctificāre.* See FRUCTI-, -FY]

fruc·to·san (fruk′tə san′, fro͝ok′-, fro͞ok′-), *n. Biochem.* any of the class of hexosans, as inulin and the like, that yield fructose upon hydrolysis. [1925–30; FRUCTOSE + -AN]

fruc·tose (fruk′tōs, fro͝ok′-, fro͞ok′-), *n. Chem., Pharm.* a yellowish to white, crystalline, water-soluble, levorotatory ketose sugar, $C_6H_{12}O_6$, sweeter than sucrose, occurring in invert sugar, honey, and a great many fruits: used in foodstuffs and in medicine chiefly in solution as an intravenous nutrient. Also called **levulose, fruit sugar.** [1860–65; FRUCT- + -OSE[2]]

fruc·to·side (fruk′tə sīd′, fro͝ok′-, fro͞ok′-), *n. Biochem.* a glycoside that yields fructose upon hydrolysis. [FRUCTOSE + -IDE]

fruc·tu·ous (fruk′cho͞o əs), *adj.* productive; fertile; profitable: *a fructuous region, rich in natural resources.* [1350–1400; ME < L *frūctuōsus,* deriv. of *frūctus* fruit; see -OUS] **—fruc′tu·ous·ly,** *adv.* **—fruc′tu·ous·ness,** *n.*

frug (fro͞og), *n., v.,* **frugged, frug·ging.** —*n.* **1.** a dance deriving from the twist. —*v.i.* **2.** to dance the frug. [1960–65; of unexplained orig.; perh. akin to FRIG] **—frug′ger,** *n.*

fru·gal (fro͞o′gəl), *adj.* **1.** economical in use or expenditure; prudently saving or sparing; not wasteful: *a frugal manager.* **2.** entailing little expense; requiring few resources; meager; scanty: *a frugal meal.* [1590–1600; < L *frūgālis* economical, equiv. to *frūg-* (s. of *frūx* produce, FRUIT) + *-ālis* -AL[1]] **—fru·gal′i·ty, fru′gal·ness,** *n.* **—fru′gal·ly,** *adv.*
—Syn. 1. thrifty, chary, provident, careful. See **economical.**

fru·gi·vore (fro͞o′jə vôr′, -vōr′), *n.* any chiefly fruit-eating organism, as certain bats. [1970–75; see FRUGIVOROUS, -VORE]

fru·giv·o·rous (fro͞o jiv′ər əs), *adj.* fruit-eating, as certain bats. [1705–15; < L *frūgi-,* comb. form of *frūx* fruit + -VOROUS]

fruit (fro͞ot), *n., pl.* **fruits,** (*esp. collectively*) **fruit,** *v.* —*n.* **1.** any product of plant growth useful to humans or animals. **2.** the developed ovary of a seed plant with its contents and accessory parts, as the pea pod, nut, tomato, or pineapple. **3.** the edible part of a plant developed from a flower, with any accessory tissues, as the peach, mulberry, or banana. **4.** the spores and accessory organs of ferns, mosses, fungi, algae, or lichen. **5.** anything produced or accruing; product, result, or effect; return or profit: *the fruits of one's labors.* **6.** *Slang (disparaging and offensive).* a male homosexual. —*v.i., v.t.* **7.** to bear or cause to bear fruit: *a tree that fruits in late summer; careful pruning that sometimes fruits a tree.* [1125–75; ME < OF < L *frūctus* enjoyment, profit, fruit, equiv. to *frūg-,* var. s. of *frui* to enjoy the produce of + *-tus* suffix of v. action] **—fruit′like′,** *adj.*

fruit·age (fro͞o′tij), *n.* **1.** the bearing of fruit: *soil additives to hasten the fruitage.* **2.** fruits collectively. **3.** product or result: *This year's fruitage was of better quality.* [1570–80; < MF *fruit(er)* to bear fruit + *-age* -AGE]

fruit·ar·i·an (fro͞o târ′ē ən), *n.* a person whose diet consists chiefly of fruit. [1890–95; FRUIT + -ARIAN, on the model of VEGETARIAN]

fruit′ bat′, any fruit-eating bat, esp. of the suborder Megachiroptera, of tropical regions throughout the Old World, typically having erect, catlike ears and large eyes adapted for night vision, and either tailless or with a rudimentary tail, the numerous species ranging in wing-span from 10 in. to 5 ft. (25 cm to 1.5 m). [1875–80]

fruit·cake (fro͞ot′kāk′), *n.* **1.** a rich cake containing dried or candied fruit, nuts, etc. **2.** *Slang.* a crazy or eccentric person; nut. [1840–50; FRUIT + CAKE]

fruit′ cup′, an assortment of fruits cut into sections or pieces and served in a cup or a glass as an appetizer or dessert. [1925–30, *Amer.*]

fruit·ed (fro͞o′tid), *adj.* **1.** having or bearing fruit. **2.** with fruit added. [1605–15; FRUIT + -ED[3]]

fruit·er (fro͞o′tər), *n.* **1.** a cargo vessel carrying fruit. **2.** a person who grows fruit. [1425–75; late ME; see FRUIT, -ER[1]]

fruit·er·er (fro͞o′tər ər), *n. Chiefly Brit.* a dealer in fruit. [1375–1425; late ME; extended form of FRUITER]

fruit′ fly′, 1. any of numerous small dipterous insects of the family Tephritidae, the larvae of which feed on the fruit of various plants. **2.** See **vinegar fly. 3.** drosophila. [1745–55]

fruit·ful (fro͞ot′fəl), *adj.* **1.** producing good results; beneficial; profitable: *fruitful investigations.* **2.** abounding in fruit, as trees or other plants; bearing fruit abundantly. **3.** producing an abundant growth, as of fruit: *fruitful soil; fruitful rain.* [1250–1300; ME; see FRUIT, -FUL] **—fruit′ful·ly,** *adv.* **—fruit′ful·ness,** *n.*
—Syn. 1, 3. See **productive. —Ant. 1.** barren.

fruit′ing bod′y, an organ that produces spores; fructification. [1915–20]

fru·i·tion (fro͞o ish′ən), *n.* **1.** attainment of anything desired; realization; accomplishment: *After years of hard work she finally brought her idea to full fruition.* **2.** enjoyment, as of something attained or realized. **3.** state of bearing fruit. [1375–1425; late ME *fruicioun* < LL *fruitiōn-* (s. of *fruitiō*) enjoyment, equiv. to L *fruit(us)* (var. of *frūctus;* see FRUIT) + *-iōn-* -ION]
—Syn. 1. consummation, accomplishment, fulfillment, achievement, completion, perfection, result.

fru·i·tive[1] (fro͞o′i tiv), *adj.* able to produce fruit or fruition; fruitful. [FRUIT(ION) + -IVE]

fru·i·tive[2] (fro͞o′i tiv), *adj.* able to enjoy or to produce enjoyment. [1625–35; < ML *fruitivus.* See FRUIT, -IVE]

fruit′ jar′, a glass jar for preserving fruit or vegetables, usually holding one pint or one quart and having an airtight cap. Cf. **Mason jar.** [1860–65, *Amer.*]

fruit′ knife′, a small knife, usually having a distinctive handle and a stainless steel blade with a sharp or serrated edge, used at table for paring and cutting fruit. [1850–55]

fruit·less (fro͞ot′lis), *adj.* **1.** useless; unproductive; without results or success: *a fruitless search for the missing treasure.* **2.** bearing no fruit; barren. [1300–50; ME; see FRUIT, -LESS] **—fruit′less·ly,** *adv.* **—fruit′·less·ness,** *n.*
—Syn. 1. futile, unavailing, vain. **2.** sterile. **—Ant. 1.** useful, profitable. **2.** fertile.

fruit·let (fro͞ot′lit), *n. Bot.* a small fruit, esp. one of those forming an aggregate fruit, as the raspberry. [1880–85; FRUIT + -LET]

fruit′ ranch′, *Western U.S.* a farm where fruit is the main produce. [1890–95, *Amer.*]

fruit′ sug′ar, *Chem.* fructose. [1885–90]

fruit′ tree′, a tree bearing edible fruit. [1570–80]

fruit·wood (fro͞ot′wo͝od′), *n.* any of various woods from fruit-bearing trees, used for cabinetmaking and the like. [1925–30; FRUIT + WOOD[1]]

fruit·y (fro͞o′tē), *adj.,* **fruit·i·er, fruit·i·est. 1.** resembling fruit; having the taste or smell of fruit. **2.** rich in flavor; pungent. **3.** excessively sweet or mellifluous; cloying; syrupy: *a specialist in fruity prose; to read poetry in a fruity voice.* **4.** *Slang.* insane; crazy. **5.** *Slang (disparaging and offensive).* homosexual. [1650–60; FRUIT + -Y[1]] **—fruit′i·ness,** *n.*

fru·men·ta·ceous (fro͞o′mən tā′shəs), *adj.* of the nature of or resembling wheat or other grain. [1660–70; < LL *frūmentāceus* of corn or grain, equiv. to L *frūment(um)* grain + *-āceus* -ACEOUS]

Fru·men·ti·us (fro͞o men′shē əs), *n.* **Saint,** A.D. c300–c380, founder of the Ethiopian Church.

fru·men·ty (fro͞o′mən tē), *n. Brit. Dial.* a dish of hulled wheat boiled in milk and seasoned with sugar, cinnamon, and raisins. [1350–1400; ME *frumentee* < OF, equiv. to *frument* grain (< L *frūmentum*) + *-ee* -Y[3]]

frump (frump), *n.* **1.** a person who is dowdy, drab, and unattractive. **2.** a dull, old-fashioned person. [1545–55; orig. uncert.] **—frump′ish,** *adj.*

frump·y (frum′pē), *adj.,* **frump·i·er, frump·i·est.** frumpish. [1740–50; FRUMP + -Y[1]] **—frump′i·ly,** *adv.* **—frump′i·ness,** *n.*

Frun·ze (fro͞on′zə; *Russ.* fro͞on′zyə), *n.* a city in and the capital of Kirghizia, in the SW Soviet Union in Asia. 533,000. Formerly, **Pishpek.**

frus·trate (frus′trāt), *v.,* **-trat·ed, -trat·ing,** *adj.* —*v.t.* **1.** to make (plans, efforts, etc.) worthless or of no avail; defeat; nullify: *The student's indifference frustrated the teacher's efforts to help him.* **2.** to disappoint or thwart (a person): *a talented woman whom life had frustrated.* —*v.i.* **3.** to become frustrated: *His trouble is that he frustrates much too easily.* —*adj.* **4.** frustrated. [1400–50; late ME < L *frustrātus,* ptp. of *frustrārī,* v. deriv. of *frustrā* in vain] **—frus′trat·er,** *n.* **—frus′trat·ing·ly,** *adv.* **—frus·tra·tive** (frus′trā tiv, -trə-), *adj.*
—Syn. 1. balk, foil, circumvent. See **thwart.**

frus·trat·ed (frus′trā tid), *adj.* **1.** disappointed; thwarted: *an announcer who was a frustrated actor.* **2.** having a feeling of or filled with frustration; dissatisfied: *His unresolved difficulty left him absolutely frustrated.* [1635–45; FRUSTRATE + -ED[2]]

frus·tra·tion (fru strā′shən), *n.* **1.** act of frustrating; state of being frustrated: *the frustration of the president's efforts.* **2.** an instance of being frustrated: *to experience a series of frustrations before completing a project.* **3.** something that frustrates, as an unresolved problem. **4.** a feeling of dissatisfaction, often accompanied by anxiety or depression, resulting from unfulfilled needs or unresolved problems. [1425–75; late ME *frustracioun* < L *frustrātiōn-* (s. of *frustrātiō*) deception, disappointment. See FRUSTRATE, -ION]

frus·tule (frus′cho͞ol), *n. Bot.* the siliceous cell wall of a diatom. [1855–60; < F < LL *frustulum,* dim. of *frustum* FRUSTUM]

frus·tu·lum (frus′tə ləm, -chə-), *n., pl.* **-la** (-lə). *Rom. Cath. Ch.* a small breakfast permitted on fast days. [1690–1700; < L; see FRUSTULE]

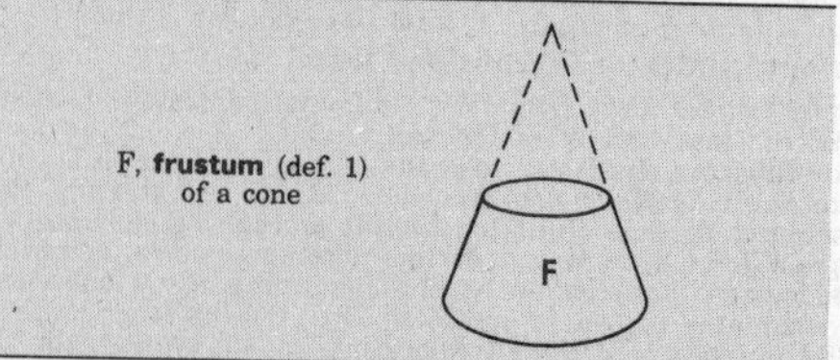

F, **frustum** (def. 1) of a cone

frus·tum (frus′təm), *n., pl.* **-tums, -ta** (-tə). *Geom.* **1.** the part of a conical solid left after cutting off a top portion with a plane parallel to the base. **2.** the part of a solid, as a cone or pyramid, between two usually parallel cutting planes. [1650–60; < L: piece, bit; prob. akin to OIr *brúid* (he) breaks, OE *brȳsan* to crush]

CONCISE ETYMOLOGY KEY: <, descended or borrowed from; >, whence; b., blend of, blended; c., cognate with; cf., compare; deriv., derivative; equiv., equivalent; imit., imitative; obl., oblique; r., replacing; s., stem; sp., spelling, spelled; resp., respelling, respelled; trans., translation; ?, origin unknown; *, unattested; ‡, probably earlier than. See the full key inside the front cover.

fru·tes·cent (fro͞o tes′ənt), *adj. Bot.* tending to be shrublike; shrubby. [1700–10; < L *frut(ex)* shrub, bush + -ESCENT] —**fru·tes′cence,** *n.*

fru·ti·cose (fro͞o′ti kōs′), *adj.* **1.** having the form of a shrub; shrublike. **2.** having branched stalks, as certain lichens. Cf. **crustose, foliose.** [1660–70; < L *fruticōsus* full of shrubs, bushy, equiv. to *frutic-* (s. of *frutex*) shrub + *-ōsus* -OSE[1]]

frwy., freeway.

fry[1] (frī), *v.,* **fried, fry·ing,** *n., pl.* **fries.** —*v.t.* **1.** to cook in a pan or on a griddle over direct heat, usually in fat or oil. **2.** *Slang.* to execute by electrocution in an electric chair. —*v.i.* **3.** to undergo cooking in fat or oil. **4.** *Slang.* to die by electrocution in an electric chair. —*n.* **5.** a dish of something fried. **6.** a piece of french-fried potato. **7.** a party or gathering at which the chief food is fried, frequently outdoors: *a fish fry.* [1250–1300; 1925–30 for def. 2; ME *frien* < AF, OF *frire* < L *frīgere* to fry] —**fry′a·ble,** *adj.*

fry[2] (frī), *n., pl.* **fry. 1.** the young of fish. **2.** the young of various other animals, as frogs. **3.** people; individuals, esp. children: *games that are fun for the small fry.* [1325–75; ME *frie, fry* seed, descendant, perh. < ON *frjō* seed; c. Sw *frö,* Goth *fraiw* seed]

Fry (frī), *n.* **Christopher,** born 1907, English playwright.

fry′ cook′, a cook who mainly prepares fried foods, as at a lunch counter.

Frye (frī), *n.* **(Herman) Northrop,** 1912–91, Canadian literary critic and educator.

fry·er (frī′ər), *n.* **1.** a person or thing that fries. **2.** something, as a young chicken, to be cooked by frying. **3.** See **deep fryer.** Also, **frier.** [1850–55; FRY[1] + -ER[1]]

fry′ing pan′, 1. a shallow, long-handled pan in which food is fried. **2. out of the frying pan into the fire,** free of one predicament but immediately in a worse one. Also, **fry-pan, fry·pan** (frī′pan′). Also called **skillet.** [1350–1400; ME *fryinge panne*]

f.s., foot-second.

FSA, Farm Security Agency.

FSH, *Biochem.* follicle-stimulating hormone: a peptide, produced by the anterior lobe of the pituitary gland, that regulates the development of the Graafian follicle in the female and stimulates the production of spermatozoa in the male.

FSLIC, See **Federal Savings and Loan Insurance Corporation.**

FSO, foreign service officer.

FSR, Field Service Regulations.

F star, *Astron.* a white to yellow star, as Canopus, Polaris, or Procyon, having a surface temperature between 6000 and 7500 K and an absorption spectrum in which the pair of ultraviolet lines of singly ionized calcium and the Balmer series of hydrogen are of about equal strength. Cf. **spectral type.**

f-stop (ef′stop′), *n. Photog.* the setting of an adjustable lens aperture, as indicated by an f number. Also, **f stop.**

Ft., forint; forints.

ft., 1. feet. **2.** (in prescriptions) **a.** let it be made. [< L *fiat*] **b.** let them be made. [< L *fiant*] **3.** foot. **4.** fort. **5.** fortification.

FTC, *U.S. Govt.* Federal Trade Commission: a board, consisting of five members, charged with investigating and enjoining illegal practices in interstate trade, as price-fixing or fraudulent advertising.

fth., fathom. Also, **fthm.**

ft-L, foot-lambert.

ft-lb, foot-pound.

ft-pdl, foot-poundal.

FTZ, free-trade zone.

Fu·ad I (fo͞o äd′), (*Ahmed Fuad Pasha*) 1868–1936, king of Egypt 1922–36.

fu·age (fyo͞o′ij), *n. Old Eng. Law.* fumage. [1755–65]

fub (fub), *v.t.,* **fubbed, fub·bing.** fob[2]. [1605–15]

fub·sy (fub′zē), *adj.,* **-si·er, -si·est.** *Brit. Dial.* short and stout. [1770–80; obs. *fubs, fub* chubby person + -Y[1]; cf. -S[4], -SY]

Fuchs (fyo͝oks), *n.* **Sir Vivian (Ernest),** born 1908, British geologist and antarctic explorer.

fuch·sia (fyo͞o′shə), *n.* **1.** a plant belonging to the genus *Fuchsia,* of the evening primrose family, including many varieties cultivated for their handsome drooping flowers. **2.** Also called **California fuchsia.** a nonwoody shrub, *Zauschneria californica,* having large crimson flowers. **3.** a bright, purplish-red color. —*adj.* **4.** of the color fuchsia: *a fuchsia dress.* [1745–55; < NL; named after Leonhard *Fuchs* (1501–66), German botanist; see -IA]

fuch·sin (fo͝ok′sin), *n.* a greenish, water-soluble, solid, coal-tar derivative, obtained by the oxidation of a mixture of aniline and the toluidines, that forms deep-red solutions: used chiefly as a dye. Also, **fuch·sine** (fo͝ok′sin, -sēn). Also called **basic fuchsin, basic magenta, magenta.** [1860–65; FUCHS(IA) + -IN[2]]

fuchs·ite (fyo͞ok′sīt, fo͝ok′-), *n. Mineral.* a bright green variety of muscovite having chromium in place of some of the aluminum. [1835–45; < G *Fuchsit;* named after J. N. von *Fuchs,* 19th-century German geologist; see -ITE[1]]

fuck (fuk), *Vulgar.* —*v.t.* **1.** to have sexual intercourse with. **2.** *Slang.* to treat unfairly or harshly. —*v.i.* **3.** to have sexual intercourse. **4.** *Slang.* to meddle (usually fol. by *around* or *with*). **5. fuck around,** *Slang.* **a.** to behave in a frivolous or meddlesome way. **b.** to engage in promiscuous sex. **6. fuck off,** *Slang.* **a.** to shirk one's duty; malinger. **b.** go away: used as an exclamation of impatience. **c.** to waste time. **7. fuck up,** *Slang.* **a.** to bungle or botch; ruin. **b.** to act stupidly or carelessly; cause trouble; mess up. —*interj.* **8.** *Slang.* (used to express anger, disgust, peremptory rejection, etc., often fol. by a pronoun, as *you* or *it.*) —*n.* **9.** an act of sexual intercourse. **10.** a partner in sexual intercourse. **11.** *Slang.* a person, esp. one who is annoying or contemptible. **12. give a fuck,** *Slang.* to care; be concerned. **13. the fuck,** *Slang.* (used as an intensifier, esp. with WH-questions, to express annoyance, impatience, etc.) [1495–1505; akin to MD *fokken* to thrust, copulate with, Sw dial. *focka* to copulate with, strike, push, *fock* penis] —**fuck′y,** *adj.*

fuck·er (fuk′ər), *n. Slang* (*vulgar*). an inconsequential, annoying, or disgusting person. [1590–1600; FUCK + -ER[1]]

fuck·head (fuk′hed′), *n. Slang* (*vulgar*). a stupid or obnoxious person. [FUCK + HEAD]

fuck·ing (fuk′ing, -in), *adj., adv. Slang* (*vulgar*). damned; confounded (used as an intensifier). [1670–80 for earlier ger. sense; 1890–95 for current sense; FUCK + -ING[2]]

fuck·off (fuk′ôf′, -of′), *n. Slang* (*vulgar*). a person who shirks responsibility or wastes time; malingerer; goldbrick. [1940–45; n. use of v. phrase *fuck off*]

fuck·up (fuk′up′), *n. Slang* (*vulgar*). **1.** a person who bungles or botches, esp. a habitual bungler. **2.** a bungle or botch. [1955–60; n. use of v. phrase *fuck up*]

fu·coid (fyo͞o′koid), *adj.* **1.** resembling or related to seaweeds of the genus *Fucus.* —*n.* **2.** a fucoid seaweed. [1830–40; FUC(US) + -OID]

fu·cus (fyo͞o′kəs), *n., pl.* **-ci** (-sī), **-cus·es.** any olive-brown seaweed or alga of the genus *Fucus,* having branching fronds and often air bladders. [1590–1600; < L < Gk *phŷkos* orchil, red color, rock lichen, rouge]

fud (fud), *n. Slang.* a fuddy-duddy. [1910–15; back formation from FUDDY-DUDDY]

fud·dle (fud′l), *v.,* **-dled, -dling,** *n.* —*v.t.* **1.** to muddle or confuse: *a jumble of sounds to fuddle the senses.* **2.** to make drunk; intoxicate. —*v.i.* **3.** to tipple. —*n.* **4.** a confused state; muddle; jumble. [1580–90; orig. uncert.]

fud·dle-dud·dle (fud′l dud′l), *v.i.,* **-dled, -dling.** *Canadian.* to depart; be off. [appar. extension of FUDDLE, after FUDDY-DUDDY, though sense is unaccounted for]

fud′dling cup′, an English earthenware drinking vessel of the 17th and 18th centuries, having the form of a cluster of three or more cups communicating at their bottoms in such a way that the entire vessel can be drained from any of them.

fud′dling glass′. See **coaching glass.**

fud·dy-dud·dy (fud′ē dud′ē, -dud′ē), *n., pl.* **-dud·dies,** *adj.* —*n.* Also, **fud′dy. 1.** a person who is stuffy, old-fashioned, and conservative. **2.** a person who is fussy or picayune about details; fussbudget. —*adj.* **3.** stuffy, old-fashioned, and conservative. **4.** fussy; picayune. [1900–05; of obscure orig.; cf. dial. (Cumberland) *duddy-fuddiel* a ragged fellow]

fudge[1] (fuj), *n.* a soft candy made of sugar, butter, milk, chocolate, and sometimes nuts. [1895–1900, *Amer.;* of uncert. orig.; the word was early in its history associated with college campuses, where fudge-making was popular; however, attempts to explain it as a derivative of FUDGE[3] (preparing the candy supposedly being an excuse to "fudge" on dormitory rules) are dubious and prob. after-the-fact speculation]

fudge[2] (fuj), *n., v.,* **fudged, fudg·ing.** —*n.* **1.** nonsense or foolishness (often used interjectionally). —*v.i.* **2.** to talk nonsense. [1690–1700; orig. uncert.; cf. FUDGE[3]]

fudge[3] (fuj), *v.,* **fudged, fudg·ing,** *n.* —*v.i.* **1.** to cheat or welsh (often fol. by *on*): *to fudge on an exam; to fudge on one's campaign promises.* **2.** to avoid coming to grips with something: *to fudge on an issue.* **3.** to exaggerate a cost, estimate, etc., in order to allow leeway for error. —*v.t.* **4.** to avoid coming to grips with (a subject, issue, etc.); evade; dodge: *to fudge a direct question.* —*n.* **5.** a small stereotype or a few lines of specially prepared type, bearing a newspaper bulletin, for replacing a detachable part of a page plate without the need to replate the entire page. **6.** the bulletin thus printed, often in color. **7.** a machine or attachment for printing such a bulletin. [1665–75; orig. uncert.; in earliest sense, "to contrive clumsily," perh. expressive var. of *fadge* to fit, agree, do (akin to ME *feien* to put together, join, OE *fēgan*); unclear if FUDGE[1] and FUDGE[2] are developments of this word or independent coinages]

Fu·e·gi·an (fyo͞o ē′jē ən, fwā′jē-), *adj.* **1.** of or belonging to Tierra del Fuego or its indigenous Indians. —*n.* **2.** a native or inhabitant of Tierra del Fuego. [1815–25; (TIERRA DEL) FUEG(O) + -IAN]

Fueh·rer (fyo͝or′ər), *n.* Führer.

fu·el (fyo͞o′əl), *n., v.,* **-eled, -el·ing** or (*esp. Brit.*) **-elled, -el·ling.** —*n.* **1.** combustible matter used to maintain fire, as coal, wood, oil, or gas, in order to create heat or power. **2.** something that gives nourishment; food. **3.** an energy source for engines, power plants, or reactors: *Kerosene is used as jet engine fuel.* **4.** something that sustains or encourages; stimulant: *Our discussion provided him with fuel for debate.* —*v.t.* **5.** to supply with fuel. —*v.i.* **6.** to obtain or replenish fuel. [1300–50; ME *fuel(le), feuel* < OF *feuaile* < VL **focālia,* neut. pl. of **focālis* of the hearth, fuel. See FOCUS, -AL[1]] —**fu′el·er, fu′el·ler,** *n.*
—**Syn. 4.** ammunition, sustenance, impetus, stimulus.

fu′el cell′, a device that produces a continuous electric current directly from the oxidation of a fuel, as that of hydrogen by oxygen. [1920–25]

fu·el-ef·fi·cient (fyo͞o′əl i fish′ənt), *adj.* producing power, heat, etc., at a rate considered optimal with regard to the amount of fuel consumed. —**fu′el-ef·fi′·cien·cy,** *n.*

fu·el-in·ject·ed (fyo͞o′əl in jek′tid), *adj.* (of an engine) having fuel injection.

fu′el injec′tion, the spraying of liquid fuel into the cylinders or combustion chambers of an engine. [1895–1900] —**fu′el-in·jec′tion,** *adj.*

fu′el injec′tor, injector (def. 2b).

fu′el oil′, an oil used for fuel, esp. one used as a substitute for coal, as crude petroleum.

fu′el rod′, *Energy.* nuclear fuel contained in a long thin-walled tube, an array of such tubes forming the core of a nuclear reactor.

Fuen·tes (fwen′tās; *Sp.* fwen′tes), *n.* **Carlos,** born 1928, Mexican writer and diplomat.

Fuer·tes (fyo͝or′tēz, -tēs, fyo͞o′ər-), *n.* **Louis Ag·as·siz** (ag′ə sē), 1874–1927, U.S. painter and naturalist.

fug (fug), *n.* stale air, esp. the humid, warm, ill-smelling air of a crowded room, kitchen, etc. [1885–90; of obscure orig.; cf. earlier Brit. slang *fogo* stench]

fu·ga·cious (fyo͞o gā′shəs), *adj.* **1.** fleeting; transitory: *a sensational story with but a fugacious claim on the public's attention.* **2.** *Bot.* falling or fading early. [1625–35; < L *fugāci-* (s. of *fugāx* apt to flee, fleet, deriv. of *fugere* to flee + -OUS] —**fu·ga′cious·ly,** *adv.* —**fu·ga′cious·ness, fu·gac·i·ty** (fyo͞o gas′i tē), *n.*

fu·gal (fyo͞o′gəl), *adj. Music.* of or pertaining to a fugue, or composed in the style of a fugue. [1850–55; FUGUE + -AL[1]] —**fu′gal·ly,** *adv.*

Fu·gard (fyo͞o′gärd, fo͞o′-), *n.* **Athol (Harold),** born 1932, South African playwright and actor.

fu·ga·to (fo͞o gä′tō, fyo͞o-), *n., pl.* **-tos.** *Music.* a section of a composition that is in fugal style but does not constitute a real fugue. [1865–70; < It; see FUGUE, -ATE[1]]

-fuge, a combining form occurring in words having the general sense "something that repels" whatever is specified by the initial element: *vermifuge.* [< F < L *-fugus,* deriv. of *fugāre* to drive away]

Fug·ger (fo͝og′ər), *n.* **Ja·kob II** (yä′kôp), ("*the Rich*"), 1459–1525, German financier, a member of a German family of bankers and merchants of the 14th to 17th centuries.

fu·gi·tive (fyo͞o′ji tiv), *n.* **1.** a person who is fleeing, from prosecution, intolerable circumstances, etc.; a runaway: *a fugitive from justice; a fugitive from a dictatorial regime.* —*adj.* **2.** having taken flight, or run away: *a fugitive slave.* **3.** fleeting; transitory; elusive: *fugitive thoughts that could not be formulated.* **4.** *Fine Arts.* changing color as a result of exposure to light and chemical substances present in the atmosphere, in other pigments, or in the medium. **5.** dealing with subjects of passing interest, as writings; ephemeral: *fugitive essays.* **6.** wandering, roving, or vagabond: *a fugitive carnival.* [1350–1400; < L *fugitīvus* fleeing, equiv. to *fugit(us)* (ptp. of *fugere* to flee) + *-īvus* -IVE; r. ME *fugitif* < OF] —**fu′gi·tive·ly,** *adv.* —**fu′gi·tive·ness, fu′gi·tiv′i·ty,** *n.*
—**Syn. 3.** transient, passing, flitting, flying, brief, temporary. **5.** momentary, evanescent, trivial, light. **6.** straying, roaming. —**Ant. 3, 4.** permanent.

fu·gle (fyo͞o′gəl), *v.i.,* **-gled, -gling.** *Archaic.* **1.** to act as a guide or model. **2.** to signal, or motion as if signaling. [1830–40; back formation from FUGLEMAN]

fu·gle·man (fyo͞o′gəl mən), *n., pl.* **-men. 1.** (formerly) a soldier placed in front of a military company as a good model during training drills. **2.** a person who heads a group, company, political party, etc.; a leader or manager. [1795–1805; < G *Flügelmann* lit., flank man]

fu·gu (fo͞o′go͞o), *n.* any of several species of puffer fish eaten as a delicacy, esp. in Japan, after the removal of the skin and certain organs which contain a deadly poison. [1905–10; < Japn]

fugue (fyo͞og), *n.* **1.** *Music.* a polyphonic composition based upon one, two, or more themes, which are enunciated by several voices or parts in turn, subjected to contrapuntal treatment, and gradually built up into a complex form having somewhat distinct divisions or stages of development and a marked climax at the end. **2.** *Psychiatry.* a period during which a person suffers from loss of memory, often begins a new life, and, upon recovery, remembers nothing of the amnesic phase. [1590–1600; < F < It *fuga* < L: flight] —**fugue′like′,** *adj.*

Füh·rer (fy′rər; *Eng.* fyo͝or′ər), *n. German.* **1.** leader. **2.** ***der Führer*** (der), the leader: title of Adolf Hitler. Also, **Fuehrer.** [1930–35]

Fu-hsi (fo͞o′shē′), *n. Chinese Legend.* a sage who taught mankind to hunt, fish, and cook.

Fu·ji (fo͞o′jē), *n.* a dormant volcano in central Japan, on Honshu island: highest mountain in Japan. 12,395 ft. (3778 m). Also called **Fu·ji·ya·ma** (fo͞o′jē yä′mə; *Japn.* fo͞o′jē yä′mä), **Fu·ji·san** (fo͞o′jē sän′).

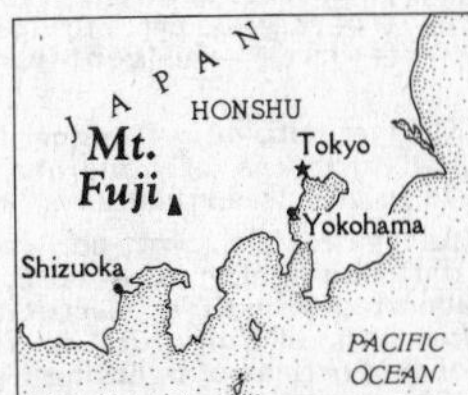

Fu·jian (fy′jyän′), *n. Pinyin.* a province in SE China, opposite Taiwan. 16,760,000; 45,845 sq. mi. (118,739 sq. km). *Cap.:* Fuzhou. Also, **Fukien.**

Fu·ji·mo·ri (fo͞o′jē môr′ē), *n.* **Alberto,** born 1938, president of Peru since 1990.

Fu·ji·sa·wa (fo͞o′jē sä′wə; *Japn.* fo͞o′jē sä′wä), *n.* a city on E Honshu, in Japan, S of Tokyo. 300,181.

Fu·ji·wa·ra (fo͞o′jē wär′ə; *Japn.* fo͞o′jē wä′rä), *n.* a member of a powerful family in Japan who exercised power as regent of the emperor, A.D. 858–1160.

Fu·kien (fo͞o′kyen′), *n.* *Older Spelling.* Fujian.

Fu·kien·ese (fo͞o′kye nēz′, -nēs′), *n.* a group of Chinese dialects, including Amoy and Taiwanese, spoken in Fukien province in southeastern China as well as in Taiwan. Also, **Fujianese.** Also called **Southern Min.** Cf. **Min.**

Fu·ku·o·ka (fo͞o′ko͞o ō′kə; *Japn.* fo͞o′ko͝o ô′kä), *n.* a city on N Kyushu, in SW Japan. 1,088,617.

Fu·ku·shi·ma (fo͞o′ko͞o shē′mə; *Japn.* fo͞o′ko͝o shē′mä), *n.* a city on N Honshu, in N Japan. 262,847.

Fu·ku·ya·ma (fo͞o′ko͞o yä′mə; *Japn.* fo͞o′ko͝o yä′mä), *n.* a city on SW Honshu, in Japan, NE of Hiroshima. 346,031.

Ful (fo͝ol), *n., pl.* **Fuls,** (*esp. collectively*) **Ful.** Fulani.

-ful, a suffix meaning "full of," "characterized by" (*shameful; beautiful; careful; thoughtful*); "tending to," "able to" (*wakeful; harmful*); "as much as will fill" (*spoonful*). [ME, OE *-full, -ful,* repr. *full, ful* FULL[1]]
—**Usage.** The plurals of nouns ending in -FUL are usually formed by adding *-s* to the suffix: *two cupfuls.* Perhaps influenced by the phrase in which a noun is followed by the adjective FULL (*both arms full of packages*), some speakers and writers pluralize such nouns by adding *-s* before the suffix: *two cupsful.*

Fu·la (fo͞o′lə, fo͝ol′ə), *n., pl.* **-las,** (*esp. collectively*) **-la.** Fulani.

Fu·lah (fo͞o′lä), *n., pl.* **-lahs,** (*esp. collectively*) **-lah.** Fulani (def. 1).

Fu·la·ni (fo͞o′lä nē, fo͞o lä′-), *n., pl.* **-nis,** (*esp. collectively*) **-ni** for 1. **1.** Also, **Fulah.** a member of a pastoral and nomadic people of mixed African and Mediterranean ancestry, scattered through W Africa from Senegal to Cameroon. **2.** the language of the Fulani, a Niger-Congo language closely related to Wolof. Also, **Ful, Fula, Peul.**

Fu′lani Em′pire, a powerful W African Muslim state that flourished in the 19th century in the area of present-day Nigeria.

Ful·bright (fo͝ol′brīt′), *n.* **1. (James) William,** 1905–95, U.S. politician: senator 1945–74. **2.** *Informal.* **a.** a grant awarded under the provisions of the Fulbright Act. **b.** a person who receives such a grant.

Ful′bright Act′, an act of Congress (1946) by which funds derived chiefly from the sale of U.S. surplus property abroad are made available to U.S. citizens for study, research, and teaching in foreign countries as well as to foreigners to engage in similar activities in the U.S. [named after J. W. FULBRIGHT]

ful·crum (fo͝ol′krəm, ful′-), *n., pl.* **-crums, -cra** (-krə), *v.* —*n.* **1.** the support, or point of rest, on which a lever turns in moving a body. **2.** any prop or support. **3.** *Zool.* any of various structures in an animal serving as a hinge or support. —*v.t.* **4.** to fit with a fulcrum; put a fulcrum on. [1665–75; < L: back-support of a couch, appar. for *fulctrum,* equiv. to *fulc(ire)* to hold up, support + *-trum* n. suffix of instrument]

ful·fil (fo͝ol fil′), *v.t.,* **-filled, -fil·ling.** fulfill.

ful·fill (fo͝ol fil′), *v.t.* **1.** to carry out, or bring to realization, as a prophecy or promise. **2.** to perform or do, as duty; obey or follow, as commands. **3.** to satisfy (requirements, obligations, etc.): *a book that fulfills a long-felt need.* **4.** to bring to an end; finish or complete, as a period of time: *He felt that life was over when one had fulfilled his threescore years and ten.* **5.** to develop the full potential of (usually used reflexively): *She realized that she could never fulfill herself in such work.* Also, **fulfil.** [bef. 1000; ME *fulfillen,* OE *fulfyllan.* See FULL[1], FILL] —**ful·fill′er,** *n.*
—**Syn. 1.** accomplish, achieve, complete, realize. **2.** execute, discharge, observe. **3.** meet, answer, fill, comply with. **4.** end, terminate, conclude.

ful·fill·ment (fo͝ol fil′mənt), *n.* **1.** the act or state of fulfilling: *to witness the fulfillment of a dream; to achieve fulfillment of one's hopes.* **2.** the state or quality of being fulfilled; completion; realization: *a vague plan that had no hope of fulfillment.* **3.** the process or business of handling and executing customer orders, as packing, shipping, or processing checks. Also, **ful·fil′ment.** [1765–75; FULFILL + -MENT]

ful·gent (ful′jənt), *adj.* shining brightly; dazzling; resplendent: *fulgent patterns of sunlight.* [1375–1425; late ME < L *fulgent-* (s. of *fulgēns,* prp. of *fulgēre*), equiv. to *fulg-* flash + *-ent-* -ENT] —**ful′gent·ly,** *adv.* —**ful′gent·ness,** *n.*

ful·gu·rant (ful′gyər ənt), *adj.* flashing like lightning. [1640–50; < L *fulgurant-* (s. of *fulgurāns,* prp. of *fulgurāre*), equiv. to *fulgur-* (see FULGURATE) + *-ant-* -ANT]

ful·gu·rate (ful′gyə rāt′), *v.,* **-rat·ed, -rat·ing.** —*v.i.* **1.** to flash or dart like lightning. —*v.t.* **2.** *Med.* to destroy (esp. an abnormal growth) by electricity. [1670–80; < L *fulgurātus,* ptp. of *fulgurāre* to flash, glitter, lighten, deriv. of *fulgur* flash of lightning] —**ful′gu·ra′tion,** *n.*

ful·gu·rat·ing (ful′gyə rā′ting), *adj.* *Med.* (of pains) sharp and piercing. [1670–80; FULGURATE + -ING[2]]

ful·gu·rite (ful′gyə rīt′), *n.* a tubelike formation in sand or rock, caused by lightning. [1825–35; < L *fulgur* (see FULGURATE) + -ITE[1]]

ful·gu·rous (ful′gyər əs), *adj.* characteristic of or resembling lightning: *the fulgurous cracking of a whip.* [1610–20; < L *fulgur-* (see FULGURATE) + -OUS]

CONCISE ETYMOLOGY KEY: <, descended or borrowed from; >, whence; b., blend of, blended; c., cognate with; cf., compare; deriv., derivative; equiv., equivalent; imit., imitative; obl., oblique; r., replacing; s., stem; sp., spelling, spelled; resp., respelling, respelled; trans., translation; ?, origin unknown; *, unattested; ‡, probably earlier than. See the full key inside the front cover.

ful·ham (fo͝ol′əm), *n.* *Archaic.* a die loaded at one corner either to favor a throw of 4, 5, or 6 (**high fulham**) or to favor a throw of 1, 2, or 3 (**low fulham**). Also, **fullam, fullom.** [1540–50; orig. uncert.]

fu·lig·i·nous (fyo͞o lij′ə nəs), *adj.* **1.** sooty; smoky: *the fuliginous air hanging over an industrial city.* **2.** of the color of soot, as dark gray, dull brown, black, etc. [1565–75; < L *fūlīginōsus* full of soot, equiv. to *fūlīgin-* (s. of *fūlīgō*) soot + *-ōsus* -OUS] —**fu·lig′i·nous·ly,** *adv.* —**fu·lig′i·nous·ness,** *n.*

full[1] (fo͝ol), *adj.,* **-er, -est,** *adv., v., n.* —*adj.* **1.** completely filled; containing all that can be held; filled to utmost capacity: *a full cup.* **2.** complete; entire; maximum: *a full supply of food for a three-day hike.* **3.** of the maximum size, amount, extent, volume, etc.: *a full load of five tons; to receive full pay.* **4.** (of garments, drapery, etc.) wide, ample, or having ample folds. **5.** abundant; well-supplied: *a yard full of litter; a cabinet full of medicine.* **6.** filled or rounded out, as in form: *a full bust.* **7.** engrossed; occupied (usually fol. by *of*): *She was full of her own anxieties.* **8.** of the same parents: *full brothers.* **9.** *Music.* ample and complete in volume or richness of sound. **10.** (of wines) having considerable body. **11.** *Baseball.* **a.** (of the count on a batter) amounting to three balls and two strikes: *He hit a slider for a homer on a full count.* **b.** having base runners at first, second, and third bases; loaded. **12.** being slightly oversized, as a sheet of glass cut too large to fit into a frame. **13.** *Poker.* of or pertaining to the three cards of the same denomination in a full house: *He won the hand with a pair of kings and sixes full.* —*adv.* **14.** exactly or directly: *The blow struck him full in the face.* **15.** very: *You know full well what I mean.* **16.** fully, completely, or entirely; quite; at least: *The blow knocked him full around. It happened full 30 years ago.* —*v.t.* **17.** *Sewing.* **a.** to make full, as by gathering or pleating. **b.** to bring (the cloth) on one side of a seam to a little greater fullness than on the other by gathering or tucking very slightly. —*v.i.* **18.** (of the moon) to become full. —*n.* **19.** the highest or fullest state, condition, or degree: *The moon is at the full.* **20. in full, a.** to or for the full or required amount. **b.** without abridgment: *The book was reprinted in full.* **21. to the full,** to the greatest extent; thoroughly: *They enjoyed themselves to the full.* [bef. 900; ME, OE *full, ful;* c. Goth *fulls,* ON *fullr,* OHG *fol* (G *voll*); akin to L *plēnus,* Gk *plḗrēs*] —**full′ness,** *n.*

full[2] (fo͝ol), *v.t.* **1.** to cleanse and thicken (cloth) by special processes in manufacture. —*v.i.* **2.** (of cloth) to become compacted or felted. [1350–1400; ME *fullen;* back formation from FULLER[1]]

full·lam (fo͝ol′əm), *n.* fulham.

full·back (fo͝ol′bak′), *n.* *Football.* **1.** a running back who lines up behind the quarterback and is farthest from the line of scrimmage. **2.** the position played by this back. **3.** (in soccer, Rugby, field hockey) a player stationed near the defended goal to carry out chiefly defensive duties. [1885–90; FULL[1] + BACK[1]]

full′ bind′ing, a complete binding of a volume in any one material, generally leather. —**full-bound** (fo͝ol′bound′), *adj.*

full′ blood′, **1.** a person or animal of unmixed ancestry; one descended of a pure breed. Cf. **purebred. 2.** relationship through both parents. [1805–15]

full-blood·ed (fo͝ol′blud′id), *adj.* **1.** of unmixed ancestry; thoroughbred: *a full-blooded Cherokee.* **2.** vigorous; virile; hearty: *full-blooded enjoyment.* [1765–75, *Amer.*] —**full′-blood′ed·ness,** *n.*

full-blown (fo͝ol′blōn′), *adj.* **1.** completely developed: *an idea expanded into a full-blown novel.* **2.** in full bloom: *a full-blown rose.* [1605–15]

full-bod·ied (fo͝ol′bod′ēd), *adj.* of full strength, flavor, richness, etc.: *full-bodied wine.* [1680–90]

full-bore (fo͝ol′bôr′, -bōr′), *Informal.* —*adj.* **1.** moving or operating at the greatest speed or with maximum power. —*adv.* **2.** to the fullest extent; with the greatest power, speed, force, etc.: *The cars drove full-bore down the straightaway.*

full′ cir′cle, to the original place, source, or state through a cycle of developments (usually used in the phrase *come full circle*). [1875–80, for literal sense]

full′-court press′ (fo͝ol′kôrt′, -kōrt′), **1.** *Basketball.* a tactic of harassing, close-guarding defense in which the team without the ball pressures the opponent man-to-man the entire length of the court in order to disrupt dribbling or passing and force a turnover. **2.** a vigorous attack or offensive.

full′ cous′in, cousin (def. 1).

full-cut (fo͝ol′kut′), *adj.* *Jewelry.* (of a brilliant) cut with 58 facets, including the table and culet.

full′ den′ture. See under **denture.**

full′ dress′, **1.** the formal attire customarily worn in the evening, usually consisting of black tailcoats and white bow ties for men, and floor-length dresses for women. **2.** a ceremonial style of dress. [1755–65]

full-dress (fo͝ol′dres′), *adj.* **1.** formal and complete in all details: *a full-dress uniform.* **2.** done or presented completely or thoroughly. [1755–65]

full-du·plex (fo͝ol′do͞o′pleks, -dyo͞o′-), *adj.* of or pertaining to the simultaneous, independent transmission of information in both directions over a two-way channel. Cf. **half-duplex.**

full·er[1] (fo͝ol′ər), *n.* a person who fulls cloth. [bef. 1000; ME; OE *fullere* < L *fullō* fuller; see -ER[1]]

full·er[2] (fo͝ol′ər), *n.* **1.** a half-round hammer used for grooving and spreading iron. **2.** a tool or part of a die for reducing the sectional area of a piece of work. **3.** a groove running along the flat of a sword blade. —*v.t.* **4.** to reduce the sectional area of (a piece of metal) with a fuller or fullers. [1810–20; orig. n., appar. FULL[1] in sense to make full, close, compact + -ER[1]]

Full·er (fo͝ol′ər), *n.* **1. George,** 1822–84, U.S. painter. **2. Melville Wes·ton** (wes′tən), 1833–1910, Chief Justice of the U.S. 1888–1910. **3. R(ichard) Buckminster,** 1895–1983, U.S. engineer, designer, and architect. **4. (Sarah) Margaret** (*Marchioness Ossoli*), 1810–50, U.S. author and literary critic. **5. Thomas,** 1608–61, English clergyman and historian.

ful·ler·ene (fo͝ol′ə rēn′), *n.* any of a class of molecules of carbon having a roughly spherical shape. [1985–90; after R. Buckminster FULLER; see -ENE]

Ful′ler rose′ bee′tle, a beetle, *Pantomorus godmani,* that feeds on the leaves of roses as well as on those of citrus and other fruit trees. [perh. named after A. S. *Fuller* (d. 1896), American horticulturist]

ful′ler's earth′, an absorbent clay, used esp. for removing grease from fabrics, in fulling cloth, as a filter, and as a dusting powder. [1515–25]

Ful·ler·ton (fo͝ol′ər tən), *n.* a city in SW California, SE of Los Angeles. 102,034.

full-faced (fo͝ol′fāst′), *adj.* **1.** having a plump or round face. **2.** facing squarely toward the spectator or in a given direction. [1600–10] —**full′face′,** *n., adv.*

full′ faith′ and cred′it, the obligation under Article IV of the U.S. Constitution for each state to recognize the public acts, records, and judicial proceedings of every other state.

full-fash·ioned (fo͝ol′fash′ənd), *adj.* knitted to conform to the shape of a body part, as of the foot or leg: *full-fashioned hosiery.* [1880–85]

full-fig·ured (fo͝ol′fig′yərd; *Brit.* fo͝ol′fig′ərd), *adj.* (of a woman) having an amply proportioned or heavy body.

full-fledged (fo͝ol′flejd′), *adj.* **1.** of full rank or standing: *a full-fledged professor.* **2.** fully developed. [1880–85]

full′ frame′, *Carpentry.* See **braced frame.**

full-fron·tal (fo͝ol′frun′tl), *adj.* **1.** showing the entire front: *full-frontal nudity.* **2.** direct; hard-hitting: *a full-frontal assault.* [1970–75]

full′ gain′er, *Diving.* a dive in which the diver takes off facing forward and performs a backward somersault, entering the water feet first and facing away from the springboard.

full-grain (fo͝ol′grān′), *adj.* (of leather) having the original grain surface intact.

full-grown (fo͝ol′grōn′), *adj.* completely grown; mature. [1660–70]

full′ house′, *Poker.* a hand consisting of three of a kind and a pair, as three queens and two tens. Also called **full′ hand′.** [1885–90]

full-length (fo͝ol′lengkth′, -length′), *adj.* **1.** of standard or customary length: *a full-length movie.* **2.** showing or accommodating the full length or height of the human body: *a full-length mirror.* [1700–10]

full-line (fo͝ol′līn′), *adj.* *Com.* of, supplying, or dealing in many related products and services, as opposed to a single or limited one.

full′ lin′ear group′, *Math.* the group of all nonsingular linear transformations mapping a finite-dimensional vector space into itself.

full′ marks′, *Brit.* full credit; due praise. [1915–20]

full′ moon′, **1.** the moon when the whole of its disk is illuminated, occurring when in opposition to the sun. **2.** the phase of the moon at this time. See diag. under **moon.** [bef. 1000; ME *ful moyne,* OE *fulles monan*]

full′-moon ma′ple (fo͝ol′mo͞on′, -mo͞on′). See **Japanese maple.**

full-mouthed (fo͝ol′mouthd′, -moutht′), *adj.* **1.** (of cattle, sheep, etc.) having a complete set of teeth. **2.** noisy; loud. [1570–80]

full′ nel′son, a hold in which a wrestler, from behind the opponent, passes each arm under the corresponding arm of the opponent and locks the arms at the fingers or wrists on the back of the opponent's neck. Cf. **nelson.**

full′ness of time′, the proper or destined time. [1550–60]

full·lom (fo͝ol′əm), *n.* fulham.

full-pow·er (fo͝ol′pou′ər), *adj.* (of a radio station) able to broadcast up to 100 mi. (166 km) under clear atmospheric conditions. Cf. **low-power.**

full′ pow′ered, (of a vessel) relying on engines for propulsion without assistance from sails. [1735–45]

full′ profes′sor, professor (def. 1). [1930–35, *Amer.*]

full′ rhyme′, *Pros.* rhyme in which the stressed vowels and all following consonants and vowels are identical, but the consonants preceding the rhyming vowels are different, as in *chain, brain; soul, pole.* Also called **perfect rhyme, rime suffisante, true rhyme.**

full-rigged (fo͝ol′rigd′), *adj.* **1.** (of a sailing vessel) rigged as a ship; square-rigged on all of three or more masts. **2.** having all equipment. [1820–30]

full′ sail′, **1.** all the sails of a vessel. **2.** with all sails set: *The ship was moving ahead full sail.* **3.** rapidly; forcefully: *He proceeded full sail despite our objections.* [1585–95] —**full′-sailed′,** *adj.*

full-scale (fo͝ol′skāl′), *adj.* **1.** having the exact size or proportions of the original: *a full-scale replica.* **2.** using all possible means, facilities, etc.; complete: *The factory began full-scale operation last month.* [1930–35]

full′ sen′tence, *Gram.* any sentence the form of which exemplifies the most frequently used structural pattern of a particular language, as, in English, any sentence that contains a subject and a predicate; a sentence from which elliptical sentences may be derived by grammatical transformations.

full-serv·ice (fo͝ol′sûr′vis), *adj.* *Com.* providing a wide range of services related to the basic line of business, as when a filling station changes tires or makes car repairs in addition to selling gasoline. [1955–60]

full-size (fo͝ol′sīz′), *adj.* **1.** of the usual or normal size of its kind: *a full-size kitchen.* **2.** (of a bed) 54 in. (137 cm) wide and 75 or 76 in. (191 or 193 cm) long; double. **3.** pertaining to or made for a full-size bed: *full-size sheets.* Cf. **king-size, queen-size, twin-size.** Also, **full′-sized′.** [1830–40]

full′ speed′, **1.** the maximum speed. **2.** *Naut.* the speed normally maintained on a passage. **3.** at maximum speed: *to move full speed ahead.*

full′ stop′, period (defs. 10, 11). [1590–1600]

full′ swing′, full operation; greatest activity: *For the first time in years the factory was in full swing. The meeting was in full swing when we arrived.*

full-term (fo͝ol′tûrm′), *adj.* **1.** of or noting the entire duration of normal pregnancy. **2.** serving the complete designated term of office: *He was not a full-term president.*

full′ tilt′, at the full potential, speed, energy, forcefulness, etc. [1590–1600]

full′ time′, the number of hours in a period, as a day, week, or month, considered customary for pursuing an activity, esp. working at a job: *The factory now operates on full time.* Cf. **part time.** [1910–15]

full-time (fo͝ol′tīm′), *adj.* **1.** working or operating the customary number of hours in each day, week, or month: *a full-time housekeeper; full-time production.* Cf. **part-time.** —*adv.* **2.** on a full-time basis. [1895–1900]

full-tim•er (fo͝ol′tī′mər), *n.* a full-time worker. [1865–70, for earlier sense; FULL-TIME + -ER[1]]

full′ trail′er, a trailer supported entirely by its own wheels. Also, **full′-trail′er.** Cf. **semitrailer.**

full′ twist′, *Diving.* a front or back dive made by a complete rotation of the body on its vertical axis. Cf. **half twist** (def. 1).

full′-wave rec′tifier (fo͝ol′wāv′), *Electronics.* a rectifier that transmits both halves of a cycle of alternating current as a direct current. Cf. **half-wave rectifier.**

full′ word′, (esp. in Chinese grammar) a word that has lexical meaning rather than grammatical meaning; a word or morpheme that functions grammatically as a contentive. Cf. **empty word.** [1890–95]

ful•ly (fo͝ol′ē, fo͝ol′lē), *adv.* **1.** entirely or wholly: *You should be fully done with the work by now.* **2.** quite or at least: *Fully half the class attended the ceremony.* [bef. 900; ME, OE. See FULL[1], -LY]

ful•mar (fo͝ol′mər), *n.* any of certain oceanic birds of the petrel family, esp. *Fulmarus glacialis,* a gull-like Arctic species. [1690–1700; orig. dial. (Hebrides) < Icel *fūl* stinking, FOUL + *mār* gull (with reference to its stench)]

ful•mi•nant (ful′mə nənt), *adj.* **1.** occurring suddenly and with great intensity or severity; fulminating. **2.** *Pathol.* developing or progressing suddenly: *fulminant plague.* [1595–1605; < L *fulminant-* (s. of *fulmināns*), prp. of *fulmināre* to FULMINATE; see -ANT]

ful•mi•nate (ful′mə nāt′), *v.,* **-nat•ed, -nat•ing,** *n.* —*v.i.* **1.** to explode with a loud noise; detonate. **2.** to issue denunciations or the like (usually fol. by *against*): *The minister fulminated against legalized vice.* —*v.t.* **3.** to cause to explode. **4.** to issue or pronounce with vehement denunciation, condemnation, or the like. —*n.* **5.** one of a group of unstable, explosive compounds derived from fulminic acid, esp. the mercury salt of fulminic acid, which is a powerful detonating agent. [1375–1425; late ME *fulminaten* < L *fulminātus* (ptp. of *fulmināre*) thundered, equiv. to *fulmin-* (s. of *fulmen*) thunderbolt, lightning + *-ātus* -ATE[1]] —**ful′mi•na′tor,** *n.* —**ful•mi•na•to•ry** (ful′mə nə tôr′ē, -tōr′ē), *adj.*

ful′minate of mer′cury, See **mercury fulminate.**

ful′minating com′pound, a fulminate.

ful′minating pow′der, **1.** powder that explodes by percussion. **2.** a fulminate. [1795–1805]

ful•mi•na•tion (ful′mə nā′shən), *n.* **1.** a violent denunciation or censure: *a sermon that was one long fulmination.* **2.** violent explosion. [1495–1505; < L *fulminātiōn-* (s. of *fulminātiō*) a thundering, fuming. See FULMINATE, -ION]

ful•mine (ful′min), *v.t., v.i.,* **-mined, -min•ing.** *Archaic.* to fulminate. [1580–90; < L *fulmināre*]

ful•min•ic (ful min′ik), *adj.* **1.** highly explosive; unstable. **2.** of or derived from fulminic acid. [1815–25; < L *fulmin-* (s. of *fulmen*) lightning, thunder + -IC]

fulmin′ic ac′id, an unstable acid, CNOH, isomeric with cyanic acid, and known only in the form of its salts. [1815–25]

ful•ness (fo͝ol′nis), *n.* fullness.

ful•some (fo͝ol′səm, ful′-), *adj.* **1.** offensive to good taste, esp. as being excessive; overdone or gross: *fulsome praise that embarrassed her deeply; fulsome décor.* **2.** disgusting; sickening; repulsive: *a table heaped with fulsome mounds of greasy foods.* **3.** excessively or insincerely lavish: *fulsome admiration.* **4.** encompassing all aspects; comprehensive: *a fulsome survey of the political situation in Central America.* **5.** abundant or copious. [1200–50; ME *fulsom.* See FULL[1], -SOME[1]] —**ful′some•ly,** *adv.* —**ful′some•ness,** *n.*

—**Usage.** In the 13th century when it was first used, FULSOME meant simply "abundant or copious." It later developed additional senses of "offensive, gross" and "disgusting, sickening," probably by association with FOUL, and still later a sense of excessiveness: *a fulsome disease; a fulsome meal, replete with too much of everything.* For some centuries FULSOME was used exclusively, or nearly so, with these unfavorable meanings.

Today, both FULSOME and FULSOMELY are also used in senses closer to the original one: *The sparse language of the new Prayer Book contrasts with the fulsome language of Cranmer's Book of Common Prayer. Later they discussed the topic more fulsomely.* These uses are often criticized on the grounds that FULSOME must always retain its connotations of "excessive" or "offensive." The common phrase *fulsome praise* is thus sometimes ambiguous in modern use.

Ful•ton (fo͝ol′tn), *n.* **1. Robert,** 1765–1815, U.S. engineer and inventor: builder of the first profitable steamboat. **2.** a city in central New York. 13,312. **3.** a city in central Missouri. 11,046. **4.** a male given name.

ful•vous (ful′vəs), *adj.* tawny; dull yellowish-gray or yellowish-brown. [1655–65; < L *fulvus* deep yellow, tawny, reddish-yellow; see -OUS]

fum•a•did•dle (fum′ə did′l, fum′ə did′l), *n.* flumadiddle. [var. of FLUMADIDDLE]

fu•mage (fyo͞o′mij), *n. Old Eng. Law.* a tax payable to the king for each hearth in every house owned by a person not exempt from church taxes and poor taxes. Also, **feuage, fuage.** [1745–55; < ML *fūmāgium.* See FUME, -AGE]

Fu′ Man•chu′ mus′tache (fo͞o′ man cho͞o′), a mustache whose ends droop to the chin. Also called **Fu′ Manchu′.** [1935–40; after the mustache worn by *Fu Manchu,* an Oriental master criminal in films of the 1920's and '30's, based on novels by British author Sax Rohmer (1883–1959)]

fu•ma•rate (fyo͞o′mə rāt′), *n. Biochem.* the salt of fumaric acid, a key chemical intermediate in the Krebs cycle. [1860–65; FUMAR(IC ACID) + -ATE[2]]

fu•mar•i•a•ceous (fyo͞o mar′ē ā′shəs), *adj.* belonging to the plant family Fumariaceae. Cf. **fumitory family.** [< *Fumariace*(ae) (*Fumari*(a) the type genus (ML *fūmāria, fūmārium* fumitory; see FUME, -ARY) + *-aceae* -ACEAE) + -OUS]

fu•mar•ic (fyo͞o mar′ik), *adj.* of or derived from fumaric acid. [< NL *Fumar*(ia) + -IC]

fumar′ic ac′id, a colorless, odorless, crystalline, slightly water-soluble solid, $C_4H_4O_4$, isomeric with maleic acid, essential to cellular respiration in most eukaryotic organisms: used in the making of synthetic resins and as a replacement for tartaric acid in beverages and baking powders. Also called **boletic acid, lichenic acid.** [1875–80]

fu•ma•role (fyo͞o′mə rōl′), *n.* a hole in or near a volcano, from which vapor rises. [1805–15; < F *fumerolle* < LL *fūmāriōlum,* dim. of L *fūmārium* smoke chamber, equiv. to *fūm*(*us*) smoke + *-ārium* -ARIUM; see -OLE[1]] —**fu•ma•rol•ic** (fyo͞o′mə rol′ik), *adj.*

fu•ma•to•ri•um (fyo͞o′mə tôr′ē əm, -tōr′-), *n., pl.* **-to•ri•a** (-tôr′ē ə, -tōr′-). an airtight structure in which plants are fumigated to destroy fungi or insects. [< NL, equiv. to L *fūmā*(*re*) to smoke (deriv. of *fūmus* smoke) + *-tōrium* -TORY[2]]

fum•ble (fum′bəl), *v.,* **-bled, -bling,** *n.* —*v.i.* **1.** to feel or grope about clumsily: *She fumbled in her purse for the keys.* **2.** *Sports.* to fumble the ball. —*v.t.* **3.** to make, handle, etc., clumsily or inefficiently: *to fumble an attempt; He fumbled his way through the crowded room.* **4.** *Sports.* to fail to hold or maintain hold on (a ball) after having touched it or carried it. —*n.* **5.** the act of fumbling: *We completed the difficult experiment without a fumble.* **6.** *Sports.* an act or instance of fumbling the ball. [1500–10; akin to Norw, Sw *fumla,* MLG *fummeln* to grope, fumble] —**fum′bler,** *n.* —**fum′bling•ly,** *adv.* —**fum′bling•ness,** *n.*

—**Syn. 3.** bungle, botch, mishandle, spoil, muff.

fume (fyo͞om), *n., v.,* **fumed, fum•ing.** —*n.* **1.** Often, **fumes.** any smokelike or vaporous exhalation from matter or substances, esp. of an odorous or harmful nature: *tobacco fumes; noxious fumes of carbon monoxide.* **2.** an irritable or angry mood: *He has been in a fume ever since the contract fell through.* —*v.t.* **3.** to emit or exhale, as fumes or vapor: *giant stacks fuming their sooty smoke.* **4.** to treat with or expose to fumes. **5.** to show fretful irritation or anger: *She always fumes when the mail is late.* —*v.i.* **6.** to rise, or pass off, as fumes: *smoke fuming from an ashtray.* **7.** to emit fumes: *The leaky pipe fumed alarmingly.* [1350–1400; ME < OF *fum* < L *fūmus* smoke, steam, fume] —**fume′less,** *adj.* —**fume′like′,** *adj.* —**fum′er,** *n.* —**fum′ing•ly,** *adv.*

—**Syn. 2.** rage, fury, agitation, storm. **5.** chafe, fret.

fu•mé (fʏ mā′), *adj. French.* smoked.

fumed (fyo͞omd), *adj.* darkened or colored by exposure to ammonia fumes, as oak and other wood. [1605–15; FUME + -ED[2]]

fu•met (fyo͞o′mit), *n.* a stock made by simmering fish, chicken, game, etc., in water, wine, or in both, often boiled down to concentrate the flavor and used as a flavoring. Also, **fu•mette** (fyo͞o met′). [1715–25; < F: fumes, odor of wine or meat, deriv. of MF *fumer* to smoke, expose to fumes]

fu•meuse (*Fr.* fʏ mœz′), *n., pl.* **-meuses** (*Fr.* -mœz′). *Fr. Furniture.* a chair of the 18th century, having a crest rail incorporating a place for pipes and tobacco. [< F: lit., smoker (fem.), equiv. to *fum*(*er*) to smoke (see FUME) + *-euse* -EUSE]

fu•mi•gant (fyo͞o′mi gənt), *n.* any volatile or volatilizable chemical compound used as a disinfectant or pesticide. [1720–30; < L *fūmigant-* (s. of *fūmigāns,* prp. of *fūmigāre*), equiv. to *fūmig-* (see FUMIGATE) + *-ant-* -ANT]

fu•mi•gate (fyo͞o′mi gāt′), *v.t.,* **-gat•ed, -gat•ing.** to expose to smoke or fumes, as in disinfecting or exterminating roaches, ants, etc. [1520–30; < L *fūmigātus,* ptp. of *fūmigāre* to smoke, fumigate, equiv. to *fūm*(*us*) smoke + *-igāre* (v. suffix based on *-ig-,* n. deriv. of *agere* to drive, do, as in *remex,* s. *remig-* oarsman, hence *remigāre* to row)] —**fu′mi•ga′tion,** *n.* —**fu•mi•ga•to•ry** (fyo͞o′mi gə tôr′ē, -tōr′ē, -gā′tə rē), *adj.*

fu•mi•ga•tor (fyo͞o′mi gā′tər), *n.* **1.** a person or thing that fumigates. **2.** a structure in which plants are fumigated to destroy insects. [1850–55, *Amer.*; FUMIGATE + -OR[2]]

fum′ing ni′tric ac′id, a colorless, yellowish, or brownish fuming corrosive liquid, usually prepared from nitric acid by the addition of excess nitrogen dioxide: used in organic synthesis for nitration, and as an oxidizer in liquid propellants for rockets. [1785–95]

fum′ing sulfu′ric ac′id. See **pyrosulfuric acid.**

fu•mi•to•ry (fyo͞o′mi tôr′ē, -tōr′ē), *n., pl.* **-ries.** any plant of the genus *Fumaria,* esp. a delicate herb, F. *officinalis,* having finely dissected, grayish leaves and spikes of purplish flowers. [1350–1400; alter. of earlier *fumiterre,* ME *fumetere* < MF < ML *fūmus terrae* lit., smoke of the earth; literal sense uncert.]

fu′mitory fam′ily, the plant family Fumariaceae, characterized by herbaceous plants having deeply cut basal or alternate leaves, flowers with four petals of which one or two are spurred or lobed, and fruit in the form of a capsule, and including the bleeding heart, Dutchman's-breeches, fumitory, and squirrel corn.

fum•y (fyo͞o′mē), *adj.,* **fum•i•er, fum•i•est.** emitting or full of fumes; fumelike. [1560–70; FUME + -Y[1]]

fun (fun), *n., v.,* **funned, fun•ning,** *adj.* —*n.* **1.** something that provides mirth or amusement: *A picnic would be fun.* **2.** enjoyment or playfulness: *She's full of fun.* **3. for** or **in fun,** as a joke; not seriously; playfully: *His insults were only in fun.* **4. like fun,** *Informal.* certainly not; of doubtful truth: *He told us that he finished the exam in an hour. Like fun he did!* **5. make fun of,** to make the object of ridicule; deride: *The youngsters made fun of their teacher.* —*v.i., v.t.* **6.** *Informal.* joke; kid. —*adj.* **7.** *Informal.* of or pertaining to fun, esp. to social fun: *a fun thing to do; really a fun person.* **8.** *Informal.* whimsical; flamboyant: *The fashions this year are definitely on the fun side.* [1675–85; dial. var. of obs. *fon* to befool. See FOND[1]]

—**Syn. 1, 2.** merriment, pleasure, play, gaiety.

Fu•na•fu•ti (fo͞o′nə fo͞o′tē), *n.* a village in and the capital of Tuvalu. 900.

fu•nam•bu•list (fyo͞o nam′byə list), *n.* a tightrope walker. [1785–95; < L *fūnambul*(*us*) ropedancer + -IST] —**fu•nam′bu•lism,** *n.*

fun′ and games′, *Informal.* frivolously diverting activity. [1915–20]

Fun•chal (*Port.* fo͞on shäl′), *n.* a seaport in and the capital of the Madeira islands, on SE Madeira: winter resort. 38,340.

func•tion (fungk′shən), *n.* **1.** the kind of action or activity proper to a person, thing, or institution; the purpose for which something is designed or exists; role. **2.** any ceremonious public or social gathering or occasion. **3.** a factor related to or dependent upon other factors: *Price is a function of supply and demand.* **4.** *Math.* **a.** Also called **correspondence, map, mapping, transformation.** a relation between two sets in which one element of the second set is assigned to each element of the first set, as the expression $y = x^2$; operator. **b.** Also called **multiple-value function.** a relation between two sets in which two or more elements of the second set are assigned to each element of the first set, as $y^2 = x^2$, which assigns to every x the two values $y = +x$ and $y = -x$. **c.** a set of ordered pairs in which none of the first elements of the pairs appears twice. **5.** *Geom.* **a.** a formula expressing a relation between the angles of a triangle and its sides, as sine or cosine. **b.** See **hyperbolic function. 6.** *Gram.* **a.** the grammatical role a linguistic form has or the position it occupies in a particular construction. **b.** the grammatical roles or the positions of a linguistic form or form class collectively. **7.** *Sociol.* the contribution made by a sociocultural phenomenon to an ongoing social system. —*v.i.* **8.** to perform a specified action or activity; work; operate: *The computer isn't functioning now. He rarely functions before noon.* **9.** to have or exercise a function; serve: *In earlier English the present tense often functioned as a future. This orange crate can function as a chair.* [1525–35; < L *functiōn-* (s. of *functiō*) a performance, execution, equiv. to *funct*(*us*) (ptp. of *fungī*) performed, executed + *-iōn-* -ION]

func•tion•a•ble (fungk′shə nə bəl), *adj.* functional (def. 3). [FUNCTION + -ABLE] —**func′tion•a•bil′i•ty,** *n.*

func•tion•al (fungk′shə nl), *adj.* **1.** of or pertaining to a function or functions: *functional difficulties in the administration.* **2.** capable of operating or functioning: *When will the ventilating system be functional again?* **3.** having or serving a utilitarian purpose; capable of serving the purpose for which it was designed: *functional architecture; a chair that is functional as well as decorative.* **4.** Also, **func′tion•al•is′tic.** (of a building or furnishing) constructed or made according to the principles of functionalism or primarily as a direct fulfillment of a material need. **5.** *Med.* without a known organic cause or structural change: *a functional disorder.* Cf. **organic** (def. 5). **6.** pertaining to an algebraic operation: *a functional symbol.* **7.** *Ling.* (of linguistic analysis, language teaching, etc.) concerned with the communicative role of language rather than, in addition to, or as the framework for its formal structure. —*n.* **8.** *Math.* a function that has a domain whose elements are functions, sets, or the like, and that assumes numerical values. [1625–35; FUNCTION + -AL[1]] —**func′tion•al′i•ty,** *n.* —**func′tion•al•ly,** *adv.*

func′tional anal′ysis, the branch of mathematics that deals with the theory of vector spaces and linear functionals. [1945–50]

func′tional cal′culus, the branch of symbolic logic that includes the sentential calculus and that deals with sentential functions and quantifiers and with logical relations between sentences containing quantifiers. Also called **predicate calculus, predicate logic.** [1930–35]

func′tional change′. See **functional shift.**

func′tional disease′, *Pathol.* a disease in which there is an abnormal change in the function of an organ, but no structural alteration in the tissues involved (opposed to *organic disease*). [1870–75]

func′tional group′, a group of atoms responsible for the characteristic behavior of the class of compounds in which the group occurs, as the hydroxyl group in alcohols. [1935–40]

func′tional illit′erate, a person with some basic education who still falls short of a minimum standard of literacy or whose reading and writing skills are inadequate to everyday needs. [1945–50] **—func′tional illit′eracy. —func′tionally illit′erate.**

func′tional imper′ative, *Sociol.* a requirement for the survival of any social system, as communication, control of conflict, or socialization.

func•tion•al•ism (fungk′shə nl iz′əm), *n.* **1.** (*usually cap.*) *Chiefly Archit., Furniture.* **a.** a design movement evolved from several previous movements or schools in Europe in the early 20th century, advocating the design of buildings, furnishings, etc., as direct fulfillments of material requirements, as for shelter, repose, or the serving of food, with the construction, materials, and purpose clearly expressed or at least not denied, and with aesthetic effect derived chiefly from proportions and finish, purely decorative effects being excluded or greatly subordinated. **b.** the doctrines and practices associated with this movement. Cf. **rationalism** (def. 4). **2.** *Psychol.* the doctrine that emphasizes the adaptiveness of the mental or behavioral processes. **3.** *Sociol.* Also called **structural functionalism.** a theoretical orientation that views society as a system of interdependent parts whose functions contribute to the stability and survival of the system. [1910–15; FUNCTIONAL + -ISM]

func•tion•al•ist (fungk′shə nl ist), *n.* **1.** a person who advocates, or works according to, the principles of functionalism. *—adj.* **2.** of or pertaining to functionalism. **3.** built or made according to the principles of Functionalism by a person associated with the movement. Also, **Functionalist.** [1910–15; FUNCTIONAL + -IST]

func•tion•al•ize (fungk′shə nl īz′), *v.t.,* **-ized, -iz•ing.** to make functional. Also, *esp. Brit.,* **func′tion•al•ise′.** [1860–65; FUNCTIONAL + -IZE] **—func′tion•al•i•za′tion,** *n.*

func′tional load′, *Ling.* the relative frequency of occurrence of words that are differentiated in one and the same position by only one distinctive feature. In English, the opposition of voiced and voiceless *th* has a low functional load being used only to distinguish such pairs as *ether* and *either,* or *wreath* and *wreathe.* Also called **func′tional yield′.**

func′tional representa′tion, *Govt.* representation in a governing body on the basis of social class or occupation.

func′tional sen′tence perspec′tive, *Ling.* the organization of a sentence in terms of the role of its elements in distinguishing between old and new information, esp. the division of a sentence into theme and rheme.

func′tional shift′, a change in the grammatical function of a word, as in the use of the noun *input* as a verb or the noun *fun* as an adjective. Also called **functional change.** [1940–45]

func•tion•ar•y (fungk′shə ner′ē), *n., pl.* **-ar•ies.** a person who functions in a specified capacity, esp. in government service; an official: *civil servants, bureaucrats, and other functionaries.* [1785–95; FUNCTION + -ARY, modeled on F *fonctionnaire*]

func′tion key′, a key on a computer terminal or microcomputer keyboard that, when pressed, causes a specific computational or mechanical operation to be carried out.

func′tion space′, *Math.* a linear space, the elements of which are functions. [1930–35]

func′tion word′, a word, as a preposition, article, auxiliary, or pronoun, that chiefly expresses grammatical relationships, has little semantic content of its own, and belongs to a small, closed class of words whose membership is relatively fixed (distinguished from *content word*). Also called **form word.** [1935–40]

func•tor (fungk′tər), *n.* **1.** that which functions. **2.** *Ling.* a function word or affix. Cf. **contentive.** [1935–40; FUNCT(ION) + -OR[2]]

fund (fund), *n.* **1.** a supply of money or pecuniary resources, as for some purpose: *a fund for his education; a retirement fund.* **2.** supply; stock: *a fund of knowledge; a fund of jewels.* **3. funds,** money immediately available; pecuniary resources: *to be momentarily without funds.* **4.** an organization created to administer or manage a fund, as of money invested or contributed for some special purpose. *—v.t.* **5.** to provide a fund to pay the interest or principal of (a debt). **6.** to convert (general outstanding debts) into a more or less permanent debt, represented by interest-bearing bonds. **7.** to allocate or provide funds for (a program, project, etc.). [1670–80; < L *fundus* bottom, estate; r. FOND[2] in most of its meanings]
—Syn. 2. store, reservoir, fount, mine, hoard.

fun•da•ment (fun′də mənt), *n.* **1.** the buttocks. **2.** the anus. **3.** a base or basic principle; underlying part; foundation. [1250–1300; < L *fundāmentum* foundation; r. ME *fondement* < OF. See FOUND[2], -MENT]

fun•da•men•tal (fun′də men′tl), *adj.* **1.** serving as, or being an essential part of, a foundation or basis; basic; underlying: *fundamental principles; the fundamental structure.* **2.** of, pertaining to, or affecting the foundation or basis: *a fundamental revision.* **3.** being an original or primary source: *a fundamental idea.* **4.** *Music.* (of a chord) having its root as its lowest note. *—n.* **5.** a basic principle, rule, law, or the like, that serves as the groundwork of a system; essential part: *to master the fundamentals of a trade.* **6.** Also called **fun′damen′tal note′, fun′damen′tal tone′.** *Music.* **a.** the root of a chord. **b.** the generator of a series of harmonics. **7.** *Physics.* the component of lowest frequency in a composite wave. [1400–50; late ME < ML *fundāmentālis* of, belonging to a foundation. See FUNDAMENT, -AL[1]] **—fun′da•men•tal′i•ty, fun′da•men′tal•ness,** *n.* **—fun′da•men′tal•ly,** *adv.*
—Syn. 1. indispensable, primary.

fundamen′tal bass′ (bās), *Music.* a bass consisting of the roots of the chords employed. [1745–55]

fun′damen′tal fre′quency, *Physics.* **1.** the lowest frequency at which a medium will freely oscillate. **2.** the frequency of the fundamental. [‡1960–65]

fun•da•men•tal•ism (fun′də men′tl iz′əm), *n.* **1.** (*sometimes cap.*) a movement in American Protestantism that arose in the early part of the 20th century in reaction to modernism and that stresses the infallibility of the Bible not only in matters of faith and morals but also as a literal historical record, holding as essential to Christian faith belief in such doctrines as the creation of the world, the virgin birth, physical resurrection, atonement by the sacrificial death of Christ, and the Second Coming. **2.** the beliefs held by those in this movement. **3.** strict adherence to any set of basic ideas or principles: *the fundamentalism of the extreme conservatives.* [1920–25, *Amer.*; FUNDAMENTAL + -ISM] **—fun′da•men′tal•ist,** *n., adj.*

fun′damen′tal law′, the organic law of a state, esp. its constitution. [1910–15]

fun′damen′tal par′ticle. See **elementary particle.** [1930–35]

fun′damen′tal se′quence, *Math.* an infinite sequence, $x_1, x_2, \ldots$, whose terms are points in E_k, in which there exists a point y such that the limit as n goes to infinity of $x_n = y$ if and only if for every $\epsilon > 0$, there exists a number N such that $i > N$ and $j > N$ implies $|x_i - x_j| < \epsilon$. Also called **Cauchy sequence, convergent sequence.** Cf. **complete** (def. 10b).

fun′damen′tal star′, *Astron.* one of a number of stars with positions that have been determined accurately and that are used as reference stars for the determination of positions of other celestial objects.

fun′damen′tal u′nit, *Physics.* See **base unit.**

fund′ed debt′, a debt, as in the form of bonds, having a long period of maturity. [1810–20]

fund-raise (fund′rāz′), *v.,* **-raised, -rais•ing.** *—v.t.* **1.** to collect by fund-raising: *The charity needs to fund-raise more than a million dollars.* *—v.i.* **2.** to engage in fund-raising. Also, **fund′raise′.**

fund-rais•er (fund′rā′zər), *n.* **1.** a person who solicits contributions or pledges. **2.** a gathering held for such solicitation: *a fund-raiser to aid the campaign of the Senate candidate.* Also, **fund′rais′er.** [1955–60]

fund-rais•ing (fund′rā′zing) *n.* the act or process of raising funds, as for nonprofit organizations or for a political cause. Also, **fund′rais′ing.** [1935–40]

fun•dus (fun′dəs), *n., pl.* **-di** (-dī). *Anat.* the base of an organ, or the part opposite to or remote from an aperture. [1745–55; < L: lit., bottom] **—fun′dic,** *adj.*

Fun•dy (fun′dē), *n.* **Bay of,** an inlet of the Atlantic in SE Canada, between New Brunswick and Nova Scotia, having swift tidal currents.

Fü•nen (fy′nən), *n.* German name of **Fyn.**

fu•ner•al (fyo͞o′nər əl), *n.* **1.** the ceremonies for a dead person prior to burial or cremation; obsequies. **2.** a funeral procession. **3. be someone's funeral,** *Informal.* to have unpleasant consequences for someone: *If you don't finish the work on time, it will be your funeral!* *—adj.* **4.** of or pertaining to a funeral: *funeral services; funeral expenses.* [1350–1400; ME (adj.) < ML *fūnerālis,* equiv. to L *fūner-,* s. of *fūnus* funeral rites + *-ālis* -AL[1]; (n.), from early 16th cent., prob. < MF *funerailles* < ML *fūnerālia,* neut. pl. of *fūnerālis*]

fu′neral direc′tor, 1. a person, usually a licensed embalmer, who supervises or conducts the preparation of the dead for burial and directs or arranges funerals. **2.** a person who owns or operates a funeral home. Also called **mortician, undertaker.** [1885–90, *Amer.*]

fu′neral home′, an establishment where the dead are prepared for burial or cremation, where the body may be viewed, and where funeral services are sometimes held. Also called **fu′neral chap′el, fu′neral church′, fu′neral par′lor, fu′neral res′idence, mortuary.** [1935–40, *Amer.*]

fu•ner•al•ize (fyo͞o′nər ə līz′), *v.t.,* **-ized, -iz•ing.** to hold or officiate at a funeral service for. Also, *esp. Brit.,* **fu′ner•al•ise′.** [1645–55 for earlier sense; FUNERAL + -IZE]

fu′neral pie′, *Pennsylvania Dutch Cookery.* a traditional pie made with a black filling of raisins and lemon juice and presented to a bereaved family.

fu•ner•ar•y (fyo͞o′nə rer′ē), *adj.* of or pertaining to a funeral or burial: *a funerary urn.* [1685–95; < LL *fūnerārius* of, relating to a funeral. See FUNERAL, -ARY]

fu•ne•re•al (fyo͞o nēr′ē əl), *adj.* **1.** of or suitable for a funeral. **2.** mournful; gloomy; dismal: *a funereal aloofness that was quite chilling.* [1715–25; < L *fūnere(us)* of, belonging to a FUNERAL + AL[1]] **—fu•ne′re•al•ly,** *adv.*

fu•nest (fyo͞o nest′), *adj.* boding or causing evil or death; fatal; disastrous. [1645–55; < F *funeste* < L *fūnestus,* deriv. of *fūnus* funeral, death]

fun′ fair′, an amusement park. [1920–25]

fun•fest (fun′fest′), *n.* a party or other gathering for fun and entertainment. [1915–20; FUN + -FEST]

Fünf•kir•chen (fynf′kēr′KHən), *n.* German name of **Pécs.**

fun•gal (fung′gəl), *adj.* fungous. [1825–35; < NL *fungālis.* See FUNGUS, -AL[1]]

fun•gi (fun′jī, fung′gī), *n.* a pl. of **fungus.**

Fun•gi (fun′jī, fung′gī), *n.* (*used with a plural v.*) *Biol.* a taxonomic kingdom, or in some classification schemes a division of the kingdom Plantae, comprising all the fungus groups and sometimes also the slime molds. Also called **Mycota.** [< NL; see FUNGUS]

fungi-, a combining form representing **fungus** in compound words: *fungicide.*

fun•gi•ble (fun′jə bəl), *adj. Law.* (esp. of goods) being of such nature or kind as to be freely exchangeable or replaceable, in whole or in part, for another of like nature or kind. [1755–65; < ML *fungibilis,* equiv. to L *fung(ī)* to perform the office of + *-ibilis* -IBLE] **—fun′•gi•bil′i•ty,** *n.*

fun•gi•cide (fun′jə sīd′, fung′gə-), *n.* a substance or preparation, as a spray or dust, used for destroying fungi. [1885–90; FUNGI- + -CIDE] **—fun′gi•cid′al,** *adj.* **—fun′gi•cid′al•ly,** *adv.*

fun•gi•form (fun′jə fôrm′, fung′gə-), *adj.* having the form of a fungus or mushroom. [1815–25; FUNGI- + -FORM]

Fun′gi Im•per•fec′ti (im′pər fek′tī), a class of fungi for which a sexually reproductive stage of the life cycle has not been found. [< NL: lit., imperfect fungi]

fun•gi•stat (fun′jə stat′, fung′gə-), *n.* a fungistatic substance or preparation. [FUNGI- + -STAT]

fun•gi•stat•ic (fun′jə stat′ik, fung′gə-), *adj.* (of a substance or preparation) inhibiting the growth of a fungus. [1920–25; FUNGI- + -STATIC] **—fun′gi•stat′i•cal•ly,** *adv.*

fun•gi•tox•ic (fun′ji tok′sik, fung′gi-), *adj.* toxic to fungi. [1950–55; FUNGI- + TOXIC] **—fun•gi•tox•ic•i•ty** (fun′ji tok sis′i tē, fung′gi-), *n.*

fun•giv•or•ous (fən jiv′ər əs), *adj.* feeding on fungi, as certain insects. [1820–30; FUNGI- + -VOROUS]

fun•go (fung′gō), *n., pl.* **-goes.** *Baseball.* **1.** (in practice sessions) a ball tossed into the air by the batter and struck as it comes down. **2.** a batted ball, esp. a fly ball, hit in this manner. **3.** Also called **fun′go bat′.** a bat used in hitting fungoes, being lighter, longer, and narrower than an ordinary baseball bat. [1865–70, *Amer.*; of obscure orig.]

fun•goid (fung′goid), *adj.* **1.** resembling a fungus; of the nature of a fungus. **2.** *Pathol.* characterized by funguslike growths. *—n.* **3.** *Pathol.* a growth having the characteristics of a fungus. [1830–40; FUNG(US) + -OID]

fun•gos•i•ty (fung gos′i tē), *n., pl.* **-ties** for 2. **1.** the condition of being fungous. **2.** a fungous excrescence. [1710–20; < L *fungōs(us)* FUNGOUS + -ITY]

fun•gous (fung′gəs), *adj.* **1.** of, pertaining to, or caused by fungi; fungal. **2.** of the nature of or resembling a fungus. [1375–1425; late ME < L *fungōsus* fungous, spongy. See FUNGUS, -OUS]

fun•gus (fung′gəs), *n., pl.* **fun•gi** (fun′jī, fung′gī), **fun•gus•es,** *adj.* *—n.* **1.** any of a diverse group of eukaryotic single-celled or multinucleate organisms that live by decomposing and absorbing the organic material in which they grow, comprising the mushrooms, molds, mildews, smuts, rusts, and yeasts, and classified in the kingdom Fungi or, in some classification systems, in the division Fungi (Thallophyta) of the kingdom Plantae. **2.** *Pathol.* a spongy, abnormal growth, as granulation tissue formed in a wound. *—adj.* **3.** fungous. [1520–30; < L: fungus, mushroom; perh. akin to Gk *spóngos, sphóngos* SPONGE] **—fun•gic** (fun′jik), *adj.* **—fun′gus•like′,** *adj.*

fun′gus bug′. See **flat bug.**

fun′gus gnat′, any of several mosquitolike insects of the family Mycetophilidae, the larvae of which feed on fungi or decaying vegetation. [1880–85]

fun′gus root′, *n.* mycorrhiza.

fun′gus stone′. See **stone fungus.**

fun′ house′, (in an amusement park) a building that is specially constructed and has devices for surprising and amusing patrons walking through. [1945–50]

fu•ni•cle (fyo͞o′ni kəl), *n. Bot.* the stalk of an ovule or seed. [1655–65; < L *fūniculus.* See FUNICULUS, -CLE[1]]

fu•nic•u•lar (fyo͞o nik′yə lər), *adj.* **1.** of or pertaining to a rope or cord, or its tension. **2.** worked by a rope or the like. *—n.* **3.** See **funicular railway.** [1655–65; < L *fūnicul(us)* (see FUNICULUS) + -AR[1]]

funic′ular rail′way, a short, very steep railway having two parallel sets of tracks, upon each of which runs a car or train raised or lowered by means of a cable that simultaneously lowers or raises the other car or train in such a way that the two are approximately counterbalanced. [1885–90]

fu•nic•u•late (fyo͞o nik′yə lit, -lāt′), *adj. Bot.* having a funicle. [1820–30; FUNICUL(US) + -ATE[1]]

fu•nic•u•lus (fyo͞o nik′yə ləs), *n., pl.* **-li** (-lī′). **1.** *Anat.* a conducting cord, as a nerve cord or umbilical cord. **2.** *Bot.* a funicle. **3.** *Entomol.* (in certain insects) the portion of the antenna between the basal segments and the club. [1655–65; < L: small rope, cord, equiv. to *fūni(s)* rope, line + *-culus* -CULE[1]]

funk[1] (fungk), *n.* **1.** cowering fear; state of great fright or terror. **2.** a dejected mood: *He's been in a funk ever since she walked out on him.* *—v.t.* **3.** to be afraid of. **4.** to frighten. **5.** to shrink from; try to shirk. *—v.i.* **6.** to shrink or quail in fear. [1735–45; perh. < early D dial. *fonck*] **—funk′er,** *n.*

funk[2] (fungk), *n.* **1.** music having a funky quality. **2.** the state or quality of being funky. **3.** a strong smell; stench. [1615–25; perh. < North F dial. *funquier, funquer* give off smoke, ONF *fungier* < VL *fūmicāre,* alter. of L *fūmigāre;* see FUMIGATE]

Funk (fo͝ongk, fungk), *n.* **Cas•i•mir** (kaz′ə mēr′), 1884–1967, U.S. biochemist, born in Poland: discovered thiamine, the first vitamin isolated.

funked (fungkt), *adj. Southern U.S.* (*chiefly Kentucky*). (of tobacco) rotten; moldy. [1890–95; *funk* punk (n.) (ME *fonk;* c. D *vonk,* G *Funke*) + -ED[3]]

fun•ki•a (fung′kē ə, fo͝ong′-), *n.* See **plantain lily.**

CONCISE ETYMOLOGY KEY: <, descended or borrowed from; >, whence; b., blend of, blended; c., cognate with; cf., compare; deriv., derivative; equiv., equivalent; imit., imitative; obl., oblique; r., replacing; s., stem; sp., spelling, spelled; resp., respelling, respelled; trans., translation; ?, origin unknown; *, unattested; ‡, probably earlier than. See the full key inside the front cover.

[1830–40; < NL; named after C. H. Funck (d. 1839), German botanist; see -IA]

funk•y[1] (fung′kē), *adj.*, **funk•i•er, funk•i•est.** overcome with great fear; terrified. [1830–40; FUNK[1] + -Y[1]]

funk•y[2] (fung′kē), *adj.*, **funk•i•er, funk•i•est. 1.** *Jazz.* having an earthy, blues-based quality or character. **2.** having an offensive smell; evil-smelling; foul. [1905–10, *Amer.*; FUNK[2] + -Y[1]] **—funk′i•ly,** *adv.* **—funk′i•ness,** *n.*

fun•nel (fun′l), *n., v.,* **-neled, -nel•ing** or (*esp. Brit.*) **-nelled, -nel•ling.** —*n.* **1.** a cone-shaped utensil with a tube at the apex for conducting liquid or other substance through a small opening, as into a bottle, jug, or the like. **2.** a smokestack, esp. of a steamship. **3.** a flue, tube, or shaft, as for ventilation. **4.** *Eastern New England.* a stovepipe. —*v.t.* **5.** to concentrate, channel, or focus: *They funneled all income into research projects.* **6.** to pour through or as if through a funnel. —*v.i.* **7.** to pass through or as if through a funnel. [1375–1425; late ME *fonel* < OPr *fonilh* (Gascon) < VL **fundibulum,* for L *infundibulum,* deriv. of *infundere* to pour in] **—fun′nel•like′,** *adj.*

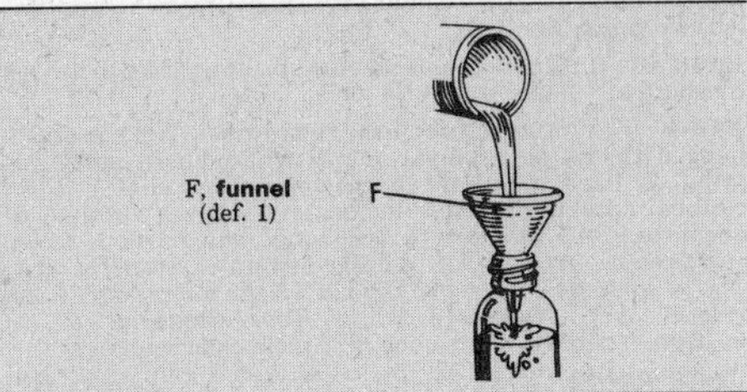

F, **funnel** (def. 1)

fun′nel cake′, a crisp, deep-fried cake, made by pouring batter through a funnel into fat or oil, usually in a spiral shape, and dusted with powdered sugar.

fun′nel cloud′, a rapidly rotating funnel-shaped cloud extending downward from the base of a cumulonimbus cloud, which, if it touches the surface of the earth, is a tornado or waterspout. Also called **pendant cloud, tornado cloud, tuba.**

fun•nel•form (fun′l fôrm′), *adj.* shaped like a funnel, as the corolla of the morning-glory; infundibuliform. [1820–30; FUNNEL + -FORM]

fun•ny[1] (fun′ē), *adj.*, **-ni•er, -ni•est,** *n., pl.* **-nies.** —*adj.* **1.** providing fun; causing amusement or laughter; amusing; comical: *a funny remark; a funny person.* **2.** attempting to amuse; facetious: *Did you really mean that or were you just being funny?* **3.** warranting suspicion; deceitful; underhanded: *We thought there was something funny about those extra charges.* **4.** *Informal.* insolent; impertinent: *Don't get funny with me, young man!* **5.** curious; strange; peculiar; odd: *Her speech has a funny twang.* —*n.* **6.** *Informal.* a funny remark or story; a joke: *to make a funny.* **7. funnies, a.** comic strips. **b.** Also called **funny paper.** the section of a newspaper reserved for comic strips, word games, etc. [1750–60; FUN + -Y[1]] **—fun′ni•ly,** *adv.* **—fun′ni•ness,** *n.*
—Syn. 1. diverting, comic, farcical, ridiculous, droll, witty, facetious, humorous. FUNNY, LAUGHABLE, LUDICROUS refer to that which excites laughter. FUNNY and LAUGHABLE are both applied to that which provokes laughter or deserves to be laughed at; FUNNY is a colloquial term loosely applied and in popular use is commonly interchangeable with the other terms: *a funny story, scene, joke; a laughable incident, mistake.* That which is LUDICROUS excites laughter by its incongruity and foolish absurdity: *The monkey's attempts to imitate the woman were ludicrous.*

fun•ny[2] (fun′ē), *n., pl.* **-nies.** a shell or light skiff rowed by one person with sculls. [1790–1800; perh. jocular use of FUNNY[1]]

fun′ny bone′, 1. the part of the elbow where the ulnar nerve passes by the internal condyle of the humerus, which when struck causes a peculiar, tingling sensation in the arm and hand; crazy bone. **2.** a sense of humor. [1830–40]

fun′ny book′, *Older Use.* See **comic book.** [1945–50]

fun′ny busi′ness, *Informal.* improper or unethical conduct, as deception or trickery: *He won't stand for any funny business here.* [1880–85, *Amer.*]

fun′ny farm′, *Slang (offensive).* a psychiatric hospital. [1960–65]

fun•ny•man (fun′ē man′), *n., pl.* **-men.** a comedian or humorist. [1840–50; FUNNY[1] + MAN[1]]

fun′ny mon′ey, *Slang.* **1.** counterfeit currency. **2.** money from undisclosed or questionable sources. **3.** currency of little value, as of a nation whose currency has been artificially inflated or recently devaluated. **4.** any foreign currency. [1940–45]

fun′ny pa′per, funny[1] (def. 7b). [1870–75, *Amer.*]

fun•ster (fun′stər), *n.* a person who creates or seeks fun, as a comedian or reveler. [1780–90; FUN + -STER]

Fun•ston (fun′stən), *n.* **Frederick,** 1865–1917, U.S. general.

fu•qa•ha (fo͞o kä′hə), *n.* pl. of **faqih.**

fur (fûr), *n., adj., v.,* **furred, fur•ring.** —*n.* **1.** the fine, soft, thick, hairy coat of the skin of a mammal. **2.** the skin of certain animals, as the sable, ermine, or beaver, covered with such a coat, used for lining, trimming, or making garments. **3.** a garment made of fur. **4.** any coating resembling or suggesting fur, as certain matter on the tongue. **5.** *Heraldry.* any conventional representation of a fur, as ermine, vair, potent, or their variations. **6. make the fur fly, a.** to cause a scene or disturbance, esp. of a violent nature; make trouble: *When the kids got mad they really made the fur fly.* **b.** to do things quickly: *She always makes the fur fly when she types.* —*adj.* **7.** of or pertaining to fur, animal skins, dressed pelts, etc.: *a fur coat; a fur trader.* —*v.t.* **8.** to line, face, or trim, with fur, as a garment. **9.** *Building Trades.* to apply furring to (a wall, ceiling, etc.). **10.** to clothe (a person) with fur. **11.** to coat with foul or deposited matter. [1300–50; ME *furre* (n.), deriv. of *furren* to trim with fur < AF *furrer,* OF *fo(u)rrer* orig. to encase, deriv. of *fuerre* sheath < Gmc; akin to OE *fōdder* case, sheath, ON *fōthr,* Gk *pōma*] **—fur′less,** *adj.*

fur., furlong; furlongs.

fu•ran (fyo͝or′an, fyo͝o ran′), *n.* a colorless, liquid, unsaturated, five-membered heterocyclic compound, C_4H_4O, obtained from furfural: used chiefly in organic synthesis. Also called **furfuran.** [1890–95; aph. form of FURFURAN]

fu•ra•zol•i•done (fyo͝or′ə zol′i dōn′), *n. Pharm.* a nitrofuran, $C_8H_7N_3O_5$, that is used in the treatment of giardiasis, and bacterial gastroenteritis and dysentery. [1950–55; prob. *fur(anyl)* + *(ox)azolid(in)one,* two of its chemical components]

fur•bear•er (fûr′bâr′ər), *n.* any furry animal, esp. one whose fur is of commercial value. Also, **fur′-bear′er.** [1905–10; FUR + BEARER] **—fur′bear′ing,** *adj.*

fur•be•low (fûr′bə lō′), *n.* **1.** a ruffle or flounce, as on a woman's skirt or petticoat. **2.** any bit of showy trimming or finery. —*v.t.* **3.** to ornament with or as if with furbelows. [1670–80; var. of FALBALA]

fur•bish (fûr′bish), *v.t.* **1.** to restore to freshness of appearance or good condition (often fol. by *up*): *to furbish a run-down neighborhood; to furbish up one's command of a foreign language.* **2.** to polish. [1350–1400; ME *furbishen* < MF *forbiss-,* long s. of *forbir* to polish, clean < Gmc; cf. OHG *furban*] **—fur′bish•er,** *n.*

Fur′bish louse′wort (fûr′bish). See under **lousewort.** [1975–80; after Kate *Furbish* (1834–1931), U.S. botanist, its discoverer]

fur•cate (*adj.* fûr′kāt, -kit; *v.* fûr′kāt), *adj., v.,* **-cat•ed, -cat•ing.** —*adj.* **1.** forked; branching. —*v.i.* **2.** to form a fork; branch. [1810–20; < ML *furcātus* cloven. See FORK, -ATE[1]] **—fur•ca•tion** (fər kā′shən), *n.*

fur•cu•la (fûr′kyə lə), *n., pl.* **-lae** (-lē′). **1.** the forked clavicular bone of a bird; wishbone. **2.** the ventral, forked appendage on the abdomen of a springtail that the insect uses in springing itself into the air. [1855–60; < L: a forked prop. See FORK, -ULE] **—fur′cu•lar,** *adj.*

fur•cu•lum (fûr′kyə ləm), *n., pl.* **-la** (-lə). furcula. [< NL]

fur′ farm′, a farm on which animals, as minks, are raised for their pelts. [1910–15] **—fur′ farm′ing.**

fur•fur (fûr′fər), *n., pl.* **fur•fur•es** (fûr′fyə rēz′, -fə-). **1.** the formation of flakelike particles on the surface of the skin, as of dandruff. **2. furfures,** these particles. [1615–25; < L: bran, scaly infection]

fur•fu•ra•ceous (fûr′fyə rā′shəs, -fə-), *adj.* **1.** of or containing bran **2.** resembling bran; branlike. **3.** scaly; scurfy. [1640–50; < LL *furfurāceus.* See FURFUR, -ACEOUS] **—fur′fu•ra′ceous•ly,** *adv.*

fur•fur•al (fûr′fyə ral′, -fə-), *n.* a colorless, oily liquid, $C_5H_4O_2$, having an aromatic odor, obtained from bran, sugar, wood, corncobs, or the like, by distillation: used chiefly in the manufacture of plastics and as a solvent in the refining of lubricating oils. Also called **fur•fur•al•de•hyde** (fûr′fyə ral′də hīd′, -fə-), **pyromucic aldehyde.** [1875–80; < L *furfur* bran + -AL[3]]

fur•fur•an (fûr′fyə ran′, -fə-), *n.* furan. [1875–80; FURFUR + -AN]

fur•fu•rol (fûr′fyər əl, -fər-), *n.* (erroneously) furfural. Also, **fur•fu•role** (fûr′fyə rōl′, -fə-). [1835–45]

Fu•ri•ae (fyo͝or′ē ē′), *n.pl. Rom. Myth.* fury (def. 3).

fu•ri•o•so (fyo͝or′ē ō′sō; *It.* fo͞o ryô′zô), *Music.* —*adj.* **1.** forceful; turbulent. —*adv.* **2.** forcefully; turbulently. [1660–70, for an earlier sense; < It: lit., furious, equiv. to *furi(a)* FURY + *-oso* -OUS]

fu•ri•ous (fyo͝or′ē əs), *adj.* **1.** full of fury, violent passion, or rage; extremely angry; enraged: *He was furious about the accident.* **2.** intensely violent, as wind or storms. **3.** of unrestrained energy, speed, etc.: *furious activity.* [1300–50; ME < L *furiōsus.* See FURY, -OUS] **—fu′ri•ous•ly,** *adv.* **—fu′ri•ous•ness,** *n.*

furl (fûrl), *v.t.* **1.** to gather into a compact roll and bind securely, as a sail against a spar or a flag against its staff. —*v.i.* **2.** to become furled. **3. furl in a body,** *Naut.* to furl (a square sail) with loose canvas gathered at the mast, so as to make a harbor furl. **4. furl in the bunt,** *Naut.* to furl (a square sail) by gathering canvas upward, so as to load the yard equally at all points. —*n.* **5.** the act of furling. **6.** something furled, as a roll. [1550–60; cf. MF *ferler* in same sense, perh. repr. OF *ferlier* to chain, fasten, equiv. to *fer* firm (< L *firmus*) + *lier* to bind (< L *ligāre*)] **—furl′a•ble,** *adj.* **—furl′er,** *n.*

furl., furlough.

fur•long (fûr′lông, -long), *n.* a unit of distance, equal to 220 yards (201 m) or ⅛ mile (0.2 km). *Abbr.:* fur. [bef. 900; ME; OE *furlang* length of a furrow. See FURROW, LONG[1]]

fur•lough (fûr′lō), *n.* **1.** *Mil.* a vacation or leave of absence granted to an enlisted person. **2.** a usually temporary layoff from work: *Many plant workers have been forced to go on furlough.* **3.** a temporary leave of absence authorized for a prisoner from a penitentiary. —*v.t.* **4.** to grant a furlough to. **5.** to lay (an employee or worker) off from work, usually temporarily. [1615–25; var. of earlier *furlogh, furloff* < D *verlof* leave, permission; current pronunciation by assoc. with DOUGH, etc.]

fur•mint (fo͝or′mint), *n.* **1.** a variety of grape from which Tokay is made. **2.** the vine bearing this grape, grown in northeastern Hungary. [< Hungarian < MF *fromenté, fourmenté* a type of grape; see FRUMENTY]

fur•nace (fûr′nis), *n., v.,* **-naced, -nac•ing.** —*n.* **1.** a structure or apparatus in which heat may be generated, as for heating houses, smelting ores, or producing steam. **2.** a place characterized by intense heat: *The volcano was a seething furnace.* **3.** (*cap.*) *Astron.* the constellation Fornax. —*v.t.* **4.** to heat (a metal piece) in a furnace. [1175–1225; ME *furneis, furnais* < OF *fornais, fournais* < L *fornāc-* (s. of *fornāx* kiln, oven), akin to *formus* warm] **—fur′nace•like′,** *adj.*

Fur•ness (fûr′nis), *n.* **Horace Howard,** 1833–1912, and his son **Horace Howard,** 1865–1930, U.S. Shakespearean scholars and editors.

fur•nish (fûr′nish), *v.t.* **1.** to supply (a house, room, etc.) with necessary furniture, carpets, appliances, etc. **2.** to provide or supply (often fol. by *with*): *The delay furnished me with the time I needed.* —*n.* **3.** paper pulp and any ingredients added to it prior to its introduction into a papermaking machine. [1400–50; late ME *furnisshen* < OF *furniss-,* long s. of *furnir* to accomplish, furnish < Gmc; cf. OHG *frumjan* to provide] **—fur′nish•er,** *n.*
—Syn. 1, 2. rig, outfit, deck out. FURNISH, APPOINT, EQUIP all refer to providing something necessary. FURNISH emphasizes the idea of providing necessary or customary services or appliances in living quarters: *to furnish board; a room meagerly furnished with a bed, desk, and a wooden chair.* APPOINT (now found only in WELL-APPOINTED) means to furnish completely with all requisites or accessories or in an elegant style: *a well-appointed house.* EQUIP means to supply with necessary materials or apparatus for some service, action, or undertaking; it emphasizes preparation: *to equip a vessel, a soldier.*

fur•nish•ing (fûr′ni shing), *n.* **1. furnishings, a.** furniture, carpeting, etc., for a house or room. **b.** articles or accessories of dress: *men's furnishings.* **2.** that with which anything is furnished. [1490–1500; FURNISH + -ING[1]]

furnit., furniture.

fur•ni•ture (fûr′ni chər), *n.* **1.** the movable articles, as tables, chairs, desks or cabinets, required for use or ornament in a house, office, or the like. **2.** fittings, apparatus, or necessary accessories for something. **3.** equipment for streets and other public areas, as lighting standards, signs, benches, or litter bins. **4.** Also called **bearer, dead metal.** *Print.* pieces of wood or metal, less than type high, set in and about pages of type to fill them out and hold the type in place in a chase. [1520–30; < F *fourniture,* deriv. of *fournir* to FURNISH] **—fur′ni•ture•less,** *adj.*

Fur•ni•vall (fûr′nə vəl), *n.* **Frederick James,** 1825–1910, English philologist and editor.

fu•ro (fo͝or′ō; *Japn.* fo͞o′RÔ), *n., pl.* **fu•ros,** *Japn.* **fu•ro.** a short, deep Japanese bathtub, often with a seat, in which a person sits upright while soaking in hot water. Also called **ofuro.** [< Japn, earlier **fu-ro* < MChin, equiv. to Chin *fēnglú* a kind of stove]

fu•ro•cou•ma•rin (fyo͝or′ō ko͞o′mə rin), *n. Biochem.* psoralen. [*furo-,* comb. form repr. FURAN or FURFURAL + COUMARIN]

fu•ror (fyo͝or′ôr, -ər), *n.* **1.** a general outburst of enthusiasm, excitement, controversy, or the like. **2.** a prevailing fad, mania, or craze. **3.** fury; rage; madness. Also, *esp. Brit.,* **fu′rore** (defs. 1, 2). [1425–75; < L: a raging; r. late ME *fureor* < MF]
—Syn. 1, 3. frenzy, uproar, commotion, turmoil.

fur•phy (fûr′fē), *n., pl.* **-phies.** *Australian.* a false report; rumor. [1910–15; after *Furphy carts* water and rubbish carts manufactured by the Furphy family of Shepparton, Victoria, and used during World War I; cf. parallel semantic development of SCUTTLEBUTT]

furred (fûrd), *adj.* **1.** having fur. **2.** made with or of fur, as garments. **3.** clad in fur or furs, as persons: *elegantly furred in chinchilla.* **4.** coated with matter, as the tongue. [1275–1325; ME; see FUR, -ED[3]]

fur•ri•er[1] (fûr′ē ər), *n.* a person who buys and sells furs, or one who makes, repairs, or cleans furs and fur garments; a fur dealer or fur dresser. [1570–80; re-formation, perh. after CLOTHIER, of earlier E, ME *furrer* < AF; see FUR, -ER[2]]

fur•ri•er[2] (fûr′ē ər), *adj.* comparative of **furry.**

fur•ri•er•y (fûr′ē ə rē), *n., pl.* **-er•ies. 1.** the business, trade, or craftsmanship of a furrier. **2.** *Archaic.* furs in general. [1760–70; FURRI(ER)[1] + -ERY]

fur•rin•er (fûr′ə nər, fur′-), *n. Dial.* a foreigner.

fur•ring (fûr′ing), *n.* **1.** the act of lining, trimming, or clothing with fur: *Furring this coat will take several weeks* **2.** the fur used: *What kind of furring would you like?* **3.** the formation of a coating of matter on something, as on the tongue: *A heavy furring could mean a high fever.* **4.** *Building Trades.* **a.** the attaching of strips of wood or the like **(fur′ring strips′)** to a wall or other surface, as to provide an even support for lath or to provide an air space between the wall and plasterwork. **b.** material used for this purpose. [1350–1400; ME; see FUR, -ING[1]]

fur•row (fûr′ō, fur′ō), *n.* **1.** a narrow groove made in the ground, esp. by a plow. **2.** a narrow groovelike or trenchlike depression in any surface: *the furrows of a wrinkled face.* —*v.t.* **3.** to make a furrow or furrows in. **4.** to make wrinkles in (the face): *to furrow one's brow.* —*v.i.* **5.** to become furrowed. [bef. 900; ME *forwe, furgh,* OE *furh;* c. OFris *furch,* OHG *fur(u)h* (G *Furche*), L *porca* ridge between furrows] **—fur′row•er,** *n.* **—fur′row•less,** *adj.* **—fur′row•like′,** *adj.* **—fur′row•y,** *adj.*

fur•ry (fûr′ē), *adj.,* **fur•ri•er, fur•ri•est. 1.** consisting of or resembling fur: *a deep, furry rug in front of the fireplace; the furry undergrowth of the forest.* **2.** covered with fur; wearing fur: *Many furry animals are in danger of becoming extinct.* **3.** obstructed or coated as if with fur: *a furry voice; a furry tongue.* **4.** *Slang.* terrifying; hair-raising. [1590–1600; FUR + -Y[1]] —**fur′ri·ly,** *adv.* —**fur′ri·ness,** *n.*

fur′ seal′, any of several eared seals, as *Callorhinus alascanus,* having a plush underfur used in making coats, trimmings, etc. [1765–75]

Fürth (fYRT), *n.* a city in S West Germany, near Nuremberg. 100,700.

fur·ther (fûr′thər), *compar. adv. and adj. of* **far** *with superl.* **fur·thest,** *v.* —*adv.* **1.** at or to a greater distance; farther: *I'm too tired to go further.* **2.** at or to a more advanced point; to a greater extent: *Let's not discuss it further.* **3.** in addition; moreover: *Further, he should be here any minute.* —*adj.* **4.** more distant or remote; farther: *The map shows it to be further than I thought.* **5.** more extended: *Does this mean a further delay?* **6.** additional; more: *Further meetings seem pointless.* —*v.t.* **7.** to help forward (a work, undertaking, cause, etc.); promote; advance; forward: *You can always count on him to further his own interests.* [bef. 900; ME *furthere,* OE *furthra;* c. G *vordere* more advanced] —**fur′ther·er,** *n.*
—**Usage.** See **farther.**

fur·ther·ance (fûr′thər əns), *n.* the act of furthering; promotion; advancement. [1400–50; late ME *fortheraunce.* See FURTHER, -ANCE]

fur′ther educa′tion, *Brit.* See **adult education.** [1895–1900]

fur·ther·more (fûr′thər môr′, -mōr′), *adv.* moreover; besides; in addition: *Furthermore, he left orders not to be disturbed.* [1150–1200; ME; see FURTHER, MORE]

fur·ther·most (fûr′thər mōst′), *adj.* most distant: *Their house is furthermost on the right.* [1350–1400; ME; see FURTHER, -MOST]

fur·thest (fûr′thist), *adj., adv. superl. of* **far** *with* **further** *as compar.* farthest.

fur·tive (fûr′tiv), *adj.* **1.** taken, done, used, etc., surreptitiously or by stealth; secret: *a furtive glance.* **2.** sly; shifty: *a furtive manner.* [1480–90; < L *furtīvus,* equiv. to *furt(um)* theft (cf. *fūr* thief) + *-īvus* -IVE] —**fur′tive·ly,** *adv.* —**fur′tive·ness,** *n.*
—**Syn. 1.** clandestine, covert. **2.** underhand, cunning.

Furt·wäng·ler (fŏŏRt′veng′lər), *n.* **Wil·helm** (vil′helm), 1886–1954, German orchestral conductor.

fu·run·cle (fyŏŏr′ung kəl), *n. Pathol.* boil[2]. [1670–80; < L *fūrunculus* petty thief, boil, equiv. to *fūr* thief (cf. FURTIVE) + *-unculus* dim. suffix extracted from derivs. of n-stems; see HOMUNCULUS] —**fu·run·cu·lar** (fyŏŏ-rung′kyə lər), **fu·run′cu·lous,** *adj.*

fu·run·cu·lo·sis (fyŏŏ rung′kyə lō′sis), *n. Pathol.* the condition characterized by the presence of boils. [1885–90; < L *fūruncul(us)* (see FURUNCLE) + -OSIS]

fu·ry (fyŏŏr′ē), *n., pl.* **-ries. 1.** unrestrained or violent anger, rage, passion, or the like: *The gods unleashed their fury on the offending mortal.* **2.** violence; vehemence; fierceness: *the fury of a hurricane; a fury of creative energy.* **3. Furies,** *Class. Myth.* minor female divinities: the daughters of Gaea who punished crimes at the instigation of the victims: known to the Greeks as the Erinyes or Eumenides and to the Romans as the Furiae or Dirae. Originally there were an indefinite number, but were later restricted to Alecto, Megaera, and Tisiphone. **4.** a fierce and violent person, esp. a woman: *She became a fury when she felt she was unjustly accused.* **5. like fury,** *Informal.* violently; intensely: *It rained like fury.* [1325–75; ME < L *furia* rage, equiv. to *fur(ere)* to be angry, rage + *-ia* -Y[2]]
—**Syn. 1.** ire, wrath. See **anger. 2.** turbulence.

furze (fûrz), *n.* gorse. Also called, *esp. Brit.,* **whin.** [bef. 1000; ME *furse, firse,* OE *fyr(e)s;* akin to Russ *pyréĭ* couch grass, Gk *pŷros* wheat, Lith dial. *pūraī* winter wheat]

fu·sain (fyōō zān′, fyōō′zān; *Fr.* fY zaN′), *n., pl.* **-sains** (-zānz′, -zānz; *Fr.* -zaN′) for 2. **1.** a fine charcoal used in drawing, made from the wood of the spindle tree. **2.** a drawing made with this charcoal. **3.** a blackish-gray, friable component of coal with a silky luster that leaves a charcoallike mark. [1865–70; < F: spindle tree, charcoal made from its wood < VL **fūsāgin-* (s. of **fūsāgō*), deriv. of L *fūsus* spindle]

fu·sar·i·um (fyōō zâr′ē əm), *n., pl.* **-sar·i·a** (-zâr′ē ə). any fungus of the genus *Fusarium,* occurring primarily in temperate regions and causing a variety of diseases in plants and animals, producing in humans a loss of fingernails and sometimes blindness. [< NL (1832), equiv. to L *fūs(us)* spindle + *-ārium* -ARY]

fusar′ium wilt′, a disease of plants, characterized by damping-off, wilting, and a brown dry rot, caused by fungi of the genus *Fusarium.*

fus·cous (fus′kəs), *adj.* of brownish-gray or dusky color. [1655–65; < L *fusc(us)* dark, tawny, dusky + -OUS]

fuse[1] (fyōōz), *n., v.,* **fused, fus·ing.** —*n.* **1.** a tube, cord, or the like, filled or saturated with combustible matter, for igniting an explosive. **2.** fuze (def. 1). **3. have a short fuse,** *Informal.* to anger easily; have a quick temper. —*v.t.* **4.** fuze (def. 3). [1635–45; < It *fuso* < L *fūsus* spindle] —**fuse′less,** *adj.* —**fuse′like′,** *adj.*

fuse[2] (fyōōz), *n., v.,* **fused, fus·ing.** —*n.* **1.** *Elect.* a protective device, used in an electric circuit, containing a conductor that melts under heat produced by an excess current, thereby opening the circuit. Cf. **circuit breaker. 2. blow a fuse,** *Informal.* to lose one's temper; become enraged: *If I'm late again, they'll blow a fuse.* —*v.t.* **3.** to combine or blend by melting together; melt. **4.** to unite or blend into a whole, as if by melting together: *The author skillfully fuses these fragments into a cohesive whole.* —*v.i.* **5.** to become liquid under the action of heat; melt: *At a relatively low temperature the metal will fuse.* **6.** to become united or blended: *The two groups fused to create one strong union.* **7.** *Chiefly Brit.* to overload an electric circuit so as to burn out a fuse. [1675–85; < L *fūsus* melted, poured, cast, ptp. of *fundere*]
—**Syn. 3.** See **melt.**

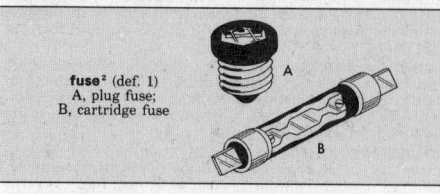

fuse[2] (def. 1)
A, plug fuse;
B, cartridge fuse

fused′ quartz′, glass made entirely from quartz: a form of silica glass. [1920–25]

fused′ sen′tence. See **run-on sentence.**

fused′ sil′ica. See **silica glass.**

fu·see (fyōō zē′), *n.* **1.** a wooden friction match having a large head, formerly used when a larger than normal flame was needed. **2.** a red flare light, used on a railroad as a warning signal to approaching trains. **3.** *Horol.* a spirally grooved, conical pulley and chain arrangement for counteracting the diminishing power of the uncoiling mainspring. **4.** fuse[1] (def. 1). Also, **fuzee.** [1580–90; < MF *fusée* spindleful, deriv. of OF *fus* spindle. See FUSE[1]]

fu·se·lage (fyōō′sə läzh′, -lij, -zə-, fyōō′sə läzh′, -zə-), *n. Aeron.* the complete central structure to which the wing, tail surfaces, and engines are attached on an airplane. [1905–10; < F, equiv. to *fusel(é)* spindle-shaped (deriv. of *fuseau* spindle; see FUSEE) + *-age* -AGE]

Fu·se·li (fyōō′zə lē), *n.* **(John) Henry** (*Johann Heinrich Füssli*), 1741–1825, English painter, illustrator, and essayist; born in Switzerland.

fu′sel oil′ (fyōō′zəl, -səl), a mixture consisting chiefly of amyl alcohols obtained as a by-product in the fermentation of grains. [1855–60; < G *Fusel* bad liquor]

Fu·shih (*Chin.* fōō′shœ′), *n. Wade-Giles.* former name of **Yanan.**

Fu·shun (fY′shYn′), *n. Pinyin, Wade-Giles.* a city in E Liaoning province, in NE China. 1,700,000.

fu·si·bil·i·ty (fyōō′zə bil′i tē), *n.* **1.** the quality of being fusible or convertible from a solid to a liquid state by heat. **2.** the degree to which a substance is fusible. [1615–25; < F *fusibilité.* See FUSIBLE, -ITY]

fu·si·ble (fyōō′zə bəl), *adj.* capable of being fused or melted. [1350–1400; ME < ML *fūsibilis.* See FUSE[2], -IBLE] —**fu′si·ble·ness,** *n.* —**fu′si·bly,** *adv.*

fu′sible met′al, any of various alloys, as of bismuth, lead, and tin, that melt at temperatures as low as 160°F (70°C), making them useful in various safety devices. Also called **fu′sible al′loy.**

fu·si·form (fyōō′zə fôrm′), *adj.* spindle-shaped; rounded and tapering from the middle toward each end, as some roots. [1740–50; < L *fūs(us)* spindle + -I- + -FORM]

fu·sil[1] (fyōō′zəl, -sil), *n.* a light flintlock musket. [1670–80; < F: musket, OF *fuisil, foisil* steel for striking fire < VL **focīlis,* deriv. of L *focus* fire. See FOCUS]

fu·sil[2] (fyōō′zəl, -sil), *adj.* **1.** formed by melting or casting; fused; founded. **2.** *Archaic.* capable of being melted; fusible. **3.** *Archaic.* melted; molten. Also, **fu·sile** (fyōō′zəl, -sil, -sīl). [1350–1400; ME < L *fūsilis* molten, fluid. See FUSE[2], -ILE]

fu·sil·ier (fyōō′zə lēr′), *n.* a member of a British regiment formerly armed with fusils. Also, **fu′si·leer′.** [1670–80; < F; see FUSIL[1], -IER[2]]

fu·sil·lade (fyōō′sə lād′, -läd′, -zə-), *n., v.,* **-lad·ed, -lad·ing.** —*n.* **1.** a simultaneous or continuous discharge of firearms. **2.** a general discharge or outpouring of anything: *a fusillade of questions.* —*v.t.* **3.** to attack or shoot by a fusillade. [1795–1805; < F, equiv. to *fusill(er)* to shoot (see FUSIL[1]) + *-ade* -ADE[1]]

Fu·sin (fōō′sin′), *n. Older Spelling.* Fuxin.

fu·sion (fyōō′zhən), *n.* **1.** the act or process of fusing; the state of being fused. **2.** that which is fused; the result of fusing: *A ballet production is the fusion of many talents.* **3.** *Politics.* **a.** a coalition of parties or factions. **b.** (*cap*) the political party resulting from such a coalition. **4.** Also called **nuclear fusion.** *Physics.* a thermonuclear reaction in which nuclei of light atoms join to form nuclei of heavier atoms, as the combination of deuterium atoms to form helium atoms. Cf. **fission** (def. 2). **5.** *Ophthalm.* **a.** Also called **binocular fusion.** the correct blending of the images of both eyes. **b.** the perception of rapid, intermittent flashes of light as a continuous beam. **6.** popular music that is a blend of two styles, esp. a combining of jazz with either rock, classical music, or such ethnic elements as Brazilian or Japanese music. **7.** *Ling.* the merging of linguistic elements, esp. morphemes, usually accompanied by a change in the form of the elements. [1545–55: < L *fūsiōn-* (s. of *fūsiō*) a pouring out, melting. See FUSE[2], -ION] —**fu′sion·al,** *adj.*

fu′sion bomb′. See **hydrogen bomb.** [1945–50]

fu·sion·ism (fyōō′zhə niz′əm), *n. Politics.* the principle, policy, or practice of fusion. [1850–55; FUSION + -ISM] —**fu′sion·ist,** *n., adj.*

fu′sion reac′tor, *Physics.* a reactor for producing atomic energy by nuclear fusion. Cf. **reactor** (def. 4).

fu·so·bac·te·ri·um (fyōō′zō bak tēr′ē əm), *n., pl.* **-te·ri·a** (-tēr′ē ə). any of several rod-shaped, anaerobic bacteria of the genus *Fusobacterium,* certain species of which are pathogenic in humans. [< NL (1922), equiv. to L *fūs(us)* spindle + NL *-o-* -O- + *bacterium* BACTERIUM]

fuss (fus), *n.* **1.** an excessive display of anxious attention or activity; needless or useless bustle: *They made a fuss over the new baby.* **2.** an argument or noisy dispute: *They had a fuss about who should wash dishes.* **3.** a complaint or protest, esp. about something relatively unimportant. —*v.i.* **4.** to make a fuss; make much ado about trifles: *You'll never finish the job if you fuss over details.* **5.** to complain esp. about something relatively unimportant. —*v.t.* **6.** to disturb, esp. with trifles; annoy; bother. [1695–1705; orig. uncert.] —**fuss′er,** *n.*
—**Syn. 1.** pother, to-do, stir, commotion. **6.** pester.
—**Ant. 1.** inactivity.

fuss′ and feath′ers, an excessively elaborate or pretentious display; ostentation. [1890–95]

fuss·box (fus′boks′), *n. South Atlantic States.* a fussbudget. [FUSS + BOX[1]]

fuss·budg·et (fus′buj′it), *n.* a fussy or needlessly fault-finding person. [1900–05, *Amer.;* FUSS + BUDGET] —**fuss′budg′et·y,** *adj.*

fuss·pot (fus′pot′), *n. New England and New York.* a fussbudget. [FUSS + POT[1]]

fuss·y (fus′ē), *adj.,* **fuss·i·er, fuss·i·est. 1.** excessively busy with trifles; anxious or particular about petty details. **2.** hard to satisfy or please: *a fussy eater.* **3.** (of clothes, decoration, etc.) elaborately made, trimmed, or decorated: *All the bric-a-brac gave the room a fussy, cluttered look.* **4.** full of details, esp. in excess: *His writing is so fussy I lose the thread of the story.* [1825–35; FUSS + -Y[1]] —**fuss′i·ly,** *adv.* —**fuss′i·ness,** *n.*
—**Syn. 2.** particular, choosy, finicky, persnickety.

fus·ta·nel·la (fus′tə nel′ə, fōō′stə-), *n.* a short stiff skirt, usually pleated, made of white cotton or linen, worn by men in some parts of the Balkans. Also, **fustinella.** [1840–50; < It < ModGk *phoustanélla,* dim. of *phoustáni* woman's dress < It *fustagno* FUSTIAN]

fus·tet (fu stet′), *n.* **1.** the smoke tree, *Cotinus coggygria.* **2.** Also called **young fustic.** the dyewood of this tree. [1815–25; < F < Pr < Sp *fustete,* by assoc. with *fuste* stick. See FUSTIC]

fus·tian (fus′chən), *n.* **1.** a stout fabric of cotton and flax. **2.** a fabric of stout twilled cotton or of cotton and low-quality wool, with a short nap or pile. **3.** inflated or turgid language in writing or speaking: *Fustian can't disguise the author's meager plot.* —*adj.* **4.** made of fustian: *a fustian coat; fustian bed linen.* **5.** pompous or bombastic, as language: *fustian melodrama.* **6.** worthless; cheap: *fustian knaves and dupes.* [1150–1200; ME < OF *fustaigne* < ML *fūstāneum,* perh. a deriv. of L *fūstis* stick, cudgel (LL: trunk; cf. FUSTY), if a trans. of L *xylinus,* Gk (Septuagint) *xýlina lína* cotton, lit., linen from wood; *Fostat,* a suburb of Cairo, has also been proposed as the source of *fūstāneum*]
—**Syn. 3.** bombast, rant, claptrap.

fus·tic (fus′tik), *n.* **1.** the wood of a large, tropical American tree, *Chlorophora tinctoria,* of the mulberry family, yielding a light-yellow dye. **2.** the tree itself. **3.** the dye. **4.** any of several other dyewoods. Also called **old fustic** (for defs. 1–3). [1425–75; late ME *fustik* < MF *fustoc* < Ar *fustuq* < Pers *pistah;* akin to Gk *pistákē* pistachio tree]

fus·ti·gate (fus′ti gāt′), *v.t.,* **-gat·ed, -gat·ing. 1.** to cudgel; beat; punish severely. **2.** to criticize harshly; castigate: *a new satire that fustigates bureaucratic shilly-shallying.* [1650–60; < LL *fūstīgātus,* ptp. of *fūstīgāre* to cudgel, deriv. of L *fūstis* cudgel; for formation, see FUMIGATE] —**fus′ti·ga′tion,** *n.* —**fus′ti·ga′tor,** *n.* —**fus·ti·ga·to·ry** (fus′ti gə tôr′ē, -tōr′ē), *adj.*

fus·ti·nel·la (fus′tə nel′ə, fōō′stə-), *n.* fustanella.

fus·ty (fus′tē), *adj.,* **-ti·er, -ti·est. 1.** having a stale smell; moldy; musty: *fusty rooms that were in need of a good airing.* **2.** old-fashioned or out-of-date, as architecture, furnishings, or the like: *They still live in that fusty, gingerbread house.* **3.** stubbornly conservative or old-fashioned; fogyish. [1350–1400; ME *fusti,* equiv. to *fust* (n.) < OF: wine cask, tree trunk (< L *fūstis* stick, pole) + -Y[1]] —**fus′ti·ly,** *adv.* —**fus′ti·ness,** *n.*
—**Syn. 1.** close, stuffy, oppressive; smelly, malodorous.

fu·su·la (fyōō′zə lə), *n., pl.* **-lae** (-lē′), **-las.** (in the spinneret of a spider) the terminal tube of a silk gland. [1905–10; < NL; see FUSE[1], -ULE]

fu·su·ma (fyōō′sə mä′), *n.* a sliding door in a Japanese house, esp. one serving as a room partition. [1875–80; < Japn]

fut., future.

Fu·ta·ba·tei (fōō tä′bä tā′), *n.* **Shi·mei** (shē mā′), (*Tatsunosuke Hasegawa*), 1864–1909, Japanese author.

fu·thark (fōō′thärk), *n.* the runic alphabet. Also, **fu′·tharc, fu·thorc, fu·thork** (fōō′thôrk). [1850–55; so called from first six letters of OE and Scand runic alphabet: *f, u, th, a* (or *o*), *r, k* (modeled on ALPHABET)]

fu·tile (fyōōt′l, fyōō′tīl), *adj.* **1.** incapable of producing any result; ineffective; useless; not successful: *Attempting to force-feed the sick horse was futile.* **2.** trifling; frivolous; unimportant. [1545–55; < L *fūtilis, futtilis* easily broken, vain, worthless, equiv. to *fūt-* (akin to *fundere* to pour, melt) + *-ilis* -ILE] —**fu′tile·ly,** *adv.* —**fu′tile·ness,** *n.*
—**Syn. 1.** See **useless.**

fu·til·i·tar·i·an (fyōō til′i târ′ē ən), *adj.* **1.** believing that human hopes are vain, and human strivings unjustified. —*n.* **2.** a person who holds this belief. [1820–30; humorous b. FUTILE and UTILITARIAN] —**fu·til′i·tar′i·an·ism,** *n.*

fu·til·i·ty (fyōō til′i tē), *n., pl.* **-ties** for 2, 3. **1.** the quality of being futile; ineffectiveness; uselessness. **2.** a trifle or frivolity: *the large collection of futilities that clutter our minds.* **3.** a futile act or event. [1615–25; < L *fūtilitās.* See FUTILE, -ITY]

CONCISE ETYMOLOGY KEY: <, descended or borrowed from; >, whence; b., blend of, blended; c., cognate with; cf., compare; deriv., derivative; equiv., equivalent; imit., imitative; obl., oblique; r., replacing; s., stem; sp., spelling, spelled; resp., respelling, respelled; trans., translation; ?, origin unknown; *, unattested; ‡, probably earlier than. See the full key inside the front cover.

fu•ton (fo͞o′ton, fyo͞o′-), *n.* a thin mattress, usually filled with layers of cotton batting and encased in cotton fabric, placed on a floor for sleeping, esp. in traditional Japanese interiors, and folded and stored during the day. Also called **shikibuton.** [1875–80; < Japn < MChin, equiv. to Chin *pùtuán* rush-mat seat]

fut•tock (fut′ək), *n. Naut.* any of a number of timbers forming the lower, more curved portion of the frame in a wooden hull. [1605–15; perh. alter. of *foothook*]

fut′tock band′, *Naut.* a metal band around a lower mast somewhat below the top, for holding the lower ends of a futtock shroud. Also called **fut′tock hoop′, fut′tock wye′** (wī), **spider band.**

fut′tock shroud′, *Naut.* any of several metal rods secured at their lower ends to a futtock band and at their upper ends to a futtock plate, connecting the lower mast to the topmast rigging. [1830–40]

fu•tu•ram•a (fyo͞o′chə ram′ə, -rä′mə), *n.* **1.** an exhibition or display that attempts to depict certain aspects or elements of life in the future. **2.** a comprehensive projection of the future. [after *Futurama* (see FUTURE, -AMA), name of an exhibit at the New York World's Fair (1939)] —**fu•tu•ram•ic** (fyo͞o′chə ram′ik), *adj.*

fu•ture (fyo͞o′chər), *n.* **1.** time that is to be or come hereafter. **2.** something that will exist or happen in time to come: *The future is rooted in the past.* **3.** a condition, esp. of success or failure, to come: *Some people believe a gypsy can tell you your future.* **4.** *Gram.* **a.** the future tense. **b.** another future formation or construction. **c.** a form in the future, as *He will come.* **5.** Usually, **futures.** speculative purchases or sales of commodities for future receipt or delivery. —*adj.* **6.** that is to be or come hereafter: *future events; on some future day.* **7.** pertaining to or connected with time to come: *one's future prospects; future plans.* **8.** *Gram.* noting or pertaining to a tense or other verb formation or construction that refers to events or states in time to come. [1325–75; ME *futur* AF, OF < L *fūtūrus* about to be (fut. participle of *esse* to be)]

Fu′ture Farm′er, a member of the Future Farmers of America.

Fu′ture Farm′ers of Amer′ica, a national organization of high-school students studying vocational agriculture. *Abbr.:* FFA

fu′ture in′terests, *Law.* interests in personal or real property, the possession and enjoyment of which are to commence at a later date.

fu•ture•less (fyo͞o′chər lis), *adj.* without a future; having no prospect of future betterment or prosperity. [1860–65; FUTURE + -LESS]

fu′ture life′, afterlife (def. 1). [1770–80]

fu′ture per′fect, *Gram.* **1.** perfect with respect to a temporal point of reference in time to come; completed with respect to a time in the future, esp. when incomplete with respect to the present. **2.** noting or pertaining to a tense or other verb formation or construction with such reference. **3.** the future perfect tense. **4.** another verb formation or construction with future perfect meaning. **5.** a form in the future perfect, as *He will have come.* [1895–1900]

fu′ture shock′, **1.** physical and psychological disturbance caused by a person's inability to cope with very rapid social and technological change. **2.** any overload of a person's or an organization's capacity for adaptation or decision making. [on the model of CULTURE SHOCK; popularized by a book of the same title (1970) by Alvin Toffler (b. 1928), U.S. journalist]

fu′tures mar′ket, a market in which futures contracts in commodities are traded.

fu•tur•ism (fyo͞o′chə riz′əm), *n.* **1.** (*sometimes cap.*) a style of the fine arts developed originally by a group of Italian artists about 1910 in which forms derived chiefly from cubism were used to represent rapid movement and dynamic motion. **2.** (*often cap.*) a style of art, literature, music, etc., and a theory of art and life in which violence, power, speed, mechanization or machines, and hostility to the past or to traditional forms of expression were advocated or portrayed. [1905–10; < It *futurismo.* See FUTURE, -ISM]

fu•tur•ist (fyo͞o′chər ist), *n.* **1.** (*sometimes cap.*) a follower of futurism, esp. an artist or writer. **2.** *Theol.* a person who maintains that the prophecies in the Apocalypse will be fulfilled in the future. Cf. **presentist, preterist. 3.** Also, **fu′tur•ol′o•gist.** a person whose occupation or specialty is the forecasting of future events, conditions, or developments. —*adj.* **4.** futuristic. [1835–45; < It *futurista.* See FUTURE, -IST]

fu•tur•is•tic (fyo͞o′chə ris′tik), *adj.* **1.** of or pertaining to the future: *a futuristic view of the world.* **2.** ahead of the times; advanced: *futuristic technology.* **3.** (*sometimes cap.*) of or pertaining to futurism: *the futuristic rejection of traditional forms.* [1910–15; FUTURE + -ISTIC] —**fu′tur•is′ti•cal•ly,** *adv.*

fu•tu•ri•ty (fyo͞o to͝or′i tē, -tyo͝or′-, -cho͝or′-, -chûr′-), *n., pl.* **-ties. 1.** future time: *Such discussion is better left to futurity.* **2.** future generations; posterity: *What will futurity say about this?* **3.** the afterlife: *the promise of eternal rest in futurity.* **4.** a future state or condition; a future event, possibility, or prospect: *We are concerned about the futurity of unsubsidized opera. His tactfulness remains more of a futurity than a reality.* **5.** the quality of being future: *the futurity of the end of the world.* **6.** Also called **futu′rity race′.** *Horse Racing.* a race, usually for two-year-olds, in which the entrants are selected long before the race is run, sometimes before the birth of the foal. [1595–1605; FUTURE + -ITY]

fu•tur•ol•o•gy (fyo͞o′chə rol′ə jē), *n.* the study or forecasting of trends or developments in science, technology, political or social structure, etc. [1945–50; FUTURE + -O- + -LOGY] —**fu•tur•o•log•i•cal** (fyo͞o′chər ə loj′i kəl), *adj.*

futz (futs), *Slang.* —*v.i.* **1.** to pass time in idleness (usually fol. by *around*). **2. futz with** or **around with,** to handle or deal with, esp. idly, reluctantly, or as a time-consuming task: *I spent all day futzing with those file folders.* —*n.* **3.** a fool; simpleton. [1930–35, *Amer.*; appar. a euphemism for FUCK; perh. b. this word and PUTZ]

Fu•xin (fy′shin′), *n. Pinyin.* a city in central Liaoning province, in NE China. 188,600. Also, **Fusin.**

fuze (fyo͞oz), *n., v.,* **fuzed, fuz•ing.** —*n.* **1.** a mechanical or electronic device to detonate an explosive charge, esp. as contained in an artillery shell, a missile, projectile, or the like. **2.** fuse[1] (def. 1). —*v.t.* **3.** Also, **fuse.** to attach a fuse or fuze to (a bomb, mine, etc.). [1635–45; var. of FUSE[1]]

fu•zee (fyo͞o zē′), *n.* fusee.

Fu•zhou (fy′jō′), *n. Pinyin.* a seaport in and the capital of Fujian province, in SE China, opposite Taiwan. 900,000. Also, **Foochow.** Formerly, **Minhow.**

fuzz[1] (fuz), *n.* **1.** loose, light, fibrous, or fluffy matter. **2.** a mass or coating of such matter: *the fuzz on a peach.* **3.** *Slang.* a man's very short haircut, similar to a crew cut. —*v.t.* **4. fuzz up,** to make unclear; confuse; bungle: *He fuzzed up the plot line with a lot of emotional nonsense.* [1595–1605; cf. D *voos* spongy, woolly]

fuzz[2] (fuz), *n., pl.* **fuzz, fuzz•es** for 2. *Slang.* **1.** the police; police officers collectively. **2.** a police officer or detective. [1925–30; of uncert. orig.]

fuzz•ball (fuz′bôl′), *n.* a puffball. [FUZZ[1] + BALL[1]]

Fuzz•bust•er (fuz′bus′tər), *Trademark.* a brand name for an electronic device that alerts the driver of an automobile to the presence of radar units used by police to measure vehicle speed.

fuzz′ tone′, a distorted, blurred effect produced electrically in the sound of an electric guitar by increased vibrations or added overtones. [1965–70]

fuzz•y (fuz′ē), *adj.,* **fuzz•i•er, fuzz•i•est. 1.** of the nature of or resembling fuzz: *a soft, fuzzy material.* **2.** covered with fuzz: *a plant with broad, fuzzy leaves.* **3.** indistinct; blurred: *A fuzzy photograph usually means you jiggled the camera.* **4.** muddleheaded or incoherent: *a fuzzy thinker; to become fuzzy after one drink.* [1590–1600; FUZZ[1] + -Y[1]] —**fuzz′i•ly,** *adv.* —**fuzz′i•ness,** *n.*
—**Syn. 3.** hazy, vague, unclear, foggy.

fuzz•y-head•ed (fuz′ē hed′id), *adj.* **1.** not given to clear thinking; foolish. **2.** giddy; light-headed.

fuzz′y set′, *Math.* a generalization of a classical set with the property that each member of a population of objects has associated with it a number, usually from 0 to 1, that indicates the degree to which the object belongs to the set. [1960–65]

f.v., on the back of the page. [< L *foliō versō*]

f value. See **f number.**

FVC, *Med.* forced vital capacity. Cf. **vital capacity.**

f.w., fresh water.

FWA, Federal Works Agency.

fwd., 1. foreword **2.** forward.

FX, foreign exchange.

fx., 1. fracture. **2.** fractured.

FY, fiscal year.

-fy, a verbal suffix meaning "to make," "cause to be," "render" (*simplify; beautify*); "to become," "be made" (*liquefy*). The suffix was introduced into English in loan words from Old French (*deify*), but is also used in the formation of new words, usually on a Latin root (*reify*). [< OF *-fier* << L *-ficāre* to do, make]

fyce (fīs), *n.* feist.

FYI, for your information.

fyke (fīk), *n. Hudson and Delaware Valleys.* a bag-shaped fish trap. [1825–35, *Amer.*; < D *fuik,* MD *fuycke;* c. OFris *fūcke*]

fyl•fot (fil′fot), *n.* a swastika. [1490–1500; var. of *fill-foot* foot filler]

Fyn (fyn), *n.* an island in S Denmark. 446,233; 1149 sq. mi. (2975 sq. km). German, **Fünen.**

fyrd (fûrd), *n.* **1.** the militia in Anglo-Saxon England. **2.** the duty to serve in this militia. [< OE *fyrd, fierd,* akin to *faran* to go, FARE]

fytte (fit), *n.* fit[3].

F.Z.S., Fellow of the Zoological Society, London. Also, **F.Z.S.L.**

CONCISE PRONUNCIATION KEY: *act, cāpe, dâre, pärt; set, ēqual; if, īce; ox, ōver, ôrder, oil, bo͝ok, bo͞ot, out; up, ûrge; child; sing; shoe; thin, that;* zh as in *treasure.* ə = *a* as in *alone, e* as in *system, i* as in *easily, o* as in *gallop, u* as in *circus;* ᵊ as in *fire* (fīᵊr), *hour* (ouᵊr). l and n can serve as syllabic consonants, as in *cradle* (krād′l), and *button* (but′n). See the full key inside the front cover.

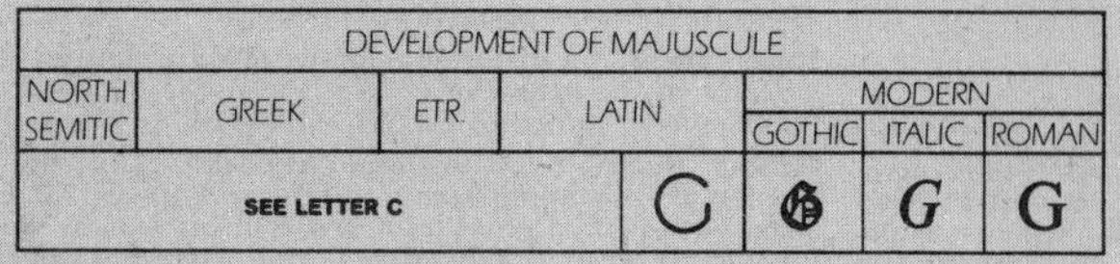

DEVELOPMENT OF MAJUSCULE
NORTH SEMITIC
GREEK
ETR.
LATIN
MODERN
GOTHIC
ITALIC
ROMAN
SEE LETTER C

DEVELOPMENT OF MINUSCULE					
ROMAN CURSIVE	ROMAN UNCIAL	CAROL. MIN.	MODERN		
			GOTHIC	ITALIC	ROMAN

The seventh letter of the English alphabet developed from North Semitic *ghimel* and Greek *gamma* (see **C**). The Etruscans, having no meaningful distinction between the *g*-sound and the *k*-sound in their language, used this symbol for both. When the distinction again had to be made in Latin, the small stroke was added to the lower curve of the C. The minuscule (g) is a scribal variant of the capital.

G, g (jē), *n., pl.* **G's** or **Gs, g's** or **gs. 1.** the seventh letter of the English alphabet, a consonant. **2.** any spoken sound represented by the letter *G* or *g*, as in *get, German*, or *camouflage*. **3.** something having the shape of a G. **4.** a written or printed representation of the letter *G* or *g*. **5.** a device, as a printer's type, for reproducing the letter *G* or *g*.

G, *pl.* **Gs** or **G's. 1.** *Slang.* grand: a sum of one thousand dollars. **2.** (*sometimes l.c.*) *Aerospace.* gravity: a unit of acceleration equal to the acceleration of gravity at the earth's surface.

G, 1. gay. **2.** *Psychol.* general intelligence. **3.** German. **4.** good.

G, *Symbol.* **1.** the seventh in order or in a series. **2.** *Music.* **a.** the fifth tone in the scale of C major or the seventh tone in the relative minor scale, A minor. **b.** a string, key, or pipe tuned to this tone. **c.** a written or printed note representing this tone. **d.** (in the fixed system of solmization) the fifth tone of the scale of C major, called *sol*. **e.** the tonality having G as the tonic note. **3.** (*sometimes l.c.*) the medieval Roman numeral for 400. Cf. **Roman numerals. 4.** *Elect.* **a.** conductance. **b.** gauss. **5.** *Physics.* constant of gravitation. See under **law of gravity. 6.** *Biochem.* **a.** glycine. **b.** guanine. **7.** general: a rating assigned to a motion picture by the Motion Picture Association of America indicating that the film is suitable for general audiences, or children as well as adults. Cf. **PG, PG-13, R** (def. 5), **X** (def. 8).

g, 1. *Psychol.* general intelligence. **2.** good. **3.** gram; grams. **4.** *Electronics.* grid.

g, *Symbol, Physics.* **1.** See **acceleration of gravity. 2.** gravity (def. 5).

G., 1. German. **2.** gourde; gourdes. **3.** (specific) gravity. **4.** Gulf.

g., 1. gauge. **2.** gender. **3.** general. **4.** generally. **5.** genitive. **6.** going back to. **7.** gold. **8.** grain; grains. **9.** gram; grams. **10.** *Football.* guard. **11.** *Brit.* guinea. **12.** gun.

Ga (gä), *n.* a Kwa language of Ghana, spoken in Accra and vicinity.

GA, 1. Gamblers Anonymous. **2.** See **General American. 3.** general of the army. **4.** Georgia (approved esp. for use with zip code).

Ga, *Symbol, Chem.* gallium.

Ga., Georgia.

G.A., 1. General Agent. **2.** General Assembly. **3.** Also, **g.a., G/A** *Insurance.* general average.

gab[1] (gab), *v.,* **gabbed, gab•bing,** *n. Informal.* —*v.i.* **1.** to talk or chat idly; chatter. —*n.* **2.** idle talk; chatter. [1780–90; appar. expressive var. of GOB[4]; cf. GABBLE] —**gab′ber,** *n.*
—**Syn. 1.** chitchat, gossip, visit; yak, rap, schmooze.

gab[2] (gab), *n. Mach.* a hook or fork that engages temporarily with a moving rod or lever. [prob. < D dial. *gabbe* notch, gash]

gab[3] (gab), *n. Scot. Slang.* gob[3].

GABA (gab′ə), *n. Biochem.* a neurotransmitter of the central nervous system that inhibits excitatory responses. [G(AMMA-)A(MINO)B(UTYRIC) A(CID)]

Gab•a•on (gab′ā ən), *n. Douay Bible.* Gibeon.

Gab•a•on•ite (gab′ā ə nīt′), *n. Douay Bible.* Gibeonite.

Ga•bar (gä′bər), *n.* an Iranian Zoroastrian. Also, **Gheber.** [< Pers < Ar *kāfir;* see KAFFIR]

gab•ar•dine (gab′ər dēn′, gab′ər dēn′), *n.* **1.** Also, **gaberdine.** a firm, tightly woven fabric of worsted, cotton, polyester, or other fiber, with a twill weave. **2.** gaberdine (def. 1). [sp. var. of GABERDINE]

Gab•bai (*Seph.* gä bī′; *Ashk.* gä′bī; *Eng.* gə bī′), *n., pl.* **Gab•ba•im** (*Seph.* gä bä ēm′; *Ashk.* gä bī′im), *Eng.* **Gab•bais.** (*sometimes l.c.*) *Hebrew.* **1.** a minor official of a synagogue, having limited ceremonial or administrative functions. **2.** (in the early Middle Ages) a government official charged with collecting taxes. [lit., treasurer]

gab•ble (gab′əl), *v.,* **-bled, -bling,** *n.* —*v.i.* **1.** to speak or converse rapidly and unintelligibly; jabber. **2.** (of hens, geese, etc.) to cackle. —*v.t.* **3.** to utter rapidly and unintelligibly. —*n.* **4.** rapid, unintelligible talk. **5.** any quick succession of meaningless sounds. [1570–80; perh. < MD *gabbelen,* or expressive formation in E; cf. GAB[1], GOB[4], -LE] —**gab′bler,** *n.*

gab•bro (gab′rō), *n., pl.* **-bros.** *Petrol.* a dark granular igneous rock composed essentially of labradorite and augite. [< It; akin to L *glaber* smooth] —**gab•bro•ic** (gə brō′ik), **gab′bro•it′ic,** *adj.* —**gab•broid** (gab′roid), *adj.*

gab•by (gab′ē), *adj.* **-bi•er, -bi•est.** talkative; garrulous. [1710–20; GAB[1] + -Y[1]] —**gab′bi•ness,** *n.*

Gab•by (gab′ē), *n.* **1.** a male given name, form of **Gabriel. 2.** a female given name, form of **Gabriella.**

Gabe (gāb), *n.* a male given name, form of **Gabriel.**

ga•belle (gə bel′), *n.* **1.** a tax; excise. **2.** *Fr. Hist.* a tax on salt, abolished in 1790. [1375–1425; ME *gabul, gabel* (prob. confused with GAVEL[2]) < MF < It *gabella* < Ar *gabālah* tax, receipt] —**ga•belled′,** *adj.*

gab•er•dine (gab′ər dēn′, gab′ər dēn′), *n.* **1.** Also, **gabardine.** a long, loose coat or frock for men, worn in the Middle Ages, esp. by Jews. **2.** gabardine (def. 1). [1510–20; < MF *gauvardine, gallevardine* < Sp *gabardina,* perh. a conflation of *gabán* (<< Ar *qabā* men's overgarment) and *tabardina,* dim. of *tabardo* TABARD]

Ga•be•ro•nes (gä′bə rō′nes, gab′ə-), *n.* former name of **Gaborone.**

Ga•bès (gä′bes), *n.* **Gulf of,** a gulf of the Mediterranean on the E coast of Tunisia.

gab•fest (gab′fest′), *n. Informal.* **1.** a gathering at which there is a great deal of conversation. **2.** a long conversation. [1895–1900, *Amer.;* GAB[1] + -FEST]

ga•bi•on (gā′bē ən), *n.* **1.** a cylinder of wickerwork filled with earth, used as a military defense. **2.** a metal cylinder filled with stones and sunk in water, used in laying the foundations of a dam or jetty. [1570–80; < MF: rough, two-handled basket < It *gabbione,* aug. of *gabbia* cage < L *cavea* cavity, cage]

ga•ble (gā′bəl), *n. Archit.* **1.** the portion of the front or side of a building enclosed by or masking the end of a pitched roof. **2.** a decorative member suggesting a gable, used esp. in Gothic architecture. **3.** Also called **ga′ble wall′.** a wall bearing a gable. [1325–75; ME < OF (of Gmc orig.); c. ON *gafl;* cf. OE *gafol, geafel* a fork] —**ga′ble•like′,** *adj.*

gable (def. 1)

Ga•ble (gā′bəl), *n.* **(William) Clark,** 1901–60, U.S. film actor.

ga•bled (gā′bəld), *adj.* **1.** provided with a gable or gables: *a gabled house.* **2.** built with a gable or gables. [1840–50; GABLE + -ED[3]]

ga′ble end′, an end wall bearing a gable. [1300–50; ME] —**ga′ble-end′ed,** *adj.*

ga′ble roof′, a roof sloping downward in two parts at an angle from a central ridge, so as to leave a gable at each end. See illus. at **roof.** [1840–50] —**ga′ble-roofed′,** *adj.*

ga′ble win′dow, a window in or under a gable. [1300–50; ME] —**ga′ble-win′dowed,** *adj.*

Ga•bo (gä′bə, -bō), *n.* **Naum** (noum), (*Naum Pevsner*), 1890–1977, U.S. sculptor, born in Russia (brother of Antoine Pevsner).

Ga•bon (gA bôN′), *n.* **1.** Official name, **Gab′onese Repub′lic.** a republic in W equatorial Africa: formerly a part of French Equatorial Africa; member of the French Community. 950,000; 102,290 sq. mi. (264,931 sq. km). *Cap.:* Libreville. **2.** an estuary in W Gabon. ab. 40 mi. (65 km) long. Also, **Gabun.**

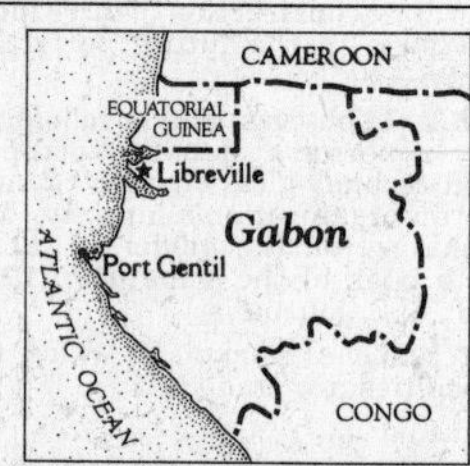

Gab•o•nese (gab′ə nēz′, -nēs′, gä′bə-), *adj., n., pl.* **-nese.** —*adj.* **1.** of or pertaining to Gabon or its inhabitants. —*n.* **2.** an inhabitant or native of Gabon. [GABON + -ESE]

ga•boon (gə bo͞on′, ga-, gä-), *n.* **1.** Also called **gaboon′ mahog′any.** the soft, reddish-brown wood of an African tree, *Aucoumea klaineana,* used for making furniture. **2.** the tree itself. Also called **okoume.** [1910–15; var. of GABON]

gaboon′ vi′per, a large, venomous snake, *Bitis gabonica,* of tropical African forests, having large retractable fangs and geometrically patterned scales of yellow, brown, and sometimes purple. [1925–30]

Ga•bor (gä′bôr, gə bôr′), *n.* **Dennis,** 1900–79, British physicist, born in Hungary: inventor of holography; Nobel prize 1971.

Ga•bo•riau (gA bô RYŌ′), *n.* **É•mile** (ā mēl′), 1835–73, French author of detective stories.

Ga•bo•ro•ne (gä′bə rō′nē, gab′ə-), *n.* a town in and the capital of Botswana, in the SE part. 59,700. Formerly, **Gaberones.**

Ga•bri•el (gā′brē əl), *n.* **1.** one of the archangels, appearing usually as a divine messenger. Dan. 8:16, 9:21; Luke 1:19, 26. **2.** *Islam.* the angel of revelation and the intermediary between God and Muhammad. **3.** a male given name.

Ga•bri•e•li (gä′brē el′ē, gab′rē-; *It.* gä′bRē e′lē), *n.* **1.** **An•dre•a** (än drā′ə; *It.* än dRe′ä), 1510–86, Italian organist and composer. **2.** his nephew, **Gio•van•ni** (jō vä′nē, jē′ə-; *It.* jô vän′nē), 1557–1612, Italian organist and composer. Also, **Ga•bri•el•li** (gä′brē el′ē, gab′rē-; *It.* gä′bRē el′lē).

Ga•bri•el•la (gā′brē el′ə, gab′rē-), *n.* a female given name. Also, **Ga′bri•el′a, Ga•bri•elle** (gā′brē el′, gab′rē-; *Fr.* gA bRē el′).

Ga•bri•lo•witsch (gä′bri luv′ich; *Russ.* gə bRyi lô′vyich), *n.* **Os•sip** (ô′syip), 1878–1936, Russian pianist and conductor, in America.

Ga•bun (gə bo͞on′), *n.* Gabon.

CONCISE ETYMOLOGY KEY: <, descended or borrowed from; >, whence; b., blend of, blended; c., cognate with; cf., compare; deriv., derivative; equiv., equivalent; imit., imitative; obl., oblique; r., replacing; s., stem; sp., spelling, spelled; resp., respelling, respelled; trans., translation; ?, origin unknown; *, unattested; ‡, probably earlier than. See the full key inside the front cover.

ga•by (gā′bē), *n., pl.* **-bies.** *Brit. Dial.* a fool. [1790–1800; orig. uncert.]

Gab•y (gab′ē), *n.* a female given name, form of **Gabriella.**

G/A con., *Insurance.* general average contribution.

gad[1] (gad), *v.,* **gad•ded, gad•ding,** *n.* —*v.i.* **1.** to move restlessly or aimlessly from one place to another: *to gad about.* —*n.* **2.** the act of gadding. [1425–75; late ME *gadden,* perh. back formation from *gadeling* companion in arms, fellow (in 16th century, vagabond, wanderer), OE *gædeling,* deriv. of *gæd* fellowship; see GATHER, -LING[1]] —**gad′der,** *n.* —**gad′ding•ly,** *adv.*

gad[2] (gad), *n.* **1.** a goad for driving cattle. **2.** a pointed mining tool for breaking up rock, coal, etc. [1175–1225; ME < ON *gaddr* spike; c. Goth *gazds*]

Gad (gad), *interj.* (used as a mild oath.) Also, **gad.** [1600–10; euphemism for GOD]

Gad (gad), *n.* **1.** a son of Zilpah. Gen. 30:11. **2.** one of the twelve tribes of Israel, traditionally descended from him. **3.** a Hebrew prophet and chronicler of the court of David. II Sam. 24:11–19.

gad•a•bout (gad′ə bout′), *n.* **1.** a person who moves about restlessly or aimlessly, esp. from one social activity to another. **2.** a person who travels often or to many different places, esp. for pleasure. [1810–20; n. use of v. phrase *gad about*]

Gad•da•fi (gə dä′fē), *n.* **Mu•am•mar (Muhammad), al-** or **el-,** (mo͞o äm′är al, el), Qadhafi.

Gad•di (gäd′dē), *n.* **Tad•de•o** (täd de′ô), 1300–66, Italian painter and architect.

G/A dep., *Insurance.* general average deposit.

gad•fly (gad′flī′), *n., pl.* **-flies. 1.** any of various flies, as a stable fly or warble fly, that bite or annoy domestic animals. **2.** a person who persistently annoys or provokes others with criticism, schemes, ideas, demands, requests, etc. [1585–95; GAD[2] + FLY[2]]

gadg•et (gaj′it), *n.* a mechanical contrivance or device; any ingenious article. [1850–55; orig. uncert.; cf. F *gâchette* the catch of a lock, sear of a gunlock] —**gadg•et•y** (gaj′i tē), *adj.*
—**Syn.** contraption; whatsis, doohickey, thingamajig.

gadg•e•teer (gaj′i tēr′), *n.* a person who invents or particularly likes using gadgets. [1935–40; GADGET + -EER]

gadg•et•ry (gaj′i trē), *n.* mechanical or electronic contrivances; gadgets: *the gadgetry of the well-equipped modern kitchen.* [1915–20; GADGET + -RY]

Ga•dhel•ic (gə del′ik), *adj., n.* Goidelic.

ga•did (gā′did), *adj.* **1.** belonging or pertaining to the cod family, Gadidae. —*n.* **2.** a gadid fish. Also, **ga•doid** (gā′doid). [1885–90; < NL *Gadidae,* equiv. to *Gad(us)* the cod genus (< Gk *gádos* a kind of fish) + *-idae* -ID[2]]

Gad•ite (gad′it), *n.* a member of the tribe of Gad. [GAD + -ITE[1]]

ga•doid (gā′doid), *adj., n.* gadid. [1835–45; < NL *Gad(us)* (see GADID) + -OID]

gad•o•lin•ite (gad′l ə nīt′), *n.* a silicate mineral from which the rare-earth metals gadolinium, holmium, and rhenium are extracted. [1795–1805; named after J. *Gadolin* (1760–1852), Finnish chemist; see -ITE[1]]

gad•o•lin•i•um (gad′l in′ē əm), *n. Chem.* a rare-earth metallic element. *Symbol:* Gd; *at. wt.:* 157.25; *at. no.:* 64. [1885–90; see GADOLINITE, -IUM] —**gad′o•lin′ic,** *adj.*

ga•droon (gə dro͞on′), *n.* **1.** *Archit.* an elaborately carved or indented convex molding. **2.** a decorative series of curved, inverted flutings, or of convex and concave flutings, as on silversmith's work. Also, **godroon.** [1715–25; < F *godron* (with final conformed to -OON), MF *goderon,* prob. deriv. of *godet* a kind of cup without base or handle (perh. < MD *kodde* billet, log; see -ET), after the ornamentation on such cups] —**ga•drooned′,** *adj.* —**ga•droon′age,** *n.*

ga•droon•ing (gə dro͞o′ning), *n.* ornamentation with gadroons. [1880–85; GADROON + -ING[1]]

Gads•bod•i•kins (gadz′bod′i kinz), *interj. Archaic.* (a euphemistic form of *God's body,* used as a mild oath.) Also, **Oddsbodikins, Odsbodikins, Odsbodkins.** [1670–80; GAD + -'s[1] + *bodikin* (BODY + -KIN) + -S[1]]

Gads•den (gadz′dən), *n.* **1. James,** 1788–1858, U.S. railroad promoter and diplomat. **2.** a city in NE Alabama. 47,565.

Gads′den Pur′chase, a tract of 45,535 sq. mi. (117,935 sq. km), now contained in New Mexico and Arizona, purchased for $10,000,000 from Mexico in 1853, the treaty being negotiated by James Gadsden.

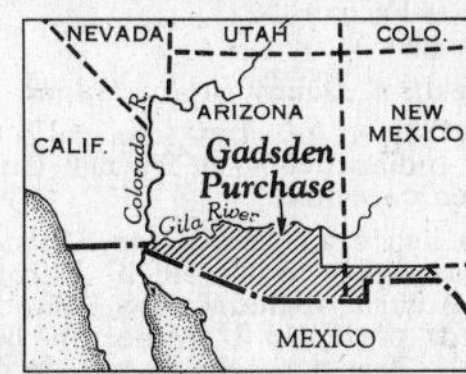

gad•wall (gad′wôl′), *n., pl.* **-walls,** (*esp. collectively*) **-wall.** a grayish-brown wild duck, *Anas strepera,* found in temperate parts of the Northern Hemisphere. [1660–70; orig. uncert.]

Gad•zooks (gad′zo͝oks′), *interj. Archaic.* (used as a mild oath.) Also, **Odzooks, Odzookers.** [1645–55; perh. repr. *God's hooks* (i.e., the nails of Christ's Cross); cf. GAD]

Gae•a (jē′ə), *n.* the ancient Greek goddess of the earth, mother of the Titans. [< Gk *gaîa* earth]

Gael (gāl), *n.* **1.** a Scottish Celt or Highlander. **2.** a Gaelic-speaking Celt. [1590–1600; < ScotGael *Gaidheal,* OIr *Goídel*]

Gael, Gaelic (def. 1). Also, **Gael.**

Gael•ic (gā′lik), *n.* **1.** a Celtic language that includes the speech of ancient Ireland and the dialects that have developed from it, esp. those usually known as Irish, Manx, and Scots Gaelic. Gaelic constitutes the Goidelic subbranch of Celtic. *Abbr.:* Gael —*adj.* **2.** of or in Gaelic. **3.** of or pertaining to the Gaels or their language. [1590–1600; GAEL + -IC (repr. ScotGael *Gaidhlig,* deriv. of *Gaidheal* GAEL)]

gaff[1] (gaf), *n.* **1.** an iron hook with a handle for landing large fish. **2.** the spur on a climbing iron, esp. as used by telephone linemen. **3.** *Naut.* a spar rising aft from a mast to support the head of a quadrilateral fore-and-aft sail (**gaff sail**). **4.** a metal spur for a gamecock. —*v.t.* **5.** to hook or land (a fish) with a gaff. [1275–1325; ME < MF *gaffe, gaff* < Pr *gaf* hook, gaff, n. deriv. of *gafar* to seize (cf. ML *gaffare*), prob. < Gmc (Visigothic) **gaff-,* perh. deriv. from base of Goth *giban* GIVE]

gaff[2] (gaf), *n.* **1.** harsh treatment or criticism: *All the gaff he took never made him bitter.* **2. stand** or **take the gaff,** *Slang.* to weather hardship or strain; endure patiently. [1895–1900, *Amer.*; cf. earlier British use: nonsense, humbug, Scots dial.: loud laugh, guffaw; of uncert. orig.; cf. GUFF]

gaff[3] (gaf), *v.t.* **1.** *Slang.* to cheat; fleece. —*v.i.* **2.** *Brit. Slang.* to gamble, esp. to indulge in petty gambling, as to toss coins. [1745–55; orig. uncert.]

gaffe (gaf), *n.* a social blunder; faux pas. [1905–10; < F: blunder, prob. special use of *gaffe* GAFF[1]]

gaf•fer (gaf′ər), *n.* **1.** the chief electrician on a motion-picture or television production. **2.** *Informal.* an old man. **3.** *Brit.* a foreman or overseer, esp. the boss of a group of physical laborers. **4.** *Glassmaking.* a master glassblower responsible for shaping glassware. [1565–75; contr. of GODFATHER]

gaf•fle (gaf′əl), *v.,* **-fled, -fling.** *New England* (*chiefly Maine*). —*v.t.* **1.** to take hold of; seize. —*v.i.* **2.** to take as one's own (used in the phrase *gaffle on to*): *I'm going to gaffle on to that last piece of pie.* [1930–35; perh. b. GAFF[1] and GRAPPLE]

Gaff•ney (gaf′nē), *n.* a city in N South Carolina. 13,453.

gaff-rigged (gaf′rigd′), *adj. Naut.* (of a sailboat) having one or more gaff sails. [1930–35]

gaff′ sail′, *Naut.* See under **gaff**[1] (def. 3). Also called **gaff′-head•ed sail′** (gaf′hed′id).

gaff′ top′sail, *Naut.* **1.** Also called **fore-and-aft topsail.** a jib-headed fore-and-aft sail set above a gaff. **2.** a quadrilateral fore-and-aft sail set above the spanker of a bark, between the gaff of the spanker and an upper gaff. [1785–95]

gaff-top′sail cat′fish (gaf′top′sāl′, -səl), a sea catfish, *Bagre marinus,* occurring in the Atlantic and the Gulf of Mexico from Cape Cod to Panama, and having the spine of the dorsal fin greatly prolonged and flattened. Also, **gaff•top′sail cat′fish.**

gag[1] (gag), *v.,* **gagged, gag•ging,** *n.* —*v.t.* **1.** to stop up the mouth of (a person) by putting something in it, thus preventing speech, shouts, etc. **2.** to restrain by force or authority from freedom of speech; silence. **3.** to fasten open the jaws of, as in surgical operations. **4.** to cause to retch or choke. **5.** *Metalworking.* to straighten or bend (a bar, rail, etc.) with a gag. —*v.i.* **6.** to retch or choke. —*n.* **7.** something put into a person's mouth to prevent speech, shouting, etc. **8.** any forced or arbitrary suppression of freedom of speech. **9.** a surgical instrument for holding the jaws open. **10.** *Metalworking.* a shaped block of steel used with a press to straighten or bend a bar, rail, etc. [1400–50; late ME *gaggen* to suffocate; perh. imit. of the sound made in choking]
—**Syn. 2.** curb, stifle, suppress.

gag[2] (gag), *n., v.,* **gagged, gag•ging.** *Informal.* —*n.* **1.** a joke, esp. one introduced into a script or an actor's part. **2.** any contrived piece of wordplay or horseplay. —*v.i.* **3.** to tell jokes or make amusing remarks. **4.** to introduce gags in acting. **5.** to play on another's credulity, as by telling false stories. —*v.t.* **6.** to introduce usually comic interpolations into (a script, an actor's part, or the like) (usually fol. by *up*). [1770–80; perh. special use of GAG[1]; cf. ON *gagg* yelp]

gag[3] (gag), *n., pl.* (*esp. collectively*) **gag,** (*esp. referring to two or more kinds or species*) **gags. 1.** a serranid game fish, *Mycteroperca microlepsis,* found along the southeastern coast of the U.S. **2.** any of several related fishes. [1880–85, *Amer.*; orig. uncert.]

ga•ga (gä′gä′), *adj. Informal.* **1.** excessively and foolishly enthusiastic: *The public went gaga over the new fashions.* **2.** ardently fond; infatuated: *He's gaga over the new girl in class.* **3.** demented; crazy; dotty. Also, **ga′-ga′.** [1915–20; < F; imit.]

ga•ga•ku (gä gä′ko͞o), *n.* **1.** the select group of Japanese men who, as both dancers and musicians, perform the bugaku. **2.** the style of music played to accompany the bugaku. [< Japn < MChin, equiv. to Chin *yǎ* elegant + *yuè* music; cf. BUGAKU]

Ga•ga•rin (gä gär′in, gə-; *Russ.* gu gä′ʀyin), *n.* **Yu•ri A•le•kse•ye•vich** (yo͝or′ē al′ik sā′ə vich; *Russ.* yo͞o′ʀyi u lyi ksye′yi vyich), 1934–68, Russian astronaut: first human being to make an orbital space flight (1961).

gage[1] (gāj), *n., v.,* **gaged, gag•ing.** —*n.* **1.** something, as a glove, thrown down by a medieval knight in token of challenge to combat. **2.** *Archaic.* a challenge. **3.** *Archaic.* a pledge or pawn. —*v.t.* **4.** *Archaic.* to pledge, stake, or wager. [1350–1400; ME < MF < Gmc; see WAGE]

gage[2] (gāj), *n., v.t.,* **gaged, gag•ing.** (chiefly in technical use) gauge. —**gag′er,** *n.*

gage[3] (gāj), *n.* greengage. [1840–50; by shortening]

Gage (gāj), *n.* **Thomas,** 1721–87, British general in America 1763–76.

gag•ger[1] (gag′ər), *n.* **1.** a person or thing that gags. **2.** an L-shaped rod for reinforcing sand in a foundry mold. [1855–60; GAG[1] + -ER[1]]

gag•ger[2] (gag′ər), *n.* a person who writes or tells gags; gagman. [1775–85; GAG[2] + -ER[1]]

gag•gle (gag′əl), *v.,* **-gled, -gling,** *n.* —*v.i.* **1.** to cackle. —*n.* **2.** a flock of geese when not flying. Cf. **skein. 3.** an often noisy or disorderly group or gathering: *a politician followed by a gaggle of supporters.* **4.** an assortment of related things. [1350–1400; ME *gagelen* (v.), *gagel* (n.); of imit. orig.]

gag′ law′, 1. any law restricting freedom of the press, free speech, or the right of petition. **2.** See **gag rule.** [1790–1800, *Amer.*]

gag•man (gag′man′), *n., pl.* **-men. 1.** a person who writes comic material for public performers. **2.** a comedian who uses a patter of jokes and funny remarks. Also, **gag•ster** (gag′stər). [1925–30, *Amer.*; GAG[2] + MAN[1]]

gag′ or′der, a court order banning reporters, attorneys, and other parties involved in a case before a court of law from reporting on or publicly disclosing anything relating to the case. [1975–80]

gag′ rule′, any rule restricting open discussion or debate concerning a given issue, esp. in a deliberative body. [1800–10, *Amer.*]

Ga•han•na (gə han′ə), *n.* a town in central Ohio. 18,001.

gahn•ite (gä′nīt), *n.* a dark-green to black mineral of the spinel group, zinc aluminate, $ZnAl_2O_4$. [1800–10; named after J. G. *Gahn* (1745–1818), Swedish chemist; see -ITE[1]]

GAI, See **guaranteed annual income.**

Gai′a hypoth′esis (gā′ə), a model of the earth as a self-regulating organism, advanced as an alternative to a mechanistic model. [1970–75; < Gk *gaîa* earth; see GAEA]

gai•e•ty (gā′i tē), *n., pl.* **-ties. 1.** the state of being gay or cheerful; gay spirits. **2.** Often, **gaieties.** merrymaking or festivity: *the gaieties of the New Year season.* **3.** showiness; finery: *gaiety of dress.* Also, **gayety.** [1625–35; < F *gaieté,* equiv. to *gai* GAY + *-té* -TY[2]]
—**Syn. 1.** merriment, mirth, glee, jollity, joyousness, liveliness, sportiveness, hilarity, vivacity, cheerfulness, joviality. **3.** brilliance, glitter, flashiness, gaudiness.
—**Ant. 1.** sadness.

gai•jin (gī′jēn; *Eng.* gī′jin), *n., pl.* **-jin** (-jēn; *Eng.* -jin). *Japanese.* an outsider; foreigner.

Gail (gāl), *n.* a female or male given name: from a Hebrew word meaning "joy."

gail•lard (gal′yərd), *n.* galliard.

Gail•lard′ Cut′ (gil yärd′, gā′lärd), an artificial cutting in the Panama Canal Zone, NW of the city of Panama: excavated for the Panama Canal. 8 mi. (13 km) long. Formerly, **Culebra Cut.** [named after Col. D. DuB. *Gaillard* (1859–1913), U.S. Army engineer]

gail•lar•di•a (gā lär′dē ə), *n.* any composite plant of the genus *Gaillardia,* including the blanket-flowers. [1885–90; < NL, named after *Gaillard* de Charentonneau, 18th-century French botanical amateur; see -IA]

gai•ly (gā′lē), *adv.* **1.** with merriment; merrily; joyfully; cheerfully. **2.** with showiness; showily. Also, **gayly.** [1350–1400; ME; see GAY, -LY]

gain[1] (gān), *v.t.* **1.** to get (something desired), esp. as a result of one's efforts: *to gain possession of an object; to gain permission to enter a country.* **2.** to acquire as an increase or addition: *to gain weight; to gain speed.* **3.** to obtain as a profit: *He gained ten dollars by this deal.* **4.** to win; get in competition: *to gain the prize.* **5.** to win (someone) to one's own side or point of view; persuade (sometimes fol. by *over*): *to gain supporters.* **6.** (of a watch or clock) to run fast by (a specified amount): *My watch gains six minutes a day.* **7.** to reach, esp. by effort; get to; arrive at: *to gain one's destination.* —*v.i.* **8.** to improve; make progress; advance: *to gain in health after an illness.* **9.** to get nearer, as in pursuit (usually fol. by *on* or *upon*): *Our horse was gaining on the favorite.* **10.** to draw away from or farther ahead of the other contestants in a race, one's pursuers, etc. (usually fol. by *on* or *upon*). **11.** (of a watch or clock) to run fast. **12. gain ground,** to progress or advance, as in value, strength, or achievement: *The company's new products are gaining ground in the city.* **13. gain time,** to arrange a postponement or delay for a particular purpose, esp. by roundabout means. —*n.* **14.** profit or advantage. **15.** an increase or advance. **16. gains,** profits or winnings. **17.** the act of gaining; acquisition. **18.** *Electronics.* **a.** a measure of the increase in signal amplitude produced by an amplifier, expressed as the ratio of output to input. **b.** the effectiveness of a directional antenna as compared with a standard, nondirectional one. **19.** the volume control of a radio, phonograph, amplifier, etc. [1425–75; late ME (n.) < MF, contr. of OF *gaaing,* n. deriv of *gaaignier* to till, earn, win < Gmc; cf. OHG *weidanōn* to hunt, forage for food] —**gain′a•ble,** *adj.*
—**Syn. 1.** procure. GAIN, ATTAIN, EARN, WIN imply obtaining a reward or something advantageous. GAIN carries the least suggestion of method or of effort expended. ATTAIN emphasizes the reaching of a goal. EARN emphasizes the exertions and labor expended that deserve reward. WIN emphasizes attainment in spite of competition or opposition. **7.** attain. **15.** addition, increment, acquisition. —**Ant. 1.** lose.

gain[2] (gān), *Carpentry.* —*n.* **1.** a notch, dado, or mortise cut into a piece of wood, as to receive another piece or to house a flap of a hinge. **2.** tusk (def. 4). **3.** a short rabbet, for receiving a flap of a butt hinge. —*v.t.* **4.** to make a gain or gains in. **5.** to fasten or support by means of a gain. [1670–80; perh. akin to obs. *gane,* OE (north) *ganian* to yawn, open]

CONCISE PRONUNCIATION KEY: act, cāpe, dâre, pärt; set, ēqual; *if,* īce; ox, ōver, ôrder, oil, bo͝ok, bo͞ot, out; up, ûrge; child; sing; shoe; thin, *th*at; zh as in *treasure.* ə = *a* as in *alone, e* as in *system, i* as in *easily, o* as in *gallop, u* as in *circus;* ᵊ as in *fire* (fīᵊr), *hour* (ouᵊr). l and n can serve as syllabic consonants, as in *cradle* (krād′l), and *button* (but′n). See the full key inside the front cover.

gain·er (gā′nər), *n.* **1.** a person or thing that gains. **2.** See **full gainer.** [1530–40; GAIN[1] + -ER[1]]

Gaines (gānz), *n.* **Edmund Pendleton,** 1777–1849, U.S. general.

Gaines·ville (gānz′vil), *n.* **1.** a city in N Florida. 81,371. **2.** a city in N Georgia. 15,280. **3.** a city in N Texas. 14,081.

gain·ful (gān′fəl), *adj.* profitable; lucrative: *gainful employment.* [1545–55; GAIN[1] + -FUL] **—gain′ful·ly,** *adv.* **—gain′ful·ness,** *n.*

gain·giv·ing (gān′giv′ing, gān giv′-), *n. Archaic.* a misgiving. [1325–75; *gain-* (ME *gein-*) against + GIVE + -ING[1]]

gain·less (gān′lis), *adj.* **1.** unprofitable. **2.** unavailing. [1630–40; GAIN[1] + -LESS] **—gain′less·ness,** *n.*

gain·ly (gān′lē), *adj.* graceful; comely; handsome. [1850–55; prob. back formation from UNGAINLY] **—gain′li·ness,** *n.*

gain·say (gān′sā′, gān sā′), *v.t.,* **-said, -say·ing. 1.** to deny, dispute, or contradict. **2.** to speak or act against; oppose. [1250–1300; ME *gainsaien.* See AGAIN, SAY[1]] **—gain′say′er,** *n.*

Gains·bor·ough (gānz′bûr′ō, -bur′ō; *Brit.* gānz′bər ə), *n.* **Thomas,** 1727–88, English painter.

Gai·ser·ic (gī′zə rik), *n.* Genseric.

gait (gāt), *n.* **1.** a manner of walking, stepping, or running. **2.** any of the manners in which a horse moves, as a walk, trot, canter, gallop, or rack. —*v.t.* **3.** to teach a specified gait or gaits to (a horse). [1500–10; Scots, ME sp. var. of GATE[1] in various senses]
—Syn. 1. walk, step, stride, bearing, carriage.

gait·ed (gā′tid), *adj.* having a specified gait (usually used in combination): *slow-gaited; heavy-gaited oxen.* [1580–90; GAIT + -ED[3]]

gait·er (gā′tər), *n.* **1.** a covering of cloth or leather for the ankle and instep and sometimes also the lower leg, worn over the shoe or boot. Cf. **upper** (def. 7). **2.** a cloth or leather shoe with elastic insertions at the sides. **3.** an overshoe with a fabric top. [1765–75; < F *guêtre,* MF *guiestre, guestre,* perh. < Frankish **wrist,* c. G *Rist* ankle, wrist. See WRIST] **—gai′ter·less,** *adj.*

Gai·thers·burg (gā′thərz bûrg′), *n.* a town in central Maryland. 26,424.

Gait·skell (gāt′skəl), *n.* **Hugh Todd Nay·lor** (nā′lər), 1906–63, English economist and statesman: Labour party leader 1955–63.

Ga·ius (gā′əs), *n.* **1.** A.D. c110–c180, Roman jurist and writer, esp. on civil law. **2.** Caius.

Gaj·du·sek (gī′do͝o shek′, -də-), *n.* **D(aniel) Carle·ton** (kärl′tən), born 1923, U.S. medical researcher, esp. on viral diseases: Nobel prize 1976.

gal[1] (gal), *n. Informal.* a girl or woman. [1785–95; orig. dial. pron. of GIRL]
—Usage. See **girl.**

gal[2] (gal), *n.* a centimeter-gram-second unit of acceleration, equal to one centimeter per second per second. [1910–15; named after GALILEO]

Gal., Galatians.

gal., gallon; gallons.

ga·la (gā′lə, gal′ə; *esp. Brit.* gä′lə), *adj.* **1.** festive; festal; showy: *Her birthday parties were always gala occasions.* —*n.* **2.** a festive occasion; celebration; special entertainment: *a gala featuring opera stars in their most famous scenes.* **3.** festal pomp or dress. [1615–25; < F < It < OF; see GALLANT]

ga·la·bi·a (jə lä′bē ə), *n.* djellabah. Also, **ga·la′bi·ya, ga·la′bi·yah, ga·la′bi·eh.** [1715–25; < Egyptian Ar *gallabiyah*]

galact-, var. of **galacto-** before a vowel: *galactagogue.*

ga·lac·tan (gə lak′tən, -tan), *n. Biochem.* any of the class of hexosans, as agar, that yield galactose upon hydrolysis. Also, **galactosan.** [1885–90; < G; see GALACT-, -ANE]

ga·lac·tic (gə lak′tik), *adj.* **1.** *Astron.* **a.** of or pertaining to a galaxy. **b.** of or pertaining to the Milky Way. **2.** immense; huge; vast: *a problem of galactic proportions.* **3.** *Physiol.* pertaining to or stimulating the secretion of milk. [1830–40; < Gk *galaktikós* milky. See GALACT-, -IC]

galac′tic clus′ter, *Astron.* See **open cluster.**

galac′tic coor′dinates, *Astron.* a system of coordinates utilizing galactic latitude and galactic longitude to define the position of a celestial body with reference to the Milky Way. [1930–35]

galac′tic equa′tor, *Astron.* the great circle on the celestial sphere that is equidistant from the galactic poles, being inclined approximately 62° to the celestial equator and lying about one degree north of the center line of the Milky Way. Also called **galac′tic cir′cle.** [1885–90]

galac′tic lat′itude, *Astron.* the angular distance from the galactic equator of a point on the celestial sphere. [1905–10]

galac′tic lon′gitude, *Astron.* the angular distance in degrees measured eastward in the galactic plane from a radius drawn from the earth as center to the constellation Sagittarius. [1910–15]

galac′tic neb′ula, *Astron.* a nebula in the Milky Way.

galac′tic plane′, *Astron.* the plane of the galactic equator. [1840–50]

CONCISE ETYMOLOGY KEY: <, descended or borrowed from; >, whence; b., blend of, blended; c., cognate with; cf., compare; deriv., derivative; equiv., equivalent; imit., imitative; obl., oblique; r., replacing; s., stem; sp., spelling, spelled; resp., respelling, respelled; trans., translation; ?, origin unknown; *, unattested; ‡, probably earlier than. See the full key inside the front cover.

galac′tic pole′, *Astron.* either of the two opposite points on the celestial sphere that are farthest north and south of the Milky Way. [1840–50]

galac′tic year′, *Astron.* the duration of a complete rotation of the Milky Way, approximately 200 million years.

ga·lac·tin (gə lak′tin), *n. Biochem.* prolactin. [1830–40; GALACT- + -IN[2]]

galacto-, a combining form meaning "milk," used in the formation of compound words: *galactopoietic.* Also, *esp. before a vowel,* **galact-.** [< Gk *galakto-,* comb. form of *galakt-,* s. of *gála* milk]

ga·lac·toid (gə lak′toid), *adj.* resembling milk; milky. [1880–85; GALACT- + -OID]

gal·ac·tom·e·ter (gal′ək tom′i tər), *n.* a lactometer. [1835–45; GALACTO- + -METER] **—gal′ac·tom′e·try,** *n.*

ga·lac·to·phore (gə lak′tə fôr′, -fōr′), *n. Anat.* a galactophorous duct. [1900–05; GALACTO- + -PHORE]

gal·ac·toph·or·ous (gal′ək tof′ər əs), *adj. Anat.* bearing milk; lactiferous. [1810–20; < Gk *galaktophóros.* See GALACTO-, -PHOROUS]

ga·lac·to·poi·et·ic (gə lak′tə poi et′ik), *adj.* **1.** increasing the secretion of milk. —*n.* **2.** a galactopoietic agent or medicine. [1655–65; GALACTO- + -POIETIC] **—ga·lac·to·poi·e·sis** (gə lak′tə poi ē′sis), *n.*

ga·lac·tor·rhe·a (gə lak′tə rē′ə), *n. Pathol.* **1.** an abnormally abundant flow of milk in a lactating woman. **2.** secretion of milk from the breast of a nonlactating person. Also, **ga·lac′tor·rhoe′a.** [1850–55; GALACTO- + -RRHEA]

ga·lac·tos·a·mine (gə lak tos′ə mēn′, -min, -tō′sə-), *n. Biochem.* an amino sugar that is a major component of glycolipids and chondroitin. [1895–1900; GALACTOSE + -AMINE]

ga·lac·to·san (gə lak′tə san′, -sən), *n.* galactan. [GALACTOSE + -AN]

ga·lac·to·scope (gə lak′tə skōp′), *n.* a lactoscope. [GALACTO- + -SCOPE]

ga·lac·tose (gə lak′tōs), *n. Chem.* a white, crystalline, water-soluble hexose sugar, $C_6H_{12}O_6$, obtained in its dextrorotatory form from milk sugar by hydrolysis and in its levorotatory form from mucilages. [1865–70; GALACT- + -OSE[2]]

ga·lac·to·se·mi·a (gə lak′tə sē′mē ə), *n. Pathol.* an inherited disorder characterized by the inability to metabolize galactose and requiring a galactose-free diet to avoid consequent mental retardation and eye, spleen, and liver abnormalities. [1930–35; GALACTOSE + -EMIA] **—ga·lac′to·se′mic,** *adj.*

ga·la·go (gə lā′gō, -lä′-), *n., pl.* **-gos.** See **bush baby.** [< NL: the genus name, of uncert. orig.]

ga·lah (gə lä′), *n.* **1.** an Australian cockatoo, *Kakatoe roseicapilla,* having rose-colored underparts. **2.** *Australian.* a fool. [1885–90; < Yuwaalaraay (Australian Aboriginal language spoken near Lightning Ridge, N New South Wales) *gilā*]

Gal·a·had (gal′ə had′), *n.* **1. Sir,** *Arthurian Romance.* the noblest and purest knight of the Round Table, son of Lancelot and Elaine: gained the Holy Grail. **2.** a man showing devotion to the highest ideals.

ga·lan·gal (gə lang′gəl), *n.* the aromatic, medicinal rhizome of certain eastern Asian plants belonging to the genus *Alpinia,* of the ginger family. [var. of GALINGALE]

gal·an·tine (gal′ən tēn′, gal′ən tēn′), *n.* a dish of boned poultry, wrapped in its skin and poached in gelatin stock, pressed, and served cold with aspic or its own jelly. Also, **galatine.** [1350–1400; ME < OF *galentine, gala(n)tine* jellied fish or other meat, perh. ult. < Dalmatian *galatina;* see GELATIN]

Ga·lá′pa·gos Is′lands (gə lä′pə gōs′; *Sp.* gä lä′pä-gôs′), an archipelago on the equator in the Pacific, ab. 600 mi. (965 km) W of and belonging to Ecuador: many unique species of animal life. 4058; 3029 sq. mi. (7845 sq. km). Also called **Colón Archipelago.** Spanish, **Archipiélago de Colón.**

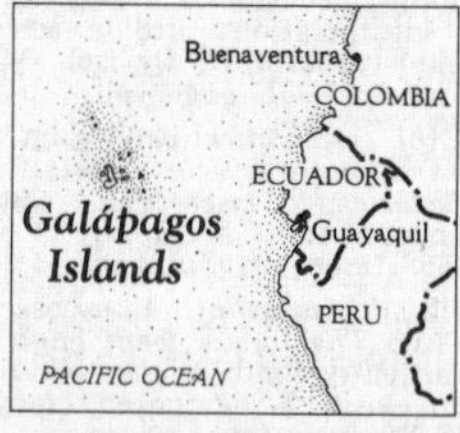

Ga·la·ta (gä′lä tä), *n.* the chief commercial section of Istanbul, Turkey.

gal·a·te·a (gal′ə tē′ə), *n.* a strong cotton fabric, plain or striped, for clothing. [1880–85; named after the 19th-century British man-of-war H.M.S. *Galatea;* the fabric was once used for children's sailor suits]

Gal·a·te·a (gal′ə tē′ə), *n. Class. Myth.* **1.** a sea nymph who was the lover of Acis. **2.** a maiden who had been an ivory statue carved by Pygmalion and brought to life by Aphrodite in response to his prayers.

Ga·la·ţi (gä läts′, -lä′tsē), *n.* a port in E Rumania, on the Danube River. 252,884. Also, **Ga·latz** (gä läts′).

Ga·la·tia (gə lā′shə, -shē ə), *n.* an ancient country in central Asia Minor: later a Roman province; site of an early Christian community. **—Ga·la′tian,** *adj., n.*

Ga·la·tians (gə lā′shənz), *n.* (*used with a singular v.*) a book in the New Testament, written to the Christians in Galatia. *Abbr.:* Gal. [GALATI(A) + -AN + -S[3]]

gal·a·tine (gal′ə tēn′, gal′ə tēn′), *n.* galantine.

gal·a·vant (gal′ə vant′, gal′ə vant′), *v.i.* gallivant.

ga·lax (gā′laks), *n.* a plant, *Galax urceolata,* of the southeastern U.S., having rounded, evergreen leaves and spikes of small white flowers. Also called **beetleweed.** [1745–55; < NL < Gk *gál(a)* milk + L *-āx* n. suffix]

gal·ax·y (gal′ək sē), *n., pl.* **-ax·ies. 1.** *Astron.* **a.** a large system of stars held together by mutual gravitation and isolated from similar systems by vast regions of space. **b.** (*usually cap.*) See **Milky Way. 2.** any large and brilliant or impressive assemblage of persons or things: *a galaxy of opera stars.* [1350–1400; ME *galaxie, galaxias* < ML *galaxia, galaxias,* ult. < Gk *galaxías kýklos* the Milky Way; see GALACTO-]

Gal·ba (gal′bə), *n.* **Ser·vi·us Sul·pi·cius** (sûr′vē əs sul-pish′əs), 5? B.C.–A.D. 69, Roman emperor A.D. 68–69.

gal·ba·num (gal′bə nəm), *n.* a gum resin with a peculiar, strong odor, obtained from certain Asian plants of the genus *Ferula,* used in incense and formerly in medicine. [1350–1400; ME < L; akin to Gk *chalbánē,* Heb *chelbenāh*]

Gal·braith (gal′brāth), *n.* **John Kenneth,** born 1908, U.S. economist, born in Canada.

Gal·cha (gal′chä), *n., pl.* **-chas,** (*esp. collectively*) **-cha.** a member of an Iranian people inhabiting the Pamirs. **—Gal′chic,** *adj.*

gale[1] (gāl), *n.* **1.** a very strong wind. **2.** *Meteorol.* a wind of 32–63 mph (14–28 m/sec). **3.** a noisy outburst: *A gale of laughter filled the room.* **4.** *Archaic.* a gentle breeze. [1540–50; perh. < Scand; cf. Norw dial. *geil* uproar, unrest, boiling]
—Syn. 3. burst, eruption, outbreak, fit, gust.

gale[2] (gāl), *n.* See **sweet gale.** [bef. 1000; ME *gail,* OE *gagel;* c. G *Gagel*]

Gale (gāl), *n.* **1. Zo·na** (zō′nə), 1874–1938, U.S. novelist, short-story writer, playwright, and poet. **2.** a female or male given name.

ga·le·a (gā′lē ə), *n., pl.* **-le·ae** (-lē ē′). **1.** *Bot.* a part of the calyx or corolla having the form of a helmet, as the upper lip of the corolla of the monkshood. **2.** *Anat.* any of several helmet-shaped structures. [1700–10; < L: helmet]

ga·le·ate (gā′lē āt′), *adj.* **1.** having a galea. **2.** helmet-shaped. Also, **ga′le·at′ed.** [1700–10; < L *galeātus* covered with a helmet, equiv. to *gale(a)* helmet + *-ātus* -ATE[1]]

ga·le·i·form (gə lē′ə fôrm′), *adj.* helmet-shaped; resembling a galea. [< L *gale(a)* helmet + -I- + -FORM]

Ga·len (gā′lən), *n.* **1.** Latin, **Ga·le·nus** (gə lē′nəs). **Claudius,** A.D. c130–c200, Greek physician and writer on medicine. **2.** any physician.

ga·le·na (gə lē′nə), *n.* a common, heavy mineral, lead sulfide, PbS, occurring in lead-gray crystals, usually cubes, and cleavable masses: the principal ore of lead. Also called **ga·le·nite** (gə lē′nīt). [1595–1605; < L: lead ore]

ga·len·ic (gə lē′nik, -len′ik), *adj.* of, pertaining to, or containing galena. [1820–30; GALEN(A) + -IC]

Ga·len·ic (gā len′ik, gə-), *adj.* **1.** of or pertaining to Galen, his principles, or his methods. **2.** (*usually l.c.*) of or pertaining to galenicals or Galenic pharmacy. [1660–70; GALEN + -IC]

ga·len·i·cal (gā len′i kəl, gə-), *n.* **1.** an herb or other vegetable drug, distinguished from a mineral or chemical drug. **2.** a crude drug, tincture, or decoction, distinguished from a preparation that has been refined. —*adj.* **3.** galenic. **4.** (*cap.*) Galenic (def. 1). **5.** Galenic (def. 2). [1645–55; GALENIC + -AL[1]]

Galen′ic phar′macy, the art or practice of preparing and dispensing galenicals.

Ga·len·ism (gā′lə niz′əm), *n.* the medical system or principles of Galen. [1865–70; GALEN + -ISM] **—Ga′len·ist,** *n.*

ga·le·rie (gal rē′, gal′ə-), *n. Gulf States (chiefly Louisiana).* gallery (def. 8). [< LaF, F: GALLERY]

galerie′ house′, (in French Louisiana) a house with its main story above the ground floor and with verandas **(galeries)** for both stories in tiers on at least one side.

Gales·burg (gālz′bûrg), *n.* a city in NW Illinois. 35,305.

gal·et (gal′it), *n., v.t.* gallet.

gale′ warn′ing, *U.S. Meteorol.* a National Weather Service warning of sustained winds at sea having speeds in the range 34–47 knots (39–54 mph, 17–24 m/sec). Cf. **warning** (def. 3). [1915–20]

gal′ Fri′day, a woman who acts as a general assistant in a business office or to an executive and has a wide variety of esp. secretarial and clerical duties. [1955–60; modeled on MAN FRIDAY]
—Usage. See **girl.**

Gal·gal (gal′gal), *n. Douay Bible.* Gilgal.

Ga·li·bi (gä lē′bē), *n., pl.* **-bis,** (*esp. collectively*) **-bi.** a member of an Indian people of French Guiana. [1890–95; < Carib; see CANNIBAL]

Ga·li·ci·a (gə lish′ē ə, -lish′ə; *for 2 also Sp.* gä lē′-thyä), *n.* **1.** a region in E central Europe: a former crown land of Austria, included in S Poland after World War I, and now partly in Ukraine. ab. 30,500 sq. mi. (79,000 sq. km). **2.** a maritime region in NW Spain: a former kingdom, and later a province. 11,256 sq. mi. (29,153 sq. km).

Ga·li·ci·an (gə lish′ē ən, -lish′ən), *adj.* **1.** of or pertaining to Galicia in NW Spain, its people, or their language. **2.** of or pertaining to Galicia in E central Europe or its people. —*n.* **3.** a native or inhabitant of Galicia in Spain. **4.** the language of Spanish Galicia, often considered a dialect of Portuguese. **5.** a native or inhabitant of Galicia in E central Europe. **6.** a Jew from Polish Galicia, esp. one speaking a Galician dialect of Yiddish.

Gal·i·le·an (gal′ə lē′ən), *adj.* **1.** of or pertaining to Galilee. —*n.* **2.** a native or inhabitant of Galilee. **3.** a

Christian. **4. the Galilean,** Jesus. [1605–15; < L *Galilae(a)* GALILEE + -AN]

Gal•i•le•an (gal′ə lā′ən, -lē′-), *adj.* of or pertaining to Galileo, his theories, or his discoveries. [1720–30; GALILE(O) + -AN]

Gal′ile′an sat′ellites, *Astron.* the four largest and brightest moons of Jupiter: Io, Europa, Ganymede, and Callisto, discovered by Galileo in 1610.

Gal′ile′an tel′escope, a refracting telescope that forms an erect image, consisting of an objective of relatively long focal length that causes light rays to converge and an eyepiece of short focal length that causes them to diverge. [1715–25]

Galile′an transforma′tion, *Physics.* the equations in classical mechanics that relate position and time in two frames of reference that are moving uniformly with respect to each other. Cf. **inertial system, relativity** (def. 2). [1905–10]

gal•i•lee (gal′ə lē′), *n.* a porch or vestibule, often on the ground floor of a tower, at the entrance of some English churches. [1585–95; < ML *galilaea* porch of a church, lit., GALILEE; perh. alluding to Galilee as a country of Gentiles (as opposed to Judaea), the porch being an area esp. associated with the laity]

Gal•i•lee (gal′ə lē′), *n.* **1.** an ancient Roman province in what is now N Israel. **2. Sea of.** Also called **Lake Tiberias.** a lake in NE Israel through which the Jordan River flows. 14 mi. (23 km) long; 682 ft. (208 m) below sea level.

Gal•i•le•o (gal′ə lā′ō, -lē′ō; *for 1 also It.* gä′lē le′ô), *n.* **1.** (*Galileo Galilei*), 1564–1642, Italian physicist and astronomer. **2.** *Aerospace.* a U.S. space probe designed to take photographs and obtain other scientific information while orbiting the planet Jupiter.

gal•i•ma•ti•as (gal′ə mā′shē əs, -mat′ē əs), *n.* confused or unintelligible talk. [1645–55; < F, word of obscure orig. first attested in Montaigne (*jargon de galimathias*)]

gal•in•gale (gal′in gāl′, -ing-), *n.* any sedge of the genus *Cyperus,* esp. an Old World species, *C. longus,* having aromatic roots. [1275–1325; ME < MF *galingal, garingal* < Ar *khalanjān* < Pers *khūlanjān*]

gal•in•so•ga (gal′in sō′gə), *n.* any of several weedy composite plants of the genus *Galinsoga,* esp. *G. ciliata* or *G. parviflora,* having small flower heads with short, sparse white rays. [< NL (1794), after Mariano M. de *Galinsoga,* Spanish botanist]

Gal•ion (gal′yən), *n.* a city in N central Ohio. 12,391.

gal•i•ot (gal′ē ət), *n. Naut.* **1.** a small galley propelled by both sails and oars. **2.** a small ketchlike sailing vessel used for trade along the coast of Germany and nearby countries. [1325–75; ME *galiote* < MF < ML *galeota,* dim. of *galea* GALLEY]

gal•i•pot (gal′ə pot′), *n.* a type of turpentine exuded on the stems of certain species of pine. Also, **gallipot.** [1785–95; < F *galipot, galipo,* perh. < OF *garipot* a species of pine tree]

gall[1] (gôl), *n.* **1.** impudence; effrontery. **2.** bile, esp. that of an animal. **3.** something bitter or severe. **4.** bitterness of spirit; rancor. **5. gall and wormwood,** bitterness of spirit; deep resentment. [bef. 900; ME; OE *galla, gealla;* c. G *Galle;* akin to L *fel,* Gk *cholḗ* gall, bile] —**Syn. 1.** nerve, audacity, brass, cheek.

gall[2] (gôl), *v.t.* **1.** to make sore by rubbing; chafe severely: *The saddle galled the horse's back.* **2.** to vex or irritate greatly: *His arrogant manner galls me.* —*v.i.* **3.** to be or become chafed. **4.** *Mach.* (of either of two engaging metal parts) to lose metal to the other because of heat or molecular attraction resulting from friction. **5.** *Metall.* (of a die or compact in powder metallurgy) to lose surface material through adhesion to the die. —*n.* **6.** a sore on the skin, esp. of a horse, due to rubbing; excoriation. **7.** something very vexing or irritating. **8.** a state of vexation or irritation. [bef. 1000; ME *galle* (n.), *gallen* (v.) perh. < MD, MLG *gall,* akin to OE *gealla* sore on a horse]

gall[3] (gôl), *n.* any abnormal vegetable growth or excrescence on plants, caused by various agents, as insects, nematodes, fungi, bacteria, viruses, chemicals, and mechanical injuries. [1350–1400; ME *galle* < MF < L *galla* gallnut. See GALL[2]]

Gall (gôl), *n.* (*Pizi*), 1840?–94, leader of the Hunkpapa Sioux: a major chief in the battle of Little Bighorn.

Gal•la (gal′ə), *n., pl.* **-las,** (*esp. collectively*) **-la.** Oromo.

gal•la•mine tri•eth•i•o•dide (gal′ə mēn′ trī eth ī′ə-did′), *Pharm.* a neuromuscular blocking drug, $C_{30}H_{60}I_3N_3O_3$, similar to curare, used as a skeletal muscle relaxant in conjunction with surgical anesthesia. [(PYRO)GALL(OL) + AMINE; TRIETH(YL) + IODIDE]

gal•lant (*adj.* gal′ənt *for 1, 3, 4;* gə lant′, -länt′, gal′ənt *for 2, 5; n.* gə lant′, -länt′, gal′ənt; *v.* gə lant′, -länt′), *adj.* **1.** brave, spirited, noble-minded, or chivalrous: *a gallant knight; a gallant rescue attempt.* **2.** exceptionally polite and attentive to women; courtly. **3.** stately; grand: *a gallant pageant.* **4.** showy, colorful, or stylish, as in dress; magnificent. **5.** amorous; amatory. —*n.* **6.** a brave, noble-minded, or chivalrous man. **7.** a man exceptionally attentive to women. **8.** a stylish and dashing man. **9.** a suitor or lover. **10.** a paramour. —*v.t.* **11.** to court or act as a lover of (a woman). **12.** to escort (a woman). —*v.i.* **13.** to attend or pay court as a gallant. [1350–1400; ME *gala(u)nt* < OF *galant,* prp. of *galer* to amuse oneself, make merry < Gallo-Rom **walāre,* deriv. of Frankish **wala* good, happy; see WELL[1], WEAL[1]] —**gal′lant•ly,** *adv.* —**gal′lant•ness,** *n.* —**Syn. 1.** valorous, courageous, heroic, bold, daring, intrepid. See **brave. 2.** chivalrous, courteous.

gal•lant•ry (gal′ən trē), *n., pl.* **-ries. 1.** dashing courage; heroic bravery; noble-minded behavior. **2.** gallant or courtly attention to women. **3.** a gallant act, action, or speech. [1600–10; < MF *galanterie,* equiv. to OF *galant* (see GALLANT) + *-erie* -RY] —**Syn. 1.** daring, valor, heroism. **2.** chivalry, courtliness. —**Ant. 1.** cowardice.

gal•late (gal′āt, gô′lāt), *n. Chem.* a salt or ester of gallic acid. [1785–95; GALL(IC ACID) + -ATE[2]]

Gal•la•tin (gal′ə tin), *n.* **1. Albert,** 1761–1849, U.S. statesman: Secretary of the Treasury 1801–13. **2.** a town in N Tennessee. 17,191.

Gal•lau•det (gal′ə det′), *n.* **Thomas Hopkins,** 1787–1851, U.S. educator of the deaf and writer.

gall•ber•ry (gôl′ber′ē, -bə rē), *n., pl.* **-ries. 1.** either of two North American shrubs, *Ilex glabra,* the inkberry, or *I. coriacea,* having glossy leaves and white flowers. **2.** the fruit of either of these shrubs. [1700–10, *Amer.;* GALL[3] + BERRY]

gall•blad•der (gôl′blad′ər), *n. Anat.* a pear-shaped, muscular sac attached to the undersurface of the right lobe of the liver, in which bile is stored and concentrated. Also, **gall′ blad′der.** [1670–80; GALL[1] + BLADDER]

Galle (gäl), *n.* a seaport in SW Sri Lanka. 72,720.

gal•le•ass (gal′ē as′), *n. Naut.* a fighting galley, lateen-rigged on three masts, used in the Mediterranean Sea from the 15th to the 18th centuries. [1535–45; < OF *galleasse, galiace* < OIt *galeaza* (Venice), aug. of *galea* GALLEY]

Ga•lle•gos (gä ye′gôs), *n.* **1. Ró•mu•lo** (rô′mo͞o lô′), 1884–1969, Venezuelan educator, statesman, and novelist: president of Venezuela 1948. **2.** See **Río Gallegos.**

gal•le•on (gal′ē ən, gal′yən), *n.* a large sailing vessel of the 15th to the 17th centuries used as a fighting or merchant ship, square-rigged on the foremast and mainmast and generally lateen-rigged on one or two after masts. [1520–30; < Sp *galeón,* aug. of *galea* GALLEY]

galleon

gal•le•ri•a (gal′ə rē′ə), *n.* **1.** a spacious passageway, court, or indoor mall, usually with a vaulted roof and lined with commercial establishments. **2.** gallery (defs. 7, 8, 9, 10). [1900–05; < It. See GALLERY]

gal•ler•y (gal′ə rē, gal′rē), *n., pl.* **-ler•ies. 1.** a raised area, often having a stepped or sloping floor, in a theater, church, or other public building to accommodate spectators, exhibits, etc. **2.** the uppermost of such areas in a theater, usually containing the cheapest seats. **3.** the occupants of such an area in a theater. **4.** the general public, esp. when regarded as having popular or uncultivated tastes. **5.** any group of spectators or observers, as at a golf match, a Congressional session, etc. **6.** a room, series of rooms, or building devoted to the exhibition and often the sale of works of art. **7.** a long covered area, narrow and open at one or both sides, used esp. as a walk or corridor. **8.** *Chiefly South Atlantic States.* a long porch or portico; veranda. **9.** a long, relatively narrow room, esp. one for public use. **10.** a corridor, esp. one having architectural importance through its scale or decorative treatment. **11.** a raised, balconylike platform or passageway running along the exterior wall of a building inside or outside. **12.** a large room or building used for photography, target practice, or other special purposes: *a shooting gallery.* **13.** a collection of art for exhibition. **14.** *Theat.* a narrow, raised platform located beyond the acting area, used by stagehands or technicians to stand on when working. **15.** *Naut.* a projecting balcony or structure on the quarter or stern of a vessel. **16.** *Furniture.* an ornamental railing or cresting surrounding the top of a table, stand, desk, etc. **17.** *Mining.* a level or drift. **18.** a small tunnel in a dam, mine, or rock, for various purposes, as inspection or drainage. **19.** a passageway made by an animal. **20.** *Fort. Obs.* an underground or covered passage to another part of a fortified position. **21. play to the gallery,** to attempt to appeal to the popular taste, as opposed to a more refined or esoteric taste: *Movies, though still playing mainly to the gallery, have taken their place as a significant art form.* [1400–50; late ME < OF *galerie* < ML *galeria,* by dissimilation or suffix replacement from *galilea, galilæa* GALILEE] —**gal′ler•ied,** *adj.* —**gal′ler•y•like′,** *adj.*

gallery (def. 16)

gal′lery for′est, a narrow strip of woods or forest along the banks of a watercourse flowing through open country. Also called **fringing forest.** [1915–20]

gal•ler•y•go•er (gal′ə rē gō′ər), *n.* a person who visits art galleries, esp. often or regularly. [1885–90; GALLERY + GOER]

gal•ler•y•ite (gal′ə rē īt′, gal′rē-), *n.* a spectator, as in a theater gallery or at a golf match. [1890–95; GALLERY + -ITE[1]]

gal′lery wire′, perforated wire or metal stripping used to support or enhance a stone mounted in a ring. Also called **gal′lery strip′.**

gal•let (gal′it), *Masonry.* —*n.* **1.** spall (def. 1). —*v.t.* **2.** to fill (a mortar joint) with gallets. Also, **galet, garret.** [1705–15; < F *galet* pebble, OF *galet, jalet,* deriv. of ONF *gal* pebble (said to be < Celtic, but MIr *gall* "pillar stone, standing stone" is only point of comparison)]

galley (def. 2a)

gal•ley (gal′ē), *n., pl.* **-leys. 1.** a kitchen or an area with kitchen facilities in a ship, plane, or camper. **2.** *Naut.* **a.** a seagoing vessel propelled mainly by oars, used in ancient and medieval times, sometimes with the aid of sails. **b.** a long rowboat, as one used as a ship's boat by a warship or one used for dragging a seine. **c.** (formerly, in the U.S. Navy) a shoal-draft vessel, variously rigged, relying mainly on its sails but able to be rowed by sweeps. **3.** *Print.* **a.** a long, narrow tray, usually of metal, for holding type that has been set. **b.** See **galley proof. c.** a rough unit of measurement, about 22 in. (56 cm), for type composition. [1250–1300; ME *galei(e)* < OF *galee, galie,* perh. < OPr *galea* < LGk *galéa, galaía*] —**gal′ley•like′,** *adj.*

gal′ley proof′, *Print.* a proof, originally one set from type in a galley, taken before the material has been made up into pages and usually printed as a single column of type with wide margins for marking corrections. [1885–90]

gal′ley slave′, 1. a person condemned to work at an oar on a galley. **2.** a drudge. [1560–70]

gal•ley-west (gal′ē west′), *adv.* **1.** *Informal.* into a state of unconsciousness, confusion, or disarray (usually used in the phrase *to knock galley-west*). —*adj.* **2.** *Northern U.S.* lopsided; cockeyed. [1870–75, *Amer.;* alter. of Brit. dial. *collywest*]

gall•fly (gôl′flī′), *n., pl.* **-flies.** any of various insects that deposit their eggs in plants, causing the formation of galls. [1815–25; GALL[3] + FLY[2]]

gall′ gnat′. See **gall midge.**

Gal•li•a (gal′ē ä), *n.* Latin name of **Gaul.**

Gal•lia•no (gal yä′nō; *It.* gäl lyä′nô), *Trademark.* a yellow, anise-flavored liqueur made in Italy.

gal•liard (gal′yərd), *n.* **1.** a spirited dance for two dancers in triple rhythm, common in the 16th and 17th centuries. Also, **gaillard.** [1525–35; < MF *gaillard,* n. use of adj.: lively, vigorous (> ME *gaillard,* late ME *galyarde*), prob. < Gallo-Rom **galia* < Celtic (cf. MIr *gal* warlike ardor, valor); see -ARD]

gal•lic[1] (gal′ik), *adj. Chem.* of or containing gallium, esp. in the trivalent state. [GALL(IUM) + -IC]

gal•lic[2] (gal′ik, gô′lik), *adj.* pertaining to or derived from plant galls: *gallic acid.* [1785–95; < F *gallique;* see GALL[3], -IC]

Gal•lic (gal′ik), *adj.* **1.** pertaining to the Gauls or Gaul. **2.** pertaining to the French or France. [1665–75; < L *Gallicus,* equiv. to *Gall(us)* a GAUL + *-icus* -IC] —**Gal′li•cal•ly,** *adv.*

gal′lic ac′id, *Chem.* a white or yellowish, crystalline, sparingly water-soluble solid, $C_7H_6O_5$, obtained from nutgalls, used chiefly in tanning and in ink dyes. [1785–95; < F *acide gallique*]

Gal•li•can (gal′i kən), *adj.* **1.** Gallic; French. **2.** *Eccles.* **a.** of or pertaining to the Roman Catholic Church in France. **b.** of or pertaining to a school or party of French Roman Catholics, before 1870, advocating the restriction of papal authority in favor of the authority of general councils, the bishops, and temporal rulers. [1590–1600; < L *Gallicānus* belonging to Gallia, Gallican, equiv. to *Gallic-* GALLIC + *-ānus* -AN]

Gal•li•can•ism (gal′i kə niz′əm), *n.* the movement or body of doctrines, chiefly associated with the Gallican church, advocating the restriction of papal authority in certain matters. Cf. **ultramontanism.** [1855–60; < F *Gallicanisme.* See GALLICAN, -ISM]

Gal·li·cism (gal′ə siz′əm), *n.* **1.** a French idiom or expression used in another language, as *Je ne sais quoi* when used in English. **2.** a feature that is characteristic of or peculiar to the French language. **3.** a custom or trait considered to be characteristically French. Also, **gal′li·cism.** [1650–60; < F *gallicisme.* See GALLIC, -ISM]

Gal·li·cize (gal′ə sīz′), *v.t., v.i.,* **-cized, -ciz·ing.** (*sometimes l.c.*) to make or become French in language, character, etc. Also, *esp. Brit.,* **gal′li·cise′.** [1765–75; < L *Gallic(us)* GALLIC + -IZE] **—Gal′li·ci·za′tion,** *n.* **—Gal′li·ciz′er,** *n.*

Gal·li-Cur·ci (gal′ē kûr′chē; *It.* gäl′lē ko͝or′chē), *n.* **A·me·li·ta** (ä′me lē′tä), 1889–1964, Italian soprano in the U.S.

Gal·li·e·nus (gal′ē ē′nəs), *n.* (*Publius Licinius Egnatius*) died A.D. 268, emperor of Rome 253–268 (son of Valerian).

gal·li·gas·kins (gal′i gas′kinz), *n.* (*used with a plural v.*) **1.** loose hose or breeches worn in the 16th and 17th centuries. **2.** loose breeches in general. **3.** leggings or gaiters, usually of leather. Also, **gallygaskins.** [1570–80; earlier *gallogascaine(s), galigascon(s),* of obscure orig.; final element is perh. GASCON (later assimilated to -KIN)]

gal·li·mau·fry (gal′ə mô′frē), *n., pl.* **-fries.** *Chiefly Literary.* **1.** a hodgepodge; jumble; confused medley. **2.** a ragout or hash. [1545–55; < MF *galimafree* kind of sauce or stew, prob. a conflation of *galer* to amuse oneself (see GALLANT) and Picard dial. *mafrer* to gorge oneself (< MD *moffelen* to eat, nosh)]

gal·li·na·cean (gal′ə nā′shən), *n.* a gallinaceous bird. [1835–45; < NL *Gallinace(ae)* name of a group (fem. pl. of L *gallināceus* (adj.) GALLINACEOUS) + -AN]

gal·li·na·ceous (gal′ə nā′shəs), *adj.* **1.** pertaining to or resembling the domestic fowls. **2.** belonging or pertaining to the order Galliformes, comprising medium-sized, mainly ground-feeding domestic or game birds, as the chicken, turkey, grouse, pheasant, and partridge. [1775–85; < L *gallināceus* pertaining to poultry, equiv. to *gallīn(a)* hen (deriv. of *gallus* cock) + *-āceus* -ACEOUS]

Ga·lli·nas (gä yē′näs), *n.* **Pun·ta** (po͞on′tä), a cape in NE Colombia: northernmost point of South America.

gall·ing (gô′ling), *adj.* that galls; chafing; irritating; vexing; exasperating. [1640–50; GALL[2] + -ING[2]] **—gall′·ing·ly,** *adv.* **—gall′ing·ness,** *n.*

gal·li·nip·per (gal′ə nip′ər), *n. Informal.* any of various insects that sting or bite, esp. a large American mosquito, *Psorophora ciliata.* [1675–85; of obscure orig.; final element appar. assimilated to NIPPER]

gal·li·nule (gal′ə no͞ol′, -nyo͞ol′), *n.* any aquatic bird of the family Rallidae, having elongated, webless toes. [1770–80; < NL *Gallinula* a genus name, LL *gallīnula* chicken, equiv. to L *gallīn(a)* hen + *-ula* -ULE]

Gal·lip′o·li Penin′sula (gə lip′ə lē), a peninsula in European Turkey, between the Dardanelles and the Aegean Sea. 60 mi. (97 km) long.

gal·li·pot[1] (gal′ə pot′), *n.* a small glazed pot used by apothecaries for medicines, confections, or the like. [1425–75; late ME *galy pott.* See GALLEY, POT[1]]

gal·li·pot[2] (gal′ə pot′), *n.* galipot.

gal·li·um (gal′ē əm), *n. Chem.* a rare, steel-gray, trivalent metallic element used in high-temperature thermometers because of its high boiling point (1983°C) and low melting point (30°C). *Symbol:* Ga; *at. wt.:* 69.72; *at. no.:* 31; *sp. gr.:* 5.91 at 20°C. [1870–75; < NL, equiv. to L *gall(us)* cock (trans. of F *coq,* from Lecoq de Boisbaudran, 19th-century French chemist) + NL *-ium* -IUM]

gal′lium ar′senide, *Chem.* a crystalline and highly toxic semiconductor, GaAs, used in light-emitting diodes, lasers, and electronic devices. [1960–65]

gal·li·vant (gal′ə vant′, gal′ə vant′), *v.i.* **1.** to wander about, seeking pleasure or diversion; gad. **2.** to go about with members of the opposite sex. Also, **galavant.** [1815–25; perh. fanciful alter. of GALLANT] **—gal′li·vant′er,** *n.*

gal·li·wasp (gal′ə wosp′), *n.* any of numerous scaly marsh lizards of the genus *Diploglossus,* inhabiting Central America and the West Indies. [1715–25; earlier *gallivache* (1683), of unexplained orig.; appar. assimilated to GALLY, WASP]

gall′ midge′, any of several dipterous insects of the family Cecidomyiidae, the larvae of which form characteristic galls on plants. Also called **gall gnat.** [1900–05]

gall′ mite′, a mite of the family Eriophyidae that feeds on plant juices, damaging buds, leaves, and twigs and causing galls and other deformities. [1880–85]

gall·nut (gôl′nut′), *n.* a nutlike gall on plants. [1565–75; GALL[3] + NUT]

CONCISE ETYMOLOGY KEY: <, descended or borrowed from; >, whence; b., blend of, blended; c., cognate with; cf., compare; deriv., derivative; equiv., equivalent; imit., imitative; obl., oblique; r., replacing; s., stem; sp., spelling, spelled; resp., respelling, respelled; trans., translation; ?, origin unknown; *, unattested; ‡, probably earlier than. See the full key inside the front cover.

Gal·lo (gal′ō), *n.* **Robert (Charles),** born 1937, U.S. scientist, specializing in cancer and AIDS research.

Gallo-, a combining form representing **Gallic** in the formation of compound words: *Gallo-Romance.* [< L, equiv. to *Gall(us)* a Gaul + -o-]

gal·lo·glass (gal′ō glas′, -gläs′), *n. Irish Hist.* a follower and supporter of or a soldier owing allegiance to an Irish chief. Also, **gallowglass.** [1505–15; < Ir *galló-glách,* equiv. to *gall* a stranger, foreigner + *óglach* a youth, soldier, servant, deriv. of OIr *óac, óc* young]

gal·lon (gal′ən), *n.* a common unit of capacity in English-speaking countries, equal to four quarts, the U.S. standard gallon being equal to 231 cubic inches (3.7853 liters), and the British imperial gallon to 277.42 cubic inches (4.546 liters). *Abbr.:* gal. [1250–1300; ME *galo(u)n, gallon* < ONF *galon,* deriv. from base of ML *gallēta* jug, bucket, of uncert. orig.]

gal·lon·age (gal′ə nij), *n.* **1.** the number of gallons of something used. **2.** the rate at which gallons of something are used. [1905–10; GALLON + -AGE]

gal·loon (gə lo͞on′), *n.* a braid or trimming of worsted, silk or rayon tinsel, gold or silver, etc., usually having scalloping along both edges. [1595–1605; < MF *galon,* OF *galonner* to adorn one's head with ribbons, deriv. of *gale* GALA] **—gal·looned′,** *adj.*

gal·loot (gə lo͞ot′), *n.* galoot.

gal·lop (gal′əp), *v.i.* **1.** to ride a horse at a gallop; ride at full speed: *They galloped off to meet their friends.* **2.** to run rapidly by leaps, as a horse; go at a gallop. **3.** to go fast, race, or hurry, as a person or time. —*v.t.* **4.** to cause (a horse or other animal) to gallop. —*n.* **5.** a fast gait of the horse or other quadruped in which, in the course of each stride, all four feet are off the ground at once. **6.** a run or ride at this gait. **7.** a rapid rate of going. **8.** a period of going rapidly. [1375–1425; late ME *galopen* (v.) < OF *galoper* < Frankish **wala hlaupan* to run well (see WELL[1], LEAP) or, alternatively, v. deriv. of **walhlaup,* equiv. to **wal* battlefield (c. OHG *wal;* see VALKYRIE) + **hlaup* run, course (deriv. of the v.)] **—gal′lop·er,** *n.*
—Syn. 3. run, rush, dash, speed, fly, scoot.

gal·lo·pade (gal′ə pād′), *n.* galop. Also, **galopade.** [1825–35; < F *galopade,* equiv. to *galop(er)* to GALLOP + *-ade* -ADE[1]]

gal·lop·ing (gal′ə ping), *adj.* **1.** at a gallop; running or moving quickly. **2.** progressing rapidly to some conclusion, as a disease: *galloping pneumonia.* **3.** growing or spreading rapidly: *galloping inflation.* [1595–1605; GALLOP + -ING[2]]

gal′loping dom′inoes, *Slang.* dice, esp. as used in the game of craps.

gal′lop rhythm′, *Pathol.* an abnormal heart rhythm characterized by three clear sounds in each beat, resembling the sound of a horse's gallop.

Gal·lo-Ro·mance (gal′ō rō mans′), *n.* the vernacular language, a development from Latin, spoken in France from about A.D. 600 to 900. *Abbr.:* Gallo-Rom.

Gal·lo·way (gal′ə wā′), *n.* **1.** a historic region in SW Scotland. **2.** one of a Scottish breed of beef cattle having a coat of curly, black hair. **3.** one of a Scottish breed of small, strong horses.

gal·low·glass (gal′ō glas′, -gläs′), *n. Irish Hist.* galloglass.

gal·lows (gal′ōz, -əz), *n., pl.* **-lows·es, -lows. 1.** a wooden frame, consisting of a crossbeam on two uprights, on which condemned persons are executed by hanging. **2.** a similar structure from which something is suspended. **3.** execution by hanging: *a crime deserving of the gallows.* **4.** Also called **gal′lows bitts′.** *Naut.* a support on the deck of a vessel, generally one of two or more, consisting of a crosspiece on two uprights, for spars, boats, etc. [bef. 900; ME *galwes,* OE *g(e)algan,* pl. of *g(e)alga* gallows; c. G *Galgen*]

gal′lows bird′, *Informal.* a person who deserves to be hanged. [1775–85]

gal′lows frame′, *Mining.* headframe. [1880–85]

gal′lows hu′mor, humor that treats serious, frightening, or painful subject matter in a light or satirical way. [1900–05]

gal′lows tree′, a gallows. Also, **gal′low tree′.** [bef. 900; ME *galwe tree,* OE *galgtrēow,* equiv. to *galg(a)* GALLOWS + *trēow* TREE]

gall·stone (gôl′stōn′), *n.* an abnormal stonelike mass, usually of cholesterol, formed in the gallbladder or bile passages. Also called **biliary calculus.** [1750–60; GALL[1] + STONE]

Gal·lup (gal′əp), *n.* **1. George Horace,** 1901–84, U.S. statistician. **2.** a city in W New Mexico. 18,161.

Gal′lup poll′, a representative sampling of public opinion or public awareness concerning a certain subject or issue. [1935–40; after G. H. GALLUP]

gal·lus·es (gal′ə siz), *n.* (*used with a plural v.*) *Older Use.* a pair of suspenders for trousers. [1825–35; var. of GALLOWS] **—gal′lused,** *adj.*

gall′ wasp′, any wasp of the family Cynipidae, the larvae of which form characteristic galls on plants. [1875–80]

gal·ly (gal′ē), *v.t.,* **-lied, -ly·ing.** *Chiefly Dial.* to frighten or scare. [1695–1705; cf. earlier *gallow,* appar. repr. OE *agælwan* to frighten]

gal·ly·gas·kins (gal′ə gas′kinz), *n.* (*used with a plural v.*) galligaskins.

Ga·lo·fa·lo (*It.* gä lô′fä lô), *n.* modern name of **Charybdis.** Also, **Garofalo.**

Ga·lois′ the′ory, (gal wä′; *Fr.* ga lwa′), *Math.* the branch of mathematics that deals with the application of the theory of finite groups to the solution of algebraic equations. [1890–95; named after Évariste Galois (1811–32), French mathematician]

ga·loot (gə lo͞ot′), *n. Slang.* an awkward, eccentric, or foolish person. Also, **galloot.** [1805–15; orig. uncert.]

gal·op (gal′əp), *n.* **1.** a lively round dance in duple time. **2.** a piece of music for, or in the rhythm of, this dance. Also called **gallopade, gal′o·pade′.** [1830–40; < F *galop;* see GALLOP]

ga·lore (gə lôr′, -lōr′), *adv.* in abundance; in plentiful amounts: *food and drink galore.* [1660–70; < Ir *go leor* enough, plenty (ScotGael *gu leòr, leòir*), equiv. to *go,* particle forming predicative adjectives and adverbs + *leór* enough (OIr *lour*)]

ga·losh (gə losh′), *n.* a waterproof overshoe, esp. a high one. Also, **ga·loshe′, golosh.** [1325–75; ME < OF *galoche,* of obscure orig.]

gals., gallons.

Gals·wor·thy (gôlz′wûr′thē, galz′-), *n.* **John,** 1867–1933, English novelist and dramatist: Nobel prize 1932.

Gal·ton (gôl′tn), *n.* **Sir Francis,** 1822–1911, English scientist and writer. **—Gal·to·ni·an** (gôl tō′nē ən), *adj.*

ga·lumph (gə lumf′), *v.i.* to move along heavily and clumsily. [1872; phonesthemic invention of Lewis Carroll, perh. b. GALLOP and TRIUMPHANT]

Ga·lup·pi (gä lo͞op′pē), *n.* **Bal·das·sa·re** (bäl′däs sä′re), ("*Il Buranello*"), 1706–85, Italian composer.

Ga·luth (*Seph.* gä lo͞ot′; *Ashk.,* gô′ləs), *n.* (*sometimes l.c.*) *Hebrew.* the forced exile of Jews, esp. from countries where they were most persecuted. Also, ***Ga·lut′, ga·lut′.*** [*gālūth* lit., exile]

galv, 1. galvanic. **2.** galvanized.

Gal·va·ni (gäl vä′nē), *n.* **Lu·i·gi** (lo͞o ē′jē), 1737–98, Italian physiologist whose experiments led to the discovery that electricity can result from chemical action.

gal·van·ic (gal van′ik), *adj.* **1.** pertaining to or produced by galvanism; producing or caused by an electric current. **2.** affecting or affected as if by galvanism; startling; shocking: *the galvanic effect of his speech.* **3.** stimulating; energizing: *Her galvanic presence brought the party to life.* [1790–1800; < F *galvanique,* named after Luigi GALVANI; see -IC] **—gal·van′i·cal·ly,** *adv.*

galvan′ic bat′tery, *Elect.* battery (def. 1a). [1795–1805]

galvan′ic cell′, *Elect.* cell (def. 7a).

galvan′ic cou′ple, *Elect.* See **voltaic couple.** [1895–1900]

galvan′ic pile′, *Elect.* See **voltaic pile.** [1795–1805]

galvan′ic skin′ response′, a change in the electrical conductivity of the skin caused by an emotional reaction to a stimulus. [1960–65]

gal·va·nism (gal′və niz′əm), *n.* **1.** *Elect.* electricity, esp. as produced by chemical action. **2.** *Med.* the therapeutic application of electricity to the body. [1790–1800; < F *galvanisme,* named after Luigi GALVANI; see -ISM]

gal·va·nize (gal′və nīz′), *v.t.,* **-nized, -niz·ing. 1.** to stimulate by or as if by a galvanic current. **2.** *Med.* to stimulate or treat (muscles or nerves) with induced direct current (distinguished from *faradize*). **3.** to startle into sudden activity; stimulate. **4.** to coat (metal, esp. iron or steel) with zinc. Also, *esp. Brit.,* **gal′va·nise′.** [1795–1805; < F *galvaniser,* named after Luigi GALVANI; see -IZE] **—gal′va·ni·za′tion,** *n.* **—gal′va·niz′er,** *n.*
—Syn. 3. rouse, stir, electrify, fire, spur, animate.

gal′vanized i′ron, iron or steel, esp. in sheets, coated with zinc to prevent rust. [1830–40]

galvano-, a combining form representing **galvanic** or **galvanism** in compound words: *galvanometer.*

gal·va·no·cau·ter·y (gal′və nō kô′tə rē, gal van′ō-), *n., pl.* **-ter·ies.** *Med.* **1.** a cautery heated by a galvanic current. **2.** cauterization by means of such a cautery. [1870–75; GALVANO- + CAUTERY]

gal·va·no·mag·net′ic effect′ (gal′və nō mag net′ik, gal van′ō-), *Elect., Physics.* any of several phenomena that occur when an electric current is passed through a conductor or semiconductor situated in a magnetic field, as the Hall effect. [GALVANO- + MAGNETIC]

gal·va·nom·e·ter (gal′və nom′i tər), *n.* an instrument for detecting the existence of small electric currents and determining their strength. [1795–1805; GALVANO- + -METER]

gal·va·nom·e·try (gal′və nom′i trē), *n.* the method or process of determining the strength of electric currents. [GALVANO- + -METRY] **—gal·va·no·met·ric** (gal′və nō me′trik, gal van′ə-), **gal′va·no·met′ri·cal,** *adj.* **—gal′va·no·met′ri·cal·ly,** *adv.*

gal·va·no·plas·tic (gal′və nō plas′tik, gal van′ō-), *adj. Print.* pertaining to reproduction by electrotypy. [1840–50; GALVANO- + -PLASTIC] **—gal′van·o·plas′ti·cal·ly,** *adv.*

gal·va·no·plas·ty (gal′və nō plas′tē, gal van′ō-), *n. Print.* electrotypy. [1865–70; GALVANO- + -PLASTY]

gal·va·no·scope (gal′və nə skōp′, gal van′ə-), *n.* an instrument for detecting the existence of an electric current and determining its direction. [1825–35; GALVANO- + -SCOPE] **—gal·va·no·scop·ic** (gal′və nə skop′ik, gal-van′ə-), *adj.* **—gal·va·nos·co·pist** (gal′və nos′kə pist), *n.* **—gal′va·nos′co·py,** *n.*

gal·va·no·tax·is (gal′və nō tak′sis, gal van′ō-), *n.* movement of an organism or any of its parts in a particular direction in response to an electric current; electrotaxis. [1895–1900; < NL; see GALVANO-, TAXIS] **—gal·va·no·tac·tic** (gal′və nō tak′tik, gal van′ō-), *adj.*

gal·va·no·ther·a·py (gal′və nō ther′ə pē, gal van′ō-), *n. Med.* treatment employing electric current. [GALVANO- + THERAPY]

Gal·ves·ton (gal′və stən), *n.* a seaport in SE Texas, on an island at the mouth of Galveston Bay. 61,902.

Gal′veston Bay′, an inlet of the Gulf of Mexico.

Gal′veston plan′. See **commission plan.** [after GALVESTON, the first U.S. city to adopt such a plan]

Gal•way (gôl′wā), *n.* **1.** a county in S Connaught, in W Republic of Ireland. 171,836; 2293 sq. mi. (5940 sq. km). **2.** its county seat: a seaport in the W part. 37,714.

Gal•we•gian (gal wē′jən), *adj.* **1.** of or pertaining to the region of Galloway, Scotland. —*n.* **2.** a native or inhabitant of Galloway. [1765–75; irreg. < ML *Galwedi(a)* GALLOWAY + -AN]

gal•yak (gal′yak), *n.* a sleek, flat fur made from lambskin or from the pelt of a young goat. Also, **gal′yac.** [of uncert. orig.]

gam[1] (gam), *n. Slang.* a person's leg, esp. an attractive female leg. [1775–85; prob. < Polari < It *gamba* leg; see JAMB[1]]

gam[2] (gam), *n., v.,* **gammed, gam•ming.** —*n.* **1.** a herd or school of whales. **2.** *Eastern New Eng., Naut.* a social meeting, visit, etc., as between whaling vessels at sea. —*v.i.* **3.** (of whales) to assemble into a herd or school. **4.** *Naut.* (of the officers and crews of two whaling vessels) to visit or converse with one another for social purposes. **5.** *Eastern New Eng.* to participate in a gam or social visit. [1840–50, *Amer.*; perh. dial. var. of GAME[1]]

Ga•ma (gam′ə; *Port.* gä′mə), *n.* **Vas•co da** (vas′kō də; *Port.* väsh′ko͝o də), c1460–1524, Portuguese navigator: discovered the sea route from Portugal around the continent of Africa to India.

ga′ma grass′ (gä′mə), an ornamental, reedlike grass, *Tripsacum dactyloides,* one of the largest in the U.S., growing from 4 to 7 ft. (1.2 to 2.1 m) high. [1825–35, *Amer.*; var. of GRAMA]

Ga•ma•li•el (gə mā′lē əl, -māl′yəl), *n.* **1.** ("*the Elder*" or "*Gamaliel I*"), died A.D. 50?, the teacher of Paul (Acts 22:3); the grandson of Hillel. **2.** his grandson ("*the Younger*" or "*Gamaliel II*"), died A.D. 115?, leader of the Jews after the destruction of Jerusalem, A.D. 70. **3.** a male given name: from Hebrew, meaning "the Lord is my reward."

Ga•may (ga mā′, gam′ā), *n.* **1.** a grape grown esp. in the Beaujolais region of France and in N California. **2.** the dry red wine made from this grape. [< F *gamay, gamet,* after *Gamay,* a village in St.-Aubin commune (Côte-d'Or), France]

gam•ba•do[1] (gam bā′dō), *n., pl.* **-dos, -does. 1.** either of a pair of large protective boots or gaiters fixed to a saddle instead of stirrups. **2.** any long gaiter or legging. [1650–60; < It *gamb(a)* leg + *-ado* -ADE[1]]

gam•ba•do[2] (gam bā′dō), *n., pl.* **-dos, -does. 1.** a spring or leap by a horse. **2.** a caper or antic. Also, **gam•bade** (gam bād′, -bäd′). [1810–20; prob. a pseudo-Sp alter. of F *gambade* a leap or spring, perh. < Pr *cambado, gambado,* equiv. to *gamb(a)* leg (see JAMB[1]) + *-ado* -ADE[1]]

gam•be•son (gam′bə sən), *n. Armor.* a quilted garment worn under mail. [1300–50; ME *ga(u)mbeson* a military tunic < OF *gambison, gambeison,* prob. < Gmc]

Gam•bet•ta (gam bet′ə; *Fr.* gäɴ be tA′), *n.* **Lé•on** (lā ôɴ′), 1838–82, French statesman.

Gam•bi•a (gam′bē ə), *n.* **1.** a river in W Africa, flowing W to the Atlantic. 500 mi. (800 km) long. **2. The,** a republic extending inland along both sides of this river: formerly a British crown colony and protectorate; gained independence 1965; member of the Commonwealth of Nations. 525,000; 4003 sq. mi. (10,368 sq. km). *Cap.:* Banjul. —**Gam′bi•an,** *adj., n.*

gam•bier (gam′bēr), *n.* an astringent extract obtained from the leaves and young shoots of a tropical Asian shrub, *Uncaria gambir,* of the madder family, used in medicine, dyeing, tanning, etc. Also, **gam′bir.** [1820–30; < Malay *gambir* the name of the plant]

Gam′bier Is′lands (gam′bēr), a group of islands in French Polynesia, belonging to the Tuamotu Archipelago. 8226; 12 sq. mi. (31 sq. km).

gam•bit (gam′bit), *n.* **1.** *Chess.* an opening in which a player seeks to obtain some advantage by sacrificing a pawn or piece. **2.** any maneuver by which one seeks to gain an advantage. **3.** a remark made to open or redirect a conversation. [1650–60; < F < Sp *gambito* or It *gambetto* (akin to OF *gambet, jambet*), equiv. to *gamb(a)* leg + *-etta* -ET]
—**Syn. 2.** ploy, stratagem, scheme, ruse.

gam•ble (gam′bəl), *v.,* **-bled, -bling,** *n.* —*v.i.* **1.** to play at any game of chance for money or other stakes. **2.** to stake or risk money, or anything of value, on the outcome of something involving chance: *to gamble on a toss of the dice.* —*v.t.* **3.** to lose or squander by betting (usually fol. by *away*): *He gambled all his hard-earned money away in one night.* **4.** to wager or risk (money or something else of value): *to gamble one's freedom.* **5.** to take a chance on; venture; risk: *I'm gambling that our new store will be a success.* —*n.* **6.** any matter or thing involving risk or hazardous uncertainty. **7.** a venture in a game of chance for stakes, esp. for high stakes. [1150–1200; ME *gamenen* to play (OE *gamenian*), with substitution of -LE for *-en;* see GAME[1]] —**gam′bler,** *n.*
—**Syn. 6.** venture, hazard, speculation, flyer.

gam′bling house′, a building for gambling, esp. for a large number of betting games. [1830–40]

gam•boge (gam bōj′, -bo͞ozh′), *n.* **1.** Also, **cambogia.** a gum resin from various Asian trees of the genus *Garcinia,* esp. *G. hanburyi,* used as a yellow pigment and as a cathartic. **2.** yellow or yellow-orange. [1625–35; < NL *gambog-* (s. of *gambogium*), var. of *cambog-,* after CAMBODIA] —**gam•bo′gi•an,** *adj.*

gam•bol (gam′bəl), *v.,* **-boled, -bol•ing** or (*esp. Brit.*) **-bolled, -bol•ling,** *n.* —*v.i.* **1.** to skip about, as in dancing or playing; frolic. —*n.* **2.** a skipping or frisking about; frolic. [1495–1505; earlier *gambold, gambald, gamba(u)de* < MF *gambade;* see GAMBADE]
—**Syn. 1.** spring, caper, frisk, romp.

gam•brel (gam′brəl), *n.* **1.** the hock of an animal, esp. of a horse. **2.** Also called **gam′brel stick′.** a wood or metal device for suspending a slaughtered animal. [1540–50; < ONF *gamberel,* akin to F *jambier* legging, *jambe* leg]

gam′brel roof′, a gable roof, each side of which has a shallower slope above a steeper one. Cf. **mansard** (def. 1). See illus. under **roof.** [1755–65, *Amer.*] —**gam′•brel-roofed′,** *adj.*

Gam•bri•nus (gam brī′nəs), *n.* a mythical Flemish king, the reputed inventor of beer.

gam•bu•sia (gam byo͞o′zhə, -zhē ə, -zē ə), *n.* any fish of the genus *Gambusia,* comprising small livebearers that feed on aquatic insect larvae and are used to control mosquitoes. [1900–05; < NL, alter. of Cuban Sp *gambusino;* see -IA]

game[1] (gām), *n., adj.,* **gam•er, gam•est,** *v.,* **gamed, gam•ing.** —*n.* **1.** an amusement or pastime: *children's games.* **2.** the material or equipment used in playing certain games: *a store selling toys and games.* **3.** a competitive activity involving skill, chance, or endurance on the part of two or more persons who play according to a set of rules, usually for their own amusement or for that of spectators. **4.** a single occasion of such an activity, or a definite portion of one: *the final game of the season; a rubber of three games at bridge.* **5.** the number of points required to win a game. **6.** the score at a particular stage in a game: *With five minutes to play, the game was 7 to 0.* **7.** a particular manner or style of playing a game: *Her game of chess is improving.* **8.** anything resembling a game, as in requiring skill, endurance, or adherence to rules: *the game of diplomacy.* **9.** a trick or strategy: *to see through someone's game.* **10.** fun; sport of any kind; joke: *That's about enough of your games.* **11.** wild animals, including birds and fishes, such as are hunted for food or taken for sport or profit. **12.** the flesh of such wild animals or other game, used as food: *a dish of game.* **13.** any object of pursuit, attack, abuse, etc.: *The new boy at school seemed to be fair game for practical jokers.* **14.** *Informal.* a business or profession: *He's in the real-estate game.* **15.** *Archaic.* fighting spirit; pluck. **16. make game of,** to make fun of; ridicule: *to make game of the weak and defenseless.* **17. play games,** to act in an evasive, deceitful, manipulative, or trifling manner in dealing with others: *Don't play games with me—I want to know if you love me or not!* **18. play the game,** *Informal.* **a.** to act or play in accordance with the rules. **b.** to act honorably or justly: *We naively assumed that our allies would continue to play the game.* —*adj.* **19.** pertaining to or composed of animals hunted or taken as game or to their flesh. **20.** having a fighting spirit; plucky. **21.** *Informal.* having the required spirit or will (often fol. by *for* or an infinitive): *Who's game for a hike through the woods?* **22. die game, a.** to die after a brave struggle. **b.** to remain steadfast or in good spirits at the moment of defeat: *He knew that as a candidate he didn't have a chance in the world, but he campaigned anyway and died game.* —*v.i.* **23.** to play games of chance for stakes; gamble. —*v.t.* **24.** to squander in gaming (usually fol. by *away*). [bef. 1000; ME *gamen,* OE *gaman;* c. OHG *gaman* glee] —**game′less,** *adj.* —**game′like′,** *adj.* —**game′ness,** *n.*
—**Syn. 3.** sport, contest, competition. **9.** scheme, artifice, stratagem, plan, plot, venture. **11, 13.** prey, quarry. **20.** brave, bold, intrepid, dauntless, fearless.

game[2] (gām), *adj.* lame: *a game leg.* [1780–90; perh. shortening of GAMMY, though change in vowel unclear]

game•bag (gām′bag′), *n.* a bag, usually of leather or canvas, for carrying game, esp. birds, killed by a hunter. [1820–30; GAME[1] + BAG]

game′ bird′, any bird hunted chiefly for sport, as a quail or pheasant, esp. such a bird that is protected by game laws. [1865–70]

game•cast (gām′kast′, -käst′), *n. Radio and Television.* the broadcast of a team sport game. [GAME[1] + (BROAD)CAST]

game•cock (gām′kok′), *n.* a rooster of a fighting breed, or one bred and trained for fighting. [1670–80; GAME[1] + COCK[1]]

game′ fish′, an edible fish capable of affording sport to the angler in its capture. [1860–65]

game′ fowl′, a domestic fowl of a breed much used for fighting. [1775–85]

game•keep•er (gām′kē′pər), *n.* a person employed, as on an estate or game preserve, to prevent poaching and provide a natural environment conducive to the propagation of game, as by thinning brush, scattering food after a snowstorm, and the like. [1660–70; GAME[1] + KEEPER] —**game′keep′ing,** *n.*

gam•e•lan (gam′ə lan′, -lən), *n.* an Indonesian orchestra consisting of bowed stringed instruments, flutes, and a great variety of percussion instruments. Also, **gam•e•lin** (gam′ə lin). [1810–20; < Javanese, equiv. to *gamel* song accompanied by a gamelan + *-an* nominalizing suffix]

game′ law′, a law enacted for the preservation of game, as by restricting the number and kinds of game that may be taken and by designating periods of the year when specified game may be taken. [1705–15]

game•ly (gām′lē), *adv.* in a game or plucky manner: *They struggled gamely.* [1860–65; GAME[1] (adj.) + -LY]

Game′ Mas′ter, the person who controls a role-playing game.

game′ of chance′, a game in which the outcome is determined by chance rather than by the skill of its players, as roulette. [1920–25]

game′ of skill′, a game in which the outcome is determined by skill rather than by chance, as chess.

game′ park′, a game preserve, esp. in Africa. [1965–70]

game′ plan′, 1. a carefully thought-out strategy or course of action, as in politics, business, or one's personal affairs. **2.** *Sports.* the overall strategy of a team for winning a specific game. [1965–70]

game′ point′, (in tennis, squash, handball, etc.) the point that if won would enable the scorer or the scorer's side to win the game. [1945–50]

gam•er (gā′mər), *n.* a person who plays games. [1610–20; GAME[1] + -ER[1]]

game′ room′, a room used for recreation, esp. for table games. [1905–10]

game′ show′, a television or radio program in which contestants answer questions or play games of skill or chance in order to win money or other prizes.

games•man (gāmz′mən), *n., pl.* **-men. 1.** a person who is skilled at manipulating events and circumstances to gain or maintain personal advantage, esp. in business or politics. **2.** a person who enjoys playing games of skill. [1930–35; GAME[1] + -S[3] + -MAN]

games•man•ship (gāmz′mən ship′), *n.* **1.** the use of methods, esp. in a sports contest, that are dubious or seemingly improper but not strictly illegal. **2.** the technique or practice of manipulating people or events so as to gain an advantage or outwit one's opponents or competitors. [1945–50; GAME[1] + -S[3] + -MANSHIP, perh. on the model of SPORTSMANSHIP]

game•some (gām′səm), *adj.* playful; frolicsome. [1300–50; ME; see GAME[1], -SOME[1]] —**game′some•ly,** *adv.* —**game′some•ness,** *n.*

game•ster (gām′stər), *n.* a gambler. [1545–55; GAME[1] + -STER]

gamet-, var. of **gameto-** before a vowel: *gametangium.*

gam•e•tan•gi•um (gam′i tan′jē əm), *n., pl.* **-gi•a** (-jē ə). *Bot.* an organ or body bearing gametes, as in mosses and liverworts. [1885–90; < NL; see GAMET-, ANGIO-, -IUM]

gam•ete (gam′ēt, gə mēt′), *n. Biol.* a mature sexual reproductive cell, as a sperm or egg, that unites with another cell to form a new organism. [1885–90; < NL *gameta* < Gk *gamet-* (s. of *gametḗ* wife, *gamétēs* husband), deriv. of *gameîn* to marry] —**ga•met•ic** (gə met′ik), **ga•me•tal** (gə mēt′l), *adj.* —**ga•met′i•cal•ly,** *adv.*

game′ the′ory, a mathematical theory that deals with strategies for maximizing gains and minimizing losses within prescribed constraints, as the rules of a card game: widely applied in the solution of various decision-making problems, as those of military strategy and business policy. Also called **theory of games.** [1950–55]

gameto-, a combining form representing **gamete:** *gametophore.* Also, *esp. before a vowel,* **gamet-.** [< NL *gamet(a)* GAMETE + -o- -o-]

ga•me•to•cide (gə mē′tə sīd′, gam′i-), *n.* a substance that kills gametes or gametocytes. [GAMETO- + -CIDE]

ga•me•to•cyte (gə mē′tə sīt′, gam′i-), *n. Biol.* a cell that produces gametes. [1895–1900; GAMETO- + -CYTE]

gam•e•to•gen•e•sis (gə mē′tə jen′ə sis, gam′i-), *n. Biol.* the development of gametes. [1895–1900; GAMETO- + -GENESIS] —**ga•me′to•gen′ic, gam•e•tog•e•nous** (gam′i toj′ə nəs), *adj.*

ga•me•to•phore (gə mē′tə fôr′, -fōr′, gam′i-), *n. Bot.* a part or structure bearing gametangia. [1890–95; GAMETO- + -PHORE] —**ga•me•to•phor•ic** (gə mē′tə fôr′ik, -for′-, gam′i-), *adj.*

ga•me•to•phyte (gə mē′tə fīt′, gam′i-), *n. Bot.* the sexual form of a plant in the alternation of generations. Cf. **sporophyte.** [1890–95; GAMETO- + -PHYTE] —**ga•me•to•phyt•ic** (gə mē′tə fit′ik, gam′i-), *adj.*

ga•me•to•thal•lus (gə mē′tə thal′əs, gam′i-), *n. Mycol.* a gamete-producing thallus. [GAMETO- + THALLUS]

game′ war′den, a public official who enforces game laws.

gam•ey (gā′mē), *adj.,* **gam•i•er, gam•i•est.** gamy.

gam•ic (gam′ik), *adj. Biol.* sexual (def. 3). [1855–60; < Gk *gamikós* bridal of marriage, equiv. to *gám(os)* marriage, wedding + *-ikos* -IC]

Ga•mi•la•raay (gä′mē lär′ī, gä′mē lär′ī), *n.* Kamilaroi.

gam•in (gam′in), *n.* a neglected boy left to run about the streets; street urchin. [1830–40; < F, orig. boy assisting a glassblower, young boy; of uncert. orig.]

gam•ine (gam′ēn, -in, ga mēn′), *n.* **1.** a neglected girl who is left to run about the streets. **2.** a diminutive or very slender girl, esp. one who is pert, impudent, or playfully mischievous. —*adj.* **3.** of or like a gamine: *a gamine personality; clothes for the gamine figure.* [1895–1900; < F; fem. of GAMIN]

gam•i•ness (gā′mē nis), *n.* **1.** the taste or odor of game, esp. when slightly tainted. **2.** gameness; pluck. **3.** squalor or lewdness. [GAMY + -NESS]

gam•ing (gā′ming), *n.* **1.** gambling. **2.** the playing of games, esp. those developed to teach something or to help solve a problem, as in a military or business situation. [1495–1505; GAME[1] + -ING[1]]

gam′ing ta′ble, a table used for gambling, esp. one designed with a game board and slots for chips. [1590–1600]

gam•ma (gam′ə), *n.* **1.** the third letter of the Greek alphabet (Γ, γ). **2.** the consonant sound represented by this letter. **3.** the third in a series of items. **4.** (*cap.*) *Astron.* a star that is usually the third brightest of a constellation: *The third brightest star in the Southern Cross is Gamma Crucis.* **5.** a unit of weight equal to one microgram. **6.** *Physics.* a unit of magnetic field strength, equal to 10^{-5} gauss. **7.** *Photog.* a measure of the degree of development of a negative or print. **8.** *Television.* an analogous numerical indication of the degree of contrast between light and dark in the reproduction of an image in television. **9.** *Chiefly Brit.* a grade showing that an individual student is in the third, or lowest, of three scholastic sections in a class. Cf. **alpha** (def. 7), **beta** (def. 8). [< Gk *gámma*]

gam′ma-a·mi·no·bu·tyr′ic ac′id (gam′ə ə mē′-nō byōō tir′ik, -am′ə nō-). See **GABA**. [1960–65; AMINO- + BUTYRIC ACID]

gam′ma glob′ulin, *Immunol.* a protein fraction of blood plasma that responds to stimulation of antigens, as bacteria or viruses, by forming antibodies: administered therapeutically in the treatment of some viral diseases. [1955–60]

gam·ma·gram (gam′ə gram′), *n.* a record of the intensity and distribution of radioactivity in tissue following the application of radioactive tracers; scintigram. [GAMMA + -GRAM[1]]

gam′ma i′ron, *Metall.* an allotrope of iron, stable between 910°C and 1400°C and having a face-centered cubic lattice. [1895–1900]

gam′ma ray′, *Physics.* **1.** a photon of penetrating electromagnetic radiation **(gam′ma radia′tion)** emitted from an atomic nucleus. **2.** a photon emitted by an electron as a result of internal conversion. **3.** electromagnetic radiation with wavelengths shorter than approximately one tenth of a nanometer. [1900–05]

gam′ma-ray astron′omy (gam′ə rā′), the branch of astronomy that deals with the study of celestial objects by means of the gamma rays that come from them. [1960–1965]

gam·mer (gam′ər), *n. Brit. Archaic.* an old woman. [1565–75; contr. of GODMOTHER; cf. GAFFER]

gam·mon[1] (gam′ən), *Backgammon.* —*n.* **1.** the game of backgammon. **2.** a victory in which the winner throws off all his or her pieces before the opponent throws off any. —*v.t.* **3.** to win a gammon over. [1720–30; perh. special use of ME *gamen* GAME[1]]

gam·mon[2] (gam′ən), *n.* **1.** a smoked or cured ham. **2.** the lower end of a side of bacon. [1480–90; < OF *gambon* ham (F *jambon*), deriv. of *gambe;* see JAMB[1]]

gam·mon[3] (gam′ən), *Brit. Informal.* —*n.* **1.** deceitful nonsense; bosh. —*v.i.* **2.** to talk gammon. **3.** to make pretense. —*v.t.* **4.** to humbug. [1710–20; perh. special use of GAMMON[1]] —**gam′mon·er,** *n.*

gam·mop·a·thy (ga mop′ə thē), *n. Immunol.* a disorder of the immune system characterized by abnormally increased levels of immunoglobulins in the blood. [GAMM(A GLOBULIN) + -O- + -PATHY]

gam·my (gam′ē), *adj.,* **-mi·er, -mi·est.** *Brit. Informal.* disabled; lame: *a gammy leg.* [1830–40; orig. dial., perh. < dial. F; cf. Normandy dial. *gambier* having bad legs, *gambie* lame, MF *gambi* bent, crooked, all ult. deriv. of LL *gamba;* see JAMB[1]]

gamo-, a combining form meaning "joined, united," "joining, union," used in the formation of compound words: *gamopetalous.* [comb. form repr. Gk *gámos* marriage]

gam·o·gen·e·sis (gam′ə jen′ə sis), *n. Biol.* sexual reproduction. [1860–65; GAMO- + -GENESIS] —**gam·o·ge·net·ic** (gam′ō jə net′ik), **gam′o·ge·net′i·cal,** *adj.* —**gam′o·ge·net′i·cal·ly,** *adv.*

gam·o·pet·al·ous (gam′ə pet′l əs), *adj. Bot.* having the petals united. [1820–30; < NL; see GAMO-, PETALOUS]

gamopetalous flower

gam·o·phyl·lous (gam′ə fil′əs), *adj. Bot.* having leaves united by their edges. [1870–75; GAMO- + -PHYLLOUS]

gam·o·sep·al·ous (gam′ə sep′ə ləs), *adj. Bot.* having the sepals united. See illus. under **calyx.** [1825–35; GAMO- + -SEPALOUS]

-gamous, a combining form with the meaning "having gametes or reproductive organs" of the kind specified by the initial element: *heterogamous;* also forming adjectives corresponding to nouns ending in **-gamy:** *endogamous.* [< Gk *-gamos* marrying; see -OUS]

Gam·ow (gam′ôf, -of), *n.* **George,** 1904–68, U.S. nuclear physicist and writer, born in Russia.

gamp (gamp), *n. Brit. Informal.* an umbrella. [1860–65; after the umbrella of Mrs. Sarah *Gamp* in Dickens' *Martin Chuzzlewit*]

gam·ut (gam′ət), *n.* **1.** the entire scale or range: *the gamut of dramatic emotion from grief to joy.* **2.** *Music.* **a.** the whole series of recognized musical notes. **b.** the major scale. [1425–75; late ME < ML; contr. of *gamma ut,* equiv. to *gamma,* used to represent the first or lowest tone (G) in the medieval scale + *ut* (later *do*); the notes of the scale (*ut, re, mi, fa, sol, la, si*) being named from a Latin hymn to St. John the Baptist: *Ut* queant laxis *re*sonare fibris. *Mi*ra gestorum *fa*muli tuorum, *Sol*ve polluti *la*bii reatum, *S*ancte *I*ohannes]
—**Syn. 1.** sweep, breadth, scope, reach, extent, field.

gam·y (gā′mē), *adj.,* **gam·i·er, gam·i·est. 1.** having the tangy flavor or odor of game: *I like the gamy taste of venison.* **2.** having the flavor or odor of game or other meat kept uncooked until slightly tainted: *The roast was still edible but was slightly gamy.* **3.** plucky; spirited. **4.** lewd or suggestive; risqué. **5.** gross or squalid; unwholesome. Also, **gamey.** [1835–45; GAME[1] + -Y[1]] —**gam′i·ly,** *adv.*

-gamy, a combining form with the meanings "marriage," "union," "fertilization, pollination," of the kind specified by the initial element: *exogamy; plastogamy; allogamy;* also forming nouns corresponding to adjectives ending in **-gamous:** *heterogamy.* [comb. form repr. Gk *-gamia* act of marrying]

gan (gan), *v.* pt. of **gin**[3].

Gand (gäN), *n.* French name of **Ghent.**

Gan·da (gan′də, gän′-), *n.* Luganda.

G&AE, *Accounting.* general and administrative expense.

gan·der (gan′dər), *n.* **1.** the male of the goose. Cf. **goose** (def. 2). **2.** *Slang.* a look: *Take a gander at his new shoes.* [bef. 1000; 1910–15 for def. 2; ME; OE *gan(d)ra;* c. MLG *ganre,* D *gander;* akin to GOOSE, G *Gans*]

Gan·der (gan′dər), *n.* a town in E Newfoundland, in Canada: airport on the great circle route between New York and northern Europe.

Gan·dha·ra (gun där′ə), *n.* **1.** an ancient region in NW India and E Afghanistan. —*adj.* **2.** Also, **Gan·dha·ran** (gun där′ən). of or pertaining to Gandhara, its inhabitants, or its art.

Gan·dhi (gän′dē, gan′-), *n.* **1. In·di·ra** (in dēr′ə), 1917–84, Indian political leader: prime minister 1966–77 and 1980–84 (daughter of Jawaharlal Nehru). **2. Mo·han·das Kar·am·chand** (mō′hən däs′ kur′əm chund′), ("*Mahatma*"), 1869–1948, Hindu religious leader, nationalist, and social reformer. **3. Ra·jiv** (rä jēv′), 1944–91, Indian political leader: prime minister 1984–89 (son of Indira).

Gan·dhi·an (gän′dē ən, gan′-), *adj.* of or pertaining to Mohandas Gandhi or to Gandhiism. [1920–25; GANDHI + -AN]

Gan′dhi cap′, a white cap, pointed in front and back and having a wide band, worn by men in India. [1920–25]

Gan·dhi·ism (gän′dē iz′əm, gan′-), *n.* the principles associated with Mohandas Gandhi, esp. his principles of noncooperation and passive resistance in gaining political and social reforms. Also, **Gan·dhism** (gän′diz əm, gan′-). Cf. **Satyagraha.** [1920–25; GANDHI + -ISM] —**Gan′dhi·ist, Gan·dhist** (gän′dist, gan′-), *n.*

G and T, See **gin and tonic.** Also, **g and t**

gan′dy danc′er (gan′dē), *Railroad Slang.* a member of a railroad section gang that lays or maintains track. [1915–20; *dancer* appar. in reference to the rhythmic movements characteristic of such work; *gandy* is of uncert. orig.]

Gan·dzha (gän′jə; *Russ.* gun jä′), *n.* a former name of **Kirovabad.**

ga·nef (gä′nəf), *n. Slang.* a thief, swindler, crook, or rascal. Also, **gonif, goniff.** [1920–25; < Yiddish < Heb *gannābh*]

Ga·ne·sha (gə nä′shə), *n.* the Hindu god of wisdom.

gang[1] (gang), *n.* **1.** a group or band: *A gang of boys gathered around the winning pitcher.* **2.** a group of youngsters or adolescents who associate closely, often exclusively, for social reasons, esp. such a group engaging in delinquent behavior. **3.** a group of people with compatible tastes or mutual interests who gather together for social reasons: *I'm throwing a party for the gang I bowl with.* **4.** a group of persons working together; squad; shift: *a gang of laborers.* **5.** a group of persons associated for some criminal or other antisocial purpose: *a gang of thieves.* **6.** a set of tools, electronic components or circuits, oars, etc., arranged to work together or simultaneously. **7.** a group of identical or related items. —*v.t.* **8.** to arrange in groups or sets; form into a gang: *to gang illustrations for more economical printing on one sheet.* **9.** to attack in a gang. —*v.i.* **10.** to form or act as a gang: *Cutthroats who gang together hang together.* **11. gang up on,** *Informal.* (of a number of persons) to unite in opposition to (a person); combine against: *The bigger boys ganged up on the smaller ones in the schoolyard.* [1300–50; ME; OE *gang, gong* manner of going, way, passage; c. OHG *gang,* ON *gangr,* Goth *gagg;* cf. GANG[2]]
—**Syn. 1.** company, crowd, crew; party, set, clique, coterie. **4.** team.

gang[2] (gang), *v.i. Chiefly Scot. and North Eng.* to walk or go. [bef. 900; ME *gangen,* OE *gangan, gongan;* c. OHG *gangan,* ON *ganga,* Goth *gaggan;* cf. GANG[1], n. deriv. from same base]

gang·bang (gang′bang′), *Slang* (*vulgar*). —*n.* **1.** Also, **gang′ bang′.** often forcible sexual intercourse engaged in by several persons successively with one passive partner. —*v.i.* **2.** to participate in such an activity. —*v.t.* **3.** to subject to a gangbang. [1950–55, *Amer.;* GANG[1] + BANG[1]] —**gang′bang′er,** *n.*

gang·board (gang′bôrd′, -bōrd′), *n. Naut.* a raised walk on a sailing ship, crossing the waist and connecting the forecastle directly with the quarterdeck. [1740–50; GANG[1] + BOARD]

gang·bust·er (gang′bus′tər), *n. Informal.* **1.** a law-enforcement officer who specializes in breaking up organized crime, often by forceful or sensational means. **2.** someone or something having great impact, usually in a positive way. **3. gangbusters,** an outstandingly successful state or situation: *I'm not looking for gangbusters, but I'd like you to pass all your courses this term.* **4. like gangbusters,** with great speed, intensity, vigor, impact, or success: *The software market was growing like gangbusters. The hockey team came on at the beginning of the season like gangbusters.* —*adj.* Often, **gangbusters. 5.** of or like a law-enforcement officer who uses rough, aggressive, or sensational tactics in fighting crime: *The undercover agents avoided the gangbusters approach.* **6.** strikingly effective or successful: *a gangbusters year for compact cars.* **7.** enthusiastic: *I'm not gangbusters over the idea.* [1935–40; GANG[1] + BUSTER]

gang′ drill′, a drilling machine having a number of separately driven vertical spindles in a row, used for drilling holes in a piece successively. Cf. **multiple drill.** [1880–85]

gang·er (gang′ər), *n. Brit.* a foreman of a gang of laborers. [1840–50; GANG[1] + ER[1]]

Gan·ges (gan′jēz), *n.* a river flowing SE from the Himalayas in N India into the Bay of Bengal: sacred to Hindus. 1550 mi. (2495 km) long. —**Gan·get·ic** (gan-jet′ik), *adj.*

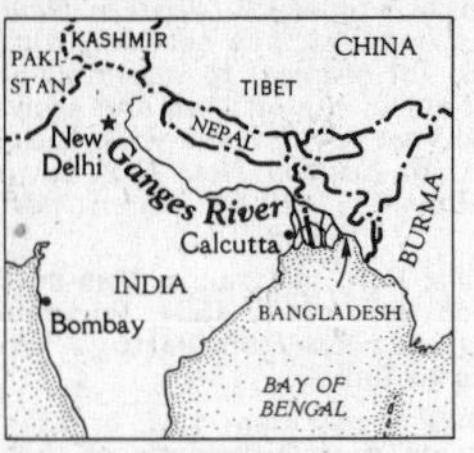

gang′ hook′, *Angling.* a hook with several points, made by joining the shanks of two or three hooks. [1625–35, *Amer.*]

gang·land (gang′land′, -lənd), *n.* the world of organized crime; criminal underworld. [1910–15, *Amer.;* GANG[1] + LAND]

gan·gle (gang′gəl), *v.i.,* **-gled, -gling.** to move awkwardly or ungracefully: *A tall, stiff-jointed man gangled past.* [1965–70; back formation from GANGLING]

gan·gli·ate (gang′glē āt′, -it), *adj.* having ganglia. Also, **gan′gli·at′ed.** [GANGLI(ON) + -ATE[1]]

gan·gli·form (gang′glə fôrm′), *adj.* having the form of a ganglion. [1675–85; GANGLI(ON) + -FORM]

gan·gling (gang′gling), *adj.* awkwardly tall and spindly; lank and loosely built. Also, **gangly.** [1800–10; akin to obs. *gangrel* gangling person; cf. GANG[1]]

gan·gli·on (gang′glē ən), *n., pl.* **-gli·a** (-glē ə), **-gli·ons. 1.** *Anat.* **a.** a mass of nerve tissue existing outside the central nervous system. **b.** any of certain masses of gray matter in the brain, as the basal ganglia. **2.** *Pathol.* a cyst or enlargement in connection with the sheath of a tendon, usually at the wrist. **3.** a center of intellectual or industrial force, activity, etc. [1675–85; < LL: a type of swelling < Gk *gánglion* a tumor under the skin, on or near a tendon] —**gan′gli·al, gan′gli·ar,** *adj.*

gan·gli·on·ate (gang′glē ə nāt′, -nit), *adj.* gangliate. Also, **gan′gli·on·at′ed.** [GANGLION + -ATE[1]]

gan·gli·on·ec·to·my (gang′glē ə nek′tə mē), *n., pl.* **-mies.** *Surg.* the excision of a ganglion. [1920–25; GANGLION + -ECTOMY]

gan·gli·on·ic (gang′glē on′ik), *adj. Anat.* of, pertaining to, or consisting of ganglia. [1820–30; GANGLION + -IC]

gan·gli·o·side (gang′glē ə sīd′), *n. Biochem.* any of a class of glycolipids, found chiefly in nerve ganglia, that upon hydrolysis yield sphingosine, neuraminic acid, a fatty acid, and a monosaccharide. [1940–45; GANGLI(ON) + -OSE[2] + -IDE]

gan·gly (gang′glē), *adj.,* **-gli·er, -gli·est.** gangling. [1870–75, *Amer.*]

Gang′ of Four′, a group of four radical members of the Chinese Communist party who were leaders of the Cultural Revolution and who were purged and imprisoned after the death of Mao Zedong: Jiang Qing (widow of Mao), Wang Hongwen, Yao Wenyuan, and Zhang Chunqiao. Cf. **Cultural Revolution, Red Guard.** [trans. of Chin *sirén bāng*]

gang·plank (gang′plangk′), *n.* a flat plank or small, movable, bridgelike structure for use by persons boarding or leaving a ship at a pier. Also called **brow, gangway.** [1840–50, *Amer.;* GANG[1] + PLANK]

gang′ plow′, a combination of two or more plows in one frame. [1840–50, *Amer.*]

gang′ rape′, an act or instance of gang-raping someone.

gang-rape (gang′rāp′), *v.t.,* **-raped, -rap·ing.** to force to have sexual intercourse with several persons.

gan·grel (gang′grəl, -rəl), *n. Brit. Dial.* **1.** a lanky, loose-jointed person. **2.** a wandering beggar; vagabond; vagrant. [1300–50; ME; See GANG[1], -REL; cf. GANGLING]

gan·grene (gang′grēn, gang grēn′), *n., v.,* **-grened, -gren·ing.** *Pathol.* —*n.* **1.** necrosis or death of soft tissue due to obstructed circulation, usually followed by decomposition and putrefaction. —*v.t., v.i.* **2.** to affect or become affected with gangrene. [1535–45; < MF *gangrene* (earlier *cancrene*) < L *gangraena* < Gk *gángraina* an eating sore] —**gan·gre·nous** (gang′grə nəs), *adj.*

gang′ saw′, a saw having several parallel blades for making simultaneous cuts. [1840–50, *Amer.*]

gang′sta rap′ (gang′stə), a type of rap music whose lyrics feature violence, sexual exploits, and the like. Also, **gang′ster rap′.** [1985–90]

gang·ster (gang′stər), *n.* a member of a gang of criminals, esp. a racketeer. [1895–1900, *Amer.;* GANG[1] + -STER]
—**Syn.** mobster, hoodlum, crook, thug; hood, goon.

gang·ster·ism (gang′stə riz′əm), *n.* **1.** the methods or behavior of gangsters. **2.** the use of tactics associated with gangsters, as intimidation or violence, in order to achieve something. [1925–30, *Amer.;* GANGSTER + -ISM]

gang′ switch′, *Elect.* a collection of switches connected to separate circuits and operating simultaneously.

Gang•tok (gung′tok′), *n.* a city in and the capital of Sikkim, in the S part. 36,768.

gangue (gang), *n.* rock or mineral matter of no value occurring with the metallic ore in a vein or deposit. [1800–10; < F < G *Gang;* see GANG[1]]

gang-up (gang′up′), *n.* an act of ganging up or uniting in opposition to someone or something. [1935–40; n. use of v. phrase *gang up (on)*]

gang•way (*n.* gang′wā′; *interj.* gang′wā′), *n.* **1.** a passageway, esp. a narrow walkway. **2.** *Naut.* **a.** an opening in the railing or bulwark of a ship, as that into which a gangplank fits. **b.** gangplank. **c.** an area of the weather deck of a ship, between the side and a deckhouse. **d.** See **accommodation ladder. 3.** *Railroads.* **a.** the space between the cab of a steam locomotive and its tender. **b.** the side entrance of a diesel or electric locomotive. **4.** *Brit.* **a.** an aisle in a theater, restaurant, etc. **b.** an aisle in the House of Commons separating the more influential members of the political parties from the younger, less influential members. **c.** a runway in a theater. **5.** a temporary path of planks, as at a building site. **6.** *Mining.* a main passage or level. **7.** Also called **logway.** the ramp up which logs are moved into a sawmill. —*interj.* **8.** clear the way! out of the way! [1680–90; GANG[1] + WAY; not continuous with OE *gangweg*] —**gang′wayed′,** *adj.*

gan•is•ter (gan′ə stər), *n.* **1.** a highly refractory, siliceous rock used to line furnaces. **2.** a synthetic product similar to this rock, made by mixing ground quartz with a bonding material. [1805–15; orig. uncert.]

gan•ja (gän′jə, gan′-), *n.* marijuana, esp. in the form of a potent preparation used chiefly for smoking. Also, **gan′jah.** [1680–90; < Hindi *gājā* hemp, the cut tops and leaves of nonfertilized female hemp plants; cf. Skt *gañjā* hemp]

gan•net (gan′it), *n.* any large, web-footed, seabird of the family Sulidae, having a sharply pointed bill, long wings, and a wedge-shaped tail, noted for its plunging dives for fish. [bef. 900; ME; OE *ganot;* akin to D *gent* GANDER]

Gan•nett (gan′it), *n.* **Henry,** 1846–1914, U.S. geographer and cartographer.

gan•oid (gan′oid), *adj.* **1.** of or pertaining to the Ganoidei, a group of mostly extinct fishes characterized by hard, bony scales, the living species of which include the paddlefishes, sturgeons, and gars. **2.** (of the scale of a fish) having a smooth, shiny surface of ganoin or a similar substance. —*n.* **3.** a ganoid fish. [1830–40; < F *ganoïde* < Gk *gán(os)* brightness + *-oïde* -OID]

gan•o•in (gan′ō in), *n. Ichthyol.* a hard, shiny, enamellike substance secreted by the corium, composing the outer layer of the scales of certain fishes. Also, **gan′o•ine.** [1855–60; GANO(ID) + -IN[2]]

Ganse•voort (ganz′vôrt, -vōrt), *n.* **Peter,** 1749–1812, U.S. general: soldier in the American Revolutionary War.

Gan•su (gän′sy′), *n. Pinyin.* a province in N central China. 12,650,000; 137,104 sq. mi. (355,099 sq. km). *Cap.:* Lanzhou. Also, **Kansu.**

gan•te•lope (gan′tl ōp′), *n. Archaic.* gauntlet[2]. [1640–50; var. of GANTLOPE]

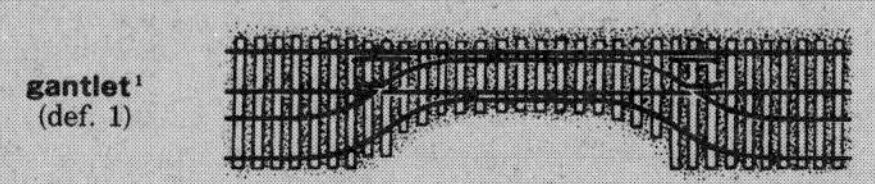
gantlet[1] (def. 1)

gant•let[1] (gant′lit, gônt′-), *n.* **1.** *Railroads.* a track construction used in narrow places, in which two parallel tracks converge so that their inner rails cross, run parallel, and diverge again, thus allowing a train to remain on its own track at all times. **2.** gauntlet[2] (defs. 1, 2, 4). —*v.t.* **3.** *Railroads.* to form or lay down as a gantlet: *to gantlet tracks.* Also, **gauntlet** (for defs. 1, 3). [1900–05; var. of GANTLOPE]

gant•let[2] (gant′lit, gônt′-), *n.* gauntlet[1]. —**gant′let•ed,** *adj.*

gant•line (gant′līn′), *n. Naut.* a rope rove through a single block hung from a mast, funnel, etc., as a means of hoisting workers, tools, flags, or the like. Also called **girtline.** [1830–40; var. of GIRTLINE]

gant•lope (gant′lōp), *n. Archaic.* gauntlet[2]. [1640–50; < Scand; cf. Sw *gatlopp,* lit., lane run, equiv. to *gat(a)* way, lane + *lopp* a running, course]

Gan•tri•sin (gan′trə sin), *Pharm., Trademark.* a brand of sulfisoxazole.

gan•try (gan′trē), *n., pl.* **-tries. 1.** a framework spanning a railroad track or tracks for displaying signals. **2.** any of various spanning frameworks, as a bridgelike portion of certain cranes. **3.** *Rocketry.* a frame consisting of scaffolds on various levels used to erect vertically launched rockets and spacecraft. **4.** a framelike stand for supporting a barrel or cask. Also, **gauntry.** [1325–75; ME *gauntre* < dial. OF *gantier* wooden stand, frame, var. of *chantier* < ML *cantārius* < L *canthērius* < Gk *kanthḗlios* packass]

Ga•nym•e•da (gə nim′i də), *n. Class. Myth.* Hebe.

Gan•y•mede (gan′ə mēd′), *n.* **1.** Also, **Gan•y•me•des** (gan′ə mē′dēz). *Class. Myth.* a Trojan youth who was abducted by Zeus and taken to Olympus, where he was made the cupbearer of the gods and became immortal. **2.** *Astron.* the largest moon of the planet Jupiter.

Ga•o (gä′ō, gou), *n.* a city in E Mali. 21,000.

GAO, See **General Accounting Office.**

gaol (jāl), *n., v.t. Brit.* jail. —**gaol′er,** *n.*

Ga•on (gä′ōn; *Seph. Heb.,* gä ôn′ *Ashk. Heb.* gä′ōn, goin), *n., pl.* **Ge•o•nim** (*Seph. Heb.* ge ô nēm′; *Ashk. Heb.* gā ō′nim), *Eng.* **Ga•ons. 1.** a title of honor for the directors of the Jewish academies at Sura and Pumbedita in Babylonia, used from the end of the 6th century A.D. to about the beginning of the 11th century. **2.** an eminent Jewish scholar noted for wisdom and knowledge of the Talmud: *the Gaon of Vilna.* [1770–80; < Heb: lit., majesty] —**Ga•on•ic** (gā on′ik), *adj.*

Gao•xiong (*Chin.* gou′shyông′), *n. Pinyin.* Kaohsiung.

gap (gap), *n., v.,* **gapped, gap•ping.** —*n.* **1.** a break or opening, as in a fence, wall, or military line; breach: *We found a gap in the enemy's line of fortifications.* **2.** an empty space or interval; interruption in continuity; hiatus: *a momentary gap in a siren's wailing; a gap in his memory.* **3.** a wide divergence or difference; disparity: *the gap between expenses and income.* **4.** a difference or disparity in attitudes, perceptions, character, or development, or a lack of confidence or understanding, perceived as creating a problem: *a communications gap.* **5.** a deep, sloping ravine or cleft through a mountain ridge. **6.** *Chiefly Midland and Southern U.S.* a mountain pass: *the Cumberland Gap.* **7.** *Aeron.* the distance between one supporting surface of an airplane and another above or below it. —*v.t.* **8.** to make a gap, opening, or breach in. —*v.i.* **9.** to come open or apart; form or show a gap. [1350–1400; ME < ON *gap* chasm] —**gap′less,** *adj.*
—**Syn. 2.** pause, interstice, break, interlude, lull.

gape (gāp, gap), *v.,* **gaped, gap•ing,** *n.* —*v.i.* **1.** to stare with open mouth, as in wonder. **2.** to open the mouth wide involuntarily, as the result of hunger, sleepiness, or absorbed attention. **3.** to open as a gap; split or become open wide. —*n.* **4.** a wide opening; gap; breach. **5.** an act or instance of gaping. **6.** a stare, as in astonishment. **7.** a yawn. **8.** *Zool.* the width of the open mouth. [1175–1225; ME < ON *gapa* to open the mouth wide; cf. G *gaffen*] —**gap′ing•ly,** *adv.*
—**Syn. 1.** See **gaze. 2, 3.** yawn.

gap•er (gā′pər), *n.* **1.** a person or thing that gapes. **2.** Also called **horse clam.** a large clam, *Tresus capax,* common on gravelly and coarse-sand beaches. [1630–40; GAPE + -ER[1]]

gapes (gāps, gaps), *n.* (*used with a singular v.*) **1.** *Vet. Pathol.* a parasitic disease of poultry and other birds, characterized by frequent gaping due to infestation of the trachea and bronchi with gapeworms. **2.** a fit of yawning. [see GAPE, -S[3]] —**gap′y,** *adj.*

gape•seed (gāp′sēd′, gap′-), *n. Brit. Dial.* **1.** a daydream or reverie. **2.** an idealistic, impossible, or unreal plan or goal. **3.** a person who gapes or stares in wonder, esp. a rustic or unworldly person who is easily awed. **4.** something that is gaped at; anything unusual or remarkable. **5. seek, plant,** or **sow gapeseed, a.** to daydream; woolgather. **b.** to plan, strive, or wish for impossible or unreal goals. [1590–1600; GAPE + SEED]

gape•worm (gāp′wûrm′, gap′-), *n.* a nematode worm, *Syngamus trachea,* that causes gapes. [1870–75; GAPE + WORM]

gap′ junc′tion, *Cell Biol.* a linkage of two adjacent cells consisting of a system of channels extending across a gap from one cell to the other, allowing the passage of ions and small molecules.

gap•o•sis (gap ō′sis), *n. Facetious.* a noticeable gap or series of gaps, as between the fastened buttons or snaps on an overly tight garment. [1950–55; GAP + -OSIS]

gap•ping (gap′ing), *n. Ling.* a rule of transformational grammar by which repeated instances of a verb are deleted from conjoined sentences, as in the deletion of *brought* from *Mary brought the bread, John the cheese, and Bill the wine.* [GAP + -ING[1]]

gap-toothed (gap′tōōtht′, -tōōthd′), *adj.* having a noticeable space between two teeth. Also, **gat-toothed.** [1560–70]

gar[1] (gär), *n., pl.* (*esp. collectively*) **gar,** (*esp. referring to two or more kinds or species*) **gars. 1.** Also called **garfish, garpike.** any predaceous freshwater fish of the genus *Lepisosteus,* of North America, covered with hard, diamond-shaped scales and having long jaws with needlelike teeth. **2.** needlefish (def. 1). [1755–65, *Amer.;* shortened form of GARFISH]

gar[1] (def. 1), *Lepisosteus osseus,* length to 5 ft. (1.5 m)

gar[2] (gär), *v.t.,* **garred, gar•ring. 1.** *Scot.* to compel or force (someone) to do something. **2.** *Scot. and North Eng. Obs.* to do, perform, or cause. [1250–1300; ME *geren, garren, gairen* < ON *gera* to do, make; akin to OE *gearwian* to prepare]

gar., garage.

G.A.R., Grand Army of the Republic.

ga•rage (gə räzh′, -räj′ *or, esp. Brit.,* gar′ij, -äzh), *n., v.,* **-raged, -rag•ing.** —*n.* **1.** a building or indoor area for parking or storing motor vehicles. **2.** a commercial establishment for repairing and servicing motor vehicles. —*v.t.* **3.** to put or keep in a garage. [1900–05; < F, equiv. to *gar(er)* to shelter (< Gmc **warôn* to take notice of; see WARE[2]) + *-age* -AGE] —**ga•rage′a•ble,** *adj.*

ga•rage•man (gə räzh′man′, -räj′- *or, esp. Brit.,* gar′ij-, -äzh-), *n., pl.* **-men.** a person who works in a garage, as a mechanic or attendant. [1915–20; GARAGE + -MAN]

garage′ sale′, a sale of used or unwanted household goods, personal items, bric-a-brac, etc., typically held in one's garage or yard. Also called **tag sale, yard sale.** [1960–65, *Amer.*]

Gar•a•mond (gar′ə mond′), *n.* a printing type designed in 1540 by Claude Garamond (c1480–1561), French type founder. [1865–70]

Gar•and (gar′ənd, gə rand′), *n.* **John C(an•tius)** (*Fr.* kän′tsyys), 1888–1974, U.S. inventor of M-1 semiautomatic rifle, born in Canada.

Gar′and ri′fle (gar′ənd, gə rand′). See **M-1.** [1935–40; named after John C. GARAND]

garb (gärb), *n.* **1.** a fashion or mode of dress, esp. of a distinctive, uniform kind: *in the garb of a monk.* **2.** wearing apparel; clothes. **3.** outward appearance or form. —*v.t.* **4.** to dress; clothe. [1585–95; < MF *garbe* graceful outline < OIt *garbo* grace < Gmc; cf. OHG *garawen,* OE *gearwian* to prepare, adorn (see GAR[2], GEAR] —**garb′less,** *adj.*
—**Syn. 1.** style, cut. **2.** clothing, dress, costume, attire.

gar•bage (gär′bij), *n.* **1.** discarded animal and vegetable matter, as from a kitchen; refuse. **2.** any matter that is no longer wanted or needed; trash. **3.** anything that is contemptibly worthless, inferior, or vile: *There's nothing but garbage on TV tonight.* **4.** worthless talk; lies; foolishness. **5.** *Slang.* any unnecessary item added to something else, as for appearance only; garnish: *I'll have an Old Fashioned, but without the garbage.* **6.** useless artificial satellites or parts of rockets floating in space, as satellites that are no longer transmitting information or rocket boosters jettisoned in flight. **7.** *Computers.* meaningless or unwanted data: *That program was not properly debugged and produced nothing but garbage.* [1400–50; late ME: discarded parts of butchered fowls; compared with *garbelage* the removal of waste from spices (< AF, OF; see GARBLE, -AGE) or OF *garbage* tax on sheaves of grain, though shift of sense, and form in first case, is unclear]
—**Syn. 2.** litter, refuse, junk, rubbish.

gar′bage can′, a container, usually of metal or plastic, for the disposal of waste matter, esp. kitchen refuse. Cf. **trash can.** [1905–10, *Amer.*]

gar•bage•man (gär′bij man′), *n., pl.* **-men.** a person employed to collect, haul away, and dispose of garbage; sanitation worker. [1885–90, *Amer.;* GARBAGE + MAN[1]]

gar•ban•zo (gär bän′zō), *n., pl.* **-zos.** chickpea (def. 1). [1750–60, *Amer.;* < Sp, alter. of OSp *arvanco;* perh. akin to L *ervum* (see ERVIL)]

gar•ble (gär′bəl), *v.,* **-bled, -bling,** *n.* —*v.t.* **1.** to confuse unintentionally or ignorantly; jumble: *to garble instructions.* **2.** to make unfair or misleading selections from or arrangement of (fact, statements, writings, etc.); distort: *to garble a quotation.* **3.** *Archaic.* to take out the best of. —*n.* **4.** the act or process of garbling. **5.** an instance of garbling; a garbled phrase, literary passage, etc. [1400–50; late ME *garbelen* to remove refuse from spices < OIt *garbellare* to sift < Ar *gharbala* < LL *crībellāre,* deriv. of *crībellum,* dim. of L *crībrum* sieve (see -ELLE); prob. influenced by GARBOIL] —**gar′ble•a•ble,** *adj.* —**gar′bler,** *n.*

Gar•bo (gär′bō), *n.* **Greta** (*Greta Lovisa Gustaffson*), 1905–90, U.S. film actress, born in Sweden.

gar′board strake′, *Naut.* the first strake on each side of a keel. [1620–30]

gar•boil (gär′boil), *n. Archaic.* confusion. [1540–50; < MF *garbouil* < OIt *garbuglio*]

gar•bol•o•gy (gär bol′ə jē), *n.* the study of the material discarded by a society to learn what it reveals about social or cultural patterns. [1976; GARB(AGE) + -O- + -LOGY] —**gar•bol′o•gist,** *n.*

Gar•cí•a Lor•ca (gär sē′ə lôr′kə; *Sp.* gär thē′ä lôr′kä, -sē′ä), **Fe•de•ri•co** (fed′ə rē′kō; *Sp.* fe′the rē′kô), 1899–1936, Spanish poet and dramatist.

Gar•cí•a Már•quez (gär sē′ə mär′kes; *Sp.* gär sē′ä mär′kes), **Ga•bri•el** (gä′brē əl, gä′brē el′; *Sp.* gä′vrē-el′), born 1928, Colombian novelist and short-story writer: Nobel prize 1982.

Gar•cí•a Mo•re•no (gär sē′ə mə rā′nō; *Sp.* gär sē′ä mô re′nô), **Ga•bri•el** (gä′brē əl, gä′brē el′; *Sp.* gä′vrē-el′), 1821–75, Ecuadorian journalist and political leader: president of Ecuador 1861–65; 1869–75.

Gar•cí•a y Í•ñi•guez (gär sē′ä ē ē′nye ges), **Ca•lix•to** (kä lēs′tô), 1839?–98, Cuban lawyer, soldier, and revolutionist.

Gar•ci•la•so de la Ve•ga (gär′sə lä′sō də lə vā′gə; *Sp.* gär′the lä′sô the lä ve′gä, gär′se-), **1.** 1503?–36, Spanish poet. **2.** ("*el Inca*") 1539?–1616, Peruvian historian and author in Spain.

gar•çon (gar sôN′), *n., pl.* **-çons** (-sôN′). *French.* **1.** (usually in direct address) a waiter in a restaurant. **2.** a boy or a young unmarried man. **3.** a male employee.

Gard (gar), *n.* a department in S France. 494,575; 2271 sq. mi. (5882 sq. km). *Cap.:* Nîmes.

Gar•da (gär′də), *n.* **Lake,** a lake in N Italy: the largest lake in Italy. 35 mi. (56 km) long; 143 sq. mi. (370 sq. km).

gar•dant (gär′dnt), *adj.* guardant.

garde-man•ger (gard män zhā′), *n., pl.* ***garde-man•ger.*** *French.* **1.** a cool room used for storing foods and for preparing certain dishes, esp. cold buffet dishes. **2.** a chef or cook who supervises the preparation of cold dishes. [lit., (that which) keeps food]

gar•den (gär′dn), *n.* **1.** a plot of ground, usually near a house, where flowers, shrubs, vegetables, fruits, or herbs are cultivated. **2.** a piece of ground or other space, commonly with ornamental plants, trees, etc., used as a park or other public recreation area: *a public garden.* **3.** a fertile and delightful spot or region. **4.** *Brit.* yard[2] (def. 1). —*adj.* **5.** pertaining to, produced in, or suitable for cultivation or use in a garden: *fresh garden vegetables; garden furniture.* **6.** garden-variety. **7. lead up** or **down the garden path,** to deceive or mislead in an enticing way; lead on; delude: *The voters had been led up the garden path too often to take a candidate's promises seriously.* —*v.i.* **8.** to lay out, cultivate,

CONCISE PRONUNCIATION KEY: act, cāpe, dâre, pärt; set, ēqual; *if,* īce; ox, ōver, ôrder, oil, bŏŏk, bōōt, out; up, ûrge; child; sing; shoe; thin, *that;* zh as in *treasure.* ə = *a* as in *alone,* e as in *system,* i as in *easily,* o as in *gallop,* u as in *circus;* ə as in *fire* (fīər), *hour* (ouər). l and n can serve as syllabic consonants, as in *cradle* (krād′l), and *button* (but′n). See the full key inside the front cover.

or tend a garden. —*v.t.* **9.** to cultivate as a garden. [1300–50; ME *gardin* < ONF *gardin,* OF *jardin* < Gmc; cf. OHG *gartin-,* G *Garten,* YARD[2]] —**gar′den·a·ble,** *adj.* —**gar′den·less,** *adj.* —**gar′den·like′,** *adj.*

Gar·den (gär′dn), *n.* **Mary,** 1877–1967, U.S. soprano.

Gar·de·na (gär dē′nə), *n.* a city in SW California, near Los Angeles. 45,165.

gar′den apart′ment, 1. an apartment on the ground floor of an apartment building having direct access to a backyard or garden. **2.** a low-level apartment building or building complex surrounded by lawns and trees, shrubbery, or gardens. [1945–50]

gar′den cen′ter, a store that sells gardening supplies, as seeds, plants, fertilizer, and tools. [1960–65]

gar′den cit′y, a residential community or section of a community with landscaped gardens, parks, and other open areas. [1840–50]

Gar′den Cit′y, 1. a city in SE Michigan, near Detroit. 35,640. **2.** a city on W Long Island, in SE New York. 22,927. **3.** a city in W Kansas. 18,256.

gar′den cress′, a peppergrass, *Lepidium sativum,* used as a salad vegetable. [1570–80]

gar·den·er (gärd′nər), *n.* **1.** a person who is employed to cultivate or care for a garden, lawn, etc. **2.** any person who gardens or is skillful in gardening. [1250–1300; ME < ONF *gardinier* (OF *jardinier*). See GARDEN, -ER[2]]

Gar′den Grove′, a city in SW California. 123,351.

gar′den he′liotrope, the common valerian, *Valeriana officinalis,* esp. when cultivated as an ornamental. [1900–05]

gar·de·nia (gär dē′nyə, -nē ə), *n.* **1.** any evergreen tree or shrub belonging to the genus *Gardenia,* of the madder family, native to the warmer parts of the Eastern Hemisphere, cultivated for its usually large, fragrant white flowers. **2.** the flower of any of these plants. [< NL (1760), after Alexander *Garden* (1730–91), American physician; see -IA]

gar·den·ing (gärd′ning), *n.* **1.** the act of cultivating or tending a garden. **2.** the work or art of a gardener. [1570–80; GARDEN + -ING[1]]

gar′den loose′strife. See under **loosestrife** (def. 1).

Gar′den of E′den, Eden.

gar′den par′ty, a party given out of doors in a garden or yard. [1865–70]

gar′den pea′, pea[1] (defs. 1–3). [1620–30]

Gar′den State′, New Jersey (used as a nickname).

gar·den-va·ri·e·ty (gär′dn və rī′i tē), *adj.* common, usual, or ordinary; unexceptional. [1925–30]

gar′den web′worm. See under **webworm.**

garde·robe (gärd′rōb′), *n.* **1.** a wardrobe or its contents. **2.** a private room, as a bedroom. **3.** (in medieval architecture) a latrine or privy. [1400–50; late ME < MF: lit., (it) keeps clothing]

Gar·di·ner (gärd′nər, gär′dn ər), *n.* **1. Samuel Rawson** (rô′sən), 1829–1902, English historian. **2. Stephen,** 1483–1555, English ecclesiastic and statesman.

Gard·ner (gärd′nər), *n.* **1. Erle Stanley** (ûrl), 1889–1970, U.S. writer of detective stories. **2. Dame Helen (Louise),** 1908–86, British educator and literary critic. **3. John (Champ·lin, Jr.)** (champ′lin), 1933–82, U.S. novelist and critic. **4. John W(illiam),** born 1912, U.S. educator and author: Secretary of Health, Education, and Welfare 1965–68. **5.** a city in N Massachusetts. 17,900. **6.** a male given name: from an Old French word meaning "gardener."

gar·dy·loo (gär′dē lo͞o′), *interj.* (a cry formerly used in Scotland to warn pedestrians when slops were about to be thrown from an upstairs window.) [1760–70; Anglicized form of F *gare (de) l'eau* beware of the water]

gare (gâr), *n.* low-grade wool fibers from the legs of sheep. [1535–45; < AF, var. of OF *gard, jart*]

Gar·eth (gar′ith), *n.* **1.** *Arthurian Romance.* nephew of King Arthur and a knight of the Round Table. **2.** a male given name.

Gar·field (gär′fēld′), *n.* **1. James Abram,** 1831–81, 20th president of the U.S., 1881. **2.** a city in NE New Jersey. 26,803. **3.** a male given name.

Gar′field Heights′, a city in NE Ohio, near Cleveland. 33,380.

gar·fish (gär′fish′), *n., pl.* (*esp. collectively*) **-fish,** (*esp. referring to two or more kinds or species*) **-fish·es.** gar[1]. [1400–50; late ME; cf. OE *gār* spear]

garg., (in prescriptions) a gargle. [< L *gargarisma*]

gar·ga·ney (gär′gə nē), *n., pl.* **-neys.** a small Old World duck, *Anas querquedula.* [1660–70; according to K. von Gesner, who introduced the term, a dial. form of It *garganello* name for various teallike ducks; ult. < LL *gargala* throat; cf. GARGLE]

Gar·gan·tu·a (gär gan′cho͞o ə), *n.* **1.** an amiable giant and king, noted for his enormous capacity for food and drink, in Rabelais' *Gargantua* and *Pantagruel.* **2.** (*italics*) a satirical novel (1534) by Rabelais. Cf. **Pantagruel.**

gar·gan·tu·an (gär gan′cho͞o ən), *adj.* gigantic; enormous; colossal: *a gargantuan task.* [1585–95; GARGANTU(A) + -AN]
—**Syn.** huge, mammoth, immense, vast, elephantine.

gar·get (gär′git), *n.* **1.** *Vet. Pathol.* inflammation of the udder of a cow; bovine mastitis. **2.** pokeweed. [1580–90; earlier, inflammation of the head or throat in livestock, appar. the same word as ME *garget, gargat* throat < MF *gargate*] —**gar′get·y,** *adj.*

CONCISE ETYMOLOGY KEY: <, descended or borrowed from; >, whence; b., blend of, blended; c., cognate with; cf., compare; deriv., derivative; equiv., equivalent; imit., imitative; obl., oblique; r., replacing; s., stem; sp., spelling, spelled; resp., respelling, respelled; trans., translation; ?, origin unknown; *, unattested; ‡, probably earlier than. See the full key inside the front cover.

gar·gle (gär′gəl), *v.,* **-gled, -gling,** *n.* —*v.i.* **1.** to wash or rinse the throat or mouth with a liquid held in the throat and kept in motion by a stream of air from the lungs. —*v.t.* **2.** to gargle (the throat or mouth). **3.** to utter with a gargling sound. —*n.* **4.** any liquid used for gargling. **5.** a gargling sound. [1520–30; < MF *gargouiller* to gargle, rattle the throat, deriv. of *gargouille* throat; perh. imit.] —**gar′gler,** *n.*

gar·goyle (gär′goil), *n.* **1.** a grotesquely carved figure of a human or animal. **2.** a spout, terminating in a grotesque representation of a human or animal figure with open mouth, projecting from the gutter of a building for throwing rain water clear of a building. [1250–1300; ME *gargoile* < OF *gargouille, gargoule* lit., throat; see GARGLE] —**gar′goyled,** *adj.*

gargoyle (def. 2)

gar·goyl·ism (gär′goi liz′əm), *n. Pathol.* a congenital abnormality characterized chiefly by dwarfism, grotesque deformities of the head, trunk, and limbs, mental retardation, and enlargement of the liver and spleen. [1935–40; GARGOYLE + -ISM]

gar·i·bal·di (gar′ə bôl′dē), *n.* **1.** a loose blouse worn by women and children in the mid-19th century, made in imitation of the red shirts worn by the soldiers of Garibaldi. **2.** a brilliant orange damselfish, *Hypsypops rubicundus,* found off the rocky coasts of southern California. [1860–65]

Gar·i·bal·di (gar′ə bôl′dē; *It.* gä′rē bäl′dē), *n.* **Giu·sep·pe** (jə sep′ē; *It.* jo͞o zep′pe), 1807–82, Italian patriot and general. —**Gar′i·bal′di·an,** *adj., n.*

gar·ish (gâr′ish, gar′-), *adj.* **1.** crudely or tastelessly colorful, showy, or elaborate, as clothes or decoration. **2.** excessively ornate or elaborate, as buildings or writings. **3.** dressed in or ornamented with bright colors. **4.** excessively bright; glaring. [1535–45; earlier *gaurish,* perh. equiv. to obs. *gaure* to stare (ME *gauren* < ON) + -ISH[1]] —**gar′ish·ly,** *adv.* —**gar′ish·ness,** *n.*
—**Syn. 1.** loud, tawdry. See **gaudy**[1].

gar·land (gär′lənd), *n.* **1.** a wreath or festoon of flowers, leaves, or other material, worn for ornament or as an honor or hung on something as a decoration: *A garland of laurel was placed on the winner's head.* **2.** a representation of such a wreath or festoon. **3.** a collection of short literary pieces, as poems and ballads; literary miscellany. **4.** *Naut.* a band, collar, or grommet, as of rope. —*v.t.* **5.** to crown with a garland; deck with garlands. [1275–1325; ME *ger(e)lande, garlande* < OF < ?] —**gar′land·less,** *adj.* —**gar′land·like′,** *adj.*

Gar·land (gär′lənd), *n.* **1. Ham·lin** (ham′lin), 1860–1940, U.S. novelist, short-story writer, and poet. **2. Judy** (*Frances Gumm*), 1922–69, U.S. singer and actress. **3.** a city in NE Texas, near Dallas. 138,857. **4.** a male or female given name.

gar′land crab′ apple′. See **American crab apple.**

gar·lic (gär′lik), *n.* **1.** a hardy plant, *Allium sativum,* of the amaryllis family whose strongly, pungent bulb is used in cookery and medicine. **2.** any of various other plants of the genus *Allium.* **3.** the bulb of such a plant, consisting of smaller bulbs, or cloves, used in cooking, sometimes in the form of a powder or flakes. **4.** the flavor or smell of this bulb. —*adj.* **5.** cooked, flavored, or seasoned with garlic: *garlic bread; garlic salt.* **6.** of or pertaining to garlic. [bef. 1000; ME *garlec,* OE *gārlēac* (*gār* spear (c. G *Ger*) + *lēac* LEEK)] —**gar′licked, gar′·lick·y,** *adj.*

gar·ment (gär′mənt), *n.* **1.** any article of clothing: *dresses, suits, and other garments.* **2.** an outer covering or outward appearance. —*v.t.* **3.** to clothe, dress, or cover. [1300–50; ME *garnement* < OF *garniment,* equiv. to *garni(r)* to GARNISH + *-ment* -MENT] —**gar′ment·less,** *adj.*
—**Syn. 1.** attire, apparel, garb, dress, costume.

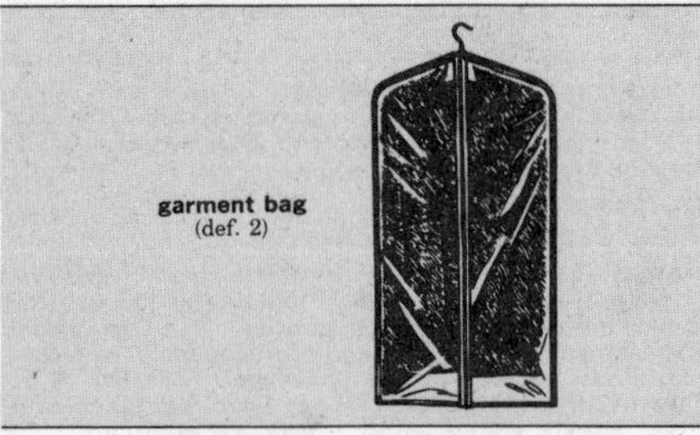
garment bag (def. 2)

gar′ment bag′, 1. a travel bag made of pliable, durable material with a handle and a zipper closure, designed to hang straight or fold double and used to carry suits, dresses, coats, or the like without crushing or wrinkling. **2.** a plastic or cloth bag with a zipper closure in which clothes can be hung in a closet, esp. for storage.

Gar′ment Dis′trict, an area in the borough of Manhattan, in New York City, including portions of Seventh Avenue and Broadway between 34th and 40th Streets and the streets intersecting them, that contains many factories, showrooms, etc., related to the design, manufacture, and wholesale distribution of clothing. Also called **Gar′ment Cen′ter.**

Gar·neau (*Fr.* GAR nō′), *n.* **Fran·çois Xa·vier** (*Fr.* FRÄN SWA′ GZA VYĀ′), 1809–66, Canadian historian.

gar·ner (gär′nər), *v.t.* **1.** to gather or deposit in or as if in a granary or other storage place. **2.** to get; acquire; earn: *He gradually garnered a national reputation as a financial expert.* **3.** to gather, collect, or hoard. —*n.* **4.** a granary or grain bin. **5.** a store or supply of anything. [1125–75; ME *garner, gerner* < OF *gernier, grenier* < L *grānārium* GRANARY; see -ER[2]]

Gar·ner (gär′nər), *n.* **John Nance** (nans), 1868–1967, vice president of the U.S. 1933–41.

gar·net (gär′nit), *n.* **1.** any of a group of hard, vitreous minerals, silicates of calcium, magnesium, iron, or manganese with aluminum or iron, varying in color: a deep-red transparent variety is used as a gem and as an abrasive. **2.** a deep-red color. [1275–1325; ME *garnet, gernate* < OF *gernate, grenade* < L *grānātum* granular; cf. POMEGRANATE] —**gar′net·like′,** *adj.*

Gar·net (gär′nit), *n.* **Henry Highland,** 1815–82, U.S. clergyman and abolitionist.

gar·net·if·er·ous (gär′ni tif′ər əs), *adj.* containing or yielding garnets. [1850–55; GARNET + -I- + -FEROUS]

gar′net jade′. See **Transvaal jade.**

gar′net pa′per, an abrasive paper coated with pulverized garnet. [1900–05]

gar·nett (gär net′), *v.t.* **1.** *Textiles.* to reduce (waste material) to its fibrous state for reuse in textile manufacturing. —*n.* **2.** a machine used in garnetting. [1885–90; after the surname *Garnett*] —**gar·nett′er,** *n.*

Gar·nett (gär′nit, gär net′), *n.* **Constance Black,** 1862–1946, English translator from Russian.

gar·ni (GAR nē′), *adj. French.* garnished.

gar·ni·er·ite (gär′nē ə rīt′), *n.* a mineral, hydrous nickel magnesium silicate, occurring in earthy, green masses: an important ore of nickel. [1875; named after Jules *Garnier* (d. 1904), French geologist; see -ITE[1]]

gar·nish (gär′nish), *v.t.* **1.** to provide or supply with something ornamental; adorn; decorate. **2.** to provide (a food) with something that adds flavor, decorative color, etc.: *to garnish boiled potatoes with chopped parsley.* **3.** *Law.* **a.** to attach (as money due or property belonging to a debtor) by garnishment; garnishee. **b.** to summon in, so as to take part in litigation already pending between others. —*n.* **4.** something placed around or on a food or in a beverage to add flavor, decorative color, etc. **5.** adornment or decoration. **6.** *Chiefly Brit.* a fee formerly demanded of a new convict or worker by the warden, boss, or fellow prisoners or workers. [1300–50; ME *garnishen* < OF *garniss-* (extended s. of *garnir, guarnir* to furnish < Gmc); cf. WARN] —**gar′nish·a·ble,** *adj.* —**gar′nish·er,** *n.*
—**Syn. 1.** embellish, ornament, beautify, trim, bedeck, bedizen, set off, enhance. **5.** ornament; garniture.

gar·nish·ee (gär′ni shē′), *v.,* **-nish·eed, -nish·ee·ing,** *n. Law.* —*v.t.* **1.** to attach (money or property) by garnishment. **2.** to serve (a person) with a garnishment. —*n.* **3.** a person served with a garnishment. [1620–30; GARNISH + -EE]

gar·nish·ment (gär′nish mənt), *n.* **1.** *Law.* **a.** a warning, served on a third party to hold, subject to the court's direction, money or property belonging to a debtor who is being sued by a creditor. **b.** a summons to a third party to appear in litigation pending between a creditor and debtor. **2.** adornment or decoration. [1540–50; GARNISH + -MENT]

gar·ni·ture (gär′ni chər, -cho͝or′), *n.* **1.** something that garnishes; decoration; adornment. **2.** *Armor.* a set of plate armor having pieces of exchange for all purposes. [1525–35; < F, equiv. to MF *garni(r)* to GARNISH + *-ture* n. suffix; see -URE]

Ga·ro·fa·lo (*It.* gä RÔ′fä lô), *n.* Galofalo.

Ga·ronne (GA RÔN′), *n.* a river in SW France, flowing NW from the Pyrenees to the Gironde River. 350 mi. (565 km) long.

ga·rote (gə rot′, -rōt′), *n., v.t.,* **-rot·ed, -rot·ing.** garrote. —**ga·rot′er,** *n.*

ga·rotte (gə rot′, -rōt′), *n., v.t.,* **-rot·ted, -rot·ting.** garrote. —**ga·rot′ter,** *n.*

gar·pike (gär′pīk′), *n.* gar[1]. [1770–80; formed after GARFISH]

gar·ret[1] (gar′it), *n.* an attic, usually a small, wretched one. [1300–50; ME *garite* watchtower < OF *garite, guerite* watchtower, deriv. of *garir, guarir* to defend, protect; see GARRISON] —**gar′ret·ed,** *adj.*

gar·ret[2] (gar′it), *n., v.t. Masonry.* gallet. [1835–45; of uncert. orig.]

Gar·rett (gar′it), *n.* a male given name, form of **Gerald.**

Gar·rick (gar′ik), *n.* **David,** 1717–79, English actor and theatrical manager.

gar·ri·son (gar′ə sən), *n.* **1.** a body of troops stationed in a fortified place. **2.** the place where such troops are stationed. **3.** any military post, esp. a permanent one. —*v.t.* **4.** to provide (a fort, town, etc.) with a garrison. **5.** to occupy (a fort, post, station, etc.) with troops. **6.** to put (troops) on duty in a fort, post, station, etc. [1250–1300; ME *garisoun* protection, stronghold < OF *garison, gareison* defense, provision, deriv. of *garir, guerir* to defend < Gmc; cf. OHG *warjan*]

Gar·ri·son (gar′ə sən), *n.* **William Lloyd,** 1805–79, U.S. leader in the abolition movement.

gar′rison cap′. See **overseas cap.** [1945–50, *Amer.*]

Gar′rison fin′ish, the finish of a race, esp. a horse race, in which the winner comes from behind to win at the last moment. [1930–35; prob. named after Edward ("Snapper") *Garrison,* 19th-century American jockey who often won in this fashion]

gar′rison house′, 1. a style of early New England

house in which the second floor projects beyond the first. **2.** blockhouse (def. 2). [1670–80]

gar′rison state′, a state in which military matters dominate economic and political life. [1935–40]

gar•rote (gə rōt′, -rot′), *n., v.,* **-rot•ed, -rot•ing.** —*n.* **1.** a method of capital punishment of Spanish origin in which an iron collar is tightened around a condemned person's neck until death occurs by strangulation or by injury to the spinal column at the base of the brain. **2.** the collarlike instrument used for this method of execution. **3.** strangulation or throttling, esp. in the course of a robbery. **4.** an instrument, usually a cord or wire with handles attached at the ends, used for strangling a victim. —*v.t.* **5.** to execute by the garrote. **6.** to strangle or throttle, esp. in the course of a robbery. Also, **garote, garotte, garrotte.** [1615–25; < Sp *garrote* or F *garrot* packing-stick < ?] —**gar•rot′er,** *n.*

gar•rotte (gə rot′, -rōt′), *n., v.t.,* **-rot•ted, -rot•ting.** garrote. —**gar•rot′ter,** *n.*

gar•ru•li•ty (gə rōō′li tē), *n.* the quality of being garrulous; talkativeness; loquacity. [1575–85; < F *garrulité* < L *garrulitās.* See GARRULOUS, -ITY]

gar•ru•lous (gar′ə ləs, gar′yə-), *adj.* **1.** excessively talkative in a rambling, roundabout manner, esp. about trivial matters. **2.** wordy or diffuse: *a garrulous and boring speech.* [1605–15; < L *garrulus* talkative, garrulous, equiv. to *garr(īre)* to chatter + *-ulus* -ULOUS] —**gar′ru•lous•ly,** *adv.* —**gar′ru•lous•ness,** *n.*
—**Syn. 1.** prating, babbling. See **talkative. 2.** verbose, prolix. —**Ant. 1.** reticent, uncommunicative, taciturn, close-mouthed.

gar•ter (gär′tər), *n.* **1.** Also called, *Brit.,* **sock suspender, suspender.** an article of clothing for holding up a stocking or sock, usually an elastic band around the leg or an elastic strap hanging from a girdle or other undergarment. **2.** a similar band worn to hold up a shirt sleeve. **3.** a leather strap for passing through a loop at the back of a boot and buckling around the leg to keep the boot from slipping. **4.** *Brit.* **a.** the badge of the Order of the Garter. **b.** membership in the Order. **c.** (*cap.*) the Order itself. **d.** (*usually cap.*) a member of the Order. —*v.t.* **5.** to fasten with a garter. [1300–50; ME < ONF *gartier,* deriv. of *garet* the bend of the knee < Celtic; cf. Welsh *gar* shank, Breton *gâr* leg] —**gar′ter•less,** *adj.*

gar′ter belt′, an undergarment of cloth or elastic, with attached garters, worn to hold up stockings.

gar′ter snake′, any of numerous harmless snakes of the genus *Thamnophis,* common in North and Central America, ranging in size from 14 to 30 in. (36 to 76 cm) and typically having three longitudinal stripes on the back. [1760–70, *Amer.*]

gar′ter stitch′, a basic knitting pattern that produces an evenly pebbled texture on both sides of the work, created by consistently knitting or purling every stitch of every row. [1905–10]

garth (gärth), *n.* **1.** Also called **cloister garth.** an open courtyard enclosed by a cloister. **2.** *Archaic.* a yard or garden. [1300–50; ME < ON *garthr* farm, farmyard, courtyard; see YARD²]

Garth (gärth), *n.* a male given name.

gar•vey (gär′vē), *n., pl.* **-veys.** a scowlike open boat, variously propelled, used by oyster and clam fishermen in Delaware Bay and off the coasts of Delaware and New Jersey. [1895–1900; prob. from a proper name]

Gar•vey (gär′vē), *n.* **Marcus (Mo•zi•ah)** (mō zī′ə), 1887–1940, Jamaican black-rights activist in the U.S. (1916–27): advocated emigration of black Americans to Africa.

Gar•y (gâr′ē, gar′ē), *n.* **1. Elbert Henry,** 1846–1927, U.S. financier and lawyer. **2.** a port in NW Indiana, on Lake Michigan. 151,953. **3.** a male given name: from an Old English word meaning "spear bearer."

gas (gas), *n., pl.* **gas•es,** *v.,* **gassed, gas•sing.** —*n.* **1.** *Physics.* a substance possessing perfect molecular mobility and the property of indefinite expansion, as opposed to a solid or liquid. **2.** any such fluid or mixture of fluids. **3.** any such fluid used as an anesthetic, as nitrous oxide: *Did the dentist give you gas for your extraction?* **4.** any such combustible fluid used as fuel: *Light the gas in the oven.* **5.** *Auto.* **a.** gasoline. **b.** Also called **gas pedal.** the foot-operated accelerator of an automotive vehicle: *Take your foot off the gas.* **6.** flatus. **7.** *Coal Mining.* an explosive mixture of firedamp with air. **8.** an aeriform fluid or a mistlike assemblage of fine particles suspended in air, used in warfare to asphyxiate, poison, or stupefy an enemy. **9.** *Slang.* **a.** empty talk. **b.** a person or thing that is very entertaining, pleasing, or successful: *The party was an absolute gas, and we loved it.* **c.** a person or thing that affects one strongly. **10. step on the gas,** *Informal.* to increase the speed of one's movement or activity; hurry: *We'd better step on the gas or we'll be late for the concert.* —*v.t.* **11.** to supply with gas. **12.** to overcome, poison, or asphyxiate with gas or fumes. **13.** to singe (yarns or fabrics) with a gas flame to remove superfluous fibers. **14.** to treat or impregnate with gas. **15.** *Slang.* **a.** to talk nonsense or falsehood to. **b.** to amuse or affect strongly: *Her weird clothes really gas me.* —*v.i.* **16.** to give off gas, as a storage battery being charged. **17.** *Slang.* **a.** to indulge in idle, empty talk. **b.** to become drunk (often fol. by *up*). **18. gas up,** to fill the gasoline tank of an automobile, truck, or other vehicle. [1650–60; coined by J. B. van Helmont (1577–1644), Flemish chemist; suggested by Gk *cháos* atmosphere] —**gas′less,** *adj.*

gas′ bacil′lus, any of several pathogenic bacilli, esp. of the genus *Clostridium,* that produce gas in infected tissue.

gas•bag (gas′bag′), *n.* **1.** a bag for holding gas, as in a balloon or dirigible. **2.** *Slang.* a talkative, boastful person; windbag. [1820–30; GAS + BAG]

gas′ black′, the soot of a natural gas flame, used in paints; fine carbon. Also called **channel black.** [1880–85]

gas′ blad′der. See **air bladder** (def. 2).

gas′ burn′er, 1. the tip, jet, or nozzle from which gas issues, as on a stove. **2.** a stove or the like that burns gas as a fuel. [1805–15]

gas′ cham′ber, an enclosure used for the execution of prisoners by means of a poisonous gas. [1935–40]

gas′ chromat′ograph, *Chem.* a chromatograph used for the separation of volatile substances. [1950–55] —**gas′ chromatog′raphy.**

gas′ coal′, a soft coal suitable for the production of gas. [1875–80]

Gas•coigne (gas′koin), *n.* **George,** 1525?–77, English poet.

Gas•con (gas′kən), *n.* **1.** a native of Gascony, France, the inhabitants of which were reputedly very boastful. **2.** (*l.c.*) a boaster or braggart. —*adj.* **3.** pertaining to Gascony or its people. **4.** (*l.c.*) boastful; bragging. [1325–75; ME *gascoyne, gascoun* < OF, ult. < L *Vascōnēs* the inhabitants of the Basque country and adjacent areas]

gas•con•ade (gas′kə nād′), *n., v.,* **-ad•ed, -ad•ing.** —*n.* **1.** extravagant boasting; boastful talk. —*v.i.* **2.** to boast extravagantly; bluster. [1700–10; < F *gasconnade,* deriv. of *gasconner* to boast, chatter. See GASCON, -ADE¹] —**gas′con•ad′er,** *n.*

gas′ con′stant, *Physics.* See **universal gas constant.**

Gas•co•ny (gas′kə nē), *n.* a former province in SW France. French, **Gas•cogne** (gA skôn′yᵊ).

Gas•coyne-Cec•il (gas′koin ses′əl), *n.* **Robert Arthur Tal•bot** (tôl′bət), **3rd Marquis of Salisbury.** See **Salisbury** (def. 1).

gas′ en′gine, an internal-combustion engine driven by a mixture of air and gas. [1870–75]

gas•e•ous (gas′ē əs, gash′əs), *adj.* **1.** existing in the state of a gas; not solid or liquid. **2.** pertaining to or having the characteristics of gas. **3.** *Informal.* lacking firmness or solidity; uncertain; not definite. **4.** gassy (defs. 1, 3). [1790–1800; GAS + -EOUS] —**gas′e•ous•ness, gas•e•i•ty** (ga sē′i tē), *n.*

gas′eous diffu′sion, *Chem.* the passage of gas through microporous barriers, a technique used for isotope separation, esp. in the preparation of fuel for nuclear reactors. [1845–50]

gas′ field′, a district yielding natural gas. [1885–90, *Amer.*]

gas-fired (gas′fīᵊrd′), *adj.* using a gas for fuel. [1885–90]

gas′ fit′ter, a person who installs gas pipes and apparatus in buildings. [1855–60]

gas′ fit′ting, 1. the work or business of a gas fitter. **2. gas fittings,** fittings for the use of illuminating gas. [1860–65]

gas′ fur′nace, 1. a furnace using gas as a fuel. **2.** a furnace for distilling gas from a solid fuel, as coal. [1870–75]

gas′ gan′grene, *Pathol.* a gangrenous infection developing in wounds, esp. deep wounds with closed spaces, caused by bacteria that form gases in the subcutaneous tissues. [1910–15]

gas-guz•zler (gas′guz′lər), *n. Informal.* an automobile that has low fuel efficiency, getting relatively few miles per gallon. Also, **gas′ guz′zler.** [1975–80] —**gas′-guz′zling,** *adj.*

gas′-guz′zler tax′, a tax imposed on the purchase price of an automobile not meeting fuel efficiency standards. [1985–90]

gash¹ (gash), *n.* **1.** a long, deep wound or cut; slash. **2.** *Slang* (*vulgar*). **a.** the vagina. **b.** *Disparaging and Offensive,* a woman considered as a sex object. —*v.t.* **3.** to make a long, deep cut in; slash. [1540–50; alter. (with *-sh* perh. from SLASH¹) of ME *garsen* < OF *garser, jarsier* (F *gercer*) to scarify, wound < VL **charaxāre* < Gk *charássein* to scratch, notch]

gash² (gash), *adj. Chiefly Scot.* **1.** wise, sagacious. **2.** neat; well-dressed; well-groomed. [1700–10; orig. uncert.]

gash³ (gash), *adj. Scot. Archaic.* dreary or gloomy in appearance. [1580–90; orig. uncert.]

gas•house (gas′hous′), *n., pl.* **-hous•es** (-hou′ziz). gasworks. [1875–80, *Amer.*; GAS + HOUSE]

gas•i•form (gas′ə fôrm′), *adj.* having the form of gas; gaseous. [1790–1800; GAS + -I- + -FORM]

gas•i•fy (gas′ə fī′), *v.t., v.i.,* **-fied, -fy•ing.** to convert into or become a gas. [1820–30; GAS + -IFY] —**gas′i•fi′a•ble,** *adj.* —**gas′i•fi•ca′tion,** *n.* —**gas′i•fi′er,** *n.*

gas′ jet′, 1. See **gas burner** (def. 1). **2.** a flame of illuminating gas. [1830–40]

Gas•kell (gas′kəl), *n.* **Mrs.** (*Elizabeth Cleghorn Stevenson Gaskell*), 1810–65, English novelist.

gas•ket (gas′kit), *n.* **1.** a rubber, metal, or rope ring, for packing a piston or placing around a joint to make it watertight. **2.** *Naut.* any of a number of light lines for securing a furled sail to a boom, gaff, or yard. [1615–25; perh. < F *garcette* a plait of rope]

gas•kin¹ (gas′kin), *n.* **1.** the part of the hind leg of a horse, or other hoofed mammal, between the stifle and the hock. See diag. under **horse. 2. gaskins,** *Obs.* hose or breeches; galligaskins. [1565–75; perh. shortened form of GALLIGASKINS]

gas•kin² (gas′kin), *n.* a gasket. Also, **gas•king** (gas′king). [1825–35; by alter.]

gas′ law′, *Physics.* See **ideal gas law.** [1895–1900]

gas•light (gas′līt′), *n.* **1.** light produced by the combustion of illuminating gas. **2.** a gas burner or gas jet for producing this kind of light. —*adj.* **3.** gaslit (def. 2). [1800–10; GAS + LIGHT¹] —**gas′light′ed,** *adj.*

gas′ liq′uor, *Chem.* See **ammonia liquor.** [1835–45]

gas•lit (gas′lit′), *adj.* **1.** having illumination provided by burning gas: *gaslit streets.* **2.** of or resembling a time, esp. the 1890's, when gaslight was widely used: *the gaslit era.* [1830–40; GAS + LIT]

gas′ log′, a gas burner in a fireplace, made to resemble a log. [1880–85, *Amer.*]

gas′ main′, a large pipe for conducting and distributing gas to lesser pipes or ducts, esp. such a pipe carrying and distributing household gas beneath the streets of a town or city. [1810–20]

gas•man (gas′man′), *n., pl.* **-men. 1.** a person who works for a company that sells or distributes household gas, esp. a person who goes from building to building reading gas meters to determine what charge is to be billed. **2.** a person who produces, distributes, or sells gas for industrial or commercial use. **3.** See **gas fitter. 4.** *Mining.* See **fire boss.** [1815–25; GAS + MAN¹]

gas′ man′tle, mantle (def. 5). [1895–1900]

gas′ mask′, a masklike device containing or attached to a component that filters the air inhaled by the wearer through charcoal and chemicals, for protecting the face and lungs against noxious gases and fumes, as in warfare or in certain industrial processes. [1910–15]

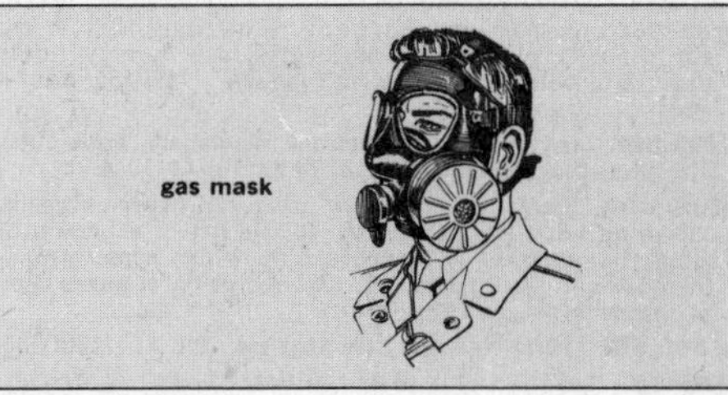
gas mask

gas′ me′ter, an apparatus for measuring and recording the amount of gas produced or consumed, esp. such an apparatus metering the amount of household gas piped into a dwelling. [1805–15]

gas•o•gene (gas′ə jēn′), *n.* gazogene.

gas•o•hol (gas′ə hôl′, -hol′), *n.* a mixture of gasoline and ethyl alcohol, generally containing no more than 10 percent alcohol, used as an alternative fuel for some automobiles. [1975–80; GAS(OLINE) + (ALC)OHOL]

gas•o•lene (gas′ə lēn′, gas′ə lēn′), *n. Now Rare.* gasoline.

gas•o•lier (gas′ə lēr′), *n.* a chandelier furnished with gaslights. [GAS + -O- + (CHANDE)LIER]

gas•o•line (gas′ə lēn′, gas′ə lēn′), *n.* a volatile, flammable liquid mixture of hydrocarbons, obtained from petroleum, and used as fuel for internal-combustion engines, as a solvent, etc. [1860–65, *Amer.*; GAS + -OL² + -INE²] —**gas′o•line′less,** *adj.* —**gas•o•lin•ic** (gas′ə lē′nik, -lin′ik), *adj.*

gas•om•e•ter (gas om′i tər), *n.* **1.** an apparatus for measuring and storing gas in a laboratory. **2.** *Brit.* a large tank or cylindrical reservoir of gas, as at a gasworks, to be piped to homes, factories, etc. [1785–95; < F *gazomètre.* See GAS, -O-, -METER]

gas•om•e•try (gas om′i trē), *n. Chem.* the measurement of gases. [1780–90; GAS + -O- + -METRY] —**gas•o•met•ric** (gas′ə me′trik), **gas′o•met′ri•cal,** *adj.* —**gas′•o•met′ri•cal•ly,** *adv.*

gas-op•er•at•ed (gas′op′ə rā′tid), *adj.* (of a firearm) using some of the exhaust gases to operate the action. [1940–45]

gasp (gasp, gäsp), *n.* **1.** a sudden, short intake of breath, as in shock or surprise. **2.** a convulsive effort to breathe. **3.** a short, convulsive utterance: *the words came out in gasps.* **4. last gasp,** the point of death; dying: *At his last gasp he confessed to the murder.* —*v.i.* **5.** to catch one's breath. **6.** to struggle for breath with the mouth open; breathe convulsively. **7.** to long with breathless eagerness; desire; crave (usually fol. by *for* or *after*). —*v.t.* **8.** to utter with gasps (often fol. by *out, forth, away,* etc.): *She gasped out the words.* **9.** to breathe or emit with gasps (often fol. by *away*). [1350–1400; ME *gaspen,* prob. OE **gāspen,* equiv. to ON *geispa;* akin to GAPE] —**gasp′ing•ly,** *adv.*
—**Syn. 5, 6.** puff, blow. See **pant.**

Gas•pé (ga spā′; *Fr.* gAs pā′), *n.* a town in SE Quebec, in E Canada on the Gaspé Peninsula. 17,261.

gas′ ped′al, *Auto.* gas (def. 5b).

Gas·pé′ Penin′sula (ga spā′; *Fr.* gas pā′), a peninsula in SE Canada, in Quebec province, between New Brunswick and the St. Lawrence River.

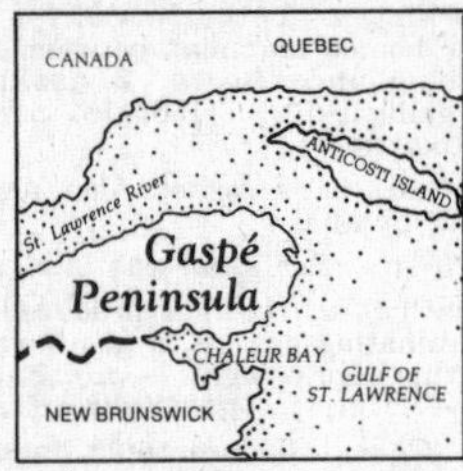

gas·per (gas′pər, gä′spər), *n. Brit. Slang.* a cigarette. [1910–15; GASP + -ER[1]]

gas·per·gou (gas′pər go͞o′), *n., pl.* **-gous,** (*esp. collectively*) **-gou.** See **freshwater drum.** [1800–10, *Amer.*; < LaF *casburgot,* F *casse-burgot,* equiv. to *cass(er)* to break + *burgeau* a kind of shellfish]

Gas·pe·ri (*It.* gäs′pe rē), *n.* **Al·ci·de De** (*It.* äl chē′de de). See **De Gasperi, Alcide.**

gas′-per·me·a·ble lens′ (gas′pûr′mē ə bəl), a semisoft contact lens, usually removed each day, that allows air to pass through to the eye and affords a wider range of vision corrections than a soft contact lens.

gas′ plant′, a plant, *Dictamnus albus,* of the rue family, native to Eurasia, having clusters of white or reddish flowers and strong-smelling foliage that emits a flammable vapor. Also called **fraxinella, dittany.**

gas′ range′, a cooking stove that uses household gas as fuel. [1880–85, *Amer.*]

gassed (gast), *adj. Slang.* drunk. [1910–15; GAS (v.) + -ED[2]]

Gas·sen·di (ga sän dē′), *n.* **Pierre** (pyer), 1592–1655, French philosopher and scientist.

gas·ser (gas′ər), *n.* **1.** *Slang.* something that is extraordinarily pleasing or successful, esp. a very funny joke. **2.** a person or thing that gasses. [1890–95; GAS + -ER[1]]

Gas·ser (gas′ər), *n.* **Herbert Spencer,** 1888–1963, U.S. physiologist: Nobel prize for medicine 1944.

gas·sing (gas′ing), *n.* **1.** an affecting, overcoming, or poisoning with gas or fumes. **2.** the act of a person or thing that gasses. **3.** a process by which something is gassed, as in fumigation. **4.** the evolution of gases during electrolysis. [GAS + -ING[1]]

gas′ sta′tion. See **service station** (def. 1). [1930–35]

gas·sy (gas′ē), *adj.,* **-si·er, -si·est. 1.** full of or containing gas. **2.** resembling gas. **3.** flatulent. **4.** *Slang.* given to idle, empty talk. [1750–60; GAS + -Y[1]] —**gas′·si·ness,** *n.*

gast (gast), *v.t. Obs.* to terrify or frighten. [bef. 1000; ME *gasten,* OE *gǣstan*]

gas′ tank′, 1. a tank containing the gasoline supply in a car, truck, or other gasoline-engine vehicle. **2.** a storage tank for gas or gasoline. [1880–85]

Gast·ar·beit·er (gäst′är′bī tər), *n., pl.* **-beit·er** (-bī tər). *German.* See **guest worker.**

gas·ter (gas′tər), *n.* (in ants, bees, wasps, and other hymenopterous insects) the part of the abdomen behind the petiole. [1905–10; < Gk *gastḗr* paunch, belly]

gast·haus (gäst′hous′), *n., pl.* **-haus·es** (-hou′ziz), **-häus·er** (-hoi′zər). a German inn or tavern. [1825–35; < G *Gasthaus* guesthouse]

gas′ thermom′eter, a device for measuring temperature by observing the change in either pressure or volume of an enclosed gas. [1875–80]

gas·tight (gas′tīt′), *adj.* **1.** not penetrable by a gas. **2.** not admitting a given gas under a given pressure. [1825–35; GAS + TIGHT] —**gas′tight′ness,** *n.*

gast·ness (gast′nis), *n. Obs.* terror or fright. [1350–1400; ME *gastnes(se),* equiv. to *gast* (ptp. of *gasten* GAST) + *-nes* -NESS]

Gas·ton (gas′tən; *Fr.* ga stôN′), *n.* a male given name.

Gas·to·ni·a (ga stō′nē ə), *n.* a city in S North Carolina, W of Charlotte. 47,333.

gastr-, var. of **gastro-** before a vowel: *gastrectomy.*

gas·tral·gi·a (ga stral′jē ə, -jə), *n.* **1.** neuralgia of the stomach. **2.** any stomach pain. [1815–25; < NL; see GASTR-, -ALGIA] —**gas·tral′gic,** *adj., n.*

gas·trec·to·my (ga strek′tə mē), *n., pl.* **-mies.** partial or total excision of the stomach. [1885–90; GASTR- + -ECTOMY]

gas·tric (gas′trik), *adj.* pertaining to the stomach. [1650–60; GASTR- + -IC]

gas′tric by′pass, a surgical procedure by which all or part of the stomach is circumvented by anastomosis to the small intestine, performed to overcome obstruction or in the treatment of morbid obesity. Also called **gastroplasty.**

gas′tric juice′, the digestive fluid, containing pepsin and other enzymes, secreted by the glands of the stomach. [1720–30]

gas′tric lavage′, *Med.* the washing out of the stomach; lavage.

CONCISE ETYMOLOGY KEY: <, descended or borrowed from; >, whence; b., blend of, blended; c., cognate with; cf., compare; deriv., derivative; equiv., equivalent; imit., imitative; obl., oblique; r., replacing; s., stem; sp., spelling, spelled; resp., respelling, respelled; trans., translation; ?, origin unknown; *, unattested; ‡, probably earlier than. See the full key inside the front cover.

gas′tric mill′, *Zool.* **1.** a gizzard in decapod crustaceans, as lobsters, crabs, and shrimps, having an arrangement of teeth and small bones for grinding food and bristles for filtering small particles. **2.** gizzard (def. 2). [1895–1900]

gas′tric ul′cer, *Pathol.* a peptic ulcer located in the stomach's inner wall, caused in part by the corrosive action of the gastric juice on the mucous membrane. [1905–10]

gas·trin (gas′trin), *n.* a hormone that stimulates the secretion of gastric juice. [1900–05; GASTR- + -IN[2]]

gas·tri·tis (ga strī′tis), *n.* inflammation of the stomach, esp. of its mucous membrane. [1800–10; < NL; see GASTR-, -ITIS] —**gas·trit·ic** (ga strit′ik), *adj.*

gastro-, a combining form meaning "stomach," used in the formation of compound words: *gastrology.* Also, *esp. before a vowel,* **gastr-.** [< Gk, comb. form of *gastḗr*]

gas·troc·ne·mi·us (gas′trok nē′mē əs, gas′trə nē′-), *n., pl.* **-mi·i** (-mē ī′). *Anat.* the largest muscle in the calf of the leg, the action of which extends the foot, raises the heel, and assists in bending the knee. [1670–80; < NL < Gk *gastroknēm(ía)* calf of the leg + L *-ius* n. suffix] —**gas′troc·ne′mi·al, gas′troc·ne′mi·an,** *adj.*

gas·tro·coel (gas′trō sēl′), *n. Embryol.* archenteron. Also, **gas′tro·coele′.** [1800–10; GASTRO- + COEL]

gas·tro·col·ic (gas′trō kol′ik), *adj. Anat.* of, pertaining to, or involving the stomach and colon. [1840–50; GASTRO- + COLIC]

gastrocol′ic omen′tum. See **greater omentum.**

gas·tro·der·mis (gas′trō dûr′mis), *n. Zool.* the inner cell layer of the body of an invertebrate. [GASTRO- + -DERMIS] —**gas′tro·der′mal,** *adj.*

gas·tro·du·o·de·nos·to·my (gas′trō do͞o′ə dn os′tə mē, -dyo͞o′-), *n., pl.* **-mies.** *Surg.* See under **gastroenterostomy.** [1885–90; GASTRO- + DUODENO- + -STOMY]

gas·tro·en·ter·i·tis (gas′trō en′tə rī′tis), *n. Pathol.* inflammation of the stomach and intestines. [1815–25; GASTROENTER(O)- + -ITIS] —**gas·tro·en·ter·it·ic** (gas′trō en′tə rit′ik), *adj.*

gastroentero-, a combination of **gastro-** and **entero-:** *gastroenterostomy.*

gas·tro·en·ter·ol·o·gy (gas′trō en′tə rol′ə jē), *n.* the study of the structure, functions, and diseases of digestive organs. [1900–05; GASTROENTERO- + -LOGY] —**gas·tro·en·ter·o·log·ic** (gas′trō en′tər ə loj′ik), **gas′·tro·en′ter·o·log′i·cal,** *adj.* —**gas′tro·en′te·rol′o·gist,** *n.*

gas·tro·en·ter·os·to·my (gas′trō en′tə ros′tə mē), *n., pl.* **-mies.** *Surg.* the making of a new passage between the stomach and the duodenum (**gastroduodenostomy**) or, esp., the jejunum (**gastrojejunostomy**). [1885–90; GASTROENTERO- + -STOMY]

gas·tro·he·pat·ic (gas′trō hi pat′ik), *adj. Anat.* of, pertaining to, or involving the stomach and the liver. [GASTRO- + HEPATIC]

gas′trohepat′ic omen′tum. See **lesser omentum.** [1825–35]

gas·tro·in·tes·ti·nal (gas′trō in tes′tə nl), *adj. Anat.* of, pertaining to, or affecting the stomach and intestines. [1825–35; GASTRO- + INTESTINAL]

gastrointes′tinal ser′ies. See **GI series.**

gas·tro·je·ju·nos·to·my (gas′trō ji jo͞o nos′tə mē), *n., pl.* **-mies.** *Surg.* See under **gastroenterostomy.** [1890–95; GASTRO- + JEJUNOSTOMY]

gas·tro·lith (gas′trə lith), *n. Pathol.* a calculous concretion in the stomach. [1850–55; GASTRO- + -LITH]

gas·trol·o·gy (ga strol′ə jē), *n.* the study of the structure, functions, and diseases of the stomach. [1800–10; GASTRO- + -LOGY] —**gas·tro·log·ic** (gas′trə loj′ik), **gas′tro·log′i·cal,** *adj.* —**gas′tro·log′i·cal·ly,** *adv.* —**gas·trol′o·gist,** *n.*

gas·tro·nome (gas′trə nōm′), *n.* a connoisseur of good food; gourmet; epicure. Also, **gas·tron·o·mer** (ga stron′ə mər), **gas·tron′o·mist.** [1815–25; < F, back formation from *gastronomie* GASTRONOMY]

gas·tron·o·my (ga stron′ə mē), *n.* **1.** the art or science of good eating. **2.** a style of cooking or eating. [1805–15; < F *gastronomie* < Gk *gastronomía.* See GASTRO-, -NOMY] —**gas·tro·nom·ic** (gas′trə nom′ik), **gas′·tro·nom′i·cal,** *adj.* —**gas′tro·nom′i·cal·ly,** *adv.*

gas·tro·plas·ty (gas′trə plas′tē), *n.* **1.** any plastic surgery on the stomach. **2.** See **gastric bypass.** [1945–50; GASTRO- + -PLASTY]

gas·tro·pod (gas′trə pod′), *n.* **1.** any mollusk of the class Gastropoda, comprising the snails, whelks, slugs, etc. —*adj.* **2.** Also, **gas·trop·o·dous** (ga strop′ə dəs). belonging or pertaining to the gastropods. [1820–30; < NL *Gast(e)ropoda* a class of mollusks. See GASTRO-, -POD]

gas·tro·scope (gas′trə skōp′), *n. Med.* a lighted flexible tubular instrument passed through the mouth for examining the esophagus, stomach, and duodenum. [1885–90; GASTRO- + -SCOPE] —**gas·tro·scop·ic** (gas′trə skop′ik), *adj.*

gas·tros·co·py (ga stros′kə pē), *n., pl.* **-pies.** *Med.* the examination with a gastroscope to detect disease. [1850–55; GASTRO- + -SCOPY]

gas·tros·to·my (ga stros′tə mē), *n., pl.* **-mies.** *Surg.* **1.** the construction of an artificial opening from the stomach through the abdominal wall, permitting intake of food or drainage of gastric contents. **2.** the opening so constructed. [1850–55; GASTRO- + -STOMY]

gas·trot·o·my (ga strot′ə mē), *n., pl.* **-mies.** *Surg.* the operation of cutting into the stomach. [1650–60; GASTRO- + -TOMY] —**gas·tro·tom·ic** (gas′trə tom′ik), *adj.*

gas·tro·trich (gas′trə trik), *n.* any of the microscopic, multicellular animals of the class or phylum Gastrotricha, of fresh or salt waters, characterized by bands of cilia on the ventral surface of the bottle-shaped or ribbony body and by a protrusible feeding apparatus at the mouth. [1935–40; < NL *Gastrotricha,* equiv. to *gastro-* GASTRO- + Gk *-tricha* neut. pl. of *-trichos* -haired, adj. deriv. of *thríx* hair] —**gas·trot·ri·chan** (gas tro′tri kən), *adj.*

gas·tro·vas·cu·lar (gas′trō vas′kyə lər), *adj. Zool.* serving for digestion and circulation, as a cavity. [1875–80; GASTRO- + VASCULAR]

gas·tru·la (gas′tro͝o lə), *n., pl.* **-las, -lae** (-lē′). *Embryol.* a metazoan embryo in an early state of germ layer formation following the blastula stage, consisting of a cuplike body of two layers of cells, the ectoderm and endoderm, enclosing a central cavity, or archenteron, that opens to the outside by the blastopore: in most animals progressing to the formation of a third cell layer, the mesoderm. [1875–80; < NL; see GASTRO-, -ULE] —**gas′tru·lar,** *adj.*

gas·tru·late (gas′tro͝o lāt′), *v.i.,* **-lat·ed, -lat·ing.** *Embryol.* to undergo gastrulation. [GASTRUL(A) + -ATE[1]]

gas·tru·la·tion (gas′tro͝o lā′shən), *n. Embryol.* **1.** the formation of a gastrula. **2.** any process, as invagination, by which a blastula or other form of embryo is converted into a gastrula. [1875–80; GASTRULATE + -ION]

gas′ tube′, an electron tube the envelope of which contains a highly rarefied gas. Also called **discharge tube.** [1805–15]

gas′ tur′bine, a turbine utilizing the gaseous products of combustion. [1900–05]

gas′ well′, a well from which natural gas is obtained. [1840–50, *Amer.*]

gas·works (gas′wûrks′), *n., pl.* **-works.** (*used with a singular v.*) a plant where heating and illuminating gas is manufactured and piped to homes and buildings. Also called **gashouse.** [1810–20; GAS + WORKS]

gat[1] (gat), *v. Archaic.* pt. of **get.**

gat[2] (gat), *n. Older Slang.* a pistol or revolver. [1900–05, *Amer.*; shortening of GATLING GUN]

gat[3] (gat), *n.* a passage or channel that extends inland from a shore through shoals, cliffs, etc. [1715–25; < ON *gat* hole, opening]

ga·ta (gä′tə), *n.* the nurse shark, *Ginglymostoma cirratum.* [< AmerSp, Sp: cat < LL *catta* CAT[1]]

gate[1] (gāt), *n., v.,* **gat·ed, gat·ing.** —*n.* **1.** a movable barrier, usually on hinges, closing an opening in a fence, wall, or other enclosure. **2.** an opening permitting passage through an enclosure. **3.** a tower, architectural setting, etc., for defending or adorning such an opening or for providing a monumental entrance to a street, park, etc.: *the gates of the walled city; the palace gate.* **4.** any means of access or entrance: *The gate to stardom is talent.* **5.** a mountain pass. **6.** any movable barrier, as at a tollbooth or a road or railroad crossing. **7.** a gateway or passageway in a passenger terminal or pier that leads to a place for boarding a train, plane, or ship. **8.** a sliding barrier for regulating the passage of water, steam, or the like, as in a dam or pipe; valve. **9.** *Skiing.* **a.** an obstacle in a slalom race, consisting of two upright poles anchored in the snow a certain distance apart. **b.** the opening between these poles, through which a competitor in a slalom race must ski. **10.** the total number of persons who pay for admission to an athletic contest, a performance, an exhibition, etc. **11.** the total receipts from such admissions. **12.** *Cell Biol.* a temporary channel in a cell membrane through which substances diffuse into or out of a cell. **13.** *Motion Pictures.* See **film gate. 14.** a sash or frame for a saw or gang of saws. **15.** *Metall.* **a.** Also called **ingate.** a channel or opening in a mold through which molten metal is poured into the mold cavity. **b.** the waste metal left in such a channel after hardening. **16.** *Electronics.* **a.** a signal that makes an electronic circuit operative or inoperative either for a certain time interval or until another signal is received. **b.** Also called **logic gate.** a circuit with one output that is activated only by certain combinations of two or more inputs. **17. get the gate,** *Slang.* to be dismissed, sent away, or rejected. **18. give (someone) the gate,** *Slang.* **a.** to reject (a person), as one's fiancé, lover, or friend. **b.** to dismiss from one's employ: *They gave him the gate because he was caught stealing.* —*v.t.* **19.** (at British universities) to punish by confining to the college grounds. **20.** *Electronics.* **a.** to control the operation of (an electronic device) by means of a gate. **b.** to select the parts of (a wave signal) that are within a certain range of amplitude or within certain time intervals. —*v.i.* **21.** *Metall.* to make or use a gate. [bef. 900; ME *gat, gate,* OE *geat* (pl. *gatu*); c. LG, D *gat* hole, breach; cf. GATE[2]]

gate[2] (gāt), *n.* **1.** *Archaic.* a path; way. **2.** *North Eng. and Scot.* habitual manner or way of acting. [1150–1200; ME < ON *gata* path; perh. akin to OE *geat* GATE[1]; cf. GAT[3]]

-gate, a combining form extracted from **Watergate,** occurring as the final element in journalistic coinages, usually nonce words, that name scandals resulting from concealed crime or other alleged improprieties in government or business: *Koreagate.*

gate′ array′, *Computers, Electronics.* See **logic array.** [1975–80]

gâ·teau (ga tō′, gä-; *Fr.* gä tō′), *n., pl.* **-teaux** (-tōz′; *Fr.* -tō′). *French Cookery.* a cake, esp. a very light sponge cake with a rich icing or filling. [1835–45; < F; OF *gastel* (cf. ME *wastel* < ONF) < Frankish **wastil,* perh. akin to OE, OS *wist* food, nourishment]

gate-crash·er (gāt′krash′ər), *n. Informal.* a person who attends or enters a social function without an invitation, a theater without a ticket, etc. [1925–30, *Amer.*]

gat·ed (gā′tid), *adj.* (of patterns in a foundry mold) linked by gates. [1620–30; GATE[1] + -ED[3]]

gate·fold (gāt′fōld′), *n. Print.* foldout (def. 1). [1960–65; GATE[1] + FOLD[1]]

gate·house (gāt′hous′), *n., pl.* **-hous·es** (-hou′ziz). **1.** a house at or over a gate, used as a gatekeeper's quarters, fortification, etc. **2.** a house or structure at the gate of a dam, reservoir, etc., with equipment or controls for regulating the flow of water. [1350–1400; ME; see GATE[1], HOUSE]

gate·keep·er (gāt′kē′pər), *n.* **1.** a person in charge of a gate, usually to supervise the traffic or flow through it. **2.** guardian; monitor: *the gatekeepers of Western culture.* [1565–75; GATE[1] + KEEPER]

gate′ leg′, *Furniture.* a leg attached to a hinged frame that can be swung out to support a drop leaf. Cf. **swing leg.** [1900–05]

gate-leg table
(18th century)

gate′-leg ta′ble (gāt′leg′), a table having drop leaves supported by gate legs. Also, **gate′-legged′ ta′·ble.** [1900–05]

gate·man (gāt′mən, -man′), *n., pl.* **-men** (-mən, -men′). a gatekeeper. [1790–1800; GATE[1] + MAN[1]]

gate·post (gāt′pōst′), *n.* the vertical post on which a gate is suspended by hinges, or the post against which the gate is closed. [1515–25; GATE[1] + POST[1]]

ga·ter (gā′tər), *n.* gator. Also, **'ga′ter.**

Gates (gāts), *n.* **Horatio,** 1728–1806, American Revolutionary general, born in England.

Gates·head (gāts′hed′), *n.* a metropolitan borough in Tyne and Wear, in NE England: seaport on the Tyne River opposite Newcastle. 222,000.

gate′ the′ory, a theory proposing that neural stimulation beyond a certain threshold level, as by application of an electric current, can overwhelm the ability of the nerve center to sense pain. [1965–70]

gate·way (gāt′wā′), *n.* **1.** an entrance or passage that may be closed by a gate. **2.** a structure for enclosing such an opening or entrance. **3.** any passage by or point at which a region may be entered: *New York soon became the gateway to America.* [1700–10; GATE[1] + WAY]

gate′way drug′, any mood-altering drug, as a stimulant or tranquilizer, that does not cause physical dependence but may lead to the use of addictive drugs, as heroin. [1985–90]

Ga·tha (gä′tə, -tä), *n. Zoroastrianism.* one of several groups of hymns **(the Gathas)** forming the oldest part of the Avesta. [< Avestan *gāthā-*; c. Skt *gāthā* song]

gath·er (gath′ər), *v.t.* **1.** to bring together into one group, collection, or place: *to gather firewood; to gather the troops.* **2.** to bring together or assemble from various places, sources, or people; collect gradually: *The college is gathering a faculty from all over the country.* **3.** to serve as a center of attention for; attract: *A good football game always gathers a crowd.* **4.** to pick or harvest (any crop or natural yield) from its place of growth or formation: *to gather fruit; to gather flowers.* **5.** to pick up piece by piece: *Gather your toys from the floor.* **6.** to pick or scoop up: *She gathered the crying child in her arms.* **7.** to collect (as taxes, dues, money owed, etc.). **8.** to accumulate; increase: *The storm gathers force. The car gathered speed.* **9.** to take by selection from among other things; sort out; cull. **10.** to assemble or collect (one's energies or oneself) as for an effort (often fol. by *up*): *He gathered up his strength for the hard job.* **11.** to learn or conclude from observation; infer; deduce: *I gather that he is the real leader.* **12.** to wrap or draw around or close: *He gathered his scarf around his neck.* **13.** to contract (the brow) into wrinkles. **14.** to draw (cloth) up on a thread in fine folds or puckers by means of even stitches. **15.** *Bookbinding.* to assemble (the printed sections of a book) in proper sequence for binding. **16.** *Naut.* to gain (way) from a dead stop or extremely slow speed. **17.** *Metalworking.* to increase the sectional area of (stock) by any of various operations. **18.** *Glassmaking.* to accumulate or collect (molten glass) at the end of a tube for blowing, shaping, etc. —*v.i.* **19.** to come together around a central point; assemble: *Let's gather round the fire and sing.* **20.** to collect or accumulate: *Clouds were gathering in the northeast.* **21.** to grow, as by accretion; increase. **22.** to become contracted into wrinkles, folds, creases, etc., as the brow or as cloth. **23.** to come to a head, as a sore in suppurating. **24. be gathered to one's fathers,** to die. —*n.* **25.** a drawing together; contraction. **26.** Often, **gathers.** a fold or pucker, as in gathered cloth. **27.** an act or instance of gathering. **28.** an amount or number gathered, as during a harvest. **29.** *Glassmaking.* a mass of molten glass attached to the end of a punty. [bef. 900; ME *gaderen,* OE *gaderian,* deriv. of *geador* together, akin to *gæd* fellowship; cf. TOGETHER, GOOD] —**gath′er·a·ble,** *adj.* —**gath′er·er,** *n.*
—**Syn. 1, 2.** accumulate, amass, garner, hoard. GATHER, ASSEMBLE, COLLECT, MUSTER, MARSHAL imply bringing or drawing together. GATHER expresses the general idea usually with no implication of arrangement: *to gather seashells.* ASSEMBLE is used of objects or facts brought together preparatory to arranging them: *to assemble data for a report.* COLLECT implies purposeful accumulation to form an ordered whole: *to collect evidence.* MUSTER, primarily a military term, suggests thoroughness in the process of collection: *to muster all one's resources.* MARSHAL, another term primarily military, suggests rigorously ordered, purposeful arrangement: *to marshal facts for effective presentation.* **4.** pluck, reap, glean, garner. **11.** assume, understand. **20.** accrete.

gath·er·ing (gath′ər ing), *n.* **1.** an assembly or meeting. **2.** an assemblage of people; group or crowd. **3.** a collection, assemblage, or compilation of anything. **4.** the act of a person or thing that gathers. **5.** something that is gathered together. **6.** a gather or a series of gathers in cloth. **7.** an inflamed and suppurating swelling. **8.** (in a flue, duct, etc.) a tapered section forming a transition between two sections, one of which has a greater area than the other. **9.** *Bookbinding.* a section in a book, usually a sheet cut into several leaves. [bef. 900; ME *gaderinge,* OE *gaderunge.* See GATHER, -ING[1]]
—**Syn. 1.** assemblage. **2.** congregation, concourse, company, throng. **7.** boil, abscess, carbuncle.

Ga·thic (gä′tik), *n.* **1.** an ancient Iranian language of the Indo-European family; the language in which the Gathas were written. Cf. **Avestan.** —*adj.* **2.** of, pertaining to, or expressed in this language. **3.** of or pertaining to the Gathas. [GATH(A) + -IC]

Gat·i·neau (gat′n ō′; *Fr.* ga tē nō′), *n.* a city in S Quebec, in E Canada, near Hull. 74,988.

gat·ing (gā′ting), *n. Cell Biol.* the process by which a channel in a cell membrane opens or closes. [GATE[1] + -ING[1]]

Gat·lin·burg (gat′lən bûrg′), *n.* a town in E Tennessee: resort. 3210.

Gat′ling gun′ (gat′ling), an early type of machine gun consisting of a revolving cluster of barrels around a central axis, each barrel being automatically loaded and fired every revolution of the cluster. [1860–65, *Amer.*; named after R. J. *Gatling* (1818–1903), U.S. inventor]

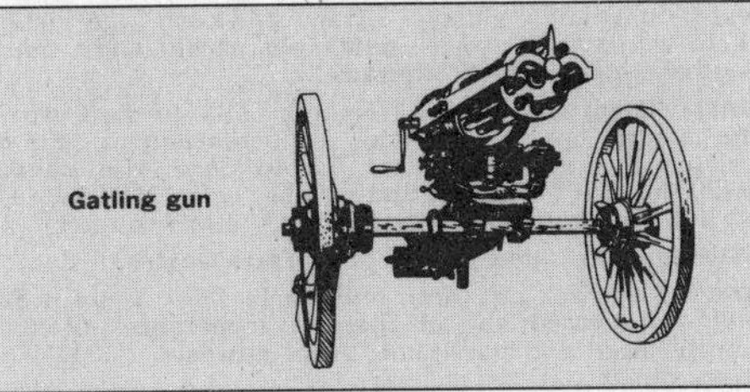
Gatling gun

ga·tor (gā′tər), *n. Southern U.S. Informal.* alligator. Also, **gater, 'gater.** [1835–45, *Amer.*; shortened form]

GATT, See **General Agreement on Tariffs and Trade.**

gat-toothed (gat′tōōtht′, -tōōthd′), *adj.* gap-toothed. [1350–1400; ME *gat tothed*]

Ga·tun (gä tōōn′), *n.* **1.** a town in the N Canal Zone of Panama. **2.** a large dam near this town. 1½ mi. (2 km) long.

Gatun′ Lake′, an artificial lake in the Canal Zone, forming part of the Panama Canal: created by the Gatun dam. 164 sq. mi. (425 sq. km). See map under **Panama Canal.**

gauche (gōsh), *adj.* lacking social grace, sensitivity, or acuteness; awkward; crude; tactless: *Their exquisite manners always make me feel gauche.* [1745–55; < F: awkward, left; MF, deriv. of *gauchir* to turn, veer < Gmc] —**gauche′ly,** *adv.* —**gauche′ness,** *n.*
—**Syn.** inept, clumsy, maladroit; coarse, gross, uncouth.

gau·che·rie (gō′shə rē′; *Fr.* gōshᵊ rē′), *n., pl.* **-ries** (-rēz′; *Fr.* -rē′). **1.** lack of social grace, sensitivity, or acuteness; awkwardness; crudeness; tactlessness. **2.** an act, movement, etc., that is socially graceless, awkward, or tactless. [1790–1800; < F; see GAUCHE, -ERY]

Gau·cher's′ disease′ (gō shāz′), *Pathol.* a rare inherited disorder of fat metabolism that causes spleen and liver enlargement, abnormal fragility and pain of the bones, and progressive neurologic disturbances, leading to early death. [after Philippe C. Ernest *Gaucher* (1854–1918), French physician, who described it]

gau·cho (gou′chō; *Sp.* gou′chô), *n., pl.* **-chos** (-chōz; *Sp.* -chôs). **1.** a native cowboy of the South American pampas, usually of mixed Spanish and Indian ancestry. **2. gauchos.** Also called **gau′cho pants′.** wide, calf-length trousers for men or women modeled after the trousers worn by South American gauchos. [1815–25; < AmerSp < Arawak *cachu* comrade]

gaud (gôd), *n.* a showy ornament or trinket. [1300–50; ME, perh. < AF, n. use of *gaudir* to rejoice < L *gaudēre* to enjoy]

gaud·er·y (gô′də rē), *n., pl.* **-er·ies. 1.** ostentatious show. **2.** finery; gaudy or showy things: *a fashionable dandy and his gaudery.* [1520–30; GAUD + -ERY]

Gau·dí i Cor·net (gou dē′ ē kôr′net), **An·to·ni** (än-tô′nē), 1852–1926, Spanish architect and designer.

gaud·y[1] (gô′dē), *adj.,* **gaud·i·er, gaud·i·est. 1.** brilliantly or excessively showy: *gaudy plumage.* **2.** cheaply showy in a tasteless way; flashy. **3.** ostentatiously ornamented; garish. [1520–30; orig. attributive use of GAUDY[2]; later taken as a deriv. of GAUD] —**gaud′i·ly,** *adv.* —**gaud′i·ness,** *n.*
—**Syn. 2.** tawdry, loud; conspicuous, obvious. GAUDY, FLASHY, GARISH, SHOWY agree in the idea of conspicuousness and, often, bad taste. That which is GAUDY challenges the eye, as by brilliant colors or evident cost, and is not in good taste: *a gaudy hat.* FLASHY suggests insistent and vulgar display, in rather a sporty manner: *a flashy necktie.* GARISH suggests a glaring brightness, or crude vividness of color, and too much ornamentation: *garish decorations.* SHOWY applies to that which is strikingly conspicuous, but not necessarily offensive to good taste: *a garden of showy flowers; a showy dress.* —**Ant. 2.** modest, sober.

gaud·y[2] (gô′dē), *n., pl.* **gaud·ies.** *Brit.* a festival or celebration, esp. an annual college feast. [1400–50; late ME < L *gaudium* joy, delight]

gauf·fer (gô′fər, gof′ər), *n., v.t.* goffer.

gauf·fer·ing (gô′fər ing, gof′ər-), *n.* goffering.

Gau·ga·me·la (gô′gə mē′lə), *n.* an ancient village in Assyria, E of Nineveh: Alexander the Great defeated Darius III here in 331 B.C. The battle is often mistakenly called "battle of Arbela."

gauge (gāj), *v.,* **gauged, gaug·ing,** *n.* —*v.t.* **1.** to determine the exact dimensions, capacity, quantity, or force of; measure. **2.** to appraise, estimate, or judge. **3.** to make conformable to a standard. **4.** to mark or measure off; delineate. **5.** to prepare or mix (plaster) with a definite proportion of plaster of Paris and mortar. **6.** to chip or rub (bricks or stones) to a uniform size or shape. —*n.* **7.** a standard of measure or measurement. **8.** a standard dimension, size, or quantity. **9.** any device or instrument for measuring, registering measurements, or testing something, esp. for measuring a dimension, quantity, or mechanical accuracy: *pressure gauge; marking gauge.* **10.** a means of estimating or judging; criterion; test. **11.** extent; scope; capacity: *trying to determine the gauge of his own strength.* **12.** *Ordn.* a unit of measure of the internal diameter of a shotgun barrel, determined by the number of spherical lead bullets of a diameter equal to that of the bore that are required to make one pound: *a twelve-gauge shotgun.* **13.** *Railroads.* the distance between the inner edges of the heads of the rails in a track, usually 4 ft. 8.5 in. (1.4 m) **(standard gauge),** but sometimes more **(broad gauge)** and sometimes less **(narrow gauge). 14.** the distance between a pair of wheels on an axle. **15.** the thickness or diameter of various, usually thin, objects, as the thickness of sheet metal or the diameter of a wire or screw. **16.** the fineness of a knitted fabric as expressed in loops per every 1.5 in. (3.8 cm): *15 denier, 60 gauge stockings.* **17.** *Naut.* the position of one vessel as being to the windward **(weather gauge)** or to the leeward **(lee gauge)** of another vessel on an approximately parallel course. **18.** *Building Trades.* the portion of the length of a slate, tile, etc., left exposed when laid in place. **19.** the amount of plaster of Paris mixed with mortar or common plaster to hasten the set. Also, *esp. in technical use,* **gage.** [1375–1425; late ME < ONF (F *jauge*) < Gmc] —**gauge′a·ble,** *adj.*
—**Syn. 2.** evaluate, assess, value, calculate.

gaug·er (gā′jər), *n.* **1.** a person or thing that gauges. **2.** a worker or inspector who checks the dimensions or quality of machined work. **3.** a customs official, collector of excise taxes, or the like. Also, *esp. in technical use,* **gager.** [1400–50; late ME < AF *gaugeour.* See GAUGE, -OR[2]]

Gau·guin (gō gaN′), *n.* **(Eu·gène Hen·ri) Paul** (œ zhen′ äN rē′ pôl), 1848–1903, French painter.

Gau·ha·ti (gou hä′tē), *n.* a city in W Assam, in E India, on the Brahmaputra River. 122,981.

Gaul (gôl), *n.* **1.** an ancient region in W Europe, including the modern areas of N Italy, France, Belgium, and the S Netherlands: consisted of two main divisions, one part S of the Alps **(Cisalpine Gaul)** and another part N of the Alps **(Transalpine Gaul). 2.** Latin, **Gallia.** a province of the ancient Roman Empire, including the territory corresponding to modern France, Belgium, the S Netherlands, Switzerland, N Italy, and Germany W of the Rhine. **3.** an inhabitant of the ancient region of Gaul. **4.** a native or inhabitant of France.

gau·lei·ter (gou′lī′tər), *n.* the leader or chief official of a political district under Nazi control. [1935–40; < G, equiv. to *Gau* region + *Leiter* director]

Gaul·ish (gô′lish), *n.* **1.** the extinct, Celtic language of ancient Gaul. —*adj.* **2.** of or pertaining to ancient Gaul, its inhabitants, or their language. [1650–60; GAUL + -ISH[1]]

Gaull·ism (gō′liz əm, gô′-), *n.* **1.** a political movement in France led by Charles de Gaulle. **2.** the principles and policies of the Gaullists. [1945–50; Charles (DE) GAULLE + -ISM]

Gaull·ist (gō′list, gô′-), *n.* **1.** a supporter of the political principles of Charles de Gaulle. **2.** a French person who supported the French resistance movement against the Nazi occupation in World War II. [1940–45; < F *Gaulliste.* See Charles DE GAULLE, -IST]

gaum (gôm, gäm), *v.t. Chiefly South Midland and Southern U.S.* to smear or cover with a gummy, sticky substance (often fol. by *up*): *My clothes were gaumed up with syrup.* [1790–1800; also Brit. dial.; of uncert. orig.]

gaum·less (gôm′lis), *adj. Chiefly Brit. Informal.* lacking in vitality or intelligence; stupid, dull, or clumsy. Also, **gormless.** [1740–50; dial. (Scots, N England) *gaum* heed, attention (ME *gome* < ON *gaumr;* akin to Goth *gaumjan* to observe) + -LESS]

gaunt (gônt), *adj.,* **-er, -est. 1.** extremely thin and bony; haggard and drawn, as from great hunger, weariness, or torture; emaciated. **2.** bleak, desolate, or grim, as places or things: *a gaunt, windswept landscape.* [1400–50; late ME, prob. < OF *gaunet, jaunet* yellowish, deriv. of *gaune, jaune* yellow < L *galbinus* greenish-yellow] —**gaunt′ly,** *adv.* —**gaunt′ness,** *n.*
—**Syn. 1.** lean, spare, scrawny, lank, angular, rawboned. See **thin.** —**Ant. 1.** stout.

Gaunt (gônt, gänt), *n.* **John of.** See **John of Gaunt.**

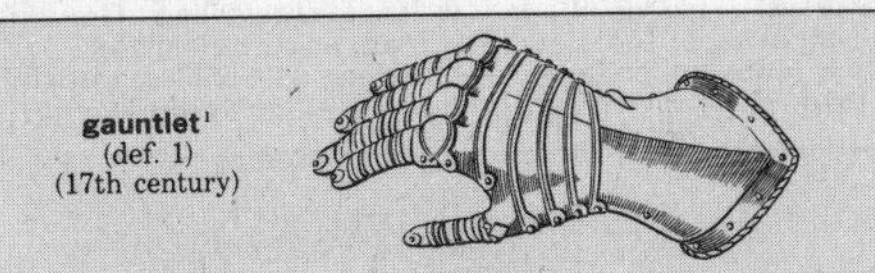
gauntlet[1]
(def. 1)
(17th century)

gaunt·let[1] (gônt′lit, gänt′-), *n.* **1.** a medieval glove, as of mail or plate, worn by a knight in armor to protect the hand. **2.** a glove with an extended cuff for the wrist. **3.** the cuff itself. **4. take up the gauntlet, a.** to accept a

CONCISE PRONUNCIATION KEY: act, cāpe, dâre, pärt; set, ēqual; if, ice; ox, ōver, ôrder, oil, bŏŏk, bōōt, out; up, ûrge; child; sing; shoe; thin, *th*at; zh as in *treasure.* ə = *a* as in *alone, e* as in *system, i* as in *easily, o* as in *gallop, u* as in *circus;* ᵊ as in *fire* (fīᵊr), *hour* (ouᵊr). l and n can serve as syllabic consonants, as in *cradle* (krād′l), and *button* (but′n). See the full key inside the front cover.

challenge to fight: *He was always willing to take up the gauntlet for a good cause.* **b.** to show one's defiance. Also, **take up the glove. 5. throw down the gauntlet, a.** to challenge. **b.** to defy. Also, **throw down the glove.** [1375–1425; late ME *gantelet* < MF, dim. of *gant* glove < Gmc **want-;* cf. ON *vǫttr*] **—gaunt′let·ed,** *adj.*

gaunt·let² (gônt′lit, gänt′-), *n.* **1.** a former punishment, chiefly military, in which the offender was made to run between two rows of men who struck at him with switches or weapons as he passed. **2.** the two rows of men administering this punishment. **3.** an attack from two or all sides. **4.** trying conditions; an ordeal. **5.** gantlet¹ (def. 1). **6. run the gauntlet,** to suffer severe criticism or tribulation. *—v.t.* **7.** gantlet¹ (def. 3). Also, **gantlet** (for defs. 1, 2, 4). [1670–80; alter. of GANTLOPE]

gaun·try (gôn′trē), *n., pl.* **-tries.** gantry.

gaup (gôp), *v.i.* gawp.

gaur (gouᵊr, gou′ər), *n., pl.* **gaurs,** (*esp. collectively*) **gaur.** a massive wild ox, *Bibos gaurus,* of southeastern Asia and the Malay Archipelago, growing to a height of 6 ft. (1.8 m) at the shoulder: now reduced in numbers. [1800–10; < Hindi < Skt *gaura*]

gauss (gous), *n. Elect.* **1.** the centimeter-gram-second unit of magnetic induction, equal to the magnetic induction of a magnetic field in which one abcoulomb of charge, moving with a component of velocity perpendicular to the field and equal to one centimeter per second, is acted on by a force of one dyne; 1 maxwell per square centimeter or 10^{-4} weber per square meter. *Symbol:* G **2.** (formerly) oersted (def. 1). [1880–85; named after K. F. GAUSS]

Gauss (gous), *n.* **Karl Frie·drich** (kärl frē′drĭkh), 1777–1855, German mathematician and astronomer. **—Gauss′i·an,** *adj.*

Gauss′ian curve′, *Statistics.* See **normal curve.** [1900–05]

Gauss′ian distribu′tion, *Statistics.* See **normal distribution.** [1965–70]

Gauss′ian im′age, *Optics.* the point in an optical system with spherical aberration at which the paraxial rays meet. Also called **Gauss′ian im′age point′.**

Gauss′ian in′teger, *Math.* a complex number of the form $a + bi$ where a and b are integers.

Gauss′ law′, *Physics.* the principle that the total electric flux of a closed surface in an electric field is equal to 4π times the electric charge inside the surface. Also, **Gauss′ law′, Gauss′s law′.** [named after K. F. GAUSS]

gauss·me·ter (gous′mē′tər), *n.* a magnetometer for measuring the intensity of a magnetic field, calibrated in gauss. [GAUSS + -METER]

Gau·ta·ma (gô′tə mə, gou′-), *n.* Buddha (def. 1). Also, **Gotama.** Also called **Gau′tama Bud′dha.**

Gau·tier (gō tyā′), *n.* **Thé·o·phile** (tā ô fēl′), 1811–72, French poet, novelist, and critic.

gauze (gôz), *n.* **1.** any thin and often transparent fabric made from any fiber in a plain or leno weave. **2.** a surgical dressing of loosely woven cotton. **3.** any material made of an open, meshlike weave, as of wire. **4.** a thin haze. [1555–65; < F *gaze* < ?] **—gauze′like′,** *adj.*

gauze′ weave′, leno (def. 1).

gauz·y (gô′zē), *adj.,* **gauz·i·er, gauz·i·est.** like gauze; transparently thin and light. [1790–1800; GAUZE + -Y¹] **—gauz′i·ly,** *adv.* **—gauz′i·ness,** *n.*

ga·vage (gə väzh′; *Fr.* GA VAZH′), *n.* forced feeding, as by a flexible tube and a force pump. [1885–90; < F, equiv. to *gav(er)* to stuff (OF (dial.) *gave* gullet, throat) + *-age* -AGE]

gave (gāv), *v.* pt. of **give.**

gav·el¹ (gav′əl), *n.* **1.** a small mallet used by the presiding officer of a meeting, a judge, etc., usually to signal for attention or order. **2.** a similar mallet used by an auctioneer to indicate acceptance of the final bid. **3.** *Masonry.* kevel. *—v.t.* **4.** to chair (a legislative session, convention, meeting, etc.). **5.** (of a presiding officer) **a.** to request or maintain (order) by striking a gavel. **b.** to begin or put into effect (a legislative session, motion, etc.) by striking a gavel. [1795–1805, *Amer.*; orig. uncert.]

gav·el² (gav′əl), *n.* feudal rent or tribute. [bef. 900; ME *govel,* OE *gafol,* akin to *giefan* to give; cf. GABELLE]

gav·el·kind (gav′əl kīnd′), *n. Eng. Law.* **1.** (originally) a tenure of land in which the tenant was liable for a rental in money or produce rather than for labor or military service. **2.** a customary system of land tenure featuring equal division of land among the heirs of the holder. **3.** the land so held. [1175–1225; ME *gavelkinde, gavlikind,* OE *gafel* GAVEL² + *(ge)cynd* KIND²]

gav′el-to-gav′el, *adj.* from the opening to the closing of a formal session or series of sessions: *gavel-to-gavel television coverage of the Congressional hearing.* [1970–75]

ga·vi·al (gā′vē əl), *n.* a large crocodilian, *Gavialis gangeticus,* of India and Pakistan, having elongated, garlike jaws: an endangered species. Also called **gharial.** [1815–25; < F < Hindi *ghariyāl*] **—ga′vi·al·oid′,** *adj.*

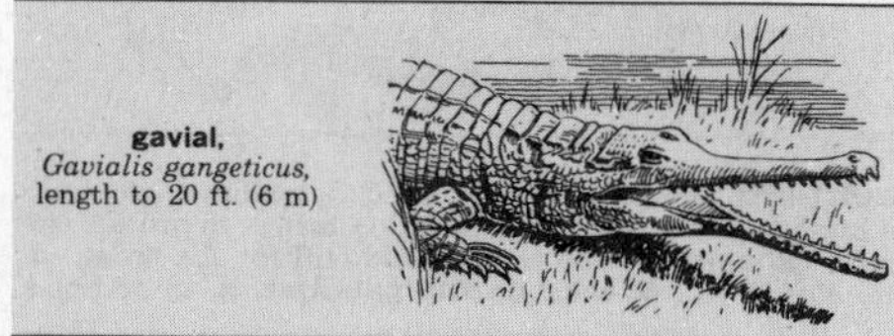

gavial, *Gavialis gangeticus,* length to 20 ft. (6 m)

CONCISE ETYMOLOGY KEY: <, descended or borrowed from; >, whence; b., blend of, blended; c., cognate with; cf., compare; deriv., derivative; equiv., equivalent; imit., imitative; obl., oblique; r., replacing; s., stem; sp., spelling, spelled; resp., respelling, respelled; trans., translation; ?, origin unknown; *, unattested; ‡, probably earlier than. See the full key inside the front cover.

Gav·in (gav′in), *n.* a male given name.

Gäv·le (yāv′le), *n.* a seaport in E Sweden. 87,378.

ga·votte (gə vot′), *n.* **1.** an old French dance in moderately quick quadruple meter. **2.** a piece of music for, or in the rhythm of, this dance, often forming one of the movements in the classical suite, usually following the saraband. Also, **ga·vot′.** [1690–1700; < F < Pr *gavoto* a mountaineer of Provence, a dance of such mountaineers, appar. deriv. of *gava* bird's crop (prob. < pre-L **gaba* throat, crop, goiter), alluding to the prevalence of goiter among the mountaineers]

gaw (gô), *n. Chiefly Scot.* a narrow, trenchlike depression, esp. a furrow in the earth or a worn or thin area in cloth. [1785–95; orig. uncert.]

G.A.W., guaranteed annual wage.

Ga·wain (gä′win, gô′-), *n. Arthurian Romance.* a knight of the Round Table: a nephew of King Arthur.

gawk (gôk), *v.i.* **1.** to stare stupidly; gape: *The onlookers gawked at arriving celebrities.* *—n.* **2.** an awkward, foolish person. [1775–85; appar. repr. OE word meaning fool, equiv. to *ga(gol)* foolish + *-oc* -OCK; used attributively in *gawk hand, gallock hand* left hand]
—Syn. 1. peer, ogle, gaze, goggle, rubberneck.

gawk·y (gô′kē), *adj.,* **gawk·i·er, gawk·i·est.** awkward; ungainly; clumsy. Also, **gawk·ish** (gô′kish). [1715–25; GAWK + -Y¹] **—gawk′i·ly, gawk′ish·ly,** *adv.* **—gawk′i·ness, gawk′ish·ness,** *n.*

gawp (gôp), *v.i. Chiefly Northern U.S.* to stare with the mouth open in wonder or astonishment; gape: *Crowds stood gawping at the disabled ship.* Also, **gaup.** [1720–30; Brit. dial., continuing obs. *galp,* ME *galpen,* perh. b. MD *galpen* to yawn and ME *gapen* to GAPE]

Gaw·ra (*Turk.* gou rä′), *n.* See **Tepe Gawra.**

gaw·sy (gô′sē), *adj. Scot. and North Eng.* **1.** (of people) well-dressed and of cheerful appearance. **2.** (of things) large and handsome. Also, **gaw′sie.** [1710–20; perh. var. of GAUDY¹; cf. -SY]

gay (gā), *adj.,* **-er, -est,** *n., adv.* *—adj.* **1.** having or showing a merry, lively mood: *gay spirits; gay music.* **2.** bright or showy: *gay colors; gay ornaments.* **3.** given to or abounding in social or other pleasures: *a gay social season.* **4.** licentious; dissipated; wanton: *The baron is a gay old rogue with an eye for the ladies.* **5.** homosexual. **6.** of, indicating, or supporting homosexual interests or issues: *a gay organization.* *—n.* **7.** a homosexual person, esp. a male. *—adv.* **8.** in a gay manner. [1275–1325; 1950–55 for def. 5; ME *gai* < OF < Gmc; cf. OHG *gāhi* fast, sudden] **—gay′ness,** *n.*
—Syn. 1. gleeful, jovial, glad, joyous, happy, cheerful, sprightly, blithe, airy, light-hearted; vivacious, frolicsome, sportive, hilarious. GAY, JOLLY, JOYFUL, MERRY describe a happy or light-hearted mood. GAY suggests a lightness of heart or liveliness of mood that is openly manifested: *when hearts were young and gay.* JOLLY indicates a good-humored, natural, expansive gaiety of mood or disposition: *a jolly crowd at a party.* JOYFUL suggests gladness, happiness, rejoicing: *joyful over the good news.* MERRY is often interchangeable with *gay: a merry disposition; a merry party;* it suggests, even more than the latter, convivial animated enjoyment. **2.** brilliant. **—Ant. 1.** unhappy, mournful.
—Usage. In addition to its original and continuing senses of "merry, lively" and "bright or showy," GAY has had various senses dealing with sexual conduct since the 17th century. A *gay woman* was a prostitute, a *gay man* a womanizer, a *gay house* a brothel. This sexual world included homosexuals too, and GAY as an adjective meaning "homosexual" goes back at least to the early 1900's. After World War II, as social attitudes toward sexuality began to change, GAY was applied openly by homosexuals to themselves, first as an adjective and later as a noun. Today, the noun often designates only a male homosexual: *gays and lesbians.* The word has ceased to be slang and is not used disparagingly. HOMOSEXUAL as a noun is sometimes used only in reference to a male.

Gay (gā), *n.* **1. John,** 1685–1732, English poet and dramatist. **2.** a female or male given name.

Ga·ya (gä′yə, gī′ə, gə yä′), *n.* a city in central Bihar, in NE India: Hindu center of pilgrimage. 179,826.

ga·yal (gə yäl′), *n., pl.* **-yals,** (*esp. collectively*) **-yal.** an ox, *Bibos frontalis,* of southeastern Asia and the Malay Archipelago, sometimes considered to be a domesticated breed of the gaur. Also called **mithan.** [1780–90; < Bengali *gayāl*]

Ga′ya Mar′e·tan (mar′i tan′), *n.* Gayomart.

ga·ya·tri (gä′yə trē′), *n. Hinduism.* a Vedic mantra expressing hope for enlightenment: recited daily by the faithful and repeated in all religious rites and ceremonies. [1835–45; < Skt *gāyatri,* deriv. of *gāyatra* song, hymn]

gay·e·ty (gā′i tē), *n., pl.* **-ties.** gaiety.

gay-feath·er (gā′feth′ər), *n.* any of several composite plants of the genus *Liatris,* esp. *L. spicata* or *L. scariosa,* having hairy leaves and long clusters of purplish flowers. [1810–20, *Amer.*]

Gayle (gāl), *n.* a female or male given name.

gay′ libera′tion, a political and social movement to combat legal and social discrimination against homosexuals. [1965–70] **—gay′ libera′tionist.**

Gay·lord (gā′lôrd′), *n.* a male given name.

Gay-Lus·sac (gā′lə sak′; *Fr.* gā ly sak′), *n.* **Jo·seph Lou·is** (jō′zəf lo͞o′ē, -səf; *Fr.* zhô zef′ lwē), 1778–1850, French chemist and physicist.

Gay′-Lussac's′ law′, *Thermodynamics.* the principle that, for relatively low pressures, the density of an ideal gas at constant pressure varies inversely with the absolute temperature of the gas. Also called **Charles' law.** Cf. **Boyle's law.** [named after J. L. GAY-LUSSAC]

gay·lus·site (gā′lə sīt′), *n.* a rare mineral, hydrated carbonate of sodium and calcium. [1826; named after J. L. GAY-LUSSAC; see -ITE¹]

gay·ly (gā′lē), *adv.* gaily.

Gay′ Nine′ties, the 1890's in the United States, a period regarded nostalgically as a decade of prosperous comfort and associated with gaslights, early bicycles and cars, and the Gibson girl.

Ga·yo·mart (gä yō′märt), *n. Zoroastrianism.* the first Aryan and the sixth creation of Ahura Mazda. Also called **Gaya Maretan.**

gay′ pow′er, the organized political influence exerted by homosexuals as a group, esp. to ensure equal rights in employment, housing, etc.

gay·wings (gā′wingz′), *n., pl.* **-wings.** See **fringed polygala.** [1840–50, *Amer.*; GAY + WING + -S³]

gaz., 1. gazette. **2.** gazetteer.

Ga·za (gä′zə, gaz′ə, gā′zə), *n.* a seaport on the Mediterranean Sea, in the Gaza Strip, adjacent to SW Israel; occupied by Israel 1967–94; since 1994 under Palestinian self-rule: ancient trade-route center. 118,300.

ga·za·bo (gə zā′bō), *n., pl.* **-bos.** *Older Slang.* a fellow; man; boy. Also, **gazebo.** [1895–1900; perh. < Sp *gazapo* sly customer, sharpie, lit., bunny, young rabbit, akin to Pg *caçapo;* Iberian Rom word of obscure orig.]

ga·za·ni·a (gə zā′nē ə), *n.* any of several composite plants of the genus *Gazania,* native to southern Africa, having showy flowers with variously colored rays. [< NL (1791), after Theodorus *Gaza* (1398–1478), Greek scholar; see -AN, -IA]

gaz·ar (gə zär′), *n.* a silk fabric of loose construction with a stiff hand.

Ga′za Strip′, a coastal area on the E Mediterranean: formerly in the Palestine mandate, occupied by Israel 1967–94; since 1994 under Palestinian self-rule.

gaze (gāz), *v.,* **gazed, gaz·ing,** *n.* *—v.i.* **1.** to look steadily and intently, as with great curiosity, interest, pleasure, or wonder. *—n.* **2.** a steady or intent look. **3. at gaze,** *Heraldry.* (of a deer or deerlike animal) represented as seen from the side with the head looking toward the spectator: *a stag at gaze.* [1350–1400; ME *gasen;* cf. Norw, Sw (dial.) *gasa* to look] **—gaze′less,** *adj.* **—gaz′er,** *n.* **—gaz′ing·ly,** *adv.*
—Syn. 1. GAZE, STARE, GAPE suggest looking fixedly at something. To GAZE is to look steadily and intently at something, esp. at that which excites admiration, curiosity, or interest: *to gaze at scenery, at a scientific experiment.* To STARE is to gaze with eyes wide open, as from surprise, wonder, alarm, stupidity, or impertinence: *to stare unbelievingly or rudely.* GAPE is a word with uncomplimentary connotations; it suggests open-mouthed, often ignorant or rustic wonderment or curiosity: *to gape at a tall building or a circus parade.*

ga·ze·bo¹ (gə zā′bō, -zē′-), *n., pl.* **-bos, -boes. 1.** a structure, as an open or latticework pavilion or summerhouse, built on a site that provides an attractive view. **2.** a small roofed structure that is screened on all sides, used for outdoor entertaining and dining. [1745–55; orig. uncert.]

ga·ze·bo² (gə zā′bō, -zē′-), *n., pl.* **-bos.** gazabo.

gaze·hound (gāz′hound′), *n.* one of any of several breeds of hounds, as the Afghan, borzoi, greyhound, Saluki, or whippet, that hunts by sighting the game rather than by scent. Also called **sighthound.** [1560–70; GAZE + HOUND¹]

ga·zelle (gə zel′), *n., pl.* **-zelles,** (*esp. collectively*) **-zelle.** any small antelope of the genus *Gazella* and allied genera, of Africa and Asia, noted for graceful movements and lustrous eyes. [1575–85; < F; OF *gazel* < Ar *ghazāla*] **—ga·zelle′like′,** *adj.*

gazelle, *Gazella subgutturosa,* 2½ ft. (0.8 m) high at shoulder; horns 14 in. (36 cm); length 4 ft. (1.2 m)

gazelle′ hound′, Saluki.

ga·zette (gə zet′), *n., v.,* **-zet·ted, -zet·ting.** *—n.* **1.** a newspaper (now used chiefly in the names of newspapers): *The Phoenix Gazette.* **2.** *Chiefly Brit.* an official government journal containing lists of government appointments and promotions, bankruptcies, etc. *—v.t.* **3.** *Chiefly Brit.* to publish, announce, or list in an official government journal. [1595–1605; < F < It *gazetta* < Venetian *gazeta,* orig. a coin (the price of the paper), dim. of *gaza* magpie]

gaz·et·teer (gaz′i tēr′), *n.* **1.** a geographical dictionary. **2.** *Archaic.* a journalist, esp. one appointed and paid by the government. [1605–15; GAZETTE + -EER]

Ga·zi·an·tep (gä′zē än tep′), *n.* a city in S Turkey in Asia. 294,950. Formerly, **Aintab.**

gaz·o·gene (gaz′ə jēn′), *n.* an apparatus for impregnating a liquid with a gas, esp. carbon dioxide. Also, **gasogene.** [1850–55; < F *gazogène.* See GAS, -O-, -GEN]

gaz·pa·cho (gə spä′chō; *Sp.* gäth pä′chô, gäs-), *n.* *Spanish Cookery.* a soup made of chopped tomatoes, cucumbers, onions, garlic, oil, and vinegar, and served cold. [1835–45; < Sp]

ga·zump (gə zump′), *Brit. Slang.* —*v.t.* **1.** to cheat (a house buyer) by raising the price, at the time a contract is to be signed, over the amount originally agreed upon. —*n.* **2.** an act of gazumping. —**ga·zump′er,** *n.* [1925–30; earlier *gazoomph,* argot word of uncert. orig.]

G.B., Great Britain.

Gba·ri (gə bär′ē), *n., pl.* **-ris,** (*esp. collectively*) **-ri.** Gwari.

G.B.E., Knight Grand Cross of the British Empire or Dame Grand Cross of the British Empire.

Gc, 1. gigacycle; gigacycles. **2.** gigacycles per second.

GCA, 1. Girls' Clubs of America. **2.** *Aeron.* See **ground-controlled approach.**

g-cal, See **gram calorie.** Also, **g-cal.**

G.C.B., Grand Cross of the Bath.

GCC, See **Gulf Cooperation Council.**

G.C.D., greatest common divisor. Also, **g.c.d.**

GCE, *Brit.* General Certificate of Education.

G.C.F., greatest common factor. See **greatest common divisor.** Also, **g.c.f.**

GCI, *Mil.* ground-controlled interception.

G clef, *Music.* See **treble clef.**

G.C.M., greatest common measure. Also, **g.c.m.**

GCR, *Mil.* ground-controlled radar.

G.C.T., Greenwich Civil Time.

GD, *Real Estate.* garbage disposal.

Gd, *Symbol, Chem.* gadolinium.

gd., 1. good. **2.** guard.

G.D., 1. Grand Duchess. **2.** Grand Duke.

Gdańsk (gdïnsk; *Eng.* gə dänsk′, -dansk′), *n.* a seaport in N Poland, on the Gulf of Danzig. 402,200. German, **Danzig.**

Gde., gourde; gourdes.

Gdn, guardian.

gDNA, genomic DNA.

GDP, gross domestic product.

GDR, German Democratic Republic. Also, **G.D.R.**

gds., goods.

Gdy·nia (gə din′ē ə, -yə; *Pol.* gdi′nyä), *n.* a seaport in N Poland, on the Gulf of Danzig. 211,900.

Ge (zhä), *n.* **1.** a family of South American Indian languages spoken in southern and eastern Brazil and northern Paraguay. **2.** a member of any of several Ge-speaking peoples.

Ge, *Symbol, Chem.* germanium.

g.e., (in bookbinding) gilt edges.

gean (gēn), *n.* See **heart cherry.** [1525–35; < MF *guigne,* of uncert. orig.]

ge·an·ti·cline (jē an′ti klīn′), *n. Geol.* an anticlinal upwarp of regional extent. [1890–95; < Gk *gê* earth + ANTICLINE] —**ge·an·ti·cli·nal** (jē an′ti klīn′l, jē′an-), *adj.*

gear (gēr), *n.* **1.** *Mach.* **a.** a part, as a disk, wheel, or section of a shaft, having cut teeth of such form, size, and spacing that they mesh with teeth in another part to transmit or receive force and motion. **b.** an assembly of such parts. **c.** one of several possible arrangements of such parts in a mechanism, as an automobile transmission, for affording different relations of torque and speed between the driving and the driven machinery, or for permitting the driven machinery to run in either direction: *first gear; reverse gear.* **d.** a mechanism or group of parts performing one function or serving one purpose in a complex machine: *steering gear.* **2.** implements, tools, or apparatus, esp. as used for a particular occupation or activity; paraphernalia: *fishing gear.* **3.** a harness, esp. of horses. **4.** *Naut.* **a.** the lines, tackles, etc., of a particular sail or spar. **b.** the personal tools, clothing, and other possessions of a sailor. **5.** portable items of personal property, including clothing; possessions: *The campers keep all their gear in footlockers.* **6.** wearing apparel; clothing: *The fashion pages of the Sunday paper are featuring the latest fall gear.* **7.** armor or arms. **8. in gear, a.** *Mach.* in the state in which gears are connected or meshed: *The car is in gear.* **b.** in proper or active working order; functioning continuously without trouble: *Every department in this company must be in gear at all times.* **9. in** or **into high gear,** in or into a state of utmost speed, activity, or efficiency: *Military rearmament moved into high gear.* **10. out of gear,** *Mach.* in the state in which gears are not connected or meshed: *The engine is out of gear.* **11. shift** or **switch gears,** to change one's attitude, course of action, methods, etc., in an abrupt, dramatic, or unexpected manner: *In the middle of the second act the play shifts gears from comedy to tragedy.* —*v.t.* **12.** to provide with or connect by gearing. **13.** to put in or into gear. **14.** to provide with gear; supply; equip. **15.** to prepare, adjust, or adapt to a particular situation, person, etc., in order to bring about satisfactory results: *The producers geared their output to seasonal demands.* —*v.i.* **16.** to fit exactly, as one part of gearing into another; come into or be in gear. **17. gear down, a.** *Auto.* to shift the transmission of a vehicle to a lower gear: *The truck driver geared down at the top of the hill.* **b.** to reduce in scope or intensity: *With less income you'll have to gear down your spending habits.* **18. gear up, a.** to make or get ready for a future event or situation: *Insiders say the senator is gearing up to run for governor.* **b.** to get or put on equipment or clothing for a particular purpose: *The hikers geared up for the long trek down the mountain.* **c.** to arouse or excite, as with enthusiasm or expectation: *The employees were geared up for a hard battle with management over working hours.* —*adj.* **19.** *Slang.* great; wonderful. [1150–1200; ME *gere* < ON *gervi, gørvi;* akin to OE *gearwe* equipment] —**gear′less,** *adj.*

—**Syn. 2.** equipment, outfit, tackle, rig.

gear·box (gēr′boks′), *n.* **1.** a transmission, as in an automobile. **2.** a shield or housing for gears. Also, **gear′ box′.** [1885–90; GEAR + BOX[1]]

gear·ing (gēr′ing), *n. Mach.* **1.** an assembly of parts, esp. a train of gears, for transmitting and modifying motion and torque in a machine. **2.** the act or process of equipping with gears. **3.** the method of installation of such gears. [1815–25; GEAR + -ING[1]]

gear′ lev′er, *Brit.* gearshift. [1900–05]

gear′ pump′. See **lobular pump.** [1920–25]

gear′ ra′tio, *Mach.* **1.** the ratio of the rotational speeds of the first and final gears in a train of gears or of any two meshing gears. **2.** the ratio of the diameters of the pitch surfaces of any two meshing gears or of the numbers of their teeth. [1905–10]

gear·set (gēr′set′), *n. Auto., Mach.* a combination of gears that mesh to provide a particular gear ratio. [GEAR + SET]

gear·shift (gēr′shift′), *n.* **1.** See **shift lever. 2.** a device for selecting, engaging, and disengaging gears for a system for the transmission of power, esp. in a motor vehicle. [1925–30, *Amer.;* GEAR + SHIFT]

gear·wheel (gēr′hwēl′, -wēl′), *n.* a wheel having teeth or cogs that engage with those of another wheel or part; cogwheel. Also, **gear′ wheel′.** [1870–75; GEAR + WHEEL]

Geb (geb), *n. Egyptian Religion.* the god of the earth and the father of Osiris and Isis. Also, **Keb.**

geb., born. [< G *geboren*]

Gê·ba (gā′bə; *Port.* zhe′bä), *n.* a river in W Africa, flowing N from NW Guinea-Bissau to the Atlantic Ocean. ab. 190 mi. (305 km) long.

Ge·ber (jē′bər), *n.* (*Jabir ibn Hayyan*) 8th-century A.D. Arab alchemist. Also, **Jabir.**

geck·o (gek′ō), *n., pl.* **geck·os, geck·oes.** any of numerous small, mostly nocturnal tropical lizards of the family Gekkonidae, usually having toe pads that can cling to smooth surfaces: the largest species, *Gekko gecko,* is sometimes kept as a pet. [1705–15; < NL *gekko* < D; orig. uncert.; alleged to be a Malay word imit. of the lizard's call.]

ged (ged), *n., pl.* (*esp. collectively*) **ged,** (*esp. referring to two or more kinds or species*) **geds.** *Scot. and North Eng.* any fish of the pike family. Also, **gedd.** [1275–1325; ME *gedde* < ON *gedda* pike]

GED, 1. general educational development. **2.** general equivalency diploma.

Ged·a·li·ah (ged′l ī′ə, gi däl′yə), *n.* the governor of Judah after its conquest by Babylon. II Kings 25:22–26.

Ge·dank′en exper′iment (gə däng′kən), *Physics.* See **thought experiment.** [< G, pl. of *Gedanke* thought]

Ged·des (ged′ēz), *n.* **1. Norman Bel** (bel), 1893–1958, U.S. industrial and stage designer and architect. **2. Sir Patrick,** 1854–1932, Scottish biologist, sociologist, and town planner.

gee[1] (jē), *interj., v.,* **geed, gee·ing.** —*interj.* **1.** (used as a word of command to a horse or other draft animal directing it to turn to the right.) **2. gee up,** (used as a word of command to a horse or other draft animal directing it to go faster.) —*v.i.* **3.** to turn to the right. —*v.t.* **4.** to turn (something) to the right. **5.** to evade. Cf. **haw**[3]. [1620–30; orig. uncert.]

gee[2] (jē), *interj. Informal.* (used to express surprise, disappointment, enthusiasm, or simple emphasis): *Gee, that's great! Gee, I can't remember the book's title.* [1890–95, *Amer.;* euphemism for JESUS]

gee[3] (jē), *v.i.,* **geed, gee·ing.** *Informal.* to agree; get along. [1690–1700; orig. uncert.]

gee[4] (jē), *n. Slang.* a sum of one thousand dollars: *a fancy car costing twenty-five gees.* Cf. **G.** [1925–30; sp. of G, abbr. for GRAND (a thousand dollars)]

gee[5] (jē), *n.* a radio navigational system by which a fix can be obtained by comparing the pulse repetition rates of high-frequency ground waves from two separate stations. [1940–45; orig. abbr. for *ground electronics engineering*]

gee·bung (jē′bung), *n.* **1.** any of various small trees or shrubs of the genus *Persoonia,* native to Australia and New Zealand, having small white or yellow flowers and fleshy, edible fruit. **2.** the fruit itself. [1820–30; < Dharuk *ji-buŋ*]

Gee·chee (gē′chē), *n.* Gullah.

gee·gaw (jē′gô, gē′-), *n.* gewgaw.

geek (gēk), *n. Slang.* **1.** a carnival performer who performs sensationally morbid or disgusting acts, as biting off the head of a live chicken. **2.** any strange or eccentric person. [1915–20; prob. var. of *geck* (mainly Scots) fool < D or LG *gek*]

Gee·long (ji lông′), *n.* a seaport in SE Australia, SW of Melbourne. 125,279.

Geel′vink Bay′ (*Du.* KHāl′vingk), former (Dutch) name of **Sarera Bay.**

geep (gēp), *n., pl.* **geep.** the hybrid offspring of a goat and a sheep. Also called **shoat.** [1970–75; G(OAT) + (SH)EEP]

geese (gēs), *n.* a pl. of **goose.**

gee-string (jē′string′), *n.* G-string. Also, **gee′ string′.**

gee′ whiz′, *Informal.* gee[2]. [1880–85, *Amer.;* appar. euphemistic alter. of JESUS, with final syllable replaced by WHIZ[1]]

gee-whiz (jē′hwiz′, -wiz′), *adj. Informal.* arousing or characterized by surprise, wonder, or triumphant achievement: *a gee-whiz technology; a gee-whiz reaction to the sight of the Grand Canyon.* [1930–35]

Ge·ez (gē ez′, gā-), *n.* a Semitic language of ancient Ethiopia, now used only as the liturgical language of the Ethiopian Church. Also, **Ge'ez′.** Also called **Ethiopic.**

gee·zer (gē′zər), *n. Slang.* an odd or eccentric man: *the old geezer who sells shoelaces on the corner.* [1880–85; var. of *guiser* (see GUISE (v.), -ER[1]), repr. dial. pron.]

ge·fil′te fish′ (gə fil′tə), *Jewish Cookery.* a forcemeat of boned fish, esp. such freshwater fish as carp, pike, or whitefish, blended with eggs, matzo meal, and seasoning, shaped into balls or sticks and simmered in a vegetable broth, and often served chilled. Also, **ge·fill′te fish′, ge·füll′te fish′, ge·ful′te fish′.** [1890–95; < Yiddish: lit., stuffed fish]

ge·gen·schein (gā′gən shīn′), *n. Astron.* a faint, elliptical patch of light in the night sky that appears opposite the sun, being a reflection of sunlight by meteoric material in space. Also called **counterglow.** Cf. **zodiacal light.** [1875–80; < G *Gegenschein* counterglow]

Ge·hen·na (gi hen′ə), *n.* **1.** the valley of Hinnom, near Jerusalem, where propitiatory sacrifices were made to Moloch. II Kings 23:10. **2.** hell (def. 1). **3.** any place of extreme torment or suffering. [< LL < Gk *Géenna* < Heb *Gē-Hinnōm* hell, short for *gē ben Hinnōm* lit., valley of the son of Hinnom]

geh·len·ite (gā′lə nīt′), *n.* a mineral, aluminum calcium silicate, occurring in prismatic crystals varying in color from gray-green to brown. [1810–20; named after A. F. *Gehlen* (1775–1815), German chemist; see -ITE[1]]

Geh·rig (ger′ig), *n.* **Henry Louis** ("*Lou*"), 1903–41, U.S. baseball player.

Gei·ger (gī′gər), *n.* **Hans** (häns), 1882–1947, German physicist.

Gei′ger count′er, an instrument for detecting ionizing radiations, consisting of a gas-filled tube in which electric-current pulses are produced when the gas is ionized by radiation, and of a device to register these pulses: used chiefly to measure radioactivity. Also called **Gei′ger-Mül′ler count′er.** [1920–25; named after H. GEIGER]

Gei′ger-Mül′ler thresh′old (gī′gər mul′ər, -myo͞o′lər), *Physics.* the minimum voltage applied to an ionization chamber, as in a Geiger counter, at which the charge collected per count is independent of the nature of the ionizing event producing the count. Also called **Gei′ger thresh′old.** [named after H. GEIGER and W. *Müller,* 20th-century German physicist]

Gei′ger-Mül′ler tube′, *Physics.* a tube functioning as an ionization chamber within a Geiger counter. Also called **Gei′ger tube′.** [1925–30; see GEIGER-MÜLLER THRESHOLD]

Gei·kie (gē′kē), *n.* **Sir Archibald,** 1835–1924, Scottish geologist.

Gei·sel (gī′zəl), *n.* **Theodor Seuss** (so͞os), ("*Dr. Seuss*"), 1904–91, U.S. humorist, illustrator, and author of children's books.

gei·sha (gā′shə, gē′-), *n., pl.* **-sha, -shas.** a Japanese woman trained as a professional singer, dancer, and companion for men. [1890–95; < Japn, equiv. to *gei* arts (< Chin) + *-sha* person (< Chin)]

Geiss′ler tube′ (gīs′lər), a sealed glass tube with platinum connections at the ends, containing rarefied gas made luminous by an electrical discharge. [1865–70; named after H. *Geissler* (1814–79), German inventor]

gei·to·nog·a·my (gīt′n og′ə mē), *n. Bot.* pollination of a flower by pollen from another flower on the same plant. Cf. **xenogamy.** [1875–80; < Gk *geitono-* (s. of *geitōn*) neighbor + -GAMY] —**gei′to·nog′a·mous,** *adj.*

gel (jel), *n., v.,* **gelled, gel·ling.** —*n.* **1.** *Physical Chem.* a semirigid colloidal dispersion of a solid with a liquid or gas, as jelly, glue, etc. **2.** *Theat.* gelatin (def. 5). **3.** *Biochem.* a semirigid polymer, as agarose, starch, cellulose acetate, or polyacrylamide, cast into slabs or cylinders for the electrophoretic separation of proteins and nucleic acids. —*v.i.* **4.** to form or become a gel. **5.** jell (def. 2). [1895–1900; shortening of GELATIN]

gel·a·da (jel′ə də, jə lä′-), *n.* a large baboonlike cliff-dwelling monkey, *Theropithecus gelada,* native to mountains of Ethiopia, having a brown coat and, in the male, a luxuriant mane: an endangered species. [1835–45; < Amharic *č'ällada;* perh. akin to the Cushitic word for the baboon; cf. Oromo *jaldeessa*]

ge·län·de·läu·fer (gə len′də loi′fər), *n. Skiing.* a participant in cross-country skiing. [1930–35; < G, equiv. to *Gelände* countryside + *Läufer* runner]

ge·län·de·sprung (gə len′də spro͝ong′; *Ger.* gə len′də shpro͝ong′), *n. Skiing.* a jump, usually over an obstacle, in which one plants both poles in the snow in advance of the skis, bends close to the ground, and propels oneself chiefly by the use of the poles. Also called **ge·län′de jump′** (gə len′də). [1930–35; < G, equiv. to *Gelände* countryside + *Sprung* jump]

Ge·la·si·us I (jə lā′shē əs, -zhē-, -zē-), **Saint,** died A.D. 496, pope 492–496.

Gelasius II, (*Giovanni de Gaeta*) died 1119, Italian ecclesiastic: pope 1118–19.

ge•la•ti (jə lä′tē), *n. Italian Cookery.* a rich ice cream, made with eggs and usually containing a relatively low percentage of butterfat. Also, **ge•la•to** (jə lä′tō). [< It, pl. of *gelato,* n. use of ptp. of *gelare* to freeze; see GELATIN]

ge•lat•i•fi•ca•tion (jə lat′ə fi kā′shən), *n.* the process of gelatinizing. [1855–60; GELAT(IN) + -I- + -FICATION]

gel•a•tin (jel′ə tn), *n.* **1.** a nearly transparent, faintly yellow, odorless, and almost tasteless glutinous substance obtained by boiling in water the ligaments, bones, skin, etc., of animals, and forming the basis of jellies, glues, and the like. **2.** any of various similar substances, as vegetable gelatin. **3.** a preparation or product in which such an animal or vegetable substance is the essential constituent. **4.** an edible jelly made of this substance. **5.** Also called **gel′atin slide′.** *Theat.* a thin sheet made of translucent gelatin colored with an aniline dye, placed over stage lights, and used as a color medium in obtaining lighting effects. Also, **gel′a•tine.** [1790–1800; < F *gélatine* < ML *gelātina,* equiv. to L *gelāt(us)* frozen, ptp. of *gelāre* (*gel-* freeze + *-ātus* -ATE[1]) + *-ina* -IN[2]]

ge•lat•i•nate (jə lat′n āt′), *v.t., v.i.,* **-nat•ed, -nat•ing.** gelatinize. [1790–1800; GELATIN + -ATE[1]] —**ge•lat′i•na′tion,** *n.*

gel′atin dy′namite, a high explosive consisting of a gelatinized mass of nitroglycerin with cellulose nitrate added. Also called **gelignite, nitrogelatin.** [1885–90]

ge•lat•i•nize (jə lat′n īz′, jel′ə tn-), *v.,* **-nized, -niz•ing.** —*v.t.* **1.** to make gelatinous. **2.** to coat with gelatin, as paper. —*v.i.* **3.** to become gelatinous. Also, **gelatinate;** *esp. Brit.,* **ge•lat′i•nise′.** [1800–10; GELATIN + -IZE] —**ge•lat′i•ni•za′tion,** *n.* —**ge•lat′i•niz′er,** *n.*

ge•lat•i•noid (jə lat′n oid′), *adj.* **1.** resembling gelatin; gelatinous. —*n.* **2.** a gelatinoid substance. [1865–70; GELATIN + -OID]

ge•lat•i•nous (jə lat′n əs), *adj.* **1.** having the nature of or resembling jelly, esp. in consistency; jellylike. **2.** pertaining to, containing, or consisting of gelatin. [1715–25; GELATIN + -OUS] —**ge•lat′i•nous•ly,** *adv.* —**ge•lat′i•nous•ness, gel•a•tin•i•ty** (jel′ə tin′i tē), *n.*

ge•la•tion[1] (je lā′shən, jə-), *n.* solidification by cold; freezing. [1850–55; < L *gelātiōn-* (s. of *gelātiō*) a freezing, equiv. to *gelāt(us)* (see GELATIN) + *-iōn-* -ION]

ge•la•tion[2] (je lā′shən, jə-), *n. Physical Chem.* the process of gelling. [1910–15; GEL + -ATION]

geld[1] (geld), *v.t.,* **geld•ed** or **gelt, geld•ing. 1.** to castrate (an animal, esp. a horse). **2.** to take strength, vitality, or power from; weaken or subdue. [1250–1300; ME *gelden* < ON *gelda*] —**geld′er,** *n.*

geld[2] (geld), *n. Eng. Hist.* **1.** a payment; tax. **2.** a tax paid to the crown by landholders under the Anglo-Saxon and Norman kings. [1600–10; < ML *geldum* payment, tribute < Gmc; cf. OE *geld,* G *Geld*]

Gel•der•land (gel′dər land′; *Du.* KHel′dəʀ länt′), *n.* a province in E Netherlands. 1,717,458; 1965 sq. mi. (5090 sq. km). *Cap.:* Arnhem. Also called **Guelders.**

geld•ing (gel′ding), *n.* **1.** a castrated male animal, esp. a horse. **2.** a eunuch. [1350–1400; ME < ON *geldingr.* See GELD[1], -ING[3]]

ge•lech•i•id (jə lek′ē id), *n.* **1.** any of numerous small moths of the family Gelechiidae, including many crop pests, as the Angoumois grain moth and potato tuberworm. —*adj.* **2.** belonging or pertaining to the gelechiids. [< NL *Gelechiidae* name of the family, equiv. to *Gelechi(a)* name of the genus (< Gk *gēlechḗs* sleeping on earth; see -IA) + *-idae* -ID[2]]

ge•lée (zhə lā′), *n.* a jellied substance, esp. a cosmetic gel or a jellied food. Also, **ge•lee′.** [< F; see JELLY]

Ge•lée (zhə lā′), *n.* **Claude** (klōd). See **Lorraine, Claude.**

gel′ electrophore′sis, *Biochem.* a technique for separating protein molecules of varying sizes in a mixture by moving them through a block of gel, as of agarose or polyacrylamide, by means of an electric field, with smaller molecules moving faster and therefore farther than larger ones.

gel•id (jel′id), *adj.* very cold; icy. [1600–10; < L *gelidus* icy cold, equiv. to *gel(um)* frost, cold + *-idus* -ID[4]] —**ge•lid•i•ty** (jə lid′i tē), **gel′id•ness,** *n.* —**gel′id•ly,** *adv.*

gel•ig•nite (jel′ig nīt′), *n.* See **gelatin dynamite.** [GEL(ATIN) + L *ign(is)* fire + -ITE[1]]

Gell-Mann (gel män′, -man′), *n.* **Murray,** born 1929, U.S. physicist: devised a system for classifying elementary particles and postulated theory of quarks; Nobel prize 1969.

gel′ min′eral, a colloidal mineral.

gel•se•mi•um (jel sē′mē əm), *n., pl.* **-mi•ums, -mi•a** (-mē ə). the dried rhizome and roots of yellow jasmine, formerly used as a sedative in the form of a powder, tincture, or fluid extract. [1870–75; < NL < It *gelsom(ino)* jasmine + L *-ium* -IUM]

Gel•sen•kir•chen (gel′zən kiʀ′KHən), *n.* a city in W Germany, in the Ruhr valley. 287,600.

gelt[1] (gelt), *v.* a pt. and pp. of **geld**[1].

gelt[2] (gelt), *n. Slang.* money. [1890–95; < Yiddish < MHG *geld* money; in earlier Brit. dial. uses < G or D; see GELD[2]]

Ge•lug•pa (ge′lo͝og′pä′), *n. Lamaism.* See **Yellow Hats.**

gem (jem), *n., v.,* **gemmed, gem•ming,** *adj.* —*n.* **1.** a cut and polished precious stone or pearl fine enough for use in jewelry. **2.** something likened to or prized as such a stone because of its beauty or worth: *His painting was the gem of the collection.* **3.** a person held in great esteem or affection. **4.** muffin (def. 1). **5.** *Print. Brit.* a 4-point type of a size between brilliant and diamond. —*v.t.* **6.** to adorn with or as with gems. —*adj.* **7.** *Jewelry.* noting perfection or very high quality: *a gem ruby.* [1275–1325; ME *gemme* < OF < L *gemma* bud, jewel; r. ME *yimme,* OE *gim(m)* < L] —**gem′like′,** *adj.*
—**Syn. 2.** treasure, prize, jewel, pearl.

CONCISE ETYMOLOGY KEY: <, descended or borrowed from; >, whence; b., blend of, blended; c., cognate with; cf., compare; deriv., derivative; equiv., equivalent; imit., imitative; obl., oblique; r., replacing; s., stem; sp., spelling, spelled; resp., respelling, respelled; trans., translation; ?, origin unknown; *, unattested; ‡, probably earlier than. See the full key inside the front cover.

Ge•ma•ra (gə mär′ə; *Seph. Heb.* gə mä ʀä′; *Ashk. Heb.* gə mô′ʀə), *n.* **1.** the section of the Talmud consisting essentially of commentary on the Mishnah. **2.** the Talmud. —**Ge•ma′ric,** *adj.* —**Ge•ma′rist,** *n.*

Ge•may•el (jə mī el′), *n.* **A•min** (ä mēn′), born 1942, Lebanese political leader: president 1982–88.

ge•mein•schaft (*Ger.* gə mīn′shäft′), *n., pl.* **-schaf•ten** (*Ger.* -shäf′tən). (*often cap.*) **1.** an association of individuals having sentiments, tastes, and attitudes in common; fellowship. **2.** *Sociol.* a society or group characterized chiefly by a strong sense of common identity, close personal relationships, and an attachment to traditional and sentimental concerns. Cf. **Gesellschaft.** [1935–40; < G: community, equiv. to *gemein* common + *-schaft* -SHIP]

gem′el bot′tle (jem′əl), a bottle consisting of two flasks set side by side with the necks curving in opposite directions. [see GIMMALS]

gem•i•nate (*v.* jem′ə nāt′; *adj., n.* jem′ə nit, -nāt′), *v.,* **-nat•ed, -nat•ing,** *adj., n.* —*v.t., v.i.* **1.** to make or become doubled or paired. —*adj.* **2.** Also, **gem′i•nat′ed.** combined or arranged in pairs; twin; coupled. —*n.* **3.** *Phonet.* a doubled consonant sound. [1590–1600; < L *geminātus* doubled (ptp. of *gemināre*), equiv. to *gemin-* double + *-ātus* -ATE[1]] —**gem′i•nate•ly,** *adv.*

gem•i•na•tion (jem′ə nā′shən), *n.* **1.** a doubling; duplication; repetition. **2.** *Phonet.* the doubling of a consonantal sound. **3.** *Rhet.* the immediate repetition of a word, phrase, etc., for rhetorical effect. [1590–1600; < L *geminātiōn-* (s. of *geminātiō*), equiv. to *gemināt(us)* (see GEMINATE) + *-iōn-* -ION]

Gem•i•ni (jem′ə nī′, -nē), *n.pl., gen.* **Gem•i•no•rum** (jem′ə nôr′əm, -nōr′-) for 1. **1.** *Astron.* the Twins, a zodiacal constellation between Taurus and Cancer containing the bright stars Castor and Pollux. **2.** *Astrol.* **a.** the third sign of the zodiac: the mutable air sign. See illus. under **zodiac. b.** a person born under this sign, usually between May 21st and June 20th. **3.** a two-person U.S. spacecraft designed for orbital rendezvous and docking: used in 1965–66 in various experiments preparatory to a landing on the moon. [1350–1400; ME < L *geminī,* pl. of *geminus*]

Ge•mi•nia•ni (je′mē nyä′nē), *n.* **Fran•ces•co** (fʀän ches′kô), c1680–1762, Italian violinist and composer.

Gem•i•nids (jem′ə nidz), *n.* (*used with a plural v.*) *Astron.* a collection of meteors making up a meteor shower **(Gem′inid me′teor show′er)** visible around December 13, having its apparent origin in the constellation Gemini. [GEMIN(I) + -ID[1] + -S[3]]

gem•i•ni•flo•rous (jem′ə nē flôr′əs, -flōr′-), *adj. Bot.* having flowers arranged in pairs. [1865–70; < L *gemin(us)* twin + -I- + -FLOROUS]

gem′ jade′. See **imperial jade.**

gem•ma (jem′ə), *n., pl.* **gem•mae** (jem′ē). **1.** a bud. **2.** *Bot.* a cell or cluster of cells, or a leaflike or budlike body, that separates from the parent plant to form a new organism, as in mosses and liverworts. [1760–70; < L: bud, GEM]

gem•ma•ceous (je mā′shəs), *adj.* of, pertaining to, or resembling gemmae. [1850–55; GEMM(A) + -ACEOUS]

gem•mate (jem′āt), *adj., v.,* **-mat•ed, -mat•ing.** *Bot., Zool.* —*adj.* **1.** having buds; increasing by budding. —*v.i.* **2.** to put forth buds; increase by budding. [1840–50; < L *gemmātus* budded, adorned with gems. See GEMMA, -ATE[1]]

gem•ma•tion (je mā′shən), *n. Biol.* reproduction by gemmae. [1750–60; < F *gemmation.* See GEMMATE, -ION]

gem•mif•er•ous (je mif′ər əs), *adj.* bearing buds or gemmae; gemmiparous. [1650–60; GEMM(A) + -I- + -FEROUS]

gem•mi•form (jem′ə fôrm′), *adj.* shaped like a bud. [GEMM(A) + -I- + -FORM]

gem•mip•a•ra (je mip′ər ə), *n.pl.* gemmiparous animals, as hydra. Also, **gem•mip•a•res** (je mip′ə rēz′). [GEMM(A) + -I- + NL *-para,* deriv. of L *parere* to bear]

gem•mip•a•rous (je mip′ər əs), *adj.* producing or reproducing by buds or gemmae. [1785–95; < NL *gemmiparus.* See GEMMA, -PAROUS] —**gem•mi•par•i•ty** (jem′ə par′i tē), *n.* —**gem•mip′a•rous•ly,** *adv.*

gem•mu•la•tion (jem′yə lā′shən), *n.* the process of reproduction by gemmules. [GEMMULE + -ATION]

gem•mule (jem′yo͞ol), *n.* **1.** *Bot.* gemma. **2.** *Zool.* an asexually produced mass of cells that is capable of developing into an animal, as a freshwater sponge. **3.** *Evolution.* one of the hypothetical living units conceived by Darwin in the theory of pangenesis as the bearers of the hereditary attributes. [1835–45; < F < L *gemmula.* See GEMMA, -ULE]

gem•mu•lif•er•ous (jem′yo͞o lif′ər əs), *adj. Zool.* producing or reproducing by gemmules. [1840–50; GEMMULE + -I- + -FEROUS]

gem•my (jem′ē), *adj.,* **-mi•er, -mi•est. 1.** having gems; set with gems. **2.** like a gem, esp. in being bright, glittering, or sparkling. [1400–50; late ME. See GEM, -Y[1]] —**gem′mi•ly,** *adv.* —**gem′mi•ness,** *n.*

gem•ol•o•gy (je mol′ə jē), *n.* the science dealing with natural and artificial gemstones. Also, **gem•mol′o•gy.** [1965–70; GEM + -O- + -LOGY] —**gem•o•log•i•cal, gem•mo•log•i•cal** (jem′ə loj′i kəl), *adj.* —**gem•ol′o•gist, gem•mol′o•gist,** *n.*

ge•mot (gə mōt′), *n.* (in Anglo-Saxon England) a legislative or judicial assembly. Also, **ge•mote′.** [OE *gemōt,* equiv. to *ge-* collective prefix + *mōt* meeting; see MOOT]

gem•pyl•id (jem pil′id), *n.* **1.** any of several fishes of the family Gempylidae, comprising the snake mackerels. —*adj.* **2.** belonging or pertaining to the gempylids. [< NL *Gempylidae* name of the family, equiv. to *Gempyl(us)* name of the genus (< Gk *gempylos* a kind of fish) + *-idae* -ID[2]]

gems (gems), *n., pl.* **gems•es** (gem′siz, -ziz). chamois (def. 1). Also, **gem•se** (gem′zə). [< G; OHG *gamiza* < LL *camoc-* (s. of *camox*)]

gems•bok (gemz′bok′), *n., pl.* **-boks,** (*esp. collectively*) **-bok.** a large antelope, *Oryx gazella,* of southern and eastern Africa, having long, straight horns and a long, tufted tail. Also, **gemsbuck.** Also called **oryx.** [1770–80; < Afrik < G *Gemsbock* male chamois. See GEMS, BUCK[1]]

gemsbok, *Oryx gazella,* 4½ ft. (1.4 m) high at shoulder; horns 3 to 4 ft. (0.9 to 1.2 m)

gems•buck (gemz′buk′), *n., pl.* **-bucks,** (*esp. collectively*) **-buck.** gemsbok.

Gem′ State′, Idaho (used as a nickname).

gem•stone (jem′stōn′), *n.* a precious or semiprecious stone that can be cut and polished for use as a gem. [bef. 1000; ME *gimstone,* OE *gimstān.* See GEM, STONE]

ge•müt•lich (gə mo͞ot′lik -mo͝ot′-; *Ger.* gə mʏt′liKH), *adj.* **1.** comfortable and pleasant; cozy. **2.** friendly; easygoing. Also, **ge•muet′lich.** [1850–55; < G; late MHG *gemüetlich,* equiv. to *gemüet(e)* (G *Gemüt*) mind, mentality (collective deriv. of *mut,* OHG *muot* courage, spirit; see MOOD[1]) + *-lich* -LY]

Ge•müt•lich•keit (gə mʏt′liKH kīt′), *n. German.* warm cordiality; comfortable friendliness; congeniality. Also, ***Ge•muet′lich•keit′.***

-gen, a combining form meaning "that which produces," used in the formation of compound words: *endogen; hydrogen.* [< F *-gène* << Gk *-genēs* born, produced; akin to L *genus,* KIN]

Gen., 1. *Mil.* General. **2.** Genesis. **3.** Geneva.

gen., 1. gender. **2.** general. **3.** genitive. **4.** genus.

ge•na (jē′nə, gen′ə), *n., pl.* **ge•nae** (jē′nē, gen′ē). *Zool., Anat.* the cheek or side region of the head. [1820–30; < L: cheek; c. Gk *génys* jaw, CHIN] —**ge′nal,** *adj.*

ge•nappe (jə nap′, zhə-), *v.t.,* **-napped, -nap•ping.** to singe (worsted yarn) in order to remove loose or protruding fibers. [1855–60; after *Genappe,* Belgium, where the yarn was originally manufactured]

genappe′ yarn′, a worsted yarn that has been genapped and made smooth and lustrous. [1890–95]

gen•darme (zhän′därm; *Fr.* zhäɴ daʀm′), *n., pl.* **-darmes** (-därmz; *Fr.* -daʀm′). **1.** a police officer in any of several European countries, esp. a French police officer. **2.** a soldier, esp. in France, serving in an army group acting as armed police with authority over civilians. **3.** (formerly) a cavalryman in charge of a French cavalry squad. [1540–50; < MF, earlier *gens d'armes,* alter. of *gent d'armes* people at arms]

gen•dar•me•rie (zhän där′mə rē; *Fr.* zhäɴ daʀ mə ʀē′), *n.* gendarmes collectively; a body of gendarmes. Also, **gen•dar′mer•y.** [1545–55; < F; see GENDARME, -ERY]

gen•der[1] (jen′dər), *n.* **1.** *Gram.* **a.** (in many languages) a set of classes that together include all nouns, membership in a particular class being shown by the form of the noun itself or by the form or choice of words that modify, replace, or otherwise refer to the noun, as, in English, the choice of *he* to replace *the man,* of *she* to replace *the woman,* of *it* to replace *the table,* of *it* or *she* to replace *the ship.* The number of genders in different languages varies from 2 to more than 20; often the classification correlates in part with sex or animateness. The most familiar sets of genders are of three classes (as masculine, feminine, and neuter in Latin and German) or of two (as common and neuter in Dutch, or masculine and feminine in French and Spanish). **b.** one class of such a set. **c.** such classes or sets collectively or in general. **d.** membership of a word or grammatical form, or an inflectional form showing membership, in such a class. **2.** sex: *the feminine gender.* **3.** *Archaic.* kind, sort, or class. [1300–50; ME < MF *gendre, genre* < L *gener-* (s. of *genus*) kind, sort] —**gen′der•less,** *adj.*

gen•der[2] (jen′dər), *v.t., v.i.* **1.** *Archaic.* to engender. **2.** *Obs.* to breed. [1300–50; ME *gendren, genderen* < MF *gendrer* < L *generāre* to beget, deriv. of *genus* GENDER[1], GENUS[1]]

gen′der bend′er, *Informal.* one, as a cross-dresser, that blurs differences between the sexes. [1980–85] —**gen′der-bend′ing,** *adj.*

gen′der gap′, the differences between women and men, esp. as reflected in social, political, intellectual, cultural, or economic attainments or attitudes. [1980–85]

gen′der iden′tity, a person's inner sense of being male or female, usually developed during early childhood as a result of parental rearing practices and societal influences and strengthened during puberty by hormonal changes. Also called **core gender identity.**

gen′der role′, the public image of being male or female that a person presents to others.

gen•der-spe•cif•ic (jen′dər spi sif′ik), *adj.* for, characteristic of, or limited to either males or females: *Left-handedness is not gender-specific.*

gene (jēn), *n.* the basic physical unit of heredity; a linear sequence of nucleotides along a segment of DNA that provides the coded instructions for synthesis of RNA, which, when translated into protein, leads to the expression of hereditary character. [1911; < G *Gen* (1909), appar. abstracted from *-gen* -GEN; introduced by Danish geneticist Wilhelm L. Johannsen (1857–1927)]

Gene (jēn), *n.* a male given name, form of **Eugene.**

geneal., genealogy.

genealog′ical rela′tionship, *Historical Ling.* See **genetic relationship.**

ge′nealog′ical tree′. See **family tree.** [1805–15]

ge•ne•al•o•gy (jē′nē ol′ə jē, -al′-, jen′ē-), *n., pl.* **-gies.** **1.** a record or account of the ancestry and descent of a person, family, group, etc. **2.** the study of family ancestries and histories. **3.** descent from an original form or progenitor; lineage; ancestry. **4.** *Biol.* a group of individuals or species having a common ancestry: *The various species of Darwin's finches form a closely knit genealogy.* [1250–1300; ME *genealogie* < MF < LL *geneălogia* < Gk *geneălogía* pedigree, equiv. to *geneá* race (see GENE) + *-logia* -LOGY] **—ge•ne•a•log•i•cal** (jē′nē ə loj′i kəl, jen′ē-), **ge′ne•a•log′ic,** *adj.* **—ge′ne•a•log′i•cal•ly,** *adv.* **—ge′ne•al′o•gist,** *n.*
—Syn. 1. See **pedigree.**

gene′ amplifica′tion, 1. an increase in the frequency of replication of a DNA segment. **2.** such an increase induced by a polymerase chain reaction. [1970–75]

gen•e•arch (jen′ē ärk′), *n.* a chief of a family or tribe. [1720–30; < Gk *geneárchēs* founder of a family, equiv. to *gene(á)* race (see GENE) + *árchēs* -ARCH]

gene′ flow′, *Ecol.* the alteration of the frequencies of alleles of particular genes in a population, resulting from interbreeding with organisms from another population having different frequencies. [1945–50]

gene′ fre′quency, the frequency of occurrence or proportions of different alleles of a particular gene in a given population. Also called **allele frequency.** [1925–30]

gene′ map′ping, *Genetics.* **1.** any of a number of methods used to construct a model of the linear sequence of genes of a particular chromosome. **2.** the act of constructing such a model. [1975–80]

gene′ pool′, the total genetic information in the gametes of all the individuals in a population. [1945–50]

gen•er•a (jen′ər ə), *n.* a pl. of **genus.**

gen•er•a•ble (jen′ər ə bəl), *adj.* capable of being generated or produced. [1350–1400; ME < L *generābi-l(is)* creative, productive, equiv. to *gener(āre)* to beget, produce (see GENDER²) + *-ābilis* -ABLE] **—gen′er•a•bil′i•ty, gen′er•a•ble•ness,** *n.*

gen•er•al (jen′ər əl), *adj.* **1.** of or pertaining to all persons or things belonging to a group or category: *a general meeting of the employees.* **2.** of, pertaining to, or true of such persons or things in the main, with possible exceptions; common to most; prevalent; usual: *the general mood of the people.* **3.** not limited to one class, field, product, service, etc.; miscellaneous: *the general public; general science.* **4.** considering or dealing with overall characteristics, universal aspects, or important elements, esp. without considering all details or specific aspects: *general instructions; a general description; a general resemblance one to another.* **5.** not specific or definite: *I could give them only a general idea of what was going on.* **6.** (of anesthesia or an anesthetic) causing loss of consciousness and abolishing sensitivity to pain throughout the body. **7.** having extended command or superior or chief rank: *the secretary general of the United Nations; the attorney general.* **—*n.*** **8.** *Mil.* **a.** *U.S. Army and Air Force.* an officer ranking above a lieutenant general and below a general of the army or general of the air force. **b.** *U.S. Army.* an officer of any of the five highest ranks: a brigadier general, major general, lieutenant general, general, or general of the army. **c.** *U.S. Marines.* an officer holding the highest rank in the corps. **d.** (in numerous armies) an officer in the highest, second, or third highest rank, as one ranking immediately below a field marshal in the British army. **9.** *Eccles.* the chief official of a religious order. **10.** something that is general; generality. **11.** *Archaic.* the general public. **12. in general, a.** with respect to the whole class referred to; as a whole: *He likes people in general.* **b.** as a rule; usually: *In general, the bus is here by 9 A.M.* [1250–1300; ME < L *generālis,* equiv. to *gener-* (s. of *genus*) GENUS + *-ālis* -AL¹] **—gen′er•al•ness,** *n.*
—Syn. 1, 2. customary, prevailing, regular, ordinary; catholic. GENERAL, COMMON, POPULAR, UNIVERSAL agree in the idea of being nonexclusive and widespread. GENERAL means belonging to, or prevailing throughout, a whole class or body collectively, irrespective of individuals: *a general belief.* COMMON means shared by all, and belonging to one as much as another: *a common interest; common fund;* but use of this sense is frequently avoided because of ambiguity of sense. POPULAR means belonging to, adapted for, or favored by the people or the public generally, rather than by a particular (esp. a superior) class: *the popular conception; a popular candidate.* UNIVERSAL means found everywhere, and with no exceptions: *a universal longing.* **5.** ill-defined, inexact, imprecise, approximate. **—Ant. 1.** special, limited. **5.** definite, exact, precise.

Gen′eral Account′ing Of′fice, *U.S. Govt.* an independent auditing and accounting agency that assists Congress and government departments and agencies and settles claims for the federal government. *Abbr.:* GAO

gen′eral admis′sion, an admission charge for unreserved seats at a theatrical performance, sports event, etc. [1945–50]

Gen′eral Agree′ment on Tar′iffs and Trade′, an international organization formed in 1948 to establish common rules governing tariffs and to eliminate restrictive trade practices. *Abbr.:* GATT

Gen′eral Amer′ican, any form of American English speech considered to show few regional peculiarities, usually including all dialects except for eastern New England, New York City, Southern, and South Midland (no longer in technical use). *Abbr.:* GA [1930–35, *Amer.*]

Gen′eral Assem′bly, 1. the legislature in some states of the U.S. **2.** the main deliberative body of the United Nations, composed of delegations from member nations. [1610–20, *Amer.*]

gen′eral av′erage, *Insurance.* any damage or loss to a ship or its cargo voluntarily sustained, as freight jettisoned in a storm, by all parties to a voyage (distinguished from *particular average*). *Abbr.:* G.A. [1690–1700]

gen′eral avia′tion, aviation including business flying, sports flying, and crop dusting.

Gen′eral Court′, 1. the state legislature of Massachusetts or New Hampshire. **2.** (in colonial New England) any of various local assemblies having both legislative and judicial powers. [1620–30, *Amer.*]

gen′eral court′-martial, a court-martial having the authority to try any offense against military law and to impose a sentence of dishonorable discharge or of death when provided by law. [1805–15]

gen•er•al•cy (jen′ər əl sē), *n.* the office or tenure of a general. [1860–65; GENERAL + -CY]

gen′eral deliv′ery, 1. a postal service that delivers mail to a specific post office where it is held for pickup by the addressee. **2.** the postal department that handles such mail. [1830–40, *Amer.*]

gen′eral dis′charge, *Mil.* **1.** a discharge from military service of a person who has served honorably but who has not met all the conditions of an honorable discharge. **2.** a certificate of such a discharge.

gen′eral elec′tion, 1. *U.S. Politics.* **a.** a regularly scheduled local, state, or national election in which voters elect officeholders. Cf. **primary** (def. 15). **b.** a state or national election, as opposed to a local election. **2.** *Brit.* an election, which must be held at any time within five years of the last election, in which constituents elect members of the House of Commons. Cf. **by-election.** [1710–20, *Amer.*]

gen′eral head′quarters, *U.S. Army.* the headquarters of the commanding officer of a large military force. *Abbr.:* GHQ, G.H.Q. [1855–60]

gen•er•al•is•si•mo (jen′ər ə lis′ə mō′), *n., pl.* **-mos.** (in certain countries) the supreme commander of the armed forces. [1615–25; < It, superl. of *generale* GENERAL]

gen•er•al•ist (jen′ər ə list), *n.* a person whose knowledge, aptitudes, and skills are applied to a field as a whole or to a variety of different fields (opposed to *specialist*). [1605–15; GENERAL + -IST]

gen•er•al•i•ty (jen′ə ral′i tē), *n., pl.* **-ties. 1.** an indefinite, unspecific, or undetailed statement: *to speak in generalities.* **2.** a general principle, rule, or law. **3.** the greater part or majority: *the generality of people.* **4.** the state or quality of being general. [1400–50; late ME *generalite* < L *generālitās.* See GENERAL, -ITY]
—Syn. 1. truism, cliché, platitude, banality.

gen•er•al•i•za•tion (jen′ər ə lə zā′shən), *n.* **1.** the act or process of generalizing. **2.** a result of this process; a general statement, idea, or principle. **3.** *Logic.* **a.** a proposition asserting something to be true either of all members of a certain class or of an indefinite part of that class. **b.** the process of obtaining such propositions. **4.** *Psychol.* **a.** Also called **stimulus generalization.** the act or process of responding to a stimulus similar to but distinct from the conditioned stimulus. **b.** Also called **response generalization.** the act or process of making a different but similar response to the same stimulus. **c.** Also called **mediated generalization.** the act or process of responding to a stimulus not physically similar to the conditioned stimulus and not previously encountered in conditioning. **d.** the act or process of perceiving similarity or relation between different stimuli, as between words, colors, sounds, lights, or feelings; the formation of a general notion. [1755–65; GENERALIZE + -ATION]

gen•er•al•ize (jen′ər ə līz′), *v.,* **-ized, -iz•ing.** **—*v.t.*** **1.** to infer (a general principle, trend, etc.) from particular facts, statistics, or the like. **2.** to infer or form (a general principle, opinion, conclusion, etc.) from only a few facts, examples, or the like. **3.** to give a general rather than a specific or special character or form to. **4.** to make general; bring into general use or knowledge. **—*v.i.*** **5.** to form general principles, opinions, etc. **6.** to deal, think, or speak in generalities. **7.** to make general inferences. Also, *esp. Brit.,* **gen′er•al•ise′.** [1745–55; GENERAL + -IZE] **—gen′er•al•iz′a•ble,** *adj.* **—gen′er•al•iz′er,** *n.*

gen′eralized coor′dinates, *Physics.* the least number of coordinates needed to specify the state of a given system. [1880–85]

gen′eralized oth′er, *Sociol.* an individual's internalized impression of societal norms and expectations.

gen′eral linguis′tics, the study of the characteristics of language in general rather than of a particular language; theoretical, rather than applied, linguistics.

gen•er•al•ly (jen′ər ə lē), *adv.* **1.** usually; commonly; ordinarily: *He generally comes home at noon.* **2.** with respect to the larger part; for the most part: *a generally accurate interpretation of the facts.* **3.** without reference to or disregarding particular persons, things, situations, etc., that may be an exception: *generally speaking.* [1250–1300; ME; see GENERAL, -LY]
—Syn. 1. See **often.** **—Ant. 1.** seldom.

gen′er•al-ob•li•ga′tion bond′ (jen′ər əl ob′li gā′shən), a bond issued by a state or city and backed by general tax revenue and the issuer's credit. Cf. **revenue bond.**

gen′eral of′ficer, *Mil.* an officer ranking above colonel. [1635–45, *Amer.*]

gen′eral of the air′ force′, the highest ranking officer in the U.S. Air Force.

gen′eral of the ar′mies, *U.S. Army.* a special rank held by John J. Pershing, equivalent to general of the army.

gen′eral of the ar′my, *U.S. Army.* the highest ranking military officer; the next rank above general. Cf. **fleet admiral.** [1940–45]

gen′eral or′ders, *Mil.* **1.** a set of permanent orders from a headquarters establishing policy for a command or announcing official acts. **2.** a set of permanent orders governing the duties and behavior of sentries on routine guard duty. Cf. **special order.** [1865–70]

gen′eral paral′ysis, *Pathol.* a syphilitic brain disorder characterized by chronic inflammation and degeneration of cerebral tissue resulting in mental and physical deterioration. Also called **gen′eral pare′sis.** [1890–95]

gen′eral part′ner, a partner with unlimited liability for the debts of the partnership. Cf. **special partner.** [1885–90, *Amer.*]

gen′eral part′nership, a partnership in which each of the partners is fully liable for the firm's debts. Cf. **limited partnership.**

Gen′eral Post′al Un′ion, former name of **Universal Postal Union.** *Abbr.:* GPU

gen′eral post′ of′fice, (in the U.S. postal system) the main post office of a city, county, etc., that also has branch post offices. *Abbr.:* G.P.O., GPO [1650–60]

gen′eral prac′tice. See **family practice.** [1815–25]

gen′eral practi′tioner, a medical practitioner whose practice is not limited to any specific branch of medicine or class of diseases. *Abbr.:* G.P. [1880–85]

gen′eral preces′sion, *Astron.* the precession that results from both lunisolar precession and planetary precession; precession of the equinoxes.

gen•er•al-pur•pose (jen′ər əl pûr′pəs), *adj.* useful in many ways; not limited in use or function: *a good general-purpose dictionary.* [1890–95]

gen′eral quar′ters, *Mil.* a condition of readiness for combat on a warship, during which crew members remain at their battle stations and have guns and ammunition ready for immediate loading.

gen′eral relativ′ity, *Physics.* See under **relativity** (def. 2).

gen′eral rule′, *Law.* See under **rule** (def. 10).

gen′eral seman′tics, a philosophical approach to language, developed by Alfred Korzybski, exploring the relationship between the form of language and its use and attempting to improve the capacity to express ideas. [1930–35]

Gen′eral Serv′ices Administra′tion, *U.S. Govt.* an independent agency, created in 1949, that manages federal property, records, construction, etc. *Abbr.:* GSA

gen′eral ses′sions, a court of general jurisdiction in criminal cases in some U.S. states. [1685–95]

gen•er•al•ship (jen′ər əl ship′), *n.* **1.** skill as commander of a large military force or unit. **2.** the rank or functions of a general. **3.** management or leadership. [1585–95; GENERAL + -SHIP]

gen′eral solu′tion, *Math.* a solution to a differential equation that contains arbitrary, unevaluated constants. Cf. **particular solution.**

gen′eral staff′, *Mil.* a group of officers who are without command and whose duty is to assist high commanders in planning and carrying out orders.

gen′eral store′, a store, usually in a rural area, that sells a wide variety of merchandise, as clothing, food, or hardware, but is not divided into departments. [1825–35, *Amer.*]

gen′eral strike′, a mass strike in all or many trades and industries in a section or in all parts of a country. [1800–10, *Amer.*]

gen′eral the′ory of relativ′ity, *Physics.* See under **relativity** (def. 2). [1930–35]

gen•er•ate (jen′ə rāt′), *v.,* **-at•ed, -at•ing.** **—*v.t.*** **1.** to bring into existence; cause to be; produce. **2.** to create by a vital or natural process. **3.** to create and distribute vitally and profusely: *He generates ideas that we all should consider. A good diplomat generates good will.* **4.** to reproduce; procreate. **5.** to produce by a chemical process. **6.** *Math.* **a.** to trace (a figure) by the motion of a point, straight line, or curve. **b.** to act as base for all the elements of a given set: *The number 2 generates the set 2, 4, 8, 16.* **7.** *Ling.* to produce or specify (a grammatical sentence or other construction or set of constructions) by the application of a rule or set of rules in a generative grammar. **—*v.i.*** **8.** to reproduce; propagate. [1350–1400; ME < L *generātus* produced, ptp. of *generāre* to beget; see GENUS]
—Syn. 1. create, evolve, originate, engender, institute.

gen•er•a•tion (jen′ə rā′shən), *n.* **1.** the entire body of individuals born and living at about the same time: *the postwar generation.* **2.** the term of years, roughly 30 among human beings, accepted as the average period between the birth of parents and the birth of their offspring. **3.** a group of individuals, most of whom are the same approximate age, having similar ideas, problems, attitudes, etc. Cf. **Beat Generation, Lost Generation.** **4.** a group of individuals belonging to a specific category at the same time: *Chaplin belonged to the generation of silent-screen stars.* **5.** a single step in natural descent, as of human beings, animals, or plants. **6.** a form, type, class, etc., of objects existing at the same time and having many similarities or developed from a common model or ancestor: *a new generation of computers.* **7.** the offspring of a certain parent or couple, considered as a step in natural descent. **8.** the act or process of generating; procreation. **9.** the state of being generated. **10.** production by natural or artificial processes; evolution, as of heat or sound. **11.** *Biol.* **a.** one complete life cycle. **b.** one of the alternate phases that complete a life cycle having more than one phase: *the gametophyte generation.* **12.** *Math.* the production of a geometrical figure by the motion of another figure. **13.** *Physics.* one of the successive sets of nuclei produced in a chain reaction. **14.** (in duplicating processes, as photocopying, film, etc.) the distance in duplicating steps that a copy is from the original work. [1250–1300; ME *generacioun* < MF < L *generātiōn-* (s. of *generātiō*). See GENERATE, -ION] **—gen′er•a′tion•al,** *adj.* **—gen′er•a′tion•al•ly,** *adv.*

genera′tion gap′, a lack of communication between one generation and another, esp. between young people and their parents, brought about by differences of tastes, values, outlook, etc. [1965–70]

Generation X, the generation born in the United States after 1960. [after the novel of the same name (1991) by Doug Coupland (born 1961)]

gen•er•a•tive (jen′ər ə tiv, -ə rā′tiv), *adj.* **1.** capable of producing or creating. **2.** pertaining to the production of offspring. **3.** *Ling.* **a.** of or pertaining to generative grammar. **b.** using rules to generate surface forms from underlying, abstract forms. [1375–1425; late ME < MF *generatif,* LL *generātīvus.* See GENERATE, -IVE] **—gen′er•a•tive•ly,** *adv.* **—gen′er•a•tive•ness,** *n.*

gen′erative gram′mar, *Ling.* **1.** a linguistic theory that attempts to describe the tacit knowledge that a native speaker has of a language by establishing a set of explicit, formalized rules that specify or generate all the possible grammatical sentences of a language, while excluding all unacceptable sentences. Cf. **transformational grammar. 2.** a set of such rules. [1955–60]

gen′erative phonol′ogy, *Ling.* a theory of phonology that uses a set of rules to derive phonetic representations from abstract underlying forms.

gen′erative seman′tics, *Ling.* a theory of generative grammar holding that the deep structure of a sentence is equivalent to its semantic representation, from which the surface structure can then be derived using only one set of rules that relate underlying meaning and surface form rather than separate sets of semantic and syntactic rules.

gen′er•a•tive-trans•for•ma′tion•al gram′mar (jen′ər ə tiv trans′fər mā′shə nl, -ə rā′tiv-), *Ling.* See **transformational-generative grammar.**

gen•er•a•tiv•ist (jen′ə rā′tə vist, -ər ə tə-), *n.* a person who follows or promotes the theories of generative grammar. [1965–70; GENERATIVE + -IST]

gen•er•a•tor (jen′ə rā′tər), *n.* **1.** a machine that converts one form of energy into another, esp. mechanical energy into electrical energy, as a dynamo, or electrical energy into sound, as an acoustic generator. **2.** a person or thing that generates. **3.** *Chem.* an apparatus for producing a gas or vapor. **4.** *Math.* **a.** an element or one of a set of elements from which a specified mathematical object can be formed by applying certain operations. **b.** an element, as a line, that generates a figure. **5.** *Computers.* a program that produces a particular type of output on demand, as random numbers, an application program, or a report. [1640–50; < L *generātor* producer, equiv. to *generā(re)* (see GENERATE) + *-tor* -TOR]

gen•er•a•trix (jen′ə rā′triks), *n., pl.* **gen•er•a•tri•ces** (jen′ə rā′trə sēz′, jen′ər ə trī′sēz). *Math.* generator (def. 4b). [1830–40; < L *generātrix* producer. See GENERATE, -TRIX]

ge•ner•ic (jə ner′ik), *adj.* Also, **ge•ner′i•cal. 1.** of, applicable to, or referring to all the members of a genus, class, group, or kind; general. **2.** of, pertaining to, or noting a genus, esp. in biology. **3.** (of a word) applicable or referring to both men and women: *a generic pronoun.* **4.** not protected by trademark registration: *"Cola" and "shuttle" are generic terms.* —*n.* **5.** a generic term. **6.** any product, as a type of food, drug, or cosmetic commonly marketed under a brand name, that is sold in a package without a brand. **7.** a wine made from two or more varieties of grapes, with no one grape constituting more than half the product (distinguished from *varietal*). [1670–80; < L *gener-* (see GENDER[1]) + -IC] **—ge•ner′i•cal•ly,** *adv.* **—ge•ner′i•cal•ness,** *n.*
—Syn. 4. general, nonproprietary, unrestricted.

gen•er•os•i•ty (jen′ə ros′i tē), *n., pl.* **-ties. 1.** readiness or liberality in giving. **2.** freedom from meanness or smallness of mind or character. **3.** a generous act: *We thanked him for his many generosities.* **4.** largeness or fullness; amplitude. [1375–1425; late ME *generosite* < L *generōsitās,* equiv. to *generōs(us)* GENEROUS + *-itās* -ITY]
—Syn. 1. munificence, bountifulness. **2.** nobleness, magnanimity. **—Ant. 1.** stinginess. **2.** pettiness.

gen•er•ous (jen′ər əs), *adj.* **1.** liberal in giving or sharing; unselfish: *a generous patron of the arts.* **2.** free from meanness or smallness of mind or character; magnanimous. **3.** large; abundant; ample: *a generous portion.* **4.** rich or strong in flavor: *a generous wine.* **5.** fertile; prolific: *generous soil.* [1580–90; < MF *généreux* < L *generōsus* of noble birth, equiv. to *gener-* (see GENDER[2]) + *-ōsus* -OUS] **—gen′er•ous•ly,** *adv.* **—gen′er•ous•ness,** *n.*
—Syn. 1. open-handed, free, unstinting. GENEROUS, CHARITABLE, LIBERAL, BOUNTIFUL, MUNIFICENT all describe persons who give to others something of value, or the acts of such persons. GENEROUS stresses the warm and sympathetic nature of the giver: *a generous gift; generous in praise of the work of others.* CHARITABLE places stress on both the goodness and kindness of the giver and the indigence or need of the receiver: *charitable assistance to the needy; a charitable person, always willing to help those less fortunate than herself.* LIBERAL, in this connection, emphasizes the size of the gift, the largesse and openhandedness of the giver: *a liberal contribution to the endowment fund.* BOUNTIFUL implies effusive, unstinted giving and a sense of abundance or plenty: *bountiful and unrestricted support for the museum; a bountiful return for his efforts.* MUNIFICENT refers to gifts or awards so large and striking as to evoke amazement or admiration: *a life income, a truly munificent reward for his loyalty; a munificent contribution, larger by far than any other.* **2.** high-minded, noble, big. **3.** plentiful, copious. **5.** fruitful. **—Ant. 1.** selfish. **2.** mean. **3.** meager. **5.** barren.

Gen•e•see (jen′ə sē′), *n.* a river flowing N from N Pennsylvania through W New York into Lake Ontario. 144 mi. (230 km) long.

ge•nes•ic (jə nes′ik, -nē′sik), *adj.* pertaining to genesis or reproduction; genetic. [GENES(IS) + -IC]

gen•e•sis (jen′ə sis), *n., pl.* **-ses** (-sēz′). an origin, creation, or beginning. [1595–1605; < L: generation, birth < Gk *génesis* origin, source]

Gen•e•sis (jen′ə sis), *n.* the first book of the Bible, dealing with the Creation and the Patriarchs. *Abbr.:* Gen. **—Ge•ne•si•ac** (jə nē′sē ak′), **Gen•e•si•a•cal** (jen′ə sī′ə kəl), **Gen′e•sit′ic,** *adj.*

-genesis, a combining form of **genesis:** *parthenogenesis.*

gene′ splic′ing, *Genetics.* See **recombinant DNA technology.** [1975–80]

gen•et[1] (jen′it, jə net′), *n.* **1.** any small, Old World carnivore of the genus *Genetta,* esp. *G. genetta,* having spotted sides and a ringed tail. **2.** the fur of such an animal. Also, **ge•nette′.** [1375–1425; late ME < OF *genette* < Ar *jarnait*]

genet[1] (def. 1), *Genetta genetta,* head and body 18 in. (46 cm); tail 18 in. (46 cm)

gen•et[2] (jen′it), *n.* jennet.

Ge•net (zhə nā′; *Fr.* zhə ne′), *n.* **Jean** (zhäɴ), 1910–86, French playwright and novelist.

Ge•nêt (zhə nā′; *Fr.* zhə ne′), *n.* **Ed•mond Charles E•douard** (ed môɴ′ sharl ā dwar′), (*"Citizen Genêt"*), 1763–1834, French minister to the U.S. in 1793.

gene′ ther′apy, *Med.* the application of genetic engineering to the transplantation of genes into human cells in order to cure a disease caused by a genetic defect, as a missing enzyme. Cf. **gene transfer.** [1970–75]

ge•neth•li•ac (jə neth′lē ak′), *adj. Astrol.* of or pertaining to birthdays or to the position of the stars at one's birth. [1575–85; < L *genethliacus* < Gk *genethliakós,* equiv. to *genéthli(os)* pertaining to one's birth (deriv. of *genéthlē* birth) + *-akos* -AC] **—gen•eth•li•a•cal•ly** (jen′ith lī′ik lē), *adv.*

ge•neth•li•al•o•gy (jə neth′lē ol′ə jē, -al′-), *n. Astrol.* the science of calculating positions of the heavenly bodies on nativities. [1650–60; < Gk *genethlialogía* casting of destinies, equiv. to *genethliá-* (comb. form of *genéthlē* birth) + *-logia* -LOGY] **—ge•neth•li•a•log•ic** (ji neth′lē ə loj′ik), **ge•neth′li•a•log′i•cal,** *adj.*

ge•net•ic (jə net′ik), *adj.* **1.** *Biol.* pertaining or according to genetics. **2.** of, pertaining to, or produced by genes; genic. **3.** of, pertaining to, or influenced by geneses or origins. Also, **ge•net′i•cal.** [1825–35; GENE(SIS) + -TIC] **—ge•net′i•cal•ly,** *adv.*

-genetic, a suffix of adjectives corresponding to nouns ending in **-genesis:** *parthenogenetic.*

genet′ic code′, the biochemical instructions that translate the genetic information present as a linear sequence of nucleotide triplets in messenger RNA into the correct linear sequence of amino acids for the synthesis of a particular peptide chain or protein. Cf. **codon, translation** (def. 9). [1960–65]

genet′ic coun′seling, the counseling of individuals with established or potential genetic problems, concerned with risks to future offspring. [1965–70]

genet′ic drift′, random changes in the frequency of alleles in a gene pool, usually of small populations. Cf. **gene flow.** [1955–60]

genet′ic engineer′ing, *Genetics.* **1.** the development and application of scientific methods, procedures, and technologies that permit direct manipulation of genetic material in order to alter the hereditary traits of a cell, organism, or population. **2.** a technique that produces unlimited amounts of otherwise unavailable or scarce biological product by introducing DNA isolated from animals or plants into bacteria and then harvesting the product from a bacterial colony, as human insulin produced in bacteria by the human insulin gene. Also called **biogenetics.** [1965–70] **—genet′ic engineer′.**

genet′ic fal′lacy, *Logic.* the fallacy of confusing questions of validity and logical order with questions of origin and temporal order. [1930–35]

genet′ic fin′gerprinting. See **DNA fingerprinting.** [1985–90] **—genet′ic fin′gerprint.**

ge•net•i•cist (jə net′ə sist), *n.* a specialist or expert in genetics. [1910–15; GENETIC + -IST]

genet′ic load′, the extent to which a population deviates from the theoretically fittest genetic constitution. [1965–70]

genet′ic map′, an arrangement of genes on a chromosome. Also called **linkage map.** [1955–60]

genet′ic mark′er, 1. any distinct inheritable indicator of identity and ancestry. **2.** See **HLA antigen. 3.** a chromosomal landmark or allele that allows for the tracing of a specific region of DNA, as in the study of recombination. Also called **marker, marker gene.** [1945–50]

genet′ic rela′tionship, *Historical Ling.* the relationship that exists between languages that have developed from a single earlier language. Also called **genealogical relationship.** [1875–80]

ge•net•ics (jə net′iks), *n.* (*used with a singular v.*) **1.** *Biol.* the science of heredity, dealing with resemblances and differences of related organisms resulting from the interaction of their genes and the environment. **2.** the genetic properties and phenomena of an organism. [see GENETIC, -ICS; term first proposed in this sense by British biologist William Bateson (1861–1926) in 1905]

genet′ic screen′ing, 1. assessment of an individual's genetic makeup to detect inheritable defects that may be transmitted to offspring. **2.** evaluation of a person's genetic makeup in an attempt to predict genetic predisposition to certain illnesses associated with a workplace environment. [1970–75]

gene′ trans′fer, *Biotech.* the insertion of copies of a gene into living cells in order to induce synthesis of the gene's product: the desired gene may be microinjected directly into the cell or it may be inserted into the core of a virus by gene splicing and the virus allowed to infect the cell for replication of the gene in the cell's DNA.

ge•ne•va (jə nē′və), *n.* Hollands. [1700–10; < D *genever* < OF *genevre* < L *jūniperus* JUNIPER]

Ge•ne•va (jə nē′və), *n.* **1.** a city in and the capital of the canton of Geneva, in SW Switzerland: seat of the League of Nations 1920–46. 155,800. **2.** a canton in SW Switzerland. 335,800; 109 sq. mi. (282 sq. km). **3. Lake of.** Also called **Lake Leman.** a lake between SW Switzerland and France. 45 mi. (72 km) long; 225 sq. mi. (583 sq. km). **4.** a city in central New York. 15,133. **5.** a female given name. French, **Genève** (for defs. 1–3).

Gene′va bands′, two bands or pendent stripes made usually of white lawn and worn at the throat as part of clerical garb, originally by the Swiss Calvinist clergy. Also called **bands.** [1880–85]

Gene′va Conven′tion, one of a series of international agreements, first made in Geneva, Switzerland, in 1864, establishing rules for the humane treatment of prisoners of war and of the sick, the wounded, and the dead in battle.

Gene′va cross′, a red Greek cross on a white background, used to distinguish ambulances, hospitals, and persons belonging to the Red Cross Society. [1885–90]

Gene′va gown′, a loose, large-sleeved, black preaching gown worn by members of the Protestant clergy: so named from its use by the Calvinist clergy of Geneva, Switzerland. [1810–20]

Ge•ne•van (jə nē′vən), *adj.* **1.** of or pertaining to Geneva, Switzerland. **2.** Calvinistic. —*n.* **3.** a native or inhabitant of Geneva, Switzerland. **4.** a Calvinist. [1555–65; GENEV(A) + -AN]

Gene′va no′menclature, *Chem.* an internationally accepted system for naming organic carbon compounds.

Ge•nève (zhə nev′), *n.* French name of **Geneva.**

Gen•e•vese (jen′ə vēz′, -vēs′), *adj., n., pl.* **-vese.** Genevan.

Gen•e•vieve (jen′ə vēv′), *n.* **1. Saint,** A.D. 422–512, French nun: patron saint of Paris. **2.** a female given name. Also, **Gene•viève** (*Fr.* zhənᵊ vyev′).

Gen•ghis Khan (jeng′gis kän′ *or, often,* geng′-), 1162–1227, Mongol conqueror of most of Asia and of E Europe to the Dnieper River. Also, **Jenghis Khan, Jenghiz Khan.**

gen•ial[1] (jēn′yəl, jē′nē əl), *adj.* **1.** warmly and pleasantly cheerful; cordial: *a genial disposition; a genial host.* **2.** favorable for life, growth, or comfort; pleasantly warm; comfortably mild: *the genial climate of Hawaii.* **3.** characterized by genius. [1560–70; < L *geniālis* festive, jovial, pleasant, equiv. to *geni(us)* tutelary deity, the spirit of social enjoyment + *-ālis* -AL[1]] **—gen′ial•ly,** *adv.* **—ge•ni•al•i•ty** (jē′nē al′i tē), **gen′ial•ness,** *n.*
—Syn. 1. friendly, hearty, pleasant, agreeable.

ge•ni•al[2] (jə nī′əl), *adj. Anat., Zool.* of or pertaining to the chin. [1825–35; < Gk *genei(on)* CHIN, deriv. of *gén(ys)* jaw (cf. L *gena*) + -AL[1]]

gen•ic (jen′ik), *adj. Biol.* of, pertaining to, resembling, or arising from a gene or genes. [1920–25; GENE + -IC]

-genic, a combining form often corresponding to nouns ending in **-gen** or **-geny,** with the following senses: "producing or causing" (*hallucinogenic*); "produced or caused by" (*cosmogenic*); "pertaining to a gene or genes" (*polygenic*); "pertaining to suitability for reproduction by a medium" (*telegenic*). Cf. **-genous.** [see -GEN, -IC]

ge•nic•u•late (jə nik′yə lit, -lāt′), *adj. Biol.* **1.** having kneelike joints or bends. **2.** bent at a joint like a knee. [1660–70; < L *geniculātus* knotted, equiv. to *genicul(um)* small knee; knot (*gen(u)* KNEE + *-i-* -I- + *-culum* -CULE[1]) + *-ātus* -ATE[1]] **—ge•nic′u•late•ly,** *adv.*

ge•nic•u•la•tion (jə nik′yə lā′shən), *n.* **1.** the state of being geniculate. **2.** a geniculate formation. [1605–15; < LL *geniculātiōn-* (s. of *geniculātiō*) a kneeling < L *geniculāt(us)* (see GENICULATE) + *-iōn-* -ION]

ge•nie (jē′nē), *n.* **1.** *Islamic Myth.* jinn. **2.** a spirit, often appearing in human form, that when summoned by a person carries out the wishes of the summoner. **3.** any spirit. [1645–55; < F *génie* < L *genius;* see GENIUS]

CONCISE ETYMOLOGY KEY: <, descended or borrowed from; >, whence; b., blend of, blended; c., cognate with; cf., compare; deriv., derivative; equiv., equivalent; imit., imitative; obl., oblique; r., replacing; s., stem; sp., spelling, spelled; resp., respelling, respelled; trans., translation; ?, origin unknown; *, unattested; ‡, probably earlier than. See the full key inside the front cover.

ge•ni•i (jē′nē ī′), *n.* a pl. of **genius.**

gen•in (jen′in), *n. Biochem.* aglycon. [1910–15; extracted from the names of aglycons, such as *sapogenin, saligenin,* etc.]

ge•nip (gə nip′), *n.* **1.** Also, **ginep.** a genipap. **2.** a tropical American tree, *Melicoccus bijugatus,* of the soapberry family, bearing a yellow, sweet, edible fruit. **3.** the fruit itself. Also called **Spanish lime** (for defs. 2, 3). [1750–60; shortened form of GENIPAP]

gen•i•pap (jen′ə pap′), *n.* **1.** a tropical American tree, *Genipa americana,* of the madder family, bearing an edible fruit used for preserves or in making beverages. **2.** the fruit itself. Also called **marmalade box.** [1605–15; < Pg *genipapo* < Tupi *ianipaba*]

ge•nis•ta (jə nis′tə), *n.* **1.** any plant belonging to the genus *Genista,* of the legume family, having showy flowers and including many species of broom. **2.** a related plant, *Cytisus canariensis,* of the Canary Islands, having loose clusters of fragrant yellow flowers. [1615–25; < NL, L: the broomplant]

genit., genitive.

gen•i•tal (jen′i tl), *adj.* **1.** of, pertaining to, or noting reproduction. **2.** of or pertaining to the sexual organs. **3.** *Psychoanal.* **a.** of or pertaining to the genital phase of psychosexual development. **b.** of or pertaining to the centering of sexual impulses and excitation on the genitalia. [1350–1400; ME <OF < L *genitālis* of birth, equiv. to *genit(us),* ptp. of *gignere* to beget + *-ālis* -AL[1]]

gen′ital her′pes, *Pathol.* a sexually transmitted disease caused by herpes simplex virus type 2, characterized primarily by transient blisters on and around the genitals. Also called **herpes genitalis.**

gen•i•ta•li•a (jen′i tā′lē ə, -tāl′yə), *n.pl. Anat.* the organs of reproduction, esp. the external organs. [1875–80; < L *genitālia,* neut. pl. of *genitālis* GENITAL] —**gen•i•tal•ic** (jen′i tal′ik), **gen′i•ta′li•al,** *adj.*

gen′ital phase′, *Psychoanal.* **1.** the final stage of psychosexual development, in which a person achieves an affectionate, mature relationship with a sexual partner. **2.** the childhood stage between 2½ and 7, marked by increased sexual and genital interest.

gen′ital ridge′, the area in the vertebrate embryo that develops into ovaries in the female and testes in the male.

gen•i•tals (jen′i tlz), *n.pl.* genitalia. [pl. n. use of GENITAL]

gen′ital warts′, *Pathol.* warts occurring in the genital and anal areas and spread mainly by sexual contact, sometimes affecting the cervix in women and associated with an increased risk of cervical cancer.

gen•i•tive (jen′i tiv), *Gram.* —*adj.* **1.** (in certain inflected languages) noting a case of nouns, pronouns, or adjectives, used primarily to express possession, measure, or origin: as *John's* hat, *week's* vacation, *duty's* call. **2.** noting an affix or other element characteristic of this case, or a word containing such an element. **3.** similar to such a case form in function or meaning. —*n.* **4.** the genitive case. **5.** a word in the genitive case. **6.** a construction noting this case or the relationship usually expressed by it. Cf. **possessive.** [1350–1400; ME < ML *genitivus,* equiv. to *genit(us)* (ptp. of *gignere* to beget) + *-īvus* -IVE] —**gen•i•ti•val** (jen′i tī′vəl), *adj.* —**gen′i•ti′val•ly,** *adv.*

genito-, a combining form representing **genital** in compound words: *genitourinary.*

gen•i•tor (jen′i tər), *n.* a parent, esp. a father. [1400–50; late ME < L, equiv. to *geni-* (var. s. of *gignere* to beget) + *-tor* -TOR; c. Gk *genétōr,* Skt *janitar-*]

gen•i•to•u•ri•nar•y (jen′i tō yŏŏr′ə ner′ē), *adj.* of or pertaining to the genital and urinary organs; urogenital. [1825–35; GENITO- + URINARY]

gen•i•ture (jen′i chər, -chŏŏr′), *n.* **1.** birth; generation. **2.** *Astrol.* nativity. [1540–50; (MF) < L *genitūra.* See GENITAL, -URE]

gen•ius (jēn′yəs), *n., pl.* **gen•ius•es** for 2, 3, 8, **gen•i•i** (jē′nē ī′) for 6, 7, 9. **1.** an exceptional natural capacity of intellect, especially as shown in creative and original work in science, art, music, etc.: *the genius of Mozart.* **2.** a person having such capacity. **3.** a person having an extraordinarily high intelligence rating on a psychological test, as an IQ above 140. **4.** natural ability or capacity; strong inclination: *a special genius for leadership.* **5.** distinctive character or spirit, as of a nation, period, or language. **6.** the guardian spirit of a place, institution, etc. **7.** either of two mutually opposed spirits, one good and the other evil, supposed to attend a person throughout life. **8.** a person who strongly influences for good or ill the character, conduct, or destiny of a person, place, or thing: *Rasputin, the evil genius of Russian politics.* **9.** genie (defs. 1, 3). [1350–1400; ME < L: tutelary deity or genius of a person; cf. GENUS]
—**Syn. 4.** gift, talent, aptitude, faculty.

ge•ni•us lo•ci (gen′i ŏŏs′ lō′kē; *Eng.* jē′nē əs lō′sī, -kī), *Latin.* **1.** guardian of a place. **2.** the distinctive character or atmosphere of a place with reference to the impression that it makes on the mind.

Genl., General.

Gen. Mtg., *Banking.* general mortgage.

Gen•na•ro (jə när′ō; *It.* jen nä′rô), *n.* **San** (san; *It.* sän), Januarius.

gen•o•a (jen′ō ə), *n.* (*sometimes cap.*) *Naut.* a large jib for cruising and racing yachts, overlapping the mainsail. Also called **gen′oa jib′, Gen′oa jib′, reaching jib.** [1930–35; after GENOA]

Gen•o•a (jen′ō ə), *n.* a seaport in NW Italy, S of Milan. 798,892. Italian, **Genova.**

Gen′oa sala′mi, a hard, garlic-flavored salami of pork and veal or, in the U.S., pork and beef.

gen•o•cide (jen′ə sīd′), *n.* the deliberate and systematic extermination of a national, racial, political, or cultural group. [1940–45; < Gk *géno(s)* race + -CIDE] —**gen′o•cid′al,** *adj.*

Gen•o•ese (jen′ō ēz′, -ēs′), *adj., n., pl.* **-ese.** —*adj.* **1.** of, pertaining to, or characteristic of Genoa or its inhabitants. —*n.* **2.** a native or inhabitant of Genoa. Also, **Gen•o•vese** (jen′ə vēz′, -vēs′). [1545–55]

gen•o•gram (jen′ə gram′, jē′nə-), *n.* a graphic representation of the personalities and interplay of generations within a family, used to identify repetitive patterns of behavior; a psychological family tree. [GEN(ERATION) + -O- + -GRAM[1]]

ge•nome (jē′nōm), *n. Genetics.* a full set of chromosomes; all the inheritable traits of an organism. Also, **ge•nom** (jē′nom). [1925–30; < G *Genom,* equiv. to *Gen* GENE + (*Chromos*)*om* CHROMOSOME] —**ge•no•mic** (ji nō′mik, -nom′ik), *adj.*

genomic DNA, a fragment or fragments of DNA produced by restriction enzymes acting on the DNA of a cell or an organism. *Abbr.:* gDNA [1985–90]

gen•o•type (jen′ə tīp′, jē′nə-), *n. Genetics.* **1.** the genetic makeup of an organism or group of organisms with reference to a single trait, set of traits, or an entire complex of traits. **2.** the sum total of genes transmitted from parent to offspring. Cf. **phenotype.** [< G *Genotypus* (1909); see GENE, -O-, -TYPE] —**gen•o•typ•ic** (jen′ə tip′ik, jē′nə-), **gen′o•typ′i•cal,** *adj.* —**gen′o•typ′i•cal•ly,** *adv.*

-genous, a suffix of adjectives corresponding to nouns with stems in **-gen:** *erogenous.* [-GEN + -OUS]

Ge•no•va (je′nô vä′), *n.* Italian name of **Genoa.**

gen•re (zhän′rə; *Fr.* zhäɴ′rᵊ), *n., pl.* **-res** (-rəz; *Fr.* -rᵊ), *adj.* —*n.* **1.** a class or category of artistic endeavor having a particular form, content, technique, or the like: *the genre of epic poetry; the genre of symphonic music.* **2.** *Fine Arts.* **a.** paintings in which scenes of everyday life form the subject matter. **b.** a realistic style of painting using such subject matter. **3.** genus; kind; sort; style. —*adj.* **4.** *Fine Arts.* of or pertaining to genre. **5.** of or pertaining to a distinctive literary type. [1760–70; < F: kind, sort; see GENDER[1]]

gen•ro (gen rō′, gen′rō), *n., pl.* **-ro.** any of the unofficial elder statesmen of Japan who influenced the government c1875–1940. [1875–80; < Japn *genrō* senior statesman (from a reference in the Book of Odes) < MChin, equiv. to Chin *yuán* original, first + *lǎo* old]

Gen•ro•ku (gen rō′kōō; *Japn.* gen rô′kŏŏ), *n.* a period of Japanese cultural history, c1675–1725, characterized by depiction of everyday secular activities of urban dwellers in fiction and woodblock prints. [< Japn, the imperial era name (official epithet) for the period 1688–1704 (< MChin, equiv. to Chin *yuán* original, first + *lù* good fortune)]

gens (jenz), *n., pl.* **gen•tes** (jen′tēz). **1.** a group of families in ancient Rome claiming descent from a common ancestor and united by a common name and common ancestral religious rites. **2.** *Anthropol.* a group tracing common descent in the male line; clan. [1840–50; < L *gēns* race, people. See GENUS, GENDER[1], GENDER[2]]

gens du monde (zhäɴ dʏ môɴd′), *French.* people of the world; leaders in society; fashionable people.

gen•seng (jen′seng′), *n.* ginseng.

Gen•ser•ic (jen′sər ik, gen′-), *n.* A.D. c390–477, king of the Vandals, conqueror in northern Africa and Italy. Also, **Gaiseric.**

gent[1] (jent), *n. Informal.* gentleman (defs. 1, 2). [1555–65; by shortening]

gent[2] (jent), *adj. Obs.* elegant; graceful. [1175–1225; ME < OF < L *genitus* begotten, born]

Gent (KHent), *n.* Flemish name of **Ghent.**

Gent., gentleman or gentlemen. Also, **gent.**

gen•ta•mi•cin (jen′tə mī′sin), *n. Pharm.* a highly toxic broad-spectrum antibiotic mixture of related aminoglycoside substances derived from the actinomycete bacterium *Micromonospora purpurea,* used in its sulfate form in the treatment of severe Gram-negative infections. [1963; resp. of *gentamycin,* prob. equiv. to GENT(IAN VIOLET) + *-a-* (as in KANAMYCIN) + -MYCIN; so called from the color of the source bacterium]

gen•teel (jen tēl′), *adj.* **1.** belonging or suited to polite society. **2.** well-bred or refined; polite; elegant; stylish. **3.** affectedly or pretentiously polite, delicate, etc. [1590–1600; < F *gentil;* see GENTLE] —**gen•teel′ly,** *adv.* —**gen•teel′ness,** *n.*

gen•teel•ism (jen tē′liz əm), *n.* a word or phrase used in place of another, supposedly less genteel term: *"Limb" is a genteelism for "leg."* [1925–30; GENTEEL + -ISM]

gen•tian (jen′shən), *n.* **1.** any of several plants of the genera *Gentiana, Gentianella,* and *Gentianopsis,* having usually blue, or sometimes yellow, white, or red, flowers, as the fringed gentian of North America, or *Gentiana lutea,* of Europe. Cf. **gentian family. 2.** any of various plants resembling the gentian. **3.** the root of *G. lutea,* or a preparation of it, used as a tonic. [1350–1400; ME *gencian* < L *gentiāna;* said to be named after *Gentius,* an Illyrian king]

gen•ti•a•na•ceous (jen′shē ə nā′shəs), *adj.* belonging to the plant family Gentianaceae. Cf. **gentian family.** [1850–55; < NL *Gentianace(ae)* name of the family (L *gentiān(a)* GENTIAN + *-aceae* -ACEAE) + -OUS]

gen′tian fam′ily, the plant family Gentianaceae, typified by herbaceous plants having simple opposite leaves, usually blue flowers with five united petals, and fruit in the form of a capsule, and including the closed gentian, fringed gentian, centaury, and marsh pink.

gen′tian vi′olet, a dye derived from rosaniline, used in chemistry as an indicator and in medicine as a fungicide, bactericide, anthelmintic, and in the treatment of burns. Also called **crystal violet, methylrosaniline chloride.** [1895–1900]

gen•tile (jen′tīl), *adj.* (*sometimes cap.*) **1.** of or pertaining to any people not Jewish. **2.** Christian, as distinguished from Jewish. **3.** *Mormon Ch.* not Mormon. **4.** heathen or pagan. **5.** (of a linguistic expression) expressing nationality or local origins. **6.** of or pertaining to a tribe, clan, people, nation, etc. —*n.* **7.** a person who is not Jewish, esp. a Christian. **8.** (among Mormons) a person who is not a Mormon. **9.** a heathen or pagan. [1350–1400; ME < L *gentīlis,* equiv. to *gent-,* s. of *gēns* GENS + *-īlis* -ILE]

gen•ti•lesse (jen′tl es′, jen′tl es′), *n.* the quality of being gentle. [1300–50; ME < MF *gentillesse,* equiv. to *gentil* (see GENTEEL, GENTLE) + *-esse* n. suffix]

gen•til•ism (jen′tl iz′əm), *n.* the quality of being a gentile, esp. heathenism; paganism. [1570–80; GENTILE + -ISM]

gen•til•i•ty (jen til′i tē), *n.* **1.** good breeding or refinement. **2.** affected or pretentious politeness or elegance. **3.** the status of belonging to polite society. **4.** members of polite society collectively. [1300–50; ME < OF *gentilite* < L *gentīlitāt-* (s. of *gentīlitās*), equiv. to *gentīl(is)* (see GENTLE) + *-itāt-* -ITY]
—**Syn. 1.** polish, grace, decorum, propriety.

gen•ti•sate (jen′tə sāt′), *n. Chem.* a salt or ester of gentisic acid. [GENTIS(IC ACID) + -ATE[2]]

gen•tis′ic ac′id (jen tis′ik, -tiz′-), *Pharm.* a crystalline, water-soluble compound, $C_7H_6O_4$, used chiefly in the form of its sodium salt as an analgesic and diaphoretic. [1875–80; GENTI(AN) + -s- connective + -IC]

gen•tle (jen′tl), *adj.,* **-tler, -tlest,** *v.,* **-tled, -tling.** —*adj.* **1.** kindly; amiable: *a gentle manner.* **2.** not severe, rough, or violent; mild: *a gentle wind; a gentle tap on the shoulder.* **3.** moderate: *gentle heat.* **4.** gradual: *a gentle slope.* **5.** of good birth or family; wellborn. **6.** characteristic of good birth; honorable; respectable: *a gentle upbringing.* **7.** easily handled or managed; tractable: *a gentle animal.* **8.** soft or low: *a gentle sound.* **9.** polite; refined: *Consider, gentle reader, my terrible predicament at this juncture.* **10.** entitled to a coat of arms; armigerous. **11.** *Archaic.* noble; chivalrous: *a gentle knight.* —*v.t.* **12.** to tame; render tractable. **13.** to mollify; calm; pacify. **14.** to make gentle. **15.** to stroke; soothe by petting. **16.** to ennoble; dignify. [1175–1225; ME *gentle, gentil(e)* < OF *gentil* highborn, noble < L *gentīlis* belonging to the same family, equiv. to *gent-* (s. of *gēns*) GENS + *-īlis* -LE] —**gen′tle•ness,** *n.* —**gen′tly,** *adv.*
—**Syn. 1.** clement, peaceful, pacific, soothing; tender, humane, lenient, merciful. GENTLE, MEEK, MILD refer to an absence of bad temper or belligerence. GENTLE has reference esp. to disposition and behavior, and often suggests a deliberate or voluntary kindness or forbearance in dealing with others: *a gentle pat; gentle with children.* MEEK implies a submissive spirit, and may even indicate undue submission in the face of insult or injustice: *meek and even servile or weak.* MILD suggests absence of harshness or severity, rather because of natural character or temperament than conscious choice: *a mild rebuke; a mild manner.* **3.** temperate. **5.** noble. **7.** manageable, docile, tame, quiet. **9.** courteous; polished. —**Ant. 1.** harsh, cruel. **2.** violent. **7.** wild, unruly.

gen′tle breeze′, *Meteorol.* a wind of 8–12 mph (4–5 m/sec). [1900–05]

gen′tle craft′, the sport of angling or fishing (usually prec. by *the*). Also called **gen′tle art′.**

gen•tle•folk (jen′tl fōk′), *n.* (*used with a plural v.*) persons of good family and breeding. Also, **gen′tle•folks′.** [1585–95; GENTLE + FOLK]

gen•tle•man (jen′tl mən), *n., pl.* **-men. 1.** a man of good family, breeding, or social position. **2.** (used as a polite term) a man: *Do you know that gentleman over there?* **3. gentlemen,** (used as a form of address): *Gentlemen, please come this way.* **4.** a civilized, educated, sensitive, or well-mannered man: *He behaved like a true gentleman.* **5.** a male personal servant, esp. of a man of social position; valet. **6.** a male attendant upon a king, queen, or other royal person, who is himself of high birth or rank. **7.** a man of good social standing, as a noble or an armigerous commoner. **8.** a man with an independent income who does not work for a living. **9.** a male member of the U.S. Senate or House of Representatives: *The chair recognizes the gentleman from Massachusetts.* **10.** *Hist.* a man who is above the rank of yeoman. [1225–75; ME; see GENTLE, MAN[1]] —**gen′tle•man•like′,** *adj.*
—**Syn. 4.** See **man.**
—**Usage.** See **lady.**

gen•tle•man-at-arms (jen′tl mən ət ärmz′), *n., pl.* **gen•tle•men-at-arms.** (in England) one of a guard of 40 gentlemen who attend the sovereign on state occasions. [1855–60]

gen•tle•man-com•mon•er (jen′tl mən kom′ə nər), *n., pl.* **gen•tle•men-com•mon•ers.** (formerly) a member of a class of commoners enjoying special privileges at Oxford University. [1680–90]

gen•tle•man-farm•er (jen′tl mən fär′mər), *n., pl.* **gen•tle•men-farm•ers. 1.** a man whose wealth or income from other sources permits him to farm for pleasure rather than for basic income. **2.** a man whose income from his farm has freed him from the necessity of physical labor. [1740–50]

gen′tleman friend′, *Older Use.* a man with whom a woman is romantically involved; suitor. [1820–30, *Amer.*]

gen•tle•man•ly (jen′tl mən lē), *adj.* like, befitting, or characteristic of a gentleman. [1375–1425; late ME; see GENTLEMAN, -LY] —**gen′tle•man•li•ness,** *n.*

gen′tleman of for′tune, an adventurer. [1880–85]

gen′tleman of the road′, 1. a highwayman. **2.** a tramp or hobo. [1720–30]

gen•tle•man-pen•sion•er (jen′tl mən pen′shə nər), *n., pl.* **gen•tle•men-pen•sion•ers.** (formerly) a gentleman-at-arms. [1620–30]

gen′tleman's gen′tleman, a valet. [1715–25]

Gen′tleman Ush′er of the Black′ Rod′. See **Black Rod** (def. 1).

gen′tlemen's agree′ment, 1. an agreement that, although unenforceable at law, is binding as a matter of personal honor. **2.** an unwritten agreement by a socially prominent clique, private club, etc., to discriminate against or refuse to accept members of certain religious, racial, national, or other groups. Also, **gen′tleman's agree′ment.** [1885–90, *Amer.*]

gen•tle•per•son (jen′tl pûr′sən), *n.* a person of good family and position; gentleman or lady. [1970–75; GENTLE(MAN) + -PERSON]
—Usage. See **-person.**

gen′tle sex′, women in general. Also, **gen′tler sex′.** [1575–85]

gen•tle•wom•an (jen′tl wo͝om′ən), *n., pl.* **-wom•en. 1.** a woman of good family, breeding, or social position **2.** a civilized, educated, sensitive, or well-mannered woman; lady. **3.** a woman who attends upon a lady of rank. **4.** a female member of the U.S. Senate or House of Representatives: *The chair recognizes the gentlewoman from Maine.* [1200–50; ME; see GENTLE, WOMAN] **—gen′tle•wom′an•ly,** *adj.*

Gen•too (jen′to͞o), *n., pl.* **-toos,** *adj. Archaic.* **—***n.* **1.** a Hindu. **2.** any of the languages of those who practice the Hindu religion, esp. Telugu. **—***adj.* **3.** of or relating to the Gentoos. [1630–40; < Pg *gentio* GENTILE]

gen′too pen′guin (jen′to͞o), a penguin, *Pygoscelis papua,* of small Antarctic islands. [1855–60; perh. GENTOO, though sense unclear]

gen•trice (jen′tris), *n. Archaic.* gentility; high birth. [1175–1225; ME *gentrise* < OF *genterise,* alter. of *gentelise,* equiv. to *gentil* GENTLE + *-ise* -ICE]

gen•tri•fi•ca•tion (jen′trə fi kā′shən), *n.* **1.** the buying and renovation of houses and stores in deteriorated urban neighborhoods by upper- or middle-income families or individuals, thus improving property values but often displacing low-income families and small businesses. **2.** an instance of gentrifying; the condition of being gentrified. [1975–80; GENTRI(FY) + -FICATION]

gen•tri•fied (jen′trə fīd′), *adj.* **1.** very or excessively refined or elegant. **2.** subjected to gentrification. [1975–80; GENTRIFY + -ED[2]]

gen•tri•fy (jen′trə fī′), *v.,* **-fied, -fy•ing.** **—***v.t.* **1.** to improve (a neighborhood) by gentrification. **—***v.i.* **2.** to undergo gentrification: *Some neighborhoods gentrify more easily than others.* [1970–75; GENTRY + -FY] **—gen′tri•fi′er,** *n.*

gen•try (jen′trē), *n.* **1.** wellborn and well-bred people. **2.** (in England) the class below the nobility. **3.** an upper or ruling class; aristocracy. **4.** those who are not members of the nobility but are entitled to a coat of arms, esp. those owning large tracts of land. **5.** (*used with a plural v.*) people, esp. considered as a specific group, class, or kind: *The polo crowd doesn't go there, but these hockey gentry do.* **6.** the state or condition of being a gentleman. [1275–1325; ME < OF *genterie.* See GENTILE, GENTLE]

gents' (jents), **the,** *Informal.* a men's room. [1920–25; see GENT[1], -S[3]]

ge•nu (jē′no͞o, -nyo͞o, jen′o͞o, -yo͞o), *n., pl.* **ge•nu•a** (jen′o͞o ə, -yo͞o ə). *Anat., Zool.* **1.** the knee. **2.** a knee-like part or bend. [1850–55; < L; c. Gk *góny* KNEE] **—ge′nu•al,** *adj.*

gen•u•flect (jen′yo͝o flekt′), *v.i.* **1.** to bend the knee or touch one knee to the floor in reverence or worship. **2.** to express a servile attitude. [1620–30; < ML *genūflectere* to bend the knee, equiv. to L *genū-,* s. of *genu* KNEE + *flectere* to bend] **—gen′u•flec′tor,** *n.*

gen•u•flec•tion (jen′yo͝o flek′shən), *n.* an act of bending the knee or touching it to the ground in reverence or worship. Also, *esp. Brit.,* **gen′u•flex′ion.** [1520–30; < ML *genūflexiōn-* (s. of *genūflexiō*). See GENUFLECT, -ION]

gen•u•ine (jen′yo͞o in), *adj.* **1.** possessing the claimed or attributed character, quality, or origin; not counterfeit; authentic; real: *genuine sympathy; a genuine antique.* **2.** properly so called: *a genuine case of smallpox.* **3.** free from pretense, affectation, or hypocrisy; sincere: *a genuine person.* **4.** descended from the original stock; pure in breed: *a genuine Celtic people.* [1590–1600; < L *genuīnus* innate, natural, equiv. to *genu-* (as in *ingenuus* native) + *-īnus* -INE[1]] **—gen′u•ine•ly,** *adv.* **—gen′u•ine•ness,** *n.*
—Syn. 1. See **authentic. 3.** true, unaffected, open, honest, forthright.
—Pronunciation. Two pronunciations of GENUINE occur, with a sharp social contrast between them. The usual educated pronunciation is (jen′yo͞o in), with the final syllable unstressed. Among some less educated speakers, especially older ones, GENUINE is commonly pronounced as (jen′yo͞o īn′), with a secondary stress on the final syllable, which has the vowel of *sign.* The latter pronunciation is sometimes used deliberately by educated speakers, as for emphasis or humorous effect.

ge•nus (jē′nəs), *n., pl.* **gen•e•ra** (jen′ər ə), **ge•nus•es. 1.** *Biol.* the usual major subdivision of a family or subfamily in the classification of organisms, usually consisting of more than one species. **2.** *Logic.* a class or group of individuals, or of species of individuals. **3.** a kind; sort; class. [1545–55; < L: race, stock, kind, gender; c. Gk *génos.* See GENS, GENDER[1], KIN]

CONCISE ETYMOLOGY KEY: <, descended or borrowed from; >, whence; b., blend of, blended; c., cognate with; cf., compare; deriv., derivative; equiv., equivalent; imit., imitative; obl., oblique; r., replacing; s., stem; sp., spelling, spelled; resp., respelling, respelled; trans., translation; ?, origin unknown; *, unattested; ‡, probably earlier than. See the full key inside the front cover.

ge′nu val′gum, *Pathol.* knock-knee. [< NL]

-geny, a combining form meaning "origin," used in the formation of compound words: *phylogeny.* [1885–90; < Gk *-geneia.* See -GEN, -Y[3]]

geo-, a combining form meaning "the earth," used in the formation of compound words: *geochemistry.* [< Gk *geō-,* comb. form of *gê* the earth]

Geo., George.

ge•o•bot•a•ny (jē′ō bot′n ē), *n.* phytogeography. [1900–05; GEO- + BOTANY] **—ge•o•bo•tan•i•cal** (jē′ō bə tan′i kəl), **ge′o•bo•tan′ic,** *adj.* **—ge′o•bo•tan′i•cal•ly,** *adv.* **—ge′o•bot′a•nist,** *n.*

ge•o•cen•tric (jē′ō sen′trik), *adj.* **1.** having or representing the earth as a center: *a geocentric theory of the universe.* **2.** using the earth or earthly life as the only basis of evaluation. **3.** viewed or measured as from the center of the earth: *the geocentric position of the moon.* [1680–90; GEO- + -CENTRIC] **—ge′o•cen′tri•cal•ly,** *adv.*

ge′ocen′tric par′allax. See under **parallax** (def. 2).

ge•o•chem•is•try (jē′ō kem′ə strē), *n.* the science dealing with the chemical changes in and the composition of the earth's crust. [1900–05; GEO- + CHEMISTRY] **—ge•o•chem•i•cal** (jē′ō kem′i kəl), *adj.* **—ge′o•chem′i•cal•ly,** *adv.* **—ge′o•chem′ist,** *n.*

ge•o•chro•nol•o•gy (jē′ō krə nol′ə jē), *n.* the chronology of the earth, as based on both absolute and relative methods of age determination. [1890–95; GEO- + CHRONOLOGY] **—ge•o•chron•o•log•ic** (jē′ō kron′l oj′ik), **ge′o•chron′o•log′i•cal,** *adj.* **—ge′o•chro•nol′o•gist,** *n.*

ge•o•chro•nom•e•try (jē′ō krə nom′i trē), *n.* the determination of the absolute age of earth materials, as by radiometric dating. [1920–25; GEO- + CHRONOMETRY] **—ge•o•chron•o•met•ric** (jē′ō kron′ə me′trik), *adj.*

ge•o•code (jē′ə kōd′), *n.* the characterization of a neighborhood, locality, etc., according to such demographic features as ethnic composition or the average income or educational level of its inhabitants, esp. as used in marketing. [GEO(GRAPHIC) + CODE]

ge•o•co•ro•na (jē′ō kə rō′nə), *n.* a belt of ionized hydrogen surrounding the earth at the outer limit of the exosphere. [1955–60; GEO- + CORONA] **—ge′o•co•ro′•nal,** *adj.*

geod., 1. geodesy. **2.** geodetic.

ge•ode (jē′ōd), *n.* **1.** a hollow concretionary or nodular stone often lined with crystals. **2.** the hollow or cavity of this. **3.** any similar formation. [1670–80; < F *géode* < L *geōdēs* < Gk *geṓdēs* earthlike. See GEO-, -ODE[1]] **—ge•od•ic** (jē od′ik), **ge•od•al** (jē ōd′l), *adj.*

ge•o•des•ic (jē′ə des′ik, -dē′sik), *adj.* **1.** Also, **ge′o•des′i•cal.** pertaining to the geometry of curved surfaces, in which geodesic lines take the place of the straight lines of plane geometry. **—***n.* **2.** See **geodesic line.** [1815–25; < F *géodésique.* See GEODESY, -IC]

ge′odes′ic dome′, a light, domelike structure developed by R. Buckminster Fuller to combine the properties of the tetrahedron and the sphere and consisting essentially of a grid of compression or tension members lying upon or parallel to great circles running in three directions in any given area, the typical form being the projection upon a sphere of an icosahedron, the triangular faces of which are filled with a symmetrical triangular, hexagonal, or quadrangular grid. [1955–60]

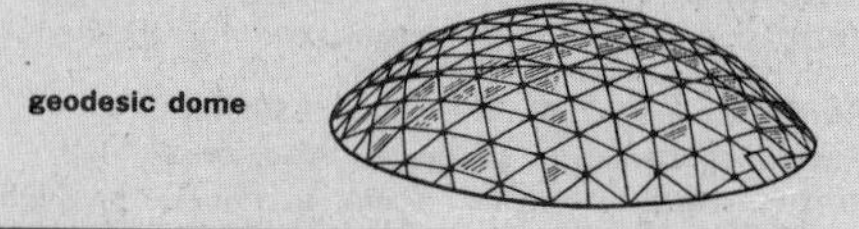
geodesic dome

ge′odes′ic line′, the shortest line lying on a given surface and connecting two given points. [1885–90]

ge•od•e•sy (jē od′ə sē), *n.* the branch of applied mathematics that deals with the measurement of the shape and area of large tracts of country, the exact position of geographical points, and the curvature, shape, and dimensions of the earth. Also, **ge•o•det•ics** (jē′ə det′iks). [1560–70; < F *géodésie* < Gk *geōdaisía,* equiv. to *geō-* GEO- + *daí(ein)* to divide + *-sia,* var. of *-ia* -IA (generalized from stems ending in *t*)] **—ge•od′e•sist,** *n.*

ge•o•det•ic (jē′ə det′ik), *adj.* **1.** pertaining to geodesy. **2.** geodesic. Also, **ge′o•det′i•cal.** [1665–75; irreg. from GEODESY; see -IC] **—ge′o•det′i•cal•ly,** *adv.*

ge′odet′ic sur′vey, a land area survey in which the curvature of the surface of the earth is taken into account. [1875–80, *Amer.*]

Ge•o•dim•e•ter (jē′ə dim′i tər), *Trademark.* a brand of distance-measuring instrument, used in surveying, that measures the change in phase of a modulated light beam when it returns to the instrument from a distant point.

ge•o•dome (jē′ə dōm′), *n.* a geodesic dome. [short for GEODESIC DOME]

ge•o•duck (go͞o′ē duk′), *n.* a very large edible clam, *Panope generosa,* of the NW coast of the U.S. Also called **gweduc.** [1880–85, *Amer.*; < Puget Salish *gʷídəq*]

ge•o•dy•nam•ics (jē′ō dī nam′iks), *n.* (*used with a singular v.*) the science dealing with dynamic processes or forces within the earth. [1880–85; GEO- + DYNAMICS] **—ge′o•dy•nam′ic, ge′o•dy•nam′i•cal,** *adj.* **—ge•o•dy•nam•i•cist** (jē′ō dī nam′ə sist), *n.*

ge•o•ec•o•nom•ics (jē′ō ek′ə nom′iks, -ē′kə-), *n.* (*used with a singular v.*) the study or application of the influence of geography on domestic and international economics. [GEO- + ECONOMICS] **—ge′o•ec′o•nom′ic, ge′o•ec′o•nom′i•cal,** *adj.* **—ge′o•ec′o•nom′i•cal•ly,** *adv.* **—ge•o•e•con•o•mist** (jē′ō i kon′ə mist), *n.*

ge•o•fact (jē′ə fakt′), *n.* a rock, bone, shell, or the like that has been modified by natural processes to appear to look like an artifact. [GEO- + (ARTI)FACT]

Geof•frey (jef′rē), *n.* a male given name: from Germanic, meaning "divine peace."

Geof′frey of Mon′mouth, 1100?–1154, English chronicler.

geog., 1. geographer. **2.** geographic; geographical. **3.** geography.

ge•og•no•sy (jē og′nə sē), *n. Archaic.* a science dealing with the constituent parts of the earth, its envelope of air and water, its crust, and the condition of its interior. [1785–95; < F *géognosie,* equiv. to *géo-* GEO- + *-gnosie* < Gk *gnôsis* knowledge] **—ge•og•nos•tic** (jē′og nos′tik), **ge′og•nos′ti•cal,** *adj.* **—ge′og•nos′ti•cal•ly,** *adv.*

ge•og•ra•pher (jē og′rə fər), *n.* a person who specializes in geographical research, delineation, and study. [1535–45; < LL *geōgraph(us)* (< Gk *geōgráphos,* equiv. to *geō-* GEO- + *gráphos* a writer; see -GRAPH) + -ER[1]]

ge•o•graph•i•cal (jē′ə graf′i kəl), *adj.* **1.** of or pertaining to geography. **2.** of or pertaining to the natural features, population, industries, etc., of a region or regions. Also, **ge′o•graph′ic.** [1550–60; < LL *geōgraphicus* (< Gk *geōgraphikós;* see GEO-, -GRAPH, -IC) + -AL[2]] **—ge′o•graph′i•cal•ly,** *adv.*

ge′ograph′ical mile′. See **nautical mile.** [1815–25]

geograph′ic deter′minism, *Sociol.* a doctrine that regards geographical conditions as the determining or molding agency of group life.

ge′ograph′ic range′, *Navig.* the distance at which a certain light, as that of a lighthouse, is visible to the eye at a given elevation, assuming that the weather is clear and that the light is sufficiently powerful to be visible from any point at which it appears above the horizon. Cf. **luminous range.**

ge•og•ra•phy (jē og′rə fē), *n., pl.* **-phies. 1.** the science dealing with the areal differentiation of the earth's surface, as shown in the character, arrangement, and interrelations over the world of such elements as climate, elevation, soil, vegetation, population, land use, industries, or states, and of the unit areas formed by the complex of these individual elements. **2.** the study of this science. **3.** the topographical features of a region, usually of the earth, sometimes of the planets. **4.** a book dealing with this science or study, as a textbook. **5.** the arrangement of features of any complex entity: *the geography of the mind.* [1535–45; < L *geōgraphia* < Gk *geōgraphía* earth description. See GEO-, -GRAPHY]

ge•o•hy•drol•o•gy (jē′ō hī drol′ə jē), *n.* hydrogeology. [1905–10; GEO- + HYDROLOGY] **—ge•o•hy•dro•log•ic** (jē′ō hī′drə loj′ik), **ge′o•hy′dro•log′i•cal,** *adj.* **—ge′o•hy′dro•log′i•cal•ly,** *adv.* **—ge′o•hy•drol′o•gist,** *n.*

ge•oid (jē′oid), *n.* **1.** an imaginary surface that coincides with mean sea level in the ocean and its extension through the continents. **2.** the geometric figure formed by this surface, an ellipsoid flattened at the poles. [1880–85; < Gk *geoeidḗs* earthlike. See GEO-, -OID] **—ge•oi′dal,** *adj.*

ge•o•i•so•therm (jē′ō ī′sə thûrm′), *n.* isogeotherm. [GEO- + ISOTHERM]

geol., 1. geologic; geological. **2.** geologist. **3.** geology.

ge•o•log•ic (jē′ə loj′ik), *adj.* of, pertaining to, or based on geology. Also, **ge′o•log′i•cal.** [1790–1800; GEOLOG(Y) + -IC] **—ge′o•log′i•cal•ly,** *adv.*

Geolog′ical Sur′vey, 1. *U.S. Govt.* a division of the Department of the Interior, created in 1879, that studies the nation's water and mineral resources, makes topographic surveys, and classifies and leases public lands. **2.** (*l.c.*) a systematic investigation of the geology of an area.

ge′olog′ic time′, the succession of eras, periods, and epochs as considered in historical geology. See table on next page. [1860–65]

ge•ol•o•gist (jē ol′ə jist), *n.* a person who specializes in geologic research and study. [1785–95; GEOLOG(Y) + -IST]

ge•ol•o•gize (jē ol′ə jīz′), *v.,* **-gized, -giz•ing.** **—***v.i.* **1.** to study geology. **—***v.t.* **2.** to examine geologically. Also, *esp. Brit.,* **ge•ol′o•gise′.** [1825–35; GEOLOG(Y) + -IZE]

ge•ol•o•gy (jē ol′ə jē), *n., pl.* **-gies. 1.** the science that deals with the dynamics and physical history of the earth, the rocks of which it is composed, and the physical, chemical, and biological changes that the earth has undergone or is undergoing. **2.** the study of this science. **3.** the geologic features and processes occurring in a given region on the earth or on a celestial body: *the geology of Mars; the geology of eastern Kentucky.* [1680–90; GEO- + -LOGY]

geom., 1. geometric; geometrical. **2.** geometry.

ge•o•mag•net•ic (jē′ō mag net′ik), *adj.* of or pertaining to geomagnetism. [1900–05; GEO- + MAGNETIC] **—ge•o•mag•ne•ti•cian** (jē′ō mag′ni tish′ən), **ge′o•mag′ne•tist,** *n.*

ge′omagnet′ic storm′. See **magnetic storm.** [1940–45]

ge•o•mag•net•ism (jē′ō mag′ni tiz′əm), *n.* **1.** the earth's magnetic field and associated phenomena. **2.** the branch of geophysics that studies such phenomena. [1935–40; GEO- + MAGNETISM]

ge•o•man•cy (jē′ə man′sē), *n.* divination by geographic features or by figures or lines. [1325–75; ME < OF *geomancie* << LGk *geōmanteía.* See GEO-, -MANCY] **—ge′o•man′cer,** *n.* **—ge′o•man′tic,** *adj.*

ge•o•med•i•cine (jē′ō med′ə sən *or, esp. Brit.,* -med′sin), *n.* the branch of medicine dealing with the effect of geography on disease. [GEO- + MEDICINE] **—ge•o•med•i•cal** (jē′ō med′i kəl), *adj.*

ge•om•e•ter (jē om′i tər), *n.* **1.** geometrician. **2.** a geometrid moth or larva. [1375–1425; late ME *gemeter* < LL *geōmeter,* for L *geōmetrēs* < Gk *geōmétrēs,* equiv.

to *geō-* GEO- + *-metrēs,* deriv. of *métron* measure; see -METER]

ge•o•met•ric (jē′ə me′trik), *adj.* Also, **ge′o•met′ri•cal.** **1.** of or pertaining to geometry or to the principles of geometry. **2.** resembling or employing the simple rectilinear or curvilinear lines or figures used in geometry. **3.** of or pertaining to painting, sculpture, or ornamentation of predominantly geometric characteristics. **4.** (*often cap.*) *Fine Arts.* **a.** pertaining to or designating a style of vase painting developed in Greece between the 10th and 8th centuries B.C., characterized chiefly by rectilinear or curvilinear shapes in abstract and human figuration, often arranged in tiers or panels around the vase. **b.** designating a style of Greek sculpture of approximately the same period, exemplified chiefly in small figurines or reliefs having a schematic and generalized treatment of the human form. —*n.* **5.** a geometric pattern, design, etc.: *an ornate and handsome geometric.* [1620–30; < L *geōmetricus* < Gk *geōmetrikós,* equiv. to *geōmétr(ēs)* (see GEOMETER) + *-ikos* -IC] —**ge′o•met′ri•cal•ly,** *adv.*

geomet′rical op′tics, the branch of optics dealing with light as rays, esp. in the study of the effects of lenses and mirrors on light beams and of their combination in optical instruments. [1830–40]

geomet′rical pace′, a pace of 5 ft. (1.5 m), representing the distance between the places at which the same foot rests on the ground in walking. Also called **great pace.** [1550–60]

ge•om•e•tri•cian (jē om′i trish′ən, jē′ə mi-), *n.* a person skilled in geometry. [1475–85; GEOMETRIC + -IAN]

ge•o•met•ri•cize (jē′ə me′trə sīz′), *v.t.,* **-cized, -ciz•ing.** to draw, design, or form in geometrical shapes or patterns. Also, *esp. Brit.,* **ge′o•met′ri•cise′.** [GEOMETRIC + -IZE] —**ge′o•met′ri•ci•za′tion,** *n.*

ge′omet′ric mean′, *Math.* the mean of *n* positive numbers obtained by taking the *n*th root of the product of the numbers: *The geometric mean of 6 and 24 is 12.*

geomet′ric progres′sion, *Math.* a sequence of terms in which the ratio between any two successive terms is the same, as the progression 1, 3, 9, 27, 81 or 144, 12, 1, ¹⁄₁₂, ¹⁄₁₄₄. Also called **geometric series.** [1550–60]

ge′omet′ric ra′tio, *Math.* the ratio of consecutive terms in a geometric progression. Also called **common ratio.** [1800–10]

ge•o•met•rics (jē′ə me′triks), *n.* (*used with a plural v.*) the geometric characteristics or features of a thing: *the geometrics of a building design.* [1960–65; see GEOMETRIC, -METRICS]

ge′omet′ric se′ries, *Math.* **1.** an infinite series of the form, $c + cx + cx^2 + cx^3 + \ldots$, where *c* and *x* are real numbers. **2.** See **geometric progression.** [1830–40]

ge•om•e•trid (jē om′i trid), *adj.* **1.** belonging or pertaining to the family Geometridae, comprising slender-bodied, broad-winged moths, the larvae of which are called measuring worms. —*n.* **2.** a geometrid moth. [1860–65; < NL *Geometridae,* equiv. to *Geometr(a)* a genus name (see GEOMETER; so called because the larva seems to measure the ground with its looping motion) + *-idae* -ID²]

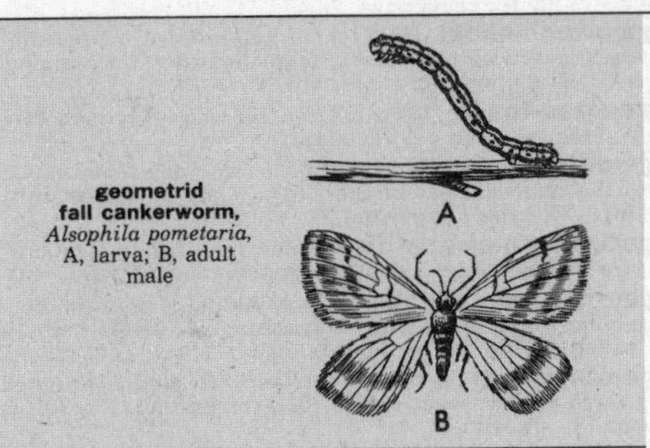

geometrid fall cankerworm, *Alsophila pometaria,* A, larva; B, adult male

ge•om•e•trize (jē om′i trīz′), *v.,* **-trized, -triz•ing.** —*v.i.* **1.** to work by geometric methods. —*v.t.* **2.** to put into geometric form. Also, *esp. Brit.,* **ge•om′e•trise′.** [1650–60; GEOMETR(Y) + -IZE] —**ge•om′e•tri•za′tion,** *n.*

ge•om•e•try (jē om′i trē), *n.* **1.** the branch of mathematics that deals with the deduction of the properties, measurement, and relationships of points, lines, angles, and figures in space from their defining conditions by means of certain assumed properties of space. **2.** any specific system of this that operates in accordance with a specific set of assumptions: *Euclidean geometry.* **3.** the study of this branch of mathematics. **4.** a book on this study, esp. a textbook. **5.** the shape or form of a surface or solid. **6.** a design or arrangement of objects in simple rectilinear or curvilinear form. [1300–50; ME < L *geōmetria* < Gk *geōmetría.* See GEO-, -METRY]

ge•o•mor•phic (jē′ə môr′fik), *adj.* **1.** of or pertaining to the form of the earth or the forms of its surface. **2.** resembling the earth in form. [1890–95; GEO- + -MORPHIC]

ge•o•mor•phol•o•gy (jē′ə môr fol′ə jē), *n.* the study of the characteristics, origin, and development of landforms. [1890–95; GEO- + MORPHOLOGY] —**ge•o•mor•pho•log•i•cal** (jē′ə môr′fə loj′i kəl), **ge′o•mor′pho•log′ic,** *adj.* —**ge′o•mor•phol′o•gist,** *n.*

ge•o•nav•i•ga•tion (jē′ō nav′i gā′shən), *n.* navigation by means of observations of terrestrial features. [1880–85; GEO- + NAVIGATION]

Ge•o•nim (*Seph.* ge ô nēm′; *Ashk.* gā ō′nim,), *n. Hebrew.* a pl. of **Gaon.** —**Ge•on•ic** (gā on′ik), *adj.*

ge•oph•a•gy (jē of′ə jē), *n.* the practice of eating earthy matter, esp. clay or chalk, as in famine-stricken areas. Also, **ge•o•pha•gia** (jē′ə fā′jə, -jē ə), **ge•oph•a•gism** (jē of′ə jiz′əm). [1840–50; GEO- + -PHAGY] —**ge•oph′a•gist,** *n.* —**ge•oph•a•gous** (jē of′ə gəs), *adj.*

ge•oph•i•lous (jē of′ə ləs), *adj.* **1.** *Zool.* terrestrial, as certain snails. **2.** *Bot.* fruiting underground. [1850–55; < NL *Geophilus* genus name; see GEO-, -PHILE, -OUS]

ge•o•phone (jē′ə fōn′), *n.* a device that is placed on or in the ground and used to detect seismic waves. [1915–20; GEO- + -PHONE]

ge•o•phys•ics (jē′ō fiz′iks), *n.* (*used with a singular v.*) the branch of geology that deals with the physics of the earth and its atmosphere, including oceanography, seismology, volcanology, and geomagnetism. [1885–90; GEO- + PHYSICS] —**ge′o•phys′i•cal,** *adj.* —**ge′o•phys′i•cal•ly,** *adv.* —**ge′o•phys′i•cist,** *n.*

ge•o•phyte (jē′ə fīt′), *n. Bot.* a plant propagated by means of underground buds. [1895–1900; GEO- + -PHYTE] —**ge•o•phyt•ic** (jē′ə fit′ik), *adj.*

ge•o•pol•i•tics (jē′ō pol′i tiks), *n.* (*used with a singular v.*) **1.** the study or the application of the influence of political and economic geography on the politics, national power, foreign policy, etc., of a state. **2.** the combination of geographic and political factors influencing or delineating a country or region. **3.** a national policy based on the interrelation of politics and geography. **4.** a Nazi doctrine that a combination of political, geographic, historical, racial, and economic factors substantiated Germany's right to expand its borders and control various strategic land masses and natural resources. Cf. **Lebensraum.** [1900–05; trans. of G *Geopolitik.* See GEO-, POLITICS] —**ge′o•pol′i•tic, ge•o•po•lit•i•cal** (jē′ō pə lit′i kəl), *adj.* —**ge′o•po•lit′i•cal•ly,** *adv.* —**ge•o•pol•i•ti•cian** (jē′ō pol′i tish′ən), **ge′o•pol′i•tist,** *n.*

ge•o•pon•ic (jē′ə pon′ik), *adj.* of or pertaining to tillage or agriculture; agricultural. [1600–10; < Gk *geōponikós* pertaining to husbandry, equiv. to *geōpón(os)* husbandman (*geō-* GEO- + *-ponos,* agentive deriv. of *pónos* work, labor + *-ikos* -IC]

ge•o•pon•ics (jē′ə pon′iks), *n.* (*used with a singular v.*) **1.** the art or science of agriculture. **2.** gardening or farming in soil. Cf. **hydroponics.** [1600–10; see GEOPONIC, -ICS]

ge•o•po•ten•tial (jē′ō pə ten′shəl), *n. Physics.* the difference between the potential energy of a mass at a given altitude and the potential energy of an identical mass at sea level, equivalent to the energy required to move the mass from sea level to the given altitude. [1910–15; GEO- + POTENTIAL]

ge•o•pres•sured (jē′ō presh′ərd), *adj.* subject to geostatic pressure. Also, **ge′o•pres′sur•ized′.** [1965–70; GEO- + PRESSURE + -ED²]

ge•o•ram•a (jē′ə ram′ə, -rä′mə), *n.* an encompassingly large, hollow globe on the inside of which is depicted a map of the earth's surface, to be viewed by a spectator within the globe. [1840–50; GEO- + (PANO)RAMA; cf. -ORAMA]

Geor•die (jôr′dē), *n. Brit.* **1.** a native of Newcastle-upon-Tyne, England. **2.** the dialect spoken by Geordies. [generic use of *Geordie,* hypocoristic form of GEORGE]

Georg•ann (jôr jan′), *n.* a female given name.

George (jôrj), *n.* **1.** a figure of St. George killing the dragon, esp. one forming part of the insignia of the Order of the Garter. **2.** *Brit. Slang.* any coin bearing the image of St. George. **3.** a word formerly used in communications to represent the letter *G.* **4.** *Brit. Slang.* an automatic pilot on an airplane.

George (jôrj; *for 4 also Ger.* gā ôr′gə), *n.* **1. David Lloyd.** See **Lloyd George, David. 2. Henry,** 1839–97, U.S. economist: advocate of a single tax. **3. Saint,** died A.D. 303?, Christian martyr: patron saint of England. **4. Ste•fan An•ton** (shte′fän än′tōn), 1868–1933, German poet. **5. Lake,** a lake in E New York. 36 mi. (58 km) long. **6.** a male given name: from a Greek word meaning "farmer."

George I, **1.** 1660–1727, king of England 1714–27. **2.** 1845–1913, king of Greece 1863–1913.

George II, **1.** 1683–1760, king of England 1727–60 (son of George I). **2.** 1890–1947, king of Greece 1922–23 and 1935–47.

George III, 1738–1820, king of England 1760–1820 (grandson of George II).

George IV, 1762–1830, king of England 1820–30 (son of George III).

George V, 1865–1936, king of England 1910–36 (son of Edward VII).

George VI, 1895–1952, king of England 1936–1952 (second son of George V; brother of Edward VIII).

Geor′ges Bank′ (jôr′jiz), a bank extending generally NE from Nantucket: fishing grounds. 150 mi. (240 km) long.

George•town (jôrj′toun′), *n.* **1.** Also, **George′ Town′.** a seaport in and the capital of the state of Penang, in NW Malaysia. 250,578. **2.** a seaport in and the capital of Guyana, at the mouth of the Demerara. 182,000. **3.** a residential section in the District of Columbia. **4.** a town in N Kentucky. 10,972. **5.** a city in E South Carolina. 10,144. **6.** a town in and the capital of the Cayman Islands, West Indies, on Grand Cayman. 3975.

Geor•gette (jôr jet′), *n.* a sheer silk or rayon crepe of dull texture. Also called **Georgette′ crepe′.** [1910–15; formerly a trademark]

Geor•gette (jôr jet′, jôr′jet), *n.* a female given name, form of **Georgia.**

Geor•gia (jôr′jə), *n.* **1.** a state in the SE United States. 5,464,265; 58,876 sq. mi. (152,489 sq. km). *Cap.:* Atlanta. *Abbr.:* GA (for use with zip code), Ga. See map on next page. **2.** Also called **Geor′gian Repub′lic.** a republic in Transcaucasia, bordering on the Black Sea, N of Turkey and Armenia: an independent kingdom for ab. 2000 years. 5,167,000; 26,872 sq. mi. (69,700 sq. km). *Cap.:* Tbilisi. See map on next page. **3. Strait of,** an inlet of the Pacific in SW Canada between Vancouver Island and the mainland. 150 mi. (240 km) long. **4.** a female given name: *George* + feminine ending *-a.*

GEOLOGIC TIME DIVISIONS

Era	Years Ago	Period	Epoch	Features and Events
Cenozoic	10,000	Quaternary	Recent	Modern humans
	2 million		Pleistocene	Widespread glacial ice (ice ages)
	10 million	Tertiary	Pliocene	Mountain uplift; cool climate; mammals increase in size and numbers
	25 million		Miocene	Widespread grasslands; grazing mammals; ape; whales
	40 million		Oligocene	Browsing mammals; sabertoothed tigers
	55 million		Eocene	Warm climate; modern birds and mammals; giant birds
	65 million		Paleocene	Mild to cool climate; age of mammals begins; primates
Mesozoic	140 million	Cretaceous		Last dinosaurs; modern insects; flowering plants
	190 million	Jurassic		Age of dinosaurs; first birds and mammals; flying reptiles
	230 million	Triassic		Active volcanoes; age of reptiles begins; first dinosaurs
Paleozoic	280 million	Permian		Conifer forests; extinctions of many marine invertebrates
	310 million	Pennsylvanian (Carboniferous)		Warm climate; swamps and coal forests; first reptiles
	345 million	Mississippian (Carboniferous)		Shallow seas, low lands; fern forests; age of amphibians begins
	405 million	Devonian		Age of fishes; first amphibians, insects, land animals
	425 million	Silurian		Shellfish abundant; first land plants, modern fungi
	500 million	Ordovician		Primitive fishes; seaweeds; fungi
	570 million	Cambrian		Age of marine invertebrates begins: shellfish, echinoderms, etc.
Precambrian	2.5 billion	Proterozoic		Bacteria; algae; primitive multicellular life
	5 billion	Archeozoic		Earth's crust solidifies; earliest life forms; blue-green algae; free oxygen

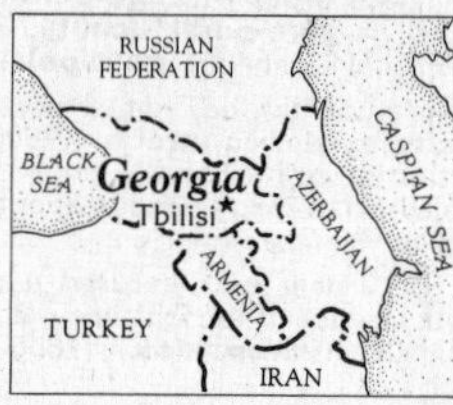

Geor·gian (jôr′jən), *adj.* **1.** of or pertaining to the period of British history from the accession of George I in 1714 to the death of George IV in 1830, or the four kings named George who reigned successively during this period. **2.** of or pertaining to the period of the reign of George V (1910–36) or to George V himself. **3.** of, noting, or designating the styles of architecture, furniture, and crafts current in England esp. from 1714 to 1811. **4.** of or pertaining to the state of Georgia in the U.S. **5.** of or pertaining to the Georgian Republic. —*n.* **6.** a person, esp. a writer, of either of the Georgian periods in England. **7.** the styles or character of either of the Georgian periods. **8.** a native or inhabitant of the state of Georgia in the U.S. **9.** a native or inhabitant of the Georgian Republic. **10.** the most important South Caucasian language, spoken principally in the Georgian Republic, and written in a distinctive script derived from the Aramaic alphabet. [GEORGE or GEORGI(A) + -AN]

Geor·gi·an·a (jôr′jē an′ə), *n.* a female given name.

Geor′gian Bay′, the NE part of Lake Huron, in Ontario, Canada. 6000 sq. mi. (15,500 sq. km).

Geor′gia pine′. See **longleaf pine.** [1790–1800, *Amer.*]

geor·gic (jôr′jik), *adj.* **1.** agricultural. —*n.* **2.** a poem on an agricultural theme. [1505–15; < L *geōrgicus* < Gk *geōrgikós,* equiv. to *geōrg(ós)* husbandman (*geō-* GEO- + *-ourgos* working, worker, akin to *érgon* WORK) + *-ikos* -IC]

Geor·gi·na (jôr jē′nə), *n.* **1.** a town in SE Ontario, in S Canada. 18,530. **2.** Also, **Geor·gine** (jôr jēn′). a female given name.

ge·o·sci·ence (jē′ō sī′əns), *n.* See **earth science.** [1940–45; GEO- + SCIENCE]

ge·o·sci·en·tist (jē′ō sī′ən tist), *n.* a specialist in earth science. [1940–45; GEO- + SCIENTIST]

ge·o·stat·ic (jē′ə stat′ik), *adj.* **1.** of or pertaining to pressure exerted by the weight of overlying rock. **2.** (of a construction) resistant to such pressure. [GEO- + STATIC]

ge·o·sta·tion·ar·y (jē′ō stā′shə ner′ē), *adj.* of or pertaining to a satellite traveling in an orbit 22,300 miles (35,900 km) above the earth's equator: at this altitude, the satellite's period of rotation, 24 hours, matches the earth's and the satellite always remains in the same spot over the earth: *geostationary orbit.* Also, **ge·o·syn·chro·nous** (jē′ō sing′krə nəs). [1960–65; GEO- + STATIONARY]

Geosta′tionary Opera′tional Environmen′tal Sat′ellite, one of a series of U.S. geostationary meteorological satellites that collect data for worldwide weather forecasting. *Abbr.:* GOES

ge·o·stroph·ic (jē′ə strof′ik, -strō′fik), *adj.* of or pertaining to the balance between the Coriolis force and the horizontal pressure force in the atmosphere. [1915–20; GEO- + STROPHIC]

ge′ostroph′ic wind′, a wind whose velocity and direction are mathematically defined by the balanced relationship of the pressure gradient force and the Coriolis force: conceived as blowing parallel to isobars. Cf. **gradient wind.** [1915–20]

ge·o·syn·cli·nal (jē′ō sin klīn′l), *adj. Geol.* pertaining to a synclinal fold that involves a relatively large part of the earth's surface. [1870–75; GEO- + SYNCLINAL]

ge·o·syn·cline (jē′ō sin′klīn), *n. Geol.* a portion of the earth's crust subjected to downward warping during a large span of geologic time; a geosynclinal fold. [1890–95; GEO- + SYNCLINE]

ge·o·tax·is (jē′ō tak′sis), *n. Biol.* oriented movement of a motile organism toward or away from a gravitational force. [1960–65; GEO- + -TAXIS] —**ge·o·tac·tic** (jē′ō tak′tik), *adj.* —**ge′o·tac′ti·cal·ly,** *adv.*

CONCISE ETYMOLOGY KEY: <, descended or borrowed from; >, whence; b., blend of, blended; c., cognate with; cf., compare; deriv., derivative; equiv., equivalent; imit., imitative; obl., oblique; r., replacing; s., stem; sp., spelling, spelled; resp., respelling, respelled; trans., translation; ?, origin unknown; *, unattested; ‡, probably earlier than. See the full key inside the front cover.

ge·o·tech·ni·cal (jē′ō tek′ni kəl), *adj.* of or pertaining to practical applications of geological science in civil engineering, mining, etc. [GEO- + TECHNICAL]

ge·o·tec·ton·ic (jē′ō tek ton′ik), *adj.* tectonic (def. 2). [1880–85; GEO- + TECTONIC]

ge·o·ther·mal (jē′ō thûr′məl), *adj.* of or pertaining to the internal heat of the earth. Also, **ge′o·ther′mic.** [1870–75; GEO- + THERMAL]

ge′other′mal gra′dient, the increase in temperature with increasing depth within the earth. [1935–40]

ge·o·trop·ic (jē′ō trop′ik, -trō′pik), *adj. Biol.* of, pertaining to, or exhibiting geotropism. [1870–75; GEO- + -TROPIC] —**ge′o·trop′i·cal·ly,** *adv.*

ge·ot·ro·pism (jē o′trə piz′əm), *n. Biol.* oriented growth with respect to the force of gravity. [1870–75; GEO- + -TROPISM]

Ge-Pa·no-Car·ib (zhā′pä′nō kar′ib), *n.* a linguistic phylum comprising a large number of aboriginal languages with scattered distribution in South America east of the Andes.

Ger., **1.** German. **2.** Germany.

ger., **1.** gerund. **2.** gerundive.

Ge·ra (gā′rä), *n.* a city in E central Germany. 124,000.

ge·rah (gē′rə), *n.* an ancient Hebrew weight and coin, equal to 1/20 of a shekel. [1525–35; < Heb *gērāh* < Akkadian *girū*]

Ge·raint (ji rānt′), *n. Arthurian Romance.* one of the knights of the Round Table, husband of Enid.

Ger·ald (jer′əld), *n.* a male given name: from Germanic words meaning "spear" and "rule."

Ger·al·dine (jer′əl dēn′), *n.* a female given name: derived from *Gerald.*

Ger·ald·ton (jer′əld tən, -əl-), *n.* a seaport in W Australia. 20,895.

ge·ra·ni·a·ceous (ji rā′nē ā′shəs), *adj.* belonging to the Geraniaceae, the geranium family of plants. Cf. **geranium family.** [< NL *Geraniace(ae)* (see GERANIUM, -ACEAE) + -OUS]

ge·ra·ni·al (ji rā′nē əl), *n.* See under **citral.** [1895–1900; GERANI(UM) + -AL[3]]

ge·ra·ni·ol (jə rā′nē ôl′, -ol′), *n. Chem.* a colorless or pale-yellow terpene alcohol, $C_{10}H_{18}O$, with a geraniumlike odor, found in rose oil, soluble in alcohol and ether, insoluble in water: used in perfumes and flavors. [< G *Geraniol* (1871); see GERANIUM, -OL[1]]

ge·ra·ni·um (ji rā′nē əm), *n.* **1.** any of numerous plants of the genus *Geranium,* which comprises the crane's-bills. **2.** the wild geranium, *G. maculatum,* of eastern North America, having loose clusters of lavender flowers. **3.** Also called **stork's-bill.** any of various plants of the allied genus *Pelargonium,* native to southern Africa, having showy flowers or fragrant leaves, widely cultivated in gardens and as houseplants. **4.** a flower of this plant. **5.** a vivid red color. [1540–50; < NL, for L *geranion* < Gk *gerá̄nion* name for various plants the fruit of which was thought to resemble a crane's bill, deriv. of *géranos* CRANE; akin to L *grūs*]

gera′nium fam′ily, the plant family Geraniaceae, typified by herbaceous plants or small shrubs having lobed leaves, showy flowers and slender, beak-shaped fruit, and including the crane's-bills, stork's-bills, and cultivated geraniums of the genus *Pelargonium.*

Ge·rar (gē′rär), *n.* an ancient city in Palestine, near the Mediterranean: now an archaeological site in Israel.

Ge·rard (jə rärd′), *n.* Also, **Gé·rard′.** a male given name, form of **Gerald.**

Gé·rard (zhā RAR′), *n.* **Comte É·tienne Mau·rice** (kôN ā tyen′ mō Rēs′), 1773–1852, French marshal under Napoleon.

ger·a·tol·o·gy (jer′ə tol′ə jē), *n. Biol.* the study of the diminution or decline of life, as in an individual animal or a species approaching extinction. [1880–85; *gerat-* (erroneously taken as the s. of Gk *gêras* old age) + -O- + -LOGY] —**ger·a·to·log·ic** (jer′ə tl oj′ik), **ger·a·tol·o·gous** (jer′ə tol′ə gəs), *adj.*

ger·ber·a (gûr′bər ə, jûr′-), *n.* any of various composite plants of the genus *Gerbera,* native to Africa and Asia, having showy, many-rayed flowers ranging from yellow to red. [< NL (Linnaeus), named after Traugott *Gerber* (d. 1743), German naturalist; see -A[2]]

ger·bil (jûr′bəl), *n.* **1.** any of numerous small burrowing rodents of the genus *Gerbillus* and related genera, of Asia, Africa, and southern Russia, having long hind legs used for jumping. **2.** Also called **tamarisk gerbil.** a jird, *Meriones unguiculatus,* that is popular as a pet. Also called **sand rat.** [1840–50; < F *gerbille* < NL *gerbillus,* dim. of *gerbo* JERBOA]

gerbil (def. 2), *Meriones unguiculatus,* head and body 6 in. (15 cm); tail 6 in. (15 cm)

Gerd (gârd), *n. Scand. Myth.* the daughter of a giant and the consort of Frey, who wooed her through his servant Skirnir. Also, **Ger·da** (gâr′də). [< ON *Gerthr,* deriv. of *garthr* fenced-in field; see GARTH]

ge·rent (jēr′ənt), *n.* a ruler or manager. [1570–80; < L *gerent-* (s. of *gerēns*), prp. of *gerere* to bear, conduct, manage, equiv. to *ger-* bear + *-ent-* -ENT]

ger·e·nuk (ger′ə nŏŏk′, gə ren′ək), *n.* a reddish-brown antelope, *Litocranius walleri,* of eastern Africa, having a long, slender neck. [1890–95; < Somali *gáránúug*]

ger·fal·con (jûr′fôl′kən, -fal′-, -fô′-), *n.* gyrfalcon.

ger·i·at·ric (jer′ē a′trik, jēr′-), *adj.* **1.** of or pertaining to geriatrics, old age, or aged persons. —*n.* **2.** *Slang.* an old person. [1925–30; < Gk *gér(ōn)* old man + -IATRIC]

ger·i·at·rics (jer′ē a′triks, jēr′-), *n.* (*used with a singular v.*) **1.** the branch of medicine dealing with the diseases, debilities, and care of aged persons. **2.** the study of the physical processes and problems of aging; gerontology. [1905–10; see GERIATRIC, -ICS] —**ger·i·a·tri·cian** (jer′ē ə trish′ən), **ger′i·at′rist,** *n.*

Gé·ri·cault (zhā Rē kō′), *n.* **(Jean Louis An·dré) Thé·o·dore** (zhäN lwē äN drā′ tā ô dôR′), 1791–1824, French painter.

Ger·la·chov·ka (ger′lä KHôf′kä), *n.* a mountain in N Slovakia: highest peak of the Carpathian Mountains. 8737 ft. (2663 m).

germ (jûrm), *n.* **1.** a microorganism, esp. when disease-producing; microbe. **2.** a bud, offshoot, or seed. **3.** the rudiment of a living organism; an embryo in its early stages. **4.** the initial stage in development or evolution, as a germ cell or ancestral form. **5.** something that serves as a source or initial stage for subsequent development: *the germ of an idea.* —*adj.* **6.** *Pathol.* of, pertaining to, or caused by disease-producing germs. [1400–50; late ME < MF *germe* < L *germen* shoot, sprout, by dissimilation from **genmen,* equiv. to *gen-* (see GENITOR, GENUS) + *-men* resultative n. suffix)] —**germ′less,** *adj.* —**germ′like′,** *adj.*
—**Syn. 4.** spark, root, bud, rudiment, seed.

Ger·maine (jər mān′; *Fr.* zheR men′), *n.* a female given name. Also, **Ger·main′.**

ger·man (jûr′mən), *adj.* **1.** having the same father and mother, as a full brother or sister (usually used in combination): *a brother-german.* **2.** born of the brother or sister of one's father or mother, as a first cousin (usually used in combination): *a cousin-german.* **3.** *Archaic.* germane. [1250–1300; ME *germain* < OF < L *germānus,* deriv of *germen;* see GERM]

Ger·man (jûr′mən), *adj.* **1.** of or pertaining to Germany, its inhabitants, or their language. —*n.* **2.** a native or inhabitant of Germany. **3.** a descendant of a native of Germany. **4.** Also called **High German.** an Indo-European language that is based on a High German dialect, is official in Germany, Austria, and Switzerland, and is also widely used as an international language for scholarship and science. *Abbr.:* G, G. **5.** *Ling.* any variety of West Germanic speech native to Germany, Austria, or Switzerland. **6.** (*usually l.c.*) an elaborate social dance resembling a cotillion. **7.** (*l.c.*) *New England and South Atlantic States.* a dancing party featuring the german. [1520–30; < L *Germānus* German; c. Gk *Germanoí* (pl.)]

Ger′man Af′rica, the former German colonies in Africa, comprising German East Africa, German Southwest Africa, Cameroons, and Togoland.

Ger′man Bap′tist Breth′ren. See **Church of the Brethren.**

Ger′man cock′roach, a common yellowish-brown cockroach, *Blatta germanica,* brought into the U.S. from Europe. Also called **crotonbug.** See illus. under **cockroach.** [1895–1900]

Ger′man Democrat′ic Repub′lic, official name of **East Germany.**

ger·man·der (jər man′dər), *n.* **1.** any of several plants or shrubs belonging to the genus *Teucrium,* of the mint family, as *T. chamaedrys,* of Europe, and *T. canadense,* of eastern North America. [1400–50; late ME < ML *germandr(e)a* < LGk *chamandryá*]

german′der speed′well, a speedwell, *Veronica chamaedrys,* having blue flowers. [1850–60]

ger·mane (jər mān′), *adj.* **1.** closely or significantly related; relevant; pertinent: *Please keep your statements germane to the issue.* **2.** *Obs.* closely related. [var. of GERMAN] —**ger·mane′ly,** *adv.* —**ger·mane′ness,** *n.*
—**Syn. 1.** related, applicable, apposite, appropriate, fitting, apt, suited.

Ger′man East′ Af′rica, a former German territory in E Africa, the area now comprised of continental Tanzania and the independent republics of Rwanda and Burundi.

Ger′man fries′, *Chiefly Northern, Midland, and Western U.S.* See **home fries.** Also called **Ger′·man-fried pota′toes.** (jûr′mən frīd′).

ger·man·ic (jər man′ik, -mā′nik), *adj. Chem.* of or containing germanium, esp. in the tetravalent state. [1885–90; GERMAN(IUM) + -IC]

Ger·man·ic (jər man′ik), *adj.* **1.** of or pertaining to the Teutons or their languages. **2.** German. **3.** of, pertaining to, or noting the Germanic branch of languages. —*n.* **4.** a branch of the Indo-European family of languages including German, Dutch, English, the Scandinavian languages, Afrikaans, Flemish, Frisian, and the extinct Gothic language. **5.** Proto-Germanic (def. 1). **6.** an ancient Indo-European language, the immediate linguistic ancestor of the Germanic languages. *Abbr.:* Gmc [1625–35; < L *Germānicus.* See GERMAN, -IC] —**Ger·man′i·cal·ly,** *adv.*

Ger·man′i·cus Cae′sar (jər man′i kəs), 15 B.C.–A.D. 19, Roman general.

Ger·man·ism (jûr′mə niz′əm), *n.* **1.** a usage, idiom, or other feature that is characteristic of the German language. **2.** a custom, manner, mode of thought, action, etc., that is characteristic of the German people. **3.** extreme partiality for or attachment to Germany, Germans, or German customs, manners, etc. [1605–15; GERMAN + -ISM]

Ger·man·ist (jûr′mə nist), *n.* a specialist in the study of German culture, literature, or linguistics. [1825–35; < G < L *Germān(ia)* GERMANY + -IST]

ger·ma·ni·um (jər mā′nē əm), *n. Chem.* a scarce, metallic, grayish-white element, normally tetravalent, used chiefly in transistors. *Symbol:* Ge; *at. wt.:* 72.59; *at. no.:* 32; *sp. gr.:* 5.36 at 20°C. [1885–90; GERMAN(Y) + -IUM]

Ger′man i′vy, a twining composite plant, *Senecio mikanioides,* native to southern Africa, having ivy-shaped leaves and clusters of yellow flowers. [1860–65]

Ger·man·ize (jûr′mə nīz′), *v.t., v.i.,* **-ized, -iz·ing. 1.** to make or become German in character, sentiment, etc. **2.** *Archaic.* to translate into German. Also, *esp. Brit.,* **Ger′man·ise′.** [1590–1600; GERMAN + -IZE] **—Ger′·man·i·za′tion,** *n.* **—Ger′man·iz′er,** *n.*

Ger′man la′pis, *Jewelry.* jasper stained blue in imitation of lapis lazuli. Also called **blue onyx.**

Ger′man mea′sles, *Pathol.* rubella. [1840–50]

Germano-, a combining form of **German:** *Germanophile.*

Ger′man O′cean, former name of the **North Sea.**

Ger·man·o·phile (jər man′ə fīl′), *n.* a person who is friendly toward or admires or studies Germany or German culture. [1860–65; GERMANO- + -PHILE]

Ger·man·o·phobe (jər man′ə fōb′), *n.* a person who hates or fears Germany, Germans, or German culture. [1910–15; GERMANO- + -PHOBE] **—Ger·man′o·pho′·bi·a,** *n.*

ger·man·ous (jər mā′nəs), *adj. Chem.* containing bivalent germanium. [GERMAN(IUM) + -OUS]

Ger′man shep′herd, one of a breed of large shepherd dogs having a coat ranging in color from gray to brindled, black-and-tan, or black, used esp. in police work and as a guide for the blind. Also called **Ger′man shep′herd dog′, Ger′man police′ dog′.** [1930–35; *shepherd* prob. as trans. of G *Schäferhund*]

German shepherd, 2 ft. (0.6 m) high at shoulder

Ger′man short′haired point′er, one of a German breed of large sporting dogs having a short hard coat, usually liver or liver and white in color, and a docked tail, used as a versatile hunting dog. [1930–35]

Ger′man sil′ver, any of various alloys of copper, zinc, and nickel, usually white and used for utensils, drawing instruments, etc.; nickel silver. [1820–30]

Ger′man South′west Af′rica, a former name of **Namibia.**

Ger·man·town (jûr′mən toun′), *n.* **1.** a NW section of Philadelphia, Pa.: American defeat by British 1777. **2.** a town in SW Tennessee. 20,459. **3.** a town in SE Wisconsin. 10,729. **4.** *Informal.* any U.S. city neighborhood heavily populated with persons of German descent.

Ger′man wire′haired point′er, one of a German breed of large sporting dogs having a harsh, wiry, flat-lying coat usually liver and white in color, a muzzle with a beard and whiskers, and a docked tail, used as a retrieving pointer. [1960–65]

Ger·ma·ny (jûr′mə nē), *n.* a republic in central Europe: after World War II divided into four zones, British, French, U.S., and Soviet, and in 1949 into East Germany and West Germany; East and West Germany were reunited in 1990. 78,420,000; 137,852 sq. mi. (357,039 sq. km). *Cap.:* Berlin. Official name, **Federal Republic of Germany.** German, **Deutschland.** Formerly, **Deutsches Reich.** Cf. **East Germany, West Germany.** See map on this page.

germ′ cell′, *Biol.* the sexual reproductive cell at any stage from the primordial cell to the mature gamete. [1850–55]

ger·men (jûr′mən), *n., pl.* **-mens, -mi·na** (-mə nə). *Archaic.* a germ. [1595–1605; < L; see GERM]

germ·free (jûrm′frē′, -frē′), *adj.* **1.** free of germs; sterile: *a germfree laboratory.* **2.** (of experimental animals) born and raised under sterile conditions. [1930–35]

ger·mi·cide (jûr′mə sīd′), *n.* an agent for killing germs or microorganisms. [1875–80; GERM + -I- + -CIDE] **—ger′mi·cid′al,** *adj.*

ger·mi·na·bil·i·ty (jûr′mə nə bil′i tē), *n. Bot.* the degree of ability of a seed to germinate or sprout. [1895–1900; GERMIN(ATE) + -ABILITY]

ger·mi·nal (jûr′mə nl), *adj.* **1.** being in the earliest stage of development: *germinal ideas.* **2.** of or pertaining to a germ or germs. **3.** of the nature of a germ or germ cell. [1800–10; (< F) < L *germin-* (s. of *germen* sprout, bud; see GERM) + -AL[1]] **—ger′mi·nal·ly,** *adv.*

Ger·mi·nal (jûr′mə nl; *Fr.* zher mē nal′), *n.* **1.** (in the French Revolutionary calendar) the seventh month of the year, extending from March 21 to April 19. **2.** (*italics*) a novel (1884) by Émile Zola. [< F; see GERMINAL]

ger′minal disk′, *Embryol.* blastodisk. [1875–80]

ger′minal ves′icle, *Embryol.* the large, vesicular nucleus of an ovum before the polar bodies are formed. [1850–55]

ger·mi·nant (jûr′mə nənt), *adj.* germinating. [1595–1605; < L *germinant-* (s. of *germināns*), prp. of *germināre* to GERMINATE; -ANT] **—ger′mi·nance, ger′mi·nan·cy,** *n.*

ger·mi·nate (jûr′mə nāt′), *v.,* **-nat·ed, -nat·ing.** —*v.i.* **1.** to begin to grow or develop. **2.** *Bot.* **a.** to develop into a plant or individual, as a seed, spore, or bulb. **b.** to put forth shoots; sprout; pullulate. **3.** to come into existence; begin. —*v.t.* **4.** to cause to develop; produce. **5.** to cause to come into existence; create. [1600–10; < L *germinātus* (ptp. of *germināre* to sprout, bud), equiv. to *germin-* (see GERMINAL) + *-ātus* -ATE[1]] **—ger·mi·na·ble** (jûr′mə nə bəl), *adj.* **—ger′mi·na′tion,** *n.* **—ger′mi·na′tor,** *n.*

ger·mi·na·tive (jûr′mə nā′tiv, -mə nə tiv), *adj.* capable of germinating, developing, or creating; of or pertaining to germination. [1700–10; GERMINATE + -IVE] **—ger′mi·na′tive·ly,** *adv.*

Ger·mis·ton (jûr′mə stən), *n.* a city in S Transvaal, in the NE Republic of South Africa. 132,273.

germ′ lay′er, one of the three primary embryonic cell layers. Cf. **ectoderm, endoderm, mesoderm.** [1875–80]

germ′line inser′tion (jûrm′līn′), *Biotech.* the insertion of cloned genes into the egg or sperm cell of an organism, using a gene transfer technique, in order to perpetuate a desired trait in its descendants, as pest-resistance in a crop plant.

germ′ plasm′, the protoplasm of the germ cells containing the chromosomes. [1885–90]

germ·proof (jûrm′pro͞of′), *adj.* not vulnerable to the action or penetration of germs. [1900–05]

germ′ the′ory, 1. *Pathol.* the theory that infectious diseases are due to the agency of germs or microorganisms. **2.** *Biol.* biogenesis. [1870–75]

germ′ war′fare. See **biological warfare.** [1935–40]

germ·y (jûr′mē), *adj.,* **germ·i·er, germ·i·est.** full of germs. [1910–15; GERM + -Y[1]] **—germ′i·ness,** *n.*

Gerns·back (gûrnz′bak), *n.* **Hugo,** 1884–1967, U.S. publisher and inventor, born in Belgium: a pioneer in science-fiction publishing.

ger·o·don·tics (jer′ə don′tiks, jēr′-), *n.* (*used with a singular v.*) the branch of dentistry dealing with aging and aged persons. Also, **ger·o·don·tia** (jer′ə don′shə, -shē ə, jēr′-). Also called **ger·o·don·tol·o·gy** (jer′ō dontol′ə jē, jēr′-). [< Gk *gêr(as)* old age + -ODONT + -ICS] **—ger′o·don′tic,** *adj.*

Gé·rôme (zhā rōm′), *n.* **Jean Lé·on** (zhäN lā ôN′), 1824–1904, French painter and sculptor.

Ge·ron·i·mo (jə ron′ə mō′), *n.* **1.** (*Goyathlay*), 1829–1909, American Apache Indian chief. —*interj.* **2.** (a battle cry used by paratroopers, esp. during World War II, on jumping from a plane.)

ge·ron·tic (jə ron′tik), *adj.* **1.** geriatric. **2.** of or pertaining to the last phase in the life cycle of an organism or in the life history of a species. [1880–85; < Gk *gerontikós* of old men, equiv. to *geront-* (s. of *gérōn* old man) + *-ikos* -IC]

geronto-, a combining form meaning "old age," used in the formation of compound words: *gerontology.* Also, *esp. before a vowel,* **geront-.** [< Gk, comb. form repr. *geront-,* s. of *gérōn* old man]

ger·on·toc·ra·cy (jer′ən tok′rə sē, jēr′-), *n., pl.* **-cies. 1.** government by a council of elders. **2.** a governing body consisting of old people. **3.** a state or government in which old people rule. [1820–30; GERONTO- + -CRACY] **—ge·ron·to·crat** (jə ron′tə krat′), *n.* **—ge·ron′to·crat′ic,** *adj.*

ge·ron·to·ge·ous (jə ron′tə jē′əs), *adj.* belonging to the Old World. [1875–80; GERONTO- + GE(O)- + -OUS]

ger·on·tol·o·gy (jer′ən tol′ə jē, jēr′-), *n.* the branch of science that deals with aging and the problems of aged persons. [1900–05; GERONTO- + -LOGY] **—ge·ron·to·log·i·cal** (jə ron′tl oj′i kəl), *adj.* **—ger′on·tol′o·gist,** *n.*

ge·ron·to·mor·pho·sis (jə ron′tə môr′fə sis), *n. Biol.* evolutionary specialization of a species to a degree that decreases its capability for further adaptation and eventually leads to its extinction. [GERONTO- + MORPHOSIS]

ge·ron·to·pho·bi·a (jə ron′tə fō′bē ə), *n.* **1.** a fear of old people. **2.** a fear of old age, esp. of growing old. [1975–80; GERONTO- + -PHOBIA]

-gerous, a combining form meaning "bearing," "producing," used in the formation of compound words: *setigerous.* [< L *-ger* bearing, deriv. of *gerere* to bear, wear; see -OUS]

Ger·ry (ger′ē), *n.* **1. El·bridge** (el′brij), 1744–1814, U.S. politician: vice president 1813–14. Cf. **gerrymander. 2.** Also, **Ger′ri.** a male or female given name.

ger·ry·man·der (jer′i man′dər, ger′-), *n.* **1.** *U.S. Politics.* the dividing of a state, county, etc., into election districts so as to give one political party a majority in many districts while concentrating the voting strength of the other party into as few districts as possible. —*v.t.* **2.** *U.S. Politics.* to subject (a state, county, etc.) to a gerrymander. [1812, *Amer.*; after E. GERRY (governor of Massachusetts, whose party redistricted the state in 1812) + (*sala*)*mander,* from the fancied resemblance of the map of Essex County, Mass., to this animal, after the redistricting] **—ger′ry·man′der·er,** *n.*

Gers (zhεr), *n.* a department in SW France. 175,366; 2429 sq. mi. (6290 sq. km). *Cap.:* Auch.

gers·dorff·ite (gerz′dôr fīt′, gers′-), *n.* a mineral, sulfide-arsenide of nickel, NiAsS, occurring in metallic, light-gray cubes. [1840–50; < G, after von *Gersdorff,* the name of a 19th-century family of mine owners in Austria; see -ITE[1]]

Ger·shom (gûr′shəm), *n.* the elder son of Moses and Zipporah. Ex. 18:3.

Gersh·win (gûrsh′win), *n.* **1. George,** 1898–1937, U.S.

CONCISE PRONUNCIATION KEY: act, cāpe, dâre, pärt; set, ēqual; if, īce; ox, ōver, ôrder, oil, bo͝ok, bo͞ot, out; up, ûrge; child; sing; shoe; thin, *th*at; zh as in *treasure.* ə = *a* as in *alone, e* as in *system, i* as in *easily, o* as in *gallop, u* as in *circus;* ᵊ as in *fire* (fīᵊr), *hour* (ouᵊr). l and n can serve as syllabic consonants, as in *cradle* (krād′l), and *button* (but′n). See the full key inside the front cover.

composer. **2. Ira,** 1896–1983, U.S. lyricist (brother of George Gershwin).

Gert (gûrt), *n.* a female given name, form of **Gertrude.** Also called **Ger·tie, Ger·ty** (gûr′tē).

ger·trude (gûr′tro͞od), *n.* a slip or underdress for infants. [1925–30, *Amer.*; special use of GERTRUDE]

Ger·trude (gûr′tro͞od), *n.* a female given name: from Germanic words meaning "spear" and "strength."

ger·und (jer′ənd), *n. Gram.* **1.** (in certain languages, as Latin) a form regularly derived from a verb and functioning as a noun, having in Latin all case forms but the nominative, as Latin *dicendī* gen., *dicendō,* dat., abl., etc., "saying." **2.** the English *-ing* form of a verb when functioning as a noun, as *writing* in *Writing is easy.* **3.** a form similar to the Latin gerund in meaning or function. [1505–15; < LL *gerundium,* L *gerundum* that which is to be carried on, equiv. to *ger(ere)* to bear, carry on + *-undum,* var. of *-endum,* gerund suffix] **—ge·run·di·al** (jə run′dē əl), *adj.* **—ge·run′di·al·ly,** *adv.* **—Usage.** See **me.**

ger·un·dive (jə run′div), *n.* **1.** (in Latin) a verbal adjective similar to the gerund in form and noting the obligation, necessity, or worthiness of the action to be done, as *legendus* in *Liber legendus est,* "The book is worth reading." *—adj.* **2.** resembling a gerund. [1375–1425; late ME < LL *gerundīvus.* See GERUND, -IVE] **—ger·un·di·val** (jer′ən dī′vəl), *adj.* **—ge·run′dive·ly,** *adv.*

ger·vais (zher vā′; *Fr.* zheʀ ve′), *n.* (*sometimes cap.*) an unsalted French cream cheese made from whole milk and cream. [1895–1900; named after Charles *Gervais* (1830–92), French cheesemaker]

Ger·ze·an (ger′zē ən, gûr′-), *adj.* of or pertaining to the predynastic, Aeneolithic culture of Upper Egypt c3600–3200 B.C., characterized by an emphasis on agriculture and fishing and the use of foreign artifacts and materials. [1920–25; El *Gerzeh* a district in Egypt + -AN]

Ge·samt·kunst·werk (gə zämt′ko͝onst′veʀk), *n. German.* total art work; an artistic creation, as the music dramas of Richard Wagner, that synthesizes the elements of music, drama, spectacle, dance, etc.

ge·schrei (gə shʀā′; *Eng.* gə shrā′, -shrī′), *n. Yiddish.* **1.** a yell; shout. **2.** an uproar. Also, ***ge·shrey′.***

Ge·sell (gə zel′), *n.* **Arnold Lucius,** 1880–1961, U.S. psychologist.

Gesell′ Devel′opmental Sched′ules, a rating system designed to evaluate the cognitive, motor, language, and social development of pre-school-age children by observing their performance on developmental tasks, as reaching, walking, and using sentences. [after A. L. GESELL, who devised them]

ge·sell·schaft (*Ger.* gə zel′shäft′), *n., pl.* **-schaf·ten** (*Ger.* -shäf′tən). (*often cap.*) **1.** an association of individuals for common goals, as for entertainment, or intellectual, cultural, or business purposes. **2.** *Sociol.* a society or group characterized chiefly by formal organization, impersonal relations, the absence of generally held or binding norms, and a detachment from traditional and sentimental concerns, and often tending to be rationalistic and secular in outlook. Cf. **Gemeinschaft.** [1935–40; < G, equiv. to *Geselle* companion + *-schaft* -SHIP]

Ges·ner (ges′nər; *Ger.* ges′nəʀ), *n.* **Kon·rad von** (kon′rad von; *Ger.* kôn′ʀät fən), 1516–65, Swiss naturalist.

ges·ne·ri·ad (ges nēr′ē ad′, jes-), *n.* any of various, chiefly tropical plants of the gesneria family. [1880–85; < NL *Gesneri(a)* a genus name (after K. von GESNER; see -IA) + -AD[1]]

gesne′ria fam′ily (ges nēr′ē ə, jes-), the plant family Gesneriaceae, characterized by herbaceous plants having a basal rosette of usually toothed leaves, tubular two-lipped flowers, and fruit in the form of a berry or capsule, and including the African violet, gloxinia, and streptocarpus. [see GESNERIAD]

Ges·sen (ges′ən), *n. Douay Bible.* Goshen (def. 1).

ges·so (jes′ō), *n., pl.* **-soes. 1.** gypsum or plaster of Paris prepared with glue for use as a surface for painting. **2.** any plasterlike preparation to prepare a surface for painting, gilding, etc. **3.** a prepared surface of plaster or plasterlike material for painting, gilding, etc. [1590–1600; < It < L *gypsum* GYPSUM]

gest (jest), *n.* **1.** a story or tale. **2.** a deed or exploit. **3.** *Archaic.* a metrical romance or history. Also, **geste.** [1250–1300; ME < OF *geste* action, exploit < L *gesta* exploits, neut. pl. ptp. of *gerere* to carry on, perform]

ge·stalt (gə shtält′, -shtôlt′, -stält′, -stôlt′), *n., pl.* **-stalts, -stal·ten** (-shtäl′tn, -shtôl′-, -stäl′-, -stôl′-). (*sometimes cap.*) *Psychol.* **1.** a configuration, pattern, or organized field having specific properties that cannot be derived from the summation of its component parts; a unified whole. **2.** an instance or example of such a unified whole. [1920–25; < G: figure, form, structure]

Gestalt′ psychol′ogy, (*sometimes l.c.*) the theory or doctrine that physiological or psychological phenomena do not occur through the summation of individual elements, as reflexes or sensations, but through gestalts functioning separately or interrelatedly. Also called **configurationism.** [1920–25]

Ge·sta·po (gə stä′pō; *Ger.* gə shtä′pō), *n.* **1.** the German state secret police during the Nazi regime, organized in 1933 and notorious for its brutal methods and operations. *—adj.* **2.** (*sometimes l.c.*) of or resembling the Nazi Gestapo, esp. in the brutal suppression of opposition: *The new regime is using gestapo tactics.* [< G *Ge(heime) Sta(ats)po(lizei)*]

CONCISE ETYMOLOGY KEY: <, descended or borrowed from; >, whence; b., blend of, blended; c., cognate with; cf., compare; deriv., derivative; equiv., equivalent; imit., imitative; obl., oblique; r., replacing; s., stem; sp., spelling, spelled; resp., respelling, respelled; trans., translation; ?, origin unknown; *, unattested; ‡, probably earlier than. See the full key inside the front cover.

ges·tate (jes′tāt), *v.,* **-tat·ed, -tat·ing.** *—v.t.* **1.** to carry in the womb during the period from conception to delivery. **2.** to think of and develop (an idea, opinion, plan, etc.) slowly in the mind. *—v.i.* **3.** to experience the process of gestating offspring. **4.** to develop slowly. [1865–70; < L *gestātus* ptp. of *gestāre* to carry about, carry in the womb, freq. of *gerere* to bear, perform]

ges·ta·tion (je stā′shən), *n.* the process, state, or period of gestating. [1525–35; < L *gestātiōn-* (s. of *gestātiō*), equiv. to *gestāt(us)* (see GESTATE) + *-iōn-* -ION] **—ges·ta′tion·al, ges·ta·tive** (jes′tə tiv, je stā′-), *adj.*

gesta′tional car′rier. See **surrogate mother** (def. 3). Also called **gesta′tional moth′er.** [1985–90]

geste (jest), *n.* gest.

ges·tic (jes′tik), *adj.* pertaining to bodily motions, esp. in dancing. Also, **ges′ti·cal.** [1755–65; obs. *gest* deportment (< MF *geste* < L *gestus* movement of the limbs, performance, equiv. to *ges-,* var. s. of *gerere* (see GEST) + *-tus* suffix of v. action) + -IC]

ges·tic·u·lant (je stik′yə lənt), *adj.* making or tending to make gestures or gesticulations: *a gesticulant speaker.* [1875–80; GESTICUL(ATE) + -ANT]

ges·tic·u·lar (je stik′yə lər), *adj.* pertaining to or characterized by gesticulation. [1840–50; < LL *gesticu-l(us)* (see GESTICULATE) + -AR[1]]

ges·tic·u·late (je stik′yə lāt′), *v.,* **-lat·ed, -lat·ing.** *—v.i.* **1.** to make or use gestures, esp. in an animated or excited manner with or instead of speech. *—v.t.* **2.** to express by gesturing. [1595–1605; < L *gesticulātus* (ptp. of *gesticulārī*), equiv. to LL (assumed in L) *gesticul(us)* gesture (dim. of *gestus;* see GESTIC, -CULE[1]) + *-ātus* -ATE[1]] **—ges·tic′u·la′tive, ges·tic·u·la·to·ry** (je stik′yə lə tôr′ē, -tōr′ē), *adj.* **—ges·tic′u·la′tor,** *n.*
—Syn. 1. gesture, motion, wave, signal.

ges·tic·u·la·tion (je stik′yə lā′shən), *n.* **1.** the act of gesticulating. **2.** an animated or excited gesture. [1595–1605; < L *gesticulātiōn-* (s. of *gesticulātiō*). See GESTICULATE, -ION]

ges·ture (jes′chər), *n., v.,* **-tured, -tur·ing.** *—n.* **1.** a movement or position of the hand, arm, body, head, or face that is expressive of an idea, opinion, emotion, etc.: *the gestures of an orator; a threatening gesture.* **2.** the use of such movements to express thought, emotion, etc. **3.** any action, courtesy, communication, etc., intended for effect or as a formality; considered expression; demonstration: *a gesture of friendship.* *—v.i.* **4.** to make or use a gesture or gestures. *—v.t.* **5.** to express by a gesture or gestures. [1375–1425; late ME < ML *gestūra* mode of action, manner, bearing, equiv. to L *gest(us)* ptp. of *gerere* to bear, carry on, perform + *-ūra* -URE] **—ges′tur·al,** *adj.* **—ges′tur·er,** *n.*

Ge·su·al·do (je′zo͞o äl′dō), *n.* **Don Car·lo** (dôn kär′-lô), **Prince of Ve·no·sa** (ve nô′zä), c1560–1613, Italian composer.

ge·sund·heit (gə zo͝ont′hīt), *interj.* (used to wish good health, esp. to a person who has just sneezed.) [1905–10, *Amer.*; < G: lit., health, equiv. to *gesund* healthy (OHG *gisunt;* see SOUND[2]) + *-heit* -HOOD]

get (get), *v.,* **got** or (*Archaic*) **gat; got** or **got·ten; get·ting,** *n.* *—v.t.* **1.** to receive or come to have possession, use, or enjoyment of: *to get a birthday present; to get a pension.* **2.** to cause to be in one's possession or succeed in having available for one's use or enjoyment; obtain; acquire: *to get a good price; to get oil by drilling; to get information.* **3.** to go after, take hold of, and bring (something) for one's own or for another's purposes; fetch: *Would you get the milk from the refrigerator for me?* **4.** to cause or cause to become, to do, to move, etc., as specified; effect: *to get one's hair cut; to get a person drunk; to get a fire to burn; to get a dog out of a room.* **5.** to communicate or establish communication with over a distance; reach: *You can always get me by telephone.* **6.** to hear or hear clearly: *I didn't get your last name.* **7.** to acquire a mental grasp or command of; learn: *to get a lesson.* **8.** to capture; seize: *Get him before he escapes!* **9.** to receive as a punishment or sentence: *to get a spanking; to get 20 years in jail.* **10.** to prevail on; influence or persuade: *We'll get him to go with us.* **11.** to prepare; make ready: *to get dinner.* **12.** (esp. of animals) to beget. **13.** *Informal.* to affect emotionally: *Her pleas got me.* **14.** to hit, strike, or wound: *The bullet got him in the leg.* **15.** *Informal.* to kill. **16.** *Informal.* to take vengeance on: *I'll get you yet!* **17.** to catch or be afflicted with; come down with or suffer from: *He got malaria while living in the tropics. She gets butterflies before every performance.* **18.** *Informal.* to puzzle; irritate; annoy: *Their silly remarks get me.* **19.** *Informal.* to understand; comprehend: *I don't get the joke. This report may be crystal-clear to a scientist, but I don't get it.* *—v.i.* **20.** to come to a specified place; arrive; reach: *to get home late.* **21.** to succeed, become enabled, or be permitted: *You get to meet a lot of interesting people.* **22.** to become or to cause oneself to become as specified; reach a certain condition: *to get angry; to get sick.* **23.** (used as an auxiliary verb fol. by a past participle to form the passive): *to get married; to get elected; to get hit by a car.* **24.** to succeed in coming, going, arriving at, visiting, etc. (usually fol. by *away, in, into, out, etc.*): *I don't get into town very often.* **25.** to bear, endure, or survive (usually fol. by *through* or *over*): *Can he get through another bad winter?* **26.** to earn money; gain. **27.** *Informal.* to leave promptly; scram: *He told us to get.* **28.** to start or enter upon the action of (fol. by a present participle expressing action): *to get moving; Get rolling.* **29. get about, a.** to move about; be active: *He gets about with difficulty since his illness.* **b.** to become known; spread: *It was supposed to be a secret, but somehow it got about.* **c.** to be socially active: *She's been getting about much more since her family moved to the city.* Also, **get around. 30. get across, a.** to make or become understandable; communicate: *to get a lesson across to students.* **b.** to be convincing about; impress upon others: *The fire chief got across forcefully the fact that turning in a false alarm is a serious offense.* **31. get ahead,** to be successful, as in business or society: *She got ahead by sheer determination.* **32. get ahead of, a.** to move forward of, as in traveling: *The taxi got ahead of her after the light changed.* **b.** to surpass; outdo: *He refused to let anyone get ahead of him in business.* **33. get along, a.** to go away; leave. **b.** See **get on. 34. get around, a.** to circumvent; outwit. **b.** to ingratiate oneself with (someone) through flattery or cajolery. **c.** to travel from place to place; circulate: *I don't get around much anymore.* **d.** See **get about. 35. get at, a.** to reach; touch: *to stretch in order to get at a top shelf.* **b.** to suggest, hint at, or imply; intimate: *What are you getting at?* **c.** to discover; determine: *to get at the root of a problem.* **d.** *Informal.* to influence by surreptitious or illegal means; bribe: *The gangsters couldn't get at the mayor.* **36. get away, a.** to escape; flee: *He tried to get away, but the crowd was too dense.* **b.** to start out; leave: *The racehorses got away from the starting gate.* **37. get away with,** to perpetrate or accomplish without detection or punishment: *Some people lie and cheat and always seem to get away with it.* **38. get back, a.** to come back; return: *When will you get back?* **b.** to recover; regain: *He got back his investment with interest.* **c.** to be revenged: *She waited for a chance to get back at her accuser.* **39. get by, a.** to succeed in going past: *to get by a police barricade.* **b.** to manage to exist, survive, continue in business, etc., in spite of difficulties. **c.** to evade the notice of: *He doesn't let much get by him.* **40. get down, a.** to bring or come down; descend: *The kitten climbed the tree, but then couldn't get down again.* **b.** to concentrate; attend: *to get down to the matter at hand.* **c.** to depress; discourage; fatigue: *Nothing gets me down so much as a rainy day.* **d.** to swallow: *The pill was so large that he couldn't get it down.* **e.** to relax and enjoy oneself completely; be uninhibited in one's enjoyment: *getting down with a bunch of old friends.* **41. get even.** See **even**[1] (def. 22). **42. get going, a.** to begin; act: *They wanted to get going on the construction of the house.* **b.** to increase one's speed; make haste: *If we don't get going, we'll never arrive in time.* **43. get in, a.** to go into a place; enter: *He forgot his key and couldn't get in.* **b.** to arrive; come: *They both got in on the same train.* **c.** to become associated with: *He got in with a bad crowd.* **d.** to be chosen or accepted, as for office, membership, etc.: *As secretary of the club, his friend made sure that he got in.* **e.** to become implicated in: *By embezzling money to pay his gambling debts quickly, he was getting in further and further.* **44. get it,** *Informal.* **a.** to be punished or reprimanded: *You'll get it for breaking that vase!* **b.** to understand or grasp something: *This is just between us, get it?* **45. get it off,** *Slang* (*vulgar*). to experience orgasm. **46. get it on, a.** *Informal.* to work or perform with satisfying harmony or energy or develop a strong rapport, as in music: *a rock group really getting it on with the audience.* **b.** *Slang* (*vulgar*). to have sexual intercourse. **47. get it up,** *Slang* (*vulgar*), to achieve an erection of the penis. **48. get off, a.** to escape the consequences of or punishment for one's actions. **b.** to help (someone) escape punishment: *A good lawyer might get you off.* **c.** to begin a journey; leave: *He got off on the noon flight.* **d.** to leave (a train, plane, etc.); dismount from (a horse); alight. **e.** to tell (a joke); express (an opinion): *The comedian got off a couple of good ones.* **f.** *Informal.* to have the effrontery: *Where does he get off telling me how to behave?* **g.** *Slang* (*vulgar*). to experience orgasm. **h.** to experience or cause to experience a high from or as if from a drug. **i.** to cause to feel pleasure, enthusiasm, or excitement: *a new rock group that gets everyone off.* **49. get off on,** *Slang.* to become enthusiastic about or excited by: *After years of indifference, she's getting off on baseball.* **50. get on** or **along, a.** to make progress; proceed; advance. **b.** to have sufficient means to manage, survive, or fare. **c.** to be on good terms; agree: *She simply can't get on with her brothers.* **d.** to advance in age: *He is getting on in years.* **51. get out, a.** to leave (often fol. by *of*): *Get out of here! We had to get out of the bus at San Antonio.* **b.** to become publicly known: *We mustn't let this story get out.* **c.** to withdraw or retire (often fol. by *of*): *He decided to get out of the dry goods business.* **d.** to produce or complete: *Let's get this work out!* **52. get over, a.** to recover from: *to get over an illness.* **b.** See **get across. 53. get round.** See **get around. 54. get the lead out.** See **lead**[2] (def. 11). **55. get there,** to reach one's goal; succeed: *He wanted to be a millionaire but he died before he got there.* **56. get through, a.** to succeed, as in meeting, reaching, or contacting by telephone (usually fol. by *to*): *I tried to call you last night, but I couldn't get through.* **b.** to complete; finish: *How he ever got through college is a mystery.* **c.** to make oneself understood: *One simply cannot get through to her.* **57. get to, a.** to get in touch or into communication with; contact: *It was too late by the time he got to the authorities.* **b.** *Informal.* to make an impression on; affect: *This music really gets to you.* **c.** to begin: *When he gets to telling stories about the war, there's no stopping him.* **58. get together, a.** to accumulate; gather: *to get together a portfolio of 20 stocks.* **b.** to congregate; meet: *The alumnae chapter gets together twice a year.* **c.** to come to an accord; agree: *They simply couldn't get together on matters of policy.* **59. get up, a.** to sit up or stand; arise. **b.** to rise from bed. **c.** to ascend or mount. **d.** to prepare; arrange; organize: *to get up an exhibit.* **e.** to draw upon; marshal; rouse: *to get up one's courage.* **f.** to acquire a knowledge of. **g.** (to a horse) go! go ahead! go faster! **h.** to dress, as in a costume or disguise: *She got herself up as an astronaut.* **i.** to produce in a specified style, as a book: *It was got up in brown leather with gold endpapers.* **60. has** or **have got, a.** to possess or own; have: *She's got a new car. Have you got the tickets?* **b.** must (fol. by an infinitive): *He's got to get to a doctor right away.* **c.** to suffer from: *Have you got a cold?* *—n.* **61.** an offspring or the total of the offspring, esp. of a male animal: *the get of a stallion.* **62.** a return of a ball, as in tennis, that would normally have resulted in a point for the opponent. **63.** *Brit. Slang.* **a.** something earned, as salary, profits, etc.: *What's your week's get?* **b.** a child born out of wedlock. [1150–1200; (v.) ME *geten* < ON *geta* to obtain, beget; c. OE *-gietan* (>ME *yeten*),

G *-gessen,* in *vergessen* to forget; (n.) ME: something gotten, offspring, deriv. of the v.] **—get′ta·ble, get′a·ble,** *adj.*

—Syn. 1, 2. GET, OBTAIN, ACQUIRE, PROCURE, SECURE imply gaining possession of something. GET may apply to coming into possession in any manner, and either voluntarily or not. OBTAIN suggests putting forth effort to gain possession, and ACQUIRE stresses the possessing after an (often prolonged) effort. PROCURE suggests the method of obtaining, as that of search or choice. SECURE, considered in bad taste as a would-be-elegant substitute for GET, is, however, when used with discrimination, a perfectly proper word. It suggests making possession sure and safe, after obtaining something by competition or the like. **2.** win, gain. **7.** apprehend, grasp. **10.** induce, dispose. **12.** engender.

—Usage. For nearly 400 years, forms of GET have been used with a following past participle to form the passive voice: *She got engaged when she was 19. He won't get accepted with those grades.* This use of GET rather than of forms of *to be* in the passive is found today chiefly in speech and informal writing.

In British English GOT is the regular past participle of GET, and GOTTEN survives only in a few set phrases, such as *ill-gotten gains.* In American English GOTTEN, although occasionally criticized, is an alternative standard past participle in most senses, especially in the senses "to receive" or "to acquire": *I have gotten* (or *got*) *all that I ever hoped for.*

HAVE or HAS GOT in the sense "must" has been in use since the early 19th century; often the HAVE or HAS is contracted: *You've got to carry your passport at all times.* The use of HAVE (or HAS) GOT in the sense of "to possess" goes back to the 15th century; it is also frequently contracted: *She's got a master's degree in biology.* These uses are occasionally criticized as redundant on the grounds that HAVE alone expresses the meaning adequately, but they are well established and fully standard in all varieties of speech and writing. In some contexts in American English, substituting GOTTEN for GOT produces a change in meaning: *She's got* (possesses) *a new job. She's gotten* (has aquired) *a new job. He's got to* (must) *attend the wedding. He's gotten to* (has been allowed or enabled to) *attend. The children have got* (are suffering from) *the measles. The children have gotten* (have caught) *the measles.* The use of GOT without HAVE or HAS to mean "must" (*I got to buy a new suit*) is characteristic of the most relaxed, informal speech and does not occur in edited writing except in representations of speech. GOTTA is a pronunciation spelling representing this use.

—Pronunciation. The pronunciation (git) for GET has existed since the 16th century. The same change is exhibited in (kin) for CAN and (yit) for YET. The pronunciation (git) is not regional and occurs in all parts of the country. It is most common as an unstressed syllable: *Let's get going!* (lets′ git gō′ing). In educated speech the pronunciation (git) in stressed syllables is rare and sometimes criticized. When GET is an imperative meaning "leave immediately," the pronunciation is usually facetious: *Now get!* (nou′ git′).

get (get), *n., pl.* **git·tin** (*Seph.* gē tēn′; *Ashk.* git′in), **gi·tim** (*Seph.* gē tēm′; *Ashk.* git′im). *Hebrew.* **1.** a legal document, executed by a rabbi or Jewish court of law, dissolving the marriage bond between husband and wife. **2.** a divorce granted in accordance with Jewish law.

ge·ta (get′ə; *Japn.* ge′tä), *n., pl.* **-ta, -tas.** a traditional Japanese wooden clog that is worn outdoors, with a thong that passes between the first two toes and with two transverse supports on the bottom of the sole. [1880–85; < Japn, perh. by ellipsis from *shita-geta,* equiv. to *shita* below, under + *-geta,* comb. form of *keta* slat, lath; or *ge* (< MChin, equiv. to Chin *xià* below) + Japn (*i*)*ta* board]

get·a·way (get′ə wā′), *n.* **1.** a getting away or fleeing; an escape. **2.** the start of a race: *a fast getaway.* **3.** a place where one escapes for relaxation, vacation, etc., or a period of time for such recreation: *a little seaside getaway; a two-week getaway in the Bahamas.* **—***adj.* **4.** used as a means of escape or fleeing: *a stolen getaway car.* **5.** used for occasional relaxation, retreat, or reclusion: *a weekend getaway house.* [1850–55; n. use of v. phrase *get away*]

Geth·sem·a·ne (geth sem′ə nē), *n.* **1.** a garden east of Jerusalem, near the brook of Kedron: scene of Jesus' agony and betrayal. Matt. 26:36. **2.** (*l.c.*) a scene or occasion of suffering; calvary. **—Geth·se·man·ic, geth·se·man·ic** (geth′sə man′ik), *adj.*

Gethsem′ane cheese′. See **Trappist cheese.**

get-out (get′out′), *n.* **1.** *Com.* the break-even point. **2.** *Chiefly Brit.* a method or maneuver used to escape a difficult or embarrassing situation; cop-out: *The scoundrel has used that get-out once too often.* **3. as all get-out,** *Informal.* in the extreme; to the utmost degree: *Once his mind is made up, he can be stubborn as all get-out.* [1880–85; n. use of v. phrase *get out*]

get·ter (get′ər), *n.* **1.** a person or thing that gets. **2.** any substance introduced into a partial vacuum, as the interior of a vacuum tube or an incandescent lamp, to combine chemically with the residual gas in order to increase the vacuum. **3.** *Chiefly Canadian.* poisoned bait used to exterminate wolves, gophers, and other pests from farm areas. [1325–75; ME; see GET, -ER[1]]

get·ter·ing (get′ər ing), *n.* the removal of residual gas from a partial vacuum by use of a getter. [1920–25; GETTER + -ING[1]]

get-to·geth·er (get′tə geth′ər), *n.* **1.** an informal and usually small social gathering. **2.** a meeting or conference. [1910–15; n. use of v. phrase *get together*]

get-tough (get′tuf′), *adj.* characterized by firmness, determination, aggressiveness, or severity: *a get-tough policy.* [1955–60]

Get·ty (get′ē), *n.* **J(ean) Paul,** 1892–1976, U.S. oil magnate and art collector.

Get·tys·burg (get′iz bûrg′), *n.* a borough in S Pennsylvania: Confederate forces defeated in a crucial battle of the Civil War fought near here on July 1–3, 1863; national cemetery and military park. 7194.

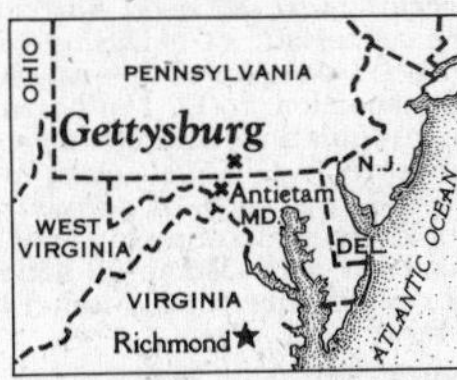

Get′tysburg Address′, the notable short speech made by President Lincoln on November 19, 1863, at the dedication of the national cemetery at Gettysburg, Pa.

get-up (get′up′), *n.* **1.** getup. **2.** get-up-and-go.

get·up (get′up′), *n. Informal.* **1.** costume; outfit: *Everyone will stare at you if you wear that getup.* **2.** arrangement or format; style: *the getup of a new cookbook.* Also, **get-up.** [1825–35; n. use of v. phrase *get up*]

get-up-and-go (get′up′ən gō′), *n.* energy, drive, and enthusiasm. [1905–10]

get-well (get′wel′), *adj.* conveying wishes for one's recovery, as from an illness: *a get-well card.*

Getz (gets), *n.* **Stan(ley),** 1927–91, U.S. jazz saxophonist.

Geu·lincx (*Flem.* gœ′lingks), *n.* **Arnold,** 1624?–69, Belgian philosopher.

ge·um (jē′əm), *n.* any plant of the genus *Geum,* comprising the avens. [1540–50; < NL; L *gaeum, geum* (in Pliny) a plant of uncert. identity]

GeV, gigaelectron volt. Also, **Gev**

gew·gaw (gyo͞o′gô, go͞o′-), *n.* something gaudy and useless; trinket; bauble. Also, **geegaw.** [1175–1225; ME *giuegaue;* gradational compound of uncert. orig.; perh. akin to MF, F *gogo* (see À GOGO)] **—gew′gawed,** *adj.*

Ge·würz·tra·mi·ner (gə vo͝orts′trə mē′nər; *Ger.* gə vʏʀts′trä mē′nəʀ), *n.* **1.** a type of white grape used in winemaking. **2.** a dry white table wine of Germany, the Alsace region of France, and northern California. [< G, equiv. to *Gewürz* spice, seasoning (deriv. of *Würze* spice; see WORT[1]) + *Traminer* a wine and grape variety of the South Tirol, after *Tramin* a wine-growing district there; see -ER[1]]

gey (gā), *adv. Scot.* considerably; very. [1805–15; var. of GAY]

gey·ser (gī′zər, -sər *for 1, 3;* gē′zər *for 2*), *n.* **1.** a hot spring that intermittently sends up fountainlike jets of water and steam into the air. **2.** *Brit. Informal.* a hot-water heater, as for a bath. **—***v.i.* **3.** to spew forth as or like a geyser: *the kettle geysering all over the stove.* [1755–65; < Icel *Geysir* name of a hot spring in Iceland, lit., gusher, deriv. of *geysa* to gush] **—gey′ser·al, gey′·ser·ic,** *adj.*

gey′ser ba′sin, an area containing a group of geysers.

gey·ser·ite (gī′zə rīt′, -sə-), *n. Petrol.* a variety of siliceous sinter deposited about the orifices of geysers and hot springs. [1805–15; GEYSER + -ITE[1]]

Ge·zer (gē′zər), *n.* an ancient Canaanite town, NW of Jerusalem.

Ge·zi·ra (jə zēr′ə), *n.* a region in central Sudan, S of Khartoum, between the Blue Nile and the White Nile: a former province.

G.F.T.U., General Federation of Trade Unions.

GG, 1. gamma globulin. **2.** great gross.

GGR, great gross.

GH, See **growth hormone.**

GHA, Greenwich hour angle.

ghain (ʀän), *n.* the nineteenth letter of the Arabic alphabet. [< Ar *ghayn*]

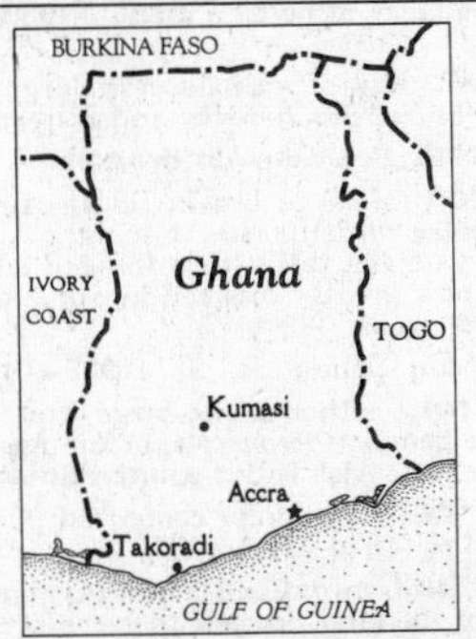

Gha·na (gä′nə, gan′ə), *n.* **1.** a republic in West Africa comprising the former colonies of the Gold Coast and Ashanti, the protectorate of the Northern Territories, and the U.N. trusteeship of British Togoland: member of the Commonwealth of Nations since 1957. 8,559,313; 91,843 sq. mi. (237,873 sq. km). *Cap.:* Accra. **2. Kingdom of,** a medieval W African empire extending from near the Atlantic coast almost to Timbuktu; flourished from about the 9th to 12th centuries. **—Gha·na·ian, Gha·ni·an** (gä′nē ən, gan′ē-), *n., adj.*

Ghar·da·ïa (gär dä′yə), *n.* a city in N Algeria. 30,167.

gha·ri·al (gur′ē əl), *n.* gavial.

ghar·ry (gar′ē), *n., pl.* **-ries.** a horse-drawn cab or carriage used in India and Egypt. Also, **ghar′ri.** [1800–10; < Hindi *gāṛī*]

ghast (gast, gäst), *adj. Archaic.* ghastly. [1350–1400; ME *gast* afraid, orig. ptp. of *gasten* GAST; cf. AGHAST]

ghast·ful (gast′fəl, gäst′-), *adj. Obs.* frightful. [1350–1400; ME *gastful;* see GHAST, -FUL]

ghast·ly (gast′lē, gäst′-), *adj.,* **-li·er, -li·est,** *adv.* **—***adj.* **1.** shockingly frightful or dreadful; horrible: *a ghastly murder.* **2.** resembling a ghost, esp. in being very pale: *a ghastly look to his face.* **3.** terrible; very bad: *a ghastly error.* **—***adv.* **4.** Also, **ghast′li·ly, ghast′i·ly.** in a ghastly manner; horribly; terribly. **5.** with a deathlike quality. [1275–1325; ME *gastly;* see GHAST, -LY] **—ghast′li·ness,** *n.*

—Syn. 2. deathlike, pallid, cadaverous.

ghat (gôt, got), *n.* (in India) **1.** a wide set of steps descending to a river, esp. a river used for bathing. **2.** a mountain pass. **3.** a mountain range or escarpment. Also, **ghaut.** [1595–1605; < Hindi *ghāṭ* < Skt *ghaṭṭa*]

Ghats (gôts, gots), *n.* (*used with a singular v.*) **1.** See **Eastern Ghats. 2.** See **Western Ghats.**

gha·zi (gä′zē), *n., pl.* **-zis. 1.** a Muslim soldier, esp. one fighting against non-Muslims. **2.** (*cap.*) a title given in Turkey to a victorious sultan, general, etc. [1745–55; < Ar *ghāzī*]

Ghaz·za·li (ga zä′lē), *n.* **Al-** (al), 1058–1111, Arab philosopher. Also, **Gha·za′li.** Also called **Al-Gazel.**

Ghe·ber (gā′bər, gē′bər), *n.* Gabar.

ghee (gē), *n.* a kind of liquid butter, used esp. in the cooking of India, made from the milk of cows or buffaloes and clarified by boiling. [1655–65; < Hindi *ghī*]

Ghel·de·rode (*Fr.* gel də ʀōd′), *n.* **Mi·chel de** (*Fr.* mē-shel′ də). See **de Ghelderode, Michel.**

Ghent (gent), *n.* a port in NW Belgium, at the confluence of the Scheldt and Lys rivers: treaty 1814. 142,551. French, **Gand.** Flemish, **Gent.**

Gheor·ghiu-Dej (gyôʀ′gyo͞o dezh′), *n.* **Gheor·ghe** (gyôʀ′ge), 1901–65, Rumanian statesman: premier 1952–55; president of the state council 1961–65.

gher·kin (gûr′kin), *n.* **1.** the small, immature fruit of a variety of cucumber, used in pickling. **2.** Also called **bur gherkin, West Indian gherkin.** the small, spiny fruit of a tropical vine, *Cucumis anguria,* of the gourd family, used in pickling. **3.** the plant yielding this fruit. **4.** a small pickle, esp. one made from this fruit. [1655–65; < D *gurken,* pl. of *gurk* (G *Gurke*) < Slav; cf. Pol *ogórek,* Czech *okurka* << Pers]

ghet·to (get′ō), *n., pl.* **-tos, -toes. 1.** a section of a city, esp. a thickly populated slum area, inhabited predominantly by members of an ethnic or other minority group, often as a result of social or economic restrictions, pressures, or hardships. **2.** (formerly, in most European countries) a section of a city in which all Jews were required to live. **3.** a section predominantly inhabited by Jews. **4.** any mode of living, working, etc., that results from stereotyping or biased treatment: *job ghettos for women; ghettos for the elderly.* [1605–15; < It, orig. the name of an island near Venice where Jews were forced to reside in the 16th century < Venetian, lit., foundry for artillery (giving the island its name), n. deriv. of *ghettare* to throw < VL **jectāre;* see JET[1]]

ghet′to blast′er, *Slang.* a large, powerful portable radio, esp. as carried and played by a pedestrian or used outdoors in an urban area.

ghet·to·ize (get′ō īz′), *v.t., v.i.,* **-ized, -iz·ing.** to place or collect in a ghetto: *New immigrants still tended to ghettoize in the cities.* Also, *esp. Brit.,* **ghet′to·ise′.** [1935–40; GHETTO + -IZE] **—ghet′to·i·za′tion,** *n.*

Ghib·el·line (gib′ə lin, -lēn′), *n.* **1.** a member of the aristocratic party in medieval Italy and Germany that supported the claims of the German emperors against the papacy: politically opposed to the Guelphs. **—***adj.* **2.** of or pertaining to the Ghibellines. [1565–75; < It *Ghibellino* < MHG **wībeling-* (G *Waiblingen*) a Hohenstaufen estate in Germany] **—Ghib′el·lin·ism,** *n.*

Ghi·ber·ti (gē beʀ′tē), *n.* **Lo·ren·zo** (lô ʀen′tsô), 1378–1455, Florentine sculptor, goldsmith, and painter.

ghib·li (gib′lē), *n.* a hot dust-bearing wind of the North African desert. [< dial. Ar *gibli* south wind, akin to Ar *qibli* lit., southern]

ghil·lie (gil′ē), *n.* a low-cut, tongueless shoe with loops instead of eyelets for the laces, which cross the instep and are sometimes tied around the ankle. Also, **gillie.** [1590–1600; see GILLIE; appar. a type of shoe orig. worn by Scottish hunting guides]

Ghior·des (gyôr′dəs, gôr′-), *n.* a Turkish rug characterized by an uneven pile produced by the Ghiordes knot. [1895–1900; var. sp. of *Gördes,* town in Turkey]

Ghior′des knot′, a hand-tied knot, used in rug weaving, in which the parallel ends of looped yarn alternate with two threads of warp, producing an uneven pile effect. Also called **Turkish knot.** Cf. **Sehna knot.** [1895–1900]

Ghir·lan·da·io (gēʀ′län dä′yô), *n.* (*Domenico di Tommaso Curradi di Doffo Bigordi*) 1449–94, Italian painter. Also, **Ghir·lan·da·jo** (gēʀ′län dä′yô).

ghirsh (gûrsh), *n.* qirsh.

ghost (gōst), *n.* **1.** the soul of a dead person, a disembodied spirit imagined, usually as a vague, shadowy or evanescent form, as wandering among or haunting living persons. **2.** a mere shadow or semblance; a trace: *He's a*

CONCISE PRONUNCIATION KEY: act, cāpe, dâre, pärt; set, ēqual; *if,* ice; ox, ōver, ôrder, oil, bo͝ok, bo͞ot, out; up, ûrge; child; sing; shoe; thin, *th*at; zh as in *treasure.* ə = *a* as in *alone, e* as in *system, i* as in *easily, o* as in *gallop, u* as in *circus;* ᵊ as in *fire* (fīᵊr), *hour* (ouᵊr). l and n can serve as syllabic consonants, as in *cradle* (ʀʀād′l), and *button* (but′n). See the full key inside the front cover.

ghost of his former self. **3.** a remote possibility: *He hasn't a ghost of a chance.* **4.** (*sometimes cap.*) a spiritual being. **5.** the principle of life; soul; spirit. **6.** *Informal.* See **ghost writer. 7.** a secondary image, esp. one appearing on a television screen as a white shadow, caused by poor or double reception or by a defect in the receiver. **8.** Also called **ghost image.** *Photog.* a faint secondary or out-of-focus image in a photographic print or negative resulting from reflections within the camera lens. **9.** an oral word game in which each player in rotation adds a letter to those supplied by preceding players, the object being to avoid ending a word. **10.** *Optics.* a series of false spectral lines produced by a diffraction grating with unevenly spaced lines. **11.** *Metalworking.* a streak appearing on a freshly machined piece of steel containing impurities. **12.** a red blood cell having no hemoglobin. **13.** a fictitious employee, business, etc., fabricated esp. for the purpose of manipulating funds or avoiding taxes: *Investigation showed a payroll full of ghosts.* **14. give up the ghost, a.** to die. **b.** to cease to function or exist. —*v.t.* **15.** to ghostwrite (a book, speech, etc.). **16.** to haunt. **17.** *Engraving.* to lighten the background of (a photograph) before engraving. —*v.i.* **18.** to ghostwrite. **19.** to go about or move like a ghost. **20.** (of a sailing vessel) to move when there is no perceptible wind. **21.** to pay people for work not performed, esp. as a way of manipulating funds. —*adj.* **22.** fabricated for purposes of deception or fraud: *We were making contributions to a ghost company.* [bef. 900; ME *goost* (n.), OE *gāst;* c. G *Geist* spirit] —**ghost′i·ly,** *adv.* —**ghost′like′,** *adj.*

—**Syn. 1.** apparition, phantom, phantasm, wraith, revenant; shade, spook. GHOST, SPECTER, SPIRIT all refer to the disembodied soul of a person. A GHOST is the soul or spirit of a deceased person, which appears or otherwise makes its presence known to the living: *the ghost of a drowned child.* A SPECTER is a ghost or apparition of more or less weird, unearthly, or terrifying aspect: *a frightening specter.* SPIRIT is often interchangeable with GHOST but may mean a supernatural being, usually with an indication of good or malign intent toward human beings: *the spirit of a friend; an evil spirit.*

ghost′ crab′, a whitish crab, *Ocypode albicans,* of sandy beaches from the eastern coast of the U.S. to Brazil. [1905–10, *Amer.*]

ghost′ dance′, a ritual dance intended to establish communion with the dead, esp. such a dance as performed by various messianic western American Indian cults in the late 19th century. [1885–90, *Amer.*]

ghost·fish (gōst′fish′), *n., pl.* **-fish·es,** (*esp. collectively*) **-fish.** wrymouth. [GHOST + FISH]

ghost′ im′age, *Photog.* ghost (def. 8). [1900–05]

ghost·ing (gō′sting), *n. Television.* the appearance of multiple images, or ghosts, on a television screen. Cf. **ghost** (def. 7) [GHOST + -ING[1]]

ghost·ly (gōst′lē), *adj.,* **-li·er, -li·est. 1.** of, characteristic of, or resembling a ghost; phantasmal; spectral. **2.** *Literary.* spiritual. [bef. 900; ME; OE *gāstlic.* See GHOST, -LY] —**ghost′li·ness,** *n.*

—**Syn. 1.** wraithlike, phantom, ghostlike, unearthly.

ghost′ moth′, swift (def. 9). [1825–35]

Ghosts (gōsts), *n.* a play (1881) by Henrik Ibsen.

ghost′ shrimp′, a shrimplike crustacean of the genus *Callianassa,* of the Pacific coast of North America, having a pinkish, transparent body.

ghost′ sto′ry, a tale in which such elements as ghostly visitations and supernatural intervention are used to further the plot and a chilling, suspenseful atmosphere. [1810–20]

ghost′ town′, a town permanently abandoned by its inhabitants, as because of a business decline or because a nearby mine has been worked out. [1870–75]

ghost·weed (gōst′wēd′), *n.* snow-on-the-mountain.

ghost′ word′, a word that has come into existence by error rather than by normal linguistic transmission, as through the mistaken reading of a manuscript, a scribal error, or a misprint. [1885–90]

ghost·write (gōst′rīt′), *v.t., v.i.,* **-wrote, -writ·ten, writ·ing.** to write as a ghost writer. [1925–30; back formation from GHOST WRITER]

ghost′ writ′er, a person who writes one or numerous speeches, books, articles, etc., for another person who is named as or presumed to be the author. Also, **ghost′·writ′er.** [1895–1900, *Amer.*]

ghoul (go͞ol), *n.* **1.** an evil demon, originally of Oriental legend, supposed to feed on human beings, and especially to rob graves, prey on corpses, etc. **2.** a grave robber. **3.** a person who revels in what is revolting. [1780–90; < Ar *ghūl*]

ghoul·ish (go͞o′lish), *adj.* **1.** strangely diabolical or cruel; monstrous: *a ghoulish and questionable sense of humor.* **2.** showing fascination with death, disease, maiming, etc.; morbid: *ghoulish curiosity.* **3.** of, pertaining to, or like a ghoul or ghouls. [1835–45; GHOUL + -ISH] —**ghoul′ish·ly,** *adv.* —**ghoul′ish·ness,** *n.*

GHQ, *Mil.* general headquarters. Also, **G.H.Q.**

GHz, gigahertz; gigahertzes.

gi (gē), *n.* a lightweight, two-piece, usually white garment worn by barefooted martial-arts participants, consisting of loose-fitting pants and a wraparound jacket with cloth belt. Also, **gie.** [1970–75; shortening of Japn *jūdō-gi* jujitsu garb, equiv. to *jūdō* JUDO + *-gi,* comb. form of *ki* to wear]

GI (jē′ī′), *n., pl.* **GI's** or **GIs,** *adj., v.,* **GI'd, GI'ing.** —*n.* **1.** a member or former member of the U.S. armed forces, esp. an enlisted soldier. —*adj.* **2.** rigidly adhering to military regulations and practices; regimented; spit-and-polish: *a platoon leader who tried to be more GI than anyone else.* **3.** of a standardized style or type issued by the U.S. armed forces: *GI shoes; GI blankets.* **4.** conforming to the regulations or practices of the U.S. armed forces: *Every recruit must get a GI haircut.* **5.** of, pertaining to, or characteristic of a U.S. enlisted person: *a typical peacetime GI complaint.* —*v.t.* **6.** to clean in preparation for inspection: *to GI the barracks.* —*v.i.* **7.** to follow military regulations and customs closely; shape up: *You'd better learn to GI if you want to be promoted.* Also, **G.I.** [1915–20; orig. abbr. of *galvanized iron,* used in U.S. Army bookkeeping in entering articles (e.g., trash cans) made of it; later extended to all articles issued (as an assumed abbrev. of *government issue*) and finally to soldiers themselves]

Gi, gilbert; gilberts.

gi., gill; gills.

G.I., 1. galvanized iron. **2.** gastrointestinal. **3.** general issue. **4.** government issue. Also, **GI, g.i.**

Gia·co·met·ti (jä′kə met′ē; *It.* jä′kô met′tē), *n.* **Alber·to** (al bâr′tō; *It.* äl beʀ′tô), 1901–66, Swiss sculptor and painter.

Giae·ver (yā′vər), *n.* **I·var** (ē′vär), born 1929, U.S. physicist, born in Norway: Nobel prize 1973.

gi·ant (jī′ənt), *n.* **1.** (in folklore) a being with human form but superhuman size, strength, etc. **2.** a person or thing of unusually great size, power, importance, etc.; major figure; legend: *a giant in her field; an intellectual giant.* **3.** (*often cap.*) *Class. Myth.* any of the Gigantes. **4.** *Mining.* monitor (def. 12). **5.** *Astron.* See **giant star.** —*adj.* **6.** unusually large, great, or strong; gigantic; huge. **7.** greater or more eminent than others. [1250–1300; ME *geant* < OF < L *gigant-* (s. of *gigās*) < Gk *Gigās;* r. OE *gigant* < L, as above] —**gi′ant·like′,** *adj.*

gi′ant ant′eater, a large, narrow-bodied anteater, *Myrmecophaga tridactyla,* having a long, tapering snout and extensile tongue, powerful front claws, and a shaggy gray coat marked with a conspicuous black band.

giant anteater, *Myrmecophaga tridactyla,* 2 ft. (0.6 m) high at shoulder; head and body 4 ft. (1.2 m); tail about 2 ft. (0.6 m)

gi′ant cane′. See under **cane** (def. 5).

gi′ant clam′, any of several huge clams of the family Tridacnidae, inhabiting the shallow waters of coral reefs in the tropical Indo-Pacific, as *Tridacna gigas:* some may weigh more than 500 lb. (225 kg). [1945–50]

gi′ant crab′, a large, deep-water Japanese spider crab, *Macrocheira kaempferi,* sometimes measuring 11 ft. (3.4 m) across from claw to claw.

gi·ant·ess (jī′ən tis), *n.* **1.** an imaginary female being of human form but superhuman size, strength, etc. **2.** any very large woman. [1350–1400; ME *geauntesse* < OF. See GIANT, -ESS]

—**Usage.** See **-ess.**

gi′ant fen′nel. See under **fennel** (def. 3). [1880–85]

gi′ant ful′mar. See **giant petrel.**

gi′ant gar′lic, 1. an Asian plant, *Allium giganteum,* of the amaryllis family, having a large, dense, round cluster of lilac-colored flowers, grown as an ornamental. **2.** rocambole.

gi′ant granadil′la. See under **granadilla** (def. 1).

gi′ant hog′weed, a tall plant, *Heracleum mantegazzianum,* of the parsley family, native to Russia and now naturalized in the U.S., having very large leaves and broad, white flower heads somewhat resembling Queen Anne's lace: can cause an allergic rash when touched by susceptible persons.

gi′ant hor′net. See under **hornet.**

gi·ant·ism (jī′ən tiz′əm), *n.* **1.** *Pathol.* gigantism. **2.** the state or quality of being a giant. [1630–40; GIANT + -ISM]

gi′ant kelp′, any of various very large kelps of the genera *Laminaria, Macrocystis,* and *Nereocystis.*

gi′ant liz′ard. See **Komodo dragon.**

gi′ant ot′ter, a large brown South American river otter, *Pteronura brasiliensis,* having a creamy chest patch and a long flat tail with a flanged border, hunted for its hide: now greatly reduced in number and endangered in some areas. [1970–75]

gi′ant pan′da, panda (def. 2). [1935–40]

gi′ant pet′rel, either of two large white or brownish petrels of the genus *Macronectes,* of the Antarctic Ocean and adjacent seas. Also called **giant fulmar.**

gi′ant pow′der, dynamite composed of nitroglycerin and kieselguhr. [1870–75, *Amer.*]

gi′ant puff′ball, a puffball, *Calvatia gigantea,* that is the largest of its kind, known to have grown to more than 5 ft. (1.6 m) in circumference.

gi′ant rag′weed. See under **ragweed.**

gi′ant reed′, a tall grass, *Arundo donax,* of southern Europe, having woody stems and a spirelike flower cluster often 2 ft. (60 cm) long. [1895–1900]

gi′ant scal′lop. See **sea scallop.**

Gi′ant's Cause′way, a large body of basalt, unusual in displaying perfect columnar jointing, exposed on a promontory on the northern coast of Northern Ireland. [1770–80]

gi′ant schnau′zer, one of a German breed of large working dogs, resembling a larger and more powerful version of the standard schnauzer, having a pepper-and-salt or pure black, wiry coat, bushy eyebrows and beard, and a docked tail set moderately high, originally developed as a cattle herder but now often used in police work. [1930–35]

gi′ant sequoi′a. See **big tree.** [1930–35]

gi′ant silk′worm moth′, any silkworm moth of the family Saturniidae.

gi′ant sla′lom, *Skiing.* a slalom race in which the course has more gates and is longer and steeper than that in a regular slalom. [1950–55]

gi′ant snail′, any land snail of the genus *Achatina* and related genera, mostly of tropical Africa, having shells up to 9 in. (23 cm) high.

gi′ant squid′, any squid of the genus *Architeuthis,* inhabiting deep ocean bottoms and sometimes attaining an arm span of 65 ft. (20 m) or more. [1935–40]

gi′ant star′, a star having a diameter of from 10 to 100 times that of the sun, as Arcturus or Aldebaran. Also, **giant.** Cf. **supergiant star.** [1910–15]

gi′ant steps′, 1. a children's game in which a leader calls upon individual players to advance toward him or her in a given number and variety of steps, the object being for one person to tag the leader and for all of them to run back to the starting line without being caught by the leader. Any player who is caught becomes the leader. **2. giant step,** the longest step that a player is capable of making in this game. Cf. **baby step, umbrella step.**

gi′ant sun′flower, a composite plant, *Helianthus giganteus,* of eastern North America, growing nearly 12 ft. (4 m) high and having very large yellow flower heads. Also called **tall sunflower.**

gi′ant tor′toise, any of several large tortoises of the genus *Geochelone,* of the Galápagos Islands and islands near Madagascar: some are endangered. [1910–15]

gi′ant wa′ter bug′. See under **water bug.**

giaour (jour), *n. Turkish.* an unbeliever; a non-Muslim, esp. a Christian. [1555–65; earlier *gower, gour* < Turk *gâvur* < Pers *gaur,* var. of *gabr* Zoroastrian, non-Muslim; sp. *giaour* < F, with *gi-* repr. Turk palatalized *g,* later taken as sp. for *j*]

gi·ar·di·a (jē är′dē ə, jär′-), *n.* any flagellate of the genus *Giardia,* parasitic in the intestines of vertebrates. [< NL, named after Alfred M. *Giard* (d. 1908), French biologist; see -IA]

gi·ar·di·a·sis (jē′är dī′ə sis, jär-), *n. Pathol.* an intestinal disorder characterized by abdominal discomfort and prolonged, intermittent diarrhea, caused by the protozoan *Giardia lamblia* and contracted by drinking untreated water, as of streams or ponds, contaminated with the feces of infected animals. Also called **beaver fever.** [1915–20; see GIARDIA, -ASIS]

Gi·auque (jē ōk′), *n.* **William Francis,** 1895–1982, U.S. chemist: Nobel prize 1949.

gib[1] (gib), *n., v.,* **gibbed, gib·bing.** —*n.* **1.** a hooked prolongation that develops during the spawning season on the lower jaw of a male salmon or trout. **2.** *Mach.* **a.** a thin, wedgelike strip of metal for controlling the area in which a moving part, as the table of a milling machine, slides. **b.** a keylike part having a head at each end, used with a matching cotter as a fastening. See diag. under **exploded view. 3.** (in carpentry or ironwork) a heavy metal strap for fastening two members together. —*v.t.* **4.** to fasten (parts) together by means of a gib. [1555–65; orig. uncert.]

gib[2] (gib), *n.* **1.** a cat, esp. a male cat. **2.** a castrated cat. [1350–1400; ME *gib(be),* short for *Gilbert* proper name]

Gib., Gibraltar.

gibbed (gibd), *adj. Vet. Med.* (of a cat) castrated. [1625–35; GIB[2] + -ED[2]]

gib·ber (jib′ər, gib′-), *v.i.* **1.** to speak inarticulately or meaninglessly. **2.** to speak foolishly; chatter. —*n.* **3.** gibbering utterance. [1595–1605; orig. uncert.; perh. freq. of *gib* (obs.) to caterwaul (see GIB[2]); sense and pronunciation influenced by assoc. with JABBER]

gib′ber·el′lic ac′id (jib′ə rel′ik, jib′-), a gibberellin $C_{18}H_{21}O_4COOH$, produced as a metabolite by the fungus *Gibberella fujikuroi,* used as a stimulator of plant growth. [1950–55; < NL *Gibberell(a)* (L *gibber* hump + *-ella* -ELLA) + -IC]

gib·ber·el·lin (jib′ə rel′in), *n. Biochem.* any of a class of growth hormones occurring in fungi and plants. [1935–40; < NL *Gibberell(a)* (see GIBBERELLIC ACID) + -IN[2]]

gib·ber·ish (jib′ər ish, gib′-), *n.* **1.** meaningless or unintelligible talk or writing. **2.** talk or writing containing many obscure, pretentious, or technical words. [1545–55; appar. GIBBER + -ISH[1], on the model of language names so formed]

—**Syn. 1.** nonsense, foolishness, babble, gabble, drivel, gobbledegook.

gib·bet (jib′it), *n., v.,* **-bet·ed, -bet·ing.** —*n.* **1.** a gallows with a projecting arm at the top, from which the bodies of criminals were formerly hung in chains and left suspended after execution. —*v.t.* **2.** to hang on a gibbet. **3.** to put to death by hanging on a gibbet. **4.** to hold up to public scorn. [1175–1225; ME < OF *gibet* (earlier, staff or cudgel), dim. of *gibe* staff, club]

gib·ble-gab·ble (gib′əl gab′əl), *n., v.,* **-bled, -bling.** —*n.* **1.** senseless chatter. —*v.i.* **2.** to engage in gibble-gabble. [1590–1600; gradational compound from GABBLE] —**gib′ble-gab′bler,** *n.*

gib·bon (gib′ən), *n.* any small, slender, long-armed arboreal anthropoid ape of the genus *Hylobates,* of the East Indies and southern Asia: all gibbon species are reduced in number and some are very rare. See illus. on next page. [1760–70; < F, name of uncert. orig. used by Buffon]

gibbon,
Hylobates lar,
length 2 ft. (0.6 m)

Gib•bon (gib′ən), *n.* **Edward,** 1737–94, English historian.

Gib•bons (gib′ənz), *n.* **1. Grin•ling** (grin′ling), 1648–1720, English woodcarver and sculptor, born in the Netherlands. **2. Orlando,** 1583–1625, English composer.

gib•bos•i•ty (gi bos′i tē), *n.* **1.** the state of being gibbous. **2.** a protuberance or swelling. [1350–1400; ME < MF *gibbosite* < ML *gibbōsitāt-* (s. of *gibbōsitās*). See GIBBOUS, -ITY]

gib•bous (gib′əs), *adj.* **1.** *Astron.* (of a heavenly body) convex at both edges, as the moon when more than half full. See diag. under **moon. 2.** humpbacked. Also, **gib•bose** (gib′ōs). [1350–1400; ME < L *gibbōsus* humped, equiv. to *gibb(a)* hump + *-ōsus* -OUS] **—gib′bous•ly, gib′bose•ly,** *adv.* **—gib′bous•ness, gib′bose•ness,** *n.*

Gibbs (gibz), *n.* **1. James,** 1682–1754, Scottish architect and author. **2. Josiah Willard,** 1839–1903, U.S. physicist. **3. Oliver Wol•cott** (wo͝ol′kət), 1822–1908, U.S. chemist and educator. **4. Sir Philip,** 1877–1962, English journalist and writer.

Gibbs′ func′tion, the thermodynamic function of a system that is equal to its enthalpy minus the product of its absolute temperture and entropy: a decrease in the function is equal to the maximum amount of work available exclusive of that due to pressure times volume change during a reversible, isothermal, isobaric process. Also called **Gibbs′ free′ en′ergy, thermodynamic potential.** [named after J. W. GIBBS]

gibbs•ite (gib′zīt), *n.* a mineral, hydrated aluminum oxide, $Al_2O_3{\cdot}3H_2O$, occurring in whitish or grayish crystals and masses: an important constituent of bauxite ore. Also called **hydrargillite.** [1815–25; named after George *Gibbs* (d. 1833), American mineralogist; see -ITE[1]]

gibe[1] (jīb), *v.,* **gibed, gib•ing,** *n.* —*v.i.* **1.** to utter mocking or scoffing words; jeer. —*v.t.,* **2.** to taunt; deride. —*n.* **3.** a taunting or sarcastic remark. Also, **jibe.** [1560–70; perh. < MF *giber* to handle roughly, shake, deriv. of *gibe* staff, billhook] **—gib′er,** *n.* **—gib′ing•ly,** *adv.*
—Syn. 1. mock, sneer, gird. **2.** ridicule, twit, fleer. **3.** sneer, scoff, jeer.

gibe[2] (jīb), *v.i., v.t.,* **gibed, gib•ing,** *n.* jibe[1].

Gib•e•on (gib′ē ən), *n.* a town in ancient Palestine, NW of Jerusalem. Josh. 9:3.

Gib•e•on•ite (gib′ē ə nīt′), *n.* one of the inhabitants of Gibeon, who were condemned by Joshua to be hewers of wood and drawers of water for the Israelites. Josh. 9. [GIBEON + -ITE[1]]

GI Bill, any of various Congressional bills enacted to provide funds for college educations, home-buying loans, and other benefits for armed-services veterans. Also called **GI Bill of Rights.**

gib•let (jib′lit), *n.* Usually, **giblets.** the heart, liver, gizzard, and the like, of a fowl. [1275–1325; ME < OF *gibelet* a stew of game; cf. F *gibelotte* rabbit stew]

Gi•bral•tar (ji brôl′tər), *n.* **1.** a British crown colony comprising a fortress and seaport located on a narrow promontory near the S tip of Spain. 29,934; 1⅞ sq. mi. (5 sq. km). **2. Rock of. a.** Ancient, **Calpe.** a long, precipitous mountain nearly coextensive with this colony: one of the Pillars of Hercules. 1396 ft. (426 m) high; 2½ mi. (4 km) long. **b.** any person or thing that has strength and endurance that can be relied on. **3. Strait of,** a strait between Europe and Africa at the Atlantic entrance to the Mediterranean. 8½–23 mi. (14–37 km) wide. **4.** any impregnable fortress or stronghold. **—Gi•bral•tar•i•an** (ji brôl târ′ē ən, jib′rôl-), *adj., n.*

Gib•ran (ji brän′), *n.* **Kah•lil** (kä lēl′), 1883–1931, Lebanese mystic, poet, and artist; in the U.S. after 1910.

Gib•son (gib′sən), *n.* a dry martini cocktail garnished with a pearl onion. [1925–30; after the surname *Gibson*]

Gib•son (gib′sən), *n.* **1. Althea,** born 1927, U.S. tennis player. **2. Charles Da•na** (dā′nə), 1867–1944, U.S. artist and illustrator. **3. Josh(ua),** 1911–47, U.S. baseball player. **4.** a male given name.

Gib′son Des′ert, a desert in W central Australia: scrub; salt marshes. ab. 85,000 sq. mi. (220,000 sq. km).

Gib′son girl′, 1. the idealized American girl of the 1890's as represented in the illustrations of Charles Dana Gibson. **2.** of, indicating, or resembling the characteristic clothing of the Gibson girl, typically a high-necked, fitted blouse or bodice with full puff sleeves and a long skirt with a flared bottom and a tightly fitted waistline. [1890–95, *Amer.*]

gi•bus (jī′bəs), *n., pl.* **-bus•es.** See **opera hat.** Also called **gi′bus hat′.** [1840–50; named after *Gibus,* 19th-century Frenchman, its inventor]

gid (gid), *n. Vet. Pathol.* a disease of cattle and esp. of sheep in which the brain or spinal cord is infested with larvae of the dog tapeworm, *Multiceps multiceps,* producing staggers. Also called **sturdy.** Cf. **water-brain.** [1550–60; back formation from GIDDY]

gid•dy (gid′ē), *adj.,* **-di•er, -di•est,** *v.,* **-died, -dy•ing.** —*adj.* **1.** affected with vertigo; dizzy. **2.** attended with or causing dizziness: *a giddy climb.* **3.** frivolous and lighthearted; impulsive; flighty: *a giddy young person.* —*v.t., v.i.* **4.** to make or become giddy. [bef. 1000; ME *gidy,* OE *gidig* mad (as var. of **gydig*), deriv. of *god* GOD, presumably orig. "possessed by a divine being"] **—gid′di•ly,** *adv.* **—gid′di•ness,** *n.*
—Syn. 1. lightheaded, vertiginous. **3.** unstable, volatile, fickle, inconstant, vacillating.

gid•dy•ap (gid′ē ap′, -up′), *interj.* (used as a command to a horse to speed up). Also, **gid•dap** (gi dap′, -dup′), **gid•dy•up** (gid′ē up′). [1920–25, *Amer.*; informal pron. of *get up*]

gid•dy-head•ed (gid′ē hed′id), *adj. Chiefly Southern U.S.* giddy (def. 1).

Gide (zhēd), *n.* **An•dré (Paul Guil•laume)** (äɴ drā′ pôl gē yōm′), 1869–1951, French novelist, essayist, poet, and critic: Nobel prize 1947.

Gid•e•on (gid′ē ən), *n.* **1.** Also called **Jerubbaal.** a judge of Israel and conqueror of the Midianites. Judges 6–8. **2.** a member of the Gideons International. **3.** a male given name: from a Hebrew word meaning "great destroyer."

Gid′e•ons Interna′tional (gid′ē ənz), an interdenominational lay society organized in 1899 to place Bibles in hotel rooms. Formerly, **Gid′eon Soci′ety.**

gie[1] (gē), *v.t., v.i.,* **gied, gied** or **gien** (gēn), **gie•ing.** *Chiefly Scot.* give.

gie[2] (gē), *n.* gi.

Giel•gud (gil′go͝od, gēl′-), *n.* **Sir (Arthur) John,** born 1904, English actor and director.

gier-ea•gle (jēr′ē′gəl), *n.* a bird, probably the Egyptian vulture, regarded as unclean. Lev. 11:18; Deut. 14:17. [1611; *gier* (< G *Geier* vulture) + EAGLE]

Gie•rek (gēr′ek; *Pol.* gye′ʀek), *n.* **Ed•ward** (ed′wərd; *Pol.* ed′värt), born 1913, Polish political leader: first secretary of the Polish Communist party 1970–80.

Gie•se•king (gē′zə king, -sə-), *n.* **Wal•ter (Wil•helm)** (wôl′tər wil′helm; *Ger.* väl′təʀ vil′helm), 1895–1956, German pianist and composer.

gift (gift), *n.* **1.** something given voluntarily without payment in return, as to show favor toward someone, honor an occasion, or make a gesture of assistance; present. **2.** the act of giving. **3.** something bestowed or acquired without any particular effort by the recipient or without its being earned: *Those extra points he got in the game were a total gift.* **4.** a special ability or capacity; natural endowment; talent: *the gift of saying the right thing at the right time.* —*v.t.* **5.** to present with as a gift; bestow gifts upon; endow with. **6.** to present (someone) with a gift: *just the thing to gift the newlyweds.* [1125–75; ME < ON *gift;* c. OE *gift* (ME *yift*) marriage gift; akin to GIVE] **—gift′less,** *adj.*
—Syn. 1. donation, contribution, offering, benefaction, endowment, bounty, boon, largess, alms, gratuity, tip, premium, allowance, subsidy, bequest, legacy, inheritance, dowry. See **present**[2]. **4.** faculty, aptitude, capability, bent, forte, genius, turn, knack.

gift•a•ble (gif′tə bəl), *adj.* **1.** suitable for a gift. —*n.* **2.** something for giving as a gift. [GIFT + -ABLE]

gift′ certif′icate, a certificate entitling the bearer to select merchandise of a specified cash value from a store, usually presented as a gift. [1940–45]

gift•ed (gif′tid), *adj.* **1.** having great special talent or ability: *the debut of a gifted artist.* **2.** having exceptionally high intelligence: *gifted children.* [1635–45; GIFT + -ED[3]] **—gift′ed•ly,** *adv.* **—gift′ed•ness,** *n.*
—Syn. 1. accomplished, talented.

gift′ of gab′, *Informal.* an aptitude for speaking fluently, glibly, or persuasively. Also, **gift′ of the gab′.** [1675–85]

gift′ of tongues′. See **speaking in tongues.** [1550–60]

gift′ tax′, a tax imposed on the transfer of money or property from one living person to another by gift, payable by the donor.

gift′ vouch′er, *Brit.* See **gift certificate.** [1960–65]

gift•ware (gift′wâr′), *n.* china, crystal, or other items suitable for gifts. [1900–05; GIFT + WARE[1]]

gift-wrap (gift′rap′), *v.,* **-wrapped** or **-wrapt, -wrap•ping,** *n.* —*v.t.* **1.** to wrap (something), as a package, with decorative paper, ribbon, etc., for presentation as a gift. —*n.* **2.** giftwrapping. Also, **gift′wrap′.** [1935–40] **—gift′-wrap′per,** *n.*

gift•wrap•ping (gift′rap′ing), *n.* decorative paper, ribbon, etc., for wrapping objects to be presented as gifts. [1945–50; GIFT + WRAPPING]

Gi•fu (gē′fo͞o′), *n.* a city on S Honshu, in central Japan. 410,368.

gig[1] (gig), *n., v.,* **gigged, gig•ging.** —*n.* **1.** a light, two-wheeled one-horse carriage. **2.** *Naut.* **a.** a light boat rowed with four, six, or eight long oars. **b.** a boat reserved for the use of the captain of a ship. **3.** something that whirls. **4.** Also called **gig mill.** a roller containing teasels, used for raising nap on a fabric. **5.** *Obs.* whirligig (def. 5). —*v.i.* **6.** to ride in a gig. **7.** to raise the nap on (a fabric). [1200–50; ME *gigge, gig* flighty girl; akin to Dan *gig* top; cf. Norw *giga* to shake about]

gig[1]
(def. 1)

gig[2] (gig), *n., v.,* **gigged, gig•ging.** —*n.* **1.** a device, commonly four hooks secured back to back, for dragging through a school of fish to hook them through the body. **2.** a spearlike device with a long, thick handle, used for spearing fish and frogs. —*v.t.* **3.** to catch or spear (a fish or frog) with a gig. —*v.i.* **4.** to catch fish or frogs with a gig. [1715–25; shortened from FISHGIG or FIZGIG]

gig[3] (gig), *n., v.,* **gigged, gig•ging.** —*n.* **1.** an official report of a minor infraction of regulations, as in school or the army; a demerit. **2.** a punishment for a minor infraction of rules. —*v.t.* **3.** to give a gig to or punish with a gig. [1940–45; orig. uncert.]

gig[4] (gig), *n., v.,* **gigged, gig•ging.** *Slang.* —*n.* **1.** a single professional engagement, usually of short duration, as of jazz or rock musicians. **2.** any job, esp. one of short or uncertain duration: *a teaching gig out west somewhere.* —*v.i.* **3.** to work as a musician, esp. in a single engagement: *He gigged with some of the biggest names in the business.* [1925–30; orig. uncert.]

giga-, a combining form meaning "billion," used in the formation of compound words: *gigabyte.* [< Gk *gígās* GIANT]

gig•a•bit (gig′ə bit′, jig′-), *n. Computers.* a measure of storage capacity and data transfer equal to 1 billion (10^9) bits. [1965–70; GIGA- + BIT[3]]

gig•a•byte (gig′ə bīt′, jig′-), *n. Computers.* a measure of storage capacity equal to 1 billion (10^9) bytes. [GIGA- + BYTE]

gi•ga•cy•cle (gig′ə sī′kəl, jig′-), *n.* one billion cycles. *Abbr.:* Gc [1955–60; GIGA- + CYCLE]

gi′ga•e•lec′tron volt′ (gig′ə i lek′tron, jig′ə-), one billion electron volts. *Abbr.:* GeV, Gev [GIGA- + ELECTRON]

gig•a•flops (gig′ə flops′, jig′-), *n.* a measure of computer speed, equal to one billion floating-point operations per second. [1985–90; see FLOPS]

gig•a•hertz (gig′ə hûrts′, jig′-), *n., pl.* **-hertz, -hertz•es.** one billion hertz. *Abbr.:* GHz [1960–65; GIGA- + HERTZ]

gi•gan•te•an (jī′gan tē′ən, ji gan′tē ən, ji-), *adj.* gigantic. [1605–15; < L *gigante(us)* of giants (*gigant-* GIANT + *-eus* adj. suffix) + -AN]

Gi•gan•tes (ji gan′tēz), *n.pl.* huge monsters, the children of Gaea, who fought the Olympians but were defeated by them.

gi•gan•tesque (jī′gan tesk′), *adj.* of a huge or gigantic size; of or suited to a giant. [1815–25; < F < It *gigantesco,* equiv. to *gigante* GIANT + *-esco* -ESQUE]

gi•gan•tic (jī gan′tik, ji-), *adj.* **1.** very large; huge: *a gigantic statue.* **2.** of, like, or befitting a giant. [1605–15; < L *gigant-* GIANT + -IC] **—gi•gan′ti•cal•ly,** *adv.* **—gi•gan′tic•ness,** *n.*
—Syn. 1. enormous, immense, prodigious, herculean, cyclopean, titanic. GIGANTIC, COLOSSAL, MAMMOTH, MONSTROUS are used of whatever is physically or metaphorically of great magnitude. GIGANTIC refers to the size of a giant, or to size or scope befitting a giant: *a gigantic stalk of corn.* COLOSSAL refers to the size of a colossus, to anything huge or vast as befitting a hero or god: *a colossal victory.* MAMMOTH refers to the size of the animal of that name and is used esp. of anything large and heavy: *a mammoth battleship.* MONSTROUS means strikingly unusual or out of the normal in some way, as in size: *a monstrous blunder.* **—Ant. 1.** tiny.

gi•gan•tism (jī gan′tiz əm, ji-, jī′gan tiz′əm), *n. Pathol.* abnormally great development in size or stature of the whole body or of parts of the body, most often due to dysfunction of the pituitary gland. Cf. **hypertrophy.** [1880–85; < L *gigant-* GIANT + -ISM]

Gi•gan•to•pi•the•cus (jī gan′tō pi thē′kəs, -pith′i kəs, ji-), *n.* a genus of extinct ape of southern Asia existing during the Pliocene and Pleistocene epochs, known only from very large fossil jaws and teeth and believed to be perhaps the biggest hominoid that ever lived. [1940–45; < NL < Gk *gigant-* (s. of *gígās*) GIANT + *-o-* -O- + *píthēkos* ape]

gi•ga•ton (gig′ə tun′, jig′-), *n.* one billion tons. *Abbr.:* GT [GIGA- + TON[1]]

gi•ga•watt (gig′ə wot′, jig′-), *n.* one billion watts. *Abbr.:* GW, Gw [1960–65; GIGA- + WATT]

gig•gle (gig′əl), *v.,* **-gled, -gling,** *n.* —*v.i.* **1.** to laugh in a silly, often high-pitched way, esp. with short, repeated gasps and titters, as from juvenile or ill-concealed amusement or nervous embarrassment. —*n.* **2.** a silly, spasmodic laugh; titter. **3.** *Slang.* an amusing experience, incident, etc.: *Going to a silly movie was always a giggle.* [1500–10; imit.; cf. D *gigelen,* G *gickeln.* See -LE] **—gig′gler,** *n.* **—gig′gling•ly,** *adv.* **—gig′gly,** *adj.*
—Syn. 1, 2. snicker, snigger, chuckle.

gig•let (gig′lit), *n.* **1.** a giddy, playful girl. **2.** *Archaic.* a lascivious woman. Also, **gig′lot.** [1300–50; ME *gig(e)lot.* See GIG[1], -LET]

CONCISE PRONUNCIATION KEY: *act, cāpe, dâre, pärt; set, ēqual; if, ice; ox, ōver, ôrder, oil, bo͝ok, bo͞ot, out; up, ûrge; child; sing; shoe; thin, that;* zh as in *treasure.* ə = *a* as in *alone, e* as in *system, i* as in *easily, o* as in *gallop, u* as in *circus;* ᵊ as in *fire* (fīᵊr), *hour* (ouᵊr). l and n can serve as syllabic consonants, as in *cradle* (krād′l), and *button* (but′n). See the full key inside the front cover.

Gi·gli (jē′lyē), *n.* **Be·nia·mi·no** (be′nyä mē′nô), 1890–1957, Italian operatic tenor.

gig′ mill′, gig[1] (def. 4). [1545–55]

GIGO (gī′gō), *n. Computers.* a rule of thumb stating that when faulty data are fed into a computer, the information that emerges will also be faulty. [1965–70; *g(arbage) i(n) g(arbage) o(ut)*]

gig·o·lo (jig′ə lō′, zhig′-), *n., pl.* **-los. 1.** a man living off the earnings or gifts of a woman, esp. a younger man supported by an older woman in return for his sexual attentions and companionship. **2.** a male professional dancing partner or escort. [1920–25; < F, masc. deriv. of *gigolette* woman of the streets or public dance halls, prob. ult. deriv. of MF *giguer* to frolic (see JIG[2]); cf. GIGLET, ME *gig(e)lot,* which may have influenced *gigolette*]

gig·ot (jig′ət, zhē gō′), *n.* **1.** a leg-of-mutton sleeve. **2.** a leg of lamb or mutton. [1520–30; < MF, appar. dim. of *gigue* fiddle (< Gmc; cf. OHG *gīga* kind of fiddle (G *Geige*), GIG[1]), so called in allusion to its shape]

gigue (zhēg), *n.* **1.** *Dance.* jig[2] (def. 1). **2.** *Music.* a dance movement often forming the conclusion of the classical suite. [1675–85; < F, prob. < E JIG[2]]

GI Joe, an enlisted soldier in the U.S. Army, esp. in World War II. [1940–45]

Gi·jón (gē hôn′; *Sp.* hē hôn′), *n.* a seaport in NW Spain, on the Bay of Biscay. 187,612.

Gil (gil), *n.* a male given name, form of **Gilbert.**

Gi·la (hē′lə), *n.* a river flowing W from SW New Mexico across S Arizona to the Colorado River. 630 mi. (1015 km) long.

Gi′la mon′ster, a large, venomous lizard, *Heloderma suspectum,* of the southwestern U.S. and northwestern Mexico, covered with beadlike scales of yellow, orange, and black. [1875–80, *Amer.*; after GILA]

Gila monster, *Heloderma suspectum,* length 16 to 20 in. (41 to 51 cm)

Gi′la wood′pecker, a dull-colored woodpecker, *Melanerpes uropygialis,* of the southwestern U.S. and Mexico. [1855–60, *Amer.*; after GILA]

gil·bert (gil′bərt), *n. Elect.* the centimeter-gram-second unit of magnetomotive force, equal to 0.7958 ampere-turns. *Abbr.:* Gi [1890–95; named after William GILBERT]

Gil·bert (gil′bərt), *n.* **1. Cass,** 1859–1934, U.S. architect. **2. Henry Franklin Bel·knap** (bel′nap), 1868–1928, U.S. composer. **3. Sir Humphrey,** 1537–83, English soldier, navigator, and colonizer in America. **4. John** (*John Pringle*), 1895–1936, U.S. film actor. **5. William,** 1544–1603, English physician and physicist: pioneer experimenter in magnetism and electricity. **6. Sir William Schwenck** (shwengk), 1836–1911, English dramatist and poet: collaborator with Sir Arthur Sullivan. **7.** a male given name: from Germanic words meaning "pledge" and "bright."

Gil′bert and El′lice Is′lands (el′is), a former British colony, comprising the Gilbert Islands (now Kiribati), the Ellice Islands (now Tuvalu), and other widely scattered islands in the central Pacific Ocean.

Gil·ber·ti·an (gil bûr′tē ən), *adj.* of, pertaining to, or characteristic of the style or humor of Sir William S. Gilbert. [1875–80; GILBERT + -IAN]

Gil′bert Is′lands, former name of **Kiribati.**

Gil Blas (*Fr.* zhēl blä′), (*Gil Blas de Santillane*) a picaresque novel (1715–35) by Le Sage.

gild[1] (gild), *v.t.,* **gild·ed** or **gilt, gild·ing. 1.** to coat with gold, gold leaf, or a gold-colored substance. **2.** to give a bright, pleasing, or specious aspect to. **3.** *Archaic.* to make red, as with blood. **4. gild the lily,** to add unnecessary ornamentation, a special feature, etc., in an attempt to improve something that is already complete, satisfactory, or ideal: *After that wonderful meal, serving a fancy dessert would be gilding the lily.* [1300–50; ME *gilden,* OE *-gyldan;* akin to GOLD] **—gild′a·ble,** *adj.*

gild[2] (gild), *n.* guild.

Gil·da (gil′də), *n.* a female given name: from an Old English word meaning "golden."

gild·ed (gil′did), *adj.* **1.** covered or highlighted with gold or something of a golden color. **2.** having a pleasing or showy appearance that conceals something of little worth. [bef. 1000; GILD[1] + -ED[2]; r. ME *gild,* OE *gegyld*]

Gild′ed Age′, the period in the U.S. c1870–98, characterized by a greatly expanding economy and the emergence of plutocratic influences in government and society.

gild·er[1] (gil′dər), *n.* a person or thing that gilds. [1275–1325; ME. See GILD[1], -ER[1]]

gil·der[2] (gil′dər), *n.* guilder.

gild·hall (gild′hôl′), *n.* guildhall.

gild·ing (gil′ding), *n.* **1.** the application of gilt. **2.** the gold leaf or other material with which something is gilded. **3.** the golden surface produced by the application of gilt. **4.** something used to create a deceptively pleasing, impressive, or alluring aspect or character. [1400–50; late ME; see GILD[1], -ING[1]]

CONCISE ETYMOLOGY KEY: <, descended or borrowed from; >, whence; b., blend of, blended; c., cognate with; cf., compare; deriv., derivative; equiv., equivalent; imit., imitative; obl., oblique; r., replacing; s., stem; sp., spelling, spelled; resp., respelling, respelled; trans., translation; ?, origin unknown; *, unattested; ‡, probably earlier than. See the full key inside the front cover.

Gil·e·ad (gil′ē əd), *n.* **1.** a district of ancient Palestine, E of the Jordan River, in present N Jordan. **2. Mount,** a mountain in NW Jordan. 3596 ft. (1096 m).

Gil·e·ad·ite (gil′ē ə dīt′), *n.* **1.** a member of a branch of the Israelite tribe descended from Manasseh. **2.** an inhabitant of ancient Gilead. [GILEAD + -ITE[1]]

Gi·lels (gi lelz′; *Russ.* gyē′lyils), *n.* **E·mil (Gri·go·rye·vich)** (ē′mil gri gôr′yə vich, ā′mil; *Russ.* e myēl′ gryi-gô′ryi vyich), 1916–85, Russian pianist.

Giles (jīlz), *n.* **1. Saint,** 8th century A.D., Athenian hermit in France. **2.** a male given name: from a Greek word meaning "shieldbearer."

gil·gai (gil′gī), *n. Australian.* **1.** a small gully or ditch. **2.** a small pond or pool of water. Also, **gil′gie.** [1895–1900; < Kamilaroi *gilgay*]

Gil·gal (gil′gal), *n.* the name of several places in ancient Palestine, esp. a site near Jericho where the Israelites encamped after crossing the Jordan. Josh. 4:19–24.

Gil·ga·mesh (gil′gə mesh′), *n.* a legendary Sumerian king, the hero of Sumerian and Babylonian epics.

gil·gul (*Seph. Heb.* gēl go͞ol′; *Ashk. Heb.* gil′go͝ol), *n., pl.* **gil·gu·lim** (*Seph. Heb.* gēl go͞o lēm′; *Ashk. Heb.* gil-go͞o′lim). *Jewish Folklore.* the soul of a dead person that passes into another living body to assume a new existence and atone for past sins. Cf. **dybbuk.** [< Yiddish *gilgl* lit., transmigration, metamorphosis < Heb *gilgul* metamorphosis, lit., rolling, revolving]

gil·guy (gil′gī′), *n.* **1.** *Naut.* a rope used as a temporary guy. **2.** any device or object not specifically named; gadget. [1865–70; orig. uncert.]

gill[1] (gil), *n.* **1.** the respiratory organ of aquatic animals, as fish, that breathe oxygen dissolved in water. **2.** Also called **lamella.** one of the radiating vertical plates on the underside of the cap of an agaric mushroom. See diag. under **mushroom. 3.** See **ground ivy. 4. green** or **white around the gills,** somewhat pale, as from being sickly, nervous, or frightened: *When he heard how much the bill was, he looked a little green around the gills.* **5. to the gills,** *Informal.* fully; completely; totally: *After that big meal we were all stuffed to the gills.* —*v.t.* **6.** to catch (fish) by the gills in a gill net. **7.** to gut or clean (fish). [1300–50; ME *gile* < Scand; cf. ON *gjǫlnar* < **gelnō;* c. Swed *gäl,* Dan *gælle,* Norw *gjelle* gill] **—gill′-less,** *adj.* **—gill′-like′,** *adj.*

gill[2] (jil), *n.* a unit of liquid measure equal to ¼ pint (118.2937 ml). [1225–75; ME *gille* < OF: vat, tub < LL *gello, gillo* water pot]

gill[3] (gil), *n. Brit.* **1.** a deep rocky cleft or wooded ravine forming the course of a stream. **2.** a stream; brook; rivulet. [1350–1400; ME *gille* < ON *gil*]

gill[4] (jil), *n.* a girl or young woman; sweetheart. [1400–50; late ME *gil(le)* generic use of *Gil(le),* short form of *Gillian;* see GILLIAN]

gill[5] (gil), *Textiles.* —*n.* **1.** a faller used in the combing process, generally for only the highest-quality fibers. —*v.t.* **2.** to comb (fibers) with a gill. [1830–40; perh. special use of GILL[1]]

Gill (gil *for 1;* jil *for 2*), *n.* **1.** a male given name. **2.** a female given name.

gill′ arch′ (gil). See **branchial arch.** [1875–80]

gill′ bar′ (gil). See **branchial arch** (def. 1).

gill′ book′ (gil). See **book gill.** [1880–85]

gill′ box′ (gil), *Textiles.* a machine having a number of gills, used in combing.

gill′ cleft′ (gil). See **branchial cleft.** [1885–90]

Gil·les·pie (gi les′pē), *n.* **John Birks** (bûrks), ("*Dizzy*"), 1917–93, U.S. jazz trumpeter and composer.

Gil·lett (ji let′), *n.* **1. Frederick Huntington,** 1851–1935, U.S. political leader: Speaker of the House 1919–25. **2.** a male given name, form of **Gilbert.**

Gil·lette (ji let′), *n.* **1. King Camp,** 1855–1932, U.S. businessman: inventor of the safety razor. **2. William (Hooker),** 1855–1937, U.S. actor and dramatist. **3.** a town in NE Wyoming. 12,134. **4.** a male given name, form of **Gilbert.**

gill′ fil′ament (gil), one of the threadlike processes forming the respiratory surface of a gill. [1840–50]

gill′ fun′gus (gil), an agaricaceous fungus; mushroom. [1925–30]

Gil·li·an (jil′ē ən, -yən), *n.* a female given name, form of **Juliana.**

gil·lie (gil′ē), *n.* **1.** *Scot.* **a.** a hunting or fishing guide. **b.** a male attendant or personal servant to a Highland chieftain. **2.** ghillie. Also, **gilly.** [1590–1600; < ScotGael *gille* lad, servant]

gill·ing (gil′ing), *n. Textiles.* the process of attenuating worsted fibers and making them parallel by using a gill box while combing. [GILL[5] + -ING[1]]

gill′ net′ (gil), a curtainlike net, suspended vertically in the water, with meshes of such a size as to catch by the gills a fish that has thrust its head through. [1790–1800, *Amer.*]

gill-net·ter (gil′net′ər), *n.* **1.** a person who uses a gill net in fishing. **2.** a boat used in fishing with a gill net. [1885–90]

gill-o·ver-the-ground (gil′ō′vər thə ground′, -ground′), *n.* See **ground ivy.** [1590–1600]

gill′ pouch′ (gil). See **branchial pouch.** [1900–05]

gill′ rak′er (gil), (in fish) one of a series of stiff projections along the inner margins of the branchial arches that prevent food particles from passing through the branchial clefts. [1875–80]

gill′ slit′ (gil). See **branchial cleft.** [1850–55]

gil·ly[1] (gil′ē), *n., pl.* **-lies.** *Scot.* gillie.

gil·ly[2] (gil′ē), *n., pl.* **-lies,** *v.,* **-lied, -ly·ing.** —*n.* **1.** a truck or wagon, esp. one used to transport the equipment of a circus or carnival. —*v.t., v.i.* **2.** to carry or be carried on a gilly. [*gill* (dial.) < ? + -Y[2]]

gil·ly·flow·er (jil′ē flou′ər), *n.* **1.** *Archaic.* any of several fragrant flowers of the genus *Dianthus,* as the carnation or clove pink. **2.** any of various other usually fragrant flowers, esp. a stock, *Matthiola incana,* of the mustard family. Also, **gil′li·flow′er.** [1300–50; alter. (by association with FLOWER) of ME *gilofre, geraflour* < OF *gilofre, girofle* < L *caryophyllum* < Gk *karyóphyllon* clove (*káryo(n)* nut + *phýllon* leaf)]

Gil·man (gil′mən), *n.* **1. Arthur,** 1837–1909, U.S. educator. **2. Daniel Coit** (koit), 1831–1908, U.S. educator.

Gi·lo·lo (jī lō′lō, ji-), *n.* Halmahera.

Gil·roy (gil′roi), *n.* a town in W California. 21,641.

Gil·son (zhēl sôɴ′), *n.* **É·tienne Hen·ry** (ā tyen′ äɴ-rē′), 1884–1978, French historian.

Gil·son·ite (gil′sə nit′), *Trademark.* uintaite. [1885–90]

gilt[1] (gilt), *v.* **1.** a pt. and pp. of **gild**[1]. —*adj.* **2.** gilded. **3.** gold in color; golden. —*n.* **4.** the thin layer of gold or other material applied in gilding. **5.** gilt-edged security.

gilt[2] (gilt), *n.* a young female swine, esp. one that has not produced a litter. [1300–50; ME *gilte* < ON *gylta*]

gilt′ bronze′, ormolu (def. 2). [1885–90]

gilt-edged (gilt′ejd′), *adj.* **1.** having the edge or edges gilded. **2.** of the highest or best quality, kind, etc. **3.** *Finance.* **a.** (of securities and bonds) of the highest rating or quality; secure. **b.** (of bonds) government backed or guaranteed. Also, **gilt′-edge′.** [1810–20]

gilt·head (gilt′hed′), *n.* any of several marine fishes having gold markings, as a sparid, *Sparus auratus,* of the Mediterranean Sea. [1545–55; GILT[1] + HEAD]

Gil·yak (gil′yäk, gil yäk′) *n.* Nivkh. [< Russ *gilyák;* of uncert. orig., perh. akin to Nivkh (Amur dial.) *kil* a name for neighboring Tungusic peoples (with the Russ n. suffix *-(y)ak,* as in *sibiryák* a Siberian)]

gim·bals (jim′bəlz, gim′-), *n.* (*used with a singular v.*) Sometimes, **gimbal.** a contrivance, consisting of a ring or base on an axis, that permits an object, as a ship's compass, mounted in or on it to tilt freely in any direction, in effect suspending the object so that it will remain horizontal even when its support is tipped. Also called **gim′·bal ring′.** [1570–80; alter. of GIMMAL]

Gim·bel (gim′bəl), *n.* **Jacob,** 1850–1922, U.S. retail merchant.

gim·crack (jim′krak′), *n.* **1.** a showy, useless trifle; gewgaw. —*adj.* **2.** showy but useless. [1325–75 for earlier sense; ME *gib(e)crake;* cf. ME *gibben* to waver (< OF *giber* to shake)]
—Syn. 1. bauble, knickknack, trinket, ornament.

gim·crack·er·y (jim′krak′ə rē), *n.* **1.** cheap, showy, useless trifles, ornaments, trinkets, etc. **2.** obvious or contrived effects, esp. in art, music, literature, etc. [1770–80; GIMCRACK + -ERY]

gim·el (gim′əl), *n.* **1.** the third letter of the Hebrew alphabet. **2.** the consonant sound represented by this letter. **3.** *Music.* gymel. [< Heb *gimel,* akin to *gāmāl* camel]

gim·let (gim′lit), *n.* **1.** a small tool for boring holes, consisting of a shaft with a pointed screw at one end and a handle perpendicular to the shaft at the other. **2.** a cocktail made with gin or vodka, sweetened lime juice, and sometimes soda water. —*v.t.* **3.** to pierce with or as if with a gimlet. **4.** Also, **gim·blet** (gim′blit). *Naut.* to rotate (a suspended anchor) to a desired position. —*adj.* **5.** able to penetrate or bore through. [1375–1425; late ME < OF *guimbelet* < Gmc; cf. MD *wimmel* WIMBLE]

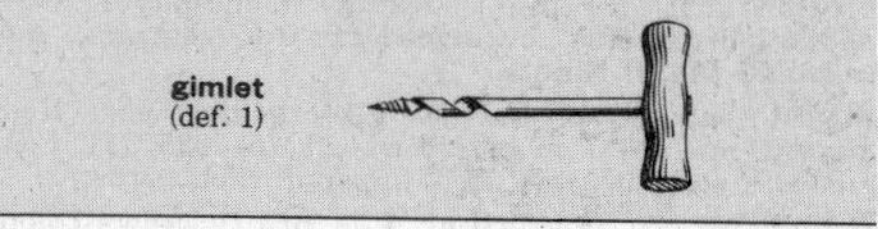

gimlet (def. 1)

gim′let eye′, 1. a sharp or piercing glance. **2.** an eye that appears to give a sharp or piercing look. [1815–25] **—gim′let-eyed′,** *adj.*

gim·mal (gim′əl, jim′əl), *n.* any of various joints for transmitting motion between rotating parts, as in a timepiece. [1520–30; alter. of *gemel* (orig. in pl.) twin, ME *gemelles* (< OF *gemeles*) < L *gemellus* (sing.), dim. of *geminus* twin]

gim·me (gim′ē), **1.** *Pron. Spelling.* give me. —*n. Slang.* **2.** *Golf.* a final short putt that a player is not required to take in informal play. **3. the gimmes, a.** reliance on or a demand for the generosity of others, esp. as one's due: *grown children with the gimmes who still expect money from their parents.* **b.** greediness. Also, **gim′·mie.** [1925–30; informal pron. of *give me*]

gim′me cap′, a visored cap decorated with the symbol or name of a product, company, etc. [1975–80; so called from its being given away as a promotional item]

gim·mick (gim′ik), *n.* **1.** an ingenious or novel device, scheme, or stratagem, esp. one designed to attract attention or increase appeal. **2.** a concealed, usually devious aspect or feature of something, as a plan or deal: *An offer that good must have a gimmick in it somewhere.* **3.** a hidden mechanical device by which a magician works a trick or a gambler controls a game of chance. **4.** *Electronics Informal.* a capacitor formed by intertwining two insulated wires. —*v.t.* **5.** to equip or embellish with unnecessary features, esp. in order to increase salability, acceptance, etc. (often fol. by *up*): *to gimmick up a sports car with chrome and racing stripes.* —*v.i.* **6.** to resort to gimmickry, esp. habitually. [1925–30, *Amer.*; orig. uncert.] **—gim′mick·er,** *n.* **—gim′mick·y,** *adj.*
—Syn. 1. stunt, plan, ruse, ploy; angle.

gim·mick·ry (gim′ik rē), *n.* **1.** the use of gimmicks. **2.** an abundance of gimmicks. Also, **gim·mick·ery** (gim′ik rē, -ik ə rē). [1950–55; GIMMICK + -RY]

gimp[1] (gimp), *n.* **1.** a flat trimming of silk, wool, or other cord, sometimes stiffened with wire, for garments, curtains, etc. **2.** a coarse thread, usually glazed, employed in lacemaking to outline designs. [1655–65; appar. < D *gimp* < ?]

gimp[2] (gimp), *n. Chiefly Northeastern U.S.* spirit, vigor, or ambition. [1900–05; orig. uncert.]

gimp[3] (gimp), *Slang.* —*n.* **1.** a limp. **2.** a person who limps; lame person. —*v.i.* **3.** to limp; walk in a halting manner: *a sprain that made her gimp for weeks.* [1920–25, *Amer.*; orig. uncert.] —**gimp′y,** *adj.*

gimp[4] (jimp), *adj. Scot. and North Eng.* jimp.

gin[1] (jin), *n.* **1.** an alcoholic liquor obtained by distilling grain mash with juniper berries. **2.** an alcoholic liquor similar to this, made by redistilling spirits with flavoring agents, esp. juniper berries, orange peel, angelica root, etc. [1705–15; shortened from GENEVA]

gin[2] (jin), *n., v.,* **ginned, gin•ning.** —*n.* **1.** See **cotton gin. 2.** a trap or snare for game. **3.** any of various machines employing simple tackle or windlass mechanisms for hoisting. **4.** a stationary prime mover having a drive shaft rotated by horizontal beams pulled by horses walking in a circle. —*v.t.* **5.** to clear (cotton) of seeds with a gin. **6.** to snare (game). [1150–1200; ME *gyn,* aph. var. of OF *engin* ENGINE] —**gin′ner,** *n.*

gin[3] (gin), *v.i., v.t.,* **gan, gun, gin•ning.** *Archaic.* to begin. [1150–1200; ME *ginnen,* OE *ginnan,* aph. var. of *onginnan, beginnen* to BEGIN]

gin[4] (jin), *n., v.,* **ginned, gin•ning.** *Cards.* —*n.* **1.** Also called **gin rummy.** a variety of rummy for two players, in which a player with 10 or fewer points in unmatched cards can end the game by laying down the hand. **2.** the winning of such a game by laying down a full set of matched cards, earning the winner a bonus of 20 or 25 points. —*v.i.* **3.** to win a game in gin by laying down a hand in which all 10 cards are included in sets. [1955–60; perh. special use of GIN[1]]

gin[5] (gin), *conj. Chiefly Scot. and Southern Appalachian.* if; whether. [1665–75; variously explained as sense development of *gien* given (see GIE, -EN[3]); as contr. of *gif* IF + AN[2] (cf. IFFEN); or as aph. form of AGAIN]

gin[6] (jin), *n. Australian Informal.* **1.** a female Aborigine. **2.** an Aboriginal wife. Also, **jin.** [1820–30; < Dharuk *di-yin*]

Gi•na (jē′nə), *n.* a female given name.

gin′ and ton′ic (jin), a drink made with gin and quinine water, served in a tall glass and usually garnished with a slice of lime or lemon. [1930–35]

Gi•nas•te•ra (hē′näs te′rä), *n.* **Al•ber•to** (äl beʀ′tô), 1916–83, Argentine composer.

gin′ block′ (jin), *Mach.* a block having a large sheave in an open metal frame, used esp. to support a cargo whip. [1870–75]

gi•nep (kə nep′, gə-), *n.* genip.

gin•gal (jin′gôl), *n.* jingal. Also, **gin′gall.**

gin•ger (jin′jər), *n.* **1.** a reedlike plant, *Zingiber officinale,* native to the East Indies but now cultivated in most tropical countries, having a pungent, spicy rhizome used in cookery and medicine. Cf. **ginger family. 2.** any of various related or similar plants. **3.** *Informal.* piquancy; animation: *plenty of ginger in their performance of the dance.* **4.** a yellowish or reddish brown. —*v.t.* **5.** to treat or flavor with ginger. **6.** *Informal.* to impart piquancy or spirit to; enliven (usually fol. by *up*): *to ginger up a talk with a few jokes.* —*adj.* **7.** flavored or made with ginger. [bef. 1000; ME *ginger, gingivere* < OF *gingivre* < L *gingiber,* for *zingiberi* < Gk *zingíberis;* r. OE *gingiber* < L, as above]

Gin•ger (jin′jər), *n.* a female given name, form of **Virginia** or **Regina.**

gin′ger ale′, a carbonated soft drink flavored with ginger extract. [1835–45]

gin′ger beer′, a soft drink similar to ginger ale but containing more ginger flavor. [1800–10]

gin•ger•bread (jin′jər bred′), *n.* **1.** a type of cake flavored with ginger and molasses. **2.** a rolled cookie similarly flavored, often cut in fanciful shapes, and sometimes frosted. **3.** elaborate, gaudy, or superfluous architectural ornamentation: *a series of gables embellished with gingerbread.* —*adj.* **4.** heavily, gaudily, and superfluously ornamented: *a gingerbread style of architecture.* [1250–1300; ME *gingebreed* (influenced by *breed* bread), var. of *gingebrad, -brat* ginger paste < OF *gingembras, -brat* preserved ginger < ML **gingi(m)brātum* a medicinal preparation (neut. ptp.), deriv. of L *gingiber* GINGER] —**gin′ger•bread′y,** *adj.*

gin′gerbread palm′. See **doom palm.** [1860–65]

gin′gerbread plum′, a tree, *Neocarya macrophylla,* of western Africa, bearing a large, edible, starchy fruit. [1820–30]

gin′ger fam′ily, the plant family Zingiberaceae, characterized by tropical, often aromatic herbaceous plants having rhizomes, long sheathing leaves, and clusters of tubular flowers, and including cardamon, ginger, and turmeric.

gin′ger group′, *Chiefly Brit.* the most active group within an organization, as a political party. [1925–30]

gin′ger jar′, a Chinese ceramic jar having a wide mouth, a globular body, and a dome-shaped cover. [1880–85]

gin′ger lil′y, any of various plants belonging to the genus *Hedychium,* of the ginger family, native to Asia, esp. the white ginger, *H. coronarium,* having white, fragrant flowers. [1895–1900]

gin•ger•ly (jin′jər lē), *adv.* **1.** with great care or caution; warily. —*adj.* **2.** cautious, careful, or wary. [1510–20; *ginger-,* perh. < MF *gensor, genzor* delicate, pretty, positive use of compar. of *gent* GENTLE; see -LY] —**gin′ger•li•ness,** *n.*
—**Syn. 1.** cautiously, carefully, prudently.

gin•ger•snap (jin′jər snap′), *n.* a small, brittle cookie flavored with ginger and molasses. Also called, *Brit.,* **gin′ger nut′.** [1795–1805; GINGER + SNAP]

gin•ger•y (jin′jə rē), *adj.* **1.** having the flavor or pungence of ginger; spicy: *gingery cookies.* **2.** piquant; sharp and lively: *gingery humor.* **3.** of the color of ginger. [1850–55; GINGER + -Y[1]]

ging•ham (ging′əm), *n.* yarn-dyed, plain-weave cotton fabric, usually striped or checked. [1605–15; < D *gingang* < Malay *gəŋgaŋ, giŋgaŋ* with space between, hence, striped]

gin•gi•va (jin jī′və, jin′jə-), *n., pl.* **-gi•vae** (-jī′vē, -jə vē′). gum[2] (def. 1). [1885–90; < L *gingīva*]

gin•gi•val (jin jī′vəl, jin′jə-), *adj.* **1.** of or pertaining to the gums. **2.** *Phonet.* alveolar. [1660–70; GINGIV(A) + -AL[1]]

gin•gi•vec•to•my (jin′jə vek′tə mē), *n., pl.* **-mies.** *Dentistry.* surgical removal of gum tissue. [GINGIV(A) + -ECTOMY]

gin•gi•vi•tis (jin′jə vī′tis), *n. Pathol.* inflammation of the gums. [1870–75; < NL; see GINGIVA, -ITIS]

gin•gly•moid (jing′glə moid′, ging′-), *adj.* of, pertaining to, or resembling a ginglymus. [1660–70; GINGLYM(US) + -OID]

gin•gly•mus (jing′glə məs, ging′-), *n., pl.* **-mi** (-mī′). *Anat.* a joint in which movement is limited to one plane. Also called **hinge joint.** [1650–60; < NL < Gk *gínglymos* hinge]

gink (gingk), *n. Slang (sometimes disparaging and offensive).* person; fellow. [1905–10, *Amer.*; orig. uncert.]

gink•go (ging′kō, jing′-), *n., pl.* **-goes.** a large shade tree, *Ginkgo biloba,* native to China, having fan-shaped leaves and fleshy seeds with edible kernels: the sole surviving species of the gymnosperm family Ginkgoaceae, which thrived in the Jurassic Period, and existing almost exclusively in cultivation. Also, **ging′ko.** Also called **maidenhair-tree.** [1765–75; < NL representation of Japn *ginkyō,* equiv. to *gin* silver (< Chin) + *kyō* apricot (< Chin)]

gin′ mill′ (jin), *Slang.* a bar or saloon, esp. a cheap or disreputable one. [1860–65, *Amer.*]

ginned (jind), *adj. Slang.* drunk; intoxicated; inebriated. [1895–1900; GIN[1] + -ED[3]]

gin•ner•y (jin′ə rē), *n., pl.* **-ner•ies.** a mill for ginning cotton. [1895–90, *Amer.*; GIN[2] + -ERY]

Gin′nie Mae′ (jin′ē), *Finance.* **1.** See **Government National Mortgage Association. 2.** a bond or certificate sold by the Government National Mortgage Association. [1970–75; formed from the initials *GNMA;* cf. FANNIE MAE]

Gin•nun•ga•gap (gin′o͝ong gä gäp′), *n. Scand. Myth.* a primordial void, filled with mists, existing between Niflheim and Muspelheim. [< ON, perh. lit., magical gap]

Gin•ny (jin′ē), *n.* a female given name, form of **Virginia** or **Genevieve.**

Gi•no (jē′nō), *n.* a male given name.

gin′ rick′ey (jin), a rickey made with gin. [1890–95, *Amer.*]

gin′ rum′my, *Cards.* gin[4] (def. 1). [1940–45]

Gins•berg (ginz′bûrg), *n.* **Allen,** 1926–97, U.S. poet associated with the Beat Generation.

gin•seng (jin′seng), *n.* **1.** any of several plants of the genus *Panax,* esp. *P. pseudoginseng,* of eastern Asia, or *P. quinquefolius,* of North America, having an aromatic root used medicinally. **2.** the root itself. **3.** a preparation made from it. Also, **genseng.** [1645–55; < Chin (Wade-Giles) *jên[2] shên[1],* (Pinyin) *rén-shēn,* equiv. to *rén* man + *shēn* name for a kind of herb]

gin′seng fam′ily, the plant family Araliaceae, characterized by often prickly herbaceous plants, trees, and shrubs having alternate leaves and dense clusters of small, whitish or greenish flowers, and including the devil's-club, ginseng, ivy, schefflera, and wild sarsaparilla.

Gin•za (gin′zə), *n.* **the,** a district in Tokyo, Japan, famous for its department stores, nightclubs, and bars.

Ginz•berg (ginz′bûrg), *n.* **Ash•er** (ash′ər), (*Achad Ha-Am, Ahad Ha-am*), 1856–1927, Hebrew philosophical writer and editor, born in Russia.

gin•zo (gin′zō), *n., pl.* **-zoes.** *Slang (disparaging and offensive).* an Italian. [1930–35; orig. uncert.; cf. GUINEA in this sense]

Gio•con•da, La (lä′ jō kon′də, jē′ə-; *It.* lä jô kôn′dä), **1.** See ***Mona Lisa.* 2.** an opera (1876) by Amilcare Ponchielli.

gio•co•so (jə kō′sō; *It.* jô kô′sô), *adj., adv. Music.* merry; playful. [1820–30; < It: playful < L *jocōsus* JOCOSE]

Gio•no (jə nō′; *Fr.* jô nō′), *n.* **Jean** (zhäɴ), 1895–1970, French novelist.

Gior•da•no (jôr dä′nō; *It.* jôʀ dä′nô), *n.* **1. Lu•ca** (lo͞o′kə; *It.* lo͞o′kä), ("*Luca Fapresto*"), 1632–1705, Italian painter. **2. Um•ber•to** (o͝om ber′tō, um-; *It.* o͞om beʀ′tô), 1867–1948, Italian composer of operas.

Gior•gio•ne (jôr jō′nē; *It.* jôʀ jô′ne), *n.* (*Giorgione de Castelfranco, Giorgio Barbarelli*) 1478?–1511, Italian painter.

Giot•to (jot′ō; *It.* jôt′tô), *n.* (*Giotto di Bondone*) 1266?–1337, Florentine painter, sculptor, and architect.

gip (jip), *v.t., v.i.,* **gipped, gip•ping,** *n.* gyp[1]. —**gip′•per,** *n.*

gi•pon (ji pon′, jip′on), *n.* jupon.

Gip•sy (jip′sē), *n., pl.* **-sies,** *adj. Chiefly Brit.* Gypsy. Also, **gip′sy.** —**gip′sy•dom,** *n.* —**gip′sy•esque′, gip′sy•ish, gip′sy•like′, gip•se′ian,** *adj.* —**gip′sy•hood′,** *n.* —**gip′sy•ism,** *n.*

gi•raffe (jə raf′ *or, esp. Brit.,* -räf′), *n.* **1.** a tall, long-necked, spotted ruminant, *Giraffa camelopardalis,* of Africa: the tallest living quadruped animal. **2.** (*cap.*) *Astron.* the constellation Camelopardalis. [1585–95; < F *girafe* < It *giraffa* < dial. Ar *zirāfah,* perh. < Pers *zurnāpā*]

giraffe,
Giraffa camelopardalis,
height 18 ft. (5.5 m)

gir•an•dole (jir′ən dōl′), *n.* **1.** a rotating and radiating firework. **2.** an ornate bracket for candelabra or the like, sometimes with a reflecting mirror at the back of the shelf. **3.** a brooch or earring consisting of a central ornament with usually three smaller ornaments hanging from it. Also, **gi•ran•do•la** (ji ran′dl ə). [1625–35; < F < It *girandola,* deriv. of *girare* to turn in a circle < L *gȳrāre,* deriv. of *gȳrus* a circle < Gk *gŷros*]

Gi•rard (jə rärd′), *n.* **Stephen, 1.** 1750–1831, U.S. merchant, banker, and philanthropist, born in France. **2.** a city in NE Ohio. 12,517.

gir•a•sol (jir′ə sôl′, -sol′), *n.* **1.** an opal that reflects light in a bright luminous glow. **2.** See **Jerusalem artichoke** (def. 1). —*adj.* **3.** (of a stone) translucent and bluish-white with reddish reflections under strong light; opalescent. Also, **gir•a•sole** (jir′ə sōl′), **girosol.** [1580–90; < It, equiv. to *gira(re)* to turn (see GIRANDOLE) + *sole* the sun; cf. PARASOL]

Gi•raud (zhē rō′), *n.* **Hen•ri Ho•no•ré** (äɴ ʀē′ ô nô-ʀā′), 1879–1949, French general.

Gi•rau•doux (zhēr′ə do͞o′, zhēr′ə do͞o′; *Fr.* zhē ʀō-do͞o′), *n.* **Jean** (zhäɴ), 1882–1944, French novelist, playwright, and diplomat.

gird[1] (gûrd), *v.t.,* **gird•ed** or **girt, gird•ing. 1.** to encircle or bind with a belt or band. **2.** to surround; enclose; hem in. **3.** to prepare (oneself) for action: *He girded himself for the trial ahead.* **4.** to provide, equip, or invest, as with power or strength. [bef. 950; ME *girden,* OE *gyrdan;* c. G *gürten*] —**gird′ing•ly,** *adv.*
—**Syn. 3.** brace, steel, fortify, strengthen.

gird[2] (gûrd), *v.i.* **1.** to gibe; jeer (usually fol. by *at*). —*v.t.* **2.** to gibe or jeer at; taunt. —*n.* **3.** a gibe. [1175–1225; ME *gyrd* a stroke, blow, hence a cutting remark, deriv. of *girden* to strike, smite < ?] —**gird′ing•ly,** *adv.*

gird•er (gûr′dər), *n.* **1.** a large beam, as of steel, reinforced concrete, or timber, for supporting masonry, joists, purlins, etc. **2.** a principal beam of wood, steel, etc., supporting the ends of joists. [1605–15; GIRD[1] + -ER[1]] —**gird′er•less,** *adj.*

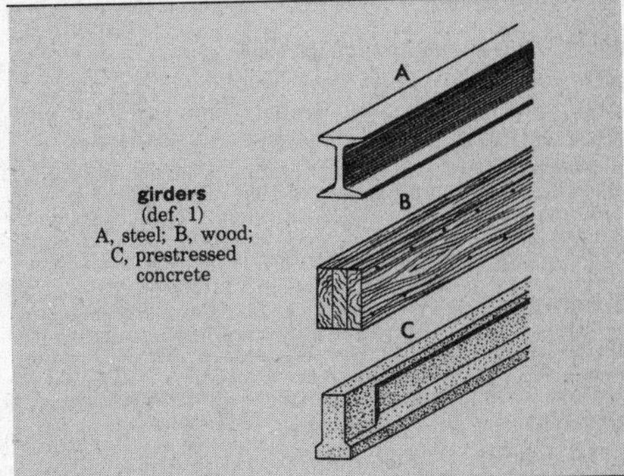

girders
(def. 1)
A, steel; B, wood;
C, prestressed
concrete

gir•dle (gûr′dl), *n., v.,* **-dled, -dling.** —*n.* **1.** a lightweight undergarment, worn esp. by women, often partly or entirely of elastic or boned, for supporting and giving a slimmer appearance to the abdomen, hips, and buttocks. **2.** a belt, cord, sash, or the like, worn about the waist. **3.** anything that encircles, confines, or limits. **4.** *Jewelry.* the edge or narrow band between the upper and lower facets of a gem. **5.** *Anat.* the bony framework that unites the upper or lower extremities to the axial skeleton. **6.** *Archit.* an ornamental band, esp. one surrounding the shaft of a column. **7.** a ring made about a tree trunk, branch, etc., by removing a band of bark. —*v.t.* **8.** to encircle with a belt; gird. **9.** to encompass; enclose; encircle. **10.** to move around (something or someone) in a circle. **11.** to cut away the bark and cambium in a ring around (a tree, branch, etc.). **12.** *Jewelry.* round (def. 51). [bef. 1000; ME; OE *gyrdel,* deriv. of *girdan* to GIRD[1]] —**gir′dle•like′,** *adj.* —**gir′dling•ly,** *adv.*
—**Syn. 3.** belt, circle, ring, band, hedge.

gir•dler (gûrd′lər), *n.* **1.** a person or thing that girdles. **2.** any of several insects, as a beetle, *Oncideres cingulata* **(twig girdler),** that cut a groove around the bark of a

CONCISE PRONUNCIATION KEY: act, cāpe, dâre, pärt; set, ēqual; if, īce; ox, ōver, ôrder, oil, bo͝ok, bo͞ot, out; up, ûrge; child; sing; shoe; thin, *th*at; zh as in *treasure.* ə = *a* as in *alone, e* as in *system, i* as in *easily, o* as in *gallop, u* as in *circus;* ᵊ as in *fire* (fīᵊr), *hour* (ouᵊr). l and n can serve as syllabic consonants, as in *cradle* (krād′l), and *button* (but′n). See the full key inside the front cover.

twig, stem, etc. **3.** a person who makes girdles. [1325–75; ME; see GIRDLE, -ER[1]]

gir′dle-tailed liz′ard (gûr′dl tāld′), any African lizard of the family Cordylidae, having a spiny tail used in defense.

Gir·gen·ti (*It.* jēr jen′tē), *n.* former name of **Agrigento.**

girl (gûrl), *n.* **1.** a female child, from birth to full growth. **2.** a young, immature woman, esp. formerly, an unmarried one. **3.** a daughter: *My wife and I have two girls.* **4.** *Informal (sometimes offensive).* a grown woman, esp. when referred to familiarly: *She's having the girls over for bridge next week.* **5.** girlfriend; sweetheart. **6.** *Often Offensive.* a female servant. **7.** *Usually Offensive.* a female employee. **8.** a female who is from or native to a given place: *She's a Missouri girl.* **9.** **girls,** (*used with a singular or plural v.*) **a.** a range of sizes from 7 to 14, for garments made for girls. **b.** a garment in this size range. **c.** the department or section of a store where these garments are sold. [1250–1300; ME *gurle, girle, gerle* child, young person; cf. OE *gyrela, gi(e)rela,* item of dress, apparel (presumably worn by the young in late OE period, and hence used as a metonym)]
—Usage. Just as many mature men, even young men, resent being referred to as *boys,* many adult women today are offended if referred to as GIRLS, or the less formal GALS. In business and professional offices, the practice of referring to one's secretary as *the girl* or *my girl,* as in *I'll have my girl look it up and call you back,* has decreased but not disappeared entirely. Such terms as THE GIRLS in reference to a group of women, GIRL or GAL FRIDAY in reference to a female secretary or assistant, and BACHELOR GIRL in reference to an unmarried woman are increasingly regarded as offensive, and WORKING GIRL in the sense "a woman who works" is declining in use. See also **lady, woman.**

girl′ Fri′day, *pl.* **girl Fridays.** See **gal Friday.** [1935–40; modeled on MAN FRIDAY]

girl·friend (gûrl′frend′), *n.* **1.** a frequent or favorite female companion; sweetheart. **2.** a female friend. Also, **girl′ friend′.** [1855–60; GIRL + FRIEND]

girl′ guide′, (*sometimes caps.*) a member of a British organization of girls (**Girl′ Guides′**) founded in England by Lord Robert S. S. Baden-Powell and his sister Lady Agnes as a sister organization of the Girl Scouts. [1905–10]

girl·hood (gûrl′ho͝od), *n.* **1.** the state or time of being a girl. **2.** girls collectively: *the nation's girlhood.* [1775–85; GIRL + -HOOD]

girl·ie (gûr′lē), *adj. Informal.* **1.** featuring nude or scantily clad young women: *a girlie show; girlie magazines.* —*n.* **2.** *Offensive.* a term of address used for a girl or woman. Also, **girly.** [1940–45; GIRL + -IE]

girl·ish (gûr′lish), *adj.* of, like, or befitting a girl or girlhood: *girlish laughter.* [1555–65; GIRL + -ISH[1]] **—girl′ish·ly,** *adv.* **—girl′ish·ness,** *n.*

girl·o (gûrl′ō), *n., pl.* **girl·os.** *Australian Informal.* a girl or young woman. [GIRL + -O]

Girl′ of the Gold′en West′, The, (Italian, *La fanciulla del West*), an opera (1910) by Giacomo Puccini.

girl′ scout′, (*sometimes caps.*) a member of an organization of girls (**Girl′ Scouts′**) founded in the U.S. in 1912 by Juliette Low that seeks to develop certain skills, as well as health, citizenship, and character. [1905–10, *Amer.*]

girl·y (gûr′lē), *adj., n., pl.* **girl·ies.** girlie.

girn[1] (gûrn), *v.i., v.t., n. Scot.* grin[1].

girn[2] (gûrn), *n., v.t. Scot.* grin[2].

gi·ro (jī′rō), *n., pl.* **-ros.** autogiro. [by shortening]

Gi·ronde (jə rond′; *Fr.* zhē RÔND′), *n.* **1.** an estuary in SW France, formed by the junction of the Garonne and Dordogne rivers. 45 mi. (72 km) long. **2.** a department in SW France. 1,061,474; 4141 sq. mi. (10,725 sq. km). *Cap.:* Bordeaux. **3. the Gironde,** the party of the Girondists.

Gi·ron·dist (jə ron′dist), *n.* **1.** *Fr. Hist.* a member of a political party (1791–93) of moderate republicans whose leaders were deputies from the department of Gironde. —*adj.* **2.** of or pertaining to the Girondists. [1785–95; < F *Girondiste.* See GIRONDE, -IST] **—Gi·ron′dism,** *n.*

gir·o·sol (jir′ə sôl′, -sōl′, -sol′), *n.* girasol.

girsh (gûrsh), *n.* qirsh.

girt[1] (gûrt), *v.* a pt. and pp. of **gird**[1].

girt[2] (gûrt), *v.t.* gird[1] (def. 1).

girt[3] (gûrt), *n., v.t.* girth.

girt[4] (gûrt), *n.* **1.** *Carpentry.* **a.** a timber or plate connecting the corner posts of an exterior wooden frame, as a braced frame, at a floor above the ground floor. **b.** a heavy beam, as for supporting the ends of rafters. **2.** *Print.* (in certain hand presses) one of a pair of leather straps having one end fastened to the bed and the other to the rounce, for drawing the bed under the platen. [1555–65; alter. of GIRTH]

girth (gûrth), *n.* **1.** the measure around anything; circumference. **2.** a band that passes underneath a horse or other animal to hold a saddle in place, esp. one having a buckle at each end for fastening to straps running from under the flaps of the saddle. See illus. under **saddle. 3.** something that encircles; a band or girdle. —*v.t.* **4.** to bind or fasten with a girth. **5.** to girdle; encircle. Also, **girt.** [1300–50; ME *girth, gerth* < ON *gerth* girdle; akin to GIRD[1]]

Gir·tin (gûr′tin), *n.* **Thomas,** 1775–1802, English painter.

CONCISE ETYMOLOGY KEY: <, descended or borrowed from; >, whence; b., blend of, blended; c., cognate with; cf., compare; deriv., derivative; equiv., equivalent; imit., imitative; obl., oblique; r., replacing; s., stem; sp., spelling, spelled; resp., respelling, respelled; trans., translation; ?, origin unknown; *, unattested; ‡, probably earlier than. See the full key inside the front cover.

girt·line (gûrt′līn′), *n. Naut.* gantline. [1760–70; GIRT[1] + LINE[1]]

GI′s (jē′īz′), *n.* **the GI's,** *Slang.* diarrhea. Also, **G.I.'s, G.I.s** [1960–65, *Amer.*; prob. for *GI shits;* see GI, -S[3]]

gi·sant (*Fr.* zhē zäN′), *n., pl.* **-sants** (*Fr.* -zäN′). a sculptured representation of a dead person in a recumbent position, usually as part of a sepulchral monument. [< F, n. use of prp. of *gésir* to lie << L *jacēre;* see -ANT]

gi·sarme (gi zärm′), *n.* guisarme.

Gis·borne (giz′bərn), *n.* a seaport on E North Island, in N New Zealand. 31,790.

Gis·card d'Es·taing (zhēs KAR des taN′; *Eng.* zhē-skär′ de stang′), **Va·lé·ry** (VA lā Rē′), born 1926, French political leader: president 1974–81.

Gi·selle (ji zel′; *Fr.* zhē zel′), *n.* **1.** (*italics*) a ballet (1841) choreographed by Jean Coralli and Jules Perrot, with musical score by Adolphe Adam. **2.** Also, **Gisele.** a female given name, form of **Elizabeth.**

GI series, gastrointestinal series: x-ray examination of the upper or lower gastrointestinal tract after barium sulfate is given rectally (**barium enema**) or orally as a contrast medium. Also called **barium x-ray.**

Gish (gish), *n.* **Dorothy,** 1898–1968, and her sister **Lillian,** born 1896, U.S. film actresses.

gis·mo (giz′mō), *n., pl.* **-mos.** *Informal.* a gadget or device: *What is this gismo supposed to do?* Also, **gizmo.** [1940–45; orig. uncert.]

Gis·sing (gis′ing), *n.* **George (Robert),** 1857–1903, English novelist.

gist (jist), *n.* **1.** the main or essential part of a matter: *What was the gist of his speech?* **2.** the ground of a legal action. [1720–30; < AF (*cest action*) *gist* (this matter) lies, 3rd sing. pres. indic. of AF, OF *gesir* to lie << L *jacēre*]
—Syn. 1. essence, point, substance, burden, kernel, import.

git (git), *v. Dial.* get.
—Pronunciation. See **get.**

Gi·ta (gē′tä), *n. Hinduism.* See **Bhagavad-Gita.**

git·a·lin (jit′ə lin, ji tä′-, ji tal′in), *n. Pharm.* a mixture of glycosides from *Digitalis purpurea,* used chiefly in the management of congestive heart failure. [(DI)GITAL(IS) + -IN[1]]

git-go (git′gō′), *n. Dial.* **1.** start; beginning: *to work hard from the git-go.* **2.** pep; energy; get-up-and-go.

gi·tim (*Seph.* gē tēm′; *Ashk.* git′im), *n. Hebrew.* a pl. of ***get.***

git·tern (git′ərn), *n.* cittern.

git·tin (*Seph.* gē tēn′; *Ashk.* git′in), *n. Hebrew.* a pl. of ***get.***

git-up-and-git (git′up′ən git′), *n. Informal.* get-up-and-go.

Giu·ba (*It.* jo͞o′bä), *n.* Juba.

Giu·ki (gyo͞o′kē), *n.* Gjuki.

Giu·kung (gyo͞o′ko͝ong), *n.* Gjukung.

Giu·lio Ro·ma·no (jo͞ol′yô RÔ. mä′nô), (*Giulio Pippi de' Giannuzzi*), 1492?–1546, Italian painter and architect.

give (giv), *v.,* **gave, giv·en, giv·ing,** *n.* —*v.t.* **1.** to present voluntarily and without expecting compensation; bestow: *to give a birthday present to someone.* **2.** to hand to someone: *Give me that plate, please.* **3.** to place in someone's care: *If you give me your coat, I'll put it in the closet.* **4.** to grant (permission, opportunity, etc.) to someone: *Give me a chance.* **5.** to impart or communicate: *to give advice; to give a cold to someone.* **6.** to set forth or show; present; offer: *He gave no reason for his lateness.* **7.** to pay or transfer possession to another in exchange for something: *They gave five dollars for the picture. He gave me the car for $800.* **8.** to furnish, provide, or proffer: *to give evidence; Let me give you my umbrella before you go out in this rain.* **9.** to provide as an entertainment or social function: *to give a New Year's Eve party.* **10.** to deal or administer: *to give a blow to someone; to give medicine to a patient.* **11.** to put forth, emit, or utter; issue: *to give a cry; to give a command.* **12.** to assign or admit as a basis of calculation or reasoning (usually used passively): *These facts being given, the argument makes sense.* **13.** to produce, yield, or afford: *to give good results; 9 × 8 gives 72; The hen gave six eggs a week.* **14.** to make, do, or perform: *to give a start; to give a lurch.* **15.** to perform or present publicly: *to give a play; to give a concert.* **16.** to cause; be responsible for (usually fol. by an infinitive): *They gave me to understand that you would be there.* **17.** to care about something to the value or extent of (something fanciful): *I don't give a hoot about his opinion.* **18.** to relinquish or sacrifice: *to give one's life for a cause.* **19.** to convey or transmit: *Give Aunt Betty my love.* **20.** to assign or allot: *Give every man a full ration of biscuits. They gave him the name of "Joseph."* **21.** to bestow (the object of one's choice) upon, as if by providence: *Give me the wide open spaces anytime.* **22.** to be connected with, as by a telephone operator: *Give me 235-7522.* **23.** to present to an audience, as an entertainer, speaker, or act: *Ladies and gentlemen, I give you the governor of Texas.* **24.** to attribute or ascribe: *to give the devil his due; After long study the critic gave the unsigned work to a minor impressionist.* **25.** to cause or occasion: *She gives me a pain in the neck.* **26.** to apply fully or freely: *He gives his free time to golf.* **27.** to award by verdict or after consideration: *A decision was given for the defendant.* **28.** to inflict as a punishment on another; punish by; impose a sentence of: *The judge gave him five years.* **29.** to pledge, offer as a pledge, or execute and deliver: *He gave her his promise. Can you give bond?* **30.** to propose as the subject of a toast (fol. by an indirect object): *Ladies and gentlemen, I give you our country.* **31.** to bear to a man; deliver (fol. by an indirect object): *She gave him a beautiful baby boy.* **32.** to sire upon a woman; father (fol. by an indirect object): *He gave her two children in the first five years of marriage.* **33.** to concede or grant, as a point in an argument. —*v.i.* **34.** to make a gift or gifts; contribute: *to give to the United Way.* **35.** to yield somewhat, as to influence or force; compromise: *We can't negotiate until each side is willing to give on some points.* **36.** to yield somewhat when subjected to weight, force, pressure, etc.: *A horsehair mattress doesn't give much.* **37.** to collapse; break down; fall apart; fail: *The antique chair gave when I sat on it.* **38.** to be warm and open in relationships with other persons: *a withdrawn person who doesn't know how to give.* **39.** *Informal.* to divulge information: *Okay now, give! What happened?* **40.** to afford a view or passage; face, open, or lead (usually fol. by *on, onto,* etc.): *The window gives on the sea. This door gives onto the hallway.* **41. give and take, a.** to compromise in order to cooperate: *A willingness to give and take is important for success in marriage.* **b.** to exchange ideas: *an informal meeting in which there would be opportunities to give and take.* **42. give away, a.** to give as a present; bestow. **b.** to present (the bride) to the bridegroom in a marriage ceremony. **c.** to expose or betray (a person). **d.** to reveal (a confidence or secret, hidden motives, true feelings, etc.): *That remark gave away his real feelings.* **43. give back,** to return (something), as to its owner; restore: *You haven't given back the books you borrowed from me.* **44. give battle.** See **battle**[1] (def. 6). **45. give birth to.** See **birth** (def. 8). **46. give ground,** to yield before superior force, as of arms or of reasoning. **47. give in, a.** to acknowledge defeat; yield. **b.** to hand in; deliver: *Please give in your timecards.* **48. give it to,** *Informal.* to reprimand or punish: *His father really gave it to him for coming home so late.* **49. give of,** to devote or contribute generously of: *to give of oneself; to give of one's abundance.* **50. give off,** to put forth; emit: *The gardenia gives off a very strong fragrance.* **51. give or take,** plus or minus a specified amount; more or less: *It will cost $20, give or take a dollar or two.* **52. give out, a.** to send out; emit. **b.** to make public; announce. **c.** to distribute; issue. **d.** to become exhausted. **e.** to become used up; fail: *The fuel gave out.* **f.** to do or express something, esp. unrestrainedly or easily: *to give out with a song.* **53. give over, a.** to put into the care of; transfer: *She gave over all her property to her daughter.* **b.** to put an end to; stop: *They will never give over their impossible dreams.* **c.** to indulge in without restraint: *She gave herself over to tears.* **d.** to devote to a specified activity: *The day was given over to relaxing in the sun.* **54. give rise to.** See **rise** (def. 55). **55. give up, a.** to abandon hope; despair. **b.** to desist from; renounce: *to give up smoking.* **c.** to surrender; relinquish. **d.** to devote (oneself) entirely to: *She gave herself up to her job and seldom saw her old friends.* **e.** *South Midland U.S.* to consider; deem: *She's given up to be the kindest woman around here.* **56. give way.** See **way** (def. 26).
—*n.* **57.** the quality or state of being resilient; springiness. [bef. 900; ME < ON *gefa* (cf. Dan *give*); r. ME *yeven, yiven,* OE *gefan, giefan;* c. D *geven,* G *geben,* Goth *giban*] **—giv′a·ble, give′a·ble,** *adj., n.* **—giv·ee′,** *n.* **—giv′er,** *n.*
—Syn. 1. offer, vouchsafe, impart, accord, furnish, provide, supply, donate, contribute. GIVE, CONFER, GRANT, PRESENT may mean that something concrete or abstract is bestowed on one person by another. GIVE is the general word: *to give someone a book, permission, etc.* CONFER usually means to give an honor or a favor; it implies courteous and gracious giving: *to confer a degree.* GRANT is limited to the idea of acceding to a request; it may apply to the bestowal of privileges, or the fulfillment of an expressed wish: *to grant a charter, a prayer, permission, etc.* PRESENT, a more formal word than GIVE, usually implies a certain ceremony in the giving: *to present a citation to a regiment.* **18.** cede, yield. **—Ant. 1.** receive.

give-and-take (giv′ən tāk′), *n.* **1.** the practice of dealing by compromise or mutual concession; cooperation. **2.** good-natured exchange of talk, ideas, etc. [1760–70]

give·a·way (giv′ə wā′), *n.* **1.** an act or instance of giving something away. **2.** something that is given away, esp. as a gift or premium: *A pocket calculator was offered as a giveaway with every new subscription to the magazine.* **3.** a radio or television program on which prizes are given away to contestants in a question-and-answer game. **4.** a tax law or other legislation designed to benefit one segment of the population, one area or state, etc.: *a giveaway that benefited only the very rich.* **5.** an unscrupulous deal, esp. one that benefits some while defrauding others. **6.** *Sports.* any careless loss of possession of a ball, puck, etc., or other offensive lapse that leads to a score by the opponent. —*adj.* **7.** constituting a giveaway: *a giveaway newspaper.* [1870–75, *Amer.*; n. use of v. phrase *give away*]

give·back (giv′bak′), *n.* **1.** (in union negotiations) a reduction in employee wages or benefits conceded by a union in exchange for other benefits or in recognition of depressed economic conditions: *Givebacks have not slowed the number of shutdowns.* **2.** something returned, rebated, etc.: *Givebacks to dealers have increased car sales.* Also, **give′-back′.** [1975–80; n. use of v. phrase *give back*]

giv·en (giv′ən), *v.* **1.** pp. of **give.** —*adj.* **2.** stated, fixed, or specified: *at a given time.* **3.** addicted or disposed (often fol. by *to*): *given to making snide remarks.* **4.** bestowed as a gift; conferred. **5.** assigned as a basis of calculation, reasoning, etc.: *Given A and B, C follows.* **6.** *Math.* known or independently determined: *a given magnitude.* **7.** (on official documents) executed and delivered as of the date shown. —*n.* **8.** an established fact, condition, factor, etc.

Gi·ven·chy (zhi väN′shē; *Fr.* zhē väN shē′), *n.* **Hubert de** (Y beR′ də), born 1927, French fashion designer.

giv′en name′, the name given to one, as distinguished from an inherited family name; first name; Christian name: *His given name is John.* [1820–30, *Amer.*]

give-up (giv′up′), *n.* **1.** something conceded or relinquished; concession: *Labor has balked at any more give-*

ups in the contract talks. **2.** *Stock Exchange.* **a.** a commission shared among two or more stockbrokers. **b.** a part of a commission that constitutes a single such share. [1965–70; n. use of v. phrase *give up*]

giv•ey (giv′ē), *adj.,* **giv•i•er, giv•i•est.** *Chiefly South Midland U.S.* **1.** (esp. of soil) moist, soft, or spongy. **2.** unsteady; rickety: *That chair is getting a little givey.* **3.** (of weather) misty, rainy, or humid; damp. [1820–30, *Amer.*; GIVE + -Y[1]; retention of *e* allows base word to be more transparent]

Gi•za (gē′zə), *n.* a city in N Egypt: a suburb of Cairo across the Nile; the ancient Egyptian pyramids and the Sphinx are located nearby. 853,700. Also, **Gi′zeh.** Also called **El Giza, El Gizeh.**

giz•mo (giz′mō), *n., pl.* **-mos.** gismo.

giz•zard (giz′ərd), *n. Zool.* **1.** Also called **ventriculus.** a thick-walled, muscular pouch in the lower stomach of many birds and reptiles that grinds food, often with the aid of ingested stones or grit. **2.** Also called **gastric mill.** a similar structure in the foregut of arthropods and several other invertebrates, often lined with chitin and small teeth. **3.** the innards or viscera collectively, esp. the intestine and stomach. [1325–75; ME *giser, gezier* (F *gésier*) < VL **gigerium*; cf. L *gigeria, gizeria* giblets, perh. ult. < Iranian; cf. Pers *jigar* liver]

giz′zard shad′, a silvery herring, *Dorosoma cepedianum,* of eastern and central U.S. waters, that has a gizzardlike stomach. [1810–20, *Amer.*]

GJ, grapefruit juice.

Gjal•lar-horn (yäl′lär hôrn′), *n. Scand. Myth.* Heimdall's horn, used to warn the gods of Ragnarok. [< ON, equiv. to *gjallar,* gen. sing of *gjǫll* noise, din (cf. *gjalla* to resound loudly, scream; c. OE *g(i)ellan* to YELL) + *horn* HORN]

Gjel•le•rup (gel′ə ro͝op), *n.* **Karl** (kärl), 1857–1919, Danish novelist: Nobel prize 1917.

Gju•ki (gyo͞o′kē), *n.* (in the *Volsunga Saga*) a king, the father of Gudrun and Gunnar and the husband of Grimhild. Also, **Giuki.** [< ON *Gjūki*; cf. OE *Gifica,* OHG *Gibicho*]

Gju•kung (gyo͞o′ko͝ong), *n.* (in the *Volsunga Saga*) any member of the family of Gjuki. Also, **Giukung.**

Gk, Greek. Also, **Gk.**

Gl, *Symbol, Chem.* glucinum.

gl., **1.** glass. **2.** gloss.

g/l, grams per liter.

gla•bel•la (glə bel′ə), *n., pl.* **-bel•lae** (-bel′ē). *Anat.* the flat area of bone between the eyebrows, used as a craniometric point. [1590–1600; < NL, fem. of L *glabellus* smooth, hairless, equiv. to *glaber* without hair, smooth + *-lus* dim. suffix; cf. CASTELLUM] —**gla•bel′•lar,** *adj.*

gla•bel•lum (glə bel′əm), *n., pl.* **-bel•la** (-bel′ə). glabella.

Gla•ber (glā′bər; *Fr.* gla bεr′), *n.* **Ra•oul** (rä o͞ol′), or **Ru•dolphe** (ro͞o dôlf′), c990–c1050, French ecclesiastic and chronicler.

gla•brate (glā′brāt, -brit), *adj.* **1.** *Zool.* glabrous. **2.** *Bot.* becoming glabrous; somewhat glabrous. [1855–60; < L *glabrātus* (ptp. of *glabrāre* to make bare, deprive of hair), equiv. to *glabr-,* s. of *glaber* without hair, smooth + *-ātus* -ATE[1]]

gla•bres•cent (glā bres′ənt), *adj. Bot.* becoming glabrous. [1855–60; < L *glabrēscent-* (s. of *glabrēscēns,* prp. of *glabrēscere* to become smooth), equiv. to *glabr-,* s. of *glaber* smooth + *-ēscent-* -ESCENT]

gla•brous (glā′brəs), *adj. Zool., Bot.* having a surface devoid of hair or pubescence. [1630–40; < L *glabr-* (s. of *glaber*) smooth, hairless + -OUS]

glace (glas), *n. Canadian (chiefly Montreal).* ice placed in a drink to cool it. [< CanF, F: ice; see GLACÉ]

gla•cé (gla sā′), *adj., v.,* **-céed, -cé•ing.** **1.** frosted or iced, as cake. **2.** candied, as fruits. —*adj.* **3.** frozen. **4.** finished with a gloss, as kid or silk. —*v.t.* **5.** to make glacé. [1840–50; < F, ptp. of *glacer* to freeze, deriv. of *glace* ice < L *glaciēs*]

Glace′ Bay′ (glās), a town in E Nova Scotia, in SE Canada, on E Cape Breton Island on the Atlantic Ocean. 21,466.

gla•cial (glā′shəl), *adj.* **1.** of or pertaining to glaciers or ice sheets. **2.** resulting from or associated with the action of ice or glaciers: *glacial terrain.* **3.** characterized by the presence of ice in extensive masses or glaciers. **4.** bitterly cold; icy: *a glacial winter wind.* **5.** happening or moving extremely slowly: *The work proceeded at a glacial pace.* **6.** icily unsympathetic or immovable: *a glacial stare; glacial indifference.* **7.** *Chem.* of, pertaining to, or tending to develop into icelike crystals: *glacial phosphoric acid.* [1650–60; < L *glaciālis* icy, equiv. to *glaci(ēs)* ice + *-ālis* -AL[1]] —**gla′cial•ly,** *adv.*
—**Syn. 4.** chill, freezing, frigid, wintry. **6.** forbidding, unfriendly, hostile.

gla′cial ace′tic ac′id, acetic acid of at least 99.5 percent concentration, solidifying at 16.7°C. [1835–45]

gla′cial drift′, *Geol.* material, as gravel, sand, or clay, transported and deposited by a glacier or by glacial meltwater. Also called **drift.** Cf. **till**[4].

gla′cial ep′och, **1.** Also called **gla′cial pe′riod, ice age.** the geologically recent Pleistocene Epoch, during which much of the Northern Hemisphere was covered by great ice sheets. **2.** any one of the Permian, Carboniferous, Cambrian, or Precambrian glaciations. [1840–50]

gla•cial•ist (glā′shə list), *n.* a person who studies geological phenomena involving the action of ice, esp. of glaciers. Also, **glaciologist.** Also called **gla′cial geol′ogist.** [1850–55; GLACIAL + -IST]

gla′cial meal′, finely ground rock material produced by the grinding action of a glacier on its bed. Also called **rock flour.**

gla′cial milk′, waters of a glacial stream in which particles of light-colored silt are suspended.

gla•ci•ate (glā′shē āt′, -sē-), *v.,* **-at•ed, -at•ing.** —*v.t.* **1.** to cover with ice or glaciers. **2.** to affect by glacial action. —*v.i.* **3.** to become frozen or covered with ice or glaciers. [1615–25; < L *glaciātus* (ptp. of *glaciāre* to freeze), equiv. to *glaci(ēs)* ice + *-ātus* -ATE[1]] —**gla′ci•a′tion,** *n.*

gla•cier (glā′shər), *n.* an extended mass of ice formed from snow falling and accumulating over the years and moving very slowly, either descending from high mountains, as in valley glaciers, or moving outward from centers of accumulation, as in continental glaciers. [1735–45; < dial. F, deriv. of OF *glace* ice < LL *glacia* (for L *glaciēs*)] —**gla′ciered,** *adj.*

Gla′cier Bay′, a national park in SE Alaska, made up of large tidewater glaciers. 4381 sq. mi. (11,347 sq. km).

gla′cier lil′y, a dogtooth violet, *Erythronium grandiflorum,* of the lily family, native to western North America, having bright yellow flowers. Also called **snow lily.**

Gla′cier Na′tional Park′, a national park in NW Montana: glaciers; lakes; forest reserve. 1534 sq. mi. (3970 sq. km).

gla′cier ta′ble, a stone slab supported over the surface of a mountain glacier by a column or columns of ice. [1855–60]

gla•ci•ol•o•gist (glā′shē ol′ə jist, -sē-), *n.* glacialist.

gla•ci•ol•o•gy (glā′shē ol′ə jē, -sē-), *n.* the branch of geology that deals with the nature, distribution, and action of glaciers and with their effect on the earth's topography. [1890–95; GLACI(ER) + -O- + -LOGY] —**gla•ci•o•log•i•cal** (glā′shē ə loj′i kəl, -sē-), **gla′ci•o•log′ic,** *adj.*

gla•cis (glā′sis, glas′is), *n., pl.* **gla•cis** (glā′sēz, -siz, glas′ēz, -iz), **gla•cis•es.** **1.** a gentle slope. **2.** *Fort.* a bank of earth in front of the counterscarp or covered way of a fort, having an easy slope toward the field or open country. [1665–75; < MF; akin to OF *glacier* to slide; cf. L *glaciāre* to make into ice; see GLACÉ]

Glack•ens (glak′ənz), *n.* **William James,** 1870–1938, U.S. painter and illustrator.

glad[1] (glad), *adj.,* **glad•der, glad•dest,** *v.,* **glad•ded, glad•ding.** —*adj.* **1.** feeling joy or pleasure; delighted; pleased: *glad about the good news; glad that you are here.* **2.** accompanied by or causing joy or pleasure: *a glad occasion; glad tidings.* **3.** characterized by or showing cheerfulness, joy, or pleasure, as looks or utterances. **4.** very willing: *I'll be glad to give him your message.* —*v.t.* **5.** *Archaic.* to make glad. [bef. 900; ME; OE *glæd*; c. ON *glathr* bright, glad, D *glad,* G *glatt* smooth; akin to L *glaber* smooth] —**glad′ly,** *adv.* —**glad′ness,** *n.*
—**Syn. 1.** elated, gratified, contented. **3.** merry, joyous, joyful, cheerful, happy, cheery. —**Ant. 1–3.** sad.

glad[2] (glad), *n.* gladiolus (def. 1). [1920–25; by shortening]

Glad•bach-Rheydt (glät′bäKH rīt′), *n.* a former city in W West Germany; now part of Mönchengladbach.

glad•den (glad′n), *v.t.* **1.** to make glad. —*v.i.* **2.** *Obs.* to be glad. [1250–1300; ME; see GLAD[1], -EN[1]] —**glad′•den•er,** *n.*
—**Syn. 1.** See **cheer.**

glade (glād), *n.* an open space in a forest. [1520–30; akin to GLAD[1], in obs. sense "bright"] —**glade′like′,** *adj.*

glad′ eye′, *Informal.* a friendly or interested glance, esp. a flirtatious one. [1910–15]

glad′ hand′, *Informal.* a hearty welcome or enthusiastic reception, esp. one that is effusive or hypocritical: *Visiting dignitaries were being given the glad hand.* [1890–95]

glad-hand (glad′hand′), *Informal.* —*v.t.* **1.** to greet warmly. **2.** to greet in an insincerely effusive manner. —*v.i.* **3.** to greet others with enthusiasm, esp. feigned enthusiasm: *The candidate spent weeks glad-handing around the state.* [1900–05] —**glad′-hand′er,** *n.*

glad•i•ate (glad′ē it, -āt′, glā′dē-), *adj. Bot.* sword-shaped. [1785–95; < L *gladi(us)* sword + -ATE[1]]

glad•i•a•tor (glad′ē ā′tər), *n.* **1.** (in ancient Rome) a person, often a slave or captive, who was armed with a sword or other weapon and compelled to fight to the death in a public arena against another person or a wild animal, for the entertainment of the spectators. **2.** a person who engages in a fight or controversy. **3.** a prizefighter. [1535–45; < L *gladiātor,* equiv. to *gladi(us)* sword + *-ātor* -ATOR]

glad•i•a•to•ri•al (glad′ē ə tôr′ē əl, -tōr′-), *adj.* of or pertaining to gladiators or to their combats. [1745–55; < L *gladiātōri(us)* (see GLADIATOR, -TORY[1]) + -AL[1]]

glad•i•o•la (glad′ē ō′lə), *n.* gladiolus (def. 1). [< L, neut. pl. treated as if fem. sing.] —**glad′i•o′lar,** *adj.*

glad•i•o•lus (glad′ē ō′ləs), *n., pl.* **-lus, -li** (-lī), **-lus•es** for 1; **-li** for 2. **1.** any plant of the genus *Gladiolus,* of the iris family, native esp. to Africa, having erect, sword-shaped leaves and spikes of flowers in a variety of colors. **2.** *Anat.* the middle and largest segment of the sternum. Cf. **manubrium** (def. 2a), **xiphisternum.** [1560–70; < L: small sword, sword lily, equiv. to *gladi(us)* sword + *-olus* -OLE[1]]

gla•di•us (glā′dē əs), *n., pl.* **-di•i** (-dē ī′). a short sword used in ancient Rome by legionaries. [1510–20; < L]

glad′ rags′, *Informal.* dressy clothes, esp. as worn to a party or other social event. [1900–05]

Glads•heim (gläts′hām), *n. Scand. Myth.* the golden palace of Odin, of which Valhalla was a part.

glad•some (glad′səm), *adj.* **1.** giving or causing joy; delightful. **2.** glad. [1325–75; ME; see GLAD[1], -SOME[1]] —**glad′some•ly,** *adv.* —**glad′some•ness,** *n.*

Glad•stone (glad′stōn′, -stən), *n.* **1.** a four-wheel pleasure carriage with a calash top, two inside seats, and dickey seats. **2.** See **Gladstone bag.** [1860–65; after W.E. GLADSTONE]

Glad•stone (glad′stōn′, -stən), *n.* **1.** **William Ew•art** (yo͞o′ərt), 1809–98, British statesman: prime minister four times between 1868 and 1894. **2.** a city in NW Missouri. 24,990.

Glad′stone bag′, a small rectangular suitcase hinged to open into two compartments of equal size. Also called **Gladstone.** [1880–85; after W.E. GLADSTONE]

Glad•ys (glad′is), *n.* a female given name.

Glag•o•lit•ic (glag′ə lit′ik), *adj.* **1.** noting or written in an alphabet, probably invented by St. Cyril in about A.D. 865, formerly used in writing Old Church Slavonic and other Slavic languages: almost completely replaced by Cyrillic starting about the 10th century. —*n.* **2.** the Glagolitic alphabet. [1860–65; < NL *glagoliticus,* equiv. to *glagolit(a),* Latinization of Serbo-Croatian *glagoljica* (ult. deriv. of OCS *glagolŭ* speech, word) + *-icus* -IC]

glaik•it (glā′kit), *adj. Chiefly Scot.* foolish; giddy; flighty. Also, **glaik′et.** [1400–50; late ME < ?]

glair (glâr), *n.* **1.** the white of an egg. **2.** a glaze or size made of egg white. **3.** any viscous substance like egg white. —*v.t.* **4.** to coat with glair. Also, **glaire.** [1300–50; ME *glaire* < OF: white of an egg < VL **clāria*; cf. L *clārus* clear]

glaire (glâr), *n., v.t.,* **glaired, glair•ing.** glair.

glair•y (glâr′ē), *adj.,* **glair•i•er, glair•i•est.** **1.** of the nature of glair; viscous. **2.** covered with glair. Also, **glair•e•ous** (glâr′ē əs). [1655–65; GLAIR + -Y[1]] —**glair′i•ness,** *n.*

glaive (glāv), *n. Archaic.* a sword or broadsword. [1250–1300; ME < OF *glaive, glai* < L *gladius* sword] —**glaived,** *adj.*

glam (glam), *adj. Informal.* glamorous. [1985–90; by shortening]

Gla•mor•gan (glə môr′gən), *n.* a historic county in SE Wales, now part of Mid, South, and West Glamorgan. Also called **Gla•mor•gan•shire** (glə môr′gən shēr′, -shər).

glam•or•ize (glam′ə rīz′), *v.t.,* **-ized, -iz•ing.** **1.** to make glamorous. **2.** to glorify or romanticize: *an adventure film that tended to glamorize war.* Also, **glam′our•ize′;** *esp. Brit.,* **glam′our•ise′.** [1935–40, *Amer.*; GLAMOR + -IZE] —**glam′or•i•za′tion,** *n.* —**glam′or•iz′er,** *n.*

glam•or•ous (glam′ər əs), *adj.* **1.** full of glamour; charmingly or fascinatingly attractive, esp. in a mysterious or magical way. **2.** full of excitement, adventure, and unusual activity: *the glamorous job of a foreign correspondent.* Also, **glam′our•ous.** [1935–40; GLAMOR + -OUS] —**glam′or•ous•ly, glam′our•ous•ly,** *adv.* —**glam′or•ous•ness, glam′our•ous•ness,** *n.*
—**Syn. 1.** captivating, beguiling, fascinating, alluring.

glam•our (glam′ər), *n.* **1.** the quality of fascinating, alluring, or attracting, esp. by a combination of charm and good looks. **2.** excitement, adventure, and unusual activity: *the glamour of being an explorer.* **3.** magic or enchantment; spell; witchery. —*adj.* **4.** suggestive or full of glamour; glamorous: *a glamour job in television; glamour stocks.* Also, **glam′or.** [1710–20; earlier *glammar,* dissimilated var. of GRAMMAR in sense of occult learning]
—**Usage.** See **-or.**

glam′our boy′, a man whose appearance or lifestyle is considered glamorous by popular standards. [1935–40]

glam′our girl′, a girl or woman whose appearance or lifestyle is considered glamorous by popular standards. [1930–35]

glam′our puss′, *Older Slang.* a person with an unusually attractive face. [1950–55]

glam′our stock′, a popular stock that rises quickly or continuously in price and attracts large numbers of investors.

glance[1] (glans, gläns), *v.,* **glanced, glanc•ing,** *n.* —*v.i.* **1.** to look quickly or briefly. **2.** to gleam or flash: *a silver brooch glancing in the sunlight.* **3.** to strike a surface or object obliquely, esp. so as to bounce off at an angle (often fol. by *off*): *The arrow glanced off his shield.* **4.** to allude briefly to a topic or subject in passing (usually fol. by *at*). —*v.t. Archaic.* **5.** to cast a glance or brief look at; catch a glimpse of. **6.** to cast or reflect, as a gleam. **7.** to throw, hit, kick, shoot, etc. (something) so that it glances off a surface or object. —*n.* **8.** a quick or brief look. **9.** a gleam or flash of light, esp. reflected light. **10.** a deflected movement or course; an oblique rebound. **11.** a passing reference or allusion; insinuation. **12.** *Cricket.* a stroke in which the batsman deflects the ball with the bat, as to leg. [1400–50; late ME *glancen* (v.), nasalized var. (perh. influenced by obs. *glent*; see GLINT) of ME *glacen* to strike a glancing blow < OF *glacier* to slip, slide < L *glaciāre* to freeze. See GLACÉ]
—**Syn. 2.** glisten, scintillate. See **flash. 3.** reflect, ricochet. **9.** glitter.

glance[2] (glans, gläns), *n.* any of various minerals having a luster that indicates a metallic nature. [1795–1805; < G *Glanz* brightness, luster]

glanc•ing (glan′sing, glän′-), *adj.* **1.** striking obliquely and bouncing off at an angle: *a glancing blow.* **2.** brief and indirect: *glancing references to his dubious past.* [1485–95; GLANCE[1] + -ING[2]] —**glanc′ing•ly,** *adv.*

glanc′ing an′gle, the angle between a ray incident on a plane surface and the surface, as of a beam of electrons incident on a crystal; the complement of the angle of incidence.

gland[1] (gland), *n.* **1.** *Anat.* **a.** a cell, group of cells, or organ producing a secretion. **b.** any of various organs or structures resembling the shape but not the function of

CONCISE PRONUNCIATION KEY: act, cāpe, dâre, pärt; set, ēqual; *if,* īce; ox, ōver, ôrder, oil, bo͝ok, bo͞ot, out; up, ûrge; child; sing; shoe; thin, *that;* zh as in *treasure.* ə = *a* as in *alone, e* as in *system, i* as in *easily, o* as in *gallop, u* as in *circus;* ə as in *fire* (fīər), *hour* (ouər). l and n can serve as syllabic consonants, as in *cradle* (krād′l), and *button* (but′n). See the full key inside the front cover.

true glands. **2.** *Bot.* a secreting organ or structure. [1685–95; < L *gland-* (s. of *glāns* acorn); cf. It *ghianda*] —**gland′less,** *adj.* —**gland′like′,** *adj.*

gland[2] (gland), *n. Mach.* **1.** a sleeve within a stuffing box, fitted over a shaft or valve stem and tightened against compressible packing in such a way as to prevent leakage of fluid while allowing the shaft or stem to move; lantern ring. **2.** See **stuffing box.** [1830–40; orig. uncert.]

glan·dered (glan′dərd), *adj. Vet. Pathol.* affected with glanders. [1660–70; GLANDER(S) + -ED[3]]

glan·ders (glan′dərz), *n.* (*used with a singular v.*) *Vet. Pathol.* a contagious disease chiefly of horses and mules but communicable to humans, caused by the bacterium *Pseudomonas mallei* and characterized by swellings beneath the jaw and a profuse mucous discharge from the nostrils. Cf. **farcy.** [1475–85; < MF *glandres* swollen glands < L *glandulae* swollen glands, lit., little acorns. See GLAND[1], -ULE] —**glan′der·ous,** *adj.*

glan·du·lar (glan′jə lər), *adj.* **1.** consisting of, containing, or bearing glands. **2.** of, pertaining to, or resembling a gland: *a glandular disorder.* **3.** visceral; instinctive. [1730–40; GLANDULE + -AR[1]] —**glan′du·lar·ly,** *adv.*

glan′dular fe′ver. See **infectious mononucleosis.**

glan·du·lous (glan′jə ləs), *adj.* glandular. [1350–1400; ME *glandelous* < L *glandulōsus* full of kernels. See GLANDULE, -OUS] —**glan′du·lous·ness,** *n.*

glans (glanz), *n., pl.* **glan·des** (glan′dēz). *Anat.* the head of the penis **(glans′ pe′nis)** or of the clitoris **(glans′ clit′oris).** [1640–50; < L *glāns* lit., acorn, beechmast; akin to Gk *bálanos*]

Glan·ville-Hicks (glan′vil hiks′), *n.* **Peggy,** born 1912, U.S. composer and music critic, born in Australia.

glare[1] (glâr), *n., v.,* **glared, glar·ing.** —*n.* **1.** a very harsh, bright, dazzling light: *in the glare of sunlight.* **2.** a fiercely or angrily piercing stare. **3.** dazzling or showy appearance; showiness. —*v.i.* **4.** to shine with or reflect a very harsh, bright, dazzling light. **5.** to stare with a fiercely or angrily piercing look. **6.** *Archaic.* to appear conspicuous; stand out obtrusively. —*v.t.* **7.** to express with a glare: *They glared their anger at each other.* [1250–1300; (v.) ME *glaren;* c. MD, MLG *glaren;* akin to GLASS (cf. OE *glæren* glassy); (n.) ME, deriv. of the v.] —**glare′less,** *adj.*
—**Syn. 1.** flare, glitter, flash. **4.** See **shine. 5.** GLARE, GLOWER, GLOAT all have connotations of emotion that accompany an intense gaze. To GLARE is to look piercingly or angrily: *A tiger glares at its prey.* To GLOWER is to look fiercely and threateningly, as from wrath; it suggests a scowl along with a glare: *to glower at a mischievous child.* To GLOAT meant originally to look with exultation, avaricious or malignant, on something or someone: *a tyrant gloating over the helplessness of his victim.* Today, however, it may simply imply inner exultation.

glare[2] (glâr), *n.* a bright, smooth surface, as of ice. [1560–70; special use of GLARE[1]]

glare′ ice′, ice having a smooth, glassy surface that reflects sunlight. [1825–35, *Amer.*]

glar·ing (glâr′ing), *adj.* **1.** shining with or reflecting a harshly bright or brilliant light. **2.** very conspicuous or obvious; flagrant: *several glaring errors in spelling.* **3.** staring in a fiercely or angrily piercing manner. **4.** excessively showy or bright; garish. [1350–1400; ME: see GLARE[1], -ING[2]] —**glar′ing·ly,** *adv.* —**glar′ing·ness,** *n.*
—**Syn. 1.** blinding. **2.** prominent, patent. See **flagrant. 4.** loud, gaudy, flashy.

Gla·rus (glär′əs, -o͞os), *n.* **1.** a canton in E central Switzerland. 35,900; 264 sq. mi. (684 sq. km). **2.** a town in and the capital of this canton, E of Lucerne. 6100.

glar·y[1] (glâr′ē), *adj.,* **glar·i·er, glar·i·est.** harshly brilliant; glaring. [1625–35; GLARE[1] + -Y[1]] —**glar′i·ness,** *n.*

glar·y[2] (glâr′ē), *adj.,* **glar·i·er, glar·i·est.** smooth and slippery, as ice. [1560–70; GLARE[2] + -Y[1]]

Gla·ser (glā′zər), *n.* **Donald A.,** born 1926, U.S. physicist: Nobel prize 1960.

Glas·gow (glas′gō, -kō; *for 2 also* glaz′gō), *n.* **1. Ellen (Anderson Ghol·son)** (gōl′sən), 1874–1945, U.S. novelist. **2.** a seaport in SW Scotland, on the Clyde River: administrative center of the Strathclyde region; shipyards. 880,617. **3.** a city in S Kentucky. 12,958.

glas·nost (glaz′nost, glaz′-; *Russ.* gläs′nəst), *n.* the declared public policy within the Soviet Union of openly and frankly discussing economic and political realities: initiated under Mikhail Gorbachev in 1985. [1980–85; < Russ *glásnost′* lit. publicity (taken to mean openness)]

Glas·pell (glas′pel), *n.* **Susan,** 1882–1948, U.S. novelist and dramatist.

glas·phalt (glas′fôlt, gläs′- *or, esp. Brit.,* -falt), *n.* a road-surfacing material composed of asphalt and crushed glass. [1965–70; b. GLASS and ASPHALT]

glass (glas, gläs), *n.* **1.** a hard, brittle, noncrystalline, more or less transparent substance produced by fusion, usually consisting of mutually dissolved silica and silicates that also contain soda and lime, as in the ordinary variety used for windows and bottles. **2.** any artificial or natural substance having similar properties and composition, as fused borax, obsidian, or the like. **3.** something made of such a substance, as a windowpane. **4.** a tumbler or other comparatively tall, handleless drinking container. **5. glasses.** Also called **eyeglasses.** a device to compensate for defective vision or to protect the eyes from light, dust, and the like, consisting usually of two glass or plastic lenses set in a frame that includes a nosepiece for resting on the bridge of the nose and two sidepieces extending over or around the ears (usually used with *pair of*). Cf. **goggle** (def. 1), **pince-nez, spectacle** (def. 3). **6.** a mirror. **7.** things made of glass, collectively; glassware. **8.** a glassful. **9.** a lens, esp. one used as a magnifying glass. **10.** a spyglass. —*adj.* **11.** made of glass. **12.** furnished or fitted with panes of glass; glazed. —*v.t.* **13.** to fit with panes of glass. **14.** cover with or encase in glass. **15.** to coat or cover with fiberglass: *to glass the hull of a boat.* **16.** to scan with a spyglass or other optical instrument. **17.** to reflect: *Trees glassed themselves in the lake.* [bef. 900; ME *glas* (n.), OE *glæs;* c. D, G *Glas*] —**glass′less,** *adj.* —**glass′like′,** *adj.*

Glass (glas, gläs), *n.* **Carter,** 1858–1946, U.S. statesman.

glass′ block′, a translucent, hollow or solid block of glass for glazing openings or constructing partitions, usually square on the face, with variously treated outer surfaces. Also called **glass′ brick′.**

glass·blow·ing (glas′blō′ing), *n.* the art or process of forming or shaping a mass of molten or heat-softened glass into ware by blowing air into it through a tube. [1820–30; GLASS + BLOWING] —**glass′blow′er,** *n.*

Glass·bor·o (glas′bûr ō, -bur ō, gläs′-), *n.* a borough in SW New Jersey. 14,574.

glass′ ceil′ing, an upper limit to professional advancement, esp. as imposed on women, that is not readily perceived or openly acknowledged. [1985–90]

glass′ cur′tain, a transparent or translucent curtain covering the interior of a window opening.

glass′ cut′ter, 1. a tool for cutting glass. **2.** a person who cuts glass into specified sizes. **3.** a person who etches designs onto or otherwise decorates the surface of glass. [1695–1705] —**glass′ cut′ting.**

glassed-in (glast′in′, gläst′-), *adj.* enclosed by glass or glass panels, as for protection or shelter: *a glassed-in shower.* [1950–55]

glass′ eel′, elver. [1830–40; so called because it is nearly transparent at an early stage]

glass eye (glas′ ī′, gläs′ ī′ *for 1;* glas′ ī′, gläs′ ī′ *for 2*), **1.** See **artificial eye. 2.** any of various fish, birds, etc., having eyes with a glassy or milky appearance. [1595–1605]

glass-faced (glas′fāst′, gläs′-), *adj.* having the front or outer surfaces covered with glass. [1600–10]

glass·fish (glas′fish′, gläs′-), *n., pl.* (*esp. collectively*) **-fish,** (*esp. referring to two or more kinds or species*) **-fish·es.** any small, transparent marine, brackish, or freshwater fishes of the genus *Chanda* (or *Ambassis*), native to Africa and the Indo-Pacific region and popular in home aquariums. [GLASS + FISH]

glass·ful (glas′fo͝ol, gläs′-), *n., pl.* **-fuls.** an amount contained by or sufficient to fill a glass or tumbler. [bef. 900; ME; OE *glæs full.* See GLASS, -FUL]
—**Usage.** See **-ful.**

glass′ gall′, sandiver. [1590–1600]

glass′ harmon′ica, a musical instrument composed of a set of graduated, revolving glass bowls, the rims of which are moistened and set in vibration by friction from the fingertips. [1905–10]

glass·house (glas′hous′, gläs′-), *n., pl.* **-hous·es** (-hou′ziz). **1.** a glassworks. **2.** *Chiefly Brit.* a greenhouse. **3.** *Brit. Informal.* a military prison. [1350–1400; ME *glas hous.* See GLASS, HOUSE]

glass·ie (glas′ē, glä′sē), *n. Marbles.* glassy (def. 4). [GLASS + -IE]

glass·ine (gla sēn′), *n.* a strong, thin, glazed, semitransparent paper, often made into small bags, used for packaging foods, for book jackets, etc. [1915–20; GLASS + -INE[1]]

glass′ jaw′, a person's jaw, esp. that of a boxer, that is vulnerable to even a light blow. [1910–15]

glass′ liz′ard, any limbless lizard of the genus *Ophisaurus,* inhabiting the eastern U.S., Europe, and Asia, having external ear openings and the ability to regenerate its long, fragile tail. Also called **glass′ snake′.**

glass·mak·ing (glas′mā′king, gläs′-), *n.* the art of making glass or glassware. [1810–20; GLASS + MAKING] —**glass′mak′er,** *n.*

glass·man (glas′mən, gläs′-), *n., pl.* **-men. 1.** a person who makes or sells glass. **2.** a glazier. [1275–1325; ME (in proper names); see GLASS, -MAN]

Glass′ Menag′erie, The, a play (1945) by Tennessee Williams.

glass′ pox′, *Pathol.* alastrim, or mild smallpox.

glass′ tank′, a reverberatory furnace in which glass is melted directly under the flames.

glass·ware (glas′wâr′, gläs′-), *n.* articles of glass, esp. drinking glasses. [1705–15; GLASS + WARE[1]]

glass′ wool′, spun glass similar to wool, used for insulation, filters, etc. [1875–80]

glass·work (glas′wûrk′, gläs′-), *n.* **1.** the manufacture of glass and glassware. **2.** articles of glass collectively; glassware. **3.** the fitting of glass; glazing. [1605–15; GLASS + WORK]

glass·work·er (glas′wûr′kər, gläs′-), *n.* a person who makes or does glasswork. [1835–45; GLASS + WORKER]

glass·works (glas′wûrks′, gläs′-), *n., pl.* **-works.** (*usually used with a singular v.*) a factory where glass is made. [1620–30; GLASS + WORKS]

glass·worm (glas′wûrm′, gläs′-), *n.* arrowworm. [1545–55; GLASS + WORM]

glass·wort (glas′wûrt′, -wôrt′, gläs′-), *n.* any of several plants of the genus *Salicornia,* of the goosefoot family, having succulent stems with rudimentary leaves, formerly used, when burned to ashes, as a source of soda for glassmaking. Also called **samphire.** [1590–1600; GLASS + WORT[2]]

glass·y (glas′ē, glä′sē), *adj.,* **glass·i·er, glass·i·est,** *n., pl.* **glass·ies.** —*adj.* **1.** resembling glass, as in transparency or smoothness. **2.** expressionless; dull: *glassy eyes; a glassy stare.* **3.** of the nature of glass; vitreous. —*n.* **4.** Also, **glassie.** *Marbles.* a marble used as a shooter. [1350–1400; ME *glasy.* See GLASS, -Y[1]] —**glass′i·ly,** *adv.* —**glass′i·ness,** *n.*

glass′y al′loy, a metal alloy having a noncrystalline, glasslike structure. Also called **metallic glass.**

glass·y-eyed (glas′ē īd′, glä′sē-), *adj.* having a dull, dazed, or uncomprehending expression; staring fixedly. [1890–95]

Glas·ton·bur·y (glas′tən ber′ē; *for 1 also* glas′tən bə rē; *for 2 also* glas′ən ber′ē), *n.* **1.** a borough of SW England, in whose vicinity the ruins of an important Iron Age lake village have been found and to which in folklore both King Arthur and Joseph of Arimathaea have been linked, the latter as the founder of the abbey there. 6773. **2.** a town in N Connecticut. 24,327.

Glas′tonbury chair′, a folding chair having legs crossed front-to-back and having arms connected to the back and to the front seat rail. [1850–55; after the abbey of *Glastonbury* in SW England, site of the original chair]

Glas·we·gian (gla swē′jən, -jē ən), *adj.* **1.** of or characteristic of Glasgow or its inhabitants. —*n.* **2.** a native or inhabitant of Glasgow. [1810–20; GLAS(GOW) + *-wegian* (extracted from GALWEGIAN)]

glatt′ ko′sher (glät), *Judaism.* **1.** prepared for eating according to the dietary laws followed by Hasidic Jews, which differ somewhat from those followed by other observers of kashruth: *glatt kosher meat.* **2.** adhering to these laws: *a glatt kosher restaurant.* **3.** (loosely) strictly kosher. [< Yiddish *glat* lit., smooth, even < MHG (G *glatt*), OHG: bright, shining; see GLAD[1]]

glau·ber·ite (glou′bə rīt′), *n.* a mineral, sodium calcium sulfate, $Na_2Ca(SO_4)_2$, often found as a deposit on the beds of salt lakes. [1800–10; < F; so called because chemically similar to GLAUBER'S SALT; see -ITE[1]]

Glau′ber's salt′ (glou′bərz), the decahydrate form of sodium sulfate, a colorless, crystalline, water-soluble solid, $Na_2SO_4·10H_2O$, used chiefly in textile dyeing and as a cathartic. Also, **Glau′ber salt′.** [1730–40; named after J. R. *Glauber* (1604–68), German chemist]

glau·ces·cent (glô ses′ənt), *adj. Bot.* becoming glaucous; somewhat glaucous. [1820–30; GLAUC- + -ESCENT] —**glau·ces′cence,** *n.*

glauco-, a combining form meaning "gray, opaque," used in the formation of compound words: *glaucophane.* Also, *esp. before a vowel,* **glauc-.** [< Gk *glauko-, glauk-,* comb. forms of *glaukós*]

glau·co·dot (glô′kə dot′), *n.* a mineral, iron and cobalt sulfarsenide, (Co,Fe)AsS, occurring in grayish-white crystals. [1840–50; < G *Glaukodot,* equiv. to *glauko-* GLAUCO- + *-dot* < Gk *dotḗr* giver]

glau·co·ma (glô kō′mə, glou-), *n. Ophthalm.* abnormally high fluid pressure in the eye, most commonly caused either by blockage of the channel through which aqueous humor drains **(open-angle glaucoma** or **chronic glaucoma)** or by pressure of the iris against the lens, which traps the aqueous humor **(angle-closure glaucoma** or **acute glaucoma).** [1635–45; < Gk *glaúkōma* opacity of the eye lens. See GLAUC-, -OMA] —**glau·co·ma·tous** (glô kō′mə təs, -kom′ə-, glou-), *adj.*

glau·co·nite (glô′kə nīt′), *n.* a greenish micaceous mineral consisting essentially of a hydrous silicate of potassium, aluminum, and iron and occurring in greensand, clays, etc. [1830–40; < Gk *glaukón,* neut. of *glaukós* (see GLAUCO-) + -ITE[1]] —**glau·co·nit·ic** (glô′kə nit′ik), *adj.*

glau·co·phane (glô′kə fān′), *n.* a sodium-rich monoclinic mineral of the amphibole family, usually metamorphic. [1840–50; GLAUCO- + -PHANE]

glau·cous (glô′kəs), *adj.* **1.** light bluish-green or greenish-blue. **2.** *Bot.* covered with a whitish bloom, as a plum. [1665–75; < L *glaucus* silvery, gray, bluish-green < Gk *glaukós.* See GLAUCO-, -OUS] —**glau′cous·ly,** *adv.*

glau′cous gull′, a large white and pale-gray gull, *Latus hyperboreus,* of Arctic regions. [1820–30]

glave (glāv), *n. Archaic.* glaive.

glaze (glāz), *v.,* **glazed, glaz·ing,** *n.* —*v.t.* **1.** to furnish or fill with glass: *to glaze a window.* **2.** to give a vitreous surface or coating to (a ceramic or the like), as by the application of a substance or by fusion of the body. **3.** to cover with a smooth, glossy surface or coating. **4.** *Cookery.* to coat (a food) with sugar, a sugar syrup, or some other glossy, edible substance. **5.** *Fine Arts.* to cover (a painted surface or parts of it) with a thin layer of transparent color in order to modify the tone. **6.** to give a glassy surface to, as by polishing. **7.** to give a coating of ice to (frozen food) by dipping in water. **8.** to grind (cutlery blades) in preparation for finishing. —*v.i.* **9.** to become glazed or glassy: *Their eyes glazed over as the lecturer droned on.* **10.** (of a grinding wheel) to lose abrasive quality through polishing of the surface from wear. —*n.* **11.** a smooth, glossy surface or coating. **12.** the substance for producing such a coating. **13.** *Ceram.* **a.** a vitreous layer or coating on a piece of pottery. **b.** the substance of which such a layer or coating is made. **14.** *Fine Arts.* a thin layer of transparent color spread over a painted surface. **15.** a smooth, lustrous surface on certain fabrics, produced by treating the material with a chemical and calendering. **16.** *Cookery.* **a.** a substance used to coat a food, esp. sugar or sugar syrup. **b.** stock cooked down to a thin paste for applying to the surface of meats. **17.** Also called **glaze′ ice′, silver frost, silver thaw, verglas;** *esp. Brit.,* **glazed′ frost′.** a thin coating of ice on terrestrial objects, caused by rain that freezes on impact. Cf. **rime**[1] (def. 1). [1325–75; ME *glasen,* deriv. of *glas* GLASS] —**glaz′i·ly,** *adv.* —**glaz′i·ness,** *n.*

glazed (glāzd), *adj.* **1.** having a surface covered with a glaze; lustrous; smooth; glassy. **2.** fitted or set with glass. **3.** having a fixed, dazed, or lifeless expression. [1520–30; GLAZE + -ED[2]]
—**Syn. 3.** glassy, dull, dim, expressionless.

CONCISE ETYMOLOGY KEY: <, descended or borrowed from; >, whence; b., blend of, blended; c., cognate with; cf., compare; deriv., derivative; equiv., equivalent; imit., imitative; obl., oblique; r., replacing; s., stem; sp., spelling, spelled; resp., respelling, respelled; trans., translation; ?, origin unknown; *, unattested; ‡, probably earlier than. See the full key inside the front cover.

glaze•ment (glāz′mənt), *n.* a waterproof glaze for a masonry wall. [GLAZE + -MENT]

glaz•er (glā′zhər), *n.* **1.** a person who applies a glaze, as to pottery, baked goods, leather, or fur. **2.** any mechanical device used to apply a glaze. [1375–1425; late ME *glauser.* See GLAZE, -ER[1]]

Gla•zer (glā′zər), *n.* **Nathan,** born 1923, U.S. sociologist.

gla•zier (glā′zhər), *n.* a person who fits windows or the like with panes of glass. [1350–1400; ME *glasier.* See GLAZE, -IER[1]]

gla′zier's point′, a small, pointed piece of sheet metal, for holding a pane of glass in a sash until the putty has hardened. Also called **glaz′ing brad′, sprig.**

gla•zier•y (glā′zhə rē), *n.* the work of a glazier; glasswork. [1835–45; GLAZIER + -Y[3]]

glaz•ing (glā′zing), *n.* **1.** the act of furnishing or fitting with glass; the business or work of a glazier. **2.** panes or sheets of glass set or made to be set in frames, as in windows, doors, or mirrors. **3.** the act of applying a glaze. **4.** the glassy surface of something glazed. [1325–75; ME; see GLAZE, -ING[1]]

glaz′ing bead′, a convex molding nailed against the edge of a pane of glass to hold it in place.

Gla•zu•nov (glaz′ə nôf′, -nof′; *Russ.* glə zo͞o nôf′), *n.* **A•le•xan•der Kon•stan•ti•no•vitch** (al′ig zan′dər, -zän′-, kon′stən tē′nə vich; *Russ.* u lyi ksändʀ′ kən-stun tyē′nə vyich), 1865–1936, Russian composer. Also, **Gla′zu•noff′.**

glb, *Math.* See **greatest lower bound.**

Gld., guilder; guilders.

gleam (glēm), *n.* **1.** a flash or beam of light: *the gleam of a lantern in the dark.* **2.** a dim or subdued light. **3.** a brief or slight manifestation or occurrence; trace: *a gleam of hope.* —*v.i.* **4.** to send forth a gleam or gleams. **5.** to appear suddenly and clearly like a flash of light. [bef. 1000; (n.) ME *glem(e),* OE *glǣm;* c. OHG *gleimo* glowworm; akin to OS *glīmo* brightness; (v.) ME, deriv. of the n. See GLIMMER, GLIMPSE] —**gleam′ing•ly,** *adv.*
—**Syn. 1.** GLEAM, GLIMMER, BEAM, RAY are terms for a stream of light. GLEAM denotes a not very brilliant, intermittent or nondirectional stream of light. GLIMMER indicates a nondirectional light that is feeble and unsteady: *a faint glimmer of moonlight.* BEAM usually means a directional, and therefore smaller, stream: *the beam from a searchlight.* RAY usually implies a still smaller amount of light than a beam, a single line of light: *a ray through a pinprick in a window shade.* **4.** shine, glimmer, flash, glitter, sparkle, beam.

gleam•y (glē′mē), *adj.,* **gleam•i•er, gleam•i•est.** gleaming. [1585–95; GLEAM + -Y[1]]

glean (glēn), *v.t.* **1.** to gather slowly and laboriously, bit by bit. **2.** to gather (grain or the like) after the reapers or regular gatherers. **3.** to learn, discover, or find out, usually little by little or slowly. —*v.i.* **4.** to collect or gather anything little by little or slowly. **5.** to gather what is left by reapers. [1350–1400; ME *glenen* < OF *glener* < LL *glennāre* << Celtic] —**glean′a•ble,** *adj.* —**glean′er,** *n.*
—**Syn. 3.** garner, deduce, infer.

glean•ing (glē′ning), *n.* **1.** the act of a person who gleans. **2. gleanings,** things found or acquired by gleaning. [1400–50; late ME *glenynge.* See GLEAN, -ING[1]]

gle•ba (glē′bə), *n., pl.* **-bae** (-bē). *Mycol.* the sporogenous tissue forming the central part of the sporophore in certain fungi, as in puffballs and stinkhorns. [1840–50; < NL, L *glēba* clod; see GLEBE] —**gle′bal,** *adj.*

glebe (glēb), *n.* **1.** Also called **glebe′ land′.** *Chiefly Brit.* the cultivable land owned by a parish church or ecclesiastical benefice. **2.** *Archaic.* soil; field. [1275–1325; ME < L *glēba, glaeba* clod of earth] —**glebe′less,** *adj.*

glee[1] (glē), *n.* **1.** open delight or pleasure; exultant joy; exultation. **2.** an unaccompanied part song for three or more voices, popular esp. in the 18th century. [bef. 900; ME; OE *glēo;* c. ON *gly;* akin to GLOW]
—**Syn. 1.** merriment, jollity, hilarity, mirth, joviality, gaiety. See **mirth.**

glee[2] (glē), *Scot. and North Eng.* —*v.i.* **1.** to squint or look with one eye. —*n.* **2.** a squint. **3.** an imperfect eye, esp. one with a cast. [1250–1300; ME *glien, gleen;* perh. < Scand; cf. ON *gljā* to shine]

glee′ club′, a chorus organized for singing choral music. [1805–15]

gleed (glēd), *n. Archaic.* a glowing coal. [bef. 950; ME *gleed(e),* OE *glēd;* c. G *Glut,* ON *glōth;* akin to GLOW]

glee•ful (glē′fəl), *adj.* full of exultant joy; merry; delighted. [1580–90; GLEE[1] + -FUL] —**glee′ful•ly,** *adv.* —**glee′ful•ness,** *n.*

gleek[1] (glēk), *v.i. Archaic.* to make a joke; jest. [1540–50; orig. uncert.]

gleek[2] (glēk), *n.* an English card game for three persons played with a 44-card pack, popular from the 16th through the 18th century. [1525–35; < MF *glic,* perh. < MD *gelic* LIKE[1]]

glee•man (glē′mən), *n., pl.* **-men.** (in medieval times) an itinerant singer; minstrel. [bef. 900; ME; OE *glēoman.* See GLEE[1], -MAN]

glee•some (glē′səm), *adj.* gleeful; merry. [1595–1605; GLEE[1] + -SOME[1]] —**glee′some•ly,** *adv.* —**glee′some•ness,** *n.*

gleet (glēt), *n.* **1.** *Pathol.* **a.** a thin, morbid discharge, as from a wound. **b.** persistent or chronic gonorrhea. **2.** Also called **nasal gleet.** *Vet. Pathol.* an inflammation of the nasal passages of a horse, producing a thick discharge. [1300–50; ME *glete* < MF *glete,* OF *glette* < L *glittus* sticky]

gleet•y (glē′tē), *adj.,* **gleet•i•er, gleet•i•est.** characteristic of or resembling gleet. [1475–85; GLEET + -Y[1]]

gleg (gleg), *adj. Scot.* quick; keen. [1250–1300; ME < ON *glǫggr;* c. OE *glēaw,* OS, OHG *glau* wise; akin to GLOW]

Gleip•nir (glāp′nir), *n. Scand. Myth.* a bond with magic properties, forged by elves, and used by the gods to bind Loki. [< ON, perh. deriv. of *gleipa* to scorn, sneer]

Glei•witz (glī′vits), *n.* German name of **Gliwice.**

glei•za•tion (glā zā′shən), *n. Geol.* the natural process of producing gley. [1935–40; GLEY + -IZATION]

glen (glen), *n.* a small, narrow, secluded valley. [1480–90; < Ir, ScotGael *gleann;* c. Welsh *glynn*] —**glen′like′,** *adj.*

Glen (glen), *n.* a male or female given name.

Glen′ Bur′nie (bûr′nē), a city in E central Maryland, near Baltimore. 37,263.

Glen′ check′. See **Glen plaid.** [1920–25] —**Glen′ checked′.**

Glen′ Cove′, a city on NW Long Island, in SE New York. 24,618.

Glen•da (glen′də), *n.* a female given name.

Glen•dale (glen′dāl′), *n.* **1.** a city in SW California, near Los Angeles. 139,060. **2.** a city in central Arizona, near Phoenix. 96,988. **3.** a town in SE Wisconsin. 13,882.

Glen′dale Heights′, a city in NE Illinois. 23,163.

Glen•do•ra (glen dôr′ə, -dōr′ə), *n.* **1.** a city in SW California, near Los Angeles. 38,654. **2.** a female given name.

Glen•dow•er (glen dou′ər, glen′dou ər), *n.* **Owen,** 1359?–1416?, Welsh rebel against Henry IV of England.

Glen′ El′lyn (el′ən), a city in NE Illinois. 23,649.

glen•gar•ry (glen gar′ē), *n., pl.* **-ries.** a Scottish cap with straight sides, a crease along the top, and sometimes short ribbon streamers at the back, worn by Highlanders as part of military dress. [1835–45; after *Glengarry,* a valley in Invernesshire, Scotland]

glengarry

Glenn (glen), *n.* **1. John (Herschel),** born 1921, U.S. astronaut and politician: first U.S. orbital space flight 1962; U.S. senator since 1975. **2.** a male or female given name.

gle•noid (glē′noid), *adj. Anat.* **1.** shallow or slightly cupped, as the articular cavities of the scapula and the temporal bone. **2.** pertaining to such a cavity. [1700–10; < Gk *glēnoeid(ḗs),* equiv. to *glḗn(ē)* pupil, eyeball + *-oeidēs* -OID]

Glen′ plaid′, **1.** a plaid pattern of muted colors or of black or gray and white, esp. one in which two dark and two light stripes alternate with four dark and four light stripes, both vertically and horizontally, forming a crossing pattern of irregular checks. **2.** a fabric having such a pattern. **3.** a garment made of such a fabric. Also called **Glen check.** [1925–30; orig. *Glenurquhart* (or *Glen Urquhart*) plaid (check, tweed, etc.), after a valley of that name in Invernesshire, Scotland]

Glen′ Rock′, a borough in NE New Jersey. 11,497.

Glens′ Falls′, a city in E New York, on the Hudson River. 15,897.

Glen•view (glen′vyo͞o′), *n.* a city in NE Illinois, near Chicago. 30,842.

Glen•wood (glen′wo͝od′), *n.* a town in SW Iowa. 10,538.

gley (glā), *n. Geol.* a mottled soil in which iron compounds have been oxidized and reduced by intermittent water saturation. Cf. **gleization.** [1925–30; < Ukrainian *gleĭ* clayey earth; c. Byelorussian, Russ dial. *gleĭ,* Serbo-Croatian *glêj;* akin to CLAY]

gli•a (glī′ə, glē′ə), *n. Anat.* neuroglia. [1885–90; < LGk *glía* glue] —**gli′al,** *adj.*

gli•a•din (glī′ə din, -dn), *n. Biochem.* **1.** a prolamin derived from the gluten of grain, as wheat or rye, used chiefly as a nutrient in high-protein diets. **2.** any prolamin. Also, **gli•a•dine** (glī′ə dēn′, -din). [1820–30; < It *gliadina.* See GLIA, -IN[2]]

glib (glib), *adj.,* **glib•ber, glib•best.** **1.** readily fluent, often thoughtlessly, superficially, or insincerely so: *a glib talker; glib answers.* **2.** easy or unconstrained, as actions or manners. **3.** *Archaic.* agile; spry. [1585–95; cf. obs. *glibbery* slippery (c. D *glibberig*)] —**glib′ly,** *adv.* —**glib′ness,** *n.*
—**Syn. 1.** talkative, loquacious; facile, smooth. See **fluent.**

Glid•den (glid′n), *n.* **Charles Jasper,** 1857–1927, U.S. businessman: a pioneer in the telephone industry.

glide (glīd), *v.,* **glid•ed, glid•ing,** *n.* —*v.i.* **1.** to move smoothly and continuously along, as if without effort or resistance, as a flying bird, a boat, or a skater. **2.** to pass by gradual or unobservable change (often fol. by *along, away, by,* etc.). **3.** to move quietly or stealthily or without being noticed (usually fol. by *in, out, along,* etc.). **4.** *Aeron.* **a.** to move in the air, esp. at an easy angle downward, with less engine power than for level flight, solely by the action of air currents and gravity, or by momentum already acquired. **b.** to fly in a glider. **5.** *Music.* to pass from one note to another without a break. —*v.t.* **6.** to cause to glide. —*n.* **7.** a gliding movement, as in dancing. **8.** a dance marked by such movements. **9.** *Music.* slur (def. 10a). **10.** *Phonet.* **a.** a speech sound having the characteristics of both a consonant and a vowel, esp. *w* in *wore* and *y* in *your,* and, in some analyses, *r* in *road* and *l* in *load;* semivowel. **b.** a transitional sound heard during the articulation linking two phonemically contiguous sounds, as the *y*-sound often heard between the *i* and *e* of *quiet.* **11.** a calm stretch of shallow, smoothly flowing water, as in a river. **12.** an act or instance of gliding. **13.** *Metall.* slip[1] (def. 56). **14.** a smooth metal plate, as on the bottom of the feet of a chair or table, to facilitate moving and to prevent scarring of floor surfaces. **15.** a metal track in which a drawer, shelf, etc., moves in or out. [bef. 900; ME *gliden* (v.), OE *glīdan;* c. G *gleiten*] —**glid′ing•ly,** *adv.*
—**Syn. 1.** flow. See **slide.** —**Ant. 1.** stick.

glide•path (glīd′path′, -päth′), *n., pl.* **-paths** (-pathz′, -päthz′, -paths′, -päths′). the course followed by an aircraft or spacecraft when descending for a landing. [1935–40; GLIDE + PATH]

glide′ plane′, *Crystall.* a symmetry element of a space group such that a reflection of the lattice with respect to the plane and a translation of the lattice parallel to the plane bring the lattice back to its original position. [1890–95]

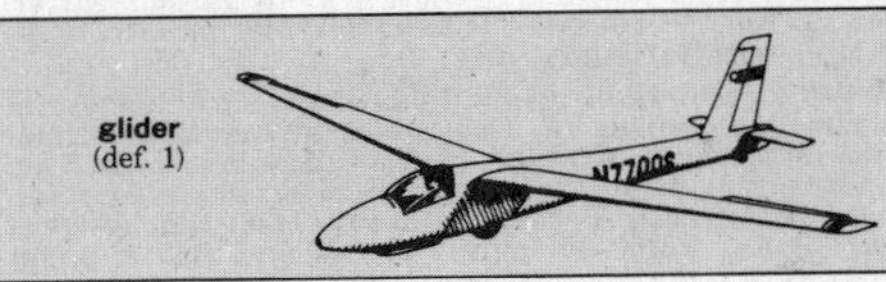
glider (def. 1)

glid•er (glī′dər), *n.* **1.** a motorless, heavier-than-air aircraft for gliding from a higher to a lower level by the action of gravity or from a lower to a higher level by the action of air currents. **2.** a porch swing made of an upholstered seat suspended from a steel framework by links or springs. **3.** a person or thing that glides. **4.** a person who pilots a glider. [1400–50; late ME; see GLIDE, -ER[1]]

glide′ slope′, *Aeron.* the angle that the glidepath of an aircraft or spacecraft makes with the horizontal. Also called **glide′ an′gle, glid′ing an′gle.** [1945–50]

glid′ing bacte′ria, bacteria that form colonies in a self-produced slime that permits them to glide, mainly inhabiting moist soils, decaying plant matter, animal waste, and rotting tree bark: some species produce brightly colored, funguslike fruiting bodies. Also called **slime bacteria, myxobacteria.**

glid′ing joint′, *Anat.* arthrodia. [1880–85]

glid′ing le′mur. See **flying lemur.**

Glière (glyeʀ), *n.* **Rein•hold Mo•ri•tzo•vich** (rīn′hôlt mô′ʀyi tsə vyich), 1875–1956, Russian composer.

glim (glim), *n.* **1.** a light or lamp. **2.** *Scot.* a little bit; small portion; scrap. [1690–1700; see GLIMPSE, GLIMMER]

glim•mer (glim′ər), *n.* **1.** a faint or unsteady light; gleam. **2.** a dim perception; inkling. —*v.i.* **3.** to shine faintly or unsteadily; twinkle, shimmer, or flicker. **4.** to appear faintly or dimly. [1300–50; ME *glimeren* to gleam; c. G *glimmern;* cf. OE *gleomu* splendor]
—**Syn. 1.** See **gleam.**

glim′mer ice′, new ice formed in cracks, holes, or depressions in older ice.

glim•mer•ing (glim′ər ing), *n.* **1.** a faint or unsteady light; glimmer. **2.** a faint glimpse or idea; inkling. —*adj.* **3.** shining faintly or unsteadily; shimmering. [1300–50; ME; see GLIMMER, -ING[1], -ING[2]] —**glim′mer•ing•ly,** *adv.*

glimpse (glimps), *n., v.,* **glimpsed, glimps•ing.** —*n.* **1.** a very brief, passing look, sight, or view. **2.** a momentary or slight appearance. **3.** a vague idea; inkling. **4.** *Archaic.* a gleam, as of light. —*v.t.* **5.** to catch or take a glimpse of. —*v.i.* **6.** to look briefly; glance (usually fol. by *at*). **7.** *Archaic.* to come into view; appear faintly. [1350–1400; ME *glimsen* (v.); c. MHG *glimsen* to glow; akin to GLIMMER] —**glimps′er,** *n.*
—**Syn. 5.** spot, spy, view, sight, espy.

glin (glin), *n., v.i.,* **glinned, glin•ning.** glinn.

Glin•ka (gling′kə; *Russ.* glyēn′kə), *n.* **Mi•kha•il I•va•no•vich** (mi kä ēl′ i vä′nə vich; *Russ.* myi ᴋʜu yēl′ ē vä′nə vyich), 1803–57, Russian composer.

glinn (glin), *Maine.* —*n.* **1.** a bright glow in the sky close to the horizon, usually taken as a portent of a storm. —*v.i.* **2.** (of the sky near the horizon) to become lighter (often fol. by *up*). Also, **glin.** [cf. Newfoundland dial. *glin, glynn, glim* glow from distant ice; appar. akin to GLIM, GLIMMER, though source of *n* is unclear]

glint (glint), *n.* **1.** a tiny, quick flash of light. **2.** gleaming brightness; luster. **3.** a brief or slight manifestation; inkling; trace. —*v.i.* **4.** to shine with a glint. **5.** to move suddenly; dart. —*v.t.* **6.** to cause to glint; reflect. [1400–50; late ME *glint,* var. of obs. *glent;* cf. Dan *glente,* Sw dial. *glänta* to glimpse, brighten]
—**Syn. 1.** gleam, glimmer. **4.** See **flash.**

gli•o•ma (glī ō′mə), *n., pl.* **-mas, -ma•ta** (-mə tə). a tumor of the brain composed of neuroglia. [1865–70; < NL; see GLIA, -OMA] —**gli•o•ma•tous** (glī ō′mə təs, -om′ə-), *adj.*

gli•o•sis (glī ō′sis), *n.* an increase in the size and number of astrocytes of the brain. [1890–1900; GLI(A) + -OSIS]

glis•sade (gli säd′, -sād′), *n., v.,* **-sad•ed, -sad•ing.** —*n.* **1.** a skillful glide over snow or ice in descending a mountain, as on skis or a toboggan. **2.** *Dance.* a sliding or gliding step. —*v.i.* **3.** to perform a glissade. [1830–40; < F, equiv. to *gliss(er)* to slip, slide + *-ade* -ADE[1]] —**glis•sad′er,** *n.*

CONCISE PRONUNCIATION KEY: act, cāpe, dâre, pärt; set, ēqual; if, īce; ox, ōver, ôrder, oil, bo͝ok, bo͞ot, out; up, ûrge; child; sing; shoe; thin, that; zh as in *treasure.* ə = *a* as in *alone, e* as in *system, i* as in *easily, o* as in *gallop, u* as in *circus;* ᵊ as in *fire* (fīᵊr), *hour* (ouᵊr). l and n can serve as syllabic consonants, as in *cradle* (krād′l), and *button* (but′n). See the full key inside the front cover.

glis·san·do (gli sän′dō), *adj., n., pl.* **-di** (-dē). *Music.* —*adj.* **1.** performed with a gliding effect by sliding one or more fingers rapidly over the keys of a piano or strings of a harp. —*n.* **2.** a glissando passage. **3.** (in string playing) a slide. [1870–75; < F *gliss(er)* to slide + It *-ando* ger. ending]

glis·ten (glis′ən), *v.i.* **1.** to reflect a sparkling light or a faint intermittent glow; shine lustrously. —*n.* **2.** a glistening; sparkle. [bef. 1000; ME *glis(t)nen* (v.), OE *glisnian,* deriv. of *glisian* to GLITTER; see -EN[1]] —**glis′·ten·ing·ly,** *adv.*
—**Syn. 1.** glimmer, gleam, glitter. GLISTEN, SHIMMER, SPARKLE refer to different ways in which light is reflected from surfaces. GLISTEN refers to a lustrous light, as from something sleek or wet, or it may refer to myriads of tiny gleams reflected from small surfaces: *Wet fur glistens. Snow glistens in the sunlight.* SHIMMER refers to the changing play of light on a (generally moving) surface, as of water or silk: *Moonbeams shimmer on water. Silk shimmers in a high light.* To SPARKLE is to give off sparks or small ignited particles, or to send forth small but brilliant gleams, sometimes by reflection: *A diamond sparkles with numerous points of light.*

glis·ter (glis′tər), *v.i. Archaic.* **1.** to glisten; glitter. —*n.* **2.** glitter; sparkle. [1350–1400; ME; akin to GLISTEN] —**glis′ter·ing·ly,** *adv.*

glitch (glich), *Slang.* —*n.* **1.** a defect or malfunction in a machine or plan. **2.** *Computers.* any error, malfunction, or problem. Cf. **bug**[1] (def. 5). **3.** a brief or sudden interruption or surge in voltage in an electric circuit. —*v.t.* **4.** to cause a glitch in: *an accident that glitched our plans.* [1960–65; perh. < Yiddish *glitsh* slippery area; cf. *glitshn,* G *glitschen* to slip, slide]

glit·ter (glit′ər), *v.i.* **1.** to reflect light with a brilliant, sparkling luster; sparkle with reflected light. **2.** to make a brilliant show. —*n.* **3.** a sparkling reflected light or luster. **4.** showy splendor. **5.** small glittering ornaments. [1300–50; ME < ON *glitra;* cf. OE *glitenian,* G *gleissen* to shine, glitter] —**glit′ter·ing·ly,** *adv.*
—**Syn. 1.** See **flash. 3.** sparkle.

glit·te·ra·ti (glit′ə rä′tē), *n.pl.* wealthy or famous people who conspicuously or ostentatiously attend fashionable events. [1935–40; b. GLITTER and LITERATI]

glit′ter ice′, ice or a sheet of ice formed on a surface by a quickly freezing rain. [1875–80]

glit·ter·y (glit′ə rē), *adj.* glittering; sparkling. [1750–60; GLITTER + -Y[1]]

glitz (glits), *Slang.* —*n.* **1.** ostentatious glitter or sophistication: *a cocktail lounge noted for its glitz.* —*v.t.* **2.** to add a showy sophistication to (often fol. by *up*): *They glitzed up the lobby with a couple of fountains and a birdcage.* [1970–75; perh. b. GLITTER and RITZ]

glitz·y (glit′sē), *adj.,* **glitz·i·er, glitz·i·est.** *Slang.* pretentiously or tastelessly showy: *a glitzy gown.* [1965–70; see GLITZ, -Y[1]] —**glitz′i·ness,** *n.*

Gli·wi·ce (glē vē′tse), *n.* a city in SW Poland. 197,000. German, **Gleiwitz.**

Gln, *Biochem.* glutamine.

gloam (glōm), *n. Archaic.* twilight; gloaming. [1815–25; back formation from GLOAMING]

gloam·ing (glō′ming), *n.* twilight; dusk. [bef. 1000; ME *gloming,* OE *glōmung,* deriv. of *glōm* twilight]

gloat (glōt), *v.i.* **1.** to look at or think about with great or excessive, often smug or malicious, satisfaction: *The opposing team gloated over our bad luck.* —*n.* **2.** an act or feeling of gloating. [1565–75; perh. akin to ON *glotta* to smile scornfully; cf. G *glotzen* to stare] —**gloat′er,** *n.* —**gloat′ing·ly,** *adv.*
—**Syn. 1.** See **glare**[1].

glob (glob), *n.* **1.** a drop or globule of a liquid. **2.** a usually rounded quantity or lump of some plastic or moldable substance: *a little glob of clay; a huge glob of whipped cream.* [1895–1900; perh. b. GLOBE and BLOB]

glob·al (glō′bəl), *adj.* **1.** pertaining to the whole world; worldwide; universal: *the dream of global peace.* **2.** comprehensive. **3.** globular; globe-shaped. **4.** of, pertaining to, or using a terrestrial or celestial globe. **5.** (of a computer operation, linguistic rule, etc.) operating on a group of similar strings, commands, etc., in a single step. [1670–80; GLOBE + -AL[1]] —**glob′al·ly,** *adv.*

glob·al·ism (glō′bə liz′əm), *n.* the attitude or policy of placing the interests of the entire world above those of individual nations. [1940–45, *Amer.;* GLOBAL + -ISM] —**glob′al·ist,** *n., adj.*

glob·al·ize (glō′bə līz′), *v.t.,* **-ized, -iz·ing.** to extend to other or all parts of the globe; make worldwide: *efforts to globalize the auto industry.* Also, *esp. Brit.,* **glob′al·ise′.** [1940–45; GLOBAL + -IZE] —**glob′al·i·za′tion,** *n.*

Glo′bal Posi′tioning Sys′tem. See **NAVSTAR Global Positioning System.** *Abbr.:* GPS

glob′al tecton′ics, earth movements and interactions on a global scale, esp. as they relate to the causes and results of the dynamics of the crustal plates and seafloor spreading. Cf. **plate tectonics.** [1965–70]

glob′al vil′lage, the world, esp. as the home of all nations and peoples living interdependently. [term introduced by the book *War and Peace in the Global Village* (1968) by Marshall McLuhan and Quentin Fiore]

glo′bal warm′ing, an increase in the earth's average atmospheric temperature that causes corresponding changes in climate and that may result from the greenhouse effect. [1975–80]

glo·bate (glō′bāt), *adj.* shaped like a globe. Also, **glo′·bat·ed.** [1840–50; < L *globātus* (ptp. of *globāre* to make into a ball). See GLOBE, -ATE[1]]

globe (glōb), *n., v.,* **globed, glob·ing.** —*n.* **1.** the planet Earth (usually prec. by *the*). **2.** a planet or other celestial body. **3.** a sphere on which is depicted a map of the earth (**terrestrial globe**) or of the heavens (**celestial globe**). **4.** a spherical body; sphere. **5.** anything more or less spherical, as a lampshade or a glass fishbowl. **6.** a golden ball traditionally borne as an emblem of sovereignty; orb. —*v.t.* **7.** to form into a globe. —*v.i.* **8.** to take the form of a globe. [1400–50; late ME < MF *globe* < L *globus* round body, ball, sphere] —**globe′like′,** *adj.*
—**Syn. 1.** See **earth.**

globe′ am′aranth, a plant, *Gomphrena globosa,* native to the Old World tropics, having dense heads of variously colored flowers that retain their color when cut. [1725–35; so called from the globose flower head]

globe′ ar′tichoke, artichoke (defs. 1, 2). [1855–60; so called from the globose flower head]

globe·fish (glōb′fish′), *n., pl.* (*esp. collectively*) **-fish,** (*esp. referring to two or more kinds or species*) **-fish·es. 1.** puffer (def. 2). **2.** See **ocean sunfish.** [1660–70]

globe·flow·er (glōb′flou′ər), *n.* any of several plants belonging to the genus *Trollius,* of the buttercup family, as *T. laxus,* of North America, having rounded, yellowish flowers. [1590–1600; GLOBE + FLOWER]

globe′ light′ning. See **ball lightning.** [1885–90]

Globe′ The′atre, a theater on the south bank of the Thames in London, 1599–1613: many of Shakespeare's plays were first produced here.

globe′ this′tle, any of various Old World, thistlelike, composite plants of the genus *Echinops,* having dense heads of tubular blue or white flowers.

globe·trot (glōb′trot′), *v.i.,* **-trot·ted, -trot·ting.** to travel throughout the world, esp. regularly or frequently. [1880–85; back formation from GLOBETROTTER]

globe·trot·ter (glōb′trot′ər), *n.* a person who travels regularly or frequently to countries all over the world. [1870–75; GLOBE + TROTTER]

globe′ valve′, a valve with a globular body, closed by a disk seating on an opening in an internal wall.

glo·big·er·i·na (glō bij′ə rī′nə, -rē′-), *n., pl.* **-nas, -nae** (-nē). any marine foraminifer of the genus *Globigerina,* having a calcareous shell, occurring either near the surface of the sea or in the mud at the bottom. [1840–50; < NL, equiv. to L *globi-* globe (comb. form of *globus*) + *-ger-* (s. of *gerere* to carry) + *-ina* -INA]

globigeri′na ooze′, a calcareous deposit occurring upon ocean beds and consisting mainly of the shells of dead foraminifers, esp. globigerina. [1875–80]

glo·bin (glō′bin), *n. Biochem.* the protein component of hemoglobin, made up of alpha and beta chains. [1875–80; < L *glob(us)* globe, sphere + -IN[2]]

glo·boid (glō′boid), *adj.* **1.** approximately globular. —*n.* **2.** a globoid figure or body. [1870–75; GLOBE + -OID]

glo·bose (glō′bōs, glō bōs′), *adj.* having the shape of a globe; globelike. [1400–50; late ME < L *globōsus* spherical, forming a globelike mass. See GLOBE, -OSE[1]] —**glo′·bose·ly,** *adv.* —**glo·bos·i·ty** (glō bos′i tē), **glo′bose·ness,** *n.*

glob·u·lar (glob′yə lər), *adj.* **1.** globe-shaped; spherical. **2.** composed of or having globules. **3.** worldwide; global. Also, **glob′u·lous.** [1650–60; < L *globul(us)* GLOBULE + -AR[1]] —**glob′u·lar′i·ty, glob′u·lar·ness,** *n.* —**glob′u·lar·ly,** *adv.*

glob′ular clus′ter, *Astron.* a comparatively older, spherically symmetrical, compact group of up to a million old stars, held together by mutual gravitation, that are located in the galactic halo and move in giant and highly eccentric orbits around the galactic center. Cf. **open cluster, stellar association.** [1855–60]

glob·ule (glob′yōōl), *n.* **1.** a small spherical body. **2.** See **Bok globule.** [1655–65; < L *globulus.* See GLOBE, -ULE]

glob·u·lif·er·ous (glob′yə lif′ər əs), *adj.* containing or producing globules. [1790–1800; GLOBULE + -I- + -FEROUS]

glob·u·lin (glob′yə lin), *n. Biochem.* **1.** any of a group of proteins, as myosin, occurring in plant and animal tissue, insoluble in pure water but soluble in dilute salt solutions and coagulable by heat. **2.** any of several groups of blood plasma proteins, divided into fractions, as alpha, beta, or gamma globulin, depending on electrophoretic mobility. [1825–35; GLOBULE + -IN[2]]

glo·bus hys·ter·i·cus (glō′bəs hi ster′i kəs), *Psychiatry.* the sensation of having a lump in the throat or difficulty in swallowing for which no medical cause can be found. [1790–95; < NL: lump of hysteria; see GLOBE, HYSTERICAL]

glo·chid (glō′kid), *n.* a short hair, bristle, or spine having a barbed tip. Also, **glo·chis** (glō′kis). [1880–90; < Gk *glōchid-,* s. of *glōchis* arrow point] —**glo·chid·i·ate** (glō kid′ē it, -āt′), *adj.*

glo·chid·i·um (glō kid′ē əm), *n., pl.* **-chid·i·a** (-kid′ē ə). **1.** glochid. **2.** the larva of a freshwater mussel of the family Unionidae that lives as a temporary parasite in the gills or on other external parts of fishes. [1895–1900; < NL < Gk *glōch(ís)* point of an arrow + *-idion* dim. suffix] —**glo·chid′i·al,** *adj.*

glockenspiel

glock·en·spiel (glok′ən spēl′, -shpēl′), *n.* a musical instrument composed of a set of graduated steel bars mounted in a frame and struck with hammers, used esp. in bands. [1815–25; < G, equiv. to *Glocken* bells + *Spiel* play]

glögg (glug, glŏŏg; *Sw.* glœg), *n.* a hot wine punch containing brandy or aquavit and flavored with almonds, raisins, cloves, and cinnamon. Also, **glogg.** [< Sw, shortening of *glödgat vin* mulled wine (*glödgat,* ptp. of *glödga* to mull, heat up, deriv. of *glöd* ember; *vin* WINE)]

glom (glom), *v.,* **glommed, glom·ming,** *n. Slang.* —*v.t.* **1.** to steal. **2.** to catch or grab. **3.** to look at. —*v.i.* **4. glom onto,** to take hold or possession of: *He wanted to glom onto some of that money.* —*n.* **5.** a look or glimpse. [1905–10, *Amer.;* cf. Scots *glaum, glam* to snatch at, *glammis* jaws of a vise, appar. < ScotGael *glàm* to grab, clutch, influenced by CLAM[2]]

glom·er·ate (glom′ər it, -ə rāt′), *adj.* compactly clustered. [1785–95; < L *glomerātus* wound or formed into a ball (ptp. of *glomerāre*), equiv. to *glomer-* (s. of *glomus*) ball-shaped mass + *-ātus* -ATE[1]]

glom·er·a·tion (glom′ə rā′shən), *n.* **1.** a glomerate condition; conglomeration. **2.** a glomerate mass. [1620–30; GLOMERATE + -ION]

glom·er·ule (glom′ə rōōl′), *n. Bot.* a cyme condensed into a headlike cluster. [1785–95; < NL *glomerulus* GLOMERULUS]

glo·mer·u·li·tis (glō mer′yə lī′tis, glə-), *n. Pathol.* inflammation of the glomeruli of the kidney. [1880–85; GLOMERUL(US) + -ITIS]

glo·mer·u·lo·ne·phri·tis (glō mer′yə lō nə frī′tis, glə-), *n. Pathol.* a kidney disease affecting the capillaries of the glomeruli, characterized by albuminuria, edema, and hypertension. [1885–90; GLOMERUL(US) + -O- + NEPHRITIS]

glo·mer·u·lus (glō mer′yə ləs, glə-), *n., pl.* **-li** (-lī′). *Anat.* **1.** a compact cluster of capillaries. **2.** Also called **Malpighian tuft.** a tuft of convoluted capillaries in the nephron of a kidney, functioning to remove certain substances from the blood before it flows into the convoluted tubule. Cf. **Bowman's capsule, Malpighian corpuscle.** [1855–60; < NL, equiv. to L *glomer-* (s. of *glomus*) ball-shaped mass + *-ulus* -ULE] —**glo·mer′u·lar,** *adj.*

Glom·ma (glôm′mä), *n.* a river in E Norway, flowing S into the Skagerrak. 375 mi. (605 km) long.

glo·mus (glō′məs), *n., pl.* **glom·er·a** (glom′ər ə), **glo·mi** (glō′mī). *Anat.* a small globular body. [1830–40; < NL, L: ball-shaped mass]

gloom (glōōm), *n.* **1.** total or partial darkness; dimness. **2.** a state of melancholy or depression; low spirits. **3.** a despondent or depressed look or expression. —*v.i.* **4.** to appear or become dark, dim, or somber. **5.** to look sad, dismal, or dejected; frown. —*v.t.* **6.** to fill with gloom; make gloomy or sad; sadden. **7.** to make dark or somber. [1300–50; ME *gloumben, glomen* to frown, perh. repr. OE **glūmian* (akin to early G *glūmen* to make turbid); see GLUM] —**gloom′ful,** *adj.* —**gloom′ful·ly,** *adv.* —**gloom′less,** *adj.*
—**Syn. 1.** shadow, shade, obscurity. **2.** dejection, despondency, sadness. —**Ant. 1.** brightness. **2.** cheerfulness.

gloom′ and doom′, an account or prediction of adversity, esp. in economic or business affairs; bad news: *full of gloom and doom about next year's trends.* —**gloom′-and-doom′,** *adj.* —**gloom′-and-doom′er,** *n.*

glooms (glōōmz), *n.pl.* the blues; melancholy (usually prec. by *the*). [1735–45; see GLOOM, -S[3]]

gloom·y (glōō′mē), *adj.,* **gloom·i·er, gloom·i·est. 1.** dark or dim; deeply shaded: *gloomy skies.* **2.** causing gloom; dismal or depressing: *a gloomy prospect.* **3.** filled with or showing gloom; sad, dejected, or melancholy. **4.** hopeless or despairing; pessimistic: *a gloomy view of the future.* [1580–90; GLOOM + -Y[1]] —**gloom′i·ly,** *adv.* —**gloom′i·ness,** *n.*
—**Syn. 1.** obscure, shadowy, dusky; lowering, threatening. **3.** downcast, downhearted, despondent, depressed, glum, dispirited. —**Ant. 3.** happy.

glop (glop), *n. Informal.* **1.** unappetizing food, esp. of a semiliquid consistency. **2.** any messy substance, esp. of a semiliquid consistency. **3.** sentimentality; mawkishness. [1940–45; expressive word akin to GOOP, GULP]

glop·py (glop′ē), *adj.,* **-pi·er, -pi·est.** marked by or full of glop. [GLOP + -Y[1]]

Glo·ri·a (glôr′ē ə, glōr′-), *n.* **1.** *Liturgy.* **a.** See **Gloria in Excelsis Deo. b.** See **Gloria Patri. c.** the response *Gloria tibi, Domine,* "Glory be to Thee, O Lord." **2.** (*l.c.*) a repetition of one of these. **3.** (*l.c.*) a musical setting for one of these. **4.** (*l.c.*) a halo, nimbus, or aureole, or an ornament in imitation of one. **5.** (*l.c.*) a fabric of silk, cotton, nylon, or wool for umbrellas, dresses, etc., often with a filling of cotton warp and yarn of other fiber. **6.** a female given name. [1150–1200; ME < L; see GLORY]

Glo·ri·a in Ex·cel·sis De·o (glôr′ē ə in ek sel′sis dā′ō, glōr′-), the hymn beginning, in Latin, *Gloria in Excelsis Deo,* "Glory be in the highest to God," and in the English version, "Glory be to God on high." Also called **great doxology, greater doxology.**

Glo·ri·a Pa·tri (glôr′ē ə pä′trē, glōr′-), the short hymn "Glory be to the Father, and to the Son, and to the Holy Ghost. As it was in the beginning, is now, and ever shall be, world without end. Amen." Also called **lesser doxology.** [< L]

glo·ri·fi·ca·tion (glôr′ə fi kā′shən, glōr′-), *n.* **1.** a glorified or more splendid form of something. **2.** the act of glorifying. **3.** the state of being glorified. **4.** exaltation to the glory of heaven. [1425–75; late ME < LL *glōrificātiōn-* (s. of *glōrificātiō*), equiv. to *glōrific(āre)* to GLORIFY + *-ātiōn-* -ATION]

glo·ri·fy (glôr′ə fī′, glōr′-), *v.t.,* **-fied, -fy·ing. 1.** to cause to be or treat as being more splendid, excellent, etc., than would normally be considered. **2.** to honor with praise, admiration, or worship; extol. **3.** to make glorious; invest with glory. **4.** to praise the glory of (God), esp. as an act of worship. [1300–50; ME < OF

CONCISE ETYMOLOGY KEY: <, descended or borrowed from; >, whence; b., blend of, blended; c., cognate with; cf., compare; deriv., derivative; equiv., equivalent; imit., imitative; obl., oblique; r., replacing; s., stem; sp., spelling, spelled; resp., respelling, respelled; trans., translation; ?, origin unknown; *, unattested; ‡, probably earlier than. See the full key inside the front cover.

glorifier < LL *glōrificāre.* See GLORY, -FY] —**glo′ri·fi′a·ble,** *adj.* —**glo′ri·fi′er,** *n.*
—**Syn. 2.** venerate, praise, worship, celebrate.

glo·ri·ole (glôr′ē ōl′, glōr′-), *n.* a halo, nimbus, or aureole. [1805–15; < L *glōriola,* equiv. to *glōri(a)* GLORY + *-ola* -OLE[1]]

glo·ri·o′sa lil′y (glôr′ē ō′sə, glōr′-), a climbing lily of the genus *Gloriosa,* native to Africa and Asia, having showy red and yellow flowers. Also called **climbing lily.** [< NL *Gloriosa* genus name; L *glōriōsa,* fem. of *glōriōsus* GLORIOUS]

glo·ri·ous (glôr′ē əs, glōr′-), *adj.* **1.** delightful; wonderful; completely enjoyable: *to have a glorious time at the circus.* **2.** conferring glory: *a glorious victory.* **3.** full of glory; entitled to great renown: *England is glorious in her poetry.* **4.** brilliantly beautiful or magnificent; splendid: *a glorious summer day.* **5.** *Archaic.* blissfully drunk. [1300–50; ME < AF, OF *glorieus* < L *glōriōsus.* See GLORY, -OUS] —**glo′ri·ous·ly,** *adv.* —**glo′ri·ous·ness,** *n.*
—**Syn. 3.** famous, famed, renowned, illustrious, noted, celebrated, eminent, distinguished. —**Ant. 1.** unpleasant, disgusting. **3.** unknown.

Glo′rious Revolu′tion. See **English Revolution.**

glo·ry (glôr′ē, glōr′ē), *n., pl.* **-ries,** *adj., v.,* **-ried, -ry·ing,** *interj.* —*n.* **1.** very great praise, honor, or distinction bestowed by common consent; renown: *to win glory on the field of battle.* **2.** something that is a source of honor, fame, or admiration; a distinguished ornament or an object of pride: *a sonnet that is one of the glories of English poetry.* **3.** adoring praise or worshipful thanksgiving: *Give glory to God.* **4.** resplendent beauty or magnificence: *the glory of autumn.* **5.** a state of great splendor, magnificence, or prosperity. **6.** a state of absolute happiness, gratification, contentment, etc.: *She was in her glory when her horse won the Derby.* **7.** the splendor and bliss of heaven; heaven. **8.** a ring, circle, or surrounding radiance of light represented about the head or the whole figure of a sacred person, as Christ or a saint; a halo, nimbus, or aureole. **9.** anticorona. **10. go to glory,** to die. Also, **go to one's glory.** —*adj.* **11. glory days** or **years,** the time of greatest achievement, popularity, success, or the like: *the glory days of radio.* —*v.i.* **12.** to exult with triumph; rejoice proudly (usually fol. by *in*): *Their father gloried in their success.* **13.** *Obs.* to boast. —*interj.* **14.** Also, **glo′ry be′.** Glory be to God (used to express surprise, elation, wonder, etc.). [1300–50; ME < OF *glorie* < L *glōria*] —**glo′ry·ing·ly,** *adv.*
—**Syn. 1.** fame, eminence, celebrity. **4.** brilliance, refulgence, effulgence. —**Ant. 1.** disgrace, obloquy.

glo′ry bush′. See **princess flower.**

glo′ry hole′, 1. *Naut.* **a.** the quarters on a ship that are occupied by the stewards or stokers. **b.** lazaretto (def. 3). **c.** any locker or enclosed space for loose gear. **2.** *Glassmaking.* an auxiliary furnace for reheating glass that has cooled during offhand blowing. **3.** *Mining.* See **draw hole.** [1830–40]

glo·ry-of-the-snow (glôr′ē əv *th*ə snō′, -snō′, glōr′-), *n., pl.* **-snows.** any of several plants belonging to the genus *Chionodoxa,* of the lily family, native to the Old World, having showy, blue, white, or pink flowers that bloom early in the spring. [1895–1900]

glo·ry-of-the-sun (glôr′ē əv *th*ə sun′, -sun′, glōr′-), *n., pl.* **-suns.** a bulbous, Chilean plant, *Leucocoryne ixioides,* of the amaryllis family, having fragrant, white or blue flowers.

glo·ry-pea (glôr′ē pē′, glōr′-), *n.* either of two trailing plants, *Clianthus formosus* or *C. puniceus,* of Australia and New Zealand, having showy red flowers. [1840–50]

gloss[1] (glos, glôs), *n.* **1.** a superficial luster or shine; glaze: *the gloss of satin.* **2.** a false or deceptively good appearance. **3.** Also, **glosser.** a cosmetic that adds sheen or luster, esp. one for the lips. —*v.t.* **4.** to put a gloss upon. **5.** to give a false or deceptively good appearance to: *to gloss over flaws in the woodwork.* [1530–40; prob. akin to D *gloos* glowing, MHG *glosen* to glow, shine, Sw dial. *glysa* to shine] —**gloss′less,** *adj.*
—**Syn. 1.** See **polish. 2.** front, pretense.

gloss[2] (glos, glôs), *n.* **1.** an explanation or translation, by means of a marginal or interlinear note, of a technical or unusual expression in a manuscript text. **2.** a series of verbal interpretations of a text. **3.** a glossary. **4.** an artfully misleading interpretation. —*v.t.* **5.** to insert glosses on; annotate. **6.** to place (a word) in a gloss. **7.** to give a specious interpretation of; explain away (often fol. by *over* or *away*): *to gloss over a serious problem with a pat solution.* —*v.i.* **8.** to make glosses. [1250–1300; (n.) ME *glose* (< OF glose) < ML *glōsa, glōza* < Gk *glôssa* word requiring explanation, lit., language, tongue; (v.) ME *glosen* < ML *glōsāre,* deriv. of *glōsa;* cf. GLOZE, reflecting OF pron. of verb] —**gloss′ing·ly,** *adv.*
—**Syn. 1.** comment, annotation. **2.** commentary, critique, exegesis, explication. **5.** explain, interpret, analyze, explicate.

gloss-, var. of **glosso-** before a vowel: *glossectomy.*

gloss., glossary.

glos·sa (glos′ə, glô′sə), *n., pl.* **glos·sae** (glos′ē, glô′sē), **glos·sas. 1.** *Anat.* the tongue. **2.** *Entomol.* one of a pair of median, sometimes fused lobes of the labium of an insect. [1885–90; < Gk *glôssa* tongue]

Glos·sa (glô′sə), *n.* **Cape,** a promontory in SW Albania.

glos·sal (glos′əl, glô′səl), *adj.* of or pertaining to the tongue. [1855–60; GLOSS(A) + -AL[1]]

glos·sa·ry (glos′ə rē, glô′sə-), *n., pl.* **-ries. 1.** a list of terms in a special subject, field, or area of usage, with accompanying definitions. **2.** such a list at the back of a book, explaining or defining difficult or unusual words and expressions used in the text. [1350–1400; ME *glossarye* < L *glōssarium* difficult word requiring explanation < Gk *glōssárion,* dim. of *glôssa* tongue, language; later taken as a collection of such words, by construing suffix as L *-ārium* -ARY; cf. GLOSS[2]] —**glos·sar·i·al** (glo sâr′ē əl, glô-), *adj.* —**glos·sar′i·al·ly,** *adv.* —**glos′sa·rist,** *n.*

glos·sa·tor (glo sā′tər, glô-), *n.* **1.** a person who writes glosses; glossarist. **2.** one of the medieval interpreters of the Roman and canon laws. [1350–1400; ME *glosator* < ML *glōssātor* commentator, equiv. to *glōssā(re)* to explain, interpret (see GLOSS[2]) + L *-tor* -TOR] —**glos·sa·to·ri·al** (glos′ə tôr′ē əl, -tōr′-, glô′sə-), *adj.*

glos·se·mat·ics (glos′ə mat′iks, glô′sə-), *n.* (*used with a singular v.*) *Ling.* a school of linguistic analysis developed by Louis Hjelmslev (1899–1965) in Copenhagen in the 1930's based on the study of the distribution of glossemes. [1935–40; GLOSSEME + *-atics,* on the model of Gk formations such as *phṓnēma* speech (s. *phōnēmat-*), adj. deriv. *phōnēmatikós* (cf. PHONEME), and the names of disciplines formed from such adjs., as MATHEMATICS] —**glos′se·mat′ic,** *adj.*

glos·seme (glos′ēm, glô′sēm), *n. Ling.* (in glossematics) an irreducible, invariant form, as a morpheme or tagmeme, that functions as the smallest meaningful unit of linguistic signaling. [1925–30; GLOSS- + -EME] —**glos·se′mic,** *adj.*

gloss·er (glos′ər, glô′sər), *n.* **1.** a person or thing that puts a gloss or shine on something. **2.** gloss[1] (def. 3). [1820–30; GLOSS[1] + -ER[1]]

glos·si·na (glo sī′nə, -sē′-, glô-), *n.* See **tsetse fly.** [1885–90; < NL: genus name, so called from its long proboscis; see GLOSS-, -INA]

glos·si·tis (glo sī′tis, glô-), *n. Pathol.* inflammation of the tongue. [1815–25; GLOSS- + -ITIS] —**glos·sit·ic** (glo sit′ik, glô-), *adj.*

gloss·me·ter (glos′mē′tər, glôs′-), *n.* an instrument for measuring the reflectivity of a surface. Also called **glos·sim·e·ter** (glo sim′i tər, glô-). [GLOSS[1] + -METER]

glosso-, a combining form meaning "tongue, word, speech," used in the formation of compound words: *glossology.* Also, **glotto-.** Also, *esp. before a vowel,* **gloss-.** [< Gk (Ionic), comb. form of *glôssa*]

glos·sog·ra·pher (glo sog′rə fər, glô-), *n.* a glossator. [1600–10; < Gk *glōssográph(os)* + -ER[1]. See GLOSSO-, -GRAPHER] —**glos·so·graph·i·cal** (glos′ə graf′i kəl, glô′sə-), *adj.* —**glos·sog′ra·phy,** *n.*

glos·so·la·li·a (glos′ə lā′lē ə, glô′sə-), *n.* incomprehensible speech in an imaginary language, sometimes occurring in a trance state, an episode of religious ecstasy, or schizophrenia. Cf. **speaking in tongues.** [1875–80; GLOSSO- + -LALIA] —**glos·sol·a·list** (glo sol′ə list, glô-), *n.*

glos·sol·o·gy (glo sol′ə jē, glô-), *n. Archaic.* linguistics. [1710–20; GLOSSO- + -LOGY] —**glos·so·log·i·cal** (glos′ə loj′i kəl, glô′sə-), *adj.* —**glos·sol′o·gist,** *n.*

glos·so·pha·ryn·ge·al (glos′ō fə rin′jē əl, -jəl, -far′in jē′əl, glô′sō-), *Anat.* —*adj.* **1.** of or pertaining to the tongue and pharynx. —*n.* **2.** See **glossopharyngeal nerve.** [1815–25; GLOSSO- + PHARYNGEAL]

glos′sopharyn′geal nerve′, *Anat.* either of the ninth pair of cranial nerves, consisting of motor fibers that innervate the muscles of the pharynx, the soft palate, and the parotid glands, and of sensory fibers that conduct impulses to the brain from the pharynx, the middle ear, and the posterior third of the tongue. [1815–25]

gloss·y (glos′ē, glô′sē), *adj.,* **gloss·i·er, gloss·i·est,** *n., pl.* **gloss·ies.** —*adj.* **1.** having a shiny or lustrous surface. **2.** having a false or deceptive appearance or air, esp. of experience or sophistication; specious. —*n.* **3.** slick[1] (def. 9). **4.** a photograph printed on glossy paper. [1550–60; GLOSS[1] + -Y[1]] —**gloss′i·ly,** *adv.* —**gloss′i·ness,** *n.*
—**Syn. 1.** shining, polished, glazed. —**Ant. 1.** dull.

gloss′y snake′, a nocturnal burrowing snake, *Arizona elegans,* of the western U.S. and northern Mexico, having smooth, glistening scales of tan with brown blotches.

-glot, a combining form with the meanings "having a tongue," "speaking, writing, or written in a language" of the kind or number specified by the initial element: *polyglot.* [< Gk (Attic) *-glōttos* -tongued, adj. deriv. of *glôtta* tongue; see GLOTTO-]

glot·tal (glot′l), *adj.* **1.** of or pertaining to the glottis. **2.** *Phonet.* articulated at the glottis. —*n.* **3.** See **glottal stop.** [1840–50; GLOTT(IS) + -AL[1]]

glot·tal′ic air′stream (glo tal′ik), *Phonet.* a current of air in the pharynx produced by the action of the glottis. [GLOTTAL + -IC]

glot·tal·ize (glot′l īz′), *v.t.,* **-ized, -iz·ing.** *Phonet.* to pronounce with glottal coarticulation. Also, *esp. Brit.,* **glot′tal·ise′.** [1945–50; GLOTTAL + -IZE] —**glot′tal·i·za′tion,** *n.*

glot·tal·ized (glot′l īzd′), *adj. Phonet.* pronounced with glottal coarticulation. [1915–20; GLOTTALIZE + -ED[2]]

glot′tal stop′, *Phonet.* **1.** a plosive consonant whose occlusion and release are accomplished chiefly at the glottis, as in the Scottish articulation of the *t*-sound of *little, bottle,* etc. **2.** a stop consonant, without release, having glottal occlusion as a secondary articulation, as in *yep* for *yes, nope* for *no.* Also called **glottal.** [1885–90]

glot·tic (glot′ik), *adj.* pertaining to the glottis; glottal. [1795–1805; < Gk *glōttikós.* See GLOTTIS, -IC]

glot·tis (glot′is), *n., pl.* **glot·tis·es, glot·ti·des** (glot′i dēz′). *Anat.* the opening at the upper part of the larynx, between the vocal cords. [1570–80; < NL < Gk (Attic) *glōttís,* deriv. of *glôtta* tongue (Ionic *glôssa;* see GLOSS[2])] —**glot·tid·e·an** (glo tid′ē ən, glô-), *adj.*

glotto-, var. of **glosso-:** *glottology.* [< Gk (Attic) *glōtto-,* comb. form of *glôtta;* see GLOTTIS]

glot·to·chro·nol·o·gy (glot′ō krə nol′ə jē, glot′ə-), *n. Ling.* the branch of lexicostatistics that studies the rate of replacement of vocabulary and attempts to determine what percentage of basic vocabulary two presently distinct but related languages share, using the information thus obtained to estimate how long ago they ceased being a single language. [1950–55; GLOTTO- + CHRONOLOGY]

glot·tog·o·ny (glo tog′ə nē), *n. Ling.* the study of the putative origin of language. [GLOTTO- + -GONY] —**glot·to·gon·ic** (glot′ō gon′ik), *adj.*

glot·tol·o·gy (glo tol′ə jē), *n. Obs.* linguistics. [1835–45; GLOTTO- + -LOGY] —**glot·to·log·ic** (glot′l oj′ik), **glot′to·log′i·cal,** *adj.* —**glot·tol′o·gist,** *n.*

Glouces·ter (glos′tər, glô′stər), *n.* **1. Duke of.** See **Humphrey. 2.** a seaport in W Gloucestershire in SW England, on the Severn River. 90,700. **3.** a seaport in NE Massachusetts. 27,768. **4.** Gloucestershire.

Glouces′ter Cit′y, a city in W New Jersey, on the Delaware River. 13,121.

Glouces·ter·shire (glos′tər shēr′, -shər, glô′stər-), *n.* a county in SW England. 487,600; 1255 sq. mi. (2640 sq. km). *Co. seat:* Gloucester. Also called **Gloucester.**

glout (gloot, glout), *v.i. Archaic.* to scowl or frown. [1400–50; late ME, of uncert. orig.]

glove (gluv), *n., v.,* **gloved, glov·ing.** —*n.* **1.** a covering for the hand made with a separate sheath for each finger and for the thumb. **2.** See **boxing glove. 3.** See **baseball glove. 4.** gauntlet[1]. **5. hand and glove.** See **hand** (def. 42). **6. handle with kid gloves.** See **kid gloves** (def. 2). **7. take up the glove.** See **gauntlet**[1] (def. 4). **8. throw down the glove.** See **gauntlet**[1] (def. 5). —*v.t.* **9.** to cover with or as if with a glove; provide with gloves. **10.** to serve as a glove for. [bef. 900; ME; OE *glōf;* c. ON *glōfi*] —**glove′less,** *adj.* —**glove′like′,** *adj.*

glove′ box′, 1. See **glove compartment. 2.** an enclosed compartment with openings to which long gloves are attached, enabling someone outside the compartment to reach inside and handle its contents without causing or incurring injury or contamination, as in a laboratory or hospital. [1855–60 for earlier sense]

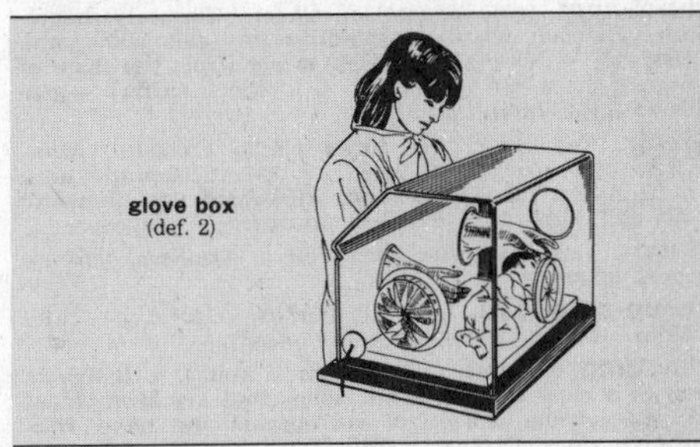
glove box (def. 2)

glove′ compart′ment, a compartment in the dashboard of an automobile for storing small items. Also called **glove box.** [1935–40]

glove·man (gluv′man′), *n., pl.* **-men.** *Baseball, Cricket.* fielder. [GLOVE + MAN[1]]

glov·er (gluv′ər), *n.* a person who makes or sells gloves. [1350–1400; ME; see GLOVE, -ER[2]]

Glov·er (gluv′ər), *n.* **John,** 1732–97, American general.

Glov·ers·ville (gluv′ərz vil′), *n.* a city in E New York. 17,836.

glove′ silk′, a warp knit fabric made of silk or nylon, used in the manufacture of gloves and undergarments.

glow (glō), *n.* **1.** a light emitted by or as if by a substance heated to luminosity; incandescence. **2.** brightness of color. **3.** a sensation or state of bodily heat. **4.** a warm, ruddy color of the cheeks. **5.** warmth of emotion or passion; ardor. —*v.i.* **6.** to emit bright light and heat without flame; become incandescent. **7.** to shine like something intensely heated. **8.** to exhibit a strong, bright color; be lustrously red or brilliant. **9.** (of the cheeks) to exhibit a healthy, warm, ruddy color. **10.** to become or feel very warm or hot. **11.** to show emotion or elation: *to glow with pride.* [bef. 1000; ME *glowen* (v.), OE *glōwan;* akin to G *glühen,* ON *glōa*]
—**Syn. 9.** flush, blush, redden.

glow′ dis′charge, *Physics.* the conduction of electricity in a low-pressure gas, producing a diffuse glow. [1835–45]

glow·er (glou′ər), *v.i.* **1.** to look or stare with sullen dislike, discontent, or anger. —*n.* **2.** a look of sullen dislike, discontent, or anger. [1350–1400; ME (Scots) *glowren* to glower; akin to MLG *glūren* to be overcast, MD *gloeren* to leer] —**glow′er·ing·ly,** *adv.*
—**Syn. 1.** See **glare**[1].

glow·fly (glō′flī′), *n., pl.* **-flies.** firefly. [1780–90; GLOW + FLY[2]]

glow·ing (glō′ing), *adj.* **1.** incandescent. **2.** rich and warm in coloring: *glowing colors.* **3.** showing the radiance of health, excitement, etc.: *glowing cheeks.* **4.** warmly favorable or complimentary: *a glowing account of her work.* [bef. 1000; ME *glowynge,* OE *glowende.* See GLOW, -ING[2]] —**glow′ing·ly,** *adv.*
—**Syn. 4.** ardent, wholehearted, enthusiastic, rapturous, unstinting.

glow′ lamp′, *Electronics.* a vacuum tube containing a gas that is ionized by the electrons, giving a visible glow. [1880–85]

glow′ plug′, *Auto., Mach.* a device for each cylinder of a diesel engine with a heating element to heat the incoming fuel and air so that combustion will take place more readily when the engine is cold. [1940–45] **—glow′-plug′,** *adj.*

glow·worm (glō′wûrm′), *n.* **1.** the wingless female or larva of the European beetle, *Lampyris noctiluca,* which emits a sustained greenish light. **2.** any of various other beetle larvae or wingless females that emit a glow rather than a flash of light. [1300–50; ME. See GLOW, WORM]

glox·in·i·a (glok sin′ē ə), *n.* **1.** any of several horticultural varieties of a plant belonging to the genus *Sinningia,* of the gesneria family, esp. *S. speciosa,* having large white, red, or purple bell-shaped flowers. **2.** any plant of the genus *Gloxinia,* of Central and South America, having bluish, white, or pink flowers. [named after Benjamin P. *Gloxin* (fl. 1785), German physician and botanist; see -IA]

gloze (glōz), *v.,* **glozed, gloz·ing,** *n.* *—v.t.* **1.** to explain away; extenuate; gloss over (usually fol. by *over*). *—v.i.* **2.** *Archaic.* to make glosses; comment. *—n.* **3.** *Archaic.* flattery or deceit. **4.** *Obs.* a specious show. [1250–1300; ME < OF *gloser* < ML *glossāre;* see GLOSS²] **—gloz′ing·ly,** *adv.*

Glu, *Biochem.* glutamic acid.

Glubb (glub), *n.* **Sir John Bag·ot** (bag′ət), ("*Glubb Pasha*"), 1897–1986, British army officer: commander of the Arab Legion in Jordan 1939–56.

gluc-, var. of **gluco-** before a vowel: *glucide.*

glu·ca·gon (glo͞o′kə gon′), *n. Biochem.* a hormone secreted by the pancreas that acts in opposition to insulin in the regulation of blood glucose levels. [1923; prob. GLUC- + Gk *ágōn* prp. of *ágein* to lead, drive; see -AGOGUE]

glu·car′ic ac′id (glo͞o kar′ik): See **saccharic acid.** [GLUC- + *-aric,* as in *saccharic*]

glu·cide (glo͞o′sīd), *n.* any of various organic compounds that consist of or contain a carbohydrate. [GLUC- + -IDE] **—glu·cid·ic** (glo͞o sid′ik), *adj.*

glu·ci·num (glo͞o sī′nəm), *n. Chem.* (formerly) beryllium. *Symbol:* Gl Also, **glu·cin·i·um** (glo͞o sin′ē əm). [1805–15; < NL < Gk *glyk(ýs)* sweet (from the taste of some of the salts) + *-in-* -IN² + L *-um* n. suffix] **—glu·cin·ic** (glo͞o sin′ik), *adj.*

Gluck (glo͝ok), *n.* **1. Alma** (*Reba Fiersohn, Mme. Efrem Zimbalist*), 1884–1938, U.S. operatic soprano, born in Rumania. **2. Chris·toph Wil·li·bald von** (kris′tôf vil′i bält′ fən), 1714–87, German operatic composer.

gluco-, var. of **glyco-:** *glucoprotein.* Also, *esp. before a vowel,* **gluc-.**

glu·co·chlo·rose (glo͞o′kō klôr′ōs, -klōr′-), *n.* chloralose. [GLUCO- + CHLOR(AL) + -OSE²]

glu·co·cor·ti·coid (glo͞o′kō kôr′ti koid′), *n. Biochem.* any of a class of steroid hormones that are synthesized by the adrenal cortex of vertebrates and have anti-inflammatory activity. [1945–50; GLUCO- + CORTIC- + -OID; cf. CORTICOSTEROID]

glu·co·gen·e·sis (glo͞o′kō jen′ə sis), *n. Biochem.* the production of glucose by the decomposition of glycogen or from any nonglucose precursor. [< NL; see GLUCO-, -GENESIS] **—glu′co·gen′ic,** *adj.*

glu·co·ki·nase (glo͞o′kō kī′nās, -nāz), *n. Biochem.* an enzyme, found in all living systems, that serves to catalyze the phosphorylation of gluconic acid. [GLUC(ONIC ACID) + -O- + KINASE]

glu·co·ne·o·gen·e·sis (glo͞o′kō nē′ə jen′ə sis), *n. Biochem.* glucose formation in animals from a noncarbohydrate source, as from proteins or fats. Also, **glyconeogenesis.** [1910–15; GLUCO- + NEO- + -GENESIS] **—glu·co·ne·o·gen·ic** (glo͞o′kō nē′ə jen′ik), **glu·co·ne·o·ge·net·ic** (glo͞o′kō nē′ō jə net′ik), *adj.*

glu·con′ic ac′id (glo͞o kon′ik), a colorless, water-soluble acid, $C_6H_{12}O_7$, obtained by the oxidation of glucose, used commercially in a 50-percent solution for cleaning metals. Also, **glyconic acid, glycogenic acid.** [1870–75; trans. of G *Glukonsäure;* see GLUC-, -ONIC]

glu·co·pro·tein (glo͞o′kō prō′tēn, -tē in), *n. Biochem.* glycoprotein.

glu·co·sa·mine (glo͞o kō′sə mēn′, -min), *n. Biochem.* an aminosugar occurring in many polysaccharides of vertebrate tissue and also as the major component of chitin. [1880–85; GLUCOSE + -AMINE]

glu·co·san (glo͞o′kə san′), *n. Biochem.* any of a number of polysaccharides that yield glucose upon hydrolysis. [1920–25; GLUCOSE + *-an,* for -ANE]

glu·cose (glo͞o′kōs), *n. Biochem.* **1.** a sugar, $C_6H_{12}O_6$, having several optically different forms, the common dextrorotatory form **(dextroglucose,** or ***d*-glucose)** occurring in many fruits, animal tissues and fluids, etc., and having a sweetness about one half that of ordinary sugar, and the rare levorotatory form **(levoglucose,** or ***l*-glucose)** not naturally occurring. **2.** Also called **starch syrup.** a syrup containing dextrose, maltose, and dextrine, obtained by the incomplete hydrolysis of starch. [1830–40; < F < Gk *glyk(ýs)* sweet + F *-ose* -OSE²] **—glu·cos′ic,** *adj.*

glu′cose tol′erance test′, *Med.* a diagnostic procedure in which a measured amount of glucose is ingested and blood samples are taken periodically as a means of detecting diabetes mellitus. [1920–25]

glu·co·side (glo͞o′kə sīd′), *n.* any of an extensive group of compounds that yield glucose and some other substance or substances when treated with a dilute acid or decomposed by a ferment or enzyme. Cf. **glycoside.** [1865–70; GLUCOSE + -IDE] **—glu′co·sid′al, glu·co·sid·ic** (glo͞o′kə sid′ik), *adj.*

glu·co·sin (glo͞o′kō sin), *n. Biochem.* any of a class of compounds, some of which are highly toxic, derived from reactions of glucose with ammonia. [GLUCOSE + -IN²]

glu·cos·u·ri·a (glo͞o′kōs yo͞o rē′ə), *n. Pathol.* glycosuria. **—glu′cos·u′ric,** *adj.*

glu′cu·ron′ic ac′id (glo͞o′kyə ron′ik, glo͞o′-), *Biochem.* an acid, $C_6H_{10}O_7$, formed by the oxidation of glucose, found combined with other products of metabolism in the blood and urine. Also, **glycuronic acid.** [1910–15; earlier *glycuronic acid,* trans. of G *Glykuronsäure;* see GLYC-, URONIC ACID]

glu·cu·ron·ide (glo͞o kyo͝or′ə nīd′), *n. Biochem.* a glycoside that yields glucuronic acid upon hydrolysis. Also, **glycuronide.** [1930–35; GLUCURON(IC ACID) + -IDE]

glue (glo͞o), *n., v.,* **glued, glu·ing.** *—n.* **1.** a hard, impure, protein gelatin, obtained by boiling skins, hoofs, and other animal substances in water, that when melted or diluted is a strong adhesive. **2.** any of various solutions or preparations of this substance, used as an adhesive. **3.** any of various other solutions or preparations that can be used as adhesives. *—v.t.* **4.** to join or fasten with glue. **5.** to cover or smear (something) with glue (sometimes fol. by *up*). **6.** to fix or attach firmly with or as if with glue; make adhere closely: *to glue a model ship together.* [1300–50; (n.) ME *glu, gleu* < OF *glu* < L *glūt-* (s. of *glūs*); c. Gk *gloiós* gum, anything sticky; (v.) ME *glywen, glewen,* deriv. of the n.] **—glue′like′,** *adj.* **—glu′er,** *n.*
—Syn. 4. paste, gum, stick, cement, plaster.

glue·ball (glo͞o′bôl′), *n. Physics.* a hypothetical object consisting of two or more gluons. Also, **gluonium.** [GLUE + BALL¹]

glue′ cell′, colloblast.

glue·pot (glo͞o′pot′), *n.* a double boiler in which glue is melted. [1475–85; GLUE + POT¹]

glue′ sniff′ing, the inhaling of the fumes of certain kinds of glue for the hallucinogenic or euphoric effect. [1960–65, *Amer.*] **—glue′ sniff′er.**

glue·y (glo͞o′ē), *adj.,* **glu·i·er, glu·i·est. 1.** like glue; viscid; sticky. **2.** full of or smeared with glue. [1350–1400; ME; see GLUE, -Y¹] **—glu′ey·ness,** *n.*

glug (glug), *v.,* **glugged, glug·ging,** *n.* *—v.i.* **1.** to make the sound of liquid pouring from a bottle. *—n.* **2.** such a sound. [1890–95; imit.]

glum (glum), *adj.,* **glum·mer, glum·mest.** sullenly or silently gloomy; dejected. [1425–75; late ME; var. of GLOOM] **—glum′ly,** *adv.* **—glum′ness,** *n.*
—Syn. moody, sulky; despondent, melancholy. GLUM, MOROSE, SULLEN, DOUR, SURLY all are adjectives describing a gloomy, unsociable attitude. GLUM describes a depressed, spiritless condition or manner, usually temporary rather than habitual: *a glum shrug of the shoulders.* MOROSE, which adds to GLUM a sense of bitterness, implies a habitual and pervasive gloominess: *a sour, morose manner; morose withdrawal from human contact.* SULLEN usually implies reluctance or refusal to speak accompanied by glowering looks expressing anger or a sense of injury: *a sullen manner, silence, look.* DOUR refers to a stern and forbidding aspect, stony and unresponsive: *dour rejection of friendly overtures.* SURLY implies gruffness of speech and manner, usually accompanied by an air of injury and ill temper: *a surly reply.*

glu·ma·ceous (glo͞o mā′shəs), *adj. Bot.* **1.** glumelike; chaffy. **2.** consisting of or having glumes. [1820–30; GLUME + -ACEOUS]

glume (glo͞om), *n. Bot.* one of the characteristic chafflike bracts of the inflorescence of grasses, sedges, etc., esp. one of the pair of bracts at the base of a spikelet. [1570–80; < L *glūma* husk enclosing a cereal grain, prob. equiv. to *glūb(ere)* to strip the bark from + **-sma* n. suffix] **—glume′like′,** *adj.*

glu·on (glo͞o′on), *n. Physics.* an unobserved massless particle with spin 1 that is believed to transmit the strong force between quarks, binding them together into baryons and mesons. [1970–75; GLUE + -ON¹]

glu·o·ni·um (glo͞o ō′nē əm), *n., pl.* **-ni·ums, -ni·a** (-nē ə). *Physics.* glueball. [cf. GLUON, CHARMONIUM]

glu·side (glo͞o′sīd), *n. Chem.* saccharin. [perh. alter. (by syncope) of GLUCOSIDE]

glut (glut), *v.,* **glut·ted, glut·ting,** *n.* *—v.t.* **1.** to feed or fill to satiety; sate: *to glut the appetite.* **2.** to feed or fill to excess; cloy. **3.** to flood (the market) with a particular item or service so that the supply greatly exceeds the demand. **4.** to choke up: *to glut a channel.* *—v.i.* **5.** to eat to satiety or to excess. *—n.* **6.** a full supply. **7.** an excessive supply or amount; surfeit. **8.** an act of glutting or the state of being glutted. [1275–1325; ME *gluten,* back formation from *glutun* GLUTTON¹] **—glut′·ting·ly,** *adv.*
—Syn. 1. surfeit, stuff, satiate. **5.** gorge, cram. **7.** surplus, excess, superabundance.

glu·ta·mate (glo͞o′tə māt′), *n.* a salt or ester of glutamic acid. [1875–80; GLUTAM(IC ACID) + -ATE²]

glu·tam′ic ac′id (glo͞o tam′ik), *Biochem.* an amino acid, $HOOCCH_2CH_2CH(NH_2)COOH$, obtained by hydrolysis from wheat gluten and sugar-beet residues, used commercially chiefly in the form of its sodium salt to intensify the flavor of meat or other food. *Abbr.:* Glu; *Symbol:* E Also, **glu′ta·min′ic ac′id** (glo͞o′tə min′ik, glo͞o′-). [1870–75; GLUT(EN) + AMIC ACID]

glu·ta·mine (glo͞o′tə mēn′, -min), *n. Biochem.* a crystalline amino acid, $HOOCCH(NH_2)CH_2CH_2CONH_2$, related to glutamic acid. *Abbr.:* Gln; *Symbol:* Q [1880–85; GLUT(EN) + -AMINE]

glu·tar·al·de·hyde (glo͞o′tə ral′də hīd′), *n. Biochem.* a nonflammable liquid, $C_5H_8O_2$, soluble in water and alcohol, toxic and an irritant, used for tanning leather and as a fixative for samples to be examined under the electron microscope. [1950–55; GLUTAR(IC ACID) + ALDEHYDE]

glu·ta·thi·one (glo͞o′tə thī′ōn), *n. Biochem.* a crystalline, water-soluble peptide of glutamic acid, cysteine, and glycine, $C_{10}H_{17}N_3O_6S$, found in blood and in animal and plant tissues, and important in tissue oxidations and in the activation of some enzymes. [1920–25; GLUTA(MIC ACID) + THI- + -ONE]

glutch (gluch), *Newfoundland.* *—v.t.* **1.** to swallow. *—n.* **2.** a mouthful. [cf. Brit. dial. *glutch,* with same sense; of uncert. orig.]

glu·te·al (glo͞o′tē əl, glo͞o tē′əl), *adj. Anat.* pertaining to the buttock muscles or the buttocks. [1795–1805; GLUTE(US) + -AL¹]

glu·te·lin (glo͞ot′l in), *n. Biochem.* any of a group of simple proteins of vegetable origin, esp. one from wheat. [1905–10; perh. alter. of *glutenin.* See GLUTEN, -IN²]

glu·ten (glo͞ot′n), *n.* **1.** the tough, viscid, nitrogenous substance remaining when the flour of wheat or other grain is washed to remove the starch. **2.** *Archaic.* glue or a gluey substance. [1590–1600; < L *glūten* glue]

glu′ten bread′, bread made from gluten flour. [1840–50]

glu′ten flour′. See **bread flour.**

glu·ten·in (glo͞ot′n in), *n.* a simple protein of cereal grains that imparts adhesive properties to flour. [1890–1900; GLUTEN + -IN¹]

glu·te·nous (glo͞ot′n əs), *adj.* **1.** like gluten. **2.** containing gluten, esp. in large amounts. [GLUTEN + -OUS]

glu·tes (glo͞o′tēz), *n.pl. Informal.* the muscles of the buttocks. [*glute* shortening of GLUTEUS + -S³]

glu·teth·i·mide (glo͞o teth′ə mīd′), *n. Pharm.* a white, crystalline, water-insoluble powder, $C_{13}H_{15}NO_2$, used as a hypnotic and sedative. [1950–55; GLUTE(N) + THI- + (A)MIDE]

glu·te·us (glo͞o′tē əs, glo͞o tē′-), *n., pl.* **-te·i** (-tē ī′, -tē′ī). *Anat.* any of several muscles of the buttocks, esp. the gluteus maximus. [1675–85; < NL < Gk *gloutó(s)* the rump + L *-eus* adj. suffix]

glu′teus max′i·mus (mak′sə məs), *pl.* **glutei max·i·mi** (mak′sə mī′). **1.** the broad, thick, outermost muscle of the buttocks, involved in the rotation and extension of the thigh. **2.** *Facetious.* the buttocks. [1900–05; < NL: largest gluteus]

glu′teus me′di·us (mē′dē əs), *pl.* **glutei me·di·i** (mē′dē ī′). the muscle of the buttocks lying between the gluteus maximus and the gluteus minimus, involved in the abduction of the thigh. [< NL: middle gluteus]

glu′teus min′i·mus (min′ə məs), *pl.* **glutei min·i·mi** (min′ə mī′). the innermost muscle of the buttocks, involved in the abduction and rotation of the thigh. [< NL: smallest gluteus]

glu·tin·ant (glo͞ot′n ənt), *n.* a nematocyst that discharges a thread covered with a sticky secretion. [1675–85; < L *glūtinant-* (s. of *glūtināns*), prp. of *glūtināre* to glue. See GLUTEN, -ANT]

glu·ti·nous (glo͞ot′n əs), *adj.* of the nature of glue; viscid; sticky. [1375–1425; late ME; < L *glūtinōsus* gluey, sticky. See GLUTEN, -OUS] **—glu′ti·nous·ly,** *adv.* **—glu′ti·nous·ness, glu·ti·nos·i·ty** (glo͞ot′n os′i tē), *n.*

glu·tose (glo͞o′tōs), *n.* an ingredient of a syrupy mixture obtained by the action of alkali on levulose or found in the unfermentable reducing portion of cane molasses. [GLU(COSE) + (FRUC)TOSE]

glut·ton¹ (glut′n), *n.* **1.** a person who eats and drinks excessively or voraciously. **2.** a person with a remarkably great desire or capacity for something: *a glutton for work; a glutton for punishment.* [1175–1225; ME *glutun* < OF *glouton* < L *gluttōn-* (s. of *gluttō*), var. of *glūtō* glutton, akin to *glūtire* to gulp down]
—Syn. 1. gourmand; gastronome; chowhound.

glut·ton² (glut′n), *n.* the wolverine, *Gulo gulo,* of Europe. [1665–75; trans. of G *Vielfrass,* equiv. to *viel* much + *frass* eating, deriv. of *fressen* (of animals) to eat]

glut·ton·ize (glut′n īz′), *v.,* **-ized, -iz·ing.** *Archaic.* *—v.i.* **1.** to eat like a glutton. *—v.t.* **2.** to feast gluttonously on. Also, *esp. Brit.,* **glut′ton·ise′.** [1650–60; GLUTTON¹ + -IZE]

glut·ton·ous (glut′n əs), *adj.* **1.** tending to eat and drink excessively; voracious. **2.** greedy; insatiable. [1300–50; ME; see GLUTTON¹, -OUS] **—glut′ton·ous·ly,** *adv.* **—glut′ton·ous·ness,** *n.*

glut·ton·y (glut′n ē), *n.* excessive eating and drinking. [1175–1225; ME *glotonie, glutonie* < OF *glotonie;* see GLUTTON¹, -Y³]
—Syn. gormandizing, intemperance, voracity.

Gly, *Biochem.* glycine.

gly·bu·ride (glī byo͝or′īd), *n. Pharm.* a hypoglycemic substance, $C_{23}H_{28}ClN_3O_5S$, used orally in the treatment of diabetes mellitus. [GLY(CO)- + *-buride,* of uncert. derivation]

glyc-, var. of **glyco-** before a vowel: *glycemia.*

glyc., (in prescriptions) glycerite. [< NL *glyceritum*]

gly·ce·mi·a (glī sē′mē ə), *n. Med.* the presence of glucose in the blood. Also, **gly·cae′mi·a.** [1900–05; GLYC- + -EMIA] **—gly·ce′mic, gly·cae′mic,** *adj.*

glyc·er·al·de·hyde (glis′ə ral′də hīd′), *n. Biochem.* a white, crystalline, water-soluble solid, $C_3H_6O_3$, that is an intermediate in carbohydrate metabolism and yields glycerol on reduction. Also called **glycer′ic al′dehyde.** [1880–85; GLYCER(IN) + ALDEHYDE]

gly·cer·ic (gli ser′ik, glis′ər ik), *adj.* of or derived from glycerol. [1860–65; GLYCER(OL) + -IC]

glycer′ic ac′id, a colorless, syrupy liquid, $C_3H_6O_4$, obtained by oxidizing glycerol. [1860–65]

glyc·er·ide (glis′ə rīd′, -ər id), *n. Chem., Biochem.* any of a group of esters obtained from glycerol by the replacement of one, two, or three hydroxyl groups with a fatty acid: the principal constituent of adipose tissue. Cf. **monoglyceride, diglyceride, triglyceride.** [1860–65; GLYCER(IN) + -IDE]

glyc·er·in (glis′ər in), *n. Chem.* glycerol. Also, **glyc·er·ine** (glis′ər in, -ə rēn′, glis′ə rēn′). [1830–40; < F *glycérine,* equiv. to Gk *glyker(ós)* sweet + *-ine* -IN²]

glyc·er·in·ate¹ (glis′ər ə nāt′), *v.t.,* **-at·ed, -at·ing.** to

CONCISE ETYMOLOGY KEY: <, descended or borrowed from; >, whence; b., blend of, blended; c., cognate with; cf., compare; deriv., derivative; equiv., equivalent; imit., imitative; obl., oblique; r., replacing; s., stem; sp., spelling, spelled; resp., respelling, respelled; trans., translation; ?, origin unknown; *, unattested; ‡, probably earlier than. See the full key inside the front cover.

impregnate with glycerin. [1895–1900; GLYCERIN + -ATE[1]]

glyc·er·in·ate[2] (glis′ər ə nāt′), *n.* any salt of glyceric acid. [GLYCERIN + -ATE[2]]

glyc·er·ite (glis′ə rīt′), *n. Pharm.* a preparation of a medicinal substance dissolved in or mixed with glycerin. [1870–75; GLYCER(IN) + -ITE[1]]

glyc·er·ol (glis′ə rôl′, -rol′), *n.* a colorless, odorless, syrupy, sweet liquid, $C_3H_8O_3$, usually obtained by the saponification of natural fats and oils: used for sweetening and preserving food, in the manufacture of cosmetics, perfumes, inks, and certain glues and cements, as a solvent and automobile antifreeze, and in medicine in suppositories and skin emollients. Also called **glycerin, glycerine.** [1880–85; GLYCER(IN) + -OL[1]]

glyc·er·ol·y·sis (glis′ə rol′ə sis), *n., pl.* **-ses** (-sēz′). chemical decomposition resulting from the interaction of a compound and glycerol. [GLYCERO(L) + -LYSIS]

glyc·er·yl (glis′ər il), *adj.* containing the glyceryl group. [1835–45; GLYCER(IN) + -YL]

glyc′eryl group′, the trivalent group $(C_3H_5)^{-3}$, derived from glycerol. Also called **glyc′eryl rad′ical.**

glyc′eryl mon·o·ac′e·tate (mon′ō as′i tāt′), acetin. [MONO- + ACETATE]

glyc′eryl tri·ni′trate (trī nī′trāt), nitroglycerin. [1890–95; TRI- + NITRATE]

glyc′eryl tri·o′le·ate (trī ō′lē āt′), olein. [1880–85; TRI- + OLEATE]

glyc′eryl tri·pal′mi·tate (trī pal′mi tāt′, -päl′-, -pä′mi-), palmitin. [TRI- + PALMITATE]

gly·cine (glī′sēn, glī sēn′), *n. Biochem.* a colorless, crystalline, sweet, water-soluble solid, H_2NCH_2COOH, the simplest amino acid: used chiefly in organic synthesis and biochemical research. *Abbr.:* Gly; *Symbol:* G Also called **aminoacetic acid, gly·co·coll** (glī′kə kol′). [1850–55; GLYC- + -INE[2]]

glyco-, a combining form with the meanings "sugar," "glucose and its derivatives," used in the formation of compound words: *glycolipid.* Also, **gluco-.** Also, *esp. before a vowel,* **glyc-.** [comb. form repr. Gk *glykýs* sweet]

gly·co·gen (glī′kə jən, -jen′), *n. Biochem.* a white, tasteless polysaccharide, $(C_6H_{10}O_5)_n$, molecularly similar to starch, constituting the principal carbohydrate storage material in animals and occurring chiefly in the liver, in muscle, and in fungi and yeasts. Also called **animal starch.** [1855–60; GLYCO- + -GEN]

gly·co·gen·e·sis (glī′kə jen′ə sis), *n. Biochem.* the formation of glycogen from monosaccharides in the body, esp. glucose. Also, **gly·cog·e·ny** (glī koj′ə nē). [1870–75; GLYCO- + -GENESIS]

gly·co·ge·net·ic (glī′kō jə net′ik), *adj. Biochem.* of or pertaining to the formation of sugar in the liver. Also, **gly·cog·e·nous** (glī koj′ə nəs). [1870–75; GLYCO- + -GENETIC]

gly·co·gen·ic (glī′kə jen′ik), *adj. Biochem.* **1.** of or pertaining to glycogen. **2.** glycogenetic. [1855–60; GLYCOGEN + -IC]

gly′cogen′ic ac′id. See **gluconic acid.** [1885–90]

gly′cogen stor′age disease′, *Pathol.* any of several inherited disorders of glycogen metabolism that result in excess accumulation of glycogen in various organs of the body. Also called **gly·co·ge·no·sis** (glī′kō jə nō′sis).

gly·col (glī′kôl, -kol), *n.* **1.** Also called **ethylene glycol, ethylene alcohol.** a colorless, sweet liquid, $C_2H_6O_2$, used chiefly as an automobile antifreeze and as a solvent. **2.** Also called **diol.** any of a group of alcohols containing two hydroxyl groups. [1855–60; GLYC(ERIN) + (ALCOH)OL]

gly·co·late (glī′kə lāt′), *n.* a salt or ester of glycolic acid. [1860–65; GLYCOL(IC ACID) + -ATE[2]]

gly·col·ic (glī kol′ik), *adj.* pertaining to or derived from glycol. Also, **gly·col′lic.** [1850–55; GLYCOL + -IC]

glycol′ic ac′id, a colorless, crystalline, water-soluble powder, $C_2H_4O_3$, that is a major substrate for photorespiration in plants: used chiefly for textile printing and dyeing and in pesticides. Also, **glycol′lic ac′id.** Also called **hydroxyacetic acid.** [1850–55]

gly·co·lip·id (glī′kə lip′id), *n. Biochem.* any of a class of lipids, comprising the cerebrosides and gangliosides, that upon hydrolysis yield galactose or a similar sugar, a fatty acid, and sphingosine or dihydrosphingosine. [1935–40; GLYCO- + LIPID]

gly·col·y·sis (glī kol′ə sis), *n. Biochem.* the catabolism of carbohydrates, as glucose and glycogen, by enzymes, with the release of energy and the production of lactic or pyruvic acid. [1890–95; GLYCO- + -LYSIS]

gly·co·lyt·ic (glī′kə lit′ik), *adj. Biochem.* of, relating to, or causing glycolysis. [1895–1900; GLYCO- + -LYTIC] **—gly′co·lyt′i·cal·ly,** *adv.*

gly·co·ne·o·gen·e·sis (glī′kō nē′ə jen′ə sis), *n. Biochem.* gluconeogenesis. [GLYCO- + NEO- + -GENESIS] **—gly·co·ne·o·ge·net·ic** (glī′kō nē′ō jə net′ik), *adj.*

gly·con′ic ac′id (glī kon′ik). See **gluconic acid.**

gly·co·pro·tein (glī′kō prō′tēn, -tē in), *n. Biochem.* any of a group of complex proteins, as mucin, containing a carbohydrate combined with a simple protein. Also, **glucoprotein.** Also called **gly·co·pep·tide** (glī′kō pep′tīd). [1905–10; GLYCO- + PROTEIN]

gly·cos·a·mi·no·gly·can (glī′kōs ə mē′nō glī′kan), *n.* any of a class of polysaccharides derived from hexosamine that form mucins when complexed with proteins: formerly called mucopolysaccharide. [1975–80; GLYCO- + (HEXO)SAMINE + -O- + *glycan* polysaccharide]

gly·co·side (glī′kə sīd′), *n. Biochem.* any of the class of compounds that yield a sugar and an aglycon upon hydrolysis. [1925–30; GLYCOSE + -IDE] **—gly·co·sid·ic** (glī′kə sid′ik), *adj.*

gly·cos·u·ri·a (glī′kōs yŏŏ rē′ə), *n. Pathol.* excretion of glucose in the urine, as in diabetes. Also, **glucosuria.** [1855–60; GLYCOSE + -URIA] **—gly′cos·u′ric,** *adj.*

gly′cu·ron′ic ac′id (glī′kyə ron′ik, glī′-), *Biochem.* See **glucuronic acid.**

gly·cur·o·nide (glī kyŏŏr′ə nīd′), *n. Biochem.* glucuronide. Also, **gly·cur·o·nid** (glī kyŏŏr′ə nid).

gly·cyl (glī′səl), *Biochem.* —*adj.* **1.** of or pertaining to a glycinic residue present in a polypeptide or protein. —*n.* **2.** the acyl radical C_2H_4NO of glycine. [1900–05; GLYC(INE) + -YL]

Glyn (glin), *n.* **1. Elinor,** 1864–1943, English writer. **2.** Also, **Glyn·is** (glin′is), **Glynn, Glynne.** a male or female given name.

gly·ox·a·line (glī ok′sə lēn′, -lin), *n.* imidazole. [1855–60; GLY(COL) + OXAL(IC) + -INE[2]]

gly·ox·y·late (glī ok′sə lāt′), *n. Biochem.* a salt or ester of glyoxylic acid. [1855–60; GLYOXYL(IC ACID) + -ATE[2]]

gly′ox·yl′ic ac′id (glī′ok sil′ik, glī′-), a water-soluble crystalline compound, $C_2H_2O_3$, that is an intermediate in photorespiration in plants. [1855–60; GLY(COL) + OX(ALIC) + -YL + -IC]

glyph (glif), *n.* **1.** a pictograph or hieroglyph. **2.** a sculptured figure or relief carving. **3.** *Archit.* an ornamental channel or groove. [1720–30; < Gk *glyph(ḗ)* carving, deriv. of *glýphein* to hollow out] **—glyph′ic,** *adj.*

glyp·tic (glip′tik), *adj.* **1.** of or pertaining to carving or engraving on gems or the like. —*n.* **2.** the act or process of producing glyptic ornaments. [1810–20; < Gk *glyptikós* of engraving, of stone carving, equiv. to *glypt(ós)* carved (verbid of *glýphein* to engrave, hollow out) + *-ikos* -IC]

glyp·tics (glip′tiks), *n.* (*used with a singular v.*) glyptography (def. 2). [1810–20; see GLYPTIC, -ICS]

glyp·to·dont (glip′tə dont′), *n.* any edentate mammal of the extinct genus *Glyptodon,* of the Pleistocene Epoch, having the body covered by a horny and bony armor. [1830–40; < NL, s. of *Glyptodon* genus name, equiv. to Gk *glypt(ós)* carved + *-odōn* (s. *-odont-*) -toothed, adj. deriv. of *odṓn* tooth]

glyptodont, genus *Glyptodon,* length about 9 ft. (2.7 m)

glyp·to·graph (glip′tə graf′, -gräf′), *n.* **1.** an engraved or carved design, as on a gem. **2.** an object, as a gem, having such a design. [< Gk *glyptó(s)* carved + -GRAPH]

glyp·tog·ra·phy (glip tog′rə fē), *n.* **1.** the description or study of engraved gems or other stones. **2.** Also called **glyptics.** the art or process of engraving on gems or the like. [1790–1800; < Gk *glyptó(s)* carved + -GRAPHY] **—glyp·tog′ra·pher,** *n.* **—glyp·to·graph·ic** (glip′tə graf′ik), *adj.*

gm., gram; grams.

G.M., 1. General Manager. **2.** Grand Marshal. **3.** Grand Master. Also, **GM**

G-man (jē′man′), *n., pl.* **G-men.** an agent for the FBI. [1920–25; prob. repr. *Government man*]

G.M.&S., general, medical, and surgical.

GMAT, 1. *Trademark.* Graduate Management Admissions Test. **2.** Greenwich Mean Astronomical Time.

Gmc, Germanic. Also, **Gmc.**

GMP, *Biochem.* guanosine monophosphate: a ribonucleotide constituent of ribonucleic acid that is the phosphoric acid ester of the nucleoside guanosine. Also called **guanylic acid.**

GMT, Greenwich Mean Time. Also, **G.M.T.**

GMW, See **gram-molecular weight.**

G.N., Graduate Nurse.

gnam′ma hole′ (nam′ə), *Australian.* a hollow in bare rock, narrow at the opening and wider at the bottom, in which water collects. Also called **namma hole.** [1900–05; < Nyungar *ŋamma*]

gnar (när), *v.i.,* **gnarred, gnar·ring.** to snarl; growl. Also, **gnarr.** [1490–1500; imit; cf. OE *gnyrran,* G *knarren, knirren,* MD *gnerren, gnorren*]

gnarl[1] (närl), *n.* **1.** a knotty protuberance on a tree; knot. —*v.t.* **2.** to twist into a knotted or distorted form. [1805–15; back formation from GNARLED] **—Syn. 2.** contort, distort.

gnarl[2] (närl), *v.i.* to growl; snarl. [1585–95; var. of GNAR]

gnarled (närld), *adj.* **1.** (of trees) full of or covered with gnarls; bent; twisted. **2.** having a rugged, weather-beaten appearance: *a gnarled old sea captain.* **3.** crabby; cantankerous. [1595–1605; var. of KNURLED]

gnarl·y (när′lē), *adj.,* **gnarl·i·er, gnarl·i·est. 1.** gnarled. **2.** *Slang.* distasteful; distressing; offensive; gross: *a comic noted for his gnarly humor.* [1820–30; GNARL[1] + -Y[1]] **—gnarl′i·ness,** *n.*

gnash (nash), *v.t.* **1.** to grind or strike (the teeth) together, esp. in rage or pain. **2.** to bite with grinding teeth. —*v.i.* **3.** to gnash the teeth. —*n.* **4.** an act of gnashing. [1490–1500; var. of obs. *gnast,* ME *gnasten;* cf. ON *gnastan* gnashing of teeth] **—gnash′ing·ly,** *adv.*

gnat (nat), *n.* **1.** any of certain small flies, esp. the biting gnats or punkies of the family Ceratopogonidae, the midges of the family Chironomidae, and the black flies of the family Simuliidae. **2.** *Brit.* mosquito. **3. strain at a gnat and swallow a camel,** to fuss about trifles while ignoring more serious matters. [bef. 900; ME; OE *gnæt(t);* c. G (dial.) *Gnatze*] **—gnat′like′,** *adj.*

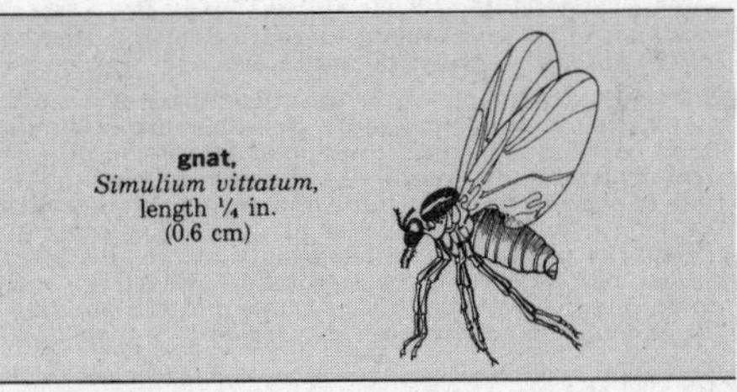

gnat, *Simulium vittatum,* length 1/4 in. (0.6 cm)

gnat·catch·er (nat′kach′ər), *n.* any tiny insect-eating, New World warbler of the genus *Polioptila,* having a long, mobile tail and a slender bill. [1835–45; GNAT + CATCHER]

gnat·eat·er (nat′ē′tər), *n.* any small, long-legged antbird of the genus *Conopophaga,* of South America. Also called **antpipit.** [GNAT + EATER]

gnath·ic (nath′ik), *adj.* of or pertaining to the jaw. Also, **gnath′al.** [1880–85; < Gk *gnáth(os)* jaw + -IC]

gnath′ic in′dex, *Craniom.* the ratio of the distance from basion to prosthion to the distance from basion to nasion, expressed in percent of the latter.

gna·thi·on (nā′thē on′, nath′ē-), *n. Craniom.* the lowest point on the anterior margin of the lower jaw in the midsaggital plane. [1885–90]

gna·thite (nā′thīt, nath′īt), *n. Anat.* any of the mouth appendages of an insect or other arthropod. [1865–70; < Gk *gnáth(os)* jaw + -ITE[1]]

gna·thon·ic (na thon′ik), *adj.* sycophantic; fawning. [1630–40; < L *gnathōnicus,* deriv. of *Gnathōn-* (s. of *Gnathō*) name of a sycophantic character in the Roman comedy *Eunuchus* by Terence; see -IC] **—gna·thon′i·cal·ly,** *adv.*

-gnathous, a combining form meaning "having a jaw" of the kind or in the position specified by the initial element: *prognathous.* [< Gk *-gnathos* -jawed, adj. deriv. of *gnáthos* jaw (akin to CHIN); see -OUS]

gnat·ty (nat′ē), *adj.,* **-ti·er, -ti·est.** infested with gnats. [1905–10; GNAT + -Y[1]]

gnaw (nô), *v.,* **gnawed, gnawed** or **gnawn, gnaw·ing.** —*v.t.* **1.** to bite or chew on, esp. persistently. **2.** to wear away or remove by persistent biting or nibbling. **3.** to form or make by so doing: *to gnaw a hole through the wall.* **4.** to waste or wear away; corrode; erode. **5.** to trouble or torment by constant annoyance, worry, etc.; vex; plague. —*v.i.* **6.** to bite or chew persistently: *The spaniel gnawed happily on a bone.* **7.** to cause corrosion: *The acid gnaws at the metal.* **8.** to cause an effect resembling corrosion: *Her mistake gnawed at her conscience.* [bef. 1000; ME *gnawen,* OE *gnagen;* c. G *nagen,* ON *gnaga*] **—gnaw′a·ble,** *adj.* **—gnaw′er,** *n.*

gnaw·ing (nô′ing), *n.* **1.** the act of a person or thing that gnaws. **2.** Usually, **gnawings.** persistent, dull pains; pangs: *the gnawings of hunger.* [1300–50; ME; see GNAW, -ING[1]] **—gnaw′ing·ly,** *adv.*

gnawn (nôn), *v.* a pp. of **gnaw.**

gneiss (nīs), *n.* a metamorphic rock, generally made up of bands that differ in color and composition, some bands being rich in feldspar and quartz, others rich in hornblende or mica. [1750–60; < G] **—gneiss′ic,** *adj.*

gneiss·oid (nī′soid), *adj.* resembling gneiss. [1840–50; GNEISS + -OID]

Gniez·no (gnyez′nô), *n.* a city in W central Poland, ENE of Posen: important in the early history of the country; 10th-century cathedral. 50,600. German, **Gnesen** (gnā′zən).

GNMA, See **Government National Mortgage Association.**

gnoc·chi (nok′ē, nō′kē; *It.* nyôk′kē), *n.* (*used with a singular or plural v.*) *Italian Cookery.* a dish of little dumplings made from potatoes, semolina, flour, or a combination of these ingredients. [1890–95; < It, pl. of *gnocco,* orig. Upper It (Veneto), perh. c. Tuscan *nocca, nocco* knuckle < Langobardic **knohha* joint; see KNUCKLE]

gnome[1] (nōm), *n.* **1.** (in folklore) one of a species of diminutive beings, usually described as shriveled little old men, that inhabit the interior of the earth and act as guardians of its treasures; troll. **2.** an expert in monetary or financial affairs; international banker or financier: *the gnomes of Zurich.* [1705–15; < F < NL *gnomus,* perh. < Gk *gnṓmē;* see GNOME[2]] **—gnom′ish,** *adj.*
—Syn. 1. See **goblin, sylph.**

gnome[2] (nōm, nō′mē), *n.* a short, pithy expression of a general truth; aphorism. [1570–80; < Gk *gnṓmē* judgment, opinion, purpose]

gno·mic[1] (nō′mik, nom′ik), *adj.* of, pertaining to, or resembling a gnome. [1805–15; GNOME[1] + -IC]

gno·mic[2] (nō′mik, nom′ik), *adj.* **1.** like or containing gnomes or aphorisms. **2.** of, pertaining to, or noting a writer of aphorisms, esp. any of certain Greek poets. Also, **gno′mi·cal.** [1805–15; < Gk *gnōmikós.* See GNOME[2], -IC] **—gno′mi·cal·ly,** *adv.*

CONCISE PRONUNCIATION KEY: act, cāpe, dâre, pärt; set, ēqual; *if,* ice; ox, ōver, ôrder, oil, bŏŏk, bŏŏt, out; up, ûrge; child; sing; shoe; thin, *that;* zh as in *treasure.* ə = *a* as in *alone, e* as in *system, i* as in *easily, o* as in *gallop, u* as in *circus;* ᵊ as in *fire* (fīᵊr), *hour* (ouᵊr). l and n can serve as syllabic consonants, as in *cradle* (krād′l), and *button* (but′n). See the full key inside the front cover.

gno•mist (nō′mist), *n.* a writer of aphorisms. [1870–75; GNOME² + -IST]

gno•mol•o•gy (nō mol′ə jē), *n.* **1.** a collection or anthology of gnomes or aphorisms. **2.** gnomic or aphoristic writing. [1635–45; < Gk *gnōmología.* See GNOME², -O-, -LOGY] —**gno•mo•log•ic** (nō′mə loj′ik), **gno′mo•log′i•cal,** *adj.* —**gno•mol′o•gist,** *n.*

gno•mon (nō′mon), *n.* **1.** the raised part of a sundial that casts the shadow; a style. See illus. under **sundial. 2.** an early astronomical instrument consisting of a vertical shaft, column, or the like, for determining the altitude of the sun or the latitude of a position by measuring the length of its shadow cast at noon. **3.** *Geom.* (formerly) the part of a parallelogram that remains after a similar parallelogram has been taken away from one of its corners. [1540–50; < L *gnōmōn* pin of a sundial < Gk *gnṓmōn* lit., interpreter, discerner]

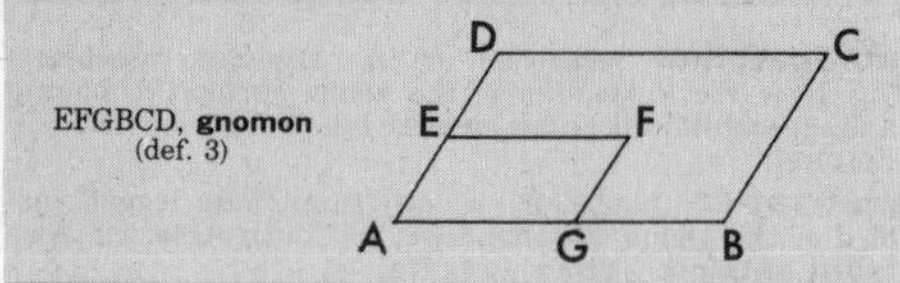

EFGBCD, **gnomon** (def. 3)

gno•mon•ic (nō mon′ik), *adj.* **1.** of or pertaining to a gnomon or to a sundial. **2.** of or pertaining to the measurement of time by a gnomon or a sundial. **3.** gnomic². Also, **gno•mon′i•cal.** [1595–1605; < L *gnōmonicus* of, belonging to a gnomon < Gk *gnōmonikós.* See GNOMON, -IC]

-gnomy, a combining form meaning "knowledge," occurring in loanwords from Greek and used in combination with other elements of Greek origin: *physiognomy.* [< LL *-gnōmia* < Gk. See GNOMON, -Y³]

gno•sis (nō′sis), *n.* knowledge of spiritual matters; mystical knowledge. [1695–1705; < NL < Gk *gnṓsis* a seeking to know, equiv. to *gnō-,* base of *gignṓskein* KNOW + *-sis* -SIS]

-gnosis, a combining form meaning "knowledge," used in the formation of compound words: *prognosis.* [< L *-gnōsis* < Gk; see GNOSIS]

Gnos•sus (nos′əs), *n.* Knossos. —**Gnos′si•an,** *adj.*

gnos•tic (nos′tik), *adj.* Also, **gnos′ti•cal. 1.** pertaining to knowledge. **2.** possessing knowledge, esp. esoteric knowledge of spiritual matters. **3.** (*cap.*) pertaining to or characteristic of the Gnostics. —*n.* **4.** (*cap.*) a member of any of certain sects among the early Christians who claimed to have superior knowledge of spiritual matters, and explained the world as created by powers or agencies arising as emanations from the Godhead. [1555–65; < LL *Gnōstici* (pl.) name of the sect < Gk *gnōstikós* (sing.) pertaining to knowledge, equiv. to *gnōst(ós)* known + *-ikos* -IC] —**gnos′ti•cal•ly,** *adv.*

-gnostic, a combination of **-gnosis** and **-ic,** used to form adjectives from stems ending in **-gnosis:** *prognostic.* [< ML *-gnōsticus* < Gk *gnōstikós* pertaining to knowledge]

Gnos•ti•cism (nos′tə siz′əm), *n. Rom. Cath. Ch.* a group of ancient heresies, stressing escape from this world through the acquisition of esoteric knowledge. [GNOSTIC + -ISM]

Gnos•ti•cize (nos′tə sīz′), *v.,* **-cized, -ciz•ing.** —*v.i.* **1.** to adopt or maintain Gnostic views. —*v.t.* **2.** to explain on Gnostic principles; give a Gnostic interpretation of or quality to. Also, **gnos′ti•cize′;** *esp. Brit.,* **Gnos′ti•cise′.** [1655–65; GNOSTIC + -IZE] —**Gnos′ti•ciz′er,** *n.*

gno•to•bi•o•sis (nō′tō bī ō′sis), *n.* an environmental condition in which germfree animals have been inoculated with strains of known microorganisms. [1945–50; < Gk *gnōt(ós)* known + -O- + -BIOSIS]

gno•to•bi•ote (nō′tō bī′ōt), *n.* a gnotobiotic animal. [< Gk *gnōt(ós)* known + -o- + *-biote,* back formation from BIOTIC]

gno•to•bi•ot•ic (nō′tō bī ot′ik), *adj.* (of germfree animals) inoculated with microorganisms of a given type. [1945–50; GNOTOBIOTE + -IC]

GNP, See **gross national product.** Also, **G.N.P.**

GnRH, See **gonadotropin releasing hormone.**

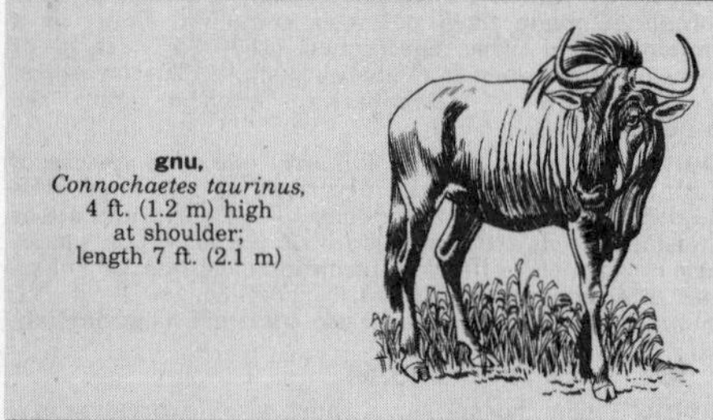
gnu, *Connochaetes taurinus,* 4 ft. (1.2 m) high at shoulder; length 7 ft. (2.1 m)

gnu (nōō, nyōō), *n., pl.* **gnus,** (*esp. collectively*) **gnu.** either of two stocky, oxlike antelopes of the genus *Connochaetes,* the silver-gray, white-bearded *C. taurinus* of the eastern African plain and the black, white-tailed *C. gnou* of central South Africa: recently near extinction, the South African gnu is now protected. Also called **wildebeest.** [1770–80; < Khoikhoi, first recorded as *t'gnu;* prob. to be identified with *≠nû* black, as applying orig. to the black wildebeest]

CONCISE ETYMOLOGY KEY: <, descended or borrowed from; >, whence; b., blend of, blended; c., cognate with; cf., compare; deriv., derivative; equiv., equivalent; imit., imitative; obl., oblique; r., replacing; s., stem; sp., spelling, spelled; resp., respelling, respelled; trans., translation; ?, origin unknown; *, unattested; ‡, probably earlier than. See the full key inside the front cover.

go¹ (gō), *v.,* **went, gone, go•ing,** *n., pl.* **goes,** *interj., adj.* —*v.i.* **1.** to move or proceed, esp. to or from something: *They're going by bus.* **2.** to leave a place; depart: *People were coming and going all the time.* **3.** to keep or be in motion; function or perform as required: *Can't you go any faster in your work?* **4.** to become as specified: *to go mad.* **5.** to continue in a certain state or condition; be habitually: *to go barefoot.* **6.** to act as specified: *Go warily if he wants to discuss terms.* **7.** to act so as to come into a certain state or condition: *to go into debt; to go to sleep.* **8.** to be known: *to go by a false name.* **9.** to reach, extend, or give access to: *Where does this door go?* **10.** to pass or elapse: *The time went fast.* **11.** to be applied, allotted, awarded, transferred, etc., to a particular recipient or purpose: *My money goes for food and rent.* **12.** to be sold: *I have a bid of two dollars. Going! Going! Gone!* **13.** to be considered generally or usually: *He's short, as basketball players go.* **14.** to conduce or tend: *This only goes to prove the point.* **15.** to result or end; turn out: *How did the game go?* **16.** to belong; have a place: *This book goes on the top shelf.* **17.** (of colors, styles, etc.) to harmonize; be compatible; be suited: *Your tweed jacket would go well with these pants.* **18.** to fit around or into; be able to be extended, contained, inserted, etc.: *This belt won't go around my waist.* **19.** to be or become consumed, spent, finished, etc.: *The cake went fast.* **20.** to be or become discarded, dismissed, put aside, forgotten, etc.: *Those practical jokes of yours have got to go!* **21.** to develop, progress, or proceed, esp. with reference to success or satisfaction: *How is your new job going?* **22.** to move or proceed with remarkable speed or energy: *Look at that airplane go!* **23.** to make a certain sound: *The gun goes bang.* **24.** to be phrased, written, or composed: *How does that song go?* **25.** to seek or have recourse for a decision, verdict, corroboration, defense, etc.; resort: *to go to court.* **26.** to become worn-out, weakened, ineffective, etc.: *His eyesight is beginning to go.* **27.** to die: *The old man went peacefully at 3 A.M.* **28.** to fail, break, or give way: *The dike might go any minute.* **29.** to come into action; begin: *Go when you hear the bell.* **30.** to make up a quantity or content; be requisite: *Sixteen ounces go to the pound.* **31.** to be able to be divided; be contained as a mathematical element: *Three goes into fifteen five times.* **32.** to contribute to an end result: *the items that go to make up the total.* **33.** to have as one's goal; intend (usually used in the present tense, fol. by an infinitive): *Their daughter is going to be a doctor.* **34.** to be permitted, approved, or the like: *Around here, anything goes.* **35.** to be authoritative; be the final word: *This is my house, and what I say goes!* **36.** to subject oneself: *Don't go to any trouble.* **37.** (used in the infinitive as an intensifier to indicate the idea of proceeding, esp. with the expectation of serious consequences): *He finally had to go ask for a loan.* **38.** *Informal.* to urinate or defecate.
—*v.t.* **39.** *Informal.* to endure or tolerate: *I can't go his preaching.* **40.** *Informal.* to risk, pay, afford, bet, or bid: *I'll go fifty dollars for a ticket, but no more.* **41.** to move or proceed with or according to; follow: *Going my way?* **42.** to share or participate in to the extent of (often fol. by a complementary substantive): *to go halves.* **43.** to yield, produce, weigh as a usable amount, or grow to: *This field will go two bales of cotton.* **44.** to assume the obligation, responsibility, or function of: *His father went bail for him.* **45.** *Informal.* to enjoy, appreciate, desire, or want: *I could go a big steak dinner right now.* **46.** *Informal.* to say; declare (usually used in speech): *I asked the clerk for my receipt, and he goes, "You don't need it."* **47. go about, a.** to occupy oneself with; perform: *The shoemaker goes about his work with a smile.* **b.** *Naut.* to change course by tacking or wearing. **48. go after,** to attempt to obtain; strive for: *You'll never get what you want if you don't go after it energetically.* **49. go against,** to be in conflict with or opposed to: *It goes against the company's policy.* **50. go ahead,** to proceed without hesitation or delay: *If you want to use my car, go ahead.* **51. go along, a.** to move or proceed. **b.** to accompany in travel. **c.** to agree; concur: *I can't go along with you on that idea.* **52. go and,** to be so thoughtless, unfortunate, or silly as to: *It was going to be a surprise but he went and told her.* **53. go ape over** or **for.** See **ape** (def. 6). **54. go around, a.** to be often in company (often fol. by *with*): *to go around with a bad crowd.* **b.** to be sufficient for all: *Is there enough food to go around?* **c.** to pass or circulate, as in transmission or communication: *The rumor is going around that he was forced to resign.* **55. go at, a.** to assault; attack. **b.** to begin or proceed vigorously: *to go at one's work with a will.* **56. go back on.** See **back²** (def. 9). **57. go bananas.** See **bananas** (def. 2). **58. go by, a.** to be disregarded or not taken advantage of: *Don't let this chance go by.* **b.** to be guided by or to rely upon: *Don't go by what she says.* **59. go down, a.** to decrease or subside, as in amount or size: *Prices went down. The swelling is going down.* **b.** to descend or sink: *When does the sun go down?* **c.** to suffer defeat: *to go down fighting.* **d.** to be accepted or believed: *This nonsense goes down as truth with many persons.* **e.** to admit of being consumed: *This food goes down easily.* **f.** to be remembered in history or by posterity. **g.** *Slang.* to happen; occur: *What's been going down since I've been away?* **h.** *Brit.* to leave a university, permanently or at the end of a term. **i.** *Bridge.* to fall short of making one's contract. **j.** *Slang* (*vulgar*). to perform fellatio or cunnilingus. **60. go down on,** *Slang* (*vulgar*). to perform fellatio or cunnilingus on. **61. go for, a.** to make an attempt at; try for: *He is going for the championship.* **b.** to assault. **c.** to favor; like: *It simply isn't the kind of life you would go for.* **d.** to be used for the purpose of or be a substitute for: *material that goes for silk.* **62. go for broke.** See **broke** (def. 7). **63. go for it,** *Informal.* to pursue a goal with determination. **64. go in for, a.** to adopt as one's particular interest; approve of; like. **b.** to occupy oneself with; engage in: *Europeans in increasing numbers are going in for camping.* **65. go into, a.** to discuss or investigate: *Let's not go into the question of whose fault it was.* **b.** to undertake as one's study or work: *to go into medicine.* **66. go in with,** to join in a partnership or union; combine with: *He asked me to go in with him on the purchase of a boat.* **67. go it alone,** to act or proceed independently, without assistance, companionship, or the like: *If you don't want to form a partnership, I'll go it alone.* **68. go native.** See **native** (def. 18). **69. go off, a.** to explode, fire, or perform or begin to function abruptly: *A gun went off in the distance.* **b.** (of what has been expected or planned) to happen: *The interview went off very badly.* **c.** to leave, esp. suddenly: *She went off without saying goodbye.* **d.** to die. **e.** to deteriorate. **f.** *Slang.* to experience orgasm. **70. go on, a.** to happen or take place: *What's going on here?* **b.** to continue: *Go on working.* **c.** to behave; act: *Don't go on like that!* **d.** to talk effusively; chatter. **e.** (used to express disbelief): *Go on, you're kidding me.* **f.** to appear onstage in a theatrical performance: *I go on in the middle of the second act.* **71. go out, a.** to come to an end, esp. to fade in popularity: *Silent movies went out as soon as the talkies were perfected.* **b.** to cease or fail to function: *The lights went out.* **c.** to participate in social activities, on dates, etc. **d.** to take part in a strike: *The printers went out yesterday in a contract dispute.* **e.** *Rummy.* to dispose of the last card in one's hand by melding it on the table. **f.** *Cards.* to achieve a point score equal to or above the score necessary to win the game. **72. go over, a.** to repeat; review. **b.** to be effective or successful: *The proposal went over very well with the trustees.* **c.** to examine: *The mechanic went over the car but found nothing wrong.* **d.** to read; scan. **73. go the whole hog,** to do something thoroughly or consistently: *If you're getting a new amplifier, why don't you go the whole hog and get new speakers and a turntable, too?* **74. go through, a.** to bear; experience. **b.** to examine or search carefully: *He went through all of his things but couldn't find the letter.* **c.** to be successful; be accepted or approved: *The proposed appropriation will never go through.* **d.** to use up; spend completely: *He went through his allowance in one day.* **75. go through with,** to persevere with to the end; bring to completion: *It was perhaps the biggest challenge of her life, and she resolved to go through with it.* **76. go to!,** *Archaic.* **a.** you don't say! I don't believe you! **b.** let's do it! come on! **77. go together, a.** to be appropriate or harmonious: *The rug and curtains don't go together.* **b.** *Informal.* to keep company; date; court: *They have gone together for two years.* **78. go to it,** *Informal.* to begin vigorously and at once. **79. go under, a.** to be overwhelmed or ruined; fail. **b.** (of a ship) to founder. **80. go up, a.** to be in the process of construction, as a building. **b.** to increase in cost, value, etc. **c.** to forget one's lines during a theatrical performance. **d.** *Brit.* to go to a university at the beginning of a term. **81. go with,** *Informal.* to keep company with; court; date: *He went with her for two semesters.* Also, **go out with. 82. let go, a.** to release one's grasp or hold: *Please let go of my arm.* **b.** to free; release. **c.** to cease to employ; dismiss: *Business was slack and many employees were let go.* **d.** to become unrestrained; abandon inhibitions: *She'd be good fun if she would just let go and enjoy herself.* **e.** to dismiss; forget; discard: *Once he has an idea, he never lets go of it.* **83. let go with,** to express or utter with abandon: *He let go with a sudden yell.* **84. let oneself go,** to free oneself of inhibitions or restraint: *Let yourself go and get mad once in a while.* **85. to go,** *Informal.* (of food) for consumption off the premises where sold: *coffee to go.*
—*n.* **86.** the act of going: *the come and go of the seasons.* **87.** energy, spirit, or animation: *a man with a lot of go.* **88.** a try at something; attempt: *to have a go at winning the prize.* **89.** a successful accomplishment; success: *to make a go of a new business.* **90.** *Informal.* a business agreement; deal; bargain: *Thirty dollars? It's a go.* **91.** *Informal.* approval or permission, as to undertake or begin something: *The boss gave us the go on the new project.* **92.** *Boxing.* a bout: *the main go.* **93. from the word "go,"** from the very start; since the beginning. **94. no go,** *Informal.* **a.** futile; useless: *We tried to get there by noon, but it was no go.* **b.** not authorized or approved to proceed; canceled or aborted: *Tomorrow's satellite launching is no go.* **95. on the go, a.** very busy; active: *She's always on the go.* **b.** while going from place to place; while traveling.
—*interj.* **96.** (in calling the start of a race) start the race; leave the starting line: *On your mark! Get set! Go!*
—*adj.* **97.** ready. **98.** functioning properly: *two minutes before the satellite is to be launched and all systems are go.* [bef. 900; ME *gon,* OE *gān;* c. OHG *gēn,* G *gehen*]
—**Syn. 1.** walk, run, travel, advance. —**Ant. 1.** stay.

go² (gō), *n.* a Japanese game for two persons, played on a board having 361 intersections on which black and white stones or counters are alternately placed, the object being to block off and capture the opponent's stones and control the larger part of the board. Also called **I-go.** [1885–90; < Japn < MChin, equiv. to Chin *gí* name for various board games]

G.O., 1. general office. **2.** general order. Also, **g.o.**

go•a (gō′ə), *n.* a gazelle, *Procapra picticaudata,* of the Tibetan plateau. [1840–50; < Tibetan *gowa* (sp. *dgo ba*)]

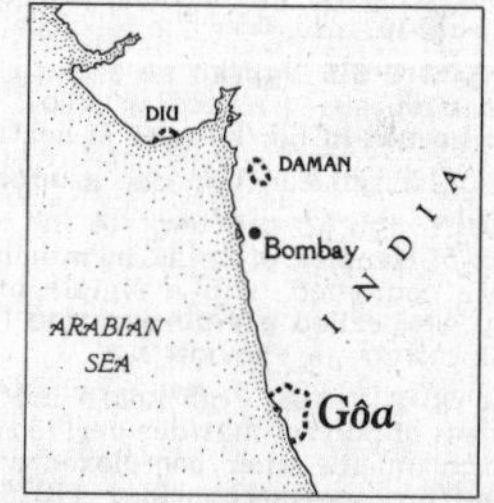

Gô•a (gō′ə), *n.* a former district in Portuguese India, on the Arabian Sea, ab. 250 mi. (400 km) S of Bombay: annexed by India December 1961; now part of the union territory of Goa, Daman, and Diu.

Go′a, Daman′, and Di′u (gō′ə), an administrative territory of India, in the W part: formerly Portuguese India; annexed by India 1961. 857,180; 1426 sq. mi. (3693 sq. km). *Cap.:* Panjim.

goad (gōd), *n.* **1.** a stick with a pointed or electrically charged end, for driving cattle, oxen, etc.; prod. **2.** anything that pricks or wounds like such a stick. **3.** something that encourages, urges, or drives; a stimulus. —*v.t.* **4.** to prick or drive with, or as if with, a goad; prod; incite. [bef. 900; ME *gode,* OE *gād;* cf. Langobardic *gaida* spearhead] —**goad′like′,** *adj.*
—**Syn. 4.** spur, push, impel.

goaf (gōf), *n., pl.* **goaves.** *Mining.* gob[1] (def. 3). [1830–40; orig. uncert.]

go-a·head (gō′ə hed′), *n.* **1.** permission or a signal to proceed: *They got the go-ahead on the construction work.* **2.** *Chiefly Hawaii and California.* a sandal held on the foot by a strap between the big toe and the next toe. —*adj.* **3.** moving forward; advancing. **4.** enterprising: *a go-ahead Yankee peddler.* [1830–40, *Amer.;* n., adj. use of v. phrase *go ahead*]

goal (gōl), *n.* **1.** the result or achievement toward which effort is directed; aim; end. **2.** the terminal point in a race. **3.** a pole, line, or other marker by which such a point is indicated. **4.** an area, basket, cage, or other object or structure toward or into which players of various games attempt to throw, carry, kick, hit, or drive a ball, puck, etc., to score a point or points. **5.** the act of throwing, carrying, kicking, driving, etc., a ball or puck into such an area or object. **6.** the score made by this act. [1275–1325; ME *gol* boundary, limit; cf. OE *gǣlan* to hinder, impede] —**goal′less,** *adj.*
—**Syn. 1.** target; purpose, object, objective, intent, intention. **2.** finish.

goal′ crease′, *Ice Hockey.* crease (def. 4). [1885–90]

goal·er (gō′lər), *n. Canadian.* goalkeeper in the game of ice hockey. [< CanF *gôleur* < E GOAL + F *-eur* -EUR]

goal·ie (gō′lē), *n.* a goalkeeper. [1920–25; GOAL + -IE]

goal·keep·er (gōl′kē′pər), *n.* (in ice hockey, field hockey, lacrosse, soccer, etc.) a player whose chief duty is to prevent the ball or puck from crossing or entering the goal. [1650–60; GOAL + KEEPER] —**goal′keep′·ing,** *n.*

goal′ kick′, *Soccer.* a free kick taken by a defensive player after the ball, having last been touched by an offensive player, has gone out of bounds over the goal line.

goal′ line′, *Sports.* the line that bounds a goal, esp. the front line. [1865–70]

goal·mouth (gōl′mouth′), *n., pl.* **-mouths** (-mouᵺz′, mouths′). the area between the goalposts directly in front of the goal in certain games, as soccer, lacrosse, and hockey. [1880–85; GOAL + MOUTH]

goal·post (gōl′pōst′), *n.* a post supporting a crossbar and, with it, forming the goal on a playing field in certain sports, as football. Also, **goal′ post′.** [1855–60]

goal·tend·er (gōl′ten′dər), *n.* a goalkeeper. [1905–10; GOAL + TENDER[3]]

goal·tend·ing (gōl′ten′ding), *n.* **1.** goalkeeping. **2.** *Basketball.* any of several violations that prevent a goal from being scored, occurring when a player interferes with a shot by touching the ball on its downward flight to the basket or while it is over, on, or within the rim of the basket. [1935–40; GOAL + TEND[2] + -ING[1]]

go·an·na (gō an′ə), *n.* any of the several large monitor lizards of the family Varanidae, of Australia, esp. *Varanus varius* and *V. giganteus,* both sometimes growing to 6 ft. (1.8 m). [1795–1805; aph. form of IGUANA]

Go′a pow′der, a brownish-yellow, odorless, crystalline powder obtained from the wood or the trunk of the Brazilian tree *Andira araroba,* used as a source of chrysarobin. Also called **araroba.** [1870–75; after GOA]

go-a·round (gō′ə round′), *n.* **1.** an act or instance of going around something, as a circle, course, or traffic pattern, and returning to the starting point. **2.** a series or pattern of occurrences; round: *After the third go-around of questions, the witness was released.* **3.** runaround (def. 1). Also, **go-round** (for defs. 2, 3). [1890–95; n. use of v. phrase *go around*]

goat, *Capra hircus,* 2½ ft. (0.8 m) high at shoulder; length 4½ ft. (1.4 m)

goat (gōt), *n.* **1.** any of numerous agile, hollow-horned ruminants of the genus *Capra,* of the family Bovidae, closely related to the sheep, found native in rocky and mountainous regions of the Old World, and widely distributed in domesticated varieties. **2.** any of various related animals, as the Rocky Mountain goat. **3.** (*cap.*) *Astron., Astrol.* the constellation or sign Capricorn. **4.** a scapegoat or victim. **5.** a licentious or lecherous man; lecher. **6. get one's goat,** *Informal.* to anger, annoy, or frustrate a person: *His arrogance gets my goat.* [bef. 900; ME *got,* OE *gāt;* c. G *Geiss*] —**goat′like′,** *adj.*

goat′ an′telope, any of several wild goats with antelopelike features, including the chamois, goral, serow, and Rocky Mountain goat. [1840–50]

goat′ cheese′, a cheese containing goat's milk, either alone or mixed with cow's milk, usually having a stronger flavor than one made of cow's milk alone.

goat·ee (gō tē′), *n.* a man's beard trimmed to a tuft or point on the chin. [1835–45, *Amer.;* GOAT (from its resemblance to a goat's tufted chin) + *-ee,* prob. as sp. var. of -Y[2], -IE, though stressed as if formed with -EE] —**goat·eed′,** *adj.*

goat·fish (gōt′fish′), *n., pl.* **-fish·es,** (*esp. collectively*) **-fish.** any tropical and subtropical marine fish of the family Mullidae, having a pair of long barbels below the mouth. Also called **red mullet.** [1630–40; GOAT + FISH]

goat′ god′, a deity with the legs and feet of a goat, as Pan or a satyr. [1875–80]

goat·herd (gōt′hûrd′), *n.* a person who tends goats. [bef. 1000; ME; OE *gāthyrde.* See GOAT, HERD[2]]

goat·ish (gō′tish), *adj.* **1.** of or like a goat. **2.** lustful; lecherous. [1520–30; GOAT + -ISH[1]] —**goat′ish·ly,** *adv.* —**goat′ish·ness,** *n.*

goat·pox (gōt′poks′), *n.* a virus disease of goats that resembles cowpox and produces lesions inside the thighs and on other hairless skin areas. Also, **goat′ pox′, goat′-pox′.** [GOAT + POX]

goats·beard (gōts′bērd′), *n.* **1.** any of several composite plants of the genus *Tragopogon,* esp. *T. pratensis,* having yellow flower heads. **2.** a plant, *Aruncus dioicus,* of the rose family, having pinnate leaves and long, slender spikes of small white flowers. [1570–80; GOAT + -'S[1] + BEARD]

goat·skin (gōt′skin′), *n.* **1.** the skin or hide of a goat. **2.** leather made from it. [1350–1400; ME; see GOAT, SKIN]

goat's-rue (gōts′ro͞o′), *n.* **1.** Also called **catgut.** a hairy American plant, *Tephrosia virginiana,* of the legume family, having yellow and pink flowers. **2.** a European plant, *Galega officinalis,* of the legume family, formerly used in medicine. [1570–80]

goat·suck·er (gōt′suk′ər), *n.* nightjar (def. 2). [1605–15; so called because formerly believed to suck the milk of goats; trans. of L *caprimulgus,* itself trans. of Gk *aigothḗlas*]

goaves (gōvz), *n. Mining.* pl. of **goaf.**

gob[1] (gob), *n.* **1.** a mass or lump. **2. gobs,** *Informal.* a large quantity: *gobs of money.* **3.** Also called **goaf.** *Mining.* waste or barren material. [1350–1400; ME *gobbe,* var. of *gobet* GOBBET]

gob[2] (gob), *n. Slang.* a sailor, esp. a seaman in the U.S. Navy. [1910–15, *Amer.;* orig. uncert.]

gob[3] (gob), *n. Slang.* the mouth. [1540–50; perh. < ScotGael *gob* mouth, beak]

gob[4] (gob), *v.i.,* **gobbed, gob·bing,** *n. Brit. Dial.* gab[1]. [1685–95]

go·bang (gō bäng′), *n.* a Japanese game played on a go board with players alternating and attempting to be first to place five counters in a row. Also, **go·ban** (gō-bän′). Also called **go-moku.** [1885–90; < Japn, equiv. to *go* GO[2] + *ban* board (< Chin)]

Go·bat (*Fr.* gô bᴀ′), *n.* **Al·bert** (*Fr.* ᴀl bᴇʀ′), 1843–1914, Swiss lawyer and statesman: Nobel peace prize 1902.

gob·bet (gob′it), *n.* **1.** a fragment or piece, esp. of raw flesh. **2.** a lump or mass. [1275–1325; ME *gobet* < OF: a mouthful, dim. of *gobe.* See -ET]

gob·ble[1] (gob′əl), *v.,* **-bled, -bling.** —*v.t.* **1.** to swallow or eat hastily or hungrily in large pieces; gulp. **2.** to seize upon eagerly (often fol. by *up*): *After being gone for so long, they gobbled up all the local news.* —*v.i.* **3.** to eat hastily. [1595–1605; prob. imit.; see GOB[1], -LE]
—**Syn. 1.** bolt, devour.

gob·ble[2] (gob′əl), *v.,* **-bled, -bling,** *n.* —*v.i.* **1.** to make the characteristic throaty cry of a male turkey. —*n.* **2.** the cry itself. [1670–80; var. of GABBLE]

gob·ble·de·gook (gob′əl dē go͝ok′), *n.* language characterized by circumlocution and jargon, usually hard to understand: *the gobbledegook of government reports.* Also, **gob′ble·dy·gook′.** [1940–45; fanciful formation from GOBBLE[2]]
—**Syn.** gibberish, doubletalk, bosh, mumbo jumbo.

gob·bler[1] (gob′lər), *n.* a male turkey. [1730–40; GOBBLE[2] + -ER[1]]

gob·bler[2] (gob′lər), *n.* a person or thing that gobbles or consumes voraciously or quickly: *a gobbler of science fiction.* [1745–55; GOBBLE[1] + -ER[1]]

gob·by (gob′ē), *adj.,* **-bi·er, -bi·est.** *Chiefly South Midland and Southern U.S.* fat. [of uncert. orig.]

Gob·e·lin (gob′ə lin, gō′bə-; *Fr.* gô blᴀɴ′), *adj.* **1.** made at the tapestry factory established in Paris in the 15th century by the Gobelins, a French family of dyers and weavers. **2.** resembling the tapestry made at the Gobelin factory. [1780–90]

go-be·tween (gō′bi twēn′), *n.* a person who acts as an agent or intermediary between persons or groups; emissary. [1590–1600; n. use of v. phrase *go between*]
—**Syn.** middleman, negotiator, deputy, envoy, liaison; mediator, arbitrator.

Go·bi (gō′bē), *n.* a desert in E Asia, mostly in Mongolia. ab. 500,000 sq. mi. (1,295,000 sq. km). Chinese, **Shamo.** —**Go′bi·an,** *adj.*

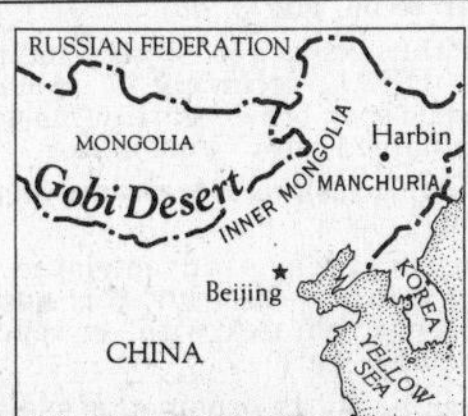

Go′bi bu′rin, a wedge-shaped engraving tool made by Pleistocene hunters on both the Asian and American sides of the Bering Strait. [after GOBI Desert, where tools and cores of a comparable type were found]

go·bi·oid (gō′bē oid′), *adj.* **1.** of or resembling a goby. —*n.* **2.** a gobioid fish. [1850–55; < L *gōbi(us)* gudgeon + -OID]

gob·let (gob′lit), *n.* **1.** a drinking glass with a foot and stem. **2.** *Archaic.* a bowl-shaped drinking vessel with no handles. [1300–50; ME *gobelet* < OF, dim. of *gobel* cup << Celtic]

gob′let cell′, *Cell Biol.* a type of epithelial cell that secretes mucin, so called after its shape. [1875–80]

gob·lin (gob′lin), *n.* a grotesque sprite or elf that is mischievous or malicious toward people. [1300–50; ME *gobelin* < MF < MHG *kobold* goblin; see KOBOLD]
—**Syn.** GOBLIN, GNOME, GREMLIN refer to supernatural beings thought to be malevolent to people. GOBLINS are demons of any size, usually in human or animal form, that are supposed to assail, afflict, and even torture human beings: *"Be thou a spirit of health or goblin damn'd, . . ."* (Shak. *Hamlet I, iv*). GNOMES are small beings, like ugly little old men, who live in the earth, guarding mines, treasures, etc. They are mysteriously malevolent and terrify human beings by causing dreadful mishaps to occur. GREMLINS are thought to disrupt machinery and are active in modern folklore.

go·bo (gō′bō), *n., pl.* **-bos, -boes.** *Motion Pictures, Television.* **1.** a screen or mat covered with a dark material for shielding a camera lens from excess light or glare. **2.** a screen or sheet of sound-absorbent material for shielding a microphone from sounds coming from a particular direction. [1925–30, *Amer.;* orig. uncert.]

go·bo·ny (gə bō′nē), *adj. Heraldry.* compony. Also, **go·bo·née** (gə bō′nā). [1605–15; obs. *gobon* slice, ME *goboun* < AF **gobon* (OF *gobet;* see GOBBET) + *-y* as in *compony*]

gob-stop·per (gob′stop′ər), *n. Brit. Slang.* a large piece of hard candy. [1925–30; see GOB[3]]

go-by (gō′bī′), *n. Informal.* a going by without notice; an intentional passing by; snub: *to give one the go-by.* [1605–15; n. use of v. phrase *go by*]

go·by (gō′bē), *n., pl.* (*esp. collectively*) **-by,** (*esp. referring to two or more kinds or species*) **-bies. 1.** any small marine or freshwater fish of the family Gobiidae, often having the pelvic fins united to form a suctorial disk. **2.** any fish of the closely related family Eleotridae, having the pelvic fins separate. [1760–70; < L *gōbius* gudgeon (sp. var. of *gōbiō* or *cōbius*) < Gk *kōbiós*]

go-cart (gō′kärt′), *n.* **1.** a small carriage for young children to ride in; stroller. **2.** a small framework with casters, wheels, etc., in which children learn to walk; walker. **3.** a handcart. **4.** kart. **5.** *Northeastern U.S.* (formerly) a small horse-drawn cart. [1680–90]

God (god), *n., v.,* **god·ded, god·ding,** *interj.* —*n.* **1.** the one Supreme Being, the creator and ruler of the universe. **2.** the Supreme Being considered with reference to a particular attribute: *the God of Islam.* **3.** (*l.c.*) one of several deities, esp. a male deity, presiding over some portion of worldly affairs. **4.** (*often l.c.*) a supreme being according to some particular conception: *the god of mercy.* **5.** *Christian Science.* the Supreme Being, understood as Life, Truth, Love, Mind, Soul, Spirit, Principle. **6.** (*l.c.*) an image of a deity; an idol. **7.** (*l.c.*) any deified person or object. **8.** (*often l.c.*) **Gods,** *Theat.* **a.** the upper balcony in a theater. **b.** the spectators in this part of the balcony. —*v.t.* **9.** (*l.c.*) to regard or treat as a god; deify; idolize. —*interj.* **10.** (used to express disappointment, disbelief, weariness, frustration, annoyance, or the like): *God, do we have to listen to this nonsense?* [bef. 900; ME, OE; c. D *god,* G *Gott,* ON *goth,* Goth *guth*]

Go·dard (gō därd′, -där′; *Fr.* gô dᴀʀ′), *n.* **1. Ben·ja·min Louis Paul** (bän zʜᴀ mᴀɴ′ lwē pôl), 1849–95, French violinist and composer. **2. Jean-Luc** (zhän-lʏk′), born 1930, French filmmaker.

Go·da·va·ri (gō dä′və rē), *n.* a river flowing SE from W India to the Bay of Bengal. 900 mi. (1450 km) long.

God-aw·ful (god′ô′fəl), *adj.* (*sometimes l.c.*) *Informal.* extremely dreadful or shocking: *What a God-awful thing to say!* [1875–80; *Amer.*]

god·child (god′chīld′), *n., pl.* **-chil·dren. 1.** a child for whom a godparent serves as sponsor at baptism. **2.** a child for whom a godparent serves as sponsor. [1175–1225; ME; see GOD, CHILD]

god·damn (god′dam′), *interj. Informal* (*sometimes offensive*). **1.** (used as an exclamation of any strong feeling, esp. of disgust or irritation, and often fol. by *it.*) —*n.* **2.** the utterance of "goddamn" in swearing or for emphasis. **3.** something of negligible value; damn: *not to give a good goddamn.* —*adj.* **4.** damned (def. 2). —*adv.* **5.** damned. —*v.t.* **6.** to curse (someone or something) as being contemptible or worthless; damn. —*v.i.* **7.** to use the word "goddamn"; swear. Also, **god′dam′.** [1400–50; late ME. See GOD, DAMN]

god·damned (god′damd′), *adj., superl.* **-damned·est** or **-damnd·est,** *adv. Informal* (*sometimes offensive*). —*adj.* **1.** damned (def. 2). **2.** (esp. in the superlative) unusually difficult to deal with; extremely complicated or peculiar. —*adv.* **3.** damned. Also, **goddamn, god′·dam′.** [1915–20; GOD + DAMNED]

god·damn·it (god′dam′it), *interj.* (*sometimes cap.*) *Informal* (*sometimes offensive*). (used to express anger, perplexity, amazement, etc.) Also, **god′dam′mit.** [GOD + DAMN + IT[1]]

God·dard (god′ərd), *n.* **Robert Hutch·ings** (huch′-ingz), 1882–1945, U.S. physicist: pioneer in rocketry.

god·daugh·ter (god′dô′tər), *n.* a female godchild. [bef. 1050; ME; OE *goddohtor.* See GOD, DAUGHTER]

God·den (god′n), *n.* **(Margaret) Ru·mer** (ro͞o′mər),

CONCISE PRONUNCIATION KEY: act, cāpe, dâre, pärt; set, ēqual; *if,* īce; ox, ōver, ôrder, oil, bo͝ok, bo͞ot, out; up, ûrge; child; sing; shoe; thin, ᵺat; zh as in *treasure.* ə = *a* as in *alone, e* as in *system, i* as in *easily, o* as in *gallop, u* as in *circus;* ᵊ as in *fire* (fīᵊr), *hour* (ouᵊr). l and n can serve as syllabic consonants, as in *cradle* (krād′l), and *button* (but′n). See the full key inside the front cover.

born 1907, English novelist and writer of children's books.

god•dess (god′is), *n.* **1.** a female god or deity. **2.** a woman of extraordinary beauty and charm. **3.** a greatly admired or adored woman. [1300–50; ME; see GOD, -ESS] —**god′dess•hood′, god′dess•ship′,** *n.*
—**Usage.** See **-ess.**

Go•de•froy de Bouil•lon (gôdᵊ frwä′ də bo͞o yôN′), c1060–1100, French crusader.

Gö•del (gœd′l), *n.* **Kurt** (kûrt), 1906–78, U.S. mathematician and logician, born in Czechoslovakia.

Gö′del's incomplete′ness the′orem, *Logic, Math.* **1.** the theorem that states that in a formal logical system incorporating the properties of the natural numbers, there exists at least one formula that can be neither proved nor disproved within the system. **2.** the corollary that the consistency of such a system cannot be proved within the system. [after K. GÖDEL, who formulated it]

go•den•dag (gō den′däg), *n.* a medieval Flemish club having a spike at the end. [< MD *goedendach* lit., good day, since it dispatched its victims quickly]

Go•des•berg (gō′des berk′), *n.* a city in W Germany, SE of Bonn. 73,512. Official name, **Bad Godesberg.**

go•det (gō det′), *n.* **1.** a triangular piece of fabric, often rounded at the top, inserted in a garment to give fullness. Cf. **gore**[3] (def. 1), **gusset** (def. 1). **2.** *Textiles.* a glass or plastic roller for guiding synthetic filaments into the centrifugal box. [1570–80 for earlier sense "drinking cup"; 1870–75 for def. 1 < MF, equiv. to *god-* (< Gmc; see COD[2]) + *-et* -ET]

go•dev•il (gō′dev′əl), *n.* **1.** a flexible, jointed apparatus forced through a pipeline to free it from obstructions. **2.** a dart dropped into a well, esp. an oil well, to explode a charge of dynamite or nitroglycerin previously placed in a desired position. **3.** *Railroads.* a handcar. **4.** a sled used to drag or carry logs, stone, etc. **5.** Also called **sled cultivator.** a cultivator that rides on wooden runners and is used on listed furrows. **6.** *Western U.S.* any exceptionally fast or effective machine or appliance: *That food processor is a real go-devil.* [1825–35, *Amer.*]

Go•dey (gō′dē), *n.* **Louis An•toine** (an′twän), 1804–78, U.S. publisher: founded the first women's magazine in the U.S. 1830.

god•fa•ther (god′fä′thər), *n.* **1.** a man who serves as sponsor for a child at baptism. **2.** any male sponsor or guardian. **3.** (*often cap.*) a powerful leader, esp. of the Mafia. **4.** a person who is regarded as the originator or principal shaper of a movement, school of thought, art form, industry, or the like: *the godfather of abstract expressionism.* —*v.t.* **5.** to act as godfather to; be sponsor or protector for. [bef. 1000; ME *godfader,* OE *godfæder.* See GOD, FATHER] —**god′fa′ther•ly,** *adj.*

God-fear•ing (god′fēr′ing), *adj.* **1.** deeply respectful or fearful of God. **2.** (*sometimes l.c.*) deeply religious; pious; devout. [1825–35]

god•for•sak•en (god′fər sā′kən, god′fər sā′-), *adj.* (*sometimes cap.*) **1.** desolate; remote; deserted: *They live in some godforsaken place 40 miles from the nearest town.* **2.** wretched; neglected; pitiable. [1855–60; GOD + FORSAKEN]
—**Syn. 1.** bleak, dreary, lonely. **2.** forlorn, miserable.

God•frey (god′frē), *n.* **1.** a male given name: from Germanic words meaning "god" and "peace." —*interj.* **2.** (*sometimes l.c.*) (used as an exclamation of surprise, anger, etc.)

God-giv•en (god′giv′ən), *adj.* **1.** given by, or coming directly from, God: *the God-given laws.* **2.** welcome; propitious; opportune. [1790–1800]

God•head (god′hed′), *n.* **1. a.** the essential being of God; the Supreme Being. **b.** the Holy Trinity of God the Father, Christ the Son, and the Holy Ghost. **2.** (*l.c.*) divinity; godhood. **3.** (*l.c.*) *Rare.* a god or goddess; deity. [1200–50; ME *godhede;* see GOD, -HEAD]

god•hood (god′ho͝od), *n.* divine character or condition; divinity. [1175–1225; ME; OE *godhād.* See GOD, -HOOD]

Go•di•va (gə dī′və), *n.* ("*Lady Godiva*"), died 1057, wife of Leofric. According to legend, she rode naked through the streets of Coventry, England, to win relief for the people from a burdensome tax.

god-king (god′king′, -king′), *n.* a human sovereign believed to be a deity or to have godlike attributes. [1860–65]

god•less (god′lis), *adj.* **1.** having or acknowledging no god or deity; atheistic. **2.** wicked; evil; sinful. [1520–30; GOD + -LESS] —**god′less•ly,** *adv.* —**god′less•ness,** *n.*

god•like (god′līk′), *adj.* like or befitting God or a god; divine. [1505–15; GOD + -LIKE] —**god′like′ness,** *n.*

god•ling (god′ling), *n.* a minor god, esp. one whose influence or authority is entirely local. [1490–1500; see GOD, -LING[1]]

god•ly (god′lē), *adj.,* **-li•er, -li•est. 1.** conforming to the laws and wishes of God; devout; pious. **2.** coming from God; divine. [bef. 1000; ME; OE *godlīc.* See GOD, -LY] —**god′li•ness,** *n.*
—**Syn. 1.** religious, saintly, holy, righteous, good.
—**Ant. 1.** wicked, impious.

God-man (god′man′, -man′), *n., pl.* **-men** for 2. **1.** Jesus Christ. **2.** (*l.c.*) a being who possesses the combined attributes of a deity and of a human; demigod. [1550–60]

god•moth•er (god′muth′ər), *n.* **1.** a woman who serves as sponsor for a child at baptism. **2.** any female sponsor or guardian. —*v.t.* **3.** to act as godmother to; sponsor. [bef. 1000; ME; OE *godmōdor.* See GOD, MOTHER[1]]

God•o•li•as (god′l ī′əs), *n. Douay Bible.* Gedaliah.

Go•dol•phin (gō dol′fin, gə-), *n.* **Sidney, 1st Earl of,** 1645–1712, English statesman and financier.

go•down (gō doun′), *n.* (in India and other countries in Asia) a warehouse or other storage place. [1580–90; < Malay *godong,* perh. < Telugu *giḍ(ḍ)angi,* Tamil *kiṭanku,* akin to *kiṭa-* to lie]

Go•dow•sky (gə dôf′skē, gô-), *n.* **Leopold,** 1870–1938, U.S. composer and pianist, born in Poland.

Go•doy Al•ca•ya•ga (*Sp.* gô thoi′ äl kä yä′gä), **Lu•ci•la** (*Sp.* lo͞o sē′lä), real name of Gabriela Mistral.

god•par•ent (god′pâr′ənt, -par′-), *n.* a godfather or godmother. [1860–65; GOD + PARENT]

go•droon (gō dro͞on′), *n.* gadroon.

God's′ a′cre, a cemetery, esp. one adjacent to a church; churchyard. [1610–20; trans. of G *Gottesacker*]

God's′ coun′try, 1. an area or region supposed to be favored by God, esp. a naturally beautiful rural area. **2.** an isolated rural area. **3.** one's native region. [1860–65; *Amer.*]

god•send (god′send′), *n.* an unexpected thing or event that is particularly welcome and timely, as if sent by God. [1805–15; earlier *God's send,* var. (by influence of SEND[1]) of *God's sond* or *sand,* ME *Godes sand* (*sand* OE: message, service)]

god•sent (god′sent′), *adj.* sent by God or as if by God: *a godsent rain.* [1150–1200; ME; See GOD, SENT]

god•ship (god′ship), *n.* **1.** the rank, character, or condition of a god. **2.** *Often Facetious.* a title used in referring to a godlike person: *A bevy of servants were on hand to attend their godship's every whim.* [1545–55; GOD + -SHIP]

god•son (god′sun′), *n.* a male godchild. [bef. 900; ME; OE *godsunu.* See GOD, SON]

God•speed (god′spēd′), *n.* good fortune; success (used as a wish to a person starting on a journey, a new venture, etc.). [1250–1300; ME, in the phrase *God spede* may God prosper (you). See GOD, SPEED]

God's′ pen′ny, *Old Eng. Law.* See **earnest money.** [1300–50; ME]

God's′ plen′ty, an abundant or overabundant quantity.

God's′ Word′, the Bible.

Godt•håb (*Dan.* gôt′hôp′), *n.* a city in and the capital of Greenland, in the SW part. 12,209.

Go•du•nov (god′n ôf′, go͝od′-; *Russ.* gə do͞o nôf′), *n.* **Bo•ris Fe•do•ro•vich** (bôr′is fi dôr′ə vich, bōr′-, bor′-; *Russ.* bu ryēs′ fyô′də rə vyich), 1552–1605, regent of Russia 1584–98 and czar 1598–1605.

God•ward (god′wərd), *adv.* **1.** Also, **God′wards.** toward God. —*adj.* **2.** directed toward God. [1350–1400; ME; see GOD, -WARD]

God•win (god′win), *n.* **1.** Also, **God•wi•ne** (god′wi nə). **Earl of the West Saxons,** died 1053, English statesman. **2. Mary Woll•stone•craft** (wo͝ol′stən kraft′, -kräft′), 1759–97, English writer. **3.** her husband **William,** 1756–1836, English political philosopher, novelist, and essayist. **4.** a male given name: from an Old English word meaning "good friend."

God•win Aus•ten (god′win ô′stin). See **K2.**

god•wit (god′wit), *n.* any of several large, widely distributed shorebirds of the genus *Limosa,* as the New World *L. haemastica* **(Hudsonian godwit),** having a long bill that curves upward slightly. [1545–55; of obscure orig.]

Goeb•bels (gœ′bəls), *n.* **Jo•seph Paul** (yō′zef poul), 1897–1945, German propaganda director for the Nazis.

go•er (gō′ər), *n.* **1.** a person or thing that goes: *We sat in the lobby watching the comers and goers.* **2.** a person who attends frequently or habitually (usually used in combination): *churchgoer; moviegoer.* [1350–1400; ME; see GO[1], -ER[1]]

Goe•ring (gâr′ing, gûr′-; *Ger.* gœ′ʀing), *n.* **Her•mann Wil•helm** (her′män vil′helm, hûr′mən wil′helm; *Ger.* her′män vil′helm). See **Göring, Hermann Wilhelm.**

goes (gōz), *v.* **1.** 3rd pers. sing. pres. indic. of **go**[1]. —*n.* **2.** pl. of **go**[1].

Goes (go͞os), *n.* **Hu•go van der** (hyo͞o′gō van dər; *Du.* hʏ′gō vän dər), c1440–82, Flemish painter.

GOES, See **Geostationary Operational Environmental Satellite.**

Goe•thals (gō′thəlz), *n.* **George Washington,** 1858–1928, U.S. major general and engineer: chief engineer of the Panama Canal 1907–14; governor of the Canal Zone 1914–16.

Goe•the (gûr′tə, *Ger.* gœ′tə), *n.* **Jo•hann Wolf•gang von** (yō′hän vôlf′gäng fən), 1749–1832, German poet, dramatist, novelist, and philosopher. —**Goe•the•an, Goe•thi•an** (gûr′tē ən, gœ′-), *adj.*

goe•thite (gō′thīt, gœ′tit), *n.* a very common mineral, iron hydroxide, $HFeO_2$, occurring in crystals, but more commonly in yellow or brown earthy masses: an ore of iron. [1815–25; named after GOETHE; see -ITE[1]]

Goetz (gets; *Ger.* gœts), *n.* **Her•mann** (heʀ′män). See **Götz, Hermann.**

go•fer (gō′fər), *n. Slang.* an employee whose chief duty is running errands. Also, **go′-fer, gopher.** [1965–70; resp. of *go for* (v. phrase), with *-er* repr. both vowel reduction in *for* and -ER[1]]

gof•fer (gof′ər), *n.* **1.** an ornamental plaiting used for frills and borders, as on women's caps. —*v.t.* **2.** to flute (a frill, ruffle, etc.), as with a heated iron. Also, **gauffer.** [1700–10; < F *gaufre* waffle < MD *wāfel* WAFFLE]

gof•fer•ing (gof′ər ing), *n.* a decorative or ornamental frill, ruffle, etc. Also, **gauffering.** [1840–50; GOFFER + -ING[1]]

Goffs•town (gofs′toun′), *n.* a town in S New Hampshire. 11,315.

go′ fish′, a card game for two or more persons similar to the game of authors.

Gog (gog), *n.* a chief prince of Meshech and Tubal who came from Magog. Ezek. 38–39.

Gog and Ma•gog (gog′ ən mā′gog), two nations led by Satan in a climactic battle at Armageddon against the kingdom of God. Rev. 20:8.

go-get•ter (gō′get′ər, -get′-), *n. Informal.* an enterprising, aggressive person. [1920–25, *Amer.;* prob. from the exhortation *Go get 'em!;* see -ER[1]] —**go′-get′ting,** *adj.*

gog•gle (gog′əl), *n., v.,* **-gled, -gling,** *adj.* —*n.* **1. goggles,** large spectacles equipped with special lenses, protective rims, etc., to prevent injury to the eyes from strong wind, flying objects, blinding light, etc. **2.** a bulging or wide-open look of the eyes; stare. —*v.i.* **3.** to stare with bulging or wide-open eyes. **4.** (of the eyes) to bulge and be wide open in a stare. **5.** to roll the eyes. **6.** (of the eyes) to roll. **7.** *Informal.* to spearfish. —*v.t.* **8.** to roll (the eyes). —*adj.* **9.** (of the eyes) rolling, bulging, or staring. [1350–1400; ME *gogelen* to look aside; cf. AGOG]

gog•gle-box (gog′əl boks′), *n. Brit. Slang.* a television set. [1955–60]

gog•gle-eye (gog′əl ī′), *n., pl.* **-eyes,** (*esp. collectively*) **-eye. 1.** See **rock bass. 2.** Also called **gog′gle-eye scad′.** See **bigeye scad.**

gog•gle-eyed (gog′əl īd′), *adj.* **1.** having bulging, wide-open, or rolling eyes, esp. in astonishment or wonderment. —*adv.* **2.** with bulging, wide-open eyes. [1350–1400; ME *gogel eied* squinting, looking sideways]

gog•gler (gog′lər), *n.* **1.** a person who stares goggle-eyed. **2.** a person who spearfishes. **3.** See **bigeye scad.** [1815–25; GOGGLE + -ER[1]]

Gogh (gō, gôKH; *Du.* KHôKH), *n.* **Vin•cent van** (vin′sənt van; *Du.* vin sent′ vän). See **van Gogh, Vincent.**

gog•let (gog′lit), *n.* (esp. in India) a long-necked container, esp. for water, usually of porous earthenware so that its contents are cooled by evaporation. Also, **guglet, gurglet.** [1690–1700; < Pg *gorgoleta* (dim. of *gorja* throat), akin to F *gargoulette* (dim. of *gargoule* throat); see GARGLE]

go-go (gō′gō′), *adj. Informal.* **1.** full of energy, vitality, or daring: *the go-go generation.* **2.** stylish, modern, or up-to-date: *the go-go social set.* **3.** of or pertaining to the music and dancing performed at discotheques or nightclubs. **4.** performing at a discotheque or nightclub. **5.** seeking large earnings quickly by trading aggessively and often speculatively in stocks: *a go-go mutual fund.* **6.** marked by swift price upswings due to excessive speculation: *a go-go stock.* **7.** being a time of great prosperity, economic growth, and optimism: *the go-go years of the 1920's.* [1960–65; redupl. of GO[1], influenced in some senses by À GOGO]

go•go (gō′gō), *n.* See **à gogo.**

go′-go danc′er, an entertainer who performs popular dances on a stage or platform for the patrons of a discotheque or nightclub. [1960–65]

Go•gol (gō′gəl; -gôl; *Russ.* gô′gəl), *n.* **Ni•ko•lai Va•si•lie•vich** (nik′ə lī′ və sēl′yə vich; *Russ.* nyi ku lī′ vu syē′lyi vyich), 1809–52, Russian novelist, short-story writer, and playwright.

goi (goi), *n., pl.* **goy•im, gois.** goy.

Goi•â•ni•a (goi ä′nē ə), *n.* a city in and the capital of Goiás, in central Brazil, SW of Brasília. 738,117.

Goi•ás (goi äs′), *n.* a state in central Brazil. 3,967,310; 247,826 sq. mi. (641,870 sq. km). *Cap.:* Goiânia.

Goi•del•ic (goi del′ik), *Ling.* —*adj.* **1.** of or belonging to Goidelic; Q-Celtic. —*n.* **2.** Also called **Q-Celtic.** the subbranch of Celtic in which the Proto-Indo-European *kw*-sound remained a velar. Irish and Scots Gaelic belong to Goidelic. Cf. **Brythonic, P-Celtic.** Also, **Gadhelic.** [1880–1885; < OIr *Goídil* GAEL + -IC]

go•ing (gō′ing), *n.* **1.** the act of leaving or departing; departure: *a safe going and quick return.* **2.** the condition of surfaces, as those of roads, for walking or driving: *After the heavy rain, the going was bad.* **3.** progress; advancement: *With such slow going, the work is behind schedule.* **4.** Usually, **goings.** behavior; conduct; deportment. —*adj.* **5.** moving or working, as machinery. **6.** active, alive, or existing. **7.** continuing to operate or do business, esp. in a successful manner: *a going company.* **8.** current; prevalent; usual: *What is the going price of good farmland in this area?* **9.** leaving; departing. **10. get going,** to begin; get started. **11. going away,** *Sports.* by a wide margin, esp. as established in the late stages of a contest: *The champion won the bout going away.* **12. going on, a.** nearly; almost: *It's going on four o'clock.* **b.** happening: *What's going on here?* **c.** continuing; lasting: *That party has been going on all night.* [1250–1300; ME; see GO[1], -ING[1], -ING[2]]

go•ing-o•ver (gō′ing ō′vər), *n., pl.* **go•ings-o•ver** (gō′ingz ō′vər). **1.** a review, examination, or investigation: *The accounts were given a thorough going-over.* **2.** a severe, thorough scolding. **3.** a sound thrashing; beating: *The hoodlums gave him a good going-over when they found him.* [1870–75, *Amer.;* n. use of v. phrase *go over*]

go•ings-on (gō′ingz on′, ôn′), *n. Informal.* **1.** conduct or behavior, esp. when open to criticism: *We had never seen such goings-on as at the last dance.* **2.** happenings; events: *The American newspaper kept her in touch with the goings-on back home.* [1765–75; n. use of prp. phrase *going on*]

go′ing to Jeru′salem. See **musical chairs.**

go′ing train′, *Horol.* the gear train for moving the hands of a timepiece or giving some other visual indication of the time. Cf. **dial train, striking train.**

goi•ter (goi′tər), *n. Pathol.* an enlargement of the thyroid gland on the front and sides of the neck, usually symptomatic of abnormal thyroid secretion, esp. hypothyroidism due to a lack of iodine in the diet. Also, *esp. Brit.,* **goi′tre.** Cf. **exophthalmic goiter.** [1615–25; < F *goitre* << L *guttur* throat]

goi•tro•gen (goi′trə jən, -jen′), *n.* any goiter-producing substance, as thiouracil. [1945–50; GOIT(E)R + -O- + -GEN]

goi•tro•gen•ic (goi′trə jen′ik), *adj.* tending to produce goiter. Also, **goi•trog•e•nous** (goi troj′ə nəs). [1925–30; GOIT(E)R + -O- + -GENIC]

goi•trous (goi′trəs), *adj. Pathol.* pertaining to or affected with goiter. [1790–1800; < F *goitreux.* See GOITER, -OUS]

go-kart (gō′kärt′), *n.* kart. [1955–60]

Gol•con•da (gol kon′də), *n.* **1.** a ruined city in S India, near the modern city of Hyderabad: capital of a former Muslim kingdom; famous for its diamond cutting. **2.** (*often l.c.*) a rich mine or other source of great wealth.

gold (gōld), *n.* **1.** a precious yellow metallic element, highly malleable and ductile, and not subject to oxidation or corrosion. *Symbol:* Au; *at. wt.:* 196.967; *at. no.:* 79; *sp. gr.:* 19.3 at 20°C. **2.** a quantity of gold coins: *to pay in gold.* **3.** a monetary standard based on this metal; gold standard. **4.** money; wealth; riches. **5.** something likened to this metal in brightness, preciousness, superiority, etc.: *a heart of gold.* **6.** a bright, metallic yellow color, sometimes tending toward brown. **7.** See **gold medal. 8.** (*cap.*) *Mil.* the code name for one of the five D-day invasion beaches, assaulted by British troops. —*adj.* **9.** consisting of gold. **10.** pertaining to gold. **11.** like gold. **12.** of the color of gold. **13.** indicating the fiftieth event of a series, as a wedding anniversary. See table under **wedding anniversary. 14.** *Music Slang.* (of a recording or record album) having sold a minimum of 1 million single records or 500,000 LPs. [bef. 900; ME, OE; c. G *Gold,* Goth *gulth*]

Gold (gōld, gôld), *n.* Nanay.

Gold (gōld), *n.* **Thomas,** born 1920, U.S. astronomer, born in Austria: formulated the steady-state theory of the universe.

Gol•da (gōl′də), *n.* a female given name.

gol•darn (gol′därn′), *n., adj., adv., v.t. Informal.* goddamn (used as a euphemism in expressions of anger, disgust, surprise, etc.). Also, **goldurn.** [1825–35]

gol•darned (gol′därnd′), *adj., superl.* **-darned•est,** *adv. Informal.* goddamned (used as a euphemism in expressions of anger, disgust, surprise, etc.). Also, **goldurned.** [1905–10; GOLDARN + -ED[2]]

Gold′bach conjec′ture (gōld′bäk), *Math.* an unproved theorem that every even integer greater than 2 can be written as the sum of two prime numbers. [1940–45]

gold′ ba′sis, a gold standard as a basis for prices.

gold′beat•er's skin′ (gōld′bē′tərz), the prepared outside membrane of the large intestine of the ox, used by goldbeaters to lay between the leaves of the metal while they beat it into gold leaf. [1700–10; GOLD + BEATER + 's[1]]

gold•beat•ing (gōld′bē′ting), *n.* the art or process of beating out gold into gold leaf. Also, **gold′ beat′ing.** [1755–65; GOLD + BEATING] —**gold′beat′er,** *n.*

gold′ bee′tle, any of several beetles having a golden luster, as a chrysomelid, *Metriona bicolor,* that feeds on morning glories and roses. Also called **goldbug.**

Gold•berg (gōld′bûrg), *n.* **1. Arthur Joseph,** 1908–90, U.S. jurist, statesman, and diplomat: associate justice of the U.S. Supreme Court 1962–65; ambassador to the U.N. 1965–68. **2. Reuben Lucius** ("*Rube*"), 1883–1970, U.S. cartoonist, whose work often depicts deviously complex and impractical inventions.

Gold•ber•ger (gōld′bûr gər), *n.* **Joseph,** 1874–1929, U.S. physician, born in Austria: discovered the cause of and treatment for pellagra.

Gold•berg•i•an (gōld bûr′gē ən), *adj.* See **Rube Goldberg.** [GOLDBERG + -IAN]

gold′ bond′, a bond payable in gold.

gold•brick (gōld′brik′), *n.* **1.** *Informal.* a brick made to look like gold, sold by a swindler. **2.** *Informal.* anything supposed to be valuable but which turns out to be worthless. **3.** Also, **gold′brick′er.** *Slang.* a person, esp. a soldier, who shirks responsibility or performs duties without proper effort or care. —*Slang. v.i.* **4.** to shirk responsibility or perform halfheartedly; loaf. —*v.t.* **5.** to swindle; cheat. [1850–55, *Amer.*; GOLD + BRICK]

gold′ bronze′, an alloy of about 90 percent copper, 5 percent zinc, 3 percent lead, and 2 percent tin.

gold•bug (gōld′bug′), *n.* **1.** *Informal.* a person, esp. an economist or politician, who supports the gold standard. **2.** *Informal.* a person who believes in buying gold bullion as a personal investment. **3.** See **gold beetle.** Also, **gold′ bug′.** [1875–80, *Amer.*]

gold′ bul′lion stand′ard, a gold standard in which gold is not coined but may be purchased at a fixed price for foreign exchange. [1930–35]

gold′ certif′icate, a former U.S. paper currency issued by the federal government for circulation from 1865 to 1933, equal to and redeemable for gold to a stated value. [1860–65, *Amer.*]

gold′ chlo′ride, a yellow to red, water-soluble compound, $AuCl_3$, used chiefly in photography, gilding ceramic ware and glass, and in the manufacture of purple of Cassius. Also called **gold trichloride.**

Gold′ Coast′, 1. a former British territory in W Africa; now a part of Ghana. **2.** a wealthy residential area along a shore, as in Florida between Miami and Palm Beach or in Chicago along the shore of Lake Michigan.

gold•crest (gōld′krest′), *n.* a Eurasian kinglet, *Regulus regulus,* having a bright yellow patch on the top of the head. [GOLD + CREST]

gold•cup (gōld′kup′), *n.* a Mexican climbing shrub, *Solandra guttata,* of the nightshade family, having cup-shaped yellow flowers marked with purple. [1570–80; GOLD + CUP]

gold′ dig′ger, 1. a person who seeks or digs for gold in a gold field. **2.** *Informal.* a woman who associates with or marries a man chiefly for material gain. [1820–30, *Amer.*]

gold′ dig′ging, 1. the work of digging for gold. **2. gold diggings,** a region where digging or seeking for gold, esp. by placer mining, is carried on. [1795–1805]

gold′ dust′, gold in fine particles. [1695–1705]

gold•en (gōl′dən), *adj.* **1.** bright, metallic, or lustrous like gold; of the color of gold; yellow: *golden hair.* **2.** made or consisting of gold. **3.** exceptionally valuable, advantageous, or fine: *a golden opportunity.* **4.** having glowing vitality; radiant: *golden youth.* **5.** full of happiness, prosperity, or vigor: *golden hours; a golden era of exploration.* **6.** highly talented and favored; destined for success: *television's golden boy.* **7.** richly soft and smooth: *a golden voice.* **8.** indicating the fiftieth event of a series: *a golden wedding anniversary.* [1225–75; ME; see GOLD, -EN[2]] —**gold′en•ly,** *adv.* —**gold′en•ness,** *n.*
—**Syn. 5.** splendid, glorious, joyous.

Gold•en (gōl′dən), *n.* a city in central Colorado. 12,237.

gold′en age′, 1. the most flourishing period in the history of a nation, literature, etc. **2.** *Class. Myth.* the first and best of the four ages of humankind; an era of peace and innocence that finally yielded to the silver age. **3.** (*usually caps.*) a period in Latin literature, 70 B.C. to A.D. 14, in which Cicero, Catullus, Horace, Vergil, Ovid, and others wrote; the first phase of classical Latin. Cf. **silver age** (def. 2). **4.** the period in life after middle age, traditionally characterized by wisdom, contentment, and useful leisure. **5.** the age at which a person normally retires. [1545–55]

gold′en ag′er (ā′jər), an elderly person, esp. one who has retired. [1960–65, *Amer.*; GOLDEN AGE + -ER[1]]

gold′en alexan′ders, a plant, *Zizia aurea,* of the parsley family, native to eastern North America, having compound leaves and umbels of yellow flowers. [ME *alisaundre* (< OF < ML), OE *alexandre* < ML (*petroselinum*) *Alexandrinum* horse-parsley (*Smyrnium olusatrum*), a synonym of *petroselinum Macedonicum* (appar. by assoc. of Macedonia with ALEXANDER THE GREAT); cf. PARSLEY]

gold′en as′ter, any North American, asterlike, composite plant of the genus *Chrysopsis,* having bright, golden-yellow flower heads, as *C. mariana,* of the eastern U.S. [1905–10, *Amer.*]

gold′en ban′tam corn′, a horticultural variety of sweet corn having yellow kernels. [1905–10, *Amer.*]

Gold′en Bough′, *Class. Myth.* a branch of mistletoe, sacred to Proserpina, that served Aeneas as a pass to the underworld.

gold′en-brown al′gae (gōl′dən broun′), a group of mostly marine, motile algae of the phylum Chlorophyta, characterized by the presence of the pigments chlorophyll, carotene, and xanthophyll, which impart golden to yellow-brown colors. [1955–60]

gold′en buck′, a dish consisting of Welsh rabbit topped with a poached egg. [1895–1900, *Amer.*]

Gold′en Bull′, an edict of Charles IV, emperor of the Holy Roman Empire, issued in 1356 and in force until the extinction of the empire in 1806, in which the selection of the emperor was entrusted to seven Electors.

gold′en calf′, 1. a golden idol set up by Aaron and worshiped by the Israelites. Ex. 32. **2.** either of two similar idols set up by Jeroboam. I Kings 12:28, 29. **3.** money or material goods as an object of worship or pursuit.

gold′en chain′, laburnum.

gold′en club′, an aquatic plant, *Orontium aquaticum,* of the arum family, native to the eastern U.S., having blue-green leaves and a clublike spadix covered with tiny yellow flowers. [1830–40; *Amer.*]

gold′en-crowned king′let (gōl′dən kround′), a yellowish-green kinglet, *Regulus satrapa,* of North America, having a yellow or orange patch on the top of the head. [1870–75, *Amer.*]

gold′en cur′rant, a western North American shrub, *Ribes aureum,* of the saxifrage family, having purplish fruit and fragrant, drooping clusters of yellow flowers that turn reddish. [1900–05, *Amer.*]

Gold′en Deli′cious, a bright yellow type of Delicious apple.

gold′en ea′gle, a large eagle, *Aquila chrysaëtos,* of the Northern Hemisphere, having golden-brown feathers on the back of the head and neck. See illus. under **raptorial.** [1780–90]

gold′en ear′drops, *pl.* **-drops.** (*used with a singular v.*) a Californian plant, *Dicentra chrysantha,* of the fumitory family, having bluish-green foliage and branched clusters of yellow flowers.

gold•en•eye (gōl′dən ī′), *n., pl.* **-eyes,** (*esp. collectively*) **-eye. 1.** either of two diving ducks, *Bucephala clangula,* of Eurasia and North America, or *B. islandica* **(Barrow's goldeneye),** of North America, having bright yellow eyes. **2.** Also called **gold′en-eyed fly′** (gōl′dən-īd′). a lacewing of the family Chrysopidae. [1670–80; GOLDEN + EYE]

gold′en fizz′, a drink containing egg yolk, gin or vodka, lemon juice, sugar, and soda water.

Gold′en Fleece′, *Class. Myth.* a fleece of pure gold, kept at Colchis by King Aeëtes from whom it was stolen by Jason and the Argonauts with the help of Aeëtes's daughter, Medea.

Gold′en Gate′, a strait in W California, between San Francisco Bay and the Pacific. 2 mi. (3.2 km) wide.

Gold′en Gate′ Bridge′, a bridge connecting N California with San Francisco peninsula. 4200-ft. (1280-m) center span.

gold′en goose′, a legendary goose that laid one golden egg a day and was killed by its impatient owner, who wanted all the gold immediately.

gold′en gram′. See under **gram[2]** (def. 2).

gold′en ham′ster, a small light-colored hamster, *Mesocricetus auratus,* native to Asia Minor and familiar as a laboratory animal and pet. See illus. under **hamster.** Also called **Syrian hamster.** [1945–50]

gold′en hand′cuffs, a series of raises, bonuses, etc., given at specified intervals or tied to the length of employment so as to keep an executive from leaving the company. [1985–90]

gold′en hand′shake, 1. a special incentive, as generous severance pay, given to an older employee as an inducement to elect early retirement. **2.** the giving or offering of such an incentive. [1955–60]

Gold′en Horde′, the army of Mongol Tartars that overran eastern Europe in the 13th century, established a khanate in Russia, and maintained suzerainty there until the 15th century.

Gold′en Horn′, an inlet of the Bosporus, in European Turkey: forms the inner part of Istanbul.

Gold′en Horse′shoe, *Canadian.* the urban and agricultural area surrounding Toronto.

gold′en ju′bilee. See under **jubilee** (def. 1).

gold′en li′on tam′arin, a monkey, *Leontopithecus rosalia rosalia,* of tropical rain forests of southeastern Brazil, having a silky golden coat and a long golden mane: threatened with extinction.

gold′en mean′, 1. the perfect moderate course or position that avoids extremes; the happy medium. **2.** See **golden section.** [1580–90]

gold′en mole′, any of several burrowing insectivores of the family Chrysochloridae, of southern Africa, the fur of which has an iridescent, often golden luster.

gold′en nem′atode, a yellowish nematode, *Heterodera rostochiensis,* that is parasitic on the roots of potatoes, tomatoes, and other solanaceous plants. [1945–50]

gold′en old′ie, (*sometimes caps.*) *Informal.* something once popular or valued that has retained its appeal or for which interest has been reawakened, esp. a popular song or record. [1965–70, *Amer.*]

gold′en o′riole, an Old World oriole, *Oriolus oriolus,* the male of which is bright yellow with black wings. [1835–45, *Amer.*]

gold′en par′achute, an employment contract or agreement guaranteeing a key executive of a company substantial severance pay and other financial benefits in the event of job loss caused by the company's being sold or merged. [1980–85]

gold′en perch′, a freshwater food fish, *Plectroplites ambiguus,* that inhabits inland waters of Australia. Also called **callop.**

gold′en pheas′ant, an Asiatic pheasant, *Chrysolophus pictus,* having brilliant scarlet, orange, gold, green, and black plumage.

gold′en plov′er, either of two plovers of the genus *Pluvialis,* having the back marked with golden-yellow spots, *P. apricaria,* of Europe, or *P. dominica,* of America. [1775–85]

gold′en pol′ypody. See **hare's-foot fern.**

gold′en rag′wort. See under **ragwort.**

gold′en rain′ tree′, an ornamental tree, *Koelreuteria paniculata,* of the soapberry family, native to China and adjacent areas, having pinnate leaves, large clusters of fragrant yellow flowers, and inflated pods containing black seeds used as beads. [1925–30]

gold′en retriev′er, one of an English breed of retrievers with a thick, flat or wavy, golden coat. [1915–20]

gold•en•rod (gōl′dən rod′), *n.* **1.** any composite plant of the genus *Solidago,* most species of which bear numerous small, yellow flower heads. **2.** a strong to vivid yellow. —*adj.* **3.** of the color goldenrod. [1560–70; GOLDEN + ROD]

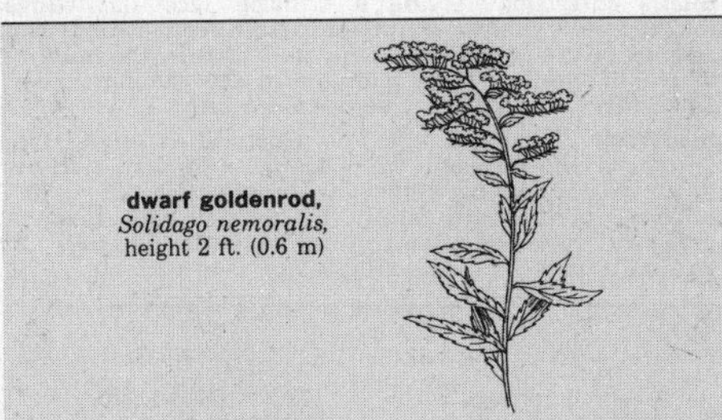

dwarf goldenrod, *Solidago nemoralis,* height 2 ft. (0.6 m)

gold′en rose′, *Rom. Cath. Ch.* a gold, bejeweled ornament in the form of a rose or spray of roses, blessed and presented by the pope in recognition of service to the Holy See.

gold′en rule′, 1. a rule of ethical conduct, usually phrased "Do unto others as you would have them do unto you," or, as in the Sermon on the Mount, "Whatsoever ye would that men should do to you, do ye even so unto them." Matt. 7:12; Luke 6:31. **2.** any philosophy, guiding principle, or ideal of behavior, as in a discipline, pursuit, or business: *The protesters agreed that their golden rule would be "no violence."* [1800–10]

gold•en•seal (gōl′dən sēl′), *n.* **1.** a plant, *Hydrastis canadensis,* of the buttercup family, having a thick yel-

CONCISE PRONUNCIATION KEY: act, cāpe, dâre, pärt; set, ēqual; *if,* īce; ox, ōver, ôrder, oil, bŏŏk, bōōt, out; up, ûrge; child; sing; shoe; thin, *that;* zh as in *treasure.* ə = *a* as in *alone, e* as in *system, i* as in *easily, o* as in *gallop, u* as in *circus;* ᵊ as in *fire* (fīᵊr), *hour* (ouᵊr). l and n can serve as syllabic consonants, as in *cradle* (krād′l), and *button* (but′n). See the full key inside the front cover.

low rootstock. **2.** Also called **hydrastis.** the rhizomes and roots of this plant, formerly used in medicine as an astringent and to inhibit bleeding. [1830–40, *Amer.*, GOLDEN + SEAL^1]

gold′en sec′tion, *Fine Arts, Math.* a ratio between two portions of a line, or the two dimensions of a plane figure, in which the lesser of the two is to the greater as the greater is to the sum of both: a ratio of approximately 0.618 to 1.000. Also called **golden mean.** [1870–75]

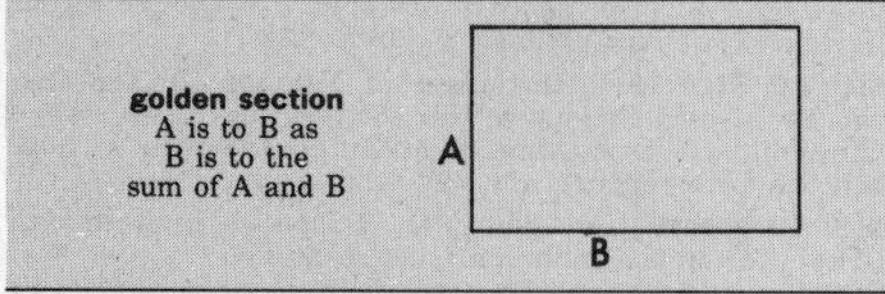

golden section
A is to B as B is to the sum of A and B

gold′en shin′er, a small, silvery freshwater minnow, *Notemigonus crysoleucas,* native to eastern North America and introduced into western North America: often used as live bait in sport fishing. [1900–05]

gold′en show′er. a tree, *Cassia fistula,* of the legume family, native to India, having long, drooping clusters of yellow flowers. Also called **pudding-pipe tree.** [1910–15]

gold′en stars′, a plant, *Bloomeria crocea,* of the amaryllis family, native to southern California, having clusters of golden-orange, starlike flowers.

Gold′en State′, California (used as a nickname).

gold′en syr′up, *Brit.* treacle (def. 1b).

gold′en this′tle. See **Spanish oyster plant.** [1590–1600]

Gold′en Tri′angle, **1.** (*sometimes l.c.*) an area of Southeast Asia encompassing parts of Burma, Laos, and Thailand, significant as a major source of opium and heroin. **2.** *Canadian.* the peninsula enclosed by Lakes Ontario, Erie, and Huron.

Gold′en Val′ley, a town in SE Minnesota. 22,775.

gold′en war′bler. See **yellow warbler.** [1870–75, *Amer.*]

gold′en wat′tle, **1.** a broad-leaved, Australian acacia, *Acacia pycnantha,* of the legume family, having short clusters of yellow flowers and yielding tanbark and a useful gum. **2.** any similar acacia, esp. *A. longifolia,* of Australia and Tasmania.

gold′en wed′ding, the fiftieth anniversary of a wedding.

gold′en years′, the years of retirement, normally after age 65. [1950–55]

gold′-ex·change′ stand′ard (gōld′iks chānj′), a monetary system in one country in which currency is maintained at a par with that of another country that is on the gold standard.

gold·eye (gōld′ī′), *n., pl.* **-eyes,** (*esp. collectively*) **-eye.** a silvery, herringlike game fish, *Hiodon alosoides,* found in the fresh waters of central North America. [GOLD + EYE]

gold′ fe′ver, greed and excitement caused by a gold rush. [1840–50]

gold′ field′, an area or district where gold is mined. [1850–55]

gold·fields (gōld′fēldz′), *n., pl.* **-fields.** any of several Californian, composite herbs of the genus *Lasthenia,* having yellow flowers. [1910–15, *Amer.*; GOLD + FIELD + -S^3]

gold-filled (gōld′fild′), *adj. Jewelry.* composed of a layer of gold backed with a base metal. Cf. **filled gold.** [1900–05]

gold·finch (gōld′finch′), *n.* **1.** a European finch, *Carduelis carduelis,* having a crimson face and wings marked with yellow. **2.** any of certain related American finches of the genus *Carduelis,* as *C. tristis,* the male of which has yellow body plumage in the summer. [bef. 1000; ME; OE *goldfinc.* See GOLD, FINCH]

gold·fish (gōld′fish′), *n., pl.* (*esp. collectively*) **-fish,** (*esp. referring to two or more kinds or species*) **-fish·es.** **1.** a small, usually yellow or orange fish, *Carassius auratus,* of the carp family, native to China, bred in many varieties and often kept in fishbowls and pools. **2.** garibaldi (def. 2). [1690–1700; GOLD + FISH]

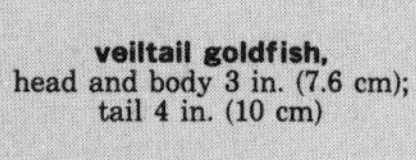

veiltail goldfish,
head and body 3 in. (7.6 cm);
tail 4 in. (10 cm)

gold′ fix′ing, *Finance.* **1.** the procedure by which the price of gold is established. **2.** the price itself, esp. as established daily in the London gold market. Also, **gold′ fix′.** Also called **fixing.**

gold′ foil′, sheets of gold slightly thicker than gold leaf. [1275–1325; ME] **—gold′-foil′,** *adj.*

Gol·di (gōl′dē, gôl′-), *n., pl.* **-dis,** (*esp. collectively*) **-di.** Nanay.

Gol′die's fern′ (gōl′dēz), a wood fern, *Dryopteris goldiana,* of northeastern North America, having large, golden-green, leathery fronds with blades that tilt backward. [after its discoverer, John *Goldie* (1793–1886), Scottish gardener and plant collector]

gold·i·locks (gōl′dē loks′), *n., pl.* **-locks.** (*used with a singular v.*) a person with golden hair. [1540–50; obs. *goldy* golden + LOCK^2 + -S^3]

Gol·ding (gōl′ding), *n.* **1. Louis,** 1895–1958, English novelist and essayist. **2. William Gerald,** born 1911, British novelist: Nobel prize 1983.

gold′ leaf′, gold in the form of very thin foil, as for gilding. [1720–30] **—gold′-leaf′,** *adj.*

Gold·man (gōld′mən), *n.* **1. Edwin Fran·ko** (frang′kō), 1878–1956, U.S. composer and bandmaster. **2. Emma,** 1869–1940, U.S. anarchist leader, born in Russia.

Gold·mark (gōld′märk′), *n.* **Karl** (kärl), 1830–1915, Hungarian composer.

gold′ med′al, a medal, traditionally of gold or gold color, awarded to a person or team finishing first in a competition, meet, or tournament; championship medal. Cf. **bronze medal, silver medal.** [1905–10] **—gold′ med′alist.**

gold′ mine′, **1.** a mine yielding gold. **2.** a source of great wealth or profit, or any desirable thing. **3.** a copious source or reserve of something required: *a gold mine of information about antiques.* [1425–75; late ME]

gold·min·er (gōld′mī′nər), *n.* a person who mines gold or works in a gold mine. [1850–55; GOLD + MINER]

gold′ min′ing, the act or process of mining gold. [1555–65]

gold′ note′, a former U.S. bank note payable in gold coin. [1865–70, *Amer.*]

Gol·do·ni (gôl dō′nē; *It.* gôl dô′nē), *n.* **Car·lo** (kär′lō; *It.* käʀ′lô), 1707–93, Italian dramatist. **—Gol·do′ni·an,** *adj.*

gold′ or′ange, *Chem.* See **methyl orange.**

Gol·dov·sky (gol dôf′skē, -dof′-; *Russ.* gul dôf′skyĕ), *n.* **Bo·ris** (bôr′is, bōr′-, bor′-; *Russ.* bu ʀyēs′), born 1908, U.S. conductor, pianist, and opera director, born in Russia.

gold′ plate′, **1.** tableware or containers made of gold. **2.** a plating, esp. electroplating, of gold.

gold-plate (gōld′plāt′), *v.t.,* **-plat·ed, -plat·ing.** **1.** to coat (base metal) with gold, esp. by electroplating. **2.** to incorporate costly features or refinements into (something) unnecessarily: *The engineers were accused of gold-plating the construction project.*

gold-plat·ing (gōld′plā′ting), *n.* **1.** the incorporation of costly and unnecessary features or refinements into a product or structure. **2.** any expensive nonessential item, convenience, or feature: *an apartment with a sauna and other gold-plating.* [1960–65]

gold′ point′, **1.** the point at which it is equally expensive to buy, sell, export, import, or exchange gold in adjustment of foreign claims or counterclaims. **2.** the melting point of gold, equal to 1036°C and used as a fixed point on the international temperature scale. [1880–85]

gold′ reserve′, the stock of gold held by a government or central bank to back its promissory notes or currency or to settle its international debts. [1865–70, *Amer.*]

gold′ rush′, a large-scale and hasty movement of people to a region where gold has been discovered, as to California in 1849. [1875–80, *Amer.*]

Golds·bor·o (gōldz′bûr′ō, -bur′ō), *n.* a city in E North Carolina. 31,871.

gold·smith (gōld′smith′), *n.* **1.** a person who makes or sells articles of gold. **2.** (formerly) such a person also acting as a banker, moneylender, etc. [bef. 1000; ME, OE. See GOLD, SMITH]

Gold·smith (gōld′smith′), *n.* **Oliver,** 1730?–74, Irish poet, playwright, essayist, and novelist.

gold′smith bee′tle, a brilliant golden scarabaeid beetle, *Cetonia aurata,* of Europe. [1850–55, *Amer.*]

gold′ stand′ard, a monetary system with gold of specified weight and fineness as the unit of value. [1825–35, *Amer.*]

gold′ star′, **1.** a gold-colored star displayed, as on a service flag, to indicate that a member of one's family, organization, or the like, was killed in war as a member of the armed forces. **2.** *Informal.* **a.** symbolic approval or recognition for outstanding merit or effort: *You get the gold star for cooking such a gourmet dinner.* **b.** anything that represents an outstanding effort or achievement: *Her promotion was the gold star she'd been working for.* [1920–25, *Amer.*] **—gold′-star′,** *adj.*

gold′ stick′, (in England) **1.** the gilded rod carried on state occasions by certain members of the royal household. **2.** the bearer of it. [1795–1805]

gold·stone (gōld′stōn′), *n.* aventurine. [1620–30; GOLD + STONE]

gold′ ther′apy, administration of gold salts as a treatment for disease, esp. rheumatoid arthritis. Also called **chrysotherapy.** [1935–40]

gold·thread (gōld′thred′), *n.* a white-flowered plant, *Coptis trifolia,* of the buttercup family, having a slender, yellow root that is sometimes used as a tonic. [1770–80, *Amer.*; GOLD + THREAD]

gold′ trichlo′ride. See **gold chloride.**

gol·durn (gol′dûrn′), *n., adj., adv., v.t. Informal.* goldarn.

gol·durned (gol′dûrnd′), *adj., superl.* **-durned·est,** *adv. Informal.* goldarned.

Gold·was·ser (gōld′vä sər, -wä-, *Ger.* gôlt′vä′səʀ), *n.* a liqueur flavored with spices, figs, lemons, and herbs, and having minute flakes of gold leaf in suspension. [1915–20; < G, equiv. to *Gold* GOLD + *Wasser* water]

Gold·wa·ter (gōld′wô′tər, -wot′ər), *n.* **Barry Morris,** born 1909, U.S. politician: U.S senator 1953–64 and 1968–87.

gold·work (gōld′wûrk′), *n.* work produced by a goldsmith. [1675–85; GOLD + WORK]

Gold·wyn (gōld′win), *n.* **Samuel** (*Samuel Goldfish*), 1882–1974, U.S. movie producer, born in Poland.

Gold·wyn·ism (gōld′wi niz′əm), *n.* a phrase or statement involving a humorous and supposedly unintentional misuse of idiom, as "Keep a stiff upper chin," esp. such a statement attributed to Samuel Goldwyn, as "Include me out." [1935–40; GOLDWYN + -ISM]

go·lem (gō′ləm, -lem), *n.* **1.** *Jewish Folklore.* a figure artificially constructed in the form of a human being and endowed with life. **2.** a stupid and clumsy person; blockhead. **3.** an automaton. [1895–1900; (< Yiddish *goylem*) < Heb *gōlem* embryo, larva, cocoon]

golf (golf, gôlf; *Brit. also* gof), *n.* **1.** a game in which clubs with wooden or metal heads are used to hit a small, white ball into a number of holes, usually 9 or 18, in succession, situated at various distances over a course having natural or artificial obstacles, the object being to get the ball into each hole in as few strokes as possible. **2.** a word used in communications to represent the letter *G.* **—***v.i.* **3.** to play golf. [1425–75; late ME; of uncert. orig.] **—golf′er,** *n.*

golf′ bag′, a bag, usually made of canvas, for carrying golf clubs and golf balls. [1890–95]

golf′ ball′, **1.** a small, white ball with a tough cover and a resilient core of rubber, used in playing golf. **2.** a ball-shaped printing element on certain electric typewriters. [1535–45]

golf′ cart′, **1.** a small, battery-powered, three- or four-wheel vehicle used for transporting one or two golfers and their equipment around a golf course. **2.** See **caddie cart.** [1950–55]

golf′ club′, **1.** any of various long-handled clubs with wooden or metal heads, for hitting the ball in golf. Cf. **iron** (def. 5), **wood^1** (def. 8). **2.** an organization of golf players or the facilities and grounds used by such an organization. [1500–10]

golf′ course′, the ground or course over which golf is played. A standard full-scale golf course has 125 to 175 acres (51 to 71 hectares), usually with 18 holes varying from 100 to 650 yd. (91 to 594 m) in length from tee to cup. Also called **golf′ links′.** [1595–1605]

Golfe du Li·on (gôlf dʏ lē ôɴ′), French name of the Gulf of Lions.

golf′ wid′ow, a woman whose husband frequently leaves her alone while he plays golf. [1915–20]

Gol·gi (gôl′jē), *n.* **Ca·mil·lo** (kä mēl′lô), 1843?–1926, Italian physician and histologist: Nobel prize for medicine 1906.

Gol′gi bod′y, *Cell Biol.* an organelle, consisting of layers of flattened sacs, that takes up and processes secretory and synthetic products from the endoplasmic reticulum and then either releases the finished products into various parts of the cell cytoplasm or secretes them to the outside of the cell. Also called **Gol′gi apparat′us.** See diag. under **cell.** [1920–25]

Gol·go·tha (gol′gə thə), *n.* **1.** a hill near Jerusalem where Jesus was crucified; Calvary. **2.** a place of suffering or sacrifice. **3.** a place of burial. Also, **gol′go·tha** (for defs. 2, 3). [1585–95; < L (Vulgate) < Gk *golgothá* < Aram *gulgaltā,* akin to Heb. *gulgōleth* skull]

gol·iard (gōl′yərd), *n.* (*sometimes cap.*) one of a class of wandering scholar-poets in Germany, France, and England, chiefly in the 12th and 13th centuries, noted as the authors of satirical Latin verse written in celebration of conviviality, sensual pleasures, etc. [1275–1325; ME < OF *goliart, goliard* drunkard, glutton, equiv. to *gole* throat (F *gueule*) + *-ard* -ARD] **—gol·iar·der·y** (gōl yär′də rē), *n.* **—gol·iar′dic,** *adj.*

Go·li·ath (gə lī′əth), *n.* **1.** the giant warrior of the Philistines whom David killed with a stone from a sling. I Sam. 17:48–51. **2.** (*usually l.c.*) a giant. **3.** (*usually l.c.*) a very large, powerful, or influential person or thing: *a neighborhood grocery competing against the supermarket goliaths.*

Goli′ath crane′, a gantry crane for heavy work, as in steel mills. [1890–95; after GOLIATH]

go·lil·la (gō lē′ə, -lēl′yə), *n.* a collar of lawn or linen, slightly rolled under at the edge and starched to stand out from the neckline, worn in Spain in the 17th century. [1665–75; < Sp, dim. of *gola* throat]

gol·li·wogg (gol′ē wog′), *n.* (*sometimes cap.*) **1.** a grotesque black doll. **2.** a grotesque person. Also, **gol′li·wog′.** [1890–95; after the name of a doll in an illustrated series of children's books by Bertha Upton (d. 1912), U.S. writer, and Florence Upton (d. 1922), illustrator]

gol·ly (gol′ē), *interj. Informal.* (used as a mild exclamation expressing surprise, wonder, puzzlement, pleasure, or the like.) [1840–50; euphemistic alter. of GOD]

gol·ly·wob·bler (gol′ē wob′lər), *n. Naut.* a very large quadrilateral staysail set between the foremast and mainmast of a schooner. [orig. uncert.]

go·losh (gə losh′), *n.* galosh.

golp (golp), *n. Heraldry.* a roundel purpure. [1555–65; perh. < Sp *golpe* a wound]

Golsch·mann (gōlsh′män), *n.* **Vlad·i·mir** (vlad′ə mēr′), 1893–1972, French orchestra conductor in the U.S.

Goltz (gôlts), *n.* **Baron Kol·mar von der** (kôl′mäʀ fən dəʀ), 1843–1916, German field marshal.

gom·been (gom bēn′), *n. Irish Eng.* usury. [1860–65; < Ir *gaimbín* interest, esp. exorbitant interest, lit., bit, small piece, dim. of *gamba* lump, hunk]

gom·been-man (gom bēn′man′), *n., pl.* **-men.** *Irish Eng.* a usurer or moneylender. [1880–85]

CONCISE ETYMOLOGY KEY: <, descended or borrowed from; >, whence; b., blend of, blended; c., cognate with; cf., compare; deriv., derivative; equiv., equivalent; imit., imitative; obl., oblique; r., replacing; s., stem; sp., spelling, spelled; resp., respelling, respelled; trans., translation; ?, origin unknown; *, unattested; ‡, probably earlier than. See the full key inside the front cover.

Gom•berg (gom′bûrg), *n.* **Moses,** 1866–1947, U.S. chemist, born in Russia.

gom•bo (gum′bō), *n., pl.* **-bos.** gumbo.

gom•broon (gom bro͞on′), *n.* a type of Persian pottery ware. [1690–1700; after *Gombroon* a town on the Persian Gulf]

Go•mel (gō′məl; *Russ.* gô′myil), *n.* a city in SE Byelorussia (Belarus) on a tributary of the Dnieper. 383,000.

go•mer (gō′mər), *n. Slang.* **1.** an undesirable hospital patient. **2.** an enemy aviator, esp. in a dogfight. [1965–70; of disputed orig.]

gom•er•el (gom′ər əl), *n. Scot. and North Eng.* a fool. Also, **gom′er•al, gom′er•il.** [1805–15; obs. *gome* man (OE *guma;* c. Goth *guma,* L *homō*) + -REL]

Gó•mez (gō′mez; *Sp.* gô′mes), *n.* **Juan Vi•cen•te** (hwän bē sen′te), 1857?–1935, Venezuelan soldier and political leader: commander in chief and dictator of Venezuela 1908–35; president of Venezuela 1908–15, 1922–29, 1931–35.

Gó•mez de la Ser•na (gô′meth *th*e lä seʀ′nä, -mes), **Ra•món** (ʀä môn′), *("Ramón"),* 1888–1963, Spanish novelist, dramatist, biographer, and critic.

gomme′ syr′up (gôm). See **simple syrup** (def. 1).

gom•mie (gom′ē), *n. Canadian Slang (chiefly the Maritime Provinces).* a fool. [Hiberno-E *gom* (akin to *gommel* < Ir *gamal* lout, simpleton) + -IE]

go•mo•ku (gô mô′ko͞o), *n.* gobang. [< Japn *gomoku(-narabe),* equiv. to *go-muku* lit., five eyes + *narabe* line up]

Go•mor•rah (gə môr′ə, -mor′ə), *n.* **1.** Also, *Douay Bible,* **Go•mor′rha.** an ancient city destroyed, with Sodom, because of its wickedness. Gen. 19:24, 25. **2.** any extremely wicked place. —**Go•mor′re•an,** *adj.*

Gom•pers (gom′pərz), *n.* **Samuel,** 1850–1924, U.S. labor leader, born in England: president of the American Federation of Labor 1886–94, 1896–1924.

gom•phi•a•sis (gom fī′ə sis), *n. Dentistry.* looseness of the teeth. [1700–10; < Gk *gomphí(os)* molar tooth + -ASIS]

gom•pho•sis (gom fō′sis), *n., pl.* **-pho•ses** (-fō′sēz). *Anat.* an immovable articulation in which one bone or part is received in a cavity in another, as a tooth in its socket. [1570–80; < NL < Gk *gomphō-,* verbid s. of *gomphoûn* to bolt together (deriv. of *gómphos* bolt, nail) + NL *-sis* -SIS; see -OSIS]

Go•mul•ka (gə mo͝ol′kə), *n.* **Wla•dy•slaw** (vlä di′släf), 1905–82, Polish political leader: First Secretary of the Polish Communist party 1956–70.

go•mu•ti (gə mo͞o′tē), *n., pl.* **-tis. 1.** Also called **gomu′ti palm′, sugar palm.** a sago palm, *Arenga pinnata,* of the East Indies, yielding palm sugar. **2.** a black, horsehairlike fiber obtained from this palm, used for making cords, ropes, cables, etc. [1805–15; prob. < dial. Malay (Moluccas) *gomuti* the stem fibers of the palm; cf. Malay *gəmuti* (sp. *gemuti*)]

gon-, var. of **gono-** before a vowel: *gonidium.*

-gon, a combining form meaning "angled," "angular," used in the formation of compound words: *polygon; pentagon.* Cf. **gonio-.** [< Gk *-gōnos,* deriv. of *gōnía* angle, akin to *góny* KNEE]

go•nad (gō′nad, gon′ad), *n. Anat.* a sex gland in which gametes are produced; an ovary or testis. [1875–80; < NL *gonad-* (s. of *gonas*), equiv. to *gon-* GON- + *-ad-* -AD[1]] —**go•nad′al, go•na•di•al** (gō nā′dē əl), **go•nad•ic** (gō nad′ik), *adj.*

go•nad•o•trope (gō nad′ə trōp′), *n. Biochem.* a gonadotropic substance. [GONAD + -O- + -TROPE]

go•nad•o•trop•ic (gō nad′ə trop′ik, -trō′pik, gon′ə-dō-), *adj. Biochem.* pertaining to substances formed in the anterior pituitary gland that affect the activity of the ovary or testis. Also, **go•nad•o•troph•ic** (gō nad′ə trof′-ik, -trō′fik, gon′ə dō-). [1930–35; GONAD + -O- + -TROPIC]

go•nad•o•tro•pin (gō nad′ə trō′pin, gon′ə dō-), *n. Biochem.* a gonadotropic substance. Also, **go•nad•o•tro•phin** (gō nad′ə trō′fin, gon′ə dō-). Cf. **chorionic gonadotropin.** [1935–40; GONADOTROP(IC) + -IN[2]]

gonadotro′pin releas′ing hor′mone, 1. *Biochem.* a peptide hormone, produced by the hypothalamus, that stimulates the anterior lobe of the pituitary gland to secrete luteinizing hormone and follicle-stimulating hormone. **2.** *Pharm.* a preparation of this hormone, used to treat precocious puberty, prostate cancer, male and female infertility, and female reproductive disorders. *Abbr.:* GnRH Also, **go•nad′o•tro′pin-re•leas′ing hor′•mone.**

Go•na•ïves (*Fr.* gô nᴀ ēv′), *n.* **1. Gulf of,** an inlet of the Caribbean Sea, between the two peninsulas of W Haiti. **2.** a seaport in W Haiti. 25,925.

go•nan•gi•um (gō nan′jē əm), *n., pl.* **-gi•a** (-jē ə), **-gi•ums.** a reproductive polyp of a colonial hydroid, giving rise asexually to medusa buds. [1870–75; < NL, equiv. to *gon-* GON- + Gk *angeîon* vessel, reservoir; see -IUM] —**go•nan′gi•al,** *adj.*

Go•nâve (gō näv′; *Fr.* gô nᴀv′), *n.* **1.** Also called **Gonâve′ Is′land.** an island in the Gulf of Gonaïves, in W Haiti. 287 sq. mi. (743 sq. km). **2. Gulf of.** Also called **Gonâve′ Gulf′.** Gonaïves (def. 1). Also, **Go•nave** (gō näv′).

Gon•çal•ves Di•as (gôɴ sôl′vis dē′äs), **An•to•nio** (ᴀɴ tô′nyo͝o), 1823–64, Brazilian poet.

Gon•cha•rov (gon′chə rôf′, -rof′; *Russ.* gən chyi ʀôf′), *n.* **I•van A•le•xan•dro•vich** (i vän′ al′ig zan′drə vich, -zän′-, ī′vən; *Russ.* ē vän′ u lyi ksän′dʀə vyich), 1812–91, Russian novelist.

Gon•court (gôɴ ko͞oʀ′; *for 2 also Eng.* gon ko͝or′), *n.* **1. Ed•mond Louis An•toine Hu•ot de** (ed môɴ′ lwē äɴ twᴀɴ′ y ō′ də), 1822–96, and his brother **Jules Al•fred Huot de** (zhyl ᴀl fʀed′), 1830–70, French art critics, novelists, and historians: collaborators until the death of Jules. **2. Prix** (pʀē; *Eng.* prē), an annual award of money made by a French literary society **(Académie Goncourt)** for the best prose work of the year.

Gond (gond), *n.* a member of an aboriginal people of Dravidian stock, in central India and the Deccan.

Gon•dar (gon′dər), *n.* a city in NW Ethiopia, N of Lake Tana: a former capital. 38,600.

Gon•di (gon′dē), *n.* a Dravidian language, the language of the Gonds.

gon•do•la (gon′dl ə *or, esp. for 1,* gon dō′lə), *n.* **1.** a long, narrow, flat-bottomed boat having a tall, ornamental stem and stern and sometimes a small cabin for passengers, rowed or poled by a single person who stands at the stern, facing forward: used esp. on the canals of Venice, Italy. **2.** a passenger compartment suspended beneath a balloon or airship. Cf. **car[1]** (def. 4). **3.** an enclosed cabin suspended from an overhead cable, used to transport passengers up and down a ski slope or over scenic or treacherous terrain. **4.** Also called **gon′dola car′.** an open railroad freight car with low sides, for transporting bulk freight and manufactured goods. **5.** a truck whose bed or trailer is a hopper, as for transporting mixed cement. **6.** a freestanding structure for displaying merchandise in a retail establishment, as a supermarket. **7.** a chair or couch having a gondola back. [1540–50; < It < Venetian, prob. < MGk *kontoúra* small boat used in coastal navigation, n. use of fem. of *kóntouros* short, clipped, lit., dock-tailed, equiv. to LGk *kont(ós), kond(ós)* short + Gk *-ouros* -tailed, adj. deriv. of *ourá* tail]

gondola (def. 1) (Venetian)

gon′dola back′, a chair or couch back curving forward and downward to form arms.

gon•do•let•ta (gon′dl et′ə), *n.* a small Venetian gondola. Also, **gon•do•let** (gon′dl et′). [1595–1605; < It, dim. of GONDOLA]

gon•do•lier (gon′dl ēr′), *n.* a person who rows or poles a gondola. [1595–1605; < It *gondoliere.* See GONDOLA, -IER[2]]

Gon•do•mar (gôn′dô mäʀ′), *n.* **Die•go Sar•mien•to de A•cu•ña** (dye′gô säʀ myen′tô *th*e ä ko͞o′nyä), **Count of,** 1567–1626, Spanish diplomat.

Gond•wa•na (gond wä′nə), *n.* a hypothetical landmass in the Southern Hemisphere that separated toward the end of the Paleozoic Era to form South America, Africa, Antarctica, and Australia. Also called **Gond•wa′na•land′.** Cf. **Laurasia.** [1870–75]

gone (gôn, gon), *v.* **1.** pp. of **go[1].** —*adj.* **2.** departed; left. **3.** lost or hopeless. **4.** ruined. **5.** that has passed away; dead. **6.** past. **7.** weak and faint: *a gone feeling.* **8.** used up. **9.** *Slang.* **a.** pregnant: *two months gone.* **b.** great; outstanding. **c.** exhilarated; inspired. **10. far gone, a.** much advanced; deeply involved. **b.** nearly exhausted; almost worn out. **c.** dying: *The rescue party finally reached the scene of the crash, but most of the survivors were already far gone.* **11. gone on,** *Informal.* infatuated with; in love with: *He is still gone on the woman who jilted him.*

gone′ away′, *Fox Hunting.* the cry uttered by the huntsman as a signal to the field that the hounds are in full cry and the hunt is on.

gone•ness (gôn′nis, gon′-), *n.* a sinking sensation; exhaustion or faintness. [1840–50, *Amer.;* GONE + -NESS]

G_1 phase, *Cell Biol.* the first growth period of the cell cycle, during interphase, in which the cell grows and cytoplasmic organelles are replicated. [*G* abbr. for *growth*]

gon•er (gô′nər, gon′ər), *n. Informal.* a person or thing that is dead, lost, or past recovery. [1840–50; GONE + -ER[1]]

Gon•er•il (gon′ər il), *n.* (in Shakespeare's *King Lear*) the elder of Lear's two faithless daughters. Cf. **Cordelia, Regan.**

Gone′ With the Wind′ (wind), a novel (1936) by Margaret Mitchell.

gon•fa•lon (gon′fə lən), *n.* **1.** a banner suspended from a crossbar, often with several streamers or tails. **2.** a standard, esp. one used by the medieval Italian republics. [1585–95; < It *gonfalone* < MF *gonfalon, gonfanon* < Gmc; see GONFANON]

gon•fa•lon•ier (gon′fə lə nēr′), *n.* **1.** the bearer of a gonfalon. **2.** a chief magistrate or some other elected official in any of several medieval Italian republics. [1580–90; < F < It *gonfaloniere.* See GONFALON, -IER[2]]

gon•fa•non (gon′fə nən), *n.* a gonfalon that hangs directly from a pole, esp. from the shaft of a lance just below the lance head. [1250–1300; ME *go(u)nfano(u)n* < OF *gunfanun, gonfanon,* OPr *gonfano* < Gmc; cf. OHG *gund* (OE *gūth*) battle, G *Fahne* flag]

gong (gông, gong), *n.* **1.** a large bronze disk, of Asian origin, having an upturned rim, that produces a vibrant, hollow tone when struck, usually with a stick or hammer that has a padded head. **2.** a shallow bell sounded by a hammer operated electrically or mechanically: *The fire-alarm system will automatically sound the gong.* **3.** (in a clock or watch) a rod or wire, either straight or bent into a spiral, on which the time is struck. **4.** *Brit. Slang.* a medal or military decoration. —*v.i.* **5.** to sound as a gong does; ring, chime, or reverberate. [1800–10; < Malay, Javanese: any suspended bossed and rimmed gong; presumably imit.] —**gong′like′,** *adj.*

gong′ buoy, *Naut.* a buoy in which one or more gongs are struck by hammers that swing freely with the motion of the buoy.

Gón•go•ra y Ar•go•te (gông′gô ʀä′ ē äʀ gô′te), **Luis de** (lwēs de), 1561–1627, Spanish poet.

Gon•go•rism (gong′gə riz′əm, gông′-), *n.* imitation of the ornate and intricate style of Góngora y Argote. [1805–15; < Sp *gongorismo.* See GÓNGORA Y ARGOTE, -ISM] —**Gon′go•rist,** *n.* —**Gon′go•ris′tic,** *adj.*

go•nid•i•um (gə nid′ē əm), *n., pl.* **-nid•i•a** (-nid′ē ə). **1.** (in algae) any one-celled asexual reproductive body, as a tetraspore or zoospore. **2.** an algal cell, or a filament of an alga, growing within the thallus of a lichen. [1835–45; < NL, equiv. to *gon-* GON- + *-idium* n. suffix] —**go•nid′i•al, go•nid′ic,** *adj.* —**go•nid′i•oid′,** *adj.*

gon•if (gon′əf), *n.* ganef. Also, **gon′iff.**

gonio-, a combining form meaning "angle," used in the formation of compound words: *goniometer.* Cf. **-gon.** [< Gk, comb. form of *gōnía*]

go•ni•om•e•ter (gō′nē om′i tər), *n.* an instrument for measuring solid angles, as of crystals. [1760–70; GONIO- + -METER] —**go•ni•o•met•ric** (gō′nē ə me′trik), **go′ni•o•met′ri•cal,** *adj.* —**go′ni•o•met′ri•cal•ly,** *adv.* —**go′•ni•om′e•try,** *n.*

go•ni•on (gō′nē on′), *n., pl.* **-ni•a** (-nē ə). *Craniom.* a point on each side of the lower jaw at the mandibular angle. [1875–80]

go•ni•o•scope (gō′nē ə skōp′), *n.* an optical instrument used for measuring the angle of the anterior chamber of the eye. [GONIO- + -SCOPE] —**go•ni•os•co•py** (gō′nē os′kə pē), *n.* —**go•ni•o•scop•ic** (gō′nē ə skop′-ik), *adj.*

go•ni•um (gō′nē əm), *n., pl.* **-ni•a** (-nē ə). *Cell Biol.* the germ cell during the phase marked by mitosis. [< NL; see GON-, -IUM]

-gonium, a combining form of **gonium:** *archegonium.*

gon•na (gô′nə; *unstressed* gə nə), *Pron. Spelling.* going to: *Are we gonna go soon?*

gono-, a combining form meaning "sexual," "reproductive," used in the formation of compound words: *gonophore.* Also, *esp. before a vowel,* **gon-.** [< Gk, comb. form of *gónos, gonḗ* seed, generation; akin to L *genus,* Skt *janas*]

gon•o•coc•cus (gon′ə kok′əs), *n., pl.* **-coc•ci** (-kok′sī, -sē). the bacterium *Neisseria gonorrhoeae,* causing gonorrhea. [1885–90; GONO- + -COCCUS] —**gon′o•coc′cal, gon•o•coc•cic** (gon′ə kok′sik), *adj.* —**gon′o•coc′coid,** *adj.*

go/no-go (gō′nō′gō′), *adj.* being or relating to a decision as to whether or not to proceed as planned or to the time at which such a decision must be made. Also, **go′-no′-go′, go or no-go.** [1940–45]

gon•o•phore (gon′ə fôr′, -fōr′), *n. Zool.* an asexually produced bud in hydrozoans that gives rise to the equivalent of a medusa. [1825–35; GONO- + -PHORE] —**gon•o•phor•ic** (gon′ə fôr′ik, -for′-), **go•noph•o•rous** (gō-nof′ər əs), *adj.*

gon•o•po•di•um (gon′ə pō′dē əm), *n., pl.* **-po•di•a** (-pō′dē ə). *Ichthyol.* the modified anal fin of a male poeciliid fish, serving as an organ of copulation. [GONO- + -PODIUM] —**gon′o•po′di•al,** *adj.*

gon•o•pore (gon′ə pôr′, -pōr′), *n. Zool.* an opening through which eggs or sperm are released, esp. in invertebrates. [1895–1900; GONO- + PORE[2]]

gon•or•rhe•a (gon′ə rē′ə), *n. Pathol.* a contagious, purulent inflammation of the urethra or the vagina, caused by the gonococcus. Also, *esp. Brit.,* **gon′or•rhoe′a.** [1540–50; < LL < Gk *gonórrhoia.* See GONO-, -RRHEA] —**gon′or•rhe′al,** *adj.* —**gon′or•rhe′ic,** *adj.*

gon•o•the•ca (gon′ə thē′kə), *n., pl.* **-cae** (-sē). *Zool.* the part of the perisarc covering a gonangium. [1860–65; GONO- + THECA] —**gon′o•the′cal,** *adj.*

-gony, a combining form meaning "production," "genesis," "origination," used in the formation of compound words: *theogony; cosmogony.* [< L *-gonia* < Gk *-goneia,* equiv. to *gón(os)* (see GON-) + *-eia* -Y[3]]

go•ny•au•lax (gō′nē ô′laks), *n.* any marine dinoflagellate of the genus *Gonyaulax,* sometimes occurring in great numbers and causing red tide. [< NL < Gk *góny* KNEE + *aûlax* furrow]

gon•y•camp•sis (gon′ə kamp′sis), *n.* abnormal curvature of the knee. [< Gk *góny* KNEE + *kámpsis* bending, curving, equiv. to *kámp(tein)* to bend + *-sis* -SIS]

go•nys (gō′nis), *n.* the ridge along the tip of the lower mandible of a bird's bill at the junction of the two joined halves, esp. prominent in gulls. [1830–40; < NL, prob. erroneously for Gk *génys* jaw] —**go•nyd•e•al, go•nyd•i•al** (gō nid′ē əl), *adj.*

Gon•zal•es (gən zä′lis), *n.* **Richard Alonzo** *("Pancho"),* born 1928, U.S. tennis player.

gon•zo (gon′zō), *Slang.* —*adj.* **1.** (of journalism, reportage, etc.) filled with bizarre or subjective ideas, commentary, or the like. **2.** crazy; eccentric. —*n.* **3.** eccentricity, weirdness, or craziness. [1970–75, *Amer.;* appar. first used in the phrase *Gonzo journalism* by U.S. journalist Hunter S. Thompson (b. 1939); perh. < It: simpleton, one easily duped (of uncert. orig.) or < Sp *ganso* a lazy or dull person, lit., goose (< Gmc; see GOOSE)]

goo (go͞o), *n. Informal.* **1.** a thick or sticky substance: *Wash that goo off your hands.* **2.** maudlin sentimentality. [1910–15, *Amer.;* perh. short for BURGOO]

goo•ber (go͞o′bər), *n. South Midland and Southern U.S.* the peanut. Also called **goo′ber pea′.** [1825–35; of Afr orig.; cf. Kimbundu *nguba* peanut]

Gooch (go͞och), *n.* **George Peabody,** 1873–1968, English historian.

good (go͝od), *adj.,* **bet•ter, best,** *n., interj., adv.* —*adj.* **1.** morally excellent; virtuous; righteous; pious: *a good man.* **2.** satisfactory in quality, quantity, or degree: *a good teacher; good health.* **3.** of high quality; excellent. **4.** right; proper; fit: *It is good that you are here. His credentials are good.* **5.** well-behaved: *a good child.* **6.** kind, beneficent, or friendly: *to do a good deed.* **7.** honorable or worthy; in good standing: *a good name.* **8.** educated and refined: *She has a good background.* **9.** financially sound or safe: *His credit is good.* **10.** genuine; not counterfeit: *a good quarter.* **11.** sound or valid: *good judgment; good reasons.* **12.** reliable; dependable; responsible: *good advice.* **13.** healthful; beneficial: *Fresh fruit is good for you.* **14.** in excellent condition; healthy: *good teeth.* **15.** not spoiled or tainted; edible; palatable: *The meat was still good after three months in the freezer.* **16.** favorable; propitious: *good news.* **17.** cheerful; optimistic; amiable: *in good spirits.* **18.** free of distress or pain; comfortable: *to feel good after surgery.* **19.** agreeable; pleasant: *Have a good time.* **20.** attractive; handsome: *She has a good figure.* **21.** (of the complexion) smooth; free from blemish. **22.** close or intimate; warm: *She's a good friend of mine.* **23.** sufficient or ample: *a good supply.* **24.** advantageous; satisfactory for the purpose: *a good day for fishing.* **25.** competent or skillful; clever: *a good manager; good at arithmetic.* **26.** skillfully or expertly done: *a really good job; a good play.* **27.** conforming to rules of grammar, usage, etc.; correct: *good English.* **28.** socially proper: *good manners.* **29.** remaining available to one: *Don't throw good money after bad.* **30.** comparatively new or of relatively fine quality: *Don't play in the mud in your good clothes.* **31.** best or most dressy: *He wore his good suit to the office today.* **32.** full: *a good day's journey away.* **33.** fairly large or great: *a good amount.* **34.** free from precipitation or cloudiness: *good weather.* **35.** *Med.* (of a patient's condition) having stable and normal vital signs, being conscious and comfortable, and having excellent appetite, mobility, etc. **36.** fertile; rich: *good soil.* **37.** loyal: *a good Democrat.* **38.** (of a return or service in tennis, squash, handball, etc.) landing within the limits of a court or section of a court. **39.** *Horse Racing.* (of the surface of a track) drying after a rain so as to be still slightly sticky: *This horse runs best on a good track.* **40.** (of meat, esp. beef) noting or pertaining to the specific grade below "choice," containing more lean muscle and less edible fat than "prime" or "choice." **41.** favorably regarded (used as an epithet for a ship, town, etc.): *the good ship Syrena.* **42. as good as.** See **as**[1] (def. 18). **43. good for, a.** certain to repay (money owed) because of integrity, financial stability, etc. **b.** the equivalent in value of: *Two thousand stamps are good for one coffeepot.* **c.** able to survive or continue functioning for (the length of time or the distance indicated): *These tires are good for another 10,000 miles.* **d.** valid or in effect for (the length of time indicated): *a license good for one year.* **e.** (used as an expression of approval): *Good for you!* **44. good full,** *Naut.* (of a sail or sails) well filled, esp. when sailing close to the wind; clean full; rap full. **45. make good, a.** to make recompense for; repay. **b.** to implement an agreement; fulfill. **c.** to be successful. **d.** to substantiate; verify. **e.** to carry out; accomplish; execute: *The convicts made good their getaway.* **46. no good,** without value or merit; worthless; contemptible: *The check was no good.*
—*n.* **47.** profit or advantage; worth; benefit: *What good will that do? We shall work for the common good.* **48.** excellence or merit; kindness: *to do good.* **49.** moral righteousness; virtue: *to be a power for good.* **50.** (esp. in the grading of U.S. beef) an official grade below that of "choice." **51. goods, a.** possessions, esp. movable effects or personal property. **b.** articles of trade; wares; merchandise: *canned goods.* **c.** *Informal.* what has been promised or is expected: *to deliver the goods.* **d.** *Informal.* the genuine article. **e.** *Informal.* evidence of guilt, as stolen articles: *to catch someone with the goods.* **f.** cloth or textile material: *top-quality linen goods.* **g.** *Chiefly Brit.* merchandise sent by land, rather than by water or air. **52. come to no good,** to end in failure or as a failure: *Her jealous relatives said that she would come to no good.* **53. for good,** finally and permanently; forever: *to leave the country for good.* Also, **for good and all.** **54. the good, a.** the ideal of goodness or morality. **b.** good things or persons collectively. **55. to the good, a.** generally advantageous: *That's all to the good, but what do I get out of it?* **b.** richer in profit or gain: *When he withdrew from the partnership, he was several thousand dollars to the good.*
—*interj.* **56.** (used as an expression of approval or satisfaction): *Good! Now we can all go home.*
—*adv.* **57.** *Informal.* well. **58. good and,** *Informal.* very; completely; exceedingly: *This soup is good and hot.* [bef. 900; ME (adj., adv., and n.); OE *gōd* (adj.); c. D *goed,* G *gut,* ON *gōthr,* Goth *goths*]
—Syn. 1. pure, moral, conscientious, meritorious, worthy, exemplary, upright. **2.** commendable, admirable. **5.** obedient, heedful. **6.** kindly, benevolent, humane, gracious, obliging. **23.** full, adequate. **24.** profitable, useful, serviceable, beneficial. **25.** efficient, proficient, capable, able, ready, suited, suitable, dexterous, expert, adroit, apt. **51.** See **property.**
—Usage. GOOD is common as an adverb in informal speech, especially after forms of *do: He did good on the test. She sees good with her new glasses.* This use does not occur in formal speech or edited writing, where the adverb WELL is used instead: *He did well on the test. She sees well with her new glasses.*
The adjective GOOD is standard after linking verbs like *taste, smell, look, feel, be,* and *seem: Everything tastes good. The biscuits smell good. You're looking good today.* When used after *look* or *feel,* GOOD may refer to spirits as well as health: *I'm feeling pretty good this morning, ready to take on the world.* WELL is both an adjective and an adverb. As an adjective used after *look, feel,* or other linking verbs, it often refers to good health: *You're looking well; we missed you while you were in the hospital.* See also **bad.**

good′ afternoon′, a conventional expression used at meeting or parting in the afternoon.

good′ behav′ior, 1. satisfactory, proper, or polite conduct. **2.** conduct conformable to law; orderly conduct: *The convict's sentence was reduced for good behavior.* **3.** proper fulfillment of the duties of an office, esp. a public office: *The incumbent could not be discharged during good behavior.*

Good′ Book′, the Bible.

good′ bud′dy, 1. *CB Radio Slang.* the operator of a CB radio; fellow operator (often used as a form of direct address while broadcasting). **2.** *Informal.* a trusted companion or colleague; friend.

good-by (go͝od′bī′), *interj., n., pl.* **-bys.** good-bye. Also, **good′by′.**

good-bye (go͝od′bī′), *interj., n., pl.* **-byes.** —*interj.* **1.** farewell (a conventional expression used at parting). —*n.* **2.** a farewell. Also, **good′bye′.** [1565–75; contr. of *God be with ye*]

good′ cheer′, 1. cheerful spirits; courage: *to be of good cheer.* **2.** feasting and merrymaking: *to make good cheer.* **3.** good food and drink: *to be fond of good cheer.*

Good′ Con′duct Med′al, *U.S. Mil.* a medal awarded an enlisted person for meritorious behavior during the period of service.

good′ day′, a conventional expression used at meeting or parting during the daytime. [1175–1225; ME]

good′ egg′, *Informal.* a person who is pleasant, agreeable, or trustworthy. [1915–20]

good′ eve′ning, a conventional expression used at meeting or parting in the evening. [1860–65]

good′ faith′, accordance with standards of honesty, trust, sincerity, etc. (usually prec. by *in*): *If you act in good faith, he'll have no reason to question your motives.* Cf. **bad faith.** [1890–95]

good′ fel′low, a friendly and pleasant person. [1175–1225; ME]

good-fel•low•ship (go͝od′fel′ō ship′), *n.* a pleasant, convivial spirit; comradeship; geniality. [1350–1400; ME]

good-for-noth•ing (go͝od′fər nuth′ing, -nuth′-), *adj.* **1.** worthless; of no use. —*n.* **2.** a worthless or useless person. [1705–15]

Good′ Fri′day, the Friday before Easter, a holy day of the Christian church, observed as the anniversary of the Crucifixion of Jesus. [1250–1300; ME]

good-heart•ed (go͝od′här′tid), *adj.* kind or generous; considerate; benevolent. Also, **good′heart′ed.** [1545–55] **—good′-heart′ed•ly, good′heart′ed•ly,** *adv.* **—good′-heart′ed•ness, good′heart′edness,** *n.*

Good′ Hope′, Cape of. See **Cape of Good Hope.**

Good•hue (go͝od′hyo͞o), *n.* **Bertram Gros•ve•nor** (grōv′nər, grō′və-), 1869–1924, U.S. architect.

good′ hu′mor, a cheerful or amiable mood. [1610–20]

good-hu•mored (go͝od′hyo͞o′mərd *or, often,* -yo͞o′-), *adj.* having or showing a pleasant, amiable mood: *a good-humored man; a good-humored remark.* Also, *esp. Brit.,* **good′-hu′moured.** [1655–65] **—good′-hu′mored•ly,** *adv.* **—good′-hu′mored•ness,** *n.*
—Syn. sunny, cheerful, affable, cheery, warm-hearted.

good•ie (go͝od′ē), *n., interj. Informal.* goody[1]. [GOOD + -IE]

good•ish (go͝od′ish), *adj.* rather good; fairly good. [1750–60; GOOD + -ISH[1]]

good′ Joe′, *Informal.* a warm-hearted, good-natured person. [1940–45]

Good-King-Hen•ry (go͝od′king′hen′rē), *n., pl.* **-ries.** a European, chenopodiaceous weed, *Chenopodium bonus-henricus,* naturalized in North America, having spinachlike leaves. Also called **mercury.** [1895–1900]

good′ life′, 1. a life abounding in material comforts and luxuries. **2.** a life lived according to the moral and religious laws of one's culture. [1945–50]

good-look•er (go͝od′lo͝ok′ər), *n. Informal.* a person with a pleasingly attractive appearance. [1890–95, *Amer.;* GOOD-LOOK(ING) or GOOD LOOK(S) + -ER[1]]

good-look•ing (go͝od′lo͝ok′ing), *adj.* of good or attractive appearance; handsome or beautiful: *a good-looking young man; a good-looking hat.* [1770–80]

good′ looks′, good or attractive personal appearance; handsomeness or beauty. [1790–1800]

good•ly (go͝od′lē), *adj.,* **-li•er, -li•est. 1.** of good or substantial size, amount, etc.: *a goodly sum.* **2.** of good or fine appearance. **3.** *Archaic.* of a good quality: *a goodly gift.* [bef. 1000; ME; OE *gōdlīc.* See GOOD, -LY] **—good′li•ness,** *n.*

good•man (go͝od′mən), *n., pl.* **-men.** *Archaic.* **1.** the master of a household; husband. **2.** (*cap.*) a title of respect used for a man below the rank of gentleman, esp. a farmer or yeoman. [1125–75; ME; see GOOD, -MAN]

Good•man (go͝od′mən), *n.* **Benjamin David** ("**Benny**"), 1909–86, U.S. jazz clarinetist and bandleader.

good′ morn′ing, a conventional expression at meeting or parting in the morning.

good′ mor′row, *Archaic.* good morning. [1350–1400; ME]

good′ na′ture, pleasant disposition; kindly nature; amiability. [1400–50; late ME]

good-na•tured (go͝od′nā′chərd), *adj.* having or showing a pleasant, kindly disposition; amiable: *a warm, good-natured person.* [1570–80] **—good′-na′tured•ly,** *adv.* **—good′-na′tured•ness,** *n.*
—Syn. agreeable, willing, cheerful, equable.

good-neigh•bor (go͝od′nā′bər), *adj.* characterized by friendly political relations and mutual aid between countries. [1925–30]

Good′ Neigh′bor Pol′icy, a diplomatic policy of the U.S., first presented in 1933 by President Roosevelt, for the encouragement of friendly relations and mutual defense among the nations of the Western Hemisphere.

good•ness (go͝od′nis), *n.* **1.** the state or quality of being good. **2.** moral excellence; virtue. **3.** kindly feeling; kindness; generosity. **4.** excellence of quality: *goodness of workmanship.* **5.** the best part of anything; essence; strength. **6.** a euphemism for God: *Thank goodness!* —*interj.* **7.** (used in expressions of surprise, alarm, etc.): *Goodness, you gave me a start! Goodness gracious!* [bef. 900; ME; OE *gōdnes.* See GOOD, -NESS]
—Syn. 2. integrity, honesty, uprightness, probity. GOODNESS, MORALITY, VIRTUE refer to qualities of character or conduct that entitle the possessor to approval and esteem. GOODNESS is the simple word for the general quality recognized in character or conduct: *Many could tell of her goodness and kindness.* MORALITY implies conformity to the recognized standards of right conduct: *a citizen of the highest morality.* VIRTUE is a rather formal word, and suggests usually GOODNESS that is consciously or steadily maintained, often in spite of temptations or evil influences: *of unassailable virtue; firm and of unwavering virtue.* **3.** benevolence, benignity, humanity. **4.** worth, value. **—Ant. 1.** badness, evil.

good′ news′, *Informal.* someone or something that is positive, encouraging, uplifting, desirable, or the like. [1970–75]

good′ night′, an expression of farewell used in parting at nighttime or when going to sleep. [1325–75; ME]

good-night (go͝od′nīt′), *n.* a farewell or leave-taking: *He said his good-nights before leaving the party.*

good′ of′fices, 1. influence, esp. with a person in a position of power: *He got the job through the good offices of his uncle.* **2.** services rendered by a mediator in a dispute. [1900–05]

good-oh (go͝od′ō), *Brit. Informal.* —*interj.* **1.** good (used as an expression of approval, agreement, or admiration). —*adv.* **2.** all right. **3.** yes. Also, **good′-o.** [1915–20]

good′ old′ boy′, *Informal.* **1.** a male who embodies the unsophisticated good fellowship and sometimes boisterous sociability regarded as typical of white males of small towns and rural areas of the South. **2.** a person who belongs to a network of friends and associates with close ties of loyalty and mutual support. Also, **good′ ol′ boy′** (ōl), **good′ ole′ boy′** (ōl). [1970–75] **—good′ old′ boy′ism.**

Good•rich (go͝od′rich), *n.* **Samuel Gris•wold** (griz′wəld, -wōld, -wôld), ("*Peter Parley*"), 1793–1860, U.S. author and publisher.

good′ Samar′itan, a person who gratuitously gives help or sympathy to those in distress. Luke 10:30–37. Also, **Good′ Samar′itan.** [1840–50]

good′ Samar′itan law′, a law that exempts from legal liability persons, sometimes only physicians, who give reasonable aid to strangers in grave physical distress.

goods′ en′gine, *Brit.* a railway locomotive used to haul a freight train.

Good′ Shep′herd, Jesus Christ. John 10:11–14.

good-sized (go͝od′sīzd′), *adj.* of ample or large size; rather large for its kind: *a good-sized pumpkin.* [1830–40]

good′ speed′, good luck; success: *to wish someone good speed.*

Good•speed (go͝od′spēd′), *n.* **Edgar Johnson,** 1871–1962, U.S. Biblical scholar and translator.

goods′ train′, *Brit.* See **freight train.** [1880–85]

goods′ wag′on, *Brit.* a heavy railroad freight car. [1885–90]

goods′ yard′, *Brit.* a railway freight yard. [1890–95]

good-tem•pered (go͝od′tem′pərd), *adj.* good-natured; amiable. [1760–70] **—good′-tem′pered•ly,** *adv.* **—good′-tem′pered•ness,** *n.*

good′ time′, *Prison Slang.* time deducted from an inmate's sentence for good behavior while in prison.

good′-time Char′lie (go͝od′tīm′), *Informal.* an affable, sociable, pleasure-loving man. Also, **good′-time Char′ley.** [1955–60]

good′ ti′tle, *Law.* See **marketable title.**

good′ use′, (in a language) standard use or usage. Also, **good′ us′age.**

good•wife (go͝od′wīf′), *n., pl.* **-wives** (-wīvz′). **1.** *Chiefly Scot.* the mistress of a household. **2.** (*cap.*) *Archaic.* a title of respect for a woman. [1275–1325; ME; see GOOD, WIFE]

good•will (go͝od′wil′), *n.* **1.** friendly disposition; benevolence; kindness. **2.** cheerful acquiescence or consent. **3.** *Com.* an intangible, salable asset arising from the reputation of a business and its relations with its customers, distinct from the value of its stock and other tangible assets. Also, **good′ will′.** [bef. 900; ME; OE *gōd willa.* See GOOD, WILL[2]]
—Syn. 1. friendliness. See **favor.**

good•will•y (go͝od′wil′ē), *n., pl.* **-will•ies,** *adj. Scot. Obs.* —*n.* **1.** a volunteer. —*adj.* **2.** liberal; generous. **3.** cordial; friendly. Also, **good′wil′ie, guidwillie.** [1525–35; GOOD + WILL[2] + -Y[1]; cf. D *goedwillig,* G *gutwillig*]

Good′win Sands′ (go͝od′win), a line of shoals at the

CONCISE ETYMOLOGY KEY: <, descended or borrowed from; >, whence; b., blend of, blended; c., cognate with; cf., compare; deriv., derivative; equiv., equivalent; imit., imitative; obl., oblique; r., replacing; s., stem; sp., spelling, spelled; resp., respelling, respelled; trans., translation; ?, origin unknown; *, unattested; ‡, probably earlier than. See the full key inside the front cover.

N entrance to the Strait of Dover, off the SE coast of England. 10 mi. (16 km) long.

good·y[1] (go͝od′ē), *n., pl.* **good·ies,** *interj. Informal.* —*n.* **1.** Usually, **goodies.** something especially attractive or pleasing, esp. cake, cookies, or candy. **2.** something that causes delight or satisfaction: *A record collector played some goodies for me on his phonograph.* —*interj.* **3.** good (used to express childish delight). Also, **goodie.** [1750–60; GOOD + -Y[2], as n. suffix]

good·y[2] (go͝od′ē), *adj.* goody-goody. [1805–15; appar. GOOD + -Y[2], with attenuating or pejorative value, prob. influenced by GOODY TWO SHOES]

good·y[3] (go͝od′ē), *n., pl.* **good·ies.** *Archaic.* a polite term of address for a woman of humble social standing. [1550–60; GOOD(WIFE) + -Y[2]; cf. HUSSY]

Good·year (go͝od′yēr′), *n.* **Charles,** 1800–60, U.S. inventor: developer of the process of vulcanizing rubber.

good·y-good·y (go͝od′ē go͝od′ē), *n., pl.* **-good·ies,** *adj.* —*n.* **1.** a person who is self-righteously, affectedly, or cloyingly good. —*adj.* **2.** self-righteously or cloyingly good; affecting goodness. [1870–75; redupl. of GOODY[2]]

good′y two′ shoes′, *pl.* **goody two shoes.** (*sometimes caps.*) a goody-goody. [after the title character of *The History of Little Goody Two-Shoes* (1765), a nursery tale perh. written by Oliver Goldsmith]

goo·ey (go͞o′ē), *adj.,* **goo·i·er, goo·i·est. 1.** like or covered with goo; sticky; viscid. **2.** *Informal.* extremely sentimental or emotionally effusive. [1905–10, *Amer.*; GOO + -EY[1]]

goof (go͞of), *Slang.* —*v.i.* **1.** to blunder; make an error, misjudgment, etc. **2.** to waste or kill time; evade work or responsibility (often fol. by *off* or *around*): *Exam week is not a time to goof off. We goofed around till train time.* —*v.t.* **3.** to spoil or make a mess of (something); botch; bungle (often fol. by *up*): *You really goofed up the job.* **4. goof on,** *Slang.* to tease, ridicule, or mock; make fun of. —*n.* **5.** a foolish or stupid person. **6.** a mistake or blunder, esp. one due to carelessness. **7.** a source of fun or cause for amusement: *We short-sheeted his bunk just for a goof.* [1915–20; appar. var. of obs. *goff* dolt < MF *goffe* awkward, stupid]

goof·ball (go͞of′bôl′), *n. Slang.* **1.** an extremely incompetent, eccentric, or silly person. **2.** a pill containing a barbiturate or a tranquilizing drug. [1935–40; GOOF + BALL[1]]

goof-off (go͞of′ôf′, -of′), *n. Slang.* a person who habitually shirks work or responsibility; idler. [1950–55; n. use of v. phrase *goof off*]

goof-up (go͞of′up′), *n. Slang.* **1.** a person who habitually makes mistakes, spoils things, gets into trouble, etc., esp. through carelessness or irresponsibility. **2.** a mistake, blunder, malfunction, or the like. Also, **goof′up′.** [1940–45; n. use of v. phrase *goof up*]

goof·y (go͞o′fē), *adj.,* **goof·i·er, goof·i·est.** *Slang.* ridiculous; silly; wacky; nutty: *a goofy little hat.* [1915–20; GOOF + -Y[1]] —**goof′i·ly,** *adv.* —**goof′i·ness,** *n.*

goog (go͝og, go͞og), *n. Australian.* an egg. [1940–45; orig. uncert.]

goo·gly (go͞o′glē), *n., pl.* **-glies.** *Cricket.* a bowled ball that swerves in one direction and breaks in the other. [1900–05; orig. uncert.]

goo·gly-eyed (go͞o′glē īd′), *adj.* goggle-eyed. [1925–30]

goo·gol (go͞o′gôl, -gol, -gəl), *n.* a number that is equal to 1 followed by 100 zeros and expressed as 10^{100}. [1935–40; introduced by U.S. mathematician Edward Kasner (1878–1955), whose nine-year-old nephew allegedly invented it]

goo·gol·plex (go͞o′gôl pleks′, -gol-, -gəl-), *n.* a number that is equal to 1 followed by a googol of zeros and expressed as $10^{10^{100}}$. [1935–40; GOOGOL + -PLEX]

goo′-goo eyes′ (go͞o′go͞o′), *Older Slang.* foolishly amorous glances: *They sat there making goo-goo eyes at each other.* [1895–1900; var. of GOGGLE-EYES]

gook[1] (go͝ok, go͞ok), *n. Informal.* **1.** guck. **2.** makeup, esp. when thickly applied: *She looks ridiculous with all that gook around her eyes.* [expressive word, perh. b. GOO and MUCK; cf. GUCK]

gook[2] (go͞ok), *n. Slang (disparaging and offensive).* **1.** a native of Southeast Asia or the South Pacific, esp. when a member of an enemy military force. **2.** any dark-skinned foreigner, esp. one from the Middle East. **3.** anyone who is offensive to others because of stupidity, coarseness, etc. [1930–35; of uncert. orig; cf. earlier *goo-goo, gugu,* as opprobrious term for a Filipino, and perh. comparable relationship of KOOK to CUCKOO]

goom·bay (go͞om′bā, go͞om′-), *n.* the style of calypso music or rhythm popular in the Bahamas. [cf. Jamaican E *gombay* a drum, said to be < Kongo *ŋgoma, ŋkumbi* drum (or a cognate Bantu word)]

goon (go͞on), *n.* **1.** *Informal.* a hired hoodlum or thug. **2.** *Slang.* **a.** a stupid, foolish, or awkward person. **b.** a roughneck. [1920–25; shortened from dial. *gooney,* var. of obs. *gony* a simpleton (< ?); influenced by the comic-strip character Alice the *Goon* in the series *Thimble Theatre* by E. C. Segar (1894–1938), American cartoonist]

goon·da (go͞on′də), *n. Anglo-Indian.* a rogue or hoodlum. Also, **gunda.** [1925–30; < Hindi *gundā*]

goon·ey (go͞o′nē), *adj.,* **goon·i·er, goon·i·est,** *n., pl.* **goon·eys, goon·ies.** goony.

goon′ey bird′ (go͞o′nē), **1.** any of several albatrosses, esp. the black-footed albatross and the Laysan albatross, occurring on islands in the Pacific Ocean, often near naval bases. **2.** *Slang.* a foolish or awkward person or thing; goon. Also, **goon′y bird′.** Also called **gooney, goony.** [1940–45; see GOON]

goon′ squad′, a group of hired thugs used to perform ruthless or violent acts. [1935–40]

goon·y (go͞o′nē), *adj.,* **goon·i·er, goon·i·est,** *n., pl.* **goon·ies.** —*adj.* **1.** *Slang.* stupid, foolish, or awkward: *a goony smile on his face.* **2.** *Informal.* of or like a goon; thuggish; brutal. —*n.* **3.** *Slang.* goon (def. 2a). **4.** See **gooney bird.** Also, **gooney.** [GOON + -Y[1]] —**goon′i·ly,** *adv.*

goop[1] (go͞op), *n. Informal.* a bad-mannered or inconsiderate person; clod; boor. [expressive coinage, appar. first used by Gelett Burgess in his book *Goops and How to Be Them* (1900)]

goop[2] (go͞op), *n. Slang.* a viscous or sticky substance; goo. [1955–60; expressive coinage akin to GLOP, GOOK[1], etc.]

goop·y (go͞o′pē), *adj.,* **goop·i·er, goop·i·est.** *Slang.* **1.** characteristic of goop; sticky, viscous. **2.** mawkishly sentimental: *a goopy love story.* [1915–20; GOOP[2] + -Y[1]]

go′ or no′-go (nō′gō′), go/no-go.

goos·an·der (go͞o san′dər), *n. Brit.* **1.** a common merganser, *Mergus merganser,* of Eurasia and North America. **2.** any merganser. [1615–25; alter. of *gossander;* perh. b. GOOSE and obs. *bergander* shelduck (< ?)]

Canada goose, *Branta canadensis,* length to 3¾ ft. (1.1 m)

goose (go͞os), *n., pl.* **geese** for 1, 2, 4, 8, 9; **goos·es** for 5–7; *v.,* **goosed, goos·ing.** —*n.* **1.** any of numerous wild or domesticated, web-footed swimming birds of the family Anatidae, esp. of the genera *Anser* and *Branta,* most of which are larger and have a longer neck and legs than the ducks. **2.** the female of this bird, as distinguished from the male, or gander. **3.** the flesh of a goose, used as food. **4.** a silly or foolish person; simpleton. **5.** *Slang.* a poke between the buttocks to startle. **6.** *Informal.* anything that energizes, strengthens, or the like: *to give the economy a badly needed goose.* **7.** a tailor's smoothing iron with a curved handle. **8.** an obsolete board game played with dice and counters in which a player whose cast falls in a square containing the picture of a goose is allowed to advance double the number of his or her throw. **9. cook someone's goose,** *Informal.* to ruin someone's hopes, plans, chances, etc.: *His goose was cooked when they found the stolen gems in his pocket.* —*v.t.* **10.** *Slang.* to poke (a person) between the buttocks to startle. **11.** *Informal.* **a.** to prod or urge to action or an emotional reaction: *The promise of time off may goose the workers and increase profits.* **b.** to strengthen or improve (often fol. by *up*): *Let's goose up the stew with some wine.* **c.** to increase; raise (often fol. by *up*): *to goose up government loans in weak industries.* **d.** to give a spurt of fuel to (a motor) to increase speed. [bef. 1000; ME *gose, goos,* OE *gōs* (pl. *gēs*); c. G *Gans,* ON *gās;* cf. Skt *haṁsa,* Gk *chḗn,* L *ānser*] —**goose′like′,** *adj.*

goose′ bar′nacle. See under **barnacle**[1] (def. 1). [1880–85]

Goose′ Bay′, an air base in S central Labrador, in Newfoundland, in E Canada, on the great circle route between New York and London: used as a fuel stop by some transatlantic airplanes. Cf. **Happy Valley-Goose Bay.**

goose·ber·ry (go͞os′ber′ē, -bə rē, go͞oz′-), *n., pl.* **-ries. 1.** the edible, acid, globular, sometimes spiny fruit of certain prickly shrubs belonging to the genus *Ribes,* of the saxifrage family, esp. *R. uva-crispa* (or *R. grossularia*). **2.** a shrub bearing this fruit. [1525–35; GOOSE + BERRY]

goose′berry gar′net, *Mineral.* grossularite.

Goose′ Creek′, a town in SE South Carolina. 17,811.

goose′ egg′, *Informal.* **1.** the numeral zero, often used to indicate the failure of a team to score in a game or unit of a game: *a pitchers' duel, with nothing but goose eggs on the scoreboard.* **2.** a lump raised by a blow, esp. on the head. [1350–1400; 1885–90, *Amer.,* for def. 1; ME: the egg of a goose]

goose·fish (go͞os′fish′), *n., pl.* (*esp. collectively*) **-fish,** (*esp. referring to two or more kinds or species*) **-fish·es.** angler (def. 3). [1800–10, *Amer.*; GOOSE + FISH]

goose′ flesh′, a rough condition of the skin, resembling that of a plucked goose, induced by cold or fear; horripilation. Also, **goose′flesh′.** Also called **goose pimples, goose′ bumps′, goose skin.** [1375–1425; late ME]

goose·foot (go͞os′fo͝ot′), *n., pl.* **-foots.** any of numerous, often weedy plants of the genus *Chenopodium,* having inconspicuous greenish flowers. [1540–50; GOOSE + FOOT]

goose′foot fam′ily, the plant family Chenopodiaceae, characterized by often weedy herbaceous plants and shrubs having simple, usually alternate leaves, small and inconspicuous flowers, and tiny, dry fruit, and including the beet, glasswort, goosefoot, Russian thistle, saltbush, and spinach.

goose·gog (go͞oz′gog), *n. Brit. Dial.* gooseberry. [1815–25; GOOSE + *gog* (< ?)]

goose′ grass′, cleavers. [1350–1400; ME]

goose′ grease′, the melted fat of the goose, used in domestic medicine as an ointment. [1400–50; late ME]

goose·herd (go͞os′hûrd′), *n.* a person who tends geese. [1200–50; ME *gos herd.* See GOOSE, HERD[2]]

goose·neck (go͞os′nek′), *n.* **1.** a curved object resembling the neck of a goose, often of flexible construction, as in the shaft of a gooseneck lamp. **2.** *Naut.* a curved piece at the foot of a boom, attached to a mast by a vertical pivot and itself having a horizontal pivot so that the boom can be pointed in a wide angle vertically or horizontally. **3.** *Carpentry.* a vertical continuation of the handrail of a flight of stairs, terminating in a short horizontal part on the top of a newel post. [1680–90; GOOSE + NECK] —**goose′necked′,** *adj.*

goose′neck lamp′, a desk lamp having a flexible shaft or stem. [1925–30]

goose′ pim′ples. See **goose flesh.** [1885–90] —**goose′-pim′ply,** *adj.*

goose′ skin′. See **goose flesh.** [1630–40]

goose′ step′, 1. a marching step of some infantries in which the legs are swung high and kept straight and stiff. **2.** a military exercise in which the body is balanced on one foot, without advancing, while the other foot is swung forward and back. [1800–10]

goose-step (go͞os′step′), *v.i.,* **-stepped, -step·ping.** to march in a goose step: *Troops goose-stepped past the reviewing stand.* [1875–80] —**goose′-step′per,** *n.*

goose·wing (go͞os′wing′), *n. Naut.* **1.** the weather clew of a square sail, held taut when the lee side of the sail is furled. **2.** either of the triangular areas of a square sail left exposed to the wind when the middle part is lashed to the yard during a gale. **3.** a triangular studdingsail. [1350–1400; ME, for literal sense. See GOOSE, WING]

goose-winged (go͞os′wingd′), *adj. Naut.* **1.** (of a square sail) having the lee clew furled while the weather clew is held taut. **2.** (of a fore-and-aft-rigged vessel) having the foresail and mainsail set on opposite sides. [1865–70; GOOSEWING + -ED[3]]

Goos·sens (go͞o′sənz), *n.* **Sir Eugene,** 1893–1962, English composer and conductor.

goos·y (go͞o′sē), *adj.,* **goos·i·er, goos·i·est. 1.** like a goose; foolish or giddy. **2.** *Informal.* **a.** ticklish; reacting very quickly to touch. **b.** nervous; jumpy; uneasy. Also, **goos′ey.** [1805–15; GOOSE + -Y[1]]

goo·zle (go͞o′zəl), *n. South Midland and Southern U.S.* gozzle.

G.O.P., Grand Old Party (an epithet of the Republican party since 1880). Also, **GOP**

go·pak (gō′pak), *n.* a folk dance of the Ukraine. Also called **hopak.** [1925–30; < Ukrainian *gopák,* deriv. of *gop* interjection uttered during such dances < Pol *hop* < G *hopp, hops,* akin to HOP[1]]

Go·pā·la (gō pä′lə), *n. Hinduism.* Krishna as a cowherd.

go·pher[1] (gō′fər), *n.* **1.** any of several ground squirrels of the genus *Citellus,* of the prairie regions of North America. **2.** See **pocket gopher. 3.** See **gopher tortoise. 4.** See **gopher snake. 5.** (*cap.*) a native or inhabitant of Minnesota (used as a nickname). —*v.i.* **6.** *Mining.* **a.** to mine unsystematically. **b.** to enlarge a hole, as in loose soil, with successively larger blasts. [1785–95; earlier *megopher, magopher* gopher tortoise; of obscure orig.; sp. copies GOPHER WOOD]

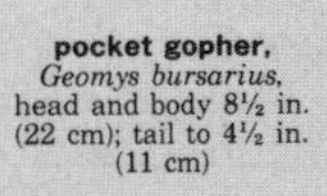

pocket gopher, *Geomys bursarius,* head and body 8½ in. (22 cm); tail to 4½ in. (11 cm)

go·pher[2] (gō′fər), *n. Slang.* gofer. [1925–30; resp. of GOFER by assoc. with GOPHER[1]]

go′pher ball′, *Baseball Slang.* a pitched ball hit for a home run: *leading the league in gopher balls.* [1945–55]

go·pher·ber·ry (gō′fər ber′ē), *n., pl.* **-ries.** See **bush huckleberry.** [GOPHER[1] + BERRY]

go′pher plant′, a spurge, *Euphorbia lathyris,* producing latex that is considered a possible source of crude oil and gasoline. Also called **gop′her weed′, caper spurge.**

go′pher snake′, 1. a bullsnake, *Pituophis melanoleucus,* of western North America, that invades burrows to prey on rodents. **2.** See **indigo snake.** [1830–40, *Amer.*]

Go′pher State′, Minnesota (used as a nickname).

go′pher tor′toise, any North American burrowing tortoise of the genus *Gopherus,* esp. *G. polyphemus,* of the southeastern U.S.: several species are now reduced in number. Also called **go′pher tur′tle, gopher.** [1785–95; see GOPHER[1]]

go′pher wood′, an unidentified wood used in building Noah's ark. Gen. 6:14. [1605–15; < Heb *gōpher*]

go·pher·wood (gō′fər wo͝od′), *n.* yellowwood. [1880–85, *Amer.*; GOPHER[1] + WOOD[1]]

go·pi (gō′pē), *n.pl. Hinduism.* female cowherds, lovers of Krishna with whom he dances at the time of the autumn moon. [< Skt]

gor (gôr), *interj. Brit. Dial.* **1.** (used as a mild oath.) **2.** (used as an exclamation of surprise or disbelief.) Also, **cor.** [see GORBLIMEY]

Go·rakh·pur (gôr′ək po͝or′, gōr′-), *n.* a city in SE Uttar Pradesh, in N India. 230,911.

go·ral (gôr′əl, gōr′-), *n.* a short-horned goat antelope, *Naemorhedus goral,* of the mountainous regions of southeastern Asia: an endangered species. [1825–35; perh. << Skt *gaura, gaur*]

Gor·ba·chev (gôr′bə chôf′, -chof′; *Russ.* gər bu-chôf′), *n.* **Mi·kha·il S(er·ge·ye·vich)** (mi kīl′ sûr gā′ə-

CONCISE PRONUNCIATION KEY: *act, cāpe, dâre, pärt; set, ēqual; if, īce; ox, ōver, ôrder, oil, bo͝ok, bo͞ot, out; up, ûrge; child; sing; shoe; thin,* that; zh *as in* treasure. ə = *a as in alone, e as in system, i as in easily, o as in gallop, u as in circus;* ə *as in fire* (fīər), *hour* (ouər). l *and* n *can serve as syllabic consonants, as in cradle* (krād′l), *and button* (but′n). *See the full key inside the front cover.*

vich, mi käl′; *Russ.* myi KHU yĕl′ syiR gye′yi vyich), born 1931, Soviet political leader: general secretary of the Communist party 1985–91; president of the Soviet Union 1988–91; Nobel peace prize 1990.

gor•bel•ly (gôr′bel′ē), *n., pl.* **-lies.** *Obs.* a protruding belly. [1510–20; perh. GORE[1] + BELLY; cf. Sw (dial.) *går-bälg*] —**gor′bel′lied,** *adj.*

gor•bli•mey (gôr blī′mē), *interj. Brit. Slang.* blimey. Also, **gor•bli′my.** Cf. **gor.** [1895–1900; reduced form of *God blind me;* for sp. with *r,* cf. ARVO, SCARPER]

Gor•cha•kov (gôr′chə kôf′, -kof′; *Russ.* gəR chyi-kôf′), *n.* **Prince A•le•ksan•der Mi•khai•lo•vich** (al′ig-zan′dər mi hī′lə vich, -zän′-; *Russ.* u lyi ksändR′ myi-KHī′lə vyich), 1798–1883, Russian statesman.

Gor•di•an (gôr′dē ən), *adj.* **1.** pertaining to Gordius, ancient king of Phrygia, who tied a knot (the **Gor′dian knot′**) that, according to prophecy, was to be undone only by the person who was to rule Asia, and that was cut, rather than untied, by Alexander the Great. **2.** resembling the Gordian knot in intricacy. **3. cut the Gordian knot,** to act quickly and decisively in a difficult situation; solve a problem boldly. [1555–65; < L *Gordi(us)* (< Gk *Górdios* Gordius) + -AN]

gor′di•an worm′ (gôr′dē ən), *Zool.* nematomorph. [after the *Gordian knot,* alluding to the tangles the worms sometimes form]

Gor•don (gôr′dn), *n.* **1. Charles George** (*"Chinese Gordon"; "Gordon Pasha"*), 1833–85, British general: administrator in China and Egypt. **2. Charles William,** real name of Ralph Connor. **3. Lord George,** 1751–93, English politician. **4. George Hamilton, 4th Earl of Aberdeen,** 1784–1860, British statesman, born in Scotland: prime minister 1852–55. **5.** a male given name: from an Old English word meaning "round hill."

Gor′don set′ter, one of a Scottish breed of medium-sized setters having a black-and-tan coat. [1860–65; after Alexander, 4th Duke of *Gordon* (1743–1827), Scottish sportsman partly responsible for developing the breed]

gore[1] (gôr, gōr), *n.* **1.** blood that is shed, esp. when clotted. **2.** murder, bloodshed, violence, etc.: *That horror movie had too much gore.* [bef. 900; ME; OE *gor* dung, dirt; c. D *goor,* OHG *gor* filth]

gore[2] (gôr, gōr), *v.t.,* **gored, gor•ing.** to pierce with or as if with a horn or tusk. [1350–1400; ME *goren;* see GORE[3]]

G, **gore**[3] (def. 2)

gore[3] (gôr, gōr), *n., v.,* **gored, gor•ing.** —*n.* **1.** a triangular piece of material inserted in a garment, sail, etc., to give it greater width or a desired shape. Cf. **godet** (def. 1), **gusset** (def. 1). **2.** one of the panels, usually tapering or shaped, making up a garment, as a skirt. **3.** a triangular tract of land, esp. one lying between larger divisions. —*v.t.* **4.** to make or furnish with a gore or gores. [bef. 900; ME; OE *gāra* corner (c. G *Gehre* gusset); cf. OE *gār* spear]

Gore (gôr, gōr), *n.* **Albert Arnold, Jr.** (*Al*), born 1948, vice president of the U.S. since 1993.

Go•re (gôr′ä, gōr′ä), *n.* a city in W Ethiopia. 8381.

Gor•en (gôr′ən), *n.* **Charles Henry,** 1901–91, U.S authority and writer on contract bridge.

Gore-Tex (gôr′teks′, gōr′-), *Trademark.* a brand of breathable, water-repellent fabric laminate used on clothing, shoes, etc.

Gor•gas (gôr′gəs), *n.* **William Crawford,** 1854–1920, U.S. physician and epidemiologist: chief sanitary officer of the Panama Canal 1904–13; surgeon general of the U.S. Army 1914–18.

gorge[1] (gôrj), *n., v.,* **gorged, gorg•ing.** —*n.* **1.** a narrow cleft with steep, rocky walls, esp. one through which a stream runs. **2.** a small canyon. **3.** a gluttonous meal. **4.** something that is swallowed; contents of the stomach. **5.** an obstructing mass: *an ice gorge.* **6.** the seam formed at the point where the lapel meets the collar of a jacket or coat. **7.** *Fort.* the rear entrance or part of a bastion or similar outwork. See diag. under **bastion. 8.** Also called **gorge hook.** a primitive type of fishhook consisting of a piece of stone or bone with sharpened ends and a hole or groove in the center for fastening a line. **9.** the throat; gullet. **10. make one's gorge rise,** to evoke violent anger or strong disgust: *The cruelty of war made his gorge rise.* —*v.t.* **11.** to stuff with food (usually used reflexively or passively): *He gorged himself. They were gorged.* **12.** to swallow, esp. greedily. **13.** to choke up (usually used passively). —*v.i.* **14.** to eat greedily. [1325–75; (v.) ME < OF *gorger,* deriv. of *gorge* throat < VL **gorga,* akin to L *gurguliō* gullet, throat, *gurges* whirlpool, eddy] —**gorge′a•ble,** *adj.* —**gorg•ed•ly** (gôr′jid lē), *adv.* —**gorg′er,** *n.*
—**Syn. 1.** defile, ravine, notch, gap. **11.** glut, cram, fill. **12.** devour. **12, 14.** bolt, gulp, gobble.

CONCISE ETYMOLOGY KEY: <, descended or borrowed from; >, whence; b., blend of, blended; c., cognate with; cf., compare; deriv., derivative; equiv., equivalent; imit., imitative; obl., oblique; r., replacing; s., stem; sp., spelling, spelled; resp., respelling, respelled; trans., translation; ?, origin unknown; *, unattested; ‡, probably earlier than. See the full key inside the front cover.

gorge[2] (gôrj), *n. Heraldry.* gurge (def. 2).

gorged (gôrjd), *adj. Heraldry.* (of a beast) represented wearing something about the neck in the manner of a collar: *a lion gules gorged with a collar or.* [1600–10; GORGE[1] + -ED[3]]

gorge′ hook′, 1. a fishhook with two barbed prongs; a hook made by fastening two hooks back to back at the shanks. **2.** gorge (def. 8). [1865–70]

gor•geous (gôr′jəs), *adj.* **1.** splendid or sumptuous in appearance, coloring, etc.; magnificent: *a gorgeous gown; a gorgeous sunset.* **2.** *Informal.* extremely good, enjoyable, or pleasant: *a gorgeous time.* [1490–1500; earlier *gorgeouse* < OF *gorgias* fashionable, elegant (< ?); see -OUS] —**gor′geous•ly,** *adv.* —**gor′geous•ness,** *n.*
—**Syn. 1.** rich, superb, grand; brilliant, resplendent, glittering, dazzling. See **magnificent.** —**Ant. 1.** poor, plain.

gor•ger•in (gôr′jər in), *n. Archit.* the neckline portion of a capital of a column, or a feature forming the junction between a shaft and its capital. Also called **necking.** [1655–65; < F, deriv. of *gorge* throat; see GORGE[1]]

gor•get (gôr′jit), *n.* **1.** a patch on the throat of a bird or other animal, distinguished by its color, texture, etc. **2.** a piece of armor for the throat. See diag. under **armor. 3.** a crescent-shaped ornament worn on a chain around the neck as a badge of rank by officers in the 17th and 18th centuries. **4.** a wimple of the Middle Ages, worn with the ends fastened in the hair. [1425–75; late ME < OF. See GORGE[1], -ET] —**gor′get•ed,** *adj.*

Gor•gi•as (gôr′jē əs), *n.* c483–c375 B.C., Greek philosopher.

Gor•gon (gôr′gən), *n.* **1.** *Class. Myth.* any of three sister monsters commonly represented as having snakes for hair, wings, brazen claws, and eyes that turned anyone looking into them to stone. Medusa, the only mortal Gorgon, was beheaded by Perseus. **2.** (*l.c.*) a mean, ugly, or repulsive woman. [1350–1400; ME < L *Gorgōn* < Gk *Gorgṓ,* deriv. of *gorgós* dreadful] —**Gor•go•ni•an** (gôr-gō′nē ən), *adj.*

gor•go•nei•on (gôr′gə nē′on), *n., pl.* **-nei•a** (-nē′ə). a representation of the head of a Gorgon, esp. that of Medusa. [1835–45; < Gk, equiv. to *Gorgōn-,* s. of *Gorgṓ* GORGON + *-eion* neut. adj. suffix]

Gor•go•ni•an (gôr gō′nē ən), *n.* **1.** any of numerous alcyonarian corals of the order Gorgonacea, having a usually branching, horny or calcareous skeleton. —*adj.* **2.** belonging or pertaining to the Gorgonacea. [1825–35; < NL *Gorgoni(a)* genus name (see GORGON, -IA) + -AN]

gor•gon•ize (gôr′gə nīz′), *v.t.,* **-ized, -iz•ing.** to affect as a Gorgon; hypnotize; petrify. Also, *esp. Brit.,* **gor′gon•ise′.** [1600–10; GORGON + -IZE]

Gor•gon•zo•la (gôr′gən zō′lə), *n.* a strongly flavored, semisoft variety of Italian milk cheese veined with mold. Also called **Gor′gonzo′la cheese′.** [1875–80; after *Gorgonzola,* Italy, a village near Milan, where it was first produced]

Gor•ham (gôr′əm), *n.* a town in SW Maine. 10,101.

go•ril•la (gə ril′ə), *n.* **1.** the largest of the anthropoid apes, *Gorilla gorilla,* terrestrial and vegetarian, of western equatorial Africa and the Kivu highlands, comprising the subspecies *G. g. gorilla* **(western lowland gorilla),** *G. g. graueri* **(eastern lowland gorilla),** and *G. g. beringei* **(mountain gorilla):** now rare. **2.** an ugly, brutish person. **3.** *Slang.* a hoodlum or thug, esp. one who threatens or inflicts violence. [1790–1800; < NL < Gk *Gorillās* (acc. pl.) name for a race of hairy women in Hanno's account of his voyage along the coast of Africa (5th century B.C.)] —**go•ril′la•like′,** *adj.* —**go•ril′li•an, go•ril•line** (gə ril′īn, -in), *adj.* —**go•ril′loid,** *adj.*

gorilla, *Gorilla gorilla,* standing height 6 ft. (1.8 m)

gor•ing (gôr′ing, gor′-), *n. Naut.* the triangular area along a leech of a square sail, created by the presence of a gore. [1620–30; GORE[3] + -ING[1]]

Gö•ring (gâr′ing, gûr′-; *Ger.* gœ′Ring), *n.* **Her•mann Wil•helm** (her′män vil′helm, hûr′mən wil′helm; *Ger.* heR′män vil′helm), 1893–1946, German field marshal and Nazi party leader. Also, **Goering.**

Go•ri•zia (gô Re′tsyä), *n.* a city in NE Italy, on the Isonzo River, N of Trieste. 43,213. German, **Görz.**

gork (gôrk), *n. Medical Slang (disparaging and offensive).* a patient whose brain has suffered severe and irreversible damage and whose vital functions are being maintained by artificial means. [1970–75; perh. back formation from *gorked* (slang) anesthetized; appar. an expressive coinage]

Gor•ki (gôr′kē; *Russ.* gôR′kyə), *n.* **1.** Also, **Gorky. Max•im** (mak′sim; *Russ.* mu ksyēm′) *(Aleksey Maksimovich Pyeshkov),* 1868–1936, Russian novelist, short-story writer, and dramatist. **2.** former name (1932–91) of **Nizhni Novgorod.**

Gor•ky (gôr′kē; *for 2 also Russ.* gôR′kyə), *n.* **1. Arshile** (är′shēl) *(Vosdanig Adoian),* 1904–48, American painter, born in Armenia. **2. Maxim.** See **Gorki, Maxim.**

Gör•litz (gœR′lits), *n.* a city in E Germany, on the Neisse River, at the Polish boundary. 79,506.

Gor•lov•ka (gôr lôf′kə, -lof′-; *Russ.* gôR′ləf kə), *n.* a city in SE Ukraine, N of Donetsk. 345,000.

gor•mand (gôr′mənd), *n.* gourmand. —**gor′mand•ism,** *n.*

gor•mand•ize (*v.* gôr′mən dīz′; *n.* gôr′mən dēz′), *v.,* **-ized, -iz•ing,** *n.* —*v.i., v.t.* **1.** to eat greedily or ravenously. —*n.* **2.** gourmandise[1]. Also, *esp. Brit.,* **gor′mand•ise′.** [1540–50; < F *gourmandise* (n.), equiv. to MF *gourmand* GOURMAND + *-ise* n. suffix later taken as v. suffix -IZE] —**gor′mand•iz′er,** *n.*

gorm•less (gôrm′lis), *adj. Chiefly Brit. Informal.* gaumless. [resp. by speakers with r-less accents]

Gor′no-Al•tai′ Auton′omous Re′gion (gôr′nō al-tī′, -äl-; *Russ.* gôR′nə ul tī′), an autonomous region in the Russian Federation, in the Altai territory bordering China and Mongolia. 192,000; 35,753 sq. mi. (92,600 sq. km). *Cap.:* Gorno-Altaisk.

Gor′no-Ba•dakh•shan′ Auton′omous Re′gion (gôr′nō bə dak shan′, -däk shän′; *Russ.* gôR′nə bə duKH shän′), an autonomous region in SE Tadzhikistan (Tajikistan). 161,000; 25,784 sq. mi. (63,700 sq. km). *Cap.:* Khorog.

go-round (gō′round′), *n.* go-around (defs. 2, 3).

gorp (gôrp), *n. Informal.* a mixture of nuts, raisins, dried fruits, seeds, or the like eaten as a high-energy snack, as by hikers and climbers. [1955–60; perh. alter. of GLOP]

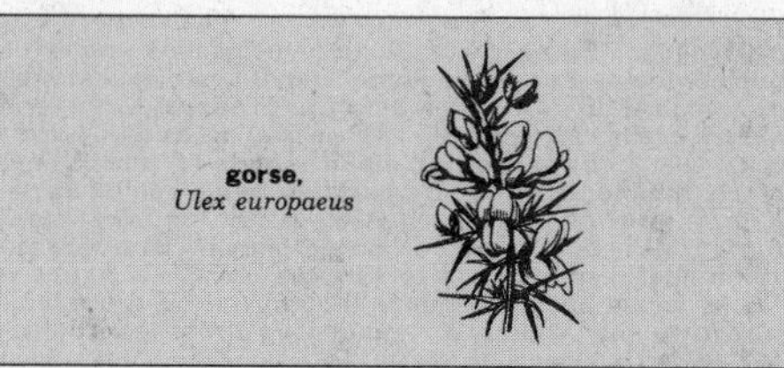
gorse, *Ulex europaeus*

gorse (gôrs), *n.* any spiny shrub of the genus *Ulex,* of the legume family, native to the Old World, esp. *U. europaeus,* having rudimentary leaves and yellow flowers and growing in waste places and sandy soil. Also called **furze;** *esp. Brit.,* **whin.** [bef. 900; ME *gorst,* OE; akin to G *Gerste,* L *hordeum* barley] —**gors′y,** *adj.*

Gor•ton (gôr′tn), *n.* **John Grey,** born 1911, Australian political leader: prime minister 1968–71.

gor•y (gôr′ē, gōr′ē), *adj.,* **gor•i•er, gor•i•est. 1.** covered or stained with gore; bloody. **2.** resembling gore. **3.** involving much bloodshed and violence: *a gory battle.* **4.** unpleasant or disagreeable: *to reveal the gory details of a divorce.* [1470–80; GORE[1] + -Y[1]] —**gor′i•ly,** *adv.* —**gor′i•ness,** *n.*

Görz (gœRts), *n.* German name of **Gorizia.**

Go•sa•la (gō sä′lə), *n.* died c484 B.C., Indian religious leader: founder of the Ajivaka sect.

gosh (gosh), *interj.* (used as an exclamation or mild oath): *Gosh, this bag is heavy!* [1750–60; euphemistic alter. of GOD]

goshawk, *Accipiter gentilis,* length 26 in. (66 cm)

gos•hawk (gos′hôk′), *n.* any of several powerful, short-winged hawks, as *Accipiter gentilis,* of Europe and America, formerly much used in falconry. [bef. 1000; ME *goshauk,* OE *gōshafoc.* See GOOSE, HAWK[1]]

Go•shen (gō′shən), *n.* **1.** a pastoral region in Lower Egypt, occupied by the Israelites before the Exodus. Gen. 45:10. **2.** a land or place of plenty and comfort. **3.** a city in N Indiana. 19,665.

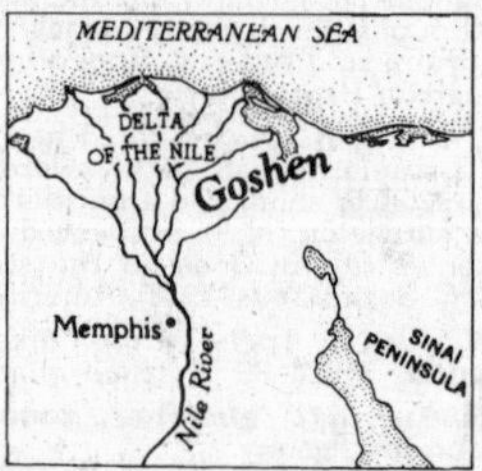

gos•ling (goz′ling), *n.* **1.** a young goose. **2.** a foolish, inexperienced person. [1375–1425; late ME *goselyng;* see GOOSE, -LING[1]; c. ON *gæslingr*]

go-slow (gō′slō′), *n. Chiefly Brit.* a work slowdown, as in sympathy with strikers or as a protest. [1925–30]

gos•more (gos′môr, -mōr), *n.* cat's-ear. [perh. alter. of GOSSAMER]

gos•pel (gos′pəl), *n.* **1.** the teachings of Jesus and the apostles; the Christian revelation. **2.** the story of

Christ's life and teachings, esp. as contained in the first four books of the New Testament, namely Matthew, Mark, Luke, and John. **3.** (*usually cap.*) any of these four books. **4.** something regarded as true and implicitly believed: *to take his report for gospel.* **5.** a doctrine regarded as of prime importance: *political gospel.* **6.** glad tidings, esp. concerning salvation and the kingdom of God as announced to the world by Christ. **7.** (*often cap.*) *Eccles.* an extract from one of the four Gospels, forming part of the Eucharistic service in certain churches. **8.** See **gospel music.** —*adj.* **9.** of, pertaining to, or proclaiming the gospel or its teachings: *a gospel preacher.* **10.** in accordance with the gospel; evangelical. **11.** of or pertaining to gospel music: *a gospel singer.* [bef. 950; ME *go(d)spell,* OE *gōdspell* (see GOOD, SPELL[2]); trans. of Gk *euangélion* good news; see EVANGEL[1]]

gos•pel•er (gos′pə lər), *n. Eccles.* a person who reads or sings the Gospel. Also, *esp. Brit.,* **gos′pel•ler.** [bef. 1000; ME; OE *gōdspellere.* See GOSPEL, -ER[1]]

gos′pel mu′sic, a now popularized form of impassioned rhythmic spiritual music rooted in the solo and responsive church singing of rural blacks in the American South, central to the development of rhythm and blues and of soul music. Also called **gospel.** [1950–55]

gos′pel side′, (in some Protestant churches) the left side of a church, facing the altar. Cf. **epistle side.** [1890–95]

gos′pel truth′, an unquestionably true statement, fact, etc. [1640–50]

Gos•plan (gos plän′), *n.* (in the Soviet Union) the official planning organization, which drew up projects embracing trade and industry, agriculture, education, and public health. [< Russ *Gosplán,* for *Gosudárstvennaya plánovaya komíssiya* State Planning Commission]

go•spo•din (gə spu dyĕn′), *n., pl.* ***-spo•da*** (-spu dä′). *Russian.* a title of respect corresponding to *Mr.*

gos•port (gos′pôrt′, -pōrt′), *n.* a flexible speaking tube for communication between separate cockpits or compartments of an aircraft. [1940–45; after *Gosport,* England]

Gos•saert (go särt′), *n.* **Jan** (yän). See **Mabuse, Jan.** Also, **Gos•sart′.**

gos•sa•mer (gos′ə mər), *n.* **1.** a fine, filmy cobweb seen on grass or bushes or floating in the air in calm weather, esp. in autumn. **2.** a thread or a web of this substance. **3.** an extremely delicate variety of gauze, used esp. for veils. **4.** any thin, light fabric. **5.** something extremely light, flimsy, or delicate. **6.** a thin, waterproof outer garment, esp. for women. —*adj.* **7.** Also, **gos•sa•mer•y** (gos′ə mə rē), **gos′sa•mered.** of or like gossamer; thin and light. [1275–1325; ME *gosesomer* (see GOOSE, SUMMER[1]); possibly first used as name for late, mild autumn, a time when goose was a favorite dish (cf. G *Gänsemonat* November), then transferred to the cobwebs frequent at that time of year]

gos•san (gos′ən, goz′-), *n.* a rust-colored deposit of mineral matter at the outcrop of a vein or orebody containing iron-bearing materials. Also called **iron hat.** [1770–80; orig. dial. (Cornwall) < Cornish, deriv. of *gōs* blood; akin to Welsh *gwaed*]

Gosse (gôs, gos), *n.* **Sir Edmund William,** 1849–1928, English poet, biographer, and critic.

gos•sip (gos′əp), *n., v.,* **-siped** or **-sipped, -sip•ing** or **-sip•ping.** —*n.* **1.** idle talk or rumor, esp. about the personal or private affairs of others: *the endless gossip about Hollywood stars.* **2.** light, familiar talk or writing. **3.** Also, **gos′sip•er, gos′sip•per.** a person given to tattling or idle talk. **4.** *Chiefly Brit. Dial.* a godparent. **5.** *Archaic.* a friend, esp. a woman. —*v.i.* **6.** to talk idly, esp. about the affairs of others; go about tattling. —*v.t.* **7.** *Chiefly Brit. Dial.* to stand godparent to. **8.** *Archaic.* to repeat like a gossip. [bef. 1050; ME *gossib, godsib(be),* OE *godsibb,* orig. godparent, equiv. to *god* GOD + *sibb* related; see SIB[1]] —**gos′sip•ing•ly,** *adv.*

—**Syn. 1.** small talk, hearsay, palaver, chitchat. GOSSIP, SCANDAL apply to idle talk and newsmongering about the affairs of others. GOSSIP is light chat or talk: *to trade gossip about the neighbors.* SCANDAL is rumor or general talk that is damaging to reputation; it is usually more or less malicious: *The town never lived down the election scandal.* **3.** chatterer, talker, gabbler, rumormonger. **6.** chatter, prattle, prate, palaver.

gos•sip•mon•ger (gos′əp mung′gər, -mong′-), *n.* a person especially fond of or addicted to gossiping. [1830–40; GOSSIP + MONGER]

gos•sip•y (gos′ə pē), *adj.* **1.** given to or fond of gossip: *a gossipy neighbor.* **2.** full of gossip: *a gossipy tabloid.* [1810–20; GOSSIP + -Y[1]] —**gos′sip•i•ness,** *n.*

gos•soon (go sōōn′), *n. Irish Eng.* a boy; lad. [1675–85; < Ir *garsún* boy < AF, OF *garçon*]

gos•sy•pol (gos′ə pôl′, -pol′), *n.* a toxic pigment, $C_{30}H_{30}O_8$, derived from cottonseed oil, made nontoxic by heating, presently under study as a potential male contraceptive and antimicrobial. [1895–1900; < NL *Gossyp(ium)* (see GOSSYPOSE) + -OL[1]]

gos•sy•pose (gos′ə pōs′), *n. Chem.* raffinose. [< NL *Gossyp(ium)* genus name (L *gossypion, gossypinum* (Pliny) cotton plant) + -OSE[2]]

got (got), *v.* **1.** a pt. and pp. of **get.** —*auxiliary verb.* **2.** *Informal.* must; have got (fol. by an infinitive).
—**Usage.** See **get.**

Go•ta•ma (gô′tə mə, gō′-), *n.* Buddha. Also, **Gautama.** Also called **Go′tama Bud′dha.**

got•cha (goch′ə), *Pron. Spelling.* got you (usually used interjectionally).

Gö•te•borg (yœ′tə bôR′yᵊ), *n.* a seaport in SW Sweden, on the Kattegat. 431,273. Also, **Gothenburg.**

Goth (goth), *n.* **1.** one of a Teutonic people who in the 3rd to 5th centuries invaded and settled in parts of the Roman Empire. **2.** a person of no refinement; barbarian. [bef. 900; ME *Gothe* < LL *Gothī* (pl.); r. OE *Gotan* (pl.) (*Gota,* sing.); c. Goth *Gut-* (in *Gut-thiuda* Goth-people)]

Goth., Gothic. Also, **Goth, goth.**

Go•tha (gō′tä), *n.* a city in S Thuringia, in SW East Germany. 58,279.

Goth•am (goth′əm, gō′thəm *for 1;* got′əm, gō′thəm *for 2*), *n.* **1.** a journalistic nickname for New York City. **2.** an English village, proverbial for the foolishness of its inhabitants. —**Goth′am•ite′,** *n.*

Goth•en•burg (goth′ən bûrg′, got′n-), *n.* Göteborg.

goth•ic (goth′ik), *adj.* **1.** (*usually cap.*) noting or pertaining to a style of architecture, originating in France in the middle of the 12th century and existing in the western half of Europe through the middle of the 16th century, characterized by the use of the pointed arch and the ribbed vault, by the use of fine woodwork and stonework, by a progressive lightening of structure, and by the use of such features as flying buttresses, ornamental gables, crockets, and foils. **2.** (*usually cap.*) pertaining to or designating the style of painting, sculpture, etc., produced between the 13th and 15th centuries, esp. in northern Europe, characterized by a tendency toward realism and interest in detail. **3.** (*cap.*) of or pertaining to Goths or their language. **4.** (*usually cap.*) of or pertaining to the music, esp. of northern Europe, of the period roughly from 1200 to 1450, including that of the Ars Antiqua, Ars Nova, and the Burgundian school. **5.** (*usually cap.*) pertaining to the Middle Ages; medieval. **6.** (*sometimes cap.*) barbarous or crude. **7.** (*often cap.*) noting or pertaining to a style of literature characterized by a gloomy setting, grotesque, mysterious, or violent events, and an atmosphere of degeneration and decay: *19th-century gothic novels.* **8.** (*cap.*) noting or pertaining to the alphabetical script introduced for the writing of Gothic by Ulfilas and derived by him from Greek uncials with the addition of some Latin and some invented letters. **9.** (*often cap.*) being of a genre of contemporary fiction typically relating the experiences of an often ingenuous heroine imperiled, as at an old mansion, where she typically becomes involved with a stern or mysterious but attractive man. —*n.* **10.** (*usually cap.*) the arts and crafts of the Gothic period. **11.** (*cap.*) the extinct Germanic language of the Goths, preserved esp. in the 4th-century translation by Ulfilas of the Bible. *Abbr.:* Goth, Goth., goth. **12.** (*often cap.*) a story, play, film, or other work in the gothic style. **13.** (*usually cap.*) *Brit.* See **black letter. 14.** (*often cap.*) a square-cut printing type without serifs or hairlines. [1605–15; < LL *Gothicus* of, pertaining to the Goths. See GOTH, -IC] —**goth′i•cal•ly,** *adv.* —**goth′ic•ness, goth•ic•i•ty** (go this′i tē), *n.*

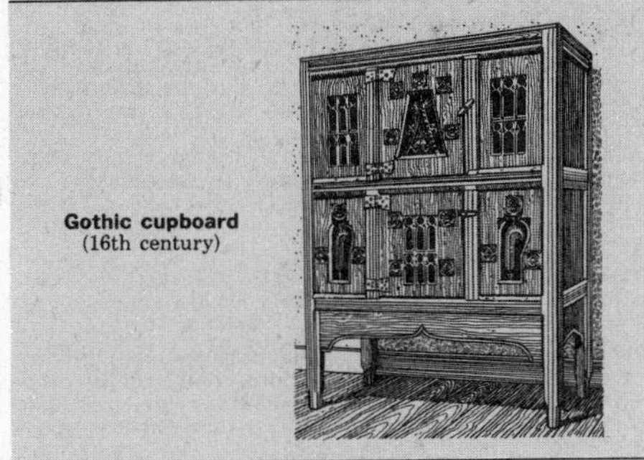
Gothic cupboard (16th century)

Goth′ic arch′, a pointed arch, esp. one having only two centers and equal radii. See illus. under **arch.** [1730–40]

Goth′ic ar′mor, white armor of the 15th century, marked esp. by much fluting and ornamentation.

Goth•i•cism (goth′ə siz′əm), *n.* **1.** conformity or devotion to the gothic style in the arts. **2.** the principles and techniques of the gothic style. **3.** (*sometimes l.c.*) barbarism; crudeness. [1700–10; GOTHIC + -ISM]

Goth•i•cize (goth′ə sīz′), *v.t.,* **-cized, -ciz•ing.** to make gothic, as in style. Also, *esp. Brit.,* **Goth′i•cise′.** [1740–50; GOTHIC + -IZE] —**Goth′i•ciz′er,** *n.*

Got•land (got′lənd; *Swed.* gôt′lund, gôl′lund), *n.* an island in the Baltic, forming a province of Sweden. 55,346; 1212 sq. mi. (3140 sq. km). *Cap.:* Visby. Also, **Gottland.** —**Got′land•er, Gott′land•er,** *n.*

go-to-meet•ing (gō′tə mēt′n, -mē′ting), *adj.* Sunday-go-to-meeting. [1780–90, *Amer.*]

go•tra (gō′trə), *n.* a Hindu clan tracing its paternal lineage from a common ancestor, usually a saint or sage. [1875–80; < Skt]

go-train (gō′trān′), *n. Canadian.* a lightweight passenger train providing rapid surface transport between a city center and the suburbs and from suburb to suburb. Also, **GO train.**

got•ta (got′ə), *Pron. Spelling.* got to; have got to.
—**Usage.** See **get.**

got•ten (got′n), *v.* a pp. of **get.**
—**Usage.** See **get.**

Göt•ter•däm•mer•ung (got′ər dam′ə rōōng′, -rung′; *Ger.* gœt′əR dem′ə Rōōng′), *n.* **1.** *German Myth.* the destruction of the gods and of all things in a final battle with evil powers: erroneous modern translation of the Old Icelandic *Ragnarǫk,* meaning "fate of the gods," misunderstood as *Ragnarökkr,* meaning "twilight of the gods." **2.** (*italics.*) the final opera of Richard Wagner's *The Ring of the Nibelung.* [1875–80; < G, equiv. to *Götter,* pl. of *Gott* GOD + *Dämmerung* twilight]

Göt•tin•gen (gœt′ing ən), *n.* a city in central Germany. 123,600.

Gott•lieb (got′lēb), *n.* **Adolph,** 1903–74, U.S. painter.

Gott•schalk (got′shôk), *n.* **Louis Mo•reau** (mô rō′, mō-), 1829–69, U.S. pianist and composer.

Gott•wald (gôt′vält), *n.* **Kle•ment** (kle′ment), 1896–1953, Czech Communist leader: prime minister 1946–48; president 1948–53.

Götz (gets; *Ger.* gœts), *n.* **Her•mann** (heR′män), 1840–76, German composer. Also, **Goetz.**

gouache (gwäsh, gōō äsh′; *Fr.* gwash), *n., pl.* **gouach•es** (gwä′shiz, gōō ä′shiz; *Fr.* gwash′) for 3. **1.** a technique of painting with opaque watercolors prepared with gum. **2.** an opaque color used in painting a gouache. **3.** a work painted using gouache. [1880–85; < F < It *guazzo* place where there is water << L *aquātiō,* deriv. of *aqua* water]

Gou•da (gou′də, gōō′-; *Du.* KHOU′dä), *n.* **1.** a city in the W Netherlands, NE of Rotterdam. 59,185. **2.** a semisoft, cream-colored cheese made in Holland from whole or partly skimmed milk.

Gou•dy (gou′dē), *n.* **Frederic William,** 1865–1947, U.S. designer of printing types.

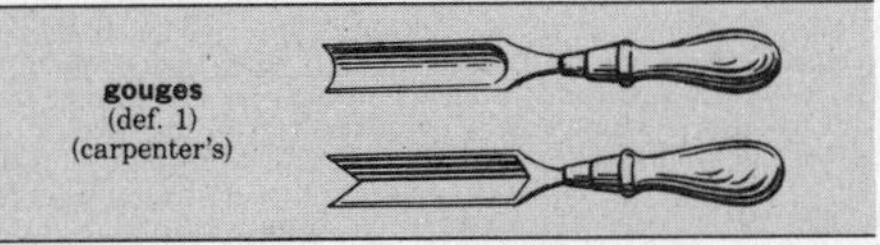
gouges (def. 1) (carpenter's)

gouge (gouj), *n., v.,* **gouged, goug•ing.** —*n.* **1.** a chisel having a partly cylindrical blade with the bevel on either the concave or the convex side. **2.** an act of gouging. **3.** a groove or hole made by gouging. **4.** an act of extortion; swindle. **5.** *Geol.* **a.** a layer of decomposed rocks or minerals found along the walls of a vein. **b.** fragments of rock that have accumulated between or along the walls of a fault. —*v.t.* **6.** to scoop out or turn with or as if with a gouge: *to gouge a channel; to gouge holes.* **7.** to dig or force out with or as if with a gouge: *to gouge out an eye.* **8.** to make a gouge in: *to gouge one's leg.* **9.** to extort from, swindle, or overcharge. —*v.i.* **10.** to engage in swindling, overcharging, or the like: *I bought my clothes there before they began gouging.* [1300–50; ME < F < LL *gu(l)bia;* cf. OPr *goja,* Sp *gubia;* perh. < Celt; cf. OIr *gulba* sting, Welsh *gylf* beak, Cornish *gilb* borer] —**goug′er,** *n.*

gou•jon (gōō′jən), *n., pl.* **-jons,** (*esp. collectively*) **-jon.** See **flathead catfish.** [1880–85, *Amer.;* < LaF, F: GUDGEON[1]]

Gou•jon (gōō zhôN′), *n.* **Jean** (zhäN), c1510–c1568, French sculptor.

gou•lash (gōō′läsh, -lash), *n.* **1.** Also called **Hungarian goulash.** a stew of beef or veal and vegetables, with paprika and other seasoning. **2.** a heterogeneous mixture; hodgepodge; jumble. **3.** a deal in bridge for producing hands of unusual distribution, in which the players arrange their cards of the previous deal by suit and the dealer, after cutting the cards, distributes them without shuffling in three rounds of five, five, and three cards each. [1865–70; < Hungarian *gulyás,* short for *gulyáshús* herdsman's meat]

Gould (gōōld), *n.* **1. Chester,** 1900–85, U.S. cartoonist: creator of the comic strip "Dick Tracy." **2. Glenn Herbert,** 1932–82, Canadian pianist and composer. **3. Jay,** 1836–92, U.S. financier. **4. Morton,** born 1913, U.S. composer and pianist.

Gou•nod (gōō′nō; *Fr.* gōō nō′), *n.* **Charles Fran•çois** (chärlz fran swä′; *Fr.* sharl fräN swa′), 1818–93, French composer.

gou•ra•mi (gŏŏ rä′mē), *n., pl.* (*esp. collectively*) **-mi,** (*esp. referring to two or more kinds or species*) **-mis. 1.** a large, air-breathing, nest-building, freshwater Asiatic fish, *Osphronemus goramy,* used for food. **2.** any of several small, air-breathing, nest-building Asiatic fishes of the genera *Trichogaster, Colisa,* and *Trichopsis,* often kept in aquariums. [1875–80; < Malay (Java dial.) *gurami* < Javanese *graméh*]

gourd (gôrd, gōrd, gŏŏrd), *n.* **1.** the hard-shelled fruit of any of various plants, esp. those of *Lagenaria siceraria* **(white-flowered gourd** or **bottle gourd),** whose dried shell is used for bowls and other utensils, and *Cucurbita pepo* **(yellow-flowered gourd),** used ornamentally. Cf. **gourd family. 2.** a plant bearing such a fruit. **3.** a dried and excavated gourd shell used as a bottle, dipper, flask, etc. **4.** a gourd-shaped, small-necked bottle or flask. **5. out of** or **off one's gourd,** *Slang.* out of one's mind; crazy. [1275–1325; ME *gourd(e), courde* < AF (OF *cöorde*) < L *cucurbita*] —**gourd′like′,** *adj.*

gourd′ cup′, a metal cup of the 16th and 17th centuries having a gourd-shaped bowl mounted on a stem.

gourde (*Fr.* gōōRd; *Eng.* gŏŏrd), *n., pl.* **gourdes** (*Fr.* gōōRd; *Eng.* gŏŏrdz). a paper money and monetary unit of Haiti, equal to 100 centimes. *Abbr.:* G., Gde. [1855–60; < F, n. use of fem. of *gourd* dull, slow, heavy < L *gurdus* dull, obtuse]

gourd′ fam′ily, the plant family Cucurbitaceae, characterized by tendril-bearing vines, either trailing or climbing and having alternate, palmately lobed leaves, often large yellow or greenish flowers, and many-seeded, fleshy fruit with a hard rind, and including the cucumber, gourd, melon, pumpkin, and squash.

gour•mand (gŏŏr mänd′, gŏŏr′mənd), *n.* **1.** a person who is fond of good eating, often indiscriminatingly and to excess. **2.** a gourmet; epicure. Also, **gormand.** [1400–50; late ME *gourmaunt* < OF *gormant* a glutton] —**gour′mand•ism,** *n.*

gour•man•dise[1] (gŏŏr′mən dēz′), *n.* unrestrained enjoyment of fine foods, wines, and the like. [< F; see GORMANDIZE]

CONCISE PRONUNCIATION KEY: act, cāpe, dâre, pärt; set, ēqual; *if,* īce; ox, ōver, ôrder, oil, bŏŏk, bōōt, out; up, ûrge; child; sing; shoe; thin, *th*at; zh as in *treasure.* ə = *a* as in *alone, e* as in *system, i* as in *easily, o* as in *gallop, u* as in *circus;* ᵊ as in *fire* (fīᵊr), *hour* (ouᵊr). l and n can serve as syllabic consonants, as in *cradle* (krād′l), and *button* (but′n). See the full key inside the front cover.

gour·man·dise^{2} (go͝or′mən dīz′), *v.i.*, **-dised, dis·ing.** *Chiefly Brit.* gourmandize.

gour·man·dize (go͝or′mən dīz′), *v.i.*, **-dized, -diz·ing.** to enjoy fine food and drink, esp. often and in lavish quantity. [1540–50; GOURMAND + -IZE] **—gour′man·diz′er,** *n.*

gour·met (go͝or mā′, go͝or′mā), *n.* **1.** a connoisseur of fine food and drink; epicure. **—***adj.* **2.** of or characteristic of a gourmet, esp. in involving or purporting to involve high-quality or exotic ingredients and skilled preparation: *gourmet meals; gourmet cooking.* **3.** elaborately equipped for the preparation of fancy, specialized, or exotic meals: *a gourmet kitchen.* [1810–20; < F; OF *gromet, grommes* valet (esp. of a wine merchant)] **—Syn. 1.** gastronome, bon vivant.

Gour·mont (go͞or môɴ′), *n.* **Re·my de** (rə mē′ də), 1858–1915, French critic and novelist.

Gour·ni·a (go͝or′nē ə), *n.* a village in NE Crete, near the site of an excavated Minoan town and palace.

gout (gout), *n.* **1.** an acute, recurrent disease characterized by painful inflammation of the joints, chiefly those in the feet and hands, and esp. in the great toe, and by an excess of uric acid in the blood. **2.** a mass or splash, as of blood; spurt. [1250–1300; ME *goute* < OF < L *gutta* a drop (of fluid); gout in the feet formerly was attributed to drops of a corrupted humor]

gout·ish (gou′tish), *adj.* susceptible to gout; gouty. [1350–1400; ME; see GOUT, -ISH^{1}]

gout·weed (gout′wēd′), *n.* a fast-spreading weed, *Aegopodium podagraria,* of the parsley family, native to Eurasia, having umbels of white flowers. Also called **bishop's-weed.** [1770–80; GOUT + WEED^{1}]

gout·y (gou′tē), *adj.*, **gout·i·er, gout·i·est. 1.** pertaining to or of the nature of gout. **2.** causing gout. **3.** diseased with or subject to gout. **4.** swollen as if from gout. [1375–1425; late ME; see GOUT, -Y^{1}] **—gout′i·ly,** *adv.* **—gout′i·ness,** *n.*

gout′y stool′, a footstool of the 18th century having a top adjustable to a variety of angles.

Gov., governor.

gov., **1.** governor. **2.** government.

gov·ern (guv′ərn), *v.t.* **1.** to rule over by right of authority: *to govern a nation.* **2.** to exercise a directing or restraining influence over; guide: *the motives governing a decision.* **3.** to hold in check; control: *to govern one's temper.* **4.** to serve as or constitute a law for: *the principles governing a case.* **5.** *Gram.* to be regularly accompanied by or require the use of (a particular form). In *They helped us,* the verb *helped* governs the objective case of the pronoun *we.* **6.** to regulate the speed of (an engine) with a governor. **—***v.i.* **7.** to exercise the function of government. **8.** to have predominating influence. [1250–1300; ME < OF *gouverner* < L *gubernāre* to steer (a ship) < Gk *kybernân* to steer] **—gov′ern·a·ble,** *adj.* **—gov′ern·a·bil′i·ty, gov′ern·a·ble·ness,** *n.* **—Syn. 1.** reign. See **rule. 2.** control, sway, influence, conduct, supervise, superintend. **—Ant. 1.** obey.

Go·ver·na·dor Va·la·da·res (gô′viʀ nə dôʀ′ vä′lə·dä′ʀis), a city in E Brazil. 125,174.

gov·ern·ance (guv′ər nəns), *n.* **1.** government; exercise of authority; control. **2.** a method or system of government or management. [1325–75; ME *governaunce* < OF < ML *gubernantia;* see GOVERN, -ANCE]

gov·ern·ess (guv′ər nis), *n.* **1.** a woman who is employed to take charge of a child's upbringing, education, etc. **2.** *Archaic.* a woman who is a ruler or governor. [1400–50; late ME *governeress* < OF *gouverneresse,* fem. of *gouverneur* GOVERNOR; see -ESS] **—gov′er·ness·y,** *adj.* **—Usage.** See **-ess.**

gov·ern·ment (guv′ərn mənt, -ər mənt), *n.* **1.** the political direction and control exercised over the actions of the members, citizens, or inhabitants of communities, societies, and states; direction of the affairs of a state, community, etc.; political administration: *Government is necessary to the existence of civilized society.* **2.** the form or system of rule by which a state, community, etc., is governed: *monarchical government; episcopal government.* **3.** the governing body of persons in a state, community, etc.; administration. **4.** a branch or service of the supreme authority of a state or nation, taken as representing the whole: *a dam built by the government.* **5.** (in some parliamentary systems, as that of the United Kingdom) **a.** the particular group of persons forming the cabinet at any given time: *The Prime Minister has formed a new government.* **b.** the parliament along with the cabinet: *The government has fallen.* **6.** direction; control; management; rule: *the government of one's conduct.* **7.** the district governed; province. **8.** See **political science. 9.** *Gram.* the established usage that requires that one word in a sentence should cause another to be of a particular form: *the government of the verb by its subject.* [1350–1400; ME < OF *governement.* See GOVERN, -MENT] **—gov·ern·men·tal** (guv′ərn men′tl, -ər men′-), *adj.* **—gov′ern·men′tal·ly,** *adv.* **—Usage.** See **collective noun.** **—Pronunciation.** Normal phonological processes are reflected in a variety of pronunciations for GOVERNMENT. Most commonly, the first (n) of (guv′ərn mənt) assimilates to the immediately following (m), with the resulting identical nasal sounds coalescing to give the pronunciation (guv′ər mənt). This pronunciation is considered standard and occurs throughout the U.S. For speakers in regions where postvocalic (r) is regularly lost, as along the Eastern Seaboard and in the South, the resulting pronunciation is (guv′ə mənt) or, with loss of the medial unstressed vowel, (guv′mənt). Further assimilation, in which the labiodental (v), in anticipation of the bilabial quality of the following (m), becomes the bilabial stop (b), leads in the South Midland and Southern U.S. to the pronunciation (gub′mənt). See **isn't.**

gov·ern·men·tal·ism (guv′ərn men′tl iz′əm, -ər men′-), *n.* the trend toward expansion of the government's role, range of activities, or power. [1840–50; GOVERNMENTAL + -ISM] **—gov′ern·men′tal·ist,** *n.*

gov·ern·ment·ese (guv′ərn mən tēz′, -tēs′, -ər mən-), *n.* complicated or obscurantist language thought to be characteristic of government bureaucratic statements; officialese. Also, **gov·ern·men·tal·ese** (guv′ərn men′tl ēz′, -ēs′, guv′ər-). [GOVERNMENT + -ESE]

Gov′ernment House′, the official residence of a colonial governor, as in a British Commonwealth country. Also, **gov′ernment house′.** [1795–1805]

gov·ern·ment-in-ex·ile (guv′ərn mənt in eg′zīl, -ek′sīl, -ər mənt-), *n.* a government temporarily moved to or formed in a foreign land by exiles who hope to establish that government in their native country after its liberation.

gov′ernment is′sue, (*often cap.*) issued or supplied by the government or one of its agencies. Also, **gov′ernment-is′sue.** [1935–40]

Gov′ernment Na′tional Mort′gage Associa′tion, a U.S. government-owned corporation whose chief function is to help finance government-guaranteed home mortgages through the sale of bonds. *Abbr.:* GNMA Also called **Ginnie Mae.**

Gov′ernment Print′ing Of′fice, *U.S. Govt.* the federal agency that prints and disseminates publications for other federal agencies. *Abbr.:* G.P.O., GPO

gov·ern·ment·y (guv′ərn mən tē, -ər mən-), *adj. Canadian Informal.* pompous. [GOVERNMENT + -Y^{1}]

gov·er·nor (guv′ər nər, -ə nər), *n.* **1.** the executive head of a state in the U.S. **2.** a person charged with the direction or control of an institution, society, etc.: *the governors of a bank; the governor of a prison.* **3.** Also called **governor general.** the representative of the crown, as in the Commonwealth of Nations. **4.** a ruler or chief magistrate appointed to govern a province, town, fort, or the like. **5.** *Mach.* a device for maintaining uniform speed regardless of changes of load, as by regulating the supply of fuel or working fluid. **6.** *Brit. Informal.* **a.** one's father. **b.** one's employer. **c.** any man of superior rank or status. [1250–1300; 1915–20 for def. 5; ME *gouernour* < OF *governeor, gouverneur* < L *gubernātōr-* (s. of *gubernātor*), equiv. to *gubernā(re)* to steer, GOVERN + *-tōr-* -TOR] **—Pronunciation.** In GOVERNOR, the process of dissimilation—the tendency for neighboring like sounds to become unlike or for one of them to disappear entirely—commonly results in the loss of the first (r) of (guv′ər nər), producing the pronunciation (guv′ə nər). This pronunciation is heard even in regions where postvocalic (r) is not usually dropped. A further loss, of the medial unstressed vowel, results in (guv′nər). All three pronunciations are standard. See **colonel, February, library.**

gov·er·nor·ate (guv′ər nər it, -nə rāt′, -ə nər-, -ə nə-), *n.* an administrative division of a country, esp. Egypt. [1895–1900; GOVERNOR + -ATE^{3}]

gov′ernor gen′eral, *pl.* **governors general, governor generals. 1.** a governor who is chief over subordinate or deputy governors. **2.** governor (def. 3). Also, **gov′er·nor-gen′er·al.** [1580–90] **—gov′er·nor-gen′er·al·ship′,** *n.*

gov′ernor's coun′cil, a council chosen to assist or inform a governor on legislative or executive matters. [1885–90, *Amer.*]

gov·er·nor·ship (guv′ər nər ship′, -ə nər-), *n.* the duties, term in office, etc., of a governor. [1635–45; GOVERNOR + -SHIP]

Gov′ernors Is′land, an island in New York Bay at the S end of the East River: U.S. military post. 2 sq. mi. (5 sq. km).

Gov′ernor Win′throp desk′, an 18th-century American desk having a slant front. Also called **Winthrop desk.** [1925–30, *Amer.*; after John WINTHROP]

Govt., government. Also, **govt.**

gow·an (gou′ən), *n. Scot. and North Eng.* any of various yellow or white field flowers, esp. the English daisy. [1560–70; earlier *gollan* < ON *gollinn* golden] **—gow′·aned,** *adj.* **—gow′an·y,** *adj.*

gowd (goud), *n. Chiefly Scot.* gold.

Gow·er (gou′ər, gôr, gōr), *n.* **John,** 1325?–1408, English poet.

gowk (gouk, gōk), *n.* **1.** *Brit. Dial.* cuckoo. **2.** a fool or simpleton. [1275–1325; ME *goke* < ON *gaukr;* c. OE *gēac,* G *Gauch*]

gown (goun), *n.* **1.** a woman's dress or robe, esp. one that is full-length. **2.** nightgown. **3.** dressing gown. **4.** See **evening gown. 5.** a loose, flowing outer garment in any of various forms, worn by a man or woman as distinctive of office, profession, or status: *an academic gown.* **6.** the student and teaching body in a university or college town. **—***v.t.* **7.** to dress in a gown. [1300–50; ME *goune* < OF < LL *gunna* fur or leather garment] **—Syn. 1.** frock. See **dress.**

gowns·man (gounz′mən), *n., pl.* **-men.** a person who wears a gown indicating office, profession, or status. [1570–80; GOWN + -'S^{1} + MAN^{1}]

gox (goks), gaseous oxygen. Cf. **lox**^{2}. [by contr. and shortening]

goy (goi), *n., pl.* **goy·im** (goi′im), **goys.** *Often Disparaging.* a non-Jewish person; gentile. Also, **goi.** [1835–45; < Yiddish < Heb *goi* nation, non-Jew, Jew ignorant of the Jewish religion] **—goy′ish,** *adj.*

Go·ya (goi′ə; *Sp.* gô′yä), *n.* **Fran·cis·co de** (fran sis′kō də; *Sp.* fräN thēs′kô de, -sēs′-), (*Francisco José de Goya y Lucientes*), 1746–1828, Spanish painter.

Go·yen (goi′ən), *n.* **Jan van** (yän vän), 1596–1656, Dutch painter.

goz·zle (goz′əl), *n. South Midland and Southern U.S.* the throat; gullet. Also, **goozle, guzzle.** [1905–10, *Amer.*; expressive word akin to GUZZLE; cf. Brit. dial. *guzzle* gutter, drain, throat]

gp, general purpose.

gp., group. Also, **Gp.**

G.P., **1.** General Practitioner. **2.** General Purpose. **3.** Gloria Patri. **4.** Graduate in Pharmacy. **5.** Grand Prix.

GPA, See **grade point average.**

gpad, gallons per acre per day.

gpcd, gallons per capita per day.

gpd, gallons per day.

gph, gallons per hour. Also, **GPH, g.p.h.**

gpm, gallons per minute. Also, **GPM, g.p.m.**

G.P.O., **1.** See **general post office. 2.** See **Government Printing Office.** Also, **GPO.**

GPS, Global Positioning System. See **NAVSTAR Global Positioning System.**

gps, gallons per second. Also, **GPS, g.p.s.**

GPU, General Postal Union. See **Universal Postal Union.**

GPU (gä′pä′o͞o′, jē′pē′yo͞o′), (in the Soviet Union) the secret-police organization (1922–23) functioning under the NKVD. Also **G.P.U.** Cf. **Cheka, NKVD.** [< Russ *G(osudárstvennoe) p(olitícheskoe) u(pravlénie)* state political directorate]

GQ, General Quarters.

gr, **1.** grain; grains. **2.** gram; grams. **3.** gross.

Gr., **1.** Grecian. **2.** Greece. **3.** Greek.

gr., **1.** grade. **2.** grain; grains. **3.** gram; grams. **4.** grammar. **5.** gravity. **6.** great. **7.** gross. **8.** group.

G.R., King George. [< L *Geōrgius Rēx*]

Graaf′i·an fol′licle (grä′fē ən), (*sometimes l.c.*) one of the small vesicles containing a developing ovum in the ovary of a mammal. [1835–45; named after Regnier de *Graaf* (d. 1673), Dutch anatomist; see -IAN]

grab^{1} (grab), *v.*, **grabbed, grab·bing,** *n.* **—***v.t.* **1.** to seize suddenly or quickly; snatch; clutch: *He grabbed me by the collar.* **2.** to take illegal possession of; seize forcibly or unscrupulously: *to grab land.* **3.** to obtain and consume quickly: *Let's grab a sandwich before going to the movie.* **4.** *Slang.* **a.** to cause a reaction in; affect: *How does my idea grab you?* **b.** to arouse the interest or excitement of: *The book was O.K., but it just didn't grab me.* **—***v.i.* **5.** to make a grasping or clutching motion (usually fol. by *at*): *He grabbed frantically at the life preserver.* **6.** (of brakes, a clutch, etc.) to take hold suddenly or with a jolting motion; bind. **—***n.* **7.** a sudden, quick grasp or snatch: *to make a grab at something.* **8.** seizure or acquisition by violent or unscrupulous means. **9.** something that is grabbed. **10.** a mechanical device for gripping objects. **11.** the capacity to hold or adhere: *The glue was so old it had lost its grab.* **12. up for grabs,** *Informal.* available to anyone willing to expend the energy to get it: *The Republican nomination for mayor was up for grabs.* [1580–90; c. MD, MLG *grabben,* Sw *grabba*] **—grab′ba·ble,** *adj.* **—Syn. 1.** grasp, grip, catch.

grab^{2} (grab), *n.* an Oriental ship having two or three masts with a square rig. [1670–80; < Ar *ghurāb* lit., raven]

grab′ bag′, **1.** a container or receptacle from which a person at a party or the like draws a gift without knowing what it is. **2.** any miscellaneous collection. [1850–55, *Amer.*]

grab′ bar′, a bar attached to a wall near a bathtub or shower to provide a handgrip for a person who is bathing.

grab·ber (grab′ər), *n.* **1.** a person or thing that grabs. **2.** *Slang.* something attention-getting or sensational. [1840–50; GRAB^{1} + -ER^{1}]

grab·ble (grab′əl), *v.i.*, **-bled, -bling. 1.** to feel or search with the hands; grope. **2.** to sprawl; scramble. [1570–80; GRAB^{1} + -LE; cf. D *grabbelen*] **—grab′bler,** *n.*

grab·by (grab′ē), *adj.*, **-bi·er, -bi·est. 1.** tending to grab or grasp for gain; greedy: *a grabby ticket scalper.* **2.** *Slang.* provoking immediate attention or interest; arresting: *a poster with some really grabby artwork.* **3.** having a capacity for or tendency toward holding, grasping, or sticking: *Car tires that are too grabby waste fuel.* [1905–10; GRAB^{1} + -Y^{1}]

gra·ben (grä′bən), *n.* a portion of the earth's crust, bounded on at least two sides by faults, that has dropped downward in relation to adjacent portions. Also called **rift valley.** Cf. **horst.** [1895–1900; < G: ditch]

grab′ rope′, *Naut.* a rope supported to afford a hold for a person walking up a gangplank, working aloft, etc. Also called **grab′ line′.**

Grac·chus (grak′əs), *n.* **1. Ga·ius Sem·pro·ni·us** (gā′əs sem prō′nē əs), 153–121 B.C., and his brother, **Ti·be·ri·us Sempronius** (tī bēr′ē əs), 163–133 B.C., Roman reformers and orators. **2. the Gracchi** (grak′ī), the brothers Gracchus.

grace (grās), *n.*, *v.*, **graced, grac·ing. —***n.* **1.** elegance or beauty of form, manner, motion, or action. **2.** a pleasing or attractive quality or endowment. **3.** favor or good will. **4.** a manifestation of favor, esp. by a superior: *It was only through the dean's grace that I wasn't expelled from school.* **5.** mercy; clemency; pardon: *an act of grace.* **6.** favor shown in granting a delay or temporary immunity. **7.** an allowance of time after a debt or bill has become payable granted to the debtor before suit can be brought against him or her or a penalty applied: *The life insurance premium is due today, but we have 31 days' grace before the policy lapses.* Cf. **grace period. 8.** *Theol.* **a.** the freely given, unmerited favor and love of God. **b.** the influence or spirit of God operat-

CONCISE ETYMOLOGY KEY: <, descended or borrowed from; >, whence; b., blend of, blended; c., cognate with; cf., compare; deriv., derivative; equiv., equivalent; imit., imitative; obl., oblique; r., replacing; s., stem; sp., spelling, spelled; resp., respelling, respelled; trans., translation; ?, origin unknown; *, unattested; ‡, probably earlier than. See the full key inside the front cover.

ing in humans to regenerate or strengthen them. **c.** a virtue or excellence of divine origin: *the Christian graces.* **d.** Also called **state of grace.** the condition of being in God's favor or one of the elect. **9.** moral strength: *the grace to perform a duty.* **10.** a short prayer before or after a meal, in which a blessing is asked and thanks are given. **11.** (*usually cap.*) a formal title used in addressing or mentioning a duke, duchess, or archbishop, and formerly also a sovereign (usually prec. by *your, his,* etc.). **12. Graces,** *Class. Myth.* the goddesses of beauty, daughters of Zeus and Eurynome, worshiped in Greece as the Charities and in Rome as the Gratiae. **13.** *Music.* See **grace note. 14. fall from grace, a.** *Theol.* to relapse into sin or disfavor. **b.** to lose favor; be discredited: *He fell from grace when the boss found out he had lied.* **15. have the grace to,** to be so kind as to: *Would you have the grace to help, please?* **16. in someone's good** (or **bad**) **graces,** regarded with favor (or disfavor) by someone. **17. with bad grace,** reluctantly; grudgingly: *He apologized, but did so with bad grace.* **18. with good grace,** willingly; ungrudgingly: *She took on the extra work with good grace.* —*v.t.* **19.** to lend or add grace to; adorn: *Many fine paintings graced the rooms of the house.* **20.** to favor or honor: *to grace an occasion with one's presence.* [1125–75; ME < OF < L *grātia* favor, kindness, esteem, deriv. of *grātus* pleasing] —**grace′like′,** *adj.*
—**Syn. 1.** attractiveness, charm, gracefulness, comeliness, ease. **4.** kindness, kindliness, love, benignity; condescension. **5.** lenity, leniency. **19.** embellish, beautify, deck, decorate, ornament; enhance, honor. —**Ant. 1.** ugliness. **4.** animosity. **5.** harshness. **19.** disfigure.

Grace (grās), *n.* **1. William Russell,** 1832–1904, U.S. financier and shipping magnate, born in Ireland: mayor of New York City 1880–88. **2.** a female given name.

grace-and-fa•vor (grās′ən fā′vər), *adj.* noting a residence owned by a noble or sovereign and bestowed by him or her upon some person for that person's lifetime. [1905–10]

grace′ cup′, **1.** a cup, as of wine, passed around at the end of the meal for the final health or toast. **2.** the drink passed. [1585–95]

grace•ful (grās′fəl), *adj.* characterized by elegance or beauty of form, manner, movement, or speech; elegant: *a graceful dancer; a graceful reply.* [1375–1425; late ME; see GRACE, -FUL] —**grace′ful•ly,** *adv.* —**grace′ful•ness,** *n.*
—**Syn.** limber, lithe, lissome.

grace•less (grās′lis), *adj.* **1.** lacking grace, pleasing elegance, or charm. **2.** without any sense of right or propriety. [1325–75; ME; see GRACE, -LESS] —**grace′less•ly,** *adv.* —**grace′less•ness,** *n.*

grace′ note′, *Music.* a note not essential to the harmony or melody, added as an embellishment, esp. an appoggiatura. [1815–25]

grace′ pe′riod, a period of time after a payment becomes due, as of a loan or life-insurance premium, before one is subject to penalties or late charges or before the loan or policy is canceled.

gra•ci•as (grä′thē äs′, -sē; *Eng.* grä′sē əs), *interj. Spanish.* thank you.

grac•ile (gras′il), *adj.* **1.** gracefully slender. **2.** slender; thin. [1615–25; < L *gracilis* slender, slight, thin] —**gra•cil•i•ty** (gra sil′i tē, grə-), **grac′ile•ness,** *n.*

grac•i•lis (gras′ə lis), *n., pl.* **-les** (-lēz′). *Anat.* a muscle in the inner side of the thigh, the action of which assists in drawing the legs inward and in bending the knee. [1605–15; < NL; L: GRACILE]

gra•ci•o•so (grä′shē ō′sō, grä′sē-; *Sp.* grä thyô′sô, -syô′-), *n., pl.* **-sos** (-sōz; *Sp.* -sôs). a buffoon or clown in Spanish comedy. [1640–50; < Sp: amiable, gracious, spirited (n. use of adj.) < L *grātiōsus* GRACIOUS]

gra•cious (grā′shəs), *adj.* **1.** pleasantly kind, benevolent, and courteous. **2.** characterized by good taste, comfort, ease, or luxury: *gracious suburban living; a gracious home.* **3.** indulgent or beneficent in a pleasantly condescending way, esp. to inferiors. **4.** merciful or compassionate: *our gracious king.* **5.** *Obs.* fortunate or happy. —*interj.* **6.** (used as an exclamation of surprise, relief, dismay, etc.) [1250–1300; ME *gracious* < OF < L *grātiōsus* amiable, equiv. to *grāti(a)* GRACE + *-ōsus* -OUS] —**gra′cious•ly,** *adv.* —**gra′cious•ness, gra•ci•os•i•ty** (grā′shē os′i tē), *n.*
—**Syn. 1.** benign, friendly, polite. See **kind**[1]. **4.** tender, clement, mild, gentle. —**Ant. 1.** churlish. **4.** cruel.

grack•le (grak′əl), *n.* **1.** any of several long-tailed American birds of the family Icteridae, esp. of the genus *Quiscalus,* having usually iridescent black plumage. **2.** any of several Old World birds of the family Sturnidae, esp. certain mynas. [1765–75; < NL *Gracula* name of genus, based on L *grāculus* jackdaw]

grad[1] (grad), *n. Informal.* a graduate. [1870–75; by shortening]

grad[2] (grad), *n.* one hundredth of a right angle. Also, **grade.** [1905–10; < F *grade* degree < L *gradus* step]

grad., **1.** *Math.* gradient. **2.** graduate. **3.** graduated.

grad•a•bil•i•ty (grā′də bil′i tē), *n. Transp.* a measure of a truck's pulling power expressed as the steepest grade the truck can climb with a full load. Also, **gradeability.** Cf. **grade** (def. 9). [1950–55; GRADE + -ABILITY]

grad•a•ble (grā′də bəl), *adj.* **1.** capable of being graded. **2.** *Gram.* (esp. of adjectives and adverbs) denoting a quality or state that can be present in varying degree or extent; capable of undergoing comparison or intensification, as *heavy—heavier, cheerful—more cheerful,* or *tall—very tall,* but not *atomic* or *dental.* [GRADE + -ABLE]

gra•date (grā′dāt), *v.,* **-dat•ed, -dat•ing.** —*v.i.* **1.** to pass by gradual or imperceptible degrees, as one color into another. —*v.t.* **2.** to cause to gradate. **3.** to arrange in grades. [1745–55; back formation from GRADATION]

gra•da•tim (grā dā′tim), *adv.* (in prescriptions) by degrees; gradually. [1575–85; < L]

gra•da•tion (grā dā′shən), *n.* **1.** any process or change taking place through a series of stages, by degrees, or in a gradual manner. **2.** a stage, degree, or grade in such a series. **3.** the passing of one tint or shade of color to another, or one surface to another, by very small degrees, as in painting or sculpture. **4.** the act of grading. **5.** ablaut. **6.** *Geol.* the leveling of a land surface, resulting from the concerted action of erosion and deposition. [1530–40; < L *gradātiōn-* (s. of *gradātiō*). See GRADE, -ATION] —**gra•da′tion•al,** *adj.* —**gra•da′tion•al•ly,** *adv.*

grade (grād), *n., v.,* **grad•ed, grad•ing.** —*n.* **1.** a degree or step in a scale, as of rank, advancement, quality, value, or intensity: *the best grade of paper.* **2.** a class of persons or things of the same relative rank, quality, etc. **3.** a step or stage in a course or process. **4.** a single division of a school classified according to the age or progress of the pupils. In the U.S., public schools are commonly divided into twelve grades below college. **5.** the pupils in such a division. **6. grades,** elementary school (usually prec. by *the*): *He first began teaching in the grades.* **7.** a letter, number, or other symbol indicating the relative quality of a student's work in a course, examination, or special assignment; mark. **8.** a classification or standard of food based on quality, size, etc.: *grade A milk.* **9.** inclination with the horizontal of a road, railroad, etc., usually expressed by stating the vertical rise or fall as a percentage of the horizontal distance; slope. **10.** *Building Trades.* Also called **grade line.** the level at which the ground intersects the foundation of a building. **11.** an animal resulting from a cross between a parent of ordinary stock and one of a pure breed. **12.** *Math.* grad[2]. **13. at grade, a.** on the same level: *A railroad crosses a highway at grade.* **b.** (of a stream bed) so adjusted to conditions of slope and the volume and speed of water that no gain or loss of sediment takes place. **14. make the grade,** to attain a specific goal; succeed: *He'll never make the grade in medical school.* **15. up to grade,** of the desired or required quality: *This shipment is not up to grade.* —*v.t.* **16.** to arrange in a series of grades; class; sort: *a machine that grades two thousand eggs per hour.* **17.** to determine the grade of. **18.** to assign a grade to (a student's work); mark: *I graded forty tests last night.* **19.** to cause to pass by degrees, as from one color or shade to another. **20.** to reduce to a level or to practicable degrees of inclination: *to grade a road.* **21.** to cross (an ordinary or low-grade animal) with an animal of a pure or superior breed. —*v.i.* **22.** to incline; slant or slope: *The road grades steeply for a mile.* **23.** to be of a particular grade or quality. **24.** to pass by degrees from one color or shade to another; blend: *See how the various colors grade into one another.* **25. grade up,** to improve (a herd, flock, etc.) by breeding with purebreds. [1505–15; < F: office < L *gradus* step, stage, degree, deriv. of *gradī* to go, step, walk]
—**Syn. 16.** classify, rank, rate, order, categorize.

-grade, a combining form meaning "walking, moving," in the manner or by the means specified by the initial element: *plantigrade.* [< L *-gradus,* comb. form repr. *gradus* step or *gradī* to walk. See GRADE, GRADIENT]

grade•a•bil•i•ty (grā′də bil′i tē), *n. Transp.* gradability.

grade′ cross′ing, an intersection of a railroad track and another track, a road, etc., at the same level. Also, *Brit.,* **level crossing.** [1885–90, *Amer.*]

grad′ed ar′ea. See **transition area.**

grade•fla•tion (grād′flā′shən), *n.* See **grade inflation.**

grade′ infla′tion, the awarding of higher grades than students deserve either to maintain a school's academic reputation or as a result of diminished teacher expectations. [1980–85]

grade′ line′, grade (def. 10).

grade•mark (grād′märk′), *n.* **1.** a symbol noting the relative quality of a product, as lumber. —*v.t.* **2.** to mark with a grademark. [GRADE + MARK[1]]

grade′ point′, *Educ.* a numerical equivalent to a received letter grade, usually 0 for F, 1 for D, 2 for C, 3 for B, and 4 for A, multiplied by the number of credits for the course: used to compute a grade point average.

grade′ point′ av′erage, *Educ.* a measure of scholastic attainment computed by dividing the total number of grade points received by the total number of credits or hours of course work taken. Also called **quality point average.** [1965–70]

grad•er (grā′dər), *n.* **1.** a person or thing that grades. **2.** a pupil of a specified grade at school: *a fourth grader.* **3.** a machine for grading. [1840–50, *Amer.*; GRADE + -ER[1]]

grade′ school′, an elementary school that has its pupils grouped or classified into grades. Also, **grad′ed school′.** [1850–55, *Amer.*]

grade-school•er (grād′sko͞o′lər), *n.* a pupil in a grade school. [GRADE SCHOOL + -ER[1]]

grade′ separa′tion, separation of the levels at which roads, railroads, paths, etc., cross one another in order to prevent conflicting rows of traffic or the possibility of accidents. [1930–35, *Amer.*]

gra•di•ent (grā′dē ənt), *n.* **1.** the degree of inclination, or the rate of ascent or descent, in a highway, railroad, etc. **2.** an inclined surface; grade; ramp. **3.** *Physics.* **a.** the rate of change with respect to distance of a variable quantity, as temperature or pressure, in the direction of maximum change. **b.** a curve representing such a rate of change. **4.** *Math.* a differential operator that, operating upon a function of several variables, results in a vector the coordinates of which are the partial derivatives of the function. *Abbr.:* grad. *Symbol:* ∇ —*adj.* **5.** rising or descending by regular degrees of inclination. **6.** progressing by walking; stepping with the feet as animals do. **7.** of a type suitable for walking or running, as the feet of certain birds; gressorial. [1635–45; < L *gradient-* (s. of *gradiēns*), prp. of *gradī* to walk, go, equiv. to *grad-* walk + *-i-* thematic vowel + *-ent-* -ENT]

gra•di•ent•er (grā′dē en′tər), *n. Survey.* an instrument on a transit for measuring angles of inclination in terms of their tangents. [1880–85; GRADIENT + -ER[1]]

gra′dient wind′ (wind), a wind with a velocity and direction that are mathematically defined by the balanced relationship of the pressure gradient force to the centrifugal force and the Coriolis force: conceived as blowing parallel to isobars. Cf. **geostrophic wind.** [1905–10]

gra•din (grā′din; *Fr.* GRA daN′), *n., pl.* **-dins** (-dinz; *Fr.* -daN′). **1.** one of a series of steps or seats raised one above another. **2.** *Eccles.* a shelf or one of a series of shelves behind and above an altar. Also, **gra•dine** (grə dēn′). [1830–40; < F: step, ledge of altar < It *gradino,* dim. of *grado* GRADE]

gra•di•om•e•ter (grā′dē om′i tər), *n. Physics.* any instrument used to measure a gradient, as the rate of change of the geomagnetic field. Cf. **gradient** (def. 3a). [1800–10; GRADI(ENT) + -O- + -METER]

grad•u•al (graj′o͞o əl), *adj.* **1.** taking place, changing, moving, etc., by small degrees or little by little: *gradual improvement in health.* **2.** rising or descending at an even, moderate inclination: *a gradual slope.* —*n.* **3.** *Eccles.* (*often cap.*) **a.** an antiphon sung between the Epistle and the Gospel in the Eucharistic service. **b.** a book containing the words and music of the parts of the liturgy that are sung by the choir. [1375–1425; late ME < ML *graduālis* pertaining to steps, *graduāle* the part of the service sung as the choir stood on the altar steps, equiv. to L *gradu(s)* step, GRADE + *-ālis* -AL[1]] —**grad′u•al•ly,** *adv.* —**grad′u•al•ness,** *n.*
—**Syn. 1.** See **slow. 2.** gentle. —**Ant. 1.** sudden. **2.** precipitous.

grad•u•al•ism (graj′o͞o ə liz′əm) *n.* **1.** the principle or policy of achieving some goal by gradual steps rather than by drastic change. **2.** *Philos.* a theory maintaining that two seemingly conflicting notions are not radically opposed, but are related by others partaking in varying degrees of the character of both. **3.** *Biol.* a tenet in evolutionary theory maintaining that species evolve slowly and continuously over long periods of geological time. Cf. **punctuated equilibrium.** [1825–35, *Amer.*; GRADUAL + -ISM] —**grad′u•al•ist,** *n., adj.* —**grad′u•al•is′tic,** *adj.*

grad•u•and (graj′o͞o and′), *n. Brit.* a student who is about to graduate or receive a degree. [1880–85; < ML *graduandus,* ger. of *graduāre* to GRADUATE]

grad•u•ate (*n., adj.* graj′o͞o it, -āt′; *v.* graj′o͞o āt′), *n., adj., v.,* **-at•ed, -at•ing.** —*n.* **1.** a person who has received a degree or diploma on completing a course of study, as in a university, college, or school. **2.** a student who holds the bachelor's or the first professional degree and is studying for an advanced degree. **3.** a cylindrical or tapering graduated container, used for measuring. —*adj.* **4.** of, pertaining to, or involved in academic study beyond the first or bachelor's degree: *graduate courses in business; a graduate student.* **5.** having an academic degree or diploma: *a graduate engineer.* —*v.i.* **6.** to receive a degree or diploma on completing a course of study (often fol. by *from*): *She graduated from college in 1985.* **7.** to pass by degrees; change gradually. —*v.t.* **8.** to confer a degree upon, or to grant a diploma to, at the close of a course of study, as in a university, college, or school: *Cornell graduated eighty students with honors.* **9.** *Informal.* to receive a degree or diploma from: *She graduated college in 1950.* **10.** to arrange in grades or gradations; establish gradation in. **11.** to divide into or mark with degrees or other divisions, as the scale of a thermometer. [1375–1425; late ME < ML *graduātus* (ptp. of *graduāre*), equiv. to *grad(us)* GRADE, step + *-u-* thematic vowel + *-ātus* -ATE[1]] —**grad′u•a′tor,** *n.*
—**Usage.** In the sense "to receive a degree or diploma" GRADUATE followed by FROM is the most common construction today: *Her daughter graduated from Yale in 1981.* The passive form WAS GRADUATED FROM, formerly insisted upon as the only correct pattern, has decreased in use and occurs infrequently today: *My husband was graduated from West Point last year.*
Even though it is condemned by some as nonstandard, the use of GRADUATE as a transitive verb meaning "to receive a degree or diploma from" is increasing in frequency in both speech and writing: *The twins graduated high school in 1974.*

grad•u•at•ed (graj′o͞o ā′tid), *adj.* **1.** characterized by or arranged in degrees, esp. successively, as according to height, depth, or difficulty: *a graduated series of lessons.* **2.** marked with divisions or units of measurement. **3.** (of a bird's tail) having the longest feathers in the center, the others being successively shorter. **4.** (of a tax) increasing along with the taxable base: *a graduated income tax.* [1645–55; GRADUATE + -ED[2]]

grad′uate nurse′, a person who has graduated from an accredited school of nursing. Also called **trained nurse.**

grad′uate school′, a school, usually a division of a university, offering courses leading to degrees more advanced than the bachelor's degree. [1890–95, *Amer.*]

grad•u•a•tion (graj′o͞o ā′shən), *n.* **1.** an act of graduating; the state of being graduated. **2.** the ceremony of conferring degrees or diplomas, as at a college or school. **3.** arrangement in degrees, levels, or ranks. [1375–1425; late ME *graduacion* < ML *graduātiōn-* (s. of *graduātiō*). See GRADUATE, -ION]

gra•dus[1] (grā′dəs), *n., pl.* **-dus•es.** *Music.* a work consisting wholly or in part of exercises of increasing difficulty. [< L: GRADE, step]

gra•dus[2] (grā′dəs), *n., pl.* **-dus•es.** a dictionary of prosody, esp. one that gives word quantities and poetic

CONCISE PRONUNCIATION KEY: act, cāpe, dâre, pärt; set, ēqual; if, īce; ox, ōver, ôrder, oil, bo͝ok, bo͞ot, out; up, ûrge; child; sing; shoe; thin, *th*at; zh as in *treasure.* ə = a as in *alone,* e as in *system,* i as in *easily,* o as in *gallop,* u as in *circus;* ə as in *fire* (fīər), *hour* (ouər). l and n can serve as syllabic consonants, as in *cradle* (krād′l), and *button* (but′n). See the full key inside the front cover.

phrases and that is intended to aid students in the writing of Latin and Greek verse. [1755–65; after *Gradus ad Parnassum* (a step to Parnassus), Latin title of a dictionary of prosody much used in English public schools during the 18th and 19th centuries]

Grae·ae (grē′ē), *n.pl. Class. Myth.* three old sea goddesses who had but one eye and one tooth among them and were the protectors of their sisters the Gorgons. Also, **Graiae.**

Grae·ci·a Mag·na (grē′shē ə mag′nə). See **Magna Graecia.**

Grae·cize (grē′sīz), *v.t., v.i.,* **-cized, -ciz·ing.** *Chiefly Brit.* Grecize. Also, **Grae′cise.** —**Grae′cism,** *n.*

Graeco-, *Chiefly Brit.* var. of **Greco-.**

Grae·co-Ro·man (grē′kō rō′mən, grek′ō-), *adj., n. Chiefly Brit.* Greco-Roman.

Graef′fe meth′od (gref′ə, graf′ə), *Math.* a method, involving the squaring of roots, for approximating the solutions to algebraic equations.

Graf (gräf), *n., pl.* **Graf·en** (gräf′fən). *German.* a count: a title of nobility in Germany, Austria, and Sweden, equivalent in rank to an English earl.

Gräf′en·berg spot′ (gräf′ən bûrg′, gref′-), a patch of tissue in the front wall of the vagina, claimed to be erectile and highly erogenous. Also called **G spot, G-spot.** [1980–85; after German-born gynecologist Ernst *Gräfenberg* (1881–1957), who is credited with first describing it]

graf·fi·ti (grə fē′tē), *n.* **1.** pl. of **graffito. 2.** (*used with a plural v.*) markings, as initials, slogans, or drawings, written, spray-painted, or sketched on a sidewalk, wall of a building or public restroom, or the like: *These graffiti are evidence of the neighborhood's decline.* **3.** (*used with a singular v.*) such markings as a whole or as constituting a particular group: *Not much graffiti appears around here these days.* [1850–55; < It, pl. of *graffito* incised inscription or design, deriv. with *-ito* -ITE[2] of *graffiare* to scratch, perh. influenced by presumed L *graphire to write; both prob. deriv. of L *graphium* stylus < Gk *grapheîon;* cf. GRAPHIC, GRAPHO-, GRAFT[1]] —**graf·fi′tist,** *n.*
—**Usage.** In formal speech and writing GRAFFITI takes a plural verb. In less formal contexts it is sometimes considered a mass noun and is used with a singular verb. The singular GRAFFITO is found mostly in archaeological and other technical writing.

graf·fi·to (grə fē′tō), *n., pl.* **-ti** (-tē). **1.** *Archaeol.* an ancient drawing or writing scratched on a wall or other surface. **2.** a single example of graffiti. [see GRAFFITI]
—**Usage.** See **graffiti.**

graft[1] (graft, gräft), *n.* **1.** *Hort.* **a.** a bud, shoot, or scion of a plant inserted in a groove, slit, or the like in a stem or stock of another plant in which it continues to grow. **b.** the plant resulting from such an operation; the united stock and scion. **c.** the place where the scion is inserted. **2.** *Surg.* a portion of living tissue surgically transplanted from one part of an individual to another, or from one individual to another, for its adhesion and growth. **3.** an act of grafting. —*v.t.* **4.** to insert (a graft) into a tree or other plant; insert a scion of (one plant) into another plant. **5.** to cause (a plant) to reproduce through grafting. **6.** *Surg.* to transplant (a portion of living tissue, as of skin or bone) as a graft. **7.** to attach as if by grafting: *an absurdity grafted onto an otherwise coherent body of thought.* **8.** *Naut.* to cover (a rope) with a weaving of rope yarn. —*v.i.* **9.** to insert scions from one plant into another. **10.** to become grafted. [1350–1400; earlier *graff,* ME *graffe, craffe* < OF *graife, greffe, graffe* < LL *graphium* hunting knife (L: stylus) < Gk *grapheion,* deriv. of *gráphein* to write; so called from the resemblance of the point of a (cleft) graft to a stylus] —**graft′er,** *n.*
—**Syn. 10.** implant, transplant, plant, join, adhere.

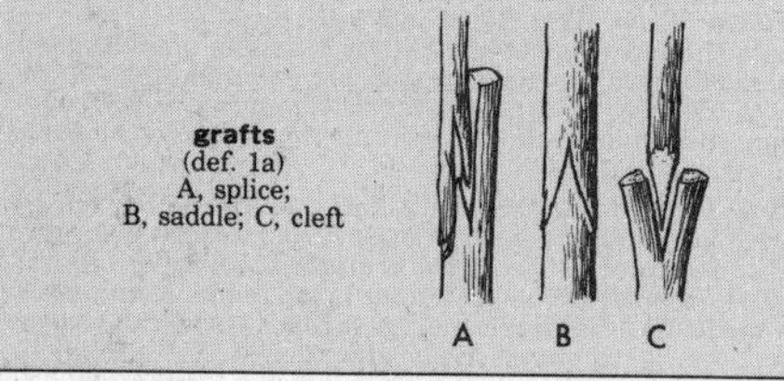

grafts
(def. 1a)
A, splice;
B, saddle; C, cleft

graft[2] (graft, gräft), *n.* **1.** the acquisition of money, gain, or advantage by dishonest, unfair, or illegal means, esp. through the abuse of one's position or influence in politics, business, etc. **2.** a particular instance, method, or means of thus acquiring gain or advantage. **3.** the gain or advantage acquired. **4.** *Brit. Slang.* work; labor. —*v.t.* **5.** to obtain by graft. —*v.i.* **6.** to practice graft. [1855–60; perh. special use of GRAFT[1]] —**graft′er,** *n.*

graft·age (graf′tij, gräf′-), *n.* the art or practice of inserting a part of one plant into another plant in such a way that the two will unite and continue their growth. [1890–95; GRAFT[1] + -AGE]

graft′ hy′brid, a hybrid plant that is produced by grafting and that exhibits characters of both the stock and the scion. [1865–70]

graft·ing (graf′ting, gräf′-), *n. Surg.* graft[1] (def. 2). [1475–85; GRAFT[1] + -ING[1]]

CONCISE ETYMOLOGY KEY: <, descended or borrowed from; >, whence; b., blend of, blended; c., cognate with; cf., compare; deriv., derivative; equiv., equivalent; imit., imitative; obl., oblique; r., replacing; s., stem; sp., spelling, spelled; resp., respelling, respelled; trans., translation; ?, origin unknown; *, unattested; ‡, probably earlier than. See the full key inside the front cover.

Graf·ton (graf′tən, gräf′-), *n.* a city in central Massachusetts. 11,238.

graft′-ver·sus-host′ disease′ (graft′vûr′səs hōst′, gräft′-), a reaction in which the cells of transplanted tissue immunologically attack the cells of the host organism, occurring esp. in bone-marrow transplants. [1970–75]

gra·ger (grä′gər), *n. Judaism.* a noise-making device, typically a small container filled with pellets and fitted with a handle, used by children each time Haman's name is said during the traditional reading of the Book of Esther on Purim. Also, **grogger.** [< Yiddish: rattle]

gra·ham (grā′əm, gram), *adj.* made of graham flour. [1825–35]

Gra·ham (grā′əm, gram), *n.* **1. Martha,** 1894–1991, U.S. dancer and choreographer. **2. Thomas,** 1805–69, Scottish chemist. **3. William Franklin** ("*Billy*"), born 1918, U.S. evangelist. **4.** a male given name: from an Old English word meaning "gray home."

gra′ham crack′er, a semisweet cracker, usually rectangular in shape, made chiefly of whole-wheat flour. [1815–25, *Amer.*]

Gra·hame (grā′əm), *n.* **Kenneth,** 1859–1932, Scottish writer, esp. of children's stories.

gra′ham flour′, unbolted wheat flour, containing all of the wheat grain; whole-wheat flour. [1825–35, *Amer.;* named after Sylvester *Graham* (1794–1851), U.S. dietary reformer]

gra·ham·ite (grā′ə mīt′), *n. Mineral.* an asphaltite with a pitch-black luster. [1865–70, *Amer.;* named after J. A. and J. L. *Graham,* 19th-century American mine-owners; see -ITE[1]]

Gra′ham Land′, a part of the British Antarctic Territory, in the N section of the Antarctic Peninsula: formerly the British name for the entire peninsula.

Gra′ham's law′ of diffu′sion, *Physical Chem.* the principle that at a given temperature and pressure the rate of diffusion of a gas is inversely proportional to the square root of its density. [1945–50; named after T. GRAHAM]

gra′ham wa′fer, *Canadian.* See **digestive biscuit.**

Grai·ae (grā′ē, grī′ē), *n.pl.* Graeae.

grail (grāl), *n.* **1.** (*usually cap.*) Also called **Holy Grail.** a cup or chalice that in medieval legend was associated with unusual powers, esp. the regeneration of life and, later, Christian purity, and was much sought after by medieval knights: identified with the cup used at the Last Supper and given to Joseph of Arimathea. **2.** (*sometimes cap.*) *Informal.* any greatly desired and sought-after objective; ultimate ideal or reward. [1300–50; ME *graiel, graile,* etc. < AF *grahel, grayel,* OF *gräel, grel* < ML *gradālis* platter, of uncert. orig.]

grain (grān), *n.* **1.** a small, hard seed, esp. the seed of a food plant such as wheat, corn, rye, oats, rice, or millet. **2.** the gathered seed of food plants, esp. of cereal plants. **3.** such plants collectively. **4.** any small, hard particle, as of sand, gold, pepper, or gunpowder. **5.** the smallest unit of weight in most systems, originally determined by the weight of a plump grain of wheat. In the U.S. and British systems, as in avoirdupois, troy, and apothecaries' weights, the grain is identical. In an avoirdupois ounce there are 437.5 grains; in the troy and apothecaries' ounces there are 480 grains (one grain equals 0.0648 gram). **6.** the smallest possible amount of anything: *a grain of truth.* **7.** the arrangement or direction of fibers in wood, or the pattern resulting from this. **8.** the direction in which the fibers of a piece of dressed wood, as a board, rise to the surface: *You should work with or across the grain, but never against.* **9.** the side of leather from which the hair has been removed. **10.** a stamped pattern that imitates the natural grain of leather: used either on leather to simulate a different type of natural leather, or on coated cloth. **11.** *Textiles.* **a.** the fibers or yarn in a piece of fabric as differentiated from the fabric itself. **b.** the direction of threads in a woven fabric in relation to the selvage. **12.** the lamination or cleavage of stone, coal, etc. **13.** *Metall.* any of the individual crystalline particles forming a metal. **14.** *Jewelry.* a unit of weight equal to 50 milligrams or ¼ carat, used for pearls and sometimes for diamonds. **15.** the size of constituent particles of any substance; texture: *sugar of fine grain.* **16.** a granular texture or appearance: *a stone of coarse grain.* **17.** a state of crystallization: *boiled to the grain.* **18.** temper or natural character: *two brothers of similar grain.* **19.** *Rocketry.* a unit of solid propellant. **20.** *Obs.* color or hue. **21. against the** or **one's grain,** in opposition to one's temper, inclination, or character: *Haggling always went against her grain.* **22. with a grain of salt.** See **salt**[1] (def. 9). —*v.t.* **23.** to form into grains; granulate. **24.** to give a granular appearance to. **25.** to paint in imitation of the grain of wood, stone, etc.: *metal doors grained to resemble oak.* **26.** to feed grain to (an animal). **27.** *Tanning.* **a.** to remove the hair from (skins). **b.** to soften and raise the grain of (leather). [1250–1300; ME *grain, grein* < OF *grain* < L *grānum* seed, grain; see CORN[1]] —**grain′er,** *n.* —**grain′less,** *adj.*
—**Syn. 6.** bit, speck, trace, jot, iota, whit, tittle.

grain′ al′cohol, alcohol (def. 1). [1920–25]

grained (grānd), *adj.* **1.** having, reduced to, consisting of, or bearing grain or grains (usually used in combination): *fine-grained sand; large-grained rice.* **2.** having a granular form, structure, or surface: *wood and other grained materials.* **3.** having an artificially produced granular texture or pattern: *grained kid.* **4.** marked by a particular quality (usually used in combination): *tough-grained journalism.* [1520–30; GRAIN + -ED[3]] —**grained·ness** (grānd′nis, grā′nid-), *n.*

grain′ el′evator, elevator (def. 4). [1850–55]

grain·field (grān′fēld′), *n.* a field in which grain is grown. [1810–20; GRAIN + FIELD]

Grain·ger (grān′jər), *n.* **Percy Al·dridge** (ôl′drij), 1882–1961, Australian pianist and composer, in the U.S. after 1915.

grain′ growth′, *Metall.* a tendency of certain grains to grow and absorb others when heated under certain conditions. [1925–30]

grain′ itch′ mite′. See **straw mite.**

grain′ refin′er, *Metall.* any chemical added to a molten metal or alloy to check grain growth.

grains (grānz), *n.* (*often used with a singular v.*) an iron instrument with barbed prongs, for spearing or harpooning fish. [1895–1900; earlier *grainse* < ON *grein* branch, division; cf. Sw *gren*]

grains′ of par′adise, the pungent, peppery seeds of an African plant, *Aframomum melegueta,* of the ginger family, used to strengthen cordials and in veterinary medicine. Also called **guinea grains, Guinea pepper.** [1490–1500]

grain′ sor′ghum, any of several varieties of sorghum, as durra or milo, having starchy seeds, grown for grain and forage. [1915–20]

grain·y (grā′nē), *adj.,* **grain·i·er, grain·i·est. 1.** resembling grain; granular. **2.** full of grains or grain. **3.** having a natural or simulated grain, as wood, wallpaper, etc. **4.** *Photog.* (of a negative or positive) having a granular appearance. [1605–15; GRAIN + -Y[1]] —**grain′i·ness,** *n.*

gral·la·to·ri·al (gral′ə tôr′ē əl, -tōr′-), *adj.* belonging or pertaining to the wading birds, as the snipes, cranes, storks, and herons, many species of which have very long legs. [1825–35; < L *grallātor* one who walks on stilts (*grall(ae)* stilts + *-ātor* -ATOR) + -IAL]

gram[1] (gram), *n.* a metric unit of mass or weight equal to 15.432 grains; one thousandth of a kilogram. *Abbr.:* g Also, *esp. Brit.,* **gramme.** [1790–1800; < F *gramme* < LL *gramma* a small weight < Gk *grámma* something drawn, a small weight]

gram[2] (gram), *n.* **1.** (in the East Indies) the chickpea used as a food for people and cattle. **2.** any of several other beans, as the mung bean, *Vigna radiata* (**green gram** or **golden gram**), or the urd, *V. mungo* (**black gram**). [1695–1705; < Pg *grão* < L *grānum* GRAIN]

Gram (gräm), *n.* (in the *Volsunga Saga*) the sword of Sigmund, broken by Odin, repaired by Regin, and used again by Sigurd in killing Fafnir. Cf. **Balmung.** [< ON *Gramr* lit., angry, evil]

-gram[1], a combining form occurring in loanwords from Greek, where it meant "something written," "drawing" (*epigram; diagram*); on this model, used in the formation of compound words (*oscillogram*). Cf. **-graph.** [< Gk *-gramma,* comb. form of *grámma* something written or drawn; akin to CARVE]

-gram[2], a combining form of **gram**[1]: *kilogram.*

-gram[3], a combining form extracted from **telegram,** used in the formation of compound words that have the general sense "message, bulletin": *culturegram; electiongram; prophecy-gram.*

gram., **1.** grammar. **2.** grammarian. **3.** grammatical.

gra·ma (grä′mə), *n.* any grass of the genus *Bouteloua,* of South America and western North America, as *B. gracilis* (**blue grama**). Also, **gram′ma.** Also called **gra′ma grass′.** [1820–30, *Amer.;* < Sp *grama* < L *grāmina,* pl. of *grāmen* grass]

gra·ma·dan (grä mä′dän, grä′mä dän′, gräm dän′), *n.* the practice advocated by followers of Mahatma Gandhi in which village landowners in India transfer the title to and the management of their property to a village assembly that represents the interests of all the villagers. Also, **gram·dan** (gräm dän′). [1955–60; < Hindi *grāmadān,* equiv. to *grāma* village + *dān* gift, donation]

gram·a·rye (gram′ə rē), *n.* occult learning; magic. Also, **gram′a·ry.** [1275–1325; ME *gramary* < OF *gramaire,* lit., GRAMMAR]

gram′ at′om, *Chem.* the quantity of an element whose weight in grams is numerically equal to the atomic weight of the element. Also called **gram′-a·tom′ic weight′** (gram′ə tom′ik, -tom′-). Cf. **Avogadro's number.** [1895–1900]

gram′ cal′orie, calorie (def. 1a). *Abbr.:* g-cal [1900–05]

gram′ equiv′alent, *Chem.* See under **equivalent weight.** [1895–1900]

gra·mer·cy (grə mûr′sē), *interj.* **1.** *Archaic.* (used as an exclamation expressing surprise or sudden strong feeling.) —*n.* **2.** *Obs.* thanks. [1300–50; ME *gramerci, grantmerci* < OF *grand merci* great thanks. See GRAND, MERCY]

gram·i·ci·din (gram′ə sīd′n), *n. Pharm.* a crystalline, water-insoluble antibiotic obtained from tyrothrycin by extraction, used chiefly in treating local infections caused by Gram-positive organisms. Also called **gramicidin D.** [1935–40; GRAM-(POSITIVE) + -I- + -CIDE + -IN[2]]

gra·min·e·ous (grə min′ē əs), *adj.* **1.** grasslike. **2.** belonging to the Gramineae family of plants. Cf. **grass family.** [1650–60; < L *grāmineus* pertaining to grass, equiv. to *grāmin-* (s. of *grāmen*) grass + *-eus* -EOUS] —**gra·min′e·ous·ness,** *n.*

gram·i·niv·o·rous (gram′ə niv′ər əs), *adj.* feeding or subsisting on grass: *a graminivorous bird.* [1730–40; < L *grāmin-* (s. of *grāmen*) grass + -I- + -VOROUS]

gram·ma·logue (gram′ə lôg′, -log′), *n.* a word symbolized by a sign or letter. [< Gk *grámma* letter + -LOGUE]

gram·mar (gram′ər), *n.* **1.** the study of the way the sentences of a language are constructed; morphology and syntax. **2.** these features or constructions themselves: *English grammar.* **3.** an account of these features; a set of rules accounting for these constructions: *a grammar of English.* **4.** *Generative Gram.* a device, as a body of rules, whose output is all of the sentences that are permissible in a given language, while excluding all those that are not permissible. **5.** See **prescriptive grammar.** **6.** knowledge or usage of the preferred or prescribed forms in speaking or writing: *She said his grammar was terrible.* **7.** the elements of any science, art, or subject. **8.** a book treating such elements. [1325–75; ME *gramery* < OF *gramaire* < L *gramatica* < Gk *grammatikḗ* (*téchnē*) GRAMMATICAL (art); see -AR²] —**gram′mar·less,** *adj.*

gram·mar·i·an (grə mâr′ē ən), *n.* **1.** a specialist or expert in grammar. **2.** a person who claims to establish or is reputed to have established standards of usage in a language. [1350–1400; ME *gramarien* < OF *gramairien.* See GRAMMAR, -IAN]

gram′mar school′, **1.** an elementary school. **2.** *Brit.* a secondary school corresponding to a U.S. high school. **3.** (formerly) a secondary school in which Latin and Greek are among the principal subjects taught. [1350–1400; ME]

gram′mar-trans·la′tion meth′od (gram′ər trans-lā′shən, -tranz-), a traditional technique of foreign-language teaching based on explicit instruction in the grammatical analysis of the target language and translation of sentences from the native language into the target language and vice versa.

gram·mat·i·cal (grə mat′i kəl), *adj.* **1.** of or pertaining to grammar: *grammatical analysis.* **2.** conforming to standard usage: *grammatical speech.* [1520–30; < L *grammatic(us)* (< Gk *grammatikós* knowing one's letters, equiv. to *grammat-,* s. of *grámma* letter + *-ikos* -IC) + -AL¹] —**gram·mat′i·cal·ly,** *adv.*

grammat′ical gen′der, *Gram.* gender based on arbitrary assignment, without regard to the referent of a noun, as in French *le livre* (masculine), "the book," and German *das Mädchen* (neuter), "the girl." Cf. **natural gender.** [1870–75]

gram·mat·i·cal·i·ty (grə mat′i kal′i tē), *n.* the state or quality of being grammatical. Also, **gram·mat·i·cal·ness** (grə mat′i kəl nis). [1960–65; GRAMMATICAL + -ITY]

gram·mat·i·cal·ize (grə mat′i kə līz′), *v.t.,* **-ized, -iz·ing.** *Ling.* **1.** to convert (a content word or part of one) into a functor, as in using OE *līc,* 'body,' as a suffix in adjectives and adverbs, such as OE *frēondlīc,* 'friendly.' **2.** to represent (semantic features) by grammatical categories, as plurality in English or gender in French. Also, *esp. Brit.,* **gra·mat′i·cal·ise′.** [1935–40; GRAMMATICAL + -IZE] —**gram·mat′i·cal·i·za′tion,** *n.*

grammat′ical mean′ing, the meaning of an inflectional morpheme or of some other syntactic device, as word order. Cf. **lexical meaning.** [1760–70]

gram·mat·i·cism (grə mat′ə siz′əm), *n. Rare.* **1.** a point or principle of grammar. **2.** a grammatical definition. [1600–10; GRAMMATIC(AL) + -ISM]

gram·ma·tol·o·gy (gram′ə tol′ə jē), *n.* the scientific study of systems of writing. [< Gk *grammat-,* s. of *grámma* letter + -O- + -LOGY]

gramme (gram), *n. Chiefly Brit.* gram¹.

gram′-molec′ular weight′. See **gram molecule.** *Abbr.:* GMW [1900–05]

gram′ mol′ecule, *Chem.* that quantity of a substance whose weight in grams is numerically equal to the molecular weight of the substance. Cf. **Avogadro's number.** [1890–95] —**gram-mo·lec·u·lar** (gram′mə lek′yə lər), **gram-mo·lar** (gram′mō′lər), *adj.*

Gram·my (gram′ē), *n., pl.* **-mys, -mies.** one of a group of statuettes awarded annually by the National Academy of Recording Arts and Sciences for outstanding achievement in various categories in the recording industry. [GRAM(OPHONE) + -Y²]

Gram-neg·a·tive (gram′neg′ə tiv), *adj.* (*often l.c.*) (of bacteria) not retaining the violet dye when stained by Gram's method. [1905–10; see GRAM'S METHOD]

Gra·mont (gRA môN′), *n.* **Phi·li·bert** (fē lē beR′), **Comte de,** 1621–1707, French courtier, soldier, and adventurer.

gram·o·phone (gram′ə fōn′), *n.* a phonograph. [1887; orig. a trademark; appar. inversion of *phonogram* now obs. name for a phonographic cylinder] —**gram·o·phon·ic** (gram′ə fon′ik), **gram′o·phon′i·cal,** *adj.* —**gram′o·phon′i·cal·ly,** *adv.*

Gram·pi·an (gram′pē ən), *n.* a region in E Scotland. 448,772; 3361 sq. mi. (8704 sq. km).

Gram·pi·ans (gram′pē ənz), *n.* **The,** (*used with a plural v.*) a range of low mountains in central Scotland, separating the Highlands from the Lowlands. Highest peak, Ben Nevis, 4406 ft. (1343 m). Also called **Gram′pian Hills′.**

Gram-pos·i·tive (gram′poz′i tiv), *adj.* (*often l.c.*) (of bacteria) retaining the violet dye when stained by Gram's method. [1905–10; see GRAM'S METHOD]

gramps (gramps), *n. Informal.* grandfather. Also, **gramp.** [1860–65; see GRANDPA, -S⁴]

gram·pus (gram′pəs), *n., pl.* **-pus·es.** **1.** a cetacean, *Grampus griseus,* of the dolphin family, widely distributed in northern seas. **2.** any of various related cetaceans, as the killer whale, *Orcinus (Orca) orca.* **3.** a giant whip scorpion common to Florida. [1520–30; earlier *grampoys,* var. (by assimilation) of *graundepose* great fish, equiv. to *graunde* GRAND + *pose, poys* < MF *pois, peis* < L *pisce-* (s. of *piscis*) fish; r. ME *gra(s)peis* < MF << L *crassus piscis* fat fish]

grampus, *Grampus griseus,* length 9 to 13 ft. (2.7 to 4 m)

Gram′-Schmidt′ orthogonaliza′tion (gram′-shmit′), *Math.* a process for constructing an orthogonal basis for a Euclidean space, given any basis for the space. [named after Jörgen Pedersen *Gram* (1850–1916), Danish mathematician, and Erhard *Schmidt* (1876–1959), German mathematician]

Gram's′ meth′od (gramz), (*sometimes l.c.*) a method of staining and distinguishing bacteria, in which a fixed bacterial smear is stained with crystal violet, treated with Gram's solution, decolorized with alcohol, counterstained with safranine, and washed with water. Cf. **Gram-negative, Gram-positive.** [named after Hans C. J. *Gram* (1853–1938), Danish bacteriologist]

Gram's′ solu′tion, (*sometimes l.c.*) a solution of iodine, potassium iodide, and water, used in staining bacteria. Cf. **Gram's method.**

Gram-var·i·a·ble (gram′vâr′ē ə bəl), *adj.* (*often l.c.*) of or pertaining to bacteria that stain irregularly with Gram's stain, being neither Gram-positive nor Gram-negative. [1955–60; see GRAM'S METHOD]

gran (gran), *n. Informal.* grandmother. [1860–65; by shortening]

gra·na (grā′nə), *n.* (in prescriptions) pl. of **granum.** [1890–95; < L]

Gra·na·da (grə nä′də; *Sp.* grä nä′thä), *n.* **1.** a medieval kingdom along the Mediterranean coast of S Spain. See map under **Castile.** **2.** a city in S Spain: the capital of this former kingdom and last stronghold of the Moors in Spain; site of the Alhambra. 190,429. **3.** a city in SW Nicaragua, near Lake Nicaragua. 40,200.

gran·a·dil·la (gran′ə dil′ə), *n.* **1.** the edible fruit of any of several species of passionflower, esp. *Passiflora edulis* (**purple granadilla**) or *P. quadrangularis* (**giant granadilla**). **2.** any of the plants yielding these fruits. Also, **grenadilla.** [1605–15; < Sp *granadilla,* dim. of *granada* pomegranate]

Gra·na·dos (grä nä′thôs), *n.* **En·ri·que** (en Rē′ke), 1867–1916, Spanish pianist and composer.

gra·na·ry (grā′nə rē, gran′ə-), *n., pl.* **-ries.** **1.** a storehouse or repository for grain, esp. after it has been threshed or husked. **2.** a region that produces great quantities of grain. [1560–70; < L *grānārium,* equiv. to *grān(um)* GRAIN + *-ārium* -ARY]

gra′nary wee′vil, a reddish-brown weevil, *Sitophilus granarius,* that infests stored grain. [1840–50, *Amer.*]

Gran·by (gran′bē), *n.* a city in S Quebec, in E Canada. 38,069.

Gran Ca·na·ria (gRän′ kä nä′Ryä), one of the Canary Islands, in the central part. 519,606; 650 sq. mi. (1685 sq. km). *Cap.:* Las Palmas. Also, **Grand Canary.**

Gran Cha·co (gRän chä′kô), an extensive subtropical region in central South America, in Argentina, Bolivia, and Paraguay. 300,000 sq. mi. (777,000 sq. km). Also called **Chaco.**

grand (grand), *adj.,* **grand·er, grand·est,** *n., pl.* **grands** for 13, **grand** for 14. —*adj.* **1.** impressive in size, appearance, or general effect: *grand mountain scenery.* **2.** stately, majestic, or dignified: *In front of an audience her manner is grand and regal.* **3.** highly ambitious or idealistic: *grand ideas for bettering the political situation.* **4.** magnificent or splendid: *a grand palace.* **5.** noble or revered: *a grand old man.* **6.** highest, or very high, in rank or official dignity: *a grand potentate.* **7.** main or principal; chief: *the grand ballroom.* **8.** of great importance, distinction, or pretension: *a man used to entertaining grand personages.* **9.** complete or comprehensive: *a grand total.* **10.** pretending to grandeur, as a result of minor success, good fortune, etc.; conceited: *Jane is awfully grand since she got promoted.* **11.** first-rate; very good; splendid: *to have a grand time; to feel grand.* **12.** *Music.* written on a large scale or for a large ensemble: *a grand fugue.* —*n.* **13.** See **grand piano.** **14.** *Informal.* an amount equal to a thousand dollars: *The cops found most of the loot, but they're still missing about five grand.* [1350–1400; 1920–25 for def. 14; ME *gra(u)nd, gra(u)nt* < OF *grant, grand* < L *grand-* (s. of *grandis*) great, large full-grown] —**grand′ly,** *adv.* —**grand′ness,** *n.*
—**Syn.** **2.** princely, regal, royal, exalted. **4.** great, large, palatial; brilliant, superb. **9.** inclusive. —**Ant.** **1.** insignificant. **2.** modest, unassuming. **3.** small; mean. **7.** minor.

grand-, a combining form used in genealogical terminology meaning "one generation more remote": *grandfather; grandnephew.* [special use of GRAND]

gran·dam (gran′dəm, -dam), *n.* **1.** a grandmother. **2.** an old woman. Also, **gran·dame** (gran′dām, -dəm). [1175–1225; ME *gra(u)ndame* < OF *grant dame.* See GRAND, DAME]

Grand′ Ar′my of the Repub′lic, an organization, founded in 1866, composed of men who served in the U.S. Army and Navy during the Civil War: its last member died in 1956. *Abbr.:* G.A.R.

grand·aunt (grand′ant′, -änt′), *n.* an aunt of one's father or mother; great-aunt. [1820–30; GRAND- + AUNT]

grand·ba·by (gran′bā′bē, grand′-), *n., pl.* **-bies.** an infant grandchild. [1915–20; GRAND- + BABY]

Grand′ Baha′ma, an island in the NW Bahamas. 25,859; 430 sq. mi. (1115 sq. km).

Grand′ Banks′, an extensive shoal SE of Newfoundland: fishing grounds. 350 mi. (565 km) long; 40,000 sq. mi. (104,000 sq. km). Also, **Grand′ Bank′.**

Grand′ Canal′, **1.** a canal in E China, extending S from Tientsin to Hangchow. 900 mi. (1450 km) long. **2.** a canal in Venice, Italy, forming the main city thoroughfare.

Grand′ Canar′y. See **Gran Canaria.**

Grand′ Can′yon, a gorge of the Colorado River in N Arizona. over 200 mi. (320 km) long; 1 mi. (1.6 km) deep.

Grand′ Can′yon Na′tional Park′, a national park in N Arizona, including part of the Grand Canyon and the area around it. 1009 sq. mi. (2615 sq. km).

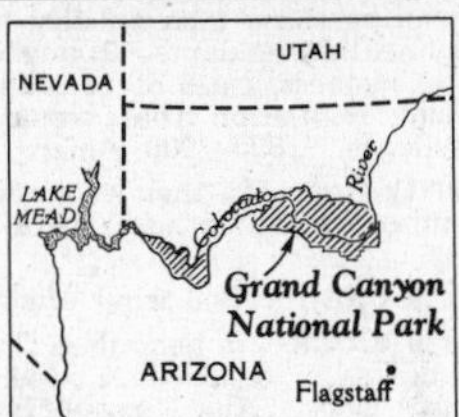

Grand′ Can′yon State′, Arizona (used as a nickname).

Grand′ Cay′man, the largest of the Cayman Islands, West Indies. 8932; 76 sq. mi. (197 sq. km).

grand·child (gran′chīld′), *n., pl.* **-chil·dren.** a child of one's son or daughter. [1580–90; GRAND- + CHILD]

grand′ chop′, (in China and India trade) a customs clearance.

grand′ climac′teric. See under **climacteric** (def. 3).

Grand′ Cou′lee (ko͞o′lē), **1.** a dry canyon in central Washington: cut by the Columbia River in the glacial period. 52 mi. (84 km) long; over 400 ft. (120 m) deep. **2.** a dam on the Columbia River at the N end of this canyon. 550 ft. (168 m) high.

grand′ coun′cil fire′, a formal gathering of camp fire members requiring a minimum attendance of three troops.

grand′ coup′, *Bridge, Whist.* the trumping of a trick that could have been taken by the winner's partner. [1870–75]

Grand Cru (*Fr.* gRäN kRY′), *pl.* **Grands Crus** (*Fr.* gRäN kRY′). *French.* See under **cru.**

grand·dad (gran′dad′), *n. Informal.* grandfather. [1810–20; GRAND- + DAD¹]

grand·dad·dy (gran′dad′ē), *n., pl.* **-dies.** *Informal.* grandfather. [1760–70; GRAND- + DADDY]

grand·daugh·ter (gran′dô′tər), *n.* a daughter of one's son or daughter. [1605–15; GRAND- + DAUGHTER]

grand′ drag′on, a high-ranking official of the Ku Klux Klan. [1865–70, *Amer.*]

grand′ dra′pery, *Theat.* a valance across the proscenium arch, forming part of the decorative frame for the stage.

grand′ duch′ess, **1.** the wife or widow of a grand duke. **2.** a woman who governs a grand duchy in her own right. **3.** a daughter of a czar or of a czar's son. [1750–60]

grand′ duch′y, a territory ruled by a grand duke or grand duchess. [1825–35]

Grand′ Duch′y of Mus′covy, Muscovy (def. 1). Also, **Grand′ Duch′y of Mos′cow.**

grand′ duke′, **1.** the sovereign of a territory called a grand duchy, ranking next below a king. **2.** a son of a czar or of a czar's son. [1685–95] —**grand′-du′cal,** *adj.*

Gran·de (grand, gran′dē, grän′dā; *Port.* gRäN′di), *n.* **Rio.** See **Rio Grande.**

Grande Char·treuse, La (*Fr.* lA gRäNd shAR trœz′), the Carthusian monastery at Grenoble, France: the chief monastery of the Carthusians until 1903.

grande dame (gran′ dam′, dām′; *Fr.* gRäNd dAm′), *pl.* **grandes dames** (gran′ damz′, dāmz′; *Fr.* gRäNd dAm′). **1.** a usually elderly woman of dignified or aristocratic bearing. **2.** a woman who is the doyenne of a specific field: *a grande dame of the American theater.* [1735–45; < F: lit., great lady]

gran·dee (gran dē′), *n.* a man of high social position or eminence, esp. a Spanish or Portuguese nobleman. [1590–1600; < Sp, Pg *grande,* with ending assimilated to -EE] —**gran·dee′ship,** *n.*

Grande′ Prai′rie (grand), a city in W Alberta, in W Canada. 17,626.

Grande-Terre (*Fr.* gRäNd teR′), *n.* See under **Guadeloupe.**

gran·deur (gran′jər, -jo͝or), *n.* **1.** the quality or state of being impressive or awesome: *the grandeur of the Rocky Mountains.* **2.** the quality or state of being lofty or elevated in conception or treatment: *the grandeur of a prose style.* **3.** the quality or state of being exalted in some deliberate way: *the grandeur of a royal court.* **4.** an instance of something that is grand: *the grandeurs of Rembrandt's paintings.* [1490–1500; < F, OF, equiv. to *grand-* GRAND + *-eur* -OR¹]
—**Syn.** **3.** stateliness, majesty; pomp, splendor.

Grand′ Falls′, former name of **Churchill Falls.**

grand·fa·ther (gran′fä′thər, grand′-), *n.* **1.** the father of one's father or mother. **2.** a forefather. **3.** the founder or originator of a family, species, type, etc.; the first of one's or its kind, or the one being longest in existence: *the grandfather of all steam locomotives.* —*v.t.* **4.** to exempt (something or someone) from new legislation, restrictions, or requirements: *The law grandfathered all banks already operating at the time of passage. He was grandfathered into the pension plan.* [1375–1425; late ME; see GRAND-, FATHER]

grand′father clause′, **1.** *U.S. Hist.* a clause in the constitutions of some Southern states after 1890 intended to permit whites to vote while disfranchising blacks: it exempted from new literacy and property qualifications for voting those men entitled to vote before 1867 and their lineal descendants. **2.** any legal provision that exempts a business, class of persons, etc., from a new government regulation that would affect prior rights and privileges. [1895–1900, *Amer.*]

grand·fa·ther·ly (gran′fä′thər lē, grand′-), *adj.* of or characteristic of a grandfather. [1815–25; GRANDFATHER + -LY]

grand′father's chair′. See **wing chair.** [1890–95]

grand′father's clock′, a pendulum floor clock having a case as tall as or taller than a person; tall-case clock; long-case clock. Also, **grand′father clock′.** [1890–95]

grandfather's clock

grand feu (*Fr.* gräN fœ′), *Ceram.* **1.** a firing of ceramics at a high temperature. **2.** the category of ceramic colors fired at high temperature. Cf. **petit feu.** [1860–65; < F: lit., great fire]

grand′ fina′le, the concluding portion of a performance or entertainment, as a musical show, rodeo, etc., usually spectacular and involving most or all of the prior participants. [1870–75]

grand′ fir′, a large fir, *Abies grandis,* of the western coast of North America, having a narrow, pointed crown and yielding a soft wood used for lumber, pulp, and boxes. Also called **lowland fir.** [1895–1900]

Grand′ Forks′, a town in E North Dakota. 43,765.

Grand·gent (gran′jənt), *n.* **Charles Hall,** 1862–1939, U.S. philologist and essayist.

Grand Gui·gnol (*Fr.* gräN gē nyôl′), **1.** a short drama stressing horror and sensationalism. **2.** of, pertaining to, or resembling such a drama. [1905–10; after *Le Grand Guignol,* small theater in Paris where such dramas were performed]

Grand′ Ha′ven, a city in W Michigan. 11,763.

gran·di·flo·ra (gran′də flôr′ə, -flōr′ə), *n.* any of several plant varieties or hybrids characterized by large showy flowers, as certain kinds of petunias, baby's breath, or roses. [1900–05; < NL, a specific epithet frequent in the names of such flowers; see GRAND, -I-, FLORA]

gran·dil·o·quence (gran dil′ə kwəns), *n.* speech that is lofty in tone, often to the point of being pompous or bombastic. [1580–90; < L *grandiloqu(us)* speaking loftily (*grandi(s)* great + *-loquus* speaking) + -ENCE]

gran·dil·o·quent (gran dil′ə kwənt), *adj.* speaking or expressed in a lofty style, often to the point of being pompous or bombastic. [1585–95; GRANDILOQU(ENCE) + -ENT] **—gran·dil′o·quent·ly,** *adv.*
—Syn. turgid, inflated, rhetorical, pretentious.
—Ant. simple, sincere.

grand′ inquis′itor, (*often caps.*) the presiding officer of a court of inquisition.

gran·di·ose (gran′dē ōs′), *adj.* **1.** affectedly grand or important; pompous: *grandiose words.* **2.** more complicated or elaborate than necessary; overblown: *a grandiose scheme.* **3.** grand in an imposing or impressive way. **4.** *Psychiatry.* having an exaggerated belief in one's importance, sometimes reaching delusional proportions, and occurring as a common symptom of mental illnesses, as manic disorder. [1830–40; < F < It *grandioso* < L *grandi(s)* grand + *-ōsus* -OSE[1]] **—gran′di·ose′ly,** *adv.* **—gran′di·ose′ness, gran·di·os·i·ty** (gran′dē os′i tē), *n.*
—Syn. 1. pretentious, extravagant, flamboyant, splashy, high-flown. **2.** GRANDIOSE, SHOWY, OSTENTATIOUS, PRETENTIOUS all refer to conspicuous outward display, either designed to attract attention or likely to do so. GRANDIOSE and SHOWY are alike in that they may suggest impressiveness that is not objectionable: *the grandiose sweep of the arch; a fresh bouquet of showy zinnias.* GRANDIOSE, however, most often implies inflation or exaggeration to the point of absurdity: *grandiose, impractical plans; a ridiculously grandiose manner.* SHOWY sometimes suggests a meretricious gaudiness or flashiness: *a showy taste in dress.* OSTENTATIOUS, which refers to behavior or manner clearly designed to impress, also has negative connotations: *an ostentatious display of wealth; an assumption of superiority too ostentatious to be ignored.* PRETENTIOUS, like the preceding term, is always derogatory, implying falseness or exaggeration in claims made or implied: *natural and straightforward, not pretentious; pretentious language designed to mask the absence of real content.*

Grand′ Is′land, a city in S Nebraska. 33,180.

grand je·té (*Fr.* gräN zhə tā′), *pl.* **grands je·tés** (*Fr.* gräN zhə tā′). *Ballet.* a jump or jeté, preceded by a grand battement or high kick, in which a dancer leaps from one leg and lands on the other. [1925–30; < F]

CONCISE ETYMOLOGY KEY: <, descended or borrowed from; >, whence; b., blend of, blended; c., cognate with; cf., compare; deriv., derivative; equiv., equivalent; imit., imitative; obl., oblique; r., replacing; s., stem; sp., spelling, spelled; resp., respelling, respelled; trans., translation; ?, origin unknown; *, unattested; ‡, probably earlier than. See the full key inside the front cover.

Grand′ Junc′tion, a city in W Colorado. 28,144.

grand′ ju′ror, a person serving on a grand jury. Also called **grand′ ju′ryman.** [1590–1600]

grand′ ju′ry, a jury, at common law, of 12 to 23 persons, designated to inquire into alleged violations of the law in order to ascertain whether the evidence is sufficient to warrant trial. [1490–1500; < AF *graund juree*]

Grand′ Kabu′ki, kabuki (def. 2).

Grand′ La′ma, the chief monk and ruler of Tibet: called the Dalai Lama since the middle of the 17th century. [1930–35]

grand′ lar′ceny, *Law.* larceny in which the value of the goods taken is above a certain legally specified amount. Also called **grand theft.** Cf. **petty larceny.** [1840–50]

grand·ma (gran′mä′, -mô′, grand′-, gram′-, gram′mə), *n. Informal.* grandmother. [1865–70; GRAND- + MA]

grand mal (gran′ mäl′, -mal′, grand′; *Fr.* gräN mal′), *Pathol.* See under **epilepsy.** [1875–80; < F: great ailment, epilepsy]

grand·mam·ma (grand′mə mä′; gran′mä′mə, grand′-, gram′-), *n. Informal.* grandmother. [1740–50; GRAND- + MAMMA[1]]

Grand′ma Mo′ses. See **Moses, Anna Mary Robertson.**

Grand′ Ma·nan′ (mə nan′), a Canadian island at the entrance to the Bay of Fundy: a part of New Brunswick; summer resort. ab. 3000; 57 sq. mi. (148 sq. km).

grand′ march′, the opening ceremonies of a formal ball, in which guests promenade into or around the ballroom. [1895–1900, *Amer.*]

Grand Mar·nier (gräN′ mär nyā′; *Fr.* gräN marnyā′), *Trademark.* a brand of French liqueur having a brandy base and an orange flavor.

Grand′ Mas′ter, 1. the head of a military order of knighthood, a lodge, fraternal order, or the like. **2.** (*often l.c.*) *Chess.* See **International Grand Master.**

Grand'Mère (*Fr.* gräN mer′), *n.* a town in S Quebec, in E Canada. 15,442.

grand·moth·er (gran′muth′ər, grand′-, gram′-), *n.* **1.** the mother of one's father or mother. **2.** a female ancestor. [1375–1425; late ME; see GRAND-, MOTHER[1]]

grand·moth·er·ly (gran′muth′ər lē, grand′-, gram′-), *adj.* of or characteristic of a grandmother. [1835–45; GRANDMOTHER + -LY] **—grand′moth′er·li·ness,** *n.*

grand′mother's clock′, a pendulum clock similar to a grandfather's clock but shorter. Also, **grand′mother clock′.** [1920–25]

Grand′ Muf′ti, 1. a Muslim religious leader. **2.** (formerly) the chief legal authority for Muslims in Jerusalem.

grand·neph·ew (gran′nef′yōō, -nev′yōō, grand′-), *n.* a son of one's nephew or niece. [1630–40; GRAND- + NEPHEW]

grand·niece (gran′nēs′, grand′-), *n.* a daughter of one's nephew or niece. [1820–30; GRAND- + NIECE]

grand′ old′ man′, a highly respected, usually elderly man who has been a major or the most important figure in a specific field for many years.

Grand′ Old′ Par′ty. See **G.O.P.**

Grand′ Ole′ Op′ry (ōl′ op′rē), a successful radio show from Nashville, Tenn., first broadcast on Nov. 28, 1925, noted for its playing of and continuing importance to country music.

grand′ op′era, a serious, usually tragic, opera in which most of the text is set to music. [1795–1805]

grand·pa (gran′pä′, -pô′, grand′-, gram′-, gram′pə), *n. Informal.* grandfather. [1885–90; GRAND- + PA]

grand·pa·pa (grand′pə pä′; gran′pä′pə, grand′-, gram′-), *n. Informal.* grandfather. [1745–55; GRAND- + PAPA]

grand·pap·py (gran′pap′ē, grand′-, gram′-), *n., pl.* **-pies.** *Dial.* grandfather. Also, **grand′pap′.** [1935–40; GRAND- + PAPPY[2]]

grand·par·ent (gran′pâr′ənt, -par′-, grand′-), *n.* a parent of a parent. [1820–30; GRAND- + PARENT] **—grand·pa·ren·tal** (gran′pə ren′tl, grand′-), *adj.* **—grand′par′ent·ing,** *n.*

grand′ pas′sion, 1. an intense or overwhelming attraction or love. **2.** the object of such feelings. [1925–30; trans. of F *grande passion*]

grand′ peniten′tiary. See under **penitentiary** (def. 3).

grand′ pian′o, a piano having the frame supported horizontally on three legs. Cf. **concert grand.** See illus. under **piano**[1]. [1790–1800]

Grand′ Prai′rie, a city in NE Texas. 71,462.

Grand Pré (gran′ prā′; *Fr.* gräN prā′), a village in central Nova Scotia, on Minas Basin: locale of Longfellow's *Evangeline.*

Grand Prix (*Fr.* gräN prē′), *pl.* **Grand Prix, Grands Prix, Grand Prixes** (*all pronounced Fr.* gräN prē′). (*sometimes l.c.*) any of various major automobile races over a long, arduous course, esp. an international car race held each year over the same course. [1905–10; < F: grand prize]

grand′ quar′ter, *Heraldry.* a quartered coat of arms, itself one of the quarters of a coat of arms. [1885–90]

Grand′ Rap′ids, 1. a city in SW Michigan: furniture factories. 181,843. **2.** noting or pertaining to mass-produced furniture of generally low quality.

gran·drelle (gran drel′), *n.* (*sometimes cap.*) a two-ply yarn made by twisting together two singles of contrasting color. [orig. obscure]

grand′ right′ and left′, a figure called in square dancing in which partners face each other, forming a small circle, and then advance around the circle by extending alternating right and left hands to pull past each new person until they reach their partners again.

Grand′ Riv′er, 1. former name of the Colorado River above its junction with the Green River in SE Utah. **2.** a river in SW Michigan, flowing W to Lake Michigan. 260 mi. (420 km) long.

grand′ rounds′, a formal hospital meeting at which physicians discuss interesting medical cases.

grand-scale (grand′skāl′), *adj.* of large proportion, extent, magnitude, etc.: *grand-scale efforts; a grand-scale approach.* [1955–60]

grand′ ser′jeanty, *Medieval Eng. Law.* serjeanty in which the tenant rendered services of a personal, honorary nature to the king, as carrying his sword or banner. Cf. **petit serjeanty.** [ME *graunte sergaunte* < AF]

grand·sire (grand′sīᵊr′), *n.* **1.** a grandfather. **2.** *Archaic.* **a.** a forefather. **b.** an aged man. [1250–1300; ME *graunt-sire* < AF. See GRAND-, SIRE]

grand′ slam′, 1. *Bridge.* the winning of all thirteen tricks of a deal. Cf. **little slam. 2.** Also, **grand′-slam′·mer.** *Baseball.* a home run with three runners on base. **3.** *Sports.* the winning by a single player of several designated major championship contests in one season, as in golf or tennis. **4.** any sweeping success or total victory. [1890–95]

grand·son (gran′sun′, grand′-), *n.* a son of one's son or daughter. [1580–90; GRAND- + SON]

grand·stand (gran′stand′, grand′-), *n., v.,* **-stand·ed, -stand·ing,** *adj.* **—***n.* **1.** the main seating area of a stadium, racetrack, parade route, or the like, usually consisting of tiers with rows of individual seats. **2.** the people sitting in these seats. **—***v.i.* **3.** to conduct oneself or perform showily or ostentatiously in an attempt to impress onlookers: *The senator doesn't hesitate to grandstand if it makes her point.* **—***adj.* **4.** situated in a grandstand: *grandstand seats.* **5.** having a vantage point resembling that of a grandstand: *From our office windows on the third floor, we had a grandstand view of the parade.* **6.** intended to impress an onlooker or onlookers: *a grandstand catch.* [1835–45; GRAND + STAND] **—grand′stand′er,** *n.*

grand′stand play′, 1. an ostentatious play, as in a sport, overemphasized deliberately to elicit applause from spectators. **2.** any action or attempt designed to win approval or to make a strong impression: *His going to work on Christmas was another of his grandstand plays.* [1890–95, *Amer.*]

Grand′ Te′ton Na′tional Park′, a national park in NW Wyoming, including a portion of the Teton Range. 148 sq. mi. (383 sq. km).

grand′ theft′. See **grand larceny.**

grand′ tier′, the first tier of boxes after the parquet circle in a large theater or opera house.

grand′ tour′, 1. an extended tour of Europe, formerly regarded as a necessary part of the education of young British gentlemen. **2.** an extended tour of any region or country. **3.** a comprehensive guided tour or inspection, as of a building, exhibit, or military installation. [1660–70]

grand′ tour′ing car′. See **GT** (def. 2). Also called **grand′ tour′ing.** [1965–70]

Grand′ Turk′, 1. an island in the Turks and Caicos Islands of the West Indies. 7 mi. (11 km) long. **2.** capital of the Turks and Caicos Islands, on Grand Turk. 2287.

grand·un·cle (grand′ung′kəl), *n.* an uncle of one's father or mother; a great-uncle. [1400–50; late ME. See GRAND-, UNCLE]

grand′ unifica′tion the′ory, *Physics.* a possible future quantum field theory that would encompass both the electroweak theory and quantum chromodynamics. *Abbr.:* GUT Also called **grand′ u′nified the′ory.** [1980–85]

Grand·view (grand′vyōō′), *n.* a town in W Missouri. 24,502.

Grand·ville (grand′vil), *n.* a town in SW Michigan. 12,412.

grand′ vizier′, the chief officer of state of various Muslim countries, as in the former Ottoman Empire.

grange (grānj), *n.* **1.** a farm, with its farmhouse and nearby buildings. **2.** *Chiefly Brit.* a country house with its various farm buildings, usually constituting the dwelling of a yeoman or gentleman farmer. **3. the Grange.** See under **Granger Movement. 4.** *Archaic.* a barn or granary. [1150–1200; ME *gra(u)nge* barn < AF < VL **grānica* (occurs in ML), equiv. to L *grān(um)* GRAIN + *-ica,* fem. of *-icus* -IC]

Grange (grānj), *n.* **Harold** (*"Red"*), born 1903, U.S. football player.

grang·er (grān′jər), *n.* **1.** *Northwestern U.S.* a farmer. **2.** (*cap.*) a member of the Granger Movement. [1125–75; ME *gra(u)nger* farm-bailiff < AF; OF *grangier.* See GRANGE, -ER[2]]

grang·er·ize (grān′jə rīz′), *v.t.,* **-ized, -iz·ing. 1.** to augment the illustrative content of (a book) by inserting additional prints, drawings, engravings, etc., not included in the original volume. **2.** to mutilate (books) in order to get illustrative material for such a purpose. Also, *esp. Brit.,* **grang′er·ise′.** [1880–85; after James Granger (1723–1776), English clergyman whose *Biographical History of England* (1769) was arranged for such illustration; see -IZE] **—grang′er·ism,** *n.* **—grang′er·i·za′tion,** *n.* **—grang′er·iz′er,** *n.*

Grang′er Move′ment, *U.S. Hist.* a campaign for state control of railroads and grain elevators, esp. in the north central states, carried on during the 1870's by members of the Patrons of Husbandry **(the Grange),** a farmers' organization that had been formed for social and cultural purposes.

Gra·ni (grä′nē), *n.* (in the *Volsunga Saga*) the horse of Sigurd.

grani-, a combining form meaning "grain," used in the formation of compound words: *granivorous.* [< L, comb. form of *grānum;* akin to CORN[1]]

Gra·ni·cus (grə nī′kəs), *n.* a river in NW Turkey, flowing N to the Sea of Marmara: battle 334 B.C. 45 mi. (70 km) long.

Gra·nit (*Sw.* grä nēt′), *n.* **Rag·nar Ar·thur** (*Sw.* räng′-när är′to͝or), born 1900, Swedish physiologist, born in Finland: Nobel prize for medicine 1967.

gra·ni·ta (grə nē′tə; *It.* grä nē′tä), *n. Italian Cookery.* frozen flavored ice. [1865–70; < It: n. use of fem. of *granito* grainy; see GRANITE]

gran·ite (gran′it), *n.* **1.** a coarse-grained igneous rock composed chiefly of orthoclase and albite feldspars and of quartz, usually with lesser amounts of one or more other minerals, as mica, hornblende, or augite. **2.** anything compared to this rock in great hardness, firmness, or durability. [1640–50; < It *granito* grainy. See GRAIN, -ITE[1]] —**gra·nit·ic** (grə nit′ik), *adj.* —**gran′ite·like′,** *adj.*

gra·ni·té (gran′i tā′, grä′ni-; *Fr.* GRA nē tā′), *n. French Cookery.* ice (def. 4). [< F]

Gran′ite Cit′y, a city in SW Illinois, near St. Louis, Missouri. 36,815.

gran′ite pa′per, paper containing fibers of various colors that give it a granitelike appearance.

Gran′ite State′, New Hampshire (used as a nickname).

gran·ite·ware (gran′it wâr′), *n.* **1.** a kind of ironware with a gray, stonelike enamel. **2.** pottery with a speckled appearance like that of granite. **3.** a semivitreous white pottery somewhat harder than earthenware. [1890–95; GRANITE + WARE[1]]

gran·it·ite (gran′i tīt′), *n.* a granite rich in biotite. [1870–75; GRANITE + -ITE[1]]

gran·it·i·za·tion (gran′i tə zā′shən), *n.* a hypothetical process of forming granite. Also called **gran·i·ti·fi·ca·tion** (gran′i tə fi kā′shən). [1890–95; GRANITIZE + -ATION]

gran·it·ize (gran′i tīz′), *v.t.,* **-ized, -iz·ing.** to subject to granitization. Also, *esp. Brit.,* **gran′it·ise′.** [1960–65; GRANITE + -IZE]

gran·it·oid (gran′i toid′), *adj.* resembling or having the texture of granite. [1785–95; GRANITE + -OID]

Gran·jon (gran′jən), *n. Print.* a style of type originally cut by the French designer Robert Granjon.

gran·ny (gran′ē), *n., pl.* **-nies,** *adj.* **-ni·er, -ni·est** for 6. —*n.* **1.** *Informal.* a grandmother. **2.** an elderly woman. **3.** a fussy person. **4.** *Chiefly Midland and Southern U.S.* a nurse or midwife. **5.** See **granny knot.** —*adj.* **6.** of, pertaining to, or thought to be like a grandmother or an elderly or old-fashioned woman: *granny notions about what's proper.* **7.** (of clothing for women or girls) being loose-fitted and having such features as high necklines, puff sleeves, long skirts, and ruffles and lace trimmings: *a granny blouse; a granny nightgown.* Also, **gran′nie.** [1655–65; GRAND(MOTHER) + -Y[2], with *-nd-* > *-nn-*]

gran′ny dress′, a loose-fitting, ankle-length dress, usually with long sleeves and a high collar and sometimes having flounces, ruffles, or lace trimming. [1905–10]

gran′ny flat′, *Brit.* a flat or apartment within or attached to a house to accommodate an elderly person, usually a grandparent.

gran′ny glass′es, eyeglasses with wirelike metal frames that sometimes sit below the bridge of the nose and often have oval lenses.

gran′ny knot′, an incorrect version of a square knot in which the bights cross each other in the wrong direction next to the end, so as to produce a knot that is insecure. See illus. under **knot.** Also, **gran′ny's knot′.** Also called **lubber's knot.** [1850–55; so called in contempt]

Gran′ny Smith′, *n.* a variety of crisp, green-skinned apple, for eating raw or for cooking. [after Maria Ann *Smith* (d. 1870), who allegedly developed the variety in the vicinity of Sydney, Australia]

grano-, a combining form representing **granite** in compound words: *granophyre.* [< G, comb. form of *Granit* granite; see -O-]

gra·no·la (grə nō′lə), *n.* a breakfast food consisting of rolled oats, brown sugar, nuts, dried fruit, etc., usually served with milk. [1870–75; orig. a trademark; cf. -OLA]

gran·o·lith (gran′l ith), *n.* a composition stone for pavements, made from crushed granite or the like and cement. [1905–10; GRANO- + -LITH] —**gran′o·lith′ic,** *adj.*

gran·o·phyre (gran′ə fīər′), *n.* a fine-grained or porphyritic granitic rock with a micrographic intergrowth of the minerals of the groundmass. [1880–85; GRANO- + -PHYRE] —**gran·o·phy·ric** (gran′ə fir′ik), *adj.*

grant (grant, gränt), *v.t.* **1.** to bestow or confer, esp. by a formal act: *to grant a charter.* **2.** to give or accord: *to grant permission.* **3.** to agree or accede to: *to grant a request.* **4.** to admit or concede; accept for the sake of argument: *I grant that point.* **5.** to transfer or convey, esp. by deed or writing: *to grant property.* **6. take for granted, a.** to accept without question or objection; assume: *Your loyalty to the cause is taken for granted.* **b.** to use, accept, or treat in a careless or indifferent manner: *A marriage can be headed for trouble if either spouse begins to take the other for granted.* —*n.* **7.** something granted, as a privilege or right, a sum of money, or a tract of land: *Several major foundations made large grants to fund the research project.* **8.** the act of granting. **9.** *Law.* a transfer of property. **10.** a geographical unit in Vermont, Maine, and New Hampshire, originally a grant of land to a person or group of people. [1175–1225; ME *gra(u)nten* < OF *graunter,* var. of *creanter* < VL **credentāre,* v. deriv. of L *crēdent-,* s. of *crēdēns,* prp. of *crēdere* to believe] —**grant′a·ble,** *adj.* —**grant′ed·ly,** *adv.* —**grant′er,** *n.*
—**Syn. 1.** award, vouchsafe. **2.** See **give. 7, 8.** concession, bequest. **8.** conveyance. —**Ant. 1, 2.** receive.

Grant (grant, gränt), *n.* **1. Cary** (*Archibald Leach*), 1904–86, U.S. actor, born in England. **2. He·ber Jed·e·di·ah** (hē′bər jed′i dī′ə), 1856–1945, U.S. president of the Mormon Church 1918–45. **3. Ulysses S(impson)** 1822–85, 18th president of the U.S. 1869–77: Union general in the Civil War. **4.** a male given name: from a Latin word meaning "large, great."

Gran·ta (gran′tə), *n.* Cam.

gran·tee (gran tē′, grän-), *n.* the receiver of a grant. [1400–50; late ME; see GRANT, -EE]

Granth (grunt), *n.* the sacred scripture of the Sikhs, original text compiled 1604. Also, **Grunth.** Also called **Adigranth, Grant′ Sa′hib** (grunt). [< Hindi < Skt *grantha* a tying together, a book]

grant-in-aid (grant′in ād′, gränt′-), *n., pl.* **grants-in-aid. 1.** a subsidy furnished by a central government to a local one to help finance a public project, as the construction of a highway or school. **2.** a financial subsidy given to an individual or institution for research, educational, or cultural purposes. [1880–85]

gran·tor (gran′tər, grän′-, gran tôr′, grän-), *n.* a person or organization that makes a grant. [1620–30; < AF; see GRANT, -OR[2]]

Grants (grants, gränts), *n.* a town in W New Mexico. 11,451.

Grant's′ gazelle′, a large gazelle, *Gazella granti,* with distinctive long curved horns, native to the eastern African plains. [after James A. *Grant* (1827–92), British explorer and Africanist]

grants·man (grants′mən, gränts′-), *n., pl.* **-men.** an expert in grantsmanship. [1965–70; back formation from GRANTSMANSHIP]

grants·man·ship (grants′mən ship′, gränts′-), *n.* skill in securing grants, as for research, from federal agencies, foundations, or the like. [1960–65, *Amer.;* GRANT + -S[3] + -MANSHIP]

Grants′ Pass′, a city in SW Oregon. 14,997.

Gran Tu·ris·mo O·mo·lo·ga·to (grän′ to͞o riz′mō ə mō′lə gä′tō, -gä′tō; *It.* grän′ to͞o rē′zmô ô mô′lô-gä′tô), (of an automobile) certified as conforming to the specifications, as fuel capacity and engine displacement, for a class of standard automobiles **(Gran′ Turis′mo)** qualified to engage in various types of competitions. *Abbr.:* GTO [1965–70; < It: certified (for) grand touring]

gran·u·lar (gran′yə lər), *adj.* **1.** of the nature of granules; grainy. **2.** composed of or bearing granules or grains. **3.** showing a granulated structure. [1785–95; GRANULE + -AR[1]] —**gran′u·lar′i·ty,** *n.* —**gran′u·lar·ly,** *adv.*

gran·u·late (gran′yə lāt′), *v.,* **-lat·ed, -lat·ing.** —*v.t.* **1.** to form into granules or grains. **2.** to raise in granules; make rough on the surface. —*v.i.* **3.** to become granular or grainy. **4.** *Pathol.* to form granulation tissue. [1660–70; GRANULE + -ATE[1]] —**gran′u·lat′er, gran′u·la′tor,** *n.* —**gran·u·la·tive** (gran′yə lā′tiv, -lə tiv), *adj.*

gran′ulated sug′ar, a coarsely ground white sugar, widely used as a sweetener.

gran·u·la·tion (gran′yə lā′shən), *n.* **1.** the act or process of granulating. **2.** a granulated condition. **3.** any of the grains of a granulated surface. **4.** *Pathol.* **a.** the formation of granulation tissue, esp. in healing. **b.** See **granulation tissue. 5.** *Astron.* one of the small, short-lived features of the sun's surface that in the aggregate give it a mottled appearance when viewed with a telescope. [1606–15; GRANULE + -ATION]

granula′tion tis′sue, *Pathol.* tissue formed in ulcers and in early wound healing and repair, composed largely of newly growing capillaries and so called from its irregular surface in open wounds; proud flesh. [1870–75]

gran·ule (gran′yo͞ol), *n.* **1.** a little grain. **2.** a small particle; pellet. **3.** a corpuscle; sporule. [1645–55; < LL *grānulum* small grain. See GRAIN, -ULE]

gran·u·lite (gran′yə līt′), *n.* a metamorphic rock composed of granular minerals of uniform size, as quartz, feldspar, or pyroxene, and showing a definite banding. [1840–50; GRANULE + -ITE[1]] —**gran·u·lit·ic** (gran′yə-lit′ik), *adj.*

gran·u·lo·blast (gran′yə lō blast′), *n. Cell Biol.* an immature granulocyte. [GRANULE + -O- + -BLAST] —**gran′u·lo·blas′tic,** *adj.*

gran·u·lo·cyte (gran′yə lō sīt′), *n. Cell Biol.* a circulating white blood cell having prominent granules in the cytoplasm and a nucleus of two or more lobes. Also called **polymorph.** [1905–10; GRANULE + -O- + -CYTE] —**gran·u·lo·cyt·ic** (gran′yə lō sit′ik), *adj.*

gran·u·lo·ma (gran′yə lō′mə), *n., pl.* **-mas, -ma·ta** (-mə tə). *Pathol.* an inflammatory tumor or growth composed of granulation tissue. [1860–65; GRANULE + -OMA] —**gran·u·lom·a·tous** (gran′yə lom′ə təs), *adj.*

granulo′ma in·gui·na′le (ing′gwə nal′ē, -nä′lē, -nä′lā), *Pathol.* a venereal disease marked by deep ulceration of the skin of the groin and external genitals, caused by the bacterium *Calymmatobacterium granulomatis.* Also called **granulo′ma ve·ne′re·um** (və nēr′ē əm). [1915–20; < NL: inguinal granuloma]

gran·u·lo·ma·to·sis (gran′yə lō mə tō′sis), *n. Pathol.* any disease characterized by the formation of numerous granulomas. [1910–15; < NL *granulomat-* (s. of *granuloma*) GRANULOMA + -OSIS]

gran·u·lo·poi·e·tin (gran′yə lō poi ēt′n, -poi′i tn), *n. Biochem.* a hormone that promotes the production of white blood cells. [GRANULE + -O- + -POIET(IC) + -IN[2]]

gran·u·lose (gran′yə lōs′), *adj.* granular. [1850–55; GRANULE + -OSE[1]]

gra·num (grā′nəm), *n., pl.* **-na** (-nə). **1.** (in prescriptions) a grain. **2.** *Bot.* one of the structural units of a chloroplast in vascular plants, consisting of layers of thylakoids. [< L]

Gran·ville (gran′vil), *n.* **1. Earl of.** See **Carteret, John. 2.** a male given name.

Gran·ville-Bar·ker (gran′vil bär′kər), *n.* **Harley,** 1877–1946, English dramatist, actor, and critic.

grape (grāp), *n.* **1.** the edible, pulpy, smooth-skinned berry or fruit that grows in clusters on vines of the genus *Vitis,* and from which wine is made. **2.** any vine bearing this fruit. **3.** a dull, dark, purplish-red color. **4. grapes,** (*used with a singular v.*) *Vet. Pathol.* **a.** tuberculosis occurring in cattle, characterized by the internal formation of grapelike clusters, esp. in the lungs. **b.** tuberculosis occurring in horses, characterized by grapelike clusters on the fetlocks. **5.** grapeshot. **6. the grape,** wine. [1200–50; ME < OF, var. of *crape* cluster of fruit or flowers, orig. hook < Gmc; cf. G *Krapf* hook and GRAPPEL, GRAPNEL] —**grape′like′,** *adj.*

grape′ fam′ily, the plant family Vitaceae, characterized by woody climbing vines with tendrils, having alternate, simple or compound leaves, and bearing clusters of small flowers and berries, and including Boston ivy, grape, grape ivy, and Virginia creeper.

grape′ fern′, any of several ferns of the genus *Botrychium,* comprising several species having grapelike clusters of sporangia.

grape·fruit (grāp′fro͞ot′), *n.* **1.** a large, roundish, yellow-skinned, edible citrus fruit having a juicy, acid pulp. **2.** the tropical or semitropical tree, *Citrus paradisi,* yielding this fruit. [1805–15; GRAPE + FRUIT, appar. from the resemblance of its clusters to those of grapes]

grape′fruit league′, *Baseball Informal.* a series of training games played by major-league teams before the opening of the season (so named because they take place in the citrus-growing South, as in Florida). [1950–55]

grape′ hy′acinth, any plant belonging to the genus *Muscari,* of the lily family, as *M. botryoides,* having globular, blue flowers resembling tiny grapes. [1725–35]

grape′ i′vy, a hairy vine, *Cissus rhombifolia,* native to tropical America, having glossy trifoliate leaves and often cultivated as a houseplant.

grape ivy, *Cissus rhombifolia*

grape·line (grap′lin), *n. Naut.* grapnel. [alter. of GRAPPLING]

grape′ phyllox′era. See under **phylloxera.**

grap·er·y (grā′pə rē), *n., pl.* **-er·ies. 1.** a building where grapes are grown. **2.** a vineyard. [1805–15; GRAPE + -ERY]

grape·shot (grāp′shot′), *n.* a cluster of small cast-iron balls formerly used as a charge for a cannon. [1740–50; GRAPE + SHOT[1]]

Grapes′ of Wrath′, The, a novel (1939) by John Steinbeck.

grape′ stake′, a post used in vineyards to support wires along which grapevines are trained. [1905–10, *Amer.*]

grape·stone (grāp′stōn′), *n.* the seed of a grape. [1580–90; GRAPE + STONE]

grape′ sug′ar, dextrose. [1825–35]

grape·vine (grāp′vīn′), *n.* **1.** a vine that bears grapes. **2.** Also called **grape′vine tel′egraph.** a person-to-person method of spreading rumors, gossip, information, etc., by informal or unofficial conversation, letter writing, or the like. **3.** a private or secret source of information. [1645–55; 1860–65, *Amer.* for def. 2; GRAPE + VINE]

Grape·vine (grāp′vīn′), *n.* a town in N Texas. 11,801.

grap·ey (grā′pē), *adj.,* **grap·i·er, grap·i·est.** grapy.

graph (graf, gräf), *n.* **1.** a diagram representing a system of connections or interrelations among two or more things by a number of distinctive dots, lines, bars, etc. **2.** *Math.* **a.** a series of points, discrete or continuous, as in forming a curve or surface, each of which represents a value of a given function. **b.** Also called **linear graph.** a network of lines connecting points. **3.** a written symbol for an idea, a sound, or a linguistic expression. —*v.t.* **4.** *Math.* to draw (a curve) as representing a given function. **5.** to represent by means of a graph. [1875–80; short for *graphic formula;* see GRAPHIC]
—**Syn. 1.** See **map.**

graph-, var. of **grapho-** before a vowel: *grapheme.*

-graph, a combining form meaning "drawn," "written" (*lithograph; monograph*); specialized in meaning to indicate the instrument rather than the written product of the instrument (*telegraph; phonograph*). [< Gk *-graphos* (something) drawn or written, one who draws or writes. See GRAPHO-]

graph·al·loy (graf′ə loi′), *n.* a compound of graphite impregnated with Babbitt metal, bronze, copper, gold, etc., used as a low-friction material. [GRAPH(ITE) + ALLOY]

graph•eme (graf′ēm), *n. Ling.* **1.** a minimal unit of a writing system. **2.** a unit of a writing system consisting of all the written symbols or sequences of written symbols that are used to represent a single phoneme. [1935–40; GRAPH- + -EME] —**gra•phe′mi•cal•ly,** *adv.*

gra•phe•mics (gra fē′miks), *n.* (*used with a singular v.*) *Ling.* the study of writing systems and of their relation to speech. [1950–55; GRAPHEME + -ICS]

graph•ic (graf′ik), *adj.* Also, **graph′i•cal. 1.** giving a clear and effective picture; vivid: *a graphic account of an earthquake.* **2.** pertaining to the use of diagrams, graphs, mathematical curves, or the like; diagrammatic. **3.** of, pertaining to, or expressed by writing: *graphic symbols.* **4.** written, inscribed, or drawn. **5.** *Geol.* (of a rock) having a texture formed by the intergrowth of certain minerals so as to resemble written characters. **6.** *Math.* pertaining to the determination of values, solution of problems, etc., by direct measurement on diagrams instead of by ordinary calculations. **7.** of or pertaining to the graphic arts. —*n.* **8.** a product of the graphic arts, as a drawing or print. **9.** a computer-generated image. [1630–40; < L *graphicus* of painting or drawing < Gk *graphikós* able to draw or paint, equiv. to *gráph(ein)* to draw, write + *-ikos* -IC; c. CARVE] —**graph′i•cal•ly,** *adv.* —**graph′i•cal•ness, graph′ic•ness,** *n.*
—**Syn. 1.** striking, telling; detailed. See **picturesque.**

-graphic, a combination of **-graph** and **-ic,** forming adjectives corresponding to nouns ending in **-graph:** *telegraphic.*

graph′ic ac′cent, any mark written above a letter, esp. one indicating stress in pronunciation, as in Spanish *rápido.*

graph′ical us′er in′terface, a software interface designed to standardize and simplify the use of computer programs, as by using a mouse to manipulate text and images on a display screen featuring icons, windows, and menus. Also called **GUI.**

graph′ic arts′, 1. Also called **graphics.** the arts or techniques, as engraving, etching, drypoint, woodcut, and other methods, by which copies of an original design are printed from a plate, block, or the like. **2.** the arts of drawing, painting, and printmaking. [1660–70]

graph′ic gran′ite, a pegmatite that has crystals of gray quartz imbedded in white or pink microcline in such a manner that they resemble cuneiform writing. [1830–40]

graph′ic nov′el, a novel in the form of comic strips. [1985–90]

graph•ics (graf′iks), *n.* **1.** (*used with a singular v.*) the art of drawing, esp. as used in mathematics, engineering, etc. **2.** (*used with a plural v.*) See **graphic arts** (def. 1). **3.** (*used with a plural v.*) *Motion Pictures, Television.* the titles, credits, subtitles, announcements, etc., shown on the screen before, or as part of, a film or television program. **4.** (*used with a singular v.*) the science of calculating by diagrams. **5.** (*used with a singular or plural v.*) *Computers.* See **computer graphics.** —*adj.* **6.** *Computers.* pertaining to pictorial information displayed, plotted, or printed by a computer: *a graphics tablet.* [1885–90; see GRAPHIC, -ICS]

graph•ite (graf′it), *n.* a very common mineral, soft native carbon, occurring in black to dark-gray foliated masses, with metallic luster and greasy feel: used for pencil leads, as a lubricant, and for making crucibles and other refractories; plumbago; black lead. [1790–1800; < G *Graphit* < Gk *gráph(ein)* to write, draw + G *-it* -ITE[1]] —**gra•phit•ic** (grə fit′ik), *adj.*

graph′ite cloth′, a nonwoven fabric made by embedding carbon fibers in a plastic bonding material, used in layers as a substitute for sheet metal, as in the construction of aircraft wings.

graph•i•tize (graf′i tīz′), *v.t.,* **-tized, -tiz•ing. 1.** to convert into graphite. **2.** to cover (the surface of an object) with graphite. Also, *esp. Brit.,* **graph′i•tise′.** [1895–1900; GRAPHITE + -IZE] —**graph′i•ti•za′tion,** *n.*

grapho-, a combining form meaning "writing," used in the formation of compound words: *graphomotor.* Also, *esp. before a vowel,* **graph-.** Cf. **-graph, -graphic, -graphy.** [< Gk, comb. form of *graphḗ;* akin to CARVE]

graph•ol•o•gy (gra fol′ə jē), *n.* **1.** the study of handwriting, esp. when regarded as an expression of the writer's character, personality, abilities, etc. **2.** *Ling.* the study of systems of writing; grammatology. [1875–80; GRAPHO- + -LOGY] —**graph•o•log•ic** (graf′ə loj′ik), **graph′o•log′i•cal,** *adj.* —**graph•ol′o•gist,** *n.*

graph•o•mo•tor (graf′ə mō′tər), *adj. Med.* pertaining to the muscular movements in writing. [GRAPHO- + MOTOR]

graph•o•phone (graf′ə fōn′), *n.* a phonograph for recording and reproducing sounds on wax records. [GRAPHO- + -PHONE] —**graph•o•phon•ic** (graf′ə fon′ik), *adj.*

Graph•o•type (graf′ə tīp′), *Trademark.* a typewriterlike machine for embossing letters upon thin sheets of metal, as for use in an addressing machine. —**graph•o•typ•ic** (graf′ə tip′ik), *adj.*

graph′ pa′per, paper printed with a pattern of straight or curved lines, esp. a grid of small squares, for plotting or drawing graphs and curves. [1925–30]

graph′ the′ory, *Math.* the branch of mathematics dealing with linear graphs. [1965–70]

-graphy, a combining form denoting a process or form of drawing, writing, representing, recording, describing, etc., or an art or science concerned with such a process: *biography; choreography; geography; orthography; photography.* [< Gk *-graphia.* See -GRAPH, -Y[3]]

CONCISE ETYMOLOGY KEY: <, descended or borrowed from; >, whence; b., blend of, blended; c., cognate with; cf., compare; deriv., derivative; equiv., equivalent; imit., imitative; obl., oblique; r., replacing; s., stem; sp., spelling, spelled; resp., respelling, respelled; trans., translation; ?, origin unknown; *, unattested; ‡, probably earlier than. See the full key inside the front cover.

grap•nel (grap′nl), *n.* **1.** a device consisting essentially of one or more hooks or clamps, for grasping or holding something; grapple; grappling iron. **2.** a small anchor with three or more flukes, used for grappling or dragging or for anchoring a small boat, as a skiff. Also called **grapeline, grap•lin, grap•line** (grap′lin). [1325–75; ME *grapnel(l),* dim. of OF *grapin,* dim. of *grape* hook, GRAPE]

grapnel (def. 2)

grap•pa (gräp′pä), *n.* an unaged brandy, originally from Italy, distilled from the pomace of a wine press. [1890–95; < It: grape stalk < Gmc; see GRAPE]

grap′pi•er cement′ (grap′ē ā′), a by-product of the calcination of hydraulic lime, having similar properties and made from ground, unslaked lumps. [1900–05; < F *grappier,* deriv. of *grappe* bunch of grapes. See GRAPE, -IER[2]]

grap•ple (grap′əl), *v.,* **-pled, -pling,** *n.* —*v.i.* **1.** to hold or make fast to something, as with a grapple. **2.** to use a grapple. **3.** to seize another, or each other, in a firm grip, as in wrestling; clinch. **4.** to engage in a struggle or close encounter (usually fol. by *with*): *He was grappling with a boy twice his size.* **5.** to try to overcome or deal (usually fol. by *with*): *to grapple with a problem.* —*v.t.* **6.** to seize, hold, or fasten with or as with a grapple. **7.** to seize in a grip, take hold of: *The thug grappled him around the neck.* —*n.* **8.** a hook or an iron instrument by which one thing, as a ship, fastens onto another; grapnel. **9.** a seizing or gripping. **10.** a grip or close hold in wrestling or hand-to-hand fighting. **11.** a close, hand-to-hand fight. [1520–30; appar. a freq. of OE *gegrǣppian* to seize; associated with GRAPNEL] —**grap′•pler,** *n.*
—**Syn. 5.** struggle, contend, wrestle, cope, tussle.

grap′ple ground′, an anchorage, esp. for small vessels.

grap′ple plant′, a procumbent, thorny plant, *Harpagophytum procumbens,* of southern Africa. Also called **wait-a-bit.** [1815–25]

grap′ple shot′, *Naut.* a grapnellike projectile fired from a gun and used as a hold for the end of a line in rescue operations or in kedging. Also called **anchor shot.** [1880–85]

grap•pling (grap′ling), *n.* grapnel. [1590–1600; GRAPPLE + -ING[1]]

grap′pling i′ron, a grapnel. Also called **grap′pling hook′.** [1530–40]

grap•to•lite (grap′tə līt′), *n.* any colonial animal of the extinct class Graptolithina, most common in the Ordovician and Silurian Periods, thought to be related to the pterobranchs. [1830–40; < Gk *graptó(s)* painted, marked with letters (v. adj. from *gráphein* to write) + -LITE] —**grap•to•lit•ic** (grap′tə lit′ik), *adj.*

grap•y (grā′pē), *adj.,* **grap•i•er, grap•i•est. 1.** of, like, or composed of grapes. **2.** tasting of grapes: *a grapy wine.* Also, **grapey.** [1350–1400; ME. See GRAPE, -Y[1]]

GRAS (gras), generally recognized as safe: a status label assigned by the FDA to a listing of substances (**GRAS′ list′**) not known to be hazardous to health and thus approved for use in foods. [1970–75]

Gras•mere (gras′mēr, gräs′-), *n.* **1.** a lake in Westmoreland, in NW England. 1 mi. (1.6 km) long. **2.** a village on this lake: Wordsworth's home 1790–1808.

grasp (grasp, gräsp), *v.t.* **1.** to seize and hold by or as if by clasping with the fingers or arms. **2.** to seize upon; hold firmly. **3.** to get hold of mentally; comprehend; understand: *I don't grasp your meaning.* —*v.i.* **4.** to make an attempt to seize, or a motion of seizing, something (usually fol. by *at* or *for*): *to grasp for an enemy's rifle.* —*n.* **5.** the act of grasping or gripping, as with the hands or arms: *to make a grasp at something.* **6.** a hold or grip: *to have a firm grasp of a rope.* **7.** one's arms or hands, in embracing or gripping: *He had it in his grasp.* **8.** one's power of seizing and holding; reach: *to have a thing within one's grasp.* **9.** hold, possession, or mastery: *to wrest power from the grasp of a usurper.* **10.** mental hold or capacity; power to understand. **11.** broad or thorough comprehension: *a good grasp of computer programming.* [1350–1400; ME *graspen, grapsen;* c. LG *grapsen;* akin to OE *gegrǣppian* to seize (see GRAPPLE)] —**grasp′a•ble,** *adj.* —**grasp′er,** *n.* —**grasp′•less,** *adj.*
—**Syn. 1.** grip, clutch; grab. See **catch. 9.** clutches. **10.** scope, comprehension. GRASP, REACH refer to the power of seizing, either concretely or figuratively. GRASP suggests actually seizing and closing the hand upon something (or, figuratively, thoroughly comprehending something) and therefore refers to what is within one's possession or immediate possibility of possession: *a good grasp of a problem; immense mental grasp.* REACH suggests a stretching out of (usually) the hand to touch, strike, or, if possible, seize something; it therefore refers to a potentiality of possession that requires an effort. Figuratively, it implies perhaps a faint conception of something still too far beyond one to be definitely and clearly understood. —**Ant. 1.** release.

grasp•ing (gras′ping, gräs′-), *adj.* **1.** greedy; avaricious: *a sly, grasping man.* **2.** being used to grasp or tending to grasp; tenacious. [1540–50; GRASP + -ING[2]] —**grasp′ing•ly,** *adv.* —**grasp′ing•ness,** *n.*
—**Syn. 1.** covetous, selfish, acquisitive, venal.

grass (gras, gräs), *n.* **1.** any plant of the family Gramineae, having jointed stems, sheathing leaves, and seedlike grains. Cf. **grass family. 2.** such plants collectively, as when cultivated in lawns or used as pasture for grazing animals or cut and dried as hay. **3.** the grass-covered ground. **4.** pasture: *Half the farm is grass.* **5.** *Slang.* marijuana. **6. grasses,** stalks or sprays of grass: *filled with dried grasses.* **7.** the season of the new growth of grass. **8. go to grass,** to retire from one's occupation or profession: *Many executives lack a sense of purpose after they have gone to grass.* **9. let the grass grow under one's feet,** to delay action, progress, etc.; become slack in one's efforts. —*v.t.* **10.** to cover with grass or turf. **11.** to feed with growing grass; pasture. **12.** to lay (something) on the grass, as for the purpose of bleaching. —*v.i.* **13.** to feed on growing grass; graze. **14.** to produce grass; become covered with grass. [bef. 900; ME *gras,* OE *græs;* c. D, G, ON, Goth *gras;* akin to GROW, GREEN] —**grass′less,** *adj.* —**grass′like′,** *adj.* —**grass′ward, grass′wards,** *adv. adj.*

Grass (gräs; *Ger.* gräs), *n.* **Gün•ter (Wil•helm)** (go͝on′tər wil′helm; *Ger.* gʏn′tər vil′helm), born 1927, German novelist, poet, and playwright.

grass′ bug′. See **rhopalid bug.**

grass′ carp′, a large carp of the genus *Ctenopharyngodon,* of southern Chinese inland waters, that grazes on water weeds. [1880–85]

grass′ cloth′, a fabric made from tough vegetable fibers, used for table linens, wall coverings, etc. Also, **grass′cloth′.** Also called **Canton linen, China grass cloth.** [1850–55]

grass′ court′, an outdoor tennis court having a grass surface. Cf. **clay court, hard court.** [1880–85]

grass•cut•ter (gras′kut′ər, gräs′-), *n.* **1.** a device used to cut grass, as a lawn mower. **2.** *Baseball.* a ground ball that travels with great speed across the infield close to and barely touching the turf. [1850–55; GRASS + CUTTER]

Grasse (gräs), *n.* **1. Fran•çois Jo•seph Paul** (fräN-swa′ zhô zef′ pôl), **Comte de** (*Marquis de Grasse-Tilly*), 1722–1788, French admiral. **2.** a city in S France, near the Mediterranean: tourist center; perfume industry. 135,330.

gras•se•rie (gras′ə rē, grä′sə-), *n.* a virus disease of silkworms, characterized by yellowness of the integument and an excessive accumulation of fluid within the body. Also called **jaundice.** [1830–40; < F, equiv. to *gras* fat (< L *crassus*) + *-erie* -ERY]

grass′ fam′ily, the large plant family Gramineae (or Poaceae), characterized by mostly herbaceous but sometimes woody plants with hollow and jointed stems, narrow sheathing leaves, petalless flowers borne in spikelets, and fruit in the form of seedlike grain, and including bamboo, sugar cane, numerous grasses, and cereal grains such as barley, corn, oats, rice, rye, and wheat.

grass′ finch′, 1. any of several Australian weaverbirds, esp. of the genus *Poephila.* **2.** the vesper sparrow. Also, **grass′finch′.** [1775–85, *Amer.*]

grass-green (gras′grēn′, gräs′-), *adj.* yellowish green.

grass′ hock′ey, *Canadian.* See **field hockey.** [1920–25]

grass•hop•per (gras′hop′ər, gräs′-), *n.* **1.** any of numerous herbivorous, orthopterous insects, esp. of the families Acrididae and Tettigoniidae, having the hind legs adapted for leaping and having chewing mouth parts, some species being highly destructive to vegetation. Cf. **locust** (def. 1), **long-horned grasshopper. 2.** a small, light airplane used on low-flying missions, as for reconnaissance. **3.** (*cap.*) *Mil.* a U.S. antipersonnel mine that jumps off the ground when activated by proximate body heat and sprays shrapnel over a lethal radius of 350 ft. (107 m). **4.** a cocktail of light cream, green crème de menthe, and white crème de menthe or crème de cacao. [1275–1325; ME; see GRASS, HOPPER]

grasshopper, *Melanoplus differentialis,* length about 1¼ in. (3.2 cm)

grass′hopper en′gine, a steam engine having a piston attached to one end of a beam that is hinged to an upright at the other end, the connecting rod being suspended from near the center of the beam. [1850–55]

grass′hopper pie′, a custardlike pie, flavored and colored with green crème de menthe and served in a graham-cracker crust.

grass′hopper spar′row, a brown and white North American sparrow, *Ammodramus savannarum,* having a buffy breast and a buzzing insectlike song. [1880–85]

grass•land (gras′land′, gräs′-), *n.* **1.** an area, as a prairie, in which the natural vegetation consists largely of perennial grasses, characteristic of subhumid and semiarid climates. **2.** land with grass growing on it, esp. farmland used for grazing or pasture. [1675–85, *Amer.;* GRASS + LAND]

Grass•man (gräs′mən, -män; *Ger.* gräs′män′), *n.* **Hermann Gün•ther** (her′män gʏn′tər), 1809–77, German mathematician and linguist.

Grass′man's law′, *Ling.* an observation, made by H. G. Grassman, that when aspirated consonants occurred in successive syllables in Sanskrit and classical Greek, one, usually the first, was unaspirated, becoming a voiced stop in Sanskrit and a voiceless stop in Greek. [1890–95]

Gras•so (gras′ō, grä′sō), *n.* **Ella T(am•bus•si)** (tambo͞o′sē), 1919–81, U.S. politician: congresswoman 1971–75; governor of Connecticut 1975–80.

grass-of-Par•nas•sus (gras′əv pär nas′əs, gräs′-), *n.* any plant belonging to the genus *Parnassia,* of the saxifrage family, growing in marshy areas, having broad, smooth leaves and a single, pale flower.

grass′ par′akeet, any of several Australian parakeets, esp. the budgerigar. [1830–40]

grass′ pink′, **1.** a pink, *Dianthus plumarius,* of Europe and Asia, having fragrant, fringed pink, purplish, or white flowers. **2.** an orchid, *Calopogon tuberosus,* having clusters of rose or purplish-pink flowers, growing in bogs of eastern North America. [1810–20, *Amer.*]

grass·plot (gras′plot′, gräs′-), *n.* a plot of ground covered with or reserved for grass. [1600–10; GRASS + PLOT]

grass·quit (gras′kwit′, gräs′-), *n.* any of several tiny finches, esp. of the genus *Tiaris,* of tropical America and the West Indies. [1840–50; GRASS + QUIT[2]]

grass′ roots′, (*used with a singular or plural v.*) **1.** the common or ordinary people, esp. as contrasted with the leadership or elite of a political party, social organization, etc.; the rank and file. **2.** the agricultural and rural areas of a country. **3.** the people inhabiting these areas, esp. as a political, social, or economic group. **4.** the origin or basis of something; the basic or primary concept, rule, part, or the like. [1910–15 *Amer.* for def. 1]

grass-roots (gras′ro͞ots′, -ro͝ots′, gräs′-), *adj.* of, pertaining to, or involving the common people, esp. as contrasted with or separable from an elite: *a grass-roots movement for nuclear disarmament.* [1910–15]

grass′ rug′, a rug woven of strong marsh grass and cotton, usually with stenciled designs.

grass′ sack′, *South Midland U.S.* a gunnysack. **—Regional Variation.** See **gunnysack.**

grass′ shears′, special shears for trimming grass that is hard to cut properly with a mower, as around the base of a tree.

grass′ ski′ing, turfskiing. [1965–70]

grass′ snake′, **1.** Also called **ring snake.** a common European snake, *Natrix natrix,* having a collar of bright orange or yellow. **2.** any of various small, slender snakes of North America, as the garter snake or green snake. [1835–45, *Amer.*]

grass′ snipe′, the pectoral sandpiper. [1870–75, *Amer.*]

grass′ sor′ghum, any of several varieties of sorghum, as Sudan grass, grown for pasturage and hay.

grass′ sponge′, a large, dark brown, commercial sponge, *Spongia graminea,* of Florida, the West Indies, and the Gulf of Mexico. [1870–75, *Amer.*]

grass′ style′, a style of Japanese calligraphy and *sumi-e* painting, characterized chiefly by free or loose brush strokes.

grass′ tree′, any Australian plant of the genus *Xanthorrhoea,* of the lily family, having a stout, woody stem bearing a tuft of long grasslike leaves and a dense flower spike. [1795–1805]

grass′ wid′ow, **1.** a woman who is separated, divorced, or lives apart from her husband. **2.** a woman whose husband is away from home frequently or for a long time, as on business or to pursue a sport or hobby. **3.** *Archaic.* **a.** a discarded mistress. **b.** a woman who has borne an illegitimate child. [1520–30; the first element perh. orig. alluding to a bed of grass, hay, or the like; cf. D *grasweduwe,* G *Strohwittwe* lit., straw-widow] **—grass′wid′ow·hood′,** *n.*

grass′ wid′ower, **1.** a man who is separated, divorced, or lives apart from his wife. **2.** a man whose wife is away from home frequently or for a long time, as on business or to pursue a sport or hobby. [1860–65]

grass·y (gras′ē, grä′sē), *adj.,* **grass·i·er, grass·i·est.** **1.** covered with grass. **2.** of, like, or pertaining to grass; grasslike. **3.** of the color of grass: *grassy green.* [1505–15; GRASS + -Y[1]] **—grass′i·ness,** *n.*

grate[1] (grāt), *n., v.,* **grat·ed, grat·ing.** **—***n.* **1.** a frame of metal bars for holding fuel when burning, as in a fireplace, furnace, or stove. **2.** a framework of parallel or crossed bars, used as a partition, guard, cover, or the like; grating. **3.** a fireplace. **—***v.t.* **4.** to furnish with a grate or grates. [1350–1400; ME < ML *grāta* a grating, var. of *crāta,* deriv. of L *crāt-* (s. of *crātis*) wickerwork, hurdle; cf. CRATE] **—grate′less,** *adj.* **—grate′like′,** *adj.*

grate[2] (grāt), *v.,* **grat·ed, grat·ing.** **—***v.i.* **1.** to have an irritating or unpleasant effect: *His constant chatter grates on my nerves.* **2.** to make a sound of, or as if of, rough scraping; rasp. **3.** to sound harshly; jar: *to grate on the ear.* **4.** to scrape or rub with rough or noisy friction, as one thing on or against another. **—***v.t.* **5.** to reduce to small particles by rubbing against a rough surface or a surface with many sharp-edged openings: *to grate a carrot.* **6.** to rub together with a harsh, jarring sound: *to grate one's teeth.* **7.** to irritate or annoy. **8.** *Archaic.* to wear down or away by rough friction. [1375–1425; late ME *graten* < OF *grater* < Gmc; cf. G *kratzen* to scratch]
—Syn. 7. vex, gall, nettle, irk, rile, bug.

G-rat·ed (jē′rā′tid), *adj.* (of a motion picture) deemed suitable for viewers of all ages: *a G-rated film.*

grate·ful (grāt′fəl), *adj.* **1.** warmly or deeply appreciative of kindness or benefits received; thankful: *I am grateful to you for your help.* **2.** expressing or actuated by gratitude: *a grateful letter.* **3.** pleasing to the mind or senses; agreeable or welcome; refreshing: *a grateful breeze.* [1545–55; obs. *grate* pleasing (< L *grātus*) + -FUL] **—grate′ful·ly,** *adv.* **—grate′ful·ness,** *n.*
—Syn. 1. obliged, indebted. GRATEFUL, THANKFUL describe an appreciative attitude for what one has received. GRATEFUL indicates a warm or deep appreciation of personal kindness as shown to one: *grateful for favors; grateful to one's neighbors for help in time of trouble.* THANKFUL indicates a disposition to express gratitude by giving thanks, as to a benefactor or to a merciful Providence; there is often a sense of deliverance as well as of appreciation: *thankful that one's life was spared in an accident; thankful for the comfort of one's general situation.* **3.** pleasant, gratifying, satisfying.

grat·er (grā′tər), *n.* **1.** a person or thing that grates. **2.** any of various kitchen devices for grating food: *a cheese grater.* [1400–50; late ME. See GRATE[2], -ER[1]]

Gra·ti·ae (grā′shē ē′), *n.pl.* grace (def. 12). [< L, pl. of *grātia* GRACE; cf. Gk *Chárites*]

Gra·ti·an (grā′shē ən, -shən), *n.* (*Flavius Gratianus*) A.D. 359–383, Roman emperor 375–383.

grat·i·cule (grat′i kyo͞ol′), *n.* **1.** *Navig.* a network of parallels and meridians on a map or chart. **2.** *Optics.* a reticle. [1885–90; < F < L *crāticula,* dim. of *crātis.* See GRATE[2], -CULE]

grat·i·fi·ca·tion (grat′ə fi kā′shən), *n.* **1.** the state of being gratified; great satisfaction. **2.** something that gratifies; source of pleasure or satisfaction. **3.** the act of gratifying. **4.** *Archaic.* a reward, recompense, or gratuity. [1590–1600; < L *grātificātiōn-* (s. of *grātificātiō*). See GRATIFY, -ATION]
—Syn. 1. pleasure, relish, delight, enjoyment, comfort.

grat·i·fy (grat′ə fī′), *v.t.,* **-fied, -fy·ing.** **1.** to give pleasure to (a person or persons) by satisfying desires or humoring inclinations or feelings: *Her praise will gratify all who worked so hard to earn it.* **2.** to satisfy; indulge; humor, as one's desires or appetites. **3.** *Obs.* to reward; remunerate. [1350–1400; ME *gratifien* < L *grātificāre,* equiv. to *grāt(us)* pleasing + *-i-* -I- + *-ficāre* -FY] **—grat′i·fi′a·ble,** *adj.* **—grat′i·fi·ed·ly** (grat′ə fī′id lē, -fīd′-), *adv.* **—grat′i·fi′er,** *n.*
—Syn. 1. please, delight, gladden. **1, 2.** See **humor.**

gra·ti·fy·ing (grat′ə fī′ing), *adj.* tending to gratify; giving or causing satisfaction; pleasing. [1605–15; GRATIFY + -ING[2]] **—grat′i·fy′ing·ly,** *adv.*
—Syn. See **interesting.**

grat·in (grat′n, grät′-; *Fr.* GRA TAN′), *n.* See **au gratin.** [1800–10; < F, MF; see GRATE[2]]

grat·i·nate (grat′n āt′), *v.t.,* **-nat·ed, -nat·ing.** to gratiné. [1900–05; GRATIN + -ATE[1]]

gra·ti·né (grat′n ā′, grät′-; *Fr.* GRA tē nā′), *v.t.,* **-néed, -né·ing.** to bake or broil (food) in au gratin style. [1930–35; < F: ptp. of *gratiner* to cook au gratin, deriv. of *gratin* orig., burnt food adhering to the sides and bottom of a pot, deriv. of *grater* to scrape; see GRATE[2]]

grat·ing[1] (grā′ting), *n.* **1.** a fixed frame of bars or the like covering an opening to exclude persons, animals, coarse material, or objects while admitting light, air, or fine material. **2.** *Physics.* See **diffraction grating.** [1605–15; GRATE[1] + -ING[1]]

grat·ing[2] (grā′ting), *adj.* **1.** irritating or unpleasant to one's feelings. **2.** (of a sound or noise) harsh, discordant, or rasping. [1555–65; GRATE[2] + -ING[2]] **—grat′ing·ly,** *adv.*

grat·is (grat′is, grä′tis), *adv.* **1.** without charge or payment; free: *The manufacturer provided an extra set of coat buttons gratis.* **—***adj.* **2.** free; gratuitous. [1400–50; late ME < L *grātis* freely, contr. of *grātiīs* with favors, graces (abl. pl. of *grātia* GRACE)]

grat·i·tude (grat′i to͞od′, -tyo͞od′), *n.* the quality or feeling of being grateful or thankful: *He expressed his gratitude to everyone on the staff.* [1400–50; late ME < ML *grātitūdin-* (s. of *grātitūdō*) thankfulness, equiv. to *grāt(us)* pleasing + *-i-* -I- + *-tūdin-* -TUDE]
—Syn. thanks, thankfulness, appreciation, gratefulness.

Grat·tan (grat′n), *n.* **Henry,** 1746–1820, Irish statesman and orator.

grat·toir (grä twär′; *Fr.* GRA TWAR′), *n., pl.* **-toirs** (-twärz′; *Fr.* -TWAR′). *Archaeol.* a flaked stone implement, usually Upper Paleolithic, retouched at the end and used probably for working wood or cleaning hides; scraper. [1870–75; < F, equiv. to *gratt(er)* to GRATE[2] + *-oir* -ORY[2]]

gra·tu·i·tous (grə to͞o′i təs, -tyo͞o′-), *adj.* **1.** given, done, bestowed, or obtained without charge or payment; free; voluntary. **2.** being without apparent reason, cause, or justification: *a gratuitous insult.* **3.** *Law.* given without receiving any return value. [1650–60; < L *grātuītus* free, freely given, spontaneous, deriv. of *grātus* thankful, received with thanks (for formation cf. FORTUITOUS); see -OUS] **—gra·tu′i·tous·ly,** *adv.* **—gra·tu′i·tous·ness,** *n.*
—Syn. 2. unnecessary, superfluous, redundant; causeless, unreasonable, groundless, unprovoked, unjustified.

gratu′itous con′tract, *Law.* a contract for the benefit of only one of the parties, the other party receiving nothing as consideration. [1650–60]

gra·tu·i·ty (grə to͞o′i tē, -tyo͞o′-), *n., pl.* **-ties.** **1.** a gift of money, over and above payment due for service, as to a waiter or bellhop; tip. **2.** something given without claim or demand. **3.** *Brit.* **a.** a bonus granted to war veterans by the government. **b.** a bonus given military personnel on discharge or retirement. [1515–25; < MF *gratuite,* equiv. to L *grātui(tus)* free + MF *-te* -TY[2]]

grat·u·lant (grach′ə lənt), *adj.* expressing gratification; congratulatory. [1425–75; late ME: joyful < L *grātulant-* (s. of *grātulāns*), equiv. to *grātul-* express joy (see GRATULATE) + *-ant-* -ANT]

grat·u·late (grach′ə lāt′), *v.,* **-lat·ed, -lat·ing.** *Archaic.* **—***v.t.* **1.** to hail with joy; express joy at. **2.** to congratulate. **—***v.i.* **3.** to express joy. [1550–60; < L *grātulātus* (ptp. of *grātulārī* to express joy), equiv. to *grātul-* express joy, congratulate, thank (deriv. of *grātus* pleasing) + *-ātus* -ATE[1]] **—grat·u·la·to·ri·ly** (grach′ə lə tôr′ə lē, -tōr′-), *adv.* **—grat′u·la·to′ry,** *adj.*

grat·u·la·tion (grach′ə lā′shən), *n.* **1.** a feeling of joy. **2.** the expression of joy. [1425–75; late ME *gratulacioun* < L *grātulātiōn-* (s. of *grātulātiō*). See GRATULATE, -ION]

Grau·bün·den (grou′byn′dən), *n.* German name of **Grisons.**

grau·pel (grou′pəl), *n.* See **snow pellets.** [1885–90; < G; dim. of *Graupe* hulled grain]

Grau·stark (grou′stärk, grô′-), *n.* a novel (1901) by George Barr McCutcheon about the romantic and melodramatic adventures of military and courtly figures in the fictional kingdom of Graustark. **—Grau·stark′i·an,** *adj.*

gra·va·men (grə vā′mən), *n., pl.* **-vam·i·na** (-vam′ə nə). *Law.* **1.** the part of an accusation that weighs most heavily against the accused; the substantial part of a charge or complaint. **2.** a grievance. [1595–1605; < LL: trouble, physical inconvenience, equiv. to L *gravā(re)* to load, weigh down (deriv. of *gravis* heavy, burdened) + *-men* n. suffix]

grave[1] (grāv), *n.* **1.** an excavation made in the earth in which to bury a dead body. **2.** any place of interment; a tomb or sepulcher: *a watery grave.* **3.** any place that becomes the receptacle of what is dead, lost, or past: *the grave of unfulfilled ambitions.* **4.** death: *O grave, where is thy victory?* **5. have one foot in the grave,** to be so frail, sick, or old that death appears imminent: *It was a shock to see my uncle looking as if he had one foot in the grave.* **6. make (one) turn** or **turn over in one's grave,** to do something to which a specified dead person would have objected bitterly: *This production of* Hamlet *is enough to make Shakespeare turn in his grave.* [bef. 1000; ME; OE *græf;* c. G *Grab;* see GRAVE[3]] **—grave′less,** *adj.* **—grave′like′,** *adj.* **—grave′ward, grave′wards,** *adv., adj.*

grave[2] (grāv; *for 4, 6 also* gräv), *adj.,* **grav·er, grav·est** for 1–3, 5, *n.* **—***adj.* **1.** serious or solemn; sober: *a grave person; grave thoughts.* **2.** weighty, momentous, or important: *grave responsibilities.* **3.** threatening a seriously bad outcome or involving serious issues; critical: *a grave situation; a grave illness.* **4.** *Gram.* **a.** unaccented. **b.** spoken on a low or falling pitch. **c.** noting or having a particular accent (`) indicating originally a comparatively low pitch (as in French *père*), distinct syllabic value (as in English *belovèd*), etc. (opposed to *acute*). **5.** (of colors) dull; somber. **—***n.* **6.** the grave accent. [1535–45; < MF < L *gravis;* akin to Gk *barýs* heavy] **—grave′ly,** *adv.* **—grave′ness,** *n.*
—Syn. 1. sedate, staid, thoughtful. GRAVE, SOBER, SOLEMN refer to the condition of being serious in demeanor or appearance. GRAVE indicates a weighty dignity, or the character, aspect, demeanor, speech, etc., of one conscious of heavy responsibilities or cares, or of threatening possibilities: *The jury looked grave while studying the evidence.* SOBER (from its original sense of freedom from intoxication, and hence temperate, staid, sedate) has come to indicate absence of levity, gaiety, or mirth, and thus to be akin to serious and grave: *as sober as a judge; a sober expression on one's face.* SOLEMN implies an impressive seriousness and deep earnestness: *The minister's voice was solemn as he announced the text.*
—Ant. 1. frivolous, gay.

grave[3] (grāv), *v.t.,* **graved, grav·en** or **graved, grav·ing.** **1.** to carve, sculpt, or engrave. **2.** to impress deeply: *graven on the mind.* [bef. 1000; ME *graven,* OE *grafan;* c. G *graben*] **—grav′er,** *n.*

grave[4] (grāv), *v.t.,* **graved, grav·ing.** *Naut.* to clean and apply a protective composition of tar to (the bottom of a ship). [1425–75; late ME; perh. akin to GRAVEL]

gra·ve[5] (grä′vā; *It.* grä′ve), *Music.* **—***adj.* **1.** slow; solemn. **—***adv.* **2.** slowly; solemnly. [1575–85; < It *grave* < L *gravis* heavy; see GRAVE[2]]

grave·clothes (grāv′klōz′, -klōthz′), *n.pl.* the clothes or wrappings in which a body is buried; cerements. [1525–35; GRAVE[1] + CLOTHES]

grave·dig·ger (grāv′dig′ər), *n.* **1.** a person whose occupation is digging graves. **2.** See **burying beetle.** [1585–95; GRAVE[1] + DIGGER]

grav·el (grav′əl), *n., v.,* **-eled, -el·ing** or (*esp. Brit.*) **-elled, -el·ling,** *adj.* **—***n.* **1.** small stones and pebbles, or a mixture of these with sand. **2.** *Pathol.* **a.** multiple small calculi formed in the kidneys. **b.** the disease characterized by such concretions. **—***v.t.* **3.** to cover with gravel. **4.** to bring to a standstill from perplexity; puzzle. **5.** *Informal.* to be a cause of irritation to. **6.** *Obs.* to run (a ship) aground, as on a beach. **—***adj.* **7.** harsh and grating: *a gravel voice.* [1250–1300; ME < OF *gravele,* dim. of *grave* sandy shore, perh. < Celt; cf. GRAVE[4], GROWAN] **—grav′el·ish,** *adj.*

grav·el-blind (grav′əl blīnd′), *adj. Literary.* more blind or dim-sighted than sand-blind and less than stone-blind. [1590–1600]

grav·el·div·er (grav′əl dī′vər), *n.* any of several eel-like fishes of the family Scytalinidae, found off the Pacific coast of North America, esp. *Scytalina cerdale,* which burrows among rocks. [GRAVEL + DIVER]

grav·el·ly (grav′ə lē), *adj.* **1.** of, like, or abounding in gravel. **2.** harsh and grating: *a gravelly voice.* [1350–1400; ME *gravelli.* See GRAVEL, -Y[1]]

Grave·ly (grāv′lē), *n.* **Samuel L(ee), Jr.,** born 1922, U.S. naval officer: first black admiral.

grav·en (grā′vən), *v.* **1.** a pp. of **grave[3].** **—***adj.* **2.** deeply impressed; firmly fixed. **3.** carved; sculptured: *a graven idol.* [1200–50; ME. See GRAVE[3], -EN[3]]

Gra·ven·ha·ge, 's (SKHRä′vən hä′KHə), a Dutch name of The Hague.

grav′en im′age, an idol. [1350–1400; ME]

grav·er (grā′vər), *n.* **1.** any of various tools for chasing, engraving, etc., as a burin. **2.** an engraver. [1350–1400; ME; see GRAVE[3], -ER[1]]

grave·rob·ber (grāv′rob′ər), *n.* **1.** a person who steals valuables from graves and tombs: *Graverobbers had emptied the Mayan tomb before archaeologists could examine its contents.* **2.** a person who steals corpses after burial, esp. for medical dissection. Also, **grave′ rob′ber.** [GRAVE[1] + ROBBER] **—grave′rob′bing,** *n.*

Graves (grāvz), *n.* **Robert (Ran·ke)** (rang′kə), 1895–1985, English poet, novelist, and critic.

Graves (grāv; *Fr.* GRAV), *n.* **1.** a wine-growing district in Gironde department, in SW France. **2.** a dry, red or white table wine produced in this region.

Graves′ disease′ (grāvz), *Pathol.* a disease characterized by an enlarged thyroid, a rapid pulse, and increased basal metabolism due to excessive thyroid secretion; exophthalmic goiter. [1865–70; named after R. J. *Graves* (1796–1853), Irish physician]

Graves·end (grāvz′end′), *n.* a seaport in NW Kent, in SE England, on the Thames River: incorporated into Gravesham 1974. 52,963.

Grave·sham (grāv′shəm), *n.* a borough in NW Kent, in SE England. 95,329.

grave·side (grāv′sīd′), *n.* **1.** the area beside a grave. —*adj.* **2.** being or conducted beside a grave: *a graveside funeral service.* [1830–40; GRAVE[1] + SIDE[1]]

grave·stone (grāv′stōn′), *n.* a stone marking a grave, usually giving the name, date of death, etc., of the person buried there. [1175–1225; ME; see GRAVE[1], STONE]

Gra·vett·i·an (grə vet′ē ən), *adj.* of, pertaining to, or characteristic of an advanced Upper Paleolithic industry of Europe dating to c25,000 B.C. and characterized by straight, blunt-backed blades. [1935–40; after *la Gravette* on the Dordogne, France; see -IAN]

grave·yard (grāv′yärd′), *n.* **1.** a burial ground, often associated with small rural churches. **2.** *Informal.* See **graveyard shift. 3.** a place in which obsolete or derelict objects are kept: *an automobile graveyard.* [1765–75; GRAVE[1] + YARD[2]]

grave′yard shift′, 1. a work shift usually beginning at about midnight and continuing for about eight hours through the early morning hours. **2.** those who work this shift. Also called **graveyard watch, lobster shift.** [1905–10, *Amer.*]

grave′yard stew′, *Slang.* See **milk toast.** [appar. so called because it was served to sick people]

grave′yard watch′, 1. See **graveyard shift. 2.** *Naut.* See **middle watch.** [1925–30]

grav·i·cem·ba·lo (grav′i chem′bə lō′, grä′vi-), *n., pl.* **-cem·ba·li** (-chem′bə lē′), **-cem·ba·los.** a harpsichord. [1855–60; < It, alter. of *clavicembalo* harpsichord (by assoc. with *grave* heavy); see CLAVICEMBALO]

grav·id (grav′id), *adj.* pregnant. [1590–1600; < L *gravidus,* equiv. to *grav(is)* burdened, loaded + *-idus* -ID[4]] —**gra·vid·i·ty** (grə vid′i tē), **grav′id·ness,** *n.* —**grav′id·ly,** *adv.*

grav·i·da (grav′i də), *n., pl.* **-das, -dae** (-dē′). *Obstet.* **1.** a woman's status regarding pregnancy; usually followed by a roman numeral designating the number of times the woman has been pregnant. **2.** a pregnant woman. Cf. **para**[5]. [1925–30; < NL, L: fem. of *gravidus* pregnant, laden; see GRAVID]

gra·vim·e·ter (grə vim′i tər), *n.* **1.** an instrument for measuring the specific gravity of a solid or liquid. **2.** Also called **gravity meter.** an instrument for measuring variations in the gravitational field of the earth by detecting differences in weight of an object of constant mass at different points on the earth's surface. [1790–1800; < F *gravimètre,* equiv. to *gravi-* (comb. form of L *gravis* heavy) + *-mètre* -METER]

grav·i·met·ric (grav′ə me′trik), *adj.* of or pertaining to measurement by weight. Also, **grav′i·met′ri·cal.** [1870–75; *gravi-* (comb. form of L *gravis* heavy) + -METRIC] —**grav′i·met′ri·cal·ly,** *adv.*

gravimet′ric anal′ysis, *Chem.* analysis by weight. Cf. **volumetric analysis.** [1930–35]

gra·vim·e·try (grə vim′i trē), *n.* the measurement of weight or density. [1855–60; *gravi-* (comb. form of L *gravis* heavy) + -METRY]

grav′ing dock′, *Naut.* an excavated shore dry dock for the repair and maintenance of ships. [1830–40]

grav′ing piece′, *Naut.* a piece of wood let into a wooden hull to replace decayed wood. [1795–1805]

grav·i·sphere (grav′ə sfēr′), *n.* the area in which the gravitational force of a celestial body is predominant. [GRAVI(TY) + SPHERE]

grav·i·tate (grav′i tāt′), *v.i.,* **-tat·ed, -tat·ing. 1.** to move or tend to move under the influence of gravitational force. **2.** to tend toward the lowest level; sink. **3.** to have a natural tendency or be strongly attracted (usually fol. by *to* or *toward*): *Musicians gravitate toward one another.* [1635–45; < NL *gravitātus* (ptp. of *gravitāre*). See GRAVITY, -ATE[1]] —**grav′i·tat′er,** *n.* —**Syn. 3.** incline, tend, lean, move.

grav·i·ta·tion (grav′i tā′shən), *n.* **1.** *Physics.* **a.** the force of attraction between any two masses. Cf. **law of gravitation. b.** an act or process caused by this force. **2.** a sinking or falling. **3.** a movement or tendency toward something or someone: *the gravitation of people toward the suburbs.* [1635–45; < NL *gravitātiōn-* (s. of *gravitātiō*). See GRAVITATE, -ION] —**grav′i·ta′tion·al,** *adj.* —**grav′i·ta′tion·al·ly,** *adv.*

gravita′tional collapse′, *Astron.* **1.** the final stage of stellar evolution in which a star collapses to a final state, as a white dwarf, neutron star, or black hole, when the star's nuclear reactions no longer generate enough pressure to balance the attractive force of gravity. **2.** the initial stage of stellar evolution in which interstellar gases and dust contract under gravity and condense into one or more stars.

grav′ita′tional con′stant, *Physics.* constant of gravitation. See under **law of gravitation.** [1900–05]

CONCISE ETYMOLOGY KEY: <, descended or borrowed from; >, whence; b., blend of, blended; c., cognate with; cf., compare; deriv., derivative; equiv., equivalent; imit., imitative; obl., oblique; r., replacing; s., stem; sp., spelling, spelled; resp., respelling, respelled; trans., translation; ?, origin unknown; *, unattested; ‡, probably earlier than. See the full key inside the front cover.

gravita′tional field′, *Physics.* **1.** the attractive effect, considered as extending throughout space, of matter on other matter. **2.** the region surrounding an astronomical body in which the force of gravitation is strong. [1915–20]

gravita′tional lens′, *Astron.* a heavy, dense body, as a galaxy, that lies along our line of sight to a more distant object, as a quasar, and whose gravitational field refracts the light of that object, splitting it into multiple images as seen from the earth. [1975–80]

grav′ita′tional mass′, *Physics.* the mass of a body as measured by its gravitational attraction for other bodies. Cf. **inertial mass.**

gravita′tional ra′dius, *Astron.* See **Schwarzschild radius.**

gravita′tional red′shift, *Physics, Astron.* (in general relativity) the shift toward longer wavelengths of electromagnetic radiation emitted by a source in a gravitational field, esp. at the surface of a massive star. Cf. **redshift.**

gravita′tional wave′, *Astron., Physics.* (in general relativity) a propagating wave of gravitational energy produced by accelerating masses, esp. during catastrophic events, as the gravitational collapse of massive stars. Also called **gravity wave.** [1895–1900]

grav·i·ta·tive (grav′i tā′tiv), *adj.* **1.** of or pertaining to gravitation. **2.** tending or causing to gravitate. [1790–1800; GRAVITATE + -IVE]

grav·i·ton (grav′i ton′), *n. Physics.* the theoretical quantum of gravitation, usually assumed to be an elementary particle that is its own antiparticle and that has zero rest mass and charge and a spin of two. Cf. **photon.** [1940–45; GRAVIT(Y) + -ON[1]]

grav·i·ty (grav′i tē), *n., pl.* **-ties. 1.** the force of attraction by which terrestrial bodies tend to fall toward the center of the earth. **2.** heaviness or weight. **3.** gravitation in general. **4.** See **acceleration of gravity. 5.** a unit of acceleration equal to the acceleration of gravity. *Symbol:* g **6.** serious or critical nature: *He seemed to ignore the gravity of his illness.* **7.** serious or dignified behavior; dignity; solemnity: *to preserve one's gravity.* **8.** lowness in pitch, as of sounds. [1500–10; < L *gravitāt-* (s. of *gravitās*) heaviness, equiv. to *grav(is)* heavy, GRAVE[2] + *-itāt-* -ITY] —**Syn. 6.** seriousness, danger, emergency, import.

grav′ity cell′, *Elect.* a cell containing two electrolytes that have different specific gravities.

grav′ity clock′, a clock driven by its own weight as it descends a rack, cord, incline, etc.

grav′ity dam′, a dam resisting the pressure of impounded water through its own weight. [1935–40]

grav′ity escape′ment, *Horol.* an escapement, used esp. in large outdoor clocks, in which the impulse is given to the pendulum by means of a weight falling through a certain distance. [1840–50]

grav′ity fault′, *Geol.* a fault along an inclined plane in which the upper side or hanging wall appears to have moved downward with respect to the lower side or footwall (opposed to *reverse fault*). Also called **normal fault.**

grav′ity feed′, 1. the supplying of fuel, materials, etc., by force of gravity. **2.** a system or device designed for this purpose. [1910–15] —**grav·i·ty-fed** (grav′i tē fed′), *adj.*

grav′ity hinge′, a hinge closing automatically by means of gravity.

grav′ity me′ter, *Geol.* gravimeter (def. 2). [1940–45]

grav′ity rail′road, a railroad depending partly on the force of gravity for motive power.

grav′ity wave′, 1. *Astron., Physics.* See **gravitational wave. 2.** a wave created by the action of gravity on local variations in the density of a stratified fluid, as the atmosphere, or at an interface between fluids of different density, as a liquid and a gas. [1875–80]

grav′ity wind′ (wind), a light wind directed downslope, occurring at night because of the cooling and densification of the air near the ground. Also called **drainage wind.** [1925–30]

grav·lax (gräv′läks), *n. Scandinavian Cookery.* boned salmon, cured by marinating in sugar, salt, pepper, and other spices, esp. dill. [1960–65; < Sw *gravlax,* Norw *gravlaks,* equiv. to *grav-* (cf. Sw *grava,* Norw *grave* to dig, bury) + *lax, laks* salmon; see LOX[1]; the salmon was orig. cured by burying it]

gra·vure (grə vyŏŏr′, grā′vyər), *n.* **1.** an intaglio process of photomechanical printing, such as photogravure or rotogravure. **2.** a print produced by gravure. **3.** the metal or wooden plate used in photogravure. [1875–80; < F, equiv. to *grav(er)* to engrave < Gmc (see GRAVE[3]) + *-ure* -URE]

gra·vy (grā′vē), *n., pl.* **-vies. 1.** the fat and juices that drip from cooking meat, often thickened, seasoned, flavored, etc., and used as a sauce for meat, potatoes, rice, etc. **2.** *Slang.* **a.** profit or money easily obtained or received unexpectedly. **b.** money illegally or dishonestly acquired, esp. through graft. **3.** something advantageous or valuable that is received or obtained as a benefit beyond what is due or expected. [1350–1400; 1905–10 for def. 2; ME *gravé, gravey* < OF *gravé,* perh. misreading of *grané* (cf. *grain* spice) < L *granātus* full of grains. See GRAIN, -ATE[1]]

gra′vy boat′, a small dish, often boat-shaped, for serving gravy or sauce. [1890–95]

gra′vy train′, *Slang.* a position in which a person or group receives excessive and unjustified money or advantages with little or no effort: *The top executives were on the gravy train with their huge bonuses.* [1925–30]

gray[1] (grā), *adj.,* **-er, -est,** *n., v.* —*adj.* **1.** of a color between white and black; having a neutral hue. **2.** dark, dismal, or gloomy: *gray skies.* **3.** dull, dreary, or monotonous. **4.** having gray hair. **5.** pertaining to old age; mature. **6.** *Informal.* pertaining to, involving, or composed of older persons: *gray households.* **7.** old or ancient. **8.** indeterminate and intermediate in character: *The tax audit concentrated on deductions in the gray area between purely personal and purely business expenses.* —*n.* **9.** any achromatic color; any color with zero chroma, intermediate between white and black. **10.** something of this color. **11.** gray material or clothing: *to dress in gray.* **12.** an unbleached and undyed condition. **13.** (*often cap.*) a member of the Confederate army in the American Civil War or the army itself. Cf. **blue** (def. 5). **14.** a horse of a gray color. **15.** a horse that appears white but is not an albino. —*v.t., v.i.* **16.** to make or become gray. Also, **grey.** [bef. 900; ME; OE *grǣg;* c. G *grau*] —**gray′ly,** *adv.* —**gray′ness,** *n.*

gray[2] (grā), *n. Physics.* the SI unit of absorbed dose, equal to the amount of ionizing radiation absorbed when the energy imparted to matter is 1 J/kg. *Abbr.:* Gy Cf. **rad.** [1975; named in honor of Louis Harold *Gray* (1905–65), English radiobiologist]

Gray (grā), *n.* **1. A·sa** (ā′sə), 1810–88, U.S. botanist. **2. Thomas,** 1716–71, English poet.

gray·back (grā′bak′), *n.* **1.** any of various marine and aquatic animals that are dark gray above and light-colored or white below, as the gray whale, the alewife, certain whitefish, and certain sandpipers. **2.** *Informal.* a Confederate soldier. [1805–15; GRAY[1] + BACK[1]]

gray·beard (grā′bērd′), *n.* **1.** *Sometimes Disparaging.* a man whose beard is gray; old man; sage. **2.** bellarmine. Also, **greybeard.** [1570–80; GRAY[1] + BEARD] —**gray′beard′ed,** *adj.*

gray′ birch′, a small, bushy birch, *Betula populifolia,* of stony or sandy areas of the eastern U.S., having grayish-white bark and triangular leaves. [1850–55, *Amer.*]

gray′ bod′y, *Physics.* any body that emits radiation at each wavelength in a constant ratio less than unity to that emitted by a black body at the same temperature.

gray′ card′, *Photog.* a card of controlled reflectance held near a subject to approximate middle tones and used as a target for an exposure meter.

gray′ cat′bird. See under **catbird.**

gray′-cheeked thrush′ (grā′chēkt′), a North American thrush, *Catharus minimus,* having olive upper parts and grayish cheeks. [1855–60, *Amer.*]

gray′ duck′, any of several ducks in which certain immature or female plumages are predominantly gray, as the gadwall and the pintail. [1880–85]

gray′ em′inence, a person who wields unofficial power, esp. through another person and often surreptitiously or privately. Also, **éminence grise.** [1940–45; trans. of F *éminence grise*]

gray·fish (grā′fish′), *n., pl.* **-fish·es,** (*esp. collectively*) **-fish.** a name used in marketing for any of several American sharks, esp. the dogfishes of the genus *Squalus.* [1785–95; GRAY[1] + FISH]

gray′ fox′, a fox, *Urocyon cinereoargenteus,* ranging from Central America through the southwestern and eastern U.S., having blackish-gray upper parts and rusty-yellowish feet, legs, and ears. [1670–80, *Amer.*]

Gray′ Fri′ar, a Franciscan friar: so called from the traditional gray habit worn by the order. [1275–1325; ME]

gray′ goods′, a woven fabric as it comes from the loom and before it has been submitted to the finishing process. Also called **greige, griege.** [1950–55]

gray-head·ed (grā′hed′id), *adj.* **1.** having gray hair. **2.** of or pertaining to old age or old people. **3.** old. Also, **grey-headed.** [1525–35]

gray·hound (grā′hound′), *n.* greyhound.

gray′ i′ron, pig iron or cast iron having much of its carbon in the form of graphite and exhibiting a gray fracture. [1655–65]

gray·ish (grā′ish), *adj.* **1.** having a tinge of gray; slightly gray: *The sky was full of dark, grayish clouds.* **2.** similar to gray: *a grayish color; a grayish purple.* Also, **greyish.** [1555–65; GRAY[1] + -ISH[1]]

gray′ jay′, a gray jay, *Perisoreus canadensis,* of northern North America, noted for its boldness in stealing food from houses, traps, camps, etc. Also called **Canada jay, camp robber, whiskey jack.** [1935–40]

Gray′ La′dy, a female worker in the American Red Cross who serves as a volunteer aide in medical services.

gray·lag (grā′lag′), *n.* a common, gray, wild goose, *Anser anser,* of Europe, that is the ancestor of most breeds of domestic goose. Also, **greylag.** [1705–15; GRAY[1] + LAG[1] (with reference to its habit of remaining longer in England before migrating than other species of the genus)]

gray·ling (grā′ling), *n.* **1.** any freshwater fish of the genus *Thymallus,* related to the trouts but having a longer and higher, brilliantly colored dorsal fin. **2.** any of several grayish or brownish satyr butterflies. [1400–50; late ME; see GRAY[1], -LING[1]]

gray·mail (grā′māl′), *n.* a means of preventing prosecution, as for espionage, by threatening to disclose government secrets during trial. [1975–80; GRAY[1] (in sense "indeterminate") + (BLACK)MAIL]

gray′ man′ganese ore′, manganite.

gray′ mar′ket, a market operating within the law but charging prices substantially below list prices or those fixed by an official agency. Cf. **black market.** [1945–50]

gray′ mat′ter, 1. *Anat.* nerve tissue, esp. of the brain and spinal cord, that contains fibers and nerve cell bodies and is dark reddish-gray. Cf. **white matter. 2.** *Informal.* brains or intellect. [1830–40]

gray′ mold′, 1. a disease of plants, characterized by a gray, furry coating on the decaying parts, caused by any of several fungi. **2.** any fungus causing this disease, as *Botrytis cinerea.*

gray′ mul′let, mullet[1] (def. 1).

gray′ nurse′ shark′, a sand shark, *Odontaspis arenarius,* abundant in S African and Australian coastal waters and estuaries. [1895–1900; see NURSE SHARK]

gray′ ox′, kouprey.

Gray′ Pan′ther, a member of an organized group of elderly people seeking to secure or protect their rights by collective action.

gray′ par′rot, an ashy-gray, African parrot, *Psittacus erithacus,* having a short, red tail, noted esp. for its ability to mimic speech. Also called **African gray.**

gray′ pine′. See **jack pine.** [1800–10, *Amer.*]

gray′ pow′er, the organized influence exerted by elderly people as a group, esp. for social or political purposes or ends. [1975–80]

grays•by (grāz′bē), *n., pl.* **-bies.** a serranid fish, *Epinephelus cruentatus,* inhabiting warm waters of the western Atlantic Ocean, having a reddish-gray body marked with vermilion spots. [orig. uncert.]

gray′ scale′, a scale of achromatic colors having several, usually ten, equal gradations ranging from white to black, used in television and photography. [1935–40]

gray′ sea′ ea′gle, a grayish-brown sea eagle, *Haliaetus albicilla,* of the Old World and Greenland, having a white tail. Also called **white-tailed sea eagle.**

Gray's′ Inn′. See under **Inns of Court** (def. 1).

gray′ skate′, a skate, *Raja batis,* of coastal seas off Great Britain.

gray′ snap′per, a snapper, *Lutjanus griseus,* of shallow waters off the coast of Florida, having a grayish-green body with a brown spot on each scale. Also called **mangrove snapper.** [1765–75, *Amer.*]

Gray•son (grā′sən), *n.* **David,** pen name of Ray Stannard Baker.

gray′ squir′rel, a common, grayish squirrel, *Sciurus carolinensis,* of eastern North America. See illus. under **squirrel.** [1615–25, *Amer.*]

gray′ trout′, a common weakfish, *Cynoscion regalis,* inhabiting Atlantic and Gulf coastal waters of the U.S. Also called **gray′ sea′ trout′.**

gray′ urn′, a smooth, urn-shaped edible mushroom, *Urnula craterium,* commonly found in North America on fallen hardwood.

gray•wacke (grā′wak′, -wak′ə), *n. Geol.* a dark-gray coarse-grained wacke. Also, **greywacke.** [1805–15; partly adapted from G *Grauwache;* see WACKE]

gray′ wa′ter, dirty water from sinks, showers, bathtubs, washing machines, and the like, that can be recycled, as for use in flushing toilets. [1975–80]

gray•weth•er (grā′weth′ər), *n.* sarsen. [1785–95; GRAY[1] + WETHER]

gray′ whale′, a grayish-black whalebone whale, *Eschrichtius robustus,* of the North Pacific, growing to a length of 50 ft. (15.2 m): now rare. [1855–60]

gray′ wolf′, a wolf, *Canis lupus,* having a grizzled, blackish, or whitish coat: formerly common in Eurasia and North America, some subspecies are now reduced in numbers or near extinction. Cf. **timber wolf.** [1805–15]

Graz (gräts), *n.* a city in SE Austria. 243,405.

graze[1] (grāz), *v.,* **grazed, graz•ing.** —*v.i.* **1.** to feed on growing grass and pasturage, as do cattle, sheep, etc. **2.** *Informal.* to eat small portions of food, as appetizers or the like, in place of a full-sized meal or to snack during the course of the day in place of regular meals. —*v.t.* **3.** to feed on (growing grass). **4.** to put cattle, sheep, etc., to feed on (grass, pastureland, etc.). **5.** to tend (cattle, sheep, etc.) while they are at pasture. [bef. 1000; ME *grasen,* OE *grasian,* deriv. of *græs* GRASS] —**graze′a•ble,** *adj.* —**graz′er,** *n.*

graze[2] (grāz), *v.,* **grazed, graz•ing,** *n.* —*v.t.* **1.** to touch or rub lightly in passing. **2.** to scrape the skin from; abrade: *The bullet just grazed his shoulder.* —*v.i.* **3.** to touch or rub something lightly, or so as to produce slight abrasion, in passing: *to graze against a rough wall.* —*n.* **4.** a grazing; a touching or rubbing lightly in passing. **5.** a slight scratch, scrape, or wound made in passing; abrasion. [1595–1605; perh. special use of GRAZE[1]; for the semantic shift cf. F *effleurer,* deriv. of *fleur* flower, in the same meaning] —**graz′er,** *n.* —**graz′•ing•ly,** *adv.*

gra•zier (grā′zhər), *n. Chiefly Brit.* a person who grazes cattle for the market. [1225–75; ME *grasier.* See GRAZE[1], -IER[1]]

graz•ing (grā′zing), *n.* **1.** pastureland; a pasture. **2.** *Informal.* the act or practice of switching television channels frequently to watch several programs. [1400–50; late ME; see GRAZE[1], -ING[1]]

gra•zi•o•so (grät′sē ō′sō; *It.* grä tsyô′zô), *Music.* —*adj.* **1.** graceful; flowing. —*adv.* **2.** gracefully; flowingly. [1800–10; < It: lit., gracious, gentle, equiv. to *grazi(a)* GRACE + *-oso* -OUS]

Gr. Br., Great Britain. Also, **Gr. Brit.**

GRE, Graduate Record Examination.

grease (*n.* grēs; *v.* grēs, grēz), *n., v.,* **greased, greas•ing.** —*n.* **1.** the melted or rendered fat of animals, esp. when in a soft state. **2.** fatty or oily matter in general; lubricant. **3.** Also called **grease′ wool′.** wool, as shorn, before being cleansed of the oily matter. **4.** Also called **grease-heel** (grēs′hēl′). *Vet. Pathol.* inflammation of a horse's skin in the fetlock region, attended with an oily secretion. **5.** *Informal.* a bribe. —*v.t.* **6.** to put grease on; lubricate: *to grease the axle of a car.* **7.** to smear or cover with grease. **8.** to cause to occur easily; smooth the way; facilitate. **9.** *Informal.* to bribe. **10. grease someone's palm.** See **palm**[1] (def. 11). [1250–1300; ME *grese, grece, greice* < AF *grece, gresse,* OF *craisse* (F *graisse*) < VL **crassia,* equiv. to L *crass(us)* fat, thick + *-ia* n. suffix] —**grease′less,** *adj.* —**grease′less•ness,** *n.* —**grease′proof′,** *adj.*

grease•ball (grēs′bôl′), *n. Slang (disparaging and offensive).* **1.** a person of Mediterranean or Latin American descent. **2.** a person having oily or slicked-back hair. **3.** greaser (def. 3). [1930–35; GREASE + BALL[1]]

grease′ cup′, oilcup. [1830–40]

grease′ gun′, a hand-operated pump for greasing bearings under pressure. [1915–20]

grease′ mon′key, *Slang.* a mechanic, esp. one who works on automobiles or airplanes. [1905–10]

grease′ paint′, **1.** an oily mixture of melted tallow or grease and a pigment, used by actors, clowns, etc., for making up their faces. **2.** theatrical makeup. [1885–90]

grease′ pen′cil, a pencil of pigment and compressed grease encased in a spiral paper strip that can be partially unwound to expose a new point and used esp. for writing on glossy surfaces.

greas•er (grē′sər), *n.* **1.** a person or thing that greases. **2.** *Slang (disparaging and offensive).* a Latin American, esp. a Mexican. **3.** *Slang.* a swaggering young tough, esp. a member of a street gang. [1635–45; GREASE + -ER[1]]

grease•wood (grēs′wo͝od′), *n.* **1.** a shrub, *Sarcobatus vermiculatus,* of the goosefoot family, growing in alkaline regions of the western U.S., containing a small amount of oil. **2.** any of various similar shrubs. **3.** See **white sage** (def. 1). **4.** *Western U.S.* mesquite. Also called **grease•bush** (grēs′bo͝osh′). [1830–40, *Amer.;* GREASE + WOOD[1]]

greas•y (grē′sē, -zē), *adj.,* **greas•i•er, greas•i•est.** **1.** smeared, covered, or soiled with grease. **2.** composed of or containing grease; oily: *greasy food.* **3.** greaselike in appearance or to the touch; slippery. **4.** insinuatingly unctuous in manner; repulsively slick; oily. **5.** *Vet. Pathol.* affected with grease. [1505–15; GREASE + -Y[1]] —**greas′i•ly,** *adv.* —**greas′i•ness,** *n.*

—**Pronunciation.** GREASY is almost always pronounced as (grē′zē), with a medial (z), in the South Midland and Southern U.S. and as (grē′sē), with a medial (s), in New England, New York State, and the Great Lakes Basin. Speakers of New Jersey and eastern Pennsylvania are divided, with some using (s) and some using (z). Standard British English reflects both (z) and (s) pronunciations and British folk speech is also divided regionally, with (z) heard in the eastern countries and (s) in the central and western ones. Both pronunciations were brought to the colonies, where the present U.S. pattern emerged.

greas′y spoon′, *Slang.* a cheap and rather unsanitary restaurant. [1920–25, *Amer.*]

great (grāt), *adj.,* **-er, -est,** *adv., n., pl.* **greats,** (*esp. collectively*) **great,** *interj.* —*adj.* **1.** unusually or comparatively large in size or dimensions: *A great fire destroyed nearly half the city.* **2.** large in number; numerous: *Great hordes of tourists descend on Europe each summer.* **3.** unusual or considerable in degree, power, intensity, etc.: *great pain.* **4.** wonderful; first-rate; very good: *We had a great time. That's great!* **5.** being such in an extreme or notable degree: *great friends; a great talker.* **6.** notable; remarkable; exceptionally outstanding: *a great occasion.* **7.** important; highly significant or consequential: *the great issues in American history.* **8.** distinguished; famous: *a great inventor.* **9.** of noble or lofty character: *great thoughts.* **10.** chief or principal: *the great hall; his greatest novel.* **11.** of high rank, official position, or social standing: *a great noble.* **12.** much in use or favor: *"Humor" was a great word with the old physiologists.* **13.** of extraordinary powers; having unusual merit; very admirable: *a great statesman.* **14.** of considerable duration or length: *We waited a great while for the train.* **15.** *Informal.* **a.** enthusiastic about some specified activity (usually fol. by *at, for,* or *on*): *He's great on reading poetry aloud.* **b.** skillful; expert (usually fol. by *at* or *on*): *He's great at golf.* **16.** being of one generation more remote from the family relative specified (used in combination): *a great-grandson.* **17. great with child,** being in the late stages of pregnancy. —*adv.* **18.** *Informal.* very well: *Things have been going great for him.* —*n.* **19.** a person who has achieved importance or distinction in a field: *She is one of the theater's greats.* **20.** great persons, collectively: *England's literary great.* **21.** (*often cap.*) **greats,** (*used with a singular v.*) Also called **great go.** *Brit. Informal.* **a.** the final examination for the bachelor's degree in the classics and mathematics, or *Literae Humaniores,* esp. at Oxford University and usually for honors. **b.** the course of study. **c.** the subject studied. —*interj.* **22.** (used to express acceptance, appreciation, approval, admiration, etc.). **23.** (used ironically or facetiously to express disappointment, annoyance, distress, etc.): *Great! We just missed the last train home.* [bef. 900; ME *greet,* OE *grēat;* c. D *groot,* G *gross*] —**great′•ness,** *n.*

—**Syn.** **1.** immense, enormous, gigantic, huge, vast, grand. GREAT, BIG, LARGE refer to size, extent, and degree. In reference to the size and extent of concrete objects, BIG is the most general and most colloquial word, LARGE is somewhat more formal, and GREAT is highly formal and even poetic, suggesting also that the object is notable or imposing: *a big tree; a large tree; a great oak; a big field; a large field; great plains.* When the reference is to degree or a quality, GREAT is the usual word: *great beauty; great mistake; great surprise;* although BIG sometimes alternates with it in colloquial style: *a big mistake; a big surprise;* LARGE is not used in reference to degree, but may be used in a quantitative reference: *a large number* (*great number*). **6.** noteworthy. **7.** weighty, serious, momentous, vital, critical. **8.** famed, eminent, noted, notable, prominent, renowned. **9.** elevated, exalted, dignified. **10.** main, grand, leading.

Great′ Ab′a•co (ab′ə kō′). See under **Abaco.**

Great′ A′jax, *Class. Myth.* Ajax (def. 1).

great′ ape′, any of several apes of the family Pongidae, characterized by a relatively hairless face with protrusive lips and by hands with complex fingerprints and flat nails, including the gorilla, chimpanzee, and orangutan. [1945–50]

Great′ Attrac′tor, a vast concentration of matter whose gravitational pull alters the direction and speed of the Milky Way and other galaxies as they spread apart in the expanding universe posited by the big bang theory. [1985–90]

great′ auk′, a large, flightless auk, *Pinguinus impennis,* of rocky islands off North Atlantic coasts: extinct since 1844. [1820–30]

great-aunt (grāt′ant′, -änt′), *n.* a grandaunt. [1650–60]

Great′ Austral′ian Bight′, a wide bay in S Australia.

Great′ Awak′ening, the series of religious revivals among Protestants in the American colonies, esp. in New England, lasting from about 1725 to 1770. [1730–40]

great′ barracu′da, a large barracuda, *Sphyraena barracuda,* of Atlantic and western Pacific seas. See illus. under **barracuda.**

Great′ Bar′rier Reef′, a coral reef parallel to the coast of Queensland, in NE Australia. 1250 mi. (2010 km) long. Also called **Barrier Reef.**

Great′ Ba′sin, a region in the Western U.S. that has no drainage to the ocean: includes most of Nevada and parts of Utah, California, Oregon, and Idaho. 210,000 sq. mi. (544,000 sq. km).

great′ bas′inet, *Armor.* a basinet having a beaver permanently attached.

Great′ Bear′, *Astron.* the constellation Ursa Major.

Great′ Bear′ Lake′, a lake in NW Canada, in the Northwest Territories. 12,275 sq. mi. (31,792 sq. km).

Great′ Bend′, a city in central Kansas. 16,608.

great′ black′-backed gull′ (blak′bakt′). See under **black-backed gull.**

great′ blue′ her′on, a large American heron, *Ardea herodias,* having bluish-gray plumage. See illus. under **heron.** [1825–35, *Amer.*]

great′ blue′ shark′. See **blue shark.**

Great′ Brit′ain, an island of NW Europe, separated from the mainland by the English Channel and the North Sea: since 1707 the name has applied politically to England, Scotland, and Wales. 46,417,600; 88,139 sq. mi. (228,280 sq. km). Cf. **United Kingdom.**

great′ bus′tard, a large bustard, *Otis tarda,* of southern and central Europe and western and central Asia, having a wingspread of about 8 ft. (2.4 m).

great′ cir′cle, **1.** a circle on a spherical surface such that the plane containing the circle passes through the center of the sphere. Cf. **small circle.** **2.** a circle of which a segment represents the shortest distance between two points on the surface of the earth. [1585–95]

great′-cir′cle sail′ing (grāt′sûr′kəl), *Navig.* sailing between two points more or less according to an arc of a great circle, in practice almost always using a series of rhumb lines of different bearings to approximate the arc, whose own bearing changes constantly unless it coincides with a meridian or the equator.

great′-cir′cle track′, the route of a ship following the arc of a great circle, appearing as a curved line on a Mercator chart and as a straight line on a gnomonic chart. [1955–60]

great•coat (grāt′kōt′), *n. Chiefly Brit.* a heavy overcoat. [1655–65; GREAT + COAT] —**great′coat′ed,** *adj.*

great′ coun′cil, **1.** (in Norman England) an assembly composed of the king's tenants in chief that served as the principal council of the realm and replaced the witenagemot. **2.** (formerly in Italy) the municipal council in some towns or cities, as in Venice. [1730–40]

great′ crest′ed fly′catcher, a North American flycatcher, *Myiarchus crinitus,* noted for its use of the castoff skins of snakes in building its nest. [1800–10]

great′ crest′ed grebe′, a large Old World grebe, *Podiceps cristatus,* having black, earlike tufts of feathers projecting backward from the top of the head. See illus. under **grebe.**

Great′ Dae′dala. See under **Daedala.**

Great′ Dane′, one of a breed of large, powerful, shorthaired dogs ranging in color from fawn to brindle, blue, black, or white with black spots. [1765–75]

Great Dane, 32 in. (81 cm) high at shoulder

Great′ Depres′sion, the economic crisis and period of low business activity in the U.S. and other countries, roughly beginning with the stock-market crash in October, 1929, and continuing through most of the 1930's.

Great′ Divide′, **1.** the continental divide of North America; the Rocky Mountains. **2.** any similar continental divide. **3.** the passage from life to death: *He crossed the Great Divide before his promise as a poet was recognized.* **4.** an important division or difference. [1860–65; *Amer.*]

Great′ Divid′ing Range′, a mountain range extending along the E coast of Australia: vast watershed region. 100 to 200 mi. (160–320 km) wide.

Great′ Dog′, *Astron.* the constellation Canis Major.

great′ doxol′ogy. See **Gloria in Excelsis Deo.** Also called **great′er doxol′ogy.**

great·en (grāt′n), *v.t.* **1.** to make greater; enlarge; increase. —*v.i.* **2.** to become greater. [1325–75; ME; see GREAT, -EN[1]]

Great′ En′trance, *Eastern Ch.* the solemn procession in which the unconsecrated Eucharistic elements are carried from the prothesis through the nave of the church and into the bema. Cf. **Little Entrance.**

Great·er (grā′tər), *adj.* designating a city or country and its adjacent area: *Greater New York; Greater Los Angeles.* [1570–80; GREAT + -ER[4]]

Great′er Antil′les. See under **Antilles.**

great′er cel′andine, celandine (def. 1).

Great′er Diony′sia, (in ancient Athens) the chief festival in honor of Dionysus, celebrated in early spring and notable for the performance of dithyrambs, tragedies, comedies, and satyr plays. Also called **City Dionysia.**

great′er Ion′ic. See under **Ionic** (def. 2).

Great′er Lon′don, London (def. 5).

Great′er Man′chester, a metropolitan county in central England, with the city of Manchester as its center. 2,708,900; 498 sq. mi. (1290 sq. km).

great′er omen′tum, *Anat.* the peritoneal fold attached to the stomach and the colon and hanging over the small intestine. Also called **caul, gastrocolic omentum.** Cf. **lesser omentum.**

great′er prai′rie chick′en. See under **prairie chicken** (def. 1).

great′er road′runner. See under **roadrunner.**

great′er scaup′. See under **scaup.**

great′er shear′water, a sooty-brown and white shearwater, *Puffinus gravis,* of eastern coasts of the Western Hemisphere.

great′er si′ren. See **mud eel.**

Great′er Sun′da Is′lands. See under **Sunda Islands.**

great′er wee′ver. See under **weever** (def. 1).

great′er yel′lowlegs. See under **yellowlegs.** [1925–30]

great′est com′mon divi′sor, the largest number that is a common divisor of a given set of numbers. *Abbr.:* G.C.D. Also called **great′est com′mon fac′tor, highest common factor.** [1920–25]

great′est-in′te·ger func′tion (grā′tist in′ti jər), the function that assigns to each real number the greatest integer less than or equal to the number. *Symbol:* [*x*]

great′est low′er bound′, a lower bound that is greater than or equal to all the lower bounds of a given set: 1 is the greatest lower bound of the set consisting of 1, 2, 3. *Abbr.:* glb Also called **infimum.**

Great′ Expecta′tions, a novel (1861) by Charles Dickens.

Great′ Falls′, a city in central Montana, on the Missouri River. 56,725.

Great′ Fes′tival, *Islam.* See **ʽId al-Adha.**

Great′ Gats′by, The (gats′bē), a novel (1925) by F. Scott Fitzgerald.

great′ go′, *Brit. Informal.* great (def. 21). [1810–20]

Great′ God′dess, The. See **Great Mother.**

great-grand·aunt (grāt′grand′ant′, -änt′), *n.* an aunt of one's grandfather or grandmother.

great-grand·child (grāt′gran′chīld′), *n., pl.* **-children.** a grandchild of one's son or daughter. [1745–55]

great-grand·daugh·ter (grāt′gran′dô′tər), *n.* a granddaughter of one's son or daughter. [1745–55]

great-grand·fa·ther (grāt′gran′fä′thər, -grand′-), *n.* a grandfather of one's father or mother. [1505–15]

great-grand·moth·er (grāt′gran′muth′ər, -grand′-, -gram′-), *n.* a grandmother of one's father or mother. [1520–30]

great-grand·neph·ew (grāt′gran′nef′yōō, -nev′yōō, -grand′-), *n.* a grandson of one's nephew or niece.

great-grand·niece (grāt′gran′nēs′, -grand′-), *n.* a granddaughter of one's nephew or niece. [1795–1805]

great-grand·par·ent (grāt′gran′pâr′ənt, -par′-, -grand′-), *n.* a grandfather or grandmother of one's father or mother. [1880–85]

great-grand·son (grāt′gran′sun′, -grand′-), *n.* a grandson of one's son or daughter. [1710–20]

great-grand·un·cle (grāt′grand′ung′kəl), *n.* an uncle of one's grandfather or grandmother. [1800–10]

great′ gray′ owl′, a large, dish-faced, gray owl, *Strix nebulosa,* of northern North America and western Eurasia, having streaked and barred plumage. [1835–45, *Amer.*]

great′ gross′, a unit of quantity equivalent to 12 gross. *Abbr.:* GGR [1525–35]

great′ guns′, 1. *Informal.* in a relentlessly energetic or successful manner: *The new president has the company going great guns.* **2.** (used as an expression of surprise, astonishment, etc.) [1870–75]

great·heart·ed (grāt′här′tid), *adj.* **1.** having or showing a generous heart; magnanimous. **2.** high-spirited; courageous; fearless: *greathearted defense of liberty.* [1350–1400; ME *grete hartyd*] —**great′heart′ed·ly,** *adv.* —**great′heart′ed·ness,** *n.*

great′ helm′, *Armor.* helm² (def. 1).

great′ horned′ owl′, a large, brown-speckled owl, *Bubo virginianus,* common in the Western Hemisphere, having prominent ear tufts. See illus. under **owl.** [1670–80]

Great′ I·dae′an Moth′er (ī dē′ən), Cybele.

Great′ Khing′an′ (KHing′än′), a mountain range in NE China: highest peak, 5000 ft. (1525 m).

great′ kis′kadee. See under **kiskadee.**

Great′ Lakes′, a series of five lakes between the U.S. and Canada, comprising Lakes Erie, Huron, Michigan, Ontario, and Superior; connected with the Atlantic by the St. Lawrence River.

Great′ Lakes′ Na′val Train′ing Cen′ter, a U.S. Navy training center in NE Illinois, S of Waukegan.

great′ lau′rel, a tall shrub, *Rhododendron maximum,* of eastern North America, having rose-pink flowers. Also called **great rhododendron, rosebay.** [1775–85, *Amer.*]

great′ lobel′ia, a North American plant, *Lobelia siphilitica,* having long, showy clusters of blue flowers.

great·ly (grāt′lē), *adv.* **1.** in or to a great degree; much: *greatly improved in health.* **2.** in a great manner. [1150–1200; ME *gretli;* see GREAT, -LY]

Great′ Miam′i, Miami (def. 2).

Great′ Mo′gul, 1. the emperor of the former Mogul Empire in India founded in 1526 by Baber. **2.** (*l.c.*) an important or distinguished person.

Great′ Moth′er, The, a vaguely defined deity symbolizing maternity, the fertility of the earth, and femininity in general; the central figure in the religions of ancient Anatolia, the Near East, and the eastern Mediterranean, later sometimes taking the form of a specific goddess, as Cybele, Rhea, or Demeter. Also called **The Great Goddess.**

Great′ Neb′ula of Ori′on. See **Orion nebula.**

Great′ Neck′, a town on NW Long Island, in SE New York. 10,800.

great-neph·ew (grāt′nef′yōō, -nev′yōō), *n.* a son of one's nephew or niece; grandnephew. [1575–85]

great-niece (grāt′nēs′), *n.* a daughter of one's nephew or niece; grandniece. [1880–85]

Great′ Ouse′, Ouse (def. 2).

great′ pace′. See **geometrical pace.**

great′ pas′tern bone′. See under **pastern.**

Great′ Plague′, the bubonic plague that occurred in London in 1665 and killed about 15 percent of the city's population. Also, **great′ plague′.**

Great′ Plains′, a semiarid region E of the Rocky Mountains, in the U.S. and Canada.

Great′ Pow′er, a nation that has exceptional military and economic strength, and consequently plays a major, often decisive, role in international affairs. [1725–35] —**Great′-Pow′er, great′-pow′er,** *adj.*

great′ prim′er, *Print.* an 18-point type of a size larger than Columbian, formerly used for Bibles. [1675–85]

Great′ Proletar′ian Cul′tural Revolu′tion. See **Cultural Revolution.**

Great′ Pyr′enees, one of a breed of large dogs having a heavy, white coat, raised originally in the Pyrenees for herding sheep and as a watchdog. [1935–40]

great′ rag′weed. See under **ragweed.**

Great′ Rebel′lion. See **English Civil War.**

Great′ Red′ Spot′, *Astron.* See **Red Spot.**

great′ rhododen′dron. See **great laurel.**

Great′ Rift′, *Astron.* a group of large dark clouds in the Milky Way between the constellations Cygnus and Sagittarius.

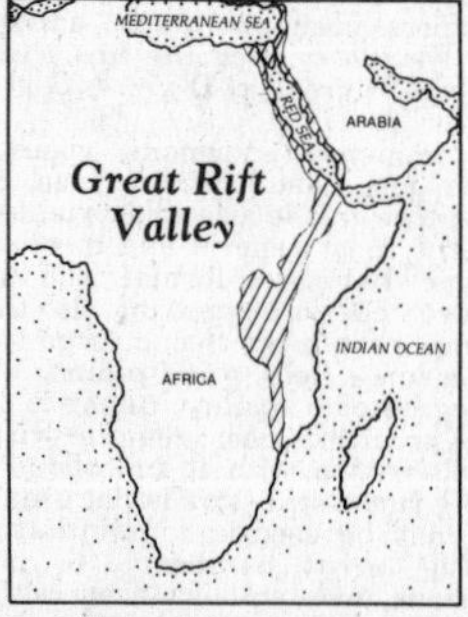

Great′ Rift′ Val′ley, a series of rift valleys running from N to S, from the Jordan Valley in SW Asia to Mozambique in SE Africa.

Great′ Rus′sian, 1. a member of the main stock of the Russian people, dwelling chiefly in the northern or central parts of the Soviet Union in Europe. **2.** the Russian language, excluding Ukrainian and Byelorussian. [1885–90]

Great′ Salt′ Des′ert, Dasht-i-Kavir.

Great′ Salt′ Lake′, a shallow salt lake in NW Utah. 2300 sq. mi. (5950 sq. km); 80 mi. (130 km) long; maximum depth 60 ft. (18 m).

Great′ Salt′ Lake′ Des′ert, an arid region in NW Utah, extending W from the Great Salt Lake to the Nevada border. 110 mi. (177 km) long; ab. 4000 sq. mi. (10,360 sq. km).

Great′ Sand′y Des′ert, 1. a desert in NW Australia, ab. 300 mi. (485 km) long; 500 mi. (800 km) wide; ab. 160,000 sq. mi. (414,400 sq. km). **2.** See **Rub'al Khali.**

Great′ Sanhed′rin, Sanhedrin (def. 1).

Great′ Schism′, a period of division in the Roman Catholic Church, 1378–1417, over papal succession, during which there were two, or sometimes three, claimants to the papal office.

Great′ Scott′, a euphemistic interjection or oath, usually expressing surprise, amazement, or the like. [1880–85; *Scott,* euphemism for GOD]

great′ seal′, 1. the principal seal of a government or state. **2.** (*caps.*) *Brit.* **a.** the Lord Chancellor, keeper of the principal seal of Great Britain. **b.** his office. [1350–1400; ME]

great′ sku′a. See under **skua** (def. 1). [1950–55]

Great′ Slave′ Lake′, a lake in NW Canada, in the Northwest Territories. 11,172 sq. mi. (28,935 sq. km).

Great′ Smok′y Moun′tains, a range of the Appalachian Mountains in North Carolina and Tennessee; most of the range is included in Great Smoky Mountains National Park. 720 sq. mi. (1865 sq. km). Highest peak, Clingman's Dome, 6642 ft. (2024 m). Also called **Smoky Mountains, Great′ Smok′ies.**

Great′ Smo′ky Moun′tains Na′tional Park′, a national park in SE Tennessee and SW North Carolina, including most of the Great Smoky Mountains: hardwood forest. 808 sq. mi. (2092 sq. km).

Great′ Soci′ety, the goal of the Democratic party under the leadership of President Lyndon B. Johnson, chiefly to enact domestic programs to improve education, provide medical care for the aged, and eliminate poverty. Cf. **Fair Deal, New Deal, New Frontier.**

great′ soil′ group′, according to a system of classification that originated in Russia, any of several broad groups of soils with common characteristics usually associated with particular climates and vegetation types. [1935–40]

Great′ Spir′it, the chief deity in the religion of many North American Indian tribes.

Great St. Bernard. See **St. Bernard, Great.**

Great′ Sun′day, *Eastern Ch.* See **Easter Sunday.** [trans. of LGk *megálē hēméra* lit., great day]

Great′ Syn′agogue, (according to Jewish tradition) a council of 120 members, established by Ezra, that directed the Jews chiefly in religious matters, c450–c200 B.C., and made significant contributions to the Jewish liturgy and Bible.

great′ tit′, an Old World titmouse, *Parus major,* yellowish green above with white cheeks. [1895–1900]

great′ toe′, *Anat.* See **big toe.**

great-un·cle (grāt′ung′kəl), *n.* a granduncle.

great′ unwashed′, the general public; the populace or masses. Also, **Great′ Unwashed′.** [1855–60]

Great′ Victo′ria Des′ert, a desert in SW central Australia. 125,000 sq. mi. (324,000 sq. km). Also called **Victoria Desert.**

Great′ Vow′el Shift′, *Ling.* a series of changes in the quality of the long vowels between Middle and Modern English as a result of which all were raised, while the high vowels (ē) and (ōō), already at the upper limit, underwent breaking to become the diphthongs (ī) and (ou).

Great′ Wall′ of Chi′na, a system of fortified walls with a roadway along the top, constructed as a defense for China against the nomads of the regions that are now Mongolia and Manchuria: completed in the 3rd century B.C., but later repeatedly modified and rebuilt. 2000 mi. (3220 km) long. Also called **Chinese Wall.**

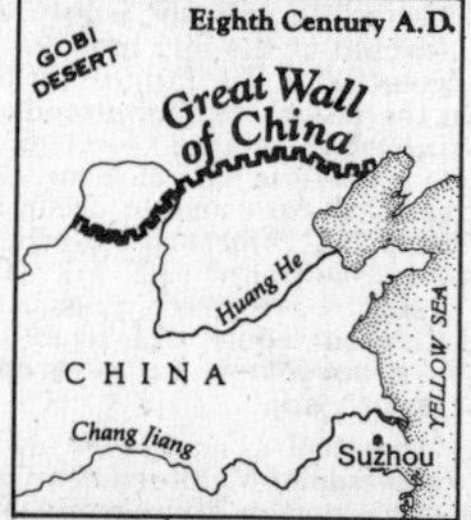

CONCISE ETYMOLOGY KEY: <, descended or borrowed from; >, whence; b., blend of, blended; c., cognate with; cf., compare; deriv., derivative; equiv., equivalent; imit., imitative; obl., oblique; r., replacing; s., stem; sp., spelling, spelled; resp., respelling, respelled; trans., translation; ?, origin unknown; *, unattested; ‡, probably earlier than. See the full key inside the front cover.

Great′ War′. See **World War I.**

Great′ Week′, *Eastern Ch.* See **Holy Week.** [1650–60; trans. of LGk *megálē hebdomás*]

great′ wheel′, *Horol.* the wheel immediately driven by the power source.

Great′ White′ Fa′ther, *Facetious.* **1.** the president of the U.S. **2.** any man who holds a position of great authority. [1915–20, *Amer.*; after the epithet supposedly used for the U.S. president by American Indians in the 19th century]

great′ white′ her′on, 1. a large white heron, *Ardea occidentalis*, of Florida and the Florida Keys. **2.** a large white egret, *Casmerodius albus*, of southeastern Europe, tropical Africa, Asia, New Zealand, and America. [1805–15]

great′ white′ shark′, a large shark, *Carcharodon carcharias*, of tropical and temperate seas, known to occasionally attack swimmers. Also called **white shark.** [1930–35]

Great′ White′ Way′, the theater district along Broadway, near Times Square in New York City.

great′ wil′low herb′, either of two tall, large-flowered willow herbs, *Epilobium angustifolium* or *E. hirsutum.*

Great′ Yar′mouth, a seaport in E Norfolk, in E England. 77,200.

great′ year′, *Astron.* See **Platonic year.** [1905–10]

Great′ Year′. See **Magnus Annus.**

Great′ Zimbab′we. See under **Zimbabwe** (def. 2).

greave (grēv), *n. Armor.* a piece of plate armor for the leg between the knee and the ankle, usually composed of front and back pieces. Also called **jamb, jambeau.** See diag. under **armor.** [1300–50; ME *greves* (pl.) < OF < ?] **—greaved,** *adj.*

greaves (grēvz), *n.* (*used with a singular or plural v.*) crackling (def. 3). [1605–15; < LG *greven;* c. OHG *griubo,* G *Grieben*]

grebe (grēb), *n.* any diving bird of the family Podicipedidae, related to the loons, but having a rudimentary tail and lobate rather than webbed toes. Cf. **great crested grebe, pied-billed grebe.** [1760–70; < F *grèbe* < ?]

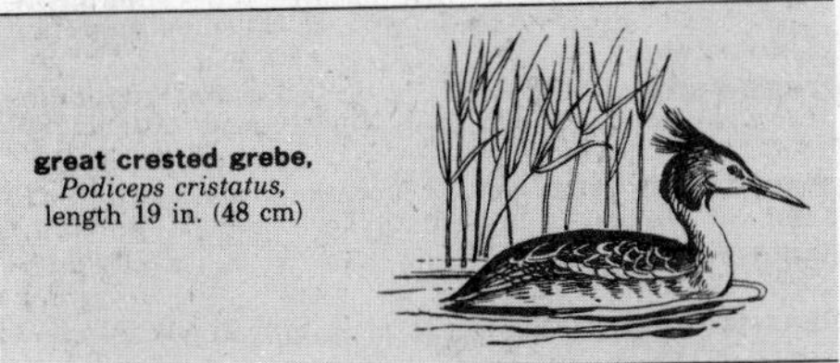

great crested grebe, *Podiceps cristatus,* length 19 in. (48 cm)

Gre·cian (grē′shən), *adj.* **1.** Greek (esp. with reference to ancient Greece). *—n.* **2.** a Greek. **3.** an expert in the Greek language or Greek literature. [1540–50; < L *Graeci(a)* GREECE + -AN]

Gre′cian bend′, (esp. in the late 19th century) a posture or walk, often considered fashionable, in which the body is bent forward from the waist.

Gre′cian pro′file, a profile distinguished by the absence of the hollow between the upper ridge of the nose and the forehead, thereby forming a straight line.

Gre·cism (grē′siz əm), *n.* **1.** the spirit of Greek thought, art, etc. **2.** adoption or imitation of this. **3.** an idiom or peculiarity of Greek. Also, *esp. Brit.,* **Graecism.** [1560–70; < ML *Graecismus,* equiv. to L *Graec(us)* GREEK + *-ismus* -ISM]

Gre·cize (grē′sīz), *v.,* **-cized, -ciz·ing.** *—v.t.* **1.** to impart Greek characteristics to. **2.** to translate into Greek. *—v.i.* **3.** to conform to what is Greek; adopt Greek speech, customs, etc. Also, **gre′cize;** *esp. Brit.,* **Graecize.** [1685–95; < L *graecizāre* to imitate the Greeks < Gk *graikízein* to speak Greek; see -IZE]

Gre·co (grek′ō; *Sp., It.* gʀe′kô), *n.* **1. Jo·sé** (hō zā′; *Sp.* hô se′), born 1918, U.S. dancer and choreographer, born in Italy. **2. El** (el). See **El Greco.**

Greco-, a combining form representing **Greek** in compound words: *Greco-Roman.* Also, *esp. Brit.,* **Graeco-.** [< L *Graec(us)* Greek + -o-]

Gre·co-Ro·man (grē′kō rō′mən, grek′ō-), *adj.* **1.** of or having both Greek and Roman characteristics: *the Greco-Roman influence.* **2.** pertaining to or designating a style of the fine arts developed in Rome or the Roman Empire from the middle of the 1st century B.C. to the early 4th century A.D., chiefly characterized by an apparent indebtedness to Greek forms or motifs modified by technological innovation, monumental scale, the combination of symbolic with narrative treatment of subject matter, and an emphasis on the commemorative aspect of a work of art. *—n.* **3.** a style of wrestling in which the contestants are forbidden to trip, tackle, and use holds below the waist. Cf. **catch-as-catch-can** (def. 1). Also, *esp. Brit.,* **Graeco-Roman.**

gree[1] (grē), *n. Chiefly Scot.* **1.** superiority, mastery, or victory. **2.** the prize for victory. **3.** *Obs.* a step. [1275–1325; ME *gre* < OF < L *gradus* step, GRADE; cf. DEGREE]

gree[2] (grē), *n. Archaic.* **1.** favor; goodwill. **2.** satisfaction, as for an injury. [1250–1300; ME *gre* < OF *gre* (F *gré*) < L *grātum* what is agreeable]

gree[3] (grē), *v.t., v.i.,* **greed, gree·ing.** *Brit. Dial.* agree. [1375–1425; late ME; see GREE[2]]

Greece (grēs), *n.* **1.** Ancient Greek, **Hellas.** Modern Greek, **Ellas.** a republic in S Europe at the S end of the Balkan Peninsula. 9,000,000; 50,147 sq. mi. (129,880 sq. km). *Cap.:* Athens. See map in next column. **2.** a city in W New York. 16,177.

greed (grēd), *n.* excessive or rapacious desire, esp. for wealth or possessions. [1600–10; back formation from GREEDY] **—greed′less,** *adj.* **—greed′some,** *adj.*
—Syn. avarice, avidity, cupidity, covetousness; voracity, ravenousness, rapacity. GREED, GREEDINESS denote an excessive, extreme desire for something, often more than one's proper share. GREED means avid desire for gain or wealth (unless some other application is indicated) and is definitely uncomplimentary in implication: *His greed drove him to exploit his workers.* GREEDINESS, when unqualified, suggests a craving for food; it may, however, be applied to all avid desires, and need not be always uncomplimentary: *greediness for knowledge, fame, praise.* **—Ant.** generosity.

greed·y (grē′dē), *adj.,* **greed·i·er, greed·i·est. 1.** excessively or inordinately desirous of wealth, profit, etc.; avaricious: *the greedy owners of the company.* **2.** having a strong or great desire for food or drink. **3.** keenly desirous; eager (often fol. by *of* or *for*): *greedy for praise.* [bef. 900; ME *gredy,* OE *grǣdig;* c. ON *gráthugr,* Goth *gredags*] **—greed′i·ly,** *adv.* **—greed′i·ness,** *n.*
—Syn. 1. grasping, rapacious, selfish. **1, 3.** See **avaricious. 2.** ravenous, voracious, gluttonous, insatiable. **3.** covetous, anxious. **—Ant. 1.** generous, unselfish.

gree·gree (grē′grē), *n.* grigri.

Greek (grēk), *adj.* **1.** of or pertaining to Greece, the Greeks, or their language. **2.** pertaining to the Greek Orthodox Church. **3.** noting or pertaining to the alphabetical script derived from a Semitic form of writing and employing some letters that originally represented consonants for vowel sounds, which was used from about the beginning of the first millennium B.C. for the writing of Greek, and from which the Latin, Cyrillic, and other alphabets were derived. *—n.* **4.** a native or inhabitant of Greece. **5.** the language of the ancient Greeks and any of the languages that have developed from it, as Hellenistic Greek, Biblical Greek, the Koine, and Modern Greek. *Abbr.:* Gk, Gk. **6.** *Informal.* anything unintelligible, as speech, writing, etc.: *This contract is Greek to me.* **7.** a member of the Greek Church. **8.** Hellenic (def. 3). **9.** a person who belongs to a Greek-letter fraternity or sorority. **10.** *Archaic.* a cheater, esp. one who cheats at cards: usually considered offensive. [bef. 900; ME; OE *Grēcas* (pl.) < L *Graecī* the Greeks (nom. pl. of *Graecus*) < Gk *Graikoí,* pl. of *Graikós* Greek] **—Greek′dom,** *n.* **—Greek′ish,** *adj.*

Greek′ cal′ends, a point or time that does not or will not exist: *She will do it on the Greek calends.* Also, **Greek′ kal′ends.**

Greek′ Cath′olic, 1. a member of the Greek Orthodox Church. **2.** a Uniat belonging to a church observing the Greek rite. [1905–10]

Greek′ Church′. See **Greek Orthodox Church** (def. 1).

Greek′ cross′, a cross consisting of an upright crossed in the middle by a horizontal piece of the same length. See illus. under **cross.** [1715–25]

Greek′ fire′, 1. an incendiary mixture of unknown composition, used in warfare in medieval times by Byzantine Greeks. **2.** any of a group of inflammable mixtures; wildfire. [1820–30]

Greek′ god′, a man who is strikingly handsome and well built. [1905–10]

Greek′-let·ter frater′nity (grēk′let′ər), a fraternity whose name consists usually of two or three Greek letters, as Sigma Delta Phi (ΣΔΦ). [1875–80, *Amer.*]

Greek′-letter soror′ity, a sorority whose name consists usually of two or three Greek letters, as Lambda Rho (ΛΡ). [1940–45, *Amer.*]

Greek′ love′, *Slang.* anal intercourse. Also called **Greek′ way′.**

Greek′ Or′thodox Church′, 1. the branch of the Orthodox Church constituting the national church of Greece. **2.** See **Orthodox Church** (def. 2).

Greek′ Reviv′al, a style of architecture, furnishings, and decoration prevalent in the U.S. and in parts of Europe in the first half of the 19th century, characterized by a more or less close imitation of ancient Greek designs and ornamented motifs. **—Greek′ Reviv′alism. —Greek′ Reviv′alist.**

Greek′ rite′, the rite of the Greek Orthodox Church and of certain Uniat churches, observed in the Greek language. Also called **Byzantine rite, Constantinopolitan rite.**

Greek′ vale′rian, any of various plants belonging to the genus *Polemonium,* of the phlox family, esp. *P. reptans,* having pinnate leaves and blue flowers. Cf. **Jacob's ladder.** [1810–20]

Gree·ley (grē′lē), *n.* **1. Horace,** 1811–72, U.S. journalist, editor, and political leader. **2.** a city in N Colorado. 53,006.

Gree·ly (grē′lē), *n.* **Adolphus Washington,** 1844–1935, U.S. general and arctic explorer.

green (grēn), *adj.,* **-er, -est,** *n., v.* *—adj.* **1.** of the color of growing foliage, between yellow and blue in the spectrum: *green leaves.* **2.** covered with herbage or foliage; verdant: *green fields.* **3.** characterized by the presence of verdure. **4.** made of green vegetables, as lettuce, spinach, endive, or chicory: *a green salad.* **5.** not fully developed or perfected in growth or condition; unripe; not properly aged: *This peach is still green.* **6.** unseasoned; not dried or cured: *green lumber.* **7.** immature in age or judgment; untrained; inexperienced: *a green worker.* **8.** simple; unsophisticated; gullible; easily fooled. **9.** fresh, recent, or new: *an insult still green in his mind.* **10.** having a sickly appearance; pale; wan: *green with fear; green with envy.* **11.** full of life and vigor; young: *a man ripe in years but green in heart.* **12.** (of wine) having a flavor that is raw, harsh, and acid, due esp. to a lack of maturity. **13.** freshly slaughtered or still raw: *green meat.* **14.** not fired, as bricks or pottery. **15.** (of cement or mortar) freshly set and not completely hardened. **16.** *Foundry.* **a.** (of sand) sufficiently moist to form a compact lining for a mold without further treatment. **b.** (of a casting) as it comes from the mold. **c.** (of a powder, in powder metallurgy) unsintered. *—n.* **17.** a color intermediate in the spectrum between yellow and blue, an effect of light with a wavelength between 500 and 570 nm; found in nature as the color of most grasses and leaves while growing, of some fruits while ripening, and of the sea. **18.** *Art.* a secondary color that has been formed by the mixture of blue and yellow pigments. **19.** green coloring matter, as paint or dye. **20.** green material or clothing: *to be dressed in green.* **21. greens, a.** fresh leaves or branches of trees, shrubs, etc., used for decoration; wreaths. **b.** the leaves and stems of plants, as spinach, lettuce, or cabbage, used for food. **c.** a blue-green uniform of the U.S. Army. **22.** grassy land; a plot of grassy ground. **23.** a piece of grassy ground constituting a town or village common. **24.** Also called **putting green.** *Golf.* the area of closely cropped grass surrounding each hole. **25.** See **bowling green. 26.** a shooting range for archery. **27.** *Informal.* See **green light** (def. 1). **28.** *Slang.* money; greenbacks (usually prec. by *the*): *I'd like to buy a new car but I don't have the green.* **29.** (*cap.*) a member of the Green party (in West Germany). **30. read the green,** to inspect a golf green, analyzing its slope and surface, so as to determine the difficulties to be encountered when putting. *—v.i., v.t.* **31.** to become or make green. **32.** *Informal.* to restore the vitality of: *Younger executives are greening corporate managements.* [bef. 900; ME, OE *grēne;* c. G *grün;* akin to GROW] **—green′age,** *n.* **—green′ly,** *adv.*

Green (grēn), *n.* **1. Henrietta Howland Robinson** (*"Hetty"*), 1835–1916, U.S. financier. **2. Henry** (*Henry Vincent Yorke*), 1905–73, English novelist. **3. John Richard,** 1837–83, English historian. **4. Julian,** born 1900, U.S. writer. **5. Paul Eliot,** 1894–1981, U.S. playwright, novelist, and teacher. **6. William,** 1873–1952, U.S. labor leader: president of the A.F.L. 1924–52. **7.** a river flowing S from W Wyoming to join the Colorado River in SE Utah. 730 mi. (1175 km) long.

green′ al′gae, any grass-green, chiefly freshwater algae of the phylum Chlorophyta, often growing on wet rocks, damp wood, or on the surface of stagnant water. [1900–05]

Green·a·way (grēn′ə wā′), *n.* **Kate** (*Catherine*), 1846–1901, English painter and author and illustrator of children's books.

green·back (grēn′bak′), *n.* a U.S. legal-tender note, printed in green on the back since the Civil War, originally issued against the credit of the country and not against gold or silver on deposit. [1860–65, *Amer.*; GREEN + BACK[1]]

green′-backed her′on (grēn′bakt′), a small, American heron, *Butorides striatus,* having glossy green wings. Also called **green heron, little green heron.**

Green′back par′ty, *U.S. Hist.* a former political party, organized in 1874, opposed to the retirement or reduction of greenbacks and favoring their increase as the only paper currency. **—Green′back′er,** *n.* **—Green′back′ism,** *n.*

green′ bag′, *Brit.* **1.** a bag or briefcase made of green cloth, formerly used by lawyers for carrying documents. **2.** *Slang.* **a.** the legal profession. **b.** a lawyer. Also, **green′-bag′.** [1670–80]

green′ bass′ (bas). See **largemouth bass.**

Green′ Bay′, 1. an arm of Lake Michigan, in NE Wisconsin. 120 mi. (195 km) long. **2.** a port in E Wisconsin at the S end of this bay. 87,899. [1810–20, *Amer.*]

green′ bean′, the immature green pod of the kidney bean, eaten as a vegetable. Also called **string bean, stringless bean.** [1940–45, *Amer.*]

green·belt (grēn′belt′), *n.* **1.** an area of woods, parks, or open land surrounding a community. **2.** Also, **green′ belt′.** a strip of land on the edge of a desert that has been planted and irrigated to keep the desert from spreading. [1930–35; GREEN + BELT]

Green·belt (grēn′belt′), *n.* a town in central Maryland. 16,000.

Green′ Beret′. See **Special Forces.**

CONCISE PRONUNCIATION KEY: act, cāpe, dâre, pärt; set, ēqual; if, ice; ox, ōver, ôrder, oil, bŏŏk, bōōt, out; up, ûrge; child; sing; shoe; thin, *th*at; zh as in *treasure.* ə = *a* as in *alone, e* as in *system, i* as in *easily, o* as in *gallop, u* as in *circus;* ə as in *fire* (fīər), *hour* (ouər). l and n can serve as syllabic consonants, as in *cradle* (krād′l), and *button* (but′n). See the full key inside the front cover.

Green•berg (grēn′bûrg), *n.* **Henry B.** (*Hank*), 1911–86, U.S. baseball player.

green•board (grēn′bôrd′, -bōrd′), *n.* a green chalkboard or blackboard. [GREEN + BOARD]

green′bot•tle fly′ (grēn′bot′l), any of several metallic-green blowflies, as *Phaenicia sericata.* Also called **green′bot′tle.** [1860–65; GREEN + BOTTLE[1]]

green•bri•er (grēn′brī′ər), *n.* catbrier. [1775–85, *Amer.*; GREEN + BRIER[1]]

green•bug (grēn′bug′), *n.* a pale-green aphid, *Schizaphis graminum,* of North America, destructive of wheat, other small grains, and alfalfa. [1705–15; GREEN + BUG[1]]

green′ card′, an official card, originally green, issued by the U.S. government to foreign nationals permitting them to work in the U.S. [1965–70] —**green′-card′er,** *n.*

green′ cin′nabar, *Chem.* See **chromic oxide.**

green′ corn′. See **sweet corn** (def. 2). [1800–10]

green′ crab′, a yellowish-green crab, *Carcinides maenas,* common in shallow waters along rocky shores. [1860–65]

Green•dale (grēn′dāl′), *n.* a town in SE Wisconsin. 16,928.

green′ drag′on. See under **dragon** (def. 8). [1810–20, *Amer.*]

Greene (grēn), *n.* **1. Graham,** 1904–91, English novelist and journalist. **2. Nathanael,** 1742–86, American Revolutionary general. **3. Robert,** 1558–92, English dramatist and poet.

green′ earth′, a pigment used in painting consisting mainly of iron silicate, characterized chiefly by its variable grayish-green hue, lack of tinting strength, and permanence. Also called **terra verde.** [1785–95]

green•er•y (grē′nə rē), *n., pl.* **-er•ies** for 2. **1.** green foliage or vegetation; verdure. **2.** a place where green plants are grown or kept. [1790–1800; GREEN + -ERY]

Greene•ville (grēn′vil), *n.* a city in E Tennessee. 14,097.

green-eyed (grēn′īd′), *adj. Informal.* jealous; envious; distrustful. [1590–1600]

green′-eyed mon′ster, jealousy: *Othello fell under the sway of the green-eyed monster.* [1595–1605]

green′ fee′. See **greens fee.**

Green•field (grēn′fēld′), *n.* **1.** a city in SE Wisconsin, near Milwaukee. 31,467. **2.** a city in NW Massachusetts. 18,436. **3.** a town in central Indiana. 11,439.

Green′field Park′, a town in S Quebec, in E Canada, near Montreal. 18,527.

green•finch (grēn′finch′), *n.* any finch of the genus *Carduelis,* of Europe and Asia, having green and yellow plumage, esp. *C. chloris* **(European greenfinch).** [1490–1500; GREEN + FINCH]

green′ fin′gers, *Brit. Informal.* See **green thumb.** [1930–35]

green′ fish′, *Newfoundland.* fish that have been split and salted but not yet cured.

green•fish (grēn′fish′), *n., pl.* **-fish•es,** (*esp. collectively*) **-fish.** opaleye. [1425–75; late ME. See GREEN, FISH]

green′ flag′, (in automobile racing) a green-colored flag that is used to signal the start of a race.

green′ flash′, a green coloration of the upper portion of the sun, caused by atmospheric refraction and occasionally seen as the sun rises above or sinks below the horizon. [1910–15]

green•fly (grēn′flī′), *n., pl.* **-flies.** an aphid, *Coloradoa rufomaculata,* that is an important pest of chrysanthemums. Also called **pale chrysanthemum aphid.** [1680–90; GREEN + FLY[2]]

green•gage (grēn′gāj′), *n.* any of several varieties of light-green plums, as *Prunus insititia italica.* [1715–25; GREEN + *Gage,* after Sir William *Gage,* 18th-century English botanist who introduced such varieties from France ca. 1725]

green′ gen′tian, *n.* a plant, *Frasera speciosa,* of the gentian family, native to the northwestern U.S., having open clusters of purple-spotted, greenish-white flowers that blend in with its leaves. Also, **deer's-tongue.**

green′ gland′, *Zool.* one of the pair of excretory organs in each side of the head region of decapod crustaceans, emptying at the base of the antennae. [1885–90]

green′ glass′, glass of low quality, colored green by impurities in the materials from which it is made. [1650–60]

green′ gram′. See under **gram**[2] (def. 2).

green•gro•cer (grēn′grō′sər), *n. Chiefly Brit.* a retailer of fresh vegetables and fruit. [1715–25]

green•gro•cer•y (grēn′grō′sə rē, -grōs′rē), *n., pl.* **-cer•ies.** *Chiefly Brit.* **1.** a greengrocer's shop. **2.** the fruits and vegetables stocked and sold in such a shop. [1800–10; GREEN + GROCERY]

green•head (grēn′hed′), *n.* a male mallard. [1805–15]

green•heart (grēn′härt′), *n.* **1.** a South American tree, *Ocotea* (or *Nectandra*) *rodiei,* of the laurel family, yielding a hard, durable wood often used for wharves and bridges and in shipbuilding. **2.** any of certain other timber trees of tropical America. **3.** their valuable greenish wood. [1750–60; GREEN + HEART]

green′ her′on. See **green-backed heron.** [1775–85]

green•horn (grēn′hôrn′), *n.* **1.** an untrained or inexperienced person. **2.** a naive or gullible person; someone who is easily tricked or swindled. **3.** *Slang.* a newly arrived immigrant; newcomer. [1425–75; late ME; see GREEN, HORN; orig. applied to cattle with green (i.e., young) horns] —**green′horn′ism,** *n.*

green•house (grēn′hous′), *n., pl.* **-hous•es** (-hou′ziz). a building, room, or area, usually chiefly of glass, in which the temperature is maintained within a desired range, used for cultivating tender plants or growing plants out of season. [1655–65; GREEN + HOUSE]

green′house effect′, **1.** an atmospheric heating phenomenon, caused by short-wave solar radiation being readily transmitted inward through the earth's atmosphere but longer-wavelength heat radiation less readily transmitted outward, owing to its absorption by atmospheric carbon dioxide, water vapor, methane, and other gases; thus, the rising level of carbon dioxide is viewed with concern. **2.** such a phenomenon on another planet. [1935–40]

green′house gas′, any of the gases whose absorption of solar radiation is responsible for the greenhouse effect, including carbon dioxide, methane, ozone, and the fluorocarbons. [1980–85]

green′house white′fly. See under **whitefly.**

green•ie (grē′nē), *n.* **1.** *Slang.* an amphetamine pill, esp. one that is green in color. **2.** *Australian Slang.* a conservationist or environmentalist, esp. one who participates in protest demonstrations. [1945–50, for def. 1; GREEN + -IE]

green•ing (grē′ning), *n.* **1.** any variety of apple whose skin is green when ripe. **2.** the return or revival of youthful characteristics: *the greening of America.* [1590–1600; GREEN + -ING[1]]

green•ish (grē′nish), *adj.* somewhat green; having a tinge of green. [1350–1400; ME; see GREEN, -ISH[1]]

green′ June′ bee′tle, a large, greenish scarab beetle, *Cotinis nitida,* of the southern U.S. Also called **figeater.**

green•keep•er (grēn′kē′pər), *n.* greenskeeper.

Green•land (grēn′lənd, -land′), *n.* a self-governing island belonging to Denmark, located NE of North America: the largest island in the world. 55,558; ab. 844,000 sq. mi. (2,186,000 sq. km); over 700,000 sq. mi. (1,800,000 sq. km) icecapped. *Cap.:* Godthåb. —**Green′land•er,** *n.* —**Green′land•ish,** *adj.*

Green′land Cur′rent, the ocean current flowing clockwise around S Greenland.

Green•land•ic (grēn lan′dik), *n.* **1.** a dialect of Inuit, spoken in Greenland. —*adj.* **2.** of or pertaining to Greenland, its inhabitants, or their language. [GREENLAND + -IC]

Green′land Sea′, a part of the Arctic Ocean, NE of Greenland and N of Iceland.

Green′land spar′, *Mineral.* cryolite.

Green′land whale′, bowhead.

Green•lawn (grēn′lôn′), *n.* a town on NW Long Island, in SE New York. 13,869.

green′ lead′ ore′ (led), pyromorphite. [1860–65]

green′ light′, **1.** a green-colored traffic light used to signal drivers, pedestrians, etc., that they may proceed. **2.** authorization; approval; permission: *The railroad has been given the green light on the proposed fare increase.*

green′ line′, (*sometimes caps.*) **1.** (in Lebanon) a demarcation line that divides predominantly Christian East Beirut and predominantly Moslem West Beirut. **2.** any similar demarcation line between two hostile communities, as between Greek and Turkish Cypriots in Nicosia.

green•ling (grēn′ling), *n.* any spiny-finned food fish of the genus *Hexagrammos,* of North Pacific coasts. [1400–50; late ME; see GREEN, -LING[1]]

green•mail (grēn′māl′), *n. Stock Exchange.* the practice of buying a large block of a company's stock in order to force a rise in stock prices or an offer by the company to repurchase that block of stock at an inflated price to thwart a possible takeover bid. [GREEN (in sense "money") + (BLACK)MAIL] —**green′mail′er,** *n.*

green′ manure′, *Agric.* **1.** a crop of growing plants, as clover and other nitrogen-fixing plants, plowed under to enrich the soil. **2.** manure that has not undergone decay. [1835–45]

green′ mold′. See **blue mold** (def. 1). [1915–20]

green′ mon′key, a common savanna monkey, *Cercopithecus aethiops sabaeus,* of West Africa, with a greenish-gray back and yellow tail. Also called **African green monkey.** [1830–40]

green′ mon′key disease′. See **Marburg disease.** [1965–70]

Green′ Moun′tain Boys′, the soldiers from Vermont in the American Revolution, originally organized by Ethan Allen around 1770 to oppose the territorial claims of New York.

Green′ Moun′tains, a mountain range in Vermont: a part of the Appalachian system. Highest peak, Mt. Mansfield, 4393 ft. (1339 m).

Green′ Moun′tain State′, Vermont (used as a nickname).

green•ness (grēn′nis), *n.* **1.** the quality or state of being green. **2.** green vegetation, grass, or the like; verdure or verdancy. **3.** lack of maturity or experience; youthfulness. **4.** the state or quality of being naive; innocence; gullibility. [bef. 900; ME, OE *grēnnes.* See GREEN, -NESS]

Green•ock (grē′nək, gren′ək), *n.* a seaport in the Strathcylde region, in SW Scotland, on the Firth of Clyde. 69,171.

green•ock•ite (grē′nə kīt′), *n.* a yellow mineral, cadmium sulfide, CdS, associated with zinc ores and used as a source of cadmium. [1840–45; named after Charles Cathcart, Lord *Greenock* (1807–43), Englishman who discovered it; see -ITE[1]]

green′ on′ion, a young onion with a slender green stalk and a small bulb, used as a table vegetable, usually raw, esp. in salads; scallion. [1930–35]

green′ o′sier, a dogwood tree, *Cornus alternifolia,* of the eastern U.S., having clusters of small white flowers and dark-blue fruit.

Green•ough (grē′nō), *n.* **Horatio,** 1805–52, U.S. sculptor.

Green′ Pa′per, *Brit.* a report presenting the policy proposals of the government, to be discussed in Parliament. [1945–50; appar. so called from the color of the paper on which they are printed]

Green′ par′ty, a liberal political party esp. in Germany focusing on environmental issues.

green′ pea′, pea[1] (defs. 1–3).

green′ peach′ a′phid, an aphid, *Myzus persicae,* that is a pest of many fruit trees, ornamentals, and vegetables and a vector of certain viral plant diseases. Also called **spinach aphid, tobacco aphid.** [1920–25]

green′ pep′per, the mild-flavored, unripe fruit of the bell or sweet pepper, *Capsicum annuum grossum,* used as a green vegetable. [1690–1700]

green′ plov′er, *Brit.* lapwing. [1700–10]

green′ pow′er, the power of money, viewed as a social force.

green′ revolu′tion, *Agric.* an increase in food production, esp. in underdeveloped and developing nations, through the introduction of high-yield crop varieties and application of modern agricultural techniques. [1965–70]

Green′ Riv′er, a town in SW Wyoming. 12,807.

Green′ Riv′er or′dinance, a local ordinance banning door-to-door selling. Also called **Green′ Riv′er law′.** [named after such an ordinance, passed in 1931 in GREEN RIVER]

green•room (grēn′ro͞om′, -ro͝om′), *n.* a lounge in a theater, broadcasting studio, or the like, for use by performers when they are not onstage, on camera, etc. [1695–1705; GREEN + ROOM, prob. so called because orig. painted green]

green•sand (grēn′sand′), *n.* a sandstone containing much glauconite, which gives it a greenish hue. [1790–1800; GREEN + SAND]

green′sand proc′ess, a process for casting iron with sand not previously heated.

Greens•bo•ro (grēnz′bûr′ō, -bur′ō), *n.* a city in N North Carolina. 155,642.

Greens•burg (grēnz′bûrg), *n.* a city in SW Pennsylvania. 17,588.

green•schist (grēn′shist′), *n. Petrol.* schist colored green by an abundance of chlorite, epidote, or actinolite. Cf. **greenstone.** [GREEN + SCHIST]

green′ sea′, *Naut.* a solid mass of water breaking over the bow or bulwark of a ship. [1825–35, *Amer.*]

greens′ fee′, a fee paid by golfers in order to play on a golf course. Also, **green fee.** [1905–10]

green•shank (grēn′shangk′), *n.* an Old World shore bird, *Tringa nebularia,* having green legs. [1760–70; GREEN + SHANK]

green•sick•ness (grēn′sik′nis), *n. Pathol.* chlorosis (def. 2). [1575–85] —**green′sick′,** *adj.*

greens•keep•er (grēnz′kē′pər), *n.* a person charged with the care and maintenance of a golf course. Also, **greenkeeper.** [GREEN + 'S[1] + KEEPER]

green′ snake′, any slender, green snake of the genus *Opheodrys,* of North America, feeding chiefly on insects. [1700–10, *Amer.*]

green′ soap′, a soap made chiefly from potassium hydroxide and linseed oil, used in treating some skin diseases. [1830–40]

Green′ Stamp′, **1.** *Trademark.* a brand of trading stamp. **2.** *CB Radio Slang.* **a.** a speeding ticket. **b.** Usually, **Green Stamps.** money; currency.

Green's′ the′orem, *Math.* one of several theorems that connect an integral in *n*-dimensional space with one in $(n - 1)$-dimensional space. [after George Green (1793–1841), English mathematician, who formulated it]

green′stick frac′ture (grēn′stik′), an incomplete fracture of a long bone, in which one side is broken and the other side is still intact. See illus. under **fracture.** [1880–85; GREEN + STICK[1]]

green•stone (grēn′stōn′), *n.* any of various altered basaltic rocks having a dark-green color caused by the presence of chlorite, epidote, etc. [1765–75; GREEN + STONE]

green′ strength′, **1.** *Foundry.* the tensile strength of greensand. **2.** *Metall.* the tensile strength of an unsintered compact.

green′ stuff′, *Slang.* paper money. [1950–55, *Amer.*]

green′ sul′fur bacte′ria, a group of green or brown bacteria of the families Chlorobiaceae and Chloroflexaceae that occur in aquatic sediments, sulfur springs, and hot springs and that utilize reduced sulfur compounds instead of oxygen.

green•sward (grēn′swôrd′), *n.* green, grassy turf. [1590–1600; GREEN + SWARD] —**green′sward′ed,** *adj.*

green′ tea′, a tea that is steamed to prevent fermentation and then rolled and dried. [1695–1705]

greenth (grēnth), *n.* green growth; verdure. [1745–55; GREEN + -TH[1]]

green′ thumb′, an exceptional aptitude for gardening or for growing plants successfully: *Houseplants pro-*

CONCISE ETYMOLOGY KEY: <, descended or borrowed from; >, whence; b., blend of, blended; c., cognate with; cf., compare; deriv., derivative; equiv., equivalent; imit., imitative; obl., oblique; r., replacing; s., stem; sp., spelling, spelled; resp., respelling, respelled; trans., translation; ?, origin unknown; *, unattested; ‡, probably earlier than. See the full key inside the front cover.

vide much pleasure for the city dweller with a green thumb. [1940–45] **—green′-thumbed′,** *adj.* **—green′-thumb′er,** *n.*

green′ tur′tle, a sea turtle, *Chelonia mydas,* common in tropical and subtropical seas, the flesh of which is used for turtle soup: now greatly reduced in number and endangered in some areas. [1650–60]

green′ veg′etable, a vegetable having green edible parts, as lettuce or broccoli. [1880–85]

green′ ver′diter. See under **verditer.**

Green•ville (grēn′vil), *n.* **1.** a city in NW South Carolina. 58,242. **2.** a city in W Mississippi, on the Mississippi River. 40,613. **3.** a city in E North Carolina. 35,740. **4.** a city in NE Texas. 22,161. **5.** a city in W Ohio. 12,999.

green′ vit′riol. See **ferrous sulfate.**

green•way (grēn′wā′), *n.* any scenic trail or route set aside for travel or recreational activities. [1970–75]

Green•wich (grin′ij, -ich, gren′- *for 1, 3;* gren′ich, grin′-, grēn′wich *for 2*), *n.* **1.** a borough in SE London, England: located on the prime meridian from which geographic longitude is measured; formerly the site of the Royal Greenwich Observatory. 209,800. **2.** a town in SW Connecticut. 59,578. **3.** *Informal.* See **Greenwich Time.**

Green′wich hour′ an′gle, hour angle measured from the meridian of Greenwich, England.

Green′wich Observ′atory. See **Royal Greenwich Observatory.**

Green′wich Time′, the time as measured on the prime meridian running through Greenwich, England: used in England and as a standard of calculation elsewhere. Also called **Green′wich Mean′ Time′, Green′wich Civ′il Time′, universal time, Universal Time.** [1840–50]

Green′wich Vil′lage (gren′ich, grin′-), a section of New York City, in lower Manhattan: inhabited and frequented by artists, writers, and students.

green′-winged teal′ (grēn′wingd′), a small freshwater duck, *Anas crecca,* of Eurasia and North America, having an iridescent green speculum in the wing. Also called, *Brit.,* **common teal.** [1630–40]

green•wood (grēn′wo͝od′), *n.* a wood or forest when green, as in summer. [1300–50; ME; see GREEN, WOOD[1]]

Green•wood (grēn′wo͝od′), *n.* **1.** a city in W South Carolina. 21,613. **2.** a city in NW Mississippi. 20,115. **3.** a town in central Indiana. 19,327.

green′ wood′pecker, a woodpecker, *Picus viridis,* of Eurasia and northern Africa, having green plumage with a yellow rump and red on the top of the head.

Greer (grēr), *n.* **1.** a town in NW South Carolina. 10,525. **2.** a female given name.

greet[1] (grēt), *v.t.* **1.** to address with some form of salutation; welcome. **2.** to meet or receive: *to be greeted by cheering crowds; to greet a proposal with boos and hisses.* **3.** to manifest itself to: *Music greeted his ear as he entered the salon.* —*v.i.* **4.** *Obs.* to give salutations on meeting. [bef. 900; ME *greten,* OE *grētan;* c. G *grüssen*] **—greet′er,** *n.*
—Syn. 1. hail, accost.

greet[2] (grēt), *Scot. and North Eng. Archaic.* —*v.i.* **1.** to grieve; lament; cry. —*v.t.* **2.** to lament; bewail. [bef. 900; ME *grete,* OE *grǣtan;* c. ON grāta, Goth *gretan*]

greet•ing (grē′ting), *n.* **1.** the act or words of a person who greets. **2.** a friendly message from someone who is absent: *a greeting from a friend in another country.* **3. greetings,** an expression of friendly or respectful regard: *Send my greetings to your family.* [bef. 900; ME, OE *grēting*e. See GREET[1], -ING[1]] **—greet′ing•less,** *adj.*

greet′ing card′, card[1] (def. 4). [1895–1900]

gre•fa (grē′fə, -fä), *n. Slang.* griefo.

Greg (greg), *n.* a male given name, form of **Gregory.**

gre•ga•le (grā gä′lā), *n.* a strong northeast wind that blows in the central and western Mediterranean area. Also, **gré•gal** (grā gäl′), **gre•gau** (grā gou′). Also called **Euroclydon.** [1795–1805; < It *grecale, gregale* < LL *Graecālis.* See GREEK, -AL[1]]

greg•a•rine (greg′ə rīn′, -ər in), *n.* **1.** a type of sporozoan parasite that inhabits the digestive and other cavities of various invertebrates and produces cysts filled with spores. —*adj.* **2.** having the characteristics of or pertaining to a gregarine or gregarines. [1865–70; < NL *Gregarina* name of type, equiv. to L *gregār(ius)* (see GREGARIOUS) + *-ina* -INE[1]]

gre•gar•i•ous (gri gâr′ē əs), *adj.* **1.** fond of the company of others; sociable. **2.** living in flocks or herds, as animals. **3.** *Bot.* growing in open clusters or colonies; not matted together. **4.** pertaining to a flock or crowd. [1660–70; < L *gregārius* belonging to a flock, equiv. to *greg-* (s. of *grex*) flock + *-ārius* -ARIOUS] **—gre•gar′i•ous•ly,** *adv.* **—gre•gar′i•ous•ness,** *n.*
—Syn. 1. social, genial, outgoing, convivial, companionable, friendly, extroverted.

Gregg (greg), *n.* **John Robert,** 1864–1948, U.S. educator: inventor of a system of shorthand.

gre•go (grē′gō, grā′-), *n., pl.* **-gos.** a short, hooded coat of thick, coarse fabric, originally worn in the eastern Mediterranean countries. [1740–50; perh. < Pg (cf. Sp *griego,* It *greco*) < L *Graecus* GREEK]

Gre•go•ri•an (gri gôr′ē ən, -gōr′-), *adj.* of or pertaining to any of the popes named Gregory, esp. Gregory I or Gregory XIII. [1590–1600; < NL *gregoriānus* of, pertaining to Pope Gregory, equiv. to LL *Gregori(us)* + L *-ānus* -AN]

Grego′rian cal′endar, the reformed Julian calendar now in use, according to which the ordinary year consists of 365 days, and a leap year of 366 days occurs in every year whose number is exactly divisible by 4 except centenary years whose numbers are not exactly divisible by 400, as 1700, 1800, and 1900. See table under **calendar.** [1640–50; named after Pope GREGORY XIII; see -IAN]

Grego′rian chant′, **1.** the plain song or cantus firmus used in the ritual of the Roman Catholic Church. **2.** a melody in this style. [1745–55; named after Pope GREGORY I; see -IAN]

Grego′rian mode′, *Music.* See **church mode.** [named after Pope GREGORY I; see -IAN]

Grego′rian tel′escope, a telescope similar in design to the Cassegrainian telescope but less widely used. [1755–65; named after James GREGORY; see -IAN]

Grego′rian wa′ter, *Rom. Cath. Ch.* a mixture of water, salt, ashes, and wine, blessed and sprinkled over the altar in the consecration of a church. [1645–55]

Greg•o•ry (greg′ə rē), *n.* **1. Lady Augusta** (*Isabella Augusta Persse*), 1852–1932, Irish dramatist. **2. Horace,** 1898–1982, U.S. poet and critic. **3. James,** 1638–75, Scottish mathematician. **4.** a male given name: from a Greek word meaning "watchful."

Gregory I, Saint (*"Gregory the Great"*), A.D. c540–604, Italian ecclesiastic: pope 590–604.

Gregory II, Saint, died A.D. 731, pope 715–731.

Gregory III, Saint, died A.D. 741, pope 731–741.

Gregory IV, died A.D. 844, pope 827–844.

Gregory V, (*Bruno of Carinthia*) died A.D. 999, German ecclesiastic: pope 996–999.

Gregory VI, (*Johannes Gratianus*) died 1048, German ecclesiastic: pope 1045–46.

Gregory VII, Saint (*Hildebrand*) c1020–85, Italian ecclesiastic: pope 1073–85.

Gregory VIII, (*Alberto de Mora* or *Alberto di Morra*) died 1187, Italian ecclesiastic: pope 1187.

Gregory IX, (*Ugolino di Segni* or *Ugolino of Anagni*) c1143–1241, Italian ecclesiastic: pope 1227–41.

Gregory X, (*Teobaldo Visconti*) c1210–76, Italian ecclesiastic: pope 1271–76.

Gregory XI, (*Pierre Roger de Beaufort*) 1330–78, French ecclesiastic: pope 1370–78.

Gregory XII, (*Angelo Correr, Corrario,* or *Corraro*) c1327–1417, Italian ecclesiastic: installed as pope in 1406 and resigned office in 1415.

Gregory XIII, (*Ugo Buoncompagni*) 1502–85, Italian ecclesiastic: pope 1572–85, educator and innovator of the modern calendar.

Gregory XIV, (*Niccolò Sfandrati*) 1535–91, Italian ecclesiastic: pope 1590–91.

Gregory XV, (*Alessandro Ludovisi*) 1554–1623, Italian ecclesiastic: pope 1621–23.

Gregory XVI, (*Bartolommeo Alberto Cappellari*) 1765–1846, Italian ecclesiastic: pope 1831–46.

Greg′ory of Nys′sa (nis′ə), **Saint,** A.D. c330–395?, Christian bishop and theologian in Asia Minor (brother of Saint Basil).

Greg′ory of Tours′, Saint, A.D. 538?–594, Frankish bishop and historian.

greige (grā, grāzh), *n.* **1.** *Textiles.* See **gray goods.** —*adj.* **2.** unbleached and undyed: *greige linen.* [1925–30; < F *grège* (of silk) raw < It *greggio* GRAY]

grei•sen (grī′zən), *n.* a hydrothermally altered rock of granitic texture composed chiefly of quartz and mica, common in the tin mines of Europe. [1875–80; < G]

gre•mi•al (grē′mē əl), *n. Eccles.* a cloth placed on the lap of the bishop, as during the celebration of Mass or when he confers orders. [1555–65; < LL *gremiālis* growing in a cluster from a stump, equiv. to L *grem(ium)* lap, bosom + *-ālis* -AL[1]]

grem•lin (grem′lin), *n.* **1.** a mischievous invisible being, said by airplane pilots in World War II to cause engine trouble and mechanical difficulties. **2.** any cause of trouble, difficulties, etc. [1925–30; of obscure orig; in its earliest attested use, an RAF term for a low-ranking officer or enlisted man; later development perh. affected by phonetic resemblance to GOBLIN]
—Syn. 1. See **goblin.**

grem•mie (grem′ē), *n. Slang.* a novice surfer or one with poor form. [1960–65; GREM(LIN) + -IE]

grem•my (grem′ē), *n., pl.* **-mies.** gremmie.

Gre•nache (grə nash′), *n.* a variety of grape used in winemaking, esp. for table wines in the Rhône Valley of France and for a type of rosé in California. [< F *grenache* < Catalan *garnatxa, granatxa,* Medieval Catalan *vernatxa* < It *vernaccia,* after *Vernazza,* a commune of the Cinque Terre, a wine-growing region of Liguria]

Gre•na•da (gri nā′də), *n.* **1.** one of the Windward Islands, in the E West Indies. **2.** an independent country comprising this island and the S Grenadines: a former British colony; gained independence 1974: scene of invasion by U.S. and Caribbean forces 1983. 107,779; 133 sq. mi. (344 sq. km). *Cap.:* St. George's. **3.** a town in central Mississippi. 12,641. **—Gre•na•di•an** (gri nā′dē ən), *adj., n.*

gre•nade (gri nād′), *n., v.,* **-nad•ed, -nad•ing.** —*n.* **1.** a small shell containing an explosive and thrown by hand or fired from a rifle or launching device. **2.** a similar missile containing a chemical, as for dispersing tear gas or fire-extinguishing substances. —*v.t.* **3.** to attack with a grenade or grenades. [1525–35; < F < Sp *granada* pomegranate, special use of *granado* having grains < L *grānātus.* See GRAIN, -ATE[1]]

grenade′ launch′er, *Mil.* a device attached to the muzzle of a rifle, permitting the firing of rifle grenades. [1955–60]

gren•a•dier (gren′ə dēr′), *n.* **1.** (in the British army) a member of the first regiment of household infantry (**Gren′adier Guards′**). **2.** (formerly) a specially selected foot soldier in certain elite units. **3.** (formerly) a soldier who threw grenades. **4.** Also called **rat-tail, rat tail.** any of several deep-sea fishes of the family Macrouridae, having an elongated, tapering tail. [1670–80; < F; see GRENADE, -IER[2]] **—gren′a•dier′i•al,** *adj.* **—gren′a•dier′ly,** *adv.* **—gren′a•dier′ship,** *n.*

gren•a•dil•la (gren′ə dil′ə), *n.* granadilla.

gren•a•dine[1] (gren′ə dēn′, gren′ə dēn′), *n.* a thin fabric of leno weave in silk, nylon, rayon, or wool. [1850–55; < F, perh. after GRANADA, Spain. See -INE[1]]

gren•a•dine[2] (gren′ə dēn′, gren′ə dēn′), *n.* a syrup made from pomegranate juice. [1700–10; < F, dim. of *grenade* pomegranate. See GRENADE, -INE[1]]

Gren•a•dines (gren′ə dēnz′, gren′ə dēnz′), *n.* (*used with a plural v.*) a chain of about 600 islands in the E West Indies in the Windward Islands: a former British colony; now divided between Grenada and St. Vincent and the Grenadines.

Gren•del (gren′dl), *n. Eng. and Scand. Myth.* the monster killed by Beowulf.

Gren•fell (gren′fel), *n.* **Sir Wilfred Thom•a•son** (tom′ə sən), 1865–1940, English physician and missionary in Labrador and Newfoundland.

Gre•no•ble (grə nō′bəl; *Fr.* grə nô′blᵊ), *n.* a city in and the capital of Isère, in SE France. 169,740.

Gren•ville (gren′vil), *n.* **1. George,** 1712–70, British statesman: prime minister 1763–65. **2.** Also, **Greynville. Sir Richard,** 1541?–91, English naval commander. **3. William Wyndham, Baron,** 1759–1834, British statesman: prime minister 1806–07 (son of George Grenville).

Gresh•am (gresh′əm), *n.* **1. Sir Thomas,** 1519?–79, English merchant and financier. **2.** a town in NW Oregon. 33,005.

Gresh′am's law′, *Econ.* the tendency of the inferior of two forms of currency to circulate more freely than, or to the exclusion of, the superior, because of the hoarding of the latter. [1855–60; named after Sir T. GRESHAM]

gres•so•ri•al (gre sôr′ē əl, -sōr′-), *adj. Zool.* adapted for walking, as the feet of some birds. [1835–45; < L *gress(us),* ptp. of *gradī* to walk + *-orial,* as in GRALLATORIAL]

Gret•a (gret′ə), *n.* a female given name, form of **Margaret.** Also, **Gret′ta.**

Gret•chen (grech′ən; *Ger.* grāt′shən), *n.* a female given name, form of **Margaret.**

Gret•na (gret′nə), *n.* a city in SE Louisiana, near New Orleans. 20,615.

Gret′na Green′, a village in S Scotland, near the English border, to which many English couples formerly eloped to be married.

Gret′na Green′ mar′riage, *Brit. Informal.* marriage without parental consent; elopement. [1860–65]

Gré•try (grā tʀē′), *n.* **An•dré Er•nest Mo•deste** (äɴ drā′ ᴇʀ nest′ mô dest′), 1741–1813, French composer.

Greuze (grœz), *n.* **Jean Bap•tiste** (zhäɴ bᴀ tēst′), 1725–1805, French painter.

Grev•ille (grev′il), *n.* **Fulke** (fo͝olk), **1st Baron Brooke,** 1554–1628, English poet and statesman.

grew (gro͞o), *v.* pt. of **grow.**

grew•some (gro͞o′səm), *adj.* gruesome. **—grew′some•ly,** *adv.* **—grew′some•ness,** *n.*

grex (greks), *n.* a numerical system for measuring the size of fibers, filaments, or yarns, based on the weight in grams of 10,000 meters of the fibrous material. [from the expression *gram per x* (ten)]

grey (grā), *adj.,* **-er, -est,** *n., v.t., v.i.* gray[1]. **—grey′ly,** *adv.* **—grey′ness,** *n.*

Grey (grā), *n.* **1. Charles, 2nd Earl,** 1764–1845, British statesman: prime minister 1830–34. **2. Sir Edward** (*Viscount Fallodon*), 1862–1933, British statesman. **3. Sir George,** 1812–98, British statesman and colonial administrator: prime minister of New Zealand 1877–79. **4. Lady Jane** (*Lady Jane Dudley*), 1537–54, descendant of Henry VII of England; executed under orders of Mary I to eliminate her as a rival for the throne. **5. Zane** (zān), 1875–1939, U.S. novelist.

grey•back (grā′bak′), *n.* grayback.

grey•beard (grā′bērd′), *n.* graybeard.

grey-head•ed (grā′hed′id), *adj.* gray-headed.

grey•hen (grā′hen′), *n. Brit.* the female of the black grouse. [1400–50; late ME. See GREY, HEN]

grey•hound (grā′hound′), *n.* **1.** one of a breed of tall, slender, short-haired dogs, noted for its keen sight and swiftness. **2.** a swift ship, esp. a fast ocean liner. Also, **grayhound.** [bef. 1000; ME *greihund, grehund, grihund,* OE *grīghund* < ON *greyhundr;* cf. ON *grey* bitch; see HOUND[1]]

greyhound (def. 1), 28 in. (71 cm) high at shoulder

grey•ish (grā′ish), *adj.* grayish.

grey•lag (grā′lag′), *n.* graylag.

Greyn•ville (gran′vil, gren′-), *n.* **Sir Richard.** See **Grenville, Sir Richard.**

CONCISE PRONUNCIATION KEY: act, cāpe, dâre, pärt; set, ēqual; if, īce; ox, ōver, ôrder, oil, bo͝ok, bo͞ot, out; up, ûrge; child; sing; shoe; thin, *that;* zh as in *treasure.* ə = a as in *alone,* e as in *system,* i as in *easily,* o as in *gallop,* u as in *circus;* ᵊ as in *fire* (fīᵊr), *hour* (ouᵊr). l and n can serve as syllabic consonants, as in *cradle* (krād′l), and *button* (but′n). See the full key inside the front cover.

grey′ plov′er, *Brit.* the black-bellied plover.

grey·wacke (grā′wak′, -wak′ə), *n.* graywacke.

GRF, See **growth hormone releasing factor.**

grib·ble (grib′əl), *n.* a small, marine isopod crustacean of the genus *Limnoria* that destroys submerged timber by boring into it. [1830–40; perh. akin to GRUB]

grice (grīs), *n. Chiefly Scot.* a pig, esp. a young or suckling pig. [1175–1225; ME *gris* < ON *griss* pig]

grid (grid), *n.* **1.** a grating of crossed bars; gridiron. **2.** *Elect.* **a.** a metallic framework employed in a storage cell or battery for conducting the electric current and supporting the active material. **b.** a system of electrical distribution serving a large area, esp. by means of high-tension lines. **3.** *Electronics.* an electrode in a vacuum tube, usually consisting of parallel wires, a coil of wire, or a screen, for controlling the flow of electrons between the other electrodes. **4.** *Survey.* a basic system of reference lines for a region, consisting of straight lines intersecting at right angles. **5.** a network of horizontal and perpendicular lines, uniformly spaced, for locating points on a map, chart, or aerial photograph by means of a system of coordinates. **6.** *Archit.* a rectangular system of coordinates used in locating the principal elements of a plan. **7.** grillage. **8.** *Football.* gridiron (def. 1). [1830–40; short for GRIDIRON]

grid′ bi′as, *Electronics.* the potential difference applied between a grid and the cathode of a vacuum tube. Also called **C-bias.** [1925–30]

grid′ capac′itor, *Electronics.* a capacitor connected in series with the grid.

grid′ cir′cuit, *Electronics.* that part of a circuit that contains the cathode and the grid of a vacuum tube. [1915–20]

grid′ cur′rent, *Electronics.* the current that moves within the vacuum tube from the grid to the cathode. [1915–20]

grid·der (grid′ər), *n. Informal.* a football player. [1925–30, *Amer.*; GRID + -ER[1]]

grid·dle (grid′l), *n., v.,* **-dled, -dling.** —*n.* **1.** a frying pan with a handle and a slightly raised edge, for cooking pancakes, bacon, etc., over direct heat. **2.** any flat, heated surface, esp. on the top of a stove, for cooking food: *a quick breakfast from the luncheonette's griddle.* **3.** *Upstate New York Older Use.* a circular lid covering an opening on the cooking surface of a wood or coal-burning stove. —*v.t.* **4.** to cook on a griddle: *Griddle two eggs for me, will you?* [1175–1225; ME *gridel, gredil* < OF *gridil, gredil;* see GRILL[1]]

grid·dle·cake (grid′l kāk′), *n.* a thin cake of batter cooked on a griddle; pancake. [1775–85; GRIDDLE + CAKE]
—Regional Variation. See **pancake.**

gride (grīd), *v.,* **grid·ed, grid·ing,** *n.* —*v.i.* **1.** to make a grating sound; scrape harshly; grate; grind. —*v.t.* **2.** to pierce or cut. —*n.* **3.** a griding or grating sound. [1350–1400; ME; metathetic var. of GIRD[2]]

grid·i·ron (grid′ī′ərn), *n.* **1.** a football field. **2.** a utensil consisting of parallel metal bars on which to broil meat or other food. **3.** any framework or network resembling a gridiron. **4.** a structure above the stage of a theater, from which hung scenery and the like are manipulated. —*v.t.* **5.** to mark off into squares or design with a network of squares. [1250–1300; ME *gridirne, gridir(e), gridere,* var. of *gridel* GRIDDLE; variants in *-irne, -ire,* etc. are associated by folk etymology with ModE var. *irne, ire* IRON]

grid′iron pen′dulum, a clock pendulum having, as part of its shaft, an arrangement of brass and steel rods having different coefficients of expansion, such that the pendulum has the same length at any temperature. [1745–55]

grid′i·ron-tailed liz′ard (grid′ī′ərn tāld′). See **zebra-tailed lizard.**

grid′ leak′, *Electronics.* a high-resistance device that permits excessive charges on the grid to leak off or escape. [1915–20]

grid·lock (grid′lok′), *n.* **1.** the stoppage of free vehicular movement in an urban area because key intersections are blocked by traffic. **2.** the blocking of an intersection by vehicular traffic entering the intersection but unable to pass through it. **3.** any situation in which nothing can move or proceed in any direction: *a financial gridlock due to high interest rates.* [1975–80, *Amer.*; GRID + LOCK[1]] **—grid′locked′,** *adj.*

grid′ road′, *Canadian.* a municipal road that follows a grid line established by the original survey of the area. [1955–60]

grid′ varia′tion, *Navig.* the angle, at any point on the surface of the earth, between the magnetic and true meridians passing through that point. Also called **grivation.**

grief (grēf), *n.* **1.** keen mental suffering or distress over affliction or loss; sharp sorrow; painful regret. **2.** a cause or occasion of keen distress or sorrow. **3. come to grief,** to suffer disappointment, misfortune, or other trouble; fail: *Their marriage came to grief after only two years.* **4. good grief,** (used as an exclamation of dismay, surprise, or relief): *Good grief, it's started to rain again!* [1175–1225; ME *gref, grief* < AF *gref;* see GRIEVE] **—grief′less,** *adj.* **—grief′less·ness,** *n.*
—Syn. 1. anguish, heartache, woe, misery; sadness, melancholy, moroseness. See **sorrow. —Ant. 1.** joy.

grief·o (grē′fō), *n. Slang.* marijuana. Also, **grefa, griffa, griffo.** [< MexSp *grifa;* cf. *grifo* marijuana user, appar. the same word as *grifo* curly-haired, tap, spigot, GRIFFIN[1] (sense development unclear, but perh. parallel to that of *kinky*); cf. GRIFFE[1], REEFER[2]]

grief-strick·en (grēf′strik′ən), *adj.* overwhelmed by grief; deeply afflicted or sorrowful. [1900–05]

Grieg (grēg; *Norw.* grig), *n.* **Ed·vard** (ed′värd; *Norw.* ed′värt), 1843–1907, Norwegian composer.

griege (grā, grāzh), *n.* See **gray goods.** [var. of GREIGE]

grie·shoch (grē′shuk; *Scot.* grē′shuкн), *n. Scot.* a bed of embers, esp. of a peat or moss fire. [1795–1805; < Scot Gael *griòsach* embers]

griev·ance (grē′vəns), *n.* **1.** a wrong considered as grounds for complaint, or something believed to cause distress: *Inequitable taxation is the chief grievance.* **2.** a complaint or resentment, as against an unjust or unfair act: *to have a grievance against someone.* [1250–1300; ME *greva(u)nce* < OF *grevance.* See GRIEVE, -ANCE]
—Syn. 1. affront, injustice, hurt, injury, distress.

griev′ance commit′tee, a group of representatives chosen from a labor union or from both labor and management to consider and remedy workers' grievances. [1925–30]

griev·ant (grē′vənt), *n.* a person who submits a complaint for arbitration. [1955–60; back formation from GRIEVANCE. See -ANT.]

grieve (grēv), *v.,* **grieved, griev·ing.** —*v.i.* **1.** to feel grief or great sorrow: *She has grieved over his death for nearly three years.* —*v.t.* **2.** to distress mentally; cause to feel grief or sorrow: *It grieves me to see you so unhappy.* **3.** *Archaic.* to oppress or wrong. [1175–1225; ME *greven, grieven* < OF *grever* < L *gravāre* to burden, deriv. of *gravis* heavy, GRAVE[2]] **—griev·ed·ly** (grē′vid-lē, grēvd′-), *adv.* **—griev′er,** *n.* **—griev′ing·ly,** *adv.*
—Syn. 1. lament, weep, bewail, bemoan; suffer. GRIEVE, MOURN imply showing suffering caused by sorrow. GRIEVE is the stronger word, implying deep mental suffering often endured alone and in silence but revealed by one's aspect: *to grieve over the loss (or death) of a friend.* MOURN usually refers to manifesting sorrow outwardly, either with or without sincerity: *to mourn publicly and wear black.* **2.** sadden, pain.

griev·ous (grē′vəs), *adj.* **1.** causing grief or great sorrow: *grievous news.* **2.** flagrant; outrageous; atrocious: *a grievous offense against morality.* **3.** full of or expressing grief; sorrowful: *a grievous cry.* **4.** burdensome or oppressive. **5.** causing great pain or suffering: *arrested for causing grievous bodily harm to someone in a bar.* [1250–1300; ME *grevous* < OF *grevo(u)s.* See GRIEVE, -OUS] **—griev′ous·ly,** *adv.* **—griev′ous·ness,** *n.*
—Syn. 1. distressing, sad, sorrowful, painful. **2.** deplorable, lamentable, calamitous, heinous, flagitious, dreadful, shameful, iniquitous. **—Ant. 1.** delightful.

griff (grif), *n.* griffin[2]. [1890–95; by shortening]

grif·fa (grē′fə, -fä), *n. Slang.* griefo.

griffe[1] (grif), *n. Chiefly Louisiana.* **1.** the offspring of a black and a mulatto. **2.** a person of mixed black and American Indian ancestry. **3.** a mulatto, esp. a woman. [1715–25, *Amer.*; < LaF < AmerSp *grifo* curly-haired]

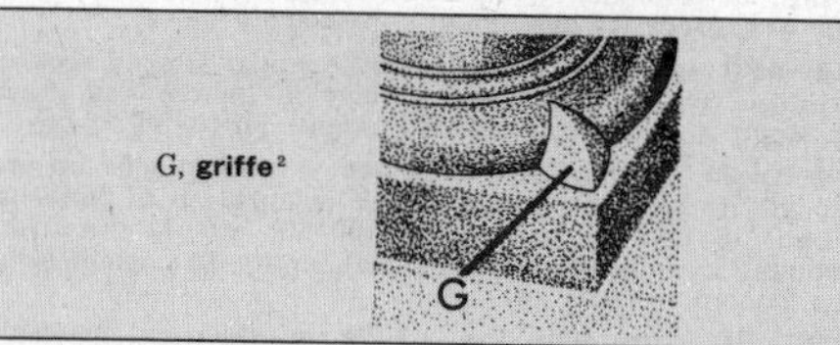

G, griffe[2]

griffe[2] (grif), *n. Archit.* an ornament at the base of a column, projecting from the torus toward a corner of the plinth. Also called **spur.** [1870–75; < F: claw < Gmc]

Grif·fes (grif′əs), *n.* **Charles Tomlinson,** 1884–1920, U.S. composer.

grif·fin[1] (grif′in), *n. Class. Myth.* a fabled monster, usually having the head and wings of an eagle and the body of a lion. Also, **griffon, gryphon.** [1300–50; ME *griffoun* < MF *grifon* < L *grȳphus* < Gk *grȳp-* (s. of *grȳps*) curled, curved, having a hooked nose] **—grif′fin·esque′,** *adj.*

griffin[1]

grif·fin[2] (grif′in), *n.* (in India and the East) a newcomer, esp. a white person from a Western country. [1785–95; orig. uncert.] **—grif′fin·age, grif′fin·hood′, grif′fin·ism,** *n.* **—grif′fin·ish,** *adj.*

Grif·fin (grif′in), *n.* **1.** a city in W Georgia. 20,728. **2.** a male given name.

Grif·fith (grif′ith), *n.* **1. D(avid Lewelyn) W(ark)** (wûrk), 1875–1948, U.S. film director and producer. **2.** a town in NW Indiana. 17,026. **3.** a male given name, form of **Griffin.**

grif·fo (grē′fō), *n. Slang.* griefo.

grif·fon[1] (grif′ən), *n.* a vulture of the genus *Gyps,* esp. *G. fulvus,* of southern Europe. [1350–1400; ME *griffoun* < F; see GRIFFIN[1]]

grif·fon[2] (grif′ən), *n.* **1.** any of several varieties of the Brussels griffon differing from each other in coloration or in the texture of the coat. Cf. **Belgian griffon, Brabançon, Brussels griffon. 2.** Also called **wirehaired pointing griffon.** one of a Dutch breed of medium-sized dogs having a coarse, steel-gray or grayish-white coat with chestnut markings, used for pointing and retrieving birds. [1820–30; < F; akin to GRIFFIN[1]]

grif·fon[3] (grif′ən), *n. Class. Myth.* griffin[1].

grift (grift), *Slang.* —*n.* **1.** (*sometimes used with a plural v.*) a group of methods for obtaining money falsely through the use of swindles, frauds, dishonest gambling, etc. **2.** money obtained from such practices. —*v.i.* **3.** to profit by the use of grift: *a man known to have grifted for many years.* —*v.t.* **4.** to obtain (money or other profit) by grift. [1910–15; perh. alter. of GRAFT[2]]

grift·er (grif′tər), *n. Slang.* **1.** a person who operates a side show at a circus, fair, etc., esp. a gambling attraction. **2.** a swindler, dishonest gambler, or the like. [1910–15; GRIFT + -ER[1]]

grig (grig), *n. North Brit. Dial.* **1.** a cricket or grasshopper. **2.** a small or young eel. **3.** a lively person. [1350–1400; ME *grig, grege;* orig. uncert.]

Gri·gnard (grēn yärd′; *Fr.* grē nyar′), *n.* **(Fran·çois Au·guste) Vic·tor** (fran swa′ ō gyst′ vēk tôr′), 1871–1935, French organic chemist: Nobel prize 1912.

Grignard′ reac′tion, *Chem.* the reaction of a Grignard reagent with any of the numerous types of compounds with which it can combine, as alcohols, acids, aldehydes, ketones, or esters: used chiefly in organic synthesis. [1900–05; see V. GRIGNARD]

Grignard′ rea′gent, *Chem.* any of the group of reagents produced by the interaction of magnesium and an organic halide, usually in the presence of an ether, and having the general formula RMgX, where R is an organic group and X is a halogen: used in the Grignard reaction. [1900–05; see V. GRIGNARD]

gri·gri (grē′grē), *n., pl.* **-gris.** an African charm, amulet, or fetish. Also, **greegree, gris-gris.** [1755–65; < F *gris-gris, grigri,* first recorded in West Africa in 1557; orig. obscure]

grill[1] (gril), *n.* **1.** a grated utensil for broiling meat, fish, vegetables, etc., over a fire; gridiron. **2.** a dish of grilled meat, fish, etc. Cf. **mixed grill. 3.** grillroom. **4.** *Philately.* a group of small pyramidal marks, embossed or impressed in parallel rows on certain U.S. and Peruvian stamps of the late 19th century to prevent erasure of cancellation marks. —*v.t.* **5.** to broil on a gridiron or other apparatus over or before a fire. **6.** to subject to severe and persistent cross-examination or questioning. **7.** to torment with heat. **8.** to mark with a series of parallel bars like those of a grill. —*v.i.* **9.** to undergo broiling. [1660–70; 1890–95 for def. 6; < F *gril* gridiron << L *crāticulum, crēāticulō,* dim. of *crātis* wickerwork, hurdle. See GRILLE]
—Syn. 5. barbecue. **6.** interrogate, probe. **7.** torture.

grill[2] (gril), *n.* grille.

gril·lade (gri läd′, -yäd′; *Fr.* grē yad′), *n., pl.* **gril·lades** (gri lädz′; *Fr.* grē yad′), *v.,* **gril·lad·ed** (gri lä′did, -yä′-), **gril·lad·ing.** —*n.* **1.** a dish or serving of broiled or grilled meat. **2.** the act of grilling. —*v.t.* **3.** *Obs.* to grill or broil (meat). [1650–60; < F: something grilled, equiv. to OF *grille* GRILL[1] + *-ade* -ADE[1]]

gril·lage (gril′ij), *n.* a framework of crossing beams used for spreading heavy loads over large areas. Also called **grid.** [1770–80; < F; see GRILLE, -AGE]

grille (def. 1)

grille (gril), *n.* **1.** a grating or openwork barrier, as for a gate, usually of metal and often of decorative design. **2.** an opening, usually covered by grillwork, for admitting air to cool the engine of an automobile or the like; radiator grille. **3.** any of various perforated screens, sheets, etc., used to cover something, as on a radio for protecting the amplifier or in cryptography for coding purposes. **4.** a ticket window covered by a grating. **5.** *Court Tennis.* a square-shaped winning opening on the hazard side of the court. Cf. **dedans** (def. 1), **winning gallery.** Also, **grill.** [1655–65; < F, OF < LL *gratīcula, L *crāticula* (cf. OPr *grazilha*), dim. of *crātis*] **—grilled,** *adj.*

gril·lé (*Fr.* grē yā′), *adj.* **1.** cooked on a grill; broiled. **2.** *Textiles.* having an ornamental bar or grate pattern across the open areas of a lace motif. Also, **gril·lée′.** [1680–90; < F: grilled; see GRILLE]

grill·er (gril′ər), *n.* **1.** a person who grills food, esp. as a cook in a restaurant. **2.** an appliance for grilling food. [1865–70; GRILL[1] + -ER[1]]

Grill·par·zer (gril′pärt′sər), *n.* **Franz** (fränts), 1791–1872, Austrian poet and dramatist.

grill·room (gril′ro͞om′, -ro͝om′), *n.* a restaurant or dining room, as in a hotel, that specializes in serving grilled meat and fish. [1905–10; GRILL[1] + ROOM]

grill·work (gril′wûrk′), *n.* material so formed as to function as or to have the appearance of a grille. [1895–1900; GRILL[2] + WORK]

grilse (grils), *n., pl.* **grils·es,** (*esp. collectively*) **grilse.** a young Atlantic salmon as it returns from the sea to fresh water for the first time. [1375–1425; late ME *grills, grilles* (pl.) < ?]

CONCISE ETYMOLOGY KEY: <, descended or borrowed from; >, whence; b., blend of, blended; c., cognate with; cf., compare; deriv., derivative; equiv., equivalent; imit., imitative; obl., oblique; r., replacing; s., stem; sp., spelling, spelled; resp., respelling, respelled; trans., translation; ?, origin unknown; *, unattested; ‡, probably earlier than. See the full key inside the front cover.

grim (grim), *adj.*, **grim•mer, grim•mest. 1.** stern and admitting of no appeasement or compromise: *grim determination; grim necessity.* **2.** of a sinister or ghastly character; repellent: *a grim joke.* **3.** having a harsh, surly, forbidding, or morbid air: *a grim man but a just one; a grim countenance.* **4.** fierce, savage, or cruel: *War is a grim business.* [bef. 900; ME, OE; c. OS, OHG *grimm,* ON *grimmr*] **—grim′ly,** *adv.* **—grim′ness,** *n.*
—Syn. 1. harsh, unyielding. **2.** frightful, horrible, dire, appalling, horrid, grisly, gruesome, hideous, dreadful. **3.** severe, stern, hard. **4.** ferocious, ruthless.
—Ant. 1. lenient. **2.** attractive. **3.** gentle.

grim•ace (grim′əs, gri mās′), *n., v.,* **-aced, -ac•ing.** *—n.* **1.** a facial expression, often ugly or contorted, that indicates disapproval, pain, etc. *—v.i.* **2.** to make grimaces. [1645–55; < F << Frankish **grima* mask (cf. GRIME, GRIM) + *-azo* < L *-āceus* -ACEOUS] **—grim′ac•er,** *n.* **—grim′ac•ing•ly,** *adv.*

Gri•mal•di (gri mäl′dē, -môl′-), *n.* **1. Joseph,** 1779–1837, English actor, mime, and clown. **2.** a walled plain in the third quadrant of the face of the moon: about 120 mi. (195 km) in diameter.

Gri•mal•di•an (gri mäl′dē ən, -môl′-), *adj.* of, pertaining to, or characteristic of an Upper Paleolithic cultural epoch in northwestern Italy. [1930–35; after the *Grimaldi* caves, Italy + -AN]

gri•mal•kin (gri mal′kin, -môl′-), *n.* **1.** a cat. **2.** an old female cat. **3.** an ill-tempered old woman. [1595–1605; appar. alter. of GRAY + *malkin,* dim. of *Maud* proper name; see -KIN]

grime (grīm), *n., v.,* **grimed, grim•ing.** *—n.* **1.** dirt, soot, or other filthy matter, esp. adhering to or embedded in a surface. *—v.t.* **2.** to cover with dirt; make very dirty; soil. [1250–1300; ME *grim;* appar. special use of OE *grīma* mask, to denote layer of dust; cf. dial. D *grijm*]

Grimes′ Gold′en (grīmz), a yellow variety of apple that ripens in late autumn. [1855–60, *Amer.;* named after Thomas P. *Grimes* of West Virginia]

Grimes′ Graves′, an area of Neolithic flint mines in Suffolk, England, comprising more than 300 mine shafts and galleries.

Grim•hild (grim′hild), *n.* (in the *Volsunga Saga*) a sorceress, the wife of Gjuki and the mother of Gudrun and Gunnar. She gave Sigurd a potion to make him forget Brynhild so that he would marry Gudrun. [< ON *Grīmhildr,* equiv. to *grīm(a)* mask + *hildr* battle]

Grim•ké (grim′kē), *n.* **Sarah Moore,** 1792–1873, and her sister **Angelina Emily,** 1805–79, U.S. abolitionists and women's-rights leaders.

Grimm (grim), *n.* **Ja•kob Lud•wig Karl** (yä′kop lo͞ot′-vikh kärl, lo͞od′-), 1785–1863, and his brother **Wil•helm Karl** (vil′helm), 1786–1859, German philologists and folklorists.

Grimm's′ law′, *Ling.* the statement of the regular pattern of consonant correspondences presumed to represent changes from Proto-Indo-European to Germanic, according to which voiced aspirated stops became voiced obstruents, voiced unaspirated stops became unvoiced stops, and unvoiced stops became unvoiced fricatives: first formulated in 1820–22 by Jakob Grimm, though the facts had been noted earlier by Rasmus Rask.

Grim′ Reap′er, the personification of death as a man or cloaked skeleton holding a scythe. [1925–30]

Grims•by (grimz′bē), *n.* **1.** a seaport in Humberside county, in E England at the mouth of the Humber estuary. 93,800. **2.** a town in SE Ontario, in S Canada, on the SW shore of Lake Ontario. 15,797.

grim•y (grī′mē), *adj.,* **grim•i•er, grim•i•est.** covered with grime; dirty: *I shook his grimy hand.* [1605–15; GRIME + -Y¹] **—grim′i•ly,** *adv.* **—grim′i•ness,** *n.*

grin¹ (grin), *v.,* **grinned, grin•ning,** *n.* *—v.i.* **1.** to smile broadly, esp. as an indication of pleasure, amusement, or the like. **2.** to draw back the lips so as to show the teeth, as a snarling dog or a person in pain. **3.** to show or be exposed through an opening, crevice, etc. *—v.t.* **4.** to express or produce by grinning: *The little boy grinned his approval of the gift.* *—n.* **5.** a broad smile. **6.** the act of producing a broad smile. **7.** the act of withdrawing the lips and showing the teeth, as in anger or pain. [bef. 1000; ME *grinnen, grennen,* OE *grennian;* c. OHG *grennan* to mutter] **—grin′ner,** *n.* **—grin′ning•ly,** *adv.*
—Syn. 1. See **laugh.**

grin² (grin), *n., v.,* **grinned, grin•ning.** *—n.* **1.** *Chiefly Scot.* a snare like a running noose. *—v.t.* **2.** to catch in a nooselike snare. [bef. 900; ME *grin(e),* OE *grin, gryn*]

grind (grīnd), *v.,* **ground** or (*Rare*) **grind•ed; grind•ing;** *n.* *—v.t.* **1.** to wear, smooth, or sharpen by abrasion or friction; whet: *to grind a lens.* **2.** to reduce to fine particles, as by pounding or crushing; bray, triturate, or pulverize. **3.** to oppress, torment, or crush: *to grind the poor.* **4.** to rub harshly or gratingly; grate together; grit: *to grind one's teeth.* **5.** to operate by turning a crank: *to grind a hand organ.* **6.** to produce by crushing or abrasion: *to grind flour.* **7.** *Slang.* to annoy; irritate; irk: *It really grinds me when he's late.* *—v.i.* **8.** to perform the operation of reducing to fine particles. **9.** to rub harshly; grate. **10.** to be or become ground. **11.** to be polished or sharpened by friction. **12.** *Informal.* to work or study laboriously (often fol. by *away*): *He was grinding away at his algebra.* **13.** *Slang.* (in a dance) to rotate the hips in a suggestive manner. Cf. **bump** (def. 11). **14. grind out, a.** to produce in a routine or mechanical way: *to grind out magazine stories.* **b.** to extinguish by rubbing the lighted end against a hard surface: *to grind out a cigarette.* *—n.* **15.** the act of grinding. **16.** a grinding sound. **17.** a grade of particle fineness into which a substance is ground: *The coffee is available in various grinds for different coffee makers.* **18.** laborious, usually uninteresting work: *Copying all the footnotes was a grind.* **19.** *Informal.* an excessively diligent student. **20.** *Slang.* a dance movement in which the hips are rotated in a suggestive or erotic manner. Cf. **bump** (def. 22). [bef. 950; ME *grinden,* OE *grindan;* akin to Goth *grinda-,* L *frendere*] **—grind′a•ble,** *adj.* **—grind′a•bil′i•ty,** *n.* **—grind′ing•ly,** *adv.*
—Syn. 2. crush, powder, comminute, pound. **3.** persecute, plague, afflict, trouble. **4.** abrade.

grin•de•li•a (grin dē′lē ə, -dēl′yə), *n.* **1.** any of various composite plants of the genus *Grindelia,* comprising the gumweeds. **2.** the dried leaves and tops of certain species of this plant, used in medicine. [1880–85, *Amer.;* named after D.H. *Grindel* (1777–1836), Russian scientist; see -IA]

grind•er (grīn′dər), *n.* **1.** a person or thing that grinds. **2.** a kitchen device or appliance for grinding food. **3.** a sharpener of tools. **4.** a molar tooth. **5.** *Chiefly New Eng. and Inland North.* See **hero sandwich. 6. grinders,** *Informal.* the teeth. [1350–1400; ME. See GRIND, -ER¹]
—Regional Variation. 5. See **hero sandwich.**

grind•er•y (grīn′də rē), *n., pl.* **-er•ies. 1.** a workshop for grinding edge tools. **2.** *Brit.* **a.** a shoemaker's or leatherworker's material and equipment. **b.** a shop where such material and equipment may be purchased. [1795–1805; GRIND + -ERY]

grind′ house′, *Slang.* **1.** a burlesque house, esp. one providing continuous entertainment at reduced prices. **2.** a movie theater that shows films throughout the day and all or most of the night.

grind′ing wheel′, a wheel composed of abrasive material, used for grinding. [1785–95]

grin•dle (grin′dl), *n.* bowfin. [1700–10, *Amer.;* < G *Gründel,* dim. of *Grund* ground, bottom]

grind′ rock′, *Southern U.S.* whetstone.

grind•stone (grīnd′stōn′), *n.* **1.** a rotating solid stone wheel used for sharpening, shaping, etc. **2.** a millstone. **3. keep** or **put one's nose to the grindstone,** to work, study, or practice hard and steadily or to cause someone to do so: *If I put my nose to the grindstone, I'll finish the job this week.* [1175–1225; ME. See GRIND, STONE]

grin•ga (gring′gə, -gä), *n.* *Usually Disparaging.* (in Latin America or Spain) a female foreigner, esp. one of U.S. or British descent. [< Sp, fem. of *gringo* GRINGO]

grin•go (gring′gō), *n., pl.* **-gos.** *Usually Disparaging.* (in Latin America or Spain) a foreigner, esp. one of U.S. or British descent. [1840–50, *Amer.;* < Sp: foreign language, foreigner, esp. English-speaking (pejorative); prob. alter. of *griego* GREEK. The belief that word is from the song "Green Grow the Lilacs," popular during U.S.-Mexican War, is without substance]

gri•ot (grē ō′, grē′ō, grē′ot), *n.* a member of a hereditary caste among the peoples of western Africa whose function is to keep an oral history of the tribe or village and to entertain with stories, poems, songs, dances, etc. [1955–60; < F, earlier *guiriot,* perh. ult. < Pg *criado* domestic servant, altered in W African coastal creoles]

grip (grip), *n., v.,* **gripped** or **gript, grip•ping.** *—n.* **1.** the act of grasping; a seizing and holding fast; firm grasp. **2.** the power of gripping: *He has a strong grip.* **3.** a grasp, hold, or control. **4.** mental or intellectual hold: *to have a good grip on a problem.* **5.** competence or firmness in dealing with situations in one's work or personal affairs: *The boss is old and is losing his grip.* **6.** a special mode of clasping hands: *Members of the club use the secret grip.* **7.** something that seizes and holds, as a clutching device on a cable car. **8.** a handle or hilt: *That knife has a very unusual grip.* **9.** a sudden, sharp pain; spasm of pain. **10.** grippe. **11.** *Older Use.* a small traveling bag. **12. a.** *Theat.* a stagehand, esp. one who works on the stage floor. **b.** *Motion Pictures, Television.* a general assistant available on a film set for shifting scenery, moving furniture, etc. **13. come to grips with, a.** to encounter; meet; cope with: *She had never come to grips with such a situation before.* **b.** to deal with directly or firmly: *We didn't come to grips with the real problem.* *—v.t.* **14.** to grasp or seize firmly; hold fast: *We gripped the sides of the boat as the waves tossed us about.* **15.** to take hold on; hold the interest of: *to grip the mind.* **16.** to attach by a grip or clutch. *—v.i.* **17.** to take firm hold; hold fast. **18.** to take hold on the mind. [bef. 900; ME, OE *gripe* grasp (n.); c. G *Griff,* OE *gripa* handful; see GRIPE] **—grip′less,** *adj.*
—Syn. 15. impress, attract, rivet, hold, fascinate.

gripe (grīp), *v.,* **griped, grip•ing,** *n.* *—v.i.* **1.** *Informal.* to complain naggingly or constantly; grumble. **2.** to suffer pain in the bowels. **3.** *Naut.* (of a sailing vessel) to tend to come into the wind; to be ardent. *—v.t.* **4.** to seize and hold firmly; grip; grasp; clutch. **5.** to produce pain in (the bowels) as if by constriction. **6.** to distress or oppress. **7.** to annoy or irritate: *His tone of voice gripes me.* **8.** to grasp or clutch, as a miser. **9.** *Naut.* to secure (a lifeboat) to a deck or against a pudding boom on davits. *—n.* **10.** the act of gripping, grasping, or clutching. **11.** *Informal.* a nagging complaint. **12.** a firm hold; clutch. **13.** a grasp; hold; control. **14.** something that grips or clutches; a claw or grip. **15.** *Naut.* **a.** a lashing or chain by which a boat is secured to a deck or in position on davits. **b.** Also called **gripe′ piece′.** a curved timber connecting the stem or cutwater of a wooden hull with the keel. **c.** the exterior angle or curve formed by this piece; forefoot. **d.** the forward end of the dished keel of a metal hull. **16.** a handle, hilt, etc. **17.** Usually, **gripes.** *Pathol.* an intermittent spasmodic pain in the bowels. [1350–1400; ME *gripen,* OE *grīpan;* c. D *grijpen,* G *griefen;* see GRIP, GROPE] **—grip′er,** *n.* **—gripe′ful,** *adj.* **—grip′ing•ly,** *adv.*
—Syn. 1. whine, mutter, carp, rail, bellyache.

grip•ey (grī′pē), *adj.,* **grip•i•er, grip•i•est.** gripy.

grip•man (grip′mən), *n., pl.* **-men.** a worker on a cable car who operates the grip, which, by grasping or releasing the moving cable, starts or stops the car. [1880–85, *Amer.;* GRIP + -MAN]

grippe (grip), *n.* *Pathol.* (formerly) influenza. [1770–80; < F, n. deriv. of *gripper* to seize suddenly < Gmc; akin to GRIP, GRIPE] **—gripp′al,** *adj.* **—grippe′like′,** *adj.*

grip•per (grip′ər), *n.* **1.** a person or thing that grips. **2.** *Print.* (in certain presses) one of a number of finger-like devices for gripping a sheet and transferring it to or from the printing surface. **3.** *Metalworking.* dog (def. 13). [1560–70; GRIP + -ER¹]

grip•ping (grip′ing), *adj.* holding the attention or interest intensely; fascinating; enthralling: *a gripping play; a gripping book.* [1620–30; GRIP + -ING²] **—grip′ping•ly,** *adv.* **—grip′ping•ness,** *n.*

grip•ple (grip′əl), *adj.* *Brit. Dial.* miserly; avaricious. [bef. 1000; ME *grip(p)el,* OE *gripul;* see GRIPE]

grip•py¹ (grip′ē), *adj.,* **-pi•er, -pi•est.** afflicted with the grippe. [GRIPPE + -Y¹]

grip•py² (grip′ē), *adj.,* **-pi•er, -pi•est.** *Chiefly Scot.* stingy; avaricious. [1800–10; GRIP + -Y¹]

grip•sack (grip′sak′), *n.* *Older Use.* a traveling bag; grip. [1875–80, *Amer.;* GRIP + SACK¹]

gript (gript), *v.* a pp. and pt. of **grip.**

grip•y (grī′pē), *adj.,* **grip•i•er, grip•i•est.** resembling or causing gripes. Also, **gripey.** [1875–80; GRIPE + -Y¹]

Gri•qua (grē′kwə, grik′wə), *n.* (in South Africa) a person of mixed ethnic or racial heritage, esp. a native of Griqualand.

Gri′qua•land East′ (grē′kwə land′, grik′wə-), a former district in S South Africa, SW of Natal.

Gri′qualand West′, a former district in S South Africa, N of the Orange River and W of the Orange Free State: diamonds found 1867.

Gris (grēs), *n.* **Juan** (hwän), (*José Vittoriano Gonzáles*), 1887–1927, Spanish painter in France.

gri•saille (gri zī′, -zāl′; *Fr.* grē zä′yᵊ), *n., pl.* **-sailles** (-zīz′, -zālz′; *Fr.* -zä′yᵊ) for 2. **1.** monochromatic painting in shades of gray. **2.** a work of art, as a painting or stained-glass window, executed in grisaille. [1840–50; < F: painted in gray monotone, equiv. to *gris* gray + *-aille* n. suffix]

Gri•sel•da (gri zel′də), *n.* **1.** a woman of exemplary meekness and patience. **2.** a female given name: from a Germanic word meaning "gray battle." [(def. 1) after a character in a tale of the same name in Boccaccio's *Decameron*]

gris•e•o•ful•vin (griz′ē ō fo͝ol′vin, -ful′-, gris′-), *n.* *Pharm.* an antibiotic, $C_{17}H_{17}ClO_6$, obtained from a species of *Penicillium,* used in the treatment of ringworm and other fungous infections of the skin. [1935–40; < NL *griseofulv(um)* epithet of a species of *Penicillium* (equiv. to ML *grīse(us)* GRISEOUS + NL *-o-* -O- + L *fulvum,* neut. of *fulvus* tawny, yellow-brown) + -IN²]

gris•e•ous (gris′ē əs, griz′-), *adj.* gray; pearl-gray. [1810–20; < ML *grīseus,* based on Gmc **gris* or **grisi* gray, perh. with suffix of L *rūbeus;* cf. OS *grîs* gray OF, F *gris* gray; see -EOUS]

gri•sette (gri zet′), *n.* a young French workingwoman. [1690–1700; < F, equiv. to *gris* gray (see GRISEOUS) + *-ette* -ETTE; orig. a cheap gray fabric, or dress made of such fabric, worn by young working women in the garment trade] **—gri•set′tish,** *adj.*

gris-gris (grē′grē), *n., pl.* **-gris** (-grēz). grigri.

gris•kin (gris′kin), *n.* *Brit.* **1.** a chop or steak, esp. a pork chop. **2.** *Archaic.* a pork loin, esp. the lean part. [1690–1700; GRICE + -KIN]

gris•ly¹ (griz′lē), *adj.,* **-li•er, -li•est. 1.** causing a shudder or feeling of horror; horrible; gruesome: *a grisly murder.* **2.** formidable; grim: *a grisly countenance.* [bef. 1150; ME; OE *grislic* horrible; c. OHG *grisenlīh*] **—gris′li•ness,** *n.*

gris•ly² (gris′lē), *adj.,* **-li•er, -li•est.** *Obs.* gristly.

gri•son (grī′sən, griz′ən), *n.* a weasellike carnivore, *Galictis vittata,* ranging from southern Mexico to Peru, having a grayish-white upper body, a distinctive white stripe across the forehead and ears, and a dark brown face, chest, and legs. [1790–1800; < F, equiv. to MF *gris* gray (see GRISEOUS) + *-on* dim. suffix]

Gri•sons (*Fr.* grē zôN′), *n.* a canton in E Switzerland. 162,900; 2747 sq. mi. (7115 sq. km). *Cap.:* Chur. German, **Graubünden.**

grist (grist), *n.* **1.** grain to be ground. **2.** ground grain; meal produced from grinding. **3.** a quantity of grain for grinding at one time; the amount of meal from one grinding. **4.** *Older Use.* a quantity or lot. **5. grist for** or **to one's mill,** something employed to one's profit or advantage, esp. something seemingly unpromising: *Every delay was so much more grist for her mill.* *—v.t.* **6.** to grind (grain). [bef. 1000; ME, OE; akin to OE *grindan* to GRIND] **—grist′er,** *n.*

gris•tle (gris′əl), *n.* cartilage, esp. in meats. [bef. 900; ME, OE; c. OFris, MLG *gristal;* akin to OE *grost* cartilage]

gris•tly (gris′lē), *adj.,* **-tli•er, -tli•est.** resembling or containing gristle; cartilaginous. [1350–1400; ME; see GRISTLE, -Y¹] **—gris′tli•ness,** *n.*

grist•mill (grist′mil′), *n.* a mill for grinding grain, esp. the customer's own grain. [1595–1605; GRIST + MILL¹] **—grist′mill′er,** *n.* **—grist′mill′ing,** *n.*

Gris•wold (griz′wôld, -wəld), *n.* **1. Erwin Nathaniel,** born 1904, U.S. lawyer and educator: dean of Harvard University Law School 1950–67. **2.** a male given name.

grit (grit), *n., v.,* **grit•ted, grit•ting.** *—n.* **1.** abrasive particles or granules, as of sand or other small, coarse impurities found in the air, food, water, etc. **2.** firmness of character; indomitable spirit; pluck: *She has a reputation for grit and common sense.* **3.** a coarse-grained siliceous rock, usually with sharp, angular grains. **4.** *Brit.* gravel. **5.** sand or other fine grainy particles eaten by fowl to aid in digestion. *—v.t.* **6.** to cause to grind or

CONCISE PRONUNCIATION KEY: act, cāpe, dâre, pärt; set, ēqual; *if,* ice; ox, ōver, ôrder, oil, bo͝ok, bo͞ot, out; up, ûrge; child; sing; shoe; thin, *that;* zh as in *treasure.* ə = a as in *alone,* e as in *system,* i as in *easily,* o as in *gallop,* u as in *circus;* ᵊ as in *fire* (fīᵊr), *hour* (ouᵊr). l and n can serve as syllabic consonants, as in *cradle* (krād′l), and *button* (but′n). See the full key inside the front cover.

grate together. —*v.i.* **7.** to make a scratchy or slightly grating sound, as of sand being walked on; grate. **8. grit one's teeth,** to show tenseness, anger, or determination by or as if by clamping or grinding the teeth together. [bef. 1000; ME *gret, griet, grit,* OE *grēot;* c. G *Griess,* ON *grjōt* pebble, boulder; see GRITS] —**grit′less,** *adj.* —**grit′ter,** *n.*
—**Syn. 2.** resolution, fortitude, courage.

grith (grith), *n. Chiefly Scot.* protection or asylum for a limited period of time, as under church or crown. [bef. 1000; ME, OE < ON *grith* asylum, protection (as in a home)]

grits (grits), *n.* (*used with a singular or plural v.*) **1.** Also called **hominy grits.** coarsely ground hominy, boiled and sometimes then fried, eaten as a breakfast dish or as a side dish with meats. **2.** grain hulled and coarsely ground. [bef. 900; ME *gryttes* (pl.), OE *gryt(t);* c. G *Grütze*]

grit·ty (grit′ē), *adj.,* **-ti·er, -ti·est. 1.** consisting of, containing, or resembling grit; sandy. **2.** resolute and courageous; plucky. [1590–1600; GRIT + -Y[1]] —**grit′ti·ly,** *adv.* —**grit′ti·ness,** *n.*

gri·va·tion (gri vā′shən, grī-), *n.* See **grid variation.** [GRI(D) + V(ARI)ATION]

griv·et (griv′it), *n.* a small Abyssinian monkey, *Cercopithecus aethiops,* with a grayish back, gray tail, black face, and dark extremities. [1855–60; orig. uncert.]

griz·zle[1] (griz′əl), *v.,* **-zled, -zling,** *adj., n.* —*v.i., v.t.* **1.** to make or become gray or partly gray. —*adj.* **2.** gray; grayish; devoid of hue. —*n.* **3.** gray or partly gray hair. **4.** a gray wig. [1350–1400; ME *grisel* < OF, deriv. of *gris* gray < Gmc; see GRISEOUS]

griz·zle[2] (griz′əl), *v.i.,* **-zled, -zling.** *Brit.* **1.** to complain; whimper; whine. **2.** to laugh or grin in mockery; sneer. [1740–50; orig. uncert.; cf. MHG *grisgramen* to gnash one's teeth, G *Griesgram* sourpuss] —**griz′zler,** *n.*

griz·zled (griz′əld), *adj.* **1.** having gray or partly gray hair. **2.** gray or partly gray. [1350–1400; ME. See GRIZZLE[1], -ED[3]]

griz·zling (griz′ling), *n. Brit.* the act of complaining or whimpering. [GRIZZLE[2] + -ING[1]]

griz·zly (griz′lē), *adj.,* **-zli·er, -zli·est,** *n., pl.* **-zlies.** —*adj.* **1.** somewhat gray; grayish. **2.** gray-haired. —*n.* **3.** See **grizzly bear. 4.** a device for screening ore, consisting of a row of iron or steel bars. [1585–95; GRIZZLE[1] + -Y[1]]

griz′zly bear′, a large North American brown bear, *Ursus (arctos) horribilis,* with coarse, gray-tipped brown fur, once widespread in the western part of the continent as far south as northern Mexico but now restricted to some regions of Alaska, western Canada, and the U.S. Rocky Mountains: a threatened species except in Alaska. Also, **grizzly.** Also called **silvertip.** Cf. **brown bear.** [1685–95]

gro., gross.

groan (grōn), *n.* **1.** a low, mournful sound uttered in pain or grief: *the groans of dying soldiers.* **2.** a deep, inarticulate sound uttered in derision, disapproval, desire, etc. **3.** a deep grating or creaking sound due to a sudden or continued overburdening, as with a great weight: *We heard the groan of the ropes as the crane lowered the heavy cargo into the ship's hold.* —*v.i.* **4.** to utter a deep, mournful sound expressive of pain or grief. **5.** to make a deep, inarticulate sound expressive of derision, disapproval, desire, etc. **6.** to make a sound resembling a groan; resound harshly: *The old stairway groaned under my weight.* **7.** to be overburdened or overloaded. **8.** to suffer greatly or lamentably: *groaning under an intolerable burden.* —*v.t.* **9.** to utter or express with groans. [bef. 900; ME *gronen,* OE *grānian;* c. G *greinen* to whine] —**groan′er,** *n.* —**groan′ing·ly,** *adv.*
—**Syn. 1.** GROAN, MOAN refer to sounds indicating deep suffering. A GROAN is a brief, strong, deep-throated sound emitted involuntarily under pressure of pain or suffering: *The wounded man groaned when they lifted him.* A MOAN is a prolonged, more or less continuous, low, inarticulate sound indicative of suffering, either physical or mental: *She was moaning after the operation. She did not weep, but moaned softly.*

groat (grōt), *n.* a silver coin of England, equal to four pennies, issued from 1279 to 1662. [1325–75; ME *groot* < MD *groot* large, name of a large coin; see GREAT]

groats (grōts), *n.* (*used with a singular or plural v.*) **1.** hulled grain, as wheat or oats, broken into fragments. **2.** hulled kernels of oats, buckwheat, or barley. [bef. 1100; ME *grotes* (pl.), OE *grot* meal; akin to GRITS]

gro·cer (grō′sər), *n.* the owner or operator of a store that sells general food supplies and certain nonedible articles of household use, as soaps and paper products. [1325–75; ME < OF *gross(i)er* wholesale merchant. See GROSS, -ER[2]]

gro·cer·y (grō′sə rē, grōs′rē), *n., pl.* **-cer·ies. 1.** Also called **gro′cery store′.** a grocer's store. **2.** Usually, **groceries;** *esp. Brit.* **grocery.** food and other commodities sold by a grocer. **3.** the business of a grocer. **4.** *Southwestern U.S.* (formerly) **a.** a saloon or bar. **b.** a liquor store. [1400–50; late ME *grocerie* < OF *grosserie.* See GROSS, -ERY]

gro·cer·y·man (grō′sə rē mən, -man′, grōs′rē-), *n., pl.* **-men** (-mən, -men′). a grocer. [1875–80]

Gro·dno (grod′nō; *Russ.* grô′dnə), *n.* a city in W Byelorussia (Belarus), on the Niemen River: formerly in Poland. 195,000.

gro·dy (grō′dē), *adj.,* **-di·er, -di·est.** *Slang.* **1.** inferior in character or quality; seedy; sleazy: *They lived for a month in a grody little shack without lights or running water.* **2.** repulsive; disgusting; nauseating. [expressive coinage, perh. reflecting GROSS (in slang sense) and MOLDY] —**gro′di·ness,** *n.*

Groe·nen·dael (grōō′nən däl′, grō′-, grā′-, gren′ən-), *n.* former name of **Belgian sheepdog.** [1920–25; after the village in Belgium where it was bred]

Groete (*Du.* KHRŌŌ′tə; *Eng.* grōt), *n.* **Ger·hard** (*Du.* KHā′RäRT; *Eng.* gâr′härt). See **Groote, Gerhard.**

Gro·fé (grō′fā, grə fā′), *n.* **Fer·de** (fûr′dē) (*Ferdinand Rudolf von Grofé*), 1892–1972, U.S. composer.

grog (grog), *n.* **1.** a mixture of rum and water, often flavored with lemon, sugar, and spices and sometimes served hot. **2.** any strong alcoholic drink. **3.** fired and crushed clay. [1760–70; from Old *Grog* (alluding to his GROGRAM cloak), the nickname of Edward Vernon (d. 1757), British admiral, who in 1740 ordered the alcoholic mixture to be served, instead of pure spirits, to sailors.]

grog·ger (grog′ər, grô′gər), *n.* grager.

grog·ger·y (grog′ə rē), *n., pl.* **-ger·ies.** a slightly disreputable barroom. [1815–25, *Amer.;* GROG + -ERY]

grog·gy (grog′ē), *adj.,* **-gi·er, -gi·est. 1.** staggering, as from exhaustion or blows: *a boxer groggy from his opponent's hard left jab.* **2.** dazed and weakened, as from lack of sleep: *Late nights always make me groggy the next morning.* **3.** *Archaic.* drunk; intoxicated. [1760–70; GROG + -Y[1]] —**grog′gi·ly,** *adv.* —**grog′gi·ness,** *n.*
—**Syn. 2.** sluggish, lethargic; woozy, dopey.

grog·ram (grog′rəm), *n.* a coarse fabric of silk, of silk and mohair or wool, or of wool, formerly in use. [1555–65; < MF *gros grain.* See GROSGRAIN]

grog·shop (grog′shop′), *n. Brit.* a saloon or barroom, esp. a cheap one. [1765–75; GROG + SHOP]

groin (groin), *n.* **1.** *Anat.* the fold or hollow on either side of the front of the body where the thigh joins the abdomen. **2.** the general region of this fold or hollow. **3.** *Archit.* the curved line or edge formed by the intersection of two vaults. See illus. under **vault[1]. 4.** Also, **groyne.** a small jetty extending from a shore to prevent beach erosion. —*v.t.* **5.** *Archit.* to form with groins. [1350–1400; earlier *grine,* ME *grinde;* cf. OE *grynde* abyss, akin to *grund* bottom, GROUND[1]]

groin·ing (groi′ning), *n.* **1.** the intersection of two vaults. **2.** the construction of groined vaults. [1645–55]

grok (grok), *v.,* **grokked, grok·king.** *Slang.* —*v.t.* **1.** to understand thoroughly and intuitively. —*v.i.* **2.** to communicate sympathetically. [coined by Robert A. Heinlein in the science-fiction novel *Stranger in a Strange Land* (1961)]

Gro·li·er (grō′lē ər; *Fr.* grô lyā′), *adj.* pertaining to a decorative design **(Gro′lier design′)** in bookbinding, consisting of bands interlaced in geometric forms. [1820–30; named after J. GROLIER DE SERVIERES]

Gro·lier de Ser·vières (grô lyā də ser vyer′), **Jean** (zhäN), 1479–1565, French bibliophile.

gro·ma (grō′mə), *n.* (in ancient Roman surveying) an instrument having a cruciform wooden frame with a plumb line at the end of each arm, used for laying out lines at right angles to existing lines. [< L *grōma, grūma,* by dissimilation < Gk *gnôma,* presumably with sense of *gnṓmōn* carpenter's square; see GNOMON]

grom·met (grom′it), *n.* **1.** *Mach.* **a.** any of various rings or eyelets of metal or the like. **b.** an insulated washer of rubber or plastic, inserted in a hole in a metal part to prevent grounding of a wire passing through the hole. **2.** *Naut.* **a.** a ring or strop of fiber or wire; becket. **b.** a ring having a thickness of three strands, made by forming a loop of a single strand, then laying the ends around the loop. **c.** a ring of fiber used as a seal or gasket, as under the head of a bolt. **3.** a washer or packing for sealing joints between sections of pipe. **4.** *Mil.* a stiff ring of rubber or metal inside the top of a service cap, designed to keep the top of the cap stretched flat. **5.** a metal-bound eyelet in cloth, sometimes used decoratively, as on a garment. —*v.t.* **6.** to fasten with a grommet. Also, **grummet.** [1620–30; < obs. F *gromette* curb of bridle < ?]

grom·well (grom′wəl), *n.* any of various often hairy plants of the genus *Lithospermum,* of the borage family, usually bearing white or yellowish flowers and smooth, white, stony nutlets. [1275–1325; ME *gromil* < OF, equiv. to *gro-* (< ?) + *mil* millet < L *milium*]

Gro·my·ko (grō mē′kō, grə-; *Russ.* gru mi′kə), *n.* **Andrei An·dre·e·vich** (un drā′ un drye′yi vyich), 1909–89, Soviet diplomat: foreign minister 1957–85, president 1985–88.

Gron·chi (grong′kē; *It.* grôn′kē), *n.* **Gio·van·ni** (jō vän′nē), 1887–1978, Italian statesman: president 1955–62.

Gro·ning·en (grō′ning ən; *Du.* KHRō′ning ən), *n.* a city in the NE Netherlands. 162,952.

groom (grōōm, grŏŏm), *n.* **1.** a bridegroom. **2.** a man or boy in charge of horses or the stable. **3.** any of several officers of the English royal household. **4.** *Archaic.* a manservant. —*v.t.* **5.** to tend carefully as to person and dress; make neat or tidy. **6.** to clean, brush, and otherwise tend (a horse, dog, etc.). **7.** to prepare for a position, election, etc.: *The mayor is being groomed for the presidency.* **8.** (of an animal) to tend (itself or another) by removing dirt, parasites, or specks of other matter from the fur, skin, feathers, etc.: often performed as a social act. [1175–1225; ME *grom* boy, groom; appar. akin to GROW] —**groom′er,** *n.* —**groom′ish,** *adj.* —**groom′ish·ly,** *adv.*
—**Syn. 7.** educate, train, coach, drill, tutor.

groom's′ cake′, a fruit cake in layers of graduated size, served at a wedding.

grooms·man (grōōmz′mən, grŏŏmz′-), *n., pl.* **-men.** a man who attends the bridegroom in a wedding ceremony. [1690–1700; GROOM + 'S[1] + -MAN]

Groot (*Du.* KHRōt; *Eng.* grōt), *n.* **1. Huig** (*Du.* hoikH) **de** (də) or **van** (vän). See **Grotius, Hugo. 2. Gerhard.** See **Groote, Gerhard.**

Groote (*Du.* KHRō′tə; *Eng.* grōt), *n.* **Ger·hard** (*Du.* KHā′RäRT; *Eng.* gâr′härt), (*Gerardus Magnus*), 1340–84, Dutch religious reformer, educator, and author: founder of the order of the Brethren of the Common Life. Also, **Groot, Groete.**

groove (grōōv), *n., v.,* **grooved, groov·ing.** —*n.* **1.** a long, narrow cut or indentation in a surface, as the cut in a board to receive the tongue of another board **(tongue-and-groove joint),** a furrow, or a natural indentation on an organism. **2.** the track or channel of a phonograph record for the needle or stylus. **3.** a fixed routine: *to get into a groove.* **4.** *Print.* the furrow at the bottom of a piece of type. See diag. under **type. 5.** *Slang.* an enjoyable time or experience. **6. in the groove,** *Slang.* **a.** in perfect functioning order. **b.** in the popular fashion; up-to-date. —*v.t.* **7.** to cut a groove in; furrow. **8.** *Slang.* **a.** to appreciate and enjoy. **b.** to please immensely. —*v.i.* **9.** *Slang.* **a.** to take great pleasure; enjoy oneself: *He was grooving on the music.* **b.** to get along or interact well. **10.** to fix in a groove. [1350–1400; ME *grofe, groof* mining shaft; c. MD *groeve,* D *groef,* G *Grube* pit, ditch; akin to GRAVE[1]] —**groove′less,** *adj.* —**groove′like′,** *adj.* —**groov′er,** *n.*
—**Syn. 3.** rut, habit, pattern.

grooved (grōōvd), *v.* **1.** pt. and pp. of **groove.** —*adj.* **2.** provided with a groove. [1785–95; GROOVE + -ED[2]]

grooved′ fric′ative, *Phonet.* a fricative, as (s), in which air is channeled through a groove along the center of the tongue. Also, **groove′ fric′ative.** Cf. **slit fricative.**

groov·y (grōō′vē), *adj.,* **groov·i·er, groov·i·est. 1.** *Slang.* highly stimulating or attractive; excellent: *groovy music; a groovy car.* **2.** inclined to follow a fixed routine. [1850–55; GROOVE + -Y[1]]

grope (grōp), *v.,* **groped, grop·ing,** *n.* —*v.i.* **1.** to feel about with the hands; feel one's way: *I had to grope around in the darkness to find the light switch.* **2.** to search blindly or uncertainly: *He seemed to be groping for an answer.* —*v.t.* **3.** to seek by or as if by groping: *to grope one's way up the dark stairs.* **4.** to touch or handle (someone) for sexual pleasure. —*n.* **5.** an act or instance of groping. **6.** *Slang.* an act or instance of sexually fondling another person. [bef. 900; ME *gropien,* OE *grāpian,* deriv. of *grāp* grasp; akin to GRIPE, GRASP]
—**Syn. 1.** fumble, probe, fish.

grop·er[1] (grō′pər), *n.* a person or thing that gropes. [1560–70; GROPE + -ER[1]]

grop·er[2] (grō′pər), *n.* a large, purplish food fish, *Achoerodus gouldii,* inhabiting waters off Australia and New Zealand, characterized by an enormous gape. [appar. alter. of GROUPER[1], perh. by assoc. with GROPE]

grop·ing (grō′ping), *adj.* **1.** moving or going about clumsily or hesitantly; stumbling. **2.** showing or reflecting a desire to understand, esp. something that proves puzzling: *a groping scrutiny; a groping expression.* [1300–50; ME; see GROPE, -ING[2]] —**grop′ing·ly,** *adv.*

Gro·pi·us (grō′pē əs; *Ger.* grō′pē ŏŏs′), *n.* **Wal·ter** (wôl′tər; *Ger.* väl′tər), 1883–1969, German architect, in the U.S. from 1937.

Grop·per (grop′ər), *n.* **William,** 1897–1977, U.S. painter.

Gros (grō), *n.* **An·toine Jean** (äN twan′ zhäN), **Baron,** 1771–1835, French painter.

gros·beak (grōs′bēk′), *n.* any of various finches having a thick, conical bill. [1670–80; < F *grosbec,* lit., large beak]

gro·schen (grō′shən), *n., pl.* **-schen. 1.** a zinc or aluminum coin of Austria, the 100th part of a schilling. **2.** a German 10-pfennig piece made of nickel. **3.** any of the silver coins of various German regions first introduced in the 13th century. [1610–20; < G; MHG *grosse, grosze* < L (*denārius*) *grossus* thick (coin); akin to GROAT]

gros de Lon·dres (grō′ də lôn′drə, lônd′; *Fr.* grō də lôN′dRᵊ), a cross-ribbed, silk dress fabric with ribs alternating in color or between coarse and fine yarn. [< F: lit., London gross; cf. GROSGRAIN]

gros de Tours (grō′ də tŏŏr′; *Fr.* grō də tōōR′), a ribbed silk fabric made with a two- or three-ply warp interlaced with organzine and tram filling. [1790–1800; < F: lit., Tours gross; cf. GROSGRAIN]

gros·grain (grō′grān′), *n.* a heavy, corded ribbon or cloth of silk or rayon. [1865–70; < F *gros grain* large grain] —**gros′grained′,** *adj.*

gros point (grō′ point′), *pl.* **gros points. 1.** a large stitch used in embroidery. Cf. **petit point** (def. 1), **tent stitch. 2.** Venetian point lace with raised work and large designs. [1860–65; < F: large point]

gross (grōs), *adj.,* **-er, -est,** *n., pl.* **gross** for 11, **gross·es** for 12, 13; *v.* —*adj.* **1.** without deductions; total, as the amount of sales, salary, profit, etc., before taking deductions for expenses, taxes, or the like (opposed to *net*): *gross earnings; gross sales.* **2.** unqualified; complete; rank: *a gross scoundrel.* **3.** flagrant and extreme: *gross injustice.* **4.** indelicate, indecent, obscene, or vulgar: *gross remarks.* **5.** lacking in refinement, good manners, education, etc.; unrefined. **6.** large, big, or bulky. **7.** extremely or excessively fat. **8.** thick; dense; heavy: *gross vegetation.* **9.** of or concerning only the broadest or most general considerations, aspects, etc. **10.** *Slang.* extremely objectionable, offensive, or disgusting: *He wore an outfit that was absolutely gross.* —*n.* **11.** a group of 12 dozen, or 144, things. *Abbr.:* gro. **12.** total income from sales, salary, etc., before any deductions (opposed to *net*). **13.** *Obs.* the main body, bulk, or mass. —*v.t.* **14.** to have, make, or earn as a total before any deductions, as of taxes, expenses, etc.: *The company grossed over three million dollars last year.* **15. gross out,** *Slang.* **a.** to disgust or offend, esp. by crude language or behavior. **b.** to shock or horrify. [1350–1400; ME < OF *gros* large (as n., *grosse* twelve dozen) < LL *gross(us)* thick, coarse] —**gross′ly,** *adv.* —**gross′ness,** *n.*
—**Syn. 3.** shameful, outrageous, heinous, grievous. See **flagrant. 4.** low, sensual, broad. **6.** massive, great.

CONCISE ETYMOLOGY KEY: <, descended or borrowed from; >, whence; b., blend of, blended; c., cognate with; cf., compare; deriv., derivative; equiv., equivalent; imit., imitative; obl., oblique; r., replacing; s., stem; sp., spelling, spelled; resp., respelling, respelled; trans., translation; ?, origin unknown; *, unattested; ‡, probably earlier than. See the full key inside the front cover.

Gross (grōs), *n.* **Chaim** (KHĭm), born 1904, U.S. sculptor and graphic artist, born in Austria.

gross′ anat′omy, the branch of anatomy that deals with structures that can be seen with the naked eye. Cf. **microanatomy, histology.** [1885–90]

gross′ domes′tic prod′uct, gross national product excluding payments on foreign investments. *Abbr.:* GDP

Grosse′ Pointe′ Farms′, a city in SE Michigan, near Detroit. 10,551.

Grosse′ Pointe′ Park′, a city in SE Michigan, near Detroit. 13,639.

Grosse′ Pointe′ Woods′, a city in SE Michigan, near Detroit. 18,886.

gross·er (grō′sər), *n. Informal.* a commercial production, as a motion picture or record, that generates a large amount of income. [1955–60; GROSS + -ER[1]]

gross′ in′come, *Accounting.* total revenue received before any deductions or allowances, as for rent, cost of goods sold, taxes, etc. Also called **gross′ rev′enue.**

gross′ na′tional prod′uct, the total monetary value of all final goods and services produced in a country during one year. *Abbr.:* GNP Cf. **national income, net national product.** [1945–50]

gross-out (grōs′out′), *n. Slang.* something that is disgustingly offensive. [1970–75; n. use of v. phrase *gross out*]

gross′ prof′it, gross receipts less the cost of goods or production but before the deduction of such other costs as rent or salaries.

gross′ ton′, **1.** *Chiefly Brit.* a long ton. See under **ton**[1] (def. 1). **2.** Also called **gross′ reg′ister ton′.** *Naut.* See under **gross tonnage.**

gross′ ton′nage, *Naut.* the total volume of a vessel, expressed in units of 100 cubic feet (**gross ton**), with certain open structures, deckhouses, tanks, etc., exempted. Also called **gross′ reg′ister ton′nage.**

gros·su·lar·ite (gros′yə lə rīt′), *n.* a mineral, calcium aluminum garnet, $Ca_3Al_2Si_3O_{12}$, occurring in gray-white to pinkish crystals. Also, **gros·su·lar** (gros′yə lər). Also called **gooseberry garnet.** [1840–50; < NL *grossulār(ia)* gooseberry (irreg. < F *groseille*) + -ITE[1]]

Gross·war·dein (grōs′vär dīn′), *n.* German name of **Oradea.**

gross′ weight′, total weight without deduction for tare, tret, or waste.

Gros·ve·nor (grōv′nər), *n.* **Gilbert Hovey,** 1875–1966, U.S. geographer, writer, and editor.

grosz (grôsh), *n., pl.* **gro·szy** (grô′shē). an aluminum coin of Poland, the 100th part of a zloty. [1945–50; < Pol < Czech *groš;* see GROSCHEN]

Grosz (grōs), *n.* **George,** 1893–1959, U.S. painter and graphic artist, born in Germany.

grot (grot), *n. Chiefly Literary.* a grotto. [1500–10; < F *grotte* < It *grotta;* see GROTTO]

Grote (grōt), *n.* **George,** 1794–1871, English historian.

Gro·tesk (grō tesk′), *n.* (in Europe) gothic (def. 12). [var. of GROTESQUE]

gro·tesque (grō tesk′), *adj.* **1.** odd or unnatural in shape, appearance, or character; fantastically ugly or absurd; bizarre. **2.** fantastic in the shaping and combination of forms, as in decorative work combining incongruous human and animal figures with scrolls, foliage, etc. —*n.* **3.** any grotesque object, design, person, or thing. [1555–65; < F < It *grottesco* (as n., *grottesca* grotesque decoration such as was appar. found in excavated dwellings), deriv. of *grotta.* See GROTTO, -ESQUE] —**gro·tesque′ly,** *adv.* —**gro·tesque′ness,** *n.*
—**Syn. 1.** distorted, deformed, weird, antic, wild. See **fantastic.**

grotesque work (16th century)

gro·tes·quer·y (grō tes′kə rē), *n., pl.* **-quer·ies. 1.** grotesque character. **2.** something grotesque. **3.** grotesque ornamental work. Also, **gro·tes′quer·ie.** [1555–65; < F *grotesquerie.* See GROTESQUE, -ERY]

Gro·ti·us (grō′shē əs), *n.* **Hugo** (*Huig De Groot*), 1583–1645, Dutch jurist and statesman. —**Gro·tian** (grō′shən, -shē ən), *adj.* —**Gro′tian·ism,** *n.*

Grot·on (grot′n), a city in SE Connecticut. 10,086.

grot·to (grot′ō), *n., pl.* **-toes, -tos. 1.** a cave or cavern. **2.** an artificial cavernlike recess or structure. [1610–20; < It *grotta* < VL **crupta,* for L *crypta* subterranean passage, chamber. See CRYPT] —**grot′toed,** *adj.* —**grot′to·like′,** *adj.*

grot·ty (grot′ē), *adj.,* **-ti·er, -ti·est.** *Slang.* seedy; wretched; dirty. [perh. GROT(ESQUE) + -Y[1], though senses do not correspond; appar. not akin to GRODY]

grouch (grouch), *v.i.* **1.** to be sulky or morose; show discontent; complain, esp. in an irritable way. —*n.* **2.** a sulky, complaining, or morose person. **3.** a sulky, irritable, or morose mood. [1890–95, *Amer.;* var. of obs. *grutch* < OF *groucher* to grumble. See GRUDGE]
—**Syn. 2.** grumbler, spoilsport, crab, killjoy.

grouch·y (grou′chē), *adj.,* **grouch·i·er, grouch·i·est.** sullenly discontented; sulky; morose; ill-tempered. [1890–95, *Amer.;* GROUCH + -Y[1]] —**grouch′i·ly,** *adv.* —**grouch′i·ness,** *n.*

Grou·chy (grōō shē′), *n.* **Em·ma·nu·el** (e mä ny el′), **Marquis de,** 1766–1847, French general.

ground[1] (ground), *n.* **1.** the solid surface of the earth; firm or dry land: *to fall to the ground.* **2.** earth or soil: *stony ground.* **3.** land having an indicated character: *rising ground.* **4.** Often, **grounds.** a tract of land appropriated to a special use: *picnic grounds; a hunting ground.* **5.** Often, **grounds.** the foundation or basis on which a belief or action rests; reason or cause: *grounds for dismissal.* **6.** subject for discussion; topic: *Sex education is forbidden ground in some school curricula.* **7.** rational or factual support for one's position or attitude, as in a debate or argument: *on firm ground; on shaky ground.* **8.** the main surface or background in painting, decorative work, lace, etc. **9.** *Fine Arts.* **a.** a coating of some substance serving as a surface for paint, ink, or other media in art: *Lead white is a traditional ground for oil paintings.* **b.** See **ground color** (def. 2). **10.** (in perception) the background in a visual field, contrasted with the figure. **11.** Also called **etching ground.** an acid-resistant substance, composed of wax, gum, and resin in varying proportions, applied to the entire surface of an etching plate and through which the design is drawn with an etching needle. **12. grounds,** dregs or sediment: *coffee grounds.* **13. grounds,** the gardens, lawn, etc., surrounding and belonging to a building. **14.** *Elect.* a conducting connection between an electric circuit or equipment and the earth or some other conducting body. **15.** *Music.* See **ground bass. 16.** *Naut.* the bottom of a body of water. **17.** the earth's solid or liquid surface; land or water. **18.** *Carpentry.* **a.** a strip of wood to which woodwork can be attached, set flush with the plaster finish of a room. **b.** a strip of wood or length of corner bead used at an opening as a stop for plasterwork. **19. break ground, a.** to plow. **b.** to begin excavation for a construction project. **c.** to begin upon or take preparatory measures for any undertaking. **20. cover ground, a.** to pass or travel over a certain area. **b.** to make a certain amount of progress in dealing with a piece of work, subject, treatise, or the like: *He talked for two hours without covering much ground.* **21. cut the ground from under,** to render (an argument, position, person, etc.) ineffective or invalid; refute: *It didn't require much effort to cut the ground from under that case.* **22. from the ground up, a.** gradually from the most elementary level to the highest level: *She learned the business from the ground up.* **b.** extensively; thoroughly: *The professor knew his subject from the ground up.* **23. gain ground, a.** to make progress; advance. **b.** to gain approval or acceptance: *The case for air-pollution control is gaining ground throughout the country.* **24. give ground,** to yield to force or forceful argument; retreat: *The disarmament talks reached an impasse when neither side would give ground on inspection proposals.* **25. hold** or **stand one's ground,** to maintain one's position; be steadfast: *The referee stood his ground, though his decision was hotly contested by the crowd.* **26. into the ground,** beyond a reasonable or necessary point: *You've stated your case, and you needn't run it into the ground.* **27. lose ground, a.** to retreat or be forced back. **b.** to lose one's advantage; suffer a reverse. **c.** to wane in popularity or acceptance; begin to fail: *Our candidate is losing ground in industrial areas.* **28. off the ground,** *Informal.* into action or well under way: *The play never got off the ground.* **29. on one's own ground,** in an area or situation that one knows well. **30. on the ground,** at the place of interest or importance; actively engaged: *Minutes after the bank robbery reporters were on the ground to get the story.* **31. shift ground,** to change position in an argument or situation. **32. suit down to the ground,** to be perfectly satisfactory; please greatly: *This climate suits me down to the ground.* **33. take the ground,** *Naut.* to become grounded at low water. **34. to ground, a.** into a den, burrow, shelter, or the like: *a fox gone to ground.* **b.** into concealment or hiding: *Rather than take the witness stand, she went to ground in another country.*
—*adj.* **35.** situated on or at, or adjacent to, the surface of the earth: *a ground attack.* **36.** pertaining to the ground. **37.** *Mil.* operating on land: *ground forces.*
—*v.t.* **38.** to lay or set on the ground. **39.** to place on a foundation; fix firmly; settle or establish; found. **40.** to instruct in elements or first principles: *to ground students in science.* **41.** to furnish with a ground or background, as on decorative work. **42.** to cover (wallpaper) with colors or other materials before printing. **43.** *Elect.* to establish a ground for (a circuit, device, etc.). **44.** *Naut.* to cause (a vessel) to run aground. **45.** *Aeron.* to restrict (an aircraft or the like) to the ground because of bad weather, the unsatisfactory condition of the aircraft, etc. **46.** to forbid (a pilot) to fly because of bad health, failure to comply with safety regulations, or the like. **47.** *Informal.* to put out of action or make unable to participate: *The quarterback was grounded by a knee injury.* **48.** *Informal.* to restrict the activities, esp. the social activities, of: *I can't go to the party—my parents have grounded me until my grades improve.*
—*v.i.* **49.** to come to or strike the ground. **50.** *Baseball.* **a.** to hit a ground ball. **b.** to ground out. **51. ground out,** *Baseball.* to be put out at first base after hitting a ground ball to the infield. [bef. 900; (n.) ME *ground, grund,* OE *grund;* c. D *grond,* G *Grund;* (v.) ME *grundien, grownden* to set on a foundation, establish, deriv. of the n.] —**ground′a·ble,** *adj.* —**ground′a·bly,** *adv.* —**ground′ed·ly,** *adv.* —**ground′ed·ness,** *n.* —**ground′ward, ground′wards,** *adv., adj.*

ground[2] (ground), *v.* **1.** a pt. and pp. of **grind.** —*adj.* **2.** reduced to fine particles or dust by grinding. **3.** (of meat, vegetables, etc.) reduced to very small pieces by putting through a food processor or grinder: *ground beef.* **4.** having the surface abraded or roughened by or as if by grinding, as in order to reduce its transparency: *ground glass.* [1755–65 for def. 2; see GROUND[1]]

ground·age (groun′dij), *n. Brit.* a tax levied on ships that anchor in a port. [1400–50; late ME *grondage.* See GROUND[1], -AGE]

ground′ alert′, *Mil.* **1.** the state of waiting for orders in or near combat airplanes ready to take to the air at once. **2.** the aircraft standing by during a ground alert. [1960–65]

ground′ bait′, chum[2] (def. 1). [1645–55]

ground′ ball′, *Baseball.* a batted ball that rolls or bounces along the ground. Also called **grounder.** Cf. **fly ball.** [1830–40, in cricket; 1855–60, *Amer.* in baseball use]

ground′ bass′ (bās), *Music.* a short fundamental bass part continually repeated throughout a movement. [1690–1700]

ground′ beam′, **1.** a reinforced concrete beam for supporting walls, joists, etc., at or near ground level, itself either resting directly upon the ground or supported at both ends by piers. **2.** groundsill.

ground′ bee′tle, any of numerous nocturnal, terrestrial beetles of the family Carabidae that feed chiefly on other insects. [1840–50]

ground·break·er (ground′brā′kər), *n.* **1.** a person who is an originator, innovator, or pioneer in a particular activity. **2.** an original idea, product, or the like that leads to or makes possible further developments, growth, improvements, etc. [GROUND[1] + BREAKER[1]]

ground·break·ing (ground′brā′king), *n.* **1.** the act or ceremony of breaking ground for a new construction project. —*adj.* **2.** of or pertaining to such a ceremony. **3.** originating or pioneering a new endeavor, field of inquiry, or the like: *Pasteur's groundbreaking work in bacteriology.* [1905–10; GROUND[1] + BREAK + -ING[1], -ING[2]]

ground′ ca′ble, *Naut.* a heavy chain for securing permanent floating moorings, as a number of mooring buoys. [1785–95]

ground′ ce′dar, a ground pine, *Lycopodium complanatum.* [1830–40, *Amer.*]

ground′ cher′ry, 1. Also called **husk tomato.** any of several plants belonging to the genus *Physalis,* of the nightshade family, the several species bearing an edible berry enclosed in an enlarged calyx. **2.** any of several European dwarf cherries, esp. *Prunus fruticosa,* of the rose family. **3.** the fruit of any of these plants. [1595–1605]

ground′ cloth′, 1. groundsheet. **2.** a covering, usually of canvas, for the floor of a stage. [1915–20]

ground′ col′or, 1. Also called **ground′ coat′.** a primary coat of paint; priming; base coat. **2.** the background color, as of a painting or decoration. [1605–15]

ground′ connec′tion, *Elect.* the conductor used to establish a ground. Also called **grounding connection.**

ground′ control′, an airport facility that supervises the movement of aircraft and ground vehicles on ramps and taxiways. [1930–35] —**ground′ control′ler.**

ground′-con·trolled approach′ (ground′kən-trōld′), *Aeron.* a system in which an observer interprets radar observations of the position of an aircraft and transmits continuous instructions to its pilot for landing. *Abbr.:* GCA Also, **ground′-con·trol′ approach′.** [1940–45]

ground′ cov′er, 1. the herbaceous plants and low shrubs in a forest, considered as a whole. **2.** any of a variety of low-growing or trailing plants used to cover the ground in areas where grass is difficult to grow, as in dense shade or on steep slopes. Also, **ground′cov′er.** [1895–1900]

ground′ crew′, ground personnel responsible for the maintenance and repair of aircraft. [1930–35]

ground′ dove′, any of several small terrestrial doves of the warmer parts of the Americas, esp. *Columbina passerina.* Also, **ground′-dove′.** [1720–30, *Amer.*]

ground′-ef·fect machine′ (ground′i fekt′). See **ACV** (def. 2). [1965–70]

ground·er (groun′dər), *n. Baseball.* See **ground ball.** [1865–70, *Amer.;* GROUND[1] + -ER[1]]

ground′ fault′, the momentary, usually accidental, grounding of a conducting wire. —**ground′-fault′,** *adj.*

ground′-fault interrupt′er, a circuit breaker that senses currents caused by ground faults and quickly shuts off power before damage can occur to generating equipment.

ground·fire (ground′fīər′), *n.* small arms fire directed against aircraft from the ground. [GROUND[1] + FIRE]

ground′ fish′. See **bottom fish.** [1855–60]

ground-fish (ground′fish′), *v.i.* bottom-fish.

ground′ floor′, 1. the floor of a building at or nearest to ground level. **2.** *Informal.* an advantageous position or opportunity in a business matter, esp. in a new enterprise: *She took the job in the new company because she wanted to get in on the ground floor.* [1595–1605]

ground′ fog′, 1. a low, often dense fog, esp. one through which the sky and clouds above can be seen. **2.** See **radiation fog.**

ground′ glass′, 1. *Optics.* glass that has had its polished surface removed by fine grinding and that is used to diffuse light. **2.** glass that has been ground into fine particles, esp. for use as an abrasive. [1840–50]

ground′ hem′lock, a prostrate yew, *Taxus canadensis,* of eastern North America, having short, flat needles and red, berrylike fruit. [1825–35, *Amer.*]

ground·hog (ground′hog′, -hôg), *n.* woodchuck. Also, **ground′ hog′.** [1650–60, *Amer.;* GROUND[1] + HOG]

Ground′hog Day′, February 2, in most parts of the U.S., the day on which, according to legend, the ground-

CONCISE PRONUNCIATION KEY: *act, cāpe, dâre, pärt; set, ēqual; if, ice; ox, ōver, ôrder, oil, bŏŏk, bōōt, out; up, ûrge; child; sing; shoe; thin, that;* zh as in *treasure.* ə = *a* as in *alone, e* as in *system, i* as in *easily, o* as in *gallop, u* as in *circus;* ᵊ as in *fire* (fīᵊr), *hour* (ouᵊr). l and n can serve as syllabic consonants, as in *cradle* (krād′l), and *button* (but′n). See the full key inside the front cover.

hog first emerges from hibernation. If it is a sunny day and the groundhog sees its shadow, six more weeks of wintry weather are predicted. [1870–75, *Amer.*]

ground′ ice′. See **anchor ice.** [1685–95]

ground′ing connec′tion, *Elect.* See **ground connection.**

ground′ itch′, a disease of the skin of the feet, caused by penetration of hookworm larvae, characterized by a blisterlike eruption and itching. [1815–25, *Amer.*]

ground′ i′vy, a creeping, aromatic plant, *Glechoma hederacea,* of the mint family, having rounded leaves and whorling clusters of small blue flowers. Also called **gill-over-the-ground.** [1300–50; ME]

ground•keep•er (ground′kē′pər), *n.* groundskeeper. [1875–80; GROUND[1] + KEEPER]

ground′ land′lord, *Chiefly Brit.* a landlord who receives ground rent. [1710–20]

ground′ lay′er. See **surface boundary layer.**

ground•less (ground′lis), *adj.* without rational basis: *groundless fears.* [bef. 900; ME: bottomless, unfathomable; OE *grundlēas.* See GROUND[1], -LESS] **—ground′less•ly,** *adv.* **—ground′less•ness,** *n.*
—Syn. baseless, unfounded, unjustified, idle.

ground′ lev′el, *Physics.* See **ground state.** [1920–25]

ground•ling (ground′ling), *n.* **1.** a plant or animal that lives on or close to the ground. **2.** any of various fishes that live at the bottom of the water. **3.** a spectator, reader, or other person of unsophisticated or uncultivated tastes; an uncritical or uncultured person. **4.** a member of a theater audience who sits in one of the cheaper seats. [1595–1605; GROUND[1] + -LING[1]]

ground′ log′, *Naut.* a lead weight attached to a line, cast overboard in shoal water and allowed to pay out freely to show the speed of a ship and the force of the current.

ground′ loop′, *Aeron.* a sharp horizontal loop performed, usually involuntarily, while touching the ground. [1920–25]

ground•mass (ground′mas′), *n.* the crystalline, granular, or glassy base or matrix of a porphyritic or other igneous rock, in which the more prominent crystals are embedded. [1875–80; GROUND[1] + MASS]

ground′ mer′istem, *Bot.* an area of primary meristematic tissue, emerging from and immediately behind the apical meristem, that develops into the pith and the cortex. [1935–40]

ground•nut (ground′nut′), *n.* **1.** Also called **wild bean, potato bean.** a twining, North American plant, *Apios americana* (or *A. tuberosa*), of the legume family, having clusters of fragrant brownish flowers and an edible tuber. **2.** any of several other plants having edible underground parts, as the peanut. **3.** *South Atlantic U.S.* peanut. [1595–1605; GROUND[1] + NUT]

ground′ observ′er, a person stationed in a position on the ground to watch, follow, and report on flights of aircraft, esp. of enemy aircraft.

ground•out (ground′out′), *n. Baseball.* a play in which a batter is put out at first base after hitting a ground ball to the infield. [1960–65; n. use of v. phrase *ground out*]

ground′ owl′, the burrowing owl. [1910–15, *Amer.*]

ground′ pea′, *South Atlantic U.S.* peanut. [1760–70]

ground′ pine′, **1.** any of several species of club moss, esp. *Lycopodium obscurum* or *L. complanatum.* **2.** a European herb, *Ajuga chamaepitys,* of the mint family, having a resinous odor. [1545–55]

ground′ pink′, a plant, *Linanthus dianthiflorus,* of southern California, having pink or white flowers.

ground′ plan′, **1.** Also called **groundplot.** the plan of a floor of a building. **2.** first or fundamental plan. [1725–35]

ground′ plane′, **1.** (in perspective drawing) the theoretical horizontal plane receding from the picture plane to the horizon, beginning at the level of the base line. **2.** *Elect.* a ground plate or an underground mesh of radial wires connected to a vertical antenna **(ground′ plane′ anten′na)** that is grounded in order to provide suitable radiation characteristics. [1825–35]

ground′ plate′, **1.** *Elect.* a metal plate for making a ground connection to the earth. **2.** *Building Trades.* groundsill. [1655–65]

ground•plot (ground′plot′), *n.* **1.** *Aeron.* a method for obtaining the position of an aircraft by multiplying its groundspeed by its time in flight and marking off the product with respect to its starting position. **2.** See **ground plan** (def. 1). [1570–80; GROUND[1] + PLOT]

ground′ plum′, **1.** a prostrate milk vetch, *Astragalus crassicarpus,* of the legume family, growing in the prairie regions of North America. **2.** its plum-shaped fruit. [1855–60, *Amer.*]

ground′ rent′, the rent at which land is let to a tenant either for a long term or perpetually. [1660–70]

ground′ rob′in, towhee. [1785–95, *Amer.*]

ground′ rod′, a metal rod embedded in the ground to make a ground connection to the earth.

ground′ row′, a long, low piece of stage scenery, built to simulate part of a landscape, a building, a fence, or the like. [1785–95, *Amer.*]

ground′ rule′, **1.** Usually, **ground rules.** basic or governing principles of conduct in any situation or field of endeavor: *the ground rules of press conferences.* **2.** *Sports.* any of certain rules specially adopted, as in baseball and softball, for dealing with situations or circumstances arising chiefly from the particular nature of the playing area or the interference of spectators. [1885–90, *Amer.*]

ground′ rule′ dou′ble, *Baseball.* a safe hit ruled for two bases according to the rules of a particular stadium, as when a fly ball bounces once in the outfield and then clears a fence. [1945–50, *Amer.*]

ground•sel[1] (ground′səl), *n.* any composite plant of the genus *Senecio,* esp. *S. vulgaris,* a common weed having clusters of small yellow disk flowers without rays. [bef. 900; ME *grundeswili(e), groundeswel,* OE *grundeswelge, gundeswelge;* cf. OE *gund* pus, *swelgan* to swallow, absorb (from its use in medicine); the *-r-* is by folk etymology from assoc. with GROUND[1]]

ground•sel[2] (ground′səl), *n.* groundsill.

ground′sel tree′, a composite shrub, *Baccharis halimifolia,* having dull, gray-green leaves and fruit with tufts of long, white hair, growing in salt marshes of eastern North America. Also called **consumption weed.** [1735–45]

ground′ shark′, any of various requiem sharks, esp. of the genus *Carcharhinus.* [1810–20]

ground•sheet (ground′shēt′), *n.* a waterproof sheet of plastic, canvas, or other durable material spread on the ground, as under a sleeping bag or in a tent, for protection against moisture. Also called **ground cloth.** [1905–10; GROUND[1] + SHEET[1]]

ground•sill (ground′sil′), *n.* the lowermost sill of a framed structure, esp. one lying close to the ground. Also, **groundsel.** Also called **ground beam, ground plate.** [1400–50; late ME *grownsel.* See GROUND[1], SILL]

grounds•keep•er (groundz′kē′pər), *n.* **1.** a person who is responsible for the care and maintenance of a particular tract of land, as an estate, a park, or a cemetery. **2.** a person in charge of maintaining a football field, baseball diamond, etc. Also, **groundkeeper.** [GROUNDS + KEEPER] **—grounds′keep′ing,** *n.*

ground′ sloth′, any of various extinct large, edentate mammals from the Pleistocene Epoch of North and South America resembling modern sloths but living on the ground rather than in trees. [1855–60]

ground′ sluice′, *Mining.* a trench, cut through a placer or through bedrock, through which a stream is diverted in order to dislodge and wash the gravel. [1865–70] **—ground′-sluic′er,** *n.*

ground•speed (ground′spēd′), *n.* the speed of an aircraft with reference to the ground. Also, **ground′ speed′.** [1915–20; GROUND[1] + SPEED]

ground′ squir′rel, any of several terrestrial rodents of the squirrel family, as of the genus *Citellus* and chipmunks of the genus *Tamias.* [1680–90, *Amer.*]

ground′ state′, *Physics.* the state of least energy of a particle, as an atom, or of a system of particles. Also called **ground level.** [1925–30]

ground′ sta′tion. See **earth station.**

ground′ stroke′, *Tennis.* a stroke made by hitting the ball after it has bounced from the ground. Cf. **volley** (def. 4b). [1890–95]

ground′ sub′stance, *Biol.* **1.** Also called **matrix.** the homogeneous substance in which the fibers and cells of connective tissue are embedded. **2.** Also called **hyaloplasm.** the clear portion of the cell cytoplasm; cytosol. [1880–85]

ground•swell (ground′swel′), *n.* **1.** a broad, deep swell or rolling of the sea, due to a distant storm or gale. **2.** any surge of support, approval, or enthusiasm, esp. among the general public: *a groundswell of political support for the governor.* [1810–20; GROUND[1] + SWELL]

ground′ tack′le, *Naut.* equipment, as anchors, chains, or windlasses, for mooring a vessel away from a pier or other fixed moorings. [1550–60]

ground-to-air (ground′to͞o âr′), *adj., adv.* surface-to-air. [1915–20]

ground-to-ground (ground′tə ground′), *adj., adv.* surface-to-surface. [1915–20]

ground′ track′, the path on the earth's surface below an aircraft, missile, rocket, or spacecraft. [1975–80]

ground′ wa′ter, the water beneath the surface of the ground, consisting largely of surface water that has seeped down: the source of water in springs and wells. Also, **ground′wa′ter.** [1885–90]

ground′ wave′, a radio wave that propagates on or near the earth's surface and is affected by the ground and the troposphere. [1925–30]

ground′ ways′, *Shipbuilding.* hardwood timbers laid end-to-end to form an inclined track on which the keel of a ship can slide during launching. [1705–15]

ground′ wire′, *Elect.* a lead from an electric apparatus to the earth or to a ground connection. [1890–95]

ground•wood (ground′wo͝od′), *n. Papermaking.* wood that has been ground for making into pulp. [1915–20; GROUND[2] + WOOD[1]]

ground′wood pulp′, wood pulp consisting of groundwood that has not been cooked or chemically treated, used for making newsprint and other poorer grades of paper. Also called **mechanical pulp.** Cf. **chemical pulp.**

ground•work (ground′wûrk′), *n.* foundation or basis: *He laid the groundwork for an international conference.* [1540–50; GROUND[1] + WORK]

ground′ ze′ro, **1.** the point on the surface of the earth or water directly below, directly above, or at which an atomic or hydrogen bomb explodes. **2.** *Informal.* the very beginning or most elementary level: *Some of the students are starting from ground zero.* [1945–50]

group (gro͞op), *n.* **1.** any collection or assemblage of persons or things; cluster; aggregation: *a group of protesters; a remarkable group of paintings.* **2.** a number of persons or things ranged or considered together as being related in some way. **3.** Also called **radical.** *Chem.* two or more atoms specifically arranged, as the hydroxyl group, –OH. Cf. **free radical.** **4.** *Ling.* **a.** (in the classification of related languages within a family) a category of a lower order than a subbranch and of a higher order than a subgroup: *the Low German group of West Germanic languages.* **b.** any grouping of languages, whether it is made on the basis of geography, genetic relationship, or something else. **5.** *Geol.* a division of stratified rocks comprising two or more formations. **6.** *Mil.* **a.** *Army.* a flexible administrative and tactical unit consisting of two or more battalions and a headquarters. **b.** *Air Force.* an administrative and operational unit subordinate to a wing, usually composed of two or more squadrons. **7.** *Music.* a section of an orchestra comprising the instruments of the same class. **8.** *Art.* a number of figures or objects shown in an arrangement together. **9.** *Math.* an algebraic system that is closed under an associative operation, as multiplication or addition, and in which there is an identity element that, on operating on another element, leaves the second element unchanged, and in which each element has corresponding to it a unique element that, on operating on the first, results in the identity element. **10.** *Gram. Chiefly Brit.* a phrase: *nominal group; verbal group.* **—*v.t.*** **11.** to place or associate together in a group, as with others. **12.** to arrange in or form into a group or groups. **—*v.i.*** **13.** to form a group. **14.** to be part of a group. [1665–75; < F *groupe* < It *gruppo* << Gmc] **—group′wise′,** *adv.*
—Syn. 12. order, organize, classify, combine.
—Usage. 1, 2. See **collective noun.**

group′ annu′ity, *Insurance.* a plan in which the members of a group, usually employees of the same company, receive annuities upon retirement.

group′ dynam′ics, **1.** the interactions that influence the attitudes and behavior of people when they are grouped with others through either choice or accidental circumstances. **2.** the study of such interactions. [1940–45]

group•er[1] (gro͞o′pər), *n., pl.* (*esp. collectively*) **-er,** (*esp. referring to two or more kinds or species*), **-ers.** any of various sea basses of the family Serranidae, esp. of the genera *Epinephelus* and *Mycteroperca,* of tropical and subtropical seas. [1680–90; < Pg *garupa,* of uncert. orig.]

group•er[2] (gro͞o′pər), *n.* **1.** a member of a group, as of tourists. **2.** *Slang.* a member of a group of usually young and single persons who rent and share a house or apartment, as at a summer resort. [1930–35; GROUP + -ER[1]]

group′ gen′itive, (in English) a construction in which the genitive ending *'s* is added to an entire phrase, esp. when added to a word other than the head of the noun phrase, as *the woman who lives across the street's* in *That is the woman who lives across the street's cat* or *the people next-door's* in *The people next-door's house is for rent.* Also called **group′ posses′sive.** [1890–95]

group′ grope′, *Slang.* sexual activity involving several people; orgy. [1965–70]

group′ home′, a substitute home, usually located in a residential neighborhood, providing foster care for orphans, delinquents, handicapped persons, or others with special needs.

group•ie (gro͞o′pē), *n. Informal.* **1.** a young person, esp. a teenage girl, who is an ardent admirer of rock musicians and may follow them on tour. **2.** an ardent fan of a celebrity or of a particular activity: *a tennis groupie.* [1965–70; GROUP + -IE]

group•ing (gro͞o′ping), *n.* **1.** an act or process of placing in groups. **2.** a set or arrangement of persons or things in a group. [1740–50; See GROUP, -ING[1], -ING[2]]

group′ insur′ance, life, accident, or health insurance available to a group of persons, as the employees of a company, under a single contract, usually without regard to physical condition or age of the individuals. [1910–15]

group•ism (gro͞o′piz əm), *n.* the tendency to conform to the general thinking and behavior of a group. [1930–35; GROUP + -ISM]

group′ life′ insur′ance, a form of life insurance available to members of a group, typically employees of a company, under a master policy. Also called **group′ life′.** [1925–30]

group′ mar′riage, (among primitive peoples) a form of marriage in which a group of males is united with a group of females to form a single conjugal unit. Also called **communal marriage.** [1895–1900]

group•oid (gro͞o′poid), *n. Math.* an algebraic system closed under a binary operation. Also called **monoid.** Cf. **group** (def. 9), **semigroup.** [GROUP + -OID]

group′ prac′tice, **1.** Also called **group′ med′icine.** the practice of medicine by an association of physicians and other health professionals who work together, usually in one suite of offices. **2.** any similar practice by an association of professional persons. **3.** *Law.* a system in which legal services are provided by a corporation retaining and paying a number of lawyers. [1940–45]

group′ representa′tion, *Govt.* representation in a governing body on the basis of interests rather than by geographical location.

group′ the′ory, the branch of mathematics that deals with the structure of mathematical groups and mappings between them. [1895–1900]

group′ ther′apy, psychotherapy in which a number of patients discuss their problems together, usually under the leadership of a therapist, using shared knowledge and experiences to provide constructive feedback about maladaptive behavior. [1940–45]

group•think (gro͞op′thingk′), *n.* **1.** the practice of approaching problems or issues as matters that are best dealt with by consensus of a group rather than by individuals acting independently; conformity. **2.** the lack of individual creativity, or of a sense of personal responsibility, that is sometimes characteristic of group interaction. [1950–55; GROUP + THINK[1], on the model of DOUBLETHINK]

group′ veloc′ity, *Physics.* the velocity of finite numbers of waves undergoing simple harmonic motion, equal to the phase velocity when it does not vary with the wavelengths of the waves. The group velocity of the set of waves produced in water when a stone is dropped is less than the velocity of the individual waves. [1885–90]

group′ work′, *Sociol.* a method, used by professional social workers, of aiding a group or members of a group toward individual adjustment and increased participation in community activity by exploiting the mechanisms of group life. [1940–45]

grouse[1] (grous), *n., pl.* **grouse, grous•es. 1.** any of numerous gallinaceous birds of the subfamily Tetraoninae. Cf. **black grouse, capercaillie, ruffed grouse, spruce grouse. 2.** *Brit.* the red grouse. [1525–35; orig. uncert.] **—grouse′less,** *adj.* **—grouse′like′,** *adj.*

ruffed grouse, *Bonasa umbellus,* length 18 in. (46 cm)

grouse[2] (grous), *v.,* **groused, grous•ing,** *n. Informal.* —*v.i.* **1.** to grumble; complain: *I've never met anyone who grouses so much about his work.* —*n.* **2.** a complaint. [1850–55; orig. uncert.; cf. GROUCH] **—grous′er,** *n.*
—Syn. 1. gripe, fret, fuss.

grouse[3] (grous), *adj. Australian Slang.* excellent; great; wonderful. [1940–45; orig. uncert.]

grout (grout), *n.* **1.** a thin, coarse mortar poured into various narrow cavities, as masonry joints or rock fissures, to fill them and consolidate the adjoining objects into a solid mass. **2.** a coat of plaster for finishing a ceiling or interior wall. **3.** Usually, **grouts.** lees; grounds. **4.** *Archaic.* **a.** coarse meal or porridge. **b. grouts,** groats. —*v.t.* **5.** to fill or consolidate with grout. **6.** to use as grout. [bef. 1150; ME; OE *grūt;* see GRITS, GROATS, GRIT] **—grout′er,** *n.*

grout′ box′, a conical object of expanded metal, buried in poured concrete with an anchor bolt held in its inner and smaller end.

grout′lock brick′ (grout′lok′), a brick chamfered on its inner angles to allow space for vertical and horizontal reinforcing rods sealed in grout. [GROUT + LOCK[1]]

grout•y (grou′tē), *adj.,* **grout•i•er, grout•i•est.** sulky; surly; bad-tempered. [1825–35; *grout* to grumble, sulk, of uncert. orig. (cf. GROUSE[2], GROUCH) + -Y[1]]

grove (grōv), *n.* **1.** a small wood or forested area, usually with no undergrowth: *a grove of pines.* **2.** a small orchard or stand of fruit-bearing trees, esp. citrus trees: *a grove of lemon trees.* [bef. 900; ME; OE *grāf*] **—groved,** *adj.* **—grove′less,** *adj.*
—Syn. 1. See **forest.**

Grove (grōv), *n.* **1. Sir George,** 1820–1900, English musicologist. **2. Robert Moses** (*"Lefty"*), 1900–75, U.S. baseball player.

Grove′ Cit′y, a town in central Ohio. 16,793.

grov•el (gruv′əl, grov′-), *v.i.,* **-eled, -el•ing** or (*esp. Brit.*) **-elled, -el•ling. 1.** to humble oneself or act in an abject manner, as in great fear or utter servility. **2.** to lie or crawl with the face downward and the body prostrate, esp. in abject humility, fear, etc. **3.** to take pleasure in mean or base things. [1585–95; back formation from obs. *groveling* (adv.), equiv. to obs. *grufe* face down (< ON *ā grūfu* face down) + -LING[2], taken to be prp.] **—grov′el•er;** *esp. Brit.,* **grov′el•ler,** *n.* **—grov′el•ing•ly;** *esp. Brit.,* **grov′el•ling•ly,** *adv.*
—Syn. 1. truckle, toady, fawn, kowtow, pander.

Gro•ver (grō′vər), *n.* a male given name.

Groves (grōvz), *n.* **1. Leslie Richard,** 1896–1970, U.S. general. **2.** a city in SE Texas. 17,090.

grow (grō), *v.,* **grew, grown, grow•ing.** —*v.i.* **1.** to increase by natural development, as any living organism or part by assimilation of nutriment; increase in size or substance. **2.** to form and increase in size by a process of inorganic accretion, as by crystallization. **3.** to arise or issue as a natural development from an original happening, circumstance, or source: *Our friendship grew from common interests.* **4.** to increase gradually in size, amount, etc.; become greater or larger; expand: *His influence has grown.* **5.** to become gradually attached or united by or as if by growth: *The branches of the trees grew together, forming a natural arch.* **6.** to come to be by degrees; become: *to grow old.* **7.** *Naut.* to lie or extend in a certain direction, as an anchor cable. —*v.t.* **8.** to cause to grow: *They grow corn.* **9.** to allow to grow: *to grow a beard.* **10.** to cover with a growth (used in the passive): *a field grown with corn.* **11. grow into, a.** to become large enough for: *He'll grow into his brother's suits before long.* **b.** to become mature or experienced enough for: *She grew into the job, although she wasn't qualified for it at first.* **12. grow on** or **upon, a.** to increase in influence or effect. **b.** to become gradually more liked or accepted by: *He didn't like tofu at first, but eventually it grew on him.* **13. grow out of, a.** to become too large or mature for; outgrow: *He has grown out of all his clothes.* **b.** to originate in; develop from: *The plan grew out of a casual conversation.* **14. grow up, a.** to be or become fully grown; attain mental or physical maturity. **b.** to come into existence; arise: *New cities grew up in the desert.* [bef. 900; ME *growen,* OE *grōwan;* c. D *groeien,* OHG *grouwan,* ON *grōa*] **—grow′a•ble,** *adj.*
—Syn. 1. develop, multiply, swell, enlarge, expand, extend. **3.** originate. **4.** wax. **8.** raise, cultivate, produce. **—Ant. 1.** decrease. **4.** wane.

Grow (grō), *n.* **Ga•lu•sha Aaron** (gə lo͞o′shə), 1822–1907, U.S. political leader: Speaker of the House 1861–63.

grow•an (grō′ən, grou′-), *n.* decomposed granite. [1745–55; < Cornish **growan* (c. Breton *grouan*), deriv. of *grou* gravel]

growed (grōd), *v. Nonstandard.* a pt. and pp. of **grow.**

grow•er (grō′ər), *n.* **1.** a person who grows something: *He is a grower of flowers and vegetables.* **2.** a person or thing that grows in a certain way: *This plant is a quick grower.* [1555–65; GROW + -ER[1]]

grow•ing (grō′ing), *adj.* **1.** becoming greater in quantity, size, extent, or intensity: *growing discontent among industrial workers.* **2.** having or showing life. [bef. 900; ME; OE *growende.* See GROW, -ING[2]] **—grow′ing•ly,** *adv.*

grow′ing degree′-day, a degree-day above 41°F (5°C), used in relation to plant growth. Cf. **cooling degree-day, heating degree-day.**

grow′ing-eq′ui•ty mort′gage (grō′ing ek′wi tē), a type of mortgage under which the interest rate is fixed but monthly payments increase annually to include more of the principal, so that the mortgage can be paid off in about half the conventional term.

grow′ing pains′, 1. dull, quasi-rheumatic pains of varying degree in the limbs during childhood and adolescence, often popularly associated with the process of growing. **2.** emotional difficulties experienced during adolescence and preadulthood. **3.** difficulties attending any new project or any rapid development of an existing project: *a city plagued with growing pains.* [1800–10]

grow′ing point′, *Bot.* the undifferentiated end of a root, shoot, or vegetative axis consisting of a single cell or group of cells that divide to form primary meristematic tissue. [1825–35]

growl (groul), *v.i.* **1.** to utter a deep guttural sound of anger or hostility: *The dog growled at the mail carrier.* **2.** to murmur or complain angrily; grumble. **3.** to rumble: *The thunder growled.* **4.** *Jazz.* to use flutter-tonguing in playing a wind instrument. —*v.t.* **5.** to express by growling. —*n.* **6.** the act or sound of growling. **7.** *Jazz.* the technique of flutter-tonguing. [1350–1400; ME *groule* to rumble (said of the bowels); c. G *grollen*] **—growl′ing•ly,** *adv.*
—Syn. 2. See **complain.**

growl•er (grou′lər), *n.* **1.** a person or thing that growls. **2.** *Informal.* a pitcher, pail, or other container brought by a customer for beer. **3.** *Brit. Slang.* a four-wheeled, horse-drawn carriage. **4.** *Elect.* an electromagnetic device consisting of two field poles, used for indicating short-circuited coils in armatures and for magnetizing or demagnetizing objects. **5.** an iceberg large enough to be a navigational hazard. [1745–55; GROWL + -ER[1]]

grow′ light′, a fluorescent light bulb designed to emit light of a wavelength conducive to plant growth.

growl•y (grou′lē), *adj.,* **growl•i•er, growl•i•est. 1.** resembling a growl in pitch and harshness: *This cold has made my voice growly.* **2.** irritable; grouchy. [1915–20; GROWL + -Y[1]] **—growl•i•ness,** *n.*

grown (grōn), *adj.* **1.** advanced in growth: *a grown boy.* **2.** arrived at full growth or maturity; adult: *a grown man.* —*v.* **3.** pp. of **grow.**

grown-up (grōn′up′), *adj.* **1.** having reached the age of maturity. **2.** characteristic of or suitable for adults: *grown-up behavior; grown-up fiction.* [1625–35; adj. use of v. phrase *grow up*] **—grown′-up′ness,** *n.*

grown•up (grōn′up′), *n.* a mature, fully grown person; adult. [1805–15; n. use of v. phrase *grow up*]

growth (grōth), *n.* **1.** the act or process, or a manner of growing; development; gradual increase. **2.** size or stage of development: *It hasn't yet reached its full growth.* **3.** completed development. **4.** development from a simpler to a more complex stage: *the growth of ritual forms.* **5.** development from another but related form or stage: *the growth of the nation state.* **6.** something that has grown or developed by or as if by a natural process: *a growth of stubborn weeds.* **7.** *Pathol.* an abnormal increase in a mass of tissue, as a tumor. **8.** origin; source; production: *onions of English growth.* —*adj.* **9.** of or denoting a business, industry, or equity security that grows or is expected to grow in value over a long period of time: *a growth industry; a growth stock.* [1550–60; see GROW, -TH[1]; prob. c. ON *grōthr*]
—Syn. 1. augmentation, expansion. **6.** result, outgrowth. **7.** excrescence. **—Ant. 1.** decline, decrease.

growth′ cone′, *Cell Biol.* a flattened area at the end of a growing axon or dendrite, having thin radiating pseudopods that function as guides for the outgrowth of embryonic nerve fibers.

growth′ fac′tor, any of various proteins that promote the growth, organization, and maintenance of cells and tissues.

growth′ fund′, a mutual fund that invests primarily in growth stocks. [1965–70]

growth′ hor′mone, any substance that stimulates or controls the growth of an organism, esp. a species-specific hormone, as the human hormone somatotropin, secreted by the anterior pituitary gland. *Abbr.:* GH [1920–25]

growth′ hor′mone releas′ing fac′tor, *Biochem.* a substance produced in the hypothalamus that regulates the release of growth hormone by the anterior pituitary gland. *Abbr.:* GRF

growth′ ring′. See **annual ring.** [1905–10]

groyne (groin), *n.* groin (def. 4).

groz′ing i′ron (grō′zing), **1.** (in plumbing) a hot iron for finishing soldered joints. **2.** a steel tool for cutting glass. [1680–90; part trans. of D *gruisijzer,* equiv. to *gruis-* (s. of *gruizen* to crush, deriv. of *gruis* grit) + *ijzer* IRON]

Groz•ny (grôz′nē; *Russ.* grô′znē), *n.* a city in and the capital of the Chechen-Ingush Autonomous Republic of the Russian Federation in Europe. 401,000.

GRU, (in the Soviet Union) the Chief Intelligence Directorate of the Soviet General Staff, a military intelligence organization founded in 1920 and functioning as a complement to the KGB. Also, **G.R.U.** [< Russ, for *Glávnoe razvédyvatel'noe upravlénie*]

grub (grub), *n., v.,* **grubbed, grub•bing.** —*n.* **1.** the thick-bodied, sluggish larva of several insects, as of a scarab beetle. **2.** a dull, plodding person; drudge. **3.** an unkempt person. **4.** *Slang.* food; victuals. **5.** any remaining roots or stumps after cutting vegetation to clear land for farming. —*v.t.* **6.** to dig; clear of roots, stumps, etc. **7.** to dig up by the roots; uproot (often fol. by *up* or *out*). **8.** *Slang.* to supply with food; feed. **9.** *Slang.* to scrounge: *to grub a cigarette.* —*v.i.* **10.** to dig; search by or as if by digging: *We grubbed through piles of old junk to find the deed.* **11.** to lead a laborious or groveling life; drudge: *It's wonderful to have money after having to grub for so many years.* **12.** to engage in laborious study. **13.** *Slang.* to eat; take food. [1250–1300; ME *grubbe* (n.), *grubben* (v.); akin to OHG *grubilōn* to dig, G *grübeln* to rack (the brain), ON *gryfia* hole, pit; see GRAVE[1], GROOVE] **—grub′ber,** *n.*

grub′ beam′, *Shipbuilding.* a curved, laminated wooden beam forming part of a rounded stern.

grub•by[1] (grub′ē), *adj.,* **-bi•er, -bi•est. 1.** dirty; slovenly: *children with grubby faces and sad eyes.* **2.** infested with or affected by grubs or larvae. **3.** contemptible: *grubby political tricks.* [1605–15; GRUB + -Y[1]] **—grub′bi•ly,** *adv.* **—grub′bi•ness,** *n.*
—Syn. 1. grimy, unkempt, messy, filthy, bedraggled.

grub•by[2] (grub′ē), *n., pl.* **-bies.** a small sculpin, *Myxocephalus aenaeus,* inhabiting waters off the coast of New England. [orig. uncert.]

grub′ hoe′, a heavy hoe for digging up roots, stumps, etc.

grub′ saw′, a handsaw for cutting stone. [1850–55]

grub•stake (grub′stāk′), *n., v.,* **-staked, -stak•ing.** —*n.* **1.** provisions, gear, etc., furnished to a prospector on condition of participating in the profits of any discoveries. **2.** money or other assistance furnished at a time of need or of starting an enterprise. —*v.t.* **3.** to furnish with a grubstake: *I grubstaked him to two mules and supplies enough for five months.* [1860–65, *Amer.*; GRUB + STAKE[2]] **—grub′stak′er,** *n.*

Grub′ Street′, 1. a street in London, England: formerly inhabited by many impoverished minor writers and literary hacks; now called Milton Street. **2.** petty and needy authors, or literary hacks, collectively.

grub•street (grub′strēt′), *adj.* **1.** produced by a hack; poor in quality: *a grubstreet book.* —*n.* **2.** See **Grub Street** (def. 2). [1640–50]

grub•worm (grub′wûrm′), *n.* grub (def. 1). [1745–55; GRUB + WORM]

grudge (gruj), *n., adj., v.,* **grudged, grudg•ing.** —*n.* **1.** a feeling of ill will or resentment: *to hold a grudge against a former opponent.* —*adj.* **2.** done, arranged, etc., in order to settle a grudge: *The middleweight fight was said to be a grudge match.* —*v.t.* **3.** to give or permit with reluctance; submit to unwillingly: *The other team grudged us every point we scored.* **4.** to resent the good fortune of (another); begrudge. —*v.i.* **5.** *Obs.* to feel dissatisfaction or ill will. [1400–50; late ME *grudgen, gruggen,* var. of *gruchen* < OF *gro(u)c(h)ier* < Gmc.; cf. MHG *grogezen* to complain, cry out] **—grudge′less,** *adj.* **—grudg′er,** *n.*
—Syn. 1. bitterness, rancor, malevolence, enmity, hatred. GRUDGE, MALICE, SPITE refer to ill will held against another or others. A GRUDGE is a feeling of resentment harbored because of some real or fancied wrong: *to hold a grudge because of jealousy; She has a grudge against him.* MALICE is the state of mind that delights in doing harm, or seeing harm done, to others, whether expressing itself in an attempt seriously to injure or merely in sardonic humor: *malice in watching someone's embarrassment; to tell lies about someone out of malice.* SPITE is petty, and often sudden, resentment that manifests itself usually in trifling retaliations: *to reveal a secret out of spite.* **4.** envy.

grudg•ing (gruj′ing), *adj.* displaying or reflecting reluctance or unwillingness: *grudging acceptance of the victory of an opponent.* [1375–1425; late ME. See GRUDGE, -ING[2]] **—grudg′ing•ly,** *adv.*

grue (gro͞o), *v.i.,* **grued, gru•ing.** *Chiefly Scot.* to shudder. [1275–1325; ME]

gru•el (gro͞o′əl), *n.* a light, usually thin, cooked cereal made by boiling meal, esp. oatmeal, in water or milk. [1275–1325; ME < MF, OF, equiv. to *gru-* (< Gmc; see GROUT) + *-el* dim. suffix]

gru•el•ing (gro͞o′ə ling, gro͞o′ling), *adj.* **1.** exhausting; very tiring; arduously severe: *the grueling Boston marathon.* —*n.* **2.** any trying or exhausting procedure or experience. Also, *esp. Brit.,* **gru′el•ling.** [1850–55; slang *gruel* punishment (n.), punish (v.) + -ING[2], -ING[1]] **—gru′el•ing•ly,** *adv.*

Gru•en•berg (gro͞o′ən bûrg′), *n.* **Louis,** 1884–1964, U.S. pianist and composer, born in Russia.

grue•some (gro͞o′səm), *adj.* **1.** causing great horror;

CONCISE PRONUNCIATION KEY: act, cāpe, dâre, pärt; set, ēqual; if, ice; ox, ōver, ôrder, oil, bo͝ok, bo͞ot, out; up, ûrge; child; sing; shoe; thin, *th*at; zh as in *treasure.* ə = *a* as in *alone, e* as in *system, i* as in *easily, o* as in *gallop, u* as in *circus;* ᵊ as in *fire* (fīᵊr), *hour* (ouᵊr). l and n can serve as syllabic consonants, as in *cradle* (krād′l), and *button* (but′n). See the full key inside the front cover.

horribly repugnant; grisly: *the site of a gruesome murder.* **2.** full of or causing problems; distressing: *a gruesome day at the office.* Also, **grewsome.** [1560–70; obs. *grue* to shudder (c. G *grauen,* D *gruwen*) + -SOME[1]] —**grue′some·ly,** *adv.* —**grue′some·ness,** *n.*

gruff (gruf), *adj.,* **-er, -est. 1.** low and harsh; hoarse: *a gruff voice.* **2.** rough, brusque, or surly: *a gruff manner.* [1525–35; < MD *grof* coarse; c. G *grob*] —**gruff′ish,** *adj.* —**gruff′ly,** *adv.* —**gruff′ness,** *n.*
—**Syn. 2.** curt. —**Ant. 2.** courteous.

gruff·y (gruf′ē), *adj.,* **gruff·i·er, gruff·i·est.** gruff. [1780–90; GRUFF + -Y[1]] —**gruff′i·ly,** *adv.* —**gruff′i·ness,** *n.*

gru·gru (grōō′grōō), *n.* **1.** any of several spiny-trunked, tropical feather palms, as *Acrocomia totai,* of tropical America, having a swollen trunk with rings of blackish spines. **2.** Also called **gru′gru grub′, gru′gru worm′.** the larva of any of several South American billbugs, as *Rhynchophorus cruentatus,* that feeds on the pith of palm trees, sugar cane, etc., and is sometimes prized as food. [1895–1900; < AmerSp *grugrú* < Carib]

gru·i·form (grōō′ə fôrm′), *adj. Ornith.* of or pertaining to birds of the order Gruiformes, including cranes, rails, and coots. [1895–1900; < NL *gruiformis,* sing. of *Gruiformes,* equiv. to *Gru-,* s. of *Grus* a genus of the order (L *grūs* CRANE) + *-iformes* -IFORMES]

grum (grum), *adj.,* **grum·mer, grum·mest.** (of a person's appearance) grim; glum; surly. [1630–40; prob. b. GRIM and GLUM] —**grum′ly,** *adv.* —**grum′ness,** *n.*

grum·ble (grum′bəl), *v.,* **-bled, -bling,** *n.* —*v.i.* **1.** to murmur or mutter in discontent; complain sullenly. **2.** to utter low, indistinct sounds; growl. **3.** to rumble: *The thunder grumbled in the west.* —*v.t.* **4.** to express or utter with murmuring or complaining. —*n.* **5.** an expression of discontent; complaint; growl. **6. grumbles,** a grumbling, discontented mood. **7.** a rumble. [1580–90; perh. freq. of OE *grymman* to wail; cf. D *grommelen,* G *grummeln,* F *grommeler* (< Gmc)] —**grum′bler,** *n.* —**grum′bling·ly,** *adv.* —**grum′bly,** *adj.*
—**Syn. 1.** See **complain.**

grume (grōōm), *n.* **1.** blood when viscous. **2.** a clot of blood. [1545–55 for sense "lump"; < LL *grūmus* hillock]

grum·met (grum′it), *n.* grommet.

gru·mous (grōō′məs), *adj.* **1.** Also, **gru·mose** (grōō′mōs). *Bot.* formed of clustered grains or granules. **2.** having or resembling grume; clotted. [1655–65; < L *grūm(us)* (see GRUME) + -OUS] —**gru′mous·ness,** *n.*

grump (grump), *n.* **1.** a person given to constant complaining. **2.** *Informal.* **the grumps,** a depressed or sulky mood. —*v.i.* **3.** to complain or sulk. [1835–45; prob. back formation from GRUMPY]

grumph·ie (grum′fē, grōōm′pē), *n. Chiefly Scot.* a familiar name for a pig. Also, **grumph′y.** [1775–85; *grumph* to grunt (imit.) + -IE]

grump·y (grum′pē), *adj.,* **grump·i·er, grump·i·est.** surly or ill-tempered; discontentedly or sullenly irritable; grouchy. Also, **grump′ish.** [1770–80; *grump* expressive word, first attested in the phrase *humps and grumps* slights and snubs + -Y[1]] —**grump′i·ly,** *adv.* —**grump′i·ness,** *n.*

Grun·dy (grun′dē), **Felix,** 1777–1840, American politician: senator 1829–38, 1839–40; attorney general 1838–39.

Grun·dy (grun′dē), *n.* **Mrs.,** a narrow-minded, conventional person who is extremely critical of any breach of propriety. [after *Mrs. Grundy,* a character mentioned in the play *Speed the Plough* (1798) by Thomas Morton (1764?–1838), English playwright] —**Grun′dy·ist, Grun′dy·ite′,** *n.*

Grun·dy·ism (grun′dē iz′əm), *n.* **1.** a prudish adherence to conventionality, esp. in personal behavior. **2.** (*l.c.*) an instance of such prudishness. [1830–40]

Grü·ne·wald (GRY′nə vält′), *n.* **Ma·thi·as** (mä tē′äs), (*Mathias Neithardt-Gothardt*), c1470–1528, German painter and architect.

grunge (grunj), *n. Slang.* **1.** dirt; filth; rubbish. **2.** something of inferior quality; trash: *He didn't know good music from grunge.* **3.** a person who works hard, usually for meager rewards; grind. **4.** a style or fashion derived from a movement in rock music: in fashion characterized by unkempt clothing and in music by aggressive, nihilistic songs. [1960–65; expressive coinage, perh. reflecting GRIME and SLUDGE; sense "grind" perh. by assoc. with DRUDGE]

grun·gy (grun′jē), *adj.,* **-gi·er, -gi·est.** *Slang.* **1.** ugly, run-down, or dilapidated: *a grungy, abandoned mill town.* **2.** dirty; filthy: *a pair of grungy sneakers.* [1965–70, *Amer.;* GRUNGE + -Y[1]] —**grun′gi·ness,** *n.*

grun·ion (grun′yən), *n.* a small, silvery food fish, *Leuresthes tenuis,* of southern California, that spawns at high tide in wet sand. [1915–20; prob. < Sp *gruñon* grunter, deriv. of *gruñir* to grunt < L *grunnire*]

Gru·nit·sky (grə nit′skē), *n.* **Nicolas,** 1913–69, African statesman: president of Togo 1963–67.

grunt (grunt), *v.i.* **1.** to utter the deep, guttural sound characteristic of a hog. **2.** to utter a similar sound. **3.** to grumble, as in discontent. —*v.t.* **4.** to express with a grunt. —*n.* **5.** a sound of grunting. **6.** *New Eng. Cookery.* a dessert, typically of cherries, peaches, or apples sweetened and spiced, and topped with biscuit dough. **7.** any food fish of the family Pomadasyidae (Haemulidae), found chiefly in tropical and subtropical seas, that emits grunting sounds. **8.** *Slang.* a soldier, esp. an infantryman. **9.** *Slang.* a common or unskilled worker; laborer. [bef. 900; ME *grunten,* OE *grunnettan,* freq. of *grunian;* c. G *grunzen,* L *grunnire*] —**grunt′ing·ly,** *adv.*

CONCISE ETYMOLOGY KEY: <, descended or borrowed from; >, whence; b., blend of, blended; c., cognate with; cf., compare; deriv., derivative; equiv., equivalent; imit., imitative; obl., oblique; r., replacing; s., stem; sp., spelling, spelled; resp., respelling, respelled; trans., translation; ?, origin unknown; *, unattested; ‡, probably earlier than. See the full key inside the front cover.

grunt·er (grun′tər), *n.* **1.** a hog. **2.** any animal or person that grunts. **3.** grunt (def. 7). [1400–50; late ME; see GRUNT, -ER[1]]

Grunth (grunt), *n.* Granth.

grunt′ing ox′, the yak.

grunt′ work′, *Slang.* work that is repetitious, often physically exhausting, and boring.

Grus (grus, grōōs), *n., gen.* **Gru·is** (grōō′is). *Astron.* the Crane, a southern constellation between Indus and Piscis Austrinus. [< L *grūs* crane; akin to Gk *géranos*]

grush·ie (grush′ē, grōō′shē), *adj. Scot.* healthy; thriving. Also, **grush.** [orig. uncert.]

grutch (gruch), *n., v.t., v.i. Brit. Dial.* grudge. [1175–1225; ME. See GRUDGE]

Gru·yère (grōō yâr′, gri-; *Fr.* GRY YER′), *n.* a firm, pale-yellow cheese, made of whole milk and having small holes, produced chiefly in France and Switzerland. Also called **Gru·yère′ cheese′.** [1795–1805; after *Gruyère* district in Switzerland where the cheese is made]

gr. wt., gross weight.

gryl·lid (gril′id), *n.* cricket[1] (def. 1). [< NL *Gryllidae* the cricket family, equiv. to *Gryll(us)* a genus (L *grillus* cricket) + *-idae* -ID[2]]

gryl·lo·blat·tid (gril′ō blat′id), *n.* a primitive insect of the order Grylloblattidea, having a soft, unpigmented wingless body with long antennae and no eyes, living under stones in moderately high mountains of the western U.S., Japan, and the U.S.S.R. [< NL *Grylloblattidae* a family of the order, equiv. to *Grylloblatt(a)* a genus (L *grill(us)* cricket + NL -o- -o- + L *blatta* cockroach) + *-idae* -ID[2]]

gryph·on (grif′ən), *n. Class. Myth.* griffin[1].

grys·bok (grīs′bok, grās′-), *n.* either of two small, usually solitary antelopes of southern Africa, *Raphicerus melanotis,* or *R. sharpei* (**Sharpe's grysbok**), having a light to dark reddish-brown coat speckled with white. [1780–90; < Afrik, equiv. to *grys* gray (< D *grijs;* see GRISEOUS) + *bok* BUCK[1]]

GS, 1. General Schedule (referring to the Civil Service job classification system). **2.** general staff. **3.** German silver.

G.S., 1. general secretary. **2.** general staff. Also, **g.s.**

GSA, 1. See **General Services Administration. 2.** Girl Scouts of America. Also, **G.S.A.**

G.S.C., General Staff Corps.

G7 (jē′sev′ən), Group of Seven: the economic alliance of Canada, France, Germany, Great Britain, Italy, Japan, and the U.S.

GSL, Guaranteed Student Loan.

G spot. See **Gräfenberg spot.** Also, **G-spot.**

GSR, 1. galvanic skin response. **2.** galvanic skin reflex.

GST, Greenwich Sidereal Time.

G star, *Astron.* a yellow star, as the sun or Capella, having a surface temperature between 5000 and 6000 K and an absorption spectrum in which the ultraviolet pair of lines of singly ionized calcium are strongest and in which the Balmer series is prominent. Cf. **spectral type.**

G-string (jē′string′), *n.* **1.** a loincloth or breechcloth, usually secured by a cord at the waist. **2.** such a garment made of a narrow strip of decorative fabric and worn by striptease entertainers. Also, **gee-string, gee string.** [1875–80, *Amer.;* orig. uncert.]

G-stro·phan·thin (jē′strə fan′thin), *n. Pharm.* ouabain. [< L *g(rātus)* + STROPHANTHIN]

G-suit (jē′sōōt′), *n.* See **anti-G suit.** Also, **g-suit.** [1940–45, *Amer.; g(ravity) suit*]

GT, 1. gigaton; gigatons. **2.** Also called **GT car, grand touring car, grand touring.** *Auto.* **a.** an automobile in the style of a coupe, usually seating two but occasionally four, and designed for comfort and high speed. **b.** a high-speed, two-door model of a four-door sedan.

gt., 1. gilt. **2.** great. **3.** (in prescriptions) a drop. [(def. 3) < L *gutta*]

Gt. Br., Great Britain. Also, **Gt. Brit.**

g.t.c., 1. good till canceled. **2.** good till countermanded. Also, **G.T.C.**

gtd., guaranteed.

GTO, See **Gran Turismo Omologato.**

GTP, *Biochem.* guanosine triphosphate: an ester of guanosine and triphosphoric acid that is an important metabolic cofactor and precursor in the biosynthesis of cyclic GMP.

GTS, gas turbine ship.

gtt., (in prescriptions) drops. [< L *guttae*]

G_2 phase, *Cell Biol.* the second growth period of the cell cycle, following DNA replication and preceding prophase, during which the cell forms the materials that make up the spindle. [1970–75; *G* abbr. for *growth*]

GU, 1. genitourinary. **2.** Guam (approved esp. for use with zip code).

gua·ca·mo·le (gwä kə mō′lē; *Sp.* gwä′kä mô′le), *n. Mexican Cookery.* a dip of mashed avocado mixed with tomato, onion, and seasonings. [1915–20; < MexSp < Nahuatl *āhuacamōlli* lit., avocado sauce; see AVOCADO, MOLE[6]]

gua·cha·ro (gwä′chə rō′), *n., pl.* **-ros.** a nocturnal, fruit-eating, South American bird, *Steatornis caripensis,* the young of which yield an oil derived from their fat. Also called **oilbird.** [1820–30; < AmerSp]

gua·co (gwä′kō), *n., pl.* **-cos. 1.** a climbing composite plant, *Mikania guaco,* of tropical America. **2.** its leaves, or a leaf extract used locally as an antidote for snakebites. [1815–25; < AmerSp]

Gua·da·la·ja·ra (gwäd′l ə här′ə; *Sp.* gwä′thä lä hä′rä), *n.* a city in and the capital of Jalisco, in W Mexico. 2,000,000.

Gua·dal·ca·nal (gwäd′l kə nal′), *n.* the largest of the Solomon Islands, in the W central Pacific: U.S. victory over the Japanese 1942–43. 23,922; ab. 2500 sq. mi. (6475 sq. km).

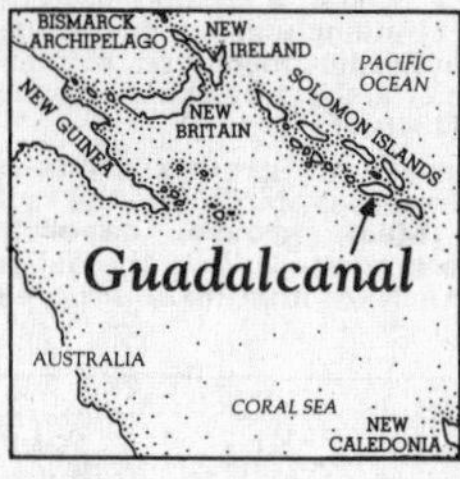

Gua·dal·qui·vir (gwä′thäl kē vēr′), *n.* a river in S Spain, flowing W to the Gulf of Cádiz. 374 mi. (602 km) long.

Gua·da·lupe Hi·dal·go (gwäd′l ōōp′ hi däl′gō, -ōō′pē; *Sp.* gwä′thä lōō′pe ē thäl′gô), a city in the Federal District of Mexico: famous shrine; peace treaty 1848. 1,182,895. Official name, **Gustavo A. Madero.**

Gua′dalupe Moun′tains, a mountain range in S New Mexico and SW Texas, part of the Sacramento Mountains. Highest peak, Guadalupe Peak, 8751 ft. (2667 m).

Gua′dalupe Moun′tains Na′tional Park′, a national park E of El Paso, Texas: limestone fossil reef. 129 sq. mi. (334 sq. km).

Gua′dalupe palm′, a fan palm, *Brahea* (or *Erythea*) *edulis,* of southern California, having long clusters of globe-shaped, black, edible fruit. [1890–95]

Gua·de·loupe (gwäd′l ōōp′), *n.* two islands (**Basse-Terre** and **Grande-Terre**) separated by a narrow channel in the Leeward Islands of the West Indies: together with five dependencies they form an overseas department of France. 334,900; 687 sq. mi. (1179 sq. km). *Cap.:* Basse-Terre.

Gua·di·a·na (*Sp.* gwä thyä′nä; *Port.* gwə dyä′nə), *n.* a river in SW Europe, flowing S from central Spain through SE Portugal to the Gulf of Cádiz. 515 mi. (830 km) long.

gua·guan·che (gwə gwän′chē), *n.* a barracuda, *Sphyraena guachanco,* found chiefly off the coast of Florida. [< AmerSp]

guai·ac (gwī′ak), *n.* **1.** Also called **guai′acum gum′, gum guaiac.** a greenish-brown resin obtained from the guaiacum tree, esp. from *Guaiacum officinale,* used in varnishes, as a food preservative, and in medicine in various tests for the presence of blood. **2.** guaiacum (def. 2). [1550–60; see GUAIACUM]

guai·a·col (gwī′ə kōl′, -kôl′), *n. Pharm.* a slightly yellowish, aromatic, crystalline substance, $C_7H_8O_2$, resembling creosote and usually obtained from guaiacum resin: used in medicine chiefly as an expectorant and local anesthetic. Also called **methylcatechol.** [1860–65; GUAIAC(UM) + -OL[2]]

guai·a·cum (gwī′ə kəm), *n.* **1.** any of several tropical American trees or shrubs belonging to the genus *Guaiacum* of the caltrop family; lignum vitae. **2.** the hard, heavy wood of such a tree; guaiac. **3.** resin obtained from such a tree; guaiac. [1525–35; < NL < Sp *guayaco, guayacán* < Taino]

Guai·ra (*Sp.* gwī′rä), *n.* See **La Guaira.**

gua·ji·ra (gwä hēr′ə; *Sp.* gwä hē′rä), *n., pl.* **-ji·ras** (-hēr′əz; *Sp.* -hē′räs). a Cuban peasant dance with shifting rhythms. [1920–25; < AmerSp: lit., peasant woman]

Guam (gwäm), *n.* an island, belonging to the U.S., in the N Pacific, E of the Philippines: the largest of the Marianas group; U.S. naval station. 84,996; 206 sq. mi. (535 sq. km). *Cap.:* Agaña. *Abbr.:* GU (for use with zip code). —**Gua·ma·ni·an** (gwä mā′nē ən), *n., adj.*

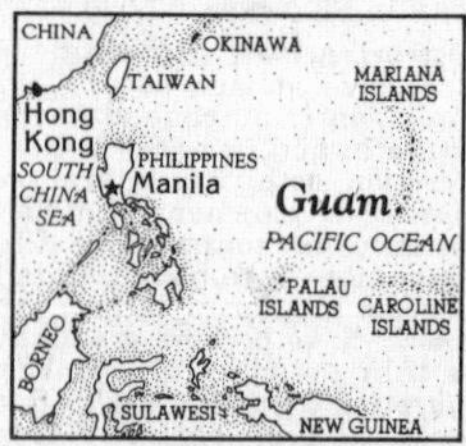

guan (gwän), *n.* a large game bird of the curassow family, common in dense woodlands of Central and South America, somewhat resembling a turkey. [1735–45; < AmerSp]

gua·na·ba·na (gwə nä′bə nə), *n.* soursop. [< Sp *guanábana* < Taino]

Gua·na·ba·ra (gwä′nə bär′ə), *n.* a state in SE Brazil. 4,296,782; 452 sq. mi. (1170 sq. km). *Cap.:* Rio de Janeiro.

gua·na·co (gwä nä′kō), *n., pl.* **-cos.** a wild South American ruminant, *Lama guanicoe,* of which the llama and alpaca are believed to be domesticated varieties: related to the camels. See illus. on next page. [1595–1605; < Sp < Quechua *wanaku*]

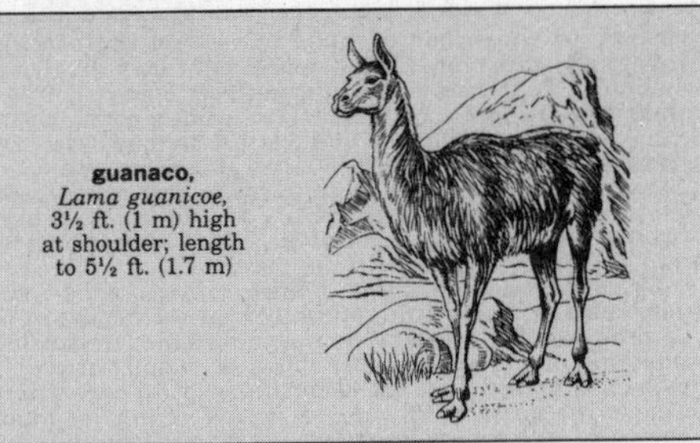
guanaco, *Lama guanicoe,* 3½ ft. (1 m) high at shoulder; length to 5½ ft. (1.7 m)

gua•na•drel (gwä′nə drel′, -drəl), *n. Pharm.* a substance, $C_{20}H_{40}N_6O_8S$, used as an antihypertensive. [perh. GUAN(IDINE) + ADRE(NERGIC) + *-l,* of uncert. derivation]

Gua•na•jua•to (gwä′nä hwä′tô), *n.* **1.** a state in central Mexico. 2,811,000; 11,805 sq. mi. (30,575 sq. km). **2.** a city in and the capital of this state: center of the silver-mining region. 65,258.

gua•nay (gwə nī′; *Sp.* gwä nī′), *n., pl.* **-nay•es** (-nī′äs; *Sp.* -nä′yes), **-nays.** a cormorant, *Phalacrocorax bougainvillii,* of islands off the coasts of Peru and Chile, a chief source of guano. Also called **guanay′ cor′morant.** [1855–60; < AmerSp *guanae,* appar. as back formation from colonial Sp *huanaes,* as pl. of *huano* GUANO, taken as the name of the bird that produced it]

Guan•dong (gwän′dông′), *n. Pinyin.* a former territory in NE China at the tip of Liaodong peninsula; leased to Japan 1905–45. Also, **Kwantung.**

guan•eth•i•dine (gwon eth′i dēn′), *n. Pharm.* a potent adrenergic neuron blocking agent, $C_{10}H_{22}N_4$, used in the treatment of hypertension. [1955–60; by insertion of ETH(YL) into GUANIDINE]

Guang•dong (gwäng′dông′), *n. Pinyin.* a province in SE China. 42,800,000; 89,344 sq. mi. (231,401 sq. km). *Cap.:* Canton. Also, **Kwangtung.**

Guang•xi Zhuang (gwäng′shē′ jwäng′), *Pinyin.* an administrative division in S China. 20,840,000; 85,096 sq. mi. (220,399 sq. km). *Cap.:* Nanning. Also, **Kwangsi Chuang.** Official name, **Guang′xi′ Zhuang′ Auton′omous Re′gion.**

Guang•zhou (*Chin.* gwäng′jō′), *n. Pinyin.* Canton.

Guang•zhou•wan (gwäng′jō′wän′), *n. Pinyin.* a former French-leased territory (1898–1945) on the SW coast of Guangdong province, in S China. ab. 190 sq. mi. (490 sq. km). Also, **Kwangchowan.**

guan•i•dine (gwan′i dēn′, -din, gwä′ni-), *n. Chem.* a colorless, crystalline, strongly alkaline, water-soluble solid, CH_5N_3, used chiefly in the manufacture of plastics, resins, rubber accelerators, and explosives. Also called **carbamidine, iminourea.** [1860–65; GUAN(O) + -ID[3] + -INE[2]]

gua•nine (gwä′nēn), *n. Biochem.* a purine base, $C_5H_5N_5O$, that is a fundamental constituent of DNA and RNA, in which it forms base pairs with cytosine. *Symbol:* G Cf. **guanosine.** [GUAN(O) + -INE[2]]

gua′nine deam′inase, *Biochem.* an enzyme, found in liver, brain, spleen, pancreas, and kidney, that converts guanine into xanthine and ammonia.

gua•no (gwä′nō), *n.* **1.** a natural manure composed chiefly of the excrement of sea birds, found esp. on islands near the Peruvian coast. **2.** any similar substance, as an artificial fertilizer made from fish. [1595–1605; < Sp: fertilizer, dung; AmerSp *huano* dung < Quechua *wanu* dung for fuel, fertilizer]

gua•no•sine (gwä′nə sēn′, -sin), *n. Biochem.* a ribonucleoside component of ribonucleic acid, comprising ribose and guanine. [1905–10; GUAN(INE) + -OSE + -INE[2]]

gua′nosine monophos′phate, *Biochem.* See **GMP.** [MONO- + PHOSPHATE]

gua′nosine triphos′phate, *Biochem.* See **GTP.**

Guan•tá•na•mo (gwän tä′nə mō′; *Sp.* gwän tä′nä-mô′), *n.* a city in SE Cuba: U.S. naval base. 129,005.

Guantá′namo Bay′, a bay on the SE coast of Cuba.

Guan•yin (gwän′yin′), *n. Buddhism.* Kwan-yin.

gua•nyl′ic ac′id (gwä nil′ik). See **GMP.** [1895–1900; GUAN(INE) + -YL + -IC]

Gua•po•ré (*Port.* gwä pŏŏ RE′; *Sp.* gwä′pô RE′), *n.* **1.** a river forming part of the boundary between Brazil and Bolivia, flowing NW to the Mamoré River. 950 mi. (1530 km) long. **2.** former name of **Rondônia.**

guar (gwär), *n.* a plant, *Cyamopsis tetragonolobus,* of the legume family, grown as a forage crop and for its seeds, which produce a gum **(guar gum)** used as a thickening agent and stabilizer in foods and pharmaceuticals and as sizing for paper and cloth. [1880–85; < Hindi *guār*]

guar., guaranteed.

gua•ra•cha (gwə rä′chə; *Sp.* gwä RÄ′chä), *n., pl.* **-chas** (-chəz; *Sp.* -chäs). **1.** a vigorous Cuban dance in triple meter. **2.** the music for this dance. [1820–30; < Sp, equiv. to OSp *guar* place + *hacha* a kind of dance]

gua•ra•na (gwär′ə nä′, gwär′ə nä′), *n.* **1.** a woody, climbing shrub *Paullinia cupana,* of the soapberry family, growing in parts of South America, having seeds that contain caffeine and are used in soft drinks. **2.** a drink containing extract of guarana seed. [1860–65; (< Pg) < Tupi]

gua•ra•ni (gwär′ə nē′, gwär′ə nē′), *n., pl.* **-ni, -nis.** a paper money and monetary unit of Paraguay, equal to 100 centimos. [1940–45; < Sp, after GUARANI]

Gua•ra•ni (gwär′ə nē′), *n., pl.* **-nis, -nies,** (*esp. collectively*) **-ni. 1.** a member of an Indian people now living principally in Paraguay. **2.** a language belonging to the Tupi-Guarani family of languages and spoken by the Guarani Indians: the chief vernacular of Paraguay. Also, **Gua′ra•ní′.**

guar•an•tee (gar′ən tē′), *n., v.,* **-teed, -tee•ing.** —*n.* **1.** a promise or assurance, esp. one in writing, that something is of specified quality, content, benefit, etc., or that it will perform satisfactorily for a given length of time: *a money-back guarantee.* **2.** guaranty (defs. 1, 2). **3.** something that assures a particular outcome or condition: *Wealth is no guarantee of happiness.* **4.** a person who gives a guarantee or guaranty; guarantor. **5.** a person to whom a guarantee is made. —*v.t.* **6.** to secure, as by giving or taking security. **7.** to make oneself answerable for (something) on behalf of someone else who is primarily responsible: *to guarantee the fulfillment of a contract.* **8.** to undertake to ensure for another, as rights or possessions. **9.** to serve as a warrant or guaranty for. **10.** to engage to protect or indemnify: *to guarantee a person against loss.* **11.** to engage (to do something). **12.** to promise (usually fol. by a clause as object): *I guarantee that I'll be there.* [1670–80; alter. of GUARANTY]

guar′anteed an′nual in′come, 1. Also called **guar′anteed in′come.** compensation provided by the government to any family or individual whose annual income falls below a specified level. **2.** See **guaranteed annual wage.** [1965–70]

guar′anteed an′nual wage′, a provision in a contract with an employer guaranteeing the employee a minimum income or work over a period of one year. Also called **annual wage.** [1935–40]

guar′anteed bond′, a bond issued by a corporation in which payment of the principal, interest, or both is guaranteed by another corporation. [1960–65]

guar′anteed stock′, stock for which dividends are guaranteed by a company other than the one issuing the stock. [1890–95]

guar•an•tor (gar′ən tôr′, -tər), *n.* **1.** a person, group, system, etc., that guarantees. **2.** a person who makes or gives a guarantee, guaranty, warrant, etc. [1850–55; GUARANT(EE) + -OR[2]]

guar•an•ty (gar′ən tē′), *n., pl.* **-ties,** *v.,* **-tied, -ty•ing.** —*n.* **1.** a warrant, pledge, or formal assurance given as security that another's debt or obligation will be fulfilled. **2.** something that is taken or presented as security. **3.** the act of giving security. **4.** a person who acts as a guarantor. —*v.t.* **5.** guarantee. [1585–95; < AF *garantie.* See WARRANT, -Y[3]]

Gua•ra•pua•va (gwä′rä pwä′vä), *n.* a city in S Brazil. 126,080.

guard (gärd), *v.t.* **1.** to keep safe from harm or danger; protect; watch over: *to guard the ruler.* **2.** to keep under close watch in order to prevent escape, misconduct, etc.: *to guard a prisoner.* **3.** to keep under control or restraint as a matter of caution or prudence: *to guard one's temper.* **4.** to provide or equip with some safeguard or protective appliance, as to prevent loss, injury, etc. **5.** *Sports.* to position oneself so as to obstruct or impede the movement or progress of (an opponent on offense): *The linebacker moved to his right to guard the end going out for a pass.* **6.** *Chess.* to protect (a piece or a square) by placing a piece in a supportive or defensive position relative to it. —*v.i.* **7.** to take precautions (usually fol. by *against*): *to guard against errors.* **8.** to give protection; keep watch; be watchful. —*n.* **9.** a person or group of persons that guards, protects, or keeps a protective or restraining watch. **10.** a person who keeps watch over prisoners or others under restraint. **11.** a body of people, esp. soldiers, charged with guarding a place from disturbance, theft, fire, etc. **12.** a close watch, as over a prisoner or other person under restraint: *to be kept under guard.* **13.** a device, appliance, or attachment that prevents injury, loss, etc. **14.** something intended or serving to guard or protect; safeguard: *insurance as a guard against disasters.* **15.** a posture of defense or readiness, as in fencing, boxing, or bayonet drill. **16.** *Football.* **a.** either of the linemen stationed between a tackle and the center. **b.** the position played by this lineman. **17.** *Basketball.* either of the players stationed in the backcourt. **18.** *Chess.* a piece that supports or defends another. **19.** *Cards.* a low card that is held with a high card of the same suit and that enables the holder to save the high card for a later trick. **20.** *Brit.* a railroad conductor. **21. Guards,** the name of certain bodies of troops in the British army. **22. off guard,** unprepared; unwary: *The blow from behind caught him off guard.* Also, **off one's guard. 23. on guard,** vigilant; wary: *on guard against dishonest merchants.* Also, **on one's guard. 24. stand guard over,** to watch over; protect: *The dog stood guard over his wounded master.* [1375–1425; late ME *garde* guardianship < OF *g(u)arde,* n. deriv. of *g(u)arder* (v.) < Gmc; see WARD] —**guard′a•ble,** *adj.* —**guard′er,** *n.* —**guard′less,** *adj.* —**guard′like′,** *adj.*
—**Syn. 1.** shield, shelter, safeguard; preserve, save. See **defend. 3.** hold, watch. **9.** defender, protector; watchman, guardian; guardsman, sentry, sentinel, patrol. **14.** defense, protection, aegis, security, safety; bulwark, shield. —**Ant. 1.** attack.

Guar•da•fui (gwär′də fwē′), *n.* **Cape,** a cape at the E extremity of Africa.

guard•ant (gär′dnt), *adj. Heraldry.* (of an animal) depicted full-faced but with the body seen from the side: *a lion guardant.* Also, **gardant.** [1565–75; < F *gardant,* prp. of *garder.* See GUARD, -ANT]

guard′ band′, *Radio.* an unassigned range of radio frequencies either just above or just below the band of frequencies required for the signal transmitted by a broadcasting station. It helps to prevent interference in receivers between signals from different stations. [1955–60]

guard′ cell′, *Bot.* either of two specialized epidermal cells that flank the pore of a stoma and usually cause it to open and close. [1870–75]

guard′ dog′, a large, aggressive dog, as a German shepherd or Doberman pinscher, trained to guard persons or property and often to attack or restrain on command. Also, **guard′dog′.** [1790–1800]

guard′ du′ty, a military assignment involving watching over or protecting a person or place or supervising prisoners. [1890–95]

guard•ed (gär′did), *adj.* **1.** cautious; careful; prudent: *to be guarded in one's speech.* **2.** protected, watched, or restrained, as by a guard. [1500–10; GUARD + -ED[2]] —**guard′ed•ly,** *adv.* —**guard′ed•ness,** *n.*
—**Syn. 1.** wary, watchful, chary, circumspect, vigilant.

guard•ee (gär′dē), *n. Brit. Informal.* guardsman (def. 3). [1900–05; GUARD + -EE]

guard′ hair′, the long, usually stiff outer hair protecting the underfur in certain animals. [1910–15]

guard•house (gärd′hous′), *n., pl.* **-hous•es** (-hou′ziz). **1.** a building used for housing military personnel on guard duty. **2.** a building used for the temporary detention of military prisoners. [1585–95; GUARD + HOUSE]

guard′house law′yer, *Mil. Slang.* a person in military service, esp. an inmate of a guardhouse or brig, who is or claims to be an authority on military law, regulations, and soldiers' rights. [1925–30]

Guar•di (gwär′dē), *n.* **Fran•ces•co** (fRän ches′kô), 1712–93, Italian painter.

guard•i•an (gär′dē ən), *n.* **1.** a person who guards, protects, or preserves. **2.** *Law.* a person who is entrusted by law with the care of the person or property, or both, of another, as a minor or someone legally incapable of managing his or her own affairs. **3.** the superior of a Franciscan convent. —*adj.* **4.** guarding; protecting: *a guardian deity.* [1375–1425; late ME *gardein* < AF. See GUARD, -IAN] —**guard′i•an•less,** *adj.*
—**Syn. 1.** protector, defender.
—**Pronunciation.** GUARDIAN is occasionally pronounced with two syllables and with stress on the final syllable: (gär dēn′). This pronunciation is now most characteristic of older, less educated speakers.

guard•i•an ad li•tem (gär′dē ən ad lī′təm), *Law.* a person appointed by a court as guardian of an infant or other person to act on his or her behalf in a particular action or proceeding. Cf. **next friend.**

guard′ian an′gel, 1. an angel believed to protect a particular person, as from danger or error. **2.** a person who looks after or is concerned with the welfare of another. [1625–35]

guard•i•an•ship (gär′dē ən ship′), *n.* **1.** the position and responsibilities of a guardian, esp. toward a ward. **2.** care; responsibility; charge. [1545–55; GUARDIAN + -SHIP]

guard′ of hon′or, a guard specially designated for welcoming or escorting distinguished guests or for accompanying a casket in a military funeral. Also called **honor guard.** [1915–20]

guard′ pin′, *Horol.* (in a lever escapement) a pin on the lever, meeting the safety roller in such a way as to prevent the lever from overbanking. See diag. under **lever escapement.** [1875–80]

guard•rail (gärd′rāl′), *n.* **1.** Also, **guard′rail′ing.** a protective railing, as along a road or stairway. **2.** *Railroads.* a rail laid parallel to a track to prevent derailment or to keep derailed rolling stock from leaving the roadbed. [1825–35; GUARD + RAIL[1]]

guard′ ring′, a ring worn tightly in front of another ring to prevent the latter from slipping off the finger. [1810–20]

guard•room (gärd′rŏŏm′, -rŏŏm′), *n.* **1.** a room used by military guards during the period they are on duty. **2.** a room in which military prisoners are kept. [1755–65; GUARD + ROOM]

guards•man (gärdz′mən), *n., pl.* **-men. 1.** a person who acts as a guard. **2.** a member of the U.S. National Guard. **3.** *Brit.* a member of any select body of troops traditionally organized to protect the person of the sovereign. [1810–20; GUARD + -S[3] or 's[1] + -MAN]

guar′ gum′. See under **guar.** [1945–50]

Gua•ri•ni (gwä rē′nē), *n.* **Gua•ri•no** (gwä rē′nô), 1624–83, Italian architect.

Guar•ne•ri (gwär nâr′ē; *It.* gwär ne′rē), *n.* **Giu•sep•pe An•to•nio** (jo͞o zep′pe än tô′nyô), (*Joseph Guarnerius*), 1683–1745, Italian violinmaker.

Guar•ne•ri•us (gwär nâr′ē əs), *n., pl.* **-us•es.** a violin made by Guarneri or by a member of his family.

Gua•ru•lhos (gwä ro͞o′lyo͝os), *n.* a city in SE Brazil, NE of São Paulo. 311,318.

Guat., Guatemala.

Gua•te•ma•la (gwä′tə mä′lə; *Sp.* gwä′te mä′lä), *n.* **1.** a republic in N Central America. 6,300,000; 42,042 sq. mi. (108,889 sq. km). **2.** Also called **Guatema′la Cit′y.** a city in and the capital of this republic. 717,322. **—Gua′•te•ma′lan,** *adj., n.*

gua•va (gwä′və), *n.* **1.** any of numerous tropical and subtropical American trees or shrubs belonging to the genus *Psidium,* of the myrtle family, esp. *P. guajava,* bearing large, yellow, round to pear-shaped fruit, and *P. littorale,* bearing smaller, yellowish to deep-red, oval fruit. **2.** the fruit, used for making jam, jelly, etc. [1545–55; < Sp *guayaba* < Arawak]

gua•ya•be•ra (gwī′ə ber′ə; *Sp.* gwä′yä be′rä), *n., pl.* **-be•ras** (-ber′əz; *Sp.* -be′räs). a sport shirt or lightweight jacket, often with several large front pockets, modeled upon a loose, smocklike shirt originally worn by men in Cuba. Also called **guayabe′ra shirt′.** [< Sp]

Gua•ya•ma (gwä yä′mä), *n.* a city in S Puerto Rico. 21,097.

Guay•a•quil (gwä′yä kēl′), *n.* **1.** a seaport in W Ecuador, on the Gulf of Guayaquil. 823,219. **2. Gulf of,** an arm of the Pacific in SW Ecuador.

Guay•mas (gwī′mäs), *n.* a seaport in NW Mexico. 84,730.

Guay•na•bo (gwī nä′bō; *Sp.* gwī nä′vô), *n.* a city in N Puerto Rico, SE of Bayamón. 65,075.

gua•yu•le (gwä yo͞o′lē, wä-; *Sp.* gwä yo͞o′le), *n., pl.* **-les** (-lēz; *Sp.* -les). **1.** a composite shrub, *Parthenium argentatum,* of the southwestern U.S. and Mexico, yielding a form of rubber. **2.** the rubber obtained from this plant. [1905–10, *Amer.*; < MexSp < Nahuatl *cuauholli* or *huauholli,* equiv. to *cuahu(itl)* tree or *huauh(tli)* amaranth + *olli* rubber]

gub•bah (gub′ə), *n. Australian.* a white person. Also, **gub** (gub). [< Australian Pidgin E, repr. *government man*]

gu•ber•nac•u•lum (go͞o′bər nak′yə ləm), *n., pl.* **-la** (-lə). *Anat., Zool.* a part or organ that directs the movement or course of another part. [1655–65; < NL, L *gubernāculum* rudder, equiv. to *gubernā(re)* to steer (see GOVERN) + *-culum* -CULE[2]] **—gu′ber•nac′u•lar,** *adj.*

gu•ber•na•to•ri•al (go͞o′bər nə tôr′ē əl, -tōr′-, gyo͞o′-), *adj.* of or pertaining to a state governor or the office of state governor. [1725–35, *Amer.*; < L *gubernātōr-* (s. of *gubernātor*) steersman, GOVERNOR + -IAL]

gu•ber•ni•ya (go͞o ber′nē ə; *Russ.* go͞o byer′nyi yə), *n.* **1.** (in the Soviet Union) an administrative division of the volosts, smaller than a district. **2.** (in Russia before 1917) an administrative division equivalent to the province. [< Russ *gubérniya,* prob. deriv. of *gubernátor* GOVERNOR (< Pol < L), by analogy with *imperátor* EMPEROR, *impériya* EMPIRE]

guck (guk, go͝ok), *n. Informal.* **1.** slime or oozy dirt: *the guck in a stagnant pond.* **2.** any oozy, sticky, or slimy substance: *a can of guck to patch the roof.* Also, **gook.** [1945–50; perh. b. GOO and MUCK]

gud•dle (gud′l), *v.,* **-dled, -dling,** *n. Scot.* —*v.t.* **1.** to catch (fish) by groping with the hands, as under rocks or along a riverbank. —*v.i.* **2.** to grope for fish under stones, along a riverbank, etc. —*n.* **3.** *Informal.* a muddled affair; mix-up; confusion. [1810–20; prob. imit.]

gude (gyd), *adj., n., interj., adv. Scot. and North Eng.* good.

Gude (gyd), *n. Scot. and North Eng.* God.

Gu•de•a (go͞o dē′ə), *n.* fl. c2250 B.C., Sumerian ruler.

gudg•eon[1] (guj′ən), *n.* **1.** a small, European, freshwater fish, *Gobio gobio,* of the minnow family, having a threadlike barbel at each corner of the mouth, used as bait. **2.** any of certain related fishes. **3.** a person who is easily duped or cheated. **4.** a bait or allurement. —*v.t.* **5.** to dupe or cheat. [1375–1425; late ME *gogion* < OF *go(u)jon* < L *gōbiōn-* (s. of *gōbiō*), var. of *gobius.* See GOBY]

gudg•eon[2] (guj′ən), *n.* **1.** *Mach.* a trunnion. **2.** a socket for the pintle of a hinge. **3.** *Naut.* a socket attached to the stern frame of a vessel, for holding the pintle of a rudder. [1350–1400; ME *gudyon* < OF *go(u)jon,* perh. ult. < LL *gu(l)bia* a chisel; see GOUGE]

gudg′eon pin′, *Brit.* See **wrist pin.** [1890–95]

Gud•munds•son (gyd′mo͞on son), *n.* **Krist•mann** (krist′män), born 1902, Icelandic novelist.

Gud•run (go͝od′ro͞on), *n.* (in the *Volsunga Saga*) the daughter of the king of the Nibelungs. Cf. **Kriemhild.** [ON *Guthrun,* equiv. to *gunn(r), guth(r)* battle + *-rún* fem. n. *suffix*]

Gue•dal•la (gwi dal′ə), *n.* **Philip,** 1889–1944, English writer.

guel′der rose′ (gel′dər), a shrub, *Viburnum opulus,* of the honeysuckle family, native to the Old World, having broad clusters of white flowers and scarlet fruit. Also called **cranberry bush, snowball bush.** [1590–1600; after GUELDERS]

Guel•ders (gel′dərz), *n.* Gelderland.

Guelph (gwelf), *n.* **1.** a member of the political party in medieval Italy and Germany that supported the sovereignty of the papacy against the German emperors: opposed to the Ghibellines. **2.** a member of a secret society in Italy in the early 19th century that opposed foreign rulers and reactionary ideas. Also, **Guelf.** [1570–80; < It *Guelfo* < MHG *Welf* name of founder of a princely German family] **—Guelph′ic, Guelf′ic,** *adj.* **—Guelph′ism, Guelf′ism,** *n.*

Guelph (gwelf), *n.* a city in SE Ontario, in S Canada. 71,207.

gue•mal (gwā′məl, gā′-), *n.* huemul.

Guen•e•vere (gwen′ə vēr′), *n.* a female given name: from a Welsh word meaning "white, fair."

gue•non (gə nôn′, -non′), *n.* any of several long-tailed African monkeys, esp. of the genus *Cercopithecus,* having a grizzled coat. [1830–40; < F < ?]

guer•don (gûr′dn), *n.* **1.** a reward, recompense, or requital. —*v.t.* **2.** to give a guerdon to; reward. [1325–75; ME < OF, var. of *werdoun* < ML *widerdonum,* alter. (prob. by assoc. with L *dōnum* gift) of OHG *widarlōn,* equiv. to *widar* again, back + *lōn* reward; c. OE *witherlēan*] **—guer′don•er,** *n.* **—guer′don•less,** *adj.*

gue•rez•a (gə rez′ə), *n.* a colobus monkey, esp. of the species *Colobus guereza.* [< Amharic *gureza* monkey, or < a related word in a Cushitic language, e.g., Oromo *gureezaa*]

Gue•rick•e (gâr′ə kē, -kə, gwâr′-; *Ger.* gy′ri kə), *n.* **Ot•to von** (ôt′ō fən), 1602–86, German physicist.

gue•ri•don (ger′ē don′; *Fr.* gā rē dôn′), *n., pl.* **-dons** (-donz′; *Fr.* -dôn′). *Fr. Furniture.* a small table or stand, as for holding a candelabrum. [1850–55; < F *guéridon,* after the proper name *Guéridon*]

gue•ril•la (gə ril′ə), *n., adj.* guerrilla. **—gue•ril′la•ism,** *n.*

gué•rite (gā rēt′; *Fr.* gā rēt′), *n., pl.* **-rites** (-rēts′; *Fr.* -rēt′). *Fr. Furniture.* a wicker chair having a tall back arched over the seat to form a hood. [1700–10; < F, MF, prob. alter. of OF *garite* watchtower; see GARRET[1]]

Guer•ni•ca (gwâr′ni kə; *Sp.* ger nē′kä), *n.* Basque town in northern Spain: bombed and destroyed 1937 by German planes helping the insurgents in the Spanish Civil War.

Guern•sey (gûrn′zē), *n., pl.* **-seys** for 2, 3. **1. Isle of,** one of the Channel Islands, in the English Channel. With adjacent islands: 51,138; 24½ sq. mi. (63 sq. km). **2.** one of a breed of dairy cattle, raised originally on the Isle of Guernsey, producing rich, golden-tinted milk. **3.** (*l.c.*) a close-fitting knitted woolen shirt worn by sailors and soccer or Rugby players. [1825–35, for def. 2]

Guern′sey lil′y, a bulbous plant, *Nerine sarniensis,* of the amaryllis family, native to southern Africa, having clusters of crimson flowers. [1655–65]

Guer•re•ro (ger re′rô), *n.* a state in S Mexico. 2,013,000; 24,885 sq. mi. (64,452 sq. km). *Cap.:* Chilpancingo.

guer•ril•la (gə ril′ə), *n.* **1.** a member of a band of irregular soldiers that uses guerrilla warfare, harassing the enemy by surprise raids, sabotaging communication and supply lines, etc. —*adj.* **2.** pertaining to such fighters or their technique of warfare: *guerrilla strongholds; guerrilla tactics.* Also, **guerilla.** [1800–10; < Sp, dim. of *guerra* war (< Gmc; cf. WAR[1]); orig. in reference to the Spanish resistance against Napoleon; the name for the struggle erroneously taken as a personal n.] **—guer•ril′la•ism,** *n.*

guerril′la the′ater, the presentation of short propaganda plays or skits, usually on sociopolitical themes, as war or repression, often on the streets or in other nontheater locations. [1965–70]

guerril′la war′fare, the use of hit-and-run tactics by small, mobile groups of irregular forces operating in territory controlled by a hostile, regular force. [1835–45]

Guesde (ged), *n.* **Jules** (zhyl), (*Mathieu Basile*), 1845–1922, French socialist leader, editor, and writer. **—Guesd′ism,** *n.* **—Guesd′ist,** *adj., n.*

guess (ges), *v.t.* **1.** to arrive at or commit oneself to an opinion about (something) without having sufficient evidence to support the opinion fully: *to guess a person's weight.* **2.** to estimate or conjecture about correctly: *to guess what a word means.* **3.** to think, believe, or suppose: *I guess I can get there in time.* —*v.i.* **4.** to form an estimate or conjecture (often fol. by *at* or *about*): *We guessed at the weight of the package.* **5.** to estimate or conjecture correctly. —*n.* **6.** an opinion that one reaches or to which one commits oneself on the basis of probability alone or in the absence of any evidence whatever. **7.** the act of forming such an opinion. **8. by guess and by gosh,** *Northern U.S.* using a combination of guesswork and reliance on luck; hit or miss. Also, **by guess and by golly.** [1300–50; (v.) ME *gessen,* perh. < Scand; cf. Sw, Dan, Norw *gissa,* MLG *gissen,* MD *gessen,* ON *geta;* (n.) ME *gesse,* deriv. of the v. See GET] **—guess′a•ble,** *adj.* **—guess′er,** *n.* **—guess′ing•ly,** *adv.*

—Syn. 1. hazard. **1, 2, 4.** GUESS, GUESS AT, CONJECTURE, SURMISE imply attempting to form an opinion as to the probable. To GUESS is to risk an opinion regarding something one does not know about, or, wholly or partly by chance, to arrive at the correct answer to a question: *to guess the outcome of a game.* GUESS AT implies more haphazard or random guessing: *to guess at the solution of a crime.* To CONJECTURE is to make inferences in the absence of sufficient evidence to establish certainty: *to conjecture the circumstances of the crime.* SURMISE implies making an intuitive conjecture that may or may not be correct: *to surmise the motives that led to it.* **3.** fancy, imagine. **6.** supposition. **—Ant. 3.** know.

guess•ti•mate (*v.* ges′tə māt′; *n.* ges′tə mit, -māt′), *v.,* **-mat•ed, -mat•ing,** *n. Informal.* —*v.t.* **1.** to estimate without substantial basis in facts or statistics. —*n.* **2.** an estimate arrived at by guesswork. Also, **guestimate.** [1935–40, *Amer.*; b. GUESS and ESTIMATE]

guess•work (ges′wûrk′), *n.* work or procedure based on or consisting of the making of guesses or conjectures. [1715–25; GUESS + WORK]

guest (gest), *n.* **1.** a person who spends some time at another person's home in some social activity, as a visit, dinner, or party. **2.** a person who receives the hospitality of a club, a city, or the like. **3.** a person who patronizes a hotel, restaurant, etc., for the lodging, food, or entertainment it provides. **4.** an often well-known person invited to participate or perform in a regular program, series, etc., as a substitute for a regular member or as a special attraction. **5.** *Zool.* an inquiline. —*v.t.* **6.** to entertain as a guest. —*v.i.* **7.** to be a guest; make an appearance as a guest: *She's been guesting on all the TV talk shows.* —*adj.* **8.** provided for or done by a guest: *a guest towel; a guest column for a newspaper.* **9.** participating or performing as a guest: *a guest conductor.* [bef. 900; ME *gest* < ON *gestr;* r. OE *gi(e)st;* c. G *Gast,* Goth *gasts,* L *hostis;* cf. HOST[1], HOST[2]] **—guest′less,** *adj.*
—Syn. 1. company. See **visitor.**

Guest (gest), *n.* **Edgar A(lbert),** 1881–1959, U.S. journalist and writer of verse, born in England.

guest′ flag′, a rectangular white flag flown at the starboard main spreader or main yardarm of a yacht when the owner is away but guests are on board.

guest•house (gest′hous′), *n., pl.* **-hous•es** (-hou′ziz). a small building, separate from a main house or establishment, for the housing of guests. [bef. 1000; ME; OE *giest hūs.* See GUEST, HOUSE]

gues•ti•mate (*v.* ges′tə māt′; *n.* ges′tə mit, -māt′) *v.t.,* **-mat•ed, -mat•ing,** *n.* guesstimate.

guest•list (gest′list′), *n.* a list of guests invited to attend a social function. [GUEST + LIST[1]]

guest′ of hon′or, 1. a person in whose honor a dinner, party, etc., is given. **2.** a distinguished person invited to a dinner, meeting, etc., esp. on some unique occasion.

guest′ room′, a room for the lodging of guests. Also, **guest′room′.** [1630–40]

guest-rope (gest′rōp′), *n. Naut.* **1.** a rope suspended from the side of a vessel or a boom as an object to which other vessels can moor, or to afford a hold for persons in such vessels. **2.** a line sent out from a vessel to a fixed object or a buoy or anchor to help the vessel in warping. **3.** a line, in addition to the towrope, to steady a boat in tow. Also, **guest′ rope′.** [1615–25; *guest* < ? + ROPE]

guest-shot (gest′shot′), *n.* an appearance as a guest, esp. on a television show.

guest′ work′er, a foreign worker permitted to work in a country, esp. in Western Europe, on a temporary basis. [1965–70; trans. of G *Gastarbeiter*]

Gueux (*Fr.* gœ), *n.* See **Les Gueux.**

Gue•va•ra (gə vär′ə; *Sp.* ge vä′rä), *n.* **Er•nes•to** (er nes′tô), ("*Che*"), 1928–67, Cuban revolutionist and political leader, born in Argentina.

Gue•var•ist (gə vär′ist), *n.* a supporter of the revolutionary theories and tactics of Ernesto Guevara. [1965–70; Ernesto GUEVAR(A) + -IST, or < Sp *guevarista*]

guff (guff), *n. Informal.* **1.** empty or foolish talk; nonsense. **2.** insolent talk. [1815–25; perh. imit.]

guf•faw (gu fô′, gə-), *n.* **1.** a loud, unrestrained burst of laughter. —*v.i.* **2.** to laugh loudly and boisterously. [1710–20; perh. imit.]

GUGB, (in the Soviet Union) the Chief Directorate for State Security, the government's secret police organization (1934–1941) functioning as part of the NKVD. Also, **G.U.G.B.** [< Russ, for *Glávnoe upravlénie gosudárstvennoĭ bezopásnosti*]

Gug•gen•heim (go͝og′ən hīm′, go͞o′gən-), *n.* **Daniel,** 1856–1930, U.S. industrialist and philanthropist.

Gug•gen•heim (go͝og′ən hīm′, go͞o′gən-), *n. Games.* category (def. 4). [from the proper name]

gug•gle (gug′əl), *v.,* **-gled, -gling,** *n.* —*v.i., v.t.* **1.** to gurgle. —*n.* **2.** a guggling sound; gurgle. [1605–15; imit.; see -LE]

gug•let (gug′lit), *n.* goglet.

GUI (go͞o′ē), *n., pl.* **GUIs, GUI's.** See **graphical user interface.**

Gui., Guiana.

Gui•an•a (gē an′ə, -ä′nə, gī an′ə), *n.* **1.** a vast tropical region in NE South America, bounded by the Orinoco, Negro, and Amazon rivers and the Atlantic. ab. 690,000 sq. mi. (1,787,000 sq. km). **2.** the coastal portion of this region, which includes Guyana, French Guiana, and Suriname. 1,263,200; 175,275 sq. mi. (453,962 sq. km). See map on next page.

Guian′a cur′rent, an ocean current flowing northwest along the northeast coast of South America.

Gui•a•nese (gē′ə nēz′, -nēs′, gī′-), *adj., n., pl.* **-nese.** —*adj.* **1.** of or pertaining to the region of Guiana, its inhabitants, or their language. —*n.* **2.** an inhabitant or native of Guiana. Also, **Gui•an•an** (gē an′ən, -ä′nən, gī an′ən). [1590–1600; GUIAN(A) + -ESE]

guib (gwib, gēb), *n.* bushbuck. [1765–75; < F *guiba,* name used by Buffon; orig. obscure]

guid•ance (gīd′ns), *n.* **1.** the act or function of guiding; leadership; direction. **2.** advice or counseling, esp. that provided for students choosing a course of study or preparing for a vocation. **3.** supervised care or assistance, esp. therapeutic help in the treatment of minor emotional disturbances. **4.** something that guides. **5.** the process by which the flight of a missile or rocket may be altered in speed and direction in response to controls situated either wholly in the projectile or partly at a base. [1765–75; GUIDE + -ANCE]
—**Syn. 1.** management, conduct, supervision, control, government.

guide (gīd), *v.,* **guid•ed, guid•ing,** *n.* —*v.t.* **1.** to assist (a person) to travel through, or reach a destination in, an unfamiliar area, as by accompanying or giving directions to the person: *He guided us through the forest.* **2.** to accompany (a sightseer) to show points of interest and to explain their meaning or significance. **3.** to force (a person, object, or animal) to move in a certain path. **4.** to supply (a person) with advice or counsel, as in practical or spiritual affairs. **5.** to supervise (someone's actions or affairs) in an advisory capacity. —*n.* **6.** a person who guides, esp. one hired to guide travelers, tourists, hunters, etc. **7.** a mark, tab, or the like, to catch the eye and thus provide quick reference. **8.** a guidebook. **9.** a book, pamphlet, etc., giving information, instructions, or advice; handbook: *an investment guide.* **10.** a guidepost. **11.** a device that regulates or directs progressive motion or action: *a sewing-machine guide.* **12.** a spirit believed to direct the utterances of a medium. **13.** *Mil.* a member of a group marching in formation who sets the pattern of movement or alignment for the rest. [1325–75; ME *giden* (v.), *gide* (n.) < OF *gui(d)er* (v.), *gui(d)e* (n.) < Gmc; akin to WIT[2]] —**guid′a•ble,** *adj.* —**guide′less,** *adj.* —**guid′er,** *n.* —**guid′ing•ly,** *adv.*
—**Syn. 1.** pilot, steer, escort. GUIDE, CONDUCT, DIRECT, LEAD imply showing the way or pointing out or determining the course to be taken. GUIDE implies continuous presence or agency in showing or indicating a course: *to guide a traveler.* To CONDUCT is to precede or escort to a place, sometimes with a degree of ceremony: *to conduct a guest to his room.* To DIRECT is to give information for guidance, or instructions or orders for a course of procedure: *to direct someone to the station.* To LEAD is to bring onward in a course, guiding by contact or by going in advance; hence, fig., to influence or induce to some course of conduct: *to lead a procession; to lead astray.* **5.** regulate, manage, govern, rule. **6.** pilot, director, conductor. **7.** sign, signal, indication, key, clue. —**Ant. 1.** follow.

guide•board (gīd′bôrd′, -bōrd′), *n.* a large board or sign, usually mounted on a post, giving directions to travelers. [1800–10; GUIDE + BOARD]

guide•book (gīd′bo͝ok′), *n.* a book of directions, advice, and information, esp. for travelers or tourists. [1805–15; GUIDE + BOOK] —**guide′book′ish, guide′•book′y,** *adj.*

guide′ cen′ter, *Mil.* a command to a marching formation to align itself behind a guide marching at the head of the formation.

guid•ed (gī′did), *adj.* **1.** accompanied by a guide: *a guided tour.* **2.** supervised or controlled: *a guided beam.* [1905–10; GUIDE + -ED[2]]

guid′ed mis′sile, an aerial missile, as a rocket, steered during its flight by radio signals, clockwork controls, etc. [1940–45]

guid′ed mis′sile cruis′er, a naval cruiser equipped with long-range guided missiles and missile launchers.

guide′ dog′. See **Seeing Eye dog.** [1930–35]

guid′ed wave′, a wave the energy of which is concentrated near a boundary or between parallel boundaries separating different materials and that has a direction of propagation parallel to these boundaries. [1920–25]

guide′ fos′sil. See **index fossil.** [1905–10]

guide′ left′, *Mil.* a command to a marching formation to align itself with a guide marching at the left side of the formation.

guide•line (gīd′līn′), *n.* **1.** any guide or indication of a future course of action: *guidelines on the government's future policy.* **2.** a lightly marked line used as a guide, as in composing a drawing, a typed page, or a line of lettering. **3.** a rope or cord that serves to guide one's steps, esp. over rocky terrain, through underground passages, etc. **4.** a rope or wire used in guiding the movement of stage scenery or curtains being raised or lowered. [1775–85, *Amer.*; GUIDE + LINE[1]]

guide•post (gīd′pōst′), *n.* **1.** a post, usually mounted on the roadside or at the intersection of two or more roads, bearing a sign for the guidance of travelers. **2.** anything serving as a guide; guideline. [1755–65; GUIDE + POST[1]]

guide′ rail′, a track or rail designed to control the movement of an object, as a door or window.

guide′ right′, *Mil.* a command to a marching formation to align itself with a guide marching at the right side of the formation.

guide′ rope′, **1.** a rope fastened, usually at an angle, to a hoisting or towing line, to guide the object being moved. **2.** *Aeron.* a long rope hung downward from a balloon and trailing along the ground, used to regulate the altitude of the balloon and to act as a brake. [1815–25]

guide•way (gīd′wā′), *n.* a structure, usually made of concrete, that is used to support and guide trains or individual vehicles that ride over it. [1875–80, for an earlier sense; GUIDE + WAY]

guide′ word′, catchword (def. 2). [1925–30]

Gui•do (gwē′dō; *It.* gwē′dô), *n.* a male given name.

Gui•do d'A•rez•zo (gwē′dô dä ʀet′tsô), (*Guido Aretinus*) (*"Fra Guittone"*), c995–1049?, Italian monk and music theorist: reformer of musical notation. —**Gui•do•ni•an** (gwi dō′nē ən), *adj.*

gui•don (gīd′n), *n. Mil.* **1.** a small flag or streamer carried as a guide, for marking or signaling, or for identification. **2.** the soldier carrying it. Cf. **colorbearer.** [1540–50; < MF < It *guidone,* equiv. to *guid(are)* to GUIDE + *-one* n. suffix]

guid•wil•lie (gʏd′wil′ē, gwēd′-), *n., adj. Scot. Obs.* goodwilly.

Gui•enne (gwē yen′), *n.* a former province in SW France. Also, **Guyenne.**

guige (gēj, gēzh), *n. Armor.* a shoulder strap attached to the inner side of a shield. [1350–1400; ME *gige* < OF *guige* extra strap for shield]

Gui•ja (gē′hä), *n.* **Lake,** a lake on the border between SE Guatemala and NW El Salvador, in Central America. ab. 20 mi. (32 km) long.

guild (gild), *n.* **1.** an organization of persons with related interests, goals, etc., esp. one formed for mutual aid or protection. **2.** any of various medieval associations, as of merchants or artisans, organized to maintain standards and to protect the interests of its members, and that sometimes constituted a local governing body. **3.** *Bot.* a group of plants, as parasites, having a similar habit of growth and nutrition. Also, **gild.** [bef. 1000; ME *gild(e)* < ON *gildi* guild, payment; r. OE *gegyld* guild; akin to G *Geld* money, Goth *-gild* tax]

guil•der (gil′dər), *n.* **1.** a silver or nickel coin and monetary unit of the Netherlands, equal to 100 cents; florin. *Abbr.:* Gld.,f.,fl. **2.** a former gold coin of the Netherlands; florin. **3.** the monetary unit of the Netherlands Antilles and Suriname, equal to 100 cents. **4.** the Austrian florin. **5.** any of various gold coins formerly issued by German states. Also, **gilder.** Also called **gulden.** [1425–75; late ME *gilder, guldren,* with intrusive *r* < MD *gulden* GULDEN]

guild•hall (gild′hôl′), *n.* (in Britain) the hall built or used by a guild or corporation for its assemblies; town hall. Also, **gildhall.** [bef. 1000; ME; OE *gegyld healle;* see GUILD, HALL]

guild•ship (gild′ship), *n.* **1.** guild (defs. 1, 2). **2.** the condition or standing of a guild member. [bef. 1000; GUILD + -SHIP; prob. not continuous with OE *gieldscipe*]

guilds•man (gildz′mən), *n., pl.* **-men.** a member of a guild. [1870–75; GUILD + 'S[1] + MAN[1]]

guild′ so′cialism, a form of socialism developed in England in the 20th century, emphasizing decentralization of industry and services with control to be vested in autonomous guilds of workers. —**guild′ so′cialist.** —**guild′-so′cial•is′tic,** *adj.* [1910–15]

guile (gīl), *n.* insidious cunning in attaining a goal; crafty or artful deception; duplicity. [1175–1225; ME < OF < Gmc; akin to WILE]
—**Syn.** trickery, fraud, craft. See **deceit.**

guile•ful (gīl′fəl), *adj.* insidiously cunning; artfully deceptive; wily. [1300–50; ME; see GUILE, -FUL] —**guile′•ful•ly,** *adv.* —**guile′ful•ness,** *n.*

guile•less (gīl′lis), *adj.* free from guile; sincere; honest; straightforward; frank. [1720–30; GUILE + -LESS] —**guile′less•ly,** *adv.* —**guile′less•ness,** *n.*
—**Syn.** artless, ingenuous, naive, unsophisticated.

Guil•ford (gil′fərd), *n.* a town in S Connecticut, on Long Island Sound. 17,375.

Gui•lin (gwē′lin′), *n. Pinyin.* a city in the NE Guangxi Zhuang region, in S China. 235,000. Also, **Kweilin.**

Guil•lain′-Bar•ré′ syn′drome (gē yan′bə rā′), *Pathol.* an uncommon, usually self-limited form of polyneuritis, occurring after a viral illness or immunization and manifested by loss of muscle strength, loss of or altered sensation and sometimes paralysis. [after French physicians Georges *Guillain* (1876–1961) and Jean Alexandre *Barré* (born 1880), who described it]

Guil•laume (*Fr.* gē yōm′), *n.* **Charles É•douard** (*Fr.* sharl ā dwar′), 1861–1938, Swiss physicist: Nobel prize 1920.

Guil•laume de Ma•chaut (gē yōm də ma shō′), 1300–77, French poet and composer.

Guille•min (gē′ə man′; *Fr.* gēyᵉ maɴ′), *n.* **Rog•er (Charles Lou•is)** (roj′ər chärlz lo͞o′ē; *Fr.* rô zhā′ sharl lwē), born 1924, U.S. physiologist, born in France: Nobel prize for medicine 1977.

guil•le•mot (gil′ə mot′), *n.* **1.** a black or brown-speckled seabird of the genus *Cepphus,* of northern seas, having a sharply pointed black bill, red legs, and white wing patches, as *C. grylle* **(black guillemot),** of the North Atlantic and the similar *C. columba* **(pigeon guillemot)** of the North Pacific. **2.** *Brit.* a murre of the genus *Uria.* [1670–80; < F, appar. dim. of *Guillaume* William]

Gui•llén (gēl yen′; *Sp.* gē lyen′), *n.* **Jor•ge** (hôʀ′he), 1893–1984, Spanish poet, in the U.S. 1940–75.

guil•loche (gi lōsh′), *n.* an ornamental pattern or border, as in architecture, consisting of paired ribbons or lines flowing in interlaced curves around a series of circular voids. [1855–60; < F: graining tool < ?]

guilloche

guil•lo•tine (gil′ə tēn′, gē′ə-; *esp. for v.* gil′ə tēn′, gē′ə-), *n., v.,* **-tined, -tin•ing.** —*n.* **1.** a device for beheading a person by means of a heavy blade that is dropped between two posts serving as guides: widely used during the French Revolution. **2.** an instrument for surgically removing the tonsils. **3.** any of various machines in which a vertical blade between two parallel uprights descends to cut or trim metal, stacks of paper, etc. —*v.t.* **4.** to behead by the guillotine. **5.** to cut with or as if with a guillotine. [1785–95; named after J. I. *Guillotin* (1738–1814), French physician who urged its use]

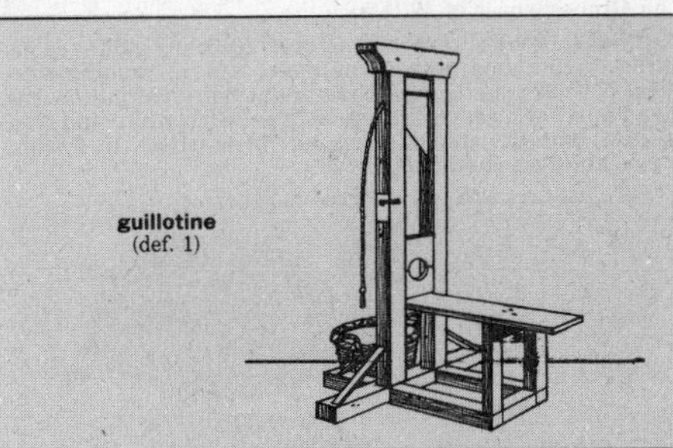
guillotine (def. 1)

guilt (gilt), *n.* **1.** the fact or state of having committed an offense, crime, violation, or wrong, esp. against moral or penal law; culpability: *He admitted his guilt.* **2.** a feeling of responsibility or remorse for some offense, crime, wrong, etc., whether real or imagined. **3.** conduct involving the commission of such crimes, wrongs, etc.: *to live a life of guilt.* [bef. 1000; ME *gilt,* OE *gylt* offense]
—**Syn. 3.** criminality. —**Ant. 1.** innocence.

guilt•less (gilt′lis), *adj.* **1.** free from guilt; innocent. **2.** having no knowledge or experience; innocent (usually fol. by *of*). **3.** destitute or devoid (usually fol. by *of*): *a house guiltless of any charm.* [1150–1200; ME; see GUILT, -LESS] —**guilt′less•ly,** *adv.* —**guilt′less•ness,** *n.*
—**Syn. 1.** See **innocent.**

guilt′ trip′, *Slang.* an experience of feeling guilt or self-reproach.

guilt•y (gil′tē), *adj.,* **guilt•i•er, guilt•i•est. 1.** having committed an offense, crime, violation, or wrong, esp. against moral or penal law; justly subject to a certain accusation or penalty; culpable: *The jury found her guilty of murder.* **2.** characterized by, connected with, or involving guilt: *guilty intent.* **3.** having or showing a sense of guilt, whether real or imagined: *a guilty conscience.* [bef. 1000; ME; OE *gyltig.* See GUILT, -Y[1]] —**guilt′i•ly,** *adv.* —**guilt′i•ness,** *n.*
—**Syn. 2.** criminal, felonious, culpable; illicit, nefarious.

guimpe (gimp, gamp), *n.* **1.** a chemisette or yoke of lace, embroidery, or other material, worn with a dress cut low at the neck. **2.** gimp[1]. **3.** a part of the habit of nuns of certain orders, consisting of a wide, stiffly starched cloth that covers the neck and shoulders. [1840–50; earlier *gimp;* see GIMP[1]]

Guin., Guinea.

Guin•ea (gin′ē), *n.* **1.** a coastal region in W Africa, extending from the Gambia River to the Gabon estuary. **2.** Formerly, **French Guinea.** an independent republic in W Africa, on the Atlantic coast. 4,800,000; ab. 96,900 sq. mi. (251,000 sq. km). *Cap.:* Conakry. **3. Gulf of,** a part of the Atlantic Ocean that projects into the W coast of Africa and extends from the Ivory Coast to Gabon. **4.** (*l.c.*) a former money of account of the United Kingdom, equal to 21 shillings: still often used in quoting fees or prices. **5.** (*l.c.*) a gold coin of Great Britain issued from 1663 to 1813, with a nominal value of 20 shillings. **6.** *Slang (disparaging and offensive).* a person of Italian birth or descent. **7.** (*l.c.*) *Horse Racing.* a person who does miscellaneous work in or around a horse stable. —**Guin′e•an,** *adj., n.*

CONCISE PRONUNCIATION KEY: act, cāpe, dâre, pärt; set, ēqual; *if,* īce; ox, ōver, ôrder, oil, bo͝ok, bo͞ot, out; up, ûrge; child; sing; shoe; thin, *that;* zh as in *treasure.* ə = *a* as in *alone, e* as in *system, i* as in *easily, o* as in *gallop, u* as in *circus;* ᵊ as in *fire* (fīᵊr), *hour* (ouᵊr). l and n can serve as syllabic consonants, as in *cradle* (krād′l), and *button* (but′n). See the full key inside the front cover.

Guin•ea-Bis•sau (gin′ē bi sou′), *n.* a republic on the W coast of Africa, between Guinea and Senegal: formerly a Portuguese overseas province; gained independence in 1974. 600,000; 13,948 sq. mi. (36,125 sq. km). *Cap.:* Bissau. Formerly, **Portuguese Guinea.**

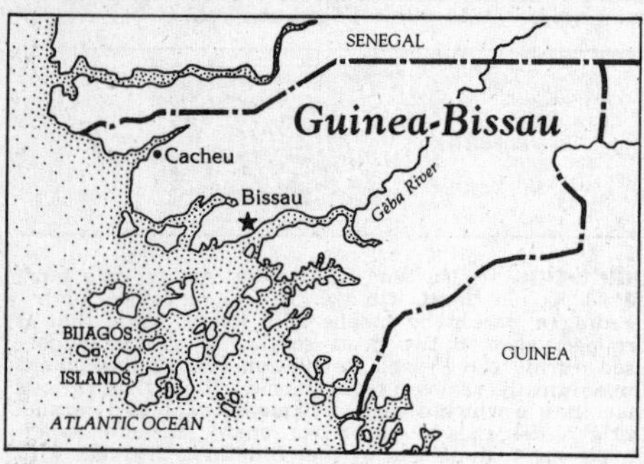

Guin′ea corn′, durra. [1665–75, *Amer.*]

Guin′ea Cur′rent, an ocean current flowing E along the Guinea coast of W Africa.

guin′ea fowl′, any of several African, gallinaceous birds of the subfamily Numidinae, esp. a common species, *Numida meleagris,* that has a bony casque on the head and dark gray plumage spotted with white and that is now domesticated and raised for its flesh and eggs. Also, **guin′ea•fowl′.** [1645–55]

guinea fowl, *Numida meleagris,* length 2 ft. (0.6 m)

guin′ea grains′. See **grains of paradise.**

guin′ea grass′, a grass, *Panicum maximum,* native to Africa, used for forage in warm regions of North and South America. [1750–60]

guin′ea hen′, **1.** the female of the guinea fowl. **2.** any member of the guinea fowl family. [1570–80]

guin′ea-hen flow′er (gin′ē hen′). See **checkered lily.** [1590–1600]

Guin′ea pep′per. See **grains of paradise.**

guin′ea pig′, **1.** a short-eared, tailless rodent of the genus *Cavia,* usually white, black, and tawny, commonly regarded as the domesticated form of one of the South American wild species of cavy: often used in scientific experiments or kept as a pet. **2.** *Informal.* the subject of any sort of experiment. [1655–65]

guinea pig, *Cavia porcellus,* length 11 in. (28 cm)

guin′ea worm′, a long, slender, roundworm, *Dracunculus medinensis,* parasitic under the skin of humans and animals, common in parts of India and Africa. Also, **Guin′ea worm′.** [1690–1700]

Guin•e•vere (gwin′ə vēr′), *n.* **1.** *Arthurian Romance.* wife of King Arthur and mistress of Lancelot. **2.** a female given name.

Guin•ness (gin′is), *n.* **Sir Alec,** born 1914, English actor.

gui•pure (gi pyŏŏr′; *Fr.* gē pyr′), *n., pl.* **-pures** (-pyŏŏrz′; *Fr.* -pyr′). **1.** any of various laces, often heavy, made of linen, silk, etc., with the pattern connected by brides rather than by a net ground. **2.** any of various laces or trimmings formerly in use, made with cords or heavy threads, metal, etc. [1835–45; < F, equiv. to *guip(er)* to cover or whip with silk, etc. (< Gmc; see WIPE, WHIP) + *-ure* -URE]

gui•ro (gwēr′ō; *Sp.* gē′rô), *n., pl.* **-ro.** a South American musical instrument consisting of a hollow gourd with serrated surface that is scraped with a stick. [1895–1900; < AmerSp *güiro,* lit., gourd, prob. < Taino]

gui•sard (gī′zərd), *n.* a person who wears a mask; mummer. [1620–30; GUISE + -ARD]

gui•sarme (gi zärm′), *n.* a shafted weapon having as a head a curved, double-edged blade with a beak at the back. Also, **gisarme.** [1200–50; ME < OF *g(u)isarme, gisarne,* prob. of Gmc orig.; cf. OHG *getisarn,* lit., weeding iron, equiv. to *get(an)* to weed (G *jäten*) + *isarn* IRON]

Guis•card (*Fr.* gēs kar′), *n.* **Ro•bert** (*Fr.* rô ber′), (*Robert de Hauteville*) c1015–85, Norman conqueror in Italy.

CONCISE ETYMOLOGY KEY: <, descended or borrowed from; >, whence; b., blend of, blended; c., cognate with; cf., compare; deriv., derivative; equiv., equivalent; imit., imitative; obl., oblique; r., replacing; s., stem; sp., spelling, spelled; resp., respelling, respelled; trans., translation; ?, origin unknown; *, unattested; ‡, probably earlier than. See the full key inside the front cover.

guise (gīz), *n., v.,* **guised, guis•ing.** —*n.* **1.** general external appearance; aspect; semblance: *an old principle in a new guise.* **2.** assumed appearance or mere semblance: *under the guise of friendship.* **3.** style of dress: *in the guise of a shepherd.* **4.** *Archaic.* manner; mode. —*v.t.* **5.** to dress; attire: *children guised as cowboys.* —*v.i.* **6.** *Scot. and North Eng.* to appear or go in disguise. [1175–1225; (n.) ME *g(u)ise* < OF < Gmc; see WISE[2]: (v.) ME *gisen,* deriv. of the n.]
—**Syn. 1.** form, shape. See **appearance.**

Guise (gēz), *n.* **1. Fran•çois de Lor•raine** (fräN swa′ də lô ren′), **2nd Duc de,** 1519–63, French general and statesman. **2.** his son, **Hen•ri I de Lorraine** (äN rē′), **Duc de,** 1550–88, French general and leader of opposition to the Huguenots.

gui•tar (gi tär′), *n.* a stringed musical instrument with a long, fretted neck, a flat, somewhat violinlike body, and typically six strings, which are plucked with the fingers or with a plectrum. [1615–25; < Sp *guitarra* < Ar *kītārah* << Gk *kithára* KITHARA]

electric guitar with amplifier
acoustic guitar

gui•tar•fish (gi tär′fish′), *n., pl.* (*esp. collectively*) **-fish,** (*esp. referring to two or more kinds or species*) **-fish•es.** any sharklike ray of the family Rhinobatidae, of warm seas, resembling a guitar in shape. [1900–05; GUITAR + FISH]

gui•tar•ist (gi tär′ist), *n.* a performer on the guitar. [1760–70; GUITAR + -IST]

guit•guit (gwit′gwit′), *n.* any of several tropical American honeycreepers. [1890–95; imit.]

Gui•try (gē′trē; *Fr.* gē trē′), *n.* **Sa•cha** (sä′shə; *Fr.* sa-sha′), 1885–1957, French actor and dramatist, born in Russia.

gui•ver (gī′vər), *n. Australian Slang.* guyver.

Gui•yang (gwē′yäng′), *n. Pinyin.* a city in and the capital of Guizhou province, in S China. 660,000. Also, **Kweiyang.**

Gui•zhou (gwē′jō′), *n. Pinyin.* **1.** Also, **Kweichow.** a province in S China. 17,140,000; 67,181 sq. mi. (173,999 sq. km). *Cap.:* Guiyang. **2.** former name of **Fengjie.**

Gui•zot (gē zō′), *n.* **Fran•çois Pierre Guil•laume** (fräN swa′ pyer gē yōm′), 1787–1874, French historian and statesman.

Gu•ja•rat (gŏŏj′ə rät′, gōō′jə-), *n.* **1.** a region in W India, N of the Narbada River. **2.** a state in W India, on the Arabian Sea. 30,930,000; 72,138 sq. mi. (186,837 sq. km). *Cap.:* Gandhinagar. Also, **Gu′je•rat′.**

Gu•ja•ra•ti (gŏŏj′ə rä′tē, gōō′jə-), *n.* an Indic language of western India. [1600–10; < Hindi < Skt *Gurjara* GUJARAT]

Gu′jarat States′, a group of former princely states, in W India: placed under a special agency (**Gu′jarat States′ A′gency**) in 1933; now divided between Gujarat and Maharashtra states.

Guj•ran•wa•la (gŏŏj′rən wä′lə, gŏŏj′-), *n.* a city in NE Pakistan. 597,000.

gu•la (gyōō′lə, gōō′-), *n., pl.* **-lae** (-lē), **-las. 1.** *Zool.* **a.** the upper part of the throat or gullet. **b.** the front or forward part of the neck. **2.** *Archit.* **a.** a molding having a large hollow, as a cavetto. **b.** ogee (def. 2). [1350–1400; ME < L: throat, gullet, appetite] —**gu′lar,** *adj.*

gu•lag (gōō′läg), *n.* (*sometimes cap.*) **1.** the system of forced-labor camps in the Soviet Union. **2.** a Soviet forced-labor camp. **3.** any prison or detention camp, esp. for political prisoners. [1970–75; < Russ *Gulág,* acronym from *Glávnoe upravlénie ispravítel′no-trudovýkh lagereí* Main Directorate of Corrective Labor Camps]

gulch (gulch), *n.* a deep, narrow ravine, esp. one marking the course of a stream or torrent. [1825–35; cf. Brit. dial. *gulch, gulsh* to run with a full stream, gush, (of land) to sink in, ME *gulchen* to spew forth, gush; expressive word akin to GULP, GUSH, etc.]

gul•den (gōōl′dn), *n., pl.* **-dens, -den.** guilder. [1590–1600; < D *gulden* (*florijin*) golden (florin)]

Gü•lek Bo•ğaz (gy lek′ bō äz′), Turkish name of the **Cilician Gates.**

gules (gyōōlz), *Heraldry.* —*n.* **1.** the tincture red. —*adj.* **2.** of the tincture red: *a lion gules.* [1300–50; ME *goules* < OF *gueules* red fur neckpiece, deriv. of *gole* throat < L *gula*]

gulf (gulf), *n.* **1.** a portion of an ocean or sea partly enclosed by land. **2.** a deep hollow; chasm or abyss. **3.** any wide separation, as in position, status, or education. **4.** something that engulfs or swallows up. —*v.t.* **5.** to swallow up; engulf. [1300–50; ME *go(u)lf* < OF *golfe* < It *golfo* < LGk *kólphos,* Gk *kólpos* bosom, lap, bay] —**gulf′like′,** *adj.* —**gulf′y,** *adj.*
—**Syn. 2.** canyon, gorge, gully, cleft, rift, split.

Gulf′ Coopera′tion Coun′cil, an association of Persian Gulf nations formed for the purpose of collective defense against aggression. *Abbr.:* GCC

Gulf′ Intracoast′al Wa′terway. See under **Intracoastal Waterway.**

Gulf•port (gulf′pôrt′, -pōrt′), *n.* **1.** a city in SE Mississippi, on the Gulf of Mexico. 39,676. **2.** a town in W Florida. 11,180.

Gulf′ States′, **1.** the states of the U.S. bordering on the Gulf of Mexico: Florida, Alabama, Mississippi, Louisiana, and Texas. **2.** Also called **Persian Gulf States.** the oil-producing countries bordering on or located near the Persian Gulf: Bahrain, Iran, Iraq, Kuwait, Oman, Qatar, Saudi Arabia, and the United Arab Emirates.

Gulf′ Stream′, **1.** a warm ocean current flowing N from the Gulf of Mexico, along the E coast of the U.S., to an area off the SE coast of Newfoundland, where it becomes the western terminus of the North Atlantic Current. **2.** See **Gulf Stream system.**

Gulf′ Stream′ sys′tem, a major ocean-current system consisting of the Gulf Stream and the Florida and North Atlantic currents. Also called **Gulf Stream.**

Gulf′ War′, a conflict (Jan.–Feb. 1991) between Iraq and the United States and its allies to expel Iraq from Kuwait.

gulf•weed (gulf′wēd′), *n.* **1.** a coarse, olive-brown, branching seaweed, *Sargassum bacciferum,* common in the Gulf Stream and tropical American seas, characterized by numerous berrylike air vessels. **2.** any seaweed of the same genus. [1665–75; GULF + WEED[1]]

gul•gul (gul′gul), *n.* a preparation of pulverized seashells and oil, applied to the wooden hull of a ship as a protection against boring worms. [orig. uncert.]

gull[1] (gul), *n.* any of numerous long-winged, web-toed, aquatic birds of the family Laridae, having usually white plumage with a gray back and wings. [1400–50; late ME *gulle,* perh. < Welsh *gŵylan,* Cornish *guilan* (cf. F *goéland* < Breton *gwelan*)] —**gull′-like′,** *adj.*

herring gull, *Larus argentatus,* length 26 in. (66 cm); wingspread 4½ ft. (1.4 m)

gull[2] (gul), *v.t.* **1.** to deceive, trick, or cheat. —*n.* **2.** a person who is easily deceived or cheated; dupe. [1540–50; perh. akin to obs. *gull* to swallow, guzzle]
—**Syn. 1.** cozen, dupe, fool, bamboozle, hoodwink.

Gul•lah (gul′ə), *n.* **1.** a member of a population of black Americans inhabiting the Sea Islands and the coastal regions of South Carolina, Georgia, and northeastern Florida. **2.** a creolized form of English spoken by the Gullahs, containing many words and grammatical features derived from African languages. [1730–40; of uncert. orig.; variously identified with ANGOLA or the *Gola,* a Liberian ethnic group]

gul•let (gul′it), *n.* **1.** the esophagus. **2.** the throat or pharynx. **3.** a channel for water. **4.** a gully or ravine. **5.** a preparatory cut in an excavation. **6.** a concavity between two sawteeth, joining them at their bases. —*v.t.* **7.** to form a concavity at the base of (a sawtooth). [1350–1400; ME *golet* < OF *goulet* << L *gula* throat; see -ET]

gul•ley[1] (gul′ē), *n., pl.* **-leys.** gully[1] (defs. 1, 2).

gul•ley[2] (gul′ē, gŏŏl′ē), *n., pl.* **-leys.** *Scot. and North Eng.* gully[2].

gul•li•ble (gul′ə bəl), *adj.* easily deceived or cheated. Also, **gul′la•ble.** [1815–25; GULL[2] + -IBLE] —**gul′li•bil′i•ty,** *n.* —**gul′li•bly,** *adv.*
—**Syn.** credulous, trusting, naive, innocent, simple.

Gul′li•ver's Trav′els (gul′ə vərz), a social and political satire (1726) by Jonathan Swift, narrating the voyages of Lemuel Gulliver to four imaginary regions: Lilliput, Brobdingnag, Laputa, and the land of the Houyhnhnms.

Gull•strand (gul′strand′; *Swed.* gŏŏl′sträNd′), *n.* **All•var** (äl′vär), 1862–1930, Swedish oculist: Nobel prize for medicine 1911.

gull′ wing′, an airplane wing that slants briefly upward from the fuselage and then extends horizontally outward. [1930–35]

gull-wing (gul′wing′), *adj.* **1.** (of an automobile door) hinged at the top and opening upward. **2.** having gull-wing doors: *a gull-wing sports car.* **3.** having or resembling airplane gull wings. [1930–35]

gul•ly[1] (gul′ē), *n., pl.* **-lies,** *v.,* **-lied, -ly•ing.** —*n.* **1.** a small valley or ravine originally worn away by running water and serving as a drainageway after prolonged heavy rains. **2.** a ditch or gutter. **3.** *Cricket.* **a.** the position of a fielder between point and slips. **b.** the fielder occupying this position. —*v.t.* **4.** to make gullies in. **5.** to form (channels) by the action of water. Also, **gulley** (for defs. 1,2). [1530–40; appar. var. of GULLET, with *-y* r. F *-et*]
—**Syn. 1.** gulch, gorge, defile, watercourse.

gul·ly² (gul′ē, gŏŏl′ē), *n., pl.* **-lies.** *Scot. and North Eng.* a knife, esp. a large kitchen or butcher knife. Also, **gulley.** [1575–85; orig. uncert.]

gul·ly·wash·er (gul′ē wosh′ər, -wô′shər), *n. Chiefly Midland and Western U.S.* a usually short, heavy rainstorm. [1815–25; GULLY¹ + WASHER]

gu·los·i·ty (gyōō los′i tē), *n.* gluttony or greediness. [1490–1500; < LL *gulōsitās,* equiv. to L *gulōs(us)* (*gul(a)* throat, appetite + *-ōsus* -OSE¹) + *itās* -ITY]

gulp (gulp), *v.i.* **1.** to gasp or choke, as when taking large drafts of a liquid. —*v.t.* **2.** to swallow eagerly, or in large drafts or morsels (often fol. by *down*): *He gulps down his food like a starving man.* **3.** to suppress, subdue, or choke back as if by swallowing: *to gulp down a sob.* —*n.* **4.** the act of gulping: *He drank the whole bottle of beer in one gulp.* **5.** the amount swallowed at one time; mouthful. [1400–50; late ME *gulpen* (v.); cf. D *gulpen,* Norw *glupa*] —**gulp′er,** *n.* —**gulp′ing·ly,** *adv.* —**gulp′y,** *adj.*
—**Syn. 2.** wolf, gobble, quaff, bolt, devour, guzzle.

gum¹ (gum), *n., v.,* **gummed, gum·ming.** —*n.* **1.** any of various viscid, amorphous exudations from plants, hardening on exposure to air and soluble in or forming a viscid mass with water. **2.** any of various similar exudations, as resin. **3.** a preparation of such a substance, as for use in the arts or bookbinding. **4.** See **chewing gum. 5.** mucilage; glue. **6.** rubber¹ (def. 1). **7.** See **gum tree. 8.** *Philately.* the adhesive by which a postage stamp is affixed. Cf. **o.g.** (def. 1). **9.** *Informal.* a rubber overshoe or boot. —*v.t.* **10.** to smear, stiffen, or stick together with gum. **11.** to clog with or as if with some gummy substance. —*v.i.* **12.** to exude or form gum. **13.** to become gummy. **14.** to become clogged with a gummy substance. **15. gum up,** *Slang.* to spoil or ruin. **16. gum up the works.** See **work** (def. 14). [1350–1400; ME *gomme* < OF < VL **gumma,* for L *gummi, cummi* < Gk *kómmi*] —**gum′less,** *adj.* —**gum′like′,** *adj.*

gum² (gum), *n., v.,* **gummed, gum·ming.** —*n.* **1.** Often, **gums.** Also called **gingiva.** the firm, fleshy tissue covering the alveolar parts of either jaw and enveloping the necks of the teeth. **2. beat one's gums,** *Slang.* to talk excessively or ineffectively. —*v.t.* **3.** to masticate (food) with the gums instead of teeth. **4.** to shape or renew the teeth of (a saw), as by grinding. [1275–1325; ME *gome,* OE *gōma* palate; akin to ON *gómr,* G *Gaumen* palate]

gum³ (gum), *interj.* **by gum,** (used as a mild oath). [1825–35; euphemism for GOD]

gum′ ammo′niac, a brownish-yellow gum resin, having an acrid taste, occurring in tearlike fragments from a plant, *Dorema ammoniacum,* of western Asia: used in porcelain ceramics and in medicine as an expectorant and counterirritant. Also called **ammoniac, ammoniacum.** [1350–1400; ME]

gum′ ar′abic, a water-soluble, gummy exudate obtained from the acacia tree, esp. *Acacia senegal,* used as an emulsifier, an adhesive, in inks, and in pharmaceuticals. Also called **acacia, gum′ aca′cia.** [1350–1400; ME]

gum·ball (gum′bôl′), *n.* a brightly colored ball of sugar-coated chewing gum. [1880–85, *Amer.*; GUM¹ + BALL¹]

gum′ band′, *Chiefly Pennsylvania and West Virginia.* a rubber band.

gum′ ben′zoin, benzoin (def. 1). Also called **gum′ ben′jamin.**

gum′ bichro′mate proc′ess, a contact printing method in which the image is formed on a coating of sensitized gum containing a suitable colored pigment and potassium or ammonium dichromate. Also called **gum′ dichro′mate proc′ess.** [1895–1900]

gum·bo (gum′bō), *n., pl.* **-bos,** *adj.* —*n.* **1.** a stew or thick soup, usually made with chicken or seafood, greens, and okra or sometimes filé as a thickener. **2.** okra. **3.** soil that becomes sticky and nonporous when wet. —*adj.* **4.** of, pertaining to, or like gumbo. [1795–1805, *Amer.*; < LaF *gombo, gumbo* < a Bantu language; cf. Umbundu *ochinggombo,* Luba *chinggombo* okra]

Gum·bo (gum′bō), *n.* (*sometimes l.c.*) a French patois spoken by blacks and Creoles in Louisiana and the French West Indies.

gum·boil (gum′boil′), *n. Pathol.* a small abscess on the gum, originating in an abscess in the pulp of a tooth. Also called **parulis.** [1745–55; GUM² + BOIL²]

gum·bo-lim·bo (gum′bō lim′bō), *n., pl.* **-lim·bos.** a tropical American tree, *Bursera simaruba,* having reddish bark and yielding a sweet, aromatic resin used in varnishes. Also called **gum elemi.** [1830–40, *Amer.*; of uncert. orig.]

gum·boot (gum′bōōt′), *n.* a rubber boot. [1840–50, *Amer.*; GUM¹ + BOOT¹]

gum·bo·til (gum′bə til), *n. Geol.* a sticky clay formed by the thorough weathering of glacial drift, the thickness of the clay furnishing means for comparing relative lengths of interglacial ages. [1915–20; GUMBO + *til,* var. of TILL⁴]

gum′ dam′mar, dammar (def. 1). [1865–70]

gum·drop (gum′drop′), *n.* a small candy made of gum arabic, gelatin, or the like, sweetened and flavored. [1855–60, *Amer.*; GUM¹ + DROP]

gum′ elas′tic, rubber¹ (def. 1). [1780–90]

gum′ el′emi, 1. elemi. **2.** gumbo-limbo. [1800–10, *Amer.*]

gum′ eras′er, a block of gummy, easily crumbled rubber used to erase smudges, pencil marks, and the like esp. from artwork.

gum′ guai′ac, guaiac.

gu·mi (gōō′mē), *n.* a spreading shrub, *Elaeagnus multiflora,* of eastern Asia, having fragrant yellowish-white flowers and edible red fruit. [< Japn]

gum·ma (gum′ə), *n., pl.* **gum·mas, gum·ma·ta** (gum′ə tə). *Pathol.* a rubbery, tumorlike lesion associated with tertiary syphilis. [1715–25; < NL; see GUM¹] —**gum′ma·tous,** *adj.*

gummed (gumd), *adj.* covered with a gummy substance. [1400–50; late ME; see GUM¹, -ED²]

gum·mite (gum′it), *n. Mineral.* a yellow to red alteration product of pitchblende and a minor ore of uranium, having a greasy luster and occurring in gumlike masses. [1865–70; orig. G *Gummit.* See GUM¹, -ITE¹]

gum·mous (gum′əs), *adj.* consisting of or resembling gum; gummy. [1660–70; < L *gummōsus,* equiv. to *gumm(i)* GUM¹ + *-ōsus* -OUS]

gum·my (gum′ē), *adj.,* **-mi·er, -mi·est. 1.** of, resembling, or of the consistency of gum; viscid; mucilaginous. **2.** covered with or clogged by gum or sticky matter. **3.** exuding gum. [1350–1400; ME; see GUM¹, -Y¹] —**gum′mi·ness,** *n.*

gum′ myr′tle, any of several trees of the genus *Angophora,* native to Australia, allied to and resembling the eucalyptus.

gump (gump), *n. Dial.* a foolish or stupid person. [1815–25; orig. uncert.]

gum′ plant′, gumweed. [1880–85, *Amer.*]

gum′ print′, *Photog.* a print made by the gum bichromate process.

gump·tion (gump′shən), *n. Informal.* **1.** initiative; aggressiveness; resourcefulness: *With his gumption he'll make a success of himself.* **2.** courage; spunk; guts: *It takes gumption to quit a high-paying job.* **3.** common sense; shrewdness. [1710–20; orig. Scots] —**gump′tion·less,** *adj.* —**gump′tious,** *adj.*

gum′ res′in, a plant exudation consisting of a mixture of gum and resin. [1705–15] —**gum′-res′i·nous,** *adj.*

Gum·ri (gŏŏm rē′), *n.* a city in NW Armenia, NW of Yerevan. 120,000. Formerly, **Aleksandropol, Leninakan.**

gum·shoe (gum′shōō′), *n., v.,* **-shoed, -shoe·ing.** —*n.* **1.** *Slang.* a detective. **2.** a shoe made of gum elastic or India rubber; rubber overshoe. **3.** sneaker (def. 1). —*v.i.* **4.** *Slang.* **a.** to work as a detective. **b.** to go softly, as if wearing rubber shoes; move or act snoopily or stealthily. [1860–65, *Amer.*; GUM¹ + SHOE]

gum′ thus′ (thus), thickened turpentine, used in certain oil paints. [*thus* < L *thūs, tūs* frankincense (see THURIFER)]

gum′ trag′acanth, tragacanth. [1565–75]

gum′ tree′, 1. any tree that exudes gum, as a eucalyptus, the sour gum, or the sweet gum. **2.** any of various other gum-yielding trees, as the sapodilla. [1670–80, *Amer.*]

gum·weed (gum′wēd′), *n.* any of various New World composite plants of the genus *Grindelia,* having yellow flower heads and covered with a viscid secretion. Also called **gum plant.** [GUM¹ + WEED¹]

gum·wood (gum′wŏŏd′), *n.* the wood of a gum tree, esp. the wood of a eucalyptus or of the sweet gum. [1675–85; GUM¹ + WOOD¹]

gun¹ (gun), *n., v.,* **gunned, gun·ning.** —*n.* **1.** a weapon consisting of a metal tube, with mechanical attachments, from which projectiles are shot by the force of an explosive; a piece of ordnance. **2.** any portable firearm, as a rifle, shotgun, or revolver. **3.** a long-barreled cannon having a relatively flat trajectory. **4.** any device for shooting something under pressure: *a paint gun; a staple gun.* **5.** *Slang.* a person whose profession is killing; professional killer: *a gangland gun.* **6.** *Brit.* a member of a shooting party. **7.** See **electron gun. 8. give the gun,** *Slang.* to put into motion or speed up: *We gave the motor the gun and drove off.* **9. jump the gun,** *Slang.* **a.** to begin a race before the starting signal. **b.** to begin prematurely; act too hastily. **10. spike someone's guns,** to frustrate or prevent someone from accomplishing a plan: *Our competitors planned a surprise reduction in their rates, but we discovered it and were able to spike their guns.* **11. stick to one's guns,** to maintain one's position in the face of opposition; stand firm: *They stuck to their guns and refused to submit.* Also, **stand by one's guns. 12. under the gun,** under pressure, as to meet a deadline or solve a problem: *We're all under the gun with these new sales quotas.* —*v.t.* **13.** to shoot with a gun (often fol. by *down*): *The guards gunned down the fleeing convict.* **14.** to cause (an engine, vehicle, aircraft, etc.) to increase in speed very quickly by increasing the supply of fuel. —*v.i.* **15.** to hunt with a gun. **16.** to shoot with a gun. **17. gun for, a.** to seek with intent to harm or kill. **b.** to seek; try earnestly to obtain: *He is gunning for a raise.* [1300–50; ME *gunne, gonne,* appar. short for AL *Gunilda, gonnyld,* name for engine of war; cf. ON *Gunna,* short for *Gunnhildr* woman's name] —**gun′less,** *adj.*

gun² (gun), *v.* pp. of **gin**³.

gun., gunnery.

gu·na (gŏŏn′ə), *n.* (in Sankhya and Vedantic philosophy) one of the three qualities of prakriti, or nature, which are passion **(rajas),** dullness or inertia **(tamas),** and goodness or purity **(sattva).** [1860–65; < Skt *guṇa* thread, quality]

gun·boat (gun′bōt′), *n.* **1.** a small, armed warship of light draft, used in ports where the water is shallow. **2.** any small ship carrying mounted guns. [1770–80; GUN¹ + BOAT]

gun′boat diplo′macy, diplomatic relations involving the use or threat of military force, esp. by a powerful nation against a weaker one. [1925–30]

gun′ brig′, a naval brig of the 18th century having from 8 to 12 guns. [1795–1805]

gun′ cam′era, an aircraft-mounted motion-picture camera recording the firing of all weapons on the gun-target line of the pilot. [1920–25]

gun′ car′riage, the structure on which a gun is mounted or moved and from which it is fired. [1760–70]

gun·cot·ton (gun′kot′n), *n.* a highly explosive cellulose nitrate, made by digesting clean cotton in a mixture of one part nitric acid and three parts sulfuric acid: used in making smokeless powder. [1840–50; GUN¹ + COTTON]

gun′ crew′, the sailors and petty officers in charge of a gun on a ship. [1860–65]

gun·da (gŏŏn′də), *n. Anglo-Indian.* goonda.

gun′ deck′, (formerly, on a warship) any deck, other than the weather deck, having cannons from end to end.

gun·di (gun′dē), *n., pl.* **-dis.** either of two small desert rodents, *Ctenodactylus gundi* or *C. vali,* of northern Africa, living in dry, rocky areas and characterized by comblike bristles on the hind feet. [< dial. Ar]

gun′ dog′, a dog trained to help a hunter, as by pointing or retrieving game. Also, **gun′dog′.** [1735–45]

gun·fight (gun′fīt′), *n.* a battle between two or more people or groups armed with guns, esp. a confrontation between two gunfighters using revolvers in the frontier days of the American West. [1650–60; GUN¹ + FIGHT]

gun·fight·er (gun′fī′tər), *n.* a person highly skilled in the use of a gun and a veteran of many gunfights, esp. one living during the frontier days of the American West. [1890–95, *Amer.*; GUN¹ + FIGHTER]

gun·fire (gun′fīər′), *n.* **1.** the firing of a gun or guns. **2.** *Mil.* the tactical use of firearms, esp. artillery, as distinguished from other weapons, as bayonets, torpedoes, or grenades. [1795–1805; GUN¹ + FIRE]

gun·flint (gun′flint′), *n.* the flint in a flintlock. [1725–35; GUN¹ + FLINT]

gunge (gunj), *n., v.,* **gunged, gung·ing.** *Brit. Informal.* —*n.* **1.** soft, sticky matter; goo. —*v.t.* **2.** to clog with gunge (often fol. by *up*). [1935–40; expressive coinage; cf. GUNK, GRUNGE]

gung-ho (gung′hō′), *Informal.* —*adj.* **1.** wholeheartedly enthusiastic and loyal; eager; zealous: *a gung-ho military outfit.* —*adv.* **2.** in a successful manner: *The business is going gung-ho.* [introduced as a training slogan in 1942 by U.S. Marine officer Evans F. Carlson (1896–1947) < Chin *gōng hé,* the abbreviated name of the Chinese Industrial Cooperative Society, taken by a literal trans. as "work together"]

Gun·ite (gun′īt), *n.* a mixture of cement, sand or crushed slag, and water, sprayed over reinforcement as a lightweight concrete construction. Also, **gun′ite.** [1910–15; formerly trademark]

gunk (gungk), *n. Informal.* any sticky or greasy residue or accumulation: *gunk on the oil filter.* [1932, *Amer.*; orig. a trademark name for a degreasing solvent]

gunk′ hole′, a quiet anchorage, as in a cove, used by small yachts. [1905–10]

gunk·y (gung′kē), *adj.,* **gunk·i·er, gunk·i·est.** *Informal.* of, pertaining to, characteristic of, or resembling gunk. [GUNK + -Y¹]

gun·lock (gun′lok′), *n.* the mechanism of a firearm by which the charge is exploded. [1645–55; GUN¹ + LOCK¹]

gun·mak·er (gun′mā′kər), *n.* a person or company that makes guns. [1350–1400; ME; see GUN¹, MAKER] —**gun′mak′ing,** *n.*

gun·man (gun′mən), *n., pl.* **-men. 1.** a person armed with or expert in the use of a gun, esp. one ready to use a gun unlawfully. **2.** a person who makes guns. [1615–25; GUN¹ + -MAN] —**gun′man·ship′,** *n.*

gun·met·al (gun′met′l), *n.* **1.** any of various alloys or metallic substances with a dark gray or blackish color or finish, used for chains, belt buckles, etc. **2.** Also called **gun′metal gray′.** a dark gray with bluish or purplish tinge. **3.** a bronze formerly much used for cannon. **4.** an alloy of 88 percent copper, 10 percent tin, and 2 percent zinc, cast or machined for use in valves, gears, and other parts. Also, **gun′ met′al.** [1535–45]

gun′ moll′, *Slang.* **1.** a female companion of a criminal. **2.** a female criminal. Also called **moll.** [1905–10; *gun* in earlier Brit. argot "thief" (see GANEF), later taken as GUN¹, which has influenced sense; cf. SON OF A GUN]

Gun·nar (gŏŏn′när, gŏŏn′ər), *n.* **1.** *Scand. Legend.* the husband of Brynhild: corresponds to Gunther in the *Nibelungenlied.* **2.** a male given name. [< ON *Gunnarr,* equiv. to *gunn* battle + *herr* master; cf. *Gundaharius,* Latinized form of a Burgundian personal name]

Gunn′ effect′ (gun), *Physics, Electronics.* the onset of microwave oscillations in a thin slice of a semiconductor when a voltage exceeding a given value is applied across the slice. [named after J. B. Gunn (b. 1928), British physicist, who discovered the effect in 1963]

gun·nel¹ (gun′l), *n.* any small eellike blenny of the family Pholididae (Pholidae), esp. *Pholis gunnellus* **(rock gunnel),** common in shallow waters of the North Atlantic. Also called **bracketed blenny.** [1680–90; orig. uncert.]

gun·nel² (gun′l), *n. Naut.* gunwale. [1425–75; ME. See GUNWALE]

gun·ner (gun′ər), *n.* **1.** a person who operates a gun or cannon. **2.** *Army.* an occupational title in the artillery. **3.** *Navy.* a person skilled in handling ammunition and gunnery equipment. **4.** *Marine Corps.* a warrant officer who may be given any one of a number of assignments. **5.** *Brit.* **a.** *Mil.* a private in the artillery. **b.** *Informal.* any officer or enlisted person assigned to the artillery. **6.** a person who hunts with a gun. [1300–50; ME; see GUN¹, -ER¹] —**gun′ner·ship′,** *n.*

gun·ner·y (gun′ə rē), *n.* **1.** the art and science of constructing and operating guns, esp. large guns. **2.** the act of firing guns. **3.** guns collectively. [1490–1500; GUN[1] + -ERY]

gun′nery ser′geant, *Marine Corps.* a noncommissioned officer ranking above a staff sergeant and below a first or master sergeant. [1960–65, *Amer.*]

gun·ning (gun′ing), *n.* **1.** the act, practice, or art of shooting with guns; gunnery. **2.** the hunting of game with guns. [1555–65; GUN[1] + -ING[1]]

gun·ny (gun′ē), *n., pl.* **-nies.** a strong, coarse material made commonly from jute, esp. for bags or sacks; burlap. [1705–15; < Hindi *goni* < Skt: sack, perh. orig. of hide; cf. GAUR]

gun·ny·sack (gun′ē sak′), *n.* a sack made of gunny or burlap. Also called **gun·ny-bag** (gun′ē bag′). [1860–65; GUNNY + SACK[1]]
—Regional Variation. CROCUS SACK, CROKER SACK, GRASS SACK, and TOWSACK are widely used in the Southern U.S. as synonyms for GUNNYSACK; CROCUS SACK is used esp. in the South Atlantic States and CROKER SACK in the Gulf States, while GRASS SACK and TOWSACK are used esp. in the South Midland U.S. BARLEY SACK is a Southwestern U.S. term, used esp. in California.

gun·pa·per (gun′pā′pər), *n. Mil.* a type of paper treated with nitric acid so that it has a composition similar to that of guncotton. [1850–55; GUN[1] + PAPER]

gun·play (gun′plā′), *n.* the exchange of gunshots, usually with intent to wound or kill. [1880–85, *Amer.*; GUN[1] + PLAY]

gun·point (gun′point′), *n.* **1.** the point or aim of a gun. **2. at gunpoint,** under threat of being shot: *He carried out the robber's orders at gunpoint.* [1955–60; GUN[1] + POINT]

gun·port (gun′pôrt′, -pōrt′), *n.* an aperture, as in a protective wall or the side of a ship, through which a gun can be aimed and fired. [1760–70; GUN[1] + PORT[4]]

gun·pow·der (gun′pou′dər), *n.* **1.** an explosive mixture, as of potassium nitrate, sulfur, and charcoal, used in shells and cartridges, in fireworks, for blasting, etc. **2.** Also called **gun′powder tea′.** a fine variety of green China tea, each leaf of which is rolled into a little ball. [1375–1425; late ME; see GUN[1], POWDER[1]] **—gun′pow′der·y,** *adj.*

Gun′powder Plot′, an unsuccessful plot to kill King James I and the assembled Lords and Commons by blowing up Parliament, November 5, 1605, in revenge for the laws against Roman Catholics. Cf. **Guy Fawkes Day.**

gun′ room′, **1.** a room in which guns are kept. **2.** *Brit.* a room on a warship for the use of junior naval officers. [1620–30]

gun·run·ning (gun′run′ing), *n.* the smuggling of guns or other ammunition into a country. [1880–85; GUN[1] + RUNNING] **—gun′run′ner,** *n.*

gun·sel (gun′səl), *n. Slang.* **1.** a criminal armed with a gun. **2.** a catamite. [1910–15; prob. < Yiddish *genzel* gosling < MHG *gensel* (dim. of *gans* goose); sense of def. 1, by influence of GUN[1]]

gun·ship (gun′ship′), *n.* a helicopter or fixed-wing airplane armed with rapid-fire guns or cannons and used to provide close air support for troops in combat. [1965–70; GUN[1] + SHIP]

gun·shot (gun′shot′), *n.* **1.** the shooting of a gun: *We heard three gunshots.* **2.** a bullet, projectile, or other shot fired from a gun. **3.** the range of a gun: *The bear was out of gunshot.* —*adj.* **4.** made by a gunshot. [1375–1425; late ME; see GUN[1], SHOT[1]]

gun-shy (gun′shī′), *adj.* **1.** frightened by the sound of a gunshot: *a gun-shy bird dog.* **2.** hesitant, wary, or distrustful, esp. because of previous unpleasant experience. [1880–85] **—gun′-shy′ness,** *n.*

gun·sling·er (gun′sling′ər), *n.* **1.** *Informal.* gunfighter. **2.** *Slang.* a person who acts in an aggressive and decisive manner, esp. in business or politics, as an investor who takes large risks in seeking large, quick gains. [1950–55; GUN[1] + SLING[1] + -ER[1]] **—gun′sling′ing,** *adj.*

gun·smith (gun′smith′), *n.* a person who makes or repairs firearms. [1580–90; GUN[1] + SMITH] **—gun′smith′ing,** *n.*

gun·stock (gun′stok′), *n.* the stock or support in which the barrel of a shoulder weapon is fixed. [1485–95; see GUN[1], STOCK]

gun′stock stile′, (in a door) a diminished stile having an oblique transition between the broader and narrower parts.

gun′ tack′le, *Naut.* a tackle composed of a fall rove through two single blocks and secured to one of them so as to secure a mechanical advantage of two or three, neglecting friction, depending on the arrangement. See diag. under **tackle.** [1785–95]

gun·ter (gun′tər), *n. Naut.* a jib-headed sail fastened to a vertical spar that is attached to a short mast, usually by two rings, in such a way that the spar can slide up the mast to spread the sail. [1670–80; named after E. GUNTER for its resemblance to an instrument using his principles]

Gun·ter (gun′tər), *n.* **Edmund,** 1581–1626, English mathematician and astronomer: inventor of various measuring instruments and scales.

Gun′ter's chain′. See under **chain** (def. 8a). [1670–80; named after E. GUNTER]

Gun·ther (gun′thər *for 1, 3;* go͝on′tər *for 2*), *n.* **1. John,** born 1901, U.S. journalist and author. **2.** (in the *Nibelungenlied*) a king of Burgundy and the husband of Brunhild, beheaded by Kriemhild in her revenge for the murder of Siegfried. Cf. **Gunnar. 3.** a male given name.

gun-tot·ing (gun′tō′ting, -tōt′n), *adj.* carrying a gun, esp. a pistol. [1910–15]

Gun·tur (go͝on to͝or′), *n.* a city in E Andhra Pradesh, in SE India. 269,991. Also, **Gun·tar** (go͝on tär′).

gun·wale (gun′l), *n. Naut.* **1.** the upper edge of the side or bulwark of a vessel. **2.** the sheer strake of a wooden vessel; the uppermost strake beneath the planksheer. Also, **gunnel.** [1325–75; ME. See GUN[1], WALE[1]; a plank so called because guns were set upon it]

gun·yah (gun′yə), *n. Australian.* **1.** an aboriginal hut or shelter. **2.** any crude bush hut or shelter. [1790–1800; < Dharuk *gu-n'i*]

Günz (gints; *Ger.* gynts), *n.* the first stage of the glaciation of Eurasia during the Pleistocene. Cf. **Nebraskan** (def. 4). [1905–10; after a region in the Alps; see WÜRM] **—Günz′i·an,** *adj.*

Guo Mo·ruo (gwô′ mô′RWô′, -zhwô′), 1892–1978, Chinese intellectual, writer, poet, scholar, and government official.

gup·py (gup′ē), *n., pl.* **-pies.** a small, freshwater topminnow, *Poecilia reticulata,* often kept in aquariums. Also called **rainbow fish.** [named after R.J.L. Guppy (1836–1916) of Trinidad, who presented specimens to the British Museum; catalogued under the NL name *Gerardinus guppyi* in 1866]

Gup·ta (go͝op′tə, gup′-), *n.* **1.** a dynasty of N India (A.D. 320–540) whose court was the center of classical Indian art and literature. **2.** the empire of this dynasty, encompassing all of N India and Gujarat.

Gur (go͝or), *n.* a branch of the Niger-Congo subfamily of languages, including Mossi and other languages spoken in Burkina Faso, Ghana, Togo, Ivory Coast, and Mali. Also called **Voltaic.**

gur·dwa·ra (gûr′dwär ə), *n.* a Sikh temple in India. [1905–10; < Panjabi *gurduārā* < Skt *gur(u)* GURU + *dvāra* door]

gurge (gûrj), *n., pl.* **gur·ges** (gûr′jēs), *v.,* **gurged, gurg·ing.** —*n.* **1.** a whirlpool. **2.** Also, **gorge.** Also called **whirlpool.** *Heraldry.* a charge covering the entire field of an escutcheon and having the form either of a spirallike scroll or of a number of concentric rings, the whole field having two tinctures. —*v.i.* **3.** to swirl like a whirlpool. [1515–25; < L *gurges* whirlpool]

gur·gi·ta·tion (gûr′ji tā′shən), *n.* a surging rise and fall; ebullient motion, as of water. [1535–45; < L *gurgitāt(us)* (ptp. of *gurgitāre* to engulf, deriv. of *gurgit-,* s. of *gurges* whirlpool; see -ATE[1]) + -ION]

gur·gle (gûr′gəl), *v.,* **-gled, -gling,** *n.* —*v.i.* **1.** to flow in a broken, irregular, noisy current: *The water gurgled from the bottle.* **2.** to make a sound as of water doing this (often used of birds or of human beings). —*v.t.* **3.** to utter or express with a gurgling sound: *The baby gurgled its delight.* —*n.* **4.** the act or noise of gurgling. [1555–65; cf. D, MLG *gorgelen,* G *gurgeln* to gargle; akin to L *gurguliō* throat] **—gur′gling·ly,** *adv.*
—Syn. 1, 2. bubble, burble, babble.

gur·glet (gûr′glit), *n.* goglet. [1790–1800; GURGLE + -ET]

Gur·kha (gûr′kə, go͝or′-), *n., pl.* **-khas,** (*esp. collectively*) **-kha. 1.** a member of a Rajput people, Hindu in religion, who achieved dominion over Nepal in the 18th century. **2.** a Nepalese soldier in the British or Indian army. [1805–15]

gur·nard (gûr′nərd), *n., pl.* (*esp. collectively*) **-nard,** (*esp. referring to two or more kinds or species*) **-nards. 1.** any marine fish of the family Triglidae, having an armored, spiny head and the front part of the pectoral fins modified for crawling on the sea bottom. **2.** See **flying gurnard.** [1275–1325; ME < OF *gornard,* prob. lit., grunter << L *grunnīre* to grunt]

gur·ney (gûr′nē), *n., pl.* **-neys.** a flat, padded table or stretcher with legs and wheels, for transporting patients or bodies. [1935–40; of unexplained orig.]

Gur·ney·ite (gûr′nē īt′), *n.* a supporter of Joseph John Gurney (1788–1847), an English Quaker, who, on a preaching tour of America, advocated Christian evangelical principles. Cf. **Wilburite.** [*Gurney* + -ITE[1]]

Gür·sel (GYR sel′), *n.* **Ce·mal** (je mäl′), 1895–1966, Turkish army officer and statesman: president 1961–66.

gursh (gûrsh), *n.* qirsh.

gu·ru (go͝or′o͞o, go͞o ro͞o′), *n.* **1.** *Hinduism.* a preceptor giving personal religious instruction. **2.** an intellectual or spiritual guide or leader. **3.** any person who counsels or advises; mentor: *The elder senator was her political guru.* **4.** a leader in a particular field: *the city's cultural gurus.* [1820–30; < Hindi *gurū* < Skt *guru* venerable, weighty] **—gu′ru·ship′,** *n.*

Gu·ryev (go͝or′yəf; *Russ.* go͞o′RYif), *n.* a port in W Kazakhstan, at the mouth of the Ural River on the Caspian Sea. 142,000.

Gus (gus), *n.* a male given name, form of **Augustus** or **Gustave.**

gush (gush), *v.i.* **1.** to flow out or issue suddenly, copiously, or forcibly, as a fluid from confinement: *Water gushed from the broken pipe.* **2.** to express oneself extravagantly or emotionally; talk effusively: *She gushed with pride over her new grandchild.* **3.** to have a sudden, copious flow, as of blood or tears. —*v.t.* **4.** to emit suddenly, forcibly, or copiously. —*n.* **5.** a sudden, copious outflow of a fluid. **6.** the fluid emitted. **7.** effusive and often insincere language or behavior. [1350–1400; ME; prob. phonesthemic in orig.; see GUST[1], RUSH[1]] **—gush′ing·ly,** *adv.*
—Syn. 1. pour, stream, flood. See **flow. 4.** spurt.

gush·er (gush′ər), *n.* **1.** a flowing oil well, usually of large capacity. **2.** a person who gushes. [1860–65; GUSH + -ER[1]]

gush·y (gush′ē), *adj.,* **gush·i·er, gush·i·est.** given to or marked by excessively effusive talk, behavior, etc. [1835–45; GUSH + -Y[1]] **—gush′i·ly,** *adv.* **—gush′i·ness,** *n.*
—Syn. emotional, enthusiastic, unrestrained, demonstrative, unreserved.

gus·set (gus′it), *n.* **1.** a small, triangular piece of material inserted into a shirt, shoe, etc., to improve the fit or for reinforcement. Cf. **godet** (def. 1), **gore**[3] (def. 1). **2.** *Civil Engin.* a plate for uniting structural members at a joint, as in a steel frame or truss. **3.** *Armor.* **a.** Also called **voider.** an area of mail backed with cloth, for defending the armpits or areas at joints. **b.** a small piece of plate armor at the armhole of a cuirass; pallet. [1375–1425; late ME < OF *gousset,* deriv. of *gousse* pod, husk]

Gus·sie (gus′ē), *n.* a female given name, form of **Augusta.** Also, **Gus′sy.**

gus·sy (gus′ē), *v.,* **-sied, -sy·ing.** *Informal.* —*v.t.* **1.** to enhance the attractiveness of in a gimmicky, showy manner (usually fol. by *up*): *a room gussied up with mirrors and lights.* —*v.i.* **2.** to dress in one's best clothes (usually fol. by *up*): *to gussy up for the ball.* [1935–40; of obscure orig.]

gust[1] (gust), *n.* **1.** a sudden, strong blast of wind. **2.** a sudden rush or burst of water, fire, smoke, sound, etc. **3.** an outburst of passionate feeling. —*v.i.* **4.** to blow or rush in gusts. [1580–90; < ON *gustr* a gust, akin to *gjōsa, gusa* to gust] **—gust′less,** *adj.*
—Syn. 1. See **wind**[1].

gust[2] (gust), *n.* **1.** *Archaic.* flavor or taste. **2.** *Obs.* enjoyment or gratification. —*v.t.* **3.** *Scot.* to taste; savor. [1400–50; late ME < L *gustus* a tasting (of food), eating a little, akin to *gustāre* to taste] **—gust′a·ble,** *adj., n.*

gus·ta·tion (gu stā′shən), *n.* **1.** the act of tasting. **2.** the faculty of taste. [1590–1600; < L *gustātiōn-* (s. of *gustātiō*), equiv. to *gustāt(us)* (ptp. of *gustāre* to taste) + *-iōn-* -ION]

gus·ta·tive (gus′tə tiv), *adj.* gustatory. [1610–20; < ML *gustātīvus,* equiv. to L *gustāt(us)* (see GUSTATION) + *-īvus* -IVE] **—gus′ta·tive·ness,** *n.*

gus·ta·to·ry (gus′tə tôr′ē, -tōr′ē), *adj.* of or pertaining to taste or tasting. [1675–85; < L *gustā(re)* to taste + -TORY[1]] **—gus′ta·to′ri·ly,** *adv.*

Gus·tave (gus′täv; *Fr.* GYS TAV′), *n.* a male given name: from a Germanic word meaning "staff of God."

Gus·ta·vo A. Ma·de·ro (go͞os tä′vô ä′ mä *th*e′Rô), official name of **Guadalupe Hidalgo.**

Gus·ta·vus (gu stā′vəs, -stä′-), *n.* a male given name, Latinized form of **Gustave.**

Gustavus I, (*Gustavus Vasa*) 1496–1560, king of Sweden 1523–60.

Gustavus II, (*Gustavus Adolphus*) (*"Lion of the North"*) 1594–1632, king of Sweden 1611–32: national military hero (grandson of Gustavus I).

Gustavus III, 1746–92, king of Sweden 1771–92: economic and legal reformer.

Gustavus IV, (*Gustavus Adolphus*) 1778–1837, king of Sweden 1792–1809 (son of Gustavus III).

Gustavus V, 1858–1950, king of Sweden 1907–50: advocate of Swedish neutrality during World Wars I and II. Also, **Gus·taf V, Gus·tav V** (gus′täv).

Gustavus VI, (*Gustaf Adolf*) 1882–1973, king of Sweden 1950–73 (son of Gustavus V). Also, **Gustav VI.**

gus·to (gus′tō), *n., pl.* **-toes. 1.** hearty or keen enjoyment, as in eating or drinking, or in action or speech in general: *to dance with gusto.* **2.** individual taste or liking. [1620–30; < It < L *gustus;* see GUST[2]]
—Syn. 1. enthusiasm, delight, relish, zest, spirit, fervor.

Gus·ton (gus′tən), *n.* **Philip,** 1912–80, U.S. abstract expressionist painter, born in Canada.

gust·y[1] (gus′tē), *adj.,* **gust·i·er, gust·i·est. 1.** blowing or coming in gusts, as wind, rain, or storms. **2.** affected or marked by gusts of wind, rain, etc.: *a gusty day.* **3.** occurring or characterized by sudden bursts or outbursts, as sound or laughter. **4.** full of meaningless, pretentious talk: *gusty speechmaking.* **5.** vigorous; hearty; zestful: *a gusty woman.* [1590–1600; GUST[1] + -Y[1]; def. 5 perh. GUST(O) + -Y[1]] **—gust′i·ly,** *adv.* **—gust′i·ness,** *n.*

gust·y[2] (gus′tē, go͞os′tē), *adj.,* **gust·i·er, gust·i·est.** *Chiefly Scot.* tasty; savory; appetizing. [1715–25; GUST[2] + -Y[1]]

gut (gut), *n., v.,* **gut·ted, gut·ting,** *adj.* —*n.* **1.** the alimentary canal, esp. between the pylorus and the anus, or some portion of it. Cf. **foregut, midgut, hindgut. 2. guts, a.** the bowels or entrails. **b.** *Informal.* courage and fortitude; nerve; determination; stamina: *Climbing that cliff takes a lot of guts.* **c.** the inner working parts of a machine or device: *The mechanic had the guts of the refrigerator laid out on the kitchen floor.* **3.** the belly; stomach; abdomen. **4.** the substance forming the case of the intestine; intestinal tissue or fiber: *sheep's gut.* **5.** a preparation of the intestines of an animal, used for various purposes, as for violin strings, tennis rackets, or fishing lines. **6.** the silken substance taken from a silkworm killed when about to spin its cocoon, used in making snells for fishhooks. **7.** a narrow passage, as a channel of water or a defile between hills. **8.** *Slang.* a gut course. **9. spill one's guts,** *Slang.* to tell all; lay oneself bare: *the famous star spills his guts in his autobiography.* —*v.t.* **10.** to take out the guts or entrails of; disembowel. **11.** to destroy the interior of: *Fire gutted the building.* **12.** to plunder (a house, city, etc.) of contents: *Invaders gutted the village.* **13.** to remove the vital or essential parts from: *The prisoner's letters were gutted by heavy censorship.* —*adj.* **14.** *Informal.* **a.** basic or essential: *to discuss the gut issues.* **b.** based on instincts or emotions: *a gut reaction; gut decisions.* [bef. 1000; ME

CONCISE ETYMOLOGY KEY: <, descended or borrowed from; >, whence; b., blend of, blended; c., cognate with; cf., compare; deriv., derivative; equiv., equivalent; imit., imitative; obl., oblique; r., replacing; s., stem; sp., spelling, spelled; resp., respelling, respelled; trans., translation; ?, origin unknown; *, unattested; ‡, probably earlier than. See the full key inside the front cover.

gut, guttes (pl.), OE *guttas* (pl.), akin to *gēotan* to pour] —**gut′like′**, *adj.*
—**Syn. 2b.** pluck.

GUT, *Physics.* grand unification theory.

gut·buck·et (gut′buk′it), *n.* jazz played in the raucous and high-spirited style of barrelhouse. [1925–30; GUT + BUCKET]

gut′ course′. See **snap course.** [1945–50]

Gu·ten·berg (gōōt′n bûrg′; *Ger.* gōōt′n berk′), *n.* **Jo·han·nes** (yō hän′əs), (*Johann Gensfleisch*), c1400–68, German printer: credited with invention of printing from movable type.

Gu′tenberg Bi′ble, an edition of the Vulgate printed at Mainz before 1456, ascribed to Gutenberg and others: probably the first large book printed with movable type.

Guth·rie (guth′rē), *n.* **1. Sir (William) Tyrone,** 1900–71, English stage director and producer. **2. Woodrow Wilson** (*"Woody"*), 1912–67, U.S. folk singer. **3.** a city in central Oklahoma: the former state capital. 10,312. **4.** a male given name.

Gu·tiér·rez Ná·je·ra (gōō tyeʀ′ʀes nä′he rä′), **Manuel** (mä nwel′), (*"El Duque Job"*), 1859–95, Mexican poet, short-story writer, and editor.

gut·less (gut′lis), *adj. Informal.* lacking courage, fortitude, or determination. [1600–10 for literal sense; GUT + -LESS] —**gut′less·ness,** *n.*

Gut′ of Can′so, Canso (def. 2).

gut·ser (gut′sər), *n. Australian Slang.* **1.** a person who eats too much and greedily. **2. come a gutser, a.** to fall over. **b.** to fail, esp. as a result of pride. [1900–05; GUTS (see GUT) + -ER[1]]

guts·y (gut′sē), *adj.,* **guts·i·er, guts·i·est.** *Informal.* **1.** having a great deal of courage or nerve: *a gutsy lampooner of the administration.* **2.** robust, vigorous, or earthy; lusty: *gutsy writing; a gutsy red wine.* [1890–95; GUTS + -Y[1]; cf. -SY] —**guts′i·ness,** *n.*

gut·ta (gut′ə), *n., pl.* **gut·tae** (gut′ē). **1.** a drop, or something resembling one. **2.** Also called **drop.** *Archit.* one of a series of pendent ornaments, generally in the form of a frustum of a cone, attached to the undersides of the mutules of the Doric entablature. [1350–1400; ME *goute, gutta* < L *gutta* a drop]

gut′tae band′, regula. [*guttae* < L, pl. of *gutta* GUTTA]

gut·ta-per·cha (gut′ə pûr′chə), *n.* **1.** the milky juice, nearly white when pure, of various Malaysian trees of the sapodilla family, esp. *Palaquium gutta.* **2.** the tough, rubberlike gum made from this and used as a dental cement, in the manufacture of golf balls, for insulating electric wires, etc. [1835–45; < Malay *gətah* (sp. *getah*) tree sap + *perca* rag, strip of cloth; perh. so called from the appearance of the sap (Malay *getah taban*) in its marketed form]

gut·tate (gut′āt), *adj. Biol.* resembling a drop; having droplike markings. Also, **gut′tat·ed.** [1820–30; < L *guttātus* speckled, spotted. See GUTTA, -ATE[1]]

gut·ta·tim (gə tā′təm, -tä′-), *adv.* (in prescriptions) drop by drop. [1685–95; < L *guttātim*]

gut·ta·tion (gu tā′shən), *n. Bot.* a process in which water in liquid form is given off by plants. [1885–90; < G; see GUTTA, -ATION]

gut·ter (gut′ər), *n.* **1.** a channel at the side or in the middle of a road or street, for leading off surface water. **2.** a channel at the eaves or on the roof of a building, for carrying off rain water. **3.** any channel, trough, or the like for carrying off fluid. **4.** a furrow or channel made by running water. **5.** *Bowling.* a sunken channel on each side of the alley from the line marking the limit of a fair delivery of the ball to the sunken area behind the pins. **6.** the state or abode of those who live in degradation, squalor, etc.: *the language of the gutter.* **7.** the white space formed by the inner margins of two facing pages in a bound book, magazine, or newspaper. —*v.i.* **8.** to flow in streams. **9.** (of a candle) to lose molten wax accumulated in a hollow space around the wick. **10.** (of a lamp or candle flame) to burn low or to be blown so as to be nearly extinguished. **11.** to form gutters, as water does. —*v.t.* **12.** to make gutters in; channel. **13.** to furnish with a gutter or gutters: *to gutter a new house.* [1250–1300; ME *gutter, goter* < AF *goutiere,* equiv. to *goutte* drop (see GOUT) + *-iere,* fem. of *-ier* -ER[2]] —**gut′ter·like′,** *adj.*

gut·ter·ing (gut′ər ing), *n.* **1.** the act of making gutters. **2.** material for making gutters. **3.** the gutters of an individual building. **4.** the melted wax or tallow of a candle. [1400–50; late ME. See GUTTER, -ING[1]]

gut·ter·snipe (gut′ər snīp′), *n.* **1.** a person belonging to or characteristic of the lowest social group in a city. **2.** a street urchin. [1855–60; GUTTER + SNIPE] —**gut′ter·snip′ish,** *adj.*

gut·ti·form (gut′ə fôrm′), *adj.* shaped like a drop. [1870–75; GUTT(A) drop (of liquid) + -I- + -FORM]

gut·tle (gut′l), *v.i., v.t.,* **-tled, -tling.** to eat greedily or voraciously; gormandize. [1645–55; GUT + -LE; cf. GUZZLE] —**gut′tler,** *n.*

gut·tur·al (gut′ər əl), *adj.* **1.** of or pertaining to the throat. **2.** harsh; throaty. **3.** *Phonet.* pertaining to or characterized by a sound articulated in the back of the mouth, as the non-English velar fricative sound (ᴋʜ). —*n.* **4.** a guttural sound. [1585–95; < NL *gutturālis* of the throat, equiv. to L *guttur* gullet, throat + *-ālis* -AL[1]] —**gut′tur·al·ly,** *adv.* —**gut′tur·al·ness, gut′tur·al′i·ty, gut′tur·al·ism,** *n.*

gut·tur·al·ize (gut′ər ə līz′), *v.,* **-ized, -iz·ing.** —*v.t.* **1.** to speak or pronounce (something) in a guttural manner. **2.** *Phonet.* to change into, pronounce as, or supplement with a guttural or gutturalized sound. —*v.i.* **3.** to speak gutturally. Also, *esp. Brit.,* **gut′tur·al·ise.** [1815–25; GUTTURAL + -IZE] —**gut′tur·al·i·za′tion,** *n.*

gut·tur·al·ized (gut′ər ə līzd′), *adj. Phonet.* pronounced with guttural coarticulation. [1875–80; GUTTURALIZE + -ED[2]]

gut·tur·o·na·sal (gut′ə rō nā′zəl), *Phonet.* —*adj.* **1.** articulated in the back of the mouth and given resonance in the nasal cavity, as the sound represented by (ng) in (ring). —*n.* **2.** a gutturonasal sound. [1870–75; GUTTUR(AL) + -O- + NASAL[1]]

gut·ty (gut′ē), *adj.,* **-ti·er, -ti·est.** *Informal.* showing spirit; plucky; gutsy: *a gutty attempt to kick a field goal.* [1935–40; GUT + -Y[1]]

gut-wrench·ing (gut′ren′ching), *adj.* involving great distress or anguish; agonizing: *a gut-wrenching decision.*

guv (guv), *n. Chiefly Brit. Informal.* **1.** term of address used to a man, esp. by a younger man, boy, employee, or social inferior. **2.** governor (def. 6). [1850–55; by shortening and resp.]

guy[1] (gī), *n., v.,* **guyed, guy·ing.** —*n.* **1.** *Informal.* a man or boy; fellow: *He's a nice guy.* **2.** Usually, **guys.** *Informal.* persons of either sex; people: *Could one of you guys help me with this?* **3.** *Chiefly Brit. Slang.* a grotesquely dressed person. **4.** (*often cap.*) *Brit.* a grotesque effigy of Guy Fawkes that is paraded through the streets and burned on Guy Fawkes Day. **5. give the guy to,** *Brit. Slang.* to escape from (someone); give (someone) the slip. —*v.t.* **6.** to jeer at or make fun of; ridicule. [1800–10; after *Guy Fawkes*]

guy[2] (gī), *n., v.,* **guyed, guy·ing.** —*n.* **1.** a rope, cable, or appliance used to guide and steady an object being hoisted or lowered, or to secure anything likely to shift its position. —*v.t.* **2.** to guide, steady, or secure with a guy or guys. [1300–50; ME *gye* < OF *guie* a guide, deriv. of *guier* to GUIDE]

Guy (gī; *Fr.* gē), *n.* a male given name: from a Germanic word meaning "woods."

Guy·a·na (gī an′ə, -ä′nə), *n.* an independent republic on the NE coast of South America: a former British protectorate; gained independence 1966; member of the Commonwealth of Nations. 800,000; 82,978 sq. mi. (214,913 sq. km). *Cap.:* Georgetown. Formerly, **British Guiana.** See map under **Guiana.** —**Guy·a·nese** (gī′ə nēz′, -nēs′), *n., adj.*

Guy·enne (gwē yen′), *n.* Guienne.

Guy′ Fawkes′ Day′ (gī′ fôks′), (in Britain) November 5, celebrating the anniversary of the capture of Guy Fawkes. Cf. **Gunpowder Plot.**

guy′ Fri′day, a man who acts as a general assistant in a business office or to an executive and has a wide variety of esp. secretarial and clerical duties. Cf. **gal Friday.**

Guy·on (gwē yôɴ′), *n.* **Madame** (*Jeanne Marie Bouvier de la Matte*), 1648–1717, French writer.

guy·ot (gē ō′), *n.* a flat-topped seamount, found chiefly in the Pacific Ocean. [1945–50; named after Arnold H. *Guyot* (1807–84), Swiss-born American geologist and geographer]

guy·ver (gī′vər), *n. Australian Slang.* affectation of speech or manner. Also, **guiver.** [1865–70; orig. obscure; perh. to be identified with dial. (N England) *givour* greedy, gluttonous, but sense shift unexplained]

Guz·mán (gōōs män′), *n.* **Mar·tín Luis** (mär tēn′ lwēs), 1887–1976, Mexican novelist, journalist, and soldier.

Guz·mán Blan·co (gōōs män′ bläng′kô), **An·to·nio** (än tô′nyô), 1829–99, Venezuelan political leader: president 1870–88.

guz·zle (guz′əl), *v.,* **-zled, -zling,** *n.* —*v.i., v.t.* **1.** to drink, or sometimes eat, greedily, frequently, or plentifully: *They spent the whole night guzzling beer.* —*n.* **2.** *South Midland and Southern U.S.* gozzle. [1570–80; orig. uncert.] —**guz′zler,** *n.*
—**Syn. 1.** swill, imbibe, swig, tope; chugalug.

g.v., gravimetric volume.

GVW, gross vehicle weight; gross vehicular weight.

GW, gigawatt; gigawatts. Also, **Gw**

Gwa·li·or (gwä′lē ôr′), *n.* **1.** a former state in central India, now part of Madhya Pradesh. **2.** a city in N Madhya Pradesh. 406,755.

Gwa·ri (gwär′ē), *n., pl.* **-ris,** (*esp. collectively*) **-ri.** a member of an agricultural people of northeastern Nigeria. Also, **Gbari.**

Gwawl (gwoul), *n. Welsh Legend.* the rival of Pwyll for the hand of Rhiannon.

gwe·duc (gōō′ē duk′), *n.* geoduck.

Gwen (gwen), *n.* a female given name, form of **Gwendolyn** or **Guenevere.**

Gwen·do·lyn (gwen′dl in), *n.* a female given name: from a Welsh word meaning "white."

Gwent (gwent), *n.* a county in S Wales. 440,100; 531 sq. mi. (1376 sq. km).

Gwe·ru (gwā′rōō), *n.* a city in central Zimbabwe. 25,000. Formerly, **Gwe·lo** (gwā′lō).

gwine (gwīn), *v. Chiefly Southern U.S. Nonstandard.* pres. part. of **go.**

Gwin·nett (gwi net′), *n.* **Button,** 1735?–77, American Revolutionary leader, born in England.

Gwyn (gwin), *n.* **Eleanor** ("*Nell*"), 1650–87, English actress: mistress of Charles II. Also, **Gwynne.**

Gwyn·edd (gwin′eth), *n.* a county in E Wales. 224,200; 1493 sq. mi. (3866 sq. km).

Gy, *Physics.* gray[2].

gybe (jīb), *v.i., v.t.,* **gybed, gyb·ing,** *n. Naut.* jibe[1].

Gy·ges (jī′jēz), *n. Gk. Myth.* **1.** Also, **Gy·es** (jī′ēz). one of the Hecatonchires. **2.** a shepherd who found a ring making its wearer invisible. Invited by the king of Lydia secretly to view his beautiful wife naked, Gyges was incited by her to kill the king and seize the throne. During his reign, allegedly, coinage was invented.

gym (jim), *n.* **1.** a gymnasium. **2.** *Informal.* See **physical education.** [1870–75; by shortening]

gym·el (jim′əl), *n. Music.* the technique, found in some medieval English music, of singing voice parts in parallel thirds. Also, **gimel.** [1350–1400; ME *gimeles, gemeles* twins < MF *gemel, gimel* twin; see GIMMAL, GEMINATE]

gym·kha·na (jim kä′nə), *n.* **1.** a field day held for equestrians, consisting of exhibitions of horsemanship and much pageantry. **2.** Also called **autocross.** a competition in which sports cars are timed as they travel on a closed, twisting course that requires much maneuvering. **3.** any of various other sporting events, as a gymnastics exhibition or surfing contest. **4.** a place where any such event is held. [1860–65; < Hindi *gẽdkhānā* lit., ball-house (influenced by GYMNASTICS)]

gymn-, var. of **gymno-** before a vowel: *gymnanthous.*

gym·nan·thous (jim nan′thəs), *adj. Bot.* achlamydeous. [1875–80; GYMN- + -ANTHOUS]

gym·na·si·a (jim nā′zē ə, -zhə), *n.* a pl. of **gymnasium.**

gym·na·si·arch (jim nā′zē ärk′), *n.* (in ancient Greece) a magistrate who superintended the gymnasia and public games in certain cities. [1650–60; < L *gymnasiarchus* master of a gymnasium < Gk *gymnasíarchos,* equiv. to *gymnási(on)* (see GYMNASIUM[1]) + *-archos* -ARCH] —**gym·na′si·arch′y,** *n.*

gym·na·si·ast[1] (jim nā′zē ast′), *n.* a gymnast. [1855–60; GYMNASI(UM)[1] + -AST]

gym·na·si·ast[2] (jim nā′zē ast′), *n.* a student in a gymnasium. [1820–30; < G < NL *gymnasiasta.* See GYMNASIUM[2], -AST]

gym·na·si·um[1] (jim nā′zē əm), *n., pl.* **-si·ums, -si·a** (-zē ə, -zhə). **1.** a building or room designed and equipped for indoor sports, exercise, or physical education. **2.** a place where Greek youths met for exercise and discussion. [1590–1600; < L: a public school for gymnastics < Gk *gymnásion* gymnastic school (deriv. of *gymnázein* to train in the nude)] —**gym·na′si·al,** *adj.*

gym·na·si·um[2] (gim nä′zē əm), *n., pl.* **-si·ums, -si·a** (-zē ə). (*often cap.*) (in continental Europe, esp. Germany) a classical school preparatory to the universities. [1685–95; < G; special use of GYMNASIUM[1]]

gym·nast (jim′nast, -nəst), *n.* a person trained and skilled in gymnastics. [1585–95; < Gk *gymnastḗs* the trainer of the athletes, equiv. to *gymnáz(ein)* (see GYMNASIUM[1]) + *-tēs* agent suffix]

gym·nas·tic (jim nas′tik), *adj.* of or pertaining to physical exercises that develop and demonstrate strength, balance, and agility, esp. such exercises performed mostly on special equipment. Also, **gym·nas′ti·cal.** [1565–75; < MF *gymnastique* < L *gymnasticus* < Gk *gymnastikós,* equiv. to *gymnáz(ein)* (see GYMNASIUM[1]) + *-tikos* -TIC] —**gym·nas′ti·cal·ly,** *adv.*

gym·nas·tics (jim nas′tiks), *n.* **1.** (*used with a plural v.*) gymnastic exercises. **2.** (*used with a singular v.*) the practice, art, or competitive sport of gymnastic exercises. **3.** (*used with a plural v.*) mental feats or other exercises of skill: *Verbal gymnastics.* [1645–55; see GYMNASTIC, -ICS]

gymno-, a combining form meaning "naked," "bare," "exposed," used in the formation of compound words: *gymnoplast.* Also, *esp. before a vowel,* **gymn-.** [< Gk, comb. form of *gymnós*]

gym·no·car·pous (jim′nə kär′pəs), *adj.* (of a fungus or lichen) having the apothecium open and attached to the surface of the thallus. Also, **gym·no·car·pic** (jim′nə kär′pik). Cf. **angiocarpous** (def. 2). [GYMNO- + -CARPOUS]

gym·no·din·i·um (jim′nə din′ē əm), *n., pl.* **-din·i·a** (-din′ē ə). any marine or freshwater dinoflagellate of the genus *Gymnodinium,* certain species of which cause red tide. [< NL, equiv. to *gymno-* GYMNO- + Gk *dīn(ein)* to whirl + NL *-ium* -IUM]

gym·nog·y·nous (jim noj′ə nəs), *adj. Bot.* having a naked ovary. [GYMNO- + -GYNOUS]

CONCISE PRONUNCIATION KEY: act, cāpe, dâre, pärt; set, ēqual; *if,* īce; ox, ōver, ôrder, oil, bŏŏk, bōōt, out; up, ûrge; child; sing; shoe; thin, *th*at; zh as in *treasure.* ə = *a* as in *alone, e* as in *system, i* as in *easily, o* as in *gallop, u* as in *circus;* ᵊ as in *fire* (fīᵊr), *hour* (ouᵊr). l and n can serve as syllabic consonants, as in *cradle* (krād′l), and *button* (but′n). See the full key inside the front cover.

gym·no·plast (jim′nə plast′), *n.* a mass of protoplasm without an enclosing wall. [GYMNO- + -PLAST]

gym·no·rhi·nal (jim′nə rīn′l), *adj.* (of a bird) having the nostrils exposed, not covered by feathers. [< NL; see GYMNO-, RHINAL]

gym·nos·o·phist (jim nos′ə fist), *n.* one of a group of Jainist philosophers, existing from ancient times to c1000, characterized by refusal to wear clothes and the abandonment of caste marks; a member of the Digambara sect. [1400–50; late ME < L *gymnosophistae* Indian ascetics < Gk *gymnosophistaí* naked philosophers. See GYMNO-, SOPHIST] **—gym·nos′o·phy,** *n.*

gym·no·sperm (jim′nə spûrm′), *n. Bot.* a vascular plant having seeds that are not enclosed in an ovary; a conifer or cycad. Cf. **angiosperm.** [1820–30; < NL *gymnospermae* name of type. See GYMNO-, -SPERM] **—gym′·no·sperm′ism,** *n.*

gym·no·sper·mous (jim′nə spûr′məs), *adj. Bot.* of or pertaining to a gymnosperm; having exposed or naked seeds. Also, **gym·no·sperm·al** (jim′nə spûr′məl), **gym·no·sperm·ic** (jim′nə spûr′mik). [1720–30; < NL *gymnospermus* < Gk *gymnóspermos.* See GYMNO-, -SPERMOUS]

gym·no·spore (jim′nə spôr′, -spōr′), *n. Bot.* a naked spore, esp. one not produced in a sporangium or one lacking a protective envelope. [1880–85; GYMNO- + -SPORE] **—gym·no·spo·rous** (jim′nə spôr′əs, -spōr′-, jim nos′pər əs), *adj.*

gym′ shoe′, a lightweight canvas shoe with a rubber sole; sneaker. [1925–30]

gym′ suit′, any outfit prescribed for wear while participating in gymnastics or sports.

GYN, 1. gynecological. **2.** gynecologist. **3.** gynecology. Also, **gyn.**

gyn-, var. of **gyno-** before a vowel: *gynarchy.*

gyn·ae·ce·um[1] (jin′ə sē′əm, gī′nə-, jī′nə-), *n., pl.* **-ce·a** (-sē′ə). (among the ancient Greeks) the part of a dwelling used by women. [1600–10; < L *gynaecēum* < Gk *gynaikeîon,* equiv. to *gynaik-* (s. of *gynḗ*) woman + *-eion* n. suffix of place]

gyn·ae·ce·um[2] (jin′ə sē′əm, gī′nə-, jī′nə-), *n., pl.* **-ce·a** (-sē′ə). *Bot.* gynoecium.

gynaeco-, *Chiefly Brit.* var. of **gyneco-:** *gynaecology.*

gy·nan·dro·morph (ji nan′drə môrf′, gī-, jī-), *n. Biol.* an individual exhibiting morphological characteristics of both sexes. [1895–1900; < Gk *gýnandro(s)* (see GYNANDROUS) + -MORPH] **—gy·nan′dro·mor′phic, gy·nan′·dro·mor′phous,** *adj.* **—gy·nan′dro·morph′ism, gy·nan′dro·mor′phy,** *n.*

gy·nan·drous (ji nan′drəs, gī-, jī-), *adj. Bot.* having stamens and pistils united in a column, as in orchids. [1800–10; < Gk *gýnandros* of doubtful sex. See GYN-, -ANDROUS]

gy·nan·dry (ji nan′drē, gī-, jī-), *n.* hermaphroditism. Also, **gy·nan′drism.** [< Gk *gýnandr(os)* (see GYNANDROUS) + -Y[3]]

gy·nan·ther·ous (ji nan′thər əs, gī-, jī-), *adj. Bot.* having the stamens converted into pistils by the action of frost, disease, or insects. [1870–75; GYN- + ANTHER + -OUS]

gyn·ar·chy (jin′ər kē, gī′nər-, jī′nər-), *n., pl.* **-chies.** government by women. [1570–80; GYN- + -ARCHY] **—gy·narch·ic** (ji när′kik, gī-, jī-), *adj.*

gyne-, var. of **gyneco-:** *gynephobia.*

gynec-, var. of **gyneco-** before a vowel: *gynecoid.*

gy·ne·cic (ji nē′sik, -nes′ik, gī-, jī-), *adj.* of or pertaining to women. [1875–80; < Gk *gynaikikós.* See GYNEC-, -IC]

gy·ne·ci·um (ji nē′sē əm, -shē-, gī-, jī-), *n., pl.* **-ci·a** (-sē ə, -shē ə). gynoecium.

gyneco-, a combining form meaning "woman," "female," used in the formation of compound words: *gynecology.* Also, *esp. Brit.,* **gynaeco-.** Also, *esp. before a vowel,* **gynec-.** Also, **gyne-, gyno-.** [< Gk, comb. form repr. *gynaik-,* s. of *gynḗ* female, woman]

gyn·e·coc·ra·cy (jin′i kok′rə sē, gī′ni-, jī′ni-), *n., pl.* **-cies.** gynarchy. [1605–15; < Gk *gynaikokratía.* See GYNECO-, -CRACY] **—gy·ne·co·crat** (ji nē′kə krat′, gī-, jī-), *n.* **—gy·ne·co·crat·ic** (ji nē′kə krat′ik, gī-, jī-; jin′i-, gī′ni-, jī′ni-), *adj.*

gyn·e·coid (jin′i koid′, gī′ni-, jī′ni-), *adj.* of or like a woman. [1905–10; GYNEC- + -OID]

gynecol., 1. gynecological. **2.** gynecology.

gy·ne·col·o·gist (gī′ni kol′ə jist, jin′i-, jī′ni-), *n.* a physician specializing in gynecology. *Abbr.:* GYN, gyn [1870–75; GYNECOLOG(Y) + -IST]

gy·ne·col·o·gy (gī′ni kol′ə jē, jin′i-, jī′ni-), *n.* the branch of medical science that deals with the health maintenance and diseases of women, esp. of the reproductive organs. *Abbr.:* GYN, gyn [1840–50; GYNECO- + -LOGY] **—gy·ne·co·log·ic** (jin′i kə loj′ik, gī′ni-, jī′ni-), **gyn′e·co·log′i·cal,** *adj.*

gyn·e·co·mas·ti·a (jin′i kō mas′tē ə, gī′ni-, jī′ni-), *n.* abnormal enlargement of the breast in a male. Also, **gyn·e·co·mas·ty** (jin′i kə mas′tē, gī′ni-, jī′ni-). [1880–85; < NL; see GYNECO-, MAST-, -IA]

gyn·e·co·mor·phous (jin′i kō môr′fəs, gī′ni-, jī′ni-), *adj.* having the form, appearance, or attributes of a female. [1860–65; < Gk *gynaikómorphos.* See GYNECO-, -MORPHOUS]

CONCISE ETYMOLOGY KEY: <, descended or borrowed from; >, whence; b., blend of, blended; c., cognate with; cf., compare; deriv., derivative; equiv., equivalent; imit., imitative; obl., oblique; r., replacing; s., stem; sp., spelling, spelled; resp., respelling, respelled; trans., translation; ?, origin unknown; *, unattested; ‡, probably earlier than. See the full key inside the front cover.

gyn·e·cop·a·thy (jin′i kop′ə thē, gī′ni-, jī′ni-), *n.* any disease occurring only in women. [GYNECO- + -PATHY] **—gyn·e·co·path·ic** (jin′i kə path′ik, gī′ni-, jī′ni-), *adj.*

gyn·e·pho·bi·a (jin′ə fō′bē ə, gī′nə-, jī′nə-), *n.* an abnormal fear of women. [GYNE- + -PHOBIA]

Gyn·er·gen (jin′ər jin, -jen′, gī′nər-, jī′nər-), *Pharm., Trademark.* a brand of ergotamine.

gyno-, var. of **gyneco-:** *gynophore.* Also, *esp. before a vowel,* **gyn-.** Cf. **gyneco-.** [< Gk, comb. form of *gynḗ*]

gyn·o·base (jin′ō bās′, gī′nō-, jī′-), *n. Bot.* an elevation of the receptacle of a flower, bearing the gynoecium. [GYNO- + BASE[1]] **—gyn′o·ba′sic,** *adj.*

gyn·o·di·oe·cious (jin′ō dī ē′shəs, gī′nō-, jī′-), *adj. Bot.* having female flowers on one plant and hermaphrodite flowers on another plant of the same species. [1875–80; GYNO- + DIOECIOUS] **—gyn′o·di·oe′cious·ly,** *adv.* **—gy·no·di·oe·cism** (jī′nō dī ē′siz əm), *n.*

gy·noe·ci·um (ji nē′sē əm, -shē-, gī-, jī-), *n., pl.* **-ci·a** (-sē ə, -shē ə). *Bot.* the pistil or pistils of a flower; the female parts. Also, **gynaeceum, gynecium.** [1600–10; < NL, irreg. < Gk *gynaikeîon; see* GYNAECEUM[1]]

gyn·o·gen·e·sis (jin′ə jen′ə sis, gī′nə-, jī′-), *n. Biol.* a type of reproduction by parthenogenesis that requires stimulation by a sperm to activate the egg into development but occurs without fusion of sperm and egg nuclei. [1920–25; GYNO- + -GENESIS]

gyn·o·mo·noe·cious (jin′ō mə nē′shəs, gī′nō-, jī′-), *adj. Bot.* having both female and hermaphrodite flowers on the same plant. [1875–80; GYNO- + MONOECIOUS] **—gyn′o·mo·noe′cious·ly,** *adv.* **—gyn·o·mo·noe·cism** (jin′ō mə nē′siz əm, gī′nō-, jī′-), *n.*

gyn·o·phore (jin′ə fôr′, -fōr′, gī′nə-, jī′-), *n. Bot.* the elongated stalk of a pistil. [1815–25; GYNO- + -PHORE] **—gyn·o·phor·ic** (jin′ə fôr′ik, -for′-, gī′nə-, jī′-), *adj.*

gyn·o·ste·gi·um (jin′ə stē′jē əm, gī′nə-, jī′-), *n., pl.* **-gi·a** (-jē ə). *Bot.* a specialized caplike mass of tissue covering a gynoecium. [1875–80; < NL; see GYNO-, STEGO-, -IUM]

gyn·o·ste·mi·um (jin′ə stē′mē əm, gī′nə-, jī′-), *n., pl.* **-mi·a** (-mē ə). *Bot.* the united stamens and pistil of an orchid. [1860–65; < NL, equiv. to *gyno-* GYNO- + Gk *stḗm(ōn)* warp, thread + NL *-ium* -IUM]

-gynous, a combining form with the meanings "of women," "of females," "having pistils or analogous organs," as specified by the initial elements: *androgynous.* [< Gk *-gynos.* See GYNO-, -OUS]

-gyny, a combining form occurring in nouns corresponding to adjectives ending in **-gynous:** *androgyny.*

Györ (dyœr), *n.* a city in NW Hungary. 119,000.

gyp[1] (jip), *v.,* **gypped, gyp·ping,** *n.* **—***v.t., v.i.* **1.** to defraud or rob by some sharp practice; swindle; cheat. **—***n.* **2.** a swindle or fraud. **3.** Also, **gyp·per** (jip′ər), **gypster.** a swindler or cheat. **4.** Also called **gypsy** an owner of racehorses who also acts as trainer and jockey. Also, **gip.** [1885–90, *Amer.;* back formation from GYPSY]

gyp[2] (jip), *n. Brit. Informal.* a male college servant, as at Cambridge and Durham. [1740–50; perh. from GYPSY]

gyp′ joint′, *Informal.* **1.** any business establishment that charges excessively for poor-quality service or goods. **2.** a gambling house in which the games are dishonestly run. [1930–35]

gyp·lure (jip′lŏŏr′), *n.* a synthetic form of the sex pheromone of the female gypsy moth, used in traps to attract males. [GYP(SY MOTH) + LURE]

gyp·o (jip′ō), *n., pl.* **gyp·os.** *Slang.* gyppo.

gyp·po (jip′ō), *n. pl.* **-pos.** *Slang.* a logger who operates on a small budget and typically gleans the timberlands already cut by larger companies. Also called **gyp′·po log′ger.** [prob. ellipsis from *gyppo logger, gyppo outfit,* etc.; *gyppo* orig., someone willing to do piecework, usually a non-union worker (prob. employed by such logging companies); see GYP[1], -O]

gyp-room (jip′rōōm′, -rŏŏm′), *n. Brit. Slang.* a pantry, esp. one attached to a student's quarters. [1870–75; see GYP[2]]

gyp·se·ous (jip′sē əs), *adj.* of or pertaining to gypsum. [1655–65; < LL *gypseus.* See GYPSUM, -EOUS]

gyp·sif·er·ous (jip sif′ər əs), *adj.* containing gypsum. [1840–50; GYPS(UM) + -I- + -FEROUS]

gyp·soph·i·la (jip sof′ə lə), *n.* any plant belonging to the genus *Gypsophila,* of the pink family, native to Mediterranean regions, having small, panicled, pink or white flowers, as baby's breath. [1765–75; < NL < Gk *gýpso(s)* chalk + *phíla* -PHILE]

gyp·ster (jip′stər), *n.* gyp[1] (def. 3). [GYP[1] + -STER]

gyp·sum (jip′səm), *n.* a very common mineral, hydrated calcium sulfate, $CaSO_4 \cdot 2H_2O$, occurring in crystals and in masses, soft enough to be scratched by the fingernail: used to make plaster of Paris, as an ornamental material, as a fertilizer, etc. [1640–50; < L: chalk < Gk *gýpsos* chalk, gypsum]

gyp′sum board′, wallboard composed primarily of gypsum and often used as sheathing.

gyp′sum plas′ter, plaster made primarily of gypsum.

Gyp·sy (jip′sē), *n., pl.* **-sies,** *adj.* **—***n.* **1.** a member of a nomadic, Caucasoid people of generally swarthy complexion, who migrated originally from India, settling in various parts of Asia, Europe, and, most recently, North America. **2.** Romany; the language of the Gypsies. **3.** (*l.c.*) a person held to resemble a gypsy, esp. in physical characteristics or in a traditionally ascribed freedom or inclination to move from place to place. **4.** (*l.c.*) *Informal.* See **gypsy cab. 5.** (*l.c.*) *Informal.* an independent, usually nonunion trucker, hauler, operator, etc. **6.** (*l.c.*) *Slang.* a chorus dancer, esp. in the Broadway theater. **7.** (*l.c.*) gyp[1] (def. 4). **—***adj.* **8.** of or pertaining to the Gypsies. **9.** (*l.c.*) *Informal.* working independently or without a license: *gypsy truckers.* Also, *esp. Brit.,* **Gipsy, gipsy.** [1505–15; back formation of *gipcyan,* aph. var. of EGYPTIAN, from a belief that Gypsies came originally from Egypt] **—gyp′sy·dom,** *n.* **—gyp′sy·esque′, gyp′sy·ish, gyp′sy·like′, gyp′se·ian,** *adj.* **—gyp′sy·hood′,** *n.* **—gyp′sy·ism,** *n.*

gyp′sy cab′, a taxicab that is licensed only to pick up passengers on call by telephone, but that often illegally seeks passengers on the street. [1960–65, *Amer.*]

gyp′sy cap′stan, *Naut.* a small capstan moved only by a motor or engine.

gyp·sy·head (jip′sē hed′), *n. Naut.* a flanged drum on a winch, for winding in lines. [GYPSY + HEAD]

gyp′sy moth′, a moth, *Porthetria dispar,* introduced into the U.S. from Europe, the larvae of which feed on the foliage of shade and other trees. [1810–20]

gyp′sy scale′, either of two scales that often form the basis of Hungarian Gypsy music.

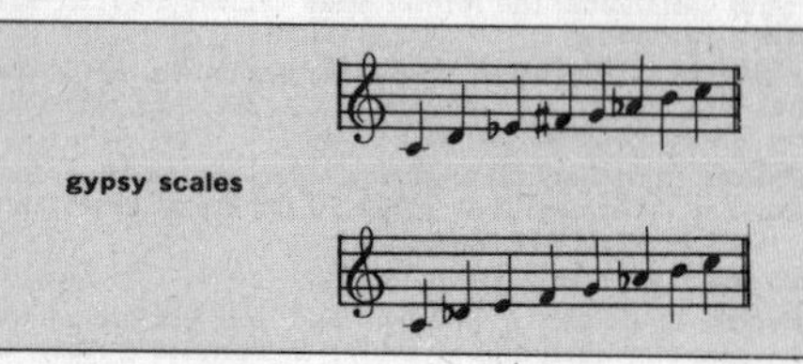

gypsy scales

gyp′sy set′ting, *Jewelry.* a setting, as on a ring, completely enclosing the girdle of the stone.

gyp′sy winch′, *Naut.* a small winch or crab. [1870–75]

gyr-, var. of **gyro-** before a vowel: *gyral.*

gy·ral (jī′rəl), *adj.* **1.** gyratory. **2.** *Anat.* of or pertaining to a gyrus. [1740–50; GYR- + -AL[1]] **—gy′ral·ly,** *adv.*

gy·rase (jī′rās, -rāz), *n. Biochem.* a bacterial enzyme that causes supercoiling of DNA. [1976; GYR- + -ASE]

gy·rate (*v.* jī′rāt, jī rāt′; *adj.* jī′rāt), *v.,* **-rat·ed, -rat·ing,** *adj.* **—***v.i.* **1.** to move in a circle or spiral, or around a fixed point; whirl. **—***adj.* **2.** *Zool.* having convolutions. [1820–30; < L *gȳrātus* (ptp. of *gȳrāre* to turn around). See GYR-, -ATE[1]] **—gy′ra·tor,** *n.*
—Syn. 1. spin, twirl, revolve, swirl, pirouette.

gy·ra·tion (jī rā′shən), *n.* the act of gyrating; circular or spiral motion; revolution; rotation; whirling. [1605–15; < LL *gȳrātiōn-* (s. of *gȳrātiō*). See GYRATE, -ION] **—gy·ra′tion·al,** *adj.*

gy·ra·to·ry (jī′rə tôr′ē, -tōr′ē), *adj.* moving in a circle or spiral; gyrating. [1810–20; GYRAT(ION) + -ORY[1]]

gyre (jīᵊr), *n.* **1.** a ring or circle. **2.** a circular course or motion. **3.** *Oceanog.* a ringlike system of ocean currents rotating clockwise in the Northern Hemisphere and counterclockwise in the Southern Hemisphere. [1560–70; < L *gȳrus* < Gk *gŷros* ring, circle]

gy·rec·to·my (jī rek′tə mē), *n., pl.* **-mies.** *Surg.* excision of a cerebral gyrus. [1945–50; GYR(US) + -ECTOMY]

gy·rene (jī′rēn, jī rēn′), *n. Slang.* a member of the U.S. Marine Corps. [1920–25; GI + (MA)RINE with altered sp.]

gyr·fal·con (jûr′fôl′kən, -fal′-, -fô′kən), *n.* a large falcon, *Falco rusticolus,* of arctic and subarctic regions, having white, gray, or blackish color phases: now greatly reduced in number. Also, **gerfalcon.** [1300–50; ME *gerfaucon, jerfacoun* < MF, OF, equiv. to *ger-* (perh. < OHG *giri* greedy) + *faucon* FALCON; cf. ON *geirfalki*]

gyrfalcon, *Falco rusticolus,* length 2 ft. (0.6 m)

gy·ri (jī′rī), *n.* pl. of **gyrus.**

gy·ro[1] (jī′rō), *n., pl.* **-ros. 1.** gyrocompass. **2.** gyroscope. [1905–10; independent use of GYRO-]

gy·ro[2] (jēr′ō, zhēr′ō; *Gk.* yē′rô), *n. Greek Cookery.* meat, usually lamb, roasted on a vertical spit, then thinly sliced, topped with onions, and usually served in a sandwich of pita bread. [1970–75; < ModGk *gŷros* lit., turn, revolution; see GYRE]

gyro-, a combining form meaning "ring," "circle," "spiral," used in the formation of compound words: *gyromagnetic; gyroscope.* Also, *esp. before a vowel,* **gyr-.** [< Gk. *gŷros* ring, n. use of *gȳrós* round]

gy·ro·com·pass (jī′rō kum′pəs), *n.* a navigational compass containing a gyroscope rotor, that, when adjusted for the latitude and speed of the vessel or aircraft, indicates the direction of true north along the surface of the earth or communicates this information to one or more gyro repeaters. Also called **gyrostatic compass.** [1905–10; GYRO(SCOPE) + COMPASS]

gy·ro·cop·ter (jī′rə kop′tər), *n.* autogiro. [1910–15; GYRO- + (HELI)COPTER]

gy·ro·fre·quen·cy (jī′rō frē′kwən sē), *n., pl.* **-cies.** *Physics.* the frequency of rotation of an electron or other charged particle in a magnetic field, directly proportional to the charge of the particle and to the field strength and inversely proportional to the mass of the particle. [1940–45; GYRO- + FREQUENCY]

gy′ro hori′zon (jī′rō), *Aeron.* See **artificial horizon** (def. 3). [1935–40]

gy•roi•dal (jī roid′l), *adj.* having a spiral arrangement. [1860–65; GYR- + -OID + -AL[1]] **—gy•roi′dal•ly,** *adv.*

gy•ro•mag•net•ic (jī′rō mag net′ik), *adj.* of or pertaining to the magnetic properties of a rotating charged particle. [1920–25; GYRO- + MAGNETIC]

gy′romagnet′ic ra′tio, *Physics.* the ratio of the magnetic moment of a rotating charged particle to its angular momentum. [1925–30]

gy•ron (jī′rən, -ron), *n. Heraldry.* a subordinary having the form of a triangle, usually equal to half a quarter of the escutcheon, with its apex at the fess point. [1565–75; < MF, OF *giron* gusset < OHG *gēro;* c. GORE[3]]

gy•ron•ny (jī ron′ē, jī′rə nē), *adj. Heraldry.* divided into a number of gyrons, usually eight: *gyronny of eight.* [1350–1400; GYRON + -Y[3]; r. ME *gerundi* < MF *gironne* having gyrons]

gy•ro•pi•lot (jī′rə pī′lət), *n. Aeron.* See **automatic pilot.** [1920–25; GYRO(SCOPE) + PILOT]

gy•ro•plane (jī′rə plān′), *n.* autogiro. [1905–10; GYRO- + PLANE[1]]

gy′ro repeat′er (jī′rō), a navigational compass, under the control of a gyroscope, that automatically indicates true north. Also called **repeater.**

gy•ro•scope (jī′rə skōp′), *n.* an apparatus consisting of a rotating wheel so mounted that its axis can turn freely in certain or all directions, and capable of maintaining the same absolute direction in space in spite of movements of the mountings and surrounding parts: used to maintain equilibrium, determine direction, etc. Also called **gyro.** [1855–60; < F; see GYRO-, -SCOPE] **—gy•ro•scop•ic** (jī′rə skop′ik), *adj.* **—gy′ro•scop′i•cal•ly,** *adv.*

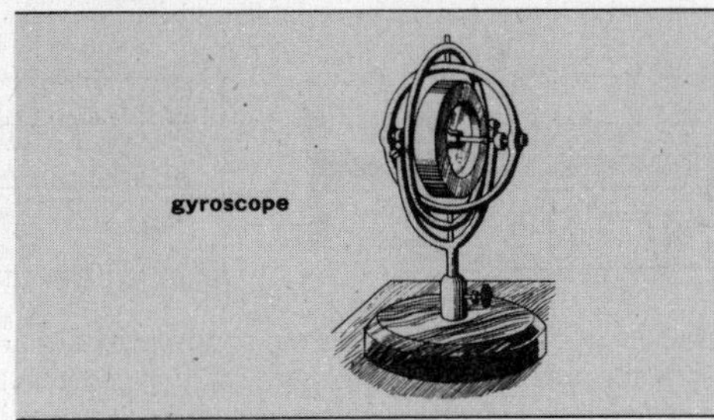

gy•rose (jī′rōs), *adj.* marked with wavy lines. [1830–40; GYR- + -OSE[1]]

gy•ro•sta•bi•lized (jī′rə stā′bə līzd′), *adj.* stabilized by means of a gyrostabilizer. [1945–50; GYRO(SCOPE) + STABILIZED]

gy•ro•sta•bi•liz•er (jī′rə stā′bə lī′zər), *n.* a device for stabilizing a seagoing vessel by counteracting its rolling motion from side to side, consisting essentially of a rotating gyroscope weighing about 1 percent of the displacement of the vessel. Also called **gy′roscop′ic sta′bilizer, stabilizer.** [1920–25; GYRO(SCOPE) + STABILIZER]

gy•ro•stat (jī′rə stat′), *n.* a modified gyroscope, consisting of a rotating wheel pivoted within a rigid case. [1875–80; GYRO- + -STAT]

gy′rostat′ic com′pass, gyrocompass.

gy•ro•stat•ics (jī′rə stat′iks), *n.* (*used with a singular v.*) *Mech.* the science that deals with the laws of rotating bodies. [GYRO- + STATICS] **—gy′ro•stat′ic,** *adj.* **—gy′ro•stat′i•cal•ly,** *adv.*

gy•ro•vague (jī′rō vāg′), *n.* a vagrant monk who wandered from one monastery to another. [1795–1805; < F < LL *gȳrovagus gȳro-*, equiv. to *gyro-* GYRO- + *vagus* strolling about; see VAGUE]

gy•rus (jī′rəs), *n., pl.* **gy•ri** (jī′rī). *Anat.* a convolution, esp. of the brain. [1835–45; < L *gȳrus;* see GYRE]

GySgt, *Marine Corps.* gunnery sergeant.

gyt•tja (yit′chä), *n. Geol.* a mud rich in organic matter, found at the bottom or near the shore of certain lakes. [1885–90; < Sw, akin to *gjuta* to pour]

gyve (jīv), *n., v.,* **gyved, gyv•ing.** *Archaic.* **—*n.* 1.** Usually, **gyves.** a shackle, esp. for the leg; fetter. **—*v.t.* 2.** to shackle. [1175–1225; ME *give* < ?]

CONCISE PRONUNCIATION KEY: act, cāpe, dâre, pärt; set, ēqual; if, īce; ox, ōver, ôrder, oil, bŏŏk, bōōt, out; up, ûrge; child; sing; shoe; thin, *th*at; zh as in *treasure.* ə = *a* as in *alone, e* as in *system, i* as in *easily, o* as in *gallop, u* as in *circus;* ə as in *fire* (fīər), *hour* (ouər). l and n can serve as syllabic consonants, as in *cradle* (krād′l), and *button* (but′n). See the full key inside the front cover.

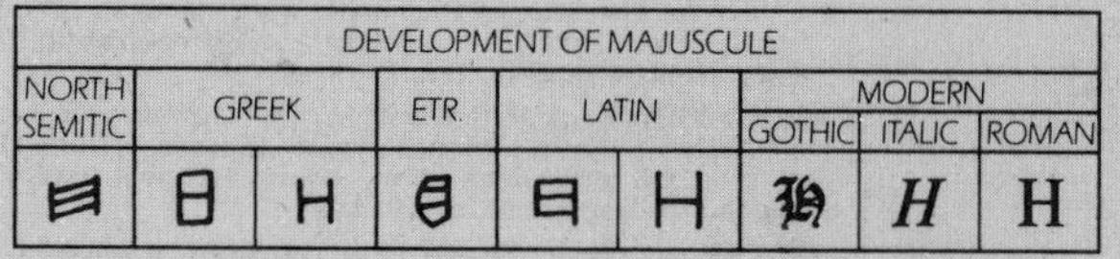

DEVELOPMENT OF MAJUSCULE
NORTH SEMITIC
GREEK
ETR.
LATIN
MODERN
GOTHIC
ITALIC
ROMAN

DEVELOPMENT OF MINUSCULE					
ROMAN CURSIVE	ROMAN UNCIAL	CAROL MIN	MODERN		
			GOTHIC	ITALIC	ROMAN
		b		*h*	h

The eighth letter of the English alphabet is traceable to North Semitic origins. In that early alphabet its pronunciation was similar to that of Scottish *ch*. In Greek, the symbol came to represent *eta* (written H). In English, this letter represents an aspirate sound, but in most Indo-European languages it has seldom been used in this way.

H, h (āch), *n., pl.* **H's** or **Hs, h's** or **hs. 1.** the eighth letter of the English alphabet, a consonant. **2.** any spoken sound represented by the letter *H* or *h*, as in *hot* or *behave*. **3.** something having the shape of an H. **4.** a written or printed representation of the letter *H* or *h*. **5.** a device, as a printer's type, for reproducing the letter *H* or *h*.

H, 1. hard. **2.** *Gram.* head. **3.** *Elect.* henry. **4.** *Slang.* heroin. **5.** high.

H, *Symbol.* **1.** the eighth in order or in a series. **2.** (*sometimes l.c.*) the medieval Roman numeral for 200. Cf. **Roman numerals. 3.** *Chem.* hydrogen. **4.** *Biochem.* histidine. **5.** *Physics.* **a.** enthalpy. **b.** horizontal component of the earth's magnetic field. **c.** See **magnetic intensity. 6.** *Music.* the letter used in German to indicate the tone B.

H[1], *Symbol, Chem.* protium. Also, **[1]H, H**[a]

H[2], *Symbol, Chem.* deuterium. Also, **[2]H, H**[b]

H[3], *Symbol, Chem.* tritium. Also, **[3]H, H**[c]

h, hard.

h, *Symbol, Physics.* See **Planck's constant.**

H., (in prescriptions) an hour. [< L *hōra*]

h., 1. harbor. **2.** hard. **3.** hardness. **4.** heavy sea. **5.** height. **6.** hence. **7.** high. **8.** *Baseball.* hit; hits. **9.** horns. **10.** hour; hours. **11.** hundred. **12.** husband. Also, **H.**

ha (hä), *interj.* (used as an exclamation of surprise, interrogation, suspicion, triumph, etc.) Also, **hah.** [1250–1300; ME; see HA-HA[1]]

hā (hä), *n.* the 26th letter of the Arabic alphabet, representing a glottal spirant consonant sound. [< Ar]

ḥā (khä), *n.* the sixth letter of the Arabic alphabet, representing a pharyngeal spirant consonant. [< Ar]

Ha, *Symbol, Chem.* hahnium.

ha, hectare; hectares.

h.a., 1. *Gunnery.* high angle. **2.** in this year. [(def. 2) < L *hōc annō*]

haaf (häf), *n.* deep-sea fishing grounds off the Shetland and Orkney Islands. [1785–95; < Scand; cf. ON *haf* sea; c. OE *hæf;* akin to HEAVE]

Haag (häkh), *n.* **Den** (den), a Dutch name of The Hague.

Haa·kon VII (hô′ko͝on), (*Prince Carl of Denmark*) 1872–1957, king of Norway 1905–57: in exile 1940–45.

haar (här), *n. Scot. and North Eng.* a thick, wet fog along the seacoast. [1665–75; north var. of HOAR]

Haar·lem (här′ləm), *n.* a city in the W Netherlands, W of Amsterdam. 157,556.

Hab., Habakkuk.

Há·ba (hä′bä), *n.* **A·lois** (ä′lois), 1893–1972, Czech composer.

Ha·bak·kuk (hə bak′ək, hab′ə kuk′, -ko͝ok′), *n.* **1.** a Minor Prophet of the 7th century B.C. **2.** a book of the Bible bearing his name. *Abbr.:* Hab. Also, *Douay Bible,* **Ha·bac′uc.**

Ha·ba·na (*Sp.* ä vä′nä), *n.* Havana.

ha·ba·ne·ra (hä′bə nâr′ə *or, often,* -nyâr′ə), *n.* **1.** a dance of Cuban origin. **2.** the music for this dance, having a slow duple meter and a rhythm similar to that of a tango. [1875–80; < Sp (*danza*) *habanera* (dance) of Havana]

CONCISE ETYMOLOGY KEY: <, descended or borrowed from; >, whence; b., blend of, blended; c., cognate with; cf., compare; deriv., derivative; equiv., equivalent; imit., imitative; obl., oblique; r., replacing; s., stem; sp., spelling, spelled; resp., respelling, respelled; trans., translation; ?, origin unknown; *, unattested; ‡, probably earlier than. See the full key inside the front cover.

Hab·da·lah (*Seph.* häv dä lä′; *Ashk.* häv dô′lə), *n. Hebrew.* Havdalah.

ha·be·as cor·pus (hā′bē əs kôr′pəs), *Law.* a writ requiring a person to be brought before a judge or court, esp. for investigation of a restraint of the person's liberty, used as a protection against illegal imprisonment. [< L: lit., have the body (first words of writ), equiv. to *habeās* 2nd sing. pres. subj. (with impv. force) of *habēre* to have + *corpus* body]

ha·ben·u·la (hə ben′yə lə), *n., pl.* **-lae** (-lē′). *Anat.* a narrow bandlike structure, as the stalk attaching the pineal gland to the thalamus. [1875–80; < L: small strip of skin, equiv. to *habēn(a)* strap, thong, rein (deriv. of *habēre* to have, hold, possess; cf. ABLE, HABIT[1]) + *-ula* -ULE] **—ha·ben′u·lar,** *adj.*

Ha·ber (hä′bər), *n.* **Fritz,** 1868–1934, German chemist: Nobel prize 1918.

hab·er·dash·er (hab′ər dash′ər), *n.* **1.** a retail dealer in men's furnishings, as shirts, ties, gloves, socks, and hats. **2.** *Chiefly Brit.* a dealer in small wares and notions. [1275–1325; ME *haberdasshere,* of obscure orig.; cf. AF *habredache* haberdashery, *hapertas* perh. a kind of cloth]

hab·er·dash·er·y (hab′ər dash′ə rē), *n., pl.* **-er·ies. 1.** a haberdasher's shop. **2.** the goods sold there. [1425–75; late ME *haberdashrye* < AF. See HABERDASHER, -Y[3]]

Ha′ber proc′ess, a process for synthesizing ammonia from gaseous nitrogen and hydrogen under high pressure and temperature in the presence of a catalyst. [named after Fritz HABER]

hab·ile (hab′il), *adj.* skillful; dexterous; adroit. [1375–1425; late ME *habyll* < L *habilis* handy, apt; see ABLE]

ha·bil·i·ment (hə bil′ə mənt), *n.* **1.** Usually, **habiliments. a.** clothes or clothing. **b.** clothes as worn in a particular profession, way of life, etc. **2. habiliments,** accouterments or trappings. [1375–1425; late ME *(h)abylement* < MF *habillement,* equiv. to *habill(er), abil(ier)* to trim a log, hence, dress, prepare (< VL **adbiliare;* see A-[5], BILLET[2]) + *-ment* -MENT] **—ha·bil·i·men·tal** (hə bil′ə men′tl), **ha·bil′i·men′ta·ry,** *adj.* **—ha·bil′i·ment′ed,** *adj.*

ha·bil·i·tate (hə bil′i tāt′), *v.,* **-tat·ed, -tat·ing.** *—v.t.* **1.** to clothe or dress. **2.** to make fit. *—v.i.* **3.** to become fit. [1595–1605; < ML *habilitātus* ptp. of *habilitāre* to make fit. See ABILITY, -ATE[1]] **—ha·bil′i·ta′tion,** *n.* **—ha·bil′i·ta′tive,** *adj.* **—ha·bil′i·ta′tor,** *n.*

Ha·bi·ma (hä bē′mə, hä′bē mä′), *n.* a Hebrew-language theater company, founded in Moscow in 1917: now the national theater of Israel. Also called **Habi′ma The′atre.**

Ha·bi·ru (hä bē′ro͞o, hä′bē ro͞o′), *n.* (*used with a plural v.*) a nomadic people mentioned in Assyro-Babylonian literature: possibly the early Hebrews. Also, **Ha·bi·ri** (hä bē′rē, hä′bē rē′). [< Akkadian *khāpiru*]

hab·it[1] (hab′it), *n.* **1.** an acquired behavior pattern regularly followed until it has become almost involuntary: *the habit of looking both ways before crossing the street.* **2.** customary practice or use: *Daily bathing is an American habit.* **3.** a particular practice, custom, or usage: *the habit of shaking hands.* **4.** a dominant or regular disposition or tendency; prevailing character or quality: *She has a habit of looking at the bright side of things.* **5.** addiction, esp. to narcotics (often prec. by *the*). **6.** mental character or disposition: *a habit of mind.* **7.** characteristic bodily or physical condition. **8.** the characteristic form, aspect, mode of growth, etc., of an organism: *a twining habit.* **9.** the characteristic crystalline form of a mineral. **10.** garb of a particular rank, profession, religious order, etc.: *a monk's habit.* **11.** the attire worn by a rider of a saddle horse. *—v.t.* **12.** to clothe; array. [1175–1225; ME < L *habitus* state, style, practice, equiv. to *habi-* (var. s. of *habēre* to have) + *-tus* verbal n. suffix; r. ME *abit* < OF]

—Syn. 2. bent, wont. **3.** See **custom. 10.** dress, costume. **12.** dress, garb, attire; deck out.

hab·it[2] (hab′it), *v.t.* **1.** *Archaic.* to dwell in. *—v.i.* **2.** *Obs.* to dwell. [1325–75; ME *habiten* < L *habitāre* to inhabit; see HABITAT]

hab·it·a·ble (hab′i tə bəl), *adj.* capable of being inhabited. [1350–1400; ME *habitābilis,* equiv. to *habitā(re)* to inhabit (see HABITAT) + *-bilis* -BLE; r. ME *abitable* < MF] **—hab′it·a·bil′i·ty, hab′it·a·ble·ness,** *n.* **—hab′it·a·bly,** *adv.*

ha·bi·tan (*Fr.* A bē täN′), *n., pl.* **-tans** (-täN′). habitant[2].

hab·i·tan·cy (hab′i tn sē), *n., pl.* **-cies. 1.** the act or fact of inhabiting; inhabitancy. **2.** the total number of inhabitants; population. [1785–95; HABIT(ANT)[1] + -ANCY]

hab·it·ant[1] (hab′i tənt), *n.* an inhabitant. [1480–90; < L *habitant-* (s. of *habitāns*), prp. of *habitāre* to inhabit. See HABITAT, -ANT]

ha·bi·tant[2] (hab′i tənt; *Fr.* A bē täN′), *n., pl.* **ha·bi·tants** (hab′i tənts; *Fr.* A bē täN′). **1.** a French settler in Canada or Louisiana, or a descendant of one, esp. a farmer. **2.** *Canadian.* a Canadian of French speech and culture, esp. one residing in the province of Quebec. [1780–90; < F, prp. of *habiter* < L *habitāre* to inhabit]

hab·i·tat (hab′i tat′), *n.* **1.** the natural environment of an organism; the kind of place that is natural for the life and growth of an organism: *a tropical habitat.* **2.** the place where a person or thing is usually found: *Paris is a major habitat of artists.* **3.** a special environment for living in over an extended period, as an underwater research vessel. **4.** habitation (def. 1). [1755–65; < L: it inhabits, 3rd sing. pres. ind. of *habitāre,* freq. of *habēre* to have, hold] **—hab·i·tal·ly** (hab′i tl ē), *adv.*

—Syn. 1. territory, range, domain, element.

hab·i·ta·tion (hab′i tā′shən), *n.* **1.** a place of residence; dwelling; abode. **2.** the act of inhabiting; occupancy by inhabitants. **3.** a colony or settlement; community: *Each of the scattered habitations consisted of a small number of huts.* [1325–75; ME *(h)abitacioun* (< AF) < L *habitātiōn-* (s. of *habitātiō*) a dwelling, equiv. to *habitāt(us)* inhabited (ptp. of *habitāre;* see HABITAT) + *-iōn-* -ION] **—hab′i·ta′tion·al,** *adj.*

—Syn. 1. lodgings, home, domicile, quarters.

hab·it·ed[1] (hab′i tid), *adj.* dressed or clothed, esp. in a habit: *habited nuns.* [1595–1605; HABIT[1] + -ED[3]]

hab·it·ed[2] (hab′i tid), *adj. Archaic.* inhabited. [HABIT[2] + -ED[2]]

hab·it-form·ing (hab′it fôr′ming), *adj.* tending to cause or encourage addiction, esp. through physiological dependence: *habit-forming drugs.* [1895–1900]

ha·bit·u·al (hə bich′o͞o əl), *adj.* **1.** of the nature of a habit; fixed by or resulting from habit: *habitual courtesy.* **2.** being such by habit: *a habitual gossip.* **3.** commonly used, followed, observed, etc., as by a particular person; customary: *She took her habitual place at the table.* [1520–30; < ML *habituālis* relating to dress, condition, or habit, equiv. to L *habitu(s)* HABIT[1] + *-ālis* -AL[1]] **—ha·bit′u·al·ly,** *adv.* **—ha·bit′u·al·ness,** *n.*

—Syn. 2. confirmed, inveterate. **3.** accustomed. See **usual. —Ant. 2.** occasional. **3.** unaccustomed.

ha·bit·u·ate (hə bich′o͞o āt′), *v.,* **-at·ed, -at·ing.** *—v.t.* **1.** to accustom (a person, the mind, etc.), as to a particular situation: *Wealth habituated him to luxury.* **2.** *Archaic.* to frequent. *—v.i.* **3.** to cause habituation, physiologically or psychologically. [1520–30; < LL *habituātus* conditioned, constituted, (ptp. of *habituāre*), equiv. to *habitu(s)* HABIT[1] + *-ātus* -ATE[1]]

—Syn. 1. familiarize, acclimate, train.

ha·bit·u·a·tion (hə bich′o͞o ā′shən), *n.* **1.** the act of habituating. **2.** the condition of being habituated. **3.** physiological tolerance to or psychological dependence on a drug, short of addiction. **4.** reduction of psychological or behavioral response occurring when a specific stimulus occurs repeatedly. [1400–50; late ME. See HABITUATE, -ION]

hab•i•tude (hab′i to͞od′, -tyo͞od′), *n.* **1.** customary condition or character: *a healthy mental habitude.* **2.** a habit or custom: *traditional habitudes of kindliness and courtesy.* **3.** *Obs.* familiar relationship. [1375–1425; late ME < MF < L *habitūdō.* See HABIT[1], -TUDE] **—hab′i•tu′di•nal,** *adj.*

ha•bit•u•é (hə bich′o͞o ā′, -bich′o͞o ā′; *Fr.* A bē twā′), *n., pl.* **ha•bit•u•és** (hə bich′o͞o āz′, -bich′o͞o āz′; *Fr.* A bē twā′). a frequent or habitual visitor to a place: *a habitué of art galleries.* [1810–20; < F, n. use of masc. ptp. of *habituer* < LL *habituāre.* See HABITUATE]

hab•i•tus (hab′i təs), *n., pl.* **-tus.** the physical characteristics of a person, esp. appearance and constitution as related to disease. [1885–90; < NL, L; see HABIT[1]]

ha•boob (hə bo͞ob′), *n.* a thick dust storm or sandstorm that blows in the deserts of North Africa and Arabia or on the plains of India. [1895–1900; < Ar *habūb*]

Ha•bor (hä′bôr, -bōr), *n.* Khabur.

Habs•burg (haps′bûrg; *Ger.* häps′bo͝ork′), *n.* Hapsburg.

ha•bu•tai (hä′bə tī′), *n.* a thin, soft, durable Japanese silk, used in the manufacture of garments. Also, **ha′bu•tae′.** [1890–95; < Japn *habutae,* equiv. to *ha* feathers (< *fa* < **pa*) + *-butae,* comb. form of *futa-e* (< *futa-f(y)e* < **puta pe*) two layers]

ha•ček (hä′chek), *n.* a diacritical mark (ˇ) placed over a letter in some languages, as Czech and Lithuanian, and in some systems of phonetic transcription, esp. to indicate that a sound is palatalized. Also, **há′ček.** Also called **wedge.** [1950–55; < Czech *háček,* dim. of *hák* hook < G; see HOOK]

Ha•chi•o•ji (hä′chē ō′jē), *n.* a city on SE Honshu, in Japan, W of Tokyo. 387,162.

ha•choo (hä cho͞o′), *interj.* ahchoo.

ha•chure (*n.* ha sho͝or′, hash′o͝or; *v.* ha sho͝or′), *n., v.,* **-chured, -chur•ing.** **—***n.* **1.** one of a series of short parallel lines drawn on a map to indicate topographic relief. **2.** shading composed of such lines; hatching. **—***v.t.* **3.** Also, **hatch.** to indicate or shade by hachures. Also, **hatchure.** [1855–60; < F; see HATCH[3], -URE]

ha•ci•en•da (hä′sē en′də; *Sp.* ä syen′dä), *n., pl.* **-das** (-dəz; *Sp.* -däs). (in Spanish America) **1.** a large landed estate, esp. one used for farming or ranching. **2.** the main house on such an estate. **3.** a stock raising, mining, or manufacturing establishment in the country. [1710–20; < Sp < L *facienda* things to be done or made, neut. pl. of *faciendus,* ger. of *facere* to DO[1], make]

Ha′ci•en′da Heights′ (hä′sē en′də, hä′-), a city in SW California, near Los Angeles. 49,422.

hack[1] (hak), *v.t.* **1.** to cut, notch, slice, chop, or sever (something) with or as with heavy, irregular blows (often fol. by *up* or *down*): *to hack down trees.* **2.** to break up the surface of (the ground). **3.** to clear (a road, path, etc.) by cutting away vines, trees, brush, or the like: *They hacked a trail through the jungle.* **4.** to damage or injure by crude, harsh, or insensitive treatment; mutilate; mangle. **5.** to reduce or cut ruthlessly; trim: *The Senate hacked the budget severely before returning it to the House.* **6.** *Slang.* to deal or cope with; handle: *He can't hack all this commuting.* **7.** *Computers.* to devise or modify (a computer program), usually skillfully. **8.** *Basketball.* to strike the arm of (an opposing ball handler): *He got a penalty for hacking the shooter.* **9.** *Brit.* to kick or kick at the shins of (an opposing player) in Rugby football. **10.** *South Midland and Southern U.S.* to embarrass, annoy, or disconcert. **—***v.i.* **11.** to make rough cuts or notches; deal cutting blows. **12.** to cough harshly, usually in short and repeated spasms. **13.** *Tennis.* **a.** to take a poor, ineffective, or awkward swing at the ball. **b.** to play tennis at a mediocre level. **14.** *Brit.* to kick or kick at an opponent's shins in Rugby football. **15. hack around,** *Slang.* to pass the time idly; indulge in idle talk. **16. hack it,** *Slang.* to handle or cope with a situation or an assignment adequately and calmly: *The new recruit just can't hack it.* **—***n.* **17.** a cut, gash, or notch. **18.** a tool, as an ax, hoe, or pick, for hacking. **19.** an act or instance of hacking; a cutting blow. **20.** a short, rasping dry cough. **21.** a hesitation in speech. **22.** *Curling.* an indentation made in the ice at the foot score, for supporting the foot in delivering the stone. **23.** *Brit.* a gash in the skin produced by a kick, as in Rugby football. [1150–1200; ME *hacken;* cf. OE *tōhaccian* to hack to pieces; c. D *hakken,* G *hacken*]
—Syn. 1. mangle, haggle. See **cut.**

hack[2] (hak), *n.* **1.** a person, as an artist or writer, who exploits, for money, his or her creative ability or training in the production of dull, unimaginative, and trite work; one who produces banal and mediocre work in the hope of gaining commercial success in the arts: *As a painter, he was little more than a hack.* **2.** a professional who renounces or surrenders individual independence, integrity, belief, etc., in return for money or other reward in the performance of a task normally thought of as involving a strong personal commitment: *a political hack.* **3.** a writer who works on the staff of a publisher at a dull or routine task; someone who works as a literary drudge: *He was one among the many hacks on Grub Street.* **4.** *Brit.* **a.** a horse kept for common hire or adapted for general work, esp. ordinary riding. **b.** a saddle horse used for transportation, rather than for show, hunting, or the like. **5.** an old or worn-out horse; jade. **6.** a coach or carriage kept for hire; hackney. **7.** *Informal.* **a.** a taxi. **b.** Also, **hackie.** a cabdriver. **8.** *Slang.* a prison guard. **—***v.t.* **9.** to make a hack of; let out for hire. **10.** to make trite or stale by frequent use; hackney. **—***v.i.* **11.** *Informal.* to drive a taxi. **12.** to ride or drive on the road at an ordinary pace, as distinguished from cross-country riding or racing. **13.** *Brit.* to rent a horse, esp. by the hour. **—***adj.* **14.** hired as a hack; of a hired sort: *a hack writer; hack work.* **15.** hackneyed; trite; banal: *hack writing.* [1680–90; short for HACKNEY]
—Syn. 2. mercenary. **3.** scribbler. **9.** lease, rent.

hack[3] (hak), *n.* **1.** a rack for drying food, as fish. **2.** a rack for holding fodder for livestock. **3.** a low pile of unburnt bricks in the course of drying. **4. at hack,** *Falconry.* (of a young hawk) being trained to fly freely but to return to a hack house or hack board for food rather than to pursue quarry. **—***v.t.* **5.** to place (something) on a hack, as for drying or feeding. **6.** *Falconry.* to train (a young hawk) by letting it fly freely and feeding it at a hack board or a hack house. [1565–75; var. of HATCH[2]]

hack•a•more (hak′ə môr′, -mōr′), *n.* **1.** a simple looped bridle, by means of which controlling pressure is exerted on the nose of a horse, used chiefly in breaking colts. **2.** *Western U.S.* any of several forms of halter used esp. for breaking horses. [1840–50, *Amer.;* alter. (by folk etym.) of Sp *jáquima* headstall < Ar *shaqīmah*]

hack•ber•ry (hak′ber′ē, -bə rē), *n., pl.* **-ries.** **1.** any of several trees or shrubs belonging to the genus *Celtis,* of the elm family, bearing cherrylike fruit. **2.** the sometimes edible fruit of such a tree. **3.** the wood of such a tree. [1775–85, *Amer.;* var. of HAGBERRY]

hack′ board′, *Falconry.* a board or platform at which hawks being flown at hack are fed. [1890–95]

hack•but (hak′but), *n.* harquebus. [1535–45; earlier *hacquebute* < MF, var. of *ha(r)quebusche* < MD *hākebusse* lit., hookgun; see HARQUEBUS] **—hack•but•eer** (hak′bə tēr′), *n.*

Hack•en•sack (hak′ən sak′), *n.* a city in NE New Jersey, near New York City. 36,039.

hack•er (hak′ər), *n.* **1.** a person or thing that hacks. **2.** *Slang.* a person who engages in an activity without talent or skill: *weekend hackers on the golf course.* **3.** *Computers Slang.* **a.** a computer enthusiast. **b.** a microcomputer user who attempts to gain unauthorized access to proprietary computer systems. [1200–50; ME (as surname); see HACK[1], -ER[1]]

hack′ ham′mer, an adzlike tool for dressing stone. [1350–1400; ME]

hack′ house′, *Falconry.* a shed where young hawks are kept and fed while at hack.

hack•ie (hak′ē), *n. Informal.* hack[2] (def. 7b). [1935–40, *Amer.;* HACK[2] + -IE]

hack•ing (hak′ing), *n.* replacement of a single course of stonework by two or more lower courses. [1400–50; late ME, in literal sense. See HACK[1], -ING[1]]

hack′ing jack′et, *Chiefly Brit.* a riding jacket having a tight waist, flared skirt, slanted pockets with flaps, and slits or vents at the sides or back. Also called **hack′ing coat′.** [1950–55]

hack•le[1] (hak′əl), *n., v.,* **-led, -ling.** **—***n.* **1.** one of the long, slender feathers on the neck or saddle of certain birds, as the domestic rooster, much used in making artificial flies for anglers. **2.** the neck plumage of a male bird, as the domestic rooster. **3. hackles, a.** the erectile hair on the back of an animal's neck: *At the sound of footsteps, the dog raised her hackles.* **b.** anger, esp. when aroused in a challenging or challenged manner: *with one's hackles up.* **4.** *Angling.* **a.** the legs of an artificial fly made with feathers from the neck or saddle of a rooster or other such bird. See diag. under **fly**[2]. **b.** See **hackle fly. 5.** a comb for dressing flax or hemp. **6. raise one's hackles,** to arouse one's anger: *Such officiousness always raises my hackles.* **—***v.t.* **7.** *Angling.* to equip with a hackle. **8.** to comb, as flax or hemp. Also, **hatchel, heckle** (for defs. 5, 8). [1400–50; late ME *hakell;* see HECKLE] **—hack′ler,** *n.*

hack•le[2] (hak′əl), *v.t.,* **-led, -ling.** to cut roughly; hack; mangle. [1570–80; HACK[1] + -LE; c. MD *hakkelen*]

hack•le•back (hak′əl bak′), *n.* See **shovelnose sturgeon.** [HACKLE[1] + BACK[1]]

hack′le fly′, *Angling.* an artificial fly made with hackles, usually without wings. Also called **hackle.** [1670–80]

hack•ly (hak′lē), *adj.* rough or jagged, as if hacked: *Some minerals break with a hackly fracture.* [1790–1800; HACKLE[2] + -Y[1]]

hack•man (hak′mən, -man′), *n., pl.* **-men** (-mən, -men′). the driver of a hack or taxi. [1790–1800, *Amer.;* HACK[2] + MAN[1]]

hack•ma•tack (hak′mə tak′), *n.* **1.** tamarack (def. 1). **2.** See **balsam poplar.** [1765–75, *Amer.;* earlier *hackmetack woods, hakmantak* dense forest or interwoven shrubbery of tamarack or other conifers; prob < Western Abenaki]

hack•ney (hak′nē), *n., pl.* **-neys,** *adj., v.* **—***n.* **1.** Also called **hackney coach.** a carriage or coach for hire; cab. **2.** a trotting horse used for drawing a light carriage or the like. **3.** a horse used for ordinary riding or driving. **4.** (*cap.*) one of an English breed of horses having a high-stepping gait. **—***adj.* **5.** let out, employed, or done for hire. **—***v.t.* **6.** to make trite, common, or stale by frequent use. **7.** to use as a hackney. [1300–50; ME *hakeney,* special use of placename *Hackney,* Middlesex, England] **—hack′ney•ism,** *n.*

Hack•ney (hak′nē), *n.* a borough of Greater London, England. 206,200.

hack′ney coach′, **1.** hackney (def. 1). **2.** a four-wheeled carriage having six seats and drawn by two horses. [1615–25]

hack•neyed (hak′nēd), *adj.* made commonplace or trite; stale; banal: *the hackneyed images of his poetry.* [1740–50; HACKNEY + -ED[2]]
—Syn. overdone, overused. See **commonplace.**

hack•saw (hak′sô′), *n.* a saw for cutting metal, consisting typically of a narrow, fine-toothed blade fixed in a frame. Also **hack′ saw′.** See illus. under **saw.** [1645–55; HACK[1] + SAW[1]]

hack•work (hak′wûrk′), *n.* writing, painting, or any professional work done for hire and usually following a formula rather than being motivated by any creative impulse. [1850–55; HACK[2] + WORK]

Hack′y Sack′ (hak′ē), *Trademark.* a small leather beanbag juggled with the feet as a game.

had (had), *v.* pt. and pp. of **have.**

ha•dal (hād′l), *adj.* **1.** of or pertaining to the greatest ocean depths, below approximately 20,000 ft. (6500 m). **2.** of or pertaining to the biogeographic region of the ocean bottom below the abyssal zone. [1955–60; HAD(ES) + -AL[1]]

Ha•da•mard (A dA mAR′), *n.* **Jacques Sa•lo•mon** (zhäk sA lô môN′), 1865–1963, French mathematician.

Had•ar (had′är, hā′där), *n.* a first magnitude star in the constellation Centaurus. [< Ar *Ḥaḍārī*]

Ha•dar (hä′där, hä′-, hä där′), *n.* a fossil site in the Afar triangle of eastern Ethiopia where *Australopithecus afarensis* was found.

ha•da•rim (KHə dä′RIm), *n. Yiddish.* pl. of ***heder.***

Ha•das (had′əs, hä′dəs), *n.* **Moses,** 1900–66, U.S. classical scholar, teacher, and author.

Ha•das•sah (hə dä′sə, hä-), *n.* a benevolent organization of Jewish women founded in New York City in 1912 by Henrietta Szold and concerned chiefly with bettering medical and educational facilities in Israel, forwarding Zionist activities in the U.S., and promoting world peace. [< Heb *hădassāh* lit., myrtle, the Hebrew name of Queen Esther; see Esther 2:7]

Had•ding•ton (had′ing tən), *n.* former name of **East Lothian.**

had•dock (had′ək), *n., pl.* (*esp. collectively*) **-dock,** (*esp. referring to two or more kinds or species*) **-docks.** **1.** a North Atlantic food fish, *Melanogrammus aeglefinus,* of the cod family. **2.** the rosefish, *Sebastes marinus.* [1275–1325; ME *haddok;* see -OCK]

Had•don (had′n), *n.* **1. Alfred Cort** (kôrt), 1855–1940, English ethnologist, anthropologist, and writer. **2.** a town in W New Jersey. 15,875.

Had•don•field (had′n fēld′), *n.* a town in SW New Jersey. 12,337.

hade (hād), *n., v.,* **had•ed, had•ing.** **—***n.* **1.** *Geol.* the angle between a fault plane and the vertical, measured perpendicular to the strike of the fault; complement of the dip. **2.** *Mining.* the inclination of a vein or seam from the vertical. **—***v.i.* **3.** (of a fault, vein, or seam) to incline from a vertical position. [1675–85; orig. uncert.]

Ha•des (hā′dēz), *n.* **1.** *Class. Myth.* **a.** the underworld inhabited by departed souls. **b.** the god ruling the underworld; Pluto. **2.** (in the Revised Version of the New Testament) the abode or state of the dead. **3.** (*often l.c.*) hell. [1590–1600] **—Ha•de•an** (hā dē′ən, hā′dē ən), *adj.*

Had•field (had′fēld′), *n.* **Sir Robert Abbott,** 1858–1940, English metallurgist and industrialist.

Ha•dhra•maut (hä′dRä môt′), *n.* a region along the S coast of the Arabian peninsula, in the People's Democratic Republic of Yemen. Also, **Ha′dra•maut′.** **—Ha•dhra•mau•tian** (hä′drə mô′shən), *adj., n.*

ha•dith (hä dēth′), *n., pl.* **-dith, -diths.** **1.** *Islam.* a traditional account of things said or done by Muhammad or his companions. **2.** (*used with a plural v.*) the entire body of such accounts. [1810–20; < Ar *ḥadīth*]

hadj (haj), *n., pl.* **hadj•es.** hajj.

hadj•i (haj′ē), *n., pl.* **hadj•is.** hajji.

Had•ley (had′lē), *n.* **1. Henry Kim•ball** (kim′bəl), 1871–1937, U.S. composer and conductor. **2.** a male or female given name.

Had′ley chest′, *U.S. Furniture.* a style of chest made c1700 in Massachusetts or Connecticut, having front rails and panels carved in low relief with elaborate tulip and leaf patterns. [after *Hadley,* Massachusetts]

had•n't (had′nt), contraction of *had not.*

Ha•dri•an (hā′drē ən), *n.* (*Publius Aelius Hadrianus*) A.D. 76–138, Roman emperor 117–138.

Hadrian I. See **Adrian I.**

Hadrian II. See **Adrian II.**

Hadrian III. See **Adrian III.**

Hadrian IV. See **Adrian IV.**

Hadrian V. See **Adrian V.**

Hadrian VI. See **Adrian VI.**

Ha′drian's Wall′, a wall of defense for the Roman province of Britain, constructed by Hadrian between Solway Firth and the mouth of the Tyne.

had•ron (had′ron), *n. Physics.* any elementary particle that is subject to the strong interaction. Hadrons are subdivided into baryons and mesons. Cf. **quark.** [1962; < Gk *hadr(ós)* thick, bulky + -ON[1]] **—ha•dron•ic** (ha dron′ik), *adj.*

CONCISE PRONUNCIATION KEY: act, cāpe, dâre, pärt; set, ēqual; if, īce; ox, ōver, ôrder, oil, bo͝ok, bo͞ot, out; up, ûrge; child; sing; shoe; thin, *th*at; zh as in *treasure.* ə = a as in *alone,* e as in *system,* i as in *easily,* o as in *gallop,* u as in *circus;* ᵊ as in *fire* (fīᵊr), *hour* (ouᵊr). l and n can serve as syllabic consonants, as in *cradle* (krād′l), and *button* (but′n). See the full key inside the front cover.

had•ro•saur (had′rə sôr′), *n.* a bipedal dinosaur of the genus *Hadrosaurus,* belonging to the ornithopod family Hadrosauridae of the late Cretaceous Period, having broad, flat jaws for scooping up water plants. Also called **duck-billed dinosaur.** [< NL *Hadrosaurus* (1858) genus name, equiv. to Gk *hadr(ós)* thick, bulky + *-o-* -O- + *saûros* -SAUR] —**had′ro•sau′ri•an,** *adj.*

hadrosaur
length 40 ft. (12 m);
height 18 ft. (5 m)

hadst (hadst), *v. Archaic.* a 2nd pers. sing. pt. of **have.**

hae (hā, ha), *v.t., auxiliary verb. Scot.* have.

Haeck•el (hek′əl), *n.* **Ernst Hein•rich** (ernst hīn′rikh), 1834–1919, German biologist and philosopher of evolution. —**Haeck•e•li•an** (he kē′lē ən), *adj., n.* —**Haeck′el•ism,** *n.*

haem-, *Chiefly Brit.* var. of **hem-:** *haemangioma.*

haema-, *Chiefly Brit.* var. of **hema-:** *haemachrome.*

haemat-, *Chiefly Brit.* var. of **hemat-:** *haematoid.*

haemato-, *Chiefly Brit.* var. of **hemato-:** *haematocyst.*

-haemia, *Chiefly Brit.* var. of **-hemia:** *leukocythaemia.*

haemo-, *Chiefly Brit.* var. of **hemo-:** *haemoglobin.*

hae•res (hēr′ēz), *n., pl.* **hae•re•des** (hi rē′dēz). *Civil Law.* heres.

haf•fet (haf′it), *n. Scot.* the part of the face above the upper jaw; the cheekbone and temple. [1505–15; earlier *halfet, halfhed,* OE *healfhēafod* sinciput, equiv. to *healf* side, part, HALF + *hēafod* HEAD]

ha•fiz (hä′fiz), *n.* a title of respect for a Muslim who knows the Koran by heart. [1655–65; < Ar *ḥāfiz* lit., a guard, one who keeps (in memory)]

Ha•fiz (hä fiz′), *n.* (*Shams ud-din Mohammed*) c1320–89?, Persian poet.

haf•ni•um (haf′nē əm, häf′-), *n. Chem.* a gray, toxic metallic element with a high melting point (over 2000°C), found in most zirconium minerals. *Symbol:* Hf; *at. wt.:* 178.49; *at. no.:* 72; *sp. gr.:* 12.1. [1923; < NL *Hafn(ia)* Copenhagen + -IUM]

haft (haft, häft), *n.* **1.** a handle, esp. of a knife, sword, or dagger. —*v.t.* **2.** to furnish with a haft or handle; set in a haft. [bef. 1000; ME; OE *hæft* handle, lit., that which is taken, grasped; c. L *captus,* G *Heft* handle]

Haf•ta•rah (*Seph. Heb.* häf tä rä′; *Ashk. Heb.* häf tô′rə, -tō′-), *n., pl. Seph. Heb.* **-ta•roth, -ta•rot** (-tä rôt′), *Ashk. Heb.* **-ta•ros** (-tô′rōs, -tō′-), *Eng.* **-ta•rahs.** *Judaism.* a portion of the Prophets that is chanted or read in the synagogue on the Sabbath and holy days immediately after the Parashah. Also, **Haphtarah.** [1890–95; < Heb *Haphṭārāh* lit., finish, ending]

hag[1] (hag), *n.* **1.** an ugly old woman, esp. a vicious or malicious one. **2.** a witch or sorceress. **3.** a hagfish. [1175–1225; ME *hagge,* OE **hægge,* akin to *hægtesse* witch, *hagorūn* spell, G *Hexe* witch] —**hag′gish, hag′like′,** *adj.*
—**Syn. 1.** harpy, harridan, virago, shrew.

hag[2] (hag, häg), *n. Brit. Dial.* **1.** bog; quagmire. **2.** a firm spot or island of firm ground in a bog or marsh. [1250–1300; ME: chasm < ON *hǫgg* a cut, ravine]

Hag., Haggai.

Ha•ga•nah (hä gä nä′), *n.* the underground Jewish militia in Palestine (1920–48) that became the national army of Israel after the partition of Palestine in 1948. [< ModHeb *hagana* lit., defense, Heb *hagannāh*]

Ha•gar (hā′gär, -gər), *n.* the mother of Ishmael. Gen. 16.

hag•born (hag′bôrn′), *adj.* born of a hag or witch. [1600–10; HAG[1] + BORN]

hag•but (hag′but), *n.* harquebus. [1535–45; var. of HACKBUT]

hag•don (hag′dən), *n. Brit. and Eastern Canada Dial.* any of various oceanic birds of the North Atlantic coasts of Europe and America, esp. the greater shearwater. [1835–45; orig. uncert.]

Ha•gen (hä′gən), *n.* a city in North Rhine-Westphalia, in W Germany. 209,200.

Ha•gen (hā′gən), *n.* **Walter,** 1892–1969, U.S. golfer.

Ha•gers•town (hā′gərz toun′), *n.* a city in NW Maryland. 34,132.

hag•fish (hag′fish′), *n., pl.* (*esp. collectively*) **-fish,** (*esp. referring to two or more kinds or species*) **-fish•es.** any eellike, marine cyclostome of the order Myxiniformes, having undeveloped eyes, a barbel-rimmed, circular mouth, and horny teeth for boring into the flesh of fishes to feed on their interior parts. See illus. in next column. [1605–15; HAG[1] + FISH]

CONCISE ETYMOLOGY KEY: <, descended or borrowed from; >, whence; b., blend of, blended; c., cognate with; cf., compare; deriv., derivative; equiv., equivalent; imit., imitative; obl., oblique; r., replacing; s., stem; sp., spelling, spelled; resp., respelling, respelled; trans., translation; ?, origin unknown; *, unattested; ‡, probably earlier than. See the full key inside the front cover.

Hag•ga•da (hə gä′də; *Seph. Heb.* hä gä dä′; *Ashk. Heb.* hä gô′də), *n., pl. Heb.* **-doth, -dot, -dos** (*Seph.* -dôt′; *Ashk.* -dōs), *Eng.* **-das.** Haggadah (def. 1).

Hag•ga•dah (hə gä′də; *Seph. Heb.* hä gä dä′; *Ashk. Heb.* hä gô′də), *n., pl. Seph. Heb.* **-doth, -dot** (-dôt′), *Ashk. Heb.* **-dos** (-dōs), *Eng.* **-das. 1.** a book containing the liturgy for the Seder service on the Jewish festival of Passover. **2.** Aggadah. [< Heb; see AGGADAH] —**hag•gad•ic** (hə gad′ik, -gä′dik), **hag•gad′i•cal,** *adj.*

hag•ga•dist (hə gä′dist), *n.* **1.** one of the writers of the Aggadah. **2.** a person who is versed in the Aggadah. [1855–60; HAGGAD(AH) + -IST] —**hag•ga•dist•ic** (hag′ə dis′tik), *adj.*

Hag•ga•i (hag′ē ī′, hag′ī), *n.* **1.** a Minor Prophet of the 6th century B.C. **2.** a book of the Bible bearing his name. *Abbr.:* Hag.

hag•gard (hag′ərd), *adj.* **1.** having a gaunt, wasted, or exhausted appearance, as from prolonged suffering, exertion, or anxiety; worn: *the haggard faces of the tired troops.* **2.** wild; wild-looking: *haggard eyes.* **3.** *Falconry.* (esp. of a hawk caught after it has attained adult plumage) untamed. —*n.* **4.** *Falconry.* a wild or untamed hawk caught after it has assumed adult plumage. [1560–70; orig., wild female hawk. See HAG[1], -ARD] —**hag′gard•ly,** *adv.* —**hag′gard•ness,** *n.*
—**Syn. 1.** emaciated, drawn, hollow-eyed. —**Ant. 1.** robust.

Hag•gard (hag′ərd), *n.* **(Sir) H(enry) Rider,** 1856–1925, English novelist.

hagged (hagd, hag′id), *adj. Brit. Dial.* **1.** haglike. **2.** haggard (defs. 1, 2). [1685–95; HAG[1] + -ED[3]]

hag•gis (hag′is), *n. Chiefly Scot.* a traditional pudding made of the heart, liver, etc., of a sheep or calf, minced with suet and oatmeal, seasoned, and boiled in the stomach of the animal. [1375–1425; late ME *hageys* < AF **hageis,* equiv. to *hag-* (root of *haguer* to chop, hash < MD *hacken* to HACK[1]) + *-eis* n. suffix used in cookery terms]

hag•gle (hag′əl), *v.,* **-gled, -gling,** *n.* —*v.i.* **1.** to bargain in a petty, quibbling, and often contentious manner: *They spent hours haggling over the price of fish.* **2.** to wrangle, dispute, or cavil: *The senators haggled interminably over the proposed bill.* —*v.t.* **3.** to mangle in cutting; hack. **4.** to settle on by haggling. **5.** *Archaic.* to harass with wrangling or haggling. —*n.* **6.** the act of haggling; wrangle or dispute over terms. [1275–1325; ME *haggen* to cut, chop (< ON *hǫggva* to HEW) + -LE] —**hag′gler,** *n.*

ha•gi•a (hä′jē ə), *n.pl. Eastern Ch.* the Eucharistic elements before or after the consecration. [< LGk, n. use of neut. pl. of Gk *hágios* holy]

hag•i•arch•y (hag′ē är′kē, hā′jē-), *n., pl.* **-arch•ies.** hagiocracy. [1820–30; HAGI- + -ARCHY]

hagio-, a combining form meaning "saint," "holy," used in the formation of compound words: *hagiography; hagiocracy.* Also, *esp. before a vowel,* **hagi-.** [< Gk, comb. form of *hágios* holy, sacred]

hag•i•oc•ra•cy (hag′ē ok′rə sē, hā′jē-), *n., pl.* **-cies. 1.** government by a body of persons esteemed as holy. **2.** a state so governed. Also, **hagiarchy.** [1840–50; HAGIO- + -CRACY]

Hag•i•og•ra•pha (hag′ē og′rə fə, hā′jē-), *n.* (*used with a singular v.*) the third of the three Jewish divisions of the Old Testament, variously arranged, but usually comprising the Psalms, Proverbs, Job, Song of Solomon, Ruth, Lamentations, Ecclesiastes, Esther, Daniel, Ezra, Nehemiah, and Chronicles. Also called **the Writings.** Cf. **Law of Moses, Prophets.** [< LL < Gk: sacred writings, equiv. to *hagio-* HAGIO- + *-grapha,* neut. pl. of *-graphos* -GRAPH]

hag•i•og•ra•pher (hag′ē og′rə fər, hā′jē-), *n.* **1.** one of the writers of the Hagiographa. **2.** a writer of lives of the saints; hagiologist. Also, **hag′i•og′ra•phist.** [1650–60; < Gk *hagiógraph(os)* + -ER[1]]

hag•i•og•ra•phy (hag′ē og′rə fē, hā′jē-), *n., pl.* **-phies.** the writing and critical study of the lives of the saints; hagiology. [1805–15; HAGIO- + -GRAPHY] —**hag•i•o•graph•ic** (hag′ē ə graf′ik, hā′jē-), **hag′i•o•graph′i•cal,** *adj.*

hag•i•ol•a•try (hag′ē ol′ə trē, hā′jē-), *n.* the worship of saints. [1800–10; HAGIO- + -LATRY] —**hag′i•ol′a•ter,** *n.* —**hag′i•ol′a•trous,** *adj.*

hag•i•ol•o•gy (hag′ē ol′ə jē, hā′jē-), *n., pl.* **-gies** for 2, 3. **1.** the branch of literature dealing with the lives and legends of the saints. **2.** a biography or narrative of a saint or saints. **3.** a collection of such biographies or narratives. [1800–10; HAGIO- + -LOGY] —**hag•i•o•log•ic** (hag′ē ə loj′ik, hā′jē-), **hag′i•o•log′i•cal,** *adj.* —**hag′i•ol′o•gist,** *n.*

hag•i•o•scope (hag′ē ə skōp′, hā′jē-), *n.* squint (def. 13). [1830–40; HAGIO- + -SCOPE] —**hag•i•o•scop•ic** (hag′ē ə skop′ik, hā′jē-), *adj.*

hag•rid•den (hag′rid′n), *adj.* worried or tormented, as by a witch. [1675–85; HAG[1] + RIDDEN]

hag•ride (hag′rīd′), *v.t.,* **-rode** or (*Archaic*) **-rid; -rid•den** or (*Archaic*) **-rid; -rid•ing.** to afflict with worry, dread, need, or the like; torment. [1655–65; HAG[1] + RIDE] —**hag′rid′er,** *n.*

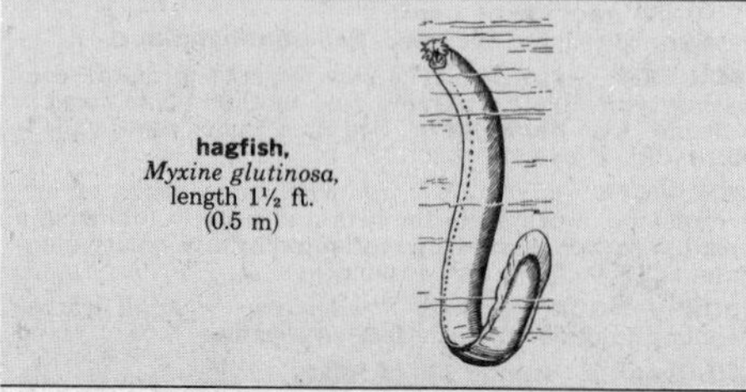
hagfish,
Myxine glutinosa,
length 1½ ft.
(0.5 m)

Hague (hāg), *n.* **The,** a city in the W Netherlands, near the North Sea: site of the government, royal residence, and of the International Court of Justice. 677,552. Dutch, **Den Haag, 's Gravenhage.**

Hague′ Peace′ Con′ference, 1. a meeting held at The Hague, Netherlands, in 1899, that established The Hague Permanent Court of Arbitration. **2.** a meeting held at The Hague, Netherlands, in 1907, that defined prisoner-of-war treatment, maritime warfare, and wartime neutrality.

hague•ton (hak′tən), *n. Armor.* acton.

Hague′ Tribu′nal, the court of arbitration for the peaceful settlement of international disputes, established at The Hague by the international peace conference of 1899: its panel of jurists nominates a list of persons from which members of the United Nations International Court of Justice are elected. Official name, **Permanent Court of Arbitration.**

hah (hä), *interj.* ha.

ha-ha[1] (hä′hä′, hä′hä′), *interj., n.* (used as an exclamation or representation of laughter, as in expressing amusement or derision.) Cf. **haw-haw.** [bef. 1000; ME, OE; of imit. orig.]

ha-ha[2] (hä′hä′), *n.* See **sunk fence.** [1705–15; < F *haha* repetitive compound based on *ha!* exclamation of surprise]

Hahn (hän), *n.* **Otto,** 1879–1968, German chemist: Nobel prize 1944.

Hah•ne•mann (hä′nə mən; *Ger.* hä′nə män′), *n.* **(Chris•tian Frie•drich) Sam•u•el** (kris′chən frē′drik sam′yo͞o əl; *Ger.* kris′tē än frē′drikh zä′mo͞o el), 1755–1843, German physician: founder of homeopathy. —**Hah•ne•mann•i•an** (hä′nə man′ē ən, -mä′nē-), *adj.* —**Hah′ne•mann′ism,** *n.*

hahn•i•um (hä′nē əm), *n. Chem.* unnilpentium. *Symbol:* Ha [1965–70; after O. HAHN; see -IUM]

Hai•da (hī′də), *n., pl.* **-das,** (*esp. collectively*) **-da** for 1. **1.** a member of an Indian people inhabiting the Queen Charlotte Islands in British Columbia and Prince of Wales Island in Alaska. **2.** the language of the Haida people, part of the Na-Dene language group.

Hai•dar•a•bad (hī′dər ə bäd′, -bad′, hī′drə-), *n.* Hyderabad.

Hai•dar A•li (hī′dər ä′lē, ä lē′), 1722–82, Islamic prince and military leader of India: ruler of Mysore 1759–82. Also, **Hyder Ali.**

Hai′ding•er fring′es (hī′ding ər), *Optics.* interference fringes produced by light passing through thick glass plates at near-normal incidence. [named after Wilhelm Karl von *Haidinger* (1795–1871), Austrian mineralogist]

Hai•duk (hī′do͝ok), *n.* **1.** one of a class of mercenary soldiers in 16th-century Hungary. **2.** an outlaw who engaged in brigandage and irregular warfare against the Turks in the Slavic regions of the Ottoman Empire. **3.** a male servant or attendant dressed in semimilitary Hungarian costume. Also, **Heyduck, Heyduke, Heyduc, Heiduc, Heiduk.** [< Hungarian *hajdúk,* pl. of *hajdú*]

Hai•fa (hī′fə), *n.* a seaport in NW Israel. 230,000.

Haig (hāg), *n.* **Douglas, 1st Earl,** 1861–1928, British field marshal: commander in chief of the British forces in France 1915–18.

Haight-Ash•bur•y (hāt′ash′ber ē, -bə rē), *n.* a district of San Francisco, in the central part of the city: a center for hippies and the drug culture in the 1960's.

haik (hīk, hāk), *n.* an oblong cloth used as an outer garment by the Arabs. Also, **haick.** [1605–15; < Ar *hā'ik, hayk,* akin to *ḥāk* weave]

hai•kai (hī′kī), *n., pl.* **-kai** for 2. *Pros.* **1.** an informal type of linked verse originated by Bashō, a 17th-century Japanese poet. **2.** a poem of this type. [1880–85; < Japn *haikai (no renga)* jesting (linked verse); earlier *fai-kai* < MChin, equiv. to Chin *páixié* jest]

Hai•kou (hī′kō′), *n. Pinyin, Wade-Giles.* a city on N Hainan island, in SE China. 500,000. Also, **Hoihow.**

hai•ku (hī′ko͞o), *n., pl.* **-ku** for 2. **1.** a major form of Japanese verse, written in 17 syllables divided into 3 lines of 5, 7, and 5 syllables, and employing highly evocative allusions and comparisons, often on the subject of nature or one of the seasons. **2.** a poem written in this form. [1895–1900; < Japn, equiv. to *hai(kai)* HAIKAI + *ku* stanza; see HOKKU]

hai′kwan′ tael′ (hī′kwän′), **1.** the customs unit in China, which is the basis for other local taels, equal to 1.20666 troy ounces of fine silver. **2.** liang. [< Chin *hǎiguān* sea customhouse]

hail[1] (hāl), *v.t.* **1.** to cheer, salute, or greet; welcome. **2.** to acclaim; approve enthusiastically: *The crowds hailed the conquerors. They hailed the recent advances in medicine.* **3.** to call out to in order to stop, attract attention, ask aid, etc.: *to hail a cab.* —*v.i.* **4.** to call out in order to greet, attract attention, etc.: *The people on land hailed as we passed in the night.* **5. hail from,** to have as one's place of birth or residence: *Nearly everyone here*

hails from the Midwest. —*n.* **6.** a shout or call to attract attention. **7.** a salutation or greeting: *a cheerful hail.* **8.** the act of hailing. **9. within hail,** within range of hearing; audible: *The mother kept her children within hail of her voice.* —*interj.* **10.** (used as a salutation, greeting, or acclamation.) [1150–1200; ME *haile,* earlier *heilen,* deriv. of *hail* health < ON *heill;* c. OE *hǣl.* See HEAL, WASSAIL] —**hail′er,** *n.*
—**Syn. 2.** cheer, applaud, honor, exalt, laud, extol.

hail[2] (hāl), *n.* **1.** showery precipitation in the form of irregular pellets or balls of ice more than ⅕ in. (5 mm) in diameter, falling from a cumulonimbus cloud (distinguished from *sleet*). **2.** a shower or storm of such precipitation. **3.** a shower of anything: *a hail of bullets.* —*v.i.* **4.** to pour down hail (often used impersonally with *it* as subject): *It hailed this afternoon.* **5.** to fall or shower as hail: *Arrows hailed down on the troops as they advanced.* —*v.t.* **6.** to pour down on as or like hail: *The plane hailed leaflets on the city.* [bef. 900; ME; OE *hægl,* var. of *hagol;* c. G *Hagel,* ON *hagl*]

Hail′ Colum′bia, *Slang.* hell (used as a euphemism): *He caught Hail Columbia for being late.* [1840–50]

Hai·le Se·las·sie I (hī′lē sə las′ē, -lä′sē), (*Ras Tafari*), 1891–1975, emperor of Ethiopia 1930–74: in exile 1936–41.

hail-fel·low (*n.* hāl′fel′ō; *adj.* hāl′fel′ō), *n.* **1.** Also, **hail′ fel′low, hail′-fel′low well′ met′.** a spiritedly sociable person; jolly companion. —*adj.* **2.** sociable; heartily genial: *His hail-fellow manner helped him to advance in the sales force.* [1570–80]

hail′ing dis′tance, 1. the distance within which the human voice can be heard: *They sailed within hailing distance of the island.* **2.** a close distance; the reach of something or someone (usually prec. by *within*): *Success is within hailing distance.* [1830–40]

Hail′ Mar′y, 1. See **Ave Maria. 2.** Also called **Hail′ Mar′y pass′, Hail′ Mar′y play′.** a long forward pass in football, esp. as a last-ditch attempt at the end of a game, where completion is considered unlikely. [1300–50; ME, trans. of ML *Ave Maria*]

hail·stone (hāl′stōn′), *n.* a pellet of hail. [bef. 1000; ME; OE *hagolstān.* See HAIL[2], STONE]

hail·storm (hāl′stôrm′), *n.* a storm with hail. [1675–85; HAIL[2] + STORM]

haim·ish (hā′mish), *adj. Slang.* homey; cozy and unpretentious. Also, **heimish.** [< Yiddish *heymish* < MHG *heimisch,* OHG *heimisc* lit., pertaining to the home; see HOME, -ISH[1]]

Hai·nan (hī′nän′), *n. Pinyin, Wade-Giles.* an island in the South China Sea, separated from the mainland by the Hainan Strait: a part of Guangdong province. 2,800,000; 13,200 sq. mi. (34,200 sq. km).

Hai′nan′ Strait′, a strait between Hainan island and Leizhou peninsula. 50 mi. (81 km) long; 15 mi. (24 km) wide. Also called **Qiongzhou Strait.**

Hai·naut (e nō′), *n.* **1.** a medieval county in territory now in SW Belgium and N France. **2.** a province in SW Belgium. 1,271,649; 1437 sq. mi. (3722 sq. km). *Cap.:* Mons.

Haines′ Cit′y (hānz), a town in central Florida. 10,799.

hain't (hānt), *Nonstandard Older Use.* ain't; have not; has not. [1830–40, *Amer.*; orig. contr. of *have not, has not* (with loss of consonant and compensatory lengthening of *a*); influenced in use by AIN'T]

Hai·phong (hī′fong′), *n.* a seaport in N Vietnam, near the Gulf of Tonkin. 1,190,900.

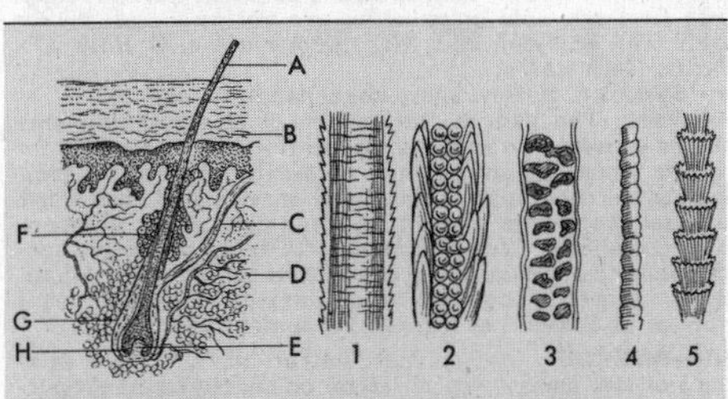

hair (def. 1)
Cross section of skin containing: A, hair; B, epidermis; C, muscle; D, dermis; E, papilla; F, sebaceous glands; G, follicle; H, root. Longitudinal sections of hairs: 1, human being; 2, sable; 3, mouse. External view: 4, mouse; 5, Indian bat

hair (hâr), *n.* **1.** any of the numerous fine, usually cylindrical, keratinous filaments growing from the skin of humans and animals; a pilus. **2.** an aggregate of such filaments, as that covering the human head or forming the coat of most mammals. **3.** a similar fine, filamentous outgrowth from the body of insects, spiders, etc. **4.** *Bot.* a filamentous outgrowth of the epidermis. **5.** cloth made of hair from animals, as camel and alpaca. **6.** a very small amount, degree, measure, magnitude, etc.; a fraction, as of time or space: *He lost the race by a hair.* **7. get in someone's hair,** *Slang.* to annoy or bother someone: *Their snobbishness gets in my hair.* **8. hair of the dog,** *Informal.* a drink of liquor, supposed to relieve a hangover: *Even a hair of the dog didn't help his aching head.* Also, **hair of the dog that bit one. 9. let one's hair down,** *Informal.* **a.** to relax; behave informally: *He finally let his hair down and actually cracked a joke.* **b.** to speak candidly or frankly; remove or reduce restraints: *He let his hair down and told them about his anxieties.* **10. make one's hair stand on end,** to strike or fill with horror; terrify: *The tales of the jungle made our hair stand on end.* **11. split hairs,** to make unnecessarily fine or petty distinctions: *To argue about whether they arrived at two o'clock or at 2:01 is just splitting hairs.* **12. tear one's hair,** to manifest extreme anxiety, grief, or anger: *He's tearing his hair over the way he was treated by them.* Also, **tear one's hair out. 13. to a hair,** perfect to the smallest detail; exactly: *The reproduction matched the original to a hair.* **14. without turning a hair,** without showing the least excitement or emotion. Also, **not turn a hair.** [bef. 900; ME *heer,* OE *hǣr* (c. D, G *haar,* ON *hār*), with vowel perh. from ME *haire* hair shirt < OF < OHG *hāria* (c. ME *here,* OE *hǣre,* ON *hǣra*)] —**hair′like′,** *adj.*

hair·ball (hâr′bôl′), *n.* a ball of hair accumulated in the stomach or intestines of a cat or other animal as a result of the animal's licking its coat. [1705–15]

hair·brained (hâr′brānd′), *adj.* harebrained.

hair·breadth (hâr′bredth′, -bretth′), *n., adj.* hairsbreadth. [1400–50; late ME *heere brede;* see HAIR, BREADTH]

hair·brush (hâr′brush′), *n.* a brush for smoothing and styling the hair. [1590–1600; HAIR + BRUSH[1]]

hair′brush cac′tus, a stout, spiny cactus, *Pachycereus pecten-aboriginum,* of Mexico, having white flowers and bristly fruits sometimes used locally as combs.

hair′ cell′, *Biol.* an epithelial cell having hairlike processes, as that of the organ of Corti. [1885–90]

hair·cloth (hâr′klôth′, -kloth′), *n.* cloth of hair from the manes and tails of horses, woven with a cotton warp, and used for interlinings of clothes, upholstery, etc. Also called **cilice.** [1490–1500; HAIR + CLOTH]

hair·col·or·ing (hâr′kul′ər ing), *n.* dye or tint for the hair. [1955–60; HAIR + COLORING]

hair·cut (hâr′kut′), *n.* **1.** an act or instance of cutting the hair. **2.** the style in which the hair is cut and worn, esp. men's hair. [1895–1900; HAIR + CUT] —**hair′cut′ter,** *n.* —**hair′cut′ting,** *n., adj.*

hair·do (hâr′do͞o′), *n., pl.* **-dos. 1.** the style in which a person's hair is cut, arranged, and worn; coiffure. **2.** the hair itself, esp. when newly or elaborately arranged. [1920–25; HAIR + DO[1]]

hair·dress·er (hâr′dres′ər), *n.* **1.** a person who arranges or cuts hair. **2.** *Chiefly Brit.* barber. [1760–70; HAIR + DRESSER[1]]

hair·dress·ing (hâr′dres′ing), *n.* **1.** the act or process of cutting, styling, or dressing hair. **2.** the vocation or occupation of a hairdresser. **3.** a style of arranging the hair; hairdo; coiffure. **4.** a preparation, as tonic, oil, pomade, or the like, applied to the hair for increased manageability. [1765–75; HAIR + DRESSING]

haired (hârd), *adj.* **1.** having hair of a specified kind (usually used in combination): *dark-haired; long-haired.* **2.** *New England* (*chiefly Maine*). angry, annoyed, or upset (often fol. by *up*): *Don't get haired up over his insults.* [1350–1400; ME *hered;* see HAIR, -ED[3]]

hair′ fol′licle, *Anat.* a small cavity in the epidermis and corium of the skin, from which a hair develops. See illus. under **hair.** [1830–40]

hair′ grass′, any of various grasses having slender stems and leaves, esp. one of the genus *Deschampsia,* as *D. flexuosa* or *D. caespitosa.* [1750–60]

hair′ hygrom′eter, a hygrometer actuated by the changes in length of a strand of human hair brought about by changes in the relative humidity. [1875–80]

hair′ im′plant, the insertion of synthetic fibers or human hair into the scalp to cover baldness. Cf. **hair transplant.** [1970–75]

hair·less (hâr′lis), *adj.* without hair; bald: *his pink hairless pate.* [1375–1425; late ME *hereles.* See HAIR, -LESS] —**hair′less·ness,** *n.*

hair·line (hâr′līn′), *n.* **1.** a very slender line. **2.** the lower edge of the hair, esp. along the upper forehead: *a hairline that slowly receded.* **3.** worsted fabric woven with very fine lines or stripes. **4.** *Print.* **a.** a very thin line on the face of a type. See illus. under **type. b.** a style of type consisting entirely of such lines. **c.** a thin rule for printing fine lines. **d.** undesirable vertical lines between letters, caused by worn matrices. —*adj.* **5.** narrow or fine as a hair: *a hairline fracture.* [1725–35; HAIR + LINE[1]]

hair′ net′, a cap of loose net, as of silk or nylon, for holding the hair in place. [1860–65]

hair·piece (hâr′pēs′), *n.* a toupee. [1935–40; HAIR + PIECE]

hair·pin (hâr′pin′), *n.* **1.** a slender U-shaped piece of wire, shell, etc., used by women to fasten up the hair or hold a headdress. —*adj.* **2.** (of a road, curve in a road, etc.) sharply curved back, as in a U shape: *a hairpin turn.* [1770–80; HAIR + PIN]

hair-rais·er (hâr′rā′zər), *n.* a story, experience, etc., that is terrifying or thrilling. [1895–1900]

hair-rais·ing (hâr′rā′zing), *adj.* terrifying or horrifying: *We had a hair-raising brush with death.* [1895–1900]

hairs·breadth (hârz′bredth′, -bretth′, -breth′), *n.* **1.** a very small space or distance: *We escaped an accident by a hairsbreadth.* —*adj.* **2.** extremely narrow or close. Also, **hair's′-breadth′, hairbreadth.** [1575–85]

hair′ seal′, any of various seals having coarse hair and no soft underfur. [1815–25]

hair′ shirt′, 1. a garment of coarse haircloth, worn next to the skin as a penance by ascetics and penitents. **2.** self-imposed punishment, suffering, sacrifice, or penance. [1730–40; cf. HAIR]

hair′ space′, *Print.* the thinnest metal space used to separate words, symbols, etc. [1835–45]

hair·split·ting (hâr′split′ing), *n.* **1.** the making of unnecessarily fine distinctions. —*adj.* **2.** characterized by such distinctions: *the hairsplitting arguments of a political debate.* [1820–30; HAIR + SPLITTING] —**hair′split′ter,** *n.*
—**Syn. 2.** quibbling, niggling, nitpicking, captious.

hair′ spray′, a liquid in an aerosol or other spray container, for holding the hair in place. Also, **hair′spray′.** [1955–60]

hair·spring (hâr′spring′), *n. Horol.* a fine, usually spiral, spring used for oscillating the balance of a timepiece. Also called **balance spring.** [1820–30]

hair·streak (hâr′strēk′), *n.* any small, dark butterfly of the family Lycaenidae, having hairlike tails on the hind wings. [1810–20; HAIR + STREAK]

hair′ stroke′, a fine line in writing or printing. [1625–35]

hair′ style′, a style of cutting, arranging, or combing the hair; hairdo; coiffure. Also, **hair′style′.** [1910–15]

hair′ styl′ist, a person who designs and arranges hair styles. Also, **hair′styl′ist.** [1930–35] —**hair′ styl′ing.** —**hair′styl′ing,** *n.*

hair′ trans′plant, the surgical transfer of clumps of skin with hair or of viable hair follicles from one site of the body to another, usually performed to correct baldness. Cf. **hair implant.** [1970–75]

hair′ trig′ger, a trigger that allows the firing mechanism of a firearm to be operated by very slight pressure. [1815–25]

hair-trig·ger (hâr′trig′ər), *adj.* easily activated or set off; reacting immediately to the slightest provocation or cause: *a hair-trigger temper.* [1885–90]

hair·weav·ing (hâr′wē′ving), *n.* the attachment of matching hair to a base of nylon thread interwoven with a person's remaining hair, to cover a bald area. Also, **hair′-weav′ing.** [1965–70; HAIR + WEAVE + -ING[1]] —**hair′weav′er,** *n.*

hair·worm (hâr′wûrm′), *n.* any small, slender worm of the family Trichostrongylidae, parasitic in the alimentary canals of various animals. [1650–60; HAIR + WORM]

hair·y (hâr′ē), *adj.,* **hair·i·er, hair·i·est. 1.** covered with hair; having much hair. **2.** consisting of or resembling hair: *moss of a hairy texture.* **3.** *Informal.* **a.** causing anxiety or fright: *a hairy trip through the rapids.* **b.** full of hardship or difficulty: *a hairy exam; a hairy illness.* [1250–1300; ME *heeri.* See HAIR, -Y[1]] —**hair′i·ness,** *n.*
—**Syn. 1.** furry, woolly, shaggy.

hair′y cell′ leuke′mia, a form of cancer in which abnormal cells with many hairlike cytoplasmic projections appear in the bone marrow, liver, spleen, and blood. Also called **leukemic reticuloendotheliosis.**

hair·y-faced (hâr′ē fāst′), *adj.* having a face covered with hair.

hair′y-tailed mole′ (hâr′ē tāld′), a blackish North American mole, *Parascalops breweri,* having a short, hairy tail. Also, **hair′y·tail′ mole′.** Also called **Brewer's mole.**

hair′y vetch′, a plant, *Vicia villosa,* of the legume family, native to Eurasia, having hairy stems and violet and white flowers, widely grown as forage and as a cover crop. Also called **winter vetch.** [1900–05]

hair′y wood′pecker, a North American woodpecker, *Picoides villosus,* resembling but larger than the downy woodpecker. [1720–30, *Amer.*]

Hai·ti (hā′tē), *n.* **1.** Formerly, **Hayti.** a republic in the West Indies occupying the W part of the island of Hispaniola. 5,000,000; 10,714 sq. mi. (27,750 sq. km). *Cap.:* Port-au-Prince. **2.** Also, **Hayti.** a former name of **Hispaniola.**

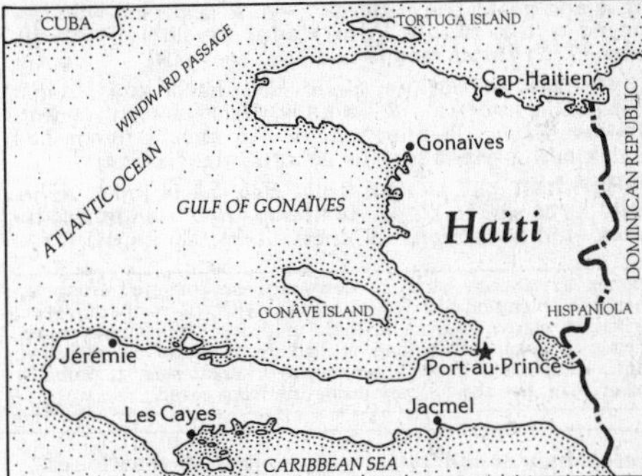

Hai·tian (hā′shən, -tē ən), *adj.* **1.** of or pertaining to Haiti or its people. —*n.* **2.** a native or inhabitant of Haiti. **3.** See **Haitian Creole.** [1795–1805; HAITI + -AN]

Hai′tian Cre′ole, the creolized French that is the native language of most Haitians. Also called **Creole, Haitian.**

haj·i (haj′ē), *n., pl.* **haj·is.** hajji.

hajj (haj), *n., pl.* **hajj·es.** the pilgrimage to Mecca, which every adult Muslim is supposed to make at least once in his or her lifetime: the fifth of the Pillars of Islam. Also, **hadj.** [1665–75; < Ar *ḥajj* pilgrimage]

haj·ji (haj′ē), *n., pl.* **haj·jis. 1.** a Muslim who has gone on a pilgrimage to Mecca. **2.** a Christian from Greece, Armenia, or any country of the Near East, who has visited the Holy Sepulcher at Jerusalem. Also, **hadji, haji.** [1600–10; < Ar *ḥajjī,* equiv. to *ḥajj* pilgrimage + *-ī* suffix of appurtenance]

CONCISE PRONUNCIATION KEY: act, cāpe, dâre, pärt; set, ēqual; if, īce; ox, ōver, ôrder, oil, bo͝ok, bo͞ot, out; up, ûrge; child; sing; shoe; thin, *th*at; zh as in *treasure.* ə = *a* as in *alone, e* as in *system, i* as in *easily, o* as in *gallop, u* as in *circus;* ᵊ as in *fire* (fīᵊr), *hour* (ouᵊr). l and n can serve as syllabic consonants, as in *cradle* (krād′l), and *button* (but′n). See the full key inside the front cover.

ha·ka·foth (*Seph.* hä kä fôt′; *Ashk.* hä′kô fōs′), *n. Hebrew.* a ceremony on Simhath Torah and on other occasions in which members of a synagogue congregation carry Torah scrolls around the synagogue seven or more times. Also, ***ha·ka·fot′, hak·ka·foth′, hak·ka·fot′.*** [Heb *haqqāphōth*, pl. of *haqqāphāh* lit., going around]

ha·ka·pik (hä′kə pik′), *n.* an implement used in seal hunting, consisting of an iron or steel hook, sometimes with a hammer opposite, mounted on a long wooden pole. [1975–80; < Norw *hakepigg*, equiv. to *hake* hook (cf. HAKE, HOOK) + *pigg* spike (akin to PIKE[1])]

hake (hāk), *n., pl.* (*esp. collectively*) **hake,** (*esp. referring to two or more kinds or species*) **hakes. 1.** any marine fish of the genus *Merluccius*, closely related to the cods, esp. *M. bilinearis*, found off the New England coast. **2.** any of several related marine fishes, esp. of the genus *Urophycis.* [1275–1325; ME; special use of OE *haca* hook; cf. MLG *haken* kipper salmon]

ha·ke·a (hä′kē ə, hä′-), *n.* any of various shrubs or trees of the genus *Hakea*, native to Australia, having evergreen, pinnate leaves and clusters of variously colored flowers. [< NL (1798) named after Christian Ludwig von *Hake* (1745–1818), German horticulturist; see -A[2]]

Ha·ken·kreuz (hä′kən kroits′), *n., pl.* ***-kreu·ze*** (-kroi′tsə), *German.* a swastika, esp. that used as the emblem of the Nazi party and the Third Reich.

ha·kham (*Seph.* khä khäm′; *Ashk.* hô′khəm), *n. Hebrew.* **1.** a wise and learned person; sage. **2.** (among Sephardic Jews) a title given to a rabbi. Also, ***ha·kam′.*** [*ḥākhām* lit., wise]

ha·kim[1] (hä kēm′), *n.* (esp. in Muslim countries) **1.** a wise or learned man. **2.** a physician; doctor. Also, **ha·keem′.** [1575–85; < Ar *hakīm* wise, wise man]

ha·kim[2] (hä′kēm), *n.* (in Muslim countries) a ruler; governor; judge. [1605–15; < Ar *hākim* governor]

Ha·kim (hä kēm′), *n.* a male given name. Also, **Ha·keem′.**

Hak·ka (hä′kə; *Chin.* häk′kä′), *n., pl.* **-kas,** (*esp. collectively*) **-ka** for 1. **1.** a member of a Chinese people originally of northern China, now widely distributed throughout southeastern China, in Taiwan and Hong Kong, and in Southeast Asia. **2.** the Chinese language spoken by the Hakka.

Hak·luyt (hak′lo͞ot), *n.* **Richard,** 1552?–1616, English geographer and editor of explorers' narratives.

Ha·ko·da·te (hä′kô dä′te), *n.* a seaport on S Hokkaido, in N Japan. 320,152.

Hal (hal), *n.* a male given name, form of **Harold.**

Hal, *Chem.* halogen.

hal-, var. of **halo-** before a vowel: *halite.*

Ha·la·cha (hä lô′khə; *Seph. Heb.* hä lä khä′; *Ashk. Heb.* hä′lô khô′), *n., pl.* **-la·chas,** *Heb.* **-la·choth, -la·chot, -la·chos** (*Seph.* -lä khôt′; *Ashk.* -lô khōs′). (*often l.c.*) Halakhah.

Ha·la·chah (hä lô′khə; *Seph. Heb.* hä lä khä′; *Ashk. Heb.* hä′lô khô′), *n., pl.* **-la·chahs,** *Heb.* **-la·choth, -la·chot, -la·chos** (*Seph.* -lä khôt′; *Ashk.* -lô khōs′). (*often l.c.*) Halakhah.

ha·la·chist (hä′lə kist, hə lä′-, hə lak′ist), *n.* halakhist.

Ha·laf·i·an (hə lä′fē ən), *adj.* **1.** of or belonging to the Neolithic culture chiefly of northern Syria, dating to the fifth millennium B.C. and characterized by adobe dwellings and polychrome pottery decorated with animal designs and geometric patterns. —*n.* **2.** a person who belonged to this culture. Also, **Ha·laf** (hə läf′). [1935–40; after (*Tell*) *Halaf* mound in Syria; see -IAN]

Ha·la·kah (hä lô′khə; *Seph. Heb.* hä lä khä′; *Ashk. Heb.* hä′lô khô′), *n., pl.* **-la·kahs,** *Heb.* **-la·koth, -la·kot, -la·kos** (*Seph.* -lä khôt′; *Ashk.* -lô khōs′). (*often l.c.*) Halakhah. —**Ha·lak·ic** (hə lä′khik, -lak′ik), *adj.*

Ha·la·khah (hä lô′khə; *Seph. Heb.* hä lä khä′; *Ashk. Heb.* hä′lô khô′), *n., pl.* **-la·khahs,** *Heb.* **-la·khoth, -la·khot, -la·khos** (*Seph.* -lä khôt′; *Ashk.* -lô khōs′) for 2. **1.** (*often l.c.*) the entire body of Jewish law and tradition comprising the laws of the Bible, the oral law as transcribed in the legal portion of the Talmud, and subsequent legal codes amending or modifying traditional precepts to conform to contemporary conditions. **2.** a law or tradition established by the Halakhah. Also, **Halakah, Halachah, Halacha.** [1855–60; < Heb *hălākhāh*, lit., way] —**Ha·la·khic** (hə lä′khik, -lak′ik), *adj.*

ha·la·khist (hä′lə kist, hə lä′-, hə lak′ist), *n.* **1.** one of the writers or compilers of the Halakhah. **2.** a person who is versed in the Halakhah. Also, **ha′la·kist, halachist.** [1880–85; HALAKH(AH) + -IST]

ha·la·la (hə lä′lə), *n., pl.* **-la, -las.** a bronze coin and monetary unit of Saudi Arabia, the 100th part of a riyal. [< Ar *halalah*]

ha·la·lah (hə lä′lə), *n., pl.* **-lah, -lahs.** halala.

Hal·as (hal′əs), *n.* **George Stanley,** 1895–1983, U.S. football coach and team owner.

ha·la·tion (hā lā′shən, ha-), *n. Photog.* a blurred effect around the edges of highlight areas in a photographic image caused by reflection and scattering of light through the emulsion from the back surface of the film support or plate. [1855–60; HAL(O) + -ATION]

ha·la·vah (hä′lə vä′), *n.* halvah.

hal·a·ze·pam (ha lā′zə pam′), *n. Pharm.* a derivative of benzodiazepine, $C_{17}H_{12}ClF_3N_2O$, used for management of anxiety disorders. [HAL- + (DI)AZEPAM]

hal·a·zone (hal′ə zōn′), *n.* a white crystalline powder, $C_7H_5Cl_2NO_4S$, having a strong chlorinelike odor, used to disinfect water. [HAL- + AZ- + -ONE]

hal·berd (hal′bərd, hôl′-, hol′-; *formerly* hô′bərd), *n.* a shafted weapon with an axlike cutting blade, beak, and apical spike, used esp. in the 15th and 16th centuries. Also, **hal·bert** (hal′bərt, hôl′-, hol′-; *formerly* hô′bərt). [1485–95; earlier *haubert* < MF *hallebarde* < MLG *helmbarde*, equiv. to *helm* handle (c. HELM[1]) + *barde* broadax (c. MHG *barte*)]

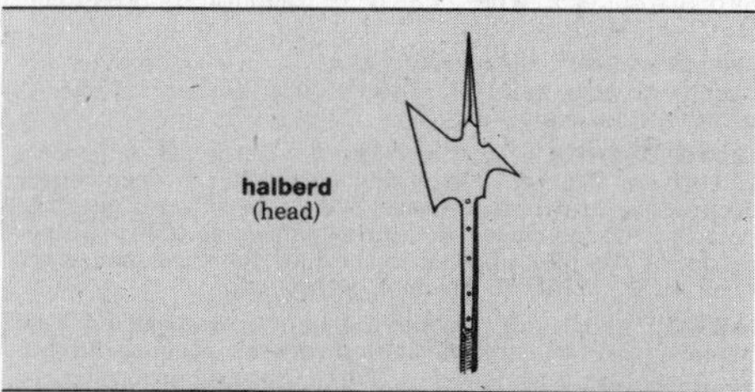
halberd (head)

hal·berd·ier (hal′bər dēr′), *n.* a soldier, guard, or attendant armed with a halberd. [1540–50; < MF *hallebardier.* See HALBERD, -IER[2]]

Hal·ci·on (hal′sē on′), *Trademark.* a benzodiazepine, used as a sleeping drug and as an anxiolytic.

hal·cy·on (hal′sē ən), *adj.* Also, **hal·cy·o·ni·an** (hal′sē-ō′nē ən), **hal·cy·on·ic** (hal′sē on′ik). **1.** calm; peaceful; tranquil: *halcyon weather.* **2.** rich; wealthy; prosperous: *halcyon times of peace.* **3.** happy; joyful; carefree: *halcyon days of youth.* **4.** of or pertaining to the halcyon or kingfisher. —*n.* **5.** a mythical bird, usually identified with the kingfisher, said to breed about the time of the winter solstice in a nest floating on the sea, and to have the power of charming winds and waves into calmness. **6.** any of various kingfishers, esp. of the genus *Halcyon.* **7.** (*cap.*) *Class. Myth.* Alcyone (def. 2). [1350–1400; < L < Gk *halkyṓn*, pseudo-etymological var. of *alkyṓn* kingfisher; r. ME *alceon, alicion* < L *alcyōn* < Gk]
—**Syn. 1.** serene, placid, pacific, untroubled.

Hal·dane (hôl′dān), *n.* **1. John Bur·don San·der·son** (bûr′dn san′dər sən), 1892–1964, English biochemist, geneticist, and writer. **2.** his father, **John Scott,** 1860–1936, Scottish physiologist and writer. **3. Richard Burdon** (*Viscount Haldane of Cloan*), 1856–1928, Scottish jurist, statesman, and writer (brother of John Scott).

Hal·di·mand (hôl′də mənd), *n.* a town in SE Ontario, in S Canada. 16,866.

Hal·dol (hal′dôl, -dol), *Pharm., Trademark.* a brand of haloperidol.

hale[1] (hāl), *adj.,* **hal·er, hal·est.** free from disease or infirmity; robust; vigorous: *hale and hearty men in the prime of life.* [bef. 1000; ME (north); OE *hāl* WHOLE] —**hale′ness,** *n.*
—**Syn. 1.** sound, healthy. —**Ant. 1.** sickly.

hale[2] (hāl), *v.t.,* **haled, hal·ing. 1.** to compel (someone) to go: *to hale a man into court.* **2.** to haul; pull. [1175–1225; ME *halen* < MF *haler* < Gmc; cf. D *halen* to pull, fetch; akin to OE *geholian* to get, G *holen* to fetch. See HAUL] —**hal′er,** *n.*

ha·le[3] (hä′lā), *n.* (in Hawaii) a simple thatched-roof dwelling. [< Hawaiian; house, building]

Hale (hāl), *n.* **1. Edward Everett,** 1822–1909, U.S. clergyman and author. **2. George El·ler·y** (el′ə rē), 1868–1938, U.S. astronomer. **3. Sir Matthew,** 1609–76, British jurist: Lord Chief Justice 1671–76. **4. Nathan,** 1755–76, American soldier hanged as a spy by the British during the American Revolution. **5. Sarah Jo·se·pha** (jō sē′fə), 1788–1879, U.S. editor and author.

Ha·le·a·ka·la (hä′lē ä′kä lä′), *n.* a dormant volcano in Hawaii, on the island of Maui. 10,032 ft. (3058 m) above sea level.

Ha′leakala′ Na′tional Park′, a national park on Maui, Hawaii: site of 21-mi. (34-km) diameter volcanic crater. 43 sq. mi. (111 sq. km).

ha·ler (hä′lər), *n.* **1.** heller[2] (def. 1). **2.** Also, **heller.** a minor coin of the Czech Republic, the 100th part of a koruna. [1930–35; < Czech *haléř* < MHG *haller*, var. of *heller* HELLER]

Hale′ tel′escope, the 200-in. (508-cm) reflector at the Palomar Observatory. [after G. E. HALE]

Ha·le·vi (hä lē′vī, -lā′vē), *n.* **Judah.** See **Judah ha-Levi.**

Ha·lé·vy (A lā vē′), *n.* **1. Fro·men·tal** (frô mäɴ tal′), (*Jacques François Fromental Élie Lévy*), 1790–1862, French composer, esp. of operas. **2.** his nephew, **Lu·do·vic** (ly dô vēk′), 1834–1908, French novelist and playwright: librettist in collaboration with Henri Meilhac.

half (haf, häf), *n., pl.* **halves** (havz, hävz), *adj., adv.* —*n.* **1.** one of two equal or approximately equal parts of a divisible whole, as an object, or unit of measure or time; a part of a whole equal or almost equal to the remainder. **2.** a quantity or amount equal to such a part (½). **3.** *Sports.* either of two equal periods of play, usually with an intermission or rest period separating them. Cf. **quarter** (def. 10). **4.** one of two; a part of a pair. **5.** *Informal.* **a.** See **half dollar. b.** the sum of 50 cents. **6.** *Baseball.* either of the two units of play into which an inning is divided, the visiting team batting in the first unit and the home team batting in the second. **7.** *Football.* a halfback. **8.** *Brit. Informal.* **a.** a half-crown coin. **b.** the sum of a half crown; two shillings, sixpence. **c.** a half pint: *He ordered a half of ale.* **9. not the half of,** a significant yet relatively minor part of something that remains to be described in full: *He accused them of being responsible for the error, and that's not the half of the story.* Also, **not half of, not half.** —*adj.* **10.** being one of two equal or approximately equal parts of a divisible whole: *a half quart.* **11.** being half or about half of anything in degree, amount, length, etc.: *at half speed; half sleeve.* **12.** partial or incomplete: *half measures.* —*adv.* **13.** in or to the extent or measure of half. **14.** in part; partly; incompletely: *half understood.* **15.** to some extent; almost: *half recovered.* **16. by half,** by very much; by far: *She was too talented by half for her routine role.* **17. half again as much** or **as many,** as much as 50 percent more: *This mug holds half again as much coffee as the smaller one.* **18. half in two,** *Southern U.S.* (*chiefly Gulf States*). in or into two parts; in half: *Cut the cake half in two.* **19. in half,** divided into halves: *The vase broke in half.* **20. not half, a.** not at all; not really: *His first attempts at painting are not half bad.* **b.** See **half** (def. 9). [bef. 900; ME; OE *h(e)alf;* c. G *Halb*, ON *halfr*, Goth *halbs*]
—**Syn. 14.** barely, somewhat, partially; sort of.
—**Note.** The lists at the bottom of this and following pages provide the spelling, syllabification, and stress for words whose meanings may be easily inferred by combining the meanings of HALF and an attached base word, or base word plus a suffix. Appropriate parts of speech are also shown. Words formed with HALF that have special meanings or uses are entered in their proper alphabetical places in the main vocabulary or as derived forms run on at the end of a main vocabulary entry.

half-and-half (haf′ən haf′, häf′ən häf′), *n.* **1.** a mixture of two things, esp. in equal or nearly equal proportions. **2.** milk and light cream combined in equal parts,

CONCISE ETYMOLOGY KEY: <, descended or borrowed from; >, whence; b., blend of, blended; c., cognate with; cf., compare; deriv., derivative; equiv., equivalent; imit., imitative; obl., oblique; r., replacing; s., stem; sp., spelling, spelled; resp., respelling, respelled; trans., translation; ?, origin unknown; *, unattested; ‡, probably earlier than. See the full key inside the front cover.

half′-a·ban′doned, *adj.*
half′-ac·cus′tomed, *adj.*
half′-ac·quaint′ed, *adj.*
half′-ac·qui·es′cent, *adj.;* **-ly,** *adv.*
half′-a′cre, *n.*
half′-ad·dressed′, *adj.*
half′-ad·mir′ing, *adj.;* **-ly,** *adv.*
half′-ad·mit′ted, *adj.;* **-ly,** *adv.*
half′-a·dream′, *adj.*
half′-a·float′, *adj.*
half′-a·fraid′, *adj.*
half′-a·greed′, *adj.*
half′-a·like′, *adj.*
half′-a·live′, *adj.*
half′-al′tered, *adj.*
half′-A·mer′i·can, *adj.*
half′-A·mer′i·can·ized′, *adj.*
half′-An′gli·cized′, *adj.*
half′-an′gri·ly, *adv.*
half′-an′gry, *adj.*
half′-an·noyed′, *adj.*
half′-an·noy′ing, *adj.;* **-ly,** *adv.*
half′-Ar′is·to·te′lian, *adj.*
half′-armed′, *adj.*
half′-a·shamed′, *adj.*
half′-a·sham′ed·ly, *adv.*
half′-A′sian, *adj., n.*
half′-A·si·at′ic, *adj.*
half′-a·sleep′, *adj.*
half′-a·wake′, *adj.*
half′-backed′, *adj.*
half′-bald′, *adj.*
half′-banked′, *adj.*
half′-bar·bar′i·an, *adj.*
half′-bare′, *adj.*
half′-bar′rel, *n.*
half′-beg′ging, *adj.*
half′-be·gun′, *adj.*
half′-be·lieved′, *adj.*
half′-be·liev′ing, *adj.*
half′-bleached′, *adj.*
half′-blind′, *adj.;* **-ly,** *adv.;* **-ness,** *n.*
half′-blown′, *adj.*
half′-blue′, *adj.*
half′-boiled′, *adj.*
half′-boil′ing, *adj.*
half′-bro′ken, *adj.*
half′-bur′ied, *adj.*
half′-burned′, *adj.*
half′-car′ried, *adj.*
half′-cen′tu·ry, *n., pl.* **-ries.**
half′-chant′ed, *adj.*
half′-Chris′tian, *adj.*
half′-civ′il, *adj.;* **-ly,** *adv.*
half′-civ′il·ized′, *adj.*
half′-clad′, *adj.*
half′-cleaned′, *adj.*
half′-clear′, *adj.;* **-ly,** *adv.*
half′-climb′ing, *adj.*
half′-closed′, *adj.*
half′-clos′ing, *adj.*
half′-clothed′, *adj.*
half′-coax′ing, *adj.;* **-ly,** *adv.*
half′-col′ored, *adj.*
half′-com·plet′ed, *adj.*
half′-con·cealed′, *adj.*
half′-con·ceal′ing, *adj.*
half′-Con·fed′er·ate, *adj.*
half′-con·fessed′, *adj.*
half′-con·gealed′, *adj.*
half′-con′quered, *adj.*
half′-con′scious, *adj.;* **-ly,** *adv.;* **-ness,** *n.*
half′-con·serv′a·tive, *adj.;* **-ly,** *adv.*
half′-con·sumed′, *adj.*
half′-con′sum·mat′ed, *adj.*
half′-con·temp′tu·ous, *adj.;* **-ly,** *adv.*
half′-con·tent′ed, *adj.;* **-ly,** *adv.;* **-ness,** *n.*
half′-con·vict′ed, *adj.*
half′-con·vinced′, *adj.*
half′-con·vinc′ing, *adj.;* **-ly,** *adv.*
half′-cooked′, *adj.*
half′-cor′date, *adj.*
half′-cor·rect′ed, *adj.*
half′-cot′ton, *adj.*
half′-count′ed, *adj.*
half′-cov′ered, *adj.*
half′-crazed′, *adj.*
half′-cra′zy, *adj.*
half′-Cre′ole, *adj.*
half′-crit′i·cal, *adj.;* **-ly,** *adv.;* **-ness,** *n.*
half′-crum′bled, *adj.*
half′-crum′bling, *adj.*
half′-cured′, *adj.*
half′-cut′, *adj.*
half′-Da′cron, *adj.*
half′-day′, *n.*
half′-dazed′, *adj.*
half′-dead′, *adj.*
half′-deaf′, *adj.*
half′-deaf′ened, *adj.*
half′-deaf′en·ing, *adj.*
half′-dec′ade, *n.*
half′-de·fi′ant, *adj.;* **-ly,** *adv.*
half′-de′i·fied′, *adj.*
half′-de·ment′ed, *adj.*
half′-dem·o·crat′ic, *adj.*
half′-de·mol′ished, *adj.*
half′-de·nud′ed, *adj.*
half′-dep′re·cat′ing, *adj.;* **-ly,** *adv.*
half′-de·served′, *adj.*
half′-de·serv′ed·ly, *adv.*
half′-de·serv′ed·ness, *n.*
half′-de·stroyed′, *adj.*
half′-de·vel′oped, *adj.*
half′-di·gest′ed, *adj.*
half′-dis·crim′i·nat′ed, *adj.*
half′-dis·crim′i·nat′ing, *adj.;* **-ly,** *adv.*
half′-dis·posed′, *adj.*
half′-di·vine′, *adj.;* **-ly,** *adv.*
half′-done′, *adj.*
half′-door′, *adj., n.*
half′-dram′, *adj., n.*
half′-dressed′, *adj.*
half′-dress′ed·ness, *n.*
half′-dried′, *adj.*
half′-drowned′, *adj.*
half′-drown′ing, *adj.*
half′-drunk′, *adj.*
half′-drunk′en, *adj.*
half′-dug′, *adj.*

esp. for table use. **3.** *Chiefly Brit.* a mixture of two malt liquors, esp. porter and ale. —*adj.* **4.** half one thing and half another. —*adv.* **5.** in two equal parts. [1705–15]

half-assed (haf′ast′, häf′-), *adj. Slang (vulgar).* **1.** insufficient or haphazard; not fully planned or developed. **2.** incompetent; lacking sufficient ability or knowledge. [1960–65; HALF + ASS² + -ED³]

half•back (haf′bak′, häf′-), *n.* **1.** *Football.* **a.** one of two backs who typically line up on each side of the fullback. **b.** the position played by such a back. **2.** (in soccer, Rugby, field hockey, etc.) a player stationed near the forward line to carry out chiefly offensive duties. [1880–85; HALF + BACK¹]

half-baked (haf′bākt′, häf′-), *adj.* **1.** insufficiently cooked. **2.** not completed; insufficiently planned or prepared: *a half-baked proposal for tax reform.* **3.** lacking mature judgment or experience; unrealistic. [1615–25]

half′ bath′, a bathroom containing only a toilet and wash basin; powder room. Also, **half′-bath′.** Also called **half′ bath′room, half′-bath′room′.** [1875–80]

half•beak (haf′bēk′, häf′-), *n.* any of several marine fishes of the family Hemiramphidae, having a greatly elongated lower jaw. [1875–80; HALF + BEAK]

half′ bind′ing, *Bookbinding.* a type of book binding consisting of a leather binding on the spine and, sometimes, the corners, with paper or cloth sides. Also called **half leather.** [1815–25]

half′-blind joint′, *Joinery.* a corner dovetail joint visible on one face only. Also called **lap dovetail joint.**

half′ blood′, the relation between persons having only one common parent. [1545–55]

half-blood (haf′blud′, häf′-), *n.* **1.** a half-breed. **2.** a person who has only one parent in common with another person, as a half sister or half brother. [1400–50; late ME *half blod*]

half-blood•ed (haf′blud′id, häf′-), *adj.* having parents of two different breeds, races, or the like. [1595–1605]

half′ board′, demi-pension (def. 1). [1970–75]

half′ boot′, a boot reaching about halfway to the knee. [1780–90]

half-bound (haf′bound′, häf′-), *adj.* bound in half binding. [1765–75]

half′-breadth′ plan′ (haf′bredth′, -bretth′, -breth′, häf′-), *Naval Archit.* a diagrammatic plan of one half of the hull of a vessel divided lengthwise amidships, showing water lines, stations, diagonals, and bow and buttock lines. Cf. **body plan, sheer plan.**

half-breed (haf′brēd′, häf′-), *Often Disparaging and Offensive.* —*n.* **1.** the offspring of parents of different racial origin, esp. the offspring of an American Indian and a white person of European heritage. —*adj.* **2.** of or pertaining to such offspring. [1750–60, *Amer.*]

half′ broth′er, brother (def. 2). [1300–50; ME]

half′ buck′, *Slang.* a half dollar; the sum of 50 cents. Also, **half-a-buck** (haf′ə buk′, häf′-). [1945–50, *Amer.*]

half-bush•el (haf′bo͝osh′əl, häf′-), *n.* a unit of dry measure equal to 2 pecks (17.6 liters).

half′ ca′dence, *Music.* a cadence ending with dominant harmony.

half-caste (haf′kast′, häf′käst′), *n.* **1.** a person of mixed race. **2.** a person of mixed European and Hindu or European and Muslim parentage. **3.** a person descended from parents of different social strata. —*adj.* **4.** of or pertaining to a half-caste. [1785–95]

half-cell (haf′sel′, häf′-), *n. Elect.* a single electrode, generally a metal, immersed in a container filled with an electrolyte, and having a specific electrical potential for a given combination of electrode and electrolyte. [1935–40]

half′ cent′, a bronze coin of the U.S., equal to one-half cent, issued at various periods between 1793 and 1857. [1780–90, *Amer.*]

half′ cock′, the position of the hammer of a firearm when held halfway between the firing and retracted positions by a mechanism so that it will not operate. [1695–1705]

half-cock (haf′kok′, häf′-), *v.t.* to set the hammer of (a firearm) at half cock. [1825–35]

half-cocked (haf′kokt′, häf′-), *adj.* **1.** (of a firearm) at the position of half cock. **2.** lacking mature consideration or enough preparation; ill-considered or ill-prepared; half-baked. **3. go off half-cocked,** to act or happen prematurely: *He went off half-cocked and told everyone the news.* Also, **go off at half cock.** [1800–10]

half′ crown′, a former silver or cupronickel coin of Great Britain equal to two shillings and sixpence: use phased out after decimalization in 1971. [1535–45]

half-cup (haf′kup′, häf′-), *n.* half of a cup, equal to 4 fluid ounces (0.1 liter) or 8 tablespoons.

half′ deck′, (in a sailing ship) the portion of the deck below the upper or spar deck and aft of the mainmast. [1620–30] —**half′-deck′er,** *n.*

half′ dime′, a silver coin of the U.S., equal to five cents, issued 1794–1805 and 1829–73. [1785–95, *Amer.*]

half′ dol′lar, **1.** a silver or cupronickel coin of the U.S., equal to 50 cents. **2.** a silver or nickel coin of Canada, equal to 50 cents. [1755–65]

half-doz•en (half′duz′ən, häf′-), *n.* **1.** one half of a dozen; six. —*adj.* **2.** considering six as a unit; consisting of six. [1375–1425; late ME]

half′-du′plex (haf′do͞o′pleks, -dyo͞o′-, häf′-), *adj.* of or pertaining to the transmission of information in opposite directions but not simultaneously. Cf. **full-duplex.**

half′ ea′gle, a gold coin of the U.S., discontinued in 1929, equal to five dollars. [1780–90, *Amer.*]

half′ gain′er, *Diving.* a dive in which the diver takes off facing forward and performs a backward half-somersault, entering the water headfirst and facing the springboard.

half-gal•lon (haf′gal′ən, häf′-), *n.* **1.** a half of a gallon, equal to 2 quarts (1.9 liters). —*adj.* **2.** holding or consisting of two quarts.

half-glass•es (haf′glas′iz, häf′glä′siz), *n.* (*used with a plural v.*) a pair of eyeglasses, often shaped like the lower half of regular eyeglasses, containing lenses to aid in reading and not suitable for distance vision.

half-har•dy (haf′här′dē, häf′-), *adj. Hort.* having moderate resistance to cold temperatures. [1815–25]

half•heart•ed (haf′här′tid, häf′-), *adj.* having or showing little enthusiasm: *a halfhearted attempt to work.* [1605–15; HALF + HEART + -ED³] —**half′heart′ed•ly,** *adv.* —**half′heart′ed•ness,** *n.*
—**Syn.** indifferent, uninterested, cold, cool, perfunctory.
—**Ant.** enthusiastic.

half′ hitch′, a knot or hitch made by forming a bight and passing the end of the rope around the standing part and through the bight. See illus. under **knot.** [1760–70]

half-hol•i•day (haf′hol′i dā′, häf′-), *n.* a holiday limited to half a working day or half an academic day. [1545–55]

half′ hose′, short hose; socks. [1850–55]

half-hour (haf′ouᵊr′, -ou′ər, häf′-), *n.* **1.** a period of 30 minutes. **2.** the midpoint between the hours: *The clock struck on the half-hour.* —*adj.* **3.** of, pertaining to, or consisting of a half-hour: *half-hour programs.* [1375–1425; late ME]

half-hour•ly (haf′ouᵊr′lē, -ou′ər-, häf′-), *adj.* **1.** half-hour (def. 3). **2.** occurring every half-hour: *a halfhourly interruption.* —*adv.* **3.** at half-hour intervals: *The bell rang halfhourly.* [1800–10; HALF + HOURLY]

half•ies (haf′ēz, hä′fēz, hav′ēz, hä′vēz), *n.pl. Informal.* halves. [HALF + -IE + -S³]

half-inch (haf′inch′, häf′-), *n.* a half of an inch, equal to 1⁄24 of a foot (1.27 centimeters). [1810–20]

half′-lap joint′ (haf′lap′, häf′-), a joint between two timbers halved together so that a flush surface results.

half′ leath′er, *Bookbinding.* See **half binding.**

half-length (haf′lengkth′, -length′, -lenth′, häf′-), *n.* **1.** something that is only half a full length or height, esp. a portrait that shows only the upper half of the body, including the hands. —*adj.* **2.** of half the complete length or height. [1690–1700]

half-life (haf′līf′, häf′-), *n., pl.* **-lives** (-līvz′). **1.** *Physics.* the time required for one half the atoms of a given amount of a radioactive substance to disintegrate. **2.** *Pharm.* the time required for the activity of a substance taken into the body to lose one half its initial effectiveness. **3.** *Informal.* a brief period during which something flourishes before dying out. Also, **half′ life′, half′-life′.** Also called **half′-life pe′riod.** [1905–10; HALF + LIFE]

half-light (haf′līt′, häf′-), *n.* light that is about half its customary brightness, or that is partially dimmed or obscured: *the half-light of early dawn; a room in half-light.* [1615–25]

half-line (haf′līn′, häf′-), *n. Math.* ray (def. 7b). [1910–15]

half-li•ter (haf′lē′tər, häf′-), *n.* a unit of capacity equal to 500 cubic centimeters. [1920–25]

half-long (haf′lông′, -long′, häf′-), *adj. Phonet.* (of a speech sound) of intermediate length; neither short nor fully long.

half-mast (haf′mast′, häf′mäst′), *n.* **1.** a position approximately halfway between the top of a mast, staff, etc., and its base. —*v.t.* **2.** to place (a flag) at half-mast, as a mark of respect for the dead or as a signal of distress. [1620–30]

half-mile (haf′mīl′, häf′-), *n.* **1.** a half of a mile (0.8 kilometer). **2.** a race of half a mile. —*adj.* **3.** measuring or running half a mile. [1595–1605]

half-mil•er (haf′mī′lər, häf′-), *n. Informal.* **1.** a half-mile race. **2.** a runner who participates or specializes in such a race. [1930–35; HALF-MILE + -ER¹]

half-moon (haf′mo͞on′, häf′-), *n.* **1.** the moon when, at either quadrature, half its disk is illuminated. **2.** the phase of the moon at this time. See diag. under **moon.** **3.** something having the shape of a half-moon or crescent. [1375–1425; late ME]

half•moon (haf′mo͞on′, häf′-), *n.* an edible fish, *Medialuna californiensis,* found in southern California, having a slate-gray body. [1490–1500; HALF + MOON]

Half′ Moon′, the ship in which Henry Hudson made his voyage to explore America in 1609.

half′ mourn′ing, **1.** a mourning garb less somber than deep mourning, usually following a period of deep mourning. **2.** the period during which it is worn. [1810–20]

half′ nel′son, *Wrestling.* a hold in which a wrestler, from behind the opponent, passes one arm under the corresponding arm of the opponent and locks the hand on the back of the opponent's neck. Cf. **nelson.** [1885–90]

half′ note′, *Music.* a note equivalent in time value to one half of a whole note; minim. See illus. under **note.** [1590–1600]

half′ pay′, **1.** half one's regular pay. **2.** a reduced amount paid to a British army or navy officer when not in actual service or after retirement. [1655–65]

half-peck (haf′pek′, häf′-), *n.* a unit of dry measure equal to 4 quarts (4.4 liters). [1745–55]

half•pen•ny (hā′pə nē, hāp′nē), *n., pl.* **half•pen•nies** for 1; **half•pence** (hā′pəns) for 2; *adj.* —*n.* **1.** a bronze coin of the United Kingdom, equal to half a penny: use phased out in 1984. **2.** the sum of half a penny. —*adj.* **3.** of the price or value of a halfpenny. **4.** of little value; worthless: *a halfpenny matter.* **5.** *Brit. Informal.* (of newspapers) sensational, esp. morbidly or offensively so. [1225–75; ME *halfpeny, halpeny.* See HALF, PENNY]

half-pike (haf′pīk′, häf′-), *n.* **1.** spontoon. **2.** a short pike formerly used by sailors boarding enemy vessels. [1590–1600]

half pint (haf′ pīnt′, häf′ *for 1;* haf′ pīnt′, häf′ *for 2, 3*), **1.** half of a pint, equal to 8 fluid ounces (1 cup) or 16 tablespoons (0.2 liter). **2.** *Informal.* a very short person. **3.** *Slang.* a person of little importance or influence. [1605–15]

half-plane (haf′plān′, häf′-), *n. Math.* the part of the plane on one side of a straight line of infinite length in the plane. [1890–95]

half-pound (haf′pound′, häf′-), *n.* a unit of weight equal to 8 ounces avoirdupois (0.227 kilogram) or 6 ounces troy or apothecaries' weight (0.187 kilogram). [1545–55]

CONCISE PRONUNCIATION KEY: *act, cāpe, dâre, pärt; set, ēqual; if, īce; ox, ōver, ôrder, oil, bo͝ok, bo͞ot, out; up, ûrge; child; sing; shoe; thin, that;* zh *as in treasure.* ə = *a* as in *alone, e* as in *system, i* as in *easily, o* as in *gallop, u* as in *circus;* ᵊ as in *fire* (fīᵊr), *hour* (ouᵊr). l and n can serve as syllabic consonants, as in *cradle* (krād′l), and *button* (but′n). See the full key inside the front cover.

half′-dy′ing, *adj.*
half′-earn′est, *adj.;* **-ly,** *adv.;* **-ness,** *n.*
half′-eat′en, *adj.*
half′-ed′u•cat′ed, *adj.*
half′-E•liz′a•be′than, *adj.*
half′-em•braced′, *adj.*
half′-em•brac′ing, *adj.;* **-ly,** *adv.*
half′-en•am′ored, *adj.*
half′-en•forced′, *adj.*
half′-Eng′lish, *adj.*
half′-e•rased′, *adj.*
half′-e•vap′o•rat′ed, *adj.*
half′-e•vap′o•rat′ing, *adj.*
half′-ex•pect′ant, *adj.;* **-ly,** *adv.*
half′-ex•ploit′ed, *adj.*
half′-ex•posed′, *adj.*
half′-false′, *adj.*
half′-fam′ished, *adj.*
half′-far′thing, *n.*
half′-fas′ci•nat′ed, *adj.*
half′-fas′ci•nat′ing, *adj.;* **-ly,** *adv.*
half′-fed′, *adj.*
half′-fem′i•nine, *adj.*
half′-fer′tile, *adj.;* **-ly,** *adv.;* **-ness,** *n.*
half′-fic•ti′tious, *adj.;* **-ly,** *adv.;* **-ness,** *n.*
half′-filled′, *adj.*
half′-fin′ished, *adj.*
half′-flat′tered, *adj.*
half′-flat′ter•ing, *adj.;* **-ly** *adv.*
half′-fold′ed, *adj.*
half′-for•giv′en, *adj.*
half′-for•got′ten, *adj.*
half′-formed′, *adj.*
half′-French′, *adj.*
half′-frown′ing, *adj.;* **-ly,** *adv.*
half′-ful•filled′, *adj.*
half′-ful•fill′ing, *adj.*
half′-full′, *adj.*
half′-fur′nished, *adj.*
half′-Ger′man, *adj.*
half′-gill′, *n.*
half′-great′, *adj.*
half′-Greek′, *adj.*
half′-grown′, *adj.*
half′-hard′, *adj.*
half′-har′vest•ed, *adj.*
half′-healed′, *adj.*
half′-heard′, *adj.*
half′-hea′then, *adj., n.*
half′-Hes′sian, *adj.*
half′-hid′den, *adj.*
half′-hol′low, *adj.*
half′-hu′man, *adj.*
half′-hun′gered, *adj.*
half′-hyp′no•tized′, *adj.*
half′-im•por′tant, *adj.;* **-ly,** *adv.*
half′-in•clined′, *adj.*
half′-in•dig′nant, *adj.;* **-ly,** *adv.*
half′-in•formed′, *adj.*
half′-in•form′ing, *adj.;* **-ly,** *adv.*
half′-in•gen′ious, *adj.;* **-ly,** *adv.;* **-ness,** *n.*
half′-in•gen′u•ous, *adj.;* **-ly,** *adv.;* **-ness,** *n.*
half′-in•her′it•ed, *adj.*
half′-in•sin′u•at′ed, *adj.*
half′-in•sin′u•at′ing, *adj.;* **-ly,** *adv.*
half′-in•stinc′tive, *adj.;* **-ly,** *adv.*
half′-in•tel•lec′tu•al, *adj.;* **-ly,** *adv.*
half′-in•tel′li•gi•ble, *adj.;* **-bly,** *adv.*
half′-in•toned′, *adj.*
half′-in•tox′i•cat′ed, *adj.*
half′-in•val′id, *adj.;* **-ly,** *adv.*
half′-I′rish, *adj.*
half′-I•tal′ian, *adj.*
half′-jelled′, *adj.*
half′-Jew′ish, *adj.*
half′-jok′ing, *adj.;* **-ly,** *adv.*
half′-jus′ti•fied′, *adj.*
half′-lan′guaged, *adj.*
half′-lan′guish•ing, *adj.*
half′-lapped′, *adj.*
half′-Lat′in•ized′, *adj.*
half′-lat′ticed, *adj.*
half′-learned′, *adj.*
half′-learn′ed•ly, *adv.*
half′-left′, *adj., n.*
half′-lib′er•al, *adj.;* **-ly,** *adv.*
half′-lin′en, *adj.*
half′-lived′, *adj.*
half′-lu′na•tic, *adj.*
half′-lunged′, *adj.*
half′-mad′, *adj.;* **-ly,** *adv.;* **-ness,** *n.*
half′-made′, *adj.*
half′-marked′, *adj.*
half′-mas′ti•cat′ed, *adj.*
half′-ma•tured′, *adj.*
half′-meant′, *adj.*
half′-men′tal, *adj.;* **-ly,** *adv.*
half′-mer′it•ed, *adj.*
half′-Mex′i•can, *adj.*
half′-mind′ed, *adj.*
half′-min′ute, *n.*
half′-mi•nute′, *adj.*
half′-mis•un•der•stood′, *adj.*
half′-Mo•ham′med•an, *adj.*
half′-month′ly, *adj.*
half′-Mos′lem, *adj.*
half′-Mu•ham′mad•an, *adj.*
half′-mum′bled, *adj.*
half′-mum′mi•fied′, *adj.*
half′-Mus′lim, *adj.*
half′-na′ked, *adj.*
half′-nor′mal, *adj.;* **-ly,** *adv.*
half′-numb′, *adj.*
half′-ny′lon, *adj.*
half′-ob•lit′er•at′ed, *adj.*
half′-of•fend′ed, *adj.*
half′-o′pened, *adj.*
half′-o•ri•en′tal, *adj.*
half′-or′phan, *n.*
half′-o′val, *adj., n.*
half′-ox′i•dized′, *adj.*
half′-pet′ri•fied′, *adj.*
half′-pipe′, *n.*
half′-play′ful, *adj.;* **-ly,** *adv.;* **-ness,** *n.*

half-quire (haf′kwīər′, häf′-), *n.* 12 uniform sheets of paper.

half′ relief′, mezzo-relievo.

half′ rest′, *Music.* a rest equal in time value to a half note. See illus. under **rest.** [1895–1900]

half′ rhyme′. See **slant rhyme.** [1820–30]

half-rod (haf′rod′, häf′-), *n.* **1.** a unit of length equal to 2¾ yards or 8¼ feet (2.515 meters). **2.** an area equal to 15⅛ square yards (12.65 square meters).

half-round (haf′round′, häf′-), *adj.* **1.** semicircular in cross section, as a molding or piece of type. —*n.* **2.** anything that is semicircular in cross section. **3.** *Print.* a curved stereotype plate. [1655–65]

half′-seas o′ver (haf′sēz′, häf′-), *Slang.* drunk; intoxicated; inebriated. [1545–55]

half-share (haf′shâr′, häf′-), *n.* **1.** a share, as in profits, equal to one half. **2.** a claim to half the income from a share of stock.

half′ shell′, either of the halves of a double-shelled creature, as of an oyster, clam, or other bivalve mollusk. [1855–60, *Amer.*]

half·sies (haf′sēz, häf′-, hav′zēz, häv′-), *n.pl. Informal.* halves. [HALF + -SY + -S³]

half′ sis′ter, sister (def. 2). [1150–1200; ME]

half′ size′, any size in women's garments designated by a fractional number from 12½ through 24½, designed for a short-waisted, full figure.

half-slip (haf′slip′, häf′-), *n.* a woman's skirtlike undergarment, usually of a straight or slightly flared shape and having a narrow elasticized waistband. [1950–55]

half′ snipe′, jacksnipe (def. 1). [1760–70]

half′ sole′, that part of the sole of a boot or shoe that extends from the shank to the end of the toe. [1860–65]

half-sole (haf′sōl′, häf′-), *v.t.,* **-soled, -sol·ing.** to repair or renew (a shoe) by putting on a new half sole. [1785–95]

half′ sov′ereign, a gold coin of the United Kingdom, discontinued in 1917, equal to 10 shillings. [1495–1505]

half-staff (haf′staf′, häf′stäf′), *n., v.t.* half-mast. [1595–1605]

half′ step′, **1.** *Music.* semitone. **2.** *Mil.* a step 15 in. (38 cm) long in quick time and 18 in. (46 cm) long in double time. [1900–05]

half′ sto′ry, *Archit.* a usable living space within a sloping roof, usually having dormer windows for lighting. [1610–20]

half-stuff (haf′stuf′, häf′-), *n.* (in a manufacturing process) any material half formed, esp. partly prepared pulp for making paper. Also, **half-stock** (haf′stok′, häf′-). [1760–70]

half′ tide′, the state or time of the tide when halfway between high water and low water. [1625–35]

half-tim·bered (haf′tim′bərd, häf′-), *adj.* (of a house or building) having the frame and principal supports of timber and the interstices filled in with masonry, plaster, or the like. Also, **half′-tim′ber.** [1840–50]

half·time (haf′tīm′, häf′-), *n.* **1.** the period indicating completion of half the time allowed for an activity, as for a football or basketball game or an examination. **2.** *Sports.* the intermission or rest period between the two halves of a football, basketball, or other game, during which spectators are often entertained by baton twirling, marching bands, or the like. —*adj.* **3.** pertaining to or taking place during a halftime: *The football fans were treated to a halftime exhibition by the marching band.* Also, **half′-time′.** [1870–75; HALF + TIME]

half′ ti′tle, **1.** Also called **bastard title.** the first printed page of certain books, appearing after the end papers and before the title page and containing only the title of the book. **2.** the title of any subdivision of a book when printed on a full page by itself. [1875–80]

half′ tone′, *Music.* semitone. [1645–55]

half·tone (haf′tōn′, häf′-), *n.* **1.** Also called **middle-tone.** (in painting, drawing, graphics, photography, etc.) a value intermediate between light and dark. **2.** *Print.* **a.** a process in which gradation of tone in an image is conveyed by first photographing the image through a screen to break up the continuous tones of the image into minute, closely spaced dots, then using the print obtained to produce a metal plate by photoengraving, and finally using the plate to reproduce the original image by letterpress or offset printing. **b.** the metal plate used in such a process. **c.** the print obtained in such a process. Cf. **line cut.** —*adj.* **3.** pertaining to, using, used in, or produced by the halftone process: *a halftone screen; a halftone print.* [1645–55; HALF + TONE]

half-track (haf′trak′, häf′-), *n.* **1.** a caterpillar tread that runs over and under the rear or driving wheels of a vehicle but is not connected with the forward wheels: used esp. on military vehicles. **2.** a motor vehicle with rear driving wheels on caterpillar treads. **3.** *Mil.* an armored vehicle equipped with half-tracks. Also, **half′-track′.** [1925–30] —**half′-tracked′,** *adj.*

half-track (def. 3)

half-truth (haf′trōōth′, häf′-), *n., pl.* **-truths** (-trōōthz). a statement that is only partly true, esp. one intended to deceive, evade blame, or the like. [1650–60]

half-turn (haf′tûrn′, häf′-), *n.* a 180-degree turn; a direct reversal of direction or orientation, as from front to back or left to right.

half-turn·ing (haf′tûr′ning, häf′-), *n. Furniture.* See **split spindle.**

half′ twist′, **1.** *Diving.* a dive made by a half rotation of the body on its long axis. Cf. **full twist. 2.** the twisting of the body in a half-turn, as in tumbling.

half′ vol′ley, (in tennis, racquets, etc.) a stroke in which the ball is hit the moment it bounces from the ground. [1875–80]

half-vol·ley (haf′vol′ē, häf′-), *v.t., v.i.,* **-leyed, -ley·ing.** to make or stroke with a half volley. [1870–75] —**half′-vol′ley·er,** *n.*

half′-wave plate′ (haf′wāv′, häf′-), *Optics.* a crystal thin enough to cause a phase difference of 180° between the ordinary and extraordinary rays of polarized light, thereby changing the direction of the plane of polarization. Cf. **quarter-wave plate.** [1900–05]

half′-wave rec′tifier, *Electronics.* a rectifier that changes only one half of a cycle of alternating current into a pulsating, direct current. Cf. **full-wave rectifier.** [1925–30] —**half′-wave rectifica′tion.**

half·way (haf′wā′, häf′-), *adv.* **1.** to half the distance; to midpoint: *The rope reaches only halfway.* **2.** almost; nearly; just about: *He halfway surrendered to their demands.* **3. meet halfway,** to compromise with; give in partially to: *They didn't comply with all our demands, but met us halfway on the more important points.* —*adj.* **4.** midway, as between two places or points. **5.** going to or covering only half or part of the full extent: *halfway measures.* [1350–1400; ME *half wei.* See HALF, WAY]

half′way house′, **1.** an inn or stopping place situated approximately midway between two places on a road. **2.** any place considered as midway in a course. **3.** a residence for former mental patients, convicts, or recovering drug users or alcoholics that serves as a transitional environment between confinement and the return to society. [1685–95]

half′ Wel′lington, a loose boot extending to just above the ankle and usually worn under the trousers.

half-wit (haf′wit′, häf′-), *n.* **1.** a person who is feeble-minded. **2.** a person who is foolish or senseless; dunderhead. [1670–80]
—**Syn. 2.** blockhead, dolt, fool, nitwit, dope, dummy, dimwit.

half-wit·ted (haf′wit′id, häf′-), *adj.* **1.** feeble-minded. **2.** foolish; stupid. [1635–45] —**half′-wit′ted·ly,** *adv.* —**half′-wit′ted·ness,** *n.*

hal·i·but (hal′ə bət, hol′-), *n., pl.* (*esp. collectively*) **-but,** (*esp. referring to two or more kinds or species*) **-buts. 1.** either of two large flatfishes, *Hippoglossus hippoglossus,* of the North Atlantic, or *H. stenolepis,* of the North Pacific, used for food. **2.** any of various other similar flatfishes. Also, **holibut.** [1350–1400; ME *halybutte,* equiv. to *haly* (var. of HOLY) + *butte* flat fish (< MD); so called because eaten on holy days. Cf. D *heilbot,* G *Heilbutt*]

Hal·i·car·nas·sus (hal′ə kär nas′əs), *n.* an ancient city of Caria, in SW Asia Minor: site of the Mausoleum, one of the seven wonders of the ancient world. —**Hal′i·car·nas′si·an, Hal′i·car·nas′se·an,** *adj.*

hal·i·cot (hal′ə kō′), *n.* haricot².

hal·ide (hal′īd, -id, hā′līd, -lid), *n.* **1.** a chemical compound in which one of the elements is a halogen. —*adj.* **2.** of, pertaining to, or characteristic of a halide. [1875–80; HAL(OGEN) + -IDE]

hal·i·dom (hal′i dəm), *n.* a holy place, as a church or sanctuary. Also, **hal·i·dome** (hal′i dōm′). [bef. 1000; ME; OE *hāligdōm.* See HOLY, -DOM]

Hal·i·fax (hal′ə faks′), *n.* **1. Earl of** (*Edward Frederick Lindley Wood*), 1881–1959, British statesman. **2.** a seaport in and the capital of Nova Scotia, in SE Canada. 117,882. **3.** a city in West Yorkshire, in N central England. 91,171.

Hal·i·go·ni·an (hal′i gō′nē ən), *adj.* **1.** of or pertaining to Halifax, Nova Scotia, or to Halifax, England. —*n.* **2.** a native or inhabitant of Halifax. [< ML *Haligoni(a)* Halifax + -AN]

hal·ite (hal′īt, hā′līt), *n.* a soft white or colorless mineral, sodium chloride, NaCl, occurring in cubic crystals with perfect cleavage; rock salt. [1865–70; HAL- + -ITE¹]

hal·i·to·sis (hal′i tō′sis), *n.* a condition of having offensive-smelling breath; bad breath. [1870–75; < NL; see HALITUS, -OSIS]

hal·i·tus (hal′i təs), *n., pl.* **-tus·es.** breath; exhalation; vapor. [1655–65; < L, equiv. to *hāl(āre)* to breathe, exhale + *-itus* suffix of v. action (prob. by analogy with *spīritus* SPIRIT)] —**ha·lit·u·os·i·ty** (hə lich′ōō os′i tē), *n.* —**ha·lit·u·ous** (hə lich′ōō əs), *adj.*

hall (hôl), *n.* **1.** a corridor or passageway in a building. **2.** the large entrance room of a house or building; vestibule; lobby. **3.** a large room or building for public gatherings; auditorium: *convention hall; concert hall.* **4.** a large building for residence, instruction, or other purposes, at a college or university. **5.** a college at a university. **6.** (in English colleges) **a.** a large room in which the members and students dine. **b.** dinner in such a room. **7.** *Brit.* a mansion or large residence, esp. one on a large estate. **8.** *Brit. Informal.* See **music hall. 9.** the chief room in a medieval castle or similar structure, used for eating, sleeping, and entertaining. **10.** the castle, house, or similar structure of a medieval chieftain or noble. **11.** *Southeastern U.S.* (*older use*). the living room or family room of a house. [bef. 900; ME; OE *heall;* c. ON *hǫll,* G *Halle;* akin to OE *helan* to cover, hide, L *cēlāre* to hide (see CONCEAL)]

Hall (hôl), *n.* **1. A·saph** (ā′səf), 1829–1907, U.S. astronomer: discovered the satellites of Mars. **2. Charles Francis,** 1821–71, U.S. Arctic explorer. **3. Charles Martin,** 1863–1914, U.S. chemist, metallurgist, and manufacturer. **4. Granville Stanley,** 1846–1924, U.S. psychologist and educator. **5. James Norman,** 1887–1951, U.S. novelist. **6. Prince,** 1748–1807, U.S. clergyman and abolitionist, born in Barbados: fought at Bunker Hill.

hal·lah (KHä′lə, hä′-), *n.* challah.

Hal·lam (hal′əm), *n.* **1. Arthur Henry,** 1811–35, English poet and essayist. **2.** his father, **Henry,** 1777–1859, English historian.

Hal·lan·dale (hal′ən dāl′), *n.* a city in SE Florida. 36,517.

Hal·le (häl′ə), *n.* a city in central Germany, NW of Leipzig. 236,044. Official name, **Hal·le an der Saal·e** (häl′ə än dər zäl′ə).

Hal·leck (hal′ik, -ək), *n.* **1. Fitz-Greene** (fits′grēn′, fits grēn′), 1790–1867, U.S. poet. **2. Henry Wa·ger** (wā′jər), 1815–72, Union general in the U.S. Civil War and writer on military subjects.

Hall′ effect′, *Physics, Elect.* the electromotive force generated in a strip of metal longitudinally conducting an electric current and subjected to a magnetic field normal to its major surface. [1900–05; named after Edwin

CONCISE ETYMOLOGY KEY: <, descended or borrowed from; >, whence; b., blend of, blended; c., cognate with; cf., compare; deriv., derivative; equiv., equivalent; imit., imitative; obl., oblique; r., replacing; s., stem; sp., spelling, spelled; resp., respelling, respelled; trans., translation; ?, origin unknown; *, unattested; ‡, probably earlier than. See the full key inside the front cover.

half′-pleased′, *adj.*
half′-pleas′ing, *adj.*
half′-plucked′, *adj.*
half′-pound′er, *n.*
half′-praised′, *adj.*
half′-prais′ing, *adj.*
half′-pres′ent, *adj.*
half′-pro·fane′, *adj.*
half′-pro·fessed′, *adj.*
half′-pro′file, *n.*
half′-pro·le·tar′i·an, *adj.*
half′-pro·test′ed, *adj.*
half′-pro·test′ing, *adj.*
half′-proved′, *adj.*
half′-prov′en, *adj.*
half′-pro·voc′a·tive, *adj.*
half′-quar′ter, *adj.*
half′-ques′tion·ing, *adj.;* **-ly,** *adv.*
half′-quix·ot′ic, *adj.*
half′-quix·ot′i·cal·ly, *adv.*
half′-rad′i·cal, *adj.;* **-ly,** *adv.*
half′-raw′, *adj.*
half′-ray′on, *adj.*
half′-re·ac′tion·ar′y, *adj.*
half′-read′, *adj.*
half′-rea′son·a·ble, *adj.;* **-bly,** *adv.*
half′-rea′son·ing, *adj.*
half′-re·bel′lious, *adj.;* **-ly,** *adv.;* **-ness,** *n.*
half′-re·claimed′, *adj.*
half′-re·clined′, *adj.*
half′-re·clin′ing, *adj.*
half′-re·fined′, *adj.*
half′-re·gained′, *adj.*
half′-re·luc′tant, *adj.;* **-ly,** *adv.*
half′-re·mon′strant, *adj.*
half′-re·pent′ant, *adj.*
half′-re·pub′li·can, *adj.*
half′-ret′i·nal, *adj.*
half′-re·vealed′, *adj.*
half′-re·versed′, *adj.*
half′-right′, *adj., n.*
half′-ripe′, *adj.*
half′-rip′ened, *adj.*
half′-rise′, *n.*
half′-roast′ed, *adj.*
half′-ro·man′tic, *adj.*
half′-ro·man′ti·cal·ly, *adv.*
half′-rot′ted, *adj.*
half′-rot′ten, *adj.*
half′-rue′ful, *adj.;* **-ly,** *adv.*
half′-ru′ined, *adj.*
half′-Rus′sian, *adj.*
half′-sag′it·tate′, *adj.*
half′-sav′age, *adj.;* **-ly,** *adv.*
half′-Scot′tish, *adj.*
half′-sec′ond, *adj., n.*
half′-sec′tion, *n.*
half′-Se·mit′ic, *adj.*
half′-sensed′, *adj.*
half′-se′ri·ous, *adj.;* **-ly,** *adv.;* **-ness,** *n.*
half′-sev′ered, *adj.*
half′-Shake·spear′e·an, *adj.*
half′-shamed′, *adj.*
half′-shared′, *adj.*
half′-sheathed′, *adj.*
half′-shod′dy, *adj.*
half′-shout′ed, *adj.*
half′-shut′, *adj.*
half′-shy′, *adj.;* **-ly,** *adv.*
half′-sib′ling, *n.*
half′-sight′ed, *adj.;* **-ly,** *adv.;* **-ness,** *n.*
half′-silk′, *adj.*
half′-sink′ing, *adj.*
half′-size′, *adj.*
half′-smil′ing, *adj.;* **-ly,** *adv.*
half′-smoth′ered, *adj.*
half′-sol′id, *adj.*
half′-souled′, *adj.*
half′-Span′ish, *adj.*
half′-spoon′ful, *adj., n.*
half′-spun′, *adj.*
half′-squad′ron, *n.*
half′-starved′, *adj.*
half′-starv′ing, *adj.*
half′-ster′ile, *adj.*
half′-stock′ing, *n.*
half′-sub·dued′, *adj.*
half′-sub·merged′, *adj.*
half′-suc·cess′ful, *adj.;* **-ly,** *adv.;* **-ness,** *n.*
half′-sung′, *adj.*
half′-sunk′, *adj.*
half′-sunk′en, *adj.*
half′-syl′la·bled, *adj.*
half′-taught′, *adj.*
half′-tear′ful, *adj.;* **-ly,** *adv.;* **-ness,** *n.*
half′-tea′spoon·ful, *adj., n.*
half′-tent′ed, *adj.*
half′-term′, *n.*
half′-the·at′ri·cal, *adj.*
half′-thought′, *adj.*
half′-trained′, *adj.*
half′-train′ing, *adj.*
half′-trans′lat·ed, *adj.*
half′-true′, *adj.*
half′-turned′, *adj.*
half′-un·der·stood′, *adj.*
half′-un·done′, *adj.*
half′-used′, *adj.*
half′-u′til·ized′, *adj.*
half′-veiled′, *adj.*
half′-vel′lum, *n.*
half′-ver′i·fied′, *adj.*
half′-vexed′, *adj.*
half′-wak′ing, *adj.*
half′-whis′pered, *adj.*
half′-whis′per·ing·ly, *adv.*
half′-white′, *adj.*
half′-wick′et, *n.*
half′-wild′, *adj.;* **-ly,** *adv.;* **-ness,** *n.*
half′-will′ful, *adj.;* **-ly,** *adv.;* **-ness,** *n.*
half′-winged′, *adj.*
half′-wom′an·ly, *adj.*
half′-won′, *adj.*
half′-wool′en, *adj.*
half′-worst′ed, *adj.*
half′-wo′ven, *adj.*
half′-writ′ten, *adj.*

H. *Hall* (1855–1938), American physicist who discovered it]

Hal·lel (hä lāl′; *Seph. Heb.* hä lel′; *Ashk. Heb.* hä′lāl), *n. Judaism.* a liturgical prayer consisting of all or part of Psalms 113–118, recited on Passover, Shavuoth, Sukkoth, Hanukkah, and Rosh Hodesh. [1695–1705; < Heb *hallēl* praise]

hal·le·lu·jah (hal′ə lo͞o′yə), *interj.* **1.** Praise ye the Lord! —*n.* **2.** an exclamation of "hallelujah!" **3.** a shout of joy, praise, or gratitude. **4.** a musical composition wholly or principally based upon the word "hallelujah." Also, **hal′le·lu′iah.** [1525–35; < Heb *halălūyāh* praise ye Yahweh; cf. ALLELUIA]

Hal·ler (*Ger.* hä′lər), *n.* **Al·brecht von** (*Ger.* äl′brekht fən), 1708–77, Swiss physiologist, botanist, and writer.

Hal·ley (hal′ē), *n.* **Edmund** or **Edmond,** 1656–1742, English astronomer.

Hal′ley's com′et (hal′ēz *or, sometimes,* hā′lēz), a comet with a period averaging 76 years. In this century it was visible to terrestrial observers just before and after reaching perihelion in 1910 and again in 1986. [named after Edmund HALLEY, who first predicted its return]

—**Pronunciation.** The most common current pronunciation for both the comet and the astronomer after whom it is named is (hal′ē). This is the pronunciation usually recommended by astronomers. However, several variant spellings of the name, including *Hailey, Haley,* and *Hawley,* were used interchangeably during the astronomer's own time, a period when spellings even of proper names were not yet fixed, and corresponding pronunciations have survived. The pronunciation (hā′lē) in particular remains associated with HALLEY'S COMET; it is less likely to be heard as a pronunciation of Edmund HALLEY.

hal·liard (hal′yərd), *n.* halyard.

Hal·lie (hal′ē), *n.* a female given name. Also, **Hal′li.**

hal·ling (hä′ling, hal′ing), *n.* a vigorous, athletic, Norwegian folk dance. [1865–70; < Norw, short for *Hallingdal* place known for this dance]

hall·mark (hôl′märk′), *n.* **1.** an official mark or stamp indicating a standard of purity, used in marking gold and silver articles assayed by the Goldsmiths' Company of London; plate mark. **2.** any mark or special indication of genuineness, good quality, etc. **3.** any distinguishing feature or characteristic: *Accuracy is a hallmark of good scholarship.* —*v.t.* **4.** to stamp or imprint (something) with a hallmark. [1715–25; Goldsmiths' *Hall,* London, the seat of the Goldsmiths' Company + MARK[1]] —**hall′mark′er,** *n.*

hal·lo (hə lō′), *interj., n., pl.* **-los,** *v.,* **-loed, -lo·ing.** —*interj.* **1.** (used to call or answer someone, or to incite dogs in hunting.) —*n.* **2.** the cry "hallo!" **3.** a shout of exultation. —*v.i.* **4.** to call with a loud voice; shout; cry, as after hunting dogs. —*v.t.* **5.** to incite or chase (something) with shouts and cries of "hallo!" **6.** to cry "hallo" to (someone). **7.** to shout (something). Also, **halloa, halloo, hallow, hillo, hilloa, hullo, hulloo.** [1560–70; var. of *hollo,* itself var. of earlier *holla* < MF *hola,* equiv. to *ho* ahoy + *la* there]

hal·loa (hə lō′, ha-), *interj., n., pl.* **-loas,** *v.i., v.t.,* **-loaed, -loa·ing.** hallo.

Hall′ of Fame′, 1. a national shrine in New York City commemorating the names of outstanding Americans. **2.** a room, building, etc., set aside to honor outstanding individuals in any profession, locality, nation, or the like. **3.** a number of individuals acclaimed as outstanding in a particular profession, field of endeavor, locality, or the like.

Hall′ of Fam′er, (*sometimes l.c.*) *Informal.* a person who has been accepted into a Hall of Fame. [HALL OF FAME + -ER[1]]

hal·loo (hə lo͞o′), *interj., n., pl.* **-loos,** *v.i., v.t.,* **-looed, -loo·ing.** hallo.

hal·low[1] (hal′ō), *v.t.* **1.** to make holy; sanctify; consecrate. **2.** to honor as holy; consider sacred; venerate: *to hallow a battlefield.* [bef. 900; ME *hal(o)wen,* OE *hālgian* (c. G *heiligen,* ON *helga*), deriv. of *hālig* HOLY] —**hal′low·er,** *n.*

hal·low[2] (hə lō′), *interj., n., v.i., v.t.* hallo.

hal·lowed (hal′ōd; *in liturgical use often* hal′ō id), *adj.* regarded as holy; venerated; sacred: *Hallowed be Thy name; the hallowed saints; our hallowed political institutions.* [bef. 900; ME *halwed;* OE (*ge*)*halgod;* see HALLOW[1] + -ED[2]] —**hal′lowed·ly,** *adv.* —**hal′lowed·ness,** *n.*

—**Syn.** blessed. See **holy.** —**Ant.** desecrated.

Hal·low·een (hal′ə wēn′, -ō ēn′, hol′-), *n.* the evening of October 31; the eve of All Saints' Day; Allhallows Eve: observed esp. by children in costumes who solicit treats, often by threatening minor pranks. Also, **Hal′low·e'en′.** [1550–60; (ALL)HALLOW(S) + E(V)EN[2]]

Hal·low·mas (hal′ō məs, -mas′), *n.* the feast of Allhallows or All Saints' Day, on November 1. [1375–1425; late ME; short for ALLHALLOWMAS]

hal·loy·site (hə loi′sīt, -zīt, ha-), *n.* a refractory clay mineral similar in composition to kaolinite. [1820–30; after Jean-Baptiste-Julien Omalius d'*Halloy* (1783–1875), Belgian geologist; with *-site* for -ITE[1], after mineral names formed from surnames ending in *s*]

Hall′ proc′ess, a process in which aluminum is refined by electrolytic reduction of alumina fused with cryolite. [after Charles Martin HALL]

halls′ of i′vy, an institution of higher learning; university or college; the academic world. [1965–70]

Hall·statt·an (hôl stat′n, häl shtät′n), *adj.* of, pertaining to, or belonging to a variously dated early period of Iron Age culture in Europe, characterized by the use of bronze, the introduction of iron, and by artistic work in pottery, jewelry, etc. Also, **Hall·stat·ti·an** (hôl stat′ē ən, häl shtät′-), **Hall·statt** (hôl′stat, häl′shtät), **Hall·stad′tan, Hall′stadt′.** Cf. **La Tène** (def. 1). [1865–70; *Hallstatt,* village in central Austria where remains were found + -AN]

hall′ tree′, a stand or post having hooks or knobs for holding coats and hats; hatrack or clothes tree. Also called **hat tree.** [1870–75, *Amer.*]

hal·lu·cal (hal′yə kəl), *adj.* of or pertaining to the hallux. [1885–90; < NL *halluc-* (s. of *hallux*) HALLUX + -AL[1]]

hal·lu·ci·nate (hə lo͞o′sə nāt′), *v.,* **-nat·ed, -nat·ing.** —*v.i.* **1.** to have hallucinations. —*v.t.* **2.** to affect with hallucinations. [1595–1605; < L *hallūcinātus,* ptp. of (*h*)*allūcinārī* to wander in mind; see -ATE[1]] —**hal·lu′ci·na′tor,** *n.*

hal·lu·ci·na·tion (hə lo͞o′sə nā′shən), *n.* **1.** a sensory experience of something that does not exist outside the mind, caused by various physical and mental disorders, or by reaction to certain toxic substances, and usually manifested as visual or auditory images. **2.** the sensation caused by a hallucinatory condition or the object or scene visualized. **3.** a false notion, belief, or impression; illusion; delusion. [1640–50; < L *hallūcinātiōn-* (s. of (*h*)*allūcinātiō*) a wandering of the mind. See HALLUCINATE, -ION] —**hal·lu′ci·na′tion·al, hal·lu·ci·na·tive** (hə lo͞o′sə nā′tiv, -nə tiv), *adj.*

—**Syn. 1.** phantasm, aberration. See **illusion.**

hal·lu·ci·na·to·ry (hə lo͞o′sə nə tôr′ē, -tōr′ē), *adj.* pertaining to or characterized by hallucination: *hallucinatory visions.* [1820–30; HALLUCINATE + -ORY[1]]

hal·lu·ci·no·gen (hə lo͞o′sə nə jən), *n.* a substance that produces hallucinations. [1950–55; HALLUCIN(ATION) + -O- + -GEN]

hal·lu·ci·no·gen·ic (hə lo͞o′sə nə jen′ik), *adj.* **1.** producing hallucinations: *a hallucinogenic drug.* **2.** of, pertaining to, or constituting a hallucinogen or hallucinogens. —*n.* **3.** a hallucinogenic substance. [1950–55; HALLUCINO(GEN) + -GENIC]

hal·lu·ci·no·sis (hə lo͞o′sə nō′sis), *n. Psychiatry.* a mental state characterized by repeated hallucinations. [1900–05; HALLUCIN(ATION) + -OSIS]

hal·lux (hal′əks), *n., pl.* **hal·lu·ces** (hal′yə sēz′). *Anat., Zool.* **1.** the first or innermost digit of the foot of humans and other primates or of the hind foot of other mammals; great toe; big toe. **2.** the comparable, usually backward-directed digit in birds. [1825–35; < LL (*h*)*allux,* for L *hallus,* by assoc. with *pollex* thumb]

hall·way (hôl′wā′), *n.* **1.** a corridor, as in a building. **2.** an entrance hall. [1875–80, *Amer.* HALL + WAY]

Hal·ly (hal′ē), *n.* a female given name.

halm (hôm), *n.* haulm.

Hal·ma·he·ra (hal′mə her′ə, häl′-), *n.* an island in NE Indonesia: the largest of the Moluccas. ab. 100,000; 6928 sq. mi. (17,944 sq. km). Also, **Hal′ma·hei′ra.** Also called **Gilolo, Jilolo.**

Halm·stad (hälm′städ′), *n.* a seaport in SW Sweden. 76,042.

ha·lo (hā′lō), *n., pl.* **-los, -loes,** *v.,* **-loed, -lo·ing.** —*n.* **1.** Also called **nimbus.** a geometric shape, usually in the form of a disk, circle, ring, or rayed structure, traditionally representing a radiant light around or above the head of a divine or sacred personage, an ancient or medieval monarch, etc. **2.** an atmosphere or quality of glory, majesty, sanctity, or the like: *the halo around Shakespeare's works; She put a halo around her son.* **3.** *Meteorol.* any of a variety of bright circles or arcs centered on the sun or moon, caused by the refraction or reflection of light by ice crystals suspended in the earth's atmosphere and exhibiting prismatic coloration ranging from red inside to blue outside (distinguished from *corona*). **4.** *Astron.* a spherical cloud of gas clusters and stars that form part of a spiral galaxy. **5.** an undesirable bright or dark ring surrounding an image on the fluorescent screen of a television tube, due to some fault either in transmission or reception. —*v.t.* **6.** to surround with a halo. —*v.i.* **7.** to form a halo. [1555–65; < L, acc. of *halōs* circle round sun or moon < Gk *hálōs* such a circle, disk, orig. threshing floor]

halo-, a combining form meaning "salt," used in the formation of compound words (*halophyte*); sometimes specialized as a combining form of **halogen** (*halothane*). Also, *esp. before a vowel,* **hal-.** [< Gk, comb. form of *háls* salt]

hal·o·bac·te·ri·a (hal′ō bak tēr′ē ə), *n.pl., sing.* **-te·ri·um** (-tēr′ē əm). rod-shaped archaebacteria, as of the genera *Halobacterium* and *Halococcus,* occurring in saline environments as the Dead Sea, salt flats, and brine, and using the pigment bacteriorhodopsin rather than chlorophyll for photosynthesis. Also called **hal·o·bac·ters** (hal′ō bak′tərz). [1975–80; HALO- + BACTERIA; cf. NL *Halobacterium* a genus of such bacteria]

hal·o·bi·ont (hal′ō bī′ont, hā′lō-), *n. Biol.* an organism that thrives in a saline environment. [1925–30; HALO- + *-biont* living (in the environment specified); see SYMBIONT] —**hal′o·bi·on′tic,** *adj.*

ha′lo blight′, a disease of plants, characterized by small, necrotic leaf or fruit lesions surrounded by a yellowish, halolike band, caused by any of several bacteria of the genus *Pseudomonas.* [1915–20]

hal·o·car·bon (hal′ə kär′bən), *n. Chem.* any of a class of compounds containing carbon, one or more halogens, and sometimes hydrogen. [1945–50; HALO- + CARBON]

hal·o·cline (hal′ə klīn′), *n.* a well-defined vertical salinity gradient in ocean or other saline water. [1955–60; HALO- + CLINE]

ha′lo effect′, 1. a predisposition to admire all of a person's actions, work, etc., because of an estimable quality or action in the past. **2.** *Psychol.* a potential inaccuracy in observation, as of a person, due to overgeneralization from a limited amount of evidence or the influence of preconceived beliefs or a priori hypotheses: *The assumption that he is an authority on the subject is a halo effect of his Ivy League manner.* **3.** any desirable side effect. [1925–30]

hal·o·gen (hal′ə jən, -jen′, hā′lə-), *n. Chem.* any of the electronegative elements, fluorine, chlorine, iodine, bromine, and astatine, that form binary salts by direct union with metals. [1835–45; HALO- + -GEN] —**ha·log·e·nous** (ha loj′ə nəs), *adj.*

hal·o·gen·ate (hal′ə jə nāt′, hā′lə-), *v.t.,* **-at·ed, -at·ing.** *Chem.* **1.** to treat or combine with a halogen. **2.** to introduce a halogen into (an organic compound). [1910–15; HALOGEN + -ATE[1]] —**hal′o·gen·a′tion** (hal′ə jenā′shən, hal oj′ə-), *n.*

hal′ogen lamp′, a gas-filled, high-intensity incandescent lamp having a tungsten filament and containing a small amount of a halogen, such as iodine, that vaporizes on heating and redeposits any evaporated tungsten particles back onto the filament: used esp. in motion-picture projectors and automobile headlights.

hal·oid (hal′oid, hā′loid), *Chem.* —*adj.* **1.** Also, **hal·o·gen·oid** (hal′ə jə noid′, hā′lə-). resembling or derived from a halogen. —*n.* **2.** a haloid salt or derivative from a halogen. [1835–45; HAL- + -OID]

ha·lo·like (hā′lō līk′), *adj.* resembling a halo. Also, **ha′lo·esque′.** [1835–45; HALO + -LIKE]

hal·o·per·i·dol (hal′ō per′i dôl′, -dol′), *n. Pharm.* a major antipsychotic agent, $C_{21}H_{23}ClFNO_2$, used in the management of schizophrenia, severe anxiety, and other behavioral disorders. [1955–60; HALO- + (PI)PERID(INE) + -OL[1]]

hal·o·phile (hal′ə fīl′), *n.* any organism, as certain halobacteria and marine bacteria, that requires a salt-rich environment for its growth and survival. [1835–45; HALO- + -PHILE] —**hal·o·phil·ic** (hal′ə fil′ik), **ha·loph·i·lous** (ha lof′ə ləs), *adj.*

hal·o·phyte (hal′ə fīt′), *n.* a plant that thrives in saline soil. [1885–90; HALO- + -PHYTE] —**hal·o·phyt·ic** (hal′ə fit′ik), *adj.*

hal·o·thane (hal′ə thān′), *n. Pharm.* a colorless liquid, $C_2HBrClF_3$, used as an inhalant for general anesthesia. [1955–60; HALO- + *-thane,* as in *fluothane*]

ha·lot·ri·chite (ha lo′trə kīt′), *n.* a mineral, iron alum, isomorphous with pickeringite, occurring in the form of yellowish fibers. [1839; HALO- + TRICHITE]

Hals (häls), *n.* **Frans** (fräns), 1581?–1666, Dutch portrait and genre painter.

Hal·sey (hôl′zē), *n.* **William Frederick** ("*Bull*"), 1882–1959, U.S. admiral.

Häl·sing·borg (hel′sing bôr′yᵊ), *n.* a seaport in SW Sweden, opposite Helsingör. 101,956.

Hal′stead-Rei′tan Neuropsycholog′ical Bat′·tery (hôl′sted rī′tan), a group of tests used in the neuropsychological assessment of cognitive functions, as attention, memory, or the ability to make abstractions. [after U.S. neuropsychologists Ward C. *Halstead* (1908–69) and Ralph M. *Reitan* (born 1922), who developed it]

Hal·sted (hôl′stid, -sted), *n.* **William Stewart** ("*Brill*"), 1852–1922, U.S. surgeon and educator.

halt[1] (hôlt), *v.i.* **1.** to stop; cease moving, operating, etc., either permanently or temporarily: *They halted for lunch and strolled about.* —*v.t.* **2.** to cause to stop temporarily or permanently; bring to a stop: *They halted operations during contract negotiations.* —*n.* **3.** a temporary or permanent stop. —*interj.* **4.** (used as a command to stop and stand motionless, as to marching troops or to a fleeing suspect.) [1615–25; from the phrase *make halt* for G *halt machen.* See HOLD[1]]

—**Syn. 2.** See **stop. 3.** cessation, suspension, standstill, stoppage.

halt[2] (hôlt), *v.i.* **1.** to falter, as in speech, reasoning, etc.; be hesitant; stumble. **2.** to be in doubt; waver between alternatives; vacillate. **3.** *Archaic.* to be lame; walk lamely; limp. —*adj.* **4.** *Archaic.* lame; limping. —*n.* **5.** *Archaic.* lameness; a limp. **6.** (*used with a plural v.*) lame people, esp. severely lamed ones (usually prec. by *the*): *the halt and the blind.* [bef. 900; ME; OE *healt;* c. OHG *halz,* ON *haltr,* Goth *halts,* akin to L *clādēs* damage, loss] —**halt′less,** *adj.*

hal·ter[1] (hôl′tər), *n.* **1.** a rope or strap with a noose or headstall for leading or restraining horses or cattle. **2.** a rope with a noose for hanging criminals; the hangman's noose; gallows. **3.** death by hanging. **4.** Also called **hal′ter top′.** a woman's top, secured behind the neck and across the back, leaving the arms, shoulders, upper-back, and often the midriff bare. —*v.t.* **5.** to put a halter on; restrain as by a halter. **6.** to hang (a person). —*adj.* **7.** (of a garment) having a neckline consisting of a cord, strap, band, or the like that is attached to or forms part of the front of a backless and sleeveless bodice and extends around the neck: *a halter dress.* [bef. 1000; ME; OE *hælfter;* c. G *Halfter*] —**hal′ter·like′,** *adj.*

hal·ter[2] (hal′tər), *n., pl.* **hal·te·res** (hal tēr′ēz). one of a pair of slender, club-shaped appendages on the hindmost body segment of a fly, serving to maintain its balance in flight. Also called **balancer.** [< NL, special use of L *halter* jumping weight < Gk *haltēr,* akin to *hállesthai,* L *salīre* to jump (see SALTANT)]

halt·er[3] (hôl′tər), *n.* a person who halts or brings to a stop. [HALT[1] + -ER[1]]

halt·er[4] (hôl′tər), *n.* a person who halts, falters, or hesitates. [1400–50; late ME; see HALT[2], -ER[1]]

halt·ing (hôl′ting), *adj.* **1.** faltering or hesitating, esp. in speech. **2.** faulty or imperfect. **3.** limping or lame: *a halting gait.* [1375–1425; late ME; see HALT[2], -ING[2]] —**halt′ing·ly,** *adv.* —**halt′ing·ness,** *n.*

Hal·tom Cit′y (hôl′təm), a city in N Texas, near Fort Worth. 29,014.

Hal′ton Hills′ (hôl′tn), a city in SE Ontario, in S Canada, near Toronto. 35,190.

ha·lutz (khä lo͞ots′), *n., pl.* ***ha·lutz·im*** (*Seph.* khä′lo͞o-

CONCISE PRONUNCIATION KEY: act, cāpe, dâre, pärt; set, ēqual; if, īce; ox, ōver, ôrder, oil, bo͝ok, bo͞ot, out; up, ûrge; child; sing; shoe; thin, *th*at; zh as in *treasure.* ə = *a* as in *alone, e* as in *system, i* as in *easily, o* as in *gallop, u* as in *circus;* ᵊ as in *fire* (fīᵊr), *hour* (ouᵊr). l and n can serve as syllabic consonants, as in *cradle* (krād′l), and *button* (but′n). See the full key inside the front cover.

tsēm′; *Ashk.* KHä lo͞o′tsim). *Hebrew.* a person who immigrates to Israel to establish or join a settlement for accomplishing tasks, as clearing the land or planting trees, that are necessary to future development of the country. Also, ***chalutz.*** [ModHeb *ḥalūṣ* lit., pioneer]

hal•vah (häl vä′, häl′vä), *n.* a sweet, candylike confection of Turkish origin, consisting chiefly of ground sesame seeds and honey. Also, **halavah, hal•va′.** [1840–50; < Yiddish *halva* < Rumanian < Turk *helva* < Ar *ḥalwā* sweet confection]

halve (hav, häv), *v.t.,* **halved, halv•ing. 1.** to divide into two equal parts. **2.** to share equally: *to halve one's rations with a stranger.* **3.** to reduce to half. **4.** *Golf.* to play (a hole, round, or match) in the same number of strokes as one's opponent. **5. halve together,** to join (two pieces of wood) by cutting from one, at the place of joining, a portion fitting to that left solid in the other. [1250–1300; ME *halven,* deriv. of HALF]

halv•ers (hav′ərz, hä′vərz), *n.pl. Midland and Southern U.S.* halves: *Let's go halvers on anything we find.* [1500–10; HALF + -ER¹ + -S³, with voicing of *f* by analogy with plural HALVES]

halves (havz, hävz), *n.* **1.** pl. of **half. 2. by halves, a.** incompletely or partially: *to do things by halves.* **b.** halfheartedly: *better not at all than by halves.* **3. go halves,** to share equally; divide evenly.

hal•yard (hal′yərd), *n.* any of various lines or tackles for hoisting a spar, sail, flag, etc., into position for use. Also, **halliard.** [1325–75; ME *halier* rope to haul with (see HALE², -IER¹) with final syllable altered by assoc. with YARD¹]

Hal•y•si•tes (hal′i si′tēz), *n.* an extinct genus comprising the chain corals. [< NL < Gk *hálys(is)* chain + *-itēs* -ITE¹]

ham¹ (ham), *n.* **1.** a cut of meat from the heavy-muscled part of a hog's rear quarter, between hip and hock, usually cured. **2.** that part of a hog's hind leg. **3.** the part of the leg back of the knee. **4.** Often, **hams.** the back of the thigh, or the thigh and the buttock together. [bef. 1000; ME *hamme,* OE *hamm* bend of the knee; c. MD, MLG *hamme,* OHG *hamma;* akin to ON *hǫm* buttock; perh. akin to Gk *knḗmē* shin, OIr *cnáim* bone]

ham² (ham), *n., v.,* **hammed, ham•ming.** —*n.* **1.** an actor or performer who overacts. **2.** an operator of an amateur radio station. —*v.i., v.t.* **3.** to act with exaggerated expression of emotion; overact. **4. ham it up,** to overact; ham. [1880–85; short for *hamfatter,* after *The Hamfat Man,* a black minstrel song celebrating an awkward man]

Ham (ham), *n.* the second son of Noah, Gen. 10:1.

Ha•ma (hä′mä, hä mä′), *n.* a city in W Syria, on the Orontes River. 137,589. Ancient, **Epiphania.** Biblical name, **Hamath.**

Ham•a•dan (ham′ə dan′; *Pers.* ha ma dän′), *n.* a city in W Iran. 124,379. Ancient, **Ecbatana.**

ham•a•dry•ad (ham′ə drī′əd, -ad), *n., pl.* **-ads, -a•des** (-ə dēz′). **1.** *Class. Myth.* a dryad who is the spirit of a particular tree. **2.** See **king cobra.** [< L, s. of *Hamādryas* wood nymph < Gk, equiv. to *hama* together with (c. SAME) + *dryás* DRYAD]

ham•a•dry′as baboon′ (ham′ə drī′əs), a baboon, *Papio (Comopithecus) hamadryas,* of Ethiopia, the male of which has a mantle of long, dark hair about the head and shoulders: held sacred by the ancient Egyptians. Also called **sacred baboon.** [1930–35; < NL *hamadryas* the specific epithet (see HAMADRYAD)]

ha•mal (hə mäl′, -môl′), *n.* (in the Middle East and Orient) a porter. Also, **hammal.** [1960–65; < Ar *ḥammāl* porter, carrier, akin to *ḥamala* to carry]

Ha•ma•mat•su (hä′mä mä′tso͞o), *n.* a city on S central Honshu, in central Japan. 490,827.

ham•a•mel•i•da•ceous (ham′ə mel′i dā′shəs, -mē′-, li-), *adj.* belonging to the Hamamelidaceae, the witch hazel family of plants. Cf. **witch hazel family.** [< NL *Hamamelidace(ae)* (*Hamamelid-,* s. of *Hamamelis* a genus < Gk *hamamēlís* kind of medlar tree; see HAMADRYAD, MELON) + -OUS]

Ha•man (hā′mən), *n.* a powerful prince at the court of Ahasuerus, who was hanged upon exposure of his plan to destroy the Jews of Persia. Esther 3–6.

ha•man•tasch (hä′mən täsh′, hum′ən-, ho͝om′-), *n., pl.* **-tasch•en** (-tä′shən). *Jewish Cookery.* a small triangular cake often made with yeast and filled with a mixture of poppy seeds and honey or with prune paste, prepared esp. for the festival of Purim. [< Yiddish *homentash,* equiv. to *homen* HAMAN + *tash* pouch, pocket (cf. MHG *tasche,* OHG *tasca;* akin to TASK)]

ha•man•tash (hä′mən täsh′, hum′ən-, ho͝om′-), *n., pl.* **-tash•en** (-tä′shən). hamantasch.

ha•mar•ti•a (hä′mär tē′ə), *n.* See **tragic flaw.** [1890–95; < Gk: a fault, equiv. to *hamart-* (base of *hamartánein* to err) + *-ia* -IA]

ha•mate (hā′māt), *adj. Anat.* **1.** hook-shaped. **2.** having a hooklike process. [1735–45; < L *hāmātus* hooked, equiv. to *hām(us)* hook + *-ātus* -ATE¹]

Ham•ble•to•ni•an (ham′bəl tō′nē ən), *n.* **1.** one of a superior strain of American trotting horses descended from the stallion *Hambletonian.* **2.** an annual harness race for three-year-old trotters, formerly held at Goshen, New York, now at DuQuoin, Illinois. [1855–60; *Amer.*]

ham•bo (häm′bo͞o), *n., pl.* **-bos.** a Swedish folk dance in three-quarter time, originating in the 16th century. [1920–25; < Sw, dial. shortening of *Hanebo* parish in Hälsingland, Sweden, after which the dance is named]

*CONCISE ETYMOLOGY KEY: <, descended or borrowed from; >, whence; b., blend of, blended; c., cognate with; cf., compare; deriv., derivative; equiv., equivalent; imit., imitative; obl., oblique; r., replacing; s., stem; sp., spelling, spelled; resp., respelling, respelled; trans., translation; ?, origin unknown; *, unattested; ‡, probably earlier than. See the full key inside the front cover.*

ham•bone (ham′bōn′), *n. Theat.* (esp. in vaudeville) a performer made up in blackface and using a stereotyped black dialect. [1850–55; HAM¹ + BONE; cf. HAM²]

Ham•born (*Ger.* häm′bôrn), *n.* Duisburg.

Ham•burg (ham′bûrg; *for 1, 2 also Ger.* häm′bo͝ork), *n.* **1.** a state in N Germany. 288 sq. mi. (746 sq. km). **2.** a city in and the capital of this state, on the Elbe River: the largest seaport in continental Europe. 1,597,500. **3.** a town in W New York. 10,582.

ham•burg•er (ham′bûr′gər), *n.* **1.** a sandwich consisting of a cooked patty of ground or chopped beef, usually in a roll or bun, variously garnished. **2.** ground or chopped beef. **3.** Also called **Ham′burg steak′.** a patty of ground or chopped beef, seasoned and fried or broiled. Also, **ham•burg** (ham′bûrg). Also called **beefburger.** [1885–90; short for *Hamburger steak;* see -ER¹]

Ham•den (ham′dən), *n.* a town in S Connecticut. 51,071.

hame (hām), *n.* either of two curved pieces lying upon the collar in the harness of an animal, to which the traces are fastened. See illus. under **harness.** [1275–1325; ME < MD]

Ha•meln (hä′məln), *n.* a city in N central Germany, on the Weser River: scene of the legend of the Pied Piper of Hamelin. 55,580. Also, **Ham•e•lin** (ham′ə lin).

hame′ tug′, a loop or short leather strap attaching a trace to a hame. See illus. under **harness.** [1785–95]

ha•metz (*Seph.* KHä mets′; *Ashk.* KHô′mits), *n. Hebrew.* **1.** a food forbidden for use by Jews during the festival of Passover, esp. a baked food, as bread or cake, made with leaven or a leavening agent. **2.** a dish, kitchen utensil, or the like used in preparing or serving such food and similarly forbidden for use during Passover. Also, ***chametz.*** [*ḥāmēṣ* lit., that which is leavened]

ham-hand•ed (ham′han′did), *adj.* clumsy, inept, or heavy-handed: *a ham-handed approach to dealing with people that hurts a lot of feelings.* Also, *esp. Brit.,* **ham-fist•ed** (ham′fis′tid). [1915–20] —**ham′hand′ed•ness;** *esp. Brit.,* **ham′fist′ed•ness,** *n.*

Ham•hung (häm′ho͝ong′), *n.* a city in central North Korea. 150,000.

Ha•mil•car Bar•ca (hə mil′kär bär′kə, ham′əl kär′), c270–228 B.C., Carthaginian general and statesman (father of Hannibal).

Ham•ill (ham′əl), *n.* **Dorothy (Stuart),** born 1956, U.S. figure-skater.

Ham•il•ton (ham′əl tən), *n.* **1. Alexander,** 1757–1804, American statesman and writer on government: the first Secretary of the Treasury 1789–97; mortally wounded by Aaron Burr in a duel. **2. Edith,** 1867–1963, U.S. classical scholar and writer. **3. Lady Emma,** (*Amy,* or *Emily, Lyon*), 1765?–1815, mistress of Viscount Nelson. **4. Sir Ian Standish Mon•teith** (mon′tēth), 1853–1947, British general. **5. Sir William,** 1788–1856, Scottish philosopher. **6. Sir William Rowan** (rō′ən), 1805–65, Irish mathematician and astronomer. **7.** former name of **Churchill River. 8. Mount,** a mountain of the Coast Range in California, near San Jose: site of Lick Observatory. 4209 ft. (1283 m). **9.** a seaport in SE Ontario, in SE Canada, on Lake Ontario. 312,003. **10.** a city on central North Island, in New Zealand. 154,606. **11.** an administrative district in the Strathclyde region, in S Scotland. 107,178; 50 sq. mi. (130 sq. km). **12.** a city in this district, SE of Glasgow. 46,376. **13.** a city in SW Ohio. 63,189. **14.** a seaport in and the capital of Bermuda. 3000. **15.** a male given name.

Ham•il•to•ni•an (ham′əl tō′nē ən), *adj.* **1.** pertaining to or advocating Hamiltonianism. —*n.* **2.** a supporter of Alexander Hamilton or Hamiltonianism. [1790–1800, *Amer.;* HAMILTON + -IAN]

Ham•il•to•ni•an•ism (ham′əl tō′nē ə niz′əm), *n.* the political principles or doctrines held by or associated with Alexander Hamilton, esp. those stressing a strong central government and protective tariffs. Cf. **federalism.** [1900–05; HAMILTONIAN + -ISM]

Ham′ilton In′let, an arm of the Atlantic in SE Labrador, an estuary of the Churchill River. 150 mi. (240 km) long.

Ha•mi•shah A•sar Bi•she•vat (*Seph. Heb.* KHä mi shä′ ä sär′ bi shə vät′, -shvät′; *Ashk. Heb.,* KHä mi shô′ ô sôr′, bi shə vät′, -shvät′, KHä mi′shə ô′sər), *Judaism.* See **Tu Bishevat.** [< Heb *ḥamishshāh ʿāsār bishbhāṭ* fifteenth of (the month) Shevat]

Ham•ite (ham′īt), *n.* **1.** a descendant of Ham. Gen. 10:1, 6–20. **2.** a member of any of various peoples of northern and eastern Africa, as the ancient Egyptians and modern Berbers. [1635–45; HAM + -ITE¹]

Ham•it•ic (ha mit′ik, hə-), *n.* **1.** (esp. formerly) the non-Semitic branches of the Afroasiatic language family. —*adj.* **2.** of or pertaining to the Hamites or Hamitic. [1880–85; HAMITE + -IC]

Ham•it•i•cized (ha mit′ə sīzd′, hə-), *adj.* exhibiting the characteristics of or influenced by speakers of Hamitic. [1910–15; HAMITIC + -IZE + -ED²]

Ham•i•to-Se•mit•ic (ham′i tō sə mit′ik), *adj., n.* Afroasiatic. [1905–10; *Hamito-,* comb. form of HAMITIC]

ham•let¹ (ham′lit), *n.* **1.** a small village. **2.** *Brit.* a village without a church of its own, belonging to the parish of another village or town. [1300–50; ME *hamelet* < MF, equiv. to *hamel* (dim. of *ham* < Gmc; see HOME) + *-et* -ET]
—**Syn. 1.** See **community.**

ham•let² (ham′lit), *n., pl.* (*esp. collectively*) **-let,** (*esp. referring to two or more kinds or species*) **-lets.** any of various sea basses of the family Serranidae, found in the warm waters of the western Atlantic Ocean, esp. the Nassau grouper. [1950–55; orig. obscure]

Ham•let (ham′lit), *n.* **1.** (*italics*) a tragedy (first printed 1603) by Shakespeare. **2.** the hero of this play, a young prince who avenges the murder of his father.

Ham•lin (ham′lin), *n.* **1. Hannibal,** 1809–91, U.S. political leader: vice president of the U.S. 1861–65. **2.** a male given name.

Hamm (häm), *n.* a city in North Rhine-Westphalia, in W Germany. 171,100.

ham•mal (hə mäl′, -môl′), *n.* hamal.

ham•mam (hə mäm′), *n.* (in Islamic countries) a communal bathhouse, usually with separate baths for men and women. [(< Turk *haman*) < Ar *ḥammām*]

Ham•mar•skjöld (hä′mər shōld′, -shəld, ham′ər-; *Sw.* häm′är shœld′), *n.* **Dag Hjal•mar** (däg yäl′mär), 1905–61, Swedish statesman: Secretary General of the United Nations 1953–61; Nobel peace prize 1961.

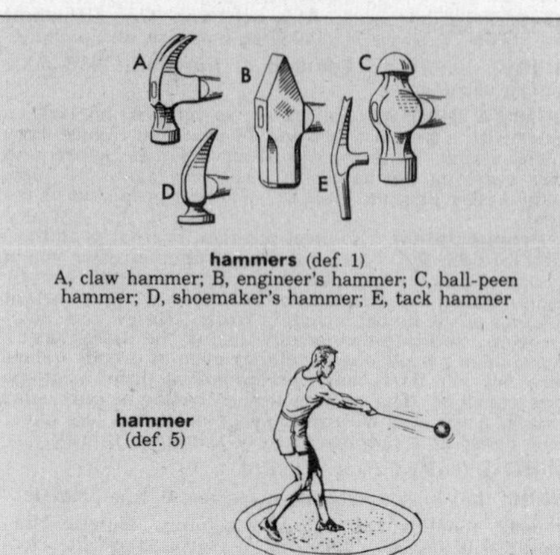

hammers (def. 1)
A, claw hammer; B, engineer's hammer; C, ball-peen hammer; D, shoemaker's hammer; E, tack hammer

hammer
(def. 5)

ham•mer (ham′ər), *n.* **1.** a tool consisting of a solid head, usually of metal, set crosswise on a handle, used for beating metals, driving nails, etc. **2.** any of various instruments or devices resembling this in form, action, or use, as a gavel, a mallet for playing the xylophone, or a lever that strikes the bell in a doorbell. **3.** *Firearms.* the part of a lock that by its fall or action causes the discharge, as by exploding the percussion cap or striking the primer or firing pin; the cock. **4.** one of the padded levers by which the strings of a piano are struck. **5.** *Track.* a metal ball, usually weighing 16 lb. (7.3 kg), attached to a steel wire at the end of which is a grip, for throwing for distance in the hammer throw. **6.** *Anat.* the malleus. **7. under the hammer,** for sale at public auction: *The old estate and all its furnishings went under the hammer.* —*v.t.* **8.** to beat or drive (a nail, peg, etc.) with a hammer. **9.** to fasten by using hammer and nails; nail (often fol. by *down, up,* etc.): *We spent the day hammering up announcements on fences and trees.* **10.** to assemble or build with a hammer and nails (often fol. by *together*): *He hammered together a small crate.* **11.** to shape or ornament (metal or a metal object) by controlled and repeated blows of a hammer; beat out: *to hammer brass; to hammer a brass bowl.* **12.** to form, construct, or make with or as if with a hammer; build by repeated, vigorous, or strenuous effort (often fol. by *out* or *together*): *to hammer out an agreement; to hammer together a plot.* **13.** to produce with or by force (often fol. by *out*): *to hammer out a tune on the piano; to hammer a home run.* **14.** to pound or hit forcefully: *to hammer someone in the jaw.* **15.** to settle (a strong disagreement, argument, etc.); bring to an end, as by strenuous or repeated effort (usually fol. by *out*): *They hammered out their differences over a glass of beer.* **16.** to present (points in an argument, an idea, etc.) forcefully or compellingly; state strongly, aggressively, and effectively (often fol. by *home*). **17.** to impress (something) as if by hammer blows: *You'll have to hammer the rules into his head.* **18.** *Brit.* **a.** (in the London stock exchange) to dismiss (a person) from membership because of default. **b.** to depress the price of (a stock). —*v.i.* **19.** to strike blows with or as if with a hammer. **20.** to make persistent or laborious attempts to finish or perfect something (sometimes fol. by *away*): *He hammered away at his speech for days.* **21.** to reiterate; emphasize by repetition (often fol. by *away*): *The teacher hammered away at the multiplication tables.* [bef. 1000; ME *hamer,* OE *hamor;* c. G *Hammer* hammer, ON *hamarr* hammer, crag; orig. made of stone; prob. akin to Russ *kámen′* stone] —**ham′mer•a•ble,** *adj.* —**ham′•mer•er,** *n.* —**ham′mer•like′,** *adj.*
—**Syn. 13, 14.** knock, bang. **14.** strike. **15.** resolve, solve, thrash, work.

Ham•mer (ham′ər), *n.* **Armand,** 1898–1990, U.S. businessman and art patron.

hammer and sickle

ham′mer and sick′le, 1. the emblem of the Soviet Union, adopted in 1923 and consisting of an insignia of a hammer with its handle across the blade of a sickle and a star above. **2.** any emblem similar to this, as the flag of Communist parties in some countries.

ham′mer and tongs′, with great vigor, determination, or vehemence: *When he starts a job he goes at it hammer and tongs.* [1700–10]
—**Syn.** hard, energetically, fiercely, wholeheartedly.

ham•mer•cloth (ham′ər klôth′, -kloth′), *n., pl.* **-cloths** (-klôthz′, -klothz′, -klôths′, -kloths′). a cloth covering for the driver's seat on a horse-drawn carriage. [1425–75; late ME *hamerclothe,* dissimilated var. of **hamelcloth* home-woven cloth, equiv. to *hamel* domestic (akin to ON *heimili* homestead) + *cloth(e)* CLOTH]

ham·mered (ham′ərd), *adj.* shaped, formed, or ornamented by a metalworker's hammer: *a hammered bowl of brass; hammered gold.* [1515–25; HAMMER + -ED[2]]

Ham·mer·fest (hä′mər fest′), *n.* a seaport in N Norway: the northernmost town in Europe. 7062.

ham·mer·head (ham′ər hed′), *n.* **1.** the part of a hammer designed for striking. **2.** a shark of the genus *Sphyrna,* esp. *S. zygaena,* having the head expanded laterally so as to resemble a double-headed hammer, sometimes dangerous to swimmers. **3.** Also called **ham·mer·kop** (ham′ər kop′). a brown heronlike African bird, *Scopus umbretta,* having the head so crested as to resemble a claw hammer. **4.** See **flatheaded borer. 5.** *Slang.* blockhead; dunce; lout. [1525–35; HAMMER + HEAD] —**ham′mer·head′ed,** *adj.*

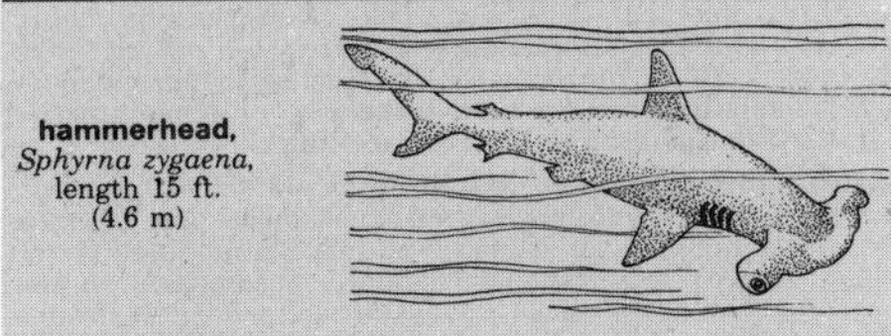
hammerhead, *Sphyrna zygaena,* length 15 ft. (4.6 m)

ham′mering glass′. See **firing glass.**

ham·mer·less (ham′ər lis), *adj.* (of a firearm) having the hammer concealed within the receiver. [1870–75; HAMMER + -LESS]

ham·mer·lock (ham′ər lok′), *n. Wrestling.* a hold in which one arm of an opponent is twisted and forced upward behind his back. Also, **ham′mer lock′.** [1895–1900; HAMMER + LOCK[1]]

ham′mer mill′, *Mining.* a mill for breaking up ore or crushing coal. [1600–10]

ham′mer pond′, an artificial pond for maintaining a head of water at a water mill. [1885–90]

Ham·mer·smith (ham′ər smith′), *n.* a borough of Greater London, England. 172,300.

Ham·mer·stein (ham′ər stīn′), *n.* **1. Oscar,** 1847?–1919, U.S. theatrical manager, born in Germany. **2.** his grandson, **Oscar II,** 1895–1960, U.S. lyricist and librettist.

ham′mer throw′, *Track.* a field event in which the hammer is thrown for distance. —**ham′mer throw′er.**

ham·mer·toe (ham′ər tō′), *n. Pathol.* **1.** a clawlike deformity of a toe, usually the second or third, in which there is a permanent flexion of the second and third joints. **2.** a toe having such a deformity. [1885–90; HAMMER + TOE]

Ham·mett (ham′it), *n.* **(Samuel) Da·shiell** (də shēl′, dash′ēl), 1894–1961, U.S. writer of detective stories.

ham·mock[1] (ham′ək), *n.* a hanging bed or couch made of canvas, netted cord, or the like, with cords attached to supports at each end. [1545–55; < Sp *hamaca* < Taino of Hispaniola] —**ham′mock·like′,** *adj.*

ham·mock[2] (ham′ək), *n.* hummock (def. 1).

Ham·mon (ham′ən), *n.* **Jupiter,** c1720–c1800, American poet.

Ham·mond (ham′ənd), *n.* **1. John Hays** (hāz), 1855–1936, U.S. engineer. **2.** a city in NW Indiana, near Chicago. 93,714. **3.** a city in SE Louisiana. 15,043.

Ham′mond or′gan, *Trademark.* a brand of musical instrument, resembling in shape an upright piano, with two keyboards and electronic tone generation.

Ham·mon·ton (ham′ən tən), *n.* a town in S New Jersey. 12,298.

Ham·mu·ra·bi (hä′mo͝o rä′bē, ham′o͝o-), *n.* 18th century B.C. or earlier, king of Babylonia. Also, **Ham·mu·ra·pi** (hä′mo͝o rä′pē, ham′o͝o-). Cf. **Code of Hammurabi.**

ham·my[1] (ham′ē), *adj.,* **-mi·er, -mi·est.** resembling ham in taste, flavor, appearance, etc. [1860–65; HAM[1] + -Y[1]]

ham·my[2] (ham′ē), *adj.,* **-mi·er, -mi·est. 1.** characteristic of a person who overacts. **2.** overacted. **3.** exaggerated. [1925–30; HAM[2] + -Y[1]] —**ham′mi·ly,** *adv.* —**ham′mi·ness,** *n.*

Hamp·den (hamp′dən, ham′-), *n.* **1. John,** 1594–1643, British statesman who defended the rights of the House of Commons against Charles I. **2. Walter** (*Walter Hampden Dougherty*), 1879–1955, U.S. actor.

ham·per[1] (ham′pər), *v.t.* **1.** to hold back; hinder; impede: *A steady rain hampered the progress of the work.* **2.** to interfere with; curtail: *The dancers' movements were hampered by their elaborate costumes.* —*n.* **3.** *Naut.* gear that, although necessary to the operations of a vessel, is sometimes in the way. [1300–50; ME *hampren;* akin to OE *hamm* enclosure, *hemm* HEM[1]] —**ham′pered·ly,** *adv.* —**ham′pered·ness,** *n.* —**ham′per·er,** *n.*
—**Syn. 1.** obstruct, encumber, trammel, clog. See **prevent.** —**Ant. 1.** further, encourage, facilitate.

ham·per[2] (ham′pər), *n.* **1.** a large basket or wickerwork receptacle, usually with a cover: *picnic hamper; clothes hamper.* **2.** *Brit.* such a basket together with its contents, esp. food. [1350–1400; ME *hampere,* var. of *hanypere* HANAPER]

Hamp·shire (hamp′shēr, -shər), *n.* **1.** Also called **Hants.** a county in S England. 1,449,700; 1460 sq. mi. (3780 sq. km). **2.** Also called **Hamp′shire Down′.** one of an English breed of sheep having a dark face, ears, and legs, noted for the rapid growth of its lambs. **3.** one of an English breed of black hogs having a broad band of white over the shoulders and front legs.

Hamp·stead (hamp′stid, -sted), *n.* a former borough of London, England, now part of Camden.

Hamp·ton (hamp′tən), *n.* **1. Lionel,** born 1913, U.S. jazz vibraphonist. **2. Wade** (wād), 1818–1902, Confederate general: U.S. senator 1879–91. **3.** a city in SE Virginia, on Chesapeake Bay. 122,617. **4.** a town in SE New Hampshire. 10,493.

Hamp′ton Roads′, a channel in SE Virginia between the mouth of the James River and Chesapeake Bay: battle between the *Monitor* and the *Virginia* 1862.

golden hamster, *Mesocricetus auratus,* length 7 in. (18 cm)

ham·ster (ham′stər), *n.* any of several short-tailed, stout-bodied, burrowing rodents, as *Cricetus cricetus,* of Europe and Asia, having large cheek pouches. [1600–10; < G; cf. OHG *hamastro,* OS *hamstra* weevil]

ham·string (ham′string′), *n., v.,* **-strung, -string·ing.** —*n.* **1.** (in humans and other primates) any of the tendons that bound the ham of the knee. **2.** (in quadrupeds) the great tendon at the back of the hock. —*v.t.* **3.** to disable by cutting the hamstring or hamstrings; cripple. **4.** to render powerless or useless; thwart: *Their efforts were hamstrung by stubborn pride.* [1555–65; HAM[1] + STRING]

Ham·sun (häm′so͝on), *n.* **Knut** (kno͞ot), 1859–1952, Norwegian novelist: Nobel prize 1920.

Ham·tramck (ham tram′ik), *n.* a city in SE Michigan, completely surrounded by the city of Detroit. 21,300.

ham·u·lus (ham′yə ləs), *n., pl.* **-li** (-lī′). a small hook or hooklike process, esp. at the end of a bone. [1720–30; < L, equiv. to *hām(us)* hook + *-ulus* -ULE] —**ham′u·lar, ham·u·late** (ham′yə lāt′), **ham·u·lose** (ham′yə-lōs′), **ham′u·lous,** *adj.*

ham·za (häm′zä), *n.* the sign used in Arabic writing to represent the glottal stop, usually written above another letter and shown in English transliterations as an apostrophe. [1935–40; < Ar *ḥamzah* lit., a squeezing together]

Han (hän), *n.* **1.** a dynasty in China, 206 B.C.–A.D. 220, with an interregnum, A.D. 9–25: characterized by consolidation of the centralized imperial state and territorial expansion. Cf. **Earlier Han, Later Han. 2.** a river flowing from central China into the Yangtze at Hankow. 900 mi. (1450 km) long. **3.** the Chinese people in general, esp. those not of Mongol, Manchu, Tibetan, or other non-Chinese extraction.

Han (hän, hun), *n., pl.* **Hans,** (*esp. collectively*) **Han** for **1. 1.** a member of a group of Indians inhabiting the Yukon River drainage basin near the Alaska-Canada border. **2.** the Athabaskan language of the Han. [< Kutchin *han-gʷičin* river dwellers]

Han·a·fi (han′ə fē), *n. Islam.* one of the four schools of Islamic law, founded by Abu Hanifa. Cf. **Hanbali, Maliki, Shafi'i.** [< Ar *Ḥanafī,* deriv. of name of founder *Abū Ḥanīfah*] —**Han′a·fite′,** *n.*

Han·a·han (han′ə han′), *n.* a city in SE South Carolina. 13,224.

han·a·per (han′ə pər), *n.* a wicker receptacle for documents. [1275–1325; ME *hanypere* < AF; MF *hanapier* case to hold a drinking vessel, deriv. of *hanap* goblet (< Gmc **hnapp* bowl; cf. OE *hnæpp,* OHG *hnapf,* ON *hnappr,* early ML *anappus, hanappum*); see -ER[2]]

ha-Na·si (hä nä sē′), *n.* **Judah.** See **Judah ha-Nasi.** Also, **Ha·na·si′.**

Han·ba·li (han′bə lē), *n. Islam.* one of the four schools of Islamic law, founded by Ahmad ibn Hanbal. Cf. **Hanafi, Maliki, Shafi'i.** [< Ar *Ḥanbalī,* deriv. of name of founder *Aḥmad ibn Ḥanbal*] —**Han′ba·lite′,** *n.*

Han′ Cit′ies, Wuhan.

Han·cock (han′kok), *n.* **1. John,** 1737–93, American statesman: first signer of the Declaration of Independence. **2. Winfield Scott,** 1824–86, Union general in the Civil War.

hand (hand), *n.* **1.** the terminal, prehensile part of the upper limb in humans and other primates, consisting of the wrist, metacarpal area, fingers, and thumb. **2.** the corresponding part of the forelimb in any of the higher vertebrates. **3.** a terminal prehensile part, as the chela of a crustacean, or, in falconry, the foot of a falcon. **4.** something resembling a hand in shape or function, as various types of pointers: *the hands of a clock.* **5.** index (def. 8). **6.** a person employed in manual labor or for general duties; worker; laborer: *a factory hand; a ranch hand.* **7.** a person who performs or is capable of performing a specific work, skill, or action: *a real hand at geometry.* **8.** skill; workmanship; characteristic touch: *a painting that shows a master's hand.* **9.** a person, with reference to ability or skill: *He was a poor hand at running a business.* **10.** a member of a ship's crew: *All hands on deck!* **11.** Often, **hands.** possession or power; control, custody, or care: *to have someone's fate in one's hands.* **12.** a position, esp. one of control, used for bargaining, negotiating, etc.: *an action to strengthen one's hand.* **13.** means, agency; instrumentality: *death by his own hand.* **14.** assistance; aid; active participation or cooperation: *Give me a hand with this ladder.* **15.** side; direction: *no traffic on either hand of the road.* **16.** style of handwriting; penmanship: *She wrote in a beautiful hand.* **17.** a person's signature: *to set one's hand to a document.* **18.** a round or outburst of applause for a performer: *to get a hand.* **19.** a promise or pledge, as of marriage: *He asked for her hand in marriage.* **20.** a linear measure equal to 4 inches (10.2 centimeters), used esp. in determining the height of horses. **21.** *Cards.* **a.** the cards dealt to or held by each player at one time. **b.** the person holding the cards. **c.** a single part of a game, in which all the cards dealt at one time are played. **22.** *Roman Law.* manus (def. 2). **23. hands,** *Manège.* skill at manipulating the reins of a horse: *To ride well, one must have good hands.* **24.** a bunch, cluster, or bundle of various leaves, fruit, etc., as a bundle of tobacco leaves tied together or a cluster of bananas. **25.** *Mach.* the deviation of a thread or tooth from the axial direction of a screw or gear, as seen from one end looking away toward the other. **26.** *Building Trades.* **a.** the position of the hinges of a door, in terms of right and left, as seen from outside the building, room, closet, etc., to which the doorway leads. **b.** the position of the hinges of a casement sash, in terms of right and left, from inside the window. **27.** Also called **handle.** the fabric properties that can be sensed by touching the material, as resilience, smoothness, or body: *the smooth hand of satin.* **28.** *Archaic.* a person considered as a source, as of information or of supply. **29. at first hand,** firsthand (def. 1). **30. at hand, a.** within reach; nearby; close by. **b.** near in time; soon. **c.** ready for use: *We keep a supply of canned goods at hand.* **31. at second hand,** See **second hand** (def. 3). **32. at the hand** or **hands of,** by the action of; through the agency of: *They suffered at the hands of their stepfather.* **33. by hand,** by using the hands, as opposed to machines; manually: *lace made by hand.* **34. change hands,** to pass from one owner to another; change possession: *The property has changed hands several times in recent years.* **35. come to hand, a.** to come within one's reach or notice. **b.** to be received; arrive: *The spring stock came to hand last week.* **36. eat out of one's hand,** to be totally submissive to another; be very attentive or servile: *That spoiled brat has her parents eating out of her hand.* **37. force one's hand,** to prompt a person to take immediate action or to reveal his or her intentions: *The criticism forced the governor's hand so that he had to declare his support of the tax bill.* **38. from hand to hand,** from one person to another; through successive ownership or possession: *The legendary jewel went from hand to hand.* **39. from hand to mouth,** improvidently; precariously; with nothing in reserve: *They looked forward to a time when they would no longer have to live from hand to mouth.* **40. give one's hand on** or **upon,** to give one's word; seal a bargain by or as if by shaking hands: *He said the goods would be delivered within a month and gave them his hand on it.* **41. hand and foot, a.** so as to hinder movement: *They tied him hand and foot.* **b.** slavishly and continually: *Cinderella had to wait on her stepsisters hand and foot.* **42. hand and glove,** very intimately associated: *Several high-ranking diplomats were found to be hand and glove with enemy agents.* Also, **hand in glove. 43. hand in hand, a.** with one's hand enclasped in that of another person. **b.** closely associated; concurrently; conjointly: *Doctors and nurses work hand in hand to save lives.* **44. hand over fist,** speedily; increasingly: *He owns a chain of restaurants and makes money hand over fist.* **45. hands down, a.** effortlessly; easily: *He won the championship hands down.* **b.** indisputably; incontestably: *It was hands down the best race I've ever seen.* **46. hands off!** don't touch, strike, or interfere! keep away from!: *Hands off my stereo!* **47. hands up!** hold your hands above your head! give up! **48. hand to hand,** in direct combat; at close quarters: *The troops fought hand to hand.* **49. have a hand in,** to have a share in; participate in: *It is impossible that she could have had a hand in this notorious crime.* **50. have one's hands full,** to have a large or excessive amount of work to handle; be constantly busy: *The personnel department has its hands full trying to process the growing number of applications.* **51. hold hands,** to join hands with another person as a token of affection: *They have been seen holding hands in public.* **52. in hand, a.** under control: *He kept the situation well in hand.* **b.** in one's possession: *cash in hand.* **c.** in the process of consideration or settlement: *regarding the matter in hand.* **53. join hands,** to unite in a common cause; combine: *The democracies must join hands in order to survive.* **54. keep one's hand in,** to continue to practice: *He turned the business over to his sons, but he keeps his hand in it. I just play enough golf to keep my hand in.* **55. lay one's hands on, a.** to obtain; acquire: *I wish I could lay my hands on a good used piano.* **b.** to seize, esp. in order to punish: *He wanted to lay his hands on the person who had backed into his car.* **c.** to impose the hands in a ceremonial fashion, as in ordination: *The bishop laid hands on the candidates.* **56. lend** or **give a hand,** to lend assistance; help out: *Lend a hand and we'll finish the job in no time.* **57. lift a hand,** to exert any effort: *She wouldn't lift a hand to help anyone.* Also, **lift a finger. 58. off one's hands, a.** out of one's charge or care: *Now, with their children grown and off their hands, they will be free to travel.* **b.** successfully completed; finished: *The lawyer planned a vacation as soon as the case was off his hands.* **59. on all hands, a.** by everyone; universally: *It was decided on all hands to take an excursion.* **b.** on every side; all around: *piercing glances on all hands.* Also, **on every hand. 60. on hand, a.** in one's possession; at one's disposal: *cash on hand.* **b.** about to occur; imminent: *A change of government may be on hand.* **c.** present: *There were not enough members on hand to constitute a quorum.* **61. on** or **upon one's hands,** under one's care or management; as one's responsibility: *He was left with a large surplus on his hands.* **62. on the other hand,** from another side or aspect; conversely: *It was an unfortunate experience, but, on the other hand, one can learn from one's mistakes.* **63. out of hand, a.** beyond control: *to let one's temper get out of hand.* **b.** without delay; at once: *The crisis obliged him to act out of hand.* **c.** no longer in process; finished: *The case has been out of hand for some time.* **d.** without consideration or deliber-

ation: *to reject a proposal out of hand.* **64. shake hands,** to clasp another's hand in greeting, congratulation, or agreement: *They shook hands on the proposed partnership.* **65. show one's hand,** to disclose or display one's true intentions or motives: *The impending revolution forced him to show his hand.* **66. sit on one's hands, a.** to be unenthusiastic or unappreciative; fail to applaud: *It was a lively show, but the audience sat on its hands.* **b.** to take no action; be passive or hesitant: *While he was being beaten, the others sat on their hands.* **67. take a hand in,** to take part in; participate in: *If the strike continues, the government will have to take a hand in the negotiations.* **68. take in hand, a.** to undertake responsibility for; assume charge: *When both parents died, an uncle took the youngster in hand.* **b.** to deal with; treat of: *We'll take the matter in hand at the next meeting.* **69. throw up one's hands,** to admit one's inadequacy, exasperation, or failure; despair: *When the general received reports of an enemy build-up, he threw up his hands.* **70. tie one's hands,** to render one powerless to act; thwart: *The provisions of the will tied his hands.* Also, **have one's hands tied. 71. tip one's hand,** to reveal one's plans or intentions before the propitious time. **72. to hand, a.** within reach; accessible or nearby. **b.** into one's possession: *A search of the attic brought some valuable antiques to hand.* **73. try one's hand (at),** to test one's skill or aptitude for: *After becoming a successful painter, he decided to try his hand at sculpture.* **74. turn** or **put one's hand to,** to set to work at; busy oneself with: *He turned his hand successfully to gardening.* **75. wash one's hands of,** to disclaim any further responsibility for; renounce interest in or support of: *I washed my hands of the entire affair.* **76. with a heavy hand, a.** with severity; oppressively: *The law will punish offenders with a heavy hand.* **b.** in a clumsy manner; awkwardly; gracelessly: *The play was directed with a heavy hand.* **77. with a high hand,** in an arrogant or dictatorial manner; arbitrarily: *He ran the organization with a high hand.*
—*v.t.* **78.** to deliver or pass with or as if with the hand. **79.** to help, assist, guide, etc., with the hand: *He handed the elderly woman across the street.* **80.** *Naut.* **a.** to take in or furl (a sail). **b.** to haul on or otherwise handle. **81. hand down, a.** to deliver (the decision of a court): *The jury handed down a verdict of guilty.* **b.** to transmit from one to another, esp. to bequeath to posterity: *The ring had been handed down from her grandmother.* **82. hand in,** to submit; present for acceptance: *She handed in her term paper after the deadline.* **83. hand in one's checks,** *Chiefly Brit.* See **cash** (def. 7). **84. hand it to,** *Informal.* to give just credit to; pay respect to: *You have to hand it to her for getting the work out.* **85. hand off,** *Football.* to hand the ball to a member of one's team in the course of a play. **86. hand on,** to transmit; pass on to a successor, posterity, etc.: *The silver service was handed on to the eldest daughter of the family.* **87. hand out,** to give or distribute; pass out: *People were handing out leaflets on every corner.* **88. hand over, a.** to deliver into the custody of another. **b.** to surrender control of: *He handed over his business to his children.*
—*adj.* **89.** of, belonging to, using, or used by the hand. **90.** made by hand. **91.** carried in or worn on the hand. **92.** operated by hand; manual. [bef. 900; ME, OE; c. D, G *Hand,* ON *hǫnd,* Goth *handus*] —**hand′like′,** *adj.*
—**Syn. 16.** script, calligraphy, longhand.

Hand (hand), *n.* **Lear·ned** (lûr′nid), 1872–1961, U.S. jurist.

hand′ ax′, 1. Also, **hand′ axe′.** a usually large, general-purpose bifacial Paleolithic stone tool, often oval or pear-shaped in form and characteristic of certain Lower Paleolithic industries. **2.** See **broad hatchet.** [bef. 1000; ME, OE]

hand·bag (hand′bag′), *n.* **1.** a bag or box of leather, fabric, plastic, or the like, held in the hand or carried by means of a handle or strap, commonly used by women for holding money, toilet articles, small purchases, etc. **2.** valise. [1860–65; HAND + BAG]

hand·ball (hand′bôl′), *n.* **1.** a game, similar to squash, played by two or four persons who strike a small ball against a wall or walls with the hand. **2.** the small, hard rubber ball used in this game. [1400–50; late ME *handballe.* See HAND, BALL[1]] —**hand′ball′er,** *n.*

hand·bar·row (hand′bar′ō), *n.* **1.** a frame with handles at each end by which it is carried. **2.** a handcart. [1400–50; late ME *handberwe.* See HAND, BARROW[1]]

hand·bas·ket (hand′bas′kit, -bä′skit), *n.* **1.** a small basket with a handle for carrying by hand. **2. go to hell in a handbasket,** to degenerate quickly and decisively: *The economy has gone to hell in a handbasket.* [1485–95; HAND + BASKET]

hand·bill (hand′bil′), *n.* a small printed notice, advertisement, or announcement, usually for distribution by hand. [1745–55; HAND + BILL[1]]

hand·blown (hand′blōn′), *adj.* (of glassware) shaped by means of a hand-held blowpipe: *handblown crystal.* Also, **hand′-blown′.** [1925–30; HAND + BLOWN]

hand·book (hand′bo͝ok′), *n.* **1.** a book of instruction or guidance, as for an occupation; manual: *a handbook of radio.* **2.** a guidebook for travelers: *a handbook of Italy.* **3.** a reference book in a particular field: *a medical handbook.* **4.** a scholarly book on a specific subject, often consisting of separate essays or articles: *a handbook of lectures on criticism.* [trans. of G *Handbuch*]

hand·bound (hand′bound′), *adj.* (of books) bound by hand. [1590–1600; HAND + BOUND[2]]

hand′ brake′, 1. a brake operated by a hand lever. Cf. **caliper** (def. 6). **2.** (in an automobile) an emergency or parking brake operated by a hand lever. [1840–50]

hand·breadth (hand′bredth′, -bretth′), *n.* a unit of linear measure from 2½ to 4 in. (6.4 to 10 cm). Also, **hand's-breadth.** [1525–35; HAND + BREADTH]

hand·car (hand′kär′), *n.* a small railroad car or platform on four wheels propelled by a mechanism worked by hand, used on some railroads for inspecting tracks and transporting workers. [1840–50, *Amer.*; HAND + CAR[1]]

hand-car·ry (hand′kar′ē), *v.t.*, **-ried, -ry·ing.** to carry or deliver by hand, as for security reasons: *The ambassador hand-carried a message from the president.* Also, **hand′car′ry.**

hand·cart (hand′kärt′), *n.* a small cart drawn or pushed by hand. [1630–40; HAND + CART]

hand·clap (hand′klap′), *n.* a clapping of the hands. [1815–25; HAND + CLAP]

hand·clasp (hand′klasp′, -kläsp′), *n.* a gripping of hands by two or more people, as in greeting, parting, making a commitment, or expressing affection. [1575–85; HAND + CLASP]

hand·craft (*n.* hand′kraft′, -kräft′; *v.* hand′kraft′, -kräft′), *n.* **1.** handicraft. —*v.t.* **2.** to make (something) by manual skill. [bef. 1000; ME; OE *handcræft.* See HANDICRAFT]

hand·craft·man (hand′kraft′mən, -kräft′-), *n., pl.* **-men.** handicraftsman. Also, **hand′crafts′man.** [HANDCRAFT + -MAN]

hand·cuff (hand′kuf′), *n.* **1.** a ring-shaped metal device that can be locked around a person's wrist, usually one of a pair connected by a short chain or linked bar; shackle: *The police put handcuffs on the suspect.* —*v.t.* **2.** to put handcuffs on. **3.** to restrain or thwart (someone) by or as if by handcuffing: *The amendments handcuffed the committee and prevented further action.* [1635–45; HAND + CUFF[1]]

H and D curve, *Photog.* See **characteristic curve.** [after Ferdinand *Hurter* (1844–98), Swiss chemist, and Vero Charles *Driffield* (1848–1915), English chemist, who jointly descibed it in 1890]

hand-de·liv·er (hand′di liv′ər), *v.t.* to deliver in person or by messenger.

hand′ drill′, a portable drill designed for two-handed operation. See illus. under **drill[1].** [1760–70]

hand·ed (han′did), *adj.* **1.** having or involving a hand or hands (usually used in combination): *two-handed backhand; a four-handed piano work.* **2.** using a particular hand (usually used in combination): *right-handed.* **3.** having, requiring, or with the number of people, workers, or players indicated (usually used in combination): *a three-handed game of poker.* **4.** manned; staffed (usually used in combination). [1520–30; HAND + -ED[3]]

hand·ed·ness (han′did nis), *n.* a tendency to use one hand more than the other. [1920–25; HANDED + -NESS]

Han·del (han′dl), *n.* **George Fri·de·ric** (frē′dər ik, -drik) (*Georg Friedrich Händel*), 1685–1759, German composer in England after 1712. Also, **Hän·del** (hen′dl). —**Han·del·i·an** (han del′ē ən, -dē′lē, -del′yən, -dēl′yən), *adj.*

hand·fast (hand′fast′, -fäst′), *n.* *Archaic.* a covenant or contract, esp. a betrothal, usually completed by a handclasp. [1150–1200; ME (ptp.), earlier *handfest* < Scand; cf. ON *handfestr,* ptp. of *handfesta* to betroth with a joining of hands, equiv. to *hand* HAND + *festa* to betroth, lit., make fast, FASTEN]

hand-feed (hand′fēd′), *v.t.*, **-fed, -feed·ing. 1.** *Agric.* to feed (animals) with apportioned amounts at regular intervals. Cf. **self-feed. 2.** to feed (an animal or person) by hand: *The students hand-fed the baby monkeys with an eyedropper.* [1795–1805]

hand·free (hand′frē′), *adj.* handsfree.

hand·ful (hand′fo͝ol), *n., pl.* **-fuls. 1.** the quantity or amount that the hand can hold: *a handful of coins.* **2.** a small amount, number, or quantity: *a handful of men.* **3.** *Informal.* a person or thing that is as much as one can manage or control: *The baby's tantrums made him a handful.* [bef. 900; ME, OE. See HAND, -FUL]
—**Usage.** See **-ful.**

hand′ glass′, 1. a small mirror with a handle. **2.** See **hand lens.** [1780–90]

hand′ grenade′, 1. a grenade or explosive shell that is thrown by hand and exploded either by impact or by means of a fuze. **2.** a grenade or glass missile containing a chemical, for extinguishing fire. [1655–65]

hand·grip (hand′grip′), *n.* **1.** the grip or clasp of a hand, as in greeting: *a firm but friendly handgrip.* **2.** a handle or similar part of an object affording a grip by the hand, as for lifting. **3. handgrips,** hand-to-hand combat. [bef. 900; ME; OE *handgripe.* See HAND, GRIP]

hand·gun (hand′gun′), *n.* any firearm that can be held and fired with one hand; a revolver or a pistol. [1400–50; late ME *handgone.* See HAND, GUN[1]]

hand-held (hand′held′), *adj.* **1.** held in the hand or hands: *a hand-held torch.* **2.** small enough to be used or operated while being held in the hand or hands: *a hand-held hair drier.* —*n.* **3.** something small enough to be used or operated while held in the hand or hands: *She traded in her bulky old movie camera for a hand-held.* Also, **hand′held′.** [1920–25]

hand·hold (hand′hōld′), *n.* **1.** a grip with the hand or hands. **2.** something to grip or take hold of, as a support or handle. [1635–45; HAND + HOLD[1]]

hand·hold·ing (hand′hōl′ding), *n.* **1.** the act of holding hands, esp. as a sign or token of affection. **2.** constant reassurance and help, esp. as an indication of one's interest or confidence: *We do a lot of handholding with our clients.* [1905–10; HAND + HOLDING]

hand′ horn′, a forerunner of the modern French horn, developed in Germany during the mid-17th century. See illus. under **horn.**

hand·i·cap (han′dē kap′), *n., v.*, **-capped, -cap·ping.** —*n.* **1.** a race or other contest in which certain disadvantages or advantages of weight, distance, time, etc., are placed upon competitors to equalize their chances of winning. **2.** the disadvantage or advantage itself. **3.** any disadvantage that makes success more difficult: *The main handicap of our business is lack of capital.* **4.** a physical or mental disability making participation in certain of the usual activities of daily living more difficult. —*v.t.* **5.** to place at a disadvantage; disable or burden: *He was handicapped by his injured ankle.* **6.** to subject to a disadvantageous handicap, as a competitor of recognized superiority. **7.** to assign handicaps to (competitors). **8.** *Sports.* **a.** to attempt to predict the winner of (a contest, esp. a horse race), as by comparing past performances of the contestants. **b.** to assign odds for or against (any particular contestant) to win a contest or series of contests: *He handicapped the Yankees at 2-to-1 to take the series from the Cardinals.* [1640–50; 1870–75 for def. 8; orig. *hand i' cap* hand in cap, referring to a drawing before a horse race]
—**Syn. 5.** hinder, impede, cripple, incapacitate.
—**Ant. 5.** aid, assist, help.

hand·i·capped (han′dē kapt′), *adj.* **1.** physically or mentally disabled. **2.** (of a contestant) marked by, being under, or having a handicap: *a handicapped player.* —*n.* **3.** (*used with a plural v.*) handicapped persons collectively (usually prec. by *the*): *increased job opportunities for the handicapped.* [1910–15; HANDICAP + -ED[2]]

hand·i·cap·per (han′dē kap′ər), *n.* **1.** *Horse Racing.* **a.** a racetrack official or employee who assigns the weight a horse must carry in a race. **b.** a person employed, as by a newspaper, to make predictions on the outcomes of horse races. **2.** a person who determines the handicaps that will be placed on competitors. [1745–55; HANDICAP + -ER[1]]

hand·i·craft (han′dē kraft′, -kräft′), *n.* **1.** manual skill. **2.** an art, craft, or trade in which the skilled use of one's hands is required. **3.** the articles made by handicraft: *a shop offering the handicraft of various South American nations.* Also, **handcraft.** [1225–75; ME *hendi craft* dexterous skill. See HANDY, CRAFT] —**hand′i·craft′ship,** *n.*

hand·i·crafts·man (han′dē krafts′mən, -kräfts′-), *n., pl.* **-men.** a person skilled in a handicraft; craftsman. [1545–55; HANDICRAFT + 'S[1] + MAN[1]] —**hand′i·crafts′man·ship′,** *n.*
—**Usage.** See **-man.**

hand·i·ly (han′di lē, -dl ē), *adv.* **1.** skillfully; dexterously; expertly: *to manage a boat handily.* **2.** conveniently: *The books were handily at his side.* **3.** easily: *We won handily.* **4.** *Midland U.S.* rightly; readily: *You can't handily blame him.* [1605–15; HANDY + -LY]

hand·i·ron (and′ī′ərn), *n.* *Dial.* andiron.

hand·i·work (han′dē wûrk′), *n.* **1.** work done by hand. **2.** the characteristic quality of a particular doer or maker: *In all of Mozart's music we discover the handiwork of a genius.* **3.** the result of work done by hand: *woven mats and other handiwork.* [bef. 1000; ME *handiwerk,* OE *handgeweorc,* var. of *handweorc* (c. G *Handwerk*). See HAND, Y-, WORK]

hand′ job′, *Slang (vulgar).* an act of masturbation.

hand·ker·chief (hang′kər chif, -chēf′), *n.* **1.** a small piece of linen, silk, or other fabric, usually square, and used esp. for wiping one's nose, eyes, face, etc., or for decorative purposes. **2.** a neckerchief or kerchief. [1520–30; HAND + KERCHIEF]

hand′kerchief ta′ble. See **corner table.** [1955–60]

hand-knit (hand′nit′), *v.*, **-knit·ted** or **-knit, -knit·ting,** *adj.* —*v.t.* **1.** to knit by hand. —*adj.* **2.** knitted by hand. [1915–20] —**hand′ knit′ter.**

hand-laun·der (hand′lôn′dər, -län′-), *v.t.* hand-wash.

han·dle (han′dl), *n., v.*, **-dled, -dling.** —*n.* **1.** a part of a thing made specifically to be grasped or held by the hand. **2.** that which may be held, seized, grasped, or taken advantage of in effecting a purpose: *The clue was a handle for solving the mystery.* **3.** *Slang.* **a.** a person's name, esp. the given name. **b.** a person's alias, nickname, or code name. **c.** a name or term by which something is known, described, or explained. **4.** the total amount wagered on an event, series of events, or for an entire season or seasons, as at a gambling casino or in horse racing: *The track handle for the day was over a million dollars.* **5.** the total amount of money taken in by a business concern on one transaction, sale, event, or series of transactions, or during a specific period, esp. by a theater, nightclub, sports arena, resort hotel, or the like. **6.** hand (def. 27). **7.** *Informal.* a way of getting ahead or gaining an advantage: *The manufacturer regards the new appliance as its handle on the Christmas market.* **8. fly off the handle,** *Informal.* to become very agitated or angry, esp. without warning or adequate reason: *I can't imagine why he flew off the handle like that.* **9. get** or **have a handle on,** to acquire an understanding or knowledge of: *Can you get a handle on what your new boss expects?* —*v.t.* **10.** to touch, pick up, carry, or feel with the hand or hands; use the hands on; take hold of. **11.** to manage, deal with, or be responsible for: *My wife handles the household accounts. This computer handles all our billing.* **12.** to use or employ, esp. in a particular manner; manipulate: *to handle color expertly in painting.* **13.** to manage, direct, train, or control: *to handle troops.* **14.** to deal with (a subject, theme, argument, etc.): *The poem handled the problem of instinct versus intellect.* **15.** to deal with or treat in a particular way: *to handle a person with tact.* **16.** to deal or trade in: *to handle dry goods.* —*v.i.* **17.** to behave or perform in a particular way when handled, directed, managed, etc.: *The troops handled well. The jet was handling poorly.* [bef. 900; (n.) ME *handel,* OE *hand(e)le,* deriv. of HAND; (v.) ME *handelen,* OE *handlian* (c. G *handlen,* ON *hǫndla* to seize); deriv. of HAND] —**han′dle·a·ble,** *adj.* —**han′dle·a·bil′i·ty,** *n.* —**han′dle·less,** *adj.*
—**Syn. 16.** sell, vend, carry, market; hawk, peddle.

han·dle·bar (han′dl bär′), *n.* **1.** Usually, **handlebars. a.** the curved steering bar of a bicycle, motorcycle, etc., placed in front of the rider and gripped by the hands.

See illus. under **bicycle. b.** See **handlebar moustache. 2.** a bar or rod, usually of metal and having a handle at one end, used for handling, guiding, or maneuvering some object. [1885–90; HANDLE + BAR[1]]

han′dlebar moustache′, a man's moustache having long, curved ends that resemble the handlebars of a bicycle. [1885–90]

han•dled (han′dld), *adj.* fitted with or having a handle or handles, esp. of a specified kind (often used in combination): *a handled pot; a long-handled knife.* [1775–85; HANDLE + -ED[3]]

hand′ lens′, a magnifying glass designed to be held in the hand. Also called **hand glass.** [1925–30]

han•dler (hand′lər), *n.* **1.** a person or thing that handles. **2.** *Boxing.* a person who assists in the training of a fighter or is the fighter's second during a fight. **3.** a person who exhibits a dog in a bench show or field trial. [1350–1400; ME. See HANDLE, -ER[1]]

hand•less (hand′lis), *adj.* **1.** without a hand or hands. **2.** clumsy; awkward: *to be handless at a task.* [1375–1425; late ME *hand(e)les.* See HAND, -LESS]

hand′ let′ter, a brass letter, mounted in a handle, for printing on the cover of a handbound book. [1885–90]

hand-let•ter (hand′let′ər), *v.t.* to print by hand: *She hand-lettered a "for sale" sign.* [1905–10]

hand′ lev′el, *Survey.* a leveling instrument held in the hand and used for approximate work at short distances.

H and L hinge, a surface-mounted hinge that when applied resembles H and L combined. Also, **HL hinge.**

han•dling (hand′ling), *n.* **1.** a touching, grasping, or using with the hands. **2.** the manner of treating or dealing with something; management; treatment. **3.** the manual or mechanical method or process by which something is moved, carried, transported, etc. —*adj.* **4.** of or pertaining to the process of moving, transporting, delivering, working with, etc.: *The factory added a 10 percent handling charge for delivery.* [bef. 1000; ME; OE *handlung* (n.). See HANDLE, -ING[1]]

hand•load (*v.* hand′lōd′; *n.* hand′lōd′), *v.t.* **1.** to load (cartridges or other ammunition) by hand. —*v.i.* **2.** to load ammunition by hand. —*n.* **3.** a cartridge or other ammunition designed to be loaded by hand. [HAND + LOAD] —**hand′load′er,** *n.*

hand′ log′, *Naut.* See **chip log.** [1955–60]

hand•loom (hand′lo͞om′), *n.* a loom operated manually, in contrast to a power loom. [1825–35; HAND + LOOM[1]]

hand•loomed (hand′lo͞omd′), *adj.* handwoven. [HANDLOOM + -ED[3]]

hand•made (hand′mād′), *adj.* made by hand, rather than by machine: *the luxury of handmade shoes.* [1605–15; HAND + MADE]

hand•maid (hand′mād′), *n.* **1.** something that is necessarily subservient or subordinate to another: *Ceremony is but the handmaid of worship.* **2.** a female servant or attendant. Also, **hand′maid′en.** [1350–1400; ME; see HAND, MAID]

hand-me-down (hand′mē doun′, han′-), *n.* **1.** an article of clothing passed on to another person after being used, outgrown, etc.: *The younger children wore the hand-me-downs of the older ones.* **2.** any item not new that is or can be used again: *Our office furniture was a collection of hand-me-downs.* —*adj.* **3.** passed along for further use by others: *some hand-me-down clothes from my older brother.* **4.** borrowed or adapted from other sources; derivative: *a street full of hand-me-down architecture.* [1870–75]

hand′ mow′er, a lawn mower that is pushed by hand (distinguished from *power mower*). [1955–60]

hand-off (hand′ôf′, -of′), *n.* **1.** *Football.* **a.** an offensive play in which a player, usually a back, hands the ball to a teammate. **b.** the ball itself during the execution of such a transfer: *He fumbled the hand-off.* **2.** *Aviation.* the condition or period in which control or surveillance of an aircraft is transferred from one control center to another. Also, **hand′off′.** [1895–1900; n. use of v. phrase *hand off*]

hand′ of writ′, *Scot.* handwriting; penmanship.

hand′ or′gan, a portable barrel organ played by means of a crank turned by hand. [1790–1800, *Amer.*]

hand•out (hand′out′), *n. Informal.* **1.** a portion of food or the like given to a needy person, as a beggar. **2.** See **press release. 3.** any printed, typed, mimeographed, or photocopied copy of information, as a speech, policy statement, or fact sheet given to reporters, attendees at a meeting, or the like. **4.** anything given away for nothing, as a free sample of a product by an advertiser. [1825–35; 1940–45 for def. 2; n. use of v. phrase *hand out*]

hand•o•ver (hand′ō′vər), *n.* the act of relinquishing property, authority, etc.: *a handover of occupied territory.* Also, **hand′-o′ver.** [n. use of v. phrase *hand over*]

hand•pick (hand′pik′), *v.t.* **1.** to pick by hand. **2.** to select personally and with care: *The boss handpicked his assistants.* [1825–35; HAND + PICK[1]]

hand′ press′, a printing press requiring hand operation. [1670–80]

hand′ pup′pet, a puppet made of a hollow head sewn or glued to material that fits over the hand, concealing the fingers and thumb, which manipulate it. [1945–50]

hand•rail (hand′rāl′), *n.* a rail serving as a support or guard at the side of a stairway, platform, etc. [1785–95; HAND + RAIL[1]]

hand-ride (hand′rīd′), *v.,* **-rode, -rid•den, -rid•ing.** —*v.t.* **1.** to ride (a horse) in a race without using a whip or spurs, urging it on with only the hands. —*v.i.* **2.** to hand-ride a horse.

hand•rub (hand′rub′), *v.t.,* **-rubbed, -rub•bing.** to rub by hand, esp. so as to polish: *Handrubbing the wood brings out the natural grain.* [HAND + RUB]

hand-run•ning (hand′run′ing), *adv.* in unbroken succession; consecutively. [1820–30]

hand•saw (hand′sô′), *n.* any common saw with a handle at one end for manual operation with one hand. See illus. under **saw**[1]. [1375–1425; late ME; see HAND, SAW[1]]

hand's-breadth (handz′bredth′, -bretth′, -breth′), *n.* hand-breadth.

hand′ screw′, 1. a screw that can be tightened by the fingers, without the aid of a tool. **2.** Also called **hand′-screw′ clamp′.** *Carpentry.* a clamp having two wooden jaws that are adjusted by two long screws. See illus. under **clamp**[1]. [1755–65]

hand′ scroll′. See under **scroll** (def. 5).

hands-down (handz′doun′), *adj.* **1.** easy: *a hands-down victory.* **2.** certain: *a book destined to be a hands-down bestseller.* [1865–70]

hand•sel (han′səl), *n., v.,* **-seled, -sel•ing** or (*esp. Brit.*) **-selled, -sel•ling.** —*n.* **1.** a gift or token for good luck or as an expression of good wishes, as at the beginning of the new year or when entering upon a new situation or enterprise. **2.** a first installment of payment. **3.** the initial experience of anything; first encounter with or use of something taken as a token of what will follow; foretaste. —*v.t.* **4.** to give a handsel to. **5.** to inaugurate auspiciously. **6.** to use, try, or experience for the first time. Also, **hansel.** [bef. 1050; ME *handselne* good-luck token, good-will gift, OE *handselen* manumission, lit., hand-gift (see HAND, SELL); c. Dan *handsel,* earnest money]

hand•set (*n.* hand′set′; *v., adj.* hand′set′, -set′), *n., v.,* **-set, -set•ting,** *adj.* —*n.* **1.** Also called **French telephone.** a telephone having a mouthpiece and earpiece mounted at opposite ends of a handle. —*v.t.* **2.** to set (type) by hand. —*adj.* **3.** (of type) set by hand. **4.** (of a publication) printed directly from type set by hand. [1915–20; HAND + SET]

hand•sew (hand′sō′), *v.t.,* **-sewed, -sewn** or **-sewed, -sew•ing.** to sew by hand. [1915–20; HAND + SEW]

hand•sewn (hand′sōn′), *adj.* sewn by hand. [1885–90; HAND + SEWN]

hands•free (handz′frē′), *adj.* not requiring the use of the hands: *handsfree telephone dialing by voice commands.* Also, **handfree.** [HAND + -S[3] + FREE]

hand•shake (hand′shāk′), *n.* **1.** a gripping and shaking of right hands by two individuals, as to symbolize greeting, congratulation, agreement, or farewell. **2.** Also, **hand′shak′ing.** *Computers.* an exchange of predetermined signals between a computer and a peripheral device or another computer, made when a connection is initially established or at intervals during data transmission, in order to assure proper synchronization. [1870–75; HAND + SHAKE]

hand•shak•er (hand′shā′kər), *n.* a person who is or is required to be overtly or ostentatiously friendly: *Politicians are often incurable handshakers.* [1900–05; HANDSHAKE + -ER[1]]

hand•shape (hand′shāp′), *n.* (in sign language) the held position of the hand and fingers in producing a particular sign. [HAND + SHAPE]

hands-off (handz′ôf′, -of′), *adj.* **1.** characterized by nonintervention or noninterference: *the new hands-off foreign policy.* **2.** remote or unfriendly; estranging: *a truculent, hands-off manner toward strangers.* [1900–05]

hand•some (han′səm), *adj.,* **-som•er, -som•est. 1.** having an attractive, well-proportioned, and imposing appearance suggestive of health and strength; good-looking: *a handsome man; a handsome woman.* **2.** having pleasing proportions, relationships, or arrangements, as of shapes, forms, or colors; attractive: *a handsome house; a handsome interior.* **3.** exhibiting skill, taste, and refinement; well-made: *a handsome story; handsome furniture.* **4.** considerable, ample, or liberal in amount: *a handsome fortune.* **5.** gracious; generous; flattering: *a handsome compliment; a handsome recommendation.* **6.** adroit and appealing; graceful: *a handsome speech.* [1350–1400; ME *handsom* easy to handle (see HAND, -SOME[1]); c. D *handzaam* tractable] —**hand′some•ish,** *adj.* —**hand′some•ness,** *n.*
—**Syn. 1.** See **beautiful. 4.** large, generous, munificent. —**Ant. 1.** ugly. **4, 5.** small, miserly.

hand•some•ly (han′səm lē), *adv.* in a handsome manner; pleasingly; successfully. [1540–50; HANDSOME + -LY]

hands-on (handz′on′, -ôn′), *adj.* **1.** characterized by or involved in active personal participation in an activity; individual and direct: *a workshop to give children hands-on experience with computers.* **2.** requiring manual operation, control, adjustment, or the like; not automatic or computerized: *The hands-on telephone switchboard is almost obsolete.* [1965–70; by analogy with HANDS-OFF]

hand•spike (hand′spīk′), *n.* a bar used as a lever. [1605–15; < D *handspaak* (see HAND, SPOKE[2]), with *-spaak* replaced by SPIKE[1]]

hand•spring (hand′spring′), *n., v.,* **-sprang, -sprung, -springing.** —*n.* **1.** an acrobatic feat in which one starts from a standing position and wheels the body forward or backward in a complete circle, landing first on the hands and then on the feet, without contact by the rest of the body. —*v.i.* **2.** to perform a handspring. Cf. **somersault.** [1870–75; HAND + SPRING]

hand•stand (hand′stand′), *n., v.,* **-stood, -stand•ing.** —*n.* **1.** an act or instance of supporting the body in a vertical position by balancing on the palms of the hands. —*v.i.* **2.** to perform a handstand. Cf. **headstand.** [1895–1900; HAND + STAND]

hand•stitch (hand′stich′), *v.t.* to stitch or sew by hand. [HAND + STITCH]

hand-tai•lor (hand′tā′lər), *v.t.* **1.** to produce (a garment or the like) by individual workmanship. **2.** to make according to individual requirements.

hand′ tight′, (of a setscrew, nut, etc.) as tight as it can be made by hand, without the aid of a tool. [1785–95]

hand-to-hand (hand′tə hand′), *adj.* close to one's adversary; at close quarters: *hand-to-hand combat.* [1400–50; late ME]

hand-to-mouth (hand′tə mouth′), *adj.* offering or providing the barest livelihood, sustenance, or support; meager; precarious: *a hand-to-mouth existence.* [1500–10]

hand′ tool′, any tool or implement designed for manual operation.

hand-tool (hand′to͞ol′), *v.t.* tool (defs. 8, 9).

hand′ truck′, truck[1] (def. 3). [1915–20]

hand-walk (hand′wôk′), *v.t. Informal.* to carry (a memorandum, check, or other document) from one person or office to another so as to assure prompt delivery.

hand•warm•er (hand′wôr′mər), *n.* a small, flat, usually pocket-size device containing material, as chemicals, hot liquids, or a battery-operated heating element, for warming the hands. [HAND + WARM + -ER[1]]

hand-wash (hand′wosh′, -wôsh′), *v.t.* to launder by hand rather than by washing machine: *to hand-wash socks in a hotel-room sink.* Also, **hand-launder.**

hand•weav•ing (hand′wē′ving), *n.* **1.** the art or technique of weaving on a handloom. **2.** the fabric produced by handweaving. [1835–45; HAND + WEAVING]

hand•wheel (hand′hwēl′, -wēl′), *n.* a wheel, as a valve wheel, turned by hand. [1930–35; HAND + WHEEL]

hand•work (hand′wûrk′), *n.* work done by hand, as distinguished from work done by machine. [bef. 1000; ME; OE *handweorc.* See HAND, WORK; cf. HANDIWORK] —**hand′ work′er.**

hand•wo•ven (hand′wō′vən), *adj.* made on a handloom; handloomed. [1875–80; HAND + WOVEN]

hand•write (hand′rīt′), *v.t.,* **-wrote** or (*Archaic*) **-writ; -writ•ten** or (*Archaic*) **-writ; writ•ing.** to write (something) by hand. [1840–50; back formation from HANDWRITING]

hand•writ•ing (hand′rī′ting), *n.* **1.** writing done with a pen or pencil in the hand; script. **2.** a style or manner of writing by hand, esp. that which characterizes a particular person; penmanship: *an eccentric handwriting.* **3.** a handwritten document; manuscript. **4. handwriting on the wall,** a premonition, portent, or clear indication, esp. of failure or disaster: *The company had ignored the handwriting on the wall and was plunged into bankruptcy.* Also, **writing on the wall.** [1375–1425; late ME *hand writyng;* see HAND + WRITING]

hand•wrought (hand′rôt′), *adj.* formed or shaped by hand, as metal objects. Also, **hand•worked** (hand′wûrkt′). [HAND + WROUGHT]

hand•y (han′dē), *adj.,* **hand•i•er, hand•i•est. 1.** within easy reach; conveniently available; accessible: *The aspirins are handy.* **2.** convenient or useful: *A typewriter is a handy thing to have in the house.* **3.** skillful with the hands; deft; dexterous: *a handy person.* **4.** easily maneuvered: *a handy ship.* [1275–1325; ME (in surnames); see HAND, -Y[1]] —**hand′i•ness,** *n.*
—**Syn. 3.** all-round; versatile. See **dexterous. 4.** manageable, wieldy; yare.

Han•dy (han′dē), *n.* **W(illiam) C(hristopher),** 1873–1958, U.S. blues composer.

hand•y-an•dy (han′dē an′dē), *n., pl.* **-dies.** a handyman. [after hero of *Handy Andy,* novel by Samuel Lover (1797–1868), Irish novelist]

hand•y-dan•dy (han′dē dan′dē), *adj. Informal.* handy (def. 2). [1575–85]

hand•y•man (han′dē man′), *n., pl.* **-men.** a person hired to do various small jobs, esp. in the maintenance of an apartment building, office building, or the like. [1870–75; HANDY + MAN[1]]
—**Usage.** See **-man.**

hand′yman's spe′cial, fixer-upper.

hand•y•per•son (han′dē pûr′sən), *n.* a person who is practiced at doing maintenance work. [HANDY(MAN) + -PERSON]
—**Usage.** See **-person.**

ha•ne•fi•yeh (hä′ne fē′ye), *n.* (in the courtyard of a mosque) a fountain for ritual washing. [< Ar *ḥanafīyah,* after the name of one of the four main schools of Islamic jurisprudence]

Han Fei-tzu (hän′ fā′dzu′), died 233 B.C., Chinese philosopher and legal theorist. Also, *Pinyin,* **Han Fei•zi** (hän′ fā′zœ′).

Han•ford (han′fərd), *n.* **1.** a city in central California. 20,958. **2.** a locality in SE Washington, on the Columbia River: site of an atomic energy plant (**Han′ford Works′**). Cf. **Richland.**

hang (hang), *v.,* **hung** or (*esp. for 4, 5, 20, 24*) **hanged; hang•ing;** *n.* —*v.t.* **1.** to fasten or attach (a thing) so that it is supported only from above or at a point near its own top; suspend. **2.** to attach or suspend so as to allow free movement: *to hang a pendulum.* **3.** to place in position or fasten so as to allow easy or ready movement. **4.** to put to death by suspending by the neck from a gallows, gibbet, yardarm, or the like. **5.** to suspend (oneself) by the neck until dead: *He hanged himself from a beam in the attic.* **6.** to fasten to a cross; crucify. **7.** to furnish or decorate with something suspended: *to hang a room with pictures.* **8.** to fasten into position; fix at a proper angle: *to hang a scythe.* **9.** to fasten or attach (wallpaper, pictures, etc.) to a wall: *to hang pictures in a room.* **10.** to suspend (something) in front of anything: *to hang curtains on a window.* **11.** *Fine Arts.* **a.** to exhibit (a painting or group of paintings): *The gallery hung his paintings in a small corner.* **b.** to put the paintings of (an art exhibition) on the wall of a gallery: *They hung the show that morning.* **12.** to attach or annex as an addition: *to hang a rider on a bill.* **13.** to attach (a door or the like) to its frame by means of hinges. **14.** to make (an idea, form, etc.) dependent on a situation, structure, concept, or the like, usually derived from another source: *He hung the meaning of his puns on the current political scene.* **15.** (of a juror) to keep (a jury) from rendering a verdict by refusing to agree with the others. **16.** *Informal.* to cause (a nickname, epithet, etc.) to become associated with a person: *Friends hung that nickname on him.* **17.** *Slang.* to hit with (a fist, blow, punch, etc.): *He hung a left on his opponent's jaw.* **18.** *Baseball.* to throw (a pitch) so that it fails to break, as a curve. **19.** *Naut.* to steady (a boat) in one place against a wind or current by thrusting a pole or the like into the bottom under the boat and allowing the wind or current to push the boat side-on against the pole. **20.** (used in mild curses and emphatic expressions, often as a euphemism for *damn*): *I'll be hanged if I do. Hang it all!* —*v.i.* **21.** to be suspended; dangle. **22.** to swing freely, as on a hinge. **23.** to incline downward, jut out, or lean over or forward: *The tree hung over the edge of the lake.* **24.** to be suspended by the neck, as from a gallows, and suffer death in this way. **25.** to be crucified. **26.** to be conditioned or contingent; be dependent: *His future hangs on the outcome of their discussion.* **27.** to be doubtful or undecided; waver or hesitate: *He hung between staying and going.* **28.** to remain unfinished or undecided; be delayed: *Let that matter hang until our next meeting.* **29.** to linger, remain, or persist: *He hung by her side, unwilling to leave.* **30.** to float or hover in the air: *Fog hung over the city.* **31.** to be oppressive, burdensome, or tedious: *guilt that hangs on one's conscience.* **32.** to remain in attention or consideration (often fol. by *on* or *upon*): *They hung on his every word.* **33.** to fit or drape in graceful lines: *That coat hangs well in back.* **34.** *Fine Arts.* **a.** to be exhibited: *His works hang in most major museums.* **b.** to have one's works on display: *Rembrandt hangs in the Metropolitan Museum of Art.* **35. hang a left** (or **right**), *Slang.* to make a left (or right) turn, as while driving an automobile: *Hang a right at the next corner.* **36. hang around** or **about,** *Informal.* **a.** to spend time in a certain place or in certain company: *He hangs around with an older crowd.* **b.** to linger about; loiter: *They had stopped working and were just hanging around to talk.* **37. hang back, a.** to be reluctant to proceed or move forward: *The older pupils went straight to the podium, but the younger ones hung back out of shyness.* **b.** to refrain from taking action; hesitate: *A forward pass would have been the best call, but the quarterback hung back because his last pass had been intercepted.* **38. hang five,** to ride a surfboard with the weight of the body forward and the toes of the forward foot curled over the front edge of the surfboard. **39. hang in,** *Slang.* to persevere: *She has managed to hang in despite years of bad luck.* Also, **hang in there. 40. hang in the balance,** to be in a precarious state or condition: *The wounded man's life hung in the balance.* **41. hang it up,** *Informal.* to quit, resign, give up, etc.: *The chief engineer is hanging it up after 40 years with the company.* **42. hang loose,** *Slang.* to remain relaxed or calm: *Try to hang loose and don't let it bother you.* **43. hang on, a.** to hold fast; cling to. **b.** to continue with effort; persevere: *If you can hang on for a month longer, you will be eligible for the bonus.* **c.** to be sustained to the point of danger, tedium, etc.: *coughs that hang on for months.* **d.** to keep a telephone line open: *Hang on, I'll see if she's here.* **e.** to wait briefly; keep calm. **44. hang one on,** *Slang.* **a.** to hit: *He hung one on the bully and knocked him down.* **b.** to become extremely drunk: *Every payday he hangs one on.* **45. hang one's head.** See **head** (def. 44). **46. hang out, a.** to lean or be suspended through an opening. **b.** *Informal.* to frequent a particular place, esp. in idling away one's free time: *to hang out in a bar.* **c.** *Informal.* to loiter in public places: *nothing to do on Saturday night but hang out.* **d.** *Informal.* to consort or appear in public with: *Who's she been hanging out with?* **e.** *Slang.* to calm down: *Hang out, Mom, I'm OK.* **f.** to wait, esp. briefly: *Hang out a minute while I get my backpack.* **g.** to suspend in open view; display: *to hang out the flag.* **47. hang over, a.** to remain to be settled; be postponed: *They will probably let the final decision hang over until next year.* **b.** to be imminent or foreboding; threaten: *Economic ruin hangs over the town.* **48. hang ten,** to ride a surfboard with the weight of the body as far forward as possible and the toes of both feet curled over the front edge of the surfboard. **49. hang together, a.** to be loyal to one another; remain united: *"We must indeed all hang together, or, most assuredly, we shall all hang separately."* **b.** to cohere: *This pancake batter doesn't hang together.* **c.** to be logical or consistent: *His version of the story does not hang together.* **50. hang tough,** *Slang.* to remain unyielding, stubborn, or inflexible: *He's hanging tough and won't change his mind.* **51. hang up, a.** to suspend by placing on a hook, peg, or hanger. **b.** to cause or encounter delay; suspend or slow the progress of: *The accident hung up the traffic for several hours.* **c.** to break a telephone connection by replacing the receiver on the hook: *She received an anonymous call, but the party hung up when she threatened to call the police.* **d.** to cause a hang-up or hang-ups in: *The experience hung her up for years.* **52. let it all hang out,** *Slang.* **a.** to be completely candid in expressing one's feelings, opinions, etc.: *She's never been one to let it all hang out.* **b.** to act or live without restraint or inhibitions.

CONCISE ETYMOLOGY KEY: <, descended or borrowed from; >, whence; b., blend of, blended; c., cognate with; cf., compare; deriv., derivative; equiv., equivalent; imit., imitative; obl., oblique; r., replacing; s., stem; sp., spelling, spelled; resp., respelling, respelled; trans., translation; ?, origin unknown; *, unattested; ‡, probably earlier than. See the full key inside the front cover.

—*n.* **53.** the way in which a thing hangs. **54.** *Informal.* the precise manner of doing, using, etc., something; knack: *to get the hang of a tool.* **55.** *Informal.* meaning or thought: *to get the hang of a subject.* **56.** *Naut.* **a.** loss of way due to adverse wind or current. **b.** a rake, as of a mast. **57.** the least degree of care, concern, etc. (used in mild curses and emphatic expressions as a euphemism for *damn*): *He doesn't give a hang about those things.* [bef. 900; fusion of 3 verbs: (1) ME, OE *hōn* to hang (transit.), c. Goth *hāhan,* orig. **haghan;* (2) ME *hang(i)en,* OE *hangian* to hang (intrans.), c. G *hangen;* (3) ME *henge* < ON *hengja* (transit.), c. G *hängen* to hang] —**hang′a·ble,** *adj.* —**hang′a·bil′i·ty,** *n.*

—**Syn. 4.** HANG, LYNCH have in common the meaning of "to put to death," but lynching is not always by hanging. HANG, in the sense of execute, is in accordance with a legal sentence, the method of execution being to suspend by the neck until dead. To LYNCH, however, implies the summary putting to death, by any method, of someone charged with a flagrant offense (though guilt may not have been proved). Lynching is done by private persons, usually a mob, without legal authority. **26.** depend, rely, rest, hinge.

—**Usage.** HANG has two forms for the past tense and past participle, HANGED and HUNG. The historically older form HANGED is now used exclusively in the sense of causing or putting to death: *He was sentenced to be hanged by the neck until dead.* In the sense of legal execution, HUNG is also quite common and is standard in all types of speech and writing except in legal documents. When legal execution is not meant, HUNG has become the more frequent form: *The prisoner hung himself in his cell.*

hang·ar (hang′ər), *n.* **1.** a shed or shelter. **2.** any relatively wide structure used for housing airplanes or airships. —*v.t., v.i.* **3.** to keep (an aircraft) in a hangar: *She spent a fortune hangaring her plane.* [1850–55; < F: shed, hangar, MF, prob. < Old Low Franconian **haimgard* fence around a group of buildings, equiv. to *haim* small village (see HAMLET) + *gard* YARD[2]]

hang·bird (hang′bûrd′), *n. Older Use.* a bird that builds a hanging nest, esp. the Baltimore oriole. [1785–95, *Amer.*; HANG + BIRD]

Hang·chow (hang′chou′; *Chin.* häng′jō′), *n. Older Spelling.* Hangzhou.

Hang′chow Bay′. See **Hangzhou Bay.**

hang·dog (hang′dôg′, -dog′), *adj.* **1.** browbeaten; defeated; intimidated; abject: *He always went about with a hangdog look.* **2.** shamefaced; guilty: *He sneaked out of the room with a hangdog expression.* **3.** suitable to a degraded or contemptible person; sneaky; furtive. —*n.* **4.** *Archaic.* a degraded, contemptible person. [1670–80; HANG + DOG]

—**Syn. 2.** ashamed, contrite, crestfallen. —**Ant. 1.** confident, assured.

hang·er (hang′ər), *n.* **1.** a shoulder-shaped frame with a hook at the top, usually of wire, wood, or plastic, for draping and hanging a garment when not in use. **2.** a part of something by which it is hung, as a loop on a garment. **3.** a contrivance on which things are hung, as a hook. **4.** *Auto.* a double-hinged device linking the chassis with the leaf springs on vehicles having solid axles. **5.** a light saber of the 17th and 18th centuries, often worn by sailors. **6.** a person who hangs something. [1400–50; late ME *hangere;* see HANG, -ER[1]]

hang·er-on (hang′ər on′, -ôn′), *n., pl.* **hang·ers-on.** a person who remains in a place or attaches himself or herself to a group, another person, etc., although not wanted, esp. in the hope or expectation of personal gain. [1540–50; n. use of v. phrase *hang on;* see -ER[1]]

—**Syn.** toady, parasite, sycophant, follower.

hang·fire (hang′fīᵊr′), *n.* a delay in the detonation of gunpowder or other ammunition, caused by some defect in the fuze. [1890–95; HANG + FIRE]

hang′ glid′er, a kitelike glider consisting of a V-shaped wing underneath which the pilot is strapped: kept aloft by updrafts and guided by the pilot's shifting body weight. [1925–30]

hang glider

hang′ glid′ing, the sport of launching oneself from a cliff or a steep incline and soaring through the air by means of a hang glider. [1970–75]

hang·ing (hang′ing), *n.* **1.** the act, an instance, or the form of capital punishment carried out by suspending one by the neck from a gallows, gibbet, or the like, until dead. **2.** Often, **hangings.** something that hangs or is hung on the walls of a room, as a drapery or tapestry. **3.** a suspending or temporary attaching, as of a painting: *a careless hanging of pictures.* —*adj.* **4.** punishable by, deserving, or causing death by hanging: *a hanging crime; a hanging offense.* **5.** inclined to inflict death by hanging: *a hanging jury.* **6.** suspended; pendent; overhanging: *a hanging cliff.* **7.** situated on a steep slope or at a height: *a hanging garden.* **8.** directed downward: *a hanging look.* **9.** made, holding, or suitable for a hanging object. [1250–1300; ME (n., adj.), OE *hangande* (adj.) See HANG, -ING[1], -ING[2]] —**hang′ing·ly,** *adv.*

hang·ing·fly (hang′ing flī′), *n., pl.* **-flies.** a small, long-legged scorpionfly of the family Bittacidae, resembling the crane fly but having four wings rather than two and hanging from leaves or twigs by the front or middle legs while using the hind legs to seize prey, mostly small flies. [HANGING + FLY[2]]

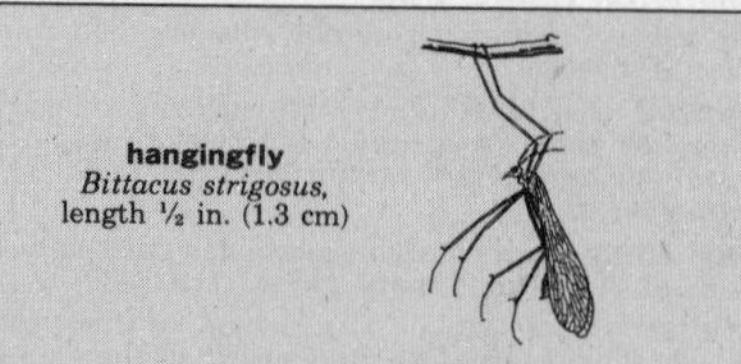
hangingfly
Bittacus strigosus,
length ½ in. (1.3 cm)

Hang′ing Gar′dens of Bab′ylon, ornamental gardens planted on the terraces of the ziggurats of ancient Babylon. Cf. **Seven Wonders of the World.**

hang′ing inden′tion, *Print.* an indention of uniform length at the beginning of each line except the first, which is flush left and of full width. [1925–30]

hang′ing lie′, *Golf.* a lie in which the ball is situated on a slope having a downward incline in the direction that the ball is to be played. [1905–10]

hang′ing post′, a post from which a door, gate, etc., is hung. Also called **hinging post.** [1785–95]

hang′ing scroll′. See under **scroll** (def. 5).

hang′ing step′, a step projecting from a wall with no real or apparent support at its outer end. [1875–80]

hang′ing stile′, 1. the stile of a door, shutter, etc., by which it is hung. **2.** the stile of a window frame from which a casement sash is hung. **3.** See **pulley stile.** Cf. **shutting stile.** [1815–25]

hang′ing val′ley, 1. a valley, the lower end of which opens high above a shore, usually caused by the rapid erosion of a cliff. **2.** a tributary valley whose mouth is set above the the floor of the main valley, usually as a result of differences in glacial erosion. [1895–1900]

hang′ing wall′, 1. *Mining.* the underside of the wall rock overlying a vein or bed of ore. Cf. **footwall** (def. 1). **2.** *Geol.* a mass of rock overhanging a fault plane. [1770–80]

hang·man (hang′mən *for 1;* hang′man′ *for 2*), *n., pl.* **-men.** for 1. **1.** a person who hangs criminals who are condemned to death; public executioner. **2.** a word game in which one player selects a word that the other player must guess by supplying each of its letters: for each incorrect guess a part of a stick figure of a hanged man is drawn. [1350–1400; ME; see HANG, MAN[1]]

hang′man's knot′, a slip noose for hanging a person, usually having eight or nine turns around the rope.

hang·nail (hang′nāl′), *n.* a small piece of partly detached skin at the side or base of the fingernail. Cf. **whitlow.** [1300–50; ME *angenayle* corn, OE *angnægl,* equiv. to *ang-* (var. of *enge* narrow, painful; c. G *eng,* see ANGER) + *nægl* callus, NAIL; modern *h-* by assoc. with HANG]

hang-on (hang′on′, -ôn′), *Informal.* —*n.* **1.** something easily attached to or mounted on another surface or object, as a turbocharger or transceiver in an automobile, a unit suspendable from shelving, or a portable soap dish. —*adj.* **2.** pertaining to or denoting such an attachment: *A clumsy hang-on unit supplied the air conditioning.* [n., adj. use of v. phrase *hang on*]

hang·out (hang′out′), *n. Informal.* a place where a person frequently visits, esp. for socializing or recreation. [1850–55, *Amer.*; n. use of v. phrase *hang out*]

hang·o·ver (hang′ō′vər), *n.* **1.** the disagreeable physical aftereffects of drunkenness, such as a headache or stomach disorder, usually felt several hours after cessation of drinking. **2.** something remaining behind from a former period or state of affairs. **3.** any aftermath of or lingering effect from a distressing experience: *the post-Watergate hangover in Washington.* [1890–95, *Amer.*; n. use of v. phrase *hang over*]

—**Syn. 1.** queasiness, sickishness, qualm, nausea.

hang·tag (hang′tag′), *n.* a tag attached to a garment or other piece of merchandise that includes information about the manufacturer or designer, the fabric or material used, the model number, care instructions, and sometimes the price. Also, **hang′-tag′.** [1950–55; HANG + TAG[1]]

Hang′town Fry′ (hang′toun′), a type of omelet to which fried oysters, bacon, and sometimes onions are added. [allegedly after *Hangtown,* a Gold Rush-era nickname of Placerville, El Dorado Co., California]

Han·gul (häng′gool), *n.* the Korean alphabetic writing system, introduced in the 15th century, containing 14 consonants and 11 vowels. [< Korean, equiv. to *han* great (but frequently taken to be *Han* < MChin, equiv. to Chin *hán* Korea) + *kŭl* writing]

hang-up (hang′up′), *n. Slang.* **1.** a preoccupation, fixation, or psychological block; complex: *His hang-up is trying to outdo his brother.* **2.** a source of annoying difficulty or burden; impediment; snag: *The most serious hang-up the project has is a shortage of funds.* **3.** a fixture, object, or decoration that can be affixed to a wall, ceiling, other objects, etc.: *He brightened up the room with flower baskets and other hang-ups.* Also, **hang′up′.** [1955–60; n. use of v. phrase *hang up*]

Hang·zhou (häng′jō′), *n. Pinyin.* a seaport in and the capital of Zhejiang province, in E China, on Hangzhou Bay. 1,100,000. Also, **Hangchow.**

Hang′zhou′ Bay′, a bay of the East China Sea. Also, **Hangchow Bay.**

Ha·ni·fah (hä nē′fə), *n.* a female given name: from an Arabic word meaning "true believer." Also, **Ha·ni′fa.**

ha·ni·wa (hä′nē wä′), *n., pl.* **-wa.** any of the terracotta models of people, animals, and houses from the

Yayoi period of Japanese culture. [1965–70; < Japn, earlier *faniwa,* equiv. to *fani* red clay + *wa* wheel]

hank (hangk), *n.* **1.** a skein, as of thread or yarn. **2.** a definite length of thread or yarn: *A hank of cotton yarn measures 840 yards.* **3.** a coil, knot, or loop: *a hank of hair.* **4.** *Naut.* a ring, link, or shackle for securing the luff of a staysail or jib to its stay or the luff or head of a gaff sail to the mast or gaff. —*v.t.* **5.** *Naut.* to fasten (a sail) by means of hanks. [1175–1225; ME < ON *hǫnk* hank, coil, skein, clasp; akin to HANG]

Hank (hangk), *n.* a male given name, form of **Henry.**

han•ker (hang′kər), *v.i.* to have a restless or incessant longing (often fol. by *after, for,* or an infinitive). [1595–1605; < early D dial. *hankeren* (c. D *hunkeren*), freq. of *hangen* to HANG] —**han′ker•er,** *n.*
—**Syn.** See **yearn.**

han•ker•ing (hang′kər ing), *n.* a longing; craving. [1655–65; HANKER + -ING¹] —**han′ker•ing•ly,** *adv.*
—**Syn.** desire, need, yearning, hunger, yen, thirst.

Han•kou (hang′kou′; *Chin.* hän′kō′), *n. Pinyin, Wade-Giles.* a former city in E Hubei province, in E China: now part of Wuhan. Also, *Older Spelling,* **Han′kow′.**

han•ky (hang′kē), *n., pl.* **-kies.** a handkerchief. Also, **han′kie.** [1890–95; HAN(D)K(ERCHIEF) + -Y²]

han•ky-pan•ky (hang′kē pang′kē), *n. Informal.* **1.** unethical behavior; deceit: *When the bank teller bought an expensive car and house, they suspected there might be some hanky-panky going on.* **2.** illicit sexual relations. Also, **han′key-pan′key, han′ky pank′.** [1835–45; rhyming compound; cf. initial *h, p* of HIGGLEDY-PIGGLEDY, HOCUS-POCUS, HODGE-PODGE, etc.]

Han•na (han′ə), *n.* **Marcus Alonzo** (*"Mark"*), 1837–1904, U.S. merchant and politician: senator 1897–1904.

Han•nah (han′ə), *n.* **1.** the mother of Samuel. I Sam. 1:20. **2.** a female given name: from a Hebrew word meaning "grace."

Han•ni•bal (han′ə bəl), *n.* **1.** 247–183 B.C., Carthaginian general who crossed the Alps and invaded Italy (son of Hamilcar Barca). **2.** a port in NE Missouri, on the Mississippi: Mark Twain's boyhood home. 18,811.

Han•no (han′ō), *n.* Carthaginian statesman, fl. 3rd century B.C.

Ha•noi (ha noi′, hə-), *n.* a city in and the capital of Vietnam, in the N part, on the Songka River. 1,443,500.

Ha•no•taux (A nô tō′), *n.* **(Al•bert Au•guste) Ga•bri•el** (Al bεR′ ō gyst′ GA bRē el′), 1853–1944, French statesman and historian.

Han•o•ver (han′ō vər), *n.* **1.** a member of the royal family that ruled Great Britain under that name from 1714 to 1901. **2.** a former province in NW Germany; now a district in Lower Saxony. 14,944 sq. mi. (38,705 sq. km). **3.** a city in and the capital of Lower Saxony, in N central Germany. 495,300. **4.** a city in S Pennsylvania. 14,890. **5.** a town in SE Massachusetts. 11,358. German, **Han•no•ver** (hä nō′vəR) (for defs. 2, 3).

Han•o•ve•ri•an (han′ō vēr′ē ən), *adj.* **1.** of or pertaining to the former ruling house of Hanover. —*n.* **2.** a supporter of the house of Hanover. [1765–75; HANOVER + -IAN]

Han′over Park′, a city in NE Illinois. 28,850.

Han′ Riv′er. See **Han Shui.**

Hans (hanz; *Ger.* häns), *n.* a male given name, Germanic form of **John.**

Han•sa (han′sə, -zə), *n.* **1.** a company or guild of merchants in a northern European medieval town. **2.** a fee paid to a merchant guild by a new member. **3.** Also called **Han′sa town′, Hansetown.** a town that is a member of the Hanseatic League. **4.** See **Hanseatic League.** [< ML; r. ME *hans, hanze* < MLG *hanse;* c. OE *hōs,* OHG, Goth *hansa* company]

Han•sard (han′sərd), *n.* the official verbatim published reports of the debates and proceedings in the British Parliament. [named after Luke *Hansard* (1752–1828) and his descendants, who compiled the reports until 1889]

Han′sa yel′low, **1.** a pigment derived from coal tar, characterized chiefly by its brilliant yellow color. **2.** See **spectra yellow.** [after HANSA (perh. pun on *enhance*)]

Hans•ber•ry (hanz′ber ē), *n.* **Lorraine,** 1930–65, U.S. playwright.

Hanse (hans), *n.* Hansa.

Han•se•at•ic (han′sē at′ik), *adj.* **1.** of or pertaining to the Hanseatic League or to any of the towns belonging to it. —*n.* **2.** any of the towns belonging to the Hanseatic League. [1605–15; < ML *Hanseāticus,* equiv. to *hanse* (< MLG; see HANSA) + *-āt-* -ATE¹ + *-icus* -IC]

Han′seat′ic League′, a medieval league of towns of northern Germany and adjacent countries for the promotion and protection of commerce. Also called **Hansa.**

Centers of the Hanseatic League

han•sel (han′səl), *n., v.t.,* **-seled, -sel•ing** or (*esp. Brit.*) **-selled, -sel•ling.** handsel.

Han•sen (hän′sən), *n.* **Pe•ter An•dre•as** (pē′təR än-dRē′äs), 1795–1874, Danish astronomer.

Han′sen's disease′, *Pathol.* leprosy. [1935–40; named after G. H. *Hansen* (1841–1912), Norwegian physician and discoverer of leprosy-causing *Mycobacterium leprae*]

Hanse•town (hans′town′), *n.* Hansa (def. 3). [1565–75; HANSE + TOWN]

Han Shui (hän′ shwē′), *Pinyin, Wade-Giles.* a river flowing from central China into the Chang Jiang at Wuhan. 900 mi. (1450 km) long. Also called **Han River.**

han•som (han′səm), *n.* **1.** a low-hung, two-wheeled, covered vehicle drawn by one horse, for two passengers, with the driver being mounted on an elevated seat behind and the reins running over the roof. **2.** any similar horse-drawn vehicle. Also called **han′som cab′.** [1850–55; named after J. A. Hansom (1803–82), English architect who designed it]

hansom

Han•son (han′sən), *n.* **1. Duane,** born 1925, U.S. artist and sculptor. **2. Howard** (*Harold*), 1896–1981, U.S. composer.

hant (hant), *v.t., v.i., n. South Midland and Southern U.S.* haunt. Also, **ha'nt.**

han't (hānt), *Older Use.* **1.** a contraction of *has not.* **2.** a contraction of *have not.*

Hants (hants), *n.* Hampshire (def. 1).

Ha•nuk•kah (hä′nə kə; *Ashk. Heb.* KHä′nə kə; *Seph. Heb.* KHä nōō kä′), *n.* a Jewish festival lasting eight days, celebrated from the 25th day of the month of Kislev to the 2nd of Tevet in commemoration of the rededication of the Temple by the Maccabees following their victory over the Syrians under Antiochus IV, characterized chiefly by the lighting of the menorah on each night of the festival. Also, **Chanukah.** Also called **Feast of Dedication, Feast of Lights.** [1890–95; < Heb *ḥănukkāh* lit., a dedicating]

han•u•man (hun′ōō män′, hä′nōō-; hun′ōō män′, hä′-nōō-), *n., pl.* **-mans** for 1. **1.** Also called **entellus.** a langur, *Presbytis (Semnopithecus) entellus,* held sacred in India. **2.** (*cap.*) *Hindu Myth.* a monkey chief who is a conspicuous figure in the Ramayana. [1805–15; < Skt *hanuman,* nom. sing. of *hanumant*]

Han Wu Ti (hän′ wōō′ dē′), (*Liu Ch'e, Liu Che*) 156–87 B.C., emperor of China 140–87. Also called **Wu Ti, Wu Di.** Also, *Pinyin,* **Han′ Wu′ Di′.**

Han•yang (hän′yäng′), *n. Pinyin, Wade-Giles.* a former city in E Hubei province, in E China: now part of Wuhan.

Han Yü (hän′ yy′), (*Han Wen-kung, Han Wengong*) A.D. 768–824, Chinese writer, poet, and philosopher. Also, *Pinyin,* **Han′ Yu′.**

hao (hou), *n.* an aluminum coin and monetary unit of Vietnam, the tenth part of a dong. [1945–50; < Vietnamese *hào*]

hao•le (hou′lē, -lā), *n.* **1.** (among Polynesian Hawaiians) a non-Polynesian, esp. a Caucasian. **2.** (formerly) a foreigner. [1835–45; < Hawaiian: white person, (earlier) foreigner, foreign]

hao•ma (hou′mə), *n.* **1.** a leafless vine, *Sarcostemma acidum,* of eastern India, yielding a sour, milky juice. **2.** Also, **homa.** *Zoroastrianism.* **a.** a sacramental drink prepared with the juice of the haoma plant, milk, and water. **b.** (*cap.*) a god personifying this sacred drink. [1885–90; < Avestan; c. SOMA²]

ha•o•ri (hou′rē; *Japn.* hä ô′Rē), *n., pl.* **-ris,** *Japn.* **-ri.** a loose, knee-length, Japanese garment resembling a coat. [< Japn, earlier *faori* or *fawori,* of uncert. etym.]

hap¹ (hap), *n., v.,* **happed, hap•ping.** —*n.* **1.** one's luck or lot. **2.** an occurrence, happening, or accident. —*v.i.* **3.** to happen: *if it so hap.* [1150–1200; ME < ON *happ* luck, chance; akin to OE *gehæp* fit, convenient; prob. akin to OCS *kobŭ* auspice, OIr *cob* victory]

hap² (hap, ap), *Chiefly Pennsylvania.* —*n.* **1.** a comforter or quilt. —*v.t.* **2.** to cover with or as with a comforter or quilt. [1350–1400; ME *happen* to cover; perh. b. *lappen* LAP² and OF *happer* to seize]

Hap (häp, KHäp), *n.* Apis (def. 1).

ha•pai (hä′pī), *Hawaii.* —*v.t.* **1.** to carry; lift. —*adj.* **2.** pregnant. [< Hawaiian *hāpai*]

hap•ax le•go•me•non (hap′aks li gom′ə non′, hā′-paks), *pl.* **hap•ax le•go•me•na** (hap′aks li gom′ə nə, hā′paks). a word or phrase that appears only once in a manuscript, document, or particular area of literature. [1880–85; < Gk *hápax legómenon* (thing) once said]

ha'-pen•ny (hā′pə nē, hāp′nē), *n., pl.* **-nies.** *Brit.* halfpenny.

hap•haz•ard (*adj., adv.* hap haz′ərd; *n.* hap′haz′ərd), *adj.* **1.** characterized by lack of order or planning, by irregularity, or by randomness; determined by or dependent on chance; aimless. —*adv.* **2.** haphazardly. —*n.* **3.** mere chance; accident. [1565–75; HAP¹ + HAZARD] —**hap•haz′ard•ness,** *n.*
—**Syn. 1.** disorganized, unsystematic, careless, slapdash, helter-skelter. —**Ant. 1.** methodical, systematic, organized.

hap•haz•ard•ly (hap haz′ərd lē), *adv.* in a haphazard manner; at random. [1885–90; HAPHAZARD + -LY]

hap•haz•ard•ry (hap haz′ər drē), *n.* **1.** haphazard character, state, or order; fortuity. **2.** haphazard items, thoughts, etc. [1930–35; HAPHAZARD + -RY]

Haph•si•ba (haf′sə bə), *n. Douay Bible.* Hephzibah (def. 1).

Haph•ta•rah (*Seph. Heb.* häf tä Rä′; *Ashk. Heb.* häf-tô′Rə, -tō′-), *n., pl.* **-ta•roth, -ta•rot, -ta•ros** (*Seph. Heb.* -tä Rôt′, *Ashk. Heb.*-tô′Rōs, -Rōt, -tō′-), **-ta•rahs.** *Judaism.* Haftarah.

Ha•pi (hä′pē, KHä′pē), *n.* Apis (def. 1).

hap•less (hap′lis), *adj.* unlucky; luckless; unfortunate. [1560–70; HAP¹ + -LESS] —**hap′less•ly,** *adv.* —**hap′less•ness,** *n.*
—**Syn.** miserable, woebegone, wretched, forlorn; pathetic, pitiable.

haplo-, a combining form meaning "single," "simple," used in the formation of compound words: *haplology.* Also, *esp. before a vowel,* **hapl-.** [< Gk, comb. form of *haplóos* single, simple; akin to L *simplex*]

hap•log•ra•phy (hap log′rə fē), *n.* the accidental omission of a letter or letter group that should be repeated in writing, as in *Missippi* for *Mississippi.* Cf. **dittography.** [1885–90; HAPLO- + -GRAPHY]

hap•loid (hap′loid), *adj.* Also, **hap•loi′dic.** **1.** single; simple. **2.** *Biol.* pertaining to a single set of chromosomes. —*n.* **3.** *Biol.* an organism or cell having only one complete set of chromosomes, ordinarily half the normal diploid number. [1905–10; HAPL- + -OID]

hap•lol•o•gy (hap lol′ə jē), *n. Ling.* the omission of one of two similar adjacent syllables or sounds in a word, as in substituting *morphonemic* for *morphophonemic* or in the pronunciation (prob′lē) for *probably.* [HAPLO- + -LOGY] —**hap•lo•log•ic** (hap′lə loj′ik), *adj.*

hap•lont (hap′lont), *n. Biol.* the haploid individual in a life cycle that has a diploid and a haploid phase. [1915–20; HAPL- + *-ont* < Gk *ont-,* s. of *ṓn* being, prp. of *eînai* to be (cf. ONTO-)]

hap•lo•phase (hap′lə fāz′), *n. Biol.* the haploid portion of an organism's life cycle. [1920–25; HAPLO- + PHASE]

hap•lo•pi•a (hap lō′pē ə), *n. Ophthalm.* normal vision (opposed to *diplopia*). [HAPL- + -OPIA]

hap•lo•sis (hap lō′sis), *n. Biol.* the production of haploid chromosome groups during meiosis. [HAPL- + -OSIS]

hap•ly (hap′lē), *adv. Archaic.* perhaps; by chance. [1325–75; ME *hapliche.* See HAP¹, -LY]

hap•pen (hap′ən), *v.i.* **1.** to take place; come to pass; occur: *Something interesting is always happening in New York.* **2.** to come to pass by chance; occur without apparent reason or design: *Don't ask me what caused it—it just happened, that's all.* **3.** to have the fortune or lot (to do or be as specified); chance: *I happened to see him on the street.* **4.** to befall, as to a person or thing: *Something dreadful has happened to me.* **5.** to meet or discover by chance (usually fol. by *on* or *upon*): *to happen on a clue to a mystery.* **6.** to be, come, go, etc., casually or by chance: *My friend happened along.* [1300–50; ME *hap(pe)nen.* See HAP¹, -EN¹]
—**Syn. 1.** betide. HAPPEN, CHANCE, OCCUR refer to the taking place of an event. HAPPEN, which originally denoted the taking place by hap or chance, is now the most general word for coming to pass: *Something has happened.* CHANCE suggests the accidental nature of an event: *It chanced to rain that day.* OCCUR is often interchangeable with HAPPEN, but is more formal, and is usually more specific as to time and event: *His death occurred the following year.*

hap•pen•chance (hap′ən chans′, -chäns′), *n.* happenstance. [1875–80; HAPPEN + CHANCE]

hap•pen•ing (hap′ə ning), *n.* **1.** something that happens; occurrence; event. **2.** an unconventional dramatic or artistically orchestrated performance, often a series of discontinuous events involving audience participation. **3.** any event considered worthwhile, unusual, or interesting. [1545–55; 1965–70 for def. 2; HAPPEN + -ING¹]
—**Syn. 1.** incident, episode, instance, affair, case.

hap•pen-so (hap′ən sō′), *n. South Midland and Southern U.S.* chance; happenstance; accident: *Meeting you today was pure happen-so.* [1900–05]

hap•pen•stance (hap′ən stans′), *n.* a chance happening or event. [1895–1900; HAPPEN + (CIRCUM)STANCE]

hap′pi coat′ (hap′ē), (*sometimes caps.*) a Japanese lounging jacket with wide, loose sleeves and often an overlapping front closure usually tied with a sash. [1875–80; < Japn, earlier *fappi,* var. of *fan-pi* < MChin, equiv. to Chin *bàn* half + *bèi* wear]

hap•pi•ly (hap′ə lē), *adv.* **1.** in a happy manner; with pleasure. **2.** by good fortune; luckily; providentially. **3.** felicitously; aptly; appropriately: *a happily turned phrase.* [1300–50; ME; see HAPPY, -LY]

hap•pi•ness (hap′ē nis), *n.* **1.** the quality or state of being happy. **2.** good fortune; pleasure; contentment; joy. [1520–30; HAPPY + -NESS]
—**Syn. 1, 2.** pleasure, joy, exhilaration, bliss, contentedness, delight, enjoyment, satisfaction. HAPPINESS, BLISS, CONTENTMENT, FELICITY imply an active or passive state of pleasure or pleasurable satisfaction. HAPPINESS results from the possession or attainment of what one considers good: *the happiness of visiting one's family.* BLISS is unalloyed happiness or supreme delight: *the bliss of perfect companionship.* CONTENTMENT is a peaceful kind of happiness in which one rests without desires, even though every wish may not have been gratified: *contentment in one's surroundings.* FELICITY is a formal

word for happiness of an especially fortunate or intense kind: *to wish a young couple felicity in life.* —**Ant. 1.** misery.

hap•py (hap′ē), *adj.,* **-pi•er, -pi•est. 1.** delighted, pleased, or glad, as over a particular thing: *to be happy to see a person.* **2.** characterized by or indicative of pleasure, contentment, or joy: *a happy mood; a happy frame of mind.* **3.** favored by fortune; fortunate or lucky: *a happy, fruitful land.* **4.** apt or felicitous, as actions, utterances, or ideas. **5.** obsessed by or quick to use the item indicated (usually used in combination): *a trigger-happy gangster. Everybody is gadget-happy these days.* [1300–50; ME; see HAP[1], -Y[1]]
—**Syn. 1.** joyous, joyful, blithe, cheerful, merry, contented, gay, blissful, satisfied. **3.** favorable, propitious; successful, prosperous. See **fortunate. 4.** appropriate, fitting, opportune, pertinent. —**Ant. 1.** sad.

hap′py dust′, *Slang.* cocaine. [1920–25]

hap•py-go-luck•y (hap′ē gō luk′ē), *adj.* trusting cheerfully to luck; happily unworried or unconcerned. [1665–75]
—**Syn.** carefree, heedless, light-hearted, insouciant.

hap′py hour′, a cocktail hour or longer period at a bar, during which drinks are served at reduced prices or with free snacks: *happy hour from 5 to 7 P.M.* [1965–70]

hap′py hunt′ing ground′, **1.** the North American Indian heaven, conceived of as a paradise of hunting and feasting for warriors and hunters. **2.** a place where one finds in abundance that which one needs or desires, or where one may pursue an activity without restriction: *New England attics are happy hunting grounds for antique collectors.* [1830–40, *Amer.*]

Hap′py Val′ley-Goose′ Bay′, a twin town in SE Labrador in Newfoundland, E Canada, consisting of an air base, Goose Bay, and its adjacent residential town of Happy Valley: used as a fuel stop by some transatlantic airplanes. 8075.

hap′py war′rior, **1.** a person who is undiscouraged by difficulties or opposition. **2.** (*cap.*) a nickname of Alfred E. Smith. [1800–10]

Haps•burg (haps′bûrg; *Ger.* häps′bŏŏrk′), *n.* a German princely family, prominent since the 13th century, that has furnished sovereigns to the Holy Roman Empire, Austria, Spain, etc. Also, **Habsburg.**

hap•ten (hap′ten), *n. Immunol.* a substance having a single antigenic determinant that can react with a previously existing antibody but cannot stimulate more antibody production unless combined with other molecules; a partial antigen. Also, **hap•tene** (hap′tēn). [1920–25; < G < Gk *hápt(ein)* to grasp + G *-en* -ENE]

hap•ter•on (hap′tə ron′), *n., pl.* **-ter•a** (-tər ə). *Biol.* a structure by which a fungus, aquatic plant, or algae colony attaches to an object; a holdfast. [1890–95; appar. a pseudo-Gk deriv. of Gk *háptein* to grasp and *-tēr* agentive suffix]

hap•tics (hap′tiks), *n.* (*used with a singular v.*) the branch of psychology that investigates cutaneous sense data. [1890–95; *haptic* < Gk *haptikós* able to grasp or perceive, equiv. to *háp(tein)* to grasp, sense, perceive + *-tikos* -TIC; see -ICS] —**hap′tic, hap′ti•cal,** *adj.*

hap•tom•e•ter (hap tom′i tər), *n.* a mechanical device for measuring the sense of touch. [< Gk *hápt(ein)* to sense, touch, grasp + -O- + -METER]

ha•pu•u (hä po͞o′o͞o), *n.* a Hawaiian tree fern, *Cibotium splendens,* the cut trunks of which are used in horticulture as pots and planters. [< Hawaiian *hāpu'u*]

Har•a•han (har′ə han′), *n.* a town in SE Louisiana. 11,384.

ha•ra-ki•ri (här′ə kēr′ē, har′ə-, har′ē-), *n.* **1.** Also called **seppuku.** ceremonial suicide by ripping open the abdomen with a dagger or knife: formerly practiced in Japan by members of the warrior class when disgraced or sentenced to death. **2.** suicide or any suicidal action; a self-destructive act: *political hara-kiri.* Also, **hari-kari.** [1855–60; < Japn, equiv. to *hara* belly (earlier *fara* < *para) + *kiri* cut]

Ha•rald V (har′əld; *Norw.* här′äl), born 1937, king of Norway since 1991.

ha•ram (hâr′əm, har′-), *n.* harem.

ha•rangue (hə rang′), *n., v.,* **-rangued, -rangu•ing.** —*n.* **1.** a scolding or a long or intense verbal attack; diatribe. **2.** a long, passionate, and vehement speech, esp. one delivered before a public gathering. **3.** any long, pompous speech or writing of a tediously hortatory or didactic nature; sermonizing lecture or discourse. —*v.t.* **4.** to address in a harangue. —*v.i.* **5.** to deliver a harangue. [1530–40; (n.) < MF *harangue* < It *ar(r)inga* speech, oration, n. deriv. of *ar(r)ingare* to speak in public, v. deriv. of *aringo* public square < Goth *hriggs RING[1]; (v.) < MF *haranguer* < It *ar(r)ingare*]

Ha•rap•pa (hə rap′ə), *n.* **1.** a village in Pakistan: site of successive cities of the Indus valley civilization. **2.** a Bronze Age culture that flourished in the Indus valley.

Ha•rap•pan (hə rap′ən), *adj.* of or pertaining to Harappa, esp. the Bronze Age culture of the Indus valley civilization. [HARAPP(A) + -AN]

Ha•rar (här′ər), *n.* a city in E Ethiopia. 58,000. Also, **Harrar.**

Ha•ra•re (hə rär′ā), *n.* a city in and the capital of Zimbabwe, in the NE part. 675,000. Formerly, **Salisbury.**

ha•rass (hə ras′, har′əs), *v.t.* **1.** to disturb persistently; torment, as with troubles or cares; bother continually; pester; persecute. **2.** to trouble by repeated attacks, incursions, etc., as in war or hostilities; harry; raid. [1610–20; < F, MF *harasser* to harry, harass, v. deriv. of *harace, harache* (in phrase *courre a la harace* pursue), equiv. to *hare* interjection used to urge hunting dogs on (< Frankish *hara here, from this side; cf. OHG *hera,* G *her,* MD *hare*) + *-asse* aug. or pejorative suffix < L *-ācea*] —**ha•rass′a•ble,** *adj.* —**ha•rass′er,** *n.* —**ha•rass′ing•ly,** *adv.* —**ha•rass′ment,** *n.*
—**Syn. 1.** badger, vex, plague, hector; torture. See **worry. 2.** molest.
—**Pronunciation.** HARASS, a 17th century French borrowing, has traditionally been pronounced (har′əs), with stress on the first syllable. A newer pronunciation, (hə ras′), has developed in North American (but not British) English. While this newer pronunciation is sometimes criticized by older educated speakers, it has become the more common one in the U.S., especially among younger educated speakers, some of whom have only minimal familiarity with the older form.

Har•bin (här′bin′), *n. Pinyin.* a city in and the capital of Heilongjiang province, in NE China. 2,000,000. Formerly, **Pinkiang.**

har•bin•ger (här′bin jər), *n.* **1.** a person who goes ahead and makes known the approach of another; herald. **2.** anything that foreshadows a future event; omen; sign: *Frost is a harbinger of winter.* **3.** a person sent in advance of troops, a royal train, etc., to provide or secure lodgings and other accommodations. —*v.t.* **4.** to act as harbinger to; herald the coming of. [1125–75; late ME *herbenger,* nasalized var. of ME *herbegere,* dissimilated var. of OF *herberg(i)ere* host, equiv. to *herberg(ier)* to shelter (< Gmc; see HARBOR) + *-iere* -ER[2]]
—**Syn. 2.** herald, forerunner, precursor, portent, indication.

har•bin•ger-of-spring (här′bin jər əv spring′), *n., pl.* **har•bin•gers-of-spring.** a North American umbelliferous herb, *Erigenia bulbosa,* having white flowers that bloom early in the spring. [1865–70]

Har•bo•na (här bō′nə), *n.* one of the seven eunuchs who served in the court of King Ahasuerus. Esther 1:10.

har•bor (här′bər), *n.* **1.** a part of a body of water along the shore deep enough for anchoring a ship and so situated with respect to coastal features, whether natural or artificial, as to provide protection from winds, waves, and currents. **2.** such a body of water having docks or port facilities. **3.** any place of shelter or refuge: *The old inn was a harbor for tired travelers.* —*v.t.* **4.** to give shelter to; offer refuge to: *They harbored the refugees who streamed across the borders.* **5.** to conceal; hide: *to harbor fugitives.* **6.** to keep or hold in the mind; maintain; entertain: *to harbor suspicion.* **7.** to house or contain. **8.** to shelter (a vessel), as in a harbor. —*v.i.* **9.** (of a vessel) to take shelter in a harbor. Also, *esp. Brit.,* **harbour.** [bef. 1150; ME *herber(we), herberge,* OE *hereborg* lodgings, quarters (*here* army + *(ge)beorg* refuge); c. G *Herberge*] —**har′bor•er,** *n.* —**har′bor•less,** *adj.* —**har′bor•ous,** *adj.*
—**Syn. 1.** HARBOR, HAVEN, PORT indicate a shelter for ships. A HARBOR may be natural or artificially constructed or improved: *a fine harbor on the eastern coast.* A HAVEN is usually a natural harbor that can be utilized by ships as a place of safety; the word is common in literary use: *a haven in time of storm; a haven of refuge.* A PORT is a HARBOR viewed esp. in its commercial relations, though it is frequently applied in the meaning of HARBOR or HAVEN also: *a thriving port; any old port in a storm.* **3.** asylum, sanctuary, retreat. **4.** protect, lodge. **6.** See **cherish.**

har•bor•age (här′bər ij), *n.* **1.** shelter for vessels, as that provided by a harbor. **2.** any shelter or lodging. **3.** a place of shelter. [1560–70; HARBOR + -AGE]

har′bor mas′ter, an official who supervises operations in a harbor area and administers its rules. [1760–70]

har′bor seal′, a small, spotted seal, *Phoca vitulina,* of the Atlantic coasts of North America and Europe and the Pacific coast of northern North America. [1760–70]

har•bor•side (här′bər sīd′), *adj.* **1.** bordering a harbor. —*adv.* **2.** in, to, or near the area bordering a harbor. [1945–50; HARBOR + SIDE[1]]

har•bour (här′bər), *n., v.t., v.i. Chiefly Brit.* harbor. —**Usage.** See **-or**[1].

hard (härd), *adj.,* **-er, -est,** *adv.,* **-er, -est,** *n.* —*adj.* **1.** not soft; solid and firm to the touch; unyielding to pressure and impenetrable or almost impenetrable. **2.** firmly formed; tight: *a hard knot.* **3.** difficult to do or accomplish; fatiguing; troublesome: *a hard task.* **4.** difficult or troublesome with respect to an action, situation, person, etc.: *hard to please; a hard time.* **5.** difficult to deal with, manage, control, overcome, or understand: *a hard problem.* **6.** involving a great deal of effort, energy, or persistence: *hard labor; hard study.* **7.** performing or carrying on work with great effort, energy, or persistence: *a hard worker.* **8.** vigorous or violent in force; severe: *a hard rain; a hard fall.* **9.** bad; unendurable; unbearable: *hard luck.* **10.** oppressive; harsh; rough: *hard treatment.* **11.** austere; severe: *a hard winter; the hard times of the Great Depression.* **12.** harsh or severe in dealing with others: *a hard master.* **13.** difficult to explain away; undeniable: *hard facts.* **14.** that can be verified; factual, as distinguished from speculation or hearsay: *hard information.* **15.** harsh or unfriendly; resentful; severe; bitter: *hard feelings; hard words.* **16.** of stern judgment or close examination; searching: *a hard look.* **17.** lacking delicacy or softness; not blurred or diffused; clear and distinct; sharp; harsh: *a hard line; a hard, bright light; hard features; a hard face.* **18.** (of a photograph) contrasty. **19.** severe or rigorous in terms: *a hard bargain.* **20.** sternly realistic; dispassionate; unsentimental: *a hard, practical man; a hard view of life.* **21.** incorrigible; disreputable; tough: *a hard character.* **22.** *Scot. and North Eng.* niggardly; stingy. **23.** in coins or paper money as distinguished from checks, securities, promissory notes, or other negotiable instruments). **24.** (of paper money or a monetary system) supported by sufficient gold reserves and easily convertible into the currency of a foreign nation. **25.** (of money) scarce or available at high interest rates: *a hard loan.* **26.** denoting assets with intrinsic value, as gold, silver, or diamonds. **27.** (of alcoholic beverages) **a.** containing more than 22.5 percent alcohol by volume, as whiskey and brandy as opposed to beer and wine. **b.** strong because of fermentation; intoxicating: *hard cider.* **28.** (of wine) tasting excessively of tannin. **29.** (of an illicit narcotic or drug) known to be physically addictive, as opium, morphine, or cocaine. **30.** (of water) containing mineral salts that interfere with the action of soap. **31.** (of bread and baked goods) **a.** having a firm, crisp crust or texture: *hard rolls.* **b.** stale or tough. **32.** (of a fabric) having relatively little nap; smooth: *Silk is a harder fabric than wool or cotton.* **33.** (of the landing of a rocket or space vehicle) executed without decelerating: *a hard landing on the moon.* Cf. **soft** (def. 28). **34.** (of a missile base) equipped to launch missiles from underground silos. **35.** (of a missile) capable of being launched from an underground silo. **36.** *Mil.* being underground and strongly protected from nuclear bombardment. **37.** *Agric.* noting wheats with high gluten content, milled for a bread flour as contrasted with pastry flour. **38.** *Phonet.* **a.** fortis. **b.** (of *c* and *g*) pronounced as (k) in *come* and (g) in *go,* rather than as in *cent, cello, suspicion, gem,* or *beige.* **c.** (of consonants in Slavic languages) not palatalized. Cf. **soft** (def. 26). **39.** (in the making of rope) noting a lay having a considerable angle to the axis of the rope; short. **40.** *Physics.* (of a beam of particles or photons) having relatively high energy: *hard x-rays.* Cf. **soft** (def. 29). **41.** (of the penis) erect. **42. hard of hearing.** See **hearing-impaired. 43. hard up,** *Informal.* **a.** urgently in need of money. **b.** feeling a lack or need: *The country is hard up for technicians and doctors.*
—*adv.* **44.** with great exertion; with vigor or violence; strenuously: *to work hard; to try hard.* **45.** earnestly, intently, or critically: *to look hard at a thing.* **46.** harshly or severely. **47.** so as to be solid, tight, or firm: *frozen hard.* **48.** with strong force or impact: *She tripped and came down hard on her back.* **49.** in a deeply affected manner; with genuine sorrow or remorse: *She took it very hard when they told her of his death.* **50.** closely; immediately: *Failure and defeat seemed hard at hand. The decision to ban students from the concerts followed hard on the heels of the riot.* **51.** to an unreasonable or extreme degree; excessively; immoderately: *He's hitting the bottle pretty hard.* **52.** *Naut.* closely, fully, or to the extreme limit: *hard aport; hard alee.* **53. be hard on,** to deal harshly with; be stern: *You are being too hard on him.* **54. hard by,** in close proximity to; near: *The house is hard by the river.* **55. hard put,** in great perplexity or difficulty; at a loss: *We were hard put to finish the examination in one hour.*
—*n.* **56.** *Naut.* a firm or paved beach or slope convenient for hauling vessels out of the water. **57.** *Brit.* **a.** a firm or solid beach or foreshore. **b.** a firm landing, jetty, or road across or adjoining the foreshore. **58.** *Brit. Slang.* See **hard labor.** [bef. 900; ME; OE *heard;* c. D *hard,* G *hart,* ON *harthr,* Goth *hardus;* akin to Gk *kratýs* strong, Ionic dial. *kártos* strength (cf. -CRACY)]
—**Syn. 1.** inflexible, rigid, compressed, compact, dense, resisting, adamantine, flinty. See **firm**[1]. **3.** toilsome, burdensome, wearisome, exhausting. HARD, DIFFICULT both describe something resistant to one's efforts or one's endurance. HARD is the general word: *hard times; It was hard to endure the severe weather.* DIFFICULT means not easy, and particularly denotes that which requires special effort or skill: *a difficult task.* **5.** complex, complicated, perplexing, puzzling, intricate, knotty, tough. **6.** arduous, onerous, laborious. **8.** stormy, tempestuous. **10.** severe, rigorous, grinding, cruel, merciless, unsparing. **12.** stern, austere, strict, exacting, relentless, obdurate, adamant; unyielding, unpitying. HARD, CALLOUS, UNFEELING, UNSYMPATHETIC imply a lack of interest in, feeling for, or sympathy with others. HARD implies insensibility, either natural or acquired, so that the plight of others makes no impression on one: *a hard taskmaster.* CALLOUS may mean the same or that one is himself or herself insensitive to hurt as the result of continued repression and indifference: *a callous answer; callous to criticism.* UNFEELING implies natural inability to feel with and for others: *an unfeeling and thoughtless remark.* UNSYMPATHETIC implies an indifference that precludes pity, compassion, or the like: *unsympathetic toward distress.* **13.** incontrovertible. —**Ant. 1.** soft. **3–6.** easy.

hard-and-fast (härd′n fast′, -fäst′), *adj.* strongly binding; not to be set aside or violated: *hard-and-fast rules.* [1865–70] —**hard′-and-fast′ness,** *n.*
—**Syn.** fixed, precise, inflexible, inviolable, rigorous, unambiguous.

har•dang•er (här dang′ər), *n.* embroidery openwork having elaborate symmetrical designs created by blocks of satin stitches within which threads of the embroidery fabric are removed. [1880–85; after *Hardanger,* an area in SW Norway where such embroidery was orig. produced]

hard-ass (härd′as′), *n. Slang (vulgar).* a person who follows rules and regulations meticulously and enforces them without exceptions. Also, **hard′ass′.**

hard-as•set (härd′as′et), *adj.* denoting an asset with intrinsic value: *diamonds and other hard-asset commodities.*

hard•back (härd′bak′), *n., adj.* hardcover. [1740–50; HARD + BACK[1]]

hard•ball (härd′bôl′), *n.* **1.** baseball, as distinguished from softball. **2. play hardball,** to act or work aggressively, competitively, or ruthlessly, as in business or politics. —*adj.* **3.** tough or ruthless: *He wasn't ready for the hardball politics of Washington.* **4.** outspoken, challenging, or difficult: *Reporters asked the president some hardball questions.* [1825–35; HARD + BALL[1]]

hard-bill (härd′bil′), *n. Ornith.* a seed-eating bird.

hard-bit•ten (härd′bit′n), *adj.* **1.** tough; stubborn. **2.** conditioned by battle or struggle: *a hard-bitten army.* **3.** grim or severe in judgment or attitude: *a hard-bitten old teacher.* **4.** hard-boiled (defs. 2, 3). [1775–85]

hard•board (härd′bôrd′, -bōrd′), *n.* a material made from wood fibers compressed into sheets, having many household and industrial uses. [1925–30; HARD + BOARD]

CONCISE ETYMOLOGY KEY: <, descended or borrowed from; >, whence; b., blend of, blended; c., cognate with; cf., compare; deriv., derivative; equiv., equivalent; imit., imitative; obl., oblique; r., replacing; s., stem; sp., spelling, spelled; resp., respelling, respelled; trans., translation; ?, origin unknown; *, unattested; ‡, probably earlier than. See the full key inside the front cover.

hard-boil (härd′boil′), *v.t.* to boil (an egg) until the yolk and white have become firm or solid. [1890–95]

hard-boiled (härd′boild′), *adj.* **1.** *Cookery.* (of an egg) boiled in the shell long enough for the yolk and white to solidify. **2.** *Informal.* tough; unsentimental: *a hard-boiled vice-squad detective.* **3.** marked by a direct, clear-headed approach; realistic: *a hard-boiled appraisal of the foreign situation.* **4.** (of detective fiction) written in a laconic, dispassionate, often ironic style for a realistic, unsentimental effect. [1715–25; 1895–80 for def. 2; HARD + BOILED] —**hard′-boiled′ness,** *n.*

hard•boot (härd′bo͞ot′), *n.* a horse-racing enthusiast. [1920–25; HARD + BOOT[1]]

hard′ bop′, an aggressive, driving, hot style of modern jazz developed by East Coast musicians in the late 1950's as a rejection of the more relaxed, cool style of West Coast jazz. Cf. **bop[1], cool jazz, modern jazz, progressive jazz.**

hard•bound (härd′bound′), *adj.* (of a book) bound with a stiff cover, usually of cloth or leather; casebound. Cf. **paperback.** [1725–35; HARD + BOUND[1]]

hard′ can′dy, candy, often fruit flavored, made by boiling together sugar and corn syrup. [1920–25]

hard′ case′, a rough, hard-bitten person. [1830–40, *Amer.*]

hard-case (härd′kās′), *adj.* rough and hard-bitten: *hard-case juvenile delinquents.* [1915–20]

hard′ cash′, actual money as distinguished from checks or credit.

hard′ cheese′, *Slang.* an unpleasant, difficult, or adverse situation: *It's hard cheese for the unskilled worker these days.* [1875–80]

hard′ ci′der. See under **cider.** [1780–90, *Amer.*]

hard′ clam′, a quahog. [1790–1800]

hard′ coal′, anthracite. [1780–90]

hard-coat•ed (härd′kō′tid), *adj.* having a coarsely textured coat, as a dog. [1895–1900]

hard′ cop′y, 1. copy, as computer output printed on paper, that can be read without using a special device (opposed to *soft copy*). **2.** copy that is finished and ready for the printer. [1885–90, *Amer.*] —**hard′-cop′y,** *adj.*

hard′ core′, 1. the permanent, dedicated, and completely faithful nucleus of a group or movement, as of a political party. **2.** an unyielding or intransigent element in a social or organizational structure, as that part of a group consisting of longtime adherents or those resistant to change. **3.** those whose condition seems to be without hope of remedy or change. [1935–40]

hard-core (härd′kôr′, -kōr′), *adj.* **1.** unswervingly committed; uncompromising; dedicated: *a hard-core segregationist.* **2.** pruriently explicit; graphically depicted: *hard-core pornography.* **3.** being so without apparent change or remedy; chronic: *hard-core inflation; hard-core unemployment.* Cf. **soft-core.** [1950–55]

hard′ court′, a tennis court having a concrete or asphalt surface. Cf. **clay court, grass court.**

hard•cov•er (härd′kuv′ər), *n.* **1.** a book bound in cloth, leather, or the like, over stiff material: *Hardcovers are more durable than paperbacks.* —*adj.* **2.** bound in cloth, leather, or the like, over stiff material: *a hardcover series.* **3.** noting or pertaining to hardcover books: *hardcover sales.* Cf. **paperback.** Also, **hardback.** [1945–50; HARD + COVER] —**hard′cov′ered,** *adj.*

hard′ cur′rency, money that is backed by gold reserves and is readily convertible into foreign currencies.

hard′ din′kum, *Australian Informal.* hard work; a difficult task.

hard′ disk′, *Computers.* See **magnetic disk** (def. 1). [1980–85]

hard′ drug′, *Pharm.* an addicting drug capable of producing severe physical or psychological dependence, as heroin. [1965–70, *Amer.*]

Har•de•ca•nute (här′də kə no͞ot′, -nyo͞ot′), *n.* 1019?–42, king of Denmark 1035–42, king of England 1040–42 (son of Canute). Also, **Hardicanute, Harthacnut.**

hard-edge (härd′ej′), *adj.* of, pertaining to, or characteristic of a style of abstract painting associated with the 1960's and marked chiefly by sharply outlined geometric or nongeometric forms. [1960–65]

hard-edged (härd′ejd′), *adj.* realistic and uncompromising: *a hard-edged documentary.* [1950–55]

hard•en (här′dn), *v.t.* **1.** to make hard or harder: *to harden steel.* **2.** to make pitiless or unfeeling: *to harden one's heart.* **3.** to make rigid or unyielding; stiffen: *The rigors of poverty hardened his personality.* **4.** to strengthen or confirm, esp. with reference to character, intentions, feelings, etc.; reinforce. **5.** to make hardy, robust, or capable of endurance; toughen. **6.** *Mil.* to reinforce the structure of (a military or strategic installation) to protect it from nuclear bombardment. —*v.i.* **7.** to become hard or harder. **8.** to become pitiless or unfeeling. **9.** to become rigid or unyielding; stiffen: *His personality hardened over the years.* **10.** to become confirmed or strengthened: *His resistance hardened.* **11.** to become inured or toughened: *The troops hardened under constant fire.* **12.** *Com.* (of a market, prices, etc.) **a.** to cease to fluctuate; firm: *When the speculators withdrew from the market, the prices hardened.* **b.** to rise higher. [1150–1200; ME; see HARD, -EN[1]] —**hard′en•a•ble,** *adj.* —**hard′en•a•bil′i•ty,** *n.*
—**Syn. 1.** solidify, indurate; petrify, ossify. **4.** fortify, steel, brace, nerve. —**Ant. 1.** soften. **4.** weaken.

Har•den (här′dn), *n.* **Sir Arthur,** 1865–1940, English biochemist: Nobel prize 1929.

Har•den•berg (här′dn berk′), *n.* Novalis.

har•den•ber•gi•a (här′dn bûr′jē ə), any vine or shrub belonging to the genus *Hardenbergia,* of the legume family, native to Australia, having evergreen foliage and long clusters of usually purplish flowers. [< NL (1837), after Franziska von *Hardenberg,* 19th century Austrian noblewoman; see -IA]

hard•ened (här′dnd), *adj.* **1.** made or become hard or harder. **2.** pitiless; unfeeling. **3.** firmly established or unlikely to change; inveterate: *a hardened criminal.* **4.** inured; toughened: *a hardened trooper.* **5.** rigid; unyielding: *a hardened attitude.* **6.** (of a missile base) equipped to launch missiles from underground silos. **7.** (of a missile) capable of being launched from an underground silo. [1325–75; ME; see HARDEN, -ED[2]]

hard•en•er (här′dn ər), *n.* **1.** a person or thing that hardens. **2.** a substance mixed with paint or other protective covering to make the finish harder or more durable. **3.** *Photog.* a chemical used to raise the melting point of an emulsion. [1605–15; HARDEN + -ER[1]]

hard•en•ing (här′dn ing), *n.* **1.** a material that hardens another, as an alloy added to iron to make steel. **2.** the process of becoming hard or rigid. [1620–30; HARDEN + -ING[1]]

hard-fa•vored (härd′fā′vərd), *adj. South Midland U.S.* (of a person) hard-featured. [1505–15]

hard-fea•tured (härd′fē′chərd), *adj.* having stern, harsh, or unattractive features. [1740–50] —**hard′-fea′tured•ness,** *n.*

hard-fist•ed (härd′fis′tid), *adj.* **1.** stingy; miserly; closefisted. **2.** tough-minded; ruthless: *hard-fisted revolutionists.* **3.** having hard or strong hands, as a laborer. Also, **hard′fist′ed.** [1650–60] —**hard′-fist′ed•ness, hard′fist′ed•ness,** *n.*

hard′ goods′. See **durable goods.** Also, **hard′•goods′.** [1930–35]

hard′ ground′, an etching ground applied to the surface of a plate held over a small flame and spread by a dabber or brayer. Cf. **soft ground** (def. 1).

hard•hack (härd′hak′), *n.* **1.** a woolly-leaved North American shrub, *Spiraea tomentosa,* of the rose family, having short, spikelike clusters of rose-colored flowers. **2.** See **shrubby cinquefoil.** [1805–15, *Amer.*; HARD + HACK[1]]

hard-hand•ed (härd′han′did), *adj.* **1.** oppressive or tyrannical; stern or cruel. **2.** having hands hardened by toil. Also, **hard′hand′ed.** [1580–90] —**hard′-hand′ed•ness, hard′hand′ed•ness,** *n.*

hard′ hat′, 1. a protective helmet of metal or plastic, esp. as worn by construction or factory workers. **2.** a uniformed soldier of a regular army, as opposed to a guerrilla. [1925–30]

hard-hat (härd′hat′), *n. Informal.* **1.** a construction worker, esp. a member of a construction workers' union. **2.** a working-class conservative. —*adj.* **3.** pertaining to or characteristic of hard-hats: *enlisting hard-hat support for his policies.* Also, **hard′hat′.** [1960–65]

hard′ head′, *Metall.* semirefined tin containing iron. Also, **hardhead.** [1510–20]

hard•head[1] (härd′hed′), *n.* **1.** a shrewd, practical person. **2.** a blockhead. **3.** a freshwater fish, *Mylopharodon conocephalus,* of California. **4.** the Atlantic croaker. See under **croaker** (def. 2). **5.** See **hardhead sponge. 6. hardheads.** a common knapweed, *Centaurea nigra.* **7.** See **hard head.** [1510–20; HARD + HEAD]

hard•head[2] (härd′hed′), *n.* an alloyed silver coin of Scotland, issued in the 16th and 17th centuries, equal to one and one-half pence and later to twopence. Also called **lion.** [1555–65; perh. (by folk etymology) < F *hardit,* after Philip III, named le *Hardi* the Bold (1245–85), king of France, who first issued the coin]

hard•head•ed (härd′hed′id), *adj.* **1.** not easily moved or deceived; practical; shrewd. **2.** obstinate; stubborn; willful. Also, **hard′-head′ed.** [1575–85] —**hard′head′•ed•ly,** *adv.* —**hard′head′ed•ness,** *n.*
—**Syn. 1.** astute, realistic, pragmatic, cool, down-to-earth.

hard′head sponge′, any of several commercial sponges, as *Spongia officinalis dura,* of the West Indies and Central America, having a harsh, fibrous, resilient skeleton. [1880–85]

hard•heart•ed (härd′här′tid), *adj.* unfeeling; unmerciful; pitiless. [1175–1225; ME *hardherted.* See HARD, -HEARTED] —**hard′heart′ed•ly,** *adv.* —**hard′heart′•ed•ness,** *n.*
—**Syn.** heartless, merciless, mean, unforgiving.

hard-hit•ting (härd′hit′ing), *adj.* **1.** striking or capable of striking with force. **2.** strikingly or effectively forceful: *a hard-hitting exposé.* [1830–40]

Har•di•ca•nute (här′də kə no͞ot′, -nyo͞ot′), *n.* Hardecanute.

har•di•hood (här′dē ho͝od′), *n.* **1.** boldness or daring; courage. **2.** audacity or impudence. **3.** strength; power; vigor: *the hardihood of youth.* **4.** hardy spirit or character; determination to survive; fortitude: *the hardihood of early settlers.* [1625–35; HARDY[1] + -HOOD]

har•di•ly (här′dl ē), *adv.* in a hardy manner: *The plants thrived hardily.* [1175–1225; ME; see HARDY[1], -LY]

har•di•ment (här′dē mənt), *n. Archaic.* hardihood. [1325–75; ME < OF; see HARDY[1], -MENT]

Har•din (här′dn), *n.* **John Wesley,** 1853–95, U.S. outlaw in the West.

har•di•ness (här′dē nis), *n.* **1.** the capacity for enduring or sustaining hardship, privation, etc.; capability of surviving under unfavorable conditions. **2.** courage; boldness; audacity. [1250–1300; ME; see HARDY[1], -NESS]

Har•ding (här′ding), *n.* **1. Chester,** 1792–1866, U.S. portrait painter. **2. Warren G(amaliel),** 1865–1923, 29th president of the U.S. 1921–23. **3.** a male given name.

hard-knock (härd′nok′), *adj.* beset with hardship.

hard′ knocks′, *Informal.* adversity or hardships.

hard′ la′bor, compulsory labor imposed upon criminals in addition to imprisonment, generally not exceeding ordinary labor in severity or amount. [1850–55]

hard-laid (härd′lād′), *adj.* describing a rope the lay of which is at a relatively great angle to its axis; short-laid.

hard′ lens′, a contact lens of rigid plastic or silicon, exerting light pressure on the cornea of the eye, used for correcting various vision problems including astigmatism. Cf. **soft lens.**

hard′ light′, *Cinematog.* directed light, esp. light whose beams are relatively parallel, producing distinct shadows and a harsher modeling effect on the subject.

hard′ line′, an uncompromising or unyielding stand, esp. in politics. [1965–70]

hard-line (härd′līn′), *adj.* adhering rigidly to a dogma, theory, or plan; uncompromising or unyielding: *hard-line union demands.* Also, **hard′line′.** [1960–65, *Amer.*]

hard-lin•er (härd′lī′nər), *n.* a person who adheres rigidly to a dogma, theory, or plan. Also, **hard′lin′er.** [1960–65; HARD-LINE + -ER[1]]

hard′ lines′, *Chiefly Brit. Slang.* tough luck; bad breaks. [1815–25]

hard•ly (härd′lē), *adv.* **1.** only just; almost not; barely: *We had hardly reached the lake when it started raining. hardly any; hardly ever.* **2.** not at all; scarcely: *That report is hardly surprising.* **3.** with little likelihood: *He will hardly come now.* **4.** forcefully or vigorously. **5.** with pain or difficulty. **6.** *Brit.* harshly or severely. **7.** hard. [1175–1225; ME; OE *heardlice.* See HARD, -LY]
—**Syn. 1.** HARDLY, BARELY, SCARCELY imply a narrow margin by which performance was, is, or will be achieved. HARDLY, though often interchangeable with SCARCELY and BARELY, usually emphasizes the idea of the difficulty involved: *We could hardly endure the winter.* BARELY emphasizes the narrowness of the margin of safety, "only just and no more": *We barely succeeded.* SCARCELY implies a very narrow margin, below satisfactory performance: *He can scarcely read.*
—**Usage. 1, 3.** HARDLY, BARELY, and SCARCELY all have a negative connotation, and the use of any of them with a negative like *can't* or *couldn't* is often condemned as a double negative and thus considered nonstandard: *I can't hardly wait.* Such constructions do occur occasionally in the speech of educated persons, often with jocular intent (*You can't hardly get that kind any more*) but are not found in formal speech or writing. When HARDLY in the sense "only just, almost not" is followed by a clause, the usual word to introduce the clause is *when: The telephone had hardly stopped ringing when* (not *than*) *the doorbell rang.* See also **double negative.**

hard′ ma′ple, *Inland North.* the sugar maple, *Acer saccharum.* [1770–80, *Amer.*]

hard′ mass′, 1. *Jewelry.* a hard glass used for imitating gemstones. **2.** (not in technical use) **a.** any glass for imitating gemstones, esp. emerald. **b.** any of certain synthetic gemstones. Also, **hard′ masse′.**

hard•mouthed (härd′mouthd′, -moutht′), *adj.* **1.** of or pertaining to a horse not sensitive to the pressure of a bit. **2.** stubborn; obstinate; self-willed. [1610–20; HARD + MOUTH + -ED[3]]

hard•ness (härd′nis), *n.* **1.** the state or quality of being hard: *the hardness of ice.* **2.** a relative degree or extent of this quality: *wood of a desirable hardness.* **3.** that quality in water that is imparted by the presence of dissolved salts, esp. calcium sulfate or bicarbonate. **4.** unfeelingness or jadedness; callousness. **5.** harshness or austerity, as of a difficult existence. **6.** *South Midland U.S.* ill will; bad feelings: *There's a lot of hardness between those two boys.* **7.** *Mineral.* the comparative ability of a substance to scratch or be scratched by another. Cf. **Mohs scale. 8.** *Metall.* the measured resistance of a metal to indention, abrasion, deformation, or machining. [bef. 900; ME *hardnes,* OE *heardnes.* See HARD, -NESS]

hard′ news′, *Journalism.* serious news of widespread import, concerning politics, foreign affairs, or the like, as distinguished from routine news items, feature stories, or human-interest stories. —**hard′-news′,** *adj.*

hard-nose (härd′nōz′), *n. Slang.* a person who is tough, practical, and unsentimental, esp. in business: *We need a hard-nose to run the department.* Also, **hard′•nose′.**

hard-nosed (härd′nōzd′), *adj. Informal.* hardheaded or tough; unsentimentally practical: *a hard-nosed labor leader.* Also, **hard′nosed′.** [1885–90]
—**Syn.** realistic, down-to-earth; intractable, rigid, stubborn, inflexible.

hard-of-hear•ing (härd′əv hēr′ing), *adj., n.* hearing-impaired. [1555–65]

hard-on (härd′on′, -ôn′), *n., pl.* **-ons.** *Slang (vulgar).* an erection of the penis. [1890–95]

Har•douin-Man•sart (AR dwan män SAR′), *n.* **Jules** (zhyl). See **Mansart, Jules Hardouin-.** Also, **Har•douin-Man•sard′.**

hard′ pal′ate. See under **palate** (def. 1). [1855–60]

hard•pan (härd′pan′), *n.* **1.** any layer of firm detrital matter, as of clay, underlying soft soil. Cf. **caliche, duricrust. 2.** hard, unbroken ground. **3.** the fundamental or basic aspect of anything; solid foundation; underlying reality: *the hardpan of mathematical theory.* [1810–20, *Amer.*; HARD + PAN[1]]

hard′ paste′, true porcelain, made with kaolin, feldspar, quartz, or petuntse. French, ***pâte dure.*** Cf. **soft paste.** [1840–50]

hard′ peach′, *Southern U.S.* a clingstone peach.

hard′ porn′, *Informal.* hard-core pornography. [1970–75]

hard-pressed (härd′prest′), *adj.* heavily burdened or

oppressed, as by overwork or financial difficulties; harried; put-upon. Also, **hard′pressed′.** [1815–25] —**Syn.** assailed, plagued, beset, bedeviled, beleaguered.

hard-put (härd′po͝ot′), *adj.* See **hard** (def. 55). [1890–95]

hard′ rock′, the original form of rock-'n'-roll, basically dependent on a consistently loud and strong beat. Cf. **soft rock.** [1965–70] —**hard′ rock′er.**

hard-rock (härd′rok′), *adj.* (loosely) of or pertaining to igneous or metamorphic rocks, as in mining **(hard′-rock min′ing)** and geology **(hard′-rock geol′ogy).** Cf. **soft-rock geology.** [1920–25]

hard′ rub′ber, rubber vulcanized with a large amount of sulfur, usually 25–35 percent, to render it stiff and comparatively inflexible. [1855–60]

hards (härdz), *n.pl.* the refuse or coarser parts of flax or hemp, separated in hackling. Also, **hurds.** [bef. 900; ME *herdes,* OE *heordan*]

hard′ sauce′, a mixture of butter and confectioners' sugar, often with flavoring and cream. [1895–1900]

hard′ sci′ence, any of the natural or physical sciences, as chemistry, biology, physics, or astronomy, in which aspects of the universe are investigated by means of hypotheses and experiments. Cf. **soft science.**

hard•scrab•ble (härd′skrab′əl), *adj.* providing or yielding meagerly in return for much effort; demanding or unrewarding: *the hardscrabble existence of mountainside farmers.* [1795–1805, *Amer.*; HARD + SCRABBLE]

hard′ sell′, a method of advertising or selling that is direct, forceful, and insistent; high-pressure salesmanship (opposed to *soft sell*). [1950–55, *Amer.*]

hard-sell (härd′sel′), *v.,* **-sold, -sell•ing,** *adj.* —*v.t., v.i.* **1.** to sell or advertise (something) in a forceful and insistent way: *to hard-sell new car models to reluctant buyers.* **2.** to convince (someone) in a forceful and insistent way: *to hard-sell customers on a new product.* —*adj.* **3.** characterized by or promoted through a hard sell: *hard-sell tactics.* [1955–60, *Amer.*]

hard-set (härd′set′), *adj.* **1.** firmly or rigidly set; fixed: *a hard-set smile.* **2.** in a difficult position: *The troops were hard-set before their supplies came.* **3.** determined; obstinate. [1400–50; late ME *harde set*]

hard-shell (härd′shel′), *adj.* Also, **hard′-shelled′. 1.** having a firm, hard shell, as a crab in its normal state; not having recently molted. **2.** rigid or uncompromising. —*n.* **3.** See **hard-shell crab.** [1790–1800]

hard′-shell clam′, quahog. [1810–20, *Amer.*]

hard′-shell crab′, a crab, esp. an edible crab, that has not recently molted and has a hard shell. [1900–05]

hard•ship (härd′ship), *n.* **1.** a condition that is difficult to endure; suffering; deprivation; oppression: *a life of hardship.* **2.** an instance or cause of this; something hard to bear, as a deprivation, lack of comfort, or constant toil or danger: *They faced bravely the many hardships of frontier life.* [1175–1225; ME; see HARD, -SHIP] —**Syn. 1.** trouble, affliction, suffering, misfortune. HARDSHIP, PRIVATION, AUSTERITY refer to a condition hard to endure. HARDSHIP applies to a circumstance in which excessive and painful effort of some kind is required, as enduring acute discomfort from cold, or battling over rough terrain. PRIVATION has particular reference to lack of food, clothing, and other necessities or comforts. AUSTERITY not only includes the ideas of privation and hardship but also implies deliberate control of emotional reactions to these. —**Ant. 1.** ease.

hard′ sign′, 1. the Cyrillic letter Ъ, ъ as used in Russian to indicate that the preceding consonant is not palatalized: not in official use since 1918. **2.** the same symbol used for the back vowel of Old Church Slavonic from which this Russian usage and phenomenon are derived.

hard′ sol′der, a solder fusing at temperatures above 1200°F (650°C). Also called **brazing alloy.** Cf. **soft solder.** [1840–50]

hard-spun (härd′spun′), *adj.* (of yarn) compactly twisted in spinning. [1905–10]

hard•stand (härd′stand′), *n.* a hard-surfaced area on which heavy vehicles or airplanes can be parked. Also, **hard•stand•ing** (härd′stan′ding). [1955–60; HARD + STAND]

hard′ stuff′, *Slang.* **1.** strongly addictive drugs. **2.** liquor with a high alcoholic content; hard liquor. [1950–55]

hard-sur•face (härd′sûr′fis), *v.t.,* **-faced, -fac•ing.** to make the surface of (something) hard or firm, as by compacting or paving it: *to hard-surface a parking area.* [1925–30, *Amer.*]

hard•tack (härd′tak′), *n.* a hard, saltless biscuit, formerly much used aboard ships and for army rations. Also called **pilot biscuit, pilot bread, ship biscuit, ship bread.** [1830–40; HARD + TACK[2]]

hard•tail (härd′tāl′), *n., pl.* **-tails,** (*esp. collectively*) **-tail.** See **blue runner.** [1880–85, *Amer.*; HARD + TAIL[1]]

hard′ tick′, any tick of the family Ixodidae, characterized by a hard shield on the back and mouth parts that project from the head. Cf. **soft tick.**

hard-tick•et (*n.* härd′tik′it; *adj.* härd′tik′it), *n.* **1.** a ticket entitling one to a reserved seat. **2.** an entertainment for which seats are reserved in advance. —*adj.* **3.** of, pertaining to, or designating an entertainment for which tickets are in great demand: *a hard-ticket musical.*

hard′ time′, 1. a period of difficulties or hardship. **2.** *Slang.* time actually served in a prison or other penal institution: *He had merely been fined before, but now was sentenced to 90 days' hard time in the county jail.* **3. give a hard time,** *Informal.* to bother, annoy, or harass: *He gave me a hard time about the money I owe him.* [1905–10]

Hard′ Times′ to′ken, any of a series of U.S. copper tokens, issued 1834–41, bearing a political inscription or advertising message and serving as currency during coin shortages.

hard•top (härd′top′), *n.* **1.** a style of car having a rigid metal top and no center posts between windows. **2.** Also called **hard′top convert′ible.** a similar style of car that is designed to resemble a convertible. [1945–50; HARD + TOP[1]]

hard•wall (härd′wôl′), *n.* a type of gypsum plaster used as a basecoat. [HARD + WALL]

hard•ware (härd′wâr′), *n.* **1.** metalware, as tools, locks, hinges, or cutlery. **2.** the mechanical equipment necessary for conducting an activity, usually distinguished from the theory and design that make the activity possible. **3.** military weapons and combat equipment. **4.** *Slang.* a weapon carried on one's person: *The rougher types were asked to check their hardware at the door.* **5.** *Computers.* the mechanical, magnetic, electronic, and electrical devices comprising a computer system, as the CPU, disk drives, keyboard, or screen. Cf. **software.** [1505–15; 1955–60 for def. 5; HARD + WARE[1]]

hard′ware cloth′, galvanized steel wire screen with a mesh usually between 0.25 and 0.5 in. (0.64 and 1.27 cm), used for coarse sieves, animal cages, and the like.

hard′ware plat′form, a group of compatible computers that can run the same software.

hard′ wa′ter, water that contains magnesium, calcium, or iron salts and therefore forms a soap lather with difficulty.

hard•wear•ing (härd′wâr′ing), *adj.* resistant to extensive wear; durable: *a pair of hardwearing jeans.* [1905–10; HARD + WEARING]

hard′ wheat′, a wheat, as durum wheat, characterized by flinty, dark-colored kernels that yield a flour used in making bread, macaroni, etc. [1805–15]

hard-wired (härd′wīrd′), *adj.* **1.** *Computers.* **a.** built into a computer's hardware and thus not readily changed. **b.** (of a terminal) connected to a computer by a direct circuit rather than through a switching network. **2.** (of electrical or electronic components) connected by hardwiring. **3.** pertaining to or being an intrinsic and relatively unmodifiable behavior pattern: *Every cricket has a hard-wired pattern of chirps.* [1970–75]

hard•wir•ing (härd′wīər′ing), *n.* **1.** a fixed connection between electrical and electronic components and devices by means of wires (as distinguished from a *wireless connection*). **2.** *Computers.* a hard-wired connection between electronic components within a computer system. Also, **hard′-wir′ing.** [1975–80; HARD + WIRING]

hard•wood (härd′wo͝od′), *n.* **1.** the hard, compact wood or timber of various trees, as the oak, cherry, maple, or mahogany. **2.** a tree yielding such wood. —*adj.* **3.** made or constructed of hardwood: *a hardwood floor.* [1560–70; HARD + WOOD[1]]

hard•work•ing (härd′wûr′king), *adj.* industrious; zealous: *a hardworking family man.* [1765–75; HARD + WORKING]

har•dy[1] (här′dē), *adj.,* **-di•er, -di•est. 1.** capable of enduring fatigue, hardship, exposure, etc.; sturdy; strong: *hardy explorers of northern Canada.* **2.** (of plants) able to withstand the cold of winter in the open air. **3.** requiring great physical courage, vigor, or endurance: *the hardiest sports.* **4.** bold or daring; courageous: *hardy soldiers.* **5.** unduly bold; presumptuous; foolhardy. [1175–1225; ME *hardi* < OF, ptp. of **hardir* to harden, make brave < Gmc; cf. Goth *-hardjan,* OHG *hartjan* to harden] —**Syn. 1.** vigorous, robust, hale, stout, sound. **4.** intrepid, resolute, brave. —**Ant. 1.** weak. **4.** timid.

har•dy[2] (här′dē), *n., pl.* **-dies.** a chisel or fuller with a square shank for insertion into a square hole **(har′dy hole′)** in a blacksmith's anvil. [1865–70; HARD + -Y[2]]

Har•dy (här′dē), *n.* **1. Godfrey Harold,** 1877–1947, English mathematician. **2. Oliver,** 1892–1957, U.S. motion-picture comedian. **3. Thomas,** 1840–1928, English novelist and poet.

har′dy agera′tum, the mistflower.

Har′dy-Wein′berg law′ (här′dē wīn′bûrg), *Genetics.* a principle stating that in an infinitely large, randomly mating population in which selection, migration, and mutation do not occur, the frequencies of alleles and genotypes do not change from generation to generation. Also called **binomial law, Har′dy-Wein′berg distribu′tion.** [1945–50; named after English mathematician G. H. HARDY and German physician Wilhelm *Weinberg* (1862–1937), who independently formulated it]

hare (hâr), *n., pl.* **hares,** (*esp. collectively*) **hare,** *v.,* **hared, har•ing.** —*n.* **1.** any rodentlike mammal of the genus *Lepus,* of the family Leporidae, having long ears, a divided upper lip, and long hind limbs adapted for leaping. **2.** any of the larger species of this genus, as distinguished from certain of the smaller ones known as rabbits. **3.** any of various similar animals of the same family. **4.** (*cap.*) *Astron.* the constellation Lepus. **5.** the player pursued in the game of hare and hounds. —*v.i.* **6.** *Chiefly Brit.* to run fast. [bef. 900; ME; OE *hara;* c. Dan *hare;* akin to G *Hase* hare, OE *hasu* gray] —**hare′like′,** *adj.*

hare′ and hounds′, an outdoor game in which certain players, the hares, start off in advance on a long run, scattering small pieces of paper, called the scent, with the other players, the hounds, following the trail so marked in an effort to catch the hares before they reach a designated point. Also called **paper chase.** [1835–45]

hare•bell (hâr′bel′), *n.* **1.** a low plant, *Campanula rotundifolia,* of the bellflower family, having narrow leaves and blue, bell-shaped flowers. **2.** a plant, *Endymion nonscriptus,* of the lily family, having long, one-sided clusters of bell-shaped flowers. [1350–1400; ME; see HARE, BELL[1]]

hare•brained (hâr′brānd′), *adj.* giddy; reckless. Also, **hairbrained.** [1545–55; HARE + BRAINED] —**hare′•brained′ly,** *adv.* —**hare′brained′ness,** *n.* —**Syn.** rattlebrained, scatterbrained, half-baked, dimwitted.

ha•reem (hä rēm′), *n.* harem.

Ha•re Krish•na (här′ē krish′nə, har′ē), a religious sect based on Vedic scriptures, whose followers engage in joyful congregational chanting of Krishna's name: founded in the U.S. in 1966. [from chanted phrase *Hare Krishna!* < Hindi *hare kṛṣṇā* O Krishna!]

hare•lip (hâr′lip′), *n.* **1.** a congenitally deformed lip, usually the upper one, in which there is a vertical fissure causing it to resemble the cleft lip of a hare. **2.** the deformity itself. Also called **cleft lip.** [1560–70; HARE + LIP] —**hare′lipped′,** *adj.*

har•em (hâr′əm, har′-), *n.* **1.** the part of a Muslim palace or house reserved for the residence of women. **2.** the women in a Muslim household, including the mother, sisters, wives, concubines, daughters, entertainers, and servants. **3.** *Animal Behav.* a social group of females, as elephant seals, accompanied or followed by one fertile male who denies other males access to the group. **4.** *Facetious or Offensive.* a group of women associated in any way with one man or household: *Father joked that he had a harem of five daughters.* Also, **haram, hareem, harim.** [1625–35; < Ar *harīm* harem, lit., forbidden]

har′em pants′, women's pants usually made of soft fabric and having full legs gathered at the ankle. [1950–55]

hare's′-foot fern′ (hârz′fo͝ot′), a fern, *Polypodium aureum,* of tropical America, having a brown, scaly rootstock and green or deep bluish-green fronds. Also called **golden polypody, rabbit's-foot fern.** [1865–70]

hare•wood (hâr′wo͝od′), *n.* the greenish-gray wood of the sycamore maple, used for making furniture. [1655–65; var. of obs. *airewood,* equiv. to obs. *aire* harewood (< dial. G *Ahre* << VL **acre,* L *acer* maple) + WOOD[1]]

Har•gei•sa (här gā′sə), *n.* a city in NW Somalia. 70,000.

Har•greaves (här′grēvz), *n.* **James,** died 1778, English inventor of spinning machinery.

Ha•ri•a•na (hur′ē ä′nə), *n.* Haryana.

har•i•cot[1] (har′ə kō′), *n.* **1.** any plant of the genus *Phaseolus,* esp. *P. vulgaris,* the kidney bean. **2.** the seed or unripe pod of any of these plants, eaten as a vegetable. [1605–15; < F, earlier *feve d'aricot,* perh. ult. < Nahuatl *ayacohtli, ayecohtli* bean, but influenced by *haricot* stew (see HARICOT[2]), in which such beans can be an ingredient]

har•i•cot[2] (har′ə kō′), *n.* a stew of lamb or mutton with turnips and potatoes. Also, **halicot.** [1605–15; < F; MF *hericot* (*de mouton*), prob. n. deriv. (perh. influenced by *écot* lopped branch) of OF *harigoter* to tear into scraps, perh. deriv., with v. suffix *-oter,* of Old Low Franconian **hariôn* to fight, make war on (see HARRY)]

ha•ri•cot vert (A RĒ KŌ VER′), *pl.* ***ha•ri•cots verts*** (A RĒ KŌ VER′). *French.* See **green bean.**

Har•i•jan (har′i jan′), *n., pl.* **-jans,** (*esp. collectively*) **-jan.** (*often l.c.*) *Hinduism.* **1.** untouchable (def. 5). **2.** a member of the group formerly known as untouchables in India: a term used by Mohandas K. Gandhi. [1930–35; < Neo-Skt *harijana* person of Hari (a name for Vishnu), hence, in Gandhi's conception, a child of God]

ha•ri-ka•ri (här′ē kär′ē, har′ē kar′ē), *n.* hara-kiri.

ha•rim (hâr′əm, har′-, ha rēm′), *n.* harem.

Har•in•gey (har′ing gā′), *n.* a borough of Greater London, England. 232,800.

hark (härk), *v.i.* **1.** to listen attentively; hearken. —*v.t.* **2.** *Archaic.* to listen to; hear. **3. hark back, a.** (of hounds) to return along the course in order to regain a lost scent. **b.** to return to a previous subject or point; revert: *He kept harking back to his early days in vaudeville.* —*n.* **4.** a hunter's shout to hounds, as to encourage them in following the scent. [1175–1225; ME *herken,* earlier *herkien,* OE **heorcian;* c. OFris *herkia, harkia;* akin to MD *harken,* MHG, G *horchen.* See HEARKEN; HEAR] —**Syn. 3b.** refer, allude; regress, retrogress.

hark•en (här′kən), *v.i., v.t.* hearken. —**hark′en•er,** *n.*

Har•kins (här′kinz), *n.* **William Draper,** 1873–1951, U.S. chemist.

Hark•ness (härk′nis), *n.* **Edward Stephan,** 1874–1940, U.S. philanthropist.

Har•lan (här′lən), *n.* **1. John Marshall,** 1833–1911, U.S. jurist: associate justice of the U.S. Supreme Court 1877–1911. **2.** his grandson, **John Marshall,** 1899–1971, U.S. jurist: associate justice of the U.S. Supreme Court 1955–71.

Har′le•ian Li′brary (här′lē ən), a large library of manuscripts collected by the British statesman Robert Harley and his son and now housed in the British Museum. [< NL *Harleiānus* of, belonging to (Robert) HARLEY; see -AN]

Har•lem (här′ləm), *n.* **1.** a section of New York City, in the NE part of Manhattan. **2.** a tidal river in New York City, between the boroughs of Manhattan and the Bronx, which, with Spuyten Duyvil Creek, connects the Hudson and East rivers. 8 mi. (13 km) long.

Har•lem•ite (här′lə mīt′), *n.* a native or inhabitant of Harlem. [1885–90; HARLEM + -ITE[1]]

Har′lem Ren′aissance, a renewal and flourishing of black literary and musical culture during the years after World War I in the Harlem section of New York City. Also called **Black Renaissance.**

har•le•quin (här′lə kwin, -kin), *n.* **1.** (*often cap.*) a comic character in commedia dell'arte and the harlequinade, usually masked, dressed in multicolored, diamond-patterned tights, and carrying a wooden sword or magic wand. **2.** a buffoon. **3.** any of various small snakes having bright diamond-pattern scales. —*adj.* **4.** fancifully varied in color, decoration, etc.: *harlequin pants.* **5.** resembling a harlequin's mask: *harlequin glasses.* [1580–90; < F, MF (*h*)*arlequin,* semantically (and in part phonetically) < It *arlecchino* < MF, phonetically continuing OF **harlequin, halequin* a malevolent spirit (cf. *mesniee Hellequin* a troop of demonic horsemen, lit., Hellequin's escort), prob. < ME **Herla king,* OE **Her(e)la cyning* King Herle, presumably a legendary figure, rendered in AL as *Herla rex;* cf. OHG *Herilo* a personal name, deriv. of *heri* armed forces] —**har′le•quin•ism,** *n.*

Harlequin (def. 1)

har•le•quin•ade (här′lə kwi nād′, -ki-), *n.* **1.** a pantomime, farce, or similar play in which Harlequin plays the principal part. **2.** buffoonery. [1770–80; < F *arlequinade.* See HARLEQUIN, -ADE[1]]

har′lequin bug′, a black stink bug, *Murgantia histrionica,* having red and yellow markings, that feeds on cabbages and other cruciferous plants. Also called **cabbage bug, calicoback, calico bug, har′lequin cab′bage bug′.** [1865–70, *Amer.*]

har′lequin duck′, a small diving duck, *Histrionicus histrionicus,* of North America and Iceland, the male of which has bluish-gray plumage marked with black, white, and chestnut. [1765–75]

har•le•quin•esque (här′lə kwi nesk′, -ki-), *adj.* in the manner of a harlequin. [1880–85; HARLEQUIN + -ESQUE]

har′lequin o′pal, a variety of opal having patches of various colors. [1870–75]

har′lequin ta′ble, a writing or dressing table having a central set of compartments that rise when drop leaves are raised.

Har•ley (här′lē), *n.* **Robert, 1st Earl of Oxford,** 1661–1724, British statesman.

Har′ley Street′, a street in London, England: noted for the eminent doctors who have offices there.

Har•lin•gen (här′lin jən), *n.* a city in S Texas. 43,543.

har•lot (här′lət), *n.* a prostitute; whore. [1175–1225; ME: young idler, rogue < OF *herlot,* of obscure orig.]

har•lot•ry (här′lə trē), *n.* prostitution. [1275–1325; ME *harlotrie.* See HARLOT, -RY]

Har•low (här′lō), *n.* **1. Jean,** 1911–37, U.S. motion-picture actress. **2.** a town in W Essex, in SE England. 80,300. **3.** a male given name.

harm (härm), *n.* **1.** physical injury or mental damage; hurt: *to do him bodily harm.* **2.** moral injury; evil; wrong. —*v.t.* **3.** to do or cause harm to; injure; damage; hurt: *to harm one's reputation.* [bef. 900; ME; OE *hearm;* c. G *Harm,* ON *harmr*] —**harm′er,** *n.*
—**Syn. 1, 2.** See **damage. 3.** maltreat, abuse.
—**Ant. 1.** benefit. **3.** help.

HARM (härm), *n. Mil.* a U.S. air-to-surface missile designed to detect and destroy radar sites by homing on their emissions. [*H*(*igh-speed*) *A*(*nti*) *R*(*adiation*) *M*(*issile*)]

har•mat•tan (här′mə tan′), *n.* (on the west coast of Africa) a dry, parching land breeze, charged with dust. [1665–75; said to be < Twi *haramata*]

harm•ful (härm′fəl), *adj.* causing or capable of causing harm; injurious: *a harmful idea; a harmful habit.* [bef. 1000; ME; OE *hearmful.* See HARM, -FUL] —**harm′ful•ly,** *adv.* —**harm′ful•ness,** *n.*
—**Syn.** hurtful, detrimental, damaging, deleterious.
—**Ant.** beneficial.

harm•less (härm′lis), *adj.* **1.** without the power or desire to do harm; innocuous: *He looks mean but he's harmless; a harmless Halloween prank.* **2.** without injury; unhurt; unharmed. **3. hold harmless,** *Law.* to relieve from responsibility or liability for any damage or loss. Also, **save harmless.** [1250–1300; ME. See HARM, -LESS] —**harm′less•ly,** *adv.* —**harm′less•ness,** *n.*
—**Syn. 1.** inoffensive, mild, innocent, unobjectionable, benign.

Har•mo•ni•a (här mō′nē ə), *n. Class. Myth.* the daughter of Ares and Aphrodite and wife of Cadmus.

har•mon•ic (här mon′ik), *adj.* **1.** pertaining to harmony, as distinguished from melody and rhythm. **2.** marked by harmony; in harmony; concordant; consonant. **3.** *Physics.* of, pertaining to, or noting a series of oscillations in which each oscillation has a frequency that is an integral multiple of the same basic frequency. **4.** *Math.* **a.** (of a set of values) related in a manner analogous to the frequencies of tones that are consonant. **b.** capable of being represented by sine and cosine functions. **c.** (of a function) satisfying the Laplace equation. —*n.* **5.** *Music.* overtone (def. 1). **6.** *Physics.* a single oscillation whose frequency is an integral multiple of the fundamental frequency. [1560–70; < L *harmonicus* < Gk *harmonikós* musical, suitable. See HARMONY, -IC] —**har•mon′i•cal•ly,** *adv.* —**har•mon′i•cal•ness,** *n.*

harmonica (def. 1)

har•mon•i•ca (här mon′i kə), *n.* **1.** Also called **mouth organ.** a musical wind instrument consisting of a small rectangular case containing a set of metal reeds connected to a row of holes, over which the player places the mouth and exhales and inhales to produce the tones. **2.** any of various percussion instruments that use graduated bars of metal or other hard material as sounding elements. [n. use of fem. of L *harmonicus* HARMONIC; in the form *armonica* (< It < L) applied by Benjamin Franklin in 1762 to a set of musical glasses; later used of other instruments]

harmon′ic anal′ysis, *Math.* **1.** the calculation of Fourier series and their generalization. **2.** the study of Fourier series and their generalization. Also called **Fourier analysis.** [1865–70]

harmon′ic con′jugates, *Math.* two points whose cross ratio with two specified points equals −1. [1880–85]

harmon′ic in′terval. See under **interval** (def. 6).

harmon′ic law′, *Astron.* See under **Kepler's laws.**

harmon′ic mean′, *Statistics.* the mean obtained by taking the reciprocal of the arithmetic mean of the reciprocals of a set of nonzero numbers. [1880–85]

harmon′ic mi′nor scale′, *Music.* See **minor scale** (def. 1). [1880–85]

harmon′ic mo′tion, *Physics.* periodic motion consisting of one or more vibratory motions that are symmetric about a region of equilibrium, as the motion of a vibrating string of a musical instrument. [1865–70]

har•mon•i•con (här mon′i kən), *n.* **1.** harmonica (def. 1). **2.** orchestrion. [1815–25; n. use of Gk *harmonikón,* neut. of *harmonikós* HARMONIC]

harmon′ic progres′sion, *Math.* a series of numbers the reciprocals of which are in arithmetic progression. [1865–70]

har•mon•ics (här mon′iks), *n. Music.* **1.** (*used with a singular v.*) the science of musical sounds. **2.** (*used with a plural v.*) the partials or overtones of a fundamental tone. Cf. **overtone** (def. 1). **3.** (*used with a plural v.*) the flageoletlike tones of a string, as a violin string, made to vibrate so as to bring out an overtone. [1700–10; see HARMONIC, -ICS]

harmon′ic se′ries, *Math.* **1.** a series in which the reciprocals of the terms form an arithmetic progression. **2.** the divergent infinite series, $1 + \frac{1}{2} + \frac{1}{3} + \frac{1}{4} + \frac{1}{5} + \ldots$ [1865–70]

harmon′ic tone′, *Music.* a tone produced by suppressing the fundamental tone and bringing into prominence one of its overtones.

har•mo•ni•ous (här mō′nē əs), *adj.* **1.** marked by agreement in feeling, attitude, or action: *a harmonious group.* **2.** forming a pleasingly consistent whole; congruous: *harmonious colors.* **3.** pleasant to the ear; tuneful; melodious. [1520–30; < Gk *harmónios* melodious, lit., fitting. See HARMONY, -OUS] —**har•mo′ni•ous•ly,** *adv.* —**har•mo′ni•ous•ness,** *n.*
—**Syn. 1.** amicable, congenial; sympathetic. **2.** concordant, congruent, consonant, consistent. —**Ant. 1, 3.** discordant.

har•mo•nist (här′mə nist), *n.* **1.** a person skilled in harmony. **2.** a person who makes a harmony, as of the Gospels. [1560–70; HARMON(Y) + -IST]

Har•mo•nist (här′mə nist), *n.* a member of a celibate religious sect that emigrated from Germany to Pennsylvania in 1803. Also, **Har′mo•nite′.** Also called **Rappist, Rappite.** [1815–25; after *Harmony,* town in Pennsylvania; see -IST]

har•mo•nis•tic (här′mə nis′tik), *adj.* **1.** pertaining to a harmonist or harmony. **2.** pertaining to the collation and harmonizing of parallel passages, as of the Gospels. [1855–60; HARMON(Y) + -ISTIC] —**har′mo•nis′ti•cal•ly,** *adv.*

har•mo•ni•um (här mō′nē əm), *n.* an organlike keyboard instrument with small metal reeds and a pair of bellows operated by the player's feet. [1840–50; Latinization of Gk *harmónion,* neut. of *harmónios* HARMONIOUS]

har•mo•nize (här′mə nīz′), *v.,* **-nized, -niz•ing.** —*v.t.* **1.** to bring into harmony, accord, or agreement: *to harmonize one's views with the new situation.* **2.** *Music.* to accompany with appropriate harmony. —*v.i.* **3.** to be in agreement in action, sense, or feeling: *Though of different political parties, all the delegates harmonized on civil rights.* **4.** to sing in harmony. Also, *esp. Brit.,* **har′mo•nise′.** [1475–85; earlier *armonise* < MF *harmoniser.* See HARMONY, -IZE] —**har′mo•niz′a•ble,** *adj.* —**har′mo•ni•za′tion,** *n.* —**har′mo•niz′er,** *n.*
—**Syn. 1.** reconcile, compose. **3.** agree, accord.

har•mo•ny (här′mə nē), *n., pl.* **-nies. 1.** agreement; accord; harmonious relations. **2.** a consistent, orderly, or pleasing arrangement of parts, congruity. **3.** *Music.* **a.** any simultaneous combination of tones. **b.** the simultaneous combination of tones, esp. when blended into chords pleasing to the ear; chordal structure, as distinguished from melody and rhythm. **c.** the science of the structure, relations, and practical combination of chords. **4.** an arrangement of the contents of the Gospels, either of all four or of the first three, designed to show their parallelism, mutual relations, and differences. [1350–1400; ME *armonye* < MF < L *harmonia* < Gk *harmonía* joint, framework, agreement, harmony, akin to *hárma* chariot, *harmós* joint, *ararískein* to join together]
—**Syn. 1.** concord, unity, peace, amity, friendship. **2.** consonance, conformity, correspondence, consistency. See **symmetry. 3.** HARMONY, MELODY in music suggest a combination of sounds from voices or musical instruments. HARMONY is the blending of simultaneous sounds of different pitch or quality, making chords: *harmony in part singing; harmony between violins and horns.* MELODY is the rhythmical combination of successive sounds of various pitch, making up the tune or air: *a tuneful melody to accompany cheerful words.*

har•most (här′most), *n.* a person serving the ancient Spartans as governor of a subject or conquered town. [1765–75; < Gk *harmostḗs,* deriv. of *harmózein* to regulate, govern, join]

har•mo•tome (här′mə tōm′), *n.* a zeolite mineral related to stilbite, occurring in twinned crystals. [1795–1805; < F < Gk *harmó(s)* joint + *-tomos* -TOME]

Harms•worth (härmz′wûrth), *n.* **1. Alfred Charles William, Viscount Northcliffe,** 1865–1922, English journalist, publisher, and politician. **2.** his brother, **Harold Sidney, 1st Viscount Roth•er•mere** (roth′ər mēr′), 1868–1940, English publisher and politician.

Har•nack (här′näk), *n.* **A•dolf von** (ä′dôlf fən), 1851–1930, German Protestant theologian, born in Estonia.

har•ness (här′nis), *n.* **1.** the combination of straps, bands, and other parts forming the working gear of a draft animal. Cf. **yoke**[1] (def. 1). **2.** (on a loom) the frame containing heddles through which the warp is drawn and which, in combination with another such frame or other frames, forms the shed and determines the woven pattern. **3.** the equipment, as straps, bolts, or gears, by which a large bell is mounted and rung. **4.** *Elect.* See **wiring harness. 5.** armor for persons or horses. **6. in double harness.** See **double harness** (def. 2). **7. in harness, a.** engaged in one's usual routine of work: *After his illness he longed to get back in harness.* **b.** together as cooperating partners or equals: *Joe and I worked in harness on our last job.* —*v.t.* **8.** to put a harness on (a horse, donkey, dog, etc.); attach by a harness, as to a vehicle. **9.** to bring under conditions for effective use; gain control over for a particular end: *to harness water power; to harness the energy of the sun.* **10.** *Archaic.* to array in armor or equipments of war. [1250–1300; ME *harneis, herneis* < OF *herneis* baggage, equipment < ON **hernest* provisions for an armed force, equiv. to *herr* army (cf. HARBOR, HERALD) + *nest* provisions for a journey] —**har′ness•er,** *n.* —**har′ness•less,** *adj.* —**har′ness•like′,** *adj.*
—**Syn. 9.** control, manage, utilize, exploit.

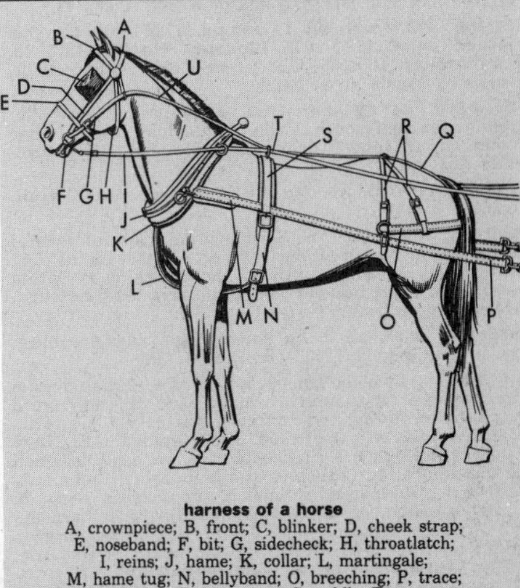

harness of a horse
A, crownpiece; B, front; C, blinker; D, cheek strap; E, noseband; F, bit; G, sidecheck; H, throatlatch; I, reins; J, hame; K, collar; L, martingale; M, hame tug; N, bellyband; O, breeching; P, trace; Q, crupper; R, hip straps; S, saddle; T, terret; U, checkrein

har′nessed an′telope, any African antelope of the genus *Tragelaphus,* esp. the bushbuck, having the body marked with white stripes and spots that resemble a harness, and, in the male, long, gently spiraling horns. [1780–90]

har′ness eye′, *Textiles.* the eyelet on a heddle or on harness cords. Cf. **mail**[2] (def. 3).

har′ness hitch′, a hitch forming a loop around a rope, esp. one formed at the end of a bowline.

har′ness horse′, **1.** a horse used for pulling vehicles. **2.** a horse used in harness racing. [1885–90]

har′ness race′, a trotting or pacing race for Standardbred horses harnessed to sulkies. [1900–05] —**har′ness rac′ing.**

Har•nett (här′nit), *n.* **William Michael,** 1848–92, U.S. painter.

Har′ney Peak′ (här′nē), a mountain in SW South Dakota: the highest peak in the Black Hills. 7242 ft. (2207 m).

Har•old (har′əld), *n.* a male given name.

Harold I, (*"Harefoot"*) died 1040, king of England 1035–40 (son of Canute).

Harold II, 1022?–66, king of England 1066: defeated by

William the Conqueror at the Battle of Hastings (son of Earl Godwin).

ha•ro•seth (*Seph.* KHä rô′set; *Ashk.* KHä rō′sis), *n. Hebrew.* a mixture of chopped nuts and apples, wine, and spices that is eaten at the Seder meal on Passover: traditionally regarded as symbolic of the mortar used by Israelite slaves in Egypt. Also, ***ha•ro′set, charoseth, charoset.*** [*ḥărōseth,* akin to *ḥarsith* pottery clay]

Ha•roun-al-Ra•schid (hä ro͞on′äl rä shēd′; *Arab.* hä-ro͞on′är′rä shēd′), *n.* See **Harun al-Rashid.**

harp (härp), *n.* **1.** a musical instrument consisting of a triangular frame formed by a soundbox, a pillar, and a curved neck, and having strings stretched between the soundbox and the neck that are plucked with the fingers. **2.** anything that resembles this instrument, esp. in having a row of parallel strings or wires, as various mechanical devices or kitchen implements for slicing cheese. **3.** a vertical metal frame shaped to bend around the bulb in a standing lamp and used to support a lamp shade. **4.** *Slang (disparaging and offensive).* a person of Irish birth or descent. **5.** Also called **harper.** any of several English coins issued for use in Ireland during the 16th and 17th centuries, bearing the figure of a harp on the reverse. **6.** *South Midland and Southern U.S.* a mouth harp; harmonica. —*v.i.* **7.** to play on a harp. **8. harp on** or **upon,** to dwell on persistently or tediously in speaking or writing: *He was always harping on the importance of taking vitamin supplements.* [bef. 900; ME *harpe,* OE *hearpe;* c. D *harp,* G *Harfe,* ON *harpa*] —**harp′like′,** *adj.*

harp (def. 1)

harp•er (här′pər), *n.* **1.** a person who plays the harp. **2.** a person who harps on a subject. **3.** *Numis.* harp (def. 5). [bef. 900; ME; OE *hearpere.* See HARP, -ER¹]

Har•per (här′pər), *n.* **1. James,** 1795–1869, and his brothers **John,** 1797–1875, **(Joseph) Wesley,** 1801–70, and **Fletcher,** 1806–77, U.S. printers and publishers. **2.** a male or female given name.

Har′pers Fer′ry (här′pərz), a town in NE West Virginia at the confluence of the Shenandoah and Potomac rivers: site of John Brown's raid 1859. 361. Also, **Har′per's Fer′ry.**

Har′per Woods′, a city in SE Michigan, near Detroit. 16,361.

harp•ing (här′ping), *n. Shipbuilding.* any of several horizontal members at the ends of a vessel for holding cant frames in position until the shell planking or plating is attached. Also, **har•pin** (här′pin), **harp•ins** (här′pinz). [1620–30; perh. HARP + -ING¹]

harp•ist (här′pist), *n.* a person who plays the harp, esp. professionally. [1605–15; HARP + -IST]

har•poon (här po͞on′), *n.* **1.** a barbed, spearlike missile attached to a rope, and thrown by hand or shot from a gun, used for killing and capturing whales and large fish. **2.** (*cap.*) *Mil.* a jet-powered, radar-guided U.S. Navy cruise missile with a high explosive warhead designed for use against surface ships and launchable from a surface vessel, submerged submarine, or aircraft. —*v.t.* **3.** to strike, catch, or kill with or as if with a harpoon. [1590–1600; < D *harpoen* << OF *harpon* a clasp, brooch, equiv. to *harp-* (< L *harpē* < Gk: hook) + *-on* dim. suffix] —**har•poon′er,** *n.* —**har•poon′like′,** *adj.*

harpoon′ gun′, a small cannon for shooting harpoons. [1810–20]

harp′ seal′, a northern earless seal, *Pagophilus groenlandicus,* with pale-yellow fur darkening to gray with age, of coasts, drifting ice, and seas of the North Atlantic Ocean, hunted for its fur. [1775–85; so called from the harplike shape of markings on the backs of adults]

harp•si•chord (härp′si kôrd′), *n.* a keyboard instrument, precursor of the piano, in which the strings are plucked by leather or quill points connected with the keys, in common use from the 16th to the 18th century, and revived in the 20th. [1605–15; < NL *harpichordium* (with intrusive *-s-* of obscure orig.). See HARP, -I-, CHORD¹] —**harp′si•chord′ist,** *n.*

harpsichord

CONCISE ETYMOLOGY KEY: <, descended or borrowed from; >, whence; b., blend of, blended; c., cognate with; cf., compare; deriv., derivative; equiv., equivalent; imit., imitative; obl., oblique; r., replacing; s., stem; sp., spelling, spelled; resp., respelling, respelled; trans., translation; ?, origin unknown; *, unattested; ‡, probably earlier than. See the full key inside the front cover.

Har•py (här′pē), *n., pl.* **-pies. 1.** *Class. Myth.* a ravenous, filthy monster having a woman's head and a bird's body. **2.** (*l.c.*) a scolding, nagging, bad-tempered woman; shrew. **3.** (*l.c.*) a greedy, predatory person. [< L *Harpyia,* sing. of *Harpyiae* < Gk *Hárpyiai* (pl.), lit., snatchers, akin to *harpázein* to snatch away] —**harp′y•like′,** *adj.*

har′py ea′gle, a large, powerful eagle, *Harpia harpyja,* of tropical America: an endangered species. [1820–30]

har•que•bus (här′kwə bəs), *n., pl.* **-bus•es.** any of several small-caliber long guns operated by a matchlock or wheel-lock mechanism, dating from about 1400. Also, **har′que•buse, har′que•buss, arquebus.** Also called **hackbut, hagbut.** [1525–35; < MF *harquebusche* (with intrusive *-r-*) < MD *hākebusse,* equiv. to *hāke* hook + *busse* gun (lit., box) < LL *buxis* for L *buxus* BOX¹]

har•que•bus•ier (här′kwə bə sēr′), *n.* a soldier armed with a harquebus. Also, **arquebusier.** [1540–50; < MF; see HARQUEBUS, -IER²]

Har•rar (här′ər), *n.* Harar.

har•ri•dan (här′i dn), *n.* a scolding, vicious woman; hag; shrew. [1690–1700; perh. alter. of F *haridelle* thin, worn-out horse, large, gaunt woman (compared with the initial element of *haras* stud farm, though derivation is unclear)]
—**Syn.** nag, virago, scold.

har•ri•er¹ (har′ē ər), *n.* **1.** a person who or thing that harries. **2.** any of several short-winged hawks of the genus *Circus* that hunt over meadows and marshes and prey on reptiles and small birds and mammals. **3.** (*cap.*) *Mil.* a one- or two-seat British-American fighter, both an attack and a reconnaissance aircraft, featuring a turbofan engine with a directable thrust that enables it to land and take off vertically. [1550–60; HARRY + -ER¹]

har•ri•er² (har′ē ər), *n.* **1.** one of a breed of medium-sized hounds, used, usually in packs, in hunting. **2.** a cross-country runner. [1535–45; special use of HARRIER¹, by assoc. with HARE]

Har•ri•et (har′ē ət), *n.* a female given name, form of **Harry.** Also, **Har′ri•ette, Har•ri•et•ta** (har′ē et′ə).

Har•ri•man (har′ə mən), *n.* **1. Edward Henry,** 1848–1909, U.S. financier and railroad magnate. **2.** his son, **W(illiam) A•ve•rell** (ā′vər əl), 1891–1986, U.S. diplomat: governor of New York 1954–58.

Har•ris (har′is), *n.* **1. Benjamin,** c1660–c1720, English journalist who published the first newspaper in America 1690. **2. Frank,** 1856–1931, U.S. writer, born in Ireland. **3. Joel Chan•dler** (chan′dlər, chän′-), 1848–1908, U.S. journalist, novelist, and short-story writer: creator of Uncle Remus. **4. Julie,** born 1925, U.S. actress. **5. Louis,** born 1921, U.S. public-opinion pollster and columnist. **6. Roy,** 1898–1979, U.S. composer. **7. Thaddeus William,** 1795–1856, U.S. entomologist: pioneer in applied entomology. **8.** a male given name.

Har•ris•burg (har′is bûrg′), *n.* a city in and the capital of Pennsylvania, in the S part, on the Susquehanna River. 53,264.

Har•ri•son (har′ə sən), *n.* **1. Benjamin,** 1726?–91, American political leader (father of William Henry Harrison). **2. Benjamin,** 1833–1901, twenty-third president of the U.S. 1889–93 (grandson of William Henry Harrison). **3. Peter,** 1716–75, English architect in the U.S. **4. William Henry,** 1773–1841, U.S. general: ninth president of the U.S. 1841. **5.** a city in SE New York. 23,046. **6.** a town in W Pennsylvania. 13,252. **7.** a town in NE New Jersey. 12,242. **8.** a male given name.

Har•ri•son•burg (har′ə sən bûrg′), *n.* a city in N Virginia. 19,671.

Har′rison red′, 1. a pigment consisting of a paratoluidine toner, characterized by its brilliant red color and tendency to bleed. **2.** pimento (def. 3). [perh. after B. *Harrison* (d. 1929), American artist]

Har′ris Tweed′, *Trademark.* a brand of heavy, handwoven woolen fabric made in the Outer Hebrides.

Har•ro•vi•an (hə rō′vē ən), *adj.* **1.** of or pertaining to Harrow. —*n.* **2.** a pupil or former pupil of Harrow. [1860–65; < NL *Harrovi(a)* Harrow + -AN]

har•row¹ (har′ō), *n.* **1.** an agricultural implement with spikelike teeth or upright disks, drawn chiefly over plowed land to level it, break up clods, root up weeds, etc. —*v.t.* **2.** to draw a harrow over (land). **3.** to disturb keenly or painfully; distress the mind, feelings, etc., of. —*v.i.* **4.** to become broken up by harrowing, as soil. [1250–1300; ME *harwe;* akin to ON *herfi* harrow, D *hark* rake, Gk *krṓpion* sickle] —**har′row•er,** *n.*

har•row² (har′ō), *v.t. Archaic.* **1.** to ravish; violate; despoil. **2.** harry (def. 2). **3.** (of Christ) to descend into (hell) to free the righteous held captive. [bef. 1000; ME *harwen, herwen,* OE *hergian* to HARRY] —**har′row•ment,** *n.*

Har•row (har′ō), *n.* **1.** a borough of Greater London, in SE England. 201,300. **2.** a boarding school for boys, founded in 1571 at Harrow-on-the-Hill, an urban district near London, England.

har•row•ing (har′ō ing), *adj.* extremely disturbing or distressing; grievous: *a harrowing experience.* [1800–10; HARROW¹ + -ING²] —**har′row•ing•ly,** *adv.*
—**Syn.** painful, agonizing, tormenting, heartbreaking.

har•rumph (hə rumf′), *v.i.* **1.** to clear the throat audibly in a self-important manner: *The professor harrumphed good-naturedly.* **2.** to express oneself gruffly. [1935–40; imit.]

har•ry (har′ē), *v.,* **-ried, -ry•ing.** —*v.t.* **1.** to harass, annoy, or prove a nuisance to by or as if by repeated attacks; worry: *He was harried by constant doubts.* **2.** to ravage, as in war; devastate: *The troops harried the countryside.* —*v.i.* **3.** to make harassing incursions. [bef. 900; ME *herien,* OE *her(g)ian* (deriv. of *here* army); c. G *verheeren,* ON *herja* to harry, lay waste]
—**Syn. 1.** molest, plague, trouble. **2.** plunder, strip, rob, pillage.

Har•ry (har′ē), *n.* a male given name, form of **Harold** or **Henry.**

harsh (härsh), *adj.* **1.** ungentle and unpleasant in action or effect: *harsh treatment; harsh manners.* **2.** grim or unpleasantly severe; stern; cruel; austere: *a harsh life; a harsh master.* **3.** physically uncomfortable; desolate; stark: *a harsh land.* **4.** unpleasant to the ear; grating; strident: *a harsh voice; a harsh sound.* **5.** unpleasantly rough, ragged, or coarse to the touch: *a harsh surface.* **6.** jarring to the eye or to the esthetic sense; unrefined; crude; raw: *harsh colors.* **7.** unpleasant to the taste or sense of smell; bitter; acrid: *a harsh flavor; a harsh odor.* [1250–1300; ME *harsk;* c. G *harsch,* Dan *harsk* rancid] —**harsh′ly,** *adv.* —**harsh′ness,** *n.*
—**Syn. 2.** brusque, hard, unfeeling, unkind, brutal, acrimonious, bad-tempered. See **stern**¹. **3.** rough. **4.** discordant, dissonant, unharmonious. **6.** unesthetic.

harsh•en (här′shən), *v.t., v.i.* to make or become harsh: *Avarice had harshened his features.* [1815–25; HARSH + -EN¹]

hars•let (härs′lit), *n. Chiefly Southern U.S.* haslet.

Har•stad (här′stä), *n.* a seaport in W Norway: herring fishing. 21,150.

hart (härt), *n., pl.* **harts,** (*esp. collectively*) **hart.** a male deer, commonly of the red deer, *Cervus elaphus,* esp. after its fifth year. [bef. 900; ME *hert,* OE *heorot;* c. D *hert,* G *Hirsch,* ON *hjǫrtr;* akin to L *cervus* stag, Gk *kóry̆s* helmet, crest]

Hart (härt), *n.* **1. Albert Bush•nell** (bo͝osh′nl), 1854–1943, U.S. editor, historian, and educator. **2. Gary (Warren),** born 1936, U.S. politician: senator 1975–87. **3. Lo•renz** (lôr′ənts, lōr′-), 1895–1943, U.S. lyricist. **4. Moss,** 1904–61, U.S. playwright and librettist. **5. William S(hakespeare),** 1872–1946, U.S. film actor.

Har•tack (här′tak), *n.* **William John, Jr.** (*"Bill"*), born 1932, U.S. jockey.

har•tal (här täl′), *n.* (in India) a closing of shops and stopping of work, esp. as a form of passive resistance. [1915–20; < Hindi *hartal,* var. of *haṭtāl,* equiv. to *hat* shop (Skt *haṭṭa*) + *tāl* locking (Skt *tālaka* lock, bolt)]

Harte (härt), *n.* **(Francis) Bret** (bret), 1839–1902, U.S. author, esp. of short stories.

har•te•beest (här′tə bēst′, härt′bēst′), *n., pl.* **-beests,** (*esp. collectively*) **-beest. 1.** any large African antelope of the genus *Alcelaphus,* having ringed horns that curve backward: some species are endangered. **2.** any of several related African antelopes, as certain species of the genus *Damaliscus.* [1780–90; < Afrik; see HART, BEAST]

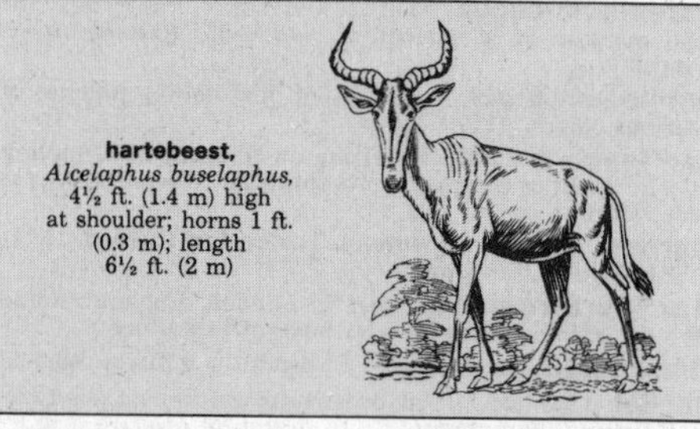
hartebeest, *Alcelaphus buselaphus,* 4½ ft. (1.4 m) high at shoulder; horns 1 ft. (0.3 m); length 6½ ft. (2 m)

Hart•ford (härt′fərd), *n.* **1. (George) Huntington, 2nd,** born 1911, U.S. businessman and patron of the arts. **2.** a port in and the capital of Connecticut, in the central part, on the Connecticut River. 136,392.

Hart′ford fern′, a climbing or sprawling fern, *Lygodium palmatum,* of the eastern U.S., having deeply lobed ivylike leaves. Also called **climbing fern.** [1895–1900, *Amer.*]

Har•tha•cnut (här′thə kə no͞ot′, -nyo͞ot′), *n.* Hardecanute.

Hart•ley (härt′lē), *n.* **1. David,** 1705–57, English physician and philosopher. **2. Mars•den** (märz′dən), 1877–1943, U.S. painter.

Hart•line (härt′līn), *n.* **Hal•dan Kef•fer** (hôl′dən kef′ər), 1903–83, U.S. physiologist: Nobel prize for medicine 1967.

Hart•mann (härt′män, -mən; *Ger.* härt′män′), *n.* **1. (Karl Ro•bert) E•du•ard von** (kärl rō′bərt ā′do͞o ärt′ fən), 1842–1906, German philosopher. **2. Ni•co•la•i** (nē′kô lä′ē, nē′kô lī′), 1882–1950, German philosopher, born in Latvia.

harts•horn (härts′hôrn′), *n.* **1.** the antler of a hart, formerly used as a source of ammonia. **2.** ammonium carbonate. [bef. 1000; ME *hertis horn,* OE *heortes horn.* See HART, 'S¹, HORN]

hart's-tongue (härts′tung′), *n.* a fern, *Phyllitis scolopendrium,* having long, leathery, wavy-edged leaves. Also, **harts′-tongue′.** [1275–1325; ME *hertis tonge.* See HART, 'S¹, TONGUE]

har•um-scar•um (hâr′əm skâr′əm, har′əm skar′əm), *adj.* **1.** reckless; rash; irresponsible: *He had a harum-scarum youth.* **2.** disorganized; uncontrolled. —*adv.* **3.** recklessly; wildly: *He ran harum-scarum all over the place.* —*n.* **4.** a reckless person. **5.** reckless or unpredictable behavior or action. [1665–75; earlier *harum-starum* rhyming compound based on obs. *hare* to harass + STARE] —**har′um-scar′um•ness,** *n.*
—**Syn. 1, 2.** erratic, impulsive, impetuous; giddy, scatterbrained.

Ha•run al-Ra•shid (hä ro͞on′ äl rä shēd′; *Arab.* hä-ro͞on′ är′rä shēd′), A.D. 764?–809, caliph of Baghdad 786–809: one of the greatest Abbasids, he was made almost a legendary hero in the *Arabian Nights.* Also, **Haroun-al-Raschid, Ha•run ar-Ra•shid** (hä ro͞on′ är′rä-shēd′; *Arab.* hä ro͞on′ är′rä shēd′).

Ha•ru•no•bu (här′o͝o nō′bo͞o; *Japn.* hä′ro͞o nô′bô′), *n.* **Su•zu•ki** (so͞o zo͞o′kē), 1720?–70, Japanese painter and printmaker.

ha•rus•pex (hə rus′peks, har′ə speks′), *n., pl.* **ha•rus•pi•ces** (hə rus′pə sēz′). (in ancient Rome) one of a class of minor priests who practiced divination, esp. from the entrails of animals killed in sacrifice. Also, **aruspex.** [1575–85; < L, equiv. to *haru-* (akin to *hīra* intestine; see CHORD[1]) + *spec-* (s. of *specere* to look at) + *-s* nom. sing. ending]

ha•rus•pi•cy (hə rus′pə sē), *n.* divination by a haruspex. Also, **ha•rus•pi•ca•tion** (hə rus′pi kā′shən). [1560–70; < L *haruspicium,* equiv. to *haruspic-* (s. of *haruspex*) + *-ium* -IUM] **—ha•rus•pi•cal** (hə rus′pi kəl), *adj.*

Har•vard (här′vərd), *n.* **1. John,** 1607–38, English clergyman in the U.S.: principal benefactor of Harvard College, now Harvard University. **2.** a city in central Massachusetts. 12,170.

Har′vard beets′, sliced or diced beets cooked in a mixture of sugar, cornstarch, vinegar, and water. [after HARVARD University]

Har′vard chair′, *Furniture.* a three-legged armchair of the late 17th century, composed of turned uprights and spindles and having a triangular seat. [after HARVARD University]

Har′vard frame′, *Trademark.* an adjustable metal bedframe having legs equipped with casters, into which a box spring may be set and to which a headboard may be attached. Also called **Har′vard bed′ frame′.**

Harve (härv), *n.* a male given name, form of **Harvey.**

har•vest (här′vist), *n.* **1.** Also, **har′vest•ing.** the gathering of crops. **2.** the season when ripened crops are gathered. **3.** a crop or yield of one growing season. **4.** a supply of anything gathered at maturity and stored: *a harvest of wheat.* **5.** the result or consequence of any act, process, or event: *The journey yielded a harvest of wonderful memories.* —*v.t.* **6.** to gather (a crop or the like); reap. **7.** to gather the crop from: *to harvest the fields.* **8.** to gain, win, acquire, or use (a prize, product, or result of any past act, process, plan, etc.). **9.** to catch, take, or remove for use: *Fishermen harvested hundreds of salmon from the river.* —*v.i.* **10.** to gather a crop; reap. [bef. 950; ME; OE *hærfest;* c. G *Herbst* autumn; akin to HARROW[1]] **—har′vest•a•ble,** *adj.* **—har′vest•a•bil′i•ty,** *n.* **—har′vest•less,** *adj.*
—Syn. 3. See **crop. 5.** accumulation, collection, product, return, proceeds.

har•ves•ter (här′və stər), *n.* **1.** a person who harvests; reaper. **2.** any of various farm machines for harvesting field crops. **3.** an orange-brown butterfly, *Feniseca tarquinius,* the larvae of which are predacious on aphids. [1580–90; HARVEST + -ER[1]]

har′vester ant′, any of several red or black ants, esp. of the genus *Pogonomyrmex,* of the southwestern U.S., that feed on and store the seeds of grasses. Also called **agricultural ant.** [1880–85]

har•vest•fish (här′vist fish′), *n., pl.* (*esp. collectively*) **-fish,** (*esp. referring to two or more kinds or species*) **-fish•es.** a butterfish of the genus *Peprilus,* esp. *P. alepidotus* of Atlantic waters. [1805–15, *Amer.*; HARVEST + FISH]

har′vest fly′. See **dog-day cicada.**

har′vest home′, 1. the bringing home of the harvest. **2.** the time of harvesting or of gathering in the harvest. **3.** an English festival celebrated at the close of the harvest. **4.** a song sung as the harvest is brought home. [1565–75]

har′vest in′dex, *Agric.* a measurement of crop yield: the weight of a harvested product as a percentage of the total plant weight of a crop. [1965–70]

har•vest•man (här′vist mən), *n., pl.* **-men. 1.** daddy-longlegs (def. 1). **2.** a person engaged in harvesting. [1400–50; late ME. See HARVEST, MAN[1]]

har′vest mite′, chigger (def. 1). [1870–75, *Amer.*]

har′vest moon′, the moon at and about the period of fullness that is nearest to the autumnal equinox. [1700–10]

har′vest mouse′, 1. an Old World field mouse, *Micromys minutus,* that builds a spherical nest among the stems of grains and other plants. **2.** any of several New World mice of the genus *Reithrodontomys* having similar habits. [1805–15]

har′vest tick′, chigger (def. 1). [1885–90]

har•vest•time (här′vist tīm′), *n.* the time of year when a crop or crops are harvested, esp. autumn. [1325–75; ME; see HARVEST, TIME]

Har•vey (här′vē), *n.* **1. William,** 1578–1657, English physician: discoverer of the circulation of the blood. **2.** a city in NE Illinois, near Chicago. 35,810. **3.** a male given name: from Germanic words meaning "army" and "battle."

Har′vey Wall′bang•er (wôl′bang′ər), a screwdriver cocktail topped with Galliano. [allegedly after an American surfer named Tom *Harvey,* who favored such a drink; but the story is unsubstantiated and may have been fabricated by marketers of Galliano]

Ha•ry•a•na (hur′ē ä′nə), *n.* a state in NW India, formed in 1966 from the S part of Punjab. 11,610,000; 17,074 sq. mi. (44,222 sq. km). *Cap.* (shared with Punjab): Chandigarh. Also, **Hariana.**

Há•ry Já•nos (*Hung.* hä′ʀi yä′nôsh), an opera (1926) by Zoltán Kodály.

Harz′ Moun′tains (härts), a range of low mountains in central Germany between the Elbe and Weser rivers. Highest peak, Brocken, 3745 ft. (1141 m).

has (haz; *unstressed* həz, əz), *v.* a 3rd pers. sing. pres. indic. of **have.**

Ha•sa (hä′sə), *n.* a region in E Saudi Arabia, on the Persian Gulf. Also, **El Hasa.**

Ha•san (hä′sən, ha san′), *n.* (*al-Hasan*), A.D. 624?–669?, Arabian caliph: son of Ali and Fatima (brother of Hussein). Also, **Hassan.**

Ha•san•lu (hä′sän lo͞o′), *n.* an archaeological site in NW Iran, S of Lake Urmia: excavated Mannaean city.

has-been (haz′bin′), *n.* a person or thing that is no longer effective, successful, popular, etc.: *She was dismissed as a has-been after directing one hit movie.* [1600–10]

Has′brouck Heights′ (haz′bro͝ok), a borough in NE New Jersey. 12,166.

Has•dru•bal (haz′dro͞o bəl, haz dro͞o′-), *n.* **1.** died 207 B.C., Carthaginian general (brother of Hannibal). **2.** died 221 B.C., Carthaginian general (brother-in-law of Hannibal).

Ha•šek (hä′shek), *n.* **Ja•ro•slav** (yä′rô släf′), 1883–1923, Czech novelist and short-story writer.

ha•sen•pfef•fer (hä′sən fef′ər), *n.* a stew of marinated rabbit meat garnished usually with sour cream. Also, **hassenpfeffer.** [1890–95; < G, equiv. to *Hasen-,* comb. form of *Hase* HARE + *Pfeffer* PEPPER]

hash[1] (hash), *n.* **1.** a dish of diced or chopped meat and often vegetables, as of leftover corned beef or veal and potatoes, sautéed in a frying pan or of meat, potatoes, and carrots cooked together in gravy. **2.** a mess, jumble, or muddle: *a hash of unorganized facts and figures.* **3.** a reworking of old and familiar material: *This essay is a hash of several earlier and better works.* **4.** *Computers.* garbage (def. 7). **5.** *Radio and Television Slang.* electrical noise on a radio or snow in a television picture caused by interfering outside sources that generate sparking. **6. make a hash of,** to spoil or botch: *The new writer made a hash of his first assignment.* **7. settle someone's hash,** *Informal.* to get rid of; subdue: *Her blunt reply really settled my hash.* —*v.t.* **8.** to chop into small pieces; make into hash; mince. **9.** to muddle or mess up: *We thought we knew our parts, but when the play began we hashed the whole thing.* **10.** to discuss or review (something) thoroughly (often fol. by *out*): *They hashed out every aspect of the issue.* **11. hash over,** to bring up again for consideration; discuss, esp. in review: *At the class reunion they hashed over their college days.* [1645–55; < F *hacher* to cut up, deriv. of *hache* ax, HATCHET]
—Syn. 6. bungle, butcher, muddle, mess up, flub. **11.** review, recall, reminisce, recollect, remember.

hash[2] (hash), *n. Slang.* hashish. [by shortening]

hash′ browns′, crisp-fried potatoes made by dicing, chopping, or mashing boiled potatoes and browning them in hot fat or oil. Also, **hash′-browns′, hash′•browns′.** Also called **hash′-browned pota′toes, hash′-brown pota′toes.** [1950–55]

Hash′e•mite King′dom of Jor′dan (hash′ə mīt′), official name of **Jordan.**

hash•er (hash′ər), *n. Slang.* a waiter or waitress, esp. in a hash house. [1835–45; HASH[1] + -ER[1]]

hash•head (hash′hed′), *n. Slang.* a hashish addict. [1945–50; HASH[2] + HEAD]

hash′ house′, *Slang.* an inexpensive restaurant, diner, or the like, that serves a limited number of short-order dishes: *We stopped for lunch at a roadside hash house.* [1865–70, *Amer.*]

Hash•i•mite (hash′ə mīt′), *n.* **1.** a member of any Arab dynasty in the Middle East founded by Husein ibn-Ali or his descendants. —*adj.* **2.** of or pertaining to the Hashimites. [1690–1700; *Hāshim* great-grandfather of Muhammad + -ITE[1]]

hash•ing (hash′ing), *n.* **1.** *Radio.* interference of signals between two stations on the same or adjacent frequencies. **2.** *Computers.* a technique for locating data in a file by applying a transformation, usually arithmetic, to a key. [HASH[1] + -ING[1]]

hash•ish (hash′ēsh, -ish, ha shēsh′, hä-), *n.* **1.** the flowering tops and leaves of Indian hemp smoked, chewed, or drunk as a narcotic and intoxicant. **2.** the dried resinous exudate of the flowering tops of this plant, containing larger amounts of the active ingredient. Also, **hash•eesh** (hash′ēsh, hä shēsh′). [1590–1600; < Ar *hashish* lit., dry vegetation (e.g., hay)]

hash′ mark′, 1. *Informal.* **a.** a service stripe. **b.** the symbol #. **2.** *Football.* the marking formed by either inbounds line intersecting with one of the lines delineating yardage between the goal lines. [1905–10]

hash-sling•er (hash′sling′ər), *n. Slang.* **1.** a waiter or waitress, esp. in a hash house. **2.** a short-order cook. [1865–70, *Amer.*]

Ha•sid (hä′sid; *Ashk. Heb.* KHô′sid; *Seph. Heb.* KHä sēd′), *n., pl.* **Ha•sid•im** (hä sid′im, hə-; *Ashk. Heb.* KHô sē′dim; *Seph. Heb.* KHä sē dēm′). *Judaism.* **1.** a member of a sect founded in Poland in the 18th century by Baal Shem-Tov and characterized by its emphasis on mysticism, prayer, ritual strictness, religious zeal, and joy. Cf. **Mitnagged. 2.** an Assidean. Also, **Hassid, Chasid, Chassid.** [< Heb *ḥāsīd* pious (person)] **—Ha•sid•ic** (hä sid′ik, hə-), *adj.*

Has•i•de•an (has′i dē′ən, hä′si-), *n. Judaism.* Assidean. Also, **Has′i•dae′an.**

Has•i•dism (has′i diz′əm, hä′si-), *n. Judaism.* the principles and practices of the Hasidim. Also, **Hassidism, Chasidism, Chassidism.** [HASID + -ISM]

Ha•ska•lah (hä′skə lä′; *Ashk. Heb.* hä skô′lə; *Seph. Heb.* hä skä lä′), *n.* an 18th–19th-century movement among central and eastern European Jews, begun in Germany under the leadership of Moses Mendelssohn, designed to make Jews and Judaism more cosmopolitan in character by promoting knowledge of and contributions to the secular arts and sciences and encouraging adoption of the dress, customs, and language of the general population. [< Heb *haskālāh* enlightenment]

has•let (has′lit, hās′-, häz′-), *n. Chiefly Southern U.S.* the heart, liver, etc., of a hog or other animal used for food. Also, **harslet.** [1300–50; ME *hastelet* < MF: roasted meat, dim. (see -LET) of *haste* spit, piece of spit-roasted meat < Gmc; cf. OE *hearstepanne* frying pan, *hierstan* to roast, fry, D *harst* sirloin; see HEARTH]

Has•mo•ne•an (haz′mə nē′ən), *n.* a member of a priestly family of Jewish rulers and leaders in Judea in the 1st and 2nd centuries B.C. Also, **Has′mo•nae′an, Asmonean, Asmonaean.** Cf. **Maccabees.** [1610–20; var. (with *h-* < Heb *kh-*) of *Asmonean* < LL *Asmōnae*(*us*) of *Hasmōn* (< Gk *Asmōnaios*) + -AN]

has•n't (haz′ənt), contraction of *has not.*
—Usage. See **contraction.**

hasp (hasp), *n.* **1.** a clasp for a door, lid, etc., esp. one passing over a staple and fastened by a pin or a padlock. —*v.t.* **2.** to fasten with or as with a hasp. [bef. 1000; ME; OE *hæsp, hæpse;* c. G *Haspe* hasp; akin to D *haspel* reel, ON *hespa* skein, hasp]

Has•sam (has′əm), *n.* **(Frederick) Childe** (child), 1859–1935, U.S. painter and etcher.

Has•san (hä′sən, ha san′), *n.* Hasan.

Hassan II, born 1929, king of Morocco since 1961.

Has•sel (hä′səl), *n.* **Odd** (ôd), 1897–1981, Norwegian chemist: Nobel prize 1969.

has•sen•pfef•fer (hä′sən fef′ər), *n.* hasenpfeffer.

Has•sid (hä′sid; *Ashk. Heb.* KHô′sid; *Seph. Heb.* KHä′-sēd), *n., pl.* **Has•sid•im** (hä sid′im, hə-; *Ashk. Heb.* KHô-sē′dim; *Seph. Heb.* KHä sē dēm′). *Judaism.* Hasid. **—Has•sid•ic** (hä sid′ik, hə-), *adj.* **—Has′sid•ism,** *n.*

has•sle (has′əl), *n., v.,* **-sled, -sling.** *Informal.* —*n.* **1.** a disorderly dispute. **2.** a problem brought about by pressures of time, money, inconvenience, etc.: *Finding a decent place to have lunch in this neighborhood is always a hassle.* —*v.i.* **3.** to dispute or quarrel: *children hassling over who has the most toys.* **4.** to take time or effort: *We don't want to hassle with all that waiting in line.* —*v.t.* **5.** to bother, annoy, or harass: *I'll do the work, so don't hassle me.* [1935–40; orig. uncert.]
—Syn. 1, 3. squabble, quarrel, row, scrap.

has•sock (has′ək), *n.* **1.** a thick, firm cushion used as a footstool or for kneeling. **2.** ottoman (def. 6). **3.** a rank tuft of coarse grass or sedge, as in a bog. [bef. 1000; ME; OE *hassuc* coarse grass]

hast (hast), *v. Archaic.* 2nd pers. sing. pres. indic. of **have.**

has•ta la vis•ta (äs′tä lä vēs′tä; *Eng.* hä′stə lə vē′-stə), *Spanish.* until I see you; until we meet; so long.

has•ta lue•go (äs′tä lwe′gô; *Eng.* hä′stə lo͞o ā′gō), *Spanish.* see you later; so long.

has•ta ma•ña•na (äs′tä mä nyä′nä; *Eng.* hä′stə mən yä′nə), *Spanish.* see you tomorrow.

has•tate (has′tāt), *adj. Bot.* (of a leaf) triangular or shaped like an arrow, with two spreading lobes at the base. [1780–90; < L *hastātus* armed with a spear, equiv. to *hast*(*a*) spear + *-ātus* -ATE[1]] **—has′tate•ly,** *adv.*

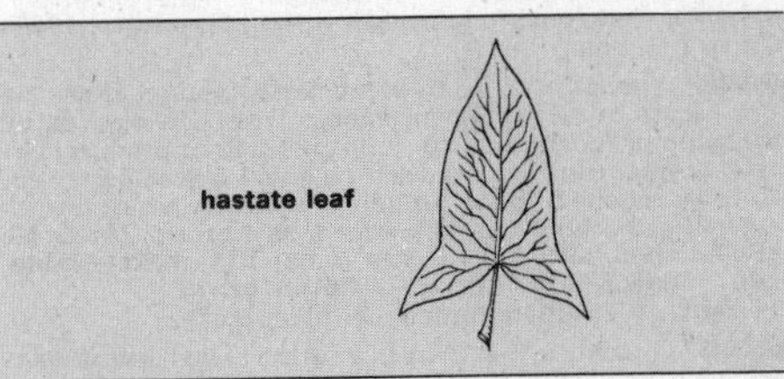
hastate leaf

haste (hāst), *n., v.,* **hast•ed, hast•ing.** —*n.* **1.** swiftness of motion; speed; celerity: *He performed his task with great haste. They felt the need for haste.* **2.** urgent need of quick action; a hurry or rush: *to be in haste to get ahead in the world.* **3.** unnecessarily quick action; thoughtless, rash, or undue speed: *Haste makes waste.* **4. make haste,** to act or go with speed; hurry: *She made haste to tell the president the good news.* —*v.i., v.t.* **5.** *Archaic.* to hasten. [1250–1300; ME < OF < Gmc; akin to OFris *hāste,* OE *hæst* violence, ON *heifst* hatred, Goth *haifsts* quarrel] **—haste′ful,** *adj.* **—haste′ful•ly,** *adv.* **—haste′less,** *adj.* **—haste′less•ness,** *n.*
—Syn. 1. See **speed. 2.** flurry, bustle, ado, urgency. **3.** precipitancy, precipitation. **—Ant. 1.** sloth.

has•ten (hā′sən), *v.i.* **1.** to move or act with haste; proceed with haste; hurry: *to hasten to a place.* —*v.t.* **2.** to cause to hasten; accelerate: *to hasten someone from a room; to hasten the arrival of a happier time.* [1565–75; HASTE + -EN[1]] **—has′ten•er,** *n.*
—Syn. 2. urge, press; expedite, quicken, speed; precipitate.

Has•tie (hā′stē), *n.* **William Henry,** 1904–76, U.S. jurist: first black judge of the U.S. Circuit Court of Appeals.

Has•tings (hā′stingz), *n.* **1. Thomas,** 1860–1929, U.S. architect. **2. Warren,** 1732–1818, British statesman: first governor general of India 1773–85. **3.** a seaport in E Sussex, in SE England: William the Conqueror defeated the Saxons near here on Senlac Hill 1066. 74,600. **4.** a city in S Nebraska. 23,045. **5.** a town in SE Minnesota. 12,827.

hast•y (hā′stē), *adj.,* **hast•i•er, hast•i•est. 1.** moving or acting with haste; speedy; quick; hurried. **2.** made or

CONCISE PRONUNCIATION KEY: act, cāpe, dâre, pärt; set, ēqual; if, īce; ox, ōver, ôrder, oil, bo͝ok, bo͞ot, out; up, ûrge; child; sing; shoe; thin, *that;* zh as in *treasure.* ə = *a* as in *alone, e* as in *system, i* as in *easily, o* as in *gallop, u* as in *circus;* ə as in *fire* (fīər), *hour* (ouər). l and n can serve as syllabic consonants, as in *cradle* (krād′l), and *button* (but′n). See the full key inside the front cover.

done with haste or speed: *a hasty visit.* **3.** unduly quick; precipitate; rash: *a hasty decision.* **4.** brief; fleeting; slight; superficial: *a hasty glance.* **5.** impatient; impetuous; thoughtless; injudicious: *hasty words.* **6.** easily irritated or angered; irascible: *a hasty temper.* [1300–50; ME < MF *hasti, hastif;* see HASTE, -IVE] **—hast′i·ly,** *adv.* **—hast′i·ness,** *n.*
—Syn. 1. swift, rapid, fast, fleet, brisk. **3.** foolhardy, reckless, headlong. **6.** testy, touchy, fiery, excitable, irritable. **—Ant. 1.** slow. **3.** deliberate.

hast′y pud′ding, 1. *New England.* cornmeal mush. **2.** *Chiefly Brit.* a dish made of flour or oatmeal stirred into seasoned boiling water or milk and quickly cooked. [1590–1600]

hat (hat), *n., v.,* **hat·ted, hat·ting.** **—***n.* **1.** a shaped covering for the head, usually with a crown and brim, esp. for wear outdoors. **2.** *Rom. Cath. Ch.* **a.** the distinctive head covering of a cardinal. **b.** the office or dignity of a cardinal. Cf. **red hat. 3. hat in hand,** humbly; respectfully: *He approached the boss, hat in hand.* **4. pass the hat,** to ask for contributions of money, as for charity; take up a collection: *The lodge members passed the hat to send underprivileged children to summer camp.* **5. take off one's hat to,** to express high regard for; praise: *We took off our hats to their courage and daring.* **6. talk through one's hat,** to speak without knowing the facts; make unsupported or incorrect statements: *He is talking through his hat when he says he'll make the team.* **7. throw** or **toss one's hat in** or **into the ring,** to become a participant in a contest, esp. to declare one's candidacy for political office: *His friends are urging him to throw his hat in the ring.* **8. under one's hat,** confidential; private; secret: *I'll tell you the real story, but keep it under your hat.* **9. wear two** or **several hats,** to function in more than one capacity; fill two or more positions: *He wears two hats, serving as the company's comptroller as well as its chief executive officer.* **—***v.t.* **10.** to provide with a hat; put a hat on. [bef. 900; ME; OE *hætt;* c. ON *hǫttr* hood; akin to HOOD[1]] **—hat′less,** *adj.* **—hat′less·ness,** *n.* **—hat′like′,** *adj.*

hat·a·ble (hā′tə bəl), *adj.* hateable.

Ha·ta·su (hə tä′sōō), *n.* Hatshepsut.

hat·band (hat′band′), *n.* **1.** a band or ribbon placed about the crown of a hat, just above the brim. **2.** a black band similarly worn as a sign of mourning. [1375–1425; late ME; see HAT, BAND[2]]

hat·box (hat′boks′), *n.* a case or box for a hat. [1785–95; HAT + BOX[1]]

hatch[1] (hach), *v.t.* **1.** to bring forth (young) from the egg. **2.** to cause young to emerge from (the egg) as by brooding or incubating. **3.** to bring forth or produce; devise; create; contrive; concoct: *to hatch a scheme.* **—***v.i.* **4.** to be hatched. **5.** to brood. **—***n.* **6.** the act of hatching. **7.** something that is hatched, as a brood. [1200–50; ME *hacchen;* akin to G *hecken* to hatch] **—hatch′a·ble,** *adj.* **—hatch′a·bil′i·ty,** *n.* **—hatch′er,** *n.*
—Syn. 1. incubate, brood. **3.** plan, plot.

hatch[2] (hach), *n.* **1.** *Naut.* **a.** Also called **hatchway.** an opening, usually rectangular, in the deck through which passengers can pass, cargo can be loaded or unloaded, etc. **b.** the cover over such an opening. **2.** an opening that serves as a doorway or window in the floor or roof of a building. **3.** the cover over such an opening. **4.** *Slang.* the throat as used for drinking: *His usual toast was a muttered "Down the hatch!"* **5.** *Aeron.* an opening or door in an aircraft. **6.** the lower half of a divided door, both parts of which can be opened separately. **7.** a small door, grated opening, or serving counter in or attached to the wall of a building, room, etc., as for a merchant's stall. **8.** a bin or compartment built into a confined space, esp. a deep storage bin. **9.** *Auto.* **a.** the cargo area in a hatchback. **b.** Also called **liftgate.** the hinged lid of a hatchback that swings upward to provide access to the cargo area. **10.** anything resembling a hatch. **11. batten down the** or **one's hatches, a.** *Naut.* prepare for stormy weather: used as a command. **b.** to prepare to meet an emergency or face a great difficulty: *The government must batten down its hatches before the election.* [bef. 1100; ME *hacche,* OE *hæcc* grating, hatch, half-gate; akin to D *hek* gate, railing]

hatch[3] (hach), *v.t.* **1.** to mark with lines, esp. closely set parallel lines, as for shading in drawing or engraving. **2.** hachure (def. 3). **—***n.* **3.** a shading line in drawing or engraving. [1470–80; earlier *hache* < MF *hacher* to cut up, deriv. of *hache* ax. See HATCHET]

Hatch′ Act′, either of two acts of Congress (1939, 1940), regulating expenditures, contributions, and procedures in political campaigns. [named after Carl A. *Hatch* (1889–1963), U.S. lawyer and politician]

hatch·back (hach′bak′), *n.* a style of automobile in which the rear deck lid and window lift open as a unit. Also called **liftback.** [1965–70; HATCH[2] + BACK[1]]

hatch′ boat′, a small fishing vessel having covered wells for holding the catch. [1865–70]

hat·check (hat′chek′), *adj.* **1.** of, noting, or engaged in the checking of hats, coats, etc., into temporary safekeeping: *a hatcheck girl.* **2.** used in checking hats, coats, etc.: *a hatcheck room.* [1915–20; HAT + CHECK]

hatch·el (hach′əl), *n., v.,* **-eled, -el·ing** or (*esp. Brit.*) **-elled, -el·ling.** **—***n.* **1.** hackle[1] (def. 5). **—***v.t.* **2.** hackle[1] (def. 8). [1275–1325; var. of earlier *hetchel,* ME *hechel;* perh. influenced by HACKLE[1]]

hatch·er·y (hach′ə rē), *n., pl.* **-er·ies.** a place for hatching eggs of hens, fish, etc., esp. a large, commercial or government site where the young are hatched, cared for, and sold or distributed. [1875–80; HATCH[1] + -ERY]

hatch·et (hach′it), *n.* **1.** a small, short-handled ax having the end of the head opposite the blade in the form of a hammer, made to be used with one hand. See illus. under **ax. 2.** a tomahawk. **3.** hatchetfish. **4. bury the hatchet,** to become reconciled or reunited; make peace. **5. take up the hatchet,** to begin or resume hostilities; prepare for or go to war: *The natives are taking up the hatchet against the enemy.* **—***v.t.* **6.** to cut, destroy, kill, etc., with a hatchet. **7.** to abridge, delete, excise, etc.: *The network censor may hatchet 30 minutes from the script.* [1300–50; 1670–80, *Amer.* for def. 4; ME *hachet* < MF *hachette,* dim. (see -ET) of *hache* ax < Frankish **hapja* kind of knife; akin to Gk *kóptein* to cut (cf. COMMA, SYNCOPE)] **—hatch′et·like′,** *adj.*

hatch′et face′, a thin face with sharp features. [1640–50] **—hatch′et-faced′,** *adj.*

hatch·et·fish (hach′it fish′), *n., pl.* (*esp. collectively*) **-fish,** (*esp. referring to two or more kinds or species*) **-fish·es. 1.** any deep-sea fishes of the genera *Argyropelicus, Sternoptyx,* and related genera, of tropical and temperate waters, having a silvery, hatchet-shaped body. **2.** Also called **flying characin.** any of several freshwater fishes of the genera *Carnegiella, Gasteropelecus,* and *Thorachocharax,* occurring from Panama to the Rio de la Plata and capable of flying short distances by rapid movements of their large pectoral fins. [1930–35; HATCHET + FISH]

hatchetfish, *Carnegiella strigata,* a freshwater gasteropelecid, length about 2½ in. (6 cm)

hatch′et job′, a maliciously destructive critique or act: *The special committee has done a hatchet job on the new proposal.* Also called **ax job.** [1940–45]

hatch′et man′, 1. a professional murderer. **2.** a writer or speaker who specializes in defamatory attacks, as on political candidates or public officials. **3.** a person whose job it is to execute unpleasant tasks for a superior, as dismissing employees. Also, **hatch′et·man′.** Also called **axman.** [1745–55, *Amer.*]

hatch·ett·ite (hach′i tīt′), *n.* a soft yellowish mineral wax, $C_{38}H_{78}$, darkening on exposure: found in bogs and coal beds. Also, **hatch·ett·ine** (hach′i tēn′, -tin). Also called **adipocerite.** [1865–70; named after Charles *Hatchett* (c1765–1847), English chemist; see -ITE[1]]

hatch·et·work (hach′it wûrk′), *n.* destruction, damage, or paring done by or as if by a hatchet. [1690–1700; HATCHET + WORK]

hatch·ing (hach′ing), *n.* hachure (def. 2). [1655–65; HATCH[3] + -ING[1]]

hatch·ling (hach′ling), *n.* a young bird, reptile, or fish recently emerged from an egg. [1895–1900; HATCH[1] + -LING[1]]

hatch·ment (hach′mənt), *n. Heraldry.* a square tablet, set diagonally, bearing the coat of arms of a deceased person. [1540–50; var. (by syncopation and aspiration) of ACHIEVEMENT]

hatchment

hatch·ure (hach′ər), *n., v.t.* hachure.

hatch·way (hach′wā′), *n.* **1.** *Naut.* hatch[2] (def. 1a). **2.** the opening of any trap door, as in a floor, ceiling, or roof. [1620–30; HATCH[2] + WAY]

hat′ dance′, a Mexican folk dance in which the man places his sombrero on the ground as an offer of love and the woman dances on the hat's brim and then places the hat on her head to indicate her acceptance of him.

hate (hāt), *v.,* **hat·ed, hat·ing,** *n.* **—***v.t.* **1.** to dislike intensely or passionately; feel extreme aversion for or extreme hostility toward; detest: *to hate the enemy; to hate bigotry.* **2.** to be unwilling; dislike: *I hate to do it.* **—***v.i.* **3.** to feel intense dislike, or extreme aversion or hostility. **—***n.* **4.** intense dislike; extreme aversion or hostility. **5.** the object of extreme aversion or hostility. [bef. 900; ME *hat(i)en,* OE *hatian* (v.); c. D *haten,* ON *hata,* Goth *hatan,* G *hassen*] **—hat′er,** *n.*
—Syn. 1. loathe, execrate; despise. HATE, ABHOR, DETEST, ABOMINATE imply feeling intense dislike or aversion toward something. HATE, the simple and general word, suggests passionate dislike and a feeling of enmity: *to hate autocracy.* ABHOR expresses a deep-rooted horror and a sense of repugnance or complete rejection: *to abhor cruelty; Nature abhors a vacuum.* DETEST implies intense, even vehement, dislike and antipathy, besides a sense of disdain: *to detest a combination of ignorance and arrogance.* ABOMINATE expresses a strong feeling of disgust and repulsion toward something thought of as unworthy, unlucky, or the like: *to abominate treachery.* **—Ant. 1.** love.

hate·a·ble (hā′tə bəl), *adj.* meriting hatred or loathing. Also, **hatable.** [1605–15; HATE + -ABLE]

hate·ful (hāt′fəl), *adj.* **1.** arousing hate or deserving to be hated: *hateful oppression.* **2.** unpleasant; dislikable; distasteful: *She found her domestic chores hateful.* **3.** full of or expressing hate; malignant; malevolent: *a hateful denunciatory speech.* [1300–50; ME; see HATE, -FUL] **—hate′ful·ly,** *adv.* **—hate′ful·ness,** *n.*
—Syn. 1. abominable, execrable, abhorrent, repugnant; invidious, loathsome. HATEFUL, OBNOXIOUS, ODIOUS, OFFENSIVE refer to something that causes strong dislike or annoyance. HATEFUL implies actually causing hatred or extremely strong dislike: *The sight of him is hateful to me.* OBNOXIOUS emphasizes causing annoyance or discomfort by objectionable qualities: *His persistence made him seem obnoxious. His piggish manners made him obnoxious to his companions.* ODIOUS emphasizes the disagreeable or displeasing: *an odious little man; odious servility.* OFFENSIVE emphasizes the distaste and resentment caused by something that may be either displeasing or insulting: *an offensive odor, remark.* **—Ant. 1.** likable, agreeable; commendable, praiseworthy.

hate′ mail′, letters, telegrams, etc., that express prejudice or disagreement in abusive or threatening terms.

hate·mon·ger (hāt′mung′gər, -mong′-), *n.* a person who kindles hatred, enmity, or prejudice in others. [HATE + MONGER] **—hate′mon′ger·ing,** *n.*

hate′ sheet′, a newspaper or other publication that consistently expresses biased hatred toward some race, nationality, religion, or other group.

hate′ speech′, speech that attacks a person or group on the basis of race, religion, gender, or sexual orientation.

Hat·field (hat′fēld′), *n.* a town in central Hertfordshire, in SE England: incorporated into Welwyn Hatfield 1974. Also called **Bishop's Hatfield.**

Hat′field-Mc·Coy′ Feud′ (hat′fēld′mə koi′), *U.S. Hist.* a blood feud between two mountain clans on the West Virginia–Kentucky border, the Hatfields of West Virginia and the McCoys of Kentucky, that grew out of their being on opposite sides during the Civil War and was especially violent during 1880–90.

hath (hath), *v. Archaic.* 3rd pers. sing. pres. indic. of **have.**

Hath·a·way (hath′ə wā′), *n.* **Anne,** 1557–1623, the wife of William Shakespeare.

hath·a-yo·ga (hath′ə yō′gə, hut′ə-), *n.* (in Yoga) a method utilizing physical exercises to control the body and attain union of the self with the Supreme Being. [< Skt]

Hath·or (hath′ôr, -ər), *n. Egyptian Relig.* the goddess of love and joy, often represented with the head, horns, or ears of a cow.

Hath·or-head·ed (hath′ər hed′id), *adj.* (of an ancient Egyptian column) having a capital in the form of the head of Hathor; Hathoric. [1900–05]

Ha·thor·ic (hə thôr′ik, -thor′-), *adj.* of or pertaining to Hathor. [1900–05; HATHOR + -IC]

Ha·tik·vah (*Seph. Heb.* hä tēk′vä; *Ashk. Heb.* hä tik′-vô; *Eng.* hä tik′və), *n.* the national anthem of Israel.

hat·pin (hat′pin′), *n.* a long pin for securing a woman's hat to her hair, often having a bulbous decorative head of colored glass, simulated pearl, or the like. [1890–95; HAT + PIN]

hat·rack (hat′rak′), *n.* a frame or stand having knobs or hooks for hanging hats. [1870–75; HAT + RACK[1]]

ha·tred (hā′trid), *n.* the feeling of one who hates; intense dislike or extreme aversion or hostility. [1125–75; ME; see HATE, -RED]
—Syn. animosity, detestation, loathing, abomination. **—Ant.** attraction, love.

Hat·shep·sut (hat shep′sōōt), *n.* 1495–75 B.C., queen of Egypt. Also, **Hatasu, Hat·shep·set** (hat shep′set).

Hat·ta (hat′ə), *n.* **Mohammed,** born 1902, Indonesian political leader: vice president of the Republic of Indonesia 1945–49, 1950–56; prime minister 1948, 1949–50.

hat·ter[1] (hat′ər), *n.* a maker or seller of hats. [1350–1400; ME; see HAT, -ER[1]]

hat·ter[2] (hat′ər), *n. Australian Informal.* **1.** a person who has become eccentric from living alone in a remote area. **2.** a person who lives alone in the bush, as a herder or prospector. [1850–55; said to be from the phrase "as mad as a hatter"]

Hat·ter·as (hat′ər əs), *n.* **Cape,** a promontory on an island off the E coast of North Carolina.

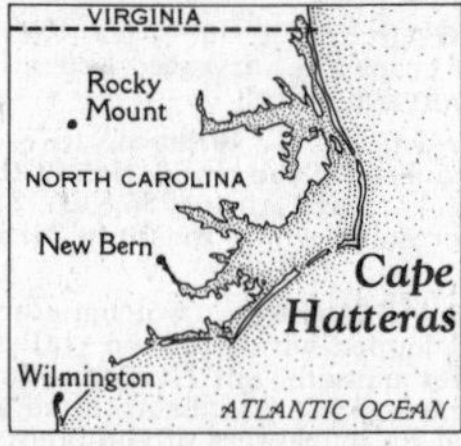

Hat·ti (hat′ē), *n.* **1.** an ancient people who lived in central Anatolia before its conquest by the Hittites. **2.** (in ancient inscriptions) the Hittites or the land of the Hittites. Also, **Khatti. —Hat′ti·an,** *n., adj.*

Hat·tic (hat′ik), *adj.* of or pertaining to the Hatti. [1920–25; HATT(I) + -IC]

Hat·ties·burg (hat′ēz bûrg′), *n.* a city in SE Mississippi. 40,865.

hat′ tree′. See **hall tree.** [1810–20, *Amer.*]

hat′ trick′, 1. *Cricket.* the knocking off by one bowler of three wickets with three successive pitches: so called because formerly such a bowler was rewarded with a hat. **2.** *Ice Hockey, Soccer.* three goals or points scored by one player in one game. **3.** *Baseball.* a series of a base hit, a two-base hit, a three-base hit, and a home run achieved in any order by one player in one game. **4.** a clever or adroitly deceptive maneuver. [1875–80; 1955–60 for def. 2]

Hat·tu·sas (hät′to͞o säs′), *n.* the capital of the ancient Hittite empire in Asia Minor: site of modern Boghazköy, Turkey. Also, **Khattusas.**

Hat·ty (hat′ē), *n.* a female given name, form of **Harriet.** Also, **Hat′tie.**

Hau·a Fte·ah (hou′ə fə tē′ə), a cave site in Cyrenaica that has produced archaeological evidence of the longest sequence of human habitation in northern Africa, extending to about 80,000 years B.P.

hau·berk (hô′bûrk), *n. Armor.* a long defensive shirt, usually of mail, extending to the knees; byrnie. [1250–1300; ME < OF *hauberc,* earlier *halberc* < Frankish **halsberg,* equiv. to **hals* neck (see HAWSE) + **berg* protection (see HARBOR); c. OHG *halsberc* OE *healsbeorg,* ON *halsbjǫrg*]

haugh (häkh, häf), *n. Scot.* a stretch of alluvial land forming part of a river valley; bottom land. [bef. 900; ME *halche, hawgh,* OE *healh* corner, nook]

haugh·ty (hô′tē), *adj.,* **-ti·er, -ti·est. 1.** disdainfully proud; snobbish; scornfully arrogant; supercilious: *haughty aristocrats; a haughty salesclerk.* **2.** *Archaic.* lofty or noble; exalted. [1520–30; obs. *haught* (sp. var. of late ME *haute* < MF < L *altus* high, with *h-* < Gmc; cf. OHG *hok* high) + -Y¹] —**haugh′ti·ly,** *adv.* —**haugh′ti·ness,** *n.*
—**Syn. 1.** lordly, disdainful, contemptuous. See **proud.**
—**Ant. 1.** humble, unpretentious, unassuming.

haul (hôl), *v.t.* **1.** to pull or draw with force; move by drawing; drag: *They hauled the boat up onto the beach.* **2.** to cart or transport; carry: *He hauled freight.* **3.** to cause to descend; lower (often fol. by *down*): *to haul down the flag.* **4.** to arrest or bring before a magistrate or other authority (often fol. by *before, in, to, into,* etc.): *He was hauled before the judge.* —*v.i.* **5.** to pull or tug. **6.** to go or come to a place, esp. with effort: *After roistering about the streets, they finally hauled into the tavern.* **7.** to do carting or transport, or move freight commercially. **8.** *Naut.* **a.** to sail, as in a particular direction. **b.** to draw or pull a vessel up on land, as for repairs or storage. **c.** (of the wind) to shift to a direction closer to the heading of a vessel (opposed to *veer*). **d.** (of the wind) to change direction, shift, or veer (often fol. by *round* or *to*). **9. haul around,** *Naut.* **a.** to brace (certain yards of a sailing vessel). **b.** (of the wind) to change in a clockwise direction. **10. haul** or **shag ass,** *Slang* (*vulgar*). to get a move on; hurry. **11. haul in with,** *Naut.* to approach. **12. haul off, a.** *Naut.* to change a ship's course so as to get farther off from an object. **b.** to withdraw; leave. **c.** *Informal.* to draw back the arm in order to strike; prepare to deal a blow: *He hauled off and struck the insolent lieutenant a blow to the chin.* **13. haul up, a.** to bring before a superior for judgment or reprimand; call to account. **b.** to come to a halt; stop. **c.** *Naut.* to change the course of (a sailing vessel) so as to sail closer to the wind. **d.** *Naut.* (of a sailing vessel) to come closer to the wind. **e.** *Naut.* (of a vessel) to come to a halt. —*n.* **14.** an act or instance of hauling; a strong pull or tug. **15.** something that is hauled. **16.** the load hauled at one time; quantity carried or transported. **17.** the distance or route over which anything is hauled. **18.** *Fishing.* **a.** the quantity of fish taken at one draft of the net. **b.** the draft of a fishing net. **c.** the place where a seine is hauled. **19.** the act of taking or acquiring something. **20.** something that is taken or acquired: *The thieves' haul included several valuable paintings.* **21. long haul, a.** a relatively great period of time: *In the long haul, he'll regret having been a school dropout.* **b.** a relatively great distance: *It's a long haul from Maine to Texas.* **c.** *Naut.* the drawing up on shore of a vessel for a relatively long period of time, as for winter storage or longer. **22. short haul, a.** a relatively small period of time: *For the short haul, he'll be able to get by on what he earns.* **b.** a relatively little distance: *The axle wouldn't break for just a short haul.* **c.** *Naut.* the drawing up on shore of a vessel for a relatively short period, as for repairs or painting. [1550–60; earlier *hall,* var. of HALE²]
—**Syn. 1.** See **draw.**

haul·age (hô′lij), *n.* **1.** the act or labor of hauling. **2.** the amount of force expended in hauling. **3.** a charge made, esp. by a railroad, for hauling equipment, commodities, etc. [1820–30; HAUL + -AGE]

haul·age·way (hô′lij wā′), *n.* a passageway by which coal, ore, etc., is hauled to the surface from an underground mine. [1905–10; HAULAGE + WAY]

haul·back (hôl′bak′), *n.* (in lumbering) a small line for pulling a cable back to its original position after it has been used to haul a log away. Also called **trip line.** [1900–05, *Amer.*; n. use of v. phrase *haul back*]

haul·er (hô′lər), *n.* **1.** a person who hauls. **2.** a commercial trucking company. **3.** a vehicle used for hauling or trucking. **4.** *Slang.* a car capable of very high speeds. [1665–75; HAUL + -ER¹]

haul·ier (hôl′yər), *n. Brit. Dial.* hauler.

haulm (hôm), *n.* **1.** stems or stalks collectively, as of grain or of peas, beans, or hops, esp. as used for litter or thatching. **2.** a single stem or stalk. Also, **halm.** [bef. 900; ME *halm,* OE *healm;* c. D, G *halm,* ON *halmr;* akin to L *culmus* stalk, Gk *kálamos* reed]

haunch (hônch, hänch), *n.* **1.** the hip. **2.** the fleshy part of the body about the hip. **3.** a hindquarter of an animal. **4.** the leg and loin of an animal, used for food. **5.** *Archit.* **a.** either side of an arch, extending from the vertex or crown to the impost. **b.** the part of a beam projecting below a floor or roof slab. [1150–1200; ME *haunche* < OF *hanche* < Gmc; cf. MD *hanke* haunch, hip, G *Hanke* haunch] —**haunched,** *adj.* —**haunch′less,** *adj.*

haunch′ bone′, the ilium or hipbone. [1350–1400; ME]

haunt (hônt, hänt; *for 10 also* hant), *v.t.* **1.** to visit habitually or appear to frequently as a spirit or ghost: *to haunt a house; to haunt a person.* **2.** to recur persistently to the consciousness of; remain with: *Memories of love haunted him.* **3.** to visit frequently; go to often: *He haunted the galleries and bars that the artists went to.* **4.** to frequent the company of; be often with: *He haunted famous men, hoping to gain celebrity for himself.* **5.** to disturb or distress; cause to have anxiety; trouble; worry: *His youthful escapades came back to haunt him.* —*v.i.* **6.** to reappear continually as a spirit or ghost. **7.** to visit habitually or regularly. **8.** to remain persistently; loiter; stay; linger. —*n.* **9.** Often, **haunts.** a place frequently visited: *to return to one's old haunts.* **10.** *Chiefly Midland and Southern U.S. and North Eng.* a ghost. [1200–50; ME *haunten* < OF *hanter* to frequent, prob. < ON *heimta* to lead home, deriv. of *heim* homewards; see HOME] —**haunt′er,** *n.*
—**Syn. 3.** frequent. **5.** obsess, beset, vex, plague.

haunt·ed (hôn′tid, hän′-), *adj.* **1.** inhabited or frequented by ghosts: *a haunted castle.* **2.** preoccupied, as with an emotion, memory, or idea; obsessed: *His haunted imagination gave him no peace.* **3.** disturbed; distressed; worried: *Haunted by doubt he again turned to law books on the subject.* [1275–1325; ME; see HAUNT, -ED²]

haunt·ing (hôn′ting, hän′-), *adj.* **1.** remaining in the consciousness; not quickly forgotten: *haunting music; haunting memories.* —*n.* **2.** the act of a person or thing that haunts; visitation. [1275–1325; ME; see HAUNT, -ING², -ING¹] —**haunt′ing·ly,** *adv.*

Haup·pauge (hä′pôg, -pog), *n.* a city on central Long Island, in SE New York. 20,960.

Haupt·mann (houpt′män′), *n.* **Ger·hart** (geR′härt), 1862–1946, German dramatist, novelist, and poet: Nobel prize 1912.

hau·ri·ant (hôr′ē ənt), *adj. Heraldry.* (of a fish) represented as erect, with the head upward: *a dolphin hauriant.* [1565–75; var. of *haurient* < L *haurient-* (s. of *hauriēns*) drawing, scooping up, prp. of *haurīre;* see HAUSTELLUM, -ANT, -ENT]

Hau·sa (hou′sä, -sə, -zə), *n., pl.* **-sas,** (*esp. collectively*) **-sa** for 1. **1.** a member of an indigenous people of northern Nigeria and southern Niger whose culture has been strongly influenced by Islam. **2.** the language of the Hausa people, belonging to the Chadic branch of the Afroasiatic family, widely used in Africa as a language of commerce. Also, **Haus′sa.**

Haus′dorff space′ (hous′dôrf, houz′-), *Math.* a topological space in which each pair of points can be separated by two disjoint open sets containing the points. [named after Felix *Hausdorff* (1868–1942), German mathematician, who first described it]

hau·sen (hô′zən; *Ger.* hou′zən), *n.* beluga (def. 1). [1735–45; < G; OHG *hūso;* see ISINGLASS]

haus·frau (hous′frou′), *n., pl.* **-fraus, -frau·en** (-frou′-ən). a housewife. [1790–1800; < G, equiv. to *Haus* HOUSE + *Frau* wife, woman]

Haus·ho·fer (hous′hō fər), *n.* **Karl,** 1860–1946, German geographer and general: political adviser to Hitler.

Hauss·mann (hous′mən; *Fr.* ōs mAN′), *n.* **Georges Eu·gène** (zhôrzh œ zhen′), **Baron,** 1809–91, French administrator who improved the landscaping, street designs, and utilities systems of Paris. —**Hauss·mann·i·za·tion** (hous′mə nə zā′shən), *n.*

haust., (in prescriptions) draught. [< L *haustus.* See HAUSTELLUM]

haus·tel·late (hô stel′it, hô′stə lāt′), *adj. Zool.* **1.** having a haustellum. **2.** adapted for sucking, as the mouthparts of certain insects. [1825–35; HAUSTELL(UM) + -ATE¹]

haus·tel·lum (hô stel′əm), *n., pl.* **haus·tel·la** (hô-stel′ə). (in certain crustaceans and insects) an organ or part of the proboscis adapted for sucking blood or plant juices. [1810–20; < NL, dim. of L *haustrum* scoop on a water wheel, equiv. to *haus-,* var. s. of *haurīre* to scoop up, draw + *-trum* suffix of instrument; for formation, see CASTELLUM]

haus·to·ri·um (hô stôr′ē əm, -stōr′-), *n., pl.* **haus·to·ri·a** (hô stôr′ē ə, -stōr′-). **1.** a projection from the hypha of a fungus into the organic matter from which it absorbs nutrients. **2.** the penetrating feeding organ of certain parasites. [1870–75; < NL, equiv. to L *haus-* (var. s. of *haurīre* to draw, scoop up) + *-tōrium* -TORY²] —**haus·to′ri·al,** *adj.*

haut·bois (hō′boi, ō′boi), *n., pl.* **-bois.** hautboy.

haut·boy (hō′boi, ō′boi), *n.* oboe. [1565–75; < MF *hautbois,* equiv. to *haut* high (see HAUGHTY) + *bois* wood (see BUSH¹)] —**haut′boy·ist,** *n.*

haute (ōt), *adj.* **1.** high-class or high-toned; fancy: *an haute restaurant that attracts a monied crowd.* **2.** high; elevated; upper. Also, **haut** (ō; *esp. before a vowel* ōt). [1780–90; generalized from *haute couture, haute cuisine,* etc.; < F, fem. of *haut* lit., high; see HAUGHTY]

haute cou·ture (ōt′ ko͞o to͝or′; *Fr.* ōt ko͞o tyR′), **1.** high fashion; the most fashionable and influential dressmaking and designing. **2.** the fashions so created. **3.** the leading dressmaking establishments in the world of fashion, considered collectively. [< F]

haute cui·sine (ōt′ kwi zēn′; *Fr.* ōt kwē zēn′), fine or gourmet cooking; food preparation as an art. [< F]

haute é·cole (ōt′ ā kōl′, -kôl′; *Fr.* ō tā kôl′), *pl.* **hautes é·coles** (ōts′ ā kōl′, -kôl′; *Fr.* ōt zā kôl′). **1.** a series of intricate steps, gaits, etc., taught to an exhibition horse. **2.** dressage (def. 2). [< F: lit., high school]

Haute-Ga·ronne (ōt gA Rôn′), *n.* a department in S France. 777,431; 2458 sq. mi. (6365 sq. km). *Cap.:* Toulouse.

Haute-Loire (ōt lwAR′), *n.* a department in central France. 205,491; 1931 sq. mi. (5000 sq. km). *Cap.:* Le Puy.

Haute-Marne (ōt mARN′), *n.* a department in E France. 212,304; 2416 sq. mi. (6255 sq. km). *Cap.:* Chaumont.

haute-piece (hōt′pēs′), *n. Armor.* a standing flange fixed to or formed on a pauldron as a protection for one side of the neck. [1490–1500; < F: lit., high piece]

Haute·rive (*Fr.* ōt Rēv′), *n.* a town in SE Quebec, in E Canada. 13,995.

Hautes-Alpes (ōt zAlp′), *n.* a department in SE France. 97,358; 2179 sq. mi. (5645 sq. km). *Cap.:* Gap.

Haute-Saône (ōt sōn′), *n.* a department in E France. 222,254; 2075 sq. mi. (5375 sq. km). *Cap.:* Vesoul.

Haute-Sa·voie (ōt sA vwä′), *n.* a department in E France. 447,795; 1775 sq. mi. (4595 sq. km). *Cap.:* Annecy.

Hautes-Py·ré·nées (ōt pē Rā nā′), *n.* a department in SW France. 227,222; 1751 sq. mi. (4535 sq. km). *Cap.:* Tarbes.

hau·teur (hō tûr′; *Fr.* ō tœR′), *n.* haughty manner or spirit; arrogance. [1620–30; < F, equiv. to *haut* high (see HAUGHTY) + *-eur* -OR¹]

Haute-Vienne (ōt vyen′), *n.* a department in central France. 352,149; 2145 sq. mi. (5555 sq. km). *Cap.:* Limoges.

haut monde (ō′ mond′; *Fr.* ō môNd′), high society. Also, **haute-monde** (ōt′mond′). [< F]

hau′ tree′ (hou), a clambering tree, *Hibiscus tileaceus,* of tropical shores, having leathery, ovate leaves and yellow flowers that turn dark red as they fade, and yielding a fiber used as cordage. Also called **mahoe, sea hibiscus.** [1910–15; < Hawaiian *hau* hau tree]

Haut-Rhin (ō RAN′), *n.* a department in NE France. 635,209; 1354 sq. mi. (3505 sq. km). *Cap.:* Colmar.

Hauts-de-Seine (ō də sen′), *n.* a department in N France. 1,438,930; 63 sq. mi. (163 sq. km). *Cap.:* Nanterre.

ha·üy·nite (ä wē′nit), *n.* a relatively rare feldspathoid mineral related to sodalite: sometimes confused with lapis lazuli. Also, **ha·üyne** (ä wēn′). [1865–70; < F *haüyne* (*Haüy* + *-(i)ne* -INE¹, after R. Haüy (1743–1822), French mineralogist) + -ITE¹]

Ha·van·a (hə van′ə), *n.* **1.** Spanish, **Habana.** a seaport in and the capital of Cuba, on the NW coast. 1,800,000. **2.** a cigar made in Cuba or of Cuban tobacco.

Ha·va·su·pai (hä′və so͞o′pī), *n., pl.* **-pais,** (*esp. collectively*) **-pai** for 1. **1.** a member of a small tribe of nomadic North American Indians now living in Arizona. **2.** the Yuman language of the Havasupai.

Hav·da·lah (*Seph.* häv dä lä′; *Ashk.* häv dô′lə), *n. Hebrew.* a religious ceremony, observed by Jews at the conclusion of the Sabbath or a festival, that consists of blessings over wine, spices, and the light of a candle. Also, ***Habdalah.*** [*habhdālāh* lit., division, separation]

have (hav; *unstressed* həv, əv; *for 26 usually* haf), *v.* and *auxiliary v., pres. sing. 1st pers.* **have,** *2nd* **have** or (*Archaic*) **hast,** *3rd* **has** or (*Archaic*) **hath,** *pres. pl.* **have;** *past sing. 1st pers.* **had,** *2nd* **had** or (*Archaic*) **hadst** or **had·dest,** *3rd* **had,** *past pl.* **had;** *past part.* **had;** *pres. part.* **hav·ing,** *n.* —*v.t.* **1.** to possess; own; hold for use; contain: *He has property. The work has an index.* **2.** to hold, possess, or accept in some relation, as of kindred or relative position: *He wanted to marry her, but she wouldn't have him.* **3.** to get, receive, or take: *to have a part in a play; to have news.* **4.** to experience, undergo, or endure, as joy or pain: *Have a good time. He had a heart attack last year.* **5.** to hold in mind, sight, etc.: *to have doubts.* **6.** to cause to, as by command or invitation: *Have him come here at five.* **7.** to be related to or be in a certain relation to: *She has three cousins. He has a kind boss.* **8.** to show or exhibit in action or words: *She had the crust to refuse my invitation.* **9.** to be identified or distinguished by; possess the characteristic of: *He has a mole on his left cheek. This wood has a silky texture.* **10.** to engage in or carry on: *to have a talk; to have a fight.* **11.** to partake of; eat or drink: *He had cake and coffee for dessert.* **12.** to permit or allow: *I will not have any talking during the concert.* **13.** to assert, maintain, or represent as being: *Rumor has it that she's going to be married.* **14.** to know, understand, or be skilled in: *to have neither Latin nor Greek.* **15.** to beget or give birth to: *to have a baby.* **16.** to hold an advantage over: *He has you there.* **17.** to outwit, deceive, or cheat: *We realized we'd been had by an expert con artist.* **18.** to control or possess through bribery; bribe. **19.** to gain possession of: *There is none to be had at that price.* **20.** to hold or put in a certain position or situation: *The problem had me stumped. They had him where they wanted him.* **21.** to exercise, display, or make use of: *Have pity on him.* **22.** to invite or cause to be present as a companion or guest: *We had Evelyn and Everett over for dinner. He has his bodyguard with him at all times.* **23.** to engage in sexual intercourse with. —*v.i.* **24.** to be in possession of money or wealth: *There are some who have and some who have not.* —*auxiliary verb.* **25.** (used with a past participle to form perfect tenses): *She has gone. It would have been an enjoyable party if he hadn't felt downcast.* **26.** to be required, compelled, or under obligation (fol. by infinitival *to,* with or without a main verb): *I have to leave now. I didn't want to study, but I had to.* **27. had better** or **best,** ought to: *You'd better go now, it's late.* **28. had rather.** See **rather** (def. 8). **29. have at,** to go at vigorously; attack: *First he decided to have at his correspondence.* **30. have done,** to cease; finish: *It seemed that they would never have done with their struggle.* **31. have had it, a.** to become weary of or disgusted with whatever one has been doing: *I've been working like a fool, but now I've had it.* **b.** to suffer defeat; fail: *He was a great pitcher, but after this season he'll have had it.* **c.** to have missed a last opportunity: *He refused to take any more excuses and told them all that they'd had it.* **d.** to become unpopular or passé: *Quiz shows have had it.* **32. have it coming,** to merit or deserve: *When they lost their fortune, everyone said that they had it coming.* **33. have it in for,** to plan or wish to do something unpleasant to; hold a grudge against: *She has it in for intelligent students who fail to use their abilities.* **34. have it out,** to come to an understanding or decision through discus-

sion or combat: *We've been in disagreement about this for a long time, and I think we should have it out, once and for all.* **35. have on, a.** to be clothed in; be wearing: *She had on a new dress.* **b.** to have arranged or planned: *What do you have on for Christmas?* **c.** to tease (a person); make the butt of a joke. Cf. **put** (def. 34). **36. have to do with, a.** to be connected or associated with: *Your lack of confidence probably had a lot to do with your not getting the job.* **b.** to deal with; be concerned with: *I will have nothing to do with their personal squabbles.* **37. to have and to hold,** to possess legally; have permanent possession of: *The house, with the mortgage finally paid, was theirs at last to have and to hold.* —*n.* **38.** Usually, **haves.** an individual or group that has wealth, social position, or other material benefits (contrasted with *have-not*). [bef. 900; ME *haven, habben,* OE *habban;* c. G *haben,* ON *hafa,* Goth *haban* to have; perh. akin to HEAVE]
—**Syn. 1.** HAVE, HOLD, OCCUPY, OWN, POSSESS mean to be, in varying degrees, in possession of something. HAVE, being the most general word, admits of the widest range of application: *to have money, rights, discretion, a disease, a glimpse, an idea; to have a friend's umbrella.* To HOLD is to have in one's grasp or one's control, but not necessarily as one's own: *to hold stakes.* To OCCUPY is to hold and use, but not necessarily by any right of ownership: *to occupy a chair, a house, a position.* To OWN is to have the full rights of property in a thing, which, however, another may be holding or enjoying: *to own a house that is rented to tenants.* POSSESS is a more formal equivalent for OWN and suggests control, and often occupation, of large holdings: *to possess vast territories.* **3.** obtain, gain, secure, procure. —**Ant. 1.** lack.
—**Usage.** See **of.**

havelock

Ha•vel (hä′vel), *n.* **Vá•clav** (väts′läf), born 1936, Czech writer and political leader: president of Czechoslovakia 1989–92; president of the Czech Republic since 1993.

have•lock (hav′lok), *n.* a cap cover with a flap hanging over the back of the neck, for protection from the sun. [1860–65, *Amer.;* named after Sir Henry *Havelock* (1795–1857), English general in India]

Have•lock (hav′lok, -lək), *n.* **1.** a town in SE North Carolina. 17,718. **2.** a male given name.

ha•ven (hā′vən), *n.* **1.** a harbor or port. **2.** any place of shelter and safety; refuge; asylum. —*v.t.* **3.** to shelter, as in a haven. [bef. 1050; ME; OE *hæfen;* c. D *haven,* G *Hafen,* ON *hǫfn;* akin to OE *hæf,* ON *haf* sea]
—**Syn. 1.** See **harbor.**

have-not (hav′not′, -not′), *n.* Usually, **have-nots.** an individual or group that is without wealth, social position, or other material benefits (contrasted with *have*). [1830–40]

have•n't (hav′ənt), contraction of *have not.*
—**Usage.** See **contraction.**

ha•ver (hā′vər), *v.i. Chiefly Brit.* to equivocate; vacillate. [1780–90; orig. uncert.]

ha•ver (KHä ver′), *n., pl.* ***ha•ve•rim*** (KHä′ve rēm′). *Hebrew.* friend; comrade; companion.

Hav•er•ford (hav′ər fərd), *n.* a township in SE Pennsylvania, near Philadelphia. 52,349.

Ha•ver•hill (hā′vər əl, -vrəl), *n.* a city in NE Massachusetts, on the Merrimack River. 46,865.

Ha•ver•ing (hā′vər ing), *n.* a borough of Greater London, England. 237,200.

ha•vers (hā′vərz), *interj. Chiefly Scot.* nonsense; poppycock. [pl. of *haver* nonsense, akin to HAVER]

hav•er•sack (hav′ər sak′), *n.* **1.** a single-strapped bag worn over one shoulder and used for carrying supplies. **2.** a soldier's bag for rations, extra clothing, etc. [1740–50; earlier *havresack* < F *havresac* < G *Habersack,* equiv. to *Haber* oats (cf. dial. E *haver* < ON *hafrar* oats) + *Sack* SACK¹]

Ha•ver′sian canal′ (hə vûr′zhən), *(sometimes l.c.) Anat.* a microscopic channel in bone, through which a blood vessel runs. [1835–45; named after Clopton *Havers* (d. 1702), English anatomist; see -IAN]

Haver′sian sys′tem, *(sometimes l.c.) Anat.* a Haversian canal and the series of concentric bony plates surrounding it. [1835–45; see HAVERSIAN CANAL]

hav•er•sine (hav′ər sīn′), *n. Trigonom.* one half the versed sine of a given angle or arc. [1870–75; HA(LF) + VER(SED) + SINE¹]

Hav•i•lah (hav′ə lä′, -lə), *n.* a female given name.

Hav•i•land (hav′ə lənd), *n.* **John,** 1792–1852, English architect, in the U.S.

hav•oc (hav′ək), *n., v.,* **-ocked, -ock•ing.** —*n.* **1.** great destruction or devastation; ruinous damage. **2. cry havoc,** to warn of danger or disaster. **3. play havoc with, a.** to create confusion or disorder in: *The wind played havoc with the papers on the desk.* **b.** to destroy; ruin: *The bad weather played havoc with our vacation plans.* —*v.t.* **4.** to work havoc upon; devastate. —*v.i.* **5.** to work havoc. [1400–50; late ME *havok* < AF (in phrase *crier havok* to cry havoc, i.e., utter the command *havoc!* as signal for pillaging), MF *havot* in same sense < Gmc] —**hav′ock•er,** *n.*
—**Syn. 1.** desolation, waste. See **ruin.**

CONCISE ETYMOLOGY KEY: <, descended or borrowed from; >, whence; b., blend of, blended; c., cognate with; cf., compare; deriv., derivative; equiv., equivalent; imit., imitative; obl., oblique; r., replacing; s., stem; sp., spelling, spelled; resp., respelling, respelled; trans., translation; ?, origin unknown; *, unattested; ‡, probably earlier than. See the full key inside the front cover.

Ha•vre (hav′ər *for 1;* hä′vrə, -vər *for 2*), *n.* **1.** a city in N Montana. 10,891. **2.** See **Le Havre.**

ha•vu•rah (*Seph., Ashk.* KHä′voo rä′; *Eng.* KHä′vŏŏ-rä′), *n., pl.* ***-roth, -rot*** (*Seph.* -rôt′; *Ashk.* -rōs′), *Eng.* **-rahs.** *Hebrew.* a Jewish fellowship, esp. an informal one that meets regularly for discussion or prayer. Also, ***chavurah.*** [*ḥăbhūrāh* lit., company, group]

haw¹ (hô), *v.i.* **1.** to utter a sound representing a hesitation or pause in speech. —*n.* **2.** a sound or pause of hesitation. Cf. **hem²** (def. 3). [1625–35; imit.]

haw² (hô), *interj.* **1.** (used as a word of command to a horse or other draft animal, usually directing it to turn to the left.) —*v.t., v.i.* **2.** to turn or make a turn to the left: *The horse refused to haw.* Cf. **gee¹.** [1835–45, *Amer.;* appar. orig. the impv. *haw!* look! of ME *hawen,* OE *hāwian;* akin to L *cavēre* to beware]

haw³ (hô), *n.* **1.** the fruit of the Old World hawthorn, *Crataegus laevigata,* or of other species of the same genus. **2.** the hawthorn. [before 1000; ME; OE *haga,* presumably identical with *haga* hedge, fence; cf. HAWTHORN]

haw⁴ (hô), *n.* the thin, protective membrane at the inner corner of the lower eyelid of a horse, dog, etc.; nictitating membrane. [1515–1525; orig. uncert.]

Haw., Hawaii.

Ha•wai•i (hə wī′ē, -wä′-, -wä′yə, hä vä′ē), *n.* **1.** a state of the United States comprising the N Pacific islands of Hawaii, Kahoolawe, Kauai, Lanai, Maui, Molokai, Niihau, and Oahu: a U.S. territory 1900–59; admitted to the Union 1959. 965,000; 6424 sq. mi. (16,715 sq. km). *Cap.:* Honolulu. *Abbr.:* HI (for use with zip code), Haw. **2.** the largest island of Hawaii, in the SE part. 63,468; 4021 sq. mi. (10,415 sq. km).

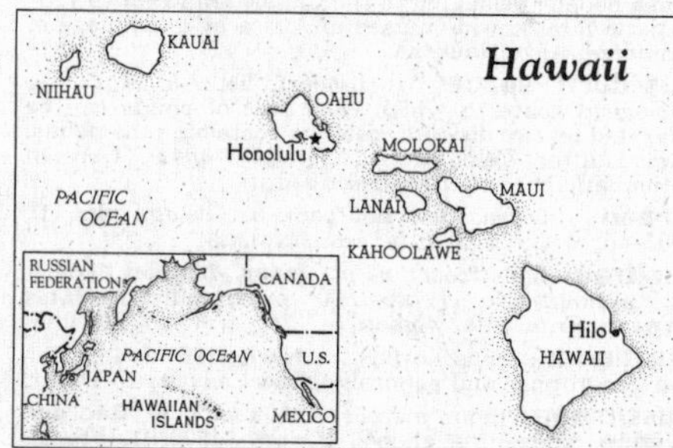

Ha•wai•ian (hə wī′ən, -wä′yən), *adj.* **1.** of or pertaining to Hawaii or the Hawaiian Islands. —*n.* **2.** a native or inhabitant of Hawaii or the Hawaiian Islands. **3.** the aboriginal language of Hawaii, a Polynesian language. [1815–25; HAWAII + -AN]

Hawai′ian Gar′dens, a town in SW California. 10,548.

Hawai′ian goose′, nene. [1825–35]

Hawai′ian guitar′, a six-to-eight-string electric guitar, fretted with a piece of metal or bone to produce a whining, glissando sound, played in a horizontal position usually resting on the performer's knees or on a stand, and much used by country music performers. Also called **steel guitar.** [1925–30]

Hawai′ian hawk′, io.

Hawai′ian high′, *Meteorol.* See **Pacific high.**

Hawai′ian hon′eycreeper, any small to medium-sized finches of the subfamily Drepanidinae, native to the Hawaiian Islands and including many rare and extinct species.

Hawai′ian Is′lands, a group of islands in the N Pacific; 2090 mi. (3370 km) SW of San Francisco: includes the eight islands comprising the state of Hawaii and volcanic, rock, and coral islets. Formerly, **Sandwich Islands.**

Hawai′ian Pid′gin, an English-based creole widely spoken in Hawaii.

Hawai′ian shirt′, a short-sleeved, loose-fitting, open-collar shirt originally worn in Hawaii, made of lightweight fabric printed in colorful, often bold designs of flowers, leaves, birds, beaches, etc. Also called **aloha shirt.** [1950–55]

Hawai′i time′. See **Alaska-Hawaii time.** Also called **Hawai′i Stand′ard Time′.** [1900–05]

Hawai′i Volca′noes Na′tional Park′, a large national park that includes the active volcanoes Kilauea and Mauna Loa on the island of Hawaii and the extinct crater Haleakala on Maui. 343 sq. mi. (890 sq. km).

Ha•wal•li (hə wä′lē), *n.* a town in E central Kuwait. 106,542.

haw•finch (hô′finch′), *n.* a European grosbeak, *Coccothraustes coccothraustes.* [1665–75; HAW¹ + FINCH]

hawg (hôg), *n., v.t., v.i. Pron. Spelling.* hog.

haw-haw (hô′hô′), *interj.* **1.** (used to represent the sound of a loud, boisterous laugh.) —*n.* **2.** a guffaw. [1825–35; imit.; see HA-HA¹]

hawk¹ (hôk), *n.* **1.** any of numerous birds of prey of the family Accipitridae, having a short, hooked beak, broad wings, and curved talons. **2.** any of several similar, unrelated birds, as the nighthawk. **3.** *Informal.* a person who preys on others, as a sharper. **4.** Also called **war hawk.** *Informal.* a person, esp. one in public office, who advocates war or a belligerent national attitude. Cf. **dove** (def. 5). **5.** any person who pursues an aggressive policy in business, government, etc. —*v.i.* **6.** to fly, or hunt on the wing, like a hawk. **7.** to hunt with hawks. [bef. 900; ME *hauk(e),* OE *hafoc;* c. OFris *havek,* OS *habuc* OHG *habuh,* ON *haukr* hawk, perh. Pol *kobuz* kind of falcon] —**hawk′like′,** *adj.*

red-tailed hawk, *Buteo jamaicensis,* length 2 ft. (0.6 m)

hawk² (hôk), *v.t.* **1.** to peddle or offer for sale by calling aloud in public. **2.** to advertise or offer for sale: *to hawk soap on television.* **3.** to spread (rumors, news, etc.). —*v.i.* **4.** to carry wares about for sale; peddle. [1470–80; back formation from HAWKER²]

hawk³ (hôk), *v.i.* **1.** to make an effort to raise phlegm from the throat; clear the throat noisily. —*v.t.* **2.** to raise by hawking: *to hawk phlegm up.* —*n.* **3.** a noisy effort to clear the throat. [1575–85; imit.; see HAW¹]

hawk⁴ (hôk), *n.* a small, square board with a handle underneath it, used by plasterers and masons to hold plaster or mortar being applied. [1350–1400; ME; perh. var. of *hache* battle-ax (see HATCHET)]

Hawk (hôk), *n. Mil.* a medium-range, mobile U.S. surface-to-air missile system. [*H(oming) A(ll the) W(ay) K(iller)*]

hawk•bill (hôk′bil′), *n.* See **hawksbill turtle.** [1775–85; HAWK¹ + BILL²]

Hawke (hôk), *n.* **Robert (James Lee),** born 1929, Australian political leader: prime minister 1983–91.

hawk•er¹ (hô′kər), *n.* a person who hunts with hawks or other birds of prey. [bef. 1000; ME; OE *hafecere.* See HAWK¹, -ER¹]

hawk•er² (hô′kər), *n.* a person who offers goods for sale by shouting his or her wares in the street or going from door to door; peddler. [1375–1425; late ME < MLG *haker* retail dealer; akin to MD *hac* in same sense; cf. HUCKSTER]

Hawk•eye (hôk′ī′), *n., pl.* **-eyes.** a native or inhabitant of Iowa (used as a nickname).

hawk-eyed (hôk′īd′), *adj.* having very keen sight: *a hawk-eyed guard.* [1810–20]

Hawk′eye State′, Iowa (used as a nickname).

hawk•ing (hô′king), *n.* the sport of hunting with hawks or other birds of prey; falconry. [1300–50; ME; see HAWK¹, -ING¹]

Haw•kins (hô′kinz), *n.* **1. Sir Anthony Hope** (*"Anthony Hope"*), 1863–1933, English novelist and playwright. **2. Coleman,** 1904–69, U.S. jazz saxophonist. **3.** Also, **Hawkyns. Sir John,** 1532–95, English slave trader and rear admiral.

hawk•ish (hô′kish), *adj.* **1.** resembling a hawk, as in appearance or behavior. **2.** advocating war or a belligerently threatening diplomatic policy. [1835–45; HAWK¹ + -ISH¹] —**hawk′ish•ly,** *adv.* —**hawk′ish•ness,** *n.*

hawk′ moth′, any of numerous moths of the family Sphingidae, noted for their very swift flight and ability to hover while sipping nectar from flowers. Also called **sphingid, sphinx moth, hummingbird moth.** [1775–85]

hawk•nose (hôk′nōz′), *n.* a nose curved like the beak of a hawk. [1525–35; back formation from *hawk-nosed;* see HAWK¹, NOSE, -ED³] —**hawk′nosed′,** *adj.*

hawk′ owl′, a gray and white diurnal owl, *Surnia ulula,* of northern parts of the Northern Hemisphere, resembling a hawk in appearance and actions. [1735–45]

Hawks (hôks), *n.* **Howard (Winchester),** 1896–1977, U.S. film director.

hawks′bill tur′tle (hôks′bil′), a sea turtle, *Eretmochelys imbricata,* the shell of which is the source of tortoise shell: an endangered species. Also called **hawks′bill′, hawkbill, tortoiseshell turtle.** [1650–60; HAWK¹ + 'S¹ + BILL²]

hawk's-eye (hôks′ī′), *n.* a dark-blue chatoyant quartz formed by the silicification of crocidolite, used for ornamental purposes. Cf. **tiger's-eye** (def. 1). [1675–85]

hawk•shaw (hôk′shô′), *n.* a detective. [1900–05; after *Hawkshaw,* a detective in the play *The Ticket of Leave Man* (1863) by Tom Taylor]

Hawks•moor (hôks′mŏŏr′), *n.* **Nicholas,** 1661–1736, English architect.

hawk•weed (hôk′wēd′), *n.* **1.** any composite plant of the genus *Hieracium,* usually bearing yellow flowers. **2.** any of various related plants. [1555–65; trans. of NL, L *hierăcium* < Gk *hierák,-* s. of *hiérāx* hawk + L *-ium* -IUM; see WEED¹]

Haw•kyns (hô′kinz), *n.* **Sir John.** See **Hawkins, Sir John.**

Ha•worth (hä′wərth, hô′-), *n.* **Sir Walter Norman,** 1883–1950, English chemist: Nobel prize 1937.

hawse (hôz, hôs), *n., v.,* **hawsed, haws•ing.** *Naut.* —*n.* **1.** the part of a bow where the hawseholes are located. **2.** a hawsehole or hawsepipe. **3.** the distance or space between the bow of an anchored vessel and the point on the surface of the water above the anchor. **4.** the relative position or arrangement of the port and starboard anchor cables when both are used to moor a vessel. **5. to hawse,** with both bow anchors out: *a ship riding to hawse.* —*v.i.* **6.** (of a vessel) to pitch heavily at anchor. [bef. 1000; ME *hals,* OE *heals* bow of a ship, lit., neck; c. ON *hals* in same senses, OFris, OS, OHG *hals* neck, throat, L *collus* (< **kolsos*)]

hawse·hole (hôz′hōl′, hôs′-), *n. Naut.* a hole in the stem or bow of a vessel for an anchor cable. [1655–65]

hawse·pipe (hôz′pīp′, hôs′-), *n. Naut.* an iron or steel pipe in the stem or bow of a vessel through which an anchor cable passes. [1860–65; HAWSE + PIPE[1]]

haw·ser (hô′zər, -sər), *n. Naut.* a heavy rope for mooring or towing. [1300–50; ME *haucer* < AF *hauceour,* equiv. to MF *hauci(er)* to hoist (< LL **altiāre* to raise, deriv. of L *altus* high; see HAUGHTY) + *-our* -OR[2], -ER[2]]

haw′ser bend′, a knot uniting the ends of two lines. [1895–1900]

haw·ser-laid (hô′zər lād′, -sər-), *adj. Ropemaking.* **1.** cable-laid (def. 1). **2.** plain-laid. [1760–70]

haw·thorn (hô′thôrn′), *n.* any of numerous plants belonging to the genus *Crataegus,* of the rose family, typically a small tree with stiff thorns, certain North American species of which have white or pink blossoms and bright-colored fruits and are cultivated in hedges. [bef. 900; ME; OE *haguthorn,* c. MD *hagedorn,* MHG *hagendorn,* ON *hagthorn.* See HAW[3], THORN] **—haw′thorn′y,** *adj.*

Haw·thorne (hô′thôrn′), *n.* **1. Nathaniel,** 1804–64, U.S. novelist and short-story writer. **2.** a city in SW California, SW of Los Angeles. 56,447. **3.** a city in NE New Jersey. 18,200.

Haw′thorne effect′, *Psychol.* a positive change in the performance of a group of persons taking part in an experiment or study due to their perception of being singled out for special consideration. [1960–65; after the *Hawthorne* Works of the Western Electric Company, Cicero, Ill., where such an effect was observed in experiments]

Haw·thorn·esque (hô′thôr nesk′), characteristic of or resembling the style, manner, or subjects of the writings of Nathaniel Hawthorne. [HAWTHORNE + -ESQUE]

hay (hā), *n.* **1.** grass, clover, alfalfa, etc., cut and dried for use as forage. **2.** grass mowed or intended for mowing. **3.** *Slang.* **a.** a small sum of money: *Twenty dollars an hour for doing very little certainly ain't hay.* **b.** money: *A thousand dollars for a day's work is a lot of hay!* **4.** *Slang.* marijuana. **5. a roll in the hay,** *Slang.* sexual intercourse. **6. hit the hay,** *Informal.* to go to bed: *It got to be past midnight before anyone thought of hitting the hay.* **7. in the hay,** in bed; retired, esp. for the night: *By ten o'clock he's in the hay.* **8. make hay of,** to scatter in disorder; render ineffectual: *The destruction of the manuscript made hay of two years of painstaking labor.* **9. make hay while the sun shines,** to seize an opportunity when it presents itself: *If you want to be a millionaire, you have to make hay while the sun shines.* Also, **make hay.** —*v.t.* **10.** to convert (plant material) into hay. **11.** to furnish (horses, cows, etc.) with hay. —*v.i.* **12.** to cut grass, clover, or the like, and store for use as forage. [bef. 900; ME; OE *hēg;* c. G *Heu,* ON *hey,* Goth *hawi.* See HEW] **—hay′ey,** *adj.*

Hay (hā), *n.* **John Milton,** 1838–1905, U.S. statesman and author.

Ha·ya·ka·wa (hä′yə kä′wə), *n.* **1. S(amuel) I(chi·ye)** (i chē′ā), 1906–92, U.S. semanticist, educator, and politician, born in Canada: senator 1977–83. **2. Ses·sue** (sesh′o͞o; *Japn.* se sho͞o′), 1889–1973, Japanese film actor.

hay·cock (hā′kok′), *n.* a small conical pile of hay stacked in a hayfield while the hay is awaiting removal to a barn. [1425–75; late ME; see HAY, COCK[3]]

Hay·den (hād′n), *n.* **Melissa** (*Mildred Herman*), born 1928, Canadian ballerina in the U.S.

Hay·dn (hīd′n), *n.* **Franz Jo·seph** (franz jō′zəf, -səf, frants; *Ger.* fʀänts yō′zef), 1732–1809, Austrian composer.

hay′ doo′dle, doodle[2].

Ha·yek (hä′yek), *n.* **Frie·drich Au·gust von** (frē′drik ô′gəst von; *Ger.* fʀē′dʀɪkн ou′go͝ost fən), 1899–1992, British economist, born in Austria: Nobel prize 1974.

Hayes (hāz), *n.* **1. Carlton J(oseph) H(untley),** 1882–1964, U.S. historian, educator, and diplomat. **2. Helen** (*Helen Hayes Brown MacArthur*), 1900–93, U.S. actress. **3. Roland,** 1887–1977, U.S. tenor. **4. Rutherford B(irchard)** (bûr′chərd), 1822–93, nineteenth president of the U.S. 1877–81.

hay′ fe′ver, *Pathol.* a type of allergic rhinitis affecting the mucous membranes of the eyes and respiratory tract, affecting susceptible persons usually during the summer, caused by pollen of ragweed and certain other plants. [1820–30]

hay·field (hā′fēld′), *n.* a field where grass, alfalfa, etc., are grown for making into hay. [1775–85; HAY + FIELD]

hay·fork (hā′fôrk′), *n.* **1.** a forklike tool for pitching hay. **2.** a machine for loading or unloading hay. [1545–55; HAY + FORK]

hay·lage (hā′lij), *n.* silage of about 40 to 50 percent moisture made from forage stored in a silo. [1955–60; HAY + (SI)LAGE]

Hay·ley (hā′lē), *n.* a female given name.

hay·lift (hā′lift′), *n.* an airlift of hay for animals that have been snowed in. [HAY + (AIR)LIFT]

hay·loft (hā′lôft′, -loft′), *n.* a loft in a stable or barn for the storage of hay. [1565–75; HAY + LOFT]

hay·mak·er (hā′mā′kər), *n.* **1.** a person or machine that cuts hay and spreads it to dry. **2.** *Slang.* a punch delivered with great force, esp. one that results in a knockout. [1400–50; 1910–15 for def. 2; late ME *heymakere.* See HAY, MAKER]

Hay·mar·ket (hā′mär′kit), *n.* **1.** a famous London market 1644–1830. **2.** a street in London, site of this market, known for its theaters. **3.** a playhouse erected in London in 1720 and still in use.

Hay′market Square′, a square in Chicago: scene of a riot (**Hay′market Ri′ot**) in 1886 between police and labor unionists.

hay·mow (hā′mou′), *n.* **1.** hay stored in a barn. **2.** hayloft. [1470–80; HAY + MOW[2]]

Haynes (hānz), *n.* **El·wood** (el′wo͝od′), 1857–1925, U.S. inventor.

Hay′-Paunce′fote Trea′ty (hā′pôns′fo͝ot), an agreement (1901) between the U.S. and Great Britain giving the U.S. the sole right to build a canal across Central America connecting the Atlantic and Pacific. Cf. **Clayton-Bulwer Treaty.** [named after J. M. HAY and Julian *Pauncefote* (1828–1902), English diplomat]

hay·rack (hā′rak′), *n.* **1.** a rack for holding hay for feeding horses or cattle. **2.** a rack or framework mounted on a wagon, for use in carrying hay, straw, or the like. **3.** the wagon and rack together. [1815–25; HAY + RACK[1]]

hay′ rake′, a farm implement used to rake hay from a swath into a windrow. Also, **hay′rake′.** [1715–25]

hay·rick (hā′rik′), *n.* **1.** *Chiefly Midland U.S.* rick[1] (def. 1). **2.** *Chiefly Brit.* a haystack. [1400–50; late ME *heyrek.* See HAY, RICK[1]]

hay·ride (hā′rīd′), *n.* a pleasure ride or outing, usually at night, by a group in an open wagon or truck partly filled with hay. [1855–60, *Amer.*; HAY + RIDE]

Hays (hāz), *n.* **1. Will (Harrison),** 1879–1954, U.S. lawyer, politician, and official of the motion-picture industry. **2.** a city in central Kansas. 16,301.

hay′-scent·ed fern′ (hā′sen′tid), a fern, *Dennstaedtia punctilobula,* of eastern North America, having brittle, yellow-green fronds. [1860–65]

hay·seed (hā′sēd′), *n.* **1.** grass seed, esp. that shaken out of hay. **2.** small bits of the chaff, straw, etc., of hay. **3.** an unsophisticated person from a rural area; yokel; hick. [1570–80; HAY + SEED]

hay′ shock′, *South Midland and Southern U.S.* a haycock.

hay·stack (hā′stak′), *n.* a stack of hay with a conical or ridged top, built up in the mowed field so as to prevent the accumulation of moisture and promote drying. Also, *esp. Brit.,* **hayrick.** [1425–75; late ME. See HAY, STACK]

Hay·ti (hā′tē), *n.* **1.** former name of **Haiti** (def. 1). **2.** Also **Haiti.** a former name of **Hispaniola.**

hay·ward (hā′wôrd′), *n.* an officer having charge of hedges and fences around a town common, esp. to keep cattle from breaking through and to impound stray cattle. [1175–1225; ME *heiward,* equiv. to *hei(e)* hedge, fence (OE *hege;* akin to HEDGE, HAW[3]) + *ward* WARD]

Hay·ward (hā′wərd), *n.* **1. Leland,** 1902–71, U.S. theatrical producer. **2.** a city in central California, SE of Oakland. 94,167.

hay·wire (hā′wīər′), *n.* **1.** wire used to bind bales of hay. —*adj. Informal.* **2.** in disorder: *The town is haywire because of the bus strike.* **3.** out of control; disordered; crazy: *The car went haywire. He's been haywire since he got the bad news.* [1900–05; HAY + WIRE]

Hay·wood (hā′wo͝od′), *n.* **1. William Dudley** ("*Big Bill*"), 1869–1928, U.S. labor leader: a founder of the Industrial Workers of the World; in the Soviet Union after 1921. **2.** a male given name.

ha·zan (*Seph.* KHä zän′; *Ashk.* KHä′zən), *n., pl.* ***ha·za·nim*** (*Seph.* KHä zä nēm′; *Ashk.* KHä zô′nim), *Eng.* **ha·zans.** *Hebrew.* a cantor of a synagogue. Also, ***hazzan, chazan, chazzan.***

haz·ard (haz′ərd), *n.* **1.** an unavoidable danger or risk, even though often foreseeable: *The job was full of hazards.* **2.** something causing unavoidable danger, peril, risk, or difficulty: *the many hazards of the big city.* **3.** the absence or lack of predictability; chance; uncertainty: *There is an element of hazard in the execution of the most painstaking plans.* **4.** *Golf.* a bunker, sand trap, or the like, constituting an obstacle. **5.** the uncertainty of the result in throwing a die. **6.** a game played with two dice, an earlier and more complicated form of craps. **7.** *Court Tennis.* any of the winning openings. **8.** (in English billiards) a stroke by which the player pockets the object ball (**winning hazard**) or his or her own ball after contact with another ball (**losing hazard**). **9. at hazard,** at risk; at stake; subject to chance: *His reputation was at hazard in his new ventures.* —*v.t.* **10.** to offer (a statement, conjecture, etc.) with the possibility of facing criticism, disapproval, failure, or the like; venture: *He hazarded a guess, with trepidation, as to her motives in writing the article.* **11.** to put to the risk of being lost; expose to risk: *In making the investment, he hazarded all his savings.* **12.** to take or run the risk of (a misfortune, penalty, etc.): *Thieves hazard arrest.* **13.** to venture upon (anything of doubtful issue): *to hazard a dangerous encounter.* [1250–1300; ME *hasard* < OF, perh. < Ar *al-zahr* the die] **—haz′ard·a·ble,** *adj.* **—haz′ard·er,** *n.* **—haz′ard·less,** *adj.*
—Syn. 1. See **danger. 3.** accident, fortuity, fortuitousness. **11.** stake, endanger, peril, imperil. **—Ant. 1.** safety.

haz·ard·ous (haz′ər dəs), *adj.* **1.** full of risk; perilous; risky: *a hazardous journey.* **2.** dependent on chance. [1570–80; HAZARD + -OUS] **—haz′ard·ous·ly,** *adv.* **—haz′ard·ous·ness,** *n.*
—Syn. 1. dangerous, unsafe. **2.** chancy, uncertain, risky, speculative. **—Ant. 1.** safe, secure. **2.** sure, certain, reliable.

haz′ardous waste′, any industrial by-product, esp. from the manufacture of chemicals, that is destructive to the environment or dangerous to the health of people or animals: *Hazardous wastes often contaminate ground water.*

haze[1] (hāz), *n., v.,* **hazed, haz·ing.** *n.* **1.** an aggregation in the atmosphere of very fine, widely dispersed, solid or liquid particles, or both, giving the air an opalescent appearance that subdues colors. **2.** vagueness or obscurity, as of the mind or perception; confused or vague thoughts, feelings, etc.: *The victims were still in a haze and couldn't describe the accident.* —*v.t., v.i.* **3.** to make or become hazy. [1700–10; perh. n. use of ME **hase;* OE *hasu,* var. of *haswa* ashen, dusky. See HAZY, HARE] **—haze′less,** *adj.*
—Syn. 2. See **cloud.**

haze[2] (hāz), *v.t.,* **hazed, haz·ing. 1.** to subject (freshmen, newcomers, etc.) to abusive or humiliating tricks and ridicule. **2.** *Chiefly Naut.* to harass with unnecessary or disagreeable tasks. [1670–80; < MF *haser* to irritate, annoy]

ha·zel (hā′zəl), *n.* **1.** any shrub or small tree belonging to the genus *Corylus,* of the birch family, having toothed, ovate leaves and bearing edible nuts, as *C. avellana,* of Europe, or *C. americana* and *C. cornuta,* of the Western Hemisphere. **2.** any of several other shrubs or trees, as an Australian shrub, *Pomaderris apetala.* **3.** the wood of any of these trees. **4.** the hazelnut or filbert. **5.** light golden brown, as the color of a hazelnut. —*adj.* **6.** of or pertaining to the hazel. **7.** made of the wood of the hazel. **8.** having a light golden-brown color. [bef. 900; ME *hasel;* OE *hæs(e)l;* c. G *Hasel,* ON *hasl,* L *corylus* hazel shrub] **—ha′zel·ly,** *adj.*

Ha·zel (hā′zəl), *n.* a female given name.

Ha′zel Crest′, a town in NE Illinois. 13,973.

ha′zel grouse′, a European woodland grouse, *Tetrastes bonasia,* somewhat resembling the North American ruffed grouse. Also called **ha′zel hen′.** [1775–85]

ha·zel·nut (hā′zəl nut′), *n.* the nut of the hazel; filbert. [bef. 900; ME *haselnote,* OE *hæselhnutu.* See HAZEL, NUT]

Ha′zel Park′, a city in SE Michigan, near Detroit. 20,914.

Ha·zel·wood (hā′zəl wo͝od′), *n.* a town in E Missouri. 12,935.

haze·me·ter (hāz′mē′tər), *n.* transmissometer. [HAZE[1] + -METER]

haz·er (hā′zər), *n.* **1.** a person or thing that hazes. **2.** a horse rider who assists in rodeo bulldogging by riding on the opposite side of the steer as the competing cowboy to keep the steer running in a straight path. [1895–1900; HAZE[2] + -ER[1]]

haz·ing (hā′zing), *n.* subjection to harassment or ridicule. [1815–25; HAZE[2] + -ING[1]]

Ha·zle·ton (hā′zəl tən), *n.* a city in E Pennsylvania. 27,318.

Haz·litt (haz′lit), *n.* **William,** 1778–1830, English critic and essayist.

Ha·zor (hä zôr′, -zōr′), *n.* an ancient city in Israel, N of the Sea of Galilee: extensive excavations; capital of Canaanite kingdom.

ha·zy (hā′zē), *adj.,* **-zi·er, -zi·est. 1.** characterized by the presence of haze; misty: *hazy weather.* **2.** lacking distinctness or clarity; vague; indefinite; obscure; confused: *a hazy idea.* [1615–25; earlier *hawsey,* metathetic var. of ME **haswy,* OE *haswig* ashen, dusky. See HAZE[1], -Y[1]] **—ha′zi·ly,** *adv.* **—ha′zi·ness,** *n.*
—Syn. 1. foggy, smoggy, overcast.

haz·zan (*Seph.* KHä zän′; *Ashk.* KHä′zən), *n., pl.* ***haz·za·nim*** (*Seph.* KHä zä nēm′; *Ashk.* KHä zô′nim), *Eng.* **haz·zans.** *Hebrew.* hazan.

Hb, *Symbol, Biochem.* hemoglobin.

h.b., *Football.* halfback.

H-beam (āch′bēm′), *n.* an I-beam having flanges the width of the web. Also called **H-bar** (āch′bär′). See illus. under **shape.**

H.B.M., His Britannic Majesty; Her Britannic Majesty.

H-bomb (āch′bom′), *n.* See **hydrogen bomb.** [1945–50, *Amer.*]

HBP, See **high blood pressure.**

HBV, See under **hepatitis B.**

H.C., 1. Holy Communion. **2.** House of Commons.

h.c., for the sake of honor. [< L *honōris causā*]

H.C.F., See **highest common factor.** Also, **h.c.f.**

hCG, See **human chorionic gonadotropin.**

H chain, *Immunol.* See **heavy chain.**

H.C.M., His Catholic Majesty; Her Catholic Majesty.

H. Con. Res., House concurrent resolution.

HCR, See **highway contract route.**

hd., 1. hand. **2.** head.

h.d., 1. heavy duty. **2.** (in prescriptions) at bedtime [< NL *hōra dēcubitūs*]

hdbk., handbook.

hdkf., handkerchief.

HDL, See **high-density lipoprotein.**

H. Doc., House document.

HDPE, See **high-density polyethylene.**

hdqrs., headquarters.

HDTV, See **high-definition television.**

hdw., hardware. Also, **hdwe.**

hdwd, hardwood.

he[1] (hē; *unstressed* ē), *pron., nom.* **he,** *poss.* **his,** *obj.* **him;** *pl. nom.* **they,** *poss.* **their** or **theirs,** *obj.* **them;** *n., pl.* **hes;** *adj.* —*pron.* **1.** the male person or animal being discussed or last mentioned; that male. **2.** anyone (without reference to sex); that person: *He who hesitates is lost.* —*n.* **3.** any male person or animal; a man: *hes and shes.* —*adj.* **4.** male (usually used in combination): *a he-*

goat. [bef. 900; ME, OE *hē* (masc. nom. sing.); c. D *hij,* OS *hē,* OHG *her* he; see HIS, HIM, SHE, HER, IT[1]]

—**Usage.** Traditionally, the masculine singular pronouns HE[1], HIS, and HIM have been used generically to refer to indefinite pronouns like *anyone, everyone,* and *someone* (*Everyone who agrees should raise his right hand*) and to singular nouns that can be applied to either sex (*painter, parent, person, teacher, writer,* etc.): *Every writer knows that his first book is not likely to be a best-seller.* This generic use is often criticized as sexist, although many speakers and writers continue the practice.

Those who object to the generic use of HE have developed various ways of avoiding it. One is to use HE/SHE or SHE/HE (or *he or she* or *she or he*) or the appropriate case forms of these pairs: *Everyone who agrees should raise his or her* (or *her or his* or *his/her* or *her/his*) *right hand.* Forms blending the feminine and masculine pronouns, as *s/he,* have not been widely adopted, probably because of confusion over how to say them.

Another solution is to change the antecedent pronoun or noun from singular to plural so that the plural pronouns THEY, THEIR, and THEM can be used: *All who agree should raise their right hands. All writers know that their first books are not likely to be bestsellers.* See also **they.**

he[2] (hā), *n.* **1.** the fifth letter of the Hebrew alphabet. **2.** any of the sounds represented by this letter. Also, **heh.** [< Heb *hē'*]

HE, high explosive.

He, *Symbol, Chem.* helium.

H.E., **1.** high explosive. **2.** His Eminence. **3.** His Excellency; Her Excellency.

head (hed), *n.* **1.** the upper part of the body in humans, joined to the trunk by the neck, containing the brain, eyes, ears, nose, and mouth. **2.** the corresponding part of the body in other animals. **3.** the head considered as the center of the intellect, as of thought, memory, understanding, or emotional control; mind; brain: *She has a good head for mathematics. Keep a cool head in an emergency.* **4.** the position or place of leadership, greatest authority, or honor. **5.** a person to whom others are subordinate, as the director of an institution or the manager of a department; leader or chief. **6.** a person considered with reference to his or her mind, disposition, attributes, status, etc.: *wise heads; crowned heads.* **7.** that part of anything that forms or is regarded as forming the top, summit, or upper end: *head of a pin; head of a page.* **8.** the foremost part or front end of anything or a forward projecting part: *head of a procession.* **9.** the part of a weapon, tool, etc., used for striking: *the head of a hammer.* **10.** a person or animal considered merely as one of a number, herd, or group: *ten head of cattle; a dinner at $20 a head.* **11.** a culminating point, usually of a critical nature; crisis or climax: *to bring matters to a head.* **12.** the hair covering the head: *to wash one's head.* **13.** froth or foam at the top of a liquid: *the head on beer.* **14.** *Bot.* **a.** any dense flower cluster or inflorescence. See illus. under **inflorescence. b.** any other compact part of a plant, usually at the top of the stem, as that composed of leaves in the cabbage or lettuce, of leafstalks in the celery, or of flower buds in the cauliflower. **15.** the maturated part of an abscess, boil, etc. **16.** a projecting point of a coast, esp. when high, as a cape, headland, or promontory. **17.** the obverse of a coin, as bearing a head or other principal figure (opposed to *tail*). **18.** one of the chief parts or points of a written or oral discourse; a main division of a subject, theme, or topic. **19.** something resembling a head in form or a representation of a head, as a piece of sculpture. **20.** the source of a river or stream. **21.** *Slang.* **a.** a habitual user of a drug, esp. LSD or marijuana (often used in combination): *feds versus the heads; an acid-head; a pot-head.* **b.** a fan or devotee (usually used in combination): *a punk-rock head; a chili head.* **22.** **heads,** *Distilling.* alcohol produced during the initial fermentation. Cf. **tail**[1] (def. 6d). **23.** headline. **24.** a toilet or lavatory, esp. on a boat or ship. **25.** *Naut.* **a.** the forepart of a vessel; bow. **b.** the upper edge of a quadrilateral sail. **c.** the upper corner of a jib-headed sail. See diag. under **sail. d.** that part of the upper end of one spar of a mast that is overlapped by a spar above; a doubling at the upper end of a spar. **e.** that part of the upper end of a mast between the highest standing rigging and the truck. **f.** crown (def. 28). **26.** *Gram.* **a.** the member of an endocentric construction that belongs to the same form class and may play the same grammatical role as the construction itself. **b.** the member upon which another depends and to which it is subordinate. In *former presidents, presidents* is head and *former* is modifier. **27.** the stretched membrane covering the end of a drum or similar musical instrument. **28.** *Mining.* a level or road driven into solid coal for proving or working a mine. **29.** *Mach.* any of various devices on machine tools for holding, moving, indexing, or changing tools or work, as the headstock or turret of a lathe. **30.** *Railroads.* railhead (def. 3). **31.** (loosely) the pressure exerted by confined fluid: *a head of steam.* **32.** Also called **pressure head.** *Hydraul.* **a.** the vertical distance between two points in a liquid, as water, or some other fluid **b.** the pressure differential resulting from this separation, expressed in terms of the vertical distance between the points. **c.** the pressure of a fluid expressed in terms of the height of a column of liquid yielding an equivalent pressure. **33.** Also called **magnetic head.** *Electronics.* the part or parts of a tape recorder that record, play back, or erase magnetic signals on magnetic tape. Cf. **erasing head, playback head, recording head. 34.** *Computers.* See **read/write head. 35.** *Photog.* **a.** a mounting for a camera, as on a tripod. **b.** the part of an enlarger that contains the light source, negative carrier, lensboard, and lens. **36.** *Slang (vulgar).* fellatio. **37.** *Archaic.* power, strength, or force progressively gathered or gradually attained. **38. by** or **down by the head,** *Naut.* so loaded as to draw more water forward than aft. **39. come to a head, a.** to suppurate, as a boil. **b.** to reach a crisis; culminate: *The struggle for power came to a head.* **40. get one's head together,** *Slang.* to have one's actions, thoughts, or emotions under control or in order: *If he'd get his head together, maybe he'd get to work on time.* **41. give head,** *Slang (vulgar).* perform fellatio. **42. give someone his** or **her head,** to permit someone to do as he or she likes; allow someone freedom of choice: *She wanted to go away to college, and her parents gave her her head.* **43. go to someone's head, a.** to make someone dizzy or drunk; overcome one with excitement: *Power went to his head. The brandy went to his head.* **b.** to make someone conceited or self-important: *Success went to his head.* **44. hang one's head,** to become dejected or ashamed: *When he realized what an unkind thing he had done, he hung his head in shame.* Also, **hide one's head. 45. head and shoulders, a.** far better, more qualified, etc.; superior: *In intelligence, he was head and shoulders above the rest of the children in the class.* **b.** *Archaic.* by force. **46. head over heels, a.** headlong, as in a somersault: *He tripped and fell head over heels into the gully.* **b.** intensely; completely: *head over heels in love.* **c.** impulsively; carelessly: *They plunged head over heels into the fighting.* **47. heads up!** *Informal.* be careful! watch out for danger! **48. head to head,** in direct opposition or competition: *The candidates will debate head to head.* **49. keep one's head,** to remain calm or poised, as in the midst of crisis or confusion: *It was fortunate that someone kept his head and called a doctor.* **50. keep one's head above water,** to remain financially solvent: *Despite their debts, they are managing to keep their heads above water.* **51. lay** or **put heads together,** to meet in order to discuss, consult, or scheme: *Neither of them had enough money for a tour of Europe, so they put their heads together and decided to find jobs there.* **52. lose one's head,** to become uncontrolled or wildly excited: *When he thought he saw an animal in the underbrush, he lost his head and began shooting recklessly.* **53. make head,** to progress or advance, esp. despite opposition; make headway: *There have been many delays, but we are at last making head.* **54. make heads roll,** to exert authority by firing or dismissing employees or subordinates: *He made heads roll as soon as he took office.* **55. not make head or tail of,** to be unable to understand or decipher: *We couldn't make head or tail of the strange story.* Also, **not make heads or tails of. 56. off the top of one's head,** candidly or extemporaneously: *Off the top of my head, I'd say that's right.* **57. one's head off,** extremely; excessively: *We screamed our heads off at that horror movie. He laughed his head off at the monkey's antics.* **58. on one's head,** as one's responsibility or fault: *Because of his reckless driving he now has the deaths of three persons on his head.* **59. out of one's head** or **mind, a.** insane; crazy. **b.** *Informal.* delirious; irrational: *You're out of your head if you accept those terms.* **60. over one's head, a.** beyond one's comprehension, ability, or resources: *The classical allusion went right over his head.* **b.** beyond one's financial resources or ability to pay: *He's lost over his head in that poker game.* **61. over someone's head,** to appeal to someone having a superior position or prior claim: *She went over her supervisor's head and complained to a vice president.* **62. pull one's head in,** *Australian Slang.* to keep quiet or mind one's own business; shut up. **63. take it into one's head,** to form a notion, purpose, or plan: *She took it into her head to study medicine.* Also, **take into one's head. 64. turn someone's head, a.** to cause someone to become smug or conceited: *Her recent success has completely turned her head.* **b.** to cause one to become foolish or confused: *A whirlwind romance has quite turned his head.*
—*adj.* **65.** first in rank or position; chief; leading; principal: *a head official.* **66.** of, pertaining to, or for the head (often used in combination): *head covering; headgear; headpiece.* **67.** situated at the top, front, or head of anything (often used in combination): *headline; headboard.* **68.** moving or coming from a direction in front of the head or prow of a vessel: *head sea; head tide; head current.* **69.** *Slang.* of or pertaining to drugs, drug paraphernalia, or drug users.
—*v.t.* **70.** to go at the head of or in front of; lead; precede: *to head a list.* **71.** to outdo or excel; take the lead in or over: *to head a race; to head one's competitors in a field.* **72.** to be the head or chief of (sometimes fol. by *up*): *to head a school; to head up a department.* **73.** to direct the course of; turn the head or front of in a specified direction: *I'll head the boat for the shore. Head me in the right direction and I'll walk to the store.* **74.** to go around the head of (a stream). **75.** to furnish or fit with a head. **76.** to take the head off; decapitate; behead. **77.** to remove the upper branches of (a tree). **78.** *Fox Hunting.* to turn aside (a fox) from its intended course. **79.** to get in front of in order to stop, turn aside, attack, etc. **80.** headline (def. 4). **81.** *Soccer.* to propel (the ball) by striking it with the head, esp. with the forehead.
—*v.i.* **82.** to move forward toward a point specified; direct one's course; go in a certain direction: *to head toward town.* **83.** to come or grow to a head; form a head: *Cabbage heads quickly.* **84.** (of a river or stream) to have the head or source where specified. **85. head off,** to go before in order to hinder the progress of; intercept: *The police headed off the fleeing driver at a railroad crossing.* [bef. 900; ME *he(v)ed,* OE *hēafod;* c. OHG *houbit,* Goth *haubith;* akin to OE *hafud-* (in *hafudland* headland), ON *hǫfuth,* L *caput* (see CAPITAL[1])] —**head′like′,** *adj.*
—**Syn. 5.** commander, superior, master, principal, superintendent, president, chairman. **65.** cardinal, foremost, supreme, main. **71.** surpass, beat. **72.** direct, command, rule, govern. —**Ant. 1.** foot. **65.** subordinate.

CONCISE ETYMOLOGY KEY: <, descended or borrowed from; >, whence; b., blend of, blended; c., cognate with; cf., compare; deriv., derivative; equiv., equivalent; imit., imitative; obl., oblique; r., replacing; s., stem; sp., spelling, spelled; resp., respelling, respelled; trans., translation; ?, origin unknown; *, unattested; ‡, probably earlier than. See the full key inside the front cover.

-head, a native English suffix meaning "state of being" (*godhead; maidenhead*), occurring in words now mostly archaic or obsolete, many being superseded by forms in **-hood.** [ME *-hede,* OE **-hǣdu,* f. of *-hād* -HOOD]

head•ache (hed′āk′), *n.* **1.** a pain located in the head, as over the eyes, at the temples, or at the base of the skull. **2.** an annoying or bothersome person, situation, activity, etc. [bef. 1000; ME; OE *hēafodece.* See HEAD, ACHE]

head•ach•y (hed′ā′kē), *adj.* **1.** having a headache. **2.** accompanied by or causing headaches: *a headachy cold.* [1820–30; HEADACHE + -Y[1]]

head′-and-tail′ light′ (hed′n tāl′), a small South American characin fish, *Hemmigrammus ocellifer,* having shiny red eyes and tail spots, often kept in aquariums. Also called **head′-and-tail′-light fish′.**

head′ arrange′ment, *Jazz, Popular Music.* a roughly outlined musical arrangement that is played from memory and is often learned by ear. [1945–50]

head′ bal′ance, headstand.

head•band (hed′band′), *n.* **1.** a band worn around the head; fillet. **2.** *Print.* a band for decorative effect at the head of a chapter or of a page in a book. **3.** a band sewed or glued to the head or tail of the back of a book, or to both, often to protect and strengthen the binding but sometimes for decoration. Cf. **tailband.** [1525–35; HEAD + BAND[2]]

head•bang•er (hed′bang′ər), *n.* metalhead. [1985–90]

head•board (hed′bôrd′, -bōrd′), *n.* a board forming the head of anything, esp. of a bed. [1720–30; HEAD + BOARD]

head•box (hed′boks′), *n.* **1.** (in a papermaking machine) the container in which cleaned pulp is collected for uniform distribution across the wire. **2.** headrail (def. 2). [HEAD + BOX[1]]

head•cheese (hed′chēz′), *n.* a seasoned loaf made of the head meat, sometimes including the tongue or brains, of a calf or pig and molded in the natural aspic of the head. [1835–45, *Amer.;* HEAD + CHEESE[1]]

head•cloth (hed′klôth′, -kloth′), *n., pl.* **-cloths** (-klôthz′, -klothz′, -klôths′, -kloths′). any cloth for covering the head, as a turban or wimple. [bef. 1000; ME *he(v)ed cloth;* OE *hēafod clath;* see HEAD, CLOTH]

head′ cold′, a form of the common cold characterized esp. by nasal congestion and sneezing. [1935–40]

head′ count′, 1. an inventory of people in a group taken by counting individuals. **2.** any count of support, strength, etc.: *a head count of senators opposing the bill.* Also, **head′count′.**

head′ dip′, a maneuver in which a surfer, by squatting and leaning forward on the surfboard, partially dips his or her head into the wall of a wave. [1960–65]

head•dress (hed′dres′), *n.* **1.** a covering or decoration for the head: *a tribal headdress of feathers.* **2.** a style or manner of arranging the hair. [1695–1705; HEAD + DRESS]

head•ed (hed′id), *adj.* **1.** having a heading or course. **2.** shaped or grown into a head. **3.** having the mentality, personality, emotional control, or quality specified, or possessing a specified number of heads (usually used in combination): *a slow-headed student; a two-headed monster.* [1325–75; ME; see HEAD, -ED[3]]

head•er (hed′ər), *n.* **1.** a person or thing that removes or puts a head on something. **2.** a reaping machine that cuts off and gathers only the heads of the grain. **3.** a chamber to which the ends of a number of tubes are connected so that water or steam may pass freely from one tube to the other. **4.** *Auto.* an exhaust manifold. **5.** *Building Trades.* **a.** a brick or stone laid in a wall or the like so that its shorter ends are exposed or parallel to the surface. Cf. **stretcher** (def. 5). **b.** a framing member crossing and supporting the ends of joists, studs, or rafters so as to transfer their weight to parallel joists, studs, or rafters. **6.** *Informal.* a plunge or dive headfirst, as into water: *He stumbled and took a header into the ditch.* **7.** *Soccer.* a pass or shot made by heading the ball. **8.** a sign that is part of or attached to the top of a rack displaying merchandise. **9.** *Computers.* a line of information placed at the top of a page for purposes of identification. [1400–50; late ME *heder.* See HEAD, -ER[1]]

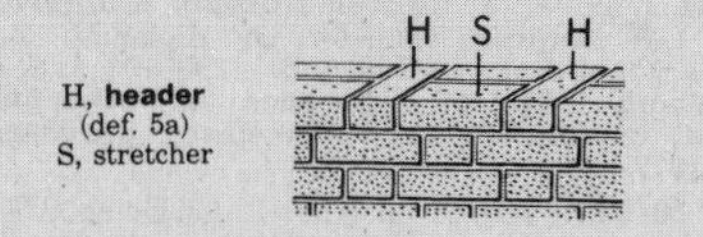

H, **header** (def. 5a)
S, stretcher

head′er bond′, a brickwork bond composed entirely of overlapping headers.

head•first (hed′fûrst′), *adv.* **1.** with the head in front or bent forward; headforemost: *He dived headfirst into the sea.* **2.** rashly; precipitately. [1820–30; HEAD + FIRST]

head•fish (hed′fish′), *n., pl.* (*esp. collectively*) **-fish,** (*esp. referring to two or more kinds or species*) **-fish•es. 1.** See **ocean sunfish. 2.** See **sharptail mola.** [1835–45, *Amer.;* HEAD + FISH]

head•fore•most (hed′fôr′mōst′, -məst, -fōr′-), *adv.* headfirst (def. 1). [1615–25; HEAD + FOREMOST]

head•frame (hed′frām′), *n.* a structure supporting the hoisting sheaves at the top of a mine shaft. Also called **gallows frame.** [1875–80; HEAD + FRAME]

head′ gate′, 1. a control gate at the upstream end of a canal or lock. **2.** a floodgate of a race, sluice, etc.

head•gear (hed′gēr′), *n.* **1.** any covering for the head, esp. a hat, cap, bonnet, etc. **2.** a protective covering for the head, as a steel helmet or football helmet. **3.** the parts of a harness about the animal's head. **4.** *Orthodontics Informal.* a device worn on the head and attached by wires and elastic bands to braces in the mouth, used to create backward tension in the process of repositioning protruding teeth. **5.** *Mining.* a headframe and its machinery. [1530–40; HEAD + GEAR]

head•hunt (hed′hunt′), *n.* **1.** a headhunting expedition: *The men left the village to go on a headhunt.* —*v.i.* **2.** to engage in headhunting. [HEAD + HUNT]

head•hunt•er (hed′hun′tər), *n.* **1.** a person who engages in headhunting. **2.** a personnel recruiter for a corporation or executive recruitment agency. **3.** an executive recruitment agency. [1850–55; HEAD + HUNTER]

head•hunt•ing (hed′hun′ting), *n.* **1.** (among certain primitive peoples) the practice of hunting down and decapitating victims and preserving their heads as trophies. **2.** the act or practice of actively searching for new employees, esp. for professionals or executives: *Every June the electronics manufacturers go headhunting among the newly graduated engineers.* **3.** the act or practice of firing without cause, esp. someone disliked: *Their periodic headhunting was a contributing factor in the company's failures.* **4.** the act or practice of trying to destroy the power, position, or influence of one's competitors or foes: *Headhunting is ferocious in advertising.* [1850–55; HEAD + HUNTING]

head•ing (hed′ing), *n.* **1.** something that serves as a head, top, or front. **2.** a title or caption of a page, chapter, etc. **3.** a section of the subject of a discourse; a main division of a topic or theme. **4.** the compass direction toward which a traveler or vehicle is or should be moving; course. **5.** an active underground mining excavation in the earth, as a drift or raise being or about to be driven. **6.** *Aeron.* the angle between the axis from front to rear of an aircraft and some reference line, as magnetic north. [1250–1300; ME *hefding.* See HEAD, -ING[1]]

head′ing course′, (in brickwork) a course of headers. Cf. **stretching course.** [1650–60]

head′ing sword′, a sword used for beheading. [1505–15]

head•lamp (hed′lamp′), *n.* headlight. Also, **head′•lamp′.** [1880–85]

head•land (hed′lənd), *n.* **1.** a promontory extending into a large body of water. **2.** a strip of unplowed land at the ends of furrows or near a fence or border. [bef. 1000; ME *hedeland,* OE *hēafodland.* See HEAD, LAND]

head•less (hed′lis), *adj.* **1.** without a head. **2.** having the head cut off; beheaded. **3.** having no leader or chief; leaderless. **4.** foolish; stupid: *a headless argument.* [bef. 1000; ME *he(ve)dles,* OE *hēafodlēas.* See HEAD, -LESS] —**head′less•ness,** *n.*

head′ let′tuce, any variety of the lettuce subspecies *Lactuca sativa capitata,* having leaves that grow in a dense rosette, esp. iceberg lettuce and Boston lettuce.

head•light (hed′līt′), *n.* a light or lamp, usually equipped with a reflector, on the front of an automobile, locomotive, etc. [1860–65, *Amer.*; HEAD + LIGHT[1]]

head•line (hed′līn′), *n., v.,* **-lined, -lin•ing.** —*n.* Also called **head. 1.** a heading in a newspaper for any written material, sometimes for an illustration, to indicate subject matter, set in larger type than that of the copy and containing one or more words and lines and often several banks. **2.** the largest such heading on the front page, usually at the top. **3.** the line at the top of a page, containing the title, pagination, etc. —*v.t.* **4.** to furnish with a headline; head. **5.** to mention or name in a headline. **6.** to publicize, feature, or star (a specific performer, product, etc.). **7.** to be the star of (a show, nightclub act, etc.) —*v.i.* **8.** to be the star of an entertainment. [1620–30; HEAD + LINE[1]]

head•lin•er (hed′lī′nər), *n.* a performer whose name appears most prominently in a program or advertisement or on a marquee; star. [1890–95; HEADLINE + -ER[1]]

head•lock (hed′lok′), *n. Wrestling.* a hold in which a wrestler locks an arm around the opponent's head. [1900–05; HEAD + LOCK[1]]

head•long (hed′lông′, -long′), *adv.* **1.** with the head foremost; headfirst: *to plunge headlong into the water.* **2.** without delay; hastily: *to plunge headlong into work.* **3.** without deliberation; rashly: *to rush headlong into battle.* —*adj.* **4.** undertaken quickly and suddenly; made precipitately; hasty: *a headlong flight.* **5.** rash; impetuous: *a headlong denunciation.* **6.** done or going with the head foremost: *a headlong dive into the pool.* [1350–1400; ME *hedlong,* earlier *hedling.* See HEAD, -LING[2]] —**head′long′ness,** *n.*

head′ louse′. See under **louse** (def. 1). [1540–50]

head•man (hed′mən, -man′), *n., pl.* **-men** (-mən, -men′). **1.** a chief or leader. **2.** headsman. [bef. 1000; ME *he(ve)dman,* OE *hēafodman.* See HEAD, MAN[1]]

head′ mar′gin, the empty space between the first line or other printed element on a page and the top of the page.

head•mas•ter (hed′mas′tər, -mä′stər), *n.* the person in charge of a private school. [1570–80; HEAD + MASTER] —**head′mas′ter•ship′,** *n.*

head•mis•tress (hed′mis′tris), *n.* a woman in charge of a private school. [1870–75; HEAD + MISTRESS] —**head′mis′tress•ship′,** *n.*
—**Usage.** See **-ess.**

head′ mon′ey, 1. a tax of so much per head or person. **2.** a reward paid for capturing or killing an outlaw, fugitive, or the like. [1520–30]

head•most (hed′mōst′ *or, esp. Brit.,* -məst), *adj.* most advanced; foremost. [1620–30; HEAD + -MOST]

head•note (hed′nōt′), *n.* a brief summary, comment, or explanation that precedes a chapter, report, etc. [1850–55; HEAD + NOTE]

head′ of state′, the person who holds the highest position in a national government: *a meeting of heads of state.*

head-on (hed′on′, -ôn′), *adj.* **1.** (of two objects) meeting with the fronts or heads foremost: *a head-on collision.* **2.** facing the direction of forward motion or alignment; frontal. **3.** characterized by direct opposition: *a head-on confrontation.* —*adv.* **4.** with the front or head foremost, esp. in a collision: *She stepped out of the front door and walked head-on into her husband.* [1830–40, *Amer.*]

head•phone (hed′fōn′), *n.* Usually, **headphones. 1.** *Audio.* a headset designed for use with a stereo system. **2.** any set of earphones. [1910–15; HEAD + -PHONE]

head•piece (hed′pēs′), *n.* **1.** a piece of armor for the head; helmet. **2.** any covering for the head. **3.** a headset. **4.** the head as the seat of the intellect; judgment. **5.** the top piece or part of any of various things. **6.** *Print.* a decorative piece at the head of a page, chapter, etc. [1520–30; HEAD + PIECE]

head•pin (hed′pin′), *n. Bowling.* the pin standing nearest to the bowler when set up, at the head or front of the triangle; the number 1 pin. [1930–35; HEAD + PIN]

head•quar•ter (hed′kwôr′tər, -kwô′-), *v.t.* **1.** to situate in headquarters. —*v.i.* **2.** to establish one's headquarters. [back formation from HEADQUARTERS]

head•quar•ters (hed′kwôr′tərz, -kwô′-), *n., pl.* **-ters.** (*used with a singular or plural v.*) **1.** a center of operations, as of the police or a business, from which orders are issued; the chief administrative office of an organization: *The operatives were always in touch with headquarters.* **2.** the offices or working location of a military commander; the place from which a commander customarily issues orders. **3.** a military unit consisting of the commander, his staff, and other assistants. [1640–50; HEAD + QUARTERS]

head•race (hed′rās′), *n.* the race, flume, or channel leading to a water wheel or the like. [1840–50; HEAD + RACE[1]]

head•rail (hed′rāl′), *n.* **1.** a railing on a sailing vessel, extending forward from abaft the bow to the back of the figurehead. **2.** Also called **headbox.** a narrow, boxlike case extending across the top of a window blind and covering the mechanical devices by which the blind operates. [1815–25; HEAD + RAIL[1]]

head′ reg′ister, the high register of the human voice. [1885–90]

head•rest (hed′rest′), *n.* **1.** a rest or support of any kind for the head. **2.** Also called **head′ restraint′.** a padded part at the top of the back of a seat, esp. in an automobile, to protect one's head against whiplash in a collision. [1850–55; HEAD + REST[1]]

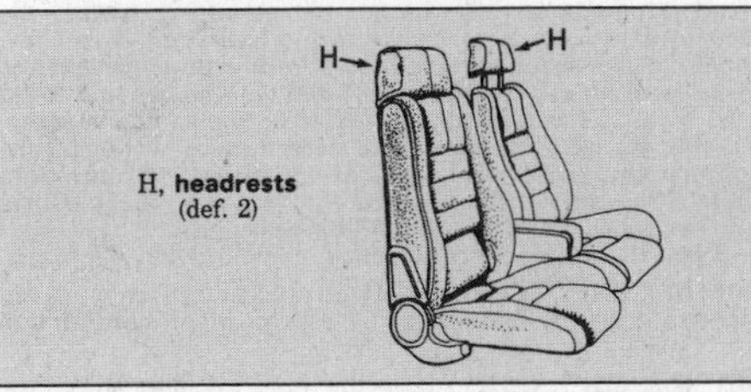

H, headrests (def. 2)

head′ rhyme′. See **beginning rhyme.** [1940–45]

head•rig (hed′rig′), *n.* (in a sawmill) the carriage and saw used in cutting a log into slabs. [HEAD + RIG[1]]

head•right (hed′rīt′), *n.* **1.** *Law.* a beneficial interest for each member of an Indian tribe in the tribal trust fund accruing from the lease of tribal oil, gas, and mineral rights, the sale of tribal lands, etc. **2.** *Amer. Hist.* a grant of land, usually 50 acres to a settler, given by certain colonies and companies in the 17th and 18th centuries. [1695–1705, *Amer.*; HEAD + RIGHT]

head•room (hed′ro͞om′, -ro͝om′), *n.* **1.** *Naut.* the clear space between two decks. **2.** Also called **headway.** clear vertical space, as between the head and sill of a doorway or between the ceiling and floor of an attic room at a certain point, esp. such height as to allow passage or comfortable occupancy. **3.** *Audio.* See **dynamic headroom.** [1850–55; HEAD + ROOM]

heads (hedz), *adj., adv.* (of a coin) with the top, or obverse, facing up: *On the first toss, the coin came up heads.* Cf. **tails.** [1675–85; HEAD + -S[1]]

head•sail (hed′sāl′; *Naut.* hed′səl), *n. Naut.* **1.** any of various jibs or staysails set forward of the foremost mast of a vessel. **2.** any sail set on a foremast, esp. on a vessel having three or more masts. [1620–30; HEAD + SAIL]

head•saw (hed′sô′), *n.* a saw that cuts and trims logs as they enter a mill. [HEAD + SAW[1]]

head′ sea′, *Naut.* a formation of waves running in a direction opposite to that of a vessel. [1885–90]

head•set (hed′set′), *n.* **1.** *Radio, Teleph.* a device consisting of one or two earphones with a headband for holding them over the ears and sometimes with a mouthpiece attached. **2.** earphones or headphones. [1920–25; HEAD + SET]

head•sheet (hed′shēt′), *n. Naut.* **1.** foresheet (def. 1). **2. headsheets,** foresheet (def. 2). [1350–1400; ME. See HEAD, SHEET[2]]

head•ship (hed′ship), *n.* the position of head or chief; chief authority; leadership; supremacy. [1575–85; HEAD + -SHIP]

head′ shop′, *Slang.* a shop selling paraphernalia of interest to drug users or associated with the use of drugs. [1965–70, *Amer.*]

head•shrink•er (hed′shring′kər), *n. Slang.* shrink (def. 9). [1945–50, *Amer.*; HEAD + SHRINK + -ER[1]]

heads•man (hedz′mən), *n., pl.* **-men.** a public executioner who beheads condemned persons. Also, **headman.** [1595–1605; HEAD + 'S[1] + MAN[1]]

head′ smut′, *Plant Pathol.* a disease of cereals and other grasses, characterized by a dark-brown, powdery mass of spores replacing the affected seed heads, caused by any of several smut fungi of the genera *Sorosporium, Sphacelotheca,* and *Ustilago.*

heads′ or tails′, 1. a gambling game in which a coin is tossed, the winner being the player who guesses which side of the coin will face up when it lands or is caught. **2.** the tossing of a coin in this manner to determine a question or choice. [1675–85]

head•spring (hed′spring′), *n.* **1.** the fountainhead or source of a stream. **2.** the source of anything. **3.** an acrobatic feat similar to a handspring, except that the head as well as the hands touch the surface before the spring back to a standing position. [1350–1400; ME *hedspring.* See HEAD, SPRING]

head•stall (hed′stôl′), *n.* that part of a bridle or halter that encompasses the head of an animal. [1425–75; late ME *hedstall.* See HEAD, STALL[1]]

head•stand (hed′stand′), *n., v.,* **-stood, -standing.** —*n.* **1.** an act or instance of supporting the body in a vertical position by balancing on the head, usually with the aid of the hands. —*v.i.* **2.** to perform a headstand. Cf. **handstand.** [1930–35; HEAD + STAND]

head′ start′, an advantage given or acquired in any competition, endeavor, etc., as allowing one or more competitors in a race to start before the others. Also, **head′start′.** [1885–90]

head•stay (hed′stā′), *n.* (on a sailing vessel) a stay leading forward from the head of the foremost mast to the stem head or the end of the bowsprit. [HEAD + STAY[3]]

head•stock (hed′stok′), *n.* the part of a machine containing or directly supporting the moving or working parts, as the assembly supporting and driving the live spindle in a lathe. See illus. under **lathe.** [1725–35; HEAD + STOCK]

head•stone (hed′stōn′), *n.* a stone marker set at the head of a grave; gravestone. [1525–35; HEAD + STONE]

head•stream (hed′strēm′), *n.* a stream that is the source, or one of the sources, of a river. [1810–20; HEAD + STREAM]

head•strong (hed′strông′, -strong′), *adj.* **1.** determined to have one's own way; willful; stubborn; obstinate: *a headstrong young man.* **2.** proceeding from or exhibiting willfulness: *a headstrong course.* [1350–1400; ME *heedstronge.* See HEAD, STRONG] —**head′strong′ly,** *adv.* —**head′strong′ness,** *n.*
—**Syn. 1.** See **willful.** —**Ant. 1.** tractable, docile.

heads′ up′, (used interjectionally to call attention to an impending danger or the need for immediate alertness). [1940–45]

heads-up (hedz′up′), *adj.* quick to grasp a situation and take advantage of opportunities; alert; resourceful. [1945–50]

head′ ta′ble, the principal table, as at a banquet or conference, often at the head of a row of tables or raised on a dais, where the presiding officer, chief speaker, guests of honor, etc., are seated.

head′ tax′, a uniform tax or surcharge imposed upon every person or every adult in a specific group, as on those entering or leaving a country or using a particular service or conveyance.

head-to-head (hed′tə hed′), *adj.* in direct personal confrontation, encounter, or exchange. [1790–1800]

head′ tone′, (in singing) a vocal tone so produced as to bring the cavities of the nose and head into sympathetic vibration.

head′ trip′, *Slang.* **1.** a mentally exhilarating or productive experience, as one in which a person's intellect or imagination seems to expand. **2.** See **ego trip.** [1970–75]

head•wait•er (hed′wā′tər), *n.* a person in charge of waiters, busboys, etc., in a restaurant or dining car. [1795–1805; HEAD + WAITER]

head•wa•ters (hed′wô′tərz, -wot′ərz), *n.pl.* the upper tributaries of a river. [1525–35; HEAD + *waters,* pl. of WATER]

head•way[1] (hed′wā′), *n.* **1.** forward movement; progress in a forward direction: *The ship's headway was slowed by the storm.* **2.** progress in general: *headway in a career.* **3.** rate of progress: *a slight headway against concerted opposition.* **4.** the time interval or distance between two vehicles, as automobiles, ships, or railroad or subway cars, traveling in the same direction over the same route. **5. make headway,** to proceed forward; advance; progress. [1700–10; (A)HEAD + WAY]

head•way[2] (hed′wā′), *n.* headroom (def. 2). [1700–10; HEAD + WAY]

head•wind (hed′wind′), *n.* a wind opposed to the course of a moving object, esp. an aircraft or other vehicle (opposed to *tailwind*). [1780–90; (A)HEAD + WIND[1]]

head•word (hed′wûrd′), *n.* **1.** a word, phrase, or the like, appearing as the heading of a chapter, dictionary or encyclopedia entry, etc. **2.** catchword (def. 2). **3.** head (def. 26). [1815–25; HEAD + WORD]

head•work (hed′wûrk′), *n.* mental labor; thought. [1830–40; HEAD + WORK] —**head′work′er,** *n.* —**head′•work′ing,** *n.*

head•y (hed′ē), *adj.,* **head•i•er, head•i•est. 1.** intoxicating: *a heady wine.* **2.** affecting the mind or senses greatly: *heady perfume.* **3.** exciting; exhilarating: *the heady news of victory.* **4.** rashly impetuous: *heady conduct.* **5.** violent; destructive: *heady winds.* **6.** clever; shrewd: *a heady scheme to win the election.* [1350–1400; ME *hevedy, hedy.* See HEAD, -Y[1]] —**head′i•ly,** *adv.* —**head′i•ness,** *n.*
—**Syn. 3.** thrilling, stirring, stimulating. —**Ant. 3.** depressing, disappointing.

heal (hēl), *v.t.* **1.** to make healthy, whole, or sound; restore to health; free from ailment. **2.** to bring to an end or conclusion, as conflicts between people or groups, usu-

CONCISE PRONUNCIATION KEY: *act, cāpe, dâre, pärt; set, ēqual; if, īce; ox, ōver, ôrder, oil, bo͝ok, bo͞ot, out; up, ûrge; child; sing; shoe; thin, that;* zh as in *treasure.* ə = *a* as in *alone, e* as in *system, i* as in *easily, o* as in *gallop, u* as in *circus;* ° as in *fire* (fī°r), *hour* (ou°r). l and n can serve as syllabic consonants, as in *cradle* (krād′l), and *button* (but′n). See the full key inside the front cover.

ally with the strong implication of restoring former amity; settle; reconcile: *They tried to heal the rift between them but were unsuccessful.* **3.** to free from evil; cleanse; purify: *to heal the soul.* —*v.i.* **4.** to effect a cure. **5.** (of a wound, broken bone, etc.) to become whole or sound; mend; get well (often fol. by *up* or *over*). [bef. 900; ME *helen,* OE *hǣlan* (c. D *helen,* G *heilen,* ON *heila,* Goth *hailjan*), deriv. of *hāl* HALE[1], WHOLE] —**heal′a·ble,** *adj.*
—**Syn. 1.** See **cure. 2.** compose, soothe. **3.** purge, disinfect. —**Ant. 1, 2.** irritate. **3.** soil, infect.

heal-all (hēl′ôl′), *n.* the self-heal, *Prunella vulgaris.* [1570–80]

heal·er (hē′lər), *n.* **1.** a person or thing that heals. **2.** See **faith healer.** [1175–1225; ME; see HEAL, -ER[1]]

heal·ing (hē′ling), *adj.* **1.** curing or curative; prescribed or helping to heal. **2.** growing sound; getting well; mending. —*n.* **3.** the act or process of regaining health: *a new drug to accelerate healing.* [bef. 1000; ME *heelyng* (adj.), *helynge* (n.), OE *hǣlinge* (n.). See HEAL, -ING[2], -ING[1]] —**heal′ing·ly,** *adv.*

heal′ing by first′ inten′tion, *Surg., Med.* See under **intention** (def. 6).

heal′ing by sec′ond inten′tion, *Surg., Med.* See under **intention** (def. 6).

health (helth), *n.* **1.** the general condition of the body or mind with reference to soundness and vigor: *good health; poor health.* **2.** soundness of body or mind; freedom from disease or ailment: *to have one's health; to lose one's health.* **3.** a polite or complimentary wish for a person's health, happiness, etc., esp. as a toast: *We drank a health to our guest of honor.* **4.** vigor; vitality: *economic health.* [bef. 1000; ME *helthe,* OE *hǣlth.* See HALE[1], WHOLE, -TH[1]] —**health′ward,** *adj., adv.*
—**Syn. 2.** vigor, vitality, strength, fitness, stamina.

health·care (helth′kâr′), *n.* Also, **health′ care′. 1.** the field concerned with the maintenance or restoration of the health of the body or mind. **2.** any of the procedures or methods employed in this field. —*adj.* Also, **health′-care′. 3.** of, pertaining to, or involved in healthcare: *healthcare workers; a healthcare center.* [HEALTH + CARE]

health′ club′, a usually private club that offers its members facilities for exercising and physical conditioning. [1960–65]

health′ code′. See under **code** (def. 3). Also called **sanitary code.**

health′ food′, any natural food popularly believed to promote or sustain good health, as by containing vital nutrients, being grown without the use of pesticides, or having a low sodium or fat content. [1880–85]

health·ful (helth′fəl), *adj.* **1.** conducive to health; wholesome or salutary: *a healthful diet.* **2.** healthy. [1350–1400; ME *helthful.* See HEALTH, -FUL] —**health′·ful·ly,** *adv.* —**health′ful·ness,** *n.*
—**Syn.** See **healthy.**

health′ insur′ance, insurance that compensates the insured for expenses or loss incurred for medical reasons, as through illness or hospitalization. [1900–05]

health′ main′tenance organiza′tion, a plan for comprehensive health services, prepaid by an individual or by a company for its employees, that provides treatment, preventive care, and hospitalization to each participating member in a central health center. *Abbr.:* HMO [1970–75]

health′ of′ficer, an official who administers laws pertaining to health, esp. sanitation. [1855–60]

health′ profes′sional, *Med.* a person trained to work in any field of physical or mental health.

health′ spa′, a resort or a special building or room where a person may exercise, swim, or otherwise condition the body.

health·y (hel′thē), *adj.,* **health·i·er, health·i·est. 1.** possessing or enjoying good health or a sound and vigorous mentality: *a healthy body; a healthy mind.* **2.** pertaining to or characteristic of good health, or a sound and vigorous mind: *a healthy appearance; healthy attitudes.* **3.** conducive to good health; healthful: *healthy recreations.* **4.** prosperous or sound: *a healthy business.* **5.** *Informal.* fairly large: *I bought a healthy number of books.* [1545–55; HEALTH + -Y[1]] —**health′i·ly,** *adv.* —**health′i·ness,** *n.*
—**Syn. 1.** hale, hearty, robust. **3.** nutritious, nourishing. HEALTHY, HEALTHFUL, SALUTARY, WHOLESOME refer to the promotion of health. HEALTHY, while applied esp. to what possesses health, is also applicable to what is conducive to health: *a healthy climate; not a healthy place to be.* HEALTHFUL is applied chiefly to what is conducive to health: *healthful diet or exercise.* SALUTARY suggests something that is conducive to well-being generally, as well as beneficial in preserving or in restoring health: *salutary effects; to take salutary measures.* It is used also to indicate moral benefit: *to have a salutary fear of devious behavior.* WHOLESOME has connotations of attractive freshness and purity; it applies to what is good for one, physically, morally, or both: *wholesome food; wholesome influences or advice.* —**Ant. 1.** sick.

Hea·ly (hē′lē), *n.* **Timothy Michael,** 1855–1931, Irish nationalist politician.

HEAO, See **High Energy Astrophysical Observatory.**

heap (hēp), *n.* **1.** a group of things placed, thrown, or lying one on another; pile: *a heap of stones.* **2.** *Informal.* a great quantity or number; multitude: *a heap of people.* **3.** *Slang.* an automobile, esp. a dilapidated one. **4. all of a heap,** *Informal.* **a.** overwhelmed with astonishment; amazed: *We were struck all of a heap upon hearing of their divorce.* **b.** suddenly; abruptly: *All of a heap the room was empty.* —*v.t.* **5.** to gather, put, or cast in a heap; pile (often fol. by *up, on, together,* etc.). **6.** to accumulate or amass (often fol. by *up* or *together*): *to heap up riches.* **7.** to give, assign, or bestow in great quantity; load (often fol. by *on* or *upon*): *to heap blessings upon someone; to heap someone with work.* **8.** to load, supply, or fill abundantly: *to heap a plate with food.* —*v.i.* **9.** to become heaped or piled, as sand or snow; rise in a heap or heaps (often fol. by *up*). [bef. 900; 1925–30 for def. 3; ME *heep,* OE *hēap;* c. D *hoop,* OHG *houf;* akin to G *Haufe*] —**heap′er,** *n.* —**heap′y,** *adj.*
—**Syn. 1.** mass, stack; accumulation, collection.

hear (hēr), *v.,* **heard** (hûrd), **hear·ing.** —*v.t.* **1.** to perceive by the ear: *Didn't you hear the doorbell?* **2.** to learn by the ear or by being told; be informed of: *to hear news.* **3.** to listen to; give or pay attention to: *They refused to hear our side of the argument.* **4.** to be among the audience at or of (something): *to hear a recital.* **5.** to give a formal, official, or judicial hearing to (something); consider officially, as a judge, sovereign, teacher, or assembly: *to hear a case.* **6.** to take or listen to the evidence or testimony of (someone): *to hear the defendant.* **7.** to listen to with favor, assent, or compliance. **8.** (of a computer) to perceive by speech recognition. —*v.i.* **9.** to be capable of perceiving sound by the ear; have the faculty of perceiving sound vibrations. **10.** to receive information by the ear or otherwise: *to hear from a friend.* **11.** to listen with favor, assent, or compliance (often fol. by *of*): *I will not hear of your going.* **12.** (of a computer) to be capable of perceiving by speech recognition. **13.** (used interjectionally in the phrase *Hear! Hear!* to express approval, as of a speech). [bef. 950; ME *heren,* OE *hēran, hieran;* c. D *horen,* G *hören,* ON *heyra,* Goth *hausjan;* perh. akin to Gk *akoúein* (see ACOUSTIC)] —**hear′a·ble,** *adj.* —**hear′er,** *n.*
—**Syn. 1, 2.** attend. HEAR, LISTEN apply to the perception of sound. To HEAR is to have such perception by means of the auditory sense: *to hear distant bells.* To LISTEN is to give attention in order to hear and understand the meaning of a sound or sounds: *to listen to what is being said; to listen for a well-known footstep.* **4.** attend. **7.** regard, heed. —**Ant. 7.** disregard.

hear·ing (hēr′ing), *n.* **1.** the faculty or sense by which sound is perceived. **2.** the act of perceiving sound. **3.** opportunity to be heard: *to grant a hearing.* **4.** an instance or a session in which testimony and arguments are presented, esp. before an official, as a judge in a lawsuit. **5.** a preliminary examination of the basic evidence and charges by a magistrate to determine whether criminal procedures, a trial, etc., are justified. **6.** earshot: *Their conversation was beyond my hearing.* [1175–1225; ME; see HEAR, -ING[1]] —**hear′ing·less,** *adj.*
—**Syn. 4.** audience, conference, consultation.

hear′ing aid′, a compact electronic amplifier worn to improve one's hearing, usually placed in or behind the ear. [1920–25]

hear′ing-ear′ dog′ (hēr′ing ēr′), a dog that has been trained to alert a hearing-impaired person to sounds, as a telephone ringing or dangerous noises. Also called **hear′ing dog′.** [1975–80; on the model of SEEING EYE DOG]

hear·ing-im·paired (hēr′ing im pârd′), *adj.* **1.** having reduced or deficient hearing ability; hard-of-hearing: *special programs for hearing-impaired persons.* —*n.* **2.** (*used with a plural v.*) hearing-impaired persons collectively (usually prec. by *the*).

heark·en (här′kən), *v.i.* **1.** *Literary.* to give heed or attention to what is said; listen. —*v.t.* **2.** *Archaic.* to listen to; hear. Also, **harken.** [1150–1200; ME *hercnen,* OE *he(o)rcnian,* suffixed form of assumed **horcian;* see HARK, -EN[1]] —**heark′en·er,** *n.*

Hearn (hûrn), *n.* **Laf·cad·i·o** (laf kad′ē ō′), ("*Koizumi Yakumo*"), 1850–1904, U.S. journalist, novelist, and essayist, born in Greece; Japanese citizen after 1894.

hear·say (hēr′sā′), *n.* **1.** unverified, unofficial information gained or acquired from another and not part of one's direct knowledge: *I pay no attention to hearsay.* **2.** an item of idle or unverified information or gossip; rumor: *a malicious hearsay.* —*adj.* **3.** of, pertaining to, or characterized by hearsay: *hearsay knowledge; a hearsay report.* [1525–35; orig. in phrase *by hear say,* trans. of MF *par ouïr dire*]
—**Syn. 1.** talk, scuttlebutt, babble, tittle-tattle.

hear′say ev′idence, *Law.* testimony based on what a witness has heard from another person rather than on direct personal knowledge or experience. [1745–55]

hear′say rule′, *Law.* the rule making hearsay evidence inadmissible.

hearse (hûrs), *n.* **1.** a vehicle for conveying a dead person to the place of burial. **2.** a triangular frame for holding candles, used at the service of Tenebrae in Holy Week. **3.** a canopy erected over a tomb. [1250–1300; ME *herse* < MF *herce* a harrow < L *hirpicem,* acc. of *hirpex*] —**hearse′like′,** *adj.*

Hearst (hûrst), *n.* **1. William Randolph,** 1863–1951, U.S. editor and publisher. **2.** his son, **William Randolph, Jr.,** born 1908, U.S. publisher and editor.

heart (härt), *n.* **1.** *Anat.* a hollow, pumplike organ of blood circulation, composed mainly of rhythmically contractile smooth muscle, located in the chest between the lungs and slightly to the left and consisting of four chambers: a right atrium that receives blood returning from the body via the superior and inferior vena cavae, a right ventricle that pumps the blood through the pulmonary artery to the lungs for oxygenation, a left atrium that receives the oxygenated blood via the pulmonary veins and passes it through the mitral valve, and a left ventricle that pumps the oxygenated blood, via the aorta, throughout the body. **2.** *Zool.* **a.** the homologous structure in other vertebrates, consisting of four chambers in mammals and birds and three chambers in reptiles and amphibians. **b.** the analogous contractile structure in invertebrate animals, as the tubular heart of the spider and earthworm. **3.** the center of the total personality, esp. with reference to intuition, feeling, or emotion: *In your heart you know I'm an honest man.* **4.** the center of emotion, esp. as contrasted to the head as the center of the intellect: *His head told him not to fall in love, but his heart had the final say.* **5.** capacity for sympathy; feeling; affection: *His heart moved him to help the needy.* **6.** spirit, courage, or enthusiasm: *His heart sank when he walked into the room and saw their gloomy faces.* **7.** the innermost or central part of anything: *Notre Dame stands in the very heart of Paris.* **8.** the vital or essential part; core: *the heart of the matter.* **9.** the breast or bosom: *to clasp a person to one's heart.* **10.** a person (used esp. in expressions of praise or affection): *dear heart.* **11.** a conventional shape with rounded sides meeting in a point at the bottom and curving inward to a cusp at the top. **12.** a red figure or pip of this shape on a playing card. **13.** a card of the suit bearing such figures. **14. hearts, a.** (*used with a singular or plural v.*) the suit so marked: *Hearts is trump. Hearts are trump.* **b.** (*used with a singular v.*) a game in which the players try to avoid taking tricks containing this suit. **15.** *Bot.* the core of a tree; the solid central part without sap or albumen. **16.** good condition for production, growth, etc., as of land or crops. **17.** Also called **core.** *Ropemaking.* a strand running through the center of a rope, the other strands being laid around it. **18. after one's own heart,** in keeping with one's taste or preference: *There's a man after my own heart!* **19. at heart,** in reality; fundamentally; basically: *At heart she is a romantic.* **20. break someone's heart,** to cause someone great disappointment or sorrow, as to disappoint in love: *The news that their son had been arrested broke their hearts.* **21. by heart,** by memory; word-for-word: *They knew the song by heart.* **22. cross one's heart,** to maintain the truth of one's statement; affirm one's integrity: *That's exactly what they told me, I cross my heart!* **23. do someone's heart good,** to give happiness or pleasure to; delight: *It does my heart good to see you again.* **24. eat one's heart out,** to have sorrow or longing dominate one's emotions; grieve inconsolably: *The children are eating their hearts out over their lost dog.* **25. from the bottom of one's heart,** with complete sincerity. Also, **from one's heart, from the heart. 26. have a heart,** to be compassionate or merciful: *Please have a heart and give her another chance.* **27. have at heart,** to have as an object, aim, or desire: *to have another's best interests at heart.* **28. have one's heart in one's mouth,** to be very anxious or fearful: *He wanted to do the courageous thing, but his heart was in his mouth.* **29. have one's heart in the right place,** to be fundamentally kind, generous, or well-intentioned: *The old gentleman may have a stern manner, but his heart is in the right place.* **30. heart and soul,** enthusiastically; fervently; completely: *They entered heart and soul into the spirit of the holiday.* **31. in one's heart of hearts,** in one's private thoughts or feelings; deep within one: *He knew, in his heart of hearts, that the news would be bad.* **32. lose one's heart to,** to fall in love with: *He lost his heart to the prima ballerina.* **33. near one's heart,** of great interest or concern to one: *It is a cause that is very near his heart.* Also, **close to one's heart. 34. not have the heart,** to lack the necessary courage or callousness to do something: *No one had the heart to tell him he was through as an actor.* **35. set one's heart against,** to be unalterably opposed to: *She had set her heart against selling the statue.* Also, **have one's heart set against. 36. set one's heart at rest,** to dismiss one's anxieties: *She couldn't set her heart at rest until she knew he had returned safely.* **37. set one's heart on,** to wish for intensely; determine on: *She has set her heart on going to Europe after graduation.* Also, **have one's heart set on. 38. take heart,** to regain one's courage; become heartened: *Her son's death was a great blow, but she eventually took heart, convinced that God had willed it.* **39. take** or **lay to heart, a.** to think seriously about; concern oneself with: *He took to heart his father's advice.* **b.** to be deeply affected by; grieve over: *She was prone to take criticism too much to heart.* **40. to one's heart's content,** until one is satisfied; as much or as long as one wishes: *The children played in the snow to their heart's content.* **41. wear one's heart on one's sleeve, a.** to make one's intimate feelings or personal affairs known to all: *She was not the kind who would wear her heart on her sleeve.* **b.** to be liable to fall in love; fall in love easily: *How lovely to be young and wear our hearts on our sleeves!* **42. with all one's heart, a.** with earnestness or zeal. **b.** with willingness; cordially: *She welcomed the visitors with all her heart.*
—*v.t.* **43.** *Archaic.* **a.** to fix in the heart. **b.** to encourage. [bef. 900; ME *herte,* OE *heorte;* c. D *hart,* G *Herz,* ON *hjarta,* Goth *hairtō;* akin to L *cor* (see CORDIAL, COURAGE), Gk *kardía* (see CARDIO-)]

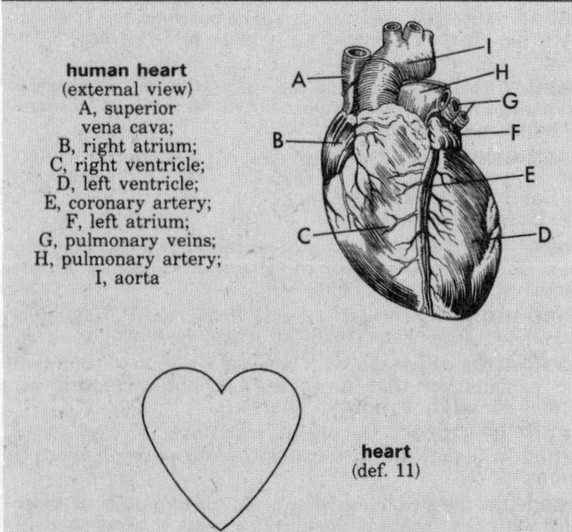

human heart (external view) A, superior vena cava; B, right atrium; C, right ventricle; D, left ventricle; E, coronary artery; F, left atrium; G, pulmonary veins; H, pulmonary artery; I, aorta

heart (def. 11)

heart·ache (härt′āk′), *n.* emotional pain or distress; sorrow; grief; anguish. [bef. 1000; ME *hert ache,* OE *heort ece;* see HEART, ACHE] —**heart′ach′ing,** *adj.*

heart′ attack′, *Pathol.* damage to an area of heart

muscle that is deprived of oxygen, usually due to blockage of a diseased coronary artery, typically accompanied by chest pain radiating down one or both arms, the severity of the attack varying with the extent and location of the damage; myocardial infarction. Cf. **coronary thrombosis.** [1925–30]

heart′ back′. See **shield back.**

heart•beat (härt′bēt′), *n. Physiol.* a pulsation of the heart, including one complete systole and diastole. [1840–50; HEART + BEAT]

heart′ block′, *Pathol.* a defect in the electrical impulses of the heart resulting in any of various arrhythmias or irregularities in the heartbeat. [1900–05]

heart•break (härt′brāk′), *n.* great sorrow, grief, or anguish. [1575–85; HEART + BREAK]

heart•break•er (härt′brā′kər), *n.* a person, event, or thing causing heartbreak. [1655–65; HEARTBREAK + -ER[1]]

heart•break•ing (härt′brā′king), *adj.* causing intense anguish or sorrow. [1600–10; HEARTBREAK + -ING[2]] **—heart′break′ing•ly,** *adv.*

heart•bro•ken (härt′brō′kən), *adj.* crushed with sorrow or grief. [1580–90; HEART + BROKEN] **—heart′•bro′ken•ly,** *adv.* **—heart′bro′ken•ness,** *n.*

heart•burn (härt′bûrn′), *n.* **1.** an uneasy burning sensation in the stomach, typically extending toward the esophagus, and sometimes associated with the eructation of an acid fluid. **2.** bitter jealousy; envy. [1590–1600; trans. of Gk *kardialgía;* see HEART, BURN[1]]

heart•burn•ing (härt′bûr′ning), *n.* rankling discontent, esp. from envy or jealousy; grudge. [1505–15; HEART + BURNING]

heart′ cam′, a cam with a single lobe having the general shape of a heart. [1870–75]

heart′ cher′ry, **1.** a large, heart-shaped variety of sweet cherry having soft flesh. **2.** the tree bearing this fruit. Also called **gean.** [1590–1600]

heart′ disease′, any condition of the heart that impairs its functioning. [1860–65]

heart•ed (här′tid), *adj.* **1.** having a specified kind of heart (now used only in combination): *hardhearted; sadhearted.* **2.** fixed or present in the heart. [1175–1225; ME *iherted.* See Y-, HEART, -ED[3]] **—heart′ed•ly,** *adv.* **—heart′ed•ness,** *n.*

heart•en (här′tn), *v.t.* to give courage or confidence to; cheer. [1520–30; HEART + -EN[1]] **—heart′en•er,** *n.* **—heart′en•ing•ly,** *adv.*

heart′ fail′ure, **1.** a condition in which the heart fatally ceases to function. **2.** Also called **congestive heart failure.** a condition in which the heart fails to pump adequate amounts of blood to the tissues, resulting in accumulation of blood returning to the heart from the veins, and often accompanied by distension of the ventricles, edema, and shortness of breath. [1890–95]

heart•felt (härt′felt′), *adj.* deeply or sincerely felt: *heartfelt sympathy.* [1725–35; HEART + FELT[1]]

heart-free (härt′frē′), *adj.* not in love. [1740–50]

hearth (härth), *n.* **1.** the floor of a fireplace, usually of stone, brick, etc., often extending a short distance into a room. **2.** home; fireside: *the joys of family and hearth.* **3.** *Metall.* **a.** the lower part of a blast furnace, cupola, etc., in which the molten metal collects and from which it is tapped out. See diag. under **blast furnace. b.** the part of an open hearth, reverberatory furnace, etc., upon which the charge is placed and melted down or refined. **4.** a brazier or chafing dish for burning charcoal. [bef. 900; ME *herth(e),* OE *he(o)rth;* c. G *Herd,* D *haard*] **—hearth′less,** *adj.*
—Syn. 2. household, abode, house.

hearth•side (härth′sīd′), *n.* fireside. [1795–1805; HEARTH + SIDE[1]]

hearth•stone (härth′stōn′), *n.* **1.** a stone forming a hearth. **2.** home; fireside; hearth. **3.** a soft stone, or a preparation of powdered stone and clay, used to whiten or scour hearths, steps, floors, etc. [1275–1325; ME *hertston.* See HEARTH, STONE]

heart•i•ly (här′tl ē), *adv.* **1.** in a hearty manner; cordially: *He was greeted heartily.* **2.** sincerely; genuinely: *He sympathized heartily with their plight.* **3.** without restraint; exuberantly; vigorously: *They laughed heartily.* **4.** with a hearty appetite: *The campers ate heartily.* **5.** thoroughly; completely: *I'm heartily sick of your complaining.* [1250–1300; ME *hertili.* See HEARTY, -LY]

heart•land (härt′land′, -lənd), *n.* **1.** the part of a region considered essential to the viability and survival of the whole, esp. a central land area relatively invulnerable to attack and capable of economic and political self-sufficiency. **2.** any central area, as of a state, nation, or continent: *a vineyard in California's heartland.* [1900–05; HEART + LAND]

heart•less (härt′lis), *adj.* **1.** unfeeling; unkind; unsympathetic; harsh; cruel: *heartless words; a heartless ruler.* **2.** *Archaic.* lacking courage or enthusiasm; spiritless; disheartened. [1300–50; ME *herteles,* OE *heortlēas.* See HEART, -LESS] **—heart′less•ly,** *adv.* **—heart′less•ness,** *n.*

heart′-lung′ machine′ (härt′lung′), a device through which blood is shunted temporarily for oxygenation during surgery, while the heart or a lung is being repaired. [1955–60]

heart′ mur′mur, *Med.* murmur (def. 3).

Heart′ of Dark′ness, a short novel (1902) by Joseph Conrad.

heart′ of palm′, the stripped terminal bud of a cabbage palm, esp. of the genus *Euterpe,* eaten in salads or as a vegetable. [1935–40, *Amer.*]

heart′ point′, *Heraldry.* See **fess point.**

heart•rend•ing (härt′ren′ding), *adj.* causing or expressing intense grief, anguish, or distress. [1680–90; HEART + RENDING] **—heart′rend′ing•ly,** *adv.*

hearts′ and flow′ers, (*used with a singular or plural v.*) maudlin sentimentality: *The play is a period piece, full of innocence abused and hearts and flowers.* [1940–45, *Amer.*]

hearts•ease (härts′ēz′), *n.* **1.** peace of mind. **2.** the pansy or other plant of the genus *Viola.* **3.** the lady's-thumb. Also, **heart's′-ease′.** [1375–1425; late ME *hertes ese.* See HEART, EASE]

heart′ shell′, **1.** any of numerous bivalve mollusks, esp. of the families Cardiidae and Carditidae, having a heart-shaped shell. **2.** the shell itself. [1745–55]

heart•sick (härt′sik′), *adj.* extremely depressed or unhappy. [1520–30; HEART + SICK[1]] **—heart′sick′en•ing,** *adj.* **—heart′sick′ness,** *n.*
—Syn. dejected, sick-at-heart, despondent, dispirited.

heart•some (härt′səm), *adj. Chiefly Scot.* **1.** giving cheer, spirit, or courage: *a heartsome wine.* **2.** cheerful; spirited. [1560–70; HEART + -SOME[1]] **—heart′some•ly,** *adv.* **—heart′some•ness,** *n.*

heart•sore (härt′sôr′, -sōr′), *adj.* heartsick. [1175–1225; ME. See HEART, SORE; cf. OE *heortsārnes* grief]

heart•stop•per (härt′stop′ər), *n.* something so frightening or emotionally gripping as to make one's heart seem to stop beating: *We didn't crash, but it was a heartstopper.* [HEART + STOPPER]

heart•strings (härt′stringz′), *n.pl.* the deepest feelings; the strongest affections: *to tug at one's heartstrings.* [1475–85; HEART + STRINGS]

heart′ tamponade′, *Pathol.* tamponade (def. 2).

heart•throb (härt′throb′), *n.* **1.** a rapid beat or pulsation of the heart. **2.** a passionate or sentimental emotion. **3.** sweetheart. [1840–50; HEART + THROB]

heart-to-heart (härt′tə härt′), *adj.* **1.** frank; sincere: *We had a heart-to-heart talk about his poor attendance.* —*n.* **2.** *Informal.* a frank talk, esp. between two persons. [1865–70]

heart′ ur′chin, an echinoderm of the order Spatangoida, having an elongate, somewhat heart-shaped outer covering. [1835–45]

heart•warm•ing (härt′wôr′ming), *adj.* gratifying; rewarding; satisfying: *a heartwarming response to his work.* [1895–1900; HEART + WARMING]

heart-whole (härt′hōl′), *adj.* **1.** not in love. **2.** wholehearted; sincere. [1425–75; late ME]

heart•wood (härt′wo͝od′), *n.* the hard central wood of the trunk of an exogenous tree; duramen. [1795–1805; HEART + WOOD[1]]

heart•worm (härt′wûrm′), *n.* **1.** a parasitic nematode, *Dirofilaria immitis,* transmitted by mosquito and invading the heart and pulmonary arteries of dogs, wolves, and foxes throughout its range in tropical, subtropical and, more recently, temperate regions around the world. **2.** the disease caused by infection with heartworm. [1885–90; HEART + WORM]

heart•y (här′tē), *adj.,* **heart•i•er, heart•i•est,** *n., pl.* **heart•ies.** —*adj.* **1.** warm-hearted; affectionate; cordial; jovial: *a hearty welcome.* **2.** genuine; sincere; heartfelt: *hearty approval; hearty dislike.* **3.** completely devoted; wholehearted: *hearty support.* **4.** exuberant; unrestrained: *hearty laughter.* **5.** violent; forceful: *a hearty push; a hearty kick.* **6.** physically vigorous; strong and well: *hale and hearty.* **7.** substantial; abundant; nourishing: *a hearty meal.* **8.** enjoying or requiring abundant food: *a hearty appetite.* **9.** (of soil) fertile. —*n. Archaic.* **10.** a brave or good fellow, esp. with reference to a shipmate. **11.** a sailor. [1350–1400; ME *herti.* See HEART, -Y[1]] **—heart′i•ness,** *n.*

heat (hēt), *n.* **1.** the state of a body perceived as having or generating a relatively high degree of warmth. **2.** the condition or quality of being hot: *the heat of an oven.* **3.** the degree of hotness; temperature: *moderate heat.* **4.** the sensation of warmth or hotness: *unpleasant heat.* **5.** a bodily temperature higher than normal: *the heat of a fever; the feeling of heat caused by physical exertion.* **6.** added or external energy that causes a rise in temperature, expansion, evaporation, or other physical change. **7.** *Physics.* a nonmechanical energy transfer with reference to a temperature difference between a system and its surroundings or between two parts of the same system. *Symbol:* Q **8.** a hot condition of the atmosphere or physical environment; hot season or weather. **9.** a period of hot weather. **10.** a sharp, pungent flavor, as that produced by strong spices. **11.** warmth or intensity of feeling; vehemence; passion: *He spoke with much heat and at great length.* **12.** maximum intensity in an activity, condition, etc.; the height of any action, situation, or the like: *the heat of battle; the heat of passion.* **13.** extreme pressure, as of events, resulting in tension or strain: *In the heat of his hasty departure he forgot his keys.* **14.** a single intense effort; a sustained, concentrated, and continuous operation: *The painting was finished at a heat.* **15.** *Slang.* intensified pressure, esp. in a police investigation. **16.** *Slang.* the police. **17.** *Slang.* armed protection, esp. a pistol, revolver, or other firearm: *All guards carry some heat.* **18.** *Sports.* **a.** a single course in or division of a race or other contest. **b.** a race or other contest in which competitors attempt to qualify for entry in the final race or contest. **19.** *Metall.* **a.** a single operation of heating, as of metal in a furnace, in the treating and melting of metals. **b.** a quantity of metal produced by such an operation. **20.** *Zool.* **a.** sexual receptiveness in animals, esp. females. **b.** the period or duration of such receptiveness: *to be in heat.* —*v.t.* **21.** to make hot or warm (often fol. by *up*). **22.** to excite emotionally; inflame or rouse with passion. —*v.i.* **23.** to become hot or warm (often fol. by *up*). **24.** to become excited emotionally. **25. heat up,** to increase or become more active or intense: *Business competition will heat up toward the end of the year.* [bef. 900; ME *hete,* OE *hǣtu;* akin to G *Hitze;* see HOT] **—heat′a•ble,** *adj.* **—heat′•ful,** *adj.* **—heat′less,** *adj.* **—heat′like′,** *adj.*
—Syn. 2. hotness, warmth. **3.** caloricity. **11.** ardor, fervor, zeal, flush, fever, excitement, impetuosity. **22.** stimulate, warm, stir, animate. **—Ant. 1.** coolness. **11.** indifference. **21.** cool.

heat′ bar′rier, *Aerospace.* See **thermal barrier.** [1950–55]

heat′ capac′ity, *Thermodynam.* the heat required to raise the temperature of a substance one degree. Cf. **specific heat.** [1900–05]

heat′ con′tent, *Thermodynam.* enthalpy.

heat′ cramp′, a cramp or muscular spasm caused by loss of water and salt following prolonged exertion in hot weather. [1935–40]

heat′ death′, *Thermodynam.* See under **entropy** (def. 3). [1925–30]

heat′ dev′il, a wavering, shimmering disturbance of air above or around a hot surface.

heat•ed (hē′tid), *adj.* **1.** made hot or hotter; warmed. **2.** excited; inflamed; vehement: *a heated discussion.* [1585–95; HEAT + -ED[2]] **—heat′ed•ly,** *adv.* **—heat′ed•ness,** *n.*
—Syn. 2. passionate, impassioned, fierce.

heat′ en′gine, *Thermodynam.* a mechanical device designed to transform part of the heat entering it into work. [1890–95]

heat′ equa′tion, *Math., Thermodynam.* a partial differential equation the solution of which gives the distribution of temperature in a region as a function of space and time when the temperature at the boundaries, the initial distribution of temperature, and the physical properties of the medium are specified.

heat•er (hē′tər), *n.* **1.** any of various apparatus for heating, esp. for heating water or the air in a room. **2.** *Electronics.* the element of a vacuum tube that carries the current for heating a cathode. **3.** *Slang.* a pistol, revolver, or other firearm. [1490–1500; HEAT + -ER[1]]

heat′ exchang′er, a device for transferring the heat of one substance to another, as from the exhaust gases to the incoming air in a regenerative furnace. [1900–05]

heat′ exhaus′tion, a condition characterized by faintness, rapid pulse, nausea, profuse sweating, cool skin, and collapse, caused by prolonged exposure to heat accompanied by loss of adequate fluid and salt from the body. Also called **heat prostration.** [1935–40]

heat′ gun′, a hand-held device that produces a flameless stream of extremely hot air, as for rapid drying or for softening paint for removal.

heath (hēth), *n.* **1.** a tract of open and uncultivated land; wasteland overgrown with shrubs. **2.** any of various low-growing evergreen shrubs common on such land, as the common heather, *Calluna vulgaris.* **3.** any plant of the genus *Erica,* or of the family Ericaceae. Cf. **heath family.** [bef. 900; ME; OE *hǣth;* c. G *Heide,* ON *heithr,* Goth *haithi;* akin to Welsh *coed* trees, wood] **—heath′less,** *adj.* **—heath′like′,** *adj.*

Heath (hēth), *n.* **Edward (Richard George),** born 1916, British statesman: prime minister 1970–74.

heath•ber•ry (hēth′ber′ē, -bə rē), *n., pl.* **-ries. 1.** crowberry. **2.** any berry found on heaths, esp. the bilberry. [bef. 1000; ME; OE *hǣth berian* (pl.); see HEATH, BERRY]

heath′ cock′, the male of the black grouse. [1580–90]

hea•then (hē′t͟hən), *n., pl.* **-thens, -then,** *adj.* —*n.* **1.** an unconverted individual of a people that do not acknowledge the God of the Bible; a person who is neither a Jew, Christian, nor Muslim; pagan. **2.** an irreligious, uncultured, or uncivilized person. —*adj.* **3.** of or pertaining to heathens; pagan. **4.** irreligious, uncultured, or uncivilized. [bef. 900; ME *hethen,* OE *hǣthen,* akin to G *Heide, heidnisch* (adj.), ON *heithingi* (n.), *heithinn* (adj.), Goth *haithno* (n.); perh. akin to HEATH] **—hea′then•dom,** *n.* **—hea′then•hood′,** *n.* **—hea′then•ness,** *n.* **—hea′then•ship′,** *n.*
—Syn. 3. heathenish, barbarous. HEATHEN, PAGAN are both applied to peoples who are not Christian, Jewish, or Muslim. HEATHEN is often distinctively applied to unenlightened or barbaric idolaters, esp. to primitive or ancient tribes: *heathen rites, idols.* PAGAN, though applied to any of the peoples not worshiping according to the three religions mentioned above, is most frequently used in speaking of the ancient Greeks and Romans: *a pagan poem; a pagan civilization.* **4.** philistine; savage. **—Ant. 4.** sophisticated, urbane, cultured.

hea•then•ish (hē′t͟hə nish), *adj.* **1.** of or pertaining to heathens: *heathenish practices of idolatry.* **2.** like or befitting heathens; barbarous. [bef. 900; OE *hǣthenisc.* See HEATHEN, -ISH[1]] **—hea′then•ish•ly,** *adv.* **—hea′•then•ish•ness,** *n.*

hea•then•ism (hē′t͟hə niz′əm), *n.* **1.** a belief or practice of heathens; idolatry. **2.** barbaric morals or behavior; barbarism. [1595–1605; HEATHEN + -ISM]

hea•then•ize (hē′t͟hə nīz′), *v.,* **-ized, -iz•ing.** —*v.t.* **1.** to make heathen. —*v.i.* **2.** to become heathen. Also, *esp. Brit.,* **hea′then•ise′.** [1675–85; HEATHEN + -IZE]

heath•er (het͟h′ər), *n.* any of various heaths, esp. *Calluna vulgaris,* of England and Scotland, having small, pinkish-purple flowers. [1300–50; sp. var. of *hether,* earlier *hedder, hadder, hather,* ME *hathir;* akin to HEATH] **—heath′ered,** *adj.*

Heath•er (het͟h′ər), *n.* a female given name.

heath•er•y (het͟h′ə rē), *adj.* **1.** of or like heather. **2.** abounding in heather. Also, **heathy.** [1525–35; HEATHER + -Y[1]] **—heath′er•i•ness,** *n.*

heath′ fam′ily, the plant family Ericaceae, characterized by evergreen or deciduous shrubs, trees, and woody plants growing in acid soil and having simple leaves, often showy flowers either solitary or in clusters, and

CONCISE PRONUNCIATION KEY: *act, cāpe, dâre, pärt; set, ēqual; if, īce; ox, ōver, ôrder, oil, bo͝ok, bo͞ot, out; up, ûrge; child; sing; shoe; thin, t͟hat;* zh as in *treasure.* ə = *a* as in *alone, e* as in *system, i* as in *easily, o* as in *gallop, u* as in *circus;* ᵊ as in *fire* (fīᵊr), *hour* (ouᵊr). l and n can serve as syllabic consonants, as in *cradle* (krād′l), and *button* (but′n). See the full key inside the front cover.

fruit in the form of a berry or capsule, and including the azalea, blueberry, cranberry, heather, madrone, mountain laurel, rhododendron, and trailing arbutus.

heath′ grass′, a European grass, *Sieglingia decumbens,* growing in spongy, wet, cold soils. Also called **heath′er grass′.**

heath′ hen′, **1.** an American gallinaceous bird, *Tympanuchus cupido cupido,* closely related to the prairie chicken: extinct. **2.** the female of the black grouse. [1585–95]

heath·y (hē′thē), *adj.,* **heath·i·er, heath·i·est.** heathery. [1400–50; late ME *hethy.* See HEATH, -Y[1]]

heat′ in′dex, a number representing the effect of temperature and humidity on humans by combining the two variables into an "apparent" temperature, introduced as a replacement for the temperature-humidity index: a temperature of 90° and relative humidity of 65 percent combine to produce a heat index of 102. *Abbr.:* H.I.

heat′ing degree′-day, a degree-day below the standard temperature of 65°F or 19°C, used in estimating fuel consumption. Cf. **cooling degree-day, growing degree-day.**

heat′ing pad′, a flexible fabric-covered pad containing insulated electrical heating elements for applying heat esp. to the body.

heat′ is′land, an urban area having higher average temperature than its rural surroundings owing to the greater absorption, retention, and generation of heat by its buildings, pavements, and human activities. [1960–65]

heat′ lamp′, a lamp fitted with an infrared bulb to supply heat esp. as part of physical therapy.

heat′ light′ning, lightning too distant for thunder to be heard, observed as diffuse flashes near the horizon on summer evenings. [1825–35, *Amer.*]

heat′ of condensa′tion, *Physics.* the heat liberated by a unit mass of gas at its boiling point as it condenses to a liquid: equal to the heat of vaporization.

heat′ of fu′sion, *Physics.* the heat absorbed by a unit mass of a given solid at its melting point that completely converts the solid to a liquid at the same temperature: equal to the heat of solidification. Cf. **latent heat.**

heat′ of solidifica′tion, *Physics.* the heat liberated by a unit mass of liquid at its freezing point as it solidifies: equal to the heat of fusion.

heat′ of sublima′tion, *Physics.* the heat absorbed by one gram or unit mass of a substance in the process of changing, at a constant temperature and pressure, from a solid to a gaseous state. Cf. **sublime** (def. 10).

heat′ of vaporiza′tion, *Physics.* the heat absorbed per unit mass of a given material at its boiling point that completely converts the material to a gas at the same temperature: equal to the heat of condensation. Cf. **latent heat.**

heat′ prostra′tion, *Med.* See **heat exhaustion.** [1935–40]

heat′ pump′, a device that uses a compressible refrigerant to transfer heat from one body, as the ground, air, or water, to another body, as a building, with the process being reversible. [1890–95]

heat′ rash′. See **prickly heat.** [1885–90]

heat′ res′ervoir, *Thermodynam.* a hypothetical body of infinitely large mass capable of absorbing or rejecting unlimited quantities of heat without undergoing appreciable changes in temperature, pressure, or density.

heat-seal (hēt′sēl′), *v.t.* to wrap in clear plastic and make airtight by applying heat to seal the edges. [1960–65]

heat′ shield′, *Aerospace.* a coating or structure that surrounds part of the nose cone or other vulnerable surfaces of a spacecraft and, by heat absorption or ablation, protects them from excessive heating during reentry. [1955–60]

heat′ sink′, **1.** *Thermodynam.* any environment or medium that absorbs heat. **2.** Also, **heat′sink′.** *Electronics.* a metallic heat exchanger designed to absorb and dissipate excess heat from one of the devices, as a transistor or resistor, in a circuit. [1935–40]

heat·stroke (hēt′strōk′), *n.* a disturbance of the temperature-regulating mechanisms of the body caused by overexposure to excessive heat, resulting in fever, hot and dry skin, and rapid pulse, sometimes progressing to delirium and coma. [1870–75; HEAT + STROKE[1]]

heat-treat (hēt′trēt′), *v.t.* to subject (a metal or alloy) to controlled heating and cooling to improve hardness or other properties. [1905–10] **—heat′ treat′ment.**

heat′ wave′, **1.** an air mass of high temperature covering an extended area and moving relatively slowly. **2.** a period of abnormally hot and usually humid weather. [1875–80]

heaume (hōm), *n.* helm[2] (def. 1). [1565–75; < MF, OF *helme* < Gmc; see HELM[2]]

heave (hēv), *v.,* **heaved** or (*esp. Naut.*) **hove; heav·ing;** *n.* **—***v.t.* **1.** to raise or lift with effort or force; hoist: *to heave a heavy ax.* **2.** to throw, esp. to lift and throw with effort, force, or violence: *to heave an anchor overboard; to heave a stone through a window.* **3.** *Naut.* **a.** to move into a certain position or situation: *to heave a vessel aback.* **b.** to move in a certain direction: *Heave the capstan around! Heave up the anchor!* **4.** to utter laboriously or painfully: *to heave a sigh.* **5.** to cause to rise and fall with or as with a swelling motion: *to heave one's chest.* **6.** to vomit; throw up: *He heaved his breakfast before noon.* **7.** to haul or pull on (a rope, cable, line, etc.), as with the hands or a capstan: *Heave the anchor cable!* **—***v.i.* **8.** to rise and fall in rhythmically alternate movements: *The ship heaved and rolled in the swelling sea.* **9.** to breathe with effort; pant: *He sat there heaving and puffing from the effort.* **10.** to vomit; retch. **11.** to rise as if thrust up, as a hill; swell or bulge: *The ground heaved and small fissures appeared for miles around.* **12.** to pull or haul on a rope, cable, etc. **13.** to push, as on a capstan bar. **14.** *Naut.* **a.** to move in a certain direction or into a certain position or situation: *heave about; heave alongside; heave in stays.* **b.** (of a vessel) to rise and fall, as with a heavy beam sea. **15.** **heave down,** *Naut.* to careen (a vessel). **16.** **heave ho** (an exclamation used by sailors, as when heaving the anchor up.) **17.** **heave in sight,** to rise to view, as from below the horizon: *The ship hove in sight as dawn began to break.* **18.** **heave out,** *Naut.* **a.** to shake loose (a reef taken in a sail). **b.** to loosen (a sail) from its gaskets in order to set it. **19.** **heave the lead.** See **lead**[2] (def. 12). **20.** **heave to, a.** *Naut.* to stop the headway of (a vessel), esp. by bringing the head to the wind and trimming the sails so that they act against one another. **b.** to come to a halt. **—***n.* **21.** an act or effort of heaving. **22.** a throw, toss, or cast. **23.** *Geol.* the horizontal component of the apparent displacement resulting from a fault, measured in a vertical plane perpendicular to the strike. **24.** the rise and fall of the waves or swell of a sea. **25.** **heaves,** (*used with a singular v.*) Also called **broken wind.** *Vet. Pathol.* a disease of horses, similar to asthma in human beings, characterized by difficult breathing. [bef. 900; ME *heven,* var. (with *-v-* from pt. and ptp.) of *hebben,* OE *hebban;* c. G *heben,* ON *hefja,* Goth *hafjan;* akin to L *capere* to take] **—heav′er,** *n.* **—heave′less,** *adj.*
—Syn. 1. elevate. See **raise. 2.** hurl, pitch, fling, cast, sling. **11.** surge, billow.

heave-ho (hēv′hō′), *n. Informal.* an act of rejection, dismissal, or forcible ejection: *The bartender gave the noisy drunk the old heave-ho.* [n. use of phrase *heave ho,* ME *havehou, hevelow*]

heav·en (hev′ən), *n.* **1.** the abode of God, the angels, and the spirits of the righteous after death; the place or state of existence of the blessed after the mortal life. **2.** (*cap.*) Often, **Heavens.** the celestial powers; God. **3.** a metonym for God (used in expressions of emphasis, surprise, etc.): *For heaven's sake!* **4.** **heavens, a.** (used interjectionally to express emphasis, surprise, etc.): *Heavens, what a cold room!* **b.** (*used with a singular v.*) a wooden roof or canopy over the outer stage of an Elizabethan theater. **5.** Usually, **heavens.** the sky, firmament, or expanse of space surrounding the earth. **6.** a place or state of supreme happiness: *She made his life a heaven on earth.* **7.** **move heaven and earth,** to do one's utmost to effect an end; make a supreme effort: *She promised to move heaven and earth to be there for our wedding anniversary.* [bef. 900; ME *heven,* OE *heofon;* c. MLG *heven;* akin to ON *himinn,* Goth *himins,* G *Himmel*] **—heav′en·less,** *adj.*

heav·en-born (hev′ən bôrn′), *adj.* of or as of heavenly origin: *the heaven-born gods.* [1585–95]

heav·en·ly (hev′ən lē), *adj.* **1.** of or in the heavens: *the heavenly bodies.* **2.** of, belonging to, or coming from the heaven of God, the angels, etc. **3.** resembling or befitting heaven; blissful; beautiful: *His home in Tahiti was a heavenly spot.* **4.** divine or celestial: *heavenly peace.* [bef. 1000; ME *hevenly,* OE *heofonlic.* See HEAVEN, -LY] **—heav′en·li·ness,** *n.*
—Syn. 4. supernal, sublime; seraphic, cherubic, angelic; blessed, beatific. **—Ant. 4.** infernal, hellish.

heav′enly bamboo′, nandina.

Heav′enly Cit′y. See **New Jerusalem.**

heav·en-sent (hev′ən sent′), *adj.* providentially opportune: *A heaven-sent rain revived the crops.* [1640–50]

heav·en·ward (hev′ən wərd), *adv.* **1.** Also, **heav′en·wards.** toward heaven. **—***adj.* **2.** directed toward heaven: *heavenward prayer.* [1200–50; ME *hevenward.* See HEAVEN, -WARD] **—heav′en·ward·ly,** *adv.* **—heav′·en·ward·ness,** *n.*

heave′-off hinge′ (hēv′ôf′, -of′). See **loose-joint hinge.**

heav·i·er-than-air (hev′ē ər thən âr′), *adj.* (of an aircraft) weighing more than the air that it displaces, hence having to obtain lift by aerodynamic means. [1900–05]

heav·i·ly (hev′ə lē), *adv.* **1.** with a great weight or burden: *a heavily loaded wagon.* **2.** in a manner suggestive of carrying a great weight; ponderously; lumberingly: *He walked heavily across the room.* **3.** in an oppressive manner: *Cares weigh heavily upon him.* **4.** severely; greatly; intensely: *to suffer heavily.* **5.** densely; thickly: *heavily wooded.* **6.** in large amounts or in great quantities; very much: *It rained heavily on Tuesday.* **7.** without animation or vigor; in a dull manner; sluggishly. [bef. 900; ME *hevyly,* OE *hefiglice.* See HEAVY, -LY]

Heav·i·side (hev′ē sīd′), *n.* **Oliver,** 1850–1925, English physicist.

Heav′iside lay′er. See **E layer.** [1910–15; named after O. HEAVISIDE]

Heav′iside u′nit func′tion, *Math.* the function that is zero for any number less than zero and that is 1 for any number greater than or equal to zero. [1935–40; named after O. HEAVISIDE]

heav·y (hev′ē), *adj.,* **heav·i·er, heav·i·est,** *n., pl.* **heav·ies,** *adv.* **—***adj.* **1.** of great weight; hard to lift or carry: *a heavy load.* **2.** of great amount, quantity, or size; extremely large; massive: *a heavy vote; a heavy snowfall.* **3.** of great force, intensity, turbulence, etc.: *a heavy sea.* **4.** of more than the usual or average weight: *a heavy person; heavy freight.* **5.** having much weight in proportion to bulk; being of high specific gravity: *a heavy metal.* **6.** of major import; grave; serious: *a heavy offense.* **7.** deep or intense; profound: *a heavy thinker; heavy slumber.* **8.** *Mil.* **a.** thickly armed or equipped with guns of large size. Cf. **heavy cruiser. b.** (of guns) of the more powerful sizes: *heavy weapons.* Cf. **heavy artillery. 9.** hard to bear; burdensome; harsh; oppressive: *heavy taxes.* **10.** hard to cope with; trying; difficult: *a heavy task.* **11.** being as indicated to an unusually great degree: *a heavy buyer.* **12.** broad, thick, or coarse; not delicate: *heavy lines drawn in charcoal.* **13.** weighted or laden: *air heavy with moisture.* **14.** fraught; loaded; charged: *words heavy with meaning.* **15.** depressed with trouble or sorrow; showing sorrow; sad: *a heavy heart.* **16.** without vivacity or interest; ponderous; dull: *a heavy style.* **17.** slow in movement or action; clumsy: *a heavy walk.* **18.** loud and deep; sonorous: *a heavy sound.* **19.** (of the sky) overcast or cloudy. **20.** exceptionally dense in substance; insufficiently raised or leavened; thick: *heavy doughnuts.* **21.** (of food) not easily digested. **22.** being in a state of advanced pregnancy; nearing childbirth: *heavy with child; heavy with young.* **23.** having a large capacity, capable of doing rough work, or having a large basic output: *a heavy truck.* **24.** producing or refining basic materials, as steel or coal, used in manufacturing: *heavy industry.* **25.** sober, serious, or somber: *a heavy part in a drama.* **26.** *Chem.* of or pertaining to an isotope of greater than normal atomic weight, as heavy hydrogen or heavy oxygen, or to a compound containing such an element, as heavy water. **27.** *Slang.* **a.** very good; excellent. **b.** very serious or important: *a really heavy relationship.* **28.** *Pros.* (of a syllable) **a.** stressed. **b.** long. **—***n.* **29.** a somber or ennobled theatrical role or character: *Iago is the heavy in* Othello. **30.** the theatrical role of a villain. **31.** an actor who plays a theatrical heavy. **32.** *Mil.* a gun of great weight or large caliber. **33.** *Slang.* a very important or influential person: *a reception for government heavies.* **—***adv.* **34.** heavily. [bef. 900; ME *hevi,* OE *hefig,* equiv. to *hef(e)* weight (akin to HEAVE) + *-ig* -Y[1]] **—heav′i·ness,** *n.*
—Syn. 1. ponderous, massive, weighty. **5.** dense. **9.** onerous, grievous, cumbersome; difficult, severe. **14.** HEAVY, MOMENTOUS, WEIGHTY refer to anything having a considerable amount of figurative weight. HEAVY suggests the carrying of a figurative burden: *words heavy with menace.* MOMENTOUS emphasizes the idea of great and usually serious consequences: *a momentous occasion, statement.* WEIGHTY, seldom used literally, refers to something heavy with importance, often concerned with public affairs, which may require deliberation and careful judgment: *a weighty matter, problem.* **15.** gloomy, mournful, dejected, despondent, downcast, downhearted. **16.** tedious, tiresome, wearisome, burdensome, boring. **17.** sluggish, lumbering. **19.** lowering, gloomy.

heav′y artil′lery, **1.** guns and howitzers of large caliber. **2.** guns and howitzers of 155-mm caliber and larger. Cf. **light artillery** (def. 2), **medium artillery.**

heav·y-beard·ed (hev′ē bēr′did), *adj.* having a thick or dark beard.

heav′y bomb′er, a large plane capable of carrying heavy bomb loads for long distances, esp. at high altitudes. Cf. **light bomber, medium bomber.** [1920–25]

heav′y chain′, *Immunol.* either of an identical pair of Y-shaped polypeptides that, together with the light chains, constitute the antibody molecule. Also called **H chain** [1960–65]

heav′y cream′, thick cream having a high percentage of butterfat.

heav′y cruis′er, a naval cruiser having 8-in. (20.3-cm) guns as its main armament. Cf. **light cruiser.**

heav·y-du·ty (hev′ē do͞o′tē, -dyo͞o′-), *adj.* **1.** providing an unusual amount of power, durability, etc.: *heavy-duty machinery; heavy-duty shoes.* **2.** very important, impressive, or serious: *heavy-duty involvement; heavy-duty questions.* [1910–15]

heav·y-foot·ed (hev′ē fo͝ot′id), *adj.* clumsy or ponderous, as in movement or expressiveness: *music that is heavy-footed and uninspired.* [1615–25] **—heav′y-foot′ed·ness,** *n.*

heav·y-hand·ed (hev′ē han′did), *adj.* **1.** oppressive; harsh: *a heavy-handed master.* **2.** clumsy; graceless: *a heavy-handed treatment of the theme.* [1625–35] **—heav′y-hand′ed·ly,** *adv.* **—heav′y-hand′ed·ness,** *n.*

heav·y-heart·ed (hev′ē här′tid), *adj.* sorrowful; melancholy; dejected. [1350–1400; ME] **—heav′y-heart′ed·ly,** *adv.* **—heav′y-heart′ed·ness,** *n.*
—Syn. depressed, sad-hearted, downcast.

heav′y hit′ter, **1.** a baseball player who makes many extra-base hits. **2.** a very important or influential person: *the secretary of state and other heavy hitters.* [1975–80] **—heav′y-hit′ter,** *adj.*

heav′y hy′drogen, **1.** either of the heavy isotopes of hydrogen, esp. deuterium. **2.** deuterium. [1930–35]

heav·y-lad·en (hev′ē lād′n), *adj.* **1.** carrying a heavy load; heavily laden: *a heavy-laden cart.* **2.** very tired or troubled; burdened: *heavy-laden with care.* [1400–50; late ME *hevy ladyn.* See HEAVY, LADEN]

heav′y met′al, **1.** any metal with a specific gravity of 5.0 or greater, esp. one that is toxic to organisms, as lead, mercury, copper, and cadmium. **2.** aggressive and heavily amplified rock music, commonly performed by groups that wear spectacular or bizarre costumes. [1860–65, for literal sense] **—heav′y-met′al,** *adj.*

heav′y min′eral oil′. See under **mineral oil.**

heav′y ni′trogen, the stable isotope of nitrogen having a mass number of 15.

heav′y ox′ygen, either of the two stable isotopes of oxygen having mass numbers of 17 and 18.

heav·y·set (hev′ē set′), *adj.* **1.** having a large body build. **2.** stout; stocky. [1920–25; HEAVY + SET]

heav′y spar′, *Mineral.* barite. [1780–90]

heav′y wa′ter, water in which hydrogen atoms have been replaced by deuterium, used chiefly as a coolant in nuclear reactors. Also called **deuterium oxide.** [1930–35]

CONCISE ETYMOLOGY KEY: <, descended or borrowed from; >, whence; b., blend of, blended; c., cognate with; cf., compare; deriv., derivative; equiv., equivalent; imit., imitative; obl., oblique; r., replacing; s., stem; sp., spelling, spelled; resp., respelling, respelled; trans., translation; ?, origin unknown; *, unattested; ‡, probably earlier than. See the full key inside the front cover.

heav•y•weight (hev′ē wāt′), *adj.* **1.** heavy in weight. **2.** of more than average weight or thickness: *a coat of heavyweight material.* **3.** noting or pertaining to a boxer, wrestler, etc., of the heaviest competitive class, esp. a professional boxer weighing more than 175 lb. (79.4 kg). **4.** of or pertaining to the weight class or division of such boxers: *a heavyweight bout.* **5.** (of a riding horse, esp. a hunter) able to carry up to 205 lb. (93 kg). **6.** designating a person, company, nation, or other entity that is extremely powerful, influential, or important: *a team of heavyweight lawyers.* —*n.* **7.** a person of more than average weight. **8.** a heavyweight boxer or wrestler. **9.** a person, company, nation, or other entity that is powerful and influential: *a price hike initiated by the heavyweights in the industry.* [1850–55; HEAVY + WEIGHT]

Heb, Hebrew (def. 2).

Heb., **1.** Hebrew. **2.** Hebrews.

Heb•bel (heb′əl), *n.* **(Chris•ti•an) Frie•drich** (kris′tē än′ frē′drikh), 1813–63, German lyric poet and playwright.

heb•do•mad (heb′də mad′), *n.* **1.** the number seven. **2.** a period of seven successive days; week. [1535–45; < L *hebdomad-* < Gk (s. of *hebdomás* week), equiv. to *hébdom(os)* seventh (see HEPTA-) + *-ad-* -AD[1]]

heb•dom•a•dal (heb dom′ə dl), *adj.* **1.** taking place, coming together, or published once every seven days; weekly: *hebdomadal meetings; hebdomadal groups; hebdomadal journals.* —*n.* **2.** a weekly magazine, newspaper, etc. Cf. **diurnal** (def. 7). [1605–15; < LL *hebdomadālis.* See HEBDOMAD, -AL[1]] —**heb•dom′a•dal•ly,** *adv.*

heb•dom•a•dar•y (heb dom′ə der′ē), *n., pl.* **-dar•ies,** *adj.* —*n.* **1.** *Rom. Cath. Ch.* a member of a church or monastery appointed for one week to sing the chapter Mass and lead in the recitation of the breviary. —*adj.* **2.** hebdomadal (def. 1). [1400–50; late ME *ebdomadarie* < LL *hebdomadārius.* See HEBDOMAD, -ARY]

he•be (hē′bē), *n.* any of various shrubs and trees belonging to the genus *Hebe,* of the figwort family, native mostly to New Zealand, having evergreen leaves and clusters or spikes of white, pink, or purple flowers. [< NL (1789), appar. after HEBE]

He•be (hē′bē), *n. Class. Myth.* a goddess of youth and spring, the daughter of Zeus and Hera, and wife of Hercules.

Hebe (hēb), *n. Slang (disparaging and offensive).* a Jew. [1930–35; shortening of HEBREW]

He•bei (hœ′bā′), *n. Pinyin.* a province in NE China. 41,410,000; 81,479 sq. mi. (211,031 sq. km). *Cap.:* Shijiazhuang. Also, **Hopeh, Hopei.** Formerly, **Chihli.**

he•be•phre•ni•a (hē′bə frē′nē ə), *n. Psychiatry.* a type of schizophrenia characterized by emotionless, incongruous, or silly behavior, intellectual deterioration, and hallucinations, frequently beginning insidiously during adolescence. [1880–85; < Gk *hēbē-* (see HEBETIC) + -PHRENIA] —**he•be•phren•ic** (hē′bə fren′ik), *adj.*

He•ber (hē′bər), *n.* **Reginald,** 1783–1826, British bishop and hymn writer.

Hé•bert (ā ber′), *n.* **Jacques Re•né** (zhäk rə nā′), (*"Père Duchesne"*), 1755–94, French journalist and revolutionary leader.

heb•e•tate (heb′i tāt′), *v.t.,* **-tat•ed, -tat•ing.** to make dull or blunt. [1565–75; < L *hebetātus* made dull or blunt (ptp. of *hebetāre*), equiv. to *hebet-* (s. of *hebes*) blunt, dull + *-ātus* -ATE[1]] —**heb′e•ta′tion,** *n.* —**heb′e•ta′tive,** *adj.*

he•bet•ic (hi bet′ik), *adj. Physiol.* pertaining to or occurring in puberty. [< Gk *hēbētikós,* equiv. to *hēbēt(ēs)* adult (*hēbē-,* var. s. of *hēbân* to reach puberty, v. deriv. of *hēbē* youth + *-tēs* agent suffix) + *-ikos* -IC]

heb•e•tude (heb′i to͞od′, -tyo͞od′), *n.* the state of being dull; lethargy. [1615–25; < LL *hebetūdō* dullness, bluntness, equiv. to L *hebet-* (s. of *hebes*) dull + *-ūdō;* see -TUDE] —**heb′e•tu′di•nous,** *adj.*

Hebr., **1.** Hebrew. **2.** Hebrews.

He•bra•ic (hi brā′ik), *adj.* of, pertaining to, or characteristic of the Hebrews, their language, or their culture. Also, **Hebrew.** [1350–1400; ME < LL *Hebraicus* < Gk *Hebraïkós,* equiv. to *Hebra(îos)* HEBREW + *-ikos* -IC; r. OE *Ebrēisc*] —**He•bra′i•cal•ly,** *adv.*

He•bra•i•cize (hi brā′ə sīz′), *v.i., v.t.,* **-cized, -ciz•ing.** Hebraize. Also, *esp. Brit.,* **He•bra′i•cise′.** [1880–85; HEBRAIC + -IZE] —**He•bra′i•ci•za′tion,** *n.* —**He•bra′i•ciz′er,** *n.*

He•bra•ism (hē′brā iz′əm, -brē-), *n.* **1.** an expression or construction distinctive of the Hebrew language. **2.** the character, spirit, principles, or practices distinctive of the Hebrew people. [1560–70; < LGk *Hebraïsmós,* equiv. to *Hebra-* (see HEBRAIZE) + *-ismos* -ISM]

He•bra•ist (hē′brā ist, -brē-), *n.* **1.** a person versed in the Hebrew language. **2.** a person imbued with the spirit of the Hebrew people or given to their principles or practices. [1745–55; HEBRA(IZE) + -IST]

He•bra•is•tic (hē′brā is′tik, -brē-), *adj.* of or pertaining to Hebraists or characterized by Hebraism or Hebraisms. Also, **He′bra•is′ti•cal.** [1840–50; HEBRAIST + -IC] —**He′bra•is′ti•cal•ly,** *adv.*

He•bra•ize (hē′brā īz′, -brē-), *v.,* **-ized, -iz•ing.** —*v.i.* **1.** to use expressions or constructions distinctive of the Hebrew language. —*v.t.* **2.** to make conformable to the spirit, character, principles, or practices of the Hebrew people. Also, **Hebraicize;** *esp. Brit.,* **He′bra•ise′.** [1635–45; < LGk *Hebraízein* to speak Hebrew, behave like a Jew. See HEBREW, -IZE] —**He′bra•i•za′tion,** *n.* —**He′bra•iz′er,** *n.*

He•brew (hē′bro͞o), *n.* **1.** a member of the Semitic peoples inhabiting ancient Palestine and claiming descent from Abraham, Isaac, and Jacob; an Israelite. **2.** a Semitic language of the Afroasiatic family, the language of the ancient Hebrews, which, although not in a vernacular use from 100 B.C. to the 20th century, was retained as the scholarly and liturgical language of Jews and is now the national language of Israel. *Abbr.:* Heb —*adj.* **3.** Hebraic. **4.** noting or pertaining to the script developed from the Aramaic and early Hebraic alphabets, used since about the 3rd century B.C. for the writing of Hebrew, and later for Yiddish, Ladino, and other languages. [bef. 1000; ME *Hebreu,* var. (with *H-* < L) of *Ebreu* < OF < ML *Ebrēus* for L *Hebraeus* < LGk *Hebraîos* < Aram *ʽIbhraij;* r. OE *Ebrēas* (pl.) < ML *Ebrēi*]

He′brew cal′endar. See **Jewish calendar.**

He•brews (hē′bro͞oz), *n.* (*used with a singular v.*) a book of the New Testament. *Abbr.:* Heb.

He′brew Scrip′tures, Bible (def. 2). Also called **He′brew Bi′ble.**

Heb•ri•des (heb′ri dēz′), *n.* (*used with a plural v.*) a group of islands **(Inner Hebrides** and **Outer Hebrides)** off the W coast of and belonging to Scotland. 29,615; ab. 2900 sq. mi. (7500 sq. km). Also called **Western Islands.** —**Heb′ri•de′an, He•brid′i•an,** *adj.*

He•bron (hē′brən), *n.* an ancient city of Palestine, formerly in W Jordan; occupied by Israel 1967–97; since 1997 under Palestinian self-rule. 38,348. Arabic, **El Khalil.**

Hec•a•te (hek′ə tē; *in Shakespeare* hek′it), *n. Class. Myth.* a goddess of the earth and Hades, associated with sorcery, hounds, and crossroads. Also, **Hekate.** [< L < Gk *hekátē,* n. use of fem. of *hékatos* far-shooting, said of Apollo as sun-god] —**Hec′a•te′an, Hec′a•tae′an,** *adj.*

hec•a•tomb (hek′ə tōm′, -to͞om′), *n.* **1.** (in ancient Greece and Rome) a public sacrifice of 100 oxen to the gods. **2.** any great slaughter: *the hecatombs of modern wars.* [1585–95; < L *hecatombē* < Gk *hekatómbē* < **hekatombwā,* equiv. to *hékaton* one hundred + **-bwā,* taken to be a deriv. of *boûs* ox (see COW[1])]

hech•sher (*Seph.* hekh sher′; *Ashk.* hekh′shər; *Eng.* hek′shər), *n., pl.* ***hech•she•rim*** (*Seph.* hekh she rēm′; *Ashk.* hekh shā′rim), *Eng.* **hech•shers.** *Hebrew.* rabbinical approval of meats and other foods that comply with the ritual requirements of Jewish dietary laws, usually issued in the form of an endorsing mark or stamp on the products so approved. Also, ***hekhsher.*** [Heb *hekhshēr*]

Hecht (hekt), *n.* **Ben,** 1894–1964, U.S. novelist and dramatist.

Hecht (hekt), *n. Gymnastics.* **1.** Also called **bird dismount.** a dismount, as from the horizontal bar, in which a gymnast releases the apparatus at the height of a backswing, sails forward with outstretched arms and legs, and lands upright on the feet. **2.** a vault over a long horse with the legs and body straight. [presumably after a gymnast named *Hecht*]

heck[1] (hek), *interj.* **1.** (used as a mild expression of annoyance, rejection, disgust, etc.): *What the heck do you care?* —*n.* **2.** something remarkable of its kind (usually used in the phrase *heck of a*): *That was a heck of an impressive speech. Have one heck of a good time.* **3. as heck** (used as a mild intensifier): *I say he's guilty as heck.* [1850–55; euphemistic alter. of HELL]

heck[2] (hek), *n.* **1.** a comblike attachment on a loom, for guiding the warp threads as they are dressed for the warp beam. **2.** a device that guides yarn onto the bobbin of a spinning wheel. **3.** a gridlike arrangement of glass or metal rods below the hooks on a Jacquard loom, used for lifting all harness eyes equally or evenly. [1300–50; ME *hekke,* OE *hecc,* var. of *hæcc* HATCH[2]]

heck•le (hek′əl), *v.,* **-led, -ling,** *n.* —*v.t.* **1.** to harass (a public speaker, performer, etc.) with impertinent questions, gibes, or the like; badger. **2.** hackle[1] (def. 8). —*n.* **3.** hackle[1] (def. 5). [1275–1325; ME *hekelen,* var. of *hechelen* to comb flax; akin to HACKLE[1], HATCHEL] —**heck′ler,** *n.*

heck•uv•a (hek′ə və), *adj., adv. Pron. Spelling.* heck of a. Cf. **heck[1]** (def. 2).

hect-, var. of **hecto-** before a vowel: *hectare.*

hec•tare (hek′târ), *n.* a unit of surface, or land, measure equal to 100 ares, or 10,000 square meters: equivalent to 2.471 acres. *Abbr.:* ha Also, **hektare.** [1800–10; < F; see HECT-, ARE[2]]

hec•tic (hek′tik), *adj.* characterized by intense agitation, excitement, confused and rapid movement, etc.: *The week before the trip was hectic and exhausting.* [1350–1400; ME < LL *hecticus* < Gk *hektikós* habitual, consumptive, adj. corresponding to *héxis* possession, state, habit, equiv. to **hech-,* base of *échein* to have + *-sis* -SIS; see -TIC; r. ME *etyk* < MF] —**hec′ti•cal•ly, hec′tic•ly,** *adv.* —**hec′tic•ness,** *n.*
—**Syn. 1.** frantic, frenzied, wild, chaotic.

hecto-, a combining form meaning "hundred," used in the formation of compound words: *hectograph; hectogram.* Also, **hect-, hekt-, hekto-.** [< F, comb. form repr. Gk *hekatón* hundred]

hec•to•cot•y•lus (hek′tə kot′l əs), *n., pl.* **-cot•y•li** (-kot′l ī′). *Zool.* a modified arm of the male of certain cephalopods that is used to transfer sperm to the female. [1850–55; < NL, equiv. to *hecto-* HECTO- + *-cotylus* < Gk *kotýlē* cup]

hec•to•gram (hek′tə gram′), *n.* a unit of mass or weight equal to 100 grams, equivalent to 3.527 ounces avoirdupois. *Abbr.:* hg Also, **hektogram;** *esp. Brit.,* **hec′to•gramme′.** [1800–10; HECTO- + -GRAM[2]]

hec•to•graph (hek′tə graf′, -gräf′), *n.* **1.** a process for making copies of a letter, memorandum, etc., from a prepared gelatin surface to which the original writing has been transferred. **2.** a machine for making such copies. —*v.t.* **3.** to copy with the hectograph. Also, **hektograph.** [1875–80; HECTO- + -GRAPH] —**hec•to•graph•ic** (hek′tə graf′ik), *adj.* —**hec•tog•ra•phy** (hek tog′rə fē), *n.*

hec•to•li•ter (hek′tə lē′tər), *n.* a unit of capacity equal to 100 liters, equivalent to 2.8378 U.S. bushels, or 26.418 U.S. gallons. *Abbr.:* hl Also, **hektoliter;** *esp. Brit.,* **hec′to•li′tre.** [1800–10; < F *hectolitre.* See HECTO-, LITER]

hec•to•me•ter (hek′tə mē′tər), *n.* a unit of length equal to 100 meters, or 328.08 feet. *Abbr.:* hm Also, **hektometer;** *esp. Brit.,* **hec′to•me′tre.** [1800–10; < F *hectomètre.* See HECTO-, -METER]

Hec•tor (hek′tər), *n.* **1.** *Class. Myth.* the eldest son of Priam and husband of Andromache: the greatest Trojan hero in the Trojan War, killed by Achilles. **2.** (*l.c.*) a blustering, domineering person; a bully. **3.** a male given name. —*v.t.* **4.** (*l.c.*) to treat with insolence; bully; torment: *The teacher hectored his students incessantly.* —*v.i.* **5.** (*l.c.*) to act in a blustering, domineering way; be a bully. [< L < Gk *Héktōr,* special use of adj. *héktōr* holding fast]
—**Syn. 4.** torture, persecute; badger, harass.

hec•to•stere (hek′tə stēr′), *n.* a unit of capacity equal to 100 steres, or 131 cubic yards. Also, **hektostere.** [1860–65; < F *hectostère.* See HECTO-, STERE]

Hec•u•ba (hek′yo͞o bə), *n. Class. Myth.* the wife of Priam.

he'd (hēd; *unstressed* ēd), **1.** contraction of *he had.* **2.** contraction of *he would.*
—**Usage.** See **contraction.**

Hed•da Gab•ler (hed′ə gab′lər), a play (1890) by Henrik Ibsen.

hed•dle (hed′l), *n.* one of the sets of vertical cords or wires in a loom, forming the principal part of the harness that guides the warp threads. [1505–15; perh. repr. OE **hefedl,* a metathetic var. of *hefeld* (ME *helde,* ModE *heald*), c. OS *hevild;* akin to ON *hafald*]

hed•en•berg•ite (hed′n bər gīt′), *n.* a contact metamorphic mineral of the pyroxene family, calcium ferrous silicate, $CaFe(SiO_3)_2$, that forms black prismatic crystals in crystalline limestone. [1815–25; named after L. *Hedenberg,* early 19th-century Swedish chemist; see -ITE[1]]

he•der (khā′dər; *Eng.* khā′dər, -hā′-), *n., pl.* ***ha•da•rim*** (khə dä′rim), *Eng.* **he•ders.** *Yiddish.* **1.** (esp. in Europe) a private Jewish elementary school for teaching children Hebrew, Bible, and the fundamentals of Judaism. **2.** (in the U.S.) See **Talmud Torah** (def. 2). Also, ***cheder.***

hedge (hej), *n., v.,* **hedged, hedg•ing.** —*n.* **1.** a row of bushes or small trees planted close together, esp. when forming a fence or boundary; hedgerow: *small fields separated by hedges.* **2.** any barrier or boundary: *a hedge of stones.* **3.** an act or means of preventing complete loss of a bet, an argument, an investment, or the like, with a partially counterbalancing or qualifying one. —*v.t.* **4.** to enclose with or separate by a hedge: *to hedge a garden.* **5.** to surround and confine as if with a hedge; restrict (often fol. by *in, about,* etc.): *He felt hedged in by the rules of language.* **6.** to protect with qualifications that allow for unstated contingencies or for withdrawal from commitment: *He hedged his program against attack and then presented it to the board.* **7.** to mitigate a possible loss by counterbalancing (one's bets, investments, etc.). **8.** to prevent or hinder free movement; obstruct: *to be hedged by poverty.* —*v.i.* **9.** to avoid a rigid commitment by qualifying or modifying a position so as to permit withdrawal: *He felt that he was speaking too boldly and began to hedge before they could contradict him.* **10.** to prevent complete loss of a bet by betting an additional amount or amounts against the original bet. **11.** *Finance.* to enter transactions that will protect against loss through a compensatory price movement. [bef. 900; ME, OE *hegge;* c. D *heg,* G *Hecke* hedge, ON *heggr* bird cherry] —**hedge′less,** *adj.*
—**Syn. 9.** evade, stall, delay, temporize, waffle.

hedge′ ap′ple, *Midland U.S.* osage orange.

hedge′ gar′lic, an erect, cruciferous herb, *Sisymbrium officinale,* having a garlicky odor.

hedge•hog (hej′hog′, -hôg′), *n.* **1.** an Old World, insect-eating mammal of the genus *Erinaceus,* esp. *E. europaeus,* having spiny hairs on the back and sides. **2.** the porcupine. **3.** *Mil.* **a.** a portable obstacle made of crossed logs in the shape of an hourglass, usually laced with barbed wire. **b.** an obstructive device consisting of steel bars, angle irons, etc., usually embedded in concrete, designed to damage and impede the boats and tanks of a landing force on a beach. [1400–50; late ME *heyghoge.* See HEDGE, HOG] —**hedge′hog′gy,** *adj.*

hedgehog, *Erinaceus europaeus,* length 9 in. (23 cm)

hedge′hog cac′tus, any of various rounded, usually spiny cacti of the genus *Echinocereus,* of the southwestern U.S. and Mexico, having bell-shaped flowers that close at night. [1875–80, *Amer.*]

hedge′hog gourd′. See **teasel gourd.**

hedge•hop (hej′hop′), *v.i.,* **-hopped, -hop•ping.** to fly an airplane at a very low altitude, as for spraying crops or for low-level bombing in warfare. [1910–15; HEDGE + HOP[1]] —**hedge′hop′per,** *n.*

hedge′ net′tle, **1.** a slender-leafed, hairy plant, *Stachys palustris,* of the mint family, abundant along roadsides and in fields and marshes, having clusters of tubular, purple flowers on a spike. **2.** any similar, related plant, esp. *S. hispida,* of wet places. [1670–80]

hedg•er (hej′ər), *n.* **1.** a person who makes or repairs hedges. **2.** a person who hedges in betting, speculating, etc. [1250–1300; ME (in surnames); see HEDGE, -ER[1]]

hedge·row (hej′rō′), *n.* a row of bushes or trees forming a hedge. [bef. 950; ME; OE *heggerewe.* See HEDGE, ROW[1]]

hedge′ spar′row, the dunnock. [1520–30]

hedg·y (hej′ē), *adj.,* **hedg·i·er, hedg·i·est.** abounding in hedges. [1590–1600; HEDGE + -Y[1]]

He·din (he dēn′), *n.* **Sven An·ders** (sven än′dərs), 1865–1952, Swedish geographer and explorer.

He·djaz (hē jaz′; *Arab.* hē zhäz′), *n.* Hijaz.

he·don·ic (hē don′ik), *adj.* **1.** of, characterizing, or pertaining to pleasure: *a hedonic thrill.* **2.** pertaining to hedonism or hedonics. [1650–60; Gk *hēdonikós* pleasurable, equiv. to *hēdon(ḗ)* pleasure + *-ikos* -IC; akin to L *suādēre* to advise, i.e., to recommend as pleasing (see SUASION, PERSUADE), SWEET] **—he·don′i·cal·ly,** *adv.*

hedon′ic cal′culus, (in utilitarianism) appraisal of possible alternative choices in terms of the amount of pleasure to be gained and pain to be avoided in each. Also called **calculus of pleasure.**

he·don·ics (hē don′iks), *n.* (*used with a singular v.*) the branch of psychology that deals with pleasurable and unpleasurable states of consciousness. [1860–65; see HEDONIC, -ICS]

he·don·ism (hēd′n iz′əm), *n.* **1.** the doctrine that pleasure or happiness is the highest good. **2.** devotion to pleasure as a way of life: *The later Roman emperors were notorious for their hedonism.* [1855–60; < Gk *hēdon(ḗ)* pleasure + -ISM]
—Syn. 2. sensualism, libertinism, debauchery, dissipation, carousal. **—Ant. 2.** puritanism, asceticism, abstemiousness, self-denial.

he·don·ist (hēd′n ist), *n.* **1.** a person whose life is devoted to the pursuit of pleasure and self-gratification. **—***adj.* **2.** Also, **he′don·is′tic.** of, pertaining to, or characteristic of a hedonist or hedonism. [1855–60; see HEDONISM, -IST] **—he′don·is′ti·cal·ly,** *adv.*

-hedral, a combining form used to form adjectives corresponding to nouns ending in **-hedron:** *polyhedral.* [-HEDR(ON) + -AL[1]]

-hedron, a combining form meaning "face," used in the names of geometrical solid figures having the form or number of faces specified by the initial element: *tetrahedron.* [< Gk *-edron,* neut. of *-edros* having bases, -sided, equiv. to *(h)édr(a)* seat, face of a geometrical form (see CATHEDRA) + *-os* adj. suffix]

Hed·y (hed′ē), *n.* a female given name: from a Greek word meaning "pleasing."

hee·bie-jee·bies (hē′bē jē′bēz), *n.* (*used with a plural v.*) *Slang.* a condition of extreme nervousness caused by fear, worry, strain, etc.; the jitters; the willies (usually prec. by *the*): *Just thinking about ghosts gives me the heebie-jeebies.* [1905–10, *Amer.*; rhyming compound coined by W. De Beck (1890–1942), American comic-strip cartoonist]

heed (hēd), *v.t.* **1.** to give careful attention to: *He did not heed the warning.* **—***v.i.* **2.** to give attention; have regard. **—***n.* **3.** careful attention; notice; observation (usually with *give* or *take*). [bef. 900; ME *heden,* OE *hēdan;* c. G *hüten* to guard, protect; akin to HOOD[1]] **—heed′er,** *n.*
—Syn. 1. note, observe, consider, mark. **3.** consideration, care; caution, vigilance, watchfulness. **—Ant. 1.** disregard, ignore.

heed·ful (hēd′fəl), *adj.* taking heed; attentive; mindful; thoughtful; careful: *She was always heedful of others' needs.* [1540–50; HEED + -FUL] **—heed′ful·ly,** *adv.* **—heed′ful·ness,** *n.*

heed·less (hēd′lis), *adj.* careless; thoughtless; unmindful: *Heedless of the danger, he returned to the burning building to save his dog.* [1570–80; HEED + -LESS] **—heed′less·ly,** *adv.* **—heed′less·ness,** *n.*
—Syn. oblivious, indifferent; negligent, uncaring, unconcerned. **—Ant.** cautious, mindful, heedful.

hee·haw (hē′hô′), *n.* **1.** the braying sound made by a donkey. **2.** rude laughter. **—***v.i.* **3.** to bray. [1805–15, *Amer.*; imit. gradational compound]

heel[1] (hēl), *n.* **1.** the back part of the human foot, below and behind the ankle. **2.** an analogous part in other vertebrates. **3.** either hind foot or hoof of some animals, as the horse. **4.** the foot as a whole: *He was hung by the heels.* **5.** the part of a stocking, shoe, or the like covering the back part of the wearer's foot. **6.** a solid, raised base or support of leather, wood, rubber, etc., attached to the sole of a shoe or boot under the back part of the foot. **7. heels,** high-heeled shoes. **8.** something resembling the back part of the human foot in position, shape, etc.: *a heel of bread.* **9.** the rear of the palm, adjacent to the wrist. **10.** the latter or concluding part of anything: *the heel of a session.* **11.** the lower end of any of various more or less vertical objects, as rafters, spars, or the sternposts of vessels. **12.** *Naut.* **a.** the after end of a keel. **b.** the inner end of a bowsprit or jib boom. **13.** the crook in the head of a golf club. **14.** *Building Trades.* the exterior angle of an angle iron. **15.** *Railroads.* the end of a frog farthest from a switch. **16.** *Hort.* the base of any part, as of a cutting or tuber, that is removed from a plant for use in the propagation of that plant. **17. at one's heels,** close behind one: *The police are at his heels.* Also, **at heel. 18. cool one's heels,** to be kept waiting, esp. because of deliberate discourtesy: *The producer let the actors who were waiting to be auditioned cool their heels in the outer office.* **19. down at the heels,** having a shabby, slipshod, or slovenly appearance. Also, **down at heel, down at the heel, out at heels, out at the heels. 20. his heels,** *Cribbage.* a jack turned up as a starter, counting two points for the dealer. **21. kick up one's heels,** to have a vigorously entertaining time; frolic: *Grandfather could still kick up his heels now and then.* **22. lay by the heels, a.** to arrest and imprison. **b.** to prevail over; render ineffectual: *Superior forces laid the invaders by the heels.* **23. on** or **upon the heels of,** closely following; in quick succession of: *On the heels of the hurricane came an outbreak of looting.* **24. show a clean pair of heels,** to leave one's pursuers or competitors behind; outrun: *The thief showed his victim a clean pair of heels.* Also, **show one's heels to. 25. take to one's heels,** to run away; take flight: *The thief took to his heels as soon as he saw the police.* **26. to heel, a.** close behind: *The dog followed the hunter to heel.* **b.** under control or subjugation: *The attackers were brought swiftly to heel.* **—***v.t.* **27.** to follow at the heels of; chase closely. **28.** to furnish with heels, as shoes. **29.** to perform (a dance) with the heels. **30.** *Golf.* to strike (the ball) with the heel of the club. **31.** to arm (a gamecock) with spurs. **—***v.i.* **32.** (of a dog) to follow at one's heels on command. **33.** to use the heels, as in dancing. **34. heel in,** to cover temporarily (the roots and most of the stem of a plant) with soil prior to permanent planting. [bef. 850; ME; OE *hēl(a);* c. D *hiel,* ON *hǣll.* See HOCK[1]] **—heel′less,** *adj.*

heel[2] (hēl), *v.i.* **1.** to incline to one side; cant; tilt: *The ship heeled in going about.* **—***v.t.* **2.** to cause to lean or cant. **—***n.* **3.** a heeling movement; a cant. [1565–75; var. of earlier *heeld,* ME *helden,* OE *hieldan* to lean, slope; akin to OE *heald,* ON *hallr* sloping]

heel[3] (hēl), *n.* a contemptibly dishonorable or irresponsible person: *We all feel like heels for ducking out on you like this.* [1910–15, *Amer.*; perh. a euphemistic shortening of *shit-heel*]

heel-and-toe (hēl′ən tō′), *adj.* noting a pace, as in walking contests, in which the heel of the front foot touches ground before the toes of the rear one leave it. [1810–20]

heel′-and-toe′ rac′ing. See **race walking.** [1820–30]

heel·ball (hēl′bôl′), *n.* a substance composed of lampblack and wax used for making rubbings or for polishing shoes. [1790–1800; HEEL[1] + BALL[1], orig. the ball or undersurface of the heel]

heel′ bone′, calcaneus. [1590–1600]

heel′ breast′, the forward side of the heel, adjoining the shank of a shoe. [1920–25]

heeled (hēld), *adj.* **1.** provided with a heel or heels. **2.** provided with money; flush or wealthy (usually used in combination): *one of the best-heeled families in town.* **3.** *Slang.* armed, esp. with a gun. [1555–65; HEEL[1] + -ED[3]]

heel·er (hē′lər), *n.* **1.** a person who heels shoes. **2.** See **ward heeler.** [1630–40; HEEL[1] + -ER[1]]

heel′ fly′. See **cattle grub.** [1875–80, *Amer.*]

heel′ing tank′, *Naut.* either of two lateral ballast tanks permitting an icebreaker to heel and crush ice to either side.

heel·piece (hēl′pēs′), *n.* **1.** *Shoemaking.* **a.** a piece of leather, wood, or other material serving as the heel of a shoe, boot, or the like. **b.** such a piece used in repairing a heel. **2.** an endpiece of anything; a terminal part. [1700–10; HEEL[1] + PIECE]

heel·plate (hēl′plāt′), *n.* a small metal plate attached to the heel of a shoe to protect it against excessive wear. [1840–50; HEEL[1] + PLATE[1]]

heel·post (hēl′pōst′), *n.* a post made to withstand strain, forming or fitted to the end of something, as the post on which a gate or door is hinged. [1840–50; HEEL[1] + POST[1]]

heel·tap (hēl′tap′), *n.* **1.** a layer of leather, metal, or the like in a shoe heel; a lift. **2.** a small portion of liquor remaining in a glass after drinking or in a bottle after decanting. **3.** dregs, sediment, or residue. [1680–90; HEEL[1] + TAP[1], TAP[2]]

Heep (hēp), *n.* **Uriah.** See **Uriah Heep.**

heer (hēr), *n.* an old unit of measure for linen and woolen yarn, equivalent to about 600 yards (550 meters). [1400–50; late ME (Scots) *her(e),* appar. to be identified with *hair(e)* HAIR]

Heer·len (hâr′lən), *n.* a city in the SE Netherlands. 71,435.

He·fei (hœ′fā′), *n. Pinyin.* a city in and the capital of Anhui province, in E China. 400,000. Also, **Hofei.**

Hef·fel·fin·ger (hef′əl fing′gər), *n.* **William Walter** ("*Pudge*"), 1867–1954, U.S. football player.

Hef′ner can′dle (hef′nər), *Optics.* a German unit of luminous intensity, equal to 0.92 of a candela. [1895–1900; named after F. von *Hefner*-Alteneck (1845–1904), German electrical engineer]

heft (heft), *n.* **1.** weight; heaviness: *It was a rather flimsy chair, without much heft to it.* **2.** significance or importance. **3.** *Archaic.* the bulk or main part. **—***v.t.* **4.** to test the weight of by lifting and balancing: *He hefted the spear for a few moments, and then flung it at the foe.* **5.** to heave; hoist. [1550–60; HEAVE + *-t,* var. of -TH[1]] **—heft′er,** *n.*

heft·y (hef′tē), *adj.,* **heft·i·er, heft·i·est. 1.** heavy; weighty: *a hefty book.* **2.** big and strong; powerful; muscular: *a hefty athlete.* **3.** impressively large or substantial: *a hefty increase in salary.* [1865–70; HEFT + -Y[1]] **—heft′i·ly,** *adv.* **—heft′i·ness,** *n.*
—Syn. 2. robust, husky, burly, stalwart.

he·gar·i (hi gar′ē, -gâr′ē, heg′ə rē), *n.* a grain sorghum having chalky white seeds. [1915–20; < Sudanese Ar *ḥijēri,* var. of Ar *ḥijārī* stonelike]

He·gel (hā′gəl), *n.* **Ge·org Wil·helm Frie·drich** (gā′ôrk vil′helm frē′drikh), 1770–1831, German philosopher.

He·ge·li·an (hā gā′lē ən, hi jē′-), *adj.* **1.** of, pertaining to, or characteristic of Hegel or his philosophical system. **—***n.* **2.** a person who accepts the philosophical principles of Hegel. **3.** an authority or expert on the writings of Hegel. [1830–40; HEGEL + -IAN]

Hege′lian dialec′tic, an interpretive method, originally used to relate specific entities or events to the absolute idea, in which some assertible proposition **(thesis)** is necessarily opposed by an equally assertible and apparently contradictory proposition **(antithesis),** the mutual contradiction being reconciled on a higher level of truth by a third proposition **(synthesis).**

He·ge·li·an·ism (hā gā′lē ə niz′əm, hi jē′-), *n.* the philosophy of Hegel and his followers, characterized by the use of the Hegelian dialectic. [1855–60; HEGELIAN + -ISM]

heg·e·mon (hej′ə mon′), *n.* a person, nation, etc., that has or exercises hegemony. [1900–05; < Gk *hēgemṓn* leader, guide]

he·gem·o·nism (hi jem′ə niz′əm), *n.* the policy or practice of hegemony to serve national interests. [1960–65; HEGEMON(Y) + -ISM] **—he·gem′o·nist,** *n., adj.* **—he·gem′o·nis′tic,** *adj.*

he·gem·o·ny (hi jem′ə nē, hej′ə mō′nē), *n., pl.* **-nies. 1.** leadership or predominant influence exercised by one nation over others, as in a confederation. **2.** leadership; predominance. **3.** (esp. among smaller nations) aggression or expansionism by large nations in an effort to achieve world domination. [1560–70; < Gk *hēgemonía* leadership, supremacy, equiv. to *hēgemon-* (s. of *hēgemṓn*) leader + *-ia* -Y[3]] **—heg·e·mon·ic** (hej′ə mon′ik), **heg′e·mon′i·cal,** *adj.*

He·gi·ra (hi jī′rə, hej′ər ə), *n.* **1.** *Islam.* Hijra. **2.** (*l.c.*) Also, **hejira.** any flight or journey to a more desirable or congenial place. [< ML < Ar; see HIJRA]

he·gu·men (hi gyōō′mən), *n. Eastern Ch.* the head of a monastery. Also, **he·gu·me·nos** (hi gyōō′mə nos′). [1655–65; < ML *hēgūmenus* < Gk *hēgoúmenos* chief, lit., leading, prp. of *hēgeîsthai* to lead]

heh (hā), *n.* he[2].

he-huck·le·ber·ry (hē′huk′əl ber′ē), *n., pl.* **-ries.** See **swamp andromeda.**

Hei·an (hā′än′), *adj.* of or pertaining to the period in Japan, A.D. 794–1185, characterized by the modification and naturalization of ideas and institutions that were earlier introduced from China. [1890–95; < Japn *heian,* earlier *feian* < MChin, equiv. to Chin *píngān* peace]

Hei·deg·ger (hī′deg ər, -di gər), *n.* **Martin,** 1889–1976, German philosopher and writer.

Hei·del·berg (hīd′l bûrg′; *Ger.* hīd′l berk′), *n.* a city in NW Baden-Württemberg, in SW Germany: university, founded 1386. 127,500.

Hei′delberg jaw′, a human lower jaw of early middle Pleistocene age found in 1907 near Heidelberg, Germany. [1910–15]

Hei′delberg man′, the primitive human being reconstructed from the Heidelberg jaw. [1925–30]

Hei·den (hīd′n), *n.* **Eric,** born 1958, U.S. speed skater.

Hei·den·stam (hā′dən stäm′), *n.* **Ver·ner von** (ver′nər fôn), 1859–1940, Swedish poet and novelist: Nobel prize 1916.

Hei·di (hī′dē), *n.* a female given name.

Hei·duc (hī′dŏŏk), *n.* Haiduk. Also, **Hei′duk.**

heif·er (hef′ər), *n.* a young cow over one year old that has not produced a calf. [bef. 900; ME *hayfre,* OE *hēa(h)f(o)re,* equiv. to *hēah* high + *-fore;* akin to Gk *póris* heifer]

Hei·fetz (hī′fits), *n.* **Ja·scha** (yä′shə), 1901–87, U.S. violinist, born in Russia.

heigh (hā, hī), *interj.* (an exclamation used to call attention, give encouragement, etc.) [1565–75]

heigh-ho (hī′hō′, hā′-), *interj.* (an exclamation of surprise, exultation, melancholy, boredom, or weariness.) [1545–55]

height (hīt), *n.* **1.** extent or distance upward: *The balloon stopped rising at a height of 500 feet.* **2.** distance upward from a given level to a fixed point: *the height from the ground to the first floor; the height of an animal at the shoulder.* **3.** the distance between the lowest and highest points of a person standing upright; stature: *She is five feet in height.* **4.** considerable or great altitude or elevation: *the height of the mountains.* **5.** Often, **heights. a.** a high place above a level; a hill or mountain: *They stood on the heights overlooking the valley.* **b.** the highest part; top; apex; summit: *In his dreams he reached the heights.* **6.** the highest point; utmost degree: *the height of power; the height of pleasure.* **7.** *Archaic.* high rank in social status. Also, **hight.** [bef. 900; ME; OE *hīehtho.* See HIGH, -TH[1]]
—Syn. 3. tallness. HEIGHT, ALTITUDE, ELEVATION refer to distance above a level. HEIGHT denotes extent upward (as from foot to head) as well as any measurable distance above a given level: *The tree grew to a height of ten feet. They looked down from a great height.* ALTITUDE usually

CONCISE ETYMOLOGY KEY: <, descended or borrowed from; >, whence; b., blend of, blended; c., cognate with; cf., compare; deriv., derivative; equiv., equivalent; imit., imitative; obl., oblique; r., replacing; s., stem; sp., spelling, spelled; resp., respelling, respelled; trans., translation; ?, origin unknown; *, unattested; ‡, probably earlier than. See the full key inside the front cover.

refers to the distance, determined by instruments, above a given level, commonly mean sea level: *altitude of an airplane.* ELEVATION implies a distance to which something has been raised or uplifted above a level: *a hill's elevation above the surrounding country, above sea level.* **5.** prominence. **6.** peak, pinnacle; acme, zenith. **—Ant. 1, 2.** depth.

—Usage. HEIGHT, and not HEIGHTH, is considered the standard English form for this word.

height·en (hīt′n), *v.t.* **1.** to increase the height of; make higher. **2.** to increase the degree or amount of; augment. **3.** to strengthen, deepen, or intensify: *to heighten the plot of a story; to heighten one's awareness; to heighten one's suffering.* **4.** to bring out the important features of, as in a drawing: *to heighten a picture with Chinese white.* —*v.i.* **5.** to become higher. **6.** to increase: *The tension heightened as the enemy forces advanced.* **7.** to brighten or become more intense. [1515–25; HEIGHT + -EN[1]] **—height′en·er,** *n.*

—Syn. 1. See **elevate.**

heighth (hītth), *n.* a nonstandard spelling of **height.**

height·ism (hī′tiz əm), *n.* discrimination or prejudice based on a person's stature, esp. discrimination against short people. [1970–75]

height-to-pa·per (hīt′tə pā′pər), *n. Print.* the standard height of type, measured from the foot to the face, in the U.S. 0.918 of an inch (2.33 cm). [1765–75]

Heil·bronn (hīl′brôn), *n.* a city in N Baden-Württemberg, in SW Germany. 110,900.

Hei·li·gen·schein (hī′li gən shīn′), *n., pl.* ***-schei·ne*** (-shī′nə). *German.* a ring of light around the shadow cast by a person's head, esp. on a dewy, sunlit lawn, caused by reflection and diffraction of light rays; halo. [lit., saint's shining light]

Hei·long Jiang (hā′lông′ jyäng′), *Pinyin.* Amur.

Hei·long·jiang (hā′lông′jyäng′), *n. Pinyin.* a province in NE China, S of the Amur River. 21,390,000; 108,880 sq. mi. (281,999 sq. km). *Cap.:* Harbin. Also, *Older Spelling,* **Hei·lung·kiang** (hā′lo͝ong′gyäng′).

Heim·dall (hām′däl′), *n. Scand. Myth.* the god of dawn and light. Also, **Heim′dal′, Heim·dallr** (hām′däl′-ər). [< ON *Heimdallr,* equiv. to *heim(r)* HOME, world + *dallr,* perh. c. OE *deall* bold, renowned]

heim·ish (hā′mish), *adj.* haimish.

Heim′lich maneu′ver (hīm′lik), an emergency rescue procedure for application to someone choking on a foreign object: the rescuer, from behind the victim, places a fist on the upper abdomen below the lowest ribs and thrusts with both hands in an inward and upward direction with sufficient force to help eject the object from the windpipe. [1970–75, *Amer.;* after Henry J. *Heimlich* (born 1920), U.S. physician who devised it]

Heimlich maneuver

Heims·kring·la (hāms′kring lä), *n. Scand. Myth.* a book of the 13th century narrating the history of the kings of Norway by Snorri Sturluson. [< ON, from *kringla heimsins* orb of the world, the first two words of the text]

Hei·ne (hī′nə), *n.* **Hein·rich** (hīn′rikh), 1797–1856, German lyric and satiric poet, journalist, and critic.

Hei′ne-Bo·rel′ the′orem (hī′nə bô rel′, -bə-), *Math.* the theorem that in a metric space every covering consisting of open sets that covers a closed and compact set has a finite collection of subsets that covers the given set. Also called **Borel-Lebesque theorem.** [named after Eduard Heine (1821–81), German mathematician and Émile *Borel* (1871–1956), French mathematician]

hei·nie[1] (hī′nē), *n. Slang (disparaging and offensive).* a German, esp. a German soldier of World War I. [1900–05; partly Anglicized form of G *Heine,* familiar var. of *Heinrich* Henry; see -IE]

hei·nie[2] (hī′nē), *n. Slang.* the buttocks. [1935–40; alter. of HINDER[2]; see -IE]

Hein·lein (hīn′līn), *n.* **Robert A(nson),** 1907–88, U.S. science-fiction writer.

hei·nous (hā′nəs), *adj.* hateful; odious; abominable; totally reprehensible: *a heinous offense.* [1325–75; ME *heynous* < MF *haineus,* equiv. to *haine* hatred (deriv. of *hair* to HATE < Gmc) + *-eus* -OUS] **—hei′nous·ly,** *adv.* **—hei′nous·ness,** *n.*

—Syn. wicked, infamous, flagrant, flagitious, atrocious, villainous, nefarious. **—Ant.** admirable.

Hein·rich (hīn′rik; *Ger.* hīn′rikh), *n.* a male given name, Germanic form of **Henry.**

Heinz (hīnz), *n.* **H(enry) J(ohn),** 1844–1919, U.S. businessman: founder of food-processing company.

heir (âr), *n.* **1.** a person who inherits or has a right of inheritance in the property of another following the latter's death. **2.** *Law.* **a.** (in common law) a person who inherits all the property of a deceased person, as by descent, relationship, will, or legal process. **b.** *Civil Law.* a person who legally succeeds to the place of a deceased person and assumes the rights and obligations of the deceased, as the liabilities for debts or the possessory rights to property. **3.** a person who inherits or is entitled to inherit the rank, title, position, etc., of another. **4.** a person or group considered as inheriting the tradition, talent, etc., of a predecessor. —*v.t.* **5.** *Chiefly South Midland and Southern U.S.* to inherit; succeed to. [1225–75; ME *eir, heir* < OF < L *hērēd-* (s. of *hērēs*); akin to Gk *chēros* bereaved] **—heir′less,** *adj.*

heir′ appar′ent, *pl.* **heirs apparent. 1.** an heir whose right is indefeasible, provided he or she survives the ancestor. **2.** a person whose succession to a position appears certain: *His popularity makes him the chief's heir apparent.* [1325–75; ME] **—heir′ appar′ency.**

heir′ at law′, *pl.* **heirs at law.** a person who inherits, or has a right of inheritance in, the real property of one who has died without leaving a valid will. [1720–30]

heir·dom (âr′dəm), *n.* heirship; inheritance. [1590–1600; HEIR + -DOM]

heir·ess (âr′is), *n.* a woman who inherits or has a right of inheritance, esp. a woman who has inherited or will inherit considerable wealth. [1650–60; HEIR + -ESS]

—Usage. See **-ess.**

heir·loom (âr′lo͞om′), *n.* **1.** a family possession handed down from generation to generation. **2.** *Law.* property neither personal nor real that descends to the heir of an estate as part of the real property. [1375–1425; late ME *heirlome.* See HEIR, LOOM[1]]

heir′ presump′tive, *pl.* **heirs presumptive.** a person who is expected to be the heir but whose expectations may be canceled by the birth of a nearer heir. [1620–30]

heir·ship (âr′ship), *n.* the position or rights of an heir; right of inheritance; inheritance. [1470–80; see HEIR, -SHIP]

Hei·sen·berg (hī′zən bûrg′; *Ger.* hī′zən berk′), *n.* **Wer·ner Karl** (ver′nər kärl), 1901–76, German physicist: Nobel prize 1932.

Hei′senberg uncer′tainty prin′ciple, *Physics.* See **uncertainty principle.** [1965–70; named after W. K. HEISENBERG]

Heiss (hīs), *n.* **Carol E(lizabeth),** born 1940, U.S. figure-skater.

heist (hīst), *Slang.* —*n.* **1.** a robbery or holdup: *Four men were involved in the armored car heist.* —*v.t.* **2.** to take unlawfully, esp. in a robbery or holdup; steal: *to heist a million dollars' worth of jewels.* **3.** to rob or hold up. [1925–30, *Amer.;* alter. of HOIST] **—heist′er,** *n.*

He·jaz (hē jaz′; *Arab.* he zhäz′), *n.* Hijaz. Also, **Hedjaz.**

He·jiang (hœ′jyäng′), *n. Pinyin.* a former province in Manchuria, in NE China. Also, **Hokiang.**

he·ji·ra (hi jī′rə, hej′ər ə), *n.* hegira (def. 2).

Hek·a·te (hek′ə tē; *in Shakespeare* hek′it), *n.* Hecate. **—Hek′a·te′an, Hek′a·tae′an,** *adj.*

hekh·sher (*Seph.* hekh sher′; *Ashk.* hekh′shər; *Eng.* hek′shər), *n., pl.* ***hekh·she·rim*** (*Seph.* hekh she rēm′; *Ashk.* hekh shā′rim), *Eng.* **hekh·shers.** *Hebrew.* hechsher.

hek·tare (hek′târ), *n.* hectare.

hekto-, var. of **hecto-:** hektometer. Also, *esp. before a vowel,* **hekt-.**

hek·to·gram (hek′tə gram′), *n.* hectogram.

hek·to·graph (hek′tə graf′, -gräf′), *n., v.t.* hectograph.

hek·to·li·ter (hek′tə lē′tər), *n.* hectoliter.

hek·to·me·ter (hek′tə mē′tər), *n.* hectometer.

hek·to·stere (hek′tə stēr′), *n.* hectostere.

Hel (hel), *n. Scand. Myth.* **1.** the goddess ruling Niflheim: a daughter of Loki and Angerboda. **2.** the home of the dead; Niflheim. [< ON; see HELL]

He′La cell′ (hel′ə), *Biol.* a vigorous strain of laboratory-cultured cells descended from a human cervical cancer, used widely in research. Also, **He′la cell′, he′la cell′.** [after *He(nrietta) La(cks),* a patient at Johns Hopkins Hospital, Baltimore, from whom the tissue was taken in 1951 prior to her death]

hé·las (ā läs′), *interj. French.* alas!

held (held), *v.* pt. and a pp. of **hold.**

Held (held), *n.* **John, Jr.,** 1889–1958, U.S. cartoonist, illustrator, and writer.

hel·den·ten·or (hel′dn ten′ər; *Ger.* hel′dn tā nōr′), *n., pl.* **-ten·ors,** *Ger.* ***-te·no·re*** (-tā nō′rə). a tenor having a brilliant, powerful voice suited to singing heroic roles, as in Wagnerian opera. Also called **heroic tenor.** [1925–30; < G, equiv. to *Helden-* comb. form of *Held* hero + *Tenor* TENOR]

Hel·en (hel′ən), *n.* **1.** Also called **Hel′en of Troy′.** *Class. Myth.* the beautiful daughter of Zeus and Leda and wife of Menelaus whose abduction by Paris was the cause of the Trojan War. **2.** a female given name. [< F *Hélène* < L *Helena* < Gk *Helénē,* of obscure orig., prob. the name of a pre-Greek vegetation goddess; often linked by folk etym. with *helénē, helánē* torch, St. Elmo's fire, an unrelated word]

Hel·e·na (hel′ə nə; *for 3 also* hə lē′nə), *n.* **1. Saint,** c247–c330, mother of Constantine I. **2.** a city in and the capital of Montana, in the W part. 23,938. **3.** a female given name, form of **Helen.**

He·lene (hə lēn′), *n.* a female given name, form of **Helen.**

Hel·ga (hel′gə), *n.* a female given name: from a Germanic word meaning "holy."

Hel·gi (hel′gē), *n. Scand. Myth.* (in the *Poetic Edda* and the *Volsunga Saga*) **1.** the son of Hjorvard and Svava, a Valkyrie. **2.** his reincarnation, the son of Sigmund and Borghild: slayer of Hunding. [< ON: masc. sing. weak form of *heilagr* HOLY, sacred]

Hel·go·land (hel′gō länt′), *n.* a German island in the North Sea. 2312; ¼ sq. mi. (0.6 sq. km). Also, **Heligoland.**

heli-[1], var. of **helio-** before a vowel: *helianthus.*

heli-[2], a combining form representing **helicopter** in compound words: *helidrop; helilift; helitaxi.* [by analysis of HELICOPTER as *heli-* (an assumed comb. form with -I-) + *-copter;* cf. COPTER]

he·li·a·cal (hi lī′ə kəl), *adj. Astron.* pertaining to or occurring near the sun, esp. applied to such risings and settings of a star as are most nearly coincident with those of the sun while yet visible. Also, **he·li·ac** (hē′lē-ak′). [1600–10; < LL *hēliac(us)* (< Gk *hēliakós;* see HELI-[1], -AC) + -AL[1]] **—he·li′a·cal·ly,** *adv.*

he·li·an·thine B (hē′lē an′thin, -thēn), *Chem.* See **methyl orange.** [HELIANTH(US) + -INE[2]]

he·li·an·thus (hē′lē an′thəs), *n., pl.* **-thus·es.** any composite plant of the genus *Helianthus,* comprising the sunflowers. [1770–80; < NL; see HELI-[1], -ANTHOUS] **—he·li·an·tha·ceous** (hē′lē ən thā′shəs), *adj.*

hel·i·borne (hel′ə bôrn′, -bōrn′), *adj.* transported by helicopter: *heliborne troops.* [1965–70; HELI-[2] + (AIR)BORNE]

helic-, var. of **helico-** before a vowel: *helical.*

hel·i·cal (hel′i kəl, hē′li-), *adj.* pertaining to or having the form of a helix; spiral. [1605–15; HELIC- + -AL[1]] **—hel′i·cal·ly,** *adv.*

hel′ical gear′, a cylindrical gear wheel whose teeth follow the pitch surface in a helical manner. [1885–90]

helical gears

hel′ical rack′, a rack having teeth set at an oblique angle to the edges. Cf. **rack**[1] (def. 5).

he·liced (hē′list, hel′ist), *adj.* decorated with spirals. [1870–75; HELIC- (cf. F *hélice*) + -ED[3]]

hel·i·ces (hel′ə sēz′), *n.* a pl. of **helix.**

hel·i·chry·sum (hel′i krī′səm, hē′li-), *n.* any of the numerous composite plants of the genus *Helichrysum,* having alternate leaves and solitary or clustered flower heads, including the strawflower. [< NL, neut. n. based on Gk *helíchrysos* a plant, prob. of this genus, equiv. to *heli-* (perh. by haplology from *heliko-* HELICO-) + *chrȳsós* gold]

hel·i·cline (hel′i klīn′), *n.* a curved ramp. [HELI(C)- + -CLINE]

helico-, a combining form meaning "spiral"; used with this meaning and as a combining form of **helix** in the formation of compound words: *helicograph.* Also, *esp. before a vowel,* **helic-.** [< Gk *heliko-,* comb. form of *hélix*]

hel·i·co·graph (hel′i kō graf′, -gräf′), *n.* an instrument for drawing helices. [1850–55; HELICO- + -GRAPH]

hel·i·coid (hel′i koid′, hē′li-), *adj.* **1.** coiled or curving like a spiral. —*n.* **2.** *Geom.* a warped surface generated by a straight line moving so as to cut or touch a fixed helix. [1690–1700; < Gk *helikoeidḗs* of spiral form. See HELIC-, -OID] **—hel′i·coi′dal,** *adj.* **—hel′i·coi′dal·ly,** *adv.*

hel·i·con (hel′i kon′, -kən), *n.* a coiled tuba carried over the shoulder and used esp. in military bands. Cf. **sousaphone.** [1520–30; prob. special use of HELICON, by assoc. with HELICO-]

helicon

Hel·i·con (hel′i kon′, -kən), *n.* a mountain in S central Greece. 5738 ft. (1749 m): regarded by ancient Greeks as the abode of Apollo and the Muses.

hel·i·copt (hel′i kopt′, hē′li-), *v.t., v.i.* helicopter. [1945–50; back formation from HELICOPTER, by false analysis as *helicopt-* + -ER[1]]

hel·i·cop·ter (hel′i kop′tər, hē′li-), *n.* **1.** any of a class of heavier-than-air craft that are lifted and sustained in the air horizontally by rotating wings or blades turning on vertical axes through power supplied by an engine. —*v.i.* **2.** to fly in a helicopter. —*v.t.* **3.** to convey in a helicopter. [1885–90; < F *hélicoptère.* See HELICO-, -PTER]

helicopter (def. 1)

hel•i•co•spore (hel′i kə spôr′, -spōr′), *n. Mycol.* a coiled cylindrical fungal spore. [HELICO- + -SPORE] —**hel•i•cos•po•rous** (hel′i kos′pər əs), *adj.*

Hel•i•go•land (hel′i gō land′), *n.* Helgoland.

he•li•o (hē′lē ō′), *n., pl.* **-li•os.** *Informal.* **1.** a heliogram. **2.** a heliograph. [by shortening]

helio-, a combining form meaning "sun," used in the formation of compound words: *heliolatry.* Also, *esp. before a vowel,* **heli-.** [< Gk, comb. form of *hḗlios* SUN]

he•li•o•cen•tric (hē′lē ō sen′trik), *adj. Astron.* **1.** measured or considered as being seen from the center of the sun. **2.** having or representing the sun as a center: *the heliocentric concept of the universe.* [1660–70; HELIO- + -CENTRIC] —**he′li•o•cen′tri•cal•ly,** *adv.* —**he•li•o•cen•tric•i•ty** (hē′lē ō sen tris′i tē), **he•li•o•cen•tri•cism** (hē′lē ō sen′trə siz′əm), *n.*

he′liocen′tric par′allax, *Astron.* See under **parallax** (def. 2). [1860–65]

He•li•o•chrome (hē′lē ə krōm′), *Trademark.* a brand of photograph reproducing directly the natural colors of a subject. —**he′li•o•chro′mic,** *adj.* —**he′li•o•chro′•my,** *n.*

he•li•o•dor (hē′lē ə dôr′), *n.* a clear yellow variety of beryl used as a gemstone. [1910–15; < G < Gk *hḗlio-* HELIO- + *dôron* gift]

He•li•o•gab•a•lus (hē′lē ə gab′ə ləs), *n.* (*Varius Avitus Bassianus*) (*"Marcus Aurelius Antoninus"*), A.D. 204–222, Roman emperor 218–222. Also, **Elagabalus.**

he•li•o•gram (hē′lē ə gram′), *n.* a message sent by a heliograph. [1880–85; HELIO- + -GRAM[1]]

he•li•o•graph (hē′lē ə graf′, -gräf′), *n.* **1.** a device for signaling by means of a movable mirror that reflects beams of light, esp. sunlight, to a distance. **2.** *Astron.* photoheliograph. **3.** *Meteorol.* an instrument for recording the duration and intensity of sunshine. **4.** *Photog., Print.* an early type of photoengraving made on a metal plate coated with sensitized asphalt. —*v.t., v.i.* **5.** to communicate by heliograph. [1815–25; HELIO- + -GRAPH] —**he•li•og•ra•pher** (hē′lē og′rə fər), *n.* —**he•li•o•graph•ic** (hē′lē ə graf′ik), **he′li•o•graph′i•cal,** *adj.* —**he′li•o•graph′i•cal•ly,** *adv.* —**he′li•og′ra•phy,** *n.*

he•li•o•gra•vure (hē′lē ō grə vyŏŏr′, -ə grā′vyŏŏr), *n.* (formerly) photoengraving. [1875–80; < F; see HELIO-, GRAVURE]

he•li•ol•a•try (hē′lē ol′ə trē), *n.* worship of the sun. [1820–30; HELIO- + -LATRY] —**he′li•ol′a•ter,** *n.* —**he′•li•ol′a•trous,** *adj.*

he•li•om•e•ter (hē′lē om′i tər), *n.* a telescope with a divided, adjustable objective, formerly used to measure small angular distances, as those between celestial bodies. [1745–55; HELIO- + -METER] —**he•li•o•met•ric** (hē′lē ə me′trik), **he′li•o•met′ri•cal,** *adj.* —**he′li•o•met′ri•cal•ly,** *adv.*

he•li•o•pause (hē′lē ə pôz′), *n. Astron.* the boundary of the heliosphere. [1970–75; HELIO- + PAUSE]

he•li•o•phyte (hē′lē ə fīt′), *n. Bot.* a plant that grows best in full sunlight. [HELIO- + -PHYTE]

He•li•op•o•lis (hē′lē op′ə lis), *n.* **1.** Biblical name, **On.** an ancient ruined city in N Egypt, on the Nile delta. **2.** ancient Greek name of **Baalbek.**

He•li•os (hē′lē os′), *n.* the ancient Greek god of the sun, represented as driving a chariot across the heavens; identified by the Romans with Sol.

he•li•o•scope (hē′lē ə skōp′), *n.* a telescope for viewing the sun, adapted to protect the eye of the viewer from the sun's glare. [1665–75; HELIO- + -SCOPE] —**he•li•o•scop•ic** (hē′lē ə skop′ik), *adj.* —**he•li•os•co•py** (hē′lē os′kə pē), *n.*

he•li•o•sphere (hē′lē ə sfēr′), *n. Astron.* the region around the sun over which the effect of the solar wind extends. [1970–75; HELIO- + -SPHERE]

he•li•o•stat (hē′lē ə stat′), *n.* an instrument consisting of a mirror moved by clockwork, for reflecting the sun's rays in a fixed direction. [1740–50; < NL *heliostata.* See HELIO-, -STAT] —**he′li•o•stat′ic,** *adj.*

he•li•o•tax•is (hē′lē ō tak′sis), *n. Biol.* movement of an organism toward or away from sunlight. [1895–1900; HELIO- + -TAXIS] —**he•li•o•tac•tic** (hē′lē ō tak′tik), *adj.*

he•li•o•ther•a•py (hē′lē ō ther′ə pē), *n.* treatment of disease by means of sunlight. [1885–90; HELIO- + THERAPY]

he•li•o•trope (hē′lē ə trōp′, hēl′yə- *or, esp. Brit.,* hel′yə-), *n.* **1.** any hairy plant belonging to the genus *Heliotropium,* of the borage family, as *H. arborescens,* cultivated for its small, fragrant purple flowers. **2.** any of various other plants, as the valerian or the winter heliotrope. **3.** any plant that turns toward the sun. **4.** a light tint of purple; reddish lavender. **5.** *Survey.* an arrangement of mirrors for reflecting sunlight from a distant point to an observation station. **6.** bloodstone. [1580–90; < MF *héliotrope* < L *hēliotropium* < Gk *hēliotrópion* (see HELIO-, -TROPE); cf. ME *elitropium, elitropius,* OE *eliotropus* < ML]

he•li•o•trop•ic (hē′lē ə trop′ik, -trō′pik), *adj. Biol.* turning or growing toward the light. [1870–75; HELIO- + -TROPIC] —**he′li•o•trop′i•cal•ly,** *adv.*

he•li•o•tro•pin (hē′lē ə trō′pin, hē′lē o′trə pin), *n.* piperonal. [1880–85; HELIOTROPE + -IN[2]]

he•li•ot•ro•pism (hē′lē o′trə piz′əm, hē′lē ə trō′pizəm), *n.* heliotropic tendency or growth. [1850–55; HELIO- + -TROPISM]

he•li•o•type (hē′lē ə tīp′), *n., v.,* **-typed, -typ•ing.** collotype. [1865–70; HELIO- + -TYPE] —**he•li•o•typ•ic** (hē′lē ə tip′ik), *adj.* —**he′li•o•typ′i•cal•ly,** *adv.*

he•li•o•zo•an (hē′lē ə zō′ən), *n.* **1.** a protozoan of the order Heliozoa, having a spherical body and radiating pseudopods. —*adj.* **2.** Also, **he•li•o•zo•ic** (hē′lē ə zō′ik). belonging or pertaining to the Heliozoa. [1890–95; < NL *Hēliozo(a)* name of the group (see HELIO-, -ZOA) + -AN]

hel•i•pad (hel′ə pad′, hē′lə-), *n.* a takeoff and landing area for helicopters, usually without commercial facilities. [1940–45; HELI-[2] + PAD[1]]

hel•i•port (hel′ə pôrt′, -pōrt′, hē′lə-), *n.* a landing place for helicopters, often on the roof of a building or in some other limited area. [1940–45; HELI-[2] + PORT[1]]

hel•i•ski•ing (hel′i skē′ing), *n.* skiing on remote mountains to which the participants are brought by helicopter. [1975–80]

hel•i•stop (hel′ə stop′, hē′lə-), *n.* a heliport. [1950–55; HELI-[2] + STOP]

he•li•um (hē′lē əm), *n.* an inert, gaseous element present in the sun's atmosphere and in natural gas, and also occurring as a radioactive decomposition product, used as a substitute for flammable gases in dirigible balloons. *Symbol:* He; *at. wt.:* 4.0026; *at. no.:* 2; *density:* 0.1785 g/l at 0°C and 760 mm pressure. [1875–80; < NL < Gk *hēli(os)* the sun + NL *-ium* -IUM]

he•lix (hē′liks), *n., pl.* **hel•i•ces** (hel′ə sēz′), **he•lix•es.** **1.** a spiral. **2.** *Geom.* the curve formed by a straight line drawn on a plane when that plane is wrapped around a cylindrical surface of any kind, esp. a right circular cylinder, as the curve of a screw. Equation: $x = a \sin\theta$, $y = a \cos\theta$, $z = b\,\theta$. **3.** *Archit.* **a.** a spiral ornament. **b.** (in a Corinthian capital) either of two scrolls issuing from a cauliculus. Cf. **Corinthian** (def. 2). **4.** *Anat.* the curved fold forming most of the rim of the external ear. See diag. under **ear.** **5.** *Biochem.* See **alpha helix.** [1555–65; < L: a spiral, a kind of ivy < Gk *hélix* anything twisted; cf. *helíssein* to turn, twist, roll]

H, **helix** (def. 3b)

hell (hel), *n.* **1.** the place or state of punishment of the wicked after death; the abode of evil and condemned spirits; Gehenna or Tartarus. **2.** any place or state of torment or misery: *They made their father's life a hell on earth.* **3.** something that causes torment or misery: *Having that cut stitched without anesthesia was hell.* **4.** the powers of evil. **5.** the abode of the dead; Sheol or Hades. **6.** extreme disorder or confusion; chaos: *The children let both dogs into the house, and all hell broke loose.* **7.** heck[1] (def. 2). **8.** a receptacle into which a tailor throws scraps. **9.** Also called **hellbox.** *Print.* a box into which a printer throws discarded type. **10.** the utterance of "hell" in swearing or for emphasis. **11. be hell on,** *Slang.* **a.** to be unpleasant to or painful for. **b.** to be harmful to: *These country roads are hell on tires.* **12. for the hell of it,** *Informal.* **a.** to see what will happen; for adventure, fun, excitement, etc.: *For the hell of it, let's just get on the next bus and see where it takes us.* **b.** with no particular purpose; for no special reason: *I called him up for the hell of it, and he offered me a job.* **13. get** or **catch hell,** *Slang.* to suffer a scolding; receive a harsh reprimand: *We'll get hell from our parents for staying out so late again.* **14. give someone hell,** *Informal.* to reprimand or reproach severely. **15. go to hell in a handbasket.** *Informal.* See **handbasket** (def. 2). **16. hell on wheels,** *Slang.* extremely demanding, fast-paced, aggressive, effective, or the like: *Our sales staff is hell on wheels when it comes to getting the most out of every account.* **17. like hell,** *Informal.* **a.** with great speed, effort, intensity, etc.: *We ran like hell to get home before the storm.* **b.** (used sarcastically or ironically to express the opposite of what is being stated): *He says the motor will never break down? Like hell it won't!* **18. play hell with,** *Slang.* to deal recklessly with; bring injury or harm to: *Snowstorms played hell with the flow of city traffic.* **19. raise hell,** *Slang.* **a.** to indulge in wild celebration. **b.** to create an uproar; object violently to: *She'll raise hell when she sees what your rabbit has done to her garden.* **20. the hell,** *Informal.* **a.** (used as an intensifier to express surprise, anger, impatience, etc.): *Why the hell can't the trains run on time?* **b.** (used sarcastically or ironically to express the opposite of what is being stated): *Are you listening to me? The hell you are!* **21. the** or **to hell with,** *Informal.* (used to express dismissal, rejection, contempt, disappointment, or the like): *If we have to walk five miles to see the view, the hell with it! He wouldn't even speak to me, so to hell with him!* **22. what the hell,** *Informal.* (used to express lack of concern or worry, indifference, abandonment, surrender, etc.): *As long as you're borrowing $100, what the hell, borrow $200.* —*interj.* **23.** (used to express surprise, irritation, disgust, etc.) —*v.* **24. hell around,** *Slang.* to live or act in a wild or dissolute manner: *All they cared about was drinking and helling around.* [bef. 900; ME, OE *hell(l);* c. OHG *hell(i)a* (G *Hölle*), ON *hel,* Goth *halja;* akin to OE *helan* to cover, hide, and to HULL[2]] —**hell′-like′,** *adj.*
—**Syn. 1.** inferno. **2.** anguish, agony, torture.
—**Ant. 1, 2.** heaven, paradise.

he'll (hēl; *unstressed* ēl, hil, il), contraction of *he will.*
—**Usage.** See **contraction.**

hel•la•cious (he lā′shəs), *adj. Slang.* **1.** remarkable; astonishing: *They're raising a hellacious amount of money in taxes.* **2.** formidably difficult: *We had a hellacious time getting here in the blizzard.* Also, **hel•la′•ceous.** [HELL + *-acious* (extracted from AUDACIOUS, SAGACIOUS, VIVACIOUS, etc.), perh. with intensive or aug. force; cf. BODACIOUS, *splendacious*]

Hel•lad•ic (he lad′ik), *adj.* of or pertaining to the Bronze Age culture on the mainland of ancient Greece c2900–1100 B.C. [1795–1805; < L *Helladicus* < Gk *Helladikós* of, from Greece, equiv. to *Hellad-* (s. of *Hellás*) Greece + *-ikos* -IC]

Hel•las (hel′əs), *n.* ancient Greek name of **Greece.**

Hel•las (hel′əs), *n.* an area in the southern hemisphere of Mars, appearing as a light region when viewed telescopically from the earth.

hell•bend•er (hel′ben′dər), *n.* **1.** a large salamander, *Cryptobranchus alleganiensis,* of rivers and streams in eastern North America, having a flat, stout body and broad head. **2.** *Informal.* a reckless or headstrong person. [1805–15, *Amer.*; HELL + BENDER]

hellbender, *Cryptobranchus alleganiensis,* length 18 in. (46 cm)

hell•bent (hel′bent′), *adj.* **1.** stubbornly or recklessly determined. **2.** going at terrific speed. —*adv.* **3.** in a hellbent manner; with reckless determination; at full speed. [1825–35, *Amer.*; HELL + BENT[1]]

hell•box (hel′boks′), *n. Print.* hell (def. 9). [1885–90; HELL + BOX[1]]

hell•broth (hel′brôth′, -broth′), *n.* a magical broth prepared for an evil purpose, as in black magic. [1595–1605; HELL + BROTH]

hell•cat (hel′kat′), *n.* **1.** a bad-tempered, spiteful woman; shrew. **2.** a woman with magic powers derived from evil sources; witch. [1595–1605; HELL + CAT[1]]

hell•div•er (hel′dī′vər), *n.* a grebe, esp. the pied-billed grebe. [1830–40, *Amer.*; HELL + DIVER]

hel•le•bore (hel′ə bôr′, -bōr′), *n.* **1.** any of several plants of the genus *Helleborus,* of the buttercup family, having basal leaves and clusters of flowers, esp. *H. niger,* the Christmas rose. **2.** any of various plants of the genus *Veratrum.* Cf. **false hellebore.** **3.** any of several poisonous or medicinal substances obtained from these plants. [1555–65; < Gk *helléboros;* r. earlier *ellebor(e),* ME *el(l)bre,* etc. < L *elleborus* < Gk]

hel•le•bo•re•in (hel′ə bôr′ē in, -bōr′-), *n.* a yellow, crystalline, water-soluble, poisonous solid, $C_{37}H_{56}O_{18}$, obtained from the rhizome and root of certain hellebores, and used in medicine chiefly as a heart stimulant. [1870–75; HELLEBORE + -IN[2]]

hel•leb•o•rin (he leb′ə rin, hel′ə bôr′in, -bōr′-), *n.* a colorless, crystalline, water-insoluble, poisonous solid, $C_{28}H_{36}O_6$, obtained from the rhizome and root of certain hellebores, and used in medicine chiefly as a purgative. [1870–75; HELLEBORE + -IN[2]]

Hel•lene (hel′ēn), *n.* a Greek. [< Gk *Héllēn*]

Hel•len•ic (he len′ik, -lē′nik), *adj.* **1.** of, pertaining to, or characteristic of the ancient Greeks or their language, culture, thought, etc., esp. before the time of Alexander the Great. Cf. **Hellenistic** (def. 3). **2.** Greek. —*n.* **3.** Also called **Greek.** a branch of the Indo-European family of languages, comprising a variety of ancient, medieval, and modern dialects and languages, all of them called Greek. **4.** Katharevusa. [1635–45; < Gk *Hellēnikós,* of, pertaining to the Greeks. See HELLENE, -IC] —**Hel•len′i•cal•ly,** *adv.*

Hel•len•ism (hel′ə niz′əm), *n.* **1.** ancient Greek culture or ideals. **2.** the imitation or adoption of ancient Greek language, thought, customs, art, etc.: *the Hellenism of Alexandrian Jews.* **3.** the characteristics of Greek culture, esp. after the time of Alexander the Great; civilization of the Hellenistic period. [1600–10; < Gk *Hellēnismós* an imitation of or similarity to the Greeks. See HELLENE, -ISM]

Hel•len•ist (hel′ə nist), *n.* **1.** a person, esp. in ancient times, adopting Greek speech, ideas, or customs. **2.** a person who admires or studies Greek civilization. [1605–15; < Gk *Hellēnistḗs.* See HELLENE, -IST]

Hel•len•is•tic (hel′ə nis′tik), *adj.* **1.** pertaining to Hellenists. **2.** following or resembling Greek usage. **3.** of or pertaining to the Greeks or their language, culture, etc., after the time of Alexander the Great, when Greek characteristics were modified by foreign elements. Cf. **Hellenic** (def. 1). **4.** of or pertaining to the architecture of Greece and Greek territories from the late 3rd century through the 1st century B.C., characterized by deviations of various sorts from the proportions and arrangements of the mature Greek orders, particularly in the attenuation of the Doric order, and by innovations in plan and ornamentation. **5.** pertaining to or designating the style of the fine arts, esp. sculpture, developed in the area conquered by Alexander the Great from the end of the 4th to the 1st century B.C., chiefly characterized by delicate and highly finished modeling, dramatic, often violent movement of forms in space, representations of extreme emotion, highly individuated characterization, and a wide variety of subject matter. Cf. **archaic** (def. 4), classical (def. 6). [1700–10; HELLENE + -ISTIC] —**Hel′·len·is′ti·cal·ly,** *adv.*

Hel·len·ize (hel′ə nīz′), *v.,* **-ized, -iz·ing.** —*v.t.* **1.** to make Greek in character. —*v.i.* **2.** to adopt Greek ideas or customs. Also, *esp. Brit.,* **Hel′len·ise′.** [1605–15; < Gk *Hellēnízein* to imitate the Greeks, speak Greek. See HELLENE, -IZE] —**Hel′len·i·za′tion,** *n.* —**Hel′len·iz′er,** *n.*

hell·er[1] (hel′ər), *n. Informal.* a noisy, rowdy, troublesome person; hellion. [1890–95, *Amer.*; short for HELL-RAISER]

hel·ler[2] (hel′ər), *n., pl.* **-lers, -ler. 1.** a former coin of various German states, usually equal to half a pfennig. **2.** a former bronze coin of Austria, the 100th part of a korona. **3.** haler (def. 2). [1565–75; < G, MHG *haller, heller,* after Schwäbisch *Hall* Swabian town where they were orig. minted; see -ER[1]]

hel·ler·i (hel′ə rī′, -rē), *n.* **1.** a brightly colored, playful topminnow that is a hybrid of *Xiphophorus helleri* and *X. maculatus,* bred for aquariums. **2.** swordtail. [1905–10; < NL *helleri* (of Heller), a specific epithet, after Carl *Heller,* 20th cent. tropical fish collector]

Hel·les (hel′is), *n.* **Cape,** a cape in European Turkey at the S end of Gallipoli Peninsula.

Hel·les·pont (hel′ə spont′), *n.* ancient name of the **Dardanelles.** —**Hel·les·pont·ine** (hel′ə spon′tin, -tīn), *adj.*

Hel·les·pon·tus (hel′ə spon′tis), *n.* an area in the southern hemisphere of Mars.

hell·fire (hel′fīᵊr′), *n.* **1.** the fire of hell. **2.** punishment in hell. **3.** (*cap.*) *Mil.* a laser-guided U.S. Army antiarmor missile designed for launch from a helicopter. [bef. 1000; ME, OE *helle fȳr;* see HELL, FIRE]

hell-fired (hel′fīᵊrd′), *adj., adv. Chiefly Midland and Southern U.S.* all-fired. [1705–15]

hell-for-leath·er (hel′fər leth′ər), *Informal.* —*adj.* **1.** characterized by reckless determination or breakneck speed: *The sheriff led the posse in a hell-for-leather chase.* —*adv.* **2.** in a hell-for-leather manner; hellbent: *motorcycles roaring hell-for-leather down the turnpike.* [1885–90]

Hell′ Gate′, a narrow channel in the East River, in New York City.

hell·gram·mite (hel′grə mīt′), *n.* the aquatic larva of a dobsonfly, used as bait in fishing. [1865–70, *Amer.*; orig. uncert.]

hell·hole (hel′hōl′), *n.* **1.** a place totally lacking in comfort, cleanliness, order, etc. **2.** a place or establishment noted for its illegal or immoral practices. [1350–1400; ME; see HELL, HOLE]

hell·hound (hel′hound′), *n.* **1.** a mythical watchdog of hell. **2.** a fiendish person. [bef. 900; ME, OE *helle hund;* see HELL, HOUND[1]]

hel·lion (hel′yən), *n. Informal.* a disorderly, troublesome, rowdy, or mischievous person. [1835–45, *Amer.*; HELL + *-ion,* as in *scullion, rapscallion*]

hell·ish (hel′ish), *adj.* **1.** of, like, or suitable to hell; infernal; vile; horrible: *It was a hellish war.* **2.** miserable; abominable; execrable: *We had a hellish time getting through traffic.* **3.** devilishly bad: *The child's behavior was hellish most of the day.* [1520–30; HELL + -ISH[1]] —**hell′ish·ly,** *adv.* —**hell′ish·ness,** *n.*

hell·kite (hel′kīt′), *n. Archaic.* a fiendishly cruel and wicked person. [1595–1605; HELL + KITE[1]]

Hell·man (hel′mən), *n.* **Lillian Florence,** 1905–84, U.S. playwright.

hel·lo (he lō′, hə-, hel′ō), *interj., n., pl.* **-los,** *v.,* **-loed, -lo·ing.** —*interj.* **1.** (used to express a greeting, answer a telephone, or attract attention.) **2.** (an exclamation of surprise, wonder, elation, etc.) —*n.* **3.** the call "hello" (used as an expression of greeting): *She gave me a warm hello.* —*v.i.* **4.** to say "hello"; to cry or shout: *I helloed, but no one answered.* —*v.t.* **5.** to say "hello" to (someone): *We helloed each other as though nothing had happened.* Also, *esp. Brit.,* **hullo.** [1865–70; var. of HALLO]

hell-rais·er (hel′rā′zər), *n. Informal.* a person who behaves in a rowdy, riotous manner, esp. habitually. [1910–15]

hell's′ bells′, *Informal.* (used interjectionally to indicate vexation or surprise.) [1910–15]

Hell's′ Kitch′en, (in New York City) a section of midtown Manhattan, west of Times Square, formerly notorious for its slums and high crime rate.

hell·uv·a (hel′ə və), *adj., adv. Pron. Spelling.* hell of a. Cf. **heck**[1] (def. 2). [1915–20]

hell′ week′, the week of hazing before initiation into a college fraternity or sorority. [1925–30, *Amer.*]

helm[1] (helm), *n.* **1.** *Naut.* **a.** a wheel or tiller by which a ship is steered. **b.** the entire steering apparatus of a ship. **c.** the angle with the fore-and-aft line made by a rudder when turned: *15-degree helm.* **2.** the place or post of control: *A stern taskmaster was at the helm of the company.* —*v.t.* **3.** to steer; direct. [bef. 900; ME *helme,* OE *helma;* c. MHG *halme, helm* handle, ON *hjalm* rudder] —**helm′less,** *adj.*

helm[2] (helm), *n.* **1.** Also, **heaume.** Also called **great helm.** a medieval helmet, typically formed as a single cylindrical piece with a flat or raised top, completely enclosing the head. **2.** *Archaic.* a helmet. —*v.t.* **3.** to furnish or cover with a helmet. [bef. 900; ME, OE; c. D, G *helm;* akin to OE *helan* to cover. See HULL[1]]

Hel·mand (hel′mənd), *n.* a river in S Asia, flowing SW from E Afghanistan to a lake in E Iran. 650 mi. (1045 km) long.

hel·met (hel′mit), *n.* **1.** any of various forms of protective head covering worn by soldiers, firefighters, divers, cyclists, etc. **2.** medieval armor for the head. **3.** (in fencing, singlestick, etc.) a protective device for the head and face consisting of reinforced wire mesh. **4.** anything resembling a helmet in form or position. [1400–50; late ME < MF *healmet, helmet,* dim. of *helme* HELM[2]] —**hel′met·ed,** *adj.* —**hel′met·like′,** *adj.*

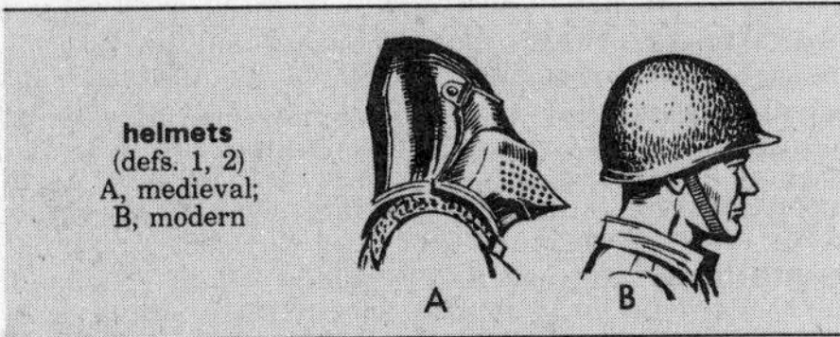

helmets (defs. 1, 2) A, medieval; B, modern

hel′meted guin′ea fowl′, the common guinea fowl in its wild state. Cf. **guinea fowl.**

hel′met lin′er, 1. a soft or padded lining for a helmet. **2.** *Mil.* a stiff, plastic head covering designed to be worn alone or under a steel helmet for protection.

hel′met shell′, 1. a predatory marine gastropod of the family Cassidae, characterized by a thick, heavy shell with a broadened outer lip. **2.** the shell of this animal, often used for making cameos. [1745–55]

Helm·holtz (helm′hōlts), *n.* **Her·mann Lud·wig Fer·di·nand von** (heʀ′män lo͞ot′vik feʀ′di nänt′ fən), 1821–94, German physiologist and physicist.

Helm′holtz func′tion, the thermodynamic function of a system that is equal to its internal energy minus the product of its absolute temperature and entropy: A decrease in the function is equal to the maximum amount of work available during a reversible isothermal process. Also called **Helm′holtz free′ en′ergy, work function.** [named after H. L. F. von HELMHOLTZ]

hel·minth (hel′minth), *n.* a worm, esp. a parasitic worm. [1850–55; < Gk *helminth-* (s. of *hélmins*) a kind of worm]

hel·min·thi·a·sis (hel′min thī′ə sis), *n. Pathol.* a disease caused by parasitic worms in the intestines. [1805–15; < NL < Gk *helminthi(ân)* to suffer from worms (see HELMINTH) + *-asis* -ASIS]

hel·min·thic (hel min′thik), *adj.* **1.** of, pertaining to, or caused by helminths. **2.** expelling intestinal worms; anthelminthic. [1695–1705; HELMINTH + -IC]

hel·min·thoid (hel min′thoid, hel′min thoid′), *adj.* shaped like a helminth; vermiform; wormlike. [1850–55; HELMINTH + -OID]

hel·min·thol·o·gy (hel′min thol′ə jē), *n.* the scientific study of worms, esp. of parasitic worms. [1810–20; HELMINTH + -O- + -LOGY] —**hel·min·tho·log·i·cal** (hel min′thə loj′i kəl), **hel·min′tho·log′ic,** *adj.* —**hel′·min·thol′o·gist,** *n.*

Hel·mont (hel′mont; *Flem.* hel′mônt), *n.* **Jan Bap·tis·ta van** (yän bäp tis′tä vän), 1579–1644, Flemish chemist and physician.

helm′ port′, the opening at the stern of a ship, through which a rudderstock passes. [1840–50]

helms·man (helmz′mən), *n., pl.* **-men.** a person who steers a ship. [1615–25; HELM[1] + 'S[1] + -MAN] —**helms′man·ship′,** *n.*

hel·o (hel′ō, hē′lō), *n., pl.* **hel·os.** *Informal.* helicopter. [HEL(ICOPTER) + -O]

Hé·lo·ïse (el′ō ēz′; *Fr.* ā lô ēz′), *n.* **1.** 1101?–64, French abbess: pupil of and secretly married to Pierre Abélard. Cf. **Abélard. 2.** a female given name, French form of **Eloise** or **Louise.**

Hel·ot (hel′ət, hē′lət), *n.* **1.** a member of the lowest class in ancient Laconia, constituting a body of serfs who were bound to the land and were owned by the state. Cf. **Perioeci, Spartiate. 2.** (*l.c.*) a serf or slave; bondman. [1570–80; < L *hēlōtēs* (pl.) < Gk *heílōtes*] —**hel′ot·age,** *n.*

hel·ot·ism (hel′ə tiz′əm, hē′lə-), *n.* **1.** the state or quality of being a helot; serfdom. **2.** *Ecol.* the subordinate organisms in an unequal symbiotic relationship. [1815–25; HELOT + -ISM]

hel·ot·ry (hel′ə trē, hē′lə-), *n.* **1.** serfdom; slavery. **2.** helots collectively. [1820–30; HELOT + -RY]

help (help), *v.t.,* **1.** to give or provide what is necessary to accomplish a task or satisfy a need; contribute strength or means to; render assistance to; cooperate effectively with; aid; assist: *He planned to help me with my work. Let me help you with those packages.* **2.** to save; rescue; succor: *Help me, I'm falling!* **3.** to make easier or less difficult; contribute to; facilitate: *The exercise of restraint is certain to help the achievement of peace.* **4.** to be useful or profitable to: *Her quick mind helped her career.* **5.** to refrain from; avoid (usually prec. by *can* or *cannot*): *He can't help doing it.* **6.** to relieve or break the uniformity of: *Small patches of bright color can help an otherwise dull interior.* **7.** to relieve (someone) in need, sickness, pain, or distress. **8.** to remedy, stop, or prevent: *Nothing will help my headache.* **9.** to serve food to at table (usually fol. by *to*): *Help her to salad.* **10.** to serve or wait on (a customer), as in a store. —*v.i.* **11.** to give aid; be of service or advantage: *Every little bit helps.* **12. cannot** or **can't help but,** to be unable to refrain from or avoid; be obliged to: *Still, you can't help but admire her.* **13. help oneself to, a.** to serve oneself; take a portion of: *Help yourself to the cake.* **b.** to take or use without asking permission; appropriate: *They helped themselves to the farmer's apples. Help yourself to any of the books we're giving away.* **14. help out,** to assist in an effort; be of aid to: *Her relatives helped out when she became ill.* **15. so help me,** (used as a mild form of the oath "so help me God") I am speaking the truth; on my honor: *That's exactly what happened, so help me.* —*n.* **16.** the act of helping; aid or assistance; relief or succor. **17.** a person or thing that helps: *She certainly is a help in an emergency.* **18.** a hired helper; employee. **19.** a body of such helpers. **20.** a domestic servant or a farm laborer. **21.** means of remedying, stopping, or preventing: *The thing is done, and there is no help for it now.* **22.** *Older Use.* helping (def. 2). —*interj.* **23.** (used as an exclamation to call for assistance or to attract attention.) [bef. 900; ME *helpen,* OE *helpan;* c. G *helfen*] —**help′a·ble,** *adj.*

—**Syn. 1.** encourage, befriend; support, second, uphold, back, abet. HELP, AID, ASSIST, SUCCOR agree in the idea of furnishing another with something needed, esp. when the need comes at a particular time. HELP implies furnishing anything that furthers one's efforts or relieves one's wants or necessities. AID and ASSIST, somewhat more formal, imply esp. a furthering or seconding of another's efforts. AID implies a more active helping; ASSIST implies less need and less help. To SUCCOR, still more formal and literary, is to give timely help and relief in difficulty or distress: *Succor him in his hour of need.* **3.** further, promote, foster. **6.** ameliorate. **7.** alleviate, cure, heal. **16.** support, backing. —**Ant. 3, 11.** hinder. **7.** afflict. **17.** hindrance.

—**Usage. 12.** HELP BUT, in sentences like *She's so clever you can't help but admire her,* has been condemned by some as the ungrammatical version of *cannot help admiring her,* but the idiom is common in all kinds of speech and writing and can only be characterized as standard.

help·er (hel′pər), *n.* **1.** a person or thing that helps or gives assistance, support, etc. **2.** an extra locomotive attached to a train at the front, middle, or rear, esp. to provide extra power for climbing a steep grade. Cf. **doubleheader, pusher** (def. 5). [1250–1300; ME; see HELP, -ER[1]]

—**Syn. 1.** aid, assistant; supporter, backer, auxiliary, ally.

helper T cell, *Immunol.* a T cell that stimulates B cells to produce antibody against a foreign substance, using lymphokines or direct contact as a signal. Also called **T helper cell.**

help·ful (help′fəl), *adj.* giving or rendering aid or assistance; of service: *Your comments were very helpful.* [1300–50; ME; see HELP, -FUL] —**help′ful·ly,** *adv.* —**help′ful·ness,** *n.*

—**Syn.** useful, convenient; beneficial, advantageous. —**Ant.** useless, inconvenient.

help·ing (hel′ping), *n.* **1.** the act of a person or thing that helps. **2.** a portion of food served to a person at one time: *That's his third helping of ice cream.* —*adj.* **3.** giving aid, assistance, support, or the like. [1175–1225; ME; see HELP, -ING[1], -ING[2]] —**help′ing·ly,** *adv.*

help′ing hand′, aid; assistance: *to give the destitute a helping hand.* [1400–50; late ME]

help′ing verb′. See **auxiliary verb.** [1815–25]

help·less (help′lis), *adj.* **1.** unable to help oneself; weak or dependent: *a helpless invalid.* **2.** deprived of strength or power; powerless; incapacitated: *They were helpless with laughter.* **3.** affording no help. [1125–75; ME; see HELP, -LESS] —**help′less·ly,** *adv.* —**help′less·ness,** *n.*

Help·mann (help′mən), *n.* **Sir Robert (Murray),** 1909–86, Australian dancer, choreographer, and actor.

help·mate (help′māt′), *n.* **1.** a companion and helper. **2.** a wife or husband. **3.** anything that aids or assists, esp. regularly: *This calculator is my constant helpmate.* [1705–15; HELP + MATE[1], by assoc. with HELPMEET]

help·meet (help′mēt′), *n.* helpmate. [from the phrase *an help meet for him* i.e., a help suitable for him, in the Authorized Version of the Bible (1611)]

Hel·sing·ør (hel′sing œʀ′), *n.* a seaport on NE Zealand, in NE Denmark: the scene of Shakespeare's *Hamlet.* 30,211. Also called **Elsinore.**

Hel·sin·ki (hel′sing kē, hel sing′-), *n.* a seaport in and the capital of Finland, on the S coast. 484,471. Swedish, **Hel·sing·fors** (hel′sing fôrz′; *Sw.* hel′sing fôsh′).

Hel′sinki Con′ference. See **Conference on Security and Cooperation in Europe.** Also called **Hel′sinki Pact′.**

hel·ter-skel·ter (hel′tər skel′tər), *adv.* **1.** in headlong and disorderly haste: *The children ran helter-skelter all over the house.* **2.** in a haphazard manner; without regard for order: *Clothes were scattered helter-skelter about the room.* —*adj.* **3.** carelessly hurried; confused: *They ran in a mad, helter-skelter fashion for the exits.* **4.** disorderly; haphazard: *Books and papers were scattered on the desk in a helter-skelter manner.* —*n.* **5.** tumultuous disorder; confusion. [1585–95; rhyming compound, perh. based on *skelt, ME *skelten* to hasten (< ?); redupl. with initial *h* parallel to HUBBLE-BUBBLE, HIGGLEDY-PIGGLEDY, etc.]

helve (helv), *n., v.,* **helved, helv·ing.** —*n.* **1.** the handle of an ax, hatchet, hammer, or the like. —*v.t.* **2.** to furnish with a helve. [bef. 900; ME; OE *h(i)elfe*] —**helv′er,** *n.*

Hel·vel·lyn (hel vel′in), *n.* a mountain in NW England. 3118 ft. (950 m).

Hel·ve·tia (hel vē′shə), *n.* **1.** an Alpine region in Roman times, corresponding to the W and N parts of Switzerland. **2.** Switzerland.

Hel·ve·tian (hel vē′shən), *adj.* **1.** of or pertaining to Helvetia or the Helvetii. **2.** Swiss. —*n.* **3.** one of the Helvetii. **4.** a Swiss. [1550–60; HELVETI(A) + -AN]

Hel·vet·ic (hel vet′ik), *n.* **1.** a Swiss Protestant; Zwinglian. —*adj.* **2.** Helvetian. [1700–10; HELVET(IA) + -IC]

Hel·ve·ti·i (hel vē′shē ī′), *n.pl.* the ancient Celtic inhabitants of Helvetia in the time of Julius Caesar. [1890–95; < L]

CONCISE PRONUNCIATION KEY: act, cāpe, dâre, pärt; set, ēqual; *if,* īce; ox, ōver, ôrder, oil, bo͝ok, bo͞ot, out; up, ûrge; child; sing; shoe; thin, *th*at; zh as in *treasure.* ə = *a* as in *alone, e* as in *system, i* as in *easily, o* as in *gallop, u* as in *circus;* ᵊ as in *fire* (fīᵊr), *hour* (ouᵊr). l and n can serve as syllabic consonants, as in *cradle* (krād′l), and *button* (but′n). See the full key inside the front cover.

Hel•vé•tius (hel vē′shəs; *Fr.* el vā syʏs′), *n.* **Claude A•dri•en** (klôd ā′drē ən; *Fr.* klōd A dʀē äɴ′), 1715–71, French philosopher.

hem[1] (hem), *v.,* **hemmed, hem•ming,** *n.* —*v.t.* **1.** to fold back and sew down the edge of (cloth, a garment, etc.); form an edge or border on or around. **2.** to enclose or confine (usually fol. by *in, around,* or *about*): *hemmed in by enemies.* —*n.* **3.** an edge made by folding back the margin of cloth and sewing it down. **4.** the edge or border of a garment, drape, etc., esp. at the bottom. **5.** the edge, border, or margin of anything. **6.** *Archit.* the raised edge forming the volute of an Ionic capital. [bef. 1000; ME *hem(m),* OE *hem,* prob. akin to *hamm* enclosure; see HOME]

hem[2] (hem), *interj., n., v.,* **hemmed, hem•ming.** —*interj.* **1.** (an utterance resembling a slight clearing of the throat, used to attract attention, express doubt, etc.) —*n.* **2.** the utterance or sound of "hem." **3.** a sound or pause of hesitation: *His sermon was full of hems and haws.* —*v.i.* **4.** to utter the sound "hem." **5.** to hesitate in speaking. **6. hem and haw, a.** to hesitate or falter: *She hemmed and hawed a lot before she came to the point.* **b.** to speak noncommittally; avoid giving a direct answer: *He hems and haws and comes out on both sides of every question.* [1520–30; imit.]

hem-, var. of **hemo-** before a vowel: *hemal.* Also, *esp. Brit.,* **haem-.** Cf. **haemat-.**

hema-, var. of **hemo-:** *hemacytometer.* Also, *esp. Brit.,* **haema-.**

he•ma•cy•tom•e•ter (hē′mə sī tom′i tər, hem′ə-), *n. Med.* hemocytometer.

he•mag•glu•ti•nate (hē′mə glo͞ot′n āt′, hem′ə-), *v.t., v.i.,* **-nat•ed, -nat•ing.** (of red blood cells) to clump. [1920–25; HEM- + AGGLUTINATE] —**he•mag•glu•tin•a•tive** (hē′mə glo͞ot′n ā′tiv, -ə tiv, hem′ə-), *adj.*

he•mag•glu•ti•na•tion (hē′mə glo͞ot′n ā′shən, hem′ə-), *n.* the clumping of red blood cells. [1905–10; HEM- + AGGLUTINATION]

he•mal (hē′məl), *adj.* **1.** Also, **hematal.** of or pertaining to the blood or blood vessels. **2.** *Zool.* noting, pertaining to, or on the side of the body ventral to the spinal axis, containing the heart and principal blood vessels. [1830–40; HEM- + -AL[1]]

he-man (hē′man′), *n., pl.* **-men.** *Informal.* a strong, tough, virile man. [1825–35, *Amer.*]

he•ma•nal•y•sis (hē′mə nal′ə sis, hem′ə-), *n., pl.* **-ses** (-sēz′). *Biochem.* an analysis, esp. of the chemical constituents, of the blood. [HEM- + ANALYSIS]

he•man•gi•o•ma (hi man′jē ō′mə), *n., pl.* **-mas, -ma•ta** (-mə tə). *Pathol.* See under **angioma.** [1885–90; < NL; see HEM-, ANGIOMA]

Hem•ans (hem′ənz, hē′mənz), *n.* **Felicia Dorothea (Browne),** 1793–1835, English poet.

he•ma•pher•e•sis (hē′mə fer′ə sis, hem′ə-), *n.* apheresis. [HEM- + APHERESIS]

hemat-, var. of **hemato-** before a vowel: *hematic.* Also, *esp. Brit.,* **haemat-.**

he•ma•tal (hē′mə tl, hem′ə-), *adj.* hemal (def. 1). [HEMAT- + -AL[1]]

he•ma•te•in (hē′mə tē′in, hem′ə-, hē′mə tēn′, hem′ə-), *n.* a reddish-brown, crystalline, slightly water-soluble solid, $C_{16}H_{12}O_6$, obtained from logwood: used chiefly as a stain in microscopy. [var. of HEMATIN]

he•ma•ther•mal (hē′mə thûr′məl, hem′ə-), *adj.* warm-blooded; homoiothermal. [1885–90; HEMA- + THERMAL]

he•mat•ic (hi mat′ik), *adj.* **1.** of or pertaining to blood; hemic. **2.** acting on the blood, as a medicine. —*n.* **3.** hematinic (def. 1). [1850–55; HEMAT- + -IC]

he•ma•tin (hē′mə tin, hem′ə-), *n.* **1.** *Biochem.* heme. **2.** (loosely) hematein. Also, **he•ma•tine** (hē′mə tēn′, -tin, hem′ə-). [1810–20; HEMAT- + -IN[2]]

he•ma•tin•ic (hē′mə tin′ik, hem′ə-), *n.* **1.** a medicine, as a compound of iron, that tends to increase the amount of hematin or hemoglobin in the blood. —*adj.* **2.** of or obtained from hematin. [1850–55; HEMATIN + -IC]

he•ma•tite (hē′mə tīt′, hem′ə-), *n.* a very common mineral, iron oxide, Fe_2O_3, occurring in steel-gray to black crystals and in red earthy masses: the principal ore of iron. [1535–45; < L *haematītes* bloodstone < Gk *haimatítēs* (*líthos*) bloodlike (stone). See HEMAT-, -ITE[1]] —**he•ma•tit•ic** (hē′mə tit′ik, hem′ə-), *adj.*

hemato-, a var. of **hemo-:** *hematogenesis.* Also, **hemat-;** *esp. Brit.,* **haemat-, haemato-.** [< NL, comb. form < Gk *haimat-,* s. of *haîma* blood]

he•mat•o•blast (hi mat′ə blast′, hē′mə tə-, hem′ə-), *n.* an immature blood cell, esp. a red blood cell. Also, **hemoblast.** [1875–80; HEMATO- + -BLAST]

he•mat•o•cele (hi mat′ə sēl′, hē′mə tə-, hem′ə-), *n. Pathol.* **1.** hemorrhage into a cavity, as the cavity surrounding the testis. **2.** such a cavity. [1720–30; HEMATO- + -CELE[2]]

he•mat•o•che•zi•a (hi mat′ō kē′zē ə, hē′mə tō-, hem′ə-), *n. Pathol.* the passage of bloody stools. [HEMATO- + Gk *chéz(ein)* to defecate + -IA]

he•mat•o•crit (hi mat′ə krit), *n.* **1.** a centrifuge for separating the cells of the blood from the plasma. **2.** Also called **hemat′ocrit val′ue.** the ratio of the volume of red blood cells to a given volume of blood so centrifuged, expressed as a percentage. [1890–95; HEMATO- + *-crit* < Gk *kritḗs* judge]

he•ma•toc•ry•al (hē′mə tok′rē əl, -tə krī′əl, hem′ə-), *adj.* cold-blooded; poikilothermal. [1865–70; HEMATO- + CRY(O)- + -AL[1]]

CONCISE ETYMOLOGY KEY: <, descended or borrowed from; >, whence; b., blend of, blended; c., cognate with; cf., compare; deriv., derivative; equiv., equivalent; imit., imitative; obl., oblique; r., replacing; s., stem; sp., spelling, spelled; resp., respelling, respelled; trans., translation; ?, origin unknown; *, unattested; ‡, probably earlier than. See the full key inside the front cover.

he•mat•o•cyst (hi mat′ə sist′, hē′mə tə-, hem′ə-), *n. Pathol.* a cyst containing blood. [1850–55; HEMATO- + -CYST]

he•mat•o•cyte (hi mat′ə sīt′, hē′mə tə-, hem′ə-), *n.* hemocyte. [HEMATO- + -CYTE]

he•ma•to•gen•e•sis (hē′mə tə jen′ə sis, hem′ə-, hi-mat′ə-), *n.* hematopoiesis. [HEMATO- + -GENESIS]

he•ma•tog•e•nous (hē′mə toj′ə nəs, hem′ə-), *adj.* **1.** originating in the blood. **2.** blood-producing. **3.** distributed or spread by way of the bloodstream, as in metastases of tumors or in infections; blood-borne. [1865–70; HEMATO- + -GENOUS]

he•ma•toid (hē′mə toid′, hem′ə-), *adj.* hemoid. [1830–40; < Gk *haimatoeidḗs.* See HEMAT-, -OID]

he•ma•tol•o•gy (hē′mə tol′ə jē, hem′ə-), *n. Med.* the study of the nature, function, and diseases of the blood and of blood-forming organs. [1805–15; HEMATO- + -LOGY] —**he•ma•to•log•ic** (hē′mə tl oj′ik, hem′ə-, hi-mat′ə-), **he′ma•to•log′i•cal,** *adj.* —**he′ma•tol′o•gist,** *n.*

he•ma•tol•y•sis (hē′mə tol′ə sis, hem′ə-), *n. Physiol.* hemolysis. [HEMATO- + -LYSIS]

he•ma•to•ma (hē′mə tō′mə, hem′ə-), *n., pl.* **-mas, -ma•ta** (-mə tə). *Pathol.* a circumscribed collection of blood, usually clotted, in a tissue or organ, caused by a break in a blood vessel. [1840–50; HEMAT- + -OMA]

he•ma•toph•a•gous (hē′mə tof′ə gəs, hem′ə-), *adj.* feeding on blood, as the vampire bat. [1850–55; HEMATO- + -PHAGOUS]

he•ma•to•phyte (hē′mə tə fīt′, hem′ə-, hi mat′ə-), *n.* a microorganism, as a bacterium, that lives in the blood. [HEMATO- + -PHYTE]

he•mat•o•poi•e•sis (hi mat′ō poi ē′sis, hē′mə tō-, hem′ə-), *n.* the formation of blood. Also, **hemopoiesis.** Also called **hematogenesis.** [1850–55; < NL *haematopoiēsis.* See HEMATO-, -POIESIS] —**he•ma•to•poi•et•ic** (hē′mə tō poi et′ik, hem′ə-), *adj.*

he•mat•o•por•phy•ri•a (hi mat′ō pôr fēr′ē ə, -fī′rē ə, hē′mə tō-, hem′ə-), *n. Pathol.* porphyria. [HEMATO- + PORPHYRIA]

he•ma•to•sis (hē′mə tō′sis, hem′ə-), *n.* **1.** hematopoiesis. **2.** *Physiol.* the conversion of venous into arterial blood; oxygenation in the lungs. [1690–1700; < NL *haematosis.* See HEMATO-, -SIS]

he•mat•o•ther•mal (hi mat′ə thûr′məl, hē′mə tə-, hem′ə-), *adj.* warm-blooded; homoiothermal. [1865–70; HEMATO- + -THERMAL]

he•ma•tox•y•lin (hē′mə tok′sə lin, hem′ə-), *n.* a colorless or pale-yellow, crystalline compound, $C_{16}H_{14}O_6 \cdot 3H_2O$, the coloring material of logwood: used as a mordant dye and as an indicator. [1840–50; HEMATO- + XYL- + -IN[2]] —**he•ma•tox•yl•ic** (hē′mə tok sil′ik, hem′ə-), *adj.*

he•mat•o•zo•on (hi mat′ə zō′on, -ən, hē′mə tə-, hem′ə-), *n., pl.* **-zo•a** (-zō′ə). a parasitic protozoan that lives in the blood. [1885–90; HEMATO- + -ZOON] —**he′ma•to•zo′al, he′ma•to•zo′ic,** *adj.*

he•ma•tu•ri•a (hē′mə to͝or′ē ə, -tyo͝or′-, hem′ə-), *n. Pathol.* the presence of blood in the urine. [1805–15; HEMAT- + -URIA] —**he′ma•tu′ric,** *adj.*

heme (hēm), *n. Biochem.* a deep-red iron-containing blood pigment, $C_{34}H_{32}N_4O_4Fe$, obtained from hemoglobin. [1920–25; shortened form of HEMATIN]

Hem′el Hemp′stead (hem′əl), a town in W Hertfordshire, in SE England. 69,371.

hem•el•y•tron (he mel′i tron′), *n., pl.* **-tra** (-trə). *Entomol.* one of the forewings of a true bug, having a hard, thick basal portion and a thinner, membranous apex. Also, **hemielytron.** [1820–30; HEM(I)- + ELYTRON] —**hem•el•y•tral** (he mel′i trəl), *adj.*

hem•er•a•lo•pi•a (hem′ər ə lō′pē ə), *n. Ophthalm.* a condition of the eyes in which sight is normal in the night or in a dim light but is abnormally poor or wholly absent in the day or in a bright light. Also called **day blindness.** [1700–10; < NL < Gk *hēmeralōp-* (s. of *hēmerálōps* having such a condition (*hēmer(a)* day + *al(aós)* blind + *-ōps* having such an appearance) + *-ia* -IA; cf. -OPIA] —**hem•er•a•lop•ic** (hem′ər ə lop′ik), *adj.*

Hem•er•o•cal•lis (hem′ər ə kal′is), *n.* the genus comprising the day lilies. [1615–25; < NL < Gk *hēmerokallís,* equiv. to *hēméra* day + *kállos* beauty]

Hem•et (hem′it), *n.* a city in SW California. 23,211.

hem•i (hem′ē), *n. Auto.* an internal-combustion engine having hemispherical combustion chambers. [shortening of HEMI-HEAD]

hemi-, a combining form meaning "half," used in the formation of compound words: *hemimorphic.* [< Gk *hēmi-* half; c. L *sēmi-* SEMI-]

-hemia, var. of **-emia** after *p, t, k: leucocythemia.*

hem•i•ac•e•tal (hem′ē as′i tal′), *n.* any of the class of organic chemical compounds having the general formula RCH(OH)OR, where R is an organic group. [1890–95; HEMI- + ACETAL]

hem•i•al•gi•a (hem′ē al′jē ə, -jə), *n. Pathol.* pain or neuralgia involving only one side of the body or head. [HEMI- + -ALGIA]

hem•i•a•nop•si•a (hem′ē ə nop′sē ə), *n. Ophthalm.* any of several conditions in which there is blindness in half of the visual field, involving one or both eyes. Also, **hem•i•a•no•pi•a** (hem′ē ə nō′pē ə), **hemiopia.** Also called **hemiscotosis.** [1880–85; HEMI- + AN-[1] + -OPSIA]

he•mic (hē′mik, hem′ik), *adj.* hematic. [1880–85; HEM- + -IC]

hem•i•cel•lu•lose (hem′i sel′yə lōs′), *n.* any of a group of gummy polysaccharides, intermediate in complexity between sugar and cellulose, that hydrolyze to monosaccharides more readily than cellulose. [1890–95; HEMI- + CELLULOSE]

hem•i•chor•date (hem′i kôr′dāt), *Zool.* —*adj.* **1.** belonging or pertaining to the chordates of the phylum Hemichordata, comprising small, widely distributed, marine animals, as the acorn worms. —*n.* **2.** a hemichordate animal, having a vertebratelike hollow nerve cord and an echinodermlike larval stage. [1880–85; < NL *Hemichordata;* see HEMI-, CHORDATE]

hem•i•cra•ni•a (hem′i krā′nē ə), *n.* **1.** pain in one side of the head. **2.** migraine. [1650–60; < LL *hēmicrānia, hēmicrānium* < Gk *hēmikrā́nion* pain on one side of the head (see HEMI-, CRANIUM)] —**hem•i•cran•ic** (hem′i kran′ik, -krā′nik), *adj.*

hem•i•cy•cle (hem′i sī′kəl), *n.* **1.** a semicircle. **2.** a semicircular structure. **3.** hemicyclium. [1595–1605; < F *hémicycle* < L *hēmicyclium* < Gk *hēmikýklion* See HEMI-, CYCLE] —**hem•i•cy•clic** (hem′i sī′klik, -sik′lik), *adj.*

hem•i•cyc•li•um (hem′i sik′lē əm), *n.* a sundial in the form of a concave quarter sphere having a rodlike gnomon lying within one radius and marked on its surface with arcs that lie in the same plane as the gnomon. Also, **hemicycle.** [< L; see HEMICYCLE]

hem•i•dem•i•sem•i•qua•ver (hem′ē dem′ē sem′ē-kwā′vər), *n. Music. Chiefly Brit.* a sixty-fourth note. [1850–55; HEMI- + DEMISEMIQUAVER]

hem•i•el•y•tron (hem′ē el′i tron′), *n., pl.* **-tra** (-trə). *Entomol.* hemelytron. —**hem′i•el′y•tral,** *adj.*

hem•i•glo•bin (hē′mi glō′bin, hem′i-; hē′mi glō′bin, hem′i-), *n. Biochem.* methemoglobin. [HEMI- + GLOBIN]

hem•i-head (hem′i hed′), *Auto.* —*n.* **1.** a cylinder head having hemispherical combustion chambers. **2.** an engine having such a cylinder head; a hemi. —*adj.* **3.** of or pertaining to such an engine: *a hemi-head V-eight.* Also, **hem′i•head′.**

hem•i•he•dral (hem′i hē′drəl), *adj.* (of a crystal) having only half the planes or faces required by the maximum symmetry of the system to which it belongs. [1830–40; HEMI- + -HEDRAL] —**hem′i•he′dral•ly,** *adv.*

hem•i•hy•drate (hem′i hī′drāt), *n. Chem.* a hydrate in which there are two molecules of the compound for each molecule of water. [1905–10; HEMI- + HYDRATE] —**hem′i•hy′drat•ed,** *adj.*

hem•i•kar•y•on (hem′i kar′ē on′), *n. Cell Biol.* a haploid nucleus. Cf. **amphikaryon.** [1920–25; HEMI- + Gk *káryon* nut] —**hem•i•kar•y•ot•ic** (hem′i kar′ē ot′-ik), *adj.*

hem•i•me•tab•o•lous (hem′ē mi tab′ə ləs), *adj. Entomol.* undergoing incomplete metamorphosis. Also, **hem•i•met•a•bol•ic** (hem′ē met′ə bol′ik). [1865–70; HEMI- + METABOLOUS] —**hem′i•me•tab′o•lism, hem′i•me•tab′o•ly,** *n.*

hem•i•mor•phic (hem′i môr′fik), *adj.* (of a crystal) having the two ends of an axis unlike in their planes or modifications; lacking a center of symmetry. [1860–65; HEMI- + -MORPHIC] —**hem′i•mor′phism, hem′i•mor′•phy,** *n.*

hem•i•mor•phite (hem′i môr′fīt), *n.* a hydrous zinc silicate mineral, $Zn_4(OH)_2Si_2O_7 \cdot H_2O$, occurring in clear, colorless orthorhombic crystals; calamine: an ore of zinc. [1865–70; HEMI- MORPH(IC) + -ITE[1]]

he•min (hē′min), *n. Biochem.* the typical, microscopic reddish-brown crystals, $C_{34}H_{32}N_4O_4FeCl$, resulting when a sodium chloride crystal, a drop of glacial acetic acid, and some blood are heated on a slide: used to indicate the presence of blood. Also called **Teichmann's crystals.** [1950–55; HEM- + -IN[2]]

Hem•ing•way (hem′ing wā′), *n.* **Ernest (Miller),** 1899–1961, U.S. novelist, short-story writer, and journalist: Nobel prize 1954.

Hem•ing•way•esque (hem′ing wā esk′), *adj.* of, pertaining to, or characteristic of Ernest Hemingway or his works. [1940–45; HEMINGWAY + -ESQUE]

hem•i•o•la (hem′ē ō′lə), *n. Music.* a rhythmic pattern of syncopated beats with two beats in the time of three or three beats in the time of two. [1590–1600; < ML *hēmiolia* < Gk *hēmiolía* the ratio of one and a half to one, fem. of *hēmiólios* half as large again, equiv. to *hēmi-* HEMI- + *(h)ól(os)* whole + *-ios* adj. suffix]

hem•i•o•pi•a (hem′ē ō′pē ə), *n. Ophthalm.* hemianopsia. [1870–75; HEMI- + -OPIA] —**hem•i•op•ic** (hem′ē-op′ik, -ō′pik), *adj.*

hem•i•pa•re•sis (hem′ē pə rē′sis, -par′ə sis), *n. Pathol.* partial paralysis affecting only one side of the body. [1890–95; HEMI- + PARESIS] —**hem•i•pa•ret•ic** (hem′ē pə ret′ik), *adj.*

hem•i•plank•ton (hem′i plangk′tən), *n.* plankton that spend part of their life cycle in a vegetative state on the sea bottom, riverbed, etc. (opposed to *holoplankton*). [HEMI- + PLANKTON] —**hem•i•plank•ton•ic** (hem′ē-plangk ton′ik), *adj.*

hem•i•ple•gi•a (hem′i plē′jē ə, -jə), *n. Pathol.* paralysis of one side of the body. [1590–1600; < NL < MGk *hēmiplēgía.* See HEMI-, -PLEGIA] —**hem•i•ple•gic** (hem′i plē′jik, -plej′ik), *adj., n.*

hem•i•pode (hem′i pōd′), *n.* See **button quail.** [1860–65; < NL *Hemipodius* name of the genus < Gk *hēmipod-* (s. of *hēmípous*) half-foot. See HEMI-, -POD] —**he•mip•o•dan** (hə mip′ə dn), *adj.*

He•mip•ter•a (hi mip′tər ə), *n.* the order comprising the true bugs. [1810–20; < NL (neut. pl.); see HEMI-, -PTEROUS]

he•mip•ter•an (hi mip′tər ən), *adj.* **1.** hemipterous. —*n.* **2.** Also, **he•mip•ter•on** (hi mip′tə ron′). a true bug; a hemipterous insect. [1875–80; HEMIPTER(A) + -AN]

he•mip•ter•ous (hi mip′tər əs), *adj.* **1.** belonging or pertaining to the Hemiptera, an order of insects having forewings that are thickened and leathery at the base and membranous at the apex, comprising the true bugs. **2.** belonging or pertaining to the order Hemiptera, in some classifications comprising the heteropterous and homopterous insects. [1810–20; HEMIPTER(A) + -OUS]

hem•i•sco•to•sis (hem′ē skə tō′sis), *n. Ophthalm.* hemianopsia. [HEMI- + SCOT- + -OSIS]

hem•i•sect (hem′i sekt′, hem′i sekt′), *v.t.* to cut into two equal parts; to bisect, esp. along a medial longitudinal plane. [1875–80; HEMI- + -SECT] —**hem′i•sec′tion,** *n.*

hem•i•sphere (hem′i sfēr′), *n.* **1.** (*often cap.*) half of the terrestrial globe or celestial sphere, esp. one of the halves into which the earth is divided. Cf. **Eastern Hemisphere, Western Hemisphere, Northern Hemisphere, Southern Hemisphere. 2.** a map or projection representing one of these halves. **3.** a half of a sphere. **4.** *Anat.* either of the lateral halves of the cerebrum or cerebellum. **5.** the area within which something occurs or dominates; sphere; realm. [1325–75; < L *hēmisphaerium* < Gk *hēmisphaírion;* r. ME *emysperie* < OF *emispere* < L]

hem•i•spher•ic (hem′i sfer′ik), *adj.* **1.** of or pertaining to a hemisphere. **2.** hemispherical (def. 1). [1575–85; HEMISPHERE + -IC]

hem•i•spher•i•cal (hem′i sfer′i kəl), *adj.* **1.** having the form of a hemisphere. **2.** hemispheric (def. 1). [1615–25; HEMI- + SPHERICAL] —**hem′i•spher′i•cal•ly,** *adv.*

hem•i•spher•oid (hem′i sfēr′oid), *n.* half of a spheroid. [1720–30; HEMI- + SPHEROID] —**hem′i•spher•oi′•dal,** *adj.*

hem•i•stich (hem′i stik′), *n. Pros.* **1.** the exact or approximate half of a stich, or poetic verse or line, esp. as divided by a caesura or the like. **2.** an incomplete line, or a line of less than the usual length. [1565–75; < LL *hēmistichium* < Gk *hēmistíchion* a half-verse. See HEMI-, STICH[1]] —**he•mis•ti•chal** (hə mis′ti kəl, hem′i-stik′əl), *adj.*

hem•i•ter•pene (hem′i tûr′pēn), *n. Chem.* See under **terpene** (def. 2). [HEMI- + TERPENE]

hem•i•trope (hem′i trōp′), *Crystall.* —*n.* **1.** twin[1] (def. 5). —*adj.* **2.** twin[1] (def. 12). [1795–1805; < F; see HEMI-, -TROPE] —**hem•i•trop•ic** (hem′i trop′ik, -trō′-pik), *adj.* —**hem′i•tro′pism, he•mit•ro•py** (hi mi′trə-pē), *n.*

hem•i•zy•gote (hem′i zī′gōt, -zig′ōt), *n. Genetics.* an individual having only one of a given pair of genes. [1930–35; HEMI- + ZYGOTE] —**hem•i•zy•gous** (hem′i-zī′gəs), *adj.*

hem•line (hem′līn′), *n.* **1.** the bottom edge of a coat, dress, skirt, etc. **2.** the level of this edge as expressed in inches from the floor: *an 18-inch hemline.* [1920–25; HEM[1] + LINE[1]]

hem•lock (hem′lok′), *n.* **1.** a poisonous plant, *Conium maculatum,* of the parsley family, having purple-spotted stems, finely divided leaves, and umbels of small white flowers, used medicinally as a powerful sedative. **2.** a poisonous drink made from this plant. **3.** any of various other plants, esp. of the genus *Cicuta,* as the water hemlock. **4.** Also called **hem′lock spruce′.** any of several coniferous trees of the genus *Tsuga,* native to the U.S., characterized by a pyramidal manner of growth. Cf. **eastern hemlock, western hemlock. 5.** the soft, light wood of a hemlock tree, used in making paper, in the construction of buildings, etc. [bef. 900; ME *hemlok, humlok,* OE *hymlic, hemlic;* perh. akin to OE *hymele* hop plant]

hem′lock loop′er, the larva of a geometrid moth, *Lambdina fiscellaria,* common in some areas of North America and a serious pest of various trees, as hemlock, Douglas fir, balsam spruce, and oak.

hem•mer (hem′ər), *n.* **1.** a person or thing that hems. **2.** a sewing-machine attachment for hemming edges. [1425–75; late ME. See HEM[1], -ER[1]]

hemo-, a combining form meaning "blood," used in the formation of compound words: *hemocyte.* Also, **hema-, hemato-;** *esp. before a vowel,* **hem-;** *esp. Brit.,* **haemo-.** [< NL, comb. form repr. Gk *haîma* blood]

he•mo•blast (hē′mə blast′, hem′ə-), *n. Anat.* hematoblast. [HEMO- + -BLAST]

he•mo•chro•ma•to•sis (hē′mə krō′mə tō′sis, hem′ə-), *n. Pathol.* a rare metabolic disorder characterized by a bronzed skin, cirrhosis, and severe diabetes, caused by the deposit in tissue, esp. of the liver and pancreas, of hemosiderin and other pigments containing iron. Also called **bronze diabetes.** [1895–1900; HEMO- + CHROMAT- + -OSIS] —**he•mo•chro•ma•tot•ic** (hē′mō krō′-mə tot′ik, hem′ō-), *adj.*

he•mo•chrome (hē′mə krōm′, hem′ə-), *n.* **1.** the red coloring matter of the blood. **2.** an oxygen-containing component of the blood. [HEMO- + -CHROME]

he•mo•coel (hē′mə sēl′, hem′ə-), *n. Anat.* a series of interconnected spaces between tissues and organs through which blood flows freely, unconfined by veins or arteries, occurring in several invertebrate groups, esp. mollusks and arthropods. [1830–40; HEMO- + -COEL]

he•mo•con•cen•tra•tion (hē′mə kon′sən trā′shən, hem′ə-), *n.* an increase in the concentration of cellular elements in the blood, resulting from loss of plasma. [1935–40; HEMO- + CONCENTRATION]

he•mo•cy•a•nin (hē′mə sī′ə nin, hem′ə-), *n. Biochem.* a blue, copper-containing respiratory pigment in the plasma of many invertebrates. [1835–45; HEMO- + CYAN-[1] + -IN[2]]

he•mo•cyte (hē′mə sīt′, hem′ə-), *n.* a blood cell. Also, **hematocyte.** [1900–05; HEMO- + -CYTE]

he•mo•cy•to•blast (hē′mə sī′tə blast′, hem′ə-), *n. Anat.* a primordial cell capable of developing into any type of blood cell. [HEMOCYTE + -O- + -BLAST] —**he′•mo•cy′to•blas′tic,** *adj.*

he•mo•cy•tom•e•ter (hē′mō sī tom′i tər, hem′ō-), *n. Med.* an instrument for counting blood cells. Also, **hemacytometer.** [1875–80; HEMO- + CYTO- + -METER]

he•mo•di•a (hi mō′dē ə), *n. Dentistry.* hypersensitivity of the teeth. [< NL *haemodia,* equiv. to Gk *haimōd(eîn)* to be set on edge, set the teeth on edge + L *-ia* -IA]

he•mo•di•al•y•sis (hē′mō dī al′ə sis, hem′ō-), *n. Biochem.* dialysis of the blood, esp. with an artificial kidney, for the removal of waste products. [1945–50; HEMO- + DIALYSIS]

he•mo•di•a•lyz•er (hē′mə dī′ə lī′zər, hem′ə-), *n. Med.* See **artificial kidney.** [1955–60; HEMO- + DIA- + -LYZE + -ER[1]]

he•mo•di•lu•tion (hē′mə di lo͞o′shən, -dī-, hem′ə-), *n.* a decreased concentration of cells and solids in blood, usually caused by an influx of fluid. [1935–40; HEMO- + DILUTION]

he•mo•dy•nam•ics (hē′mō dī nam′iks, hem′ō-), *n.* (*used with a singular v.*) the branch of physiology dealing with the forces involved in the circulation of the blood. [1855–60; HEMO- + DYNAMICS] —**he′mo•dy•nam′ic,** *adj.*

he•mo•flag•el•late (hē′mə flaj′ə lāt′, hem′ə-), *n.* a flagellate protozoan, esp. of the genera *Trypanosoma* and *Leishmania,* that is parasitic in the blood. [1905–10; HEMO- + FLAGELLATE]

he•mo•ge•ni•a (hē′mō jē′nē ə, -jēn′yə, hem′ō-), *n. Pathol.* pseudohemophilia. [HEMO- + -GEN + -IA]

he•mo•glo•bin (hē′mə glō′bin, hem′ə-), *n. Biochem.* the oxygen-carrying pigment of red blood cells that gives them their red color and serves to convey oxygen to the tissues: occurs in reduced form **(deoxyhemoglobin)** in venous blood and in combination with oxygen **(oxyhemoglobin)** in arterial blood. *Symbol:* Hb Cf. **heme.** [1865–70; earlier *hematoglobulin.* See HEMO-, GLOBULIN] —**he′mo•glo′bic, he′mo•glo′bin•ous,** *adj.*

he•mo•glo•bi•nu•ri•a (hē′mə glō′bə no͝or′ē ə, -nyo͝or′-, hem′ə-), *n. Pathol.* the presence of hemoglobin pigment in the urine. [1865–70; HEMOGLOBIN + -URIA] —**he′mo•glo′bi•nu′ric,** *adj.*

he•mo•gram (hē′mə gram′, hem′ə-), *n.* a graphic record of the cellular elements of the blood. [1925–30; HEMO- + -GRAM[1]]

he•moid (hē′moid), *adj.* resembling blood; hematoid. [1885–90; HEM- + -OID]

he•mo•lymph (hē′mə limf′, hem′ə-), *n. Anat.* a fluid in the body cavities and tissues of invertebrates, in arthropods functioning as blood and in some other invertebrates functioning as lymph. [1880–85; HEMO- + LYMPH] —**he•mo•lym•phat•ic** (hē′mō lim fat′ik, hem′ō-), *adj.*

he•mol•y•sin (hi mol′i sin, hē′mə lī′-, hem′ə-), *n. Immunol.* a substance, as an antibody, that in cooperation with complement causes dissolution of red blood cells. [1895–1900; HEMO- + LYSIN]

he•mol•y•sis (hi mol′ə sis), *n.* the breaking down of red blood cells with liberation of hemoglobin. Also called **hematolysis.** [1885–90; HEMO- + -LYSIS] —**he•mo•lyt•ic** (hē′mə lit′ik, hem′ə-), *adj.*

hemolyt′ic ane′mia, *Pathol.* an anemic condition characterized by the destruction of red blood cells: seen in some drug reactions and in certain infectious and hereditary disorders. [1935–40]

he•mo•lyze (hē′mə līz′, hem′ə-), *v.,* **-lyzed, -lyz•ing.** —*v.t.* **1.** to subject (red blood cells) to hemolysis. —*v.i.* **2.** to undergo hemolysis. [1900–05; HEMO- + -LYZE]

Hé•mon (ā môN′), *n.* **Louis** (lwē), 1880–1913, Canadian novelist, born in France.

he•mo•phile (hē′mə fīl′, hem′ə-), *n.* **1.** a hemophiliac. **2.** a hemophilic bacterium. —*adj.* **3.** hemophilic. [HEMO- + -PHILE]

he•mo•phil•i•a (hē′mə fil′ē ə, -fēl′yə, hem′ə-), *n.* any of several X-linked genetic disorders, symptomatic chiefly in males, in which excessive bleeding occurs owing to the absence or abnormality of a clotting factor in the blood. [1850–55; < NL; see HEMO- -PHILIA]

he•mo•phil•i•ac (hē′mə fil′ē ak′, -fē′lē-, hem′ə-), —*n.* **1.** Also, **hemophile.** a person having hemophilia. —*adj.* **2.** hemophilic (def. 1.). [1895–1900; HEMOPHILI(A) + -AC]

he•mo•phil•ic (hē′mə fil′ik, hem′ə-), *adj.* **1.** characteristic of or affected by hemophilia. **2.** (of bacteria) developing best in a culture containing blood, or in blood itself. [1860–65; HEMOPHIL(IA) + -IC]

he•mo•phil•i•oid (hē′mə fil′ē oid′, hem′ə-), *adj.* (of a disease) resembling hemophilia, but having a different genetic or acquired cause. [HEMOPHIL(IA) + -OID]

He•moph•i•lus (hi mof′ə ləs), *n. Bacteriol.* a genus of rod-shaped, parasitic, hemophilic bacteria, certain species of which, as *H. influenzae* or *H. suis,* are pathogenic for humans and animals. [< NL (1917); see HEMO-, -PHILOUS]

he•mo•pho•bi•a (hē′mə fō′bē ə, hem′ə-), *n. Psychiatry.* an abnormal fear of blood. [1885–90; < NL; see HEMO-, -PHOBIA]

he•mo•poi•e•sis (hē′mə poi ē′sis, hem′ə-), *n.* hematopoiesis. —**he•mo•poi•et•ic** (hē′mə poi et′ik, hem′ə-), *adj.* [HEMO- + -POIESIS]

he•mop•ty•sis (hi mop′tə sis), *n. Pathol.* the expectoration of blood or bloody mucus. [1640–50; < NL, equiv. to *hemo-* HEMO- + Gk *ptýsis* spitting, cf. *ptýein* to spit]

hem•or•rhage (hem′ər ij, hem′rij), *n., v.,* **-rhaged, -rhag•ing.** —*n.* **1.** a profuse discharge of blood, as from a ruptured blood vessel; bleeding. **2.** the loss of assets, esp. in large amounts. **3.** any widespread or uncontrolled loss or diffusion. —*v.i.* **4.** to bleed profusely. **5.** to lose assets, esp. in large amounts. —*v.t.* **6.** to lose (assets): *a company that was hemorrhaging money.* [1665–75; < L *haemorrhagia* < Gk *haimorrhagía.* See HEMO-, -RRHAGIA] —**hem•or•rhag•ic** (hem′ə raj′ik), *adj.*

hem′orrhag′ic fe′ver, *Pathol.* any of several arbovirus infections, as dengue, characterized by fever, chills, and malaise followed by hemorrhages of capillaries, sometimes leading to kidney failure and death.

hem′orrhag′ic mea′sles, *Pathol.* See **black measles.**

hemorrhag′ic septice′mia, *Vet. Pathol.* an acute infectious disease of animals, caused by the bacterium *Pasteurella multocida,* and characterized by fever, catarrhal symptoms, pneumonia, and general blood infection. Also called **pasteurellosis.**

hem•or•rhoid (hem′ə roid′, hem′roid), *n.* Usually, **hemorrhoids.** *Pathol.* an abnormally enlarged vein mainly due to a persistent increase in venous pressure, occurring inside the anal sphincter of the rectum and beneath the mucous membrane **(internal hemorrhoid)** or outside the anal sphincter and beneath the surface of the anal skin **(external hemorrhoid).** Also called **pile.** [1350–1400; ME *emoroides* (pl.) < L *haemorrhoid(a)* < Gk *haimorroḯda* (adj.) discharging blood] —**hem′or•rhoi′dal,** *adj.*

hem•or•rhoid•ec•to•my (hem′ə roi dek′tə mē), *n., pl.* **-mies.** the surgical removal of hemorrhoids. [1915–20; HEMORRHOID + -ECTOMY]

he•mo•sid•er•in (hē′mō sid′ər in, hem′ō-), *n. Biochem.* a yellowish-brown protein containing iron, derived chiefly from hemoglobin and found in body tissue and phagocytes, esp. as the result of disorders in iron metabolism and the breakdown of red blood cells. [1895–1900; HEMO- + SIDER- + -IN[2]]

he•mos•ta•sis (hi mos′tə sis, hē′mə stā′sis, hem′ə-), *n. Med.* **1.** the stoppage of bleeding. **2.** the stoppage of the circulation of blood in a part of the body. **3.** stagnation of blood in a part. Also, **he•mo•sta•sia** (hē′mə stā′-zhə, -zhē ə, -zē ə, hem′ə-). [1835–45; < NL; see HEMO-, STASIS]

he•mo•stat (hē′mə stat′, hem′ə-), *n.* an instrument or agent used to compress or treat bleeding vessels in order to arrest hemorrhage. [1895–1900; shortened form of HEMOSTATIC]

he•mo•stat•ic (hē′mə stat′ik, hem′ə-), *adj. Med.* **1.** arresting hemorrhage, as a drug; styptic. **2.** pertaining to stagnation of the blood. —*n.* **3.** a hemostatic agent or substance. [1700–10; HEMO- + STATIC]

he•mo•ther•a•peu•tics (hē′mə ther′ə pyo͞o′tiks, hem′ə-), *n.* (*used with a singular v.*) *Med.* hemotherapy. [HEMO- + THERAPEUTICS]

he•mo•ther•a•py (hē′mə ther′ə pē, hem′ə-), *n. Med.* therapy by means of blood, serum, or plasma transfusion. Also, **hemotherapeutics.** [HEMO- + THERAPY]

he•mo•tox•in (hē′mə tok′sin, hem′ə-), *n.* a toxin, as cobra venom, that causes a hemolytic reaction. [HEMO- + TOXIN] —**he′mo•tox′ic,** *adj.*

he•mo•troph (hē′mə trof′, -trōf′, hem′ə-), *n. Embryol.* the material from the maternal bloodstream and placenta that nourishes a mammalian embryo. Also, **he•mo•trophe** (hē′mə trōf′, hem′ə-, hi mo′trə fē). [HEMO- + -TROPH] —**he•mo•troph•ic** (hē′mə trof′ik, -trō′fik, hem′ə-), *adj.*

hemp (hemp), *n.* **1.** Also called **Indian hemp, marijuana.** a tall, coarse plant, *Cannabis sativa,* that is native to Asia but naturalized or cultivated in many parts of the world and is the source of a valuable fiber as well as drugs such as marijuana and hashish. Cf. **cannabis. 2.** the tough fiber of this plant, used for making rope, coarse fabric, etc. **3.** any of various plants resembling hemp. **4.** any of various fibers similar to hemp. **5.** a narcotic drug, as marijuana or hashish, prepared from the hemp plant. [bef. 1000; ME; OE *henep, hænep;* c. G *Hanf,* Gk *kánnabis*] —**hemp′like′,** *adj.*

hemp′ ag′rimony, a European composite plant, *Eupatorium cannabinum,* having dull purplish flowers. [1770–80]

Hem•pel (hem′pəl), *n.* **Carl Gustav,** born 1905, U.S. philosopher, born in Germany.

hemp•en (hem′pən), *adj.* **1.** of, like, or pertaining to hemp. **2.** made of hemp. [1325–75; ME *hempyn.* See HEMP, -EN[2]]

hemp′ net′tle, a coarse weed of the genus *Galeopsis,* of the mint family, resembling hemp in appearance and having bristly hairs like the nettle. [1795–1805]

hemp•seed (hemp′sēd′), *n.* the seed of hemp, used as food for birds. [1275–1325; ME; see HEMP, SEED]

Hemp•stead (hemp′sted, hem′-), *n.* a village on W Long Island, in SE New York. 40,404.

hemp′ tree′. See **chaste tree.** [1540–50]

hemp•y (hem′pē), *adj. Scot.* mischievous; often in trouble for mischief. [1400–50; late ME *hempi* made of hemp (see HEMP, -Y[1]); hence, fit for hanging by a hemp rope, and, by attenuation, mischievous]

hem•stitch (hem′stich′), *v.t.* **1.** to hem along a line from which threads have been drawn out, stitching the cross threads into a series of little groups. **2.** to simulate hand hemstitching by piercing the material with a large machine needle and then stitching around the perforations. —*n.* **3.** the stitch used or the needlework done in hemstitching. [1830–40; HEM[1] + STITCH[1]] —**hem′•stitch′er,** *n.*

hen (hen), *n.* **1.** the female of the domestic fowl. **2.** the female of any bird, esp. of a gallinaceous bird. **3.** *Informal* (*often disparaging and offensive*). a woman, esp. a busybody or gossip. [bef. 1000; ME; OE *hen(n)* (cf. OE *hana* cock); c. G *Henne;* akin to L *canere* to sing] —**hen′like′,** *adj.* —**hen′nish,** *adj.*

He•nan (hœ′nän′), *n. Pinyin.* **1.** a province in E China. 50,320,000; 64,479 sq. mi. (167,000 sq. km). *Cap.:* Zhengzhou. **2.** former name of **Luoyang.** Also, **Honan.**

hen-and-chick•ens (hen′ən chik′ənz), *n., pl.* **hens-and-chickens.** any of several succulent plants that grow in clusters or colonies formed by runners or off-

CONCISE PRONUNCIATION KEY: act, cāpe, dâre, pärt; set, ēqual; *if,* ice; ox, ōver, ôrder, oil, bo͝ok, bo͞ot, out; up, ûrge; child; sing; shoe; thin, *th*at; zh as in *treasure.* ə = *a* as in *alone, e* as in *system, i* as in *easily, o* as in *gallop, u* as in *circus;* ᵊ as in *fire* (fīᵊr), *hour* (ouᵊr). l and n can serve as syllabic consonants, as in *cradle* (krād′l), and *button* (but′n). See the full key inside the front cover.

shoots, as those of the genera *Echeveria* and *Sempervivum*. Cf. **houseleek.** [1785–95]

hen•bane (hen′bān′), *n.* an Old World plant, *Hyoscyamus niger*, of the nightshade family, having sticky, hairy fetid foliage and greenish-yellow flowers, and possessing narcotic and poisonous properties esp. destructive to domestic fowls. [1250–1300; ME; see HEN, BANE]

hen•bit (hen′bit′), *n.* a common weed, *Lamium amplexicaule*, of the mint family, having rounded leaves and small purplish flowers. [1570–80; HEN + BIT²]

hence (hens), *adv.* **1.** as an inference from this fact; for this reason; therefore: *The eggs were very fresh and hence satisfactory.* **2.** from this time; from now: *They will leave a month hence.* **3.** from this source or origin. **4.** *Archaic.* **a.** from this place; from here; away: *The inn is but a quarter mile hence.* **b.** from this world or from the living: *After a long, hard life they were taken hence.* **c.** henceforth; from this time on. —*interj.* **5.** *Obs.* depart (usually used imperatively). [1225–75; ME *hens, hennes*, equiv. to *henne* (OE *heonan*) + *-es* -s¹]

hence•forth (hens′fôrth′, -fōrth′; hens′fôrth′, -fōrth′), *adv.* from now on; from this point forward. Also, **hence•for•ward** (hens′fôr′wərd, -fōr′-; hens′-fôr′wərd, -fōr′-). [1300–50; ME *hennes forward;* see HENCE, FORTH]

Hench (hench), *n.* **Philip Show•al•ter** (shō′ôl tər), 1896–1965, U.S. physician: Nobel prize for medicine 1950.

hench•man (hench′mən), *n., pl.* **-men. 1.** an unscrupulous and ruthless subordinate, esp. a criminal: *The leader of the gang went everywhere accompanied by his henchmen.* **2.** an unscrupulous supporter or adherent of a political figure or cause, esp. one motivated by the hope of personal gain: *Hitler and his henchmen.* **3.** a trusted attendant, supporter, or follower. **4.** *Obs.* a squire or page. [1325–75; ME *henchman, henshman, henksman, hengestman*, OE *hengest* stallion (c. G *Hengst*) + *man* MAN¹] —**hench′man•ship′,** *n.*
—**Syn. 2.** flunky, lackey, cohort.

hen•coop (hen′ko͞op′, -ko͝op′), *n.* a large cage or coop for housing poultry. [1690–1700; HEN + COOP]

hendeca-, a combining form meaning "eleven," used in the formation of compound words: *hendecahedron.* [comb. form repr. Gk *héndeka* eleven, equiv. to *hén* one (neut. of *heîs*) + *déka* TEN]

hen•dec•a•gon (hen dek′ə gon′), *n.* a polygon having 11 angles and 11 sides. [1695–1705; HENDECA- + -GON] —**hen•de•cag•o•nal** (hen′də kag′ə nl), *adj.*

hen•dec•a•he•dron (hen dek′ə hē′drən, hen′dek-), *n., pl.* **-drons, -dra** (-drə). a solid figure having 11 faces. [HENDECA- + -HEDRON] —**hen•dec•a•he•dral** (hen-dek′ə hē′drəl, hen′dek-), *adj.*

hen•dec•a•syl•lab•ic (hen dek′ə si lab′ik, hen′dek-), *adj.* **1.** having 11 syllables. —*n.* **2.** a hendecasyllable. [1720–30; HENDECASYLLABLE + -IC]

hen•dec•a•syl•la•ble (hen dek′ə sil′ə bəl, hen′dek ə-sil′-), *n.* a word or line of verse of 11 syllables. [1740–50; < L *hendecasyllabus* < Gk *hendekasýllabos.* See HENDECA-, SYLLABLE]

Hen•der•son (hen′dər sən), *n.* **1. Arthur,** 1863–1935, British statesman and labor leader: Nobel peace prize 1934. **2. David Brem•ner** (brem′nər), 1840–1906, U.S. political leader: Speaker of the House 1899–1903. **3. Fletcher** (*"Smack"*), 1898–1952, U.S. jazz pianist, arranger, and bandleader. **4.** a city in NW Kentucky, on the Ohio River. 24,834. **5.** a city in SE Nevada, near Las Vegas. 24,363. **6.** a city in N North Carolina. 13,522. **7.** a town in E Texas. 11,473.

Hen•der•son•ville (hen′dər sən vil′), *n.* a city in S Tennessee. 26,561.

hen•di•a•dys (hen di′ə dis), *n. Rhet.* a figure in which a complex idea is expressed by two words connected by a copulative conjunction: "to look with eyes and envy" instead of "with envious eyes." [1580–90; < ML; alter. of Gk phrase *hèn dià dyoîn* one through two, one by means of two]

Hen•don (hen′dən), *n.* a former borough, now part of Barnet, a city in Middlesex, in SE England, NW of London.

Hen•drick (hen′drik), *n.* a male given name, form of **Henry.**

Hen•dricks (hen′driks), *n.* **Thomas Andrews,** 1819–85, vice president of the U.S. 1885.

hen•e•quen (hen′ə kin), *n.* the fiber of an agave, *Agave fourcroydes*, of Yucatán, used for making ropes, coarse fabrics, etc. Also, **hen′e•quin.** [1875–80; < AmerSp *henequén*, earlier *geniquén, jeniquén, heniquén*, perh. < an indigenous language of Hispaniola, where the word was allegedly first used]

hen′ fruit′, *Facetious.* a hen's egg or eggs. [1850–55, *Amer.*]

henge (henj), *n. Archaeol.* a Neolithic monument of the British Isles, consisting of a circular area enclosed by a bank and ditch and often containing additional features including one or more circles of upright stone or wood pillars: probably used for ritual purposes or for marking astronomical events, as solstices and equinoxes. [1730–40; back formation from STONEHENGE, ME *Stanenges, Stanheng*, equiv. to *stan* STONE + *-heng*, prob. orig. "something hanging"; cf. HINGE]

Heng•e•lo (heng′ə lō′), *n.* a city in the E Netherlands. 75,990.

Hen•gist (heng′gist, hen′jist), *n.* died A.D. 488?, chief of the Jutes: with his brother Horsa led the Teutonic invasion of southern Britain c440. Also, **Hen′gest.**

Heng•yang (hœng′yäng′), *n. Pinyin, Wade-Giles.* a city in E central Hunan province, in E China. 240,000. Formerly, *Older Spelling,* **Heng•chow** (hœng′jō′).

hen′ har′rier, *Brit.* See **northern harrier.** [1555–65]

hen′ hawk′. See **chicken hawk** (def. 1). [1800–10, *Amer.*]

hen•house (hen′hous′), *n., pl.* **-hous•es** (-hou′ziz). a shelter for poultry. [1505–15; HEN + HOUSE]

Hen•ie (hen′ē), *n.* **Sonja,** 1912–69, U.S. figure-skater and film actress, born in Norway.

Hen′le's loop′ (hen′lēz). See **loop of Henle.** [1880–85]

Hen•ley (hen′lē), *n.* **1. William Ernest,** 1849–1903, English poet, critic, and editor. **2.** Henley-on-Thames.

Hen•ley-on-Thames (hen′lē on temz′), *n.* a city in SE Oxfordshire, in S England: annual rowing regatta. 31,744. Also called **Henley.**

hen•na (hen′ə), *n., v.,* **-naed, -na•ing.** —*n.* **1.** an Asian shrub or small tree, *Lawsonia inermis*, of the loosestrife family, having elliptic leaves and fragrant flowers. **2.** a reddish-orange dye or cosmetic made from the leaves of this plant. **3.** a color midway between red-brown and orange-brown. —*v.t.* **4.** to tint or dye with henna. [1590–1600; < Ar *hinnā′*]

Hen•ne•pin (hen′ə pin; *Fr.* en paN′), *n.* **Louis** (lwē), 1640?–1701?, Belgian Roman Catholic missionary and explorer in America.

hen•ner•y (hen′ə rē), *n., pl.* **-ner•ies.** a place where poultry is kept or raised. [1855–60; HEN + -ERY]

hen•nin (hen′in), *n.* a conical or heart-shaped hat, sometimes extremely high, with a flowing veil or piece of starched linen about the crown, worn by women in the 15th century. Also called **steeple headdress.** [1850–55; < F, MF, perh. < MD *henninck* rooster, from a fancied resemblance of the hat to a rooster's comb]

He•noch (hē′nək), *n. Douay Bible.* Enoch (defs. 1, 2).

hen′ of the woods′, a large, grayish-brown, edible fungus, *Polyporus frondosus*, forming a mass of overlapping caps at the base of trees and somewhat resembling a hen. Also, **hen′-of-the-woods′.**

hen•o•the•ism (hen′ə thē iz′əm), *n.* **1.** the worship of a particular god, as by a family or tribe, without disbelieving in the existence of others. **2.** ascription of supreme divine attributes to whichever one of several gods is addressed at the time. [1855–60; < Gk *heno-*, comb. form of *hén* one (neut. of *heîs*) + THEISM] —**hen′o•the′ist,** *n.* —**hen′o•the•is′tic,** *adj.*

hen′ par′ty, *Informal.* a party or gathering for women only. [1880–85]

hen•pecked (hen′pekt′), *adj.* browbeaten, bullied, or intimidated by one's wife: *a henpecked husband who never dared to contradict his wife.* [1670–80; HEN + PECK + -ED²] —**hen′peck′ing,** *n.*

Hen•ri (hen′rē), *n.* **Robert,** 1865–1929, U.S. painter.

hen•ri•et•ta (hen′rē et′ə), *n.* a fine wool fabric constructed in twill weave, formerly made of silk warp and worsted filling. [1850–55; after *Henrietta* Maria (1609–69), queen consort of Charles I of England]

Hen•ri•et•ta (hen′rē et′ə), *n.* a female given name, form of **Henry.**

hen•ry (hen′rē), *n., pl.* **-ries, -rys.** *Elect.* the SI unit of inductance, equal to that of a closed circuit in which an electromotive force of one volt is produced by a current varying at a rate of one ampere per second. *Abbr.:* H [1890–95; after J. HENRY]

Hen•ry (hen′rē), *n.* **1. Joseph,** 1797–1878, U.S. physicist. **2. O.,** pen name of William Sidney Porter. **3. Patrick,** 1736–99, American patriot, orator, and statesman. **4. Cape,** a cape in SE Virginia at the mouth of the Chesapeake Bay. **5. Fort.** See **Fort Henry. 6.** a male given name: from Germanic words meaning "home" and "kingdom."

Hen•ry (hen′rē), *n.* a .44 caliber lever-action repeating rifle, marketed in the U.S. in the early 1860's, using metallic cartridges and a tubular magazine capable of holding 16 rounds. [after Benjamin Tyler *Henry* (1821–98), U.S. inventor who designed it]

Henry I, 1. (*"Henry the Fowler"*) A.D. 876?–936, king of Germany 919–936: first of the Saxon kings. **2.** (*"Beauclerc"*) 1068–1135, king of England 1100–35 (son of William the Conqueror). **3.** 1008–60, king of France 1031–60.

Henry II, 1. (*"Henry the Saint"*) 973–1024, king of Germany 1002–24 and emperor of the Holy Roman Empire 1014–24. **2.** (*"Curtmantle"*) 1133–89, king of England 1154–89: first king of the Plantagenet line (grandson of Henry I of England). **3.** 1519–59, king of France 1547–59 (son of Francis I).

Henry III, 1. 1017–56, king of Germany 1039–56 and emperor of the Holy Roman Empire 1046–56 (son of Conrad II). **2.** 1207–72, king of England 1216–72 (son of John). **3.** 1551–89, king of France 1574–89 (son of Henry II of France).

Henry IV, 1. 1050–1106, emperor of the Holy Roman Empire and king of Germany 1056–1106. **2.** (*Bolingbroke*) (*"Henry of Lancaster"*) 1367–1413, king of England 1399–1413 (son of John of Gaunt). **3.** (*"Henry of Navarre"; "Henry the Great"*) 1553–1610, king of France 1589–1610: first of the French Bourbon kings. **4.** (*italics*) a two-part drama (Part 1, 1597?; Part 2, 1597–98?) by Shakespeare.

Henry V, 1. 1086–1125, king of Germany 1106–25 and emperor of the Holy Roman Empire 1111–25 (son of Henry IV). **2.** 1387–1422, king of England 1413–22 (son of Henry IV of Bolingbroke). **3.** (*italics*) a drama (1598–99) by Shakespeare.

Henry VI, 1. 1165–97, king of Germany 1190–97; king of Sicily 1194–97; emperor of the Holy Roman Empire 1191–97 (son of Frederick I). **2.** 1421–71, king of England 1422–61, 1470–71 (son of Henry V). **3.** (*italics*) a three-part drama (Part 1, 1591–92; Part 2, 1590?; Part 3, 1590?) by Shakespeare.

Henry VII, 1. (*"Henry of Luxembourg"*) 1275?–1313, king of Germany 1309–13 and emperor of the Holy Roman Empire 1312–13. **2.** (*Henry Tudor*) 1457–1509, king of England 1485–1509: first king of the house of Tudor.

Henry VIII, 1. (*"Defender of the Faith"*) 1491–1547, king of England 1509–47 (son of Henry VII). **2.** (*italics*) a drama (1612–13?) by Shakespeare.

Hen′ry of Por′tugal, (*"the Navigator"*) 1394–1460, prince of Portugal: sponsor of geographic explorations.

Hen′ry's law′, *Thermodynam.* the principle that at a constant temperature the concentration of a gas dissolved in a fluid with which it does not combine chemically is almost directly proportional to the partial pressure of the gas at the surface of the fluid. Cf. **partial pressure.** [1885–90; named after William *Henry* (1774–1836), English chemist who devised it]

Hens•lowe (henz′lō), *n.* **Philip,** died 1616, English theater manager.

Hen•son (hen′sən), *n.* **Matthew Alexander,** 1866–1955, U.S. arctic explorer: accompanied Peary to North Pole 1909.

hent (hent), *v.t.,* **hent, hent•ing.** *Archaic.* to seize. [bef. 1000; ME *henten*, OE *hentan*]

hen′ tracks′, *Slang.* illegible or barely legible handwriting. Also called **hen′ scratch′es.** [1905–10, *Amer.*]

Hen•ty (hen′tē), *n.* **George Alfred,** 1832–1902, English journalist and novelist.

Hen•ze (hen′tsə), *n.* **Hans Wer•ner** (häns ver′nər), born 1926, German composer.

he•or•tol•o•gy (hē′ôr tol′ə jē), *n.* the study of the history and significance of the feasts and seasons in the ecclesiastical calendar. [1900–05; < Gk *heort(ḗ)* a feast, festival + -O- + -LOGY]

hep¹ (hep), *adj. Older Slang.* hip⁴. [1900–05, *Amer.*]

hep² (hut, hup, hep), *interj.* one (used in counting cadence while marching).

hep•a•rin (hep′ə rin), *n.* **1.** *Biochem.* a polysaccharide, present in animal tissues, esp. the liver, and having anticoagulent properties. **2.** *Pharm.* a commercial form of this substance, obtained from domesticated food animals: used in medicine to prevent or dissolve blood clots. [1915–20; < Gk *hêpar* the liver + -IN²]

hepat-, var. of **hepato-** before a vowel: *hepatoma.*

hep•a•tec•to•my (hep′ə tek′tə mē), *n., pl.* **-mies.** excision of part of the liver. [1895–1900; HEPAT- + -ECTOMY]

he•pat•ic (hi pat′ik), *adj.* **1.** of or pertaining to the liver. **2.** acting on the liver, as a medicine. **3.** liver-colored; dark reddish-brown. **4.** *Bot.* belonging or pertaining to the liverworts. —*n.* **5.** a medicine acting on the liver. **6.** a liverwort. [1350–1400; ME *epatik* << L *hēpaticus* < Gk *hēpatikós.* See HEPATO-, -IC]

he•pat•i•ca (hi pat′i kə), *n.* any plant belonging to the genus *Hepatica*, of the buttercup family, having heart-shaped leaves and delicate purplish, pink, or white flowers. [1540–50; < ML: liverwort, n. use of fem. of L *hēpaticus* HEPATIC]

hep•a•ti•tis (hep′ə tī′tis), *n. Pathol.* inflammation of the liver, caused by a virus or a toxin and characterized by jaundice, liver enlargement, and fever. [1720–30; < Gk *hēpatîtis.* See HEPAT-, -ITIS]

hepatitis A, *Pathol.* a normally minor form of hepatitis caused by an RNA virus that does not persist in the blood: usually transmitted by ingestion of contaminated food or water. Also called **infectious hepatitis.** [1970–75]

hepatitis B, *Pathol.* a form of hepatitis caused by a DNA virus (**hepatitis B virus,** or **HBV**) that persists in the blood, characterized by a long incubation period: usually transmitted by sexual contact or by injection or ingestion of infected blood or other bodily fluids. Also called **serum hepatitis.** [1970–75]

hepatitis C, *Pathol.* a form of hepatitis with clinical effects similar to those of hepatitis B, caused by a blood-borne retrovirus (**hepatitis C virus**) that may be of the hepatitis non-A, non-B type.

hep′ati′tis del′ta, *Pathol.* a severe form of hepatitis caused by an incomplete virus (**delta virus**) that links to the hepatitis B virus for its replication. Also called **delta hepatitis.**

hepatitis non-A, non-B, *Pathol.* a disease of the liver that is clinically indistinguishable from hepatitis B but is caused by a retrovirus or retroviruslike agent. Also called **non-A, non-B hepatitis.**

hepato-, a combining form meaning "liver," used in the formation of compound words: *hepatotoxin.* Also, *esp. before a vowel,* **hepat-.** [comb. form repr. Gk *hēpat-*, s. of *hêpar* liver]

hep•a•to•cel•lu•lar (hep′ə tō sel′yə lər, hi pat′ō-), *adj.* pertaining to or affecting liver cells. [1934–40; HEPATO- + CELLULAR]

hep•a•to•cyte (hep′ə tə sīt′, hi pat′ə-), *n.* a cell of the main tissue of the liver; liver cell. [1960–65; HEPATO- + -CYTE]

hep•a•to•ma (hep′ə tō′mə), *n., pl.* **-mas, -ma•ta** (-mə tə). *Pathol.* a tumor of the liver. [1925–30; HEPAT- + -OMA]

hep•a•to•meg•a•ly (hep′ə tō meg′ə lē, hi pat′ə-), *n. Pathol.* an abnormal enlargement of the liver, usually associated with liver disease or heart failure. [1890–95; HEPATO- + -MEGALY]

hep•a•to•pan•cre•as (hep′ə tō pan′krē əs, -pang′-, hi pat′ə-), *n. Anat.* a large gland of shrimps, lobsters, and crabs that combines the functions of a liver and pancreas. [1880–85; HEPATO- + PANCREAS] —**hep•a•to•pan•cre•at•ic** (hep′ə tō pan′krē at′ik, -pang′-, hi pat′ə-), *adj.*

hep•a•to•por′tal sys′tem (hep′ə tō pôr′tl, -pōr′-, hi pat′ə-), *Anat.* a vascular arrangement in vertebrates

CONCISE ETYMOLOGY KEY: <, descended or borrowed from; >, whence; b., blend of, blended; c., cognate with; cf., compare; deriv., derivative; equiv., equivalent; imit., imitative; obl., oblique; r., replacing; s., stem; sp., spelling, spelled; resp., respelling, respelled; trans., translation; ?, origin unknown; *, unattested; ‡, probably earlier than. See the full key inside the front cover.

through which blood is transported into the liver from capillaries of the stomach, spleen, duodenum, pancreas, and intestines. Cf. **portal system.** [HEPATO- + PORTAL[2]]

hep·a·tos·co·py (hep′ə tos′kə pē), *n., pl.* **-pies.** **1.** medical examination of the liver. **2.** examination of the livers of sacrificed animals as a technique of divination. [1720–30; HEPATO- + -SCOPY]

Hep·burn (hep′bûrn′), *n.* **Katharine,** born 1909, U.S. actress.

Hep′burn sys′tem, a widely used system of Romanization of Japanese devised by James Curtis Hepburn (1815–1911). [1935–40]

hep·cat (hep′kat′), *n. Older Slang.* **1.** a performer or admirer of jazz, esp. swing. **2.** a person who is hep; hipster. [1930–35; *Amer.*; HEP[1] + CAT[1]]

He·phaes·tus (hi fes′təs), *n.* the ancient Greek god of fire, metalworking, and handicrafts, identified by the Romans with Vulcan.

Heph·zi·bah (hef′zə bə, -sə-), *n.* **1.** the wife of Hezekiah and the mother of Manasseh. II Kings 21:1. **2.** a name applied to Jerusalem, possibly as denoting its prophesied restoration to the Jews after the Captivity. Isa. 62:4. Cf. **Beulah** (def. 1). **3.** Also, **Hep·si·ba** (hep′sə bə). a female given name.

hepped (hept), *adj. Informal.* hipped[2]. [HEP[1] + -ED[2]]

Hep·ple·white (hep′əl hwīt′, -wīt′), *n.* **1. George,** died 1786, English furniture designer and cabinetmaker. —*adj.* **2.** noting the style prevailing in English furniture c1780–c95, as illustrated in designs published by the firm of George Hepplewhite in 1788, reflecting Adam and Louis XVI influences. [1895–1900]

Hepplewhite chair

hepta-, a combining form meaning "seven," used in the formation of compound words: *heptahedron.* Also, *esp. before a vowel,* **hept-.** [< Gk, comb. form of *heptá* seven; c. L *septem;* akin to OE *seofon* SEVEN]

hep·ta·chlor (hep′tə klôr′, -klōr′), *n.* a highly toxic, light-tan, waxy solid, $C_{10}H_5Cl_7$, formerly used as an insecticide. [1945–50; HEPTA- + CHLOR-[2]]

hep·ta·chord (hep′tə kôrd′), *n.* **1.** a musical scale of seven notes. **2.** an interval of a seventh. **3.** an ancient Greek stringed instrument. [1720–30; < Gk *heptáchordos.* See HEPTA-, CHORD[1]]

hep·tad (hep′tad), *n.* **1.** the number seven. **2.** a group of seven. **3.** *Chem.* an element, atom, or group having a valence of seven. [1650–60; < Gk *heptad-* (s. of *heptás*). See HEPTA-, -AD[1]]

hep·ta·gon (hep′tə gon′), *n.* a polygon having seven angles and seven sides. [1560–70; < Gk *heptágōnos* seven-cornered. See HEPTA-, -GON]

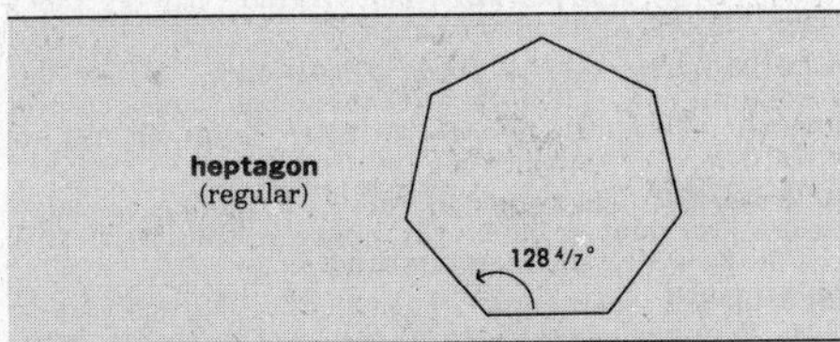

heptagon (regular)

hep·tag·o·nal (hep tag′ə nl), *adj.* having seven sides or angles. [1605–15; HEPTAGON + -AL[1]]

hep·ta·he·dron (hep′tə hē′drən), *n., pl.* **-drons, -dra** (-drə). a solid figure having seven faces. [1650–60; HEPTA- + -HEDRON] —**hep′ta·he′dral, hep′ta·he′dri·cal,** *adj.*

hep·ta·hy·drate (hep′tə hī′drāt), *n.* a hydrate that contains seven molecules of water, as magnesium sulfate, $MgSO_4·7H_2O$. [1870–75; HEPTA- + HYDRATE] —**hep′ta·hy′drat·ed,** *adj.*

hep·tam·er·ous (hep tam′ər əs), *adj.* consisting of or divided into seven parts. [1780–90; HEPTA- + -MEROUS]

hep·tam·e·ter (hep tam′i tər), *n. Pros.* a verse of seven metrical feet. [1895–1900; < ML *heptametrum* < Gk *heptámetron* a verse of seven feet. See HEPTA-, METER[2]] —**hep·ta·met·ri·cal** (hep′tə me′tri kəl), *adj.*

hep·tane (hep′tān), *n.* any of nine isomeric hydrocarbons, C_7H_{16}, of the alkane series, some of which are obtained from petroleum: used in fuels as solvents, and as chemical intermediates. [1870–75; HEPT- + -ANE]

hep′tane·di·o′ic ac′id (hep′tān dī ō′ik), *Chem.* See **pimelic acid.**

hep·tan·gu·lar (hep tang′gyə lər), *adj.* having seven angles. [1700–10; HEPT- + ANGULAR]

hep·ta·none (hep′tə nōn′), *n. Chem.* any of three isomeric ketones, $C_{11}H_{14}O$, derived from heptane. [HEPTANE + -ONE]

hep·tar·chy (hep′tär kē), *n., pl.* **-chies.** **1.** (*often cap.*) the seven principal concurrent Anglo-Saxon kingdoms supposed to have existed in the 7th and 8th centuries. **2.** government by seven persons. **3.** an allied group of seven states or kingdoms, each under its own ruler. [1570–80; HEPT- + -ARCHY] —**hep′tarch, hep′tar·chist,** *n.* —**hep·tar′chic, hep·tar′chi·cal, hep·tar′·chal,** *adj.*

hep·ta·stich (hep′tə stik′), *n. Pros.* a strophe, stanza, or poem consisting of seven lines or verses. [1880–85; HEPTA- + STICH[1]]

hep·ta·syl·la·ble (hep′tə sil′ə bəl), *n.* a word or line of verse of seven syllables. [1750–60; HEPTA- + SYLLABLE] —**hep·ta·syl·lab·ic** (hep′tə si lab′ik), *adj., n.*

Hep·ta·teuch (hep′tə to͞ok′, -tyo͞ok′), *n.* the first seven books of the Old Testament. [< LL *Heptateuchos* < LGk *Heptáteuchos* the first seven books of the Old Testament, equiv. to Gk *hepta-* HEPTA- + *teûchos* a book]

hep·tath·lon (hep tath′lən, -lon), *n.* an athletic contest for women comprising seven different track-and-field events and won by the contestant amassing the highest total score. [1985–90; HEPT- + (DEC)ATHLON]

hep·ta·va·lent (hep′tə vā′lənt), *adj. Chem.* septivalent. [HEPTA- + -VALENT]

hep·tode (hep′tōd), *n. Electronics.* a vacuum tube containing seven electrodes, usually a plate, a cathode, a control electrode, and four grids. [1930–35; HEPT- + -ODE[2]]

hep·tose (hep′tōs), *n. Chem.* any monosaccharide containing seven carbon atoms. [< G *Heptose* (1890); see HEPTA-, -OSE[2]]

Hep·zi·bah (hep′zə bə, -sə-), *n.* a female given name.

her (hûr; *unstressed* hər, ər), *pron.* **1.** the objective case of **she:** *We saw her this morning. Give this book to her.* **2.** the possessive case of **she** (used as an attributive adjective): *Her coat is the one on the chair. I'm sorry about her leaving.* Cf. **hers.** **3.** the dative case of **she:** *I gave her the book.* **4.** *Informal.* (used instead of the pronoun *she* in the predicate after the verb *to be*): *It's her. It isn't her.* —*n.* **5.** *Slang.* a female: *Is the new baby a her or a him?* [bef. 900; ME *her(e),* OE *hire,* gen. and dat. of *hēo* she (fem. of *hē* HE[1])]
—**Usage.** See **he**[1], **me.**

her., **1.** heraldic. **2.** heraldry.

He·ra (hēr′ə, her′ə), *n.* the ancient Greek queen of heaven, a daughter of Cronus and Rhea and the wife and sister of Zeus. Also, **Here.** Cf. **Juno.**

Her·a·cle·a (her′ə klē′ə), *n.* an ancient city in S Italy, near the Gulf of Taranto: Roman defeat 280 B.C.

Her·a·cles (her′ə klēz′), *n.* **1.** Hercules (def. 1). **2.** Also called **Her′acles Fu′rens** (fyo͝or′ənz). (*italics*) a tragedy (420? B.C.) by Euripides. [< Gk *Hēraklês,* lit., having the glory of Hera, equiv. to *Hḗra* HERA + *-klēs,* akin to *kléos* glory, fame] —**Her′a·cle′an,** *adj.*

Her·a·clid (her′ə klid), *n., pl.* **Her·a·cli·dae** (her′ə klī′dē). a person claiming descent from Hercules, esp. one of the Dorian aristocracy of Sparta. —**Her·a·cli·dan** (her′ə klīd′n), *adj.*

Her·a·cli·dae (her′ə klī′dē), *n.* a drama (429? B.C.) by Euripides. Also, ***Her′a·clei′dae.*** Also called ***Children of Hercules.***

Her·a·cli·te·an (her′ə klī′tē ən, -klī tē′-), *adj.* **1.** of or pertaining to Heraclitus or his philosophy. —*n.* **2.** a person who believes in or advocates the philosophy of Heraclitus. Also, **Her·a·clit·ic** (her′ə klit′ik). [1785–95; < L *Hēraclīte(us)* (< Gk *Hērakleíteios*) + -AN]

Her·a·cli·te·an·ism (her′ə klī′tē ə niz′əm, -klī tē′-), *n.* the philosophy of Heraclitus, maintaining the perpetual change of all things, the only abiding thing being the logos, or orderly principle, according to which the change takes place. [1880–85; HERACLITEAN + -ISM]

Her·a·cli·tus (her′ə klī′təs), *n.* ("*the Obscure*") c540–c470 B.C., Greek philosopher.

Her·a·cli·us (her′ə klī′əs, hi rak′lē əs), *n.* A.D. 575?–641, Byzantine emperor 610–641.

He·ra·klei·on (ē rä′klē ôn), *n.* Greek name of **Candia.**

her·ald (her′əld), *n.* **1.** (formerly) a royal or official messenger, esp. one representing a monarch in an ambassadorial capacity during wartime. **2.** a person or thing that precedes or comes before; forerunner; harbinger: *the returning swallows, those heralds of spring.* **3.** a person or thing that proclaims or announces. **4.** (in the Middle Ages) an officer who arranged tournaments and other functions, announced challenges, marshaled combatants, etc. and to regulate the use of armorial bearings. **5.** an official intermediate in rank between a king-of-arms and a pursuivant, in the Heralds' College in England or the Heralds' Office in Scotland. —*v.t.* **6.** to give news or tidings of; announce; proclaim: *a publicity campaign to herald a new film.* **7.** to indicate or signal the coming of; usher in. [1300–50; ME *herau(l)d* < OF *herau(l)t* < Frankish *heriwald, equiv. to *heri army + *wald commander (see WIELD). Cf. name HAROLD]
—**Syn. 7.** publicize, ballyhoo, tout.

he·ral·dic (he ral′dik, hə-), *adj.* of, pertaining to, or characteristic of heralds or heraldry: *heraldic form; heraldic images; heraldic history; a heraldic device.* [1765–75; HERALD + -IC] —**he·ral′di·cal·ly,** *adv.*

her·ald·ry (her′əl drē), *n., pl.* **-ries.** **1.** the science of armorial bearings. **2.** the art of blazoning armorial bearings, of settling the rights of persons to bear arms or to use certain bearings, of tracing and recording genealogies, of recording honors, and of deciding questions of precedence. **3.** the office or duty of a herald. **4.** a heraldic device, or a collection of such devices. **5.** a coat of arms; armorial bearings. **6.** heraldic symbolism. **7.** heraldic pomp or ceremony: *The coronation was marked by all the magnificence of heraldry.* [1350–1400; ME. See HERALD, -RY] —**her′ald·ist,** *n.*

Her′alds' Col′lege, a royal corporation in England, instituted in 1483, concerned chiefly with armorial bearings, genealogies, honors, and precedence. Also called **College of Arms.**

Her′alds' Of′fice, the official heraldic authority of Scotland. Also called **Lyon Office of Arms, Lyon Office.**

her′ald's trick′, *Heraldry.* See **engraver's trick.**

He·rat (he rät′), *n.* a city in NW Afghanistan. 62,000.

Hé·rault (ā rō′), *n.* a department in S France. 648,202; 2403 sq. mi. (6225 sq. km). *Cap.:* Montpellier.

herb (ûrb *or, esp. Brit.,* hûrb), *n.* **1.** a flowering plant whose stem above ground does not become woody. **2.** such a plant when valued for its medicinal properties, flavor, scent, or the like. **3.** Often, **the herb.** *Slang.* marijuana. **4.** *Archaic.* herbage. **5. give it the herbs,** *Australian Slang.* to use full power, esp. in accelerating a car. [1250–1300; ME *herbe* < OF *erbe, herbe* < L *herba*] —**herb′less,** *adj.* —**herb′like′,** *adj.*

Herb (hûrb), *n.* a male given name, form of **Herbert.**

her·ba·ceous (hûr bā′shəs, ûr-), *adj.* **1.** of, pertaining to, or characteristic of an herb; herblike. **2.** (of plants or plant parts) **a.** not woody. **b.** having the texture, color, etc., of an ordinary foliage leaf. [1640–50; < L *herbāceus* grassy, like grass, equiv. to *herb(a)* grass, herbs + *-āceus* -ACEOUS] —**her·ba′ceous·ly,** *adv.*

herb·age (ûr′bij, hûr′-), *n.* **1.** nonwoody vegetation. **2.** the succulent parts, leaves and stems, of herbaceous plants. **3.** *Law.* the right to pasture one's cattle on another's land. **4.** *Brit.* vegetation grazed by animals; pasturage. [1350–1400; ME < F; see HERB, -AGE] —**her′·baged,** *adj.*

herb·al (ûr′bəl, hûr′-), *adj.* **1.** of, pertaining to, or consisting of herbs. —*n.* **2.** a book about herbs or plants, usually describing their medicinal values. **3.** a herbarium. [1510–20; < ML *herbālis* of, belonging to grass or herbs. See HERB, -AL[1]]

herb·al·ist (hûr′bə list, ûr′-), *n.* **1.** a person who collects or deals in herbs, esp. medicinal herbs. **2.** See **herb doctor.** **3.** an author of an herbal. **4.** (formerly) a botanist. [1585–95; HERBAL + -IST]

herb′al tea′, a tea made of dried herbs and spices and usually containing no caffeine. Also called **herb tea.**

her·bar·i·um (hûr bâr′ē əm, ûr-), *n., pl.* **-bar·i·ums, -bar·i·a** (-bâr′ē ə). **1.** a collection of dried plants systematically arranged. **2.** a room or building in which such a collection is kept. [1770–80; < LL, equiv. to L *herb(a)* HERB, green vegetation + *-ārium* -ARIUM] —**her·bar′i·al,** *adj.*

Her·bart (her′bärt), *n.* **Jo·hann Frie·drich** (yō′hän frē′drikh), 1776–1841, German philosopher and educator.

herb′ ben′net, a European plant, *Geum urbanum,* of the rose family, having yellow flowers and an aromatic, astringent root. [1775–85]

herb′ doc′tor, a person who practices healing by the use of herbs. Also called **herbalist.** [1850–55]

Her·bert (hûr′bərt), *n.* **1. George,** 1593–1633, English clergyman and poet. **2. Victor,** 1859–1924, U.S. composer and orchestra conductor, born in Ireland. **3.** a male given name: from Old English words meaning "army" and "bright."

herb·i·cide (hûr′bə sīd′, ûr′-), *n.* a substance or preparation for killing plants, esp. weeds. [1895–1900; HERB + -I- + -CIDE] —**her′bi·cid′al,** *adj.*

her·bi·vore (hûr′bə vôr′, -vōr′), *n.* a herbivorous animal. [1850–55; < NL *herbivora;* see HERB, -I-, -VORE]

her·biv·o·rous (hûr biv′ər əs, ûr-), *adj.* feeding on plants. [1655–65; < NL *herbivorus;* see HERB, -I-, -VOROUS] —**her·bi·vor·i·ty** (hûr′bə vôr′i tē, -vor′-), *n.* —**her·biv′o·rous·ly,** *adv.*

Her·block (hûr′blok), *n.* See **Block, Herbert Lawrence.**

herb-of-grace (ûrb′əv grās′, hûrb′-), *n., pl.* **herbs-of-grace.** *Archaic.* rue[2]. [1540–50; so called from the assoc. of RUE[2] (the plant name) with RUE[1] (repent, repentance)]

her·bol·o·gy (hûr bol′ə jē, ûr-), *n.* the study or collecting of herbs, esp. as a hobby. [HERB + -O- + -LOGY] —**her·bol′o·gist,** *n.*

her·bo·rist (hûr′bər ist, ûr′-), *n.* herbalist. [< MF *herboriste,* irreg. < L *herb(a)* HERB + MF *-iste* -IST]

her·bo·rize (hûr′bə rīz′, ûr′-), *v.i.,* **-rized, -riz·ing.** botanize. Also, *esp. Brit.,* **her′bo·rise′.** [1655–65; < F *herboriser,* equiv. to *herbor(iste)* HERBORIST + *-iser* -IZE]

herb′ Par′is, *pl.* **herbs Paris.** a European plant, *Paris quadrifolia,* of the lily family, formerly used in medicine. [1560–70; < ML *herba paris* < ?]

herb′ pa′tience, *pl.* **herbs patience.** a European plant, *Rumex patientia,* of the buckwheat family, naturalized in North America, having long, wavy-margined, basal leaves used for salads. Also called **spinach dock.**

herb′ Rob′ert, *pl.* **herbs Robert.** a wild geranium, *Geranium robertianum,* having fernlike, scented leaves and reddish-purple flowers. Also called **red shanks.** [1250–1300; ME < ML *herba Roberti* Robert's herb]

herb′ tea′. See **herbal tea.**

herb·y (ûr′bē, hûr′bē), *adj.,* **herb·i·er, herb·i·est.** **1.** abounding in herbs or grass. **2.** of, pertaining to, or characteristic of an herb or herbs in taste or appearance. [1545–55; HERB + -Y[1]]

Her·ce·go·vi·na (her′tse gô′vi nä), *n.* Herzegovina.

Her·cu·la·ne·um (hûr′kyə lā′nē əm), *n.* an ancient city in SW Italy, on the Bay of Naples: buried along with Pompeii by the eruption of Mount Vesuvius in A.D. 79; partially excavated. —**Her′cu·la′ne·an, Her·cu·la·nen·sian** (hûr′kyə lə nen′shən, -sē ən), *adj.*

CONCISE PRONUNCIATION KEY: act, cāpe, dâre, pärt; set, ēqual; *if,* ice; ox, ōver, ôrder, oil, bo͝ok, bo͞ot, out; up, ûrge; child; sing; shoe; thin, *th*at; zh as in *treasure.* ə = *a* as in *alone,* e as in *system,* i as in *easily,* o as in *gallop,* u as in *circus;* ᵊ as in *fire* (fīᵊr), *hour* (ouᵊr). l and n can serve as syllabic consonants, as in *cradle* (krād′l), and *button* (but′n). See the full key inside the front cover.

her•cu•le•an (hûr′kyə lē′ən, hûr kyo͞o′lē ən), *adj.* **1.** requiring the great strength of a Hercules; very hard to perform: *Digging the tunnel was a herculean task.* **2.** having enormous strength, courage, or size. **3.** (*cap.*) of or pertaining to Hercules or his labors. [1590–1600; < L *Hercule(us)* of, belonging to HERCULES + -AN]
—Syn. 1. prodigious, arduous, onerous, formidable.

Her•cu•les (hûr′kyə lēz′), *n., gen.* **-cu•lis** (-kyə lis) for 2. **1.** Also, **Heracles.** Also called **Alcides.** *Class. Myth.* a celebrated hero, the son of Zeus and Alcmene, possessing exceptional strength: among his many adventures were the twelve labors for his cousin Eurystheus, performed in order to gain immortality. Cf. **labors of Hercules. 2.** *Astron.* a northern constellation, between Lyra and Corona Borealis. [< L *Herculēs, Herclēs* < Gk; see HERACLES]

Her′cules bee′tle, a large Neotropical rhinoceros beetle, *Dynastes hercules.* [1830–40]

Hercules beetle, *Dynastes hercules,* length 5 in. (13 cm)

Her•cu•les-club (hûr′kyə lēz klub′), *n.* **1.** a prickly tree, *Zanthoxylum clava-herculis,* of the rue family, having a medicinal bark and berries. **2.** Also called **angelica tree, devil's-walking-stick.** a prickly shrub, of the ginseng family, *Aralia spinosa,* having a medicinal bark and root. Also called **prickly ash.** [1680–90]

Her′cules' Pil′lars. See **Pillars of Hercules.**

her•cy•nite (hûr′sə nīt′), *n.* a black oxide mineral, $FeAl_2O_4$, of the spinel group. [< G *Hercynit* (1839), equiv. to L *Hercyn(ia silva)* the Hercynian Forest (referring to the Erz Mountains and other wooded ranges N of the Danube) + G *-it* -ITE[1]]

herd[1] (hûrd), *n.* **1.** a number of animals kept, feeding, or traveling together; drove; flock: *a herd of cattle; a herd of sheep; a herd of zebras.* **2.** *Sometimes Disparaging.* a large group of people: *The star was mobbed by a herd of autograph seekers.* **3.** any large quantity: *a herd of bicycles.* **4. the herd,** the common people; masses; rabble: *He had no opinions of his own, but simply followed the herd.* **5. ride herd on,** to have charge or control of; maintain discipline over: *He rode herd on 40 students in each class.* *—v.i.* **6.** to unite or go in a herd; assemble or associate as a herd. [bef. 1000; ME; OE *heord;* c. Goth *hairda,* G *Herde*]
—Syn. 1. See **flock**[1]. **2.** crowd, mob.
—Usage. See **collective noun.**

herd[2] (hûrd), *n.* **1.** a herdsman (usually used in combination): *a cowherd; a goatherd; a shepherd.* *—v.t.* **2.** to tend, drive, or lead (cattle, sheep, etc.). **3.** to conduct or drive (a group of people) to a destination: *The teacher herded the children into the classroom.* [bef. 900; ME *herd(e), hirde,* OE *hierde;* c. Goth *hairdeis,* G *Hirt(e)*; deriv. of HERD[1]]
—Syn. 2. guard, protect, watch.

herd•er (hûr′dər), *n.* a person in charge of a herd, esp. of cattle or sheep. [1625–35; HERD[2] + -ER[1]]

Her•der (hẽr′dər), *n.* **Jo•hann Gott•fried von** (yō′hän gôt′frēt fən), 1744–1803, German philosopher and poet.

her•dic (hûr′dik), *n.* a low-hung carriage with two or four wheels, having the entrance at the back and the seats at the sides. [1880–85, *Amer.*; named after P. *Herdic,* 19th-century American, the inventor]

herd′ing dog′, one of any of several breeds of dogs used originally for herding livestock, including the Belgian sheepdog, collie, German shepherd, and Old English sheepdog.

herd′ in′stinct, the impulse or tendency toward clustering or acting in a group, esp. the presumed instinct toward or need for gregariousness and conformity. [1905–10]

herd's-grass (hûrdz′gras′, -gräs′), *n.* timothy or redtop, used for hay or pasture. [1730–40, *Amer.*; named after John *Herd,* who in 1700 found it growing in New Hampshire]

herds•man (hûrdz′mən), *n., pl.* **-men. 1.** a herder; the keeper of a herd, esp. of cattle or sheep. **2.** (*cap.*) *Astron.* the constellation Boötes. [1595–1605; HERD[1] + -'S[1] + -MAN; cf. earlier *herdman,* ME *hird-man,* OE *hyrdemann*]

here (hēr), *adv.* **1.** in this place; in this spot or locality (opposed to *there*): *Put the pen here.* **2.** to or toward this place; hither: *Come here.* **3.** at this point; at this juncture: *Here the speaker paused.* **4.** (used to call attention to some person or thing present, or to what the speaker has, offers, brings, or discovers): *Here is your paycheck. My friend here knows the circumstances.* **5.** present (used to answer a roll call). **6.** in the present life or existence (often fol. by *below*): *We want but little here below.* **7.** under consideration, in this instance or case: *The matter here is of grave concern to us all.* **8. here and now,** at the present moment; without delay; immediately: *We must tend to the matter here and now.* **9. here and there, a.** in this place and in that; at various times or places: *He worked here and there, never for long in one town.* **b.** hither and thither: *We drove here and there in the darkness, hoping to find the right roads.* **10. here goes,** (used to express resolution in beginning a bold or unpleasant action): *You've dared me to dive from the highest board, so here goes!* **11. here's to,** hail to; salutations to: *Here's to a long and happy life! Here's to you!* **12. neither here nor there,** without relevance or importance; immaterial: *The fact that her family has no money is neither here nor there.* *—n.* **13.** this place: *It's only a short distance from here.* **14.** this world; this life; the present: *The here and the hereafter are equal mysteries to all people.* **15. here and now,** the immediate present (usually prec. by *the*): *You can't live only in the here and now.* **16. up to here with, a.** having a surfeit of: *I'm up to here with work.* **b.** at a high point of annoyance with: *Everyone is up to here with his constant complaining.* *—adj.* **17.** (used for emphasis, esp. after a noun modified by a demonstrative adjective): *this package here.* *—interj.* **18.** (often used to command attention, give comfort, etc.) now; all right: *Here, let me try it. Here, don't cry.* [bef. 900; ME; OE *hēr;* c. G *hier,* ON, Goth *hēr*]
—Usage. 17. See **there.**

He•re (hēr′ē), *n.* Hera.

here•a•bout (hēr′ə bout′), *adv.* about this place; in this neighborhood. Also, **here′a•bouts′.** [1175–1225; ME; see HERE, ABOUT]

here•af•ter (hēr af′tər, -äf′-), *adv.* **1.** after this in time or order; at some future time; farther along. **2.** in the time to follow; from now on: *Hereafter I will not accept their calls.* **3.** in the life or world to come. **4.** hereinafter. *—n.* **5.** a life or existence after death; the future beyond mortal existence. **6.** time to come; the future. [bef. 900; ME; OE *hēræfter.* See HERE, AFTER]

here•at (hēr at′), *adv.* **1.** at this time; when this happened. **2.** by reason of this; because of this. [1350–1400; ME *here at.* See HERE, AT[1]]

here•a•way (hēr′ə wā′), *adv. Dial.* hereabout. Also, **here′a•ways′.** [1350–1400; ME. See HERE, AWAY]

here•by (hēr bī′, hēr′bī′), *adv.* **1.** by this, or the present, declaration, action, document, etc.; by means of this; as a result of this: *I hereby resign as president of the class.* **2.** *Obs.* nearby. [1200–50; ME. See HERE, BY]

he•re•des (hi rē′dēz), *n.* pl. of **heres.**

He•re•dia (*Sp.* e re′thyä; *for 1 also Fr.* ā rā dyA′), *n.* **1. Jo•sé Ma•ri•a de** (*Sp.* hô se′ mä rē′ä the), 1842–1905, French poet, born in Cuba. **2.** a city in central Costa Rica, N of San José. 25,652.

he•red•i•ta•ble (hə red′i tə bəl), *adj.* heritable. [1400–50; late ME < MF < LL *hērēdit(āre)* to inherit, deriv. of L *hērēd-* (s. of *hērēs*) HEIR + MF *-able* -ABLE] **—he•red′i•ta•bil′i•ty,** *n.* **—he•red′i•ta•bly,** *adv.*

her•e•dit•a•ment (her′i dit′ə mənt), *n. Law.* any inheritable estate or interest in property. [1425–75; late ME < ML *hērēditāmentum,* deriv. of LL *hērēditāre.* See HEREDITABLE, -MENT]

he•red•i•tar•i•an (hə red′i târ′ē ən), *n.* **1.** a person who believes that differences between individuals or groups, including moral and intellectual attributes, are predominantly determined by genetic factors (opposed to *environmentalist*). *—adj.* **2.** characteristic of or based on such belief: *hereditarian theories.* [1880–85; HEREDIT(Y) or HEREDIT(ARY) + -ARIAN] **—he•red′i•tar′i•an•ism,** *n.*

he•red•i•tar•y (hə red′i ter′ē), *adj.* **1.** passing, or capable of passing, naturally from parent to offspring through the genes: *Blue eyes are hereditary in our family.* Cf. **congenital. 2.** of or pertaining to inheritance or heredity: *a hereditary title.* **3.** existing by reason of feeling, opinions, or prejudices held by predecessors: *a hereditary enemy.* **4.** *Law.* **a.** descending by inheritance. **b.** transmitted or transmissible in the line of descent by force of law. **c.** holding title, rights, etc., by inheritance: *a hereditary proprietor.* **5.** *Math.* **a.** (of a collection of sets) signifying that each subset of a set in the collection is itself a set in the collection. **b.** of or pertaining to a mathematical property, as containing a greatest integer, applicable to every subset of a set that has the property. [1375–1425; late ME < L *hērēditārius* relating to inheritance, equiv. to *hērēdit(ās)* inheritance, HEREDITY + *-ārius* -ARY] **—he•red•i•tar•i•ly** (hi red′i târ′ə lē, -red′i ter′-), *adv.* **—he•red′i•tar′i•ness,** *n.*
—Syn. 1, 2. See **innate. 3.** ancestral, traditional.

he•red•i•ty (hə red′i tē), *n., pl.* **-ties.** *Biol.* **1.** the transmission of genetic characters from parents to offspring: it is dependent upon the segregation and recombination of genes during meiosis and fertilization and results in the genesis of a new individual similar to others of its kind but exhibiting certain variations resulting from the particular mix of genes and their interactions with the environment. **2.** the genetic characters so transmitted. Cf. **congenital.** [1530–40; < MF *heredite* < L *hērēditāt-* (s. of *hērēditās*) inheritance, equiv. to *hērēd-* (s. of *hērēs*) HEIR + *-itāt-* -ITY]

Her•e•ford (hûr′fərd, her′ə- *for 1, 2;* her′ə fərd *for 3, 5;* hûr′fərd *for 4*), *n.* **1.** one of an English breed of red beef cattle having a white face and white body markings. **2.** one of an American breed of red hogs having white markings. **3.** a city in Hereford and Worcester, in W England: cathedral. 47,300. **4.** a town in N Texas. 15,853. **5.** Herefordshire.

Her′e•ford and Worces′ter (her′ə fərd), a county in W England. 585,600; 1516 sq. mi. (3926 sq. km).

Her•e•ford•shire (her′ə fərd shēr′, -shər), *n.* a former county in W England, now part of Hereford and Worcester.

here•in (hēr in′), *adv.* **1.** in or into this place. **2.** in this fact, circumstance, etc.; in view of this. [bef. 1000; ME; OE *hērinne.* See HERE, IN]

here•in•af•ter (hēr′in af′tər, -äf′-), *adv.* afterward in this document, statement, etc. Also, **here•in•be•low** (hēr′in bi lō′). [1580–90; HEREIN + AFTER]

here•in•be•fore (hēr′in bi fôr′, -fōr′), *adv.* before in this document, statement, etc. Also, **here•in•a•bove** (hēr′ in ə buv′). [1680–90; HEREIN + BEFORE]

here•in•to (hēr in′to͞o, hēr′in to͞o′), *adv.* **1.** into this place. **2.** into this matter or affair. [1585–95; HERE + INTO]

he•rem (*Seph.* KHE′REM; *Ashk.* KHÄ′rəm), *n. Hebrew.* the most severe form of excommunication, formerly used by rabbis in sentencing wrongdoers, usually for an indefinite period of time. Also, ***cherem.*** [*ḥerem* lit., banishment]

here•of (hēr uv′, -ov′), *adv.* **1.** of this: *upon the receipt hereof.* **2.** concerning this: *more hereof later.* [bef. 1050; ME, OE *hēr of.* See HERE, OF[1]]

here•on (hēr on′, -ôn′), *adv.* hereupon. [bef. 1000; ME *her on,* OE *hēron.* See HERE, ON]

He•re•ro (hə râr′ō), *n., pl.* **-ros,** (*esp. collectively*) **-ro** for 1. **1.** a member of an indigenous people of Namibia, Botswana, and Angola. **2.** the Bantu language of the Herero.

he•res (hēr′ēz), *n., pl.* **he•re•des** (hi rē′dēz). *Civil Law.* an heir. Also, **haeres.** [< L *hērēs* HEIR]

here's (hērz), contraction of *here is.*
—Usage. See **contraction.**

he•re•si•arch (hə rē′zē ärk′, -sē-, her′ə sē-), *n.* a leader in heresy; the leader of a heretical sect. [1615–25; < LL *haeresiarcha* < Gk *hairesiárchēs* the leader of a school, equiv. to *haíresi(s)* HERESY + *-archēs* -ARCH]

he•re•si•mach (hə rē′zə mak′, -sə-, her′ə sə-), *n.* a person engaged in combating heresy and heretics. [1815–25; < LGk *hairesimáchos,* equiv. to Gk *haíresi(s)* HERESY + *mách(ē)* quarrel, battle (see -MACHY) + *-os* n. suffix]

he•re•si•og•ra•phy (hə rē′zē og′rə fē, -sē-, her′ə sē-), *n., pl.* **-phies.** a treatise on heresy. [1635–45; HERESY + -O- + -GRAPHY] **—he•re′si•og′ra•pher,** *n.*

he•re•si•ol•o•gist (hə rē′zē ol′ə jist, -sē-, her′ə sē-), *n.* a person who studies or writes about heresies. [1700–10; HERESY + -O- + -LOG(Y) + -IST]

he•re•si•ol•o•gy (hə rē′zē ol′ə jē, -sē-, her′ə sē-), *n., pl.* **-gies** for 2. **1.** the study of heresies. **2.** a heresiography. [1855–60; HERESY + -O- + -LOGY]

her•e•sy (her′ə sē), *n., pl.* **-sies. 1.** opinion or doctrine at variance with the orthodox or accepted doctrine, esp. of a church or religious system. **2.** the maintaining of such an opinion or doctrine. **3.** *Rom. Cath. Ch.* the willful and persistent rejection of any article of faith by a baptized member of the church. **4.** any belief or theory that is strongly at variance with established beliefs, customs, etc. [1175–1225; ME *heresie* < OF *eresie* < L *haeresis* school of thought, sect < Gk *haíresis,* lit., act of choosing, deriv. of *haireîn* to choose]
—Syn. 4. dissent, iconoclasm, dissension.

her•e•tic (*n.* her′i tik; *adj.* her′i tik, hə ret′ik), *n.* **1.** a professed believer who maintains religious opinions contrary to those accepted by his or her church or rejects doctrines prescribed by that church. **2.** *Rom. Cath. Ch.* a baptized Roman Catholic who willfully and persistently rejects any article of faith. **3.** anyone who does not conform to an established attitude, doctrine, or principle. *—adj.* **4.** heretical. [1300–50; ME *heretik* < MF *heretique* < LL *haereticus* < Gk *hairetikós* able to choose (LGk: heretical), equiv. to *hairet(ós)* that may be taken (verbal adj. of *haireîn* to choose) + *-ikos* -IC]
—Syn. 1. apostate, backslider, recreant, protestant. **3.** dissenter, skeptic, freethinker.

he•ret•i•cal (hə ret′i kəl), *adj.* of, pertaining to, or characteristic of heretics or heresy. [1375–1425; late ME < ML *haereticālis.* See HERETIC, -AL[1]] **—he•ret′i•cal•ly,** *adv.* **—he•ret′i•cal•ness,** *n.*
—Syn. unorthodox, unconventional, dissident, radical.

here•to (hēr to͞o′), *adv.* to this matter, document, subject, etc.; regarding this point: *attached hereto; agreeable hereto.* Also, **here•un•to** (hēr un′to͞o, hēr′un to͞o′). [1125–75; ME *herto.* See HERE, TO]

here•to•fore (hēr′tə fôr′, -fōr′), *adv.* before this time; until now. [1300–50; ME *heretoforn,* equiv. to *here* HERE + *toforn,* OE *tōforan* (*tō* TO + *foran* before; see FORE[1])]

here•un•der (hēr un′dər), *adv.* **1.** under or below this; subsequent to this. **2.** under authority of this. [1175–1225; ME; see HERE, UNDER]

here•up•on (hēr′ə pon′, -pôn′), *adv.* **1.** upon or on this. **2.** immediately following this. [1125–75; ME *herupon.* See HERE, UPON]

here•with (hēr with′, -with′), *adv.* **1.** along with this. **2.** by means of this; hereby. [bef. 1050; ME *herwith,* OE *hērwith.* See HERE, WITH[1]]

Her•ges•hei•mer (hûr′gəs hī′mər), *n.* **Joseph,** 1880–1954, U.S. novelist.

He•ring (hā′RING), *n.* **E•wald** (ā′vält), 1834–1918, German physiologist and psychologist.

her•i•ot (her′ē ət), *n. Eng. Law.* a feudal service or tribute, originally of borrowed military equipment and later of a chattel, due to the lord on the death of a tenant. [bef. 900; ME *heriot, heriet,* OE *heregeate, heregeatu, heregeatwa* war gear, equiv. to *here* army + *geate,* etc., equipment; c. ON *gǫtvar* (pl.)]

He•ri•sau (*Ger.* hā′Ri zou′), *n.* a town in and the capital of Appenzell Ausser Rhoden, in NE Switzerland. 14,000. French, **He•ri•sau** (ā Rē zō′).

her•it•a•ble (her′i tə bəl), *adj.* **1.** capable of being inherited; inheritable; hereditary. **2.** capable of inheriting. [1325–75; ME < MF, equiv. to *herit(er)* to inherit + *-able* -ABLE. See HEIR, HEREDITY] **—her′it•a•bil′i•ty,** *n.* **—her′it•a•bly,** *adv.*

her•it•age (her′i tij), *n.* **1.** something that comes or belongs to one by reason of birth; an inherited lot or portion: *a heritage of poverty and suffering; a national heritage of honor, pride, and courage.* **2.** something reserved for one: *the heritage of the righteous.* **3.** *Law.* **a.** something that has been or may be inherited by legal descent or succession. **b.** any property, esp. land, that devolves by right of inheritance. [1175–1225; ME < MF, equiv. to *heriter* to inherit + *-age* -AGE; see HEIR]
—Syn. 1. estate, patrimony. See **inheritance.**

her•it•ance (her′i tns), *n. Archaic.* inheritance.

CONCISE ETYMOLOGY KEY: <, descended or borrowed from; >, whence; b., blend of, blended; c., cognate with; cf., compare; deriv., derivative; equiv., equivalent; imit., imitative; obl., oblique; r., replacing; s., stem; sp., spelling, spelled; resp., respelling, respelled; trans., translation; ?, origin unknown; *, unattested; ‡, probably earlier than. See the full key inside the front cover.

[1350–1400; ME *herita(u)nce* < MF *heritance,* equiv. to *herit(er)* to inherit + *-ance* -ANCE; see HEIR]

her•i•tor (her′i tər), *n.* inheritor. [1375–1425; late ME alter. of ME *heriter* < MF *heritier* < L *hērēditārius* HEREDITARY]

Her•ki•mer (hûr′kə mər), *n.* **Nicholas,** 1728–77, American Revolutionary general.

herk•y-jerk•y (hûr′kē jûr′kē), *adj.* progressing in a fitfully jerky or irregular manner: *a herky-jerky home movie shown on an old projector.* [1955–60; rhyming compound based on JERK[1], -Y[1]]

herl (hûrl), *n.* **1.** a barb of a feather, used esp. in dressing anglers' flies. **2.** an artificial fly dressed with a herl. [1300–50; ME; c. MLG *herle, harle,* LG *harl* fibre, hair of flax or hemp]

herm (hûrm), *n.* a monument consisting of a four-sided shaft tapering inward from top to bottom and bearing a head or bust; those of Hermes usually had an erect penis, which passersby stroked for luck. Also, **herma.** Cf. **term** (def. 10). [1570–80; < L *hermēs* < Gk *hermês* statue of Hermes]

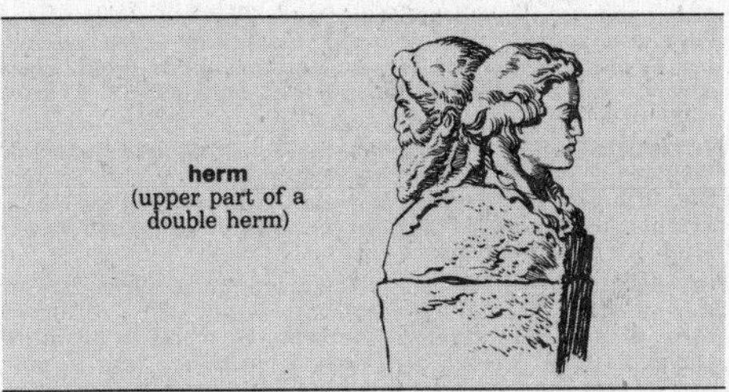
herm
(upper part of a double herm)

her•ma (hûr′mə), *n., pl.* **-mae** (-mē), **-mai** (-mī). herm. **—her•mae•an** (hər mē′ən), *adj.*

Her•man (hûr′mən), *n.* **1. Woodrow** (*"Woody"*), 1913–87, U.S. jazz saxophonist, clarinetist, and bandleader. **2.** a male given name: from Old English words meaning "army" and " man."

Her′mann-Mau•guin′ sym′bol (hûr′mən mō gan′, her′män-), *Crystall.* a notation for indicating a particular point group. [after Carl *Hermann* (1898–1961), German crystallographer and Charles *Mauguin* (1878–1937), French crystallographer]

her•maph•ro•dite (hûr maf′rə dīt′), *n.* **1.** an individual in which reproductive organs of both sexes are present. Cf. **pseudohermaphrodite. 2.** *Biol.* an organism, as an earthworm or plant, having normally both the male and female organs of generation. **3.** a person or thing in which two opposite qualities are combined. *—adj.* **4.** of, pertaining to, or characteristic of a hermaphrodite. **5.** combining two opposite qualities. **6.** *Bot.* monoclinous. [1350–1400; ME *hermofrodite* < L *hermaphrodītus* < Gk *hermaphróditos* hemaphrodite, name of the son of Hermes and Aphrodite] **—her•maph•ro•dit•ic** (hûr maf′rə dit′ik), **her•maph′ro•dit′i•cal, her•maph•ro•dit•ish** (hûr maf′rə dī′tish), *adj.* **—her•maph′ro•dit′i•cal•ly,** *adv.*

hermaph′rodite brig′, a two-masted sailing vessel, square-rigged on the foremast and fore-and-aft-rigged on the mainmast. Also called **brigantine.** [1830–40]

hermaphrodite brig

her•maph•ro•dit•ism (hûr maf′rə dī tiz′əm), *n.* the condition of being a hermaphrodite. Also, **her•maph•ro•dism** (hûr maf′rə diz′əm). [1800–10; HERMAPHRODITE + -ISM]

her•ma•type (hûr′mə tīp′), *n.* reef-building coral. [1975–80; < Gk *hérma* reef + -TYPE] **—her•ma•typ•ic** (hûr′mə tip′ik), *adj.*

her•me•neu•tic (hûr′mə nōō′tik, -nyōō′-), *adj.* of or pertaining to hermeneutics; interpretative; explanatory. Also, **her′me•neu′ti•cal.** [1800–10; < Gk *hermēneutikós* of, skilled in, interpreting, equiv. to *hermēneú(ein)* to make clear, interpret (deriv. of *hermēneús* an interpreter, itself deriv. of *Hermês* HERMES) + *-tikos* -TIC] **—her′me•neu′ti•cal•ly,** *adv.*

her•me•neu•tics (hûr′mə nōō′tiks, -nyōō′-), *n.* (*used with a singular v.*) **1.** the science of interpretation, esp. of the Scriptures. **2.** the branch of theology that deals with the principles of Biblical exegesis. [1730–40; see HERMENEUTIC, -ICS]

Her•mes (hûr′mēz), *n.* **1.** the ancient Greek herald and messenger of the gods and the god of roads, commerce, invention, cunning, and theft. Cf. **Mercury. 2.** *Astron.* a small asteroid that in 1937 approached within 485,000 mi. (780,000 km) of the earth, the closest approach of an asteroid ever observed.

Her′mes Trismegis′tus, a name variously ascribed by Neoplatonists and others to an Egyptian priest or to the Egyptian god Thoth, to some extent identified with the Grecian Hermes: various mystical, religious, philosophical, astrological, and alchemical writings were ascribed to him. [< ML < Gk *Hermês Trismégistos* Hermes thrice greatest]

her•met•ic (hûr met′ik), *adj.* **1.** made airtight by fusion or sealing. **2.** not affected by outward influence or power; isolated. **3.** (*sometimes cap.*) of, pertaining to, or characteristic of occult science, esp. alchemy. **4.** (*cap.*) of or pertaining to Hermes Trismegistus or the writings ascribed to him. Also, **her•met′i•cal.** [1630–40; < ML *hermēticus* of, pertaining to Hermes Trismegistus, equiv. to L *Hermē(s)* HERMES + *-ticus* -TIC]

her•met•i•cal•ly (hûr met′ik lē), *adv.* so as to be airtight: *hermetically sealed.* [1595–1605; HERMETIC + -ALLY]

Her•met•i•cism (hûr met′ə siz′əm), *n.* (*sometimes l.c.*). **1.** the body of ideas set forth in Hermetic writings. **2.** adherence to the ideas expressed in Hermetic writings. **3.** the occult sciences, esp. alchemy. Also, **Her•me•tism.** (hûr′mi tiz′əm). [1890–95; HERMETIC + -ISM] **—Her•met′i•cist,** *adj., n.*

Her•mi•o•ne (hûr mī′ə nē′), *n.* **1.** the daughter of Menelaus and Helen. **2.** a female given name.

her•mit (hûr′mit), *n.* **1.** a person who has withdrawn to a solitary place for a life of religious seclusion. **2.** any person living in seclusion; recluse. **3.** *Zool.* an animal of solitary habits. **4.** *Ornith.* any of numerous hummingbirds of the genera *Glaucis* and *Phaethornis,* having curved bills and dull-colored rather than iridescent plumage. **5.** a spiced molasses cookie often containing raisins or nuts. **6.** *Obs.* a beadsman. [1175–1225; ME *ermite, hermite, heremite* < OF < LL *erēmīta* < Gk *erēmī́tēs* living in a desert, equiv. to *erēm(ia)* desert (deriv. of *erêmos* desolate) + *-ītēs* -ITE[1]] **—her•mit′ic, her•mit′i•cal, her′mit•ish,** *adj.* **—her•mit′i•cal•ly,** *adv.* **—her′mit•like′,** *adj.* **—her′mit•ry, her′mit•ship′,** *n.*
—Syn. 1. eremite, monastic, anchorite, cenobite.

her•mit•age (hûr′mi tij *or, for 3,* er′mi täzh′), *n.* **1.** the habitation of a hermit. **2.** any secluded place of residence or habitation; retreat; hideaway. **3.** (*cap.*) a palace in Leningrad built by Catherine II and now used as an art museum. [1250–1300; ME < OF. See HERMIT, -AGE]

her′mit crab′, any of numerous crabs, esp. of the genera *Pagurus* and *Eupagurus,* that protect their soft uncovered abdomen by occupying the castoff shell of a univalve mollusk. [1725–35]

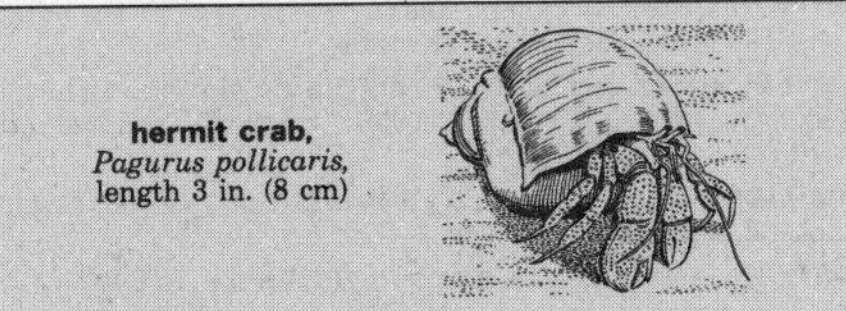
hermit crab,
Pagurus pollicaris,
length 3 in. (8 cm)

Her•mite (hər mēt′; *Fr.* ᴇʀ mēt′), *n.* **Charles** (sʜᴀʀl), 1822–1901, French mathematician.

Her•mi′tian con′jugate (hər mē′shən), *Math.* adjoint (def. 2). [1960–65; after C. HERMITE; see -IAN]

Hermi′tian ma′trix, *Math.* a matrix, whose entries are complex numbers, equal to the transpose of the matrix whose entries are the conjugates of the entries of the given matrix. [1925–30; after C. HERMITE; see -IAN]

Her′mit King′dom, Korea during the period, c1637–c1876, when it was cut off from contact with all countries except China.

Hermit of St. Augustine, *Rom. Cath. Ch.* a member of an order of mendicant friars, founded in 1256. [1700–10]

her′mit thrush′, a North American thrush, *Hylocichla guttata,* noted for its complex and appealing song. [1805–15, *Amer.*]

Her•mod (her′mōōd, -mŏŏd), *n. Scand. Myth.* a son of Odin who rode to Hel to negotiate for the return of Balder to Asgard.

Her•mon (hûr′mən), *n.* **Mount,** a mountain in SW Syria, in the Anti-Lebanon range. 9232 ft. (2814 m).

Her•mo′sa Beach′ (hər mō′sə), a city in SW California, near Los Angeles. 18,070.

Her•mo•si•llo (ᴇʀ′mô sē′yô), *n.* a city in and the capital of Sonora, in NW Mexico. 281,300.

hern[1] (hûrn), *n. Dial.* heron.

hern[2] (hûrn, hûr′ən), *pron. Nonstandard.* hers (def. 2). Also, **her'n.** [ME *hiren;* by assoc. with *my, mine, thy, thine,* etc.]

Her•nán•dez (ᴇʀ nän′des), *n.* **Jo•sé** (hô se′), 1834–86, Argentine poet.

Hern•don (hûrn′dən), *n.* **William Henry, 1.** 1818–91, U.S. law partner and biographer of Abraham Lincoln. **2.** a town in NE Virginia. 11,449.

Herne (hûrn), *n.* **1. James A(hern)** (ə hûrn′), 1839–1901, U.S. actor and playwright. **2.** a city in W Germany, in the Ruhr region. 174,200.

her•ni•a (hûr′nē ə), *n., pl.* **-ni•as, -ni•ae** (-nē ē′). *Pathol.* the protrusion of an organ or tissue through an opening in its surrounding walls, esp. in the abdominal region. Cf. **hiatus hernia, strangulated hernia.** [1350–1400; ME < L: a rupture; akin to *hīra* gut; see HARUSPEX] **—her′ni•al,** *adj.*

her•ni•ate (hûr′nē āt′), *v.i.,* **-at•ed, -at•ing.** to protrude abnormally from an enclosed cavity or from the body so as to constitute a hernia. [1875–80; HERNI(A) + -ATE[1]] **—her′ni•a′tion,** *n.*

her′niated disk′, *Pathol.* an abnormal protrusion of a spinal disk between vertebrae, most often in the lumbar region of the spine, causing pain due to pressure on spinal nerves. Also called **ruptured disk, slipped disk.**

hernio-, a combining form representing **hernia** in compound words: *herniotomy.*

her•ni•o•plas•ty (hûr′nē ə plas′tē), *n., pl.* **-ties.** *Surg.* an operation for the repair of a hernia. [HERNIO- + -PLASTY]

her•ni•or•rha•phy (hûr′nē ôr′ə fē, -or′-), *n., pl.* **-phies.** *Surg.* correction of a hernia by a suturing procedure. [1915–20; HERNIO- + -RRHAPHY]

her•ni•ot•o•my (hûr′nē ot′ə mē), *n., pl.* **-mies.** *Surg.* correction of a hernia by a cutting procedure. [1805–15; HERNIO- + -TOMY]

hern•shaw (hûrn′shô), *n. Brit. Dial.* a heron. [1555–65; var. of dial. *heronsew,* ME < MF *heronceau, heroncel,* dim. of *heron* HERON]

he•ro (hēr′ō), *n., pl.* **-roes;** for 5 also **-ros. 1.** a man of distinguished courage or ability, admired for his brave deeds and noble qualities. **2.** a person who, in the opinion of others, has heroic qualities or has performed a heroic act and is regarded as a model or ideal: *He was a local hero when he saved the drowning child.* **3.** the principal male character in a story, play, film, etc. **4.** *Class. Myth.* **a.** a being of godlike prowess and beneficence who often came to be honored as a divinity. **b.** (in the Homeric period) a warrior-chieftain of special strength, courage, or ability. **c.** (in later antiquity) an immortal being; demigod. **5.** See **hero sandwich. 6.** the bread or roll used in making a hero sandwich. [1605–15; back formation from ME *heroes* (pl.) < L *hērōs* (sing.), *hērōes* (pl.) < Gk *hḗrōs, hḗrōes*] **—he′ro•like′,** *adj.*
—Syn. 3. lead, star. **—Ant. 3.** villain, heavy.

He•ro (hēr′ō), *n.* **1.** *Class. Myth.* a priestess of Aphrodite who drowned herself after her lover Leander drowned while swimming the Hellespont to visit her. **2.** Also, **Heron.** (*Hero of Alexandria*) fl. 1st century A.D., Greek scientist.

Her•od (her′əd), *n.* (*"the Great"*) 73?–4 B.C., king of Judea 37–4.

Her′od A•grip′pa (ə grip′ə), (*Julius Agrippa*) c10 B.C.–A.D. 44, king of Judea 41–44 (grandson of Herod the Great).

Her′od An′ti•pas (an′ti pas′), died after A.D. 39, ruler of Galilee, A.D. 4–39: ordered the execution of John the Baptist and participated in the trial of Jesus.

He•ro•di•an (hə rō′dē ən), *adj.* **1.** of or pertaining to Herod the Great, his family, or its partisans. *—n.* **2.** a partisan of the house of Herod. **3.** a member of a political group that supported the dynasty of Herod and opposed Jesus. [< LL (Vulgate) *Hērōdiānī* (pl.); see HEROD, -IAN]

He•ro•di•as (hə rō′dē əs), *n.* the second wife of Herod Antipas and the mother of Salome: she told Salome to ask Herod for the head of John the Baptist.

He•rod•o•tus (hə rod′ə təs), *n.* 484?–425? B.C., Greek historian.

he•ro•ic (hi rō′ik), *adj.* Also, **he•ro′i•cal. 1.** of, pertaining to, or characteristic of a hero or heroine. **2.** suitable to the character of a hero in size or concept; daring; noble: *a heroic ambition.* **3.** having or displaying the character or attributes of a hero; extraordinarily bold, altruistic, determined, etc.: *a heroic explorer.* **4.** having or involving recourse to boldness, daring, or extreme measures: *Heroic measures were taken to save his life.* **5.** dealing with or describing the deeds, attributes, etc., of heroes, as in literature. **6.** of, pertaining to, or characteristic of the heroes of antiquity: *heroic mythology.* **7.** used in heroic poetry. Cf. **heroic verse. 8.** resembling heroic poetry in language or style; grandiloquent. **9.** (of style or language) lofty; extravagant; grand. **10.** larger than life-size: *a statue of heroic proportions.* *—n.* **11.** Usually, **heroics.** See **heroic verse. 12. heroics, a.** flamboyant or extravagant language, sentiment, or behavior, intended to seem heroic. **b.** heroic action or behavior. [1540–50; < L *hērōicus* < Gk *hērōïkós* of, pertaining to a hero; cf. late ME *heroical, heroicus;* see HERO, -IC] **—he•ro′i•cal•ly,** *adv.* **—he•ro′i•cal•ness, he•ro′ic•ness, he•ro•ic•i•ty** (hēr′ō is′i tē), *n.*
—Syn. 2, 3. dauntless, valiant, valorous, gallant, brave, courageous. **8.** epic. **—Ant. 1–3.** cowardly.

hero′ic age′, 1. one of the five periods in human history, when, according to Hesiod, gods and demigods performed heroic and glorious deeds. **2.** any period in the history of a nation, esp. in ancient Greece and Rome, when great heroes of legend lived: *Achilles, Agamemnon, and others of Greece's heroic age.* [1825–35]

hero′ic cou′plet, *Pros.* a stanza consisting of two rhyming lines in iambic pentameter, esp. one forming a rhetorical unit and written in an elevated style, as, *Know then thyself, presume not God to scan / The proper study of Mankind is Man.* [1900–05]

hero′ic dra′ma, Restoration tragedy, esp. that popular in England c1660–1700, using highly rhetorical language and written in heroic couplets.

he•ro•i•cize (hi rō′ə sīz′), *v.t.,* **-cized, -ciz•ing.** heroize. Also, *esp. Brit.,* **he•ro′i•cise′.** [HEROIC + -IZE]

he•ro•i•com•ic (hi rō′i kom′ik), *adj.* blending heroic and comic elements: *a heroicomic poem.* Also, **he•ro′i•com′i•cal.** [1705–15; HEROI(C) + COMIC]

hero′ic po′em, a poem written in an epic style using lines of iambic pentameter. [1685–95]

hero′ic quat′rain, *Pros.* a poetic stanza consisting of four lines of iambic pentameter rhyming alternately. Also called **elegiac quatrain.**

hero′ic stan′za. See **elegiac stanza.** [1920–25]

hero′ic ten′or, *Music.* heldentenor.

hero′ic verse′, a form of verse adapted to the treatment of heroic or exalted themes: in classical poetry, dactylic hexameter; in English and German, iambic pen

CONCISE PRONUNCIATION KEY: act, cāpe, dâre, pärt; set, ēqual; if, īce; ox, ōver, ôrder, oil, bŏŏk, bōōt, out; up, ûrge; child; sing; shoe; thin, *th*at; zh as in *treasure.* ə = *a* as in *alone, e* as in *system, i* as in *easily, o* as in *gallop, u* as in *circus;* ᵊ as in *fire* (fīᵊr), *hour* (ouᵊr). l and n can serve as syllabic consonants, as in *cradle* (krād′l), and *button* (but′n). See the full key inside the front cover.

tameter; and in French, the Alexandrine. An example of heroic verse is *Achilles' wrath, to Greece the direful spring / Of woes unnumbered, heavenly goddess, sing!* [1610–20]

her•o•in (her′ō in), *n. Pharm.* a white, crystalline, narcotic powder, $C_{21}H_{23}NO_5$, derived from morphine, formerly used as an analgesic and sedative: manufacture and importation of heroin are now controlled by federal law in the U.S. because of the danger of addiction. Also called **diacetylmorphine, diamorphine.** [1895–1900; formerly trademark; < G *Heroin* < Gk *hērō-*, s. of *hḗrōs* HERO + G *-in* -IN[2]; allegedly so called from the feelings of power and euphoria which it stimulates]

her•o•ine (her′ō in), *n.* **1.** a woman of distinguished courage or ability, admired for her brave deeds and noble qualities. **2.** the principal female character in a story, play, film, etc. [1650–60; < L *hērōinē* < Gk *hērōínē*, fem. of *hḗrōs* HERO; see -INE[2]]

her•o•ism (her′ō iz′əm), *n.* **1.** the qualities or attributes of a hero or heroine: *He showed great heroism in battle.* **2.** heroic conduct; courageous action: *Pat's returning into the burning building was true heroism.* [1660–70; HERO + -ISM; cf. F *héroïsme*]
—Syn. 1. intrepidity, valor, prowess, gallantry, bravery, courage, daring, fortitude. **—Ant. 1.** cowardice, timidity.

he•ro•ize (hēr′ō īz′), *v.t.*, **-ized, -iz•ing.** to make a hero of: *a war film that heroizes the warrior.* Also, **heroicize;** *esp. Brit.,* **he′ro•ise′.** [1730–40; HERO + -IZE] **—he′ro•iz•a′tion,** *n.*

Hé•rold (ā rôld′), *n.* **Louis Joseph** (lwē zhô zef′), 1791–1833, French composer.

her•on (her′ən), *n.* any of numerous long-legged, long-necked, usually long-billed birds of the family Ardeidae, including the true herons, egrets, night herons, and bitterns. [1275–1325; ME *heiro(u)n, hero(u)n* < MF *hairon* (F *héron*) < Gmc; cf. OHG *heigir*]

great blue heron, *Ardea herodias,* height 4 to 5 ft. (1.2 to 1.5 m); length 4¼ ft. (1.3 m)

He•ron (hē′ron), *n.* Hero (def. 2).

her•on•ry (her′ən rē), *n., pl.* **-ries.** a place where a colony of herons breeds. [1610–20; HERON + -RY]

her•on's-bill (her′ənz bil′), *n.* stork's-bill (def. 1). [1570–80]

he′ro sand′wich, a large sandwich, usually consisting of a small loaf of bread or long roll cut in half lengthwise and containing a variety of ingredients, as meat, cheese, lettuce, and tomatoes. Also called **hero.** [1950–55, *Amer.*]
—Regional Variation. The terms HERO SANDWICH and HERO, once largely associated with the New York City and Northern New Jersey area, are now too widely spread to warrant a specific regional label. This same sandwich is also called a SUBMARINE or a SUB, esp. in the Northeastern and North Midland U.S., although this use has spread south along the Atlantic coast and as far west as Los Angeles. TORPEDO, though less common, has also spread to various regions.
The sandwich is called a GRINDER, chiefly in New England and the Inland North, though this use has spread to the South and West. SPUKY is restricted to the Boston area, while WEDGE is a common synonym in Rhode Island and coastal Connecticut. HOAGY (or HOAGIE) is used chiefly in New Jersey and Pennsylvania, esp. Philadelphia, though it too has spread to other regions.
POOR BOY is chiefly New Orleans use, originally referring to a somewhat different sandwich in which distinct sections of fillings represented the courses of a meal. CUBAN SANDWICH, usually referring to a grilled sandwich with ham, pork, cheese, etc., is chiefly used in Southern Florida as well as the New York City area.

He′ro's for′mula (hēr′ōz), *Geom.* the formula for the area of a triangle when the sides are given: for a triangle with sides *a, b,* and *c,* the area is equal to $\sqrt{s(s-a)(s-b)(s-c)}$, where *s* is equal to one half the perimeter of the triangle. [named after HERO of Alexandria]

he′ro wor′ship, 1. a profound reverence for great people or their memory. **2.** extravagant or excessive admiration for a personal hero. [1765–75]

he•ro-wor•ship (hēr′ō wûr′ship), *v.t.*, **-shiped, -ship•ing** or (*esp. Brit.*) **-shipped, -ship•ping.** to feel or express hero worship for. [1880–85] **—he′ro-wor′ship•er,** *n.*

herp., herpetology. Also, **herpet.**

her•pan•gi•na (hûr′pan jī′nə, hər pan′jə nə), *n. Pathol.* an infectious disease, esp. of children, characterized by a sudden occurrence of fever, loss of appetite, and throat ulcerations, caused by a Coxsackie virus. [HERP(ES) + ANGINA]

her•pes (hûr′pēz), *n. Pathol.* **1.** any of several diseases caused by herpesvirus, characterized by eruption of blisters on the skin or mucous membranes. Cf. **chickenpox, genital herpes, oral herpes, shingles. 2.** herpesvirus. [1375–1425; late ME < NL: cutaneous eruption < Gk *hérpēs,* lit., a creeping (akin to *hérpein* to creep, spread); c. L *serpēns* SERPENT]

her′pes gen•i•ta′lis (jen′i tā′lis). See **genital herpes.** [1905–10; < NL: genital herpes]

her′pes la•bi•a′lis (lā′bē ā′lis). See **oral herpes.** [1805–15; < NL: labial herpes]

her′pes sim′plex (sim′pleks), either of two herpes diseases caused by a herpesvirus that infects humans and some other animals and produces small, transient blisters on the skin or mucous membranes, one type of virus (**herpes simplex virus type 1,** or **HSV-1**) usually associated with oral herpes but also causing genital herpes and the other (**herpes simplex virus type 2,** or **HSV-2**) usually causing genital herpes. [1905–10; < NL: lit., simple herpes]

her•pes•vi•rus (hûr′pēz vī′rəs), *n., pl.* **-rus•es.** a DNA-containing virus of the family Herpesviridae, certain members of which cause such diseases in humans as oral and genital herpes, infectious mononucleosis, chickenpox, and shingles. Cf. **herpes simplex, varicella-zoster virus, Epstein-Barr virus, cytomegalovirus.** [1920–25; < NL; see HERPES, VIRUS]

her′pes zos′ter (zos′tər), *Pathol.* shingles. [1800–10; < NL: lit., belt herpes]

her′pes zos′ter vi′rus. See **varicella zoster virus.**

her•pet•ic (hər pet′ik), *adj. Pathol.* of, pertaining to, or caused by herpes. [1775–85; < Gk *herpēt-*, s. of *hérpēs* (see HERPES) + -IC]

herpetol., 1. herpetology. **2.** herpetological.

her•pe•tol•o•gy (hûr′pi tol′ə jē), *n.* the branch of zoology dealing with reptiles and amphibians. [1815–25; < Gk *herpetó(n)* a creeping thing (cf. *hérpein* to creep) + -LOGY; cf. SERPENT] **—her•pe•to•log•ic** (hûr′pi tl oj′ik), **her′pe•to•log′i•cal,** *adj.* **—her′pe•to•log′i•cal•ly,** *adv.* **—her′pe•tol′o•gist,** *n.*

Herr (heʀ; *Eng.* hâr), *n., pl.* **Her•ren** (heʀ′ən; *Eng.* hâr′ən). the conventional German title of respect and term of address for a man, corresponding to *Mr.* or in direct address to *sir.* [< G]

Her•ren•volk (heʀ′ən fôlk′), *n., pl.* ***-völ•ker*** (-fœl′kəʀ). *German.* See **master race.**

Her•re•ra (eʀ ʀe′ʀä), *n.* **Fran•cis•co de** (fʀän thēs′kô the), (*"el Viejo"*), 1576–1656, Spanish painter and etcher.

Her•rick (her′ik), *n.* **1. Robert,** 1591–1674, English poet. **2. Robert,** 1868–1938, U.S. novelist.

Her•rin (her′in), *n.* a town in S Illinois. 10,040.

her•ring (her′ing), *n., pl.* (*esp. collectively*) **-ring,** (*esp. referring to two or more kinds or species*) **-rings. 1.** an important food fish, *Clupea harengus harengus,* found in enormous shoals in the North Atlantic. **2.** a similar fish, *Clupea harengus pallasii,* of the North Pacific. **3.** any fish of the family Clupeidae, including herrings, shads, and sardines. **4.** any of various fishes resembling the herring but of unrelated families. [bef. 900; ME *hering,* OE *hǣring;* c. G *Häring*] **—her′ring•like′,** *adj.*

herringbone (def. 1)

her•ring•bone (her′ing bōn′), *n.* **1.** a pattern consisting of adjoining vertical rows of slanting lines, any two contiguous lines forming either a V or an inverted V, used in masonry, textiles, etc. **2.** *Textiles.* **a.** Also called **chevron, chevron weave, her′ringbone weave′.** a type of twill weave having this pattern. **b.** a fabric constructed with this weave. **c.** a garment made from such a fabric, esp. a suit. **3.** *Skiing.* a method of going up a slope in which a skier sets the skis in a form resembling a V, and, placing weight on the inside edges, advances the skis by turns using the poles from behind for push and support. *—adj.* **4.** having or resembling herringbone: *herringbone tweed.* [1645–55; HERRING + BONE]

her′ringbone bond′, a brickwork bond in which the exposed brickwork is bonded to the heart of the wall by concealed courses of bricks laid diagonally to the faces of the wall in a herringbone pattern, with the end of each brick butting against the side of the adjoining brick.

her′ringbone bridg′ing, *Carpentry.* See **cross bridging.** Also called **her′ringbone strut′ting.**

her′ringbone gear′, a helical gear having teeth that lie on the pitch cylinder in a V-shaped form so that one half of each tooth is on a right-handed helix and the other half on a left-handed helix. Also called **double-helical gear.**

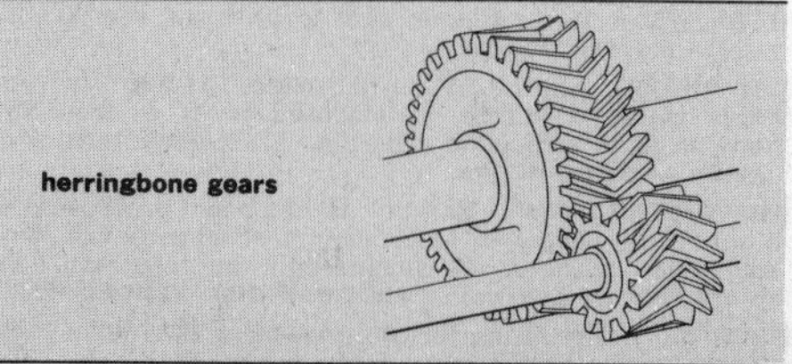
herringbone gears

her′ringbone stitch′, a type of cross-stitch in embroidery similar to the catch stitch in sewing, consisting of an overlapped V-shaped stitch that when worked in a continuous pattern produces a twill-weave effect.

her•ring•chok•er (her′ing chō′kər), *n. Canadian Slang.* a native or resident of any of the Maritime Provinces but especially of New Brunswick. [1895–1900; HERRING + CHOKER]

her′ring gull′, a common, large gull, *Larus argentatus,* of the Northern Hemisphere. See illus. under **gull.** [1820–30, *Amer.*]

Her•ri•ot (e ʀyō′), *n.* **É•douard** (ā dwaʀ′), 1872–1957, French statesman, political leader, and author.

Herr•mann (hûr′mən), *n.* **Bernard,** 1911–75, U.S. conductor and composer.

Herrn•hut•er (hârn′hōō′tər, hern′-), *n.* Moravian (def. 4). [< G, equiv. to *Herrnhut* lit., Lord's safekeeping, a town near Dresden, Germany + *-er* -ER[1]]

her•ry (her′ē), *v.t., v.i.,* **-ried, -ry•ing.** *Scot.* harry. **—her′ry•ment,** *n.*

hers (hûrz), *pron.* **1.** a form of the possessive case of **she** used as a predicate adjective: *The red umbrella is hers. Are you a friend of hers?* **2.** that or those belonging to her: *Hers is the biggest garden on the block. Hers are the yellow ones.* [1300–50; ME *hirs,* equiv. to *hire* HER + -S 'S[1]]

Her•schel (hûr′shəl, hâr′-), *n.* **1. Sir John Frederick William,** 1792–1871, English astronomer. **2.** his father, **Sir William** (Friedrich Wilhelm Herschel), 1738–1822, English astronomer, born in Germany. **3.** Also, **Her′•shel.** a male given name.

her•self (hər self′), *pron.* **1.** an emphatic appositive of **her** or **she:** *She herself wrote the letter.* **2.** a reflexive form of **her:** *She supports herself.* **3.** (used in absolute constructions): *Herself still only a child, she had to take care of her four younger brothers.* **4.** (used as the object of a preposition or as the direct or indirect object of a verb): *She gave herself a facial massage. He asked her for a picture of herself.* **5.** (used in comparisons after *as* or *than*): *She found out that the others were even more nervous than herself.* **6.** her normal or customary self: *After a few weeks of rest, she will be herself again.* [bef. 1000; ME *hire-selfe,* OE *hire self.* See HER, SELF]
—Usage. See **myself.**

Her•sey (hûr′sē, -zē), *n.* **John Richard,** 1914–93, U.S. journalist, novelist, and educator.

Her•shey (hûr′shē), *n.* **1. Alfred Day,** born 1908, U.S. biologist: helped lay the foundation of modern molecular genetics; Nobel prize for medicine 1969. **2. Lewis B(laine),** 1893–1977, U.S. Army general: director of the Selective Service System 1941–70. **3. Milton Snave•ly** (snāv′lē), 1857–1945, U.S. businessman: founder of chocolate manufacturing company. **4.** a town in central Pennsylvania. 13,249.

Her•sko•witz (hûr′skə vits), *n.* **Melville (Jean),** 1895–1963, American anthropologist.

her•sto•ry (hûr′stə rē, hûrs′trē), *n., pl.* **-ries.** history (used esp. in feminist literature and in women's studies as an alternative form to distinguish or emphasize the particular experience of women). [1975–80]

Her•ter (hûr′tər), *n.* **Christian Archibald,** 1895–1966, U.S. politician: Secretary of State 1959–61.

Hert•ford (här′fərd, härt′fərd), *n.* **1.** a city in and the county seat of Hertfordshire, in SE England. 20,379. **2.** Hertfordshire.

Hert•ford•shire (här′fərd shēr′, -shər, härt′-), *n.* a county in SE England. 938,100; 631 sq. mi. (1635 sq. km). Also called **Hertford, Herts** (härts, hûrts).

Her•to•gen•bosch, 's (*Du.* seʀ′tō ᴋʜən bôs′). See **'s Hertogenbosch.**

hertz (hûrts), *n., pl.* **hertz, hertz•es.** the SI unit of frequency, equal to one cycle per second. *Abbr.:* Hz [1925–30; named after H. R. HERTZ]

Hertz (hûrts, hârts; *Ger.* herts), *n.* **1. Gu•stav** (gōōs′täf), 1887–1975, German physicist: Nobel prize 1925. **2. Hein•rich Ru•dolph** (hīn′ʀɪᴋʜ ʀōō′dôlf), 1857–94, German physicist. **—Hertz•i•an** (hûrt′sē ən, hârt′-), *adj.*

Hertz′ effect′, *Physics.* the effect of ultraviolet radiation in lowering the sparking voltage across a spark gap: an example of photoelectric effect. [after H. R. HERTZ]

Hertz′ian wave′, *Physics.* an electromagnetic wave produced by oscillations in an electric circuit, as a radio wave: first investigated by H. R. Hertz. [1895–1900]

Her•tzog (*Du.* heʀ′tsôᴋʜ), *n.* **James Barry Mun•nik** (mœn′ək), South African statesman and general: prime minister 1924–39.

Hertz′sprung-Rus′sell di′agram (hârt′sprŏŏng-rus′əl), *Astron.* the graph showing the absolute magnitude plotted against the surface temperature for a group of stars. Also called **H-R diagram.** [after Danish astronomer Ejnar *Hertzsprung* (1873–1967) and H. N. RUSSELL, who compiled the data on which it is based]

Herz•berg (hûrts′bûrg), *n.* **Ger•hard** (gâr′härd, -härt), born 1904, Canadian physicist, born in Germany: Nobel prize for chemistry 1971.

Her•ze•go•vi•na (her′tsə gō vē′nə), *n.* a historic region in SE Europe: a former Turkish province; a part of Austria-Hungary 1878–1914; now part of Bosnia and Herzegovina. Serbo-Croatian, **Hercegovina. —Her′ze•go•vi′ni•an,** *adj., n.*

Her•zl (her′tsəl; *Eng.* hûrt′səl, hârt′-), *n.* **The•o•dor** (tā′ô dôʀ′), 1860–1904, Hungarian-born Austrian Jewish writer and journalist: founder of the political Zionist movement.

Her•zog (hûrt′sog, hûr′zog; *Fr.* eʀ zôg′ *for* 2), *n.* **1. Cha•im** (ᴋʜī′im), born 1918, Israeli political leader: president since 1983. **2. Maurice,** born 1919, French mountaineer: climbed Annapurna 1950.

he's (hēz; *unstressed* ēz), **1.** contraction of *he is.* **2.** contraction of *he has.*
—Usage. See **contraction.**

CONCISE ETYMOLOGY KEY: <, descended or borrowed from; >, whence; b., blend of, blended; c., cognate with; cf., compare; deriv., derivative; equiv., equivalent; imit., imitative; obl., oblique; r., replacing; s., stem; sp., spelling, spelled; resp., respelling, respelled; trans., translation; ?, origin unknown; *, unattested; ‡, probably earlier than. See the full key inside the front cover.

he/she (hē′shē′), a combined form used as a singular nominative pronoun to denote a person of either sex: *Each student may begin when he/she is ready.* [1975–80] —**Usage.** See **he**[1].

Hesh·van (hesh′vən, -vän, ᴋʜesh′-), *n.* the second month of the Jewish calendar. Also, **Cheshvan.** Also called **Marheshvan, Marcheshvan.** Cf. **Jewish calendar.** [1825–35; < Heb (*mar*)*ḥeshwān*]

He·si·od (hē′sē əd, hes′ē-), *n.* fl. 8th century B.C., Greek poet. —**He·si·od·ic** (hē′sē od′ik, hes′ē-), *adj.*

hes·i·tan·cy (hez′i tən sē), *n., pl.* **-cies.** hesitation; indecision or disinclination. Also, **hes′i·tance.** [1610–20; < L *haesitantia.* See HESITANT, -ANCY]

hes·i·tant (hez′i tənt), *adj.* **1.** hesitating; undecided, doubtful, or disinclined. **2.** lacking readiness of speech. [1640–50; < L *haesitant-* (s. of *haesitāns*), prp. of *haesitāre* to falter, hesitate, equiv. to *haes*(*us*), ptp. of *haerēre* to stick, hold fast + *-it-* freq. suffix + *-ant-* -ANT] —**hes′i·tant·ly,** *adv.*

hes·i·tate (hez′i tāt′), *v.i.,* **-tat·ed, -tat·ing. 1.** to be reluctant or wait to act because of fear, indecision, or disinclination: *She hesitated to take the job.* **2.** to have scruples or doubts; be unwilling: *He hesitated to break the law.* **3.** to pause: *I hesitated before reciting the next line.* **4.** to falter in speech; stammer: *Embarrassment caused the speaker to hesitate.* [1615–25; < L *haesitātus,* ptp. of *haesitāre.* See HESITANT, -ATE[1]] —**hes′i·tat′er, hes′i·ta′tor,** *n.* —**hes′i·tat′ing·ly,** *adv.*
—**Syn. 1.** waver, vacillate, falter. **3.** demur, delay.
—**Ant. 1.** decide. **3.** hasten.

hes·i·ta·tion (hez′i tā′shən), *n.* **1.** the act of hesitating; a delay due to uncertainty of mind or fear: *His hesitation cost him the championship.* **2.** a state of doubt or uncertainty. **3.** a halting or faltering in speech. [1615–25; < L *haesitātiōn-* (s. of *haesitātiō*). See HESITATE, -ION]
—**Syn. 2.** hesitancy, indecision, irresolution, vacillation. **3.** stammer.

hes′ita′tion waltz′, a waltz based on the frequent use of a step that consists of a pause and glide. [1910–15]

hes·i·ta·tive (hez′i tā′tiv), *adj.* characterized by hesitation; hesitating. [1785–95; HESITATE + -IVE] —**hes′i·ta′tive·ly,** *adv.*

Hes·per (hes′pər), *n.* Hesperus.

Hes·per·e (hes′pə rē′), *n. Class. Myth.* one of the Hesperides.

Hes·pe·ri·an (he spēr′ē ən), *adj.* **1.** western; occidental. **2.** of or pertaining to the Hesperides. —*n.* **3.** a native or inhabitant of a western land. [1540–50; < L *Hesperi*(*us*) of, toward the West (< Gk *hespérios* western, deriv. of *hésperos* evening, HESPERUS) + -AN]

Hes·per·i·des (he sper′i dēz′), *n.* **1.** *Class. Myth.* **a.** (*used with a plural v.*) nymphs, variously given as three to seven in number, who guarded with the dragon Ladon the golden apples that were the wedding gift of Gaea to Hera. **b.** (*used with a singular v.*) the garden where the golden apples were grown. **c.** (*used with a plural v.*) See **Islands of the Blessed. 2.** (*italics*) (*used with a plural v.*) a collection of poems (1648) by Robert Herrick. [see HESPERUS, -IDES] —**Hes·per·id·i·an** (hes′pə rid′ē ən), *adj.*

hes·per·i·din (he sper′i din), *n. Biochem.* a crystallizable, bioflavinoid glycoside, $C_{28}H_{34}O_{15}$, occurring in most citrus fruits, esp. in the spongy envelope of oranges and lemons. [1830–40; < NL; see HESPERIDES, -IN[2]]

hes·per·id·i·um (hes′pə rid′ē əm), *n., pl.* **-per·id·i·a** (-pə rid′ē ə). *Bot.* the fruit of a citrus plant, as an orange. [1865–70; < NL; see HESPERIDIN, -IUM] —**hes·per·i·date** (he sper′i dāt′), **hes′per·id′e·ous,** *adj.*

hes·per·i·nos (es pe′Rē nôs′; *Eng.* hes′pər ə nos′, hes′pər ə nos′), *n. Gk. Orth. Ch.* vespers (def. 1). [< LGk, Gk *hesperinós* pertaining to evening, equiv. to *hésper*(*os*) evening (see HESPERUS) + *-inos* -INE[1]]

hes·per·or·nis (hes′pə rôr′nis), *n.* a toothed aquatic bird of the extinct genus *Hesperornis,* fossils of which are found in rocks of Cretaceous age in Kansas, having the rear legs modified for swimming and reaching a length of more than 4 ft. (1.2 m). [< NL (1872) < Gk *Hésper*(*os*) HESPERUS + *órnis* bird]

Hes·per·us (hes′pər əs), *n.* an evening star, esp. Venus. Also, **Hesper.** [1350–1400; ME < L < Gk *hésperos* evening, western; akin to WEST, L *vesper* VESPER]

Hess (hes), *n.* **1. Dame Myra,** 1890–1965, English pianist. **2. Victor Francis,** 1883–1964, U.S. physicist, born in Austria: Nobel prize 1936. **3. Walter Rudolf,** 1881–1973, Swiss physiologist: Nobel prize for medicine 1949. **4. (Wal·ther Rich·ard) Ru·dolf** (väl′tər ʀɪᴋʜ′ärt ʀo͞o′dôlf), 1894–1987, German official in the Nazi party.

Hes·se (hes′ə *for 1;* hes *for 2*), *n.* **1. Her·mann** (heʀ′män), 1877–1962, German novelist and poet: Nobel prize 1946. **2.** German, **Hes·sen** (hes′ən). a state in central Germany. 5,508,000; 8150 sq. mi. (21,110 sq. km). *Cap.:* Wiesbaden.

Hes′sel·man en′gine (hes′əl mən), a low-compression oil engine requiring a spark for ignition. [after Swedish engineer Knut Jonas Elias *Hesselman* (1877–1957), its inventor]

Hesse-Nas·sau (hes′nas′ô), *n.* a former state in W Germany, now part of Hesse. German, **Hes·sen-Nas·sau** (hes′ən näs′ou).

Hes·sian (hesh′ən), *adj.* **1.** of or pertaining to the state of Hesse or its inhabitants. —*n.* **2.** a native or inhabitant of Hesse. **3.** a Hessian mercenary used by England during the American Revolution. **4.** a hireling or ruffian. **5.** (*l.c.*) burlap. **6.** Also called **Hes′sian and′iron.** (in the U.S.) an andiron having as an upright the figure of a Hessian soldier of the Revolutionary War. [1670–80; HESSE, Germany + -IAN]

Hes′sian boots′, knee-high tasseled boots, fashionable in England in the early 19th century. [1800–10]

Hes′sian fly′, a small fly, *Phytophaga destructor,* the larvae of which feed on the stems of wheat and other grasses. [1780–90, *Amer.*]

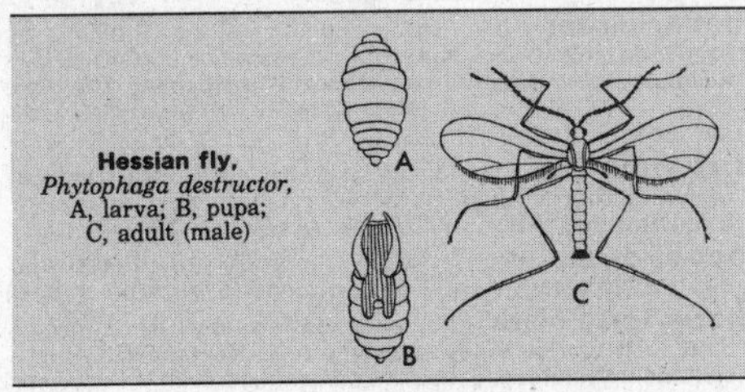

Hessian fly, *Phytophaga destructor,* A, larva; B, pupa; C, adult (male)

hess·ite (hes′īt), *n.* a rare mineral, silver telluride, Ag_2Te, found in silver ores: sometimes contains gold. [1840–50; named after G. H. Hess, 19th-century Swiss chemist; see -ITE[1]]

hes·so·nite (hes′ə nīt′), *n. Mineral.* essonite. [< Gk *hḗsson-* (s. of *hḗssōn*) less, inferior + -ITE[1]]

hest (hest), *n. Archaic.* behest. [bef. 1150; ME *hest*(*e*), OE *hǣs;* akin to *hātan* to bid]

Hes·ter (hes′tər), *n.* a female given name, form of **Esther.**

Hes·ti·a (hes′tē ə), *n.* the ancient Greek goddess of the hearth. Cf. **Vesta.**

Hes·ton and I·sle·worth (hes′tən; ī′zəl wûrth′), a former borough, now part of Hounslow, in SE England, near London.

Hes·y·chast (hes′i kast′), *n.* one of a sect of mystics that originated in the 14th century among the monks on Mt. Athos, Greece. [1825–35; < ML *hesychasta* < Gk *hēsychastḗs* a recluse, equiv. to *hēsycház*(*ein*) to be quiet, be still (v. deriv. of *hḗsychos* quiet, still) + *-tēs* agent suffix] —**Hes′y·chast′ic,** *adj.*

he·tae·ra (hi tēr′ə), *n., pl.* **-tae·rae** (-tēr′ē). **1.** a highly cultured courtesan or concubine, esp. in ancient Greece. **2.** any woman who uses her beauty and charm to obtain wealth or social position. Also, **hetaira.** [1810–20; < Gk *hetaíra* (fem.) companion] —**he·tae′ric,** *adj.*

he·tae·rism (hi tēr′iz əm), *n.* **1.** concubinage. **2.** a social system in which the women are considered common property. Also, **he·tai·rism** (hi tīᵊr′iz əm). [1855–60; HETAER(A) + -ISM] —**he·tae′rist,** *n.* —**het·ae·ris·tic** (het′ə ris′tik), *adj.*

he·tai·ra (hi tīᵊr′ə), *n., pl.* **-tai·rai** (-tī′rī). hetaera. —**he·tai′ric,** *adj.*

het·er·o (het′ə rō′), *adj., n., pl.* **-er·os.** —*adj.* **1.** *Chem.* of or pertaining to an atom other than carbon, particularly in a cyclic compound. **2.** *Informal.* heterosexual. —*n.* **3.** *Informal.* a heterosexual person. [1930–35 for def. 2; (in def. 1) by shortening of HETEROATOM; (in def. 2) by shortening of HETEROSEXUAL; see -O]

hetero-, a combining form meaning "different," "other," used in the formation of compound words: *heterocyclic.* Also, *esp. before a vowel,* **heter-.** [comb. form of Gk *héteros* the other of two, other, different]

het·er·o·ar·o·mat·ic (het′ə rō ar′ə mat′ik), *n. Chem.* a heterocyclic aromatic compound. [1955–60; HETERO- + AROMATIC]

het·er·o·at·om (het′ə rō at′əm), *n. Chem.* an atom other than carbon in the ring structure of a heterocyclic compound. [1895–1900; HETERO- + ATOM]

het·er·o·aux·in (het′ə rō ôk′sin), *n. Biochem.* See **indoleacetic acid.** [1930–35; HETERO- + AUXIN]

het·er·o·cer·cal (het′ər ə sûr′kəl), *adj. Ichthyol.* having an unequally divided tail, characteristic of sharks, rays, and skates. Cf. **diphycercal, homocercal.** [1830–40; HETERO- + Gk *kérk*(*os*) a tail + -AL[1]] —**het·er·o·cer·cal·i·ty** (het′ər ō sər kal′i tē), *n.*

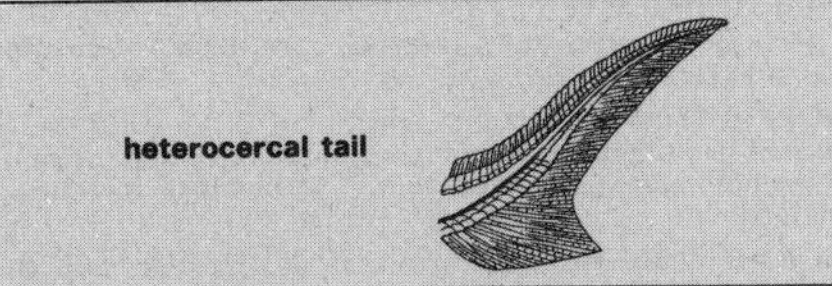
heterocercal tail

het·er·o·chro·mat·ic (het′ər ə krō mat′ik, -ō krə-), *adj.* **1.** of, having, or pertaining to more than one color. Cf. **homochromatic. 2.** having a pattern of mixed colors. **3.** *Genetics.* of or pertaining to heterochromatin. Also, **heterochrome.** [1890–95; HETERO- + CHROMATIC] —**het·er·o·chro·ma·tism** (het′ər ə krō′mə tiz′əm), *n.*

het·er·o·chro·ma·tin (het′ər ə krō′mə tin), *n. Genetics.* the dense, highly stainable part of a chromosome. Cf. **euchromatin.** [1930–35; HETERO- + CHROMATIN]

het·er·o·chrome (het′ər ə krōm′), *adj.* heterochromatic. [1930–35; HETERO- + -CHROME]

het·er·o·chro·mo·some (het′ər ə krō′mə sōm′), *n. Genetics.* See **sex chromosome.** [1900–05; HETERO- + CHROMOSOME]

het·er·o·chro·mous (het′ər ə krō′məs), *adj.* of different colors. [1835–45; HETERO- + CHROMOUS]

het·er·och·ro·ny (het′ə rok′rə nē), *n. Biol.* a genetic shift in timing of the development of a tissue or anatomical part, or in the onset of a physiological process, relative to an ancestor. [1875–80; HETERO- + CHRON- + -Y[3]; cf. G *Heterochron*] —**het·er·o·chron·ic** (het′ər ə kron′ik), **het′er·och′ro·nis′tic, het′er·och′ro·nous,** *adj.*

het·er·och·tho·nous (het′ə rok′thə nəs), *adj.* not indigenous; foreign (opposed to *autochthonous*): *heterochthonous flora and fauna.* [1890–95; HETERO- + Gk *chthṓn* the earth, land, country + -OUS]

het·er·o·clite (het′ər ə klīt′), *adj.* Also, **het·er·o·clit·ic** (het′ər ə klit′ik), **het′er·o·clit′i·cal. 1.** irregular or abnormal; anomalous. **2.** *Gram.* irregular in inflection; having inflected forms belonging to more than one class of stems. —*n.* **3.** a person or thing that deviates from the ordinary rule or form. **4.** *Gram.* a heteroclite word. [1570–80; < MF < LL *heteroclitus* < Gk *heteróklitos,* equiv. to *hetero-* HETERO- + *-klitos,* verbid of *klínein* to bend, inflect]

het·er·o·cy·clic (het′ər ə sī′klik, -sik′lik), *adj. Chem.* **1.** of or pertaining to the branch of chemistry dealing with cyclic compounds in which at least one of the ring members is not a carbon atom (contrasted with *homocyclic*). **2.** noting such compounds, as ethylene oxide, C_2H_4O. [1895–1900; HETERO- + CYCLIC] —**het·er·o·cy·cle** (het′ər ə sī′kəl), *n.*

het·er·o·cyst (het′ər ə sist′), *n. Bacteriol.* one of the enlarged nitrogen-fixing cells occurring along the filaments in some blue-green algae. [1870–75; HETERO- + CYST]

het·er·o·dac·ty·lous (het′ə rō dak′tə ləs), *adj. Ornith.* having the first and fourth toes directed backward, and the second and third forward, as in trogons. Also, **het′er·o·dac′tyl.** [1850–55; HETERO- + -DACTYLOUS]

het·er·o·dox (het′ər ə doks′), *adj.* **1.** not in accordance with established or accepted doctrines or opinions, esp. in theology; unorthodox. **2.** holding unorthodox doctrines or opinions. [1610–20; < Gk *heteródoxos* of another opinion, equiv. to *hetero-* HETERO- + *dóx*(*a*) opinion (cf. *dokeîn* to think, suppose) + *-os* adj. suffix] —**het′er·o·dox′ly,** *adv.*

het·er·o·dox·y (het′ər ə dok′sē), *n., pl.* **-dox·ies. 1.** heterodox state or quality. **2.** a heterodox opinion, view, etc. [1645–55; < Gk *heterodoxía.* See HETERODOX, -Y[3]]

het·er·o·dyne (het′ər ə dīn′), *adj., v.,* **-dyned, -dyn·ing.** *Radio.* —*adj.* **1.** noting or pertaining to a method of changing the frequency of an incoming radio signal by adding it to a signal generated within the receiver to produce fluctuations or beats of a frequency equal to the difference between the two signals. —*v.i.* **2.** to produce a heterodyne effect. —*v.t.* **3.** to mix (a frequency) with a different frequency so as to achieve a heterodyne effect. [1905–10; HETERO- + *-dyne* < Gk *dýnamis* power]

het·er·oe·cism (het′ə rē′siz əm), *n. Biol.* the development of different stages of a parasitic species on different host plants. [1870–75; HETER- + Gk *oik*(*ía*) house + -ISM] —**het·er·oe·cious** (het′ə rē′shəs), *adj.* —**het′er·oe′cious·ly,** *adv.*

het·er·o·gam·ete (het′ər ə gam′ēt, -ə rō gə mēt′), *n. Cell Biol.* either of a pair of conjugating gametes differing in form, size, structure, or sex. Cf. **isogamete.** [1895–1900; HETERO- + GAMETE]

het·er·o·ga·met·ic (het′ə rō gə met′ik), *adj. Genetics.* (of a species or individual organism) having two unlike gametes. Cf. **homogametic.** [1905–10; HETERO- + GAMETIC]

het·er·og·a·mous (het′ə rog′ə məs), *adj.* **1.** *Genetics.* having unlike gametes, or reproducing by the union of such gametes (opposed to *isogamous*). **2.** *Bot.* having flowers or florets of two sexually different kinds (opposed to *homogamous*). [1830–40; HETERO- + -GAMOUS]

het·er·og·a·my (het′ə rog′ə mē), *n.* heterogamous state. [1870–75; HETERO- + -GAMY]

het·er·o·ge·ne·i·ty (het′ə rō jə nē′i tē), *n.* the quality or state of being heterogeneous; composition from dissimilar parts; disparateness. [1635–45; < ML *heterogeneitās.* See HETEROGENEOUS, -ITY]

het·er·o·ge·ne·ous (het′ər ə jē′nē əs, -jēn′yəs), *adj.* **1.** different in kind; unlike; incongruous. **2.** composed of parts of different kinds; having widely dissimilar elements or constituents: *The party was attended by a heterogeneous group of artists, politicians, and social climbers.* **3.** *Chem.* (of a mixture) composed of different substances or the same substance in different phases, as solid ice and liquid water. [1615–25; < ML *heterogeneus* < Gk *heterogenḗs.* See HETERO-, GENE, -OUS] —**het′er·o·ge′ne·ous·ly,** *adv.* —**het′er·o·ge′ne·ous·ness,** *n.*
—**Syn. 2.** varied, diverse. —**Ant. 2.** homogeneous.

het·er·o·gen·e·sis (het′ər ə jen′ə sis), *n. Biol.* **1.** Also, **het·er·og·e·ny** (het′ə roj′ə nē). alternation of generations, esp. the alternation of parthenogenetic and sexual generations. **2.** abiogenesis. [1850–55; HETERO- + -GENESIS]

het·er·o·ge·net·ic (het′ə rō jə net′ik), *adj.* of, pertaining to, or characterized by heterogenesis. Also, **het·er·o·gen·ic** (het′ər ə jen′ik). [1870–75; HETERO- + -GENETIC] —**het′er·o·ge·net′i·cal·ly,** *adv.*

het·er·og·e·nous (het′ə roj′ə nəs), *adj. Biol., Pathol.* having its source or origin outside the organism; having a foreign origin. [1685–95; HETERO- + -GENOUS]

het·er·og·o·nous (het′ə rog′ə nəs), *adj.* **1.** *Bot.* of or pertaining to monoclinous flowers of two or more kinds occurring on different individuals of the same species, the kinds differing in the relative length of stamens and pistils (opposed to *homogonous*). **2.** heterogynous. **3.** of, pertaining to, or characterized by heterogony. Also, **het·er·o·gon·ic** (het′ər ə gon′ik). [1865–70; HETERO- + Gk *gón*(*os*) race, descent, birth + -OUS] —**het′er·og′o·nous·ly,** *adv.*

het·er·og·o·ny (het′ə rog′ə nē), *n. Biol.* **1.** the alternation of dioecious and hermaphroditic individuals in successive generations, as in certain nematodes. **2.** the

CONCISE PRONUNCIATION KEY: act, cāpe, dâre, pärt; set, ēqual; if, īce; ox, ōver, ôrder, oil, bo͝ok, bo͞ot, out; up, ûrge; child; sing; shoe; thin, *th*at; zh as in *treasure.* ə = *a* as in *alone, e* as in *system, i* as in *easily, o* as in *gallop, u* as in *circus;* ᵊ as in *fire* (fīᵊr), *hour* (ouᵊr). l and n can serve as syllabic consonants, as in *cradle* (krād′l), and *button* (but′n). See the full key inside the front cover.

alternation of parthenogenetic and sexual generations. [1865–70; HETERO- + -GONY]

het•er•o•graft (het′ər ə graft′, -gräft′), *n. Surg.* xenograft. [1905–10; HETERO- + GRAFT[1]]

het•er•og•ra•phy (het′ə rog′rə fē), *n.* **1.** spelling different from that in current use. **2.** the use of the same letter or combination of letters to represent different sounds, as, in English, the use of *s* in *sit* and *easy.* [1775–85; HETERO- + -GRAPHY] —**het•er•o•graph•ic** (het′ər ə graf′ik), **het′er•o•graph′i•cal,** *adj.*

het•er•og•y•nous (het′ə roj′ə nəs), *adj. Zool.* having females of two different kinds, one sexual and the other abortive or neuter, as ants. [1850–55; HETERO- + -GYNOUS]

het•er•o•kar•y•on (het′ər ə kar′ē on′, -ən), *n., pl.* **-kar•y•a** (-kar′ē ə). *Biol.* a cell containing two or more nuclei of differing genetic constitutions. [1940–45; HETERO- + Gk *káryon* nut, kernel; cf. KARYO-]

het•er•o•kar•y•o•sis (het′ər ə kar′ē ō′sis), *n. Biol.* condition in which a binucleate or multinucleate cell contains genetically dissimilar nuclei. [1915–20; HETERO- + KARYO- + -SIS] —**het•er•o•kar•y•ot•ic** (het′ər ə kar′ē-ot′ik), *adj.*

het•er•o•lec•i•thal (het′ər ə les′ə thəl), *adj. Embryol.* having an unequal distribution of yolk, as certain eggs or ova. [1890–95; HETERO- + LECITHAL]

het•er•ol•o•gous (het′ə rol′ə gəs), *adj.* **1.** *Biol.* of different origin; pertaining to heterology. **2.** *Med., Pathol.* consisting of dissimilar tissue, as that of another species or that of a tumor. **3.** *Immunol.* pertaining to an antigen that elicits a reaction in a nonspecific antibody. [1815–25; HETERO- + -LOGOUS]

het•er•ol•o•gy (het′ə rol′ə jē), *n.* **1.** *Biol.* the lack of correspondence of apparently similar organic structures as the result of unlike origins of constituent parts. **2.** *Pathol.* abnormality; structural difference from a type or normal standard. [1850–55; HETERO- + -LOGY]

het•er•om•er•ous (het′ə rom′ər əs), *adj.* having or consisting of parts that differ in quality, number of elements, or the like: *a heteromerous flower.* [1820–30; HETERO- + -MEROUS]

het•er•o•me•tab•o•lous (het′ə rō mi tab′ə ləs), *adj. Entomol.* undergoing development in which the young are born adultlike in form, often maturing without a pupal stage. Also, **het•er•o•met•a•bol•ic** (het′ə rō met′-ə bol′ik). [HETERO- + METABOL(IC) + -OUS] —**het′er•o•me•tab′o•lism, het′er•o•me•tab′o•ly,** *n.*

het•er•o•mor•phic (het′ər ə môr′fik), *adj.* **1.** *Biol.* dissimilar in shape, structure, or magnitude. **2.** *Entomol.* undergoing complete metamorphosis; possessing varying forms. [1860–65; HETERO- + -MORPHIC] —**het′-er•o•mor′phism, het′er•o•mor′phy,** *n.*

het•er•on•o•mous (het′ə ron′ə məs), *adj.* **1.** subject to or involving different laws. **2.** pertaining to or characterized by heteronomy. **3.** *Biol.* subject to different laws of growth or specialization. [1815–25; HETERONOM(Y) + -OUS] —**het′er•on′o•mous•ly,** *adv.*

het•er•on•o•my (het′ə ron′ə mē), *n.* the condition of being under the domination of an outside authority, either human or divine. [1815–25; HETERO- + -NOMY]

het•er•o•nym (het′ər ə nim), *n.* a word spelled the same as another but having a different sound and meaning, as *lead* (to conduct) and *lead* (a metal). [1880–85; < LGk *heterṓnymos.* See HETERO-, -ONYM]

het•er•on•y•mous (het′ə ron′ə məs), *adj.* **1.** of, pertaining to, or characteristic of a heteronym. **2.** having different names, as a pair of correlatives: *Father and son are heteronymous relatives.* [1725–35; < LGk *heterṓnymos* having a different name. See HETERONYM, -OUS] —**het′er•on′y•mous•ly,** *adv.*

Het•er•o•ou•si•an (het′ə rō o͞o′sē ən, -ou′sē ən), *Eccles.* —*n.* **1.** a person who believes the Father and the Son to be unlike in substance or essence; an Arian (opposed to *Homoousian*). —*adj.* **2.** of or pertaining to the Heteroousians or their doctrine. [1670–80; < LGk *heteroousí(os)* (Gk *hetero-* HETERO- + *ousí(a)* nature, essence + *-os* adj. suffix) + -AN]

het•er•o•phil (het′ər ə fil), *adj.* **1.** Also, **het′er•o•phil′ic.** *Immunol.* (of an antibody) having an affinity for an antigen other than its specific antigen. —*n.* **2.** *Cell Biol.* a neutrophil. Also, **het•er•o•phile** (het′ər ə fīl′). [1915–20; HETERO- + -PHIL]

het•er•oph•o•ny (het′ə rof′ə nē), *n. Music.* the simultaneous performance of the same melodic line, with slight individual variations, by two or more performers. [1940–45; HETERO- + -PHONY] —**het•er•o•phon•ic** (het′-ər ə fon′ik), *adj.*

het•er•o•pho•ri•a (het′ər ə fôr′ē ə, -fōr′-), *n. Ophthalm.* a latent strabismus of one or both eyes. [1885–90; HETERO- + Gk *-phoria* a carrying, equiv. to *-phor(os)* -PHOROUS + *-ia* -IA] —**het•er•o•phor•ic** (het′ər ə fôr′-ik, -for′-), *adj.*

het•er•o•phyl•lous (het′ər ə fil′əs), *adj. Bot.* having different kinds of leaves on the same plant. [1820–30; HETERO- + -PHYLLOUS] —**het′er•o•phyl′ly,** *n.*

het•er•o•phyte (het′ər ə fīt′), *n. Bot.* a plant that secures its nutrition directly or indirectly from other organisms; a parasite or saprophyte. Cf. **autophyte.** [HETERO- + -PHYTE] —**het•er•o•phyt•ic** (het′ər ə fit′ik), *adj.*

het•er•o•pla•sia (het′ər ə plā′zhə, -zhē ə, -zē ə), *n. Pathol.* the replacement of normal cells by abnormal cells, as in cancer. [HETERO- + -PLASIA]

het•er•o•plas•ty (het′ər ə plas′tē), *n., pl.* **-ties.** *Surg.* the repair of lesions with tissue from another individual or species. [1850–55; HETERO- + -PLASTY] —**het′er•o•plas′tic,** *adj.*

het•er•o•po•lar (het′ər ə pō′lər), *adj. Chem.* polar (def. 4). [1895–1900; HETERO- + POLAR] —**het•er•o•po•lar•i•ty** (het′ə rō pō lar′i tē), *n.*

het•er•op•ter•ous (het′ə rop′tər əs), *adj.* belonging or pertaining to the Heteroptera, in some classifications a suborder of hemipterous insects comprising the true bugs. [1890–95; < NL *Heteropter(a)* + -OUS. See HETERO-, -PTEROUS]

het•er•op•tics (het′ə rop′tiks), *n.* (*used with a singular v.*) incorrect or perverted perception of what is seen; hallucinatory vision. [1705–15; HETER- + OPTICS]

het•er•o•sex (het′ər ə seks′), *n. Informal.* heterosexuality. [HETERO- + SEX, on the model of HETEROSEXUAL]

het•er•o•sex•ism (het′ər ə sek′siz əm), *n.* a prejudiced attitude or discriminatory practices against homosexuals by heterosexuals. [HETERO(SEXUAL) + SEXISM] —**het′er•o•sex′ist,** *n., adj.*

het•er•o•sex•u•al (het′ər ə sek′sho͞o əl *or, esp. Brit.,* -seks′yo͞o-), *adj.* **1.** of, pertaining to, or exhibiting heterosexuality. **2.** *Biol.* pertaining to the opposite sex or to both sexes. —*n.* **3.** a heterosexual person. [1890–95; HETERO- + SEXUAL]

het•er•o•sex•u•al•i•ty (het′ər ə sek′sho͞o al′i tē *or, esp. Brit.,* -seks′yo͞o-), *n.* sexual feeling or behavior directed toward a person or persons of the opposite sex. [1895–1900; HETERO- + SEXUALITY]

het•er•o•sis (het′ə rō′sis), *n. Genetics.* the increase in growth, size, fecundity, function, yield, or other characters in hybrids over those of the parents. Also called **hybrid vigor.** [1910–15; < LGk *hetérōsis* an alteration. See HETERO-, -SIS]

het•er•os•po•rous (het′ə ros′pə rəs, het′ər ə spôr′əs, -spōr′-), *adj. Bot.* having more than one kind of spore. [1870–75; HETERO- + -SPOROUS]

het•er•os•po•ry (het′ə ros′pə rē), *n. Bot.* the production of both microspores and megaspores. [1895–1900; HETERO- + -SPORE + -Y[3]]

het•er•os•tra•can (het′ə ros′trə kən), *n. Paleontol.* any of several ostracoderms of the order Heterostraci, from the Silurian and Devonian Periods, having the anterior part of the body enclosed in bony plates. [< NL *Heterostrac(i)* (pl.) name of the order, equiv. to *heter-* HETER- + Gk *ostrak(ón)* (sing.) shell + -AN]

het•er•o•styled (het′ər ə stīld′), *adj.* (of a plant) having styles of different forms or lengths in the flowers. Also, **het′er•o•sty′lous.** [1870–75; HETERO- + -STYLE[1] + -ED[3]]

het•er•o•tac•tic (het′ər ə tak′tik), *adj.* of, pertaining to, or characterized by heterotaxis. Also, **het′er•o•tac′•tous, het•er•o•tax•ic** (het′ər ə tak′sik). [HETERO- + Gk *takt(ós)* fixed, ordered, arranged (cf. *tássein* to arrange) + -IC]

het•er•o•tax•is (het′ər ə tak′sis), *n.* abnormal or irregular arrangement, as of parts of the body, geological strata, etc. Also, **het•er•o•tax•i•a** (het′ər ə tak′sē ə), **het′er•o•tax′y.** [HETERO- + -TAXIS]

het•er•o•tel•ic (het′ər ə tel′ik, -tē′lik), *adj.* (of an entity or event) having the purpose of its existence or occurrence outside of or apart from itself. Cf. **autotelic.** [1900–05; HETERO- + TEL-[2] + -IC] —**het′er•o•tel′ism,** *n.*

het•er•o•thal•lic (het′ər ə thal′ik), *adj. Mycol.* **1.** having mycelia of two unlike types, both of which must participate in the sexual process. Cf. **homothallic** (def. 1). **2.** dioecious. [1900–05; HETERO- + THALLIC] —**het′-er•o•thal′lism,** *n.*

het•er•o•to•pi•a (het′ər ə tō′pē ə), *n. Pathol.* **1.** misplacement or displacement, as of an organ. **2.** the formation of tissue in a part where its presence is abnormal. Also, **het•er•ot•o•py** (het′ə rot′ə pē). [< NL; see HETERO-, TOP-, -IA] —**het•er•o•top•ic** (het′ər ə top′ik), **het′er•ot′o•pous,** *adj.*

het•er•o•trich (het′ər ə trik), *n.* any ciliate of the suborder Heterotricha, having the body covered uniformly with short cilia. [< NL *Heterotricha* name of the order. See HETERO-, -TRICHA] —**het•er•ot•ri•chous** (het′ə ro′trə kəs), *adj.*

het•er•o•troph (het′ər ə trof′, -trōf′), *n. Biol.* an organism requiring organic compounds for its principal source of food. Cf. **autotroph.** [1895–1900; HETERO- + -TROPH]

het•er•o•troph•ic (het′ər ə trof′ik, -trō′fik), *adj. Biol.* capable of utilizing only organic materials as a source of food. [1890–95; HETERO- + -TROPHIC]

het•er•o•typ•ic (het′ər ə tip′ik), *adj. Biol.* of or pertaining to the first or reductional division in meiosis. Also, **het′er•o•typ′i•cal.** Cf. **homeotypic.** [1885–90; HETERO- + -TYPIC]

het•er•o•zy•go•sis (het′ə rō zī gō′sis), *n. Biol.* the state of being a heterozygote. [1900–05; HETERO- + ZYGOSIS]

het•er•o•zy•gote (het′ər ə zī′gōt, -zig′ōt), *n. Genetics.* a hybrid containing genes for two unlike forms of a characteristic, and therefore not breeding true to type. [1900–05; HETERO- + ZYGOTE]

het•er•o•zy•gous (het′ər ə zī′gəs), *adj. Biol.* **1.** having dissimilar pairs of genes for any hereditary characteristic. **2.** of or pertaining to a heterozygote. Also, **het•er•o•zy•got•ic** (het′ə rō zī got′ik). [1900–05; HETERO- + Gk *zygós,* adj. deriv. of *zygón* yolk; see -OUS] —**het•er•o•zy•gos•i•ty** (het′ə rō zī gos′i tē), *n.*

heth (het, hes; *Seph. Heb.* KHET; *Ashk. Heb* KHES), *n.* **1.** the eighth letter of the Hebrew alphabet. **2.** the sound represented by this letter. Also, **cheth.** [1895–1900; < Heb *ḥeth* lit., enclosure]

He•tian (*Chin.* hœ′tyän′), *n. Pinyin.* Hotan.

het•man (het′mən), *n., pl.* **-mans. 1.** the title assumed by the chief of Ukrainian Cossacks of the Dnieper River region, with headquarters at Zaporozhe. **2.** ataman. [1700–10; < Ukrainian *hét'man* < Pol *hetman* < an eastern dial. form of MHG *houbetman* leader, chief (G *Hauptmann* captain; cf. G dial. (Silesia) *Hettmann, Hötmann;* see HEAD, MAN[1])]

het•man•ate (het′mə nāt′), *n.* the authority, rule, or domain of a hetman. Also called **het′man•ship′.** [1875–80; HETMAN + -ATE[3]]

HETP, *Chem.* See **hexaethyl tetraphosphate.**

Het•ty (het′ē), *n.* a female given name, form of **Hester** or **Esther.** Also, **Het′tie.**

het′ up′ (het), *Informal.* **1.** indignant; irate; upset: *She was really het up about the new city tax.* **2.** enthusiastic: *John is suddenly het up about racing cars.* [1920–25; *het,* archaic or dial. ptp. of *heat* + UP]

heu•cher•a (hyo͞o′kər ə), *n.* any of various North American plants belonging to the genus *Heuchera,* of the saxifrage family, having clusters of small, cup-shaped flowers, esp. the alumroots. Cf. **coral bells.** [< NL (Linnaeus), after Johann Heinreich von *Heucher* (1677–1747), German botanist; see -A[2]]

heu•land•ite (hyo͞o′lən dīt′), *n.* a white or transparent, colorless mineral of the zeolite family, hydrous calcium aluminum silicate, $CaAl_2Si_7O_{18}·6H_2O$, occurring in basic volcanic rocks in the form of crystals with a pearly luster. [1815–25; named after Henry *Heuland,* 19th-century English mineral collector; see -ITE[1]]

Heu•ne•burg (hyo͞o′nə bûrg′), *n. Archaeol.* an excavated prehistoric site in SW West Germany, near Ulm, consisting chiefly of a great early Iron Age fortification dating mostly to the second half of the first millennium B.C. and indicating that the inhabitants carried on an extensive trade with cities in the eastern Mediterranean.

heu•ri•ge (hoi′ri gə), **1.** a local white wine made in the Vienna region of Austria and drunk when it is very young. **2.** a Viennese inn or tavern where such wine is served and often made. [1930–35; < G (dial.): new, new wine]

heu•ris•tic (hyo͝o ris′tik *or, often,* yo͝o-), *adj.* **1.** serving to indicate or point out; stimulating interest as a means of furthering investigation. **2.** encouraging a person to learn, discover, understand, or solve problems on his or her own, as by experimenting, evaluating possible answers or solutions, or by trial and error: *a heuristic teaching method.* **3.** of, pertaining to, or based on experimentation, evaluation, or trial-and-error methods. **4.** *Computers, Math.* pertaining to a trial-and-error method of problem solving used when an algorithmic approach is impractical. —*n.* **5.** a heuristic method of argument. **6.** the study of heuristic procedure. [1815–25; < NL *heuristicus,* equiv. to Gk *heur(ískein)* to find out, discover + L *-isticus* -ISTIC] —**heu•ris′ti•cal•ly,** *adv.*

Heus′ler al′loy (hyo͞os′lər; *Ger.* hois′lər), any of various alloys of manganese and other nonferromagnetic metals that exhibit ferromagnetism. [named after Conrad *Heusler,* 19th-century German mining engineer and chemist]

he•ve•a (hē′vē ə), *n.* See **Pará rubber.** [1875–80; < NL < F *hevé,* perh. < an indigenous language of French Guiana]

He•ve′li•an ha′lo (hə vā′lē ən), a faint white halo with an angular radius of 90° that is occasionally seen around the sun or the moon, thought to be caused by the reflection and refraction of sunlight by ice crystals. [after J. HEVELIUS; see -IAN]

He•ve•li•us (hə vā′lē əs; *Ger.* hā vā′lē o͝os′), *n.* **Johannes** (*Johann Hewel* or *Hewelke*), **1.** 1611–87, Polish astronomer: charted the moon's surface and discovered four comets. **2.** a walled plain in the second quadrant of the face of the moon: about 100 mi. (160 km) in diameter.

He•ve•sy (he′ve shē), *n.* **Ge•org von** (ge ôrg′ vôn), 1885–1966, Hungarian chemist: Nobel prize 1943.

hew (hyo͞o *or, often,* yo͞o), *v.,* **hewed, hewed** or **hewn, hew•ing.** —*v.t.* **1.** to strike forcibly with an ax, sword, or other cutting instrument; chop; hack. **2.** to make, shape, smooth, etc., with cutting blows: *to hew a passage through the crowd; to hew a statue from marble.* **3.** to sever (a part) from a whole by means of cutting blows (usually fol. by *away, off, out, from,* etc.): *to hew branches from the tree.* **4.** to cut down; fell: *to hew wood; trees hewed down by the storm.* —*v.i.* **5.** to strike with cutting blows; cut: *He hewed more vigorously each time.* **6.** to uphold, follow closely, or conform (usually fol. by *to*): *to hew to the tenets of one's political party.* [bef. 900; ME *hewen,* OE *hēawan;* c. G *hauen,* ON *hǫggva;* akin to HAGGLE] —**hew′a•ble,** *adj.* —**hew′er,** *n.*
—**Syn. 1.** See **cut. 2.** form.

HEW, See **Department of Health, Education, and Welfare.**

hew′ers of wood′ and draw′ers of wa′ter, performers of menial tasks. Josh. 9:21.

Hew•ish (hyo͞o′ish *or, often,* yo͞o′-), *n.* **Antony,** born 1924, British astronomer: discovered pulsars; Nobel prize for physics 1974.

Hew•lett (hyo͞o′lit *or, often,* yo͞o′-), *n.* **Maurice Henry,** 1861–1923, English novelist, poet, and essayist.

hewn (hyo͞on *or, often,* yo͞on), *adj.* **1.** felled and roughly shaped by hewing: *hewn logs.* **2.** given a rough surface: *hewn stone.* [1300–50; ME *hewen,* ptp. of HEW]

hex[1] (heks), *v.t.* **1.** to bewitch; practice witchcraft on: *He was accused of hexing his neighbors' cows because they suddenly stopped giving milk.* —*n.* **2.** spell; charm: *With all this rain, somebody must have put a hex on our picnic.* **3.** a witch. [1820–30; < G *Hexe* witch; see HAG[1]] —**hex′er,** *n.*

hex[2] (heks), *adj. Informal.* **1.** hexagonal: *a bolt with a matching washer and hex nut.* **2.** hexadecimal (def. 1). [1920–25; by shortening]

CONCISE ETYMOLOGY KEY: <, descended or borrowed from; >, whence; b., blend of, blended; c., cognate with; cf., compare; deriv., derivative; equiv., equivalent; imit., imitative; obl., oblique; r., replacing; s., stem; sp., spelling, spelled; resp., respelling, respelled; trans., translation; ?, origin unknown; *, unattested; ‡, probably earlier than. See the full key inside the front cover.

hex., **1.** hexagon **2.** hexagonal.

hexa-, a combining form meaning "six," used in the formation of compound words: *hexapartite.* Also, *esp. before a vowel,* **hex-.** [comb. form repr. Gk *héx* SIX]

hex·a·ba·sic (hek′sə bā′sik), *adj.* containing six hydrogen atoms capable of being replaced or ionized: *a hexabasic acid.* [1875–80; HEXA- + BASIC]

hex·a·chlo·ride (hek′sə klôr′īd, -klōr′-), *n.* a chloride containing six atoms of chlorine. [1875–80; HEXA- + CHLORIDE]

hex·a·chlo·ro·eth·ane (hek′sə klôr′ō eth′ān, -klōr′-), *n.* a colorless crystalline compound, C_2Cl_6, with a camphorlike odor, soluble in alcohol and ether, insoluble in water: used in organic synthesis and pyrotechnics, as a retarding agent in fermentation, and as a solvent. Also called **carbon hexachloride, perchloroethane.** [1895–1900; HEXA- + CHLOROETHANE]

hex·a·chlo·ro·phene (hek′sə klôr′ə fēn′, -klōr′-), *n.* a white, crystalline powder, $C_{13}Cl_6H_6O_2$, insoluble in water: used as an antibacterial agent chiefly in toothpastes and soaps. [1945–50; HEXA- + CHLORO-[2] + -PHENE]

hex·a·chord (hek′sə kôrd′), *n. Music.* a diatonic series of six tones having, in medieval music, a half step between the third and fourth tones and whole steps between the others. [1685–95; < LGk *hexáchordos* having six strings. See HEXA-, CHORD[1]]

hex′a·co·sa·no′ic ac′id (hek′sə kō sə nō′ik, hek′-sə-). See **cerotic acid.** [HEXA- + Gk *(eí)kos(i)* twenty + -ANE + -O- + -IC]

hex·ad (hek′sad), *n.* **1.** the number six. **2.** a group or series of six. [1650–60; < LL *hexad-* (s. of *hexas*) < Gk *hexad-* (s. of *hexás*) unit of six, equiv. to *héx* SIX + *-ad* -AD[1]] —**hex·ad′ic,** *adj.*

hex′a·dec·a·no′ic ac′id (hek′sə dek′ə nō′ik, hek′-sə-). See **palmitic acid.** [1900–05; HEXA- + DEC(A)- + -ANE + -O- + -IC]

hex·a·dec·i·mal (hek′sə des′ə məl), *adj. Computers, Math.* **1.** Also, **hex.** of or pertaining to a numbering system that uses 16 as the radix, employing the numerals 0 through 9 and representing digits greater than 9 with the letters A through F. **2.** relating to or encoded in a hexadecimal system, esp. for use by a digital computer. [1950–55; HEXA- + DECIMAL]

hex·a·em·er·on (hek′sə em′ə ron′), *n.* **1.** the six days of the Creation. **2.** a written account of them, esp. the Biblical account. Gen. 1. **3.** a treatise on them. Also, **hexahemeron, hexameron.** [1585–95; < LL < Gk *hexaémeron* period of six days, neut. of *hexaémeros* of six days (adj.), equiv. to *hexa-* HEXA- + *(h)ēmér(a)* day + *-os* n. suffix] —**hex′a·em′er·ic,** *adj.*

hex·a·eth′yl tetraphos′phate (hek′sə eth′əl), a yellow, very poisonous liquid, $(C_2H_5O)_6P_4O_7$, soluble in water, used as an insecticide. Also called **HETP** [1945–50; HEXA- + ETHYL]

hex·a·fluor·ide (hek′sə flŏŏr′īd, -flôr′-, -flōr′-), *n.* a fluoride containing six atoms of fluorine. [HEXA- + FLUORIDE]

hex·a·gon (hek′sə gon′, -gən), *n.* a polygon having six angles and six sides. [1560–70; < Gk *hexágōnon.* See HEXA-, -GON]

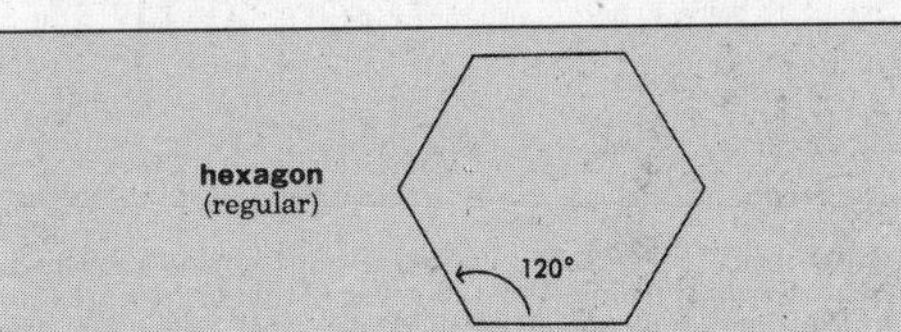

hexagon (regular)

hex·ag·o·nal (hek sag′ə nl), *adj.* **1.** of, pertaining to, or having the form of a hexagon. **2.** having a hexagon as a base or cross section: *a hexagonal prism.* **3.** divided into hexagons, as a surface. **4.** *Crystall.* noting or pertaining to a system of crystallization in which three equal axes intersect at angles of 60° on one plane, and the fourth axis, of a different length, intersects them perpendicularly. [1565–75; HEXAGON + -AL[1]] —**hex·ag′o·nal·ly,** *adv.*

hex·a·gram (hek′sə gram′), *n.* **1.** a six-pointed starlike figure formed of two equilateral triangles placed concentrically with each side of a triangle parallel to a side of the other and on opposite sides of the center. **2.** *Geom.* a figure of six lines. [1860–65; see HEXA-, -GRAM[1]] —**hex′a·gram′moid,** *adj., n.*

hexagram (def. 1)

hex·a·he·dron (hek′sə hē′drən), *n., pl.* **-drons, -dra** (-drə). a solid figure having six faces, as a cube. See illus. under **cube.** [1565–75; < Gk *hexáedron.* See HEXA-, -HEDRON] —**hex′a·he′dral,** *adj.*

hex·a·hem·er·on (hek′sə hem′ə ron′), *n.* hexaemeron. —**hex′a·hem′er·ic,** *adj.*

hex·a·hy·drate (hek′sə hī′drāt), *n.* a hydrate that contains six molecules of water, as magnesium chloride, $MgCl_2{\cdot}6H_2O$. [1905–10; HEXA- + HYDRATE] —**hex′a·hy′drat·ed,** *adj.*

hex·a·hy·dric (hek′sə hī′drik), *adj. Chem.* (esp. of alcohols and phenols) hexahydroxy. [1880–85; HEXA- + -HYDRIC]

hex·a·hy·dro·an·i·line (hek′sə hī′drō an′l in′), *n. Chem.* cyclohexylamine. [HEXA- + HYDRO-[2] + ANILINE]

hex·a·hy·dro·ben·zene (hek′sə hī′drō ben′zēn, -ben zēn′), *n. Chem.* cyclohexane. [HEXA- + HYDRO-[2] + BENZENE]

hex·a·hy·dro·thy·mol (hek′sə hī′drə thī′môl, -mol), *n. Chem.* menthol. [HEXA- + HYDRO-[2] + THYMOL]

hex·a·hy·drox·y (hek′sə hī drok′sē), *adj.* (of a molecule) containing six hydroxyl groups. [HEXA- + HYDROXY]

hex·a·hy·drox·y·cy·clo·hex·ane (hek′sə hī drok′-sē sī′klə hek′sān), *n. Chem.* inositol. [HEXAHYDROXY + CYCLOHEXANE]

hex·am·er·al (hek sam′ər əl), *adj.* hexamerous. [1875–80; HEXAMER(OUS) + -AL[1]]

hex·am·er·on (hek sam′ə ron′), *n.* hexaemeron.

hex·am·er·ous (hek sam′ər əs), *adj.* **1.** consisting of or divided into six parts. **2.** *Zool.* having a radially symmetrical arrangement of organs in six groups. **3.** *Bot.* having six members in each whorl. [1855–60; < LL *hexamerus* < Gk *hexámeros* of six parts, equiv. to *hexa-* HEXA- + *mér(os)* share, part + *-os* adj. suffix (see -OUS)] —**hex·am·er·ism** (hek sam′ə riz′əm), *n.*

hex·am·e·ter (hek sam′i tər), *Pros.* —*n.* **1.** a dactylic line of six feet, as in Greek and Latin epic poetry, in which the first four feet are dactyls or spondees, the fifth is ordinarily a dactyl, and the last is a trochee or spondee, with a caesura usually following the long syllable in the third foot. **2.** any line of verse in six feet, as in English poetry. —*adj.* **3.** consisting of six metrical feet. [1540–50; < L < Gk *hexámetros* of six measures, equiv. to *hexa-* HEXA- + *métr(on)* measure + *-os* adj. suffix] —**hex·a·met·ric** (hek′sə me′trik), **hex′a·met′ri·cal, hex·am′e·tral,** *adj.*

hex·a·me·tho·ni·um (hek′sə mə thō′nē əm), *n. Pharm.* a compound, $C_{10}H_{24}N_2$, used in the treatment of severe hypertension to lower blood pressure and increase blood flow by blocking transmission of nerve impulses that constrict blood vessels. [1945–50; HEXA- + METH(YL) + (AMM)ONIUM]

hex·a·meth·yl·ene (hek′sə meth′ə lēn′), *n. Chem.* cyclohexane. [1885–90; HEXA- + METHYLENE]

hex·a·meth·yl·ene·tet·ra·mine (hek′sə meth′ə-lēn te′trə mēn′), *n.* a white, crystalline, water-soluble powder, $C_6H_{12}N_4$, used as a vulcanization accelerator, an absorbent in gas masks, in the manufacture of the explosive RDX and synthetic resins, and in medicine as a diuretic and urinary antiseptic. Also called **hex·a·mine** (hek′sə mēn′), **methenamine.** [1885–90; HEXAMETHYLENE + TETR(A)- + -AMINE]

hex·a·naph·thene (hek′sə naf′thēn, -nap′-), *n. Chem.* cyclohexane. [HEXA- + NAPHTHENE]

hex·ane (hek′sān), *n.* any of five isomeric hydrocarbons having the formula C_6H_{14}, of the alkane series, some of which are obtained from petroleum: used as solvents and chemical intermediates and in fuels. [1875–80; HEX- + -ANE]

hex′ane·di·o′ic ac′id (hek′sān dī ō′ik, hek′-). See **adipic acid.** [HEX- + (BUT)ANE + DI(CARB)O(XYL)IC ACID]

hex·an·gu·lar (hek sang′gyə lər), *adj.* having six angles. [1655–65; HEX- + ANGULAR] —**hex·an′gu·lar·ly,** *adv.*

hex·a·ni·trate (hek′sə nī′trāt), *n.* any compound containing six nitrate groups. [HEXA- + NITRATE]

hex′a·no′ic ac′id (hek′sə nō′ik, hek′sə-). See **caproic acid.** [1925–30; HEXANE + -O- + -IC]

hex·a·par·tite (hek′sə pär′tīt), *adj.* sexpartite. [HEXA- + PARTITE]

hex·a·pla (hek′sə plə), *n.* (*often cap.*) an edition of a book, esp. the Old Testament, containing six versions or texts in parallel columns, esp. the edition compiled by Origen. [1600–10; < Gk *Hexaplâ* (title of Origen's edition), neut. pl. of *hexaploûs, hexaplóos* sixfold, equiv. to *hexa-* HEXA- + *-ploûs, -ploos* -FOLD] —**hex′a·plar, hex·a·plar·ic** (hek′sə plar′ik), **hex·a·plar·i·an** (hek′sə-plâr′ē ən), *adj.*

hex·a·ploid (hek′sə ploid′), *Biol.* —*adj.* **1.** having a chromosome number that is six times the haploid number. —*n.* **2.** a hexaploid cell or organism. Cf. **polyploid.** [1915–20; HEXA- + -PLOID] —**hex′a·ploi′dy,** *n.*

hex·a·pod (hek′sə pod′), *n.* **1.** a six-legged arthropod of the class Insecta (formerly Hexapoda); an insect. —*adj.* **2.** having six feet. [1660–70; < Gk *hexapod-* (s. of *hexápous*) six-footed. See HEXA-, -POD] —**hex·ap·o·dous** (hek sap′ə dəs), *adj.*

hex·ap·o·dy (hek sap′ə dē), *n., pl.* **-dies.** *Pros.* a measure consisting of six feet. [1835–45; < Gk *hexapod-* (see HEXAPOD) + -Y[3]] —**hex·a·pod·ic** (hek′sə pod′ik), *adj.*

hex·ar·chy (hek′sär kē), *n., pl.* **-chies.** a group of six allied states or kingdoms each under its own ruler. [1790–1800; HEX- + -ARCHY]

hex·a·stich (hek′sə stik′), *n. Pros.* a strophe, stanza, or poem consisting of six lines. Also, **hexastichon.** [1605–15; shortened form of HEXASTICHON] —**hex·a·stich·ic** (hek′sə stik′ik), *adj.*

hex·as·ti·chon (hek sas′ti kon′), *n., pl.* **-cha** (-kə). hexastich. [1570–80; < Gk *hexástichon,* neut. of *hexástichos* of six lines. See HEXA-, STICH[1]]

hex·a·syl·la·ble (hek′sə sil′ə bəl), *n.* a word or line of verse of six syllables. [HEXA- + SYLLABLE] —**hex·a·syl·lab·ic** (hek′sə si lab′ik), *adj.*

Hex·a·teuch (hek′sə tŏŏk′, -tyŏŏk′), *n.* the first six books of the Old Testament. [1875–80; HEXA- + (PENTA)TEUCH] —**Hex′a·teuch′al,** *adj.*

hex·a·va·lent (hek′sə vā′lənt), *adj. Chem.* having a valence of six. Also, **sexavalent, sexivalent.** [1885–90; HEXA- + -VALENT]

hex·o·ki·nase (hek′sə kī′nās, -nāz), *n. Biochem.* an enzyme that catalyzes the phosphorylation of hexose sugars. [1925–30; HEXO(SE) + KINASE]

hex·one (hek′sōn), *n. Chem.* **1.** any of various organic ketones containing six atoms of carbon in the molecule. **2.** See **methyl isobutyl ketone.** [1895–1900; HEX- + -ONE]

hex·os·a·mine (hek sos′ə mēn′), *n. Biochem.* any hexose derivative in which a hydroxyl group is replaced by an amino group. [1910–15; HEXOSE + -AMINE]

hex·o·san (hek′sə san′), *n.* any of a group of hemicelluloses that hydrolyze to hexoses. [1890–95; HEXOSE + -AN]

hex·ose (hek′sōs), *n.* any of a class of sugars containing six atoms of carbon, including glucose and fructose. [1890–95; HEX- + -OSE[2]]

hex′ sign′, any of various magical symbols of usually stylized design, as those painted on barns by the Pennsylvania Dutch for protection against evil spirits and now sometimes used for purely decorative purposes. Also called **hex′ mark′.**

hex sign

hex·yl (hek′sil), *adj.* containing a hexyl group. [1865–70; HEX- + -YL] —**hex·yl′ic,** *adj.*

hex′yl group′, any of five univalent, isomeric groups having the formula $C_6H_{13}-$. Also called **hex′yl rad′ical.**

hex·yl·res·or·cin·ol (hek′sil rə zôr′sə nôl′, -nol′), *n. Pharm.* white or yellowish-white, needle-shaped crystals, $C_{12}H_{18}O_2$, used chiefly as an antiseptic and for the expulsion of intestinal worms. [1920–25; HEXYL + RESORCINOL]

hey (hā), *interj.* **1.** (used as an exclamation to call attention or to express pleasure, surprise, bewilderment, etc.) **2.** *Southern U.S. Informal.* hello: used as a greeting. [1150–1200; ME *hei*]

hey·day[1] (hā′dā′), *n.* **1.** the stage or period of greatest vigor, strength, success, etc.; prime: *the heyday of the vaudeville stars.* **2.** *Archaic.* high spirits. Also, **hey′·dey′.** [1580–90; var. of HIGH DAY, appar. by confusion with HEYDAY[2]]

hey·day[2] (hā′dā), *interj. Archaic.* (used as an exclamation of cheerfulness, surprise, wonder, etc.) [1520–30; rhyming compound based on HEY; r. *heyda* < G *hei da* hey there]

Hey·duck (hī′dŏŏk), *n.* Haiduk. Also, **Hey′duke, Hey′duc.**

Hey·er·dahl (hā′ər däl′), *n.* **Thor** (tŏŏr), born 1914, Norwegian ethnologist and author.

Hey·mans (hī′mənz; *Fr.* ā mäɴs′), *n.* **Cor·neille** (kôr-ne′yᵊ), 1892–1968, Belgian physiologist: Nobel prize for medicine 1938.

Hey·rov·ský (hā′rôf skē), *n.* **Ja·ro·slav** (yä′rô släf), 1890–1967, Czech chemist: Nobel prize 1959.

hey′ rube′, **1.** (used as a call to rally circus or carnival personnel in a fight, esp. in a fight with townspeople). **2.** a fight between townspeople and the members of a circus or carnival. [1880–85]

Hey·se (hī′zə), *n.* **Paul (Jo·hann von)** (poul yō′hän fən), 1830–1914, German playwright, novelist, poet, and short-story writer: Nobel prize 1910.

Hey·ward (hā′wərd), *n.* **Du·Bose** (də bōz′), 1885–1940, U.S. playwright, novelist, and poet.

Hey·wood (hā′wŏŏd), *n.* **1. John,** 1497?–1580?, English dramatist and epigrammatist. **2. Thomas,** 1573?–1641, English dramatist, poet, and actor. **3.** a male given name.

Hez·e·ki·ah (hez′ə kī′ə), *n.* a king of Judah of the 7th and 8th centuries B.C. II Kings 18. [< Heb *ḥizqiyyāh* lit., Yahweh strengthens]

HF, See **high frequency.**

Hf, *Symbol, Chem.* hafnium.

hf., half.

hf. bd., half-bound.

HG, **1.** High German. **2.** *Brit.* Home Guard.

Hg, *Symbol, Chem.* mercury. [< NL *hydrargyrum,* for L *hydrargyrus* (by analogy with AURUM, ARGENTUM, etc.) < Gk *hydrárgyros* lit., liquid silver (*hydr-* HYDR-[1] + *árgyros* silver)]

hg, hectogram; hectograms.

H.G., **1.** High German (def. 1). **2.** His Grace; Her Grace.

hGH, human growth hormone.

hgt., height.

CONCISE PRONUNCIATION KEY: *act, cāpe, dâre, pärt; set, ēqual; if, īce; ox, ōver, ôrder, oil, bŏŏk, bōōt, out; up, ûrge; child; sing; shoe; thin, that;* zh as in *treasure.* ə = *a* as in *alone, e* as in *system, i* as in *easily, o* as in *gallop, u* as in *circus;* ᵊ as in *fire* (fīᵊr), *hour* (ouᵊr). l and n can serve as syllabic consonants, as in *cradle* (krād′l), and *button* (but′n). See the full key inside the front cover.

hgwy., highway.

H.H., **1.** His Highness; Her Highness. **2.** His Holiness.

hhd, hogshead; hogsheads.

HH.D., Doctor of Humanities.

HHFA, Housing and Home Finance Agency.

H-hinge (āch′hinj′), *n.* a strap hinge having the form of an H with the joint in the crossbar. [1720–30; H (from the form) + HINGE]

H-hour (āch′ou°r′, -ou′ər), *n.* the time, usually unspecified, set for the beginning of a planned attack. [H (for *hour*) + HOUR; cf. D-DAY]

HHS, See **Department of Health and Human Services.**

hi[1] (hī), *interj.* (used as an exclamation of greeting); hello! [1425–75; late ME *hy,* perh. var. of *hei* HEY]

hi[2] (hī), *adj.* an informal, simplified spelling of **high:** *hi fidelity.*

HI, Hawaii (approved esp. for use with zip code).

H.I., **1.** Hawaiian Islands. **2.** *Meteorol.* heat index.

Hi·a·le·ah (hī′ə lē′ə), *n.* a city in SE Florida, near Miami: racetrack. 145,254.

hi·a·tus (hī ā′təs), *n., pl.* **-tus·es, -tus. 1.** a break or interruption in the continuity of a work, series, action, etc. **2.** a missing part; gap or lacuna: *Scholars attempted to account for the hiatus in the medieval manuscript.* **3.** any gap or opening. **4.** *Gram., Pros.* the coming together, with or without break or slight pause, and without contraction, of two vowels in successive words or syllables, as in *see easily.* **5.** *Anat.* a natural fissure, cleft, or foramen in a bone or other structure. [1555–65; < L *hiātus* opening, gap, equiv. to *hiā(re)* to gape, open + *-tus* suffix of v. action] **—hi·a′tal,** *adj.*
—Syn. 3. break, interval, space.

hia′tus her′nia, *Pathol.* an abnormal condition in which part of the stomach protrudes upward through the esophageal cleft in the diaphragm, sometimes causing a backflow of acid stomach contents into the esophagus. Also, **hia′tal her′nia.**

Hi·a·wath·a (hī′ə woth′ə, -wô′thə, hē′ə-), *n.* the central figure of *The Song of Hiawatha* (1855), a poem by Henry Wadsworth Longfellow: named after a legendary Indian chief, fl. c1570.

hi·ba·chi (hi bä′chē), *n.* a small Japanese-style charcoal brazier covered with a grill, usually used for outdoor cooking. [1860–65; < Japn, equiv. to *hi* fire (earlier *fi(y)* < **poi*) + *-bachi* comb. form of *hachi* pot, earlier *fati* < MChin, akin to Chin *bō* monk's bowl; perh. < Pali *patta* < Skt *pātra* drinking vessel]

hi·ba·ku·sha (hē′bə ko͞o′shə; *Japn.* hē bä′ko͞o shä′), *n., pl.* **-shas, -sha.** a survivor of either of the atomic bomb attacks on Hiroshima and Nagasaki, Japan, in 1945. [< Japn, equiv. to *hibaku* bombed (*hi-* suffer + *baku-* burst open, explode < MChin, equiv. to Chin *bèi bào*) + *-sha* person < MChin, equiv. to Chin *chě*]

Hib·bing (hib′ing), *n.* a town in NE Minnesota: iron mining. 21,193.

hi·ber·nac·u·lum (hī′bər nak′yə ləm), *n., pl.* **-la** (-lə). **1.** a protective case or covering, esp. for winter, as of an animal or a plant bud. **2.** winter quarters, as of a hibernating animal. Also, **hi·ber·nac·le** (hī′bər nak′əl). [1690–1700; < L *hībernāculum* winter residence, equiv. to *hīberna(re)* (see HIBERNATE) + *-culum* -CULE[2]]

hi·ber·nal (hī bûr′nl), *adj.* of or pertaining to winter; wintry. [1620–30; < L *hībernālis,* equiv. to *hībern(us)* wintry + *-ālis* -AL[1]; akin to *hiems* winter (see HIEMAL)]

hi·ber·nate (hī′bər nāt′), *v.i.,* **-nat·ed, -nat·ing. 1.** to spend the winter in close quarters in a dormant condition, as bears and certain other animals. **2.** to withdraw or be in seclusion; retire. **3.** to winter in a place with a milder climate: *Each winter finds us hibernating in Florida.* [1795–1805; < L *hībernātus* (ptp. of *hībernāre* to spend the winter). See HIBERNAL, -ATE[1]] **—hi′ber·na′tion,** *n.* **—hi′ber·na′tor,** *n.*

Hi·ber·ni·a (hī bûr′nē ə), *n. Latin.* Ireland.

Hi·ber·ni·an (hī bûr′nē ən), *adj.* **1.** of, pertaining to, or characteristic of Ireland or its inhabitants; Irish. *—n.* **2.** a native of Ireland. [1625–35; HIBERNI(A) + -AN]

Hi·ber·ni·cism (hī bûr′nə siz′əm), *n.* an idiom or characteristic peculiar to Irish English or to the Irish. Also, **Hi·ber·ni·an·ism** (hī bûr′nē ə niz′əm). [1750–60; < ML *Hibernic(us)* Hibernian (*Hibern(ia)* Hibernia + *-icus* -IC) + -ISM]

Hi·ber·ni·cize (hī bûr′nə sīz′), *v.t.,* **-cized, -ciz·ing.** to make Irish in character. Also, *esp. Brit.,* **Hi·ber′ni·cise′.** [1805–15; < ML *Hibernic(us)* (see HIBERNICISM) + -IZE]

Hi·ber·no-Eng·lish (hī bûr′nō ing′glish *or, often,* -lish), *n.* **1.** Also called **Anglo-Irish.** the English language as spoken in Ireland. *—adj.* **2.** of or pertaining to Hiberno-English.

Hi·ber·no-Sax·on (hī bûr′nō sak′sən), *adj.* **1.** having the characteristics of both the Irish and English; Anglo-Irish. **2.** pertaining to or designating the style of art, esp. of manuscript illumination, developed principally during the 7th and 8th centuries A.D. in the monastic scriptoria founded by Irish missionaries, characterized chiefly by the use of zoomorphic forms elaborated in interlaced patterns and often set within a symmetrically balanced framework of geometric shapes; Anglo-Irish. Cf. **Celto-Germanic.** [1935–40; *Hiberno-* comb. form of HIBERNIAN]

CONCISE ETYMOLOGY KEY: <, descended or borrowed from; >, whence; b., blend of, blended; c., cognate with; cf., compare; deriv., derivative; equiv., equivalent; imit., imitative; obl., oblique; r., replacing; s., stem; sp., spelling, spelled; resp., respelling, respelled; trans., translation; ?, origin unknown; *, unattested; ‡, probably earlier than. See the full key inside the front cover.

hi·bis·cus (hī bis′kəs, hi-), *n., pl.* **-cus·es. 1.** Also called **China rose.** a woody plant, *Hibiscus rosa-sinensis,* of the mallow family, having large, showy flowers: the state flower of Hawaii. **2.** any of numerous other plants, shrubs, or trees of the genus *Hibiscus,* characterized by lobate or dentate leaves and usually profusely blooming flowers. [1700–10; < NL, L < Gk *hibískos* mallow]

hic (hik), *interj.* (an onomatopoeic word used to imitate or represent a hiccup.)

hic·cup (hik′up, -əp), *n., v.,* **-cuped** or **-cupped, -cup·ing** or **-cup·ping.** *—n.* **1.** a quick, involuntary inhalation that follows a spasm of the diaphragm and is suddenly checked by closure of the glottis, producing a short, relatively sharp sound. **2.** Usually, **hiccups.** the condition of having such spasms: *She got the hiccups just as she began to speak.* **3.** *Informal.* a minor difficulty, interruption, setback, etc.: *a hiccup in the stock market.* *—v.i.* **4.** to make the sound of a hiccup: *The motor hiccuped as it started.* **5.** to have the hiccups. **6.** *Informal.* to experience a temporary decline, setback, interruption, etc.: *There was general alarm when the economy hiccuped.* Also, **hic·cough** (hik′up, -əp). [1570–80; alter. of *hocket, hickock,* equiv. to HIC + -OCK; akin to LG *hick* hiccup; see HOCKET]

hic et u·bi·que (hēk′ et o͞o bē′kwe; *Eng.* hik′ et yo͞o bī′kwē), *Latin.* here and everywhere.

Hich·ens (hich′ənz), *n.* **Robert Smythe** (smīth, smith), 1864–1950, English novelist.

hic ja·cet (hēk′ yä′ket; *Eng.* hik′ jā′set), *Latin.* here lies (often used to begin epitaphs on tombstones).

hick (hik), *n.* **1.** an unsophisticated, boorish, and provincial person; rube. *—adj.* **2.** pertaining to or characteristic of hicks: *hick ideas.* **3.** located in a rural or culturally unsophisticated area: *a hick town.* [1555–65; after *Hick,* familiar form of *Richard*]

hick·ey (hik′ē), *n., pl.* **-eys. 1.** *Slang.* **a.** a pimple. **b.** a reddish mark left on the skin by a passionate kiss. **2.** any device or gadget whose name is not known or is momentarily forgotten. **3.** *Elect.* a fitting used to mount a lighting fixture in an outlet box or on a pipe or stud. **4.** a tool used to bend tubes and pipes. Also, **hick′ie.** [1905–10; *Amer.*; of obscure orig.; senses under def. 1 perh. a separate word, though the development "device > defective device > defect, blemish, mark" is also possible; cf. DOOHICKEY]

hick′-joint point′ing (hik′joint′), *Masonry.* pointing having raked joints filled flush with the face of the masonry with a finish mortar. [1875–80]

Hick·ok (hik′ok), *n.* **James Butler** ("*Wild Bill*"), 1837–76, U.S. frontiersman.

hick·o·ry (hik′ə rē, hik′rē), *n., pl.* **-ries. 1.** any of several North American trees belonging to the genus *Carya,* of the walnut family, certain species of which bear edible nuts or yield a valuable wood. Cf. **pecan, shagbark. 2.** the wood of any of these trees. **3.** a switch, stick, etc., of this wood. **4.** *Baseball Slang.* a baseball bat. **5.** Also called **hick′ory cloth′, hick′ory stripe′.** a strong fabric of twill construction, used chiefly in the manufacture of work clothes. [1610–20, *Amer.*; earlier *pohickery* < Virginia Algonquian (E sp.) *pocohiquara* a milky drink prepared from hickory nuts]

Hick·o·ry (hik′ə rē, hik′rē), *n.* a city in W North Carolina. 20,757.

Hick′ory Hills′, a town in NE Illinois. 13,778.

hick′ory pine′. See **bristlecone pine.** [1880–85, *Amer.*]

Hicks (hiks), *n.* **1. Edward,** 1780–1849, U.S. painter. **2. Sir John Richard,** born 1904, British economist: Nobel prize 1972.

Hicks·ite (hik′sīt), *n.* a member of the liberal body of Quakers in the U.S., who asserted the sufficiency of the Inner Light in religious life. [1825–35, *Amer.*; after Elias *Hicks* (1748–1830), American Quaker preacher; see -ITE[1]]

hicks·ville (hiks′vil), *n. Slang.* a backward, provincial place; backwater. [HICK + -S[3] + *-ville,* extracted from place names; cf. SQUARESVILLE]

Hicks·ville (hiks′vil), *n.* a town on W Long Island, in SE New York. 43,245.

Hicks′ yew′, a hybrid yew, *Taxus media hicksii,* having a columnar manner of growth. [after *Hicks* nurseries in Westbury, New York]

hick·wall (hik′wôl′), *n. Brit. Dial.* any of certain European woodpeckers, esp. the green woodpecker. [1400–50; late ME *hygh-whele,* orig. imit.]

hick·y (hik′ē), *adj.,* **hick·i·er, hick·i·est.** *Informal.* hick (def. 2). [HICK + -Y[1]] **—hick′i·ness,** *n.*

hick·y-horse (hik′ē hôrs′), *n. South Atlantic States (chiefly North Carolina).* a seesaw. [*hicky* of unclear orig.]

hic re·qui·es·cit in pa·ce (hēk′ re′kwe e′shet ēn pä′che), *Latin.* here rests in peace: a phrase used on tombstones before the name of the deceased.

hid (hid), *v.* pt. and a pp. of **hide**[1].

hi·dal·go (hi dal′gō; *Sp.* ē thäl′gô), *n., pl.* **-gos** (-gōz; *Sp.* -gôs). **1.** a man of the lower nobility in Spain. **2.** (in Spanish America) a man who owns considerable property or is otherwise esteemed. [1585–95; < Sp, contr. of *hijo dalgo,* OSp *fijo dalgo* a noble, a person with property, a son with something < L *filius* son + *dē* from + *aliquō* something] **—hi·dal′go·ism, hi·dal·gism** (hi-dal′jiz əm), *n.*

Hi·dal·go (hi dal′gō; *Sp.* ē thäl′gô), *n.* **1. Juan** (hwän), c1600–85, Spanish composer and harpist. **2.** a state in central Mexico. 1,409,000; 8057 sq. mi. (20,870 sq. km). *Cap.:* Pachuca.

Hi·dal·go y Cos·til·la (ē thäl′gô ē kôs tē′yä), **Miguel** (mē gel′), 1753–1811, Mexican priest, patriot, and revolutionist.

Hi·dat·sa (hē dät′sä), *n., pl.* **-sas,** (*esp. collectively*) **-sa** for 1. **1.** a member of a Siouan people dwelling on the Missouri River. **2.** the Siouan language of the Hidatsa tribe.

hid·den (hid′n), *adj.* **1.** concealed; obscure; covert: *hidden meaning; hidden hostility.* *—v.* **2.** pp. of **hide**[1]. **—hid′den·ly,** *adv.* **—hid′den·ness,** *n.*
—Syn. 1. secret, veiled; occult.

hid′den agen′da, an often duplicitously undisclosed plan or motive. [1985–90]

hid·den·ite (hid′n īt′), *n. Mineral.* a rare, transparent variety of spodumene, colored yellow-green to emerald-green by chromium: used as a gem. [after William E. *Hidden* (1853–1918), U.S. mineralogist, who discovered it in 1879; see -ITE[1]]

hid′den tax′, any tax paid by a manufacturer, supplier, or seller that is added to the consumer price.

hide[1] (hīd), *v.,* **hid, hid·den** or **hid, hid·ing,** *n.* *—v.t.* **1.** to conceal from sight; prevent from being seen or discovered: *Where did she hide her jewels?* **2.** to obstruct the view of; cover up: *The sun was hidden by the clouds.* **3.** to conceal from knowledge or exposure; keep secret: *to hide one's feelings.* *—v.i.* **4.** to conceal oneself; lie concealed: *He hid in the closet.* **5. hide out,** to go into or remain in hiding: *After breaking out of jail, he hid out in a deserted farmhouse.* *—n.* **6.** *Brit.* a place of concealment for hunting or observing wildlife; hunting blind. [bef. 900; ME *hiden,* OE *hȳdan*; c. OFris *hūda,* Gk *keúthein* to conceal] **—hid′a·ble,** *adj.* **—hid′a·bil′i·ty,** *n.* **—hid′er,** *n.*
—Syn. 1. screen, mask, cloak, veil, shroud, disguise. HIDE, CONCEAL, SECRETE mean to put out of sight or in a secret place. HIDE is the general word: *to hide one's money or purpose; A dog hides a bone.* CONCEAL, somewhat more formal, is to cover from sight: *A rock concealed them from view.* SECRETE means to put away carefully, in order to keep secret: *The spy secreted the important papers.* **3.** disguise, dissemble, suppress. **—Ant. 1.** reveal, display.

hide[2] (hīd), *n., v.,* **hid·ed, hid·ing.** *—n.* **1.** the pelt or skin of one of the larger animals (cow, horse, buffalo, etc.), raw or dressed. **2.** *Informal.* **a.** the skin of a human being: *Get out of here or I'll tan your hide!* **b.** safety or welfare: *He's only worried about his own hide.* **3.** *Australia and New Zealand Informal.* impertinence; impudence. **4. hide nor hair,** a trace or evidence, as of something missing: *They didn't find hide nor hair of the murder weapon.* Also, **hide or hair.** *—v.t.* **5.** *Informal.* to administer a beating to; thrash. **6.** to protect (a rope, as a boltrope of a sail) with a covering of leather. [bef. 900; ME; OE *hȳd*; c. D *huid,* ON *hūth,* Dan, Sw *hud,* OHG *hūt* (G *Haut*), L *cutis* skin, CUTIS; see HIDE[1]] **—hide′less,** *adj.*
—Syn. 1. See **skin.**

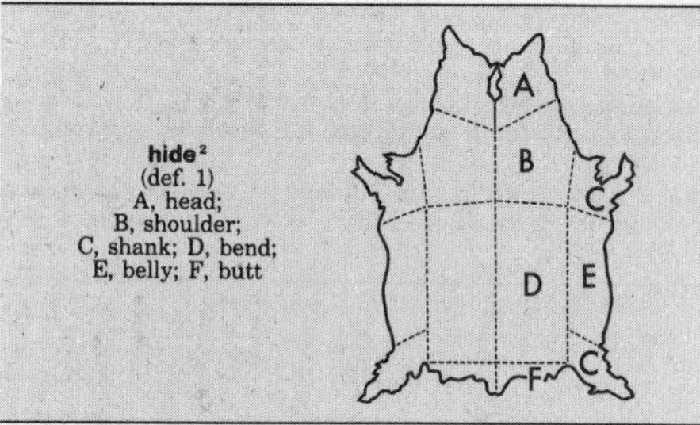

hide[2] (def. 1) A, head; B, shoulder; C, shank; D, bend; E, belly; F, butt

hide[3] (hīd), *n. Old Eng. Law.* a unit of land measurement varying from 60 to 120 acres (24 to 49 hectares) or more, depending upon local usage. [bef. 900; ME; OE *hīd(e), hīg(i)d* portion of land, family; akin to L *cīvis* citizen, Gk *keîmai* to lie, abide]

Hide-A-Bed (hīd′ə bed′), *Trademark.* a brand of hideaway bed.

hide-and-seek (hīd′n sēk′), *n.* one of a variety of children's games in which, according to specified rules, one player gives the others a chance to hide and then attempts to find them. Also called **hide-and-go-seek** (hīd′n gō sēk′). [1665–75]

hide·a·way (hīd′ə wā′), *n.* **1.** a place to which a person can retreat for safety, privacy, relaxation, or seclusion; refuge: *His hideaway is in the mountains.* **2.** See **hideaway bed.** *—adj.* **3.** hidden; concealed; *a hideaway compartment for luggage.* [1870–75; n., adj. use of v. phrase (transit.) *hide (something) away* or (intransit.) *hide away*]

hide′away bed′, a sofa, loveseat, etc., that can be converted into a bed, usually by folding out a concealed mattress and springs.

hide·bound (hīd′bound′), *adj.* **1.** narrow and rigid in opinion; inflexible: *a hidebound pedant.* **2.** oriented toward or confined to the past; extremely conservative: *a hidebound philosopher.* **3.** (of a horse, cow, etc.) having the back and ribs bound tightly by the hide. [1550–60; HIDE[2] + -BOUND[1]] **—hide′bound′ness,** *n.*

hid·e·ous (hid′ē əs), *adj.* **1.** horrible or frightful to the senses; repulsive; very ugly: *a hideous monster.* **2.** shocking or revolting to the moral sense: *a hideous crime.* **3.** distressing; appalling: *the hideous expense of moving one's home to another city.* [1275–1325; ME *hidous* < OF *hisdos,* equiv. to *hisde* horror, fright (perh. < OHG **egisida,* akin to *egisôn, agison* to frighten) + *-os* -OUS] **—hid′e·ous·ly,** *adv.* **—hid′e·ous·ness, hid·e·os·i·ty** (hid′ē os′i tē), *n.*
—Syn. 1, 2. grisly, grim; repellent, detestable, odious, monstrous, dreadful, appalling, ghastly. **—Ant. 1.** attractive, pleasing.

hide·out (hīd′out′), *n.* a safe place for hiding, esp. from the law. Also, **hide′-out′.** [1870–75; n. use of v. phrase *hide out*]

hid·ey-hole (hī′dē hōl′), *n. Informal.* a nook or cranny used as a hiding place. [1810–20; HIDE[1] + -EY[2] + HOLE]

Hi·de·yo·shi (hē′de yô′shē), *n.* **To·yo·to·mi** (tô′yô-tô′mē), 1536–98, Japanese general and statesman: prime minister and dictator of Japan 1585–98.

hid·ing[1] (hī′ding), *n.* **1.** act of concealing; concealment: *to remain in hiding.* **2.** a secret refuge or means of concealment. [1250–1300; ME; see HIDE[1], -ING[1]]

hid′ing[2] (hī′ding), *n. Informal.* a severe beating; flogging; thrashing. [1800–10; HIDE[2] + -ING[1]]

hid·ro·poi·e·sis (hid′rō poi ē′sis, hī′drō-), *n.* the production of sweat. [*hidro-*, erroneously for Gk *hidrōto-*, comb. form of *hidrṓs sweat* + *poíēsis* making; see POESY] —**hid·ro·poi·et·ic** (hid′rō poi et′ik, hī′drō-), *adj.*

hi·dro·sis (hi drō′sis, hī-), *n.* the excessive production of sweat. [1890–95; < Gk *hídrōsis* sweating, equiv. to *hidrō-*, var. s. of *hidroûn* to sweat, v. deriv. of *hidrṓs* sweat + *-sis* -SIS] —**hi·drot·ic** (hi drot′ik, hī-), *adj.*

hi·dy (hī′dē), *interj. South Midland U.S.* howdy[1] (used as a greeting).

hie (hī), *v.,* **hied, hie·ing** or **hy·ing.** —*v.i.* **1.** to hasten; speed; go in haste. —*v.t.* **2.** to hasten (oneself): *Hie yourself down to this once-in-a-lifetime sale!* [bef. 900; ME *hien, hyen,* OE *hīgian* to strive; c. D *hijgen* to pant, Gk *kíein* to go; L *ciēre* to cause to go]

hie·la·mon (hē′lə mən), *n. Australian.* a shield made of wood or bark. [1790–1800; < Dharuk *(h)i-li-mang*]

hi·e·mal (hī′ə məl), *adj.* of or pertaining to winter; wintry. [1550–60; < L *hiemālis* pertaining to winter, equiv. to *hiem(s)* winter (akin to Gk *chiṓn* snow, *cheimṓn* winter, Skt *hima* cold, frost, snow) + *-ālis* -AL[1]; see HIBERNAL]

hier-, var. of **hiero-** before a vowel: *hierarchy.*

hi·er·arch (hī′ə rärk′, hī′rärk), *n.* **1.** a person who rules or has authority in sacred matters; high priest. **2.** a person having high position or considerable authority. **3.** one of a body of officials or minor priests in certain ancient Greek temples. [1480–90; < ML *hierarcha* < Gk *hierárchēs* steward of sacred rites, equiv. to *hier-* HIER- + *-archēs* -ARCH] —**hi′er·ar′chal,** *adj.*

hi·er·ar·chi·cal (hī′ə rär′ki kəl, hī rär′-), *adj.* of, belonging to, or characteristic of a hierarchy. Also, **hi′er·ar′chic.** [1425–75; late ME. See HIERARCH, -ICAL] —**hi′er·ar′chi·cal·ly,** *adv.*

hi·er·ar·chism (hī′ə rär′kiz əm, hī′rär kiz′-), *n.* hierarchical principles, rule, or influence. [1840–50; HIERARCH(Y) + -ISM] —**hi′er·ar′chist,** *n.*

hi·er·ar·chize (hī′ə rär kīz′, hī′rär-), *v.t.,* **-chized, -chiz·ing.** to arrange in a hierarchy. Also, *esp. Brit.,* **hi′er·ar·chise′.** [1880–85; HIERARCH(Y) + -IZE]

hi·er·ar·chy (hī′ə rär′kē, hī′rär-), *n., pl.* **-chies. 1.** any system of persons or things ranked one above another. **2.** government by ecclesiastical rulers. **3.** the power or dominion of a hierarch. **4.** an organized body of ecclesiastical officials in successive ranks or orders: *the Roman Catholic hierarchy.* **5.** one of the three divisions of the angels, each made up of three orders, conceived as constituting a graded body. **6.** Also called **celestial hierarchy.** the collective body of angels. **7.** government by an elite group. **8.** *Ling.* the system of levels according to which a language is organized, as phonemic, morphemic, syntactic, or semantic. [1300–50; < ML *hierarchia* < LGk *hierarchía* rule or power of the high priest, equiv. to *hier-* HIER- + *archía* -ARCHY; r. ME *jerarchie* < MF *ierarchie* < ML *ierarchia,* var. of *hierarchia*]

hi·er·at·ic (hī′ə rat′ik, hī rat′-), *adj.* **1.** Also, **hi′er·at′i·cal.** of or pertaining to priests or the priesthood; sacerdotal; priestly. **2.** noting or pertaining to a form of ancient Egyptian writing consisting of abridged forms of hieroglyphics, used by the priests in their records. **3.** noting or pertaining to certain styles in art in which the representations or methods are fixed by or as if by religious tradition. **4.** highly restrained or severe in emotional import: *Some of the more hieratic sculptures leave the viewer curiously unmoved.* —*n.* **5.** ancient Egyptian hieratic writing. [1650–60; < L *hierāticus* < Gk *hierātikós* pertaining to the priesthood, priestly, equiv. to *hierā-*, var. s. of *hierâsthai* to perform priestly functions (v. deriv. of *hierós* sacred; see HIERO-) + *-ikos* -IC, with *-t-* by analogy with derivatives from agent nouns in *-tēs* (cf. ATHLETE, ATHLETIC)] —**hi′er·at′i·cal·ly,** *adv.*

hiero-, a combining form meaning "sacred," "priestly," used in the formation of compound words: *hierocracy.* Also, *esp. before a vowel,* **hier-.** [< Gk *hieró(s)* holy, sacred]

hi·er·oc·ra·cy (hī′ə rok′rə sē, hī rok′-), *n., pl.* **-cies.** rule or government by priests or ecclesiastics. [1785–95; HIERO- + -CRACY] —**hi·er·o·crat·ic** (hī′ər ə krat′ik, hī′rə-), **hi′er·o·crat′i·cal,** *adj.*

hi·er·o·dea·con (hī′ər ə dē′kən, hī′rə-), *n. Eastern Ch.* a monk who is also a deacon. [HIERO- + DEACON]

hi·er·o·dule (hī′ər ə do͞ol′, -dyo͞ol′, hī′rə-), *n.* a slave in service in an ancient Greek temple. [1825–35; < Gk *hieródoulos* temple slave, equiv. to *hieró(n)* temple + *doûlos* slave] —**hi′er·o·du′lic,** *adj.*

hi·er·o·glyph·ic (hī′ər ə glif′ik, hī′rə-), *adj.* Also, **hi′er·o·glyph′i·cal. 1.** designating or pertaining to a pictographic script, particularly that of the ancient Egyptians, in which many of the symbols are conventionalized, recognizable pictures of the things represented. **2.** inscribed with hieroglyphic symbols. **3.** hard to decipher; hard to read. —*n.* **4.** Also, **hi′er·o·glyph′.** a hieroglyphic symbol. **5.** Usually, **hieroglyphics.** hieroglyphic writing. **6.** a figure or symbol with a hidden meaning. **7. hieroglyphics,** handwriting, figures, characters, code, etc., difficult to decipher: *the confusing hieroglyphics of advanced mathematics.* [1575–85; < LL *hieroglyphicus* < Gk *hieroglyphikós* pertaining to sacred writing. See HIERO-, GLYPHIC] —**hi′er·o·glyph′i·cal·ly,** *adv.*

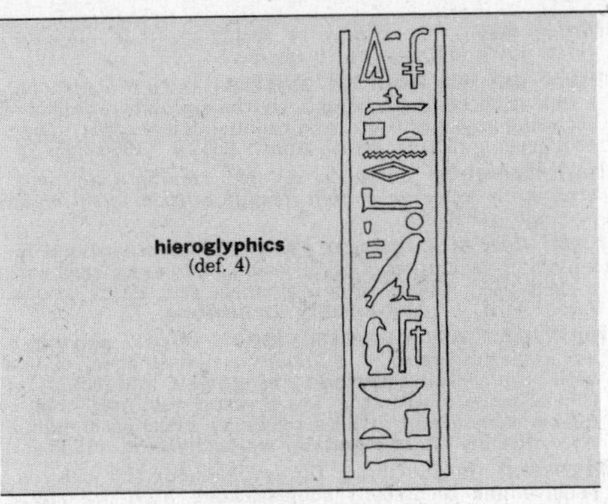

hieroglyphics (def. 4)

Hi′eroglyph′ic Hit′tite, an extinct language of the Anatolian branch of Indo-European, written in a pictographic script in Syria c1200–c600 B.C.: the same language as written in cuneiform in Anatolia is known as Luwian.

hi·er·o·glyph·ist (hī′ər ə glif′ist, hī′rə-, hī′ə rog′lə-fist, hī rog′-), *n.* **1.** a person who studies hieroglyphics; hieroglyphologist. **2.** a person who writes in hieroglyphics. [1820–30; HIEROGLYPH(ICS) + -IST]

hi·er·o·gly·phol·o·gy (hī′ər ə gli fol′ə jē, hī′rə-), *n.* the study of hieroglyphic writing. [HIEROGLYPH(ICS) + -O- + -LOGY] —**hi′er·o·gly·phol′o·gist,** *n.*

hi·er·o·gram (hī′ər ə gram′, hī′rə-), *n.* a sacred symbol, as an emblem, pictograph, or the like. [1650–60; HIERO- + -GRAM[1]]

hi·er·o·gram·mat (hī′ər ə gram′ət, -at, hī′rə-), *n.* a writer of hierograms. Also, **hi·er·o·gram·mate** (hī′ər ə-gram′it, -āt, hī′rə-). [1670–80; < Gk *hierogrammateús* sacred scribe, equiv. to *hiero-* HIERO- + *grammateús* scribe; see GRAPH] —**hi·er·o·gram·mat·ic** (hī′ər ə grə-mat′ik, hī′rə-), **hi′er·o·gram·mat′i·cal,** *adj.* —**hi′er·o·gram′ma·tist,** *n.*

hi·er·ol·a·try (hī′ə rol′ə trē, hī rol′-), *n.* worship or veneration of saints or sacred things. Cf. **hagiology.** [1805–15; HIERO- + -LATRY]

hi·er·ol·o·gy (hī′ə rol′ə jē, hī rol′-), *n.* **1.** literature or learning regarding sacred things. **2.** hagiological literature or learning. [1830–40; HIERO- + -LOGY] —**hi·er·o·log·ic** (hī′ər ə loj′ik, hī′rə-), **hi′er·o·log′i·cal,** *adj.* —**hi′er·ol′o·gist,** *n.*

hi·er·o·monk (hī′ər ə mungk′, hī′rə-), *n. Eastern Ch.* a monk who is also a priest. [1775–85; partial trans. of LGk or MGk *hieromónachos.* See HIERO-, MONK]

hi·er·on (hī′ə ron′, hī′ron), *n., pl.* **-er·a** (-ər ə). (in ancient Greece) a temple or a sacred place. [< Gk *hierón*]

Hi·er·o·nym·ic (hī′ər ə nim′ik, hī′rə-), *adj.* of or pertaining to St. Jerome. Also, **Hi′er·o·nym′i·an.** [1650–60; < L *Hieronym(us)* Jerome + -IC]

Hi·er·on·y·mite (hī′ə ron′ə mīt′, hī ron′-), *n.* a member of a congregation of hermits named after St. Jerome. [1720–30; < L *Hieronym(us)* Jerome + -ITE[1]]

Hi·er·on·y·mus (hī′ə ron′ə məs, hī ron′-), *n.* **Eu·se·bi·us** (yo͞o sē′bē əs). See **Jerome, Saint.**

hi·er·o·phant (hī′ər ə fant′, hī′rə-, hī er′ə-), *n.* **1.** (in ancient Greece) an official expounder of rites of worship and sacrifice. **2.** any interpreter of sacred mysteries or esoteric principles; mystagogue. [1670–80; < LL *hierophanta* < Gk *hierophántēs,* equiv. to *hiero-* HIERO- + *-phántēs,* deriv. of *phaínein* to show, make known] —**hi′er·o·phan′tic,** *adj.* —**hi′er·o·phan′ti·cal·ly,** *adv.*

hi·er·ur·gy (hī′ə rûr′jē, hī′rûr-), *n., pl.* **-gies.** a holy act or rite of worship. [1670–80; < Gk *hierourgía,* deriv. of *hierourgós* ritually sacrificing priest. See HIER-, -URGY] —**hi′er·ur′gi·cal,** *adj.*

hi·fa·lu·tin (hī′fə lo͞ot′n), *adj.* highfalutin. Also, **hi′fa·lu′tin′.**

hi-fi (hī′fī′), *n.* **1.** See **high fidelity. 2.** a phonograph, radio, or other sound-reproducing apparatus possessing high fidelity. —*adj.* **3.** of, pertaining to, or characteristic of such apparatus; high-fidelity. [1945–50, *Amer.*; shortened form of HIGH FIDELITY]

Hi·ga·shi·o·sa·ka (hē gä′shē ô′sä kä′; *Eng.* hi gä′-shē ō sä′kə), *n.* a city on S Honshu, in Japan, W of Osaka. 521,635.

Hi·ga·shi·ya·ma (hē gä′shē yä′mə; *Japn.* hē gä′shē-yä′mä), *adj.* of or pertaining to the period of Japanese art history, esp. during the second half of the 15th century, influenced by Zen Buddhism and characterized by architectural simplicity and monochrome painting. [after a section of Kyoto, where the shogun Ashikaga Yoshimasa (reigned 1436–90) spent his last years]

Hig·gin·son (hig′in sən), *n.* **Thomas Wentworth Stor·row** (stor′ō), 1823–1911, U.S. clergyman, author, and social reformer.

hig·gle (hig′əl), *v.i.,* **-gled, -gling.** to bargain, esp. in a petty way; haggle. [1625–35; appar. var. of HAGGLE]

hig·gle·dy-pig·gle·dy (hig′əl dē pig′əl dē), *adv.* **1.** in a jumbled, confused, or disorderly manner; helter-skelter. —*adj.* **2.** confused; jumbled. [1590–1600; rhyming compound of uncert. orig.]

hig·gler (hig′lər), *n.* a peddler or huckster. [1630–40; HIGGLE + -ER[1]]

Higgs′ bos′on (higz), *Physics.* a hypothetical type of heavy, electrically neutral particle with zero spin. Also called **Higgs′ par′ticle.** [named after Peter W. Higgs (born 1929), English physicist, who hypothesized its existence]

high (hī), *adj.,* **-er, -est,** *adv.,* **-er, -est,** *n.* —*adj.* **1.** having a great or considerable extent or reach upward or vertically; lofty; tall: *a high wall.* **2.** having a specified extent upward: *The apple tree is now 20 feet high.* **3.** situated above the ground or some base; elevated: *a high platform; a high ledge.* **4.** exceeding the common degree or measure; strong; intense: *high speed; high color.* **5.** expensive; costly; dear: *The price of food these days is much too high.* **6.** exalted in rank, station, eminence, etc.; of exalted character or quality: *a high official; high society.* **7.** *Music.* **a.** acute in pitch. **b.** a little sharp, or above the desired pitch. **8.** produced by relatively rapid vibrations; shrill: *the high sounds of crickets.* **9.** extending to or from an elevation: *a high dive.* **10.** great in quantity, as number, degree, or force: *a high temperature; high cholesterol.* **11.** *Relig.* **a.** chief; principal; main: *the high altar of a church.* **b.** High Church. **12.** of great consequence; important; grave; serious; *the high consequences of such a deed; high treason.* **13.** haughty; arrogant: *He took a high tone with his subordinates.* **14.** advanced to the utmost extent or to the culmination: *high tide.* **15.** elevated; merry or hilarious: *high spirits; a high old time.* **16.** rich; extravagant; luxurious: *They have indulged in high living for years.* **17.** *Informal.* intoxicated with alcohol or narcotics: *He was so high he couldn't stand up.* **18.** remote: *high latitude; high antiquity.* **19.** extreme in opinion or doctrine, esp. religious or political: *a high Tory.* **20.** designating or pertaining to highland or inland regions. **21.** having considerable energy or potential power. **22.** *Auto.* of, pertaining to, or operating at the gear transmission ratio at which the speed of the engine crankshaft and of the drive shaft most closely correspond: *high gear.* **23.** *Phonet.* (of a vowel) articulated with the upper surface of the tongue relatively close to some portion of the palate, as the vowels of *eat* and *it,* which are high front, and those of *boot* and *put,* which are high back. Cf. **close** (def. 58), **low**[1] (def. 30). **24.** (of meat, esp. game) tending toward a desirable or undesirable amount of decomposition; slightly tainted: *He likes his venison high.* **25.** *Metall.* containing a relatively large amount of a specified constituent (usually used in combination): *high-carbon steel.* **26.** *Baseball.* (of a pitched ball) crossing the plate at a level above the batter's shoulders: *The pitch was high and outside.* **27.** *Cards.* **a.** having greater value than other denominations or suits. **b.** able to take a trick; being a winning card. **c.** being or having a winning combination: *Whose hand is high?* **28.** *Naut.* noting a wind of force 10 on the Beaufort scale, equal to a whole gale. **29. high on,** *Informal.* enthusiastic or optimistic about; having a favorable attitude toward or opinion of.
—*adv.* **30.** at or to a high point, place, or level. **31.** in or to a high rank or estimate: *He aims high in his political ambitions.* **32.** at or to a high amount or price. **33.** in or to a high degree. **34.** luxuriously; richly; extravagantly: *They have always lived high.* **35.** *Naut.* as close to the wind as is possible while making headway with sails full. **36. fly high,** to be full of hope or elation: *His stories began to sell, and he was flying high.* **37. high and dry, a.** (of a ship) grounded so as to be entirely above water at low tide. **b.** in a deprived or distressing situation; deserted; stranded: *We missed the last bus and were left high and dry.* **38. high and low,** in every possible place; everywhere: *The missing jewelry was never found, though we searched high and low for it.*
—*n.* **39.** *Auto.* high gear: *He shifted into high when the road became level.* **40.** *Informal.* See **high school. 41.** *Meteorol.* a pressure system characterized by relatively high pressure at its center. Cf. **anticyclone, low**[1] (def. 48). **42.** a high or the highest point, place, or level; peak: *a record high for unemployment.* **43.** *Slang.* **a.** a euphoric state induced by alcohol, drugs, etc. **b.** a period of sustained excitement, exhilaration, or the like: *After winning the lottery he was on a high for weeks.* **44.** *Cards.* the ace or highest trump out, esp. in games of the all fours family. **45. on high, a.** at or to a height; above. **b.** in heaven. **c.** having a high position, as one who makes important decisions: *the powers on high.* [bef. 900; ME *heigh,* var. of *hegh, hey, heh,* OE *hēah, hēh;* c. D *hoog,* OHG *hōh* (G *hoch*), ON *hār,* Sw *hög,* Goth *hauhs,* Lith *kaũkas* swelling, *kaukarà* hill]
—**Syn. 1.** HIGH, LOFTY, TALL, TOWERING refer to something that has considerable height. HIGH is a general term, and denotes either extension upward or position at a considerable height: *six feet high; a high shelf.* LOFTY denotes imposing or even inspiring height: *lofty crags.* TALL is applied either to something that is high in proportion to its breadth, or to anything higher than the average of its kind: *a tall tree, building.* TOWERING is applied to something that rises to a great or conspicuous height as compared with something else: *a towering mountain.* **6.** elevated, eminent, prominent, distinguished. **12.** capital. —**Ant. 1.** low.

high′ and might′y, 1. in a self-important, grandiose, or arrogant manner: *They talk high and mighty, but they owe everyone in town.* **2.** persons who are members of or identify with the higher social strata of society, esp. those who are powerful or arrogant. [1150–1200; ME: title of dignity]

high-and-might·y (hī′ən mī′tē, -ənd-), *adj.* haughty; arrogant. —**high′-and-might′i·ness,** *n.*

high·ball (hī′bôl′), *n.* **1.** a drink of whiskey mixed with club soda or ginger ale and served with ice in a tall glass. **2.** *Railroads.* **a.** a signal to start a train, given with the hand or with a lamp. **b.** a signal for a train to move at full speed. **3.** *Mil. Slang.* a hand salute. —*v.i.* **4.** *Slang.* to move at full speed. —*v.t.* **5.** to signal to (the engineer of a train) to proceed. [1880–85, *Amer.*; HIGH + BALL[1]]

high′ bar′, *Gymnastics.* See **horizontal bar.**

high′ beam′, an automobile headlight beam providing bright, long-range illumination of a darkened road and chiefly for use in driving in nonurban areas. Also, **high′·beam′.** Cf. **low beam.** [1935–40]

CONCISE PRONUNCIATION KEY: *act, cāpe, dâre, pärt; set, ēqual; if, īce; ox, ōver, ôrder, oil, bo͝ok, bo͞ot, out; up, ûrge; child; sing; shoe; thin, that;* zh as in *treasure.* ə = *a* as in *alone, e* as in *system, i* as in *easily, o* as in *gallop, u* as in *circus;* ᵊ as in *fire* (fīᵊr), *hour* (ouᵊr). l and n can serve as syllabic consonants, as in *cradle* (krād′l), and *button* (but′n). See the full key inside the front cover.

high•bind•er (hī′bīn′dər), *n.* **1.** a swindler; confidence man; cheat. **2.** a dishonest political official or leader. **3.** a member of a secret Chinese band or society employed in U.S. cities in blackmail, assassination, etc. **4.** a ruffian or rowdy. [1800–10, *Amer.*; appar. HIGH + BINDER; literal sense is unclear]

high′ blood′ pres′sure, elevation of the arterial blood pressure or a condition resulting from it; hypertension. *Abbr.:* HBP [1915–20]

high′ blow′er, a horse that produces a blowing sound when exhaling. [1825–35]

high′ board′, a diving board three meters above the water.

high•born (hī′bôrn′), *adj.* of high rank by birth. [1250–1300; ME; see HIGH, BORN]

high•boy (hī′boi′), *n. U.S. Furniture.* a tall chest of drawers on legs. Also called **high′ chest′.** [1890–95]

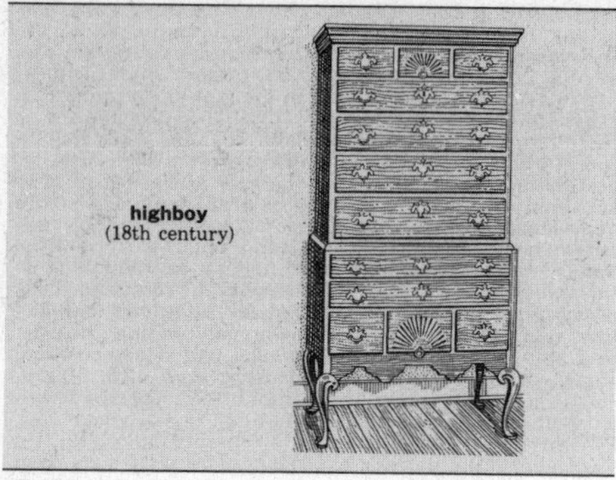

highboy (18th century)

high•bred (hī′bred′), *adj.* **1.** of superior breed. **2.** characteristic of superior breeding: *highbred manners.* [1665–75; HIGH + BRED]

high•brow (hī′brou′), *n.* **1.** a person of superior intellectual interests and tastes. **2.** a person with intellectual or cultural pretensions; intellectual snob. **3.** the crestfish. —*adj.* **4.** Also, **high′browed′.** of, pertaining to, or characteristic of a highbrow. [1895–1900; HIGH + BROW] —**high′brow′ism,** *n.*
—**Syn. 4.** intellectual, scholarly, cultured; bookish, snobbish, pseudointellectual.

high′bush blue′berry (hī′bŏŏsh′), a spreading, bushy shrub, *Vaccinium corymbosum,* of eastern North America, having small, urn-shaped, white or pinkish flowers, and bluish-black edible fruit, growing about 10 ft. (3 m) high. [1910–15, *Amer.*; HIGH + BUSH[1]]

high′bush cran′berry, a shrub, *Viburnum trilobum,* of northern North America, having broad clusters of white flowers and edible scarlet berries. Also called **cranberry bush, cranberry tree.** [1795–1805, *Amer.*]

high′bush huck′leberry. See **black huckleberry.** [1885–90, *Amer.*]

high′-card pool′ (hī′kärd′), *Cards.* See **red dog.**

high•chair (hī′châr′), *n.* a tall chair having arms and very long legs and usually a removable tray for food, for use by a very young child during meals. [1840–50; HIGH + CHAIR]

High′ Church′, (*sometimes l.c.*) (in the Anglican church) emphasizing the Catholic tradition, esp. in adherence to sacraments, rituals, and obedience to church authority. Cf. **Anglo-Catholic.** [1695–1705] —**High′ Church′man.**

high-class (hī′klas′, -kläs′), *adj.* of a type superior in quality or degree: *a high-class hotel.* [1860–65]

high-col•ored (hī′kul′ərd), *adj.* **1.** deep in color; vivid. **2.** flushed or red; florid: *a high-colored complexion.* [1920–25]

high′ com′edy, comedy dealing with polite society, characterized by sophisticated, witty dialogue and an intricate plot. Cf. **low comedy.** [1890–95]

high′ command′, **1.** the leadership or highest authority of a military command or other organization. **2.** the highest headquarters of a military force. [1915–20]

high′ commis′sioner, **1.** a representative of one sovereign member of the Commonwealth of Nations in the country of another, having a rank and responsibilities generally similar to those of an ambassador. **2.** the chief of a special international commission or other organization. **3.** the head of government in a mandate, protectorate, possession, or the like. [1880–85]

high′ con′cept, a simple and often striking idea or premise, as of a story or film, that lends itself to easy promotion and marketing. [1980–85]

high′-count′, *adj.* (of a woven fabric) having a relatively high number of warp and filling threads per square inch. [1925–30]

High′ Court′, **1.** See **Supreme Court. 2.** a superior court. [1250–1300; ME]

High′ Court′ of Jus′tice. See under **Supreme Court of Judicature.**

high•dad•dy (hī′dad′ē), *n., pl.* **-dies.** *U.S. Furniture.* a highboy having no drawers in the supporting frame. [HIGH + DADDY]

CONCISE ETYMOLOGY KEY: <, descended or borrowed from; >, whence; b., blend of, blended; c., cognate with; cf., compare; deriv., derivative; equiv., equivalent; imit., imitative; obl., oblique; r., replacing; s., stem; sp., spelling, spelled; resp., respelling, respelled; trans., translation; ?, origin unknown; *, unattested; ‡, probably earlier than. See the full key inside the front cover.

high′ day′, **1.** a holy or festal day. **2.** heyday[1]. [1150–1200; ME *heye dai* feast day]

high′-def•i•ni′tion tel′evision (hī′def′ə nish′ən), a television system having twice the standard number of scanning lines per frame and producing a sharper image, and greater picture detail. *Abbr.:* HDTV [1980–85]

high-den•si•ty (hī′den′si tē), *adj.* having a high concentration: *entering a high-density market with a new product.* [1950–55]

high′-den′sity lipopro′tein, a blood constituent involved in the transport of cholesterol and associated with a decreased risk of atherosclerosis and heart attack. *Abbr.:* HDL Cf. **low-density lipoprotein.**

high′-den′sity polyeth′ylene, *Chem.* polyethylene consisting mainly of linear, or unbranched, chains with high crystallinity and melting point, and density of 0.96 or more, produced at low pressure and used chiefly for containers and articles made by injection molding. *Abbr.:* HDPE Cf. **low-density polyethylene.** [1955–60]

high-end (hī′end′), *adj. Informal.* being the most expensive and technically sophisticated: *high-end stereo equipment.*

High′ En′ergy Astrophys′ical Observ′atory, one of a series of three U.S. satellites launched (1977–79) into orbit around the earth and equipped with instruments for studying high-energy phenomena, as x-rays, gamma rays, and cosmic rays. *Abbr.:* HEAO

high′-en′er•gy phys′ics (hī′en′ər jē), the branch of particle physics that deals with the collisions of particles accelerated to such high energies that new elementary particles are created by the collisions. [1960–65]

high′er ap′sis. See under **apsis.**

high′er arith′metic, arithmetic (def. 2).

high′er crit′icism, the study of the Bible having as its object the establishment of such facts as authorship and date of composition, as well as determination of a basis for exegesis. Cf. **lower criticism.** [1830–40]

high′er educa′tion, education beyond high school, esp. that provided by colleges and graduate and professional schools. Also called **high′er learn′ing.** [1865–70]

high′er law′, an ethical or religious principle considered as taking precedence over the laws of society, and to which one may appeal in order to justify disobedience to a constitution or enacted law with which it conflicts. [1835–45, *Amer.*]

high′er mathemat′ics, the advanced portions of mathematics, customarily considered as embracing all beyond ordinary arithmetic, geometry, algebra, and trigonometry.

high•er-up (hī′ər up′), *n. Informal.* a person in a position of higher authority in an organization; superior. [1910–15, *Amer.*; n. use of adj. phrase *higher up*]

high′est com′mon fac′tor, *Math.* See **greatest common divisor.** *Abbr.:* H.C.F.

high′ explo′sive, a class of explosive, as TNT, in which the reaction is so rapid as to be practically instantaneous, used in shells and bombs. [1875–80] —**high′-explo′sive,** *adj.*

high•fa•lu•tin (hī′fə lo͞ot′n), *adj. Informal.* pompous; bombastic; haughty; pretentious. Also, **high′fa•lu′tin′, hifalutin, hifalutin′, high•fa•lu•ting** (hī′fə lo͞o′ting, -lo͞ot′n). [1830–40; HIGH + *falutin* (perh. orig. *flutin,* var. of *fluting,* prp. of FLUTE)]

high′ fash′ion. See **haute couture.** [1940–45] —**high′-fash′ion,** *adj.*

high′ fidel′ity, *Electronics.* sound reproduction over the full range of audible frequencies with very little distortion of the original signal. Also called **hi-fi.** [1930–35] —**high′-fi•del′i•ty,** *adj.*

high′ fi′nance, large-scale financial transactions or institutions. [1900–05]

high-five (hī′fīv′), *n.* a gesture of greeting, good-fellowship, or triumph in which one person slaps the upraised palm of the hand against that of another.

high•fli•er (hī′flī′ər), *n.* **1.** a person who is extravagant or goes to extremes in aims, pretensions, opinions, etc. **2.** a person or thing that flies high. **3.** a stock, often speculative, whose price moves up or down widely. Also, **high′-fli′er, high′fly′er, high′-fly′er.** [1680–90; HIGH + FLIER]

high-flown (hī′flōn′), *adj.* **1.** extravagant in aims, pretensions, etc. **2.** pretentiously lofty; bombastic: *We couldn't endure his high-flown oratory.* [1640–50]
—**Syn. 2.** florid, flowery, magniloquent, grandiloquent.

high•fly•ing (hī′flī′ing), *adj.* **1.** moving upward to or along at a considerable height: *highflying planes.* **2.** extravagant or extreme in aims, opinions, etc.; unduly lofty: *highflying ideas about life.* **3.** having a high cost or perceived value: *the highflying glamour stocks.* Also, **high′-fly′ing.** [1575–85; HIGH + FLYING]

high′ fre′quency, the range of frequencies in the radio spectrum between 3 and 30 megahertz. [1890–95] —**high′-fre′quen•cy,** *adj.*

high′ ful′ham. See under **fulham.**

High′ Ger′man, **1.** the group of West Germanic languages that in A.D. c400–c500 underwent the second consonant shift described by Grimm's Law. *Abbr.:* HG **2.** German (def. 4). [1700–10]

high-grade (hī′grād′), *adj., v.,* **-grad•ed, -grad•ing.** —*adj.* **1.** of excellent or superior quality. **2.** (of ore) yielding a relatively large amount of the metal for which it is mined. —*v.t.* **3.** to steal (rich ore) from a mine. [1875–80] —**high′-grad′er,** *n.*

high-hand•ed (hī′han′did), *adj.* condescending or presumptuous; overbearing; arbitrary: *He has a high-handed manner.* [1625–35] —**high′-hand′ed•ly,** *adv.* —**high′-hand′ed•ness,** *n.*

high′ hat′, **1.** See **top hat. 2.** *Slang.* See **table tripod.** [1885–90]

high-hat (hī′hat′), *v.,* **-hat•ted, -hat•ting,** *adj. Informal.* —*v.t.* **1.** to snub or treat condescendingly. —*adj.* **2.** snobbish; disdainful; haughty. [1915–20; v., adj. use of HIGH HAT] —**high′-hat′ter,** *n.*

high′-hat′ cym′bals, *Music.* a pair of cymbals mounted on a rod so that the upper cymbal can be lifted and dropped on the lower by means of a pedal.

high•hole (hī′hōl′), *n.* flicker[2]. Also, **high•hold•er** (hī′hōl′dər). [1785–95; earlier *highwale, hewhole,* var. of HICKWALL]

High′ Ho′ly Day′, *Judaism.* either of two holy days of special significance, Rosh Hashanah or Yom Kippur. Also called **High′ Hol′iday.**

high′ horse′, a haughty attitude or temper; a contemptuous manner. [1375–1425; late ME]

high′ hur′dles, *Track.* a race in which runners leap over hurdles 42 in. (107 cm) high. Cf. **low hurdles.**

high•jack (hī′jak′), *v.t., v.i., n.* hijack.

high•jack•er (hī′jak′ər), *n.* hijacker.

high′ jinks′, *Informal.* boisterous celebration or merrymaking; unrestrained fun: *The city is full of conventioneers indulging in their usual high jinks.* Also, **hijinks.** [1760–70; see JINK]
—**Syn.** horseplay, skylarking.

high′ jump′, *Track.* **1.** a field event in which athletes, using a running start, compete in jumping for height over a crossbar supported by two upright poles. **2.** a jump for height made in this event. [1890–95]

high-jump (hī′jump′), *v.i.* **1.** to participate in the high jump; compete as a high jumper. —*v.t.* **2.** to clear or attempt to clear (a specified height) in a high jump.

high′ jump′er, *Track.* a participant in the high jump.

high′ key′, *Motion Pictures.* a style of lighting that is bright, even, and produces little contrast between light and dark areas of the scene. [1915–20]

high-key (hī′kē′), *adj.* (of a photograph) having chiefly light tones, usually with little tonal contrast (distinguished from *low-key*). [1915–20]

high-keyed (hī′kēd′), *adj.* very nervous or excitable; high-strung.

high•land (hī′lənd), *n.* **1.** an elevated region; plateau: *He moved to a highland far from the river.* **2. highlands,** a mountainous region or elevated part of a country. —*adj.* **3.** of, pertaining to, or characteristic of highlands. [bef. 1000; ME; OE *hēahlond.* See HIGH, LAND]
—**Syn. 1.** uplands, heights, mesa, tableland.

High•land (hī′lənd), *n.* **1.** a region in N Scotland, including a number of the Inner Hebrides. 182,044; 9710 sq. mi. (25,148 sq. km). **2.** a city in NW Indiana, near Chicago. 25,935. **3.** *Brit.* See **West Highland.**

High•land•er (hī′lən dər), *n.* **1.** a Gael inhabiting the Highlands of Scotland. **2.** a soldier of a Highland regiment. **3.** (*l.c.*) an inhabitant of any highland region. [1625–35; HIGHLAND + -ER[1]]

High′land fling′, fling (def. 17). [1865–70]

High′land Park′, **1.** a city in NE Illinois, on Lake Michigan. 30,611. **2.** a city in SE Michigan, within the city limits of Detroit. 27,909. **3.** a town in central New Jersey. 13,396.

High•lands (hī′ləndz), *n.* (*used with a singular v.*) a mountainous region in N Scotland, N of the Grampians.

high-lev•el (hī′lev′əl), *adj.* **1.** undertaken by or composed of participants having a high status: *a high-level meeting.* **2.** having senior authority or high status: *high-level personnel.* **3.** (of a programming language) based on a vocabulary of Englishlike statements for writing program code rather than the more abstract instructions typical of assembly language or machine language. **4.** *Mil.* (of aerial warfare) undertaken at or from a high altitude: *high-level bombing.* [1875–80]

high′-level lan′guage, *Computers.* a problem-oriented programming language, as COBOL, FORTRAN, or PL/1, that uses English-like statements and symbols to create sequences of computer instructions and identify memory locations, rather than the machine-specific individual instruction codes and numerical addresses employed by machine language. [1965–70]

high•life (hī′līf′), *n.* an expensive, glamorous, or elegant style of living. [1755–65; HIGH + LIFE]

high•light (hī′līt′), *v.,* **-light•ed, -light•ing,** *n.* —*v.t.* **1.** to emphasize or make prominent. **2.** to create highlights in (a photograph or engraving). —*n.* **3.** Also, **high′ light′.** an important, conspicuous, memorable, or enjoyable event, scene, part, or the like: *the highlight of the concert series.* **4.** the area of most intense light on a represented form, as in a painting or photograph. [1850–55, *Amer.*; HIGH + LIGHT[1]] —**high′light′er,** *n.*
—**Syn. 1.** stress, accent, underline, feature.

high•light•er (hī′lī′tər), *n.* **1.** a cosmetic used to emphasize some part of the face, as the eyes or the cheekbones. **2.** a felt-tip pen with a wide nib for highlighting passages of printed material in a soft, transparent color. [1965–70; HIGHLIGHT + -ER[1]]

high′light half′tone, dropout (def. 7).

high•line (hī′līn′), *n. Print., Journalism.* kicker (def. 9). [1885–90, for an earlier sense; HIGH + LINE[1]]

high′ liv′er, *Informal.* a person who lives extravagantly or luxuriously. [1880–85]

high-low (hī′lō′ *for 1, 3;* hī′lō′ *for 2*), *n.* **1.** a game of poker in which both high and low hands are eligible to win, the pot usually being split between the players with the highest and lowest hands. **2.** Also, **high′low′.** an ankle-high, laced shoe. **3.** *Chiefly Bridge.* a signal for one's partner to lead a suit, conveyed by playing a high card and then a lower card in that suit. [1795–1805]

high-low-jack (hī′lō′jak′), *n.* See **all fours** (def. 2). [1805–15]

high•ly (hī′lē), *adv.* **1.** in or to a high degree; extremely: *highly amusing; highly seasoned food.* **2.** with high appreciation or praise; admiringly: *to speak highly of a person.* **3.** more than adequately; generously: *a* *highly paid consultant.* [bef. 900; ME *heihliche,* OE *hēalīce.* See HIGH, -LY]

High′ Mass′, *Rom. Cath. Ch.* a Mass celebrated according to the complete rite, in which the liturgy is sung by the celebrant. Cf. **Low Mass.** [1100–50; ME, late OE]

high′ mill′ing, a process for making fine flour, in which the grain is alternately ground and sifted a number of times. Cf. **low milling.**

high-mind•ed (hī′mīn′did), *adj.* having or showing high, exalted principles or feelings. [1495–1505] —**high′-mind′ed•ly,** *adv.* —**high′-mind′ed•ness,** *n.* —**Syn.** principled, honest, fair, ethical, idealistic, scrupulous. See **noble.**

high-muck-a-muck (hī′muk′ə muk′, -muk′ə muk′), *n.* an important, influential, or high-ranking person, esp. one who is pompous or conceited. Also, **high-muck•y-muck** (hī′muk′ē muk′, -muk′ē muk′), **high-muck•e•ty-muck** (hī′muk′i tē muk′, -muk′i tē muk′). Also called **muck-a-muck.** [1855–60; < Chinook Jargon *hayo makamak* lit., plenty to eat, much food, perh. extended derisively to Indians of high status with much disposable wealth, as for potlatches; *hayo* < Nootka *ḥayo* ten (the base of various measures with suffixes for specific countable nouns); *mak(a)mak* eat, food < Nootka *ma·ḥo·ma(q-)* part of whale meat between blubber and flesh]

high-necked (hī′nekt′), *adj.* (of a garment) high at the neck. [1835–45]

high•ness (hī′nis), *n.* **1.** the quality or state of being high; loftiness. **2.** (*cap.*) a title of honor given to members of a royal family (usually prec. by *His, Her, Your,* etc.). [bef. 900; ME *heyenes,* OE *hēanes.* See HIGH, -NESS]

high′ noon′, **1.** the exact moment of noon. **2.** the high point of a stage or period; peak; pinnacle: *a book written at the high noon of his career.* **3.** *Informal.* a crisis or confrontation. [1350–1400; ME]

high-oc•tane (hī′ok′tān), *adj.* **1.** noting a gasoline with a relatively high octane number, characterized by high efficiency and freedom from knock. **2.** *Informal.* forceful or intense; dynamic; high-powered: *high-octane efforts to obliterate the competition.* [1930–35]

high′-oc′cu•pan•cy ve′hicle lane′ (hī′ok′yə pən-sē). See **diamond lane.**

high-pitched (hī′pitcht′), *adj.* **1.** *Music.* played or sung at a high pitch. **2.** emotionally intense: *a high-pitched argument.* **3.** (of a roof) having an almost vertical slope; steep. [1585–95]

high′ place′, (in ancient Semitic religions) a place of worship, usually a temple or altar on a hilltop.

High′ Point′, a city in central North Carolina. 64,107.

high′ pol′ymer, *Chem.* a polymer composed of a large number of monomers.

high-pow•er (hī′pou′ər), *adj.* **1.** (of a rifle) of a sufficiently high muzzle velocity and using a heavy enough bullet to kill large game. **2.** high-powered. [1890–95]

high-pow•ered (hī′pou′ərd), *adj.* **1.** extremely energetic, dynamic, and capable: *high-powered executives.* **2.** of a forceful and driving character: *high-powered selling techniques.* **3.** capable of a high degree of magnification: *a high-powered microscope.* **4.** very powerful. [1900–05]

high-pres•sure (hī′presh′ər), *adj., v.,* **-sured, -sur•ing.** —*adj.* **1.** having or involving a pressure above the normal: *high-pressure steam.* **2.** vigorous; persistent; aggressive: *high-pressure salesmanship.* —*v.t.* **3.** to employ aggressively forceful and unrelenting sales tactics on (a prospective customer): *high-pressured into buying a car.* [1815–25]

high-priced (hī′prīst′), *adj.* expensive; costly: *a high-priced camera.* [1785–95] —**Syn.** See **expensive.**

high′ priest′, **1.** a chief priest. **2.** *Judaism.* (from Aaronic times to about the 1st century A.D.) the priest ranking above all other priests and the only one permitted to enter the holy of holies. **3.** *Informal.* a person in a high position of power or influence, esp. one who is revered as a preeminent authority or interpreter: *the high priest of the young painters.* [1350–1400; ME *heiye prest*]

high′ priest′hood, **1.** the condition or office of a high priest. **2.** high priests collectively. [1525–35]

high′ pro′file, a deliberately conspicuous manner of living or operating. [1965–70] —**high′-pro′file,** *adj.*

high-proof (hī′pro͞of′), *adj.* containing a high percentage of alcohol: *high-proof spirits.*

high′ relief′, *Sculpture.* sculptured relief in which volumes are strongly projected from the background. See illus. under **relief**[2]. [1875–80]

High′ Ren′aissance, a style of art developed in Italy in the late 15th and early 16th centuries, chiefly characterized by an emphasis on draftsmanship, schematized, often centralized compositions, and the illusion of sculptural volume in painting. Cf. **Early Renaissance, Venetian** (def. 2). [1925–30]

high-res•o•lu•tion (hī′rez′ə lo͞o′shən), *adj.* **1.** having or capable of producing an image characterized by fine detail: *high-resolution photography; high-resolution lens.* **2.** *Computers.* of or pertaining to CRTs, printers, or other output devices that produce images that are sharp and finely detailed rather than blurry and inexact (opposed to *low-resolution*). [1945–50]

high-rise (hī′rīz′), *adj.* **1.** (of a building) having a comparatively large number of stories and equipped with elevators: *a high-rise apartment house.* **2.** of, pertaining to, or characteristic of high-rise buildings. **3.** of or being a small-wheeled bicycle with high handlebars and a banana-shaped seat. —*n.* **4.** Also, **high′ rise′, high-riser.** a high-rise apartment or office building. Also, **high′rise′.** [1950–55]

high-ris•er (hī′rī′zər), *n.* **1.** a couch or single bed with a mattress and frame concealed beneath, which, when pulled all the way out, lift up to the level of the upper cushion or mattress and lock into place to form a double bed. **2.** a high-rise bicycle. **3.** high-rise (def. 4).

high•road (hī′rōd′), *n.* **1.** *Chiefly Brit.* a main road; highway. **2.** an easy or certain course: *the highroad to success.* [1700–10; HIGH + ROAD]

high′ roll′er, *Informal.* **1.** a person who gambles for large stakes, as in a casino. **2.** a person who spends money freely for entertainment and extravagant living. **3.** a corporation or governmental agency that invests or spends freely or recklessly. Also, **high′roll′er.** [1880–85]

high-roll•ing (hī′rō′ling), *adj. Informal.* gambling, spending, or living extravagantly or recklessly: *high-rolling gamblers; a high-rolling investor.*

high′ school′, a school attended after elementary school or junior high school and usually consisting of grades 9 or 10 through 12. [1815–25] —**high′-school′,** *adj.* —**high′ school′er.**

high′ sea′, **1.** the sea or ocean beyond the three-mile limit or territorial waters of a country. **2.** Usually, **high seas. a.** the open, unenclosed waters of any sea or ocean; common highway. **b.** *Law.* the area within which transactions are subject to court of admiralty jurisdiction. [bef. 1100; ME; OE *hēah-sǣ*] —**high′-sea′,** *adj.*

high′ sign′, a gesture, glance, or facial expression used as a surreptitious signal to warn, admonish, or inform. [1900–05]

high′ soci′ety, society (def. 9). [1915–20]

high-sound•ing (hī′soun′ding), *adj.* having an impressive or pretentious sound; grand: *the high-sounding titles of minor officials.* [1550–60]

high-speed (hī′spēd′), *adj.* **1.** designed to operate or operating at a high speed: *a high-speed drill.* **2.** *Photog.* suitable for minimum light exposure: *high-speed film; a high-speed lens.* [1870–75]

high′-speed steel′, an especially hard, heat-resistant steel for use in lathe tools and for other applications involving high friction and wear. [1925–30]

high-spir•it•ed (hī′spir′i tid), *adj.* **1.** characterized by energetic enthusiasm, elation, vivacity, etc. **2.** boldly courageous; mettlesome. [1625–35] —**high′-spir′it•ed•ly,** *adv.* —**high′-spir′it•ed•ness,** *n.*

high′ spir′its, a mood of joy, elation, etc.; vivacity.

high-step (hī′step′), *v.,* **-stepped, -step•ping.** —*v.i.* **1.** to walk or run by raising the legs higher than normal. —*v.t.* **2.** to approach or step over by high-stepping. [1840–50]

high-step•ping (hī′step′ing), *adj.* **1.** seeking unrestrained pleasure, as by frequenting night clubs, parties, etc.; leading a wild and fast life: *a high-stepping young crowd.* **2.** (of a horse) moving with the leg raised high. [1840–50] —**high′-step′per,** *n.*

high-stick•ing (hī′stik′ing), *Ice Hockey.* the act of holding the blade of the stick above shoulder level, usually resulting in a penalty. [1945–50; *high stick* + -ING[1]]

high-strung (hī′strung′), *adj.* at great tension; highly excitable or nervous; edgy: *high-strung nerves; a high-strung person.* [1740–50] —**Syn.** tense, temperamental; jumpy, edgy, uptight.

high′ style′, the most up-to-date, elegant, or exclusive fashion, esp. in clothing. [1935–40] —**high′-style,** *adj.*

hight[1] (hīt), *adj. Archaic.* called or named: *Childe Harold was he hight.* [bef. 900; ME; OE *heht,* reduplicated preterit of *hātan* to name, call, promise, command (c. G *heissen* to call, be called, mean); akin to BEHEST]

hight[2] (hīt), *n.* height.

high′ ta′ble, *Brit.* the table in the dining hall of a college, reserved for senior members of the college and distinguished guests. [1300–50; ME]

high•tail (hī′tāl′), *v.i. Informal.* **1.** to go away or leave rapidly: *Last we saw of him, he was hightailing down the street.* **2. hightail it,** hurry; rush; scamper: *Hightail it down to the grocery store and buy some bread for lunch.* [1885–90, *Amer.*; HIGH + TAIL[1], in reference to the raised tails of fleeing animals, as deer or rabbits]

High′ Ta′tra. See **Tatra Mountains.**

high′ tea′, *Brit.* a late afternoon or early evening meal similar to a light supper. [1825–35]

high-tech (hī′tek′), *n.* **1.** See **high technology. 2.** a style of interior design using industrial, commercial, and institutional fixtures, equipment, and materials, as metal warehouse shelving, factory lamps, and exposed pipes, or incorporating other elements having the stark, utilitarian appearance characteristic of industrial design. —*adj.* **3.** of, pertaining to, or suggesting high-tech or high technology. [1970–75; by shortening]

high′ technol′ogy, any technology requiring the most sophisticated scientific equipment and advanced engineering techniques, as microelectronics, data processing, genetic engineering, or telecommunications (opposed to *low technology*). [1965–70] —**high′-tech•nol′o•gy,** *adj.*

high-ten•sion (hī′ten′shən), *adj. Elect.* subjected to or capable of operating under relatively high voltage: *high-tension wire.* [1910–15]

high-test (hī′test′), *adj.* (of gasoline) boiling at a relatively low temperature. [1955–60]

high-tick•et (hī′tik′it), *adj. Informal.* big-ticket.

high′ tide′, **1.** the tide at its highest level of elevation. **2.** the time of high water. **3.** a culminating point: *the high tide of the revolution.* [bef. 1000; ME; OE]

high′ time′, the appropriate time or past the appropriate time: *It's high time he got out of bed.*

high-toned (hī′tōnd′), *adj.* **1.** having high principles; dignified. **2.** having or aspiring to good taste, high standards, or refinement: *He writes for a high-toned literary review.* **3.** affectedly stylish or genteel. Also, **high′-tone′.** [1770–80]

high′ top′, a sneaker that covers the ankle. [1980–85]

high′ trea′son, treason against the sovereign or state. [1350–1400; ME]

high•ty-tigh•ty (hī′tē tī′tē), *adj., n.* hoity-toity.

high-up (hī′up′), *adj., n., pl.* **-ups.** —*adj.* **1.** holding a high position or rank. —*n.* **2.** a person holding a high position or rank; higher-up. [1865–70; n., adj. use of *high up*]

high-volt•age (hī′vōl′tij), *adj.* **1.** operating on or powered by high voltage: *a high-voltage generator.* **2.** *Informal.* dynamic; powerful: *a high-voltage theatrical entrepreneur.* [1965–70]

high•wall (hī′wôl′), *n.* the unexcavated face of exposed overburden and coal in a surface mine. [HIGH + WALL]

high′ wa′ter, **1.** water at its greatest elevation, as in a river. **2.** See **high tide.** [1545–55]

high′-wa′ter mark′ (hī′wô′tər, -wot′ər), **1.** a mark showing the highest level reached by a body of water. **2.** the highest point of anything; acme: *Her speech was the high-water mark of the conference.* [1545–55]

high′ wa′ters, (*used with a plural v.*) *Slang.* trousers short enough to expose the ankles, esp. as worn by growing children whom they earlier fit. Also called **flooders.** [1855–60, *Amer.*]

high•way (hī′wā′), *n.* **1.** a main road, esp. one between towns or cities: *the highway between Los Angeles and Seattle.* **2.** any public road or waterway. **3.** any main or ordinary route, track, or course. [bef. 900; ME *heyewei,* OE *heiweg.* See HIGH, WAY] —**Syn. 1.** expressway, freeway, thruway, interstate.

high′way con′tract route′, a route for carrying mail over the highway between designated points, given on contract to a private carrier and often requiring, in rural areas, delivery to home mailboxes. *Abbr.:* HCR Formerly, **star route.**

high•way•man (hī′wā′mən), *n., pl.* **-men.** (formerly) a holdup man, esp. one on horseback, who robbed travelers along a public road. [1640–50; HIGHWAY + -MAN]

high′way rob′bery, **1.** robbery committed on a highway against travelers, as by a highwayman. **2.** *Informal.* a price or fee that is unreasonably high; exorbitant charge. [1770–80] —**high′way rob′ber.**

high′ wine′, Often, **high wines.** *Distilling.* a distillate containing a high percentage of alcohol. [1350–1400; ME]

high′ wire′, a tightrope stretched very high above the ground. [1880–85]

high-wrought (hī′rôt′), *adj.* highly agitated; overwrought. [1595–1605]

high′ yel′low, *Slang* (*disparaging and offensive*). a light-skinned black person. Also, **high′ yal′ler** (yal′ər). [1920–25] —**high′-yel′low,** *adj.*

H.I.H., His Imperial Highness; Her Imperial Highness.

Hii•u•maa (hē′o͞o mä′), *n.* an island in the Baltic, E of and belonging to Estonia. 373 sq. mi. (965 sq. km). Danish, **Dagö.**

hi•jack (hī′jak′), *v.t.* **1.** to steal (cargo) from a truck or other vehicle after forcing it to stop: *to hijack a load of whiskey.* **2.** to rob (a vehicle) after forcing it to stop: *They hijacked the truck before it entered the city.* **3.** to seize (a vehicle) by force or threat of force. **4.** to skyjack. —*v.i.* **5.** to engage in such stealing or seizing. —*n.* **6.** an act or instance of hijacking. Also, **highjack.** [1920–25, *Amer.*; back formation from HIJACKER]

hi•jack•er (hī′jak′ər), *n.* a person who hijacks. Also, **highjacker.** [1885–90, *Amer.*; HIGH(WAYMAN) + *jacker,* appar. JACK[1] to hunt by night with aid of a jack light + -ER[1]]

Hi•jaz (hē jaz′; *Arab.* hē zhäz′), *n.* a region in Saudi Arabia bordering on the Red Sea, formerly an independent kingdom: contains the Islamic holy cities of Medina and Mecca. ab. 150,000 sq. mi. (388,500 sq. km). *Cap.:* Mecca. Also, **Hedjaz, Hejaz.**

hi•jinks (hī′jingks′), *n.* (*used with a plural v.*) See **high jinks.**

Hij•ra (hij′rə), *n.* (*sometimes l.c.*) *Islam.* **1.** the flight of Muhammad from Mecca to Medina to escape persecution A.D. 622: regarded as the beginning of the Muslim Era. **2.** the Muslim Era itself. Also, **Hegira, Hij′rah.** [< Ar *hijrah* flight, departure]

hike (hīk), *v.,* **hiked, hik•ing,** *n.* —*v.i.* **1.** to walk or march a great distance, esp. through rural areas, for pleasure, exercise, military training, or the like. **2.** to move up or rise, as out of place or position (often fol. by *up*): *My shirt hikes up if I don't wear a belt.* **3.** *Naut.* to hold oneself outboard on the windward side of a heeling sailboat to reduce the amount of heel. —*v.t.* **4.** to move, draw, or raise with a jerk (often fol. by *up*): *to hike up one's socks.* **5.** to increase, often sharply and unexpectedly: *to hike the price of milk.* —*n.* **6.** a long walk or march for recreational activity, military training, or the like. **7.** an increase or rise, often sharp and unexpected: *a hike in wages.* **8. take a hike,** *Slang.* to go away because one's company is not desired. [1800–10; perh. dial. var. of HITCH[1]] —**hik′er,** *n.* —**Syn. 1.** tramp, ramble, trek, trudge, backpack.

hi•lar•i•ous (hi lâr′ē əs, -lar′-, hī-), *adj.* **1.** arousing great merriment; extremely funny: *a hilarious story; a hilarious old movie.* **2.** boisterously merry or cheerful: *a hilarious celebration.* **3.** merry; cheerful. [1815–25; < L *hilar(is), hilar(us)* cheerful (< Gk *hilarós*) + -IOUS] —**hi•lar′i•ous•ly,** *adv.* —**hi•lar′i•ous•ness,** *n.* —**Syn. 2.** lively, jolly, rollicking, high-spirited. —**Ant. 2.** sad, serious, solemn.

hi•lar•i•ty (hi lar′i tē, -lâr′-, hī-), *n.* **1.** cheerfulness;

CONCISE PRONUNCIATION KEY: act, cāpe, dâre, pärt; set, ēqual; if, īce; ox, ōver, ôrder, oil, bo͝ok, bo͞ot, out; up, ûrge; child; sing; shoe; thin, *th*at; zh as in *treasure.* ə = *a* as in *alone, e* as in *system, i* as in *easily, o* as in *gallop, u* as in *circus;* ᵊ as in *fire* (fīᵊr), *hour* (ouᵊr). l and n can serve as syllabic consonants, as in *cradle* (krād′l), and *button* (but′n). See the full key inside the front cover.

merriment; mirthfulness. **2.** boisterous gaiety or merriment. [1560–70; earlier *hilaritie* < L *hilaritās,* equiv. to *hilari(s)* (see HILARIOUS) + *-tās* -TY[2]]
—Syn. 2. See **mirth.**

Hi·lar·i·us (hi lâr′ē əs), *n.* **Saint,** died A.D. 468, pope 461–468. Also, **Hil·a·rus** (hil′ər əs), **Hilary.**

Hil·a·ry (hil′ə rē), *n.* **1.** See **Hilarius, Saint. 2.** Also, **Hi·laire** (hi lâr; *Fr.* ē leʀ′). a male or female given name: from a Latin word meaning "cheerful."

Hil′ary of Poitiers′, Saint, A.D. c300–368, French bishop and theologian. French, **Hi·laire de Poi·tiers** (ē leʀ′ də pwa tyā′).

Hil·bert (hil′bərt; *Ger.* hil′bəʀt), *n.* **Da·vid** (dā′vid; *Ger.* dä′vit), 1862–1943, German mathematician.

Hil′bert space′, *Math.* a complete infinite-dimensional vector space on which an inner product is defined. [1935–40; named after D. HILBERT]

Hil·da (hil′də), *n.* a female given name: from a Germanic word meaning "maid of battle."

Hil·de·brand (hil′də brand′), *n.* See **Gregory VII, Saint.** **—Hil′de·bran′di·an,** *adj., n.* **—Hil·de·brand·ine** (hil′də bran′din, -dīn), *adj.*

Hil·de·brand (hil′də brand′), *n. German Myth.* a hero in the *Nibelungenlied.* [< ON *Hildibrandr,* equiv. to *hildr* battle + *brandr* sword]

Hil·de·garde (hil′də gärd′), *n.* a female given name: from Germanic words meaning "battle" and "protector." Also, **Hil′de·gard′.**

Hil·des·heim (hil′des hīm′), *n.* a city in N central Germany. 103,400.

hil·ding (hil′ding), *n. Archaic.* a contemptible person. [1575–85; perh. to be identified with ME *heldinge, hilding* bending, swerving aside, OE *hylding,* equiv. to *hyld(an)* to bend, incline + *-ing* -ING[1]]

hill (hil), *n.* **1.** a natural elevation of the earth's surface, smaller than a mountain. **2.** an incline, esp. in a road: *This old jalopy won't make it up the next hill.* **3.** an artificial heap, pile, or mound: *a hill made by ants.* **4.** a small mound of earth raised about a cultivated plant or a cluster of such plants. **5.** the plant or plants so surrounded: *a hill of potatoes.* **6.** *Baseball.* mound[1] (def. 4). **7. go over the hill,** *Slang.* **a.** to break out of prison. **b.** to absent oneself without leave from one's military unit. **c.** to leave suddenly or mysteriously: *Rumor has it that her husband has gone over the hill.* **8. over the hill, a.** relatively advanced in age. **b.** past one's prime. **9. the Hill.** See **Capitol Hill.** —*v.t.* **10.** to surround with hills: *to hill potatoes.* **11.** to form into a hill or heap. [bef. 1000; ME; OE *hyll;* c. MD *hille,* L *collis* hill; cf. L *culmen* top, peak (see COLUMN, CULMINATE), *celsus* lofty, very high, Goth *hallus* rock, Lith *kálnas* mountain, Gk *kolōnós* hill, *kolophṓn* summit (see COLOPHON)] **—hill′er,** *n.*
—Syn. 1. eminence, prominence; mound, knoll, hillock; foothill. **—Ant. 1.** hollow, valley.

Hill (hil), *n.* **1. Ambrose Pow·ell** (pou′əl), 1825–65, Confederate general in the U.S. Civil War. **2. Archibald Viv·i·an** (viv′ē ən), 1886–1977, English physiologist: Nobel prize for medicine 1922. **3. James Jerome,** 1838–1916, U.S. railroad builder and financier, born in Canada.

Hil·la (hil′ə), *n.* a city in central Iraq, S of Baghdad. 84,704. Also, **Al-Hillah.**

Hil·la·ry (hil′ə rē), *n.* **1. Sir Edmund P.,** born 1919, New Zealand mountain climber who scaled Mt. Everest 1953. **2.** a male or female given name.

hill·bil·ly (hil′bil′ē), *n., pl.* **-lies,** *adj.* —*n.* **1.** *Often Disparaging and Offensive.* a person from a backwoods or other remote area, esp. from the mountains of the southern U.S. —*adj.* **2.** of, like, or pertaining to hillbillies: *hillbilly humor.* [1895–1900, *Amer.;* HILL + BILLY]

hill′billy mu′sic, 1. folk music combined with elements of popular music in which the banjo, fiddle, and guitar are principal instruments: a type of music that originated in mountain regions of the southern U.S. **2.** country-and-western music. [1950–55]

hill′ climb′, a racing event for motorcycles or automobiles in which competitors drive up a hilly course one at a time, the winner having the fastest time. [1900–05]

Hill′crest Heights′ (hil′krest′), a city in central Maryland, near Washington, D.C. 17,021.

Hil·lel (hil′el, -āl, -əl, hi lāl′; *Seph. Heb.* hē lel′), *n.* ("*ha-Zaken*") c60 B.C.–A.D. 9?, Palestinian rabbi, president of the Sanhedrin and interpreter of Biblical law: first to formulate definitive hermeneutic principles. Cf. **Beth Hillel.**

Hil′lel Founda′tion, a national organization, founded in 1924 by the B'nai B'rith, that institutes and administers programs designed to enrich the religious, cultural, and social life of Jewish college students. [named after HILLEL]

Hil·ler (hil′ər), *n.* **Dame Wendy,** born 1912, British actress.

Hil·ling·don (hil′ing dən), *n.* a borough of Greater London, England. 232,200.

Hil·lis (hil′is), *n.* **Margaret,** born 1921, U.S. symphonic orchestra conductor.

Hill·man (hil′mən), *n.* **Sidney,** 1887–1946, U.S. labor leader, born in Lithuania.

hill′ my′na, an Asian bird of the genus *Gracula,* of the starling family Sturnidae, esp. *G. religiosa,* that has glossy black plumage and yellow neck wattles and is easily tamed and taught to mimic speech. [1885–90]

hil·lo (hil′ō, hi lō′), *interj., n., pl.* **-los,** *v.i., v.t.,* **-loed, -lo·ing.** hallo.

CONCISE ETYMOLOGY KEY: <, descended or borrowed from; >, whence; b., blend of, blended; c., cognate with; cf., compare; deriv., derivative; equiv., equivalent; imit., imitative; obl., oblique; r., replacing; s., stem; sp., spelling, spelled; resp., respelling, respelled; trans., translation; ?, origin unknown; *, unattested; ‡, probably earlier than. See the full key inside the front cover.

hil·loa (hi lō′), *interj., n., pl.* **-loas,** *v.i., v.t.,* **-loaed, -loa·ing.** hallo.

hill·ock (hil′ək), *n.* a small hill. [1350–1400; ME *hilloc.* See HILL, -OCK] **—hill′ocked, hill′ock·y,** *adj.*

hill′ of beans′, *Informal.* something of trifling value; virtually nothing at all: *The problem didn't amount to a hill of beans.* [1860–65]

Hills·bor·o (hilz′bûr ō, -bur ō), *n.* a town in NW Oregon. 27,664.

Hills·bor·ough (hilz′bûr′ō, -bur′ō), *n.* a town in W California. 10,451.

Hills·dale (hilz′dāl′), *n.* a town in NE New Jersey. 10,495.

hill·side (hil′sīd′), *n.* the side or slope of a hill. [1350–1400; ME; OE *hyll sīde*]

Hill·side (hil′sīd′), *n.* a township in NE New Jersey. 21,440.

hill·site (hil′sīt′), *n.* a location or site on the side or top of a hill. [1870–75; HILL + SITE]

hill′ sta′tion, a village, post, or the like, esp. in S Asia, at a high altitude where government officials and others can be stationed to escape the great heat of tropical summers. [1875–80]

hill·top (hil′top′), *n., v.,* **-topped, -top·ping.** —*n.* **1.** the top or summit of a hill. —*v.i.* **2.** *Fox Hunting.* **a.** to follow the progress of a hunt on horseback but without jumping. **b.** to follow the hunt on foot or in an automobile. [1375–1425; late ME. See HILL, TOP[1]] **—hill′top′·per,** *n.*

hill·y (hil′ē), *adj.,* **hill·i·er, hill·i·est. 1.** full of hills; having many hills: *hilly country.* **2.** resembling a hill; elevated; steep. [1350–1400; ME; OE *hyllic.* See HILL, -Y[1]] **—hill′i·ness,** *n.*

Hill·yer (hil′yər), *n.* **Robert (Sil·li·man)** (sil′i mən), 1895–1961, U.S. poet and critic.

Hi·lo (hē′lō), *n.* a seaport on E Hawaii island, in SE Hawaii. 35,269.

hilt (hilt), *n.* **1.** the handle of a sword or dagger. **2.** the handle of any weapon or tool. **3. to the hilt,** to the maximum extent or degree; completely; fully: *to play the role to the hilt.* Also, **up to the hilt.** —*v.t.* **4.** to furnish with a hilt. [bef. 900; ME, OE *hilt(e);* c. MD *hilt(e),* ON *hjalt,* OHG *helza* handle of a sword]

Hil·ton (hil′tn), *n.* **1. Conrad (Nicholson),** 1887–1979, U.S. hotel owner and developer. **2. James,** 1900–54, English novelist.

hi·lum (hī′ləm), *n., pl.* **-la** (-lə). **1.** *Bot.* **a.** the mark or scar on a seed produced by separation from its funicle or placenta. **b.** the nucleus of a granule of starch. **2.** *Mycol.* a mark or scar on a spore at the point of attachment to the spore-bearing structure. **3.** *Anat.* the region at which the vessels, nerves, etc., enter or emerge from a part. [1650–60; < NL; L: little thing, trifle; see NIL] **—hi′lar,** *adj.*

Hil·ver·sum (hil′vər səm), *n.* a city in central Netherlands. 92,141.

him (him), *pron.* **1.** the objective case of *he,* used as a direct or indirect object: *I'll see him tomorrow. Give him the message.* **2.** *Informal.* (used instead of the pronoun *he* in the predicate after the verb *to be*): *It's him. It isn't him.* **3.** *Informal.* (used instead of the pronoun *his* before a gerund): *We were surprised by him wanting to leave.* —*n.* **4.** *Informal.* a male: *Is the new baby a her or a him?* [bef. 900; ME, OE, dat. of *hē* HE[1]]
—Usage. See **he**[1]**, me.**

H.I.M., His Imperial Majesty; Her Imperial Majesty.

Hi·ma·chal Pra·desh (hi mä′chəl prə dāsh′), a state in N India. 3,750,000; 10,904 sq. mi. (28,241 sq. km). *Cap.:* Simla.

Him′ala′yan tahr′. See under **tahr.**

Him·a·la·yas (him′ə lā′əz, hi mäl′yəz), *n.* **the,** a mountain range extending about 1500 mi. (2400 km) along the border between India and Tibet. Highest peak, Mt. Everest, 29,028 ft. (8848 m). Also called the **Him′a·la′ya, Him′ala′ya Moun′tains. —Him′a·la′yan,** *adj.*

Hi·ma·lia (hi mäl′yə), *n. Astron.* a small natural satellite of the planet Jupiter. [appar. for Gk *himalís* an epithet of Demeter]

hi·mat·i·on (hi mat′ē on′), *n., pl.* **-mat·i·a** (-mat′ē ə). *Gk. Antiq.* a garment consisting of a rectangular piece of cloth thrown over the left shoulder and wrapped about the body. [1840–50; < Gk *himátion,* equiv. to *himat-,* var. of *heimat-* (s. of *heîma*) dress, garment (akin to VEST, WEAR) + *-ion* dim. suffix]

Hi·me·ji (hē′me jē′), *n.* a city on SW Honshu, in S Japan, W of Kobe. 446,255.

Himm·ler (him′lər; *Ger.* him′lər), *n.* **Hein·rich** (hīn′riᴋʜ), 1900–45, German Nazi leader and chief of the secret police.

him·self (him self′; *medially often* im self′), *pron.* **1.** an emphatic appositive of **him** or **he:** *He himself spoke to the men.* **2.** a reflexive form of **him:** *He cut himself.* **3.** (used in absolute constructions): *Himself the soul of honor, he included many rascals among his intimates.* **4.** (used as the object of a preposition or as the direct or indirect object of a verb): *The old car had room only for himself and three others.* **5.** (used in comparisons after *as* or *than*): *His wife is as stingy as himself.* **6.** his normal or customary self: *He is himself again.* **7.** *Irish Eng.* a man of importance, esp. the master of the house: *Himself will be wanting an early dinner.* [bef. 900; ME *him selven,* OE *him selfum,* dat. sing. of *hē self* he himself; see HIM, SELF]
—Usage. See **myself.**

Him·yar·ite (him′yə rīt′), *n.* **1.** one of an ancient people of southern Arabia speaking a Semitic language. **2.** a descendant of these people. —*adj.* **3.** Himyaritic. [1835–45; < Ar *ḥimyar* (name of a tribe and an old dynasty of Yemen) + -ITE[1]]

Him·yar·it·ic (him′yə rit′ik), *adj.* **1.** of or pertaining to the Himyarites and to the remains of their civilization. —*n.* **2.** a Semitic language anciently spoken in southern Arabia: extinct by 1100. [1850–55; HIMYARITE + -IC]

hin (hin), *n.* an ancient Hebrew unit of liquid measure equal to about one and one half gallons (5.7 liters). [1350–1400; ME < L (Vulgate) < Gk (Septuagint) < Heb *hīn* < Egyptian *hnw* a liquid measure, lit., jar]

Hi·na·ya·na (hē′nə yä′nə), *n.* earlier of the two great schools of Buddhism, still prevalent in Sri Lanka, Burma, Thailand, and Cambodia, emphasizing personal salvation through one's own efforts. Also called **Theravada.** Cf. **Mahayana.** [1865–70; < Skt, equiv. to *hīna* lesser, inferior + *yāna* vehicle]

Hi·na·ya·nist (hē′nə yä′nist), *n.* a Buddhist of the Hinayana school. Also called **Theravadin.** [1905–10; HINAYAN(A) + -IST]

hinc·ty (hingk′tē), *adj.,* **-ti·er, -ti·est.** *Slang.* conceited or snobbish. Also, **hinkty.** [1920–25; of obscure orig.; cf. *-cty* in DICTY]

hind[1] (hīnd), *adj.* situated in the rear or at the back; posterior: *the hind legs of an animal.* [1300–50; ME *hinde;* cf. OE *hindan* (adv.) from behind, at the back; c. G *hinten;* see BEHIND, HINDER[2]]
—Syn. See **back**[1]**.**

hind[2] (hīnd), *n., pl.* **hinds,** (*esp. collectively*) **hind. 1.** *Zool.* the female of the deer, chiefly the red deer, esp. in and after the third year. **2.** any of several speckled serranid fishes of the genus *Epinephelus,* found in the warmer waters of the western Atlantic Ocean. [bef. 900; ME, OE; c. D *hinde,* ON, Dan, Sw *hind,* OHG *hinta* (G, LG *Hinde*)]

hind[3] (hīnd), *n.* **1.** a peasant or rustic. **2.** *Scot. and North Eng.* a farm laborer. [bef. 1000; alter. of ME *hine* (pl.) servants, OE (Anglian) *hīne, hī(g)na,* gen. of *hīgan* (West Saxon *hīwan*) members of a household, domestics; see HIDE[3]]

Hind, Hindustani (def. 1).

Hind., 1. Hindi. **2.** Hindu. **3.** Hindustan. **4.** Hindustani.

Hind·a·fell (hin′də fel′), *n.* Hindfell.

hind·brain (hīnd′brān′), *n. Anat.* the most posterior of the three primary divisions of the brain in the embryo of a vertebrate or the part of the adult brain derived from this tissue, including the cerebellum, pons, and medulla oblongata; rhombencephalon. [1885–90; HIND[1] + BRAIN]

hind′ clip′ping. See **back clipping.**

Hin·de·mith (hin′də mith, -mit), *n.* **Paul,** 1895–1963, U.S. composer, born in Germany.

Hin·den·burg (hin′dən bûrg′; *Ger.* hin′dən bŏŏʀk′), *n.* **1. Paul von** (pôl von; *Ger.* poul fən), (*Paul von Beneckendorff und von Hindenburg*), 1847–1934, German field marshal; 2nd president of Germany 1925–34. **2.** German name of **Zabrze.**

Hin′denburg line′, a line of elaborate fortifications established by the German army in World War I, near the French-Belgian border, from Lille SE to Metz. [1915–20; named after P. von HINDENBURG]

hin·der[1] (hin′dər), *v.t.* **1.** to cause delay, interruption, or difficulty in; hamper; impede: *The storm hindered our progress.* **2.** to prevent from doing, acting, or happening; stop: *to hinder a man from committing a crime.* —*v.i.* **3.** to be an obstacle or impediment. [bef. 1000; ME *hindren,* OE *hindrian* to hold back, equiv. to *hinder* HINDER[2] + *-ian* causative v. suffix] **—hin′der·er,** *n.* **—hin′der·ing·ly,** *adv.*
—Syn. 1. encumber, obstruct, trammel. **2.** block, thwart. See **prevent. —Ant. 1.** encourage.

hind·er[2] (hīn′dər), *adj.* **1.** situated at the rear or back; posterior: *the hinder part of a carcass.* —*n.* **2.** *Chiefly Northern and North Midland U.S.* the buttocks. [1250–1300; ME; cf. OE *hinder* (adv.) behind; c. G *hinter* (prep.) behind]

Hind·fell (hind′fəl), *n.* (in the *Volsunga Saga*) the mountain on whose fiery top Brynhild slept until awakened by Sigurd. Also, **Hindafell.** Cf. **Isenstein.** [< ON *Hindarfjall* mountain of the hinds, equiv. to *hindar,* pl. of *hind* HIND[2] + *fjall* mountain (cf. FELL[5])]

hind·gut (hīnd′gut′), *n.* **1.** *Zool.* **a.** the last portion of the vertebrate alimentary canal, between the cecum and the anus, involved mainly with water resorption and with the storage and elimination of food residue; the large intestine. **b.** the posterior colon of arthropods, composed of ectodermal, chitin-lined tissue. **2.** *Embryol., Zool.* the posterior part of the embryonic alimentary canal from which the colon and rectum develop. Cf. **foregut, midgut.** [1875–80; HIND[1] + GUT]

Hin·di (hin′dē), *n.* **1.** the most widely spoken of the modern Indic vernaculars, esp. its best-known variety, Western Hindi. **2.** a literary language derived from Hindustani, used by Hindus. [1790–1800; < Hindi, Urdu, equiv. to Pers *Hind, Hindu* (cf. Skt *Sindhu* the river Indus; sense extended to "region of the Indus, SIND") + *-ī* suffix of appurtenance; r. *Hinduee* < Pers *Hinduī*]

hind·most (hīnd′mōst′ *or, esp. Brit.,* -məst), *adj.* furthest behind or nearest the rear; last. [1325–75; ME. See HIND[1], -MOST]

Hin·doo (hin′dōō), *n., pl.* **-doos,** *adj.* Hindu.

Hin·doo·ism (hin′dōō iz′əm), *n.* Hinduism.

Hin·doo·sta·ni (hin′dōō stä′nē, -stan′ē), *n., adj.* Hindustani. Also, **Hin·do·sta·ni** (hin′dō stä′nē, -stan′ē).

hind·quar·ter (hīnd′kwôr′tər, -kwō′-), *n.* **1.** the posterior end of a halved carcass of beef, lamb, etc., sectioned usually between the twelfth and thirteenth ribs. **2. hindquarters,** the rear part of an animal. [1880–85; HIND[1] + QUARTER]

hin·drance (hin′drəns), *n.* **1.** an impeding, stopping, preventing, or the like. **2.** the state of being hindered.

3. a person or thing that hinders. [1400–50; late ME *hinderaunce.* See HINDER[1], -ANCE] **—Syn.** 3. impediment, encumbrance, obstruction, check; restraint. See **obstacle.** **—Ant.** 3. aid.

hind′ shank′. See under **shank** (def. 4).

hind·sight (hīnd′sīt′), *n.* recognition of the realities, possibilities, or requirements of a situation, event, decision etc., after its occurrence. [1850–55; HIND[1] + SIGHT]

hind′ tit′, *Slang.* the worst or least valuable part; that left over after the best is taken or apportioned.

Hin·du (hin′do͞o), *n.* **1.** a person, esp. of northern India, who adheres to Hinduism. *—adj.* **2.** of or pertaining to Hindus or Hinduism. Also, **Hindoo.** [1655–65; < Pers *Hindū* Indian (adj., n.), equiv. to *Hind* (see HINDI) + *-ū* adj. suffix]

Hin′du-Ar′a·bic nu′merals (hin′do͞o ar′ə bik). See **Arabic numerals.**

Hin′du cal′endar, a lunisolar calendar that governs all Hindu and most Indian festivals, known from about 1000 B.C. and subsequently modified during the 4th and 6th centuries A.D. Cf. **calendar.**

Hin·du·ism (hin′do͞o iz′əm), *n.* the common religion of India, based upon the religion of the original Aryan settlers as expounded and evolved in the Vedas, the Upanishads, the Bhagavad-Gita, etc., having an extremely diversified character with many schools of philosophy and theology, many popular cults, and a large pantheon symbolizing the many attributes of a single god. Buddhism and Jainism are outside the Hindu tradition but are regarded as related religions. Also, **Hindooism.** [1820–30; HINDU + -ISM]

Hin·du·ize (hin′do͞o īz′), *v.t.,* **-ized, -iz·ing.** to convert to or bring under the influence of Hinduism. Also, *esp. Brit.,* **Hin′du·ise′.** [1855–60; HINDU + -IZE]

Hin′du Kush′, a mountain range in S Asia, mostly in NE Afghanistan, extending W from the Himalayas. Highest peak, Tirich Mir, 25,230 ft. (7690 m). Also called **Hin′du Kush′ Moun′tains.**

Hin·dus (hin′dəs), *n.* **Maurice Ger·schon** (gûr′shən), 1891–1969, U.S. writer, born in Russia.

Hin·du·stan (hin′do͝o stän′, -stan′), *n.* **1.** Persian name of India, esp. the part N of the Deccan. **2.** the predominantly Hindu areas of India, as contrasted with the predominantly Muslim areas of Pakistan. Cf. **India.**

Hin·du·sta·ni (hin′do͝o stä′nē, -stan′ē), *n.* **1.** a standard language and lingua franca of northern India based on a dialect of Western Hindi spoken around Delhi. *Abbr.:* Hind Cf. **Hindi** (def. 2), **Urdu.** *—adj.* **2.** of or pertaining to Hindustan, its people, or their languages. Also, **Hindoostani, Hindostani.** [1610–20; < Hindi, Urdu < Pers, equiv. to *Hindūstān* region of the Indus, SIND (*Hindū* HINDU + *stān* country) + *-ī* suffix of appurtenance]

hind·ward (hīnd′wərd), *adv., adj.* backward. [bef. 1100; ME; OE *hinde-weard* (adj.). See HIND[1], -WARD]

hind′ wing′, the second, posterior, or metathoracic wing of an insect. [1930–35]

Hines (hīnz), *n.* **1. Earl** (*"Fatha"*), 1905–83, U.S. jazz pianist. **2. Jerome,** born 1921, U.S. basso.

Hines·ville (hīnz′vil), *n.* a town in SE Georgia. 11,309.

hinge (hinj), *n., v.,* **hinged, hing·ing.** *—n.* **1.** a jointed device or flexible piece on which a door, gate, shutter, lid, or other attached part turns, swings, or moves. **2.** a natural anatomical joint at which motion occurs around a transverse axis, as that of the knee or a bivalve shell. **3.** that on which something is based or depends; pivotal consideration or factor. **4.** Also called **mount.** *Philately.* a gummed sticker for affixing a stamp to a page of an album, so folded as to form a hinge, allowing the stamp to be raised to reveal the text beneath. *—v.i.* **5.** to be dependent or contingent on, or as if on, a hinge (usually fol. by *on* or *upon*): *Everything hinges on his decision.* *—v.t.* **6.** to furnish with or attach by a hinge or hinges. **7.** to attach as if by a hinge. **8.** to make or consider as dependent upon; predicate: *He hinged his action on future sales.* [1250–1300; ME *henge;* c. LG *heng(e),* MD *henge* hinge; akin to HANG] **—hinge′less,** *adj.* **—hinge′like′,** *adj.* **—Syn. 5.** rest, swing, pivot, depend.

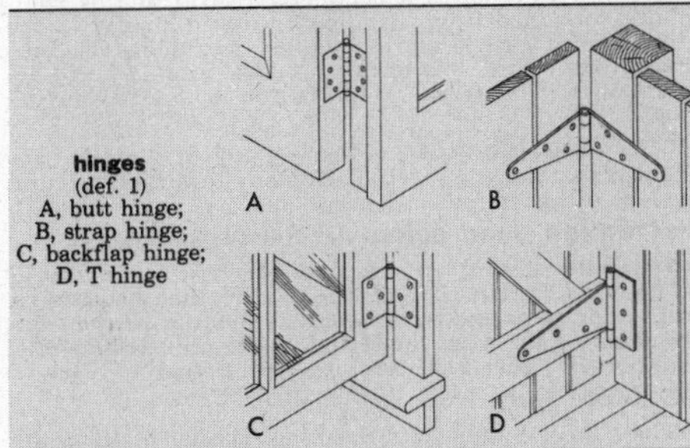

hinges (def. 1) A, butt hinge; B, strap hinge; C, backflap hinge; D, T hinge

hinge′ joint′, *Anat.* ginglymus. [1795–1805]

Hing·ham (hing′əm), *n.* a city in SE Massachusetts. 20,339.

hing′ing post′. See **hanging post.**

hink·ty (hingk′tē), *adj.,* **-ti·er, -ti·est.** *Slang.* hincty.

hin·ny (hin′ē), *n., pl.* **-nies.** the offspring of a male horse and a female donkey. Cf. **mule**[1] (defs. 1, 2). [1680–90; obs. *hinne* (< L *hinnus;* akin to Gk *ginnos* mule) + -Y[2]]

hi·no′ki cy′press (hi nō′kē), an evergreen tree, *Chamaecyparis obtusa,* of Japan, having scalelike leaves and orange-brown cones, grown for timber and as an ornamental. [1720–30; < Japn *hi-no-ki,* equiv. to *hi* cypress (earlier *f(y)i* < **pi*) + *no* grammatical particle + *ki(y)* tree (earlier **koi*)]

Hins·dale (hinz′dāl′), *n.* a city in NE Illinois, near Chicago. 16,726.

Hin·shel·wood (hin′shəl wo͝od′), *n.* **Sir Cyril Norman,** 1897–1967, English chemist: Nobel prize 1956.

hint (hint), *n.* **1.** an indirect, covert, or helpful suggestion; clue: *Give me a hint as to his identity.* **2.** a very slight or hardly noticeable amount; soupçon: *a hint of garlic in the salad dressing.* **3.** perceived indication or suggestion; note; intimation: *a hint of spring in the air.* **4.** *Obs.* an occasion or opportunity. *—v.t.* **5.** to give a hint of: *gray skies hinting a possible snowfall.* *—v.i.* **6.** to make indirect suggestion or allusion; subtly imply (usually fol. by *at*): *The article hinted at corruption in the mayor's office.* [1595–1605; (n.) orig., opportunity, occasion, appar. var. of obs. *hent* grasp, act of seizing, deriv. of the v.: to grasp, take, ME *henten,* OE *hentan;* (v.) deriv. of the n.] **—hint′er,** *n.*
—Syn. 1. allusion, insinuation, innuendo; memorandum, reminder; inkling. **5.** imply. HINT, INTIMATE, INSINUATE, SUGGEST denote the conveying of an idea to the mind indirectly or without full or explicit statement. To HINT is to convey an idea covertly or indirectly, but intelligibly: *to hint that one would like a certain present; to hint that bits of gossip might be true.* To INTIMATE is to give a barely perceptible hint, often with the purpose of influencing action: *to intimate that something may be possible.* To INSINUATE is to hint artfully, often at what one would not dare to say directly: *to insinuate something against someone's reputation.* SUGGEST denotes particularly recalling something to the mind or starting a new train of thought by means of association of ideas: *The name doesn't suggest anything to me.* **—Ant. 5.** express, declare.

hin·ter·land (hin′tər land′), *n.* **1.** Often, **hinterlands.** the remote or less developed parts of a country; back country: *The hinterlands are usually much more picturesque than the urban areas.* **2.** the land lying behind a coastal region. **3.** an area or sphere of influence in the unoccupied interior claimed by the state possessing the coast. **4.** an inland area supplying goods, esp. trade goods, to a port. [1885–90; < G: lit., hinder land, i.e., land behind]

Hin·ton (hin′tn, -tən), *n.* **1. Christopher, Baron Hinton of Bankside,** born 1901, British nuclear engineer. **2. William Augustus,** 1883–1959, U.S. medical researcher and educator.

hip[1] (hip), *n., adj., v.,* **hipped, hip·ping.** *—n.* **1.** the projecting part of each side of the body formed by the side of the pelvis and the upper part of the femur and the flesh covering them; haunch. **2.** See **hip joint. 3.** *Archit.* the inclined projecting angle formed by the junction of a sloping side and a sloping end, or of two adjacent sloping sides, of a roof. See illus. under **roof. 4.** *Furniture.* knee (def. 6). **5. shoot from the hip,** *Informal.* to speak or act bluntly or rashly, without deliberation or prudence: *Diplomats are trained to conduct themselves with discretion, and not to shoot from the hip.* **6. smite hip and thigh,** to attack unmercifully; overcome. Judg. 15:8. *—adj.* **7.** (esp. of a garment) extending to the hips; hiplength: *hip boots.* *—v.t.* **8.** (esp. of livestock) to injure or dislocate the hip of. **9.** *Archit.* to form (a roof) with a hip or hips. [bef. 1000; ME *hipe, hupe,* OE *hype;* c. OHG *huf* (G *Hüfte* hip), Goth *hups* hip, loin; cf. Gk *kýbos* CUBE, the hollow above the hips (of cattle), L *cubitus* elbow (see CUBIT)] **—hip′less,** *adj.* **—hip′like′,** *adj.*

hip[2] (hip), *n.* the ripe fruit of a rose, esp. of a wild rose. [bef. 900; ME *hepe,* OE *hēope* hip, briar; c. OHG *hiufo* bramble]

hip[3] (hip), *interj.* (used as a cheer or in signaling for cheers): *Hip, hip, hurrah!* [1745–55; orig. uncert.]

hip[4] (hip), *adj.,* **hip·per, hip·pest,** *n., v.,* **hipped, hip·ping.** *Slang.* *—adj.* **1.** familiar with or informed about the latest ideas, styles, developments, etc.: *My parents aren't exactly hip, you know.* **2.** considered aware of or attuned to what is expected, esp. with a casual or knowing air; cool: *The guy was not at all hip—a total nerd.* **3.** in agreement or willing to cooperate; going along: *We explained our whole plan, and she was hip.* *—n.* **4.** Also, **hip′ness.** the condition or state of being hip. **5.** a hipster or hippie. *—v.t.* **6.** to make or keep aware or informed. Also, **hep.** [1900–05; earlier *hep;* of disputed orig.] **—hip′ly,** *adv.*

hip[5] (hip), *n.* hyp.

HIP (äch′ī′pē′ *or, sometimes,* hip), Health Insurance Plan.

hip·bone (hip′bōn′), *n.* **1.** See **innominate bone. 2.** the ilium. [1350–1400; ME; see HIP[1], BONE]

hip′ boot′, a hip-high boot, usually of rubber, worn by fishermen, firefighters, etc. [1890–95, *Amer.*]

hip′ dyspla′sia, *Vet. Pathol.* a genetic disorder, typically affecting young dogs of medium- to large-sized breeds, characterized by alteration and malformation of the hip joint.

hip-hop (hip′hop′), *Slang.* *—n.* **1.** the popular subculture of big-city teenagers, which includes rap music, break dancing, and graffiti art. **2.** See **rap music.** *—adj.* **3.** of, pertaining to, or characteristic of this subculture: *the hip-hop generation.* [1985–90]

hip·hug·ger (hip′hug′ər), *adj.* **1.** (of a garment) having a close-fitting waistline placed at the hip rather than at the natural waist: *hiphugger jeans.* *—n.* **2. hiphuggers,** trousers having this type of waistline. [1965–70; HIP[1] + HUG + -ER[1]]

hip′ joint′, a ball-and-socket joint between the head of the femur and the innominate bone. [1785–95]

hip·length (hip′lengkth′, -length′), *adj.* reaching to or covering the hips, as clothing: *a hiplength sweater.* [1920–25; HIP[1] + LENGTH]

hipp-, var. of **hippo-** before a vowel: *hipparch.*

Hip·par·chus (hi pär′kəs), *n.* **1.** died 514 B.C., tyrant of Athens 527–514. **2.** c190–c125 B.C., Greek astronomer.

hipped[1] (hipt), *adj.* **1.** having hips. **2.** having the hips as specified (usually used in combination): *broad-hipped; narrow-hipped.* **3.** (esp. of livestock) having the hip injured or dislocated. **4.** *Archit.* formed with a hip or hips, as a roof. [1500–10; HIP[1] + -ED[3]]

hipped[2] (hipt), *adj. Informal.* greatly interested or preoccupied, almost to an irrational extent; obsessed (usually fol. by *on*): *He's hipped on learning to play the tuba.* [1915–20; HIP[4] + -ED[3]]

Hip·pi·as (hip′ē əs), *n.* fl. 6th century B.C., tyrant of Athens (brother of Hipparchus, son of Pisistratus).

hip·pie (hip′ē), *n.* a person, esp. of the late 1960's, who rejected established institutions and values and sought spontaneity, direct personal relations expressing love, and expanded consciousness, often expressed externally in the wearing of casual, folksy clothing and of beads, headbands, used garments, etc. Also, **hippy.** Cf. **flower child.** [1950–55, *Amer.;* HIP[4] + -IE]

hip·pie·dom (hip′ē dəm), *n.* the lifestyle and world of hippies, esp. in the 1960's. [1965–70, *Amer.;* HIPPIE + -DOM]

hip·po (hip′ō), *n., pl.* **-pos.** *Informal.* hippopotamus. [by shortening]

Hip·po (hip′ō), *n.* See **Hippo Regius.**

hippo-, a combining form appearing in loanwords from Greek, where it meant "horse" (*hippodrome*); on this model, used in the formation of compound words (*hippology*). Also, *esp. before a vowel,* **hipp-.** [< Gk: comb. form of *híppos;* c. L *equus,* OIr *ech,* OE *eoh,* Skt *aśvas,* Lith *ašvà*]

hip·po·cam·pal (hip′ə kam′pəl), *adj. Anat.* of or pertaining to the hippocampus. [1830–40; HIPPOCAMP(US) + -AL[1]]

hip′pocam′pal gy′rus, *Anat.* a convolution on the inner surface of the temporal lobe of the cerebrum, bordering the hippocampus. Also called **hippocam′pal convolu′tion.** [1880–85]

hip·po·cam·pus (hip′ə kam′pəs), *n., pl.* **-pi** (-pī, -pē). **1.** *Class. Myth.* a sea horse with two forefeet, and a body ending in the tail of a dolphin or fish. **2.** *Anat.* an enfolding of cerebral cortex into the lateral fissure of a cerebral hemisphere, having the shape in cross section of a sea horse. [1600–10; < L < Gk *hippókampos,* equiv. to *hippo-* HIPPO- + *kámpos* sea monster]

hip·po·cras (hip′ə kras′), *n.* an old medicinal cordial made of wine mixed with spices. [1325–75; ME *ypocras,* appar. short for *ypocras wyn* (trans. of ML *vīnum hippocraticum;* so called because clarified by filtering through a strainer named after Hippocrates); ME *ypocras* < OF: HIPPOCRATES < ML *Hippocrās,* alter. of L *Hippocratēs,* on model of words like *cīvitās* (nom.), *cīvitātis* (gen.)]

Hip·poc·ra·tes (hi pok′rə tēz′), *n.* (*"Father of Medicine"*) c460–c377 B.C., Greek physician. **—Hip·po·crat·ic** (hip′ə krat′ik), **Hip′po·crat′i·cal,** *adj.*

Hip′pocrat′ic oath′, an oath embodying the duties and obligations of physicians, usually taken by those about to enter upon the practice of medicine. [1740–50]

Hip·po·crene (hip′ə krēn′, hip′ə krē′nē), *n.* a spring on Mount Helicon sacred to the Muses and regarded as a source of poetic inspiration. **—Hip′po·cre′ni·an,** *adj.*

hip·po·drome (hip′ə drōm′), *n.* **1.** an arena or structure for equestrian and other spectacles. **2.** (in ancient Greece and Rome) an oval track for horse races and chariot races. [1540–50; < L *hippodromos* < Gk *hippódromos,* equiv. to *hippo-* HIPPO- + *drómos* -DROME] **—hip·po·drom·ic** (hip′ə drom′ik), *adj.*

hip·po·griff (hip′ə grif′), *n.* a fabulous creature resembling a griffin but having the body and hind parts of a horse. Also, **hip′po·gryph′.** [1645–55; earlier *hippogryph,* Latinized < It *ippogrifo.* See HIPPO-, GRIFFIN[1]]

hip·pol·o·gy (hi pol′ə jē), *n.* the study of horses. [1850–55; HIPPO- + -LOGY] **—hip·po·log·i·cal** (hip′ə loj′i kəl), *adj.* **—hip·pol′o·gist,** *n.*

Hip·pol·y·ta (hi pol′i tə), *n. Class. Myth.* a queen of the Amazons, variously said to have been killed by Hercules or to have been conquered and married by Theseus.

Hip·pol·y·tus (hi pol′i təs), *n.* Also, **Hip·pol·y·tos** (hi pol′i təs, -tos′). *Class. Myth.* the son of Theseus who was falsely accused by his stepmother, Phaedra, of raping her after he had rejected her advances and who was killed by Poseidon in response to the plea of Theseus.

Hip·pom·e·nes (hi pom′ə nēz′), *n. Class. Myth.* the successful suitor of Atalanta.

hip·poph·a·gist (hi pof′ə jist), *n.* a person who eats horseflesh. [1855–60; HIPPOPHAG(Y) + -IST]

hip·poph·a·gy (hi pof′ə jē), *n.* the practice of eating horseflesh. Also, **hip·poph·a·gism.** [1820–30; HIPPO- + -PHAGY] **—hip·poph·a·gous** (hi pof′ə gəs), *adj.*

hip·po·phile (hip′ə fīl′, -fil), *n.* one who loves horses. [1850–55; HIPPO- + -PHILE]

hip·po·pot·a·mus (hip′ə pot′ə məs), *n., pl.* **-mus·es, -mi** (-mī′). a large herbivorous mammal, *Hippopotamus amphibius,* having a thick hairless body, short legs, and a large head and muzzle, found in and near the rivers, lakes, etc., of Africa, and able to remain under water for a considerable time. See illus. on next page. [1555–65; < L < Gk *hippopótamos,* earlier *híppos potámios* lit., riv-

CONCISE PRONUNCIATION KEY: act, cāpe, dâre, pärt; set, ēqual; *if,* īce; ox, ōver, ôrder, oil, bo͝ok, bo͞ot, out; up, ûrge; child; sing; shoe; thin, *th*at; zh as in *treasure.* ə = *a* as in *alone, e* as in *system, i* as in *easily, o* as in *gallop, u* as in *circus;* ᵊ as in *fire* (fīᵊr), *hour* (ouᵊr). l and n can serve as syllabic consonants, as in *cradle* (krād′l), and *button* (but′n). See the full key inside the front cover.

erine horse (term used by Herodotus in his account of the Egyptian hippopotamus); cf. ME *ypotame, ypotamos, ypotanus* < OF *ypotame* < ML *ypotamus*] **—hip·po·po·tam·ic** (hip′ə pə tam′ik), **hip·po·po·ta·mi·an** (hip′ə pə-tā′mē ən), *adj.*

hippopotamus, *Hippopotamus amphibius,* 4½ ft. (1.4 m) high at shoulder; length 13 ft. (4 m)

Hip·po Re·gi·us (hip′ō rē′jē əs), a seaport of ancient Numidia: St. Augustine was bishop here A.D. 395–430; the site of modern Annaba, in Algeria. Also called **Hippo.**

Hip·po Za·ry·tus (hip′ō zə rī′təs), ancient name of **Bizerte.**

hip·pus (hip′əs), *n. Med.* spasmodic contraction of the pupil of the eye. [1675–85; < NL < Gk *híppos* horse, complaint of the eye]

-hippus, var. of **hippo-** as final element of compounds: *eohippus.* [< L < Gk *-hippos*]

hip·py[1] (hip′ē), *adj.,* **-pi·er, -pi·est.** having big hips. [1890–95; HIP[1] + -Y[1]]

hip·py[2] (hip′ē), *n., pl.* **-pies.** hippie. [HIP[4] + -Y[2]]

hip′ roof′, *Archit.* a roof with sloping ends and sides; a hipped roof. See illus. under **roof.** [1720–30] **—hip′-roofed′,** *adj.*

hip·shot (hip′shot′), *adj.* **1.** having the hip dislocated. **2.** having one hip lower than the other: *a Greek statue in hipshot pose.* [1630–40; HIP[1] + SHOT[2]]

hip·ster[1] (hip′stər), *n. Slang.* **1.** a person who is hip. **2.** hepcat. **3.** a person, esp. during the 1950's, characterized by a particularly strong sense of alienation from most established social activities and relationships. [1935–40, *Amer.*; HIP[4] + -STER]

hip·ster[2] (hip′stər), *n.* **1. hipsters,** *Chiefly Brit.* hiphugger (def. 2). **2.** Often, **hipsters.** hiphugger underpants for women and girls. [1960–65; HIP[1] + -STER]

hip·ster·ism (hip′stə riz′əm), *n.* the style of life of a hipster. [1955–60, *Amer.*; HIPSTER[1] + -ISM]

hir·a·ble (hīər′ə bəl), *adj.* able to be hired; fit for hiring. Also, **hire′a·ble.** [1860–65; HIRE + -ABLE] **—hir′a·bil′i·ty,** *n.*

hi·ra·ga·na (hēr′ə gä′nə; *Japn.* hē′Rä gä′nä), *n.* the cursive and more widely used of the two Japanese syllabaries. Cf. **katakana.** [1815–25; < Japn, equiv. to *hira* ordinary (earlier *f(y)ira* < **pira*) + *-gana,* comb. form of *kana* KANA]

Hi·ra·ka·ta (hē rä′kä tä′), *n.* a city on S Honshu, in Japan, NE of Osaka. 353,360.

Hi·ram (hī′rəm), *n.* **1.** a king of Tyre in the 10th century B.C. I Kings 5. **2.** a male given name: from a Hebrew word meaning "noble."

Hi·ra·nu·ma (hē Rä′nŏŏ mä′), *n.* **Baron Ki·i·chi·ro** (kē ē′chē Rô′), 1867?–1952, Japanese statesman.

hir·cine (hûr′sīn, -sin), *adj.* **1.** of, pertaining to, or resembling a goat. **2.** having a goatish odor. **3.** lustful; libidinous. [1650–60; < L *hircinus* of a goat, equiv. to *hirc(us)* goat + *-inus* -INE[1]]

hire (hīər), *v.,* **hired, hir·ing,** *n., adj.* **—***v.t.* **1.** to engage the services of (a person or persons) for wages or other payment: *to hire a clerk.* **2.** to engage the temporary use of at a set price; rent: *to hire a limousine.* **3. hire on,** to obtain employment; take a job: *They hired on as wranglers with the rodeo.* **4. hire out,** to offer or exchange one's services for payment: *He hired himself out as a handyman.* **—***n.* **5.** the act of hiring. **6.** the state or condition of being hired. **7.** the price or compensation paid or contracted to be paid for the temporary use of something or for personal services or labor; pay: *The laborer is worthy of his hire.* **8.** *Informal.* a person hired or to be hired: *Most of our new hires are college-educated.* **9. for hire,** available for use or service in exchange for payment. Also, **on hire.** **—***adj.* **10.** *Brit.* available for hire; rental: *a hire car.* [bef. 1000; (v.) ME *hiren,* OE *hȳrian* (c. D *huren,* LG *hüren,* OFris *hēra*); (n.) ME; OE *hȳr;* c. D *huur,* LG *hüre* (whence D *hyre,* Sw *hyra,* G *Heuer*), Fris *hēre*] **—hir·ee′,** *n.* **—hir′er,** *n.*

—Syn. 1. employ. **2.** lease. HIRE, CHARTER, RENT refer to paying money for the use of something. HIRE is a general word, most commonly applied to paying money for labor or services, but is also used in reference to paying for the temporary use of automobiles (usually with a chauffeur), halls, etc.; in New England, it is used in speaking of borrowing money on which interest is to be paid (to distinguish from borrowing from a friend, who would not accept any interest): *to hire a gardener, a delivery truck, a hall for a convention.* CHARTER formerly meant to pay for the use of a vessel, but is now applied with increasing frequency to leasing any conveyance for the use of a group: *to charter a boat, a bus, a plane.* RENT is used in the latter sense, also, but is usually applied to paying a set sum once or at regular intervals for the use of a dwelling, room, personal effects, an automobile (which one drives oneself), etc.: *to rent a business building.* **7.** rent, rental; stipend, wages, salary.

hired′ gun′, *Informal.* **1.** a person hired to kill someone, as a gunfighter or professional killer. **2.** a person hired to bear arms and fight for another, as a bodyguard or mercenary. **3.** a person, as a politician or lobbyist, skilled at attaining power for others. **4.** a person hired to resolve difficult problems or disputes or to handle complex legal or business problems. [1965–70]

CONCISE ETYMOLOGY KEY: <, descended or borrowed from; >, whence; b., blend of, blended; c., cognate with; cf., compare; deriv., derivative; equiv., equivalent; imit., imitative; obl., oblique; r., replacing; s., stem; sp., spelling, spelled; resp., respelling, respelled; trans., translation; ?, origin unknown; *, unattested; ‡, probably earlier than. See the full key inside the front cover.

hired′ hand′, **1.** a hired laborer, esp. on a farm or ranch; farm hand or ranch hand. **2.** an employee. [1810–20, *Amer.*]

hire·ling (hīər′ling), *n.* **1.** a person who works only for pay, esp. in a menial or boring job, with little or no concern for the value of the work. **—***adj.* **2.** serving for pay only. **3.** venal; mercenary. [bef. 1000; late ME *hirlyng,* OE *hȳrling.* See HIRE, -LING[1]]

—Syn. 1. menial, minion, flunky, lackey, retainer.

hire′-pur′chase sys′tem (hīər′pûr′chəs), *Brit.* a system of payment for a commodity in regular installments while using it. Also called **hire′-pur′chase.** [1895–1900]

hi-res (hī′rez′), *adj. Computers Informal.* high-resolution (def. 2). [by shortening]

hir′ing hall′, an employment office operated by a union for placing members in jobs. [1930–35]

Hi·ro·hi·to (hēr′ō hē′tō; *Japn.* hē′Rô hē′tô), *n.* ("*Showa*") 1901–89, emperor of Japan 1926–89.

Hi·ro·shi·ge (hēr′ō shē′gä; *Japn.* hē′Rô shē′ge), *n.* **An·do** (än′dô′), ("*Tokube*"), 1797–1858, Japanese painter.

Hi·ro·shi·ma (hēr′ō shē′mə, hi rō′shə mə; *Japn.* hē′-Rô shē′mä), *n.* a seaport on SW Honshu, in SW Japan: first military use of atomic bomb August 6, 1945. 899,394.

Hirsch (hûrsh), *n.* **John Stephen,** born 1930, Canadian stage director, born in Hungary.

hir·sute (hûr′sōōt, hûr sōōt′), *adj.* **1.** hairy; shaggy. **2.** *Bot., Zool.* covered with long, rather stiff hairs. **3.** of, pertaining to, or characteristic of hair. [1615–25; < L *hirsūtus* rough, shaggy, bristly; akin to HORRID] **—hir′sute·ness,** *n.*

—Syn. 1. pilose, unshaved, bearded, bushy, woolly, furry.

hir·sut·ism (hûr′sōō tiz′əm, hûr sōō′tiz-), *n. Med.* excessive hairiness, esp. in women. [1925–30; HIRSUTE + -ISM]

hir·su·tu·lous (hûr sōō′chə ləs), *adj.* hirtellous. [HIRSUTE + -ULOUS]

hir·tel·lous (hûr tel′əs), *adj.* minutely hirsute. Also, **hirsutulous.** [< L *hirt(us)* hairy + NL *-ellus* dim. adj. suffix; see -OUS]

hir·u·din (hir′yə din, hir′ə-, hi rōōd′n), *n.* a gray or white, water-soluble acidic polypeptide obtained from the buccal gland of leeches, used in medicine chiefly as an anticoagulant. [1900–05; formerly trademark]

Hir·u·din·e·a (hir′ŏŏ din′ē ə), *n.* the class comprising the leeches. [< NL; see HIRUDINEAN]

hir·u·din·e·an (hir′ŏŏ din′ē ən), *n.* **1.** any annelid worm of the class Hirudinea, comprising the leeches. **—***adj.* **2.** belonging or pertaining to the Hirudinea. [1825–35; < NL *Hirudine(a)* (L *hirūdin-* (s. of *hirūdō*) leech + *-ea,* neut. pl. of *-eus* adj. suffix) + -AN]

hi·ru·di·noid (hi rōōd′n oid′), *adj.* of, pertaining to, or resembling a leech. [HIRUDIN(EAN) + -OID]

hi·run·dine (hi run′din, -dīn), *adj.* of, pertaining to, or resembling the swallow. [1825–35; < LL *hirundineus* of a swallow, equiv. to *hirundin-* (s. of *hirundō*) swallow + *-eus* adj. suffix; see -EOUS]

his (hiz; *unstressed* iz), *pron.* **1.** the possessive form of **he** (used as an attributive or predicative adjective): *His coat is the brown one. This brown coat is his. Do you mind his speaking first?* **2.** that or those belonging to him: *His was the cleverest remark of all. I borrowed a tie of his.* [bef. 900; ME, OE, gen. of *hē* HE[1]]

—Usage. See **he**[1], **me.**

His, *Biochem.* histidine.

his-and-her (hiz′ən hûr′), *adj.* denoting two matching or identical items, one intended for use by a male and the other by a female: *his-and-her towels in the bathroom; his-and-her sweatshirts.* Also, **his′-and-hers′.** [1945–50]

hisn (hiz′ən), *pron. Nonstandard.* his (def. 2). Also, **his'n.** [1350–1400; ME *hysene;* cf. HERN[2]]

His·pa·ni·a (hi spā′nē ə, -spän′yə), *n. Latin.* Spain.

His·pan·ic (hi span′ik), *adj.* **1.** Spanish. **2.** Latin American: *the United States and its Hispanic neighbors.* **—***n.* **3.** Also, **Hispano.** Also called **Hispan′ic Amer′ican.** an American citizen or resident of Spanish or Latin-American descent. [1575–85; < L *hispānicus.* See HISPANIA, -IC] **—His·pan′i·cal·ly,** *adv.*

His·pan·i·cism (hi span′ə siz′əm), *n.* an idiom peculiar to Spanish. [1830–40; HISPANIC + -ISM]

His·pan·i·cist (hi span′ə sist), *n.* Hispanist. [HISPANIC + -IST]

His·pan·i·cize (hi span′ə sīz′), *v.t.,* **-cized, -ciz·ing.** (*sometimes l.c.*) **1.** to make Spanish or Latin American, as in character, custom, or style. **2.** to bring under Spanish or Latin-American domination or influence. Also, *esp. Brit.,* **His·pan′i·cise′.** [1875–80; HISPANIC + -IZE] **—His·pan′i·ci·za′tion,** *n.*

his·pa·ni·dad (ēs pä′nē thäth′), *n.* (*often cap.*) *Spanish.* hispanism, esp. as directed toward political objectives.

His·pan·io·la (his′pən yō′lə; *Sp.* ēs′pän yô′lä), *n.* an island in the West Indies, comprising the republic of Haiti and the Dominican Republic. 29,843 sq. mi. (77,293 sq. km). Formerly, **Haiti, Hayti, Santo Domingo, San Domingo.**

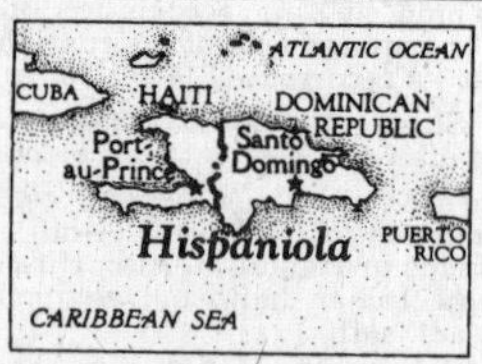

his·pa·nism (his′pə niz′əm), *n.* (*often cap.*) **1.** a movement in Latin America for the promotion of Spanish or of native culture and influence. Cf. ***hispanidad.*** **2.** a word, phrase, feature, etc., associated with Spain or Latin America. [1945–50; < Sp *hispanismo,* equiv. to *hispan(o)* Spanish (see HISPANO-) + *-ismo* -ISM]

His·pa·nist (his′pə nist), *n.* a specialist in the Spanish or Portuguese language or in Spanish or Latin-American literature or culture. Also, **Hispanicist.** [1930–35; < Sp *hispanista,* equiv. to *hispan(o)* (see HISPANO-) + *-ista* -IST]

His·pa·no (hi span′ō, -spä′nō), *n.* Hispanic (def. 3).

Hispano-, a combining form representing **Spain** or **Spanish** in compound words: *Hispano-American.* [< L *Hispān(us)* pertaining to *Hispānia* the Iberian Peninsula + -O-]

his·pid (his′pid), *adj. Bot., Zool.* rough with stiff hairs, bristles, or minute spines. [1640–50; < L *hispidus* rough, shaggy; akin to HIRSUTE] **—his·pid′i·ty,** *n.*

his·pid·u·lous (hi spij′ə ləs), *adj. Bot., Zool.* covered with stiff, short hairs. [1850–55; HISPID + -ULOUS]

hiss (his), *v.i.* **1.** to make or emit a sharp sound like that of the letter *s* prolonged, as a snake does, or as steam does when forced under pressure through a small opening. **2.** to express disapproval or contempt by making this sound: *The audience hissed when the actor forgot his lines.* **—***v.t.* **3.** to express disapproval of by hissing: *The audience hissed the controversial play.* **4.** to silence or drive away by hissing (usually fol. by *away, down,* etc.): *They hissed down the author when he tried to speak.* **5.** to utter with a hiss. **—***n.* **6.** a hissing sound, esp. one made in disapproval. [1350–1400; ME *hissen;* prob. imit.; cf. OE *hyscan* to jeer at, rail (deriv. of *husc* jeering; c. OS, OHG *hosc*)] **—hiss′er,** *n.* **—hiss′ing·ly,** *adv.*

—Syn. 2, 4. boo, razz, heckle.

Hiss (his), *n.* **Alger,** born 1904, U.S. public official, accused of espionage 1948 and imprisoned for perjury 1950–54.

His·sar·lik (hi sär lik′), *n.* the modern name of the site of ancient Troy.

his·self (hi self′, hiz-), *pron. Nonstandard.* himself. [1350–1400; ME; see HIS, SELF]

hiss·ing (his′ing), *n.* **1.** the act of emitting a hiss. **2.** the sound of a hiss. **3.** *Archaic.* an occasion or object of scorn. [1350–1400; ME; see HISS, -ING[1]]

hist (st, sst; *spelling pron.* hist), *interj.* (a sibilant exclamation used to attract attention). [1595–1605; repr. in writing the sound sequence *st*]

hist-, var. of **histo-** before a vowel: *histidine.*

hist., **1.** histology. **2.** historian. **3.** historical. **4.** history.

His·ta·drut (his tä drōōt′), *n.* a labor federation in Israel, founded in 1920.

his·tam·i·nase (hi stam′ə nās′, -nāz′), *n. Biochem., Pharm.* an enzyme that catalyzes the decomposition of histamine, used in treating allergies. [1925–30; HISTAMINE + -ASE]

his·ta·mine (his′tə mēn′, -min), *n.* **1.** *Physiol.* a histidine-derived amine compound that is released mainly by damaged mast cells in allergic reactions, causing dilation and permeability of blood vessels and lowering blood pressure. **2.** *Pharm.* a commercial form of this compound, obtained from histidine and used chiefly in the diagnosis of gastric and circulatory functions. Cf. **antihistamine.** Also, **his·ta·min** (his′tə min). [1910–15; HIST(IDINE) + -AMINE] **—his·ta·min·ic** (his′tə min′ik), *adj.*

his′tamine block′er, *Pharm.* any of various substances that act at a specific receptor site to block certain actions of histamine.

his′tamine head′ache. See **cluster headache.**

his·ti·dine (his′ti dēn′, -din), *n. Biochem.* an essential amino acid, $C_3H_3N_2CH_2CH(NH_2)COOH$, that is a constituent of proteins and is important as the iron-binding site in hemoglobin. Also, **his·ti·din** (his′ti din). *Abbr.:* His; *Symbol:* H [1895–1900; HIST- + -ID[3] + -INE[2]]

his·ti·oid (his′tē oid′), *adj.* histoid.

histo-, a combining form meaning "tissue," used in the formation of compound words: *histology.* Also, *esp. before a vowel,* **hist-.** [< Gk, comb. form of *histós* web (of a loom), tissue]

his·to·blast (his′tə blast′), *n. Biol.* a cell or group of cells capable of forming tissue. [1885–90; HISTO- + -BLAST]

his·to·chem·is·try (his′tə kem′ə strē), *n.* the branch of science dealing with the chemical components of cellular and subcellular tissue. [1860–65; HISTO- + CHEMISTRY] **—his·to·chem·i·cal** (his′tə kem′i kəl), *adj.* **—his′to·chem′i·cal·ly,** *adv.*

his·to·com·pat·i·bil·i·ty (his′tō kəm pat′ə bil′i tē), *n. Immunol.* the condition of having antigenic similarities such that cells or tissues transplanted from one (the donor) to another (the recipient) are not rejected. Cf. **major histocompatibility complex.** [1945–50; HISTO- + COMPATIBILITY] —**his′to·com·pat′i·ble,** *adj.*

histocompatibil′ity an′tigen, *Immunol.* any antigen on the surface of tissue or blood cells that provokes the immune response and subsequent rejection when transplanted to an individual of a different antigenic type, thus determining whether the tissues or organs of a donor and recipient are histocompatible. [1965–70]

his·to·gen (his′tə jən, -jen′), *n. Bot.* a region in a plant in which tissues differentiate. [1920–25; HISTO- + -GEN]

his·to·gen·e·sis (his′tə jen′ə sis), *n. Biol.* the origin and development of tissues. [1850–55; HISTO- + -GENESIS] —**his·to·ge·net·ic** (his′tə jə net′ik), *adj.* —**his′to·ge·net′i·cal·ly,** *adv.*

his·to·gram (his′tə gram′), *n. Statistics.* a graph of a frequency distribution in which rectangles with bases on the horizontal axis are given widths equal to the class intervals and heights equal to the corresponding frequencies. [1890–95; HISTO- + -GRAM[1]]

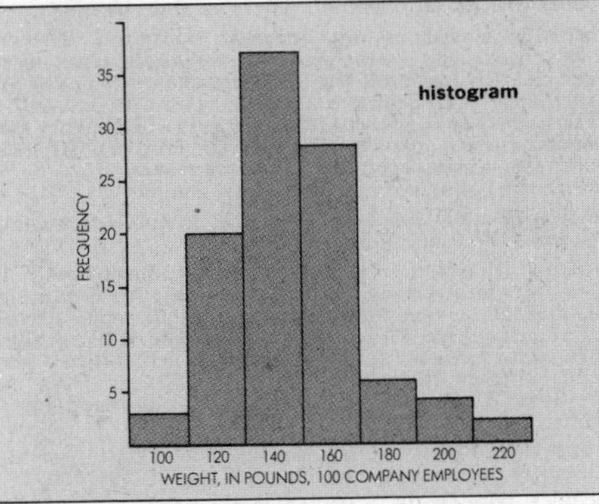

his·tog·ra·phy (hi stog′rə fē), *n., pl.* **-phies.** a treatise on or description of organic tissues. [1885–90; HISTO- + -GRAPHY] —**his·tog′ra·pher,** *n.* —**his·to·graph·ic** (his′tə graf′ik), *adj.* —**his′to·graph′i·cal·ly,** *adv.*

his·toid (his′toid), *adj.* **1.** *Pathol.* resembling normal tissue in structure. **2.** similar to or derived from one kind of tissue. Also, **histioid.** [1870–75; HIST- + -OID]

his·tol·o·gist (hi stol′ə jist), *n.* a specialist in histology. [1855–60; HISTOLOG(Y) + -IST]

his·tol·o·gy (hi stol′ə jē), *n.* **1.** the branch of biology dealing with the study of tissues. **2.** the structure, esp. the microscopic structure, of organic tissues. [1840–50; HISTO- + -LOGY] —**his·to·log·i·cal** (his′tl oj′i kəl), **his′to·log′ic,** *adj.* —**his′to·log′i·cal·ly,** *adv.*

his·tol·y·sis (hi stol′ə sis), *n.* disintegration or dissolution of organic tissues. [1855–60; HISTO- + -LYSIS] —**his·to·lyt·ic** (his′tl it′ik), *adj.*

his·to·mor·phol·o·gy (his′tō môr fol′ə jē), *n.* histology. [HISTO- + MORPHOLOGY] —**his·to·mor·pho·log·i·cal** (his′tə môr′fə loj′i kəl), *adj.* —**his′to·mor′pho·log′i·cal·ly,** *adv.*

his·tone (his′tōn), *n. Biochem.* any of a group of five small basic proteins, occurring in the nucleus of eukaryotic cells, that organize DNA strands into nucleosomes by forming molecular complexes around which the DNA winds. [1880–85; HIST- + -ONE]

his·to·pa·thol·o·gy (his′tō pə thol′ə jē), *n.* the science dealing with the histological structure of abnormal or diseased tissue; pathological histology. [1895–1900; HISTO- + PATHOLOGY] —**his·to·path·o·log·ic** (his′tə path′ə loj′ik), **his′to·path′o·log′i·cal,** *adj.* —**his′to·pa·thol′o·gist,** *n.*

his·to·phys·i·ol·o·gy (his′tə fiz′ē ol′ə jē), *n.* the branch of physiology dealing with tissues. [1885–90; HISTO- + PHYSIOLOGY] —**his·to·phys·i·o·log·i·cal** (his′tə fiz′ē ə loj′i kəl), *adj.*

his·to·plas·mo·sis (his′tō plaz mō′sis), *n. Pathol.* an infectious disease of the reticuloendothelial system, caused by the fungus *Histoplasma capsulatum* and characterized by fever, anemia, and emaciation. [1940–45; < NL, equiv. to *Histoplasm(a)* name of the genus (see HISTO-, -PLASM) + *-ōsis* -OSIS]

his·to·ri·an (hi stôr′ē ən, -stōr′-), *n.* **1.** an expert in history; authority on history. **2.** a writer of history; chronicler. [1400–50; late ME. See HISTORY, -AN]

his·tor·ic (hi stôr′ik, -stor′-), *adj.* **1.** well-known or important in history: *a historic building; historic occasions.* **2.** historical (defs. 1–5). [1605–15; < L *historicus* < Gk *historikós* historical, scientific, equiv. to *histor(ía)* inquiry (see HISTORY) + *-ikos* -IC]
—**Syn. 1.** notable, renowned, famous, famed, memorable.

his·tor·i·cal (hi stôr′i kəl, -stor′-), *adj.* **1.** of, pertaining to, treating, or characteristic of history or past events: *historical records; historical research.* **2.** based on or reconstructed from an event, custom, style, etc., in the past: *a historical reenactment of the battle of Gettysburg.* **3.** having once existed or lived in the real world, as opposed to being part of legend or fiction or as distinguished from religious belief: *to doubt that a historical Camelot ever existed; a theologian's study of the historical Jesus.* **4.** narrated or mentioned in history; belonging to the past. **5.** noting or pertaining to analysis based on a comparison among several periods of development of a phenomenon, as in language or economics. **6.** historic (def. 1). [1375–1425; late ME < L *historic(us)* HISTORIC + -AL[1]] —**his·tor′i·cal·ly,** *adv.* —**his·tor′i·cal·ness,** *n.*
—**Syn. 3.** documented, authentic, factual, attested.

histor′ical geol′ogy, the branch of geology dealing with the history of the earth. [1920–25]

histor′ical linguis′tics, the study of changes in a language or group of languages over a period of time. Also called **diachronic linguistics.** [1920–25]

histor′ical mate′rialism, (in Marxist theory) the doctrine that all forms of social thought, as art or philosophy, and institutions, as the family or the state, develop as a superstructure founded on an economic base; that they reflect the character of economic relations and are altered or modified as a result of class struggles; that each ruling economic class produces the class that will destroy or replace it; and that dialectical necessity requires the eventual withering away of the state and the establishment of a classless society: the body of theory, in dialectical materialism, dealing with historical process and social causation. Cf. **economic determinism.** [1920–25]

histor′ical meth′od, the process of establishing general facts and principles through attention to chronology and to the evolution or historical course of what is being studied. [1835–45]

histor′ical nov′el, a narrative in novel form, characterized chiefly by an imaginative reconstruction of historical events and personages. [1820–30]

histor′ical pres′ent, *Gram.* the present tense used in narrating a past event as if happening at the time of narration. [1960–65]

histor′ical school′, 1. a school of economists that arose in Germany in the 19th century in reaction to the principles of the classical economists, and that maintained that the factors making up an economy are variable and develop out of social institutions. **2.** *Law.* the school of jurists who maintain that law is not to be regarded so much as resulting from commands of sovereigns as from historical and social circumstances. [1890–95]

histor′ical sociol′ogy, the sociological study of the origins and development of societies and of other social phenomena that seeks underlying laws and principles.

his·tor·i·cism (hi stôr′ə siz′əm, -stor′-), *n.* **1.** a theory that history is determined by immutable laws and not by human agency. **2.** a theory that all cultural phenomena are historically determined and that historians must study each period without imposing any personal or absolute value system. **3.** a profound or excessive respect for historical institutions, as laws or traditions. **4.** a search for laws of historical evolution that would explain and predict historical phenomena. [1890–95; HISTORIC + -ISM; cf. G *Historismus*] —**his·tor′i·cist,** *n., adj.*

his·to·ric·i·ty (his′tə ris′i tē), *n.* historical authenticity. [1875–80; prob. < F *historicité.* See HISTORIC, -ITY]

his·tor·i·cize (hi stôr′ə siz′, -stor′-), *v.,* **-cized, -cizing.** —*v.i.* **1.** to interpret something as a product of historical development. —*v.t.* **2.** to narrate as history; render historic. Also, *esp. Brit.,* **his·tor′i·cise′.** [1840–50; HISTORIC + -IZE]

his·to·ried (his′tə rēd, his′trēd), *adj.* abounding in notable history; having an illustrious past; storied: *Italy is a richly historied land.* [1810–20; HISTORY + -ED[3]]

his·to·ri·og·ra·pher (hi stôr′ē og′rə fər, -stōr′-), *n.* **1.** a historian, esp. one appointed to write an official history of a group, period, or institution. **2.** an official historian, as of a court, institution, or cultural or learned society. [1485–95; < L *historiograph(us)* < Gk *historiográphos* (see HISTORY, -O-, -GRAPH) + -ER[1]] —**his·to′ri·og′ra·pher·ship′,** *n.*

his·to·ri·og·ra·phy (hi stôr′ē og′rə fē, -stōr′-), *n., pl.* **-phies. 1.** the body of literature dealing with historical matters; histories collectively. **2.** the body of techniques, theories, and principles of historical research and presentation; methods of historical scholarship. **3.** the narrative presentation of history based on a critical examination, evaluation, and selection of material from primary and secondary sources and subject to scholarly criteria. **4.** an official history: *medieval historiographies.* [1560–70; < MF *historiographie* < Gk *historiographía.* See HISTORY, -O-, -GRAPHY] —**his·to·ri·o·graph·ic** (hi stôr′ē ə graf′ik, -stōr′-), **his·to′ri·o·graph′i·cal,** *adj.* —**his·to′ri·o·graph′i·cal·ly,** *adv.*

his·to·ry (his′tə rē, his′trē), *n., pl.* **-ries. 1.** the branch of knowledge dealing with past events. **2.** a continuous, systematic narrative of past events as relating to a particular people, country, period, person, etc., usually written as a chronological account; chronicle: *a history of France; a medical history of the patient.* **3.** the aggregate of past events. **4.** the record of past events and times, esp. in connection with the human race. **5.** a past notable for its important, unusual, or interesting events: *a ship with a history.* **6.** acts, ideas, or events that will or can shape the course of the future; immediate but significant happenings: *Firsthand observers of our space program see history in the making.* **7.** a systematic account of any set of natural phenomena without particular reference to time: *a history of the American eagle.* **8.** a drama representing historical events: *Shakespeare's comedies, histories, and tragedies.* [1350–1400; ME *historie* < L *historia* < Gk *historía* learning or knowing by inquiry, history; deriv. of *hístōr* one who knows or sees (akin to WIT, VIDEO, VEDA)]
—**Syn. 2.** record, annals. See **narrative.**

his·to·sol (his′tə sôl′, -sol′), *n.* a worldwide soil type rich in organic matter, as peat, esp. prevalent in wet, poorly drained areas. [1970–75; HISTO- + -SOL]

his·to·tome (his′tə tōm′), *n.* a microtome. [HISTO- + -TOME]

his·tri·on·ic (his′trē on′ik), *adj.* Also, **his′tri·on′i·cal. 1.** of or pertaining to actors or acting. **2.** deliberately affected or self-consciously emotional; overly dramatic, in behavior or speech. —*n.* **3.** an actor. [1640–50; < LL *histriōnicus* of actors, equiv. to *histriōn-* (s. of *histriō*) actor (said to be < Etruscan) + *-icus* -IC] —**his′tri·on′i·cal·ly,** *adv.*

his·tri·on·ics (his′trē on′iks), *n.* (*used with a singular or plural v.*) **1.** dramatic representation; theatricals; acting. **2.** behavior or speech for effect, as insincere or exaggerated expression of an emotion; dramatics; operatics: *Cut out the histrionics—we know you're not really mad.* [1860–65; see HISTRIONIC, -ICS]

hit (hit), *v.,* **hit, hit·ting,** *n.* —*v.t.* **1.** to deal a blow or stroke to: *Hit the nail with the hammer.* **2.** to come against with an impact or collision, as a missile, a flying fragment, a falling body, or the like: *The car hit the tree.* **3.** to reach with a missile, a weapon, a blow, or the like, as one throwing, shooting, or striking: *Did the bullet hit him?* **4.** to succeed in striking: *With his final shot he hit the mark.* **5.** *Baseball.* **a.** to make (a base hit): *He hit a single and a home run.* **b.** bat[1] (def. 14). **6.** to drive or propel by a stroke: *to hit a ball onto the green.* **7.** to have a marked effect or influence on; affect severely: *We were all hit by the change in management.* **8.** to assail effectively and sharply (often fol. by *out*): *The speech hits out at warmongering.* **9.** to request or demand of: *He hit me for a loan.* **10.** to reach or attain (a specified level or amount): *Prices are expected to hit a new low. The new train can hit 100 mph.* **11.** to be published in or released to; appear in: *When will this report hit the papers? What will happen when the story hits the front page?* **12.** to land on or arrive in: *The troops hit the beach at 0800. When does Harry hit town?* **13.** to give (someone) another playing card, drink, portion, etc.: *If the dealer hits me with an ace, I'll win the hand. Bartender, hit me again.* **14.** to come or light upon; meet with; find: *to hit the right road.* **15.** to agree with; suit exactly: *I'm sure this purple shirt will hit Alfred's fancy.* **16.** to solve or guess correctly; come upon the right answer or solution: *You've hit it!* **17.** to succeed in representing or producing exactly: *to hit a likeness in a portrait.* **18.** *Informal.* to begin to travel on: *Let's hit the road. What time shall we hit the trail?*
—*v.i.* **19.** to strike with a missile, a weapon, or the like; deal a blow or blows: *The armies hit at dawn.* **20.** to come into collision (often fol. by *against, on,* or *upon*): *The door hit against the wall.* **21.** *Slang.* to kill; murder. **22.** (of an internal-combustion engine) to ignite a mixture of air and fuel as intended: *This jalopy is hitting on all cylinders.* **23.** to come or light (usually fol. by *upon* or *on*): *to hit on a new way.* **24. hit it off,** *Informal.* to be congenial or compatible; get along; agree: *We hit it off immediately with the new neighbors. She and her brother had never really hit it off.* **25. hit off, a.** to represent or describe precisely or aptly: *In his new book he hits off the American temperament with amazing insight.* **b.** to imitate, esp. in order to satirize. **26. hit on,** *Slang.* to make persistent sexual advances to: *guys who hit on girls at social events.* **27. hit out, a.** to deal a blow aimlessly: *a child hitting out in anger and frustration.* **b.** to make a violent verbal attack: *Critics hit out at the administration's new energy policy.* **28. hit the books,** *Slang.* to study hard; cram. **29. hit the bottle,** *Slang.* See **bottle** (def. 4). **30. hit the high spots, a.** to go out on the town; go nightclubbing: *We'll hit the high spots when you come to town.* **b.** to do something in a quick or casual manner, paying attention to only the most important or obvious facets or items: *When I clean the house I hit the high spots and that's about all. This course will hit the high spots of ancient history.* **31. hit up,** *Slang.* **a.** to ask to borrow money from: *He hit me up for ten bucks.* **b.** to inject a narcotic drug into a vein.
—*n.* **32.** an impact or collision, as of one thing against another. **33.** a stroke that reaches an object; blow. **34.** a stroke of satire, censure, etc.: *a hit at complacency.* **35.** *Baseball.* See **base hit. 36.** *Backgammon.* **a.** a game won by a player after the opponent has thrown off one or more men from the board. **b.** any winning game. **37.** a successful stroke, performance, or production; success: *The play is a hit.* **38.** *Slang.* a dose of a narcotic drug. **39.** *Computers.* (in information retrieval) an instance of successfully locating an item of data in the memory bank of a computer. **40.** *Slang.* a killing, murder, or assassination, esp. one carried out by criminal prearrangements. **41. hit or miss,** without concern for correctness or detail; haphazardly: *The paint job had been done hit or miss.* [bef. 1100; 1865–70, *Amer.* for def. 5a; ME *hitten,* OE *hittan;* perh. < Scand; cf. ON *hitta* to come upon (by chance), meet with] —**hit′less,** *adj.* —**hit′ta·ble,** *adj.* —**hit′ter,** *n.*
—**Syn. 1.** See **strike, beat. 33, 35, 37.** See **blow**[1].

hit-and-miss (hit′n mis′), *adj.* sometimes successful or rewarding and sometimes not. [1895–1900]

hit-and-run (hit′n run′), *adj., v.,* **-ran, -run·ning.** —*adj.* **1.** guilty of fleeing the scene of an accident or injury one has caused, esp. a vehicular accident, thereby attempting to evade being identified and held responsible: *a hit-and-run driver.* **2.** involving or resulting from such action or conduct: *hit-and-run fatalities.* **3.** *Baseball.* pertaining to or noting a play in which, to get a head start, a base runner begins to run to the next base as the pitcher delivers the ball to the batter, who must try to hit it in order to protect the runner. **4.** marked by taking flight immediately after a quick, concentrated attack: *a hit-and-run raid.* —*v.i.* **5.** *Baseball.* to attempt or execute a hit-and-run play. [1895–1900, *Amer.*] —**hit′-and-run′ner,** *n.*

hit′ bats′man, *Baseball.* a batter who, having been struck by a pitch, is awarded first base.

hitch[1] (hich), *v.t.* **1.** to fasten or tie, esp. temporarily, by means of a hook, rope, strap, etc.; tether: *Steve hitched the horse to one of the posts.* **2.** to harness (an animal) to a vehicle (often fol. by *up*). **3.** to raise with jerks (usually fol. by *up*); hike up: *to hitch up one's trousers.* **4.** to move or draw (something) with a jerk. **5.** *Slang.* to bind by marriage vows; unite in marriage; marry: *They got hitched in '79.* **6.** to catch, as on a projection; snag: *He hitched his jeans on a nail and tore them.* —*v.i.* **7.** to stick, as when caught. **8.** to fasten

CONCISE PRONUNCIATION KEY: act, cāpe, dâre, pärt; set, ēqual; *if,* ice; ox, ōver, ôrder, oil, bo͝ok, bo͞ot, out; up, ûrge; child; sing; shoe; thin, *that;* zh as in *treasure.* ə = *a* as in *alone, e* as in *system, i* as in *easily, o* as in *gallop, u* as in *circus;* ᵊ as in *fire* (fīᵊr), *hour* (ouᵊr). l and n can serve as syllabic consonants, as in *cradle* (krād′l), and *button* (but′n). See the full key inside the front cover.

oneself or itself to something (often fol. by *on*). **9.** to move roughly or jerkily: *The old buggy hitched along.* **10.** to hobble or limp. **11. hitch up,** to harness an animal to a wagon, carriage, or the like. —*n.* **12.** the act or fact of fastening, as to something, esp. temporarily. **13.** any of various knots or loops made to attach a rope to something in such a way as to be readily loosened. Cf. **bend**[1] (def. 18). **14.** *Mil. Slang.* a period of military service: *a three-year hitch in the Navy.* **15.** an unexpected difficulty, obstacle, delay, etc.: *a hitch in our plans for the picnic.* **16.** a hitching movement; jerk or pull. **17.** a hitching gait; a hobble or limp. **18.** a fastening that joins a movable tool to the mechanism that pulls it. **19.** *Mining.* **a.** a fault having a throw less than the thickness of a coal seam being mined. **b.** a notch cut in a wall or the like to hold the end of a stull or other timber. [1400–50; 1840–50 for def. 5; late ME *hytchen,* of obscure orig.] —**hitch′er,** *n.*
—**Syn. 1.** attach, connect, hook. **2.** yoke. **15.** hindrance, catch, impediment. —**Ant. 1.** loose, loosen.

hitch[2] (hich), *n.* a minnow, *Lavinia exilicauda,* inhabiting streams in the area of San Francisco and the Sacramento River basin. [orig. uncert.]

hitch[3] (hich), *v.i., v.t., n. Informal.* hitchhike. [1865–70; by shortening] —**hitch′er,** *n.*

Hitch·cock (hich′kok), *n.* **1. Sir Alfred (Joseph),** 1899–1980, U.S. film and television director and producer, born in England. **2. Thomas, Jr.** (*Tommy*), 1900–44, U.S. polo player.

Hitch′cock chair′, *U.S. Furniture.* a side chair of the early 19th century that has turned legs, a turned crest rail, and one or more slats in the back, and that is painted or stenciled in colors or gold on black. [1920–30, *Amer.*; named after L. A. *Hitchcock,* 1795–1852, American furniture maker]

hitch·hike (hich′hīk′), *v.,* **-hiked, -hik·ing,** *n.* —*v.i.* **1.** to travel by standing on the side of the road and soliciting rides from passing vehicles. —*v.t.* **2.** to ask for or get (a ride) by hitchhiking. —*n.* **3.** an act or instance of hitchhiking. [1920–25, *Amer.*; HITCH[1] + HIKE] —**hitch′·hik′er,** *n.*

hitch′ing post′, a post to which horses, mules, etc., are tied. [1835–45]

hi-tech (hī′tek′), *n., adj. Informal.* high-tech.

hith·er (hith′ər), *adv.* **1.** to or toward this place: *to come hither.* **2. hither and thither,** in various quarters; here and there: *They scurried hither and thither to escape the rain.* **3. hither and yon,** from here to over there, esp. to a farther place; in or to a great many places: *He looked hither and yon for the coin. She went hither and yon in search of an answer.* —*adj.* **4.** being on this or the closer side; nearer: *the hither side of the meadow.* [bef. 900; ME, OE *hider;* c. ON *hethra,* L *citer* on this side]

hith·er·most (hith′ər mōst′ *or, esp. Brit.,* -məst), *adj.* nearest in this direction. [1555–65; HITHER + -MOST]

hith·er·to (hith′ər to͞o′), *adv.* **1.** up to this time; until now: *a fact hitherto unknown.* **2.** to here. [1175–1225; ME *hiderto.* See HITHER, TO]

hith·er·ward (hith′ər wərd), *adv.* hither. Also, **hith′·er·wards.** [bef. 1100; ME, OE *hiderward.* See HITHER, -WARD]

Hit·ler (hit′lər), *n.* **Ad·olf** (ad′olf, ā′dolf; *Ger.* ä′dôlf), (*Adolf Schicklgruber*) ("*der Führer*"), 1889–1945, Nazi dictator of Germany, born in Austria: Chancellor 1933–45; dictator 1934–45.

Hit·ler·ism (hit′lə riz′əm), *n.* the doctrines, principles, and practices of the Nazi party, esp. as developed by Hitler; Nazism. [1925–30; HITLER + -ISM]

Hit·ler·ite (hit′lə rīt′), *n.* **1.** an advocate or a follower of Hitlerism. —*adj.* **2.** of or pertaining to Hitler or Hitlerism. [1925–30; HITLER + -ITE[1]]

hit′ list′, *Slang.* **1.** a list of persons singled out as targets for murder. **2.** a list of people or programs to be acted against or disposed of. [1970–75]

hit′ man′, *Slang.* **1.** a hired killer, esp. a professional killer from the underworld. **2.** See **hatchet man** (def. 3). Also, **hit′man′.** [1965–70, *Amer.*]

hit-or-miss (hit′ər mis′), *adj.* careless; inattentive; haphazard: *The professor criticized the hit-or-miss quality of our research.* [1600–10]

hit′ parade′, **1.** a listing or category of popular songs ranked according to their popularity with listeners, usually as shown by sales of records. **2.** any sequential listing of popular or favorite persons or things. [1935–40]

hit-run (hit′run′), *adj.* hit-and-run (defs. 1, 2, 4).

hit-skip (hit′skip′), *adj.* hit-and-run (defs. 1, 2).

hit′ squad′, *Slang.* **1.** a team of hit men, as one organized for the purpose of assassinating a political figure. **2.** a group of political terrorists. [1975–80]

Hit·tite (hit′īt), *n.* **1.** a member of an ancient people who established a powerful empire in Asia Minor and Syria, dominant from about 1900 to 1200 B.C. **2.** an extinct language of the Anatolian branch of Indo-European, preserved in cuneiform inscriptions of the second millennium B.C. Cf. **Hieroglyphic Hittite.** —*adj.* **3.** of, pertaining to, or belonging to the Hittites or their language. [1600–10; < Heb *ḥitt(īm)* Hittite (cf. Hittite *Khatti*) + -ITE[1]]

Hit·tit·ol·o·gy (hit′ĭ tol′ə jē), *n.* the study of Hittite language and culture. [1950–55; HITTITE + -O- + -LOGY]

HIV, human immunodeficiency virus. See under **AIDS virus.**

CONCISE ETYMOLOGY KEY: <, descended or borrowed from; >, whence; b., blend of, blended; c., cognate with; cf., compare; deriv., derivative; equiv., equivalent; imit., imitative; obl., oblique; r., replacing; s., stem; sp., spelling, spelled; resp., respelling, respelled; trans., translation; ?, origin unknown; *, unattested; ‡, probably earlier than. See the full key inside the front cover.

hive (hīv), *n., v.,* **hived, hiv·ing.** —*n.* **1.** a shelter constructed for housing a colony of honeybees; beehive. **2.** the colony of bees inhabiting a hive. **3.** something resembling a beehive in structure or use. **4.** a place swarming with busy occupants: *a hive of industry.* **5.** a swarming or teeming multitude. —*v.t.* **6.** to gather into or cause to enter a hive. **7.** to shelter as in a hive. **8.** to store up in a hive. **9.** to store or lay away for future use or enjoyment. —*v.i.* **10.** (of bees) to enter a hive. **11.** to live together in or as in a hive. **12. hive off,** *Brit.* to become transferred from the main body of a commercial enterprise through the agency of new ownership. [bef. 900; ME; OE *hȳf;* akin to ON *hūfr* ship's hull, L *cūpa* vat] —**hive′less,** *adj.* —**hive′like′,** *adj.* —**hiv′er,** *n.*
—**Syn. 4.** hub, center.

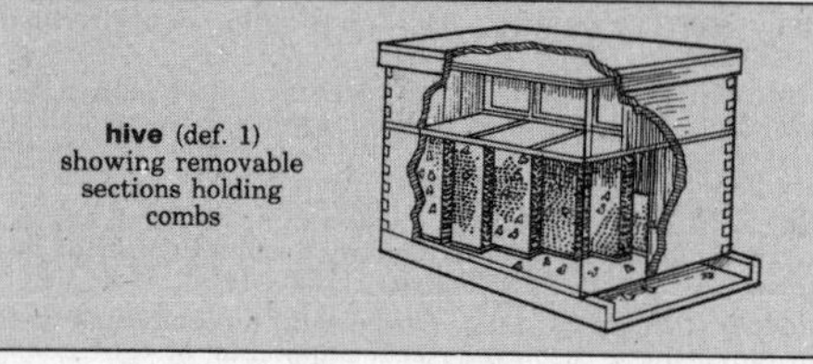
hive (def. 1) showing removable sections holding combs

hives (hīvz), *n.* (*used with a singular or plural v.*) *Pathol.* any of various eruptive conditions of the skin, as the wheals of urticaria. [1490–1500; orig. Scots; of obscure orig.]

Hi·vite (hī′vīt), *n.* a member of an ancient people inhabiting Canaan, conquered by the Israelites.

H.J., here lies. [< L *hīc jacet*]

H.J. Res., House joint resolution.

H.J.S., here lies buried. [< L *hīc jacet sepultus*]

HK, Hong Kong.

hl, hectoliter; hectoliters.

H.L., House of Lords.

HLA, *Immunol.* human leukocyte antigen: any of a complex of genetically determined antigens, occurring on the surface of almost every human cell, by which one person's cells can be distinguished from another's and the histocompatibility and genetic likeness of any two persons can be established: the major histocompatibility antigen of humans. Cf. **MHC.** [1965–70]

HLA antigen, *Immunol.* an antigen of the HLA group, designated by a letter (HLA-A, HLA-B, etc.) according to the chromosome locus on which the controlling HLA gene appears and additionally by a number (HLA-A1, HLA-A2, etc.) according to the order of discovery and identification.

HLA gene, *Immunol.* any of a complex of genes, located on human chromosome 6, that govern the expression of HLA. Cf. **MHC.**

HLBB, Home Loan Bank Board.

HL hinge. See **H and L hinge.**

h'm (hmm), *interj.* (used typically to express thoughtful absorption, hesitation, doubt, or perplexity.) Also, **hmm.**

hm, hectometer; hectometers.

H.M., **1.** Her Majesty. **2.** His Majesty.

HMAS, **1.** Her Majesty's Australian Ship. **2.** His Majesty's Australian Ship.

HMCS, **1.** Her Majesty's Canadian Ship. **2.** His Majesty's Canadian Ship.

HMF, **1.** Her Majesty's Forces. **2.** His Majesty's Forces.

HMMV, Humvee. [1985–90]

HMO, See **health maintenance organization.**

Hmong (hmông), *n., pl.* **Hmongs,** (*esp. collectively*) **Hmong.** Miao.

H.M.S., **1.** Her Majesty's Service. **2.** His Majesty's Service. **3.** Her Majesty's Ship. **4.** His Majesty's Ship.

ho[1] (hō), *interj.* **1.** (used as a call to attract attention, sometimes specially used after a word denoting a destination): *Westward ho! Land ho!* **2.** (used as an exclamation of surprise or delight.) [1250–1300; ME]

ho[2] (hō), *interj.* (used as a command to a horse to stop.) [1300–50; ME < OF. See WHOA]

HO (hō), *n.* (in police use) habitual offender.

Ho, *Symbol, Chem.* holmium.

H.O., Head Office; Home Office.

ho., house.

Ho·a·binh·i·an (hō′ə bin′ē ən), *n. Archaeol.* of, pertaining to, or typifying a middle to late Stone Age culture found in southeast Asia that is characterized chiefly by agricultural village settlements. [1940–45; < F *hoabinhien,* after *Hoà-binh* province, Vietnam, where remains typifying the culture were first found; see -IAN]

ho·ac·tzin (hō akt′sin, wäkt′sin), *n.* hoatzin.

Hoad (hōd), *n.* **Lew(is Alan),** 1934–94, Australian tennis player.

hoa·gy (hō′gē), *n., pl.* **-gies.** *New Jersey and Pennsylvania* (*chiefly Philadelphia*). a hero sandwich. Also, **hoa′gie.** [1965–70, *Amer.*; a number of anecdotal hypotheses have been advanced as to the orig. of the word, most claiming it to be derivative of *hog,* either in reference to pork as an ingredient, or as an epithet for a person capable of eating such a sandwich, or alluding to *Hog Island,* an industrial and shipping area of South Philadelphia; but corroborating evidence is lacking; see -IE]
—**Regional Variation.** See **hero sandwich.**

hoar (hôr, hōr), *n.* **1.** hoarfrost; rime. **2.** a hoary coating or appearance. —*adj.* **3.** hoary. [bef. 900; ME *hor,* OE *hār;* c. ON *hārr* gray with age, OFris *hēr* gray, OHG *hēr* old (G *hehr* august, sublime)]

hoard (hôrd, hōrd), *n.* **1.** a supply or accumulation that is hidden or carefully guarded for preservation, future use, etc.: *a vast hoard of silver.* —*v.t.* **2.** to accumulate for preservation, future use, etc., in a hidden or carefully guarded place: *to hoard food during a shortage.* —*v.i.* **3.** to accumulate money, food, or the like, in a hidden or carefully guarded place for preservation, future use, etc. [bef. 900; ME *hord(e),* OE *hord;* c. ON *hodd,* OHG *hort,* Goth *huzd* treasure; see HIDE[1], HIDE[2]] —**hoard′er,** *n.*
—**Syn. 1.** stockpile, reserve, cache, store, stock.

hoard·ing[1] (hôr′ding, hōr′-), *n.* **1.** the act of a person who hoards. **2. hoardings,** things that are hoarded. [1585–95; HOARD + -ING[1]]

hoard·ing[2] (hôr′ding, hōr′-), *n.* **1.** a temporary fence enclosing a construction site. **2.** *Brit.* a billboard. [1815–25; obs. *hoard* (<< OF *hourd(e)* palisade made of hurdles < Gmc; cf. G *Hürde* hurdle) + -ING[1]]

Hoare (hôr, hōr), *n.* **Sir Samuel John Gur·ney** (gûr′nē), **1st Viscount Tem·ple·wood** (tem′pəl wo͝od′), 1880–1959, British statesman.

hoar·frost (hôr′frôst′, -frost′, hōr′-), *n.* frost (def. 2). [1250–1300; ME *hor-frost.* See HOAR, FROST]

hoar·hound (hôr′hound′, hōr′-), *n.* horehound.

hoarse (hôrs, hōrs), *adj.* **hoars·er, hoars·est.** **1.** having a vocal tone characterized by weakness of intensity and excessive breathiness; husky: *the hoarse voice of the auctioneer.* **2.** having a raucous voice. **3.** making a harsh, low sound. [1350–1400; ME *hors* < ON **hārs* (assumed var. of *hāss*); r. ME *hoos,* OE *hās,* c. OHG *heis,* OS *hēs*] —**hoarse′ly,** *adv.* —**hoarse′ness,** *n.*
—**Syn. 1.** harsh, grating; throaty, rough.

hoars·en (hôr′sən, hōr′-), *v.t., v.i.* to make or become hoarse. [1740–50; HOARSE + -EN[1]]

hoar·y (hôr′ē, hōr′ē), *adj.,* **hoar·i·er, hoar·i·est.** **1.** gray or white with age: *an old dog with a hoary muzzle.* **2.** ancient or venerable: *hoary myths.* **3.** tedious from familiarity; stale: *Please don't tell that hoary joke at dinner again tonight.* [1520–30; HOAR + -Y[1]] —**hoar′i·ly,** *adv.* —**hoar′i·ness,** *n.*
—**Syn. 1.** grizzled, grizzly; hoar. **2.** old, dated, aged; venerated, revered.

hoar·y-head·ed (hôr′ē hed′id, hōr′-), *adj.* having the gray or white hair of advanced age. [1590–1600]

hoar′y mar′mot, a large marmot, *Marmota caligata,* living in mountainous areas of Siberia and northwestern North America and having a heavy, yellow-gray body, short black limbs, and black and white head and shoulders. [1775–85]

ho·at·zin (hō at′sin, wät′sin), *n.* a blue-faced, crested bird, *Opisthocomus hoazin,* of the Amazon and Orinoco forests, having as a nestling a large, temporary claw on the second and third digits of the forelimb, for climbing among the tree branches. Also, **hoactzin.** [1655–65; << Nahuatl *huāctzin, huāhtzin* name for several hen-sized birds of the Valley of Mexico, appar. applied indiscriminately by early naturalists to similar New World birds]

hoatzin, *Opisthocomus hoazin,* length 25 in. (64 cm)

hoax (hōks), *n.* **1.** something intended to deceive or defraud: *The Piltdown man was a scientific hoax.* —*v.t.* **2.** to deceive by a hoax; hoodwink. [1790–1800; perh. contr. of HOCUS] —**hoax′er,** *n.*
—**Syn. 1.** deception, fraud, fake, imposture, humbug.

hob[1] (hob), *n., v.,* **hobbed, hob·bing.** —*n.* **1.** a projection or shelf at the back or side of a fireplace, used for keeping food warm. **2.** a rounded peg or pin used as a target in quoits and similar games. **3.** a game in which such a peg is used. **4.** *Mach.* a milling cutter for gear and sprocket teeth, splines, threads, etc., having helically arranged teeth and fed across the work as the work is rotated. —*v.t., v.i.* **5.** *Mach.* to cut with a hob. [1505–15; var. of obs. *hub* hob (in a fireplace); perh. identical with HUB] —**hob′ber,** *n.*

hob[2] (hob), *n.* **1.** a hobgoblin or elf. **2. play hob with,** to do mischief or harm to: *The child played hob with my radio, and now it won't work at all.* **3. raise hob,** to cause a destructive commotion; behave disruptively: *They raised such hob with their antagonistic questions that the meeting broke up.* [1275–1325; ME, special use of *Hob,* for ROBERT or ROBIN] —**hob′like′,** *adj.*

Ho·ban (hō′bən), *n.* **James,** c1762–1831, U.S. architect, born in Ireland: designed the White House.

Ho·bart (hō′bərt *or, for 1, 4,* -bärt; hō′bärt *for 2*), *n.* **1. Gar·ret Augustus** (gar′it), 1844–99, U.S. lawyer and politician: vice president of the U.S. 1897–99. **2.** a seaport on and the capital of Tasmania, SE of Australia. 128,603. **3.** a city in NW Indiana. 22,987. **4.** a male given name.

Hob·be·ma (hob′ə mə; *Du.* hô′bə mä), *n.* **Mein·dert** (mīn′dərt), 1638–1709, Dutch painter.

Hobbes (hobz), *n.* **Thomas,** 1588–1679, English philosopher and author.

Hobbes·i·an (hob′zē ən), *n.* **1.** a person who believes in or advocates the principles of Thomas Hobbes. —*adj.* **2.** of, pertaining to, or recalling the principles of Thomas Hobbes. [1770–80; HOBBES + -IAN]

Hob·bism (hob′iz əm), *n.* the doctrines of, or those attributed to, Hobbes, esp. the doctrine of absolute submission to a royal sovereign in order to avoid the anarchic disorder resulting from the uncontrolled competition of individual interests. [1675–85; HOBB(ES) + -ISM] —**Hob′bist,** *n.* —**Hob·bis′ti·cal,** *adj.*

hob·ble (hob′əl), *v.,* **-bled, -bling,** *n.* —*v.i.* **1.** to walk lamely; limp. **2.** to proceed irregularly and haltingly: *His verses hobble with their faulty meters.* —*v.t.* **3.** to cause to limp: *His tight shoes hobbled him.* **4.** to fasten together the legs of (a horse, mule, etc.) by short lengths of rope to prevent free motion. **5.** to impede; hamper the progress of. —*n.* **6.** an act of hobbling; an uneven, halting gait; a limp. **7.** a rope, strap, etc., used to hobble an animal. **8. hobbles,** a leg harness for controlling the gait of a pacer. **9.** *Archaic.* an awkward or difficult situation. [1300–50; ME *hobelen,* appar. akin to *hob* protuberance, uneven ground, and to D *hobbelen,* G *hoppeln* to jolt] —**hob′bler,** *n.*
—**Syn. 5.** hinder, restrict, frustrate, cramp. —**Ant. 5.** aid, assist, benefit.

hob·ble·bush (hob′əl bo͝osh′), *n.* a North American shrub, *Viburnum alnifolium,* of the honeysuckle family, having flat-topped clusters of white flowers and red-to-black berrylike fruit. Also called **American wayfaring tree.** [1810–20, *Amer.;* HOBBLE + BUSH[1]; so called from the fact that it obstructs the way with its branches]

hob·ble·de·hoy (hob′əl dē hoi′), *n.* an awkward, ungainly youth. [1530–40; var. of *hoberdyhoy,* alliterative compound, equiv. to *hoberd* (var. of *Roberd* Robert) + -Y[2] + *-hoy* for BOY (*b* > *h* for alliteration; see HOB[2])]

hob′ble skirt′, a woman's skirt that is very narrow at the bottom, causing the wearer to walk with short, mincing steps. [1910–15]

Hobbs (hobz), *n.* a city in New Mexico. 28,794.

hob·by[1] (hob′ē), *n., pl.* **-bies. 1.** an activity or interest pursued for pleasure or relaxation and not as a main occupation: *Her hobbies include stamp-collecting and woodcarving.* **2.** a child's hobbyhorse. **3.** *Archaic.* a small horse. **4. ride a hobby,** to concern oneself excessively with a favorite notion or activity. Also, **ride a hobbyhorse.** [1325–75; ME *hoby(n),* prob. for *Robin,* or *Robert* (cf. HOB[2]), used as horse's name, as in DOBBIN] —**hob′by·ist,** *n.* —**hob′by·less,** *adj.*

hob·by[2] (hob′ē), *n., pl.* **-bies.** a small Old World falcon, *Falco subbuteo,* formerly flown at such small game as larks. [1400–50; late ME *hoby* < MF *hobé,* suffixal var. of MF, OF *hobel* (cf. F *hobereau*), prob. n. deriv. of *hobeler* to skirmish, harass, perh. < MD *hob(b)elen* to turn, roll; cf. D *hobbelen* to rock, jolt (cf. HOBBLE)]

Hob·by (hob′ē), *n.* **Oveta Culp** (kulp), born 1905, U.S. newspaper publisher and government official: first director of Women's Army Corps 1942–45; first Secretary of Health, Education, and Welfare 1953–55.

hob·by·horse (hob′ē hôrs′), *n.* **1.** a stick with a horse's head, or a rocking horse, ridden by children. **2.** a figure of a horse, attached at the waist of a performer in a morris dance, pantomime, etc. **3.** a pet idea or project. [1550–60; HOBBY[1] + HORSE]

hob·gob·lin (hob′gob′lin), *n.* **1.** something causing superstitious fear; a bogy. **2.** a mischievous goblin. **3.** (*cap.*) Puck (def. 1). [1520–30; HOB[2] + GOBLIN]

hob·nail (hob′nāl′), *n.* **1.** a large-headed nail for protecting the soles of heavy boots and shoes. **2.** a small allover pattern consisting of small tufts, as on fabrics, or of small studs, as on glass. [1585–95; HOB[1] + NAIL]

hob·nailed (hob′nāld′), *adj.* **1.** furnished with hobnails. **2.** rustic or loutish. [1590–1600; HOBNAIL + -ED[3]]

hob·nob (hob′nob′), *v.,* **-nobbed, -nob·bing,** *n.* —*v.i.* **1.** to associate on very friendly terms (usually fol. by *with*): *She often hobnobs with royalty.* **2.** *Archaic.* to drink together. —*n.* **3.** a friendly, informal chat. [1595–1605; from the phrase *hab or nab* lit., have or have not, OE *habban* to have + *nabban* not to have (*ne* not + *habban* to have)]

ho·bo (hō′bō), *n., pl.* **-bos, -boes. 1.** a tramp or vagrant. **2.** a migratory worker. [1885–90, *Amer.;* orig. uncert.] —**ho′bo·ism,** *n.*

Ho·bo·ken (hō′bō kən), *n.* a seaport in NE New Jersey, opposite New York City. 42,460.

Ho·brecht (hō′brekt; *Du.* hō′brekht), *n.* **Ja·cob** (jā′kəb; *Du.* yä′kôp). See **Obrecht, Jacob.**

Hob·son (hob′sən), *n.* **Richmond Pear·son** (pēr′sən), 1870–1937, U.S. naval officer and politician.

Hob·son-Job·son (hob′sən job′sən), *n.* the alteration of a word or phrase borrowed from a foreign language to accord more closely with the phonological and lexical patterns of the borrowing language, as in English *hoosegow* from Spanish *juzgado.* [1625–35; Anglo-Indian rendering of Ar *yā Ḥasan, yā Husayn* lament uttered during ta'ziyah; an example of such an alteration]

Hob′son's choice′ (hob′sənz), the choice of taking either that which is offered or nothing; the absence of a real alternative. [1640–50; after Thomas *Hobson* (1544–1631), of Cambridge, England, who rented horses and gave his customer only one choice, that of the horse nearest the stable door]

Hoc·cleve (hok′lēv), *n.* **Thomas,** 1370–1450, English poet. Also, **Occleve.**

Hoch·hei·mer (hok′hī′mər; *Ger.* hôkh′hī′mər), *n.* a Rhine wine produced at Hochheim, near Mainz, West Germany.

Ho Chi Minh (hō′ chē′ min′), 1890?–1969, North Vietnamese political leader: president of North Vietnam 1954–69.

Ho′ Chi′ Minh′ Cit′y, a seaport in S Vietnam. 3,460,500. Formerly, **Saigon.**

Ho′ Chi′ Minh′ Trail′, a network of jungle paths winding from North Vietnam through Laos and Cambodia into South Vietnam, used as a military route by North Vietnam to supply the Vietcong during the Vietnam War.

hock[1] (hok), *n.* **1.** the joint in the hind leg of a horse, cow, etc., above the fetlock joint, corresponding anatomically to the ankle in humans. See diag. under **horse. 2.** a corresponding joint in a fowl. —*v.t.* **3.** to hamstring. [1375–1425; var. of dial. *hough,* ME *ho(u)gh,* appar. back formation from late ME *hokschyn,* etc., OE *hōhsinu* hock (lit., heel) sinew; see HEEL[1]]

hock[2] (hok), *n. Chiefly Brit.* any white Rhine wine. [1615–25; short for *Hockamore* HOCHHEIMER]

hock[3] (hok), *v.t.* **1.** pawn. —*n.* **2.** the state of being deposited or held as security; pawn: *She was forced to put her good jewelry in hock.* **3.** the condition of owing; debt: *After the loan was paid, he was finally out of hock.* [1855–60, *Amer.;* < D *hok* kennel, sty, pen, (informal) miserable place to live, prison] —**hock′er,** *n.*

hock·et (hok′it), *n.* a technique in medieval musical composition in which two or three voice parts are given notes or short phrases in rapid alternation, producing an erratic, hiccuping effect. [1250–1300; ME *hoket* hitch < MF *hocquet* hiccup, sudden interruption, equiv. to *hoc-* (imit.) + *-et* dim. suffix; see HICCUP]

hock·ey (hok′ē), *n.* **1.** See **ice hockey. 2.** See **field hockey.** [1520–30; earlier *hockie,* perh. equiv. to *hock-* HOOK + *-ie* -IE]

hock′ey skate′, a tubular ice skate having a shorter blade than a racing skate and often having a reinforced shoe for protection. Cf. **racing skate, tubular skate.**

hock′ey stick′, the stick used in field hockey or ice hockey. [1840–50]

Hock·ing (hok′ing), *n.* **William Ernest,** 1873–1966, U.S. philosopher.

hock·le (hok′əl), *v.,* **-led, -ling,** *n.* —*v.i.* **1.** (of a rope) to have the yarns spread and kinked through twisting in use. —*n.* **2.** the spreading and kinking of the yarns in a rope strand. [perh. HOCK[1] + -LE]

hock′ leg′, *Furniture.* a leg similar to a cabriole leg, but having a straight perpendicular section between the upper, convex section and the foot.

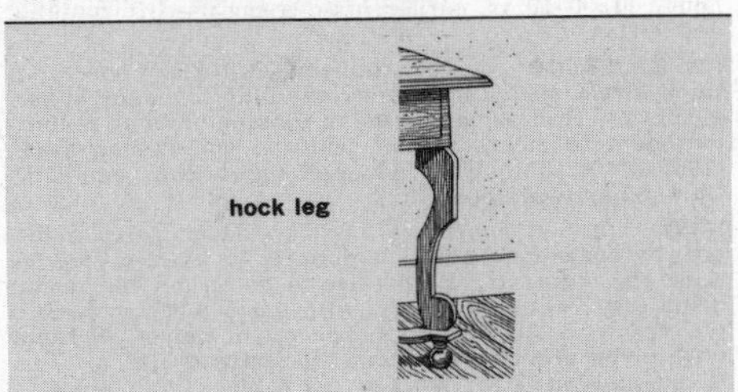
hock leg

Hock·ney (hok′nē), *n.* **David,** born 1937, British artist.

hock·shop (hok′shop′), *n.* a pawnshop. [1870–75; HOCK[3] + SHOP]

ho·cus (hō′kəs), *v.t.,* **-cused, -cus·ing** or (*esp. Brit.*) **-cussed, -cus·sing. 1.** to play a trick on; hoax; cheat. **2.** to stupefy with drugged liquor. **3.** to drug (liquor). [1665–75; short for HOCUS-POCUS]

ho·cus-po·cus (hō′kəs pō′kəs), *n., v.,* **-cused, -cus·ing** or (*esp. Brit.*) **-cussed, -cus·sing.** —*n.* **1.** a meaningless chant or expression used in conjuring or incantation. **2.** a juggler's trick; sleight of hand. **3.** trickery; deception. **4.** unnecessarily mysterious or elaborate activity or talk to cover up a deception, magnify a simple purpose, etc. —*v.t.* **5.** to play tricks on or with. —*v.i.* **6.** to perform tricks; practice trickery or deception. [1615–25; pseudo-Latin rhyming formula used by jugglers and magicians]
—**Syn. 3.** deceit, dishonesty, hanky-panky, double-dealing.

hod (hod), *n.* **1.** a portable trough for carrying mortar, bricks, etc., fixed crosswise on top of a pole and carried on the shoulder. **2.** a coal scuttle. [1565–75; perh. later var. of ME *hot* basket for carrying earth]

ho-dad (hō′dad′), *n.* **1.** a nonsurfer who spends time at beaches masquerading as a surfer. **2.** a poor surfer. [perh. HO[1] + DAD[1]]

hod′ car′rier, a mason's assistant whose work is to carry hods of materials to the mason. Also called **hodman.** [1765–75]

Ho·dei·da (ho͞o dā′dä), *n.* a seaport in W Yemen, on the Red Sea. 155,110.

Hodg·en·ville (hoj′ən vil′), *n.* a town in central Kentucky: birthplace of Abraham Lincoln. 2459.

hodge·podge (hoj′poj′), *n.* a heterogeneous mixture; jumble. [1615–25; var. of HOTCHPOTCH]
—**Syn.** conglomeration, miscellany, muddle, mess.

Hodg·kin (hoj′kin), *n.* **1. Sir Alan Lloyd,** born 1914, English biophysicist: Nobel prize for medicine 1963. **2.** his cousin, **Dorothy Mary Crow·foot** (krō′fo͝ot′), 1910–94, English chemist: Nobel prize 1964.

Hodg′kin's disease′, a type of cancer characterized by progressive chronic inflammation and enlargement of the lymph nodes of the neck, armpit, groin, and mesentery, by enlargement of the spleen and occasionally of the liver and the kidneys, and by lymphoid infiltration along the blood vessels. [1860–65; after Thomas *Hodgkin* (1798–1866), London physician who described it]

hod·man (hod′mən), *n., pl.* **-men.** See **hod carrier.** [1580–90; HOD + MAN[1]]

Hód·me·ző·vá·sár·hely (hōd′me zœ vä′shär hā), *n.* a city in SE Hungary. 53,000.

hod·o·graph (hod′ə graf′, -gräf′), *n. Math., Mech.* the figure described by the extremity of a vector that has a fixed origin and a position vector equal to the velocity of a moving particle. [1840–50; < Gk *hod(ós)* way + -O- + -GRAPH]

hoe (hō), *n., v.,* **hoed, hoe·ing.** —*n.* **1.** a long-handled implement having a thin, flat blade usually set transversely, used to break up the surface of the ground, destroy weeds, etc. **2.** any of various implements of similar form, as for mixing plaster or mortar. —*v.t.* **3.** to dig, scrape, weed, cultivate, etc., with a hoe. —*v.i.* **4.** to use a hoe. [1325–75; ME *howe* < OF *houe* < Gmc; cf. MD *houwe,* OHG *houwa* mattock; akin to HEW] —**ho′er,** *n.* —**hoe′like′,** *adj.*

Hoe (hō), *n.* **1. Richard,** 1812–86, U.S. inventor and manufacturer of printing-press equipment. **2.** his father, **Robert,** 1784–1833, U.S. manufacturer of printing presses.

hoe·cake (hō′kāk′), *n. South Midland and Southern U.S.* an unleavened cake made with flour or corn meal: originally baked on a hoe but now usually cooked on a griddle. [1735–45, *Amer.;* HOE + CAKE]
—**Regional Variation.** See **pancake.**

hoe·down (hō′doun′), *n.* **1.** a community dancing party typically featuring folk and square dances accompanied by lively hillbilly tunes played on the fiddle. **2.** the hillbilly or country music typical of a hoedown. [1835–45, *Amer.;* HOE + DOWN[1]]

Hoek van Hol·land (ho͞ok vän hôl′änt). See **Hook of Holland.**

Hoe·nir (hœ′nir), *n. Scand. Myth.* a god, one of the Aesir, companion of Odin and Loki, hostage to the Vanir.

hof·brau (hof′brou′), *n.* an informal, German-style restaurant or tavern. [by shortening of *Hofbrauhaus* (< G: lit., court brewery), a typical name for such restaurants]

Ho·fei (*Chin.* hu′fā′), *n. Wade-Giles.* Hefei.

Ho·fer (hō′fər), *n.* **An·dre·as** (än drā′əs), 1767–1810, Tyrolese patriot.

Hof·fa (hof′ə), *n.* **James Rid·dle** (rid′l), ("*Jimmy*"), 1913–75?, U.S. labor leader: president of the International Brotherhood of Teamsters 1957–71; disappeared 1975.

Hoff·man (hof′mən), *n.* **Mal·vi·na** (mal vē′nə), 1887–1966, U.S. sculptor.

Hoff′man Estates′, a city in NE Illinois. 38,258.

Hoff·mann (hof′mən), *n.* **1. E(rnst) T(he·o·dor) A(ma·de·us) (Wil·helm)** (ernst tā′ô dôr′ ä′mä dā′o͞os vil′helm), 1776–1822, German author, composer, and illustrator. **2. Jo·sef** (jō′zəf, -səf), 1870–1956, Viennese architect and designer, born in Czechoslovakia.

Hof·mann (hof′mən; *Ger., Pol.* hôf′män), *n.* **1. Au·gust Wil·helm von** (ou′go͝ost vil′helm fən), 1818–92, German chemist. **2. Hans,** 1880–1966, U.S. painter, born in Germany. **3. Jo·sef (Cas·i·mir)** (jō′zəf kaz′ə mir), 1876–1957, U.S. pianist and composer, born in Poland.

Hof·manns·thal (hôf′mäns täl′), *n.* **Hu·go von** (ho͞o′gō fən), 1874–1929, Austrian poet, playwright, and librettist.

Hof·stadt·er (hof′stat′ər, -stä′tər), *n.* **1. Richard,** 1916–70, U.S. historian. **2. Robert,** 1915–90, U.S. physicist: Nobel prize 1961.

Ho·fuf (ho͞o fo͞of′), *n.* a city in E Saudi Arabia. 100,000. Also, **Hufuf.** Also called **Al Hufuf.**

hog (hôg, hog), *n., v.,* **hogged, hog·ging.** —*n.* **1.** a hoofed mammal of the family Suidae, order Artiodactyla, comprising boars and swine. **2.** a domesticated swine weighing 120 lb. (54 kg) or more, raised for market. **3.** a selfish, gluttonous, or filthy person. **4.** *Slang.* **a.** a large, heavy motorcycle. **b.** an impressively large luxury automobile. **5.** Also, **hogg, hogget.** *Brit.* **a.** a sheep about one year old that has not been shorn. **b.** the wool shorn from such a sheep. **c.** any of several other domestic animals, as a bullock, that are one year old. **6.** *Railroads Slang.* a locomotive. **7.** a machine for shredding wood. **8.** *Curling.* a stone that stops before reaching the hog score. **9. go the whole hog,** to proceed or indulge completely and unreservedly: *We went the whole hog and took a cruise around the world.* Also, **go whole hog. 10. live high off** or **on the hog,** to be in prosperous circumstances. Also, **eat high off the hog.** —*v.t.* **11.** to appropriate selfishly; take more than one's share of. **12.** to arch (the back) upward like that of a hog. **13.** roach[3] (def. 3). **14.** (in machine-shop practice) to cut deeply into (a metal bar or slab) to reduce it to a shape suitable for final machining. **15.** to shred (a piece of wood). —*v.i.* **16.** *Naut.* (of a hull) to have less than the proper amount of sheer because of structural weakness; arch. Cf. **sag** (def. 6a). [1300–50; ME; cf. OE *hogg-* in place-names; perh. < Celtic; cf. Welsh *hwch,* Cornish *hogh* swine] —**hog′like′,** *adj.*

hog (def. 2) (domestic) 2⅓ ft. (0.7 m) high at shoulder; length 4½ ft. (1.4 m)

ho·gan (hō′gôn, -gən), *n.* a Navajo Indian dwelling constructed of earth and branches and covered with mud or sod. [1870–75, *Amer.;* < Navajo *hooghan* hogan, home]

Ho·gan (hō′gən), *n.* **Ben,** born 1912, U.S. golfer.

Ho·garth (hō′gärth), *n.* **William,** 1697–1764, English painter and engraver. —**Ho·garth′i·an,** *adj.*

Ho′garth chair′, *Eng. Furniture.* a Queen Anne

CONCISE PRONUNCIATION KEY: act, cāpe, dâre, pärt; set, ēqual; *if,* īce; ox, ōver, ôrder, oil, bo͝ok, bo͞ot, out; up, ûrge; child; sing; shoe; thin, *th*at; zh as in *treasure.* ə = *a* as in *alone, e* as in *system, i* as in *easily, o* as in *gallop, u* as in *circus;* ° as in *fire* (fī°r), *hour* (ou°r). l and n can serve as syllabic consonants, as in *cradle* (krād′l), and *button* (but′n). See the full key inside the front cover.

chair having a solid splat and cabriole legs, all pieces having a cyma curve or outline. [after W. HOGARTH; perh. from the fact that it typified the Hogarth line]

HO gauge (āch′ō′) a model railroad gauge of 5/8 in. (16 mm). [*h(alf) O* gauge]

hog·back (hôg′bak′, hog′-), *n. Geol.* a long, sharply crested ridge, generally formed of steeply inclined strata that are especially resistant to erosion. [1655–65; HOG + BACK[1]]

hog-backed (hôg′bakt′, hog′-), *adj.* cambered, as the ridge of a roof, a hill, etc. [1645–55]

hog·chok·er (hôg′chō′kər, hog′-), *n.* a sole, *Trinectes maculatus,* found in coastal streams from Maine to Texas and south to Panama. [1850–55, *Amer.*; so called to indicate that the fish is worthless, even as food for hogs]

hog′ chol′era, *Vet. Pathol.* an acute, usually fatal, highly contagious disease of swine caused by an RNA virus of the genus *Pestivirus,* characterized by high fever, lack of appetite, diarrhea, and lethargy. Also called **swine fever.** [1855–60, *Amer.*]

hog·fish (hôg′fish′, hog′-), *n., pl.* (*esp. collectively*) **-fish,** (*esp. referring to two or more kinds or species*) **-fish·es. 1.** a large wrasse, *Lachnolaimus maximus,* of the western Atlantic Ocean, used for food. **2.** any of various other fishes having a fancied resemblance to a hog, as the pigfish and logperch. [1590–1600; trans. of ML *porcopiscis* PORPOISE. See HOG, FISH]

hog′ fu′el, wood chips or shavings, residue from sawmills, etc., used for fuel, landfill, animal feed, and surfacing paths and running tracks.

hogg (hôg, hog), *n. Brit.* hog (def. 5).

Hogg (hog), *n.* **James** (*"the Ettrick Shepherd"*), 1770–1835, Scottish poet.

hog·ger (hô′gər, hog′ər), *n.* **1.** a person or thing that hogs. **2.** Also called **hog′head′.** *Railroads Slang.* a locomotive engineer. [1865–70, *Amer.*; HOG + -ER[1]]

hog·ger·y (hô′gə rē, hog′ə-), *n., pl.* **-ger·ies. 1.** piggery. **2.** slovenly or greedy behavior. [1810–20; HOG + -ERY]

hog·get (hog′it), *n. Brit.* hog (def. 5). [1300–50; ME. See HOG, -ET]

hog·gish (hô′gish, hog′ish), *adj.* **1.** like or befitting a hog. **2.** selfish; gluttonous; filthy. [1425–75; late ME. See HOG, -ISH[1]] —**hog′gish·ly,** *adv.* —**hog′gish·ness,** *n.*

hog′ heav′en, *Slang.* heaven (def. 6).

hog′ Lat′in. See **pig Latin.** [1800–10]

Hog·ma·nay (hog′mə nā′), *n. Scot.* **1.** the eve of New Year's Day. **2.** (*l.c.*) a gift given on Hogmanay. [1670–80; orig. uncert.]

hog·mol·ly (hôg′mol′ē, hog′-), *n., pl.* **-lies,** (*esp. collectively*) **-ly.** See **hog sucker.** [1885–90, *Amer.*; HOG + *molly,* alter. of MULLET]

hog′-nosed skunk′ (hôg′nōzd′, hog′-), *n.* **1.** Also called **badger skunk, rooter skunk.** a large, naked-muzzled skunk, *Conepatus mesoleucus,* common in the southwestern U.S. and Mexico, having a black coat with one broad white stripe down the back and tail. **2.** Also called **conepati.** any similar New World skunk of the genus *Conepatus.*

hog′nose snake′ (hôg′nōz′, hog′-), any harmless North American snake of the genus *Heterodon,* the several species having an upturned snout and noted for flattening the head or playing dead when disturbed. [1730–40, *Amer.*; HOG + NOSE]

hog·nut (hôg′nut′, hog′-), *n.* **1.** the nut of the brown hickory, *Carya glabra.* **2.** the tree itself. **3.** the pignut. **4.** the earthnut, *Conopodium denudatum,* of Europe. [1765–75; HOG + NUT]

hog′ pea′nut, a twining plant, *Amphicarpaea bracteata,* of the legume family, bearing pods that ripen in or on the ground. [1855–60, *Amer.*]

hog·pen (hôg′pen′, hog′-), *n.* pigpen (def. 1). [1685–95; HOG + PEN[2]]

hog′ plum′. See **yellow mombin.** [1690–1700]

hog′ score′, *Curling.* a line at each end of the rink, parallel to the foot score and usually 7 yd. (6.4 m) in advance of the tee. [1780–90]

hogs·head (hôgz′hed′, hogz′-), *n.* **1.** a large cask, esp. one containing from 63 to 140 gallons (238 to 530 liters). **2.** any of various units of liquid measure, esp. one equivalent to 63 gallons (238 liters). *Abbr.:* hhd [1350–1400; ME *hoggeshed,* lit., hog's head; unexplained]

hog′ suck′er, any of several suckers of the genus *Hypentelium,* inhabiting cool streams of eastern North America and characterized by a broad head that is concave above. Also called **hogmolly.** [1880–85, *Amer.*]

hog·tie (hôg′tī′, hog′-), *v.t.,* **-tied, -ty·ing. 1.** to tie (an animal) with all four feet together. **2.** to hamper or thwart: *Repeated delays hogtied the investigation.* [1890–95, *Amer.*; HOG + TIE]

Hogue (*Fr.* ôg), *n.* **La** (lᴀ). See **La Hogue.**

hog·wash (hôg′wosh′, -wôsh′, hog′-), *n.* **1.** refuse given to hogs; swill. **2.** any worthless stuff. **3.** meaningless or insincere talk, writing, etc.; nonsense; bunk. [1400–50; 1900–05, for def 2; late ME. See HOG, WASH]

hog·weed (hôg′wēd′, hog′-), *n.* **1.** any coarse weed with composite flower heads, esp. the cow parsnip. **2.** See **giant hogweed.** [1700–10; HOG + WEED[1]]

hog-wild (hôg′wīld′, hog′-), *adj.* wildly or intemperately enthusiastic or excited. [1900–05, *Amer.*]

CONCISE ETYMOLOGY KEY: <, descended or borrowed from; >, whence; b., blend of, blended; c., cognate with; cf., compare; deriv., derivative; equiv., equivalent; imit., imitative; obl., oblique; r., replacing; s., stem; sp., spelling, spelled; resp., respelling, respelled; trans., translation; ?, origin unknown; *, unattested; ‡, probably earlier than. See the full key inside the front cover.

Ho·hen·lin·den (hō′ən lin′dən), *n.* a village in S West Germany, in Bavaria, near Munich: French victory over the Austrians 1800. 2000.

Ho·hen·lo·he (hō′ən lō′ə), *n.* a member of a German princely family, fl. 12th to 19th centuries.

Ho·hen·stau·fen (hō′ən shtou′fən), *n.* a member of the royal family that ruled in Germany from 1138 to 1208 and from 1215 to 1254, and in Sicily from 1194 to 1266. [1890–95]

Ho·hen·zol·lern (hō′ən zol′ərn; *Ger.* hō′ən tsôl′əʀn), *n.* a member of the royal family that ruled in Rumania from 1866 to 1947, in Prussia from 1701 to 1918, and in the German Empire from 1871 to 1918. [1890–95]

Hoh·hot (hō′hōt′), *n.* a city in and the capital of Inner Mongolia, in N China. 700,000. Also, **Huhehot, Huhehaote.** Formerly, **Kweihwa, Kweisui.**

Ho·ho·kam (hə hō′kəm), *adj.* **1.** of, belonging to, or characteristic of an American Indian culture of the central and southern deserts of Arizona, about A.D. 450–1450, roughly contemporaneous with the Anasazi culture to the north. —*n.* **2.** the Hohokam culture. [coined by U.S. anthropologist J.W. Fewkes < Pima-Papago *huhugam* those who are gone, a term applied to the ancient inhabitants of the pueblo ruins]

ho-hum (hō′hum′, -hum′), *interj.* **1.** (an exclamation expressing boredom, weariness, or contempt.) —*adj.* **2.** dull, boring, or routine; so-so: *a ho-hum performance.* [1920–25]

hoicks (hoiks, hīks), *interj. Rare.* yoicks. [1600–10]

hoi·den (hoid′n), *n., adj.* hoyden. —**hoi′den·ish,** *adj.*

Hoi·how (hoi′hou′, -hō′), *n. Older Spelling.* Haikou.

hoi pol·loi (hoi′ pə loi′), the common people; the masses (often preceded by *the*). [1815–25; < Gk: the many]

hoise (hoiz), *v.t.,* **hoised** or **hoist, hois·ing.** *Archaic.* to hoist. [1500–10; cf. earlier *hissa* a cry used in hauling, and HUZZA]

hoi′sin sauce′ (hoi′sin, hoi sin′), *Chinese Cookery.* a thick, sweet, spicy condiment containing soybeans, sugar, garlic, and chili peppers, used in cooking or as an accompaniment to meat, fish, or poultry, esp. Peking duck. [1960–65; < dial. Chin (Guangdong) *hóisin,* equiv. to Chin *hǎixiān* seafood]

hoist (hoist *or, sometimes,* hīst), *v.t.* **1.** to raise or lift, esp. by some mechanical appliance: *to hoist a flag; to hoist the mainsail.* **2.** to raise to one's lips and drink; drink (esp. beer or whiskey) with gusto: *Let's go hoist a few beers.* **3.** *Archaic.* a pt. and pp. of **hoise. 4. hoist with** or **by one's own petard.** See **petard** (def. 4). —*n.* **5.** an apparatus for hoisting, as a block and tackle, a derrick, or a crane. **6.** act of hoisting; a lift: *Give that sofa a hoist at your end.* **7.** *Naut.* **a.** the vertical dimension amidships of any square sail that is hoisted with a yard. Cf. **drop** (def. 28). **b.** the distance between the hoisted and the lowered position of such a yard. **c.** the dimension of a fore-and-aft sail along the luff. **d.** a number of flags raised together as a signal. **8.** (on a flag) **a.** the vertical dimension as flown from a vertical staff. **b.** the edge running next to the staff. Cf. **fly** (def. 36b). [1540–50; later var. of HOISE, with *-t* as in AGAINST, etc.] —**hoist′er,** *n.*
—**Syn. 1.** elevate. See **raise.** —**Ant. 1.** lower.

hoi·ty-toi·ty (hoi′tē toi′tē), *adj.* **1.** assuming airs; pretentious; haughty. **2.** giddy; flighty. —*n.* **3.** giddy behavior. [1660–70; rhyming compound based on *hoit* to romp, riot (now obs.)]

Ho·jo (hō′yō), *n.* a member of a powerful family in Japan that ruled as regents in the name of the shoguns during the period 1203–1333.

Ho·kan (hō′kən), *n.* a proposed genetic grouping of American Indian languages comprising otherwise unclassified language families and isolates of California, the U.S. Southwest, and Mexico, including Yana, Pomo, Chumash, and Yuman.

hoke (hōk), *v.,* **hoked, hok·ing,** *n.* —*v.t.* **1.** to alter or manipulate so as to give a deceptively or superficially improved quality or value (usually fol. by *up*): *a political speech hoked up with phony statistics.* —*n.* **2.** hokum. [1930–35; back formation from HOKEY or HOCUM]

hok·ey (hō′kē), *adj.* **hok·i·er, hok·i·est. 1.** cloyingly sentimental; mawkish. **2.** obviously contrived, esp. to win popular appeal or support; phony. [1815–25; irreg. HOK(UM) + -Y[1]] —**hok′ey·ness, hok′i·ness,** *n.*

ho·key-po·key (hō′kē pō′kē), *n.* **1.** hocus-pocus; trickery. **2.** ice cream as formerly sold by street vendors. [1840–50; var. of HOCUS-POCUS]

Ho·kiang (hō′kyäng′; *Chin.* hu′gyäng′), *n. Older Spelling.* Hejiang.

Ho·kin·son (hō′kin sən), *n.* **Helen,** c1900–49, U.S. cartoonist.

Hok·kai·do (hôk′kī dō′; *Eng.* ho kī′dō), *n.* a large island in N Japan. 5,660,000; 30,303 sq. mi. (78,485 sq. km). Formerly, **Yezo.**

hok·ku (hô′ko͞o, hok′o͞o), *n., pl.* **-ku.** *Pros.* **1.** the opening verse of a linked verse series. **2.** haiku. [1895–1900; < Japn, equiv. to *hok* opening, first + *ku* stanza; earlier *fot-ku* < MChin, equiv. to Chin *fā* depart + *jù* phrase]

ho·kum (hō′kəm), *n.* **1.** out-and-out nonsense; bunkum. **2.** elements of low comedy introduced into a play, novel, etc., for the laughs they may bring. **3.** sentimental matter of an elementary or stereotyped kind introduced into a play or the like. **4.** false or irrelevant material introduced into a speech, essay, etc., in order to arouse interest, excitement, or amusement. [1915–20, *Amer.*; prob. b. HOCUS-POCUS and BUNKUM]

Ho·ku·sai (hō′kə sī′, hō′kə sī′; *Japn.* hô′ko͝o sī′), *n.* **Ka·tsu·shi·ka** (kä′tso͝o shē′kä), 1760–1849, Japanese painter and illustrator.

hol-, var. of **holo-** before a vowel: *holiatry.*

hol·an·dric (hol an′drik, hō-), *adj. Genetics.* of or pertaining to a heritable trait appearing only in males (opposed to *hologynic*). [1925–30; HOL- + Gk *andrikós* masculine, equiv. to *andr-* (s. of *anḗr* man) + *-ikos* -IC]

Hol·arc·tic (ho lärk′tik, -är′tik, hō-), *adj. Zoogeog.* belonging or pertaining to a geographical division comprising the Nearctic and Palearctic regions. [1883; HOL(O)- + ARCTIC]

Hol·bein (hōl′bīn; *Ger.* hôl′bīn), *n.* **1. Hans** (häns), (*"the elder"*), 1465?–1524, German painter. **2.** his son, **Hans** (*"the younger"*), 1497?–1543, German painter who worked chiefly in England.

Hol·brook (hōl′bro͝ok), *n.* **1.** a city on central Long Island, in SE New York. 24,382. **2.** a city in E Massachusetts. 11,140.

HOLC, Home Owners' Loan Corporation. Also, **H.O.L.C.**

hold[1] (hōld), *v.,* **held; held** or (*Archaic*) **hold·en; hold·ing;** *n.* —*v.t.* **1.** to have or keep in the hand; keep fast; grasp: *She held the purse in her right hand. He held the child's hand in his.* **2.** to set aside; reserve or retain: *to hold merchandise until called for; to hold a reservation.* **3.** to bear, sustain, or support, as with the hands or arms, or by any other means. **4.** to keep in a specified state, relation, etc.: *The preacher held them spellbound.* **5.** to detain: *The police held him at the station house.* **6.** to engage in; preside over; carry on: *to hold a meeting.* **7.** to keep back from action; hinder; restrain: *Fear held him from acting.* **8.** to have the ownership or use of; keep as one's own; occupy: *to hold political office.* **9.** to contain or be capable of containing: *This bottle holds a quart.* **10.** to bind or make accountable to an obligation: *We will hold you to your promise to pay back the money.* **11.** to have or keep in the mind; think or believe: *We hold this belief.* **12.** to regard or consider: *to hold a person responsible.* **13.** to decide legally. **14.** to consider of a certain value; rate: *We held her best of all the applicants.* **15.** to keep forcibly, as against an adversary: *Enemy forces held the hill.* **16.** to point, aim, or direct: *He held a gun on the prisoner. The firefighter held a hose on the blaze.* **17.** *Music.* to sustain (a note, chord, or rest). **18.** to omit from the usual order or combination: *Give me a burger well-done—hold the pickle.* —*v.i.* **19.** to remain or continue in a specified state, relation, etc.: *Hold still while I take your picture.* **20.** to remain fast; adhere; cling: *Will this button hold?* **21.** to keep or maintain a grasp on something. **22.** to maintain one's position against opposition; continue in resistance. **23.** to agree or side (usually fol. by *with*): *to hold with new methods.* **24.** to hold property by some tenure; derive title (usually fol. by *by, from, in,* or *of*). **25.** to remain attached, faithful, or steadfast (usually fol. by *to*): *to hold to one's purpose.* **26.** to remain valid; be in force: *The rule does not hold.* **27.** to refrain or forbear (usually used imperatively). **28. hold back, a.** to restrain or check: *Police held back the crowd.* **b.** to retain possession of; keep back: *He held back ten dollars.* **c.** to refrain from revealing; withhold: *to hold back information.* **d.** to refrain from participating or engaging in some activity: *He held back from joining in the singing because he felt depressed.* **e.** *Photog.* dodge (def. 2). **29. hold down, a.** to restrain; check: *Hold down that noise!* **b.** to continue to hold and manage well: *She held down that job for years.* **30. hold forth, a.** to extend or offer; propose. **b.** to talk at great length; harangue: *When we left, he was still holding forth on World War II.* **31. hold in, a.** to restrain; check; curb. **b.** to contain oneself; exercise restraint: *He was raging inside, but held himself in for fear of saying something he would regret.* **32. hold off, a.** to keep at a distance; resist; repel. **b.** to postpone action; defer: *If you hold off applying for a passport, you may not get one in time.* **33. hold on, a.** to keep a firm grip on. **b.** to keep going; continue. **c.** to maintain, as one's opinion or position. **d.** to stop; halt (usually used imperatively): *Hold on now! That isn't what I meant at all.* **e.** to keep a telephone connection open by not hanging up the receiver: *The operator asked us to hold on while the number we'd dialed was being checked.* **34. hold one's own.** See **own** (def. 5). **35. hold one's peace.** See **peace** (def. 12). **36. hold one's tongue.** See **tongue** (def. 25). **37. hold out, a.** to present; offer. **b.** to stretch forth; extend: *Hold out your hand.* **c.** to continue to exist; last: *Will the food hold out?* **d.** to refuse to yield or submit: *The defenders held out for weeks.* **e.** to withhold something expected or due: *He was suspected of holding out information important to the case.* **38. hold over, a.** to keep for future consideration or action; postpone. **b.** to remain in possession or in office beyond the regular term. **c.** to remain beyond the arranged period: *The movie was held over for a week.* **d.** *Music.* to prolong (a tone) from one measure to the next. **39. hold up, a.** to offer; give: *She held up his father as an example to follow.* **b.** to present to notice; expose: *to hold someone up to ridicule.* **c.** to hinder; delay: *The plane's departure was held up because of the storm.* **d.** to stop by force in order to rob. **e.** to support; uphold: *to hold up farm prices.* **f.** to stop; halt: *They held up at the gate.* **g.** to maintain one's position or condition; endure: *They held up through all their troubles.* **40. hold water.** See **water** (def. 17). **41. hold with, a.** to be in agreement with; concur with: *I don't hold with his pessimistic views.* **b.** to approve of; condone: *They won't hold with such a travesty of justice.*
—*n.* **42.** an act of holding fast by a grasp of the hand or by some other physical means; grasp; grip: *Take hold. Do you have a hold on the rope?* **43.** something to hold a thing by, as a handle; something to grasp, esp. for support. **44.** something that holds fast or supports something else. **45.** an order reserving something: *to put a hold on a library book.* **46.** *Finance.* a security purchased or recommended for long-term growth. **47.** a controlling force or dominating influence: *to have a hold on a person.* **48.** *Wrestling.* a method of seizing an opponent and keeping him in control: *a toe hold.* **49.** *Music.* fermata. **50.** a pause or delay, as in a continuing series: *a hold in the movements of a dance.* **51.** a prison or prison cell. **52.** a receptacle for something: *a basket used as a hold for letters.* **53.** *Rocketry.* a halt in the prelaunch countdown, either planned or unexpectedly called, to allow correction of one or more faults in the rocket or missile. **54.** a fortified place; stronghold. **55.** (on telephones with two or more lines) a feature that enables a person to maintain a connection on one line while

answering another line. **56. get hold of, a.** to get a hold on: *Get hold of the railing.* **b.** to communicate with, esp. by telephone: *If she's not at home, try to get hold of her at the office.* **57. no holds barred,** without limits, rules, or restraints. **58. on hold, a.** in or into a state of temporary interruption or suspension: *The project will be put on hold until funds become available.* **b.** *Telecommunications.* in or into a state of temporary interruption in a telephone connection: *I'm putting you on hold to answer another call.* Cf. **call waiting.** [bef. 900; ME *holden,* OE *h(e)aldan;* c. OFris, ON *halda,* OS, Goth *haldan,* OHG *haltan* (G *halten*)] **—hold′a•ble,** *adj.*
—Syn. 8. possess, own. See **have. 9.** See **contain. 11.** embrace, espouse, have. See **maintain. 12.** deem, esteem, judge. **19.** persist, last, endure. **20.** stick.

hold[2] (hōld), *n.* **1.** *Naut.* **a.** the entire cargo space in the hull of a vessel. **b.** the cargo space in the hull of a vessel between the lowermost deck and the bottom. **c.** any individual compartment of such cargo spaces, closed by bulkheads and having its own hatchway. **2.** *Aviation.* the cargo compartment of an aircraft. [1585–95; var. of HOLE; c. D *hol* hole, hold]

hold•all (hōld′ôl′), *n.* a container for holding odds and ends. [1850–55; HOLD[1] + ALL]

hold•back (hōld′bak′), *n.* **1.** the iron or strap on the shaft of a horse-drawn vehicle to which the breeching of the harness is attached, enabling the horse to hold back or to back the vehicle. **2.** a device for restraining or checking, as a doorstop or tieback. **3.** a stop or delay: *a holdback in negotiations.* **4.** a withholding: *the holdback of a day's pay.* **5.** something, as a planned expenditure or allotment, that is withheld or deferred. [1575–85; n. use of v. phrase *hold back*]

hold′ but′ton, a button on a telephone that enables someone to interrupt an incoming call temporarily in order to answer another call.

hold•down (hōld′doun′), *n.* **1.** a clamp for holding a metal piece, as a sheet being deep-drawn, to prevent distortion or movement. **2.** restraint or limitation short of reduction, esp. on costs: *a substantial holddown on military spending.* [1885–90; n. use of v. phrase *hold down*]

hold 'em (hōld′ əm), a form of poker in which each player is dealt two cards face down and then makes the best five-card hand by combining these with three of five communal cards that are dealt to the center of the table.

hold•en (hōl′dən), *v. Archaic.* a pp. of **hold.**

Hol•den (hōl′dən), *n.* a city in central Massachusetts. 13,336.

hold•er (hōl′dər), *n.* **1.** something that holds or secures: *a pencil holder.* **2.** a person who has the ownership, possession, or use of something; owner; tenant. **3.** *Law.* a person who has the legal right to enforce a negotiable instrument. [1300–50; ME *haldere.* See HOLD[1], -ER[1]] **—hold′er•ship′,** *n.*

Höl′der condi′tion (hel′dər; *Ger.* hœl′dəʀ), *Math.* See **Lipschitz condition.** [after German mathematician Ludwig Otto *Hölder* (1859–1937)]

hold′er in due′ course′, a person who has received a negotiable instrument in good faith and without notice that it is overdue, that there is any prior claim, or that there is a defect in the title of the person who negotiated it. [1890–95]

Höl•der•lin (hœl′dəʀ lēn′), *n.* **Jo•hann Chris•ti•an Frie•drich** (yō′hän kʀis′tē än′ frē′dʀiкн), 1770–1843, German poet.

hold•fast (hōld′fast′, -fäst′), *n.* **1.** something used to hold or secure a thing in place; a catch, hook, clamp, etc. **2.** *Bot., Mycol.* any of several rootlike or suckerlike organs or parts serving for attachment. [1550–60; n. use of v. phrase *hold fast*]

hold•ing (hōl′ding), *n.* **1.** the act of a person or thing that holds. **2.** a section of land leased or otherwise tenanted, esp. for agricultural purposes. **3.** a company owned by a holding company. **4.** Often, **holdings.** legally owned property, esp. stocks, bonds, or real estate. **5. holdings,** *Library Science.* the entire collection of books, periodicals, and other materials in a library. **6.** *Sports.* the illegal obstruction of an opponent, as in football, basketball, or ice hockey, by use of the hands, arms, or stick. [1175–1225; ME *holding.* See HOLD[1], -ING[1]]

hold′ing com′pany, *Finance.* a company that controls other companies through stock ownership but that usually does not engage directly in their productive operations (distinguished from *parent company*). [1905–10]

hold′ing fur′nace, *Metall.* a small furnace for holding molten metal produced in a larger melting furnace at a desired temperature for casting.

hold′ing pat′tern, 1. a traffic pattern for aircraft at a specified location **(hold′ing point′)** where they are ordered to remain until permitted to land or proceed. **2.** a state or period in which no progress or change is made or planned. [1950–55]

hold′ing tank′, 1. a tank for the temporary storage of a substance. **2.** Also called **hold′ing pen′.** tank (def. 4). [1970–75]

hold•out (hōld′out′), *n.* **1.** an act or instance of holding out. **2.** a person who delays signing a contract in hopes of gaining more favorable terms: *The basketball star was a holdout until they offered more money.* **3.** a person who declines to participate, cooperate, agree, etc.: *Aside from one or two holdouts, everyone contributed.* [1890–95; n. use of v. phrase *hold out*]

hold•o•ver (hōld′ō′vər), *n.* **1.** a person or thing remaining from a former period. **2.** *Print.* overset that can be kept for future use. [1885–1890, *Amer.*; n. use of v. phrase *hold over*]

hold•up (hōld′up′), *n.* **1.** a forcible stopping and robbing of a person. **2.** a stop or delay in the progress of something: *There was a holdup in the construction of the bridge.* **3.** an instance of being charged excessively. [1830–40, *Amer.*; n. use of v. phrase *hold up*]

hold′up man′, a person who commits an armed robbery. [1955–60]

hole (hōl), *n., v.,* **holed, hol•ing.** **—*n.* 1.** an opening through something; gap; aperture: *a hole in the roof; a hole in my sock.* **2.** a hollow place in a solid body or mass; a cavity: *a hole in the ground.* **3.** the excavated habitation of an animal; burrow. **4.** a small, dingy, or shabby place: *I couldn't live in a hole like that.* **5.** a place of solitary confinement; dungeon. **6.** an embarrassing position or predicament: *to find oneself in a hole.* **7.** a cove or small harbor. **8.** a fault or flaw: *They found serious holes in his reasoning.* **9.** a deep, still place in a stream: *a swimming hole.* **10.** *Sports.* **a.** a small cavity, into which a marble, ball, or the like is to be played. **b.** a score made by so playing. **11.** *Golf.* **a.** the circular opening in a green into which the ball is to be played. **b.** a part of a golf course from a tee to the hole corresponding to it, including fairway, rough, and hazards. **c.** the number of strokes taken to hit the ball from a tee into the hole corresponding to it. **12.** *Informal.* opening; slot: *The radio program was scheduled for the* P.M. *hole. We need an experienced person to fill a hole in our accounting department.* **13.** *Metalworking.* (in wire drawing) one reduction of a section. **14.** *Electronics.* a mobile vacancy in the electronic structure of a semiconductor that acts as a positive charge carrier and has equivalent mass. **15.** *Aeron.* an air pocket that causes a plane or other aircraft to drop suddenly. **16. burn a hole in one's pocket,** to urge one to spend money quickly: *His inheritance was burning a hole in his pocket.* **17. hole in the wall,** a small or confining place, esp. one that is dingy, shabby, or out-of-the-way: *Their first shop was a real hole in the wall.* **18. in a** or **the hole, a.** in debt; in straitened circumstances: *After Christmas I am always in the hole for at least a month.* **b.** *Baseball, Softball.* pitching or batting with the count of balls or balls and strikes to one's disadvantage, esp. batting with a count of two strikes and one ball or none. **c.** *Stud Poker.* being the card or one of the cards dealt face down in the first round: *a king in the hole.* **19. make a hole in,** to take a large part of: *A large bill from the dentist made a hole in her savings.* **20. pick a hole** or **holes in,** to find a fault or flaw in: *As soon as I presented my argument, he began to pick holes in it.* **—*v.t.* 21.** to make a hole or holes in. **22.** to put or drive into a hole. **23.** *Golf.* to hit the ball into (a hole). **24.** to bore (a tunnel, passage, etc.). **—*v.i.* 25.** to make a hole or holes. **26. hole out,** *Golf.* to strike the ball into a hole: *He holed out in five, one over par.* **27. hole up, a.** to go into a hole; retire for the winter, as a hibernating animal. **b.** to hide, as from pursuers, the police, etc.: *The police think the bank robbers are holed up in Chicago.* [bef. 900; ME; OE *hol* hole, cave, orig. neut. of *hol* (adj.) HOLLOW; c. G *hohl* hollow] **—hole′less,** *adj.* **—hol′ey,** *adj.*
—Syn. 1, 2. pit, hollow, concavity. HOLE, CAVITY, EXCAVATION refer to a hollow place in anything. HOLE is the common word for this idea: *a hole in turf.* CAVITY is a more formal or scientific term for a hollow within the body or in a substance, whether with or without a passage outward: *a cavity in a tooth; the cranial cavity.* An EXCAVATION is an extended hole made by digging out or removing material: *an excavation before the construction of a building.* **3.** den, cave; lair, retreat. **4.** hovel, shack.

hole-and-cor•ner (hōl′ən kôr′nər), *adj.* **1.** secretive; clandestine; furtive: *The political situation was full of hole-and-corner intrigue.* **2.** trivial and colorless: *She was living a hole-and-corner existence of daily drudgery.* Also, **hole-in-cor•ner** (hōl′in kôr′nər). [1825–35]

hole′ card′, 1. *Stud Poker.* the card dealt face down in the first round of a deal. **2.** something held in reserve until it can be used to advantage. [1905–10, *Amer.*]

hole-high (hōl′hī′), *adj. Golf.* (of a ball) lying on a point almost even with the hole. [1895–1900]

hole′ in one′, *Golf.* ace (def. 8a). [1930–35]

hole•proof (hōl′pro͞of′), *adj.* **1.** (of fabric or an article of clothing) designed or made so as to prevent holes. **2.** constructed so as to prevent evasion or subterfuge: *a holeproof document.* [1910–15; HOLE + -PROOF]

hole′ saw′. See **crown saw.** [1960–65]

Hol•guín (ôl gēn′), *n.* a city in NE Cuba. 131,656.

Hol Ha•mo•ed (*Seph.* кнôl′ hä mô ed′; *Ashk.* кнôl′ hä mō′äd, -moid′), *Hebrew.* the period between the first and last two days of Passover or Sukkoth, consisting of four days during Passover and five days during Sukkoth and having less than full festival status. Also, ***Chol Hamoed.*** [*ḥōl hammō'ēdh* lit., the secular part of the feast]

Ho•li (hō′lē), *n.* the Hindu spring festival. [1905–10; < Hind *holī* < Prakrit *holiyā* < Skt *holikā*]

ho•li•a•try (hō′lē a′trē, hō lī′ə-), *n.* holism (def. 2). [HOL- + -IATRY]

hol•i•but (hol′ə bət), *n., pl.* (*esp. collectively*) **-but,** (*esp. referring to two or more kinds or species*) **-buts.** halibut.

-holic, var. of **-aholic:** *chocoholic.*

hol•i•day (hol′i dā′), *n.* **1.** a day fixed by law or custom on which ordinary business is suspended in commemoration of some event or in honor of some person. **2.** any day of exemption from work (distinguished from *working day*). **3.** a time or period of exemption from any requirement, duty, assessment, etc.: *New businesses may be granted a one-year tax holiday.* **4.** a religious feast day; holy day, esp. any of several usually commemorative holy days observed in Judaism. **5.** Sometimes, **holidays.** *Chiefly Brit.* a period of cessation from work or one of recreation; vacation. **6.** an unintentional gap left on a plated, coated, or painted surface. **—*adj.* 7.** of or pertaining to a festival; festive; joyous: *a holiday mood.* **8.** suitable for a holiday: *holiday attire.* **—*v.i.* 9.** *Chiefly Brit.* to vacation: *to holiday at the seaside.* [bef. 950; ME; OE *hāligdæg.* See HOLY, DAY]
—Syn. 2. vacation, break.

Hol•i•day (hol′i dā′), *n.* **Billie** (*"Lady Day"*), 1915–59, U.S. jazz singer.

hol•i•day•er (hol′i dā′ər), *n.* vacationer. [1885–90; HOLIDAY + -ER[1]]

hol•i•day•mak•er (hol′i dā mā′kər), *n. Brit.* vacationer. [1830–40; HOLIDAY + MAKER]

ho•li•er-than-thou (hō′lē ər t͟hən t͟hou′), *adj.* **1.** obnoxiously pious; sanctimonious; self-righteous. **—*n.* 2.** a person who is obnoxiously pious or self-righteous. [1910–15]

ho•li•ly (hō′lə lē), *adv.* in a pious, devout, or sacred manner. [1150–1200; ME; *halilïy.* See HOLY, -LY]

ho•li•ness (hō′lē nis), *n.* **1.** the quality or state of being holy; sanctity. **2.** (*cap.*) a title of the pope, formerly used also of other high ecclesiastics (usually prec. by *His* or *Your*). [bef. 900; ME *holynesse,* OE *hālignes.* See HOLY, -NESS]
—Syn. 1. blessedness, godliness, saintliness.

Hol•ins•hed (hol′inz hed′, hol′in shed′), *n.* **Raphael,** died c1580, English chronicler. Also, **Hollingshead.**

ho•lism (hō′liz əm), *n. Philos.* **1.** the theory that whole entities, as fundamental components of reality, have an existence other than as the mere sum of their parts. Cf. **organicism** (def. 1). **2.** Also, **holiatry.** *Med.* care of the entire patient in all aspects. **3.** *Psychol.* any psychologic system postulating that the human mind must be studied as a unit rather than as a sum of its individual parts. [HOL- + -ISM; term introduced by J.C. Smuts in *Holism and Evolution* (1926)] **—ho′list,** *n.*

ho•lis•tic (hō lis′tik), *adj.* **1.** incorporating the concept of holism in theory or practice: *holistic psychology.* **2.** identifying with principles of holism in a system of therapeutics, esp. one considered outside the mainstream of scientific medicine, as naturopathy or chiropractic, and usually involving nutritional measures. [1926; HOL(ISM) + -ISTIC] **—ho•lis′ti•cal•ly,** *adv.*

Hol•land (hol′ənd), *n.* **1. John Philip,** 1840–1914, Irish inventor in the U.S. **2. Sir Sidney (George),** 1893–1961, New Zealand political leader: prime minister 1949–57. **3.** the Netherlands. **4.** a medieval county and province on the North Sea, corresponding to the modern North and South Holland provinces of the Netherlands. **5.** a city in W Michigan. 26,281. **6.** *Textiles.* **a.** a cotton cloth treated to produce an opaque finish, as for window shades. **b.** See **Holland finish.**

hol′lan•daise sauce′ (hol′ən dāz′, hol′ən dāz′), a sauce of egg yolks, butter, lemon juice, and seasonings. [1905–10; < F *sauce hollandaise* Dutch sauce]

Hol•land•er (hol′ən dər), *n.* a native or inhabitant of the Netherlands. [1540–50; HOLLAND + -ER[1]]

Hol′land fin′ish, an oil and sizing or starch finish applied to cotton fabrics to increase their opacity and strength. Also called **Holland.**

Hol•lan•di•a (ho lan′dē ə), *n.* former name of **Jayapura.**

Hol•lands (hol′əndz), *n.* (*used with a singular v.*) a gin, originally made in Holland, in which the juniper is mixed in the mash. Also called **Hol′land gin′.** [1705–15; < D *hollandsch* (*genever*) Dutch (gin)]

hol•ler[1] (hol′ər), *v.i.* **1.** to cry aloud; shout; yell: *Quit hollering into the phone.* **—*v.t.* 2.** to shout or yell (something): *He hollered insults back into the saloon.* **—*n.* 3.** a loud cry used to express pain or surprise, to attract attention, to call for help, etc. [1690–1700, *Amer.*; var. of *holla* (see HALLO)]

hol•ler[2] (hol′ər), *n. South Midland and Southern U.S.* a hollow. [1835–45, *Amer.*]

Hol′ler•ith code′ (hol′ə rith), *Computers.* a system for coding data into punched cards, in which each horizontal row is assigned a different value, and letters, numbers, or special characters are encoded as combinations of these values in a vertical column. [1946; named after Herman *Hollerith* (1860–1929), U.S. inventor of the system]

Hol•ley (hol′ē), *n.* **Robert William,** born 1922, U.S. biochemist: Nobel prize for medicine 1968.

Hol•lings•head (hol′ingz hed′), *n.* Holinshed.

Hol•lis•ter (hol′ə stər), *n.* a town in W California. 11,488.

Hol•lis•ton (hol′ə stən), *n.* a city in NE Massachusetts. 12,622.

hol•low (hol′ō), *adj.,* **-er, -est,** *n., v., adv.* **—*adj.* 1.** having a space or cavity inside; not solid; empty: *a hollow sphere.* **2.** having a depression or concavity: *a hollow surface.* **3.** sunken, as the cheeks or eyes. **4.** (of sound) not resonant; dull, muffled, or deep: *a hollow voice.* **5.** without real or significant worth; meaningless: *a hollow victory.* **6.** insincere or false: *hollow compliments.* **7.** hungry; having an empty feeling: *I feel absolutely hollow, so let's eat.* **—*n.* 8.** an empty space within anything; a hole, depression, or cavity. **9.** a valley: *They took the sheep to graze in the hollow.* **10.** *Foundry.* a concavity connecting two surfaces otherwise intersecting at an obtuse angle. **—*v.t.* 11.** to make hollow (often fol. by *out*): *to hollow out a log.* **12.** to form by making something hollow (often fol. by *out*): *to hollow a place in the sand; boats hollowed out of logs.* **—*v.i.* 13.** to become hollow. **—*adv.* 14.** in a hollow manner: *The politician's accusations rang hollow.* **15. beat all hollow,** to surpass or outdo completely: *His performance beat the others all hollow.* Also, **beat hollow.** [bef. 900; ME *holw(e), holow,* OE *holh* a hollow place; akin to HOLE] **—hol′low•ly,** *adv.* **—hol′low•ness,** *n.*
—Syn. 5. vain, empty, futile, pointless.

hol′low back′, *Bookbinding.* a paper tube or roll, almost flattened, having one side glued to the back of a book and the other to the inside of the spine. **—hol′•low-backed′,** *adj.*

CONCISE PRONUNCIATION KEY: act, cāpe, dâre, pärt; set, ēqual; if, ice; ox, ōver, ôrder, oil, bo͝ok, bo͞ot, out; up, ûrge; child; sing; shoe; thin, t͟hat; zh as in *treasure.* ə = *a* as in *alone, e* as in *system, i* as in *easily, o* as in *gallop, u* as in *circus;* ᵊ as in *fire* (fīᵊr), *hour* (ouᵊr). l and n can serve as syllabic consonants, as in *cradle* (krād′l), and *button* (but′n). See the full key inside the front cover.

hol·low-eyed (hol′ō īd′), *adj.* having sunken eyes. [1520–30]

hol·low-forge (hol′ō fôrj′, -fōrj′), *v.t.*, **-forged, -forg·ing.** to produce (a tube or vessel) by trepanning a hole in a forging and expanding it with further forging on a mandrel.

hol·low-ground (hol′ō ground′), *adj.* ground so as to produce a concave surface or surfaces behind a cutting edge: *the hollow-ground blade of an ice skate.* [1880–85]

hol′low leg′, an ability or inclination to drink large quantities of alcoholic beverages, esp. without evident drunkenness.

hol′low new′el, a narrow wellhole in a winding staircase.

hol′low sea′, an ocean wave formation in which the rise from troughs to crests is very steep. [1720–30]

hol′low tile′, tile (def. 5). [1910–15]

hol·low·ware (hol′ō wâr′), *n.* silver dishes, as serving dishes, having some depth (distinguished from *flatware*). Also, **hol′lo·ware′.** [1675–85; HOLLOW + WARE[1]]

hol·lus·chick (hol′əs chik′), *n., pl.* **-chick·ie** (-chik′ē). a young male fur seal. [1870–75; earlier *holluschickie* collective pl., by folk etym. < Russ *kholostyakí*, pl. of *kholostyák* lit., bachelor]

hol·ly (hol′ē), *n., pl.* **-lies. 1.** any of numerous trees or shrubs of the genus *Ilex*, as *I. opaca* **(American holly),** the state tree of Delaware, or *I. aquifolium* **(English holly),** having glossy, spiny-toothed leaves, small, whitish flowers, and red berries. **2.** the foliage and berries, used for decoration, esp. during the Christmas season. [bef. 1150; ME *holi(e), holyn,* OE *hole(g)n;* c. Welsh *celyn,* Ir *cuillean;* akin to D, G *hulst,* F *houx* (< OHG *hulis*)]

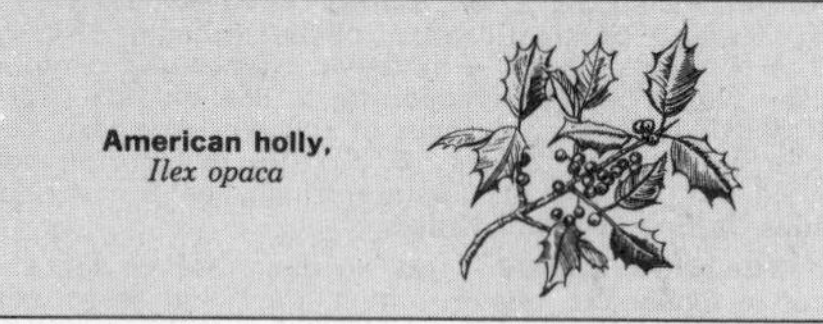
American holly, *Ilex opaca*

Hol·ly (hol′ē), *n.* a female or male given name.

hol·ly·hock (hol′ē hok′, -hôk′), *n.* any of several plants belonging to the genus *Alcea* (or *Althaea*), of the mallow family, native to Eurasia, esp. *A. rosea,* a tall plant having a long cluster of showy, variously colored flowers. [1225–75; ME *holihoc,* equiv. to *holi* HOLY + *hoc* mallow, OE *hocc*]

hol′ly oak′. See **holm oak.** [1590–1600]

Hol·ly·wood (hol′ē wo͝od′), *n.* **1.** the NW part of Los Angeles, Calif.: center of the American motion-picture industry. **2.** a city in SE Florida, near Miami: seaside resort. 117,188. —**Hol′ly·wood·ite′, Hol′ly·wood′er,** *n.*

Hol′lywood bed′, a bed consisting of a metal frame, box spring, mattress, and headboard, but lacking a footboard. [1945–50]

Hol·ly·wood·i·an (hol′ē wo͝od′ē ən, hol′ē wo͝od′-), *n.* **1.** a person who works for the motion-picture industry located in Hollywood, Calif. **2.** a person born or living in Hollywood, Calif. —*adj.* **3.** of, suitable to, or characteristic of the motion-picture industry or of the people who work in it, esp. in Hollywood, Calif. [1930–35; HOLLYWOOD + -IAN]

Hol·ly·wood·ish (hol′ē wo͝od′ish), *adj.* of, pertaining to, or resembling Hollywood, Hollywoodians, or the products of Hollywood and the motion-picture industry. [1925–30; HOLLYWOOD + -ISH[1]]

holm[1] (hōm), *n. Brit. Dial.* **1.** a low, flat tract of land beside a river or stream. **2.** a small island, esp. one in a river or lake. [bef. 1000; ME; OE *holm;* c. ON *holm* islet, Dan *holm,* Sw *holme* a small island, G *Holm* hill, island, L *columen, culmen* summit; see HILL]

holm[2] (hōm), *n.* See **holm oak.** [1350–1400; ME, by dissimilation from *holn,* OE *holen* HOLLY]

Holm (hōlm), *n.* **Han·ya** (hän′yə), born 1895?, U.S. dancer, choreographer, and teacher; born in Germany.

Hol·man (hōl′mən), *n.* **Nathan** (*"Nat"*), born 1896, U.S. basketball player and coach.

Hol·man Hunt (hōl′mən hunt′), **(William).** See **Hunt, William Holman.**

Holmes (hōmz, hōlmz), *n.* **1. John Haynes** (hānz), 1879–1964, U.S. clergyman. **2. Oliver Wen·dell** (wen′dl), 1809–94, U.S. poet, novelist, essayist, and physician. **3.** his son, **Oliver Wendell,** 1841–1935, U.S. jurist: associate justice of the U.S. Supreme Court 1902–32. **4. Sherlock,** a detective in many mystery stories by Sir Arthur Conan Doyle.

Holmes′ light′, a canister, attached to a life buoy or float, containing calcium carbonate and calcium phosphide, which ignite spontaneously on contact with the water, emitting conspicuous fire and smoke. [prob. from the surname *Holmes*]

hol·mic (hōl′mik), *adj. Chem.* of or containing the element holmium. [HOLM(IUM) + -IC]

hol·mi·um (hōl′mē əm), *n. Chem.* a rare-earth, trivalent element found in gadolinite. *Symbol:* Ho; *at. wt.:* 164.930; *at. no.:* 67. [< NL (1879), equiv. to *Holm(ia)* Stockholm + *-ium* -IUM]

holm′ oak′, an evergreen oak, *Quercus ilex,* of southern Europe, having foliage resembling that of the holly. [1590–1600]

holo-, a combining form meaning "whole," "entire," used in the formation of compound words: *holomorphic.* [< Gk, comb. form of *hólos*]

hol·o·blas·tic (hol′ə blas′tik, hō′lə-), *adj. Embryol.* (of certain eggs) undergoing total cleavage, resulting in equal blastomeres. Cf. **meroblastic.** [1870–75; *holoblast* (HOLO- + -BLAST) + -IC] —**ho′lo·blas′ti·cal·ly,** *adv.*

Hol·o·caine (hol′ə kān′, hō′lə-), *Pharm., Trademark.* a brand of phenacaine.

hol·o·car·pic (hol′ə kär′pik, hō′lə-), *adj.* (of a fungus) having the entire thallus converted into fruiting bodies. Also, **hol′o·car′pous.** Cf. **eucarpic.** [1915–20; HOLO- + -CARPIC]

hol·o·caust (hol′ə kôst′, hō′lə-), *n.* **1.** a great or complete devastation or destruction, esp. by fire. **2.** a sacrifice completely consumed by fire; burnt offering. **3.** (*usually cap.*) the systematic mass slaughter of European Jews in Nazi concentration camps during World War II (usually prec. by *the*). **4.** any mass slaughter or reckless destruction of life. [1200–50; ME < LL *holocaustum* (Vulgate) < Gk *holókauston* (Septuagint), neut. of *holókaustos* burnt whole. See HOLO-, CAUSTIC] —**hol′o·caus′tal,** *adj.* —**hol′o·caus′tic,** *adj.*
—**Syn. 1.** inferno, conflagration, ruin, havoc, ravage.

Hol·o·cene (hol′ə sēn′, hō′lə-), *Geol.* —*adj.* **1.** recent (def. 4). —*n.* **2.** recent (def. 5). [1895–1900; HOLO- + -CENE]

hol·o·crine (hol′ə krin, -krīn′, hō′lə-), *adj.* **1.** (of a gland) releasing a secretion that is a product of disintegrating cells. **2.** (of a secretion) released by such a gland. [1900–05; HOLO- + *-crine* < Gk *krínein* to separate]

hol·o·en·zyme (hol′ō en′zīm), *n.* an enzyme complete in both its apoenzyme and coenzyme components. [1940–45; HOLO- + ENZYME]

Hol·o·fer·nes (hol′ə fûr′nēz, hō′lə-), *n.* (in the Book of Judith) a general, serving Nebuchadnezzar, who was killed by Judith.

ho·log·a·mous (hə log′ə məs), *adj. Biol.* of or pertaining to an organism having reproductive cells similar in size and structure to the somatic cells. [1920–25; HOLO- + -GAMOUS]

hol·o·go·nid·i·um (hol′ō gə nid′ē əm, hō′lō-), *n., pl.* **-nid·i·a** (-nid′ē ə). *Bot., Mycol.* soredium. [< NL; see HOLO-, GONIDIUM]

hol·o·gram (hol′ə gram′, hō′lə-), *n. Optics.* a negative produced by exposing a high-resolution photographic plate, without camera or lens, near a subject illuminated by monochromatic, coherent radiation, as from a laser: when it is placed in a beam of coherent light a true three-dimensional image of the subject is formed. Also called **holograph.** [1945–50; HOLO- + -GRAM[1]]

hol·o·graph[1] (hol′ə graf′, -gräf′, hō′lə-), *adj.* **1.** Also, **hol·o·graph·ic** (hol′ə graf′ik, hō′lə-), **hol′o·graph′i·cal.** wholly written by the person in whose name it appears: *a holograph letter.* —*n.* **2.** a holograph writing, as a deed, will, or letter. [1650–60; < LL *holographus* < LGk *hológraphos.* See HOLO-, -GRAPH]

hol·o·graph[2] (hol′ə graf′, -gräf′, hō′lə-), *v.t.* **1.** to make by the use of holography. —*n.* **2.** an image produced by holography. **3.** *Optics.* hologram. [1965–70; back formation from HOLOGRAPHY] —**ho·log·ra·pher** (hə log′rə fər), *n.* —**hol·o·graph·ic** (hol′ə graf′ik, hō′lə-), *adj.* —**hol′o·graph′i·cal·ly,** *adv.*

hol′ograph′ic will′, *Law.* a will that is entirely in the handwriting of the testator: in some states recognized as valid without the attestation of witnesses. Cf. **nuncupative will.** [1890–95]

ho·log·ra·phy (hə log′rə fē), *n.* the process or technique of making holograms. [1795–1805; HOLO- + -GRAPHY]

hol·o·gyn·ic (hol′ə jin′ik, -gī′nik, -jī′-, hō′lə-), *adj. Genetics.* of or pertaining to a heritable trait appearing only in females (opposed to *holandric*). [1945–50; HOLO- + GYN- + -IC]

hol·o·he·dral (hol′ə hē′drəl, hō′lə-), *adj.* (of a crystal) having all the planes or faces required by the maximum symmetry of the system to which it belongs. [1830–40; HOLO- + -HEDRAL] —**hol′o·he′dry, hol′o·he′drism,** *n.*

hol·o·lith (hol′ə lith, hō′lə-), *n. Jewelry.* a ring made from a single piece of stone. [HOLO- + -LITH]

hol·o·me·tab·o·lous (hol′ō mi tab′ə ləs, hō′lō-), *adj. Entomol.* undergoing complete metamorphosis. Also, **hol·o·met·a·bol·ic** (hol′ō met′ə bol′ik, hō′lō-). [1865–70; HOLO- + Gk *metabólos;* see METABOLISM, -OUS] —**hol′o·me·tab′o·lism, hol′o·me·tab′o·ly,** *n.*

hol·o·mor·phic (hol′ə môr′fik, hō′lə-), *adj. Math.* analytic (def. 5). [1875–80; HOLO- + -MORPHIC] —**hol′o·mor′phism, hol′o·mor′phy,** *n.*

Ho·lon (KHô lôn′), *n.* a city in W central Israel: a suburb of Tel Aviv. 130,900.

Hol·o·phane (hol′ə fān′, hō′lə-), *Trademark.* a brand of glass having a surface pattern of small, lenslike areas for even diffusion of light.

hol·o·phote (hol′ə fōt′, hō′lə-), *n.* an apparatus by which practically all the light from a lighthouse lamp or the like is thrown in a desired direction. [1840–50; back formation from *holophotal* (HOLO- + *-photal*); see PHOTIC, -AL[1]]

hol·o·phrase (hol′ə frāz′, hō′lə-), *n.* a word functioning as a phrase or sentence, as the imperative *Go!* [1895–1900; HOLO- + PHRASE]

ho·loph·ra·sis (hə lof′rə sis), *n., pl.* **-ses** (-sēz′). the expression of the ideas of a phrase or sentence in one word; polysynthesis: *a language characterized by holophrasis.* [1865–70; HOLO- + Gk *phrásis;* see PHRASE]

hol·o·phras·tic (hol′ə fras′tik, hō′lə-), *adj.* **1.** using or consisting of a single word that functions as a phrase or sentence. **2.** characterized by holophrasis; polysynthetic: *a holophrastic language.* [1855–60; HOLO- + *-phrastic;* see PERIPHRASTIC]

hol·o·phyt·ic (hol′ə fit′ik, hō′lə-), *adj.* (of a plant) obtaining energy by synthesizing inorganic substances; autotrophic. [1880–85; HOLO- + *-phytic;* see -PHYTE, -IC] —**hol·o·phyte** (hol′ə fīt′, hō′lə-), *n.*

hol·o·plank·ton (hol′ə plangk′tən, hō′lə-), *n.* plankton that spend their entire life cycle as free-swimming organisms (opposed to *hemiplankton*). [HOLO- + PLANKTON] —**hol·o·plank·ton·ic** (hol′ō plangk ton′ik, hō′lō-), *adj.*

hol·op·neus·tic (hol′əp no͞o′stik, -nyo͞o′-, hō′ləp-), *adj.* having all the spiracles open, as the tracheal systems of most insects. [1890–95; HOLO- + Gk *pneustikós* pertaining to breathing, equiv. to *pneust(ós)* verbid of *pneîn* to breathe (see PNEUMA) + *-ikos* -IC]

hol·o·ser·i·ceous (hol′ə si rish′əs, hō′lə-), *adj. Bot., Zool.* covered with short, silky hairs. [1825–35; HOLO- + SERICEOUS]

hol·o·thu·ri·an (hol′ə tho͝or′ē ən, hō′lə-), *n.* **1.** any echinoderm of the class Holothuroidea, comprising the sea cucumbers. —*adj.* **2.** belonging or pertaining to the Holothuroidea. Also, **hol·o·thu·ri·oid** (hol′ə tho͝or′ē oid′). [1835–45; < NL *Holothuri(a)* genus name (pl. of L *holothūrium* < Gk *holothoúrion* kind of zoophyte, equiv. to *holo-* HOLO- + *-thourion* < ?) + -AN]

hol·o·type (hol′ə tīp′, hō′lə-), *n. Biol.* the type specimen used in the original description of a species. [1895–1900; HOLO- + -TYPE] —**hol·o·typ·ic** (hol′ə tip′ik, hō′lə-), *adj.*

hol·o·zo·ic (hol′ə zō′ik, hō′lə-), *adj. Biol.* feeding on solid food particles in the manner of most animals. [1880–85; HOLO- + *-zoic* < Gk *zōikós* of animals, equiv. to *zō(ē)* life + *-ikos* -IC]

holp (hōlp), *v. South Midland and Southern U.S. Nonstandard.* a pt. of **help.**

hol·pen (hōl′pən), *v. Nonstandard.* a pp. of **help.**

hols (holz), *n.pl.* Sometimes, **hol.** *Brit. Informal.* holiday (def. 5). [by shortening]

Holst (hōlst), *n.* **Gus·tav Theodore** (go͝os′täv), 1874–1934, English composer.

Hol·stein (hōl′stīn, -stēn; *for 2 also Ger.* hōl′shtīn′), *n.* **1.** Also called **Hol·stein-Frie·sian** (hōl′stīn frē′zhən, -stēn-). one of a breed of black-and-white dairy cattle, raised originally in North Holland and Friesland, that yields large quantities of milk having a low content of butterfat. **2.** a region in N Germany, at the base of the peninsula of Jutland: a former duchy. Cf. **Schleswig-Holstein.** [1860–65]

Holstein, *Bos taurus,* 4 ft. (1.2 m) high at shoulder length 12 ft. (3.7 m)

hol·ster (hōl′stər), *n.* **1.** a sheathlike carrying case for a firearm, attached to a belt, shoulder sling, or saddle. —*v.t.* **2.** to put or put back in a holster: *to holster a gun.* [1655–65; < D; c. Goth *hulistr,* ON *hulstr* sheath; akin to OE *helan* to hide]

holt (hōlt), *n. Archaic.* **1.** a wood or grove. **2.** a wooded hill. [bef. 900; ME *holte,* OE *holt;* c. D *hout,* ON *holt,* G *Holz* wood; akin to Gk *kládos* twig (see CLADO-), OIr *caill* wood]

Holt (hōlt), *n.* **1. Harold Edward,** 1908–67, Australian political leader: prime minister 1966–67. **2.** a town in central Michigan. 10,097.

Hol′ter mon′itor (hōl′tər), a portable electrocardiograph worn by a patient over an extended period of time to assess the effects on heart function of activities of daily living. [after Norman J. *Holter* (born 1914), U.S. physicist, its developer]

ho·lus-bo·lus (hō′ləs bō′ləs), *adv.* all at once; altogether. [1840–50; mock-Latin rhyming compound based on phrase *whole bolus.* See WHOLE, BOLUS]

ho·ly (hō′lē), *adj.,* **-li·er, -li·est,** *n., pl.* **-lies.** —*adj.* **1.** specially recognized as or declared sacred by religious use or authority; consecrated: *holy ground.* **2.** dedicated or devoted to the service of God, the church, or religion: *a holy man.* **3.** saintly; godly; pious; devout: *a holy life.* **4.** having a spiritually pure quality: *a holy love.* **5.** entitled to worship or veneration as or as if sacred: *a holy relic.* **6.** religious: *holy rites.* **7.** inspiring fear, awe, or grave distress: *The director, when angry, is a holy terror.* —*n.* **8.** a place of worship; sacred place; sanctuary. [bef. 900; ME *holi,* OE *hālig,* var. of *hāleg,* equiv. to *hāl* WHOLE + *-eg* -Y[1]; c. D, G *heilig,* ON *heilagr*]
—**Syn. 1.** blessed. HOLY, SACRED, CONSECRATED, HALLOWED imply possession of a sanctity that is the object of religious veneration. HOLY refers to the divine, that which has its sanctity directly from God or is connected with Him: *Remember the Sabbath day to keep it holy.* Something that is SACRED, while sometimes accepted as entitled to religious veneration, may have its sanctity from human authority: *a sacred oath.* Something that is CONSECRATED is specially or formally dedicated to some religious use: *a life consecrated to service.* Something that is HALLOWED has been made holy by being worshiped: *a hallowed shrine.* **4.** spiritual. —**Ant. 3, 4.** corrupt, impious.

Ho′ly Alli′ance, a league formed by the principal sovereigns of Europe in 1815 with the professed object of promoting Christian brotherhood but the practical object of repressing democratic revolutions and institutions. The English and Turkish rulers and Pope Pius VII did not join the league.

Ho′ly Ark′, *Judaism.* a cabinet in a synagogue set into or against the wall that faces eastward toward Jerusalem, for keeping the scrolls of the Torah.

Ho′ly Bi′ble, Bible (def. 1).

ho′ly bread′, **1.** bread used in a Eucharistic service, both before and after consecration. **2.** *Eastern Ch.* eulogia (def. 1). **3.** *Gk. Orth. Ch.* antidoron (def. 1). [1250–1300; ME]

ho′ly cats′, *Slang.* (used to express surprise, wonder, or confusion.)

Ho′ly Cit′y, (*sometimes l.c.*) **1.** a city regarded as particularly sacred by the adherents of a religious faith, as Jerusalem by Jews and Christians, Mecca and Medina by Muslims, and Varanasi by Hindus. **2.** heaven. [1350–1400; ME]

ho′ly clo′ver, sainfoin.

Ho′ly Commun′ion, communion (def. 1). [1885–90]

ho′ly cow′, *Slang.* (used to express bewilderment, surprise, or astonishment.) [1920–25]

Ho′ly Cross′, Mount of the, a peak in central Colorado, in the Sawatch Range: snow-filled, cross-shaped crevasses. 14,005 ft. (4269 m).

ho′ly day′, a consecrated day or religious festival, esp. one other than Sunday. [see HOLIDAY]

ho′ly day′ of obliga′tion, **1.** a day on which Roman Catholics are duty-bound to attend Mass and abstain from certain kinds of work. **2.** a day on which Episcopalians are expected to take communion. [1930–35]

Ho′ly Fam′ily, a representation in art of Mary, Joseph, and the infant Jesus.

Ho′ly Fa′ther, *Rom. Cath. Ch.* a title of the pope. [1375–1425; late ME]

Ho′ly Ghost′, the third person of the Trinity. Also called **Holy Spirit.** [bef. 900; ME; OE]

Ho′ly Grail′, grail. Also, **ho′ly grail′.** [1580–90]

ho′ly grass′, any of several fragrant grasses of the genus *Hierochloë,* esp. *H. odorata,* the vanilla grass. [1770–80]

Hol•y•head (hol′ē hed′), *n.* a seaport on Holy Island in NW Wales. 10,940.

Hol′yhead Is′land, former name of **Holy Island** (def. 2).

Ho′ly In′nocents' Day′, December 28, a day of religious observance commemorating the slaughter of the children of Bethlehem by Herod's order. Also called **Innocents' Day.**

Ho′ly Is′land, **1.** Also called **Lindisfarne.** an island off the E coast of Northumberland, England. 3 mi. (4.8 km) long. **2.** Formerly, **Holyhead Island.** an island off the W coast of Anglesey, in NW Wales. 7 mi. (11 km) long.

Ho′ly Joe′, *Slang.* **1.** a chaplain, esp. in the U.S. armed forces. **2.** a minister or priest. **3.** a sanctimonious or overly pious person. [1870–75]

Ho′ly Lamb′, *Heraldry.* See **paschal lamb** (def. 4).

Ho′ly Land′, Palestine (def. 1).

ho′ly mack′erel, *Slang.* (used as an exclamation to express surprise or wonder.) [1795–1805]

ho′ly mo′ly (mō′lē), *Slang.* (used as an exclamation to express surprise or astonishment.) [*moly* coined as rhyming twin to HOLY, on the model of *holy cow, holy smoke,* etc.]

ho′ly Mo′ses, *Slang.* (used as an exclamation to express surprise or wonder.) [1850–55]

Ho′ly Moth′er, honorific title of the Virgin Mary, often applied by analogy to the Roman Catholic Church.

Ho′ly Mys′teries, (*sometimes l.c.*) the liturgy in the Eastern Church.

Hol•yoake (hōl′yōk, hō′lē ōk′), *n.* **Sir Keith Jack•a** (jak′ə), 1904–83, New Zealand political leader: prime minister 1957, 1960–72; governor general 1977–80.

Ho′ly Of′fice, *Rom. Cath. Ch.* a congregation founded in 1542 to succeed the suppressed Inquisition and entrusted with matters pertaining to faith and morals, as the judgment of heresy, the application of canonical punishment, and the examination of books and prohibition of those held dangerous to faith and morals. [1720–30]

ho′ly of ho′lies, **1.** a place of special sacredness. **2.** the innermost chamber of the Biblical tabernacle and the Temple in Jerusalem, in which the ark of the covenant was kept. **3.** *Eastern Ch.* the bema. [1350–1400; ME, trans. of LL *sanctum sanctōrum* (Vulgate), trans. of Gk *tò hágion tôn hagíōn,* itself trans. of Heb *qōdesh haqqodāshīm*]

ho′ly oil′, **1.** consecrated oil; chrism. **2.** (esp. in the Eastern Church) oil that has been in contact with a sacred object, as a relic, and is used in certain rites. [1350–1400; ME]

Hol•yoke (hōl′yōk, hō′lē ōk′), *n.* a city in S Massachusetts, on the Connecticut River. 44,678.

Ho′ly One′, **1.** God. Isa. 10:20. **2.** Jesus Christ, esp. as the Messiah. Mark 1:24; Acts 3:14. [1525–35]

ho′ly or′ders, **1.** the rite or sacrament of ordination. **2.** the rank or status of an ordained Christian minister. **3.** the major degrees or grades of the Christian ministry. [1350–1400; ME]

Ho′ly Roll′er, *Disparaging and Offensive.* a member of a Pentecostal sect: so called from the frenetic religiosity expressed during services. **—Ho′ly Roll′erism.**

Ho′ly Ro′man Em′pire, a Germanic empire located chiefly in central Europe that began with the coronation of Charlemagne as Roman emperor in A.D. 800 (or, according to some historians, with the coronation of Otto the Great, king of Germany, in A.D. 962) and ended with the renunciation of the Roman imperial title by Francis II in 1806, and was regarded theoretically as the continuation of the Western Empire and as the temporal form of a universal dominion whose spiritual head was the pope.

Ho′ly Rood′, **1.** the cross on which Jesus died. **2.** (*l.c.*) a crucifix, esp. one above a rood screen. [bef. 1150; ME; OE]

Ho′ly Sac′rament, sacrament (def. 2).

Ho′ly Sat′urday, the Saturday in Holy Week. [1350–1400; ME]

Ho′ly Scrip′ture, Scripture (def. 1). Also, **Ho′ly Scrip′tures.**

Ho′ly See′, **1.** *Rom. Cath. Ch.* the see of Rome; the office or jurisdiction of the pope. **2.** the papal court. [1755–65]

Ho′ly Sep′ulcher, the sepulcher in which the body of Jesus lay between His burial and His resurrection. [1175–1225; ME]

Ho′ly Spir′it, **1.** the spirit of God. **2.** the presence of God as part of a person's religious experience. **3.** See **Holy Ghost.** [1350–1400; ME]

ho•ly•stone (hō′lē stōn′), *n., v.,* **-stoned, -ston•ing.** —*n.* **1.** a block of soft sandstone used in scrubbing the decks of a ship. —*v.t.* **2.** to scrub with a holystone. [1815–25; HOLY + STONE; perh. orig. jocular or profane]

ho′ly syn′od, *Eastern Ch.* the governing council of an autocephalous church, composed of bishops and presided over by the patriarch or another prelate. [1760–70]

ho′ly this′tle, lady's-thistle. [1590–1600]

Ho′ly Thurs′day, **1.** See **Ascension Day.** **2.** the Thursday in Holy Week; Maundy Thursday. [1150–1200; ME; OE]

ho•ly•tide (hō′lē tīd′), *n.* a time of religious observances. [bef. 1100; ME *holi tid,* OE *hālig tīd.* See HOLY, TIDE[1]]

Ho′ly Trin′ity, Trinity (def. 1). [bef. 1050; ME]

ho′ly war′, a war waged for what is supposed or proclaimed to be a holy purpose, as the defense of faith. [1685–95]

ho′ly wa′ter, water blessed by a priest. [bef. 900; ME *haliwater,* OE *hāligwæter*]

ho′ly wa′ter sprin′kler. See **morning star** (def. 2). Also, **ho′ly wa′ter sprin′kle.** [1840–50]

Ho′ly Week′, the week preceding Easter Sunday. [1700–10; trans. of It *settimana santa*]

Ho′ly Writ′, the Scriptures. [bef. 1000; ME *holi writ,* OE *hālige writu* (pl.)]

Ho′ly Year′, *Rom. Cath. Ch.* a jubilee year. [1920–25]

hom-, var. of **homo-** before a vowel: *homonym.*

ho•ma (hō′mə), *n.* haoma (def. 2).

hom•age (hom′ij, om′-), *n.* **1.** respect or reverence paid or rendered: *In his speech he paid homage to Washington and Jefferson.* **2.** the formal public acknowledgment by which a feudal tenant or vassal declared himself to be the man or vassal of his lord, owing him fealty and service. **3.** the relation thus established of a vassal to his lord. **4.** something done or given in acknowledgment or consideration of the worth of another: *a Festschrift presented as an homage to a great teacher.* [1250–1300; ME (*h*)*omage* < OF, equiv. to (*h*)*ome* man (< L *hominem,* acc. of *homō;* see HOMO) + *-age* -AGE]
—**Syn. 1.** deference, obeisance; honor, tribute. **3.** fidelity, loyalty, devotion. **—Ant. 1.** irreverence. **3.** disloyalty.

hom•ag•er (hom′ə jər, om′-), *n.* a vassal. [1350–1400; ME *omager* < AF. See HOMAGE, -ER[2]]

hom•a•lo•graph•ic (hom′ə lə graf′ik), *adj.* homolographic. [< Gk *homalō*(*s*) even, regular + GRAPHIC]

hom•bre[1] (om′bər), *n. Cards.* omber.

hom•bre[2] (om′brā, -brē), *n.* man; fellow; guy: *That sheriff is a mean hombre.* [1830–40; < Sp, by dissimilation and intrusion of *b* < VL **omne,* for L *hominem,* acc. of *homō* man, HOMO]

hom•burg (hom′bûrg), *n.* a man's felt hat with a soft crown dented lengthwise and a slightly rolled brim. [1890–95; after *Homburg,* Germany, where it was first manufactured]

home (hōm), *n., adj., adv., v.,* **homed, hom•ing.** —*n.* **1.** a house, apartment, or other shelter that is the usual residence of a person, family, or household. **2.** the place in which one's domestic affections are centered. **3.** an institution for the homeless, sick, etc.: *a nursing home.* **4.** the dwelling place or retreat of an animal. **5.** the place or region where something is native or most common. **6.** any place of residence or refuge: *a heavenly home.* **7.** a person's native place or own country. **8.** (in games) the destination or goal. **9.** a principal base of operations or activities: *The new stadium will be the home of the local football team.* **10.** *Baseball.* See **home plate.** **11.** *Lacrosse.* one of three attack positions nearest the opposing goal. **12. at home, a.** in one's own house or place of residence. **b.** in one's own town or country. **c.** prepared or willing to receive social visits: *We are always at home to her.* **d.** comfortable; at ease: *She has a way of making everyone feel at home.* **e.** well-informed; proficient: *to be at home in the classics.* **f.** played in one's hometown or on one's own grounds: *The Yankees played two games at home and one away.* —*adj.* **13.** of, pertaining to, or connected with one's home or country; domestic: *home products.* **14.** principal or main: *the corporation's home office.* **15.** reaching the mark aimed at: *a home thrust.* **16.** *Sports.* played in a ball park, arena, or the like, that is or is assumed to be the center of operations of a team: *The pitcher didn't lose a single home game all season.* Cf. **away** (def. 14). —*adv.* **17.** to, toward, or at home: *to go home.* **18.** deep; to the heart: *The truth of the accusation struck home.* **19.** to the mark or point aimed at: *He drove the point home.* **20.** *Naut.* **a.** into the position desired; perfectly or to the greatest possible extent: *sails sheeted home.* **b.** in the proper, stowed position: *The anchor is home.* **c.** toward its vessel: *to bring the anchor home.* **21. bring home to,** to make evident to; clarify or emphasize for: *The irrevocability of her decision was brought home to her.* **22. home and dry,** *Brit. Informal.* having safely achieved one's goal. **23. home free, a.** assured of finishing, accomplishing, succeeding, etc.: *If we can finish more than half the work today, we'll be home free.* **b.** certain to be successfully finished, accomplished, secured, etc.: *With most of the voters supporting it, the new law is home free.* **24. write home about,** to comment especially on; remark on: *The town was nothing to write home about.* —*v.i.* **25.** to go or return home. **26.** (of guided missiles, aircraft, etc.) to proceed, esp. under control of an automatic aiming mechanism, toward a specified target, as a plane, missile, or location (often fol. by *in on*): *The missile homed in on the target.* **27.** to navigate toward a point by means of coordinates other than those given by altitudes. **28.** to have a home where specified; reside. —*v.t.* **29.** to bring or send home. **30.** to provide with a home. **31.** to direct, esp. under control of an automatic aiming device, toward an airport, target, etc. [bef. 900; ME *hom,* OE *hām* (n. and adv.); c. D *heim,* ON *heimr,* Dan *hjem,* Sw *hem,* G *Heim* home, Goth *haims* village; akin to HAUNT]
—Syn. 1. abode, dwelling, habitation; domicile. See **house. 2.** hearth, fireside. **3.** asylum.

Home (hyōōm), *n.* **Lord.** See **Douglas-Home.**

home′ base′, **1.** *Baseball.* See **home plate.** **2.** home (def. 9). **3.** home (def. 8). [1850–55, *Amer.*]

home•bod•y (hōm′bod′ē), *n., pl.* **-bod•ies.** a person who prefers pleasures and activities that center around the home. [1815–25, *Amer.;* HOME + BODY]

home•bound[1] (hōm′bound′), *adj.* going home: *homebound commuters.* [1880–85; HOME + BOUND[4]]

home•bound[2] (hōm′bound′), *adj.* confined to one's home, esp. because of illness. [1880–85; HOME + BOUND[1]]

home•boy (hōm′boi′), *n.* **1.** a person from the same locality as oneself. **2.** *Slang.* a close friend or fellow gang member. [1895–1900; *Amer.*]

home•bred (hōm′bred′), *adj.* bred or raised at home; native; indigenous; domestic. [1580–90; HOME + BRED]

home-brew (hōm′brōō′), *n.* beer or other alcoholic beverage made at home. [1850–55] **—home′-brewed′,** *adj.*

home•build•er (hōm′bil′dər), *n.* **1.** a person whose occupation is homebuilding. **2.** a commercial firm or company for homebuilding. [1880–85; HOME + BUILDER]

home•build•ing (hōm′bil′ding), *n.* **1.** the designing or constructing of houses. —*adj.* **2.** of, pertaining to, or associated with homebuilding: *the homebuilding industry.* [1815–25; HOME + BUILDING]

home•buy•er (hōm′bī′ər), *n.* a person who buys or expects to buy a house. [1965–70; HOME + BUYER]

home-care (hōm′kâr′), *adj.* of, pertaining to, or designating care, esp. medical care, given or received at home: *a member of the hospital's home-care staff.*

home′ cen′ter, a large store that specializes in a wide range of materials and supplies for home improvements or repairs. Also called **home′-cen′ter store′.** [1965–70, *Amer.*]

home•com•ing (hōm′kum′ing), *n.* **1.** a return to one's home; arrival at home. **2.** an annual event held by a college, university, or high school for visiting alumni. [1325–75; 1930–35 for def. 2; ME *homcomyng;* r. ME *hamcume,* OE *hāmcyme,* equiv. to *hām* HOME + *cyme* arrival; see COME, -ING[1]] **—home′com′er,** *n.*

home′ comput′er, a microcomputer used in the home. [1975–80]

home′ ec′ (ek), *Informal.* See **home economics.** [by shortening]

home′ econom′ics, **1.** the art and science of home management. **2.** a college curriculum usually including studies in nutrition, the purchase, preparation, and service of food, interior design, clothing and textiles, child development, family relationships, and household economics. [1895–1900, *Amer.*] **—home′ econ′omist.**

home′ entertain′ment, the aggregate of appliances, as stereo systems, television, videocassette recorders, or computers, used for diversion in the home.

home′ fries′, sliced, boiled potatoes, fried in butter or shortening. Also called **home′ fried′ pota′toes, cottage fried potatoes, country fries.** [1950–55]

home′ front′, the civilian sector of a nation at war when its armed forces are in combat abroad. [1915–20] —**home′-front′,** *adj.*

home′ ground′, an area, locality, or subject with which one is intimately familiar: *Baseball and football are home ground for this sports-loving community.*

home·grown (hōm′grōn′), *adj.* **1.** grown or produced at home or in a particular region for local consumption: *homegrown tomatoes.* **2.** native or characteristic of a region: *homegrown musicians.* [1820–30]

home′ guard′, a volunteer force used for meeting local emergencies when the regular armed forces are needed elsewhere. [1735–45]

home′ keys′. See under **home row.**

home·land (hōm′land′, -lənd), *n.* **1.** one's native land. **2.** a region created or considered as a state by or for a people of a particular ethnic origin: *the Palestinian homeland.* **3.** any of the thirteen racially and ethnically based regions created in South Africa by the South African government as nominally independent tribal ministates to which blacks are assigned. [1660–70]

home·less (hōm′lis), *adj.* **1.** without a home: *a homeless child.* —*n.* **2. the homeless,** persons who lack permanent housing. [1605–15; HOME + -LESS] —**home′·less·ly,** *adv.* —**home′less·ness,** *n.*

home·like (hōm′līk′), *adj.* like or suggestive of home; familiar; warmly comfortable. [1810–20; HOME + -LIKE] —**Syn.** See **homely.**

home·ly (hōm′lē), *adj.,* **-li·er, -li·est. 1.** lacking in physical attractiveness; not beautiful; unattractive: *a homely child.* **2.** not having elegance, refinement, or cultivation. **3.** proper or suited to the home or to ordinary domestic life; plain; unpretentious: *homely food.* **4.** commonly seen or known. [1300–50; ME *homly.* See HOME, -LY] —**home′li·ness,** *n.*
—**Syn. 1, 2, 3.** SIMPLE, HOMELY (HOMEY), HOMELIKE, PLAIN imply absence of adornment or embellishment. Something that is SIMPLE is not elaborate or complex: *a simple kind of dress.* In the United States, HOMELY usually suggests absence of natural beauty: *an unattractive person almost homely enough to be called ugly.* In England, the word suggests a wholesome simplicity without artificial refinement or elegance; since it characterizes that which is comfortable and attractive, it is equivalent to HOMEY: *a homely cottage.* HOMELIKE also emphasizes comfort and attractiveness, but it conveys less strongly than does HOMEY a sense of intimate security: *a homelike interior, arrangement, atmosphere.* Something that is PLAIN has little or no adornment: *expensive but plain clothing.*

home·made (hōm′mād′), *adj.* **1.** made or prepared at home, locally, or by the maker's own efforts: *The restaurant's pastry is homemade.* **2.** made in one's own country; domestic. **3.** made, contrived, or assembled by oneself; not professionally made or done: *the plain look of homemade furniture.* [1650–60; HOME + MADE]

home·mak·er (hōm′mā′kər), *n.* **1.** a person who manages the household of his or her own family, esp. as a principal occupation. **2.** a person employed to manage a household and do household chores for others, as for the sick or elderly. [1885–90; HOME + MAKER] —**Usage. 1.** See **housewife.**

home·mak·ing (hōm′mā′king), *n.* **1.** the establishment or management of a home; duties of a homemaker. —*adj.* **2.** of or pertaining to the management of a home: *homemaking tasks.* [1885–90; HOME + MAKING]

home′ mis′sion, a religious mission operating within the country or territories of the supporting church. [1830–40] —**home′ mis′sionary.**

homeo-, a combining form meaning "similar," used in the formation of compound words: *homeostatic.* Also, **homoeo-, homoio-.** [< Gk *homoio-,* comb. form of *hómoios* similar, like]

ho′me·o·box gene′ (hō′mē ə boks′), any of a group of genes whose function is to divide the early embryo into bands of cells with the potential to become specific organs or tissues. [1985–90; HOMEO- + BOX[1]]

home′ of′fice, 1. the main office of a company. **2.** (*caps.*) the governmental department in Great Britain dealing with domestic matters, as elections, naturalization, and the control of police.

ho·me·o·morph (hō′mē ə môrf′), *n.* any of the crystalline minerals characterized by a particular kind of homeomorphism. [HOMEO- + MORPH]

ho·me·o·mor·phism (hō′mē ə môr′fiz əm), *n.* **1.** similarity in crystalline form but not necessarily in chemical composition. **2.** *Math.* a function between two topological spaces that is continuous, one-to-one, and onto, and the inverse of which is continuous. Also called **topological transformation.** [1850–55; HOMEOMORPH + -ISM] —**ho′me·o·mor′phic, ho′me·o·mor′phous,** *adj.*

ho·me·o·path·ic (hō′mē ə path′ik), *adj.* **1.** of, pertaining to, or according to the principles of homeopathy. **2.** practicing or advocating homeopathy. [1815–25; HOMEO- + -PATHIC] —**ho′me·o·path′i·cal·ly,** *adv.*

ho′meopath′ic mag′ic. See **imitative magic.**

ho·me·op·a·thist (hō′mē op′ə thist), *n.* a person who practices or favors homeopathy. Also, **ho·me·o·path** (hō′mē ə path′). [1820–30; HOMEO- + -PATH + -IST]

ho·me·op·a·thy (hō′mē op′ə thē), *n.* the method of treating disease by drugs, given in minute doses, that would produce in a healthy person symptoms similar to those of the disease (opposed to *allopathy*). [1820–30; HOMEO- + -PATHY]

ho·me·o·pla·sia (hō′mē ō plā′zhə, -zhē ə, -zē ə), *n.* *Med.* the formation, as in healing, of new tissue that is similar to the existing tissue. [HOMEO- + -PLASIA] —**ho·me·o·plas·tic** (hō′mē ə plas′tik), *adj.*

ho·me·o·sta·sis (hō′mē ə stā′sis), *n.* **1.** the tendency of a system, esp. the physiological system of higher animals, to maintain internal stability, owing to the coordinated response of its parts to any situation or stimulus tending to disturb its normal condition or function. **2.** *Psychol.* a state of psychological equilibrium obtained when tension or a drive has been reduced or eliminated. [1925–30; HOMEO- + STASIS] —**ho·me·o·stat·ic** (hō′mē ə stat′ik), *adj.* —**ho′me·o·stat′i·cal·ly,** *adv.*

ho·me·o·tel·eu·ton (hō′mē ō tel′yə ton′), *n.* *Rhet.* a series of words with the same or similar endings. [1580–90; < Gk, n. use of neut. of *homoiotéleutos* ending alike, equiv. to *homoio-* HOMEO- + *-teleutos,* adj. der. of *teleutḗ* end, close]

ho·me·o·ther·a·py (hō′mē ə ther′ə pē), *n.* *Med.* therapy for a disease by means of an agent that is similar to but not identical with the causative agent of the disease. [HOMEO- + THERAPY] —**ho·me·o·ther·a·peu·tic** (hō′mē ə ther′ə pyōō′tik), *adj.*

ho·me·o·therm (hō′mē ə thûrm′), *n.* homoiotherm. [1890–95]

ho·me·o·ther·mal (hō′mē ə thûr′məl), *adj.* homoiothermal. [1865–70; HOMEO- + THERMAL] —**ho′me·o·ther′my, ho′me·o·ther′mism,** *n.*

ho·me·o·typ·ic (hō′mē ə tip′ik), *adj.* *Cell Biol.* of or pertaining to the second division in meiosis. Also, **ho′·me·o·typ′i·cal.** Cf. **heterotypic.** [1885–90; HOMEO- + TYPE + -IC]

home·own·er (hōm′ō′nər), *n.* a person who owns a home. [1940–45] —**home′own′ing,** *adj.*

home′owner's pol′icy, *Insurance.* a form of home insurance that provides compensation for damage, loss, or injury of property, personal belongings, or persons due to fire, theft, accidents, etc. Also called **home′·owner's insur′ance.**

home·place (hōm′plās′), *n.* a person's birthplace or family home. [1730–40, *Amer.*; HOME + PLACE]

home′ plate′, *Baseball.* the base at which the batter stands and which a base runner must reach safely in order to score a run, typically a five-sided slab of rubber set at the front corner of the diamond. Also called **home, the plate, home base.** [1870–75, *Amer.*]

home′ port′, 1. the port where a ship is registered. **2.** the port out of which a ship is operated but not necessarily registered. [1890–95]

hom·er[1] (hō′mər), *n.* **1.** *Baseball.* See **home run. 2.** See **homing pigeon.** —*v.i.* **3.** *Baseball.* to hit a home run: *The catcher homered in the ninth with one on to take the game.* [1865–70; HOME + -ER[1]]

ho·mer[2] (hō′mər), *n.* a Hebrew unit of capacity equal to ten baths in liquid measure or ten ephahs in dry measure. Also called **kor.** [1525–35; < Heb *ḥōmer* lit., heap]

Ho·mer (hō′mər), *n.* **1.** 9th-century B.C. Greek epic poet: reputed author of the *Iliad* and *Odyssey.* **2. Winslow,** 1836–1910, U.S. painter and illustrator. **3.** a male given name.

home′ range′, *Ecol.* the area in which an animal normally lives. [1880–85]

Ho·mer·ic (hō mer′ik), *adj.* **1.** of, pertaining to, or suggestive of Homer or his poetry. **2.** of heroic dimensions; grand; imposing: *Homeric feats of exploration.* [1765–75; < L *Homēricus* < Gk *Homērikós,* equiv. to *Hómēr(os)* HOMER + *-ikos* -IC] —**Ho·mer′i·cal·ly,** *adv.*

Homer′ic laugh′ter, loud, hearty laughter, as of the gods.

Homer′ic sim′ile. See **epic simile.**

home·room (hōm′rōōm′, -rŏŏm′), *n.* **1.** a classroom in which pupils in the same grade or division of a grade meet at certain times under the supervision of a teacher, who takes attendance and administers other school business. **2.** (in an elementary school) the classroom in which pupils in the same grade or division of a grade receive instruction in all subjects except those requiring special facilities. **3.** the pupils in a particular homeroom. Also, **home′ room′.** [1910–15, *Amer.*; HOME + ROOM]

home′ row′, (in touch typing) the row on a typewriter or computer keyboard that contains the keys **(home keys)** to which four fingers of each hand return as a base, on a QWERTY keyboard being A, S, D, and F for the left hand and J, K, L, and the semicolon for the right.

home′ rule′, self-government in local matters by a city, province, state, colony, or the like. [1855–60]

home′ rul′er, an advocate of home rule. [1875–80]

home′ run′, *Baseball.* a hit that enables a batter, without the aid of a fielding error, to score a run by making a nonstop circuit of the bases. [1855–60, *Amer.*]

home·school·ing (hōm′skōō′ling), *n.* the practice of teaching one's own children at home. [1985–90]

home′ scrap′, *Metall.* scrap steel reprocessed in the steel mill in which it was produced.

home′ screen′, television. [1965–70]

Home′ Sec′retary, *Brit.* the secretary of state for the Home Office. [1790–1800]

home·sick (hōm′sik′), *adj.* sad or depressed from a longing for home or family while away from them for a long time. [1790–1800; HOME + SICK[1]] —**home′sick′·ness,** *n.*

home′ sign′, 1. any idiosyncratic system of gestural communication used by a deaf person. **2.** a single idiosyncratic form that is incorporated into a standard sign language.

home·site (hōm′sīt′), *n.* **1.** a plot of land for a home. **2.** the home on such a plot of land. [1910–15]

home·spun (hōm′spun′), *adj.* **1.** spun or made at home: *homespun cloth.* **2.** made of such cloth: *homespun clothing.* **3.** plain; unpolished; unsophisticated; simple; rustic: *homespun humor.* —*n.* **4.** a plain-weave cloth made at home, or of homespun yarn. **5.** any cloth of similar appearance. **6.** a rustic person. [1580–90; HOME + SPUN]

home·stall (hōm′stôl′), *n.* *Brit.* **1.** *Dial.* a farmyard. **2.** *Obs.* a homestead. [bef. 1000; ME *homstal,* OE *hāmsteall.* See HOME, STALL[1]]

home′ stand′, a series of consecutive sports events, as baseball games, played in a team's own stadium. [1960–65]

home·stead (hōm′sted, -stid), *n.* **1.** a dwelling with its land and buildings, occupied by the owner as a home and exempted by a homestead law from seizure or sale for debt. **2.** any dwelling with its land and buildings where a family makes its home. **3.** a tract of land acquired under the Homestead Act. **4.** a house in an urban area acquired under a homesteading program. —*v.t.* **5.** to acquire or settle on (land) as a homestead: *Pioneers homesteaded the valley.* —*v.i.* **6.** to acquire or settle on a homestead: *They homesteaded many years ago.* [bef. 1000; OE *hāmstede* (not found in ME). See HOME, STEAD]

Home·stead (hōm′sted, -stid), *n.* a town in S Florida. 20,668.

Home′stead Act′, a special act of Congress (1862) that made public lands in the West available to settlers without payment, usually in lots of 160 acres, to be used as farms.

home·stead·er (hōm′sted′ər), *n.* **1.** the owner or holder of a homestead. **2.** a settler under the Homestead Act. [1860–65, *Amer.*; HOMESTEAD + -ER[1]]

home·stead·ing (hōm′sted′ing), *n.* **1.** an act or instance of establishing a homestead. **2.** a federal program to improve deteriorating urban areas by offering abandoned or foreclosed houses to persons who agree to repair them and live in them for a specified number of years. Also called **home′steading pro′gram, urban homesteading.** [1890–95, for earlier sense "homestead"; HOMESTEAD + -ING[1]]

home′stead law′, 1. any law exempting homesteads from seizure or sale for debt. **2.** any law making public lands available to settlers to be used as farms. **3.** any of various state laws granting special property tax exemptions or other privileges to homesteaders. [1840–50, *Amer.*]

home·stretch (hōm′strech′), *n.* **1.** the straight part of a racetrack from the last turn to the finish line. Cf. **backstretch. 2.** the final phase of any endeavor: *The political campaign is in the homestretch.* [1835–45, *Amer.*; HOME + STRETCH]

home′ stud′y, instruction in a subject given by mail and addressed to a student's home.

home·town (hōm′toun′), *n.* **1.** the town or city in which a person lives or was born, or from which a person comes. —*adj.* **2.** of or pertaining to a hometown: *a hometown welcome.* [1910–15, *Amer.*; HOME + TOWN]

home′ truth′, an indisputable fact or basic truth, esp. one whose accuracy may cause discomfort or embarrassment. [1705–15]

home′ vid′eo, 1. a videotape recorded by camcorder generally for noncommercial use, esp. for viewing at home. **2.** the business of renting or selling prerecorded videocassettes for viewing esp. at home.

home·ward (hōm′wərd), *adv.* **1.** Also, **home′wards.** toward home. —*adj.* **2.** directed toward home: *his homeward way.* [bef. 900; ME *homward,* OE *hāmweard.* See HOME, -WARD]

Home·wood (hōm′wŏŏd′), *n.* **1.** a city in central Alabama, near Birmingham. 21,271. **2.** a city in NE Illinois. 19,724.

home·work (hōm′wûrk′), *n.* **1.** schoolwork assigned to be done outside the classroom (*distinguished from classwork*). **2.** paid work done at home, as piecework. **3.** thorough preparatory study of a subject: *to do one's homework for the next committee meeting.* [1675–85]

home·work·er (hōm′wûr′kər, -wûr′-), *n.* **1.** a person who works at home for pay, esp. a pieceworker. **2.** houseworker. [1900–05; HOME + WORKER]

hom·ey (hō′mē), *adj.,* **hom·i·er, hom·i·est.** comfortably informal and inviting; cozy; homelike: *a homey little inn.* Also, **homy.** [1850–55; HOME + -Y[1]] —**hom′ey·ness, hom′i·ness,** *n.*
—**Syn.** See **homely.**

hom·i·cid·al (hom′ə sīd′l, hō′mə-), *adj.* **1.** of or pertaining to homicide. **2.** having a tendency to commit homicide. [1715–25; HOMICIDE + -AL[1]] —**hom′i·cid′al·ly,** *adv.*

hom·i·cide (hom′ə sīd′, hō′mə-), *n.* **1.** the killing of one human being by another. **2.** a person who kills another; murderer. [1325–75; ME < MF < L *homicīdium* a killing, *homicīda* killer, equiv. to *homi-* (comb. form of *homō* man) + *-cīdium, -cīda* -CIDE]

hom·i·let·ic (hom′ə let′ik), *adj.* **1.** of or pertaining to preaching or to homilies. **2.** of the nature of a homily. **3.** of or pertaining to homiletics. Also, **hom′i·let′i·cal.** [1635–45; < Gk *homilētikós* affable, equiv. to *homilē-* (var. s. of *homileîn* to converse with; see HOMILY) + *-tikos* -TIC] —**hom′i·let′i·cal·ly,** *adv.*

hom·i·let·ics (hom′ə let′iks), *n.* (*used with a singular v.*) the art of preaching; the branch of practical theology that treats of homilies or sermons. [1820–30; see HOMILETIC, -ICS]

ho·mil·i·ar·y (ho mil′ē er′ē), *n., pl.* **-ar·ies.** a collection of homilies. [1835–45; < ML *homīliārium* < Gk *homīlí(a)* HOMILY + L *-ārium* -ARY]

hom•i•list (hom′ə list), *n.* a person who writes or delivers homilies. [1610–20; HOMIL(Y) + -IST]

hom•i•ly (hom′ə lē), *n., pl.* **-lies. 1.** a sermon, usually on a Biblical topic and usually of a nondoctrinal nature. **2.** an admonitory or moralizing discourse. **3.** an inspirational saying or cliché. [1545–55; < LL *homīlia* < Gk *homīlía* assembly, sermon, equiv. to *hómīl(os)* crowd (*hom(oû)* together + *-ilos,* masc. comb. form of *ílē* (fem.) crowd) + *-ia* -Y[3]; r. ME *omelie* < MF < L, as above]

hom•ing (hō′ming), *adj.* **1.** capable of returning home, usually over a great distance: *We saw the homing birds at dusk.* **2.** guiding or directing homeward or to a destination, esp. by mechanical means: *the homing instinct; a homing beacon.* [1860–65; HOME + -ING[2]]

hom′ing device′, a mechanism incorporated into a guided missile, airplane, etc., that aims it toward its objective. [1930–35]

hom′ing pi′geon, any pigeon used to carry messages and equipped by training and breeding to fly home, sometimes from great distances. [1885–90]

hom•i•nid (hom′ə nid), *n. Anthropol.* any of the modern or extinct bipedal primates of the family Hominidae, including all species of the genera *Homo* and *Australopithecus.* See illus. in next columns. Also, **homonid, ho•min•i•an** (hō min′ē ən). [1885–90; < NL *Hominidae,* equiv. to L *homin-* (s. of *homō*) man (see HOMO) + *-idae* -ID[2]]

hom•i•nine (hom′ə nīn′), *adj.* resembling or characteristic of humans. [1880–85; < L *homin-* (s. of *homō*) man (see HOMO) + -INE[1]]

hom•i•ni•za•tion (hom′ə nə zā′shən), *n.* the evolution of the human traits that set the genus *Homo* apart from its primate ancestors. [1950–55; < L *homin-* (s. of *homō* man (see HOMO) + -IZATION]

hom•i•noid (hom′ə noid′), *n. Anthropol.* a member of the biological superfamily Hominoidea, including all modern great apes and humans and a number of their extinct ancestors and relatives. [1925–30; < L *homin-* (s. of *homō*) man (see HOMO) + -OID]

hom•i•ny (hom′ə nē), *n.* whole or ground hulled corn from which the bran and germ have been removed by bleaching the whole kernels in a lye bath **(lye hominy)** or by crushing and sifting **(pearl hominy).** [1620–30, *Amer.*; < Virginia Algonquian (E sp.) *uskatahomen, usketchamun* a nominalized pass. v., lit., that which is treated (in the way specified by the unidentified initial element), here prob. that which is ground or beaten]

hom′iny grits′, grits (def. 1). [1790–1800; *Amer.*]

homme (ôm), *n., pl.* ***hommes*** (ôm). *French.* **1.** a man. **2.** a human being.

homme d'af•faires (ôm dᴀ fεʀ′), *pl.* ***hommes d'af•faires*** (ôm dᴀ fεʀ′). *French.* a businessman.

homme du monde (ôm dʏ mônd′), *pl.* ***hommes du monde*** (ôm dʏ mônd′). *French.* a man of the world; a sophisticate.

Hom•mel (hom′əl), *n.* a walled plain in the fourth quadrant of the face of the moon: about 75 mi. (120 km) in diameter.

hom•mock (hom′ək), *n.* hummock (def. 3).

hom•mos (hŏŏm′əs), *n.* hummus.

ho•mo (hō′mō), *n., pl.* **-mos.** *Slang (disparaging and offensive).* a homosexual. [by shortening]

Ho•mo (hō′mō), *n.* **1.** (*italics*) the genus of bipedal primates that includes modern humans and several extinct forms, distinguished by their large brains and a dependence upon tools. Cf. **archaic *Homo.*** **2.** *Informal.* (*sometimes l.c.*) **a.** a member of the genus *Homo.* **b.** the species *Homo sapiens* or one of its members. [1590–1600; < L *homō* man; OL *hemō* the earthly one (see HUMUS); akin to L *hūmānus* HUMAN; c. OE *guma,* OIr *duine,* Welsh *dyn* man, Lith *žmônės* men]

homo-, a combining form appearing in loanwords from Greek, where it meant "same" (*homology*); on this model, used in the formation of compound words (*homomorphic*). Also, *esp. before a vowel,* **hom-.** [< Gk, comb. form of *homós* one and the same; akin to Skt *sama-;* see SAME]

ho•mo•cen•tric (hō′mə sen′trik, hom′ə-), *adj.* **1.** having a common center; concentric. **2.** diverging from or converging to the same point: *homocentric rays.* Also, **ho′mo•cen′tri•cal.** [1615–25; HOMO- + -CENTRIC] **—ho′mo•cen′tri•cal•ly,** *adv.* **—ho•mo•cen•tric•i•ty,** (hō′mō sen tris′i tē, hom′ō-), *n.*

ho•mo•cer•cal (hō′mə sûr′kəl, hom′ə-), *adj. Ichthyol.* having an equally divided tail, characteristic of adult modern bony fishes. Cf. **diphycercal, heterocercal.** [1830–40; HOMO- + *cerc-* (< Gk *kérkos* tail) + -AL[1]] **—ho•mo•cer•cy** (hō′mə sûr′sē, hom′ə-), **ho•mo•cer•cal•i•ty** (hō′mə sər kal′i tē, hom′ə-), *n.*

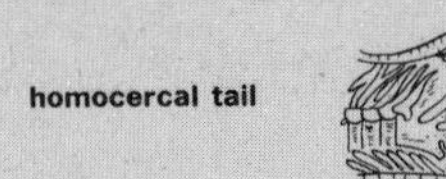
homocercal tail

ho•mo•chro•mat•ic (hō′mə krō mat′ik, -krə-, hom′ə-), *adj.* of or pertaining to one hue; monochromatic. Also, **homochrome.** Cf. **heterochromatic.** [1905–10; HOMO- + CHROMATIC] **—ho•mo•chro•ma•tism** (hō′mə krō′mə tiz′əm, hom′ə-), *n.*

ho•mo•chrome (hō′mə krōm′, hom′ə-), *adj.* homochromatic. [< Gk *homóchrōmos,* equiv. to. *homo-* HOMO- + *-chrōmos* (*chrôm(a)* color + *-os* adj. suffix); see CHROMA]

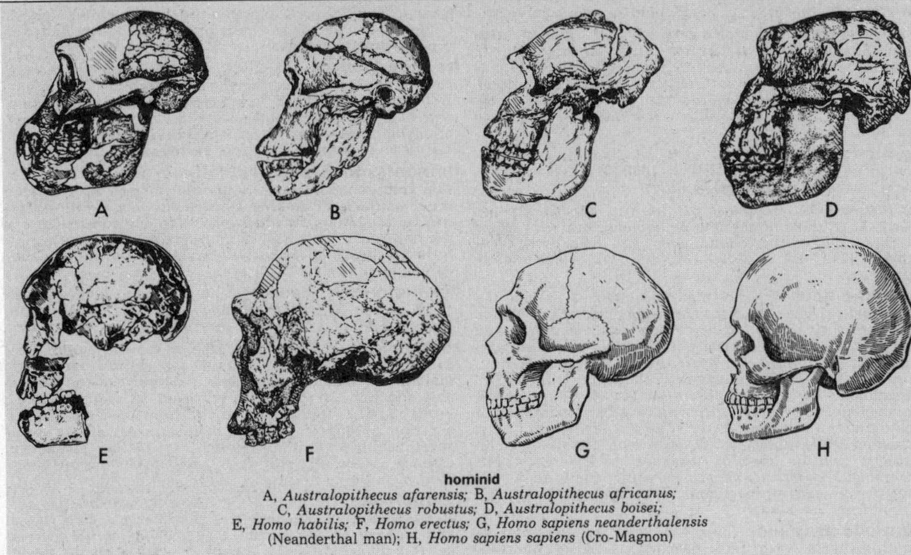

hominid
A, *Australopithecus afarensis;* B, *Australopithecus africanus;* C, *Australopithecus robustus;* D, *Australopithecus boisei;* E, *Homo habilis;* F, *Homo erectus;* G, *Homo sapiens neanderthalensis* (Neanderthal man); H, *Homo sapiens sapiens* (Cro-Magnon)

ho•mo•chro•mous (hō′mə krō′məs, hom′ə-), *adj. Bot., Zool.* being all of one color, as a composite flower or flower head. [1835–45; HOMOCHROME + -OUS] **—ho•mo•chro•my** (hō′mə krō′mē, hom′ə-), *n.*

ho•moch•ro•nous (hō mok′rə nəs, ho-), *adj.* (of a genetic character) occurring at the same age or period in the offspring as in the parent. [1875–80; < Gk *homóchronos* of the same time. See HOMO-, CHRON-, -OUS]

ho•mo•cy•clic (hō′mə sī′klik, -sik′lik, hom′ə-), *adj. Chem.* of or noting a cyclic compound having atoms of only one element, usually carbon, in the ring (contrasted with *heterocyclic*). Also, **isocyclic.** [1900–05; HOMO- + CYCLIC]

ho•mo•dyne (hō′mə dīn′, hom′ə-), *adj. Radio.* of or pertaining to reception by a device that generates a varying voltage of the same or nearly the same frequency as the incoming carrier wave and combines it with the incoming signal for detection. [1925–30; HOMO- + DYNE]

homoeo-, var. of **homeo-:** *homoeopathy.*

Ho•mo e•rec•tus (hō′mō i rek′təs), **1.** an extinct species of the human lineage, formerly known as *Pithecanthropus erectus,* having upright stature and a well-evolved postcranial skeleton, but with a smallish brain, low forehead, and protruding face. See illus. under **hominid. 2.** a fossil belonging to this species. Cf. **Arago man, Java man, Peking man.** [1970–75; < NL: upright man]

ho•mo•e•rot•i•cism (hō′mō i rot′ə siz′əm), *n.* a tendency to be sexually aroused by a member of the same sex. Also, **ho•mo•er•o•tism** (hō′mō er′ə tiz′əm). [1915–20; HOMO- + EROTICISM] **—ho•mo•e•rot•ic** (hō′mō i-rot′ik), *adj.*

ho•mo•ga•met•ic (hō′mō gə met′ik, hom′ō-), *adj. Genetics.* producing only one type of gamete with respect to sex chromosomes. Cf. **heterogametic.** [1905–10; HOMO- + GAMETIC]

ho•mog•a•mous (hō mog′ə məs), *adj.* **1.** *Bot.* **a.** having flowers or florets that do not differ sexually (opposed to *heterogamous*). **b.** having the stamens and pistils maturing simultaneously (opposed to *dichogamous*). **2.** *Biol.* pertaining to the interbreeding of individuals with like characteristics. [1835–45; HOMO- + -GAMOUS]

ho•mog•a•my (hō mog′ə mē), *n.* **1.** the state of being homogamous. **2.** interbreeding of individuals with like characteristics. [1870–75; HOMO- + -GAMY]

ho•mog•e•nate (hə moj′ə nāt′, -nit, hō-), *n.* a mixture that has been homogenized. [1940–45; HOMOGE-N(IZE) + -ATE[1]]

ho•mo•ge•ne•i•ty (hō′mə jə nē′i tē, hom′ə-), *n.* composition from like parts, elements, or characteristics; state or quality of being homogeneous. Also, **ho•mo•ge•ne•ous•ness** (hō′mə jē′nē əs nis, -jēn′yəs-, hom′ə-). [1615–25; < ML *homogeneitās,* equiv. to *homogene(us)* HOMOGENEOUS + *-itās* -ITY]

ho•mo•ge•ne•ous (hō′mə jē′nē əs, -jēn′yəs, hom′ə-), *adj.* **1.** composed of parts or elements that are all of the same kind; not heterogeneous: *a homogeneous population.* **2.** of the same kind or nature; essentially alike. **3.** *Math.* **a.** having a common property throughout: *a homogeneous solid figure.* **b.** having all terms of the same degree: *a homogeneous equation.* **c.** relating to a function of several variables that becomes multiplied by some power of a constant when each variable is multiplied by that constant: x^2y^3 *is a homogeneous expression of degree 5.* **d.** relating to a differential equation in which a linear combination of derivatives is set equal to zero. [1635–45; < ML *homogeneus,* equiv. to *homogene-* (s. of Gk *homogenḗs* of the same kind; see HOMO-, GENE) + *-us* -OUS] **—ho′mo•ge′ne•ous•ly,** *adv.*
—Syn. 1. unvarying, unmixed, alike, similar, identical.

ho•mo•gen•e•sis (hō′mə jen′ə sis, hom′ə-), *n. Biol.* reproduction in which the offspring resemble the parents and undergo the same cycle of development. [1855–60; HOMO- + -GENESIS]

ho•mo•ge•net•ic (hō′mə jə net′ik, hom′ə-), *adj. Biol.* **1.** pertaining to or characterized by homogenesis. **2.** homogenous (def. 1). Also, **ho′mo•ge•net′i•cal.** [1865–70; HOMO- + GENETIC] **—ho′mo•ge•net′i•cal•ly,** *adv.*

ho•mog•e•nize (hə moj′ə nīz′, hō-), *v.,* **-nized, -niz•ing.** **—***v.t.* **1.** to form by blending unlike elements; make homogeneous. **2.** to prepare an emulsion, as by reducing the size of the fat globules in (milk or cream) in order to distribute them equally throughout. **3.** to make uniform or similar, as in composition or function: *to homogenize school systems.* **4.** *Metall.* to subject (metal) to high temperature to ensure uniform diffusion of components. **—***v.i.* **5.** to become homogenized. Also, *esp. Brit.,* **ho•mog′e•nise′.** [1885–90; HOMOGEN(EOUS) + -IZE] **—ho•mog′e•ni•za′tion,** *n.* **—ho•mog′e•niz′er,** *n.*

ho•mog•e•nous (hə moj′ə nəs, hō-), *adj.* **1.** *Biol.* corresponding in structure because of a common origin. **2.** homogeneous. **3.** homoplastic. [1865–70; HOMO- + -GENOUS]

ho′mo•gen•tis′ic ac′id (hō′mə jen tis′ik, -tiz′-, hō′-), an intermediate compound in the metabolism of tyrosine and of phenylalanine, found in excess in the blood and urine of persons affected with alkaptonuria. Also called **alkapton.** [1890–95; HOMO- + GENTISIC ACID]

ho•mog•e•ny (hə moj′ə nē, hō-), *n. Biol.* correspondence in form or structure, owing to a common origin. [1620–30; < Gk *homogéneia* community of origin. See HOMO-, -GENY]

ho•mog•o•nous (hə mog′ə nəs, hō-), *adj. Bot.* pertaining to monoclinous flowers that do not differ in the relative length of stamens and pistils (opposed to *heterogonous*). [1877; HOMO- + *-gonous* < Gk *-gonos* generating; see -GONY, -OUS] **—ho•mog′o•nous•ly,** *adv.*

ho•mog•o•ny (hə mog′ə nē, hō-), *n. Bot.* state of being homogonous. [HOMO- + -GONY]

ho•mo•graft (hō′mə graft′, -gräft′, hom′ə-), *n. Surg.* allograft. [1920–25; HOMO- + GRAFT[1]]

hom•o•graph (hom′ə graf′, -gräf′, hō′mə-), *n.* a word of the same written form as another but of different meaning and usually origin, whether pronounced the same way or not, as *bear*[1] "to carry; support" and *bear*[2] "animal" or *lead*[1] "to conduct" and *lead*[2] "metal." [1800–10; HOMO- + -GRAPH] **—hom•o•graph•ic** (hom′ə-graf′ik, hō′mə-), *adj.*
—Syn. See **homonym.**

Ho•mo hab•i•lis (hō′mō hab′ə ləs), **1.** an extinct species of upright East African hominid having some advanced humanlike characteristics, dated as being from about 1.5 million to more than 2 million years old and proposed as an early form of *Homo* leading to modern humans. See illus. under **hominid. 2.** a fossil belonging to this species. [1965–70; < NL: adaptable man]

homoio-, var. of **homeo-:** *homoiothermal.*

ho•moi•o•therm (hō moi′ə thûrm′), *n.* a homoiothermal animal. Also, **homeotherm, homotherm.** [1890–95; back formation from HOMOIOTHERMAL]

ho•moi•o•ther•mal (hō moi′ə thûr′məl, hō′moi-), *adj.* having a body temperature that is relatively constant and mostly independent of the temperature of the environment; warm-blooded (opposed to *poikilothermal*). Also, **homeothermal, homothermal.** [1865–70; HOMOIO- + THERMAL] **—ho•moi′o•ther′my, ho′moi•o•ther′mism,** *n.*

Ho•moi•ou•si•an (hō′moi ōō′sē ən, -ou′-), *n.* **1.** a member of a 4th-century A.D. church party that maintained that the essence of the Son is similar to, but not the same as, that of the Father. **—***adj.* **2.** relating to the Homoiousians or their doctrine. [1725–35; < LGk *homoioúsi(os)* of like substance (*homoi-* HOMOIO- + *ousí(a)* substance, essence + *-os* adj. suffix) + -AN] **—Ho′moi•ou′si•an•ism,** *n.*

ho•mo•lec•i•thal (hō′mə les′ə thəl), *adj. Embryol.* having a fairly uniform distribution of yolk, as certain eggs or ova having relatively little yolk. [1890–95; HOMO- + LECITHAL]

ho•mo•log (hō′mə lôg′, -log′, hom′ə-), *n.* homologue.

ho•mol•o•gate (hə mol′ə gāt′, hō-), *v.t.*, **-gat•ed, -gat•ing.** **1.** to approve; confirm or ratify. **2.** to register (a specific make of automobile in general production) so as to make it eligible for international racing competition. [1635–45; < ML *homologātus* (ptp. of *homologāre* < Gk *homologeîn* to agree to, allow); see -ATE[1]] **—ho•mol′o•ga′tion,** *n.*

ho•mo•log•i•cal (hō′mə loj′i kəl, hom′ə-), *adj.* homologous. Also, **ho′mo•log′ic.** [1840–50; HOMOLOG(Y) + -ICAL] **—ho′mo•log′i•cal•ly,** *adv.*

ho•mol•o•gize (hə mol′ə jīz′, hō-), *v.*, **-gized, -giz•ing.** *—v.t.* **1.** to make or show to be homologous. *—v.i.* **2.** to be homologous; correspond. Also, *esp. Brit.,* **ho•mol′o•gise′.** [1710–20; HOMOLOG(OUS) + -IZE] **—ho•mol′o•giz′er,** *n.*

ho•mol•o•gous (hə mol′ə gəs, hō-), *adj.* **1.** having the same or a similar relation; corresponding, as in relative position or structure. **2.** corresponding in structure and in origin, but not necessarily in function: *The wing of a bird and the foreleg of a horse are homologous.* **3.** having the same alleles or genes in the same order of arrangement: *homologous chromosomes.* **4.** *Chem.* of the same chemical type, but differing by a fixed increment of an atom or a constant group of atoms: *Methyl and ethyl alcohols are homologous.* **5.** *Immunol.* pertaining to an antigen and its specific antibody. [1650–60; < ML *homologus* < Gk *homólogos* agreeing, equiv. to *homo-* HOMO- + *-logos* proportional, equiv. to *log-* (s. of *lógos* proportion; see LOGOS) + *-os* -OUS]

hom•o•lo•graph•ic (hom′ə lə graf′ik), *adj.* representing parts with like proportions. Also, **homalographic.** [1860–65; var. of HOMALOGRAPHIC]

homolograph′ic projec′tion, *Cartog.* an equal-area projection in which the proportion between regions of unequal area is correctly shown. Also called **Mollweide projection.** [1860–65]

ho•mo•logue (hō′mə lôg′, -log′, hom′ə-), *n.* **1.** something homologous. **2.** *Chem.* any member of a homologous series of organic compounds: *Ethane is a homologue of the alkane series.* Also, **homolog.** [1840–50; < F < Gk *homólogon,* neut. of *homólogos* HOMOLOGOUS]

ho•mo•lo•gu•me•na (hō′mō lə gōō′mə nə, -gyōō′-), *n.* (*used with a singular v.*) the books in the New Testament generally held as authoritative and canonical by the early church. Also, **ho•mo•lo•gou•me•na** (hō′mō lə-gōō′mə nə). Cf. **antilegomena.** [< Gk *homologoúmena,* neut pl. pass. prp. of *homologeîn* to agree to, allow; see HOMOLOGOUS]

ho•mol•o•gy (hə mol′ə jē, hō-), *n., pl.* **-gies.** **1.** the state of being homologous; homologous relation or correspondence. **2.** *Biol.* **a.** a fundamental similarity based on common descent. **b.** a structural similarity of two segments of one animal based on a common developmental origin. **3.** *Chem.* the similarity of organic compounds of a series in which each member differs from its adjacent compounds by a fixed increment, as by CH_2. **4.** *Math.* a classification of figures according to certain topological properties. [1650–60; < Gk *homología* agreement, equiv. to *homólog(os)* HOMOLOGOUS + *-ia* -Y[3]]

ho•mol′o•sine projec′tion (hə mol′ə sin, -sīn′, hō-), *Cartog.* an equal-area projection of the world, distorting ocean areas in order to minimize the distortion of the continents. [1920–25; HOMOLO(GRAPHIC) + SINE[1]]

ho•mo•mor•phic (hō′mə môr′fik, hom′ə-), *adj. Math.* pertaining to two sets that are related by a homomorphism. [1865–70; HOMO- + -MORPHIC]

ho•mo•mor•phism (hō′mə môr′fiz əm, hom′ə-), *n.* **1.** *Biol.* correspondence in form or external appearance but not in type of structure or origin. **2.** *Bot.* possession of perfect flowers of only one kind. **3.** *Zool.* resemblance between the young and the adult. **4.** *Math.* an into map between two sets that preserves relations between elements. Also, **ho′mo•mor′phy.** [1865–70; HOMO- + -MORPH + -ISM] **—ho′mo•mor′phous,** *adj.*

hom•o•nid (hom′ə nid), *n. Anthropol.* hominid.

hom•o•nym (hom′ə nim), *n.* **1.** homophone (def. 1). **2.** a word the same as another in sound and spelling but different in meaning, as *chase* "to pursue" and *chase* "to ornament metal." **3.** (loosely) homograph. **4.** a namesake. **5.** *Biol.* a name given to a species or genus that has been assigned to a different species or genus and that is therefore rejected. [1635–45; < L *homōnymum* < Gk *homṓnymon,* neut. of *homṓnymos* HOMONYMOUS] **—hom′o•nym′ic,** *adj.* **—hom′o•nym′i•ty,** *n.*

—Syn. 1, 2, 3. HOMONYM, HOMOPHONE, and HOMOGRAPH designate words that are identical to other words in spelling or pronunciation, or both, while differing from them in meaning and usually in origin. HOMOPHONES are words that sound alike, whether or not they are spelled differently. The words *pear* "fruit," *pare* "cut off," and *pair* "two of a kind" are HOMOPHONES that are different in spelling; *bear* "carry; support" and *bear* "animal" are HOMOPHONES that are spelled alike. HOMOGRAPHS are words that are spelled identically but may or may not share a pronunciation. *Spruce* "tree" and *spruce* "neat" are HOMOGRAPHS, but so are *row* (rō) "line" and *row* (rou) "fight" as well as *sewer* (sōō′ər) "conduit for waste" and *sewer* (sō′ər) "person who sews." HOMONYMS are, in the strictest sense, both HOMOPHONES and HOMOGRAPHS, alike in spelling *and* pronunciation, as the two forms *bear.* HOMONYM, however, is used more frequently than HOMOPHONE, a technical term, when referring to words with the same pronunciation without regard to spelling. HOMONYM is also used as a synonym of HOMOGRAPH. Thus, it has taken on a broader scope than either of the other two terms and is often the term of choice in a nontechnical context.

CONCISE ETYMOLOGY KEY: <, descended or borrowed from; >, whence; b., blend of, blended; c., cognate with; cf., compare; deriv., derivative; equiv., equivalent; imit., imitative; obl., oblique; r., replacing; s., stem; sp., spelling, spelled; resp., respelling, respelled; trans., translation; ?, origin unknown; *, unattested; ‡, probably earlier than. See the full key inside the front cover.

ho•mon•y•mous (hə mon′ə məs, hō-), *adj.* of the nature of homonyms; having the same name. [1615–25; < L *homōnymus* < Gk *homṓnymos* of the same name, equiv. to *hom(o)-* HOMO- + *-ōnymos* named, adj. deriv. of *ónyma* name, -ONYM (for vowel lengthening see ANONYMOUS); see -OUS] **—ho•mon′y•mous•ly,** *adv.*

homon′ymous construc′tion, *Gram.* a construction that consists of the same morphemes in the same order as those of another construction, as *Flying planes can be dangerous,* in which *planes* in one construction is the object of *flying,* and in another the subject of *can;* a terminal string of formatives having two or more structural descriptions.

ho•mon•y•my (hə mon′ə mē, hō-), *n.* homonymous state. [1545–55; < LL *homōnymia* < Gk *homōnymía,* equiv. to *homṓnym(os)* HOMONYMOUS + *-ia* -Y[3]]

Ho•mo•ou•si•an (hō′mō ōō′sē ən, -ou′-, hom′ō-), *n.* **1.** a member of a 4th-century A.D. church party that maintained that the essence or substance of the Father and the Son is the same (opposed to *Heteroousian*). *—adj.* **2.** of or pertaining to the Homoousians or their doctrine. [1555–65; < LGk *homooúsi(os)* of the same substance (Gk *hom(o)-* HOMO- + *ousí(a)* substance, essence + *-os* adj. suffix) + -AN] **—Ho′mo•ou′si•an•ism,** *n.*

ho•mo•phile (hō′mə fīl′), *n.* **1.** a homosexual. *—adj.* **2.** advocating or supportive of the interests, civil rights, and welfare of homosexuals; gay: *a homophile activist organization.* [1955–60; HOMO- + -PHILE, on the model of HOMOSEXUAL]

ho•mo•phobe (hō′mə fōb′), *n.* a person who fears or hates homosexuals and homosexuality. [HOMO(SEXUAL) + -PHOBE]

ho•mo•pho•bi•a (hō′mə fō′bē ə), *n.* unreasoning fear of or antipathy toward homosexuals and homosexuality. [1955–60; HOMO(SEXUAL) + -PHOBIA] **—ho′mo•pho′bic,** *adj.*

hom•o•phone (hom′ə fōn′, hō′mə-), *n.* **1.** *Phonet.* a word pronounced the same as another but differing in meaning, whether spelled the same way or not, as *heir* and *air.* **2.** a written element that represents the same spoken unit as another, as *ks,* a homophone of *x* in English. [1615–25; back formation from HOMOPHONOUS]

—Syn. See **homonym.**

hom•o•phon•ic (hom′ə fon′ik, hō′mə-), *adj.* **1.** having the same sound. **2.** *Music.* having one part or melody predominating (opposed to *polyphonic*). [1875–80; < Gk *homóphōn(os)* (see HOMOPHONOUS) + -IC] **—hom′o•phon′i•cal•ly,** *adv.*

ho•moph•o•nous (hə mof′ə nəs, hō-), *adj.* identical in pronunciation. [1745–55; < Gk *homóphōnos* of the same sound; see HOMO-, PHON-, -OUS]

ho•moph•o•ny (hə mof′ə nē, hō-), *n.* **1.** the quality or state of being homophonic. **2.** homophonic music. [1770–80; < Gk *homophōnía* unison, equiv. to *homóphōn(os)* HOMOPHONOUS + *-ia* -Y[3]]

ho•mop•la•sy (hə mop′lə sē, hō′mə plas′ē, -plā′sē, hom′ə-), *n. Biol.* correspondence in form or structure, owing to a similar environment. [1865–70; HOMO- + -PLASY] **—ho•mo•plas•tic** (hō′mə plas′tik, hom′ə-), *adj.*

ho•mo•ploid (hō′mə ploid′, hom′ə-), *adj. Genetics.* of an organism or a cell whose set of chromosomes exhibits the same degree of ploidy as an organism or cell with which it is compared.

ho•mo•po•lar (hō′mə pō′lər, hom′ə-), *adj. Chem.* **1.** of uniform polarity; not separated or changed into ions; not polar in activity. **2.** *Elect.* unipolar (def. 1). [1880–85; HOMO- + POLAR] **—ho•mo•po•lar•i•ty** (hō′mə pō-lar′i tē, hom′ə-), *n.*

ho•mo•pol•y•mer (hō′mə pol′ə mər, hom′ə-), *n. Chem.* a polymer consisting of a single species of monomer, as polyadenylic acid or polyglutamic acid. [1945–50; HOMO- + POLYMER]

ho•mop•ter•an (hə mop′tər ən, hō-), *adj.* **1.** homopterous. *—n.* **2.** a homopterous insect. [1835–45; see HOMOPTEROUS, -AN]

ho•mop•ter•ous (hə mop′tər əs, hō-), *adj.* belonging or pertaining to the Homoptera, an order of insects closely related to the hemipterous insects (in some classifications a suborder of Hemiptera) but having membranous forewings and hind wings, including the aphids, cicadas, leafhoppers, planthoppers, and scale insects. [1820–30; < NL *Homopter(a)* (neut. pl. of *homopterus* < Gk *homópteros*) + -OUS. See HOMO-, -PTEROUS]

ho•mor•gan•ic (hō′môr gan′ik, hom′ôr-), *adj. Phonet.* (of two or more speech sounds) having the same place of articulation, as *p, b,* and *m,* which are all bilabial. [1850–55; HOM(O)- + ORGANIC]

Ho•mo sa•pi•ens (hō′mō sā′pē ənz), **1.** (*italics*) the species of bipedal primates to which modern humans belong, characterized by a brain capacity averaging 1400 cc (85 cubic in.) and by dependence upon language and the creation and utilization of complex tools. **2.** humankind. [1795–1805; < NL: rational man]

Ho′mo sa′piens sa′piens, the subspecies of the genus *Homo* in which modern humans are classified.

ho•mo•sce•das•tic (hō′mə si das′tik, hom′ə-), *adj. Statistics.* having the same variance. [1900–05; HOMO- + Gk *skedastikós* able to disperse, equiv. to *skedast(ós)* dispersable (verbid of *skedannýnai* to scatter, disperse) + *-ikos* -IC]

ho•mo•sex•u•al (hō′mə sek′shōō əl *or, esp. Brit.,* -seks′yōō-), *adj.* **1.** of, pertaining to, or exhibiting homosexuality. **2.** of, pertaining to, or noting the same sex. *—n.* **3.** a homosexual person. [1890–95; HOMO- + SEXUAL]

—Usage. See **gay.**

ho•mo•sex•u•al•i•ty (hō′mə sek′shōō al′i tē, *or, esp. Brit.,* -seks′yōō-), *n.* sexual desire or behavior directed toward a person or persons of one's own sex. [1890–95; HOMO- + SEXUALITY]

ho•mos•po•rous (hə mos′pər əs, hō-, hō′mə spôr′əs, -spōr′-), *adj. Bot.* having the spores of one kind only. [1885–90; HOMO- + SPORE + -OUS]

ho•mos•po•ry (hə mos′pə rē, hō-), *n.* the production of a single kind of spore, neither microspore nor megaspore. [1900–05; HOMO- + SPORE + -Y[3]]

ho•mo•styled (hō′mō stīld′), *adj.* (of a plant) having styles of the same form or length in all flowers. Also, **ho′mo•sty′lous, ho′mo•sty′lic.** [1875–80; HOMO- + STYLED] **—ho′mo•styl′ism, ho′mo•sty′ly,** *n.*

ho•mo•tax•is (hō′mə tak′sis, hom′ə-), *n.* a similarity of arrangement, as of geologic strata or fossil assemblages that have the same relative position but are not necessarily contemporaneous. Also, **ho′mo•tax′y.** [1860–65; HOMO- + -TAXIS] **—ho′mo•tax′ic, ho•mo•tax•i•al** (hō′mə tak′sē əl, hom′ə-), *adj.* **—ho′mo•tax′i•al•ly,** *adv.*

ho•mo•thal•lic (hō′mə thal′ik, hom′ə-), *adj. Mycol.* **1.** having all mycelia alike, the opposite sexual functions being performed by different cells of a single mycelium. Cf. **heterothallic** (def. 1). **2.** monoecious. [1900–05; HOMO- + THALL(US) + -IC] **—ho′mo•thal′lism,** *n.*

ho•mo•therm (hō′mə thûrm′, hom′ə-), *n.* homoiotherm. [1930–35]

ho•mo•ther•mal (hō′mə thûr′məl, hom′ə-), *adj.* homoiothermal. **—ho′mo•ther′my, ho′mo•ther′mism,** *n.* [1885–90]

ho•mo•thet•ic (hō′mə thet′ik, hom′ə-), *adj. Geom.* similar; similarly placed. [1875–80; HOMO- + THETIC] **—ho•moth•e•ty** (hə moth′i tē, hō-), *n.*

homothet′ic transforma′tion, *Math.* See **similarity transformation** (def. 1).

ho•mot•o•py (hə mot′ə pē, hō-), *n., pl.* **-pies.** *Math.* the relation that exists between two mappings in a topological space if one mapping can be deformed in a continuous way to make it coincide with the other. [1915–20; HOMO- + *-topy* (< Gr *tóp(os)* place + -Y[3], or < NL *-topia*)]

ho•mo•trans•plant (hō′mō trans′plant′, -plänt′, hom′ō-), *n.* allograft. [1925–30; HOMO- + TRANSPLANT]

ho•mo•type (hō′mə tīp′, hom′ə-), *n. Biol.* an organ or part having a structure similar to that of another organ or part; homologue. [1830–40; HOMO- + TYPE]

ho•mo•typ•ic (hō′mə tip′ik, hom′ə-), *adj. Biol.* **1.** of or pertaining to a homotype. **2.** homeotypic. Also, **ho′mo•typ′i•cal.** [1885–90; HOMOTYPE + -IC]

ho′mo•va•nil′lic ac′id (hō′mō və nil′ik, hom′ō-, hō′mō-, hom′ō-), *Biochem.* the end product of dopamine metabolism, $C_9H_{10}O_4$, found in human urine. [HOMO- + VANILLIC]

ho•mo•zy•go•sis (hō′mə zī gō′sis, -zi-, hom′ə-), *n. Biol.* the state of being a homozygote. [1900–05; HOMO- + Gk *zýgōsis;* see ZYGO-, -OSIS]

ho•mo•zy•gote (hō′mə zī′gōt, -zig′ōt, hom′ə-), *n. Biol.* an organism with identical pairs of genes with respect to any given pair of hereditary characters, and therefore breeding true for that character. [1900–05; HOMO- + ZYGOTE]

ho•mo•zy•gous (hō′mə zī′gəs, hom′ə-), *adj. Biol.* **1.** having identical pairs of genes for any given pair of hereditary characteristics. **2.** of or pertaining to a homozygote. Also, **ho•mo•zy•got•ic** (hō′mō zī got′ik, hom′ō-). [1900–05; HOMO- + Gk *-zygos;* see ZYGO-, -OUS] **—ho•mo•zy•gos•i•ty** (hō′mō zī gos′i tē, -zi-, hom′ō-), *n.*

Homs (hôms), *n.* a city in W Syria. 215,526.

ho•mun•cu•lus (hə mung′kyə ləs, hō-), *n., pl.* **-li** (-lī′). **1.** an artificially made dwarf, supposedly produced in a flask by an alchemist. **2.** a fully formed, miniature human body believed, according to some medical theories of the 16th and 17th centuries, to be contained in the spermatozoon. **3.** a diminutive human being. **4.** the human fetus. [1650–60; < L, equiv. to *homun-* (var. of *homin-,* s. of *homō* man; see HOMO) + *-culus* -CULE[1]] **—ho•mun′cu•lar,** *adj.*

hom•y (hō′mē), *adj.,* **hom•i•er, hom•i•est.** homey.

hon (hun), *n. Informal.* honey (def. 6). [1905–10; shortened form of HONEY]

Hon., **1.** Honorable. **2.** Honorary.

hon., **1.** honor. **2.** honorable. **3.** honorably. **4.** honorary.

Ho•nan (hō′nan′; *Chin.* hœ′nän′), *n.* **1.** *Wade-Giles.* Henan. **2.** (*usually l.c.*) *Textiles.* **a.** a pongee fabric made from the filaments of the wild silkworm. **b.** a lustrous fabric simulating pongee and woven from fibers other than silk.

hon•cho (hon′chō), *n., pl.* **-chos,** *v. Slang.* *—n.* **1.** a leader, esp. an assertive leader; chief. *—v.t.* **2.** to organize, supervise, or be the leader of: *She volunteered to honcho the new project.* [1945–50; < Japn *hanchō* squad or group leader, equiv. to *han* squad (< MChin, equiv. to Chin *bān*) + *-chō* eldest, chief (< MChin, equiv. to Chin *zhǎng*)]

Hond., Honduras.

hon•da (hon′də), *n.* an eye at one end of a lariat through which the other end is passed to form a lasso, noose, etc. [1885–90, *Amer.;* < Sp: sling < L *funda,* perh. akin to Gk *sphendónē*]

Hon•do (hon′dō; *for 1 also Japn.* hôn′dô; *for 2 also Sp.* ôn′dô), *n.* **1.** Honshu. **2.** a river flowing NE from Guatemala along the border of Belize and Mexico to the Caribbean Sea. 150 mi. (240 km) long.

Hon•du•ras (hon dŏŏr′əs, -dyŏŏr′-; *Sp.* ôn dōō′räs), *n.* **1.** a republic in NE Central America. 3,036,004; 43,277 sq. mi. (112,087 sq. km). See map on next page. *Cap.:*

Tegucigalpa. **2. Gulf of,** an arm of the Caribbean Sea, bordered by Belize, Guatemala, and Honduras. —**Hon·du′ran, Hon·du·ra·ne·an, Hon·du·ra·ni·an** (hon′də rā′-nē ən), *adj., n.*

hone[1] (hōn), *n., v.,* **honed, hon·ing.** —*n.* **1.** a whetstone of fine, compact texture for sharpening razors and other cutting tools. **2.** a precision tool with a mechanically rotated abrasive tip, for enlarging holes to precise dimensions. —*v.t.* **3.** to sharpen on a hone: *to hone a carving knife.* **4.** to enlarge or finish (a hole) with a hone. **5.** to make more acute or effective; improve; perfect: *to hone one's skills.* [bef. 950; ME (n.); OE *hān* stone, rock; c. ON *hein* hone; akin to CONE] —**hon′er,** *n.*

hone[2] (hōn), *v.i.,* **honed, hon·ing. 1.** *South Midland and Southern U.S.* to yearn; long: *to hone for the farm life; to hone after peach pie.* **2.** *Archaic.* to moan and groan. [1590–1600; < AF **honer;* OF *hogner* to grumble, growl < Gmc; cf. OS *hōnian* to abuse, revile]

Ho·neck·er (hō′ni kər; *Ger.* hō′nek ər), *n.* **E·rich** (er′ik; *Ger.* ā′riкн), 1912–94, East German Communist leader: chairman of the Council of State 1976–89.

Ho·neg·ger (hon′i gər, hō′neg′ər; *Fr.* ô ne ger′), *n.* **Ar·thur** (är′thər; *Fr.* ar tōōr′), 1892–1955, Swiss composer, born in France.

hon·est (on′ist), *adj.* **1.** honorable in principles, intentions, and actions; upright and fair: *an honest person.* **2.** showing uprightness and fairness: *honest dealings.* **3.** gained or obtained fairly: *honest wealth.* **4.** sincere; frank: *an honest face.* **5.** genuine or unadulterated: *honest commodities.* **6.** respectable; having a good reputation: *an honest name.* **7.** truthful or creditable: *honest weights.* **8.** humble, plain, or unadorned. **9.** *Archaic.* chaste; virtuous. [1250–1300; ME *honeste* < MF < L *honestus* honorable, equiv. to *hones-* (var. s. of *honōs*) HONOR + *-tus* adj. suffix] —**hon′est·ness,** *n.*
—**Syn. 1.** just, incorruptible, trusty, trustworthy. **2.** fair. **4.** straightforward, candid. **5, 9.** pure. —**Ant. 1.** dishonest, corrupt.

hon′est In′jun (in′jən), (used to emphasize the truth of a statement; sometimes considered offensive). Also, **hon′est In′jun.** [1870–75, *Amer.*]

Hon′est John′, 1. *Informal.* **a.** an honest, sincere man. **b.** a man so trusting and innocent that he may be easily cheated or deceived. **2.** a surface-to-surface, single-stage U.S. artillery rocket. [1930–35]

hon·est·ly (on′ist lē), *adv.* **1.** in an honest manner. **2.** with honesty. —*interj.* **3.** (used to express mild exasperation, disbelief, dismay, etc.): *Honestly! I want to finish this work and you keep interrupting.* [1300–50; ME. See HONEST, -LY]

hon·est-to-good·ness (on′ist tə go͝od′nis), *adj.* **1.** real or genuine. —*adv.* **2.** really, truly, or genuinely. Also, **hon·est-to-God** (on′ist tə god′). [1915–20]

hon·es·ty (on′ə stē), *n., pl.* **-ties. 1.** the quality or fact of being honest; uprightness and fairness. **2.** truthfulness, sincerity, or frankness. **3.** freedom from deceit or fraud. **4.** *Bot.* a plant, *Lunaria annua,* of the mustard family, having clusters of purple flowers and semitransparent, satiny pods. **5.** *Obs.* chastity. [1300–50; ME *honeste* < MF < L *honestās.* See HONEST, -TY[2]]
—**Syn. 1.** integrity, probity, rectitude. See **honor. 2.** candor, veracity. —**Ant. 1.** dishonesty.

hone·wort (hōn′wûrt′, -wôrt′), *n.* any plant of the genus *Cryptotaenia,* of the parsley family, esp. *C. canadensis,* having clusters of small white flowers. [1625–35; *hone* (< ?) + WORT[2]]

hon·ey (hun′ē), *n., pl.* **hon·eys,** *adj., v.,* **hon·eyed** or **hon·ied, hon·ey·ing.** —*n.* **1.** a sweet, viscid fluid produced by bees from the nectar collected from flowers, and stored in nests or hives as food. **2.** this substance as used in cooking or as a spread or sweetener. **3.** the nectar of flowers. **4.** any of various similarly sweet, viscid products produced by insects or in other ways. **5.** something sweet, delicious, or delightful: *the honey of flattery.* **6.** *Informal.* a person for whom one feels love or deep affection; sweetheart; darling. **7.** (*sometimes cap.*) an affectionate or familiar term of address (sometimes offensive when used to strangers, casual acquaintances, subordinates, etc., esp. by a male to a female). **8.** *Informal.* something of esp. high quality, degree of excellence, etc.: *That's a honey of a computer.* —*adj.* **9.** of, like, or pertaining to honey; sweet. **10.** containing honey or flavored or sweetened with honey. —*v.t.* **11.** *Informal.* to talk flatteringly or endearingly to (often fol. by *up*). **12.** to sweeten or flavor with or as if with honey. —*v.i.* **13.** *Informal.* to use flattery, endearing terms, etc., in an effort to obtain something (often fol. by *up*): *They always got what they wanted by honeying up to their grandfather.* [bef. 900; ME *hony,* OE *hunig;* c. D, G *honig,* ON *hunang;* akin to Gk *knēkós* pale yellow, tawny] —**hon′ey·ful,** *adj.* —**hon′ey·less,** *adj.* —**hon′ey·like′,** *adj.*

hon′ey ant′, any of several ants, esp. of the genus *Myrmecocystus,* that feed on honeydew or nectar and store the excess juices in the bodies of certain worker ants. [1865–70]

hon′ey badg′er, ratel. [1880–85]

hon′ey bear′, 1. a kinkajou. **2.** See **sun bear.** [1830–40]

hon·ey·bee (hun′ē bē′), *n.* any bee that collects and stores honey, esp. *Apis mellifera.* Also, **hon′ey bee′.** [1560–70; HONEY + BEE[1]]

hon′ey buck′et, *Facetious Older Use.* a container for excrement, as in an outdoor toilet. [1930–35]

hon′ey bun′, 1. Also called **sticky bun.** a sweet spiral-shaped bun, usually with cinnamon, raisins, and nuts, coated with honey or butter and brown sugar. **2.** Also, **hon′ey·bun′.** *Informal.* honey (def. 6, 7). [1895–1900, *Amer.*]

hon·ey·bunch (hun′ē bunch′), *n. Informal.* honey (def. 6, 7). [1900–05; HONEY + BUNCH]

hon′ey buz′zard, a long-tailed Old World hawk, *Pernis apivorus,* that feeds on the larvae of bees as well as on small rodents, reptiles, and insects. [1665–75]

hon·ey·comb (hun′ē kōm′), *n.* **1.** a structure of rows of hexagonal wax cells, formed by bees in their hive for the storage of honey, pollen, and their eggs. **2.** a piece of this containing honey and chewed as a sweet. **3.** anything whose appearance suggests such a structure, esp. in containing many small units or holes: *The building was a honeycomb of offices and showrooms.* **4.** the reticulum of a ruminant. **5.** *Textiles.* **a.** Also called **waffle cloth.** a fabric with an embossed surface woven in a pattern resembling a honeycomb. **b.** the characteristic weave of such a fabric. —*adj.* **6.** having the structure or appearance of a honeycomb. —*v.t.* **7.** to cause to be full of holes; pierce with many holes or cavities: *an old log honeycombed with ant burrows.* **8.** to penetrate in all parts: *a city honeycombed with vice.* [bef. 1050; ME *huny-comb,* OE *hunigcamb.* See HONEY, COMB[1]]

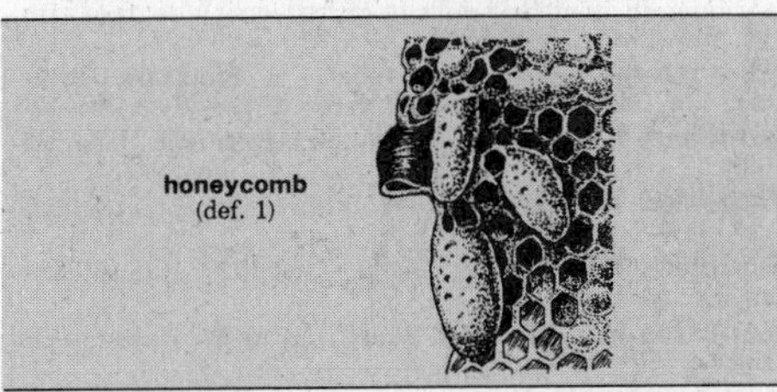
honeycomb (def. 1)

hon′eycomb tripe′, a part of the inner lining of the stomach of the steer, calf, hog, or sheep, resembling a honeycomb in appearance and considered a table delicacy. Cf. **plain tripe.**

hon′eycomb work′, *Archit.* See **stalactite work.** [1890–95]

hon·ey·creep·er (hun′ē krē′pər), *n.* **1.** any of several small, usually brightly colored birds, related to the tanagers and wood warblers, of tropical and semitropical America. **2.** See **Hawaiian honeycreeper.** [1880–85; HONEY + CREEPER]

hon·ey·dew (hun′ē do͞o′, -dyo͞o′), *n.* **1.** See **honeydew melon. 2.** the sweet material that exudes from the leaves of certain plants in hot weather. **3.** a sugary material secreted by aphids, leafhoppers, scale insects, psyllids, and other homopterous insects. [1570–80; HONEY + DEW] —**hon′ey·dewed′,** *adj.*

hon′eydew mel′on, a variety of the winter melon, *Cucumis melo inodorus,* having a smooth, pale-green rind and sweet, juicy, light-green flesh. [1915–20]

hon′ey eat′er, any of numerous oscine birds of the family Meliphagidae, chiefly of Australasia, having a bill and tongue adapted for extracting the nectar from flowers. Also, **hon′ey·eat′er.** [1725–35]

hon·eyed (hun′ēd), *adj.* **1.** containing, consisting of, or resembling honey: *honeyed drinks.* **2.** flattering or ingratiating: *honeyed words.* **3.** pleasantly soft; dulcet or mellifluous: *honeyed tones.* Also, **honied.** [1325–75; ME *honyede.* See HONEY, -ED[3]] —**hon′eyed·ly,** *adv.* —**hon′eyed·ness,** *n.*

hon′ey gild′ing, gilding of ceramics with a mixture of gold leaf and honey, later fired to fix the gold.

hon′ey guide′, any of several small, usually dull-colored birds of the family Indicatoridae, of Africa and southern Asia, certain species of which are noted for their habit of leading people or animals to nests of honeybees in order to feed on the honey, larvae, and wax of the nests after they have been broken open. Also, **hon′ey·guide′.** [1780–90]

hon′ey lo′cust, a thorny North American tree, *Gleditsia triacanthos,* of the legume family, having small, compound leaves and pods with a sweet pulp. Also called **black locust, three-thorned acacia.** [1735–45, *Amer.*]

hon′ey mesquite′, a thorny drought-resistant tree, *Prosopis glandulosa,* of the legume family, native to the southwestern U.S., having clusters of yellow flowers. [1885–90, *Amer.*]

hon·ey·moon (hun′ē mo͞on′), *n.* **1.** a vacation or trip taken by a newly married couple. **2.** the month or so following a marriage. **3.** any period of blissful harmony: *Their entire 60 years of marriage was one long honeymoon.* **4.** any new relationship characterized by an initial period of harmony and goodwill: *The honeymoon between Congress and the new president was over.* —*v.i.* **5.** to spend one's honeymoon (usually fol. by *in* or *at*). [1540–50; HONEY + MOON] —**hon′ey·moon′er,** *n.*

hon′eymoon bridge′, *Cards.* any of several varieties of bridge for two players.

hon′ey mush′room, the edible mushroom of the oak-root fungus, *Armillariella mellea.* Cf. **oak-root rot.** [1935–40]

hon′ey palm′, coquito.

hon·ey·pot (hun′ē pot′), *n.* a pot, as of glass or silver, for storing and serving honey. Also, **hon′ey pot′.** [1425–75; late ME. See HONEY, POT[1]]

hon′ey stom′ach, the crop of an ant, bee, or other hymenopterous insect, serving as a reservoir for honeydew and nectar, esp. the enlarged crop of a honeybee in which nectar is acted on by enzymes to form honey. Also called **hon′ey sac′.**

hon·ey·suck·er (hun′ē suk′ər), *n.* **1.** a bird that feeds on the nectar of flowers. **2.** See **honey eater.** [1765–75; HONEY + SUCKER]

hon·ey·suck·le (hun′ē suk′əl), *n.* any upright or climbing shrub of the genus *Diervilla,* esp. *D. lonicera,* cultivated for its fragrant white, yellow, or red tubular flowers. [1225–75; ME *honiesoukel,* equiv. to *honisouke* (OE *hunigsūce;* see HONEY, SUCK) + *-el* -LE] —**hon′ey·suck′led,** *adj.*

hon′eysuckle fam′ily, the plant family Caprifoliaceae, typified by shrubs and woody vines having opposite leaves, clusters of usually flaring, narrow, tubular flowers, and various types of fruit, and including the elder, honeysuckle, snowberry, twinflower, and viburnum.

hon′eysuckle or′nament, anthemion. [1860–65]

hon·ey-sweet (hun′ē swēt′), *adj.* sweet as honey. [bef. 1000; ME *hony sweete,* OE *hunig swēte*]

hon′ey wag′on, *Facetious Older Use.* **1.** a wagon or truck for collecting and carrying excrement or manure. **2.** a manure spreader, as on a farm. **3.** a truck or trailer containing several toilets and used as a mobile rest room. Also called **hon′ey truck′.** [1910–15]

hon·ey·wort (hun′ē wûrt′, -wôrt′), *n.* a plant, *Cerinthe retorta,* of Greece, having bluish-green leaves and purple-tipped yellow flowers. [1590–1600; HONEY + WORT[2], so called because its flowers yield much honey]

hong (hong), *n.* **1.** (in China) a group of rooms or buildings forming a warehouse, factory, etc. **2.** one of the factories under foreign ownership formerly maintained at Canton. [1720–30; < dial. Chin (Guangdong) *hòhng,* equiv. to Chin *háng* row of shops]

hong·i (hong′ē), *n. New Zealand.* a Maori greeting in which noses are pressed together. [1840–45; < Maori]

Hong Kong (hong′ kong′), **1.** a British crown colony comprising Hong Kong island (29 sq. mi.; 75 sq. km), Kowloon peninsula, nearby islands, and the adjacent mainland in SE China **(New Territories):** reverted to Chinese sovereignty in 1997. 5,761,400; 404 sq. mi. (1046 sq. km). *Cap.:* Victoria. **2.** Victoria (def. 4). Also, **Hong′·kong′.** Also called **Xianggang.** —**Hong′ Kong′er.** —**Hong′kong′ite,** *n.*

Hong·wu (hông′wo͞o′), *n. Pinyin.* (*Zhu Yuanzhang*) Hung-wu.

Ho·ni·a·ra (hō′nē är′ə), *n.* a city in and the capital of the Solomon Islands, N Guadalcanal. 11,191.

hon·ied (hun′ēd), *adj.* honeyed.

ho·ni soit qui mal y pense (ô nē swa′ kē mal ē päns′), *French.* shamed be the person who thinks evil of it: motto of the Order of the Garter.

honk (hongk, hôngk), *n.* **1.** the cry of a goose. **2.** any similar sound, as of an automobile horn. —*v.i.* **3.** to emit a honk. **4.** to cause an automobile horn to sound: *He drove up in front of the house and honked.* —*v.t.* **5.** to cause (an automobile horn) to sound: *The driver honked his horn impatiently.* [1790–1800, *Amer.*; imit.]

honk·er[1] (hong′kər, hông′-), *n.* **1.** a person or thing that honks. **2.** *Informal.* a goose. [1835–45, *Amer.*; HONK + -ER[1]]

hon·ker[2] (hong′kər, hông′-), *n. Slang (disparaging and offensive).* honky. [perh. HONK(Y) + -ER[1]]

hon·key (hong′kē, hông′-), *n., pl.* **-keys.** *Slang (disparaging and offensive).* honky.

hon·ky (hong′kē, hông′-), *n., pl.* **-kies.** *Slang (disparaging and offensive).* a white person. Also, **hon′kie, honkey, honker.** [1945–50, *Amer.*; perh. alter of HUNKY[2]]

honk·y-tonk (hong′kē tongk′, hông′kē tôngk′), *n.* **1.** a cheap, noisy, and garish nightclub or dance hall. —*adj.* **2.** Also, **honk·y-tonk·y** (hong′kē tong′kē, hông′-kē tông′-). **3.** of, pertaining to, or characteristic of a honky-tonk: *a honky-tonk atmosphere.* **4.** characterized by or having a large number of honky-tonks: *the honky-tonk part of town.* **5.** *Music.* noting a style of ragtime piano-playing characterized by a strict two-four or four-four bass, either contrapuntal or chordal, and a melody embellished with chords and syncopated rhythms, typically performed on a piano whose strings have been muffled and given a tinny sound. —*v.i.* **6.** to visit or frequent honky-tonks. [1890–95, *Amer.*; rhyming compound based on HONK] —**honk′y-tonk′er,** *n.*

Hon·o·lu·lu (hon′ə lo͞o′lo͞o), *n.* a seaport in and the capital of Hawaii, on S Oahu. 365,048.

hon•or (on′ər), *n.* **1.** honesty, fairness, or integrity in one's beliefs and actions: *a man of honor.* **2.** a source of credit or distinction: *to be an honor to one's family.* **3.** high respect, as for worth, merit, or rank: *to be held in honor.* **4.** such respect manifested: *a memorial in honor of the dead.* **5.** high public esteem; fame; glory: *He has earned his position of honor.* **6.** the privilege of being associated with or receiving a favor from a respected person, group, organization, etc.: *to have the honor of serving on a prize jury; I have the honor of introducing this evening's speaker.* **7.** Usually, **honors.** evidence, as a special ceremony, decoration, scroll, or title, of high rank, dignity, or distinction: *political honors; military honors.* **8.** (*cap.*) a deferential title of respect, esp. for judges and mayors (prec. by *His, Her, Your,* etc.). **9. honors, a.** special rank or distinction conferred by a university, college, or school upon a student for eminence in scholarship or success in some particular subject. **b.** an advanced course of study for superior students. Cf. **honors course. 10.** chastity or purity in a woman. **11.** Also called **honor card.** *Cards.* **a.** *Bridge.* any of the five highest trump cards, as an ace, king, queen, jack, or ten in the trump suit, or any of the four aces in a no-trump contract. Cf. **honor trick. b.** *Whist.* any of the four highest trump cards, as an ace, king, queen, or jack in the trump suit. **12.** *Golf.* the privilege of teeing off before the other player or side, given after the first hole to the player or side that won the previous hole. **13. be on** or **upon one's honor,** to accept and acknowledge personal responsibility for one's actions: *West Point cadets are on their honor not to cheat on an exam.* **14. do honor to, a.** to show respect to. **b.** to be a credit to: *Such good students would do honor to any teacher.* **15. do the honors,** to serve or preside as host, as in introducing people, or carving or serving at table: *Father did the honors at the family Thanksgiving dinner.* —*v.t.* **16.** to hold in honor or high respect; revere: *to honor one's parents.* **17.** to treat with honor. **18.** to confer honor or distinction upon: *The university honored him with its leadership award.* **19.** to worship (the Supreme Being). **20.** to show a courteous regard for: *to honor an invitation.* **21.** *Com.* to accept or pay (a draft, check, etc.): *All credit cards are honored here.* **22.** to accept as valid and conform to the request or demands of (an official document). **23.** (in square dancing) to meet or salute with a bow. —*adj.* **24.** of, pertaining to, or noting honor. Also, *esp. Brit.,* **honour.** [1150–1200; (n.) ME (*h*)*on*(*o*)*ur* < AF (OF (*h*)*onor, onur*) < L *honōr-* (s. of *honor,* earlier *honōs*); (v.) ME < AF (*h*)*on*(*o*)*urer* < L *honōrāre,* deriv. of *honor*] —**hon′or•er,** *n.* —**hon′or•less,** *adj.*
—**Syn. 1.** probity, uprightness. HONOR, HONESTY, INTEGRITY, SINCERITY refer to the highest moral principles and the absence of deceit or fraud. HONOR denotes a fine sense of, and a strict conformity to, what is considered morally right or due: *a high sense of honor; on one's honor.* HONESTY denotes the presence of probity and particularly the absence of deceit or fraud, esp. in business dealings: *uncompromising honesty and trustworthiness.* INTEGRITY indicates a soundness of moral principle that no power or influence can impair: *a man of unquestioned integrity and dependability.* SINCERITY implies absence of dissimulation or deceit, and a strong adherence to truth: *His sincerity was evident in every word.* **3.** deference, homage; reverence, veneration. HONOR, CONSIDERATION, DISTINCTION refer to the regard in which one is held by others. HONOR suggests a combination of liking and respect: *His colleagues held him in great honor.* CONSIDERATION suggests honor because of proved worth: *a man worthy of the highest consideration.* DISTINCTION suggests particular honor because of qualities or accomplishments: *She achieved distinction as a violinist at an early age.* **5.** distinction. **16.** esteem, venerate. —**Ant. 1.** dishonor, dishonesty.

hon•or•a•ble (on′ər ə bəl), *adj.* **1.** in accordance with or characterized by principles of honor; upright: *They were all honorable men.* **2.** of high rank, dignity, or distinction; noble, illustrious, or distinguished. **3.** worthy of honor and high respect; estimable; creditable. **4.** bringing honor or credit; consistent with honor. **5.** (*cap.*) **a.** (used as a title of respect for certain ranking government officials.) **b.** *Brit.* (used as a title of courtesy for children of peers ranking below a marquis.) *Abbr.:* Hon. [1300–50; ME *hono*(*u*)*rable* < AF (MF *honorable*) < L *honōrābilis.* See HONOR, -ABLE] —**hon′or•a•ble•ness,** *n.* —**hon′or•a•bly,** *adv.*
—**Syn. 1.** honest, noble, just. —**Ant. 1.** ignoble.

hon′orable dis′charge, *Mil.* **1.** a discharge from military service of a person who has fulfilled obligations efficiently, honorably, and faithfully. **2.** a certificate of such a discharge.

hon′orable men′tion, a citation conferred on a contestant, exhibit, etc., having exceptional merit though not winning a top honor or prize. [1865–70]

hon′orable or′dinary, *Heraldry.* any of the ordinaries believed to be among those that are oldest or that were the source of the other ordinaries, as the chief, pale, fess, bend, chevron, cross, and saltire.

hon•or•and (on′ə rand′), *n.* the recipient of an honor, esp. an honorary university degree. [1945–50; < L *honōrandus,* ger. of *honōrāre* to HONOR]

hon•o•rar•i•um (on′ə râr′ē əm), *n., pl.* **-rar•i•ums, -rar•i•a** (-râr′ē ə). **1.** a payment in recognition of acts or professional services for which custom or propriety forbids a price to be set: *The mayor was given a modest honorarium for delivering a speech to our club.* **2.** a fee for services rendered by a professional person. [1650–60; < L *honōrārium* fee paid on taking office, n. use of neut. of *honōrārius* HONORARY]

hon•or•ar•y (on′ə rer′ē), *adj.* **1.** given for honor only, without the usual requirements, duties, privileges, emoluments, etc.: *The university presented the new governor with an honorary degree.* **2.** holding a title or position conferred for honor only: *an honorary president.* **3.** (of an obligation) depending on one's honor for fulfillment. **4.** conferring or commemorating honor or distinction. **5.** given, made, or serving as a token of honor: *an honorary gift.* [1605–15; < L *honōrārius* relating to honor. See HONOR, -ARY] —**hon•or•ar•i•ly** (on′ə râr′ə lē), *adv.*

hon′orary can′on, a priest attached to a cathedral but not entitled to receive a stipend or to vote in the chapter. Cf. **minor canon.**

hon•or-bound (on′ər bound′), *adj.* bound by or placed under the obligation of honor: *She felt honor-bound to defend her friend.*

hon′or bright′, *Informal.* upon my honor; really and truly: *I did sweep the floor, honor bright.* [1810–20]

hon′or camp′, a prison work camp operating on an honor system.

hon′or card′, honor (def. 11).

hon•or•ee (on′ə rē′), *n.* a person who receives an honor, award, or special recognition. [HONOR + -EE]

hon′or guard′. See **guard of honor.** [1920–25]

hon•or•if•ic (on′ə rif′ik), *adj.* **1.** Also, **hon′or•if′i•cal.** doing or conferring honor. **2.** conveying honor, as a title or a grammatical form used in speaking to or about a superior, elder, etc. —*n.* **3.** (in certain languages, as Chinese and Japanese) a class of forms used to show respect, esp. in direct address. **4.** a title or term of respect. [1640–50; < L *honōrificus* honor-making. See HONOR-, -I-, -FIC] —**hon′or•if′i•cal•ly,** *adv.*

ho•no•ris cau•sa (ō nō′ris kou′sä; *Eng.* o nôr′is kô′zə, o nōr′-), *Latin.* as a sign of respect (usually describing an honorary college or university degree). [lit., for the sake of honor]

Ho•no•ri•us (hō nôr′ē əs, -nōr′-), *n.* **Fla•vi•us** (flā′vē-əs), A.D. 384–423, Roman emperor of the West 395–423.

Honorius I, died A.D. 638, Italian ecclesiastic: pope 625–638.

Honorius II, (*Lamberto Scannabecchi*) died 1130, Italian ecclesiastic: pope 1124–30.

Honorius III, (*Cencio Savelli*) died 1227, Italian ecclesiastic: pope 1216–27.

Honorius IV, (*Giacomo Savelli*) 1210–87, Italian ecclesiastic: pope 1285–87.

hon′or point′, *Heraldry.* a point midway between the heart point and top of an escutcheon. Also called **collar point, color point.** [1600–10]

hon′or roll′, **1.** a list of students who have earned grades above a specific average during a semester or school year. Cf. **dean's list. 2.** a list of names, usually on a plaque in a public place, of local citizens who have served or died in the armed services. [1905–10]

hon′ors course′, a course in a university or college consisting largely of independent research terminating in a dissertation or a comprehensive examination, and earning for the student who passes it a degree with distinction.

hon′or soci′ety, (in a college, university, or secondary school) a student society that admits members on the basis of academic merit and, sometimes, worthwhile contributions in extracurricular activities. [1925–30]

hon′ors of war′, privileges granted to a surrendering force, as of marching out of their camp or entrenchments with all their arms and with their colors flying. [1805–15]

hon′or sys′tem, a system whereby the students at a school, the inmates in a prison, etc., are put on their honor to observe certain rules in order to minimize administrative supervision or to promote honesty. [1900–05, *Amer.*]

hon′or trick′, *Bridge.* (in certain bidding systems) a high card or set of high cards that can reasonably be expected to take a trick, the total worth of such cards in a hand being the basis for evaluating its strength and bidding. [1930–35]

hon•our (on′ər), *n., v.t., adj. Chiefly Brit.* honor.
—**Usage.** See **-or**[1].

Hon•shu (hon′sho͞o; *Japn.* hôn′sho͞o), *n.* an island in central Japan: chief island of the country. 95,580,000; 88,851 sq. mi. (230,124 sq. km). Also called **Hondo.**

hooch[1] (ho͞och), *n. Slang.* **1.** alcoholic liquor. **2.** liquor illicitly distilled and distributed. Also, **hootch.** [1895–1900; shortening of HOOCHINOO]

hooch[2] (ho͞och), *n. Mil. Slang.* **1.** a thatched hut of southeast Asia. **2.** any living quarters, as a barracks. **3.** (esp. during the Korean War) **a.** a prostitute's dwelling. **b.** any place, as a house, room, or shack, where a serviceman sets up housekeeping with a local woman. Also, **hootch, hooch′ie.** [1950–55 prob. < Japn *uchi* house (by back formation, construing *-i* as -Y[2]); initial *h* perh. by assoc. with HUT or < Ryukyuan dial. form of *uchi* with prothetic *h*-]

Hooch (hōch; *Du.* hōKH), *n.* **Pie•ter de** (pē′tər də; *Du.* pē′təR də), 1629?–88?, Dutch painter. Also, **Hoogh.**

hoo•chi•noo (ho͞o′chə no͞o′, ho͞o′chə no͞o′), *n., pl.* **-noos.** a type of distilled liquor made by Alaskan Indians. Also, **hootchinoo.** [1875–80, *Amer.*; orig. the name of a Tlingit village on Admiralty Island, Alaska, reputed to be a source of illicit liquor; alter. of Tlingit *xucnu·wú* lit., brown bear's fort (*xú·c* brown bear + *nu·w* fortified place)]

hood[1] (ho͝od), *n.* **1.** a soft or flexible covering for the head and neck, either separate or attached to a cloak, coat, or the like. **2.** something resembling or suggesting such a covering, esp. in shape, as certain petals or sepals. **3.** the hinged, movable part of an automobile body covering the engine. **4.** *Brit.* the roof of a carriage. **5.** a metal cover or canopy for a stove, ventilator, etc. **6.** *Falconry.* a cover for the entire head of a hawk, used when the bird is not in pursuit of game. **7.** an ornamental ruffle or fold on the back of the shoulders of an academic gown, jurist's robe, etc. **8.** a crest or band of color on the head of certain birds and animals. —*v.t.* **9.** to furnish with a hood. **10.** to cover with or as if with a hood. [bef. 900; 1925–30, *Amer.* for def. 3; ME *hode,* OE *hōd;* c. OFris *hōde,* D *hoed,* G *Hut* HAT] —**hood′less,** *adj.* —**hood′like′,** *adj.*

hood[2] (ho͝od, ho͞od), *n. Slang.* a hoodlum. [1925–30; by shortening]

′hood (ho͝od), *n. Slang.* neighborhood. [1985–90; by shortening]

Hood (ho͝od), *n.* **1. John Bell,** 1831–79, Confederate general in the U.S. Civil War. **2. Raymond Math•ew•son** (math′yo͞o sən), 1881–1934, U.S. architect. **3. Robin.** See **Robin Hood. 4. Thomas,** 1799–1845, English poet and humorist. **5. Mount,** a volcanic peak in N Oregon, in the Cascade Range. 11,253 ft. (3430 m).

-hood, a native English suffix denoting state, condition, character, nature, etc., or a body of persons of a particular character or class, formerly used in the formation of nouns: *childhood; likelihood; knighthood; priesthood.* [ME *-hode, -hod,* OE *-hād* (c. G *-heit*), special use of *hād* condition, state, order, quality, rank]

hood•ed (ho͝od′id), *adj.* **1.** having, or covered with, a hood: *a hooded jacket.* **2.** hood-shaped. **3.** *Zool.* having on the head a hoodlike formation, crest, arrangement of colors, or the like. **4.** *Bot.* cucullate. [1400–50; late ME *hodid.* See HOOD[1], -ED[3]] —**hood′ed•ness,** *n.*

hood′ed crow′, a European crow, *Corvus corone cornix,* having a gray body and black head, wings, and tail. [1490–1500]

hood′ed seal′, a large seal, *Cystophora cristata,* the male of which has a large, distensible, hoodlike sac on the head. Also called **bladdernose.** [1860–65]

hood′ed top′, *Eng. Furniture.* a top to a secretary, chest, etc., following in outline a single- or double-curved pediment on the front of the piece. Cf. **bonnet top, dome top.**

hood′ed war′bler, a wood warbler, *Wilsonia citrina,* of the U.S., olive-green above, yellow below, and having a black head and throat with a yellow face. [1835–45]

hood•ie (ho͝od′ē; *Scot.* ho͞o′dē), *n. Scot.* the hooded crow. Also called **hood′ie crow′.** [1780–90; HOOD[1] + -IE]

hood•lum (ho͞od′ləm, ho͝od′-), *n.* **1.** a thug or gangster. **2.** a young street ruffian, esp. one belonging to a gang. [1870–75, *Amer.*; prob. < dial. G; cf. Swabian derivatives of *Hudel* rag, e.g. *hudelum* disorderly, *hudellam* weak, slack *Hudellump*(*e*) rags, slovenly, careless person, and related words in other dialects] —**hood′lum•ish,** *adj.* —**hood′lum•ism,** *n.*

hood•man-blind (ho͝od′mən blīnd′), *n. Archaic.* See **blindman's buff.** [1555–65]

hood′ mold′ing, a molding or dripstone over a door or window. Also, **hood′ mold′.** [1835–45]

hoo•doo (ho͞o′do͞o), *n., pl.* **-doos,** *v.,* **-dooed, -doo•ing.** —*n.* **1.** voodoo. **2.** bad luck. **3.** a person or thing that brings bad luck. **4.** *Geol.* a pillar of rock, usually of fantastic shape, left by erosion. —*v.t.* **5.** to bring or cause bad luck to. [1870–75, *Amer.*; appar. var of VOODOO]

hoo•doo•ism (ho͞o′do͞o iz′əm), *n.* the practice of or belief in voodoo. [1880–85, *Amer.*; HOODOO + -ISM]

hood•wink (ho͝od′wingk′), *v.t.* **1.** to deceive or trick. **2.** *Archaic.* to blindfold. **3.** *Obs.* to cover or hide. [1555–65; HOOD[1] + WINK] —**hood′wink′a•ble,** *adj.* —**hood′•wink′er,** *n.*
—**Syn. 1.** dupe, cheat, swindle, gyp.

hoo•ey (ho͞o′ē), *Informal.* —*interj.* **1.** (used to express disapproval or disbelief): *Hooey! You know that's not true.* —*n.* **2.** silly or worthless talk, writing, ideas, etc.; nonsense; bunk: *That's a lot of hooey and you know it!* [1920–25, *Amer.*; orig. uncert.]

hoof (ho͝of, ho͞of), *n., pl.* **hoofs** or **hooves** for 1, 2, 4; **hoof** for 3, 5; *v.* —*n.* **1.** the horny covering protecting the ends of the digits or encasing the foot in certain animals, as the ox and horse. See diag. under **horse. 2.** the entire foot of a horse, donkey, etc. **3.** *Older Use.* a hoofed animal, esp. one of a herd. **4.** *Informal.* the human foot. **5. on the hoof,** (of livestock) not butchered; live: *The city youngsters were seeing lambs on the hoof for the first time.* —*v.t.* **6.** *Slang.* to walk (often fol. by *it*): *Let's hoof it to the supermarket.* —*v.i.* **7.** *Slang.* to dance, esp. to tap-dance: *He's been hoofing at the Palladium.* [bef. 1000; ME (n.); OE *hōf;* c. OFris *hōf,* D *hoef,* G *Huf,* ON *hōfr;* cf. Skt *śaphas*] —**hoof′i•ness,** *n.* —**hoof′less,** *adj.* —**hoof′like′,** *adj.*

hoof′-and-mouth′ disease′ (ho͝of′ən mouth′, ho͞of′-). See **foot-and-mouth disease.** [1880–85, *Amer.*]

hoof•beat (ho͝of′bēt′, ho͞of′-), *n.* the sound made by an animal's hoof in walking, running, etc. [1840–50; HOOF + BEAT]

hoof•bound (ho͝of′bound′, ho͞of′-), *adj.* (of horses and other hoofed animals) having the heels of the hoofs dry and contracted, causing lameness. [1590–1600; HOOF + -BOUND[1]]

hoofed (ho͝oft, ho͞oft), *adj.* having hoofs; ungulate. [1505–15; HOOF + -ED[3]]

hoof•er (ho͝of′ər, ho͞o′fər), *n. Slang.* a professional dancer, esp. a tap dancer. [1920–25, *Amer.*; HOOF + -ER[1]]

hoof′ foot′, *Furniture.* pied-de-biche.

hoof•print (ho͝of′print′, ho͞of′-), *n.* the impression made by an animal's hoof. [1795–1805; HOOF + PRINT]

Hoogh (*Du.* hōKH), *n.* **Pie•ter de** (*Du.* pē′tər də). See **Hooch, Pieter de.**

Hoogh•ly (ho͞og′lē), *n.* a river in NE India, in W Bengal: the westernmost channel by which the Ganges enters the Bay of Bengal. 120 mi. (195 km) long. Also, **Hugli.**

hoo-ha (*n.* ho͞o′hä′; *interj.* ho͞o′hä′), *Informal.* —*n.* **1.** an uproarious commotion. —*interj.* **2.** (used to express mock surprise or excitement.) Also, **hoo′-hah′.** [1930–

35; prob. < Yiddish *hu-ha* to-do, uproar, exclamation of surprise; cf. Pol *hu-ha* exclamation of joy]

hook[1] (ho͝ok), *n.* **1.** a curved or angular piece of metal or other hard substance for catching, pulling, holding, or suspending something. **2.** a fishhook. **3.** anything that catches; snare; trap. **4.** something that attracts attention or serves as an enticement: *The product is good but we need a sales hook to get people to buy it.* **5.** something having a sharp curve, bend, or angle at one end, as a mark or symbol. **6.** a sharp curve or angle in the length or course of anything. **7.** a curved arm of land jutting into the water; a curved peninsula: *Sandy Hook.* **8.** a recurved and pointed organ or appendage of an animal or plant. **9.** a small curved catch inserted into a loop to form a clothes fastener. **10.** *Sports.* **a.** the path described by a ball, as in baseball, bowling, or golf, that curves in a direction opposite to the throwing hand or to the side of the ball from which it was struck. **b.** a ball describing such a path. **11.** *Boxing.* a short, circular punch delivered with the elbow bent. **12.** *Music.* **a.** Also called **pennant.** a stroke or line attached to the stem of eighth notes, sixteenth notes, etc. **b.** an appealing melodic phrase, orchestral ornament, refrain, etc., often important to a popular song's commercial success. **13.** *Metalworking.* an accidental short bend formed in a piece of bar stock during rolling. **14. hooks,** *Slang.* hands or fingers: *Get your hooks off that cake!* **15.** *Underworld Jargon.* a pickpocket. **16.** Also called **deck hook.** *Naut.* a triangular plate or knee that binds together the stringers and plating at each end of a vessel. **17. by hook or by crook,** by any means, whether just or unjust, legal or illegal. Also, **by hook or crook. 18. get** or **give the hook,** *Informal.* to receive or subject to a dismissal: *The rumor is that he got the hook.* **19. hook, line, and sinker,** *Informal.* entirely; completely: *He fell for the story—hook, line, and sinker.* **20. off the hook, a.** out of trouble; released from some difficulty: *This time there was no one around to get him off the hook.* **b.** free of obligation: *His brother paid all his bills and got him off the hook.* **21. on one's own hook,** *Informal.* on one's own initiative or responsibility; independently. **22. on the hook,** *Slang.* **a.** obliged; committed; involved: *He's already on the hook for $10,000.* **b.** subjected to a delaying tactic; waiting: *We've had him on the hook for two weeks now.* —*v.t.* **23.** to seize, fasten, suspend from, pierce, or catch hold of and draw with or as if with a hook. **24.** to catch (fish) with a fishhook. **25.** *Slang.* to steal or seize by stealth. **26.** *Informal.* to catch or trick by artifice; snare. **27.** (of a bull or other horned animal) to catch on the horns or attack with the horns. **28.** to catch hold of and draw (loops of yarn) through cloth with or as if with a hook. **29.** to make (a rug, garment, etc.) in this fashion. **30.** *Sports.* to hit or throw (a ball) so that a hook results. **31.** *Boxing.* to deliver a hook with: *The champion hooked a right to his opponent's jaw.* **32.** *Rugby.* to push (a ball) backward with the foot in scrummage from the front line. **33.** to make hook-shaped; crook. —*v.i.* **34.** to become attached or fastened by or as if by a hook. **35.** to curve or bend like a hook. **36.** *Sports.* **a.** (of a player) to hook the ball. **b.** (of a ball) to describe a hook in course. **37.** *Slang.* to depart hastily: *We'd better hook for home.* **38. hook it,** *Slang.* to run away; depart; flee: *He hooked it when he saw the truant officer.* **39. hook up, a.** to fasten with a hook or hooks. **b.** to assemble or connect, as the components of a machine: *to hook up a stereo system.* **c.** to connect to a central source, as of power or water: *The house hasn't been hooked up to the city's water system yet.* **d.** *Informal.* to join or become associated with: *He never had a decent job until he hooked up with this company.* [bef. 900; 1830–40, *Amer.* for def. 19; ME *hoke* (n. and v.), OE *hōc* (n.); c. D *hoek* hook, angle, corner; akin to G *Haken,* ON *haki*] —**hook′less,** *adj.* —**hook′like′,** *adj.*

hook[2] (ho͝ok), *v.i. Slang.* to work as a prostitute. [back formation from HOOKER[1]]

hook·ah (ho͝ok′ə), *n.* a tobacco pipe of Near Eastern origin with a long, flexible tube by which the smoke is drawn through a jar of water and thus cooled. Also, **hook′a.** Also called **narghile.** [1755–65; < Ar *ḥuqqah* box, vase, pipe for smoking]

hookah

hook′ and eye′, 1. a two-piece clothes fastener, usually of metal, consisting of a hook that catches onto a loop or bar. **2.** a three-piece latching device consisting of a hook attached to a screw eye or an eyebolt and a separate screw eye or eyebolt that the hook engages as it bridges a gap, as one between a door and a jamb or a gate and a gatepost. **3.** Also called **eyehook.** the two-piece portion of such a device consisting of a hook and a screw eye. [1620–30]

hook′ and lad′der, a fire engine, usually a tractor-trailer, fitted with long, extensible ladders and other equipment. Also called **hook′-and-lad′der truck′, ladder truck.** [1825–35, *Amer.*]

hook′-and-lad′der com′pany (ho͝ok′ən lad′ər), a company of firefighters equipped with a hook-and-ladder truck. Also called **ladder company.** [1815–25, *Amer.*]

hook′ bolt′, a bolt bent in a hooklike form at one end and threaded for a nut at the other. [1920–25]

hook′ check′, *Ice Hockey.* a maneuver for depriving an opponent of the puck by seizing it in the crook of one's stick. Cf. **check**[1] (def. 42). [1935–40]

Hooke (ho͝ok), *n.* **Robert,** 1635–1703, English philosopher, microscopist, and physicist.

hooked (ho͝okt), *adj.* **1.** bent like a hook; hook-shaped. **2.** having a hook or hooks. **3.** made with a hook or by hooking. **4.** *Informal.* **a.** addicted to narcotic drugs. **b.** slavishly interested in, devoted to, or obsessed with: *He was hooked on television.* **5.** *Slang.* married. [bef. 1000; ME *hoked,* OE *hōcede.* See HOOK[1], -ED[2], -ED[3]] —**hook·ed·ness** (ho͝ok′id nis), *n.*

hooked′ rug′, a rug made by drawing loops of yarn or cloth through a foundation of burlap or the like, to form a pattern. [1875–80, *Amer.*]

hook·er[1] (ho͝ok′ər), *n.* **1.** a person or thing that hooks. **2.** *Slang.* prostitute. **3.** *Slang.* a large drink of liquor. **4.** *Slang.* a concealed problem, flaw, or drawback; a catch. **5.** *Rugby.* a player who hooks the ball in the front line of scrummage. **6.** (*cap.*) *Offensive.* an Amish Mennonite. [1560–70; 1835–45, *Amer.* for def. 2; HOOK[1] + -ER[1]]

hook·er[2] (ho͝ok′ər), *n. Naut.* **1.** *Slang.* any old-fashioned or clumsy vessel. **2.** any fishing vessel working with hooks and lines rather than nets. [1635–45; < D *hoeker,* equiv. to *hoek* HOOK[1] + *-er* -ER[1]]

Hook·er (ho͝ok′ər), *n.* **1. Joseph,** 1814–79, Union general in the U.S. Civil War. **2. Richard,** 1554?–1600, English author and clergyman. **3. Thomas,** 1586?–1647, English Puritan clergyman: one of the founders of the colony of Connecticut.

Hook′er's green′, 1. a medium green to strong yellowish green. **2.** a nonpermanent pigment consisting of Prussian blue mixed with gamboge, characterized chiefly by its green color. [1850–55; named after W. *Hooker* (d. 1832), English illustrator]

Hooke's′ law′, *Physics.* the law stating that the stress on a solid substance is directly proportional to the strain produced, provided the stress is less than the elastic limit of the substance. [1850–55; named after R. HOOKE who formulated it]

hook·ey (ho͝ok′ē), *n.* hooky[1].

hook·nose (ho͝ok′nōz′), *n.* a curved nose; aquiline nose. [1680–90; HOOK[1] + NOSE] —**hook′nosed′,** *adj.*

Hook′ of Hol′land, a cape and the harbor it forms in the SW Netherlands. Dutch, **Hoek van Holland.** [1785–95]

Hooks (ho͝oks), *n.* **Benjamin Lawson,** born 1925, U.S. lawyer, clergyman, and civil-rights advocate: executive director of the NAACP since 1977–93.

hook′ shot′, *Basketball.* a shot with one hand in which a player extends the shooting arm to the side and brings it back over the head toward the basket while releasing the ball. [1940–45]

hook·swing·ing (ho͝ok′swing′ing), *n.* a ritualistic torture, practiced among the Mandan Indians, in which a voluntary victim was suspended from hooks attached to the flesh of the back. [1890–95; HOOK[1] + SWING[1] + -ING[1]]

hook·tend·er (ho͝ok′ten′dər), *n.* (in lumbering) the supervisor of a rigging crew. [1905–10; HOOK[1] + TENDER[3]]

hook·up (ho͝ok′up′), *n.* **1.** an act or instance of hooking up. **2.** an assembly and connection of parts, components, or apparatus into a circuit, network, machine, or system. **3.** the circuit, network, machine, or system so formed. **4.** a device or connection, as a plug, hose, or pipe, for conveying electricity, a water supply, etc., from a source to a user: *Some campsites have electrical hookups for trailers.* **5.** *Informal.* an association, alliance, or cooperative effort: *A closer hookup of Caribbean nations would be good for international trade.* [1900–05, *Amer.*; n. use of v. phrase *hook up*]

hook·worm (ho͝ok′wûrm′), *n.* **1.** any of certain blood-sucking nematode worms, as *Ancylostoma duodenale* and *Necator americanus,* parasitic in the intestine of humans and other animals. **2.** Also called **hook′worm disease′.** a disease caused by hookworms, which may enter the body by ingestion or through the skin of the feet or legs, causing abdominal pain, nausea, and, if untreated, severe anemia. [1900–05; HOOK[1] + WORM] —**hook′worm′y,** *adj.*

hook·y[1] (ho͝ok′ē), *n.* unjustifiable absence from school, work, etc. (usually used in the phrase *play hooky*): *On the first warm spring day the boys played hooky to go fishing.* Also, **hookey.** [1840–50, *Amer.*; perh. alter. of phrase *hook it* escape, make off]

hook·y[2] (ho͝ok′ē), *adj.,* **hook·i·er, hook·i·est. 1.** full of hooks. **2.** hook-shaped. [1545–55; HOOK[1] + -Y[1]]

hoo·li·gan (ho͞o′li gən), *n.* **1.** a ruffian or hoodlum. —*adj.* **2.** of or like hooligans. [1895–1900; perh. after the Irish surname *Hooligan,* but corroborating evidence is lacking] —**hoo′li·gan·ism,** *n.*

hoo·ly (ho͞o′lē, hy′lē), *Scot.* —*adj.* **1.** cautious; gentle. —*adv.* **2.** cautiously; gently. Also, **huly.** [1300–50; ME *holy,* appar. < Scand; cf. ON *hōfligr* moderate]

hoop (ho͞op, ho͝op), *n.* **1.** a circular band or ring of metal, wood, or other stiff material. **2.** such a band for holding together the staves of a cask, tub, etc. **3.** a large ring of iron, wood, plastic, etc., used as a plaything for a child to roll along the ground. **4.** a circular or ringlike object, part, figure, etc. **5.** the shank of a finger ring. **6.** *Croquet.* a wicket. **7.** a circular band of stiff material used to expand and display a woman's skirt. **8.** See **hoop skirt. 9.** *Basketball Informal.* **a.** the metal ring from which the net is suspended; rim. **b.** the metal ring and net taken together; the basket. **c.** the game of basketball. **10.** a decorative band, as around a mug or cup. **11.** See **hoop iron.** —*v.t.* **12.** to bind or fasten with or as if with a hoop or hoops. **13.** to encircle; surround. [1125–75; ME *hope, hoop,* late OE *hōp;* c. D *hoep*] —**hoop′less,** *adj.* —**hoop′like′,** *adj.*

hoop′ back′, *Furniture.* **1.** a chair back having the uprights and crest rail in a continuous arched form. **2.** See **bow back.** [1900–05]

hoop-de-do (ho͞op′dē do͞o′, -do͞o′, ho͝op′-), *n. Informal.* whoop-de-do.

hoop·er (ho͞o′pər, ho͝op′ər), *n.* a person who makes or puts hoops on barrels, tubs, etc.; a cooper. [1375–1425; late ME. See HOOP, -ER[1]]

hoop′ i′ron, iron in the form of thin strips for bonding masonry, holding barrels together, etc. [1810–20]

hoop·la (ho͞op′lä), *n. Informal.* **1.** bustling excitement or activity; commotion; hullabaloo; to-do. **2.** sensational publicity; ballyhoo. **3.** speech or writing intended to mislead or to obscure an issue. [1865–70; < F *houp-là!* command (as to a child) to move, take a step]

hoop·man (ho͞op′mən, ho͝op′-), *n., pl.* **-men.** *Sports Slang.* a basketball player. [1680–90 for sense "acrobat"; HOOP + -MAN]

hoo·poe (ho͞o′po͞o), *n.* any Old World bird of the family Upupidae, esp. *Upupa epops,* of Europe, having an erectile, fanlike crest. [1660–70; var. of obs. *hoopoop* (imit.); c. LG *huppup;* cf. L *upupa*]

hoopoe, *Upupa epops,* length 11 in. (28 cm)

hoop′-pet·ti·coat narcis′sus (ho͞op′pet′ē kōt′, ho͝op′-). See **petticoat narcissus.** [1885–90]

hoop′ pine′. See **Moreton Bay pine.** [1880–85]

hoop′ skirt′, 1. a woman's skirt made to stand out and drape in a stiff bell-like shape from the waist by an undergarment framework of flexible hoops connected by tapes. **2.** the framework for such a skirt. Also called **hoop.** [1855–60, *Amer.*]

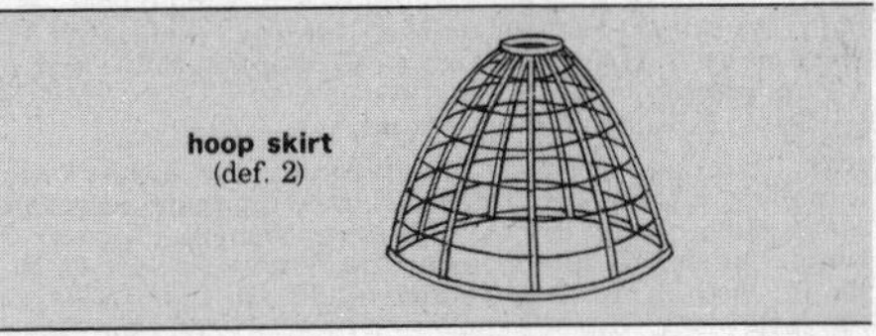
hoop skirt (def. 2)

hoop′ snake′, any of several harmless snakes, as the mud snake and rainbow snake, fabled to take its tail in its mouth and roll along like a hoop. [1775–85, *Amer.*]

hoop·ster (ho͞op′stər, ho͝op′-), *n. Sports Slang.* a basketball player. [HOOP + -STER]

hoo·ray (ho͝o rā′), *interj., v.i., n.* hurrah. Also, **hoo·rah** (ho͝o rä′).

hoose·gow (ho͞os′gou), *n. Slang.* a jail. Also, **hoos′·gow.** [1860–65, *Amer.*; < MexSp *jusgado* jail (Sp: court of justice, orig. ptp. of *juzgar* to judge) < L *jūdicātum,* equiv. to *jūdic-* (s. of *jūdex*) JUDGE + *-ātum* -ATE[1]]

Hoo·sier (ho͞o′zhər), *n.* **1.** a native or inhabitant of Indiana (used as a nickname). **2.** (*usually l.c.*) any awkward, unsophisticated person, esp. a rustic. [1920–30, *Amer;* of uncert. orig.] —**Hoo′sier·dom,** *n.*

Hoo′sier cab′inet, a tall kitchen cabinet mass-produced during the early part of the 20th century, usually of oak, featuring an enameled work surface, storage bins, a flour sifter, etc.

Hoo′sier State′, Indiana (used as a nickname).

hoot[1] (ho͞ot), *v.i.* **1.** to cry out or shout, esp. in disapproval or derision. **2.** to utter the cry characteristic of an owl. **3.** to utter a similar sound. **4.** *Chiefly Brit.* to blow a horn or whistle; toot. —*v.t.* **5.** to assail with shouts of disapproval or derision: *The fans hooted the umpire.* **6.** to drive out, off, or away by hooting. **7.** to express in hoots: *The crowd hooted its disagreement with the speaker.* —*n.* **8.** the cry of an owl. **9.** any similar sound, as an inarticulate shout. **10.** a cry or shout, esp. of disapproval or derision. **11.** *Brit.* a horn, siren, or whistle, esp. a factory whistle. **12.** *Informal.* the least bit of concern, interest, or thought; trifle: *I don't give a hoot.* **13.** *Slang.* an extremely funny person, situation, or event: *Your mother's a hoot when she tells about her escapades in boarding school.* [1150–1200; ME *hoten, huten, houten* (v.); perh. imit.] —**hoot′ing·ly,** *adv.* —**Syn. 1, 5.** jeer, boo, hiss. **5.** razz.

hoot[2] (ho͞ot), *interj. Scot. and North Eng.* (used as an expression of impatience, dissatisfaction, objection, or dislike.) [1675–85; cf. Sw *hut,* Welsh *hwt,* Ir *ut* begone!]

hootch (ho͞och), *n.* hooch.

hoot·chi·noo (ho͞o′chə no͞o′, ho͞o′chə no͞o′), *n., pl.* **-noos.** hoochinoo.

hootch·y-kootch·y (ho͞o′chē ko͞o′chē), *n., pl.* **-kootch·ies.** cooch. Also, **hoot′chie-koot′chie, hoot′chy-kootch′.** [1895–1900; orig. uncert.]

CONCISE PRONUNCIATION KEY: act, cāpe, dâre, pärt; set, ēqual; if, ice; ox, ōver, ôrder, oil, bo͝ok, bo͞ot, out; up, ûrge; child; sing; shoe; thin, *th*at; zh as in *treasure.* ə = *a* as in *alone, e* as in *system, i* as in *easily, o* as in *gallop, u* as in *circus;* ə as in *fire* (fīər), *hour* (ouər). l and n can serve as syllabic consonants, as in *cradle* (krād′l), and *button* (but′n). See the full key inside the front cover.

hoot•en•an•ny (ho͞ot′n an′ē, ho͞ot′nan′-), *n., pl.* **-nies.** **1.** a social gathering or informal concert featuring folk singing and, sometimes, dancing. **2.** an informal session at which folk singers and instrumentalists perform for their own enjoyment. **3.** *Older Use.* a thingumbob. [1910–15; orig. uncert.]

hoot•er (ho͞o′tər), *n.* **1.** a person or thing that hoots. **2.** *Brit.* a car horn. **3.** *Brit. Slang.* the nose. [1665–75; HOOT[1] + -ER[1]]

Hoo•ton (ho͞ot′n), *n.* **Ear•nest Albert** (ûr′nist), 1887–1954, U.S. anthropologist and writer.

hoot′ owl′, any of various owls that hoot. [1880–85, *Amer.*]

hoo•ver (ho͞o′vər), *v.t.* (*often cap.*) *Chiefly Brit.* to clean with a vacuum cleaner. [1925–30; after the trademark of a vacuum cleaner manufacturer]

Hoo•ver (ho͞o′vər), *n.* **1. Herbert (Clark),** 1874–1964, 31st president of the U.S. 1929–33. **2. J(ohn) Edgar,** 1895–1972, U.S. government official: director of the FBI 1924–72. **3.** a town in N central Alabama. 15,064.

hoo′ver a′pron (ho͞o′vər), a dresslike coverall for women that ties at the waist. [1945–50, *Amer.*; named after H. HOOVER, so called from its popularity during his term as food administrator]

Hoo′ver Dam′, official name of **Boulder Dam.**

Hoo•ver•ville (ho͞o′vər vil′), *n.* a collection of huts and shacks, as at the edge of a city, housing the unemployed during the 1930's. [H. HOOVER + *-ville,* suffix in place names (< F: city < L; see VILLA)]

hooves (ho͝ovz, ho͞ovz), *n.* a pl. of **hoof.**

hop[1] (hop), *v.,* **hopped, hop•ping,** *n.* —*v.i.* **1.** to make a short, bouncing leap; move by leaping with all feet off the ground. **2.** to spring or leap on one foot. **3.** *Informal.* to make a short, quick trip, esp. in an airplane: *He hopped up to Boston for the day.* **4.** *Informal.* to travel or move frequently from one place or situation to another (usually used in combination): *to island-hop; to job-hop.* **5.** *Informal.* to dance. —*v.t.* **6.** to jump over; clear with a hop: *The sheep hopped the fence.* **7.** *Informal.* to board or get onto a vehicle: *to hop a plane.* **8.** *Informal.* to cross in an airplane: *We hopped the Atlantic in five hours.* **9. hop to it,** *Informal.* to begin to move, become active, or do something immediately: *You'd better hop to it if you intend to buy groceries before the market closes.* Also, **hop to.** —*n.* **10.** an act of hopping; short leap. **11.** a leap on one foot. **12.** a journey, esp. a short trip by air. **13.** *Informal.* a dance or dancing party. **14.** a bounce or rebound of a moving object, as a ball: *She caught the ball on the first hop.* [bef. 1000; ME *hoppen* (v.), OE *hoppian;* c. G *hopfen,* ON *hoppa*] —**hop′ping•ly,** *adv.*
—**Syn. 1.** jump, spring, bound.

hop[2] (hop), *n., v.,* **hopped, hop•ping.** —*n.* **1.** any twining plant of the genus *Humulus,* bearing male flowers in loose clusters and female flowers in conelike forms. **2. hops,** the dried ripe cones of the female flowers of this plant, used in brewing, medicine, etc. **3.** *Older Slang.* a narcotic drug, esp. opium. —*v.t.* **4.** to treat or flavor with hops. **5. hop up,** *Slang.* **a.** to excite; make enthusiastic: *They hopped the crowd up with fiery speeches.* **b.** to add to the power of: *The kids hopped up the motor of their jalopy.* **c.** to stimulate by narcotics. [1400–50; late ME *hoppe* < MD *hoppe* (D *hop*); c. OHG *hopfo* (G *Hopfen*)]

ho•pak (hō′pak), *n.* gopak.

Ho•pat•cong (hə pat′kông, -kong), *n.* a town in N New Jersey. 15,531.

hop′ clo′ver, a trefoil, *Trifolium campestre,* having withered, yellow flowers that resemble the strobiles of a hop. [1670–80]

hope (hōp), *n., v.,* **hoped, hop•ing.** —*n.* **1.** the feeling that what is wanted can be had or that events will turn out for the best: *to give up hope.* **2.** a particular instance of this feeling: *the hope of winning.* **3.** grounds for this feeling in a particular instance: *There is little or no hope of his recovery.* **4.** a person or thing in which expectations are centered: *The medicine was her last hope.* **5.** something that is hoped for: *Her forgiveness is my constant hope.* —*v.t.* **6.** to look forward to with desire and reasonable confidence. **7.** to believe, desire, or trust: *I hope that my work will be satisfactory.* —*v.i.* **8.** to feel that something desired may happen: *We hope for an early spring.* **9.** *Archaic.* to place trust; rely (usually fol. by *in*). **10. hope against hope,** to continue to hope, although the outlook does not warrant it: *We are hoping against hope for a change in her condition.* [bef. 900; (n.) ME; OE *hopa;* c. D *hoop,* G *Hoffe;* (v.) ME *hopen,* OE *hopian*] —**hop′er,** *n.* —**hop′ing•ly,** *adv.*
—**Syn. 1.** expectancy, longing. **8.** See **expect.**

Hope (hōp), *n.* **1. Anthony,** pen name of Sir Anthony Hope Hawkins. **2. Bob** (*Leslie Townes Hope*), born 1903, U.S. comedian, born in England. **3. John,** 1868–1936, U.S. educator. **4.** a town in SW Arkansas. 10,290. **5.** a female given name.

hope′ chest′, (esp. formerly) a chest or the like in which a young woman collected clothing, linens, and other articles in anticipation of marriage. [1910–15]

Hope′ dia′mond, a sapphire-blue Indian diamond, the largest blue diamond in the world, weighing 44.5 carats and supposedly cut from a bigger diamond that was once part of the French crown jewels: now in the Smithsonian Institution. [after Henry Philip *Hope* (d. 1839), English gem collector, who once owned it]

hope•ful (hōp′fəl), *adj.* **1.** full of hope; expressing hope: *His hopeful words stimulated optimism.* **2.** exciting hope; promising advantage or success: *a hopeful prospect.* —*n.* **3.** a person who shows promise or aspires to success: *the Democratic presidential hopeful.* [1560–70; HOPE + -FUL] —**hope′ful•ness,** *n.*
—**Syn. 1.** expectant; sanguine, optimistic, confident.

hope•ful•ly (hōp′fə lē), *adv.* **1.** in a hopeful manner: *We worked hopefully and energetically, thinking we might finish first.* **2.** it is hoped; if all goes well: *Hopefully, we will get to the show on time.* [1630–40; HOPEFUL + -LY]
—**Usage.** Although some strongly object to its use as a sentence modifier, HOPEFULLY meaning "it is hoped (that)" has been in use since the 1930's and is fully standard in all varieties of speech and writing: *Hopefully, tensions between the two nations will ease.* This use of HOPEFULLY is parallel to that of *certainly, curiously, frankly, regrettably,* and other sentence modifiers.

hope′ful mon′ster, *Biol.* a hypothetical individual organism that, by means of a fortuitous macromutation permitting an adaptive shift to a new mode of life, becomes the founder of a new type of organism and a vehicle of macroevolution. [1933; phrase introduced by German geneticist Richard B. Goldschmidt (1879–1958)]

Ho•peh (hō′pā′; *Chin.* hu′bā′), *n.* *Older Spelling.* Hebei. Also, *Wade-Giles,* **Ho′pei′.**

hope•less (hōp′lis), *adj.* **1.** providing no hope; beyond optimism or hope; desperate: *a hopeless case of cancer.* **2.** without hope; despairing: *hopeless grief.* **3.** impossible to accomplish, solve, resolve, etc.: *Balancing my budget is hopeless.* **4.** not able to learn or act, perform, or work as desired; inadequate for the purpose: *As a bridge player, you're hopeless.* [1560–70; HOPE + -LESS] —**hope′less•ly,** *adv.* —**hope′less•ness,** *n.*
—**Syn. 1.** irremediable, remediless, incurable. **2.** forlorn, disconsolate, dejected. HOPELESS, DESPAIRING, DESPONDENT, DESPERATE all describe an absence of hope. HOPELESS is used of a feeling of futility and passive abandonment of oneself to fate: *Hopeless and grim, he still clung to the cliff.* DESPAIRING refers to the loss of hope in regard to a particular situation, whether important or trivial; it suggests an intellectual judgment concerning probabilities: *despairing of victory; despairing of finding his gloves.* DESPONDENT always suggests melancholy and depression; it refers to an emotional state rather than to an intellectual judgment: *Despondent over ill health, he killed himself. She became despondent and suspicious.* DESPERATE conveys a suggestion of recklessness resulting from loss of hope: *As the time grew shorter, he became desperate.* It may also refer to something arising from extreme need or danger: *a desperate remedy; a desperate situation.* DESPAIRING and DESPONDENT may apply only to feelings.

Hope•well (hōp′wel, -wəl), *n.* a city in E Virginia, on the James River. 23,397.

Hope•well (hōp′wel, -wəl), *adj. Archaeol.* of or pertaining to an advanced mound-building and agricultural Amerindian culture 100 B.C.–A.D. 400, centered in Ohio and Illinois and characterized by geometric earthworks, many large conical or dome-shaped burial mounds, corded and stamped pottery, ornamental knives and tobacco pipes, and the extensive trading of raw materials and artifacts. Also, **Hope•well′i•an.** [after Cloud *Hopewell,* owner (ca. 1890) of a farm in Ross Co., Ohio, on which tumuli characterizing the culture were excavated]

hop•head (hop′hed′), *n. Older Slang.* a narcotics addict, esp. an opium addict. [1910–15; HOP[2] + HEAD]

hop′ horn′beam, any of several Eurasian and North American trees of the genus *Ostrya,* of the birch family, esp. *O. virginiana,* bearing hoplike fruiting clusters. [1775–85, *Amer.*]

Ho•pi (hō′pē), *n., pl.* **-pis,** (*esp. collectively*) **-pi** for 1. **1.** a member of a Pueblo Indian people of northern Arizona. **2.** a Uto-Aztecan language, the language of the Hopi Indians. [1875–80, *Amer.*; < Hopi *hópi* a Hopi person, lit., good, peaceable]

Hop•kins (hop′kinz), *n.* **1. Sir Frederick Gow•land** (gou′lənd), 1861–1947, English physician and biochemist: Nobel prize for medicine 1929. **2. Gerard Man•ley** (man′lē), 1844–89, English poet. **3. Harry Lloyd,** 1890–1946, U.S. government administrator and social worker. **4. Johns,** 1795–1873, U.S. financier and philanthropist. **5. Mark,** 1802–87, U.S. clergyman and educator. **6.** a city in SE Minnesota. 15,336.

Hop•kins•i•an•ism (hop kin′zē ə niz′əm), *n.* a modified Calvinism taught by Samuel Hopkins (1721–1803), that emphasized the sovereignty of God, the importance of His decrees, and the necessity of submitting to His will, accepting even damnation, if required, for His glory, and holding that ethics is merely disinterested benevolence. [1805–15, *Amer.*; *Hopkins* + -IAN + -ISM] —**Hop•kin′si•an, Hop•kin•so•ni•an** (hop′kin sō′nē ən), *adj., n.*

Hop•kin•son (hop′kin sən), *n.* **Francis,** 1737–91, American statesman and satirist.

Hop•kins•ville (hop′kinz vil′), *n.* a city in S Kentucky. 27,318.

Hop•les (hop′lēz), *n. Class. Myth.* a son of Ion.

hop•lite (hop′līt), *n.* a heavily armed foot soldier of ancient Greece. [1720–30; < Gk *hoplítēs,* equiv. to *hó-pl(on)* piece of armor, particularly the large shield + *-ītēs* -ITE[1]] —**hop•lit•ic** (hop lit′ik), *adj.*

hop-o'-my-thumb (hop′ə mī thum′), *n.* a very small person, as a midget or dwarf. [1520–30; n. use of impv. phrase *hop on my thumb*]

Hop•pe (hop′ē), *n.* **Willie (William Frederick),** 1887–1959, U.S. billiards player.

hopped-up (hopt′up′), *adj. Slang.* **1.** excited; enthusiastic; exuberant, esp. overexuberant. **2.** having an engine with added power: *a hopped-up jalopy.* **3.** stimulated by narcotics; drugged; doped. [1920–25]

hop•per (hop′ər), *n.* **1.** a person or thing that hops. **2.** *Informal.* a person who travels or moves frequently from one place or situation to another (usually used in combination): *a two-week tour designed for energetic city-hoppers.* **3.** any of various jumping insects, as grasshoppers or leafhoppers. **4.** *Australian.* kangaroo. **5.** a funnel-shaped chamber or bin in which loose material, as grain or coal, is stored temporarily, being filled through the top and dispensed through the bottom. **6.** *Railroads.* See **hopper car. 7.** *U.S. Politics.* a box into which a proposed legislative bill is dropped and thereby officially introduced. **8.** one of the pieces at each side of a hopper casement. **9. in the hopper,** *Informal.* in preparation; about to be realized: *Plans for the class reunion are in the hopper.* [1200–50; ME; see HOP[1], -ER[1]]

Hop•per (hop′ər), *n.* **1. Edward,** 1882–1967, U.S. painter and etcher. **2. Grace Murray,** 1906–92, U.S. naval officer and computer scientist. **3. (William) De Wolf** (də wo͝olf), 1858–1935, U.S. actor.

hop′per barge′, a barge for disposing of garbage, dredged material, etc., having hoppers in the bottom through which such cargo can be dumped. Also called **dump scow.** [1890–95]

hop′per car′, *Railroads.* a freight car, usually open at the top and containing one or more hoppers so that bulk cargo can be quickly discharged through its bottom. [1860–65, *Amer.*]

hop′per case′ment, a casement with a sash hinged at the bottom. Also called **hop′per light′, hop′per vent′, hop′per win′dow, hospital light, hospital window.** [1835–45]

hop′per dredge′, a self-propelled dredge having compartments in which the dredged material can be carried and dumped through hoppers. [1895–1900]

hop′per frame′, a window frame having one or more upper sashes hinged at the bottoms and opening inward.

hop•ping (hop′ing), *adj.* **1.** working energetically; busily engaged: *He kept the staff hopping in order to get the report finished.* **2.** going from one place or situation to another of a similar specified type (usually used in combination): *restaurant-hopping.* **3. hopping mad,** furious; enraged: *He was hopping mad when his daughter dropped out of college.* [1665–75; HOP[1] + -ING[2]]

hop′ping John′ (hop′in, -ing), (*sometimes l.c.*) *Southern U.S.* a dish of black-eyed peas, rice, bacon or ham, and red pepper or other seasoning: traditionally served on New Year's Day because of the superstition that black-eyed peas bring good luck for the New Year. [1830–40, *Amer.*]

hop•ple (hop′əl), *v.t.,* **-pled, -pling.** to hobble; tether. [1580–90; HOP[1] + -LE]

hop•sack•ing (hop′sak′ing), *n.* **1.** bagging made chiefly of hemp and jute. **2.** Also, **hop•sack** (hop′sak′). a coarse fabric made of cotton, wool, or other fibers and similar to burlap, used in the manufacture of wearing apparel. [1880–85; HOP[2] + SACKING]

hop•scotch (hop′skoch′), *n.* **1.** a children's game in which a player tosses or kicks a small flat stone, beanbag, or other object into one of several numbered sections of a diagram marked on the pavement or ground and then hops on one foot over the lines from section to section and picks up the stone or object, usually while standing on one foot in an adjacent section. —*v.i. Informal.* **2.** to jump or leap from one place to another: *Small birds hopscotched on the lawn.* **3.** to journey quickly and directly from one usually far place to another: *ambassadors hopscotching from Moscow to Paris to London.* **4.** to move or pass through something, as a geographical area or a field of endeavor, making many brief stops: *The candidate hopscotched through four states in two days.* **5.** to shift from one thing to another quickly or abruptly: *The story hopscotches from the present to the past in a confusing way.* —*v.t. Informal.* **6.** to jump or leap over. **7.** to cross over (a large area or distance) in one continuous action: *She hopscotches the country in her private plane.* **8.** to cross or travel through erratically or abruptly. [1795–1805; HOP[1] + SCOTCH[1]]

hop′, skip′, and a jump′, a short distance: *The laundry is just a hop, skip, and a jump away.* Also, **hop′, skip′, and jump′.** [1750–60]

hop′, step′, and jump′, *Track.* See **triple jump.** [1710–20]

hop•toad (hop′tōd′), *n. Chiefly Northeastern U.S.* a toad. [1820–30, *Amer.*; HOP[1] + TOAD]

hop•tree (hop′trē′), *n.* any of several North American shrubs or small trees belonging to the genus *Ptelea,* of the citrus family, esp. *P. trifoliata,* having trifoliate leaves and roundish, waferlike fruit. [1855–60, *Amer.*; HOP[2] + TREE]

hop•vine (hop′vīn′), *n.* **1.** the twining stem of the hop plant. **2.** the plant itself. [1700–10; HOP[2] + VINE]

hor., 1. horizon. **2.** horizontal. **3.** horology.

ho•ra (hôr′ə, hōr′ə), *n.* a traditional Rumanian and Israeli round dance. [1875–80; < ModHeb *hōrāh* < Rumanian *horă* < Turk *hora*]

Hor•ace (hôr′is, hor′-), *n.* **1.** (*Quintus Horatius Flaccus*) 65–8 B.C., Roman poet and satirist. **2.** a male given name.

Ho•rae (hôr′ē, hōr′ē), *n.pl. Class. Myth.* goddesses of the seasons, of cyclical death and rebirth, and sometimes of social order, usually given as three in number, with the names Dike (Justice), Eunomia (Order), and Irene (Peace). [< L *Hōrae* lit., hours]

ho•ral (hôr′əl, hōr′-), *adj.* of or pertaining to an hour or hours; hourly. [1615–25; < LL *hōrālis,* equiv. to L *hōr(a)* HOUR + *-ālis* -AL[1]]

ho•ra•ry (hôr′ə rē, hōr′-), *adj. Archaic.* **1.** pertaining to an hour; indicating the hours: *the horary circle.* **2.** occurring every hour; hourly. [1610–20; < ML *hōrārius,* equiv. to *hōr(a)* HOUR + *-ārius* -ARY]

ho′rary astrol′ogy, a method through which the answer to a question is sought by casting and interpreting a horoscope for the precise moment one learns of an event, problem, career opportunity, etc. [1825–35]

CONCISE ETYMOLOGY KEY: <, descended or borrowed from; >, whence; b., blend of, blended; c., cognate with; cf., compare; deriv., derivative; equiv., equivalent; imit., imitative; obl., oblique; r., replacing; s., stem; sp., spelling, spelled; resp., respelling, respelled; trans., translation; ?, origin unknown; *, unattested; ‡, probably earlier than. See the full key inside the front cover.

Ho•ra•tian (hə rā′shən, hô-, hō-), *adj.* **1.** of or pertaining to Horace. **2.** *Pros.* **a.** of, pertaining to, or resembling the poetic style or diction of Horace. **b.** of, pertaining to, or noting a Horatian ode. [1740–50; < L *Horātiānus,* equiv. to *Horāti(us)* HORACE + *-ānus* -AN]

Hora′tian ode′, *Pros.* an ode consisting of several stanzas all of the same form. Also called **Lesbian ode, Sapphic ode.** Cf. **Pindaric ode.**

Ho•ra•ti•o (hə rā′shē ō′, hô-, hō-), *n.* a male given name.

Hora′tio Al′ger, of or characteristic of the heroes in the novels of Horatio Alger, who begin life in poverty and achieve success and wealth through honesty, hard work, and virtuous behavior: *the Horatio Alger story of his rise in the business world.* [1920–25]

Ho•ra•tius (hə rā′shəs, hô-, hō-), *n.* (*Publius Horatius Cocles*) *Rom. Legend.* a hero celebrated for his defense of the bridge over the Tiber against the Etruscans.

horde (hôrd, hōrd), *n., v.,* **hord•ed, hord•ing.** —*n.* **1.** a large group, multitude, number, etc.; a mass or crowd: *a horde of tourists.* **2.** a tribe or troop of Asian nomads. **3.** any nomadic group. **4.** a moving pack or swarm of animals: *A horde of mosquitoes invaded the camp.* —*v.i.* **5.** to gather in a horde: *The prisoners horded together in the compound.* [1545–55; earlier also *hord, horda* << Czech, Pol *horda* < Ukrainian dial. *gordá,* Ukrainian *ordá,* ORuss (orig. in *Zolotaya orda* the Golden Horde), via Mongolian or directly < Turkic *ordu, orda* royal residence or camp (later, any military encampment, army); cf. URDU]
—**Syn. 1.** mob, herd, throng.

hor•de•in (hôr′dē in), *n. Biochem.* a simple protein of the prolamin class, found in barley grain. [1820–30; < F *hordéine* < L *horde(um)* barley + F *-ine* -IN[2]]

hor•de•o•lum (hôr dē′ə ləm), *n., pl.* **-la** (-lə). *Pathol.* sty[2]. [1800–10; < NL, alter. of LL *hordeolus,* equiv. to L *horde(um)* barley + *-olus, -olum* -OLE[1]]

Ho•reb (hôr′eb, hōr′-), *n. Bible.* a mountain sometimes identified with Mount Sinai.

hore•hound (hôr′hound′, hōr′-), *n.* **1.** an Old World plant, *Marrubium vulgare,* of the mint family, having downy leaves and small, whitish flowers, and containing a bitter, medicinal juice that is used as an expectorant, vermifuge, and laxative. **2.** any of various plants of the mint family. **3.** a brittle candy or lozenge flavored with horehound extract. Also, **hoarhound.** [bef. 1000; ME *horehune,* OE *hārhūne,* equiv. to *hār* gray, HOAR + *hūne* horehound]

hor. interm., (in prescriptions) at intermediate hours. [< L *hōrā intermediīs*]

Ho•rite (hôr′īt, hōr′-), *n.* **1.** an ancient people of Edom living in the region of the Dead Sea, possibly identical with the Hurrians. **2.** a member of this people.

ho•ri•zon (hə rī′zən), *n.* **1.** the line or circle that forms the apparent boundary between earth and sky. **2.** *Astron.* **a.** the small circle of the celestial sphere whose plane is tangent to the earth at the position of a given observer, or the plane of such a circle **(sensible horizon). b.** the great circle of the celestial sphere whose plane passes through the center of the earth and is parallel to the sensible horizon of a given position, or the plane of such a circle **(celestial horizon). 3.** the limit or range of perception, knowledge, or the like. **4.** Usually, **horizons.** the scope of a person's interest, education, understanding, etc.: *His horizons were narrow.* **5.** *Geol.* a thin, distinctive stratum useful for stratigraphic correlation. **6.** any of the series of distinctive layers found in a vertical cross section of any well-developed soil. [1540–50; < L *horīzōn* < Gk *horízōn* (*kýklos*) bounding (circle), equiv. to *horíz(ein)* to bound, limit + *-ōn* prp. suffix (nom. sing.); r. ME *orizonte* < MF < L *horizontem,* acc. of *horīzōn*]
—**Syn. 4.** world, perspective, domain, viewpoint.

Hori′zon Club′, a division of Camp Fire, Inc., for members of high-school age.

hori′zon dis′tance, 1. *Television.* the distance of the farthest point on the earth's surface visible from a transmitting antenna. **2.** *Radio.* the distance on the earth's surface reached by a direct wave: due to atmospheric refraction, sometimes greater than the distance to the visible horizon.

ho•ri•zon•less (hə rī′zən lis), *adj.* **1.** lacking or without a horizon. **2.** without hope; hopeless. [HORIZON + -LESS]

hor•i•zon•tal (hôr′ə zon′tl, hor′-), *adj.* **1.** at right angles to the vertical; parallel to level ground. **2.** flat or level: *a horizontal position.* **3.** being in a prone or supine position; recumbent: *His bad back has kept him horizontal for a week.* **4.** near, on, or parallel to the horizon. **5.** of or pertaining to the horizon. **6.** measured or contained in a plane parallel to the horizon: *a horizontal distance.* **7.** (of material on a printed page, pieces on a game board, etc.) extending across, from the left to the right of the viewer. **8.** of or pertaining to a position or individual of similar status: *He received a horizontal promotion to a different department, retaining his old salary and title.* **9.** *Econ.* of or pertaining to companies, affiliates, divisions, etc., that perform the same or similar functions or produce the same or similar products: *Through horizontal mergers the company monopolized its field.* —*n.* **10.** anything horizontal, as a plane, direction, or object. [1545–55; < L *horizont-* (s. of *horīzōn*) HORIZON + -AL[1]] —**hor•i•zon•tal•i•ty** (hôr′i zon tal′i tē, hor′-), **hor′i•zon′tal•ness,** *n.* —**hor′i•zon′tal•ly,** *adv.*

hor′izon′tal bar′, *Gymnastics.* **1.** a bar fixed in a position parallel to the floor or ground, for use in chinning and other exercises. **2.** an event in gymnastic competitions, judged on strength and grace while performing specific movements on such a bar. Also called **high bar.** [1820–30]

horizon′tal mobil′ity, *Sociol.* **1.** movement from one position to another within the same social level, as changing jobs without altering occupational status, or moving between social groups having the same social status. **2.** cultural diffusion within the same social level, as the spread of fashion within one economic class. Cf. **vertical mobility.**

hor′izon′tal sta′bilizer, *Aeron.* the horizontal surface, usually fixed, of an aircraft empennage, to which the elevator is hinged. Also called, *esp. Brit.,* **tail plane.**

hor′izon′tal un′ion, a labor union organized by skills or trades of its members rather than by industries. [1945–50]

hor•me (hôr′mē), *n. Psychol.* activity directed toward a goal; purposive effort. [1910–15; < Gk *hormḗ* impetus, impulse] —**hor′mic,** *adj.*

hor′mic the′ory, *Psychol.* a theory that holds all behavior to be purposive, whether conscious or unconscious. [1955–60; HORM(E) + -IC]

Hor•mi•gue•ros (ôR′mē ge′Rôs), *n.* a city in W Puerto Rico, S of Mayagüez. 12,031.

Hor•mis•das (hôr miz′dəs), *n.* **Saint,** died A.D. 523, pope 514–523.

hor•mone (hôr′mōn), *n.* **1.** *Biochem.* any of various internally secreted compounds, as insulin or thyroxine, formed in endocrine glands, that affect the functions of specifically receptive organs or tissues when transported to them by the body fluids. **2.** *Pharm.* a synthetic substance used in medicine to act like such a compound when introduced into the body. **3.** *Bot.* Also called **phytohormone.** any of various plant compounds, as auxin or gibberellin, that control growth and differentiation of plant tissue. [1900–05; < Gk *hormôn* (prp. of *hormân* to set in motion, excite, stimulate), equiv. to *horm(ḗ)* HORME + *-ōn* prp. suffix, with ending assimilated to -ONE] —**hor•mo′nal, hor•mon•ic** (hôr mon′ik, -mō′nik), *adj.*

Hor•muz (hôr mo͞oz′, hôr′muz), *n.* **Strait of,** a strait between Iran and the United Arab Emirates, connecting the Persian Gulf and the Gulf of Oman. Also, **Ormuz.**

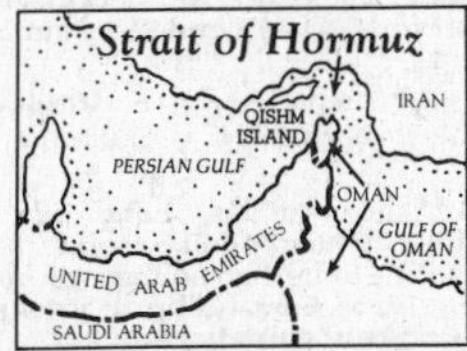

horn (hôrn), *n.* **1.** one of the bony, permanent, hollow paired growths, often curved and pointed, that project from the upper part of the head of certain ungulate mammals, as cattle, sheep, goats, or antelopes. **2.** a similar growth, sometimes of hair, as the median horn or horns on the snout of the rhinoceros, or the tusk of the narwhal. **3.** antler. **4.** a process projecting from the head of an animal and suggestive of such a growth, as a feeler, tentacle, or crest. **5.** the bony substance of which such animal growths are composed. **6.** any similar substance, as that forming tortoise shell, hoofs, nails, or corns. **7.** an article made of the material of an animal horn or like substance, as a thimble, spoon, or shoehorn. **8.** any projection or extremity resembling the horn of an animal. **9.** something resembling or suggesting an animal horn: *a drinking horn.* **10.** a part resembling an animal horn attributed to deities, demons, etc.: *the devil's horn.* **11.** Usually, **horns.** the imaginary projections on a cuckold's brow. **12.** *Music.* **a.** a wind instrument, originally formed from the hollow horn of an animal but now usually made of brass or other metal or plastic. **b.** See **French horn. 13.** something used as or resembling such a wind instrument. **14.** *Slang.* a trumpet. **15.** an instrument for sounding a warning signal: *an automobile horn.* **16.** *Aeron.* any of certain short, armlike levers on the control surfaces of an airplane. **17.** *Radio.* **a.** a tube of varying cross section used in some loudspeakers to couple the diaphragm to the sound-transmitting space. **b.** *Slang.* a loudspeaker. **18.** *Slang.* a telephone or radiotelephone: *I've been on the horn all morning.* **19.** the high protuberant part at the front and top of certain saddles; a pommel, esp. a high one. **20.** *Carpentry.* (in a door or window frame) that part of a jamb extending above the head. **21.** one of the curved extremities of a crescent, esp. of the crescent moon. **22.** a crescent-shaped tract of land. **23.** a pyramidal mountain peak, esp. one having concave faces carved by glaciation. **24.** a symbol of power or strength, as in the Bible: *a horn of salvation.* **25.** each of the alternatives of a dilemma. **26.** the narrow, more pointed part of an anvil. **27.** *Metalworking.* a projection at the side of the end of a rolled sheet or strip, caused by unevenness of the roll due to wear. **28.** *Horol.* (in a lever escapement) either of the two prongs at the end of the lever fork guarding against overbanking when the guard pin is in the crescent. **29. blow** (or **toot**) **one's own horn,** *Informal.* to publicize or boast about one's abilities or achievements: *He's a bright fellow, but likes to blow his own horn too much.* **30. draw** or **pull in one's horns,** to restrain oneself or become less belligerent; retreat: *Since he lost so much gambling, he's drawn in his horns a bit.* **31. lock horns,** to conflict, quarrel, or disagree: *The administration and the staff locked horns over the proposed measures.* **32. on the horns of a dilemma,** confronted with two equally disagreeable choices.
—*v.t.* **33.** to cuckold. **34.** to butt or gore with the horns. **35.** *Shipbuilding.* to set up (a frame or bulkhead of a vessel being built) at a proper angle to the keel with due regard to the inclination of the keel on the ways; plumb. **36. horn in,** *Informal.* to thrust oneself forward obtrusively; intrude or interrupt: *Every time we try to have a private conversation, the boss horns in.*
—*adj.* **37.** made of horn. [bef. 900; ME *horn(e)* (n.), OE *horn;* c. D *horen,* ON, Dan, Sw *horn,* G *Horn,* Goth *haurn,* L *cornu* CORNU, Ir, Welsh *corn;* akin to Gk *kéras* horn (see CERAT-)] —**horn′ish,** *adj.* —**horn′less,** *adj.* —**horn′less•ness,** *n.* —**horn′like′,** *adj.*

horn (def. 12) (French horn)

Horn (hôrn), *n.* **Cape.** See **Cape Horn.**

horn•beam (hôrn′bēm′), *n.* any North American shrub or tree belonging to the genus *Carpinus,* of the birch family, yielding a hard, heavy wood, as *C. caroliniana* **(American hornbeam).** [1570–80; HORN + BEAM]

horn•bill (hôrn′bil′), *n.* any large bird of the family Bucerotidae, of the Old World tropics, characterized by a very large bill usually surmounted by a horny protuberance. [1765–75; HORN + BILL[2]]

horn•blende (hôrn′blend′), *n.* a dark-green to black mineral of the amphibole group, calcium magnesium iron and hydroxyl aluminosilicate. [1760–70; < G; see HORN, BLENDE] —**horn•blen′dic,** *adj.*

horn′blende schist′, *Petrog.* a variety of schist containing needles of hornblende that lie in parallel planes. [1815–25]

horn•book (hôrn′bo͝ok′), *n.* **1.** a leaf or page containing the alphabet, religious materials, etc., covered with a sheet of transparent horn and fixed in a frame with a handle, formerly used in teaching children to read. **2.** a primer or book of rudiments. [1580–90; HORN + BOOK]

horn′ chair′, a chair, esp. of the late 19th-century U.S., having a frame made from steer, elk, buffalo, or other animal horns.

Horne (hôrn), *n.* **Marilyn,** born 1934, U.S. mezzo-soprano.

horned (hôrnd), *adj.* **1.** having horns (often used in combination): *a horned beast; blunt-horned.* **2.** having or wearing a horn-shaped protuberance, ornament, or the like: *the horned crags.* **3.** having a crescent-shaped part or form. [1250–1300; ME; see HORN, -ED[3]] —**horn•ed•ness** (hôr′nid nis), *n.*

horned′ di′nosaur, ceratopsian.

horned′ frog′, 1. any of various frogs having a marked protuberance on the head, cheek, or upper eyelid. **2.** Also called **horny frog.** *Chiefly Southwestern U.S.* a horned lizard. [1825–35]

horned′ lark′, a lark, *Eremophila alpestris,* of the Northern Hemisphere, having a tuft of feathers on each side of the crown of the head. [1835–45]

horned′ liz′ard, an insectivorous iguanid lizard of the genus *Phrynosoma,* of western North America, having hornlike spines on the head and a flattened body covered with spiny scales. Also called **horned′ toad′.** [1805–15, *Amer.*]

Texas horned lizard, *Phrynosoma cornutum,* length to 7 in. (18 cm)

horned′ oak′ gall′, a small, round tumor, formed around wasp eggs laid in the branches of a pin oak tree, that disrupts the flow of nutrients to the tree, with consequent defoliation and death. Also called **oak gall.**

horned′ pop′py. See **horn poppy.** [1540–50]

horned′ pout′, a bullhead, esp. the brown bullhead. Also called **hornpout.** [1830–40]

horned′ scream′er, a screamer, *Anhima cornuta,* of tropical South America, having a long, slender hornlike process projecting from the forehead. [1775–85]

horned′ scull′y (skul′ē), *Mil.* a tapered block of concrete with projecting steel rails, placed under water to tear holes in the bottoms of boats.

horned′ vi′per, a highly venomous viper, *Cerastes cerastes,* of northern Africa and extreme southwestern Asia, having a process resembling a horn just above each eye. [1760–70]

horned′ whiff′. See under **whiff**[2].

Hor•nell (hôr nel′), *n.* a city in S New York. 10,234.

Hor′ner's meth′od (hôr′nərz), *Math.* a technique, involving successive substitutions, for approximating the real roots of an equation with real coefficients. [1835–45; named after William G. Horner (d. 1837), English mathematician who invented it]

hor•net (hôr′nit), *n.* any large, stinging paper wasp of the family Vespidae, as *Vespa crabro* **(giant hornet),** in-

CONCISE PRONUNCIATION KEY: act, cāpe, dâre, pärt; set, ēqual; *if,* īce; ox, ōver, ôrder, oil, bo͝ok, bo͞ot, out; up, ûrge; child; sing; shoe; thin, *th*at; zh as in *treasure.* ə = a as in *alone,* e as in *system,* i as in *easily,* o as in *gallop,* u as in *circus;* ᵊ as in *fire* (fīᵊr), *hour* (ouᵊr). l and n can serve as syllabic consonants, as in *cradle* (krād′l), and *button* (but′n). See the full key inside the front cover.

troduced into the U.S. from Europe, or *Vespula maculata* **(bald-faced hornet** or **white-faced hornet),** of North America. [bef. 900; ME *harnete,* OE *hyrnet(u);* c. OHG *hornaz* (>G *Horniss*); akin to HORN]

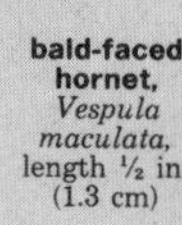
bald-faced hornet, *Vespula maculata,* length ½ in. (1.3 cm)

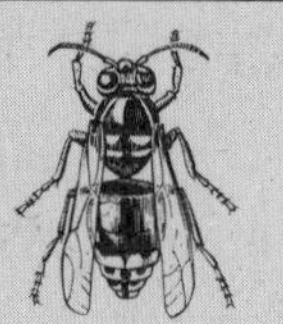

hor′net's nest′, a large amount of activity, trouble, hostility, or animosity: *His investigation stirred up a hornet's nest, resulting in major shifts in personnel.* [1730–40]

Hor•ney (hôr′nī), *n.* **Karen,** 1885–1952, U.S. psychiatrist and author, born in Germany.

horn•fels (hôrn′felz), *n.* a dark, fine-grained metamorphic rock, the result of recrystallization of siliceous or argillaceous sediments by contact metamorphism. [1850–55; < G, equiv. to *Horn* HORN + *Fels* rock, cliff]

horn′ fly′, a small bloodsucking fly, *Haematobia irritans,* that is a pest, esp. of cattle. [1700–10, *Amer.*]

Horn•ie (hôr′nē), *n. Scot.* Satan.

hor•ni•to (hôr nē′tō; *Sp.* ôR nē′tô), *n., pl.* **-tos** (-tōz; *Sp.* -tôs). *Geol.* a low oven-shaped mound of congealed lava, common in some volcanic districts, emitting hot smoke and vapors in the final stages of activity. [1820–30; < Sp, equiv. to *horn(o)* oven (< L *furnus, fornus;* see FURNACE) + *-ito* dim. suffix]

horn-mad (hôrn′mad′), *adj.* furiously enraged; intensely angry. [1570–80] **—horn′-mad′ness,** *n.*

horn′ of plen′ty, 1. cornucopia. **2.** *Mycol.* an edible trumpet-shaped chanterelle, *Craterellus cornucopiodes,* commonly found under certain trees of eastern North America and the Pacific coast. [1580–90; trans. of LL *cornūcōpia.* See CORNUCOPIA]

horn•pipe (hôrn′pīp′), *n.* **1.** an English folk clarinet having one ox horn concealing the reed and another forming the bell. **2.** a lively jiglike dance, originally to music played on a hornpipe, performed usually by one person, and traditionally a favorite of sailors. **3.** a piece of music for or in the style of such a dance. [1350–1400; ME. See HORN, PIPE¹]

horn′ pop′py, a European plant, *Glaucium flavum,* of the poppy family, having yellow flowers, naturalized along sandy shores in eastern North America. Also, **horned poppy.** Also called **sea poppy.** [1850–55]

horn•pout (hôrn′pout′), *n.* See **horned pout.** [by shortening]

horn-rimmed (hôrn′rimd′), *adj.* having the frames or rims made of horn or tortoise shell, or plastic that simulates either of these: *horn-rimmed glasses.* [1890–95]

horn-rims (hôrn′rimz′, -rimz′), *n.pl.* horn-rimmed eyeglasses. [1925–30]

Horns•by (hôrnz′bē), *n.* **Rogers,** 1896–1963, U.S. baseball player and manager.

horn′ sil′ver, *Mineral.* cerargyrite. [1760–70; trans. of G *Hornsilber*]

horn-spread (hôrn′spred′), *n.* (of a horned creature) the distance between the outermost tips of the horns.

horn•stone (hôrn′stōn′), *n. Archaic.* a variety of quartz resembling flint. [1720–30; trans. of G *Hornstein*]

horn•swog•gle (hôrn′swog′əl), *v.t.,* **-gled, -gling.** *Slang.* to swindle, cheat, hoodwink, or hoax. [1815–25 orig. uncert.]

horn•tail (hôrn′tāl′), *n.* any of various wasplike insects of the family Siricidae, the females of which have a hornlike ovipositor. [1880–85; HORN + TAIL¹]

horn′ tim′ber, *Naut.* a timber, often one of several, rising from the sternpost of a wooden vessel to support the overhang of the stern.

horn•worm (hôrn′wûrm′), *n.* the larva of any of several hawk moths, having a hornlike process at the rear of the abdomen. [1670–80, *Amer.*; HORN + WORM]

horn•wort (hôrn′wûrt′, -wôrt′), *n.* any aquatic plant of the genus *Ceratophyllum,* found in ponds and slow streams. [1795–1805; HORN + WORT²]

horn•y (hôr′nē), *adj.,* **horn•i•er, horn•i•est. 1.** consisting of a horn or a hornlike substance; corneous. **2.** having a horn or horns or hornlike projections; horned. **3.** hornlike as a result of hardening; callous: *horny hands.* **4.** *Slang (vulgar).* **a.** lustful. **b.** sexually excited. **5.** *Archaic.* semiopaque or somewhat translucent, like horn. [1350–1400; ME; see HORN, -Y¹] **—horn′i•ly,** *adv.* **—horn′i•ness,** *n.*

horn′y cor′al, a gorgonian.

horn′y frog′, *Chiefly Southwestern U.S.* See **horned frog.**

horol., horology.

hor•o•loge (hôr′ə lōj′, -loj′, hor′-), *n.* any instrument for indicating the time, esp. a sundial or an early form of clock. [1375–1425; late ME < L *hōrologium* HOROLOGIUM; r. ME *orloge* < MF < L, as above]

hor•o•log•ic (hôr′ə loj′ik, hor′-), *adj.* **1.** of or pertaining to horology. **2.** of or pertaining to horologes. Also, **hor′o•log′i•cal.** [1655–65; < LL *hōrologicus* < Gk *hōrologikós,* equiv. to *hōrolog-* (see HOROLOGIUM) + *-ikos* -IC] **—hor′o•log′i•cal•ly,** *adv.*

ho•rol•o•gist (hô rol′ə jist, hō-), *n.* **1.** an expert in horology. **2.** a person who makes clocks or watches. Also, **ho•rol′o•ger.** [1790–1800; HOROLOGE + -IST]

hor•o•lo•gi•um (hôr′ə lō′jē əm, hor′-), *n., pl.* **-gi•a** (-jē ə). **1.** a building supporting or containing a timepiece, as a clock tower. **2.** (*cap.*) *Astron.* the Clock, a small southern constellation between Eridanus and Dorado. [1655–65; < L < Gk *hōrológion,* equiv. to *hōrológ(os)* timeteller (*hōro-,* comb. form of *hṓra* HOUR + *-log-,* var. s. of *légein* to speak, tell + *-os* adj. suffix) + *-ion* dim. suffix]

ho•rol•o•gy (hô rol′ə jē, hō-), *n.* the art or science of making timepieces or of measuring time. [1810–20; < Gk *hōro-* (comb. form of *hṓra* HOUR) + -LOGY]

ho•rop•ter (hə rop′tər, hô-), *n. Ophthalm.* a projection of the points in the visual field corresponding to the aggregate of points registering on the two retinas. [1695–1705; < Gk *hór(os)* boundary + *optḗr* one that looks] **—hor•op•ter•ic** (hôr′op ter′ik), *adj.*

hor•o•scope (hôr′ə skōp′, hor′-), *n.* **1.** a diagram of the heavens, showing the relative position of planets and the signs of the zodiac, for use in calculating births, foretelling events in a person's life, etc. See illus. under **zodiac. 2.** a prediction of future events or advice for future behavior based on such a diagram. [bef. 1050; ME, OE *horoscopus* < L < Gk *hōroskópos,* equiv. to *hōro-* (comb. form of *hṓra* HOUR) + *skópos* -SCOPE] **—hor•o•scop•ic** (hôr′ə skop′ik, -skō′pik, hor′ə-), *adj.*

ho•ros•co•py (hô ros′kə pē, hō-), *n. Archaic.* the casting or taking of horoscopes. [1645–55; HOROSCOPE + -Y³] **—hor•o•scop•er** (hôr′ə skō′pər, hor′-), **ho•ros•co•pist** (hô ros′kə pist, hō-, hôr′ə skō′pist, hor′-), *n.*

hor•o•tel•ic (hôr′ə tel′ik), *adj. Biol.* of or pertaining to evolution at a rate standard for a given group of plants or animals. Cf. **bradytelic, tachytelic.** [< Gk *hóro(s)* boundary + *tél(os)* end, consummation + -IC] **—hor′o•tel′y,** *n.*

Hor•o•witz (hôr′ə wits, hor′), *n.* **Vlad•i•mir** (vlad′ə mēr′, vla dē′mēr), born 1904, U.S. pianist, born in Russia.

hor•ren•dous (hô ren′dəs, ho-), *adj.* shockingly dreadful; horrible: *a horrendous crime.* [1650–60; < L *horrendus* dreadful, to be feared (ger. of *horrēre* to bristle, shudder), equiv. to *horr-* (akin to HIRSUTE) + *-endus* ger. suffix] **—hor•ren′dous•ly,** *adv.*
—Syn. appalling, frightful, hideous.

hor•rent (hôr′ənt, hor′-), *adj.* bristling; standing erect like bristles. [1660–70; < L *horrent-* (s. of *horrēns,* prp. of *horrēre* to stand on end, bristle with fear), equiv. to *horr-* (see HORRENDOUS) + *-ent-* -ENT]

hor•ri•ble (hôr′ə bəl, hor′-), *adj.* **1.** causing or tending to cause horror; shockingly dreadful: *a horrible sight.* **2.** extremely unpleasant; deplorable; disgusting: *horrible living conditions.* [1275–1325; ME *(h)orrible* < OF < L *horribilis,* equiv. to *horr-* (s. of *horrēre* to stand on end, bristle with fear) + *-ibilis* -IBLE] **—hor′ri•ble•ness,** *n.* **—hor′ri•bly,** *adv.*
—Syn. 1. terrible, awful, appalling, frightful; hideous, grim, ghastly, shocking, revolting, repulsive, horrid, horrendous, horrifying, repellent. **—Ant. 1.** attractive.

hor•rid (hôr′id, hor′-), *adj.* **1.** such as to cause horror; shockingly dreadful; abominable. **2.** extremely unpleasant or disagreeable: *horrid weather; She thought her uncle was horrid.* **3.** *Archaic.* shaggy or bristling; rough. [1580–90; < L *horridus* bristling, rough, equiv. to *horr-* (s. of *horrēre* to stand on end, bristle) + *-idus* -ID⁴] **—hor′rid•ly,** *adv.* **—hor′rid•ness,** *n.*
—Syn. 2. nasty, vile, odious, abominable.

hor•rif•ic (hô rif′ik, ho-), *adj.* causing horror. [1645–55; < L *horrificus,* equiv. to *horri-* (comb. form of *horrēre* to bristle with fear) + *-ficus* -FIC] **—hor•rif′i•cal•ly,** *adv.*

hor•ri•fied (hôr′ə fīd′, hor′-), *adj.* **1.** showing or indicating great shock or horror: *a horrified gasp; a horrified expression.* **2.** accompanied or characterized by a feeling of horror: *horrified interest.* **3.** struck with horror; shocked: *horrified and outraged spectators.* [1830–40; HORRIFY + -ED²] **—hor•ri•fied•ly** (hôr′ə fīd′lē, -fī′id-, hor′-), *adv.*

hor•ri•fy (hôr′ə fī′, hor′-), *v.t.,* **-fied, -fy•ing. 1.** to cause to feel horror; strike with horror: *The accident horrified us all.* **2.** to distress greatly; shock or dismay: *She was horrified by the price of the house.* [1785–95; < L *horrificāre* to cause horror, equiv. to *horri-* (comb. form of *horrēre* to bristle with fear; see HORRENDOUS) + *-ficāre* -FY] **—hor′ri•fi•ca′tion,** *n.* **—hor′ri•fy′ing•ly,** *adv.*
—Syn. frighten, terrify; repel, appall.

hor•rip•i•late (hô rip′ə lāt′, ho-), *v.t.,* **-lat•ed, -lat•ing.** to produce horripilation on. [1615–25; < L *horripilātus* (ptp. of *horripilāre* to become bristly). See HORRIFY, PILE³, -ATE¹]

hor•rip•i•la•tion (hô rip′ə lā′shən, ho-), *n.* a bristling of the hair on the skin from cold, fear, etc.; goose flesh. [1615–25; < LL *horripilātiōn-* (s. of *horripilātiō*). See HORRIPILATE, -ION]

hor•ror (hôr′ər, hor′-), *n.* **1.** an overwhelming and painful feeling caused by something frightfully shocking, terrifying, or revolting; a shuddering fear: *to shrink back from a mutilated corpse in horror.* **2.** anything that causes such a feeling: *killing, looting, and other horrors of war.* **3.** such a feeling as a quality or condition: *to have known the horror of slow starvation.* **4.** a strong aversion; abhorrence: *to have a horror of emotional outbursts.* **5.** *Informal.* something considered bad or tasteless: *That wallpaper is a horror. The party was a horror.* **6. horrors,** *Informal.* **a.** See **delirium tremens. b.** extreme depression. *—adj.* **7.** inspiring or creating horror, loathing, aversion, etc.: *The hostages told horror stories of their year in captivity.* **8.** centered upon or depicting terrifying or macabre events: *a horror movie.* *—interj.* **9. horrors,** (used as a mild expression of dismay, surprise, disappointment, etc.) [1520–30; < L *horror,* equiv. to *horr-* (s. of *horrēre* to bristle with fear; see HORRENDOUS) + *-or* -OR¹; r. ME *orrour* < AF < L *horrōr-,* s. of *horror*]
—Syn. 1. dread, dismay, consternation. See **terror. 4.** loathing, antipathy, detestation, hatred, abomination. **—Ant. 1.** serenity. **4.** attraction.

hor′ror sto′ry, 1. a story, movie, etc., that entertains or fascinates by shocking or frightening, esp. by an emphasis on bloodshed or supernatural forces. **2.** *Informal.* a distressing experience: *the horror stories of child abuse.*

hor•ror-struck (hôr′ər struk′, hor′-), *adj.* stricken with horror; horrified; aghast. Also, **hor•ror-strick•en** (hôr′ər strik′ən, hor′-). [1805–15]

Hor•sa (hôr′sə), *n.* **1.** died A.D. 455, Jutish chief (brother of Hengist). **2.** *Mil.* a British glider of World War II designed to land troops or equipment in airborne operations.

hors con•cours (ôR kôN kōōR′), *French.* **1.** noting an artist, architect, or the like, not competing or not qualified to compete for the prizes in an exhibit or competition. **2.** noting or pertaining to a work or project submitted by such a person to an exhibit or competition. [lit., out (of the) competition]

hors de com•bat (ôR də kôN bA′), *French.* out of the fight; disabled; no longer able to fight.

hors d'oeu•vre (ôr dûrv′; *Fr.* ôR dœ′vRᵊ), *pl.* **hors d'oeuvre, hors d'oeuvres** (ôr dûrvz′; *Fr.* ôR dœ′vRᵊ). **1.** a small bit of appetizing food, as spicy meat, fish, cheese, or a preparation of chopped or creamed foods, often served on crackers or small pieces of toast, for eating at cocktail parties or other gatherings where drinks are served with no other food. **2.** an appetizer, as a relish or more elaborate preparation, served before or as the first course of a meal. [1705–15; < F: outside of the main course]

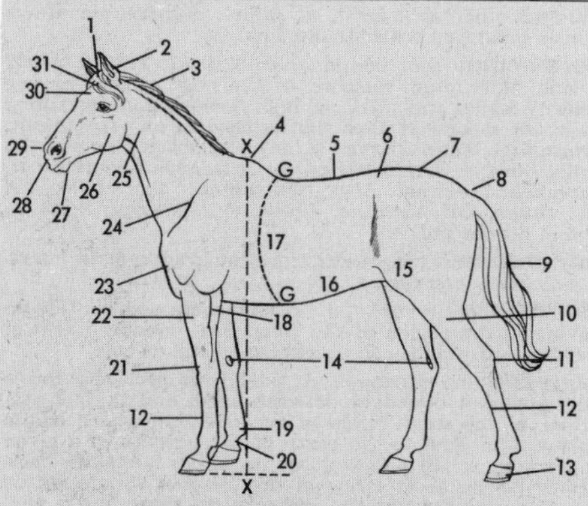

horse (def. 1)
1, poll; 2, ear; 3, mane; 4, withers; 5, back; 6, loin; 7, croup; 8, dock; 9, tail; 10, gaskin; 11, hock; 12, cannon or shank; 13, hoof; 14, chestnut; 15, stifle; 16, belly; 17, ribs; 18, elbow; 19, fetlock; 20, pastern; 21, knee; 22, forearm; 23, chest; 24, shoulder; 25, neck; 26, cheek; 27, chin; 28, muzzle; 29, nostril; 30, forehead; 31, forelock; GG, girth; XX, height

horse (hôrs), *n., pl.* **hors•es,** (*esp. collectively*) **horse,** *v.,* **horsed, hors•ing,** *adj.* *—n.* **1.** a large, solid-hoofed, herbivorous quadruped, *Equus caballus,* domesticated since prehistoric times, bred in a number of varieties, and used for carrying or pulling loads, for riding, and for racing. **2.** a fully mature male animal of this type; stallion. **3.** any of several odd-toed ungulates belonging to the family Equidae, including the horse, zebra, donkey, and ass, having a thick, flat coat with a narrow mane along the back of the neck and bearing the weight on only one functioning digit, the third, which is widened into a round or spade-shaped hoof. **4.** something on which a person rides, sits, or exercises, as if astride the back of such an animal: *rocking horse.* **5.** Also called **trestle.** a frame, block, etc., with legs, on which something is mounted or supported. **6.** *Gymnastics.* **a.** See **vaulting horse. b.** See **pommel horse. 7.** *Carpentry.* carriage (def. 7). **8.** soldiers serving on horseback; cavalry: *a thousand horse.* **9.** *Slang.* a man; fellow. **10.** Often, **horses.** *Informal.* horsepower. **11. horses,** *Slang.* the power or capacity to accomplish something, as by having enough money, personnel, or expertise: *Our small company doesn't have the horses to compete against a giant corporation.* **12.** *Chess Informal.* a knight. **13.** *Slang.* a crib, translation, or other illicit aid to a student's recitation; trot; pony. **14.** *Mining.* a mass of rock enclosed within a lode or vein. **15.** *Naut.* traveler (def. 6b). **16.** *Shipbuilding.* a mold of a curved frame, esp. one used when the complexity of the curves requires laying out at full size. **17.** *Slang.* heroin. **18. back the wrong horse,** to be mistaken in judgment, esp. in backing a losing candidate. **19. beat** or **flog a dead horse,** to attempt to revive a discussion, topic, or idea that has waned, been exhausted, or proved fruitless. **20. from the horse's mouth,** *Informal.* on good authority; from the original or a trustworthy source: *I have it straight from the horse's mouth that the boss is retiring.* **21. hold one's horses,** *Informal.* to check one's impulsiveness; be patient or calm: *Hold your horses! I'm almost ready.* **22. horse of another color,** something entirely different. Also, **horse of a different color. 23. look a gift horse in the mouth,** to be critical of a gift. **24. To horse!** Mount your horse! Ride! *—v.t.* **25.** to provide with a horse or horses. **26.** to set on horseback. **27.** to set or carry on a person's back or on one's own back. **28.** *Carpentry.* to cut notches for steps into (a carriage beam). **29.** to move with great

CONCISE ETYMOLOGY KEY: <, descended or borrowed from; >, whence; b., blend of, blended; c., cognate with; cf., compare; deriv., derivative; equiv., equivalent; imit., imitative; obl., oblique; r., replacing; s., stem; sp., spelling, spelled; resp., respelling, respelled; trans., translation; ?, origin unknown; *, unattested; ‡, probably earlier than. See the full key inside the front cover.

physical effort or force: *It took three men to horse the trunk up the stairs.* **30.** *Slang.* **a.** to make (a person) the target of boisterous jokes. **b.** to perform boisterously, as a part or a scene in a play. **31.** *Naut.* **a.** to caulk (a vessel) with a hammer. **b.** to work or haze (a sailor) cruelly or unfairly. **32.** *Archaic.* to place (someone) on a person's back, in order to be flogged. —*v.i.* **33.** to mount or go on a horse. **34.** (of a mare) to be in heat. **35.** *Vulgar.* to have coitus. **36. horse around,** *Slang.* to fool around; indulge in horseplay. —*adj.* **37.** of, for, or pertaining to a horse or horses: *the horse family; a horse blanket.* **38.** drawn or powered by a horse or horses. **39.** mounted or serving on horses: *horse troops.* **40.** unusually large. [bef. 900; (n.) ME, OE *hors;* c. ON *hross,* D *ros,* G *Ross* (MHG *ros,* OHG *hros*); (v.) ME *horsen* to provide with horses, OE *horsian,* deriv. of the n.] —**horse′less,** *adj.* —**horse′like′,** *adj.*

horse-and-bug•gy (hôrs′ən bug′ē), *adj.* **1.** of or pertaining to the last few generations preceding the invention of the automobile: *vivid recollections of horse-and-buggy days.* **2.** old-fashioned; outmoded: *horse-and-buggy methods.* [1925–30, *Amer.*]

horse•back (hôrs′bak′), *n.* **1.** the back of a horse. **2.** *Geol.* a low, natural ridge of sand or gravel; an esker. Cf. **hogback.** —*adv.* **3.** on horseback: *to ride horseback.* —*adj.* **4.** made or given in a casual or speculative way; approximate or offhand: *a horseback estimate on the construction costs.* [1350–1400; ME. See HORSE, BACK[1]]

horse′ balm′, a lemon-scented plant, *Collinsonia canadensis,* of eastern North America, having small yellow flowers. Also called **horseweed, richweed.** [1780–90, *Amer.*]

horse′ bean′. See **fava bean.** [1675–85]

horse′ block′, a step or block of stone, wood, etc., for getting on or off a horse or in or out of a vehicle. [1745–55]

horse′ brass′, a brass ornament, originally intended for the harness of a horse.

horse•brier (hôrs′brī′ər), *n.* catbrier. [1830–40, *Amer.;* HORSE + BRIER[1]]

horse•car (hôrs′kär′), *n.* **1.** a streetcar drawn by a horse or horses. **2.** a railroad car or a truck fitted with stalls for the transportation of horses. [1825–35, *Amer.;* HORSE + CAR[1]]

horse′ chest′nut, 1. a tree, *Aesculus hippocastanum,* native to the Old World, having digitate leaves and upright clusters of white flowers. **2.** the shiny, brown, nutlike seed of this tree or of other trees of the genus *Aesculus.* [1590–1600; trans. of NL *castanea equina;* so named from its use in treating respiratory diseases of horses]

horse′ clam′, gaper. [1830–40, *Amer.*]

horse•cloth (hôrs′klôth′, -kloth′), *n., pl.* **-cloths** (-klôthz′, -klothz′, -klôths′, -kloths′). a cloth used to cover a horse, or as part of its trappings. [1520–30; HORSE + CLOTH]

horse-col•lar (hôrs′kol′ər), *Slang.* —*n.* **1.** (esp. in baseball) a score of zero. —*v.t.* **2.** to prevent (an opposing baseball team or batter) from scoring or making a base hit.

horse′ conch′, a marine gastropod, *Pleuroploca gigantea,* having a yellowish, spired shell that grows to a length of 2 ft. (0.6 m). [1865–70, *Amer.*]

horse-cop•er (hôrs′kō′pər), *n. Brit.* coper. [1675–85]

horse′ corn′, *Midland U.S.* field corn. [1570–80]

horse-faced (hôrs′fāst′), *adj.* having a large face with lantern jaws and large teeth. [1665–75]

horse•feath•ers (hôrs′feth′ərz), *Slang.* —*n.* **1.** (*used with a singular or plural v.*) something not worth considering. —*interj.* **2.** rubbish; nonsense; bunk (used to express contemptuous rejection). [1925–30, *Amer.;* HORSE + FEATHERS, as euphemism for HORSESHIT]

horse•fish (hôrs′fish′), *n., pl.* (*esp. collectively*) **-fish,** (*esp. referring to two or more kinds or species*) **-fish•es.** moonfish (def. 1). [1635–45; HORSE + FISH]

horse•flesh (hôrs′flesh′), *n.* **1.** the flesh of a horse. **2.** horses collectively, esp. for riding, racing, etc. [1490–1500; HORSE + FLESH]

horse′ fly′, any bloodsucking, usually large fly of the family Tabanidae, esp. of the genus *Tabanus,* a serious pest of horses, cattle, etc. [1350–1400; ME *horsfleeye*]

horse fly, *Tabanus americanus,* length to 1⅛ in. (2.8 cm)

horse′ gen′tian, any weedy North American plant of the genus *Triosteum,* of the honeysuckle family, esp. *T. perfoliatum,* having stalkless leaves and purplish-brown flowers and bearing orange fruits. Also called **tinker's weed.** [1835–45, *Amer.*]

horse′ guard′, a black and yellow sand wasp, *Bembix carolina,* of the southern U.S., preying on flies that gather around horses and cattle. [1790–1800]

Horse′ Guards′, 1. a body of cavalry serving as a guard. **2.** a cavalry brigade from the household troops of the British monarch. [1635–45]

horse•hair (hôrs′hâr′), *n.* **1.** a hair or the hair of a horse, esp. from the mane or tail. **2.** a sturdy, glossy fabric woven of this hair. —*adj.* **3.** of or pertaining to horsehair: *a horsehair mattress.* [1275–1325; ME *hors here.* See HORSE, HAIR] —**horse′haired′,** *adj.*

horse′hair-blight fun′gus (hôrs′hâr′blīt′), a fungal parasite, *Marasmius equicrinis,* that causes a disease of certain tropical plants, esp. tea.

horse′hair fun′gus, an edible white, striated, umbrella-capped mushroom, *Marasmius rotula,* commonly found in eastern North America.

horse′hair worm′, any long, slender worm of the phylum Nematomorpha, developing parasitically on insects and crustaceans, and free-living as adults in streams and ponds. Also called **gordian worm, nematomorph.** [1745–55]

horse•head (hôrs′hed′), *n., pl.* **-heads,** (*esp. collectively*) **-head.** moonfish (def. 1). [1880–85; HORSE + HEAD]

Horse′head Neb′ula, a dark nebula in the constellation Orion, composed of opaque cosmic dust and resembling the head of a horse.

horse•hide (hôrs′hīd′), *n.* **1.** the hide of a horse. **2.** leather made from the hide of a horse. **3.** *Slang.* a baseball. —*adj.* **4.** made of horsehide. [1375–1425; late ME. See HORSE, HIDE[2]]

horse′ lat′itudes, the latitudes, approximately 30° N and S, forming the edges of the trade-wind belt, characterized by high atmospheric pressure with calms and light variable winds. [1765–75; prob. as trans. of Sp *golfo de las yeguas* lit., mares' sea; explanation of the literal sense remains uncert., despite numerous hypotheses]

horse•laugh (hôrs′laf′, -läf′), *n.* **1.** a loud, coarse laugh, esp. of derision. —*v.i.* **2.** to utter a horselaugh. [1705–15; HORSE + LAUGH] —**horse′laugh′ter,** *n.*

horse•leech (hôrs′lēch′), *n.* a large leech, as *Haemopis marmoratis,* that infests the mouth and nasal passages of horses. [1400–50; late ME *horsleych.* See HORSE, LEECH]

horse′less car′riage (hôrs′lis), an automobile: *The horse and buggy were eventually replaced by the horseless carriage.* [1890–95]

horse′ mack′erel, 1. See **bluefin tuna. 2.** See **jack mackerel.** [1695–1705]

horse•man (hôrs′mən), *n., pl.* **-men. 1.** a person who is skilled in riding a horse. **2.** a person on horseback. **3.** a person who owns, breeds, trains, or tends horses. [1175–1225; ME *horsman.* See HORSE, -MAN]

horse•man•ship (hôrs′mən ship′), *n.* **1.** the art, ability, skill, or manner of a horseman. **2.** equitation. [1555–65; HORSEMAN + -SHIP]

horse′ marine′, 1. (formerly) a marine mounted on horseback or a cavalryman doing duty on shipboard. **2.** a person out of his or her proper or natural place. [1810–20]

horse•mint (hôrs′mint′), *n.* **1.** a wild mint, *Mentha longifolia,* introduced into America from Europe, having spikes of lilac flowers. **2.** any of various other wild mints as the New World *Monarda punctata.* [1225–75; ME; see HORSE, MINT[1]]

horse′ mush′room, a smooth, edible, large white-capped mushroom, *Agaricus arvensis,* that has the odor of anise, common in North American meadows and fields. [1865–70]

horse′ net′tle, a large, prickly North American weed, *Solanum carolinense,* of the nightshade family, having violet to white flowers in a few clusters. [1810–20, *Amer.*]

horse′ op′era, a television or radio program or motion picture about the Wild West, often presented serially and usually dealing with adventures of cowboys, gunmen, gold prospectors, etc. Cf. **Western** (def. 8).

horse′ par′lor, a gambling room where people can bet on horse races with a bookmaker.

horse′ pis′tol, a large pistol formerly carried by horsemen. [1695–1705]

horse•play (hôrs′plā′), *n.* rough or boisterous play or pranks. [1580–90; HORSE + PLAY] —**horse′play′ful,** *adj.*

horse•play•er (hôrs′plā′ər), *n.* a habitual bettor on horse races. [1945–50; HORSE + PLAYER]

horse•pow•er (hôrs′pou′ər), *n.* **1.** a foot-pound-second unit of power, equivalent to 550 foot-pounds per second, or 745.7 watts. **2.** *Informal.* the capacity to achieve or produce; strength or talent: *The university's history faculty is noted for its intellectual horsepower.* [1800–10; HORSE + POWER]

horse•pow•er-hour (hôrs′pou′ər ouᵊr′, -ou′ər), *n.* a foot-pound-second unit of energy or work, equal to the work done by a mechanism with a power output of one horsepower over a period of one hour. [1895–1900]

horse•pox (hôrs′poks′), *n. Vet. Pathol.* a disease in horses caused by a virus and characterized by eruptions in the mouth and on the skin. [1650–60; HORSE + POX]

horse′ race′, 1. a contest of speed among horses that either are ridden by jockeys or pull sulkies and their drivers. **2.** any formidable contest or competition: *The primary election is expected to be a horse race among four opponents.* —**horse′ rac′ing.**

horse•rad•ish (hôrs′rad′ish), *n.* **1.** a cultivated plant, *Armoracia rusticana,* of the mustard family, having small, white flowers. **2.** the pungent root of this plant, ground and used as a condiment and in medicine. **3.** the condiment itself, sometimes moistened with vinegar or mixed with ground beets. —*adj.* **4.** of or containing ground horseradish as a flavoring: *brisket of beef with horseradish sauce.* [1590–1600; HORSE + RADISH]

horse′radish perox′idase, *Histol.* an enzyme, isolated from horseradish, that when microinjected can be detected by the colored products of the reaction it catalyzes, used as a tracer, as in tracing the route of a motor neuron from the cell body in the spinal cord to the muscle it innervates.

horse′radish tree′, a tropical tree, *Moringa pterygosperma,* having fragrant white flowers and seeds yielding a commercially useful oil. Cf. **ben**[2]. [1855–60]

horse′ rake′, a large-wheeled rake drawn by a horse. [1810–20, *Amer.*]

horse′'s ass′, *Slang* (*vulgar*). a stupid or foolish person.

horse′ sense′, common sense. [1825–35, *Amer.*]

horse•shit (hôrs′shit′, hôrsh′-), *Slang* (*vulgar*). —*n.* **1.** nonsense, lies, or exaggeration. **2.** tedious, annoying, or unreasonable chores, demands, regulations, or the like. —*interj.* **3.** (used to express disbelief, incredulity, etc.) [HORSE + SHIT]

horse•shoe (hôrs′sho͞o′, hôrsh′-), *n., v.,* **-shoed, -shoe•ing,** *adj.* —*n.* **1.** a U-shaped metal plate, plain or with calks, nailed to a horse's hoof to protect it from being injured by hard or rough surfaces. **2.** something U-shaped, as a valley, river bend, or other natural feature: *We picnicked in the middle of a horseshoe of trees.* **3. horseshoes,** (*used with a singular v.*) a game in which horseshoes or other U-shaped pieces of metal, plastic, etc., are tossed at an iron stake 30 or 40 ft. (9 or 12 m) away in order to encircle it or to come closer to it than one's opponent. —*v.t.* **4.** to put a horseshoe or horseshoes on. —*adj.* **5.** having the shape of a horseshoe; U-shaped: *a horseshoe bend in the river.* [1350–1400; ME. See HORSE, SHOE] —**horse′sho′er,** *n.*

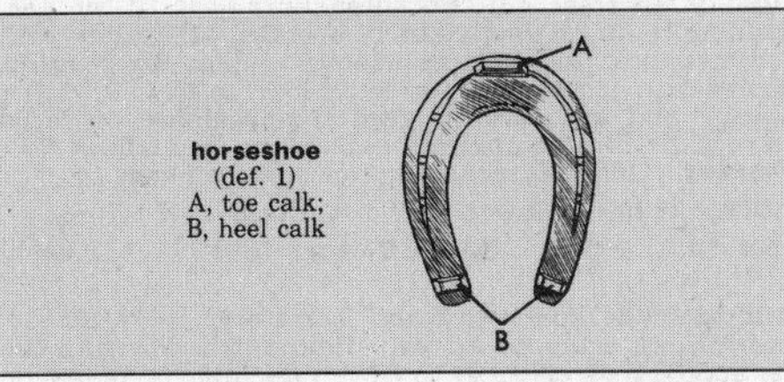

horseshoe (def. 1) A, toe calk; B, heel calk

horse′shoe arch′, an arch with the intrados widening above the springing and then narrowing to a rounded crown. Also called **Moorish arch.** See illus. under **arch.** [1805–15]

horse′shoe back′, *Furniture.* a bow back having a slight outward splay at its bottom.

horse′shoe crab′, a large marine arthropod, *Limulus polyphemus,* of shallow coastal waters of eastern North America and eastern Asia, having both compound and simple eyes, book gills, a stiff tail, and a brown carapace curved like a horseshoe: a living fossil related to the woodlouse. Also called **king crab.** [1765–75]

horseshoe crab, *Limulus polyphemus,* length of carapace 1 ft. (0.3 m); tail 9 in. (23 cm)

horse′shoe mag′net, a horseshoe-shaped permanent magnet. [1775–85]

horse′ show′, a competitive display of the capabilities and qualities of horses and their riders or handlers, usually held as an annual event. [1855–60, *Amer.*]

horse′'s mouth′, *Informal.* See **horse** (def. 20). [1925–30]

horse′'s neck′, a drink of whiskey and ginger ale, served with ice and garnished with a spiral of lemon peel on the rim of the glass. [1900–05, *Amer.*]

horse′'s tail′. See **burro's tail.** [1870–75]

horse′ sting′er, *Chiefly Brit. Dial.* a dragonfly. [1765–75]

horse′ tail′, a ponytail. [1870–75]

horse•tail (hôrs′tāl′), *n.* **1.** Also called **scouring rush.** any nonflowering plant of the genus *Equisetum,* having hollow, jointed stems. **2.** a horse's tail formerly used as a Turkish military standard or as an ensign of a pasha, the number of tails increasing with the rank. [1350–1400; ME *horse tayle.* See HORSE, TAIL[1]]

horse′tail ag′aric, the shaggy-mane. Also called **horse′tail mush′room.**

horse′tail tree′, beefwood (def. 1). [1880–85]

horse′ trade′, 1. a shrewdly conducted exchange, as of favors or objects, usually resulting from or accompanied by very close bargaining. **2.** an exchanging or trading of horses. [1840–50, *Amer.*]

horse-trade (hôrs′trād′), *v.i.,* **-trad•ed, -trad•ing.** to bargain or trade shrewdly. [1820–30, *Amer.*]

horse′ trad′er, 1. a person who is shrewd and clever at bargaining. **2.** a person who trades in horses. [1800–10, *Amer.*]

horse′ trad′ing, the act or fact of conducting a shrewd exchange or engaging in a horse trade; bargaining. [1820–30, *Amer.*]

horse•weed (hôrs′wēd′), *n.* **1.** a North American composite weed, *Erigeron canadensis,* having narrow, hairy leaves and clusters of very small greenish-white flowers. **2.** See **horse balm.** **3.** any of various other common weeds with small yellow flowers. [1780–90, *Amer.*; HORSE + WEED[1]]

horse•whip (hôrs′hwip′, -wip′), *n., v.,* **-whipped, -whip•ping.** —*n.* **1.** a whip for controlling horses. —*v.t.* **2.** to beat with a horsewhip. [1300–50; ME. See HORSE, WHIP] —**horse′whip′per,** *n.*

horse•wom•an (hôrs′wo͝om′ən), *n., pl.* **-wom•en. 1.** a woman who rides on horseback. **2.** a woman who is skilled in managing or riding horses. [1555–65; HORSE + WOMAN] —**horse′wom′an•ship′,** *n.*

hors•ey (hôr′sē), *adj.,* **hors•i•er, hors•i•est.** horsy.

hors•i•ly (hôr′sə lē), *adv.* in a horsy manner. [HORSY + -LY]

hor. som., (in prescriptions) at bedtime. [< L *hōrā somnī* at the hour of sleep]

horst (hôrst), *n.* a portion of the earth's crust, bounded on at least two sides by faults, that has risen in relation to adjacent portions. Cf. **graben.** [1890–95; < G: thicket; c. HURST]

Horst′ Wes′sel song′ (hôrst′ ves′əl), the official song of the Nazi party in Germany from 1933 to 1945. Also called ***Horst′ Wes′sel lied′.***

hors•y (hôr′sē), *adj.,* **hors•i•er, hors•i•est. 1.** of, pertaining to, or characteristic of a horse. **2.** dealing with or interested in horses, horseback riding, fox hunting, horse racing, etc.: *the horsy set in local society.* **3.** rather heavy and awkward in general appearance or facial structure: *That heavy coat makes you look horsy.* Also, **horsey.** [1585–95; HORSE + -Y[1]] —**hors′i•ness,** *n.*

hort., 1. horticultural. **2.** horticulture.

Hor•ta (hôr′tə), *n.* **Baron Victor,** 1861?–1947, Belgian architect.

hor•ta•tive (hôr′tə tiv), *adj.* hortatory. [1600–10; < L *hortātīvus,* equiv. to *hortāt(us),* ptp. of *hortārī* to incite to action, freq. of *horīrī* to encourage (akin to YEARN) + *-īvus* -IVE] —**hor′ta•tive•ly,** *adv.*

hor•ta•to•ry (hôr′tə tôr′ē, -tōr′ē), *adj.* urging to some course of conduct or action; exhorting; encouraging: *a hortatory speech.* [1580–90; < LL *hortātōrius* encouraging, equiv. to *hortā(rī)* (see HORTATIVE) + *-tōrius* -TORY[1]] —**hor′ta•to′ri•ly,** *adv.*

Hor•tense (hôr′tens), *n.* a female given name.

Hor•tense′ de Beauharnais′ (*Fr.* ôʀ täɴs′). See **Beauharnais, Eugénie Hortense de.**

Hor•thy (hôʀ′tē), *n.* **Mi•klós von Nagy-bá•nya** (mik′lōsh fôn nod′yᵊ bä′nyo), 1863–1957, Hungarian admiral: regent of Hungary 1920–44.

hor•ti•cul•ture (hôr′ti kul′chər), *n.* **1.** the cultivation of a garden, orchard, or nursery; the cultivation of flowers, fruits, vegetables, or ornamental plants. **2.** the science and art of cultivating such plants. [1670–80; < L *hort(us)* garden + (AGR)ICULTURE] —**hor′ti•cul′tur•al,** *adj.* —**hor′ti•cul′tur•ist,** *n.*

hor•tus sic•cus (hôr′təs sik′əs), a collection of dried plants; herbarium. [1680–90; < L: dry garden; see GARDEN, SACK[3]]

hor. un. spatio, (in prescriptions) at the end of one hour. [< L *hōrae ūnius spatiō*]

Ho•rus (hôr′əs, hōr′-), *n. Egyptian Relig.* a solar deity, regarded as either the son or the brother of Isis and Osiris, and usually represented as a falcon or as a man with the head of a falcon. [< LL *Hōrus* < Gk *Hôros* < Egyptian *ḥr*]

Hos., Hosea.

ho•san•na (hō zan′ə), *interj., n., pl.* **-nas,** *v.,* **-naed, -na•ing.** —*interj.* **1.** (an exclamation, originally an appeal to God for deliverance, used in praise of God or Christ.) —*n.* **2.** a cry of "hosanna." **3.** a shout of praise or adoration; an acclamation. —*v.t.* **4.** to praise, applaud, etc.: *The critics hosannaed his new play.* [< LL *(h)ōsanna* < Gk *ōsanná* < Heb *hōsh(i) ʿāh nnā* save, we pray; r. ME, OE *osanna* < LL, as above]

hose (hōz), *n., pl.* **hose** for 2, 3; **hos•es** for 1, 4, 5; (*Archaic*) **hos•en** (hō′zən); *v.,* **hosed, hos•ing.** —*n.* **1.** a flexible tube for conveying a liquid, as water, to a desired point: *a garden hose; a fire hose.* **2.** (*used with a plural v.*) an article of clothing for the foot and lower part of the leg; stocking or sock. **3.** (of men's attire in former times) **a.** an article of clothing for the leg, extending from about the knee to the ankle and worn with knee breeches. **b.** (*used with a plural v.*) knee breeches. **c.** (*used with a plural v.*) tights, as were worn with, and usually attached to, a doublet. **4.** *Brit. Dial.* a sheath, or sheathing part, as that enclosing a kernel of grain. **5.** *Golf.* hosel. —*v.t.* **6.** to water, wash, spray, or drench by means of a hose (often fol. by *down*): *to hose the garden; to hose down the ship's deck.* **7.** *Slang.* **a.** to cheat, trick, or take advantage of. **b.** to defeat decisively. **c.** to reject. **d.** *Chiefly Mil.* to attack or assault (an area) in order to gain control quickly (sometimes fol. by *down*). [bef. 1100; (n.) ME, OE; c. D *hoos,* ON *hosa,* G *Hose;* (v.) ME: to provide with hose, deriv. of the n.] —**hose′less,** *adj.* —**hose′like′,** *adj.*

Ho•se•a (hō zē′ə, -zā′ə), *n.* **1.** a Minor Prophet of the 8th century B.C. **2.** a book of the Bible bearing his name. *Abbr.:* Hos. [< Heb *hōshēaʿ,* lit., salvation, help]

hose•cock (hōz′kok′), *n.* a threaded exterior faucet, as for attaching a garden hose. Also called **sillcock.** [HOSE + COCK[1]]

Ho•sein (ho͞o sān′), *n.* Hussein (def. 1).

ho•sel (hō′zəl), *n. Golf.* the socket in the club head of an iron that receives the shaft. Also called **hose.** [1895–1900; HOSE + *-el* dim. suffix]

CONCISE ETYMOLOGY KEY: <, descended or borrowed from; >, whence; b., blend of, blended; c., cognate with; cf., compare; deriv., derivative; equiv., equivalent; imit., imitative; obl., oblique; r., replacing; s., stem; sp., spelling, spelled; resp., respelling, respelled; trans., translation; ?, origin unknown; *, unattested; ‡, probably earlier than. See the full key inside the front cover.

Ho•sha•na Rab•bah (*Seph. Heb.* hô shä nä′ ʀä bä′; *Ashk. Heb.* hō shä′nô ʀä′bô), the seventh day of the Jewish festival of Sukkoth, occurring on the twenty-first day of Tishri and having a special liturgy containing a series of invocations to God for forgiveness and salvation. Also, **Hosha′nah Rab′bah.** [< Heb *hōsh(i) ʿāh nnā* save, we pray + *rabbā* the myriad, multitude]

ho•sier (hō′zhər), *n.* a person who makes or deals in hose or stockings or goods knitted or woven like hose. [1375–1425; late ME *hosiare.* See HOSE, -IER[1]]

ho•sier•y (hō′zhə rē), *n.* **1.** stockings or socks of any kind. **2.** the business of a hosier. [1780–90; HOSIER + -Y[3]]

hos•ing (hō′zing), *n. Slang.* **1.** an act or instance of being taken advantage of or cheated. **2.** an act or instance of being attacked or defeated decisively; drubbing: *Small investors took a hosing in the recent stock-market decline.* [HOSE + -ING[1]]

hosp., hospital.

hos•pice (hos′pis), *n.* **1.** a house of shelter or rest for pilgrims, strangers, etc., esp. one kept by a religious order. **2.** *Med.* **a.** a health-care facility for the terminally ill that emphasizes pain control and emotional support for the patient and family, typically refraining from taking extraordinary measures to prolong life. **b.** a similar program of care and support for the terminally ill at home. [1810–20; < F < L *hospitium* HOSPITIUM]

hos•pi•ta•ble (hos′pi tə bəl, ho spit′ə bəl), *adj.* **1.** receiving or treating guests or strangers warmly and generously: *a hospitable family.* **2.** characterized by or betokening warmth and generosity toward guests or strangers: *a hospitable smile.* **3.** favorably receptive or open (usually fol. by *to*): *to be hospitable to new ideas; a climate hospitable to the raising of corn.* [1560–70; < L *hospitā(re)* to receive as guest (cf. L *hospitārī* to be a guest; see HOSPITIUM) + -BLE] —**hos′pi•ta•ble•ness,** *n.* —**hos′pi•ta•bly,** *adv.*

hos•pi•tal (hos′pi tl), *n.* **1.** an institution in which sick or injured persons are given medical or surgical treatment. **2.** a similar establishment for the care of animals. **3.** a repair shop for specific portable objects: *violin hospital; doll hospital.* **4.** *Brit.* an institution supported by charity or taxes for the care of the needy, as an orphanage or old people's home. [1250–1300; ME *hospitale* < ML, n. use of neut. of L *hospitālis* hospitable, equiv. to *hospit-* (see HOSPITIUM) + *-ālis* -AL[1]]

hos′pital bed′, a bed having side rails that can be raised or lowered and a mattress base in three jointed sections so that the head, foot, or middle may be raised by a crank or motor, allowing a patient to lie in various positions, as a therapeutic aid or for comfort. [1815–25]

hos′pital cor′ner, a fold on a bed sheet or blanket made by tucking the foot or head of the sheet straight under the mattress with the ends protruding and then making a diagonal fold at the side corner of the sheet and tucking this under to produce a triangular corner.

Hos•pi•tal•er (hos′pi tl ər), *n.* **1.** a member of the religious and military order **(Knights Hospitalers** or **Knights of St. John of Jerusalem)** originating about the time of the first Crusade (1096–99) and taking its name from a hospital at Jerusalem. **2.** (*l.c.*) a person, esp. a member of a religious order, devoted to the care of the sick or needy in hospitals. Also, **Hos′pi•tal•ler.** [1350–1400; HOSPITAL + -ER[1]; r. ME *hospitalier* < MF < ML *hospitālārius;* see -IER[2]]

Hos•pi•ta•let (ôs′pē tä let′), *n.* a city in NE Spain, near Barcelona. 241,978.

hos′pital gan′grene, *Pathol.* a contagious, often fatal gangrene, esp. involving amputation stumps and war wounds, occurring usually in crowded, ill-kept hospitals, and caused by putrefactive bacteria. [1805–15]

hos•pi•tal•ism (hos′pi tl iz′əm), *n.* **1.** hospital conditions having an adverse effect on patients. **2.** the adverse mental and physical effects caused by such conditions. **3.** the physiological and psychological consequences of living in a hospital, nursing home, etc. [1865–70; HOSPITAL + -ISM]

hos•pi•tal•i•ty (hos′pi tal′i tē), *n., pl.* **-ties. 1.** the friendly reception and treatment of guests or strangers. **2.** the quality or disposition of receiving and treating guests and strangers in a warm, friendly, generous way. [1325–75; ME *hospitalite* < MF < L *hospitālitās,* equiv. to *hospitāli(s)* (see HOSPITAL) + *-tās* -TY[2]]
—**Syn. 2.** warmth, cordiality, geniality, friendliness.

hospital′ity suite′, a suite or room, as in a hotel or convention center, rented by a business firm, political candidate, or the like, to meet and entertain clients, potential customers, etc. Also called **hospital′ity room′.** [1960–65]

hos•pi•tal•i•za•tion (hos′pi tl ə zā′shən), *n.* **1.** the act, process, or state of being hospitalized. **2.** the period during which a person is hospitalized: *to extend one's hospitalization.* **3.** See **hospitalization insurance.** [1905–10; HOSPITALIZE + -ATION]

hospitaliza′tion insur′ance, insurance to cover, in whole or in part, the hospital bills of a subscriber or of his or her dependents.

hos•pi•tal•ize (hos′pi tl īz′), *v.t.,* **-ized, -iz•ing.** to place in a hospital for medical care or observation: *The doctor hospitalized grandfather as soon as she checked his heart.* Also, *esp. Brit.,* **hos′pi•tal•ise′.** [1900–05; HOSPITAL + -IZE]

hos′pital light′. See **hopper casement.** Also called **hos′pital win′dow.**

hos•pi•tal•man (hos′pi tl mən), *n., pl.* **-men.** *U.S. Navy.* an enlisted person working as a hospital assistant; corpsman. [1820–30; HOSPITAL + MAN[1]]

hos′pital ship′, a ship built to serve as a hospital, esp. used to treat the wounded in wartime and accorded safe passage by international law. [1675–85]

hos′pital train′, a military train equipped to transport wounded troops to a hospital. [1870–75]

hos•pi•ti•um (ho spish′ē əm), *n., pl.* **hos•pi•ti•a** (ho-spish′ē ə). a hospice. [1640–50; < L: hospitable reception, entertainment, place of entertainment, equiv. to *hospit-* (s. of *hospes*) host, guest, stranger + *-ium* -IUM]

hos•po•dar (hos′pə där′), *n.* a former title of governors or princes of Wallachia and Moldavia. [1620–30; < Rumanian < Ukrainian *gospodár′* lit., lord; cf. Russ Church Slavonic *gospodarĭ* (c. Czech *hospodář,* Serbo-Croatian *gospòdār*), equiv. to *gospodĭ* lord + *-arĭ* n. suffix; *gospodĭ* perh. < **gos(tĭ)-potĭ,* hence c. L *hospes* (see HOST[1]), though *d* for *t* unexplained]

host[1] (hōst), *n.* **1.** a person who receives or entertains guests at home or elsewhere: *the host at a theater party.* **2.** a master of ceremonies, moderator, or interviewer for a television or radio program. **3.** a person, place, company, or the like, that provides services, resources, etc., as for a convention or sporting event: *Our city would like to serve as host for the next Winter Olympics.* **4.** the landlord of an inn. **5.** a living animal or plant from which a parasite obtains nutrition. **6.** *Surg.* the recipient of a graft. Cf. **donor** (def. 2). —*v.t.* **7.** to be the host at (a dinner, reception, etc.): *He hosted a reception for new members.* **8.** to act as host to: *The vice president hosted the foreign dignitaries during their visit.* **9.** to act as master of ceremonies, moderator, or interviewer for: *to host a popular talk show.* —*v.i.* **10.** to perform the duties or functions of a host. [1250–1300; ME *(h)oste* (n.) < MF < L *hospit-* (s. of *hospes*) host, guest, stranger, perh. < **hosti-pot(i)s* or **hos-pot(i)s,* equiv. to *hos(ti)-* comb. form of *hostis* stranger (see HOST[2]) + *-pot(i)s,* akin to *potis* having the power to, *posse* to be able (see POTENT) (hence, "one granting hospitality, one in charge of guests"); cf., with different initial elements, Gk *despótēs* master, DESPOT, Lith *viẽšpats* lord] —**host′less,** *adj.* —**host′ship,** *n.*

host[2] (hōst), *n.* **1.** a multitude or great number of persons or things: *a host of details.* **2.** an army. [1250–1300; ME *(h)oste* < OF < L *hostis* stranger, enemy; akin to GUEST]
—**Syn. 1.** swarm, crowd, drove, throng, horde, myriad.

Host (hōst), *n. Eccles.* the bread or wafer consecrated in the celebration of the Eucharist. [1275–1325; ME *hoste* < LL *hostia* Eucharistic wafer (L: victim, sacrifice); r. ME *oyst* < MF *oiste* < LL, as above]

hos•ta (hō′stə, hos′tə), *n.* any of various plants belonging to the genus *Hosta,* of the lily family, which includes the plantain lily. [< NL (1797), after Nicolaus Thomas *Host* (1761–1834), Austrian botanist; see -A[2]]

hos•tage (hos′tij), *n., v.,* **-taged, -tag•ing.** —*n.* **1.** a person given or held as security for the fulfillment of certain conditions or terms, promises, etc., by another. **2.** *Archaic.* a security or pledge. **3.** *Obs.* the condition of a hostage. —*v.t.* **4.** to give (someone) as a hostage: *He was hostaged to the Indians.* [1225–75; ME < OF *hostage* (*h-* by assoc. with *(h)oste* HOST[2]), *ostage* << VL **obsidāticum* state of being a hostage < L *obsid-* (s. of *obses*) hostage (equiv. to *ob-* OB- + *sid-* SIT) + *-āticum* -AGE] —**hos′tage•ship′,** *n.*

host′ comput′er, the main computer in a network: controls or performs certain functions for other computers.

hos•tel (hos′tl), *n., v.*-**teled, -tel•ing** or (*esp. Brit.*) **-telled, -tel•ling.** —*n.* **1.** Also called **youth hostel.** an inexpensive, supervised lodging place for young people on bicycle trips, hikes, etc. **2.** *Brit.* a residence hall at a university. **3.** an inn. —*v.i.* **4.** to travel, lodging each night at a hostel. [1200–50; ME *(h)ostel* < OF < LL *hospitāle* guest room. See HOSPITAL]

hos•tel•er (hos′tl ər), *n.* **1.** a person who operates a hostel. **2.** a person who stays at a hostel or goes hosteling. Also, *esp. Brit.,* **hos′tel•ler.** [1250–1300; ME; see HOSTEL, -ER[2]; akin to OF *hostelier*]

hos•tel•ry (hos′tl rē), *n., pl.* **-ries.** an inn or hotel. [1350–1400; ME *hostelrye,* var. of *hostelerie* < MF. See HOSTEL, -RY]

hos′tel school′, (in Canada) one of a series of boarding schools operated by the federal government in the northern territories for Indian and Eskimo students.

host•ess (hō′stis), *n.* **1.** a woman who receives and entertains guests in her own home or elsewhere. **2.** a woman employed in a restaurant or place of amusement to receive, seat, or assist patrons. **3.** a woman who acts as master of ceremonies, moderator, or interviewer for a television or radio program; host. **4.** a woman employed by an airline, railroad, bus company, etc., to see that passengers are comfortable throughout a trip, usually receiving and seating them, and sometimes serving them refreshments. **5.** a woman who manages a resort or hotel or who directs its social activities. **6.** See **taxi dancer.** —*v.t.* **7.** to be the hostess at (a reception, dinner, etc.): *She will hostess a shower for the new bride.* **8.** to act as hostess at, to, or for: *She volunteered to hostess the garden club next season.* —*v.i.* **9.** to perform the duties or functions of a hostess. [1250–1300; ME *(h)ostesse* < OF. See HOST[1], -ESS] —**host′ess•ship′,** *n.*
—**Usage.** See **-ess.**

host′ess gown′, a robe or housecoat worn by women for informal entertaining at home. [1935–40]

hos•tile (hos′tl *or, esp. Brit.,* -tīl), *adj.* **1.** of, pertaining to, or characteristic of an enemy: *a hostile nation.* **2.** opposed in feeling, action, or character; antagonistic: *hostile criticism.* **3.** characterized by antagonism. **4.** not friendly, warm, or generous; not hospitable. —*n.* **5.** a person or thing that is antagonistic or unfriendly. **6.** *Mil.* an enemy soldier, plane, ship, etc. [1585–95; < L *hostīlis,* equiv. to *hostis* enemy (see HOST[2]) + *-īlis* -ILE] —**hos′tile•ly,** *adv.*
—**Syn. 1.** warlike, aggressive. **2.** adverse, averse, contrary. HOSTILE, INIMICAL indicate that which characterizes an enemy or something injurious to one's interests. HOSTILE applies to the spirit, attitude, or action of an enemy: *They showed a hostile and menacing attitude.* INIMICAL applies to an antagonistic or injurious tendency or influence: *Their remarks were inimical to his reputation.* —**Ant. 1, 2.** friendly. **3.** sympathetic.

hos′tile fire′, *Insurance.* an unintentional fire, from which any resulting loss can be claimed as an insurance liability (opposed to *friendly fire*).

hos•til•i•ty (ho stil′i tē), *n., pl.* **-ties. 1.** a hostile state, condition, or attitude; enmity; antagonism; unfriendliness. **2.** a hostile act. **3.** opposition or resistance to an idea, plan, project, etc. **4. hostilities, a.** acts of warfare. **b.** war. [1375–1425; late ME *hostilite* < L *hostīlitās.* See HOSTILE, -ITY]
—Syn. 1. animosity, animus, ill will, hatred. **4.** fighting, conflict. **—Ant. 1.** friendliness. **4.** peace.

hos•tler (hos′lər, os′lər), *n.* **1.** a person who takes care of horses, esp. at an inn. **2.** an employee who moves and services trains, buses, or other vehicles after their regular runs or who does the maintenance work on large machines. [1350–1400; ME; var. of HOSTELER] **—hos′tler•ship′,** *n.*

host•ly (hōst′lē), *adj.* of or proper to a host: *the hostly qualities of consideration and generosity.* [1890–95; HOST + -LY]

host-spe•cif•ic (hōst′spi sif′ik), *adj.* capable of living solely on or in one species of host, as a parasite that infests only chickens. [1965–70]

hot (hot), *adj.,* **hot•ter, hot•test,** *adv., v.,* **hot•ted, hot•ting,** *n.* **—***adj.* **1.** having or giving off heat; having a high temperature: *a hot fire; hot coffee.* **2.** having or causing a sensation of great bodily heat; attended with or producing such a sensation: *He was hot with fever.* **3.** creating a burning sensation, as on the skin or in the throat: *This ointment is hot, so apply it sparingly.* **4.** sharply peppery or pungent: *Is this mustard hot?* **5.** having or showing intense or violent feeling; ardent; fervent; vehement; excited: *a hot temper.* **6.** *Informal.* having a strong enthusiasm; eager: *a hot baseball fan.* **7.** *Slang.* **a.** sexually aroused; lustful. **b.** sexy; attractive. **8.** violent, furious, or intense: *the hottest battle of the war.* **9.** strong or fresh, as a scent or trail. **10.** absolutely new; fresh: *a dozen new mystery stories hot from the press.* **11.** requiring immediate delivery or correspondence; demanding priority: *The hot freight must be delivered by 10:00 A.M. tomorrow, or we'll lose the contract.* **12.** *Slang.* skillful in a reckless or daring way: *a hot pilot.* **13.** following very closely; close: *to be hot on the trail of a thief.* **14.** (of colors) extremely intense: *hot pink.* **15.** *Informal.* popular and commercially successful; in demand; marketable: *The Beatles were a hot group in the 1960's.* **16.** *Slang.* extremely lucky, good, or favorable: *a hot poker hand.* **17.** *Slang.* (in sports and games) playing well or winningly; scoring effectively: *a hot pitcher.* **18.** *Slang.* funny; absurd: *That's a hot one!* **19.** *Games.* close to the object or answer that is being sought. **20.** *Informal.* extremely exciting or interesting; sensational or scandalous: *a hot news story.* **21.** *Jazz.* **a.** (of music) emotionally intense, propulsive, and marked by aggressive attack and warm, full tone. **b.** (of a musician) skilled in playing hot jazz. **22.** *Informal.* (of a vehicle) capable of attaining extremely high speeds: *a hot new jet plane.* **23.** *Slang.* **a.** stolen recently or otherwise illegal and dangerous to possess: *hot TV's.* **b.** wanted by the police. **c.** dangerous. **24.** *Informal.* in the mood to perform exceedingly well, or rapidly, as during a burst of creative work: *Finish writing that story while you're still hot.* **25.** actively conducting an electric current or containing a high voltage: *a hot wire.* **26.** of, pertaining to, or noting radioactivity. **27.** *Metalworking.* noting any process involving plastic deformation of a metal at a temperature high enough to permit recrystallization due to the strain: *hot working.* **28. get hot,** *Slang.* (in sports and games) to become very effective or successful; score or win repeatedly or easily. **29. hot and bothered,** *Informal.* excited, aroused, or flustered: *This mistake isn't worth getting hot and bothered about.* Also, **all hot and bothered. 30. hot under the collar.** See **collar** (def. 16). **31. make it hot for,** *Informal.* to make something unpleasant for; cause trouble for: *Ever since their argument the principal has been making it hot for the new teacher.*
—*adv.* **32.** in a hot manner; hotly. **33.** while hot: *Garnish the potatoes with parsley and serve hot.* **34.** *Metalworking.* at a temperature high enough to permit recrystallization: *The wire was drawn hot.* **35. hot and heavy,** *Informal.* in an intense, vehement, or passionate manner: *They argued hot and heavy for 20 minutes.*
—*v.t., v.i.* **36.** *Chiefly Brit. Informal.* to heat; warm (usually fol. by *up*).
—*n.* **37. the hots,** *Slang.* intense sexual desire or attraction. [bef. 1000; 1920–25 for def. 23; ME *ho(o)t,* OE *hāt;* c. D *heet,* ON *heitr,* Sw *het,* Dan *hed,* G *heiss*] **—hot′ly,** *adv.* **—hot′ness,** *n.*
—Syn. 1. heated; fiery, burning, scorching; scalding, boiling; torrid, sultry. **4.** biting, piquant, sharp, spicy. **5.** fervid; fiery, passionate, intense, excitable, impetuous; angry, furious, irate, violent. **—Ant. 1.** cold.

hot′ air′, *Informal.* empty, exaggerated, or pretentious talk or writing: *His report on the company's progress was just so much hot air.* [1835–45 for literal sense]

Ho•tan (hō′tän′), *n. Pinyin.* **1.** an oasis in W China, in SW Xinjiang. **2.** the chief city in this oasis. 50,000. Also, **Hetian, Hotien, Khotan.**

hot′ bed′, *Metalworking.* an area having rails or rolls on which rolled pieces are laid to cool. [1620–30]

hot•bed (hot′bed′), *n., v.,* **-bed•ded, -bed•ding. —***n.* **1.** a bottomless, boxlike, usually glass-covered structure and the bed of earth it covers, heated typically by fermenting manure or electrical cables, for growing plants out of season. **2.** a place or environment favoring rapid growth or spread, esp. of something disliked or unwanted: *a hotbed of disease.* **3.** *Slang.* a bed shared by two or more persons in shifts, each sleeping in it for or at a designated time and then vacating it for the next occupant. **—***v.i.* **4.** *Slang.* to share a bed in shifts, so that it is always occupied. [1620–30; HOT + BED]

hot-blood•ed (hot′blud′id), *adj.* **1.** excitable; impetuous. **2.** ardent, passionate, or virile. **3.** adventuresome, exciting, or characterized by adventure and excitement. **4.** (of livestock) of superior or pure breeding. **5.** (of horses) being a Thoroughbred or having Arab blood. [1590–1600] **—hot′-blood′ed•ness,** *n.*

hot•box (hot′boks′), *n. Railroads.* a journal box overheated by excessive friction of an axle as a result of inadequate lubrication or the presence of foreign matter. Also, **hot′ box′.** [1835–45; HOT + BOX[1]]

hot′-bulb′ en′gine (hot′bulb′), a low-compression oil engine requiring a heated bulb or cap for ignition. [1910–15]

hot′ but′tered rum′, a drink made with rum, hot water, and sugar, served with a lump of butter in a mug.

hot-but•ton (hot′but′n), *adj.* exciting strong feelings; highly charged; emotional: *hot-button issues.* [1985–90]

hot′ cake′, 1. a pancake or griddlecake. **2. sell** or **go like hot cakes,** to be disposed of very quickly and effortlessly, esp. in quantity: *His record sold like hot cakes on the first day after its release.* [1675–85, *Amer.*]
—Regional Variation. 1. See **pancake.**

hot′ cap′, a plastic or paper bag or small tentlike structure placed over plants in early spring to protect them from frost.

hot′-cath′ode tube′ (hot′kath′ōd), *Electronics.* See **thermionic tube.** [1910–15]

hotch (hoch), *Scot. and North Eng.* **—***v.i.* **1.** to fidget; shift one's weight from one foot to the other. **—***v.t.* **2.** to cause to fidget or shiver. [1350–1400; ME (north) *hotchen;* akin to D *hotsen* to jolt, dial. G *hotzen* to move up and down, F *hocher* to jog, shake (OF *hochier* < Gmc)]

hot•cha (hä′chä, -chə), *interj. Older Slang.* (used as an expression of approval or delight, now often used facetiously.) [1930–35; of uncert. orig.]

Hotch•kiss (hoch′kis), *n.* **Hazel.** See **Wightman, Hazel Hotchkiss.**

hotch•pot (hoch′pot′), *n. Law.* the bringing together of shares or properties in order to divide them equally, esp. when they are to be divided among the children of a parent dying intestate. [1250–1300; ME *hochepot* < AF, lit., shake-pot. See HOTCH, POT[1]]

hotch•potch (hoch′poch′), *n.* **1.** a thick soup or stew of vegetables or meat, often thickened with barley. **2.** *Brit.* hodgepodge. **3.** *Law.* a hotchpot. [1350–1400; ME *hoche poche,* rhyming var. of HOTCHPOT]

hot′ cock′les, a children's game in which a blindfolded player is hit by one of the other players and then tries to guess which one did the hitting. [1540–50]

hot′ cold′-working, metalworking at considerable heat but below the temperature at which the metal recrystallizes: a form of cold-working. [‡1960–65]

hot′ comb′, a comb or comblike appliance heated electrically and used to arrange or style the hair. [1965–70]

hot-comb (hot′kōm′), *v.t.* to arrange or style (the hair) with a hot comb.

hot′ cor′ner, *Baseball.* See **third base** (def. 2). [1900–05]

hot′ cross′ bun′, a bun with a cross of frosting on it, eaten chiefly during Lent. [1725–35]

hot′-dip′ coat′ing (hot′dip′), the process of coating sheets of iron or steel with molten zinc. Also called **hot galvanizing.** [1920–25]

hot-dipped (hot′dipt′), *adj.* coated by being dipped into molten tin or zinc. [1935–40]

hot′ dog′, 1. a frankfurter. **2.** a sandwich consisting of a frankfurter in a split roll, usually eaten with mustard, sauerkraut, or relish. **3.** Also, **hot′dog′, hot′ dog′ger, hot′dog′ger, hot′-dog′ger.** *Informal.* **a.** a person who performs complex, showy, and sometimes dangerous maneuvers, esp. in surfing or skiing. **b.** a show-off, esp. in sports. **4.** *Informal.* (used to express great joy or delight.) [1895–1900, *Amer.*]

hot-dog (hot′dôg′, -dog′), *v.,* **-dogged, -dog•ging,** *adj. Informal.* **—***v.i.* **1.** to perform unusual or very intricate maneuvers in a sport, esp. surfing or skiing. **2.** to perform in a recklessly or flamboyantly skillful manner, as in a sport or athletic activity; show off. **—***adj.* **3.** skillful or excellent, as in sports performance. **4.** of, indicating, or for a type of sports activity, esp. surfing or skiing, in which intricate and potentially dangerous stunts are performed. **5.** intended or done to draw attention; showy or sensational. Also, **hot′dog′.**

hot-dog•ging (hot′dô′ging, -dog′ing), *n. Informal.* the act of one who hot-dogs; the performance of intricate, daring, or flamboyant stunts. Also, **hot′-dog′ging.** [1960–65; HOT-DOG + -ING[1]]

hot-draw (hot′drô′), *v.t.,* **-drew, -drawn, -draw•ing.** *Metalworking.* to draw (wire, tubing, etc.) at a temperature high enough to permit recrystallization. [1895–1900]

ho•tel (hō tel′), *n.* **1.** a commercial establishment offering lodging to travelers and sometimes to permanent residents, and often having restaurants, meeting rooms, stores, etc., that are available to the general public. **2.** (*cap.*) *Mil.* the NATO name for a class of nuclear-powered Soviet ballistic missile submarine armed with up to six single-warhead missiles. **3.** a word used in communications to represent the letter *H.* [1635–45; < F *hôtel,* OF *hostel* HOSTEL] **—ho•tel′less,** *adj.*
—Syn. 1. hostelry, hostel, guesthouse, motel. HOTEL, HOUSE, INN, TAVERN refer to establishments for the lodging or entertainment of travelers and others. HOTEL is the common word, suggesting a more or less commodious establishment with up-to-date appointments, although this is not necessarily true: *the best hotel in the city; a cheap hotel near the docks.* The word HOUSE is often used in the name of a particular hotel, the connotation being wealth and luxury: *the Parker House; the Palmer House.* INN suggests a place of homelike comfort and old-time appearance or ways; it is used for quaint or archaic effect in the names of some public houses and hotels in the U.S.: *the Pickwick Inn; the Wayside Inn.* A TAVERN, like the English PUBLIC HOUSE, is a house where liquor is sold for drinking on the premises; until recently it was archaic or dialectal in the U.S., but has been revived to substitute for *saloon,* which had unfavorable connotations: *Taverns are required to close by two o'clock in the morning.* The word has also been used in the sense of INN, esp. in New England, ever since Colonial days: *Wiggins Tavern.*

Hô•tel des In•va•lides (ō tel dā zaN va lēd′), a military hospital built in Paris in the 17th and 18th centuries by Libéral Bruant and J. H. Mansart: famous for its chapel dome, the tomb of Napoleon, and as a military museum.

hô•tel de ville (ō tel′ də vēl′), *pl.* ***hô•tels de ville*** (ō tel′ də vēl′). *French.* a city hall. [lit., mansion of the city]

hô•tel-Dieu (ō tel dyœ′), *n. pl.* ***hô•tels-Dieu*** (ō tel-dyœ′). *French.* a hospital. [lit., mansion of God]

ho•te•lier (ō′təl yā′, hōt′l ēr′), *n.* a manager or owner of a hotel or inn. [1900–05; < F *hôtelier;* see HOTEL, -IER[2]]

ho•tel•keep•er (hō tel′kē′pər), *n.* a manager or owner of a hotel. [1820–30, *Amer.;* HOTEL + KEEPER]

ho•tel•man (hō tel′mən, -man′), *n., pl.* **-men** (-mən, -men′). hotelkeeper. [1915–20; HOTEL + MAN[1]]

hotel′ rack′, rack[6] (def. 2).

hot′ flash′, a sudden, temporary sensation of heat experienced by some women during menopause. Also called **hot′ flush′.** [1905–10]

hot•foot (hot′fo͝ot′), *n., pl.* **-foots,** *v., adv.* **—***n.* **1.** a practical joke in which a match, inserted surreptitiously between the sole and upper of the victim's shoe, is lighted and allowed to burn down. **—***v.i.* **2.** *Informal.* to go in great haste; walk or run hurriedly or rapidly (often fol. by *it*): *to hotfoot it to the bus stop.* **—***adv.* **3.** with great speed in going; in haste. [1250–1300; ME *hot fot* (adv.). See HOT, FOOT]

hot′ gal′vanizing. See **hot-dip coating.**

hot•head (hot′hed′), *n.* an impetuous or short-tempered person. [1650–60; HOT + HEAD]

hot•head•ed (hot′hed′id), *adj.* **1.** hot or fiery in spirit or temper; impetuous; rash: *Hotheaded people shouldn't drive cars.* **2.** easily angered; quick to take offense. [1635–45; HOT + HEAD + -ED[3]] **—hot′head′ed•ly,** *adv.* **—hot′head′ed•ness,** *n.*

hot•house (hot′hous′), *n., pl.* **-hous•es** (-hou′ziz), *adj.* **—***n.* **1.** an artificially heated greenhouse for the cultivation of tender plants. **—***adj.* **2.** of, pertaining to, or noting a plant grown in a hothouse, or so fragile as to be capable of being grown only in a hothouse. **3.** overprotected, artificial, or unnaturally delicate. [1505–15; HOT + HOUSE]

hot′house lamb′, a lamb born in the fall or early winter, usually reared indoors, specially fed, and marketed when from 9 to 16 weeks of age.

Ho•tien (hō′tyen′), *n. Wade-Giles.* Hotan.

hot′ lick′, *Jazz.* lick (def. 17). [1930–35]

hot′ light′, *Television.* a powerful light used in television production.

hot′ line′, 1. a direct telecommunications link, as a telephone line or Teletype circuit, enabling immediate communication between heads of state in an international crisis: *the hot line between Washington and Moscow.* **2.** a telephone service enabling people to talk confidentially with someone about a personal problem or crisis. **3.** a telephone line providing customers or clients with direct access to a company or professional service. Also, **hotline.** [1950–55]

hot•line (hot′līn′), *n.* **1.** See **hot line. —***adj.* **2.** *Chiefly Canadian.* of or pertaining to a radio program that receives telephone calls from listeners on the air. [1950–55; HOT + LINE[1]]

hot•lin•er (hot′lī′nər), *n.* **1.** a person who speaks to callers on a telephone hot line. **2.** Also, **hot′-lin′er.** *Chiefly Canadian.* a radio broadcaster who accepts calls on the air from individuals using a telephone hot line set up for that purpose. [1970–75; HOT LINE + -ER[1]]

hot′ met′al, *Print.* metallic type and printing elements produced by a casting machine; foundry type. Also called **hot type.** Cf. **cold type.** [1955–60]

hot′ mon′ey, *Informal.* funds transferred suddenly from one country to another chiefly to avoid depreciation in value or to take advantage of higher interest rates. [1925–30]

hot′ pack′, 1. a hot towel, dressing, or the like, applied to the body to reduce swelling, relieve pain, etc. **2.** Also called **hot′ pack′ meth′od.** a method of canning food by cooking it and packing it while hot in jars or cans, then sterilizing in boiling water or steam. Cf. **cold pack.**

hot pants (hot′ pants′ *for 1;* hot′ pants′ *for 2*), **1.** very brief and usually tight-fitting shorts for women and girls, first popularized in the early 1970's. **2.** *Slang.* strong sexual desire. [1965–70]

hot′ pep′per, 1. any of variously shaped pungent peppers of the genus *Capsicum,* containing large amounts of capsaicin and usually having thin walls. **2.** a plant bearing such a pepper. [1940–45]

hot′ plate′, 1. a portable appliance for cooking, formerly heated by a gas burner placed underneath it, now heated chiefly by an electrical unit in the appliance. **2.** a hot meal, usually consisting of meat, potato, and a vegetable, served all on one plate and usually at a set price at a restaurant or lunch counter. **3.** a plate that can retain heat in order to keep food hot. [1835–45]

hot′ pot′, *Chiefly Brit.* mutton or beef cooked with potatoes in a covered pot. [1690–1700]

hot′ pota′to, **1.** *Informal.* a situation or issue that is difficult, unpleasant, or risky to deal with. **2.** *Brit. Informal.* a baked potato. [1840–50]

hot-press (hot′pres′), *n.* **1.** a machine applying heat in conjunction with mechanical pressure, as for producing a smooth surface on paper or for expressing oil. —*v.t.* **2.** to subject to treatment in a hot-press. [1625–35] —**hot′-press′er,** *n.*

hot′ press′ing, a method of forming alloy steels or specialized ceramics from compound powders by the application of heat and pressure in a mold. [1735–45]

hot′ rod′, *Slang.* an automobile specially built or altered for fast acceleration and increased speed. [1940–45, *Amer.*]

hot-rod (hot′rod′), *v.,* **-rod·ded, -rod·ding.** *Slang.* —*v.i.* **1.** to drive a hot rod. **2.** to drive very fast. —*v.t.* **3.** to drive (a vehicle) very fast. **4.** to adapt (a vehicle or its engine) for increased speed. [1945–50]

hot′ rod′der, *Slang.* **1.** a driver or builder of hot rods. **2.** a fast and reckless driver. Also, **hot′-rod′der.** [1945–50, *Amer.*]

hot-roll (hot′rōl′, -rōl′), *v.t. Metalworking.* to roll (metal) at a heat high enough to permit recrystallization. [1875–80]

hot′ sauce′, any of several highly spiced, pungent condiments, esp. one containing some type of pepper or chili.

hot′ seat′, *Slang.* **1.** See **electric chair. 2.** a highly uncomfortable or embarrassing situation: *I'm in the hot seat because of the contract I lost.* [1915–20]

hot′ shit′, *Slang (vulgar).* **1.** a person who behaves in a showy or conceited manner; hotshot. **2.** (used to express enthusiasm or approval.) [1970–75]

hot′ shoe′, *Photog.* a bracket on a camera body that provides support and electrical contact for an electronic flash attachment. [1970–75]

hot-short (hot′shôrt′), *adj.* (of steel or wrought iron) brittle when heated, usually due to high sulfur content. [1790–1800; HOT + SHORT, as in RED-SHORT] —**hot′-short′ness,** *n.*

hot shot (hot′ shot′ *for 1;* hot′ shot′ *for 2*), **1.** incandescent shot fired to set enemy ships or buildings on fire. **2.** hotshot (defs. 4, 6). [1595–1605]

hot·shot (hot′shot′), *Slang.* —*adj.* **1.** highly successful and aggressive: *a hotshot lawyer; a hotshot account exec.* **2.** displaying skill flamboyantly: *a hotshot ballplayer.* **3.** moving, going, or operating without a stop; fast: *a hotshot express.* —*n.* **4.** an impressively successful or skillful and often vain person. **5.** *Railroads.* an express freight train. **6.** a firefighter. Also, **hot shot** (for defs. 4, 6). [1595–1605; HOT + SHOT[1]]

hot′ spot′, **1.** a country or region where dangerous or difficult political situations exist or may erupt, esp. where a war, revolution, or a belligerent attitude toward other countries exists or may develop: *In the 1960's, Vietnam became a hot spot.* **2.** *Informal.* any area or place of known danger, intrigue, dissension, or instability. **3.** *Informal.* a nightclub. **4.** *Photog.* an area of a negative or print revealing excessive light on that part of the subject. **5.** a section of forest or woods where fires frequently occur. **6.** an area hotter than the surrounding surface, as on the shell of a furnace. **7.** *Physics.* an area of abnormally high radioactivity. **8.** *Geol.* a region of molten rock below and within the lithosphere that persists long enough to leave a record of uplift and volcanic activity at the earth's surface. Cf. **plume** (def. 10). **9.** *Genetics.* a chromosome site or a section of DNA having a high frequency of mutation or recombination. **10.** *Vet. Pathol.* a moist, raw sore on the skin of a dog or cat caused by constant licking of an irritation from an allergic reaction, tangled coat, fleas, etc. Also, **hot′spot′.** [1925–30, *Amer.*]

hot-spot (hot′spot′), *v.t.,* **-spot·ted, -spot·ting.** to stop (a forest fire) at a hot spot. [1950–55; v. use of HOT SPOT]

hot′ spring′, a thermal spring having water warmer than 98°F (37°C): the water is usually heated by emanation from or passage near hot or molten rock. Cf. **warm spring.** [1660–70]

Hot′ Springs′, **1.** a city in central Arkansas: adjoins a national park **(Hot′ Springs′ Na′tional Park′)** noted for its thermal mineral springs. 35,166. **2.** a resort village in W Virginia: site of international conference (forerunner of Food and Agriculture Organization of the United Nations) in 1943 to aid agricultural and food supply adjustments after World War II.

hot·spur (hot′spûr′), *n.* an impetuous or reckless person; a hothead. [1425–75; late ME; after Sir Henry Percy, to whom it was applied as a nickname] —**hot′·spurred′,** *adj.*

hot′-stove′ league′ (hot′stōv′), devotees of a sport, esp. baseball, who meet for off-season talks. [1950–55]

hot′ stuff′, *Slang.* **1.** a person or thing of exceptional interest or merit. **2.** something unconventional, sensational, or daring: *This movie is hot stuff.* **3.** a person who is erotically stimulating or is easily aroused sexually. [1750–60]

hot′ switch′, *Radio and Television.* a rapid transfer from one point of origin to another during a broadcast.

hot·sy-tot·sy (hot′sē tot′sē), *adj. Slang.* about as right as can be; perfect: *Everything is just hotsy-totsy.* [1925–30; allegedly coined by Billie De Beck (d. 1942), U.S. cartoonist]

hot′ tear′ (târ), a crack formed in hot metal during cooling, caused by an improper pouring temperature or undue restraint. [1930–35]

hot-tem·pered (hot′tem′pərd), *adj.* easily angered; short-tempered.

Hot·ten·tot (hot′n tot′), *n.* Khoikhoi. [1670–80; < Afrik; orig. uncert.] —**Hot′ten·tot′ic,** *adj.*

Hot′tentot's bread′, **1.** elephant's-foot. **2.** the edible rhizome of this plant. [1725–35]

hot·ter[1] (hot′ər), *v.i. Scot. and North Eng.* **1.** to vibrate up and down; shake, totter, or rattle, as a plate on a shelf. **2.** to stammer. [1790–1800; < early D dial. *hotteren,* freq. with *-er-* of MD *hotten* to shake; akin to HOTCH]

hot·ter[2] (hot′ər), *adj.* comp. of **hot.**

hot′ tod′dy, toddy (def. 1).

hot′ tub′, a wooden tub, usually large enough to accommodate several persons, that is filled with hot aerated water and often equipped with a thermostat and whirlpool: used for recreation or physical therapy and often placed out of doors, as on a porch. [1970–75, *Amer.*] —**hot′-tub′ber,** *n.* —**hot′-tub′bing,** *n.*

hot′ type′, *Print.* See **hot metal.**

hot′ war′, open military conflict; an armed conflict between nations: *The increasing tension in the Middle East could lead to a hot war.* [1945–50; by analogy with COLD WAR]

hot′ wa′ter, *Informal.* trouble; a predicament: *His skipping classes will get him into real hot water when exam time comes.* [1530–40]

hot′-wa′ter bag′ (hot′wô′tər, -wot′ər), a bag, usually of rubber, for holding hot water to apply warmth to some part of the body, as the feet. Also called **hot′-wa′·ter bot′tle.**

hot′ well′, a tank or reservoir in which hot water is collected before being recirculated, esp. condensed steam about to be returned to a boiler. [1350–1400; ME]

hot-wire (*v.* hot′wīᵊr′; *adj.* hot′wīᵊr′), *v.,* **-wired, -wir·ing,** *adj.* —*v.t.* **1.** *Slang.* to start the engine of (a motor vehicle) by short-circuiting the ignition. —*adj.* **2.** *Elect., Engin.* depending for its operation on the lengthening or increasing resistance of a wire when it is heated: *hot-wire anemometer; hot-wire microphone.* [1950–55]

hot-work (hot′wûrk′), *v.t.* to work (metal) at a temperature high enough to permit recrystallization. [1895–1900]

hou·ba·ra (ho͞o bär′ə), *n.* a bustard, *Chlamydotis undulata,* of northern Africa and western Asia, having long black and white plumes on each side of the neck. [1820–30; < Ar *hubārā*]

hou·dah (hou′də), *n.* howdah.

Hou·dan (ho͞o′dan), *n.* one of a French breed of chickens having a V-shaped comb, five toes, and mottled or black plumage. [1870–75; after *Houdan,* village near Paris where these hens were bred]

Hou·di·ni (ho͞o dē′nē), *n.* **Harry** (*Erich Weiss*), 1874–1926, U.S. magician.

Hou·don (o͞o dôN′), *n.* **Jean An·toine** (zhäN äN-twAN′), 1741–1828, French sculptor.

hough (hok; *Scot.* hokH), *n.* **1.** *Scot.* hock[1] (defs. 1, 2). —*v.t.* **2.** *Scot.* to hamstring. —*v.i.* **3.** *Brit. Dial. Obs.* to clear the throat; hack. [1300–50; ME; see HOCK[1]]

Hough (huf), *n.* **Emerson,** 1857–1923, U.S. novelist.

Hou·ma (ho͞o′mə), *n.* a city in S Louisiana. 32,602.

hound[1] (hound), *n.* **1.** one of any of several breeds of dogs trained to pursue game either by sight or by scent, esp. one with a long face and large drooping ears. **2.** *Informal.* any dog. **3.** a mean, despicable person. **4.** *Informal.* an addict or devotee: *an autograph hound.* **5.** one of the pursuers in the game of hare and hounds. **6.** **follow the hounds,** *Fox Hunting.* to participate in a hunt, esp. as a member of the field. **7.** **ride to hounds,** *Fox Hunting.* to participate in a hunt, whether as a member of the field or of the hunt staff. —*v.t.* **8.** to hunt or track with hounds, or as a hound does; pursue. **9.** to pursue or harass without respite: *Her little brother wouldn't stop hounding her.* **10.** to incite (a hound) to pursuit or attack; urge on. **11.** *Informal.* to incite or urge (a person) to do something (usually fol. by *on*). [bef. 900; ME *h(o)und,* OE *hund;* c. D *hond,* ON *hundr,* Dan, Sw *hund,* G *Hund,* Goth *hunds;* akin to L *canis,* Gk *kýōn* (gen. *kynós*), Skt *śván* (gen. *śunas*), OIr *cú* (gen. *con*), Welsh *ci* (pl. *cwn*), Tocharian A *kū,* Lith *šuõ*] —**hound′er,** *n.* —**hound′ish, hound′y,** *adj.* —**hound′·like′,** *adj.*
—**Syn. 8.** dog, follow, chase, trail; tail. **9.** pester, annoy, persecute, bully.

hound[2] (hound), *n.* **1.** *Naut.* either of a pair of fore-and-aft members at the lower end of the head of a mast, for supporting the trestletrees, that support an upper mast at its heel. Cf. **cheek** (def. 12). **2.** a horizontal bar or brace, usually one of a pair, for strengthening the running gear of a horse-drawn wagon or the like. [1175–1225; ME *hūn* < ON *hūnn* knob at the masthead]

hound′ dog′, **1.** *Chiefly Southern U.S. Dial.* hound[1] (def. 1). **2.** (*cap.*) *Mil.* a jet-propelled air-to-ground missile designed to be launched from B-52 aircraft and having nuclear capability. [1640–50, *Amer.*]

hound·ing (houn′ding), *n. Naut.* **1.** the portion of a lower mast between the cheeks or hounds and the deck. **2.** the portion of an upper mast between the cap of the mast below and the hounds above. **3.** the part of a bowsprit projecting beyond the stem. [1850–55; HOUND[2] + -ING[1]]

hound's-tongue (houndz′tung′), *n.* any of various plants belonging to the genus *Cynoglossum,* of the borage family, esp. *C. officinale,* having coarse, tongue-shaped leaves, dull purple flowers, and prickly nutlets. [bef. 1000; ME; OE *hundestunge,* trans. of L *cynoglōssos* < Gk *kynóglōssos, kynóglōsson* (adj.) lit., dog-tongued]

hound's′ tooth′, a pattern of broken or jagged checks, used on a variety of fabrics. Also called **hound's′-tooth check′.** [1935–40]

hound's tooth

hound's-tooth (houndz′to͞oth′), *adj.* woven or printed with a pattern of broken or jagged checks: *a hound's-tooth jacket.* [1955–60]

houn·skull (houn′skul′), *n. Armor.* a snoutlike, usually conical, visor attached to a basinet of the 14th century. [HOUND[1] + SKULL]

Houns·low (hounz′lō), *n.* a borough of Greater London, England. 203,300.

Hou·phouet-Boi·gny (*Fr.* o͞o fwä′bwä nyē′), *n.* **Fé·lix** (*Fr.* fā lēks′), born 1905, Ivory Coast political leader: president since 1960.

houppe·lande (ho͞op′länd, -land), *n.* (in the Middle Ages) a robe or long tunic, belted or with a fitted bodice, usually having full trailing sleeves and often trimmed or lined with fur. Also, **houpe′lande.** [1350–1400; ME *hopeland* < MF < ?]

hour (ouᵊr, ou′ər), *n.* **1.** a period of time equal to one twenty-fourth of a mean solar or civil day and equivalent to 60 minutes: *He slept for an hour.* **2.** any specific one of these 24 periods, usually reckoned in two series of 12, one series from midnight to noon and the second from noon to midnight, but sometimes reckoned in one series of 24, from midnight to midnight: *He slept for the hour between 2 and 3 A.M. The hour for the bombardment was between 1300 and 1400.* **3.** any specific time of day; the time indicated by a timepiece: *What is the hour?* **4.** a short or limited period of time: *He savored his hour of glory.* **5.** a particular or appointed time: *What was the hour of death? At what hour do you open?* **6.** a customary or usual time: *When is your dinner hour?* **7.** the present time: *the man of the hour.* **8.** **hours, a.** time spent in an office, factory, or the like, or for work, study, etc.: *The doctor's hours were from 10 to 4. What an employee does after hours is his or her own business.* **b.** customary time of going to bed and getting up: *to keep late hours.* **c.** (in the Christian church) the seven stated times of the day for prayer and devotion. **d.** the offices or services prescribed for these times. **e.** a book containing them. **9.** distance normally covered in an hour's traveling: *We live about an hour from the city.* **10.** *Astron.* a unit of measure of right ascension representing 15°, or the twenty-fourth part of a great circle. **11.** a single period, as of class instruction or therapeutic consultation, usually lasting from 40 to 55 minutes. Cf. **clock-hour. 12.** *Educ.* Also called **credit hour.** one unit of academic credit, usually representing attendance at one scheduled period of instruction per week throughout a semester, quarter, or term. **13.** **the Hours,** *Class. Myth.* the Horae. **14.** **one's hour, a.** Also, **one's last hour.** the instant of death: *The sick man knew that his hour had come.* **b.** any crucial moment. —*adj.* **15.** of, pertaining to, or noting an hour. [1175–1225; ME *(h)oure* < AF; OF *(h)ore* < L *hōra* < Gk *hṓrā* time, season] —**hour′less,** *adj.*

hour′ an′gle, *Astron.* the angle, measured westward through 360°, between the celestial meridian of an observer and the hour circle of a celestial body. Cf. **sidereal hour angle.** [1830–40]

hour′ cir′cle, *Astron.* a great circle on the celestial sphere passing through the celestial poles and containing a point on the celestial sphere, as a star or the vernal equinox. Also called **circle of declination.** [1665–75]

hour·glass (ouᵊr′glas′, -gläs′, ou′ər-), *n.* **1.** an instrument for measuring time, consisting of two bulbs of glass joined by a narrow passage through which a quantity of sand or mercury runs in just an hour. —*adj.* **2.** having a notably slim or narrow waist, midsection, or joining segment: *She has an hourglass figure.* [1505–15; HOUR + GLASS]

hourglass (def. 1)

hour′ hand′, the hand that indicates the hours on a clock or watch. [1660–70]

hou·ri (ho͝or′ē, houᵊr′ē, hou′ə rē), *n., pl.* **-ris.** one of the beautiful virgins provided in paradise for all faithful Muslims. [1730–40; < F < Pers *hūrī* < Ar *ḥūr* pl. of *ḥaurā′* gazelle-eyed (woman)]

hour·long (ouᵊr′lông′, -long′, ou′ər-), *adj.* lasting an hour: *an hourlong interview.* Also, **hour′-long′.** [1795–1805; HOUR + LONG[1] (def. 37)]

hour·ly (ouᵊr′lē, ou′ər-), *adj.* **1.** of, pertaining to, occurring, or done each successive hour: *hourly news reports.* **2.** computed or totaled in terms of an hour; using an hour as a basic unit of reckoning: *hourly wages.* **3.** hired to work for wages by the hour: *hourly workers.* **4.** frequent; continual. —*adv.* **5.** every hour; hour by hour. **6.** at each hour or during every hour. **7.** frequently; continually. [1425–75; late ME; see HOUR, -LY]

Hou·sa·ton·ic (ho͞o′sə ton′ik), *n.* a river flowing S from NW Massachusetts through SW Connecticut to Long Island Sound near Stratford, Connecticut. 148 mi. (240 km) long.

house (*n., adj.* hous; *v.* houz), *n., pl.* **hous·es** (hou′ziz), *v.,* **housed, hous·ing,** *adj.* —*n.* **1.** a building in which

CONCISE ETYMOLOGY KEY: <, descended or borrowed from; >, whence; b., blend of, blended; c., cognate with; cf., compare; deriv., derivative; equiv., equivalent; imit., imitative; obl., oblique; r., replacing; s., stem; sp., spelling, spelled; resp., respelling, respelled; trans., translation; ?, origin unknown; *, unattested; ‡, probably earlier than. See the full key inside the front cover.

people live; residence for human beings. **2.** a household. **3.** (*often cap.*) a family, including ancestors and descendants: *the great houses of France; the House of Hapsburg.* **4.** a building for any purpose: *a house of worship.* **5.** a theater, concert hall, or auditorium: *a vaudeville house.* **6.** the audience of a theater or the like. **7.** a place of shelter for an animal, bird, etc. **8.** the building in which a legislative or official deliberative body meets. **9.** (*cap.*) the body itself, esp. of a bicameral legislature: *the House of Representatives.* **10.** a quorum of such a body. **11.** (*often cap.*) a commercial establishment; business firm: *the House of Rothschild; a publishing house.* **12.** a gambling casino. **13.** the management of a commercial establishment or of a gambling casino: *rules of the house.* **14.** an advisory or deliberative group, esp. in church or college affairs. **15.** a college in an English-type university. **16.** a residential hall in a college or school; dormitory. **17.** the members or residents of any such residential hall. **18.** *Informal.* a brothel; whorehouse. **19.** *Brit.* a variety of lotto or bingo played with paper and pencil, esp. by soldiers as a gambling game. **20.** Also called **parish.** *Curling.* the area enclosed by a circle 12 or 14 ft. (3.7 or 4.2 m) in diameter at each end of the rink, having the tee in the center. **21.** *Naut.* any enclosed shelter above the weather deck of a vessel: *bridge house; deck house.* **22.** *Astrol.* one of the 12 divisions of the celestial sphere, numbered counterclockwise from the point of the eastern horizon. **23. bring down the house,** to call forth vigorous applause from an audience; be highly successful: *The children's performances brought down the house.* **24. clean house.** See **clean** (def. 46). **25. dress the house,** *Theat.* **a.** to fill a theater with many people admitted on free passes; paper the house. **b.** to arrange or space the seating of patrons in such a way as to make an audience appear larger or a theater or nightclub more crowded than it actually is. **26. keep house,** to maintain a home; manage a household. **27. like a house on fire** or **afire,** very quickly; with energy or enthusiasm: *The new product took off like a house on fire.* **28. on the house,** as a gift from the management; free: *Tonight the drinks are on the house.* **29. put** or **set one's house in order, a.** to settle one's affairs. **b.** to improve one's behavior or correct one's faults: *It is easy to criticize others, but it would be better to put one's own house in order first.* —*v.t.* **30.** to put or receive into a house, dwelling, or living quarters: *More than 200 students were housed in the dormitory.* **31.** to give shelter to; harbor; lodge: *to house flood victims in schools.* **32.** to provide with a place to work, study, or the like: *This building houses our executive staff.* **33.** to provide storage space for; be a receptacle for or repository of: *The library houses 600,000 books.* **34.** to remove from exposure; put in a safe place. **35.** *Naut.* **a.** to stow securely. **b.** to lower (an upper mast) and make secure, as alongside the lower mast. **c.** to heave (an anchor) home. **36.** *Carpentry.* **a.** to fit the end or edge of (a board or the like) into a notch, hole, or groove. **b.** to form (a joint) between two pieces of wood by fitting the end or edge of one into a dado of the other. —*v.i.* **37.** to take shelter; dwell. —*adj.* **38.** of, pertaining to, or noting a house. **39.** for or suitable for a house: *house paint.* **40.** of or being a product made by or for a specific retailer and often sold under the store's own label: *You'll save money on the radio if you buy the house brand.* **41.** served by a restaurant as its customary brand: *the house wine.* [bef. 900; (n.) ME *h(o)us,* OE *hūs;* c. D *huis,* LG *huus,* ON *hūs,* G *Haus,* Goth *-hūs* (in *gudhūs* temple); (v.) ME *housen,* OE *hūsian,* deriv. of the n.]
—**Syn. 1.** domicile. HOUSE, DWELLING, RESIDENCE, HOME are terms applied to a place to live in. DWELLING is now chiefly poetic, or used in legal or technical contexts, as in a lease or in the phrase *multiple dwelling.* RESIDENCE is characteristic of formal usage and often implies size and elegance of structure and surroundings: *the private residence of the king.* These two terms and HOUSE have always had reference to the structure to be lived in. HOME has recently taken on this meaning and become practically equivalent to HOUSE, the new meaning tending to crowd out the older connotations of family ties and domestic comfort. See also **hotel.**

House (hous), *n.* **Edward Man•dell** (man′dl), ("*Colonel House*"), 1858–1938, U.S. diplomat.

house′ a′gent, *Brit.* **1.** a real-estate agent. **2.** a renting agent or a rent collector. [1835–45]

house′ arrest′, confinement of an arrested person to his or her residence or to a public place, as a hospital, instead of in a jail: *He was under house arrest until the day of his trial.* [1935–40]

house•boat (hous′bōt′), *n.* **1.** a flat-bottomed, barge-like boat fitted for use as a floating dwelling but not for rough water. —*v.i.* **2.** to travel or live on a houseboat. [1780–90; HOUSE + BOAT] —**house′boat′er,** *n.*

houseboat (def. 1)

house•bound (hous′bound′), *adj.* restricted to the house, as by bad weather or illness. [1875–80; HOUSE + -BOUND[1]]

house•boy (hous′boi′), *n.* houseman (def. 1). [1895–1900; HOUSE + BOY]

house•break (hous′brāk′), *v.t.,* **-broke, -bro•ken, -break•ing.** to train (a pet) to excrete outdoors or in a specific place. [1895–1900; HOUSE + BREAK]

house•break•er (hous′brā′kər), *n.* **1.** a person who breaks into and enters a house with a felonious intent. **2.** *Brit.* **a.** a worker or wrecking company that demolishes houses and buildings, as to make room for new construction. **b.** a person who buys doors, paneled walls, etc., from standing houses, to sell as antiques; a person who dismantles a house of its valuable parts before it is torn down. [1275–1325; ME. See HOUSE, BREAKER[1]] —**house′break′ing,** *n.*

house•bro•ken (hous′brō′kən), *adj.* (of a pet) trained to avoid excreting inside the house or in improper places. [1895–1900; HOUSE + BROKEN]

house′ call′, a professional visit, as by a doctor or sales representative, to the home of a patient or customer. [1955–60]

house•carl (hous′kärl′), *n.* a member of the household troops or bodyguard of a Danish or early English king or noble. [bef. 1050; ME; late OE *hūscarl* < Dan *hūskarl.* See HOUSE, CARL]

house•clean (hous′klēn′), *v.t.* **1.** to subject (a house, room, etc.) to housecleaning. —*v.i.* **2.** to engage in housecleaning. [1860–65; back formation from HOUSECLEANING] —**house′clean′er,** *n.*

house•clean•ing (hous′klē′ning), *n.* **1.** the act of cleaning a house, room, etc., and its furnishings, esp. the act of cleaning thoroughly and completely. **2.** the act of improving or reforming by weeding out excess or corrupt personnel or of revising methods of operation. [1860–65; HOUSE + CLEANING]

house•coat (hous′kōt′), *n.* a woman's robe or dress-like garment in various lengths, for casual wear about the house. [1915–20; HOUSE + COAT]

house′ coun′sel, *Law.* a lawyer drawing a full-time salary from a corporation that he or she represents.

house′ crick′et, a dark brown cricket, *Acheta domesticus,* having a light-colored head with dark crossbands, commonly occurring throughout North America and Europe, where it may be an indoor pest. [1765–75]

house′ crow′, a black and gray crow, *Corvus splendens,* of India.

house′ cur′tain. See **act curtain.**

house′ detec′tive, an employee of a department store, hotel, etc., employed to prevent thefts, violations of regulations, or other forms of misconduct on the part of patrons. [1895–1900, *Amer.*]

house′ dick′, *Slang.* See **house detective.** [1940–45, *Amer.*]

house′ doc′tor. See **house physician.**

house•dress (hous′dres′), *n.* a relatively simple and inexpensive dress suitable for housework. [1895–1900]

housed′ string′ (houzd), *Carpentry.* a string of a stair **(housed′ stair′)** receiving the ends of the risers or treads in a series of housings.

house•fa•ther (hous′fä′thər), *n.* a man responsible for a group of young people, as students, living in a dormitory, hostel, etc. [1545–55; HOUSE + FATHER; cf. L *paterfamilias*]

house′ finch′, a small common finch, *Carpodacus mexicanus,* originally of the western U.S. and Mexico and now widely distributed: the males have a red forehead, throat, breast, and rump. [1865–70, *Amer.*]

house′ flag′, a flag flown by a merchant ship, bearing the emblem of its owners or operators. [1880–85]

house•fly (hous′flī′), *n., pl.* **-flies.** a medium-sized, gray-striped fly, *Musca domestica,* common around human habitations in nearly all parts of the world. Also, **house′ fly′.** [1400–50; late ME; see HOUSE, FLY[2]]

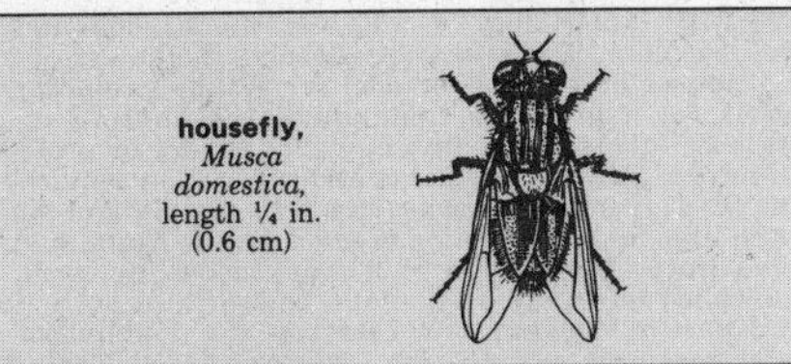
housefly, *Musca domestica,* length ¼ in. (0.6 cm)

house•ful (hous′fo͝ol), *n., pl.* **-fuls. 1.** as many as a house will accommodate: *a houseful of weekend guests.* **2.** as much as a house will hold: *He had several housefuls of furniture.* [1250–1300; ME. See HOUSE, -FUL] —**Usage.** See **-ful.**

house′ fun′gus. See **dry rot fungus.**

house′ fur′nishings, the furnishings of a household, as rugs, chairs, or draperies. [1900–05]

house•guest (hous′gest′), *n.* a person staying with a household as a guest for one night or longer. [1920–25]

house•hold (hous′hōld′, -ōld′), *n.* **1.** the people of a house collectively; a family including its servants. —*adj.* **2.** of or pertaining to a household: *household furniture.* **3.** for use in maintaining a home, esp. for use in cooking, cleaning, laundering, repairing, etc., in the home: *a household bleach.* **4.** common or usual; ordinary. [1350–1400; ME *houshold.* See HOUSE, HOLD[1]]

house′hold ammo′nia, diluted ammonia, often having a small quantity of detergent, used for cleaning.

house′hold art′, any of the skills necessary to the efficient running of a household, as cooking or keeping a family budget. [1920–25]

house′hold cav′alry, (in Britain) cavalry units forming part of the ceremonial guard of the monarch.

house′hold effects′, privately owned goods consisting chiefly of furniture, appliances, etc., for keeping house. Also called **house′hold goods′.** Cf. **personal effects.** [1890–95]

house•hold•er (hous′hōl′dər, -ōl′-), *n.* **1.** a person who holds title to or occupies a house. **2.** the head of a family. [1350–1400; ME *housholdere.* See HOUSE, HOLDER] —**house′hold′er•ship′,** *n.*

house′hold god′, a god presiding over and protecting the home, esp. in the religion of ancient Rome. Cf. **lares and penates.** [1605–15]

house′hold knight′, bachelor (def. 5).

house′hold troops′, troops guarding or attending a sovereign or a sovereign's residence. [1705–15]

house′hold word′, a familiar name, phrase, saying, etc.; byword: *The advertising campaign is designed to make this new product a household word.* [1590–1600]

house•hus•band (hous′huz′bənd), *n.* a man who is married to a working wife and who stays home to manage their household. [1965–70; HOUSE(WIFE) + HUSBAND]

house•keep (hous′kēp′), *v.i.,* **-kept, -keep•ing.** to keep or maintain a house. [1835–45; back formation from HOUSEKEEPING]

house•keep•er (hous′kē′pər), *n.* **1.** a person, often hired, who does or directs the domestic work and planning necessary for a home, as cleaning or buying food. **2.** an employee of a hotel, hospital, etc., who supervises the cleaning staff. [1375–1425; late ME *houskeper.* See HOUSE, KEEPER] —**house′keep′er•like′,** *adj.*

house•keep•ing (hous′kē′ping), *n.* **1.** the maintenance of a house or domestic establishment. **2.** the management of household affairs. **3.** the management, care, and servicing of property and equipment of an industrial or commercial building or organization. **4.** the ongoing routine, procedures, operations, and management of a commercial enterprise, government, organization, or the like. **5.** *Computers.* system tasks, as initialization and managing peripheral devices, that must be done to permit a computer program to execute properly but that do not directly contribute to program output. [1530–40; HOUSE + KEEPING]

hou•sel (hou′zəl), *n., v.,* **-seled, -sel•ing** or (*esp. Brit.*) **-selled, -sel•ling.** *Archaic.* —*n.* **1.** the Eucharist. **2.** the act of administering or receiving the Eucharist. —*v.t.* **3.** to administer the Eucharist to. [bef. 900; (n.) ME; OE *hūsl* the Eucharist, prob. orig. offering; c. ON *hūsl,* Goth *hunsl* sacrifice, offering; (v.) ME *houselen,* OE *hūslian,* deriv. of the n.]

House•lan•der (hous′lən dər), *n.* **Car•yll** (kar′əl), 1901–54, English writer on Roman Catholicism.

house•leek (hous′lēk′), *n.* **1.** Also called **old-man-and-old-woman.** a succulent plant, *Sempervivum tectorum,* of the stonecrop family, native to Europe, having reddish flowers and leaves forming dense basal rosettes. **2.** any other plant of the genus *Sempervivum.* [1325–75; ME *howsleke.* See HOUSE, LEEK]

house•less (hous′lis), *adj.* **1.** without a house or houses. **2.** homeless. [1350–1400; ME *housles.* See HOUSE, -LESS] —**house′less•ness,** *n.*

house•lights (hous′līts′), *n.pl.* the lamps providing illumination of the auditorium or seating area of a theater. [1915–20; HOUSE + LIGHT[1] + -S[3]]

house•line (hous′līn′), *n. Naut.* light cordage used for seizing. [1760–70; HOUSE + LINE[1]]

house•maid (hous′mād′), *n.* a female servant employed in general domestic work in a home, esp. to do housework. [1685–95; HOUSE + MAID]

house′maid's knee′, *Pathol.* inflammation of the bursa over the front of the kneecap. [1825–35]

house•man (hous′man′, -mən), *n., pl.* **-men** (-men′, -mən). **1.** a male servant who performs general duties in a home, hotel, etc. **2.** a man employed to maintain order, as in a bar or gambling casino; bouncer. **3.** See **house detective. 4.** one who represents the management in a gambling house. **5.** *Brit.* a medical intern at a hospital. [1790–1800; HOUSE + MAN[1]]

house′ man′ager, a business manager responsible for managing a theater and its staff. [1905–10]

house′ mark′, a trademark that appears on and identifies all of a company's products.

house′ mar′tin, a small European swallow, *Delichon urbica,* that builds its nest under the eaves of houses.

house•mas•ter (hous′mas′tər, -mä′stər), *n.* a man who is in charge of a house or a dormitory in a private school for boys. [1875–80; HOUSE + MASTER] —**house′•mas′ter•ship′,** *n.*

house•mate (hous′māt′), *n.* **1.** a person with whom one shares a house or other residence. **2.** a sexual partner with whom one shares a house or other living quarters without being married. [1800–10; HOUSE + MATE[1]]

house′ moss′, *Dial.* dust ball or dust balls. —**Regional Variation.** See **dust ball.**

house•moth•er (hous′muth′ər), *n.* a woman in charge of a residence, esp. for children, students, or young women, who acts as hostess, chaperon, and occasionally as housekeeper. [1830–40; HOUSE + MOTHER[1]] —**house′moth′er•ly,** *adj.*

house′ mouse′, a brownish-gray Old World mouse, *Mus musculus,* now common in the U.S. in or near houses. See illus. under **mouse.** [1825–35]

house′ mu′sic, an up-tempo style of disco music characterized by deep bass rhythms, piano or synthesizer melodies, and soul-music singing, sometimes with elements of rap music. [1985–90; prob. after the Ware*house,* a dance club in Chicago]

house′ of assem′bly, the legislature or the lower house of the legislature in certain countries of the Commonwealth of Nations. [1645–55]

house′ of assigna′tion, a brothel. [1825–35, *Amer.*]

House′ of Ber•nar′da Al′ba, The (bər när′də äl′bə), (Spanish, *La Casa de Bernarda Alba*), a drama (1941) by Federico García Lorca.

House′ of Bur′gesses, the assembly of representatives in colonial Virginia.

house′ of cards′, a structure or plan that is insubstantial and subject to imminent collapse, as a structure made by balancing playing cards against each other: *The scheme is so overly complicated that it's likely to prove to be just another house of cards.* [1900–05]

House′ of Com′mons, the elective, lower house of the Parliament of Great Britain and Northern Ireland, Canada, and various other countries in the Commonwealth of Nations.

house′ of correc′tion, a place for the confinement and reform of persons convicted of minor offenses and not regarded as confirmed criminals. [1625–35]

House′ of Coun′cilors, the upper house of the Japanese diet. Formerly, **House of Peers.**

House′ of Del′egates, the lower house of the General Assembly in Virginia, West Virginia, and Maryland.

house′ of deten′tion, **1.** a place maintained by the civil authorities for persons charged with a crime, and sometimes for witnesses, awaiting trial. **2.** See **detention home.**

house′ of God′, **1.** Also called **house of worship, house of prayer.** a building devoted to religious worship; a church, synagogue, temple, chapel, etc. **2.** Also, **House′ of God′.** *Islam.* Ka'ba.

house′ of ill′ repute′, a house of prostitution; whorehouse; brothel. Also called **house′ of ill′ fame′.** [1720–30]

House′ of Keys′, the lower house of the legislature of the Isle of Man.

House′ of Lords′, the nonelective, upper house of the British Parliament, comprising the lords spiritual and lords temporal.

House′ of Peers′, former name of the Japanese House of Councilors.

house′ of prayer′ (prâr). See **house of God.** [1575–85]

house′ of prostitu′tion, a brothel. [1540–50]

House′ of Represen′tatives, the lower legislative branch in many national and state bicameral governing bodies, as in the United States, Mexico, and Japan.

house′ of stud′y. See **Beth Midrash.** Also, **House′ of Stud′y.** [1925–30]

House′ of the Sev′en Ga′bles, The, a novel (1851) by Hawthorne.

house′ of wor′ship. See **house of God.**

house′ or′gan, a periodical issued by a business or other establishment for its employees, customers, and other interested readers, presenting news about the firm, its products, and its personnel. [1905–10]

house′ paint′er, a person whose occupation is painting houses. [1680–90]

house•par•ent (hous′pâr′ənt, -par′-), *n.* **1.** one of a married couple responsible for a group of young people, as students, living in a dormitory, hostel, etc., sometimes acting solely as an advisor, but often serving as host or hostess, chaperon, housekeeper, etc. **2.** a housemother or housefather. [1950–55; HOUSE + PARENT]

house′ par′ty, **1.** the entertainment of guests for one or more nights at one's home, a fraternity or sorority house, etc. **2.** the guests at such an affair or party: *The house party goes sailing today.* Also, **house′par′ty.** [1875–80]

house•per•son (hous′pûr′sən), *n.* someone who manages a household; househusband or housewife. [1970–75; HOUSE(WIFE) + -PERSON]
—Usage. See **-person.**

house•phone (hous′fōn′), *n.* a telephone, used for making calls within a hotel or apartment house, that does not have a direct line to an exchange and whose calls are routed through the building's switchboard. [HOUSE + PHONE¹]

house′ physi′cian, a resident physician in a hospital, hotel, or other public institution. Also called **house doctor.** [1745–55]

house′ place′, (in medieval architecture) a room common to all the inhabitants of a house, as a hall. [1805–15]

house•plant (hous′plant′, -plänt′), *n.* an ornamental plant that is grown indoors or adapts well to indoor culture. [1870–75; HOUSE + PLANT]

house-rais•ing (hous′rā′zing), *n.* a gathering of persons in a rural community to help one of its members build a house. [1695–1705, *Amer.*]

house•room (hous′ro͞om′, -ro͝om′), *n.* lodging or accommodation in a house. [1580–90; HOUSE + ROOM]

house′ rule′, a rule that is used in a game only in a specific place, as a particular casino, or only among a certain group of players. [1945–50]

house′ seat′, one of a number of seats in a theater that the management reserves for special guests, friends of the producer or cast, etc. [1945–50]

house•sit (hous′sit′), *v.i.,* **-sat, -sit•ting.** to take care of a house or residence while the owner or occupant is temporarily away, esp. by living in it. Also, **house′-sit′.** [1975–80; HOUSE + SIT¹, on the model of BABY-SIT] **—house′ sit′ter. —house′-sit′ter,** *n.*

house′ slip′per, a slipper worn in the house or indoors, often distinguished from a bedroom slipper by having a back and heel.

house′ snake′, **1.** any African snake of the genus *Boaedon,* some species of which are important mouse and rat catchers in areas of human habitation. **2.** See **milk snake. 3.** See **rat snake.** [1735–45]

house′ spar′row, a small, hardy, buffy-brown and gray bird, *Passer domesticus,* of Europe, introduced into America, Australia, etc. Also called **English sparrow.** [1665–75]

house′ sur′geon, a surgeon who lives in a hospital in which he or she is on call. [1815–25]

house-to-house (hous′tə hous′), *adj.* **1.** conducted from one house to the next: *a house-to-house survey.* **2.** door-to-door (def. 1). [1855–60]

house•top (hous′top′), *n.* **1.** the top or roof of a house. **2. from the housetops,** publicly; generally: *The day I got my promotion I wanted to shout it from the housetops.* [1520–30; HOUSE + TOP¹]

house′ trail′er, a trailer fitted with accommodations for sleeping, eating, washing, etc. Cf. **mobile home.** [1935–40]

house-train (hous′trān′), *v.t. Brit.* to housebreak. [1920–25]

house-trained (hous′trānd′), *adj. Brit.* housebroken. [1920–25]

House′ Un-Amer′ican Activ′ities Commit′tee, an investigative committee of the U.S. House of Representatives. Originally created in 1938 to inquire into subversive activities in the U.S., it was reestablished in 1945 as the Committee on Un-American Activities, renamed in 1969 as the Committee on Internal Security, and abolished in 1975. *Abbr.:* HUAC

house•wares (hous′wârz′), *n.pl.* articles of household equipment, as kitchen utensils, or glassware. [1920–25; HOUSE + WARE¹ + -S³]

house•warm•ing (hous′wôr′ming), *n.* a party to celebrate a person's or family's move to a new home. [1570–80; HOUSE + WARMING]

house•wife (hous′wīf′ *or, usually,* huz′if *for* 2), *n., pl.* **-wives** (-wīvz′), *v.,* **-wifed, -wif•ing.** **—***n.* **1.** a married woman who manages her own household, esp. as her principal occupation. **2.** *Brit.* a sewing box; a small case or box for needles, thread, etc. **—***v.t., v.i.* **3.** *Archaic.* to manage with efficiency and economy, as a household. [1175–1225; ME *hus(e)wif.* See HOUSE, WIFE]
—Usage. 1. HOUSEWIFE is offensive to some, perhaps because of an implied contrast with *career woman* (*just a housewife*) and perhaps because it defines an occupation in terms of a woman's relation to a man. *Homemaker* is a common substitute.

house•wife•ly (hous′wīf′lē), *adj.* of, like, or befitting a housewife. [1300–50; ME. See HOUSEWIFE, -LY] **—house′wife′li•ness,** *n.*

house•wif•er•y (hous′wī′fə rē, -wīf′rē), *n.* the function or work of a housewife; housekeeping. [1400–50; late ME *huswyfery.* See HOUSEWIFE, -ERY]

house•work (hous′wûrk′), *n.* the work of cleaning, cooking, etc., to be done in housekeeping. [1570–80; HOUSE + WORK]

house•work•er (hous′wûr′kər), *n.* a paid employee in a home, as a maid or cook. [HOUSE + WORKER]

house•wreck•er (hous′rek′ər), *n.* wrecker (def. 4). [1895–1900; HOUSE + WRECKER]

house′ wren′, a common American wren, *Troglodytes aedon,* that nests around houses. See illus. under **wren.** [1800–10, *Amer.*]

house•y-house•y (hou′sē hou′sē), *n. Brit. Informal.* house (def. 19). [see HOUSE, -Y²]

hous•ing¹ (hou′zing), *n.* **1.** any shelter, lodging, or dwelling place. **2.** houses collectively. **3.** the act of one who houses or puts under shelter. **4.** the providing of houses for a group or community: *the housing of an influx of laborers.* **5.** anything that covers or protects. **6.** *Mach.* a fully enclosed case and support for a mechanism. **7.** *Carpentry.* the space made in one piece of wood, or the like, for the insertion of another. **8.** *Naut.* **a.** Also called **bury.** the portion of a mast below the deck. **b.** Also called **bury.** the portion of a bowsprit aft of the forward part of the stem of a vessel. **c.** the doubling of an upper mast. **9.** a niche for a statue. [1250–1300; ME *husing.* See HOUSE, -ING¹]
—Syn. 5. covering, casing, shield, sheath.

hous•ing² (hou′zing), *n.* **1.** a covering of cloth for the back and flanks of a horse or other animal, for protection or ornament. **2. housings.** the trappings on a horse. [1635–45; cf. earlier *house,* ME *hous(e), houc(e)* in same sense < OF *houce* < Gmc **hulfti-* (cf. ML *hultia*), akin to MD *hulfte* cover for bow and arrow, MHG *hulft* covering; -ING¹ added by assoc. with HOUSE, HOUSING¹]

hous′ing devel′opment, a group of houses or apartments, usually of the same size and design, often erected on a tract of land by one builder and controlled by one management. [1950–55]

hous′ing estate′, *Brit.* See **housing development.** [1915–20]

hous′ing proj′ect, a publicly built and operated housing development, usually intended for low- or moderate-income tenants, senior citizens, etc. Also called **project.** [1935–40]

hous′ing start′, **1.** an instance of beginning the construction of a dwelling. **2. housing starts,** the nationwide number of such instances per period used esp. in the U.S. as an indication of economic growth or decline: *Housing starts were up 600,000 in April.*

Hous•man (hous′mən), *n.* **A(lfred) E(dward),** 1859–1936, English poet and classical scholar.

Hous•say (o͞o sī′), *n.* **Ber•nar•do Al•ber•to** (ber när′thô äl ver′tô), 1887–1971, Argentine physiologist: Nobel prize for medicine 1947.

Hous•ton (hyo͞o′stən), *n.* **1. Sam(uel),** 1793–1863, U.S. soldier and political leader: president of the Republic of Texas 1836–38. **2.** a city in SE Texas: a port on a ship canal, ab. 50 mi. (80 km) from the Gulf of Mexico. 1,594,086.

hous•to•ni•a (ho͞o stō′nē ə), *n.* any North American plant, belonging to the genus *Houstonia,* of the madder family, esp. *H. caerulea,* the common bluet. [1755–65; < NL, named after Dr. W. *Houston* (d. 1733), British botanist; see -IA]

Hous•to•ni•an (hyo͞o stō′nē ən), *n.* a native or resident of Houston, Texas. [HOUSTON + -IAN]

Hou•yhn•hnm (ho͞o in′əm, hwin′əm, win′-), *n.* (in Swift's *Gulliver's Travels*) one of a race of horses endowed with reason, who rule the Yahoos, a race of degraded, brutish creatures having human form. [1726; appar. echoic; cf. WHINNY]

HOV, high-occupancy vehicle.

hove (hōv), *v.* pt. and pp. of **heave.**

hov•el (huv′əl, hov′-), *n., v.,* **-eled, -el•ing** or (*esp. Brit.*) **-elled, -el•ling.** **—***n.* **1.** a small, very humble dwelling house; a wretched hut. **2.** any dirty, disorganized dwelling. **3.** an open shed, as for sheltering cattle or tools. **—***v.t.* **4.** to shelter or lodge as in a hovel. [1375–1425; late ME *hovell,* of uncert. orig.]

ho•ven (hō′vən), *Vet. Pathol.* **—***adj.* **1.** affected with bloat. **—***n.* **2.** bloat (def. 5). [1545–55; special use of ptp. of HEAVE]

hov•er (huv′ər, hov′-), *v.i.* **1.** to hang fluttering or suspended in the air: *The helicopter hovered over the building.* **2.** to keep lingering about; wait near at hand. **3.** to remain in an uncertain or irresolute state; waver: *to hover between life and death.* **—***n.* **4.** the act or state of hovering. [1350–1400; ME *hoveren,* freq. of *hoven* to hover < ?] **—hov′er•er,** *n.* **—hov′er•ing•ly,** *adv.*
—Syn. 1. See **fly¹. 3.** falter, pause, fluctuate.

hov•er•craft (huv′ər kraft′, -kräft′, hov′-), *n., pl.* **-craft.** *Chiefly Brit.* See **ACV.** Also, **Hov′er•craft′.** [HOVER + CRAFT]

hov′ering ac′cent, *Pros.* indeterminacy as to which of two consecutive syllables in a line of verse bears the metrical stress, as in any of the first three feet of *Slow, slow, / fresh fount, / keep time / with my / salt tears.*

hov′ering act′, *Internat. Law.* **1.** an act forbidding or restricting the loitering of foreign or domestic vessels within the prescribed limits of a coastal nation. **2.** an act stipulating that foreign vessels may be boarded and their shipping manifests checked by the appropriate government officials beyond the three-mile limit of a coastal nation.

hov′ering ves′sel, a vessel in territorial waters apparently collaborating in illicit operations.

Hov•er•train (huv′ər trān′, hov′-), *n.* **1.** an experimental high-speed British train that rides on a cushion of air and is propelled by a linear motor. **2.** (*l.c.*) aerotrain. [1960–65; HOVER + TRAIN]

Hov•ey (huv′ē), *n.* **Richard,** 1864–1900, U.S. poet.

Ho•vha•ness (hō vä′nis), *n.* **Alan,** born 1911, U.S. composer.

how¹ (hou), *adv.* **1.** in what way or manner; by what means?: *How did the accident happen?* **2.** to what extent, degree, etc.?: *How damaged is the car?* **3.** in what state or condition?: *How are you?* **4.** for what reason; why?: *How can you talk such nonsense?* **5.** to what effect; with what meaning?: *How is one to interpret his action?* **6.** what?: *How do you mean? If they don't have vanilla, how about chocolate?* **7.** (used as an intensifier): *How seldom I go there!* **8.** by what title or name?: *How does one address the president?* **9.** at what price: *How are the new cars going, cheaper than last year's models?* **10.** by what amount or in what measure or quantity?: *How do you sell these toma'oes?* **11.** in what form or shape?: *How does the demon appear in the first act of the opera?* **12. and how!** *Informal.* certainly! you bet!: *Am I happy? And how!* **13. Here's how,** *Informal.* (used as a toast). **14. how come?** *Informal.* how is it that? why?: *How come you never visit us anymore?* **15. how so?** how does it happen to be so? why?: *You haven't any desire to go? How so?* **—***conj.* **16.** the manner or way in which: *He couldn't figure out how to solve the problem.* **17.** about the manner, condition, or way in which: *Be careful how you act.* **18.** in whatever manner or way; however: *You can travel how you please.* **19.** *Informal.* that: *He told us how he was honest and could be trusted.* **—***n.* **20.** a question concerning the way or manner in which something is done, achieved, etc.: *a child's unending whys and hows.* **21.** a way or manner of doing something: *to consider all the hows and wherefores.* **22.** a word formerly used in communications to represent the letter *H.* [bef. 900; ME *how, hu,* OE *hū;* c. OFris *hū, ho,* D *hoe;* akin to G *wie* (OHG *hweo*), Goth *hwaiwa*]

how² (hou), *interj. Facetious.* (used as a greeting in imitation of American Indian speech.) [1810–20; of uncert. orig.]

how³ (hou), *n., adj. Scot. and North Eng.* howe.

How•ard (hou′ərd), *n.* **1. Catherine,** c1520–42, fifth wife of Henry VIII. **2. Sir Ebenezer,** 1850–1928, English town planner. **3. Henry.** See **Surrey, Henry Howard, Earl of. 4. Leslie** (*Leslie Stainer*), 1893–1943, English actor. **5. Roy Wilson,** 1883–1964, U.S. editor and newspaper publisher. **6. Sidney (Coe)** (kō), 1891–1939, U.S. playwright and short-story writer. **7.** a male given name: from a Germanic word meaning "brave heart."

how•be•it (hou bē′it), *adv.* **1.** *Archaic.* nevertheless. **—***conj.* **2.** *Obs.* although. [1350–1400; ME *how be it* however it may be; parallel to ALBEIT]

how•dah (hou′də), *n.* (in the East Indies) a seat or platform for one or more persons, commonly with a railing and a canopy, placed on the back of an elephant. Also, **houdah.** [1765–75; < Hindi *haudah* < Ar *hawdaj*]

how•die (hou′dē, o͞o′-; hō′dē, ō′dē), *n. Scot. and North Eng. Slang.* a midwife. Also, **howdy.** [orig. uncert.]

how′ do′, *Dial.* how do you do. [1885–90]

how′ do you do′, (used as a conventional greeting).

*CONCISE ETYMOLOGY KEY: <, descended or borrowed from; >, whence; b., blend of, blended; c., cognate with; cf., compare; deriv., derivative; equiv., equivalent; imit., imitative; obl., oblique; r., replacing; s., stem; sp., spelling, spelled; resp., respelling, respelled; trans., translation; ?, origin unknown; *, unattested; ‡, probably earlier than. See the full key inside the front cover.*

how-do-you-do (hou′də yə do͞o′), *n., pl.* **-dos.** *Informal.* **1.** a greeting; salutation: *a how-do-you-do fit for a king.* **2.** an awkward or unpleasant event or situation: *It's a fine how-do-you-do that they've refused to help us out.* Also, **how-de-do** (hou′dē do͞o′). [1625–35]

how·dy[1] (hou′dē), *n., pl.* **-dies,** *interj. Informal.* hello; how do you do (used as an expression of greeting). [1820–30; from the phrase *how do ye?*]

how·dy[2] (hou′dē), *n., pl.* **-dies.** *Slang.* howdie.

howe (hou), *Scot. and North Eng.* —*n.* **1.** a hole. **2.** the hold of a ship. **3.** a hollow; dell. —*adj.* **4.** hollow. **5.** deep. Also, **how.** [1325–75; ME (north and Scots), alter. of *holl;* see HOLLOW]

Howe (hou), *n.* **1. Elias,** 1819–67, U.S. inventor of the sewing machine. **2. Gordon** (*Gordie*), born 1928, Canadian ice-hockey player. **3. Julia Ward,** 1819–1910, U.S. writer and reformer: author of the *Battle Hymn of the Republic* (wife of Samuel Gridley Howe). **4. Richard** (*Earl Howe*) (*"Black Dick"*), 1726–99, British admiral (brother of William Howe). **5. Samuel Grid·ley** (grid′lē), 1801–76, U.S. surgeon and humanitarian. **6. William, 5th Viscount,** 1729–1814, British general in the American Revolutionary War.

how·e'er (hou âr′), *adv., conj.* however.

how·el (hou′əl), *n.* a channel cut along the inside edge of a barrel stave to receive the barrelhead. [1795–1805; perh. < Dan *hövl* < MLG *hövel;* c. G *Hobel* kind of plane]

How·ells (hou′əlz), *n.* **William Dean,** 1837–1920, U.S. author, critic, and editor.

how·ev·er (hou ev′ər), *adv.* **1.** nevertheless; yet; on the other hand; in spite of that: *We have not yet won; however, we shall keep trying.* **2.** to whatever extent or degree; no matter how: *However much you spend, I will reimburse you.* **3.** in whatever manner: *You may travel however you please.* **4.** how; how under the circumstances: *However did you manage?* —*conj.* **5.** in whatever way, manner, or state: *Arrange your hours however you like.* [1350–1400; ME *hou-ever.* See HOW[1], EVER] —**Syn. 1.** See **but**[1].

howff (houf, ouf; hōf, ōf), *Scot.* —*n.* **1.** an abode; a familiar shelter or resort. —*v.i.* **2.** to reside. **3.** to visit a familiar haunt. [1555–65; orig. uncert.]

how·itz·er (hou′it sər), *n. Ordn.* a cannon having a comparatively short barrel, used esp. for firing shells at a high angle of elevation, as for reaching a target behind cover or in a trench. [1685–95; earlier *hauwitzer* < D *houvietser,* equiv. to *houviets-* (< G *Haubitze,* MHG *haufnitz* < Czech *houfnice* slingshot) + *-er* -ER[1]]

howl (houl), *v.i.* **1.** to utter a loud, prolonged, mournful cry, as that of a dog or wolf. **2.** to utter a similar cry in distress, pain, rage, etc.; wail. **3.** to make a sound like an animal howling: *The wind howls through the trees.* **4.** *Informal.* to go on a spree; enjoy oneself without restraint. —*v.t.* **5.** to utter with howls: *to howl the bad news.* **6.** to drive or force by howls (often fol. by *down*): *to howl down the opposition.* —*n.* **7.** the cry of a dog, wolf, etc. **8.** a cry or wail, as of pain, rage, or protest. **9.** a sound like wailing: *the howl of the wind.* **10.** a loud, scornful laugh or yell. **11.** something that causes a laugh or a scornful yell, as a joke or funny or embarrassing situation. [1300–50; ME *hulen, houlen* (v.); c. D *huilen,* LG *hülen,* G *heulen,* Dan *hyle;* akin to ON *ȳla*]

How′land Is′land (hou′lənd), an island in the central Pacific, near the equator: U.S. meteorological station and airfield. 1 sq. mi. (2.6 sq. km).

howl·er (hou′lər), *n.* **1.** a person, animal, or thing that howls. **2.** Also called **howl′er mon′key.** any large tropical American monkey of the genus *Alouatta,* the males of which make a howling noise: some species are endangered. **3.** a mistake, esp. an embarrassing one in speech or writing, that evokes laughter. **4.** *Informal.* something that makes a piercing and often prolonged noise, as an alarm. [1790–1800; HOWL + -ER[1]]

howl·et (hou′lit), *n. Brit. Dial.* an owl or owlet. [1425–75; late ME; perh. < F *hulotte* wood-owl, perh. deriv. of MF *huler* to howl < Gmc; see HOWL]

howl·ing (hou′ling), *adj.* **1.** producing or uttering a howling noise: *a howling mob.* **2.** desolate, dismal, or dreary: *a howling wilderness.* **3.** *Informal.* very great; tremendous: *a howling success.* [1250–1300; ME *houlinge* (ger.); see HOWL, -ING[2]] —**howl′ing·ly,** *adv.*

howl′ing der′vishes, Rifa'iya. [1885–90]

How·rah (hou′rä), *n.* a city in W Bengal, in E India, on the Hooghly River opposite Calcutta. 599,740.

how·so·ev·er (hou′sō ev′ər), *adv.* **1.** to whatsoever extent or degree. **2.** in whatsoever manner. [1275–1325; ME; see HOW[1], SO[1], EVER]

how-to (hou′to͞o′), *adj., n., pl.* **-tos.** —*adj.* **1.** giving or pertaining to basic instructions and directions to the layperson on the methods for doing or making something, esp. as a hobby or for practical use: *a how-to book on photography.* —*n.* **2.** a set of step-by-step instructions for accomplishing a certain task or reaching a certain objective: *a how-to for fixing a leaky faucet.* **3.** the basic principles or approach for doing something: *the how-to of investing in real estate.* [1925–30] —**how′-to′er,** *n.*

Hox′ gene′ (hoks), any of a class of genes that determines the basic structure and orientation of an organism. [1993; *Hox,* contr. of *Homeobox,* the sequence of base pairs making up such a gene]

Hox·ha (hô′jä), *n.* **En·ver** (en′vər), 1908–85, Albanian political leader: premier 1944–54, First Secretary of the Central Committee 1954–1985.

hoy[1] (hoi), *n. Naut.* **1.** a heavy barge used in harbors. **2.** a vessel of the 17th and 18th centuries, usually sloop-rigged, used for fishing and coastal trading. [1485–95; < MD *hoey*]

hoy[2] (hoi), *interj.* **1.** (used as an exclamation to attract attention.) —*n.* **2.** a shout or hail. [1350–1400; ME; var. of HEY]

hoy·a (hoi′ə), *n.* any shrubby climbing plant of the genus *Hoya,* of the milkweed family, esp. the wax plant, *H. carnosa,* a pot plant with waxy white flowers. [< NL, named after Thomas *Hoy* (ca. 1750–1822), English gardener; see -A[2]]

hoy·den (hoid′n), *n.* **1.** a boisterous, bold, and carefree girl; a tomboy. —*adj.* **2.** boisterous; rude. Also, **hoiden.** [1585–95; perh. < MD *heyden* boor, HEATHEN] —**hoy′·den·ish,** *adj.* —**hoy′den·ism,** *n.*

Hoyle (hoil), *n.* **1. Edmond,** 1672–1769, English authority and writer on card games. **2. Sir Fred,** born 1915, British astronomer, mathematician, and educator. **3. according to Hoyle,** according to the rules or to the authority; correctly.

Hoyt (hoit), *n.* a male given name: from a Germanic word meaning "glee."

hp, horsepower.

H.P., 1. *Elect.* high power. **2.** high pressure. **3.** horsepower. Also, **h.p., HP**

HPV, human papilloma virus.

H.Q., headquarters. Also, **h.q., HQ**

HR, 1. home run. **2.** House of Representatives.

Hr., Herr.

hr., hour; hours. Also, **h.**

H.R., House of Representatives.

h.r., home run. Also, **hr**

HRA, Health Resources Administration.

Hra·dec Krá·lo·vé (hrä′dets krä′lô ve), a town in the N Czech Republic, on the Elbe River: Austrians defeated by Prussians in Battle of Sadowa 1866. 95,588. German, **Königgrätz.**

H-R diagram (āch′är′), *Astron.* See **Hertzsprung-Russell diagram.**

Hrd·lič·ka (hûrd′lich kə; *Czech.* hrd′lich kä), *n.* **A·leš** (ä′lesh), 1869–1943, U.S. anthropologist, born in Czechoslovakia.

H.R.E., 1. Holy Roman Emperor. **2.** Holy Roman Empire.

Hreid·mar (hrād′mär), *n.* (in the *Volsunga Saga*) the father of Fafnir, Otter, and Regin. He demanded wergild from the gods for killing Otter, and was killed by Fafnir when he got it.

H. Rept., House report.

H. Res., House resolution.

H.R.H., 1. His Royal Highness. **2.** Her Royal Highness.

H.R.I.P., here rests in peace. [< L *hīc requiēscit in pāce*]

Hrolf (hrolf), *n.* Rollo (def. 1).

Hrot·svi·tha (hrōt svē′tä), *n.* c935–c1000, German nun, poet, and dramatist. Also, **Hrot·swi′tha, Roswitha.**

Hroz·ný (hrôz′nē), *n.* **Frie·drich** (*Ger.* frē′driKH) or **Be·dřich** (*Czech.* be′drzhiKH), 1879–1952, Czech archaeologist and orientalist.

hrs., hours.

Hr·vat·ska (KHR′vät skä), *n.* Croatian name of **Croatia.**

H.S., 1. High School. **2.** *Brit.* Home Secretary.

h.s., 1. in this sense. [< L *hōc sensū*] **2.** (in prescriptions) at bedtime. [< L *hōrā somnī* at the hour of sleep]

H.S.H., 1. His Serene Highness. **2.** Her Serene Highness.

Hsia (shyä), *n.* a legendary dynasty in China, the traditional dates of which are 2205–1766 B.C. Also, **Xia.** [1905–10]

Hsia·men (*Chin.* shyä′mun′), *n. Wade-Giles.* Xiamen.

Hsiang (shyäng), *n.* a Chinese language spoken in Hunan province in southern China.

Hsiang·t'an (*Chin.* shyäng′tän′), *n. Wade-Giles.* Xiangtan.

Hsi Chiang (*Chin.* shē′ jyäng′), *Wade-Giles.* See **Xi Jiang.**

hsien (shyun), *n., pl.* **hsien. 1.** (in popular Chinese religion) one of a group of benevolent spirits promoting good in the world. **2.** (in China) a county or district. [1965–70; < Chin (Wade-Giles) *hsien*[1], (pinyin) *xiān* hermit, wizard]

hsing shêng (shing′ shung′), the process by which many Chinese characters were formed through the combination of two symbols, one phonographic and one logographic, into a single character. [< Chin (Wade-Giles) *hsing*[2] *shêng*[1], (pinyin) *xíngshēng* shape and sound (of voice)]

Hsin·hai·lien (*Chin.* shin′hī′lyun′), *n. Wade-Giles.* Xinhailian.

Hsin·hsiang (*Chin.* shin′shyäng′), *n. Wade-Giles.* Xinxiang.

Hsin Hsüeh (shēn′ shye′), *Chinese.* See **School of Mind.**

Hsi·ning (shē′ning′), *n. Wade-Giles.* Xining.

Hsin·king (shin′ging′), *n. Older Spelling.* former name of **Changchun.**

H.S.M., 1. His Serene Majesty. **2.** Her Serene Majesty.

HST, Hawaii Standard Time. Also, **H.S.T., h.s.t.**

H-stretch·er (āch′strech′ər), *n. Furniture.* a stretcher having the form of an H.

Hsüan Chiao (shyän′ jyou′), Taoism (def. 2).

Hsüan Tsung (shyän′ dzo͝ong′), A.D. 685–762, Chinese emperor of the Tang dynasty 712–756.

Hsüan T'ung (shyän′ do͝ong′). See **Pu-yi, Henry.**

Hsü·chou (*Chin.* shy′jō′), *n. Wade-Giles.* Xuzhou.

HSV-1, See under **herpes simplex.** Also, **HSV-I.**

HSV-2, See under **herpes simplex.** Also, **HSV-II.**

HT, 1. *Sports.* halftime. **2.** halftone. **3.** Hawaii time. **4.** *Elect.* high tension. **5.** high tide. **6.** at this time. [< L *hōc tempore*] **7.** under this title. [< L *hōc titulō*]

ht., height.

h.t., at this time. [< L *hōc tempore*]

HTLV, human T-cell lymphotropic virus: any of a family of retroviruses associated with certain leukemias and immune system deficiencies.

HTLV-1, human T-cell lymphotropic virus type 1: a type of retrovirus that causes a rare form of leukemia, primarily occurring in southern Japan and the Caribbean islands. Also, **HTLV-I.**

HTLV-2, human T-cell lymphotropic virus type 2: a type of retrovirus that has been associated with hairy cell leukemia. Also, **HTLV-II.**

HTLV-3, human T-cell lymphotropic virus type 3. See under **AIDS virus.** Also, **HTLV-III.**

Hts., Heights (used in placenames).

HUAC (hyo͞o′ak), *n.* See **House Un-American Activities Committee.**

Hua Guo·feng (hwä′ gwô′fung′), born 1920?, Chinese Communist leader: premier 1976–80.

Huai·nan (hwī′nän′), *n. Pinyin, Wade-Giles.* a city in central Anhui province, in E China. 350,000. Also, **Hwainan.**

Huam·bo (*Port.* wäm′bô), *n.* a city in central Angola. 67,000. Formerly, **Nova Lisboa.**

Huan·ca·yo (wäng kä′yô), *n.* a city in central Peru, on the Mantaro River. 126,754.

Huang Hai (hwäng′ hī′), *Pinyin, Wade-Giles.* See **Yellow Sea.**

Huang He (hwäng′ hœ′), *Pinyin.* a river flowing from W China into the Gulf of Bohai. 2800 mi. (4510 km) long. See map under **Chang Jiang.** Also, **Hwang Ho.** Also called **Yellow River.**

Huang Ti (hwäng′ dē′), the legendary first emperor of China. Also, *Pinyin,* **Huang′ Di′.** Also called **Yellow Emperor.**

Huá·nu·co (wä′no͞o kô′), *n.* a city in central Peru. 33,300.

hua·pan·go (wə päng′gō, -pang′-; *Sp.* wä päng′gô), *n., pl.* **-gos** (-gōz; *Sp.* -gôs). a fast, rhythmic dance of Mexico, for couples. [< MexSp, after *Huapango,* town near Veracruz, Mexico, where this dance originated]

hua·ra·che (wə rä′chē; *Sp.* wä rä′che), *n., pl.* **-ches** (-chēz; *Sp.* -ches). a Mexican sandal having the upper woven of leather strips. [1885–90; < MexSp < Tarascan *kʷarači*]

hua·ra·cho (wə rä′chō; *Sp.* wä rä′chô), *n., pl.* **-chos** (-chōz; *Sp.* -chôs). huarache. [1890–95, *Amer.*]

Huás·car (wäs′kär), *n.* 1495?–1533, Inca prince of Peru (half brother of Atahualpa; son of Huayna Capac).

Huas·ca·rán (wäs′kä rän′), *n.* a mountain in W Peru, in the Andes. 22,205 ft. (6768 m).

Huas·tec (wäs′tek), *n., pl.* **-tecs,** (*esp. collectively*) **-tec** for 1. **1.** a member of an Indian people of Mexico. **2.** the Mayan language of the Huastecs. [1835–45; < MexSp *huasteco* < Nahuatl *huāxtēcatl* person from *Huāxtlān,* equiv. to *huāx(in)* a tropical tree + *-tlān* locative suffix, *-tēcatl* suffix of ethnic names] —**Huas·tec′an,** *adj.*

Huay·na Ca·pac (wī′nä kä′päk), c1450–1527?, Inca ruler of Peru 1493?–1527? (father of Atahualpa and Huascar). Also, **Huai′na Ca′pac.**

hub (hub), *n., v.,* **hubbed, hub·bing.** —*n.* **1.** the central part of a wheel, as that part into which the spokes are inserted. **2.** the central part or axle end from which blades or spokelike parts radiate on various devices, as on a fan or propeller. **3.** a center around which other things revolve or from which they radiate; a focus of activity, authority, commerce, etc.; core. **4. the Hub,** Boston, Mass. (used as a nickname). **5.** the peg or hob used as a target in quoits and similar games. **6.** any one of the holes in an electrical panel, into which connections may be plugged. **7.** *Coining.* a design of hardened steel in relief, used as a punch in making a die. **8.** *Survey.* a stake bearing a tack used to mark a theodolite position. **9.** *Metalworking.* a die forced into a metal blank. —*v.t.* **10.** *Metalworking.* to stamp (a metal blank) with a hub. [1505–15; perh. var. of HOB[1]] —**Syn. 3.** core, pivot, heart.

hub-and-spoke (hub′ən spōk′), *adj.* of or designating a system of air transportation by which local flights carry passengers to one major regional airport where they can board long-distance or other local flights for their final destinations. [1980–85]

hub·ba hub·ba (hub′ə hub′ə), *Slang.* (an exclamation of admiration, approval, or enthusiasm, used esp. by G.I.'s of World War II as a shout in appreciation of a pretty girl.) [1940–45, *Amer.;* orig. uncert.; much speculation has been devoted to the original sense and origin of this expression; the foreign sources proposed (e.g., Arabic, Chinese, Spanish) are generally improbable and lack supporting evidence]

Hub·bard (hub′ərd), *n.* **Elbert Green,** 1856–1915, U.S. author, editor, and printer.

Hub′bard squash′, a variety of winter squash having a green or yellow skin and yellow flesh. [1865–70, *Amer.;* after the surname *Hubbard*]

hub·ble (hub′əl), *n.* **1.** a small hump, as on the surface of ice or a road. **2.** *Scot. and North Eng.* **a.** a heap; pile. **b.** a tumult; hubbub; uproar. [perh. < early D *hobbel* knot, bump; akin to *heuvel* hill]

Hub·ble (hub′əl), *n.* **Edwin Powell,** 1889–1953, U.S. astronomer: pioneer in extragalactic research.

hub·ble-bub·ble (hub′əl bub′əl), *n.* **1.** a simple form of the hookah, in which the smoke passes through water, causing a bubbling sound. **2.** a bubbling sound. **3.** an uproar; turmoil. [1625–35; rhyming compound based on BUBBLE]

Hub′ble's con′stant, *Astron.* the ratio of the recessional velocity of galaxies to their distance from the sun, with current measurements of its value ranging from 50 to 100 km/sec per megaparsec. [1950–55; after E. P. HUBBLE]

Hub′ble's law′, *Astron.* the law that the velocity of recession of distant galaxies from our own is proportional to their distance from us. [1930–35; named after E. P. HUBBLE, discoverer of the relationship]

Hub′ble Space′ Tel′escope, *Aerospace.* See **Space Telescope.**

hub•bly (hub′lē), *adj.* of uneven surface; rough: *hubbly ice; a hubbly road.* [1865–70, *Amer.*; perh. HUB (in the sense of protuberance) + -LY; c. D *hobbelig* rugged]

hub•bub (hub′ub), *n.* **1.** a loud, confused noise, as of many voices: *There was quite a hubbub in the auditorium after the announcement.* **2.** tumult; uproar. [1545–55; appar. of Ir orig.; akin to ScotGael cry *ububl* (redupl. of *ub!*) expressing aversion or contempt] —**Syn. 1.** See **noise. 2.** disturbance, disorder, confusion. —**Ant. 1.** quiet. **2.** calm.

hub•by (hub′ē), *n., pl.* **-bies.** *Informal.* husband. [1680–90; by shortening and alter.; see -Y[2]]

hub•cap (hub′kap′), *n.* a removable cover for the center area of the exposed side of an automobile wheel, covering the axle. [1900–05; HUB + CAP[1]]

Hu•bei (hʏ′bā′), *n. Pinyin.* a province in central China. 33,710,000; 72,394 sq. mi. (187,500 sq. km). *Cap.:* Wuhan. Also, **Hupeh, Hupei.**

Hu•bert (hyōō′bərt), *n.* a male given name: from Germanic words meaning "mind" and "bright."

Hu•ber•tus•burg (hyōō bûr′təs bûrg′; *Ger.* hōō bᴇʀ′-tōōs bōōʀk′), *n.* a castle in S East Germany, in the former province of Saxony, E of Leipzig: treaty ending the Seven Years' War signed here 1763.

Hub•li (hŏŏb′lē), *n.* a city in W Karnataka, in SW India. 379,166.

hu•bris (hyōō′bris, hōō′-), *n.* excessive pride or self-confidence; arrogance. Also, **hybris.** Cf. **sophrosyne.** [1880–85; < Gk *hýbris* insolence] —**hu•bris′tic,** *adj.*

huck•a•back (huk′ə bak′), *n.* toweling of linen or cotton, of a distinctive absorbent weave. Also called **huck.** [1680–90; orig. uncert.]

huck•le (huk′əl), *n.* the hip or haunch. [1520–30; obs. *huck* hip, haunch (< ?) + -LE]

huck•le•ber•ry (huk′əl ber′ē), *n., pl.* **-ries. 1.** the dark-blue or black edible berry of any of various shrubs belonging to the genus *Gaylussacia* of the heath family. **2.** a shrub bearing such fruit. **3.** blueberry (def. 1). [1660–70, *Amer.*; perh. alter. of HURTLEBERRY]

Huck′leberry Finn′ (fin), (*The Adventures of Huckleberry Finn*) a novel (1884) by Mark Twain.

huck•le•bone (huk′əl bōn′), *n.* **1.** hipbone. **2.** knucklebone (def. 2). [1475–85; HUCKLE + BONE]

huck•ster (huk′stər), *n.* **1.** a retailer of small articles, esp. a peddler of fruits and vegetables; hawker. **2.** a person who employs showy methods to effect a sale, win votes, etc.: *the crass methods of political hucksters.* **3.** a cheaply mercenary person. **4.** *Informal.* **a.** a persuasive and aggressive salesperson. **b.** a person who works in the advertising industry, esp. one who prepares aggressive advertising for radio and television. —*v.t., v.i.* **5.** to deal, as in small articles, or to make petty bargains: *to huckster fresh corn; to huckster for a living.* **6.** to sell or promote in an aggressive and flashy manner. [1150–1200; ME *huccstere* (perh. c. MD *hokester*), equiv. to *hucc-* HAGGLE (c. dial. G *hucken* to huckster) + *-stere* -STER] —**huck′ster•ism,** *n.* —**huck′ster•ish,** *adj.*

huck•ster•er (huk′stər ər), *n. Archaic.* huckster.

HUD (hud), *n.* Department of Housing and Urban Development.

Hud•ders•field (hud′ərz fēld′), *n.* a town in West Yorkshire, in N central England. 130,060.

hud•dle (hud′l), *v.,* **-dled, -dling,** *n.* —*v.i.* **1.** to gather or crowd together in a close mass. **2.** to crouch, curl up, or draw oneself together. **3.** *Football.* to get together in a huddle. **4.** to confer or consult; meet to discuss, exchange ideas, or make a decision. —*v.t.* **5.** to heap or crowd together closely. **6.** to draw (oneself) closely together, as in crouching; nestle (often fol. by *up*). **7.** *Chiefly Brit.* to do hastily and carelessly (often fol. by *up, over,* or *together*). **8.** to put on (clothes) with careless haste (often fol. by *on*). —*n.* **9.** a closely gathered group, mass, or heap; bunch. **10.** *Football.* a gathering of the offensive team in a close circle or line behind the line of scrimmage for instructions, signals, etc., from the team captain or quarterback, usually held before each offensive play. **11.** a conference, or consultation, esp. a private meeting to discuss serious matters: *The labor representatives have been in a huddle for two hours.* **12.** confusion or disorder. [1570–80; *hud-* (weak grade of root found in HIDE[1]) + -LE; r. ME *hoder,* equiv. to *hod-* (var. *hud-*) + *-er* -ER[6]] —**hud′dler,** *n.* —**hud′•dling•ly,** *adv.*

Hud•dle•ston (hud′l stən), *n.* **(Ernest Urban) Trevor,** born 1913, English Anglican bishop and missionary in Africa.

Hu•di•bras•tic (hyōō′də bras′tik, *or, often,* yōō′-), *adj.* **1.** of, pertaining to, or resembling the style of Samuel Butler's *Hudibras* (published 1663–78), a mock-heroic poem written in tetrameter couplets. **2.** of a playful burlesque style. —*n.* **3.** a Hudibrastic couplet or stanza. [1705–15; *Hudibras* + -TIC] —**Hu′di•bras′ti•cal•ly,** *adv.*

Hud•son (hud′sən), *n.* **1. Henry,** died 1611?, English navigator and explorer. **2. William Henry,** 1841–1922, English naturalist and author. **3.** a river in E New York, flowing S to New York Bay. 306 mi. (495 km) long. **4.** a town in central Massachusetts. 16,408. **5.** a town in S New Hampshire. 14,022. **6.** a steam locomotive having a four-wheeled front truck, six driving wheels, and a four-wheeled rear truck. See table under **Whyte classification.**

Hud′son Bay′, a large inland sea in N Canada. 850 mi. (1370 km) long; 600 mi. (965 km) wide; 400,000 sq. mi. (1,036,000 sq. km).

Hud•so′ni•an god′wit (hud sō′nē ən). See under **godwit.** [1855–60; HUDSON (BAY) + -IAN]

Hud′son Riv′er school′, *Fine Arts.* a group of American painters of the mid-19th century whose works are characterized by a highly romantic treatment of landscape, esp. along the Hudson River.

Hud′son's Bay′ blan′ket, *Trademark.* a heavyweight, boldly striped blanket made of wool. [1895–1900]

Hud′son's Bay′ Com′pany, a company chartered in England in 1670 to carry on fur trading with the Indians in North America.

Hud′son seal′, muskrat fur that has been plucked and dyed to give the appearance of seal. [1915–20]

Hud′son Strait′, a strait connecting Hudson Bay and the Atlantic. 450 mi. (725 km) long; 100 mi. (160 km) wide.

hue[1] (hyōō *or, often,* yōō), *n.* **1.** a gradation or variety of a color; tint: *pale hues.* **2.** the property of light by which the color of an object is classified as red, blue, green, or yellow in reference to the spectrum. **3.** color: *all the hues of the rainbow.* **4.** form or appearance. **5.** complexion. [bef. 900; ME *hewe,* OE *hīw* form, appearance, color; c. ON *hý* bird's down, Sw *hy* skin, complexion, Goth *hiwi* form, appearance; akin to OE *hār* gray (see HOAR)] —**hue′less,** *adj.*

hue[2] (hyōō), *n.* outcry, as of pursuers; clamor. [1200–50; ME *hu(e)* < MF: a hoot, outcry (whence *huer* to hoot, cry out)]

Hué (hwā), *n.* a seaport in central Vietnam: former capital of Annam. 200,000.

hue′ and cry′, **1.** *Early Eng. Law.* the pursuit of a felon or an offender with loud outcries or clamor to give an alarm. **2.** any public clamor, protest, or alarm: *a general hue and cry against the war.* [1250–1300; ME, trans. of AF *hu et cri.* See HUE[2], CRY]

hueb•ner•ite (hyōōb′nə rīt′ *or, often,* yōōb′-), *n.* a reddish-brown mineral of the wolframite group, manganese tungstate, $MnWO_4$, a minor ore of tungsten. [after Adolph *Huebner,* 19th-century German metallurgist; see -ITE[1]]

hued (hyōōd *or, often,* yōōd), *adj.* having the hue or color as specified (usually used in combination): *many-hued; golden-hued.* [bef. 1000; ME *hewed,* OE *(ge)hīwod.* See HUE[1], -ED[3]]

Huel•va (wel′vä), *n.* a seaport in SW Spain, near the Gulf of Cádiz. 96,689.

hue•mul (wā mōōl′), *n.* a yellowish-brown deer of the genus *Hippocamelus,* of South America: the two species are endangered. Also called **Andean deer, guemal.** [1800–10; < AmerSp *güemul* < Araucanian *huemul*]

Huer•ta (wer′tə; *Sp.* weʀ′tä), *n.* **Vic•to•ria•no** (bēk′tô-ʀyä′nô), 1854–1916, Mexican general: provisional president of Mexico 1913–14.

hue•vos ran•che•ros (*Eng.* wā′vōs rän châr′ōs, ran-; *Sp.* we′vôs rän che′ʀôs), a Latin American dish of eggs, usually fried or poached, topped with a spicy tomato sauce and sometimes served on a fried corn tortilla with the addition of vegetables and cheese. [< AmerSp: eggs cooked in a country or ranch style]

Hu•ey (hyōō′ē *or, often,* yōō′ē), *n.* a male given name, form of **Hugh.**

Hu•ey•town (hyōō′ē toun′ *or, often,* yōō′-), *n.* a town in central Alabama. 13,309.

huff (huf), *n.* **1.** a mood of sulking anger; a fit of resentment: *Just because you disagree, don't walk off in a huff.* —*v.t.* **2.** to give offense to; make angry. **3.** to treat with arrogance or contempt; bluster at; hector or bully. **4.** *Checkers.* to remove (a piece) from the board as a penalty for failing to make a compulsory capture. —*v.i.* **5.** to take offense; speak indignantly. **6.** to puff or blow; breathe heavily. **7.** to swell with pride or arrogance; swagger or bluster. [1575–85; imit.; see PUFF] —**Syn. 1.** temper, passion, pique, pet.

Huff-Duff (huf′duf′), *n.* a method used by the Allies in World War II for locating enemy submarines and other naval or land targets through simultaneous bearings on their radio transmissions. [vocalization of the abbr. *h.f.d.f.* for *high-frequency direction finder*]

huff•ish (huf′ish), *adj.* **1.** peevish; irritable. **2.** swaggering; insolent; bullying. [1745–55; HUFF + -ISH[1]] —**huff′ish•ly,** *adv.* —**huff′ish•ness,** *n.*

huff•y (huf′ē), *adj.,* **huff•i•er, huff•i•est. 1.** easily offended; touchy. **2.** offended; sulky: *a huffy mood.* **3.** snobbish; haughty. [1670–80; HUFF + -Y[1]] —**huff′i•ly,** *adv.* —**huff′i•ness,** *n.*
—**Syn. 2.** surly, sullen, resentful, petulant.

Hu•fuf (hōō fōōf′), *n.* Hofuf.

hug (hug), *v.,* **hugged, hug•ging,** *n.* —*v.t.* **1.** to clasp tightly in the arms, esp. with affection; embrace. **2.** to cling firmly or fondly to; cherish: *to hug an opinion.* **3.** to keep close to, as in sailing, walking, or in moving along or alongside of: *to hug the shore; to hug the road.* —*v.i.* **4.** to cling together; lie close. —*n.* **5.** a tight clasp with the arms; embrace. [1560–70; perh. < ON *hugga* to soothe, console; akin to OE *hogian* to care for] —**hug′•ger,** *n.* —**hug′ging•ly,** *adv.*

huge (hyōōj *or, often,* yōōj), *adj.,* **hug•er, hug•est. 1.** extraordinarily large in bulk, quantity, or extent: *a huge ship; a huge portion of ice cream.* **2.** of unbounded extent, scope, or character; limitless: *the huge genius of Mozart.* [1225–75; ME *huge, hoge* < OF *ahuge, ahoge* enormous, equiv. to *a-* A-[5] + *hoge* height < Gmc; cf. ON *haugr* hill (see HIGH)] —**huge′ly,** *adv.* —**huge′•ness,** *n.*
—**Syn. 1.** mammoth, gigantic, colossal; vast; stupendous; bulky. HUGE, ENORMOUS, IMMENSE, TREMENDOUS imply great magnitude. HUGE implies massiveness, bulkiness, or even shapelessness: *a huge mass of rock; a huge collection of antiques.* ENORMOUS, literally out of the norm, applies to what exceeds in extent, magnitude, or degree, a norm or standard: *an enormous iceberg.* TREMENDOUS, in informal use, applies to anything so huge as to be astonishing or to inspire awe: *a tremendous amount of equipment.* IMMENSE, literally not measurable, is particularly applicable to what is exceedingly great, without reference to a standard: *immense buildings.* All are used figuratively: *a huge success; enormous curiosity; tremendous effort; immense joy.* —**Ant. 1.** small, tiny, diminutive.
—**Pronunciation.** See **human.**

Hü•gel (hyōō′gəl *or, often,* yōō′-), *n.* **Baron Friedrich von,** 1852–1925, English theologian and writer.

huge•ous (hyōō′jəs *or, often,* yōō′-), *adj.* huge. [1520–30; HUGE + -OUS] —**huge′ous•ly,** *adv.* —**huge′•ous•ness,** *n.*

hug•ga•ble (hug′ə bəl), *adj.* evoking a desire to hug close; inviting a close embrace; cuddly: *a huggable little baby.* [1895–1900; HUG + -ABLE]

hug•ger-mug•ger (hug′ər mug′ər), *n.* **1.** disorder or confusion; muddle. **2.** secrecy; reticence: *Why is there such hugger-mugger about the scheme?* —*adj.* **3.** secret or clandestine. **4.** disorderly or confused. —*v.t.* **5.** to keep secret or concealed; hush up. —*v.i.* **6.** to act secretly. [1520–30; earlier *hucker-mucker,* rhyming compound based on *mucker,* ME *mokeren* to hoard]

hug•ger-mug•ger•y (hug′ər mug′ə rē), *n., pl.* **-ger•ies.** hugger-mugger (defs. 1, 2). [HUGGER-MUGGER + -Y[3]]

Hug•gins (hug′inz), *n.* **Charles Bren•ton** (bren′tn), born 1901, U.S. surgeon and medical researcher, born in Canada: Nobel prize 1966.

Hugh (hyōō *or, often,* yōō), *n.* a male given name: from a Germanic word meaning "heart, mind."

Hugh′ Ca′pet. See **Capet, Hugh.**

Hughes (hyōōz *or, often,* yōōz), *n.* **1. Charles Evans,** 1862–1948, U.S. jurist and statesman: Chief Justice of the U.S. 1930–41. **2. Howard (Ro•bard)** (rō′bärd), 1905–76, U.S. businessman, motion-picture producer, and aviator. **3. (John) Lang•ston** (lang′stən), 1902–67, U.S. novelist and poet. **4. Rupert,** 1872–1956, U.S. novelist and biographer. **5. Ted,** born 1930, English poet: poet laureate since 1984. **6. Thomas,** 1822–96, English novelist, reformer, and jurist. **7. William Morris,** 1864–1952, Australian statesman, born in Wales: prime minister 1915–23.

Hugh•ie (hyōō′ē *or, often,* yōō′ē), *n.* a male given name, form of **Hugh.**

Hu•gi (hyōō′gē, hōō′- *or, often,* yōō′-), *n. Scand. Myth.* a young man, a personification of thought, who defeated Thialfi in a race.

Hu•gin (hyōō′gin, hōō′- *or, often,* yōō′-), *n. Scand. Myth.* one of the two ravens of Odin that brought him news from the whole world. Cf. **Munin.** [< ON *Huginn,* equiv. to *hugi* mind, thought + *(i)nn* definite article]

Hug•li (hōōg′lē), *n.* Hooghly.

hug-me-tight (hug′mē tīt′), *n.* a woman's short, warm, close-fitting jacket, usually knitted or crocheted and often sleeveless. [1855–60, *Amer.*]

Hu•go (hyōō′gō *or, often,* yōō′-; *Fr.* ʏ gō′), *n.* **1. Vic•tor (Ma•rie, Viscount)** (vik′tər mə rē′; *Fr.* vēk tôʀ′ ma ʀē′), 1802–85, French poet, novelist, and dramatist. **2.** a male given name.

Hu•gue•not (hyōō′gə not′ *or, often,* yōō′-), *n.* a member of the Reformed or Calvinistic communion of France in the 16th and 17th centuries; a French Protestant. [1555–65; < F, perh. b. *Hugues* (name of a political leader in Geneva) and *eidgenot,* back formation from *eidgenots,* Swiss var. of G *Eidgenoss* confederate, lit., oath comrade] —**Hu′gue•not′ic,** *adj.* —**Hu′gue•not•ism,** *n.*

huh (hu), *interj.* (used as an exclamation of surprise, bewilderment, disbelief, contempt, or interrogation.) [1600–10]

Hu Han-min (hōō′ hän′min′), 1879–1936, Chinese nationalist revolutionary. Also, **Hu′ Han′min′.**

Hu•he•hot (hōō′hā′hōt′), *n.* Hohhot. Also, *Pinyin,* **Hu•he•hao•te** (hōō′hœ′hou′tœ′).

hu•ia (hōō′yə), *n.* an apparently extinct, crowlike bird, *Heteralocha acutirostris,* of New Zealand, noted for the completely different bill shapes of the male and female. [1835–45; < Maori *hūia*]

Hui•do•bro (wē ᴛʜô′vʀô), *n.* **Vi•cen•te** (bē sen′te), 1893–1948, Chilean poet.

Hui•la (wē′lä), *n.* **Mount,** a volcano in central Colombia. 18,700 ft. (5700 m).

hui•sa•che (wē sä′chē), *n.* a tropical and subtropical New World shrub, *Acacia farnesiana,* of the legume family, having clusters of fragrant, deep-yellow flower heads. Also called **cassie, popinac, sponge tree.** [1830–40, *Amer.*; < MexSp < Nahuatl *huixachi,* equiv. to *hui(tztli)* thorn + *(i)xachi* a large amount, many]

Hui Tsung (hwē′ dzŏŏng′), *n.* 1082–1135, emperor of China 1101–26: painter and patron of art. Also, *Pinyin,* **Hui Zong** (hwē′ zông′).

Hui•tzi•lo•poch•tli (wē′tsē lō pōch′tlē), *n.* the Aztec god of war and of the sun. Also, **Uitzilopochtli.** [< Nahuatl *Huitzilōpōchtli,* equiv. to *huītzil(in)* hummingbird + *ōpōchtli* left-hand side]

Hui•zhou (hwē′jō′), *n. Pinyin.* a city in S Guangdong province, in SE China, E of Canton. 73,000. Also, *Wade-*

CONCISE ETYMOLOGY KEY: <, descended or borrowed from; >, whence; b., blend of, blended; c., cognate with; cf., compare; deriv., derivative; equiv., equivalent; imit., imitative; obl., oblique; r., replacing; s., stem; sp., spelling, spelled; resp., respelling, respelled; trans., translation; ?, origin unknown; *, unattested; ‡, probably earlier than. See the full key inside the front cover.

Giles, **Hui′chou′;** *Older Spelling,* **Waichow.** Formerly, *Pinyin, Wade-Giles,* **Hui•yang** (hwē′yäng′).

Huk (ho͝ok), *n., pl.* **Huks. 1.** a member of the Hukbong Mapagpalaya ng Bayan **(People's Liberation Army),** a Communist agrarian revolutionary group in central Luzon in the Philippines. **2.** a member of the Hukbalahap, an anti-Japanese resistance group in central Luzon during World War II. [shortening of Tagalog *hukbo* army]

Hu•la-Hoop, (ho͞o′lə ho͞op′), *Trademark.* a brand name for a tubular plastic hoop, about 4 ft. (1.2 m) in diameter, for rotating about the body by swinging the hips, used for physical exercise or in children's play: introduced in the 1950's.

hu•la-hu•la (ho͞o′lə ho͞o′lə), *n.* a sinuous Hawaiian native dance with intricate arm movements that tell a story in pantomime, usually danced to rhythmic drumming and accompanied by chanting. Also called **hu′la.** [1815–25; < Hawaiian]

hu′la skirt′, 1. a skirt made of long stems of grass bound to a waistband, worn typically by a Hawaiian hula dancer. **2.** an imitation of this skirt made of any material. [1925–30]

hul•dre (ho͝ol′dər), *n. Scand. Myth.* one of a race of sirens, living in the woods, seductive but dangerous. Also, **hul′der.** [< ON *Huld* name of a witch, prob. akin to *hulda* secrecy, hiding, deriv. from base of *hel;* see HELL, HULL[1]]

hulk (hulk), *n.* **1.** the body of an old or dismantled ship. **2.** a ship specially built to serve as a storehouse, prison, etc., and not for sea service. **3.** a clumsy-looking or unwieldy ship or boat. **4.** a bulky or unwieldy person, object, or mass. **5.** the shell of a wrecked, burned-out, or abandoned vehicle, building, or the like. —*v.i.* **6.** to loom in bulky form; appear as a large, massive bulk (often fol. by *up*): *The bus hulked up suddenly over the crest of the hill.* **7.** *Brit. Dial.* to lounge, slouch, or move in a heavy, loutish manner. [bef. 1000; ME *hulke,* OE *hulc;* perh. < ML *hulcus* < Gk *holkás* trading vessel, orig., towed ship]

hulk•ing (hul′king), *adj.* heavy and clumsy; bulky. [1690–1700; HULK + -ING[2]]
—**Syn.** massive, cumbersome, ponderous.

hulk•y (hul′kē), *adj.,* **hulk•i•er, hulk•i•est.** hulking. [1775–85; HULK + -Y[1]]

hull[1] (hul), *n.* **1.** the husk, shell, or outer covering of a seed or fruit. **2.** the calyx of certain fruits, as the strawberry. **3.** any covering or envelope. —*v.t.* **4.** to remove the hull of. **5.** *Midland U.S.* to shell (peas or beans). [bef. 1000; ME; OE *hulu* husk, pod; akin to OE *helan* to cover, hide, L *cēlāre* to hide, CONCEAL, Gk *kalýptein* to cover up (see APOCALYPSE). See HALL, HELL, HOLE] —**hull′er,** *n.*
—**Syn. 1.** skin, pod, peel, rind, shuck.

hull[2] (hul), *n.* **1.** the hollow, lowermost portion of a ship, floating partially submerged and supporting the remainder of the ship. **2.** *Aeron.* **a.** the boatlike fuselage of a flying boat on which the plane lands or takes off. **b.** the cigar-shaped arrangement of girders enclosing the gasbag of a rigid dirigible. **3. hull down,** (of a ship) sufficiently far away, or below the horizon, that the hull is invisible. **4. hull up,** (of a ship) sufficiently near, or above the horizon, that the hull is visible. —*v.t.* **5.** to pierce (the hull of a ship), esp. below the water line. —*v.i.* **6.** to drift without power or sails. [1350–1400; ME; special use of HULL[1]] —**hull′-less,** *adj.*

Hull (hul), *n.* **1. Cor•dell** (kôr′del, kôr del′), 1871–1955, U.S. statesman: Secretary of State 1933–44; Nobel peace prize 1945. **2. Robert Marvin** (*Bobby*), born 1939, Canadian ice-hockey player. **3. William,** 1753–1825, U.S. general. **4.** Official name, **Kingston-upon-Hull.** a seaport in Humberside, in E England, on the Humber River. 279,700. **5.** a city in SE Canada, on the Ottawa River opposite Ottawa. 61,039.

hul•la•ba•loo (hul′ə bə lo͞o′), *n., pl.* **-loos.** a clamorous noise or disturbance; uproar. [1750–60; appar. var. of *haloobaloo,* rhyming compound based on Scots *baloo* lullaby]

hull′ bal′ance, (of a sailing ship) the property of maintaining satisfactory trim and steering qualities when heeled at a normal angle.

hull′ effi′ciency, *Naval Archit.* the ratio of the quantity of work required to tow a certain hull at a given speed to that required to drive it with a certain propeller: used in propeller design.

hull′ gird′er, *Naval Archit.* the theoretical box girder formed by the continuous longitudinal members of the hull of a ship, providing resistance to hogging and sagging. [‡1945–50]

Hull′ House′, a settlement house in Chicago, Ill., founded in 1889 by Jane Addams.

hull•ing (hul′ing), *n.* material for the framework and shell of the hull of a ship. [1400–50; late ME (ger.). See HULL[2], -ING[1]]

hul•lo (hə lō′), *interj., n., pl.* **-los,** *v.i., v.t.,* **-loed, -lo•ing. 1.** hallo. **2.** *Chiefly Brit.* hello.

hul•loa (hu lō′, hul′ō), *interj., n., pl.* **-loas,** *v.i., v.t.,* **-loaed, -loa•ing.** *Chiefly Brit.* hello.

hul•loo (hu lo͞o′, hul′o͞o), *interj., n., pl.* **-loos,** *v.i., v.t.,* **-looed, -loo•ing.** hallo.

hul•ly gul•ly (hul′ē gul′ē), a dance that is a modification of the frug. Also, **hul′ly-gul′ly.** [1960–65; orig. uncert.]

hu•ly (ho͞o′lē, hʏ′lē), *adj., adv. Scot.* hooly.

hum (hum), *v.,* **hummed, hum•ming,** *n., interj.* —*v.i.* **1.** to make a low, continuous, droning sound. **2.** to give forth an indistinct sound of mingled voices or noises. **3.** to utter an indistinct sound in hesitation, embarrassment, dissatisfaction, etc.; hem. **4.** to sing with closed lips, without articulating words. **5.** to be in a state of busy activity: *The household hummed in preparation for the wedding.* **6.** *Brit. Slang.* to have a bad odor, as of stale perspiration. —*v.t.* **7.** to sound, sing, or utter by humming: *to hum a tune.* **8.** to bring, put, etc., by humming: *to hum a child to sleep.* —*n.* **9.** the act or sound of humming; an inarticulate or indistinct murmur; hem. **10.** *Audio.* an unwanted low-frequency sound caused by power-line frequencies in any audio component. —*interj.* **11.** (an inarticulate sound uttered in contemplation, hesitation, dissatisfaction, doubt, etc.) [1300–50; ME; ult. imit.; c. G *hummen* to hum; cf. HUMBLEBEE]
—**Syn. 5.** bustle, buzz.

Hu•ma•cao (o͞o′mä kou′), *n.* a city in E Puerto Rico. 19,147.

hu•man (hyo͞o′mən *or, often,* yo͞o′-), *adj.* **1.** of, pertaining to, characteristic of, or having the nature of people: *human frailty.* **2.** consisting of people: *the human race.* **3.** of or pertaining to the social aspect or character of people: *human affairs.* **4.** sympathetic; humane: *a warmly human understanding.* —*n.* **5.** a human being. [1350–1400; earlier *humain(e), humayn(e),* ME < MF *humain* < L *hūmānus,* equiv. to *hūm-* (see HOMO) + *-ānus* -AN; sp. *human* predominant from early 18th century] —**hu′man•like′,** *adj.* —**hu′man•ness,** *n.*
—**Syn. 1.** HUMAN, HUMANE may refer to that which is, or should be, characteristic of human beings. In thus describing characteristics, HUMAN may refer to good and bad traits of a person alike (*human kindness; human weakness*). When emphasis is placed upon the latter, HUMAN is thought of as contrasted to DIVINE: *To err is human, to forgive divine. He was only human.* HUMANE (the original spelling of HUMAN, and since 1700 restricted in meaning) takes into account only the nobler or gentler aspects of people and is often contrasted to their more ignoble or brutish aspect. A HUMANE person is benevolent in treating fellow humans or helpless animals; the word once had also connotations of courtesy and refinement (hence, the application of HUMANE to those branches of learning intended to refine the mind).
—**Pronunciation.** Pronunciations of words like HUMAN, HUGE, etc., with the initial (h) deleted: (yo͞o′mən), (yo͞oj), while sometimes criticized, are heard from speakers at all social and educational levels, including professors, lawyers, and other public speakers.

hu′man be′ing, 1. any individual of the genus *Homo,* esp. a member of the species *Homo sapiens.* **2.** a person, esp. as distinguished from other animals or as representing the human species: *living conditions not fit for human beings; a very generous human being.* [1855–60]

hu′man chorion′ic gonadotro′pin, *Biochem.* See **chorionic gonadotropin** (def. 1). *Abbr.:* hCG

Hu′man Com′edy, The, (French, *La Comédie Humaine*), a collected edition of tales and novels in 17 volumes (1842–48) by Honoré de Balzac.

hu•mane (hyo͞o mān′ *or, often,* yo͞o-), *adj.* **1.** characterized by tenderness, compassion, and sympathy for people and animals, esp. for the suffering or distressed: *humane treatment of horses.* **2.** of or pertaining to humanistic studies. [orig. stress var. of HUMAN, restricted to above senses from 18th century; cf. GERMANE, GERMAN] —**hu•mane′ly,** *adv.* —**hu•mane′ness,** *n.*
—**Syn. 1.** merciful, kind, kindly, kindhearted, tender, compassionate, gentle, sympathetic; benevolent, benignant, charitable. See **human.** —**Ant. 1.** brutal.

hu′man ecol′ogy, ecology (def. 2). [1930–35]

hu′man engineer′ing, an applied science that coordinates the design of devices, systems, and physical working conditions with the capacities and requirements of the worker. Also called **ergonomics, hu′man-fac′tors engineer′ing** (hyo͞o′mən fak′tərz *or, often,* yo͞o′-). [1930–35, *Amer.*]

humane′ soci′ety, (*often cap.*) an organization devoted to promoting humane ideals, esp. with reference to the treatment of animals. [1770–80]

Hu′man Ge′nome Proj′ect, a federally funded U.S. scientific project to identify both the genes and the entire sequence of DNA base pairs that make up the human genome. [1985–90]

hu′man growth′ hor′mone, *Biochem.* somatotropin. *Abbr.:* hGH [1970–75]

hu•man•ics (hyo͞o man′iks *or, often,* yo͞o-), *n.* (*used with a singular v.*) the study of the nature or affairs of humankind. [1860–65; HUMAN + -ICS]

hu′man immunodefi′ciency vi′rus. See under **AIDS virus.** *Abbr.:* HIV

hu′man-in′terest sto′ry (hyo͞o′mən in′tər ist, -trist *or, often,* yo͞o′-), a story or report, as in a newspaper or on a newscast, designed to engage attention and sympathy by enabling one to identify readily with the people, problems, and situations described. [1925–30]

hu•man•ism (hyo͞o′mə niz′əm *or, often,* yo͞o′-), *n.* **1.** any system or mode of thought or action in which human interests, values, and dignity predominate. **2.** devotion to or study of the humanities. **3.** (*sometimes cap.*) the studies, principles, or culture of the humanists. **4.** *Philos.* a variety of ethical theory and practice that emphasizes reason, scientific inquiry, and human fulfillment in the natural world and often rejects the importance of belief in God. [1805–15; HUMAN + -ISM]

hu•man•ist (hyo͞o′mə nist *or, often,* yo͞o′-), *n.* **1.** a person having a strong interest in or concern for human welfare, values, and dignity. **2.** a person devoted to or versed in the humanities. **3.** a student of human nature or affairs. **4.** a classical scholar. **5.** (*sometimes cap.*) any one of the scholars of the Renaissance who pursued and disseminated the study and understanding of the cultures of ancient Rome and Greece, and emphasized secular, individualistic, and critical thought. **6.** (*sometimes cap.*) a person who follows a form of scientific or philosophical humanism. —*adj.* **7.** of or pertaining to human affairs, nature, welfare, or values. **8.** (*sometimes cap.*) of or pertaining to the humanities or classical scholarship, esp. that of the Renaissance humanists. **9.** of or pertaining to philosophic or scientific humanism. [1580–90; < It *umanista.* See HUMAN, -IST] —**hu′man•is′tic,** *adj.* —**hu′man•is′ti•cal•ly,** *adv.*

hu•man•i•tar•i•an (hyo͞o man′i târ′ē ən *or, often,* yo͞o-), *adj.* **1.** having concern for or helping to improve the welfare and happiness of people. **2.** of or pertaining to ethical or theological humanitarianism. —*n.* **3.** a person actively engaged in promoting human welfare and social reforms, as a philanthropist. **4.** a person who professes ethical or theological humanitarianism. [1810–20; HUMANIT(Y) + -ARIAN]

hu•man•i•tar•i•an•ism (hyo͞o man′i târ′ē ə niz′əm *or, often,* yo͞o-), *n.* **1.** humanitarian principles or practices. **2.** *Ethics.* **a.** the doctrine that humanity's obligations are concerned wholly with the welfare of the human race. **b.** the doctrine that humankind may become perfect without divine aid. **3.** *Theol.* the doctrine that Jesus Christ possessed a human nature only. [1825–35; HUMANITARIAN + -ISM] —**hu•man′i•tar′i•an•ist,** *n.*

hu•man•i•ty (hyo͞o man′i tē *or, often,* yo͞o-), *n., pl.* **-ties. 1.** all human beings collectively; the human race; humankind. **2.** the quality or condition of being human; human nature. **3.** the quality of being humane; kindness; benevolence. **4. the humanities, a.** the study of classical languages and classical literature. **b.** the Latin and Greek classics as a field of study. **c.** literature, philosophy, art, etc., as distinguished from the sciences. **d.** the study of literature, philosophy, art, etc. [1350–1400; ME *humanite* < L *hūmānitās.* See HUMAN, -ITY]
—**Syn. 3.** sympathy, tenderness, goodwill. —**Ant. 3.** inhumanity, unkindness.

hu•man•ize (hyo͞o′mə nīz′ *or, often,* yo͞o′-), *v.,* **-ized, -iz•ing.** —*v.t.* **1.** to make humane, kind, or gentle. **2.** to make human. —*v.i.* **3.** to become human or humane. Also, *esp. Brit.,* **hu′man•ise′.** [1595–1605; HUMAN + -IZE] —**hu′man•i•za′tion,** *n.* —**hu′man•iz′er,** *n.*

hu•man•kind (hyo͞o′mən kīnd′, -kīnd′ *or, often,* yo͞o′-), *n.* human beings collectively; the human race. [1635–45; from the phrase *human kind;* modeled on *mankind*]

hu′man leu′kocyte an′tigen, *Immunol.* See **HLA.**

hu•man•ly (hyo͞o′mən lē *or, often,* yo͞o′-), *adv.* **1.** in a human manner. **2.** by human means. **3.** within the limits of human knowledge and capability: *Is it humanly possible to predict the future?* **4.** from or according to the viewpoint of humankind. [1605–15; HUMAN + -LY]

hu′man na′ture, 1. the psychological and social qualities that characterize humankind, esp. in contrast with other living things. **2.** *Sociol.* the character of human conduct, generally regarded as produced by living in primary groups. [1735–45]

hu•man•oid (hyo͞o′mə noid′ *or, often,* yo͞o′-), *adj.* **1.** having human characteristics or form; resembling human beings. —*n.* **2.** a humanoid being: *to search for humanoids in outer space.* [1915–20; HUMAN + -OID]

hu′man papillo′ma vi′rus, a species of virus that causes genital warts. *Abbr.:* HPV

hu′man rela′tions, the study of group behavior for the purpose of improving interpersonal relationships, as among employees. [1915–20]

hu′man resources′, people, esp. the personnel employed by a given company, institution, or the like.

hu′man resourc′es depart′ment. See **personnel department.**

hu′man rights′, fundamental rights, esp. those believed to belong to an individual and in whose exercise a government may not interfere, as the rights to speak, associate, work, etc. [1785–95]

hu′man serv′ices, programs or facilities for meeting basic health, welfare, and other needs of a society or group, as of the poor, sick, or elderly.

human T-cell lymphotropic virus. See **HTLV.**

human T-cell lymphotropic virus type 3, HTLV-3. See under **AIDS virus.** Also, **human T-cell lymphotropic virus type III.**

hu•ma•num est er•ra•re (ho͞o mä′no͞om est ᴇʀ rä′ʀᴇ; *Eng.* hyo͞o mā′nəm est e râr′ē, -mä′-), *Latin.* to err is human.

Hu•mash (*Seph.* ᴋʜo͞o mäsh′; *Ashk.* ᴋʜo͝o′məsh), *n., pl.* ***Hu•ma•shim*** (*Seph.* ᴋʜo͞o mä shēm′; *Ashk.* ᴋʜo͞o mô′shim). *Hebrew.* the Pentateuch. Also, ***Chumash.*** [*ḥummāsh,* akin to *ḥāmēsh* five]

Hu•ma•yun (ho͞o mä′yo͞on), *n.* 1508–56, Mogul emperor of Hindustan 1530–56 (son of Baber).

Hum•ber (hum′bər), *n.* an estuary of the Ouse and Trent rivers in E England. 37 mi. (60 km) long.

Hum•ber•side (hum′bər sīd′), *n.* a county in NE England. 848,200; 1356 sq. mi. (3525 sq. km).

Hum•bert I (hum′bərt), (*Umberto I*) 1844–1900, king of Italy 1878–1900.

hum•ble (hum′bəl, um′-), *adj.,* **-bler, -blest,** *v.,* **-bled, -bling.** —*adj.* **1.** not proud or arrogant; modest: *to be humble although successful.* **2.** having a feeling of insignificance, inferiority, subservience, etc.: *In the presence of so many world-famous writers I felt very humble.* **3.** low in rank, importance, status, quality, etc.; lowly: *a humble home.* **4.** courteously respectful: *In my humble opinion you are wrong.* **5.** low in height, level, etc.; small in size: *a humble member of the galaxy.* —*v.t.* **6.** to lower in condition, importance, or dignity; abase. **7.** to destroy the independence, power, or will of. **8.** to make meek: *to humble one's heart.* [1200–50; ME (*h*)*umble* < OF < L *humilis* lowly, insignificant, on the ground. See HUMUS, -ILE] —**hum′ble•ness,** *n.* —**hum′bler,** *n.* —**hum′bling•ly,** *adv.* —**hum′bly,** *adv.*
—**Syn. 1.** unpretending, unpretentious. **2.** submissive, meek. **3.** unassuming, plain, common, poor. **4.** polite. **6.** mortify, shame, abash. **7.** subdue, crush, break. HUMBLE, DEGRADE, HUMILIATE suggest lowering or causing to seem lower. To HUMBLE is to bring down the pride of another or to reduce him or her to a state of abase-

CONCISE PRONUNCIATION KEY: act, cāpe, dâre, pärt; set, ēqual; if, īce; ox, ōver, ôrder, oil, bo͝ok, bo͞ot, out; up, ûrge; child; sing; shoe; thin, that; zh as in *treasure.* ə = *a* as in *alone, e* as in *system, i* as in *easily, o* as in *gallop, u* as in *circus;* ə as in *fire* (fīər), *hour* (ouər). l and n can serve as syllabic consonants, as in *cradle* (krād′l), and *button* (but′n). See the full key inside the front cover.

ment: *to humble an arrogant enemy.* To DEGRADE is to demote in rank or standing, or to reduce to a low level in dignity: *to degrade an officer; to degrade oneself by lying.* To HUMILIATE is to make others feel or appear inadequate or unworthy, esp. in some public setting: *to humiliate a sensitive person.* **—Ant. 1, 2.** proud. **3.** noble, exalted. **4.** rude, insolent. **6.** elevate. **8.** exalt.

hum•ble•bee (hum′bəl bē′), *n. Chiefly Brit.* bumblebee. [1400–50; late ME *humbul-be;* akin to D *hommel* drone, G *Hummelbiene* kind of wild-bee, MLG *homelbe;* prob. akin to HUM]

hum′ble pie′, **1.** humility forced upon someone, often under embarrassing conditions; humiliation. **2.** *Obs.* a pie made of the viscera and other inferior parts of deer or the like. **3. eat humble pie,** to be forced to apologize humbly; suffer humiliation: *He had to eat humble pie and publicly admit his error.* [1640–50; earlier phrase *an umble pie,* erroneous for *a numble pie;* see NUMBLES]

hum′ble plant′. See **sensitive plant** (def. 1). [1655–65]

Hum•boldt (hum′bōlt; *for 1, 2, also Ger.* ho͝om′bôlt), *n.* **1. Frie•drich Hein•rich A•lex•an•der** (frē′drɪkh hīn′rɪkh ä′lek sän′dər), **Baron von** (fən), 1769–1859, German naturalist, writer, and statesman. **2.** his brother, **(Karl) Wil•helm** (kärl vil′helm), **Baron von,** 1767–1835, German philologist and diplomat. **3.** a town in NW Tennessee. 10,209.

Hum′boldt Cur′rent. See **Peru Current.**

hum•bug (hum′bug′), *n., v.,* **-bugged, -bug•ging,** *interj.* **—***n.* **1.** something intended to delude or deceive. **2.** the quality of falseness or deception. **3.** a person who is not what he or she claims or pretends to be; impostor. **4.** something devoid of sense or meaning; nonsense: *a humbug of technical jargon.* **5.** *Brit.* a variety of hard mint candy. **—***v.t.* **6.** to impose upon by humbug or false pretense; delude; deceive. **—***v.i.* **7.** to practice humbug. **—***interj.* **8.** nonsense! [1730–40; orig. uncert.] **—hum′bug′ger,** *n.*
—Syn. 1. imposition. **2.** pretense, sham. **3.** pretender, deceiver, charlatan, swindler, quack, confidence man. **6.** cheat, swindle, trick, fool, dupe.

hum•bug•ger•y (hum′bug′ə rē), *n.* pretense; sham. [1825–35; HUMBUG + -ERY]

hum•ding•er (hum′ding′ər), *n. Informal.* a person, thing, action, or statement of remarkable excellence or effect. [1885–90; HUM + DING[1] + -ER[1]]

hum•drum (hum′drum′), *adj.* **1.** lacking variety; boring; dull: *a humdrum existence.* **—***n.* **2.** humdrum character or routine; monotony. **3.** monotonous or tedious talk. **4.** *Archaic.* a dull, boring person. [1545–55; earlier *humtrum,* rhyming compound based on HUM] **—hum′•drum′ness,** *n.*
—Syn. 1. tedious, routine, mundane, tiresome.

Hume (hyo͞om *or, often,* yo͞om), *n.* **David,** 1711–76, Scottish philosopher and historian.

hu•mec•tant (hyo͞o mek′tənt *or, often,* yo͞o-), *n.* **1.** a substance that absorbs or helps another substance retain moisture, as glycerol. **—***adj.* **2.** moistening; diluting. **3.** of or pertaining to a humectant or humectants. [1650–60; < L *hūmectant-* (s. of *(h)ūmectāns*), prp. of *(h)ūmectāre* to moisten, equiv. to *(h)ūmect(us)* moist, damp (see HUMID) + *-ant-* -ANT]

hu•mer•al (hyo͞o′mər əl *or, often,* yo͞o′-), *adj.* **1.** *Anat., Zool.* of or pertaining to the humerus or brachium. **2.** of or pertaining to the shoulder. [1605–15; < L *(h)umer(us)* HUMERUS + -AL[1]; cf. LL *(h)umerāle* shoulder covering, cape]

hu′meral veil′, *Eccles.* a fringed scarf, usually white and ornamented in the middle, worn over the shoulders by a priest or subdeacon during certain parts of a High Mass. [1850–55]

hu•mer•us (hyo͞o′mər əs *or, often,* yo͞o′-), *n., pl.* **-mer•i** (-mə rī′). *Anat.* **1.** the long bone in the arm of humans extending from the shoulder to the elbow. See diagrams under **shoulder, skeleton. 2.** brachium. **3.** *Zool.* a corresponding bone, structure, or region in the forelimbs of other animals or in the wings of birds or insects. [1350–1400; ME < L *(h)umerus* shoulder; c. Gk *ômos,* Goth *ams,* Skt *ámsas*]

hu•mic (hyo͞o′mik *or, often,* yo͞o′-), *adj. Chem.* of or noting a substance, as an acid, obtained from humus. [1835–45; < L *hum(us)* ground, mould + -IC]

hu′mic ac′id, a brown, melanin-tinted mixture of polymers, found in lignite, peat, and soils, where it acts as a cation exchange agent: used in drilling fluids and inks. [1835–45]

hu•mic•o•lous (hyo͞o mik′ə ləs *or, often,* yo͞o-), *adj. Biol.* of or pertaining to organisms that live in or on soil. [< L *hum(us)* earth (see HUMUS) + -I- + -COLOUS]

hu•mid (hyo͞o′mid *or, often,* yo͞o′-), *adj.* containing a high amount of water or water vapor; noticeably moist: *humid air; a humid climate.* [1375–1425; late ME < L *(h)ūmidus,* equiv. to *(h)ūm(ēre)* to be moist + *-idus* -ID[4]] **—hu′mid•ly,** *adv.* **—hu′mid•ness,** *n.*
—Syn. dank, wet. See **damp.**

hu•mid•i•fi•er (hyo͞o mid′ə fī′ər *or, often,* yo͞o-), *n.* **1.** a device for increasing the amount of water vapor in the air of a room or building, consisting of a container for water and a vaporizer. **2.** any device for regulating the amount of water vapor in a specific container or area. [1880–85; HUMIDIFY + -ER[1]]

hu•mid•i•fy (hyo͞o mid′ə fī′ *or, often,* yo͞o-), *v.t.,* **-fied, -fy•ing.** to make humid. [1880–85; HUMID + -IFY] **—hu•mid′i•fi•ca′tion,** *n.*

hu•mid•i•stat (hyo͞o mid′ə stat′ *or, often,* yo͞o-), *n.* an instrument for measuring and controlling humidity. [1905–10; HUMID + -I- + -STAT]

hu•mid•i•ty (hyo͞o mid′i tē *or, often,* yo͞o-), *n.* **1.** humid condition; moistness; dampness. **2.** See **relative humidity. 3.** an uncomfortably high amount of relative humidity: *It's not the heat, it's the humidity that tires me out.* [1350–1400; ME *humydite* < L *(h)ūmiditās.* See HUMID, -ITY]

hu•mi•dor (hyo͞o′mi dôr′ *or, often,* yo͞o′-), *n.* a container or storage room for cigars or other preparations of tobacco, fitted with means for keeping the tobacco suitably moist. [1900–05; HUMID + -OR[2]]

hu•mi•fi•ca•tion (hyo͞o′mə fi kā′shən, *or, often,* yo͞o′-), *n.* the formation of humus. [1895–1900; HUM(US) + -I- + -FICATION]

hu•mi•fied (hyo͞o′mə fīd′, *or, often,* yo͞o′-), *adj.* transformed into humus. [1905–10; HUM(US) + -IFY + -ED[2]]

hu•mil•i•ate (hyo͞o mil′ē āt′ *or, often,* yo͞o-), *v.t.,* **-at•ed, -at•ing.** to cause (a person) a painful loss of pride, self-respect, or dignity; mortify. [1525–35; < LL *humiliātus* (ptp. of *humiliāre* to humble), equiv. to L *humili(s)* HUMBLE + *-ātus* -ATE[1]] **—hu•mil′i•a′tor,** *n.* **—hu•mil•i•a•to•ry** (hyo͞o mil′ē ə tôr′ē, -tōr′ē *or, often,* yo͞o-), **hu•mil′i•a′tive,** *adj.*
—Syn. dishonor, disgrace, shame; degrade, abase, debase. See **humble. —Ant.** exalt, honor.

hu•mil•i•at•ing (hyo͞o mil′ē ā′ting *or, often,* yo͞o-), *adj.* lowering the pride, self-respect, or dignity of a person; mortifying: *Such a humiliating defeat was good for his overblown ego.* [1750–60; HUMILIATE + -ING[2]] **—hu•mil′i•at′ing•ly,** *adv.*

hu•mil•i•a•tion (hyo͞o mil′ē ā′shən *or, often,* yo͞o-), *n.* **1.** an act or instance of humiliating or being humiliated. **2.** the state or feeling of being humiliated; mortification. [1350–1400; ME < LL *humiliātiōn-* (s. of *humiliātiō*). See HUMILIATE, -ION]
—Syn. 2. degradation, dishonor. See **shame.**

hu•mi•lis (hyo͞o′mə lis *or, often,* yo͞o′-), *adj.* (of a cumulus cloud) having a small, flattened appearance. [< NL, L: low, HUMBLE]

hu•mil•i•ty (hyo͞o mil′i tē *or, often,* yo͞o-), *n.* the quality or condition of being humble; modest opinion or estimate of one's own importance, rank, etc. [1275–1325; ME *humilite* < L *humilitās.* See HUMBLE, -TY[2]]
—Syn. lowliness, meekness, submissiveness. **—Ant.** pride.

hu•mint (hyo͞o′mint *or, often,* yo͞o′-), *n.* the gathering of political or military intelligence through secret agents. Cf. **comint, elint, sigint.** [1975–80; *hum(an) int(elligence)*]

Hum•ism (hyo͞o′miz əm *or, often,* yo͞o′-), *n.* the philosophy or principles of David Hume, esp. his epistemological skepticism. [1855–60; HUME + -ISM]

hu•mi•ture (hyo͞o′mi chər, -cho͝or′ *or, often,* yo͞o′-), *n.* **1.** a measure of the discomfort most people feel because of the combined effects of atmospheric temperature and humidity; variously defined as Fahrenheit temperature plus some function of vapor pressure. **2.** (formerly) the average of the Fahrenheit temperature and the relative humidity. [HUMI(DITY) + (TEMPERA)TURE]

hum•ma•ble (hum′ə bəl), *adj.* (of a piece of music) able to be hummed easily; melodic; tuneful. [1940–45; HUM + -ABLE] **—hum′ma•bil′i•ty,** *n.*

hum•mer (hum′ər), *n.* **1.** a person or thing that hums. **2.** *Slang.* humdinger. **3.** a hummingbird. [1595–1605; HUM + -ER[1]]

hum•ming (hum′ing), *adj.* **1.** making a droning sound; buzzing. **2.** very busy; briskly active: *a humming office.* [1570–80; HUM + -ING[2]] **—hum′ming•ly,** *adv.*

hummingbird, *Archilochus colubris,* length 3½ in. (8.9 cm)

hum•ming•bird (hum′ing bûrd′), *n.* a very small nectar-sipping New World bird of the family Trochilidae, characterized by the brilliant, iridescent plumage of the male, a slender bill, and narrow wings, the extremely rapid beating of which produces a humming sound: noted for their ability to hover and to fly upward, downward, and backward in a horizontal position. [1625–35, *Amer.*; HUMMING + BIRD]

hum′mingbird moth′. See **hawk moth.** [1840–50, *Amer.*]

hum•mock (hum′ək), *n.* **1.** Also, **hammock.** an elevated tract of land rising above the general level of a marshy region. **2.** a knoll or hillock. **3.** Also, **hommock.** a ridge in an ice field. [1545–55; *humm-* (akin to HUMP) + -OCK] **—hum′mock•y,** *adj.*

hum•mus (ho͝om′əs), *n. Middle Eastern Cookery.* a paste or dip made of chickpeas mashed with oil, garlic, lemon juice, and tahini and usually eaten with pita. Also, **hommos.** [< dial. Ar *ḥummuṣ, ḥəmmoṣ* chickpeas]

hu•mon•gous (hyo͞o mung′gəs, -mong′- *or, often,* yo͞o-), *adj. Slang.* extraordinarily large. Also, **humungous.** [1965–70, *Amer.*; expressive coinage, perh. reflecting HUGE and MONSTROUS, with stress pattern of TREMENDOUS]

hu•mor (hyo͞o′mər *or, often,* yo͞o′-), *n.* **1.** a comic, absurd, or incongruous quality causing amusement: *the humor of a situation.* **2.** the faculty of perceiving what is amusing or comical: *He is completely without humor.* **3.** an instance of being or attempting to be comical or amusing; something humorous: *The humor in his joke eluded the audience.* **4.** the faculty of expressing the amusing or comical: *The author's humor came across better in the book than in the movie.* **5.** comical writing or talk in general; comical books, skits, plays, etc. **6. humors,** peculiar features; oddities; quirks: *humors of life.* **7.** mental disposition or temperament. **8.** a temporary mood or frame of mind: *The boss is in a bad humor today.* **9.** a capricious or freakish inclination; whim or caprice; odd trait. **10.** (in medieval physiology) one of the four elemental fluids of the body, blood, phlegm, black bile, and yellow bile, regarded as determining, by their relative proportions, a person's physical and mental constitution. **11.** any animal or plant fluid, whether natural or morbid, as the blood or lymph. **12. out of humor,** displeased; dissatisfied; cross: *The chef is feeling out of humor again and will have to be treated carefully.* **—***v.t.* **13.** to comply with the humor or mood of in order to soothe or make content or more agreeable: *to humor a child.* **14.** to adapt or accommodate oneself to. Also, *esp. Brit.,* **humour.** [1300–50; ME *(h)umour* < AF < L *(h)ūmōr-* (s. of *(h)ūmor*) moisture, fluid (medical L: body fluid), equiv. to *(h)ūm(ēre)* to be wet (see HUMID) + *-ōr-* -OR[1]] **—hu′mor•ful,** *adj.* **—hu′mor•less,** *adj.* **—hu′•mor•less•ly,** *adv.* **—hu′mor•less•ness,** *n.*
—Syn. 4. HUMOR, WIT refer to an ability to perceive and express a sense of the clever or amusing. HUMOR consists principally in the recognition and expression of incongruities or peculiarities present in a situation or character. It is frequently used to illustrate some fundamental absurdity in human nature or conduct, and is generally thought of as more kindly than wit: *a genial and mellow type of humor; his biting wit.* WIT is a purely intellectual manifestation of cleverness and quickness of apprehension in discovering analogies between things really unlike, and expressing them in brief, diverting, and often sharp observations or remarks. **9.** fancy, vagary. **13.** HUMOR, GRATIFY, INDULGE imply attempting to satisfy the wishes or whims of (oneself or others). To HUMOR is to comply with a mood, fancy, or caprice, as in order to satisfy, soothe, or manage: *to humor an invalid.* To GRATIFY is to please by satisfying the likings or desires: *to gratify someone by praising him.* INDULGE suggests a yielding to wishes that perhaps should not be given in to: *to indulge an unreasonable demand; to indulge an irresponsible son.* **—Ant. 13.** discipline, restrain.

hu•mor•al (hyo͞o′mər əl *or, often,* yo͞o′-), *adj. Physiol.* of, pertaining to, or proceeding from a fluid of the body. [1375–1425; late ME < ML *hūmōrālis.* See HUMOR, -AL[1]]

hu′moral immu′nity, *Immunol.* See **antibody-mediated immunity.**

hu•mor•esque (hyo͞o′mə resk′ *or, often,* yo͞o′-), *n.* a musical composition of humorous or capricious character. [1875–80; HUMOR + -ESQUE, modeled on G *Humoreske*] **—hu′mor•esque′ly,** *adv.*

hu•mor•ist (hyo͞o′mər ist *or, often,* yo͞o′-), *n.* **1.** a person who is skillful in the use of humor, as in writing, talking, or acting. **2.** a person with an active sense of humor. [1590–1600; < F *humoriste,* equiv. to *humour* (< E) + *-iste* -IST. Cf. It *(h)umorista* capricious, subject to humors] **—hu′mor•is′tic, hu′mor•is′ti•cal,** *adj.*

hu•mor•ous[1] (hyo͞o′mər əs *or, often,* yo͞o′-), *adj.* **1.** characterized by humor; funny; comical: *a humorous anecdote.* **2.** having or showing the faculty of humor; droll; facetious: *a humorous person.* [1570–80; HUMOR + -OUS] **—hu′mor•ous•ly,** *adv.* **—hu′mor•ous•ness,** *n.*
—Syn. 1. ludicrous, laughable. **2.** jocose, jocular, comic, comical. HUMOROUS, WITTY, FACETIOUS, WAGGISH imply something that arises from cleverness or a sense of fun. HUMOROUS implies a genuine sense of fun and the comic, impersonal, or gently personal: *a humorous version of an incident; a humorous view of life.* WITTY implies quickness to perceive the amusing, striking, or unusual and to express it cleverly and entertainingly; it sometimes becomes rather sharp and unkind, particularly in quick repartee of a personal nature: *a witty and interesting companion; to be witty at someone else's expense.* FACETIOUS suggests a desire or attempt to be jocular or witty but not to be taken seriously: *a facetious remark.* WAGGISH suggests the spirit of sly mischief and roguery of the constant joker, with no harm intended: *a waggish good humor.* **—Ant. 1, 2.** solemn, sober, serious.

hu•mor•ous[2] (hyo͞o′mər əs *or, often,* yo͞o′-), *adj.* **1.** *Archaic.* moist; wet. **2.** pertaining or due to the bodily humors. [1375–1425; late ME < LL *(h)ūmōrōsus;* see HUMOR, -OUS]

hu•mour (hyo͞o′mər), *n., v.t., Chiefly Brit.* humor.
—Usage. See **-or[1].**

hump (hump), *n.* **1.** a rounded protuberance, esp. a fleshy protuberance on the back, as that due to abnormal curvature of the spine in humans, or that normally present in certain animals, as the camel or bison. **2.** *Physical Geog.* **a.** a low, rounded rise of ground; hummock. **b.** a mountain or mountain range. **3.** *Railroads.* (in a switchyard) a raised area down which cars pushed to its crest roll by gravity and momentum for automatic sorting through a series of preset switches. **4.** *Slang (vulgar).* **a.** an act or instance of coitus. **b.** a partner in coitus. **5. the hump, a.** *Brit. Slang.* a fit of depression or bad humor: *to get the hump.* **b.** *(cap.)* (in World War II) the Himalayas. **6. over the hump,** past the most difficult, time-consuming, or dangerous part or period: *The doctor says she's over the hump now and should improve steadily.* **—***v.t.* **7.** to raise (the back) in a hump; hunch: *The cat humped its back.* **8.** *Railroads.* to sort (cars) by means of a hump. **9.** *Informal.* to exert (oneself) in a great effort. **10.** *Slang (vulgar).* to have sexual intercourse with. **11.** *Slang.* **a.** to place or bear on the back or shoulder. **b.** to carry or haul. **c.** to load or unload; lift. **—***v.i.* **12.** to rise in a hump. **13.** *Informal.* to exert oneself; hustle or hurry. **14.** *Slang (vulgar).* to engage in sexual intercourse. [1700–10; prob. abstracted from HUMPBACKED] **—hump′er,** *n.* **—hump′less,** *adj.*

hump•back (hump′bak′), *n.* **1.** a back that is humped in a convex position. **2.** kyphosis. **3.** the humpback whale. [1690–1700; appar. back formation from HUMPBACKED]

hump•backed (hump′bakt′), *adj.* having a hump on the back. [1675–85; b. *huckbacked* (*huck* haunch + BACKED) and *crumpbacked* (OE *crump* crooked + BACKED)]

hump′back salm′on, a pink salmon inhabiting North Pacific waters: so-called because of the hump that appears behind the head of the male when it is ready for spawning. Also called **humpy, humpie.** [1800–10, *Amer.*]

hump′back whale′, a large whalebone whale of the genus *Megaptera* having long narrow flippers, and noted for its habit of arching deeply as it dives: once abundant in coastal waters, it is now rare but its numbers are increasing. [1715–25]

humped (humpt), *adj.* having a hump. [1705–15; HUMP + -ED[3]]

humped′ cat′tle, any of several breeds of domestic cattle developed from the Indian species *Bos indicus* and characterized by a hump of fat and muscle over the shoulders.

Hum•per•dinck (ho͝om′pər dingk′; *Eng.* hum′pər-dingk′), *n.* **Eng•el•bert** (eng′əl bert′; *Eng.* eng′gəl-bûrt′), 1854–1921, German composer.

humph (*an inarticulate expression resembling a snort; spelling pron.* humf), *interj.* **1.** (used to indicate disbelief, contempt, etc.) —*v.i., v.t.* **2.** to utter by or as if by expressing "humph." [1675–85]

Hum•phrey (hum′frē), *n.* **1.** (*Duke of Gloucester*) 1391–1447, English soldier and statesman (youngest son of Henry IV). **2. Doris,** 1895–1958, U.S. dancer, choreographer, and teacher. **3. Hubert H(oratio),** 1911–78, U.S. politician: vice president 1965–69. **4.** a male given name: from Germanic words meaning "high" and "peace."

Hump•ty Dump•ty (hump′tē dump′tē), **1.** an egg-shaped character in a Mother Goose nursery rhyme that fell off a wall and could not be put together again. **2.** (*sometimes l.c.*) something that has been damaged severely and usually irreparably. [rhyming compound based on *humpty;* see HUMP, -ED[3], -Y[2]]

hump•y[1] (hum′pē), *adj.,* **hump•i•er, hump•i•est. 1.** full of humps. **2.** resembling a hump; humplike. [1700–10; HUMP + -Y[1]] —**hump′i•ness,** *n.*

hum•py[2] (hum′pē), *n., pl.* **-pies.** *Australian.* any crude Aborigine hut or shelter, esp. a shanty built at the edge of a town. [1840–50; < Tharapal (Australian Aboriginal language spoken between Moreton Bay and Wide Bay, S Queensland), recorded as *umpi* (*h* intrusive)]

hump•y[3] (hum′pē), *n., pl.* **hump•ies.** See **humpback salmon.** Also, **hump′ie.** [HUMP(BACK) + -Y[2]]

hu•mu•hu•mu•nu•ku•nu•ku•a•pu•a•a (ho͞o′mo͞o-ho͞o′mo͞o no͞o′ko͞o no͞o′ko͞o ä′po͞o ä′ä), *n.* either of two triggerfishes, esp. *Rhinecantus aculeatus,* of Indo-Pacific coral reefs. [< Hawaiian: pig-snouted triggerfish (*humuhumu* triggerfish + *nukunuku,* redupl. of *nuku* snout + *a* like + *pua'a* pig)]

Hu•mu•lin (hyo͞o′myə lin *or, often,* yo͞o′-), *Pharm., Trademark.* a brand of human insulin produced by genetically engineered bacteria.

hu•mu•lon (hyo͞o′myə lon′ *or, often,* yo͞o′-), *n.* a bitter constituent of hops, $C_{21}H_{30}O_5$, having antibiotic properties. Also, **hu•mu•lone** (hyo͞o′myə lōn′ *or, often,* yo͞o′-). [1915–20; < NL *Humul(us)* genus name (special use of ML: hop plant < Gmc; cf. ON *humall,* OE *hymele*) + *-on* -ONE]

hu•mun•gous (hyo͞o mung′gəs *or, often,* yo͞o-), *adj. Slang.* humongous.

hu•mus (hyo͞o′məs *or, often,* yo͞o′-), *n.* the dark organic material in soils, produced by the decomposition of vegetable or animal matter and essential to the fertility of the earth. [1790–1800; < L: earth, ground; akin to Gk *chamaí* on the ground, *chthṓn* earth, Skt *kṣam-,* Lith *žẽmė,* Serbo-Croatian *zèmlja* ground, earth; cf. CHAMELEON, CHTHONIAN, ZEMSTVO; see HOMO]

Hum•vee (hum′vē) *n.* a military vehicle that combines the features of a jeep with those of a light truck. [1985–1990; from the pronunciation of the initials HMMWV for *H(igh) M(obility) M(ultipurpose) W(heeled) V(ehicle)*]

Hun (hun), *n.* **1.** a member of a nomadic and warlike Asian people who devastated or controlled large parts of eastern and central Europe and who exercised their greatest power under Attila in the 5th century A.D. **2.** (*often l.c.*) a barbarous, destructive person; vandal. **3.** *Disparaging and Offensive.* **a.** a German soldier in World War I or II. **b.** a German. [bef. 900; 1895–1900 for def. 3b; sing. of *Huns,* OE *Hūnas;* c. ON *Hūnar;* akin to LL *Hunnī*] —**Hun′like′,** *adj.*

Hú′na Bay′ (ho͞o′nə), an inlet of the Greenland Sea on the NW coast of Iceland.

Hu•nan (ho͞o′nän′), *n.* **1.** *Pinyin, Wade-Giles.* a province in S China. 37,810,000; 81,274 sq. mi. (210,500 sq. km). *Cap.:* Changsha. **2.** Also, **Hu•nam** (ho͞o′näm′). *Chinese Cookery.* a style of cooking from this province, characterized esp. by the use of hot peppers.

hunch (hunch), *v.t.* **1.** to thrust out or up in a hump; arch: *to hunch one's back.* **2.** to shove, push, or jostle. —*v.i.* **3.** to thrust oneself forward jerkily; lunge forward. **4.** to stand, sit, or walk in a bent posture. —*n.* **5.** a premonition or suspicion; guess: *I have a hunch he'll run for reelection.* **6.** a hump. **7.** a push or shove. **8.** a lump or thick piece. [1590–1600; 1900–05 for def. 5; appar. var. of obs. *hinch* to push, shove, kick < ?]
—**Syn. 5.** surmise, feeling, theory, conjecture.

hunch•back (hunch′bak′), *n.* **1.** a person whose back is humped in a convex position because of abnormal spinal curvature. Cf. **kyphosis, kyphoscoliosis. 2.** humpback (def. 1). [1705–15; back formation from HUNCHBACKED]

hunch•backed (hunch′bakt′), *adj.* humpbacked. [1590–1600; b. *huckbacked* see (HUMPBACKED) and *bunch-backed*]

Hunch′back of No′tre Dame′, The, (French, *Notre Dame de Paris*), a novel (1831) by Victor Hugo.

hund., hundred; hundreds.

hun•dred (hun′drid), *n., pl.* **-dreds,** (*as after a numeral*) **-dred,** *adj.* —*n.* **1.** a cardinal number, ten times ten. **2.** a symbol for this number, as 100 or C. **3.** a set of this many persons or things: *a hundred of the men.* **4. hundreds,** a number between 100 and 999, as in referring to an amount of money: *hundreds of dollars.* **5.** *Informal.* **a.** a hundred-dollar bill. **b.** the sum of one hundred dollars. **6.** (formerly) an administrative division of an English county. **7.** a similar division in colonial Pennsylvania, Delaware, and Virginia, and in present-day Delaware. **8.** Also called **hundred's place.** *Math.* **a.** (in a mixed number) the position of the third digit to the left of the decimal point. **b.** (in a whole number) the position of the third digit from the right. —*adj.* **9.** amounting to one hundred in number. [bef. 950; ME, OE (c. OFris *hundred,* OS *hundred,* ON *hundrath,* D *honderd,* G *hundert*), equiv. to *hund* 100 (c. Goth *hund;* akin to L *centum,* Gk *hekatón,* Avestan *satəm,* Skt *śatám,* OCS *sŭto,* Lith *šimtas*) + *-red* tale, count, akin to Goth *rathjan* to reckon (see READ[1])]

Hun′dred Days′, 1. the period from March 20 to June 28, 1815, between the arrival of Napoleon in Paris, after his escape from Elba, and his abdication after the battle of Waterloo. **2.** a special session of Congress from March 9, 1933 to June 16, 1933, called by President Franklin D. Roosevelt, in which important social legislation was enacted.

Hun′dred Flow′ers, the 1957 political campaign in the People's Republic of China to encourage greater freedom of intellectual expression, initiated by Mao Zedong under the slogan "Let a hundred flowers bloom, let a hundred schools of thought contend." [trans. of Chin *bǎihuā* (*qífàng*) lit., (let bloom) a hundred flowers]

hun•dred•fold (hun′drid fōld′), *adj.* **1.** a hundred times as great or as much. **2.** comprising a hundred parts or members. —*adv.* **3.** in a hundredfold measure. [1125–75; ME *hundredfald.* See HUNDRED, -FOLD]

hun•dred-per•cent•er (hun′drid pər sen′tər), *n.* a completely patriotic, sometimes jingoistic person. [1925–30, *Amer.*]

hun′dred's place′, *Math.* hundred (def. 8).

hun•dredth (hun′dridth, -dritth), *adj.* **1.** next after the ninety-ninth; being the ordinal number for 100. **2.** being one of 100 equal parts. —*n.* **3.** a hundredth part, esp. of one (1/100). **4.** the hundredth member of a series. **5.** Also called **hun′dredth's place′.** (in decimal notation) the position of the second digit to the right of the decimal point. [1250–1300; ME. See HUNDRED, -TH[2]]

hun•dred•weight (hun′drid wāt′), *n., pl.* **-weights,** (*as after a numeral*) **-weight. 1.** Also called **cental, quintal.** a unit of avoirdupois weight commonly equivalent to 100 pounds (45.359 kilograms) in the U.S. *Abbr.:* cwt **2.** cental (def. 2). [1570–80; HUNDRED + WEIGHT]

Hun′dred Years′ War′, the series of wars between England and France, 1337–1453, in which England lost all its possessions in France except Calais.

Hun•e•ker (hun′i kər), *n.* **James (Gib•bons)** (gib′ənz), 1860–1921, U.S. music critic and writer.

hung (hung), *v.* **1.** pt. and pp. of **hang. 2. hung over,** *Informal.* suffering the effects of a hangover: *On New Year's Day the houseguests were all hung over.* Also, **hungover. 3. hung up,** *Informal.* **a.** detained unavoidably. **b.** stymied or baffled by a problem. **c.** *Baseball, Softball.* (of a base runner) trapped between bases and in danger of being tagged out. **4. hung up on,** *Slang.* **a.** obsessed by: *a clerk hung up on petty details.* **b.** infatuated with. —*adj.* **5.** *Slang* (*vulgar*). (of a male) having very large genitals.
—**Usage.** See **hang.**

Hung., **1.** Also, **Hung** Hungarian. **2.** Hungary.

Hun•gar•i•an (hung gâr′ē ən), *adj.* **1.** of, pertaining to, or characteristic of Hungary, its people, or their language. —*n.* **2.** a native or inhabitant of Hungary. Cf. **Magyar. 3.** Also called **Magyar.** the language of Hungary, of the Uralic family of languages. [1545–55; HUNGARY + -AN]

Hungar′ian brome′grass, a pasture grass, *Bromus inermis,* native to Europe, having smooth blades. Also called **awnless bromegrass.**

Hungar′ian gou′lash, goulash (def. 1).

Hungar′ian point′er, vizsla.

Hun•ga•ry (hung′gə rē), *n.* a republic in central Europe. 10,672,000; 35,926 sq. mi. (93,050 sq. km). *Cap.:* Budapest. Hungarian, **Magyarország.**

hun•ger (hung′gər), *n.* **1.** a compelling need or desire for food. **2.** the painful sensation or state of weakness caused by the need of food: *to collapse from hunger.* **3.** a shortage of food; famine. **4.** a strong or compelling desire or craving: *hunger for power.* **5. from hunger,** *Slang.* deplorably bad; dreadful: *The styles in coats this winter are from hunger.* Also, **strictly from hunger.** —*v.i.* **6.** to feel hunger; be hungry. **7.** to have a strong desire. —*v.t.* **8.** *Rare.* to subject to hunger. [bef. 900; ME; OE *hungor;* c. G *Hunger*] —**hun′ger•ing•ly,** *adv.*
—**Syn. 4.** appetite, greed, lust, itch.

hun•ger•ly (hung′gər lē), *adj. Archaic.* marked by a hungry look. [1350–1400; ME *hongerliche.* See HUNGER, -LY]

hun′ger strike′, a deliberate refusal to eat, undertaken in protest against imprisonment, improper treatment, objectionable conditions, etc. [1885–90]

hun•ger-strike (hung′gər strīk′), *v.i.,* **-struck, -strik•ing.** to go on a hunger strike. [1910–15] —**hun′ger strik′er.**

hung′ ju′ry, a jury that cannot agree on a verdict. [1840–50, *Amer.*]

Hung•nam (ho͞ong′näm′), *n.* a seaport in W North Korea. 150,000.

hung•o•ver (hung′ō′vər), *adj.* hung (def. 2). [1945–50]

hun•gry (hung′grē), *adj.* **-gri•er, -gri•est. 1.** having a desire, craving, or need for food; feeling hunger. **2.** indicating, characteristic of, or characterized by hunger: *He approached the table with a hungry look.* **3.** strongly or eagerly desirous. **4.** lacking needful or desirable elements; not fertile; poor: *hungry land.* **5.** marked by a scarcity of food: *The depression years were hungry times.* **6.** *Informal.* aggressively ambitious or competitive, as from a need to overcome poverty or past defeats: *a hungry investment firm looking for wealthy clients.* [bef. 950; ME, OE *hungrig.* See HUNGER, -Y[1]] —**hun′gri•ly,** *adv.* —**hun′gri•ness,** *n.*
—**Syn. 1.** ravenous, famishing, starving. HUNGRY, FAMISHED, STARVED describe a condition resulting from a lack of food. HUNGRY is a general word, expressing various degrees of eagerness or craving for food: *hungry between meals; desperately hungry after a long fast; hungry as a bear.* FAMISHED denotes the condition of one reduced to actual suffering from want of food, but sometimes is used lightly or in an exaggerated statement: *famished after being lost in a wilderness; simply famished* (*hungry*). STARVED denotes a condition resulting from long-continued lack or insufficiency of food, and implies enfeeblement, emaciation, or death (originally death from any cause, but now death from lack of food): *He looks thin and starved. By the end of the terrible winter, thousands had starved* (*to death*). It is also used as a humorous exaggeration: *I only had two sandwiches, pie, and some milk, so I'm simply starved* (*hungry*). —**Ant. 1.** sated, satiated, surfeited.

Hung′tow Is′land (ho͝ong′tō′), an island off the SE coast of Taiwan. 8 mi. (13 km) long.

hung-up (hung′up′), *adj. Slang.* **1.** beset with psychological problems. **2.** worried; anxious; concerned.

Hung-wu (ho͝ong′wo͞o′), *n.* (*Chu Yüan-chang*) 1328–98, emperor of China 1368–98: founder of the Ming dynasty.

hunk (hungk), *n.* **1.** a large piece or lump. **2.** *Slang.* **a.** a handsome man with a well-developed physique. **b.** a large or fat person. [1805–15; < D dial. *hunke*]
—**Syn. 1.** block, gobbet, clod, wad, gob.

hun•ker (hung′kər), *v.i.* **1.** to squat on one's heels (often fol. by *down*). **2.** *Informal.* **a.** to hunch: *The driver hunkered over the steering wheel.* **b.** to hide, hide out, or take shelter (usually fol. by *down*): *The escaped convicts hunkered down in a cave in the mountains.* **c.** to hold resolutely or stubbornly to a policy, opinion, etc., when confronted by criticism, opposition, or unfavorable circumstances (usually fol. by *down*): *Though all the evidence was against him, he hunkered down and refused to admit his guilt.* **3.** *Slang.* to lumber along; walk or move slowly or aimlessly. —*n.* **4. hunkers,** one's haunches. **5. on one's hunkers, a.** *Brit. Informal.* squatting on one's heels. **b.** suffering a period of poverty, bad luck, or the like. [1710–20; appar. *hunk* (perh. nasalized var. of *huck* haunch; akin to ON *hūka* to crouch) + -ER[6]]

Hun•ker (hung′kər), *n.* a member of the conservative faction in the Democratic party in New York State, 1845–48. Cf. **Barnburner.** [1835–45, *Amer.;* orig. uncert.] —**Hun′ker•ism,** *n.* —**Hun′ker•ous,** *adj.* —**Hun′ker•ous•ness,** *n.*

Hunk•pa•pa (hungk′pä pə), *n., pl.* **-pas,** (*esp. collectively*) **-pa.** a member of a North American Indian people belonging to the Teton branch of the Dakota.

hunks (hungks), *n.* (*used with a singular or plural v.*) **1.** a crabbed, disagreeable person. **2.** a covetous, stingy person; miser. [1595–1605; orig. uncert.; cf. -S[4]]

hunk•y[1] (hung′kē), *adj. Slang.* **1.** satisfactory; well; right. **2.** even; leaving no balance. [1860–65, *Amer.;* orig. uncert.]

hunk•y[2] (hung′kē), *n., pl.* **hunk•ies.** (*sometimes cap.*) *Slang* (*disparaging and offensive*). a person of Hungarian or Slavic descent, esp. an unskilled or semiskilled worker. Also, **hunk′ie.** [1895–1900; perh. HUNG(ARIAN) (with devoicing of *-g-,* influenced by HUNK) + -Y[2]; cf. BOHUNK]

hunk•y[3] (hung′kē), *adj.,* **hunk•i•er, hunk•i•est.** *Slang.* (of a male) having a handsome, well-developed physique. [1910–15; HUNK + -Y[1]]

hunk•y-do•ry (hung′kē dôr′ē, -dōr′ē), *adj. Slang.* about as well as one could wish or expect; satisfactory; fine; OK. [1865–70; HUNKY[1] + *dory* < ?]

Hun•nish (hun′ish), *adj.* **1.** of or pertaining to the Huns. **2.** (*sometimes l.c.*) barbarous; destructive. [1810–20; HUN + -ISH[1]] —**Hun′nish•ness,** *n.*

hunt (hunt), *v.t.* **1.** to chase or search for (game or other wild animals) for the purpose of catching or killing. **2.** to pursue with force, hostility, etc., in order to capture (often fol. by *down*): *They hunted him down and hanged him.* **3.** to search for; seek; endeavor to obtain or find (often fol. by *up* or *out*): *to hunt up the most promising candidates for the position.* **4.** to search (a place) thoroughly. **5.** to scour (an area) in pursuit of game. **6.** to use or direct (a horse, hound, etc.) in chasing game. **7.** *Change Ringing.* to alter the place of (a bell) in a hunt. —*v.i.* **8.** to engage in the pursuit, capture, or killing of wild animals for food or in sport. **9.** to make a search or quest (often fol. by *for* or *after*). **10.** *Change Ringing.* to alter the place of a bell in its set according to certain rules. —*n.* **11.** an act or practice of hunting game or other wild animals. **12.** a search; a seeking or endeavor to find. **13.** a pursuit. **14.** a group of persons associated for the purpose of hunting; an association of hunters. **15.** an area hunted over. **16.** *Change Ringing.* a regularly varying order of permutations in the ringing of a group of from five to twelve bells. [bef. 1000; (v.) ME *hunten,* OE *huntian,* deriv. of *hunta* hunter, akin to *hentan* to pursue; (n.) ME, deriv. of the v.] —**hunt′a·ble,** *adj.* —**hunt′ed·ly,** *adv.*
—**Syn. 1.** pursue, track.

Hunt (hunt), *n.* **1. (James Henry) Leigh** (lē), 1784–1859, English essayist, poet, and editor. **2. Richard Morris,** 1828–95, U.S. architect. **3. (William) Holman** (hōl′mən), 1827–1910, English painter. **4. William Morris,** 1824–79, U.S. painter (brother of Richard Morris Hunt).

hunt′ and peck′, a slow and inefficient method of typing by looking for each key separately before striking it: used by untrained typists. Also, **hunt′-and-peck′.** Cf. **touch system.** [1935–40]

hunt·a·way (hunt′ə wā′), *Australian.* —*n.* **1.** a sheep dog. —*adj.* **2.** (of a dog) trained to herd sheep. [1910–15; n., adj. use of v. phrase *hunt away*]

hunt′ board′, 1. *Eng. Furniture.* a semicircular drinking table, often having a groove serving as a guide for coasters and a well for unopened bottles. **2.** *U.S. Furniture.* a high sideboard table, often without drawers, used for serving breakfast before and a collation after a hunt. Also called **hunt table.**

hunt′ box′. See **hunting box.**

hunt′ but′ton, *Fox Hunting.* a button engraved with the insignia of one's hunt and worn on the coat and vest as part of the hunt uniform. See diag. under **pink coat.**

hunt·er (hun′tər), *n.* **1.** a person who hunts game or other wild animals for food or in sport. **2.** a person who searches for or seeks something: *a fortune hunter.* **3.** a horse specially trained for quietness, stamina, and jumping ability in hunting. **4.** an animal, as a dog, trained to hunt game. **5.** (*cap.*) *Astron.* the constellation Orion. **6.** Also called **hunting watch.** a watch with a hunting case. **7.** See **hunter green.** [1200–50; ME *huntere.* See HUNT, -ER[1]] —**hunt′er·like′,** *adj.*

Hun·ter (hun′tər), *n.* **1. John,** 1728–93, Scottish surgeon, physiologist, and biologist. **2. Robert Mer·cer Tal·ia·ferro** (mûr′sər tol′ə vər), 1809–87, U.S. political leader: Speaker of the House 1839–41. **3.** a male given name.

hunt·er-gath·er·er (hun′tər gath′ər ər), *n. Anthropol.* a member of a group of people who subsist by hunting, fishing, or foraging in the wild.

hunt′er green′, a dark green color of yellowish cast. Also, **hunt′er's green′.** Also called **hunter.** [1870–75]

hunt·er-kill·er (hun′tər kil′ər), *adj.* of or pertaining to a combined naval air and fleet force operating to seek out and destroy enemy submarines.

hunt′er-kill′er sat′ellite, a satellite designed to seek out and destroy a nearby enemy satellite by exploding itself into a cloud of high-speed metal fragments. [1975–80]

hunt′er's moon′, the first full moon following the harvest moon in late September or early October.

hunt′er's pink′, a brilliant red often used for the jackets of hunters.

hunt′er's robe′, *Bot.* pothos.

hunt′er's sauce′, chasseur (def. 4).

hunt′er tri′als, a test for hunters held under the auspices of a hunt, in which the course is laid with obstacles to simulate actual hunting conditions.

hunt·ing (hun′ting), *n.* **1.** the act of a person, animal, or thing that hunts. **2.** *Elect.* the periodic oscillating of a rotating electromechanical system about a mean space position, as in a synchronous motor. —*adj.* **3.** of, for, engaged in, or used while hunting: *a hunting cap.* [bef. 950; ME *huntung* (n.), OE *huntung*(e). See HUNT, -ING[1], -ING[2]]

hunt′ing box′, *Chiefly Brit.* a hunting lodge or house near or in a hunting area for use during the hunting season. Also called **hunt box.** [1790–1800]

hunt′ing case′, a watchcase with a hinged cover to protect the crystal.

hunt′ing chair′, a chair having a sliding frame in front serving as a footrest.

Hunt′ing Dogs′, *Astron.* the constellation Canes Venatici.

Hun·ting·don·shire (hun′ting dən shēr′, -shər), *n.* a former county in E England, now part of Cambridgeshire. Also called **Hun′ting·don, Hunts.**

CONCISE ETYMOLOGY KEY: <, descended or borrowed from; >, whence; b., blend of, blended; c., cognate with; cf., compare; deriv., derivative; equiv., equivalent; imit., imitative; obl., oblique; r., replacing; s., stem; sp., spelling, spelled; resp., respelling, respelled; trans., translation; ?, origin unknown; *, unattested; ‡, probably earlier than. See the full key inside the front cover.

hunt′ing ground′, a section or area for hunting game. [1650–60, *Amer.*]

hunt′ing horn′, *Music.* the earliest form of the modern horn, consisting of a conical tube coiled in a circle for carrying over the shoulder, and having a flaring bell and a trumpetlike mouthpiece. [1685–95]

hunt′ing knife′, a large, sharp knife, usually with a handle shaped to fit a firm grip and a blade with a slight curve toward the tip, that is used to skin and cut up game, or sometimes to dispatch it. [1795–1805, *Amer.*]

hunt′ing leop′ard, the cheetah. [1775–85]

hunt′ing sword′, a short, light saber of the 18th century, having a straight or slightly curved blade.

Hun·ting·ton (hun′ting tən), *n.* **1. Collis Potter,** 1821–1900, U.S. railroad developer. **2. Samuel,** 1731–96, U.S. statesman: governor of Connecticut 1786–96. **3.** a city in W West Virginia, on the Ohio River. 63,684. **4.** a city in NE Indiana. 16,202. **5.** a male given name: from an Old English family name, meaning "hunting estate."

Hun′tington Beach′, a city in SW California, SE of Los Angeles. 170,505.

Hun′tington Park′, a city in SW California, near Los Angeles. 46,223.

Hun′tington's chore′a, *Pathol.* a hereditary disease of the central nervous system characterized by brain deterioration and loss of control over voluntary movements, the symptoms usually appearing in the fourth decade of life. Also called **Hun′tington's disease′.** [named after George S. *Huntington* (1850–1916), U.S. physician, who described it in 1872]

Hun′tington Sta′tion, a town on W Long Island, in SE New York. 21,727.

hunt′ing watch′, hunter (def. 6). [1835–45]

hunt′ress (hun′tris), *n.* **1.** a woman who hunts. **2.** a mare used as a hunting horse. [1350–1400; ME *hunteresse.* See HUNTER, -ESS]
—**Usage.** See **-ess.**

Hunts (hunts), *n.* Huntingdonshire.

hunts·man (hunts′mən), *n., pl.* **-men. 1.** the member of a hunt staff who manages the hounds during the hunt. **2.** a hunter. [1560–70; HUNT + 's[1] + MAN[1]] —**hunts′·man·ship′,** *n.*

hunts·man's-cup (hunts′mənz kup′), *n.* a common pitcher plant, *Sarracenia purpurea.* [1840–50]

hunt's-up (hunts′up′), *n.* (formerly) a call played on a hunting horn in the morning to rouse and assemble the participants in a hunt. [1530–40; from phrase *(the) hunt is up*]

Hunts·ville (hunts′vil), *n.* **1.** a city in N Alabama: rocket and missile center. 142,513. **2.** a city in E Texas. 23,936. **3.** a town in SE Ontario, in S Canada: summer resort. 11,467.

hunt′ ta′ble. See **hunt board.**

Hun·tun (ho͞on′do͞on′), *n.* a mythical Chinese being personifying chaos.

Hu·nya·di (ho͝o′nyo dē), *n.* **Já·nos** (yä′nôsh), 1387?–1456, Hungarian soldier and national hero. Also, **Hu′nya·dy.**

Hu′on pine′ (hyo͞o′on *or, often,* yo͞o′-), a coniferous tree, *Dacrydium franklinii,* of Tasmania, having very small cones and yielding timber. [1810–20; named after the *Huon* river in Tasmania]

Hu·pa (ho͞o′pə), *n.* an Athabaskan Indian language of NW California.

Hu·peh (ho͞o′pā′; *Chin.* ho͞o′be′), *n. Older Spelling.* Hubei. Also, *Wade-Giles,* **Hu·pei** (ho͞o′bā′).

hup·pah (*Seph.* KHO͞O pä′; *Ashk.* KHO͝O′pə; *Eng.* ho͝op′ə), *n., pl. Seph.* ***hup·poth, hup·pot*** (KHO͞O pôt′), *Ashk.* ***hup·pos*** (KHO͞O pōs′), *Eng.* **hup·pahs.** *Hebrew.* a canopy under which the Jewish marriage ceremony is performed. Also, ***chuppah.***

hur·cheon (hûr′chən), *n. Chiefly Scot.* **1.** a hedgehog. **2.** an urchin. [1275–1325; ME *hirchoun,* var. of *urchun* URCHIN]

hur·dies (hûr′dēz), *n.pl. Scot.* the buttocks. [1525–35; orig. uncert.]

hur·dle (hûr′dl), *n., v.,* **-dled, -dling.** —*n.* **1.** a portable barrier over which contestants must leap in certain running races, usually a wooden frame with a hinged inner frame that swings down under impact to prevent injury to a runner who does not clear it. **2. hurdles,** (*used with a singular v.*) a race in which contestants must leap over a number of such barriers placed at specific intervals around the track. Cf. **high hurdles, low hurdles. 3.** any of various vertical barriers, as a hedge, low wall, or section of fence, over which horses must jump in certain types of turf races, as a steeplechase, but esp. an artificial barrier. **4.** a difficult problem to be overcome; obstacle. **5.** *Chiefly Brit.* a movable rectangular frame of interlaced twigs, crossed bars, or the like, as for a temporary fence. **6.** a frame or sled on which criminals, esp. traitors, were formerly drawn to the place of execution. —*v.t.* **7.** to leap over (a hurdle, barrier, fence, etc.), as in a race. **8.** to master (a difficulty, problem, etc.); overcome. **9.** to construct with hurdles; enclose with hurdles. —*v.i.* **10.** to leap over a hurdle or other barrier. [bef. 900; ME *hirdel, hurdel* (n.), OE *hyrdel,* equiv. to *hyrd-* + *-el* n. suffix; cf. G *Hürde* hurdle; akin to L *crātis* hurdle, wickerwork, Gk *kýrtos* basket, cage, Skt *kṛt* spin] —**hur′dler,** *n.*

hurds (hûrdz), *n.pl.* hards.

hur·dy-gur·dy (hûr′dē gûr′dē, -gûr′-), *n., pl.* **-gur·dies. 1.** a barrel organ or similar musical instrument played by turning a crank. **2.** a lute- or guitar-shaped stringed musical instrument sounded by the revolution against the strings of a rosined wheel turned by a crank. [1740–50; var. of Scots *hirdy-girdy* uproar, influenced by HURLY-BURLY] —**hur′dy-gur′dist, hur′dy-gur′dy·ist,** *n.*

hurdy-gurdy (def. 2)

hurl (hûrl), *v.t.* **1.** to throw or fling with great force or vigor. **2.** to throw or cast down. **3.** to utter with vehemence: *to hurl insults at the umpire.* —*v.i.* **4.** to throw a missile. **5.** *Baseball.* to pitch a ball. —*n.* **6.** a forcible or violent throw; fling. [1175–1225; ME *hurlen,* equiv. to *hur-* (perh. akin to HURRY) + *-len* -LE; akin to LG *hurreln* to toss, Fris *hurreln* to roar (said of the wind), dial. G *hurlen* to roll, rumble (said of thunder)] —**hurl′·er,** *n.*
—**Syn. 1.** cast, pitch.

hurl·ey (hûr′lē), *n., pl.* **hurl·eys, hurl·ies.** *Brit.* **1.** the game of hurling. **2.** the leather-covered ball used in hurling. **3.** the stick used in hurling, similar to a field hockey stick but with a wide, flat blade. **4.** *Informal.* a club or cudgel. Also, **hurly.** [1815–25; HURL + *-ey,* as in HOCKEY]

hurl·ing (hûr′ling), *n.* **1.** the act of throwing or casting, esp. with great force or strength. **2.** a traditionally Irish game played by two teams of 15 players each on a rectangular field 140 yards (128 m) long, points being scored by hitting, pushing, carrying, or throwing the leather-covered ball between the goalposts at the opponent's end of the field with a wide-bladed stick resembling a hockey stick. **3.** (in parts of Britain, esp. Cornwall) a traditional, rural game in which two groups of players, using methods similar to those of football, vie for possession of a ball or other object and try to carry or hurl it into their own parish, village, farm, etc. [1350–1400; ME; see HURL, -ING[1]]

hurl·y (hûr′lē), *n., pl.* **hurl·ies. 1.** commotion; hurly-burly. **2.** *Brit.* hurley. [1590–1600]

hurl·y-burl·y (hûr′lē bûr′lē, -bûr′-), *n., pl.* **-burl·ies,** *adj.* —*n.* **1.** noisy disorder and confusion; commotion; uproar; tumult. —*adj.* **2.** full of commotion; tumultuous. [1520–30; alter. of *hurling (and) burling,* rhyming phrase based on HURLING in its (now obs.) sense of tumult, uproar]

Hu·rok (hyo͝or′ok *or, often,* yo͝or′-), *n.* **Sol(omon),** 1888–1974, U.S. impresario, born in Russia.

Hu·ron (hyo͝or′ən, -on *or, often,* yo͝or′-), *n.* **1.** a member of an Indian tribe, the northwestern member of the Iroquoian family, living west of Lake Huron. **2.** an Iroquoian language, the language of the Huron Indians. **3. Lake,** a lake between the U.S. and Canada: second largest of the Great Lakes. 23,010 sq. mi. (59,595 sq. km). **4.** a city in E South Dakota. 13,000. [1625–35, *Amer.*]

hur·rah (hə rä′, -rô′), *interj.* **1.** (used as an exclamation of joy, exultation, appreciation, encouragement, or the like.) —*v.i.* **2.** to shout "hurrah." —*n.* **3.** an exclamation of "hurrah." **4.** hubbub; commotion; fanfare. **5.** a colorful or tumultuous event; spectacle or celebration: *We celebrated the centennial with a three-day hurrah.* **6. last** or **final hurrah,** a final moment or occasion of glory or achievement: *The new play will be her last hurrah as an actress before she retires.* Also, **hur·ray** (hə rā′), **hooray, hoorah.** [1680–90; < G *hurra*]

Hur·ri (ho͝or′ē), *n., pl.* **-ris,** (*esp. collectively*) **-ri,** *adj.* Hurrian.

Hur·ri·an (ho͝or′ē ən), *n.* **1.** a member of an ancient people, sometimes identified with the Horites, who lived in the Middle East during the 2nd and 3rd millenniums B.C. and who established the Mitanni kingdom about 1400 B.C. **2.** the extinct language of the Hurrians, written in a syllabic, cuneiform script but not known to be related to any other language. —*adj.* **3.** of or pertaining to the Hurrians or their language. [1910–15; < Heb *ḥōrī* Horite + -AN]

hur·ri·cane (hûr′i kān′, hur′- *or, esp. Brit.,* -kən), *n.* **1.** a violent, tropical, cyclonic storm of the western North Atlantic, having wind speeds of or in excess of 72 mph (32 m/sec). Cf. **tropical cyclone, typhoon. 2.** a storm of the most intense severity. **3.** anything suggesting a violent storm. **4.** (*cap.*) *Mil.* a single-seat British fighter plane of World War II, fitted with eight .303 caliber machine guns and with a top speed in excess of 300 mph (480 km/h). [1545–55; < Sp *huracán* < Taino *hurakán*]

hur′ricane deck′, a deck at the top of a passenger steamer, having a roof supported by light scantlings. [1825–35, *Amer.*] —**hur′ri·cane-decked′,** *adj.*

hur·ri·cane-force wind (hûr′i kān′fôrs′ wind′, -fōrs′, hur′- *or, esp. Brit.,* -kən-), a wind, not necessarily a hurricane, having a speed of more than 72 mph (32 m/sec): the strongest of the winds.

hur′ricane lamp′, a candlestick or oil lantern protected against drafts or winds by a glass chimney. Also, called **hur′ricane lan′tern.** [1890–95]

hur′ricane warn′ing, *Meteorol.* a storm warning given for winds with speeds exceeding 63 knots (72 mph, 32 m/sec) when the source of the winds is a tropical cyclone. Cf. **storm warning.**

hur·ried (hûr′ēd, hur′-), *adj.* **1.** moving or working rapidly, esp. forced or required to hurry, as a person. **2.** characterized by or done with hurry; hasty: *a hurried meal.* [1660–70; HURRY + -ED[2]] —**hur′ried·ly,** *adv.* —**hur′ried·ness,** *n.*
—**Syn. 2.** hectic, slapdash, haphazard.

hur·ry (hûr′ē, hur′ē), *v.*, **-ried, -ry·ing,** *n., pl.* **-ries.** —*v.i.* **1.** to move, proceed, or act with haste (often fol. by *up*): *Hurry, or we'll be late. Hurry up, it's starting to rain.* —*v.t.* **2.** to drive, carry, or cause to move or perform with speed. **3.** to hasten; urge forward (often fol. by *up*). **4.** to impel or perform with undue haste: *to hurry someone into a decision.* —*n.* **5.** a state of urgency or eagerness: *to be in a hurry to meet a train.* **6.** hurried movement or action; haste. [1580–90; expressive word of uncert. orig., cf. ME *horyed* (attested once) rushed, impelled, MHG *hurren* to move quickly] —**hur′ry·ing·ly,** *adv.*
—**Syn. 1.** See **rush**[1]. **2.** hasten. **3.** accelerate, quicken; expedite, hustle. **6.** celerity; expedition, dispatch; speed, quickness; bustle, ado. —**Ant. 3.** delay, slow. **6.** deliberation.

hur·ry-scur·ry (hûr′ē skûr′ē, hur′ē skur′ē), *n., adv., adj.* —*n.* **1.** headlong, disorderly haste; hurry and confusion. —*adv.* **2.** with hurrying and scurrying. **3.** confusedly; in a bustle. —*adj.* **4.** characterized by headlong, disorderly flight or haste. Also, **hur′ry-skur′ry.** [1725–35]

hur·ry-up (hûr′ē up′, hur′-), *adj.* characterized by speed or the need for speed; quick: *a hurry-up meal; a hurry-up phone call.* [1885–90; adj. use of v. phrase *hurry up*]

hur·sin·ghar (hûr′sing gär′), *n.* See **night jasmine** (def. 1). [< Hindi *hārsingār, hārsinghār*]

Hurst (hûrst), *n.* **1. Fannie,** 1889–1968, U.S. novelist and short-story writer. **2.** a city in N Texas. 31,420.

hurt (hûrt), *v.*, **hurt, hurt·ing,** *n., adj.* —*v.t.* **1.** to cause bodily injury to; injure: *He was badly hurt in the accident.* **2.** to cause bodily pain to or in: *The wound still hurts him.* **3.** to damage or decrease the efficiency of (a material object) by striking, rough use, improper care, etc.: *Moths can't hurt this suit because it's mothproof. Dirty oil can hurt a car's engine.* **4.** to affect adversely; harm: *to hurt one's reputation; It wouldn't hurt the lawn if you watered it more often.* **5.** to cause mental pain to; offend or grieve: *She hurt his feelings by not asking him to the party.* —*v.i.* **6.** to feel or suffer bodily or mental pain or distress: *My back still hurts.* **7.** to cause bodily or mental pain or distress: *The blow to his pride hurt most.* **8.** to cause injury, damage, or harm. **9.** to suffer want or need. —*n.* **10.** a blow that inflicts a wound; bodily injury or the cause of such injury. **11.** injury, damage, or harm. **12.** the cause of mental pain or offense, as an insult. **13.** *Heraldry.* a roundel azure. —*adj.* **14.** physically injured: *The hurt child was taken to the hospital.* **15.** offended; unfavorably affected: *hurt pride.* **16.** suggesting that one has been offended or is suffering in mind: *Take that hurt look off your face!* **17.** damaged: *hurt merchandise.* [1150–1200; (v.) ME *hurten, hirten, herten* to injure, damage, stumble, knock together, appar. < OF *hurter* to knock (against), oppose (cf. F *heurter,* orig. dial.), prob. a v. deriv. of Frankish **hûrt* ram, c. ON *hrútr;* (n.) ME < OF, deriv. of the v.] —**hurt′a·ble,** *adj.* —**hurt′er,** *n.*
—**Syn. 3.** mar, impair. **5.** afflict, wound. **6.** ache. **10.** See **injury. 12.** cut, slight.

hurt·ful (hûrt′fəl), *adj.* causing hurt or injury; injurious; harmful. [1520–30; HURT + -FUL] —**hurt′ful·ly,** *adv.* —**hurt′ful·ness,** *n.*
—**Syn.** destructive, pernicious; noxious.

hur·tle (hûr′tl), *v.*, **-tled, -tling,** *n.* —*v.i.* **1.** to rush violently; move with great speed: *The car hurtled down the highway.* **2.** to move or go noisily or resoundingly, as with violent or rapid motion: *The sound was deafening, as tons of snow hurtled down the mountain.* **3.** *Archaic.* to strike together or against something; collide. —*v.t.* **4.** to drive violently; fling; dash. **5.** *Archaic.* to dash against; collide with. —*n.* **6.** *Archaic.* clash; collision; shock; clatter. [1175–1225; ME *hurtle,* equiv. to *hurt(en)* (see HURT) + *-le* -LE]
—**Syn. 1.** speed, fly, race, rush, shoot.

hur·tle·ber·ry (hûr′tl ber′ē), *n., pl.* **-ries.** whortleberry. [1425–75; late ME *hurtil beri*]

hurt·less (hûrt′lis), *adj.* **1.** unhurt; uninjured. **2.** harmless; innocuous. [1350–1400; ME *hurtles.* See HURT, -LESS] —**hurt′less·ly,** *adv.* —**hurt′less·ness,** *n.*

Hus (hus; *Czech.* hŏŏs), *n.* **Jan** (jan; *Czech.* yän). See **Huss, John.**

Hu·sain (hŏŏ sīn′, -sän′), *n.* Hussein (def. 1).

Hu·sák (hŏŏ′säk; *Eng.* hōō′sak), *n.* **Gus·táv** (gŏŏs′täf), 1913–91, Czechoslovak political leader: first secretary of the Communist party 1969–87; president 1975–89.

Hu·sayn ′A·lī Mīr·zā (hŏŏ sän′ ä′lē mēr′zä, ä lē′), 1817–92, Persian religious leader: founder of Bahā′ī. Also called **Bahaullah.**

husb., husbandry.

hus·band (huz′bənd), *n.* **1.** a married man, esp. when considered in relation to his wife. **2.** *Brit.* a manager. **3.** *Archaic.* a prudent or frugal manager. —*v.t.* **4.** to manage, esp. with prudent economy. **5.** to use frugally; conserve: *to husband one's resources.* **6.** *Archaic.* **a.** to be or become a husband to; marry. **b.** to find a husband for. **c.** to till; cultivate. [bef. 1000; ME *husband(e),* OE *hūsbonda* master of the house < ON *hūsbōndi,* equiv. to *hūs* HOUSE + *bōndi* (*bō-,* var. of *bū-* dwell (see BOOR) + *-nd* prp. suffix + *-i* inflectional ending)] —**hus′band·er,** *n.* —**hus′band·less,** *adj.*
—**Syn. 5.** preserve, save, store, hoard.

hus·band·age (huz′bən dij), *n.* the fees and commissions of a ship's manager. [1800–10; HUSBAND + -AGE]

hus·band·man (huz′bənd mən), *n., pl.* **-men.** a farmer. [1300–50; ME *husbondeman.* See HUSBAND, MAN[1]]

hus·band·ry (huz′bən drē), *n.* **1.** the cultivation and production of edible crops or of animals for food; agriculture; farming. **2.** the science of raising crops or food animals. **3.** careful or thrifty management; frugality, thrift, or conservation. **4.** the management of domestic affairs or of resources generally. [1250–1300; ME *housebondrie.* See HUSBAND, -RY]

Hu·sein ibn-A·li (hŏŏ sīn′ ib′ən ä′lē, -ä lē′; hŏŏ-sän′), 1856–1931, 1st king of Hejaz 1916–24.

hush (hush), *interj.* **1.** (used as a command to be silent or quiet.) —*v.i.* **2.** to become or be silent or quiet: *They hushed as the judge walked in.* —*v.t.* **3.** to make silent; silence. **4.** to suppress mention of; keep concealed (often fol. by *up*): *They hushed up the scandal.* **5.** to calm, quiet, or allay: *to hush someone's fears.* —*n.* **6.** silence or quiet, esp. after noise. **7.** *Phonet.* either of the sibilant sounds (sh) and (zh). —*adj.* **8.** *Archaic.* silent; quiet. [1350–1400; appar. back formation from *husht* WHIST[2] (ME *huissht*), the *-t* being taken for ptp. suffix] —**hush·ed·ly** (hush′id lē, husht′lē), *adv.* —**hush′ful,** *adj.* —**hush′ful·ly,** *adv.*
—**Syn. 6.** peace, stillness, tranquillity.

hush·a·by (hush′ə bī′), *interj.* hush (used as a command to be silent): *Hushaby, baby.* [1790–1800; HUSH + (LULL)ABY]

hush-hush (hush′hush′), *adj.* highly secret or confidential: *a hush-hush political investigation.* [1915–20; redupl. based on HUSH]

Hu Shih (hōō′ shœ′), 1891–1962, Chinese scholar and diplomat. Also, *Pinyin,* **Hu′ Shi′.**

hush′ mon′ey, a bribe to keep someone silent about something, esp. to keep the receiver from exposing a scandal. [1700–10]

hush′ pup′py, *Chiefly Southern U.S.* a small, unsweetened cake or ball of cornmeal dough fried in deep fat. [1915–20, *Amer.*; allegedly so called because such cakes were fed to dogs to keep them from begging for scraps while other dishes were cooked]

husk (husk), *n.* **1.** the dry external covering of certain fruits or seeds, esp. of an ear of corn. **2.** the enveloping or outer part of anything, esp. when dry or worthless. —*v.t.* **3.** to remove the husk from. [1350–1400; ME *huske,* equiv. to *hus-* (akin to OE *hosu* pod, husk) + *-ke,* weak var. of -OCK] —**husk′er,** *n.* —**husk′like′,** *adj.*

husk·ing (hus′king), *n.* **1.** Also called **shucking.** the act of removing husks, esp. those of corn. **2.** See **husking bee.** [1685–95, *Amer.*; HUSK + -ING[1]]

husk′ing bee′, a gathering of farm families or friends to husk corn, usually as part of a celebration or party. [1800–10]

Hus·kis·son (hus′kə sən), *n.* **William,** 1770–1830, British statesman and financier.

husk′ toma′to. See **ground cherry** (def. 1). [1890–95, *Amer.*]

husk·y[1] (hus′kē), *adj.*, **husk·i·er, husk·i·est,** *n., pl.* **husk·ies.** —*adj.* **1.** big and strong; burly. **2.** (of the voice) having a semiwhispered vocal tone; somewhat hoarse, as when speaking with a cold or from grief or passion. **3.** like, covered with, or full of husks. **4.** made in a size meant for the larger or heavier than average boy: *size 18 husky pants.* **5.** for, pertaining to, or wearing clothing in this size: *the husky department; husky boys.* —*n.* **6.** a size of garments meant for the larger or heavier than average boy. [1545–55; HUSK + -Y[1]] —**husk′i·ly,** *adv.* —**husk′i·ness,** *n.*
—**Syn. 1.** robust, brawny, strapping. **2.** harsh, gruff, rasping, throaty.

husk·y[2] (hus′kē), *n., pl.* **husk·ies.** *Informal.* a big, strong person. [1865–70; n. use of HUSKY[1], with the suffix taken as -Y[2]]

husk·y[3] (hus′kē), *n., pl.* **husk·ies.** (*sometimes cap.*) **1.** See **Eskimo dog. 2.** See **Siberian Husky. 3.** *Canadian Slang.* **a.** an Inuit. **b.** the language of the Inuit. [1870–75; by ellipsis from *husky dog, husky breed;* cf. Newfoundland and Labrador dial. *Husky* a Labrador Inuit, earlier *Huskemaw, Uskemaw,* ult. < the same Algonquian source as ESKIMO]

Huss (hus; *Czech.* hŏŏs), *n.* **John,** 1369?–1415, Czech religious reformer and martyr. Also, **Hus.**

hus·sar (hŏŏ zär′), *n.* **1.** (originally) one of a body of Hungarian light cavalry formed during the 15th century. **2.** a member of a class of similar troops, usually with striking or flamboyant uniforms, in European armies. [1525–35; < Hungarian *huszár* < Serbo-Croatian *hùsār* brigand, pirate < ML *cursārius* CORSAIR]

Hus·sein (hŏŏ sän′), *n.* **1.** Also **Hosein, Husain.** (*al-Husayn*), A.D. 629?–680, Arabian caliph, the son of Ali and Fatima and the brother of Hasan. **2. Sad·dam** (sä-däm′) (*at-Takriti*), born 1937, Iraqi political leader: president since 1979.

Hus·sein I, born 1935, king of Jordan since 1953.

Hus·serl (hŏŏs′ərl), *n.* **Ed·mund (Gus·tav Al·brecht)** (et′mŏŏnt gŏŏs′täf äl′brekht), 1859–1938, German philosopher born in Austria.

Huss·ite (hus′īt), *n.* **1.** a member of the religious reformist and nationalistic movement initiated by John Huss in Bohemia in the late 14th century. —*adj.* **2.** of or pertaining to John Huss or the Hussites. [1525–35; HUSS + -ITE[1]] —**Huss′it·ism,** *n.*

hus·sy (hus′ē, huz′ē), *n., pl.* **-sies. 1.** a brazen or immoral woman. **2.** a mischievous, impudent, or ill-behaved girl. [1520–30; earlier *hussive* HOUSEWIFE]
—**Syn. 1.** trollop, slut. **2.** baggage, minx.

hus·tings (hus′tingz), *n.* (*used with a singular or plural v.*) **1.** (before 1872) the temporary platform on which candidates for the British Parliament stood when nominated and from which they addressed the electors. **2.** any place from which political campaign speeches are made. **3.** the political campaign trail. **4.** Also called **hus′tings court′.** a local court in certain parts of Virginia. [bef. 1050; ME, OE < ODan *hūs-thing* house meeting. See HOUSE, THING[2]]

hus·tle (hus′əl), *v.*, **-tled, -tling,** *n.* —*v.i.* **1.** to proceed or work rapidly or energetically: *to hustle about putting a house in order.* **2.** to push or force one's way; jostle or shove. **3.** to be aggressive, esp. in business or other financial dealings. **4.** *Slang.* to earn one's living by illicit or unethical means. **5.** *Slang.* (of a prostitute) to solicit clients. —*v.t.* **6.** to convey or cause to move, esp. to leave, roughly or hurriedly: *They hustled him out of the bar.* **7.** to pressure or coerce (a person) to buy or do something: *to hustle the customers into buying more drinks.* **8.** to urge, prod, or speed up: *Hustle your work along.* **9.** to obtain by aggressive or illicit means: *He could always hustle a buck or two from some sucker.* **10.** to beg; solicit. **11.** to sell in or work (an area), esp. by high-pressure tactics: *The souvenir venders began hustling the town at dawn.* **12.** to sell aggressively: *to hustle souvenirs.* **13.** to jostle, push, or shove roughly. **14.** *Slang.* to induce (someone) to gamble or to promote (a gambling game) when the odds of winning are overwhelmingly in one's own favor. **15.** *Slang.* to cheat; swindle: *They hustled him out of his savings.* **16.** *Slang.* **a.** (of a prostitute) to solicit (someone). **b.** to attempt to persuade (someone) to have sexual relations. **c.** to promote or publicize in a lively, vigorous, or aggressive manner: *an author hustling her new book on the TV talk shows.* —*n.* **17.** energetic activity, as in work. **18.** discourteous shoving, pushing, or jostling. **19.** *Slang.* **a.** an inducing by fraud, pressure, or deception, esp. of inexperienced or uninformed persons, to buy something, to participate in an illicit scheme, dishonest gambling game, etc. **b.** such a product, scheme, gambling game, etc. **20.** *Informal.* a competitive struggle: *the hustle to earn a living.* **21.** a fast, lively, popular ballroom dance evolving from Latin American, swing, rock, and disco dance styles, with a strong basic rhythm and simple step pattern augmented by strenuous turns, breaks, etc. [1675–85; < D *husselen,* var. of *hutselen* to shake, equiv. to *hutsen* to shake + *-el-* -LE]

hus·tler (hus′lər), *n.* **1.** an enterprising person determined to succeed; go-getter. **2.** *Slang.* a person who employs fraudulent or unscrupulous methods to obtain money; swindler. **3.** *Informal.* an expert gambler or game player who seeks out challengers, esp. unsuspecting amateur ones, in order to win money from them: *He earned his living as a pool hustler.* **4.** *Slang.* a prostitute. **5.** a person who hustles. [1815–25; HUSTLE + -ER[1]]

Hus·ton (hyōō′stən *or, often,* yōō′-), *n.* **1. John,** 1906–87, U.S. film director and writer. **2.** his father, **Walter,** 1884–1950, U.S. actor, born in Canada.

hut (hut), *n., v.,* **hut·ted, hut·ting.** —*n.* **1.** a small or humble dwelling of simple construction, esp. one made of natural materials, as of logs or grass. **2.** a simple roofed shelter, often with one or two sides left open. **3.** *Mil.* a wooden or metal structure for the temporary housing of troops. —*v.t.* **4.** to furnish with a hut as temporary housing; billet. —*v.i.* **5.** to lodge or take a shelter in a hut. [1645–55; < F *hutte* < Frankish, c. OS *hutta,* OHG *hutt(e)a* < WGmc **hudjā;* akin to HIDE[1]] —**hut′like′,** *adj.*
—**Syn. 1.** shed, hovel.

hutch (huch), *n.* **1.** a pen or enclosed coop for small animals: *rabbit hutch.* **2.** a chest, cupboard, bin, etc., for storage. **3.** any of various chestlike cabinets, raised on legs and having doors or drawers in front, sometimes with open shelves above. **4.** a small cottage, hut, or cabin. **5.** a baker's kneading trough. [1275–1325; ME *hucche,* var. of *whucce,* OE *hwicce* chest; not akin to OF *huge, huche* (*ch* form appar. by contamination with English word)]
—**Syn. 1.** cage, enclosure, cote.

Hutch·ins (huch′inz), *n.* **Robert Maynard,** 1899–1977, U.S. educator and college president.

Hutch·in·son (huch′in sən), *n.* **1. Anne Mar·bur·y** (mär′bə rē), 1591–1643, American religious liberal, born in England: banished from Massachusetts 1637. **2. Thomas,** 1711–80, American colonial administrator: royal governor of Massachusetts 1769–74; in exile from England after 1774. **3.** a city in central Kansas, on the Arkansas River. 40,284.

hut·ment (hut′mənt), *n.* an encampment of huts. [1885–90; HUT + -MENT]

Hut·ter·ite (hut′ə rīt′, hŏŏt′-), *n.* a member of an Anabaptist sect following the principles of Jacob Hutter (d. 1536) of Moravia and practicing community of goods. [1635–45; Jacob *Hutter* + -ITE[1]] —**Hut·ter·i·an** (hə tēr′ē ən, hŏŏ-), *adj.*

Hu·tu (hōō′tōō), *n., pl.* **-tus,** (*esp. collectively*) **-tu.** a member of a Bantu farming people of Rwanda and Burundi, in central Africa.

hutz·pa (KHŏŏt′spə, hŏŏt′-), *n. Slang.* chutzpa. Also, **hutz′pah.**

Hux·lei·an (huks′lē ən, huks lē′ən), *adj.* **1.** of, pertaining to, or characteristic or suggestive of Aldous Huxley or his writings. **2.** of or pertaining to Thomas Henry Huxley, his biological work, or his writings. Also, **Hux′ley·an.** [1885–90; HUXLEY + -AN]

Hux·ley (huks′lē), *n.* **1. Al·dous (Leonard)** (ôl′dəs), 1894–1963, English novelist, essayist, and critic. **2. Sir Andrew Fielding,** born 1918, English physiologist: Nobel prize for medicine 1963 (half brother of Aldous and Sir Julian Sorell). **3. Sir Julian Sor·ell** (sor′əl), 1887–1975, English biologist and writer (brother of Aldous). **4. Thomas Henry,** 1825–95, English biologist and writer (grandfather of Aldous and Sir Julian Sorell Huxley).

Hu Yao·bang (hy′ you′bäng′), born 1915, Chinese Communist leader: general secretary of the Chinese Communist Party 1980–87.

Huy·gens (hī′gənz, hoi′-; *Du.* hoi′gəns), *n.* **Chris·tian** (kris′chən; *Du.* kris′tē än′), 1629–95, Dutch mathematician, physicist, and astronomer. Also, **Huy′ghens.**

Huy′gens eye′piece, *Optics.* an eyepiece consisting of two plano-convex lenses, the plane sides of which both face the eye. [1830–40; named after C. HUYGENS]

CONCISE PRONUNCIATION KEY: *act, cāpe, dâre, pärt; set, ēqual; if, īce; ox, ōver, ôrder, oil, bŏŏk, bōōt, out; up, ûrge; child; sing; shoe; thin, that;* zh as in *treasure.* ə = *a* as in *alone, e* as in *system, i* as in *easily, o* as in *gallop, u* as in *circus;* ° as in *fire* (fī°r), *hour* (ou°r). l and n can serve as syllabic consonants, as in *cradle* (krād′l), and *button* (but′n). See the full key inside the front cover.

Huy′gens prin′ciple, *Optics, Physics.* the principle that all points on a wave front of light are sources of secondary waves and that surfaces tangential to these waves define the position of the wave front at any point in time. [1830–40; named after C. HUYGENS]

Huys•mans (wēs mäns′), *n.* **Jo•ris Karl** (zhō rēs′ kärl), (*Charles Marie Georges Huysmans*), 1848–1907, French novelist.

huz•zah (hə zä′), *interj.* **1.** (used as an exclamation of joy, applause, appreciation, etc.) hurrah! —*n.* **2.** the exclamation "huzzah." **3.** an instance of giving praise or applause; accolade: *The newspaper's review was one big huzzah for the new movie.* —*v.i.* **4.** to shout "huzzah." —*v.t.* **5.** to salute with huzzahs. Also, **huz•za′.** [1565–75; var. of earlier *hussa, hissa* sailors' cry; see HOISE]

H.V., 1. high velocity. **2.** high voltage. Also, **h.v.**

HVAC, heating, ventilating, and air conditioning.

HVDC, high-voltage direct current.

HVP, See **hydrolyzed vegetable protein.** Also, **H.V.P.**

hvy., heavy.

HW, 1. *Real Estate.* hardwood. **2.** high water. **3.** hot water (heat).

Hwai•nan (hwī′nän′), *n. Older Spelling.* Huainan.

hwan (hwän, wän), *n., pl.* **hwan.** a former monetary unit of South Korea. [< Korean, the reading of a character used as a graphic synonym of *wŏn* (< MChin, equiv. to Chin *yuán* YUAN)]

Hwang Hai (hwäng′ hī′), *Older Spelling.* See **Yellow Sea.**

Hwang Ho (hwäng′ hō′; *Chin.* hwäng′ hu′), *Older Spelling.* See **Huang He.** Also called **Yellow River.** See map under **Chang Jiang.**

HWM, high-water mark. Also, **H.W.M., h.w.m.**

hwy, highway. Also, **hwy.**

Hy (hī), *n.* a male given name, form of **Hiram.**

hy., *Elect.* (formerly) henry.

hy•a•cinth (hī′ə sinth), *n.* **1.** a bulbous plant, *Hyacinthus orientalis,* of the lily family, widely cultivated for its cylindrical cluster of fragrant flowers in a variety of colors. **2.** any of various similar or related plants, as the grape hyacinth or the water hyacinth. **3.** a plant fabled to have sprung from the blood of Hyacinthus and variously identified as iris, gladiolus, larkspur, etc. **4.** *Mineral.* a reddish-orange zircon. **5.** a gem of the ancients, held to be the amethyst or sapphire. Also called **jacinth** for defs. 3–5. [1545–55; < L *hyacinthus* < Gk *hyákinthos* blue larkspur, also a gem of blue color; cf. JACINTH]

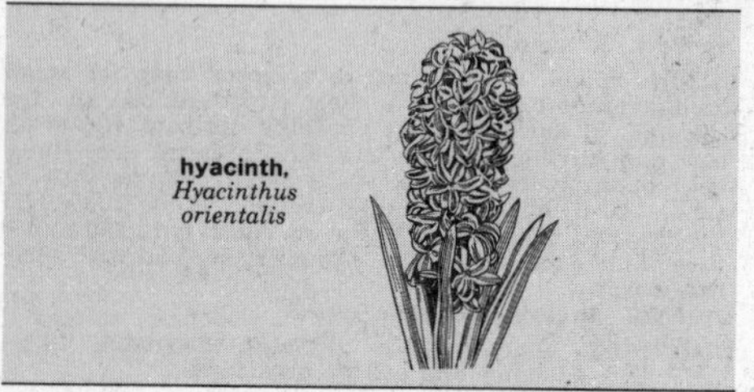
hyacinth, *Hyacinthus orientalis*

hy′acinth bean′, an Old World tropical vine, *Dolichos lablab,* of the legume family, having purple or white flowers and black or white seeds in a papery, beaked pod. Also called **bonavist, lablab.**

hy•a•cin•thin (hī′ə sin′thin), *n. Chem.* phenylacetaldehyde. [HYACINTH + -IN[2]]

hy•a•cin•thine (hī′ə sin′thin, -thīn), *adj.* **1.** of or like the hyacinth. **2.** adorned with hyacinths. [1650–60; < L *hyacinthinus* < Gk *hyakínthinos.* See HYACINTH, -INE[1]]

Hy•a•cin•thus (hī′ə sin′thəs), *n. Class. Myth.* a youth loved but accidentally killed by Apollo: from the youth's blood sprang the hyacinth.

Hy•a•des (hī′ə dēz′), *n.* (*used with a plural v.*) **1.** *Astron.* a group of stars comprising a moving cluster in the constellation Taurus, supposed by the ancients to indicate the approach of rain when they rose with the sun. **2.** *Class. Myth.* a group of nymphs and sisters of the Pleiades who nurtured the infant Dionysus and were placed among the stars as a reward. Also, **Hy•ads** (hī′adz). [1350–1400; ME *Hiades* < L < Gk, equiv. to *hý(ein)* to rain + *-ades,* pl. of *-as* -AD]

hy•ae•na (hī ē′nə), *n.* hyena. —**hy•ae′nic,** *adj.*

hyal-, var. of **hyalo-** before a vowel: *hyalite.*

hy•a•line (*n.* hī′ə lēn′, -lin; *adj.* hī′ə lin, -līn′), *n.* **1.** Also, **hy•a•lin** (hī′ə lin). *Biochem.* **a.** a horny substance found in hydatid cysts, closely resembling chitin. **b.** a structureless, transparent substance found in cartilage, the eye, etc., resulting from the pathological degeneration of tissue. **2.** something glassy or transparent. —*adj.* **3.** of or pertaining to hyaline. **4.** glassy or transparent. **5.** of or pertaining to glass. **6.** amorphous; not crystalline. [1655–65; < LL *hyalinus* < Gk *hyálinos* of glass. See HYAL-, -INE[1]]

hy′aline cart′ilage, *Anat.* the typical, translucent form of cartilage, containing little fibrous tissue. [1850–55]

hy′aline mem′brane disease′. *Pathol.* See **respiratory distress syndrome.** [1950–55]

hy•a•lin•i•za•tion (hī′ə lə nə zā′shən), *n. Pathol.* a condition in which normal tissue deteriorates into a homogeneous, translucent material. [1915–20; HYALINIZE + -ATION]

hy•a•lin•ize (hī′ə lə nīz′), *v.i.,* **-ized, -iz•ing.** to become hyaline. Also, *esp. Brit.,* **hy′a•lin•ise′.** [1925–30; HYALINE + -IZE]

hy•a•lite (hī′ə līt′), *n.* a colorless variety of opal, sometimes transparent like glass, and sometimes whitish and translucent. [1785–95; HYAL- + -ITE[1]]

hyalo-, a combining form meaning "glass," used in the formation of compound words: *hyaloplasm.* Also, *esp. before a vowel,* **hyal-.** [< Gk, comb. form of *hýalos* glass]

hy•a•lo•graph (hī′ə lə graf′, -gräf′), *n.* an instrument used in hyalography. [HYALO- + -GRAPH]

hy•a•log•ra•phy (hī′ə log′rə fē), *n.* the technique of writing or engraving on glass. [HYALO- + -GRAPHY] —**hy′a•log′ra•pher,** *n.*

hy•a•loid (hī′ə loid′), *n.* **1.** See **hyaloid membrane.** —*adj.* **2.** glassy; hyaline. [1660–70; < Gk *hyaloeidḗs* like glass. See HYAL-, -OID]

hy′aloid mem′brane, the delicate, pellucid, and nearly structureless membrane enclosing the vitreous humor of the eye. [1825–35]

hy•al•o•mere (hī al′ə mēr′, hī′ə lə-), *n. Cell Biol.* the transparent part of a blood platelet, surrounding the chromomere. [1935–40; HYALO- + -MERE]

hy•al•o•phane (hī al′ə fān′, hī′ə lə-), *n. Mineral.* a variety of orthoclase in which some of the potassium is replaced by barium. [1850–55; HYALO- + -PHANE]

hy•al•o•plasm (hī al′ə plaz′əm, hī′ə lə-), *n. Cell Biol.* See **ground substance.** [1885–90; HYALO- + -PLASM] —**hy•al′o•plas′mic,** *adj.*

hy′a•lu•ron′ic ac′id (hī′ə lo͝o ron′ik, hī′-), *Biochem.* a mucopolysaccharide serving as a viscous medium in the tissues of the body and as a lubricant in joints. [1930–35; HYAL(OID) (in reference to the vitreous humor, from which it was first isolated) + URONIC]

hy•a•lu•ron•i•dase (hī′ə lo͝o ron′i dās′, -dāz′), *n.* **1.** *Biochem.* a mucolytic enzyme found in the testes, in snake venom, and in hemolytic streptococci and certain other bacteria, that decreases the viscosity of the intercellular matrix by breaking down hyaluronic acid. **2.** *Pharm.* a commercial form of this substance, used chiefly to promote the diffusion of intradermally injected drugs. [1935–40; HYALURON(IC) + *-id-* (by analogy with AMIDASE, PEPTIDASE, etc.) + -ASE]

Hy•an′nis Port′ (hī an′is), a town in SE Massachusetts, on Nantucket Sound: summer resort.

HY antigen (āch′wī′), *Immunol.* an antigen encoded by a gene on the Y (male) chromosome, active in the development of male structures. [1975–80; *H(uman) Y (chromosome)*]

Hy•atts•ville (hī′əts vil′), *n.* a city in central Maryland. 12,709.

hy•brid (hī′brid), *n.* **1.** the offspring of two animals or plants of different breeds, varieties, species, or genera, esp. as produced through human manipulation for specific genetic characteristics. **2.** a person or group of persons reflecting the interaction of two unlike cultures, traditions, etc. **3.** anything derived from heterogeneous sources, or composed of elements of different or incongruous kinds: *a hybrid of the academic and business worlds.* **4.** a word composed of elements originally drawn from different languages, as *television,* whose components come from Greek and Latin. —*adj.* **5.** bred from two distinct races, breeds, varieties, species, or genera. **6.** composite; formed or composed of heterogeneous elements. **7.** composed of elements originally drawn from different languages, as a word. [1595–1605; < L *hybrida, hibrida* a crossbred animal]
—**Syn. 5.** HYBRID, MONGREL refer to animals or plants of mixed origin. HYBRID is the scientific term: *hybrid corn; a hybrid variety of sheep.* MONGREL, used originally of dogs to denote the offspring of crossings of different breeds, is now extended to other animals and to plants; it is usually deprecatory, as denoting mixed, nondescript, or degenerate breed or character: *a mongrel pup.* —**Ant. 5.** purebred, thoroughbred.

hy′brid chip′, *Electronics.* an integrated circuit that comprises both diffused active devices and thin-film components. Also called **hy′brid in′tegrated cir′cuit.**

hy′brid comput′er, a computer system containing both analog and digital hardware. [1965–70]

hy′brid corn′, 1. a crossbred corn, esp. the grain of corn developed by hybridization of repeatedly self-pollinated, and therefore genetically pure, varieties. **2.** a plant grown from the grain of this corn.

hy•brid•ism (hī′bri diz′əm), *n.* **1.** Also, **hy•brid•i•ty** (hī brid′i tē). the quality or condition of being hybrid. **2.** the production of hybrids. [1835–45; HYBRID + -ISM]

hy•brid•ize (hī′bri dīz′), *v.,* **-ized, -iz•ing.** —*v.t.* **1.** to cause to produce hybrids; cross. **2.** to breed or cause the production of (a hybrid). **3.** to form in a hybrid manner. —*v.i.* **4.** to produce hybrids. **5.** to cause the production of hybrids by crossing. **6.** to form a double-stranded nucleic acid of two single strands of DNA or RNA, or one of each, by allowing the base pairs of the separate strands to form complementary bonds. **7.** to fuse two cells of different genotypes into a hybrid cell. Also, *esp. Brit.,* **hy′brid•ise′.** [1835–45; HYBRID + -IZE] —**hy′brid•iz′a•ble,** *adj.* —**hy′brid•i•za′tion,** *n.* —**hy′brid•ist, hy′brid•iz′er,** *n.*

hy•brid•o•ma (hī′bri dō′mə), *n., pl.* **-mas.** *Biotech.* a hybrid cell made in the laboratory by fusing a normal cell with a cancer cell, usu. a myeloma or lymphoma, in order to combine desired features of each, as the ability of the cancer cell to multiply rapidly with the ability of the normal cell to dictate the production of a specific antibody. Cf. **monoclonal antibody.** [1975–80; HYBRID + -OMA]

hy′brid perpet′ual, a type of cultivated rose bred from varieties having vigorous growth and more or less recurrent bloom. [1840–50]

hy′brid tea′, a type of cultivated rose originally produced chiefly by crossing the tea rose and the hybrid perpetual. [1885–90]

hy′brid vig′or, heterosis. [1915–20]

hy•bris (hī′bris), *n.* hubris. —**hy•bris′tic,** *adj.*

hyd., 1. hydraulics. **2.** hydrostatics.

hy•dan•to•in (hī dan′tō in), *n. Pharm.* a colorless, needlelike, crystalline compound, $C_3H_4N_2O_2$, used in the synthesis of pharmaceutical substances and resins. [1865–70; HYD(ROGEN) + (ALL)ANTOIN]

hy•da•thode (hī′də thōd′), *n. Bot.* a specialized leaf structure through which water is exuded. [< G *Hydathode* (1894) < Gk *hydat-,* s. of *hýdōr* water + *hodós* way, path; cf. -ODE[2], CATHODE]

hy•da•tid (hī′də tid), *Pathol.* —*n.* **1.** a cyst with watery contents that is produced in humans and animals by a tapeworm in the larval state; cysticerus. **2.** a cystic vestige of an embryonic feature. —*adj.* **3.** Also, **hy′da•tid′i•nous.** of or pertaining to a hydatid. **4.** containing or affected by hydatids. [1675–85; < Gk *hydatid-* (s. of *hydatís*) watery vesicle]

Hyde (hīd), *n.* **1. Douglas,** 1860–1949, Irish author and statesman: president of Ireland. 1938–45. **2. Edward.** See **Clarendon, Edward Hyde.**

Hyde′ Park′, 1. a public park in London, England. **2.** a village in SE New York, on the Hudson: site of the estate and burial place of Franklin D. Roosevelt and Eleanor Roosevelt. 2550

Hy•der•a•bad (hī′dər ə bäd′, -bad′, hī′drə-), *n.* **1.** a former state in S India, now part of Andhra Pradesh. **2.** a city in and the capital of Andhra Pradesh, India, in the W part. 1,796,339. **3.** a city in SE Pakistan, on the Indus River. 795,000. Also, **Haidarabad.**

Hy•der A•li (hī′dər ä′lē, ä lē′). See **Haidar Ali.**

hyd•no•car•pate (hid′nō kär′pāt), *n.* a salt or ester of hydnocarpic acid. [1900–05; HYDNOCARP(IC ACID) + -ATE[2]]

hyd′no•car′pic ac′id (hid′nō kär′pik, hid′-), *Pharm.* an acid, $C_{16}H_{28}O_2$, obtained from chaulmoogra oil, and used in the treatment of leprosy. [1900–05; < Gk *hýdno(n)* truffle + *karp(ós)* fruit + -IC]

hydr-[1], var. of **hydro-**[1] before a vowel: *hydrant.*

hydr-[2], var. of **hydro-**[2] before a vowel: *hydride.*

hy•dra (hī′drə), *n., pl.* **-dras, -drae** (-drē) for 1–3, *gen.* **-drae** (-drē) for 4. **1.** (*often cap.*) *Class. Myth.* a water or marsh serpent with nine heads, each of which, if cut off, grew back as two; Hercules killed this serpent by cauterizing the necks as he cut off the heads. **2.** any freshwater polyp of the genus *Hydra* and related genera, having a cylindrical body with a ring of tentacles surrounding the mouth, and usually living attached to rocks, plants, etc., but also capable of detaching and floating in the water. **3.** a persistent or many-sided problem that presents new obstacles as soon as one aspect is solved. **4.** (*cap.*) *Astron.* the Sea Serpent, a large southern constellation extending through 90° of the sky, being the longest of all constellations. [1325–75; < L < Gk *hýdrā* water serpent (r. ME *ydre* < MF < L); see OTTER]

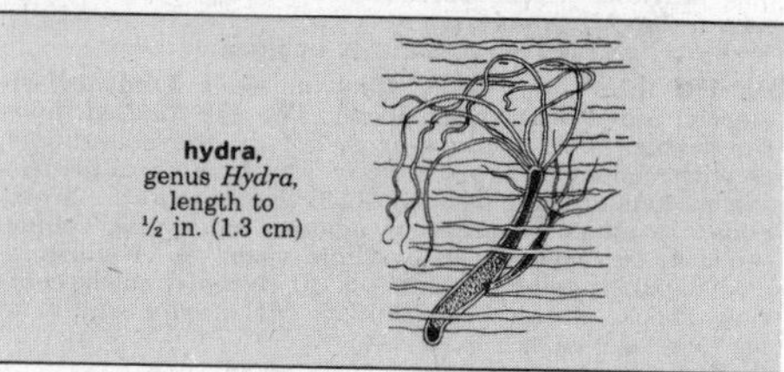
hydra, genus *Hydra,* length to ½ in. (1.3 cm)

hy•drac•id (hī dras′id), *n.* an acid that does not contain oxygen, as hydrochloric acid, HCl. [1820–30; HYDR-[2] + ACID]

hy•drae•mi•a (hī drē′mē ə), *n. Med.* hydremia.

hy•dra•gogue (hī′drə gôg′, -gog′), *adj.* **1.** causing the discharge of watery fluid, as from the bowels. —*n.* **2.** Also, **hy′dra•gog′.** *Pharm.* a hydragogue agent. [1630–40; < L *hydragōgus* < Gk *hydragōgós* water-conveying, equiv. to *hydr-* HYDR-[1] + *agōgós* leading, guiding (see -AGOGUE)]

hy•dra-head•ed (hī′drə hed′id), *adj.* **1.** containing many problems, difficulties, or obstacles. **2.** having many branches, divisions, facets, etc. [1590–1600]

hy•dral•a•zine (hī dral′ə zēn′), *n. Pharm.* a white crystalline powder, $C_8H_8N_4$, that dilates blood vessels and is used in the treatment of hypertension. [1950–55; HYDR-[2] + (PHTH)AL(IC) + AZINE]

hy•dran•gea (hī drān′jə, -jē ə, -dran′-), *n.* any shrub belonging to the genus *Hydrangea,* of the saxifrage family, several species of which are cultivated for their large, showy flower clusters of white, pink, or blue. [< NL (Linnaeus) < Gk *hydr-* HYDR-[1] + NL *angea,* fem. n. based on Gk *angeîon* vessel; so called from cup-shaped seed capsule]

hy•drant (hī′drənt), *n.* **1.** an upright pipe with a spout, nozzle, or other outlet, usually in the street, for drawing water from a main or service pipe, esp. for fighting fires. **2.** a water faucet. [1800–10, *Amer.*; HYDR-[1] + -ANT]

hy•dranth (hī′dranth), *n. Zool.* the terminal part of a hydroid polyp that bears the mouth and tentacles and contains the stomach region. [1870–75; HYDR(A) + Gk *ánth(os)* flower]

hy•drarch (hī′drärk), *adj. Ecol.* (of a sere) originating in a wet habitat. [1910–15; HYDR-[1] + -ARCH]

hy•drar•gil•lite (hī drär′jə līt′), *n. Mineral.* gibbsite. [1795–1805; HYDR-[1] + ARGILLITE]

CONCISE ETYMOLOGY KEY: <, descended or borrowed from; >, whence; b., blend of, blended; c., cognate with; cf., compare; deriv., derivative; equiv., equivalent; imit., imitative; obl., oblique; r., replacing; s., stem; sp., spelling, spelled; resp., respelling, respelled; trans., translation; ?, origin unknown; *, unattested; ‡, probably earlier than. See the full key inside the front cover.

hy·drar·gy·rism (hī drär′jə riz′əm), *n. Pathol.* mercurialism. Also, **hy·drar·gyr·i·a** (hī′drär jir′ē ə), **hy·drar·gy·ri·a·sis** (hī drär′jə rī′ə sis). [HYDRARGYR(UM) + -ISM]

hy·drar·gy·rum (hī drär′jər əm), *n.* mercury. [1555–65; < NL, equiv. to L *hydrargyr(us)* (< Gk *hydrárgyros* mercury, equiv. to *hydr-* HYDR-[1] + *árgyros* silver) + *-um,* on model of *aurum,* etc.] —**hy·drar·gyr·ic** (hī′drär jir′ik), *adj.*

hy·drase (hī′drās, -drāz), *n. Biochem.* any of the class of enzymes that catalyze the addition of a water molecule into a compound without causing hydrolysis. [1940–45; HYDR-[1] + -ASE]

hy·dras·tine (hī dras′tēn, -tin), *n. Pharm.* an alkaloid, $C_{21}H_{21}NO_6$, that is extracted from the roots of goldenseal and forms prismatic crystals: used as an astringent and to inhibit uterine bleeding. [1875–80; HYDRAST(IS) + -INE[2]]

hy·dras·ti·nine (hī dras′tə nēn′, -nin), *n. Pharm.* a white, crystalline, poisonous alkaloid, $C_{11}H_{13}NO_3$, synthesized from hydrastine: used to arrest bleeding, esp. in the uterus. [1885–90; HYDRASTINE + -INE[2]]

hy·dras·tis (hī dras′tis), *n.* goldenseal (def. 2). [< NL (Linnaeus), the genus name < Gk *hydr-* HYDR-[1] + NL *-astis* < ?]

hy·drate (hī′drāt), *n., v.,* **-drat·ed, -drat·ing.** —*n.* **1.** any of a class of compounds containing chemically combined water. In the case of some hydrates, as washing soda, $Na_2CO_3 \cdot 10H_2O$, the water is loosely held and is easily lost on heating; in others, as sulfuric acid, $SO_3 \cdot H_2O$, or H_2SO_4, it is strongly held as water of constitution. —*v.t., v.i.* **2.** to combine chemically with water. [1795–1805; HYDR-[1] + -ATE[2]] —**hy·dra′tion,** *n.*

hy·drat·ed (hī′drā tid), *adj.* **1.** chemically combined with water in its molecular form. **2.** (of paper pulp) beaten until gelatinous for making into water-resistant paper. [1800–10; HYDRATE + -ED[2]]

hy′drated alu′mina. See **aluminum hydroxide.**

hy′drated lime′. See **slaked lime.**

hydra′tion num′ber, the number of molecules of water with which an ion can combine in an aqueous solution of given concentration. [HYDRATE + -ION]

hy·dra·tor (hī′drā tər), *n.* **1.** something that hydrates. **2.** a compartment or drawer, as in a refrigerator, for keeping perishable foods fresh and preventing moisture loss. [HYDRATE + -OR[2]]

hydraul., hydraulics.

hy·drau·lic (hī drô′lik, -drol′ik), *adj.* **1.** operated by, moved by, or employing water or other liquids in motion. **2.** operated by the pressure created by forcing water, oil, or another liquid through a comparatively narrow pipe or orifice. **3.** of or pertaining to water or other liquids in motion. **4.** of or pertaining to hydraulics. **5.** hardening under water, as a cement. [1620–30; < L *hydraulicus* < Gk *hydraulikós* of a water organ. See HYDRAULUS, -IC] —**hy·drau′li·cal·ly,** *adv.*

hydrau′lic accu′mulator, 1. an apparatus in which gas, usually air, is used as a cushion or shock absorber in a hydraulic system. **2.** (in a hydraulic system) an apparatus for storing energy. [1875–80]

hydrau′lic brake′, a brake operated by fluid pressures in cylinders and connecting tubular lines. [1870–75]

hydrau′lic cement′, cement that can solidify under water. [1850–55]

hydrau′lic cou′pling. See **fluid coupling.**

hydrau′lic flu′id, a fluid, usually of low viscosity, as oil, used in a hydraulic system. [1940–45]

hydrau′lic lift′, an elevator operated by fluid pressure, esp. one used for raising automobiles in service stations and garages.

hydrau′lic min′ing, placer mining using a pressurized stream of water. Also called **hy·drau·lick·ing** (hī drô′li king, -drol′i king). [1855–60, *Amer.*]

hydrau′lic mo′tor, a motor that converts the kinetic or potential energy of a fluid into mechanical energy.

hydrau′lic pile′, *Building Trades.* a hollow pile through which a jet of water is forced to wash away the ground beneath.

hydrau′lic press′, a machine permitting a small force applied to a small piston to produce, through fluid pressure, a large force on a large piston. [1850–55]

hydrau′lic ra′dius, the ratio of the cross-sectional area to the perimeter of a pipe, outlet, or the like, through which a fluid is flowing. [1875–80]

hydrau′lic ram′, a device by which the energy of descending water is utilized to raise a part of the water to a height greater than that of the source. [1800–10]

hy·drau·lics (hī drô′liks, -drol′iks), *n.* (*used with a singular v.*) the science that deals with the laws governing water or other liquids in motion and their applications in engineering; practical or applied hydrodynamics. [1665–75; see HYDRAULIC, -ICS]

hydrau′lic torque′ convert′er, an apparatus in which a fluid, usually oil, transmits torque from one shaft to another, producing a different torque in the other shaft. Cf. **fluid coupling.**

hy·drau·lus (hī drô′ləs), *n., pl.* **-li** (-lī), **-lus·es.** a pipe organ of ancient Greece and Rome using water pressure to maintain the air supply. [1870–75; < L < Gk *hýdraulos* water organ, equiv. to *hydr-* HYDR-[1] + *aulós* pipe]

hy·dra·zine (hī′drə zēn′), *n.* **1.** Also called **diamine.** a colorless, oily, fuming liquid, N_2H_4, that is a weak base in solution and forms a large number of salts resembling ammonium salts: used chiefly as a reducing agent and a jet-propulsion fuel. **2.** a class of substances derived by replacing one or more hydrogen atoms in hydrazine by an organic group. [1885–90; HYDR-[2] + AZ- + -INE[2]]

hy·dra·zo·ate (hī′drə zō′āt), *n.* a salt of hydrazoic acid; azide. [1905–10; HYDRAZO(IC ACID) + -ATE[2]]

hy·dra·zo·ic (hī′drə zō′ik), *adj.* noting or pertaining to hydrazoic acid; triazoic. [1890–95; HYDR-[2] + AZ- + -IC]

hy′drazo′ic ac′id, a colorless, very explosive, poisonous liquid, HN_3, having a penetrating odor and irritating to the eyes and mucous membranes. Also called **azoimide.** [1890–95]

hy·dra·zone (hī′drə zōn′), *n.* any of a class of compounds containing the group $>C{=}NNH_2$. [1885–90; HYDR-[2] + AZ- + (KET)ONE]

hy·dre·mi·a (hī drē′mē ə), *n. Med.* the state of having an excess of water in the blood. Also, **hydraemia.** [HYDR-[1] + -EMIA] —**hy·dre′mic,** *adj.*

hy·dric[1] (hī′drik), *adj.* pertaining to or containing hydrogen. [1850–55; HYDR-[2] + -IC]

hy·dric[2] (hī′drik), *adj.* of, pertaining to, or adapted to a wet or moist environment. [1925–30; HYDR-[1] + -IC]

-hydric, a combining form of **hydric**[1]: *hexahydric.*

hy·dride (hī′drīd, -drid), *n.* a binary compound formed by hydrogen and another, usually more electropositive, element or group, as sodium hydride, NaH, or methyl hydride, CH_4. [1840–50; HYDR-[2] + -IDE]

hy·dril·la (hī dril′ə), *n.* a submerged aquatic plant, *Hydrilla verticillata,* native to the Old World, that has become a pest weed in U.S. lakes and waterways. [< NL (1814), the genus name, equiv. to L *hydr(a)* HYDRA + *-illa* dim. suffix]

hy·dri·od·ic (hī′drē od′ik), *adj.* of or derived from hydriodic acid. [1810–20; HYDR-[2] + IODIC]

hy′driod′ic ac′id, a colorless corrosive liquid, HI, an aqueous solution of hydrogen iodide. [1810–20]

hy·dro (hī′drō), *n., pl.* **-dros** for 2, 3, *adj.* —*n.* **1.** *Informal.* hydroelectric power. **2.** *Informal.* hydroplane. **3.** *Brit.* **a.** a bathhouse, hotel, or resort catering to people taking mineral-water health cures; spa. **b.** an establishment furnishing hydrotherapy. —*adj.* **4.** *Informal.* of, pertaining to, or furnishing water, water power, or hydroelectricity: *funds for new hydro projects.* [1880–85; by shortening of compounds with HYDRO-[1] (cf. -O); (def. 4) HYDRO-[1] analyzed as an adj.]

hydro-[1], a combining form meaning "water," used in the formation of compound words: *hydroplane; hydrogen.* Also, *esp. before a vowel,* **hydr-**[1]. [< Gk, comb. form of *hýdōr* water]

hydro-[2] a combining form representing **hydrogen** in compound words, denoting esp. a combination of hydrogen with some negative element or radical: *hydrobromic.* Also, *esp. before a vowel,* **hydr-**[2].

hy·dro·a (hī drō′ə), *n. Pathol.* any skin condition characterized by red vesicular areas. [< NL < Gk *hidrōia* (pl.) heat spots (lit., sweat eggs), equiv. to *hidr(ṓs)* sweat + *-ōia,* pl. of *ōión* egg; *-y-* of NL < *hydr-* HYDR-[1]]

hy·dro·aer·o·bics (hī′drō â rō′biks), *n.* (*used with a plural verb*) aerobic exercises performed in water, as in a swimming pool. [HYDRO- + AEROBICS]

hy·dro·air·plane (hī′drō âr′plān′), *n.* a hydroplane. [1905–10; HYDRO-[1] + AIRPLANE]

hy·dro·bi·ol·o·gy (hī′drō bī ol′ə jē), *n.* the study of aquatic organisms. [1925–30; HYDRO-[1] + BIOLOGY] —**hy·dro·bi·o·log·i·cal** (hī′drə bī′ə loj′i kəl), **hy′dro·bi′o·log′ic,** *adj.* —**hy′dro·bi′o·log′i·cal·ly,** *adv.* —**hy′dro·bi·ol′o·gist,** *n.*

hy·dro·bomb (hī′drə bom′), *n.* an aerial torpedo equipped with a rocket engine that propels it after the torpedo has entered the water. [HYDRO-[1] + BOMB]

hy·dro·bro·mic (hī′drə brō′mik), *adj. Chem.* of or derived from hydrobromic acid. [1830–40; HYDRO-[2] + BROMIC]

hy′drobro′mic ac′id, a colorless or faintly yellow corrosive liquid, HBr, an aqueous solution of hydrogen bromide. [1830–40]

hy·dro·bro·mide (hī′drə brō′mīd, -mid), *n.* a salt formed by the direct union of hydrobromic acid and an organic base, esp. an alkaloid, usually more soluble than the base. [1875–80; HYDROBROM(IC) + -IDE]

hy·dro·car·bon (hī′drə kär′bən, hī′drə kär′-), *n.* any of a class of compounds containing only hydrogen and carbon, as an alkane, methane, CH_4, an alkene, ethylene, C_2H_4, an alkyne, acetylene, C_2H_2, or an aromatic compound, benzene, C_6H_6. [1820–30; HYDRO-[2] + CARBON] —**hy·dro·car′bo·na′ceous,** *adj.*

hy·dro·cele (hī′drə sēl′), *n. Pathol.* an accumulation of serous fluid, usually about the testis. [1590–1600; < L < Gk *hydrokḗlē.* See HYDRO-[1], -CELE[1]]

hy·dro·cel·lu·lose (hī′drə sel′yə lōs′), *n.* a gelatinous substance obtained by the partial hydrolysis of cellulose, used chiefly in the manufacture of paper, mercerized cotton, and viscose rayon. [1875–80; HYDRO-[1] + CELLULOSE]

hy·dro·ce·phal·ic (hī′drō sə fal′ik), *adj. Pathol.* of or pertaining to hydrocephalus. Also, **hy·dro·ceph·a·lous** (hī′drə sef′ə ləs). [1805–15; HYDROCEPHAL(US) + -IC]

hy·dro·ceph·a·loid (hī′drə sef′ə loid′), *adj. Pathol.* resembling hydrocephalus. [1835–45; HYDROCEPHAL(US) + -OID]

hy·dro·ceph·a·lus (hī′drə sef′ə ləs), *n. Pathol.* an accumulation of serous fluid within the cranium, esp. in infancy, due to obstruction of the movement of cerebrospinal fluid, often causing great enlargement of the head; water on the brain. Also, **hy·dro·ceph·a·ly** (hī′drə sef′ə lē). [1660–70; < LL *hydrocephalus* (*morbus*) water-headed (sickness), trans. of Gk *tò hydroképhalon* (*páthos*). See HYDRO-[1], -CEPHALOUS]

hy·dro·chlo·ric (hī′drə klôr′ik, -klōr′-), *adj.* of or derived from hydrochloric acid. [1810–20; HYDRO-[2] + CHLORIC]

hy′drochlo′ric ac′id, a colorless or faintly yellow, corrosive, fuming liquid, HCl, used chiefly in chemical and industrial processes. [1825–35]

hy·dro·chlo·ride (hī′drə klôr′id, -id, -klōr′-), *n.* a salt, esp. of an alkaloid, formed by the direct union of hydrochloric acid with an organic base that makes the organic constituent more soluble. [1820–30; HYDRO-[2] + CHLORIDE]

hy·dro·chlo·ro·thi·a·zide (hī′drə klôr′ə thī′ə zīd′, -klōr′-), *n. Pharm.* a crystalline, water-insoluble powder, $C_7H_8ClN_3O_4S_2$, used as a diuretic and in the treatment of hypertension. [1955–60; HYDRO-[2] + CHLOROTHIAZIDE]

hy′dro·cin·nam′ic ac′id (hī′drō si nam′ik, -drəsin′ə mik, hī′-), a white crystalline compound, $C_9H_{10}O_2$, with a floral odor, used in perfumes and flavoring. [HYDRO-[2] + CINNAMIC]

hy′drocinnam′ic al′dehyde, a colorless liquid, $C_9H_{10}O$, having a floral odor, used in perfumery and flavoring. Also, **hy·dro·cin·na·mal·de·hyde** (hī′drōsin′ə mal′də hīd′).

hy·dro·col·loid (hī′drə kol′oid), *n.* a substance that forms a colloid when combined with water. [1925–30; HYDRO-[1] + COLLOID] —**hy·dro·col·loi·dal** (hī′drō kə loid′l), *adj.*

hy·dro·cool·ing (hī′drō ko͞o′ling), *n.* the process or technique of arresting the ripening of fruits and vegetables after harvesting by immersion in ice water. [1940–45; HYDRO-[1] + COOL + -ING[1]]

hy·dro·cor·al (hī′drə kôr′əl, -kor′-), *n.* any colonial marine animal of the hydrozoan order Stylasterina having a calcareous skeleton resembling that of the true corals. [< NL *Hydrocorallia* or *Hydrocorallinae;* see HYDRO-[1], CORAL, CORALLINE]

hy·dro·cor·ti·sone (hī′drə kôr′tə zōn′, -sōn′), *n.* **1.** *Biochem.* a steroid hormone, $C_{21}H_{30}O_5$, of the adrenal cortex, active in carbohydrate and protein metabolism. **2.** *Pharm.* Also called **cortisol.** a powerful anti-inflammatory drug, $C_{21}H_{30}O_5$, used in the treatment of shock, allergies, certain forms of arthritis, and other conditions. [1950–55; HYDRO-[2] + CORTISONE]

hy·dro·crack·er (hī′drə krak′ər), *n.* a high-pressure processing unit used for hydrocracking. [1960–65; HYDROCRACK(ING) + -ER[1]]

hy·dro·crack·ing (hī′drə krak′ing), *n.* the cracking of petroleum or the like in the presence of hydrogen. [1935–40; HYDRO-[2] + CRACKING]

hy·dro·cy·an·ic (hī′drō sī an′ik), *adj.* of or derived from hydrocyanic acid. [1810–20; HYDRO-[2] + CYANIC]

hy′drocyan′ic ac′id, a colorless, highly poisonous liquid, HCN, an aqueous solution of hydrogen cyanide. Also called **prussic acid.** [1810–20]

hy·dro·de·sul·fu·ri·za·tion (hī′drō dē sul′fyər ə-zā′shən, -fər ə-), *n.* desulfurization by catalytic agents of the sulfur-rich hydrocarbons obtained from petroleum or the like during cracking or hydrocracking. Also, **hy′·dro·de·sul′phur·i·za′tion.** [1945–50; HYDRO-[2] + DESULFURIZATION]

Hy·dro·Di·u·ril (hī′drō dī′ər il), *Pharm., Trademark.* a brand of hydrochlorothiazide.

hy·dro·dy·nam·ic (hī′drō dī nam′ik, -di-), *adj.* **1.** pertaining to forces in or motions of liquids. **2.** of or pertaining to hydrodynamics. [1770–80; HYDRO-[1] + DYNAMIC] —**hy′dro·dy·nam′i·cal·ly,** *adv.*

hy·dro·dy·nam·i·cist (hī′drō dī nam′ə sist, -di-), *n.* a specialist in hydrodynamics. [1960–65; HYDRODYNAMIC(S) + -IST]

hy·dro·dy·nam·ics (hī′drō dī nam′iks, -di-), *n.* (*used with a singular v.*) the branch of fluid dynamics that deals with liquids, including hydrostatics and hydrokinetics. Also called **hydromechanics.** [HYDRO-[1] + DYNAMICS]

hy·dro·e·lec·tric (hī′drō i lek′trik), *adj.* pertaining to the generation and distribution of electricity derived from the energy of falling water or any other hydraulic source. [1825–35; HYDRO-[1] + ELECTRIC] —**hy·dro·e·lec·tric·i·ty** (hī′drō i lek tris′i tē, -ē′lek-), *n.*

hy·dro·fluor·ic (hī′drə flo͞or′ik, -flôr′-, -flōr′-), *adj.* of or derived from hydrofluoric acid. [1815–25; HYDRO-[2] + -FLUORIC]

hy′drofluor′ic ac′id, a colorless, fuming, corrosive liquid, HF, an aqueous solution of hydrogen fluoride, used chiefly for etching glass. [1815–25]

hydrofoil (def. 2b)

hy·dro·foil (hī′drə foil′), *n.* **1.** *Naval Archit.* a surface form creating a thrust against water in a direction perpendicular to the plane approximated by the surface. **2.** *Naut.* **a.** a winglike member having this form, designed to lift the hull of a moving vessel. **b.** a vessel equipped with hydrofoils. [1915–20; HYDRO-[1] + FOIL[2]]

hy·dro·form·ing (hī′drə fôr′ming), *n.* the production of high-octane aromatic compounds for motor fuels by catalytic reforming of naphthas in the presence of hydrogen. [1931; HYDRO-[2] + (RE)FORMING]

CONCISE PRONUNCIATION KEY: act, cāpe, dâre, pärt; set, ēqual; if, īce; ox, ōver, ôrder, oil, bo͝ok, bo͞ot, out; up, ûrge; child; sing; shoe; thin, *th*at; zh as in *treasure.* ə = *a* as in *alone, e* as in *system, i* as in *easily, o* as in *gallop, u* as in *circus;* ᵊ as in *fire* (fīᵊr), *hour* (ouᵊr). l and n can serve as syllabic consonants, as in *cradle* (krād′l), and *button* (but′n). See the full key inside the front cover.

hy·dro·for·myl·a·tion (hī′drə fôr′mə lā′shən), *n.* the addition of a hydrogen atom and the formyl group to a double bond of a hydrocarbon by reaction with a mixture of carbon monoxide and hydrogen in the presence of a catalyst. [1945–50; HYDRO-[2] + FORMYL + -ATION]

hy·dro·frac·tur·ing (hī′drə frak′chə ring), *n.* a method of increasing the permeability of rocks penetrated by an oil or gas well by pumping in water and sand under pressure to open up cracks in the rocks. [1970–75; HYDRO-[1] + FRACTURE + -ING[1]]

hy·dro·gel (hī′drə jel′), *n.* a gel whose liquid constituent is water. [1890–95; HYDRO-[1] + GEL]

hy·dro·gen (hī′drə jən), *n.* a colorless, odorless, flammable gas that combines chemically with oxygen to form water: the lightest of the known elements. *Symbol:* H; *at. wt.:* 1.00797; *at. no.:* 1; *density:* 0.0899 g/l at 0°C and 760 mm pressure. [1785–95; < F *hydrogène.* See HYDRO-[1], -GEN]

hy·dro·gen·ate (hī′drə jə nāt′, hī droj′ə-), *v.t.,* **-at·ed, -at·ing.** to combine or treat with hydrogen, esp. to add hydrogen to the molecule of (an unsaturated organic compound). Also, **hydrogenize.** [1800–10; HYDROGEN + -ATE[1]] —**hy′dro·gen·a′tion,** *n.*

hy′drogen bomb′, a bomb, more powerful than an atomic bomb, that derives its explosive energy from the thermonuclear fusion reaction of hydrogen isotopes. Also called **H-bomb, fusion bomb, thermonuclear bomb.** [1945–50]

hy′drogen bond′, a type of chemical bond in which a hydrogen atom that has a covalent link with one of the electronegative atoms (F, N, O) forms an electrostatic link with another electronegative atom in the same or another molecule. [1920–25]

hy′drogen bro′mide, a colorless gas, HBr, having a pungent odor: the anhydride of hydrobromic acid. [1895–1900]

hy′drogen chlo′ride, a colorless gas, HCl, having a pungent odor: the anhydride of hydrochloric acid. [1865–70]

hy′drogen cy′anide, a colorless poisonous gas, HCN, having a bitter almondlike odor: in aqueous solution it forms hydrocyanic acid. [1880–85]

hy′drogen elec′trode, a standard reference electrode with a potential of zero, used in pH measurements, consisting of a platinum-black surface covered with hydrogen bubbles. [1895–1900]

hy′drogen fluor′ide, a colorless corrosive gas, HF, the anhydride of hydrofluoric acid, used chiefly as a catalyst and in the fluorination of hydrocarbons. [1905–10]

hy′drogen i′odide, a colorless gas, HI, having a suffocating odor: the anhydride of hydriodic acid. [1895–1900]

hy′drogen i′on, ionized hydrogen of the form H^+, found in aqueous solutions of all acids. [1895–1900]

hy·dro·gen·ize (hī′drə jə nīz′, hī droj′ə-), *v.t.,* **-ized, -iz·ing.** hydrogenate. Also, *esp. Brit.,* **hy′dro·gen·ise′.** [HYDROGEN + -IZE] —**hy′dro·gen·i·za′tion,** *n.*

hy·dro·gen·ol·y·sis (hī′drō jə nol′ə sis), *n., pl.* **-ses** (-sēz′). decomposition of a compound resulting from its interaction with hydrogen. [1930–35; HYDROGEN + -O- + -LYSIS]

hy·drog·e·nous (hī droj′ə nəs), *adj.* of or containing hydrogen. [1785–95; HYDROGEN + -OUS]

hy′drogen perox′ide, a colorless, unstable, oily liquid, H_2O_2, an aqueous solution of which is used chiefly as an antiseptic and a bleaching agent. [1870–75]

hy′drogen sul′fide, a colorless, flammable, water-soluble, cumulatively poisonous gas, H_2S, having the odor of rotten eggs: used chiefly in the manufacture of chemicals, in metallurgy, and as a reagent in laboratory analysis. Also called **sulfureted hydrogen.** [1870–75]

hy·dro·ge·ol·o·gy (hī′drō jē ol′ə jē), *n.* the science dealing with the occurrence and distribution of underground water. Also called **hydrology, geohydrology.** [1815–25; HYDRO-[1] + GEOLOGY] —**hy·dro·ge·o·log·i·cal** (hī′drə jē′ə loj′i kəl), **hy′dro·ge′o·log′ic,** *adj.* —**hy′dro·ge·ol′o·gist,** *n.*

hy·dro·graph (hī′drə graf′, -gräf′), *n.* a graph of the water level or rate of flow of a body of water as a function of time, showing the seasonal change. [1890–95; HYDRO-[1] + -GRAPH]

hy·drog·ra·phy (hī drog′rə fē), *n.* **1.** the science of the measurement, description, and mapping of the surface waters of the earth, with special reference to their use for navigation. **2.** those parts of a map, collectively, that represent surface waters. [1550–60; HYDRO-[1] + -GRAPHY] —**hy·drog′ra·pher,** *n.* —**hy·dro·graph·ic** (hī′drə graf′ik), **hy′dro·graph′i·cal,** *adj.* —**hy′dro·graph′i·cal·ly,** *adv.*

hy·droid (hī′droid), *adj.* **1.** noting or pertaining to that form of hydrozoan that is asexual and grows into branching colonies by budding. —*n.* **2.** the phase of a hydrozoan coelenterate that consists of polyp forms usually growing as an attached colony. [1860–65; HYDR(A) + -OID]

hy·dro·ki·net·ic (hī′drō ki net′ik, -kī-), *adj.* **1.** pertaining to the motion of liquids. **2.** of or pertaining to hydrokinetics. Also, **hy′dro·ki·net′i·cal.** [1870–75; HYDRO-[1] + KINETIC]

hy·dro·ki·net·ics (hī′drō ki net′iks, -kī-), *n.* (*used with a singular v.*) the branch of hydrodynamics that deals with the laws governing liquids or gases in motion. [1870–75; see HYDROKINETIC, -ICS]

HYDROLANT (hī′drə lant′), *n.* an urgent warning of navigational dangers in the Atlantic Ocean, issued by the U.S. Navy Hydrographic Office. Cf. **HYDROPAC.** [HYDRO-[1] + (AT)LANT(IC)]

hy·dro·lase (hī′drə lās′, -lāz′), *n. Biochem.* an enzyme that catalyzes hydrolysis. Also called **hy·dro·lyst** (hī′drə list). [1920–25; HYDR-[1] + -OL[1] + -ASE]

hy′drolog′ic cy′cle, the natural sequence through which water passes into the atmosphere as water vapor, precipitates to earth in liquid or solid form, and ultimately returns to the atmosphere through evaporation. [1955–60; HYDROLOG(Y) + -IC]

hy·drol·o·gy (hī drol′ə jē), *n.* **1.** the science dealing with the occurrence, circulation, distribution, and properties of the waters of the earth and its atmosphere. **2.** hydrogeology; geohydrology. [1755–65; HYDRO-[1] + -LOGY] —**hy·dro·log·ic** (hī′drə loj′ik), **hy′dro·log′i·cal,** *adj.* —**hy′dro·log′i·cal·ly,** *adv.* —**hy·drol′o·gist,** *n.*

hy·drol·y·sate (hī drol′ə sāt′), *n.* any compound formed by hydrolysis. [1910–15; HYDROLYS(IS) + -ATE[2]]

hy·drol·y·sis (hī drol′ə sis), *n., pl.* **-ses** (-sēz′). chemical decomposition in which a compound is split into other compounds by reacting with water. [1875–80; HYDRO-[1] + -LYSIS]

hy·dro·lyte (hī′drə līt′), *n.* a substance subjected to hydrolysis. [1875–80; HYDRO-[1] + -LYTE[1]]

hy·dro·lyt·ic (hī′drə lit′ik), *adj.* producing, noting, or resulting in hydrolysis. [1870–75; HYDRO-[1] + -LYTIC]

hy·dro·lyze (hī′drə līz′), *v.t., v.i.,* **-lyzed, -lyz·ing.** to subject or be subjected to hydrolysis. Also, *esp. Brit.,* **hy′dro·lyse′.** [1875–80; HYDRO(LYSIS) + -LYZE] —**hy′·dro·lyz′a·ble,** *adj.* —**hy′dro·ly·za′tion,** *n.* —**hy′dro·lyz′er,** *n.*

hy′drolyzed veg′etable pro′tein, a vegetable protein broken down into amino acids and used as a food additive to enhance flavor, esp. in soups, sauces, and processed meats. *Abbr.:* HVP, H.V.P.

hy·dro·mag·net·ics (hī′drō mag net′iks), *n.* (*used with a singular v.*) magnetohydrodynamics. [1950–55; HYDRO-[1] + MAGNETICS]

hy·dro·man·cy (hī′drə man′sē), *n.* divination by means of the motions or appearance of water. [1585–95; earlier *hydromantie, -cie* (< MF) << LGk *hydromanteía* divination by water; r. ME *ydromancye* < MF *ydromancie* < L. See HYDRO-[1], -MANCY] —**hy′dro·manc′er,** *n.* —**hy′dro·man′tic,** *adj.*

hy·dro·me·chan·ics (hī′drō mə kan′iks), *n.* (*used with a singular v.*) hydrodynamics. [1815–25; HYDRO-[1] + MECHANICS] —**hy′dro·me·chan′i·cal,** *adj.*

hy·dro·me·du·sa (hī′drō mi do͞o′sə, -zə, -dyo͞o′-), *n., pl.* **-sae** (-sē). the medusa form of a hydrozoan. [1885–90; < NL; see HYDRA, -O-, MEDUSA] —**hy′dro·me·du′·san,** *adj.*

hy·dro·mel (hī′drə mel′), *n.* a liquor consisting of honey and water that, when fermented, becomes mead. [1555–65; < L < Gk *hydrómeli,* equiv. to *hydro-* HYDRO-[1] + *méli* honey; r. late ME *ydromel* < ML (var. of *hydromel*)]

hy·dro·met·al·lur·gy (hī′drə met′l ûr′jē), *n.* the technique or process of extracting metals at ordinary temperatures by leaching ore with liquid solvents. [1885–90; HYDRO-[1] + METALLURGY] —**hy′dro·met′al·lur′gi·cal,** *adj.*

hy·dro·me·te·or (hī′drə mē′tē ər, -ôr′), *n.* liquid water or ice in the atmosphere in various forms, as rain, ice crystals, hail, fog, or clouds. Cf. **lithometeor.** [1855–60; HYDRO-[1] + METEOR]

hy·dro·me·te·or·ol·o·gy (hī′drə mē′tē ə rol′ə jē), *n.* the study of atmospheric water, esp. precipitation, as it affects agriculture, water supply, flood control, power generation, etc. [1860–65; HYDRO-[1] + METEOROLOGY] —**hy′dro·me′te·or·ol′o·gist,** *n.* —**hy·dro·me·te·or·o·log·i·cal** (hī′drə mē′tē ər ə loj′i kəl), *adj.*

hy·drom·e·ter (hī drom′i tər), *n.* an instrument for determining the specific gravity of a liquid, commonly consisting of a graduated tube weighted to float upright in the liquid whose specific gravity is being measured. [1665–75; HYDRO-[1] + METER] —**hy·dro·met·ric** (hī′drə-me′trik), **hy′dro·met′ri·cal,** *adj.* —**hy·drom′e·try,** *n.*

hy·dro·mor·phic (hī′drə môr′fik), *adj.* of or pertaining to soil having characteristics that are developed when there is excess water all or part of the time. [1935–40; HYDRO-[1] + -MORPHIC]

hy·dro·mulch (hī′drə mulch′), *v.t.* to spread mulch on (a field, garden, etc.) in a stream of water propelled through a hose. [HYDRO-[1] + MULCH]

hy·dro·naut (hī′drə nôt′, -not′), *n.* a person trained to work in deep-sea vessels for research and rescue purposes. [1965–70, *Amer.*; HYDRO-[1] + (AERO)NAUT]

hy·dro·ne·phro·sis (hī′drō nə frō′sis), *n. Pathol.* dilation of the branches and pelvic cavity of the kidney, caused by an accumulation of urine resulting from obstruction of normal outflow. [1840–50; HYDRO-[1] + NEPHROSIS]

hy·dron·ic (hī dron′ik), *adj.* of or pertaining to a heating system for a building in which the medium for carrying heat throughout the structure is circulating water, esp. when the circulation is aided by a pump. [1945–50; prob. HYDR-[1] + (ELECTR)ONIC]

hy·dro·ni·tro·gen (hī′drə nī′trə jən), *n.* a chemical compound containing only hydrogen and nitrogen. [HYDRO-[2] + NITROGEN]

hy·dro′ni·um i′on (hī drō′nē əm), the hydrogen ion bonded to a molecule of water, H_3O^+, the form in which hydrogen ions are found in aqueous solution. Also called **oxonium ion.** [< G *Hydronium* (1907), contr. of *Hydroxonium;* see HYDRO-[2], OXONIUM ION]

HYDROPAC (hī′drə pak′), *n.* an urgent warning of navigational dangers in the Pacific Ocean, issued by the U.S. Navy Hydrographic Office. Cf. **HYDROLANT.** [HYDRO-[1] + PAC(IFIC)]

hy·drop·a·thy (hī drop′ə thē), *n.* the curing of disease by the internal and external use of water. [1835–45; HYDRO-[1] + -PATHY] —**hy·dro·path·ic** (hī′drə path′ik), **hy′dro·path′i·cal,** *adj.* —**hy·drop′a·thist, hy′dro·path′,** *n.*

hy·dro·per·ox·ide (hī′drō pə rok′sīd), *n.* any chemical compound having the general formula, ROOH, where R is an element or an organic group. [1920–25; HYDRO-[2] + PEROXIDE]

hy·dro·phane (hī′drə fān′), *n.* a partly translucent variety of opal, which becomes more translucent or transparent when immersed in water. [1775–85; HYDRO-[1] + -PHANE] —**hy·droph·a·nous** (hī drof′ə nəs), *adj.*

hy·dro·phil·ic (hī′drə fil′ik), *adj. Chem.* **1.** having a strong affinity for water. —*n.* **2.** See **soft lens.** [1900–05; HYDRO-[1] + -PHILIC]

hy·droph·i·lous (hī drof′ə ləs), *adj. Bot.* **1.** pollinated by the agency of water. **2.** hydrophytic. [1850–55; < NL *hydrophilus.* See HYDRO-[1], -PHILOUS] —**hy·droph′i·ly,** *n.*

hy·dro·phobe (hī′drə fōb′), *n. Chem.* a hydrophobic substance. [1920–25; HYDRO-[1] + -PHOBE]

hy·dro·pho·bi·a (hī′drə fō′bē ə), *n.* **1.** rabies. **2.** an abnormal or unnatural dread of water. [1540–50; < LL < Gk *hydrophobía.* See HYDRO-[1], -PHOBIA]

hy·dro·pho·bic (hī′drə fō′bik), *adj.* **1.** of or pertaining to hydrophobia. **2.** *Chem.* having little or no affinity for water. Cf. **oleophilic.** [1640–50; HYDROPHOBE + -IC] —**hy·dro·pho·bic·i·ty** (hī′drə fō bis′i tē), *n.*

hy·dro·phone (hī′drə fōn′), *n.* **1.** a device for locating sources of sound under water, as for detecting submarines by the noise of their engines. **2.** an instrument employing the principles of the microphone, used to detect the flow of water through a pipe. **3.** *Med.* an instrument used in auscultation, whereby sounds are intensified through a column of water. [1855–60; HYDRO-[1] + -PHONE]

hy·dro·phyl·la·ceous (hī′drō fi lā′shəs), *adj.* belonging to the Hydrophyllaceae, the waterleaf family of plants. Cf. **waterleaf family.** [< NL *Hydrophyllace(ae)* (*Hydrophyll(um)* the type genus (see HYDRO-[1], -PHYLL) + *-aceae* -ACEAE) + -OUS]

hy·dro·phyte (hī′drə fīt′), *n.* a plant that grows in water or very moist ground; an aquatic plant. [1825–35; HYDRO-[1] + -PHYTE] —**hy·dro·phyt·ic** (hī′drə fit′ik), *adj.* —**hy′dro·phyt′ism,** *n.*

hy·drop·ic (hī drop′ik), *adj. Pathol.* dropsical. Also, **hy·drop′i·cal.** [1580–90; < L *hydrōpicus* < Gk *hydrōpikós,* equiv. to *hydrōp-* (s. of *hýdrōps*) HYDROPS + *-ikos* -IC; r. ME *ydropike* < OF < L] —**hy·drop′i·cal·ly,** *adv.*

hy·dro·plane (hī′drə plān′), *n., v.,* **-planed, -plan·ing.** —*n.* **1.** a seaplane. **2.** an attachment to an airplane enabling it to glide on the water. **3.** a light, high-powered boat, esp. one with hydrofoils or a stepped bottom, designed to plane along the surface of the water at very high speeds. **4.** a horizontal rudder for submerging or elevating a submarine. —*v.i.* **5.** to skim over water in the manner of a hydroplane. **6.** to travel in a hydroplane. **7.** Also, **aquaplane.** (of a vehicular tire or vehicle) to ride on a film of water on a wet surface with a resulting decrease in braking and steering effectiveness. [1900–05; HYDRO-[1] + PLANE[1]]

hy·dro·plan·er (hī′drə plā′nər), *n.* a person who pilots a hydroplane, esp. a professional speedboat racer. [HYDROPLANE + -ER[1]]

hy·dro·pneu·ma·ti·za·tion (hī′drə no͞o′mə tə zā′shən, -nyo͞o′-), *n.* utilization of air pressure in the housing of a water turbine to keep the level of water that has been used from rising to interfere with the rotor blades. [HYDRO-[1] + PNEUMAT- + -IZATION]

hy·dro·pon·ics (hī′drə pon′iks), *n.* (*used with a singular v.*) the cultivation of plants by placing the roots in liquid nutrient solutions rather than in soil; soilless growth of plants. Cf. **aeroculture, geoponics** (def. 2). [1935–40; HYDRO-[1] + (GEO)PONICS] —**hy′dro·pon′ic,** *adj.* —**hy′dro·pon′i·cal·ly,** *adv.* —**hy·drop·o·nist** (hī drop′ə nist), **hy′dro·pon′i·cist,** *n.*

hy·dro·pow·er (hī′drə pou′ər), *n.* hydroelectric power. [1930–35; HYDRO-[1] + POWER]

hy·drops (hī′drops), *n.* (*used with a singular v.*) *Pathol.* (formerly) edema. Also called **hy·drop·sy** (hī′drop sē). [1700–10; < L *hydrōps* < Gk *hýdrōps* DROPSY, equiv. to *hydr-* HYDR-[1] + *-ōps* appearance (lit., eye, face), appar. by confusion with *ópsis* appearance] —**hy·drop′tic,** *adj.*

hy·dro·qui·none (hī′drō kwi nōn′, -drə kwin′ōn), *n. Chem.* a white, crystalline compound, $C_6H_6O_2$, formed by the reduction of quinone: used chiefly in photography and to inhibit autoxidation reactions. Also called **hy·dro·quin·ol** (hī′drə kwin′ôl, -ol), **quinol.** [1860–65; HYDRO-[1] + QUINONE]

hy·dro·rhi·za (hī′drə rī′zə), *n., pl.* **-zae** (-zē). the rootlike base of a hydroid colony, by which it is attached to the substratum. [1860–65; < NL; see HYDRO-[1], -RHIZA] —**hy′dro·rhi′zal,** *adj.*

hydros., hydrostatics.

hy·dro·scope (hī′drə skōp′), *n.* an optical device for viewing objects below the surface of water. [1670–80; HYDRO-[1] + -SCOPE] —**hy·dro·scop·ic** (hī′drə skop′ik), **hy′dro·scop′i·cal,** *adj.* —**hy·dro·sco·pic·i·ty** (hī′drə-skō pis′i tē), *n.*

hy·dro·seed (hī′drə sēd′), *v.t.* to sow (a field, lawn, etc.) with seed by distribution in a stream of water propelled through a hose. [HYDRO-[1] + SEED]

hy·dro·sere (hī′drə sēr′), *n. Ecol.* a sere originating in water. [1925–30; HYDRO-[1] + SERE[2]]

hy·dro-ski (hī′drō skē′), *n., pl.* **-skis.** a hydrofoil attached to a seaplane to aid in takeoffs and landings. [1950–55]

hy·dro·sol (hī′drə sôl′, -sol′), *n. Physical Chem.* a colloidal suspension in water. [1860–65; HYDRO-[1] + SOL(UTION)]

CONCISE ETYMOLOGY KEY: <, descended or borrowed from; >, whence; b., blend of, blended; c., cognate with; cf., compare; deriv., derivative; equiv., equivalent; imit., imitative; obl., oblique; r., replacing; s., stem; sp., spelling, spelled; resp., respelling, respelled; trans., translation; ?, origin unknown; *, unattested; ‡, probably earlier than. See the full key inside the front cover.

hy·dro·so·ma (hī′drə sō′mə), *n., pl.* **-ma·ta** (-mə tə). *Zool.* hydrosome. [< NL]

hy·dro·some (hī′drə sōm′), *n. Zool.* the entire body of a compound hydrozoan. [1860–65; *hydro-* (comb. form repr. HYDRA) + -SOME³]

hy·dro·sphere (hī′drə sfēr′), *n.* the water on or surrounding the surface of the globe, including the water of the oceans and the water in the atmosphere. [1885–90; HYDRO-¹ + -SPHERE]

hy·dro·stat (hī′drə stat′), *n.* **1.** an electrical device for detecting the presence of water, as from overflow or leakage. **2.** any of various devices for preventing injury to a steam boiler when its water sinks below a certain level. [1855–60; HYDRO-¹ + -STAT]

hy·dro·stat·ic (hī′drə stat′ik), *adj.* of or pertaining to hydrostatics. Also, **hy′dro·stat′i·cal.** [1665–75; HYDRO-¹ + STATIC] **—hy′dro·stat′i·cal·ly,** *adv.*

hy·dro·stat·ics (hī′drə stat′iks), *n.* (*used with a singular v.*) the branch of hydrodynamics that deals with the statics of fluids, usually confined to the equilibrium and pressure of liquids. [1650–60; see HYDROSTATIC, -ICS]

hy·dro·sul·fate (hī′drə sul′fāt), *n.* a salt formed by the direct union of sulfuric acid with an organic base, esp. an alkaloid, and usually more soluble than the base. Also, **hy′dro·sul′phate.** [1820–30; HYDRO-² + SULFATE]

hy·dro·sul·fide (hī′drə sul′fīd, -fid), *n.* a compound containing the univalent group –HS. Also, **hy′dro·sul′·phide.** [1840–50; HYDRO-² + SULFIDE]

hy·dro·sul·fite (hī′drə sul′fīt), *n. Chem.* **1.** hyposulfite (def. 1). **2.** See **sodium hydrosulfite.** Also, **hy′·dro·sul′phite.** [1860–65; HYDROSULF(UROUS) + -ITE¹]

hy·dro·sul·fu·rous (hī′drō sul fyŏŏr′əs, -drə sul′fər-əs), *adj.* hyposulfurous. Also, **hy′dro·sul·phu′rous.** [1850–55; HYDRO-² + SULFUROUS]

hy·dro·tax·is (hī′drə tak′sis), *n. Biol.* oriented movement toward or away from water. [1895–1900; HYDRO-¹ + -TAXIS] **—hy·dro·tac·tic** (hī′drə tak′tik), *adj.*

hy·dro·the·ca (hī′drə thē′kə), *n., pl.* **-cae** (-kē). *Zool.* the part of the perisarc covering a hydranth. [1870–75; < NL; see HYDRO-¹, THECA] **—hy′dro·the′cal,** *adj.*

hy·dro·ther·a·peu·tics (hī′drō ther′ə pyōō′tiks), *n.* (*used with a singular v.*) hydrotherapy. [1835–45; HYDRO-¹ + THERAPEUTICS] **—hy′dro·ther′a·peu′tic,** *adj.*

hy·dro·ther·a·py (hī′drə ther′ə pē), *n.* **1.** the branch of therapeutics that deals with the curative use of water. **2.** the treatment of physical disability, injury, or illness by immersion of all or part of the body in water to facilitate movement, promote wound healing, relieve pain, etc., usually under the supervision of a trained therapist. [1875–80; HYDRO-¹ + THERAPY] **—hy′dro·ther′a·pist,** *n.*

hy·dro·ther·mal (hī′drə thûr′məl), *adj. Geol.* noting or pertaining to the action of hot, aqueous solutions or gases within or on the surface of the earth. [1840–50; HYDRO-¹ + THERMAL] **—hy′dro·ther′mal·ly,** *adv.*

hy′drother′mal vent′, *Oceanog., Geol.* an opening on the floor of the sea from which hot, mineral-rich solutions issue. Cf. **vent¹** (def. 2).

hy·dro·tho·rax (hī′drə thôr′aks, -thōr′-), *n. Pathol.* the presence of serous fluid in one or both pleural cavities. [1785–95; HYDRO-¹ + THORAX] **—hy·dro·tho·rac·ic** (hī′drō thə ras′ik), *adj.*

hy·dro·trop·ic (hī′drə trop′ik, -trō′pik), *adj. Biol.* turning or tending in a particular direction with reference to moisture. [1915–20; HYDRO-¹ + -TROPIC]

hy·drot·ro·pism (hī dro′trə piz′əm), *n. Biol.* oriented growth in response to water. [1880–85; HYDRO-¹ + -TROPISM]

hy·drous (hī′drəs), *adj.* **1.** containing water. **2.** *Chem.* containing water or its elements in some kind of union, as in hydrates or hydroxides. [1820–30; HYDR-¹ + -OUS]

hy·drox·ide (hī drok′sīd, -sid), *n.* a chemical compound containing the hydroxyl group. [1820–30; HYDR-² + OXIDE]

hydrox′ide i′on, the anion OH^-. Also called **hydroxyl ion.** [1950–55]

hydroxy-, a combining form used in the names of chemical compounds in which the hydroxyl group is present: *hydroxyketone.*

hy·drox′y·a·ce′tic ac′id (hī drok′sē ə sē′tik, -ə set′ik, -drok′-). See **glycolic acid.** [HYDROXY- + ACETIC]

hydrox′y ac′id, 1. an organic acid containing both a carboxyl and a hydroxyl group. **2.** any of a class of organic acids containing a hydroxyl group and showing properties of both an alcohol and an acid. [1895–1900]

hy·drox·y·ap·a·tite (hī drok′sē ap′ə tīt′), *n.* a mineral, $Ca_{10}(PO_4)_6OH_2$, that is the principal storage form of calcium and phosphorus in bone. [1910–15; HYDROXY- + APATITE]

hy·drox·y·ben·zene (hī drok′si ben′zēn, -ben zēn′), *n.* phenol (def. 1). [HYDROXY- + BENZENE]

hy·drox′y·bu·tyr′ic ac′id (hī drok′sē byōō tir′ik, -drok′-), *Biochem.* See **ketone body.** [1875–80; HYDROXY- + BUTYRIC]

hy·drox·y·chlo·ro·quine (hī drok′si klôr′ə kwēn′, -kwin, -klōr′-), *n. Pharm.* a colorless crystalline solid, $C_{18}H_{26}ClN_3O$, used in the treatment of malaria, lupus erythematosus, and rheumatoid arthritis. [HYDROXY- + CHLOROQUINE]

hy·drox·y·ke·tone (hī drok′si kē′tōn), *n.* a ketone containing a hydroxyl group. [HYDROXY- + KETONE]

hy·drox·yl (hī drok′səl), *adj.* containing the hydroxyl group. Also, **hy·drox′y.** [1865–70; HYDR-² + OX(Y)- + -YL] **—hy·drox·yl·ic,** (hī′drok sil′ik), *adj.*

hy·drox·yl·a·mine (hī drok′sə lə mēn′, -səl am′in), *n.* an unstable, weakly basic, crystalline compound, NH_3O, used as a reducing agent, analytical reagent, and chemical intermediate. [1865–70; HYDROXYL + -AMINE]

hy·drox·y·lase (hī drok′sə lās′, -lāz′), *n. Biochem.* any enzyme that catalyzes the introduction of a hydroxyl group into a substance. [1950–55; HYDROXYL + -ASE]

hydrox′yl group′, the univalent group –OH, as in inorganic compounds, such as sodium hydroxide, NaOH, or as in organic compounds, such as ethyl alcohol, C_2H_6O. Also called **hydrox′yl rad′ical.** [1880–85]

hydrox′yl i′on. See **hydroxide ion.**

hy·drox·y·naph·tha·lene (hī drok′si naf′thə lēn′, -nap′-), *n.* naphthol. [HYDROXY- + NAPHTHALENE]

hy·drox·y·pro·line (hī drok′si prō′lēn, -lin), *n. Biochem.* a nutritionally nonessential amino acid, $C_5H_9NO_3$, found chiefly in collagen. [1900–05; HYDROXY- + PROLINE]

hy·drox·y·u·re·a (hī drok′sē yŏŏ rē′ə, -yŏŏr′ē ə), *n. Pharm.* a synthetic compound, $CH_4N_2O_2$, used in cancer therapy. [1945–50; HYDROXY- + UREA]

hy·drox·y·zine (hī drok′sə zēn′), *n. Pharm.* an antihistaminic compound, $C_{21}H_{27}ClN_2O_2$, used in the treatment of allergy, nausea, and anxiety. [1955–60; HYDROXY- + (PIPERA)ZINE]

hy·dro·zinc·ite (hī′drō zing′kīt), *n. Mineral.* a hydrous zinc carbonate, $Zn_5(CO_3)_2(OH)_6$, an important ore of zinc in some localities. [1850–55; < G *Hydrozinkit;* see HYDRO-, ZINCITE]

hy·dro·zo·an (hī′drə zō′ən), *n.* **1.** any freshwater or marine coelenterate of the class Hydrozoa, including free-swimming or attached types, as the hydra, in which one developmental stage, either the polyp or medusa, is absent, and colonial types, as the Portuguese man-of-war, in which both medusa and polyp stages are present in a single colony. *—adj.* **2.** belonging or pertaining to the Hydrozoa. [1875–80; < NL *Hydrozo(a)* (see HYDRO-¹, -ZOA) + -AN]

Hy·drus (hī′drəs), *n., gen.* **-dri** (-drī). *Astron.* the Water Snake, a southern constellation between Eridanus and Octans. [< L < Gk *hýdros* water serpent]

hy·e·na (hī ē′nə), *n.* a doglike carnivore of the family Hyaenidae, of Africa, southwestern Asia, and south central Asia, having a coarse coat, a sloping back, and large teeth and feeding chiefly on carrion, often in packs. Also, **hyaena.** Cf. **brown hyena, spotted hyena, striped hyena.** [1350–1400; ME *hiena* < ML *hyēna,* L *hyaena* < Gk *hýaina,* equiv. to *hy-* (s. of *hŷs*) hog + *-aina* fem. suffix; r. ME *hyane, hyene* < MF *hiene* < L] **—hy·e′·nic, hy·e·nine** (hī ē′nīn, -nin), *adj.*

spotted hyena, *Crocuta crocuta,* 3 ft. (0.9 m) high at shoulder; head and body 4½ ft. (1.4 m); tail 1 ft. (0.3 m)

hy·e·noid (hī ē′noid), *adj.* resembling a hyena. Also called **hy·e·ni·form** (hī ē′nə fôrm′). [1940–45; HYEN(A) + -OID]

hy·e·tal (hī′i tl), *adj.* of or pertaining to rain or rainfall. [1860–65; HYET- + -AL¹]

hyeto-, a combining form meaning "rain," used in the formation of compound words: *hyetology.* Also, *esp. before a vowel,* **hyet-.** [comb. form repr. Gk *hyetós* rain, deriv. of *hýein* to rain]

hy·et·o·graph (hī et′ə graf′, -gräf′, hī′i tə-), *n.* a map or chart showing the average rainfall for the localities represented. [HYETO- + -GRAPH]

hy·e·tog·ra·phy (hī′i tog′rə fē), *n.* the study of the annual and geographical distribution of rainfall. [1840–50; HYETO- + -GRAPHY] **—hy·e·to·graph·ic** (hī′i tə graf′ik), **hy′e·to·graph′i·cal,** *adj.* **—hy′e·to·graph′i·cal·ly,** *adv.*

hy·e·tol·o·gy (hī′i tol′ə jē), *n.* the branch of meteorology dealing with precipitation. [HYETO- + -LOGY] **—hy·e·to·log·i·cal** (hī′i tl oj′i kəl), *adj.* **—hy′e·tol′o·gist,** *n.*

Hy·gie·ia (hī jē′ə), *n. Class. Myth.* the ancient Greek goddess of health. [< Gk, late var. of *Hygíeia,* personification of *hygíeia* health, equiv. to *hygiḗ(s)* healthy + *-ia* -IA] **—Hy·gie′ian,** *adj.*

hy·giene (hī′jēn), *n.* **1.** Also, **hygienics.** the science that deals with the preservation of health. **2.** a condition or practice conducive to the preservation of health, as cleanliness. [1590–1600; < F *hygiène* < NL *hygieina* < Gk *hygieinḗ* (*téchnē*) healthful (art), fem. of *hygieinós* healthful, equiv. to *hygiḗ(s)* healthy + *-inos* -INE¹]

hy·gi·en·ic (hī′jē en′ik, hī jen′-, -jē′nik), *adj.* **1.** conducive to good health; healthful; sanitary. **2.** of or pertaining to hygiene. Also, **hy′gi·en′i·cal.** [1825–35; HYGIENE + -IC] **—hy′gi·en′i·cal·ly,** *adv.*
—Syn. 1. See **sanitary.**

hy·gi·en·ics (hī′jē en′iks, hī jen′-, -jē′niks), *n.* (*used with a singular v.*) hygiene (def. 1). [1850–55; HYGIENE + -ICS]

hy·gien·ist (hī jē′nist, -jen′ist, hī′jē nist), *n.* **1.** an expert in hygiene. **2.** See **dental hygienist.** Also, **hy·ge·ist, hy·gie·ist** (hī′jē ist). [1835–45; HYGIENE + -IST]

Hy·gi·nus (hi jī′nəs), *n.* **Saint,** died A.D. 140, pope 136–140.

hy·gric (hī′grik), *adj.* of or pertaining to moisture. [1900–05; < Gk *hygr(os)* wet, moist + -IC]

hygro-, a combining form meaning "wet," "moist," "moisture," used in the formation of compound words: *hygrometer.* [< Gk, comb. form of *hygrós* wet, moist]

hy·gro·gram (hī′grə gram′), *n.* the record made by a hygrograph. [HYGRO- + -GRAM¹]

hy·gro·graph (hī′grə graf′, -gräf′), *n.* a self-recording hygrometer. [1860–65; HYGRO- + -GRAPH]

hy·grom·e·ter (hī grom′i tər), *n.* any instrument for measuring the water-vapor content of the atmosphere. [1660–70; HYGRO- + -METER]

hy·gro·met·ric (hī′grə me′trik), *adj.* of or pertaining to the hygrometer or hygrometry. [1785–95; HYGRO- + -METRIC] **—hy′gro·met′ri·cal·ly,** *adv.*

hy·grom·e·try (hī grom′i trē), *n.* the branch of physics that deals with the measurement of the humidity of air and gases. [1775–85; HYGRO- + -METRY]

hy·gro·phyte (hī′grə fīt′), *n.* **1.** a plant that thrives in wet or very moist ground. **2.** a hydrophyte. [1900–05; HYGRO- + -PHYTE] **—hy·gro·phyt·ic** (hī′grə fit′ik), **hy·groph·i·lous** (hī grof′ə ləs), *adj.*

hy·gro·scope (hī′grə skōp′), *n.* an instrument that indicates the approximate humidity of the air. [1655–65; HYGRO- + -SCOPE]

hy·gro·scop·ic (hī′grə skop′ik), *adj.* absorbing or attracting moisture from the air. [1765–75; HYGROSCOPE + -IC] **—hy′gro·scop′i·cal·ly,** *adv.* **—hy·gro·sco·pic·i·ty** (hī′grə skō pis′i tē), *n.*

hy·gro·ther·mo·graph (hī′grə thûr′mə graf′, -gräf′), *n.* an instrument for recording temperature and relative humidity. [1925–30; HYGRO- + THERMOGRAPH]

Hy·gro·ton (hī′grə ton), *Pharm., Trademark.* a brand of chlorthalidone.

hy·ing (hī′ing), *v.* pp. of **hie.**

Hyk·sos (hik′sōs, -sos), *n.* a nomadic people who conquered and ruled ancient Egypt between the 13th and 18th dynasties, c1700–1580 B.C.: believed to have been a Semitic people that originally migrated into Egypt from Asia. [1595–1605; < Gk *Hyksṓs,* perh. < Egyptian *ḥg(ʾ)* ruler + *ḫʾst* foreign land]

hy·la (hī′lə), *n.* a tree frog of the genus *Hyla.* [< NL (1768), the genus name; L *Hyla,* vocative of *Hylās* Hylas, a companion of Hercules, alluding to the classical legend of his death in a fountain and the repeated cries made by those seeking him (fancifully compared to the choral calling of frogs of this genus)]

hylo-, a combining form meaning "wood," "matter," used in the formation of compound words: *hylophagous; hylotheism.* [< Gk, comb. form of *hýlē* wood, matter]

hy·lo·mor·phic (hī′lə môr′fik), *adj. Philos.* (of a creature) composed of corporeal and spiritual matter. [1885–90; HYLOMORPH(ISM) + -IC]

hy·lo·mor·phism (hī′lə môr′fiz əm), *n. Philos.* the theory that every physical object is composed of two principles, an unchanging prime matter and a form deprived of actuality with every substantial change of the object. [1885–90; HYLO- + -MORPHISM] **—hy′lo·mor′·phist,** *n.*

hy·loph·a·gous (hī lof′ə gəs), *adj.* xylophagous (def. 1). [< Gk *hylophágos.* See HYLO-, -PHAGOUS]

hy·lo·the·ism (hī′lə thē′iz əm), *n.* any philosophical doctrine identifying a god or gods with matter. [1820–30; HYLO- + THEISM] **—hy′lo·the′ist,** *n., adj.* **—hy′lo·the·is′tic, hy′lo·the·is′ti·cal,** *adj.*

hy·lo·trop·ic (hī′lə trop′ik, -trō′pik), *adj. Physical Chem.* (of a substance) capable of undergoing a change in phase, as from a liquid to a gas, with no change in the original proportions of its constituents. [HYLO- + -TROPIC]

hy·lo·zo·ism (hī′lə zō′iz əm), *n. Philos.* the doctrine that matter is inseparable from life, which is a property of matter. [1670–80; HYLO- + *zo-* (s. of Gk *zōḗ*) life + -ISM] **—hy′lo·zo′ic,** *adj.* **—hy′lo·zo′ist,** *n.* **—hy′lo·zo·is′tic,** *adj.* **—hy′lo·zo·is′ti·cal·ly,** *adv.*

Hy·man (hī′mən), *n.* a male given name.

hy·men (hī′mən), *n. Anat.* a fold of mucous membrane partly closing the external orifice of the vagina in a virgin. [1605–15; < LL *hymēn* < Gk *hymḗn* skin, membrane, the virginal membrane]

Hy·men (hī′mən), *n.* the ancient Greek god of marriage.

hy·me·ne·al (hī′mə nē′əl), *adj.* **1.** of or pertaining to marriage. *—n.* **2.** *Archaic.* marriage song. [1595–1605; < L *hymenae(us)* (< Gk *hyménaios* wedding song, equiv. to *Hymen* HYMEN + *-aios* pertaining to) + -AL¹]

hy·me·ni·um (hī mē′nē əm), *n., pl.* **-ni·a** (-nē ə). *Mycol.* the sporogenous layer in a fungus, composed of asci or basidia often interspersed with various sterile structures, as paraphyses. [1820–30; < NL; see HYMEN, -IUM] **—hy·me′ni·al,** *adj.*

hymeno-, a combining form appearing in loanwords from Greek, where it meant "membrane" (*hymenopteron*); on this model, used in the formation of compound words (*hymenotomy*). [< Gk, comb. form of *hymḗn* membrane, hymen]

hy·me·nop·ter·an (hī′mə nop′tər ən), *adj.* **1.** hymenopterous. *—n.* **2.** Also, **hy′me·nop′ter.** a hymenopterous insect. [1875–80; HYMENOPTER + -AN]

hy·me·nop·ter·on (hī′mə nop′tə ron′), *n., pl.* **-ter·a** (-tər ə). hymenopteran. [1875–80; < Gk, neut. sing. of *hymenópteros* HYMENOPTEROUS]

hy·me·nop·ter·ous (hī′mə nop′tər əs), *adj.* belonging or pertaining to the Hymenoptera, an order of insects having, when winged, four membranous wings, and comprising the wasps, bees, ants, ichneumon flies, and sawflies. [1805–15; < Gk *hymenópteros.* See HYMENO-, -PTEROUS]

hy·men·ot·o·my (hī′mə not′ə mē), *n., pl.* **-mies.** incision of the hymen. [1850–55; HYMENO- + -TOMY]

CONCISE PRONUNCIATION KEY: act, cāpe, dâre, pärt; set, ēqual; if, ice; ox, ōver, ôrder, oil, bŏŏk, bōōt, out; up, ûrge; child; sing; shoe; thin, *th*at; zh as in *treasure.* ə = *a* as in *alone, e* as in *system, i* as in *easily, o* as in *gallop, u* as in *circus;* ᵊ as in *fire* (fīᵊr), *hour* (ouᵊr). l and n can serve as syllabic consonants, as in *cradle* (krād′l), and *button* (but′n). See the full key inside the front cover.

Hy·met·tus (hī met′əs), *n.* a mountain in SE Greece, near Athens. 3370 ft. (1027 m). —**Hy·met′ti·an, Hy·met′tic,** *adj.*

Hy·mie (hī′mē), *n. Slang (disparaging and offensive).* a Jew. [HYM(AN) or Yiddish *khaim* a male personal name (< Heb *ḥayyīm* lit., life) + -IE]

hymn (him), *n.* **1.** a song or ode in praise or honor of God, a deity, a nation, etc. **2.** something resembling this, as a speech, essay, or book in praise of someone or something. —*v.t.* **3.** to praise or celebrate in a hymn; express in a hymn. —*v.i.* **4.** to sing hymns. [bef. 1000; < L *hymnus* < Gk *hýmnos* song in praise of gods or heroes; r. ME *ymne* (< OF) and OE *ymn* (< LL *ymnus*)] —**hymn·er** (him′ər, -nər), *n.* —**hymn′like′,** *adj.*
—**Syn. 1.** anthem, psalm, paean.

hym·nal (him′nl), *n.* **1.** Also called **hymn·book** (him′bo͝ok′). a book of hymns for use in a religious service. —*adj.* **2.** of or pertaining to hymns. [1535–45; (in def. 1) < ML *hymnāle,* n. use of neut. of *hymnālis* (adj.); (in def. 2) < ML *hymnālis;* see HYMN, -AL[1], -AL[2]]

hym′nal stan′za. See **common measure** (def. 2).

hym·na·ry (him′nə rē), *n., pl.* **-ries.** a hymnal. [1885–90; < ML *hymnārium.* See HYMN, -ARY]

hym·nist (him′nist), *n.* a composer of hymns. [1615–25; HYMN + -IST]

hym·no·dy (him′nə dē), *n.* **1.** the singing or the composition of hymns or sacred songs. **2.** hymns collectively, esp. the collective hymns of a specific religion, place, or period. [1705–15; < ML *hymnōdia* < Gk *hymnōidía* chanting of a hymn, equiv. to *hýmn(os)* HYMN + *ōidía* singing (*aoid-* sing (see ODE) + *-ia* -IA)] —**hym·nod·i·cal** (him nod′i kəl), *adj.* —**hym′no·dist,** *n.*

hym·nol·o·gy (him nol′ə jē), *n.* **1.** the study of hymns, their history, classification; etc. **2.** the composition of hymns. **3.** hymns collectively. [1630–40; HYMN + -O- + -LOGY] —**hym·no·log·ic** (him′nl oj′ik), **hym′no·log′i·cal,** *adj.* —**hym′no·log′i·cal·ly,** *adv.* —**hym·nol′o·gist,** *n.*

hy·oid (hī′oid), *Anat., Zool.* —*adj.* **1.** Also, **hy·oi′dal, hy·oi′de·an.** noting or pertaining to a U-shaped bone at the root of the tongue in humans, or a corresponding bone or collection of bones in animals. —*n.* **2.** the hyoid bone. See diag. under **larynx.** [1700–10; < NL *hyoīdes* < Gk *hyoeidḗs,* shaped like the letter hypsilon (i.e. upsilon), equiv. to *hy-* (deriv. of letter name *hŷ,* var. of *ŷ;* see UPSILON) + *-oeidēs* -OID]

hy·ol·i·thid (hī ol′i thid), *n.* **1.** any invertebrate of the extinct genus *Hyolithes,* most common in the Cambrian Period, having a limy, univalve shell, and thought to be related to the pteropods. —*adj.* **2.** belonging or pertaining to *Hyolithes.* [< NL *Hyolith(es)* (see HYOID, -LITH) + -ID[2]]

hy·os·cine (hī′ə sēn′, -sin), *n. Pharm.* scopolamine. [1870–75; HYOSC(YAMUS) + -INE[2]]

hy·os·cy·a·mine (hī′ə sī′ə mēn′, -min), *n. Pharm.* a poisonous alkaloid, $C_{17}H_{23}NO_3$, obtained from henbane and other solanaceous plants, used as a sedative, analgesic, mydriatic, and antispasmodic. [1855–60; HYOSCYAM(US) + -INE[2]]

hy·os·cy·a·mus (hī′ə sī′ə məs), *n.* the dried leaves, with or without the tops, of the henbane, *Hyoscyamus niger,* containing the alkaloids hyoscyamine and scopolamine, used in medicine. [1700–10; < NL < Gk *hyoskýamos,* equiv. to *hyós* (gen. of *hŷs* hog) + *kýamos* bean]

hyp (hip), *n. Archaic.* hypochondria. Also, **hip.** [by shortening]

hyp-, var. of **hypo-** before a vowel: *hypalgesia.*

hyp., **1.** hypotenuse. **2.** hypothesis. **3.** hypothetical.

hyp·a·byss·al (hip′ə bis′əl, hī′pə-), *adj. Geol.* **1.** (of an igneous rock) intermediate in texture between coarse-grained intrusive rocks and fine-grained extrusive rocks. **2.** noting any of various minor intrusions, as dikes and sills, that have crystallized under conditions intermediate between plutonic and extrusive. [1890–95; HYP- + ABYSSAL]

hyp·aes·the·sia (hip′əs thē′zhə, -zhē ə, -zē ə, hī′pəs-), *n. Pathol.* hypesthesia.

hy·pae·thral (hi pē′thrəl, hī-), *adj.* hypethral.

hyp·al·ge·si·a (hip′al jē′zē ə, -sē ə, hī′pal-), *n.* decreased sensitivity to pain (opposed to *hyperalgesia*). Also, **hy·pal·gia** (hi pal′jə, -jē ə, hī-). [1880–85; HYP- + ALGESIA] —**hyp′al·ge′sic,** *adj.*

hy·pal·la·ge (hi pal′ə jē, hī-), *n. Rhet.* the reversal of the expected syntactic relation between two words, as in "her beauty's face" for "her face's beauty." [1580–90; < L < Gk *hypallagḗ* interchange, equiv. to *hyp-* HYP- + *allagḗ* change (*all-* ALL- + *ag-* (s. of *ágein* to lead; see -AGOGUE) + *-ē* n. suffix)]

Hyp·a·nis (hip′ə nis), *n.* ancient name of the **Kuban.**

hy·pan·thi·um (hi pan′thē əm, hī-), *n., pl.* **-thi·a** (-thē ə). *Bot.* a cup-shaped or tubular body formed by the conjoined sepals, petals, and stamens. [1850–55; < NL, equiv. to *hyp-* HYP- + *anthium* < Gk *ánthion* (*ánth(os)* flower + *-ion* dim. suffix)] —**hy·pan′thi·al,** *adj.*

hy·pas·pist (hi pas′pist, hī-), *n.* a shield bearer, esp. one of a special unit of light infantry in the Macedonian army. [1820–30; < Gk *hypaspistḗs* shield bearer, equiv. to *hyp-* HYP- + *aspis* shield + *-tēs* n. suffix]

Hy·pa·tia (hī pā′shə, -pat′ē ə), *n.* A.D. c370–415, Greek philosopher renowned for her beauty.

hype[1] (hīp), *v.,* **hyped, hyp·ing,** *n. Informal.* —*v.t.* **1.** to stimulate, excite, or agitate (usually fol. by *up*): *She was hyped up at the thought of owning her own car.* **2.** to create interest in by flamboyant or dramatic methods; promote or publicize showily: *a promoter who knows how to hype a prizefight.* **3.** to intensify (advertising, promotion, or publicity) by ingenious or questionable claims, methods, etc. (usually fol. by *up*). **4.** to trick; gull. —*n.* **5.** exaggerated publicity; hoopla. **6.** an ingenious or questionable claim, method, etc., used in advertising, promotion, or publicity to intensify the effect. **7.** a swindle, deception, or trick. [1925–30, *Amer.;* in sense "to trick, swindle," of uncert. orig.; subsequent senses perh. by reanalysis as a shortening of HYPERBOLE]

hype[2] (hīp), *n. Slang.* **1.** a hypodermic needle. **2.** a drug addict, esp. one who uses a hypodermic needle. [shortening of HYPODERMIC; cf. HYPO[1]]

hyped-up (hīpt′up′), *adj. Informal.* intensively or excessively stimulated or exaggerated: *an economy hyped-up by arms spending.* [1945–50]

hy·per[1] (hī′pər), *Informal.* —*adj.* **1.** overexcited; overstimulated; keyed up. **2.** seriously or obsessively concerned; fanatical; rabid: *She's hyper about noise pollution.* **3.** hyperactive. —*n.* **4.** a person who is hyper. [1970–75; prob. independent use of HYPER-]

hy·per[2] (hī′pər), *n. Informal.* a person who promotes or publicizes events, people, etc., esp. one who uses flamboyant or questionable methods; promoter; publicist. [1910–15, *Amer.,* for an earlier sense; HYPE[1] + -ER[1]]

hyper-, a prefix appearing in loanwords from Greek, where it meant "over," usually implying excess or exaggeration (*hyperbole*); on this model used, especially as opposed to **hypo-,** in the formation of compound words (*hyperthyroid*). Cf. **super-.** [Gk, repr. *hypér* over, above; c. L *super* (see SUPER-); akin to OVER]
—**Note.** The lists at the bottom of this and following pages provide the spelling, syllabification, and stress for words whose meanings may easily be inferred by combining the meanings of HYPER- and an attached base word, or base word plus a suffix. Appropriate parts of speech are also shown. Words prefixed by HYPER- that have special meanings or uses are entered in their proper alphabetical places in the main vocabulary or as derived forms run on at the end of a main vocabulary entry.

hy·per·a·cid·i·ty (hī′pər ə sid′i tē), *n. Pathol.* excessive acidity, as of the gastric juice. [1895–1900; HYPER- + ACIDITY] —**hy·per·ac·id** (hī′pər as′id), *adj.*

hy·per·ac·tive (hī′pər ak′tiv), *adj.* **1.** unusually or abnormally active: *a company's hyperactive growth; the child's hyperactive imagination.* **2.** (of children) displaying exaggerated physical activity sometimes associated with neurologic or psychologic causes. **3.** hyperkinetic. [1865–70; HYPER- + ACTIVE] —**hy·per·ac·tion** (hī′pər ak′shən), *n.* —**hy′per·ac′tive·ly,** *adv.*

hy·per·ac·tiv·i·ty (hī′pər ak tiv′i tē), *n.* **1.** the condition of being hyperactive. **2.** hyperkinesia. [1885–90; HYPERACTIVE + -ITY]

hy·per·ad·e·no·sis (hī′pər ad′n ō′sis), *n. Pathol.* abnormal enlargement of the glands, esp. of the lymph nodes. [HYPER- + ADEN- + -OSIS]

hy·per·ae·mi·a (hī′pər ē′mē ə), *n. Pathol.* hyperemia.

hy·per·aes·the·sia (hī′pər əs thē′zhə, -zhē ə, -zē ə), *n. Pathol.* hyperesthesia.

hy·per·al·do·ster·o·nism (hī′pər al′dō ster′ə niz′əm, -al dos′tər ə-), *n. Pathol.* aldosteronism. [1950–55; HYPER- + ALDOSTERONE + -ISM]

hy·per·al·ge·si·a (hī′pər al jē′zē ə, -sē ə), *n.* an exaggerated sense of pain (opposed to *hypalgesia*). Also, **hy·per·al·gi·a** (hī′pər al′jē ə, -jə). [1895–1900; HYPER- + ALGESIA] —**hy′per·al·ge′sic, hy·per·al·get·ic** (hī′pər al jet′ik), *adj.*

hy·per·al·i·men·ta·tion (hī′pər al′ə men tā′shən), *n. Med.* **1.** overfeeding. **2.** See **total parenteral nutrition.** [1965–70; HYPER- + ALIMENTATION]

hy·per·an·a·ki·ne·sia (hī′pər an′ə ki nē′zhə, -zhē ə, -zē ə, -kī-), *n.* abnormally active mechanical movement, esp. of the stomach or intestine. Also, **hy·per·an·a·ci·ne·sia** (hī′pər an′ə si nē′zhə, -zhē ə, -zē ə), **hy·per·an·a·ki·ne·sis** (hī′pər an′ə ki nē′sis, -kī-). [HYPER- + ANA- + Gk *-kīnēsia,* deriv. of *kī́nēsis* movement; see KINESTHESIA]

hy·per·a·phi·a (hī′pər ā′fē ə), *n. Pathol.* abnormal sensitivity to touch. [HYPER- + Gk *aph(ḗ)* touch + -IA] —**hy·per·aph·ic** (hī′pər af′ik), *adj.*

hy·per·bar·ic (hī′pər bar′ik), *adj. Med.* **1.** (of an anesthetic) having a specific gravity greater than that of cerebrospinal fluid. Cf. **hypobaric. 2.** pertaining to or utilizing gaseous pressure greater than normal, esp. for administering oxygen in the treatment of certain diseases. [1925–30; HYPER- + BARIC[2]]

hy′perbar′ic cham′ber, a steel vessel in which atmospheric pressure can be raised or lowered by air compressors, used to treat divers or pilots afflicted with aeroembolism and to provide high-oxygen environments for certain medical treatments and operations. Also called **recompression chamber, decompression chamber.** [1960–65]

hy·per·ba·ton (hī pûr′bə ton′), *n., pl.* **-ba·tons, -ba·ta** (-bə tə). *Rhet.* the use, esp. for emphasis, of a word order other than the expected or usual one, as in "Bird thou never wert." [1570–80; < L < Gk: transposition, lit., overstepping, deriv. of neut. of *hyperbatós,* equiv. to *hyper-* HYPER- + *ba-* (s. of *baínein* to walk, step) + *-tos* verbal adj. suffix; cf. BASIS] —**hy·per·bat·ic** (hī′pər bat′ik), *adj.* —**hy′per·bat′i·cal·ly,** *adv.*

hy·per·bil·i·ru·bi·ne·mi·a (hī′pər bil′ə ro͞o′bə nē′mē ə), *n. Pathol.* an abnormally high level of bilirubin in the blood, manifested by jaundice, anorexia, and malaise, occurring in association with liver disease and certain hemolytic anemias. Cf. **physiologic jaundice.** [1920–25; HYPER- + BILIRUBIN + -EMIA]

hy·per·bo·la (hī pûr′bə lə), *n. Geom.* the set of points in a plane whose distances to two fixed points in the plane have a constant difference; a curve consisting of two distinct and similar branches, formed by the intersection of a plane with a right circular cone when the plane makes a greater angle with the base than does the generator of the cone. *Equation:* $x^2/a^2 - y^2/b^2 = \pm 1$. See diag. under **conic section.** [1660–70; < NL < Gk *hyperbolḗ* the geometrical term, lit., excess. See HYPERBOLE]

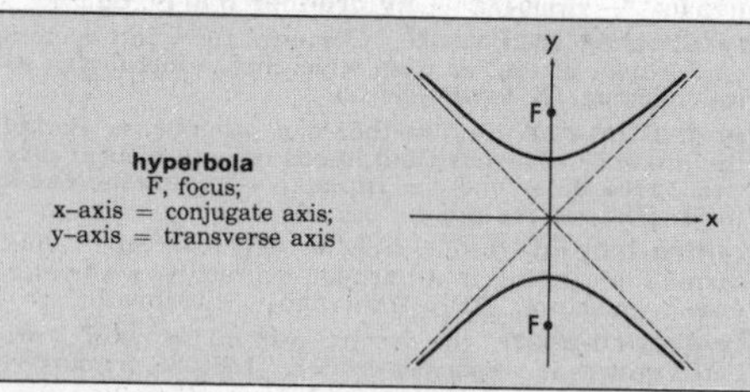

hyperbola
F, focus;
x-axis = conjugate axis;
y-axis = transverse axis

hy·per·bo·le (hī pûr′bə lē), *n. Rhet.* **1.** obvious and intentional exaggeration. **2.** an extravagant statement or figure of speech not intended to be taken literally, as "to wait an eternity." Cf. **litotes.** [1520–30; < Gk *hyperbolḗ* excess, exaggeration, throwing beyond, equiv. to *hyper-* HYPER- + *bolḗ* throw]
—**Syn. 2.** overstatement. —**Ant. 2.** understatement.

hy·per·bol·ic (hī′pər bol′ik), *adj.* **1.** having the nature of hyperbole; exaggerated. **2.** using hyperbole; exaggerating. **3.** *Math.* **a.** of or pertaining to a hyperbola. **b.** derived from a hyperbola, as a hyperbolic function. Also, **hy′per·bol′i·cal.** [1640–50; HYPERBOLE OR HYPERBOL(A) + -IC] —**hy′per·bol′i·cal·ly,** *adv.*

hy′perbol′ic func′tion, *Math.* a function of an angle expressed as a relationship between the distances from a point on a hyperbola to the origin and to the coordinate axes, as hyperbolic sine or hyperbolic cosine: often expressed as combinations of exponential functions. [1885–90]

hyperbol′ic geom′etry, *Geom.* the branch of non-

CONCISE ETYMOLOGY KEY: <, descended or borrowed from; >, whence; b., blend of, blended; c., cognate with; cf., compare; deriv., derivative; equiv., equivalent; imit., imitative; obl., oblique; r., replacing; s., stem; sp., spelling, spelled; resp., respelling, respelled; trans., translation; ?, origin unknown; *, unattested; ‡, probably earlier than. See the full key inside the front cover.

hy′per·ab·sorp′tion, *n.*
hy′per·ac′cu·ra·cy, *n.*
hy′per·ac′cu·rate, *adj.;* **-ly,** *adv.;* **-ness,** *n.*
hy′per·a·cous′tics, *n.*
hy′per·a·cu′i·ty, *n.*
hy′per·a·cute′, *adj.;* **-ly,** *adv.;* **-ness,** *n.*
hy′per·ad′i·pose′, *adj.*
hy′per·ad′i·pos′i·ty, *n.*
hy′per·aes′thete, *n.*
hy′per·ag′gre·gate′, *v.,* **-gat·ed, -gat·ing.**
hy′per·ag·gres′sive, *adj.;* **-ly,** *adv.;* **-ness,** *n.*
hy′per·a·lert′, *adj.*
hy′per·al′ka·lin′i·ty, *n.*
hy′per·al′tru·ism, *n.*
hy′per·al′tru·ist, *n.*
hy′per·al′tru·is′tic, *adj.*
hy′per·an′a·bol′ic, *adj.*
hy′per·a·nab′o·lism, *n.*
hy′per·an·ar′chic, *adj.*
hy′per·an′ar·chy, *n.*
hy′per·an·gel′ic, *adj.*
hy′per·an·gel′i·cal, *adj.;* **-ly,** *adv.*
hy′per·ar′chae·o·log′i·cal, *adj.*
hy′per·ar′id, *adj.*
hy′per·a·ware′, *adj.;* **-ness,** *n.*
hy′per·bar′bar·ism, *n.*
hy′per·bar′bar·ous, *adj.;* **-ly,** *adv.;* **-ness,** *n.*
hy′per·brach′y·ce·phal′ic, *adj.*
hy′per·brach′y·ceph′a·ly, *n.*
hy′per·bran′chi·al, *adj.*
hy′per·bru′tal, *adj.;* **-ly,** *adv.*
hy′per·car′bu·ret′ed, *adj.*
hy′per·car′nal, *adj.;* **-ly,** *adv.*
hy′per·ca·tab′o·lism, *n.*
hy′per·ca·thar′sis, *n.*
hy′per·ca·thar′tic, *adj.*
hy′per·cau′tious, *adj.;* **-ly,** *adv.;* **-ness,** *n.*
hy′per·chlo′ri·na′tion, *n.*
hy′per·civ′i·li·za′tion, *n.*
hy′per·civ′i·lized′, *adj.*
hy′per·clas′si·cal, *adj.*
hy′per·clas′si·cal′i·ty, *n.*
hy′per·cli′max, *n.*
hy′per·co·ag′u·la·bil′i·ty, *n.*
hy′per·co·ag′u·la·ble, *adj.*
hy′per·com·pos′ite, *adj.*
hy′per·con′cen·tra′tion, *n.*
hy′per·con′fi·dence, *n.*
hy′per·con′fi·dent, *adj.;* **-ly,** *adv.*
hy′per·con·form′ist, *n.*
hy′per·con·form′i·ty, *n.*
hy′per·con′sci·en′tious, *adj.;* **-ly,** *adv.;* **-ness,** *n.*
hy′per·con·serv′a·tism, *n.*
hy′per·con·serv′a·tive, *adj., n.;* **-ly,** *adv.;* **-ness,** *n.*
hy′per·con′sti·tu′tion·al, *adj.;* **-ly,** *adv.*
hy′per·con′sti·tu′tion·al·ism, *n.*
hy′per·cy′a·no′sis, *n.*
hy′per·cy′a·not′ic, *adj.*
hy′per·de′i·fi·ca′tion, *n.*
hy′per·de′i·fy′, *v.t.,* **-fied, -fy·ing.**
hy′per·del′i·ca·cy, *n.*
hy′per·del′i·cate, *adj.;* **-ly,** *adv.;* **-ness,** *n.*
hy′per·de·li′cious, *adj.;* **-ly,** *adv.;* **-ness,** *n.*
hy′per·dem′o·crat′ic, *adj.*
hy′per·de·vel′oped, *adj.*
hy′per·de·vel′op·ment, *n.*
hy′per·de·vel′op·men′tal, *adj.*
hy′per·di′a·bol′i·cal, *adj.;* **-ly,** *adv.;* **-ness,** *n.*
hy′per·di′as·tol′ic, *adj.*
hy′per·di·crot′ic, *adj.*
hy′per·di′cro·tism, *n.*
hy′per·dis·ten′tion, *n.*
hy′per·di·vi′sion, *n.*
hy′per·dol′i·cho·ce·phal′ic, *adj.*
hy′per·dol′i·cho·ceph′a·ly, *n.*
hy′per-Do′ri·an, *adj.*
hy′per·el′e·gance, *n.*
hy′per·el′e·gan·cy, *n.*
hy′per·el′e·gant, *adj.;* **-ly,** *adv.*
hy′per·em′e·sis, *n.*
hy′per·e·met′ic, *adj.*
hy′per·e·mo′tion·al, *adj.;* **-ly,** *adv.*
hy′per·e·mo′tion·al′i·ty, *n.*
hy′per·e·mo′tive, *adj.;* **-ly,** *adv.;* **-ness,** *n.*
hy′per·e′mo·tiv′i·ty, *n.*
hy′per·em′pha·size′, *v.t.,* **-sized, -siz·ing.**
hy′per·en′er·get′ic, *adj.*
hy′per·en′er·gy, *n.*
hy′per·en·thu′si·asm, *n.*
hy′per·en·thu′si·as′tic, *adj.*
hy′per·en·thu′si·as′ti·cal·ly, *adv.*
hy′per·er′e·thism, *n.*
hy′per·es′thete, *n.*
hy′per·eth′i·cal, *adj.;* **-ly,** *adv.;* **-ness,** *n.*
hy′per·ex′al·ta′tion, *n.*

Euclidean geometry that replaces the parallel postulate of Euclidean geometry with the postulate that two distinct lines may be drawn parallel to a given line through a point not on the given line. Cf. **Riemannian geometry.** [1870–75]

hyperbol′ic parab′oloid, *Geom.* a paraboloid that can be put into a position such that its sections parallel to one coordinate plane are hyperbolas, with its sections parallel to the other two coordinate planes being parabolas. Cf. **elliptic paraboloid.** [1835–45]

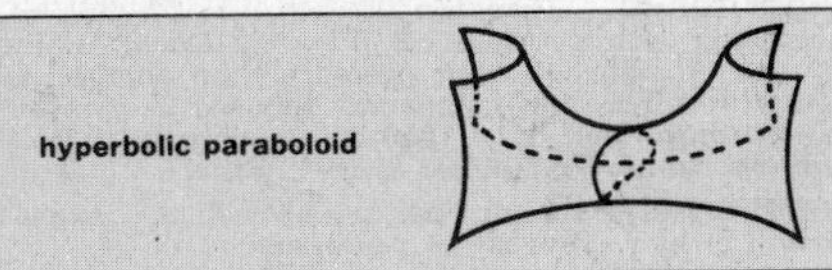

hy•per•bo•lism (hī pûr′bə liz′əm), *n.* the use of hyperbole. [1645–55; HYPERBOLE + -ISM]

hy•per•bo•lize (hī pûr′bə līz′), *v.,* **-lized, -liz•ing.** —*v.i.* **1.** to use hyperbole; exaggerate. —*v.t.* **2.** to represent or express with hyperbole or exaggeration. Also, *esp. Brit.,* **hy•per′bo•lise′.** [1590–1600; HYPERBOLE + -IZE]

hy•per•bo•loid (hī pûr′bə loid′), *n. Math.* a quadric surface having a finite center and some of its plane sections hyperbolas. Equation: $x^2/a^2 + y^2/b^2 - z^2/c^2 = 1$. [1720–30; HYPERBOL(A) + -OID] —**hy•per′bo•loi′dal,** *adj.*

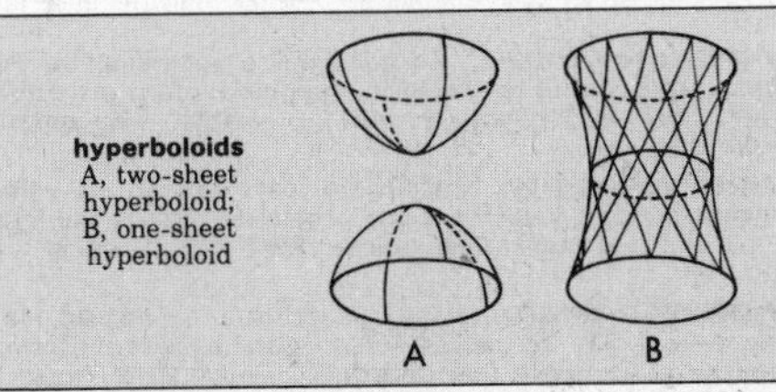

hyperboloids A, two-sheet hyperboloid; B, one-sheet hyperboloid

Hy•per•bo•re•an (hī′pər bôr′ē ən, -bōr′-, -bə rē′-), *n.* **1.** *Class. Myth.* one of a people supposed to live in a land of perpetual sunshine and abundance beyond the north wind. **2.** an inhabitant of an extreme northern region. —*adj.* **3.** of or pertaining to the Hyperboreans. **4.** (*l.c.*) of, pertaining to, or living in a far northern region. [< L *hyperbore(us)* < Gk *hyperbóreos* beyond the north wind, northern, polar (*hyper-* HYPER- + *boréas* the north, the north wind) + -AN; see BOREAS]

hy•per•cal•ce•mi•a (hī′pər kal sē′mē ə), *n. Pathol.* an abnormally large amount of calcium in the blood. Also, **hy′per•cal•cae′mi•a.** [1920–25; < NL; see HYPER-, CALC-, -EMIA]

hy•per•cal•ci•u•ri•a (hī′pər kal′si yo͝or′ē ə), *n. Pathol.* an abnormally high amount of calcium in the urine. Also, **hy•per•cal•ci•nu•ri•a** (hī′pər kal′sə no͝or′ē ə, -nyo͝or′-). [1925–30; HYPER- + CALCI- + -URIA]

hy•per•cat•a•lec•tic (hī′pər kat′l ek′tik), *adj. Pros.* (of a line of verse) containing an additional syllable after the last dipody or foot. Cf. **acatalectic** (def. 2), **catalectic.** [1695–1705; < LL *hypercatalēcticus,* equiv. to Gk *hyperkatálēkt(os)* + L *-icus* -IC; see HYPER-, CATALECTIC]

hy•per•cat•a•lex•is (hī′pər kat′l ek′sis), *n., pl.* **-cat•a•lex•es** (-kat′l ek′sēz). *Pros.* the addition of one or more syllables after the final foot in a line of verse. [1885–1890; see HYPERCATALECTIC, -SIS]

hy•per•charge (hī′pər chärj′), *n. Physics.* **1.** a quantum number assigned to baryons and mesons, equal to $B + S$, where B is the baryon number and S is the strangeness. **2.** the quantum number equal to $B + S + C$, where C is the charm. [1955–60; HYPER- + CHARGE]

hy•per•chlor•hy•dri•a (hī′pər klôr hī′drē ə, -klōr-), *n. Pathol.* excessive secretion of hydrochloric acid in the stomach. [1890–95; HYPER- + CHLOR-² + HYDR-² + -IA]

hy•per•cho•les•ter•ol•e•mi•a (hī′pər kə les′tər ə lē′mē ə), *n. Pathol.* **1.** the presence of an excessive amount of cholesterol in the blood. **2.** See **familial hypercholesterolemia.** Also, **hy•per•cho•les•ter•e•mi•a** (hī′pər kə les′tə rē′mē ə). [1890–95; < NL; see HYPER-, CHOLESTEROL, -EMIA]

hy•per•cho•li•a (hī′pər kō′lē ə), *n. Pathol.* abnormally large secretion of bile. [HYPER- + CHOL- + -IA]

hy•per•con•scious (hī′pər kon′shəs), *adj.* acutely aware. [HYPER- + CONSCIOUS] —**hy′per•con′scious•ly,** *adv.* —**hy′per•con′scious•ness,** *n.*

hy•per•cor•rect (hī′pər kə rekt′), *adj.* **1.** overly correct; excessively fastidious; fussy: *hypercorrect manners.* **2.** of, pertaining to, or characterized by hypercorrection. [1920–25; HYPER- + CORRECT] —**hy′per•cor•rect′ly,** *adv.*. —**hy′per•cor•rect′ness,** *n.*

hy•per•cor•rec•tion (hī′pər kə rek′shən), *n. Ling.* **1.** the use of an inappropriate pronunciation, grammatical form, or usage, resulting usually from overgeneralizing in an effort to replace seemingly incorrect forms with correct ones, as the substitution of *between you and I* for *between you and me,* by analogy with *you and I* as the subject of a sentence. **2.** the form so substituted. Cf. **hyperform, hyperurbanism.** [1930–35; HYPER- + CORRECTION]

hy•per•crit•ic (hī′pər krit′ik), *n.* a person who is excessively or captiously critical. [1625–35; < NL *hypercriticus.* See HYPER-, CRITIC]

hy•per•crit•i•cal (hī′pər krit′i kəl), *adj.* excessively or meticulously critical; overcritical. [1595–1605; HYPER- + CRITICAL] —**hy′per•crit′i•cal•ly,** *adv.*

hy•per•crit•i•cism (hī′pər krit′ə siz′əm), *n.* criticism that is unduly harsh. [1670–80; HYPER- + CRITICISM]

hy•per•dac•tyl•i•a (hī′pər dak til′ē ə), *n.* the presence of extra fingers or toes. Also, **hy•per•dac•tyl•ism** (hī′pər dak′tl iz′əm), **hy•per•dac•ty•ly** (hī′pər dak′tl ē). [1900–05; HYPER- + NL *-dactylia* -DACTYLY]

hy•per•du•li•a (hī′pər do͞o lē′ə, -dyo͞o-), *n. Rom. Cath. Theol.* the veneration offered to the Virgin Mary as the most exalted of creatures. Cf. **dulia, latria.** [1520–30; < ML; see HYPER-, DULIA] —**hy•per•du•lic** (hī′pər do͞o′lik, -dyo͞o′-), **hy′per•du′li•cal,** *adj.*

hy•per•e•mi•a (hī′pər ē′mē ə), *n. Pathol.* an abnormally large amount of blood in any part of the body. Also, **hyperaemia.** [1830–40; HYPER- + -EMIA] —**hy′•per•e′mic,** *adj.*

hy•per•es•the•sia (hī′pər əs thē′zhə, -zhē ə, -zē ə), *n. Pathol.* an abnormally acute sense of pain, heat, cold, or touch; algesia. Also, **hyperaesthesia.** Cf. **hypesthesia.** [1840–50; HYPER- + -ESTHESIA] —**hy•per•es•thet•ic** (hī′pər əs thet′ik), *adj.*

hy•per•eu•tec•toid (hī′pər yo͞o tek′toid), *adj. Metall.* **1.** (of an alloy) having more of the alloying element than the eutectoid composition. **2.** (of steel) having more carbon than the 0.8 percent of eutectoid steel. [1910–15; HYPER- + EUTECTOID]

hy•per•ex•cit•a•bil•i•ty (hī′pər ik sī′tə bil′i tē), *n. Pathol., Psychol.* an excessive reaction to stimuli. [HYPER- + EXCITABILITY] —**hy′per•ex•cit′a•ble,** *adj.*

hy•per•ex•ten•sion (hī′pər ik sten′shən), *n.* the extension of a part of the body beyond normal limits. [1880–85; HYPER- + EXTENSION]

hy′per•fine′ struc′ture (hī′pər fīn′, hī′-), *Physics.* the splitting of the lines of an atomic spectrum, produced by the angular momentum of the nucleus of the atom. Cf. **fine structure.** [1925–30; HYPER- + FINE¹]

hy′per•fo′cal dis′tance (hī′pər fō′kəl, hī′-), *Photog.* the distance, at a given f number, between a camera lens and the nearest point (**hy′perfo′cal point′**) having satisfactory definition when focused at infinity. [1900–05; HYPER- + FOCAL]

hy•per•form (hī′pər fôrm′), *n. Ling.* a pronunciation or grammatical form or usage produced by hypercorrection. Cf. **hypercorrection, hyperurbanism.** [1930–35; HYPER- + FORM]

hy•per•func•tion (hī′pər fungk′shən), *n. Pathol.* abnormally increased function, esp. of glands or other organs. [1905–10; HYPER- + FUNCTION]

hy•per•ga•lac•ti•a (hī′pər gə lak′tē ə), *n. Pathol.* an abnormally large secretion of milk. Also, **hy•per•gal•ac•to•si•a** (hī′pər gal′ak tō′sē ə), **hy•per•gal•ac•to•sis** (hī′pər gal′ak tō′sis). [HYPER- + GALACT- + -IA]

hy•per•ga•my (hī pûr′gə mē), *n.* the practice among Hindu women of marrying into a caste at least as high as their own. [1880–85; HYPER- + -GAMY] —**hy•per′ga•mous,** *adj.*

hy′per•ge•o•met′ric distribu′tion (hī′pər jē′ə me′trik, hī′-), *Math.* a system of probabilities associated with finding a specified number of elements, as 5 white balls, from a given number of elements, as 10 balls, chosen from a set containing 2 kinds of elements of known quantity, as 15 white balls and 20 black balls. [1945–50; HYPER- + GEOMETRIC]

hy′pergeomet′ric equa′tion, *Math.* a differential equation of the form, $(x^2-x)\ d^2y/d^2x + [(a+b+1)x-c]\ dy/dx + abx=0$, where a, b, and c are arbitrary constants.

hy′pergeomet′ric func′tion, *Math.* a function that is a solution to a hypergeometric equation.

hy•per•gly•ce•mi•a (hī′pər glī sē′mē ə), *n. Pathol.* an abnormally high level of glucose in the blood. Also, **hy′per•gly•cae′mi•a.** [1890–95; < NL; see HYPER-, GLYCEMIA] —**hy′per•gly•ce′mic,** *adj.*

hy•per•gol (hī′pər gôl′, -gol′), *n.* any hypergolic agent. [1945–50; HYP(ER)- + ERG- + -OL²]

hy•per•gol•ic (hī′pər gô′lik, -gol′ik), *adj.* (esp. of rocket-fuel propellant constituents) igniting spontaneously upon contact with a complementary substance. [1945–50; HYP(ER)- + ERG- + -OL² + -IC]

hy•per•hi•dro•sis (hī′pər hi drō′sis), *n. Pathol.* abnormally excessive sweating. Also, **hy•per•i•dro•sis** (hī′pər i drō′sis). [1850–55; HYPER- + HIDROSIS]

hy•per•in•flate (hī′pər in flāt′), *v.t.,* **-flat•ed, -flat•ing.** to subject to hyperinflation: *hyperinflated prices.*

hy•per•in•fla•tion (hī′pər in flā′shən), *n.* extreme or excessive inflation. [1925–30; HYPER- + INFLATION] —**hy′per•in•fla′tion•ar′y,** *adj.*

hy•per•in•su•lin•ism (hī′pər in′sə li niz′əm, -ins′yə-), *n. Pathol.* excessive insulin in the blood, resulting in hypoglycemia. [1920–25; HYPER- + INSULIN + -ISM]

Hy•pe•ri•on (hī pēr′ē ən), *n.* **1.** *Class. Myth.* a Titan, the father of Helios, Selene, and Eos. **2.** *Astron.* a natural satellite of the planet Saturn. [< L < Gk *Hyperíōn,* equiv. to *hyper-* HYPER- + *iōn* going; see ION]

hy•per•ir•ri•ta•bil•i•ty (hī′pər ir′i tə bil′i tē), *n.* extreme irritability. [1910–15; HYPER- + IRRITABILITY] —**hy′per•ir′ri•ta•ble,** *adj.*

hy•per•ka•le•mi•a (hī′pər kə lē′mē ə), *n. Pathol.* an abnormally high concentration of potassium in the blood. [1945–50; HYPER- + NL *kal(ium)* potassium (see ALKALI, -IUM) + -EMIA] —**hy′per•ka•le′mic,** *adj.*

hy•per•ker•a•to•sis (hī′pər ker′ə tō′sis), *n.* **1.** *Pathol.* **a.** proliferation of the cells of the cornea. **b.** a thickening of the horny layer of the skin. **2.** Also called **x-disease.** *Vet. Pathol.* a disease of cattle resulting from their physical contact with or eating of objects or food contaminated by wood preservatives or machinery lubricants containing highly chlorinated naphthalenes, characterized by thickening and hardening of the skin, abnormal secretion of tears and saliva, and diarrhea. [1835–45; < NL; see HYPER-, KERATOSIS] —**hy•per•ker•a•tot•ic** (hī′pər ker′ə tot′ik), *adj.*

hy•per•ki•ne•sia (hī′pər ki nē′zhə, -zhē ə, -zē ə, -kī-), *n.* **1.** *Pathol.* an abnormal amount of uncontrolled muscular action; spasm. **2.** *Psychiatry.* a disorder occurring in children and adolescents, characterized by excessive activity, extreme restlessness, impulsivity, and a short attention span. Also, **hy•per•ki•ne•sis** (hī′pər ki nē′sis, -kī-). [1840–50; HYPER- + -KINESIA] —**hy•per•ki•net•ic** (hī′pər ki net′ik, -kī-), *adj.*

hy•per•li•pe•mi•a (hī′pər li pē′mē ə, -lī-), *n.* excessive amounts of fat and fatty substances in the blood; lipemia. Also, **hy•per•lip•i•de•mi•a** (hī′pər lip′i dē′mē ə, -lī′pi-). [1890–95; HYPER- + LIPEMIA] —**hy′per•li•pe′•mic, hy′per•lip′i•de′mic,** *adj.*

hy•per•lip•o•pro•tein•e•mi•a (hī′pər lip′ə prō′tē nē′mē ə, -prō′tē ə-, -lī′pə-), *n. Pathol.* any of various disorders of lipoprotein metabolism, usually characterized by abnormally high levels of cholesterol and certain lipoproteins in the blood. [1965–70; HYPER- + LIPOPROTEIN + -EMIA]

hy•per•mar•ket (hī′pər mär′kit), *n. Chiefly Brit.* a combined supermarket and department store. [1965–70; HYPER- + MARKET, trans. of F *hypermarché,* on the model of *supermarché* SUPERMARKET]

hy•per•me•di•a (hī′pər mē′dē ə), *n.* (*usually used with a singular v.*) a system in which various forms of information, as data, text, graphics, video, and audio, are linked together by a hypertext program. [1985–90]

hy•per•meg•a•so•ma (hī′pər meg′ə sō′mə), *n. Pathol.* gigantism. [HYPER- + MEGA- + SOMA¹]

hy•per•me•ter (hī pûr′mi tər), *n. Pros.* a verse or line containing additional syllables after those proper to the meter. [1650–60; HYPER- + -METER] —**hy•per•met•ric** (hī′pər me′trik), **hy′per•met′ri•cal,** *adj.*

CONCISE PRONUNCIATION KEY: act, cāpe, dâre, pärt; set, ēqual; if, īce; ox, ōver, ôrder, oil, bo͝ok, bo͞ot, out; up, ûrge; child; sing; shoe; thin, *th*at; zh as in *treasure.* ə = a as in *alone,* e as in *system,* i as in *easily,* o as in *gallop,* u as in *circus;* ᵊ as in *fire* (fīᵊr), *hour* (ouᵊr). l and n can serve as syllabic consonants, as in *cradle* (krād′l), and *button* (but′n). See the full key inside the front cover.

hy′per•ex•cit′ed, *adj.*
hy′per•ex•cite′ment, *n.*
hy′per•ex•cur′sive, *adj.;* **-ly,** *adv.;* **-ness,** *n.*
hy′per•fas•tid′i•ous, *adj.;* **-ly,** *adv.;* **-ness,** *n.*
hy′per•fed′er•al•ist, *n.*
hy′per•fem′i•nine, *adj.;* **-ly,** *adv.;* **-ness,** *n.*
hy′per•fem′i•nin′i•ty, *n.*
hy′per•flex′i•bil′i•ty, *n.*
hy′per•flex′i•ble, *adj.;* **-ble•ness,** *n.;* **-bly,** *adv.*
hy′per•flex′ion, *n.*
hy′per•func′tion•al, *adj.;* **-ly,** *adv.*
hy′per•gen′e•sis, *n.*
hy′per•ge•net′ic, *adj.*
hy′per•ge•net′i•cal, *adj.;* **-ly,** *adv.;* **-ness,** *n.*
hy′per•gram•mat′i•cal, *adj.;* **-ly,** *adv.;* **ness,** *n.*
hy′per•hi•drot′ic, *adj.*
hy′per•hi•lar′i•ous, *adj.;* **-ly,** *adv.;* **-ness,** *n.*
hy′per•hi•lar′i•ty, *n.*
hy′per•hy•poc′ri•sy, *n.*
hy′per•i•de′al•ist, *n.*
hy′per•i•de′al•is′tic, *adj.*
hy′per•i•de′al•is′ti•cal•ly, *adv.*
hy′per•im•mune′, *adj.*
hy′per•im•mu′ni•ty, *n.*
hy′per•im′mu•ni•za′tion, *n.*
hy′per•im′mu•nize′, *v.t.,* **-nized, -niz•ing.**
hy′per•in′ge•nu′i•ty, *n.*
hy′per•in′ner•va′tion, *adj.*
hy′per•in′tel•lec′tu•al, *adj.;* **-ly,** *adv.;* **-ness,** *n.*
hy′per•in•tel′li•gence, *n.*
hy′per•in•tel′li•gent, *adj.;* **-ly,** *adv.*
hy′per•in•tense′, *adj.;* **-ly,** *adv.;* **-ness,** *n.*
hy′per•ka•tab′o•lism, *n.*
hy′per•lac•ta′tion, *n.*
hy′per•le′thal, *adj.*
hy′per•le•thar′gic, *adj.*
hy′per•leth′ar•gy, *n.*
hy′per•log′i•cal, *adj.;* **-ly,** *adv.;* **-ness,** *n.*
hy′per•log′i•cal′i•ty, *n.*
hy′per•lus′trous, *adj.;* **-ly,** *adv.;* **-ness,** *n.*
hy′per•mag′i•cal, *adj.;* **-ly,** *adv.*
hy′per•ma′ni•a, *n.*
hy′per•man′ic, *adj.*
hy′per•mas′cu•line, *adj.;* **-ly,** *adv.;* **-ness,** *n.*
hy′per•mas′cu•lin′i•ty, *n.*
hy′per•med′i•ca′tion, *n.*
hy′per•met′a•bol′ic, *adj.*
hy′per•me•tab′o•lism, *n.*
hy′per•met′a•phor′ic, *adj.*
hy′per•met′a•phor′i•cal, *adj.*
hy′per•met′a•phys′i•cal, *adj.*
hy′per•mil′i•tant, *adj.;* **-ly,** *adv.*
hy′per•mi•rac′u•lous, *adj.;* **-ly,** *adv.;* **-ness,** *n.*
hy′per•mod′ern, *adj.*
hy′per•mod′ern•ist, *n.*
hy′per•mo•dern′i•ty, *n., pl.* **-ties.**
hy′per•mod′est, *adj.;* **-ly,** *adv.;* **-ness,** *n.*
hy′per•mor′al, *adj.;* **-ly,** *adv.*
hy′per•mo•ral′i•ty, *n.*
hy′per•mu′ta•bil′i•ty, *n.*
hy′per•mu′ta•ble, *adj.;* **-ble•ness,** *n.;* **-bly,** *adv.*
hy′per•mys′ti•cal, *adj.;* **-ly,** *adv.;* **-ness,** *n.*
hy′per•na′tion•al•is′tic, *adj.*
hy′per•nat′u•ral, *adj.;* **-ly,** *adv.;* **-ness,** *n.*
hy′per•neu•rot′ic, *adj.*
hy′per•ni•trog′e•nous, *adj.*
hy′per•nor′mal, *adj.;* **-ly,** *adv.;* **-ness,** *n.*
hy′per•nor•mal′i•ty, *n.*
hy′per•nu•tri′tion, *n.*
hy′per•nu′tri•tive, *adj.*
hy′per•ob•tru′sive, *adj.;* **-ly,** *adv.;* **-ness,** *n.*
hy′per•or•gan′ic, *adj.*
hy′per•or•gan′i•cal•ly, *adv.*
hy′per•or′tho•dox′, *adj.*
hy′per•or′tho•dox′y, *n.*
hy′per•or•thog′na•thous, *adj.*
hy′per•ox′y•gen•ate′, *v.t.,* **-at•ed, -at•ing.**
hy′per•ox′y•gen•a′tion, *n.*
hy′per•ox′y•gen•ize′, *v.t.,* **-ized, -iz•ing.**
hy′per•par′ox•ysm, *n.*
hy′per•pa•thet′ic, *adj.*
hy′per•pa•thet′i•cal, *adj.;* **-ly,** *adv.*
hy′per•pa′tri•ot′ic, *adj.*
hy′per•pa′tri•ot′i•cal•ly, *adv.*

hy·per·mi·cro·so·ma (hī′pər mī′krə sō′mə), *n.* dwarfishness. [< NL; see HYPER-, MICROSOME]

hy·perm·ne·sia (hī′pərm nē′zhə), *n.* the condition of having an unusually vivid or precise memory. [1880–90; HYPER- + (A)MNESIA] —**hy′perm·ne′sic** (-nē′sik, -zik), *adj.*

hy·per·mo·til·i·ty (hī′pər mō til′i tē), *n. Pathol.* excessive motility of the stomach or intestine (opposed to *hypomotility*). [1890–95; HYPER- + MOTILITY]

hy·per·na·tre·mi·a (hī′pər nə trē′mē ə), *n. Pathol.* an abnormally high concentration of sodium in the blood. Also, **hy·per·nat·ro·ne·mi·a** (hī′pər na′trə nē′mē ə). [1930–35; HYPER- + NATR(IUM) + -EMIA]

hy·per·on (hī′pə ron′), *n. Physics.* any baryon with strangeness other than zero, esp. one with a relatively long lifetime. [1950–55; HYPER- + -ON[1]]

hy·per·o·pi·a (hī′pər ō′pē ə), *n. Ophthalm.* a condition of the eye in which parallel rays are focused behind the retina, distant objects being seen more distinctly than near ones; farsightedness (opposed to *myopia*). Also called **hy·per·me·tro·pi·a** (hī′pər mi trō′pē ə). [1880–85; HYPER- + -OPIA] —**hy·per·op·ic** (hī′pər op′ik, -ō′pik), *adj.*

hy·per·os·mi·a (hī′pər oz′mē ə), *n. Pathol.* an abnormally acute sense of smell. [HYPER- + -OSMIA] —**hy′per·os′mic,** *adj.*

hy·per·os·te·og·e·ny (hī′pər os′tē oj′ə nē), *n. Pathol.* excessive bone development. [HYPER- + OSTEO- + -GENY]

hy·per·os·to·sis (hī′pər o stō′sis), *n. Pathol.* abnormal development of bony tissue. [1825–35; HYPER- + OSTOSIS] —**hy·per·os·tot·ic** (hī′pər o stot′ik), *adj.*

hy·per·o·var·i·a (hī′pər ō vâr′ē ə), *n. Pathol.* precocious sexuality in girls due to abnormally heavy ovarian secretion. Also, **hy·per·o·var·i·an·ism** (hī′pər ō vâr′ē ə niz′əm), **hy·per·o·va·rism** (hī′pər ō′və riz′əm). [HYPER- + NL *ovaria,* deriv. of *ovarium* OVARY; see -A[2]]

hy·per·ox·e·mi·a (hī′pər ok sē′mē ə), *n. Pathol.* abnormal acidity of the blood. [HYPER- + OX(Y)-[1] + -EMIA]

hy·per·ox·ide (hī′pə rok′sīd, -sid), *n. Chem.* superoxide. [1850–55; HYPER- + OXIDE]

hy·per·par·a·site (hī′pər par′ə sīt′), *n. Biol.* an organism that is parasitic on or in another parasite. [1825–35; HYPER- + PARASITE] —**hy·per·par·a·sit·ic** (hī′pər par′ə sit′ik), *adj.* —**hy′per·par′a·sit·ism,** *n.*

hy·per·par·a·thy·roid·ism (hī′pər par′ə thī′roi diz′əm), *n. Pathol.* overactivity of the parathyroid gland, characterized by softening of the bones, with consequent pain, tenderness, and a tendency to spontaneous fractures, and by muscular weakness and abdominal cramps. [1915–20; HYPER- + PARATHYROID + -ISM]

hy·per·pha·gi·a (hī′pər fā′jē ə, -jə), *n. Pathol., Psychiatry.* bulimia. [1940–45; HYPER- + -PHAGIA] —**hy·per·phag·ic** (hī′pər faj′ik, -fā′jik), *adj.*

hy·per·phys·i·cal (hī′pər fiz′i kəl), *adj.* being above or beyond the physical; immaterial; supernatural. [1590–1600] —**hy′per·phys′i·cal·ly,** *adv.*

hy·per·pi·tu·i·ta·rism (hī′pər pi to͞o′i tə riz′əm, -tyo͞o′-), *n. Pathol.* **1.** overactivity of the pituitary gland. **2.** a resultant condition, as gigantism or acromegaly. [1905–10; HYPER- + PITUITAR(Y) + -ISM]

hy·per·plane (hī′pər plān′, hī′pər plān′), *n. Math.* a subspace of a vector space that has dimension one less than the dimension of the vector space. [1900–05]

hy·per·pla·sia (hī′pər plā′zhə, -zhē ə, -zē ə), *n. Pathol., Biol.* **1.** abnormal multiplication of cells. **2.** enlargement of a part due to an abnormal numerical increase of its cells. [1860–65; HYPER- + -PLASIA] —**hy·per·plas·tic** (hī′pər plas′tik), *adj.*

hy·per·ploid (hī′pər ploid′), *Biol.* —*adj.* **1.** having a chromosome number that is greater than but not a multiple of the diploid number. —*n.* **2.** a hyperploid cell or organism. [1925–30; HYPER- + -PLOID] —**hy′per·ploid′y,** *n.*

hy·perp·ne·a (hī′pərp nē′ə, hī′pər nē′ə), *n. Pathol.* abnormally deep or rapid respiration. Also, **hy′perp·noe′a.** [1855–60; < NL, equiv. to *hyper-* HYPER- + *-pnea* -PNEA]

hy·per·po·lar·ize (hī′pər pō′lə rīz′), *v.,* **-ized, -iz·ing.** *Physiol.* —*v.t.* **1.** to increase the difference in electric potential across (a cell membrane). —*v.i.* **2.** to undergo such an increase. Also, *esp. Brit.,* **hy′per·po′lar·ise′.** [1945–50; HYPER- + POLARIZE] —**hy′per·po′lar·i·za′tion,** *n.*

CONCISE ETYMOLOGY KEY: <, descended or borrowed from; >, whence; b., blend of, blended; c., cognate with; cf., compare; deriv., derivative; equiv., equivalent; imit., imitative; obl., oblique; r., replacing; s., stem; sp., spelling, spelled; resp., respelling, respelled; trans., translation; ?, origin unknown; *, unattested; ‡, probably earlier than. See the full key inside the front cover.

hy·per·pot·as·se·mi·a (hī′pər pot′ə sē′mē ə), *n. Pathol.* hyperkalemia. [1930–35; HYPER- + POTASS(IUM) + -EMIA] —**hy′per·pot′as·se′mic,** *adj.*

hy·per·py·rex·i·a (hī′pər pī rek′sē ə), *n. Pathol.* an abnormally high fever. [1865–70; HYPER- + PYREXIA] —**hy·per·py·ret·ic** (hī′pər pī ret′ik), **hy′per·py·rex′i·al,** *adj.*

hy·per·se·cre·tion (hī′pər si krē′shən), *n. Pathol.* an excessive secretion. [1860–65; HYPER- + SECRETION]

hy·per·sen·si·tive (hī′pər sen′si tiv), *adj.* **1.** excessively sensitive: *to be hypersensitive to criticism.* **2.** allergic to a substance to which persons do not normally react. [1870–75; HYPER- + SENSITIVE] —**hy′per·sen′si·tive·ness, hy′per·sen′si·tiv′i·ty,** *n.*

hy·per·sen·si·tize (hī′pər sen′si tīz′), *v.t.,* **-tized, -tiz·ing.** **1.** *Photog.* to treat (a film or emulsion) so as to increase its speed. **2.** *Pathol.* to strongly heighten a reaction upon reexposure to a particular antigen. Also, *esp. Brit.,* **hy′per·sen′si·tise′.** [1895–1900; HYPERSENSIT(IVE) + -IZE] —**hy′per·sen′si·ti·za′tion,** *n.*

hy·per·sex·u·al (hī′pər sek′sho͞o əl *or, esp. Brit.,* -seks′yo͞o-), *adj.* **1.** unusually or excessively active in or concerned with sexual matters. —*n.* **2.** a person who is hypersexual. [1940–45; HYPER- + SEXUAL] —**hy′per·sex′u·al′i·ty,** *n.* —**hy′per·sex′u·al·ly,** *adv.*

hy·per·som·ni·a (hī′pər som′nē ə), *n. Pathol.* a tendency to sleep excessively. [1875–80; HYPER- + (IN)SOMNIA] —**hy′per·som′ni·ac′,** *n.*

hy·per·son·ic (hī′pər son′ik), *adj.* noting or pertaining to speed that is at least five times that of sound in the same medium. [1935–40; HYPER- + SONIC]

hy·per·space (hī′pər spās′), *n. Math.* a Euclidean space of dimension greater than three. [1865–70; HYPER- + SPACE] —**hy·per·spa·tial** (hī′pər spā′shəl), *adj.*

hy·per·sphere (hī′pər sfēr′, hī′pər sfēr′), *n. Math.* the generalization of a sphere to more than three dimensions. [1965–70; HYPER- + SPHERE] —**hy·per·spher·i·cal** (hī′pər sfer′i kəl), *adj.*

hy·per·splen·ism (hī′pər splē′niz əm, -splen′iz-), *n. Pathol.* an abnormal condition characterized by an enlarged spleen that prematurely destroys red blood cells or platelets. Also called **hy·per·sple·ni·a** (hī′pər splē′nē ə). [1910–15; HYPER- + SPLEN- + -ISM] —**hy′per·sple′nic,** *adj.*

hy·per·stat·ic (hī′pər stat′ik), *adj.* redundant (def. 5b). [1925–30; HYPER- + STATIC]

hy·per·sthene (hī′pərs thēn′), *n. Mineral.* a dark iron magnesium silicate, an orthorhombic pyroxene containing more than 14 percent ferrous oxide. Cf. **bronzite, enstatite.** [1800–10; HYPER- + Gk *sthénos* strength, might; r. *hyperstene* < F *hyperstène*] —**hy·per·sthen·ic** (hī′pərs then′ik), *adj.*

hy·per·sur·face (hī′pər sûr′fis), *n.* a mathematical object that generalizes the concept of surface from three-dimensional Euclidean space to hyperspace. [1905–10]

hy·per·sus·cep·ti·ble (hī′pər sə sep′tə bəl), *adj. Pathol.* hypersensitive (def. 2). [1905–10; HYPER- + SUSCEPTIBLE] —**hy′per·sus·cep′ti·bil′i·ty,** *n.*

hy·per·tense (hī′pər tens′), *adj.* extremely or abnormally tense, excitable, or snappish. [HYPER- + TENSE[1], or as back formation from HYPERTENSION] —**hy′per·tense′ly,** *adv.* —**hy′per·tense′ness,** *n.*

hy·per·ten·sion (hī′pər ten′shən), *n.* **1.** *Pathol.* **a.** elevation of the blood pressure, esp. the diastolic pressure. **b.** an arterial disease characterized by this condition. **2.** excessive or extreme emotional tenseness. [1890–95; HYPER- + TENSION]

hy·per·ten·sive (hī′pər ten′siv), *adj.* **1.** characterized by or causing high blood pressure. —*n.* **2.** a person who has high blood pressure. [1900–05]

hy·per·text (hī′pər tekst′), *n.* a method of storing data through a computer program that allows a user to create and link fields of information at will and to retrieve the data nonsequentially. [1970–75]

hy·per·ther·mi·a (hī′pər thûr′mē ə), *n.* **1.** *Pathol.* abnormally high fever. **2.** *Med.* treatment of disease by the induction of fever, as by the injection of foreign protein or the application of heat. Also, **hy·per·ther·my** (hī′pər thûr′mē). [1885–90; < NL; see HYPER-, THERM-, -IA]

hy·per·thy·mi·a (hī′pər thī′mē ə), *n. Psychiatry.* **1.** a condition characterized by extreme overactivity. **2.** exaggerated emotionalism. [HYPER- + -THYMIA]

hy·per·thy·roid (hī′pər thī′roid), *adj. Pathol.* **1.** of, pertaining to, or having hyperthyroidism. **2.** characterized by extreme intensity, emotionalism, or lack of restraint: *hyperthyroid journalism.* [1915–20]

hy·per·thy·roid·ism (hī′pər thī′roi diz′əm), *n. Pathol.* **1.** overactivity of the thyroid gland. **2.** a condition resulting from this, characterized by increased metabolism and exophthalmos. [1895–1900; HYPER- + THYROID + -ISM]

hy·per·to·ni·a (hī′pər tō′nē ə), *n. Pathol.* increased rigidity, tension, and spasticity of the muscles. [1835–45; HYPER- + -TONIA]

hy·per·ton·ic (hī′pər ton′ik), *adj.* **1.** *Physiol.* of or pertaining to hypertonia. **2.** *Physical Chem.* noting a solution of higher osmotic pressure than another solution with which it is compared (opposed to *hypotonic*). Cf. **isotonic** (def. 1). [1850–55; HYPERTON(IA) + -IC] —**hy·per·to·nic·i·ty** (hī′pər tō nis′i tē), *n.*

hy·per·tri·cho·sis (hī′pər tri kō′sis), *n.* excessive growth of hair. [HYPER- + TRICHOSIS]

hy·per·tro·phy (hī pûr′trə fē), *n., pl.* **-phies,** *v.,* **-phied, -phy·ing.** —*n.* **1.** abnormal enlargement of a part or organ; excessive growth. **2.** excessive growth or accumulation of any kind. —*v.t., v.i.* **3.** to affect with or undergo hypertrophy. [1825–35; HYPER- + -TROPHY] —**hy·per·troph·ic** (hī′pər trof′ik, -trō′fik), *adj.*

hy·per·ur·ban·ism (hī′pər ûr′bə niz′əm), *n. Ling.* a pronunciation or grammatical form or usage produced by a speaker of one dialect according to an analogical rule formed by comparison of the speaker's own usage with that of another, more prestigious, dialect and often applied in an inappropriate context, esp. in an effort to avoid sounding countrified, rural, or provincial, as in the pronunciation of the word *two* (to͞o) as (tyo͞o). Cf. **hypercorrection, hyperform.** [1920–25; HYPER- + URBAN + -ISM]

hy·per·u·ri·ce·mi·a (hī′pər yo͝or′ə sē′mē ə), *n. Pathol.* an excess of uric acid in the blood, often producing gout. [1890–95; HYPER- + URIC- + -EMIA] —**hy′per·u′ri·ce′mic,** *adj.*

hy·per·ve·loc·i·ty (hī′pər və los′i tē), *n., pl.* **-ties.** extremely high velocity, as of projectiles, space vehicles, or accelerated nuclear particles. [1945–50; HYPER- + VELOCITY]

hy·per·ven·ti·late (hī′pər ven′tl āt′), *v.,* **-lat·ed, -lat·ing.** —*v.i.* **1.** to be afflicted with hyperventilation; breathe abnormally fast and deep. —*v.t.* **2.** to cause (a patient) to breathe more rapidly and deeply than normal. [1930–35; back formation from HYPERVENTILATION]

hy·per·ven·ti·la·tion (hī′pər ven′tl ā′shən), *n.* **1.** excessively rapid and deep breathing. **2.** a condition characterized by abnormally prolonged and rapid breathing, resulting in decreased carbon dioxide levels and increased oxygen levels that produce faintness, tingling of the extremities, and, if continued, alkalosis and loss of consciousness. [1925–30; HYPER- + VENTILATION]

hy·per·vi·ta·mi·no·sis (hī′pər vī′tə mə nō′sis), *n. Pathol.* an abnormal condition caused by an excessive intake of vitamins. [1925–30; HYPER- + VITAMIN + -OSIS]

hy′per·weak′ force′ (hī′pər wēk′, hī′-), *Physics.* a hypothetical force that transforms quarks into leptons and vice versa at high energies. [HYPER- + WEAK]

hyp·es·the·sia (hip′əs thē′zhə, -zhē ə, -zē ə, hī′pəs-), *n. Pathol.* an abnormally weak sense of pain, heat, cold, or touch. Also, **hypaesthesia, hypoesthesia.** Cf. **hyperesthesia.** [HYP- + ESTHESIA] —**hyp·es·the·sic** (hip′əs thē′zik, -sik, hī′pəs-), *adj.*

hy·pe·thral (hi pē′thrəl, hī-), *adj.* (of a classical building) wholly or partly open to the sky. Also, **hypaethral.** Cf. **clithral.** [< L *hypaethr(us)* (< Gk *hýpaithros,* equiv. to *hyp-* HYP- + *aîthros* clear sky; see ETHER) + -AL[1]]

hy·pha (hī′fə), *n., pl.* **-phae** (-fē). (in a fungus) one of the threadlike elements of the mycelium. [1865–70; < NL < Gk *hyphḗ* WEB] —**hy′phal,** *adj.*

hy·phe·ma (hī fē′mə), *n. Pathol.* hemorrhage in the anterior chamber of the eye, usually caused by trauma. [< Gk *hýphaim(os)* bloodshot (*hyp-* HYP- + -(*h*)*aimos,* deriv. of *haîma* blood) + -A[2]]

hy·phen (hī′fən), *n.* **1.** a short line (-) used to connect the parts of a compound word or the parts of a word divided for any purpose. —*v.t.* **2.** hyphenate. [1595–1605; < LL < Gk *hyphén* (adv.) together, deriv. of *hyph' hén* (prep. phrase), equiv. to *hyp(ó)* under (see HYPO-) + *hén,* neut. of *heîs* one] —**hy·phen·ic** (hī fen′ik), *adj.*

hy·phen·ate (*v.* hī′fə nāt′; *adj., n.* hī′fə nit, -nāt′), *v.,* **-at·ed, -at·ing,** *adj., n.* —*v.t.* **1.** to join by a hyphen. **2.** to write or divide with a hyphen. —*adj.* **3.** of or pertaining to something of distinct form or origin that has been joined; connected by a hyphen. —*n.* **4.** *Informal.* a person working or excelling in more than one craft or

hy′per·pa′tri·ot·ism, *n.*
hy′per·per·fec′tion, *n.*
hy′per·per′i·stal′sis, *n.*
hy′per·per′i·stal′tic, *adj.*
hy′per·per′son·al, *adj.;* **-ly,** *adv.*
hy′per·pig′men·ta′tion, *n.*
hy′per·pig′ment·ed, *adj.*
hy′per·pol′y·syl·lab′ic, *adj.*
hy′per·pol′y·syl·lab′i·cal·ly, *adv.*
hy′per·prog′na·thous, *adj.*
hy′per·prom′is·cu′i·ty, *n.*
hy′per·pro·mis′cu·ous, *adj.;* **-ly,** *adv.;* **-ness,** *n.*
hy′per·pro·phet′ic, *adj.*
hy′per·pro·phet′i·cal, *adj.;* **-ly,** *adv.*
hy′per·pure′, *adj.;* **-ly,** *adv.;* **-ness,** *n.*
hy′per·pur′ist, *n.*
hy′per·pur′i·ty, *n.*
hy′per·ra′tion·al, *adj.;* **-ly,** *adv.*
hy′per·re·ac′tive, *adj.*
hy′per·re′ac·tiv′i·ty, *n.*
hy′per·re′al·ism, *n.*
hy′per·re′al·ist, *n.*
hy′per·re′al·is′tic, *adj.*
hy′per·re′al·ize′, *v.t.,* **-ized, -iz·ing.**
hy′per·res′o·nance, *n.*
hy′per·res′o·nant, *adj.;* **-ly,** *adv.*
hy′per·re·spon′sive, *adj.;* **-ly,** *adv.;* **-ness,** *n.*
hy′per·rhyth′mic, *adj.*
hy′per·rhyth′mi·cal, *adj.;* **-ly,** *adv.;* **-ness,** *n.*
hy′per·ri·dic′u·lous, *adj.;* **-ly,** *adv.;* **-ness,** *n.*
hy′per·rit′u·al·ism, *n.*
hy′per·rit′u·a·lis′tic, *adj.*
hy′per·ro·man′tic, *adj.*
hy′per·ro·man′ti·cal·ly, *adv.*
hy′per·ro·man′ti·cism, *n.*
hy′per·saint′ly, *adj.*
hy′per·sa′line, *adj.*
hy′per·sa·lin′i·ty, *n.*
hy′per·sal′i·va′tion, *n.*
hy′per·scep′ti·cal, *adj.;* **-ly,** *adv.;* **-ness,** *n.*
hy′per·scho·las′tic, *adj.*
hy′per·scho·las′ti·cal·ly, *adv.*
hy′per·scru′pu·los′i·ty, *n.*
hy′per·scru′pu·lous, *adj.;* **-ly,** *adv.;* **-ness,** *n.*
hy′per·sen′si·bil′i·ty, *n.*
hy′per·sen′su·al, *adj.;* **-ly,** *adv.;* **-ness,** *n.*
hy′per·sen′su·al·ism, *n.*
hy′per·sen′su·al′i·ty, *n.*
hy′per·sen′su·ous, *adj.;* **-ly,** *adv.;* **-ness,** *n.*
hy′per·sen′ti·men′tal, *adj.;* **-ly,** *adv.*
hy′per·so′cial, *adj.;* **-ly,** *adv.*
hy′per·som′no·lence, *n.*
hy′per·som′no·lent, *adj.;* **-ly,** *adv.*
hy′per·so·phis′ti·cat′ed, *adj.;* **-ly,** *adv.*
hy′per·so·phis′ti·ca′tion, *n.*
hy′per·spec′u·la′tive, *adj.;* **-ly,** *adv.;* **-ness,** *n.*
hy′per·stim′u·la′tion, *n.*
hy′per·stim′u·la′tive, *adj.*
hy′per·sto′i·cal, *adj.*
hy′per·sub′tle, *adj.;* **-ness,** *n.*
hy′per·sub′tle·ty, *n.*
hy′per·sug·ges′ti·bil′i·ty, *n.*
hy′per·sug·ges′ti·ble, *adj.;* **-ble·ness,** *n.;* **-bly,** *adv.*
hy′per·sus·pi′cious, *adj.;* **-ly,** *adv.;* **-ness,** *n.*
hy′per·sys·tol′ic, *adj.*
hy′per·tech′ni·cal, *adj.;* **-ly,** *adv.;* **-ness,** *n.*
hy′per·tech′ni·cal′i·ty, *n.*
hy′per·ther′mal, *adj.;* **-ly,** *adv.*
hy′per·tor′rid, *adj.;* **-ly,** *adv.;* **-ness,** *n.*
hy′per·tox′ic, *adj.*
hy′per·tox·ic′i·ty, *n.*
hy′per·trag′ic, *adj.*
hy′per·trag′i·cal, *adj.;* **-ly,** *adv.*
hy′per·trop′i·cal, *adj.*
hy′per·var′i·a·bil′i·ty, *n.*
hy′per·var′i·a·ble, *adj.;* **-bly,** *adv.*
hy′per·vas′cu·lar, *adj.*
hy′per·vas′cu·lar′i·ty, *n.*
hy′per·ve·nos′i·ty, *n.*
hy′per·vig′i·lance, *n.*
hy′per·vig′i·lant, *adj.;* **-ly,** *adv.;* **-ness,** *n.*
hy′per·vir′u·lent, *adj.;* **-ly,** *adv.*
hy′per·vis·cos′i·ty, *n.*
hy′per·vis′cous, *adj.*
hy′per·vi′tal·i·za′tion, *n.*
hy′per·vi′tal·ize′, *v.t.,* **-ized, -iz·ing.**
hy′per·vo·lu′mi·nous, *adj.;* **-ly,** *adv.;* **-ness,** *n.*

occupation: *He's a film-industry hyphenate, usually listed as a writer-director-producer.* [1850–55; HYPHEN + -ATE[1]] —**hy′phen·a′tion,** *n.*

hy·phen·at·ed (hī′fə nā′tid), *adj. Informal.* of, pertaining to, or designating a person, group, or organization of mixed origin or identity: *an Irish-American club and other hyphenated organizations.* [1890–95; HYPHENATE + -ED[2]]

hy·phen·ize (hī′fə nīz′), *v.t.,* **-ized, -iz·ing.** hyphenate. Also, *esp. Brit.,* **hy′phen·ise′.** [1850–55; HYPHEN + -IZE] —**hy′phen·i·za′tion,** *n.*

hy·pho·po·di·um (hī′fə pō′dē əm), *n., pl.* **-di·a** (-dē ə). (in a fungus) a specialized hyphal branch, composed of one or two usually lobed cells, serving for attachment and for the absorption of food. [< NL; see HYPHA, -O-, -PODIUM]

hyp·na·gog·ic (hip′nə goj′ik, -gō′jik), *adj.* **1.** of or pertaining to drowsiness. **2.** inducing drowsiness. [1885–90; < F *hypnagogique;* see HYPN-, -AGOGUE, -IC]

hyp′nagog′ic state′, *Psychol.* the drowsy period between wakefulness and sleep, during which fantasies and hallucinations often occur.

hypno-, a combining form meaning "sleep," "hypnosis," used in the formation of compound words: *hypnotherapy.* Also, *esp. before a vowel,* **hypn-.** [< Gk *hýpno(s)* sleep; see HYPNOS]

hyp·no·a·nal·y·sis (hip′nō ə nal′ə sis), *n.* a method of psychoanalysis in which a patient is put into hypnosis in an attempt to secure analytic data, free associations, and early emotional reactions. [1915–20; HYPNO- + ANALYSIS] —**hyp·no·an·a·lyt·ic** (hip′nō an′l it′ik), *adj.*

hyp·no·dra·ma (hip′nə drä′mə, -dram′ə), *n. Psychiatry.* the acting out of a traumatic experience, under hypnosis, by a person undergoing psychotherapy. [1965–70; HYPNO- + DRAMA]

hyp·no·gen·e·sis (hip′nə jen′ə sis), *n.* induction of the hypnotic state. [1885–90; HYPNO- + -GENESIS] —**hyp·no·ge·net·ic** (hip′nō jə net′ik), *adj.*

hyp·no·graph (hip′nə graf′, -gräf′), *n.* an instrument that measures activities of the human body during sleep. [HYPNO- + -GRAPH]

hyp·noi·dal (hip noid′l), *adj. Psychol.* characterizing a state that resembles mild hypnosis but that is usually induced by other than hypnotic means. Also, **hyp′noid.** [1895–1900; HYPN- + -OID + -AL[1]]

hyp·nol·o·gy (hip nol′ə jē), *n.* the science dealing with the phenomena of sleep. [1885–90; HYPNO- + -LOGY] —**hyp·no·log·ic** (hip′nl oj′ik), **hyp′no·log′i·cal,** *adj.* —**hyp·nol′o·gist,** *n.*

hyp·none (hip′nōn), *n. Chem.* acetophenone. [1885–90; < F; see HYPN-, -ONE]

hyp·no·pe·di·a (hip′nə pē′dē ə), *n.* See **sleep learning.** [1930–35; HYPNO- + Gk *paideía* child-rearing, education, deriv. of *paîs,* s. *paid-* child]

hyp·no·pom·pic (hip′nə pom′pik), *adj. Psychol.* of or pertaining to the semiconscious state prior to complete wakefulness. [1900–05; HYPNO- + Gk *pomp(ḗ)* sending away (see POMP) + -IC]

Hyp·nos (hip′nos), *n.* the ancient Greek god of sleep. [< Gk *hýpnos* sleep; c. OE *swefn,* L *somnus,* Welsh *hun;* cf. SOPOR]

hyp·no·sis (hip nō′sis), *n., pl.* **-ses** (-sēz). **1.** an artificially induced trance state resembling sleep, characterized by heightened susceptibility to suggestion. **2.** hypnotism. [1875–80; HYPN(OTIC) + -OSIS]

hyp·no·ther·a·py (hip′nō ther′ə pē), *n.* treatment of a symptom, disease, or addiction by means of hypnotism. [1895–1900; HYPNO- + THERAPY] —**hyp′no·ther′a·pist,** *n.*

hyp·not·ic (hip not′ik), *adj.* **1.** of or pertaining to hypnosis or hypnotism. **2.** inducing or like something that induces hypnosis. **3.** susceptible to hypnotism, as a person. **4.** inducing sleep. —*n.* **5.** an agent or drug that produces sleep; sedative. **6.** a person who is susceptible to hypnosis. **7.** a person under the influence of hypnotism. [1680–90; < LL *hypnōticus* < Gk *hypnōtikós* sleep-inducing, narcotic, equiv. to *hypnō-* (var. s. of *hypnoûn* to put to sleep; see HYPNOS) + *-tikos* -TIC] —**hyp·not′i·cal·ly,** *adv.*

hyp·no·tism (hip′nə tiz′əm), *n.* **1.** the science dealing with the induction of hypnosis. **2.** the act of hypnotizing. **3.** hypnosis. [shortening of *neuro-hypnotism,* term introduced by British surgeon James Braid (1795–1860) in 1842; see HYPNOTIC, -ISM] —**hyp′no·tist,** *n.* —**hyp′·no·tis′tic,** *adj.*

hyp·no·tize (hip′nə tīz′), *v.,* **-tized, -tiz·ing.** —*v.t.* **1.** to put in the hypnotic state. **2.** to influence, control, or direct completely, as by personal charm, words, or domination: *The speaker hypnotized the audience with his powerful personality.* **3.** to frighten or startle so that movement is impossible: *The headlights hypnotized the deer and it just stood staring at the oncoming car.* —*v.i.* **4.** to practice hypnosis; put or be able to put others into a hypnotic state. Also, *esp. Brit.,* **hyp′no·tise′.** [1843; see HYPNOTISM, -IZE] —**hyp′no·tiz′a·ble,** *adj.* —**hyp′·no·tiz′a·bil′i·ty,** *n.*

hy·po[1] (hī′pō), *n., pl.* **-pos,** *v. Informal* —*n.* **1.** a hypodermic syringe or injection. **2.** a stimulus or boost. —*v.t.* **3.** to administer a hypodermic injection to. **4.** to stimulate by or as if by administering a hypodermic injection. **5.** to increase, boost, or augment: *to hypo the car's power by installing a bigger engine.* [by shortening of HYPODERMIC; sense "stimulate" perh. by assoc. with HYPE[1]; see -O]

hy·po[2] (hī′pō), *n.* See **sodium thiosulfate.** [1860–65; shortening of HYPOSULFITE]

hy·po[3] (hī′pō), *n. Archaic.* hypochondria. [by shortening]

hypo-, a prefix appearing in loanwords from Greek, where it meant "under" (*hypostasis*); on this model used, especially as opposed to **hyper-,** in the formation of compound words (*hypothyroid*). Also, *esp. before a vowel,* **hyp-.** [< Gk, comb. form of *hypó* under (prep.), below (adv.); c. L *sub* (see SUB-); cf. UP]

hy·po·a·cid·i·ty (hī′pō ə sid′i tē), *n. Pathol.* acidity in a lesser degree than is usual or normal, as of the gastric juice. [1895–1900; HYPO- + ACIDITY] —**hy·po·ac·id** (hī′pō as′id), *adj.*

hy·po·a·de·ni·a (hī′pō ə dē′nē ə), *n. Pathol.* a deficiency of glandular activity. [HYPO- + ADEN- + -IA]

hy·po·a·dre·nal·ism (hī′pō ə drēn′l iz′əm, -ə dren′-), *n.* underactivity of the adrenal gland, as in Addison's disease. Also, **hy·po·a·dre·ni·a** (hī′pō ə drē′nē ə). [HYPO- + ADRENAL + -ISM]

hy′po·ae·o′li·an mode′ (hī′pō ē ō′lē ən, hī′-), *Music.* a plagal church mode represented on the white keys of a keyboard instrument by an ascending scale from E to E, with the final on A. [< LL *hypoaeoli(us)* + -AN; see HYPO-, AEOLIAN]

hy·po·al·bu·min·e·mi·a (hī′pō al byōō′mə nē′mē ə), *n. Pathol.* an abnormally small quantity of albumin in the blood. [1935–40; < NL; see HYPO-, ALBUMIN, -EMIA]

hy·po·al·i·men·ta·tion (hī′pō al′ə men tā′shən), *n. Pathol.* insufficient or inadequate nourishment. Also called **subalimentation.** [HYPO- + ALIMENTATION]

hy·po·al·ler·gen·ic (hī′pō al′ər jen′ik), *adj.* designed to reduce or minimize the possibility of an allergic response, as by containing relatively few or no potentially irritating substances: *hypoallergenic cosmetics.* Also, **hy′po·al′ler·gen′ic.** [1950–55; HYPO- + ALLERGENIC]

hy·po·bar·ic (hī′pə bar′ik), *adj. Med.* (of an anesthetic) having a specific gravity lower than that of cerebrospinal fluid. Cf. **hyperbaric** (def. 1). [1925–30; HYPO- + Gk *bár(os)* weight + -IC]

hy·po·ba·rop·a·thy (hī′pō bə rop′ə thē), *n. Pathol.* a condition produced in high altitudes, caused by diminished air pressure and reduced oxygen intake; mountain sickness. [HYPO- + BARO- + -PATHY]

hy·po·ba·sis (hī′pō bā′sis), *n., pl.* **-ses** (-sēz). *Archit.* **1.** the lowermost distinctively treated part of a base. **2.** a lower base beneath an upper and more important one. [HYPO- + BASIS]

hy·po·blast (hī′pə blast′), *n. Embryol.* **1.** the endoderm. **2.** the cells entering into the inner layer of a young gastrula, capable of becoming endoderm and, to a certain extent, mesoderm. [1820–30; HYPO- + -BLAST] —**hy′po·blas′tic,** *adj.*

hy·po·bran·chi·al (hī′pə brang′kē əl), *adj. Zool.* situated below the gills or beneath the branchial arches. [1840–50; HYPO- + BRANCHIAL]

hy·po·cal·ce·mi·a (hī′pō kal sē′mē ə), *n. Pathol.* an abnormally small amount of calcium in the blood. [1920–25; HYPO- + CALC- + -EMIA]

hy·po·caust (hī′pə kôst′, hip′ə-), *n.* a hollow space or system of channels in the floor or walls of some ancient Roman buildings that provided a central heating system by receiving and distributing the heat from a furnace. [1670–80; < L *hypocaustum* < Gk *hypókauston* room heated from below, equiv. to *hypo-* HYPO- + *kaustón,* neut. of *kaustós* (verbal adj.) heated, burned; see CAUSTIC]

hy·po·cen·ter (hī′pə sen′tər), *n. Geol.* focus (def. 5). [1900–05; HYPO- + CENTER]

hy·po·chlo·rite (hī′pə klôr′īt, -klōr′-), *n.* a salt or ester of hypochlorous acid. [1840–50; HYPO- + CHLORITE[2]]

hy·po·chlo·rous (hī′pə klôr′əs, -klōr′-), *adj.* of or derived from hypochlorous acid. [1835–45; HYPO- + CHLOROUS]

hy′pochlo′rous ac′id, a weak, unstable acid, HOCl, existing only in solution and in the form of its salts, used as a bleaching agent and disinfectant. [1835–45]

hy·po·cho·les·ter·e·mi·a (hī′pō kə les′tə rē′mē ə), *n. Pathol.* an abnormally low amount of cholesterol in the blood. Also, **hy·po·cho·les·ter·o·le·mi·a** (hī′pō kə-les′tər ə lē′mē ə). [HYPO- + CHOLESTER(OL) + -EMIA]

hy·po·chon·dri·a (hī′pə kon′drē ə), *n.* **1.** Also, **hy·po·chon·dri·a·sis** (hī′pō kən drī′ə sis). *Psychiatry.* an excessive preoccupation with one's health, usually focusing on some particular symptom, as cardiac or gastric problems. **2.** excessive worry or talk about one's health. [1555–65; < LL < Gk, neut. pl. of *hypochóndrios* pertaining to the upper abdomen (supposed seat of melancholy), equiv. to *hypo-* HYPO- + *chóndr(os)* ensiform cartilage + *-ios* adj. suffix]

hy·po·chon·dri·ac (hī′pə kon′drē ak′), *adj.* **1.** Also, **hy·po·chon·dri·a·cal** (hī′pō kən drī′ə kəl). *Psychiatry.* **a.** pertaining to or suffering from hypochondria. **b.** produced by hypochondria. **2.** *Anat., Zool.* of or pertaining to the hypochondrium. —*n.* **3.** *Psychiatry.* a person suffering from or subject to hypochondria. **4.** a person who worries or talks excessively about his or her health. [1605–15; < NL *hypochondriacus* < Gk *hypochondriakós* affected in the upper abdomen. See HYPOCHONDRIA, -AC] —**hy′po·chon·dri′a·cal·ly,** *adv.*

hy·po·chon·dri·um (hī′pə kon′drē əm), *n., pl.* **-dri·a** (-drē ə). *Anat.* either of two regions of the abdomen, situated on each side of the epigastrium and above the lumbar regions. [1690–1700; < NL < Gk *hypochóndrion* abdomen. See HYPOCHONDRIA, -IUM]

hy·po·chro·mi·a (hī′pə krō′mē ə), *n. Pathol.* **1.** an anemic condition due to a deficiency of hemoglobin in the red blood cells. **2.** insufficient color or pigmentation. [1885–90; HYPO- + NL *-chromia* < LGk *-chrōmia,* Gk *-chrōm(os)* colored (deriv. of *chróma* color; see CHROMA) + -IA] —**hy′po·chro′mic,** *adj.*

hy′pochro′mic ane′mia, *Pathol.* an anemia characterized by an abnormally low concentration of hemoglobin in the red blood cells, often due to iron deficiency. [1920–25; HYPO- + CHROMIC]

hy·poc·o·rism (hī pok′ə riz′əm, hi-), *n.* **1.** a pet name. **2.** the practice of using a pet name. **3.** the use of forms of speech imitative of baby talk, esp. by an adult. [1840–50; < Gk *hypokórisma* pet name. See HYPOCORISTIC, -ISM]

hy·po·co·ris·tic (hī′pə kə ris′tik, hip′ə-), *adj.* endearing, as a pet name, diminutive, or euphemism. [1600–10; < Gk *hypokoristikós* diminutive, equiv. to *hypokor(ízesthai)* to play the child, call by endearing names (*hypo-* HYPO- + *kor-* child (cf. *kórē* girl, *kóros* boy)) + *-istikos* -ISTIC] —**hy′po·co·ris′ti·cal·ly,** *adv.*

hy·po·cot·yl (hī′pə kot′l), *n. Bot.* the part of a plant embryo directly below the cotyledons, forming a connection with the radicle. See diag. under **cotyledon.** [1875–80; HYPO- + COTYL(EDON)] —**hy′po·cot′y·lous,** *adj.*

hy·po·cri·nism (hī′pə krī′niz əm), *n. Pathol.* an abnormal condition caused by insufficient secretion from a gland, esp. an endocrine gland. Also, **hy·po·crin·i·a** (hī′pə krin′ē ə). [HYPO- + (ENDO)CRINE + -ISM]

hy·poc·ri·sy (hi pok′rə sē), *n., pl.* **-sies.** **1.** a pretense of having a virtuous character, moral or religious beliefs or principles, etc., that one does not really possess. **2.** a pretense of having some desirable or publicly approved attitude. **3.** an act or instance of hypocrisy. [1175–1225; ME *ipocrisie* < OF < LL *hypocrisis* < Gk *hypókrisis* play acting, equiv. to *hypokrī(nesthai)* to play a part, explain (*hypo-* HYPO- + *krínein* to distinguish, separate) + *-sis* -SIS; *h-* (reintroduced in 16th century) < L and Gk] —**Syn. 1.** See **deceit.**

hyp·o·crite (hip′ə krit), *n.* **1.** a person who pretends to have virtues, moral or religious beliefs, principles, etc., that he or she does not actually possess, esp. a person whose actions belie stated beliefs. **2.** a person who feigns some desirable or publicly approved attitude, esp. one whose private life, opinions, or statements belie his or her public statements. [1175–1225; ME *ipocrite* < OF < LL *hypocrita* < Gk *hypokritḗs* a stage actor, hence one who pretends to be what he is not, equiv. to *hypokrī(nesthai)* (see HYPOCRISY) + *-tēs* agent suffix] —**hyp′o·crit′i·cal,** *adj.* —**hyp′o·crit′i·cal·ly,** *adv.*
—**Syn.** deceiver, dissembler, pretender, pharisee.

hy·po·cy·cloid (hī′pə sī′kloid), *n. Geom.* a curve generated by the motion of a point on the circumference of a circle that rolls internally, without slipping, on a given circle. [1835–45; HYPO- + CYCLOID] —**hy′po·cy·cloi′dal,** *adj.*

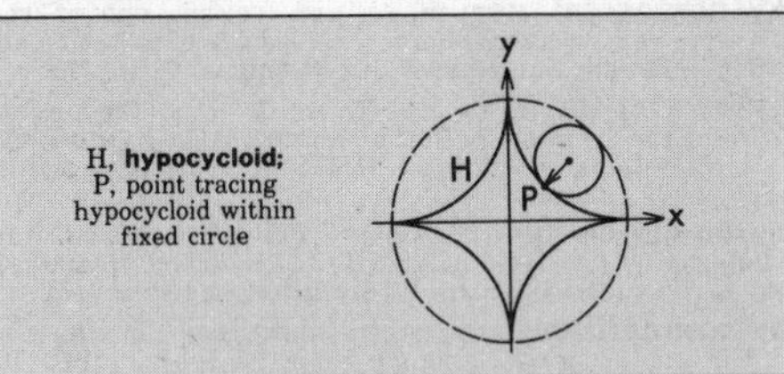

H, hypocycloid; P, point tracing hypocycloid within fixed circle

hy·po·der·ma (hī′pə dûr′mə), *n. Bot., Zool.* hypodermis. [1820–30; HYPO- + -DERMA]

hy·po·der·mic (hī′pə dûr′mik), *adj.* **1.** characterized by the introduction of medicine or drugs under the skin: *hypodermic injection.* **2.** introduced under the skin: *a hypodermic medication.* **3.** pertaining to parts under the skin. **4.** stimulating; energizing. —*n.* **5.** a hypodermic remedy. **6.** a hypodermic injection. **7.** See **hypodermic syringe.** **8.** the administration of drugs into subcutaneous body tissues. [1860–65; HYPODERM(A) + -IC] —**hy′po·der′mi·cal·ly,** *adv.*

hypoder′mic nee′dle, a hollow needle used to inject solutions subcutaneously. [1905–10]

hypoder′mic syringe′, a small glass piston or barrel syringe having a detachable, hollow needle for use in injecting solutions subcutaneously. Also called **syringe.** [1890–95]

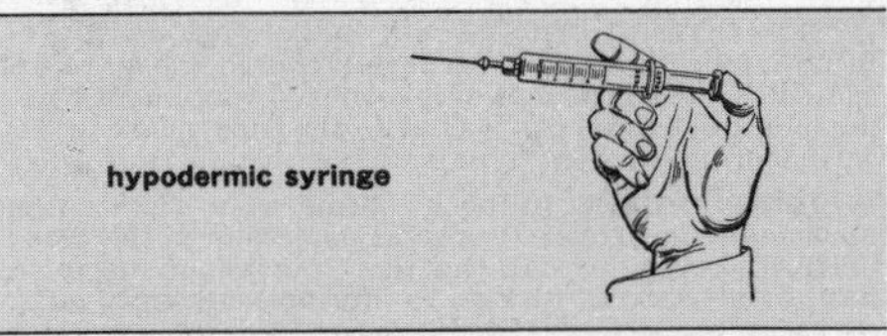
hypodermic syringe

hy·po·der·mis (hī′pə dûr′mis), *n.* **1.** *Zool.* an underlayer of epithelial cells in arthropods and certain other invertebrates that secretes substances for the overlying cuticle or exoskeleton. **2.** *Bot.* a tissue or layer of cells beneath the epidermis. Also, **hy′po·derm′.** [1865–70; HYPO- + -DERMIS] —**hy′po·der′mal,** *adj.*

hy′po·do′ri·an mode′ (hī′pō dôr′ē ən, -dōr′-, hip′-ō-, hī′pō-, hip′ō-), *Music.* a plagal church mode represented on the white keys of a keyboard instrument by an ascending scale from A to A, with the final on D. [< LL *hypodōri(us)* (< Gk *hypodṓrion*) + -AN; see HYPO-, DORIAN]

hy·po·dy·nam·i·a (hī′pō dī nam′ē ə, -nā′mē ə, -di-), *n. Pathol.* diminished strength; adynamia. [< NL, equiv. to *hypo-* HYPO- + Gk *dýnam(is)* power + *-ia* -IA] —**hy·po·dy·nam·ic** (hī′pō dī nam′ik), *adj.*

hy·po·es·the·sia (hī′pō es thē′zhə, -zhē ə, -zē ə), *n.* hypesthesia. [HYPO- + ESTHESIA]

CONCISE PRONUNCIATION KEY: *act, cāpe, dâre, pärt; set, ēqual; if, īce; ox, ōver, ôrder, oil, bŏŏk, bōōt, out; up, ûrge, child; sing; shoe; thin, that;* zh as in *treasure.* ə = *a* as in *alone, e* as in *system, i* as in *easily, o* as in *gallop, u* as in *circus;* ᵊ as in *fire* (fīᵊr), *hour* (ouᵊr). l and n can serve as syllabic consonants, as in *cradle* (krād′l), and *button* (but′n). See the full key inside the front cover.

hy·po·eu·tec·toid (hī′pō yo͞o tek′toid), *adj.* (of steel) having less carbon than the 0.8 percent of eutectoid steel. [1910–15; HYPO- + EUTECTOID]

hy·po·func·tion (hī′pō fungk′shən), *n. Pathol.* abnormally diminished function, esp. of glands or other organs. [1900–05; HYPO- + FUNCTION]

hy·po·gas·tric (hī′pə gas′trik), *adj.* of, pertaining to, or situated in the hypogastrium. [1605–15; < NL *hypogastricus.* See HYPOGASTRIUM, -IC]

hy′pogas′tric ar′tery, *Anat.* See **iliac artery** (def. 3). [1790–1800]

hy·po·gas·tri·um (hī′pə gas′trē əm), *n., pl.* **-tri·a** (-trē ə). *Anat.* the lower and median part of the abdomen. [1675–85; < NL < Gk *hypogástrion,* equiv. to *hypo-* HYPO- + *gastríon* (*gastr-,* s. of *gastḗr* paunch + *-ion* dim. suffix)]

hy·po·ge·al (hī′pə jē′əl, hip′ə-), *adj.* underground; subterranean. Also, **hy′po·gae′al, hy′po·ge′ous, hy′·po·gae′ous.** [1680–90; < L *hypogē(us)* (< Gk *hypógeios* underground, subterranean, equiv. to *hypo-* HYPO- + *gê* earth + *-ios* adj. suffix) + -AL[1]]

hy·po·gene (hī′pə jēn′, hip′ə-), *adj. Geol.* **1.** formed beneath the earth's surface, as granite (opposed to *epigene*). **2.** formed by ascending solutions, as mineral or ore deposits (opposed to *supergene*). [1825–35; HYPO- + *-gene,* var. of -GEN] —**hy·po·gen·ic** (hī′pə jen′ik, hip′ə-), *adj.*

hy·po·gen·e·sis (hī′pə jen′ə sis), *n. Pathol.* underdevelopment of an organ or function, esp. in the embryo. [HYPO- + GENESIS] —**hy·po·ge·net·ic** (hī′pō jə net′ik), *adj.*

hy·pog·e·nous (hī poj′ə nəs, hi-), *adj.* growing beneath, or on the undersurface, as fungi on leaves. [1870–75; HYPOGENE + -OUS]

hy·po·ge·um (hī′pə jē′əm, hip′ə-), *n., pl.* **-ge·a** (-jē′ə). **1.** *Anc. Archit.* the underground part of a building, as a vault. **2.** an underground burial chamber. [1700–10; < L *hypogēum* < Gk *hypógeion* underground chamber (neut. of *hypógeios* underground), equiv. to *hypo-* HYPO- + *gê* earth + *-ion* neut. adj. suffix]

hy·po·glos·sal (hī′pə glos′əl, -glô′səl), *Anat.* —*adj.* **1.** situated under the tongue. —*n.* **2.** See **hypoglossal nerve.** [1825–35; HYPO- + Gk *glôss(a)* tongue (see GLOSS[2]) + -AL[1]]

hy′poglos′sal nerve′, *Anat.* either one of the twelfth pair of cranial nerves, consisting of motor fibers that innervate the muscles of the tongue. [1840–50]

hy·po·glot·tis (hī′pə glot′is), *n.* **1.** *Anat.* the underside of the tongue. **2.** *Pathol.* ranula. Also, **hy·po·glos·sis** (hī′pə glos′is, -glô′sis). [1650–60; < Gk *hypoglōttís.* See HYPO-, GLOTTIS]

hy·po·gly·ce·mi·a (hī′pō glī sē′mē ə), *n. Pathol.* an abnormally low level of glucose in the blood. [1890–95; HYPO- + GLYC- + -EMIA] —**hy′po·gly·ce′mic,** *adj.*

hy·pog·na·thous (hī pog′nə thəs), *adj.* having the lower jaw or mandible longer than the upper. [1870–75; HYPO- + -GNATHOUS] —**hy·pog′na·thism,** *n.*

hy·po·gon·ad·ism (hī′pə gō′na diz′əm, -gon′a-), *n. Pathol.* **1.** diminished hormonal or reproductive functioning in the testes or the ovaries. **2.** a manifestation of this, as delayed pubescence or Klinefelter's syndrome. Also, **hy·po·go·nad·i·a** (hī′pō gō nad′ē ə). [1915–20; HYPO- + GONAD + -ISM]

hy·pog·y·nous (hī poj′ə nəs, hi-), *adj. Bot.* **1.** situated on the receptacle beneath the pistil and free of the ovary, as stamens, petals, or sepals. **2.** having stamens, sepals, or petals so arranged. [1815–25; HYPO- + -GYNOUS] —**hy·pog′y·ny,** *n.*

hy·po·hi·dro·sis (hī′pō hi drō′sis, -hī-), *n. Pathol.* abnormally diminished sweating. [HYPO- + HIDROSIS]

hy′poid gear′ (hī′poid), a gear resembling a bevel gear in form but designed to mesh with a similar gear in such a way that their axes would not intersect, one axis crossing over the other at approximately a right angle. [1925–30; HYP(ERBOL)OID]

hy′po·i·o′ni·an mode′ (hī′pō ī ō′nē ən, hip′ō-, hī′pō-, hip′ō-), *Music.* a plagal church mode represented on the white keys of a keyboard instrument by an ascending scale from G to G, with the final on C. [HYPO- + L *Ion(ius)* IONIAN + -IAN]

hy·po·ka·le·mi·a (hī′pō kā lē′mē ə), *n. Pathol.* an abnormally low concentration of potassium in the blood. [1945–50; HYPO- + NL *kal(ium)* potassium (deriv. of *kali,* as in ALKALI) + -EMIA] —**hy′po·ka·le′mic,** *adj.*

hy·po·ki·ne·si·a (hī′pō ki nē′zhə, -zhē ə, -zē ə, -kī-), *n. Pathol.* abnormally diminished muscular function or mobility. Also, **hy·po·ki·ne·sis** (hī′pō ki nē′sis, -kī-). [1885–90; HYPO- + -KINESIA] —**hy·po·ki·net·ic** (hī′pō-ki net′ik, -kī-), *adj.*

hy·po·lim·ni·on (hī′pə lim′nē on′, -nē ən, hip′ə-), *n., pl.* **-ni·a** (-nē ə). (in certain lakes) the layer of water below the thermocline. [1905–10; HYPO- + Gk *límn(ē)* lake + *-ion* dim. n. suffix] —**hy·po·lim·net·ic** (hī′pō-lim net′ik, hip′ō-), **hy′po·lim′ni·al,** *adj.*

hy·po·lith·ic (hī′pə lith′ik, hip′ə-), *adj.* growing beneath rocks. [HYPO- + LITHIC]

hy′po·lyd′i·an mode′ (hī′pō lid′ē ən, hip′ō-, hī′pō-, hip′ō-), *Music.* a plagal church mode represented on the white keys of a keyboard instrument by an ascending scale from C to C, with the final on F. [1835–45; trans. of Gk *hypolýdios tónos;* see HYPO-, LYDIAN MODE]

hy·po·ma·ni·a (hī′pə mā′nē ə, -mān′yə), *n. Psychiatry.* a mania of low intensity. [1880–85; HYPO- + -MANIA] —**hy·po·man·ic** (hī′pə man′ik), *adj., n.*

hy′po·mix·o·lyd′ian mode′ (hī′pō mik′sə lid′ē ən, hip′ō-, hī′pō-, hip′ō-), *Music.* a plagal church mode represented on the white keys of a keyboard instrument by an ascending scale from D to D, with the final on G. [1895–1900; HYPO- + MIXOLYDIAN MODE]

hy·po·mo·til·i·ty (hī′pə mō til′i tē), *n. Pathol.* abnormally slow motility, as of the stomach or intestine (opposed to *hypermotility*). [1895–1900; HYPO- + MOTILITY]

hy·po·my·o·to·ni·a (hī′pə mī′ə tō′nē ə), *n.* abnormally diminished muscular tone. [HYPO- + MYOTONIA]

hy·po·nas·ty (hī′pə nas′tē), *n. Bot.* increased growth along the lower surface of a plant or plant part, causing it to bend upward. [1870–75; HYPO- + Gk *nast(ós)* pressed close, compact + -Y[3]] —**hy′po·nas′tic,** *adj.* —**hy′po·nas′ti·cal·ly,** *adv.*

hy·po·ni·trite (hī′pō nī′trīt), *n.* a salt or ester of hyponitrous acid. [1840–50; HYPONITR(OUS ACID) + -ITE[1]]

hy·po·ni·trous (hī′pə nī′trəs), *adj.* of or derived from hyponitrous acid. [1820–30; HYPO- + NITROUS]

hy′poni′trous ac′id, an unstable, crystalline acid, $H_2N_2O_2$. [1820–30]

hy·po·nym (hī′pə nim), *n. Ling.* a term that denotes a subcategory of a more general class: *"Chair" and "table" are hyponyms of "furniture."* Cf. **superordinate** (def. 4). [1960–65; HYP- + -ONYM, or as back formation from HYPONYMY] —**hy·pon·y·mous** (hī pon′ə məs), *adj.*

hy·pon·y·my (hī pon′ə mē), *n. Ling.* the state or quality of being a hyponym. [1950–55; HYP- + *-onymy* (see -ONYM, -Y[3]), on the model of HOMONYMY, SYNONYMY]

hy·po·pha·lan·gism (hī′pō fə lan′jiz əm), *n.* the condition of having fewer than the normal number of phalanges per finger or toe. [1910–15; HYPO- + PHALANGE + -ISM]

hy·po·phar·ynx (hī′pə far′ingks), *n., pl.* **-pha·ryn·ges** (-fə rin′jēz), **-phar·ynx·es. 1.** *Entomol.* a tongue-like lobe on the floor of the mouth in many insects. **2.** *Anat.* the lower part of the pharynx. [1820–30; HYPO- + PHARYNX]

hy·po·phloe·o·dal (hī′pə flē′ə dl, hip′ə-), *adj.* living or growing beneath bark, as insect larvae. Also, **hy′po·phloe·o·dic, hy′po·phloe′ous.** [HYPO- + Gk *phloiōd(ēs)* like bark (*phloi(ós)* bark + *-ōdēs* -ODE[1]) + -AL[1]; see PHLOEM]

hy·po·pho·ne·sis (hī′pō fə nē′sis, -fō-), *n. Med.* a sound of less than usual intensity in percussion or auscultation. [HYPO- + -PHONE + -SIS]

hy·po·pho·ni·a (hī′pə fō′nē ə), *n. Pathol.* an abnormally weak voice due to lack of coordination of the speech muscles. [HYPO- + -PHONIA]

hy·po·phos·phate (hī′pə fos′fāt), *n.* a salt or ester of hypophosphoric acid. [1860–65; HYPOPHOSPHOR(IC ACID) + -ATE[2]]

hy·po·phos·phite (hī′pə fos′fīt), *n.* a salt of hypophosphorous acid, as sodium hypophosphite, NaH_2PO_2. [1810–20; HYPO- + PHOSPHITE]

hy·po·phos·phor·ic (hī′pə fos fôr′ik, -for′-), *adj.* of or derived from hypophosphoric acid. [1850–55; HYPO- + PHOSPHORIC]

hy′pophosphor′ic ac′id, a tetrabasic acid, $H_4P_2O_6$, produced by the slow oxidation of phosphorus in moist air. [1850–55]

hy·po·phos·phor·ous (hī′pə fos′fər əs, -fos fôr′əs, -fōr′-), *adj.* of or derived from hypophosphorous acid. [1810–20; HYPO- + PHOSPHOROUS]

hy′pophos′phorous ac′id, a colorless or yellowish, water-soluble, liquid, monobasic acid, H_3PO_2, having a sour odor, and used as a reducing agent. [1810–20]

hy′po·phryg′i·an mode′ (hī′pō frij′ē ən, hip′ō-, hī′pō-, hip′ō-), *Music.* a plagal church mode represented on the white keys of a keyboard instrument by an ascending scale from B to B, with the final on E. [trans. of Gk *hypophrýgia harmonía;* see HYPO-, PHRYGIAN MODE]

hy·poph·y·ge (hī pof′i jē, hi-), *n.* apophyge (def. 2). [< Gk *hypophygḗ* flight from under, evasion, equiv. to *hypo-* HYPO- + *phygḗ* flight; see APOPHYGE]

hy·po·phyl·lous (hī′pə fil′əs, hip′ə-), *adj.* growing on the undersurface of leaves, as a fungus. [1850–55; HYPO- + -PHYLLOUS]

hy·poph·y·sec·to·my (hī pof′ə sek′tə mē, hi-), *n., pl.* **-mies.** *Surg.* excision of the pituitary gland. [1905–10; HYPOPHYS(IS) + -ECTOMY]

hy·poph·y·sis (hī pof′ə sis, hi-), *n., pl.* **-ses** (-sēz′). *Anat.* See **pituitary gland.** [1700–10; < Gk *hypóphysis* outgrowth (from below), equiv. to *hypophý(ein)* to grow beneath (*hypo-* HYPO- + *phýein* to grow, BE) + *-sis* -SIS] —**hy·poph·y·se·al, hy·poph·y·si·al** (hī pof′ə sē′əl, -zē′-, hi-), *adj.*

hy·po·pi·e·sis (hī′pō pī ē′sis), *n. Pathol.* abnormally low arterial blood pressure; hypotension. Also, **hy·po·pi·e·sia** (hī′pō pī ē′zhə, -zē ə, -shə, -sē ə). [HYPO- + Gk *piésis* a squeezing]

hy·po·pi·tu·i·ta·rism (hī′pō pi to͞o′i tə riz′əm, -tyo͞o′-), *n. Pathol.* **1.** abnormally diminished activity of the pituitary gland, esp. of the anterior lobe. **2.** the condition produced by this, characterized by obesity, retention of adolescent traits, sterility, amenorrhea, and, in extreme cases, dwarfism. [1905–10; HYPO- + PITUITAR(Y) + -ISM]

hy·po·pla·sia (hī′pə plā′zhə, -zhē ə, -zē ə), *n.* **1.** *Pathol.* abnormal deficiency of cells or structural elements. **2.** (in plants) inability to mature properly owing to a disease or inadequate supply of nutrients. Also, **hy·po·plas·ty** (hī′pə plas′tē). [1895–1900; HYPO- + -PLASIA] —**hy′·po·plas′tic,** *adj.*

hy·po·ploid (hī′pə ploid′), *Biol.* —*adj.* **1.** having a chromosome number that is less than the diploid number. —*n.* **2.** a hypoploid cell or organism. [1925–30; HYPO- + -PLOID] —**hy′po·ploid′y,** *n.*

hy·pop·ne·a (hī pop′nē ə, hi-), *n. Pathol.* abnormally shallow and slow breathing. [HYPO- + -PNEA]

hy·po·po·tas·se·mi·a (hī′pō pə ta sē′mē ə), *n. Pathol.* hypokalemia. [1930–35; < NL; see HYPO-, POTASSIUM, -EMIA] —**hy′po·po·tas·se′mic,** *adj.*

hy·po·prax·i·a (hī′pə prak′sē ə), *n. Pathol.* abnormally decreased activity; listlessness. [HYPO- + NL *-praxia* < Gk *prâx(is)* action (see PRAXIS) + NL *-ia* -IA]

hy·po·pro·tein·e·mi·a (hī′pə prō′tē nē′mē ə, -tē ə nē′-), *n. Pathol.* an abnormally low concentration of protein in the blood. [1930–35; HYPO- + PROTEIN + -EMIA]

hy·po·py·on (hī pō′pē on′, hi-), *n. Ophthalm.* an effusion of pus into the anterior chamber of the eye. [1650–60; HYPO- + Gk *pýon* pus, discharge from a sore]

hy·por·che·ma (hī′pər kē′mə), *n., pl.* **-ma·ta** (-mə tə). a lively choral ode sung in ancient Greece in honor of Apollo or Dionysus. [1595–1605; < Gk *hypórchēma,* equiv. to *hyp-* HYP- + *orchē-* (var. s. of *orcheîsthai* to dance with or to music; see ORCHESTRA) + *-ma* neut. n. suffix] —**hy·por·che·mat·ic** (hī′pər kē mat′ik), *adj.*

hy·po·se·cre·tion (hī′pō si krē′shən), *n.* a diminished secretion. [1905–10; HYPO- + SECRETION]

hy·po·sen·si·tiv·i·ty (hī′pō sen′si tiv′i tē), *n., pl.* **-ties.** *Pathol.* low or diminished sensitivity to stimulation. [HYPO- + SENSITIVITY] —**hy′po·sen′si·tive,** *adj.*

hy·po·sen·si·tize (hī′pə sen′si tīz′), *v.t.,* **-tized, -tiz·ing.** *Med.* to cause (a person) to become less sensitive to (a substance producing an allergic reaction); desensitize. Also, *esp. Brit.,* **hy′po·sen′si·tise′.** [1930–35; HYPO- + SENSITIZE] —**hy′po·sen′si·ti·za′tion,** *n.*

Hy·po·spray (hī′pō sprā′), *Trademark.* a brand name for an instrument, similar to a hypodermic syringe, but using no needle, for forcing extremely fine jets of a solution through the unbroken skin.

hy·pos·ta·sis (hī pos′tə sis, hi-), *n., pl.* **-ses** (-sēz′). **1.** *Metaphys.* **a.** something that stands under and supports; foundation. **b.** the underlying or essential part of anything as distinguished from attributes; substance, essence, or essential principle. **2.** *Theol.* **a.** one of the three real and distinct substances in the one undivided substance or essence of God. **b.** a person of the Trinity. **c.** the one personality of Christ in which His two natures, human and divine, are united. **3.** *Med.* **a.** the accumulation of blood or its solid components in parts of an organ or body due to poor circulation. **b.** such sedimentation, as in a test tube. [1580–90; < LL < Gk *hypóstasis* that which settles at the bottom; substance, nature, essence, equiv. to *hypo-* HYPO- + *stásis* standing, STASIS]

hy·pos·ta·size (hī pos′tə sīz′, hi-), *v.t.,* **-sized, -siz·ing.** to assume the reality of (an idea, proposition, etc.); hypostatize. Also, *esp. Brit.,* **hy·pos′ta·sise′.** [1800–10; HYPOSTAS(IS) + -IZE]

hy·po·stat·ic (hī′pə stat′ik), *adj.* **1.** of or pertaining to a hypostasis; fundamental. **2.** *Theol.* pertaining to or constituting a distinct personal being or substance. **3.** *Med.* being in a condition of hypostasis. **4.** *Genetics.* (of a nonallelic gene) masked by another gene. Also, **hy′po·stat′i·cal.** [1670–80; < Gk *hypostatikós* pertaining to substance, equiv. to *hypostat(ós)* placed under, giving support (*hypo-* HYPO- + *sta-* STAND + *-tos* verbal adj. suffix) + *-ikos* -IC] —**hy′po·stat′i·cal·ly,** *adv.*

hy·pos·ta·tize (hī pos′tə tīz′, hi-), *v.t.,* **-tized, -tiz·ing.** to treat or regard (a concept, idea, etc.) as a distinct substance or reality. Also, *esp. Brit.,* **hy·pos′ta·tise′.** [1820–30; < Gk *hypostat(ós)* (see HYPOSTATIC) + -IZE] —**hy·pos′ta·ti·za′tion,** *n.*

hy·pos·the·ni·a (hī′pos thē′nē ə), *n.* abnormal lack of strength; weakness. [HYPO- + STHENIA] —**hy·pos·then·ic** (hī′pos then′ik), *adj.*

hy·po·stome (hī′pə stōm′), *n. Zool.* any of several parts or organs of the mouth, as the labrum of a crustacean. [1860–65; HYPO- + -STOME] —**hy′po·sto′mi·al,** *adj.*

hy·po·style (hī′pə stīl′, hip′ə-), *Archit.* —*adj.* **1.** having many columns carrying the roof or ceiling: *a hypostyle hall.* —*n.* **2.** a hypostyle structure. [1825–35; < Gk *hypóstȳlos* resting on pillars, equiv. to *hypo-* HYPO- + *-stȳlos* -STYLE[2]]

hy·po·sul·fite (hī′pə sul′fīt), *n.* **1.** Also called **hydrosulfite.** a salt of hyposulfurous acid. **2.** See **sodium thiosulfate.** Also, **hy′po·sul′phite.** [1820–30; HYPO- + SULFITE]

hy·po·sul·fur·ous (hī′pə sul fyo͝or′əs, -sul′fər əs), *adj.* of or derived from hyposulfurous acid. Also, **hydrosulfurous, hy′po·sul·phur′ous.** [1810–20; HYPO- + SULFUROUS]

hy′posulfur′ous ac′id, an acid, $H_2S_2O_4$, next in a series below sulfurous acid, known only in solution or in the form of its salts. [1810–20]

hy·po·tax·is (hī′pə tak′sis), *n. Gram.* dependent relation or construction, as of clauses; syntactic subordination. [1880–85; < Gk *hypótaxis* subjection, equiv. to *hypo-* HYPO- + *-taxis* -TAXIS] —**hy·po·tac·tic** (hī′pə-tak′tik, hip′ə-), *adj.*

hy·po·ten·sion (hī′pə ten′shən), *n. Pathol.* **1.** decreased or lowered blood pressure. **2.** a disease or condition characterized by this symptom. Also called **low blood pressure.** [1890–95; HYPO- + TENSION]

hy·po·ten·sive (hī′pō ten′siv), *adj.* **1.** characterized by or causing low blood pressure, as shock. —*n.* **2.** a hypotensive person or agent. [1900–05; HYPOTENS(ION) + -IVE]

hy·pot·e·nuse (hī pot′n o͞os′, -yo͞os′), *n. Geom.* the side of a right triangle opposite the right angle. See illus. on next page. Also, **hypothenuse.** [1565–75; earlier *hypotenusa* < L *hypotēnūsa* < Gk *hypoteínousa* (*grammḗ*) subtending (line) (fem. prp. of *hypoteínein* to subtend), equiv. to *hypo-* HYPO- + *tein-* stretch (see THIN) + *-ousa* fem. prp. suffix]

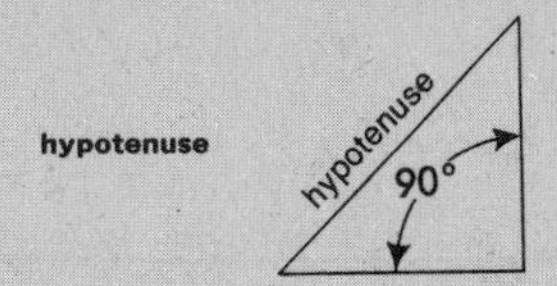

hypoth., 1. hypothesis. 2. hypothetical.

hy•po•thal•a•mus (hī′pə thal′ə məs), *n., pl.* **-mi** (-mī′). *Anat.* a region of the brain, between the thalamus and the midbrain, that functions as the main control center for the autonomic nervous system by regulating sleep cycles, body temperature, appetite, etc., and that acts as an endocrine gland by producing hormones, including the releasing factors that control the hormonal secretions of the pituitary gland. [1895–1900; < NL; see HYPO-, THALAMUS] —**hy•po•tha•lam•ic** (hī′pō thə lam′ik, hip′ō-), *adj.*

hy•po•thal•lus (hī′pə thal′əs, hip′ə-), *n., pl.* **-thal•li** (-thal′ī). 1. a layer of hyphae rimming the thallus of certain lichens. 2. a filmlike residue at the base of the sporangia of certain slime molds. [1850–55; < NL; see HYPO-, THALLUS]

hy•poth•ec (hī poth′ik, hi-), *n.* 1. *Roman and Civil Law.* a mortgage or security held by a creditor on the property of a debtor without possession of it, created either by agreement or by operation of law. 2. (in some modern legal systems) a security interest created in immovable property. [1585–95; earlier *hypotheca* < LL < Gk *hypothḗkē* deposit, pledge, mortgage (akin to *hypotithénai* to deposit as pledge). See HYPO-, THECA]

hy•poth•e•car•y (hī poth′i ker′ē, hi-), *adj.* 1. of or pertaining to a hypothec. 2. created or secured by a hypothec. [1650–60; HYPOTHEC + -ARY]

hy•poth•e•cate[1] (hī poth′i kāt′, hi-), *v.t.,* **-cat•ed, -cat•ing.** 1. to pledge to a creditor as security without delivering over; mortgage. 2. to put in pledge by delivery, as stocks given as security for a loan. [1675–85; < ML *hypothēcātus,* ptp. of *hypothēcāre.* See HYPOTHEC, -ATE[1]] —**hy•poth′e•ca′tion,** *n.* —**hy•poth′e•ca′tor,** *n.*

hy•poth•e•cate[2] (hī poth′i kāt′, hi-), *v.i., v.t.,* **-cat•ed, -cat•ing.** hypothesize. [1905–10; < Gk *hypothḗk(ē)* suggestion, counsel (akin to *hypotithénai* to assume, suppose) + -ATE[1]] —**hy•poth′e•cat′er,** *n.*

hy•po•the•ci•um (hī′pə thē′shē əm, -sē əm), *n., pl.* **-ci•a** (-shē ə, -sē ə). *Mycol.* the layer of hyphal tissue directly beneath the hymenium of an apothecium. [1865–70; HYPO- + THECIUM] —**hy′po•the′ci•al,** *adj.*

hy•poth•e•nar (hī poth′ə när′, -nər, hī′pə thē′nər), *Anat.* —*n.* 1. the fleshly prominence on the palm at the base of the little finger. —*adj.* 2. of, pertaining to, or situated on the hypothenar. [1700–10; HYPO- + THENAR]

hy•poth•e•nuse (hī poth′ə no͞os′, -nyo͞os′), *n.* hypotenuse.

hy•po•ther•mal (hī′pə thûr′məl), *adj.* 1. lukewarm; tepid. 2. characterized by subnormal body temperature. 3. *Geol.* (of mineral deposits) formed at great depths and high temperatures. [1895–1900; HYPO- + THERMAL]

hy•po•ther•mi•a (hī′pə thûr′mē ə), *n.* 1. *Pathol.* subnormal body temperature. 2. *Med.* the artificial reduction of body temperature to slow metabolic processes, as for facilitating heart surgery. [1885–90; HYPO- + THERM- + -IA] —**hy′po•ther′mic,** *adj.*

hy•poth•e•sis (hī poth′ə sis, hi-), *n., pl.* **-ses** (-sēz′). 1. a proposition, or set of propositions, set forth as an explanation for the occurrence of some specified group of phenomena, either asserted merely as a provisional conjecture to guide investigation (**working hypothesis**) or accepted as highly probable in the light of established facts. 2. a proposition assumed as a premise in an argument. 3. the antecedent of a conditional proposition. 4. a mere assumption or guess. [1590–1600; < Gk *hypóthesis* basis, supposition. See HYPO-, THESIS] —**hy•poth′e•sist,** *n.*
—**Syn.** 1. See **theory.**

hy•poth•e•size (hī poth′ə sīz′, hi-), *v.,* **-sized, -siz•ing.** —*v.i.* 1. to form a hypothesis. —*v.t.* 2. to assume by hypothesis. Also, **hypothecate;** *esp. Brit.,* **hy•poth′e•sise′.** [1730–40; HYPOTHES(IS) + -IZE] —**hy•poth′e•siz′er,** *n.*

hy•po•thet•i•cal (hī′pə thet′i kəl), *adj.* 1. assumed by hypothesis; supposed: *a hypothetical case.* 2. of, pertaining to, involving, or characterized by hypothesis: *hypothetical reasoning.* 3. given to making hypotheses. 4. *Logic.* a. (of a proposition) highly conjectural; not well supported by available evidence. b. (of a proposition or syllogism) conditional. —*n.* 5. a hypothetical situation, instance, etc.: *The Secretary of Defense refused to discuss hypotheticals with the reporters.* Also, **hy′po•thet′ic** (defs. 1–4). [1580–90; < Gk *hypothetik(ós)* supposed (*hypo-* HYPO- + *the-* put (base of *tithénai* to put, DO[1]) + *-tikos* -TIC) + -AL[1]] —**hy′po•thet′i•cal•ly,** *adv.*
—**Syn.** 1. suppositional, theoretical, speculative.

hy•po•thet′i•co-de•duc′tive meth′od (hī′pəthet′i kō di duk′tiv), *Logic.* a method in which a hypothetical model based on observations is proposed and is then tested by the deduction of consequences from the model. [1925–30; HYPOTHETIC(AL) + -O- + DEDUCTIVE, prob. as trans. of It *ipotetico-deduttivo*]

hy•po•thy•roid•ism (hī′pə thī′roi diz′əm), *n. Pathol.* 1. deficient activity of the thyroid gland. 2. the condition produced by a deficiency of thyroid secretion, resulting in goiter, myxedema, and, in children, cretinism. [1900–05; HYPO- + THYROID + -ISM] —**hy′po•thy′roid,** *adj.*

hy•po•ton•ic (hī′pə ton′ik), *adj.* 1. *Physiol.* (of tissue) having less than the normal tone. 2. *Physical Chem.* noting a solution of lower osmotic pressure than another solution with which it is compared (opposed to *hypertonic*). Cf. **isotonic** (def. 1). [1890–95; HYPO- + TONIC] —**hy•po•to•nic•i•ty** (hī′pō tō nis′i tē), *n.*

hy•po•tra•che•li•um (hī′pō trə kē′lē əm), *n., pl.* **-li•a** (-lē ə). (on a classical column) any member, as a necking, between the capital and the shaft. Cf. **trachelium.** [1555–65; < L < Gk *hypotrachḗlion.* See HYPO-, TRACHELIUM]

hy•po•trich (hī′pə trik), *n.* any ciliate of the suborder Hypotricha, having cilia chiefly on the ventral surface. [< NL *Hypotricha;* see HYPO-, -TRICHA] —**hy•pot•rich•ous** (hī po′tri kəs), *adj.*

hy•po•ty•po•sis (hī′pə tī pō′sis), *n. Rhet.* lifelike description of a thing or scene. [1575–85; < Gk *hypotýpōsis* outline, copy pattern, equiv. to *hypo-* HYPO- + *typōsis* forming, molding (*týp(os)* beat, impression, mold + *-ōsis* -OSIS)]

hy′po•vo•le′mic shock′ (hī′pō və lē′mik, hī′-), a type of shock caused by reduced blood volume, as from massive bleeding or dehydration. Cf. **cardiogenic shock, anaphylactic shock.** [1960–65; HYPO- + VOL(UME) + -EM(IA) + -IC]

hy•po•xan•thine (hī′pə zan′thēn, -thin), *n.* a white, crystalline, almost water-soluble, alkaloidal purine derivative, $C_5H_4N_4O$, found in animal and vegetable tissues: used chiefly in biochemical research. [1835–45; HYPO- + XANTHINE] —**hy′po•xan′thic,** *adj.*

hy•pox•e•mi•a (hī′pok sē′mē ə), *n. Pathol.* inadequate oxygenation of the blood. Also, **hy•pox′i•a.** [1885–90; HYP- + OX(Y)- + -EMIA] —**hy′pox•e′mic, hy•pox′•ic,** *adj.*

hy•po•zeug•ma (hī′pə zo͞og′mə), *n. Rhet.* the use of a succession of subjects with a single predicate. [1580–90; HYPO- + ZEUGMA]

hy•po•zeux•is (hī′pə zo͞ok′sis), *n. Rhet.* the use of a series of parallel clauses, each of which has a subject and predicate, as in "I came, I saw, I conquered." [1580–90; < LL < LGk, equiv. to Gk *hypozeug(nýnai)* to put under the yoke (*hypo-* HYPO- + *zeugnýnai* to yoke, deriv. of *zeûgos* YOKE) + *-sis* -SIS]

hypso-, a combining form meaning "height," "altitude," used in the formation of compound words: *hypsometer.* Also, **hypsi-.** [< Gk, comb. form of *hýpsos* height; akin to HYPO-, UP]

hyp•sog•ra•phy (hip sog′rə fē), *n.* 1. a branch of geography that deals with the measurement and mapping of the topography of the earth above sea level. 2. topographical relief, esp. as represented on a map. [1880–85; HYPSO- + -GRAPHY] —**hyp•so•graph•ic** (hip′sə graf′ik), **hyp′so•graph′i•cal,** *adj.*

hyp•som•e•ter (hip som′i tər), *n.* thermobarometer (def. 1). [1860–65; HYPSO- + -METER]

hyp•som•e•try (hip som′i trē), *n.* vertical control in mapping; the establishment of elevations or altitudes. [1560–70; HYPSO- + -METRY] —**hyp•so•met•ric** (hip′səme′trik), **hyp′so•met′ri•cal,** *adj.* —**hyp′so•met′ri•cal•ly,** *adv.* —**hyp•som′e•trist,** *n.*

hy•ra•co•the•ri•um (hī′rə kō thēr′ē əm), *n., pl.* **-the•ri•a** (-thēr′ē ə). eohippus. [< NL (1840): a genus name; see HYRAX, -O-, -THERE]

hy•rax (hī′raks), *n., pl.* **-rax•es, -ra•ces** (-rə sēz′). any of several species of small mammals of the order Hyracoidea, of Africa and the Mediterranean region, having short legs, ears, and tail, and hooflike nails on the toes. Also called **dassie, das.** [1825–35; < NL < Gk *hýrax* (gen. *hýrakos*) shrewmouse]

Hyr•ca•ni•a (hər kā′nē ə), *n.* an ancient province of the Persian empire, SE of the Caspian Sea. —**Hyr•ca′•ni•an,** *adj.*

hy•son (hī′sən), *n.* a Chinese green tea dried and prepared from twisted leaves, esp. of the early crop (**young hyson**). [1730–40; < dial. Chin (Guangdong) *héichēun,* akin to Chin *xīchūn* (blooming) spring]

hys•sop (his′əp), *n.* 1. any of several aromatic herbs belonging to the genus *Hyssopus,* of the mint family, esp. *H. officinalis,* native to Europe, having clusters of small blue flowers. 2. any of several related or similar plants, esp. of the genera *Agastache* or *Gratiola.* 3. *Bible.* a plant, perhaps the origan, whose twigs were used in ceremonial sprinkling. [bef. 900; ME, OE *ysope* < LL *ysōpus,* for L *hyssōpus* < Gk *hýssōpos* < Sem (cf. Heb *ēzōbh*); conformed to L or Gk from mid-16th century]

hyster-, var. of **hystero-** before a vowel: *hysterectomy.*

hys•ter•ec•to•mize (his′tə rek′tə mīz′), *v.t.,* **-mized, -miz•ing.** to remove the uterus from by surgery. Also, *esp. Brit.,* **hys′ter•ec′to•mise′.** [HYSTERECTOM(Y) + -IZE]

hys•ter•ec•to•my (his′tə rek′tə mē), *n., pl.* **-mies.** *Surg.* excision of the uterus. [1885–90; HYSTER- + -ECTOMY]

hys•ter•e•sis (his′tə rē′sis), *n. Physics.* 1. the lag in response exhibited by a body in reacting to changes in the forces, esp. magnetic forces, affecting it. Cf. **magnetic hysteresis.** 2. the phenomenon exhibited by a system, often a ferromagnetic or imperfectly elastic material, in which the reaction of the system to changes is dependent upon its past reactions to change. [1795–1805; < Gk *hystérēsis* deficiency, state of being behind or late, hence inferior, equiv. to *hysterē-,* var. s. of *hystereîn* to come late, lag behind, v. deriv. of *hýsteros* coming behind + *-sis* -SIS] —**hys•ter•et•ic** (his′tə ret′ik), **hys•ter•e•si•al** (his′tə rē′sē əl), *adj.* —**hys′ter•et′i•cal•ly,** *adv.*

hystere′sis loss′, *Physics.* the loss of energy by conversion to heat in a system exhibiting hysteresis. [1890–95]

hys•te•ri•a (hi ster′ē ə, -stēr′-), *n.* 1. an uncontrollable outburst of emotion or fear, often characterized by irrationality, laughter, weeping, etc. 2. *Psychoanal.* a psychoneurotic disorder characterized by violent emotional outbreaks, disturbances of sensory and motor functions, and various abnormal effects due to autosuggestion. 3. *Psychiatry.* See **conversion disorder.** Cf. **mass hysteria.** [1795–1805; HYSTER(IC) + -IA]

hys•ter•ic (hi ster′ik), *n.* 1. Usually, **hysterics.** a fit of uncontrollable laughter or weeping; hysteria. 2. a person subject to hysteria. —*adj.* 3. hysterical. [1650–60; < L *hystericus* < Gk *hysterikós,* suffering in the womb, hysterical (reflecting the Greeks' belief that hysteria was peculiar to women and caused by disturbances in the uterus); see HYSTERO-, -IC]

hys•ter•i•cal (hi ster′i kəl), *adj.* 1. of, pertaining to, or characterized by hysteria. 2. uncontrollably emotional. 3. irrational from fear, emotion, or an emotional shock. 4. causing hysteria. 5. suffering from or subject to hysteria. 6. causing unrestrained laughter; very funny: *Oh, that joke is hysterical!* [1605–15; < L *hysteric(us)* HYSTERIC + -AL[1]] —**hys•ter′i•cal•ly,** *adv.*
—**Syn.** 6. hilarious, uproarious, laughable, ludicrous.

hystero-, a combining form meaning "uterus," used in the formation of compound words: *hysterotomy.* Also, *esp. before a vowel,* **hyster-.** [< Gk, comb. form repr. Gk *hystéra* womb, uterus]

hys•ter•o•gen•ic (his′tər ə jen′ik), *adj. Med.* inducing hysteria. [1885–90; HYSTER(IA) + -O- + -GENIC] —**hys•ter•og•e•ny** (his′tə roj′ə nē), *n.*

hys•ter•oid (his′tə roid′), *adj.* resembling hysteria. Also, **hys′ter•oi′dal.** [1850–55; HYSTER(IA) + -OID]

hys•ter•on prot•er•on (his′tə ron′ prot′ə ron′). *Rhet.* a figure of speech in which the logical order of two elements in discourse is reversed, as in "bred and born" for "born and bred." [1555–65; < LL < Gk *hýsteron* (neut. of *hýsteros*) latter + *próteron* (neut. of *próteros*) former]

hys•ter•ot•o•my (his′tə rot′ə mē), *n., pl.* **-mies.** *Surg.* the operation of cutting into the uterus, as in a Cesarean. [1700–10; HYSTERO- + -TOMY]

hyte (hīt), *adj. Scot. Archaic.* insane; mad. [1715–25; orig. uncert.]

Hythe (hīth), *n.* a town in E Kent, in SE England: one of the Cinque Ports. 11,949.

hy•ther•graph (hī′thər graf′, -gräf′), *n.* a climatic graph showing relationships between temperature and humidity or temperature and precipitation. [1915–20; HY(DR)-[1] + -THER(M) + -GRAPH]

hy•zone (hī′zōn), *n. Chem.* triatomic hydrogen, H_3. [HY(DROGEN) + (O)ZONE]

Hz, Hertz; hertzes.

CONCISE PRONUNCIATION KEY: act, cāpe, dâre, pärt; set, ēqual; if, īce; ox, ōver, ôrder, oil, bo͝ok, bo͞ot, out; up, ûrge; child; sing; shoe; thin, *th*at; zh as in *treasure.* ə = *a* as in *alone, e* as in *system, i* as in *easily, o* as in *gallop, u* as in *circus;* ᵊ as in *fire* (fīᵊr), *hour* (ouᵊr). l and n can serve as syllabic consonants, as in *cradle* (krād′l), and *button* (but′n). See the full key inside the front cover.

DEVELOPMENT OF MAJUSCULE								
NORTH SEMITIC	GREEK		ETR.	LATIN		MODERN		
						GOTHIC	ITALIC	ROMAN
ⵋ	⟨	I	I	I	I	𝕴	*I*	I

I

DEVELOPMENT OF MINUSCULE					
ROMAN CURSIVE	ROMAN UNCIAL	CAROL. MIN.	MODERN		
			GOTHIC	ITALIC	ROMAN
I	I	ı	i	*i*	i

The ninth letter of the English alphabet developed from the North Semitic consonant *yodh* (**y**), which became the Greek vowel *iota* (ι). Originally, it was much like a Z in form, acquiring its present shape in Greek. The minuscule (i) was first written with a dot in early Medieval Latin to distinguish it from the *n* (written ıı), the *m* (written ııı), and other letters written with similar vertical strokes.

I, i (ī), *n., pl.* **I's** or **Is, i's** or **is. 1.** the ninth letter of the English alphabet, a vowel. **2.** any spoken sound represented by the letter *I* or *i*, as in *big, nice,* or *ski.* **3.** something having the shape of an I. **4.** a written or printed representation of the letter *I* or *i.* **5.** a device, as a printer's type, for reproducing the letter *I* or *i.*

I (ī), *pron., nom.* **I,** *poss.* **my** or **mine,** *obj.* **me;** *pl. nom.* **we,** *poss.* **our** or **ours,** *obj.* **us;** *n., pl.* **I's.** —*pron.* **1.** the nominative singular pronoun, used by a speaker in referring to himself or herself. —*n.* **2.** (used to denote the narrator of a literary work written in the first person singular). **3.** *Metaphys.* the ego. [bef. 900; ME *ik, ich, i;* OE *ic, ih;* c. G *ich,* ON *ek,* L *ego,* Gk *egṓ,* OCS *azŭ,* Lith *aš,* Skt *ahám*]
—**Usage.** See **me.**

I, interstate (used with a number to designate an interstate highway): *I-95.*

I, *Symbol.* **1.** the ninth in order or in a series. **2.** (*sometimes l.c.*) the Roman numeral for 1. Cf. **Roman numerals. 3.** *Chem.* iodine. **4.** *Biochem.* isoleucine. **5.** *Elect.* current. **6.** *Logic.* See **particular affirmative.**

i, *Math.* **1.** Also called **imaginary unit.** the imaginary number $\sqrt{-1}$. **2.** a unit vector on the *x*-axis of a coordinate system.

I, *Symbol, Physics.* isotopic spin.

i-, var. of **y-.**

-i-, the typical ending of the first element of compounds of Latin words, as **-o-** is of Greek words, but often used in English with a first element of any origin, if the second element is of Latin origin: *cuneiform; Frenchify.*

I., **1.** Independent. **2.** Island; Islands. **3.** Isle; Isles.

i., **1.** imperator. **2.** incisor. **3.** interest. **4.** intransitive. **5.** island. **6.** isle; isles.

-ia, a noun suffix having restricted application in various fields, as in names of diseases (*malaria; anemia*), place names (*Italia; Rumania*), names of Roman feasts (*Lupercalia*), Latin or Latinizing plurals (*Amphibia; insignia; Reptilia*), and in other loanwords from Latin (*militia*). [< NL, L, Gk, equiv. to *-i-* (formative or connective) or *-i-* (Gk *-ei-*) + *-a,* fem. sing. or neut. pl. n. or adj. ending]

IA, Iowa (approved esp. for use with zip code).

Ia., Iowa.

i.a., in absentia.

IAAF, International Amateur Athletic Federation.

I•a•coc•ca (ī′ə kō′kə), *n.* **Lee** (*Lido Anthony*), born 1924, U.S. automobile executive.

IADB, 1. Inter-American Defense Board. **2.** Inter-American Development Bank.

IAEA, International Atomic Energy Agency.

I•a•go (ē ä′gō), *n.* the villain in Shakespeare's *Othello.*

-ial, var. of **-al**[1]: *grallatorial.* [extracted from L loanwords in which *-ālis* -AL[1] is joined to stems ending in *i;* cf. FILIAL, IMPERIAL]

I•al•y•sus (ī al′ə səs, ē al′-), *n.* an ancient Mycenaean city on the island of Rhodes. Also, **I•al′y•sos.**

IAMAW, International Association of Machinists and Aerospace Workers.

i•amb (ī′am, ī′amb), *n. Pros.* a foot of two syllables, a short followed by a long in quantitative meter, or an unstressed followed by a stressed in accentual meter, as in *Come live / with me / and be / my love.* [1835–45; short for IAMBUS]

i•am•bic (ī am′bik), *adj.* **1.** *Pros.* **a.** pertaining to the iamb. **b.** consisting of or employing an iamb or iambs. **2.** *Gk. Lit.* noting or pertaining to satirical poetry written in iambs. —*n.* **3.** *Pros.* **a.** an iamb. **b.** Usually, **iambics.** a verse or poem consisting of iambs. **4.** *Gk. Lit.* a satirical poem in this meter. [1565–75; < L *iambicus* < Gk *iambikós.* See IAMBUS, -IC] —**i•am′bi•cal•ly,** *adv.*

i•am•bus (ī am′bəs), *n., pl.* **-bi** (-bī), **-bus•es.** iamb. [1580–90; < L < Gk *íambos*]

I•an (ē′ən, ē′än, ī′ən), *n.* a male given name, Scottish form of **John.**

-ian, a suffix with the same meaning and properties as **-an; -ian** is now the more productive of the two suffixes in recent coinages, esp. when the base noun ends in a consonant: *Orwellian; Washingtonian.* [extracted from L loanwords in which *-ānus* -AN is joined to stems ending in *i*]

-iana. See **-an, -ana.** [< L, neut. pl. of *-iānus* -IAN]

I•ap•e•tus (ī ap′i təs, ē ap′-), *n.* **1.** *Class. Myth.* a Titan, son of Uranus and Gaea. **2.** *Astron.* a natural satellite of the planet Saturn.

I•a•pig•i•a (ē′ə pij′ē ə, ī′ə-), *n.* an area in the southern hemisphere of Mars.

iar•o•vize (yär′ə vīz′), *v.t.,* **-vized, -viz•ing.** jarovize. Also, *esp. Brit.,* **iar′o•vise′.** —**iar′o•vi•za′tion,** *n.*

IAS, 1. *Aeron.* indicated air speed. **2.** Institute for Advanced Studies.

Ia•şi (yäsh, yä′shē), *n.* Rumanian name of **Jassy.**

-iasis, a noun suffix occurring in loanwords from Greek: *psoriasis.* Cf. **-asis.** [< Gk, equiv. to *-iā-* v. formative + *-sis* -SIS]

IAT, international atomic time.

IATA, International Air Transport Association.

i•at•ric (ī a′trik, ē a′-), *adj.* of or pertaining to a physician or medicine; medical. Also, **i•at′ri•cal.** [1850–55; < Gk *iātrikós* of healing, equiv. to *iātr(ós)* healer (see IATRO-) + *-ikos* -IC]

-iatrics, a combining form occurring in compound words that have the general sense "healing, medical practice," with the initial element usually denoting the type of person treated: *geriatrics; pediatrics.* [-IATR(Y) + -ICS]

iatro-, a combining form meaning "healer," "medicine," "healing," used in the formation of compound words: *iatrogenic.* [< Gk, comb. form of *iātrós* healer, equiv. to *iâ(sthai)* to heal + *-tros* n. suffix]

i•at•ro•chem•is•try (ī a′trə kem′ə strē, ē a′-), *n.* (in the 16th and 17th centuries) the study of chemistry in relation to the physiology, pathology, and treatment of disease. [1820–30; IATRO- + CHEMISTRY; cf. NL *iatrochymista, iatrochymicus*] —**i•at•ro•chem•i•cal** (ī a′trə kem′i kəl, ē a′-), *adj.* —**i•at′ro•chem′i•cal•ly,** *adv.* —**i•at′ro•chem′ist,** *n.*

i•at•ro•gen•ic (ī a′trə jen′ik, ē a′-), *adj.* (of a medical disorder) caused by the diagnosis, manner, or treatment of a physician. [1920–25; IATRO- + -GENIC] —**i•at•ro•ge•nic•i•ty** (ī a′trō jə nis′i tē, ē a′-), *n.*

-iatry, a combining form occurring in compound words that have the general sense "healing, medical practice," with the initial element usually denoting the area treated: *podiatry; psychiatry.* [< Gk *iātreía* healing. See IATRO-, -Y[3]]

IATSE, International Alliance of Theatrical Stage Employees (and Moving Picture Machine Operators of the U.S. and Canada).

ib., ibidem.

i•ba•da (ē bä′dä, -də), *n.* any of the religious duties of a Muslim, including the recital of the creed, the five daily recitals of prayers, the Ramadan fast, almsgiving, and the pilgrimage to Mecca. [< Ar *'ibādah* act of devotion, worship]

I•ba•dan (ē bä′dän, ē bäd′n), *n.* a city in SW Nigeria. 800,000.

I•ba•di (i bä′dē), *n. Islam.* a North African Kharijite. [< Ar, equiv. to *'Abd Allāh ibn Ibāḍ,* 7th-century Muslim ascetic + *-ī* suffix of appurtenance]

I•ba•gué (ē′vä ge′), *n.* a city in W central Colombia. 200,000.

I•ban (ē bän′), *n., pl.* **I•bans,** (*esp. collectively*) **I•ban. 1.** Also called **Sea Dayak.** a member of any of several Dayak tribes of Sarawak. **2.** the Austronesian language, closely related to Malay, spoken by the Iban. Cf. **Land Dayak.**

I•bá•ñez (ē vän′yeth), *n.* **Vi•cen•te Blas•co** (bē then′te bläs′kô). See **Blasco Ibáñez, Vicente.**

I-bar (ī′bär′), *n.* an I-beam used for structural support, as in buildings or bridges. [1885–90]

IBC, international business company.

IBD, See **inflammatory bowel disease.**

I-beam (ī′bēm′), *n.* a rolled or extruded metal beam having a cross section resembling an I. See illus. under **shape.** [1890–95]

I•be•ri•a (ī bēr′ē ə), *n.* **1.** Also called **Ibe′rian Penin′•sula.** a peninsula in SW Europe, comprising Spain and Portugal. **2.** an ancient region S of the Caucasus in the S Soviet Union; modern Georgia.

I•be•ri•an (ī bēr′ē ən), *adj.* **1.** of or pertaining to Iberia in SW Europe, its inhabitants, or their language. **2.** of or pertaining to ancient Iberia in the Caucasus or its inhabitants. —*n.* **3.** one of the ancient inhabitants of Iberia in Europe, from whom the Basques are supposed to be descended. **4.** the language of the ancient Iberians of SW Europe, not known to be related to any other language. **5.** one of the ancient inhabitants of Iberia in Asia. [1595–1605; IBERI(A) + -AN]

I•be•ro-Mau•ru•si•an (ī bēr′ō mô ro͞o′zē ən, -zhən), *adj.* of or pertaining to an Epipaleolithic culture of northwestern Africa that preceded the Capsian culture and was once erroneously thought to have originated in southwestern Europe; characterized by the use of backed bladelets, occupation of the maritime plain, and the hunting of the Barbary sheep. [< F *ibéromaurusien* (1909), equiv. to *ibér(ique)* Iberian + *-o-* -O- + L *Maurūs(ius)* pertaining to Mauretania (akin to *Maurus;* see MOOR) + *-ien* -IAN]

I•bert (ē bεʀ′), *n.* **Jacques Fran•çois An•toine** (zhäk fräɴ swa′ äɴ twan′), 1890–1962, French composer.

I•ber•ville, d' (dē bεʀ vēl′), **Pierre le Moyne** (pyεʀ lə mwaɴ′), **Sieur,** 1661–1706, French naval officer, born in Canada: founder of the first French settlement in Louisiana, 1699.

IBEW, International Brotherhood of Electrical Workers.

i•bex (ī′beks), *n., pl.* **i•bex•es, ib•i•ces** (ib′ə sēz′, ī′bə-), (*esp. collectively*) **i•bex.** any of several wild goats of the genus *Capra,* inhabiting mountainous regions of Eurasia and North Africa, having long, recurved horns. [1600–10; < L]

ibex, genus *Capra,* about 3 ft. (0.9 m) high at shoulder; horns to 3 ft. (0.9 m); length 4½ ft. (1.4 m)

CONCISE ETYMOLOGY KEY: <, descended or borrowed from; >, whence; b., blend of, blended; c., cognate with; cf., compare; deriv., derivative; equiv., equivalent; imit., imitative; obl., oblique; r., replacing; s., stem; sp., spelling, spelled; resp., respelling, respelled; trans., translation; ?, origin unknown; *, unattested; ‡, probably earlier than. See the full key inside the front cover.

IBF, international banking facilities.

I·bi·bi·o (ib′ə bē′ō), *n., pl.* **-bi·os,** (*esp. collectively*) **-bi·o** for 1. **1.** a member of a people of southeastern Nigeria. **2.** the Benue-Congo language of the Ibibio people, very closely related to Efik.

ibid. (ib′id), ibidem.

i·bi·dem (i bē′dem; *Eng.* ib′i dəm, i bī′dəm, i bē′-), *adv. Latin.* in the same book, chapter, page, etc. [lit., in the aforementioned place]

-ibility, var. of **-ability:** *reducibility.* [< L *-ibilitāt-*, equiv. to *-ibili(s)* -IBLE + *-tāt-* -TY[2]]

i·bis (ī′bis), *n., pl.* **i·bis·es,** (*esp. collectively*) **i·bis. 1.** any of several large wading birds of the family Threskiornithidae, of warm temperate and tropical regions, related to the herons and storks, and characterized by a long, thin, downward-curved bill. Cf. **sacred ibis. 2.** any of certain similar birds belonging to the stork family Ciconiidae, esp. the wood stork, *Mycteria americana.* [1350–1400; ME < L *ibis* < Gk *îbis* < Egyptian *hb*]

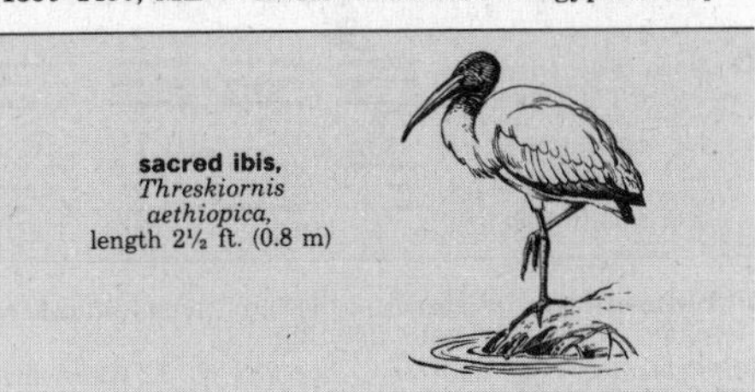

sacred ibis, *Threskiornis aethiopica,* length 2½ ft. (0.8 m)

I·bi·za (ē vē′thä, -sä; *Eng.* i bē′zə), *n.* a Spanish island in the SW Balearic Islands, in the W Mediterranean Sea. 209 sq. mi. (541 sq. km). Also, **Iviza.**

I·bi′zan hound′ (i bē′zən, -zän), one of a breed of medium-sized, tall, swift hunting hounds with a short, usually red and white coat, bred originally by the Pharaohs of ancient Egypt but today found chiefly in the Balearic Islands and other areas of Spain. Also called **Ibi′zan Po·den′co** (pə deng′kō, pō-). [1945–50; IBIZ(A) + -AN]

-ible, var. of **-able,** occurring in words borrowed from Latin (*credible; horrible; visible*), or modeled on the Latin type (*reducible*). [< L *-ibil(is)* or *-ībil(is)*, equiv. to *-i-* or *-ī-* thematic vowel + *-bilis* -BLE]

Ib·lis (ib′lis), *n. Islamic Myth.* an evil spirit or devil, the chief of the wicked jinn. [< Ar *iblīs* < Gk *diábolos* (see DEVIL); *di-* lost by confusion with Aram *di-* of]

-ibly, var. of **-ably:** *credibly; visibly.* [-IBLE + -LY]

ibn (ib′ən), (*often cap.*) son of (used in Arabic personal names): *ibn Saud.* [< Ar: son (of); cf. BEN[4]]

ibn ʿA·ra·bi (ib′ən ä rä′bē), ("Animator of the Religion"), 1165–1240, Islamic philosopher, theologian, and mystic.

ibn Ga·bi·rol (ib′ən gä bē′RÔl), *n.* Arabic name of **Avicebrón.** Also, **ibn′-Ga·bi′ral.**

ibn Han·bal (ib′ən han′bal), **Ah·mad** (ä′məd), A.D. 780–855, Islamic legist and traditionist, founder of the Hanbali school of law, one of four such schools in Islam.

ibn Khal·dun (ib′ən KHäl do͞on′), *n.* **Abd-al-Rah·man** (äb däl RÄ′män), 1332–1406, Arab historian and philosopher.

ibn Rushd (ib′ən Ro͝osht′), *n.* Arabic name of **Averroës.**

ibn Sa·ud (ib′ən sä o͞od′), *n.* **Ab·dul-A·ziz** (äb do͞ol′ä-zēz′), 1880–1953, king of Saudi Arabia 1932–53 (father of Saud ibn Abdul-Aziz).

ibn Si·na (ib′ən sē′nä), *n.* Arabic name of **Avicenna.**

I·bo (ē′bō), *n., pl.* **I·bos,** (*esp. collectively*) **I·bo. 1.** a member of an indigenous black people of southeastern Nigeria, renowned as traders and for their art. **2.** the language of the Ibo, a Kwa language. Also, **Igbo.**

i·bo·ga·ine (i bō′gə ēn′), *n. Pharm.* an alkaloid, $C_{20}H_{26}N_2O$, obtained from an African shrub, *Tabernanthe iboga,* having antidepressant and hallucinogenic properties. [< F *ibogaïne* (1901) < NL *iboga* the shrub's specific epithet (said to be < an indigenous language of the Congo) + F *-ine* -INE[2]]

I·bot′a priv′et (i bō′tə), a Japanese spreading shrub, *Ligustrum obtusifolium,* of the olive family, having hairy leaves and nodding white flower clusters. [< Japn *ibota* wax tree]

IBR, infectious bovine rhinotracheitis.

Ib·ra·him Pa·sha (ib′rä hēm′ pä′shä), 1789–1848, Egyptian general: governor of Syria 1833–40 (son of Mehemet Ali).

Ib·sen (ib′sən; *Norw.* ip′sən), *n.* **Hen·rik** (hen′rik), 1828–1906, Norwegian dramatist and poet.

Ib·sen·ism (ib′sə niz′əm), *n.* **1.** a manner or style of dramatic structure or content characteristic of Ibsen. **2.** attachment to or advocacy of Ibsen's dramatic style and social ideas. [1885–90; IBSEN + -ISM]

I.B.T.C.W.H., International Brotherhood of Teamsters, Chauffeurs, Warehousemen, and Helpers of America.

i·bu·pro·fen (ī′byo͞o prō′fən, ī byo͞o′prō fen′), *n. Pharm.* a white powder, $C_{13}H_{18}O_2$, used esp. in the treatment of rheumatoid arthritis and osteoarthritis as an anti-inflammatory, analgesic, and antipyretic. [1965–70; by contr., rearrangement and resp. of *isobutylphenyl propionic acid,* the chemical name]

Ib·y·cus (ib′i kəs), *n.* fl. c540 B.C., Greek poet.

-ic, 1. a suffix forming adjectives from other parts of speech, occurring originally in Greek and Latin loanwords (*metallic; poetic; archaic; public*) and, on this model, used as an adjective-forming suffix with the particular senses "having some characteristics of" (opposed to the simple attributive use of the base noun) (*balletic; sophomoric*); "in the style of" (*Byronic; Miltonic*); "pertaining to a family of peoples or languages" (*Finnic; Semitic; Turkic*). **2.** *Chem.* a suffix, specialized in opposition to **-ous,** used to show the higher of two valences: *ferric chloride.* **3.** a noun suffix occurring chiefly in loanwords from Greek, where such words were originally adjectival (*critic; magic; music*). [ME *-ic, -ik* < L *-icus;* in many words repr. the cognate Gk *-ikos* (directly or through L); in some words r. *-ique* < F < L *-icus*]

IC, 1. *pl.* **ICs.** See **immediate constituent. 2.** *Electronics.* integrated circuit. **3.** intensive care.

I.C., Jesus Christ. [< L *I(ēsus) C(hristus)*]

I·ça (ē′sä), *n.* Portuguese name of **Putumayo.**

ICA, 1. International Cooperation Administration. **2.** (United States) International Communication Agency: existed 1978–82.

-ical, a combination of **-ic** and **-al**[1], used in forming adjectives from nouns (*rhetorical*), providing synonyms to words ending in **-ic** (*poetical*), and providing an adjective with additional meanings to those in the **-ic** form (*economical*). [ME < L *-icālis.* See -IC, -AL[1]]

-ically, a suffix used to form adverbs from adjectives ending in **-ic** (*terrifically*) and **-ical** (*poetically; magically*).

ICAO, International Civil Aviation Organization.

I·car·i·a (i kâr′ē ə, ī kâr′-; *Gk.* ē′kä RĒ′ä), *n.* **1.** Also, **Ikaria.** a Greek island in the Aegean Sea: a part of the Southern Sporades group. 7702; 99 sq. mi. (256 sq. km). **2.** any of the former Utopian communities founded by the followers of Étienne Cabet, esp. the one established at Nauvoo, Illinois, in 1849.

I·car·i·an (i kâr′ē ən, ī kâr′-), *adj.* **1.** of or like Icarus. **2.** of or pertaining to Icaria or its inhabitants. —*n.* **3.** an inhabitant of Icaria. [1585–95; < L *Īcari(us)* (< Gk *Ikários* of ICARUS) + -AN]

Icar′ian Sea′, the part of the Aegean Sea between Turkey and the Greek islands of Patmos and Leros.

Ic·a·rus (ik′ər əs, ī′kər-), *n.* **1.** Also, **Ikaros.** *Class. Myth.* a youth who attempted to escape from Crete with wings of wax and feathers but flew so high that his wings melted from the heat of the sun, and he plunged to his death in the sea. **2.** *Astron.* an asteroid whose eccentric orbit brings it closer to the sun than any other known asteroid.

ICBM, See **intercontinental ballistic missile.** Also, **I.C.B.M.**

ICC, Indian Claims Commission.

I.C.C., 1. International Control Commission. **2.** See **Interstate Commerce Commission.** Also, **ICC**

ice (īs), *n., v.,* **iced, ic·ing,** *adj.* —*n.* **1.** the solid form of water, produced by freezing; frozen water. **2.** the frozen surface of a body of water. **3.** any substance resembling frozen water: *camphor ice.* **4.** a frozen dessert made of sweetened water and fruit juice. **5.** *Brit.* See **ice cream. 6.** icing, as on a cake. **7.** reserve; formality: *The ice of his manner betrayed his dislike of the new ambassador.* **8.** *Slang.* **a.** a diamond or diamonds. **b.** protection money paid to the police by the operator of an illicit business. **c.** a fee that a ticket broker pays to a theater manager in order to receive a favorable allotment of tickets. **9. break the ice, a.** to succeed initially; make a beginning. **b.** to overcome reserve, awkwardness, or formality within a group, as in introducing persons: *The chairman broke the ice with his warm and very amusing remarks.* **10. cut no ice,** *Informal.* to have no influence or importance; fail to impress: *Her father's position cuts no ice with me.* **11. on ice,** *Informal.* **a.** with a good chance of success or realization: *Now that the contract is on ice we can begin operating again.* **b.** out of activity, as in confinement or imprisonment. **c.** in a state of abeyance or readiness: *Let's put that topic on ice for the moment.* **12. on thin ice,** in a precarious or delicate situation: *You may pass the course, but you're on thin ice right now.* Also, **skating on thin ice.** —*v.t.* **13.** to cover with ice. **14.** to change into ice; freeze. **15.** to cool with ice, as a drink. **16.** to cover (cake, sweet rolls, etc.) with icing; frost. **17.** to refrigerate with ice, as air. **18.** to make cold, as if with ice. **19.** to preserve by placing on ice. **20.** *Ice Hockey.* (esp. in Canada) to put (a team) into formal play. **21.** *Slang.* **a.** to settle or seal; make sure of, as by signing a contract: *We'll ice the deal tomorrow.* **b.** to make (a business arrangement) more attractive by adding features or benefits: *The star pitcher wouldn't sign his new contract until the team iced it with a big bonus.* **c.** to kill, esp. to murder: *The mobsters threatened to ice him if he went to the police.* **22.** *Sports Slang.* to establish a winning score or insurmountable lead in or otherwise assure victory in (a game or contest): *Her second goal iced the game.* —*v.i.* **23.** to change to ice; freeze: *The sherbet is icing in the refrigerator.* **24.** to be coated with ice (often fol. by *up*): *The windshield has iced up.* **25. ice it,** *Slang.* stop it; that's enough: *You've been complaining all day, so ice it.* **26. ice the puck,** *Ice Hockey.* to hit the puck to the far end of the rink, esp. from the defensive area across the offensive area. —*adj.* **27.** of or made of ice: *ice shavings; an ice sculpture.* **28.** for holding ice and food or drink to be chilled: *an ice bucket; an ice chest.* **29.** on or done on the ice: *ice yachting.* [bef. 900; 1905–10 for def. 8a; ME, OE *īs;* c. G *Eis,* ON *íss*] —**ice′less,** *adj.* —**ice′like′,** *adj.*

-ice, a suffix of nouns, indicating state or quality, appearing in loanwords from French: *notice.* [ME *-ice, -ise* < OF < L *-itius, -itia, -itium* abstract n. suffix]

Ice., 1. Iceland. **2.** Icelandic.

ice′ age′, *Geol.* (*often caps.*) the glacial epoch, esp. the Pleistocene Epoch. [1870–75]

ice′ an′chor, a large, hooklike device for setting in ice to anchor a vessel or to provide a hold for a hawser in warping it along. Also called **ice drag.** [1765–75]

ice′ a′pron, a structure built in a river upstream from a bridge pier or the like for protection against drifting ice. [1865–70]

ice′ ax′, a mountaineering tool combining an adzlike blade and a pick on the head of a long wooden handle, with a spike on the end, used for cutting into ice and for support on icy surfaces. [1810–20]

ice′ bag′, a waterproof bag to be filled with ice and applied to the head or another part of the body to be cooled. Also called **ice pack.** [1880–85]

ice·berg (īs′bûrg), *n.* **1.** a large floating mass of ice, detached from a glacier and carried out to sea. **2.** *Informal.* an emotionally cold person. **3.** *Australian Informal.* a person who swims or surfs regularly in winter. [1765–75; half Anglicization, half adoption of D *ijsberg* ice mountain; c. G *Eisberg,* Sw *isberg*]

ice′berg let′tuce, a variety of lettuce having a cabbagelike head of crisp leaves. [1890–95]

ice·blink (īs′blingk′), *n.* a yellowish luminosity near the horizon or on the underside of a cloud, caused by the reflection of light from sea ice. Also called **blink.** Cf. **snowblink.** [1765–75; ICE + BLINK; cf. D *ijsblink*]

ice·boat (īs′bōt′), *n.* **1.** a vehicle for rapid movement on ice, usually consisting of a T-shaped frame on three runners driven by a fore-and-aft sailing rig or, sometimes, by an engine operating a propeller. **2.** a boat for breaking a navigable channel through ice; icebreaker. [1745–55; ICE + BOAT]

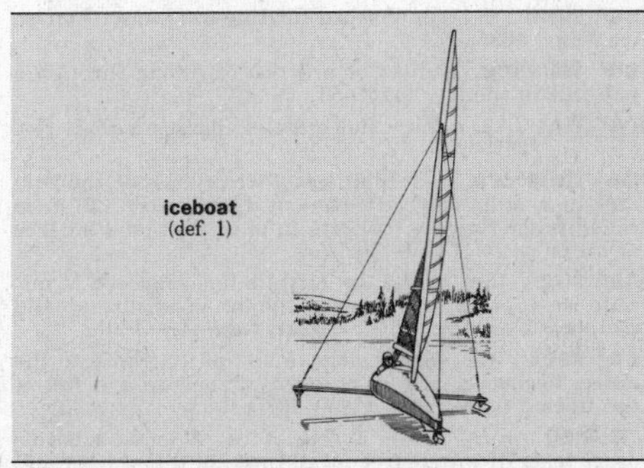

iceboat (def. 1)

ice·boat·er (īs′bō′tər), *n.* a person who races iceboats, esp. as a hobby or in competition. [1960–65; ICEBOAT + -ER[1]] —**ice′boat′ing,** *n.*

ice·bound (īs′bound′), *adj.* **1.** held fast or hemmed in by ice; frozen in: *an icebound ship.* **2.** obstructed or shut off by ice: *an icebound harbor.* [1650–60; ICE + -BOUND[1]]

ice·box (īs′boks′), *n.* **1.** an insulated cabinet or chest with a partition for ice, used for preserving or cooling food, beverages, etc. **2.** *Older Use.* an electric or gas refrigerator. **3.** *Naut.* an enclosed area in the bottom of a vessel through which sea water can be pumped up for use in the condenser in icy waters. **4.** *Slang.* an isolation cell in a prison. [1830–40; ICE + BOX[1]]

ice′box cake′, a confection made from such prepared ingredients as cookies or whipped cream that requires no additional baking but is chilled in a refrigerator before serving.

ice·break·er (īs′brā′kər), *n.* **1.** *Naut.* a ship specially built for breaking navigable passages through ice. **2.** an opening remark, action, etc., designed to ease tension or relieve formality: *A mild joke can be a good icebreaker.* **3.** a tool or machine for chopping ice into small pieces. [1810–20, *Amer.*; ICE + BREAKER[1]]

ice·cap (īs′kap′), *n.* a thick cover of ice over an area, sloping in all directions from the center. [1850–55; ICE + CAP[1]]

ice′ cave′, a cave containing ice that remains unmelted during all or most of the year. [1895–1900]

ice′ chest′, an insulated, boxlike container that can be filled with ice and used to cool beverages, preserve food, etc. [1835–45, *Amer.*]

ice-cold (īs′kōld′), *adj.* **1.** cold as ice: *Her feet were ice-cold.* **2.** without warmth of feeling or manner; unemotional; passionless: *an ice-cold reception.* [bef. 1000; OE *īs-calde;* unrecorded in ME]
—**Syn. 1.** icelike, freezing, icy, frozen.

ice′ cream′, a frozen food containing cream or milk and butterfat, sugar, flavoring, and sometimes eggs. [1735–45]

ice′-cream cone′ (īs′krēm′), **1.** a thin, crisp, hollow conical wafer for holding one or more scoops of ice cream. **2.** such a cone with the ice cream it contains. [1900–05]

ice′-cream par′lor chair′, a side chair made of heavy wire with a round wooden seat, esp. for use at a table. Also called **ice′-cream chair′.** [1945–50]

ice′-cream so′cial, *Chiefly Northern, North Midland, and Western U.S.* a social gathering, usually to raise money for a local church or school, where ice cream is the principal refreshment. [1895–1900, *Amer.*]

CONCISE PRONUNCIATION KEY: act, cāpe, dâre, pärt; set, ēqual; if, īce; ox, ōver, ôrder, oil, bo͝ok, bo͞ot, out; up, ûrge; child; sing; shoe; thin, *th*at; zh as in *treasure.* ə = *a* as in *alone, e* as in *system, i* as in *easily, o* as in *gallop, u* as in *circus;* ᵊ as in *fire* (fīᵊr), *hour* (ouᵊr). l and n can serve as syllabic consonants, as in *cradle* (krād′l), and *button* (but′n). See the full key inside the front cover.

ice′-cream suit′, a man's lightweight summer suit of white or a finely striped or solid pastel color. [1885–90, *Amer.*]

ice′-cream sup′per, *South Midland and Southern U.S.* an ice-cream social held in the late afternoon or early evening. [1890–95, *Amer.*]

ice′ crys′tals, *Meteorol.* precipitation consisting of small, slowly falling crystals of ice. Also called **ice needles.** [1840–50]

ice′ cube′, a small cube of ice, as one made in a special tray in the freezing compartment of a refrigerator or by an ice-making machine. [1915–20]

iced (īst), *adj.* **1.** covered with ice. **2.** cooled by means of ice: *iced tea.* **3.** *Cookery.* covered with icing. [1680–90; ICE + -ED², -ED³]

ice′ danc′ing, a competitive ice-skating event in which a couple, using basic skating figures and not being permitted to use lifts, performs choreographed movements to music, based on traditional ballroom dances. [1920–25]

ice′ dock′, *Naut.* an enclosed basin in icy waters in which a vessel may lie to avoid being crushed.

ice′ drag′, *Naut.* See **ice anchor.**

ice•fall (īs′fôl′), *n.* **1.** a jumbled mass of ice in a glacier. **2.** a mass of ice overhanging a precipice. **3.** a falling of ice from a glacier, iceberg, etc. [1810–20; ICE + FALL]

ice′ feath′ers, a delicate structure of crystals of ice that builds on the windward side of objects. Also called **frost feathers.**

ice′ field′, a large sheet of floating ice, larger than an ice floe. [1685–95]

ice′ fish′ing, the act or practice of fishing through a hole cut in the ice. [1745–55]

ice′ floe′, **1.** a large flat mass of floating ice. **2.** floe (def. 1). [1810–20]

ice′ flow′ers, **1.** formations of ice crystals on the surface of a still, slowly freezing body of water. **2.** Also called **frost flowers.** delicate tufts of frost on a surface of ice or snow. [1905–10]

ice′ fog′, (esp. in the far north) a fog composed of minute ice crystals that form in the air in extremely cold temperatures. Also called **frozen fog.** [1855–60]

ice′ foot′, (in polar regions) a belt of ice frozen to the shore, formed chiefly as a result of the rise and fall of the tides. Cf. **fast ice.** [1850–55]

ice-free (īs′frē′), *adj.* **1.** free of ice. **2.** (of a harbor or other body of water) free at all times of the year of any ice that would impede navigation. [1890–95]

ice′ front′, the forward section or seaward edge of an ice shelf. [1855–60]

ice′ hock′ey, a game played on ice between two teams of six skaters each, the object being to score goals by shooting a puck into the opponents' cage using a stick with a wooden blade set at an obtuse angle to the shaft. [1880–85]

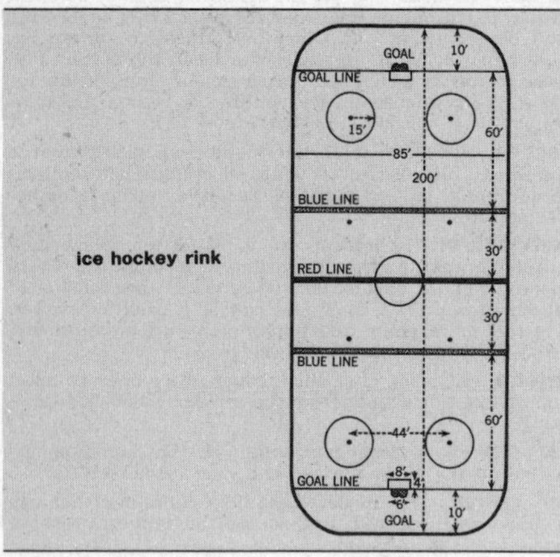

ice hockey rink

ice•house (īs′hous′), *n., pl.* **-hous•es** (-hou′ziz). a building for storing ice. [1680–90; ICE + HOUSE]

ice′ is′land, a tabular iceberg in the arctic region. [1770–80]

ice′ jam′, **1.** an obstruction of broken river ice in a narrow part of a channel. **2.** a mass of lake or sea ice broken and piled up against the shore by wind pressure. [1840–50]

ice•kha•na (īs′kä′nə), *n.* an auto-racing competition testing driving skills on a frozen lake. [ICE + (GYM)KHANA]

Icel., **1.** Iceland. **2.** Icelandic. Also, **Icel**

Ice•land (īs′lənd), *n.* **1.** a large island in the N Atlantic between Greenland and Scandinavia. 39,698 sq. mi. (102,820 sq. km). **2.** a republic including this island and several smaller islands: formerly Danish; independent since 1944. 219,033. *Cap.:* Reykjavik. —**Ice•land•er** (īs′lan′dər, -lən dər), *n.*

CONCISE ETYMOLOGY KEY: <, descended or borrowed from; >, whence; b., blend of, blended; c., cognate with; cf., compare; deriv., derivative; equiv., equivalent; imit., imitative; obl., oblique; r., replacing; s., stem; sp., spelling, spelled; resp., respelling, respelled; trans., translation; ?, origin unknown; *, unattested; ‡, probably earlier than. See the full key inside the front cover.

Ice•lan•dic (īs lan′dik), *adj.* **1.** of or pertaining to Iceland, its inhabitants, or their language. —*n.* **2.** the language of Iceland, a North Germanic language. *Abbr.:* Icel. [1665–75; ICELAND + -IC]

Ice′land moss′, an edible lichen, *Cetraria islandica,* of arctic regions, containing a starchlike substance used in medicine. [1795–1805]

Ice′land spar′, a transparent variety of calcite that is double-refracting and is used as a polarizer. [1820–30]

ice•mak•er (īs′mā′kər), *n.* an appliance for making ice, esp. ice cubes: *Some refrigerators have built-in icemakers.* [1765–75 for an earlier sense; ICE + MAKER]

ice•man (īs′man′), *n., pl.* **-men.** a man whose business is gathering, storing, selling, or delivering ice. [1835–45; ICE + MAN¹]

Ice′man Com′eth, The, a play (1946) by Eugene O'Neill.

ice′ milk′, a frozen food similar to ice cream but made with skim milk. [1835–45; ICE + MILK]

ice′ nee′dles, *Meteorol.* See **ice crystals.** [1925–30]

I•ce•ni (ī sē′nī), *n.* (*used with a singular or plural v.*) an ancient Celtic tribe of eastern England, whose queen, Boadicea, headed an insurrection against the Romans in A.D. 61. —**I•ce•nic** (ī sē′nik), *adj.*

ice-out (īs′out′), *n. Northern New Eng.* the breaking up of ice on lakes and streams during spring thaw. [1965–70]

ice′ pack′, **1.** See **pack ice.** **2.** See **ice bag.** [1850–55]

ice′ pel′lets, *Meteorol.* precipitation consisting of particles of ice less than 0.2 in. (5 mm) in diameter, occurring either as frozen raindrops or as small hailstones. Cf. **hail²** (def. 1), **sleet, snow pellets.**

ice′ pick′, a sharp-pointed tool for chipping or cutting ice. [1860–65]

ice′ plant′, a plant, *Mesembryanthemum crystallinum,* native to the Mediterranean region, having fleshy leaves that are covered with glistening vesicles and are sometimes eaten as greens. [1745–55]

ice′ point′, the temperature at which a mixture of ice and air-saturated water at a pressure of one atmosphere is in equilibrium, represented by 0°C and 32°F. Cf. **steam point.** [1900–05]

ice•quake (īs′kwāk′), *n.* a disturbance, esp. a vibration or series of vibrations, caused by the breaking up of large ice masses. [1890–95; ICE + (EARTH)QUAKE]

ice′ rain′, freezing rain.

ice′ ram′part, a mound of earth or stones formed by the action of ice against the shore of a lake, stream, etc. [1900–05]

ice′ run′, the rapid breaking up or fragmentation of river ice in spring or early summer. [1895–1900]

ice•scape (īs′skāp′), *n.* a landscape covered with ice or with snow and ice: *the limitless icescapes of Antarctica.* [1900–05; ICE + -SCAPE]

ice-scoured (īs′skouᵊrd′, -skou′ərd), *adj. Physical Geog.* noting an area having surface features resulting from scouring by an advancing ice sheet during glaciation. [1935–40]

ice′ sheet′, **1.** a broad, thick sheet of ice covering an extensive area for a long period of time. **2.** a glacier covering a large fraction of a continent. [1870–75]

ice′ shelf′, an ice sheet projecting into coastal waters so that the end floats. [1910–15]

ice′ show′, **1.** entertainment in which a company of ice skaters exhibit their skills to musical accompaniment. **2.** a company of ice skaters providing such entertainment. [1945–50]

ice′ skate′, **1.** a shoe fitted with a metal blade for skating on ice. **2.** skate¹ (def. 3). [1895–1900]

ice-skate (īs′skāt′), *v.i.,* **-skat•ed, -skat•ing.** to skate on ice. [1945–50; v. use of ICE SKATE] —**ice′ skat′er.**

ice′ sta′tion, a camp or base in an isolated part of the Arctic or Antarctic, manned by specialists to monitor the weather, geological formations, wildlife, etc. [1965–70]

ice′ storm′, a storm of freezing rain and widespread glaze formation. [1875–80]

ice′ tongs′, **1.** a small pair of tongs for serving ice cubes. **2.** tongs for handling a large block of ice. [1855–60]

ice′ tongue′, a section of ice projecting from the base of a glacier. [1890–95]

ice-up (īs′up′), *n.* freeze (def. 37). [1965–70; n. use of v. phrase *ice up*]

ice′ wa′ter, **1.** water chilled with or as if with ice. **2.** melted ice. [1715–25]

ICF, *Physics.* inertial confinement fusion: an experimental method for producing controlled thermonuclear energy by focusing laser beams onto a pellet containing deuterium and tritium.

ich (ik), *n.* a disease of tropical fishes, characterized by small, white nodules on the fins, skin, and eyes, caused by a ciliate protozoan, *Ichthyophthirius multifiliis.* Also called **ichthyophthirius, ichthyophthirius disease.** [short for ICHTHYOPHTHIRIUS]

Ich•a•bod (ik′ə bod′), *n.* a male given name: from a Hebrew word meaning "without honor."

I•chang (ē′chäng′), *n. Wade-Giles.* Yichang.

ich dien (ɪᴋʜ dēn′), *German.* I serve: traditional motto of the Prince of Wales.

I•chi•ka•wa (ē chē′kä wä′), *n.* a city on E Honshu, in Japan, NE of Tokyo. 364,244.

I Ching (ē′ jing′), an ancient Chinese book of divination, in which 64 pairs of trigrams are shown with various interpretations. Also called ***Book of Changes.***

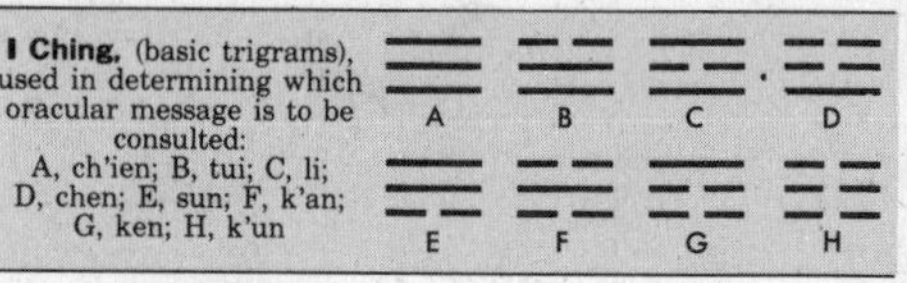

I Ching, (basic trigrams), used in determining which oracular message is to be consulted: A, ch'ien; B, tui; C, li; D, chen; E, sun; F, k'an; G, ken; H, k'un

I•chi•no•mi•ya (ē′chē nô′mē yä′), *n.* a city on central Honshu, in central Japan. 253,138.

ich•neu•mon (ik no͞o′mən, -nyo͞o′-), *n.* **1.** Also called **African mongoose.** a slender, long-tailed mongoose, *Herpestes ichneumon,* inhabiting Africa and southern Europe, and believed by the ancient Egyptians to devour crocodile eggs. **2.** See **ichneumon fly.** [1565–75; < L < Gk *ichneúmōn* tracker, equiv. to *ichneú(ein)* to track (see ICHNO-) + *-mōn* agent suffix]

ichneu′mon fly′, any of numerous wasplike insects of the family Ichneumonidae, the larvae of which are parasitic on caterpillars and immature stages of other insects. Also, **ich•neu′mon•fly′.** [1705–15]

ichno-, a combining form meaning "track," "footstep," used in the formation of compound words: *ichnology.* [< Gk, comb. form of *íchnos*]

ich•nol•o•gy (ik nol′ə jē), *n.* the branch of paleontology concerned with the study of fossilized tracks, trails, burrows, borings, or other trace fossils as evidence of the occurrence or behavior of the organisms that produced them. [1850–55; ICHNO- + -LOGY] —**ich•no•log•i•cal** (ik′nl oj′i kəl), *adj.*

i•chor (ī′kôr, ī′kər), *n.* **1.** *Class. Myth.* an ethereal fluid flowing in the veins of the gods. **2.** *Pathol.* an acrid, watery discharge, as from an ulcer or wound. [1630–40; < LL *ichōr* (in medical sense) < Gk *ichṓr*] —**i•chor•ous** (ī′kər əs), *adj.*

ichth., ichthyology.

ich•tham•mol (ik tham′ôl, -ol; ik′thə môl′, -mol′), *n. Pharm.* a viscous, reddish-brown to brownish-black substance, obtained by the destructive distillation of bituminous shales, used in medicine chiefly as an antiseptic, analgesic, and local stimulant in skin disorders. [1905–10; ICHTH(YO)- (from *ichthyosulfonate*) + AM-M(ONIUM) + -OL¹]

ich•thy•ic (ik′thē ik), *adj.* piscine. [1835–45; < Gk *ichthyikós* fishy. See ICHTHY-, -IC]

ichthyo-, a combining form meaning "fish," used in the formation of compound words: *ichthyology.* Also, *esp. before a vowel,* **ichthy-.** [< Gk, comb. form of *ichthŷs* fish]

Ich•thy•o•cen•taur (ik′thē ə sen′tôr), *n. Class. Myth.* a sea creature with a human head and torso, the legs of a horse, and the tail of a fish. [< Gk *ichthyokéntauros.* See ICHTHYO-, CENTAUR]

ich•thy•o•fau•na (ik′thē ə fô′nə), *n.* the indigenous fish of a region. [1880–85; ICHTHYO- + FAUNA]

ich•thy•oid (ik′thē oid′), *adj.* **1.** Also, **ich′thy•oi′dal.** fishlike. —*n.* **2.** any fishlike vertebrate. [1850–55; < Gk *ichthyoeidḗs.* See ICHTHY-, -OID]

Ich•thy•ol (ik′thē ôl′, -ol′), *Pharm., Trademark.* a brand of ichthammol.

ichthyol., ichthyology.

ich•thy•o•lite (ik′thē ə līt′), *n.* a fossil fish. [1820–30; ICHTHYO- + -LITE] —**ich•thy•o•lit•ic** (ik′thē ə lit′ik), *adj.*

ich•thy•ol•o•gy (ik′thē ol′ə jē), *n.* the branch of zoology dealing with fishes. [1640–50; ICHTHYO- + -LOGY] —**ich•thy•o•log•ic** (ik′thē ə loj′ik), **ich′thy•o•log′i•cal,** *adj.* —**ich′thy•o•log′i•cal•ly,** *adv.* —**ich′thy•ol′o•gist,** *n.*

ich•thy•oph•a•gist (ik′thē of′ə jist), *n.* a person who eats or subsists on fish. [1720–30; ICHTHYOPHAG(Y) + -IST]

ich•thy•oph•a•gy (ik′thē of′ə jē), *n.* the practice of eating or subsisting on fish. [1650–60; ICHTHYO- + -PHAGY] —**ich•thy•oph•a•gous** (ik′thē of′ə gəs), *adj.*

ich•thy•oph•thir•i•us (ik′thē of thēr′ē əs), *n.* ich. Also called **ichthyophthir′ius disease′.** [< NL, the protozoan genus causing the disease, equiv. to *ichthyo-* ICHTHYO- + *-phthirius* < Gk *phtheír* louse]

Ich•thy•or•nis (ik′thē ôr′nis), *n.* an extinct genus of toothed birds having vertebrae resembling those of fishes. [< NL (1872) < Gk *ichthy-* ICHTHY- + *órnis* bird]

ich•thy•o•sar•co•tox•in (ik′thē ō sär′kō tok′sin), *n.* a term applied to any poison found in the flesh of poisonous fishes. [ICHTHYO- + SARCO- + TOXIN]

ich•thy•o•saur (ik′thē ə sôr′), *n.* any fishlike marine reptile of the extinct order Ichthyosauria, ranging from 4 to 40 ft. (1.2 to 12 m) in length and having a round, tapering body, a large head, four paddlelike flippers, and a vertical caudal fin. [1820–30; see ICHTHYOSAURUS] —**ich′thy·o·sau′ri·an,** *adj., n.* —**ich′thy·o·sau′roid,** *adj.*

ichthyosaur, *Stenopterygius quadriscissus,* length 3 to 30 ft. (0.9 to 9 m)

ich·thy·o·saur·us (ik′thē ə sôr′əs), *n., pl.* **-us·es.** ichthyosaur. [1825–35; < NL; see ICHTHYO-, -SAURUS]

ich·thy·o·sis (ik′thē ō′sis), *n. Pathol.* a hereditary skin disease in which the epidermis continuously flakes off in large scales or plates. [1805–15; < NL; see ICHTHY-, -OSIS] —**ich·thy·ot·ic** (ik′thē ot′ik), *adj.*

-ician, a suffix forming personal nouns denoting occupations: *beautician; mortician.* [extracted from *musician, physician,* etc., derived with -IAN, from words ending in -IC]

i·ci·cle (ī′si kəl), *n.* **1.** a pendent, tapering mass of ice formed by the freezing of dripping water. **2.** a thin strip of paper, plastic, or foil, usually silvery, for hanging on a Christmas tree as decoration. **3.** a cold, unemotional person. [bef. 1000; ME *isikel,* OE *isgicel,* equiv. to *is* ICE + *gicel* icicle; akin to ON *jǫkul* mass of ice, glacier] —**i′ci·cled,** *adj.*

i·ci·ly (ī′sə lē), *adv.* in an icy manner: *I received him icily because of the harsh way he had treated me.* [1840–50; ICY + -LY] —**i′ci·ness,** *n.*

ic·ing (ī′sing), *n.* **1.** a sweet, creamy spread, as of confectioners' sugar, butter, and flavoring, for covering cakes, cookies, etc.; frosting. **2.** *Meteorol.* a coating of ice on a solid object. Cf. **glaze, rime**[1]. **3.** *Aviation.* the freezing of atmospheric moisture on the surface of an aircraft. **4.** *Ice Hockey.* the act of a player shooting the puck from the defensive half of the rink over the opponent's goal line, but not into the goal, as a defensive maneuver to keep the puck out of the reach of attacking opponents, resulting in a penalty against the defensive team if the puck is then next touched by an opponent other than the goalkeeper. **5. icing on the cake.** See **frosting** (def. 5). [1760–70; ICE + -ING[1]]

ICJ, International Court of Justice.

ick (ik), *interj.* (used as an expression of distaste or repugnance.)

ick·er (ik′ər), *n. Scot.* the fruit-bearing spike of any cereal plant, esp. an ear of corn. [1505–15; Scots form of EAR[2], continuing OE *æhher, eher* (Northumbrian dial.)]

Ick·es (ik′ēz), *n.* **Harold (Le Claire)** (lə klâr), 1874–1952, U.S. lawyer and statesman.

ick·y (ik′ē), *adj.,* **ick·i·er, ick·i·est.** *Informal.* **1.** repulsive or distasteful. **2.** excessively sweet or sentimental. **3.** unsophisticated or old-fashioned. **4.** sticky; viscid. [1930–35, *Amer.; ick* (of uncert. orig.) + -Y[1]] —**ick′i·ness,** *n.*
—**Syn. 1.** revolting, nasty. **3.** gummy, gooey, gucky.

i·con (ī′kon), *n.* **1.** a picture, image, or other representation. **2.** *Eastern Ch.* a representation of some sacred personage, as Christ or a saint or angel, painted usually on a wood surface and venerated itself as sacred. **3.** a sign or representation that stands for its object by virtue of a resemblance or analogy to it. **4.** *Computers.* a picture or symbol that appears on a monitor and is used to represent a command, as a file drawer to represent filing. Also, **eikon, ikon** (for defs. 1, 2). [1565–75; < L < Gk *eikṓn* likeness, image, figure]
—**Syn. 2.** See **image.**

i·con·ic (ī kon′ik), *adj.* **1.** of, pertaining to, or characteristic of an icon. **2.** *Art.* (of statues, portraits, etc.) executed according to a convention or tradition. Also, **i·con′i·cal.** [1650–60; < L *īconicus* < Gk *eikonikós,* equiv. to *eikon-* (s. of *eikṓn*) ICON + *-ikos* -IC] —**i·con′i·cal·ly,** *adv.* —**i·co·nic·i·ty** (ī′kə nis′i tē), *n.*

I·co·ni·um (ī kō′nē əm), *n.* ancient name of **Konya.**

icono-, a combining form meaning "image," "likeness," used in the formation of compound words: *iconology.* Also, *esp. before a vowel,* **icon-.** [< L < Gk *eikono-,* comb. form of *eikṓn* ICON]

i·con·o·clasm (ī kon′ə klaz′əm), *n.* the action or spirit of iconoclasts. [1790–1800; ICONOCL(AST) + *-asm* on model of such pairs as *enthusiast: enthusiasm*]

i·con·o·clast (ī kon′ə klast′), *n.* **1.** a breaker or destroyer of images, esp. those set up for religious veneration. **2.** a person who attacks cherished beliefs, traditional institutions, etc., as being based on error or superstition. [1590–1600; < ML *iconoclastēs* < MGk *eikonoklástēs,* equiv. to Gk *eikono-* ICONO- + *-klastēs* breaker, equiv. to *klas-* (var. s. of *klân* to break) + *-tēs* agent n. suffix] —**i·con′o·clas′tic,** *adj.* —**i·con′o·clas′ti·cal·ly,** *adv.*
—**Syn. 2.** nonconformist, rebel, dissenter, radical.

i·con·o·graph·ic (ī kon′ə graf′ik), *adj.* of or pertaining to iconography. Also, **i·con′o·graph′i·cal.** [1850–55; ICONO- + -GRAPHIC]

i·co·nog·ra·phy (ī′kə nog′rə fē), *n., pl.* **-phies. 1.** symbolic representation, esp. the conventional meanings attached to an image or images. **2.** subject matter in the visual arts, esp. with reference to the conventions regarding the treatment of a subject in artistic representation. **3.** the study or analysis of subject matter and its meaning in the visual arts; iconology. **4.** a representation or a group of representations of a person, place, or thing, as a portrait or a collection of portraits. [1620–30; < ML *īconographia* < Gk *eikonographía.* See ICONO-, -GRAPHY] —**i·con·o·graph** (ī kon′ə graf′, -gräf′), *n.* —**i′co·nog′ra·pher,** *n.*

i·co·nol·a·try (ī′kə nol′ə trē), *n.* the worship or adoration of icons. [1615–25; ICONO- + -LATRY] —**i′co·nol′a·ter,** *n.* —**i′co·nol′a·trous,** *adj.*

i·co·nol·o·gy (ī′kə nol′ə jē), *n.* **1.** the historical analysis and interpretive study of symbols or images and their contextual significance; iconography. **2.** the study of icons or symbolic representations. [1720–30; ICONO- + -LOGY] —**i·con·o·log·i·cal** (ī kon′l oj′i kəl, ī′kə nl-), *adj.* —**i′co·nol′o·gist,** *n.*

i·con·o·phile (ī kon′ə fīl′), *n.* a connoisseur of icons or images. [1880–85; ICONO- + -PHILE] —**i·co·noph·i·lism** (ī′kə nof′ə liz′əm), *n.*

i·con·o·scope (ī kon′ə skōp′), *n.* a television camera tube in which a beam of high-velocity electrons scans a photoemissive mosaic. Cf. **orthicon.** [1930–35; formerly trademark; see ICONO-, -SCOPE]

i·co·nos·ta·sis (ī′kə nos′tə sis), *n., pl.* **-ses** (-sēz′). *Eastern Ch.* a partition or screen on which icons are placed, separating the sanctuary from the main part of the church. Also, **i·con·o·stas** (ī kon′ə stas′). [1825–35; < MGk; see ICONO-, STASIS]

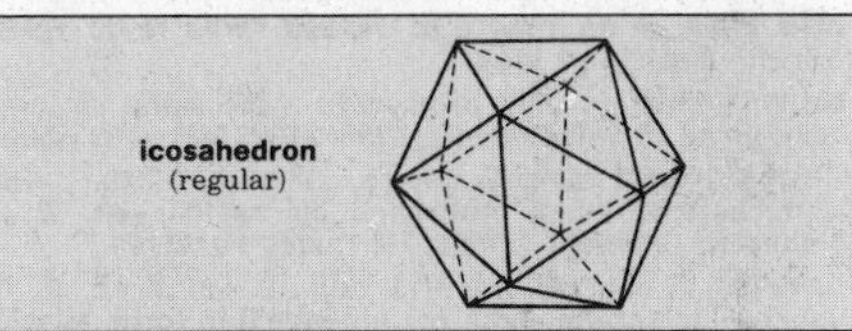
icosahedron (regular)

i·co·sa·he·dron (ī kō′sə hē′drən, ī kos′ə-), *n., pl.* **-drons, -dra** (-drə). a solid figure having 20 faces. [1560–70; < Gk *eikosáedron,* equiv. to *eikosa-* (var. of *eikosi-,* comb. form of *eíkosi* twenty) + *-edron* -HEDRON] —**i·co′sa·he′dral,** *adj.*

i·co·si·tet·ra·he·dron (ī kō′si te′trə hē′drən, ī kos′ə-), *n., pl.* **-drons, -dra** (-drə). a solid figure having 24 faces. [1825–35; < Gk *eikosi-* (comb. form of *eíkosi* twenty) + TETRAHEDRON]

-ics, a suffix of nouns that denote a body of facts, knowledge, principles, etc., usually corresponding to adjectives ending in **-ic** or **-ical:** *ethics; physics; politics; tactics.* [pl. of -IC, repr. L *-ica* (< Gk *-ika,* neut. pl. of *-ikos*), as in *rhētórica* (pl.) rhetoric book]
—**Usage.** Nouns ending in -ICS that name fields of study, sciences, arts, professions, or the like are usually not preceded by an article and are used with a singular verb: *Acoustics* (the science) *deals with sound. Politics* (the art of government) *fascinates me.* In certain uses, often when preceded by a determiner like *the, his, her,* or *their,* most of these nouns can take a plural verb: *The acoustics* (the sound-reflecting qualities) *of the hall are splendid. Their politics* (political opinions) *have antagonized everyone.*

ICSH, 1. interstitial-cell stimulating hormone: a hormone produced by the anterior lobe of the pituitary gland that, in the male, stimulates the interstitial cells of the testes to produce testosterone; chemically identical to luteinizing hormone of the female. **2.** *Pharm.* a commercial form of this substance, obtained from the pituitary glands of pigs and sheep.

ic·ter·ic (ik ter′ik), *adj. Pathol.* pertaining to or affected with icterus; jaundiced. Also, **ic·ter′i·cal.** [1590–1600; < L *ictericus* < Gk *ikterikós,* equiv. to *íkter(os)* jaundice + *-ikos* -IC]

ic·ter·us (ik′tər əs), *n. Pathol.* jaundice (def. 1). [1700–10; < L < Gk *íkteros* jaundice, a yellow bird said to cure jaundice when seen]

Ic·ti·nus (ik′tī nəs), *n.* fl. mid-5th century B.C., Greek architect, a designer of the Parthenon.

ic·tus (ik′təs), *n., pl.* **-tus·es, -tus. 1.** *Pros.* rhythmical or metrical stress. **2.** *Pathol.* **a.** an epileptic seizure. **b.** a stroke, esp. a cerebrovascular accident. [1700–10; < L: stroke, thrust, equiv. to *ic(ere)* to strike with a weapon + *-tus* suffix of v. action] —**ic′tic,** *adj.*

ICU, See **intensive care unit.**

i·cy (ī′sē), *adj.,* **i·ci·er, i·ci·est. 1.** made of, full of, or covered with ice: *icy roads.* **2.** resembling ice. **3.** cold: *icy winds.* **4.** without warmth of feeling; coldly unfriendly; frigid: *an icy stare.* [bef. 900; ME *isy,* OE *īsig.* See ICE, -Y[1]]
—**Syn. 4.** cold, distant, cool, chilly.

id (id), *n. Psychoanal.* the part of the psyche, residing in the unconscious, that is the source of instinctive impulses that seek satisfaction in accordance with the pleasure principle and are modified by the ego and the superego before they are given overt expression. [1920–25; < L *id* it, as a trans. of G *Es,* special use of *es* it, as a psychoanalytic term]

ID (ī′dē′), a means of identification, as a card or bracelet containing official or approved identification information.

ID, 1. Idaho (approved esp. for use with zip code). **2.** Also, **i.d.** inside diameter.

I'd (īd), contraction of *I would* or *I had.*
—**Usage.** See **contraction.**

-id[1], a suffix of nouns that have the general sense "offspring of, descendant of," occurring originally in loanwords from Greek (*Atreid; Nereid*), and productive in English on the Greek model, esp. in names of dynasties, with the dynasty's founder as the base noun (*Abbasid; Attalid*), and in names of periodic meteor showers, with the base noun usually denoting the constellation or other celestial object in which the shower appears (*Perseid*). [< L *-id-,* s. of *-is* < Gk: fem. patronymic suffix; or < L *-idēs* < Gk: masc. patronymic suffix]

-id[2], a suffix occurring in English derivatives of modern Latin taxonomic names, esp. zoological families and classes; such derivatives are usually nouns denoting a single member of the taxon or adjectives with the sense "pertaining to" the taxon: *arachnid; canid.* [< Gk *-idēs* -ID[1], as sing. of NL *-ida* -IDA or *-idae* -IDAE]

-id[3], var. of **-ide:** *lipid.*

-id[4], a suffix occurring in descriptive adjectives borrowed from Latin, often corresponding to nouns ending in **-or**[1]: *fetid; humid; pallid.* [< L *-idus*]

ID., (in Iraq) dinar; dinars.

Id., Idaho.

id., idem.

I.D., 1. identification. **2.** identity. **3.** *Mil.* Infantry Division. **4.** Intelligence Department. [1950–55]

I·da (ī′də), *n.* **1. Mount,** a mountain in W Turkey, in NW Asia Minor, SE of ancient Troy. 5810 ft. (1771 m). Turkish, **Kazdağ. 2.** Modern, **Mount Psiloriti.** the highest mountain in Crete. 8058 ft. (2456 m). **3.** a female given name: from a Germanic word meaning "happy."

IDA, International Development Association.

-ida, *Zool.* a suffix of the names of orders and classes: *Arachnida.* [< NL, taken as neut. pl. of L *-idēs* offspring of < Gk; see -ID[1]]

Ida., Idaho.

-idae, *Zool.* a suffix of the names of families: *Canidae.* [< NL, L < Gk *-idai,* pl. of *-idēs* offspring of; akin to -ID[1]]

I·dae·an (ī dē′ən), *adj.* of, pertaining to, associated with, or inhabiting Mount Ida in Asia Minor or Crete. [1580–90; < L *Idae(us)* (< Gk *Idaîos* Idaean) + -AN]

I·da·ho (ī′də hō′), *n.* a state in the NW United States. 943,935; 83,557 sq. mi. (216,415 sq. km). *Cap.:* Boise. *Abbr.:* ID (for use with zip code), Id., Ida. —**I·da·ho·an** (ī′də hō′ən, ī′də hō′-), *adj., n.*

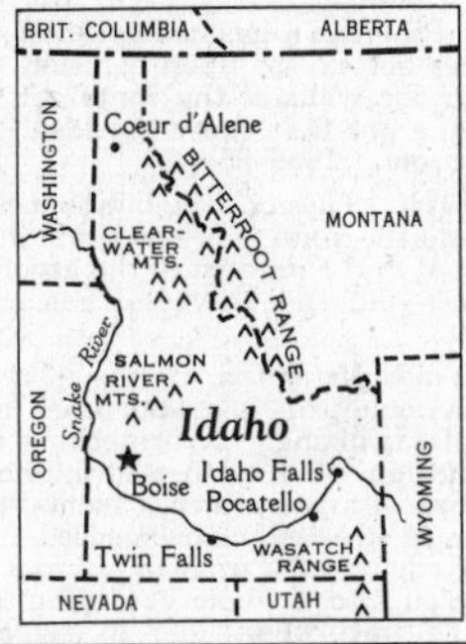

I′daho Falls′, a city in E Idaho. 39,590.

′Id al-Ad·ha (id′ al äd hä′), a major festival of Islam, beginning on the tenth day of the last month of the calendar and lasting for four days, usually characterized by the sacrificing of a sheep, whose flesh is divided among relatives and friends in memory of the ransom of Ishmael with a ram. Also called **Great Festival.**

IDB, industrial development bond.

ID bracelet. See **identification bracelet.**

ID card. See **identification card.** [1960–65]

id·dhi (id′dē), *n. Pali.* siddhi.

-ide, a suffix used in the names of chemical compounds: *bromide.* Also, **-id.** [extracted from OXIDE]

i·de·a (ī dē′ə, ī dēə′), *n.* **1.** any conception existing in the mind as a result of mental understanding, awareness, or activity. **2.** a thought, conception, or notion: *That is an excellent idea.* **3.** an impression: *He gave me a general idea of how he plans to run the department.* **4.** an opinion, view, or belief: *His ideas on raising children are certainly strange.* **5.** a plan of action; an intention: *the idea of becoming an engineer.* **6.** a groundless supposition; fantasy. **7.** *Philos.* **a.** a concept developed by the mind. **b.** a conception of what is desirable or ought to be; ideal. **c.** (*cap.*) *Platonism.* Also called **form.** an archetype or pattern of which the individual objects in any natural class are imperfect copies and from which they derive their being. **d.** *Kantianism.* See **idea of pure reason. 8.** *Music.* a theme, phrase, or figure. **9.** *Obs.* **a.** a likeness. **b.** a mental image. [1400–50; < LL < Gk *idéa* form, pattern, equiv. to *ide-* (s. of *ideîn* to see) + *-a* fem. n. ending; r. late ME *idee* < MF < LL, as above; akin to WIT[1]] —**i·de′a·less,** *adj.*
—**Syn. 1, 2.** IDEA, THOUGHT, CONCEPTION, NOTION refer to a product of mental activity. IDEA, although it may refer to thoughts of any degree of seriousness or triviality, is commonly used for mental concepts considered more important or elaborate: *We pondered the idea of the fourth dimension. The idea of his arrival frightened me.* THOUGHT, which reflects its primary emphasis on the mental process, may denote any concept except the more weighty and elaborate ones: *I welcomed his thoughts on the subject. A thought came to him.* CONCEPTION suggests a thought that seems complete, individual, recent, or somewhat intricate: *The architect's conception delighted them.* NOTION suggests a fleeting, vague, or imperfect thought: *a bare notion of how to proceed.* **4.** sentiment, judgment.

i·de·a·is·tic (ī dē′ə is′tik, ī′dē ə-, ī′dē is′-), *adj.* of ideas, esp. in their abstract or symbolic character. [IDEA + -ISTIC]

CONCISE PRONUNCIATION KEY: act, cāpe, dâre, pärt; set, ēqual; if, īce; ox, ōver, ôrder, oil, bŏŏk, bo͞ot, out; up, ûrge; child; sing; shoe; thin, *th*at; zh as in *treasure.* ə = *a* as in *alone, e* as in *system, i* as in *easily, o* as in *gallop, u* as in *circus;* ᵊ as in *fire* (fīᵊr), *hour* (ouᵊr). l and n can serve as syllabic consonants, as in *cradle* (krād′l), and *button* (but′n). See the full key inside the front cover.

i•de•al (ī dē′əl, ī dēl′), *n.* **1.** a conception of something in its perfection. **2.** a standard of perfection or excellence. **3.** a person or thing conceived as embodying such a conception or conforming to such a standard, and taken as a model for imitation: *Thomas Jefferson was his ideal.* **4.** an ultimate object or aim of endeavor, esp. one of high or noble character: *He refuses to compromise any of his ideals.* **5.** something that exists only in the imagination: *To achieve the ideal is almost hopeless.* **6.** *Math.* a subring of a ring, any element of which when multiplied by any element of the ring results in an element of the subring. —*adj.* **7.** conceived as constituting a standard of perfection or excellence: *ideal beauty.* **8.** regarded as perfect of its kind: *an ideal spot for a home.* **9.** existing only in the imagination; not real or actual: *Nature is real; beauty is ideal.* **10.** advantageous; excellent; best: *It would be ideal if she could accompany us as she knows the way.* **11.** based upon an ideal or ideals: *the ideal theory of numbers.* **12.** *Philos.* pertaining to a possible state of affairs considered as highly desirable. **c.** pertaining to or of the nature of idealism. [1605–15; < LL *ideālis.* See IDEA, -AL[1]] —**i•de′al•ness,** *n.*
—**Syn. 1, 2.** epitome. IDEAL, EXAMPLE, MODEL refer to something considered as a standard to strive toward or something considered worthy of imitation. An IDEAL is a concept or standard of perfection, existing merely as an image in the mind, or based upon a person or upon conduct: *We admire the high ideals of a religious person. Sir Philip Sidney was considered the ideal in gentlemanly conduct.* An EXAMPLE is a person or the conduct or achievements of a person regarded as worthy of being followed or imitated in a general way; or sometimes, as properly to be avoided: *an example of courage; a bad example to one's children.* A MODEL is primarily a physical shape to be closely copied, but is also a pattern for exact imitation in conduct or character: *They took their leader as a model.* **4.** intention, objective. **7.** perfect, consummate, complete. **9.** illusory, imaginary, fanciful, fantastic.

ide′al gas′, *Physics.* a gas composed of molecules on which no forces act except upon collision with one another and with the walls of the container in which the gas is enclosed; a gas that obeys the ideal gas law. Also called **perfect gas.** [1890–95]

ide′al gas′ law′, *Physics.* the law that the product of the pressure and the volume of one gram molecule of an ideal gas is equal to the product of the absolute temperature of the gas and the universal gas constant. Also called **gas law.**

i•de•al•ism (ī dē′ə liz′əm), *n.* **1.** the cherishing or pursuit of high or noble principles, purposes, goals, etc. **2.** the practice of idealizing. **3.** something idealized; an ideal representation. **4.** *Fine Arts.* treatment of subject matter in a work of art in which a mental conception of beauty or form is stressed, characterized usually by the selection of particular features of various models and their combination into a whole according to a standard of perfection. Cf. **naturalism** (def. 2), **realism** (def. 3a). **5.** *Philos.* **a.** any system or theory that maintains that the real is of the nature of thought or that the object of external perception consists of ideas. **b.** the tendency to represent things in an ideal form, or as they might or should be rather than as they are, with emphasis on values. [1790–1800; IDEAL + -ISM, prob. modeled on G *Idealismus*]

i•de•al•ist (ī dē′ə list), *n.* **1.** a person who cherishes or pursues high or noble principles, purposes, goals, etc. **2.** a visionary or impractical person. **3.** a person who represents things as they might or should be rather than as they are. **4.** a writer or artist who treats subjects imaginatively. **5.** a person who accepts the doctrines of idealism. —*adj.* **6.** idealistic. [1695–1705; IDEAL + -IST]
—**Syn. 2.** romantic, dreamer, stargazer.

i•de•al•is•tic (ī dē′ə lis′tik, ī′dē ə-), *adj.* of or pertaining to idealism or idealists. Also, **i•de′al•is′ti•cal.** [1820–30; IDEALIST + -IC] —**i•de′al•is′ti•cal•ly,** *adv.*

i•de•al•i•ty (ī′dē al′i tē), *n., pl.* **-ties.** **1.** ideal quality or character. **2.** capacity to idealize. **3.** *Philos.* existence only in idea and not in reality. [1695–1705; IDEAL + -ITY]

i•de•al•i•za•tion (ī dē′ə lə zā′shən), *n.* **1.** the act or process of idealizing something. **2.** *Psychoanal.* a mental mechanism, operating consciously or unconsciously, in which one person overestimates an admired attribute of another. [1790–1800; IDEALIZE + -ATION]

i•de•al•ize (ī dē′ə līz′), *v.,* **-ized, -iz•ing.** —*v.t.* **1.** to make ideal; represent in an ideal form or character; exalt to an ideal perfection or excellence. —*v.i.* **2.** to represent something in an ideal form. Also, *esp. Brit.,* **i•de′al•ise′.** [1780–90; IDEAL + -IZE] —**i•de′al•iz′er,** *n.*

ide′alized im′age, *Psychol.* **1.** a personal standard of perfection against which one's actual thinking, behavior, and appearance are compared. **2.** an exaggerated and unrealistic view of one's virtues and abilities.

i•de•al•ly (ī dē′ə lē), *adv.* **1.** in accordance with an ideal; perfectly. **2.** in theory or principle. **3.** in idea, thought, or imagination. [1590–1600; IDEAL + -LY]

ide′al of pure′ rea′son, *Kantianism.* God, seen as an idea of pure reason unifying the personal soul with the cosmos.

ide′al point′, *Math.* the point at infinity in projective geometry at which parallel lines intersect. [1875–80]

ide′al type′, a construct abstracted from experience in which individual elements are combined to form a whole that is conceptually independent of empirical factors or variables, but against which particular examples of the appropriate class found in life can be measured. [1925–30]

CONCISE ETYMOLOGY KEY: <, descended or borrowed from; >, whence; b., blend of, blended; c., cognate with; cf., compare; deriv., derivative; equiv., equivalent; imit., imitative; obl., oblique; r., replacing; s., stem; sp., spelling, spelled; resp., respelling, respelled; trans., translation; ?, origin unknown; *, unattested; ‡, probably earlier than. See the full key inside the front cover.

ide′a man′, a person who is capable of and responsible for providing original ideas. [1935–40]

i•de•a•mon•ger (ī dē′ə mung′gər, -mong′-), *n.* a person who originates and promotes or deals in ideas. [1830–40; IDEA + MONGER]

ide′a of pure′ rea′son, *Kantianism.* any of the three undemonstrable entities (a personal soul, a cosmos, and a supreme being) implicit in the fact of a subject and an object of knowledge, and in the need for some principle uniting them. Cf. **ideal of pure reason.**

i•de•ate (*v.* ī′dē āt′, ī dē′āt; *n.* ī′dē āt′, ī dē′it), *v.,* **-at•ed, -at•ing,** *n.* —*v.t.* **1.** to form an idea, thought, or image of. —*v.i.* **2.** to form ideas; think. —*n.* **3.** ideatum. [1600–10; IDE(A) + -ATE[1]] —**i•de•a•tive** (ī dē′ə tiv, ī′dē ā′-), *adj.*

i•de•a•tion (ī′dē ā′shən), *n.* the process of forming ideas or images. [1820–30; IDEATE + -ION]

i•de•a•tion•al (ī′dē ā′shə nl), *adj.* of, pertaining to, or involving ideas or concepts. [1850–55; IDEATION + -AL[1]] —**i′de•a′tion•al•ly,** *adv.*

i•de•a•tum (ī′dē ā′təm, ē′dē-), *n., pl.* **-ta** (-tə). (in epistemology) the object of knowledge as known by the mind. Cf. **datum** (def. 3). [1700–10; < NL *ideātum,* equiv. to L *ide(a)* IDEA + *-ātum,* neut. of *-ātus* -ATE[1]]

i•dée fixe (ē dā fēks′), *pl.* ***i•dées fixes*** (ē dā fēks′), *French.* See **fixed idea.**

i•dem (ī′dem, id′em), *pron., adj.* the same as previously given or mentioned. [1350–1400; ME < L *idem*]

i•dem•po•tent (ī′dəm pōt′nt, id′əm-), *Math.* —*adj.* **1.** unchanged when multiplied by itself. —*n.* **2.** an idempotent element. [1865–70; IDEM + POTENT[1]]

i•den•tic (ī den′tik, i den′-), *adj.* **1.** identical. **2.** *Diplomacy.* (of action, notes, etc.) identical in form, as when two or more governments deal simultaneously with another government. [1640–50; < ML *identicus* the same, equiv. to LL *ident(itās)* IDENTITY + *-icus* -IC]

i•den•ti•cal (ī den′ti kəl, i den′-), *adj.* **1.** similar or alike in every way: *The two cars are identical except for their license plates.* **2.** being the very same; selfsame: *This is the identical room we stayed in last year.* **3.** agreeing exactly: *identical opinions.* [1610–20; < ML *identic(us)* IDENTIC + -AL[1]] —**i•den′ti•cal•ly,** *adv.* —**i•den′ti•cal•ness,** *n.*
—**Syn. 3.** congruous, congruent, equal, matching.

iden′tical proposi′tion, *Logic.* a proposition in which the subject and predicate have the same meaning, as, "That which is mortal is not immortal." [1635–45]

iden′tical rhyme′, *Pros.* **1.** rhyme created by the repetition of a word. **2.** See **rime riche.**

iden′tical twin′, one of a pair of twins who develop from a single fertilized ovum and therefore have the same genotype, are of the same sex, and usually resemble each other closely. Cf. **fraternal twin.** [1885–90]

i•den•ti•fi•ca•tion (ī den′tə fi kā′shən, i den′-), *n.* **1.** an act or instance of identifying; the state of being identified. **2.** something that identifies a person, animal, or thing: *He carries identification with him at all times.* **3.** *Sociol.* acceptance as one's own of the values and interests of a social group. **4.** *Psychol.* **a.** a process by which one ascribes to oneself the qualities or characteristics of another person. **b.** (in psychoanalytic theory) the transference or reaction to one person with the feelings or responses relevant to another, as the identification of a teacher with a parent. **c.** perception of another as an extension of oneself. [1635–45; IDENTI(FY) + -FICATION]
—**Syn. 1.** association, connection, affiliation.

identifica′tion brace′let, a bracelet, usually of metal links, having an identification plate for the name of the wearer. Also called **ID bracelet.** [1965–70]

identifica′tion card′, a card giving identifying data about a person, as full name, address, age, and color of hair and eyes, and often containing a photograph: for use as identification at a place of employment, school, club, etc. Also called **ID card.** [1905–10]

identifica′tion tag′, either of two oblong metal tags, issued to armed forces personnel, on which are impressed the serial number, name, etc., of the person to whom it is issued, and carried on or about the person at all times. [1915–20]

identifica′tion thread′. See **rogue's yarn.**

i•den•ti•fy (ī den′tə fī′, i den′-), *v.,* **-fied, -fy•ing.** —*v.t.* **1.** to recognize or establish as being a particular person or thing; verify the identity of: *to identify handwriting; to identify the bearer of a check.* **2.** to serve as a means of identification for: *His gruff voice quickly identified him.* **3.** to make, represent to be, or regard or treat as the same or identical: *They identified Jones with the progress of the company.* **4.** to associate in name, feeling, interest, action, etc. (usually fol. by *with*): *He preferred not to identify himself with that group.* **5.** *Biol.* to determine to what group (a given specimen) belongs. **6.** *Psychol.* to associate (one or oneself) with another person or a group of persons by identification. —*v.i.* **7.** to experience psychological identification: *The audience identified with the play's characters.* [1635–45; < ML *identificāre,* equiv. to *identi(tās)* IDENTITY + *-ficāre* -FY] —**i•den′ti•fi′a•ble,** *adj.* —**i•den′ti•fi′a•bil′i•ty, i•den′ti•fi′a•ble•ness,** *n.* —**i•den′ti•fi′er,** *n.*
—**Syn. 1.** distinguish, place, know, determine.

I•den•ti-Kit (ī den′ti kit′, i den′-), *Trademark.* a brand name for a kit containing drawings of hairlines, eyes, noses, chins, etc., in a wide variety of shapes and sizes, used by law-enforcement agencies to construct a composite picture of a suspect from descriptions provided by witnesses.

i•den•ti•ty (ī den′ti tē, i den′-), *n., pl.* **-ties.** **1.** the state or fact of remaining the same one or ones, as under varying aspects or conditions: *The identity of the fingerprints on the gun with those on file provided evidence that he was the killer.* **2.** the condition of being oneself or itself, and not another: *He doubted his own identity.* **3.** condition or character as to who a person or what a thing is: *a case of mistaken identity.* **4.** the state or fact of being the same one as described. **5.** the sense of self, providing sameness and continuity in personality over time and sometimes disturbed in mental illnesses, as schizophrenia. **6.** exact likeness in nature or qualities: *an identity of interests.* **7.** an instance or point of sameness or likeness: *to mistake resemblances for identities.* **8.** *Logic.* an assertion that two terms refer to the same thing. **9.** *Math.* **a.** an equation that is valid for all values of its variables. **b.** Also called **identity element, unit element, unity.** an element in a set such that the element operating on any other element of the set leaves the second element unchanged. **c.** the property of a function or map such that each element is mapped into itself. **d.** the function or map itself. **10.** *Australian Informal.* an interesting, famous, or eccentric resident, usually of long standing in a community. [1560–70; < LL *identitās,* equiv. to L *ident(idem)* repeatedly, again and again, earlier **idem et idem* (*idem* neut. of *īdem* the same + *et* and) + *-itās* -ITY]
—**Syn. 5.** individuality, personality, distinctiveness, uniqueness.

iden′tity card′, a card for identifying the bearer, giving name, address, and other personal data. [1895–1900]

iden′tity cri′sis, **1.** a period or episode of psychological distress, often occurring in adolescence but sometimes in adulthood, when a person seeks a clearer sense of self and an acceptable role in society. **2.** confusion as to goals and priorities: *The company is undergoing an identity crisis.* [1950–55]

iden′tity el′ement, *Math.* identity (def. 9b). [1900–05]

iden′tity ma′trix, *Math.* a matrix that has 1 in each position on the main diagonal and 0 in all other positions. [1940–45]

ideo-, a combining form representing **idea** in compound words: *ideology.* [IDE(A) + -O-]

id•e•o•gram (id′ē ə gram′, ī′dē-), *n.* **1.** a written symbol that represents an idea or object directly rather than a particular word or speech sound, as a Chinese character. **2.** a written symbol, as 7, =, &; logogram. [1830–40; IDEO- + -GRAM[1]]

id•e•o•graph (id′ē ə graf′, -gräf′, ī′dē-), *n.* an ideogram. [1825–35; IDEO- + -GRAPH] —**id•e•o•graph•ic** (id′ē ə graf′ik, ī′dē-), **id′e•o•graph′i•cal,** *adj.* —**id′e•o•graph′i•cal•ly,** *adv.*

id•e•og•ra•phy (id′ē og′rə fē, ī′dē-), *n.* the use of ideograms. [1830–40; IDEO- + -GRAPHY]

i•de•o•log•ic (ī′dē ə loj′ik, id′ē-), *adj.* **1.** of or pertaining to ideology. **2.** speculative; visionary. Also, **i′de•o•log′i•cal.** [1855–60; IDEOLOG(Y) + -IC] —**i′de•o•log′i•cal•ly,** *adv.*

i•de•ol•o•gist (ī′dē ol′ə jist, id′ē-), *n.* **1.** an expert in ideology. **2.** a person who deals with systems of ideas. **3.** a person advocating a particular ideology. **4.** a visionary. [1790–1800; IDEOLOG(Y) + -IST]

i•de•ol•o•gize (ī′dē ol′ə jīz′, id′ē-), *v.t.,* **-gized, -giz•ing.** **1.** to explain or express ideologically: *to ideologize a political opinion.* **2.** to cause to comply with or yield to a particular ideology. Also, *esp. Brit.,* **i′de•ol′o•gise′.** [1855–60; IDEOLOG(Y) + -IZE]

i•de•o•logue (ī′dē ə lôg′, -log′, id′ē-, ī dē′-), *n.* a person who zealously advocates an ideology. [1805–15; < F *idéologue;* see IDEO-, -LOGUE]

i•de•ol•o•gy (ī′dē ol′ə jē, id′ē-), *n., pl.* **-gies.** **1.** the body of doctrine, myth, belief, etc., that guides an individual, social movement, institution, class, or large group. **2.** such a body of doctrine, myth, etc., with reference to some political and social plan, as that of fascism, along with the devices for putting it into operation. **3.** *Philos.* **a.** the study of the nature and origin of ideas. **b.** a system that derives ideas exclusively from sensation. **4.** theorizing of a visionary or impractical nature. [1790–1800; IDEO- + -LOGY; cf. F *idéologie*]

i•de•o•mo•tor (ī′dē ə mō′tər, id′ē ə-), *adj. Psychol.* of or pertaining to involuntary motor activity caused by an idea. Cf. **sensorimotor** (def. 1). [1865–70; IDEO- + MOTOR] —**i′de•o•mo′tion,** *n.*

ides (īdz), *n.* (*used with a singular or plural v.*) (in the ancient Roman calendar) the fifteenth day of March, May, July, or October, and the thirteenth day of the other months. [1300–50; ME < OF < L *īdūs* (fem. pl.); r. ME *idus* < L]

-ides, a Greek plural suffix appearing in scientific names: *cantharides.* [< Gk, pl. of *-is,* suffix of source or origin. See -ID[1]]

id est (id est′), *Latin.* See **i.e.**

-idia, pl. of **-idion** or **-idium.**

-idine, a suffix added to the name of another chemical compound to form the name of another compound derived from or related to the first. [-IDE + -INE[2]]

idio-, a combining form meaning "proper to one," "peculiar," used in the formation of compound words: *idiomorphic.* [< Gk, comb. form of *ídios* (one's) own, personal, private, separate, distinct]

id•i•o•blast (id′ē ə blast′), *n. Bot.* a cell that differs greatly from the surrounding cells or tissue. [1880–85; IDIO- + -BLAST] —**id′i•o•blas′tic,** *adj.*

id•i•o•chro•mat•ic (id′ē ə krō mat′ik, -ō krə-), *adj.* (of a mineral) deriving a characteristic color from its capacity to absorb certain light rays. Cf. **allochromatic.** [IDIO- + CHROMATIC]

id•i•oc•ra•sy (id′ē ok′rə sē), *n., pl.* **-sies.** idiosyncrasy. [1675–85; < Gk *idiokrāsía,* equiv. to *idio-* IDIO- + *-krāsia,* equiv. to *krâs(is)* mixture (see CRASIS) + *-ia* -Y[3]; see IDIOSYNCRASY] —**id•i•o•crat•ic** (id′ē ə krat′ik), **id′i•o•crat′i•cal,** *adj.* —**id′i•o•crat′i•cal•ly,** *adv.*

id•i•o•cy (id′ē ə sē), *n., pl.* **-cies.** **1.** utterly senseless or foolish behavior; a stupid or foolish act, statement, etc. **2.** *Psychol.* the state of being an idiot. [1520–30; ID-IO(T) + -CY; cf. Gk *idiōteía* uncouthness]
—**Syn. 1.** foolishness, inanity, folly.

id•i•o•dy•nam•ic (id′ē ō dī nam′ik), *adj.* of, pertaining to, or conforming to the theories of idiodynamics. [IDIO- + DYNAMIC]

id·i·o·dy·nam·ics (id′ē ō dī nam′iks), *n.* (*used with a singular v.*) a system of beliefs in psychology emphasizing the role of the personality in choosing stimuli and in organizing responses. [IDIO- + DYNAMICS]

id·i·o·glos·si·a (id′ē ə glos′ē ə, -glô′sē ə), *n.* **1.** a private form of speech invented by one child or by children who are in close contact, as twins. **2.** a pathological condition characterized by speech so distorted as to be unintelligible. [1890–95; < Gk *idióglōss(os)* of distinct or peculiar tongue (*idio-* IDIO- + *-glōssos,* adj. deriv. of *glôssa* tongue) + *-ia* -IA] —**id·i·o·glot·tic** (id′ē ə glot′ik), *adj.*

id·i·o·graph (id′ē ə graf′, -gräf′), *n.* a mark or signature characteristic of a particular person, organization, etc.; trademark. Cf. **logotype** (def. 2). [1615–25; < LGk *idiógraphon,* n. use of neut. of Gk *idiógraphos* self-written. See IDIO-, -GRAPH]

id·i·o·graph·ic (id′ē ə graf′ik), *adj. Psychol.* pertaining to or involving the study or explication of individual cases or events (opposed to *nomothetic*). [1905–10; IDIO- + -GRAPHIC]

id·i·o·lect (id′ē ə lekt′), *n. Ling.* a person's individual speech pattern. Cf. **dialect** (def. 1). [1945–50; IDIO- + *-lect,* as in DIALECT]

id·i·om (id′ē əm), *n.* **1.** an expression whose meaning is not predictable from the usual meanings of its constituent elements, as *kick the bucket* or *hang one's head,* or from the general grammatical rules of a language, as *the table round* for *the round table,* and that is not a constituent of a larger expression of like characteristics. **2.** a language, dialect, or style of speaking peculiar to a people. **3.** a construction or expression of one language whose parts correspond to elements in another language but whose total structure or meaning is not matched in the same way in the second language. **4.** the peculiar character or genius of a language. **5.** a distinct style or character, in music, art, etc.: *the idiom of Bach.* [1565–75; < L *idiōma* < Gk *idíōma* peculiarity, specific property equiv. to *idiō-* (var. s. of *idioûsthai* to make one's own, appropriate, v. deriv. of *idiós;* see IDIO-) + *-ma* n. suffix of result]
—**Syn. 1.** See **phrase.**

id·i·o·mat·ic (id′ē ə mat′ik), *adj.* **1.** peculiar to or characteristic of a particular language or dialect: *idiomatic French.* **2.** containing or using many idioms. **3.** having a distinct style or character, esp. in the arts: *idiomatic writing; an idiomatic composer.* Also, **id′i·o·mat′i·cal.** [1705–15; < LGk *idiōmatikós,* equiv. to *idiōmat-* (s. of *idíōma*) IDIOM + *-ikos* -IC] —**id′i·o·mat′i·cal·ly,** *adv.* —**id′i·o·mat′i·cal·ness, id·i·o·ma·tic·i·ty** (id′ē ō mə tis′i tē), *n.*

id·i·o·mor·phic (id′ē ə môr′fik), *adj.* **1.** Also, **euhedral.** (in a rock) noting or pertaining to a mineral constituent having its own characteristic outward crystalline form unaltered by the other constituents of the rock; automorphic. **2.** having its own characteristic form. [1885–90; < Gk *idiómorph(os)* having an individual form (see IDIO-, -MORPHOUS) + -IC] —**id′i·o·mor′phi·cal·ly,** *adv.* —**id′i·o·mor′phism,** *n.*

-idion, a diminutive suffix occurring in loanwords from Greek: *enchiridion.* Cf. **-idium.** [< Gk]

id·i·o·path·ic (id′ē ə path′ik), *adj. Pathol.* of unknown cause, as a disease. [1660–70; IDIO- + -PATHIC] —**id′i·o·path′i·cal·ly,** *adv.*

id·i·op·a·thy (id′ē op′ə thē), *n., pl.* **-thies.** a disease not preceded or occasioned by any known morbid condition. [1630–40; < NL *idiopathīa* < Gk *idiopátheia* disease or affection of local origin. See IDIO-, -PATHY]

id·i·o·plasm (id′ē ə plaz′əm), *n. Biol.* See **germ plasm.** [1885–90; IDIO- + -PLASM] —**id′i·o·plas′mic, id·i·o·plas·mat·ic** (id′ē ō plaz mat′ik), *adj.*

id·i·o·syn·cra·sy (id′ē ə sing′krə sē, -sin′-), *n., pl.* **-sies. 1.** a characteristic, habit, mannerism, or the like, that is peculiar to an individual. **2.** the physical constitution peculiar to an individual. **3.** a peculiarity of the physical or the mental constitution, esp. susceptibility toward drugs, food, etc. Cf. **allergy** (def. 1). Also, **idiocrasy.** [1595–1605; < Gk *idiosynkrāsía,* equiv. to *idio-* IDIO- + *syn-* SYN- + *krâs(is)* a blending + *-ia* -Y[3]] —**id·i·o·syn·crat·ic** (id′ē ō sin krat′ik, -sing-), *adj.* —**id′i·o·syn·crat′i·cal·ly,** *adv.*
—**Syn. 1.** peculiarity, quirk. See **eccentricity.**

id·i·ot (id′ē ət), *n.* **1.** an utterly foolish or senseless person. **2.** *Psychol.* a person of the lowest order in a former classification of mental retardation, having a mental age of less than three years old and an intelligence quotient under 25. [1250–1300; ME < L *idiōta* < Gk *idiṓtēs* private person, layman, person lacking skill or expertise, equiv. to *idiō-* (lengthened var. of *idio-* IDIO-, perh. by analogy with *stratiṓtēs* professional soldier, deriv. of *stratiá* army) + *-tēs* agent n. suffix]
—**Syn. 1.** fool, half-wit; imbecile; dolt, dunce, numskull.

id′iot board′, *Television Slang.* a mechanical apparatus, as a projector or a continuous roll of paper, for prompting a performer during a program. [1950–55]

id′iot box′, *Slang.* a television set; television. [1955–60]

id′iot card′, *Television Slang.* See **cue card.** [1955–60]

id·i·ot·ic (id′ē ot′ik), *adj.* **1.** of, pertaining to, or characteristic of an idiot. **2.** senselessly foolish or stupid: *an idiotic remark.* Also, **id′i·ot′i·cal.** [1705–15; < LL *idiōticus* < Gk *idiōtikós* private, ignorant. See IDIOT, -IC] —**id′i·ot′i·cal·ly,** *adv.* —**id′i·ot′i·cal·ness,** *n.*
—**Syn.** half-witted, imbecilic, fatuous, inane, asinine.

id·i·ot·ism[1] (id′ē ə tiz′əm), *n.* **1.** idiotic conduct or action. **2.** idiocy. [1585–95; IDIOT + -ISM]

id·i·ot·ism[2] (id′ē ə tiz′əm), *n. Obs.* an idiom. [1580–90; < L *idiōtismus* < Gk *idiōtismós* a vulgar phrase, peculiar way of speaking]

id·i·ot·ize (id′ē ə tīz′), *v.t.,* **-ized, -iz·ing.** to make a fool of; make idiotic. Also, *esp. Brit.,* **id′i·ot·ise′.** [1710–20; IDIOT + -IZE]

id·i·ot-proof (id′ē ət proof′), *adj.* built, organized, written, etc., in such a way as to be usable by or understandable to any person of average intelligence or skill: *an idiot-proof camera.* [‡1975–80]

id·i·o·trop·ic (id′ē ə trop′ik, -trō′pik), *adj. Psychiatry.* of or characterized by introspection; introspective. [< Gk *idiótrop(os)* turned or turning to one's own (see IDIO-, -TROPE) + -IC]

id·i·ot sa·vant (id′ē ət sa vänt′, sə vant′, sav′ənt; *Fr.* ē dyō SA VÄN′), *pl.* **id·i·ot sa·vants,** *Fr.* ***id·i·ots sa·vants*** (ē dyō SA VÄN′). *Psychiatry.* a mentally defective person with an exceptional skill or talent in a special field, as a highly developed ability to play music or to solve complex mathematical problems mentally at great speed. [1925–30; < F: lit., learned idiot]

id′iot's delight′, *Slang.* any variety of the card game solitaire.

id·i·o·type (id′ē ə tīp′), *n. Immunol.* the molecular arrangement of amino acids unique to the antigen-binding site of a particular antibody. [1969; back formation from *idiotypic* or *idiotypy,* on the model of *allotypy;* see IDIO-, ALLOTYPE] —**id·i·o·typ·ic** (id′ē ə tip′ik), *adj.* —**id·i·o·typ·y** (id′ē ə tī′pē), *n.*

-idium, a diminutive suffix, corresponding to **-idion,** used in zoological, biological, botanical, anatomical, and chemical terms: *peridium.* [< L < Gk *-idion* -IDION]

i·dle (īd′l), *adj.,* **i·dler, i·dlest,** *v.* **i·dled, i·dling,** *n.* —*adj.* **1.** not working or active; unemployed; doing nothing: *idle workers.* **2.** not spent or filled with activity: *idle hours.* **3.** not in use or operation; not kept busy: *idle machinery.* **4.** habitually doing nothing or avoiding work; lazy. **5.** of no real worth, importance, or significance: *idle talk.* **6.** having no basis or reason; baseless; groundless: *idle fears.* **7.** frivolous; vain: *idle pleasures.* **8.** meaningless; senseless: *idle threats.* **9.** futile; unavailing: *idle rage.* —*v.i.* **10.** to pass time doing nothing. **11.** to move, loiter, or saunter aimlessly: *to idle along the avenue.* **12.** (of a machine, engine, or mechanism) to operate at a low speed, disengaged from the load. —*v.t.* **13.** to pass (time) doing nothing (often fol. by *away*): *to idle away the afternoon.* **14.** to cause (a person) to be idle: *The strike idled many workers.* **15.** to cause (a machine, engine, or mechanism) to idle: *I waited in the car while idling the engine.* —*n.* **16.** the state or quality of being idle. **17.** the state of a machine, engine, or mechanism that is idling: *a cold engine that stalls at idle.* [bef. 900; 1915–20 for def. 12; ME, OE *īdel* (adj.) empty, trifling, vain, useless; c. G *eitel*] —**i′dle·ness,** *n.* —**i′dly,** *adv.*
—**Syn. 1.** sluggish. IDLE, INDOLENT, LAZY, SLOTHFUL apply to a person who is not active. To be IDLE is to be inactive or not working at a job. The word is sometimes derogatory, but not always, since one may be relaxing temporarily or may be idle through necessity: *pleasantly idle on a vacation; to be idle because one is unemployed or because supplies are lacking.* The INDOLENT person is naturally disposed to avoid exertion: *indolent and slow in movement; an indolent and contented fisherman.* The LAZY person is averse to exertion or work, and esp. to continued application; the word is usually derogatory: *too lazy to earn a living; incurably lazy.* SLOTHFUL denotes a reprehensible unwillingness to carry one's share of the burden: *so slothful as to be a burden on others.* **5.** worthless, trivial, trifling. **7.** wasteful. **11.** See **loiter. 13.** waste. —**Ant. 1.** busy, industrious. **5.** important, worthwhile.

i′dle gear′, a gear placed between a driving and a driven gear to transmit motion between them. Also, **i′dler gear′.**

i′dle pul′ley, *Mach.* a loose pulley made to press or rest on a belt in order to tighten or guide it. Also, **i′dler pul′ley.** Also called **idle wheel.** [1885–1890]

i·dler (īd′lər), *n.* **1.** a person who passes time in a lazy or unproductive way. **2.** *Mach.* an idle gear, wheel, or pulley. **3.** *Railroads.* an empty freight car placed under the projecting end of a long object carried by the next car, so that the latter can be connected with another part of the train. **4.** *Naut.* See **day man** (def. 2). [1525–35; IDLE + -ER[1]]

i·dlesse (īd′les), *n.* idleness. [1590–1600; IDLE + *-esse,* as in *finesse,* etc.]

i′dle wheel′, *Mach.* **1.** a wheel for transmitting power and motion between a driving and a driven part, either by friction or by means of teeth. **2.** See **idle pulley.** [1795–1805]

I
I, idle wheel (def. 1)

I·dle·wild (īd′l wīld′), *n.* former name of **John F. Kennedy International Airport.**

I·do (ē′dō), *n.* a revised and simplified form of Esperanto, introduced in 1907. [< Esperanto: lit., offspring, equiv. to *id-* (< Gk; see -IDES) + *-o* n. ending] —**I′do·ism,** *n.* —**I′do·ist,** *n.* —**I′do·is′tic,** *adj.*

i·do·crase (ī′də krās′, id′ə-), *n. Mineral.* vesuvianite. [1795–1805; < F < Gk *eîdo(s)* form + *krâsis* mixture]

i·dol (īd′l), *n.* **1.** an image or other material object representing a deity to which religious worship is addressed. **2.** *Bible.* **a.** an image of a deity other than God. **b.** the deity itself. **3.** any person or thing regarded with blind admiration, adoration, or devotion: *Madame Curie had been her childhood idol.* **4.** a mere image or semblance of something, visible but without substance, as a phantom. **5.** a figment of the mind; fantasy. **6.** a false conception or notion; fallacy. [1200–50; ME < LL *īdōlum* < Gk *eídōlon* image, idol, deriv. of *eîdos* shape, form]
—**Syn. 1.** See **image. 3.** favorite, darling, pet.

i·dol·a·ter (ī dol′ə tər), *n.* **1.** Also, **i·dol·ist** (īd′l ist). a worshiper of idols. **2.** a person who is an immoderate admirer; devotee. [1350–1400; ME *idolatrer,* equiv. to *idolatr(ie)* IDOLATRY + *-er* -ER[2]; *-rer* > *-er* by dissimilation]

i·dol·a·trous (ī dol′ə trəs), *adj.* **1.** worshiping idols. **2.** blindly adoring. **3.** of or pertaining to idolatry. [1540–50; IDOLATR(Y) + -OUS] —**i·dol′a·trous·ly,** *adv.* —**i·dol′a·trous·ness,** *n.*

i·dol·a·try (ī dol′ə trē), *n., pl.* **-tries. 1.** the religious worship of idols. **2.** excessive or blind adoration, reverence, devotion, etc. [1200–50; ME *idolatrie* < ML *īdōlatrīa,* by haplology from LL *īdōlolatrīa* Gk (NT) *eidōlolatreía.* See IDOL -LATRY]
—**Syn. 2.** obsession, madness, mania.

i·dol·ism (īd′l iz′əm), *n.* **1.** idolatry. **2.** idolizing. [1600–10; IDOL + -ISM]

i·dol·ize (īd′l īz′), *v.,* **-ized, -iz·ing.** —*v.t.* **1.** to regard with blind adoration, devotion, etc. **2.** to worship as a god. —*v.i.* **3.** to practice idolatry: *to idolize as did ancient Greece and Rome.* Also, *esp. Brit.,* **i′dol·ise′.** [1590–1600; IDOL + -IZE] —**i′dol·i·za′tion,** *n.* —**i′dol·iz′er,** *n.*
—**Syn. 1.** adore, treasure, worship, dote upon.

i·do·ne·ous (ī dō′nē əs), *adj.* appropriate; fit; suitable; apt. [1605–15; < L *idōneus;* see -OUS] —**i·do·ne·i·ty** (id′n ē′i tē), **i·do′ne·ous·ness,** *n.*

I′ doubt′ it′, a card game, the object of which is to rid oneself of all cards, in which the first player places aces face down on the table and the others follow, in turn, with cards of the next lower rank, adding at will other cards, except that if such deception is successfully challenged, the player must pick up all the cards then on the table.

i·dox·ur·i·dine (ī′doks yŏŏr′i dēn′), *n. Pharm.* a thymidine analogue, $C_9H_{11}IN_2O_5$, used topically for the ocular treatment of herpes simplex keratitis. [contr. and rearrangement of *2′-deoxy-5-iodouridine* the chemical name]

IDP, 1. integrated data processing: the processing of information by systematic techniques that reduce human intervention to a minimum and that employ a language common to all the machines in the system. Cf. **ADP, EDP. 2.** International Driving Permit.

I·dris I (ī′dris, ī drēs′), (*Mohammed Idris Senussi*), 1890–1983, king of Libya 1951–69.

Id·u·mae·a (id′yŏŏ mē′ə), *n.* Greek name of **Edom.** Also, **Id′u·me′a.** —**Id′u·mae′an, Id′u·me′an,** *adj., n.*

I·dun (ē′thŏŏn), *n. Scand. Myth.* a goddess, keeper of the apples of youth and wife of Bragi; abducted by the giant Thjazi, from whom she was rescued. Also, **Ithun, Ithunn.** [< ON *Ithunn;* perh. deriv. of *ith* deed, feat]

i·dyll (īd′l), *n.* **1.** a poem or prose composition, usually describing pastoral scenes or events or any charmingly simple episode, appealing incident, or the like. **2.** a simple descriptive or narrative piece in verse or prose. **3.** material suitable for such a work. **4.** an episode or scene of idyllic charm. **5.** a brief or inconsequential romantic affair. **6.** *Music.* a composition, usually instrumental, of a pastoral or sentimental character. Also, **i′dyl.** [1595–1605; < L *idyllium* < Gk *eidýllion* short pastoral poem, equiv. to *eíd(os)* form + *-yllion* dim. suffix]

i·dyl·lic (ī dil′ik), *adj.* **1.** suitable for or suggestive of an idyll; charmingly simple or rustic: *his idyllic life in Tahiti.* **2.** of, pertaining to, or characteristic of an idyll. [1855–60; IDYLL + -IC] —**i·dyl′li·cal·ly,** *adv.*
—**Syn. 1.** unspoiled, sylvan, pastoral, arcadian.

i·dyl·list (īd′l ist), *n.* a writer of idylls. Also, **i′dyl·ist.** [1790–1800; IDYLL + -IST]

I′dylls of the King′, The, a series of poems by Tennyson, based on Arthurian legend.

IE, Indo-European.

-ie, var. of **-y**[2].

I.E., 1. Indo-European. **2.** Industrial Engineer.

i.e., that is. [< L *id est*]

I.E.E.E., Institute of Electrical and Electronics Engineers. Also, **IEEE**

-iensis, var. of **-ensis.** [generalized from derivatives of L or NL stems ending in *-i-*]

IEP, Individualized Educational Program.

Ie·per (*Flemish.* ē′pər), *n.* Ypres.

-ier[1], var. of **-er**[1], usually in nouns designating trades: *collier; clothier; furrier; glazier.* [ME *-ier(e),* var. of *-yer(e)* (cf. -YER), equiv. to *-i-* v. stem ending + *-ere* -ER[1], prob. reinforced by OF *-ier* < L *-ārius* -ARY (cf. SOLDIER)]

-ier[2], a noun suffix occurring mainly in loanwords from French, often simply a spelling variant of **-eer,** with which it is etymologically identical (*bombardier; brigadier; financier; grenadier*); it is also found on an older and semantically more diverse group of loanwords that have stress on the initial syllable (*barrier; courier; courtier; terrier*). Recent loanwords from French may maintain the modern French pronunciation with loss of the final *r* sound (*croupier; dossier; hotelier*). [< F, OF < L *-ārius, -āria, -ārium* -ARY; cf. -AIRE, -EER, -ER[2]]

Ie·ya·su (ē′ye yä′sŏŏ), *n.* Iyeyasu.

if (if), *conj.* **1.** in case that; granting or supposing that; on condition that: *Sing if you want to. Stay indoors if it*

rains. I'll go if you do. **2.** even though: *an enthusiastic if small audience.* **3.** whether: *He asked if I knew Spanish.* **4.** (used to introduce an exclamatory phrase): *If only Dad could see me now!* **5.** when or whenever: *If it was raining, we had to play inside.* —*n.* **6.** a supposition; uncertain possibility: *The future is full of ifs.* **7.** a condition, requirement, or stipulation: *There are too many ifs in his agreement.* **8. ifs, ands, or buts,** reservations, restrictions, or excuses: *I want that job finished today, and no ifs, ands, or buts.* [bef. 900; ME, var. of *yif,* OE *gif, gef;* akin to ON *ef* if, Goth *ibai* whether, OHG *iba* condition, stipulation]
—**Syn. 1, 2.** IF, PROVIDED, PROVIDING imply a condition on which something depends. IF is general. It may be used to indicate suppositions or hypothetical conditions (often involving doubt or uncertainty): *If you like, we can go straight home. If I had known, I wouldn't have gone.* IF may mean even though: *If I am wrong, you are not right.* It may mean whenever: *If I do not understand, I ask questions.* PROVIDED always indicates some stipulation: *I will subscribe ten dollars provided (on the condition) that you do, too. Provided he goes, we can go along.* PROVIDING means the same as PROVIDED, that is, just in case some certain thing should happen: *We will buy the house, providing (provided) we can get a mortgage.*
—**Usage.** IF meaning "whether," as in *I haven't decided if I'll go,* is sometimes criticized, but the usage has been established in standard English for a long time.

if, *Radio.* See **intermediate frequency.** Also, **IF**

IFA, *Med.* See **immunofluorescence assay.**

IFALP, International Federation of Air Line Pilots Associations.

IFC, 1. International Finance Corporation. **2.** International Fisheries Commission (U.S. and Canada). **3.** International Freighting Corporation.

if′-come′ bet′ (if′kum′). See **pyramid bet.**

I·fe (ē′fā), *n.* **1.** a town in SW Nigeria. 176,000. **2.** a male or female given name: from a Yoruba word meaning "love."

IFF, *Mil.* Identification, Friend or Foe: a system of transmitters and transponders that uses coded signals to distinguish between friendly and hostile aircraft.

iff, *Math.* if and only if.

if·fen (if′ən), *conj. Dial.* if. [1930–35; IF + *-en,* of uncert. orig., perh. AN² (hence a var. of archaic *an if*) or *in′* (see -ING²), extracted from conjunctional uses of *considering, excepting,* etc.; cf. GIN⁵]

if·fy (if′ē), *adj.,* **-fi·er, -fi·est.** *Informal.* **1.** full of unresolved points or questions: *an iffy situation.* **2.** doubtful; questionable: *An early decision on this is iffy.* [1915–20; IF + -Y¹] —**if′fi·ness,** *n.*
—**Syn. 1.** doubtful, unsettled, uncertain, speculative.

I.F.L.W.U., International Fur and Leather Workers' Union.

If·ni (ēf′nē), *n.* a former Spanish enclave on the W coast of Morocco, ceded to Morocco 1969.

I formation (ī), *Football.* an offensive alignment in which the backs are positioned in line directly behind the quarterback. [1950–55]

-iformes, a combining form used in taxonomic names of animals, esp. orders of birds and fish, meaning "having the form of": *Beryciformes; Passeriformes.* [< NL, pl. of *-iformis;* see -I-, -FORM]

I.F.S., Irish Free State.

I·fu·gao (ē′fo͞o gou′), *n., pl.* **-gaos,** *(esp. collectively)* **-gao.** a member of an agricultural people who inhabit Luzon, in the Philippines.

-ify, var. of **-fy** after a consonant: *intensify.* [ME *-ifien* < MF *-ifier* < L *-ificāre,* equiv. to *-i-* -I- + *-ficāre* -FY]

Ig, immunoglobulin.

I.G., 1. Indo-Germanic. **2.** Inspector General.

IgA, *Immunol.* immunoglobulin A: a class of antibodies predominant in respiratory and alimentary tract secretions and in saliva and tears, functioning as the body's first line of defense against invading foreign substances esp. by neutralizing viral antigens and by preventing the adherence of bacteria to mucous membrane surfaces. [1960–65]

Ig·bo (ig′bō), *n., pl.* **-bos,** *(esp. collectively)* **-bo.** Ibo.

IgD, *Immunol.* immunoglobulin D: a class of antibodies present as an antigen receptor on most cell surfaces and predominant on human B cells. [1960–65]

IgE, *Immunol.* immunoglobulin E: a class of antibodies most abundant in tissue spaces, involved in the expulsion of intestinal parasites and causing allergic reactions by activating the release of histamines and leukotrienes in response to certain foreign antigens. [1960–65]

IgG, *Immunol.* immunoglobulin G: a class of circulating antibodies predominant in serum, produced by plasma cells and memory cells in response to pathogens and other foreign substances, able to pass through the placental wall to the fetal circulation to impart immune defense for the period of infancy. [1960–65]

I·glau (*Ger.* ē′glou), *n.* Jihlava.

ig·loo (ig′lo͞o), *n., pl.* **-loos. 1.** an Eskimo house, being a dome-shaped hut usually built of blocks of hard snow. **2.** *Informal.* any dome-shaped construction thought to resemble an igloo: *immense silos topped with steel igloos.* **3.** *Mil.* a dome-shaped building for the storage of rockets or other munitions. **4.** an excavation made by a seal in the snow over its breathing hole in the ice. Also, **ig′lu.** [1855–60; < Inuit *iglu* house]

CONCISE ETYMOLOGY KEY: <, descended or borrowed from; >, whence; b., blend of, blended; c., cognate with; cf., compare; deriv., derivative; equiv., equivalent; imit., imitative; obl., oblique; r., replacing; s., stem; sp., spelling, spelled; resp., respelling, respelled; trans., translation; ?, origin unknown; *, unattested; ‡, probably earlier than. See the full key inside the front cover.

igloo (def. 1)

IgM, *Immunol.* immunoglobulin M: a class of short-term circulating and secretory antibodies existing as an aggregate of five antibody molecules, having a high affinity for viruses. [1960–65]

ign., 1. ignition. **2.** unknown. [(def. 2) < L *ignōtus*]

Ig·na·tius (ig nā′shəs), *n.* **1. Saint** (*Ignatius Theophorus*), A.D. c40–107?, bishop of Antioch and Apostolic Father. **2. Saint** (*Nicetas*), A.D. 799?–878, patriarch of Constantinople 846–858, 867–878.

Igna′tius of Loyo′la, Saint. See **Loyola, Saint Ignatius.**

ig·ne·ous (ig′nē əs), *adj.* **1.** *Geol.* produced under conditions involving intense heat, as rocks of volcanic origin or rocks crystallized from molten magma. **2.** of, pertaining to, or characteristic of fire. [1655–65; < L *igneus,* equiv. to *ign(is)* fire + *-eus* -EOUS]

ig·nes·cent (ig nes′ənt), *adj.* **1.** emitting sparks of fire, as certain stones when struck with steel. **2.** bursting into flame. —*n.* **3.** an ignescent substance. [1820–30; < L *ignēscent-* (s. of *ignēscēns*), prp. of *ignēscere* to catch fire, equiv. to *ign(is)* fire + *-ēscent-* -ESCENT]

ig·nim·brite (ig′nim brīt′), *n. Petrol.* a fine-grained volcanic rock consisting mainly of welded shards of feldspar and quartz. Also called **welded tuff.** [1932; < L *ign(is)* fire + *imbr-,* s. of *imber* rain, shower + -ITE¹]

ig·nis fat·u·us (ig′nis fach′o͞o əs), *pl.* **ig·nes fat·u·i** (ig′nēz fach′o͞o ī′). **1.** Also called **friar's lantern, will-o'-the-wisp.** a flitting phosphorescent light seen at night, chiefly over marshy ground, and believed to be due to spontaneous combustion of gas from decomposed organic matter. **2.** something deluding or misleading. [1555–65; < ML: lit., foolish fire]

ig·nite (ig nīt′), *v.,* **-nit·ed, -nit·ing.** —*v.t.* **1.** to set on fire; kindle. **2.** *Chem.* to heat intensely; roast. —*v.i.* **3.** to take fire; begin to burn. [1660–70; < L *ignītus* (ptp. of *ignīre* to set on fire, ignite), equiv. to *ign(is)* fire + *-ītus* -ITE²] —**ig·nit′a·ble, ig·nit′i·ble,** *adj.* —**ig·nit′a·bil′i·ty, ig·nit′i·bil′i·ty,** *n.*
—**Syn. 1.** See **kindle.**

ig·nit·er (ig nī′tər), *n.* **1.** a person or thing that ignites. **2.** *Electronics.* the carborundum rod used to initiate the discharge in an ignitron tube. [1880–85; IGNITE + -ER¹]

ig·ni·tion (ig nish′ən), *n.* **1.** the act or fact of igniting; state of being ignited. **2.** a means or device for igniting. **3.** (in an internal-combustion engine) the process that ignites the fuel in the cylinder. [1605–15; ML *ignītiōn-* (s. of *ignītiō*) a setting on fire. See IGNITE, -ION]

igni′tion coil′, (in an automotive ignition system) a transformer consisting of two wire windings or coils in which low-voltage direct current is fed through the primary winding to generate high-voltage spark pulses in the secondary winding. Also called **coil.** [1895–1900]

igni′tion in′terlock, *Auto.* interlock (def. 10).

igni′tion point′, *Chem.* See **autoignition point.** Also called **igni′tion tem′perature.** [1885–90]

igni′tion sys′tem, the system in an internal-combustion engine that produces the spark to ignite the mixture of fuel and air: includes the battery, ignition coil, distributor, spark plugs, and associated switches and wiring. [1900–05]

ig·ni·tron (ig nī′tron, ig′ni tron), *n. Electronics.* a cathode-arc vacuum tube with an auxiliary electrode projecting into a pool of mercury: it conducts current when the anode is positive. [1930–35; IGNI(TER) + -TRON]

ig·no·ble (ig nō′bəl), *adj.* **1.** of low character, aims, etc.; mean; base: *his ignoble purposes.* **2.** of low grade or quality; inferior. **3.** not noble; of humble descent or rank. **4.** *Falconry.* noting any hawk with short wings that chases or rakes after the quarry. [1400–50; late ME < L *ignōbilis* unknown, inglorious, equiv. to *in-* IN-³ + OL *gnōbilis* (L *nōbilis*) NOBLE] —**ig′no·bil′i·ty, ig·no′ble·ness,** *n.* —**ig·no′bly,** *adv.*
—**Syn. 1.** degraded, dishonorable, ignominious, contemptible. **3.** lowly, obscure, plebeian, peasant. —**Ant. 1.** honorable. **2.** superior.

ig·no·min·i·ous (ig′nə min′ē əs), *adj.* **1.** marked by or attended with ignominy; discreditable; humiliating: *an ignominious retreat.* **2.** bearing or deserving ignominy; contemptible. [1375–1425; late ME < L *ignōminiōsus.* See IGNOMINY, -OUS] —**ig′no·min′i·ous·ly,** *adv.* —**ig′no·min′i·ous·ness,** *n.*
—**Syn. 1.** degrading, disgraceful, dishonorable, shameful. **2.** despicable, ignoble.

ig·no·min·y (ig′nə min′ē, ig nom′ə nē), *n., pl.* **-min·ies** for 2. **1.** disgrace; dishonor; public contempt. **2.** shameful or dishonorable quality or conduct or an instance of this. [1530–40; < L *ignōminia,* equiv. to *ig-* (for *in-* IN-³, appar. by assoc. with *ignōbilis* IGNOBLE, *ignōtus* unknown, etc.; cf. COGNOMEN) + *nōmin-* (s. of *nōmen*) NAME + *-ia* -Y³]
—**Syn. 1.** disrepute, discredit, shame, obloquy, opprobrium. See **disgrace.** —**Ant. 1.** credit, honor.

ig·no·ra·mus (ig′nə rā′məs, -ram′əs), *n., pl.* **-mus·es.** an extremely ignorant person. [1570–80; < L *ignōrāmus* we ignore (1st pers. pl. pres. indic. of *ignōrāre* to be ignorant of, IGNORE); hence name of an ignorant lawyer in the play *Ignoramus* (1615) by the English playwright G. Ruggle, whence current sense]
—**Syn.** simpleton, fool, dunce, know-nothing.

ig·no·rance (ig′nər əns), *n.* the state or fact of being ignorant; lack of knowledge, learning, information, etc. [1175–1225; ME < L *ignōrantia.* See IGNORE, -ANCE]

ig·no·rant (ig′nər ənt), *adj.* **1.** lacking in knowledge or training; unlearned: *an ignorant man.* **2.** lacking knowledge or information as to a particular subject or fact: *ignorant of quantum physics.* **3.** uninformed; unaware. **4.** due to or showing lack of knowledge or training: *an ignorant statement.* [1325–75; ME *ignora(u)nt* < L *ignōrant-* (s. of *ignōrāns*), prp. of *ignōrāre* to IGNORE; see -ANT] —**ig′no·rant·ly,** *adv.* —**ig′no·rant·ness,** *n.*
—**Syn. 1.** uninstructed, untutored, untaught. IGNORANT, ILLITERATE, UNLETTERED, UNEDUCATED mean lacking in knowledge or in training. IGNORANT may mean knowing little or nothing, or it may mean uninformed about a particular subject: *An ignorant person can be dangerous. I confess I'm ignorant of mathematics.* ILLITERATE originally meant lacking a knowledge of literature or similar learning, but is most often applied now to one unable to read or write: *necessary training for illiterate soldiers.* UNLETTERED emphasizes the idea of being without knowledge of literature: *unlettered though highly trained in science.* UNEDUCATED refers especially to lack of schooling or to lack of access to a body of knowledge equivalent to that learned in schools: *uneducated but highly intelligent.* **2.** unenlightened. —**Ant. 1.** literate. **2.** learned.

ig·no·ra·ti·o e·len·chi (ig′nə rā′shē ō′ i leng′kī, -kē), *Logic.* the fallacy of offering proof irrelevant to the proposition in question. [1580–90; < L *ignōrātiō elenchī* lit., ignorance of the refutation; see ELENCHUS]

ig·nore (ig nôr′, -nōr′), *v.t.,* **-nored, -nor·ing. 1.** to refrain from noticing or recognizing: *to ignore insulting remarks.* **2.** *Law.* (of a grand jury) to reject (a bill of indictment), as on the grounds of insufficient evidence. [1605–15; < L *ignōrāre* to not know, disregard, v. deriv. of *ignārus* ignorant, unaware (with *-ō-* perh. from *ignōtus* unknown), equiv. to *in-* IN-³ + *gnārus* knowing, acquainted (with); akin to *(g)nōscere* to KNOW¹] —**ig·nor′a·ble,** *adj.* —**ig·nor′er,** *n.*
—**Syn. 1.** overlook; slight, disregard, neglect. —**Ant. 1.** notice, regard.

I-go (ē′gō′), *n.* go². [< Japn; see GO²]

Ig·o·rot (ig′ə rōt′, ē′gə-), *n., pl.* **-rots,** *(esp. collectively)* **-rot.** a member of a people of the Malay stock in northern Luzon in the Philippines, comprising various tribes, some noted as headhunters.

I·graine (i grān′), *n. Arthurian Romance.* the mother of King Arthur.

i·gua·na (i gwä′nə), *n.* **1.** a large, arboreal lizard, *Iguana iguana,* native to Central and South America, having stout legs and a crest of spines from neck to tail. **2.** any of various related lizards of the genera *Iguana, Ctenosaura, Conolophus,* and *Amblyrhynchus.* [1545–55; < Sp < Arawak *iwana*]

iguana, *Iguana iguana,* length to 6 ft. (1.8 m)

i·gua·nid (i gwä′nid), *n.* **1.** any of numerous lizards of the family Iguanidae, of the New World, Madagascar, and several islands of the South Pacific, comprising terrestrial, semiaquatic, and arboreal species typically with a long tail and, in the male, a bright throat patch, including the anoles, collared lizards, earless lizards, horned lizards, and iguanas. —*adj.* **2.** belonging or pertaining to the iguanids. [< NL *Iguanidae,* equiv. to *Iguan(a)* name of genus (see IGUANA) + *-idae* -ID²]

i·guan·o·don (i gwä′nə don′, i gwan′ə-), *n.* a plant-eating dinosaur of the genus *Iguanodon* that lived in Europe early in the Cretaceous Period and grew to a length of from 15 to 30 ft. (4.5 to 9 m) and walked erect on its hind feet. [< NL (1825) < Sp *iguan(a)* IGUANA + Gk *odṓn,* var. of *odoús* TOOTH]

I·guas·sú (ē′gwä so͞o′), *n.* a river in S Brazil, flowing W to the Paraná River. 380 mi. (610 km) long. Also, **I′gua·çu′.**

I′guassú Falls′, a waterfall on the Iguassú River, on the boundary between Brazil and Argentina. 210 ft. (64 m) high. Also, **I′guaçu Falls′.** Formerly, **Victoria Falls.**

I′-head en′gine (ī′hed′), an internal-combustion engine with both intake and exhaust valves placed directly above the piston. Also called **overhead-valve engine, valve-in-head engine.**

IHL, International Hockey League.

ihp, See **indicated horsepower.** Also, **IHP**

ih·ram (ē räm′), *n.* the dress worn by male Muslims on their pilgrimage to Mecca, consisting of two white cotton cloths, one worn round the waist, the other over the left shoulder. [1695–1705; < Ar *iḥrām* lit., prohibition]

IHS, 1. Jesus. [< LL < Gk: partial transliteration of the first three letters of *Iēsoûs* Jesus] **2.** Jesus Savior of Men. [< ML *Iēsus Hominum Salvātor*] **3.** in this sign (the cross) shalt thou conquer. [< L *In Hōc Signō Vincēs*] **4.** in this (cross) is salvation. [< L *In Hōc Salūs*]

i·i·wi (ē ē′wē), *n.* a Hawaiian honeycreeper, *Vestiaria coccinea,* having a red body, black wings, and a deeply curved pinkish-red bill. [1885–90; < Hawaiian *'i'iwi,* deriv. of *'iwi* reddish; cf. earlier *eeeeve* (1779)]

IJ (ī), *n.* an inland arm of the Ijsselmeer in the Netherlands: Amsterdam located on its S side. Also, **Ij.**

I·jaw (ē′jô), *n., pl.* **I·jaws,** *(esp. collectively)* **I·jaw.** Ijo.

ij•ma‘ (ij mä′), *n. Islam.* the consensus of all believers on the rightness of a belief or practice. [< Ar *ijmā‘*]

I•jo (ē′jō), *n., pl.* **I•jos,** (*esp. collectively*) **I•jo** for 1. **1.** a member of an indigenous people of the Niger delta in southern Nigeria. **2.** the Niger-Congo language of the Ijo. Also, **Ijaw.**

IJs•sel (ī′səl), *n.* a river in the central Netherlands, flowing N to the IJsselmeer: a branch of the Rhine River. 70 mi. (110 km) long. Also, **Ijs′sel.**

IJs•sel•meer (ī′səl mâr′), *n.* a lake in the NW Netherlands: created by the diking of the Zuider Zee. 465 sq. mi. (1204 sq. km). Also, **Ijs′sel•meer′.**

ij•ti•had (ij′ti häd′), *n.* (in Islamic law) the use of reason to arrive at a knowledge of truth in religious matters. [< Ar]

I•ka•ri•a (i kâr′ē ə, ī kâr′-; *Gk.* ē′kä rē′ä), *n.* Icaria.

Ik•a•ros (ik′ər əs, -ə ros′), *n. Class. Myth.* Icarus.

i•kat (ē′kät), *n.* **1.** a method of printing woven fabric by tie-dyeing the warp yarns **(warp ikat),** the weft yarns **(weft ikat),** or both **(double ikat)** before weaving. **2.** a fabric made by this method. [1930–35; < Malay: to tie, bind]

Ike (ik), *n.* See **Eisenhower, Dwight David.**

i•ke•ba•na (ik′ə bä′nə; *Japn.* ē′ke bä′nä), *n.* the Japanese art of arranging flowers. [1900–05; < Japn, equiv. to *ike(y)* to make live, causative of *ik-* live (< **ika-i*) + *-bana* comb. form of *hana* flower (earlier *fana* < **pana*)]

I•ke•da (ē ke′dä), *n.* **Ha•ya•to** (hä yä′tô), 1899–1965, Japanese statesman: prime minister 1960–64.

Ike′ jack′et, *Informal.* Eisenhower jacket.

Ikh•na•ton (ik nät′n), *n.* See **Amenhotep IV.** Also, **Akhnaton.**

i•kon (ī′kon), *n.* icon (defs. 1, 2).

IL, Illinois (approved esp. for use with zip code).

Il, *Symbol, Chem.* illinium.

il-[1], var. of **in-**[2] (by assimilation) before *l: illation.*

il-[2], var. of **in-**[3] (by assimilation) before *l: illogical.*

-il, var. of **-ile:** *civil.*

il., **1.** illustrated. **2.** illustration.

IL-1, *Immunol.* See **interleukin 1.**

IL-2, *Immunol, Pharm.* See **interleukin 2.**

IL-3, *Immunol.* See **interleukin 3.**

I•la (ē′lə), *n.* a town in SW Nigeria. 155,000.

ILA, **1.** International Law Association. **2.** International Longshoremen's Association. Also, **I.L.A.**

i•lang-i•lang (ē′läng ē′läng), *n.* ylang-ylang.

il Du•ce (ēl dōō′chā; *It.* ēl dōō′che), duce (def. 2).

ile-, var. of **ileo-** before a vowel: *ileac.*

-ile, a suffix of adjectives expressing capability, susceptibility, liability, aptitude, etc.: *agile; docile; ductile; fragile; prehensile; volatile.* Also, **-il.** [< L *-ilis, -īlis*]

Ile, *Biochem.* isoleucine.

il•e•ac[1] (il′ē ak′), *adj.* of or pertaining to the ileum. [ILE- + -AC, on model of *iliac*]

il•e•ac[2] (il′ē ak′), *adj.* of or pertaining to ileus. [1815–25; ILE(US) + -AC, on model of *iliac*]

Île de France (ēl də fräns′), **1.** a former province in N France, including Paris and the region around it. **2.** former name of **Mauritius.**

Île du Dia•ble (ēl dʏ dyä′blᵊ), French name of **Devil's Island.**

il•e•i•tis (il′ē ī′tis), *n. Pathol.* inflammation of the ileum. [1850–55; ILE- + -ITIS]

ileo-, a combining form representing **ileum** in compound words: *ileostomy.* Also, *esp. before a vowel,* **ile-.** [< NL]

il•e•o•ce•cal (il′ē ō sē′kəl), *adj. Anat.* of, pertaining to, or involving the ileum and cecum. [1840–50; ILEO- + CECAL]

il•e•o•co•li•tis (il′ē ō kə lī′tis, -kō-), *n. Pathol.* inflammation of the mucous membrane of the ileum and colon. [1885–90; ILEO- + COLITIS]

il•e•o•co•los•to•my (il′ē ō kə los′tə mē), *n., pl.* **-mies.** the surgical formation of an artificial opening between the ileum and the colon. [1885–90; ILEO- + COLOSTOMY]

il•e•os•to•my (il′ē os′tə mē), *n., pl.* **-mies.** *Surg.* **1.** the construction of an artificial opening from the ileum through the abdominal wall, permitting drainage of the contents of the small intestine. **2.** the opening so constructed. [1885–90; ILEO- + -STOMY]

I•le•sha (i lā′shə), *n.* a town in SW Nigeria. 224,000.

Il•e•tin (il′i tin), *Pharm., Trademark.* a brand of insulin (def. 2).

il•e•um (il′ē əm), *n., pl.* **il•e•a** (il′ē ə). **1.** *Anat.* the third and lowest division of the small intestine, extending from the jejunum to the cecum. See diag. under **intestine. 2.** *Zool.* the anterior portion of the hindgut of an insect or other arthropod. [1675–85; < NL, ML *ileum,* var. of L *īlia* (neut. pl.) side of the body between hips and groin, guts, appar. by confusion with L *ileus* ILEUS] **—il′e•al,** *adj.*

il•e•us (il′ē əs), *n. Pathol.* intestinal obstruction characterized by lack of peristalsis and leading to severe colicky pain and vomiting. [1700–10; < L *īleus* colic < Gk *eileós,* equiv. to *eile-* (s. of *eílein* to roll) + *-os* n. suffix]

i•lex[1] (ī′leks), *n.* See **holm oak.** [1350–1400; ME < L]

i•lex[2] (ī′leks), *n.* **1.** any tree or shrub of the genus *Ilex.* **2.** a holly. [1555–65; < NL, L *īlex* ILEX[1]]

Il•ford (il′fərd), *n.* a former borough in SE England, now part of Redbridge, Greater London.

I.L.G.W.U., International Ladies' Garment Workers' Union. Also, **ILGWU**

I•lhé•us (ē lye′ōōs), *n.* a seaport in E Brazil. 100,687.

il•i•ac (il′ē ak′), *adj.* of, pertaining to, or situated near the ilium. [1510–20; ILI(UM) + -AC]

il′iac ar′tery, *Anat.* **1.** Also called **common iliac artery.** either of two large arteries that conduct blood to the pelvis and the legs. **2.** Also called **external iliac artery.** the outer branch of an iliac artery that becomes the femoral artery. **3.** Also called **hypogastric artery, internal iliac artery.** the inner branch of an iliac artery that conducts blood to the gluteal region. [1830–40]

Il•i•ad (il′ē əd), *n.* **1.** (*italics*) a Greek epic poem describing the siege of Troy, ascribed to Homer. **2.** (*sometimes l.c.*) any similar poem; a long narrative. **3.** (*often l.c.*) a long series of woes, trials, etc. [< L *Iliad-* (s. of *Ilias*) < Gk, equiv. to *Ili(on)* Troy + *-ad-* -AD] **—Il•i•ad•ic** (il′ē ad′ik), *adj.*

Il•i•es•cu (il′ē es′kōō), *n.* **Ion** (yôn), born 1930, Rumanian political leader: president since 1989.

ilio-, a combining form representing **ilium** in compound words: *iliofemoral.*

Il•i•on (il′ē ən, -on′), *n.* Greek name of ancient **Troy.**

-ility, a combination of **-ile** and **-ity,** used to form abstract nouns from adjectives with stems in **-ile:** *agility; civility; ability.* [< F *-ilité* < L *-ilitās;* see -ILE, -ITY]

il•i•um (il′ē əm), *n., pl.* **il•i•a** (il′ē ə). *Anat.* the broad, upper portion of either hipbone. See diag. under **pelvis.** [1705–1710; < NL, special use of ML *īlium,* as sing. of L *īlia;* see ILEUM]

Il•i•um (il′ē əm), *n.* Latin name of ancient **Troy.**

ilk[1] (ilk), *n.* **1.** family, class, or kind: *he and all his ilk.* **2. of that ilk, a.** (in Scotland) of the same family name or place: *Ross of that ilk,* i.e., *Ross of Ross.* **b.** of the same class or kind. **—***adj.* **3.** same. [bef. 900; ME *ilke,* OE *ilca* (pronoun) the same, equiv. to demonstrative *i* (c. Goth *is* he, L *is* that) + a reduced form of *lic* LIKE[1]; cf. WHICH, SUCH]

ilk[2] (ilk), *Chiefly Scot.* **—***pron.* **1.** each. **—***adj.* **2.** each; every. [bef. 900; ME *ilk,* north var. of *ilch,* OE *ylc* (pronoun) EACH]

il•ka (il′kə), *adj., Chiefly Scot.* every; each. [1150–1200; ME; orig. phrase *ilk a* each one. See ILK[2], A[1]]

ill (il), *adj.,* **worse, worst,** *n., adv.* **—***adj.* **1.** of unsound physical or mental health; unwell; sick: *She felt ill, so her teacher sent her to the nurse.* **2.** objectionable; unsatisfactory; poor; faulty: *ill manners.* **3.** hostile; unkindly: *ill feeling.* **4.** evil; wicked; bad: *of ill repute.* **5.** unfavorable; adverse: *ill fortune.* **6.** of inferior worth or ability; unskillful; inexpert: *an ill example of scholarship.* **7. ill at ease,** socially uncomfortable; nervous: *They were ill at ease because they didn't speak the language.* **—***n.* **8.** an unfavorable opinion or statement: *I can speak no ill of her.* **9.** harm or injury: *His remarks did much ill.* **10.** trouble, distress, or misfortune: *Many ills befell him.* **11.** evil: *to know the difference between good and ill.* **12.** sickness or disease. **—***adv.* **13.** in an ill manner. **14.** unsatisfactorily; poorly: *It ill befits a man to betray old friends.* **15.** in a hostile or unfriendly manner. **16.** unfavorably; unfortunately. **17.** with displeasure or offense. **18.** faultily; improperly. **19.** with difficulty or inconvenience; scarcely: *Buying a new car is an expense we can ill afford.* [1150–1200; ME *ill(e)* (n. and adj.) < ON *illr* (adj.) ill, bad]
—Syn. 1. unhealthy, ailing, diseased, afflicted. ILL, SICK mean being in bad health, not being well. ILL is the more formal word. In the U.S. the two words are used practically interchangeably except that SICK is always used when the word modifies the following noun: *He looks sick (ill); a sick person.* In England, SICK is not interchangeable with ILL, but usually has the connotation of nauseous: *She got sick and threw up.* SICK, however, is used before nouns just as in the U.S.: *a sick man.* **4.** wrong, iniquitous. See **bad**[1]. **9.** hurt, pain, affliction, misery. **10.** calamity. **11.** depravity. **12.** illness, affliction. **14.** badly. **—Ant. 1.** well, healthy. **4.** good.

I'll (il), contraction of *I will.*
—Usage. See **contraction.**

Ill., Illinois.

ill., **1.** illustrated. **2.** illustration. **3.** illustrator. **4.** most illustrious. [(def. 4) < L *illustrissimus*]

ill-ad•vised (il′əd vīzd′), *adj.* acting or done without due consideration; imprudent: *an ill-advised remark.* [1585–95] **—ill-ad•vis•ed•ly** (il′əd vī′zid lē), *adv.*
—Syn. unwise, shortsighted, ill-judged, senseless.

I•llam•pu (ē yäm′pōō), *n.* a peak of Mount Sorata. Cf. **Sorata.**

il•la•tion (i lā′shən), *n.* **1.** the act of inferring. **2.** an inference; conclusion. [1525–35; < LL *illātiōn-* (s. of *illātiō*) a carrying in, equiv. to L *illāt(us)* suppletive ptp. of *inferre* to bring in, bear in (*il-* IL-[1] + *lātus* brought, earlier **tlātus;* see TOLERATE) + *-iōn-* -ION]

il•la•tive (il′ə tiv, i lā′tiv), *adj.* **1.** of, pertaining to, or expressing illation; inferential: *an illative word such as "therefore."* **2.** *Gram.* noting a case, as in Finnish, whose distinctive function is to indicate place into or toward which. **—***n.* **3.** *Gram.* the illative case. [1585–95; < LL *illātīvus,* equiv. to *illāt-* (see ILLATION) + *-īvus* -IVE] **—il′la•tive•ly,** *adv.*

il•laud•a•ble (i lô′də bəl), *adj.* unworthy of praise; not laudable. [1580–90; < LL *illaudābilis.* See IL-[2], LAUDABLE] **—il•laud′a•bly,** *adv.*

ill-be•ing (il′bē′ing), *n.* state or condition of lacking health, solvency, etc. [1830–40; modeled on WELL-BEING]

ill-bod•ing (il′bō′ding), *adj.* foreboding evil; inauspicious; unlucky: *ill-boding stars.* [1585–95]

ill-bred (il′bred′), *adj.* showing lack of good social breeding; unmannerly; rude. [1615–25]

ill-con•ceived (il′kən sēvd′), *adj.* badly conceived or planned: *an ill-conceived project.*

ill-con•di•tioned (il′kən dish′ənd), *adj.* **1.** in a surly or bad mood, state, etc. **2.** not in a good or peak condition. [1605–15] **—ill′-con•di′tioned•ness,** *n.*

ill-con•sid•ered (il′kən sid′ərd), *adj.* lacking thorough consideration; ill-suited; unwise. [1825–35]

ill-de•fined (il′di fīnd′), *adj.* badly or inadequately defined; vague: *He confuses the reader with ill-defined terms and concepts.* [1865–70]

ill-dis•posed (il′di spōzd′), *adj.* **1.** unfriendly, unsympathetic, or having a negative attitude, as toward another person or an idea. **2.** having an objectionable disposition. [1400–50; late ME] **—ill-dis•pos•ed•ness** (il′di spō′zid nis, -spōzd′-), *n.*

Ille (ēl), *n.* a river in Ille-et-Vilaine in W France, flowing S to Rennes.

Ille-et-Vi•laine (ēl e vē len′), *n.* a department in W France. 702,199; 2700 sq. mi. (7000 sq. km). *Cap.:* Rennes.

il•le•gal (i lē′gəl), *adj.* **1.** forbidden by law or statute. **2.** contrary to or forbidden by official rules, regulations, etc.: *The referee ruled that it was an illegal forward pass.* **—***n.* **3.** *Informal.* See **illegal alien.** [1620–30; < ML *illēgālis.* See IL-[2], LEGAL] **—il•le′gal•ly,** *adv.*
—Syn. 1. unlawful; illegitimate; illicit; unlicensed. ILLEGAL, UNLAWFUL, ILLEGITIMATE, ILLICIT, CRIMINAL can all describe actions not in accord with law. ILLEGAL refers most specifically to violations of statutes or, in organized athletics, codified rules: *an illegal seizure of property; an illegal block (in football).* UNLAWFUL means not sanctioned by or according to law: *an unlawful claim to the inheritance; to take unlawful advantage of the trading situation.* ILLEGITIMATE means lacking legal or traditional right or rights: *an illegitimate child; illegitimate use of privileged knowledge.* ILLICIT, which originally meant simply "not permitted," now most often applies to matters regulated by law with specific emphasis on the way things are carried out: *illicit conversion of property; an illicit attempt to control the market.* CRIMINAL most often refers to violation of the statutes of penal as opposed to civil law. All felonies are criminal as are all crimes sometimes punishable by death such as murder, arson, and kidnapping: *a criminal act.*

ille′gal al′ien, **1.** a foreigner who has entered or resides in a country unlawfully or without the country's authorization. **2.** a foreigner who enters the U.S. without an entry or immigrant visa, esp. a person who crosses the border by avoiding inspection or who overstays the period of time allowed as a visitor, tourist, or businessperson. Cf. **resident alien.** Also called **ille′gal im′migrant.**

il•le•gal•i•ty (il′ē gal′i tē), *n., pl.* **-ties. 1.** illegal condition or quality; unlawfulness. **2.** an illegal act. [1630–40; < ML *illēgālitās.* See ILLEGAL, -ITY]

il•le•gal•ize (i lē′gə līz′), *v.t.,* **-ized, -iz•ing.** to make illegal. [1810–20; ILLEGAL + -IZE] Also, *esp. Brit.,* **il•le′•gal•ise′.** **—il•le′gal•i•za′tion,** *n.*

ille′gal proce′dure, *Football.* a penalty assessed against the offensive team for a technical rules violation, as in assuming an illegal formation.

il•leg•i•ble (i lej′ə bəl), *adj.* not legible; impossible or hard to read or decipher because of poor handwriting, faded print, etc. [1605–15; IL-[2] + LEGIBLE] **—il•leg′i•bil′i•ty, il•leg′i•ble•ness,** *n.* **—il•leg′i•bly,** *adv.*

il•le•git (il′i jit′), *adj. Informal.* dishonest or unprincipled. [1910–15; by shortening from ILLEGITIMATE]

il•le•git•i•ma•cy (il′i jit′ə mə sē), *n., pl.* **-cies.** the state or quality of being illegitimate. [1670–80; ILLEGITIM(ATE) + -ACY]

il•le•git•i•mate (*adj., n.* il′i jit′ə mit; *v.* il′i jit′ə māt′), *adj., n., v.,* **-mat•ed, -mat•ing.** **—***adj.* **1.** born of parents who are not married to each other; born out of wedlock: *an illegitimate child.* **2.** not legitimate; not sanctioned by law or custom. **3.** unlawful; illegal: *an illegitimate action.* **4.** irregular; not in good usage. **5.** *Logic.* not in accordance with the principles of valid inference. **6.** *Obs.* (formerly, in London) **a.** of or pertaining to stage plays in which musical numbers were inserted because of laws that gave only a few theaters the exclusive right to produce straight dramas. **b.** acting in or producing such productions. **—***n.* **7.** a person recognized or looked upon as illegitimate. **—***v.t.* **8.** to declare illegitimate. [1530–40; IL-[2] + LEGITIMATE] **—il′le•git′i•mate•ly,** *adv.* **—il′•le•git′i•mate•ness, il′le•git′i•ma′tion,** *n.*
—Syn. 2, 3. See **illegal.**

il•le•git•i•ma•tize (il′i jit′ə mə tīz′), *v.t.,* **-tized, -tiz•ing.** to make illegitimate: *The decree illegitimatized his heirs.* Also, *esp. Brit.,* **il•le•git′i•ma•tise′.** [1805–15; ILLEGITIMATE + -IZE]

il•le•git•i•mize (il i jit′ə mīz′), *v.t.,* **-mized, -miz•ing.** Also, *esp. Brit.,* **il•le•git′i•mise′.** illegitimatize.

ill-e•quipped (il′i kwipt′), *adj.* **1.** badly or inadequately equipped: *an ill-equipped army.* **2.** ill-prepared: *a student ill-equipped to begin calculus.* [1955–60]

ill′ fame′, bad reputation, esp. in sexual matters. **—ill′-famed′,** *adj.*

ill-fat•ed (il′fā′tid), *adj.* **1.** destined, as though by fate, to an unhappy or unfortunate end: *an ill-fated voyage.* **2.** bringing bad fortune. [1700–10]
—Syn. 1. doomed, hapless, ill-starred, jinxed.

ill-fa•vored (il′fā′vərd), *adj.* **1.** unpleasant in appearance; homely or ugly. **2.** offensive; unpleasant; objectionable. Also, *esp. Brit.,* **ill′-fa′voured.** [1520–30] **—ill′-fa′vored•ly,** *adv.* **—ill′-fa′vored•ness,** *n.*

ill-fit•ted (il′fit′id), *adj.* **1.** badly or uncomfortably fitted: *an ill-fitted denture.* **2.** ill-suited: *His health made him ill-fitted for hard labor.*

ill-formed (il′fôrmd′), *adj.* **1.** badly formed. **2.** *Ling.* not conforming to the rules of a given language; ungrammatical (opposed to *well-formed*). [1665–75] **—ill-form•ed•ness** (il′fôr′mid nis, -fôrmd′-), *n.*

ill-found•ed (il′foun′did), *adj.* based on weak evidence, illogical reasoning, or the like: *an ill-founded theory.* [1665–75]

ill-got•ten (il′got′n), *adj.* acquired by dishonest, improper, or evil means: *ill-gotten gains.* [1545–55]

ill′ hu′mor, a disagreeable or surly mood. [1560–70] **—ill′-hu′mored,** *adj.* **—ill′-hu′mored•ly,** *adv.* **—ill′-hu′mored•ness,** *n.*

I•llí•a (ē yē′ä), *n.* **Ar•tu•ro** (är to͞o′rô), 1900–83, Argentine physician and statesman: president 1963–66.

il•lib•er•al (i lib′ər əl, i lib′rəl), *adj.* **1.** narrowminded; bigoted. **2.** *Archaic.* **a.** not generous in giving; miserly; niggardly; stingy. **b.** *Chiefly Literary.* without culture or refinement; unscholarly; vulgar. [1525–35; < L *illīberālis.* See IL-², LIBERAL] **—il•lib′er•al′i•ty, il•lib′er•al•ness, il•lib′er•al•ism,** *n.* **—il•lib′er•al•ly,** *adv.*
—Syn. 1. biased, intolerant, hidebound, small-minded.

il•lic•it (i lis′it), *adj.* **1.** not legally permitted or authorized; unlicensed; unlawful. **2.** disapproved of or not permitted for moral or ethical reasons. [1645–55; < L *illicitus.* See IL-², LICIT] **—il•lic′it•ly,** *adv.* **—il•lic′it•ness,** *n.*
—Syn. 1. illegitimate, prohibited. See **illegal.**

I•lli•ma•ni (ē′yē mä′nē), *n.* a mountain in W Bolivia, in the Andes, near La Paz. 21,188 ft. (6458 m).

il•lim•it•a•ble (i lim′i tə bəl), *adj.* not limitable; limitless; boundless. [1590–1600; IL-² + LIMITABLE] **—il•lim′•it•a•bil′i•ty, il•lim′it•a•ble•ness,** *n.* **—il•lim′it•a•bly,** *adv.*

ill•in′ (il′in), *adj. Slang.* foolish; crazy (used esp. in the phrase *be illin′*). [1980–85; appar. from ILL]

ill-in•formed (il′in fôrmd′), *adj.* lacking adequate or proper knowledge or information, as in one particular subject or in a variety of subjects: *The public is ill-informed of the danger.* [1815–25]

il•lin•i•um (i lin′ē əm), *n. Chem.* (formerly) promethium. *Symbol:* Il [1925–30; named after ILLINOIS; see -IUM]

Il•li•noi•an (il′ə noi′ən), *n.* **1.** *Geol.* the third stage of the glaciation of North America during the Pleistocene. **2.** Illinoisan. *—adj.* **3.** *Geol.* of or pertaining to the Illinoian stage. **4.** Illinoisan. [1825–35, *Amer.*; ILLINOI(S) + -AN]

Il•li•nois (il′ə noi′, -noiz′), *n.* **1.** a state in the central United States: a part of the Midwest. 11,418,461; 56,400 sq. mi. (146,075 sq. km). *Cap.:* Springfield. *Abbr.:* IL (for use with zip code), Ill. **2.** a river flowing SW from NE Illinois to the Mississippi River: connected by a canal with Lake Michigan. 273 mi. (440 km) long.
—Pronunciation. The pronunciation of ILLINOIS with a final (z), which occurs chiefly among less educated speakers, is least common in Illinois itself, increasing in frequency as distance from the state increases.

Il•li•nois (il′ə noi′ *or, sometimes,* -noiz′), *n., pl.* **-nois** (-noi′, -noiz′). **1.** a member of a confederacy of North American Indians of Algonquian stock, formerly occupying Illinois and adjoining regions westward. **2.** the Algonquian language of the Illinois and Miami Indians. [1715–25, *Amer.*; < F, earlier *Erinioüai, Ilinoués,* etc. < an unidentified Algonquian language, appar. lit., one who sounds normal (i.e., speaks an Algonquian language), if equiv. to Proto-Algonquian **elen-* ordinary + **-we·* make sound]

Il•li•nois•an (il′ə noi′ən *or, sometimes,* -noi′zən), *n.* **1.** a native or inhabitant of Illinois. *—adj.* **2.** of or pertaining to Illinois or its inhabitants. Also, **Illinoian, Il′li•nois′i•an.** [ILLINOIS + -AN]

ill-in•ten•tioned (il′in ten′shənd), *adj.* having malicious intentions: *an ill-intentioned criticism.*

il•liq•uid (i lik′wid), *adj.* (of an asset) not readily convertible into cash; not liquid. [1685–95; IL-² + LIQUID] **—il′li•quid′i•ty,** *n.* **—il•liq′uid•ly,** *adv.*

il•lite (il′īt), *n.* any of a group of clay minerals, hydrous potassium aluminosilicates, characterized by a three-layer micalike structure and a gray, light green, or yellowish-brown color. [1937; ILL(INOIS) + -ITE¹] **—il•lit•ic** (i lit′ik), *adj.*

il•lit•er•a•cy (i lit′ər ə sē), *n., pl.* **-cies** for 3. **1.** a lack of ability to read and write. **2.** the state of being illiterate; lack of any or enough education. **3.** a mistake in writing or speaking, felt to be characteristic of an illiterate or semiliterate person: *a letter that was full of illiteracies.* [1650–60; ILLITER(ATE) + -ACY]

il•lit•er•ate (i lit′ər it), *adj.* **1.** unable to read and write: *an illiterate group.* **2.** having or demonstrating very little or no education. **3.** showing lack of culture, esp. in language and literature. **4.** displaying a marked lack of knowledge in a particular field: *He is musically illiterate.* *—n.* **5.** an illiterate person. [1550–60; < L *illiterātus* unlettered. See IL-², LITERATE] **—il•lit′er•ate•ly,** *adv.* **—il•lit′er•ate•ness,** *n.*
—Syn. 1. See **ignorant.**

il•lit•e•ra•ti (i lit′ə rä′tē, -rā′tī), *n.pl. Informal.* illiterate or ignorant people. [1780–90; b. ILLITERATE and LITERATI]

ill-judged (il′jujd′), *adj.* injudicious; unwise. [1710–20]

ill-kempt (il′kempt′), *adj.* unkempt.

ill-look•ing (il′lo͝ok′ing), *adj. Older Use.* **1.** ugly. **2.** sinister. [1625–35]

ill-man•nered (il′man′ərd), *adj.* having bad or poor manners; impolite; discourteous; rude. [1375–1425; late ME; see ILL, MANNERED] **—ill′-man′nered•ly,** *adv.* **—ill′-man′nered•ness,** *n.*
—Syn. unpolished, crude, uncivil.

ill′ na′ture, unkindly or unpleasant disposition. [1685–95]

ill-na•tured (il′nā′chərd), *adj.* having or showing an unkindly or unpleasant disposition. [1625–35] **—ill′-na′tured•ly,** *adv.* **—ill′-na′tured•ness,** *n.*
—Syn. cranky, petulant, sulky, morose, gloomy, sour. See **cross.** **—Ant.** kindly, amiable.

ill•ness (il′nis), *n.* **1.** unhealthy condition; poor health; indisposition; sickness. **2.** *Obs.* wickedness. [1490–1500; ILL + -NESS]
—Syn. 1. ailment, affliction, infirmity.

il•lo•cu•tion•ar•y (il′ə kyo͞o′shə ner′ē), *adj. Philos., Ling.* pertaining to a linguistic act performed by a speaker in producing an utterance, as suggesting, warning, promising, or requesting. Cf. **locutionary, perlocutionary.** [1950–55; IL-¹ + LOCUTION + -ARY] **—il′lo•cu′tion,** *n.*

il•log•ic (i loj′ik), *n.* the state or quality of being illogical; illogicality. [1855–60; IL-² + LOGIC]

il•log•i•cal (i loj′i kəl), *adj.* not logical; contrary to or disregardful of the rules of logic; unreasoning: *an illogical reply.* [1580–90; IL-² + LOGICAL] **—il•log′i•cal•ly,** *adv.* **—il•log′i•cal•ness,** *n.*
—Syn. unsound, absurd, preposterous.

il•log•i•cal•i•ty (i loj′i kal′i tē), *n., pl.* **-ties. 1.** illogic. **2.** an example of illogic: *an argument notable for its illogicalities.* [1820–30; ILLOGICAL + -ITY]

ill-o•mened (il′ō′mənd), *adj.* having or attended by bad omens; ill-starred. [1675–85]

ill-pre•pared (il′pri pârd′), *adj.* badly or inadequately prepared or trained: *ill-prepared job applicants; The hotel was ill-prepared for so many guests.*

ill-sort•ed (il′sôr′tid), *adj.* badly matched; poorly arranged. [1685–95]

ill-spent (il′spent′), *adj.* misspent; wasted.

ill-starred (il′stärd′), *adj.* **1.** doomed to misfortune or disaster; ill-fated; unlucky: *an ill-starred enterprise.* **2.** disastrous: *an ill-starred marriage.* [1595–1605]

ill-suit•ed (il′so͞o′tid), *adj.* not suitable; inappropriate.
—Syn. unsuitable, inapt. **—Ant.** suitable, apt.

ill′ tem′per, bad or irritable disposition. [1595–1605] **—ill′-tem′pered,** *adj.* **—ill′-tem′pered•ly,** *adv.* **—ill′-tem′pered•ness,** *n.*

ill-timed (il′tīmd′), *adj.* badly timed; inopportune. [1685–95]

ill-treat (il′trēt′), *v.t.* to treat badly; maltreat; abuse. [1695–1705] **—ill′-treat′ment,** *n.*

il•lume (i lo͞om′), *v.t.,* **-lumed, -lum•ing.** *Archaic.* to illuminate. [1595–1605; short for ILLUMINE]

il•lu•mi•na•ble (i lo͞o′mə nə bəl), *adj.* capable of being illuminated. [1720–30; < L *illūminābilis.* See ILLUMINE, -ABLE] **—il•lu′mi•na•bil′i•ty,** *n.*

il•lu•mi•nance (i lo͞o′mə nəns), *n. Optics.* illumination (def. 6). [1940–45; ILLUMIN(ATE) + -ANCE]

il•lu•mi•nant (i lo͞o′mə nənt), *n.* an illuminating agent or material. [1635–45; < L *illūminant-* (s. of *illūmināns*) prp. of *illūmināre* to light up, brighten, equiv. to *illūmin-* (see ILLUMINE) + *-ant-* -ANT]

il•lu•mi•nate (*v.* i lo͞o′mə nāt′; *adj., n.* i lo͞o′mə nit, -nāt′), *v.,* **-nat•ed, -nat•ing,** *adj., n.* *—v.t.* **1.** to supply or brighten with light; light up. **2.** to make lucid or clear; throw light on (a subject). **3.** to decorate with lights, as in celebration. **4.** to enlighten, as with knowledge. **5.** to make resplendent or illustrious: *A smile illuminated her face.* **6.** to decorate (a manuscript, book, etc.) with colors and gold or silver, as was often done in the Middle Ages. *—v.i.* **7.** to display lights, as in celebration. **8.** to become illuminated. *—adj.* **9.** *Archaic.* illuminated. **10.** *Obs.* enlightened. *—n.* **11.** *Archaic.* a person who is or affects to be specially enlightened. [1400–50; late ME < L *illūminātus* (ptp. of *illūmināre* to light up, brighten). See ILLUMINE, -ATE¹] **—il•lu′mi•nat′ing•ly,** *adv.*
—Syn. 2. clarify, explain, elucidate.

il•lu•mi•na•ti (i lo͞o′mə nä′tē, -nā′tī), *n.pl., sing.* **-to** (-tō). **1.** persons possessing, or claiming to possess, superior enlightenment. **2.** (*cap.*) a name given to different religious societies or sects because of their claim to superior enlightenment. [1590–1600; < L *illūminātī,* pl. of *illūminātus* enlightened; see ILLUMINATE]

il•lu•mi•nat•ing (i lo͞o′mə nā′ting), *adj.* **1.** giving or casting light. **2.** informative; enlightening. [1555–65; ILLUMINATE + -ING²]

il•lu•mi•na•tion (i lo͞o′mə nā′shən), *n.* **1.** an act or instance of illuminating. **2.** the fact or condition of being illuminated. **3.** a decoration of lights, usually colored lights. **4.** Sometimes, **illuminations.** an entertainment, display, or celebration using lights as a major feature or decoration. **5.** intellectual or spiritual enlightenment. **6.** Also called **illuminance, intensity of illumination.** *Optics.* the intensity of light falling at a given place on a lighted surface; the luminous flux incident per unit area, expressed in lumens per unit of area. **7.** a supply of light: *a source of illumination.* **8.** decoration of a manuscript or book with a painted design in color, gold, etc. **9.** a design used in such decoration. [1300–50; ME < ML *illūminātiōn-* (s. of *illūminātiō*) spiritual enlightenment (L: illustriousness, glory) See ILLUMINATE, -ION] **—il•lu′mi•na′tion•al,** *adj.*
—Syn. 5. knowledge, revelation, insight, wisdom.

il•lu•mi•na•tive (i lo͞o′mə nā′tiv, -nə tiv), *adj.* giving light; illuminating. [1635–45; ILLUMINATE + -IVE]

il•lu•mi•na•tor (i lo͞o′mə nā′tər), *n.* **1.** a person or thing that illuminates. **2.** a device for illuminating, as a light source with a lens or mirror for concentrating light. **3.** a person who paints manuscripts, books, etc., with designs in color, gold, or the like. [1475–85; < LL *illūminātor,* equiv. to *illūminā(re)* (see ILLUMINE) + *-tor* -TOR]

il•lu•mine (i lo͞o′min), *v.t., v.i.,* **-mined, -min•ing.** to illuminate. [1300–50; ME *illuminen* < L *illūmināre* to light up, equiv. to *il-* IL-¹ + *lūmin-* (s. of *lūmen*) light + *-ā-* thematic vowel + *-re* inf. suffix] **—il•lu′mi•na•ble,** *adj.*

il•lu•mi•nism (i lo͞o′mə niz′əm), *n.* **1.** the doctrines or claims of Illuminati. **2.** a doctrine of enlightenment. [1790–1800; ILLUMIN(ATI) + -ISM] **—il•lu′mi•nist,** *n.*

il•lu•mi•nom•e•ter (i lo͞o′mə nom′i tər), *n.* an instrument for measuring illumination. [1890–95; ILLUMIN(ATION) + -O- + -METER]

illus., 1. illustrated. **2.** illustration.

ill-use (*v.* il′yo͞oz′; *n.* il′yo͞os′), *v.,* **-used, -us•ing,** *n.* *—v.t.* **1.** to treat badly, unjustly, unjustly, cruelly, etc. *—n.* **2.** Also, **ill′-us′age.** bad, unjust, or cruel treatment. [1835–45]

il•lu•sion (i lo͞o′zhən), *n.* **1.** something that deceives by producing a false or misleading impression of reality. **2.** the state or condition of being deceived; misapprehension. **3.** an instance of being deceived. **4.** *Psychol.* a perception, as of visual stimuli **(optical illusion),** that represents what is perceived in a way different from the way it is in reality. **5.** a very thin, delicate tulle of silk or nylon having a cobwebbed appearance, for trimmings, veilings, and the like. **6.** *Obs.* the act of deceiving; deception; delusion. [1300–50; ME < L *illūsiōn-* (s. of *illūsiō*) irony, mocking, equiv. to *illūs(us)* ptp. of *illūdere* to mock, ridicule (*il-* IL-¹ + *lūd-* play (see LUDICROUS) + *-tus* ptp. suffix, with *dt* > *s*) + *-iōn-* -ION] **—il•lu′•sioned,** *adj.*
—Syn. 1. aberration, fantasy, chimera. ILLUSION, HALLUCINATION, DELUSION refer to false perceptions or ideas. An ILLUSION is a false mental image produced by misinterpretation of things that actually exist: *A mirage is an illusion produced by reflection of light against the sky.* A HALLUCINATION is a perception of a thing or quality that has no physical counterpart: *Under the influence of LSD, Terry had hallucinations that the living-room floor was rippling.* A DELUSION is a persistent false belief: *A paranoiac has delusions of persecution.*

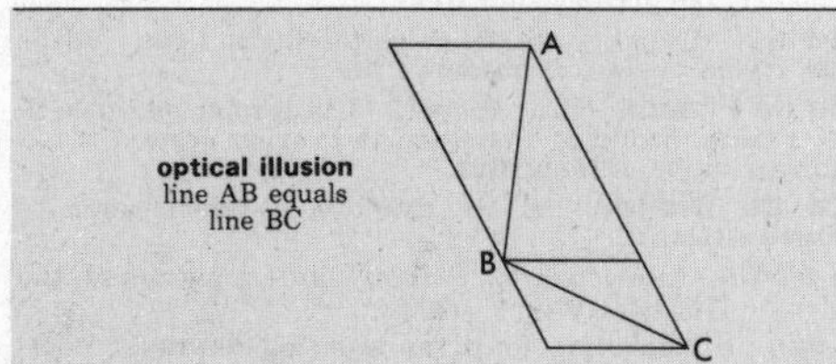

il•lu•sion•ar•y (i lo͞o′zhə ner′ē), *adj.* of, pertaining to, or characterized by illusions; deceptive; misleading. Also, **il•lu′sion•al.** [1885–90; ILLUSION + -ARY]

il•lu•sion•ism (i lo͞o′zhə niz′əm), *n.* **1.** a technique of using pictorial methods in order to deceive the eye. Cf. **trompe l'oeil. 2.** *Philos.* a theory or doctrine that the material world is an illusion. [1835–45; ILLUSION + -ISM] **—il•lu′sion•is′tic,** *adj.*

il•lu•sion•ist (i lo͞o′zhə nist), *n.* **1.** a conjurer or magician who creates illusions, as by sleight of hand. **2.** an adherent of illusionism. [1835–45; ILLUSION + -IST]

il•lu•sive (i lo͞o′siv), *adj.* illusory. [1670–80; ILLUS(ORY) + -IVE] **—il•lu′sive•ly,** *adv.* **—il•lu′sive•ness,** *n.*

il•lu•so•ry (i lo͞o′sə rē, -zə-), *adj.* **1.** causing illusion; deceptive; misleading. **2.** of the nature of an illusion; unreal. [1590–1600; < LL *illūsōrius,* equiv. to *illūd(ere)* to mock, ridicule (see ILLUSION) + *-tōrius* -TORY¹] **—il•lu′so•ri•ly,** *adv.* **—il•lu′so•ri•ness,** *n.*
—Syn. 1. fallacious, specious, false. **2.** imaginary; visionary, fancied.

illust., 1. illustrated. **2.** illustration.

il•lus•trate (il′ə strāt′, i lus′trāt), *v.,* **-trat•ed, -trat•ing.** *—v.t.* **1.** to furnish (a book, magazine, etc.) with drawings, pictures, or other artwork intended for explanation, elucidation, or adornment. **2.** to make clear or intelligible, as by examples or analogies; exemplify. **3.** *Archaic.* to enlighten. *—v.i.* **4.** to clarify one's words, writings, etc., with examples: *To prevent misunderstandings, let me illustrate.* [1520–30; < L *illustrātus* ptp. of *illustrāre* to illuminate, make clear, give glory to. See IL-¹, LUSTER¹, -ATE¹] **—il′lus•trat′a•ble,** *adj.*

il•lus•trat•ed (il′ə strā′tid), *adj.* **1.** containing pictures, drawings, and other illustrations: *an illustrated book.* *—n.* **2.** *Brit.* a magazine or newspaper regularly containing many photographs or drawings. [1825–35; ILLUSTRATE + -ED²]

il•lus•tra•tion (il′ə strā′shən), *n.* **1.** something that illustrates, as a picture in a book or magazine. **2.** a com-

parison or an example intended for explanation or corroboration. **3.** the act or process of illuminating. **4.** the act of clarifying or explaining; elucidation. **5.** *Archaic.* illustriousness; distinction. [1325–75; ME < L *illustrātiōn-* (s. of *illustrātiō*) the act of making vivid, illustrating. See ILLUSTRATE, -ION]
—Syn. 2. explication. See **case**[1].

il·lus·tra·tion·al (il′ə strā′shə nl), *adj.* **1.** of, pertaining to, or characteristic of illustrations: *illustrational art.* **2.** used for purposes of illustration; serving to illustrate; illustrative. [1880–85; ILLUSTRATION + -AL[1]]

il·lus·tra·tive (i lus′trə tiv, il′ə strā′tiv), *adj.* serving to illustrate; explanatory: *illustrative examples.* [1635–45; ILLUSTRATE + -IVE] **—il·lus′tra·tive·ly,** *adv.*

il·lus·tra·tor (il′ə strā′tər, i lus′trā tər), *n.* **1.** an artist who makes illustrations: *an illustrator of children's books.* **2.** a person or thing that illustrates. [1590–1600; < LL, equiv. to *illustrā(re)* to ILLUSTRATE + *-tor* -TOR]

il·lus·tri·ous (i lus′trē əs), *adj.* **1.** highly distinguished; renowned; famous: *an illustrious leader.* **2.** glorious, as deeds or works: *many illustrious achievements.* **3.** *Obs.* luminous; bright. [1560–70; < L *illustri(s)* bright, clear, famous (equiv. to *illustr(āre)* to brighten (see IL-[1], LUSTER[1]) + *-is* adj. suffix) + -OUS] **—il·lus′tri·ous·ly,** *adv.* **—il·lus′tri·ous·ness,** *n.*
—Syn. 1. celebrated, eminent, famed.

il·lu·vi·al (i lo͞o′vē əl, i lo͞ov′yəl), *adj.* of or pertaining to illuviation or illuvium. [1920–25; < L *illuvi(ēs)* mud, flood, lit., what washes or is washed in (*il-* IL-[1] + *-luv-*, comb. form of *lavere* to wash + *-iēs* n. suffix) + -AL[1]; see ALLUVIAL]

il·lu·vi·ate (i lo͞o′vē āt′), *v.i.,* **-at·ed, -at·ing. 1.** to undergo illuviation. **2.** to produce illuviation. [< L *illuvi(ēs)* mud (see ILLUVIAL) + -ATE[1]]

il·lu·vi·a·tion (i lo͞o′vē ā′shən), *n.* the accumulation in one layer of soil of materials that have been leached out of another layer. [1925–30; ILLUVI(AL) + -ATION]

il·lu·vi·um (i lo͞o′vē əm), *n., pl.* **-vi·ums, -vi·a** (-vē ə). the material accumulated through illuviation. [< L *illuv(iēs)* (see ILLUVIAL) + -IUM, on the model of ALLUVIUM, L *diluvium* DELUGE, etc.]

ill′ will′, hostile feeling; malevolence; enmity: *to harbor ill will against someone.* [1250–1300; ME] **—ill-willed** (il′wild′), *adj.*
—Syn. hatred, hostility, animosity, antipathy, unfriendliness. **—Ant.** benevolence.

ill-wish·er (il′wish′ər), *n.* a person who wishes misfortune to another. [1600–10]

il·ly (il′ē, il′lē), *adv.* ill. [1540–50; ILL + -LY]

Il·lyr·i·a (i lēr′ē ə), *n.* an ancient country along the E coast of the Adriatic.

Il·lyr·i·an (i lēr′ē ən), *adj.* **1.** of or pertaining to Illyria. —*n.* **2.** a native or inhabitant of Illyria. **3.** the extinct language of the Illyrians, an Indo-European language of uncertain relationship within the Indo-European language family. [1545–55; ILLYRI(A) + -AN]

Il·lyr·i·cum (i lēr′i kəm), *n.* a Roman province in ancient Illyria.

Il·ma·ri·nen (ēl′mä rē′nən), *n. Finnish Legend.* one of the heroes of the *Kalevala.*

il·men·ite (il′mə nīt′), *n.* a very common black mineral, iron titanate, $FeTiO_3$, occurring in crystals but more commonly massive. [1820–30; after the *Ilmen* Mountains (Russ *Il′ménskie góry*) in the southern Urals, where it was first identified; see -ITE[1]]

ILO, See **International Labor Organization.** Also, **I.L.O.**

I·lo·ca·no (ē′lō kä′nō), *n., pl.* **-nos,** (*esp. collectively*) **-no. 1.** a member of a people of Luzon in the Philippines. **2.** the Austronesian language of the Ilocano. Also, **Ilokano.** [1830–40; < Sp, equiv. to *Ilok(o)* the Ilocano name for themselves + *-ano* -AN]

I·lo·i·lo (ē′lō ē′lō), *n.* a seaport on S Panay, in the central Philippines. 244,827.

I·lo·ka·no (ē′lō kä′nō), *n., pl.* **-nos,** (*esp. collectively*) **-no.** Ilocano.

I·lo·rin (i lôr′in), *n.* a town in W central Nigeria. 282,000.

I·lo·ty·cin (ī′lō tī′sin), *Pharm., Trademark.* a brand of erythromycin (def. 1).

I.L.P., Independent Labour Party.

Il Pen·se·ro·so (il pen′sə rō′sō; *It.* ēl pen′se RÔ′sô), a poem (1632) by John Milton. Cf. ***L'Allegro.***

ILS, *Aeron.* instrument landing system.

Il·se (il′sə), *n.* a female given name, form of **Elizabeth.**

ILTF, International Lawn Tennis Federation.

Il Tro·va·to·re (il trō′və tôr′ē; *It.* ēl TRÔ′vä tô′RE), an opera (1853) by Giuseppe Verdi.

I.L.W.U., International Longshoremen's and Warehousemen's Union.

I'm (īm), contraction of *I am.*
—Usage. See **contraction.**

im-[1], var. of **in-**[2] before *b, m, p: imbrute; immigrate; impassion.*

im-[2], var. of **in-**[3] before *b, m, p: imbalance; immoral; imperishable.*

im-[3], var. of **in-**[1] before *b, m, p: imbed; immure; impose.*

-im, a plural ending occurring in loanwords from Hebrew: *cherubim.* [< Heb]

I.M., Isle of Man.

im·age (im′ij), *n., v.,* **-aged, -ag·ing.** —*n.* **1.** a physical likeness or representation of a person, animal, or thing, photographed, painted, sculptured, or otherwise made visible. **2.** an optical counterpart or appearance of an object, as is produced by reflection from a mirror, refraction by a lens, or the passage of luminous rays through a small aperture and their reception on a surface. **3.** a mental representation; idea; conception. **4.** *Psychol.* a mental representation of something previously perceived, in the absence of the original stimulus. **5.** form; appearance; semblance: *We are all created in God's image.* **6.** counterpart; copy: *That child is the image of his mother.* **7.** a symbol; emblem. **8.** the general or public perception of a company, public figure, etc., esp. as achieved by careful calculation aimed at creating widespread goodwill. **9.** a type; embodiment: *Red-faced and angry, he was the image of frustration.* **10.** a description of something in speech or writing: *Keats created some of the most beautiful images in the language.* **11.** *Rhet.* a figure of speech, esp. a metaphor or a simile. **12.** an idol or representation of a deity: *They knelt down before graven images.* **13.** *Math.* the point or set of points in the range corresponding to a designated point in the domain of a given function. **14.** *Archaic.* an illusion or apparition. —*v.t.* **15.** to picture or represent in the mind; imagine; conceive. **16.** to make an image of; portray in sculpture, painting, etc. **17.** to project (photographs, film, etc.) on a surface: *Familiar scenes were imaged on the screen.* **18.** to reflect the likeness of; mirror. **19.** to set forth in speech or writing; describe. **20.** to symbolize; typify. **21.** to resemble. **22.** *Informal.* to create an image for (a company, public figure, etc.): *The candidate had to be imaged before being put on the campaign trail.* **23.** to transform (data) into an exact replica in a different form, as changing digital data to pixels for display on a CRT or representing a medical scan of a body part in digital form. [1175–1225; (n.) ME < OF *image, imagene* (*-ene* appar. construed as suffix) < L *imāgin-*, s. of *imāgō* a copy, likeness, equiv. to *im-* (cf. IMITATE) + *-āgō* n. suffix; (v.) ME: to form a mental picture < OF *imagier,* deriv. of *image*] **—im′age·a·ble,** *adj.* **—im′ag·er,** *n.*
—Syn. 1, 12. IMAGE, ICON, IDOL refer to material representations of persons or things. An IMAGE is a representation as in a statue or effigy, and is sometimes regarded as an object of worship: *to set up an image of Apollo; an image of a saint.* An ICON, in the Greek or Eastern Orthodox Church, is a representation of Christ, an angel, or a saint, in painting, relief, mosaic, or the like: *At least two icons are found in each church.* An IDOL is an image, statue, or the like representing a deity and worshiped as such: *a wooden idol; The heathen worship idols.* It may be used figuratively: *to make an idol of wealth.* **2.** likeness, figure, representation. **3.** notion. **6.** facsimile. **—Ant. 6.** original.

im′age dissec′tor, a form of television camera tube in which an electron image produced by a photoemitting surface is focused in the plane of an aperture and deflected past the aperture to achieve scanning. Also called **dissector tube.** [1930–35]

im·age·mak·er (im′ij mā′kər), *n.* a person, as a publicist, who specializes in creating images for companies, political candidates, etc. Also, **im′age-mak′er.** [1925–30; IMAGE + MAKER]

im′age or′thicon, *Television.* a camera tube, more sensitive than the orthicon, in which an electron image generated by a photocathode is focused on one side of a target that is scanned on its other side by a beam of low-velocity electrons to produce the output signal. [1940–45]

im·age·ry (im′ij rē, im′i jə rē), *n., pl.* **-ries. 1.** the formation of mental images, figures, or likenesses of things, or of such images collectively: *the dim imagery of a dream.* **2.** pictorial images. **3.** the use of rhetorical images. **4.** figurative description or illustration; rhetorical images collectively. **5.** *Psychol.* mental images collectively, esp. those produced by the action of imagination. [1275–1325; ME *imagerie* < OF. See IMAGE, -ERY] **—im·a·ge·ri·al** (im′ə jēr′ē əl), *adj.* **—im′a·ge′ri·al·ly,** *adv.*

im′age tube′, an electron tube that receives a pattern of radiation, as infrared, ultraviolet, or x-ray, on a photosensitive surface and reproduces the pattern on a fluorescent screen. Also called **im′age-con·vert·er tube′** (im′ij kən vûr′tər). [1935–40]

im·ag·i·na·ble (i maj′ə nə bəl), *adj.* capable of being imagined or conceived. [1325–75; ME < LL *imāginābilis,* equiv. to L *imāginā(rī)* to IMAGINE + *-bilis* -BLE] **—i·mag′i·na·ble·ness,** *n.* **—i·mag′i·na·bly,** *adv.*

i·ma·gi·nal (i mā′gə nl, i mä′-), *adj. Entomol.* of, pertaining to, or having the form of an imago. [1875–80; < NL *imāgin-*, s. of *imāgō* IMAGO + -AL[1]]

im·ag·i·nar·y (i maj′ə ner′ē), *adj., n., pl.* **-ries.** —*adj.* **1.** existing only in the imagination or fancy; not real; fancied: *an imaginary illness; the imaginary animals in the stories of Dr. Seuss.* —*n.* **2.** *Math.* See **imaginary number.** [1350–1400; ME < L *imāginārius,* equiv. to *imāgin-*, (s. of *imāgō*) IMAGE + *-ārius* -ARY] **—im·ag′i·nar′i·ly,** *adv.* **—im·ag′i·nar′i·ness,** *n.*
—Syn. 1. fanciful, visionary, shadowy, chimerical, baseless, illusory. **—Ant. 1.** real.

imag′inary ax′is, *Math.* the vertical axis in an Argand diagram.

imag′inary num′ber, *Math.* Also called **imaginary, pure imaginary number.** a complex number having its real part equal to zero. [1905–10]

imag′inary part′, *Math.* the coefficient *b* in the complex number *a* + *bi.* Cf. **real part.** [1925–30]

imag′inary u′nit, *Math.* the complex number *i.* [1905–10]

im·ag·i·na·tion (i maj′ə nā′shən), *n.* **1.** the faculty of imagining, or of forming mental images or concepts of what is not actually present to the senses. **2.** the action or process of forming such images or concepts. **3.** the faculty of producing ideal creations consistent with reality, as in literature, as distinct from the power of creating illustrative or decorative imagery. Cf. **fancy** (def. 2). **4.** the product of imagining; a conception or mental creation, often a baseless or fanciful one. **5.** ability to face and resolve difficulties; resourcefulness: *a job that requires imagination.* **6.** *Psychol.* the power of reproducing images stored in the memory under the suggestion of associated images **(reproductive imagination)** or of recombining former experiences in the creation of new images directed at a specific goal or aiding in the solution of problems **(creative imagination). 7.** (in Kantian epistemology) synthesis of data from the sensory manifold into objects by means of the categories. **8.** *Archaic.* a plan, scheme, or plot. [1300–50; ME < L *imāginātiōn-* (s. of *imāginātiō*) fancy, equiv. to *imāgināt(us)* ptp. of *imāginārī* to IMAGINE (*imāgin-*, s. of *imāgō* IMAGE + *-ātus* -ATE[1]) + *-iōn-* -ION] **—i·mag′i·na′tion·al,** *adj.*
—Syn. 3. See **fancy. 5.** ingenuity, enterprise, thought.

im·ag·i·na·tive (i maj′ə nə tiv, -nā′tiv), *adj.* **1.** characterized by or bearing evidence of imagination: *an imaginative tale.* **2.** of, pertaining to, or concerned with imagination. **3.** given to imagining, as persons. **4.** having exceptional powers of imagination. **5.** lacking truth; fanciful. [1350–1400; ME < ML *imāginātivus* imaginary, imaginative, equiv. to L *imāgināt(us)* imagined (see IMAGINATION) + *-ivus* -IVE; r. ME *imaginatif* < MF < ML, as above] **—i·mag′i·na·tive·ly,** *adv.* **—i·mag′i·na·tive·ness,** *n.*
—Syn. 1. creative, inventive, clever, ingenious.

im·ag·ine (i maj′in), *v.,* **-ined, -in·ing.** —*v.t.* **1.** to form a mental image of (something not actually present to the senses). **2.** to think, believe, or fancy: *He imagined the house was haunted.* **3.** to assume; suppose: *I imagine they'll be here soon.* **4.** to conjecture; guess: *I cannot imagine what you mean.* **5.** *Archaic.* to plan, scheme, or plot. —*v.i.* **6.** to form mental images of things not present to the senses; use the imagination. **7.** to suppose; think; conjecture. [1300–50; ME *imaginen* < MF *imaginer* < L *imāginārī,* equiv. to *imāgin-* (s. of *imāgō*) IMAGE + *-ā-* thematic vowel + *-rī* inf. ending] **—i·mag′in·er,** *n.*
—Syn. 1. image, picture. IMAGINE, CONCEIVE, CONCEIVE OF, REALIZE refer to bringing something before the mind. To IMAGINE is, literally, to form a mental image of something: *to imagine yourself in London.* To CONCEIVE is to form something by using one's imagination: *How has the author conceived the first act of his play?* To CONCEIVE OF is to comprehend through the intellect something not perceived through the senses: *Wilson conceived of a world free from war.* To REALIZE is to make an imagined thing real or concrete to oneself, to grasp fully its implications: *to realize the extent of one's folly.*

im·ag·i·neer (i maj′ə nēr′), *n.* a person who practices or is skilled in imagineering. [b. IMAGINE and ENGINEER]

im·ag·i·neer·ing (i maj′ə nēr′ing), *n.* the implementing of creative ideas into practical form. [b. IMAGINE and ENGINEERING]

im·ag·ing (im′ə jing), *n.* **1.** *Psychol.* a technique in which one uses mental images to control bodily processes and thus ease pain or to succeed in some endeavor that one has visualized in advance. **2.** *Med.* the use of computerized axial tomography, sonography, or other specialized techniques and instruments to obtain pictures of the interior of the body, esp. those including soft tissues. [1660–70 for earlier sense "imagination"; IMAGE + -ING[1]]

im·ag·ism (im′ə jiz′əm), *n. Literature.* **1.** (*often cap.*) a theory or practice of a group of poets in England and America between 1909 and 1917 who believed that poetry should employ the language of common speech, create new rhythms, have complete freedom in subject matter, and present a clear, concentrated, and precise image. **2.** a style of poetry that employs free verse and the patterns and rhythms of common speech. [1910–15; IMAGE + -ISM] **—im′ag·ist,** *n., adj.* **—im′ag·is′tic,** *adj.* **—im′ag·is′ti·cal·ly,** *adv.*

i·ma·go (i mā′gō, i mä′-), *n., pl.* **-goes, -gi·nes** (-gə nēz′). **1.** *Entomol.* an adult insect. **2.** *Psychoanal.* an idealized concept of a loved one, formed in childhood and retained unaltered in adult life. [1790–1800; < NL, L *imāgō;* see IMAGE]

i·mam (i mäm′), *n. Islam.* **1.** the officiating priest of a mosque. **2.** the title for a Muslim religious leader or chief. **3.** one of a succession of seven or twelve religious leaders, believed to be divinely inspired, of the Shi'ites. Also, **i·maum** (i mäm′, i môm′). [1605–15; < Ar *imām* leader, guide] **—i·mam′ship,** *n.*

i·mam·ate (i mä′māt), *n.* **1.** the office of an imam. **2.** the region or territory governed by an imam. [1720–30; IMAM + -ATE[3]]

i·mam·ba·rah (i mäm′bä′rä), *n. Islam.* (in India) **1.** a building, rooms, etc., used by Shi'ites for ceremonies, esp. during the first 10 days of Muharram. **2.** a large tomb. Also, **i·maum′ba′ra, i·maum′bar′ra, i·mam′ba′ra.** [1830–40; < Hindi *imāmbārā* < Ar *imām* IMAM + Hindi *bārā* enclosure; cf. Skt *vāṭa* fence, enclosure]

I·mam·ite (i mä′mīt), *n. Islam.* a member of the principal sect of Shi'ah, believing in a succession of twelve divinely inspired imams, beginning with Ali and ending with Muhammad al-Muntazar (d. A.D. c880), who supposedly retired to a cave, later to return as the Mahdi. Also, **I·ma·mi** (i mä′mē). Also called **Twelver.** [IMAM + -ITE[1]]

i·ma·ret (i mär′et), *n.* (in Turkey) a hospice for pilgrims, travelers, etc. [1605–15; < Turk < Ar *'imārah* building]

I·ma′ri ware′ (i mär′ē), Japanese porcelain noted for its rich floral underglaze decoration in iron-red, blue, and gold, and later copied in China and Europe. [1900–05 after a locale in western Saga prefecture (Kyushu) which was the sole market selling this porcelain during the Edo period]

im·bal·ance (im bal′əns), *n.* **1.** the state or condition of lacking balance, as in proportion or distribution. **2.** faulty muscular or glandular coordination. [1895–1900; IM-[2] + BALANCE]

im·be·cile (im′bə sil, -səl *or, esp. Brit.,* -sēl′), *n.* **1.**

CONCISE PRONUNCIATION KEY: act, cāpe, dâre, pärt; set, ēqual; *if,* ice; ox, ōver, ôrder, oil, bo͝ok, bo͞ot, out; up, ûrge; child; sing; shoe; thin, *that;* zh as in *treasure.* ə = *a* as in *alone, e* as in *system, i* as in *easily, o* as in *gallop, u* as in *circus;* ᵊ as in *fire* (fīᵊr), *hour* (ouᵊr). l and n can serve as syllabic consonants, as in *cradle* (krād′l), and *button* (but′n). See the full key inside the front cover.

Psychol. a person of the second order in a former classification of mental retardation, above the level of idiocy, having a mental age of seven or eight years and an intelligence quotient of 25 to 50. **2.** a dunce; blockhead; dolt. —*adj.* **3.** mentally feeble. **4.** showing mental feebleness or incapacity. **5.** stupid; silly; absurd. **6.** *Archaic.* weak or feeble. [1540–50; earlier *imbecill* < L *imbēcillus* weak; *-ile* r. *-ill* by confusion with suffix -ILE] —**im′be·cile·ly,** *adv.*

im·be·cil·ic (im′bə sil′ik), *adj.* **1.** of, pertaining to, or characteristic of an imbecile. **2.** contemptibly stupid, silly, or inappropriate: *an imbecilic suggestion.* [1915–20; IMBECILE + -IC]
—**Syn. 2.** idiotic, stupid, asinine.

im·be·cil·i·ty (im′bə sil′i tē), *n., pl.* **-ties. 1.** *Psychol.* the state of being an imbecile. **2.** an instance or point of weakness; feebleness; incapability. **3.** stupidity; silliness; absurdity. **4.** an instance of this. [1525–35; earlier *imbecillity* < L *imbēcillitās.* See IMBECILE, -ITY]

im·bed (im bed′), *v.t.,* **-bed·ded, -bed·ding.** embed.

im·bed·ding (im bed′ing), *n. Math.* embedding.

im·bibe (im bīb′), *v.,* **-bibed, -bib·ing.** —*v.t.* **1.** to consume (liquids) by drinking; drink: *He imbibed great quantities of iced tea.* **2.** to absorb or soak up, as water, light, or heat: *Plants imbibe moisture from the soil.* **3.** to take or receive into the mind, as knowledge, ideas, or the like: *to imbibe a sermon; to imbibe beautiful scenery.* —*v.i.* **4.** to drink, esp. alcoholic beverages: *Just a soft drink for me—I don't imbibe.* **5.** to absorb liquid or moisture. **6.** *Archaic.* to soak or saturate; imbue. [1350–1400; < L *imbibere* to drink in, equiv. to *im-* IM-[1] + *bibere* to drink; r. ME *enbiben* < MF *embiber* < L, as above] —**im·bib′er,** *n.*
—**Syn. 1.** swallow. See **drink.**

im·bi·bi·tion (im′bə bish′ən), *n.* **1.** act of imbibing. **2.** *Physical Chem.* the absorption of solvent by a gel. **3.** *Photog.* (in color printing) absorption of dye by gelatin, as in the dye-transfer process. [1425–75; late ME; see IMBIBE, -ITION] —**im′bi·bi′tion·al,** *adj.*

im·bit·ter (im bit′ər), *v.t.* embitter. —**im·bit′ter·er,** *n.* —**im·bit′ter·ment,** *n.*

im·bod·y (im bod′ē), *v.t.,* **-bod·ied, -bod·y·ing.** embody. —**im·bod′i·ment,** *n.*

im·bold·en (im bōl′dn), *v.t.* embolden.

im·bos·om (im bŏŏz′əm, -bōō′zəm), *v.t.* embosom.

im·bow·er (im bou′ər), *v.t., v.i.* embower.

im·brac·er·y (im brā′sə rē), *n., pl.* **-er·ies.** *Law.* embracery.

im·bran·gle (im brang′gəl), *v.t.,* **-gled, -gling.** embrangle.

im·brex (im′breks, -briks), *n., pl.* **-bri·ces** (-brə sēz′, -bri kās′). **1.** a convex tile, used esp. in ancient Rome to cover joints in a tile roof. **2.** *Archit.* one of the scales in ornamental imbrication. [1855–60; < L, equiv. to *imbr-* (s. of *imber*) rainstorm + *-ex* n. suffix]

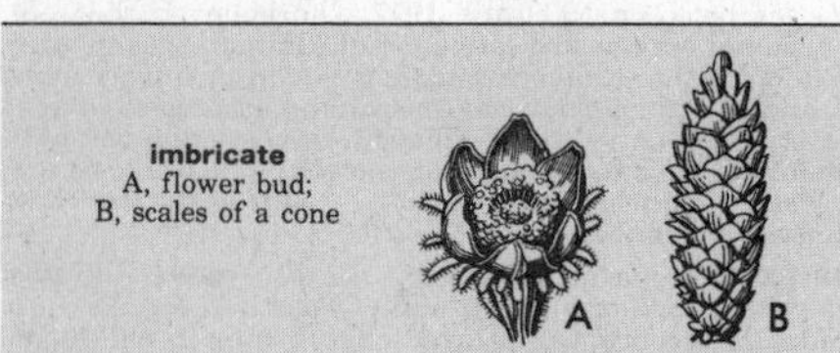

imbricate
A, flower bud;
B, scales of a cone

im·bri·cate (*adj.* im′bri kit, -kāt′; *v.* im′bri kāt′), *adj., v.,* **-cat·ed, -cat·ing.** —*adj.* **1.** overlapping in sequence, as tiles or shingles on a roof. **2.** of, pertaining to, or resembling overlapping tiles, as decoration or drawings. **3.** *Biol.* overlapping like tiles, as scales or leaves. **4.** characterized by or as if by overlapping shingles. —*v.t., v.i.* **5.** to overlap, as tiles or shingles. [1650–60; < LL *imbricātus* tiled with imbrices, shaped like such a tile or tiling, equiv. to *imbric-* (s. of *imbrex*) IMBREX + *-ātus* -ATE[1]] —**im′bri·cate·ly,** *adv.* —**im′bri·ca′tive,** *adj.*

im·bri·ca·tion (im′bri kā′shən), *n.* **1.** an overlapping, as of tiles or shingles. **2.** a decoration or pattern resembling this. **3.** *Surg.* overlapping of layers of tissue in the closure of wounds or in the correction of defects. **4.** *Geol.* shingling. [1640–50; IMBRICATE + -ION]

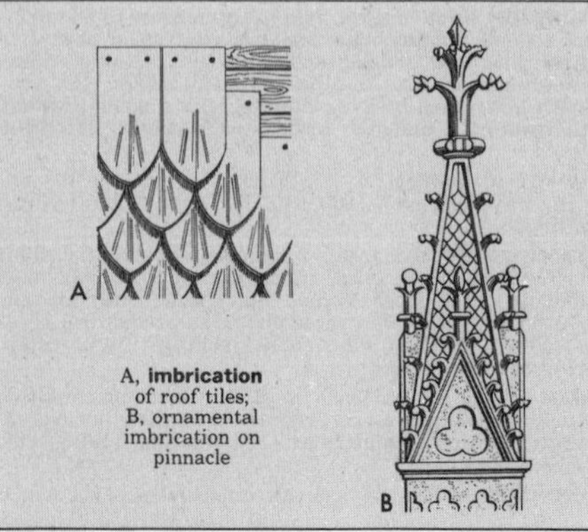

A, **imbrication** of roof tiles;
B, ornamental imbrication on pinnacle

CONCISE ETYMOLOGY KEY: <, descended or borrowed from; >, whence; b., blend of, blended; c., cognate with; cf., compare; deriv., derivative; equiv., equivalent; imit., imitative; obl., oblique; r., replacing; s., stem; sp., spelling, spelled; resp., respelling, respelled; trans., translation; ?, origin unknown; *, unattested; ‡, probably earlier than. See the full key inside the front cover.

im·bro·glio (im brōl′yō), *n., pl.* **-glios. 1.** a misunderstanding, disagreement, etc., of a complicated or bitter nature, as between persons or nations. **2.** an intricate and perplexing state of affairs; a complicated or difficult situation. **3.** a confused heap. Also, **embroglio.** [1740–50; < It, deriv. of *imbrogliare* to EMBROIL]

im·brown (im broun′), *v.t., v.i.* embrown.

im·brue (im brōō′), *v.t.,* **-brued, -bru·ing. 1.** to stain: *He refused to imbrue his hands with the blood of more killing.* **2.** to impregnate or imbue (usually fol. by *with* or *in*): *They are imbrued with the follies of youth.* Also, **embrue.** [1400–50; late ME *enbrewen* < MF *embreuver* to cause to drink in, soak, drench < VL **imbiberāre,* deriv. of L *imbibere* to IMBIBE] —**im·brue′ment,** *n.*

im·brute (im brōōt′), *v.t., v.i.,* **-brut·ed, -brut·ing.** to degrade or sink to the level of a brute. Also, **embrute.** [1625–35; IM-[1] + BRUTE] —**im·brute′ment,** *n.*

im·bue (im byōō′), *v.t.,* **-bued, -bu·ing. 1.** to impregnate or inspire, as with feelings, opinions, etc.: *The new political leader was imbued with the teachings of Mahatma Gandhi.* **2.** to saturate or impregnate with moisture, color, etc. **3.** to imbrue. [1545–55; < L *imbuere* to wet, drench] —**im·bue′ment,** *n.*
—**Syn. 1.** charge, infect, fire. **2.** permeate, infuse, tincture, soak.

IMCO, Inter-Governmental Maritime Consultive Organization.

I·me·na (i mā′nə), *n.* a female given name: from an Arabic word meaning "faith."

IMF, See **International Monetary Fund.** Also, **I.M.F.**

im·id·az·ole (im′id az′ōl, -id ə zōl′), *n. Chem.* a colorless, crystalline, water-soluble, heterocyclic compound, $C_3H_4N_2$, used chiefly in organic synthesis. Also called **glyoxaline.** [1890–95; IMIDE + AZOLE]

im·ide (im′īd, im′id), *n. Chem.* a compound derived from ammonia by replacement of two hydrogen atoms by acidic groups, characterized by the =NH group. [1840–50; alter. of AMIDE] —**i·mid·ic** (i mid′ik), *adj.*

im·i·do (im′i dō′), *adj. Chem.* containing the imido group. [1880–85; independent use of IMIDO-]

imido-, a combining form representing **imide** in compound words: *imidogen.*

i·mid·o·gen (i mid′ə jən, -jen′, i mē′də-), *n.* the imido group, esp. in an uncombined state. [1840–50; IMIDO- + -GEN]

im′ido group′, *Chem.* **1.** the bivalent group =NH linked to one or two acid groups. **2.** (erroneously) the imino group. Also called **im′ido rad′ical.**

i·mine (i mēn′, im′in), *n. Chem.* a compound containing the =NH group united with a nonacid group. [1880–85; alter. of AMINE]

im·i·no (im′ə nō′), *adj. Chem.* containing the imino group. [1900–05; independent use of IMINO-]

imino-, a combining form representing **imine** in compound words: *iminourea.*

im′ino group′, *Chem.* the bivalent group =NH not linked to any acid group. Also called **im′ino rad′ical.** Cf. **imido group.** [1905–10]

i·mi·no·u·re·a (i mē′nō yŏŏ rē′ə, -yŏŏr′ē ə, im′ə nō-), *n. Chem.* guanidine. [IMINO- + UREA]

im·ip·ra·mine (i mip′rə mēn′), *n. Pharm.* a tricyclic antidepressant, $C_{19}H_{24}N_2$, used for the symptomatic relief of depression. [1955–60; contr. and rearrangement of *iminodibenzyl* and *aminopropyl,* components of the chemical name]

imit., 1. imitation. **2.** imitative.

im·i·ta·ble (im′i tə bəl), *adj.* capable or worthy of being imitated: *She has many good, imitable qualities.* [1540–50; < L *imitābilis,* equiv. to *imitā(ri)* to IMITATE + *-bilis* -BLE] —**im′i·ta·bil′i·ty, im′i·ta·ble·ness,** *n.*

im·i·tate (im′i tāt′), *v.t.,* **-tat·ed, -tat·ing. 1.** to follow or endeavor to follow as a model or example: *to imitate an author's style; to imitate an older brother.* **2.** to mimic; impersonate: *The students imitated the teacher behind her back.* **3.** to make a copy of; reproduce closely. **4.** to have or assume the appearance of; simulate; resemble. [1525–35; < L *imitātus* ptp. of *imitāri* to copy, presumably a freq. akin to the base of *imāgō* IMAGE] —**im′i·ta′tor,** *n.*
—**Syn. 2.** ape, mock. **3.** IMITATE, COPY, DUPLICATE, REPRODUCE all mean to follow or try to follow an example or pattern. IMITATE is the general word for the idea: *to imitate someone's handwriting, behavior.* To COPY is to make a fairly exact imitation of an original creation: *to copy a sentence, a dress, a picture.* To DUPLICATE is to produce something that exactly resembles or corresponds to something else; both may be originals: *to duplicate the terms of two contracts.* To REPRODUCE is to make a likeness or reconstruction of an original: *to reproduce a 16th-century theater.*

im·i·ta·tion (im′i tā′shən), *n.* **1.** a result or product of imitating. **2.** the act of imitating. **3.** a counterfeit; copy. **4.** a literary composition that imitates the manner or subject of another author or work. **5.** *Biol.* mimicry. **6.** *Psychol.* the performance of an act whose stimulus is the observation of the act performed by another person. **7.** *Sociol.* the copying of patterns of activity and thought of other groups or individuals. **8.** *Art.* **a.** (in Aristotelian aesthetics) the representation of an object or an action as it ought to be. **b.** the representation of actuality in art or literature. **9.** *Music.* the repetition of a melodic phrase at a different pitch or key from the original or in a different voice part. —*adj.* **10.** designed to imitate a genuine or superior article or thing: *imitation leather.* **11.** *Jewelry.* noting an artificial gem no part of which is of the true gemstone. Cf. **assembled, synthetic** (def. 5). [1350–1400; ME < L *imitātiōn-* (s. of *imitātiō*). See IMITATE, -ION] —**im′i·ta′tion·al,** *adj.*

im′ita′tion dou′blet, *Jewelry.* **1.** a doublet formed entirely of glass. **2.** an imitation gem made from a single piece of glass.

im·i·ta·tive (im′i tā′tiv), *adj.* **1.** imitating; copying; given to imitation. **2.** of, pertaining to, or characterized by imitation. **3.** *Biol.* mimetic. **4.** made in imitation of something; counterfeit. **5.** onomatopoeic. [1575–85; < LL *imitātivus.* See IMITATE, -IVE] —**im′i·ta′tive·ly,** *adv.* —**im′i·ta′tive·ness,** *n.*

im′itative mag′ic, magic that attempts to control the universe through the mimicking of a desired event, as by stabbing an image of an enemy in an effort to destroy him or her or by performing a ritual dance imitative of the growth of food in an effort to secure an abundant supply; a branch of sympathetic magic based on the belief that similar actions produce similar results. Also called **homeopathic magic.** Cf. **contagious magic.**

im·mac·u·late (i mak′yə lit), *adj.* **1.** free from spot or stain; spotlessly clean: *immaculate linen.* **2.** free from moral blemish or impurity; pure; undefiled. **3.** free from fault or flaw; free from errors: *an immaculate text.* **4.** *Biol.* having no spots or colored marks; unicolor. [1400–50; late ME < L *immaculātus* unspotted. See IM-[2], MACULATE] —**im·mac·u·la·cy** (i mak′yə lə sē), **im·mac′u·late·ness,** *n.* —**im·mac·u·late·ly,** *adv.*
—**Syn. 2.** irreproachable, blameless, unimpeachable, unexceptionable.

Immac′ulate Concep′tion, *Rom. Cath. Ch.* the dogma of the unique privilege by which the Virgin Mary was conceived in her mother's womb without the stain of original sin through the anticipated merits of Jesus Christ. Cf. **virgin birth** (def. 1). [1680–90]

im·mane (i mān′), *adj. Archaic.* **1.** vast in size; enormous. **2.** inhumanly cruel. [1595–1605; < L *immānis* brutal, frightful, enormous, equiv. to *im-* IM-[2] + *-mānis,* appar. akin to *mānus* good; see MANES] —**im·mane′ly,** *adv.* —**im·mane′ness,** *n.*

im·ma·nent (im′ə nənt), *adj.* **1.** remaining within; indwelling; inherent. **2.** *Philos.* (of a mental act) taking place within the mind of the subject and having no effect outside of it. Cf. **transeunt. 3.** *Theol.* (of the Deity) indwelling the universe, time, etc. Cf. **transcendent** (def. 3). [1525–35; < LL *immanent-* (s. of *immanēns*), prp. of *immanēre* to stay in, equiv. to *im-* IM-[1] + *man(ēre)* to stay + *-ent-* -ENT; see REMAIN] —**im′ma·nence, im′·ma·nen·cy,** *n.* —**im′ma·nent·ly,** *adv.*
—**Syn. 1.** innate, inborn, intrinsic. —**Ant. 1.** extrinsic, acquired, superimposed.

im·ma·nent·ism (im′ə nən tiz′əm), *n.* the belief that the Deity indwells and operates directly within the universe or nature. [1905–10; IMMANENT + -ISM] —**im′·ma·nent·ist,** *adj., n.*

Im·man·u·el (i man′yōō əl), *n.* **1.** the name of the Messiah as prophesied by Isaiah, often represented in Christian exegesis as being Jesus Christ. Isa. 7:14. **2.** a male given name. [< Heb *'immānū'ēl* lit., God is with us]

im·ma·te·ri·al (im′ə tēr′ē əl), *adj.* **1.** of no essential consequence; unimportant. **2.** not pertinent; irrelevant. **3.** not material; incorporeal; spiritual. [1350–1400; ME < ML *immāteriālis.* See IM-[2], MATERIAL] —**im′ma·te′·ri·al·ly,** *adv.* —**im′ma·te′ri·al·ness,** *n.*

im·ma·te·ri·al·ism (im′ə tēr′ē ə liz′əm), *n.* **1.** the doctrine that there is no material world, but that all things exist only in and for minds. **2.** the doctrine that only immaterial substances or spiritual beings exist. [1705–15; IMMATERIAL + -ISM, modeled on *materialism*] —**im′ma·te′ri·al·ist,** *n.*

im·ma·te·ri·al·i·ty (im′ə tēr′ē al′i tē), *n., pl.* **-ties** for 2. **1.** state or character of being immaterial. **2.** something immaterial. [1560–70; IMMATERIAL + -ITY]

im·ma·te·ri·al·ize (im′ə tēr′ē ə līz′), *v.t.,* **-ized, -iz·ing.** to make immaterial. Also, *esp. Brit.,* **im′ma·te′ri·al·ise′.** [1655–65; IMMATERIAL + -IZE]

im·ma·ture (im′ə chŏŏr′, -tŏŏr′, -tyŏŏr′, -chûr′), *adj.* **1.** not mature, ripe, developed, perfected, etc. **2.** emotionally undeveloped; juvenile; childish. **3.** *Physical Geog.* youthful (def. 5). **4.** *Archaic.* premature. [1540–50; < L *immātūrus* unripe, hence, untimely. See IM-[2], MATURE] —**im′ma·ture′ly,** *adv.* —**im′ma·ture′·ness,** *n.*
—**Syn. 2.** callow, puerile, babyish.

im·ma·tu·ri·ty (im′ə chŏŏr′i tē, -tŏŏr′-, -tyŏŏr′-, -chûr′-), *n., pl.* **-ties** for 2. **1.** a state or condition of being immature: *the immaturity of one's behavior; the immaturity of a country's technology.* **2.** an immature action or attitude. [1530–40; IMMATURE + -ITY, prob. reflecting L *immātūritās* untimely haste, unripeness]

im·meas·ur·a·ble (i mezh′ər ə bəl), *adj.* incapable of being measured; limitless: *the immeasurable vastness of the universe.* [1350–1400; ME *immesurable.* See IM-[2], MEASURABLE] —**im·meas′ur·a·bil′i·ty, im·meas′ur·a·ble·ness,** *n.* —**im·meas′ur·a·bly,** *adv.*

im·me·di·a·cy (i mē′dē ə sē), *n., pl.* **-cies. 1.** the state, condition, or quality of being immediate. **2.** Often, **immediacies.** an immediate need: *the immediacies of everyday living.* **3.** *Philos.* **a.** immediate presence of an object of knowledge to the mind, without any distortions, inferences, or interpretations, and without involvement of any intermediate agencies. **b.** the direct content of the mind as distinguished from representation or cognition. [1595–1605; IMMEDI(ATE) + -ACY]

im·me·di·ate (i mē′dē it), *adj.* **1.** occurring or accomplished without delay; instant: *an immediate reply.* **2.** following or preceding without a lapse of time: *the immediate future.* **3.** having no object or space intervening; nearest or next: *in the immediate vicinity.* **4.** of or pertaining to the present time or moment: *our immediate plans.* **5.** without intervening medium or agent; direct: *an immediate cause.* **6.** having a direct bearing: *immediate consideration.* **7.** very close in relationship: *my immediate family.* **8.** *Philos.* directly intuited. [1525–35; < ML *immediātus.* See IM-[2], MEDIATE (adj.)] —**im·me′di·ate·ness,** *n.*
—**Syn. 1.** instantaneous. **3.** close, proximate.

imme′diate annu′ity, an annuity bought with a single premium, with payments to the annuitant to begin at the end of one payment period, as a month or a year. Cf. **deferred annuity.**

imme′diate constit′uent, *Gram.* one of the usually two largest constituents of a construction: The immediate constituents of *He ate his dinner* are *he* and *ate his dinner;* of *ate his dinner* are *ate* and *his dinner;* etc. *Abbr.:* IC Cf. **ultimate constituent.** [1930–35]

im·me·di·ate·ly (i mē′dē it lē), *adv.* **1.** without lapse of time; without delay; instantly; at once: *Please telephone him immediately.* **2.** with no object or space intervening. **3.** closely: *immediately in the vicinity.* **4.** without intervening medium or agent; concerning or affecting directly. —*conj.* **5.** *Chiefly Brit.* the moment that; as soon as. [1375–1425; late ME; see IMMEDIATE, -LY]
—Syn. 1. instantaneously, forthwith. IMMEDIATELY, INSTANTLY, DIRECTLY, PRESENTLY were once close synonyms, all denoting complete absence of delay or any lapse of time. IMMEDIATELY and INSTANTLY still almost always have that sense and usually mean at once: *He got up immediately. She responded instantly to the request.* DIRECTLY is usually equivalent to soon, in a little while rather than at once: *You go ahead, we'll join you directly.* PRESENTLY changes sense according to the tense of the verb with which it is used. With a present tense verb it usually means now, at the present time: *The author presently lives in San Francisco. She is presently working on a new novel.* In some contexts, especially those involving a contrast between the present and the near future, PRESENTLY can mean soon or in a little while: *She is at the office now but will be home presently.* **—Ant. 1.** later.

im·me·di·a·tism (i mē′dē ə tiz′əm), *n. U.S. Hist.* a policy for the immediate abolition of slavery. [1815–25; IMMEDIATE + -ISM] **—im·me′di·a·tist,** *n.*

im·med·i·ca·ble (i med′i kə bəl), *adj.* incurable. [1525–35; < L *immedicābilis* incurable. See IM-², MEDICABLE] **—im·med′i·ca·ble·ness,** *n.* **—im·med′i·ca·bly,** *adv.*

Im·mel·mann (im′əl män′, -mən), *n.* a maneuver in which an airplane makes a half loop, then resumes its normal, level position by making a half roll: used to gain altitude while turning to fly in the opposite direction. Also called **Im′melmann turn′.** [1915–20; after Max *Immelmann* (1890-1916), German aviator of World War I, who is said to have devised it]

im·me·mo·ri·al (im′ə môr′ē əl, -mōr′-), *adj.* extending back beyond memory, record, or knowledge: *from time immemorial.* [1595–1605; < ML *immemoriālis.* See IM-², MEMORIAL] **—im′me·mo′ri·al·ly,** *adv.*
—Syn. timeless, ancient, ageless, olden.

im·mense (i mens′), *adj.* **1.** vast; huge; very great: *an immense territory.* **2.** immeasurable; boundless. **3.** *Informal.* splendid: *You did an immense job getting the project started.* [1400–50; late ME < L *immēnsus,* equiv. to *im-* IM-² + *mēnsus* ptp. of *mētīrī* to measure] **—im·mense′ly,** *adv.* **—im·mense′ness,** *n.*
—Syn. 1. extensive. See **huge.**

im·men·si·ty (i men′si tē), *n.* **1.** vastness; enormous extent: *the immensity of the Roman empire.* **2.** the state or condition of being immense. [1400–50; late ME < L *immēnsitās.* See IMMENSE, -ITY]

im·men·su·ra·ble (i men′shər ə bəl, -sər ə-), *adj.* immeasurable. [1525–35; < LL *immēnsūrābilis.* See IM-², MENSURABLE] **—im·men′su·ra·bil′i·ty, im·men′su·ra·ble·ness,** *n.*

im·merge (i mûrj′), *v.,* **-merged, -merg·ing.** —*v.i.* **1.** to plunge, as into a fluid. **2.** to disappear by entering into any medium, as the moon into the shadow of the sun. —*v.t.* **3.** *Archaic.* to immerse. [1605–15; < L *immergere* to dip, plunge, sink into. See IM-¹, MERGE] **—im·mer′gence,** *n.*

im·merse (i mûrs′), *v.t.,* **-mersed, -mers·ing. 1.** to plunge into or place under a liquid; dip; sink. **2.** to involve deeply; absorb: *She is totally immersed in her law practice.* **3.** to baptize by immersion. **4.** to embed; bury. [1595–1605; < L *immersus,* ptp. of *immergere;* see IMMERGE] **—im·mers′i·ble,** *adj.*
—Syn. 1. immerge, duck, douse. See **dip**¹. **2.** engage.
—Ant. 4. disinter.

im·mersed (i mûrst′), *adj.* **1.** plunged or sunk in or as if in a liquid. **2.** *Biol.* somewhat or wholly sunk in the surrounding parts, as an organ. **3.** *Bot.* growing under water. [1660–70; IMMERSE + -ED²]

im·mer·sion (i mûr′zhən, -shən), *n.* **1.** an act or instance of immersing. **2.** state of being immersed. **3.** state of being deeply engaged or involved; absorption. **4.** baptism in which the whole body of the person is submerged in the water. **5.** Also called **ingress.** *Astron.* the entrance of a heavenly body into an eclipse by another body, an occultation, or a transit. Cf. **emersion** (def. 1). —*adj.* **6.** concentrating on one course of instruction, subject, or project to the exclusion of all others for several days or weeks; intensive: *an immersion course in conversational French.* [1425–75; late ME < LL *immersiōn-* (s. of *immersiō*) a dipping in. See IMMERSE, -ION]

immer′sion foot′, *Pathol.* an abnormal condition of the foot caused by prolonged exposure to water, characterized by pathological changes in the skin, blood vessels, nerves, and muscles. [1940–45]

immer′sion heat′er, a small electric coil used to heat a liquid, as a cup of water, in which it is immersed. Also called **immer′sion coil′.** [1910–15]

im·mer·sion·ism (i mûr′zhə niz′əm, -shə-), *n.* **1.** the doctrine that immersion is essential to Christian baptism. **2.** the practice of baptism by immersion. [1835–45; IMMERSION + -ISM] **—im·mer′sion·ist,** *n.*

immer′sion objec′tive, *Optics.* a microscope objective of high resolving power in which the space between the front lens and the cover glass is filled with an oil whose index of refraction is close to that of the objective and the cover glass. Also called **immer′sion lens′, oil-immersion objective.**

im·mesh (i mesh′), *v.t.* enmesh.

im·me·thod·i·cal (im′ə thod′i kəl), *adj.* not methodical; without method or system. [1595–1605; IM-² + METHODICAL] **—im′me·thod′i·cal·ly,** *adv.* **—im′me·thod′i·cal·ness,** *n.*

im·mie (im′ē), *n. Informal.* agate (def. 2). [*im(itation marble)* + -IE]

im·mi·grant (im′i grənt), *n.* **1.** a person who migrates to another country, usually for permanent residence. **2.** an organism found in a new habitat. —*adj.* **3.** of or pertaining to immigrants and immigration: *a department for immigrant affairs.* **4.** immigrating. [1780–90, *Amer.;* < L *immigrant-* (s. of *immigrāns*), prp. of *immigrāre* to move into. See IM-¹, MIGRANT]

im·mi·grate (im′i grāt′), *v.,* **-grat·ed, -grat·ing.** —*v.i.* **1.** to come to a country of which one is not a native, usually for permanent residence. **2.** to pass or come into a new habitat or place, as an organism. —*v.t.* **3.** to introduce as settlers: *to immigrate cheap labor.* [1615–25; < L *immigrātus* (ptp. of *immigrāre* to move into). See IM-¹, MIGRATE] **—im′mi·gra′tor,** *n.*
—Syn. 1. See **migrate.**

im·mi·gra·tion (im′i grā′shən), *n.* **1.** the act of immigrating. **2.** a group or number of immigrants. [1650–60; IM-¹ + MIGRATION] **—im′mi·gra′tion·al, im·mi·gra·to·ry** (im′ə grə tôr′ē, -tōr′ē), *adj.*

Immigra′tion and National′ity Act′. See **McCarran-Walter Act.**

im·mi·nence (im′ə nəns), *n.* **1.** Also, **im′mi·nen·cy.** the state or condition of being imminent or impending: *the imminence of war.* **2.** something that is imminent, esp. an impending evil or danger. [1600–10; < LL *imminentia.* See IMMINENT, -ENCE]

im·mi·nent (im′ə nənt), *adj.* **1.** likely to occur at any moment; impending: *Her death is imminent.* **2.** projecting or leaning forward; overhanging. [1520–30; < L *imminent-* (s. of *imminēns*), prp. of *imminēre* to overhang, equiv. to *im-* IM-¹ + *-min-* from a base meaning "jut out, project, rise" (cf. EMINENT, MOUNT²) + *-ent-* -ENT] **—im′mi·nent·ly,** *adv.* **—im′mi·nent·ness,** *n.*
—Syn. 1. near, at hand. IMMINENT, IMPENDING, THREATENING all may carry the implication of menace, misfortune, disaster, but they do so in differing degrees. IMMINENT may portend evil: *an imminent catastrophe,* but also may mean simply "about to happen": *The merger is imminent.* IMPENDING has a weaker sense of immediacy and threat than IMMINENT: *Real tax relief legislation is impending,* but it too may be used in situations portending disaster: *impending social upheaval; to dread the impending investigation.* THREATENING almost always suggests ominous warning and menace: *a threatening sky just before the tornado struck.* **—Ant. 1.** distant, remote.

im·min·gle (i ming′gəl), *v.t., v.i.,* **-gled, -gling.** to mingle in; intermingle. [1600–10; IM-³ + MINGLE]

im·mis·ci·ble (i mis′ə bəl), *adj.* not miscible; incapable of being mixed. [1665–75; IM-² + MISCIBLE] **—im·mis′ci·bil′i·ty,** *n.* **—im·mis′ci·bly,** *adv.*

im·mit·i·ga·ble (i mit′i gə bəl), *adj.* not mitigable; not to be mitigated. [1570–80; < LL *immītigābilis.* See IM-², MITIGABLE] **—im·mit′i·ga·bil′i·ty,** *n.* **—im·mit′i·ga·bly,** *adv.*

im·mit·tance (i mit′ns), *n. Elect.* impedance or admittance, used when the distinction between the two is not relevant. [1945–50; IM(PEDANCE) + (AD)MITTANCE]

im·mix (i miks′), *v.t.,* **-mixed** or **-mixt, -mix·ing.** to mix in; mingle. [1400–50; back formation from ME *immixt(e)* mixed in < L *immixtus* ptp. of *immiscēre* to blend, equiv. to *im-* IM-¹ + *mix-* (see MIX) + *-tus* ptp. suffix]

im·mix·ture (i miks′chər), *n.* **1.** the act of immixing. **2.** the state of being immixed; involvement. [1855–60; < L *immixt(us)* blended (see IMMIX) + -URE; see MIXTURE]

im·mo·bile (i mō′bəl, -bēl), *adj.* **1.** incapable of moving or being moved. **2.** not mobile or moving; motionless. [1300–50; ME < L *immōbilis.* See IM-², MOBILE]

im·mo·bil·i·ty (im′ō bil′i tē), *n.* the quality or condition of being immobile or irremovable. [1375–1425; late ME < LL *immōbilitās.* See IM-², MOBILITY]

im·mo·bi·lize (i mō′bə līz′), *v.t.,* **-lized, -liz·ing. 1.** to make immobile or immovable; fix in place. **2.** to prevent the use, activity, or movement of: *The hurricane immobilized the airlines.* **3.** to deprive of the capacity for mobilization: *The troops were immobilized by the enemy.* **4.** *Med.* to prevent, restrict, or reduce normal movement in (the body, a limb, or a joint), as by a splint, cast, or prescribed bed rest. **5.** to render (an opponent's strategy) ineffective; stymie. **6.** *Finance.* **a.** to establish a monetary reserve by withdrawing (specie) from circulation. **b.** to create fixed capital in place of (circulating capital). Also, *esp. Brit.,* **im·mo′bi·lise′.** [1870–75; IMMOBILE + -IZE; see MOBILIZE and cf. F *immobiliser*] **—im·mo′bi·li·za′tion,** *n.* **—im·mo′bi·liz′er,** *n.*

im·mod·er·a·cy (i mod′ər ə sē), *n.* immoderation. [1675–85; IMMODER(ATE) + -ACY]

im·mod·er·ate (i mod′ər it), *adj.* **1.** not moderate; exceeding just or reasonable limits; excessive; extreme. **2.** *Obs.* intemperate. **3.** *Obs.* without bounds. [1350–1400; ME < L *immoderātus.* See IM-², MODERATE] **—im·mod′er·ate·ly,** *adv.* **—im·mod′er·ate·ness,** *n.*
—Syn. 1. exorbitant, unreasonable; inordinate; extravagant.

im·mod·er·a·tion (i mod′ə rā′shən), *n.* lack of moderation. [1535–45; < L *immoderātiōn-* (s. of *immoderātiō*). See IM-², MODERATION]

im·mod·est (i mod′ist), *adj.* **1.** not modest in conduct, utterance, etc.; indecent; shameless. **2.** not modest in assertion or pretension; forward; impudent. [1560–70; < L *immodestus* unrestrained, immoderate. See IM-², MODEST] **—im·mod′est·ly,** *adv.* **—im·mod′es·ty,** *n.*
—Syn. 2. vain, exaggerated, inflated.

Im·mo·ka·lee (i mō′kə lē′), *n.* a town in S Florida. 11,038.

im·mo·late (im′ə lāt′), *v.t.,* **-lat·ed, -lat·ing. 1.** to sacrifice. **2.** to kill as a sacrificial victim, as by fire; offer in sacrifice. **3.** to destroy by fire. [1540–50; < L *immolātus,* ptp. of *immolāre* to sprinkle with holy meal prior to sacrificing, sacrifice, equiv. to *im-* IM-¹ + *mol(a)* sacrificial barley cake, lit., millstone (see MILL¹) + *-ātus* -ATE¹] **—im′mo·la′tor,** *n.*

im·mo·la·tion (im′ə lā′shən), *n.* **1.** an act or instance of immolating. **2.** the state of being immolated. **3.** a sacrifice. [1525–35; < L *immolātiōn-* (s. of *immolātiō*) offering, sacrifice. See IMMOLATE, -ION]

im·mor·al (i môr′əl, i mor′-), *adj.* **1.** violating moral principles; not conforming to the patterns of conduct usually accepted or established as consistent with principles of personal and social ethics. **2.** licentious or lascivious. [1650–60; IM-² + MORAL] **—im·mor′al·ly,** *adv.*
—Syn. bad, wicked, dissolute, dissipated, profligate. IMMORAL, ABANDONED, DEPRAVED describe one who makes no attempt to curb self-indulgence. IMMORAL, referring to conduct, applies to one who acts contrary to or does not obey or conform to standards of morality; it may also mean licentious and perhaps dissipated. ABANDONED, referring to condition, applies to one hopelessly, and usually passively, sunk in wickedness and unrestrained appetites. DEPRAVED, referring to character, applies to one who voluntarily seeks evil and viciousness. IMMORAL, AMORAL, NONMORAL, and UNMORAL are sometimes confused with one another. IMMORAL means not moral and connotes evil or licentious behavior. AMORAL, NONMORAL, and UNMORAL, virtually synonymous although the first is by far the most common form, mean utterly lacking in morals (either good or bad), neither moral nor immoral. However, since, in some contexts, there is a stigma implicit in a complete lack of morals, being amoral, nonmoral, or unmoral is sometimes considered just as reprehensible as being immoral.

im·mor·al·ism (i môr′ə liz′əm, i mor′-), *n. Philos.* indifference toward or opposition to conventional morality. [1905–10; IMMORAL + -ISM] **—im·mor′al·ist,** *n.*

im·mo·ral·i·ty (im′ə ral′i tē, im′ô-), *n., pl.* **-ties. 1.** immoral quality, character, or conduct; wickedness; evilness. **2.** sexual misconduct. **3.** an immoral act. [1560–70; IMMORAL + -ITY]

im·mor·al·ize (i môr′ə līz′, i mor′-), *v.t.,* **-ized, -iz·ing.** to make or cause to be immoral. Also, *esp. Brit.,* **im·mor′al·ise′.** [1745–55; IMMORAL + -IZE]

im·mor·tal (i môr′tl), *adj.* **1.** not mortal; not liable or subject to death; undying: *our immortal souls.* **2.** remembered or celebrated through all time: *the immortal words of Lincoln.* **3.** not liable to perish or decay; imperishable; everlasting. **4.** perpetual; lasting; constant: *an immortal enemy.* **5.** of or pertaining to immortal beings or immortality. **6.** (of a laboratory-cultured cell line) capable of dividing indefinitely. —*n.* **7.** an immortal being. **8.** a person of enduring fame: *Bach, Milton, El Greco, and other immortals.* **9. the Immortals,** the 40 members of the French Academy. **10.** (*often cap.*) any of the gods of classical mythology. [1325–75; ME (adj.) < L *immortālis.* See IM-², MORTAL] **—im·mor′tal·ly,** *adv.*
—Syn. 8. giant, titan, genius.

im·mor·tal·i·ty (im′ôr tal′i tē), *n.* **1.** immortal condition or quality; unending life. **2.** enduring fame. [1300–50; ME *immortalite* < L *immortālitās.* See IMMORTAL, -ITY]

im·mor·tal·ize (i môr′tl īz′), *v.t.,* **-ized, -iz·ing. 1.** to bestow unending fame upon; perpetuate. **2.** to make immortal; endow with immortality. Also, *esp. Brit.,* **im·mor′tal·ise′.** [1560–70; IMMORTAL + -IZE] **—im·mor′ta·liz′a·ble,** *adj.* **—im·mor′tal·i·za′tion,** *n.* **—im·mor′tal·iz′er,** *n.*

im·mor·telle (im′ôr tel′), *n.* an everlasting plant or flower, esp. *Xeranthemum annuum.* [1825–35; < F, n. use of fem. of *immortel* IMMORTAL; see -ELLE]

im·mo·tile (i mōt′l), *adj.* not able to move; not motile. [1870–75; IM-² + MOTILE] **—im·mo·til·i·ty** (im′ō til′i tē), *n.*

im·mov·a·ble (i mo͞o′və bəl), *adj.* **1.** incapable of being moved; fixed; stationary. **2.** incapable of being influenced by feeling; emotionless: *an immovable heart; an immovable tyrant.* **3.** incapable of being moved from one's purpose, opinion, etc.; steadfast; unyielding. **4.** not subject to change; unalterable. **5.** not moving; motionless. **6.** *Law.* **a.** not liable to be removed, or permanent in place. **b.** (of property) real, as distinguished from personal. **7.** not changing from one date to another in different years: *Christmas is an immovable feast.* —*n.* **8.** something immovable. **9. immovables,** *Law.* lands and the appurtenances thereof, as trees and buildings. Also, **im·move′a·ble.** [1325–75; ME *immevable, immovable;* see IM-², MOVABLE] **—im·mov′a·bil′i·ty, im·mov′a·ble·ness,** *n.* **—im·mov′a·bly,** *adv.*
—Syn. 3. obdurate, inflexible, unbending, adamant.

im·mune (i myo͞on′), *adj.* **1.** protected from a disease or the like, as by inoculation. **2.** of or pertaining to the production of antibodies or lymphocytes that can react with a specific antigen: *immune reaction.* **3.** exempt or protected: *immune from punishment.* **4.** not responsive or susceptible: *immune to new ideas.* —*n.* **5.** a person who is immune. [1400–50; late ME < L *immūnis* exempt, equiv. to *im-* IM-² + *-mūnis;* see COMMON]

immune′ com′plex, an aggregate of an antigen and its specific antibody. [1970–75]

immune′ response′, any of the body's immunologic reactions to an antigen. [1950–55]

immune′ se′rum, a serum containing naturally or

CONCISE PRONUNCIATION KEY: act, cāpe, dâre, pärt; set, ēqual; *if,* ice; ox, ōver, ôrder, oil, bo͝ok, bo͞ot, out; up, ûrge; child; sing; shoe; thin, *th*at; zh as in *treasure.* ə = *a* as in *alone, e* as in *system, i* as in *easily, o* as in *gallop, u* as in *circus;* ᵊ as in *fire* (fīᵊr), *hour* (ouᵊr). l and n can serve as syllabic consonants, as in *cradle* (krād′l), and *button* (but′n). See the full key inside the front cover.

artificially produced antibodies to a given antigen, obtained from human or animal sources. [1900–05]

immune′ sys′tem, *Anat.* a diffuse, complex network of interacting cells, cell products, and cell-forming tissues that protects the body from pathogens and other foreign substances, destroys infected and malignant cells, and removes cellular debris: the system includes the thymus, spleen, lymph nodes and lymph tissue, stem cells, white blood cells, antibodies, and lymphokines. [1960–65]

im·mu·ni·ty (i myo͞o′ni tē), *n., pl.* **-ties.** **1.** the state of being immune from or insusceptible to a particular disease or the like. **2.** the condition that permits either natural or acquired resistance to disease. **3.** the ability of a cell to react immunologically in the presence of an antigen. **4.** exemption from any natural or usual liability. **5.** exemption from obligation, service, duty, or liability to taxation, jurisdiction, etc.: *The ambassador claimed diplomatic immunity when they arrested him for reckless driving.* **6.** *Law.* exemption from criminal prosecution or legal liability or punishment on certain conditions. **7.** special privilege. **8.** *Eccles.* **a.** the exemption of ecclesiastical persons and things from secular or civil liabilities, duties, and burdens. **b.** a particular exemption of this kind. [1350–1400; ME *immunite* < L *immūnitās.* See IMMUNE, -ITY]
—**Syn. 4.** See **exemption. 5.** franchise, license, liberty, prerogative. —**Ant. 1.** susceptibility. **4, 5.** liability.

immu′nity bath′, *Law.* the giving of testimony that is self-incriminating in order to avail oneself of the immunity granted a witness. Cf. **use immunity.** [1965–70]

im·mu·ni·za·tion (im′yə nə zā′shən, i myo͞o′-), *n.* **1.** the fact or process of becoming immune, as against a disease. **2.** *Finance.* a method of protection against fluctuating bond interest rates by investing in securities having different yields and terms. [1890–95; IMMUNIZE + -ATION]

im·mu·nize (im′yə nīz′, i myo͞o′nīz), *v.t.,* **-nized, -niz·ing. 1.** to make immune. **2.** to render harmless or ineffective; neutralize. **3.** *Law.* to grant (a witness) immunity. Also, *esp. Brit.,* **im′mu·nise′.** [1890–95; IMMUNE + -IZE] —**im′mu·niz′er,** *n.*

immuno-, a combining form representing **immune** or **immunity** in compound words: *immunology.*

im·mu·no·ad·sorb·ent (im′yə nō ad sôr′bənt, -zôr′-, i myo͞o′-), *n. Immunol.* immunosorbent. [1970–75; IMMUNO- + ADSORBENT]

im·mu·no·as·say (im′yə nō ə sā′, -as′ā, i myo͞o′-), *n.* any laboratory method for detecting a substance by using an antibody reactive with it. [1955–60; IMMUNO- + ASSAY] —**im′mu·no·as·say′a·ble,** *adj.*

im·mu·no·bi·ol·o·gy (im′yə nō bī ol′ə jē, i myo͞o′-), *n.* the study of the immune response and the biological aspects of immunity to disease. [1955–60; IMMUNO- + BIOLOGY] —**im·mu·no·bi·o·log·ic** (im′yə nō bī′ə loj′ik, i myo͞o′-), **im′mu·no·bi′o·log′i·cal,** *adj.* —**im′mu·no·bi·ol′o·gist,** *n.*

im·mu·no·chem·is·try (im′yə nō kem′ə strē, i myo͞o′-), *n.* the study of the chemistry of immunologic substances and reactions. [1905–10; IMMUNO- + CHEMISTRY] —**im′mu·no·chem′i·cal,** *adj.* —**im′mu·no·chem′i·cal·ly,** *adv.* —**im′mu·no·chem′ist,** *n.*

im·mu·no·com·pe·tent (im′yə nō kom′pi tnt, i myo͞o′-), *adj.* having the potential for immunologic response; capable of developing immunity after exposure to antigen. [1970–75; IMMUNO- + COMPETENT] —**im′mu·no·com′pe·tence,** *n.*

im·mu·no·cy·to·chem·is·try (im′yə nō sī′tō kem′ə strē, i myo͞o′-), *n.* the detection of chemical components of cells by means of antibodies coupled to substances that can be made visible. [1965–70; IMMUNO- + CYTO- + CHEMISTRY] —**im′mu·no·cy′to·chem′i·cal,** *adj.* —**im′mu·no·cy′to·chem′i·cal·ly,** *adv.*

im·mu·no·de·fi·cien·cy (im′yə nō di fish′ən sē, i myo͞o′-), *n., pl.* **-cies.** impairment of the immune response, predisposing to infection and certain malignancies. [1970–75; IMMUNO- + DEFICIENCY] —**im′mu·no·de·fi′cient,** *adj.*

im·mu·no·di·ag·no·sis (im′yə nō dī′əg nō′sis, i myo͞o′-), *n., pl.* **-ses** (-sēz). serodiagnosis. [IMMUNO- + DIAGNOSIS]

im·mu·no·di·ag·nos·tics (im′yə nō dī′əg nos′tiks, i myo͞o′-), *n.* (*used with a singular v.*) the determination of immunologic characteristics of individuals, cells, and other biologic entities. [IMMUNO- + DIAGNOSTICS]

im·mu·no·dif·fu·sion (im′yə nō di fyo͞o′zhən, i myo͞o′-), *n.* any of various analytical techniques that involve antigen and antibody solutions diffusing toward each other in a gel until antibody binds specifically to antigen to form a precipitate. [1955–60; IMMUNO- + DIFFUSION]

im·mu·no·e·lec·tro·pho·re·sis (im′yə nō i lek′trō fə rē′sis, i myo͞o′-), *n.* a technique for the separation and identification of mixtures of proteins, consisting of electrophoresis followed by immunodiffusion. [1955–60; IMMUNO- + ELECTROPHORESIS] —**im·mu·no·e·lec·tro·pho·ret·ic** (im′yə nō i lek′trō fə ret′ik, i myo͞o′-), *adj.*

im·mu·no·fluo·res·cence (im′yə nō flo͞o res′əns, -flô-, -flō-, i myo͞o′-), *n.* any of various techniques for detecting an antigen or antibody in a sample by coupling its specifically interactive antibody or antigen to a fluorescent compound, mixing with the sample, and observing the reaction under an ultraviolet-light microscope. [1955–60; IMMUNO- + FLUORESCENCE] —**im′mu·no·fluo·res′cent,** *adj.*

immunofluores′cence as′say, *Med.* a diagnostic blood test using the technique of immunofluorescence. *Abbr.:* IFA

im·mu·no·gen (i myo͞o′nə jən, -jen′), *n.* any substance or cell introduced into the body in order to generate an immune response. [1955–60; IMMUNO- + -GEN]

im·mu·no·ge·net·ics (im′yə nō jə net′iks, i myo͞o′-), *n.* (*used with a singular v.*) **1.** the branch of immunology dealing with the study of immunity in relation to genetic makeup. **2.** the study of genetic relationships among animals by comparison of immunologic reactions. [1935–40; IMMUNO- + GENETICS] —**im′mu·no·ge·net′ic, im′mu·no·ge·net′i·cal,** *adj.*

im·mu·no·gen·ic (im′yə nō jen′ik, i myo͞o′nə-), *adj.* causing or capable of producing an immune response. [1930–35; IMMUNO- + -GENIC] —**im′mu·no·gen′i·cal·ly,** *adv.* —**im·mu·no·ge·nic·i·ty** (im′yə nō jə nis′i tē, i myo͞o′-), *n.*

im·mu·no·glob·u·lin (im′yə nō glob′yə lin, i myo͞o′-), *n.* **1.** any of several classes of structurally related proteins that function as antibodies or receptors and are found in plasma and other body fluids and in the membrane of certain cells. Cf. **IgA, IgD, IgE, IgG,** and **IgM. 2.** the fraction of the blood serum containing antibodies. **3.** an antibody. *Abbr.:* Ig [1955–60; IMMUNO- + GLOBULIN]

im·mu·no·he·ma·tol·o·gy (im′yə nō hē′mə tol′ə jē, -hem′ə-, i myo͞o′-), *n.* the study of blood and blood-forming tissue in relation to the immune response. [1945–50; IMMUNO- + HEMATOLOGY] —**im·mu·no·he·ma·to·log·ic** (im′yə nō hē′mə tl oj′ik, -hem′ə-, i myo͞o′-), **im′mu·no·he′ma·to·log′i·cal,** *adj.*

im·mu·no·his·to·chem·is·try (im′yə nō his′tō kem′ə strē, i myo͞o′-), *n.* the application of immunologic techniques to the chemical analysis of cells and tissues. Cf. **immunocytochemistry.** [IMMUNO- + HISTOCHEMISTRY] —**im′mu·no·his′to·chem′i·cal,** *adj.* —**im′mu·no·his′to·chem′i·cal·ly,** *adv.*

im·mu·no·his·tol·o·gy (im′yə nō hi stol′ə jē, i myo͞o′-), *n.* the microscopic study of tissues with the aid of antibodies that bind to tissue components and reveal their presence. [IMMUNO- + HISTOLOGY] —**im·mu·no·his·to·log·ic** (im′yə nō his′tl oj′ik, i myo͞o′-), **im′mu·no·his′to·log′i·cal,** *adj.* —**im′mu·no·his′to·log′i·cal·ly,** *adv.*

immunol., immunology.

im·mu·nol·o·gy (im′yə nol′ə jē), *n.* the branch of science dealing with the components of the immune system, immunity from disease, the immune response, and immunologic techniques of analysis. [1905–10; IMMUNO- + -LOGY] —**im·mu·no·log·ic** (im′yə nl oj′ik, i myo͞o′-), **im′mu·no·log′i·cal,** *adj.* —**im′mu·no·log′i·cal·ly,** *adv.* —**im′mu·nol′o·gist,** *n.*

im·mu·no·pa·thol·o·gy (im′yə nō pə thol′ə jē, i myo͞o′-), *n.* the study of diseases having an immunologic or allergic basis. [1955–60; IMMUNO- + PATHOLOGY] —**im·mu·no·path·o·log·i·cal** (im′yə nō path′ə loj′i kəl, i myo͞o′-), **im′mu·no·path′o·log′ic,** *adj.* —**im′mu·no·path′o·log′i·cal·ly,** *adv.* —**im′mu·no·pa·thol′o·gist,** *n.*

im·mu·no·pre·cip·i·ta·tion (im′yə nō pri sip′i tā′shən, i myo͞o′-), *n.* the separation of an antigen from a solution by the formation of a large complex with its specific antibody. [1965–70; IMMUNO- + PRECIPITATION]

im·mu·no·sorb·ent (im′yə nō sôr′bənt, -zôr′-, i myo͞o′-), *n. Immunol.* an insoluble surface to which a specific antibody is attached for the purpose of removing the corresponding antigen from a solution or suspension. Also called **immunoadsorbent.** [1970–75; shortening of IMMUNOADSORBENT]

im·mu·no·sup·press (im′yə nō sə pres′, i myo͞o′-), *v.t., v.i.* to suppress the normal immune response. [1965–70; back formation from IMMUNOSUPPRESSION or IMMUNOSUPPRESSIVE]

im·mu·no·sup·pres·sion (im′yə nō sə presh′ən, i myo͞o′-), *n. Pathol.* the inhibition of the normal immune response because of disease, the administration of drugs, or surgery. [1960–65; IMMUNO- + SUPPRESSION] —**im′mu·no·sup·pressed′,** *adj.*

im·mu·no·sup·pres·sive (im′yə nō sə pres′iv, i myo͞o′-), *Pharm.* —*adj.* **1.** capable of causing immunosuppression: *immunosuppressive drugs.* —*n.* **2.** *Pharm.* Also, **im·mu·no·sup·pres·sor** (im′yə nō sə pres′ər, i myo͞o′-). any substance that results in or effects immunosuppression. [1960–65; IMMUNO- + SUPPRESSIVE]

im·mu·no·ther·a·py (im′yə nō ther′ə pē, i myo͞o′-), *n., pl.* **-pies.** treatment designed to produce immunity to a disease or enhance the resistance of the immune system to an active disease process, as cancer. [1905–10; IMMUNO- + THERAPY] —**im·mu·no·ther·a·peu·tic** (im′yə nō ther′ə pyo͞o′tik, i myo͞o′-), *adj.*

im·mu·no·tox·in (im′yə nō tok′sin, i myo͞o′-), *n. Immunol.* a monoclonal antibody linked to a toxin with the intention of destroying a specific target cell while leaving adjacent cells intact. [IMMUNO- + TOXIN]

im·mure (i myo͝or′), *v.t.,* **-mured, -mur·ing. 1.** to enclose within walls. **2.** to shut in; seclude or confine. **3.** to imprison. **4.** to build into or entomb in a wall. **5.** *Obs.* to surround with walls; fortify. [1575–85; < ML *immūrāre,* equiv. to L *im-* IM-[1] + *-mūrāre,* v. deriv. of *mūrus* wall (cf. MURAL)] —**im·mure′ment, im·mu·ra·tion** (im′yə rā′shən), *n.*

im·mu·ta·ble (i myo͞o′tə bəl), *adj.* not mutable; unchangeable; changeless. [1375–1425; late ME < L *immūtābilis.* See IM-[2], MUTABLE] —**im·mu′ta·bil′i·ty, im·mu′ta·ble·ness,** *n.* —**im·mu′ta·bly,** *adv.*

Im·o·gene (im′ə jēn′), *n.* a female given name. Also, **Im·o·gen** (im′ə jen′, -jən).

imp (imp), *n.* **1.** a little devil or demon; an evil spirit. **2.** a mischievous child. **3.** *Archaic.* a scion or offshoot of a plant or tree. **4.** *Archaic.* an offspring. —*v.t.* **5.** *Falconry.* **a.** to graft (feathers) into a wing. **b.** to furnish (a wing, tail, etc.) with feathers, as to make good losses or deficiencies and improve powers of flight. **6.** *Archaic.* to add a piece to; mend or repair. [bef. 900; (n.) ME *impe,* OE *impa, impe* shoot, graft < LL *impotus, imputus* grafted shoot < Gk *émphytos* planted, implanted, v. adj. of *emphȳein* to implant (*em-* EM-[2] + *phȳein* to bring forth); (v.) ME *impen* to plant, graft, OE *impian, geimpian,* deriv. of the n. (cf. OHG *impfōn, impitōn* > G *impfen* to inoculate); sense "demon" < phrase *imp of the devil*]
—**Syn. 2.** scamp, rascal, brat, devil.

IMP, International Match Point.

Imp., **1.** Emperor. [< L *Imperātor*] **2.** Empress. [< L *Imperātrīx*]

imp., **1.** imperative. **2.** imperfect. **3.** imperial. **4.** impersonal. **5.** implement. **6.** import. **7.** important. **8.** imported. **9.** importer. **10.** imprimatur. **11.** in the first place. [< L *imprīmis*] **12.** imprint. **13.** improper. **14.** improved. **15.** improvement.

im·pact (*n.* im′pakt; *v.* im pakt′), *n.* **1.** the striking of one thing against another; forceful contact; collision: *The impact of the colliding cars broke the windshield.* **2.** an impinging: *the impact of light on the eye.* **3.** influence; effect: *the impact of Einstein on modern physics.* **4.** an impacting; forcible impinging: *the tremendous impact of the shot.* **5.** the force exerted by a new idea, concept, technology, or ideology: *the impact of the industrial revolution.* —*v.t.* **6.** to drive or press closely or firmly into something; pack in. **7.** to fill up; congest; throng: *A vast crowd impacted St. Peter's Square.* **8.** to collide with; strike forcefully: *a rocket designed to impact the planet Mars.* **9.** to have an impact or effect on; influence; alter: *The decision may impact your whole career. The auto industry will be impacted by the new labor agreements.* —*v.i.* **10.** to have impact or make contact forcefully: *The ball impacted against the bat with a loud noise.* **11.** to have an impact or effect: *Increased demand will impact on sales.* [1775–85; (n. and v.) back formation from IMPACTED]
—**Usage.** The verb IMPACT has developed the transitive sense "to have an impact or effect on" (*The structured reading program has done more to impact the elementary schools than any other single factor*) and the intransitive sense "to have an impact or effect" (*The work done at the computer center will impact on the economy of Illinois and the nation*). Although recent, the new uses are entirely standard and most likely to occur in formal speech and writing.

im′pact cra′ter, *Astron., Geol.* crater (def. 2). [1890–95]

im·pact·ed (im pak′tid), *adj.* **1.** tightly or immovably wedged in. **2.** *Dentistry.* noting a tooth so confined in its socket as to be incapable of normal eruption. **3.** driven together; tightly packed. **4.** densely populated or crowded; overcrowded: *an impacted school district.* [1675–85; obs. *impact* adj. (< L *impāctus* ptp. of *impingere* to fasten, cause to collide, strike, equiv. to *im-* IM-[1] + *pag-,* var. s. of *pangere* to drive in, plant firmly + *-tus* ptp. suffix) + -ED[2]; see IMPINGE]

im·pact·er (im pak′tər), *n.* **1.** a person or thing that impacts. **2.** See **impact wrench.** Also, **im·pac′tor.** [1915–20; IMPACT + -ER[1]]

im′pact extru′sion, *Metalworking.* an extrusion process in which a slug of cold metal in a shallow die cavity is formed by the action of a rapidly moving punch that forces the metal through the die or back around the punch. [1930–35]

im·pac·tion (im pak′shən), *n.* **1.** an act or instance of impacting. **2.** the state of being impacted; close fixation. **3.** *Dentistry.* the condition in which a tooth is impacted. [1730–40; < LL *impāctiōn-* (s. of *impāctiō*), equiv. to L *impāct*(*us*), ptp. of *impingere* (see IMPACTED) + *-iōn-* -ION]

im·pact·ite (im pak′tīt, im′pak tīt′), *n.* a glassy or crystalline material composed of slag and meteoric materials, produced by the impact of a meteorite striking the earth. [1935–40; IMPACT + -ITE[1]]

im·pac·tive (im pak′tiv), *adj.* **1.** caused by impact: *impactive pain.* **2.** compelling or impressive: *He was deeply moved by the impactive force of the performance.* [1930–35; IMPACT + -IVE]

im′pact param′eter, (in nuclear physics) the perpendicular distance from the original center of a set of scattering particles to the original line of motion of a particle being scattered.

im′pact wrench′, an electric or pneumatic power wrench with interchangeable toolhead attachments, used for installing and removing nuts, bolts, and screws. Also called **impacter, impactor.**

im·pair (im pâr′), *v.t.* **1.** to make or cause to become worse; diminish in ability, value, excellence, etc.; weaken or damage: *to impair one's health; to impair negotiations.* —*v.i.* **2.** to grow or become worse; lessen. —*n.* **3.** *Archaic.* impairment. [1250–1300; ME *empairen, empeiren* to make worse < MF *empeirer,* equiv. to *em-* IM-[1] + *peirer* to make worse < LL *pējōrāre,* equiv. to L *pējōr-,* s. of *pējor* worse + *-ā-* thematic vowel + *-re* inf. suffix; cf. PEJORATIVE] —**im·pair′a·ble,** *adj.* —**im·pair′er,** *n.* —**im·pair′ment,** *n.*
—**Syn. 1.** See **injure.** —**Ant. 1.** repair.

im·pair (an per′), *adj. French.* noting any odd number, esp. in roulette. Cf. ***pair.***

im·paired (im pârd′), *adj.* **1.** weakened, diminished, or damaged: *impaired hearing; to rebuild an impaired bridge.* **2.** functioning poorly or inadequately: *Consumption of alcohol results in an impaired driver.* [IMPAIR + -ED[2]]

im·pal·a (im pal′ə, -pä′lə), *n., pl.* **-pal·as,** (*esp. collectively*) **-pal·a.** an African antelope, *Aepyceros melampus,* the male of which has ringed, lyre-shaped horns. See illus. on next page. [1870–75; < Zulu, or a cognate word in another Nguni dial.]

CONCISE ETYMOLOGY KEY: <, descended or borrowed from; >, whence; b., blend of, blended; c., cognate with; cf., compare; deriv., derivative; equiv., equivalent; imit., imitative; obl., oblique; r., replacing; s., stem; sp., spelling, spelled; resp., respelling, respelled; trans., translation; ?, origin unknown; *, unattested; ‡, probably earlier than. See the full key inside the front cover.

impala, *Aepyceros melampus,* 2½ ft. (0.8 m) high at shoulder; horns 2 ft. (0.6 m); head and body 4½ ft. (1.4 m); tail 1 ft. (0.3 m)

im•pale (im pāl′), *v.t.,* **-paled, -pal•ing. 1.** to fasten, stick, or fix upon a sharpened stake or the like. **2.** to pierce with a sharpened stake thrust up through the body, as for torture or punishment. **3.** to fix upon, or pierce through with, anything pointed. **4.** to make helpless as if pierced through. **5.** *Archaic.* to enclose with or as if with pales or stakes; fence in; hem in. **6.** *Heraldry.* **a.** to marshal (two coats of arms, as the family arms of a husband and wife) on an escutcheon party per pale. **b.** (of a coat of arms) to be combined with (another coat of arms) in this way. Also, **empale** (for defs. 1–5). [1545–55; < ML *impālāre,* equiv. to L *im-* IM-[1] + *pāl(us)* PALE[2] + *-ā-* thematic vowel + *-re* inf. ending] **—im•pal′er,** *n.* **—im•pale′ment,** *n.*

im•pal•pa•ble (im pal′pə bəl), *adj.* **1.** not palpable; incapable of being perceived by the sense of touch; intangible. **2.** difficult for the mind to grasp readily or easily: *impalpable distinctions.* **3.** (of powder) so fine that when rubbed between the fingers no grit is felt. [1500–10; IM-[2] + PALPABLE] **—im•pal′pa•bil′i•ty,** *n.* **—im•pal′pa•bly,** *adv.*

im•pa•na•tion (im′pə nā′shən), *n. Theol.* the doctrine that the body and blood of Christ are in the bread and wine after consecration. [1540–50; < ML *impānātiōn-* (s. of *impānātiō*), equiv. to L *im-* IM-[1] + *pan(is)* bread + *-ātiōn-* -ATION]

im•pan•el (im pan′l), *v.t.,* **-eled, -el•ing** or (*esp. Brit.*) **-elled, -el•ling. 1.** to enter on a panel or list for jury duty. **2.** to select (a jury) from the panel. **3.** to enter names on a panel or other official list. Also, **empanel.** [1375–1425; late ME *empanellen* < AF *empaneller.* See EM-[1], PANEL] **—im•pan′el•ment,** *n.*

im•par (im′pär), *adj. Anat.* unpaired; azygous. [1375–1425 for earlier n. sense "odd number," 1525–35 for current sense; late ME < L *impār* unequal. See IM-[2], PAR]

im•par•a•dise (im par′ə dīs′), *v.t.,* **-dised, -dis•ing.** to enrapture. [1585–95; IM-[1] + PARADISE]

im•par•i•pin•nate (im par′ə pin′āt), *adj. Bot.* odd-pinnate. [1840–50; < NL *imparipinnātus.* See IMPAR, -I-, PINNATE]

im•par•i•syl•lab•ic (im par′ə si lab′ik), *adj.* (of a noun) not composed of the same number of syllables in all of its inflected forms, as Latin *corpus, corporis.* [1720–30; IMPAR + -I- + SYLLABIC]

im•par•i•ty (im par′i tē), *n., pl.* **-ties.** lack of parity or equality; disparity, difference, or inequality. [1555–65; < LL *imparitās.* See IM-[2], PARITY[1]]

im•park (im pärk′), *v.t.* **1.** to enclose or shut up, as in a park. **2.** to enclose (land) as a park. [1275–1325; ME < AF *emparker.* See IM-[1], PARK] **—im′par•ka′tion,** *n.*

im•parl (im pärl′), *v.i. Law.* to confer with the opposing party in a lawsuit with a view to settling the dispute amicably, out of court. [1425–75; late ME *emparlen* < MF *emparler,* equiv. to *em-* EM-[1] + *parler* to speak; see PARLIAMENT]

im•par•lance (im pär′ləns), *n. Law.* **1.** an extension of time granted to one party in a lawsuit to plead or to settle the dispute amicably. **2.** a request for, or the permission granting, such a continuance. [1570–80; < AF **emparlaunce,* equiv. to MF *emparl(er)* to IMPARL + *-aunce* -ANCE]

im•part (im pärt′), *v.t.* **1.** to make known; tell; relate; disclose: *to impart a secret.* **2.** to give; bestow; communicate: *to impart knowledge.* **3.** to grant a part or share of. *—v.i.* **4.** to grant a part or share; give. [1425–75; late ME < L *impartīre* to share. See IM-[1], PART] **—im•part′a•ble,** *adj.* **—im′par•ta′tion, im•part′ment,** *n.* **—im•part′er,** *n.*
—Syn. 1. reveal, divulge. See **communicate. 2.** grant, cede, confer. **—Ant. 1.** conceal.

im•par•tial (im pär′shəl), *adj.* not partial or biased; fair; just: *an impartial judge.* [1585–95; IM-[2] + PARTIAL] **—im•par•ti•al•i•ty** (im pär′shē al′i tē), **im•par′tial•ness,** *n.* **—im•par′tial•ly,** *adv.*
—Syn. unbiased, unprejudiced, equitable. See **fair**[1]. **—Ant.** biased.

im•part•i•ble (im pär′tə bəl), *adj.* not partible; indivisible. [1350–1400; ME < LL *impartībilis* indivisible. See IM-[2], PARTIBLE] **—im•part′i•bil′i•ty,** *n.* **—im•part′i•bly,** *adv.*

im•pass•a•ble (im pas′ə bəl, -pä′sə-), *adj.* **1.** not passable; not allowing passage over, through, along, etc.: *Heavy snow made the roads impassable.* **2.** unable to be surmounted: *an impassable obstacle to further negotiations.* **3.** (of currency) unable to be circulated: *He tore the bill in half, making it impassable.* [1560–70; IM-[2] + PASSABLE] **—im•pass′a•bil′i•ty, im•pass′a•ble•ness,** *n.* **—im•pass′a•bly,** *adv.*

im•passe (im′pas, im pas′), *n.* **1.** a position or situation from which there is no escape; deadlock. **2.** a road or way that has no outlet; cul-de-sac. [1850–55; < F, equiv. to *im-* IM-[2] + *-passe,* s. of *passer* to PASS]
—Syn. 1. stalemate, standstill, standoff, dead end.

im•pas•si•ble (im pas′ə bəl), *adj.* **1.** incapable of suffering pain. **2.** incapable of suffering harm. **3.** incapable of emotion; impassive. [1300–50; ME < LL *impassibilis.* See IM-[2], PASSIBLE] **—im•pas′si•bil′i•ty, im•pas′si•ble•ness,** *n.* **—im•pas′si•bly,** *adv.*

im•pas•sion (im pash′ən), *v.t.* to fill, or affect strongly, with intense feeling or passion; inflame; excite. [1585–95; < It *impassionare.* See IM-[1], PASSION]

im•pas•sion•ate (im pash′ə nit), *adj.* filled with passion; impassioned. [1595–1605; IMPASSION + -ATE[1]] **—im•pas′sion•ate•ly,** *adv.*

im•pas•sioned (im pash′ənd), *adj.* filled with intense feeling or passion; passionate; ardent. [1595–1605; IMPASSION + -ED[2]] **—im•pas′sioned•ly,** *adv.* **—im•pas′sioned•ness,** *n.*
—Syn. emotional, vehement, fervent, fiery. **—Ant.** apathetic.

im•pas•sive (im pas′iv), *adj.* **1.** without emotion; apathetic; unmoved. **2.** calm; serene. **3.** unconscious; insensible. **4.** not subject to suffering. [1660–70; IM-[2] + PASSIVE] **—im•pas′sive•ly,** *adv.* **—im•pas′sive•ness, im•pas•siv•i•ty** (im′pa siv′i tē), *n.*
—Syn. 1. emotionless, phlegmatic, stoical, indifferent, undisturbed, unperturbed. **2.** tranquil, unruffled, composed. **4.** unaffected; unflinching.

im•paste (im pāst′), *v.t.,* **-past•ed, -past•ing.** *Obs.* to cover with or enclose in a paste. [1540–50; < It *impastare.* See IM-[1], PASTE] **—im•pas•ta•tion** (im′pa stā′shən), *n.*

im•pas•to (im pas′tō, -pä′stō), *n. Painting.* **1.** the laying on of paint thickly. **2.** the paint so laid on. **3.** enamel or slip applied to a ceramic object to form a decoration in low relief. [1775–85; < It, n. deriv. of *impastare* to IMPASTE]

im•pa•tience (im pā′shəns), *n.* **1.** lack of patience. **2.** eager desire for relief or change; restlessness. **3.** intolerance of anything that thwarts, delays, or hinders. [1175–1225; ME *impacience* < L *impatientia.* See IM-[2], PATIENCE]

im•pa•tiens (im pā′shənz), *n., pl.* **-tiens.** any of numerous plants belonging to the genus *Impatiens,* of the balsam family, having irregular flowers in which the calyx and corolla are not clearly distinguishable and bearing fruit that bursts open to scatter the seeds. [1880–85; < NL, L *impatiēns* not enduring, not tolerating (see IMPATIENT); alluding to the plant's quick release of seeds upon slight contact; cf. the familiar name *touch-me-not*]

im•pa•tient (im pā′shənt), *adj.* **1.** not patient; not accepting delay, opposition, pain, etc., with calm or patience. **2.** indicating lack of patience: *an impatient answer.* **3.** restless in desire or expectation; eagerly desirous. **4. impatient of,** intolerant of: *impatient of any interruptions.* [1350–1400; ME *impacient* < L *impatient-* (s. of *impatiēns*) not enduring, not tolerating. See IM-[2], PATIENT] **—im•pa′tient•ly,** *adv.* **—im•pa′tient•ness,** *n.*
—Syn. 1. uneasy, unquiet. **1, 2.** irritable, testy, fretful, violent, hot; curt, brusque, abrupt. **3.** hasty, impetuous, precipitate, sudden. **—Ant. 1.** calm.

im•pawn (im pôn′), *v.t. Archaic.* to put in pawn; pledge. [1590–1600; IM-[1] + PAWN[1]]

im•peach (im pēch′), *v.t.* **1.** to accuse (a public official) before an appropriate tribunal of misconduct in office. **2.** *Chiefly Law.* to challenge the credibility of: *to impeach a witness.* **3.** to bring an accusation against. **4.** to call in question; cast an imputation upon: *to impeach a person's motives.* **5.** to call to account. *—n.* **6.** *Obs.* impeachment. [1350–1400; ME *empechen, enpeshen* < AF *empecher* < LL *impedicāre* to fetter, trap, equiv. to L *im-* IM-[1] + *pedic(a)* a fetter (deriv. of *pēs* FOOT) + *-ā-* thematic vowel + *-re* inf. suffix] **—im•peach′er,** *n.*
—Syn. 4. question, challenge, impugn.

im•peach•a•ble (im pē′chə bəl), *adj.* **1.** making one subject to impeachment, as misconduct in office. **2.** liable to be impeached. [1495–1505; IMPEACH + -ABLE] **—im•peach′a•bil′i•ty,** *n.*

im•peach•ment (im pēch′mənt), *n.* **1.** the impeaching of a public official before an appropriate tribunal. **2.** (in Congress or a state legislature) the presentation of formal charges against a public official by the lower house, trial to be before the upper house. **3.** demonstration that a witness is less worthy of belief. **4.** the act of impeaching. **5.** the state of being impeached. [1350–1400; ME *empechement* < AF. See IMPEACH, -MENT]

im•pearl (im pûrl′), *v.t.* **1.** to form into drops resembling pearls. **2.** to adorn with pearls or pearllike drops. [1580–90; IM-[1] + PEARL[1]; cf. F *emperler*]

im•pec•ca•ble (im pek′ə bəl), *adj.* **1.** faultless; flawless; irreproachable: *impeccable manners.* **2.** not liable to sin; incapable of sin. [1525–35; < L *impeccābilis* faultless, sinless. See IM-[2], PECCABLE] **—im•pec′ca•bil′i•ty,** *n.* **—im•pec′ca•bly,** *adv.*
—Syn. 1. unassailable, unexceptionable.

im•pe•cu•ni•ous (im′pi kyōō′nē əs), *adj.* having little or no money; penniless; poor. [1590–1600; IM-[2] + obs. *pecunious* wealthy < L *pecūniōsus,* equiv. to *pecūni(a)* wealth + *-ōsus* -OUS] **—im′pe•cu′ni•ous•ly,** *adv.* **—im′pe•cu′ni•ous•ness, im•pe•cu•ni•os•i•ty** (im′pi kyōō′nē os′i tē), *n.*
—Syn. destitute, poverty-stricken. See **poor.**

im•ped•ance (im pēd′ns), *n.* **1.** *Elect.* the total opposition to alternating current by an electric circuit, equal to the square root of the sum of the squares of the resistance and reactance of the circuit and usually expressed in ohms. *Symbol:* Z **2.** Also called **mechanical impedance.** *Physics.* the ratio of the force on a system undergoing simple harmonic motion to the velocity of the particles in the system. **3.** something that impedes; an obstacle or hindrance. [1886; IMPEDE + -ANCE; term introduced by O. Heaviside]

imped′ance match′ing, *Elect.* the technique of choosing or adjusting electric circuits and components so that the impedance of the load is equal to the internal impedance of the power source, thereby optimizing the power transfer from source to load. [1925–30]

im•pede (im pēd′), *v.t.,* **-ped•ed, -ped•ing.** to retard in movement or progress by means of obstacles or hindrances; obstruct; hinder. [1595–1605; < L *impedīre* to entangle, lit., to snare the feet. See IM-[1], PEDI-[1]] **—im•ped′er,** *n.* **—im•ped•i•bil•i•ty** (im pē′də bil′i tē, -ped′ə-), *n.* **—im•ped′i•ble,** *adj.* **—im•ped′ing•ly,** *adv.*
—Syn. slow, delay, check, stop, block, thwart. See **prevent. —Ant.** advance, encourage.

im•ped•i•ment (im ped′ə mənt), *n.* **1.** obstruction; hindrance; obstacle. **2.** any physical defect that impedes normal or easy speech; a speech disorder. **3.** *Chiefly Eccles. Law.* a bar, usually of blood or affinity, to marriage: *a diriment impediment.* **4.** Usually, **impediments.** impedimenta. [1350–1400; ME < L *impedīmentum.* See IMPEDE, -MENT] **—im•ped•i•men•tal** (im ped′ə men′tl), **im•ped′i•men′ta•ry,** *adj.*
—Syn. 1. bar, encumbrance, check. See **obstacle. —Ant. 1.** help, encouragement.

im•ped•i•men•ta (im ped′ə men′tə), *n.pl.* baggage or other things that retard one's progress, as supplies carried by an army: *the impedimenta of the weekend skier.* [1590–1600; < L, pl. of *impedīmentum* IMPEDIMENT]

im•pel (im pel′), *v.t.,* **-pelled, -pel•ling. 1.** to drive or urge forward; press on; incite or constrain to action. **2.** to drive or cause to move onward; propel; impart motion to. [1375–1425; late ME *impellen* < L *impellere* to strike against, set in motion (transit.), equiv. to *im-* IM-[1] + *pellere* to strike, move (something); akin to PULSE[1]]
—Syn. 1. actuate. See **compel. —Ant. 1.** restrain.

im•pel•lent (im pel′ənt), *adj.* **1.** impelling: *an impellent power; an impellent cause.* *—n.* **2.** something that impels; an impelling agency or force. [1610–20; < L *impellent-* (s. of *impellēns*), prp. of *impellere* to set in motion. See IMPEL, -ENT]

im•pel•ler (im pel′ər), *n.* **1.** a person or thing that impels. **2.** a rotor for transmitting motion, as in a centrifugal pump, blower, turbine, or fluid coupling. [1675–85; IMPEL + -ER[1]]

im•pend (im pend′), *v.i.* **1.** to be imminent; be about to happen. **2.** to threaten or menace: *He felt that danger impended.* **3.** *Archaic.* to hang or be suspended; overhang (usually fol. by *over*). [1580–90; < L *impendēre* to hang over, threaten. See IM-[1], PEND]

im•pend•ent (im pen′dənt), *adj.* impending. [1585–95; < L *impendent-* s. of *impendēns* prp. of *impendēre* to hang over, threaten. See IMPEND, -ENT] **—im•pend′ence, im•pend′en•cy,** *n.*

im•pend•ing (im pen′ding), *adj.* **1.** about to happen; imminent: *their impending marriage.* **2.** imminently threatening or menacing: *an impending storm.* **3.** *Archaic.* overhanging. [1675–85; IMPEND + -ING[2]]
—Syn. 1. See **imminent.**

im•pen•e•tra•bil•i•ty (im pen′i trə bil′i tē, im′pen-), *n.* **1.** the state or quality of being impenetrable. **2.** *Physics.* that property of matter by virtue of which two bodies cannot occupy the same space simultaneously. [1655–65; IMPENETR(ABLE) + -ABILITY]

im•pen•e•tra•ble (im pen′i trə bəl), *adj.* **1.** not penetrable; that cannot be penetrated, pierced, entered, etc. **2.** inaccessible to ideas, influences, etc. **3.** incapable of being understood; inscrutable; unfathomable: *an impenetrable mystery.* **4.** *Physics.* possessing impenetrability. [1425–75; late ME *impenetrabel* < L *impenetrābilis.* See IM-[2], PENETRABLE] **—im•pen′e•tra•ble•ness,** *n.* **—im•pen′e•tra•bly,** *adv*
—Syn. 3. incomprehensible, mysterious, obscure, hidden. **—Ant. 3.** clear, lucid.

im•pen•i•tent (im pen′i tənt), *adj.* not feeling regret about one's sin or sins; obdurate. [1525–35; < LL *impaenitent-* (s. of *impaenitēns*) unrepentant. See IM-[2], PENITENT] **—im•pen′i•tence, im•pen′i•ten•cy, im•pen′i•tent•ness,** *n.* **—im•pen′i•tent•ly,** *adv.*
—Syn. unrepentant, uncontrite, hardened.

imper., imperative.

im•per•a•ti•val (im per′ə tī′vəl), *adj.* of, pertaining to, or characteristic of the grammatical imperative. [1870–75; IMPERATIVE + -AL[1]] **—im•per′a•ti′val•ly,** *adv.*

im•per•a•tive (im per′ə tiv), *adj.* **1.** absolutely necessary or required; unavoidable: *It is imperative that we leave.* **2.** of the nature of or expressing a command; commanding. **3.** *Gram.* noting or pertaining to the mood of the verb used in commands, requests, etc., as in *Listen! Go!* Cf. **indicative** (def. 2), **subjunctive** (def. 1). *—n.* **4.** a command. **5.** something that demands attention or action; an unavoidable obligation or requirement; necessity: *It is an imperative that we help defend friendly nations.* **6.** *Gram.* **a.** the imperative mood. **b.** a verb in this mood. **7.** an obligatory statement, principle, or the like. [1520–30; < LL *imperātīvus,* equiv. to L *imperāt(us)* ptp. of *imperāre* to impose, order, command (*im-* IM-[1] + *-per-* (comb. form of *parāre* to furnish (with), produce, obtain, PREPARE) + *-ātus* -ATE[1]) + *-īvus* -IVE] **—im•per′a•tive•ly,** *adv.* **—im•per′a•tive•ness,** *n.*
—Syn. 1. inescapable; indispensable, essential; exigent, compelling.

im•per•a•tor (im′pə rä′tər, -rä′tôr, -rā′tər), *n.* **1.** an absolute or supreme ruler. **2.** (in Imperial Rome) emperor. **3.** (in Republican Rome) a temporary title accorded a victorious general. [1570–80; < L *imperātor;* see EMPEROR] **—im•per•a•to•ri•al** (im per′ə tôr′ē əl, -tōr′-), *adj.* **—im•per′a•to′ri•al•ly,** *adv.* **—im′pe•ra′tor•ship′,** *n.*

im•per•cep•ti•ble (im′pər sep′tə bəl), *adj.* **1.** very slight, gradual, or subtle: *the imperceptible slope of the road.* **2.** not perceptible; not perceived by or affecting the senses. *—n.* **3.** something not capable of being perceived by the senses: *metaphysical speculation about imperceptibles.* [1520–30; < ML *imperceptibilis.* See IM-[2], PERCEPTIBLE] **—im′per•cep′ti•bil′i•ty, im′per•cep′ti•ble•ness,** *n.* **—im′per•cep′ti•bly,** *adv.*
—Syn. 2. hidden, unperceivable, undetectable.

CONCISE PRONUNCIATION KEY: act, cāpe, dâre, pärt; set, ēqual; *if,* īce; ox, ōver, ôrder, oil, bŏŏk, bōōt, out; up, ûrge; child; sing; shoe; thin, *th*at; zh as in *treasure.* ə = *a* as in *alone, e* as in *system, i* as in *easily,* o as in *gallop, u* as in *circus;* ° as in *fire* (fī°r), *hour* (ou°r). l and n can serve as syllabic consonants, as in *cradle* (krād′l), and *button* (but′n). See the full key inside the front cover.

im·per·cep·tion (im′pər sep′shən), *n.* lack of perception. [1655–65; IM-[2] + PERCEPTION]

im·per·cep·tive (im′pər sep′tiv), *adj.* not perceptive; lacking perception. [1655–65; IM-[2] + PERCEPTIVE] —**im′per·cep·tiv′i·ty, im′per·cep′tive·ness,** *n.*

im·per·cip·i·ent (im′pər sip′ē ənt), *adj.* lacking perception; imperceptive. [1805–15; IM-[2] + PERCIPIENT] —**im′per·cip′i·ence,** *n.*

imperf., imperfect.

im·per·fect (im pûr′fikt), *adj.* **1.** of, pertaining to, or characterized by defects or weaknesses: *imperfect vision.* **2.** not perfect; lacking completeness: *imperfect knowledge.* **3.** *Gram.* noting action or state still in process at some temporal point of reference, particularly in the past. **4.** *Law.* being without legal effect or support; unenforceable. **5.** *Bot.* (of a flower) diclinous. **6.** *Music.* of or relating to the interval of a major or minor third or sixth. Cf. **perfect** (def. 12a). —*n. Gram.* **7.** the imperfect tense. **8.** another verb formation or construction with imperfect meaning. **9.** a form in the imperfect, as Latin *portābam,* "I was carrying." [1300–50; < L *imperfectus* unfinished (see IM-[2], PERFECT); r. ME *imparfit* < MF *imparfait* < L, as above] —**im·per′fect·ly,** *adv.* —**im·per′fect·ness,** *n.*
—**Syn. 1.** defective, faulty. **2.** incomplete, underdeveloped; immature. —**Ant. 2.** complete, developed.

imper′fect contri′tion. See under **contrition** (def. 2).

imper′fect fun′gus, a fungus for which only the asexual reproductive stage is known, as any fungus of the Fungi Imperfecti. [1890–95]

im·per·fect·i·ble (im′pər fek′tə bəl), *adj.* that cannot be perfected. [1865–70; IM-[2] + PERFECTIBLE] —**im′per·fect′i·bil′i·ty,** *n.*

im·per·fec·tion (im′pər fek′shən), *n.* **1.** an imperfect detail; flaw: *a law full of imperfections.* **2.** the quality or condition of being imperfect. [1350–1400; ME *imperfeccio(u)n* < LL *imperfectiōn-* (s. of *imperfectiō*) incompleteness. See IM-[2], PERFECTION]

im·per·fec·tive (im′pər fek′tiv), *Gram.* —*adj.* **1.** noting an aspect of the verb, as in Russian, that indicates incompleteness of the action or state at a temporal point of reference. —*n.* **2.** the imperfective aspect. **3.** a verb in this aspect. [1670–80; IMPERFECT + -IVE]

imper′fect rhyme′, *Pros.* See **slant rhyme.**

imper′fect stage′, *Mycol.* a phase in the life cycle of certain fungi in which either no spores or asexual spores, as conidia, are produced. [1890–95]

im·per·fo·rate (im pûr′fər it, -fə rāt′), *adj.* **1.** Also, **im·per′fo·rat′ed.** not perforate; having no perforation. **2.** *Philately.* (of a number of stamps joined together) lacking the perforations usually separating individual stamps. —*n.* **3.** an imperforate stamp. [1665–75; IM-[2] + PERFORATE] —**im·per′fo·ra′tion,** *n.*

Im·pe·ria (ēm pe′ʀyä), *n.* a seaport in NW Italy. 41,874.

im·pe·ri·al[1] (im pēr′ē əl), *adj.* **1.** of, like, or pertaining to an empire. **2.** of, like, or pertaining to an emperor or empress. **3.** characterizing the rule or authority of a sovereign state over its dependencies. **4.** of the nature or rank of an emperor or supreme ruler. **5.** of a commanding quality, manner, aspect, etc. **6.** domineering; imperious. **7.** befitting an emperor or empress; regal; majestic; very fine or grand; magnificent. **8.** of special or superior size or quality, as various products and commodities. **9.** (of weights and measures) conforming to the standards legally established in Great Britain. —*n.* **10.** a size of printing or drawing paper, 22 × 30 in. (56 × 76 cm) in England, 23 × 33 in. (58 × 84 cm) in America. **11. imperial octavo,** a size of book, about 8¼ × 11½ in. (21 × 29 cm), untrimmed, in America, and 7½ × 11 in. (19 × 28 cm), untrimmed, in England. *Abbr.:* imperial 8vo **12. imperial quarto,** *Chiefly Brit.* a size of book, about 11 × 15 in. (28 × 38 cm), untrimmed. *Abbr.:* imperial 4to **13.** the top of a carriage, esp. of a diligence. **14.** a case for luggage carried there. **15.** a member of an imperial party or of imperial troops. **16.** an emperor or empress. **17.** any of various articles of special size or quality. **18.** an oversized bottle used esp. for storing Bordeaux wine, equivalent to 8 regular bottles or 6 l (6.6 qt.). [1325–75; ME < LL *imperiālis,* equiv. to L *imperi(um)* IMPERIUM + *-ālis* -AL[1]; r. ME *emperial* < MF < LL, as above] —**im·pe′ri·al·ly,** *adv.* —**im·pe′ri·al·ness,** *n.*
—**Syn. 6.** despotic, high-handed, authoritarian.

imperial[2]

im·pe·ri·al[2] (im pēr′ē əl), *n.* a small, pointed beard beneath the lower lip. [1835–45; < F *impériale,* n. use of fem. of *impérial* IMPERIAL[1]]

im·pe·ri·al[3] (im pēr′ē əl), *n.* a Russian gold coin originally worth 10 rubles and from 1897 to 1917 worth 15 rubles. [1830–40; < Russ *imperiál* << ML *imperiālis* a coin, n. use of LL *imperiālis* IMPERIAL[1]]

CONCISE ETYMOLOGY KEY: <, descended or borrowed from; >, whence; b., blend of, blended; c., cognate with; cf., compare; deriv., derivative; equiv., equivalent; imit., imitative; obl., oblique; r., replacing; s., stem; sp., spelling, spelled; resp., respelling, respelled; trans., translation; ?, origin unknown; *, unattested; ‡, probably earlier than. See the full key inside the front cover.

Impe′rial Beach′, a city in SW California, near San Diego. 22,689.

Impe′rial bush′el. See under **bushel**[1] (def. 1).

impe′rial ea′gle, a brown eagle, *Aquila heliaca,* of Asia and southern Europe: the subspecies *A. heliaca adalberti* is endangered.

impe′rial gal′lon, a British gallon equivalent to 1⅕ U.S. gallons, or 277.42 cubic inches. [1830–40]

im·pe·ri·al·ism (im pēr′ē ə liz′əm), *n.* **1.** the policy of extending the rule or authority of an empire or nation over foreign countries, or of acquiring and holding colonies and dependencies. **2.** advocacy of imperial interests. **3.** an imperial system of government. **4.** imperial government. **5.** *Brit.* the policy of so uniting the separate parts of an empire with separate governments as to secure for certain purposes a single state. [1855–60; IMPERIAL[1] + -ISM] —**im·pe′ri·al·ist,** *n., adj.* —**im·pe′ri·al·is′tic,** *adj.* —**im·pe′ri·al·is′ti·cal·ly,** *adv.*

impe′rial jade′, transparent jadeite of gem quality; a true jade. Also called **gem jade.**

impe′rial moth′, a yellow moth, *Eacles imperialis,* having a diagonal band of pinkish brown or purple: the hairy larvae feed on the leaves of hickory, oak, etc. [1900–05]

impe′rial pres′idency, (*sometimes caps.*) a U.S. presidency that is characterized by greater power than the Constitution allows. [1970–75]

Impe′rial Val′ley, an irrigated agricultural region in SE California, adjacent to Mexico, formerly a part of the Colorado Desert: it is largely below sea level and contains the Salton Sink.

im·per·il (im per′əl), *v.t.,* **-iled, -il·ing** or (*esp. Brit.*) **-illed, -il·ling.** to put in peril or danger; endanger. [1590–1600; IM-[1] + PERIL] —**im·per′il·ment,** *n.*
—**Syn.** risk, jeopardize, hazard, chance.

im·pe·ri·ous (im pēr′ē əs), *adj.* **1.** domineering in a haughty manner; dictatorial; overbearing: *an imperious manner; an imperious person.* **2.** urgent; imperative: *imperious need.* [1535–45; < L *imperiōsus* commanding, tyrannical, equiv. to *imperi(um)* IMPERIUM + *-ōsus* -OUS] —**im·pe′ri·ous·ly,** *adv.* —**im·pe′ri·ous·ness,** *n.*
—**Syn. 1.** tyrannical, despotic, arrogant. **2.** necessary. —**Ant. 1.** submissive. **2.** unnecessary.

im·per·ish·a·ble (im per′i shə bəl), *adj.* not subject to decay; indestructible; enduring. [1640–50; IM-[2] + PERISHABLE] —**im·per′ish·a·bil′i·ty, im·per′ish·a·ble·ness,** *n.* —**im·per′ish·a·bly,** *adv.*

im·pe·ri·um (im pēr′ē əm), *n., pl.* **-pe·ri·a** (-pēr′ē ə), **-pe·ri·ums. 1.** command; supreme power. **2.** area of dominion; sphere of control or monopoly; empire. **3.** a nation having or exerting supreme power; superpower. **4.** *Law.* the right to command the force of the state in order to enforce the law. [1645–55; < L: supreme administrative power, authority, empire, equiv. to *imper(āre)* to rule (see IMPERATIVE) + *-ium* -IUM]

im·per·ma·nent (im pûr′mə nənt), *adj.* not permanent or enduring; transitory. [1645–55; IM-[2] + PERMANENT] —**im·per′ma·nence, im·per′ma·nen·cy,** *n.* —**im·per′ma·nent·ly,** *adv.*
—**Syn.** fleeting, temporary, ephemeral, evanescent.

im·per·me·a·ble (im pûr′mē ə bəl), *adj.* **1.** not permeable; impassable. **2.** *Chem., Geol.* (of porous substances, rocks, etc.) not permitting the passage of a fluid through the pores, interstices, etc. [1690–1700; < LL *impermeābilis.* See IM-[2], PERMEABLE] —**im·per′me·a·bil′i·ty, im·per′me·a·ble·ness,** *n.* —**im·per′me·a·bly,** *adv.*

im·per·mis·si·ble (im′pər mis′ə bəl), *adj.* not permissible or allowable; unallowable. [1855–60; IM-[2] + PERMISSIBLE] —**im′per·mis′si·bil′i·ty,** *n.*

impers., impersonal.

im·per·son·al (im pûr′sə nl), *adj.* **1.** not personal; without reference or connection to a particular person: *an impersonal remark.* **2.** having no personality; devoid of human character or traits: *an impersonal deity.* **3.** lacking human emotion or warmth: *an impersonal manner.* **4.** *Gram.* **a.** (of a verb) having only third person singular forms and rarely if ever accompanied by an expressed subject, as Latin *pluit* "it is raining," or regularly accompanied by an empty subject word, as English *to rain* in *It is raining.* **b.** (of a pronoun or pronominal reference) indefinite, as French *on* "one." —*n.* **5.** *Gram.* an impersonal verb or pronoun. [1510–20; < LL *impersōnālis.* See IM-[2], PERSONAL] —**im·per′son·al·ly,** *adv.*

im·per·son·al·ism (im pûr′sə nl iz′əm), *n.* **1.** the practice of maintaining impersonal relations with individuals or groups. **2.** impersonality. [1895–1900; IMPERSONAL + -ISM]

im·per·son·al·i·ty (im pûr′sə nal′i tē), *n., pl.* **-ties** for 6. **1.** absence of human character or of the traits associated with the human character: *He feared the impersonality of a mechanized world.* **2.** absence or reduction of concern for individual needs or desires: *the impersonality of a very large institution.* **3.** lack of emotional involvement: *His work reflected a certain impersonality.* **4.** lack of a personal agent or of a known personal agent: *the impersonality of folk art.* **5.** the quality of not being concerned with particular persons: *the impersonality and universality of his interests.* **6.** something that is impersonal. [1760–70; IMPERSONAL + -ITY]

im·per·son·al·ize (im pûr′sə nl īz′), *v.t.,* **-ized, -iz·ing.** to make impersonal: *The dial system impersonalized the telephone.* Also, *esp. Brit.,* **im·per′son·al·ise′.** [1875–80; IMPERSONAL + -IZE] —**im·per′son·al·i·za′tion,** *n.*

im·per·son·ate (*v.* im pûr′sə nāt′; *adj.* im pûr′sə nit, -nāt′), *v.,* **-at·ed, -at·ing,** *adj.* —*v.t.* **1.** to assume the character or appearance of; pretend to be: *He was arrested for impersonating a police officer.* **2.** to mimic the voice, mannerisms, etc., of (a person) in order to entertain. **3.** to act or play the part of; personate. **4.** *Archaic.* to represent in personal or bodily form; personify; typify. —*adj.* **5.** embodied in a person; invested with personality. [1615–25; IM-[1] + PERSON + -ATE[1]] —**im·per′son·a′tion,** *n.*

im·per·son·a·tor (im pûr′sə nā′tər), *n.* **1.** a person who pretends to be another. **2.** an actor who impersonates specific persons or types of persons as a form of entertainment. **3.** See **female impersonator.** [1850–55; IMPERSONATE + -OR[2]]

im·per·ti·nence (im pûr′tn əns), *n.* **1.** unmannerly intrusion or presumption; insolence. **2.** impertinent quality or action. **3.** something impertinent, as an act or statement. **4.** an impertinent person. **5.** irrelevance, inappropriateness, or absurdity. [1595–1605; IMPERTIN(ENCY) + -ENCE]

im·per·ti·nen·cy (im pûr′tn ən sē), *n., pl.* **-cies.** impertinence. [1580–90; < ML *impertinentia.* See IMPERTINENT, -ENCY]

im·per·ti·nent (im pûr′tn ənt), *adj.* **1.** intrusive or presumptuous, as persons or their actions; insolently rude; uncivil: *a brash, impertinent youth.* **2.** not pertinent or relevant; irrelevant: *an impertinent detail.* **3.** *Archaic.* inappropriate, incongruous, or absurd. **4.** *Obs.* (of persons) trivial, silly, or absurd. [1350–1400; ME < LL *impertinent-* (s. of *impertinēns*) not belonging. See IM-[2], PERTINENT] —**im·per′ti·nent·ly,** *adv.* —**im·per′ti·nent·ness,** *n.*
—**Syn. 1.** fresh, bold, insulting, officious, saucy, pert, brazen. IMPERTINENT, IMPUDENT, INSOLENT refer to bold, rude, and arrogant behavior. IMPERTINENT, from its primary meaning of not pertinent and hence inappropriate or out of place, has come to imply often an unseemly intrusion into what does not concern one, or a presumptuous rudeness toward one entitled to deference or respect: *an impertinent interruption, question, manner toward a teacher.* IMPUDENT suggests a bold and shameless impertinence: *an impudent speech, young rascal.* INSOLENT suggests insulting or arrogantly contemptuous behavior: *unbearably insolent toward those in authority.* —**Ant. 1.** polite.

im·per·turb·a·ble (im′pər tûr′bə bəl), *adj.* incapable of being upset or agitated; not easily excited; calm: *imperturbable composure.* [1490–1500; < LL *imperturbābilis.* See IM-[2], PERTURBABLE] —**im′per·turb′a·bil′i·ty, im′per·turb′a·ble·ness,** *n.* —**im′per·turb′a·bly,** *adv.*
—**Syn.** composed, collected, impassive, cool, unmoved.

im·per·tur·ba·tion (im′pər tər bā′shən), *n.* freedom from perturbation; tranquillity; calmness. [1640–50; < LL *imperturbātiōn-* (s. of *imperturbātiō*). See IM-[2], PERTURBATION]

im·per·vi·ous (im pûr′vē əs), *adj.* **1.** not permitting penetration or passage; impenetrable: *The coat is impervious to rain.* **2.** incapable of being injured or impaired: *impervious to wear and tear.* **3.** incapable of being influenced, persuaded, or affected: *impervious to reason; impervious to another's suffering.* Also, **im·per·vi·a·ble** (im pûr′vē ə bəl). [1640–50; < L *impervius.* See IM-[2], PERVIOUS] —**im·per′vi·ous·ly,** *adv.* —**im·per′vi·ous·ness,** *n.*
—**Syn. 3.** invulnerable, closed.

im·pe·ti·go (im′pi tī′gō), *n. Pathol.* a contagious skin disease, esp. of children, usually caused by streptococcal bacteria, marked by a superficial pustular eruption, particularly on the face. [1350–1400; ME < L *impetīgō,* equiv. to *impet(ere)* to make for, attack (see IMPETUS) + *-īgō,* as in *vertīgō* VERTIGO] —**im·pe·tig·i·nous** (im′pi tij′ə nəs), *adj.*

im·pe·trate (im′pi trāt′), *v.t.,* **-trat·ed, -trat·ing. 1.** to obtain by entreaty. **2.** to entreat; ask for. [1525–35; < L *impetrātus* ptp. of *impetrāre* to obtain by asking, equiv. to *im-* IM-[1] + *-petrā(re),* comb. form of *patrāre* to bring to completion, accomplish, deriv. of *pater* FATHER + *-tus* ptp. suffix] —**im′pe·tra′tion,** *n.* —**im′pe·tra′tive, im·pe·tra·to·ry** (im′pi trə tôr′ē, -tōr′ē), *adj.* —**im′pe·tra′tor,** *n.*

im·pet·u·os·i·ty (im pech′o͞o os′i tē), *n., pl.* **-ties** for 2. **1.** the quality or condition of being impetuous. **2.** an impetuous action. [1575–85; < LL *impetuōs(us)* IMPETUOUS + -ITY]

im·pet·u·ous (im pech′o͞o əs), *adj.* **1.** of, pertaining to, or characterized by sudden or rash action, emotion, etc.; impulsive: *an impetuous decision; an impetuous person.* **2.** having great impetus; moving with great force; violent: *the impetuous winds.* [1350–1400; ME < AF < LL *impetuōsus,* equiv. to L *impetu(s)* IMPETUS + *-ōsus* -OUS] —**im·pet′u·ous·ly,** *adv.* —**im·pet′u·ous·ness,** *n.*
—**Syn. 1.** eager, headlong. IMPETUOUS, IMPULSIVE both refer to persons who are hasty and precipitate in action, or to actions not preceded by thought. IMPETUOUS suggests eagerness, violence, rashness: *impetuous vivacity; impetuous desire; impetuous words.* IMPULSIVE emphasizes spontaneity and lack of reflection: *an impulsive act of generosity.* —**Ant. 1.** planned, careful.

im·pe·tus (im′pi təs), *n., pl.* **-tus·es. 1.** a moving force; impulse; stimulus: *The grant for building the opera house gave impetus to the city's cultural life.* **2.** (broadly) the momentum of a moving body, esp. with reference to the cause of motion. [1650–60; < L: an attack, lit., a rushing into, perh. by haplology from **impetitus* (though the expected form would be **impetītus;* see APPETITE), equiv. to *impeti-,* var. s. of *impetere* to attack (*im-* IM-[1] + *petere* to make for, assault) + *-tus* suffix of v. action]
—**Syn. 1.** stimulation, spur, boost.

impf., imperfect.

imp. gal., imperial gallon.

Imp·hal (imp′hul), *n.* a city in and the capital of Manipur state, in NE India. 100,605.

im·pi (im′pē), *n., pl.* **-pies, -pis.** (in South African history) a unit of Zulu warriors; regiment. [1875–80; < Zulu: impi, armed force, battle]

im·pi·e·ty (im pī′i tē), *n., pl.* **-ties. 1.** lack of piety; lack of reverence for God or sacred things; irreverence. **2.** lack of dutifulness or respect. **3.** an impious act, practice, etc. [1300–50; ME *impietie* < L *impietās,* equiv. to *impi(us)* IMPIOUS + *-etās*, var., after vowels, of *-itās* -ITY]

im•pinge (im pinj′), *v.*, **-pinged, -ping•ing.** —*v.i.* **1.** to make an impression; have an effect or impact (usually fol. by *on* or *upon*): *to impinge upon the imagination; social pressures that impinge upon one's daily life.* **2.** to encroach; infringe (usually fol. by *on* or *upon*): *to impinge on another's rights.* **3.** to strike; dash; collide (usually fol. by *on, upon,* or *against*): *rays of light impinging on the eye.* —*v.t.* **4.** *Obs.* to come into violent contact with. [1525–35; < ML *impingere* to strike against, drive at, equiv. to L *im-* IM-[1] + *-pingere,* comb. form of *pangere* to fasten, drive in, fix; see IMPACT] —**im•ping′ent,** *adj.* —**im•ping′er,** *n.* —**im•pinge′ment,** *n.*

im•pi•ous (im′pē əs, im pī′-), *adj.* **1.** not pious or religious; lacking reverence for God, religious practices, etc.; irreligious; ungodly. **2.** disrespectful. [1565–75; < L *impius.* See IM-[2], PIOUS] —**im′pi•ous•ly,** *adv.* —**im′pi•ous•ness,** *n.*
—**Syn. 1.** sacrilegious, blasphemous, irreverent.

imp•ish (im′pish), *adj.* **1.** mischievous. **2.** of, pertaining to, or characteristic of an imp. [1645–55; IMP + -ISH[1]] —**imp′ish•ly,** *adv.* —**imp′ish•ness,** *n.*

im•plac•a•ble (im plak′ə bəl, -plā′kə-), *adj.* not to be appeased, mollified, or pacified; inexorable: *an implacable enemy.* [1375–1425; late ME < L *implācābilis.* See IM-[2], PLACABLE] —**im•plac′a•bil′i•ty, im•plac′a•ble•ness,** *n.* —**im•plac′a•bly,** *adv.*
—**Syn.** unappeasable, unbending, merciless. See **inflexible.**

im•pla•cen•tal (im′plə sen′tl), *adj.* **1.** *Zool.* having no placenta, as a monotreme or marsupial. —*n.* **2.** an implacental mammal. Also, **im•pla•cen•tate** (im′plə sen′tāt). [1830–40; IM-[2] + PLACENTAL]

im•plant (*v.* im plant′, -plänt′; *n.* im′plant′, -plänt′), *v.t.* **1.** to put or fix firmly: *to implant sound principles in a child's mind.* **2.** to plant securely. **3.** *Med.* to insert or graft (a tissue, organ, or inert substance) into the body. —*n.* **4.** *Med.* **a.** any device or material, esp. of an inert substance, used for repairing or replacing part of the body. **b.** medication or radioactive material inserted into tissue for sustained therapy. **c.** implantation (def. 1). **5.** *Dentistry.* **a.** an artificial tooth that has been inserted permanently into the jaw. **b.** a metal framework attached to the bones of the jaw for supporting artificial teeth. [1535–45; IM-[1] + PLANT] —**im•plant′er,** *n.*

im•plant•a•ble (im plan′tə bəl, -plän′-), *adj.* **1.** capable of being implanted. **2.** pertaining to a device, as a micropump or porous polymer membrane, for surgical insertion under the skin for the controlled release of a drug. —*n.* **3.** *Surg.* a material, foreign to the body, that can be implanted without undue risk of rejection. [1955–60; IMPLANT + -ABLE]

im•plan•ta•tion (im′plan tā′shən), *n.* **1.** the act of implanting. **2.** the state of being implanted. **3.** *Pathol.* **a.** the movement of cells to a new region. **b.** metastasis, when spontaneous. **4.** *Med.* the application of solid medicine underneath the skin. **5.** *Embryol.* the attachment of the early embryo to the lining of the uterus. [1570–80; IMPLANT + -ATION]

im•plan•tol•o•gy (im′plan tol′ə jē), *n.* the branch of dentistry dealing with the permanent implantation or attachment of artificial teeth in the jaw. [IMPLANT + -O- + -LOGY] —**im′plan•tol′o•gist,** *n.*

im•plau•si•ble (im plô′zə bəl), *adj.* not plausible; not having the appearance of truth or credibility: *an implausible alibi.* [1595–1605; IM-[2] + PLAUSIBLE] —**im•plau′si•bil′i•ty, im•plau′si•ble•ness,** *n.* —**im•plau′si•bly,** *adv.*
—**Syn.** unlikely, improbable, unbelievable.

im•plead (im plēd′), *v.t.*, **-plead•ed** or **-plead** (-pled′) or **-pled, -plead•ing. 1.** to sue in a court of law. **2.** to bring (a new party) into an action because he or she is or may be liable to the impleading party for all or part of the claim against that party. **3.** to accuse; impeach. **4.** *Archaic.* to plead (a suit). [1250–1300; late ME *impleden,* ME *empleden* < AF *empleder.* See IM-[1], PLEAD] —**im•plead′a•ble,** *adj.*

im•plead•er (im plē′dər), *n. Law.* a procedural method by which an original party to an action may bring in and make a claim against a third party in connection with the claim made against the original party. Also called **third party procedure.** [1570–80; IMPLEAD + -ER[1]]

im•ple•ment (*n.* im′plə mənt; *v.* im′plə ment′, -mənt), *n.* **1.** any article used in some activity, esp. an instrument, tool, or utensil: *agricultural implements.* **2.** an article of equipment, as household furniture, clothing, ecclesiastical vestments, or the like. **3.** a means; agent: *human beings as an implement of divine plan.* —*v.t.* **4.** to fulfill; perform; carry out: *Once in office, he failed to implement his campaign promises.* **5.** to put into effect according to or by means of a definite plan or procedure. **6.** to fill out or supplement. **7.** to provide with implements. [1425–75; late ME < LL *implēmentum* a filling up, equiv. to L *implē(re)* to fill up (*im-* IM-[1] + *plēre* to FILL) + *-mentum* -MENT] —**im′ple•ment′a•ble,** *adj.* —**im′ple•men′tal,** *adj.* —**im′ple•men•ta′tion,** *n.* —**im′ple•ment′er, im′ple•men′tor,** *n.*
—**Syn. 1.** See **tool.**

im•pli•cate (im′pli kāt′), *v.t.*, **-cat•ed, -cat•ing. 1.** to show to be also involved, usually in an incriminating manner: *to be implicated in a crime.* **2.** to imply as a necessary circumstance, or as something to be inferred or understood. **3.** to connect or relate to intimately; affect as a consequence: *The malfunctioning of one part of the nervous system implicates another part.* **4.** *Archaic.* to fold or twist together; intertwine; interlace. [1530–40; < L *implicātus* ptp. of *implicāre* to interweave, equiv. to *im-* IM-[1] + *plicā(re)* to PLY[2] + *-ātus* -ATE[1]]
—**Syn. 1.** See **involve.**

im•pli•ca•tion (im′pli kā′shən), *n.* **1.** something implied or suggested as naturally to be inferred or understood: *to resent an implication of dishonesty.* **2.** the act of implying: *His implication of immediate changes surprised us.* **3.** the state of being implied: *to know only by implication.* **4.** *Logic.* the relation that holds between two propositions, or classes of propositions, in virtue of which one is logically deducible from the other. **5.** the act of implicating: *the implication of his accomplices.* **6.** the state of being implicated: *We heard of his implication in a conspiracy.* **7.** Usually, **implications.** relationships of a close or intimate nature; involvements: *the religious implications of ancient astrology.* [1400–50; late ME *implicacio(u)n* < L *implicātiōn-* (s. of *implicātiō*) an interweaving, equiv. to *implicāt(us)* (see IMPLICATE) + *-iōn-* -ION] —**im′pli•ca′tion•al,** *adj.*
—**Syn. 7.** associations, connections.

im•pli•ca•tive (im′pli kā′tiv, im plik′ə tiv), *adj.* tending to implicate or imply; characterized by or involving implication. [1580–90; IMPLICATE + -IVE] —**im′pli•ca′tive•ly,** *adv.*

im•pli•ca•to•ry (im′pli kə tôr′ē, -tōr′ē), *adj.* implicative. [1635–45; IMPLICATE + -ORY[1]]

im•pli•ca•ture (im′pli kə chər), *n. Philos., Ling.* potential inference that is not logical entailment. Cf. **conversational implicature.** [IMPLICATE + -URE]

im•plic•it (im plis′it), *adj.* **1.** implied, rather than expressly stated: *implicit agreement.* **2.** unquestioning or unreserved; absolute: *implicit trust; implicit obedience; implicit confidence.* **3.** potentially contained (usually fol. by *in*): *to bring out the drama implicit in the occasion.* **4.** *Math.* (of a function) having the dependent variable not explicitly expressed in terms of the independent variables, as $x^2 + y^2 = 1$. Cf. **explicit** (def. 5). **5.** *Obs.* entangled. [1590–1600; < L *implicitus* involved, obscure, var. ptp. of *implicāre.* See IMPLICATE, -ITE[2]] —**im•plic′it•ly,** *adv.* —**im•plic′it•ness, im•plic′i•ty,** *n.*
—**Syn. 2.** inherent, complete, total.

implic′it differentia′tion, *Math.* a method of finding the derivative of an implicit function by taking the derivative of each term with respect to the independent variable while keeping the derivative of the dependent variable with respect to the independent variable in symbolic form and then solving for that derivative. [1890–95]

implic′it func′tion the′orem, *Math.* a theorem that gives conditions under which a function written in implicit form can be written in explicit form.

im•plied (im plīd′), *adj.* involved, indicated, or suggested without being directly or explicitly stated; tacitly understood: *an implied rebuke; an implied compliment.* [1520–30; IMPLY + -ED[2]] —**im•pli•ed•ly** (im plī′id lē), *adv.*

implied′ consent′, *Law.* a manifestation of consent to something through conduct, including inaction or silence. [1965–70]

implied′ war′ranty, a warranty not stated explicitly by the seller of merchandise or real property but presumed for reasons of commercial or legal custom (distinguished from *express warranty*). [1930–35]

im•plode (im plōd′), *v.*, **-plod•ed, -plod•ing.** —*v.i.* **1.** to burst inward (opposed to *explode*). —*v.t.* **2.** *Phonet.* to pronounce by implosion. [1880–85; IM-[1] + (EX)PLODE]

im•plore (im plôr′, -plōr′), *v.*, **-plored, -plor•ing.** —*v.t.* **1.** to beg urgently or piteously, as for aid or mercy; beseech; entreat: *They implored him to go.* **2.** to beg urgently or piteously for (aid, mercy, pardon, etc.): *implore forgiveness.* —*v.i.* **3.** to make urgent or piteous supplication. [1530–40; < L *implōrāre,* equiv. to *im-* IM-[1] + *plōrāre* to lament] —**im•plor′a•ble,** *adj.* —**im′plo•ra′tion,** *n.* —**im•plor•a•to•ry** (im plôr′ə tôr′ē, -plōr′ə tōr′ē), *adj.* —**im•plor′er,** *n.* —**im•plor′ing•ly,** *adv.* —**im•plor′ing•ness,** *n.*
—**Syn. 2.** crave, beg, solicit. —**Ant. 2.** spurn, reject.

im•plo•sion (im plō′zhən), *n.* **1.** the act of imploding; a bursting inward (opposed to *explosion*). **2.** *Phonet.* **a.** the occlusive phase of stop consonants. **b.** (of a stop consonant) the nasal release heard in the common pronunciation of *eaten, sudden,* or *mitten,* in which the vowel of the final syllable is greatly reduced. **c.** the ingressive release of a suction stop. Cf. **plosion.** [1875–80; IM-[1] + (EX)PLOSION]

implo′sion ther′apy, *Psychiatry.* a form of behavior therapy involving intensive recollection and review of anxiety-producing situations or events in a patient's life in an attempt to develop more appropriate responses to similar situations in the future. Also called **implo′sive ther′apy.**

im•plo•sive (im plō′siv), *Phonet.* —*adj.* **1.** characterized by a partial vacuum behind the point of closure. —*n.* **2.** an implosive stop. [1875–80; IM-[1] + (EX)PLOSIVE] —**im•plo′sive•ly,** *adv.*

im•plu•vi•um (im plo͞o′vē əm), *n., pl.* **-vi•a** (-vē ə). a basin or tank within a compluvium. [1805–15; < L, equiv. to *impluv-,* base of *impluere* to rain (upon, into) (*im-* IM-[1] + *pluere* to rain; cf. PLUVIAL) + *-ium* -IUM]

im•ply (im plī′), *v.t.*, **-plied, -ply•ing. 1.** to indicate or suggest without being explicitly stated: *His words implied a lack of faith.* **2.** (of words) to signify or mean. **3.** to involve as a necessary circumstance: *Speech implies a speaker.* **4.** *Obs.* to enfold. [1325–75; ME *implien, emplien* < MF *emplier* < L *implicāre;* see IMPLICATE]
—**Syn. 3.** assume, include.
—**Usage.** See **infer.**

im•po•lite (im′pə līt′), *adj.* not polite or courteous; discourteous; rude: *an impolite reply.* [1605–15; < L *impolītus* rough, unpolished. See IM-[2] POLITE] —**im′po•lite′ly,** *adv.* —**im′po•lite′ness,** *n.*
—**Syn.** disrespectful; uncivil; insolent; boorish, ill-mannered, rough.

im•pol•i•tic (im pol′i tik), *adj.* not politic, expedient, or judicious. [1590–1600; IM-[2] + POLITIC] —**im•pol′i•tic•ly,** *adv.* —**im•pol′i•tic•ness,** *n.*

im•pon•der•a•bil•i•a (im pon′dər ə bil′ē ə, -bil′yə), *n.pl.* imponderables: *the imponderabilia surrounding human life.* [1920–25; < NL, neut. pl. of ML *imponderābilis* IMPONDERABLE]

im•pon•der•a•ble (im pon′dər ə bəl), *adj.* **1.** not ponderable; that cannot be precisely determined, measured, or evaluated. —*n.* **2.** an imponderable thing, force, agency, etc. [1785–95; < ML *imponderābilis.* See IM-[2], PONDERABLE] —**im•pon′der•a•bil′i•ty, im•pon′der•a•ble•ness,** *n.* —**im•pon′der•a•bly,** *adv.*

im•pone (im pōn′), *v.t.*, **-poned, -pon•ing.** *Obs.* to wager; stake. [1520–30; < L *impōnere* to put in or upon, impose, equiv. to *im-* IM-[1] + *pōnere* to put, place; see POSE[1]]

im•port (*v.* im pôrt′, -pōrt′; *n.* im′pôrt, -pōrt), *v.t.* **1.** to bring in (merchandise, commodities, workers, etc.) from a foreign country for use, sale, processing, reexport, or services. **2.** to bring or introduce from one use, connection, or relation into another: *foreign bodies imported into the blood; foodstuffs imported from the farm.* **3.** to convey as meaning or implication; signify: *Her words imported a change of attitude.* **4.** to involve as a necessary circumstance; imply: *Religion imports belief.* **5.** *Archaic.* to be of consequence or importance to; concern. —*v.i.* **6.** to be of consequence or importance; matter. —*n.* **7.** something that is imported from abroad; an imported commodity or article. **8.** the act of importing or bringing in; importation, as of goods from abroad: *the import of foreign cars.* **9.** consequence or importance: *matters of great import.* **10.** meaning; implication; purport: *He felt the import of her words.* [1400–50; late ME *importen* < L *importāre.* See IM-[1], PORT[5]] —**im•port′a•ble,** *adj.* —**im•port′a•bil′i•ty,** *n.* —**im•port′er,** *n.*
—**Syn. 10.** significance, sense.

im•por•tance (im pôr′tns), *n.* **1.** the quality or state of being important; consequence; significance. **2.** important position or standing; personal or social consequence. **3.** consequential air or manner: *an air of bustling importance.* **4.** *Obs.* an important matter. **5.** *Obs.* importunity. **6.** *Obs.* import or meaning. [1495–1505; < ML *importantia.* See IMPORTANT, -ANCE]
—**Syn. 1.** moment, weight, concern. IMPORTANCE, CONSEQUENCE, SIGNIFICANCE, MOMENT all signify something valuable, influential, or worthy of note. IMPORTANCE is the most general of these, assigning exceptional or notable value or influence to a person or thing: *the importance of Einstein's discoveries.* CONSEQUENCE may suggest outstanding personal quality or position, or it may suggest importance because of results to be produced: *a woman of consequence in world affairs; an event of great consequence for our future.* SIGNIFICANCE can be used interchangeably with *importance* or *consequence,* but it carries also the implication of importance that is not readily or immediately recognized: *The significance of the discovery only became clear years later.* MOMENT, on the other hand, almost always refers to immediately apparent, self-evident importance: *a change of great moment for the nation's political system.*

Impor′tance of Be′ing Ear′nest, The, a comedy (1895) by Oscar Wilde.

im•por•tant (im pôr′tnt), *adj.* **1.** of much or great significance or consequence: *an important event in world history.* **2.** mattering much (usually fol. by *to*): *details important to a fair decision.* **3.** entitled to more than ordinary consideration or notice: *an important exception.* **4.** prominent or large: *He played an important part in national politics.* **5.** of considerable influence or authority, as a person or position: *an important scientist.* **6.** having social position or distinction, as a person or family: *important guests.* **7.** pompous; pretentious: *When speaking, he assumes an important attitude that offends his audience.* **8.** *Obs.* importunate. [1580–90; < ML *importānt-* (s. of *importāns* prp. of *importāre* to be of consequence, weigh, L: to carry in, import), equiv. to *im-* IM-[1] + *port-* PORT[5] + *-ant-* -ANT; see IMPORT] —**im•por′tant•ly,** *adv.*
—**Usage.** Both MORE IMPORTANT and MORE IMPORTANTLY occur at the beginning of a sentence in all varieties of standard English: *More important* (or *More importantly*), *her record as an administrator is unmatched.* Today, MORE IMPORTANTLY is the more common, even though some object to its use on the grounds that MORE IMPORTANT is an elliptical form of "What is more important" and that the adverb IMPORTANTLY could not occur in such a construction. MORE IMPORTANTLY probably developed by analogy with other sentence-modifying adverbs, as *curiously, fortunately,* and *regrettably.*

im•por•ta•tion (im′pôr tā′shən, -pōr-), *n.* **1.** the act of importing. **2.** something imported. [1595–1605; IMPORT + -ATION]

import′ed cur′rantworm. See under **currantworm.** [1890–95]

im•por•tee (im′pôr tē′, -pōr-), *n.* an imported person or thing. [1855–60; IMPORT + -EE]

im•por•tu•na•cy (im pôr′chə nə sē), *n.* the quality or condition of being importunate; importunateness. [1540–50; IMPORTUN(ATE) + -ACY]

im•por•tu•nate (im pôr′chə nit), *adj.* **1.** urgent or persistent in solicitation, sometimes annoyingly so. **2.** pertinacious, as solicitations or demands. **3.** troublesome; annoying: *importunate demands from the children for attention.* [1520–30; IMPORTUNE (adj.) + -ATE[1]] —**im•por′tu•nate•ly,** *adv.* —**im•por′tu•nate•ness,** *n.*

im•por•tune (im′pôr to͞on′, -tyo͞on′, im pôr′chən), *v.*, **-tuned, -tun•ing,** *adj.* —*v.t.* **1.** to press or beset with solicitations; demand with urgency or persistence. **2.** to make improper advances toward (a person). **3.** to beg for (something) urgently or persistently. **4.** *Obs.* to annoy. **5.** *Obs.* to press; impel. —*v.i.* **6.** to make urgent or persistent solicitations. **7.** to make improper advances toward another person. —*adj.* **8.** importunate. [1350–1400; ME (adj.) < L *importūnus* unsuitable, troublesome, relentless; see IM-[2], OPPORTUNE] —**im•por′tune′ly,** *adv.* —**im′por•tun′er,** *n.*

—Syn. 1, 3. beseech, entreat, implore, supplicate, solicit. **6.** plead.

im·por·tu·ni·ty (im′pôr to͞o′ni tē, -tyo͞o′-), *n., pl.* **-ties** for 2. **1.** the state or quality of being importunate; persistence in solicitation. **2. importunities,** importunate solicitations or demands. [1425–75; late ME *importunite* < L *importūnitās.* See IMPORTUNE, -ITY]

im·pose (im pōz′), *v.,* **-posed, -pos·ing.** *—v.t.* **1.** to lay on or set as something to be borne, endured, obeyed, fulfilled, paid, etc.: *to impose taxes.* **2.** to put or set by or as if by authority: *to impose one's personal preference on others.* **3.** to obtrude or thrust (oneself, one's company, etc.) upon others. **4.** to pass or palm off fraudulently or deceptively: *He imposed his pretentious books on the public.* **5.** *Print.* to lay (type pages, plates, etc.) in proper order on an imposing stone or the like and secure in a chase for printing. **6.** to lay on or inflict, as a penalty. **7.** *Archaic.* to put or place on something, or in a particular place. **8.** *Obs.* to lay on (the hands) ceremonially, as in confirmation or ordination. *—v.i.* **9.** to make an impression on the mind; impose one's or its authority or influence. **10.** to obtrude oneself or one's requirements, as upon others: *Are you sure my request doesn't impose?* **11.** to presume, as upon patience or good nature. **12. impose on** or **upon, a.** to thrust oneself offensively upon others; intrude. **b.** to take unfair advantage of; misuse (influence, friendship, etc.). **c.** to defraud; cheat; deceive: *A study recently showed the shocking number of confidence men that impose on the public.* [1475–85; late ME < MF *imposer,* equiv. to *im-* IM-[1] + *poser* to POSE[1]; see also POSE[2]] **—im·pos′a·ble,** *adj.* **—im·pos′er,** *n.*

—Syn. 3. force, foist.

im·pos·ing (im pō′zing), *adj.* very impressive because of great size, stately appearance, dignity, elegance, etc.: *Notre Dame, Rheims, and other imposing cathedrals of France.* [1645–55; IMPOSE + -ING[2]] **—im·pos′ing·ly,** *adv.* **—im·pos′ing·ness,** *n.*

—Syn. dignified, majestic, lofty, grand, august.

impos′ing stone′, *Print.* a slab, formerly of stone but now usually of metal, on which pages of type or plates are imposed and on which type correcting in the page is done. Also called **impos′ing ta′ble.** [1720–30]

im·po·si·tion (im′pə zish′ən), *n.* **1.** the laying on of something as a burden or obligation. **2.** something imposed, as a burden or duty; an unusual or extraordinarily burdensome requirement or task. **3.** the act of imposing by or as if by authority. **4.** an instance of imposing upon a person: *He did the favor but considered the request an imposition.* **5.** the act of imposing fraudulently or deceptively on others; imposture. **6.** the ceremonial laying on of hands, as in confirmation or ordination. **7.** *Print.* the arrangement of page plates in proper order on a press for printing a signature. **8.** the act of putting, placing, or laying on. [1325–75; ME *imposicioun* < LL *impositiōn-* (s. of *impositiō*), equiv. to *imposit(us)* ptp. of *impōnere* to place upon, impose (*im-* IM-[1] + *posi-,* var. s. of *pōnere* to put + *-tus* ptp. suffix) + *-iōn-* -ION]

im·pos·si·bil·i·ty (im pos′ə bil′i tē, im′pos-), *n., pl.* **-ties** for 2. **1.** condition or quality of being impossible. **2.** something impossible. [1350–1400; ME *impossibilite* < LL *impossibilitās.* See IM-[2], POSSIBILITY]

im·pos·si·ble (im pos′ə bəl), *adj.* **1.** not possible; unable to be, exist, happen, etc. **2.** unable to be done, performed, effected, etc.: *an impossible assignment.* **3.** incapable of being true, as a rumor. **4.** not to be done, endured, etc., with any degree of reason or propriety: *an impossible situation.* **5.** utterly impracticable: *an impossible plan.* **6.** hopelessly unsuitable, difficult, or objectionable. [1250–1300; ME < L *impossibilis.* See IM-[2], POSSIBLE] **—im·pos′si·ble·ness,** *n.* **—im·pos′si·bly,** *adv.*

—Syn. 6. unbearable, intolerable, unmanageable.

im·post[1] (im′pōst), *n.* **1.** a tax; tribute; duty. **2.** a customs duty. **3.** *Horse Racing.* the weight assigned to a horse in a race. *—v.t.* **4.** to determine customs duties on, according to the kind of imports. [1560–70; < ML *impostus* a tax, n. use of L *impostus,* var. of *impositus* imposed; see IMPOSITION] **—im′post·er,** *n.*

im·post[2] (im′pōst), *n. Archit.* **1.** the point of springing of an arch; spring. **2.** an architectural feature immediately beneath this point. See diag. under **arch.** [1655–65; < F *imposte* < It *imposta* < L: fem. of *impostus* (ptp.); see IMPOST[1]]

im′post block′, dosseret. [1900–05]

im·pos·tor (im pos′tər), *n.* a person who practices deception under an assumed character, identity, or name. Also, **im·post′er.** [1580–90; < LL, equiv. to L *impos(i)-,* var. s. of *impōnere* to deceive, place on (see IMPONE) + *-tor* -TOR]

im·pos·ture (im pos′chər), *n.* **1.** the action or practice of imposing fraudulently upon others. **2.** deception using an assumed character, identity, or name, as by an impostor. **3.** an instance or piece of fraudulent imposition. [1530–40; < LL *impostūra,* equiv. to L *impost(us)* ptp. of *impōnere* (see IMPOSTOR, IMPONE) + *-ūra* -URE] **—im·pos·trous** (im pos′trəs), **im·pos′tur·ous,** *adj.*

—Syn. 3. fraud, hoax, swindle, deception, humbug, cheat.

im·po·sure (im pō′zhər), *n.* the act of imposing: *the imposure of a decree.* [1675–85; IMPOSE + -URE]

im·po·tence (im′pə təns), *n.* **1.** the condition or quality of being impotent; weakness. **2.** chronic inability to attain or sustain an erection for the performance of a sexual act. **3.** sterility, esp. in the male. **4.** *Obs.* lack of self-restraint. Also, **im′po·ten·cy, im′po·tent·ness.** [1375–1425; late ME, var. (see -ENCE) of *impotencie* < L *impotentia* want of self-control, weakness. See IM-[2], POTENCY]

im·po·tent (im′pə tənt), *adj.* **1.** not potent; lacking power or ability. **2.** utterly unable (to do something). **3.** without force or effectiveness. **4.** lacking bodily strength or physically helpless. **5.** (of a male) unable to attain or sustain a penile erection. **6.** (esp. of a male) sterile. **7.** *Obs.* without restraint. *—n.* **8.** an impotent person: *therapy for sexual impotents.* [1350–1400; ME < L *impotent-* (s. of *impotēns*) without power over oneself or others. See IM-[2], POTENT[1]] **—im′po·tent·ly,** *adv.*

—Syn. 1, 2. powerless, helpless. **3.** ineffectual, ineffective, feeble, weak.

im·pound (*v.* im pound′; *n.* im′pound), *v.t.* **1.** to shut up in a pound or other enclosure, as a stray animal. **2.** to confine within an enclosure or within limits: *water impounded in a reservoir.* **3.** to seize and retain in custody of the law, as a document for evidence. *—n.* **4.** money, property, etc., that has been impounded: *a sale of impounds by the police department.* [1545–55; IM-[3] + POUND[3]] **—im·pound′a·ble,** *adj.* **—im·pound′er,** *n.*

im·pound·ment (im pound′mənt), *n.* **1.** a body of water confined within an enclosure, as a reservoir. **2.** the act of impounding: *the impoundment of alien property.* **3.** the condition of being impounded. Also, **im·pound′age.** [1655–65; IMPOUND + -MENT]

im·pov·er·ish (im pov′ər ish, -pov′rish), *v.t.* **1.** to reduce to poverty: *a country impoverished by war.* **2.** to make poor in quality, productiveness, etc.; exhaust the strength or richness of: *Bad farming practices impoverished the soil.* [1400–50; late ME *empoverishen* < MF *empovriss-* (long s. of *empovrir*), equiv. to *em-* EM-[1] + *povre* POOR + *-iss* -ISH[2]] **—im·pov′er·ish·er,** *n.* **—im·pov′er·ish·ment,** *n.*

—Syn. 2. deplete, drain; weaken, enervate, fatigue, cripple. **—Ant. 1, 2.** enrich.

im·pov·er·ished (im pov′ər isht, -pov′risht), *adj.* **1.** reduced to poverty. **2.** (of a country, area, etc.) having few trees, flowers, birds, wild animals, etc. **3.** deprived of strength, vitality, creativeness, etc.: *an impoverished attempt at humor.* [1625–35; IMPOVERISH + -ED[2]]

—Syn. 1. See **poor.**

im·prac·ti·ca·ble (im prak′ti kə bəl), *adj.* **1.** not practicable; incapable of being put into practice with the available means: *an impracticable plan.* **2.** unsuitable for practical use or purposes, as a device or material. **3.** (of ground, places, etc.) impassable. **4.** (of persons) hard to deal with because of stubbornness, stupidity, etc. [1645–55; IM-[2] + PRACTICABLE] **—im·prac′ti·ca·bil′i·ty, im·prac′ti·ca·ble·ness,** *n.* **—im·prac′ti·ca·bly,** *adv.*

im·prac·ti·cal (im prak′ti kəl), *adj.* **1.** not practical or useful. **2.** not capable of dealing with practical matters; lacking sense. **3.** idealistic. **4.** impracticable. [1860–65; IM-[2] + PRACTICAL] **—im·prac′ti·cal′i·ty, im·prac′ti·cal·ness,** *n.*

im·pre·cate (im′pri kāt′), *v.t.,* **-cat·ed, -cat·ing.** to invoke or call down (evil or curses), as upon a person. [1605–15; < L *imprecātus* ptp. of *imprecārī* to invoke, pray to or for, equiv. to *im-* IM-[1] + *prec-* PRAY + *-ātus* -ATE[1]] **—im′pre·ca′tor,** *n.* **—im′pre·ca·to·ry,** *adj.*

—Syn. curse, execrate, anathematize, accurse, denunciate. **—Ant.** bless.

im·pre·ca·tion (im′pri kā′shən), *n.* **1.** the act of imprecating; cursing. **2.** a curse; malediction. [1575–85; < L *imprecātiōn-* (s. of *imprecātiō*), equiv. to *imprecāt(us)* (see IMPRECATE) + *-iōn-* -ION]

im·pre·cise (im′prə sīs′), *adj.* not precise; not exact; vague or ill-defined. [1795–1805; IM-[2] + PRECISE] **—im′pre·cise′ly,** *adv.* **—im·pre·ci·sion** (im′prə sizh′ən), **im′pre·cise′ness,** *n.*

im·preg·na·ble[1] (im preg′nə bəl), *adj.* **1.** strong enough to resist or withstand attack; not to be taken by force, unconquerable: *an impregnable fort.* **2.** not to be overcome or overthrown: *an impregnable argument.* [1400–50; late ME *impregnable, imprenable* < MF, equiv. to *im-* IM-[2] + *prenable* PREGNABLE] **—im·preg′na·bil′i·ty, im·preg′na·ble·ness,** *n.* **—im·preg′na·bly,** *adv.*

—Syn. 1. invulnerable. **1, 2.** See **invincible. 2.** unassailable. **—Ant. 1.** vulnerable.

im·preg·na·ble[2] (im preg′nə bəl), *adj.* susceptible to impregnation, as an egg. [IMPREGN(ATE) + -ABLE]

im·preg·nate (*v.* im preg′nāt, im′preg nāt′; *adj.* im-preg′nit, -nāt), *v.,* **-nat·ed, -nat·ing,** *adj.* *—v.t.* **1.** to make pregnant; get with child or young. **2.** to fertilize. **3.** to cause to be infused or permeated throughout, as with a substance; saturate: *to impregnate a handkerchief with cheap perfume.* **4.** to fill interstices with a substance. **5.** to furnish with some actuating or modifying element infused or introduced; imbue, infect; tincture. *—adj.* **6.** impregnated. [1535–45; < LL *impraegnātus* ptp. of *impraegnāre* to fertilize, impregnate, equiv. to *im-* IM-[1] + *praegn-* (see PREGNANT) + *-ātus* -ATE[1]] **—im′preg·na′tion,** *n.* **—im·preg′na·tor,** *n.* **—im·preg·na·to·ry** (im preg′nə tôr′ē, -tōr′ē), *adj.*

—Syn. 3. permeate, infuse, penetrate.

im·pre·sa (im prā′zə), *n., pl.* **-sas, -se** (-zā). *Obs.* **1.** a device or emblem. **2.** a motto. Also, **im·prese** (im-prēz′). [1580–90; < It: lit., undertaking, n. use of fem. of *impreso,* ptp. of *imprendere* to undertake; see EMPRISE]

im·pre·sa·ri·o (im′prə sär′ē ō′, -sâr′-), *n., pl.* **-ri·os.** **1.** a person who organizes or manages public entertainments, esp. operas, ballets, or concerts. **2.** any manager, director, or the like. [1740–50; < It, equiv. to *impres(a)* IMPRESA + *-ario* -ARY]

im·pre·scrip·ti·ble (im′pri skrip′tə bəl), *adj. Law.* not subject to prescription. [1555–65; < ML *imprescriptibilis.* See IM-[2], PRESCRIPTIBLE] **—im′pre·scrip′ti·bil′i·ty,** *n.* **—im′pre·scrip′ti·bly,** *adv.*

im·press[1] (*v.* im pres′; *n.* im′pres), *v.,* **-pressed** or (*Archaic*) **-prest; -press·ing;** *n.* *—v.t.* **1.** to affect deeply or strongly in mind or feelings; influence in opinion: *He impressed us as a sincere young man.* **2.** to fix deeply or firmly on the mind or memory, as ideas or facts: *to impress the importance of honesty on a child.* **3.** to urge, as something to be remembered or done: *She impressed the need for action on them.* **4.** to press (a thing) into or on something. **5.** to impose a particular characteristic or quality upon (something): *The painter impressed his love of garish colors upon the landscape.* **6.** to produce (a mark, figure, etc.) by pressure; stamp; imprint: *The king impressed his seal on the melted wax.* **7.** to apply with pressure, so as to leave a mark. **8.** to subject to or mark by pressure with something. **9.** to furnish with a mark, figure, etc., by or as if by stamping. **10.** *Elect.* to produce (a voltage) or cause (a voltage) to appear or be produced on a conductor, circuit, etc. *—v.i.* **11.** to create a favorable impression; draw attention to oneself: *a child's behavior intended to impress.* *—n.* **12.** the act of impressing. **13.** a mark made by or as by pressure; stamp; imprint. **14.** a distinctive character or effect imparted: *writings that bear the impress of a strong personality.* [1325–75; ME < L *impressus* ptp. of *imprimere* to press into or upon, impress, equiv. to *im-* IM-[1] + *pressus* ptp. of *premere* (comb. form *-primere*) to PRESS[1]; see PRINT] **—im·press′er,** *n.*

—Syn. 1. move, sway, disturb; persuade.

im·press[2] (*v.* im pres′; *n.* im′pres), *v.,* **-pressed** or (*Archaic*) **-prest; -press·sing;** *n.* *—v.t.* **1.** to press or force into public service, as sailors. **2.** to seize or take for public use. **3.** to take or persuade into service by forceful arguments: *The neighbors were impressed into helping the family move.* *—n.* **4.** impressment. [1590–1600; IM-[1] + PRESS[2]]

im·press·i·ble (im pres′ə bəl), *adj.* capable of being impressed; impressionable. [1620–30; IMPRESS[1] + -IBLE] **—im·press′i·bil′i·ty, im·press′i·ble·ness,** *n.* **—im·press′i·bly,** *adv.*

im·pres·sion (im presh′ən), *n.* **1.** a strong effect produced on the intellect, feelings, conscience, etc. **2.** the first and immediate effect of an experience or perception upon the mind; sensation. **3.** the effect produced by an agency or influence. **4.** a notion, remembrance, belief, etc., often of a vague or indistinct nature: *He had a general impression of lights, voices, and the clinking of silver.* **5.** a mark, indentation, figure, etc., produced by pressure. **6.** an image in the mind caused by something external to it. **7.** the act of impressing; state of being impressed. **8.** *Dentistry.* a mold taken, in plastic materials or plaster of Paris, of teeth and the surrounding tissues. **9.** an imitation of the voice, mannerisms, and other traits of a person, esp. a famous person, as by an entertainer: *The comedian did a hilarious impression of the president.* **10.** *Chiefly Print.* **a.** the process or result of printing from type, plates, etc. **b.** a printed copy from type, a plate, an engraved block, etc. **c.** one of a number of printings made at different times from the same set of type, without alteration (distinguished from *edition*). **d.** the total number of copies of a book, pamphlet, etc., printed at one time from one setting of type or from one set of plates. **11.** *Metalworking.* a portion of a die having in reverse the intended form of an object to be forged. [1325–75; ME *impressio(u)n* < L *impressiōn-* (s. of *impressiō*), equiv. to *impress(us)* (see IMPRESS[1]) + *-iōn-* -ION] **—im·pres′sion·al,** *adj.* **—im·pres′sion·al·ly,** *adv.* **—im·pres′sion·less,** *adj.*

—Syn. 2. impact, imprint. **4.** feeling.

im·pres·sion·a·ble (im presh′ə nə bəl, -presh′nə-), *adj.* **1.** easily impressed or influenced; susceptible: *an impressionable youngster.* **2.** capable of being impressed. [1825–35; IMPRESSION + -ABLE; cf. F *impressionnable*] **—im·pres′sion·a·bil′i·ty, im·pres′sion·a·ble·ness,** *n.* **—im·pres′sion·a·bly,** *adv.*

—Syn. 1. receptive, responsive, suggestible.

im·pres·sion·ism (im presh′ə niz′əm), *n.* **1.** *Fine Arts.* **a.** (*usually cap.*) a style of painting developed in the last third of the 19th century, characterized chiefly by short brush strokes of bright colors in immediate juxtaposition to represent the effect of light on objects. **b.** a manner of painting in which the forms, colors, or tones of an object are lightly and rapidly indicated. **c.** a manner of sculpture in which volumes are partially modeled and surfaces roughened to reflect light unevenly. **2.** a theory and practice in literature that emphasizes immediate aspects of objects or actions without attention to details. **3.** a late-19th-century and early-20th-century style of musical composition in which lush harmonies, subtle rhythms, and unusual tonal colors are used to evoke moods and impressions. [1880–85; IMPRESSION + -ISM; cf. G *Impressionismus,* F *impressionnisme*]

im·pres·sion·ist (im presh′ə nist), *n.* **1.** a person who follows or adheres to the theories, methods, and practices of impressionism, esp. in the fields of painting, music, or literature. **2.** an entertainer who does impressions. *—adj.* **3.** (*usually cap.*) *Fine Arts.* of, pertaining to, or characteristic of Impressionism: *Impressionist paintings; Impressionist artists.* [1875–80; < F *impressionniste.* See IMPRESSION, -IST] **—im·pres′sion·is′tic,** *adj.* **—im·pres′sion·is′ti·cal·ly,** *adv.*

im·pres·sive (im pres′iv), *adj.* having the ability to impress the mind; arousing admiration, awe, respect, etc.; moving; admirable: *an impressive ceremony; an impressive appearance.* [1585–95; IMPRESS[1] + -IVE] **—im·pres′sive·ly,** *adv.* **—im·pres′sive·ness,** *n.*

—Syn. imposing, awesome.

im·press·ment (im pres′mənt), *n.* the act of impressing people or property into public service or use. [1780–90; IMPRESS[2] + -MENT]

im·pres·sure (im presh′ər), *n. Archaic.* impression. [1590–1600; IMPRESS[1] + -URE, modeled on PRESSURE]

im·prest[1] (im′prest), *n.* an advance of money; loan. [1560–70; prob. n. use of obs. v. *imprest* to advance money to < It *imprestare* < L *im-* IM-[1] + *praestāre* to be responsible for (*prae-* PRE- + *stāre* to STAND, influenced in sense by *praes,* s. *praed-* guarantor, one acting as surety)]

im·prest[2] (im prest′), *v. Archaic.* pt. and pp. of **impress.**

im′prest fund′, a fund of petty cash.

im·pri·ma·tur (im′pri mä′tər, -mā′-, -prī-), *n.* **1.** an official license to print or publish a book, pamphlet, etc., esp. a license issued by a censor of the Roman Catholic

CONCISE ETYMOLOGY KEY: <, descended or borrowed from; >, whence; b., blend of, blended; c., cognate with; cf., compare; deriv., derivative; equiv., equivalent; imit., imitative; obl., oblique; r., replacing; s., stem; sp., spelling, spelled; resp., respelling, respelled; trans., translation; ?, origin unknown; *, unattested; ‡, probably earlier than. See the full key inside the front cover.

Church. Cf. **nihil obstat.** **2.** sanction or approval; support: *Our plan has the company president's imprimatur.* [1630–40; < NL: let it be printed, L: let it be made by pressing upon (something); see IMPRESS[1]]

im•pri•mis (im prī′mis, -prē′-), *adv.* in the first place. [1425–75; late ME < L, contr. of phrase *in prīmīs* in the first place, above all]

im•print (*n.* im′print; *v.* im print′), *n.* **1.** a mark made by pressure; a mark or figure impressed or printed on something. **2.** any impression or impressed effect: *He left the imprint of his thought on all succeeding scholars.* **3.** *Bibliog.* **a.** the name of a book's publisher printed on the title page or elsewhere, usually with the place and date of publication. **b.** the statement of such information in a bibliographic description of a printed work. **c.** a name, title, or other designation by which all or certain specific books of a publisher are identified. **4.** any marketing name used by a company or organization for a product line; brand or label. **5.** the printer's name and address as indicated on any printed matter. —*v.t.* **6.** to impress (a quality, character, distinguishing mark, etc.). **7.** to produce (a mark) on something by pressure. **8.** to bestow, as a kiss. **9.** to fix firmly on the mind, memory, etc. **10.** *Animal Behav., Psychol.* to acquire or establish by imprinting. **11.** to make an imprint upon. —*v.i.* **12.** to make an impression; have an effect. [1325–75; IM-[1] + PRINT; r. ME *empreynten* < MF *empreinter*, deriv. of *empreinte*, fem. ptp. of *empreindre* < L *imprimere* to IMPRESS[1]]

im•print•er (im prin′tər), *n.* **1.** a person or thing that imprints. **2.** a machine or device that imprints something onto another surface: *an imprinter for writing the amounts on payroll checks.* [1540–50; IMPRINT + -ER[1]]

im•print•ing (im prin′ting), *n. Animal Behav., Psychol.* rapid learning that occurs during a brief receptive period, typically soon after birth or hatching, and establishes a long-lasting behavioral response to a specific individual or object, as attachment to parent, offspring, or site. [1937; IMPRINT + -ING[1], trans. of G *Prägung*, K. Lorenz's term]

im•pris•on (im priz′ən), *v.t.* to confine in or as if in a prison. [1250–1300; ME *enprisonen* < OF *enprisoner*, equiv. to *en-* EN-[1] + *prison* PRISON + *-er* inf. suffix] —**im•pris′on•a•ble,** *adj.* —**im•pris′on•er,** *n.* —**im•pris′on•ment,** *n.*
—**Syn. 1.** incarcerate, jail, restrain.

im•prob•a•bil•i•ty (im prob′ə bil′i tē, im′prob-), *n., pl.* **-ties** for 2. **1.** the quality or condition of being improbable; unlikelihood. **2.** something improbable or unlikely. [1590–1600; IMPROBABLE + -ITY]

im•prob•a•ble (im prob′ə bəl), *adj.* not probable; unlikely to be true or to happen: *Rain is improbable tonight.* [1590–1600; < L *improbābilis*. See IM-[2], PROBABLE] —**im•prob′a•bly,** *adv.* —**im•prob′a•ble•ness,** *n.*
—**Syn.** questionable, doubtful, implausible.

im•promp•tu (im promp′to͞o, -tyo͞o), *adj.* **1.** made or done without previous preparation: *an impromptu address to the unexpected crowds.* **2.** suddenly or hastily prepared, made, etc.: *an impromptu dinner.* **3.** improvised; having the character of an improvisation. —*adv.* **4.** without preparation: *verses written impromptu.* —*n.* **5.** something impromptu; an impromptu speech, musical composition, performance, etc. **6.** a character piece for piano common in the 19th century and having, despite its title, a clear-cut form. [1660–70; < F < L *in promptū* in readiness; see IN, PROMPT]
—**Syn. 1.** See **extemporaneous.**

im•prop•er (im prop′ər), *adj.* **1.** not proper; not strictly belonging, applicable, correct, etc.; erroneous: *He drew improper conclusions from the scant evidence.* **2.** not in accordance with propriety of behavior, manners, etc.: *improper conduct at a funeral.* **3.** unsuitable or inappropriate, as for the purpose or occasion: *improper attire for a formal dance.* **4.** abnormal or irregular: *improper functioning of the speech mechanism.* [1535–45; < L *improprius*. See IM-[2], PROPER] —**im•prop′er•ly,** *adv.* —**im•prop′er•ness,** *n.*
—**Syn. 1–3.** inapplicable, unsuited, unfit. **2.** indecorous. IMPROPER, INDECENT, UNBECOMING, UNSEEMLY are applied to that which is unfitting or not in accordance with propriety. IMPROPER has a wide range, being applied to whatever is not suitable or fitting, and often specifically to what does not conform to the standards of conventional morality: *improper diet; improper behavior in church; improper language.* INDECENT, a strong word, is applied to what is offensively contrary to standards of propriety and esp. of modesty: *indecent behavior, literature.* UNBECOMING is applied to what is esp. unfitting in the person concerned: *conduct unbecoming a minister.* UNSEEMLY is applied to whatever is unfitting or improper under the circumstances: *unseemly mirth.* —**Ant. 1, 3.** fitting, suitable. **2.** proper.

improp′er frac′tion, *Math.* a fraction having the numerator greater than the denominator. [1535–45]

Im•pro•pe•ri•a (im′pro pēr′ē ə), *n.* (*used with a plural v.*) reproach (def. 8). [1875–80; < LL, pl. of *improperium*, equiv. to L *improper(āre)* to blame (appar. an unlearned conflation of *improbāre* to express disapproval and *improprius* incorrect or *improperus* not hastening) + *-ium* -IUM]

improp′er in′tegral, *Math.* **1.** Also called **infinite integral.** a definite integral in which one or both of the limits of integration is infinite. **2.** a definite integral in which the integrand becomes infinite at a point or points in the interval of integration. [1940–45]

im•pro•pri•e•ty (im′prə prī′i tē), *n., pl.* **-ties** for 4, 5. **1.** the quality or condition of being improper; incorrectness. **2.** inappropriateness; unsuitableness. **3.** unseemliness; indecorousness. **4.** an erroneous or unsuitable expression, act, etc. **5.** an improper use of a word or phrase. [1605–15; < LL *improprietās*. See IM-[2], PROPRIETY]

im•prov (im′prov), *n. Informal.* improvisation. [by shortening]

im•prove (im pro͞ov′), *v.,* **-proved, -prov•ing.** —*v.t.* **1.** to bring into a more desirable or excellent condition: *He took vitamins to improve his health.* **2.** to make (land) more useful, profitable, or valuable by enclosure, cultivation, etc. **3.** to increase the value of (real property) by betterments, as the construction of buildings and sewers. **4.** to make good use of; turn to account: *He improved the stopover by seeing a client with offices there.* —*v.i.* **5.** to increase in value, excellence, etc.; become better: *The military situation is improving.* **6.** to make improvements, as by revision, addition, or change: *None of the younger violinists have been able to improve on his interpretation of that work.* [1425–75; late ME *improuen, emprouen* < AF *emprouer* to turn (something) into profit, deriv. of phrase *en prou* into profit, equiv. to *en* (see EN-[1]) + *prou*, OF *prou, preu* < LL *prōde (est)*, by reanalysis of L *prōdest* (it) is beneficial, of use, with *prōde* taken as a neut. n. (cf. PROUD); *v* by assoc. with PROVE, APPROVE] —**im•prov′a•ble,** *adj.* —**im•prov′a•bil′i•ty, im•prov′a•ble•ness,** *n.* —**im•prov′a•bly,** *adv.* —**im•prov′ing•ly,** *adv.*
—**Syn. 1.** amend, emend. IMPROVE, AMELIORATE, BETTER imply bringing to a more desirable state. IMPROVE usually implies remedying a lack or a felt need: *to improve a process, oneself (as by gaining more knowledge).* AMELIORATE, a formal word, implies improving oppressive, unjust, or difficult conditions: *to ameliorate working conditions.* To BETTER is to improve conditions which, though not bad, are unsatisfying: *to better an attempt, oneself (gain a higher salary).* —**Ant. 1, 5.** worsen.

im•prove•ment (im pro͞ov′mənt), *n.* **1.** an act of improving or the state of being improved. **2.** a change or addition by which a thing is improved. **3.** a person or thing that represents an advance on another in excellence or achievement: *The new landlord is a great improvement over his greedy predecessor.* **4.** a bringing into a more valuable or desirable condition, as of land or real property; betterment. **5.** something done or added to real property that increases its value. **6.** profitable use, as of a period of time. [1400–50; late ME *improuement* < AF *emprouement* something profitable (especially exploitation of land). See IMPROVE, -MENT]
—**Syn. 3.** refinement, betterment, advancement. **4.** enhancement, repair.

im•prov•er (im pro͞o′vər), *n.* **1.** a person or thing that improves. **2.** a substance or agent added to improve a food, esp. as a preservative. [1640–50; IMPROVE + -ER[1]]

im•prov•i•dent (im prov′i dənt), *adj.* **1.** not provident; lacking foresight; incautious; unwary. **2.** neglecting to provide for future needs. [1505–15; IM-[2] + PROVIDENT] —**im•prov′i•dence,** *n.* —**im•prov′i•dent•ly,** *adv.*
—**Syn. 1.** thoughtless, careless, imprudent, heedless. **2.** shiftless, thriftless, unthrifty, wasteful, prodigal. —**Ant. 1.** prudent. **2.** economical.

im•prov•i•sa•tion (im prov′ə zā′shən, im′prə və-), *n.* **1.** an act of improvising. **2.** something improvised. [1780–90; IMPROVISE + -ATION] —**im•prov′i•sa′tion•al,** *adj.*

im•prov•i•sa•tor (im prov′ə zā′tər, im′prə və-), *n.* a person who improvises; improviser. [1785–95; IMPROVISE + -ATOR; cf. It *improvvisatore*]

im•pro•vi•sa•to•ry (im′prə vī′zə tôr′ē, -tōr′ē, -viz′ə-), *adj.* of, pertaining to, or characteristic of an improvisation or improvisator. Also, **im•prov•i•sa•to•ri•al** (im prov′ə zə tôr′ē əl, -tōr′-). [1800–10; IMPROVISATOR + -Y[1]; see -ORY[1]] —**im•prov′i•sa•to′ri•al•ly,** *adv.*

im•pro•vise (im′prə vīz′), *v.,* **-vised, -vis•ing.** —*v.t.* **1.** to compose and perform or deliver without previous preparation; extemporize: *to improvise an acceptance speech.* **2.** to compose, play, recite, or sing (verse, music, etc.) on the spur of the moment. **3.** to make, provide, or arrange from whatever materials are readily available: *We improvised a dinner from yesterday's leftovers.* —*v.i.* **4.** to compose, utter, execute, or arrange anything extemporaneously: *When the actor forgot his lines he had to improvise.* [1820–30; < F *improviser*, or its source, It *improvisare* (later *improvvisare*), v. deriv. of *improvviso* improvised < L *imprōvīsus*, equiv. to *im-* IM-[2] + *prōvīsus* ptp. of *prōvidēre* to see beforehand, prepare, provide for (a future circumstance). See PROVISO] —**im′pro•vis′er, im′pro•vi′sor,** *n.*

im•pro•vised (im′prə vīzd′), *adj.* made or said without previous preparation: *an improvised skit.* [1830–40; IMPROVISE + -ED[2]] —**im•pro•vis•ed•ly** (im′prə vī′zid lē), *adv.*
—**Syn.** unpremeditated, unrehearsed, unprepared. See **extemporaneous.** —**Ant.** rehearsed.

im•prov•vi•sa•to•re (ēm′prôv vē′zä tô′re), *n., pl.* **-ri** (-rē). *Italian.* an improvisator, esp. a person who extemporizes verse.

im•pru•dent (im pro͞od′nt), *adj.* not prudent; lacking discretion; incautious; rash. [1350–1400; ME < L *imprūdent-* (s. of *imprūdēns*) unforeseeing, rash. See IM-[2], PRUDENT] —**im•pru′dence, im•pru′dent•ness, im•pru′den•cy,** *n.* —**im•pru′dent•ly,** *adv.*
—**Syn.** unwise, indiscreet, ill-advised.

imp•son•ite (imp′sə nīt′), *n.* a black variety of asphaltite with a jagged fracture. [1900–05; named after *Impson*, valley in Oklahoma; see -ITE[1]]

im•pu•dence (im′pyə dəns), *n.* **1.** the quality or state of being impudent; effrontery; insolence. **2.** impudent conduct or language. **3.** *Obs.* lack of modesty; shamelessness. Also, **im′pu•den•cy.** [1350–1400; ME < L *impudentia* shamelessness. See IMPUDENT, -ENCE]
—**Syn. 1.** impertinence, rudeness; brass, brazenness, face, lip, boldness, presumption, sauce, pertness; nerve, gall. —**Ant. 1.** courtesy.

im•pu•dent (im′pyə dənt), *adj.* **1.** of, pertaining to, or characterized by impertinence or effrontery: *The student was kept late for impudent behavior.* **2.** *Obs.* shameless or brazenly immodest. [1350–1400; ME < L *impudent-* (s. of *impudēns*) shameless, equiv. to *im-* IM-[2] + *pud-* (base of *pudēre* to feel shame; cf. PUDENDUM) + *-ent-* -ENT] —**im′pu•dent•ly,** *adv.* —**im′pu•dent•ness,** *n.*
—**Syn. 1.** insulting, rude, saucy, pert; presumptuous, fresh, brazen. See **impertinent.** —**Ant. 1.** courteous.

im•pu•dic•i•ty (im′pyo͝o dis′i tē), *n.* immodesty. [1520–30; < MF *impudicité* < L *impudic(us)* immodest (*im-* IM-[2] + *pudīcus* modest; see IMPUDENT) + MF *-ité* -ITY]

im•pugn (im pyo͞on′), *v.t.* **1.** to challenge as false (another's statements, motives, etc.); cast doubt upon. **2.** *Archaic.* to assail (a person) by words or arguments; vilify. **3.** *Obs.* to attack (a person) physically. [1325–75; ME *impugnen* < MF *impugner* < L *impugnāre* to attack, equiv. to *im-* IM-[1] + *pugnāre* to fight, deriv. of *pugnus* fist; see PUGNACIOUS] —**im•pugn′a•ble,** *adj.* —**im•pugn′a•bil′i•ty,** *n.* —**im•pugn′er,** *n.* —**im•pugn′ment,** *n.*
—**Syn. 1.** attack, asperse, malign, criticize, censure.

im•pu•is•sant (im pyo͞o′ə sənt, im′pyo͞o is′ənt, im-pwis′ənt), *adj.* lacking strength; feeble; weak. [1620–30; < MF; see IM-[2], PUISSANT] —**im•pu′is•sance,** *n.*

im•pulse (im′puls), *n.* **1.** the influence of a particular feeling, mental state, etc.: *to act under a generous impulse; to strike out at someone from an angry impulse.* **2.** sudden, involuntary inclination prompting to action: *to be swayed by impulse.* **3.** an instance of this. **4.** a psychic drive or instinctual urge. **5.** an impelling action or force, driving onward or inducing motion. **6.** the effect of an impelling force; motion induced; impetus given. **7.** *Physiol.* a progressive wave of excitation over a nerve or muscle fiber, having either a stimulating or inhibitory effect. **8.** *Mech.* the product of the average force acting upon a body and the time during which it acts, equivalent to the change in the momentum of the body produced by such a force. **9.** *Elect.* a single, usually sudden, flow of current in one direction. —*adj.* **10.** marked by or acting on impulse: *an impulse buyer.* **11.** bought or acquired on impulse: *To reduce expenses, shun impulse items when shopping.* [1640–50; < L *impulsus* pressure, impulse, equiv. to *im-* IM-[1] + *pul-* (var. s. of *pellere* to push) + *-sus*, var. of *-tus* suffix of v. action]

im′pulse tur′bine, a turbine moved by free jets of fluid striking the blades of the rotor together with the axial flow of fluid through the rotor. Cf. **reaction turbine.** [1880–85]

im•pul•sion (im pul′shən), *n.* **1.** the act of impelling, driving onward, or pushing. **2.** the resulting state or effect; impulse; impetus. **3.** the inciting influence of some feeling or motive; mental impulse. **4.** a constraining or inciting action exerted on the mind or conduct: *divine impulsion.* [1400–50; late ME < L *impulsiōn-* (s. of *impulsiō*) incitement. See IMPULSE, -ION]

im•pul•sive (im pul′siv), *adj.* **1.** actuated or swayed by emotional or involuntary impulses: *an impulsive child.* **2.** having the power or effect of impelling; characterized by impulsion: *impulsive forces.* **3.** inciting to action: *the impulsive effects of a revolutionary idea.* **4.** *Mech.* (of forces) acting momentarily; not continuous. [1375–1425 for an earlier sense; 1545–55 for current senses; late ME *impulsif* < ML *impulsīvus*. See IMPULSE, -IVE] —**im•pul′sive•ly,** *adv.* —**im•pul′sive•ness, im′•pul•siv′i•ty,** *n.*
—**Syn. 1.** rash, quick, hasty. See **impetuous.**

im•pu•ni•ty (im pyo͞o′ni tē), *n.* **1.** exemption from punishment. **2.** immunity from detrimental effects, as of an action. [1525–35; < L *impūnitās*, equiv. to *im-* IM-[2] + *pūnitās* punishment (*pūn-* (s. of *punire* to PUNISH) + *-itās* -ITY); see PUNITIVE]
—**Syn.** See **exemption.**

im•pure (im pyo͝or′), *adj.* **1.** not pure; mixed with extraneous matter, esp. of an inferior or contaminating nature: *impure water and air.* **2.** modified by admixture, as color. **3.** mixed or combined with something else: *an impure style of architecture.* **4.** regarded by a religion as unclean, as animals or things. **5.** not morally pure or proper; unchaste or obscene: *impure thoughts.* **6.** marked by foreign and unsuitable or objectionable elements or characteristics, as a style of art or of literary expression. [1530–40; < L *impūrus*. See IM-[2], PURE] —**im•pure′ly,** *adv.* —**im•pure′ness,** *n.*
—**Syn. 5.** coarse, vulgar, improper, licentious.

im•pu•ri•ty (im pyo͝or′i tē), *n., pl.* **-ties** for 2. **1.** the quality or state of being impure. **2.** Often, **impurities.** something that is or makes impure: *After the flood the authorities warned against impurities in the drinking water.* [1400–50; late ME *impurite* < L *impūritās*. See IMPURE, -ITY]
—**Syn. 1.** contamination, pollution, taint.

im•pu•ta•tion (im′pyo͝o tā′shən), *n.* **1.** the act of imputing. **2.** an attribution, as of fault or crime; accusation. [1535–45; < LL *imputātiōn-* (s. of *imputātiō*), equiv. to L *imputāt(us)* ptp. of *imputāre* to ascribe, IMPUTE + *-iōn-* -ION]

im•pute (im pyo͞ot′), *v.t.,* **-put•ed, -put•ing.** **1.** to attribute or ascribe: *The children imputed magical powers to the old woman.* **2.** to attribute or ascribe (something discreditable), as to a person. **3.** *Law.* to ascribe to or charge (a person) with an act or quality because of the conduct of another over whom one has control or for whose acts or conduct one is responsible. **4.** *Theol.* to attribute (righteousness, guilt, etc.) to a person or persons vicariously; ascribe as derived from another. **5.** *Obs.* to charge (a person) with fault. [1325–75; ME *imputen* < L *imputāre*, equiv. to *im-* IM-[1] + *putāre* to assess, reckon, think; see PUTATIVE] —**im•put′a•ble,** *adj.* —**im•put•a•tive** (im pyo͞o′tə tiv), *adj.* —**im•put′a•tive•ly,** *adv.* —**im•put′a•tive•ness,** *n.* —**im•put′ed•ly,** *adv.* —**im•put′er,** *n.*
—**Syn. 1.** See **attribute.**

im•put•ed (im pyo͞o′tid), *adj.* estimated to have a certain cash value, although no money has been received or credited. [1905–10; IMPUTE + -ED[2]]

im•pu•tres•ci•ble (im′pyo͞o tres′ə bəl), *adj.* not liable to decomposition or putrefaction; incorruptible: *a tan-*

ning process to make skins imputrescible. [1650–60; < LL *imputrescibilis.* See IM-², PUTRESCIBLE]

impv., imperative.

i·mu (ē′mo͞o), *n. Hawaii.* a usually large, covered cooking pit in which food is cooked by means of heated stones. [< Hawaiian]

Im·u·ran (im′yə ran′), *Pharm., Trademark.* a brand of azathioprine.

in (in), *prep., adv., adj., n., v.,* **inned, in·ning.** —*prep.* **1.** (used to indicate inclusion within space, a place, or limits): *walking in the park.* **2.** (used to indicate inclusion within something abstract or immaterial): *in politics; in the autumn.* **3.** (used to indicate inclusion within or occurrence during a period or limit of time): *in ancient times; a task done in ten minutes.* **4.** (used to indicate limitation or qualification, as of situation, condition, relation, manner, action, etc.): *to speak in a whisper; to be similar in appearance.* **5.** (used to indicate means): *sketched in ink; spoken in French.* **6.** (used to indicate motion or direction from outside to a point within) into: *Let's go in the house.* **7.** (used to indicate transition from one state to another): *to break in half.* **8.** (used to indicate object or purpose): *speaking in honor of the event.* **9. in that,** because; inasmuch as: *In that you won't have time for supper, let me give you something now.* —*adv.* **10.** in or into some place, position, state, relation, etc.: *Please come in.* **11.** on the inside; within. **12.** in one's house or office. **13.** in office or power. **14.** in possession or occupancy. **15.** having the turn to play, as in a game. **16.** *Baseball.* (of an infielder or outfielder) in a position closer to home plate than usual; short: *The third baseman played in, expecting a bunt.* **17.** on good terms; in favor: *He's in with his boss, but he doubts it will last.* **18.** in vogue; in style: *He says straw hats will be in this year.* **19.** in season: *Watermelons will soon be in.* **20. be in for,** to be bound to undergo something, esp. a disagreeable experience: *We are in for a long speech.* **21. in for it,** *Slang.* about to suffer chastisement or unpleasant consequences, esp. of one's own actions or omissions: *I forgot our anniversary again, and I'll be in for it now.* Also, *Brit.,* **for it. 22. in with,** on friendly terms with; familiar or associating with: *They are in with all the important people.* —*adj.* **23.** located or situated within; inner; internal: *the in part of a mechanism.* **24.** *Informal.* **a.** in favor with advanced or sophisticated people; fashionable; stylish: *the in place to dine; Her new novel is the in book to read this summer.* **b.** comprehensible only to a special or ultrasophisticated group: *an in joke.* **25.** well-liked; included in a favored group. **26.** inward; incoming; inbound: *an in train.* **27.** plentiful; available. **28.** being in power, authority, control, etc.: *a member of the in party.* **29.** playing the last nine holes of an eighteen-hole golf course (opposed to *out*): *His in score on the second round was 34.* —*n.* **30.** Usually, **ins.** persons in office or political power (distinguished from *outs*). **31.** a member of the political party in power: *The election made him an in.* **32.** pull or influence; a social advantage or connection: *He's got an in with the senator.* **33.** (in tennis, squash, handball, etc.) a return or service that lands within the in-bounds limits of a court or section of a court (opposed to *out*). —*v.t.* *Brit. Dial.* **34.** to enclose. [bef. 900; 1925–30 for def. 32; ME, OE; c. G, D, OFris, OS, Goth *in,* ON *ī,* L *in,* Gk *en,* Lith *į*]

IN, Indiana (approved esp. for use with zip code).

In, *Symbol, Chem.* indium.

in-¹, a prefix representing English *in* (*income; indwelling; inland,* etc.), but used also as a verb-formative with transitive, intensive, or sometimes little apparent force (*intrust; inweave,* etc.). It often assumes the same forms as **in-²,** such as **en-, em-, im-³.** [ME, OE; see IN]

in-², a prefix of Latin origin meaning primarily "in," but used also as a verb-formative with the same force as **in-¹** (*incarcerate; incantation*). Also, **il-, im-, ir-.** Cf. **em-, en-.** [< L, comb. form of *in* (prep.); c. IN]

in-³, a prefix of Latin origin, corresponding to English *un-,* having a negative or privative force, freely used as an English formative, esp. of adjectives and their derivatives and of nouns (*inattention; indefensible; inexpensive; inorganic; invariable*). It assumes the same phonetic phases as **in-²** (*impartial; immeasurable; illiterate; irregular,* etc.). In French, it became *en-* and thus occurs unfelt in such words as *enemy* (French *ennemi,* Latin *inimicus,* lit., not friendly). Also, **il-, im-, ir-.** [< L; akin to AN-¹, A-⁶, UN-¹]
—**Syn.** The prefixes IN- and UN- may both have, among other uses, a negative force. IN- is the form derived from Latin, and is therefore used in learned words or in words derived from Latin or (rarely) Greek: *inaccessible, inaccuracy, inadequate,* etc. UN- is the native form going back to Old English, used in words of native origin, and sometimes used in combination with words of other origins if these words are in common use: *unloving, ungodly, unfeeling, unnecessary, unsafe.*

-in¹, a suffix, occurring in adjectives of Greek and Latin origin, meaning "pertaining to," and (in nouns thence derived) also imitated in English (*coffin; cousin,* etc.). [ME *-in, -ine* < OF < L *-inus, -ina, -inum* < Gk *-inos, -inē, -inon*]

-in², a noun suffix used in a special manner in chemical and mineralogical nomenclature (*glycerin; acetin,* etc.). In spelling, usage wavers between *-in* and *-ine.* In chemistry a certain distinction of use is attempted, basic substances having the termination *-ine* rather than *-in* (*aconitine; aniline,* etc.), and *-in* being restricted to certain neutral compounds, glycerides, glucosides, and proteids (*albumin; palmitin,* etc.), but this distinction is not always observed. [< NL *-ina.* See -INE²]

CONCISE ETYMOLOGY KEY: <, descended or borrowed from; >, whence; b., blend of, blended; c., cognate with; cf., compare; deriv., derivative; equiv., equivalent; imit., imitative; obl., oblique; r., replacing; s., stem; sp., spelling, spelled; resp., respelling, respelled; trans., translation; ?, origin unknown; *, unattested; ‡, probably earlier than. See the full key inside the front cover.

-in³, a suffixal use of the adverb **in,** extracted from **sit-in,** forming compound nouns, usually from verbs, referring to organized protests through or in support of the named activity (*kneel-in; chain-in; be-in*) or, more generally, to any organized social or cultural activity (*cook-in; sing-in*).

in., inch; inches.

I·na (ī′nə), *n.* a female given name.

-ina¹, a suffix used in the formation of nouns of various types, esp. female proper names, musical instruments, compositions, etc.: *Wilhelmina; sonatina.* Cf. **-in², -ine².** [< L *-ina,* fem. of *-inus*]

-ina², a suffix used in taxonomic names in biology: *Euglenoidina; Nemertina.* [< NL, neut. pl. of L *-īnus* or Gk *-inos;* cf. -IN¹, -INE¹]

in·a·bil·i·ty (in′ə bil′i tē), *n.* lack of ability; lack of power, capacity, or means: *his inability to make decisions.* [1400–50; late ME *inabilite* < ML *inhabilitās.* See IN-³, ABILITY]
—**Syn.** incapability, incapacity, impotence, incompetence. See **disability.**

in ab·sen·tia (in ab sen′shə, -shē ə, -tē ə), *Latin.* in absence.

in·ac·ces·si·ble (in′ək ses′ə bəl), *adj.* not accessible; unapproachable. [1545–55; < LL *inaccessibilis.* See IN-³, ACCESSIBLE] —**in′ac·ces′si·bil′i·ty, in′ac·ces′si·ble·ness,** *n.* —**in′ac·ces′si·bly,** *adv.*
—**Syn.** unreachable, remote, unattainable.

in·ac·cu·ra·cy (in ak′yər ə sē), *n., pl.* **-cies** for 1. **1.** something inaccurate; error. **2.** the quality or state of being inaccurate. [1750–60; IN-³ + ACCURACY]
—**Syn. 1.** mistake, blunder, slip, inexactitude. **2.** incorrectness, erroneousness, inexactness.

in·ac·cu·rate (in ak′yər it), *adj.* not accurate; incorrect or untrue. [1730–40; IN-³ + ACCURATE] —**in·ac′cu·rate·ly,** *adv.* —**in·ac′cu·rate·ness,** *n.*
—**Syn.** inexact, loose; erroneous, wrong, faulty.

in·ac·tion (in ak′shən), *n.* absence of action; idleness. [1700–10; IN-³ + ACTION]

in·ac·ti·vate (in ak′tə vāt′), *v.t.,* **-vat·ed, -vat·ing. 1.** to make inactive: *The bomb was inactivated.* **2.** *Immunol.* to stop the activity of (certain biological substances). [1905–10; INACTIVE + -ATE¹] —**in·ac′ti·va′tion,** *n.*

in·ac·tive (in ak′tiv), *adj.* **1.** not active: *an inactive volcano.* **2.** sedentary or passive: *an inactive life.* **3.** sluggish; indolent. **4.** *Mil.* not on active duty. **5.** *Chem.* **a.** inert; unreactive. **b.** noting a compound that has no effect on polarized light. [1715–25; IN-³ + ACTIVE] —**in·ac′tive·ly,** *adv.* —**in′ac·tiv′i·ty, in·ac′tive·ness,** *n.*
—**Syn. 1.** unmoving, immobile, inoperative. **1, 2.** INACTIVE, DORMANT, INERT, SLUGGISH, TORPID suggest lack of activity. INACTIVE indicates absence of action, indisposition to activity, or cessation of activity: *an inactive compound, life, file of papers.* DORMANT suggests the quiescence or inactivity of that which sleeps but may be roused to action: *a dormant volcano.* INERT suggests the condition of dead matter, with no inherent power of motion or action; it may also mean unable to move, or heavy and hard to move: *an inert mass; inert from hunger.* SLUGGISH expresses slowness of natural activity or of that which does not move readily or vigorously: *a sluggish stream, brain.* TORPID suggests a state of suspended physical powers, a condition particularly of animals that hibernate: *Snakes are torpid in cold weather.* **3.** lazy, idle, slothful. —**Ant. 1–3.** lively.

in·ad·e·qua·cy (in ad′i kwə sē), *n., pl.* **-cies** for 2. **1.** Also, **in·ad·e·quate·ness** (in ad′i kwit nis). the state or condition of being inadequate; insufficiency. **2.** something inadequate; defect: *The plan has many inadequacies.* [1780–90; INADEQU(ATE) + -ACY]

in·ad·e·quate (in ad′i kwit), *adj.* **1.** not adequate or sufficient; inept or unsuitable. **2.** *Psychiatry.* ineffectual in response to emotional, social, intellectual, and physical demands in the absence of any obvious mental or physical deficiency. [1665–75; IN-³ + ADEQUATE] —**in·ad′e·quate·ly,** *adv.*
—**Syn. 1.** inapt, incompetent; incommensurate; defective, imperfect, incomplete. —**Ant. 1.** sufficient.

in·ad·mis·si·ble (in′əd mis′ə bəl), *adj.* not admissible; not allowable: *Such evidence would be inadmissible in any court.* [1770–80; IN-³ + ADMISSIBLE] —**in′ad·mis′si·bil′i·ty,** *n.* —**in′ad·mis′si·bly,** *adv.*

in·ad·vert·ence (in′əd vûr′tns), *n.* **1.** the quality or condition of being inadvertent; heedlessness. **2.** the act or effect of inattention; an oversight. [1560–70; < ML *inadvertentia.* See INADVERTENCY, -ENCE]

in·ad·vert·en·cy (in′əd vûr′tn sē), *n., pl.* **-cies.** inadvertence. [1585–95; < ML *inadvertentia,* equiv. to L *in-* IN-³ + *advert-* turn to (see ADVERT¹) + *-entia* -ENCY]

in·ad·vert·ent (in′əd vûr′tnt), *adj.* **1.** unintentional: *an inadvertent insult.* **2.** not attentive; heedless. **3.** of, pertaining to, or characterized by lack of attention. [1645–55; abstracted from INADVERTENCE, INADVERTENCY; see -ENT] —**in′ad·vert′ent·ly,** *adv.*
—**Syn. 2.** inattentive. **3.** thoughtless, careless, negligent.

in·ad·vis·a·ble (in′əd vī′zə bəl), *adj.* not advisable; inexpedient; unwise. [1865–70; IN-³ + ADVISABLE] —**in′ad·vis′a·bil′i·ty, in′ad·vis′a·ble·ness,** *n.* —**in′ad·vis′a·bly,** *adv.*
—**Syn.** imprudent, impolitic, risky. —**Ant.** advisable, prudent, expedient.

-inae, *Zool.* a suffix of the names of subfamilies. [< NL, L, fem. pl. of *-inus;* see -INE¹]

in ae·ter·num (in ī ter′no͝om; *Eng.* in ē tûr′nəm), *Latin.* forever.

in·al·ien·a·ble (in āl′yə nə bəl, -ā′lē ə-), *adj.* not alienable; not transferable to another or capable of being repudiated: *inalienable rights.* [1635–45; IN-³ + ALIENABLE] —**in·al′ien·a·bil′i·ty, in·al′ien·a·ble·ness,** *n.* —**in·al′ien·a·bly,** *adv.*
—**Syn.** inviolable, absolute, unassailable, inherent.

in·al·ter·a·ble (in ôl′tər ə bəl), *adj.* unalterable. [1535–45; IN-³ + ALTERABLE] —**in·al′ter·a·bil′i·ty, in·al′ter·a·ble·ness,** *n.* —**in·al′ter·a·bly,** *adv.*

in·am·o·ra·ta (in am′ə rä′tə, in′am-), *n., pl.* **-tas.** a woman who loves or is loved; female sweetheart or lover. [1645–55; < It *innamorata* (fem.); see INAMORATO]

in·am·o·ra·to (in am′ə rä′tō, in′am-), *n., pl.* **-tos.** a man who loves or is loved; male sweetheart or lover. [1585–95; < It *innamorato,* masc. ptp. of *innamorare* to inflame with love. See ENAMOR]

in-and-in (in′ənd in′, -ən-), *adv.* repeatedly within the same family, strain, etc.: *to breed stock in-and-in.* [1620–30]

in-and-out (in′ənd out′, -ən-), *adj.* **1.** in or participating in a particular job, investment, etc., for a short time and then out, esp. after realizing a quick profit. —*n.* **2.** *Manège.* an obstacle consisting of two fences placed too far apart to be cleared in one jump and too close together to allow more than one or two strides between.

in′-and-out′ bond′, *Masonry.* a stonework or brickwork bond having headers and stretchers alternating vertically.

in-and-out·er (in′ənd ou′tər, -ən-), *n.* a person who is by turns in and out of a particular situation, condition, venture, investment, etc. [1900–05; *in and out* + -ER¹]

in·ane (i nān′), *adj.* **1.** lacking sense, significance, or ideas; silly: *inane questions.* **2.** empty; void. —*n.* **3.** something that is empty or void, esp. the void of infinite space. [1655–65; < L *inānis*] —**in·ane′ly,** *adv.*
—**Syn. 1.** pointless. See **foolish.**

in·an·i·mate (in an′ə mit), *adj.* **1.** not animate; lifeless. **2.** spiritless; sluggish; dull. **3.** *Ling.* belonging to a syntactic category or having a semantic feature that is characteristic of words denoting objects, concepts, and beings regarded as lacking perception and volition (opposed to *animate*). [1555–65; < LL *inanimātus.* See IN-³, ANIMATE] —**in·an′i·mate·ly,** *adv.* —**in·an′i·mate·ness, in·an·i·ma·tion** (in an′ə mā′shən), *n.*
—**Syn. 1.** inorganic, vegetable, mineral; inert, dead. **2.** inactive, dormant, torpid.

in·a·ni·tion (in′ə nish′ən), *n.* **1.** exhaustion from lack of nourishment; starvation. **2.** lack of vigor; lethargy. [1350–1400; ME < LL *inānitiōn-* (s. of *inānitiō*). See INANE, -ITION]

in·an·i·ty (i nan′i tē), *n., pl.* **-ties** for 2. **1.** lack of sense, significance, or ideas; silliness. **2.** something inane. **3.** shallowness; superficiality. [1595–1605; < L *inānitās.* See INANE, -ITY]

in·ap·par·ent (in′ə par′ənt, -pâr′-), *adj.* not apparent. [1620–30; IN-³ + APPARENT] —**in′ap·par′ent·ly,** *adv.*

in·ap·peas·a·ble (in′ə pē′zə bəl), *adj.* not appeasable; that cannot be appeased: *inappeasable anger.* [1830–40; IN-³ + APPEASABLE]

in·ap·pe·tence (in ap′i təns), *n.* lack of appetite. Also, **in·ap′pe·ten·cy.** [1685–95; IN-³ + APPETENCE] —**in·ap′pe·tent,** *adj.*

in·ap·pli·ca·ble (in ap′li kə bəl), *adj.* not applicable; unsuitable. [1650–60; IN-³ + APPLICABLE] —**in·ap′pli·ca·bil′i·ty, in·ap′pli·ca·ble·ness,** *n.* —**in·ap′pli·ca·bly,** *adv.*
—**Syn.** irrelevant, inapposite.

in·ap·po·site (in ap′ə zit), *adj.* not apposite; not pertinent. [1655–65; IN-³ + APPOSITE] —**in·ap′po·site·ly,** *adv.* —**in·ap′po·site·ness,** *n.*

in·ap·pre·ci·a·ble (in′ə prē′shē ə bəl, -shə bəl), *adj.* imperceptible; insignificant: *an inappreciable difference.* [1780–90; IN-³ + APPRECIABLE] —**in′ap·pre′ci·a·bly,** *adv.*

in·ap·pre·ci·a·tive (in′ə prē′shē ə tiv, -ā′tiv, -shə-tiv), *adj.* not appreciative; lacking in appreciation. [1895–1900; IN-³ + APPRECIATIVE] —**in′ap·pre′ci·a′tive·ly,** *adv.* —**in′ap·pre′ci·a′tive·ness,** *n.*

in·ap·pre·hen·sion (in′ap ri hen′shən), *n.* lack of apprehension. [1735–45; IN-³ + APPREHENSION]

in·ap·pre·hen·sive (in′ap ri hen′siv), *adj.* **1.** not apprehensive (often fol. by *of*). **2.** without apprehension. [1645–55; IN-³ + APPREHENSIVE] —**in′ap·pre·hen′sive·ly,** *adv.* —**in′ap·pre·hen′sive·ness,** *n.*

in·ap·proach·a·ble (in′ə prō′chə bəl), *adj.* **1.** not approachable. **2.** without rival. [1820–30; IN-³ + APPROACHABLE] —**in′ap·proach′a·bil′i·ty,** *n.* —**in′ap·proach′a·bly,** *adv.*

in·ap·pro·pri·ate (in′ə prō′prē it), *adj.* not appropriate; not proper or suitable: *an inappropriate dress for the occasion.* [1795–1805; IN-³ + APPROPRIATE] —**in′ap·pro′pri·ate·ly,** *adv.* —**in′ap·pro′pri·ate·ness,** *n.*
—**Syn.** improper, unsuitable, inapt, unfitting.

in·apt (in apt′), *adj.* **1.** not apt or fitting. **2.** without aptitude or capacity. [1735–45; IN-³ + APT] —**in·apt′ly,** *adv.* —**in·apt′ness,** *n.*
—**Syn. 1.** unsuited, unsuitable, inappropriate, unfit, inapposite. **2.** incapable, clumsy, awkward. —**Ant. 1.** appropriate. **2.** capable.

in·ap·ti·tude (in ap′ti to͞od′, -tyo͞od′), *n.* **1.** lack of aptitude; unfitness. **2.** unskillfulness; lack of dexterity. [1610–20; IN-³ + APTITUDE]

in·arch (in ärch′), *v.t. Hort.* to graft by uniting a growing branch to a stock without separating the branch from its parent stock. [1620–30; IN-² + ARCH¹]

inarching

in·ar·gu·a·ble (in är′gyo͞o ə bəl), *adj.* not arguable: *Her conclusion is so obvious as to be inarguable.* [1870–75; IN-[3] + ARGUABLE] —**in·ar′gu·a·bly,** *adv.*

I·na·ri (in′ə rē, -är ē; *Fin.* i′nä ri), *n.* **Lake,** a lake in NE Finland. ab. 500 sq. mi. (1295 sq. km).

in·ar·tic·u·late (in′är tik′yə lit), *adj.* **1.** lacking the ability to express oneself, esp. in clear and effective speech: *an inarticulate public speaker.* **2.** unable to use articulate speech: *inarticulate with rage.* **3.** not articulate; not uttered or emitted with expressive or intelligible modulations: *His mouth stuffed, he could utter only inarticulate sounds.* **4.** not fully expressed or expressible: *a voice choked with inarticulate agony.* **5.** *Anat., Zool.* not jointed; having no articulation or joint. [1595–1605; < LL *inarticulātus.* See IN-[3], ARTICULATE] —**in′ar·tic′u·late·ly,** *adv.* —**in′ar·tic′u·late·ness,** *n.*
—**Syn. 2.** mute, dumb.

in·ar·tis·tic (in′är tis′tik), *adj.* **1.** not artistic; unaesthetic. **2.** lacking in artistic sense or appreciation. Also, **in′ar·tis′ti·cal.** [1855–60; IN-[3] + ARTISTIC] —**in′ar·tis′ti·cal·ly,** *adv.*

in·as·much as (in′əz much′ əz, az′), **1.** in view of the fact that; seeing that; since. **2.** insofar as; to such a degree as. [1250–1300; ME *in as much(e) as*]
—**Syn. 1.** See **because.**

in·at·ten·tion (in′ə ten′shən), *n.* **1.** lack of attention; negligence. **2.** an act of neglect. [1700–10; IN-[3] + ATTENTION]

in·at·ten·tive (in′ə ten′tiv), *adj.* not attentive; negligent. [1735–45; IN-[3] + ATTENTIVE] —**in′at·ten′tive·ly,** *adv.* —**in′at·ten′tive·ness,** *n.*
—**Syn.** heedless, oblivious, unmindful, preoccupied.

in·au·di·ble (in ô′də bəl), *adj.* not audible; incapable of being heard. [1595–1605; IN-[3] + AUDIBLE] —**in·au′di·bil′i·ty, in·au′di·ble·ness,** *n.* —**in·au′di·bly,** *adv.*

in·au·gu·ral (in ô′gyər əl, -gər əl), *adj.* **1.** of or pertaining to an inauguration: *Harding's inaugural address.* **2.** marking the beginning of a new venture, series, etc.: *the inaugural run of the pony express.* —*n.* **3.** an address, as of a president, at the beginning of a term of office. **4.** an inaugural ceremony: *to attend the presidential inaugural.* [1680–90; obs. *inaugure* (< L *inaugurāre* to INAUGURATE) + -AL[1], -AL[2]]

in·au·gu·rate (in ô′gyə rāt′, -gə-), *v.t.,* **-rat·ed, -rat·ing. 1.** to make a formal beginning of; initiate; commence; begin: *The end of World War II inaugurated the era of nuclear power.* **2.** to induct into office with formal ceremonies; install. **3.** to introduce into public use by some formal ceremony: *Airmail service between Washington, D.C., and New York City was inaugurated in 1918.* [1595–1605; < L *inaugurātus* ptp. of *inaugurāre* to consecrate by augury (a person chosen for priesthood or other office), lit., to take auguries). See IN-[2], AUGUR, -ATE[1]] —**in·au′gu·ra′tor,** *n.*

in·au·gu·ra·tion (in ô′gyə rā′shən, -gə-), *n.* an act or ceremony of inaugurating. [1560–70; < LL *inaugurātiōn-* (s. of *inaugurātiō*). See INAUGURATE, -ION.]

Inaugura′tion Day′, the day on which the President of the United States is inaugurated, being January 20 of every year following a year whose number is divisible by four. Prior to the Twentieth Amendment to the Constitution (ratified February 6, 1933), it was March 4.

in·aus·pi·cious (in′ô spish′əs), *adj.* not auspicious; boding ill; ill-omened; unfavorable. [1585–95; IN-[3] + AUSPICIOUS] —**in′aus·pi′cious·ly,** *adv.* —**in′aus·pi′cious·ness,** *n.*
—**Syn.** unpropitious, ill-timed, unpromising.

in·au·then·tic (in′ô then′tik), *adj.* not authentic: *inauthentic Indian jewelry mass-produced in a factory.* [1855–60; IN-[3] + AUTHENTIC] —**in′au·then′ti·cal·ly,** *adv.* —**in·au·then·tic·i·ty** (in′ô then tis′i tē, -thən-), *n.*

in-bas·ket (in′bas′kit, -bä′skit), *n.* in-box. [1935–40]

in-be·tween (in′bi twēn′), *n.* Also, **in′-be·tween′er. 1.** a person or thing that is between two extremes, two contrasting conditions, etc.: *yeses, noes, and in-betweens; a tournament for professional, amateur, and in-between.* **2.** a person who handles the intermediary steps, as in a manufacturing or sales process. —*adj.* **3.** being between one thing, condition, etc., and another: *a coat for in-between weather.* [1805–15] —**in′-be·tween′ness,** *n.*

in·board (in′bôrd′, -bōrd′), *adj.* **1.** located nearer the longitudinal axis or center, as of an airplane: *the inboard section of a wing.* **2.** located inside a hull or aircraft: *a motorboat with an inboard engine.* **3.** (of a motorboat) having the motor inboard. —*adv.* **4.** inside or toward the longitudinal axis or center of a hull, aircraft, machine, etc. Cf. **outboard** (def. 4). —*n.* **5.** an inboard motor. **6.** a boat equipped with an inboard motor. [1840–50; orig. phrase *in board*]

in·board-out·board (in′bôrd′out′bôrd′, in′bōrd′out′bōrd′), *adj.* **1.** Also, **outdrive, stern-drive.** (of a motorboat) having an inboard engine connected to a maneuverable outboard drive-shaft unit. —*n.* **2.** an inboard-outboard motor. **3.** a boat equipped with such a motor. *Abbr.:* I/O Also called **outdrive, stern drive** (for defs. 2, 3).

in·bond (in′bond′), *adj. Masonry.* composed mainly or entirely of headers (opposed to *outbond*). [1835–45; IN-[1] + BOND[1]]

in·born (in′bôrn′), *adj.* naturally present at birth; innate. [bef. 1000; ME; OE *inboren* native, indigenous; see IN-[1], BORN]
—**Syn.** inbred, inherent, natural, native, congenital, inherited, hereditary. See **innate.** —**Ant.** acquired, learned.

in·bound (in′bound′), *adj.* inward bound: *inbound ships.* [1890–95; IN-[1] + -BOUND[2]]

in·bounds (in′boundz′), *adj.* **1.** *Sports.* being within the boundaries of a court or field. **2.** *Basketball.* of or pertaining to passing the ball onto the court from out of bounds. [1960–65; adj. use of prep. phrase *in bounds*]

in′bounds′ line′, *Football.* one of two broken lines, parallel to the sidelines and running the length of the field, to which the ball is brought when it goes beyond the sidelines.

in-box (in′boks′), *n.* a boxlike tray, basket, or the like, as on a desk, for holding incoming mail, messages, or work.

in·breathe (in′brēth′, in brēth′), *v.t.,* **-breathed, -breath·ing. 1.** to breathe in; inhale. **2.** to inspire; infuse with. [1350–1400; ME; see IN-[1], BREATHE]

in·bred (in′bred′), *adj.* **1.** naturally inherent; innate; native: *her inbred grace.* **2.** resulting from or involved in inbreeding. [1585–95; ptp. of INBREED]
—**Syn. 1.** inborn, constitutional, instinctive.

in·breed (in′brēd′, in brēd′), *v.,* **-bred, -breed·ing.** —*v.t.* **1.** to breed (individuals of a closely related group) repeatedly. **2.** to breed within; engender. —*v.i.* **3.** to engage in or undergo inbreeding. [1590–1600; IN-[1] + BREED]

in·breed·ing (in′brē′ding), *n. Biol.* the mating of closely related individuals, as cousins, sire-daughter, brother-sister, or self-fertilized plants, which tends to increase the number of individuals that are homozygous for a trait and therefore increases the appearance of recessive traits. [1835–45; INBREED + -ING[1]]

in·built (in′bilt′), *adj.* built-in (def. 2). [1920–25; IN-[1] + BUILT]

Inc., incorporated.

inc., 1. engraved. [< L *incisus*] **2.** inclosure. **3.** included. **4.** including. **5.** inclusive. **6.** income. **7.** incorporated. **8.** increase. **9.** incumbent.

In·ca (ing′kə), *n.* **1.** a member of any of the dominant groups of South American Indian peoples who established an empire in Peru prior to the Spanish conquest. **2.** a ruler or member of the royal family in the Incan empire. [1585–95; < Sp < Quechua *inka* ruler of the Inca state] —**In·ca·ic** (ing kā′ik, in-), *adj.* —**In′can,** *n., adj.*

In·ca·bloc (ing′kə blok′), *Horol., Trademark.* a brand of shockproof mounting in a watch that allows for slight longitudinal and lateral play of either end of the balance staff.

in·cage (in kāj′), *v.t.,* **-caged, -cag·ing.** encage.

in·cal·cu·la·ble (in kal′kyə lə bəl), *adj.* **1.** very numerous or great. **2.** unable to be calculated; beyond calculation. **3.** incapable of being forecast or predicted; undeterminable. **4.** uncertain; unsure. [1785–95; IN-[3] + CALCULABLE] —**in·cal′cu·la·bil′i·ty, in·cal′cu·la·ble·ness,** *n.* —**in·cal′cu·la·bly,** *adv.*
—**Syn. 3.** unpredictable, unforeseeable.

in·ca·les·cent (in′kə les′ənt), *adj.* increasing in heat or ardor. [1670–80; < L *incalēscent-* (s. of *incalēscēns*) prp. of *incalēscere* to become warm, glow. See IN-[2], CALESCENT] —**in′ca·les′cence,** *n.*

in′ cam′era, *Law.* See **camera** (def. 4). [1870–75; < NL: lit., in a chamber; see CAMERA]

in·can·desce (in′kən des′), *v.i., v.t.,* **-desced, -desc·ing.** to glow or cause to glow with heat. [1870–75; back formation from INCANDESCENT]

in·can·des·cence (in′kən des′əns), *n.* **1.** the emission of visible light by a body, caused by its high temperature. Cf. **luminescence. 2.** the light produced by such an emission. **3.** the quality of being incandescent. [1650–60; INCANDESC(ENT) + -ENCE]

in·can·des·cent (in′kən des′ənt), *adj.* **1.** (of light) produced by incandescence. **2.** glowing or white with heat. **3.** intensely bright; brilliant. **4.** brilliant; masterly; extraordinarily lucid: *an incandescent masterpiece; incandescent wit.* **5.** aglow with ardor, purpose, etc.: *the incandescent vitality of youth.* [1785–95; < L *incandēscent-* (s. of *incandēscēns*), prp. of *incandēscere* to glow. See IN-[2], CANDESCENT] —**in′can·des′cent·ly,** *adv.*
—**Syn. 5.** electrifying, brilliant, dynamic.

in′candes′cent lamp′, a lamp that emits light due to the glowing of a heated material, esp. the common device in which a tungsten filament enclosed within an evacuated glass bulb is rendered luminous by the passage of an electric current through it. Cf. **fluorescent lamp.** [1880–85]

in·can·ta·tion (in′kan tā′shən), *n.* **1.** the chanting or uttering of words purporting to have magical power. **2.** the formula employed; a spell or charm. **3.** magical ceremonies. **4.** magic; sorcery. **5.** repetitious wordiness used to conceal a lack of content; obfuscation: *Her prose too often resorts to incantation.* [1350–1400; ME < LL *incantātiōn-* (s. of *incantātiō*), equiv. to *incantāt(us)* ptp. of *incantāre* to put a spell on, bewitch (see ENCHANT, -ATE[1]) + *-iōn-* -ION] —**in′can·ta′tion·al, in·can·ta·to·ry** (in kan′tə tôr′ē, -tōr′ē), *adj.* —**in′can·ta′tor,** *n.*
—**Syn. 4.** witchcraft, black magic, wizardry.

in·ca·pa·ble (in kā′pə bəl), *adj.* **1.** not capable. **2.** not having the necessary ability, qualification, or strength to perform some specified act or function: *As an administrator, he is simply incapable.* **3.** without ordinary capability; incompetent. **4. incapable of, a.** not having the ability, qualification, or strength for (a specified act or function). **b.** not open to; not susceptible to or admitting: *These materials are incapable of exact measurement.* **c.** legally unqualified for. —*n.* **5.** a thoroughly incompetent person, esp. one of defective mentality. [1585–95; < LL *incapābilis.* See IN-[3], CAPABLE] —**in·ca′pa·bil′i·ty, in·ca′pa·ble·ness,** *n.* —**in·ca′pa·bly,** *adv.*
—**Syn. 1.** INCAPABLE, INCOMPETENT, INEFFICIENT, UNABLE are applied to a person or thing that is lacking in ability, preparation, or power for whatever is to be done. INCAPABLE usually means inherently lacking in ability or power: *incapable of appreciating music; a bridge incapable of carrying heavy loads.* INCOMPETENT, generally used only of persons, means unfit or unqualified for a particular task: *incompetent as an administrator.* INEFFICIENT means wasteful in the use of effort or power: *an inefficient manager; inefficient methods.* UNABLE usually refers to a temporary condition of inability to do some specific thing: *unable to relax, to go to a concert.* **2.** impotent, unqualified. —**Ant. 1.** able.

in·ca·pac·i·tant (in′kə pas′i tənt), *n.* something, as a chemical spray, that incapacitates an individual: *to use incapacitants for riot control.* [1960–65; INCAPACIT(ATE) + -ANT]

in·ca·pac·i·tate (in′kə pas′i tāt′), *v.t.,* **-tat·ed, -tat·ing. 1.** to deprive of ability, qualification, or strength; make incapable or unfit; disable. **2.** *Law.* to deprive of the legal power to act in a specified way or ways. [1650–60; INCAPACIT(Y) + -ATE[1]] —**in′ca·pac′i·ta′tion,** *n.*
—**Syn. 1.** cripple, handicap, sideline.

in·ca·pac·i·tat·ed (in′kə pas′i tā′tid), *adj.* unable to act, respond, or the like (often used euphemistically when one is busy or otherwise occupied): *He can't come to the phone now—he's incapacitated.* [1795–1805; INCAPACITATE + -ED[2]]

in·ca·pac·i·ty (in′kə pas′i tē), *n.* **1.** lack of ability, qualification, or strength; incapability. **2.** *Law.* lack of the legal power to act in a specified way or ways. [1605–15; < LL *incapācitās.* See IN-[3], CAPACITY]

in·cap·su·late (in kap′sə lāt′, -syo͞o-), *v.t., v.i.,* **-lat·ed, -lat·ing.** encapsulate. —**in·cap′su·la′tion,** *n.*

in·car·cer·ate (*v.* in kär′sə rāt′; *adj.* in kär′sər it, -sə rāt′), *v.,* **-at·ed, -at·ing,** *adj.* —*v.t.* **1.** to imprison; confine. **2.** to enclose; constrict closely. —*adj.* **3.** imprisoned. [1520–30; < ML *incarcerātus* ptp. of *incarcerāre* to imprison, equiv. to *in-* IN-[2] + *carcer* prison + *-ātus* -ATE[1]] —**in·car′cer·a′tion,** *n.* —**in·car′cer·a′tive,** *adj.* —**in·car′cer·a′tor,** *n.*
—**Syn. 1.** jail, immure, intern.

in·car·di·nate (in kär′dn āt′), *v.t.,* **-nat·ed, -nat·ing. 1.** to institute as a cardinal. **2.** to institute as chief presbyter or priest in a particular church or place. [1600–10; < ML *incardinātus* ptp. of *incardināre* to appoint, to make a cardinal, equiv. to *in* -IN-[2] + *cardin-* (see CARDINAL) + *-ātus* -ATE[1]] —**in·car′di·na′tion,** *n.*

in·car·na·dine (in kär′nə din′, -din, -dēn′), *adj., n., v.,* **-dined, -din·ing.** —*adj.* **1.** blood-red; crimson. **2.** flesh-colored; pale pink. —*n.* **3.** an incarnadine color. —*v.t.* **4.** to make incarnadine. [1585–95; < MF, fem. of *incarnadin* flesh-colored < It *incarnatino,* equiv. to *incarnat(o)* made flesh (see INCARNATE) + *-ino* -INE[1]; see CARNATION]

in·car·nate (*adj.* in kär′nit, -nāt; *v.* in kär′nāt), *adj., v.,* **-nat·ed, -nat·ing.** —*adj.* **1.** embodied in flesh; given a bodily, esp. a human, form: *a devil incarnate.* **2.** personified or typified, as a quality or idea: *chivalry incarnate.* **3.** flesh-colored or crimson. —*v.t.* **4.** to put into or represent in a concrete form, as an idea: *The building incarnates the architect's latest theories.* **5.** to be the embodiment or type of: *Her latest book incarnates the literature of our day.* **6.** to embody in flesh; invest with a bodily, esp. a human, form: *a man who incarnated wisdom and compassion.* [1350–1400; late ME < LL *incarnātus* ptp. of *incarnāre* to make into flesh, equiv. to *in-* IN-[2] + *carn-* flesh (see CARNAL) + *-ātus* -ATE[1]]

in·car·na·tion (in′kär nā′shən), *n.* **1.** an incarnate being or form. **2.** a living being embodying a deity or spirit. **3.** assumption of human form or nature. **4. the Incarnation,** (*sometimes l.c.*) *Theol.* the doctrine that the second person of the Trinity assumed human form in the person of Jesus Christ and is completely both God and man. **5.** a person or thing regarded as embodying or exhibiting some quality, idea, or the like: *The leading dancer is the incarnation of grace.* **6.** the act of incarnating. **7.** state of being incarnated. [1250–1300; ME *incarnacion* < LL *incarnātiōn-* (s. of *incarnātiō*) equiv. to *incarnāt(us)* INCARNATE + *-iōn-* -ION] —**in′car·na′tion·al,** *adj.*

in·case (in kās′), *v.t.,* **-cased, -cas·ing.** encase. —**in·case′ment,** *n.*

in·cau·tion (in kô′shən), *n.* lack of caution; heedlessness; carelessness. [1705–15; IN-[3] + CAUTION]

in·cau·tious (in kô′shəs), *adj.* not cautious; careless; reckless; heedless. [1695–1705; IN-[3] + CAUTIOUS; cf. L *incautus* in same sense] —**in·cau′tious·ly,** *adv.* —**in·cau′tious·ness,** *n.*
—**Syn.** rash, brash, hotheaded, headstrong.

in·cen·di·a·rism (in sen′dē ə riz′əm), *n.* **1.** the act or practice of an arsonist; malicious burning. **2.** inflammatory behavior; agitation. [1665–75; INCENDIAR(Y) + -ISM]

in·cen·di·ar·y (in sen′dē er′ē), *adj., n., pl.* **-ar·ies.** —*adj.* **1.** used or adapted for setting property on fire: *incendiary bombs.* **2.** of or pertaining to the criminal setting on fire of property. **3.** tending to arouse strife, sedition, etc.; inflammatory: *incendiary speeches.* **4.** tending to inflame the senses: *an incendiary extravaganza of music and dance.* —*n.* **5.** a person who deliberately sets fire to buildings or other property, as an arsonist. **6.** *Mil.* a shell, bomb, or grenade containing napalm, thermite, or some other substance that burns with an intense heat. **7.** a person who stirs up strife, sedition, etc.; an agitator. [1600–10; < L *incendiārius,* equiv. to *incendi(um)* a fire (*incend(ere)* to kindle (*in-* IN-[2] + *-cendere,* transit. v. from base of *candēre* to shine, be hot; see CANDENT, CANDID, CANDOR) + *-ium* -IUM) + *-ārius* -ARY]

in·cense[1] (in′sens), *n., v.,* **-censed, -cens·ing.** —*n.* **1.** an aromatic gum or other substance producing a sweet odor when burned, used in religious ceremonies, to enhance a mood, etc. **2.** the perfume or smoke arising from such a substance when burned. **3.** any pleasant perfume or fragrance. **4.** homage or adulation. —*v.t.* **5.** to perfume with incense. **6.** to burn incense for. —*v.i.* **7.** to burn or offer incense. [1250–1300; ME < LL *incēnsum,* lit., something kindled, neut. of *incēnsus* (ptp. of *incendere* to set on fire), equiv. to *incend-* (see INCENDIARY) + *-tus* ptp. suffix; r. ME *ansens, ensenz* < OF < LL as above]

CONCISE PRONUNCIATION KEY: act, cāpe, dâre, pärt; set, ēqual; if, īce; ox, ōver, ôrder, oil, bo͝ok, bo͞ot, out; up, ûrge; child; sing; shoe; thin, *th*at; zh as in *treasure.* ə = a as in *alone,* e as in *system,* i as in *easily,* o as in *gallop,* u as in *circus;* ᵊ as in *fire* (fīᵊr), *hour* (ouᵊr). l and n can serve as syllabic consonants, as in *cradle* (krād′l), and *button* (but′n). See the full key inside the front cover.

in·cense[2] (in sens′), *v.t.*, **-censed, -cens·ing.** to inflame with wrath; make angry; enrage. [1400–50; late ME *incensen* < L *incēnsus* (see INCENSE[1]); r. ME *encensen* < AF < L, as above] **—in·cense′ment,** *n.*
—Syn. anger, exasperate, provoke, irritate. See **enrage.**

in′cense ce′dar, **1.** any of several coniferous trees of the genus *Libocedrus* (or *Calocedrus*), esp. *L. decurrens,* of the western U.S., growing to a height of 150 ft. (50 m). **2.** the aromatic, close-grained wood of this tree, used to make pencils, chests, closet linings, etc. [1865–70, *Amer.*]

in′cense tree′, any of various trees, as *Boswellia carteri* or those of the genus *Protium,* yielding an aromatic gum resin that is burned as incense. [1580–90]

in·cen·ter (in′sen′tər), *n. Geom.* the center of an inscribed circle; that point where the bisectors of the angles of a triangle or of a regular polygon intersect. [1900–05; IN-[1] + CENTER]

in·cen·tive (in sen′tiv), *n.* **1.** something that incites or tends to incite to action or greater effort, as a reward offered for increased productivity. **—*adj.*** **2.** inciting, as to action; stimulating; provocative. [1400–50; late ME < LL *incentīvus* provocative, L: setting the tune, equiv. to *incent(us)* (ptp. of *incinere* to play (an instrument, tunes); *in-* IN-[2] + *-cinere,* comb. form of *canere* to sing) + *-īvus* -IVE] **—in·cen′tive·ly,** *adv.*
—Syn. 1. stimulus, spur, incitement, impulse, encouragement; goad, prod. See **motive.**

incen′tive pay′, additional pay, a higher wage, or a bonus paid to promote the productivity of an employee. Also called **incen′tive wage′.** [1955–60]

in·cept (in sept′), *v.t.* to take in; ingest. [1560–70; < L *inceptus* ptp. of *incipere* to begin, undertake, equiv. to *in-* IN-[2] + *cep-* (comb. form of *cap-* take; see CAPTIVE) + *-tus* ptp. suffix; sense "take in" by literal trans. of prefix and base] **—in·cep′tor,** *n.*

in·cep·tion (in sep′shən), *n.* **1.** beginning; start; commencement. **2.** *Brit.* **a.** the act of graduating or earning a university degree, usually a master's or doctor's degree, esp. at Cambridge University. **b.** the graduation ceremony; commencement. [1375–1425; late ME *incepcion* < L *inceptiōn-* (s. of *inceptiō*), equiv. to *incept(us)* begun (see INCEPT) + *-iōn-* -ION]
—Syn. 1. origin, outset, source, root, conception.

in·cep·ti·sol (in sep′tə sôl′, -sol′), *n.* a soil so young that horizons have just begun to form: esp. prevalent in tundra areas. [1970–75; INCEPT(ION) + -I- + -SOL]

in·cep·tive (in sep′tiv), *adj.* **1.** beginning; initial. **2.** *Gram.* (of a derived verb, or of an aspect in verb inflection) expressing the beginning of the action indicated by the underlying verb, as Latin verbs in *-scō,* which generally have inceptive force, as *calēscō* "become or begin to be hot" from *caleō* "be hot." **—*n.*** *Gram.* **3.** the inceptive aspect. **4.** a verb in this aspect. [1605–15; < LL *inceptīvus.* See INCEPT, -IVE] **—in·cep′tive·ly,** *adv.*
—Syn. 1. inchoative, embryonic, nascent.

in·cer·ti·tude (in sûr′ti to͞od′, -tyo͞od′), *n.* **1.** uncertainty or doubtfulness. **2.** instability or insecurity: *The incertitude of his position in life caused him to postpone marriage.* [1595–1605; < LL *incertitūdō.* See IN-[3], CERTITUDE]

in·ces·sant (in ses′ənt), *adj.* continuing without interruption; ceaseless; unending: *an incessant noise.* [1425–75; late ME *incessaunte* < LL *incessant-,* equiv. to L *in-* IN-[3] + *cessant-* (s. of *cessāns*), prp. of *cessāre* to stop work; see CEASE, -ANT] **—in·ces′san·cy, in·ces′sant·ness,** *n.* **—in·ces′sant·ly,** *adv.*
—Syn. unceasing, constant, continuous, never-ending, perpetual; eternal, everlasting; relentless, unrelenting, unremitting. **—Ant.** intermittent.

in·cest (in′sest), *n.* **1.** sexual intercourse between closely related persons. **2.** the crime of sexual intercourse, cohabitation, or marriage between persons within the degrees of consanguinity or affinity wherein marriage is legally forbidden. [1175–1225; ME < L *incestus* (n.) sexual impurity, deriv. of *incestus* (adj.) profane, sexually impure (*in-* IN-[3] + *-cestus* comb. form of *castus* CHASTE), by analogy with v. nouns derived with *-tus*]

in·ces·tu·ous (in ses′cho͞o əs), *adj.* **1.** involving incest. **2.** guilty of incest. **3.** being so close or intimate as to prevent proper functioning: *an incestuous relationship between organized crime and government.* [1525–35; < LL *incestuōsus,* equiv. to L *incestu-* s. of *incestus* INCEST + *-ōsus* -OUS] **—in·ces′tu·ous·ly,** *adv.* **—in·ces′tu·ous·ness,** *n.*

inch[1] (inch), *n.* **1.** a unit of length, 1/12 foot, equivalent to 2.54 centimeters. **2.** a very small amount of anything; narrow margin: *to win by an inch; to avert disaster by an inch.* **3. by inches, a.** narrowly; by a narrow margin: *escaped by inches.* **b.** Also, **inch by inch.** by small degrees or stages; gradually: *The miners worked their way through the narrow shaft inch by inch.* **4. every inch,** in every respect; completely: *That horse is every inch a thoroughbred.* **5. within an inch of,** nearly; close to: *He came within an inch of getting killed in the crash.* **—*v.t., v.i.*** **6.** to move by inches or small degrees: *We inched our way along the road.* [bef. 1000; ME; OE *ynce* < L *uncia* twelfth part, inch, ounce. See OUNCE[1]]

inch[2] (inch), *n. Scot.* a small island near the seacoast. [1375–1425; late ME < ScotGael *innse,* gen. of *innis* island, OIr *inis,* c. Welsh *ynys*]

inch·meal (inch′mēl), *adv.* by inches; inch by inch; little by little. [1520–30; INCH[1] + -MEAL]

in·cho·ate (in kō′it, -āt *or, esp. Brit.,* in′kō āt′), *adj.* **1.** not yet completed or fully developed; rudimentary. **2.** just begun; incipient. **3.** not organized; lacking order: *an inchoate mass of ideas on the subject.* [1525–35; < L *inchoātus,* var. of *incohātus* ptp. of *incohāre* to begin, start work on, perh. equiv. to *in-* -IN-[2] + *coh(um)* hollow of a yoke into which the pole is fitted + *-ātus* -ATE[1]] **—in·cho′ate·ly,** *adv.* **—in·cho′ate·ness,** *n.*

CONCISE ETYMOLOGY KEY: <, descended or borrowed from; >, whence; b., blend of, blended; c., cognate with; cf., compare; deriv., derivative; equiv., equivalent; imit., imitative; obl., oblique; r., replacing; s., stem; sp., spelling, spelled; resp., respelling, respelled; trans., translation; ?, origin unknown; *, unattested; ‡, probably earlier than. See the full key inside the front cover.

in·cho·a·tion (in′kō ā′shən), *n.* a beginning; origin. [1520–30; < LL *inchoātiōn-* (s. of *inchoātiō*). See INCHOATE, -ION]

in·cho·a·tive (in kō′ə tiv), *Gram.* **—*adj.*** **1.** inceptive. **—*n.*** **2.** an inceptive. [1520–30; < LL *inchoātīvum* (*verbum*) inceptive (verb). See INCHOATE, -IVE]

inch′ of mer′cury, a unit of atmospheric pressure, being the pressure equal to that exerted by a column of mercury one inch high under standard conditions of temperature and gravity: 33.864 millibars. *Abbr.:* in. Hg [1825–35]

In·chon (in′chon′), *n.* a seaport in W South Korea. 799,982. Formerly, **Chemulpo.**

inch′ plant′, **1.** any of several creeping or sprawling tropical American plants of the genus *Callisia,* having sometimes fragrant flowers in a variety of colors. **2.** See **wandering Jew** (def. 2). [1890–95, *Amer.*]

inch-pound (inch′pound′), *n.* one-twelfth of a foot-pound. *Abbr.:* in-lb

inch·worm (inch′wûrm′), *n.* measuringworm. [1860–65; INCH[1] + WORM]

in·ci·dence (in′si dəns), *n.* **1.** the rate or range of occurrence or influence of something, esp. of something unwanted: *the high incidence of heart disease in men over 40.* **2.** a falling upon, affecting, or befalling; occurrence: *The incidence of murder that Sunday afternoon shocked the sleepy village.* **3.** *Optics, Physics.* **a.** the striking of a ray of light, beam of electrons, etc., on a surface, or the direction of striking. **b.** See **angle of incidence** (def. 1). **4.** the fact or the manner of being incident. **5.** *Geom.* partial coincidence of two figures, as of a line and a plane containing it. [1375–1425; late ME < LL *incidentia.* See INCIDENT, -ENCE]

in·ci·dent (in′si dənt), *n.* **1.** an individual occurrence or event. **2.** a distinct piece of action, or an episode, as in a story or play. **3.** something that occurs casually in connection with something else. **4.** something appertaining or attaching to something else. **5.** an occurrence of seemingly minor importance, esp. involving nations or factions between which relations are strained and sensitive, that can lead to serious consequences, as an outbreak of hostilities or a war: *border incident; international incident.* **6.** an embarrassing occurrence, esp. of a social nature. **—*adj.*** **7.** likely or apt to happen (usually fol. by *to*). **8.** naturally appertaining: *hardships incident to the life of an explorer.* **9.** conjoined or attaching, esp. as subordinate to a principal thing. **10.** falling or striking on something, as light rays. [1375–1425; late ME < MF < ML *incident-* (s. of *incidēns* a happening, n. use of prp. of L *incidere* to befall), equiv. to L *in-* IN-[2] + *-cid-* (comb. form of *cad-* fall) + *-ent-* -ENT; cf. CADENCE] **—in′ci·dent·less,** *adj.*
—Syn. 1. happening. See **event.**

in·ci·den·tal (in′si den′tl), *adj.* **1.** happening or likely to happen in an unplanned or subordinate conjunction with something else. **2.** incurred casually and in addition to the regular or main amount: *incidental expenses.* **3.** likely to happen or naturally appertaining (usually fol. by *to*). **—*n.*** **4.** something incidental, as a circumstance. **5. incidentals,** minor expenses. [1610–20; INCIDENT + -AL[1]] **—in′ci·den′tal·ness,** *n.*
—Syn. 1. casual, chance, fortuitous; contingent. **—Ant. 1.** fundamental.

in·ci·den·tal·ly (in′si den′tl ē *or, for 1,* -dent′lē), *adv.* **1.** apart or aside from the main subject of attention, discussion, etc.; by the way; parenthetically. **2.** in an incidental manner. [1655–65; INCIDENTAL + -LY]

in′ciden′tal mu′sic, music intended primarily to point up or accompany parts of the action of a play or to serve as transitional material between scenes. [1860–65]

in·ci·en·so (in′sē en′sō), *n.* a shrubby, composite desert plant, *Encelia farinosa,* of the southwestern U.S., having silvery leaves and clusters of yellow flowers. [1920–25, *Amer.;* < Sp: INCENSE]

in·cin·er·ate (in sin′ə rāt′), *v.t.,* **-at·ed, -at·ing.** to burn or reduce to ashes; cremate. [1545–55; < ML *incinerātus* (ptp. of *incinerāre*) < L *in-* IN-[2] + *ciner-* (s. of *cinis*) ashes + *-ātus* -ATE[1]] **—in·cin′er·a′tion,** *n.*

in·cin·er·a·tor (in sin′ə rā′tər), *n.* a furnace or apparatus for burning trash, garbage, etc., to ashes. [1880–85; INCINERATE + -OR[2]]

in·cip·i·en·cy (in sip′ē ən sē), *n.* the state or condition of being incipient. Also, **in·cip′i·ence.** [1810–20; INCIPI(ENT) + -ENCY]

in·cip·i·ent (in sip′ē ənt), *adj.* beginning to exist or appear; in an initial stage: *an incipient cold.* [1580–90; < L *incipient-* (s. of *incipiēns,* prp. of *incipere* to take in hand, begin), equiv. to *in-* IN-[2] + *-cipi-* (comb. form of *capi-* take) + *-ent-* -ENT] **—in·cip′i·ent·ly,** *adv.*
—Syn. beginning, nascent, developing.

in·ci·pit (in′si pit; *Lat.* ing′ki pit), *n.* **1.** the introductory words or opening phrases in the text of a medieval manuscript or an early printed book. **2.** *Music.* the first words of a chanted liturgical text, as that of a Gregorian chant or certain medieval motets. [1895–1900; < L: (here) begins, 3rd sing. pres. indic. of *incipere*]

in·cir·cle (in′sûr′kəl), *n. Geom.* a circle inscribed within a triangle. [1880–85; IN-[1] + CIRCLE]

in·cise (in sīz′), *v.t.,* **-cised, -cis·ing.** **1.** to cut into; cut marks, figures, etc., upon. **2.** to make (marks, figures, etc.) by cutting; engrave; carve. [1535–45; < L *incīsus* ptp. of *incīdere* to carve, cut into, equiv. to *in-* IN-[2] + *cīd-* cut + *-tus* ptp. suffix, with *-dt-* > *-s-*]

in·cised (in sīzd′), *adj.* **1.** cut into: *the incised material.* **2.** made by cutting: *an incised pattern.* **3.** *Med.* made or cut cleanly, as if surgically; not ragged: *an incised wound.* **4.** (of a leaf) sharply, deeply, and somewhat irregularly notched. [1590–1600; INCISE + -ED[2]]

in·ci·sion (in sizh′ən), *n.* **1.** a cut, gash, or notch. **2.** the act of incising. **3.** a cutting into, esp. for surgical purposes. **4.** incisiveness; keenness. [1350–1400; ME < L *incīsiōn-* (s. of *incīsiō*). See INCISE, -ION]

in·ci·sive (in sī′siv), *adj.* **1.** penetrating; cutting; biting; trenchant: *an incisive tone of voice.* **2.** remarkably clear and direct; sharp; keen; acute: *an incisive method of summarizing the issue.* **3.** adapted for cutting or piercing. **4.** of or pertaining to the incisors: *the incisive teeth.* [1520–30; < ML *incīsīvus.* See INCISE, -IVE] **—in·ci′sive·ly,** *adv.* **—in·ci′sive·ness,** *n.*
—Syn. 1. acid, mordant; sarcastic, sardonic.

in·ci·sor (in sī′zər), *n. Dentistry.* any of the four anterior teeth in each jaw, used for cutting and gnawing. See illus. under **tooth.** [1665–75; < NL: lit., cutter, equiv. to L *incīd(ere)* to INCISE + *-tor* -TOR, with *-dt-* > *-s-*]

in·ci·so·ry (in sī′zə rē), *adj.* adapted for cutting, as the incisor teeth. [1585–95; INCISOR + -Y[1]]

in·cis·ure (in sizh′ər), *n. Anat.* a notch, as in a bone or other structure. [1590–1600; < L *incīsūra.* See INCISE, -URE] **—in·cis′ur·al,** *adj.*

in·cite (in sīt′), *v.t.,* **-cit·ed, -cit·ing.** to stir, encourage, or urge on; stimulate or prompt to action: *to incite a crowd to riot.* [1475–85; < L *incitāre,* equiv. to *in-* IN-[2] + *citāre* to start up, EXCITE; see CITE] **—in·cit′a·ble,** *adj.* **—in·cit′ant,** *adj., n.* **—in·ci·ta·tion** (in′sī tā′shən, -si-), *n.* **—in·cit′er,** *n.* **—in·cit′ing·ly,** *adv.*
—Syn. instigate, provoke, goad, spur, arouse, exhort; fire; induce. INCITE, ROUSE, PROVOKE, INFLAME are verbs meaning to goad or inspire an individual or a group to take some action or to express some feeling. INCITE and ROUSE are similar in that, although they can imply in some contexts abrasive or inflammatory arousal of violent or uncontrolled behavior, neither necessarily does so. INCITE means simply to induce activity, of whatever kind: *incited to greater effort by encouragement; incited to riot.* ROUSE has an underlying sense of awakening: *to rouse the apathetic soldiers to a determination to win; to rouse the inattentive public to an awareness of the danger.* PROVOKE implies a sense of challenge or irritation along with arousal and often suggests a resultant anger or violence: *provoked by scathing references to his accomplishments; to provoke a wave of resentment.* INFLAME, with its root sense to set afire, implies a resultant intensity and passion: *to inflame a mob by fiery speeches; He was inflamed to rage by constant frustration.* **—Ant.** discourage.

in·cite·ment (in sīt′mənt), *n.* **1.** the act of inciting. **2.** the state of being incited. **3.** motive; incentive. [1585–95; INCITE + -MENT; cf. L *incitāmentum*]

in·ci·vil·i·ty (in′sə vil′i tē), *n., pl.* **-ties** for 2. **1.** the quality or condition of being uncivil; discourteous behavior or treatment. **2.** an uncivil act. [1575–85; < LL *incīvilitās.* See IN-[3], CIVILITY] **—in·civ·il** (in siv′əl), *adj.*
—Syn. 1. rudeness, boorishness, uncouthness. **2.** discourtesy.

incl., **1.** inclosure. **2.** including. **3.** inclusive.

in·clasp (in klasp′, -kläsp′), *v.t.* enclasp.

in·clem·ent (in klem′ənt), *adj.* **1.** (of the weather, the elements, etc.) severe, rough, or harsh; stormy. **2.** not kind or merciful. [1615–25; < L *inclēment-,* equiv. to *in-* IN-[3] + *clēment-* (s. of *clēmēns*) CLEMENT] **—in·clem′en·cy, in·clem′ent·ness,** *n.* **—in·clem′ent·ly,** *adv.*

in·clin·a·ble (in klī′nə bəl), *adj.* **1.** having a mental tendency in a certain direction. **2.** favorable. **3.** capable of being inclined. [1400–50; late ME; see INCLINE, -ABLE]

in·cli·na·tion (in′klə nā′shən), *n.* **1.** a disposition or bent, esp. of the mind or will; a liking or preference: *Much against his inclination, he was forced to resign.* **2.** something to which one is inclined: *In sports his inclination is tennis.* **3.** the act of inclining; state of being inclined. **4.** a tendency toward a certain condition, action, etc.: *the door's inclination to stick.* **5.** deviation or amount of deviation from a normal, esp. horizontal or vertical, direction or position. **6.** an inclined surface. **7.** *Geom.* **a.** the angle between two lines or two planes. **b.** the angle formed by the x-axis and a given line. **8.** *Astron.* **a.** the angle between the orbital plane of a planet and another given plane, usually the ecliptic. **b.** the angle between the equatorial and orbital planes of a planet. **9.** *Magnetism.* dip (def. 32). [1350–1400; ME *inclinacioun* < L *inclīnātiōn-* (s. of *inclīnātiō*), equiv. to *inclīnāt(us)* ptp. of *inclīnāre* (see INCLINE, -ATE[1]) + *-iōn-* -ION] **—in′cli·na′tion·al,** *adj.*
—Syn. 1. leaning, tendency; propensity, proclivity, predilection, predisposition, penchant. **5, 6.** slope, slant, rise, fall, grade, pitch. **6.** ramp. **—Ant. 1.** dislike.

in·cli·na·to·ry (in klī′nə tôr′ē, -tōr′ē), *adj.* characterized by inclination. [1605–15; < L *inclīnāt(us)* (see INCLINATION) + -ORY[1]] **—in·cli′na·to′ri·ly,** *adv.*

in·cline (*v.* in klīn′; *n.* in′klīn, in klīn′), *v.,* **-clined, -clin·ing,** *n.* **—*v.t.*** **1.** to deviate from the vertical or horizontal; slant. **2.** to have a mental tendency, preference, etc.; be disposed: *We incline to rest and relaxation these days.* **3.** to tend, in a physical sense; approximate: *The flowers incline toward blue.* **4.** to tend in character or in course of action: *a political philosophy that inclines toward the conservative.* **5.** to lean; bend. **—*v.t.*** **6.** to dispose (a person) in mind, habit, etc. (usually fol. by *to*): *His attitude did not incline me to help him.* **7.** to bow, nod, or bend (the head, body, etc.): *He inclined his head in greeting.* **8.** to cause to lean or bend in a particular direction. **9. incline one's ear,** to listen, esp. willingly or favorably: *to incline one's ear to another's plea.* **—*n.*** **10.** an inclined surface; slope; slant. **11.** *Railroads.* **a.** Also called **inclined plane, in′cline plane′.** a cable railroad, the gradient of which is approximately 45°. **b.** any railroad or portion of a railroad, the gradient of which is too steep for ordinary locomotive adhesion alone to be effective. **12.** *Mining.* **a.** an angled shaft following a dipping vein. **b.** an inclined haulageway. [1300–50; ME *inclinen* < L *inclīnāre,* equiv. to *in-* IN-[2] + *-clīnāre* to bend (see LEAN[1]); r. ME *enclinen* < MF < L, as above] **—in·clin′er,** *n.*
—Syn. 1. lean, slope, rise, fall, pitch. **2.** tend, lean. **3, 4.** verge, veer.

in·clined (in klīnd′), *adj.* **1.** deviating in direction from the horizontal or vertical; sloping. **2.** disposed; of a mind (usually fol. by *to*): *He was inclined to stay.* **3.** having a physical tendency; leaning. **4.** tending in a direction that makes an angle with anything else. [1350–1400; ME *enclyned.* See INCLINE, -ED[2]]

inclined′ plane′, 1. one of the simple machines, a plane surface inclined to the horizon, or forming with a horizontal plane any angle but a right angle. Cf. **machine** (def. 4b). **2.** incline (def. 11a). [1700–10]

in·clin·ing (in klī′ning), *n.* **1.** inclination; disposition. **2.** *Archaic.* people who are sympathetic to a person or cause. [1300–50; ME *enclynynge.* See INCLINE, -ING[1]]

in·cli·nom·e·ter (in′klə nom′i tər), *n.* **1.** *Aeron.* an instrument for measuring the angle an aircraft makes with the horizontal. **2.** *Physics.* See **dip needle.** [1835–45; INCLINE + -O- + -METER]

in·clip (in klip′), *v.t.,* **-clipped, -clip·ping.** *Archaic.* to grasp or enclose. [1600–10; IN-[1] + CLIP[2] (v.)]

in·close (in klōz′), *v.t.,* **-closed, -clos·ing.** enclose. —**in·clos′er,** *n.*

in·clo·sure (in klō′zhər), *n.* enclosure.

in·clude (in klōōd′), *v.t.,* **-clud·ed, -clud·ing. 1.** to contain, as a whole does parts or any part or element: *The package includes the computer, program, disks, and a manual.* **2.** to place in an aggregate, class, category, or the like. **3.** to contain as a subordinate element; involve as a factor. [1375–1425; late ME < L *inclūdere* to shut in, equiv. to *in-* IN-[2] + *-clūdere,* comb. form of *claudere* to shut (cf. CLOSE)] —**in·clud′a·ble, in·clud′i·ble,** *adj.*
—**Syn. 1.** embody. INCLUDE, COMPREHEND, COMPRISE, EMBRACE imply containing parts of a whole. To INCLUDE is to contain as a part or member, or among the parts and members, of a whole: *The list includes many new names.* To COMPREHEND is to have within the limits, scope, or range of references, as either a part or the whole number of items concerned: *The plan comprehends several projects.* To COMPRISE is to consist of, as the various parts serving to make up the whole: *This genus comprises 50 species.* EMBRACE emphasizes the extent or assortment of that which is included: *The report embraces a great variety of subjects.* —**Ant. 1.** exclude, preclude.

in·clud·ed (in klōō′did), *adj.* **1.** being part of the whole; contained; covered: *Breakfast is included in the price of the room.* **2.** *Bot.* not projecting beyond the mouth of the corolla, as stamens or a style. **3.** enclosed. [1545–55; INCLUDE + -ED[2]] —**in·clud′ed·ness,** *n.*

in·cluse (in′klōōs), *n.* recluse (def. 2). [1375–1425; late ME < L *inclūsus,* ptp. of *inclūdere* to enclose, shut in, equiv. to *inclūd-* (see INCLUDE) + *-tus* ptp. suffix, with *-dt-* > *-s-*]

in·clu·sion (in klōō′zhən), *n.* **1.** the act of including. **2.** the state of being included. **3.** something that is included. **4.** *Biol.* a body suspended in the cytoplasm, as a granule. **5.** *Mineral.* a solid body or a body of gas or liquid enclosed within the mass of a mineral. **6.** *Petrog.* xenolith. **7.** *Logic, Math.* the relationship between two sets when the second is a subset of the first. [1590–1600; 1945–50 for def. 7; < L *inclūsiōn-* (s. of *inclūsiō*) a shutting in, equiv. to *inclūs(us)* (see INCLUSE) + *-iōn-* -ION]

in·clu·sion·ar·y (in klōō′zhə ner′ē), *adj.* (of zoning, housing programs, etc.) stipulating that a certain percentage of new housing will be priced within the reach of middle-income buyers or renters. [INCLUSION + -ARY]

inclu′sion bod′y, *Pathol.* a particle that takes a characteristic stain, found in a virus-infected cell. [1920–25]

inclu′sion com′plex, *Chem.* a solid solution in which molecules of one compound occupy places in the crystal lattice of another compound. Cf. **adduct** (def. 2). Also called **inclu′sion com′pound.**

inclu′sion map′, *Math.* a map of a set to itself in which each element of a given subset of the set is mapped to itself. [1945–50]

in·clu·sive (in klōō′siv), *adj.* **1.** including the stated limit or extremes in consideration or account: *from 6 to 37 inclusive.* **2.** including a great deal, or including everything concerned; comprehensive: *an inclusive art form; an inclusive fee.* **3.** that includes; enclosing; embracing. **4.** *Gram.* (of the first person plural) including the person or persons spoken to, as *we* in *Shall we dance?* Cf. **exclusive** (def. 12). **5. inclusive of,** including; also taking into account: *Europe, inclusive of the British Isles, is negotiating new trade agreements.* [1400–50; late ME < ML *inclūsīvus,* equiv. to L *inclūs(us)* (see INCLUSE) + *-īvus* -IVE] —**in·clu′sive·ly,** *adv.* —**in·clu′sive·ness,** *n.*
—**Syn. 2.** overall, general, all-encompassing. **3.** including, comprising.

inclu′sive disjunc′tion, *Logic.* See under **disjunction** (def. 2a). [1940–45]

inclu′sive fit′ness, *Biol.* the fitness of an individual organism as measured in terms of the survival and reproductive success of its kin, each relative being valued according to the probability of shared genetic information, an offspring or sibling having a value of 50 percent and a cousin 25 percent.

in·co·er·ci·ble (in′kō ûr′sə bəl), *adj.* **1.** not coercible. **2.** *Physics.* (of a gas) incapable of being reduced to a liquid form by pressure. [1700–10; IN-[3] + COERCIBLE]

in·cog (in kog′), *adj., adv., n. Informal.* incognita or incognito. [1690–1700; by shortening]

in·cog·i·tant (in koj′i tənt), *adj.* **1.** thoughtless; inconsiderate. **2.** not having the faculty of thought. [1620–30; < L *incōgitant-,* equiv. to *in-* IN-[3] + *cōgitant-* (s. of *cōgitāns*), prp. of *cōgitāre* to think; see COGITATE, -ANT] —**in·cog′i·tant·ly,** *adv.*

in·cog·ni·ta (in′kog nē′tə, in kog′ni-), *adj., adv.* **1.** (of a woman or girl) incognito. —*n.* **2.** a woman or girl who is incognita. [1660–70; < It; fem. of INCOGNITO]

in·cog·ni·to (in′kog nē′tō, in kog′ni tō′), *adj., adv., n., pl.* **-tos** for 3, 5. —*adj.* **1.** having one's identity concealed, as under an assumed name, esp. to avoid notice or formal attentions. —*adv.* **2.** with the real identity concealed: *to travel incognito.* —*n.* **3.** a person who is incognito. **4.** the state of being incognito. **5.** the disguise or character assumed by an incognito. [1630–40; < It < L *incognitus* unknown, equiv. to *in-* IN-[3] + *cognitus,* ptp. of *cognōscere* to get to know; see COGNITION, KNOW[1]]
—**Syn. 1.** disguised, undisclosed, unidentified.

in·cog·ni·zant (in kog′nə zənt), *adj.* not cognizant; without knowledge or awareness; unaware (usually fol. by *of*). [1830–40; IN-[3] + COGNIZANT] —**in·cog′ni·zance,** *n.*

in·co·her·ence (in′kō hēr′əns, -her′-), *n.* **1.** the quality or state of being incoherent. **2.** something incoherent; an incoherent statement, article, speech, etc. [1605–15; IN-[3] + COHERENCE]

in·co·her·en·cy (in′kō hēr′ən sē, -her′-), *n., pl.* **-cies.** incoherence. [1675–85; IN-[3] + COHERENCY]

in·co·her·ent (in′kō hēr′ənt, -her′-), *adj.* **1.** without logical or meaningful connection; disjointed; rambling: *an incoherent sentence.* **2.** characterized by such thought or language, as a person: *incoherent with rage.* **3.** not coherent or cohering: *an incoherent mixture.* **4.** lacking physical cohesion; loose: *incoherent dust.* **5.** lacking unity or harmony of elements: *an incoherent public.* **6.** lacking congruity of parts; uncoordinated. **7.** different or incompatible by nature, as things. **8.** *Physics.* (of a wave) having a low degree of coherence. Cf. **coherent** (def. 4). [1620–30; IN-[3] + COHERENT] —**in′co·her′ent·ly,** *adv.*
—**Syn. 1.** confused, irrational, muddled.

in·com·bus·ti·ble (in′kəm bus′tə bəl), *adj.* **1.** not combustible; incapable of being burned; fireproof. —*n.* **2.** an incombustible substance. [1425–75; late ME < ML *incombustibilis.* See IN-[3], COMBUSTIBLE] —**in′com·bus′ti·bil′i·ty, in′com·bus′ti·ble·ness,** *n.* —**in′com·bus′ti·bly,** *adv.*

in·come (in′kum), *n.* **1.** the monetary payment received for goods or services, or from other sources, as rents or investments. **2.** something that comes in as an addition or increase, esp. by chance. **3.** *Archaic.* a coming in. [1250–1300; ME: lit., that which has come in, n. use of *incomen* (ptp. of *incomen* to come in), OE *incuman;* see IN, COME] —**in′come·less,** *adj.*
—**Syn. 1.** interest, salary, wages, annuity, gain, return, earnings. —**Ant. 1.** outgo, expenditure.

in′come account′, 1. an account maintained for a particular item of revenue or income. **2.** Also called **profit and loss account.** a summary account for income and expenditures, used in closing the ledger. [1865–70]

in′come bond′, a bond without a guaranteed amount of interest payment, such payment being usually made only out of earnings. [1885–90]

in′come main′tenance, a government program that provides financial assistance to needy people so that they can maintain a certain income level. [1970–75]

in·com·er (in′kum′ər), *n.* **1.** a person who comes in. **2.** *Chiefly Brit.* an immigrant. **3.** an intruder. **4.** a successor. **5.** *Hunting.* a duck, pheasant, etc., that flies toward the shooter. [1520–30; IN + COMER]

in′comes pol′icy, a government policy to curb inflation that relies on voluntary compliance rather than on mandatory wage, price, or profit controls. [1955–60]

in′come state′ment, an accounting of income and expenses that indicates a firm's net profit or loss over a certain period of time, usually one year.

in′come tax′, a tax levied on incomes, esp. an annual government tax on personal incomes. [1790–1800]

in·com·ing (in′kum′ing), *adj.* **1.** coming in; arriving: *the incoming tide.* **2.** newly arrived or received: *incoming mail; incoming orders.* **3.** succeeding, as an officeholder: *the incoming mayor.* **4.** accruing, as profit. **5.** entering, beginning, etc.: *all incoming students.* **6.** *Chiefly Brit.* immigrant. **7.** *Scot.* ensuing. —*n.* **8.** the act of coming in; arrival; advent: *the incoming of spring.* **9.** Usually, **incomings.** funds received; revenue. [1275–1325; ME; see IN, COMING]

in·com·men·su·ra·ble (in′kə men′sər ə bəl, -shər-), *adj.* **1.** not commensurable; having no common basis, measure, or standard of comparison. **2.** utterly disproportionate. **3.** *Math.* (of two or more quantities) having no common measure. —*n.* **4.** something that is incommensurable. **5.** *Math.* one of two or more incommensurable quantities. [1550–60; < LL *incommēnsūrābilis.* See IN-[3], COMMENSURABLE] —**in′com·men′su·ra·bil′i·ty, in′com·men′su·ra·ble·ness,** *n.* —**in′com·men′su·ra·bly,** *adv.*

in·com·men·su·rate (in′kə men′sər it, -shər-), *adj.* **1.** not commensurate; disproportionate; inadequate: *Our income is incommensurate to our wants.* **2.** incommensurable. [1640–50; IN-[3] + COMMENSURATE] —**in′com·men′su·rate·ly,** *adv.* —**in′com·men′su·rate·ness,** *n.*

in·com·mode (in′kə mōd′), *v.t.,* **-mod·ed, -mod·ing. 1.** to inconvenience or discomfort; disturb; trouble. **2.** to impede; hinder. [1510–20; < L *incommodāre,* deriv. of *incommodus* inconvenient, equiv. to *in-* IN-[3] + *commodus* suitable; see COMMODE]
—**Syn. 1.** discommode. **2.** delay, obstruct. —**Ant. 1.** help. **2.** expedite.

in·com·mo·di·ous (in′kə mō′dē əs), *adj.* inconvenient, as not affording sufficient space or room; uncomfortable: *incommodious hotel accommodations.* [1545–55; IN-[3] + COMMODIOUS] —**in′com·mo′di·ous·ly,** *adv.* —**in′com·mo′di·ous·ness,** *n.*

in·com·mod·i·ty (in′kə mod′i tē), *n., pl.* **-ties.** disadvantage; inconvenience. [1400–50; late ME < L *incommoditās.* See INCOMMODE, -ITY]

in·com·mu·ni·ca·ble (in′kə myōō′ni kə bəl), *adj.* **1.** incapable of being communicated, imparted, shared, etc. **2.** not communicative; taciturn. [1560–70; < LL *incommūnicābilis.* See IN-[3], COMMUNICABLE] —**in′com·mu′ni·ca·bil′i·ty, in′com·mu′ni·ca·ble·ness,** *n.* —**in′com·mu′ni·ca·bly,** *adv.*

in·com·mu·ni·ca·do (in′kə myōō′ni kä′dō), *adj.* (esp. of a prisoner) deprived of any communication with others. [1835–45, *Amer.;* < Sp *incomunicado.* See IN-[3], COMMUNICATE]

in·com·mu·ni·ca·tive (in′kə myōō′ni kə tiv, -kā′-), *adj.* not communicative; reserved; uncommunicative. [1660–70; IN-[3] + COMMUNICATIVE] —**in′com·mu′ni·ca·tive·ly,** *adv.* —**in′com·mu′ni·ca·tive·ness,** *n.*

in·com·mut·a·ble (in′kə myōō′tə bəl), *adj.* **1.** not exchangeable. **2.** unchangeable; unalterable. [1400–50; late ME < L *incommūtābilis.* See IN-[3], COMMUTABLE] —**in′com·mut′a·bil′i·ty, in′com·mut′a·ble·ness,** *n.* —**in′com·mut′a·bly,** *adv.*

in·com·pact (in′kəm pakt′), *adj.* not compact; loose. [1610–20; IN-[3] + COMPACT[1]] —**in′com·pact′ly,** *adv.* —**in′com·pact′ness,** *n.*

in·com·pa·ra·ble (in kom′pər ə bəl, -prə bəl), *adj.* **1.** beyond comparison; matchless or unequaled: *incomparable beauty.* **2.** not comparable; incapable of being compared to each other, as two unlike objects or qualities, or to one or more others. [1375–1425; late ME < L *incomparābilis.* See IN-[3], COMPARABLE] —**in·com′pa·ra·bil′i·ty, in·com′pa·ra·ble·ness,** *n.* —**in·com′pa·ra·bly,** *adv.*
—**Syn. 1.** peerless, unrivaled, inimitable. —**Ant. 1.** ordinary, mediocre.

in·com·pat·i·ble (in′kəm pat′ə bəl), *adj.* **1.** not compatible; unable to exist together in harmony: *She asked for a divorce because they were utterly incompatible.* **2.** contrary or opposed in character; discordant: *incompatible colors.* **3.** that cannot coexist or be conjoined. **4.** *Logic.* **a.** (of two or more propositions) unable to be true simultaneously. **b.** (of two or more attributes of an object) unable to belong to the object simultaneously; inconsistent. **5.** (of positions, functions, ranks, etc.) unable to be held simultaneously by one person. **6.** *Med.* of or pertaining to biological substances that interfere with one another physiologically, as different types of blood in a transfusion. **7.** *Pharm.* of or pertaining to drugs that interfere with one another chemically or physiologically and therefore cannot be mixed or prescribed together. —*n.* **8.** Usually, **incompatibles.** incompatible persons or things. **9.** an incompatible drug or the like. **10. incompatibles,** *Logic.* **a.** two or more propositions that cannot be true simultaneously. **b.** two or more attributes that cannot simultaneously belong to the same object. [1555–65; < ML *incompatibilis.* See IN-[3], COMPATIBLE] —**in′com·pat′i·bil′i·ty, in′com·pat′i·ble·ness,** *n.* —**in′com·pat′i·bly,** *adv.*
—**Syn. 1.** unsuitable, unsuited. See **inconsistent. 1, 2.** inharmonious. **2.** contradictory.

in·com·pe·tence (in kom′pi təns), *n.* **1.** the quality or condition of being incompetent; lack of ability. **2.** *Law.* the condition of lacking power to act with legal effectiveness. Also, **in·com′pe·ten·cy.** [1655–65; var. (with -ENCE for -ENCY) of earlier *incompetency.* See INCOMPETENT, -CY]

in·com·pe·tent (in kom′pi tənt), *adj.* **1.** not competent; lacking qualification or ability; incapable: *an incompetent candidate.* **2.** characterized by or showing incompetence: *His incompetent acting ruined the play.* **3.** *Law.* **a.** being unable or legally unqualified to perform specified acts or to be held legally responsible for such acts. **b.** inadmissible, as evidence. —*n.* **4.** an incompetent person; a mentally deficient person. **5.** *Law.* a person lacking power to act with legal effectiveness. [1590–1600; < LL *incompetent-* (s. of *incompetēns*) unsuitable. See IN-[3], COMPETENT] —**in·com′pe·tent·ly,** *adv.*
—**Syn. 1.** unqualified, inadequate, unfit. See **incapable.** —**Ant. 1.** able, qualified.

in·com·plete (in′kəm plēt′), *adj.* **1.** not complete; lacking some part. **2.** *Football.* (of a forward pass) not completed; not caught by a receiver. **3.** *Engin.* noting a truss the panel points of which are not entirely connected so as to form a system of triangles. Cf. **complete** (def. 8), **redundant** (def. 5c). **4.** *Logic, Philos.* **a.** (of an expression or symbol) meaningful only in a specific context. **b.** (of a set of axioms) such that there is at least one true proposition (able to be formulated in terms of the basic ideas of a given system) that is not deducible from the set. Cf. **complete** (def. 7). —*n.* **5.** *Educ.* a temporary grade indicating that a student has not fulfilled one or more of the essential requirements for a course: *If I don't hand in my term paper for last semester's English course, the professor is going to change my incomplete to an F.* [1350–1400; ME < LL *incomplētus.* See IN-[3], COMPLETE] —**in′com·plete′ly,** *adv.* —**in′com·plete′ness,** *n.*
—**Syn. 1.** unfinished, partial, fragmentary.

in′complete dom′inance, the appearance in a heterozygote of a trait that is intermediate between either of the trait's homozygous phenotypes. Also called **semidominance.**

in′complete frac′ture, a fracture extending partly across the bone.

in·com·ple·tion (in′kəm plē′shən), *n.* **1.** the state of being incomplete; incompleteness. **2.** *Football.* an incomplete forward pass. [1795–1805; IN-[3] + COMPLETION]

in·com·pli·ant (in′kəm plī′ənt), *adj.* **1.** not compliant; unyielding. **2.** not pliant. [1640–50; IN-[3] + COMPLIANT] —**in′com·pli′ance, in′com·pli′an·cy,** *n.* —**in′com·pli′ant·ly,** *adv.*

in·com·pre·hen·si·ble (in′kom pri hen′sə bəl, in kom′-), *adj.* **1.** impossible to understand or comprehend; unintelligible. **2.** *Archaic.* limitless; not limited or capable of being limited. [1300–50; ME < L *incomprehēnsibilis.* See IN-[3], COMPREHENSIBLE] —**in′com·pre·**

CONCISE PRONUNCIATION KEY: *act, cāpe, dâre, pärt; set, ēqual; if, īce; ox, ōver, ôrder, oil, bŏŏk, bōōt, out; up, ûrge; child; sing; shoe; thin, that;* zh as in *treasure.* ə = a as in *alone,* e as in *system,* i as in *easily,* o as in *gallop,* u as in *circus;* ᵊ as in *fire* (fīᵊr), *hour* (ouᵊr). l and n can serve as syllabic consonants, as in *cradle* (krād′l), and *button* (but′n). See the full key inside the front cover.

hen′si·bil′i·ty, in′com·pre·hen′si·ble·ness, *n.* **—in′·com·pre·hen′si·bly,** *adv.*
—Syn. 1. baffling, bewildering, obscure.

in·com·pre·hen·sion (in′kom pri hen′shən, in-kom′-), *n.* lack of comprehension or understanding: *The audience listened politely but with incomprehension.* [1595–1605; IN-[3] + COMPREHENSION]

in·com·pre·hen·sive (in′kom pri hen′siv, in kom′-), *adj.* **1.** not comprehensive. **2.** not comprehending readily; having a slow or inadequate mental grasp. [1645–55; IN-[3] + COMPREHENSIVE] **—in′com·pre·hen′sive·ly,** *adv.* **—in′com·pre·hen′sive·ness,** *n.*

in·com·press·i·ble (in′kəm pres′ə bəl), *adj.* not compressible. [1720–30; IN-[3] + COMPRESSIBLE] **—in′·com·press′i·bil′i·ty,** *n.* **—in′com·press′i·bly,** *adv.*

in·com·put·a·ble (in′kəm pyo͞o′tə bəl), *adj.* incapable of being computed; incalculable. [1600–10; IN-[3] + COMPUTABLE] **—in′com·put′a·bly,** *adv.*

in·con·ceiv·a·ble (in′kən sē′və bəl), *adj.* **1.** not conceivable; unimaginable; unthinkable **2.** unbelievable; incredible. [1625–35; IN-[3] + CONCEIVABLE] **—in′con·ceiv′a·bil′i·ty, in′con·ceiv′a·ble·ness,** *n.* **—in′con·ceiv′a·bly,** *adv.*

in·con·clu·sive (in′kən klo͞o′siv), *adj.* **1.** not conclusive; not resolving fully all doubts or questions: *inconclusive evidence.* **2.** without final results or outcome: *inconclusive experiments.* [1680–90; IN-[3] + CONCLUSIVE] **—in′con·clu′sive·ly,** *adv.* **—in′con·clu′sive·ness,** *n.*
—Syn. unsettled, indecisive, indefinite.

in·con·den·sa·ble (in′kən den′sə bəl), *adj.* not condensable; incapable of being condensed. Also, **in′con·den′si·ble.** [1730–40; IN-[3] + CONDENSABLE] **—in′con·den′sa·bil′i·ty, in′con·den′si·bil′i·ty,** *n.*

in·con·dite (in kon′dit, -dīt), *adj.* **1.** ill-constructed; unpolished: *incondite prose.* **2.** crude; rough; unmannerly. [1530–40; < L *inconditus,* equiv. to *in-* IN-[3] + *conditus* ptp. of *condere* to put in, restore (*con-* CON- + *-di-* put, set + *-tus* ptp. suffix)]

in·con·du·cive (in′kən do͞o′siv, -dyo͞o′-), *adj.* not conducive; tending to be harmful or injurious: *inconducive to the public good.* [1840–50; IN-[3] + CONDUCIVE]

In·co·nel (ing′kə nel′), *Trademark.* an alloy of nickel, chromium, and iron that is highly resistant to high temperatures and corrosion.

in·con·form·i·ty (in′kən fôr′mi tē), *n.* lack of conformity; failure or refusal to conform; nonconformity. [1585–95; IN-[3] + CONFORMITY]

in·con·gru·ent (in kong′gro͞o ənt, in′kən gro͞o′-, -kəng-), *adj.* not congruent. [1525–35; < L *incongruent-* (s. of *incongruēns*) inconsistent. See IN-[3], CONGRUENT] **—in·con′gru·ence,** *n.* **—in·con′gru·ent·ly,** *adv.*

in·con·gru·i·ty (in′kən gro͞o′i tē, -kəng-), *n., pl.* **-ties** for 2. **1.** the quality or condition of being incongruous. **2.** something incongruous. [1525–35; < LL *incongruitās.* See IN-[3], CONGRUITY]

in·con·gru·ous (in kong′gro͞o əs), *adj.* **1.** out of keeping or place; inappropriate; unbecoming: *an incongruous effect; incongruous behavior.* **2.** not harmonious in character; inconsonant; lacking harmony of parts: *an incongruous mixture of architectural styles.* **3.** inconsistent: *actions that were incongruous with their professed principles.* [1605–15; < L *incongruus* inconsistent. See IN-[3], CONGRUOUS] **—in·con′gru·ous·ly,** *adv.* **—in·con′·gru·ous·ness,** *n.*
—Syn. 1. discrepant, unsuitable, ridiculous, ludicrous, absurd. **2.** inharmonious, discordant. **3.** contrary, contradictory. See **inconsistent.** **—Ant. 1.** becoming, appropriate. **2.** consonant. **3.** consistent.

in·con·nu (in′kə no͞o′, -nyo͞o′, ing′-; *Fr.* AN kô NY′), *n., pl.* **-nus** (-no͞oz′, -nyo͞oz′; *Fr.* -NY′), (*esp. collectively for 2*) **-nu. 1.** a person who is unknown; stranger. **2.** Also called **sheefish.** a game fish, *Stenodus leucichthys,* of fresh or brackish northern waters. [1800–10; < F: lit., unknown, equiv. to *in-* IN-[3] + *connu,* ptp. of *connaître* to know, be acquainted with < L *cognōscere;* see COGNITION]

in·con·scient (in kon′shənt), *adj.* unconscious. [1880–85; IN-[3] + *conscient* conscious (< F *conscient*) < L *conscient-,* s. of *consciēns,* prp. of *conscire,* orig., to have on one's conscience, equiv. to *con-* CON- + *scire* to know] **—in·con′scient·ly,** *adv.*

in·con·sec·u·tive (in′kən sek′yə tiv), *adj.* not consecutive. [1830–40; IN-[3] + CONSECUTIVE] **—in′con·sec′u·tive·ly,** *adj.* **—in′con·sec′u·tive·ness,** *n.*

in·con·se·quent (in kon′si kwent′, -kwənt), *adj.* **1.** characterized by lack of proper sequence in thought, speech, or action. **2.** characterized by lack of logical sequence; illogical; inconsecutive: *inconsequent reasoning.* **3.** irrelevant: *an inconsequent remark.* **4.** not following from the premises: *an inconsequent deduction.* **5.** not in keeping with the general character or design; inconsistent: *inconsequent ornamentation.* **6.** without worth or consequence; trivial: *a frivolous, inconsequent young man.* [1570–80; < LL *inconsequent-* (s. of *inconsequēns*) not following. See IN-[3], CONSEQUENT] **—in·con′se·quence′, in·con′se·quent′ness,** *n.* **—in·con′se·quent′ly,** *adv.*

in·con·se·quen·tial (in′kon si kwen′shəl, in kon′-), *adj.* **1.** of little or no importance; insignificant; trivial. **2.** inconsequent; illogical. **3.** irrelevant. [1615–25; IN-[3] + CONSEQUENTIAL] **—in′con·se·quen′ti·al′i·ty,** *n.* **—in′con·se·quen′tial·ly,** *adv.*

in·con·sid·er·a·ble (in′kən sid′ər ə bəl), *adj.* **1.** small, as in value, amount, or size. **2.** not worth consideration or notice; trivial. [1590–1600; IN-[3] + CONSIDERABLE] **—in′con·sid′er·a·ble·ness,** *n.* **—in′con·sid′er·a·bly,** *adv.*

in·con·sid·er·ate (in′kən sid′ər it), *adj.* **1.** without due regard for the rights or feelings of others: *It was inconsiderate of him to keep us waiting.* **2.** acting without consideration; thoughtless; heedless. **3.** overhasty; rash; ill-considered: *slovenly, inconsiderate reasoning.* [1425–75; late ME < L *inconsīderātus.* See IN-[3], CONSIDERATE] **—in′con·sid′er·ate·ly,** *adv.* **—in′con·sid′er·ate·ness, in′con·sid′er·a′tion,** *n.*
—Syn. 1. insensitive, uncaring, rude.

in·con·sist·en·cy (in′kən sis′tən sē), *n., pl.* **-cies** for 2. **1.** the quality or condition of being inconsistent. **2.** an inconsistent thing, action, remark, etc. Also, **in′con·sist′ence.** [1640–50; IN-[3] + CONSISTENCY]

in·con·sist·ent (in′kən sis′tənt), *adj.* **1.** lacking in harmony between the different parts or elements; self-contradictory: *an inconsistent story.* **2.** lacking agreement, as one thing with another or two or more things in relation to each other; at variance: *a summary that is inconsistent with the previously stated facts.* **3.** not consistent in principles, conduct, etc.: *He's so inconsistent we never know if he'll be kind or cruel.* **4.** acting at variance with professed principles. **5.** *Logic.* incompatible (def. 4b). [1640–50; IN-[3] + CONSISTENT] **—in′con·sist′·ent·ly,** *adv.*
—Syn. 1. incoherent. **2.** discrepant, disagreeing, irreconcilable. INCONSISTENT, INCOMPATIBLE, INCONGRUOUS refer to things that are out of keeping with each other. That which is INCONSISTENT involves variance, discrepancy, or even contradiction, esp. from the point of view of truth, reason, or logic: *His actions are inconsistent with his statements.* INCOMPATIBLE implies incapability of close association or harmonious relationship, as from differences of nature, character, temperament, and the like: *actions incompatible with honesty of purpose; qualities that make two people incompatible.* Something that is INCONGRUOUS is inappropriate or out of keeping, often to the point of being ridiculous or absurd: *Incongruous characters or situations frequently provide a basis for comedy.*

in·con·sol·a·ble (in′kən sō′lə bəl), *adj.* not consolable; that cannot be comforted; disconsolate: *She was inconsolable when her son died.* [1590–1600; < L *inconsōlābilis.* See IN-[3], CONSOLABLE] **—in′con·sol′a·bil′i·ty, in′con·sol′a·ble·ness,** *n.* **—in′con·sol′a·bly,** *adv.*

in·con·so·nant (in kon′sə nənt), *adj.* not consonant or in accord. [1650–60; IN-[3] + CONSONANT] **—in·con′·so·nance,** *n.* **—in·con′so·nant·ly,** *adv.*

in·con·spic·u·ous (in′kən spik′yo͞o əs), *adj.* not conspicuous, noticeable, or prominent. [1615–25; < L *inconspicuus.* See IN-[3], CONSPICUOUS] **—in′con·spic′u·ous·ly,** *adv.* **—in′con·spic′u·ous·ness,** *n.*
—Syn. unnoticeable, unobtrusive, unostentatious.

in·con·stant (in kon′stənt), *adj.* not constant; changeable; fickle; variable: *an inconstant friend.* [1375–1425; late ME *inconstaunt* < L *inconstant-* (s. of *inconstāns*) changeable. See IN-[3], CONSTANT] **—in·con′stan·cy,** *n.* **—in·con′stant·ly,** *adv.*
—Syn. moody, capricious, vacillating, wavering; undependable, unstable, unsettled, uncertain; mutable, mercurial, volatile. See **fickle.** **—Ant.** steady.

in·con·sum·a·ble (in′kən so͞o′mə bəl), *adj.* not consumable; incapable of being consumed. [1640–50; IN-[3] + CONSUMABLE] **—in′con·sum′a·bly,** *adv.*

in·con·test·a·ble (in′kən tes′tə bəl), *adj.* not contestable; not open to dispute; incontrovertible: *incontestable proof.* [1665–75; IN-[3] + CONTESTABLE] **—in′con·test′a·bil′i·ty, in′con·test′a·ble·ness,** *n.* **—in′con·test′a·bly,** *adv.*

in′contest′able clause′, a clause in a life-insurance or health-insurance policy stating that the insurer cannot contest the policy after a stated period of time.

in·con·ti·nent (in kon′tn ənt), *adj.* **1.** unable to restrain natural discharges or evacuations of urine or feces. **2.** unable to contain or retain (usually fol. by *of*): *incontinent of temper.* **3.** lacking in moderation or self-control, esp. of sexual desire. **4.** unceasing or unrestrained: *an incontinent flow of talk.* [1350–1400; ME < L *incontinent-* (s. of *incontinēns*). See IN-[3], CONTINENT (adj.)] **—in·con′ti·nence, in·con′ti·nen·cy,** *n.*

in·con·ti·nent·ly[1] (in kon′tn ənt lē), *adv.* without exercising continence. [1545–55; INCONTINENT + -LY]

in·con·ti·nent·ly[2] (in kon′tn ənt lē), *adv. Archaic.* immediately; at once; straightaway. [1475–85; late ME *incontinent,* in same sense (< MF < LL *in continentī* (*tempore*) in continuous (time), i.e., without pause; see CONTINENT) + -LY]

in·con·trol·la·ble (in′kən trō′lə bəl), *adj.* not controllable; uncontrollable. [1590–1600; IN-[3] + CONTROLLABLE] **—in′con·trol′la·bly,** *adv.*

in·con·tro·vert·i·ble (in′kon trə vûr′tə bəl, in kon′-), *adj.* not controvertible; not open to question or dispute; indisputable: *absolute and incontrovertible truth.* [1640–50; IN-[3] + CONTROVERTIBLE] **—in′con·tro·vert′i·bil′i·ty, in′con·tro·vert′i·ble·ness,** *n.* **—in′con·tro·vert′i·bly,** *adv.*
—Syn. incontestable, undeniable, unquestionable.

in·con·ven·ience (in′kən vēn′yəns), *n., v.,* **-ienced, -ienc·ing.** **—***n.* **1.** the quality or state of being inconvenient. **2.** an inconvenient circumstance or thing; something that causes discomfort, trouble, etc. **—***v.t.* **3.** to put to inconvenience or trouble; incommode: *He inconvenienced everyone by his constant telephoning.* [1350–1400; ME < LL *inconvenientia.* See IN-[3], CONVENIENCE]

in·con·ven·ien·cy (in′kən vēn′yən sē), *n., pl.* **-cies.** inconvenience. [1400–50; late ME: mishap, danger; see INCONVENIENCE, -Y[3]]

in·con·ven·ient (in′kən vēn′yənt), *adj.* **1.** not easily accessible or at hand: *The phone is in an inconvenient place.* **2.** inopportune; untimely: *an inconvenient time for a visit.* **3.** not suiting one's needs or purposes: *The house has an inconvenient floor plan.* [1325–75; ME < L *inconvenient-* (s. of *inconveniēns*) not suiting. See IN-[3], CONVENIENT] **—in′con·ven′ient·ly,** *adv.*
—Syn. 3. annoying, awkward, bothersome.

in·con·vert·i·ble (in′kən vûr′tə bəl), *adj.* **1.** (of paper money) not capable of being converted into specie. **2.** not interchangeable. [1640–50; < LL *inconvertibilis* not alterable. See IN-[3], CONVERTIBLE] **—in′con·vert′i·bil′i·ty, in′con·vert′i·ble·ness,** *n.* **—in′con·vert′i·bly,** *adv.*

in·con·vin·ci·ble (in′kən vin′sə bəl), *adj.* not convincible; incapable of being convinced. [1665–75; IN-[3] + CONVINCIBLE] **—in′con·vin′ci·bil′i·ty,** *n.* **—in′con·vin′ci·bly,** *adv.*

in·co·or·di·nate (in′kō ôr′dn it), *adj.* not coordinate; not coordinated. Also, **in′co-or′di·nate.** [1885–90; IN-[3] + COORDINATE]

in·co·or·di·na·tion (in′kō ôr′dn ā′shən), *n.* lack of coordination. Also, **in′co-or′di·na′tion.** [1875–80; IN-[3] + COORDINATION]

incor., incorporated. Also, **incorp.**

in·cor·po·ra·ble (in kôr′pər ə bəl), *adj.* able to be incorporated. [1600–10; < LL *incorpor(āre)* to embody + -ABLE. See INCORPORATE[1]]

in·cor·po·rate[1] (*v.* in kôr′pə rāt′; *adj.* in kôr′pər it, -prit), *v.,* **-rat·ed, -rat·ing,** *adj.* **—***v.t.* **1.** to form into a legal corporation. **2.** to put or introduce into a body or mass as an integral part or parts: *to incorporate revisions into a text.* **3.** to take in or include as a part or parts, as the body or a mass does: *His book incorporates his earlier essay.* **4.** to form or combine into one body or uniform substance, as ingredients. **5.** to embody: *His book incorporates all his thinking on the subject.* **6.** to form into a society or organization. **—***v.i.* **7.** to form a legal corporation. **8.** to unite or combine so as to form one body. **—***adj.* **9.** legally incorporated, as a company. **10.** combined into one body, mass, or substance. **11.** *Archaic.* embodied. [1350–1400; ME < LL *incorporātus* ptp. of *incorporāre* to embody, incarnate. See IN-[2], CORPORATE] **—in·cor′po·ra′tion,** *n.* **—in·cor′po·ra′tive,** *adj.*
—Syn. 4. embody, assimilate.

in·cor·po·rate[2] (in kôr′pər it, -prit), *adj. Archaic.* not embodied; incorporeal. [1525–35; < LL *incorporātus* not embodied. See IN-[3], CORPORATE]

in·cor·po·rat·ed (in kôr′pə rā′tid), *adj.* **1.** formed or constituted as a legal corporation. **2.** combined in one body; made part of. [1590–1600; INCORPORATE[1] + -ED[2]] **—in·cor′po·rat′ed·ness,** *n.*

incor′porated bar′, *Law.* See **integrated bar.**

in·cor·po·ra·tion (in kôr′pə rā′shən), *n.* **1.** the act of incorporating or the state of being incorporated. **2.** the act of forming a legal corporation. **3.** *Gram.* the inclusion of the object or object reference within the inflected verb form, a type of word-formation frequent in American Indian languages. **4.** *Psychoanal.* the adoption of the views or characteristics of others, occurring in children as part of learning and maturation and in adults as a defense mechanism. Cf. **introjection.** [1350–1400; ME *incorporacioun* < LL *incorporātiō-* (s. of *incorporātiō*), equiv. to *incorporāt(us)* (see INCORPORATE[1]) + *-iōn* -ION]

in·cor·po·ra·tor (in kôr′pə rā′tər), *n.* **1.** one of the signers of the articles or certificate of legal incorporation. **2.** one of the persons to whom the charter is granted in a corporation created by special act of the legislature. **3.** a person who incorporates. [1820–30; INCORPORATE + -OR[2]]

in cor·po·re (in KÔR′pō RE′; *Eng.* in kôr′pə rē), *Latin.* in body; in substance.

in·cor·po·re·al (in′kôr pôr′ē əl, -pōr′-), *adj.* **1.** not corporeal or material; insubstantial. **2.** of, pertaining to, or characteristic of nonmaterial beings. **3.** *Law.* without material existence but existing in contemplation of law, as a franchise. [1525–35; < L *incorpore(us)* + -AL[1]. See IN-[3], CORPOREAL] **—in′cor·po′re·al′i·ty,** *n.* **—in′cor·po′re·al·ly,** *adv.*
—Syn. 1. bodiless, spiritual, immaterial.

in·cor·po·re·i·ty (in′kôr pə rē′i tē), *n.* the quality of being incorporeal; disembodied existence or entity; incorporeality. [1595–1605; < ML *incorporeitās,* equiv. to L *incorpore(us)* incorporeal + *-itās* -ITY]

incorr., incorrect.

in·cor·rect (in′kə rekt′), *adj.* **1.** not correct as to fact; inaccurate; wrong: *an incorrect statement.* **2.** improper, unbecoming, or inappropriate: *incorrect behavior; incorrect attire.* **3.** not correct in form, use, or manner: *an incorrect copy.* [1400–50; late ME < L *incorrectus* not corrected. See IN-[3], CORRECT] **—in′cor·rect′ly,** *adv.* **—in′cor·rect′ness,** *n.*
—Syn. 1. erroneous, inexact; untrue. **2.** unsuitable. **3.** faulty.

in·cor·ri·gi·ble (in kôr′i jə bəl, -kor′-), *adj.* **1.** not corrigible; bad beyond correction or reform: *incorrigible behavior; an incorrigible liar.* **2.** impervious to constraints or punishment; willful; unruly; uncontrollable: *an incorrigible child; incorrigible hair.* **3.** firmly fixed; not easily changed: *an incorrigible habit.* **4.** not easily swayed or influenced: *an incorrigible optimist.* **—***n.* **5.** a person who is incorrigible. [1300–50; ME < L *incorrigibilis.* See IN-[3], CORRIGIBLE] **—in·cor′ri·gi·bil′i·ty, in·cor′ri·gi·ble·ness,** *n.* **—in·cor′ri·gi·bly,** *adv.*

in·cor·rupt (in′kə rupt′), *adj.* **1.** not corrupt; not debased or perverted; morally upright. **2.** not to be corrupted; incorruptible. **3.** not vitiated by errors or alterations. **4.** *Obs.* free from decomposition or putrefaction. Also, **in′cor·rupt′ed.** [1300–50; ME < L *incorruptus* unspoiled. See IN-[3] + CORRUPT] **—in′cor·rupt′ly,** *adv.* **—in′cor·rupt′ness,** *n.*

in·cor·rupt·i·ble (in′kə rup′tə bəl), *adj.* **1.** not corruptible: *incorruptible integrity.* **2.** that cannot be perverted or bribed: *incorruptible by money.* **3.** that will not dissolve, disintegrate, decay, etc.: *an incorruptible metal.* [1300–50; ME < LL *incorruptibilis.* See IN-[3], CORRUPTIBLE] **—in′cor·rupt′i·bil′i·ty, in′cor·rupt′i·ble·ness,** *n.* **—in′cor·rupt′i·bly,** *adv.*
—Syn. 1. upright, righteous, unbribable.

CONCISE ETYMOLOGY KEY: <, descended or borrowed from; >, whence; b., blend of, blended; c., cognate with; cf., compare; deriv., derivative; equiv., equivalent; imit., imitative; obl., oblique; r., replacing; s., stem; sp., spelling, spelled; resp., respelling, respelled; trans., translation; ?, origin unknown; *, unattested; ‡, probably earlier than. See the full key inside the front cover.

in·cor·rup·tion (in′kə rup′shən), *n. Archaic.* the quality or condition of being incorrupt. [1350–1400; ME < LL *incorruptiōn-* (s. of *incorruptiō*). See IN-[3], CORRUPTION]

incr., **1.** increase. **2.** increased. **3.** increasing.

in·cras·sate (*v.* in kras′āt; *adj.* in kras′it, -āt), *v.,* **-sat·ed, -sat·ing,** *adj.* —*v.t.* **1.** *Pharm.* to make (a liquid) thicker by addition of another substance or by evaporation. —*adj.* **2.** Also, **in·cras′sat·ed.** *Bot., Entomol.* thickened or swollen. [1595–1605; < LL *incrassātus* ptp. of *incrassāre* to fatten, make thick. See IN-[2], CRASS, -ATE[1]] —**in′cras·sa′tion,** *n.* —**in·cras′sa·tive,** *adj.*

in·crease (*v.* in krēs′; *n.* in′krēs), *v.,* **-creased, -creas·ing,** *n.* —*v.t.* **1.** to make greater, as in number, size, strength, or quality; augment; add to: *to increase taxes.* —*v.i.* **2.** to become greater, as in number, size, strength, or quality: *Sales of automobiles increased last year.* **3.** to multiply by propagation. **4.** to wax, as the moon. —*n.* **5.** growth or augmentation in numbers, size, strength, quality, etc.: *the increase of crime.* **6.** the act or process of increasing. **7.** that by which something is increased. **8.** the result of increasing. **9.** produce of the earth. **10.** product; profit; interest. **11.** *Obs.* **a.** multiplication by propagation; production of offspring. **b.** offspring; progeny. [1275–1325; ME *incresen, encresen* < AF *encres-,* MF *encreiss-,* s. of *encreistre* < L *incrēscere,* equiv. to *in-* IN-[2] + *crēscere* to grow; see CRESCENT] —**in·creas′a·ble,** *adj.* —**in·creas·ed·ly** (in krē′sid lē), *adv.*
—**Syn. 1.** expand, extend, prolong. INCREASE, AUGMENT, ENLARGE may all mean to make larger. To INCREASE means to make greater, as in quantity, extent, degree: *to increase someone's salary; to increase the velocity; to increase the (degree of) concentration.* ENLARGE means to make greater in size, extent, or range: *to enlarge a building, a business, one's conceptions.* AUGMENT, a more formal word, means to make greater, esp. by addition from the outside: *to augment one's income (by doing extra work).* **3.** expand, grow, develop, swell. **6.** enlargement, expansion. —**Ant. 1, 3.** decrease.

in·creas·er (in krē′sər), *n.* **1.** a person or thing that increases. **2.** (in plumbing) a coupling increasing in diameter at one end. Cf. **reducer** (def. 3). [1520–30; INCREASE + -ER[1]]

in·creas·ing (in krē′sing), *adj.* **1.** growing larger or greater; enlarging; augmenting. **2.** *Math.* (of a function) having the property that for any two points in the domain such that one is larger than the other, the image of the larger point is greater than or equal to the image of the smaller point; nondecreasing. Cf. **decreasing** (def. 2). [1590–1600; see INCREASE, -ING[2]] —**in·creas′ing·ly,** *adv.*

in·cre·ate (in′krē āt′, in krē′it), *adj.* **1.** not created; uncreated. **2.** existing without having been created. [1375–1425; late ME *increat* < LL *increātus* not made. See IN-[3], CREATE] —**in′cre·ate′ly,** *adv.*

in·cred·i·ble (in kred′ə bəl), *adj.* **1.** so extraordinary as to seem impossible: *incredible speed.* **2.** not credible; hard to believe; unbelievable: *The plot of the book is incredible.* [1375–1425; late ME < L *incredibilis.* See IN-[3], CREDIBLE] —**in·cred′i·bil′i·ty, in·cred′i·ble·ness,** *n.* —**in·cred′i·bly,** *adv.*
—**Syn. 2.** farfetched, astonishing, preposterous.

in·cre·du·li·ty (in′kri do͞o′li tē, -dyo͞o′-), *n.* the quality or state of being incredulous; inability or unwillingness to believe. [1400–50; late ME *incredulite* < L *incrēdulitās.* See INCREDULOUS, -ITY]
—**Syn.** disbelief, skepticism, doubt. —**Ant.** faith.

in·cred·u·lous (in krej′ə ləs), *adj.* **1.** not credulous; disinclined or indisposed to believe; skeptical. **2.** indicating or showing unbelief: *an incredulous smile.* [1525–35; < L *incrēdulus.* See IN-[3], CREDULOUS] —**in·cred′u·lous·ly,** *adv.* —**in·cred′u·lous·ness,** *n.*
—**Syn.** unbelieving. See **doubtful.**

in·cre·ment (in′krə mənt, ing′-), *n.* **1.** something added or gained; addition; increase. **2.** profit; gain. **3.** the act or process of increasing; growth. **4.** an amount by which something increases or grows: *a weekly increment of $25 in salary.* **5.** one of a series of regular additions: *You may make deposits in increments of $500.* **6.** *Math.* **a.** the difference between two values of a variable; a change, positive, negative, or zero, in an independent variable. **b.** the increase of a function due to an increase in the independent variable. [1375–1425; late ME < L *incrēmentum* an increase, equiv. to *incrē(scere)* to grow (see INCREASE) + *-mentum* -MENT] —**in·cre·men·tal** (in′krə men′tl, ing′-), *adj.* —**in′cre·men′tal·ly,** *adv.*

in·cre·men·tal·ism (in′krə men′tl iz′əm, ing′-), *n.* a policy of making changes, esp. social changes, by degrees; gradualism. [1965–70; INCREMENTAL + -ISM] —**in′cre·men′tal·ist,** *n., adj.*

incremen′tal repeti′tion, *Pros.* repetition, with variation, of a refrain or other part of a poem, esp. a ballad. [1915–20]

in·cres·cent (in kres′ənt), *adj.* increasing or waxing, as the moon. [1565–75; < L *incrēscent-* (s. of *incrēscēns* prp. of *incrēscere* to grow), equiv. to *in-* IN-[2] + *crēsc-* grow + *-ent-* -ENT] —**in·cres′cence,** *n.*

in·cre·tion (in krē′shən), *n. Physiol.* **1.** a substance, as a hormone, that is secreted internally. **2.** the process of such secretion. [IN-[2] + (SE)CRETION] —**in·cre′tion·ar′y, in·cre·to·ry** (in′kri tôr′ē, -tōr′ē), *adj.*

in·crim·i·nate (in krim′ə nāt′), *v.t.,* **-nat·ed, -nat·ing. 1.** to accuse of or present proof of a crime or fault: *He incriminated both men to the grand jury.* **2.** to involve in an accusation; cause to be or appear to be guilty; implicate: *His testimony incriminated his friend. He feared incriminating himself if he answered.* **3.** to charge with responsibility for all or part of an undesirable situation, harmful effect, etc.: *to incriminate cigarettes as a cause of lung cancer.* [1720–30; < LL *incrīminātus* ptp. of *incrīmināre* to accuse. See IN-[2], CRIMINATE] —**in·crim′i·na′tion,** *n.* —**in·crim′i·na′tor,** *n.* —**in·crim·i·na·to·ry** (in krim′ə nə tôr′ē, -tōr′ē), *adj.*

in·cross (in′krôs′, -kros′), *n. Genetics.* a mating between organisms that are both homozygous for the same allele. [IN-[1] + CROSS]

in·cross·bred (in′krôs′bred′, -kros′-), *adj. Genetics.* of or pertaining to the progeny that result from crossing inbred lines or varieties. [IN-[1] + CROSSBRED]

in-crowd (in′kroud′), *n.* in-group (def. 1). [1965–70]

in·crust (in krust′), *v.t.* **1.** to cover or line with a crust or hard coating. **2.** to form into a crust. **3.** to deposit as a crust. —*v.i.* **4.** to form a crust: *They scraped off the barnacles that always incrusted on the ship's hull.* Also, **encrust.** [1635–45; < L *incrustāre.* See IN-[2], CRUST] —**in·crust′ant,** *adj., n.*

in·crus·ta·tion (in′kru stā′shən), *n.* **1.** an incrusting or being incrusted. **2.** a crust or coat of anything on the surface of a body; covering, coating, or scale. **3.** the inlaying or addition of enriching materials on or to a surface or an object. **4.** the enriching materials inlaid on or added to a surface or an object. Also, **encrustation.** [1600–10; < L *incrustātiōn-* (s. of *incrustātiō*). See IN-[2], CRUST, -ATION]

in·cu·bate (in′kyə bāt′, ing′-), *v.,* **-bat·ed, -bat·ing.** —*v.t.* **1.** to sit upon (eggs) for the purpose of hatching. **2.** to hatch (eggs), as by sitting upon them or by artificial heat. **3.** to maintain at a favorable temperature and in other conditions promoting development, as cultures of bacteria or prematurely born infants. **4.** to develop or produce as if by hatching; give form to: *His brain was incubating schemes for raising money.* —*v.i.* **5.** to sit upon eggs. **6.** to undergo incubation. **7.** to develop; grow; take form: *A plan was slowly incubating in her mind.* [1635–45; < L *incubātus* ptp. of *incubāre* to lie or recline on, to sit on (eggs), equiv. to *in-* IN-[2] + *cub(āre)* to sit, lie down + *-ātus* -ATE[1]; cf. INCUMBENT, CONCUBINE] —**in′cu·ba′tive,** *adj.*

in·cu·ba·tion (in′kyə bā′shən, ing′-), *n.* **1.** the act or process of incubating. **2.** the state of being incubated. **3.** See **incubation period.** [1605–15; < L *incubātiōn-* (s. of *incubātiō*). See INCUBATE, -ION] —**in′cu·ba′tion·al, in·cu·ba·to·ry** (in′kyə bə tôr′ē, -tōr′ē, ing′-), *adj.*

incuba′tion patch′, a highly vascular, featherless area developed on the abdomen of certain brooding birds that is in direct contact with eggs during incubation and provides additional warmth. Also called **brood patch.** [1950–55]

incuba′tion pe′riod, *Pathol.* the period between infection and the appearance of signs of a disease. [1875–80]

in·cu·ba·tor (in′kyə bā′tər, ing′-), *n.* **1.** an apparatus in which eggs are hatched artificially. **2.** an enclosed apparatus in which prematurely born infants are kept in controlled conditions, as of temperature, for protection and care. **3.** an apparatus in which media inoculated with microorganisms are cultivated at a constant temperature. **4.** a person or thing that incubates. [1855–60; < LL: lit., one who lies in or upon (something). See INCUBATE, -TOR]

in·cu·bous (in′kyə bəs, ing′-), *adj.* (of leaves) overlapping, with the upper part of each leaf covering the base of the leaf above it. Cf. **succubous.** [1855–60; < L *incub(āre)* to lie upon (see INCUBATE) + -OUS]

in·cu·bus (in′kyə bəs, ing′-), *n., pl.* **-bi** (-bī′), **-bus·es. 1.** an imaginary demon or evil spirit supposed to descend upon sleeping persons, esp. one fabled to have sexual intercourse with women during their sleep. Cf. **succubus** (def. 1). **2.** a nightmare. **3.** something that weighs upon or oppresses one like a nightmare. [1175–1225; ME < LL: a nightmare induced by such a demon, n. deriv. of L *incubāre* to lie upon; see INCUBATE]

in·cu·des (in kyo͞o′dēz), *n.* a pl. of **incus.**

in·cul·cate (in kul′kāt, in′kul kāt′), *v.t.,* **-cat·ed, -cat·ing. 1.** to implant by repeated statement or admonition; teach persistently and earnestly (usually fol. by *upon* or *in*): *to inculcate virtue in the young.* **2.** to cause or influence (someone) to accept an idea or feeling (usually fol. by *with*): *Socrates inculcated his pupils with the love of truth.* [1540–50; < L *inculcātus* ptp. of *inculcāre* to trample, impress, stuff in, equiv. to *in-* IN-[2] + *culc-* (var., in noninitial position, of *calc-,* s. of *calx* heel) + *-ātus* -ATE[1]] —**in′cul·ca′tion,** *n.* —**in·cul·ca·tive** (in kul′kə tiv), **in·cul′ca·to′ry,** *adj.* —**in·cul′ca·tor,** *n.*
—**Syn. 1.** instill, infix, ingrain.

in·cul·pa·ble (in kul′pə bəl), *adj.* not culpable; blameless; guiltless. [1485–95; < LL *inculpābilis.* See IN-[3], CULPABLE] —**in·cul′pa·bil′i·ty, in·cul′pa·ble·ness,** *n.* —**in·cul′pa·bly,** *adv.*

in·cul·pate (in kul′pāt, in′kul pāt), *v.t.,* **-pat·ed, -pat·ing. 1.** to charge with fault; blame; accuse. **2.** to involve in a charge; incriminate. [1790–1800; < LL *inculpātus* ptp. of *inculpāre* to blame, equiv. to L *in-* IN-[2] + *culp(a)* fault + *-ātus* -ATE[1]; cf. CULPABLE] —**in′cul·pa′tion,** *n.* —**in·cul·pa·to·ry** (in kul′pə tôr′ē, -tōr′ē), *adj.*
—**Ant. 1, 2.** exonerate.

in·cult (in kult′), *adj.* wild; rude; unrefined. [1590–1600; < L *incultus,* equiv. to *in-* IN-[3] + *cultus* ptp. of *colere* to till, CULTIVATE]

in·cul·tu·ra·tion (in kul′chə rā′shən), *n.* enculturation.

in·cum·ben·cy (in kum′bən sē), *n., pl.* **-cies** for 2–5. **1.** the quality or state of being incumbent. **2.** the position or term of an incumbent. **3.** something that is incumbent. **4.** a duty or obligation: *my incumbencies as head of the organization.* **5.** *Archaic.* an incumbent weight or mass. [1600–10; INCUMB(ENT) + -ENCY]

in·cum·bent (in kum′bənt), *adj.* **1.** holding an indicated position, role, office, etc., currently: *the incumbent officers of the club.* **2.** obligatory (often fol. by *on* or *upon*): *a duty incumbent upon me.* **3.** *Archaic.* resting, lying, leaning, or pressing on something: *incumbent upon the cool grass.* —*n.* **4.** the holder of an office: *The incumbent was challenged by a fusion candidate.* **5.** *Brit.* a person who holds an ecclesiastical benefice. [1375–1425; late ME (n.) < L *incumbent-* (s. of *incumbēns* prp. of *incumbere* to lie or lean upon, equiv. to *in-* IN-[2] + *cumb-* (nasalized var. of *cub-* sit, lie; see INCUBUS) + *-ent-* -ENT] —**in·cum′bent·ly,** *adv.*

in·cum·ber (in kum′bər), *v.t.* encumber.

in·cum·brance (in kum′brəns), *n.* encumbrance.

in·cu·na·ble (in kyo͞o′nə bəl), *n.* a book constituting part of a collection of incunabula. [1885–90; < F < L *incūnābulum.* See INCUNABULA]

in·cu·nab·u·la (in′kyo͝o nab′yə lə, ing′-), *n.pl., sing.* **-lum** (-ləm). **1.** extant copies of books produced in the earliest stages (before 1501) of printing from movable type. **2.** the earliest stages or first traces of anything. [1815–25; < L: straps holding a baby in a cradle, earliest home, birthplace, prob. equiv. to **incūnā(re)* to place in a cradle (*in-* IN-[2] + **-cūnāre,* v. deriv. of *cūnae* cradle) + *-bula,* pl. of *-bulum* suffix of instrument; def. 1 as trans. of G *Wiegendrucke*] —**in′cu·nab′u·lar,** *adj.*

in·cur (in kûr′), *v.t.,* **-curred, -cur·ring. 1.** to come into or acquire (some consequence, usually undesirable or injurious): *to incur a huge number of debts.* **2.** to become liable or subject to through one's own action; bring or take upon oneself: *to incur his displeasure.* [1400–50; late ME < L *incurrere* to run into, come upon, equiv. to *in-* IN-[2] + *currere* to run; see CURRENT] —**in·cur′ra·ble,** *adj.*
—**Syn. 2.** arouse, incite, provoke.

in·cur·a·ble (in kyo͝or′ə bəl), *adj.* **1.** not curable; that cannot be cured, remedied, or corrected: *an incurable disease.* **2.** not susceptible to change: *his incurable pessimism.* —*n.* **3.** a person suffering from an incurable disease. [1300–50; ME < LL *incūrābilis.* See IN-[3], CURABLE] —**in·cur′a·bil′i·ty, in·cur′a·ble·ness,** *n.* —**in·cur′a·bly,** *adv.*
—**Syn. 2.** unflagging, incorrigible, relentless.

in·cu·ri·ous (in kyo͝or′ē əs), *adj.* **1.** not curious; not inquisitive or observant; inattentive; indifferent. **2.** *Archaic.* lacking care or attention; careless; negligent. **3.** *Archaic.* deficient in interest or novelty. [1560–70; < L *incūriōsus.* See IN-[3], CURIOUS] —**in·cu·ri·os·i·ty** (in′kyo͝or ē os′i tē), **in·cu′ri·ous·ness,** *n.* —**in·cu′ri·ous·ly,** *adv.*
—**Syn. 1.** uninterested, apathetic, unconcerned.

in·cur·rence (in kûr′əns, -kur′-), *n.* the act of incurring, bringing on, or subjecting oneself to something. [1650–60; INCURR(ENT) + -ENCE]

in·cur·rent (in kûr′ənt, -kur′-), *adj.* carrying or relating to an inward current. [1555–65; < L *incurrent-* (s. of *incurrēns*), prp. of *incurrere.* See INCUR, -ENT]

in·cur·sion (in kûr′zhən, -shən), *n.* **1.** a hostile entrance into or invasion of a place or territory, esp. a sudden one; raid: *The bandits made brief incursions on the village.* **2.** a harmful inroad. **3.** a running in: *the incursion of sea water.* [1400–50; late ME < L *incursiōn-* (s. of *incursiō*) raid, equiv. to *incurs(us)* (ptp. of *incurrere* to INCUR) + *-iōn-* -ION; see EXCURSION]
—**Syn. 1.** sortie, foray, attack.

in·cur·sive (in kûr′siv), *adj.* making incursions. [1585–95; INCURS(ION) + -IVE]

in·cur·vate (*adj.* in′kûr vāt′, in kûr′vit; *v.* in′kûr vāt′, in kûr′vāt), *adj., v.,* **-vat·ed, -vat·ing.** —*adj.* **1.** curved, esp. inward. —*v.t.* **2.** to make curved; turn from a straight line or course; curve, esp. inward. [1570–80; < L *incurvātus,* ptp. of *incurvāre.* See INCURVE, -ATE[1]] —**in·cur·va·ture** (in kûr′və chər), **in′cur·va′tion,** *n.*

in·curve (in kûrv′), *v.i., v.t.,* **-curved, -curv·ing.** to curve or cause to curve inward. [1600–10; < L *incurvāre* to bend in, curve. See IN-[2], CURVE]

in·cus (ing′kəs), *n., pl.* **in·cu·des** (in kyo͞o′dēz) for 1; **in·cus** for 2. **1.** *Anat.* the middle one of a chain of three small bones in the middle ear of humans and other mammals. Cf. **malleus, stapes.** See diag. under **ear. 2.** Also called **anvil, anvil cloud, anvil top, thunderhead.** the spreading, anvil-shaped, upper portion of a mature cumulonimbus cloud, smooth or slightly fibrous in appearance. [1660–70; < NL, L *incūs* anvil, equiv. to *in-cūd-* (s. of *incūdere* to hammer, beat upon) + *-s* nom. sing. ending; see INCUSE] —**in·cu·date** (ing′kyə dāt′, -dit, in′-), **in·cu·dal** (ing′kyə dl, in′-), *adj.*

in·cuse (in kyo͞oz′, -kyo͞os′), *adj., n., v.,* **-cused, -cus·ing.** —*adj.* **1.** hammered or stamped in, as a figure on a coin. —*n.* **2.** an incuse figure or impression. —*v.t.* **3.** to stamp or hammer in, as a design or figure in a coin. [1810–20; < L *incūsus* ptp. of *incūdere* to indent with a hammer, equiv. to *in-* IN-[2] + *cūd-* beat (akin to HEW) + *-tus* ptp. suffix]

Ind (ind), *n.* **1.** *Literary.* India. **2.** *Obs.* the Indies. [1175–1225; ME *Inde* before a vowel: *indamine.*]

ind-, var. of **indo-** before a vowel: *indamine.*

IND, *Pharm.* See **investigative new drug.**

Ind., **1.** India. **2.** Also, **Ind** Indian (def. 2). **3.** Indiana. **4.** Indies.

ind., **1.** independence. **2.** independent. **3.** index. **4.** indicated. **5.** indicative. **6.** indigo. **7.** indirect. **8.** industrial. **9.** industry.

in d., (in prescriptions) daily. [< L *in diēs*]

I.N.D., in the name of God. [< L *in nōmine Dei*]

in·da·ba (in dä′bä), *n.* a conference or consultation between or with native peoples of South Africa. [1890–95; < Zulu *indaba, izindaba* (with implosive *b*) matter for discussion, affair, account]

in·da·gate (in′də gāt′), *v.t.,* **-gat·ed, -gat·ing.** *Archaic.* to investigate; research. [1615–25; < L *indāgātus,* ptp. of *indāgāre* to track down, v. deriv. of *indāgō* ring of beaters, nets, etc., for trapping game, equiv. to *ind-,* by-form of *in-* IN-[2] (see ENDO-) + *-āgō,* deriv. of *agere* to

CONCISE PRONUNCIATION KEY: act, cāpe, dâre, pärt; set, ēqual; if, īce; ox, ōver, ôrder, oil, bo͝ok, bo͞ot, out; up, ûrge; child; sing; shoe; thin, *th*at; zh as in *treasure.* ə = *a* as in *alone, e* as in *system, i* as in *easily, o* as in *gallop, u* as in *circus;* ª as in *fire* (fīªr), *hour* (ouªr). l and n can serve as syllabic consonants, as in *cradle* (krād′l), and *button* (but′n). See the full key inside the front cover.

drive (cf. AMBAGES)] —**in′da·ga′tion,** *n.* —**in′da·ga′·tive,** *adj.* —**in′da·ga′tor,** *n.*

in·da·mine (in′də mēn′, -min), *n. Chem.* any of a series of basic organic compounds, the simplest having the formula $C_{12}H_{11}N_3$, which form bluish and greenish salts, used in the manufacture of dyes. Cf. **quinonimine.** [1885–90; IND- + AMINE]

In·dan·threne (in dan′thrēn), *Trademark.* a blue, crystalline, water-insoluble solid, $C_{28}H_{14}H_2O_4$, used as a dye for cotton and as a pigment in paints and enamels.

in·dap·a·mide (in dap′ə mīd′), *n. Pharm.* a thiazide-related compound, $C_{16}H_{16}ClN_3O_3S$, used in the treatment of hypertension and edema. [*ind(oline)* (see INDOLE, -INE[2]) + *-ap-* of uncert. derivation + AMIDE]

Ind.E., Industrial Engineer.

in·debt·ed (in det′id), *adj.* **1.** committed or obligated to repay a monetary loan: *He was indebted to his friend for a large sum.* **2.** obligated for favors or kindness received: *He was indebted to her for nursing him through pneumonia.* [1175–1225; IN-[2] + DEBT + -ED[2]; r. ME *endetted* < OF *endetté,* ptp. of *endetter* to involve in debt (see EN-[1])]
—**Syn. 1.** bound. **2.** beholden, grateful.

in·debt·ed·ness (in det′id nis), *n.* **1.** the state of being indebted. **2.** an amount owed. **3.** debts collectively. [1640–50; INDEBTED + -NESS]

in·de·cen·cy (in dē′sən sē), *n., pl.* **-cies** for 4. **1.** the quality or condition of being indecent. **2.** impropriety or immodesty. **3.** obscenity or indelicacy. **4.** an indecent act, remark, etc. [1580–90; < L *indecentia.* See INDECENT, -ENCY]

in·de·cent (in dē′sənt), *adj.* **1.** offending against generally accepted standards of propriety or good taste; improper; vulgar: *indecent jokes; indecent language; indecent behavior.* **2.** not decent; unbecoming or unseemly: *indecent haste.* [1555–65; < L *indecent-* (s. of *indecēns*) unseemly. See IN-[3], DECENT] —**in·de′cent·ly,** *adv.*
—**Syn. 1.** distasteful, immodest, indecorous, indelicate; coarse, outrageous, rude, gross; obscene, filthy, lewd, licentious. See **improper. 2.** inappropriate. —**Ant. 2.** appropriate; becoming.

inde′cent assault′, a sexual offense, other than rape, committed by one person against another. [1860–65]

inde′cent expo′sure, *Law.* the intentional exposure of one's body's privates in a manner that gives offense against accepted or prescribed behavior. [1850–55]

in·de·cid·u·ate (in′di sij′o͞o it, -āt′), *adj.* **1.** *Zool.* not deciduate. **2.** *Bot.* having permanent leaves. [1875–80; IN-[3] + DECIDUATE]

in·de·cid·u·ous (in′di sij′o͞o əs), *adj. Bot.* **1.** not deciduous, as leaves. **2.** (of trees) evergreen. [1640–50; IN-[3] + DECIDUOUS]

in·de·ci·pher·a·ble (in′di sī′fər ə bəl), *adj.* **1.** not decipherable; illegible. **2.** not understandable; incomprehensible. [1795–1805; IN-[3] + DECIPHERABLE] —**in′·de·ci′pher·a·bil′i·ty, in′de·ci′pher·a·ble·ness,** *n.* —**in′de·ci′pher·a·bly,** *adv.*

in·de·ci·sion (in′di sizh′ən), *n.* inability to decide. [1755–65; IN-[3] + DECISION]

in·de·ci·sive (in′di sī′siv), *adj.* **1.** characterized by indecision, as persons; irresolute; undecided. **2.** not decisive or conclusive: *a severe but indecisive battle.* **3.** lacking definition; vague or indistinct: *the indecisive outline of the distant hills.* [1720–30; IN-[3] + DECISIVE] —**in′de·ci′sive·ly,** *adv.* —**in′de·ci′sive·ness,** *n.*
—**Syn. 1.** vacillating, hesitant, wavering.

indecl., indeclinable.

in·de·clin·a·ble (in′di klī′nə bəl), *adj. Gram.* not capable of being declined; having no inflected forms: used esp. of a word belonging to a form class most of whose members are declined, as the Latin adjective *decem,* "ten." [1400–50; late ME < L *indēclīnābilis* unchangeable, inflexible. See IN-[3], DECLINABLE] —**in′de·clin′a·ble·ness,** *n.* —**in′de·clin′a·bly,** *adv.*

in·de·com·pos·a·ble (in′dē kəm pō′zə bəl), *adj.* incapable of being decomposed. [1805–15; IN-[3] + DECOMPOSABLE] —**in′de·com·pos′a·ble·ness,** *n.*

in·dec·o·rous (in dek′ər əs, in′di kôr′əs, -kōr′-), *adj.* not decorous; violating generally accepted standards of good taste or propriety; unseemly. [1670–80; < L *indecōrus.* See IN-[3], DECOROUS] —**in·dec′o·rous·ly,** *adv.* —**in·dec′o·rous·ness,** *n.*
—**Syn.** indecent, improper, inappropriate.

in·de·co·rum (in′di kôr′əm, -kōr′-), *n.* **1.** indecorous behavior or character. **2.** something indecorous. [1565–75; < L, n. use of neut. of *indecōrus* INDECOROUS]

in·deed (in dēd′), *adv.* **1.** in fact; in reality; in truth; truly (used for emphasis, to confirm and amplify a previous statement, to indicate a concession or admission, or, interrogatively, to obtain confirmation): *Indeed, it did rain as hard as predicted. Did you indeed finish the work?* —*interj.* **2.** (used as an expression of surprise, incredulity, irony, etc.): *Indeed! I can scarcely believe it.* [1300–50; ME; orig. phrase *in deed*]

indef., indefinite.

in·de·fat·i·ga·ble (in′di fat′i gə bəl), *adj.* incapable of being tired out; not yielding to fatigue; untiring. [1580–90; < L *indēfatīgābilis* untiring, equiv. to *in-* IN-[3] + *dēfatīgā(re)* to tire out (see DE-, FATIGUE) + *-bilis* -BLE] —**in′de·fat′i·ga·bil′i·ty, in′de·fat′i·ga·ble·ness,** *n.* —**in′de·fat′i·ga·bly,** *adv.*
—**Syn.** tireless, inexhaustible, persevering.

in·de·fea·si·ble (in′di fē′zə bəl), *adj.* not defeasible; not to be annulled or made void; not forfeitable. [1540–50; IN-[3] + DEFEASIBLE] —**in′de·fea′si·bil′i·ty, in′de·fea′si·ble·ness,** *n.* —**in′de·fea′si·bly,** *adv.*

in·de·fect·i·ble (in′di fek′tə bəl), *adj.* **1.** not defectible; not liable to defect or failure. **2.** not liable to fault or imperfection; faultless. [1650–60; IN-[3] + DEFECTIBLE] —**in′de·fect′i·bil′i·ty,** *n.* —**in′de·fect′i·bly,** *adv.*

in·de·fen·si·ble (in′di fen′sə bəl), *adj.* **1.** not justifiable; inexcusable: *indefensible behavior.* **2.** incapable of being protected or defended against attack: *an indefensible town.* **3.** incapable of being defended against criticism or denial; untenable: *indefensible argument.* [1520–30; IN-[3] + DEFENSIBLE] —**in′de·fen′si·bil′i·ty, in′de·fen′si·ble·ness,** *n.* —**in′de·fen′si·bly,** *adv.*
—**Syn. 2.** vulnerable, defenseless, unprotected.

in·de·fin·a·ble (in′di fī′nə bəl), *adj.* **1.** not definable; not readily identified, described, analyzed, or determined. —*n.* **2.** something that cannot be defined: *the indefinables of great musicianship.* [1800–10; IN-[3] + DEFINABLE] —**in′de·fin′a·ble·ness,** *n.* —**in′de·fin′a·bly,** *adv.*

in·def·i·nite (in def′ə nit), *adj.* **1.** not definite; without fixed or specified limit; unlimited: *an indefinite number.* **2.** not clearly defined or determined; not precise or exact: *an indefinite boundary; an indefinite date in the future.* **3.** *Gram.* **a.** See **indefinite article. b.** See **indefinite pronoun. 4.** *Bot.* **a.** very numerous or not easily counted, as stamens. **b.** (of an inflorescence) indeterminate. [1520–30; < L *indēfīnītus.* See IN-[3], DEFINITE] —**in·def′i·nite·ly,** *adv.* —**in·def′i·nite·ness,** *n.*
—**Syn. 1.** unspecified; indeterminate. **2.** imprecise, inexact, indistinct, confusing, vague, uncertain. —**Ant. 1, 2.** determinate. **2.** clear, specific.

indef′inite ar′ticle, *Gram.* an article, as English *a, an,* that denotes class membership of the noun it modifies without particularizing it. [1720–30]

indef′inite in′tegral, *Math.* a representation, usually in symbolic form, of any function whose derivative is a given function. Also called **antiderivative.** [1875–80]

indef′inite pro′noun, *Gram.* a pronoun, as English *some, any, somebody,* that leaves unspecified the identity of its referent. [1720–30]

indef′inite rel′ative clause′, a relative clause with an indefinite relative pronoun as subordinating word, as *what they said* in *We heard what they said.*

indef′inite rel′ative pro′noun, a relative pronoun without an antecedent, as *whoever* in *They gave tickets to whoever wanted them.*

in·de·his·cent (in′di his′ənt), *adj. Bot., Mycol.* not dehiscent; not opening at maturity. [1825–35; IN-[3] + DEHISCENT] —**in′de·his′cence,** *n.*

in·de·lib·er·ate (in′di lib′ər it), *adj.* done without care; special planning or deliberation; unintentional. [1610–20; IN-[3] + DELIBERATE] —**in′de·lib′er·ate·ly,** *adv.* —**in′de·lib′er·ate·ness, in′de·lib′er·a′tion,** *n.*

in·del·i·ble (in del′ə bəl), *adj.* **1.** making marks that cannot be erased, removed, or the like: *indelible ink.* **2.** that cannot be eliminated, forgotten, changed, or the like: *the indelible memories of war; the indelible influence of a great teacher.* [1520–30; < ML *indēlībilis;* r. *indeleble* < L *indēlēbilis* indestructible. See IN-[3], DELE, -BLE] —**in·del′i·bil′i·ty, in·del′i·ble·ness,** *n.* —**in·del′i·bly,** *adv.*

in·del·i·ca·cy (in del′i kə sē), *n., pl.* **-cies** for 2. **1.** the quality or condition of being indelicate. **2.** something indelicate, as language or behavior. [1705–15; IN-[3] + DELICACY]

in·del·i·cate (in del′i kit), *adj.* **1.** offensive to a sense of generally accepted propriety, modesty, or decency; improper, unrefined, or coarse: *indelicate language.* **2.** not delicate; lacking delicacy; rough. [1735–45; IN-[3] + DELICATE] —**in·del′i·cate·ly,** *adv.* —**in·del′i·cate·ness,** *n.*
—**Syn. 1.** indecorous, untactful, gauche, rude.

in·dem·ni·fi·ca·tion (in dem′nə fi kā′shən), *n.* **1.** the act of indemnifying; state of being indemnified. **2.** something that serves to indemnify; compensation. [1725–35; INDEMNI(TY) + -FICATION] —**in·dem·nif·i·ca·to·ry** (in′dem nif′ə kə tôr′ē, -tōr′ē), *adj.*
—**Syn. 2.** payment, amends, reparation, indemnity.

in·dem·ni·fy (in dem′nə fī′), *v.t.,* **-fied, -fy·ing. 1.** to compensate for damage or loss sustained, expense incurred, etc. **2.** to guard or secure against anticipated loss; give security against (future damage or liability). [1605–15; < L *indemni(s)* without loss (see INDEMNITY) + -FY] —**in·dem′ni·fi′er,** *n.*
—**Syn. 1.** recompense, reimburse, repay.

in·dem·ni·tee (in dem′ni tē′), *n.* a person or company that receives indemnity. [INDEMNIT(Y) + -EE]

in·dem·ni·tor (in dem′ni tər), *n.* a person or company that gives indemnity. [INDEMNIT(Y) + -OR[2]]

in·dem·ni·ty (in dem′ni tē), *n., pl.* **-ties. 1.** protection or security against damage or loss. **2.** compensation for damage or loss sustained. **3.** something paid by way of such compensation. **4.** protection, as by insurance, from liabilities or penalties incurred by one's actions. **5.** legal exemption from penalties attaching to unconstitutional or illegal actions, granted to public officers and other persons. [1425–75; late ME *indem(p)nite* < L *indemnitās,* equiv. to *indemni(s)* without loss (*in-* IN-[3] + *-demn-,* comb. form of *damn-* (s. of *damnum* loss; see DAMN) + *-is* adj. suffix) + *-tās* -TY[2]]

in·de·mon·stra·ble (in′di mon′strə bəl, in dem′ən-), *adj.* not demonstrable; incapable of being demonstrated or proved. [1560–70; IN-[3] + DEMONSTRABLE] —**in′de·mon′stra·bil′i·ty, in′de·mon′stra·ble·ness,** *n.* —**in′·de·mon′stra·bly,** *adv.*

in·dene (in′dēn), *n. Chem.* a colorless, liquid hydrocarbon, C_9H_8, obtained from coal tar by fractional distillation: used in synthesizing resins. [1885–90; IND- + -ENE]

in·dent[1] (*v.* in dent′; *n.* in′dent, in dent′), *v.t.* **1.** to form deep recesses in: *The sea indents the coast.* **2.** to set in or back from the margin, as the first line of a paragraph. **3.** to sever (a document drawn up in duplicate) along an irregular line as a means of identification. **4.** to cut or tear the edge of (copies of a document) in an irregular way. **5.** to make toothlike notches in; notch. **6.** to indenture, as an apprentice. **7.** *Brit.* to draw an order upon. **8.** *Chiefly Brit.* to order, as commodities. —*v.i.* **9.** to form a recess. **10.** *Chiefly Brit.* to make out an order or requisition in duplicate. **11.** *Obs.* **a.** to draw upon a person or thing for something. **b.** to enter into an agreement by indenture; make a compact. —*n.* **12.** a toothlike notch or deep recess; indentation. **13.** an indention. **14.** an indenture. **15.** *Amer. Hist.* a certificate issued by a state or the federal government at the close of the Revolutionary War for the principal or interest due on the public debt. **16.** *Brit.* a requisition for stores. [1350–1400; ME; back formation from *indented* having toothlike notches, ME < ML *indentātus,* equiv. to L *in-* IN-[2] + *dentātus* DENTATE; see -ED[2]] —**in·dent′er, in·den′tor,** *n.*

in·dent[2] (*v.* in dent′; *n.* in′dent, in dent′), *v.t.* **1.** to dent; press in so as to form a dent: *to indent a pattern on metal.* **2.** to make or form a dent in: *The wooden stairs had been indented by horses' hooves.* —*n.* **3.** a dent. [1300–50; ME; see IN-[2], DENT[1]]

in·den·ta·tion (in′den tā′shən), *n.* **1.** a cut, notch, or deep recess: *various bays and indentations.* **2.** a series of incisions or notches: *the indentation of a maple leaf.* **3.** a notching or being notched. **4.** indention (defs. 1, 2). [1715–25; INDENT[1] + -ATION]

in·den·tion (in den′shən), *n.* **1.** the indenting of a line or lines in writing or printing. **2.** the blank space left by indenting. **3.** the act of indenting; state of being indented. **4.** *Archaic.* an indentation or notch. [1755–65; INDENT[1] + -ION]

in·den·ture (in den′chər), *n., v.,* **-tured, -tur·ing.** —*n.* **1.** a deed or agreement executed in two or more copies with edges correspondingly indented as a means of identification. **2.** any deed, written contract, or sealed agreement. **3.** a contract by which a person, as an apprentice, is bound to service. **4.** any official or formal list, certificate, etc., authenticated for use as a voucher or the like. **5.** the formal agreement between a group of bondholders and the debtor as to the terms of the debt. **6.** indentation. —*v.t.* **7.** to bind by indenture, as an apprentice. **8.** *Archaic.* to make a depression in; indent; wrinkle; furrow. [1275–1325; ME < ML *indentūra.* See INDENT[1], -URE] —**in·den′ture·ship′,** *n.*

inden′tured serv′ant, *Amer. Hist.* a person who came to America and was placed under contract to work for another over a period of time, usually seven years, esp. during the 17th to 19th centuries. Generally, indentured servants included redemptioners, victims of religious or political persecution, persons kidnapped for the purpose, convicts, and paupers. [1665–75]

in·de·pend·ence (in′di pen′dəns), *n.* **1.** Also, **independency.** the state or quality of being independent. **2.** freedom from the control, influence, support, aid, or the like, of others. **3.** *Archaic.* a competency. [1630–40; INDEPEND(ENT) + -ENCE]
—**Syn. 1.** See **freedom.**

In·de·pend·ence (in′di pen′dəns), *n.* **1.** a city in W Missouri: starting point of the Santa Fe and Oregon trails. 111,806. **2.** a town in SE Kansas. 10,598.

Independ′ence Day′, July 4, a U.S. holiday commemorating the adoption of the Declaration of Independence on July 4, 1776. Also called **Fourth of July.**

In′depend′ence Hall′, the building in Philadelphia where the Declaration of Independence was signed.

independ′ence of path′, *Math.* the property of a function for which the line integral has the same value along all curves between two specified points.

in·de·pend·en·cy (in′di pen′dən sē), *n., pl.* **-cies. 1.** independence (def. 1). **2.** a territory not under the control of any other power. **3.** (*cap.*) *Eccles.* **a.** the principle that the individual congregation or church is an autonomous and equalitarian society free from any external ecclesiastical control. **b.** the polity based on this principle. [1605–15; INDEPEND(ENT) + -ENCY]

in·de·pend·ent (in′di pen′dənt), *adj.* **1.** not influenced or controlled by others in matters of opinion, conduct, etc.; thinking or acting for oneself: *an independent thinker.* **2.** not subject to another's authority or jurisdiction; autonomous; free: *an independent businessman.* **3.** not influenced by the thought or action of others: *independent research.* **4.** not dependent; not depending or contingent upon something else for existence, operation, etc. **5.** not relying on another or others for aid or support. **6.** rejecting others' aid or support; refusing to be under obligation to others. **7.** possessing a competency: *to be financially independent.* **8.** sufficient to support a person without his having to work: *an independent income.* **9.** executed or originating outside a given unit, agency, business, etc.; external: *an independent inquiry.* **10.** working for oneself or for a small, privately owned business. **11.** expressive of a spirit of independence; self-confident; unconstrained: *a free and independent citizen.* **12.** free from party commitments in voting: *the independent voter.* **13.** *Math.* (of a quantity or function) not depending upon another for its value. **14.** *Gram.* capable of standing syntactically as a complete sentence: *an independent clause.* Cf. **dependent** (def. 4), **main**[1] (def. 4). **15.** *Logic.* **a.** (of a set of propositions) having no one proposition deducible from the others. **b.** (of a proposition) belonging to such a set. **16.** *Statistics.* See **statistically independent. 17.** (*cap.*) *Eccles.* of or pertaining to the Independents. **18. independent of,** irrespective of; regardless of: *Independent of monetary considerations, it was a promising position.* —*n.* **19.** an independent person or thing. **20.** a small, privately owned business: *The conglomerates are buying up the independents.* **21.** *Politics.* a person who votes for candidates, measures, etc., in accordance with his or her own judgment and without regard to the endorsement of, or the positions taken by, any party. **22.** (*cap.*) *Eccles.* an adherent of Independency. **23.** *Brit.* a

Congregationalist. [1605–15; IN-³ + DEPENDENT] **—in′de·pend′ent·ly,** *adv.*

independ′ent assort′ment, *Genetics.* See **law of independent assortment.** [1945–50]

in′depend′ent au′dit, an audit of a company conducted by accountants from an outside accounting firm (distinguished from *internal audit*).

in′depend′ent ax′iom, *Logic, Math.* in a set of axioms, one that cannot be proved by using the others in the set. [1900–05]

in·de·pen·den·tis·ta (ēn′de pen′den tēs′tä), *n., pl.* ***-tas*** (-täs). *Spanish.* (esp. in Latin America) a person who supports or works toward political independence, esp. one supporting radical changes in an existing government or from an existing system of government.

independ′ent suspen′sion, an automotive suspension system in which each wheel is attached to the frame independently, so that a road bump affecting one wheel has no effect on the others. [1925–30]

in′depend′ent var′iable, *Math.* a variable in a functional relation whose value determines the value or values of other variables, as x in the relation $y = 3x^2$. Cf. **dependent variable.** [1850–55]

in-depth (in′depth′), *adj.* **1.** extensive, thorough, or profound: *an in-depth analysis of the problem.* **2.** well-balanced or fully developed. [1960–65]

In·der·al (in′də rôl′, -rol′), *Pharm., Trademark.* a brand of propranolol.

in·de·scrib·a·ble (in′di skrī′bə bəl), *adj.* not describable; too extraordinary for description: *a scene of indescribable confusion; indescribable euphoria.* [1785–95; IN-³ + DESCRIBABLE] **—in′de·scrib′a·bil′i·ty, in′de·scrib′a·ble·ness,** *n.* **—in′de·scrib′a·bly,** *adv.*
—Syn. overwhelming, indefinable, unutterable.

in·de·struct·i·ble (in′di struk′tə bəl), *adj.* not destructible; that cannot be destroyed. [1665–75; < LL *indēstrūctibilis.* See IN-³, DESTRUCTIBLE] **—in′de·struct′i·bil′i·ty, in′de·struct′i·ble·ness,** *n.* **—in′de·struct′i·bly,** *adv.*
—Syn. unbreakable, permanent, enduring.

in·de·ter·mi·na·ble (in′di tûr′mə nə bəl), *adj.* **1.** not determinable; incapable of being ascertained. **2.** incapable of being decided or settled. [1480–90; < LL *indēterminābilis.* See IN-³, DETERMINABLE] **—in′de·ter′mi·na·ble·ness,** *n.* **—in′de·ter′mi·na·bly,** *adv.*

in·de·ter·mi·na·cy (in′di tûr′mə nə sē), *n.* the condition or quality of being indeterminate; indetermination. [1640–50; INDETERMIN(ATE) + -ACY]

indeter′minacy prin′ciple, *Physics.* See **uncertainty principle.** [1925–30]

in·de·ter·mi·nate (in′di tûr′mə nit), *adj.* **1.** not determinate; not precisely fixed in extent; indefinite; uncertain. **2.** not clear; vague. **3.** not established. **4.** not settled or decided. **5.** *Math.* **a.** (of a quantity) undefined, as *0/0.* **b.** (of an equation) able to be satisfied by more than one value for each unknown. **6.** *Bot.* (of an inflorescence) having the axis or axes not ending in a flower or bud, thus allowing further elongation. **—***n.* **7.** *Math.* something whose value is not specified: used esp. in abstract algebra; a variable. [1350–1400; ME < LL *indēterminātus.* See IN-³, DETERMINATE] **—in′de·ter′mi·nate·ly,** *adv.* **—in′de·ter′mi·nate·ness,** *n.*
—Syn. 2. ambiguous.

in′deter′minate sen′tence, *Criminal Law.* a penalty, imposed by a court, that has relatively wide limits or no limits, as one of imprisonment for one to ten years. [1870–75]

in·de·ter·mi·na·tion (in′di tûr′mə nā′shən), *n.* **1.** the quality or condition of being indeterminate. **2.** an unsettled state, as of the mind. [1610–20; INDETERMINATE + -ION]

in·de·ter·min·ism (in′di tûr′mə niz′əm), *n. Philos.* **1.** the doctrine that human actions, though influenced somewhat by preexisting psychological and other conditions, are not entirely governed by them but retain a certain freedom and spontaneity. **2.** the theory that the will is to some extent independent of the strength of motives, or may itself modify their strength in choice. [1870–75; IN-³ + DETERMINISM] **—in′de·ter′min·ist,** *n., adj.* **—in′de·ter′min·is′tic,** *adj.*

in·dex (in′deks), *n., pl.* **-dex·es, -di·ces** (-də sēz′), *v.* **—***n.* **1.** (in a nonfiction book, monograph, etc.) a more or less detailed alphabetical listing of names, places, and topics along with the numbers of the pages on which they are mentioned or discussed, usually included in or constituting the back matter. **2.** a sequential arrangement of material, esp. in alphabetical or numerical order. **3.** something used or serving to point out; a sign, token, or indication: *a true index of his character.* **4.** something that directs attention to some fact, condition, etc.; a guiding principle. **5.** a pointer or indicator in a scientific instrument. **6.** a piece of wood, metal, or the like, serving as a pointer or indicator. **7.** *Computers.* **a.** a value that identifies and is used to locate a particular element within a data array or table. **b.** a reference table that contains the keys or references needed to address data items. **8.** Also called **fist, hand.** *Print.* a sign in the shape of a hand with extended index finger, used to point out a particular note, paragraph, etc. **9.** a light, smooth cardboard stock. **10.** the forefinger. **11.** a number or formula expressing some property, ratio, etc., of something indicated: *index of growth; index of intelligence.* **12.** *Statistics.* See **index number.** **13.** *Econ.* See **price index.** **14.** *Algebra.* **a.** an exponent. **b.** the integer n in a radical $\sqrt[n]{}$ defining the n-th root: $\sqrt[3]{7}$ *is a radical having index three.* **c.** a subscript or superscript indicating the position of an object in a series of similar objects, as the subscripts 1, 2, and 3 in the series x_1, x_2, x_3. **d.** See **winding number.** **15.** *Horol.* a leverlike regulator for a hairspring. **16.** *(cap.) Rom. Cath. Ch.* **a.** See ***Index Librorum Prohibitorum.*** **b.** See ***Index Expurgatorius.*** **17.** *(usually cap.)* any list of forbidden or otherwise restricted material deemed morally or politically harmful by authorities: *an Index of disapproved books relating to Communism.* **18.** *Optics.* See **index of refraction.** **19.** *Obs.* **a.** a table of contents. **b.** a preface or prologue. **—***v.t.* **20.** to provide with an index, as a book. **21.** to enter in an index, as a name or topic. **22.** to serve to indicate: *warm breezes indexing the approach of spring.* **23.** to place (a book) on an official list as politically or morally harmful: *The commissar insisted on indexing the book.* **24.** to rotate (work) on a milling machine in order to repeat the milling operation at a new position. **25.** *Econ.* to adjust (wages, taxes, etc.) automatically according to changes in the cost-of-living level or another economic indicator, esp. to offset inflation. [1350–1400; ME < L: informer, pointer, equiv. to *in-* IN-² + *-dec-* (comb. form of *dic-,* show, declare, INDICATE; akin to TEACH) + *-s* nom. sing. ending] **—in′dex·a·ble,** *adj.* **—in′dex·er,** *n.* **—in·dex′i·cal,** *adj.* **—in·dex′i·cal·ly,** *adv.* **—in′dex·less,** *adj.*

in·dex·a·tion (in′dek sā′shən), *n. Econ.* the automatic adjustment of wages, taxes, pension benefits, interest rates, etc., according to changes in the cost of living or another economic indicator, esp. to compensate for inflation. [INDEX + -ATION]

in′dex card′, a card, often relatively small, as 3 × 5 in. (7.6 × 12.7 cm), used in noting or recording information and usually filed in an index. [1925–30]

in′dex crime′, a crime included in the yearly crime statistics of the Federal Bureau of Investigation. [1965–70; so called because it provides an *index* of the general level of criminal activity]

In·dex Ex·pur·ga·to·ri·us (in′deks ik spûr′gə tôr′ē əs, -tōr′-), *pl.* ***In·di·ces Ex·pur·ga·to·ri·i*** (in′də sēz′ ikspûr′gə tôr′ē ī′, -tōr′-). *Rom. Cath. Ch.* a list of books now included in the *Index Librorum Prohibitorum,* forbidden to be read except from expurgated editions. [< NL: lit., expurgatory index]

in′dex fin′ger, forefinger. [1840–50]

in′dex fos′sil, *Geol., Paleontol.* a widely distributed fossil, of narrow range in time, regarded as characteristic of a given geological formation, used esp. in determining the age of related formations. Also called **guide fossil.** [1895–1900]

in′dex fund′, a fund, as a mutual fund or pension fund, with a portfolio that contains many of the securities listed in a major stock index in order to match the performance of the stock market generally. [1975–80]

in′dexing serv′ice, a service that indexes the contents of a number of publications for use in printed or machine-readable form. [INDEX + -ING²]

In·dex Li·bro·rum Pro·hib·i·to·rum (in′deks lī-brôr′əm prō hib′i tôr′əm, -brōr′əm prō hib′i tōr′-, lē-), *pl.* ***In·di·ces Li·bro·rum Pro·hib·i·to·rum*** (in′də sēz′ lī brôr′əm prō hib′i tôr′əm, -brōr′əm prō hib′i tōr′-, lē-). *Rom. Cath. Ch.* a list of books forbidden to be read except from expurgated editions or by special permission. Cf. ***Index Expurgatorius.*** [< NL: index of prohibited books]

in·dex-link (in′deks lingk′), *v.t. Chiefly Brit. Econ.* index (def. 25). [1965–70]

in′dex num′ber, *Statistics.* a quantity whose variation over a period of time measures the change in some phenomenon. Also called **index.** [1870–75]

in′dex of lead′ing in′dicators, *Econ.* See **leading indicators.**

in′dex of refrac′tion, *Optics.* a number indicating the speed of light in a given medium as either the ratio of the speed of light in a vacuum to that in the given medium **(absolute index of refraction)** or the ratio of the speed of light in a specified medium to that in the given medium **(relative index of refraction).** *Symbol:* n Also called **index, refractive index.** [1820–30]

in′dex plate′, *Mach.* a plate perforated with rows of different numbers of equally spaced holes as a guide for indexing work. [1815–25]

in′dex set′, *Math.* a set whose elements are used to indicate the order of the elements of a sequence, series, etc.

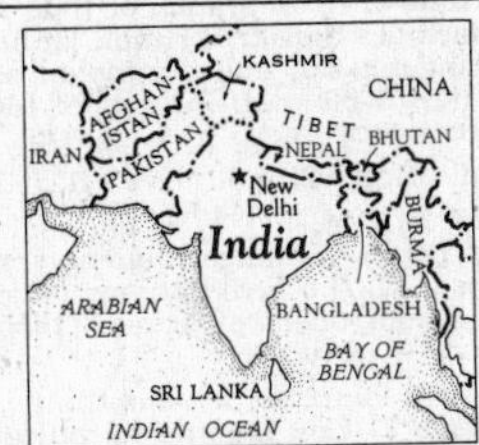

In·di·a (in′dē ə), *n.* **1.** Hindi, **Bharat.** a republic in S Asia: a union comprising 25 states and 7 union territories; formerly a British colony; gained independence Aug. 15, 1947; became a republic within the Commonwealth of Nations Jan. 26, 1950. 844,000,000; 1,246,880 sq. mi. (3,229,419 sq. km). *Cap.:* New Delhi. **2.** a subcontinent in S Asia, occupied by Bangladesh, Bhutan, the Republic of India, Nepal, Pakistan, and Sikkim. [< L < Gk *India,* equiv. to *Ind(ós)* the Indus river (< OPers *Hindu* lit., the river; c. Skt *sindhu*) + *-ia* -IA]

In·di·a (in′dē ə), *n.* a word used in communications to represent the letter *I.* [1950–55]

In′dia chintz′, a sturdy, heavyweight fabric constructed in a figured weave, used esp. in upholstery. Also called **In′dia cot′ton.**

In′dia drug′get, drugget (def. 1).

In′dia ink′, *(sometimes l.c.)* **1.** a black pigment consisting of lampblack mixed with glue or size. **2.** a liquid ink from this. Also called **Chinese ink.** [1655–65]

In·di·an (in′dē ən), *n.* **1.** Also called **American Indian, Amerind, Amerindian, Native American.** a member of the aboriginal people of America or of any of the aboriginal North or South American stocks, usually excluding the Eskimos. **2.** any of the indigenous languages of the American Indians. *Abbr.:* Ind **3.** a member of any of the peoples native to or inhabiting India or the East Indies. **4.** a citizen of the Republic of India. **5.** *Slang.* a person who performs a required task or carries out the instructions of superiors: *We have too many chiefs and not enough Indians.* **6.** *Astron.* the constellation Indus. **—***adj.* **7.** of, pertaining to, or characteristic of the American Indians or their languages. **8.** of, pertaining to, or characteristic of India or the East Indies. **9.** made of Indian corn: *Indian meal.* **10.** *Zoogeog.* oriental (def. 3). **11.** *Phytogeog.* belonging or pertaining to a geographical division comprising India south of the Himalayas, and Pakistan and Sri Lanka. [1350–1400; < ML *Indiānus;* r. ME *Indien* < OF < ML as above. See INDIA, -AN]
—Usage. Because Christopher Columbus mistakenly believed that the Caribbean island on which he had landed was the subcontinent of India, he called the inhabitants INDIANS. Eventually, that name was applied to almost all the indigenous, non-European inhabitants of North and South America. In modern times INDIAN may refer to an inhabitant of the subcontinent of India or of the East Indies, to a citizen of the Republic of India, or to a member of an aboriginal American people.
In the 18th century the term *American Indian* came to be used for the aboriginal inhabitants of the United States and Canada; it now includes the aboriginal peoples of South America as well. (When necessary, further distinctions are made with such terms as *North American Indian* and *South American Indian.*) The terms *Amerindian* and *Amerind* subsequently developed in the attempt to reduce ambiguity. For some, especially among North American Indians, the preferred designation is *Native American.* All these terms appear in edited writing. Whether one or several will gain ascendancy over the others remains to be seen.
The only pre-European inhabitants of North America to whom INDIAN or other terms using the word INDIAN are not applied are the Eskimos or Inuit. See **Eskimo.**

In·di·an·a (in′dē an′ə), *n.* **1.** **Robert** *(Robert Clarke),* born 1928, U.S. painter of pop art. **2.** a state in the central United States: a part of the Midwest. 5,490,179; 36,291 sq. mi. (93,995 sq. km). *Cap.:* Indianapolis. *Abbr.:* IN (for use with zip code), Ind. **3.** a city in W central Pennsylvania. 16,051. **— In′di·an′an, In·di·an·i·an** (in′dē an′ē ən), *adj., n.*

In′dian′a bal′lot, a ballot on which the candidates are listed in separate columns by party. Also called **party-column ballot.** Cf. **Massachusetts ballot, office-block ballot.**

In′diana Dunes′ Na′tional Lake′shore, a shore area in N Indiana, on Lake Michigan: established in 1966 for recreation and conservation purposes; comprising shoreline, dunes, bogs, and forests. 14 sq. mi. (36 sq. km).

In′dian a′gency, headquarters of an Indian agent. [1815–25, *Amer.*]

In′dian a′gent, an official representing the U.S. government in dealing with an Indian tribe or tribes. [1705–15]

In′dian al′mond, a Malayan tree, *Terminalia catappa,* having edible seeds, planted widely in the tropics as a street tree. [1885–90]

In·di·an·ap·o·lis (in′dē ə nap′ə lis), *n.* a city in and the capital of Indiana, in the central part. 700,807.

Indianapolis 500, a 500-mile oval-track race for rear-engine cars having particular specifications, held annually in Indianapolis, Ind.

In′dian bal′sam. See **Peru balsam.**

In′dian bean′, catalpa. [1835–45, *Amer.*]

In′dian bi′son, the gaur.

In′dian bread′, **1.** See **corn bread.** **2.** tuckahoe (def. 1). [1645–55, *Amer.*]

In′dian bread′root, breadroot. [1850–55]

In′dian club′, a metal or wooden club shaped like a large bottle, swung singly or in pairs for exercising the arms. [1855–60]

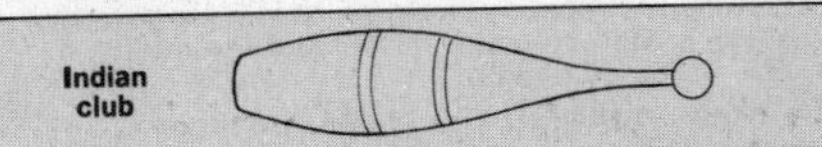

In′dian co′bra, a highly venomous cobra, *Naja naja,* common in India, having markings resembling a pair of spectacles on the back of the hood. Also called **spectacled cobra.** See illus. under **cobra.**

In′dian corn′, **1.** corn¹ (def. 1). **2.** any primitive corn with variegated kernels, often used for decorative purposes. **3.** any coarse variety of corn grown for fodder. [1610–20, *Amer.*]

In′dian coun′try, (esp. during the U.S. westward migration) any region where one was likely to encounter Indians, esp. hostile Indians. [1690–1700, *Amer.*]

In′dian cress′, a nasturtium, *Tropaeolum majus,* of South America, having red-spotted or red-striped, yellow-orange flowers, the young flower buds and fruits being used as seasoning. [1590–1600]

In′dian cu′cumber root′, a North American plant, *Medeola virginiana,* of the lily family, having whorled leaves, nodding, greenish-yellow flowers, and an edible root. Also called **In′dian cu′cumber.** [1775–85, *Amer.*]

In′dian cur′rant, a shrub, *Symphoricarpos orbiculatus,* of the honeysuckle family, found from South Dakota and Texas to the eastern coast of the U.S., having hairy leaves, inconspicuous white flowers, and reddish-purple fruit. Also called **coralberry.** [1775–85, *Amer.*]

In′dian Des′ert. See **Thar Desert.**

In′dian el′ephant. See under **elephant.** [1600–10]

In′dian Em′pire, British India and the Indian states ruled by native princes but under indirect British control: dissolved in 1947 and absorbed into India and Pakistan.

In′dian fig′, a bushy or treelike cactus, *Opuntia ficus-indica,* of central Mexico, having large yellow flowers and juicy, red, edible fruit. [1585–95]

In′dian file′, in single file. [1750–60, *Amer.*]

In′dian giv′er, *Informal* (*sometimes offensive*). a person who gives a gift and then takes it back. [1825–35] —**In′dian giv′ing.**

In′dian haw′thorn, a southern Chinese evergreen shrub, *Raphiolepis indica,* of the rose family, having shiny, leathery leaves and pinkish-white flowers in loose clusters.

In′dian hemp′, **1.** a North American dogbane, *Apocynum cannabinum,* having erect clusters of greenish-white flowers and a root with laxative and emetic properties. **2.** hemp (def. 1). [1610–20, *Amer.*]

In′dian ink′, (*sometimes l.c.*) *Brit.* See **India ink.**

In·di·an·ism (in′dē ə niz′əm), *n.* **1.** action or policy for promoting the interests of Indians, esp. American Indians. **2.** a word or usage considered to be characteristic of Indians, esp. American Indians. [1645–55; INDIAN + -ISM] —**In′di·an·ist,** *n., adj.*

In′dian ju′jube, an Indian evergreen shrub or small tree, *Ziziphus mauritiana,* of the buckthorn family, having leaves that are rusty-hairy on the underside and small, round, red, acid fruit. Also called **cottony jujube.**

In′dian lic′orice, a woody tropical vine, *Abrus precatorius,* of the legume family, having extremely poisonous scarlet and black seeds that are used for beads and a root used as a substitute for licorice. Also called **crab's-eye, rosary pea.** [1885–90]

In′dian lo′tus, a southern Asian lotus, *Nelumbo nucifera,* of the water lily family, having fragrant pink or rose flowers. Also called **East Indian lotus, Egyptian lotus, sacred lotus.** [1900–05]

In′dian mal′low, **1.** Also called **velvetleaf.** an Asian plant, *Abutilon theophrasti,* of the mallow family, having velvety leaves and yellow flowers: it is cultivated in China for its jutelike fiber and has become naturalized as a weed in North America. **2.** any of certain related species.

In′dian meal′, *Chiefly Brit.* cornmeal (def. 1). [1625–35, *Amer.*]

In′dian mil′let, **1.** durra. **2.** See **pearl millet.** [1785–95, *Amer.*]

In′dian mul′berry, a small tree, *Morinda citrifolia,* of the madder family, found from India to Australasia, having shiny leaves, white flowers, and fleshy, yellowish fruit, yielding red and yellow dyes. Also called **al.**

In′dian Mu′tiny. See **Sepoy Rebellion.**

In′dian O′cean, an ocean S of Asia, E of Africa, and W of Australia. 28,357,000 sq. mi. (73,444,630 sq. km).

In·di·a·no·la (in′dē ə nō′lə), *n.* a town in central Iowa. 10,843.

In′dian paint′brush, any of several semiparasitic plants belonging to the genus *Castilleja,* of the figwort family, as *C. linariaefolia,* of the western U.S.: the state flower of Wyoming. [1890–95, *Amer.*]

In′dian paint′ fun′gus, a common woody hoof-shaped fungus, *Echinodontium tinctorium,* found on conifers in western North America and believed to have been used as a dye by Pacific Northwest Indians.

In′dian phys′ic, **1.** See **American ipecac.** **2.** See **bowman's root.** [1730–40, *Amer.*]

In′dian pipe′, a leafless, pearly white, saprophytic plant, *Monotropa uniflora,* of North America and Asia, having a solitary white flower and resembling a tobacco pipe. [1785–95, *Amer.*]

In′dian poke′. See **false hellebore.** [1775–85, *Amer.*]

In′dian pud′ding, a sweet baked pudding made of cornmeal, molasses, milk, and various spices. [1715–25, *Amer.*]

In′dian red′, **1.** earth of a yellowish-red color, found esp. in the Persian Gulf, that serves as a pigment and as a polish for gold and silver objects. **2.** a pigment of that color prepared by oxidizing the salts of iron. [1745–55]

In′dian rice′, the wild rice plant. [1815–25]

In′dian Run′ner, one of a breed of domestic ducks.

In′dian san′icle. See **white snakeroot.**

In′dian silk′. See **India silk.** [1790–1800, *Amer.*]

In′dian States′ and A′gencies, the 560 former semidependent states and agencies in India and Pakistan: all except Kashmir were incorporated into the republics of India and Pakistan (1947–49). Also called **Native States.**

In′dian straw′berry, a plant, *Duchesnea indica,* of the rose family, native to India, having yellow flowers and inedible fruit resembling strawberries. Also called **mock strawberry.**

In′dian sum′mer, a period of mild, dry weather, usually accompanied by a hazy atmosphere, occurring usually in late October or early November and following a period of colder weather. [1770–80, *Amer.*]

In′dian Ter′ritory, a former territory of the U.S.: now in E Oklahoma. ab. 31,000 sq. mi. (80,000 sq. km).

In′dian tobac′co, a common American plant, *Lobelia inflata,* of the lobelia family, having small, blue flowers and inflated capsules. [1610–20]

In′dian tur′nip, **1.** the jack-in-the-pulpit. **2.** its root. [1800–10, *Amer.*]

In′dian war′rior, a lousewort, *Pedicularis densiflora,* of the western U.S., having densely clustered red flowers. [1900–05, *Amer.*]

In′dian wolf′, a wolf, *Canis lupus pallipes,* of Asia south of the Himalayas.

In·di·an-wres·tle (in′dē ən res′əl), *v.,* **-tled, -tling.** —*v.i.* **1.** to engage in Indian wrestling: *to Indian-wrestle for the city championship.* —*v.t.* **2.** to contend with (another person) in Indian wrestling: *to Indian-wrestle any and all challengers.* [1935–40] —**In′di·an-wres′tler,** *n.*

In′dian wres′tling, **1.** See **arm wrestling.** **2.** a form of wrestling in which two opponents clasp each other's right or left hand and, placing the corresponding feet side by side, attempt to unbalance each other. **3.** a form of wrestling in which two opponents, lying side by side on their backs and in opposite directions, lock near arms and raise and lock corresponding legs, with each attempting to force the other's leg down until one opponent is unable to remain lying flat. [1910–15, *Amer.*]

In′dian yel′low, **1.** Also called **purree, snowshoe.** an orange-yellow color. **2.** *Painting.* **a.** Also called **purree.** a yellow pigment formerly derived from the urine of cows fed on mango leaves. **b.** a pigment derived from coal tar, characterized chiefly by its yellow color and permanence. [1865–70]

In′dia pa′per, **1.** a fine, thin, opaque paper made in the Orient, used chiefly in the production of thin-paper editions and for impressions of engravings. **2.** See **Bible paper.** [1760–70]

In′dia print′, a plain-weave cotton fabric from India with brillantly colored block-print designs, or a fabric resembling this.

In′dia rub′ber, **1.** rubber[1] (def. 1). **2.** a rubber eraser. **3.** a rubber overshoe. Also, **in′dia rub′ber.** [1780–90]

In′dia silk′, a soft, lightweight fabric constructed in plain weave, woven chiefly in India. Also, **Indian silk.** [1750–60]

In′dia wheat′, a buckwheat, *Fagopyrum tataricum,* of India, having loose clusters of greenish or yellowish flowers, grown for soil improvement. Also called **duck-wheat.** [1855–60]

In·dic (in′dik), *adj.* **1.** of or pertaining to India; Indian. **2.** of or pertaining to Indic; Indo-Aryan. —*n.* **3.** a subgroup of the Indo-Iranian branch of Indo-European languages that includes Sanskrit, Hindi, Urdu, Bengali, and many other languages of India, Pakistan, and Sri Lanka; Indo-Aryan. [1875–80; < L *Indicus* of India < Gk *Indikós.* See INDIA, -IC]

indic., **1.** indicating. **2.** indicative. **3.** indicator.

in·di·can (in′di kən), *n.* **1.** a glucoside, $C_{14}H_{17}NO_6$, that occurs in plants yielding indigo and from which indigo is obtained. **2.** *Biochem.* indoxyl potassium sulfate, $C_8H_6NO_4SK$, a component of urine. [1855–60; < L *indic(um)* INDIGO + -AN]

in·di·cant (in′di kənt), *n.* **1.** something that indicates; indicator. —*adj.* **2.** *Obs.* serving to indicate; indicative. [1600–10; < L *indicant-* (s. of *indicāns,* prp. of *indicāre* to point, make known), equiv. to *indic-* (see INDICATE) + *-ant-* -ANT]

in·di·cate (in′di kāt′), *v.t.,* **-cat·ed, -cat·ing.** **1.** to be a sign of; betoken; evidence; show: *His hesitation really indicates his doubt about the venture.* **2.** to point out or point to; direct attention to: *to indicate a place on a map.* **3.** to show, as by measuring or recording; make known: *The thermometer indicates air temperature.* **4.** to state or express, esp. briefly or in a general way; signal: *He indicated his disapproval but did not go into detail.* **5.** *Med.* **a.** (of symptoms) to point out (a particular remedy, treatment, etc.) as suitable or necessary. **b.** to show the presence of (a condition, infection, etc.). [1645–55; < L *indicātus* ptp. of *indicāre* to point, make known equiv. to *indic-* (s. of *index*) INDEX + *-ātus* -ATE[1]] —**in·di·cat′a·ble,** *adj.* —**in·dic·a·to·ry** (in dik′ə tôr′ē, -tōr′ē), *adj.*
—**Syn.** **3.** register, reveal, record.

in′dicated horse′power, the horsepower of a reciprocating engine as shown by an indicator record. *Abbr.:* ihp, IHP [1870–75]

in·di·ca·tion (in′di kā′shən), *n.* **1.** anything serving to indicate or point out, as a sign or token. **2.** *Med.* a special symptom or the like that points out a suitable remedy or treatment or shows the presence of a disease. **3.** an act of indicating. **4.** the degree marked by an instrument. [1535–45; < L *indicātiōn-* (s. of *indicātiō*). See INDICATE, -ION]
—**Syn.** **1.** hint, intimation, portent.

in·dic·a·tive (in dik′ə tiv), *adj.* **1.** showing, signifying, or pointing out; expressive or suggestive (usually fol. by *of*): *behavior indicative of mental disorder.* **2.** *Gram.* noting or pertaining to the mood of the verb used for ordinary objective statements, questions, etc., as the verb *plays* in *John plays football.* Cf. **imperative** (def. 3), **subjunctive** (def. 1). —*n. Gram.* **3.** the indicative mood. **4.** a verb in the indicative. [1520–30; < LL *indicātīvus.* See INDICATE, -IVE] —**in·dic′a·tive·ly,** *adv.*

in·di·ca·tor (in′di kā′tər), *n.* **1.** a person or thing that indicates. **2.** a pointing or directing device, as a pointer on the dial of an instrument to show pressure, temperature, speed, volume, or the like. **3.** an instrument that indicates the condition of a machine or the like. **4.** an instrument for measuring and recording variations of pressure in the cylinder of an engine. **5.** *Chem.* **a.** a substance, as litmus, that indicates the presence or concentration of a certain constituent. **b.** a substance often used in a titration to indicate the point at which the reaction is complete. **6.** *Ecol.* a plant or animal that indicates, by its presence in a given area, the existence of certain environmental conditions. [1660–70; < ML *indicātor,* equiv. to L *indicā(re)* to INDICATE + *-tor* -TOR]

in·di·ces (in′də sēz′), *n.* a pl. of **index.**

in·di·ci·a (in dish′ē ə), *n.pl., sing.* **-ci·um.** **1.** a postal marking used rather than a stamp or a regular cancellation on each item in a large shipment of prepaid mail. **2.** Often, **indicium. a.** a printed message or instruction, esp. one stamped on a package: *an indicium of "bulk mail."* **b.** an indication or token. [1615–25; < L, pl. of *indicium* INDICIUM]

in·di·cial (in dish′əl), *adj.* **1.** of, pertaining to, or resembling an indication; indicative: *behavior indicial of a personality disorder.* **2.** of, pertaining to, or resembling an index or an index finger. [1840–50; INDICI(A) + -AL[1]] —**in·di′cial·ly,** *adv.*

indi′cial equa′tion, *Math.* an equation that is obtained from a given linear differential equation and that indicates whether a solution in power series form exists for the differential equation.

in·di·ci·um (in dish′ē əm), *n., pl.* **-di·ci·a** (-dish′ē ə), **-di·ci·ums.** indicia (def. 2). [1615–25; < L: disclosure, sign, indication, equiv. to *indic(āre)* to make known (see INDICATE) + *-ium* -IUM]

in·dic·o·lite (in dik′ə līt′), *n. Mineral.* a dark-blue tourmaline, used as a gem. [1800–10; < F; see INDIGO, -LITE]

in·dict (in dīt′), *v.t.* **1.** (of a grand jury) to bring a formal accusation against, as a means of bringing to trial: *The grand jury indicted him for murder.* **2.** to charge with an offense or crime; accuse of wrongdoing; castigate; criticize: *He tends to indict everyone of plotting against him.* [1620–30; var. sp. (< ML) of INDITE] —**in·dict·ee′,** *n.* —**in·dict′er, in·dict′or,** *n.*

in·dict·a·ble (in dī′tə bəl), *adj.* **1.** liable to being indicted, as a person. **2.** making a person liable to indictment, as an offense. [1700–10; INDICT + -ABLE] —**in·dict′a·bil′i·ty,** *n.* —**in·dict′a·bly,** *adv.*

in·dic·tion (in dik′shən), *n.* **1.** a proclamation made every 15 years in the later Roman Empire, fixing the valuation of property to be used as a basis for taxation. **2.** a tax based on such valuation. **3.** Also called **cycle of indiction.** the recurring fiscal period of 15 years in the Roman Empire, long used for dating ordinary events. Cf. **lustrum.** **4.** a specified year in this period. **5.** the number indicating it. [1350–1400; ME *indiccio(u)n* < L *indictiōn-* (s. of *indictiō*) announcement, equiv. to *indict(us)* ptp. of *indīcere* to announce, proclaim + *-iōn-* -ION] —**in·dic′tion·al,** *adj.*

in·dict·ment (in dīt′mənt), *n.* **1.** an act of indicting. **2.** *Law.* a formal accusation initiating a criminal case, presented by a grand jury and usually required for felonies and other serious crimes. **3.** any charge, accusation, serious criticism, or cause for blame. **4.** the state of being indicted. [1275–1325; INDICT + -MENT; r. ME *enditement* < AF (see INDITE)]

in·die (in′dē), *Informal.* —*n.* **1.** an independently owned business: *to work for an indie.* —*adj.* **2.** (of a person) self-employed; (of a business) privately owned: *an indie film producer.* [1940–45; IND(EPENDENT) + -IE]

In·dienne (an′dē en′; *Fr.* AN dyen′), *adj.* **1.** (of food) prepared or seasoned in East Indian style, as with curry. —*n.* **2.** (*l.c.*) a lightweight cotton fabric printed or painted in imitation of fabrics made in India. [1875–80, *Amer.*; < F *à l'indienne*; see INDIAN]

In·dies (in′dēz), *n.* **the. 1.** (*used with a plural v.*) See **West Indies** (def. 1). **2.** (*used with a plural v.*) See **East Indies** (def. 1). **3.** (*used with a singular v.*) a region in and near S and SE Asia; India, Indochina, and the East Indies.

in·dif·fer·ence (in dif′ər əns, -dif′rəns), *n.* **1.** lack of interest or concern: *We were shocked by their indifference toward poverty.* **2.** unimportance; little or no concern: *Whether or not to attend the party is a matter of indifference to him.* **3.** the quality or condition of being indifferent. **4.** mediocre quality; mediocrity. [1400–50; late ME, var. of *indifferency* < L *indifferentia.* See INDIFFERENT, -ENCE, -ENCY]
—**Syn.** **1.** INDIFFERENCE, UNCONCERN, LISTLESSNESS, APATHY, INSENSIBILITY all imply lack of feeling. INDIFFERENCE denotes an absence of feeling or interest; UNCONCERN, an absence of concern or solicitude, a calm or cool indifference in the face of what might be expected to cause uneasiness or apprehension; LISTLESSNESS, an absence of inclination or interest, a languid indifference to what is going on about one; APATHY, a profound intellectual and emotional indifference suggestive of faculties either naturally sluggish or dulled by emotional disturbance, mental illness, or prolonged sickness; INSENSIBILITY, an absence of capacity for feeling or of susceptibility

CONCISE ETYMOLOGY KEY: <, descended or borrowed from; >, whence; b., blend of, blended; c., cognate with; cf., compare; deriv., derivative; equiv., equivalent; imit., imitative; obl., oblique; r., replacing; s., stem; sp., spelling, spelled; resp., respelling, respelled; trans., translation; ?, origin unknown; *, unattested; ‡, probably earlier than. See the full key inside the front cover.

to emotional influences. **—Ant. 1.** eagerness, responsiveness.

in·dif·fer·en·cy (in dif′ər ən sē, -dif′rən-), *n. Archaic.* indifference. [1400–50; late ME; see INDIFFERENCE]

in·dif·fer·ent (in dif′ər ənt, -dif′rənt), *adj.* **1.** without interest or concern; not caring; apathetic: *his indifferent attitude toward the suffering of others.* **2.** having no bias, prejudice, or preference; impartial; disinterested. **3.** neither good nor bad in character or quality; average; routine: *an indifferent specimen.* **4.** not particularly good, important, etc.; unremarkable; unnotable: *an indifferent success; an indifferent performance.* **5.** of only moderate amount, extent, etc. **6.** not making a difference, or mattering, one way or the other. **7.** immaterial or unimportant. **8.** not essential or obligatory, as an observance. **9.** making no difference or distinction, as between persons or things: *indifferent justice.* **10.** neutral in chemical, electric, or magnetic quality. **11.** *Biol.* not differentiated or specialized, as cells or tissues. **—n. 12.** an ethically or morally indifferent act. **13.** a person who is indifferent, esp. in matters of religion or politics. **—adv. 14.** *Archaic.* indifferently: *I am indifferent well.* [1350–1400; ME (adj.) < L *indifferent-* (s. of *indifferēns*). See IN-[3], DIFFERENT] **—in·dif′fer·ent·ly,** *adv.*
—Syn. 4. mediocre, undistinguished, uninspired, commonplace.

in·dif·fer·ent·ism (in dif′ər ən tiz′əm, -dif′rən-), *n.* **1.** systematic indifference. **2.** adiaphorism. **3.** the principle or opinion that differences of religious belief are essentially unimportant. **4.** *Philos.* the doctrine that each entity is essentially unique and at the same time essentially the same as all other entities of its kind. [1820–30; < F *indifférentisme.* See INDIFFERENT, -ISM] **—in·dif′fer·ent·ist,** *n.*

in·di·gence (in′di jəns), *n.* seriously impoverished condition; poverty. [1325–75; ME < L *indigentia* need. See INDIGENT, -ENCE]
—Syn. privation, need, want, penury. **—Ant.** wealth.

in·di·gene (in′di jēn′), *n.* a person or thing that is indigenous or native; native; autochthon. Also, **in·di·gen** (in′di jən). [1590–1600; < MF < L *indigena* a native. See INDIGENOUS]

in·dig·e·nize (in dij′ə nīz′), *v.t.,* **-nized, -niz·ing. 1.** to make indigenous. **2.** to increase local participation in or ownership of: *to indigenize foreign-owned companies.* **3.** to adapt (beliefs, customs, etc.) to local ways. Also, *esp. Brit.,* **in·dig′e·nise′.** [1950–55; INDIGEN(OUS) + -IZE] **—in·dig′e·ni·za′tion,** *n.*

in·dig·e·nous (in dij′ə nəs), *adj.* **1.** originating in and characteristic of a particular region or country; native (often fol. by *to*): *the plants indigenous to Canada; the indigenous peoples of southern Africa.* **2.** innate; inherent; natural (usually fol. by *to*): *feelings indigenous to human beings.* [1640–50; < L *indigen(a)* native, original inhabitant (*indi-,* by-form of *in-* IN-[2] (cf. INDAGATE) + *-gena,* deriv. from base of *gignere* to bring into being; cf. GENITAL, GENITOR) + -OUS] **—in·dig′e·nous·ly,** *adv.* **—in·dig′e·nous·ness, in·di·gen·i·ty** (in′di jen′i tē), *n.*
—Syn. 1. autochthonous, aboriginal, natural. **—Ant. 1.** foreign, alien.

in·di·gent (in′di jənt), *adj.* **1.** lacking food, clothing, and other necessities of life because of poverty; needy; poor; impoverished. **2.** *Archaic.* **a.** deficient in what is requisite. **b.** destitute (usually fol. by *of*). **—n. 3.** a person who is indigent. [1350–1400; ME < L *indigent-* (s. of *indigēns*) prp. of *indigēre* to need, lack, be poor, equiv. to *ind-* by-form of *in-* IN-[2] (cf. INDAGATE) + *-ig-* (comb. form of *egēre* to need, lack) + *-ent-* -ENT] **—in′di·gent·ly,** *adv.*
—Syn. 1. necessitous, penurious, distressed.

in·di·gest·ed (in′di jes′tid, -dī-), *adj.* **1.** without arrangement or order. **2.** unformed or shapeless. **3.** not digested; undigested. **4.** not duly considered. [1585–95; IN-[3] + DIGESTED]

in·di·gest·i·ble (in′di jes′tə bəl, -dī-), *adj.* not digestible; not easily digested. [1520–30; < LL *indigestibilis.* See IN-[3], DIGESTIBLE] **—in′di·gest′i·bil′i·ty, in′di·gest′i·ble·ness,** *n.* **—in′di·gest′i·bly,** *adv.*

in·di·ges·tion (in′di jes′chən, -dī-), *n.* **1.** uncomfortable inability or difficulty in digesting food; dyspepsia. **2.** an instance or case of indigestion. [1400–50; late ME < LL *indīgestiōn-* (s. of *indīgestiō*). See IN-[2], DIGESTION]

in·di·ges·tive (in′di jes′tiv, -dī-), *adj.* accompanied by or suffering from indigestion; dyspeptic. [1625–35; IN-[3] + DIGESTIVE]

in·dign (in dīn′), *adj.* **1.** *Archaic.* unworthy. **2.** *Obs.* unbecoming or disgraceful. [1400–50; late ME *indigne* < MF < L *indignus,* equiv. to *in-* IN-[3] + *dignus* worthy; see DIGNITY]

in·dig·nant (in dig′nənt), *adj.* feeling, characterized by, or expressing strong displeasure at something considered unjust, offensive, insulting, or base: *indignant remarks; an indignant expression on his face.* [1580–90; < L *indignant-* (s. of *indignāns,* prp. of *indignārī* to deem unworthy, take offense), equiv. to *in-* IN-[3] + *dign-,* s. of *dignus* worthy + *-ant-* -ANT] **—in·dig′nant·ly,** *adv.*
—Syn. angry, resentful, infuriated, mad.

in·dig·na·tion (in′dig nā′shən), *n.* strong displeasure at something considered unjust, offensive, insulting, or base; righteous anger. [1325–75; ME *indignacio(u)n* < L *indignātiōn-* (s. of *indignātiō*), equiv. to *indignāt(us)* ptp. of *indignārī* to be indignant, take offense + *-iōn-* -ION; see INDIGNANT]
—Syn. resentment, exasperation, wrath, ire, choler. See **anger. —Ant.** calm.

in·dig·ni·ty (in dig′ni tē), *n., pl.* **-ties. 1.** an injury to a person's dignity; slighting or contemptuous treatment; humiliating affront, insult, or injury. **2.** *Obs.* disgrace or disgraceful action. [1575–85; < L *indignitās* unworthiness, equiv. to *indign(us)* INDIGN + *-itās* -ITY]
—Syn. 1. outrage. See **insult.**

in·di·go (in′di gō′), *n., pl.* **-gos, -goes,** *adj.* **—n. 1.** a blue dye obtained from various plants, esp. of the genus *Indigofera,* or manufactured synthetically. **2.** See **indigo blue** (def. 2). **3.** any of numerous hairy plants belonging to the genus *Indigofera,* of the legume family, having pinnate leaves and clusters of usually red or purple flowers. **4.** a color ranging from a deep violet blue to a dark, grayish blue. **—adj. 5.** Also called **indigo-blue, indigotic.** of the color indigo. [1545–55; < Sp or Pg, var. of *índico* < L *indicum* < Gk *indikón,* n. use of neut. of *Indikós* INDIC]

in′digo blue′, 1. indigo (def. 4). **2.** Also called **indigo, indigotin.** a dark-blue, water-insoluble, crystalline powder, $C_{16}H_{10}N_2O_2$, having a bronzelike luster, the essential coloring principle of which is contained along with other substances in the dye indigo and which can be produced synthetically. [1705–15] **—in′di·go-blue′,** *adj.*

in′digo bunt′ing, a North American bunting, *Passerina cyanea,* the male of which is indigo. Also called **in′digo bird′, in′digo finch′.** [1775–85, *Amer.*]

in·di·goid (in′di goid′), *adj.* **1.** of or pertaining to that group of vat dyes that have a molecular structure similar to that of indigo. **—n. 2.** an indigoid substance. [1905–10; INDIG(O) + -OID]

in′digo snake′, a large, deep-blue or brown harmless snake, *Drymarchon corais,* ranging from the southern U.S. to South America and invading burrows to prey on small mammals: the eastern subspecies *D. corais couperi* is now greatly reduced in number. Also called **gopher snake.** [1880–85, *Amer.*]

in·di·got·ic (in′di got′ik), *adj.* indigo (def. 5). [1830–40; INDIGO + -TIC]

in·dig·o·tin (in dig′ə tin, in′di gōt′n), *n.* See **indigo blue** (def. 2). [1830–40; INDIGOT(IC) + -IN[2]]

In·di·o (in′dē ō′), *n.* a town in S California. 21,611.

in·di·rect (in′də rekt′, -dī-), *adj.* **1.** not in a direct course or path; deviating from a straight line; roundabout: *an indirect course in sailing.* **2.** coming or resulting otherwise than directly or immediately, as effects or consequences: *an indirect advantage.* **3.** not direct in action or procedure: *His methods are indirect but not dishonest.* **4.** not straightforward; devious; deceitful: *He is known as a shady, indirect fellow.* **5.** not direct in bearing, application, force, etc.: *indirect evidence.* **6.** of, pertaining to, or characteristic of indirect discourse: *an indirect quote.* **7.** not descending in a direct line of succession, as a title or inheritance. [1350–1400; ME < ML *indirēctus.* See IN-[3], DIRECT] **—in′di·rect′ly,** *adv.* **—in′di·rect′ness,** *n.*
—Syn. 2. incidental, unintentional, secondary.

in′direct address′, *Computers.* the address in a storage location that contains the actual machine address of a data item or of other information, as the next instruction, or that contains another indirect address. Cf. **direct address.**

in′direct cost′, a business cost that is not directly accountable to a particular function or product; a fixed cost, as a land tax or the like. [1905–10]

in′direct dis′course, discourse consisting not of an exact quotation of a speaker's words but of a version transformed from them for grammatical inclusion in a larger sentence. *He said he was hungry* is an example of indirect discourse. Cf. **direct discourse.**

in′direct ev′idence. See **circumstantial evidence.** [1815–25]

in′direct free′ kick′, *Soccer.* a free kick from which a goal cannot be scored until after the ball has been touched by at least one player other than the kicker.

in′direct′ ini′tiative, a procedure in which a statute or amendment proposed by popular petition must receive legislative consideration before being submitted to the voters.

in·di·rec·tion (in′də rek′shən, -dī-), *n.* **1.** indirect action or procedure. **2.** a roundabout course or method. **3.** a lack of direction or goal; aimlessness: *His efforts were marked by indirection and indecisiveness.* **4.** deceitful or dishonest dealing. [1585–95; INDIRECT + -ION, modeled on DIRECTION]

in′direct la′bor, labor performed, as by maintenance and clerical workers, that is not considered in computing costs per unit of production. Cf. **direct labor.**

in′direct light′ing, reflected or diffused light, used esp. in interiors to avoid glare or shadows. [1920–25]

in′direct ob′ject, a word or group of words representing the person or thing with reference to which the action of a verb is performed, in English generally coming between the verb and the direct object and paraphrasable as the object of a preposition, usually *to* or *for,* following the direct object, as *the boy* in *He gave the boy a book.* [1875–80]

in′direct pri′mary, *U.S. Politics.* a primary in which members of a party elect delegates to a party convention that in turn elects the party's candidates. Cf. **direct primary.**

in′direct proof′, an argument for a proposition that shows its negation to be incompatible with a previously accepted or established premise.

in′direct tax′, a tax levied indirectly, as one levied on commodities before they reach the consumer but ultimately paid by the consumer as part of the market price. [1795–1805]

in·dis·cern·i·ble (in′di sûr′nə bəl, -zûr′-), *adj.* not discernible; that cannot be seen or perceived clearly; imperceptible. [1625–35; IN-[3] + DISCERNIBLE] **—in′dis·cern′i·ble·ness, in′dis·cern′i·bil′i·ty,** *n.* **—in′dis·cern′i·bly,** *adv.*

in·dis·cerp·ti·ble (in′di sûrp′tə bəl), *adj.* not discerptible; indivisible. [1650–60; IN-[3] + DISCERPTIBLE]

in·dis·ci·pline (in dis′ə plin), *n.* **1.** lack of discipline or control: *a campus problem of student indiscipline.* **2.** an instance of this. [1775–85; IN-[3] + DISCIPLINE] **—in·dis′ci·plin′a·ble,** *adj.* **—in·dis′ci·plined,** *adj.*

in·dis·cov·er·a·ble (in′di skuv′ər ə bəl), *adj.* not discoverable. [1630–40; IN-[3] + DISCOVERABLE]

in·dis·creet (in′di skrēt′), *adj.* not discreet; lacking prudence, good judgment, or circumspection: *an indiscreet remark.* [1375–1425; late ME *indiscret* (prob. < MF) < L *indiscrētus* undivided; see INDISCRETE] **—in′dis·creet′ly,** *adv.* **—in′dis·creet′ness,** *n.*
—Syn. imprudent, incautious, impolitic.

in·dis·crete (in′di skrēt′, in dis′krēt), *adj.* **1.** not discrete; not divided into parts. **2.** *Math.* trivial (def. 4). [1600–10; < L *indiscrētus* undivided. See IN-[3], DISCRETE]

in·dis·cre·tion (in′di skresh′ən), *n.* **1.** lack of discretion; imprudence. **2.** an indiscreet act, remark, etc. [1300–50; ME < LL *indiscrētiōn-* (s. of *indiscrētiō*). See IN-[3], DISCRETION] **—in′dis·cre′tion·ar′y,** *adj.*

in·dis·crim·i·nate (in′di skrim′ə nit), *adj.* **1.** not discriminating; lacking in care, judgment, selectivity, etc.: *indiscriminate in one's friendships.* **2.** not discriminate; haphazard; thoughtless: *indiscriminate slaughter.* **3.** not kept apart or divided; thrown together; jumbled: *an indiscriminate combination of colors and styles.* [1590–1600; IN-[3] + DISCRIMINATE (adj.)] **—in′dis·crim′i·nate·ly,** *adv.* **—in′dis·crim′i·nate·ness,** *n.*
—Syn. 1. See **miscellaneous. 3.** mixed.

in·dis·crim·i·nat·ing (in′di skrim′ə nā′ting), *adj.* not discriminating. [1745–55; IN-[3] + DISCRIMINATING] **—in′dis·crim′i·nat′ing·ly,** *adv.*

in·dis·crim·i·na·tion (in′di skrim′ə nā′shən), *n.* **1.** an act or instance of not discriminating. **2.** the quality or condition of being indiscriminate or of not discriminating; lack of discrimination. [1640–50; IN-[3] + DISCRIMINATION] **—in′dis·crim′i·na′tive,** *adj.*

in·dis·cuss·i·ble (in′di skus′ə bəl), *adj.* unsuitable for or not subject or open to discussion; not negotiable. Also, **in′dis·cuss′a·ble.** [1890–95; IN-[3] + DISCUSSIBLE]

in·dis·pen·sa·ble (in′di spen′sə bəl), *adj.* **1.** absolutely necessary, essential, or requisite: *an indispensable member of the staff.* **2.** incapable of being disregarded or neglected: *an indispensable obligation.* **—n. 3.** a person or thing that is indispensable. [1525–35; < ML *indispēnsābilis* not subject to dispensation. See IN-[3], DISPENSABLE] **—in′dis·pen′sa·bil′i·ty, in′dis·pen′sa·ble·ness,** *n.* **—in′dis·pen′sa·bly,** *adv.*
—Syn. 1. needed. See **necessary.**

in·dis·pose (in′di spōz′), *v.t.,* **-posed, -pos·ing. 1.** to make ill, esp. slightly. **2.** to put out of the proper condition for something; make unfit: *The long tennis match indisposed me for any further physical activity that day.* **3.** to render averse or unwilling; disincline: *His anger indisposed him from helping.* [1650–60; back formation from INDISPOSED]

in·dis·posed (in′di spōzd′), *adj.* **1.** sick or ill, esp. slightly: *to be indisposed with a cold.* **2.** disinclined or unwilling; averse: *indisposed to help.* [1375–1425; late ME: out of order, not suitable. See IN-[3], DISPOSED] **—in·dis·pos·ed·ness** (in′di spō′zid nis, -spōzd′-), *n.*
—Syn. 1. unwell. **2.** reluctant, loath.

in·dis·po·si·tion (in′dis pə zish′ən), *n.* **1.** state of being indisposed. **2.** a slight illness. **3.** disinclination; unwillingness. [1400–50; late ME; see IN-[3], DISPOSITION]

in·dis·put·a·ble (in′di spyōō′tə bəl, in dis′pyə-), *adj.* **1.** not disputable or deniable; uncontestable. *indisputable evidence.* **2.** unquestionably real, valid, or the like. [1545–55; < LL *indisputābilis.* See IN-[3], DISPUTABLE] **—in′dis·put′a·bil′i·ty, in′dis·put′a·ble·ness,** *n.* **—in′dis·put′a·bly,** *adv.*
—Syn. 1. incontrovertible, incontestable, undeniable, unquestionable; evident, apparent, obvious, certain. **—Ant. 1.** questionable; uncertain.

in·dis·sol·u·ble (in′di sol′yə bəl), *adj.* **1.** not dissoluble; incapable of being dissolved, decomposed, undone, or destroyed. **2.** firm or stable. **3.** perpetually binding or obligatory. [1535–45; < L *indissolūbilis.* See IN-[3], DISSOLUBLE] **—in′dis·sol′u·bil′i·ty, in′dis·sol′u·ble·ness,** *n.* **—in′dis·sol′u·bly,** *adv.*

in·dis·tinct (in′di stingkt′), *adj.* **1.** not distinct; not clearly marked or defined: *indistinct markings.* **2.** not clearly distinguishable or perceptible, as to the eye, ear, or mind: *He heard an indistinct muttering.* **3.** not distinguishing clearly: *After the accident he suffered from indistinct vision and faulty hearing.* [1520–30; < L *indistinctus.* See IN-[3], DISTINCT] **—in′dis·tinct′ly,** *adv.* **—in′dis·tinct′ness,** *n.*
—Syn. 2. blurred, clouded, dim.

in·dis·tinc·tive (in′di stingk′tiv), *adj.* **1.** without distinctive characteristics. **2.** incapable of or not making a distinction; undiscriminating. [1840–50; IN-[3] + DISTINCTIVE] **—in′dis·tinc′tive·ly,** *adv.* **—in′dis·tinc′tive·ness,** *n.*

in·dis·tin·guish·a·ble (in′di sting′gwi shə bəl), *adj.* **1.** not distinguishable. **2.** indiscernible; imperceptible. [1600–10; IN-[3] + DISTINGUISHABLE] **—in′dis·tin′guish·a·ble·ness, in′dis·tin′guish·a·bil′i·ty,** *n.* **—in′dis·tin′guish·a·bly,** *adv.*

in·dite (in dīt′), *v.t.,* **-dit·ed, -dit·ing. 1.** to compose or write, as a poem. **2.** to treat in a literary composition. **3.** *Obs.* to dictate. **4.** *Obs.* to prescribe. [1325–75; ME *enditen* < OF *enditer* < VL **indictāre,* deriv. of L *indictus* ptp. of *indicere* to announce, proclaim. See IN-[2], DICTUM] **—in·dite′ment,** *n.* **—in·dit′er,** *n.*

in·di·um (in′dē əm), *n. Chem.* a rare metallic element, soft, white, malleable, and easily fusible, found combined in various ore minerals, esp. sphalerite: so called from

CONCISE PRONUNCIATION KEY: act, cāpe, dâre, pärt; set, ēqual; *if,* ice; ox, ōver, ôrder, oil, bŏŏk, bōōt, out; up, ûrge; child; sing; shoe; thin, *that;* zh as in *treasure.* ə = *a* as in *alone, e* as in *system, i* as in *easily, o* as in *gallop, u* as in *circus;* ə as in *fire* (fīər), *hour* (ouər). l and n can serve as syllabic consonants, as in *cradle* (krād′l), and *button* (but′n). See the full key inside the front cover.

the two indigo-blue lines in its spectrum. *Symbol:* In; *at. wt.:* 114.82; *at. no.:* 49; *sp. gr.:* 7.3 at 20°C. [1860–65; < NL, equiv. to *ind(icum)* INDIGO + *-ium* -IUM]

individ., individual. Also, **indiv.**

in•di•vid•u•al (in′də vij′o͞o əl), *n.* **1.** a single human being, as distinguished from a group. **2.** a person: *a strange individual.* **3.** a distinct, indivisible entity; a single thing, being, instance, or item. **4.** a group considered as a unit. **5.** *Biol.* **a.** a single organism capable of independent existence. **b.** a member of a compound organism or colony. **6.** *Cards.* a duplicate-bridge tournament in which each player plays the same number of hands in partnership with every other player, individual scores for each player being kept for each hand. —*adj.* **7.** single; particular; separate: *to number individual copies of a limited edition.* **8.** intended for the use of one person only: *to serve individual portions of a pizza.* **9.** of, pertaining to, or characteristic of a particular person or thing: *individual tastes.* **10.** distinguished by special, singular, or markedly personal characteristics; exhibiting unique or unusual qualities: *a highly individual style of painting.* **11.** existing as a distinct, indivisible entity, or considered as such; discrete: *individual parts of a tea set.* **12.** of which each is different or of a different design from the others: *a set of individual coffee cups.* [1375–1425; late ME < ML *indīviduālis,* equiv. to L *indīvidu(us)* indivisible (*in-* IN-³ + *divid(ere)* to DIVIDE + *-uus* deverbal adj. suffix) + *-ālis* -AL¹]
—**Syn. 2.** See **person.**
—**Usage. 1, 2.** As a synonym for *person,* INDIVIDUAL is standard, occurring in all varieties of speech and writing: *Three individuals entered the room, each carrying a sheaf of papers.* Some object to this use, insisting that INDIVIDUAL can mean only "a single human being, as distinguished from a group": *An individual may have concerns that are ignored by his or her party.*

in•di•vid•u•al•ism (in′də vij′o͞o ə liz′əm), *n.* **1.** a social theory advocating the liberty, rights, or independent action of the individual. **2.** the principle or habit of or belief in independent thought or action. **3.** the pursuit of individual rather than common or collective interests; egoism. **4.** individual character; individuality. **5.** an individual peculiarity. **6.** *Philos.* **a.** the doctrine that only individual things are real. **b.** the doctrine or belief that all actions are determined by, or at least take place for, the benefit of the individual, not of society as a whole. [1825–35; INDIVIDUAL + -ISM]

in•di•vid•u•al•ist (in′də vij′o͞o ə list), *n.* **1.** a person who shows great independence or individuality in thought or action. **2.** an advocate of individualism. [1830–40; INDIVIDUAL + -IST] —**in′di•vid′u•al•is′tic,** *adj.* —**in′di•vid′u•al•is′ti•cal•ly,** *adv.*

in•di•vid•u•al•i•ty (in′də vij′o͞o al′i tē), *n., pl.* **-ties. 1.** the particular character, or aggregate of qualities, that distinguishes one person or thing from others; sole and personal nature: *a person of marked individuality.* **2. individualities,** individual characteristics. **3.** a person or thing of individual or distinctive character. **4.** state or quality of being individual; existence as a distinct individual. **5.** the interests of the individual as distinguished from the interests of the community. **6.** *Archaic.* state or quality of being indivisible or inseparable. [1605–15; INDIVIDUAL + -ITY]
—**Syn. 1.** See **character.**

in•di•vid•u•al•ize (in′də vij′o͞o ə līz′), *v.t.,* **-ized, -iz•ing. 1.** to make individual or distinctive; give an individual or distinctive character to. **2.** to mention, indicate, or consider individually; specify; particularize. Also, *esp. Brit.,* **in′di•vid′u•al•ise′.** [1630–40; INDIVIDUAL + -IZE] —**in′di•vid′u•al•i•za′tion,** *n.* —**in′di•vid′u•al•iz′er,** *n.*

in′divid′ual lib′erty, the liberty of an individual to exercise freely those rights generally accepted as being outside of governmental control.

in•di•vid•u•al•ly (in′də vij′o͞o ə lē), *adv.* **1.** one at a time; separately: *The delegates were introduced individually.* **2.** personally: *Each of us is individually responsible.* **3.** in an individual or personally unique manner: *Her interpretation was individually conceived.* [1590–1600; INDIVIDUAL + -LY]

in′divid′ual med′ley, *Swimming.* a race in which the total distance is either divided into three equal portions, in which each swimmer uses the backstroke for the first portion, the breaststroke for the second portion, and the freestyle for the third, or the total distance is divided into four equal portions, in which each swimmer uses the butterfly stroke for the first portion and then the other strokes used follow the same pattern as in the three-part medley. Cf. **medley relay** (def. 2). [1945–50]

individ′ual retire′ment account′, a plan that permits individuals to set aside savings that are tax free until retirement. *Abbr.:* IRA Cf. **Keogh plan.**

in•di•vid•u•ate (in′də vij′o͞o āt′), *v.,* **-at•ed, -at•ing.** —*v.t.* **1.** to form into an individual or distinct entity. **2.** to give an individual or distinctive character to; individualize. —*v.i.* **3.** to make distinctions: *to individuate among one's students.* **4.** to become individualized or distinctive: *With maturity, the artist individuated.* [1605–15; < ML *individuātus* ptp. of *individuāre* to make individual. See INDIVIDUAL, -ATE¹] —**in′di•vid′u•a′tor,** *n.*

in•di•vid•u•a•tion (in′də vij′o͞o ā′shən), *n.* **1.** the act of individuating. **2.** state of being individuated; individual existence; individuality. **3.** *Philos.* the determination or contraction of a general nature to an individual mode of existence; development of the individual from the general. [1620–30; INDIVIDUATE + -ION]

CONCISE ETYMOLOGY KEY: <, descended or borrowed from; >, whence; b., blend of, blended; c., cognate with; cf., compare; deriv., derivative; equiv., equivalent; imit., imitative; obl., oblique; r., replacing; s., stem; sp., spelling, spelled; resp., respelling, respelled; trans., translation; ?, origin unknown; *, unattested; ‡, probably earlier than. See the full key inside the front cover.

in•di•vis•i•ble (in′də viz′ə bəl), *adj.* **1.** not divisible; not separable into parts; incapable of being divided: *one nation indivisible.* —*n.* **2.** something indivisible. [1350–1400; ME < LL *indīvīsibilis.* See IN-³, DIVISIBLE] —**in′di•vis′i•bil′i•ty, in′di•vis′i•ble•ness,** *n.* —**in′di•vis′i•bly,** *adv.*

indo-, a combining form representing **indigo** in compound words: *indophenol.* Also, *esp. before a vowel,* **ind-.**

Indo-, a combining form representing **India** in compound words: *Indo-European.* [< L *Ind(us)* or Gk *Ind(ós)* + -o-]

In•do-Ar•y•an (in′dō âr′ē ən, -yən, -ar′-; -är′yən), *n.* **1.** a member of a people of India who are Indo-European in speech and Caucasoid in physical characteristics. **2.** Indic (def. 3). —*adj.* **3.** Indic (def. 2). **4.** of, pertaining to, or characteristic of the Indo-Aryans. [1840–50]

In′do-Aus•tral′ian Plate′ (in′dō ô strāl′yən), *Geol.* a major tectonic division of the earth's crust, comprising India and the Australian continent and adjacent subocéanic basins (the Tasman, South Australian, Mid-Indian, Cocos, and Australian basins); separated from the Eurasian Plate by the Java Trench, from the Pacific Plate by the Tonga-Kermadec Trench, and from the African Plate by a series of mid-ocean ridges (the Carlsberg, Mid-Indian, and Southeast Indian ridges).

In•do•chi•na (in′dō chī′nə), *n.* a peninsula in SE Asia, between the Bay of Bengal and the South China Sea, comprising Vietnam, Cambodia, Laos, Thailand, W Malaysia, and Burma (Myanmar). Also called **Farther India.** Cf. **French Indochina.**

In•do•chi•nese (in′dō chī nēz′, -nēs′), *adj., n., pl.* **-nese.** —*adj.* **1.** of or pertaining to Indochina or its inhabitants. **2.** Sino-Tibetan (no longer current). —*n.* **3.** an inhabitant of Indochina. **4.** Sino-Tibetan (no longer current). [1835–45]

in•doc•ile (in dos′il), *adj.* not willing to receive teaching, training, or discipline; fractious; unruly. [1595–1605; < L *indocilis.* See IN-³, DOCILE]

In•do•cin (in′də sin), *Pharm., Trademark.* a brand of indomethacin.

in•doc•tri•nate (in dok′trə nāt′), *v.t.,* **-nat•ed, -nat•ing. 1.** to instruct in a doctrine, principle, ideology, etc., esp. to imbue with a specific partisan or biased belief or point of view. **2.** to teach or inculcate. **3.** to imbue with learning. [1620–30; IN-² + ML *doctrīnātus* ptp. of *doctrīnāre* to teach; see DOCTRINE, -ATE¹] —**in•doc′tri•na′tion,** *n.* —**in•doc′tri•na′tor,** *n.*
—**Syn. 1.** brainwash, propagandize.

In•do-Eu•ro•pe•an (in′dō yo͝or′ə pē′ən), *n.* **1.** a large, widespread family of languages, the surviving branches of which include Italic, Slavic, Baltic, Hellenic, Celtic, Germanic, and Indo-Iranian, spoken by about half the world's population: English, Spanish, German, Latin, Greek, Russian, Albanian, Lithuanian, Armenian, Persian, Hindi, and Hittite are all Indo-European languages. Cf. **family** (def. 14). **2.** Proto-Indo-European (def. 1). **3.** a member of any of the peoples speaking an Indo-European language. —*adj.* **4.** of or belonging to Indo-European. **5.** speaking an Indo-European language: *an Indo-European people.* [1805–15]

In•do-Eu•ro•pe•an•ist (in′dō yo͝or′ə pē′ə nist), *n.* a linguist specializing in the study, esp. the comparative study, of the Indo-European languages. [1925–30; INDO-EUROPEAN + -IST]

In•do-Ger•man•ic (in′dō jər man′ik), *adj., n.* Indo-European (no longer current). [1825–35]

In•do-Hit•tite (in′dō hit′īt), *n.* a language family in which Proto-Anatolian and Proto-Indo-European are considered coordinate. Cf. **Hittite** (def. 2). [1925–30]

In•do-I•ra•ni•an (in′dō i rā′nē ən, -i rä′-, -ī rā′-), *n.* **1.** a branch of the Indo-European family of languages, including the Indic and Iranian subgroups. —*adj.* **2.** of or belonging to Indo-Iranian. [1875–80]

in•dole (in′dōl), *n. Chem.* a colorless to yellowish solid, C_8H_7N, having a low melting point and a fecal odor, found in the oil of jasmine and clove and as a putrefaction product from animals' intestines: used in perfumery and as a reagent. [1865–70; IND- + -OLE²]

in′dole•a•ce′tic ac′id (in′dōl ə sē′tik, -set′ik, in′-), *Biochem.* a crystalline, water-insoluble powder, $C_{10}H_9NO_2$, a natural plant hormone, used esp. for stimulating growth and root formation in plant cutting. Also called **beta-indoleacetic acid, heteroauxin.** [1885–90; INDOLE + ACETIC]

in′dole•bu•tyr′ic ac′id (in′dōl byo͞o tir′ik, in′-), *Biochem.* a white or yellowish, crystalline, water-insoluble powder, $C_{12}H_{13}O_2N$, a plant hormone similar to indoleacetic acid and used for the same purposes. [1935–40; INDOLE + BUTYRIC]

in•do•lence (in′dl əns), *n.* the quality or state of being indolent. [1595–1605; < L *indolentia* freedom from pain; see INDOLENT, -ENCE]

in•do•lent (in′dl ənt), *adj.* **1.** having or showing a disposition to avoid exertion; slothful. **2.** *Pathol.* causing little or no pain; inactive or relatively benign: *an indolent ulcer that is not painful and is slow to heal.* [1655–65; < LL *indolent-* (s. of *indolēns*), equiv. to *in-* IN-³ + *dolent-* (s. of *dolēns*) prp. of *dolēre* to be painful, be in pain; see DOLE², -ENT] —**in′do•lent•ly,** *adv.*
—**Syn. 1.** slow, inactive, sluggish, torpid. See **idle.**

in•do•log•e•nous (in′dl oj′ə nəs), *adj. Biochem.* producing or causing the production of indole. [INDOLE + -O- + -GENOUS]

In•do-Ma•lay•an (in′dō mə lā′ən), *adj.* of Indian and Malayan origin, sponsorship, etc. [1865–70]

in•do•meth•a•cin (in′dō meth′ə sin), *n. Pharm.* a substance, $C_{19}H_{16}ClNO_4$, with anti-inflammatory, antipyretic, and analgesic properties: used in the treatment of certain kinds of arthritis and gout. [1963; INDO(LE) + METH(YL) + AC(ETIC) + -IN²]

in•dom•i•ta•ble (in dom′i tə bəl), *adj.* that cannot be subdued or overcome, as persons, will, or courage; unconquerable: *an indomitable warrior.* [1625–35; < LL *indomitābilis* < L *indomit(us)* untamed (*in-* IN-³ + *domitus,* ptp. of *domāre* to subdue, tame, bring under control) + *-ābilis* -ABLE; cf. L *indomābilis*] —**in•dom′i•ta•bil′i•ty, in•dom′i•ta•ble•ness,** *n.* —**in•dom′i•ta•bly,** *adv.*
—**Syn.** unyielding. See **invincible.** —**Ant.** yielding.

In•do•ne•sia (in′də nē′zhə, -shə, -zē ə, -dō-), *n.* **1.** See **East Indies** (def. 1). **2. Republic of.** Formerly, **Netherlands East Indies, Dutch East Indies.** a republic in the Malay Archipelago consisting of 13,677 islands, including Sumatra, Java, Sulawesi, the S part of Borneo, the W part of New Guinea, the Moluccas, the Lesser Sunda Islands, Bali, and Madura: gained independence from the Netherlands in 1949. 179,100,000; 741,098 sq. mi. (1,919,443 sq. km). *Cap.:* Jakarta. [INDO- + Gk *nês(os)* island + -IA]

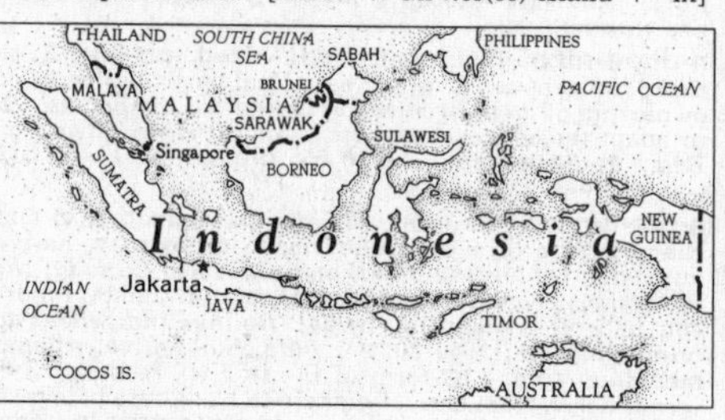

In•do•ne•sian (in′də nē′zhən, -shən, -zē ən, -dō-), *n.* **1.** a member of the ethnic group consisting of the natives of Indonesia, the Filipinos, and the Malays of Malaysia. **2.** a member of a population supposed to have been resident in the Malay Archipelago before the Malays, and believed to constitute one element of the present mixed population of Malaysia and perhaps Polynesia. **3.** Official name, **Bahasa Indonesia.** an Indonesian language that is based on the form of Malay spoken in Java and has the status of official language in the Republic of Indonesia. **4.** the westernmost branch of the Austronesian family of languages, including Malay, Indonesian, Tagalog, and Malagasy. —*adj.* **5.** of or pertaining to the Malay Archipelago. **6.** of or pertaining to Indonesia, the Indonesians, or their languages. [1840–50; INDONESI(A) + -AN]

in•door (in′dôr′, -dōr′), *adj.* occurring, used, etc., in a house or building, rather than out of doors: *indoor games.* [1705–15; aph. var. of *within-door,* orig. phrase *within (the) door,* i.e., inside the house]

in′door base′ball, softball played indoors. [1885–90, *Amer.*]

in•door-out•door (in′dôr′out′dôr′, in′dōr′out′dōr′), *adj.* designed or constructed to be used either indoors or outdoors: *indoor-outdoor carpeting.*

in•doors (in dôrz′, -dōrz′), *adv.* in or into a house or building: *We stayed indoors during the storm.* [1780–90; INDOOR + -S¹]

in′door soc′cer, a form of soccer played indoors by two teams of six players each, usually on a hockey rink covered with a temporary floor with walls to keep the ball in play, in which a player who commits a foul is penalized by suspension from play for a certain amount of time, as in hockey.

In•do-Pa•cif•ic (in′dō pə sif′ik), *adj.* **1.** of or pertaining to the areas of the Indian and Pacific oceans off the coast of SE Asia. —*n.* **2.** a proposed linguistic family including all the non-Austronesian languages of the Pacific. [1875–80]

in•do•phe•nol (in′dō fē′nôl, -nol), *n. Chem.* **1.** a quinonimine derivative that is the parent substance of the blue and green indophenol dyes. **2.** any derivative of this compound. **3.** any of various related dyes. [1890–95; INDO- + PHENOL]

In•dore (in dôr′), *n.* **1.** a former state in central India: now part of Madhya Pradesh. **2.** a city in W Madhya Pradesh, in central India. 572,622.

in•dorse (in dôrs′), *v.t.,* **-dorsed, -dors•ing.** endorse.

in•dox•yl (in dok′sil), *n. Chem.* a crystalline compound, C_8H_7NO, that is obtained by the hydrolysis of indican and is readily oxidized to furnish indigo. [1885–90; IND- + (HYDR)OXYL]

In•dra (in′drə), *n.* **1.** *Hinduism.* the chief of the Vedic gods, the god of rain and thunder. See illus. on next page. **2.** a male given name.

Indra
(def. 1)

in•draft (in′draft′, -dräft′), *n.* **1.** an inward flow or current, as of air or water. **2.** *Archaic.* an instance of being drawn in; inward attraction. Also, *esp. Brit.,* **in′•draught′.** [1560–70; IN-[1] + DRAFT]

in•drawn (in′drôn′), *adj.* **1.** reserved; introspective: *a quiet, indrawn man.* **2.** made with the breath drawn in: *an indrawn sigh.* [1745–55; IN[1]- + DRAWN]

In•dre (ɑɴ′dRᵊ), *n.* a department in central France. 248,523; 2667 sq. mi. (6910 sq. km). *Cap.:* Châteauroux.

In•dre-et-Loire (ɑɴ drā lwaR′), *n.* a department in W central France. 478,601; 2378 sq. mi. (6160 sq. km). *Cap.:* Tours.

in•dri (in′drē), *n., pl.* **-dris.** a short-tailed lemur, *Indri indri,* of Madagascar, about 2 ft. (60 cm) in length: an endangered species. [1830–40; < F *indri* < Malagasy *indry* look!, wrongly taken as animal's name]

in•du•bi•ta•ble (in do͞o′bi tə bəl, -dyo͞o′-), *adj.* that cannot be doubted; patently evident or certain; unquestionable. [1615–25; < L *indubitābilis.* See IN-[3], DUBITABLE] —**in•du′bi•ta•bil′i•ty, in•du′bi•ta•ble•ness,** *n.* —**in•du′bi•ta•bly,** *adv.*

induc., induction.

in•duce (in do͞os′, -dyo͞os′), *v.t.,* **-duced, -duc•ing. 1.** to lead or move by persuasion or influence, as to some action or state of mind: *to induce a person to buy a raffle ticket.* **2.** to bring about, produce, or cause: *That medicine will induce sleep.* **3.** *Physics.* to produce (an electric current) by induction. **4.** *Logic.* to assert or establish (a proposition about a class of phenomena) on the basis of observations on a number of particular facts. **5.** *Genetics.* to increase expression of (a gene) by inactivating a negative control system or activating a positive control system; derepress. **6.** *Biochem.* to stimulate the synthesis of (a protein, esp. an enzyme) by increasing gene transcription. [1325–75; ME < L *indūcere* to lead or bring in, introduce, equiv. to *in-* IN-[2] + *dūcere* to lead; cf. ADDUCE, DEDUCE, REDUCE] —**in•duc′i•ble,** *adj.*
—**Syn. 1.** actuate, prompt, incite, urge, spur. See **persuade.** —**Ant. 1.** dissuade.

induced′ drag′, *Aeron.* the drag force generated in the production of lift. [1925–30]

induced′ ra′dioactiv′ity, *Physics.* See **artificial radioactivity.** [1895–1900]

induced′ topol′ogy, *Math.* See **relative topology.**

in•duce•ment (in do͞os′mənt, -dyo͞os′-), *n.* **1.** the act of inducing. **2.** the state of being induced. **3.** something that induces, motivates, or persuades; incentive. [1585–95; INDUCE + -MENT]
—**Syn. 3.** stimulus, spur, incitement; attraction, lure. See **motive.**

in•duc•er (in do͞o′sər, -dyo͞o′-), *n.* **1.** *Biochem.* a substance that has the capability of activating genes within a cell. **2.** *Embryol.* a part that influences differentiation of another part. [1545–55, for an earlier sense; INDUCE + -ER[1]]

in•duct (in dukt′), *v.t.* **1.** to install in an office, benefice, position, etc., esp. with formal ceremonies: *The committee inducted her as president.* **2.** to introduce, esp. to something requiring special knowledge or experience; initiate (usually fol. by *to* or *into*): *They inducted him into the mystic rites of the order.* **3.** to take (a draftee) into military service; draft. **4.** to bring in as a member: *to induct a person into a new profession.* [1350–1400; ME < L *inductus* ptp. of *indūcere,* equiv. to *induc-* (see INDUCE) + *-tus* ptp. suffix]

in•duct•ance (in duk′təns), *n. Elect.* **1.** that property of a circuit by which a change in current induces, by electromagnetic induction, an electromotive force. *Symbol:* L Cf. **inductive coupling, mutual inductance, self-inductance. 2.** inductor (def. 1). [1885–90; INDUCT + -ANCE]

in•duc•tee (in′duk tē′, in duk-), *n.* **1.** a person inducted into military service. **2.** a person inducted into an organization. [1940–45, *Amer.;* INDUCT + -EE]

in•duc•tile (in duk′til), *adj.* not ductile; not pliable or yielding. [1730–40; IN-[3] + DUCTILE] —**in′duc•til′i•ty,** *n.*

in•duc•tion (in duk′shən), *n.* **1.** the act of inducing, bringing about, or causing: *induction of the hypnotic state.* **2.** the act of inducting; introduction; initiation. **3.** formal installation in an office, benefice, or the like. **4.** *Logic.* **a.** any form of reasoning in which the conclusion, though supported by the premises, does not follow from them necessarily. **b.** the process of estimating the validity of observations of part of a class of facts as evidence for a proposition about the whole class. **c.** a conclusion reached by this process. **5.** Also called **mathematical induction.** *Math.* a method of proving a given property true for a set of numbers by proving it true for 1 and then true for an arbitrary positive integer by assuming the property true for all previous positive integers and applying the principle of mathematical induction. **6.** a presentation or bringing forward, as of facts or evidence. **7.** *Elect., Magnetism.* the process by which a body having electric or magnetic properties produces magnetism, an electric charge, or an electromotive force in a neighboring body without contact. Cf. **electromagnetic induction, electrostatic induction. 8.** *Embryol.* the process or principle by which one part of the embryo influences the differentiation of another part. **9.** *Biochem.* the synthesis of an enzyme in response to an increased concentration of its substrate in the cell. **10.** an introductory unit in literary work, esp. in an early play; prelude or scene independent of the main performance but related to it. **11.** *Archaic.* a preface. [1350–1400; ME *induccio(u)n* < L *inductiōn-* (s. of *inductiō*). See INDUCT, -ION] —**in•duc′tion•less,** *adj.*

induc′tion coil′, *Elect.* a transformer for producing high-voltage alternating current from a low-voltage direct current, consisting essentially of two concentric coils with a common soft-iron core, a primary coil with relatively few windings of heavy wire, and a secondary coil with many turns of fine wire. Excitation of the primary coil by rapidly interrupted or variable current induces high voltage in the secondary coil. Also called **Ruhmkorff coil.** [1875–80]

induc′tion fur′nace, *Metall.* a type of electric furnace used for melting a charge of scrap by the heat produced by its own electrical resistance. [1905–10]

induc′tion heat′ing, a method of heating a conducting material, as metal in a furnace, by using electromagnetic induction to establish a current in the material. [1915–20]

induc′tion mo′tor, a type of electric motor in which alternating current from a power source is fed through a primary winding and induces a current in a secondary winding, with the parts arranged so that the resulting magnetic field causes a movable rotor to rotate with respect to a fixed stator. Cf. **linear induction motor.**

in•duc•tive (in duk′tiv), *adj.* **1.** of, pertaining to, or involving electrical or magnetic induction. **2.** operating by induction: *an inductive machine.* **3.** of, pertaining to, or employing logical induction: *inductive reasoning.* **4.** *Embryol.* eliciting the action of an embryonic inducer. **5.** serving to induce; leading or influencing (usually fol. by *to*). **6.** introductory. [1600–10; < LL *inductīvus.* See INDUCT, -IVE] —**in•duc′tive•ly,** *adv.* —**in•duc′tive•ness,** *n.*
—**Syn. 3.** See **deductive.**

induc′tive cou′pling, *Elect.* the coupling between two electric circuits through inductances linked by a common changing magnetic field. Cf. **inductance, mutual inductance.**

induc′tive react′ance, *Elect.* the opposition of inductance to alternating current, equal to the product of the angular frequency of the current times the self-inductance. *Symbol:* X_L Cf. **capacitive reactance.** [1910–15]

in•duc•tor (in duk′tər), *n.* **1.** Also called **inductance.** *Elect.* a coil used to introduce inductance into an electric circuit. **2.** a person who inducts, as into office. [1645–55; < ML: importer, instigator, LL: schoolmaster, equiv. to L *indūc(ere)* (see INDUCE) + *-tor* -TOR]

in•duc•to•ther•my (in duk′tə thûr′mē), *n. Med.* the production of fever by means of electromagnetic induction. [formerly trademark]

in•due (in do͞o′, -dyo͞o′), *v.t.,* **-dued, -du•ing.** endue.

in•dulge (in dulj′), *v.,* **-dulged, -dulg•ing.** —*v.i.* **1.** to yield to an inclination or desire; allow oneself to follow one's will (often fol. by *in*): *Dessert came, but I didn't indulge. They indulged in unbelievable shopping sprees.* —*v.t.* **2.** to yield to, satisfy, or gratify (desires, feelings, etc.): *to indulge one's appetite for sweets.* **3.** to yield to the wishes or whims of; be lenient or permissive with: *to indulge a child.* **4.** to allow (oneself) to follow one's will (usually fol. by *in*): *to indulge oneself in reckless spending.* **5.** *Com.* to grant an extension of time, for payment or performance, to (a person, company, etc.) or on (a bill, note, etc.). [1630–40; < L *indulgēre* to be lenient (toward), accede, take pleasure (in)] —**in•dulg′er,** *n.* —**in•dulg′ing•ly,** *adv.*
—**Syn. 3.** pamper, favor. See **humor.**

in•dul•gence (in dul′jəns), *n., v.,* **-genced, -genc•ing.** —*n.* **1.** the act or practice of indulging; gratification of desire. **2.** the state of being indulgent. **3.** indulgent allowance or tolerance. **4.** a catering to someone's mood or whim; humoring: *The sick man demanded indulgence as his due.* **5.** something indulged in: *Her favorite indulgence was candy.* **6.** *Rom. Cath. Ch.* a partial remission of the temporal punishment, esp. purgatorial atonement, that is still due for a sin or sins after absolution. Cf. **plenary indulgence. 7.** *Eng. and Scot. Hist.* (in the reigns of Charles II and James II) a grant by the king to Protestant dissenters and Roman Catholics freeing them from certain penalties imposed, by legislation, because of their religion. **8.** *Com.* an extension, through favor, of time for payment or performance. —*v.t.* **9.** *Rom. Cath. Ch.* to provide with an indulgence: *an indulgenced pilgrimage to Rome.* [1325–75; ME < L *indulgentia.* See INDULGE, -ENCE]
—**Syn. 3.** sufferance, forbearance, allowance.

in•dul•gen•cy (in dul′jən sē), *n., pl.* **-cies.** indulgence. [1540–50; < L *indulgentia;* see INDULGE, -ENCY]

in•dul•gent (in dul′jənt), *adj.* characterized by or showing indulgence; benignly lenient or permissive: *an indulgent parent.* [1500–10; < L *indulgent-* (s. of *indulgēns*), prp. of *indulgēre* to INDULGE; see -ENT] —**in•dul′gent•ly,** *adv.*
—**Syn.** forbearing, easygoing, tolerant.

in•du•line (in′dyə lēn′, -lin, in′dl ēn′), *n.* any of a large class of dyes yielding colors similar to indigo. [1880–85; IND- + -ULE + -INE[2]]

in•dult (in dult′), *n. Rom. Cath. Ch.* a dispensation granted often temporarily by the pope, permitting a deviation from church law. [1525–35; < ML *indultum* n. use of neut. of *indultus,* ptp. of *indulgēre* to INDULGE]

in•du•men•tum (in′do͞o men′təm, -dyo͞o-), *n., pl.* **-ta** (-tə), **-tums.** *Bot., Zool.* a dense, hairy covering. [1840–50; < NL; L: garment, covering, equiv. to L *indu(ere)* to put on, don (*ind-,* by-form of *in-* IN[2] + *-uere,* from a v. base **eu-* or **ou-* (> *ū-*), akin to OCS *obuti,* Lith *aũti* to put on (shoes); cf. EXUVIAE) + *-mentum* -MENT]

in•du•na (in do͞o′nə), *n.* an official functionary of a king or chief in South African Bantu societies. [1870–75; < Zulu]

in•du•pli•cate (in do͞o′plə kit, -kāt′, -dyo͞o′-), *adj. Bot.* folded or rolled inward: said of the parts of the calyx or corolla when the edges are bent abruptly toward the axis, or of leaves in vernation when the edges are rolled inward and then arranged about the axis without overlapping. Also, **in•du′pli•ca′tive.** [1820–30; IN-[2] + DUPLICATE] —**in•du′pli•ca′tion,** *n.*

in•du•rate (*v.* in′do͝o rāt′, -dyo͝o-; *adj.* in′do͝o rit, -dyo͝o-; in do͝or′it, -dyo͝or′-), *v.,* **-rat•ed, -rat•ing,** *adj.* —*v.t.* **1.** to make hard; harden, as rock, tissue, etc.: *Cold indurates the soil.* **2.** to make callous, stubborn, or unfeeling: *transgressions that indurate the heart.* **3.** to inure; accustom: *to indurate oneself to privation and suffering.* **4.** to make enduring; confirm; establish: *to indurate custom through practice.* —*v.i.* **5.** to become hard; harden. **6.** to become established or confirmed. —*adj.* **7.** hardened; unfeeling; callous; inured. [1375–1425; late ME *indurat* < L *indūrātus* ptp. of *indūrāre* to harden. See IN-[2], DURE[1], -ATE[1]]

in•du•ra•tion (in′do͝o rā′shən, -dyo͝o-), *n.* **1.** the act of indurating. **2.** the state of being indurated. **3.** *Geol.* **a.** lithification. **b.** hardening of rock by heat or pressure. **4.** *Pathol.* **a.** a hardening of an area of the body as a reaction to inflammation, hyperemia, or neoplastic infiltration. **b.** an area or part of the body that has undergone such a reaction. [1350–1400; ME < LL *indūrātiōn-* (s. of *indūrātiō*) a hardening. See INDURATE, -ION] —**in′•du•ra′tive,** *adj.*

In•dus (in′dəs), *n.* a river in S Asia, flowing from W Tibet through Kashmir and Pakistan to the Arabian Sea. 1900 mi. (3060 km) long.

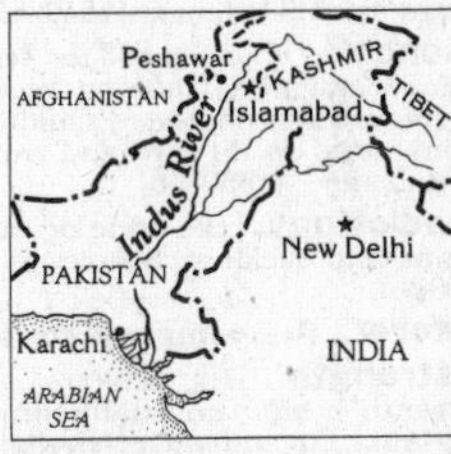

In•dus (in′dəs), *n., gen.* **-di** (-dī). *Astron.* the Indian, a southern constellation between Grus and Pavo. [< NL, L]

indus., **1.** industrial. **2.** industry.

In′dus civiliza′tion. See **Indus valley civilization.**

in•du•si•ate (in do͞o′zē it, -zhē-, -dyo͞o′-), *adj.* having an indusium. [1820–30; < L *indūsiātus,* equiv. to *indūsi(um)* INDUSIUM + *-ātus* -ATE[1]]

in•du•si•um (in do͞o′zē əm, -zhē əm, -dyo͞o′-), *n., pl.* **-si•a** (-zē ə, -zhē ə). **1.** *Bot., Mycol.* any of several structures having a netlike or skirtlike shape, as the membranous overgrowth covering the sori in ferns. **2.** *Anat., Zool.* **a.** an enveloping layer or membrane. **b.** a thin layer of gray matter on the corpus callosum. [1700–10; < NL; L: kind of tunic, perh. < Gk *éndys(is)* dressing, dress (*endý(ein)* to put on + *-sis* -SIS) + L *-ium,* for Gk *-ion* n. suffix] —**in•du′si•al,** *adj.*

in•dus•tri•al (in dus′trē əl), *adj.* **1.** of, pertaining to, of the nature of, or resulting from industry: *industrial production; industrial waste.* **2.** having many and highly developed industries: *an industrial nation.* **3.** engaged in an industry or industries: *industrial workers.* **4.** of or pertaining to the workers in industries: *industrial training.* **5.** used in industry: *industrial diamonds: industrial fabrics.* **6.** noting or pertaining to industrial life insurance. —*n.* **7.** an industrial product: *diamonds classed as industrials and nonindustrials.* **8.** a company engaged in industrial enterprises. **9.** an employee in some industry, esp. a manufacturing industry. **10. industrials,** stocks and bonds of industrial companies. [1580–90; INDUSTRY + -AL[1]] —**in•dus′tri•al•ly,** *adv.* —**in•dus′tri•al•ness,** *n.*

indus′trial arts′, the methods of using tools and machinery, as taught in secondary and technical schools. [1840–50]

indus′trial design′, the art that deals with the design problems of manufactured objects, including problems of designing such objects with consideration for available materials and means of production, of designing packages, bottles, etc., for manufactured goods, and of graphic design for manufactured objects, packages, etc. [1930–35] —**indus′trial design′er.**

indus′trial disease′. See **occupational disease** (def. 1). [1905–10]

indus′trial engineer′ing, engineering applied to the planning, design, and control of industrial operations. [1970–75] —**indus′trial engineer′.**

indus′trial es′pionage, the stealing of technological or commercial research data, blueprints, plans, etc., as by a person in the hire of a competing company. [1960–65]

indus′trial estate′, *Brit.* industrial park. [1950–55]

indus′trial insur′ance. See **industrial life insurance.** [1910–15]

in•dus•tri•al•ism (in dus′trē ə liz′əm), *n.* an economic organization of society built largely on mechanized industry rather than agriculture, craftsmanship, or commerce. [1825–35; INDUSTRIAL + -ISM]

in•dus•tri•al•ist (in dus′trē ə list), *n.* **1.** a person who owns or is involved in the management of an industrial enterprise. —*adj.* **2.** of, pertaining to, or characterized by industrialism. [1860–65; INDUSTRIAL + -IST]

in•dus•tri•al•ize (in dus′trē ə līz′), *v.*, **-ized, -iz•ing.** —*v.t.* **1.** to introduce industry into (an area) on a large scale. **2.** to convert to the ideals, methods, aims, etc., of industrialism. —*v.i.* **3.** to undergo industrialization. **4.** to follow or espouse industrialism. Also, *esp. Brit.*, **in•dus′tri•al•ise′.** [1880–85; INDUSTRIAL + -IZE] —**in•dus′tri•al•i•za′tion,** *n.*

indus′trial life′ insur′ance, life insurance having a relatively low face value in which premiums are paid weekly or monthly to an agent.

indus′trial park′, an industrial complex, typically in a suburban or rural area and set in parklike surroundings with such facilities as parking lots, restaurants, and recreation areas. Also called **business park.** [1950–55]

indus′trial psychol′ogy, the application of psychological principles and techniques to business and industrial problems, as in the selection of personnel or development of training programs. [1915–20]

indus′trial rela′tions, **1.** the dealings or relations of an industrial concern with its employees, with labor in general, with the public, etc. **2.** the administration of such relations, esp. to maintain goodwill for an industrial concern. [1900–05]

indus′trial revolu′tion, (*sometimes caps.*) the totality of the changes in economic and social organization that began about 1760 in England and later in other countries, characterized chiefly by the replacement of hand tools with power-driven machines, as the power loom and the steam engine, and by the concentration of industry in large establishments. [1840–50]

indus′trial school′, **1.** a school for teaching one or more branches of industry; trade or vocational school. **2.** a school for educating neglected children or juvenile delinquents committed to its care and training them to some form of industry. [1850–55]

indus′trial sociol′ogy, the sociological study of social relationships and social structures in business settings. [1945–50]

indus′trial store′. See **company store.**

in•dus•tri•al-strength (in dus′trē əl strengkth′, -strength′, -strenth′), *adj.* unusually strong, potent, or the like: heavy-duty: *an industrial-strength soap.*

indus′trial un′ion, a labor union composed of workers in various trades and crafts within one industry. [1920–25]

Indus′trial Work′ers of the World′, an international industrial labor union, considered radical by many, that was organized in Chicago in 1905 and that disintegrated after 1920. *Abbr.:* I.W.W., IWW Cf. **Wobbly.**

in•dus•tri•ous (in dus′trē əs), *adj.* **1.** working energetically and devotedly; hard-working; diligent: *an industrious person.* **2.** *Obs.* skillful. [1525–35; < L *industrius* diligent, assiduous, OL *indostruus*, perh. equiv. to *indo-*, by-form of *in-* IN[2] + *-struus*, n. deriv. of *struere* to arrange, devise, hence with presumed original sense "devising inwardly, secretly"] —**in•dus′tri•ous•ly,** *adv.* —**in•dus′tri•ous•ness,** *n.*
—**Syn. 1.** assiduous, sedulous, energetic. See **busy.**
—**Ant. 1.** lazy, indolent.

in•dus•try (in′də strē), *n., pl.* **-tries** for 1, 2, 7. **1.** the aggregate of manufacturing or technically productive enterprises in a particular field, often named after its principal product: *the automobile industry; the steel industry.* **2.** any general business activity; commercial enterprise: *the Italian tourist industry.* **3.** trade or manufacture in general: *the rise of industry in Africa.* **4.** the ownership and management of companies, factories, etc.: *friction between labor and industry.* **5.** systematic work or labor. **6.** energetic, devoted activity at any work or task; diligence: *Her teacher praised her industry.* **7.** *Archaeol.* an assemblage of artifacts regarded as unmistakably the work of a single prehistoric group. [1475–85; earlier *industrie* < L *industria*, n. use of fem. of *industrius* INDUSTRIOUS]
—**Syn. 6.** application, effort, assiduity, industriousness.

in•dus•try•wide (*adj.* in′də strē wīd′; *adv.* in′də strē-wīd′), *adj.* **1.** from, covering, or affecting an entire industry: *industrywide profits.* —*adv.* **2.** throughout an industry. [1945–50; INDUSTRY + -WIDE]

In′dus val′ley civiliza′tion, an ancient civilization that flourished in the Indus River valley, from about 2500 to 1500 B.C.: extensive archaeological excavations at the main sites of Mohenjo-Daro and Harappa in Pakistan. Also called **Indus civilization.**

in•dwell (in dwel′), *v.*, **-dwelt, -dwell•ing.** —*v.t.* **1.** to inhabit. **2.** to possess (a person), as a moral principle or motivating force: *compassion that indwells the heart.* —*v.i.* **3.** to dwell (usually fol. by *in*). **4.** to abide within, as a guiding force, motivating principle, etc. (usually fol. by *in*): *a divine spirit indwelling in nature and the universe.* [1350–1400; ME *indwellen.* See IN-[1], DWELL] —**in′dwell′er,** *n.*

in′dwelling cath′eter, a hollow tube left implanted in a body canal or organ, esp. the bladder, to promote drainage. [1930–35]

In•dy (in′dē), *Informal.* —*n.* **1.** Indianapolis, Ind. **2.** the Indianapolis 500. —*adj.* **3.** of or pertaining to the Indianapolis 500: *an Indy race car.* [IND(IANAPOLIS) + -Y[2]]

In•dy, d′ (daN dē′), **Vin•cent** (vaN säN′), 1851–1931, French composer.

Indy 500, *Informal.* See **Indianapolis 500.**

-ine[1], a suffix of adjectives of Greek or Latin origin, meaning "of or pertaining to," "of the nature of," "made of," "like": *asinine; crystalline; equine; marine.* Cf. **-in**[1]. [< L *-īnus, -inus* < Gk *-inos*]

-ine[2], **1.** a suffix, of no assignable meaning, appearing in nouns of Greek, Latin, or French origin: *doctrine; famine; routine.* **2.** a noun suffix used particularly in chemical terms (*bromine; chlorine*), and esp. in names of basic substances (*amine; aniline; caffeine; quinine; quinoline*). Cf. **-in**[2]. **3.** a suffix of feminine nouns (*heroine*), given names (*Clementine*), and titles (*landgravine*). Cf. **-ina.** [< F < L *-ina*, orig. fem. of *-inus*; also repr. Gk *-inē*, fem. n. suffix]

in•e•bri•ant (in ē′brē ənt, i nē′-), *n.* **1.** an intoxicant. —*adj.* **2.** inebriating; intoxicating. [1810–20; < L *inēbriant-* (s. of *inēbrians*, prp. of *inēbriāre* to make drunk), equiv. to *in-* IN-[2] + *ēbri(us)* drunk + *-ant-* -ANT]

in•e•bri•ate (*v.* in ē′brē āt′, i nē′-; *n., adj.* in ē′brē it, i nē′-), *v.*, **-at•ed, -at•ing,** *n., adj.* —*v.t.* **1.** to make drunk; intoxicate. **2.** to exhilarate, confuse, or stupefy mentally or emotionally. —*n.* **3.** an intoxicated person. **4.** a habitual drunkard. —*adj.* **5.** Also, **in•e′bri•at′ed.** drunk; intoxicated. [1400–50; late ME < L *inēbriātus* ptp. of *inēbriāre* to make drunk, equiv. to *in-* IN-[2] + *ēbri(us)* drunk + *-ātus* -ATE[1]] —**in•e′bri•a′tion,** *n.*
—**Syn. 4.** See **drunkard.**

in•e•bri•e•ty (in′i brī′i tē), *n.* drunkenness; intoxication. [1780–90; IN-[2] + obs. *ebriety* < L *ēbrietās*, equiv. to *ēbri(us)* drunk + *-etās*, var. of *-itās* -ITY]

in•ed•i•ble (in ed′ə bəl), *adj.* not edible; unfit to be eaten. [1815–25; IN-[3] + EDIBLE] —**in•ed′i•bil′i•ty,** *n.*

in•ed•i•ta (in ed′i tə), *n.pl.* unpublished literary works. [1885–90; < L, neut. pl. of *inēditus* not made known, equiv. to *in-* IN-[3] + *ēditus* (ptp. of *ēdere* to publish, lit., put or give out); see EDITION]

in•ed•it•ed (in ed′i tid), *adj.* **1.** unpublished. **2.** not edited. [1750–60; IN-[3] + EDIT + -ED[2]]

in•ed•u•ca•ble (in ej′o͝o kə bəl), *adj.* incapable of being educated, esp. because of some condition, as mental retardation or emotional disturbance. [1880–85; IN-[3] + EDUCABLE] —**in•ed′u•ca•bil′i•ty,** *n.*

in•ed•u•ca•tion (in ej′o͝o kā′shən), *n.* lack of education. [1795–1805; IN-[3] + EDUCATION]

in•ef•fa•ble (in ef′ə bəl), *adj.* **1.** incapable of being expressed or described in words; inexpressible: *ineffable joy.* **2.** not to be spoken because of its sacredness; unutterable: *the ineffable name of the deity.* [1400–50; late ME < L *ineffābilis.* See IN-[3], EFFABLE] —**in•ef′fa•bil′i•ty, in•ef′fa•ble•ness,** *n.* —**in•ef′fa•bly,** *adv.*
—**Syn. 2.** unspeakable.

in•ef•face•a•ble (in′i fā′sə bəl), *adj.* not effaceable or eradicable; indelible: *an ineffaceable impression.* [1795–1805; IN-[3] + EFFACEABLE] —**in′ef•face′a•bil′i•ty,** *n.* —**in′ef•face′a•bly,** *adv.*

in•ef•fec•tive (in′i fek′tiv), *adj.* **1.** not effective; not producing results; ineffectual: *ineffective efforts; ineffective remedies.* **2.** inefficient or incompetent; incapable: *an ineffective manager.* **3.** lacking in artistic effect, as a literary work, theatrical production, or painting. [1645–55; IN-[3] + EFFECTIVE] —**in′ef•fec′tive•ly,** *adv.* —**in′ef•fec′tive•ness,** *n.*

in•ef•fec•tu•al (in′i fek′cho͞o əl), *adj.* **1.** not effectual; without satisfactory or decisive effect: *an ineffectual remedy.* **2.** unavailing; futile: *His efforts to sell the house were ineffectual.* **3.** powerless; impotent. [1375–1425; late ME; see IN-[3], EFFECTUAL] —**in′ef•fec′tu•al′i•ty, in′ef•fec′tu•al•ness,** *n.* —**in′ef•fec′tu•al•ly,** *adv.*
—**Syn. 2.** ineffective, fruitless, pointless, abortive. See **useless. 3.** feeble, weak.

in•ef•fi•ca•cious (in′ef i kā′shəs), *adj.* not able to produce the desired effect; ineffective. [1650–60; IN-[3] + EFFICACIOUS] —**in′ef•fi•ca′cious•ly,** *adv.* —**in′ef•fi•ca′cious•ness, in•ef•fi•cac•i•ty** (in′ef i kas′i tē), *n.*

in•ef•fi•ca•cy (in ef′i kə sē), *n.* lack of power or capacity to produce the desired effect. [1605–15; < LL *inefficācia.* See IN-[3], EFFICACY]

in•ef•fi•cien•cy (in′i fish′ən sē), *n., pl.* **-cies** for 2. **1.** the quality or condition of being inefficient; lack of efficiency. **2.** an instance of inefficiency: *This work is riddled with inefficiencies.* [1740–50; INEFFICI(ENT) + -ENCY]

in•ef•fi•cient (in′i fish′ənt), *adj.* **1.** not efficient; unable to effect or achieve the desired result with reasonable economy of means. **2.** lacking in ability, incompetent. [1740–50; IN-[3] + EFFICIENT] —**in′ef•fi′cient•ly,** *adv.*
—**Syn. 2.** See **incapable.**

in•e•gal•i•tar•i•an (in′i gal′i târ′ē ən), *adj.* not egalitarian; lacking in or disdaining equality. [1935–40; IN-[3] + EGALITARIAN]

in•e•las•tic (in′i las′tik), *adj.* **1.** not elastic; lacking flexibility or resilience; unyielding. **2.** *Econ.* relatively unresponsive to changes, as demand when it fails to increase in proportion to a decrease in price. Cf. **elastic** (def. 6). [1740–50; IN-[3] + ELASTIC] —**in•e•las•tic•i•ty** (in′i la stis′i tē), *n.*
—**Syn. 1.** inflexible; rigid, uncompromising.

inelas′tic colli′sion, *Mech.* a collision in which the total kinetic energy of the colliding bodies or particles is not the same after the collision as it was before (opposed to *elastic collision*).

in•el•e•gance (in el′i gəns), *n.* **1.** the quality or state of being inelegant; lack of elegance. **2.** something that is inelegant or ungraceful. [1720–30; INELEG(ANT) + -ANCE]

in•el•e•gan•cy (in el′i gən sē), *n., pl.* **-cies.** inelegance. [1720–30; INELEG(ANT) + -ANCY]

in•el•e•gant (in el′i gənt), *adj.* not elegant; lacking in refinement, gracefulness, or good taste. [1500–10; < L *inēlegant-* (s. of *inēlegāns*). See IN-[3], ELEGANT] —**in•el′e•gant•ly,** *adv.*

in•el•i•gi•ble (in el′i jə bəl), *adj.* **1.** not eligible; not permitted or suitable: *Employees are ineligible in this contest.* **2.** legally disqualified to hold an office. **3.** legally disqualified to function as a juror, voter, witness, etc., or to become the recipient of a privilege. —*n.* **4.** a person who is ineligible, as a suitor or team member. [1760–70; IN-[3] + ELIGIBLE] —**in•el′i•gi•bil′i•ty, in•el′i•gi•ble•ness,** *n.* —**in•el′i•gi•bly,** *adv.*
—**Syn. 1.** disqualified, unsuitable.

in•el•o•quent (in el′ə kwənt), *adj.* not eloquent. [1520–30; < LL *inēloquent-* (s. of *inēloquēns*). See IN-[3], ELOQUENT] —**in•el′o•quence,** *n.* —**in•el′o•quent•ly,** *adv.*

in•e•luc•ta•ble (in′i luk′tə bəl), *adj.* incapable of being evaded; inescapable: *an ineluctable destiny.* [1615–25; < L *inēluctābilis*, equiv. to *in-* IN-[3] + *ēluctā(rī)* to force a way out or over, surmount (*ē-* E- + *luctārī* to wrestle) + *-bilis* -BLE] —**in′e•luc′ta•bil′i•ty,** *n.* —**in′e•luc′ta•bly,** *adv.*
—**Syn.** inevitable, unavoidable.

in•e•lud•i•ble (in′i lo͞o′də bəl), *adj.* not eludible; inescapable. [1655–65; IN-[3] + ELUDE + -IBLE] —**in′e•lud′i•bly,** *adv.*

in•e•nar•ra•ble (in′i nar′ə bəl), *adj.* incapable of being described or narrated. [1400–50; late ME < L *inēnarrābilis*, equiv. to *in-* IN-[3] + *ēnarrābilis* describable, explicable; see E-, NARRATE, -BLE]

in•ept (in ept′, i nept′), *adj.* **1.** without skill or aptitude for a particular task or assignment; maladroit: *He is inept at mechanical tasks. She is inept at dealing with people.* **2.** generally awkward or clumsy; haplessly incompetent. **3.** inappropriate; unsuitable; out of place. **4.** absurd or foolish: *an inept remark.* [1595–1605; < L *ineptus*, equiv. to *in-* IN-[3] + *-eptus*, comb. form of *aptus* APT] —**in•ept′ly,** *adv.* —**in•ept′ness,** *n.*
—**Syn. 1.** unskillful, bungling. **4.** stupid, pointless, inane. —**Ant. 1.** suited.

in•ept•i•tude (in ep′ti to͞od′, -tyo͞od′, i nep′-), *n.* **1.** quality or condition of being inept. **2.** an inept act or remark. [1605–15; < L *ineptitūdō.* See INEPT, -I-, -TUDE]

in•e•qual•i•ty (in′i kwol′i tē), *n., pl.* **-ties.** **1.** the condition of being unequal; lack of equality; disparity: *inequality of size.* **2.** social disparity: *inequality between the rich and the poor.* **3.** disparity or relative inadequacy in natural endowments: *a startling inequality of intellect, talents, and physical stamina.* **4.** injustice; partiality. **5.** unevenness, as of surface. **6.** an instance of unevenness. **7.** variableness, as of climate. **8.** *Astron.* **a.** any component part of the departure from uniformity in astronomical phenomena, esp. in orbital motion. **b.** the amount of such a departure. **9.** *Math.* a statement that two quantities are unequal, indicated by the symbol $\neq$; alternatively, by the symbol $<$, signifying that the quantity preceding the symbol is less than that following, or by the symbol $>$, signifying that the quantity preceding the symbol is greater than that following. [1375–1425; late ME < L *inaequālitās.* See IN-[3], EQUALITY]

in•e•qui•lat•er•al (in′ē kwə lat′ər əl), *adj.* not equilateral; having unequal sides. [1655–65; IN-[3] + EQUILATERAL] —**in′e•qui•lat′er•al•ly,** *adv.*

in•eq•ui•ta•ble (in ek′wi tə bəl), *adj.* not equitable; unjust or unfair: *an inequitable decision.* [1660–17; IN-[3] + EQUITABLE] —**in•eq′ui•ta•ble•ness,** *n.* —**in•eq′ui•ta•bly,** *adv.*

in•eq•ui•ty (in ek′wi tē), *n., pl.* **-ties** for 2. **1.** lack of equity; unfairness; favoritism or bias. **2.** an unfair circumstance or proceeding. [1550–60; IN-[3] + EQUITY]

in•e•qui•valve (in ē′kwə valv′), *adj.* (of a bivalve mollusk) having the valves of the shell unequal in shape and size. [1770–80; IN-[3] + EQUI- + VALVE]

in•e•rad•i•ca•ble (in′i rad′i kə bəl), *adj.* not eradicable; not capable of being eradicated, rooted out, or completely removed. [1810–20; IN-[3] + ERADICABLE] —**in′e•rad′i•ca•ble•ness,** *n.* —**in′e•rad′i•ca•bly,** *adv.*

in•e•ras•a•ble (in′i rā′sə bəl), *adj.* not erasable; incapable of being erased or effaced. [1805–15; IN-[3] + ERASABLE] —**in′e•ras′a•ble•ness,** *n.* —**in′e•ras′a•bly,** *adv.*

in•er•ran•cy (in er′ən sē, -ûr′-), *n.* **1.** lack of error; infallibility. **2.** the belief that the Bible is free from error in matters of science as well as those of faith. Cf. **creationism** (def. 3). [1810–20; INERR(ANT) + -ANCY]

in•er•rant (in er′ənt, -ûr′-), *adj.* free from error; infallible. [1645–55; < L *inerrant-*, equiv. to *in-* IN-[3] + *errant-*, s. of *errāns* prp. of *errāre* to wander, ERR; see -ANT] —**in•er′ran•cy,** *n.* —**in•er′rant•ly,** *adv.*

in•er•rat•ic (in′i rat′ik), *adj.* not erratic or wandering; fixed: *an inerratic star.* [1645–55; IN-[3] + ERRATIC]

in•ert (in ûrt′, i nûrt′), *adj.* **1.** having no inherent power of action, motion, or resistance (opposed to *active*): *inert matter.* **2.** *Chem.* having little or no ability to react, as nitrogen that occurs uncombined in the atmosphere. **3.** *Pharm.* having no pharmacological action, as the excipient of a pill. **4.** inactive or sluggish by habit or nature. [1640–50; < L *inert-* (s. of *iners*) unskillful, equiv. to *in-* IN-[3] + *-ert-*, comb. form of *art-* (s. of *ars*) skill; see ART[1]] —**in•ert′ly,** *adv.* —**in•ert′ness,** *n.*
—**Syn. 1.** immobile, unmoving, lifeless, motionless. **4.** See **inactive.**

in•ert•ance (in ûr′tns, i nûr′-), *n. Acoustics.* the effect of inertia in an acoustic system, an impeding of the

CONCISE ETYMOLOGY KEY: <, descended or borrowed from; >, whence; b., blend of, blended; c., cognate with; cf., compare; deriv., derivative; equiv., equivalent; imit., imitative; obl., oblique; r., replacing; s., stem; sp., spelling, spelled; resp., respelling, respelled; trans., translation; ?, origin unknown; *, unattested; ‡, probably earlier than. See the full key inside the front cover.

transmission of sound through the system. Also called **acoustic inertance, acoustic mass.** [INERT + -ANCE]

inert′ gas′, *Chem.* See **noble gas.** [1900–05]

in·er·tia (in ûr′shə, i nûr′-), *n.* **1.** inertness, esp. with regard to effort, motion, action, and the like; inactivity; sluggishness. **2.** *Physics.* **a.** the property of matter by which it retains its state of rest or its velocity along a straight line so long as it is not acted upon by an external force. **b.** an analogous property of a force: *electric inertia.* **3.** *Med.* lack of activity, esp. as applied to a uterus during childbirth when its contractions have decreased or stopped. [1705–15; < L: lack of skill, slothfulness. See INERT, -IA] —**in·er′tial,** *adj.*
—**Syn. 1.** torpor, inaction, laziness.

iner′tial guid′ance, *Navig.* a guidance system for an aerospace vehicle, in which self-contained devices determine the vehicle's course on the basis of the directions and magnitudes of the accelerations it undergoes in flight. Also called **iner′tial naviga′tion.** Cf. **celestial guidance, command guidance.** [1950–55]

iner′tial mass′, *Physics.* **1.** the mass of a body as determined by the second law of motion from the acceleration of the body when it is subjected to a force that is not due to gravity. **2.** the measure of the property of inertia. Cf. **Eötvös experiment, inertia** (def. 2a), **gravitational mass.**

iner′tial sys′tem, *Physics.* a frame of reference in which a body remains at rest or moves with constant linear velocity unless acted upon by forces: any frame of reference that moves with constant velocity relative to an inertial system is itself an inertial system. Also called **iner′tial ref′erence frame′.** Cf. **law of motion.** [1950–55]

iner′tial up′per stage′, a U.S. two-stage, solid-propellant rocket used to boost a relatively heavy spacecraft from a low earth orbit into a planetary trajectory or an elliptical transfer orbit. *Abbr.:* IUS Cf. **payload assist module.**

in·es·cap·a·ble (in′ə skā′pə bəl), *adj.* incapable of being escaped, ignored, or avoided; ineluctable: *inescapable responsibilities.* [1785–95; IN-[3] + ESCAPABLE] —**in′·es·cap′a·ble·ness,** *n.* —**in′es·cap′a·bly,** *adv.*

in es·se (in es′e; *Eng.* in es′ē), *Latin.* in being; in actuality; in actual existence (contrasted with *in posse*).

in·es·sen·tial (in′i sen′shəl), *adj.* **1.** not essential; not necessary; nonessential. **2.** without essence; insubstantial. —*n.* **3.** that which is not essential. [1670–80; IN-[3] + ESSENTIAL] —**in′es·sen′ti·al′i·ty,** *n.*

in·es·sive (in es′iv), *Gram.* —*adj.* **1.** noting a case, as in Finnish, whose distinctive function is to indicate place in or within which. —*n.* **2.** the inessive case. [1885–90; < L *iness(e)* to be in, at, or on (*in-* IN-[2] + *esse* to be; see IS) + -IVE]

in·es·ti·ma·ble (in es′tə mə bəl), *adj.* **1.** incapable of being estimated or assessed. **2.** too large or great to be estimated or appreciated: *The flood caused inestimable damage.* **3.** of incalculable value; valuable beyond measure; priceless: *jewels of inestimable worth.* [1350–1400; ME < L *inaestimābilis.* See IN-[3], ESTIMABLE] —**in·es′ti·ma·bil′i·ty, in·es′ti·ma·ble·ness,** *n.* —**in·es′ti·ma·bly,** *adv.*

in·ev·i·ta·ble (in ev′i tə bəl), *adj.* **1.** unable to be avoided, evaded, or escaped; certain; necessary: *an inevitable conclusion.* **2.** sure to occur, happen, or come; unalterable: *The inevitable end of human life is death.* —*n.* **3.** that which is unavoidable. [1400–50; late ME < L *inēvītābilis.* See IN-[3], EVITABLE] —**in·ev′i·ta·bil′i·ty, in·ev′i·ta·ble·ness,** *n.* —**in·ev′i·ta·bly,** *adv.*

in·ex·act (in′ig zakt′), *adj.* not exact; not strictly precise or accurate. [1820–30; IN-[3] + EXACT] —**in′ex·act′·ly,** *adv.* —**in′ex·act′ness,** *n.*

in·ex·act·i·tude (in′ig zak′ti to͞od′, -tyo͞od′), *n.* **1.** the quality or state of being inexact or inaccurate; inexactness. **2.** an instance of this. [1780–90; < F; see IN-[3], EXACTITUDE]

in·ex·cus·a·ble (in′ik skyo͞o′zə bəl), *adj.* incapable of being excused or justified. [1375–1425; late ME < L *inexcūsābilis;* see IN-[3], EXCUSABLE] —**in′ex·cus′a·bil′i·ty, in′ex·cus′a·ble·ness,** *n.* —**in′ex·cus′a·bly,** *adv.*
—**Syn.** unpardonable, unforgivable, intolerable.

in·ex·er·tion (in′ig zûr′shən), *n.* lack of exertion; inaction. [1785–95; IN-[3] + EXERTION]

in·ex·haust·i·ble (in′ig zôs′tə bəl), *adj.* **1.** not exhaustible; incapable of being depleted: *an inexhaustible supply.* **2.** untiring; tireless: *an inexhaustible runner.* [1595–1605; < L *inexhaust(us)* not exhausted (see IN-[3], EXHAUST) + -IBLE] —**in′ex·haust′i·bil′i·ty, in′ex·haust′i·ble·ness,** *n.* —**in′ex·haust′i·bly,** *adv.*

in·ex·ist·ent (in′ig zis′tənt), *adj.* not existent; having no existence; nonexistent. [1640–50; < LL *inexistent-* (s. of *inexistēns*) not existing. See IN-[3], EXISTENT]

in·ex·o·ra·ble (in ek′sər ə bəl), *adj.* **1.** unyielding; unalterable: *inexorable truth; inexorable justice.* **2.** not to be persuaded, moved, or affected by prayers or entreaties: *an inexorable creditor.* [1545–55; < L *inexōrābilis.* See IN-[3], EXORABLE] —**in·ex′o·ra·bil′i·ty, in·ex′o·ra·ble·ness,** *n.* —**in·ex′o·ra·bly,** *adv.*
—**Syn. 2.** unbending; severe, relentless, unrelenting, implacable, merciless, cruel, pitiless. See **inflexible.** —**Ant. 2.** flexible; merciful.

in·ex·pe·di·ent (in′ik spē′dē ənt), *adj.* not expedient; not suitable, judicious, or advisable. [1600–10; IN-[3] + EXPEDIENT] —**in′ex·pe′di·ence, in′ex·pe′di·en·cy,** *n.* —**in′ex·pe′di·ent·ly,** *adv.*

in·ex·pen·sive (in′ik spen′siv), *adj.* not expensive; not high in price; costing little. [1830–40; IN-[3] + EXPENSIVE] —**in′ex·pen′sive·ly,** *adv.* —**in′ex·pen′sive·ness,** *n.*
—**Syn.** See **cheap.** —**Ant.** costly.

in·ex·pe·ri·ence (in′ik spēr′ē əns), *n.* **1.** lack of experience. **2.** lack of knowledge, skill, or wisdom gained from experience. [1590–1600; < LL *inexperientia.* See IN-[3] EXPERIENCE]

in·ex·pe·ri·enced (in′ik spēr′ē ənst), *adj.* not experienced; lacking knowledge, skill, or wisdom gained from experience. [1620–30; INEXPERIENCE + -ED[2]]
—**Syn.** untrained, unskilled, inexpert, unpracticed; raw, green, naive, uninitiated.

in·ex·pert (in eks′pûrt, in′ik spûrt′), *adj.* not expert; unskilled. [1400–50; late ME < L *inexpertus.* See IN-[3], EXPERT] —**in·ex′pert·ly,** *adv.* —**in·ex′pert·ness,** *n.*

in·ex·pi·a·ble (in eks′pē ə bəl), *adj.* **1.** not to be expiated; not allowing for expiation or atonement: *an inexpiable crime.* **2.** *Obs.* implacable: *inexpiable hate.* [1560–70; < L *inexpiābilis.* See IN-[3], EXPIABLE] —**in·ex′·pi·a·ble·ness,** *n.* —**in·ex′pi·a·bly,** *adv.*

in·ex·plain·a·ble (in′ik splā′nə bəl), *adj.* not explainable; incapable of being explained; inexplicable. [1615–25; IN-[3] + EXPLAINABLE]

in·ex·pli·ca·ble (in ek′spli kə bəl, in′ik splik′ə bəl), *adj.* not explicable; incapable of being accounted for or explained. [1375–1425; late ME < L *inexplicābilis.* See IN-[3], EXPLICABLE] —**in·ex′pli·ca·bil′i·ty, in·ex′pli·ca·ble·ness,** *n.* —**in·ex′pli·ca·bly,** *adv.*
—**Syn.** unaccountable, mysterious, mystifying.

in·ex·plic·it (in′ik splis′it), *adj.* not explicit or clear; not clearly stated. [1795–1805; < L *inexplicitus* not straightforward. See IN-[3], EXPLICIT] —**in′ex·plic′it·ly,** *adv.* —**in′ex·plic′it·ness,** *n.*

in·ex·plo·sive (in′ik splō′siv), *adj.* not explosive; incapable of exploding or being exploded. [1865–70; IN-[3] + EXPLOSIVE]

in·ex·press·i·ble (in′ik spres′ə bəl), *adj.* **1.** not expressible; incapable of being uttered or described in words: *a scene of inexpressible beauty.* —*n.* **2. inexpressibles,** *Archaic.* trousers; pants. [1615–25; IN-[3] + EXPRESSIBLE] —**in′ex·press′i·bil′i·ty, in′ex·press′i·ble·ness,** *n.* —**in′ex·press′i·bly,** *adv.*

in·ex·pres·sive (in′ik spres′iv), *adj.* **1.** not expressive; lacking in expression. **2.** *Obs.* inexpressible. [1645–55; IN-[3] + EXPRESSIVE] —**in′ex·pres′sive·ly,** *adv.* —**in′ex·pres′sive·ness,** *n.*

in·ex·pug·na·ble (in′ik spug′nə bəl), *adj.* incapable of being taken by force; impregnable; unconquerable. [1375–1425; late ME < L *inexpugnābilis,* equiv. to *in-* IN-[3] + *expugnābilis* (*expugnā(re)* to take by storm (*ex-* EX-[1] + *pugnāre* to fight) + *-bilis* -BLE)] —**in′ex·pug′·na·bil′i·ty, in′ex·pug′na·ble·ness,** *n.* —**in′ex·pug′na·bly,** *adv.*

in·ex·pung·i·ble (in′ik spun′jə bəl), *adj.* that cannot be expunged, erased, or obliterated; inextirpable. Also, **in′ex·punge′a·ble.** [1885–90; IN-[3] + EXPUNGE + -IBLE)] —**in′ex·pung′i·bil′i·ty,** *n.*

in·ex·ten·si·ble (in′ik sten′sə bəl), *adj.* not extensible; incapable of being extended or stretched. [1830–40; IN-[3] + EXTENSIBLE] —**in′ex·ten′si·bil′i·ty,** *n.*

in ex·ten·so (in eks ten′sō; *Eng.* in ik sten′sō), *Latin.* at full length.

in·ex·tin·guish·a·ble (in′ik sting′gwi shə bəl), *adj.* not extinguishable: *an inextinguishable fire.* [1500–10; IN-[3] + EXTINGUISHABLE] —**in′ex·tin′guish·a·bly,** *adv.*

in·ex·tir·pa·ble (in′ik stûr′pə bəl), *adj.* incapable of being extirpated: *inextirpable disease.* [1425–75; late ME < L *inexstirpābilis.* See IN-[3], EXTIRPATE, -BLE]

in ex·tre·mis (in eks tre′mēs; *Eng.* in ik strē′mis), *Latin.* **1.** in extremity. **2.** near death.

in·ex·tri·ca·ble (in ek′stri kə bəl, in′ik strik′ə-), *adj.* **1.** from which one cannot extricate oneself: *an inextricable maze.* **2.** incapable of being disentangled, undone, loosed, or solved: *an inextricable knot.* **3.** hopelessly intricate, involved, or perplexing: *inextricable confusion.* [1375–1425; late ME < L *inextricābilis.* See IN-[3], EXTRICABLE] —**in·ex′tri·ca·bil′i·ty, in·ex′tri·ca·ble·ness,** *n.* —**in·ex′tri·ca·bly,** *adv.*

I·nez (ī′nez, ī nez′, ē′nez, ē nez′), *n.* a female given name, form of **Agnes.**

INF (inf), *n.* European-based U.S. nuclear weapons capable of striking the Soviet Union and Soviet ones that can hit Western Europe. [*I(ntermediate-range) N(uclear) F(orces)*]

inf, *Math.* infimum.

Inf., **1.** infantry. **2.** infuse. [(def. 2) < L *infunde*]

inf., **1.** infantry. **2.** inferior. **3.** infield. **4.** infielder. **5.** infinitive. **6.** infinity. **7.** infirmary. **8.** information. **9.** below; after. [< L *infrā*] **10.** (in prescriptions) **a.** infuse. [< L *infunde*] **b.** an infusion. [< L *infūsum*]

in f., in the end; finally. [< L *in fine*]

in·fal·li·ble (in fal′ə bəl), *adj.* **1.** absolutely trustworthy or sure: *an infallible rule.* **2.** unfailing in effectiveness or operation; certain: *an infallible remedy.* **3.** not fallible; exempt from liability to error, as persons, their judgment, or pronouncements: *an infallible principle.* **4.** *Rom. Cath. Ch.* immune from fallacy or liability to error in expounding matters of faith or morals by virtue of the promise made by Christ to the Church. —*n.* **5.** an infallible person or thing. [1375–1425; late ME < ML *infallibilis.* See IN-[3], FALLIBLE] —**in·fal′li·bil′i·ty, in·fal′li·ble·ness,** *n.* —**in·fal′li·bly,** *adv.*
—**Syn. 1, 2.** See **reliable.**

in·fa·mous (in′fə məs), *adj.* **1.** having an extremely bad reputation: *an infamous city.* **2.** deserving of or causing an evil reputation; shamefully malign; detestable: *an infamous deed.* **3.** *Law.* **a.** deprived of certain rights as a citizen, as a consequence of conviction of certain offenses. **b.** of or pertaining to offenses involving such deprivation. [1350–1400; ME < L *infām(is)* (see INFAMY) + -OUS] —**in′fa·mous·ly,** *adv.* —**in′fa·mous·ness,** *n.*
—**Syn. 1.** disreputable, ill-famed, notorious. **2.** disgraceful, scandalous; nefarious, odious, wicked, shocking, vile, base, heinous, villainous. —**Ant. 1.** reputable. **2.** praiseworthy, admirable.

in·fa·my (in′fə mē), *n., pl.* **-mies** for 3. **1.** extremely bad reputation, public reproach, or strong condemnation as the result of a shameful, criminal, or outrageous act: *a time that will live in infamy.* **2.** infamous character or conduct. **3.** an infamous act or circumstance. **4.** *Law.* loss of rights, incurred by conviction of an infamous offense. [1425–75; late ME *infamye* < L *infāmia,* equiv. to *infām(is)* ill-famed (*in-* IN-[3] + *fām(a)* FAME + *-is* adj. suffix) + *-ia* -Y[3]]
—**Syn. 1.** disrepute, obloquy, odium, opprobrium, shame. See **disgrace.** —**Ant. 1.** credit, honor.

in·fan·cy (in′fən sē), *n., pl.* **-cies. 1.** the state or period of being an infant; very early childhood, usually the period before being able to walk; babyhood. **2.** the corresponding period in the existence of anything; very early stage: *Space science is in its infancy.* **3.** infants collectively. **4.** *Law.* the period of life to the age of majority, 21 years at common law but now usually 18; minority; nonage. [1485–95; < L *infantia.* See INFANT, -CY]

in·fant (in′fənt), *n.* **1.** a child during the earliest period of its life, esp. before he or she can walk; baby. **2.** *Law.* a person who is not of full age, esp. one who has not reached the age of 18 years; a minor. **3.** a beginner, as in experience or learning; novice: *The new candidate is a political infant.* **4.** anything in the first stage of existence or progress. —*adj.* **5.** of or pertaining to infants or infancy: *infant years.* **6.** being in infancy: *an infant king.* **7.** being in the earliest stage: *an infant industry.* **8.** of or pertaining to the legal state of infancy; minor. [1350–1400; < L *infant-* (s. of *infāns*) small child, lit., one unable to speak, equiv. to *in-* IN-[3] + *-fāns,* prp. of *fārī* to speak; r. ME *enfaunt* < AF < L, as above] —**in′fant·hood′,** *n.* —**in′fant·like′,** *adj.*

in·fan·ta (in fan′tə), *n.* **1.** a daughter of the king of Spain or of Portugal. **2.** an infante's wife. [1595–1605; < Sp or Pg; fem. of INFANTE]

in′fant ap′nea. See under **apnea.**

in·fan·te (in fan′tā), *n.* any son of the king of Spain or of Portugal who is not heir to the throne. [1545–55; < Sp or Pg; see INFANT]

in·fan·ti·cide (in fan′tə sīd′), *n.* **1.** the act of killing an infant. **2.** the practice of killing newborn infants. **3.** a person who kills an infant. [1650–60; (def. 1) < LL *infanticīdium;* (def. 2) < LL *infanticīda.* See INFANT, -I-, -CIDE] —**in·fan′ti·cid′al,** *adj.*

in·fan·tile (in′fən tīl′, -til), *adj.* **1.** characteristic of or befitting an infant; babyish; childish: *infantile behavior.* **2.** of or pertaining to infants or infancy: *infantile diseases.* **3.** *Physical Geog.* youthful (def. 5). [1690–1700; < L *infantīlis.* See INFANT, -ILE] —**in·fan·til·i·ty** (in′fən til′i tē), *n.*
—**Syn. 1.** puerile, immature, weak. See **childish.** —**Ant. 1.** adult, mature.

in′fantile au′tism, *Psychol.* a disorder appearing in children before the age of two and a half, characterized by lack of interest in others, impaired communication skills, and bizarre behavior, as ritualistic acts and excessive attachment to objects.

in′fantile paral′ysis, *Pathol.* poliomyelitis. [1835–45]

in·fan·ti·lism (in′fən tl iz′əm, -tī liz′-, in fan′tl iz′-əm), *n.* **1.** the persistence in an adult of markedly childish anatomical, physiological, or psychological characteristics. **2.** an infantile act, trait, etc., esp. in an adult. **3.** a speech disorder characterized by speech and voice patterns that are typical of very young children. [1890–95; INFANTILE + -ISM]

in·fan·til·ize (in′fən tl īz′, -tī līz′, in fan′tl īz′), *v.t.,* **-ized, -iz·ing. 1.** to keep in or reduce to an infantile state. **2.** to treat or regard as infantile or immature. Also, *esp. Brit.,* **in·fan′til·ise′.** [1940–45; INFANTILE + -IZE, or by back formation from *infantilization*] —**in′·fan·til·i·za′tion,** *n.*

in·fan·tine (in′fən tīn′, -tin), *adj.* infantile. [1595–1605; INFANT + -INE[1], modeled on MF *enfantin*]

in·fan·try (in′fən trē), *n., pl.* **-tries. 1.** soldiers or military units that fight on foot, in modern times typically with rifles, machine guns, grenades, mortars, etc., as weapons. **2.** a branch of an army composed of such soldiers. [1570–80; < It *infanteria,* equiv. to *infante* boy, foot-soldier (see INFANT) + *-ria* -RY]

in·fan·try·man (in′fən trē mən), *n., pl.* **-men.** a soldier of the infantry. [1880–85; INFANTRY + MAN[1]]
—**Usage.** See **-man.**

in′fants′ school′, *Brit.* kindergarten. [1815–25]

in·farct (in′färkt′, in färkt′), *n. Pathol.* a localized area of tissue, as in the heart or kidney, that is dying or dead, having been deprived of its blood supply because of an obstruction by embolism or thrombosis. [1870–75; < NL *infarctus,* n. use of ptp. of L *infarcīre* (var. of *infercīre*) to stuff, equiv. to *in-* IN-[2] + *farc(ire)* to stuff, fill (see FARCE) + *-tus* ptp. suffix] —**in·farct′ed,** *adj.*

in·farc·tion (in färk′shən), *n. Pathol.* **1.** the formation of an infarct. **2.** an infarct. [1680–90; INFARCT + -ION]

in·fare (in′fâr′), *n. Older Use.* a party or reception for a newly married couple. [bef. 1000; ME; OE *infær* a going in. See IN-[1], FARE]

in·fat·u·ate (*v.* in fach′o͞o āt′; *adj., n.* in fach′o͞o it, -āt′), *v.,* **-at·ed, -at·ing,** *adj., n.* —*v.t.* **1.** to inspire or possess with a foolish or unreasoning passion, as of love. **2.** to affect with folly; make foolish or fatuous. —*adj.* **3.** infatuated. —*n.* **4.** a person who is infatuated. [1425–75; late ME < L *infatuātus,* ptp. of *infatuāre.* See IN-[2], FATUOUS, -ATE[1]] —**in·fat′u·a′tor,** *n.*

in·fat·u·a·tion (in fach′o͞o ā′shən), *n.* **1.** the state of being infatuated. **2.** the act of infatuating. **3.** foolish or all-absorbing passion or an instance of this: *a mere infatuation that will not last.* **4.** the object of a person's in-

CONCISE PRONUNCIATION KEY: act, cāpe, dâre, pärt; set, ēqual; *if,* ice; ox, ōver, ôrder, oil, bo͝ok, bo͞ot, out; up, ûrge; child; sing; shoe; thin, *th*at; zh as in *treasure.* ə = *a* as in *alone,* e as in *system,* i as in *easily,* o as in *gallop,* u as in *circus;* ᵊ as in *fire* (fīᵊr), *hour* (ouᵊr). l and n can serve as syllabic consonants, as in *cradle* (krād′l), and *button* (but′n). See the full key inside the front cover.

fatuation: *When I was a kid, my infatuation was stamp collecting.* [1640–50; < LL *infatuātiōn-* (s. of *infatuātiō*). See INFATUATE, -ION]

in·fau·na (in′fô′nə), *n., pl.* **-nas, -nae** (-nē). the aggregate of organisms that burrow into and live in the bottom deposits of the ocean. [1910–15; IN-[1] + FAUNA; cf. EPIFAUNA] **—in′fau′nal,** *adj.*

in·fea·si·ble (in fē′zə bəl), *adj.* not feasible; impracticable. [1525–35; IN-[3] + FEASIBLE] **—in·fea′si·bil′i·ty, in·fea′si·ble·ness,** *n.*

in·fect (in fekt′), *v.t.* **1.** to affect or contaminate (a person, organ, wound, etc.) with disease-producing germs. **2.** to affect with disease. **3.** to taint or contaminate with something that affects quality, character, or condition unfavorably: *to infect the air with poison gas.* **4.** to corrupt or affect morally: *The news of the gold strike infected him with greed.* **5.** to imbue with some pernicious belief, opinion, etc. **6.** to affect so as to influence feeling or action: *His courage infected the others.* **7.** to affect with a computer virus. **8.** *Law.* to taint with illegality, or expose to penalty, forfeiture, etc. *—v.i.* **9.** to become infected. *—adj.* **10.** *Archaic.* infected. [1350–1400; ME *infecten* < L *infectus* (ptp. of *inficere* to immerse in dye, discolor, taint, poison), equiv. to *in-* IN-[2] + *-fec-*, comb. form of *facere* to DO[1], make (see FACT) + *-tus* ptp. suffix] **—in·fect′ant,** *adj.* **—in·fect′ed·ness,** *n.* **—in·fec′tor, in·fect′er,** *n.*
—Syn. 5. damage, corrupt. **6.** touch, stir, arouse.

in·fec·tee (in′fek tē′, in fek-), *n.* a person who has been infected, esp. with a disease. [INFECT + -EE]

in·fec·tion (in fek′shən), *n.* **1.** an act or fact of infecting; state of being infected. **2.** an infecting with germs of disease, as through the medium of infected insects, air, water, or clothing. **3.** an infecting agency or influence. **4.** an infectious disease: *Is this infection very dangerous?* **5.** the condition of suffering an infection. **6.** corruption of another's opinions, beliefs, moral principles, etc.; moral contamination. **7.** an influence or impulse passing from one to another and affecting feeling or action. **8.** *Gram.* (in Celtic languages) assimilation in which a vowel is influenced by a following vowel or semivowel; umlaut. [1350–1400; ME *infeccio(u)n* < LL *infectiōn-* (s. of *infectiō*). See INFECT, -ION]

in·fec·tious (in fek′shəs), *adj.* **1.** communicable by infection, as from one person to another or from one part of the body to another: *infectious diseases.* **2.** causing or communicating infection. **3.** tending to spread from one to another: *infectious laughter.* **4.** *Law.* capable of contaminating with illegality; exposing to seizure or forfeiture. **5.** *Obs.* diseased. [1535–45; INFECT(ION) + -IOUS] **—in·fec′tious·ly,** *adv.* **—in·fec′tious·ness,** *n.*
—Syn. 1. catching. See **contagious.**

infec′tious ane′mia of hors′es, *Vet. Pathol.* See **swamp fever** (def. 2). Also called **equine infectious anemia.**

infec′tious bo′vine rhi·no·tra·che·i′tis (rī′nō-trā′kē ī′tis), *Vet. Pathol.* an infectious disease of cattle, characterized by inflammation and congestion of the respiratory passages and caused by a herpes virus. *Abbr.:* IBR Also called **red nose.** [RHINO- + TRACHEITIS]

infec′tious ca′nine hepati′tis. See **Rubarth's disease.**

infec′tious ectrome′lia, *Vet. Pathol.* ectromelia (def. 2).

infec′tious hepati′tis. See **hepatitis A.** [1940–45]

infec′tious la·ryn′go·tra·che·i′tis (lə ring′gō-trā′kē ī′tis, -ring′-), *Vet. Pathol.* a viral disease of adult chickens, characterized by inflammation and hemorrhage of the larynx and trachea and, in many cases, resulting in asphyxiation. [LARYNGO- + TRACHEITIS]

infec′tious mononucleo′sis, *Pathol.* an acute, infectious form of mononucleosis associated with Epstein-Barr virus, characterized by sudden fever and a benign swelling of lymph nodes. Also called **glandular fever.** [1915–20]

in·fec·tive (in fek′tiv), *adj.* infectious. [1350–1400; ME < ML *infectivus.* See INFECT, -IVE] **—in·fec′tive·ness, in′fec·tiv′i·ty,** *n.*

in·fe·cund (in fē′kənd, -fek′ənd), *adj.* not fecund; unfruitful; barren. [1375–1425; late ME *infecounde* < L *infēcundus.* See IN-[3], FECUND] **—in·fe·cun·di·ty** (in′fi-kun′di tē), *n.*

in·fe·lic·i·tous (in′fə lis′i təs), *adj.* **1.** inapt, inappropriate, or awkward; malapropos: *an infelicitous remark.* **2.** not felicitous, happy, or fortunate; unhappy. [1825–35; IN-[3] + FELICITOUS] **—in′fe·lic′i·tous·ly,** *adv.*

in·fe·lic·i·ty (in′fə lis′i tē), *n., pl.* **-ties** for 3, 5. **1.** the quality or state of being unhappy; unhappiness. **2.** misfortune; bad luck. **3.** an unfortunate circumstance; misfortune. **4.** inaptness, inappropriateness, or awkwardness, as of action or expression. **5.** something inapt or infelicitous: *infelicities of style.* [1350–1400; ME *infelicite* < L *infēlīcitās.* See IN-[3], FELICITY]

in·fer (in fûr′), *v.,* **-ferred, -fer·ring.** *—v.t.* **1.** to derive by reasoning; conclude or judge from premises or evidence: *They inferred his displeasure from his cool tone of voice.* **2.** (of facts, circumstances, statements, etc.) to indicate or involve as a conclusion; lead to. **3.** to guess; speculate; surmise. **4.** to hint; imply; suggest. *—v.i.* **5.** to draw a conclusion, as by reasoning. [1520–30; < L *inferre,* equiv. to *in-* IN-[2] + *ferre* to bring, carry, BEAR[1]] **—in·fer′a·ble, in·fer′i·ble, in·fer′ri·ble,** *adj.* **—in·fer′a·bly,** *adv.* **—in·fer′rer,** *n.*
—Syn. 1. deduce, reason, guess.
—Usage. INFER has been used to mean "to hint or suggest" since the 16th century by speakers and writers of unquestioned ability and eminence: *The next speaker criticized the proposal, inferring that it was made solely to embarrass the government.* Despite its long history, many 20th-century usage guides condemn the use, maintaining that the proper word for the intended sense is IMPLY and that to use INFER is to lose a valuable distinction between the two words.
Although the claimed distinction has probably existed chiefly in the pronouncements of usage guides, and although the use of INFER to mean "to suggest" usually produces no ambiguity, the distinction too has a long history and is widely observed by many speakers and writers.

CONCISE ETYMOLOGY KEY: <, descended or borrowed from; >, whence; b., blend of, blended; c., cognate with; cf., compare; deriv., derivative; equiv., equivalent; imit., imitative; obl., oblique; r., replacing; s., stem; sp., spelling, spelled; resp., respelling, respelled; trans., translation; ?, origin unknown; *, unattested; ‡, probably earlier than. See the full key inside the front cover.

in·fer·ence (in′fər əns, -frəns), *n.* **1.** the act or process of inferring. **2.** something that is inferred: *to make rash inferences.* **3.** *Logic.* **a.** the process of deriving the strict logical consequences of assumed premises. **b.** the process of arriving at some conclusion that, though it is not logically derivable from the assumed premises, possesses some degree of probability relative to the premises. **c.** a proposition reached by a process of inference. [1585–95; < ML *inferentia.* See INFER, -ENCE]

in·fer·en·tial (in′fə ren′shəl), *adj.* of, pertaining to, by, or dependent upon inference. [1650–60; < ML *inferenti(a)* INFERENCE + -AL[1]] **—in′fer·en′tial·ly,** *adv.*

in·fe·ri·or (in fēr′ē ər), *adj.* **1.** lower in station, rank, degree, or grade (often fol. by *to*): *a rank inferior to colonel.* **2.** lower in place or position; closer to the bottom or base: *descending into the inferior regions of the earth.* **3.** of comparatively low grade; poor in quality; substandard: *an inferior product.* **4.** less important, valuable, or worthy: *B+ bonds are inferior to AAA bonds.* **5.** acting or performing in a way that is comparatively poor or mediocre: *an inferior observer of human nature.* **6.** *Bot.* **a.** situated below some other organ. **b.** (of a calyx) inserted below the ovary. **c.** (of an ovary) having a superior calyx. **7.** *Anat.* (of an organ or part) **a.** lower in place or position; situated beneath another. **b.** toward the feet. Cf. **superior** (def. 9). **8.** *Astron.* lying below the horizon: *the inferior part of a meridian.* **9.** *Print.* written or printed low on a line of text, as the "2" in H_2O; subscript. Cf. **superior** (def. 10). *—n.* **10.** a person inferior to another or others, as in rank or merit. **11.** Also called **subscript.** *Print.* a letter, number, or symbol written or printed low on a line of text. Cf. **superior** (def. 12). [1400–50; late ME < L, equiv. to *infer(us)* lower (cf. UNDER) + *-ior* comp. suffix] **—in·fe·ri·or·i·ty** (in fēr′ē-ôr′i tē, -or′-), *n.* **—in·fe′ri·or·ly,** *adv.*
—Syn. 3. mediocre, low-quality, second-rate.

infe′rior conjunc′tion, *Astron.* the alignment of an inferior planet between the sun and the earth. Cf. **superior conjunction.** [1825–35]

infe′rior goods′, *Econ.* commodities that are less in demand as consumer income rises. Cf. **superior goods.**

inferior′ity com′plex, 1. *Psychiatry.* intense feeling of inferiority, producing a personality characterized either by extreme reticence or, as a result of overcompensation, by extreme aggressiveness. **2.** lack of self-esteem; feeling of inadequacy; lack of self-confidence. [1920–25]

infe′rior o′vary, *Bot.* an ovary positioned below the receptacle of a flower, as in members of the iris family. [1875–80]

infe′rior plan′et, *Astron.* either of the two planets whose orbits are inside the orbit of the earth: Venus and Mercury. Cf. **superior planet.**

infe′rior ve′na ca′va. See under **vena cava.** Also called **postcava.** [1830–40]

in·fer·nal (in fûr′nl), *adj.* **1.** hellish; fiendish; diabolical: *an infernal plot.* **2.** extremely troublesome, annoying, etc.; outrageous: *an infernal nuisance.* **3.** of, inhabiting, or befitting hell. **4.** *Class. Myth.* of or pertaining to the underworld. [1325–75; ME < LL *infernālis,* equiv. to L *infern(us)* situated below, of the underworld (see INFERIOR) + *-ālis* -AL[1]] **—in′fer·nal′i·ty,** *n.* **—in·fer′nal·ly,** *adv.*
—Syn. 2. devilish, cursed, monstrous.

infer′nal machine′, a concealed or disguised explosive device intended to destroy life or property.

in·fer·no (in fûr′nō; *for 3 also It.* ēn fer′nô), *n., pl.* **-nos. 1.** hell; the infernal regions. **2.** a place or region that resembles hell: *The ironworks was an inferno of molten steel and half-naked bodies.* **3.** (*cap., italics*) the first part of Dante's *Divine Comedy,* depicting hell and the suffering of the damned. Cf. **paradise** (def. 7), **purgatory** (def. 2). [1825–35; < It < LL *infernus* hell, n. use of L *infernus;* see INFERNAL]
—Syn. 2. furnace, hellhole, oven.

in·fe·ro·an·te·ri·or (in′fə rō an tēr′ē ər), *adj.* below and in front. [1840–50; INFER(IOR) + -O- + ANTERIOR]

in·fer·tile (in fûr′tl *or, esp. Brit.,* -tīl), *adj.* not fertile; unproductive; sterile; barren: *infertile soil.* [1590–1600; < L *infertilis.* See IN-[3], FERTILE] **—in·fer′tile·ly,** *adv.* **—in′fer·til′i·ty, in·fer′tile·ness,** *n.*

in·fest (in fest′), *v.t.* **1.** to live in or overrun to an unwanted degree or in a troublesome manner, esp. as predatory animals or vermin do: *Sharks infested the coastline.* **2.** to be numerous in, as anything undesirable or troublesome: *the cares that infest the day.* **3.** *Archaic.* to harass. [1375–1425; late ME < L *infestāre* to assail, molest, deriv. of *infestus* hostile] **—in·fest′er,** *n.*

in·fes·ta·tion (in′fe stā′shən), *n.* **1.** the act of infesting; state of being infested. **2.** a harassing or troublesome invasion: *an infestation of ants.* [1375–1425; late ME *infestacio(u)n* < LL *infestātiōn-* (s. of *infestātiō*). See INFEST, -ATION]

in·fib·u·la·tion (in fib′yə lā′shən), *n.* **1.** the stitching together of the vulva, often after a clitoridectomy, leaving a small opening for the passage of urine and menstrual blood. **2.** the similar stitching of the prepuce. [1640–50; (< F) < L *infibulāt(us),* ptp. of *infibulāre* to fasten the prepuce with a clasp (*in-* IN-[2] + *fibulāre* to fasten, v. deriv. of *fibula* FIBULA) + -ion- -ION]

in·fi·del (in′fi dl, -del′), *n.* **1.** *Relig.* **a.** a person who does not accept a particular faith, esp. Christianity. **b.** (in Christian use) an unbeliever, esp. a Muslim. **c.** (in Muslim use) a person who does not accept the Islamic faith; kaffir. **2.** a person who has no religious faith; unbeliever. **3.** (loosely) a person who disbelieves or doubts a particular theory, belief, creed, etc.; skeptic. *—adj.* **4.** not accepting a particular faith, esp. Christianity or Islam; heathen. **5.** without religious faith. **6.** due to or manifesting unbelief: *infidel ideas.* **7.** rejecting the Christian religion while accepting no other; not believing in the Bible or any Christian divine revelation. **8.** Also, **in·fi·del·ic** (in′fi del′ik). of, pertaining to, or characteristic of unbelievers or infidels. [1425–75; late ME < LL *infidēlis* unbelieving, L: unfaithful, treacherous. See IN-[3], FEAL]
—Syn. 1–3. See **atheist.**

in·fi·del·i·ty (in′fi del′i tē), *n., pl.* **-ties. 1.** marital disloyalty; adultery. **2.** unfaithfulness; disloyalty. **3.** lack of religious faith, esp. Christian faith. **4.** a breach of trust or a disloyal act; transgression. [1375–1425; late ME < L *infidēlitās,* equiv. to *infidēli(s)* unfaithful (see INFIDEL) + *-tās* -TY[2]]

in·field (in′fēld′), *n.* **1.** *Baseball.* **a.** the diamond. **b.** the positions played by the first baseman, second baseman, third baseman, and shortstop, taken collectively. **c.** the infielders considered as a group (contrasted with *outfield*). **2.** *Track, Horse Racing.* the area enclosed by a track. **3.** *Agric.* **a.** the part of the land of a farm nearest the farmhouse. **b.** land regularly tilled. Cf. **outfield** (def. 3). [1600–10; IN-[1] + FIELD]

in·field·er (in′fēl′dər), *n. Baseball.* any of the four defensive players stationed around the infield. [1865–70, *Amer.;* INFIELD + -ER[1]]

in′field hit′, *Baseball.* a base hit that does not reach the outfield. [1910–15]

in′field out′, *Baseball.* a put-out recorded by a member of the infield. [1925–30]

in·fight·ing (in′fī′ting), *n.* **1.** fighting at close range. **2.** fighting between rivals, people closely associated, members of a group, etc.; internecine contention. **3.** free-for-all fighting. [1810–20; IN-[1] + FIGHTING] **—in′·fight′er,** *n.*

in·fill (in′fil′), *v.t.* **1.** to fill in: *The old stream beds have been infilled with sediment.* *—n.* **2.** the planned conversion of empty lots, underused or rundown buildings, and other available space in densely built-up urban and suburban areas for use as sites for commercial buildings and housing, frequently as an alternative to overdevelopment of rural areas. *—adj.* **3.** of, pertaining to, or involving the use of infill in urban planning: *infill condominium projects; infill office buildings and retail space.* Also, **in′-fill′.** [1875–80; IN-[1] + FILL]

in·fil·trate (in fil′trāt, in′fil trāt′), *v.,* **-trat·ed, -trat·ing,** *n.* *—v.t.* **1.** to filter into or through; permeate. **2.** to cause to pass in by filtering. **3.** to move into (an organization, country, territory, or the like) surreptitiously and gradually, esp. with hostile intent: *The troops infiltrated the enemy lines.* **4.** to pass a small number of (soldiers, spies, or the like) into a territory or organization clandestinely and with hostile or subversive intent: *The intelligence agency infiltrated three spies into the neighboring country.* *—v.i.* **5.** to pass into or through a substance, place, etc., by or as by filtering. **6.** *Pathol.* to penetrate tissue spaces or cells. *—n.* **7.** something that infiltrates. **8.** *Pathol.* any substance penetrating tissues or cells and forming a morbid accumulation. [1750–60; IN-[2] + FILTRATE] **—in·fil·tra·tive** (in′fil trā′tiv, in fil′-trə-), *adj.* **—in·fil·tra·tor** (in′fil trā′tər, in fil′trā-), *n.*

in·fil·tra·tion (in′fil trā′shən), *n.* **1.** the act or process of infiltrating. **2.** the state of being infiltrated. **3.** something that infiltrates; an infiltrate. **4.** *Mil.* **a.** a method of attack in which small bodies of soldiers or individual soldiers penetrate the enemy's line at weak or unguarded points in order to assemble behind the enemy position and attack it from the rear, harass enemy rear-area installations, etc. **b.** a system of transporting troops or vehicles at extended and irregular intervals so as to avoid enemy observation or attack, esp. from the air. **5.** *Geol.* the seepage of water into soil or rock. Cf. **percolation** (def. 3). [1790–1800; INFILTRATE + -ION]

infiltra′tion capac′ity, the maximum rate at which a soil in a given condition will absorb water. Also called **infiltra′tion rate′.** [1930–35]

infiltra′tion gal′lery, a conduit, built in permeable earth, for collecting ground water.

in·fil·trom·e·ter (in′fil trom′i tər), *n.* a device used to measure the infiltration capacity of a soil. [1935–40; INFILTR(ATION) + -O- + -METER]

in·fi·mum (in fī′məm, -fē′-), *n. Math.* See **greatest lower bound.** *Abbr.:* inf [1935–40; < L, n. use of neut. of *infimus* lowest (superl. of *inferus* low)]

infin., infinitive.

in·fi·nite (in′fə nit), *adj.* **1.** immeasurably great: *an infinite capacity for forgiveness.* **2.** indefinitely or exceedingly great: *infinite sums of money.* **3.** unlimited or unmeasurable in extent of space, duration of time, etc.: *the infinite nature of outer space.* **4.** unbounded or unlimited; boundless; endless: *God's infinite mercy.* **5.** *Math.* **a.** not finite. **b.** (of a set) having elements that can be put into one-to-one correspondence with a subset that is not the given set. *—n.* **6.** something that is infinite. **7.** *Math.* an infinite quantity or magnitude. **8.** the boundless regions of space. **9. the Infinite** or **the Infinite Being,** God. [1350–1400; ME < L *infinītus* boundless. See IN-[3], FINITE] **—in′fi·nite·ly,** *adv.* **—in′fi·nite·ness,** *n.*
—Syn. 1. enormous, immense, tremendous. **—Ant. 1.** small, limited.

in′finite baf′fle, *Audio.* a loudspeaker enclosure that totally separates sound emanating from the rear of the speaker cone from sound emanating in front, so as to prevent mutual interference.

in′finite dec′imal, *Math.* See **nonterminating decimal.** [1790–1800]

in′finite in′tegral, *Math.* See **improper integral** (def. 1).

in′finite prod′uct, *Math.* a sequence of numbers in which an infinite number of terms are multiplied together.

in′finite re′gress, *Philos.* causal or logical relationship of terms in a series without the possibility of a term initiating the series. [1830–40]

in′finite se′ries, *Math.* a sequence of numbers in which an infinite number of terms are added successively in a given pattern; the sequence of partial sums of a given sequence. [1790–1800]

in•fin•i•tes•i•mal (in′fin i tes′ə məl), *adj.* **1.** indefinitely or exceedingly small; minute: *infinitesimal vessels in the circulatory system.* **2.** immeasurably small; less than an assignable quantity: *to an infinitesimal degree.* **3.** of, pertaining to, or involving infinitesimals. —*n.* **4.** an infinitesimal quantity. **5.** *Math.* a variable having zero as a limit. [1645–55; < NL *infinitēsim(us),* equiv. to L *infinit(us)* INFINITE + *-ēsimus* suffix of ordinal numerals + -AL[1]] —**in′fin•i•tes′i•mal′i•ty, in′fin•i•tes′i•mal•ness,** *n.* —**in′fin•i•tes′i•mal•ly,** *adv.*

in′finites′imal cal′culus, the differential calculus and the integral calculus, considered together. [1795–1805]

in•fin•i•ti•val (in′fin i tī′vəl), *adj. Gram.* of or pertaining to the infinitive. [1865–70; INFINITIVE + -AL[1]] —**in′fin•i•ti′val•ly,** *adv.*

in•fin•i•tive (in fin′i tiv), *Gram.* —*n.* **1.** a verb form found in many languages that functions as a noun or is used with auxiliary verbs, and that names the action or state without specifying the subject, as French *venir* "to come," Latin *esse* "to be," *fuisse* "to have been." **2.** (in English) the simple or basic form of the verb, as *come, take, eat, be,* used after auxiliary verbs, as in *I didn't come, He must be,* or this simple form preceded by a function word, as *to* in *I want to eat.* —*adj.* **3.** consisting of or containing an infinitive: *an infinitive construction. Abbr.:* infin. [1425–75; late ME < LL *infinītīvus* indefinite, equiv. to *in-* IN-[3] + *fīnītīvus* definite; see FINITE, -IVE] —**in•fin′i•tive•ly,** *adv.*

infin′itive clause′, *Gram.* a clause containing an infinitive as its main or only verb form, as *to speak clearly* in *Try to speak clearly.* Also called **infin′itive phrase′.**

in•fin•i•tize (in fin′i tīz′), *v.t.,* **-tized, -tiz•ing.** to free from limitations of space, time, circumstance, etc.; cause to become infinite. Also, *esp. Brit.,* **in•fin′i•tise′.** [1910–15; INFINITE + -IZE]

in•fin•i•tude (in fin′i to͞od′, -tyo͞od′), *n.* **1.** infinity: *divine infinitude.* **2.** an infinite extent, amount, or number. [1635–45; INFIN(ITE) + *-itude,* on the model of MAGNITUDE, MULTITUDE]

in•fin•i•ty (in fin′i tē), *n., pl.* **-ties. 1.** the quality or state of being infinite. **2.** something that is infinite. **3.** infinite space, time, or quantity. **4.** an infinite extent, amount, or number. **5.** an indefinitely great amount or number. **6.** *Math.* **a.** the assumed limit of a sequence, series, etc., that increases without bound. **b.** infinite distance or an infinitely distant part of space. **7.** *Photog.* **a.** a distance between a subject and the camera so great that rays of light reflected from the subject may be regarded as parallel. **b.** a distance setting of the camera lens beyond which everything is in focus. [1350–1400; ME *infinite* < L *infinitās,* equiv. to *in-* IN-[3] + *fīni(s)* boundary (see FINISH) + *-tās* -TY[2]]

in•firm (in fûrm′), *adj.* **1.** feeble or weak in body or health, esp. because of age; ailing. **2.** unsteadfast, faltering, or irresolute, as persons or the mind; vacillating: *infirm of purpose.* **3.** not firm, solid, or strong: *an infirm support.* **4.** unsound or invalid, as an argument or a property title. —*v.t.* **5.** to invalidate. [1325–75; ME *infirme* < L *infirmus.* See IN-[3], FIRM[1]] —**in•firm′ly,** *adv.* —**in•firm′ness,** *n.*
—**Syn. 1, 3, 4.** weak. **2.** wavering, indecisive. **3.** rickety, tottering, shaky, unsteady. —**Ant. 1, 2, 3.** strong.

in•fir•mar•i•an (in′fər mâr′ē ən), *n.* (in a religious house) a person who nurses the sick. [1660–70; INFIRM(ARY) + -ARIAN]

in•fir•ma•ry (in fûr′mə rē), *n., pl.* **-ries. 1.** a place for the care of the infirm, sick, or injured; hospital or facility serving as a hospital: *a school infirmary.* **2.** a dispensary. [1425–75; late ME < ML *infirmāria.* See INFIRM, -ARY]

in•fir•mi•ty (in fûr′mi tē), *n., pl.* **-ties** for 1, 3. **1.** a physical weakness or ailment: *the infirmities of age.* **2.** quality or state of being infirm; lack of strength. **3.** a moral weakness or failing. [1325–75; ME *infirmite* < L *infirmitās.* See INFIRM, -ITY]
—**Syn. 3.** flaw, defect, fault.

in•fix (*v.* in fiks′, in′fiks′; *n.* in′fiks′), *v.t.* **1.** to fix, fasten, or drive in: *He infixed the fatal spear.* **2.** to implant: *to infix a habit.* **3.** to instill (a fact, idea, etc.) in the mind or memory; impress. **4.** *Gram.* to add as an infix. —*v.i.* **5.** *Gram.* (of a linguistic form) to admit an infix. —*n.* **6.** *Gram.* an affix that is inserted within the body of the element to which it is added, as Latin *m* in *accumbō* "I lie down," as compared with *accubui* "I lay down." [1495–1505; < L *infixus* ptp. of *infīgere* to fasten in. See IN-[2], FIX] —**in•fix•ion** (in fik′shən), *n.*
—**Syn. 3.** inculcate.

infl., **1.** influence. **2.** influenced.

in fla•gran•te de•lic•to (in flə gran′tē di lik′tō), See **flagrante delicto.**

in•flame (in flām′), *v.,* **-flamed, -flam•ing.** —*v.t.* **1.** to kindle or excite (passions, desires, etc.). **2.** to arouse to a high degree of passion or feeling: *His harangue inflamed the rabble.* **3.** to incite or rouse, as to violence: *His words inflamed the angry mob to riot.* **4.** (of an emotion, as rage) to cause to redden or grow heated: *Uncontrollable rage inflamed his face.* **5.** to cause inflammation in: *Her eyes were inflamed with crying.* **6.** to raise (the blood, bodily tissue, etc.) to a morbid or feverish heat. **7.** to set aflame, ablaze, or afire; set on fire. **8.** to redden with or as with flames: *The setting sun inflames the sky.* —*v.i.* **9.** to burst into flame; take fire. **10.** to be kindled, as passion. **11.** to become hot with passion, as the heart. **12.** to become excessively affected with inflammation. Also, **enflame.** [1300–50; IN-[2] + FLAME; r. ME *enflammen* < MF *enflammer* < L *inflammāre* to kindle] —**in•flam•ed•ness** (in flā′mid nis), *n.* —**in•flam′er,** *n.* —**in•flam′ing•ly,** *adv.*
—**Syn. 1–3.** See **incite. 7.** See **kindle.** —**Ant. 2.** cool, soothe.

in•flam•ma•ble (in flam′ə bəl), *adj.* **1.** capable of being set on fire; combustible; flammable. **2.** easily aroused or excited, as to passion or anger; irascible: *an inflammable disposition.* —*n.* **3.** something inflammable. [1595–1605; < ML *inflammābilis,* equiv. to L *inflammā(re)* to INFLAME + *-bilis* -BLE] —**in•flam′ma•bil′i•ty, in•flam′ma•ble•ness,** *n.* —**in•flam′ma•bly,** *adv.*
—**Syn. 2.** fiery, volatile, choleric.
—**Usage.** INFLAMMABLE and FLAMMABLE both mean "combustible." INFLAMMABLE is the older by about 200 years. FLAMMABLE now has certain technical uses, particularly as a warning on vehicles carrying combustible materials, because of a belief that some might interpret the intensive prefix IN- of INFLAMMABLE as a negative prefix and thus think the word means "noncombustible." INFLAMMABLE is the word more usually used in nontechnical and figurative contexts: *The speaker ignited the inflammable emotions of the crowd.*

in•flam•ma•tion (in′flə mā′shən), *n.* **1.** *Pathol.* redness, swelling, pain, tenderness, heat, and disturbed function of an area of the body, esp. as a reaction of tissues to injurious agents. **2.** the act or fact of inflaming. **3.** the state of being inflamed. [1525–35; < L *inflammātiōn-* (s. of *inflammātiō*), equiv. to *inflammāt(us)* (ptp. of *inflammāre;* see INFLAME, -ATE[1]) + *-iōn-* -ION]

in•flam•ma•to•ry (in flam′ə tôr′ē, -tōr′ē), *adj.* **1.** tending to arouse anger, hostility, passion, etc.: *inflammatory speeches.* **2.** *Pathol.* of or caused by inflammation. [1725–35; < L *inflammāt(us)* (see INFLAMMATION) + -ORY[1]] —**in•flam′ma•to′ri•ly,** *adv.*
—**Syn. 1.** fiery, incendiary, provocative.

inflam′matory bow′el disease′, any intestinal inflammatory disease, esp. Crohn's disease and ulcerative colitis, of unknown cause. *Abbr.:* IBD

in•flat•a•ble (in flā′tə bəl), *adj.* **1.** capable of being inflated. **2.** designed or built to be inflated before use. —*n.* **3.** an inflatable object, device, or structure, esp. a small rubber boat that is inflated with air. [1875–80; INFLATE + -ABLE]

in•flate (in flāt′), *v.,* **-flat•ed, -flat•ing.** —*v.t.* **1.** to distend; swell or puff out; dilate: *The king cobra inflates its hood.* **2.** to cause to expand or distend with air or gas: *to inflate a balloon.* **3.** to puff up with pride, satisfaction, etc. **4.** to elate. **5.** *Econ.* to expand (money, prices, an economy, etc.) unduly in amount, value, or size; affect with inflation. —*v.i.* **6.** to become inflated. **7.** to increase, esp. suddenly and substantially: *The $10 subscription has inflated to $25.* [1470–80; < L *inflātus* ptp. of *inflāre* to blow on or into, puff out, equiv. to *in-* IN-[2] + *flā-* BLOW[2] + *-tus* ptp. suffix] —**in•flat′er, in•fla′tor,** *n.*
—**Syn. 1.** See **expand.** —**Ant. 1.** deflate.

in•flat•ed (in flā′tid), *adj.* **1.** distended with air or gas; swollen. **2.** puffed up, as with pride. **3.** turgid or bombastic: *his inflated prose.* **4.** unduly increased in level: *inflated costs.* **5.** *Econ.* unduly expanded in amount, value, or size; characterized by inflation. **6.** *Bot.* hollow and enlarged or swelled out: *inflated perianth.* [1645–55; INFLATE + -ED[2]] —**in•flat′ed•ly,** *adv.* —**in•flat′ed•ness,** *n.*

in•fla•tion (in flā′shən), *n.* **1.** *Econ.* a persistent, substantial rise in the general level of prices related to an increase in the volume of money and resulting in the loss of value of currency (opposed to *deflation*). **2.** the act of inflating. **3.** the state of being inflated. [1300–50; ME *inflacio(u)n* < L *inflātiōn-* (s. of *inflātiō*). See INFLATE, -ION]

in•fla•tion•ar•y (in flā′shə ner′ē), *adj.* of, pertaining to, reflective of, or causing inflation: *inflationary prices.* [1915–20; INFLATION + -ARY]

infla′tionary spi′ral, *Econ.* See under **spiral** (def. 7). [1930–35]

infla′tionary u′niverse, *Astron.* a version of the big bang theory in which the universe underwent very rapid growth during the first fraction of a second before it settled down to its current rate of expansion.

in•fla•tion•ism (in flā′shə niz′əm), *n.* the policy or practice of inflation through expansion of currency or bank deposits. [1915–20; INFLATION + -ISM]

in•fla•tion•ist (in flā′shə nist), *n.* an advocate of inflation through expansion of currency or bank deposits. [1865–70, *Amer.;* INFLATION + -IST]

in•flect (in flekt′), *v.t.* **1.** to modulate (the voice). **2.** *Gram.* **a.** to apply inflection to (a word). **b.** to recite or display all or a distinct set of the inflections of (a word); decline or conjugate. **3.** to bend; turn from a direct line or course. **4.** *Bot.* to bend in. —*v.i.* **5.** *Gram.* to be characterized by inflection. [1375–1425; late ME *inflecten* < L *inflectere* to bend in, equiv. to *in-* IN-[2] + *flectere* to bend, curve; cf. FLEX] —**in•flect′ed•ness,** *n.* —**in•flec′tive,** *adj.* —**in•flec′tor,** *n.*

in•flec•tion (in flek′shən), *n.* **1.** modulation of the voice; change in pitch or tone of voice. **2.** Also, **flection.** *Gram.* **a.** the process or device of adding affixes to or changing the shape of a base to give it a different syntactic function without changing its form class. **b.** the paradigm of a word. **c.** a single pattern of formation of a paradigm: *noun inflection; verb inflection.* **d.** the change in the shape of a word, generally by affixation, by means of which a change of meaning or relationship to some other word or group of words is indicated. **e.** the affix added to produce this change, as the *-s* in *dogs* or the *-ed* in *played.* **f.** the systematic description of such processes in a given language, as in *serves* from *serve, sings* from *sing,* and *harder* from *hard* (contrasted with *derivation*). **3.** a bend or angle. **4.** *Math.* a change of curvature from convex to concave or vice versa. Also, *esp. Brit.,* **inflexion.** [1525–35; var. sp. of *inflexion* < L *inflexiōn-* (s. of *inflexiō*) a bending. See INFLECT, -ION] —**in•flec′tion•less,** *adj.*

in•flec•tion•al (in flek′shə nl), *adj.* **1.** of, pertaining to, or used in inflection: *an inflectional ending.* **2.** *Ling.* pertaining to or noting a language, as Latin, characterized by the use of inflection, esp. morphemic fusion or irregular morphophonemic alternation. Cf. **agglutinative** (def. 2), **isolating.** [1825–35; INFLECTION + -AL[1]] —**in•flec′tion•al•ly,** *adv.*

inflec′tion point′, *Math.* a point on a curve at which the curvature changes from convex to concave or vice versa. Also called **flex point, point of inflection.** [1715–25]

in•flexed (in flekst′), *adj. Bot., Zool.* inflected; bent or folded downward or inward: *an inflexed leaf.* [1655–65; < L *inflex(us),* ptp. of *inflectere* to bend in (see INFLECT) + -ED[2]]

in•flex•i•ble (in flek′sə bəl), *adj.* **1.** not flexible; incapable of or resistant to being bent; rigid: *an inflexible steel rod.* **2.** of a rigid or unyielding temper, purpose, will, etc.; immovable: *an inflexible determination.* **3.** not permitting change or variation; unalterable: *inflexible rules.* [1350–1400; ME < L *inflexibilis* rigid, unbending. See IN-[3], FLEXIBLE] —**in•flex′i•bil′i•ty, in•flex′i•ble•ness,** *n.* —**in•flex′i•bly,** *adv.*
—**Syn. 1.** unbendable, stiff. **2.** rigorous, stern, unrelenting, unremitting, stubborn, obstinate, intractable, obdurate, unbending, adamant. INFLEXIBLE, RELENTLESS, IMPLACABLE, INEXORABLE imply having the quality of not being turned from a purpose. INFLEXIBLE means unbending, adhering undeviatingly to a set plan, purpose, or the like: *inflexible in interpretation of rules; an inflexible will.* RELENTLESS suggests so pitiless and unremitting a pursuit of purpose as to convey a sense of inevitableness: *as relentless as the passing of time.* IMPLACABLE means incapable of being placated or appeased: *implacable in wrath.* INEXORABLE means unmoved by prayer or entreaty: *inexorable in demanding payment.* **3.** undeviating. —**Ant. 2.** amenable.

in•flex•ion (in flek′shən), *n. Chiefly Brit.* inflection.

in•flict (in flikt′), *v.t.* **1.** to impose as something that must be borne or suffered: *to inflict punishment.* **2.** to impose (anything unwelcome): *The regime inflicted burdensome taxes on the people.* **3.** to deal or deliver, as a blow. [1520–30; < L *inflictus* ptp. of *infligere* to strike or dash against, equiv. to *in-* IN-[2] + *flig-* (s. of *fligere* to beat down) + *-tus* ptp. suffix] —**in•flict′a•ble,** *adj.* —**in•flict′er, in•flic′tor,** *n.* —**in•flic′tive,** *adj.*

in•flic•tion (in flik′shən), *n.* **1.** the act of inflicting. **2.** something inflicted, as punishment or suffering. [1525–35; < LL *inflictiōn-* (s. of *inflictiō*). See INFLICT, -ION]

in-flight (in′flīt′), *adj.* done, served, or shown during an air voyage: *an in-flight movie.* Also, **in′flight′.** [1940–45]

in•flo•res•cence (in′flô res′əns, -flō-, -flə-), *n.* **1.** a flowering or blossoming. **2.** *Bot.* **a.** the arrangement of flowers on the axis. **b.** the flowering part of a plant. **c.** a flower cluster. **d.** flowers collectively. [1750–60; < NL *inflōrēscentia* < LL *inflōrēscent-* (s. of *inflōrēscēns* prp. of *inflōrēscere* to BLOOM. See IN-[2], FLORA, -ESCENT, -ENCE] —**in′flo•res′cent,** *adj.*

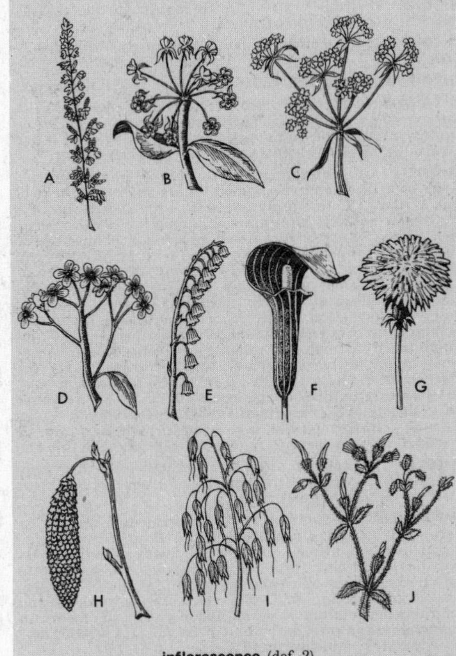

inflorescence (def. 2)
A, spike of heather, *Calluna vulgaris;* B, simple umbel of milkweed, *Asclepias syriaca;* C, compound umbel of water parsnip, *Sium cicutaefolium;* D, corymb of red chokeberry, *Aronia arbutifolia;* E, raceme of lily of the valley, *Convallaria majalis;* F, spadix of jack-in-the-pulpit, *Arisaema triphyllum;* G, head of dandelion, *Taraxacum officinale;* H, male ament of birch, genus *Betula;* I, panicle of oats, *Avena sativa;* J, cyme of chickweed, genus *Cerastium*

CONCISE PRONUNCIATION KEY: act, cāpe, dâre, pärt; set, ēqual; if, īce; ox, ōver, ôrder, oil, bo͝ok, bo͞ot, out; up, ûrge; child; sing; shoe; thin, *th*at; zh as in *treasure.* ə = *a* as in *alone, e* as in *system, i* as in *easily, o* as in *gallop, u* as in *circus;* ª as in *fire* (fīªr), *hour* (ouªr). l and n can serve as syllabic consonants, as in *cradle* (krād′l), and *button* (but′n). See the full key inside the front cover.

in•flow (in′flō′), *n.* something that flows in; influx. [1645–55; IN-[1] + FLOW]

in•flu•ence (in′flo͞o əns), *n., v.,* **-enced, -enc•ing.** —*n.* **1.** the capacity or power of persons or things to be a compelling force on or produce effects on the actions, behavior, opinions, etc., of others: *He used family influence to get the contract.* **2.** the action or process of producing effects on the actions, behavior, opinions, etc., of another or others: *Her mother's influence made her stay.* **3.** a person or thing that exerts influence: *He is an influence for the good.* **4.** *Astrol.* **a.** the radiation of an ethereal fluid from the stars, regarded as affecting human actions and destinies. **b.** the exercise of occult power by the stars, or such power as exercised. **5.** the exercise of similar power by human beings. **6.** *Obs.* influx. **7. under the influence,** *Law.* less than drunk but with one's nervous system impaired: *He was driving while under the influence.* Also, **under the influence of intoxicating liquor.** —*v.t.* **8.** to exercise influence on; affect; sway: *to influence a person.* **9.** to move or impel (a person) to some action: *Outside factors influenced her to resign.* [1325–75; ME < ML *influentia* stellar emanation, equiv. to L *influent-* (see INFLUENT) + *-ia* -Y[3]; see -ENCE] —**in′flu•ence•a•ble,** *adj.* —**in′flu•enc•er,** *n.*
—**Syn. 2.** sway, rule. See **authority. 8.** impress, bias, direct, control. **9.** incite, rouse, arouse, induce, persuade.

in′fluence ped′dler, a person who arranges to obtain favors, as government contracts, from high officials on behalf of others for a fee. [1945–50, *Amer.*] —**in′fluence ped′dling.**

in•flu•ent (in′flo͞o ənt), *adj.* **1.** flowing in. —*n.* **2.** a tributary. **3.** *Ecol.* a plant or animal that has an important effect on the biotic balance in a community. [1400–50; late ME < L *influent-* (s. of *influēns*) inflowing. See IN-[2], FLUENT]

in•flu•en•tial (in′flo͞o en′shəl), *adj.* **1.** having or exerting influence, esp. great influence: *influential educators.* —*n.* **2.** a person who exerts or can exert strong influence. [1560–70; < ML *influenti(a)* stellar emanation (see INFLUENCE) + -AL[1]] —**in′flu•en′tial•ly,** *adv.*
—**Syn. 1.** consequential, forceful, important.

in•flu•en•za (in′flo͞o en′zə), *n.* **1.** *Pathol.* an acute, commonly epidemic disease, occurring in several forms, caused by numerous rapidly mutating viral strains and characterized by respiratory symptoms and general prostration. Cf. **flu. 2.** *Vet. Pathol.* an acute, contagious disease occurring in horses and swine, characterized by fever, depression, and catarrhal inflammations of the eyes, nasal passages, and bronchi, and caused by a virus. [1735–45; < It < ML *influentia* INFLUENCE] —**in′flu•en′zal,** *adj.* —**in′flu•en′za•like′,** *adj.*

in•flux (in′fluks′), *n.* **1.** act of flowing in. **2.** an inflow (opposed to *outflux*): *an influx of tourists.* **3.** the place at which one stream flows into another or into the sea. **4.** the mouth of a stream. [1620–30; < NL or ML *influxus,* v. noun of L *influere* to flow in. See IN-[2], FLUX]
—**Syn. 2.** incursion, inpouring, entry.

in•fo (in′fō), *n. Informal.* information. [1910–15; by final shortening]

in•fold[1] (in fōld′), *v.t.* enfold.

in•fold[2] (in fōld′), *v.t., v.i.* to invaginate (defs. 2–4). [IN-[1] + FOLD[1]; cf. ENFOLD]

in•fold•ing (in fōl′ding), *n.* invagination. [INFOLD[2] + -ING[1]]

in•fo•mer•cial (in′fə mûr′shəl, -fō-), *n.* informercial.

in•fo•pre•neur (in′f′ō prə nûr′, -no͝or′, -nyo͝or′), *n.* a person whose business is gathering, processing, and providing information to advertising, marketing, and other firms. [1985–90; INFO(RMATION) + (ENTRE)PRENEUR]

in•form[1] (in fôrm′), *v.t.* **1.** to give or impart knowledge of a fact or circumstance to: *He informed them of his arrival.* **2.** to supply (oneself) with knowledge of a matter or subject: *She informed herself of all the pertinent facts.* **3.** to give evident substance, character, or distinction to; pervade or permeate with manifest effect: *A love of nature informed his writing.* **4.** to animate or inspire. **5.** *Obs.* **a.** to train or instruct. **b.** to make known; disclose. **c.** to give or impart form to. —*v.i.* **6.** to give information; supply knowledge or enlightenment: *a magazine that entertains more than it informs.* **7. inform on,** to furnish incriminating evidence about (someone) to an authority, prosecuting officer, etc.: *He informed on his accomplices.* [1275–1325; ME *informen* < L *infōrmāre* to form, shape, equiv. to *in-* IN-[2] + *fōrmāre* to FORM; r. ME *enfourmen* < MF *enfourmer* < L, as above] —**in•form′a•ble,** *adj.* —**in•form′ing•ly,** *adv.*
—**Syn. 1.** apprise; notify, advise, tell. **2.** acquaint.

in•form[2] (in fôrm′), *adj. Obs.* without form; formless. [1545–55; < L *informis* formless, deformed, equiv. to *in-* IN-[3] + *-formis* -FORM]

in•for•mal (in fôr′məl), *adj.* **1.** without formality or ceremony; casual: *an informal visit.* **2.** not according to the prescribed, official, or customary way or manner; irregular; unofficial: *informal proceedings.* **3.** suitable to or characteristic of casual and familiar, but educated, speech or writing. **4.** *Gram.* characterizing the second singular pronominal or verbal form, or its use, in certain languages: *the informal* tu *in French.* [1595–1605; IN-[3] + FORMAL[1]] —**in•for′mal•ly,** *adv.*
—**Syn. 1.** natural, easy. **3.** See **colloquial.**

in•for•mal•i•ty (in′fôr mal′i tē), *n., pl.* **-ties** for 2. **1.** the state of being informal; absence of formality. **2.** an informal act. [1590–1600; IN-[3] + FORMALITY]

in•form•ant (in fôr′mənt), *n.* **1.** a person who informs or gives information; informer. **2.** a person who supplies social or cultural data in answer to the questions of an investigator. **3.** *Ling.* a native speaker of a language who supplies utterances and forms for one analyzing or learning the language. [1655–65; < L *infōrmant-* (s. of *infōrmāns*) prp. of *infōrmāre.* See INFORM[1], -ANT]
—**Syn. 1.** source, adviser, tipster.

in for•ma pau•pe•ris (in fôr′mə pô′pə ris), *Law.* without liability for court costs and court fees: *permission to sue in forma pauperis.* [1585–95; < L: as a pauper]

in•for•mat•ics (in′fər mat′iks), *n.* (*used with a singular v.*) the study of information processing; computer science. [trans. of Russ *informátika* (1966); see INFORMATION, -ICS]

in•for•ma•tion (in′fər mā′shən), *n.* **1.** knowledge communicated or received concerning a particular fact or circumstance; news: *information concerning a crime.* **2.** knowledge gained through study, communication, research, instruction, etc.; factual data: *His wealth of general information is amazing.* **3.** the act or fact of informing. **4.** an office, station, service, or employee whose function is to provide information to the public: *The ticket seller said to ask information for a timetable.* **5.** See **Directory Assistance. 6.** *Law.* **a.** an official criminal charge presented, usually by the prosecuting officers of the state, without the interposition of a grand jury. **b.** a criminal charge, made by a public official under oath before a magistrate, of an offense punishable summarily. **c.** the document containing the depositions of witnesses against one accused of a crime. **7.** (in information theory) an indication of the number of possible choices of messages, expressible as the value of some monotonic function of the number of choices, usually the logarithm to the base 2. **8.** *Computers.* **a.** important or useful facts obtained as output from a computer by means of processing input data with a program: *Using the input data, we have come up with some significant new information.* **b.** data at any stage of processing (input, output, storage, transmission, etc.). [1350–1400; ME: instruction, teaching, a forming of the mind < ML, L: idea, conception. See INFORM[1], -ATION] —**in′for•ma′tion•al,** *adj.*
—**Syn. 1.** data, facts, intelligence, advice. **2.** INFORMATION, KNOWLEDGE, WISDOM are terms for human acquirements through reading, study, and practical experience. INFORMATION applies to facts told, read, or communicated that may be unorganized and even unrelated: *to pick up useful information.* KNOWLEDGE is an organized body of information, or the comprehension and understanding consequent on having acquired and organized a body of facts: *a knowledge of chemistry.* WISDOM is a knowledge of people, life, and conduct, with the facts so thoroughly assimilated as to have produced sagacity, judgment, and insight: *to use wisdom in handling people.*

informa′tion o′verload, *Psychol.* an excess of incoming information, as might confront a pedestrian on a crowded city street, that forces one to be selective in the information received and retained.

informa′tion proc′essing. See **data processing.**

informa′tion retriev′al, the systematic storage and recovery of data, as from a file, card catalog, or the memory bank of a computer. *Abbr.:* IR [1945–50]

informa′tion sci′ence, the study of the nature, collection, and management of information and of its uses, esp. involving computer storage and retrievals.

informa′tion the′ory, the mathematical theory concerned with the content, transmission, storage, and retrieval of information, usually in the form of messages or data, and esp. by means of computers. [1945–50]

in•form•a•tive (in fôr′mə tiv), *adj.* giving information; instructive: *an informative book.* Also, **in•form•a•to•ry** (in fôr′mə tôr′ē, -tōr′ē). [1375–1425; late ME: formative < ML *infōrmātīvus,* equiv. to L *infōrmāt(us)* (ptp. of *infōrmāre* to INFORM[1]) + *-ivus* -IVE] —**in•form′a•tive•ly,** *adv.* —**in•form′a•tive•ness,** *n.*

inform′atory dou′ble, *Bridge.* a double intended to inform one's partner that one has a strong hand and to urge a bid regardless of the strength of his or her hand. Also called **takeout double.** Cf. **business double.** [1925–30; INFORMAT(ION) + -ORY[1]]

in•formed (in fôrmd′), *adj.* having or prepared with information or knowledge; apprised: *an informed audience that asked intelligent questions.* [1400–50; late ME; see INFORM, -ED[2]] —**in•form•ed•ly** (in fôr′mid lē), *adv.*

informed′ consent′, a patient's consent to a medical or surgical procedure or to participation in a clinical study after being properly advised of the relevant medical facts and the risks involved. [1965–70]

in•form•er (in fôr′mər), *n.* **1.** a person who informs against another, esp. for money or other reward. **2.** a person who informs or communicates information or news; informant. [1350–1400; ME; see INFORM[1], -ER[1]]

in•for•mer•cial (in′fər mur′shəl, -fə-), *n. Radio and Television.* a commercial that informs or instructs, esp. in an original and entertaining manner: *an informercial on making Christmas decorations using the sponsor's brand of glue.* Also, **infomercial.** [b. INFORMATION and COMMERCIAL]

inform′ing gun′, a gun fired by a warship to signal its intention to search a merchant vessel. Also called **affirming gun.**

in•for•tu•nate (in fôr′chə nit), *adj. Obs.* of or pertaining to infortune. [1350–1400; ME < L *infortūnātus,* equiv. to *in-* IN-[3] + *fortūnātus* FORTUNATE] —**in•for′tu•nate•ly,** *adv.* —**in•for′tu•nate•ness,** *n.*

in•for•tune (in fôr′chən), *n.* **1.** *Astrol.* a planet or aspect of evil influence, esp. Saturn or Mars. **2.** *Obs.* misfortune. [1325–75; ME (see IN-[3], FORTUNE), trans. of L *infortūnium*]

in•fo•tain•ment (in′fə tān′mənt), *n.* edutainment. [INFO(RMATION) + (ENTER)TAINMENT]

in•fra (in′frə), *adv.* below, esp. when used in referring to parts of a text. Cf. **supra.** [1730–40; < L *infrā;* cf. UNDER]

infra-, a prefix meaning "below," used, with second elements of any origin, in the formation of compound words: *infrasonic; infrared.* [< L, repr. *infrā,* adv. or prep.]

in•fract (in frakt′), *v.t.* to break, violate, or infringe (a law, commitment, etc.). [1790–1800; < L *infrāctus* ptp. of *infringere* to BREAK, bend, weaken (see INFRINGE), equiv. to *in-* IN-[2] + *frag-* (var. s. of *frangere* to break; see FRANGIBLE) + *-tus* ptp. suffix] —**in•frac′tor,** *n.*

in•frac•tion (in frak′shən), *n.* **1.** breach; violation; infringement: *an infraction of the rules.* **2.** *Med.* an incomplete fracture of a bone. [1615–25; < L *infrāctiōn-* (s. of *infrāctiō*). See INFRACT, -ION]
—**Syn. 1.** See **breach.**

in•fra dig (in′frə dig′), beneath one's dignity. [1815–25; < L *infrā dignitātem*]

in•fra•hu•man (in′frə hyo͞o′mən *or, often,* -yo͞o′-), *adj.* less than human; subhuman. [1870–75; INFRA- + HUMAN]

in•fra•lap•sar•i•an (in′frə lap sâr′ē ən), *n.* **1.** a person who believes in infralapsarianism. —*adj.* **2.** of or pertaining to infralapsarians or infralapsarianism. [1725–35; INFRA- + L *laps(us)* a fall (see LAPSE) + -ARIAN]

in•fra•lap•sar•i•an•ism (in′frə lap sâr′ē ə niz′əm), *n. Theol.* the doctrine, held by Augustinians and by many Calvinists, that God planned the Creation, permitted the Fall, elected a chosen number, planned their redemption, and suffered the remainder to be eternally punished (opposed to *supralapsarianism*). [1840–50; INFRALAPSARIAN + -ISM]

in•fra•mar•gin•al (in′frə mär′jə nl), *adj.* below the margin; submarginal. [1855–60; INFRA- + MARGINAL]

in•fran•gi•ble (in fran′jə bəl), *adj.* **1.** that cannot be broken or separated; unbreakable: *infrangible moral strength.* **2.** that cannot be infringed or violated; inviolable: *an infrangible rule.* [1590–1600; < LL *infrangibilis.* See IN-[3], FRANGIBLE] —**in•fran′gi•bil′i•ty, in•fran′gi•ble•ness,** *n.* —**in•fran′gi•bly,** *adv.*

in•fra•red (in′frə red′), *n.* **1.** the part of the invisible spectrum that is contiguous to the red end of the visible spectrum and that comprises electromagnetic radiation of wavelengths from 800 nm to 1 mm. —*adj.* **2.** noting or pertaining to the infrared or its component rays: *infrared radiation.* Cf. **ultraviolet.** Also, **in′fra-red′.** [1825–35; INFRA- + RED[1]]

in′frared′ astron′omy, the study of infrared radiation emitted by celestial objects. [1960–65]

in′frared gal′axy, *Astron.* a galaxy that radiates strongly in the infrared portion of the electromagnetic spectrum. [1965–70]

in′frared star′, *Astron.* a star radiating strongly in the infrared portion of the electromagnetic spectrum.

in•fra•son•ic (in′frə son′ik), *adj.* noting or pertaining to a sound wave with a frequency below the audio-frequency range. [1925–30; INFRA- + SONIC]

in•fra•son•ics (in′frə son′iks), *n.* (*used with a singular v.*) the branch of science that deals with infrasonic phenomena. [1965–70; see INFRASONIC, -ICS]

in•fra•sound (in′frə sound′), *n.* sound with frequencies below the audible range. [1925–30; INFRA- + SOUND[1]]

in•fra•spe•cif•ic (in′frə spi sif′ik), *adj.* of or pertaining to a subdivision of a species, as a subspecies, variety, or cultivar. [1935–40; INFRA- + SPECIFIC]

in•fra•struc•ture (in′frə struk′chər), *n.* **1.** the basic, underlying framework or features of a system or organization. **2.** the fundamental facilities and systems serving a country, city, or area, as transportation and communication systems, power plants, and schools. **3.** the military installations of a country. [1925–30; INFRA + STRUCTURE] —**in′fra•struc′tur•al,** *adj.*

in•fre•quen•cy (in frē′kwən sē), *n.* state of being infrequent. Also, **in•fre′quence.** [1590–1600; < L *infrequentia* fewness. See INFREQUENT, -ENCY]

in•fre•quent (in frē′kwənt), *adj.* **1.** happening or occurring at long intervals or rarely: *infrequent visits.* **2.** not constant, habitual, or regular: *an infrequent visitor.* **3.** not plentiful or many: *infrequent opportunities for advancement.* **4.** far apart in space. [1525–35; < L *infrequent-* (s. of *infrequēns*). See IN-[3], FREQUENT] —**in•fre′quent•ly,** *adv.*
—**Syn. 1, 3.** scarce, rare, uncommon.

in•fringe (in frinj′), *v.,* **-fringed, -fring•ing.** —*v.t.* **1.** to commit a breach or infraction of; violate or transgress: *to infringe a copyright; to infringe a rule.* —*v.i.* **2.** to encroach or trespass (usually fol. by *on* or *upon*): *Don't infringe on his privacy.* [1525–35; < L *infringere* to break, weaken, equiv. to *in-* IN-[2] + *-fringere,* comb. form of *frangere* to BREAK] —**in•fring′er,** *n.*
—**Syn. 1.** break, disobey. **2.** poach. See **trespass.**

in•fringe•ment (in frinj′mənt), *n.* **1.** a breach or infraction, as of a law, right, or obligation; violation; transgression. **2.** an act of infringing. [1585–95; INFRINGE + -MENT]

in•fu•la (in′fyə lə), *n., pl.* **-lae** (-lē′). one of the two embroidered lappets of the miter of a bishop. [1600–10; < ML, L: band, priest's headband]

in•fun•dib•u•li•form (in′fun dib′yə lə fôrm′), *adj. Bot.* funnel-shaped. [1745–55; INFUNDIBUL(UM) + -I- + -FORM]

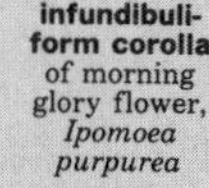

infundibuliform corolla of morning glory flower, *Ipomoea purpurea*

CONCISE ETYMOLOGY KEY: <, descended or borrowed from; >, whence; b., blend of, blended; c., cognate with; cf., compare; deriv., derivative; equiv., equivalent; imit., imitative; obl., oblique; r., replacing; s., stem; sp., spelling, spelled; resp., respelling, respelled; trans., translation; ?, origin unknown; *, unattested; ‡, probably earlier than. See the full key inside the front cover.

in·fun·dib·u·lum (in′fun dib′yə ləm), *n., pl.* **-la** (-lə). *Anat.* **1.** a funnel-shaped organ or part. **2.** a funnel-shaped extension of the hypothalamus connecting the pituitary gland to the base of the brain. **3.** a space in the right ventricle at the base of the pulmonary artery. [1700–10; < NL, L: funnel, equiv. to *infundi-* (s. of *infundere* to pour into; see IN-[2], FOUND[3]) + *-bulum* instrumental suffix; cf. INFUSE] **—in′fun·dib′u·lar, in·fun·dib·u·late** (in′fun dib′yə lāt′), *adj.*

in·fu·ri·ate (*v.* in fyŏŏr′ē āt′; *adj.* in fyŏŏr′ē it), *v.,* **-at·ed, -at·ing,** *adj.* **—***v.t.* **1.** to make furious; enrage. **—***adj.* **2.** *Archaic.* infuriated. [1660–70; < ML *infuriātus* ptp. of *infuriāre* to madden, enrage. See IN-[2], FURY, -ATE[1]] **—in·fu′ri·ate·ly,** *adv.* **—in·fu′ri·a′tion,** *n.*
—Syn. 1. anger. See **enrage.**

in·fu·ri·at·ing (in fyŏŏr′ē ā′ting), *adj.* causing or tending to cause anger or outrage; maddening: *His delay is infuriating.* [1880–85; INFURIATE + -ING[2]] **—in·fu′ri·at′ing·ly,** *adv.*

in·fus·cate (in fus′kāt, -kit), *adj. Entomol.* darkened with a fuscous or brownish tinge. Also, **in·fus′cat·ed.** [1640–50; < L *infuscātus* ptp. of *infuscāre* to darken, discolor. See IN-[2], FUSCOUS, -ATE[1]]

in·fuse (in fyōōz′), *v.,* **-fused, -fus·ing.** **—***v.t.* **1.** to introduce, as if by pouring; cause to penetrate; instill (usually fol. by *into*): *The energetic new principal infused new life into the school.* **2.** to imbue or inspire (usually fol. by *with*): *The new coach infused the team with enthusiasm.* **3.** to steep or soak (leaves, bark, roots, etc.) in a liquid so as to extract the soluble properties or ingredients. **4.** *Obs.* to pour in. **—***v.i.* **5.** to undergo infusion; become infused: *Leave the solution to infuse overnight.* [1375–1425; late ME < L *infūsus* ptp. of *infundere* to pour into. See IN-[2], FUSE[2]] **—in·fus′er,** *n.*
—Syn. 1. ingrain; inculcate.

in·fu·si·ble[1] (in fyōō′zə bəl), *adj.* not fusible; incapable of being fused or melted. [1545–55; IN-[3] + FUSIBLE] **—in·fu′si·bil′i·ty, in·fu′si·ble·ness,** *n.*

in·fu·si·ble[2] (in fyōō′zə bəl), *adj.* capable of being infused. [1650–60; INFUSE + -IBLE]

in·fu·sion (in fyōō′zhən), *n.* **1.** the act or process of infusing. **2.** something that is infused. **3.** a liquid extract, as tea, prepared by steeping or soaking. **4.** *Pharm.* **a.** the steeping or soaking of a crude drug in water. **b.** the liquid so prepared. **5.** *Med.* **a.** the introduction of a saline or other solution into a vein. **b.** the solution used. [1400–50; late ME < L *infūsiōn-* (s. of *infūsiō*). See INFUSE, -ION]

in·fu·sion·ism (in fyōō′zhə niz′əm), *n. Theol.* the doctrine that the soul existed in a previous state and is infused into the body at conception or birth. [1880–85; INFUSION + -ISM] **—in·fu′sion·ist,** *n.*

in·fu·sive (in fyōō′siv), *adj.* capable of infusing; inspiring. [1620–30; INFUSE + -IVE]

In·fu·so·ri·a (in′fyŏŏ sôr′ē ə, -sōr′-), *n.pl.* **1.** protozoans of the phylum Ciliophora (or class Ciliata). **2.** (formerly) any of various microscopic organisms found in infusions of decaying organic matter. [1780–90; < NL, neut. pl. of *infūsōrius.* See INFUSE, -ORY[1]]

in·fu·so·ri·al (in′fyŏŏ sôr′ē əl, -sōr′-), *adj.* pertaining to, containing, or consisting of infusorians: *infusorial earth.* [1840–50; INFUSORI(A) + -AL[1]]

in·fu·so·ri·an (in′fyŏŏ sôr′ē ən, -sōr′-), *n.* **1.** any of the Infusoria. **—***adj.* **2.** infusorial. [1855–60; INFUSORI(A) + -AN]

in fu·tu·ro (in fŏŏ tōō′rō; *Eng.* in fyŏŏ tŏŏr′ō, -tyŏŏr′ō), *Latin.* in the future.

-ing[1], a suffix of nouns formed from verbs, expressing the action of the verb or its result, product, material, etc. (*the art of building; a new building; cotton wadding*). It is also used to form nouns from words other than verbs (*offing; shirting*). Verbal nouns ending in *-ing* are often used attributively (*the printing trade*) and in forming compounds (*drinking song*). In some compounds (*sewing machine*), the first element might reasonably be regarded as the participial adjective, **-ing**[2], the compound thus meaning "a machine that sews," but it is commonly taken as a verbal noun, the compound being explained as "a machine for sewing." Cf. **-ing**[2]. [ME; OE *-ing, -ung*]

-ing[2], a suffix forming the present participle of verbs, (*walking; thinking*), such participles being often used as participial adjectives: *warring factions.* Cf. **-ing**[1]. [ME *-ing, -inge*; the var. *-in* (usually represented in sp. as *-in′*) continues ME *-inde, -ende,* OE *-ende*]
—Pronunciation. The common suffix -ING[2] can be pronounced in modern English as either (-ing) or (-in), with either the velar nasal consonant (ng), symbolized in IPA as [ŋ], or the alveolar nasal consonant (n), symbolized in IPA as [n]. The (-in) pronunciation therefore reflects the use of one nasal as against another and not, as is popularly supposed, "dropping the *g,*" since no actual *g*-sound is involved.
Many speakers use both pronunciations, depending on the speed of utterance and the relative formality of the occasion, with (-ing) considered the more formal variant. For some educated speakers, especially in the southern United States and Britain, (-in) is in fact the more common pronunciation, while for other educated speakers, (-ing) is common in virtually all circumstances. In response to correction from perceived authorities, many American speakers who would ordinarily use (-in) at least some of the time make a conscious effort to say (-ing), even in informal circumstances.

-ing[3], a native English suffix, meaning "one belonging to," "of the kind of," "one descended from," and sometimes having a diminutive force, formerly used in the formation of nouns: *farthing; shilling; bunting; gelding; whiting.* Cf. **-ling**[1]. [ME, OE *-ing*; c. ON *-ingr, -ungr,* Goth *-ings*]

in·gate (in′gāt′), *n. Metall.* gate[1] (def. 15). [1855–60; IN + GATE[1]]

in·gath·er (in′gath ər, in gath′ər), *v.t.* **1.** to gather or bring in, as a harvest. **—***v.i.* **2.** to collect; assemble. [1565–75; IN-[1] + GATHER] **—in′gath′er·er,** *n.*

in·gath·er·ing (in′gath′ər ing), *n.* **1.** a gathering in, esp. of farm products; harvest. **2.** a gathering together, as of persons; assembly. [1525–35; IN-[1] + GATHERING]

Inge (inj *for 1;* ing *for 2*), *n.* **1. William (Mot·ter)** (mot′ər), 1913–73, U.S. playwright. **2. William Ralph,** 1860–1954, Anglican clergyman, scholar, and author: dean of St. Paul's 1911–34.

In·ge·low (in′jə lō′), *n.* **Jean,** 1820–97, English poet and novelist.

Ing·e·mar (ing′gə mär′), *n.* a male given name.

in·gem·i·nate (in jem′ə nāt′), *v.t.,* **-nat·ed, -nat·ing.** to repeat; reiterate. [1585–95; < L *ingeminātus* ptp. of *ingemināre* to repeat, redouble. See IN-[2], GEMINATE] **—in·gem′i·na′tion,** *n.*

in·gen·er·ate[1] (in jen′ər it), *adj.* not generated; self-existent. [1650–60; < LL *ingenerātus* not begotten. See IN-[3], GENERATE]

in·gen·er·ate[2] (*v.* in jen′ə rāt′; *adj.* in jen′ər it), *v.,* **-at·ed, -at·ing,** *adj.* **—***v.t.* **1.** to engender; produce. **—***adj.* **2.** inborn; innate. [1525–35; < L *ingenerātus* ptp. of *ingenerāre* to engender, produce, implant. See IN-[2], GENERATE] **—in·gen′er·ate·ly,** *adv.* **—in·gen′er·a′tion,** *n.*

in·gen·ious (in jēn′yəs), *adj.* **1.** characterized by cleverness or originality of invention or construction: *an ingenious machine.* **2.** cleverly inventive or resourceful: *an ingenious press agent.* **3.** *Obs.* **a.** intelligent; showing genius. **b.** ingenuous. [1375–1425; late ME < L *ingeniōsus,* equiv. to *ingeni(um)* natural disposition, cleverness (*in-* IN-[2] + *gen-* (base of *gignere* to bring into being; cf. GENITOR) + *-ium* -IUM) + *-ōsus* -OUS] **—in·gen′ious·ly,** *adv.* **—in·gen′ious·ness,** *n.*
—Syn. 2. bright, gifted, able, resourceful; adroit.
—Ant. 2. unskillful.
—Usage. INGENIOUS and INGENUOUS are now distinct from each other and are not synonyms. INGENIOUS means "characterized by cleverness" or "cleverly inventive," as in contriving new explanations or methods: *an ingenious device; ingenious designers.* INGENUOUS means "candid" or "innocent": *an ingenuous and sincere statement; a thug with the ingenuous eyes of a choirboy.*

in·gé·nue (an′zhə nōō′, -nyōō′; *Fr.* aN zhā ny′), *n., pl.* **-nues** (-nōōz′, -nyōōz′; *Fr.* -ny′). **1.** the part of an artless, innocent, unworldly girl or young woman, esp. as represented on the stage. **2.** an actress who plays such a part or specializes in playing such parts. Also, **in′ge·nue′.** [1840–50; < F, fem. of *ingénu* < L *ingenuus* native, inborn, etc.; see INGENUOUS]

in·ge·nu·i·ty (in′jə nōō′i tē, -nyōō′-), *n., pl.* **-ties** for 3. **1.** the quality of being cleverly inventive or resourceful; inventiveness: *a designer of great ingenuity.* **2.** cleverness or skillfulness of conception or design: *a device of great ingenuity.* **3.** an ingenious contrivance or device. **4.** *Obs.* ingenuousness. [1590–1600; < L *ingenuitās* innate virtue, etc. (see INGENUOUS, -ITY); current senses by assoc. with INGENIOUS]

in·gen·u·ous (in jen′yōō əs), *adj.* **1.** free from reserve, restraint, or dissimulation; candid; sincere. **2.** artless; innocent; naive. **3.** *Obs.* honorable or noble. [1590–1600; < L *ingenuus* native, free-born, honorable, frank, equiv. to *in-* IN-[2] + *gen-* (base of *gignere*; see INGENIOUS) + *-uus* deverbal adj. suffix; see -OUS] **—in·gen′u·ous·ly,** *adv.* **—in·gen′u·ous·ness,** *n.*
—Syn. 1. frank, straightforward, open. **2.** guileless.
—Usage. See **ingenious.**

In·ger·soll (ing′gər sôl′, -sol′, -səl), *n.* **Robert Green,** 1833–99, U.S. lawyer, political leader, and orator.

in·gest (in jest′), *v.t.* **1.** to take, as food, into the body (opposed to *egest*). **2.** *Aeron.* to draw (foreign matter) into the inlet of a jet engine, often causing damage to the engine. [1610–20; < L *ingestus* ptp. of *ingerere* to throw or pour into. See IN-[2], GEST] **—in·gest′i·ble,** *adj.* **—in·ges′tion,** *n.* **—in·ges′tive,** *adj.*

in·ges·ta (in jes′tə), *n.pl.* substances ingested. [1720–30; < NL, neut. pl. of L *ingestus.* See INGEST]

in·ges·tant (in jes′tənt), *n.* something that is ingested, esp. a substance that may be associated with an allergic reaction. [INGEST + -ANT]

in·gle (ing′gəl), *n. Chiefly Brit. Dial.* **1.** a fire burning in a hearth. **2.** a fireplace; hearth. [1500–10; < ScotGael *aingeal* fire]

in·gle·nook (ing′gəl nŏŏk′), *n.* a corner or nook near a fireplace; chimney corner. [1765–75; INGLE + NOOK]

in·gle·side (ing′gəl sīd′), *n. Chiefly Brit. Dial.* a fireside. [1740–50; INGLE + SIDE[1]]

In·gle·wood (ing′gəl wŏŏd′), *n.* a city in SW California, near Los Angeles. 94,245.

in·glo·ri·ous (in glôr′ē əs, -glōr′-), *adj.* **1.** shameful; disgraceful: *inglorious retreat.* **2.** not famous or honored. [1565–75; < L *inglōrius.* See IN-[3], GLORIOUS] **—in·glo′ri·ous·ly,** *adv.* **—in·glo′ri·ous·ness,** *n.*
—Syn. 1. dishonorable, ignominious. **—Ant. 1.** admirable, praiseworthy.

Ing·mar (ing′mär), *n.* a male given name.

in·goal (in′gōl′), *n. Rugby.* the area at either end of the field between the goal line and the dead-ball line. [1895–1900]

In God′ We′ Trust′, 1. a motto appearing on U.S. currency. **2.** motto of Florida. [1860–65]

in·go·ing (in′gō′ing), *adj.* going in; entering. [1300–50; ME; see IN-[1], GOING]

in·got (ing′gət), *n.* **1.** a mass of metal cast in a convenient form for shaping, remelting, or refining. **—***v.t.* **2.** to make ingots of; shape into ingots. [1350–1400; ME: lit., (something) poured in, equiv. to *in-* IN-[1] + *got(e)* a stream, OE **gota,* akin to *gēotan* to flow; c. G *giessen,* Goth *giutan,* ON *gjōta* to pour]

in′got i′ron, an iron of high purity made by a basic open-hearth process. [1875–80]

in·graft (in graft′, -gräft′), *v.t.* engraft. **—in·graft′ment, in′graf·ta′tion,** *n.*

in·grain (*v.* in grān′; *adj., n.* in′grān′), *v.t.* **1.** to implant or fix deeply and firmly, as in the nature or mind. **—***adj.* **2.** ingrained; firmly fixed. **3.** (of fiber or yarn) dyed in a raw state, before being woven or knitted. **4.** made of fiber or yarn so dyed: *ingrain fabric.* **5.** (of carpets) made of ingrain yarn and so woven as to show a different pattern on each side; reversible. **—***n.* **6.** yarn, wool, etc., dyed before manufacture. **7.** an ingrain carpet. Also, **engrain** (for defs. 1, 2). [1760–70; orig. phrase (*dyed*) *in grain* (i.e., with kermes)]
—Syn. 1. infuse, inculcate, imbue.

in·grained (in grānd′, in′grānd′), *adj.* **1.** firmly fixed; deep-rooted; inveterate: *ingrained superstition.* **2.** wrought into or through the grain or fiber. Also, **engrained.** [1590–1600; INGRAIN + -ED[2]] **—in·grain·ed·ly** (in grā′nid lē, -grānd′-), *adv.* **—in·grain′ed·ness,** *n.*

In·gram (ing′grəm), *n.* a male given name.

in·grate (in′grāt), *n.* **1.** an ungrateful person. **—***adj.* **2.** *Archaic.* ungrateful. [1350–1400; ME *ingrat* < L *ingrātus* ungrateful. See IN-[3], GRATEFUL] **—in′grate·ly,** *adv.*

in·gra·ti·ate (in grā′shē āt′), *v.t.,* **-at·ed, -at·ing.** to establish (oneself) in the favor or good graces of others, esp. by deliberate effort (usually fol. by *with*): *He ingratiated himself with all the guests.* [1615–25; perh. < L *in grātiam* into favor, after It *ingraziare.* See IN, GRACE, -ATE[1]] **—in·gra′ti·a′tion,** *n.* **—in·gra·ti·a·to·ry** (in grā′shē ə tôr′ē, -tōr′ē), *adj.*

in·gra·ti·at·ing (in grā′shē ā′ting), *adj.* **1.** charming; agreeable; pleasing. **2.** deliberately meant to gain favor: *an ingratiating manner.* [1635–45; INGRATIATE + -ING[2]] **—in·gra′ti·at′ing·ly,** *adv.*

in·grat·i·tude (in grat′i tōōd′, -tyōōd′), *n.* the state of being ungrateful; unthankfulness. [1175–1225; ME < ML *ingrātitūdō.* See IN-[3], GRATITUDE]

in·gre·di·ent (in grē′dē ənt), *n.* **1.** something that enters as an element into a mixture: *Flour, eggs, and sugar are the main ingredients in the cake.* **2.** a constituent element of anything; component: *the ingredients of political success.* [1425–75; late ME < L *ingredient-* (s. of *ingrediēns*), prp. of *ingredī* to go or step into, commence, equiv. to *in-* IN-[2] + *-gredient-* going; see GRADIENT]
—Syn. 1. See **element.** **—Ant.** whole.

In·gres (aN′grᵊ), *n.* **Jean Au·guste Do·mi·nique** (zhäN ō gyst′ dô mē nēk′), 1780–1867, French painter.

in·gress (in′gres), *n.* **1.** the act of going in or entering. **2.** the right to enter. **3.** a means or place of entering; entryway. **4.** *Astron.* immersion (def. 5). [1400–50; late ME < L *ingressus* a going in, commencing, equiv. to *ingred-,* s. of *ingredī* to go or step into, commence (see IN-[2], GRADIENT) + *-tus* suffix of v. action, with *-dt-* > *-ss-*] **—in·gres·sion** (in gresh′ən), *n.*

in·gres·sive (in gres′iv), *adj.* **1.** of, pertaining to, or involving ingress. **2.** *Phonet.* (of a speech sound) produced with air being taken into the mouth, as some clicks (opposed to *egressive*). [INGRESS + -IVE] **—in·gres′sive·ly,** *adv.* **—in·gres′sive·ness,** *n.*

In·grid (ing′grid), *n.* a female given name.

in-group (in′grōōp′), *n.* **1.** a narrow exclusive group; clique. **2.** *Sociol.* a group of people sharing similar interests and attitudes, producing feelings of solidarity, community, and exclusivity. Cf. **out-group.** Also, **in′group′.** [1905–10; IN-[1] + GROUP]

in·grow·ing (in′grō′ing), *adj.* **1.** growing into the flesh: *an ingrowing nail.* **2.** growing within or inward. [1865–70; IN-[1] + GROWING]

in·grown (in′grōn′), *adj.* **1.** having grown into the flesh: *an ingrown toenail.* **2.** grown within or inward. [1660–70; IN-[1] + GROWN]

in·growth (in′grōth′), *n.* **1.** growth inward. **2.** something formed by growth inward. [1865–70; IN-[1] + GROWTH]

in·gui·nal (ing′gwə nl), *adj.* of, pertaining to, or situated in the groin. [1675–85; < L *inguinālis* of the groin, equiv. to *inguin-* (s. of *inguen*) swelling in the groin, groin (c. Gk *adḗn* gland; cf. ADENOID) + *-ālis* -AL[1]]

in′guinal her′nia, *Pathol.* a common type of hernia in which a loop of the intestine protrudes directly through a weak area of the abdominal wall in the groin region.

in·gulf (in gulf′), *v.t.* engulf.

in·gur·gi·tate (in gûr′ji tāt′), *v.,* **-tat·ed, -tat·ing.** **—***v.t.* **1.** to swallow greedily or in great quantity, as food. **2.** to engulf; swallow up: *The floodwaters ingurgitated trees and houses.* **—***v.i.* **3.** to drink or eat greedily; guzzle; swill. [1560–70; < L *ingurgitātus* ptp. of *ingurgitāre* to fill, flood, drench with a stream of liquid, equiv. to *in-* IN-[2] + *gurgit-* (s. of *gurges*) whirlpool, flood + *-ātus* -ATE[1]] **—in·gur′gi·ta′tion,** *n.*

In·gush (in gōōsh′), *n., pl.* **-gush·es,** (*esp. collectively*) **-gush** for 1. **1.** a member of a Sunni Muslim people living mainly in the Soviet Union, closely related to the Chechen. **2.** the Caucasian language of the Ingush.

Ing·ve·on·ic (ing′vē on′ik), *adj.* of or pertaining to Old English, Old Frisian, and Old Saxon, taken collectively. Also, **Ing′vae·on′ic, Ing·wae·on·ic, Ing·we·on·ic** (ing′wē on′ik). [1930–35; after L *Ingvaeōnēs* (Pliny), *Ingaevōnēs* (Tacitus) a Germanic tribal group, taken to mean "adherents of **Ingwaz,*" prob. a god; cf. OE *Ing* name of a rune, ON *Ing-* element in personal names; see -IC]

INH, *Pharm.* See **isonicotinic acid hydrazide.**

in•hab•it (in hab′it), *v.t.* **1.** to live or dwell in (a place), as people or animals: *Small animals inhabited the woods.* **2.** to exist or be situated within; dwell in: *Weird notions inhabit his mind.* —*v.i.* **3.** *Archaic.* to live or dwell, as in a place. [1325–75; < L *inhabitāre,* equiv. to *in-* IN-[2] + *habitāre* to dwell (see HABIT[2]); r. ME *enhabiten* < MF *enhabiter* < L as above] —**in•hab′it•a•ble,** *adj.* —**in•hab′it•a•bil′i•ty,** *n.* —**in•hab′i•ta′tion,** *n.*
—**Syn. 1, 2.** reside, occupy, tenant, populate.

in•hab•it•an•cy (in hab′i tn sē), *n., pl.* **-cies. 1.** place of residence; habitation. **2.** residency; occupancy. Also, **in•hab′it•ance.** [1675–85; INHABIT(ANT) + -ANCY]

in•hab•it•ant (in hab′i tənt), *n.* a person or animal that inhabits a place, esp. as a permanent resident. [1400–50; late ME < L *inhabitant-* (s. of *inhabitāns*) dwelling in. See INHABIT, -ANT]
—**Syn.** dweller, denizen.

in•hab•it•ed (in hab′i tid), *adj.* having inhabitants; occupied; lived in or on: *an inhabited island.* [1490–1500; INHABIT + -ED[2]] —**in•hab′it•ed•ness,** *n.*

in•hab•it•er (in hab′i tər), *n. Archaic.* inhabitant. [1400–50; late ME; see INHABIT, -ER[1]]

in•hal•ant (in hā′lənt), *n.* **1.** a medicine, allergen, or other substance that is inhaled. **2.** any volatile substance, as nitrous oxide, butyl nitrite, toluene, gasoline, or paint thinner, capable of being inhaled, sometimes abused for its intoxicating effect. **3.** inhaler. —*adj.* **4.** used for inhaling. [1815–25; INHALE + -ANT]

in•ha•la•tion (in′hə lā′shən), *n.* **1.** an act or instance of inhaling. **2.** an inhalant. [1615–25; INHALE + -ATION]

in•ha•la•tor (in′hə lā′tər), *n.* an apparatus designed to mix carbon dioxide and oxygen, esp. for use in artificial respiration. [1925–30, *Amer.*; INHALE + -ATOR]

in•hale (in hāl′), *v.,* **-haled, -hal•ing.** —*v.t.* **1.** to breathe in; draw in by breathing: *to inhale the polluted air.* —*v.i.* **2.** to breathe in, esp. the smoke of cigarettes, cigars, etc.: *Do you inhale when you smoke?* [1715–25; IN-[2] + (EX)HALE]

in•hal•er (in hā′lər), *n.* **1.** an apparatus or device used in inhaling medicinal vapors, anesthetics, etc. **2.** a respirator. **3.** a person who inhales. [1770–80; INHALE + -ER[1]]

In•ham•ba•ne (in′yəm bä′nə), *n.* a seaport in SE Mozambique. 70,000.

in•har•mon•ic (in′här mon′ik), *adj.* not harmonic; dissonant. [1820–30; IN-[3] + HARMONIC] —**in•har•mo•ny** (in här′mə nē), *n.*

in•har•mo•ni•ous (in′här mō′nē əs), *adj.* **1.** not harmonious; discordant; unmelodious. **2.** not congenial or compatible; discordant; disagreeing: *It was unpleasant to spend an evening with such an inharmonious group.* [1705–15; IN-[3] + HARMONIOUS] —**in′har•mo′ni•ous•ly,** *adv.* —**in′har•mo′ni•ous•ness,** *n.*

in•haul (in′hôl′), *n. Naut.* any of various lines for hauling a sail, spar, etc., inward or inboard in order to stow it after use. Also, **in′haul′er.** [1855–60; IN-[1] + HAUL]

inher., inheritance.

in•here (in hēr′), *v.i.,* **-hered, -her•ing.** to exist permanently and inseparably in, as a quality, attribute, or element; belong intrinsically; be inherent: *the advantages that inhere in a democratic system.* [1580–90; < L *inhaerēre,* equiv. to *in-* IN-[2] + *haerēre* to stick]

in•her•ence (in hēr′əns, -her′-), *n.* **1.** the state or fact of inhering or being inherent. **2.** *Philos.* the relation of an attribute to its subject. [1570–80; < ML *inhaerentia.* See INHERENT, -ENCE]

in•her•en•cy (in hēr′ən sē, -her′-), *n., pl.* **-cies** for 2. **1.** inherence. **2.** something inherent. [1595–1605; < ML *inhaerentia.* See INHERENT, -ENCY]

in•her•ent (in hēr′ənt, -her′-), *adj.* **1.** existing in someone or something as a permanent and inseparable element, quality, or attribute: *an inherent distrust of strangers.* **2.** *Gram.* standing before a noun. **3.** inhering; infixed. [1570–80; < L *inhaerent-* (s. of *inhaerēns*), prp. of *inhaerēre* to INHERE; see -ENT] —**in•her′ent•ly,** *adv.*
—**Syn. 1.** innate, native, inbred, ingrained. See **essential.**

in•her•it (in her′it), *v.t.* **1.** to take or receive (property, a right, a title, etc.) by succession or will, as an heir: *to inherit the family business.* **2.** to receive as if by succession from predecessors: *the problems the new government inherited from its predecessors.* **3.** to receive (a genetic character) by the transmission of hereditary factors. **4.** to succeed (a person) as heir. **5.** to receive as one's portion; come into possession of: *to inherit his brother's old clothes.* —*v.i.* **6.** to take or receive property or the like by virtue of being heir to it. **7.** to receive qualities, powers, duties, etc., as by inheritance (fol. by *from*). **8.** to have succession as heir. [1275–1325; ME *en(h)erit(i)en* < MF *enheriter* < LL *inhērēditāre* to make heir. See IN-[3], HEREDITARY]

in•her•it•a•ble (in her′i tə bəl), *adj.* **1.** capable of being inherited. **2.** capable of inheriting; qualified to inherit. [1375–1425; late ME < AF; see IN-[2], HERITABLE] —**in•her′it•a•bil′i•ty, in•her′it•a•ble•ness,** *n.* —**in•her′it•a•bly,** *adv.*

in•her•it•ance (in her′i təns), *n.* **1.** something that is or may be inherited; property passing at the owner's death to the heir or those entitled to succeed; legacy. **2.** the genetic characters transmitted from parent to offspring, taken collectively. **3.** something, as a quality, characteristic, or other immaterial possession, received from progenitors or predecessors as if by succession: *an inheritance of family pride.* **4.** the act or fact of inheriting by succession, as if by succession, or genetically: *to receive property by inheritance.* **5.** portion; birthright; heritage: *Absolute rule was considered the inheritance of kings.* **6.** *Obs.* right of possession; ownership. [1375–1425; ME *enheritaunce* < AF. See INHERIT, -ANCE]
—**Syn. 1.** patrimony; bequest. INHERITANCE, HERITAGE denote something inherited. INHERITANCE is the common term for property or any possession that comes to an heir: *He received the farm as an inheritance from his parents.* HERITAGE indicates something that is bequeathed to a subsequent generation by an individual or by society: *our cultural heritage from Greece and Rome.*

inher′itance tax′, a tax levied on the right of an heir to receive a decedent's property, the rate being a percentage of the value of the property. Also called **death tax;** *Brit.,* **death duty.** Cf. **estate tax.** [1835–45]

in•her•i•tor (in her′i tər), *n.* a person who inherits; heir. [1400–50; late ME *enheritour, -er.* See INHERIT, -OR[2]]

in•her•i•trix (in her′i triks), *n., pl.* **in•her•i•tri•ces** (in her′i trī′sēz). *Law* a woman who inherits; heiress. Also, **in•her•i•tress** (in her′i tris). [1475–85; INHERI(TOR) + -TRIX]
—**Usage.** See **-trix, -ess.**

in•he•sion (in hē′zhən), *n.* the state or fact of inhering; inherence. [1625–35; < LL *inhaesiōn-* (s. of *inhaesiō*), equiv. to L *inhaes(us)* ptp. of *inhaerēre* to INHERE + *-iōn-* -ION]

in. Hg, *Meteorol.* inch of mercury.

in•hib•in (in hib′in), *Biochem.* a hormone, found in semen, that acts on the pituitary gland to decrease FSH. [1980–85; INHIB(IT) + -IN[2]]

in•hib•it (in hib′it), *v.t.* **1.** to restrain, hinder, arrest, or check (an action, impulse, etc.). **2.** to prohibit; forbid. **3.** *Psychol.* to consciously or unconsciously suppress or restrain (psychologically or sociologically unacceptable behavior). **4.** *Chem.* to decrease the rate of action of or stop (a chemical reaction). [1425–75; late ME *inhibiten* < L *inhibitus,* ptp. of *inhibēre* to restrain, equiv. to *in-* IN-[2] + *-hibēre,* comb. form of *habēre* to have, hold] —**in•hib′it•a•ble,** *adj.* —**in•hib•i•to•ry** (in hib′i tôr′ē, -tōr′ē), **in•hib′i•tive,** *adj.*
—**Syn. 1.** repress, discourage, obstruct. **2.** interdict. See **forbid.**

in•hib•it•ed (in hib′i tid), *adj.* **1.** overly restrained. **2.** *Psychol.* suffering from inhibition. [1960–65; INHIBIT + ED[2]]

in•hi•bi•tion (in′i bish′ən, in′hi-), *n.* **1.** the act of inhibiting. **2.** the state of being inhibited. **3.** something that inhibits; constraint. **4.** *Psychol.* **a.** the blocking or holding back of one psychological process by another. **b.** inappropriate conscious or unconscious restraint or suppression of behavior, as sexual behavior, often due to guilt or fear produced by past punishment, or sometimes considered a dispositional trait. **5.** *Physiol.* **a.** a restraining, arresting, or checking of the action of an organ or cell. **b.** the reduction of a reflex or other activity as the result of an antagonistic stimulation. **c.** a state created at synapses making them less excitable by other sources of stimulation. **6.** *Chem.* a stoppage or decrease in the rate of action of a chemical reaction. **7.** *Eng. Eccles. Law.* an order, esp. from a bishop, suspending a priest or an incumbent from the performance of duties. [1350–1400; ME *inhibicio(u)n* < L *inhibitiōn-* (s. of *inhibitiō*). See INHIBIT, -ION]

in•hib•i•tor (in hib′i tər), *n.* **1.** a person or thing that inhibits. **2.** *Chem.* a substance that decreases the rate of or stops completely a chemical reaction. **3.** any impurity in a mineral that prevents luminescence. Cf. **activator** (def. 3). **4.** *Rocketry.* an inert antioxidant used with solid propellants to inhibit burning on certain surfaces. Also, **in•hib′it•er.** [1865–70; INHIBIT + -OR[2]]

in hoc sig•no vin•ces (in hōk′ sig′nō wing′kās; *Eng.* in hok′ sig′nō vin′sēz), *Latin.* in this sign shalt thou conquer: motto used by Constantine the Great, from his vision, before battle, of a cross bearing these words.

in•hold•ing (in′hōl′ding), *n.* a tract of land under private ownership within a national park. [IN-[1] + HOLDING] —**in′hold′er,** *n.*

in•ho•mo•ge•ne•i•ty (in hō′mə jə nē′i tē, -hom′ə-), *n.* **1.** lack of homogeneity. **2.** something that is not homogeneous. [1895–1900; IN-[3] + HOMOGENEITY] —**in•ho•mo•ge•ne•ous** (in′hō mə jē′nē əs, -hom ə-), *adj.* —**in′•ho•mo•ge′ne•ous•ly,** *adv.*

in•hos•pi•ta•ble (in hos′pi tə bəl, in′ho spit′ə bəl), *adj.* **1.** not inclined to, or characterized by, hospitality, as persons or actions; unfriendly. **2.** (of a region, climate, etc.) not offering shelter, favorable conditions, etc.; barren: *an inhospitable rocky coast.* [1560–70; < MF < ML *inhospitābilis.* See IN-[3], HOSPITABLE] —**in•hos′pi•ta•ble•ness,** *n.* —**in•hos′pi•ta•bly,** *adv.*

in•hos•pi•tal•i•ty (in′hos pi tal′i tē, in hos′-), *n.* lack of hospitality; inhospitable attitude toward or treatment of visitors, guests, etc. [1560–70; < L *inhospitālitās.* See IN-[3], HOSPITALITY]

in-house (*adj.* in′hous′; *adv.* in′hous′), *adj., adv.* within, conducted within, or utilizing an organization's own staff or resources rather than external or nonstaff facilities: *in-house research; Was the ad created in-house or by an outside advertising agency?* [1955–60]

in•hu•man (in hyōō′mən *or, often,* -yōō′-), *adj.* **1.** lacking qualities of sympathy, pity, warmth, compassion, or the like; cruel; brutal: *an inhuman master.* **2.** not suited for human beings. **3.** not human. [1475–85; < L *inhūmānus;* r. late ME *inhumain* < MF < L. See IN-[3], HUMAN] —**in•hu′man•ly,** *adv.* —**in•hu′man•ness,** *n.*
—**Syn. 1.** unfeeling, unsympathetic, cold, callous, hard, savage, brutish.

in•hu•mane (in′hyōō mān′ *or, often,* -yōō-), *adj.* not humane; lacking humanity, kindness, compassion, etc. [1590–1600; var. of INHUMAN; see IN-[3], HUMANE] —**in′•hu•mane′ly,** *adv.*

in•hu•man•i•ty (in′hyōō man′i tē *or, often,* -yōō-), *n., pl.* **-ties** for 2. **1.** the state or quality of being inhuman or inhumane; cruelty. **2.** an inhuman or inhumane act. [1470–80; earlier *inhumanite* < L *inhūmānitās.* See INHUMAN, -ITY]
—**Syn. 1.** savagery, brutality, brutishness.

in•hume (in hyōōm′ *or, often,* -yōōm′), *v.t.,* **-humed, -hum•ing.** to bury; inter. [1610–20; < ML *inhumāre,* equiv. to L *in-* IN-[2] + *-humāre,* deriv. of *humus* earth (see HUMUS); cf. EXHUME] —**in′hu•ma′tion,** *n.* —**in•hum′er,** *n.*

in•im•i•cal (i nim′i kəl), *adj.* **1.** adverse in tendency or effect; unfavorable; harmful: *a climate inimical to health.* **2.** unfriendly; hostile: *a cold, inimical gaze.* Also, **in•im′i•ca•ble.** [1635–45; < L *inimic(us)* unfriendly, hostile (see ENEMY) + -AL[1]] —**in•im′i•cal•ly,** *adv.* —**in•im′i•cal•ness, in•im′i•cal′i•ty,** *n.*
—**Syn. 1.** noxious. **2.** antagonistic. See **hostile.**
—**Ant. 2.** friendly.

in•im•i•ta•ble (i nim′i tə bəl), *adj.* incapable of being imitated or copied; surpassing imitation; matchless. [1525–35; < L *inimitābilis.* See IN-[3], IMITABLE] —**in•im′i•ta•bil′i•ty, in•im′i•ta•ble•ness,** *n.* —**in•im′i•ta•bly,** *adv.*

in•i•on (in′ē ən), *n. Craniom.* a point at the external occipital protuberance of the skull. [1805–15; < NL < Gk *iníon* nape of the neck, equiv. to *in-* (s. of *ís*) fiber, sinew + *-ion* dim. suffix]

in•iq•ui•tous (i nik′wi təs), *adj.* characterized by injustice or wickedness; wicked; sinful. [1720–30; INIQUIT(Y) + -OUS] —**in•iq′ui•tous•ly,** *adv.* —**in•iq′ui•tous•ness,** *n.*
—**Syn.** flagitious, nefarious, perverse, evil, base, unjust, wrong. —**Ant.** righteous.

in•iq•ui•ty (i nik′wi tē), *n., pl.* **-ties. 1.** gross injustice or wickedness. **2.** a violation of right or duty; wicked act; sin. [1300–50; ME < L *inīquitās* unevenness, unfairness, equiv. to *inīqu(us)* uneven, unfair (*in-* IN-[3] + *-iquus,* comb. form of *aequus* even, EQUAL) + *-itās* -ITY]
—**Syn. 1.** evildoing, infamy, depravity, knavery.

init., initial.

in•i•tial (i nish′əl), *adj., n., v.,* **-tialed, -tial•ing** or (*esp. Brit.*) **-tialled, -tial•ling.** —*adj.* **1.** of, pertaining to, or occurring at the beginning; first: *the initial step in a process.* **2.** *Phonet.* occurring at the beginning of a word or syllable, as the (k) sound of *kite, chasm,* or *quay.* —*n.* **3.** an initial letter, as of a word. **4.** the first letter of a proper name. **5.** a letter of extra size or an ornamental character used at the beginning of a chapter or other division of a book, manuscript, or the like. —*v.t.* **6.** to mark or sign with an initial or the initials of one's name, esp. as a token of preliminary or informal approval. [1520–30; < L *initiālis,* equiv. to *initi(um)* beginning (*init-,* n. deriv. of *inire* to enter, begin; *in-* IN-[2] + *īre* to go; cf. COMES) + *-ium* -IUM) + *-alis* -AL[1]] —**in•i′tial•er,** *n.* —**in•i′tial•ly,** *adv.*

ini′tial code′. See under **zip code.**

in•i•tial•ism (i nish′ə liz′əm), *n.* **1.** a name or term formed from the initial letters of a group of words and pronounced as a separate word, as *NATO* for *North Atlantic Treaty Organization;* an acronym. **2.** a set of initials representing a name, organization, or the like, with each letter pronounced separately, as *FBI* for *Federal Bureau of Investigation.* **3.** the practice of using initials or forming words from initials. [1895–1900; INITIAL + -ISM]

in•i•tial•ize (i nish′ə līz′), *v.t.,* **-ized, -iz•ing.** *Computers.* **1.** to set (variables, counters, switches, etc.) to their starting values at the beginning of a program or subprogram. **2.** to clear (internal memory, a disk, etc.) of previous data in preparation for use. Also, *esp. Brit.,* **in•i′•tial•ise′.** [1955–60; INITIAL + -IZE]

ini′tial rhyme′. See **beginning rhyme.** [1830–40]

Ini′tial Teach′ing Al′phabet, a writing system based on an expanded English alphabet, consisting of 43 characters representing different phonemes of spoken English, used for teaching beginners to read. *Abbr.:* I.T.A., i.t.a. Also called **augmented roman.**

in•i•ti•ate (*v.* i nish′ē āt′; *adj., n.* i nish′ē it, -āt′), *v.,* **-at•ed, -at•ing,** *adj., n.* —*v.t.* **1.** to begin, set going, or originate: *to initiate major social reforms.* **2.** to introduce into the knowledge of some art or subject. **3.** to admit or accept with formal rites into an organization or group, secret knowledge, adult society, etc. **4.** to propose (a measure) by initiative procedure: *to initiate a constitutional amendment.* —*adj.* **5.** initiated; begun. **6.** admitted into an organizaton or group, secret knowledge, etc. **7.** introduced to the knowledge of a subject. —*n.* **8.** a person who has been initiated. [1595–1605; < L *initiātus* ptp. of *initiāre,* equiv. to *initi(um)* (see INITIAL) + *-ātus* -ATE[1]] —**in•i′ti•a′tor,** *n.*
—**Syn. 1.** commence; introduce, inaugurate, open. See **begin. 2.** teach, instruct, indoctrinate, train. —**Ant. 1.** conclude.

in•i•ti•a•tion (i nish′ē ā′shən), *n.* **1.** formal admission or acceptance into an organization or club, adult status in one's community or society, etc. **2.** the ceremonies or rites of admission. Cf. **rite of passage. 3.** the act of initiating. **4.** the fact of being initiated. [1575–85; < L *initiātiōn-* (s. of *initiātiō*). See INITIATE, -ION]

in•i•ti•a•tive (i nish′ē ə tiv, i nish′ə-), *n.* **1.** an introductory act or step; leading action: *to take the initiative in making friends.* **2.** readiness and ability in initiating action; enterprise: *to lack initiative.* **3.** one's personal, responsible decision: *to act on one's own initiative.* **4.** *Govt.* **a.** a procedure by which a specified number of voters may propose a statute, constitutional amendment, or ordinance, and compel a popular vote on its adoption. Cf. **referendum** (def. 1). **b.** the general right or ability to present a new bill or measure, as in a legislature. —*adj.* **5.** of or pertaining to initiation; serving to initiate: *Initi-*

ative steps were taken to stop manufacture of the drug. [1785–95; INITIATE + -IVE] —**in·i′ti·a·tive·ly,** *adv.*
—**Syn. 2.** leadership, forcefulness, dynamism.

in·i·ti·a·to·ry (i nish′ē ə tôr′ē, -tōr′ē), *adj.* **1.** introductory; initial: *an initiatory step toward a treaty.* **2.** serving to initiate or admit into a society, club, etc. [1605–15; INITIATE + -ORY[1]] —**in·i·ti·a·to·ri·ly** (i nish′ē ə tôr′ə lē, -tōr′-; i nish′ē ə tôr′ə lē, -tōr′-), *adv.*

in·ject (in jekt′), *v.t.* **1.** to force (a fluid) into a passage, cavity, or tissue: *to inject a medicine into the veins.* **2.** to introduce (something new or different): *to inject humor into a situation.* **3.** to introduce arbitrarily or inappropriately; intrude. **4.** to interject (a remark, suggestion, etc.), as into conversation. [1590–1600; < L *injectus* ptp. of *in(j)icere* to throw in, equiv. to *in-* IN-[2] + *-jec-* (comb. form of *jac-* throw) + *-tus* ptp. suffix]

inject., (in prescriptions) an injection. [< L *injectiō*]

in·ject·a·ble (in jek′tə bəl), *adj.* **1.** capable of being injected. —*n.* **2.** a pharmaceutical preparation that can be injected. [1965–70; INJECT + -ABLE]

in·jec·tant (in jek′tənt), *n.* a substance injected through the skin, as bee-sting venom or penicillin administered by injection, that causes an allergic reaction. [1945–50; INJECT + -ANT]

in·jec·tion (in jek′shən), *n.* **1.** the act of injecting. **2.** something that is injected. **3.** a liquid injected into the body, esp. for medicinal purposes, as a hypodermic or an enema. **4.** state of being hyperemic or bloodshot. **5.** *Math.* a one-to-one function. **6.** Also called **insertion.** *Aerospace.* the process of putting a spacecraft into orbit or some other desired trajectory. [1535–45; < L *injectiōn-* (s. of *injectiō*). See INJECT, -ION]

injec′tion mold′ing, a method of forming thermoplastic or thermoset plastic, metal, or ceramic material by injection into a closed mold. [1935–40]

in·jec·tor (in jek′tər), *n.* **1.** a person or thing that injects. **2.** *Mach.* **a.** a device for injecting feedwater into a boiler against high pressure by means of a jet of steam. **b.** Also called **fuel injector.** a mechanism consisting of a pump, valves, and nozzles for spraying fuel into the cylinders of an internal-combustion engine. [1735–45; INJECT + -OR[2]]

in-joke (in′jōk′), *n.* a joke that can be understood or appreciated only by the members of a limited group of people. [1960–65]

in·ju·di·cious (in′jo͞o dish′əs), *adj.* not judicious; showing lack of judgment; unwise; imprudent; indiscreet: *an injudicious decision.* [1640–50; IN-[3] + JUDICIOUS] —**in′ju·di′cious·ly,** *adv.* —**in′ju·di′cious·ness,** *n.*

In·jun (in′jən), *n. Often Offensive.* an American Indian. [1805–15; var. of INDIAN, with assibilated *d*; cf. CAJUN]

in·junc·tion (in jungk′shən) *n.* **1.** *Law.* a judicial process or order requiring the person or persons to whom it is directed to do a particular act or to refrain from doing a particular act. **2.** an act or instance of enjoining. **3.** a command; order; admonition. [1520–30; < LL *injunctiōn-* (s. of *injunctiō*), equiv. to L *injunct(us)* (ptp. of *injungere* to join to; see ENJOIN) + *-iōn-* -ION] —**in·junc′tive,** *adj.* —**in·junc′tive·ly,** *adv.*

in·jure (in′jər), *v.t.,* **-jured, -jur·ing. 1.** to do or cause harm of any kind to; damage; hurt; impair: *to injure one's hand.* **2.** to do wrong or injustice to. **3.** to wound or offend: *to injure a friend's feelings.* [1575–85; back formation from INJURY (n.); r. *injury* (v.)] —**in′jur·a·ble,** *adj.* —**in′jur·er,** *n.*
—**Syn. 1.** spoil, ruin, break, mar. INJURE, IMPAIR mean to harm or damage something. INJURE is a general term referring to any kind or degree of damage: *to injure one's spine; to injure one's reputation.* To IMPAIR is to make imperfect in any way, often with a suggestion of progressive deterioration and of permanency in the result: *One's health is impaired by overwork.* **2.** maltreat, abuse. —**Ant. 1.** benefit.

in·ju·ri·ous (in jo͝or′ē əs), *adj.* **1.** harmful, hurtful, or detrimental, as in effect: *injurious eating habits.* **2.** doing or involving injury or wrong, as to another: *injurious behavior.* **3.** insulting; abusive; defamatory; offensive: *an injurious statement.* [1375–1425; late ME < L *injūrius* or *injūriōsus.* See INJURY, -OUS] —**in·ju′ri·ous·ly,** *adv.* —**in·ju′ri·ous·ness,** *n.*
—**Syn. 1.** damaging, deleterious, pernicious; baneful, destructive, ruinous. **2.** unjust, wrongful, prejudicial, inequitable. **3.** derogatory, slanderous, libelous. —**Ant. 1.** beneficial. **3.** complimentary.

in·ju·ry (in′jə rē), *n., pl.* **-ju·ries. 1.** harm or damage that is done or sustained: *to escape without injury.* **2.** a particular form or instance of harm: *an injury to one's shoulder; an injury to one's pride.* **3.** wrong or injustice done or suffered. **4.** *Law.* any wrong or violation of the rights, property, reputation, etc., of another for which legal action to recover damages may be made. **5.** *Obs.* injurious speech; calumny. [1350–1400; ME *injurie* < L *injūria* unlawful conduct, injustice, equiv. to *in-* IN-[3] + *jūr-,* s. of *jūs* right, law (see JUS, JUST[1]) + *-ia* -IA]
—**Syn. 1.** destruction, ruin, impairment, mischief. **1–3.** INJURY, HURT, WOUND refer to impairments or wrongs. INJURY, originally denoting a wrong done or suffered, is hence used for any kind of evil, impairment, or loss, caused or sustained: *physical injury; injury to one's reputation.* HURT suggests esp. physical injury, often bodily injury attended with pain: *a bad hurt from a fall.* A WOUND is usually a physical hurt caused by cutting, shooting, etc., or an emotional hurt: *a serious wound in the shoulder; to inflict a wound by betraying someone's trust.* —**Ant. 1.** benefit.

in·jus·tice (in jus′tis), *n.* **1.** the quality or fact of being unjust; inequity. **2.** violation of the rights of others; unjust or unfair action or treatment. **3.** an unjust or unfair act; wrong. [1350–1400; ME < MF < L *injūstitia.* See IN-[3], JUSTICE]

ink (ingk), *n.* **1.** a fluid or viscous substance used for writing or printing. **2.** a dark, protective fluid ejected by the cuttlefish and other cephalopods. —*v.t.* **3.** to mark, stain, cover, or smear with ink: *to ink one's clothes.* **4.** *Slang.* to sign one's name to (an official document): *We expect to ink the contract tomorrow.* [1200–50; ME *inke, enke* < OF *enque* < LL *encautum,* var. of *encaustum* < Gk *énkauston* purple ink, n. use of neut. of *énkaustos* burnt in. See ENCAUSTIC] —**ink′er,** *n.* —**ink′less,** *adj.* —**ink′like′,** *adj.*

ink′ ball′, *Print.* one of a pair of heavy pads of horsehair and cotton covered with sheepskin or buckskin and equipped with a handle, used before the invention of the ink roller for dabbing ink on type for printing. [1810–20]

ink·ber·ry (ingk′ber′ē, -bə rē), *n., pl.* **-ries. 1.** Also called **gallberry.** a shrub, *Ilex glabra,* having leathery, evergreen leaves and black berries. **2.** the pokeweed. **3.** the berry of either plant. [1755–65, *Amer.*; INK + BERRY]

ink′blot test′ (ingk′blot′), any of various psychological tests in which varied patterns formed by blotted ink are interpreted by the subject. Cf. **Rorschach test.** [1925–30; INK + BLOT[1]]

Ink·er·man (ing′kər män′), *n.* a town in S Crimea, in S Ukraine: Russian defeat by the English and French 1854.

ink′ foun′tain, the part of a printing press that stores ink and feeds it to the rollers. [1870–75]

ink·horn (ingk′hôrn′), *n.* a small container of horn or other material, formerly used to hold writing ink. [1350–1400; ME; see INK, HORN]

ink′horn term′, an obscure, affectedly or ostentatiously erudite borrowing from another language, esp. Latin or Greek. [1535–45]

in-kind (in′kīnd′), *adj.* **1.** paid or given in goods, commodities, or services instead of money: *in-kind welfare programs.* **2.** paying or returning something of the same kind as that received or offered.

ink′-jet print′ing (ingk′jet′), a high-speed typing or printing process in which charged droplets of ink issuing from nozzles are directed onto paper under computer control. Also called **jet printing.** [1975–80] —**ink′-jet print′er.**

in·kle (ing′kəl), *n.* **1.** a linen tape used for trimmings. **2.** the linen thread or yarn from which this tape is made. [1535–45; orig. uncert.]

in′kle loom′, a simple narrow loom used for weaving long decorative tapes and bands. [1840–50]

ink·ling (ingk′ling), *n.* **1.** a slight suggestion or indication; hint; intimation: *They hadn't given us an inkling of what was going to happen.* **2.** a vague idea or notion; slight understanding: *They didn't have an inkling of how the new invention worked.* [1505–15; obs. *inkle* to hint (ME *inklen*) + -ING[1]; akin to OE *inca* suspicion]

ink·stand (ingk′stand′), *n.* **1.** a small stand, usually on a desk, for holding ink, pens, etc. **2.** a small container for ink. [1765–75; INK + STAND]

Ink·ster (ingk′stər), *n.* a city in SE Michigan, near Detroit. 35,190.

ink·well (ingk′wel′), *n.* a small container for ink. Also called, *esp. Brit.,* **ink·pot** (ingk′pot′). [1870–75; INK + WELL[2]]

ink·wood (ingk′wo͝od′), *n.* a tropical tree, *Exothea paniculata,* of the soapberry family, yielding a hard, reddish-brown wood. [1885–90; INK + WOOD[1]]

ink·y (ing′kē), *adj.,* **ink·i·er, ink·i·est. 1.** black as ink: *inky shadows.* **2.** resembling ink: *The solution was an inky liquid.* **3.** stained with ink: *inky fingers.* **4.** of or pertaining to ink. **5.** consisting of or containing ink. **6.** written with ink. [1575–85; INK + -Y[1]] —**ink′i·ness,** *n.*

ink′y cap′, any mushroom of the genus *Coprinus,* esp. *C. atramentarius,* characterized by gills that disintegrate into blackish liquid after the spores mature. [1920–25]

in·lace (in lās′), *v.t.,* **-laced, -lac·ing.** enlace.

in·laid (in′lād′, in lād′), *adj.* **1.** set into the surface of something: *an inlaid design on a chest.* **2.** decorated or made with a design set into the surface: *an inlaid table.* [1590–1600; ptp. of INLAY]

in·land (*adj.* in′lənd; *adv., n.* in′land′, -lənd), *adj.* **1.** pertaining to or situated in the interior part of a country or region: *inland cities.* **2.** *Brit.* domestic or internal: *inland revenue.* —*adv.* **3.** in or toward the interior of a country. —*n.* **4.** the interior part of a country. [bef. 950; ME, OE; see IN-[1], LAND]

in′land bill′, a bill of exchange drawn and payable, actually or on its face, in the same jurisdiction, as in the same country or state. Cf. **foreign bill.** [1675–85]

in·land·er (in′lən dər), *n.* a person living inland. [1600–10; INLAND + -ER[1]]

in′land marine′ insur′ance, insurance chiefly covering risks to goods and means of transportation involved in the transporting of goods overland or by inland waterways. Cf. **ocean marine insurance.**

In′land Sea′, a sea in SW Japan, enclosed by the islands of Honshu, Shikoku, and Kyushu. 240 mi. (385 km) long.

in·laut (in′lout′), *n., pl.* **-lau·te** (-lou′tə), **-lauts.** *Ling.* **1.** medial position in a word, esp. as a conditioning environment in sound change. **2.** a sound in this position. Cf. **anlaut, auslaut.** [1890–95; < G, equiv. to *in-* IN-[1] + *Laut* sound]

in-law (in′lô′), *n.* a relative by marriage. [1890–95; back formation from MOTHER-IN-LAW, BROTHER-IN-LAW, etc.]

in·law (in lô′, in′lô′), *v.t. Law.* to restore (an outlaw) to the benefits and protection of the law. [bef. 1000; ME *inlawen,* OE *inlagian.* See IN-[1], LAW] —**in′law′ry,** *n.*

in·lay (*v.* in′lā′, in′lā′; *n.* in′lā′), *v.,* **-laid, -lay·ing,** *n.* —*v.t.* **1.** to decorate (an object) with layers of fine materials set in its surface: *to inlay a chest with lighter wood.* **2.** to insert or apply (layers of fine materials) in the surface of an object: *to inlay marble in a tabletop.* **3.** *Hort.* to place (a fitted scion) into a prepared stock, as in a method of grafting. —*n.* **4.** inlaid work. **5.** a layer of fine material inserted in something else, esp. for ornament. **6.** a design or decoration made by inlaying. **7.** *Dentistry.* a filling of metal, porcelain, or the like, that is first shaped to fit a cavity and then cemented into it. **8.** *Hort.* See **inlay graft. 9.** the act or process of inlaying. [1590–1600; IN-[1] + LAY[1]] —**in′lay′er,** *n.*

in′lay graft′, *Hort.* a graft in which the scion is matched into a place in the stock from which a piece of corresponding bark has been removed. Also called **inlay.**

in-lb, inch-pound.

in·let (*n.* in′let, -lit; *v.* in′let′, in let′), *n., v.,* **-let, -let·ting.** —*n.* **1.** an indentation of a shoreline, usually long and narrow; small bay or arm. **2.** a narrow passage between islands. **3.** a place of admission; entrance. **4.** something put in or inserted. —*v.t.* **5.** to put in; insert. [1250–1300; ME; see IN, LET[1]]

in·li·er (in′lī′ər), *n. Geol.* an outcrop of a formation completely surrounded by rocks of younger age. Cf. **outlier.** [1855–60; IN + (OUT)LIER]

in li·mi·ne (in lē′mi ne; *Eng.* in lim′ə nē), *Latin.* on the threshold; at the outset.

in-line (in′lin′, in′līn′), *adj.* (of an internal-combustion engine) having the cylinders ranged side by side in one or more rows along the crankshaft. [1925–30]

in·line (in′līn′), *n. Print.* an ornamented type with a line of white or of a contrasting color running just inside the edge and following the contour of each letter. [1920–25; IN + LINE[1]]

in′-line skate′ (in′līn′), a roller skate with typically four hard-rubber wheels in a straight line resembling the blade of an ice skate. [1985–90] —**in′-line skat′er.** —**in′-line skat′ing.**

in loc. cit., in the place cited. [< L *in locō citātō*]

in lo·co (in lō′kō), *Latin.* in place; in the proper place.

in lo·co pa·ren·tis (in lō′kō pä ren′tēs; *Eng.* in lō′kō pə ren′tis), *Latin.* in the place or role of a parent.

in·ly (in′lē), *adv.* **1.** inwardly. **2.** intimately; deeply. [bef. 900; ME *inliche,* OE *inlīce.* See IN, -LY]

in·mate (in′māt′), *n.* **1.** a person who is confined in a prison, hospital, etc. **2.** *Archaic.* a person who dwells with others in the same house. [1580–90; IN-[1] + MATE[1]]

in me·di·as res (in me′di äs′ res′; *Eng.* in mē′dē as′ rēz′, in mā′dē äs′ rās′), *Latin.* in the middle of things.

in mem., in memoriam.

in me·mo·ri·am (in mə môr′ē əm, -mōr′-), in memory (of); to the memory (of); as a memorial (to). [1840–50; < L]

in·mesh (in mesh′), *v.t.* enmesh.

in·mi·grant (in′mī′grənt), *n.* **1.** a person who in-migrates. —*adj.* **2.** entering from another part of one's country or home territory. [1940–45, *Amer.*]

in-mi·grate (in′mī′grāt), *v.i.,* **-grat·ed, -grat·ing.** to move or settle into a different part of one's country or home territory. [1940–45] —**in′-mi·gra′tion,** *n.*

in·most (in′mōst′ *or, esp. Brit.,* -məst), *adj.* **1.** situated farthest within: *the inmost recesses of the forest.* **2.** most intimate or secret: *one's inmost thoughts.* [bef. 900; ME (see IN-[1], -MOST); r. *inmest,* OE *innemest,* equiv. to *innewithin* + *-mest* -MOST]

inn (in), *n.* **1.** a commercial establishment that provides lodging, food, etc., for the public, esp. travelers; small hotel. **2.** a tavern. **3.** (*cap.*) *Brit.* **a.** any of several buildings in London formerly used as places of residence for students, esp. law students. Cf. **Inns of Court. b.** a legal society occupying such a building. [bef. 1000; ME, OE *in(n)* house; akin to ON *inni* (adv.) within, in the house] —**inn′less,** *adj.*
—**Syn. 1.** hostelry. See **hotel.**

Inn (in), *n.* a river in central Europe, flowing from S Switzerland through Austria and Germany into the Danube. 320 mi. (515 km) long.

inn·age (in′ij), *n.* **1.** the quantity of goods remaining in a container when received after shipment. Cf. **outage** (def. 4). **2.** *Aeron.* the amount of fuel remaining in the fuel tanks of an aircraft following a flight. Cf. **outage** (def. 5). [IN + -AGE]

in·nards (in′ərdz), *n.* (*used with a plural v.*) **1.** the internal parts of the body; entrails or viscera. **2.** the internal mechanism, parts, structure, etc., of something; the interior of something: *an engine's innards.* [1815–25; var. of *inwards,* n. use of INWARD]

in·nate (i nāt′, in′āt), *adj.* **1.** existing in one from birth; inborn; native: *innate musical talent.* **2.** inherent in the essential character of something: *an innate defect in the hypothesis.* **3.** originating in or arising from the intellect or the constitution of the mind, rather than learned through experience: *an innate knowledge of good and evil.* [1375–1425; late ME < L *innātus* inborn, ptp. of *innāscī* to be born, arise, equiv. to *in-* IN-[2] + *nāscī* to be born; cf. NASCENT, NATIVITY] —**in·nate′ly,** *adv.* —**in·nate′ness,** *n.*
—**Syn. 1.** natural, congenital. INNATE, INBORN, CONGENITAL, HEREDITARY describe qualities, characteristics, or possessions acquired before or at the time of birth. INNATE, of Latin origin, and INBORN, a native English word, share the literal basic sense "existing at the time of birth," and they are interchangeable in most contexts: *innate* (or *inborn*) *stodginess, agility, gracefulness.* CONGENITAL refers most often to characteristics acquired during fetal development, especially defects or undesirable conditions: *a congenital deformity; congenital blindness.* HEREDITARY describes qualities or things passed on from ancestors, either through the genes or by social or legal means: *Hemophilia is a hereditary condition; a hereditary title.*

innate′ness hypoth′esis, *Psycholinguistics.* the theory that humans are biologically equipped with a knowledge of certain universal elements of language structure that is brought into play in the course of native-language acquisition. Also called **nativism.**

in•ner (in′ər), *adj.* **1.** situated within or farther within; interior: *an inner door.* **2.** more intimate, private, or secret: *the inner workings of the organization:* **3.** of or pertaining to the mind or spirit; mental; spiritual: *the inner life.* **4.** not obvious; hidden or obscure: *an inner meaning.* [bef. 900; ME; OE *innera,* comp. based on the adv. *inne* within, inside; see INMOST, -ER[4]] **—in′ner•ly,** *adv., adj.* **—in′ner•ness,** *n.*

in′ner automor′phism, *Math.* an automorphism that maps an element *x* into an element of the form axa^{-1} where a^{-1} is the inverse of *a.* Cf. **outer automorphism.**

in′ner bar′, *Eng. Law.* a body of the King's Counsel or Queen's Counsel who sit and plead inside the dividing bar in the court, ranking above the junior counsel. Cf. **outer bar.**

in′ner bar′rister, *Eng. Law.* a barrister belonging to the inner bar. Cf. **outer barrister.**

in′ner cir′cle, a small, intimate, and often influential group of people. [1870–75]

in′ner cit′y, an older part of a city, densely populated and usually deteriorating, inhabited mainly by poor, often minority, groups. Cf. **central city.** [1960–65]

in•ner-di•rect•ed (in′ər di rek′tid, -dī-), *adj.* guided by internalized values rather than external pressures. Cf. **other-directed.** [1945–50] **—in′ner-di•rec′tion,** *n.*

in′ner ear′. See **internal ear.** [1920–25]

In′ner Heb′rides. See under **Hebrides.**

in′ner jib′, *Naut.* a headsail immediately forward of a forestaysail or fore-topmast staysail.

In′ner Light′, (in Quakerism) the light of Christ in the soul of every person, considered as a guiding force. Also called **Inner Word, Inward Light, Christ Within.** [1855–60]

in′ner man′, **1.** a person's spiritual or intellectual being. **2.** the stomach or appetite: *a hearty meal to satisfy the inner man.*

in′ner mis′sion, a movement, originating in the early 19th century within the evangelical churches of Germany and later spreading through Europe and America, that ministered chiefly to the material and spiritual needs of the poor and of social outcasts.

In′ner Mongo′lia, an administrative division in NE China, adjoining the Mongolian People's Republic. 8,500,000; 174,000 sq. mi. (450,660 sq. km). *Cap.:* Hohhot. Also called **Neimenggu, Nei Mongol.** Official name, **In′ner Mongo′lia Auton′omous Re′gion.**

in•ner•most (in′ər mōst′ or, *esp. Brit.,* -məst), *adj.* **1.** farthest inward; inmost. **2.** most intimate or secret: *one's innermost beliefs.* —*n.* **3.** the innermost part. [1375–1425; late ME; see INNER, -MOST]

in′ner plan′et, *Astron.* any of the four planets closest to the sun: Mercury, Venus, the earth, or Mars. Also called **terrestrial planet.** Cf. **outer planet.** [1950–55]

in′ner prod′uct, *Math.* **1.** Also called **dot product, scalar product.** the quantity obtained by multiplying the corresponding coordinates of each of two vectors and adding the products, equal to the product of the magnitudes of the vectors and the cosine of the angle between them. **2.** the integral of the product of two real-valued functions. **3.** the integral of the product of the first of two complex-valued functions and the conjugate of the second. **4.** a complex-valued function of two vectors taken in order, whose domain is a vector space. [1915–20]

in′ner sanc′tum, sanctum (def. 2).

in•ner•sole (in′ər sōl′), *n.* insole. [1890–95; INNER + SOLE[2]]

in•ner•spring (in′ər spring′), *adj.* having or characterized by a large number of enclosed coil springs within an overall padding: *innerspring construction.* [1925–30; INNER + SPRING]

In′ner Tem′ple, **1.** See under **Inns of Court** (def. 1). **2.** See under **temple**[1] (def. 10).

in′ner tube′, a doughnut-shaped, flexible rubber tube inflated inside a tire to bear the weight of a vehicle. Also called **tube.** [1890–95]

in•ner-tub•er (in′ər to͞o′bər, -tyo͞o′-), *n.* tuber[2] (def. 2).

in•ner-tub•ing (in′ər to͞o′bing, -tyo͞o′-), *n.* tubing (def. 4).

in•ner•vate (i nûr′vāt, in′ər vāt′), *v.t.,* **-vat•ed, -vat•ing.** **1.** to communicate nervous energy to; stimulate through nerves. **2.** to furnish with nerves; grow nerves into. [1865–70; IN-[2] + NERVE + -ATE[1]]

in•ner•va•tion (in′ər vā′shən), *n.* **1.** the act of innervating; state of being innervated. **2.** *Anat.* the distribution of nerves to a part. [1825–35; INNERVATE + -ION] **—in′ner•va′tion•al,** *adj.*

in•nerve (i nûrv′), *v.t.,* **-nerved, -nerv•ing.** to supply with nervous energy; invigorate; animate. [1820–30; IN-[2] + NERVE]

In′ner Word′. See **Inner Light.**

in-ness (in′nis), *n. Informal.* **1.** the state or quality of being fashionable: *the in-ness of his new wardrobe.* **2.** the state or quality of being part of a select or exclusive group: *her in-ness with the literary crowd.*

In•ness (in′is), *n.* **George,** 1825–94, and his son **George,** 1854–1926, U.S. painters.

inn•hold•er (in′hōl′dər), *n.* innkeeper. [1425–75; late ME; see INN, HOLDER]

in•nie (in′ē), *n. Informal.* **1.** a person who belongs to an in-group, esp. a fashionable or select one. **2.** a concave or nonprotruding navel. **3.** a person who has such a navel. [IN + -IE]

in•ning (in′ing), *n.* **1.** *Baseball.* a division of a game during which each team has an opportunity to score until three outs have been made against it. **2.** a similar opportunity to score in certain other games, as horseshoes. **3.** an opportunity for activity; a turn: *Now the opposition will have its inning.* **4. innings,** (*used with a singular v.*) **a.** *Cricket.* a unit of play in which each team has a turn at bat, the turn of a team ending after ten players are put out or when the team declares. **b.** land reclaimed, esp. from the sea. **5.** the act of reclaiming marshy or flooded land. **6.** enclosure, as of wasteland. **7.** the gathering in of crops. [bef. 900; ME *inninge,* OE *innung* a getting in, equiv. to *inn(ian)* to go in + *-ung* -ING[1]]

inn•keep•er (in′kē′pər), *n.* a person who owns or manages an inn or, sometimes, a hotel. [1540–50; INN + KEEPER]

in•no•cence (in′ə səns), *n.* **1.** the quality or state of being innocent; freedom from sin or moral wrong. **2.** freedom from legal or specific wrong; guiltlessness: *The prisoner proved his innocence.* **3.** simplicity; absence of guile or cunning; naiveté. **4.** lack of knowledge or understanding. **5.** harmlessness; innocuousness. **6.** chastity. **7.** an innocent person or thing. **8.** bluet (def. 1). **9.** See **blue-eyed Mary.** [1300–50; ME < L *innocentia.* See INNOCENT, -ENCE]

in•no•cen•cy (in′ə sən sē), *n., pl.* **-cies.** innocence (defs. 1–6). [1325–75; ME; var. of INNOCENCE; see -ENCY]

in•no•cent (in′ə sənt), *adj.* **1.** free from moral wrong; without sin; pure: *innocent children.* **2.** free from legal or specific wrong; guiltless: *innocent of the crime.* **3.** not involving evil intent or motive: *an innocent misrepresentation.* **4.** not causing physical or moral injury; harmless: *innocent fun.* **5.** devoid (usually fol. by *of*): *a law innocent of merit.* **6.** having or showing the simplicity or naiveté of an unworldly person; guileless; ingenuous. **7.** uninformed or unaware; ignorant. —*n.* **8.** an innocent person. **9.** a young child. **10.** a guileless person. **11.** a simpleton or idiot. **12.** Usually, **innocents.** (*used with a singular v.*) bluet (def. 1). [1150–1200; ME < L *innocent-* (s. of *innocēns*) harmless, equiv. to *in-* IN-[3] + *nocēns* prp. of *nocēre* to harm; see -ENT; cf. NOXIOUS] **—in′no•cent•ly,** *adv.*
—**Syn. 1.** sinless, virtuous; faultless, impeccable, spotless, immaculate. **2.** INNOCENT, BLAMELESS, GUILTLESS imply freedom from the responsibility of having done wrong. INNOCENT may imply having done no wrong at any time, and having not even a knowledge of evil: *an innocent victim.* BLAMELESS denotes freedom from blame, esp. moral blame: *a blameless life.* GUILTLESS denotes freedom from guilt or responsibility for wrongdoing, usually in a particular instance: *guiltless of a crime.* **6.** simple, naive, unsophisticated, artless. —**Ant. 1, 2.** guilty.

In•no•cent I (in′ə sənt), **Saint,** died A.D. 417, Italian ecclesiastic: pope 401–417.

Innocent II, (*Gregorio Papareschi*) died 1143, Italian ecclesiastic: pope 1130–43.

Innocent III, (*Giovanni Lotario de' Conti*) 1161?–1216, Italian ecclesiastic: pope 1198–1216.

Innocent IV, (*Sinbaldo de Fieschi*) c1180–1254, Italian ecclesiastic: pope 1243–54.

Innocent V, (*Pierre de Tarentaise*) c1225–76, French ecclesiastic: pope 1276.

Innocent VI, (*Étienne Aubert*) died 1362, French jurist and ecclesiastic: pope 1352–62.

Innocent VII, (*Cosimo de' Migliorati*) 1336–1406, Italian ecclesiastic: pope 1404–06.

Innocent VIII, (*Giovanni Battista Cibò*) 1432–92, Italian ecclesiastic: pope 1484–92.

Innocent IX, (*Giovanni Antonio Facchinetti*) 1519–91, Italian ecclesiastic: pope 1591.

Innocent X, (*Giambattista Pamfili*) 1574–1655, Italian ecclesiastic: pope 1644–55.

Innocent XI, (*Benedetto Odescalchi*) 1611–89, Italian ecclesiastic: pope 1676–89.

Innocent XII, (*Antonio Pignatelli*) 1615–1700, Italian ecclesiastic: pope 1691–1700.

Innocent XIII, (*Michelangelo Conti*) 1655–1724, Italian ecclesiastic: pope 1721–24.

In′nocents' Day′. See **Holy Innocents' Day.**

in•noc•u•ous (i nok′yo͞o əs), *adj.* **1.** not harmful or injurious; harmless: *an innocuous home remedy.* **2.** not likely to irritate or offend; inoffensive; *an innocuous remark.* **3.** not interesting, stimulating, or significant; pallid; insipid: *an innocuous novel.* [1590–1600; < L *innocuus.* See IN-[3], NOCUOUS] **—in•noc′u•ous•ly,** *adv.* **—in•noc′u•ous•ness, in•no•cu•i•ty** (in′ə kyo͞o′i tē), *n.*

in•nom•i•nate (i nom′ə nit), *adj.* having no name; nameless; anonymous. [1630–40; < LL *innōminātus* unnamed. See IN-[3], NOMINATE]

innom′inate ar′tery, *Anat.* See **brachiocephalic artery.** [1865–70]

innom′inate bone′, *Anat.* either of the two bones forming the sides of the pelvis, each consisting of three consolidated bones, the ilium, ischium, and pubis. See diag. under **pelvis.** [1700–10]

innom′inate vein′, *Anat.* See **brachiocephalic vein.** [1875–80]

in•nom•i•ne (in nom′ə nā′, -nē′, -nō′mə nā′), *n. Music.* any of various English polyphonic instrumental compositions of the 16th and 17th centuries using an antiphon for Trinity Sunday as a cantus firmus. [1630–40; < L phrase *in nōmine* in (the) name (of the Trinity or one of its members), a liturgical formula]

in•no•vate (in′ə vāt′), *v.,* **-vat•ed, -vat•ing.** —*v.i.* **1.** to introduce something new; make changes in anything established. —*v.t.* **2.** to introduce (something new) for or as if for the first time: *to innovate a computer operating system.* **3.** *Archaic.* to alter. [1540–50; < L *innovātus* ptp. of *innovāre* to renew, alter, equiv. to *in-* IN-[2] + *novātus* (*novā(re)* to renew, v. deriv. of *novus* NEW + *-tus* ptp. suffix)] **—in′no•va′tor,** *n.* **—in′no•va•to′ry,** *adj.*

in•no•va•tion (in′ə vā′shən), *n.* **1.** something new or different introduced: *numerous innovations in the high-school curriculum.* **2.** the act of innovating; introduction of new things or methods. [1540–50; < LL *innovātiōn-* (s. of *innovātiō*). See INNOVATE, -ION] **—in′no•va′tion•al,** *adj.*

in•no•va•tive (in′ə vā′tiv), *adj.* tending to innovate or characterized by innovation. [1600–10; INNOVATE + -IVE] **—in′no•va′tive•ly,** *adv.* **—in′no•va′tive•ness,** *n.*

in•nox•ious (i nok′shəs), *adj.* harmless; innocuous. [1615–25; < L *innoxius.* See IN-[3], NOXIOUS] **—in•nox′ious•ly,** *adv.* **—in•nox′ious•ness,** *n.*

Inns•bruck (inz′bro͝ok; *Ger.* ins′brʊ͝ok), *n.* a city in W Austria, on the Inn river. 116,100.

Inns′ of Court′, **1.** the four voluntary legal societies in England (**Lincoln's Inn,** the **Inner Temple,** the **Middle Temple,** and **Gray's Inn**) that have the exclusive privilege of calling candidates to the English bar after they have received such instruction and taken such examinations as the Inns provide. **2.** the buildings owned and used by the Inns.

in•nu•en•do (in′yo͞o en′dō), *n., pl.* **-dos, -does.** **1.** an indirect intimation about a person or thing, esp. of a disparaging or a derogatory nature. **2.** *Law.* **a.** a parenthetic explanation or specification in a pleading. **b.** (in an action for slander or libel) the explanation and elucidation of the words alleged to be defamatory. **c.** the word or expression thus explained. [1555–65; < L: a hint, lit., by signaling, abl. of *innuendum,* ger. of *innuere* to signal, equiv. to *in-* IN-[2] + *nuere* to nod]
—**Syn. 1.** insinuation, imputation.

In•nu•it (in′o͞o it, -yo͞o-), *n., pl.* **-its,** (*esp. collectively*) **-it.** Inuit.

in•nu•mer•a•ble (i no͞o′mər ə bəl, i nyo͞o′-), *adj.* **1.** very numerous. **2.** incapable of being counted; countless. Also, **in•nu′mer•ous.** [1300–50; ME < L *innumerābilis* countless, innumerable, equiv. to *in-* IN-[3] + *numerābilis* that can be counted or numbered (*numerā(re)* to count + *-bilis* -BLE)] **—in•nu′mer•a•ble•ness, in•nu′mer•a•bil′i•ty,** *n.* **—in•nu′mer•a•bly,** *adv.*
—**Syn. 1.** See **many. 2.** numberless.

in•nu•mer•ate (i no͞o′mər it, i nyo͞o′-), *adj.* **1.** unfamiliar with mathematical concepts and methods; unable to use mathematics; not numerate. —*n.* **2.** an innumerate person. [1959; IN-[3] + NUMERATE] **—in•nu′mer•a•cy,** *n.*

in•nu•tri•tion (in′no͞o trish′ən, -nyo͞o-), *n.* lack of nutrition. [1790–1800; IN-[3] + NUTRITION] **—in′nu•tri′tious,** *adj.*

I•no (ī′nō, ē′nō), *n. Class. Myth.* a sea goddess who rescued Odysseus from drowning by giving him a magic veil.

in•ob•serv•ance (in′əb zûr′vəns), *n.* **1.** lack of attention; inattention; heedlessness: *drowsy inobservance.* **2.** failure to observe a custom, rule, law, or the like; nonobservance: *inobservance of the Sabbath.* [1605–15; < L *inobservantia.* See IN-[3], OBSERVANCE] **—in′ob•serv′ant,** *adj.* **—in′ob•serv′ant•ly,** *adv.*

in•ob•tru•sive (in′əb tro͞o′siv), *adj.* unobtrusive. [1790–1800; IN-[3] + OBTRUSIVE]

in•oc•u•la•ble (i nok′yə lə bəl), *adj.* capable of being inoculated. [1840–50; INOCUL(ATE) + -ABLE] **—in•oc′u•la•bil′i•ty,** *n.*

in•oc•u•lant (i nok′yə lənt), *n.* inoculum. [1910–15; INOCUL(ATE) + -ANT]

in•oc•u•late (i nok′yə lāt′), *v.,* **-lat•ed, -lat•ing.** —*v.t.* **1.** to implant (a disease agent or antigen) in a person, animal, or plant to produce a disease for study or to stimulate disease resistance. **2.** to affect or treat (a person, animal, or plant) in this manner. **3.** to introduce (microorganisms) into surroundings suited to their growth, as a culture medium. **4.** to imbue (a person), as with ideas. **5.** *Metall.* to treat (molten metal) chemically to strengthen the microstructure. —*v.i.* **6.** to perform inoculation. [1400–50; late ME < L *inoculātus* ptp. of *inoculāre* to graft by budding, implant, equiv. to *in-* IN-[2] + *-oculā-* (s. of *-oculāre* to graft, deriv. of *oculus* eye, bud) + *-tus* ptp. suffix] **—in•oc′u•la•tive** (i nok′yə lā′tiv, -yə lə-), *adj.* **—in•oc′u•la′tor,** *n.*
—**Syn. 4.** indoctrinate, infuse.

in•oc•u•la•tion (i nok′yə lā′shən), *n.* **1.** the act or process of inoculating. **2.** an instance of inoculating. [1400–50; late ME < L *inoculātiōn-* (s. of *inoculātiō*) an engrafting. See INOCULATE, -ION]

in•oc•u•lum (i nok′yə ləm), *n., pl.* **-la** (-lə). the substance used to make an inoculation. [1900–05; < NL, equiv. to *inocul(āre)* to INOCULATE + *-um* n. suffix]

in•o•dor•ous (in ō′dər əs), *adj.* not odorous; odorless. [1660–70; < L *inodōrus.* See IN-[3], ODOROUS] **—in•o′dor•ous•ly,** *adv.* **—in•o′dor•ous•ness,** *n.*

in•of•fen•sive (in′ə fen′siv), *adj.* **1.** causing no harm, trouble, or annoyance: *a mild, inoffensive man.* **2.** not objectionable, as to the senses: *an inoffensive odor.* [1590–1600; IN-[3] + OFFENSIVE] **—in′of•fen′sive•ly,** *adv.* **—in′of•fen′sive•ness,** *n.*
—**Syn. 1.** harmless, innocuous, unoffending.

in•of•fi•cious (in′ə fish′əs), *adj. Law.* being inconsistent with moral duty and natural affection. [1595–1605; < L *inofficiōsus.* See IN-[3], OFFICIOUS] **—in′of•fi′cious•ness, in•of•fi•ci•os•i•ty** (in′ə fish′ē os′i tē), *n.*

in′offi′cious will′, *Law.* a will inconsistent with the moral duty and natural affection of the testator, esp. one denying the legitimate heirs the portions of the estate to

CONCISE ETYMOLOGY KEY: <, descended or borrowed from; >, whence; b., blend of, blended; c., cognate with; cf., compare; deriv., derivative; equiv., equivalent; imit., imitative; obl., oblique; r., replacing; s., stem; sp., spelling, spelled; resp., respelling, respelled; trans., translation; ?, origin unknown; *, unattested; ‡, probably earlier than. See the full key inside the front cover.

which they are legally entitled. Also called **in′offi′cious tes′tament.** Cf. **officious will.** [1655–65]

in om·ni·a pa·ra·tus (in ōm′nē ä′ pä rä′to͞os; *Eng.* in om′nē ə pə rā′təs), *Latin.* prepared for all things.

I·nö·nü (i nœ ny′), *n.* **Is·met** (is met′), (*Ismet Paşa*), 1884–1973, president of Turkey 1938–50; prime minister 1923–24, 1925–37, 1961–65.

in·op·er·a·ble (in op′ər ə bəl, -op′rə bəl), *adj.* **1.** not operable or practicable. **2.** *Med.* not admitting of a surgical operation because the pathological condition is not amenable to cure by surgery or because of undue risk. Cf. **operable** (def. 1). [1885–90; IN-³ + OPERABLE]

in·op·er·a·tive (in op′ər ə tiv, -op′rə tiv, -op′ə rā′tiv), *adj.* **1.** not operative; not in operation. **2.** without effect: *inoperative remedies.* **3.** no longer in effect; void; canceled: *The earlier rule is now inoperative.* [1625–35; IN-³ + OPERATIVE] —**in·op′er·a·tive·ness,** *n.*

in·o·per·cu·late (in′ō pûr′kyə lit, -lāt′), *adj. Zool., Bot.* having no operculum. [1825–35; IN-³ + OPERCULATE]

in·op·por·tune (in op′ər to͞on′, -tyo͞on′), *adj.* not opportune; inappropriate; inconvenient; untimely or unseasonable: *an inopportune visit.* [1525–35; < LL *inopportūnus.* See IN-³, OPPORTUNE] —**in·op′por·tune′ly,** *adv.* —**in·op′por·tune′ness, in·op′por·tu′ni·ty,** *n.*

in·or·di·nate (in ôr′dn it), *adj.* **1.** not within proper or reasonable limits; immoderate; excessive: *He drank an inordinate amount of wine.* **2.** unrestrained in conduct, feelings, etc.: *an inordinate admirer of beauty.* **3.** disorderly; uncontrolled. **4.** not regulated; irregular: *inordinate hours.* [1350–1400; ME *inordinat* < L *inordinātus* disordered, equiv. to *in-* IN-³ + *ordinātus* orderly, appointed; see ORDINATE, ORDAIN] —**in·or′di·nate·ly,** *adv.* —**in·or′di·nate·ness,** *n.*
—**Syn. 1.** extreme, exorbitant, outrageous, unreasonable, disproportionate. —**Ant. 1.** reasonable.

inorg., inorganic.

in·or·gan·ic (in′ôr gan′ik), *adj.* **1.** not having the structure or organization characteristic of living bodies. **2.** not characterized by vital processes. **3.** *Chem.* noting or pertaining to compounds that are not hydrocarbons or their derivatives. Cf. **organic** (def. 1). **4.** not fundamental or related; extraneous. [1785–95; IN-³ + ORGANIC] —**in′or·gan′i·cal·ly,** *adv.*

in′organ′ic chem′istry, the branch of chemistry dealing with inorganic compounds. [1840–50]

in·or·gan·i·za·tion (in ôr′gə nə zā′shən), *n.* lack of organization. [1830–40; IN-³ + ORGANIZATION]

in·os·cu·late (in os′kyə lāt′), *v.i., v.t.,* **-lat·ed, -lat·ing.** **1.** to unite by openings, as arteries in anastomosis. **2.** to connect or join so as to become or make continuous, as fibers; blend. **3.** to unite intimately. [1665–75; IN-² + OSCULATE] —**in·os′cu·la′tion,** *n.*

in·o·sil·i·cate (in′ə sil′i kit, -kāt′, ī′nə-), *n. Mineral.* any silicate having a structure consisting of paired parallel chains of tetrahedral silicate groups, every other of which shares an oxygen atom with a group of the other chain, the ratio of silicon to oxygen being 4 to 11. Cf. **cyclosilicate, nesosilicate, sorosilicate, tektosilicate.** [< Gk *īno-* (comb. form of *ís* fiber, sinew) + SILICATE]

in·o·si·tol (i nō′si tôl′, -tōl′, ī nō′-), *n.* **1.** *Biochem.* a compound, $C_6H_{12}O_6$, derivative of cyclohexane, widely distributed in plants and seeds as phytin, and occurring in animal tissue and in urine: an essential growth factor for animal life, present in the vitamin B complex. **2.** *Pharm.* the commercial form of this compound, a white, sweet, crystalline solid, used chiefly to promote epithelialization of the cervix after infection or injury. Also called **hexahydroxycyclohexane.** [1890–95; *inosite* (< Gk *īn-,* s. of *ís* fiber, sinew + -OSE² + -ITE¹) + -OL¹]

i·no·trop·ic (ē′nə trop′ik, -trō′pik, ī′nə-), *adj. Physiol.* influencing the contractility of muscular tissue. [1900–05; < Gk *īno-* (comb. form of *ís* fiber, sinew) + -TROPIC]

in·ox·i·diz·a·ble (in ok′si dī′zə bəl), *adj. Chem.* not susceptible to oxidation. [1860–65; IN-³ + OXIDIZABLE]

in·paint (in′pānt′), *v.t.* to restore (a painting) by repainting damaged, faded, or obliterated sections. [IN-¹ + PAINT] —**in′paint′ing,** *n.*

in pais (in pā′), *Law.* outside of court; without legal proceedings. [< AF: in (the) country]

in pa·ri de·lic·to (in par′ī di lik′tō), *Law.* in equal fault; equally culpable or blameworthy. [< L]

in·pa·tient (in′pā′shənt), *n.* a patient who stays in a hospital while receiving medical care or treatment. [1750–60; IN-¹ + PATIENT]

in per·so·nam (in pər sō′nam), *Law.* (of a legal proceeding or judgment) directed against a party or parties, rather than against property. Cf. **in rem.** [1880–85; < L]

in pet·to (ēn pet′tô; *Eng.* in pet′ō), *Italian.* (of cardinals whom the pope appoints but does not disclose in consistory) not disclosed. [lit., in (the) breast]

in·phase (in′fāz′), *adj. Elect.* having the same phase. [1910–15; orig. phrase *in phase*]

in·pour (in pôr′, -pōr′), *v.i., v.t.* to pour in. [1880–85; IN-¹ + POUR]

in prae·sen·ti (in prī sen′tē; *Eng.* in prē zen′tī, -tē), *Latin.* at the present time.

In Praise′ of Fol′ly, (Latin, *Moriae Encomium*), a prose satire (1509) by Erasmus, written in Latin and directed against theologians and church dignitaries.

in prin·ci·pi·o (in prin ki′pi ō; *Eng.* in prin sip′ē ō′), *Latin.* at or in the beginning; at first.

in pro·pri·a per·so·na (in prō′prē ə pər sō′nə), *Law.* represented by oneself and not by an attorney. *Abbr.:* in pro. per. [1645–55; < L: in one's own person]

in·put (in′po͝ot′), *n., adj., v.,* **-put·ted** or **-put, -put·ting.** —*n.* **1.** something that is put in. **2.** the act or process of putting in. **3.** the power or energy supplied to a machine. **4.** the current or voltage applied to an electric or electronic circuit or device. Cf. **output** (def. 4). **5.** *Computers.* **a.** data to be entered into a computer for processing. **b.** the process of introducing data into the internal storage of a computer. **6.** contribution of information, ideas, opinions, or the like: *Before making a decision we need your input.* **7.** the available data for solving a technical problem. **8.** *Scot.* a monetary contribution, as to charity. —*adj.* **9.** of or pertaining to data or equipment used for input: *The keyboard is my computer's main input device.* —*v.t.* **10.** *Computers.* to enter (data) into a computer for processing. **11.** to contribute (ideas, information, or suggestions) to a project, discussion, etc. [1745–55; IN-¹ + PUT]

in·put/out·put (in′po͝ot′out′po͝ot′), *Computers. n.* **1.** the process of input or output, encompassing the devices, techniques, media, and data used: *A good first step in designing a program is to define the input/output.* —*adj.* **2.** pertaining to input or output: *Early input/output devices were slow. Abbr.:* I/O [1910–15]

in·quar·ta·tion (in′kwôr tā′shən), *n.* (in assaying) the addition of silver to a gold-silver alloy in order to facilitate the parting of the gold by nitric acid. [1880–85; perh. < F *inquartation.* See IN-², QUARTER, -ATION]

in·quest (in′kwest), *n.* **1.** a legal or judicial inquiry, usually before a jury, esp. an investigation made by a coroner into the cause of a death. **2.** the body of people appointed to hold such an inquiry, esp. a coroner's jury. **3.** the decision or finding based on such inquiry. **4.** an investigation or examination. [1250–1300; ME < ML *inquēsta,* equiv. to L *in-* IN-² + *quaesīta,* pl. (taken in ML as fem. sing.) of *quaesītum* question (see QUEST); r. ME *enqueste* < AF < ML, as above]
—**Syn. 1.** hearing, inquisition.

in·qui·et (in kwī′ət), *v.t. Archaic.* to destroy the peace of; disturb; disquiet. [1375–1425; late ME *inquieten* < L *inquiētāre.* See IN-³, QUIET¹]

in·qui·e·tude (in kwī′i to͞od′, -tyo͞od′), *n.* **1.** restlessness or uneasiness; disquietude. **2. inquietudes,** disquieting thoughts: *beset by myriad inquietudes.* [1400–50; late ME < LL *inquiētūdō.* See IN-³, QUIETUDE]

in·qui·line (in′kwə līn′, -lin), *n.* **1.** *Zool.* an animal living in the nest, burrow, or body of another animal. —*adj.* **2.** of the nature of an inquiline. [1635–45; < L *inquilīnus* tenant, equiv. to *in-* IN-² + *-quil-,* comb. form (noninitially before a front vowel) of *colere* to live in (see -COLOUS) + *-īnus* -INE¹] —**in·qui·lin·i·ty** (in′kwə lin′i tē), *n.* —**in·qui·li·nous** (in′kwə lī′nəs), *adj.*

in·quire (in kwīər′), *v.,* **-quired, -quir·ing.** —*v.i.* **1.** to seek information by questioning; ask: *to inquire about a person.* **2.** to make investigation (usually fol. by *into*): *to inquire into the incident.* —*v.t.* **3.** to seek to learn by asking: *to inquire a person's name.* **4.** *Obs.* to seek. **5.** *Obs.* to question (a person). **6. inquire after,** to ask about the state of health or condition of: *Friends have been calling all morning to inquire after you.* Also, **enquire.** [1250–1300; ME < L *inquīrere* to seek for (see IN-², QUERY); r. ME *enqueren* < OF *enquerre* < L, as above] —**in·quir′a·ble,** *adj.* —**in·quir′er,** *n.*
—**Syn. 1–3.** investigate, examine, query. INQUIRE, ASK, QUESTION imply that a person addresses another to obtain information. ASK is the general word: *to ask what time it is.* INQUIRE is more formal and implies asking about something specific: *to inquire about a rumor.* To QUESTION implies repetition and persistence in asking; it often applies to legal examination or investigation: *to question the survivor of an accident.* Sometimes it implies doubt: *to question a figure, an account.*

in·quir·ing (in kwīər′ing), *adj.* **1.** seeking facts, information, or knowledge: *an inquiring mind.* **2.** curious; probing; inquisitive in seeking facts: *an inquiring reporter.* **3.** scrutinizing; questioning: *He looked at his father with inquiring eyes.* [1595–1605; INQUIRE + -ING²] —**in·quir′ing·ly,** *adv.*

in·quir·y (in kwīər′ē, in′kwə rē), *n., pl.* **-quir·ies.** **1.** a seeking or request for truth, information, or knowledge. **2.** an investigation, as into an incident: *a Congressional inquiry into the bribery charges.* **3.** the act of inquiring or of seeking information by questioning; interrogation. **4.** a question; query. Also, **enquiry.** [1400–50; INQUIRE + -Y³; r. late ME *enquery*]
—**Syn. 1.** study, scrutiny, exploration. See **investigation.** —**Ant. 4.** answer, reply.

in·qui·si·tion (in′kwə zish′ən, ing′-), *n.* **1.** an official investigation, esp. one of a political or religious nature, characterized by lack of regard for individual rights, prejudice on the part of the examiners, and recklessly cruel punishments. **2.** any harsh, difficult, or prolonged questioning. **3.** the act of inquiring; inquiry; research. **4.** an investigation, or process of inquiry. **5.** a judicial or official inquiry. **6.** the finding of such an inquiry. **7.** the document embodying the result of such inquiry. **8.** (*cap.*) *Rom. Cath. Ch.* **a.** a former special tribunal, engaged chiefly in combating and punishing heresy. Cf. **Holy Office. b.** See **Spanish Inquisition.** [1350–1400; ME *inquisicio(u)n* < L *inquīsītiōn-* (s. of *inquīsītiō*), equiv. to *inquīsīt(us)* ptp. of *inquīrere* to INQUIRE + *-iōn-* -ION] —**in′qui·si′tion·al,** *adj.*
—**Syn. 5.** inquest, hearing.

in·qui·si·tion·ist (in′kwə zish′ə nist, ing′-), *n.* an inquisitor. [1880–85; INQUISITION + -IST]

in·quis·i·tive (in kwiz′i tiv), *adj.* **1.** given to inquiry, research, or asking questions; eager for knowledge; intellectually curious: *an inquisitive mind.* **2.** unduly or inappropriately curious; prying. —*n.* **3.** an inquisitive person: *thick curtains to frustrate inquisitives.* [1350–1400; < LL *inquīsītīvus,* equiv. to L *inquīsīt(us)* (see INQUISITION) + *-īvus* -IVE; r. ME *inquisitif* < MF < LL, as above] —**in·quis′i·tive·ly,** *adv.* —**in·quis′i·tive·ness,** *n.*
—**Syn. 2.** See **curious.** —**Ant. 1, 2.** uninterested.

in·quis·i·tor (in kwiz′i tər), *n.* **1.** a person who makes an inquisition. **2.** a questioner, esp. an unduly curious or harsh one. **3.** a person who investigates in an official capacity. **4.** a member of the Inquisition. [1495–1505; < L *inquīsītor,* equiv. to *inquīsī-,* var. s. of *inquīrere* to INQUIRE + *-tor* -TOR]

in·quis·i·to·ri·al (in kwiz′i tôr′ē əl, -tōr′-), *adj.* **1.** of or pertaining to an inquisitor or inquisition. **2.** exercising the office of an inquisitor. **3.** *Law.* **a.** pertaining to a trial with one person or group inquiring into the facts and acting as both prosecutor and judge. **b.** pertaining to secret criminal prosecutions. **4.** resembling an inquisitor in harshness or intrusiveness. **5.** inquisitive; prying. [1755–65; < ML *inquīsītōri(us)* (L *inquīsītōr-,* s. of *inquīsītor* INQUISITOR + *-ius* adj. suffix) + -AL¹] —**in·quis′i·to′ri·al·ly,** *adv.* —**in·quis′i·to′ri·al·ness,** *n.*

in·quis·i·tress (in kwiz′i tris), *n.* a woman who makes an inquisition. [1720–30; INQUISIT(O)R + -ESS]
—**Usage.** See **-ess.**

in·ra·di·us (in′rā′dē əs), *n., pl.* **-di·i** (-dē ī′), **-di·us·es.** *Geom.* the radius of the circle inscribed in a triangle. [IN + RADIUS]

in re (in rē′, rā′), in the matter of. [1875–80; < L]

in rem (in rem′), *Law.* (of a legal proceeding or judgment) directed against a thing, rather than against a person, as a legal proceeding for the recovery of property. Cf. **in personam.** [1880–85; < L: lit., against (the) thing]

in-res·i·dence (in rez′i dəns), *adj.* assigned to a staff position in an institution such as a college or university, while allowed sufficient time to pursue one's own professional work, study, or research (usually used in combination): *a poet-in-residence at the university.* [1835–45]

I.N.R.I., Jesus of Nazareth, King of the Jews. [< LL *Iēsus Nazarēnus, Rēx Iūdaeōrum*]

in·rig·ger (in′rig′ər), *n.* a rowboat having oarlocks on the gunwales. [1890–95; IN + RIGGER, modeled on OUTRIGGER]

in·ro (in′rō), *n., pl.* **-ro.** a small lacquer box with compartments for medicines, cosmetics, etc., worn on the waist sash of the traditional Japanese costume. [1610–20; < Japn *inrō* < MChin, equiv. to Chin *yìn* signature seal, chop + *lǒng* round lidded container; the inro was originally used to carry one's chop]

in·road (in′rōd′), *n.* **1.** a damaging or serious encroachment: *inroads on our savings.* **2.** a sudden hostile or predatory incursion; raid; foray. [1540–50; IN-¹ + ROAD]

in·rush (in′rush′), *n.* a rushing or pouring in. [1810–20; IN-¹ + RUSH¹] —**in′rush′ing,** *n., adj.*

INS, 1. Immigration and Naturalization Service. **2.** International News Service, a news-gathering agency: merged in 1958 with United Press to form United Press International. Also, **I.N.S.**

ins., 1. inches. **2.** *Chiefly Brit.* inscribed. **3.** inspector. **4.** insulated. **5.** insurance.

in sae·cu·la sae·cu·lo·rum (in sī′ko͞o lä′ sī′ko͞o-lō′ro͝om; *Eng.* in sek′yə lə sek′yə lôr′əm, -lōr′-), *Latin.* for ever and ever. [lit., for ages of ages]

in·sal·i·vate (in sal′ə vāt′), *v.t.,* **-vat·ed, -vat·ing.** to mix with saliva, as food. [1850–55; IN-² + SALIVATE] —**in·sal′i·va′tion,** *n.*

in·sa·lu·bri·ous (in′sə lo͞o′brē əs), *adj.* unfavorable to health; unwholesome. [1630–40; < L *insalūbri(s)* + -OUS. See IN-³, SALUBRIOUS] —**in′sa·lu′bri·ous·ly,** *adv.* —**in·sa·lu·bri·ty** (in′sə lo͞o′bri tē), *n.*

ins′ and outs′, 1. physical characteristics, as windings and turnings, nooks, or recesses: *the ins and outs of a subterranean passage.* **2.** intricacies; particulars; peculiarities: *the ins and outs of the tax laws.* [1880–85]

in·sane (in sān′), *adj.* **1.** not sane; not of sound mind; mentally deranged. **2.** of, pertaining to, or characteristic of a person who is mentally deranged: *insane actions; an insane asylum.* **3.** utterly senseless: *an insane plan.* [1550–60; < L *insānus.* See IN-³, SANE] —**in·sane′ly,** *adv.* —**in·sane′ness,** *n.*
—**Syn. 1.** demented; lunatic, crazed, crazy; maniacal. **3.** foolish, irrational. See **mad.**

in·san·i·tar·y (in san′i ter′ē), *adj.* unsanitary. [1870–75; IN-³ + SANITARY] —**in·san′i·tar′i·ness,** *n.*

in·san·i·ta·tion (in san′i tā′shən), *n.* lack of sanitation or sanitary regulation; unclean or unhealthy condition. [1880–85; IN-³ + SANITATION]

in·san·i·ty (in san′i tē), *n., pl.* **-ties.** **1.** the condition of being insane; a derangement of the mind. **2.** *Law.* such unsoundness of mind as affects legal responsibility or capacity. **3.** *Psychiatry.* (formerly) psychosis. **4.** extreme folly; senselessness; foolhardiness. [1580–90; < L *insānitās.* See IN-³, SANITY]
—**Syn. 1.** dementia, lunacy, madness, craziness, mania, aberration.

in·sa·tia·ble (in sā′shə bəl, -shē ə-), *adj.* not satiable; incapable of being satisfied or appeased: *insatiable hunger for knowledge.* [1400–50; late ME *insaciable* < L *insatiābilis;* see IN-³, SATIABLE] —**in·sa′tia·bil′i·ty, in·sa′tia·ble·ness,** *n.* —**in·sa′tia·bly,** *adv.*
—**Syn.** voracious, unquenchable, bottomless.

in·sa·ti·ate (in sā′shē it), *adj.* insatiable: *insatiate greed.* [1500–10; < L *insatiātus* not filled. See IN-³, SATIATE] —**in·sa′ti·ate·ly,** *adv.* —**in·sa′ti·ate·ness, in·sa·ti·e·ty** (in′sə tī′i tē, in sā′shi tē, -sā′shē i-), *n.*

in·scribe (in skrīb′), *v.t.,* **-scribed, -scrib·ing.** **1.** to address or dedicate (a book, photograph, etc.) informally to a person, esp. by writing a brief personal note in or on it. **2.** to mark (a surface) with words, characters, etc., esp. in a durable or conspicuous way. **3.** to write, print, mark, or engrave (words, characters, etc.). **4.** to enroll, as on an official list. **5.** *Geom.* to draw or delineate (one figure) within another figure so that the inner lies entirely within the boundary of the outer, touching it at as many points as possible: *to inscribe a circle in a square.*

6. *Brit.* **a.** to issue (a loan) in the form of shares with registered stockholders. **b.** to sell (stocks). **c.** to buy (stocks). [1545–55; < L *inscrībere,* equiv. to *in-* IN-[2] + *scrībere* to write; see SCRIBE[1]] —**in·scrib′a·ble,** *adj.* —**in·scrib′a·ble·ness,** *n.* —**in·scrib′er,** *n.*

in·scrip·tion (in skrip′shən), *n.* **1.** something inscribed. **2.** a historical, religious, or other record cut, impressed, painted, or written on stone, brick, metal, or other hard surface. **3.** a brief, usually informal dedication, as of a book or a work of art. **4.** a note, as a dedication, that is written and signed by hand in a book. **5.** the act of inscribing. **6.** *Pharm.* the part of a prescription indicating the drugs and the amounts to be mixed. **7.** *Brit.* **a.** an issue of securities or stocks. **b.** a block of shares in a stock, as bought or sold by one person. **8.** Also called **legend.** *Numis.* the lettering in the field of a coin, medal, etc. [1350–1400; ME *inscripcio(u)n* < L *inscrīptiōn-* (s. of *inscrīptiō*), equiv. to *inscrīpt(us)* (ptp. of *inscrībere* to INSCRIBE) + *-iōn-* -ION] —**in·scrip′tion·al,** *adj.* —**in·scrip′tion·less,** *adj.*

in·scrip·tive (in skrip′tiv), *adj.* of, pertaining to, or of the nature of an inscription. [1730–40; < L *inscrīpt(us)* ptp. of *inscrībere* (see INSCRIPTION) + -IVE] —**in·scrip′·tive·ly,** *adv.*

in·scroll (in skrōl′), *v.t.* enscroll.

in·scru·ta·ble (in skro͞o′tə bəl), *adj.* **1.** incapable of being investigated, analyzed, or scrutinized; impenetrable. **2.** not easily understood; mysterious; unfathomable: *an inscrutable smile.* **3.** incapable of being seen through physically; physically impenetrable: *the inscrutable depths of the ocean.* [1400–50; late ME < LL *inscrūtābilis.* See IN-[3], SCRUTABLE] —**in·scru′ta·bil′i·ty, in·scru′·ta·ble·ness,** *n.* —**in·scru′ta·bly,** *adv.*
—**Syn. 1.** hidden, incomprehensible, undiscoverable. See **mysterious.** —**Ant. 1.** comprehensible.

in·sculp (in skulp′), *v.t. Archaic.* to carve in or on something; engrave. [1400–50; late ME < L *insculpere,* equiv. to *in-* IN-[2] + *sculpere* to carve; see SCULPTOR]

in·seam (in′sēm′), *n.* **1.** an inside or inner seam of a garment, esp. the seam of a trouser leg that runs from the crotch down to the bottom of the leg. —*adj.* **2.** of or pertaining to such a seam: *inseam measurements.* **3.** (of a pocket) placed at or sewn to an opening in the seam of a garment, usually the side seam, so as to lie completely inside the garment. [1905–10; IN-[1] + SEAM]

in·sect (in′sekt), *n.* **1.** any animal of the class Insecta, comprising small, air-breathing arthropods having the body divided into three parts (head, thorax, and abdomen), and having three pairs of legs and usually two pairs of wings. **2.** any small arthropod, such as a spider, tick, or centipede, having a superficial, general similarity to the insects. Cf. **arachnid. 3.** a contemptible or unimportant person. —*adj.* **4.** of, pertaining to, like, or used for or against insects: *an insect bite; insect powder.* [1595–1605; < L *insectum,* n. use of neut. of *insectus* ptp. of *insecāre* to incise, cut (cf. SEGMENT); trans. of Gk *éntomon* insect, lit., notched or incised one; see ENTOMO-] —**in·sec·ti·val** (in′sek tī′vəl), *adj.*

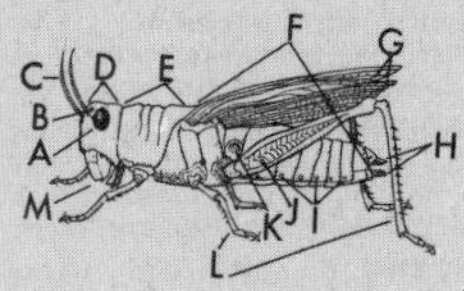

insect (grasshopper)
A, compound eye; B, simple eye; C, antenna; D, head; E, thorax; F, abdomen; G, wings; H, ovipositor; I, spiracle; J, femur; K, ears; L, legs; M, palpus

In·sec·ta (in sek′tə), *n.* the class comprising the insects. [1570–80; < NL, L, pl. of *insectum* INSECT]

in·sec·tar·i·um (in′sek târ′ē əm), *n., pl.* **-tar·i·ums, -tar·i·a** (-târ′ē ə). a place in which a collection of living insects is kept, as in a zoo. [1880–85; < NL; see INSECT, -ARIUM]

in·sec·tar·y (in′sek ter′ē), *n., pl.* **-tar·ies.** a laboratory for the study of live insects, their life histories, effects on plants, reaction to insecticides, etc. [1885–90; var. of INSECTARIUM; see -ARY]

in·sec·ti·cide (in sek′tə sīd′), *n.* **1.** a substance or preparation used for killing insects. **2.** the act of killing insects. [1860–65; INSECT + -I- + -CIDE] —**in·sec′ti·cid′al,** *adj.*

in·sec·ti·fuge (in sek′tə fyo͞oj′), *n.* a substance or preparation for driving off insects. [INSECT + -I- + -FUGE]

in·sec·tile (in sek′til), *adj.* **1.** pertaining to or like an insect. **2.** consisting of insects. [1605–15; INSECT + -ILE]

In·sec·tiv·o·ra (in′sek tiv′ər ə), *n.* the order comprising the insectivores. [1830–40; < NL, neut. pl. of *insectivorus* INSECTIVOROUS]

in·sec·ti·vore (in sek′tə vôr′, -vōr′), *n.* **1.** an insectivorous animal or plant. **2.** any mammal of the order Insectivora, comprising the moles, shrews, and Old World hedgehogs. [1860–65; back formation from INSECTIVOROUS; see -VORE]

in·sec·tiv·o·rous (in′sek tiv′ər əs), *adj.* **1.** adapted to feeding on insects. **2.** *Bot.* having specialized leaves or leaf parts capable of trapping and digesting insects, as the Venus's-flytrap, the pitcher plants, and the sundews. [1655–65; < NL *insectivorus.* See INSECT, -I-, -VOROUS]

in·sec·tol·o·gy (in′sek tol′ə jē), *n.* entomology. [1760–70; INSECT + -O- + -LOGY] —**in′sec·tol′o·ger,** *n.*

in′sect wax′, *Chem.* See **Chinese wax.** [1850–55]

in·se·cure (in′si kyo͝or′), *adj.* **1.** subject to fears, doubts, etc.; not self-confident or assured: *an insecure person.* **2.** not confident or certain; uneasy; anxious: *He was insecure about the examination.* **3.** not secure; exposed or liable to risk, loss, or danger: *an insecure stock portfolio.* **4.** not firmly or reliably placed or fastened: *an insecure ladder.* [1640–50; < ML *insēcūrus.* See IN-[3], SECURE] —**in′se·cure′ly,** *adv.* —**in′se·cure′ness,** *n.*
—**Syn. 3.** risky. See **uncertain.**

in·se·cu·ri·ty (in′si kyo͝or′i tē), *n., pl.* **-ties. 1.** lack of confidence or assurance; self-doubt: *He is plagued by insecurity.* **2.** the quality or state of being insecure; instability: *the insecurity of her financial position.* **3.** something insecure: *the many insecurities of life.* [1640–50; < ML *insēcūritās.* See INSECURE, -ITY]
—**Syn. 2.** precariousness, shakiness, vulnerability.

in·sel·berg (in′səl bûrg′, -zəl-), *n. Physical Geog.* monadnock (def. 1). [1895–1900; < G, equiv. to *Insel* island + *Berg* mountain]

in·sem·i·nate (in sem′ə nāt′), *v.t.,* **-nat·ed, -nat·ing. 1.** to inject semen into (the female reproductive tract); impregnate. **2.** to sow; implant seed into. **3.** to sow as seed in something; implant: *to inseminate youth with new ideas.* [1615–25; < L *insēminātus* ptp. of *insēmināre* to implant, impregnate, equiv. to *in-* IN-[2] + *sēmināre* to sow, deriv. of *sēmen* seed (cf. SEMEN) + *-tus* ptp. suffix)] —**in·sem′i·na′tion,** *n.*

in·sem·i·na·tor (in sem′ə nā′tər), *n. Vet. Med.* a technician who introduces prepared semen into the genital tract of breeding animals, esp. cows and mares, for artificial insemination. [1940–45; INSEMINATE + -OR[2]]

in·sen·sate (in sen′sāt, -sit), *adj.* **1.** not endowed with sensation; inanimate: *insensate stone.* **2.** without human feeling or sensitivity; cold; cruel; brutal. **3.** without sense, understanding, or judgment; foolish. [1510–20; < LL *insēnsātus* irrational. See IN-[3], SENSATE] —**in·sen′·sate·ly,** *adv.* —**in·sen′sate·ness,** *n.*
—**Syn. 1.** lifeless, inorganic. **2.** insensible. **3.** stupid, irrational, senseless, witless, dumb.

in·sen·si·ble (in sen′sə bəl), *adj.* **1.** incapable of feeling or perceiving; deprived of sensation; unconscious, as a person after a violent blow. **2.** without or not subject to a particular feeling or sensation: *insensible to shame; insensible to the cold.* **3.** unaware; unconscious; inappreciative: *We are not insensible of your kindness.* **4.** not perceptible by the senses; imperceptible: *insensible transitions.* **5.** unresponsive in feeling. **6.** not susceptible of emotion or passion; void of any feeling. **7.** not endowed with feeling or sensation, as matter; inanimate. [1350–1400; ME < L *insēnsibilis.* See IN-[3], SENSIBLE] —**in·sen′si·bly,** *adv.* —**in·sen′si·bil′i·ty,** *n.*
—**Syn. 5, 6.** apathetic, unfeeling, indifferent, cool; dull, passionless, emotionless, torpid.

in·sen·si·tive (in sen′si tiv), *adj.* **1.** deficient in human sensibility, acuteness of feeling, or consideration; unfeeling; callous: *an insensitive person.* **2.** not physically sensitive: *insensitive skin.* **3.** not affected by physical or chemical agencies or influences: *insensitive to light.* **4.** not readily responsive or aware: *insensitive to the needs of the peasants.* [1600–10; IN-[3] + SENSITIVE] —**in·sen′si·tive·ness, in·sen′si·tiv′i·ty,** *n.*

in·sen·ti·ent (in sen′shē ənt, -shənt), *adj.* not sentient; without sensation or feeling; inanimate. [1755–65; IN-[3] + SENTIENT] —**in·sen′ti·ence, in·sen′ti·en·cy,** *n.*

insep., inseparable.

in·sep·a·ra·ble (in sep′ər ə bəl, -sep′rə-), *adj.* **1.** incapable of being separated, parted, or disjoined: *inseparable companions.* —*n.* Usually, **inseparables. 2.** inseparable objects, qualities, etc. **3.** inseparable companions or friends. [1350–1400; ME < L *inseparābilis.* See IN-[3], SEPARABLE] —**in·sep′a·ra·bil′i·ty, in·sep′·a·ra·ble·ness,** *n.* —**in·sep′a·ra·bly,** *adv.*

in·sert (*v.* in sûrt′; *n.* in′sûrt), *v.t.* **1.** to put or place in: *to insert a key in a lock.* **2.** to introduce or cause to be introduced into the body of something: *to insert an extra paragraph in an article.* —*n.* **3.** something inserted or to be inserted. **4.** an extra leaf or section, printed independently, for binding or tipping into a book or periodical, esp. a leaf or section consisting of an illustration or advertisement printed on different paper. **5.** any small picture, device, etc., surrounded partly or completely by body type. **6.** a paper, circular, etc., placed within the folds of a newspaper or the leaves of a book, periodical, etc. **7.** *Motion Pictures, Television.* a cut-in. [1520–30; < L *insertus* ptp. of *inserere* to put in, insert, equiv. to *in-* IN-[2] + *ser-* (s. of *serere* to link together) + *-tus* ptp. suffix] —**in·sert′a·ble,** *adj.* —**in·sert′er,** *n.*

in·sert·ed (in sûr′tid), *adj.* **1.** *Bot.* (esp. of the parts of a flower) attached to or growing out of some part. **2.** *Anat.* having an insertion, as a muscle, tendon, or ligament; attached, as the end of a muscle that moves a bone. [1590–1600; INSERT + -ED[2]]

in·ser·tion (in sûr′shən), *n.* **1.** the act of inserting: *the insertion of a coin in a vending machine.* **2.** something inserted: *an insertion in the middle of a paragraph.* **3.** *Bot., Zool.* **a.** the manner or place of attachment, as of an organ. **b.** attachment of a part or organ, with special reference to the site or manner of such attachment. **4.** lace, embroidery, or the like, to be sewn at each edge between parts of other material. **5.** *Aerospace.* injection (def. 6). [1570–80; < LL *insertiōn-* (s. of *insertiō*). See INSERT, -ION] —**in·ser′tion·al,** *adj.*

in-serv·ice (in sûr′vis, in′sûr′-), *adj.* taking place while one is employed: *an in-service training program.* [1925–30]

in·ses·so·ri·al (in′sə sôr′ē əl, -sōr′-), *adj.* **1.** adapted for perching, as a bird's foot. **2.** habitually perching, as a bird. **3.** of or pertaining to birds that perch. [1830–40; < NL *Insessor(es)* the perching birds (L: perchers, equiv. to *insed-,* var. s. of *insidēre* to settle on (*in-* IN-[2] + *sidere* to sit down) + *-tōrēs,* pl. of *-tor* -TOR) + -IAL]

in·set (*n.* in′set′; *v.* in set′), *n., v.,* **-set, -set·ting.** —*n.* **1.** something inserted; insert. **2.** a small picture, map, etc., inserted within the border of a larger one. **3.** influx. **4.** the act of setting in. **5.** a piece of cloth or other material set into a garment, usually as an ornamental panel. —*v.t.* **6.** to set in or insert, as an inset: *to inset a panel in a dress.* **7.** to insert an inset in: *to inset a mounting with jewels.* [bef. 900; ME *insetten* to insert, OE *insettan* to initiate; see IN-[1], SET] —**in′set′ter,** *n.*

in′set ini′tial, *Print.* an initial letter, esp. of the first word of a chapter or other section of a book, magazine, etc., larger than the body type and occupying two or more lines in depth, causing body type to be set around it. Also called **drop initial.**

in·sev·er·a·ble (in sev′ər ə bəl, -sev′rə-), *adj.* unable to be severed or separated: *an inseverable alliance.* [1655–65; IN-[3] + SEVERABLE] —**in·sev′er·a·bly,** *adv.*

in·sheathe (in shēth′), *v.t.,* **-sheathed, -sheath·ing.** ensheathe. Also, **in·sheath** (in shēth′).

in·shore (in′shôr′, -shōr′), *adj.* **1.** close or closer to the shore. **2.** lying near the shore; operating or carried on close to the shore: *inshore fishing.* —*adv.* **3.** toward the shore: *They went closer inshore.* [1695–1705; IN-[1] + SHORE[1]]

in·shrine (in shrīn′), *v.t.,* **-shrined, -shrin·ing.** enshrine.

in·side (*prep.* in′sīd′, in′sīd′; *adv.* in′sīd′; *n.* in′sīd′; *adj.* in′sīd′, in′-, in′sīd′), *prep.* **1.** on the inner side or part of; within: *inside the circle; inside the envelope.* **2.** prior to the elapse of; within: *He promised to arrive inside an hour.* —*adv.* **3.** in or into the inner part: *Please go inside.* **4.** indoors: *They play inside on rainy days.* **5.** within one's heart, reason, etc.; by true nature; basically: *I know inside that he's not guilty. Inside, she's really very shy.* **6.** *Slang.* in prison. **7. inside of,** *Informal.* within the space or period of: *Our car broke down again inside of a mile.* —*n.* **8.** the inner or internal part; interior: *the inside of the house.* **9.** the inner side or surface: *the inside of the hand; He pinned the money to the inside of his jacket.* **10.** Usually, **insides.** *Informal.* the inner parts of the body, esp. the stomach and intestines: *The coffee scalded my insides.* **11.** a select or inner circle of power, prestige, etc.: *a man on the inside.* **12.** the shortest of several parallel, curving tracks or lanes; the part of an oval track closest to the inner rail: *The horse came up fast on the inside.* **13.** the inward nature, mind, feelings, etc. **14.** *Slang.* confidential or secret information. **15.** an inside passenger or place in a coach, carriage, etc. **16. inside out, a.** with the inner side reversed to face the outside. **b.** thoroughly; completely. —*adj.* **17.** situated or being on or in the inside; interior; internal: *an inside seat.* **18.** acting, employed, done, or originating within a building or place: *He used to work on the dock but now he has an inside job.* **19.** derived from the inner circle of those concerned in and having private knowledge of a situation: *inside information.* **20.** *Baseball.* (of a pitched ball) passing between home plate and the batter: *The pitch was low and inside.* [1350–1400; ME; see IN, SIDE[1]]
—**Syn. 8.** INSIDE, INTERIOR both refer to the inner part or space within something. INSIDE is a common word, and is used with reference to things of any size, small or large: *the inside of a pocket.* INTERIOR, somewhat more formal, denotes the inner part or the space or regions within; it usually suggests considerable size or extent, and sometimes a richness of decoration: *the interior of a country, of the earth, of a cathedral.* —**Ant. 8.** outside, exterior.

in′side cal′iper, a caliper whose legs turn outward so that it can accurately measure inside dimensions, as the inside diameter of a pipe. See illus. under **caliper.**

in′side for′ward, *Soccer.* one of two attacking players whose usual position is between the center forward and one of the wings. [1895–1900]

in′side job′, a crime committed by or in collusion with a person or persons closely associated with the victim: *The robbery seemed an inside job, because there was no evidence of forced entry.* [1905–10]

in′side loop′, *Aeron.* a loop during which the top of the airplane is on the inner side of the curve described by the course of flight. Cf. **outside loop.**

in·sid·er (in′sī′dər), *n.* **1.** a person who is a member of a group, organization, society, etc. **2.** a person belonging to a limited circle of persons who understand the actual facts in a situation or share private knowledge: *Insiders knew that the president would veto the bill.* **3.** a person who has some special advantage or influence. **4.** a person in possession of corporate information not generally available to the public, as a director, an accountant, or other officer or employee of a corporation. [1820–30; INSIDE + -ER[1]]

in′sider trad′ing, the illegal buying and selling of securities by persons acting on privileged information. [1965–70] —**in′sider trad′er.**

in′side straight′, 1. *Poker.* a set of four cards, as the five, seven, eight, and nine, requiring one card of a denomination next above or below the second or third ranking cards of the set to make a straight. **2. draw to an inside straight,** to build up hopes for something that has little or no chance of happening.

in′side track′, 1. the inner, or shorter, track of a racecourse. **2.** an advantageous position in a competitive situation. [1855–60, *Amer.*]

in·sid·i·ous (in sid′ē əs), *adj.* **1.** intended to entrap or beguile: *an insidious plan.* **2.** stealthily treacherous or deceitful: *an insidious enemy.* **3.** operating or proceeding in an inconspicuous or seemingly harmless way but actually with grave effect: *an insidious disease.* [1535–45; < L *insidiōsus* deceitful, equiv. to *insidi(ae)* (pl.) an ambush (deriv. of *insidēre* to SIT in or on) + *-ōsus* -OUS] —**in·sid′i·ous·ly,** *adv.* —**in·sid′i·ous·ness,** *n.*
—**Syn. 1.** corrupting. **2.** artful, cunning, wily, subtle, crafty.

in·sight (in′sīt′), *n.* **1.** an instance of apprehending the true nature of a thing, esp. through intuitive understanding: *an insight into 18th-century life.* **2.** penetrating mental vision or discernment; faculty of seeing into inner character or underlying truth. **3.** *Psychol.* **a.** an understanding of relationships that sheds light on or helps solve a problem. **b.** (in psychotherapy) the recogni-

tion of sources of emotional difficulty. **c.** an understanding of the motivational forces behind one's actions, thoughts, or behavior; self-knowledge. [1150–1200; ME; see IN-[1], SIGHT]
—Syn. 2. perception, apprehension, intuition, understanding, grasp.

in•sight•ful (in′sīt′fəl), *adj.* characterized by or displaying insight; perceptive. [1905–10; INSIGHT + -FUL] **—in′sight′ful•ly,** *adv.* **—in′sight′ful•ness,** *n.*

in•sig•ne (in sig′nē), *n.* **1.** sing. of **insignia. 2.** insignia.

in•sig•ni•a (in sig′nē ə), *n., formally a pl. of* **insigne,** *but usually used as a sing. with pl.* **-ni•a** *or* **-ni•as. 1.** a badge or distinguishing mark of office or honor: *a military insignia.* **2.** a distinguishing mark or sign of anything: *an insignia of mourning.* Also, **insigne.** [1640–50; < L, pl. of *insigne* mark, badge, n. use of neut. of *insignis* distinguished (by a mark); see IN-[2], SIGN]
—Usage. INSIGNIA, originally the plural of Latin *insigne,* began to be used as a singular in the 18th century, and the plural INSIGNIAS appeared shortly thereafter. All uses—INSIGNIA as a singular or plural and INSIGNIAS as a plural—are fully standard. The singular INSIGNE still occurs, but INSIGNIA is more common.

in•sig•nif•i•cance (in′sig nif′i kəns), *n.* the quality or condition of being insignificant; lack of importance or consequence. [1690–1700; INSIGNIFIC(ANCY) + -ANCE]

in•sig•nif•i•can•cy (in′sig nif′i kən sē), *n., pl.* **-cies** for 2. **1.** insignificance. **2.** an insignificant person or thing. [1645–55; INSIGNIFIC(ANT) + -ANCY]

in•sig•nif•i•cant (in′sig nif′i kənt), *adj.* **1.** unimportant, trifling, or petty: *Omit the insignificant details.* **2.** too small to be important: *an insignificant sum.* **3.** of no consequence, influence, or distinction: *a minor, insignificant bureaucrat.* **4.** without weight of character; contemptible: *an insignificant fellow.* **5.** without meaning; meaningless: *insignificant sounds.* **—n. 6.** a word, thing, or person without significance. [1620–30; IN-[3] + SIGNIFICANT] **—in′sig•nif′i•cant•ly,** *adv.*
—Syn. 2. trifling, minute, minuscule, picayune.

in•sin•cere (in′sin sēr′), *adj.* not sincere; not honest in the expression of actual feeling; hypocritical. [1625–35; < L *insincērus* tainted, dishonest; see IN-[3], SINCERE] **—in′sin•cere′ly,** *adv.*
—Syn. deceitful, disingenuous, guileful, two-faced.

in•sin•cer•i•ty (in′sin ser′i tē), *n., pl.* **-ties** for 2. **1.** the quality of being insincere; lack of sincerity; hypocrisy; deceitfulness. **2.** an instance of being insincere: *He recalled their many past insincerities.* [1540–50; IN-[3] + SINCERITY]

in•sin•u•ate (in sin′yōō āt′), *v.,* **-at•ed, -at•ing.** **—*v.t.* 1.** to suggest or hint slyly: *He insinuated that they were lying.* **2.** to instill or infuse subtly or artfully, as into the mind: *to insinuate doubts through propaganda.* **3.** to bring or introduce into a position or relation by indirect or artful methods: *to insinuate oneself into favor.* **—*v.i.* 4.** to make insinuations. [1520–30; < L *insinuātus,* ptp. of *insinuāre* to work in, instill. See IN-[2], SINUOUS, -ATE[1]] **—in•sin•u•a•tive** (in sin′yōō ā′tiv, -yōō ə-), **in•sin•u•a•to•ry** (in sin′yōō ə tôr′ē, -tōr′ē), *adj.* **—in•sin′u•a′tive•ly,** *adv.* **—in•sin′u•a′tor,** *n.*
—Syn. 1. See **hint. 2.** introduce, inject, inculcate.

in•sin•u•at•ing (in sin′yōō ā′ting), *adj.* **1.** tending to instill doubts, distrust, etc.; suggestive: *an insinuating letter.* **2.** gaining favor or winning confidence by artful means: *an insinuating manner.* [1585–95; INSINUATE + -ING[2]] **—in•sin′u•at′ing•ly,** *adv.*

in•sin•u•a•tion (in sin′yōō ā′shən), *n.* **1.** an indirect or covert suggestion or hint, esp. of a derogatory nature: *She made nasty insinuations about her rivals.* **2.** covert or artful suggestion or hinting, as of something implied: *His methods of insinuation are most ingenious.* **3.** subtle or artful instillment into the mind. **4.** the art or power of stealing into the affections and pleasing; ingratiation: *He made his way by flattery and insinuation.* **5.** *Archaic.* a slow winding, worming, or stealing in. **6.** *Obs.* an ingratiating act or speech. [1520–30; < L *insinuātiōn-* (s. of *insinuātiō*). See INSINUATE, -ION]

in•sip•id (in sip′id), *adj.* **1.** without distinctive, interesting, or stimulating qualities; vapid: *an insipid personality.* **2.** without sufficient taste to be pleasing, as food or drink; bland: *a rather insipid soup.* [1610–20; < L *insipidus,* equiv. to *in-* IN-[3] + *-sipidus,* comb. form of *sapidus* SAPID] **—in′si•pid′i•ty, in•sip′id•ness,** *n.* **—in•sip′id•ly,** *adv.*
—Syn. 1, 2. flat, dull, uninteresting. **2.** tasteless, bland.

in•sip•i•ence (in sip′ē əns), *n. Archaic.* lack of wisdom; foolishness. [1375–1425; late ME < L *insipientia* foolishness, equiv. to *insipient-* s. of *insipiēns* foolish (*in-* IN-[3] + *-sipient-,* comb. form of *sapient-* SAPIENT) + *-ia;* see -ENCE] **—in•sip′i•ent,** *adj.* **—in•sip′i•ent•ly,** *adv.*

in•sist (in sist′), *v.i.* **1.** to be emphatic, firm, or resolute on some matter of desire, demand, intention, etc.: *He insists on checking every shipment.* **2.** to lay emphasis in assertion: *to insist on the justice of a claim.* **3.** to dwell with earnestness or emphasis (usually fol. by *on* or *upon*): *to insist on a point in a discussion.* **—*v.t.* 4.** to assert or maintain firmly: *He insists that he saw the ghosts.* **5.** to demand or persist in demanding: *I insist that you see this thing through.* [1580–90; < L *insistere* to stand still on, persist in, equiv. to *in-* IN-[2] + *sistere* to STAND, make stand, reduplicated deriv. from base of *stāre* to stand] **—in•sist′er,** *n.* **—in•sist′ing•ly,** *adv.*
—Syn. 5. urge, require.

in•sist•ence (in sis′təns), *n.* **1.** the act or fact of insisting. **2.** the quality of being insistent. [1605–15; INSIST + -ENCE]

in•sist•en•cy (in sis′tən sē), *n., pl.* **-cies.** insistence. [1855–60; INSIST + -ENCY]

in•sist•ent (in sis′tənt), *adj.* **1.** earnest or emphatic in dwelling upon, maintaining, or demanding something; persistent; pertinacious. **2.** compelling attention or notice: *an insistent tone.* [1615–25; < L *insistent-* (s. of *insistēns*), prp. of *insistere.* See INSIST, -ENT] **—in•sist′ent•ly,** *adv.*

in si•tu (in sī′tōō, -tyōō, sē′-; *Latin.* in sit′ōō), **1.** situated in the original, natural, or existing place or position: *The archaeologists were able to date the vase because it was found in situ.* **2.** *Med.* **a.** in place or position; undisturbed. **b.** in a localized state or condition: *carcinoma in situ.* [1730–40; < L *in situ* lit., in place]

in•snare (in snâr′), *v.t.,* **-snared, -snar•ing.** ensnare. **—in•snare′ment,** *n.* **—in•snar′er,** *n.*

in•so•bri•e•ty (in′sə brī′i tē), *n.* lack of sobriety or moderation; intemperance; drunkenness. [1605–15; IN-[3] + SOBRIETY]

in•so•cia•ble (in sō′shə bəl), *adj.* unsociable. [1575–85; < L *insociābilis.* See IN-[3], SOCIABLE] **—in•so′cia•bil′i•ty,** *n.* **—in•so′cia•bly,** *adv.*

in•so•far (in′sə fär′, -sō-), *adv.* to such an extent (usually fol. by *as*): *I will do the work insofar as I am able.* [1590–1600; orig. phrase *in so far*]

insol., insoluble.

in•so•late (in′sō lāt′), *v.t.,* **-lat•ed, -lat•ing.** to expose to the sun's rays; treat by exposure to the sun's rays. [1615–25; < L *insōlātus* ptp. of *insōlāre* to place in the sun. See IN-[2], SOLI-[2], -ATE[1]]

in•so•la•tion[1] (in′sō lā′shən), *n.* exposure to the sun's rays, esp. as a process of treatment. [1605–15; < L *insōlātiōn-* (s. of *insōlātiō*). See INSOLATE, -ION]

in•so•la•tion[2] (in′sō lā′shən), *n. Meteorol.* solar radiation received at the earth's surface. [*in*(*coming*) *sol*(*ar radi*)*ation*]

in•sole (in′sōl′), *n.* **1.** the inner sole of a shoe or boot. **2.** a thickness of material laid as an inner sole within a shoe, esp. for comfort. [1850–55; IN + SOLE[2]]

in•so•lence (in′sə ləns), *n.* **1.** contemptuously rude or impertinent behavior or speech. **2.** the quality or condition of being insolent. [1350–1400; ME < L *insolentia.* See INSOLENT, -ENCE]

in•so•lent (in′sə lənt), *adj.* **1.** boldly rude or disrespectful; contemptuously impertinent; insulting: *an insolent reply.* **—n. 2.** an insolent person. [1350–1400; ME < L *insolent-* (s. of *insolēns*) departing from custom, equiv. to *in-* IN-[3] + *sol-* (s. of *solēre* to be accustomed) + *-ent-* -ENT] **—in′so•lent•ly,** *adv.*
—Syn. 1. brazen; contemptuous. See **impertinent.**

in•sol•u•bil•ize (in sol′yə bə līz′), *v.t.,* **-ized, -iz•ing.** to make incapable of dissolving: *a resin insolubilized by heat.* [1895–1900; < L *insolūbil*(*is*) INSOLUBLE + -IZE] **—in•sol′u•bi•li•za′tion,** *n.*

in•sol•u•ble (in sol′yə bəl), *adj.* **1.** incapable of being dissolved: *insoluble salts.* **2.** incapable of being solved or explained: *an insoluble problem.* [1350–1400; < L *insolūbilis;* r. ME *insoluble* < MF *insoluble* < L. See IN-[3], SOLUBLE] **—in•sol′u•bil′i•ty, in•sol′u•ble•ness,** *n.* **—in•sol′u•bly,** *adv.*

in•solv•a•ble (in sol′və bəl), *adj.* incapable of being solved or explained; insoluble. [1640–50; IN-[3] + SOLVABLE] **—in•solv′a•bil′i•ty,** *n.* **—in•solv′a•bly,** *adv.*

in•sol•ven•cy (in sol′vən sē), *n.* the condition of being insolvent; bankruptcy. [1650–60; INSOLV(ENT) + -ENCY]

in•sol•vent (in sol′vənt), *adj.* **1.** not solvent; unable to satisfy creditors or discharge liabilities, either because liabilities exceed assets or because of inability to pay debts as they mature. **2.** pertaining to bankrupt persons or bankruptcy. **—n. 3.** a person who is insolvent. [1585–95; IN-[3] + SOLVENT]
—Syn. 1. penniless, destitute, impoverished, bankrupt.

in•som•ni•a (in som′nē ə), *n.* inability to obtain sufficient sleep, esp. when chronic; difficulty in falling or staying asleep; sleeplessness. [1685–95; < L, equiv. to *insomn*(*is*) sleepless (*in-* IN-[3] + *somn*(*us*) sleep + *-is* adj. suffix) + *-ia* -IA] **—in•som′ni•ous,** *adj.*

in•som•ni•ac (in som′nē ak′), *n.* **1.** a person who suffers from insomnia. **—*adj.* 2.** having insomnia: *a nervous, insomniac person.* **3.** of, pertaining to, or causing insomnia. [1905–10; INSOMNI(A) + -AC]

in•som•no•lence (in som′nl əns), *n.* sleeplessness; insomnia: *a troubled week of insomnolence.* Also, **in•som•no•len•cy** (in som′nl ən sē). [1815–25; IN-[3] + SOMNOLENCE] **—in•som′no•lent,** *adj.* **—in•som′no•lent•ly,** *adv.*

in•so•much (in′sə much′, -sō-), *adv.* **1.** to such an extent or degree; so (usually fol. by *that*). **2.** inasmuch (usually fol. by *as*). [1350–1400; ME; orig. phrase *in so much*]

in•sou•ci•ance (in sōō′sē əns; *Fr.* AN sōō syäNs′), *n.* the quality of being insouciant; lack of care or concern; indifference. [1790–1800; < F; see INSOUCIANT, -ANCE]

in•sou•ci•ant (in sōō′sē ənt; *Fr.* AN sōō syäN′), *adj.* free from concern, worry, or anxiety; carefree; nonchalant. [1820–30; < F, equiv. to *in-* IN-[3] + *souciant* prp. of *soucier* to worry < VL **sollicitāre,* for L *sollicitāre* to disturb; see SOLICITOUS] **—in•sou′ci•ant•ly,** *adv.*
—Syn. lighthearted, debonair, jaunty, breezy.

in•soul (in sōl′), *v.t.* ensoul.

insp., inspector.

in•span (in span′), *v.t.,* **-spanned, -span•ning.** *South Africa.* to yoke or harness. [1825–35; < Afrik; see IN-[1], SPAN[2]]

in•spect (in spekt′), *v.t.* **1.** to look carefully at or over; view closely and critically: *to inspect every part of the motor.* **2.** to view or examine formally or officially: *The general inspected the troops.* [1615–25; < L *inspectus,* ptp. of *inspicere* to look into, inspect. See IN-[2], SPECIES] **—in•spect′a•ble,** *adj.* **—in•spect′a•bil′i•ty,** *n.* **—in•spect′ing•ly,** *adv.*
—Syn. 1. examine, scrutinize, investigate, study.

in•spec•tion (in spek′shən), *n.* **1.** the act of inspecting or viewing, esp. carefully or critically: *an inspection of all luggage on the plane.* **2.** formal or official viewing or examination: *an inspection of the troops.* [1350–1400; ME *inspeccio*(*u*)*n* < L *inspectiōn-* (s. of *inspectiō*). See INSPECT, -ION] **—in•spec′tion•al,** *adj.*
—Syn. 2. See **examination.**

inspec′tion arms′, a position in military drill in which the missile chamber of a weapon is open for inspection. [1880–85]

in•spec•tive (in spek′tiv), *adj.* **1.** given to inspection; watchful; attentive. **2.** of or pertaining to inspection. [1600–10; < LL *inspectīvus.* See INSPECT, -IVE]

in•spec•tor (in spek′tər), *n.* **1.** a person who inspects. **2.** an officer appointed to inspect. **3.** a police officer usually ranking next below a superintendent. [1595–1605; < L, equiv. to *inspec-,* var. s. of *inspicere* (see INSPECT) + *-tor* -TOR] **—in•spec′to•ral, in•spec•to•ri•al** (in′spek tôr′ē əl, -tōr′-), *adj.* **—in•spec′tor•ship′,** *n.*

in•spec•tor•ate (in spek′tər it), *n.* **1.** the office or function of an inspector. **2.** a body of inspectors. **3.** a district under an inspector. [1755–65; INSPECTOR + -ATE[3]]

In•spec•tor-Gen•er•al, The (in spek′tər jen′ər əl), a comedy (1836) by Gogol.

in•sphere (in sfēr′), *v.t.,* **-sphered, -spher•ing.** ensphere.

in•spir•a•ble (in spīər′ə bəl), *adj.* capable of being inspired. [1650–60; INSPIRE + -ABLE]

in•spi•ra•tion (in′spə rā′shən), *n.* **1.** an inspiring or animating action or influence: *I cannot write poetry without inspiration.* **2.** something inspired, as an idea. **3.** a result of inspired activity. **4.** a thing or person that inspires. **5.** *Theol.* **a.** a divine influence directly and immediately exerted upon the mind or soul. **b.** the divine quality of the writings or words of a person so influenced. **6.** the drawing of air into the lungs; inhalation. **7.** the act of inspiring; quality or state of being inspired. [1275–1325; ME *inspiracio*(*u*)*n* < LL *inspīrātiōn-* (s. of *inspīrātiō*). See INSPIRE, -ATION]
—Syn. 1. stimulus, incitement.

in•spi•ra•tion•al (in′spə rā′shə nl), *adj.* **1.** imparting inspiration. **2.** under the influence of inspiration; inspired. **3.** of or pertaining to inspiration. [1830–40; INSPIRATION + -AL[1]] **—in′spi•ra′tion•al•ly,** *adv.*

in•spir•a•to•ry (in spīər′ə tôr′ē, -tōr′ē), *adj.* of or pertaining to inspiration or inhalation. [1765–75; < L *inspīrāt*(*us*) ptp. of *inspīrāre* (see INSPIRE, -ATE[1]) + -ORY[1]]

in•spire (in spīər′), *v.,* **-spired, -spir•ing.** **—*v.t.* 1.** to fill with an animating, quickening, or exalting influence: *His courage inspired his followers.* **2.** to produce or arouse (a feeling, thought, etc.): *to inspire confidence in others.* **3.** to fill or affect with a specified feeling, thought, etc.: *to inspire a person with distrust.* **4.** to influence or impel: *Competition inspired her to greater efforts.* **5.** to animate, as an influence, feeling, thought, or the like, does: *They were inspired by a belief in a better future.* **6.** to communicate or suggest by a divine or supernatural influence: *writings inspired by God.* **7.** to guide or control by divine influence. **8.** to prompt or instigate (utterances, acts, etc.) by influence, without avowal of responsibility. **9.** to give rise to, bring about, cause, etc.: *a philosophy that inspired a revolution.* **10.** to take (air, gases, etc.) into the lungs in breathing; inhale. **11.** *Archaic.* **a.** to infuse (breath, life, etc.) by breathing (usually fol. by *into*). **b.** to breathe into or upon. **—*v.i.* 12.** to give inspiration. **13.** to inhale. [1300–50; ME *inspiren* < L *inspīrāre* to breathe upon or into, equiv. to *in-* IN-[2] + *spīrāre* to breathe] **—in•spir•a•tive** (in spīər′ə tiv, in′spi rā′tiv), *adj.* **—in•spir′er,** *n.* **—in•spir′ing•ly,** *adv.*

in•spired (in spīərd′), *adj.* **1.** aroused, animated, or imbued with the spirit to do something, by or as if by supernatural or divine influence: *an inspired poet.* **2.** resulting from such inspiration: *an inspired poem; an inspired plan.* **3.** inhaled: *inspired air.* [1400–50; late ME; see INSPIRE, -ED[2]] **—in•spir•ed•ly** (in spī′rid lē, -spīərd′-), *adv.*

in•spir•it (in spir′it), *v.t.* to infuse spirit or life into; enliven. Also, **enspirit.** [1600–10; IN-[2] + SPIRIT] **—in•spir′it•er,** *n.* **—in•spir′it•ing•ly,** *adv.* **—in•spir′it•ment,** *n.*

in•spis•sate (in spis′āt), *v.t., v.i.,* **-sat•ed, -sat•ing.** to thicken, as by evaporation; make or become dense. [1620–30; < LL *inspissātus* ptp. of *inspissāre* to thicken, equiv. to L *in-* IN-[2] + *spissā*(*re*) to thicken (deriv. of *spissus* thick) + *-tus* ptp. suffix] **—in′spis•sa′tion,** *n.* **—in′spis•sa′tor,** *n.*

inst., **1.** instant (def. 11). **2.** instantaneous. **3.** (*usually cap.*) institute. **4.** (*usually cap.*) institution. **5.** instructor. **6.** instrument. **7.** instrumental.

in•sta•bil•i•ty (in′stə bil′i tē), *n.* **1.** the quality or state of being unstable; lack of stability or firmness. **2.** the tendency to behave in an unpredictable, changeable, or erratic manner: *emotional instability.* [1375–1425; late ME *instabilite* < L *instabilitās.* See IN-[3], STABILITY]

instabil′ity line′, *Meteorol.* a nonfrontal line of convective activity in the atmosphere, usually several hundred miles long but of relatively brief duration.

in•sta•ble (in stā′bəl), *adj.* not stable; unstable. [1375–1425; late ME < L *instabilis.* See IN-[3], STABLE[2]]

in•stal (in stôl′), *v.t.,* **-stalled, -stal•ling.** install.

in•stall (in stôl′), *v.t.* **1.** to place in position or connect for service or use: *to install a heating system.* **2.** to establish in an office, position, or place: *to install oneself in new quarters.* **3.** to induct into an office or the like with ceremonies or formalities. Also, **instal.** [1375–1425; late ME < ML *installāre.* See IN-[2], STALL[1]] **—in•stall′er,** *n.*
—Syn. 3. invest, instate, receive.

CONCISE PRONUNCIATION KEY: act, cāpe, dâre, pärt; set, ēqual; if, īce; ox, ōver, ôrder, oil, bŏŏk, bōōt, out; up, ûrge; child; sing; shoe; thin, *th*at; zh as in *treasure.* ə = *a* as in *alone, e* as in *system, i* as in *easily, o* as in *gallop, u* as in *circus;* ᵊ as in *fire* (fīᵊr), *hour* (ouᵊr). l and n can serve as syllabic consonants, as in *cradle* (krād′l), and *button* (but′n). See the full key inside the front cover.

in•stal•la•tion (in′stə lā′shən), *n.* **1.** something installed, as machinery or apparatus placed in position or connected for use. **2.** the act of installing. **3.** the fact of being installed. **4.** *Mil.* any more or less permanent post, camp, station, base, or the like, for the support or carrying on of military activities. [1600–10; < ML *installātiōn-* (s. of *installātiō*). See INSTALL, -ATION]

in•stall•ment[1] (in stôl′mənt), *n.* **1.** any of several parts into which a debt or other sum payable is divided for payment at successive fixed times: *to pay for furniture in monthly installments.* **2.** a single portion of something furnished or issued by parts at successive times: *a magazine serial in six installments.* Also, **in•stal′ment.** [1725–35; IN-[2] + obs. (*e*)*stallment,* equiv. to *estall* to arrange payment on an installment plan (perh. < AF) + -MENT]

in•stall•ment[2] (in stôl′mənt), *n.* **1.** the act of installing. **2.** the fact of being installed; installation. Also, **in•stal′ment.** [1580–90; INSTALL + -MENT]

install′ment plan′, a system for paying for an item in fixed amounts at specified intervals. [1875–80]

In•sta•mat•ic (in′stə mat′ik), *Trademark.* a brand name for a pocket-size, fixed-focus, snapshot camera.

in•stance (in′stəns), *n., v.,* **-stanced, -stanc•ing.** —*n.* **1.** a case or occurrence of anything: *fresh instances of oppression.* **2.** an example put forth in proof or illustration: *to cite a few instances.* **3.** *Law.* the institution and prosecution of a case. **4.** *Archaic.* urgency in speech or action. **5.** *Obs.* an impelling motive. **6. at the instance of,** at the urging or suggestion of: *He applied for the assistantship at the instance of his professor.* **7. for instance,** as an example; for example: *If you were to go to Italy, for instance, you would get a different perspective on our culture.* —*v.t.* **8.** to cite as an instance or example. **9.** to exemplify by an instance. —*v.i.* **10.** to cite an instance. [1300–50; ME < L *instantia* presence, urgency (ML: case, example). See INSTANT, -ANCE]
—**Syn. 2.** See **case**[1].

in•stan•cy (in′stən sē), *n.* **1.** quality of being instant; urgency; pressing nature. **2.** immediateness. [1505–15; < L *instantia.* See INSTANCE, -ANCY]

in•stant (in′stənt), *n.* **1.** an infinitesimal or very short space of time; a moment: *They arrived not an instant too soon.* **2.** the point of time now present or present with reference to some action or event. **3.** a particular moment: *at the instant of contact.* **4.** a food or beverage, esp. coffee, specially processed for quick preparation. **5.** *Older Use.* the present or current month. —*adj.* **6.** succeeding without any interval of time; prompt; immediate: *instant relief from a headache.* **7.** pressing or urgent: *instant need.* **8.** noting a food or beverage requiring a minimal amount of time and effort to prepare, as by heating or the addition of milk or water, before being served or used: *instant coffee; instant pudding.* **9.** occurring, done, or prepared with a minimal amount of time and effort; produced rapidly and with little preparation: *an instant book; instant answers; instant history.* **10.** designed to act or produce results quickly or immediately: *an instant lottery.* **11.** *Older Use.* of the present month: *your letter of the 12th instant. Abbr.:* inst. Cf. **proximo, ultimo. 12.** present; current: *the instant case before the court.* —*adv.* **13.** instantly. [1350–1400; 1910–15; for def. 8; ME < L *instant-* (s. of *instāns*) prp. of *instāre* to be present, urgent, equiv. to *in-* IN-[2] + *-stā-* STAND + *-nt-* prp. suffix]
—**Syn. 1.** second, twinkling, flash, jiffy, trice. See **minute**[1].

in•stan•ta•ne•ous (in′stən tā′nē əs), *adj.* **1.** occurring, done, or completed in an instant: *an instantaneous response.* **2.** existing at or pertaining to a particular instant: *the instantaneous position of the rocket.* [1645–55; < ML *instantāneus.* See INSTANT, -AN, -EOUS] —**in•stan•ta•ne•i•ty** (in stan′tn ē′i tē, in′stən tə nē′-), **in′•stan•ta′ne•ous•ness,** *n.* —**in′stan•ta′ne•ous•ly,** *adv.*
—**Syn. 1.** immediate, sudden, abrupt.

in′stanta′neous sound′ pres′sure, *Physics.* See **sound pressure** (def. 1).

in′stant cam′era, a usually portable camera that produces a finished picture shortly after each exposure. Cf. **Polaroid** (def. 2). [1960–65]

in•stan•ter (in stan′tər), *adv.* immediately; at once. [1680–90; < L: urgently, insistently, equiv. to *instan(t-)* INSTANT + *-ter* adv. suffix]

in•stan•ti•ate (in stan′shē āt′), *v.t.,* **-at•ed, -at•ing.** to provide an instance of or concrete evidence in support of (a theory, concept, claim, or the like). [1945–50; < L *instanti(a)* (taken as comb. form of INSTANCE) + -ATE] —**in•stan′ti•a′tion,** *n.* —**in•stan′ti•a′tive,** *adj.*

in•stant•ize (in′stən tīz′), *v.t.,* **-ized, -iz•ing.** to make (foods or other products) available in instant or easily prepared form. Also, *esp. Brit.,* **in′stant•ise′.** [1960–65; INSTANT + -IZE]

in•stant•ly (in′stənt lē), *adv.* **1.** immediately; at once. **2.** urgently. —*conj.* **3.** as soon as; directly: *I recognized her instantly she entered the room.* [1375–1425; late ME; see INSTANT, -LY]
—**Syn. 1.** forthwith. See **immediately.**

in′stant photog′raphy, photography using an instant camera. [1975–80]

in′stant re′play, 1. Also called, *Brit.,* **action replay.** *Television.* **a.** the recording and immediate rebroadcasting of a segment of a live television broadcast, esp. of a sports event: *an instant replay of the touchdown pass.* **b.** a segment recorded and immediately rebroadcast. **2.** *Informal.* the repetition, review, or reenactment of something immediately or soon after its initial occurrence. [1965–70, *Amer.*]

in•star[1] (in′stär), *n.* an insect in any one of its periods of postembryonic growth between molts. [1890–95; < NL, L *instar* equivalent, counterpart]

in•star[2] (in stär′), *v.t.,* **-starred, -star•ring. 1.** to set with or as if with stars. **2.** *Archaic.* **a.** to place as a star. **b.** to make a star of. [1585–95; IN-[1] + STAR]

in•state (in stāt′), *v.t.,* **-stat•ed, -stat•ing. 1.** to put or place in a certain state or position, as in an office; install. **2.** *Obs.* to endow with something. [1595–1605; IN-[2] + STATE (n.); see REINSTATE] —**in•state′ment,** *n.*

in sta•tu quo (in stä′tōō kwō′; *Eng.* in stā′tyōō kwō′, stach′ōō), *Latin.* in the state in which (anything was or is).

in•stau•ra•tion (in′stô rā′shən), *n.* **1.** renewal; restoration; renovation; repair. **2.** *Obs.* an act of instituting something; establishment. [1595–1605; < L *instaurātiōn-* (s. of *instaurātiō*) a renewing, repeating. See IN-[2], STORE, -ATION] —**in•stau•ra•tor** (in′stô rā′tər), *n.*

in•stead (in sted′), *adv.* **1.** as a substitute or replacement; in the place or stead of someone or something: *We ordered tea but were served coffee instead.* **2.** in preference; as a preferred or accepted alternative: *The city has its pleasures, but she wished instead for the quiet of country life.* **3. instead of,** in place of; in lieu of: *You can use milk instead of cream in this recipe.* [1175–1225; ME; orig. phrase *in stead* in place]

in•step (in′step′), *n.* **1.** the arched upper surface of the human foot between the toes and the ankle. **2.** the part of a shoe, stocking, etc., covering this surface. **3.** the front of the hind leg of a horse, cow, etc., between the hock and the pastern joint; cannon. [1520–30; appar. IN-[1] + STEP]

in•sti•gate (in′sti gāt′), *v.t.,* **-gat•ed, -gat•ing. 1.** to cause by incitement; foment: *to instigate a quarrel.* **2.** to urge, provoke, or incite to some action or course: *to instigate the people to revolt.* [1535–45; < L *instīgātus* ptp. of *instīgāre* to goad on, impel, equiv. to *in-* IN-[2] + *-stīg-* goad, prick (akin to STIGMA, STICK[2]) + *-ātus* -ATE[1]] —**in′sti•gat′ing•ly,** *adv.* —**in′sti•ga′tive,** *adj.* —**in′•sti•ga′tor, in•sti•gant** (in′sti gənt), *n.*
—**Syn. 1.** arouse, provoke. **2.** induce, stimulate, encourage, push; initiate, start.

in•sti•ga•tion (in′sti gā′shən), *n.* **1.** the act of instigating; incitement. **2.** an incentive. [1375–1425; late ME < L *instīgātiōn-* (s. of *instīgātiō*). See INSTIGATE, -ION]

in•stil (in stil′), *v.t.,* **-stilled, -stil•ling.** instill.

in•still (in stil′), *v.t.* **1.** to infuse slowly or gradually into the mind or feelings; insinuate; inject: *to instill courtesy in a child.* **2.** to put in drop by drop. [1525–35; < L *instillāre,* equiv. to *in-* IN-[2] + *stillāre* to drip; see DISTILL] —**in•still′er,** *n.* —**in•still′ment,** *n.*
—**Syn. 1.** inculcate, introduce.

in•stil•la•tion (in′stə lā′shən), *n.* **1.** the act of instilling. **2.** something instilled. [1530–40; < L *instillātiōn-* (s. of *instillātiō*), equiv. to *instillāt(us)* ptp. of *instillāre* to INSTILL + *-iōn-* -ION]

in•stil•la•tor (in′stə lā′tər), *n. Med.* an apparatus for putting liquid drop by drop into a cavity. [1825–35; INSTILL + -ATOR]

in•stinct[1] (in′stingkt), *n.* **1.** an inborn pattern of activity or tendency to action common to a given biological species. **2.** a natural or innate impulse, inclination, or tendency. **3.** a natural aptitude or gift: *an instinct for making money.* **4.** natural intuitive power. [1375–1425; late ME < L *instinctus* prompting, instigation, enthusiasm, equiv. to **insting(uere)* (*in-* IN-[2] + **sting(u)ere* presumably, to prick; see DISTINCT) + *-tus* suffix of v. action]
—**Syn. 3.** genius, knack, faculty, talent.

in•stinct[2] (in stingkt′), *adj.* **1.** filled or infused with some animating principle (usually fol. by *with*): *instinct with life.* **2.** *Obs.* animated by some inner force. [1530–40; < L *instinctus* excited, roused, inspired, ptp. of **insting(u)ere;* see INSTINCT[1]]

in•stinc•tive (in stingk′tiv), *adj.* **1.** of, pertaining to, or of the nature of instinct. **2.** prompted by or resulting from or as if from instinct; natural; unlearned: *an instinctive will to survive.* Also, **in•stinc•tu•al** (in stingk′chōō əl). [1640–50; INSTINCT[1] + -IVE] —**in•stinc′tive•ly, in•stinc′tu•al•ly,** *adv.*
—**Syn. 2.** spontaneous, intuitive, unpremeditated.

in•sti•tute (in′sti tōōt′, -tyōōt′), *v.,* **-tut•ed, -tut•ing,** *n.* —*v.t.* **1.** to set up; establish; organize: *to institute a government.* **2.** to inaugurate; initiate; start: *to institute a new course in American literature.* **3.** to set in operation: *to institute a lawsuit.* **4.** to bring into use or practice: *to institute laws.* **5.** to establish in an office or position. **6.** *Eccles.* to assign to or invest with a spiritual charge, as of a parish. —*n.* **7.** a society or organization for carrying on a particular work, as of a literary, scientific, or educational character. **8.** the building occupied by such a society. **9.** *Educ.* **a.** an institution, generally beyond the secondary school level, devoted to instruction in technical subjects, usually separate but sometimes organized as a part of a university. **b.** a unit within a university organized for advanced instruction and research in a relatively narrow field of subject matter. **c.** a short instructional program set up for a special group interested in a specialized field or subject. **10.** an established principle, law, custom, or organization. **11. institutes, a.** an elementary textbook of law designed for beginners. **b.** (*cap.*) Also called **In′stitutes of Justin′ian.** an elementary treatise on Roman law in four books, forming one of the four divisions of the Corpus Juris Civilis. **12.** something instituted. [1275–1325; ME < L *institūtus* ptp. of *instituere* to set, put up, establish, equiv. to *in-* IN-[2] + *-stitū-* (comb. form of *statū-,* s. of *statuere* to make STAND) + *-tus* ptp. suffix]

in•sti•tut•er (in′sti tōō′tər, -tyōō′-), *n.* institutor.

in•sti•tu•tion (in′sti tōō′shən, -tyōō′-), *n.* **1.** an organization, establishment, foundation, society, or the like, devoted to the promotion of a particular cause or program, esp. one of a public, educational, or charitable character: *This college is the best institution of its kind.* **2.** the building devoted to such work. **3.** a public or private place for the care or confinement of inmates, esp. mental patients or other disabled or handicapped persons. **4.** *Sociol.* a well-established and structured pattern of behavior or of relationships that is accepted as a fundamental part of a culture, as marriage: *the institution of the family.* **5.** any established law, custom, etc. **6.** any familiar, long-established person, thing, or practice; fixture. **7.** the act of instituting or setting up; establishment: *the institution of laws.* **8.** *Eccles.* **a.** the origination of the Eucharist, and enactment of its observance, by Christ. **b.** the investment of a member of the clergy with a spiritual charge. [1350–1400; ME < L *institūtiōn-* (s. of *institūtiō*). See INSTITUTE, -ION]

in•sti•tu•tion•al (in′sti tōō′shə nl, -tyōō′-), *adj.* **1.** of, pertaining to, or established by institution. **2.** of or pertaining to organized establishments, foundations, societies, or the like, or to the buildings devoted to their work. **3.** of the nature of an institution. **4.** characterized by the blandness, drabness, uniformity, and lack of individualized attention attributed to large institutions that serve many people: *institutional food.* **5.** (of advertising) having as the primary object the establishment of goodwill and a favorable reputation rather than the immediate sale of the product. **6.** pertaining to institutes or principles, esp. of jurisprudence. [1610–20; INSTITUTION + -AL[1]] —**in′sti•tu′tion•al•ly,** *adv.*

in•sti•tu•tion•al•ism (in′sti tōō′shə nl iz′əm, -tyōō′-), *n.* **1.** the system of institutions or organized societies devoted to public, charitable, or similar purposes. **2.** strong attachment to established institutions, as of religion. **3.** the policy or practice of using public institutions to house and care for people considered incapable of caring for themselves. **4.** the belief or policy that a church must maintain institutions of education, welfare, etc., for its members. [1860–65; INSTITUTIONAL + -ISM] —**in′sti•tu′tion•al•ist,** *n.*

in•sti•tu•tion•al•ize (in′sti tōō′shə nl īz′, -tyōō′-), *v.t.,* **-ized, -iz•ing. 1.** to make institutional. **2.** to make into or treat as an institution: *the danger of institutionalizing racism.* **3.** to place or confine in an institution, esp. one for the care of mental illness, alcoholism, etc. Also, *esp. Brit.,* **in′sti•tu′tion•al•ise′.** [1860–65; INSTITUTIONAL + -IZE] —**in′sti•tu′tion•al•i•za′tion,** *n.*

in•sti•tu•tion•ar•y (in′sti tōō′shə ner′ē, -tyōō′-), *adj.* **1.** of or pertaining to an institution or institutions; institutional. **2.** of or pertaining to institution, esp. ecclesiastical institution. [1640–50; INSTITUTION + -ARY]

in•sti•tu•tive (in′sti tōō′tiv, -tyōō′-), *adj.* tending or intended to institute or establish. [1620–30; INSTITUTE + -IVE] —**in′sti•tu′tive•ly,** *adv.*

in•sti•tu•tor (in′sti tōō′tər, -tyōō′-), *n.* **1.** a person who institutes or founds. **2.** *Prot. Episc. Ch.* a person who institutes a minister into a parish or church. Also, **instituter.** [1540–50; < LL *institūtor,* equiv. to *institū-,* s. of *instituere* to INSTITUTE + *-tor* -TOR]

instr., 1. instructor. **2.** instrument. **3.** instrumental.

in•stroke (in′strōk′), *n.* **1.** a stroke in an inward direction. **2.** (in an engine) the stroke during which the piston moves into the cylinder. [1885–90; IN + STROKE[1]]

in•struct (in strukt′), *v.t.* **1.** to furnish with knowledge, esp. by a systematic method; teach; train; educate. **2.** to furnish with orders or directions; direct; order; command: *The doctor instructed me to diet.* **3.** to furnish with information; inform; apprise. **4.** *Law.* (of a judge) to guide (a jury) by outlining the legal principles involved in the case under consideration. [1375–1425; late ME < L *instructus* ptp. of *instruere* to equip, train, set in order, equiv. to *in-* IN-[2] + *struc-* (var. s. of *struere* to put together) + *-tus* ptp. suffix] —**in•struct′ed•ly,** *adv.* —**in•struct′ed•ness,** *n.* —**in•struct′i•ble,** *adj.*
—**Syn. 1.** tutor, coach; drill, discipline; indoctrinate; school. See **teach. 2.** prescribe. **3.** enlighten.

in•struc•tion (in struk′shən), *n.* **1.** the act or practice of instructing or teaching; education. **2.** knowledge or information imparted. **3.** an item of such knowledge or information. **4.** Usually, **instructions.** orders or directions: *The instructions are on the back of the box.* **5.** the act of furnishing with authoritative directions. **6.** *Computers.* a command given to a computer to carry out a particular operation. [1375–1425; late ME *instruccio(u)n* < L *instructiōn-* (s. of *instructiō*). See INSTRUCT, -ION] —**in•struc′tion•al,** *adj.*
—**Syn. 1.** tutoring, coaching; training, drill, exercise; indoctrination; schooling. **5.** command, mandate.

in•struc•tive (in struk′tiv), *adj.* **1.** serving to instruct or inform; conveying instruction, knowledge, or information; enlightening. **2.** *Gram.* noting a case, as in Finnish, whose distinctive function is to indicate means by which. [1605–15; INSTRUCT + -IVE] —**in•struc′tive•ly,** *adv.* —**in•struc′tive•ness,** *n.*

in•struc•tor (in struk′tər), *n.* **1.** a person who instructs; teacher. **2.** a teacher in a college or university who ranks below an assistant professor. [1425–75; late ME < L, equiv. to *instruc-,* var. s. of *instruere* (see INSTRUCT) + *-tor* -TOR] —**in•struc•to•ri•al** (in′struk tôr′ē əl, -tōr′-), *adj.* —**in•struc′tor•ship′,** *n.*
—**Syn. 1.** tutor, schoolmaster, preceptor, pedagogue.

in•struc•tress (in struk′tris), *n.* a woman who instructs; teacher. [1620–30; INSTRUCT(O)R + -ESS]
—**Usage.** See **-ess.**

in•stru•ment (in′strə mənt), *n.* **1.** a mechanical tool or implement, esp. one used for delicate or precision work: *surgical instruments.* **2.** a contrivance or apparatus for producing musical sounds: *a stringed instrument.* **3.** a means by which something is effected or done; agency: *an instrument of government.* **4.** a device for measuring the present value of a quantity under observation. **5.** a mechanical or electronic measuring device, esp. one used in navigation: *landing a plane by instruments.* **6.** a formal legal document, as a draft or bond: *negotiable instruments.* **7.** a person used by another merely as a means to some private end; tool or dupe. —*v.t.* **8.** to equip with instruments, as a machine or manufacturing process: *to instrument a space vehicle.* **9.** to arrange a composition for musical instruments; orchestrate. [1250–1300; ME < L *instrūmentum* equip-

ment, equiv. to *instrū-*, s. of *instruere* to equip (see INSTRUCT) + *-mentum* -MENT; see INSTRUCT]
—**Syn. 1.** See **tool.**

in•stru•men•tal (in′strə men′tl), *adj.* **1.** serving or acting as an instrument or means; useful; helpful. **2.** performed on or written for a musical instrument or instruments: *instrumental music.* **3.** of or pertaining to an instrument or tool. **4.** *Gram.* **a.** (in certain inflected languages, as Old English and Russian) noting or pertaining to a case having as its distinctive function the indication of means or agency, as Old English *beseah blithe andweitan* "looked with a happy countenance." **b.** noting the affix or other element characteristic of this case, or a word containing such an element. **c.** similar to such a case form in function or meaning, as the Latin instrumental ablative, *gladiō,* "by means of a sword." **d.** (in case grammar) pertaining to the semantic role of a noun phrase that indicates the inanimate, nonvolitional, immediate cause of the action expressed by a verb, as *the rock* in *The rock broke the window* or in *I broke the window with the rock.* —*n.* **5.** *Gram.* **a.** the instrumental case. **b.** a word in the instrumental case. **c.** a construction of similar meaning. **6.** a musical composition played by an instrument or a group of instruments. Cf. **vocal** (def. 8). [1350–1400; ME < ML *instrūmentālis.* See INSTRUMENT, -AL[1]] —**in′stru•men′tal•ly,** *adv.*
—**Syn. 1.** implemental, effectual, effective.

instrumen′tal condi′tioning, *Psychol.* conditioning (def. 1). [1935–40]

in•stru•men•tal•ism (in′strə men′tl iz′əm), *n. Philos.* the variety of pragmatism developed by John Dewey, maintaining that the truth of an idea is determined by its success in the active solution of a problem and that the value of ideas is determined by their function in human experience. [1905–10; INSTRUMENTAL + -ISM]

in•stru•men•tal•ist (in′strə men′tl ist), *n.* **1.** a person who plays a musical instrument. **2.** an advocate of instrumentalism. —*adj.* **3.** of, pertaining to, or advocating instrumentalism. [1815–25; INSTRUMENTAL + -IST]

in•stru•men•tal•i•ty (in′strə men tal′i tē), *n., pl.* **-ties** for 1, 3. **1.** the quality or state of being instrumental. **2.** the fact or function of serving some purpose. **3.** a means or agency. [1645–55; INSTRUMENTAL + -ITY]

in•stru•men•ta•tion (in′strə men tā′shən), *n.* **1.** the arranging of music for instruments, esp. for an orchestra. **2.** the list of instruments for which a composition is scored. **3.** the use of, or work done by, instruments. **4.** instrumental agency; instrumentality. **5.** the science of developing, manufacturing, and utilizing instruments, esp. those used in science and industry. [1835–45; INSTRUMENT (v.) + -ATION]

in•stru•ment•ed (in′strə men′tid), *adj.* equipped with instruments to perform specified functions, as testing, measurement, or control: *an instrumented railroad car.* [1945–50; INSTRUMENT + -ED[3]]

in′strument fly′ing, the control and navigation of an aircraft by reference to its gauges, with no or only limited visual reference outside the cockpit. [1925–30]

in′strument land′ing, an aircraft landing accomplished by use of gauges on the instrument panel and ground-based radio equipment, with limited reference to outside visual signals. [1935–40]

in′strument pan′el, 1. Also called **in′strument board′.** a panel on which are mounted an array of dials, lights, and gauges that monitor the performance of a machine or device, as an airplane. **2.** *Auto.* dashboard (def. 1). [1930–35]

in′strument sta′tion, *Survey.* station (def. 14a).

in•sub•or•di•nate (in′sə bôr′dn it), *adj.* **1.** not submitting to authority; disobedient: *an insubordinate soldier.* **2.** not lower. —*n.* **3.** a person who is insubordinate. [1840–50; IN-[3] + SUBORDINATE] —**in′sub•or′di•nate•ly,** *adv.* —**in′sub•or′di•na′tion,** *n.*
—**Syn. 1.** refractory, defiant, insolent.

in•sub•stan•tial (in′səb stan′shəl), *adj.* **1.** not substantial or real; lacking substance: *an insubstantial world of dreams.* **2.** not solid or firm; weak; flimsy. **3.** not substantial in amount or size; inconsiderable: *an insubstantial sum.* [1600–10; < LL *insubstantiālis.* See IN-[3], SUBSTANTIAL] —**in′sub•stan′ti•al′i•ty,** *n.* —**in′•sub•stan′tial•ly,** *adv.*

in•suf•fer•a•ble (in suf′ər ə bəl), *adj.* not to be endured; intolerable; unbearable: *their insufferable insolence.* [1525–35; IN-[3] + SUFFERABLE] —**in•suf′fer•a•ble•ness,** *n.* —**in•suf′fer•a•bly,** *adv.*

in•suf•fi•cien•cy (in′sə fish′ən sē), *n., pl.* **-cies** for 2. **1.** deficiency in amount, force, power, competence, or fitness; inadequacy: *insufficiency of supplies.* **2.** an instance of this. **3.** inability of an organ or other part of the body to function normally: *cardiac insufficiency.* Also, **in′suf•fi′cience.** [1375–1425; late ME < LL *insufficientia.* See INSUFFICIENT, -ENCY]

in•suf•fi•cient (in′sə fish′ənt), *adj.* **1.** not sufficient; lacking in what is necessary or required: *an insufficient answer.* **2.** deficient in force, quality, or amount; inadequate: *insufficient protection.* [1350–1400; ME < LL *insufficient-* (s. of *insufficiēns*). See IN-[3], SUFFICIENT] —**in′suf•fi′cient•ly,** *adv.*
—**Syn. 1.** inadequate, scanty, deficient.

in•suf•flate (in suf′lāt, in′sə flāt′), *v.t.,* **-flat•ed, -flat•ing. 1.** to blow or breathe (something) in. **2.** *Med.* to blow (air or a medicinal substance) into some opening or upon some part of the body. **3.** *Eccles.* to breathe upon, esp. upon one being baptized or upon the water of baptism. [1650–60; < LL *insufflātus* ptp. of *insufflāre* to blow into or on. See IN-[2], SUFFLATE] —**in′suf•fla′tion,** *n.* —**in′suf•fla′tor,** *n.*

in•su•la (in′sə lə, ins′yə-), *n., pl.* **-lae** (-lē′). *Anat.* a group of convolutions situated at the base of the lateral fissure of the brain. Also called **Island of Reil.** [1825–35; < NL, L: island; cf. ISLE]

in•su•lant (in′sə lənt, ins′yə-), *n.* an insulating material, as used in building trades. [1930–35; INSUL(ATE) + -ANT]

in•su•lar (in′sə lər, ins′yə-), *adj.* **1.** of or pertaining to an island or islands: *insular possessions.* **2.** dwelling or situated on an island. **3.** forming an island: *insular rocks.* **4.** detached; standing alone; isolated. **5.** of, pertaining to, or characteristic of islanders. **6.** narrow-minded or illiberal; provincial: *insular attitudes toward foreigners.* **7.** *Pathol.* occurring in or characterized by one or more isolated spots, patches, or the like. **8.** *Anat.* pertaining to an island of cells or tissue, as the islets of Langerhans. —*n.* **9.** an inhabitant of an island; islander. [1605–15; < LL *insulāris.* See INSULA, -AR[1]] —**in′su•lar•ism,** *n.* —**in′su•lar′i•ty,** *n.* —**in′su•lar•ly,** *adv.*

In′sular Celt′ic, a partly geographical, partly genetic grouping of Celtic languages that consists of those spoken in the British Isles in ancient times and those descended from them. Cf. **Continental Celtic.**

in•su•lar•ize (in′sə lə rīz′, ins′yə-), *v.t.,* **-ized, -iz•ing.** to make into an island or represent as insular. Also, *esp. Brit.,* **in′su•lar•ise′.** [1890–95; INSULAR + -IZE]

in•su•late (in′sə lāt′, ins′yə-), *v.t.,* **-lat•ed, -lat•ing. 1.** to cover, line, or separate with a material that prevents or reduces the passage, transfer, or leakage of heat, electricity, or sound: *to insulate an electric wire with a rubber sheath; to insulate a coat with down.* **2.** to place in an isolated situation or condition; segregate. [1530–40; < L *insulātus* made into an island. See INSULA, -ATE[1]]

in•su•la•tion (in′sə lā′shən, ins′yə-), *n.* **1.** material used for insulating. **2.** the act of insulating. **3.** the state of being insulated. [1790–1800; INSULATE + -ION]

in•su•la•tive (in′sə lā′tiv, ins′yə-), *adj.* serving to protect or insulate: *glassware shipped in insulative packing.* [1940–45; INSULATE + -IVE]

in•su•la•tor (in′sə lā′tər, ins′yə-), *n.* **1.** *Elect.* **a.** a material of such low conductivity that the flow of current through it is negligible. **b.** insulating material, often glass or porcelain, in a unit form designed so as to support a charged conductor and electrically isolate it. **2.** a person or thing that insulates. [1795–1805; INSULATE + -OR[2]]

in•su•lin (in′sə lin, ins′yə-), *n.* **1.** *Biochem.* a polypeptide hormone, produced by the beta cells of the islets of Langerhans of the pancreas, that regulates the metabolism of glucose and other nutrients. **2.** *Pharm.* any of several commercial preparations of this substance, each of which allows a particular rate of absorption into the system: genetically engineered or obtained from the pig or ox pancreas, and used in the treatment of diabetes to restore the normal ability of the body to utilize sugars and other carbohydrates. [1910–15; INSUL(A) + -IN[2]]

in′su•lin-co•ma ther′apy (in′sə lin kō′mə, ins′yə-), *Psychiatry.* a former treatment for mental illness, esp. schizophrenia, employing insulin-induced hypoglycemia as a method for producing convulsive seizures. Also called **in′su•lin-shock ther′apy** (in′sə lin shok′, ins′yə-).

in′su•lin-de•pendent diabe′tes (in′sə lin di pen′dənt, in′syə-), *Pathol.* See under **diabetes.**

in•su•lin•ize (in′sə lə nīz′, ins′yə-), *v.t.,* **-ized, -iz•ing.** to treat with insulin. Also, *esp. Brit.,* **in′su•lin•ise′.** [1925–30; INSULIN + -IZE] —**in′su•li•na′tion,** *n.*

in•su•li•no•ma (in′sə lə nō′mə, ins′yə-), *n., pl.* **-mas, -ma•ta** (-mə tə). *Pathol.* a benign tumor of the insulin-secreting cells of the pancreas that may produce signs of hypoglycemia. Also, **in•su•lo•ma** (in′sə lō′mə, ins′yə-). Also called **islet cell adenoma.** [1950–55; INSULIN + -OMA]

in′sulin pump′, an external battery-powered device that injects insulin into the body at a programmed rate to control diabetes.

in′sulin shock′, *Pathol.* a state of collapse caused by a decrease in blood sugar resulting from the administration of excessive insulin. Also called **in′sulin reac′tion.** [1920–25]

In•sull (in′səl), *n.* **Samuel,** 1859–1938, U.S. public utilities magnate, born in England.

in•sult (*v.* in sult′; *n.* in′sult), *v.t.* **1.** to treat or speak to insolently or with contemptuous rudeness; affront. **2.** to affect as an affront; offend or demean. **3.** *Archaic.* to attack; assault. —*v.i.* **4.** *Archaic.* to behave with insolent triumph; exult contemptuously (usually fol. by *on, upon,* or *over*). —*n.* **5.** an insolent or contemptuously rude action or remark; affront. **6.** something having the effect of an affront: *That book is an insult to one's intelligence.* **7.** *Med.* **a.** an injury or trauma. **b.** an agent that inflicts this. **8.** *Archaic.* an attack or assault. [1560–70; < L *insultāre* to jump on, insult, equiv. to *in-* IN-[2] + *-sultāre,* comb. form of *saltāre* to jump; see SALTANT] —**in•sult′a•ble,** *adj.* —**in•sult′er,** *n.*
—**Syn. 1.** offend, scorn, injure, abuse. **5.** offense, outrage. INSULT, INDIGNITY, AFFRONT, SLIGHT imply an act that injures another's honor, self-respect, etc. INSULT implies such insolence of speech or manner as deeply humiliates or wounds one's feelings and arouses to anger. INDIGNITY is esp. used of inconsiderate, contemptuous treatment toward one entitled to respect. AFFRONT implies open disrespect or offense shown, as it were, to the face. SLIGHT may imply inadvertent indifference or disregard, which may also indicate ill-concealed contempt. —**Ant. 1, 5.** compliment.

in•sul•ta•tion (in′səl tā′shən), *n. Archaic.* insult. [1505–15; < L *insultātiōn-* (s. of *insultātiō*), equiv. to *insultāt(us)* ptp. of *insultāre* to INSULT + *-iōn-* -ION]

in•sult•ing (in sul′ting), *adj.* giving or causing insult; characterized by affronting rudeness, insolence, etc. [1585–95; INSULT + -ING[2]] —**in•sult′ing•ly,** *adv.*
—**Syn.** rude, discourteous, abusive, derogatory, offensive, nasty.

in•su•per•a•ble (in so͞o′pər ə bəl), *adj.* incapable of being passed over, overcome, or surmounted: *an insuperable barrier.* [1300–50; ME < L *insuperābilis.* See IN-[3], SUPERABLE] —**in•su′per•a•bil′i•ty, in•su′per•a•ble•ness,** *n.* —**in•su′per•a•bly,** *adv.*

in•sup•port•a•ble (in′sə pôr′tə bəl, -pōr′-), *adj.* **1.** not endurable; unbearable; insufferable: *insupportable pain.* **2.** incapable of support or justification, as by evidence or collected facts: *an insupportable accusation.* [1520–30; < LL *insupportābilis.* See IN-[3], SUPPORTABLE] —**in′sup•port′a•ble•ness, in′sup•port′a•bil′i•ty,** *n.* —**in′sup•port′a•bly,** *adv.*

in•sup•press•i•ble (in′sə pres′ə bəl), *adj.* incapable of being suppressed; irrepressible: *his insuppressible humor.* [1600–10; IN-[3] + SUPPRESSIBLE] —**in′sup•press′i•bly,** *adv.*

in•sur•a•ble (in sho͝or′ə bəl, -shûr′-), *adj.* capable of being or proper to be insured, as against loss or harm. [1800–10; INSURE + -ABLE] —**in•sur′a•bil′i•ty,** *n.*

in•sur•ance (in sho͝or′əns, -shûr′-), *n.* **1.** the act, system, or business of insuring property, life, one's person, etc., against loss or harm arising in specified contingencies, as fire, accident, death, disablement, or the like, in consideration of a payment proportionate to the risk involved. **2.** coverage by contract in which one party agrees to indemnify or reimburse another for loss that occurs under the terms of the contract. **3.** the contract itself, set forth in a written or printed agreement or policy. **4.** the amount for which anything is insured. **5.** an insurance premium. **6.** any means of guaranteeing against loss or harm: *Taking vitamin C is viewed as an insurance against catching colds.* —*adj.* **7.** of or pertaining to a score that increases a team's lead and insures that the lead will be held if the opposing team should score once more: *The home run gave the team an insurance run, making the score 7-5.* [1545–55; INSURE + -ANCE]

in•sur•ant (in sho͝or′ənt, -shûr′-), *n.* a person who takes out an insurance policy. [1850–55; INSURE + -ANT]

in•sure (in sho͝or′, -shûr′), *v.,* **-sured, -sur•ing.** —*v.t.* **1.** to guarantee against loss or harm. **2.** to secure indemnity to or on, in case of loss, damage, or death. **3.** to issue or procure an insurance policy on or for. **4.** ensure (defs. 1–3). —*v.i.* **5.** to issue or procure an insurance policy. [1400–50; late ME; var. of ENSURE]
—**Syn. 1.** warrant. **4.** assure.

in•sured (in sho͝ord′, -shûrd′), *n.* the person, group, or organization whose life or property is covered by an insurance policy. [1675–85; INSURE + -ED[2]]

in•sur•er (in sho͝or′ər, -shûr′-), *n.* **1.** a person or company that contracts to indemnify another in the event of loss or damage; underwriter. **2.** a person or thing that insures. **3.** a person who sells insurance. [1645–55; INSURE + -ER[1]]

in•sur•gence (in sûr′jəns), *n.* an act of rebellion; insurrection; revolt. [1840–50; INSURG(ENT) + -ENCE]

in•sur•gen•cy (in sûr′jən sē), *n., pl.* **-cies** for 4. **1.** the state or condition of being insurgent. **2.** insurrection against an existing government, usually one's own, by a group not recognized as having the status of a belligerent. **3.** rebellion within a group, as by members against leaders. **4.** insurgence. [1795–1805; INSURG(ENT) + -ENCY]

in•sur•gent (in sûr′jənt), *n.* **1.** a person who rises in forcible opposition to lawful authority, esp. a person who engages in armed resistance to a government or to the execution of its laws; rebel. **2.** a member of a section of a political party that revolts against the methods or policies of the party. —*adj.* **3.** of or characteristic of an insurgent or insurgents. **4.** surging or rushing in: *The insurgent waves battered the shore.* [1755–65; < L *insurgent-* (s. of *insurgēns*) prp. of *insurgere* to get up, ascend, rebel. See IN-[2], SURGE, -ENT]
—**Syn. 3.** rebellious, revolutionary, mutinous.

insur′ing clause′, the clause in an insurance policy setting forth the kind and degree of coverage granted by the insurer.

in•sur•mount•a•ble (in′sər moun′tə bəl), *adj.* incapable of being surmounted, passed over, or overcome; insuperable: *an insurmountable obstacle.* [1690–1700; IN-[3] + SURMOUNTABLE] —**in′sur•mount′a•bil′i•ty, in′sur•mount′a•ble•ness,** *n.* —**in′sur•mount′a•bly,** *adv.*

in•sur•rec•tion (in′sə rek′shən), *n.* an act or instance of rising in revolt, rebellion, or resistance against civil authority or an established government. [1425–75; late ME < LL *insurrēctiōn-* (s. of *insurrēctiō*), equiv. to *insurrēct(us)* (ptp. of *insurgere;* see INSURGENT) + *-iōn-* -ION] —**in′sur•rec′tion•al,** *adj.* —**in′sur•rec′tion•al•ly,** *adv.* —**in′sur•rec′tion•ism,** *n.* —**in′sur•rec′tion•ist,** *n.*
—**Syn.** insurgency, uprising, mutiny.

in•sur•rec•tion•ar•y (in′sə rek′shə ner′ē), *adj., n., pl.* **-ar•ies.** —*adj.* **1.** of, pertaining to, or of the nature of insurrection. **2.** given to or causing insurrection. —*n.* **3.** a person who takes part in an insurrection; rebel; insurgent. [1790–1800; INSURRECTION + -ARY]

in•sur•rec•tion•ize (in′sə rek′shə nīz′), *v.t.,* **-ized, -iz•ing. 1.** to cause insurrection in (a country or the like). **2.** to rouse (a person, group, or people) to insurgent action. Also, *esp. Brit.,* **in′sur•rec′tion•ise′.** [1815–25; INSURRECTION + -IZE]

in•sus•cep•ti•ble (in′sə sep′tə bəl), *adj.* not susceptible; incapable of being influenced or affected (usually fol. by *of* or *to*): *insusceptible of flattery; insusceptible to infection.* [1595–1605; IN-[3] + SUSCEPTIBLE] —**in′sus•cep′ti•bil′i•ty,** *n.* —**in′sus•cep′ti•bly,** *adv.*

in•swept (in′swept′), *adj.* tapering or narrowing at the front or tip, as an airplane wing. [1905–10; adj. use of v. phrase *swept in*]

in•swing•er (in′swing′ər), *n. Cricket.* a bowled ball that veers from off side to leg side. Cf. **outswinger.** [1915–20; IN + SWINGER]

int., 1. interest. **2.** interim. **3.** interior. **4.** interjection.

CONCISE PRONUNCIATION KEY: *act, cāpe, dâre, pärt; set, ēqual; if, īce; ox, ōver, ôrder, oil, bo͝ok, bo͞ot, out; up, ûrge; child; sing; shoe; thin, that;* zh as in *treasure.* ə = *a* as in *alone, e* as in *system, i* as in *easily, o* as in *gallop, u* as in *circus;* ᵊ as in *fire* (fīᵊr), *hour* (ouᵊr). l and n can serve as syllabic consonants, as in *cradle* (krād′l), and *button* (but′n). See the full key inside the front cover.

5. internal. 6. international. 7. interpreter. 8. interval. 9. intransitive.

in·tact (in takt′), *adj.* **1.** not altered, broken, or impaired; remaining uninjured, sound, or whole; untouched; unblemished: *The vase remained intact despite rough handling.* **2.** not changed or diminished; not influenced or swayed: *Despite misfortune, his faith is still intact.* **3.** complete or whole, esp. not castrated or emasculated. **4.** having the hymen unbroken; virginal. [1400–50; late ME < L *intāctus* untouched, equiv. to *in-* IN-³ + *tāctus*, ptp. of *tangere* to touch] —**in·tact′ly,** *adv.* —**in·tact′ness,** *n.*
—**Syn. 1.** See **complete.**

in·tagl·io (in tal′yō, -täl′-; *It.* ēn tä′lyô), *n., pl.* **-tagl·ios,** *It.* **-ta·gli** (-tä′lyē), *v.* —*n.* **1.** incised carving, as opposed to carving in relief. **2.** ornamentation with a figure or design sunk below the surface. **3.** a gem, seal, piece of jewelry, or the like, cut with an incised or sunken design. **4.** an incised or countersunk die. **5.** a figure or design so produced. **6.** a process in which a design, text, etc., is engraved into the surface of a plate so that when ink is applied and the excess is wiped off, ink remains in the grooves and is transferred to paper in printing, as in engraving or etching. **7.** an impression or printing from such a design, engraving, etc. —*v.t.* **8.** to incise or display in intaglio. [1635–45; < It, deriv. of *intagliare* to cut in, engrave, equiv. to *in-* IN-² + *tagliare* to cut < LL *tāliāre*, deriv. of L *tālea* a cutting; see TALLY]

in·take (in′tāk′), *n.* **1.** the place or opening at which a fluid is taken into a channel, pipe, etc. **2.** an act or instance of taking in: *an intake of oxygen.* **3.** something that is taken in. **4.** a quantity taken in: *an intake of 50 gallons a minute.* **5.** a narrowing; contraction. [1515–25; n. use of v. phrase *take in*]

in′take man′ifold, a collection of tubes through which the fuel-air mixture flows from the carburetor or fuel injector to the intake valves of the cylinders of an internal-combustion engine.

in′take valve′, a valve in the cylinder head of an internal-combustion engine that opens at the proper moment in the cycle to allow the fuel-air mixture to be drawn into the cylinder. [1960–65]

in·tan·gi·ble (in tan′jə bəl), *adj.* **1.** not tangible; incapable of being perceived by the sense of touch, as incorporeal or immaterial things; impalpable. **2.** not definite or clear to the mind: *intangible arguments.* **3.** (of an asset) existing only in connection with something else, as the goodwill of a business. —*n.* **4.** something intangible, esp. an intangible asset: *Intangibles are hard to value.* [1630–40; < ML *intangibilis.* See IN-³, TANGIBLE] —**in·tan′gi·bil′i·ty, in·tan′gi·ble·ness,** *n.* —**in·tan′gi·bly,** *adv.*
—**Syn. 2.** vague, elusive, fleeting.

in·tar·si·a (in tär′sē ə), *n.* an art or technique of decorating a surface with inlaid patterns, esp. of wood mosaic, developed during the Renaissance. Also, **tarsia.** [1860–65; alter. (influenced by It *tarsia*) of It *intarsio*, deriv. of *intarsiare* to inlay, equiv. to *in-* IN-² + *tarsiare* < Ar *tarṣī'* an inlay, incrustation; see TARSIA] —**in·tar·si·ate** (in tär′sē āt′, -it), *adj.*

in·tar·sist (in tär′sist), *n.* a person who creates in or practices intarsia. [INTARS(IA) + -IST]

in·te·ger (in′ti jər), *n.* **1.** *Math.* one of the positive or negative numbers 1, 2, 3, etc., or zero. Cf. **whole number.** **2.** a complete entity. [1500–10; < L: untouched, hence, undivided, whole, equiv. to *in-* IN-³ + *-teg-* (comb. form of *tag-*, base of *tangere* to touch) + *-er* adj. suffix]

in·te·ger vi·tae (in′te geʀ wē′tī; *Eng.* in′ti jər vī′tē, vē′tī), *Latin.* blameless in life; innocent.

in·te·gra·ble (in′ti grə bəl), *adj. Math.* capable of being integrated, as a mathematical function or differential equation. [1720–30; INTEGR(ATE) + -ABLE] —**in′te·gra·bil′i·ty,** *n.*

in·te·gral (in′ti grəl, in teg′rəl), *adj.* **1.** of, pertaining to, or belonging as a part of the whole; constituent or component: *integral parts.* **2.** necessary to the completeness of the whole: *This point is integral to his plan.* **3.** consisting or composed of parts that together constitute a whole. **4.** entire; complete; whole: *the integral works of a writer.* **5.** *Arith.* pertaining to or being an integer; not fractional. **6.** *Math.* pertaining to or involving integrals. —*n.* **7.** an integral whole. **8.** *Math.* **a.** Also called **Riemann integral.** the numerical measure of the area bounded above by the graph of a given function, below by the *x*-axis, and on the sides by ordinates drawn at the endpoints of a specified interval; the limit, as the norm of partitions of the given interval approaches zero, of the sum of the products of the function evaluated at a point in each subinterval times the length of the subinterval. **b.** a primitive. **c.** any of several analogous quantities. Cf. **improper integral, line integral, multiple integral, surface integral.** [1545–55; < ML *integrālis.* See INTEGER, -AL¹] —**in′te·gral′i·ty,** *n.* —**in′te·gral·ly,** *adv.*
—**Syn. 2.** essential, indispensable, requisite.

in′tegral cal′culus, the branch of mathematics that deals with integrals, esp. the methods of ascertaining indefinite integrals and applying them to the solution of differential equations and the determining of areas, volumes, and lengths. [1720–30]

in′tegral curve′, *Math.* a curve that is a geometric representation of a functional solution to a given differential equation.

in′tegral domain′, *Math.* a commutative ring in which the cancellation law holds true. [1935–40]

in′tegral equa′tion, *Math.* an equation in which an integral involving a dependent variable appears. [1795–1805]

in′tegral func′tion, *Math. Chiefly Brit.* an entire function. [1810–20]

in·te·gral·ism (in′ti grə liz′əm), *n.* the belief that one's religious convictions should dictate one's political and social actions. [1870–75; INTEGRAL + -ISM]

in′tegral test′, *Math.* the theorem that a given infinite series converges if the function whose value at each integer is the corresponding term in the series is decreasing, tends to zero, and results in a finite number when integrated from one to infinity.

in·te·grand (in′ti grand′), *n. Math.* the expression to be integrated. [1895–1900; < L *integrandum*, n. use of neut. of *integrandus*, ger. of *integrāre* to INTEGRATE]

in·te·grant (in′ti grənt), *adj.* **1.** making up or being a part of a whole; constituent. —*n.* **2.** an integrant part. **3.** a solid, rigid sheet of building material composed of several layers of the same or of different materials. [1630–40; < L *integrant-* (s. of *integrāns*) prp. of *integrāre* to INTEGRATE. See INTEGER, -ANT]

in·te·graph (in′ti graf′, -gräf′), *n.* integrator (def. 2). [1880–85; b. INTEGRATE and -GRAPH]

in·te·grate (in′ti grāt′), *v.,* **-grat·ed, -grat·ing.** —*v.t.* **1.** to bring together or incorporate (parts) into a whole. **2.** to make up, combine, or complete to produce a whole or a larger unit, as parts do. **3.** to unite or combine. **4.** to give or cause to give equal opportunity and consideration to (a racial, religious, or ethnic group or a member of such a group): *to integrate minority groups in the school system.* **5.** to combine (educational facilities, classes, and the like, previously segregated by race) into one unified system; desegregate. **6.** to give or cause to give members of all races, religions, and ethnic groups an equal opportunity to belong to, be employed by, be customers of, or vote in (an organization, place of business, city, state, etc.): *to integrate a restaurant; to integrate a country club.* **7.** *Math.* to find the integral of. **8.** to indicate the total amount or the mean value of. —*v.i.* **9.** to become integrated. **10.** to meld with and become part of the dominant culture. **11.** *Math.* **a.** to perform the operation of integration. **b.** to find the solution to a differential equation. [1630–40; < L *integrātus* ptp. of *integrāre* to renew, restore. See INTEGER, -ATE¹] —**in′te·gra′tive,** *adj.*
—**Syn. 2.** merge, unify, fuse, mingle.

in·te·grat·ed (in′ti grā′tid), *adj.* **1.** combining or coordinating separate elements so as to provide a harmonious, interrelated whole: *an integrated plot; an integrated course of study.* **2.** organized or structured so that constituent units function cooperatively: *an integrated economy.* **3.** having, including, or serving members of different racial, religious, and ethnic groups as equals: *an integrated school.* Cf. **segregated.** **4.** *Sociol.* of or pertaining to a group or society whose members interact on the basis of commonly held norms or values. **5.** *Psychol.* characterized by integration. [1580–90; INTEGRATE + -ED²]

in′tegrated bar′, *Law.* (in some states) a system of bar associations to which all lawyers are required to belong. Also called **incorporated bar.**

in′tegrated cir′cuit, *Electronics.* a circuit of transistors, resistors, and capacitors constructed on a single semiconductor wafer or chip, in which the components are interconnected to perform a given function. *Abbr.:* IC Also called **microcircuit.** [1955–60]

in′tegrated da′ta proc′essing. See **IDP.** [1960–65]

in′tegrated fire′ control′, *Mil.* an electronic system that locates and tracks a target, computes the data, and employs a weapon to destroy it.

in′tegrated op′tics, an assembly of miniature optical elements of a size comparable to those used in electronic integrated circuits. [1970–75]

in′tegrated pest′ man′agement, *Agric.* an ecological approach to pest management that combines understanding the causes of pest outbreaks, manipulating the crop ecosystem for pest control, and monitoring pest populations and their life cycles to determine if and when the use of pesticides is indicated. *Abbr.:* IPM

in′tegrating fac′tor, *Math.* a factor that upon multiplying a differential equation with the right-hand side equal to zero makes the equation integrable, usually by making the resulting expression an exact differential of some function. [1855–60]

in·te·gra·tion (in′ti grā′shən), *n.* **1.** an act or instance of combining into an integral whole. **2.** an act or instance of integrating a racial, religious, or ethnic group. **3.** an act or instance of integrating an organization, place of business, school, etc. **4.** *Math.* the operation of finding the integral of a function or equation, esp. solving a differential equation. **5.** behavior, as of an individual, that is in harmony with the environment. **6.** *Psychol.* the organization of the constituent elements of the personality into a coordinated, harmonious whole. **7.** *Genetics.* coadaptation (def. 2). [1610–20; INTEGRATE + -ION; cf. L *integrātiō* renewal]
—**Syn. 1.** combination, blending, fusing.

integra′tion by parts′, *Math.* a method of evaluating an integral by use of the formula, $\int u dv = uv - \int v du$.

in·te·gra·tion·ist (in′ti grā′shə nist), *n.* **1.** a person who believes in, supports, or works for social integration. —*adj.* **2.** pertaining to, favoring, or being conducive to social integration. [1950–55; INTEGRATION + -IST]

in·te·gra·tor (in′ti grā′tər), *n.* **1.** a person or thing that integrates. **2.** Also called **integraph.** an instrument for performing numerical integrations. [1875–80; INTEGRATE + -OR²]

in·teg·ri·ty (in teg′ri tē), *n.* **1.** adherence to moral and ethical principles; soundness of moral character; honesty. **2.** the state of being whole, entire, or undiminished: *to preserve the integrity of the empire.* **3.** a sound, unimpaired, or perfect condition: *the integrity of a ship's hull.* [1400–50; late ME *integrite* < L *integritās.* See INTEGER, -ITY]
—**Syn. 1.** rectitude, probity, virtue. See **honor.**

in·teg·u·ment (in teg′yə mənt), *n.* **1.** a natural covering, as a skin, shell, or rind. **2.** any covering, coating, enclosure, etc. [1605–15; < L *integumentum* a covering. See IN-², TEGUMENT]
—**Syn. 1.** cortex, involucre, involucrum.

in·teg·u·men·ta·ry (in teg′yə men′tə rē), *adj.* of, pertaining to, or like an integument. [1835–45; INTEGUMENT + -ARY]

in·tel·lect (in′tl ekt′), *n.* **1.** the power or faculty of the mind by which one knows or understands, as distinguished from that by which one feels and that by which one wills; the understanding; the faculty of thinking and acquiring knowledge. **2.** capacity for thinking and acquiring knowledge, esp. of a high or complex order; mental capacity. **3.** a particular mind or intelligence, esp. of a high order. **4.** a person possessing a great capacity for thought and knowledge. **5.** minds collectively, as of a number of persons or the persons themselves. [1350–1400; ME < L *intellēctus*, equiv. to *intelleg(ere)* to understand + *-tus* suffix of v. action; see INTELLIGENT]
—**Syn. 1.** reason, sense, brains. See **mind.**

in·tel·lec·tion (in′tl ek′shən), *n.* **1.** the action or process of understanding; the exercise of the intellect; reasoning. **2.** a particular act of the intellect. **3.** a conception or idea as the result of such an act; notion; thought. [1400–50; late ME < ML *intellēctiōn-* (s. of *intellēctiō*). See INTELLECT, -ION]

in·tel·lec·tive (in′tl ek′tiv), *adj.* **1.** having power to understand; intelligent; cognitive. **2.** of or pertaining to the intellect. [1375–1425; late ME < L *intellēctīvus.* See INTELLECT, -IVE] —**in′tel·lec′tive·ly,** *adv.*

in·tel·lec·tu·al (in′tl ek′cho͞o əl), *adj.* **1.** appealing to or engaging the intellect: *intellectual pursuits.* **2.** of or pertaining to the intellect or its use: *intellectual powers.* **3.** possessing or showing intellect or mental capacity, esp. to a high degree: *an intellectual person.* **4.** guided or developed by or relying on the intellect rather than upon emotions or feelings; rational. **5.** characterized by or suggesting a predominance of intellect: *an intellectual way of speaking.* —*n.* **6.** a person of superior intellect. **7.** a person who places a high value on or pursues things of interest to the intellect or the more complex forms and fields of knowledge, as aesthetic or philosophical matters, esp. on an abstract and general level. **8.** an extremely rational person; a person who relies on intellect rather than on emotions or feelings. **9.** a person professionally engaged in mental labor, as a writer or teacher. **10. intellectuals,** *Archaic.* **a.** the mental faculties. **b.** things pertaining to the intellect. [1350–1400; ME < L *intellēctuālis*, equiv. to *intellēctu-*, s. of *intellēctus* INTELLECT + *-ālis* -AL¹] —**in′tel·lec′tu·al·ly,** *adv.*
—**Syn. 1, 2.** mental. **3.** See **intelligent.**

in·tel·lec·tu·al·ism (in′tl ek′cho͞o ə liz′əm), *n.* **1.** devotion to intellectual pursuits. **2.** the exercise of the intellect. **3.** excessive emphasis on abstract or intellectual matters, esp. with a lack of proper consideration for emotions. **4.** *Philos.* **a.** the doctrine that knowledge is wholly or chiefly derived from pure reason. **b.** the belief that reason is the final principle of reality. [1820–30; INTELLECTUAL + -ISM] —**in′tel·lec′tu·al·ist,** *n.* —**in′tel·lec′tu·al·is′tic,** *adj.* —**in′tel·lec′tu·al·is′ti·cal·ly,** *adv.*

in·tel·lec·tu·al·i·ty (in′tl ek′cho͞o al′i tē), *n., pl.* **-ties.** **1.** the quality or state of being intellectual. **2.** intellectual character or power. [1605–15; < LL *intellēctuālitās.* See INTELLECTUAL, -ITY]

in·tel·lec·tu·al·ize (in′tl ek′cho͞o ə līz′), *v.,* **-ized, -iz·ing.** —*v.t.* **1.** to seek or consider the rational content or form of. **2.** to make intellectual. **3.** to analyze (something) intellectually or rationally. **4.** to ignore the emotional or psychological significance of (an action, feeling, dream, etc.) by an excessively intellectual or abstract explanation. —*v.i.* **5.** to talk or write intellectually; reason; philosophize: *to intellectualize about world problems.* Also, *esp. Brit.,* **in′tel·lec′tu·al·ise′.** [1810–20; INTELLECTUAL + -IZE] —**in′tel·lec′tu·al·i·za′tion,** *n.* —**in′tel·lec′tu·al·iz′er,** *n.*

in′tellec′tual prop′erty, *Law.* property that results from original creative thought, as patents, copyright material, and trademarks. [1840–45, *Amer.*]

in·tel·li·gence (in tel′i jəns), *n.* **1.** capacity for learning, reasoning, understanding, and similar forms of mental activity; aptitude in grasping truths, relationships, facts, meanings, etc. **2.** manifestation of a high mental capacity: *He writes with intelligence and wit.* **3.** the faculty of understanding. **4.** knowledge of an event, circumstance, etc., received or imparted; news; information. **5.** the gathering or distribution of information, esp. secret information. **6.** *Govt.* **a.** information about an enemy or a potential enemy. **b.** the evaluated conclusions drawn from such information. **c.** an organization or agency engaged in gathering such information: *military intelligence; naval intelligence.* **7.** interchange of information: *They have been maintaining intelligence with foreign agents for years.* **8.** *Christian Science.* a fundamental attribute of God, or infinite Mind. **9.** (*often cap.*) an intelligent being or spirit, esp. an incorporeal one, as an angel. [1350–1400; ME < L *intelligentia.* See INTELLIGENT, -ENCE]
—**Syn. 1.** See **mind.** **2.** discernment, reason, acumen, aptitude, penetration. —**Ant. 2.** stupidity.

intel′ligence a′gency, a government department charged with obtaining intelligence, or information, esp. for use by the armed forces. Also called **intel′ligence bu′reau, intel′ligence depart′ment, intelligence office.** [1895–1900] —**intel′ligence a′gent.**

intel′ligence of′fice, 1. See **intelligence agency.** **2.** *Obs.* an employment agency for the placement of domestic help. [1685–95]

intel′ligence of′ficer, a military officer responsible for collecting and processing data on hostile forces, weather, and terrain. [1880–85]

intel′ligence quo′tient, *Psychol.* an intelligence test score that is obtained by dividing mental age, which reflects the age-graded level of performance as derived

CONCISE ETYMOLOGY KEY: <, descended or borrowed from; >, whence; b., blend of, blended; c., cognate with; cf., compare; deriv., derivative; equiv., equivalent; imit., imitative; obl., oblique; r., replacing; s., stem; sp., spelling, spelled; resp., respelling, respelled; trans., translation; ?, origin unknown; *, unattested; ‡, probably earlier than. See the full key inside the front cover.

from population norms, by chronological age and multiplying by 100: a score of 100 thus indicates a performance at exactly the normal level for that age group. *Abbr.:* IQ Cf. **achievement quotient.** [1920–25]

in·tel·li·genc·er (in tel′i jən sər), *n.* **1.** a person or thing that conveys information. **2.** an informer; spy. [1570–80; INTELLIGENCE + -ER²]

intel′ligence test′, *Psychol.* any of various tests, as the Wechsler Adult Intelligence Scale or the Stanford-Binet test, designed to measure the intellectual capacity of a person. Cf. **achievement test.** [1910–15]

in·tel·li·gent (in tel′i jənt), *adj.* **1.** having good understanding or a high mental capacity; quick to comprehend, as persons or animals: *an intelligent student.* **2.** displaying or characterized by quickness of understanding, sound thought, or good judgment: *an intelligent reply.* **3.** having the faculty of reasoning and understanding; possessing intelligence: *intelligent beings in outer space.* **4.** *Computers.* pertaining to the ability to do data processing locally; smart: *An intelligent terminal can edit input before transmission to a host computer.* Cf. **dumb** (def. 8). **5.** *Archaic.* having understanding or knowledge (usually fol. by *of*). [1500–10; < L *intelligent-* (s. of *intelligēns,* prp. of *intelligere,* var. of *intellegere* to understand, lit., choose between), equiv. to *in-tel-* (var. of *inter-* INTER-) + *-lig-* (comb. form of *leg-,* s. of *legere* to pick up, choose; cf. LECTION) + *-ent-* -ENT] —**in·tel′li·gent·ly,** *adv.*
—**Syn. 1.** bright. INTELLIGENT, INTELLECTUAL describe distinctive mental capacity. INTELLIGENT often suggests a natural quickness of understanding: *an intelligent reader.* INTELLECTUAL implies not only having a high degree of understanding, but also a capacity and taste for the higher forms of knowledge: *intellectual interests.* **2.** astute, clever, alert, bright, apt, discerning, shrewd, smart. See **sharp.** —**Ant. 1, 2.** stupid.

in·tel·li·gen·tial (in tel′i jen′shəl), *adj.* **1.** of or pertaining to the intelligence or understanding. **2.** endowed with intelligence. **3.** conveying information. [1605–15; < L *intelligenti(a)* INTELLIGENCE + -AL¹]

in·tel·li·gent·si·a (in tel′i jent′sē ə, -gent′-), *n.pl.* intellectuals considered as a group or class, esp. as a cultural, social, or political elite. [1905–10; < Russ *intelligéntsia* < L *intelligentia* INTELLIGENCE]

in·tel·li·gi·bil·i·ty (in tel′i jə bil′i tē), *n., pl.* **-ties** for 2. **1.** the quality or condition of being intelligible; capability of being understood. **2.** something intelligible. [1600–10; INTELLIGIBLE + -ITY]

in·tel·li·gi·ble (in tel′i jə bəl), *adj.* **1.** capable of being understood; comprehensible; clear: *an intelligible response.* **2.** *Philos.* apprehensible by the mind only; conceptual. [1350–1400; ME < L *intelligibilis,* equiv. to *intellig-* (see INTELLIGENT) + *-ibilis* -IBLE] —**in·tel′li·gi·ble·ness,** *n.* —**in·tel′li·gi·bly,** *adv.*
—**Syn. 1.** distinct, lucid, coherent.

In·tel·sat (in tel′sat′, in′tel-), *n.* **1.** a global communications satellite network under international control. **2.** a communications satellite launched by this organization. Also, **INTELSAT** [1965–70; *In(ternational) Tel(ecommunications) Sat(ellite Organization)*]

in·tem·er·ate (in tem′ər it), *adj.* inviolate; undefiled; unsullied; pure. [1485–95; < L *intemerātus,* equiv. to *in-* IN-³ + *temerā(re)* to violate, desecrate + *-tus* ptp. suffix] —**in·tem′er·ate·ly,** *adv.* —**in·tem′er·ate·ness,** *n.*

in·tem·per·ance (in tem′pər əns, -prəns), *n.* **1.** excessive or immoderate indulgence in alcoholic beverages. **2.** excessive indulgence of appetite or passion. **3.** lack of moderation or due restraint, as in action or speech. **4.** an act or instance of any of these: *a long series of intemperances.* [1400–50; late ME < L *intemperantia.* See IN-³, TEMPERANCE]

in·tem·per·ate (in tem′pər it, -prit), *adj.* **1.** given to or characterized by excessive or immoderate indulgence in alcoholic beverages. **2.** immoderate in indulgence of appetite or passion. **3.** not temperate; unrestrained; unbridled. **4.** extreme in temperature, as climate. [1400–50; late ME < L *intemperātus.* See IN-³, TEMPERATE] —**in·tem′per·ate·ly,** *adv.* —**in·tem′per·ate·ness,** *n.*

in·tend (in tend′), *v.t.* **1.** to have in mind as something to be done or brought about; plan: *We intend to leave in a month.* **2.** to design or mean for a particular purpose, use, recipient, etc.: *a fund intended for emergency use only.* **3.** to design to express or indicate, as by one's words; refer to. **4.** (of words, terms, statements, etc.) to mean or signify. **5.** *Archaic.* to direct (the eyes, mind, etc.). —*v.i.* **6.** to have a purpose or design. **7.** *Obs.* to set out on one's course. [1250–1300; < L *intendere* to stretch towards, aim at (see IN-², TEND¹); r. ME *entenden* < OF *entendre* < L, as above] —**in·tend′er,** *n.*
—**Syn. 1.** contemplate, expect, aim, purpose. INTEND, MEAN, DESIGN, PROPOSE imply knowing what one wishes to do and setting this as a goal. TO INTEND is to have in mind something to be done or brought about: *No offense was intended.* MEAN is a less formal word than INTEND but otherwise a close synonym: *He means to go away.* DESIGN implies planning to effect a particular result: *to design a plan for Christmas decorations.* PROPOSE suggests setting up a program for oneself or offering it to others for consideration: *We propose to beautify our city.*

in·tend·ance (in ten′dəns), *n.* **1.** an administrative department, esp. one in the government system introduced by the French statesman Richelieu during the 17th century, or the officials in charge of it. **2.** the official quarters of an intendant. **3.** the function of an intendant; superintendence; intendancy. [1730–40; < F; see INTENDANT, -ANCE]

in·tend·an·cy (in ten′dən sē), *n., pl.* **-cies. 1.** the office or function of an intendant. **2.** a body of intendants. **3.** Also, **intendency.** a district under the charge of an intendant. [1590–1600; INTEND(ANT) + -ANCY]

in·tend·ant (in ten′dənt), *n.* **1.** a person who has the direction or management of some public business, the affairs of an establishment, etc.; a superintendent. **2.** the title of various government officials, esp. administrators serving under the French, Spanish, or Portuguese monarchies. [1645–55; < F < L *intendent-* (s. of *intendēns*) prp. of *intendere* to stetch, make an effort (for), attend (to). See INTEND, -ANT]

in·tend·ed (in ten′did), *adj.* **1.** purposed; designed; intentional: *an intended snub.* **2.** prospective: *one's intended wife.* —*n.* **3.** *Informal.* the person one plans to marry; one's fiancé or fiancée. [1570–80; INTEND + -ED²] —**in·tend′ed·ly,** *adv.* —**in·tend′ed·ness,** *n.*

in·tend·en·cy (in ten′dən sē), *n., pl.* **-cies.** intendancy (def. 3).

in·tend·ing (in ten′ding), *adj.* designing or aiming to be; prospective or aspiring: *intending surgeons.* [1650–60; INTEND + -ING²]

in·tend·ment (in tend′mənt), *n.* **1.** *Law.* the true or correct meaning of something. **2.** intention; design; purpose. [1350–1400; INTEND + -MENT; r. ME *entendement* < MF < ML *intendimentum*]

in·ten·er·ate (in ten′ə rāt′), *v.t.,* **-at·ed, -at·ing.** to make soft or tender; soften. [1585–95; IN-² + L *tener* TENDER¹ + -ATE¹] —**in·ten′er·a′tion,** *n.*

intens, *Gram.* intensifier. Also, **intens**

intens., 1. intensifier. **2.** intensive.

in·tense (in tens′), *adj.* **1.** existing or occurring in a high or extreme degree: *intense heat.* **2.** acute, strong, or vehement, as sensations, feelings, or emotions: *intense anger.* **3.** of an extreme kind; very great, as in strength, keenness, severity, or the like: *an intense gale.* **4.** having a characteristic quality in a high degree: *The intense sunlight was blinding.* **5.** strenuous or earnest, as activity, exertion, diligence, or thought: *an intense life.* **6.** exhibiting a high degree of some quality or action. **7.** having or showing great strength, strong feeling, or tension, as a person, the face, or language. **8.** susceptible to strong emotion; emotional: *an intense person.* **9.** (of color) very deep: *intense red.* **10.** *Photog.* dense (def. 4). [1350–1400; ME < L *intēnsus,* var. of *intentus* INTENT², ptp. of *intendere* to INTEND. See IN-², TENSE¹] —**in·tense′ly,** *adv.* —**in·tense′ness,** *n.*
—**Syn. 2.** fervent, passionate, ardent, strong.

in·ten·si·fi·er (in ten′sə fī′ər), *n.* **1.** a person or thing that intensifies. **2.** *Gram.* a word, esp. an adverb, or other linguistic element that indicates, and usually increases, the degree of emphasis or force to be given to the element it modifies, as *very* or *somewhat;* intensive adverb. **3.** a ram-operated device for increasing hydraulic pressure. [1825–35; INTENSIFY + -ER¹]

in·ten·si·fy (in ten′sə fī′), *v.,* **-fied, -fy·ing.** —*v.t.* **1.** to make intense or more intense. **2.** to make more acute; strengthen or sharpen. **3.** *Photog.* to increase the density and contrast of (a negative) chemically. —*v.i.* **4.** to become intense or more intense. [1810–20; INTENSE + -IFY] —**in·ten′si·fi·ca′tion,** *n.*
—**Syn. 1, 2.** deepen, quicken, concentrate. See **aggravate.** —**Ant. 1.** alleviate, weaken.

in·ten·sion (in ten′shən), *n.* **1.** intensification; increase in degree. **2.** intensity; high degree. **3.** relative intensity; degree. **4.** exertion of the mind; determination. **5.** *Logic.* (of a term) the set of attributes belonging to all and only those things to which the given term is correctly applied; connotation; comprehension. Cf. **extension** (def. 12). [1595–1605; < L *intēnsiōn-* (s. of *intēnsiō*). See INTENSE, -ION] —**in·ten′sion·al,** *adj.* —**in·ten′sion·al·ly,** *adv.*

in·ten·si·tom·e·ter (in ten′si tom′i tər), *n.* a device used to measure x-ray intensity in radiography in order to determine correct exposure time. [INTENSIT(Y) + -O- + -METER]

in·ten·si·ty (in ten′si tē), *n., pl.* **-ties. 1.** the quality or condition of being intense. **2.** great energy, strength, concentration, vehemence, etc., as of activity, thought, or feeling: *He went at the job with great intensity.* **3.** a high or extreme degree, as of cold or heat. **4.** the degree or extent to which something is intense. **5.** a high degree of emotional excitement; depth of feeling: *The poem lacked intensity and left me unmoved.* **6.** the strength or sharpness of a color due esp. to its degree of freedom from admixture with its complementary color. **7.** *Physics.* magnitude, as of energy or a force per unit of area, volume, time, etc. **8.** *Speech.* **a.** the correlate of physical energy and the degree of loudness of a speech sound. **b.** the relative carrying power of vocal utterance. [1655–65; INTENSE + -ITY]
—**Syn. 5.** passion, emotion, energy, vigor.

in·ten·sive (in ten′siv), *adj.* **1.** of, pertaining to, or characterized by intensity: *intensive questioning.* **2.** tending to intensify; intensifying. **3.** *Med.* **a.** increasing in intensity or degree. **b.** instituting treatment to the limit of safety. **4.** noting or pertaining to a system of agriculture involving the cultivation of limited areas, and relying on the maximum use of labor and expenditures to raise the crop yield per unit area (opposed to *extensive*). **5.** requiring or having a high concentration of a specified quality or element (used in combination): *Coal mining is a labor-intensive industry.* **6.** *Gram.* indicating increased emphasis or force. *Certainly* is an intensive adverb. *Myself* in *I did it myself* is an intensive pronoun. —*n.* **7.** something that intensifies. **8.** *Gram.* an intensive element or formation, as *-self* in *himself,* or Latin *-tō* in *iac-tō,* "I hurl" from *iacō,* "I throw." [1400–50; late ME < ML *intēnsivus.* See INTENSE, -IVE] —**in·ten′sive·ly,** *adv.* —**in·ten′sive·ness,** *n.*

inten′sive care′, the use of specialized equipment and personnel for continuous monitoring and care of the critically ill. [1960–65]

inten′sive care′ u′nit, the specialized center in a hospital where intensive care is provided. *Abbr.:* ICU [1960–65]

in·tent¹ (in tent′), *n.* **1.** something that is intended; purpose; design; intention: *The original intent of the committee was to raise funds.* **2.** the act or fact of intending, as to do something: *criminal intent.* **3.** *Law.* the state of a person's mind that directs his or her actions toward a specific object. **4.** meaning or significance. **5. to** or **for all intents and purposes,** for all practical purposes; practically speaking; virtually: *The book is, to all intents and purposes, a duplication of earlier efforts.* [1175–1225; ME < LL *intentus* an aim, purpose, L: a stretching out (*inten(dere)* to INTEND + *-tus* suffix of v. action); r. ME *entent(e)* < OF < LL, as above]
—**Syn. 1.** See **intention. 2.** aim, plan, plot.

in·tent² (in tent′), *adj.* **1.** firmly or steadfastly fixed or directed, as the eyes or mind: *an intent gaze.* **2.** having the attention sharply focused or fixed on something: *intent on one's job.* **3.** determined or resolved; having the mind or will fixed on some goal: *intent on revenge.* **4.** earnest; intense: *an intent person.* [1600–10; < L *intentus* taut, intent, ptp. of *intendere* to INTEND; cf. INTENSE] —**in·tent′ly,** *adv.* —**in·tent′ness,** *n.*
—**Syn. 1, 2.** concentrated. **3.** resolute, set. —**Ant. 3.** irresolute.

in·ten·tion (in ten′shən), *n.* **1.** an act or instance of determining mentally upon some action or result. **2.** the end or object intended; purpose. **3. intentions, a.** purpose or attitude toward the effect of one's actions or conduct: *a bungler with good intentions.* **b.** purpose or attitude with respect to marriage: *Our friends are beginning to ask what our intentions are.* **4.** the act or fact of intending. **5.** *Logic.* **a.** Also called **first intention, primary intention.** reference by signs, concepts, etc., to concrete things, their properties, classes, or the relationships among them. **b.** Also called **second intention, secondary intention.** reference to properties, classes, or the relationships among first intentions. **6.** *Surg., Med.* a manner or process of healing, as in the healing of a lesion or fracture without granulation **(healing by first intention)** or the healing of a wound by granulation after suppuration **(healing by second intention). 7.** meaning or significance: *The intention of his words was clear.* **8.** the person or thing meant to benefit from a prayer or religious offering. **9.** *Archaic.* intentness. [1300–50; ME *intencio(u)n* < L *intentiōn-* (s. of *intentiō*). See INTENT², -ION] —**in·ten′tion·less,** *adj.*
—**Syn. 2.** goal. INTENTION, INTENT, PURPOSE all refer to a wish that one means to carry out. INTENTION is the general word: *His intention is good.* INTENT is chiefly legal or literary: *attack with intent to kill.* PURPOSE implies having a goal or determination to achieve something: *Her strong sense of purpose is reflected in her studies.*

in·ten·tion·al (in ten′shə nl), *adj.* **1.** done with intention or on purpose; intended: *an intentional insult.* **2.** of or pertaining to intention or purpose. **3.** *Metaphys.* **a.** pertaining to an appearance, phenomenon, or representation in the mind; phenomenal; representational. **b.** pertaining to the capacity of the mind to refer to an existent or nonexistent object. **c.** pointing beyond itself, as consciousness or a sign. [1520–30; INTENTION + -AL¹] —**in·ten′tion·al′i·ty,** *n.* —**in·ten′tion·al·ly,** *adv.*
—**Syn. 1.** designed, planned. See **deliberate.** —**Ant. 1.** accidental.

inten′tional foul′, *Basketball.* a foul deliberately committed by a defensive player to stop play, tactically conceding the penalty of having the fouled player attempt the awarded foul shots in return for possession of the ball.

in·ten·tioned (in ten′shənd), *adj.* having particular or specified intentions (often used in combination): *a well-intentioned person.* [1640–50; INTENTION + -ED³]

inten′tion move′ment, *Ethology.* behavior that is preparatory to another behavior, as a crouch before a leap. [1945–50]

in·ter (in tûr′), *v.t.,* **-terred, -ter·ring. 1.** to place (a dead body) in a grave or tomb; bury. **2.** *Obs.* to put into the earth. [1275–1325; ME *enteren* < MF *enterrer,* prob. < VL **interrāre,* deriv. of *terra* earth; see IN-²]

inter-, a prefix occurring in loanwords from Latin,

CONCISE PRONUNCIATION KEY: act, cāpe, dâre, pärt; set, ēqual; if, īce; ox, ōver, ôrder, oil, bŏŏk, bŏŏt, out; up, ûrge; child; sing; shoe; thin, *that;* zh as in *treasure.* ə = *a* as in *alone, e* as in *system, i* as in *easily, o* as in *gallop, u* as in *circus;* ᵊ as in *fire* (fīᵊr), *hour* (ouᵊr). l and n can serve as syllabic consonants, as in *cradle* (krād′l), and *button* (but′n). See the full key inside the front cover.

in′ter·ab·sorp′tion, *n.*
in′ter·ac′a·dem′ic, *adj.*
in′ter·ac′a·dem′i·cal·ly, *adv.*
in′ter·ac·ces′so·ry, *adj.*
in′ter·ac·cuse′, *v.t.,* **-cused, -cus·ing.**
in′ter·a·dap′tion, *n.*
in′ter·ad′di·tive, *adj.*
in′ter·af·fil′i·a′tion, *n.*
in′ter·Af′ri·can, *adj.*
in′ter·age′, *adj.*
in′ter·a′gent, *n.*
in′ter·ag·glu′ti·nate′, *v.i.,* **-nat·ed, -nat·ing.**
in′ter·ag·glu′ti·na′tion, *n.*
in′ter·a·gree′, *v.t.,* **-greed, -gree·ing.**
in′ter·a·gree′ment, *n.*
in′ter·a′lar, *adj.*
in′ter·al·lel′ic, *adj.*
in′ter·al·li′ance, *n., adj.*
in′ter·al·ve′o·lar, *adj.*
in′ter·am′bu·la′crum, *n., pl.* **-cra.**
in′ter-An·de′an, *adj.*
in′ter·an′gu·lar, *adj.*
in′ter·an′i·mate′, *v.t.,* **-mat·ed, -mat·ing.**
in′ter·an′i·ma′tion, *n.*
in′ter·an′nu·al, *adj.;* **-ly,** *adv.*
in′ter·an′nu·lar, *adj.*
in′ter·an·tag′o·nism, *n.*
in′ter·a·poph′y·sal, *adj.*
in′ter·ap′o·phys′e·al, *adj.*
in′ter·ap′pli·ca′tion, *n.*
in′ter·ar′bo·ra′tion, *n.*
in′ter·arch′, *v.i.*
in′ter·ar·tic′u·lar, *adj.*
in′ter·ar·tis′tic, *adj.*
in′ter·ar′y·te′noid, *adj.*
in′ter·as·so′ci·a′tion, *n.*
in′ter·as·sure′, *v.t.,* **-sured, -sur·ing.**
in′ter·as′ter·oi′dal, *adj.*
in′ter·as′tral, *adj.*
in′ter·a′tri·al, *adj.*
in′ter·at·tri′tion, *n.*
in′ter·au′lic, *adj.*
in′ter·au′ral, *adj.*
in′ter·au·ric′u·lar, *adj.*
in′ter·a·vail′a·bil′i·ty, *n.*
in′ter·a·vail′a·ble, *adj.*
in′ter·ax′i·al, *adj.*
in′ter·ax′il·lar′y, *adj.*
in′ter·ax′is, *n., pl.* **-ax·es.**
in′ter·bal′ance, *n., v.t.,* **-anced, -anc·ing.**
in′ter·band′ed, *adj.*
in′ter·bank′, *adj.*
in′ter·ba′sin, *adj.*
in′ter·bed′, *adj.*
in′ter·be·hav′ior, *n.*
in′ter·be·hav′ior·al, *adj.;* **-ly,** *adv.*
in′ter·bel·lig′er·ent, *adj.*

where it meant "between," "among," "in the midst of," "mutually," "reciprocally," "together," "during" (*intercept; interest*); on this model, used in the formation of compound words (*intercom; interdepartmental*). [ME < L (in some words r. ME *entre-* < MF < L *inter-*), comb. form of *inter* (prep. and adv.); see INTERIOR]
—**Note.** The list starting at the bottom of the previous page provides the spelling, syllabification, and stress for words whose meanings may be easily inferred by combining the meanings of INTER- and an attached base word, or base word plus a suffix. Appropriate parts of speech are also shown. Words prefixed by INTER- that have special meanings or uses are entered in their proper alphabetical places in the main vocabulary or as derived forms run on at the end of a main vocabulary entry.

inter., 1. intermediate. 2. interrogation. 3. interrogative.

in•ter•a•bang (in ter′ə bang′), *n.* interrobang.

in•ter•ac•i•nous (in′tər as′ə nəs), *adj. Anat.* situated between the acini of a gland or lung. [1875–80; INTER- + ACINOUS]

in•ter•act (in′tər akt′), *v.i.* to act one upon another. [1740–50; INTER- + ACT]

in•ter•ac•tant (in′tər ak′tənt), *n.* **1.** a person or thing that interacts. **2.** *Chem.* reactant (def. 2). [1945–50; INTERACT + -ANT]

in•ter•ac•tion (in′tər ak′shən), *n.* **1.** reciprocal action, effect, or influence. **2.** *Physics.* **a.** the direct effect that one kind of particle has on another, in particular, in inducing the emission or absorption of one particle by another. **b.** the mathematical expression that specifies the nature and strength of this effect. [1825–35; INTER- + ACTION] —**in′ter•ac′tion•al,** *adj.*

in•ter•ac•tion•ism (in′tər ak′shə niz′əm), *n. Philos.* a theory that the mind and the body may each affect the other. [1900–05; INTERACTION + -ISM] —**in′ter•ac′tion•ist,** *n., adj.*

in•ter•ac•tive (in′tər ak′tiv), *adj.* **1.** acting one upon or with the other. **2.** of or pertaining to a two-way system of electronic communications, as by means of television or computer: *interactive communications between families using two-way cable television.* **3.** (of a computer program or system) interacting with a human user, often in a conversational way, to obtain data or commands and to give immediate results or updated information: *For many years airline reservations have been handled by interactive computer systems.* [1825–35; INTER- + ACTIVE] —**in′ter•ac′tive•ly,** *adv.*

in′terac′tive fic′tion, an adventure or mystery story, usually presented as a video game or book, in which the player or reader is given choices as to how the storyline is to develop or the mystery is to be solved. [1975–80]

in•ter•a•gen•cy (in′tər ā′jən sē, in′-), *adj.* made up of, involving, or representing two or more government agencies: *interagency cooperation.* [1965–70; INTER- + AGENCY]

in•ter a•li•a (in′teʀ ä′li ä′; *Eng.* in′tər ā′lē ə, ä′lē ə), *Latin.* among other things.

in•ter a•li•os (in′teʀ ä′li ōs′; *Eng.* in′tər ā′lē ōs′, ä′lē-), *Latin.* among other persons.

in•ter-Al•lied (in′tər ə līd′), *adj.* between or among allied nations, esp. the Allies of World War I. Also, **in′•ter•al•lied′.** [1915–20]

in•ter-A•mer•i•can (in′tər ə mer′i kən), *adj.* of or pertaining to some or all of the countries of North, Central, and South America. [1935–40]

in•ter•a•tom•ic (in′tər ə tom′ik), *adj.* between atoms. [1860–65; INTER- + ATOMIC]

in•ter•bed•ded (in′tər bed′id), *adj.* (of a rock, mineral, etc.) lying between beds or strata of a different rock or mineral; interstratified. [1870–75; INTER- + BED + -ED³]

in•ter•blend (in′tər blend′), *v.t., v.i.,* **-blend•ed** or **-blent, -blend•ing.** to blend one with another. [1585–95; INTER- + BLEND]

in′ter•block gap′ (in′tər blok′), *Computers.* the area or space separating consecutive blocks of data or consecutive physical records on an external storage medium. Cf. **interrecord gap.** [INTER- + BLOCK]

in•ter•bor•ough (in′tər bûr′ō, -bur′ō), *adj.* **1.** between boroughs. **2.** of, pertaining to, or located in two or more boroughs. —*n.* **3.** a transportation system operating between boroughs. [1900–05; INTER- + BOROUGH]

in•ter•brain (in′tər brān′), *n.* the diencephalon. [1885–90; INTER- + BRAIN]

in•ter•breed (in′tər brēd′), *v.,* **-bred, -breed•ing.** —*v.t.* **1.** to crossbreed (a plant or animal). **2.** to cause to breed together. —*v.i.* **3.** to crossbreed. **4.** to breed or mate with a closely related individual, as in a small, closed population. [1855–60; INTER- + BREED]

CONCISE ETYMOLOGY KEY: <, descended or borrowed from; >, whence; b., blend of, blended; c., cognate with; cf., compare; deriv., derivative; equiv., equivalent; imit., imitative; obl., oblique; r., replacing; s., stem; sp., spelling, spelled; resp., respelling, respelled; trans., translation; ?, origin unknown; *, unattested; ‡, probably earlier than. See the full key inside the front cover.

in•ter•ca•lar•y (in tûr′kə ler′ē, in′tər kal′ə rē), *adj.* **1.** interpolated; interposed. **2.** inserted or interpolated in the calendar, as an extra day or month. **3.** having such an inserted day, month, etc., as a particular year. [1605–15; < L *intercalārius,* equiv. to *intercal(āre)* to INTERCALATE + *-ārius* -ARY] —**in•ter′ca•lar′i•ly,** *adv.*

inter′calary mer′istem, *Bot.* meristem in the internode of a stem.

in•ter•ca•late (in tûr′kə lāt′), *v.t.,* **-lat•ed, -lat•ing. 1.** to interpolate; interpose. **2.** to insert (an extra day, month, etc.) in the calendar. [1605–15; < L *intercalātus* ptp. of *intercalāre* to insert a day or month into the calendar, equiv. to *inter-* INTER- + *calā-* (s. of *calāre* to proclaim) + *-tus* ptp. suffix] —**in•ter′ca•la′tive,** *adj.*
—**Syn. 1.** interject, introduce, insinuate.

in•ter•ca•la•tion (in tûr′kə lā′shən), *n.* **1.** the act of intercalating; insertion or interpolation, as in a series. **2.** something that is intercalated; interpolation. [1570–80; < L *intercalātiōn-* (s. of *intercalātiō*). See INTERCALATE, -ION]

in′ter•car′di•nal point′ (in′tər kär′dn l, in′-), any of the four points of the compass midway between the cardinal points; northeast, southeast, southwest, or northwest. [1905–10; INTER- + CARDINAL]

in•ter•cede (in′tər sēd′), *v.i.,* **-ced•ed, -ced•ing. 1.** to act or interpose in behalf of someone in difficulty or trouble, as by pleading or petition: *to intercede with the governor for a condemned man.* **2.** to attempt to reconcile differences between two people or groups; mediate. **3.** *Rom. Hist.* (of a tribune or other magistrate) to interpose a veto. [1570–80; < L *intercēdere.* See INTER-, CEDE] —**in′ter•ced′er,** *n.*
—**Syn. 1, 2.** intervene.

in•ter•cel•lu•lar (in′tər sel′yə lər), *adj.* situated between or among cells. [1825–35; INTER- + CELLULAR]

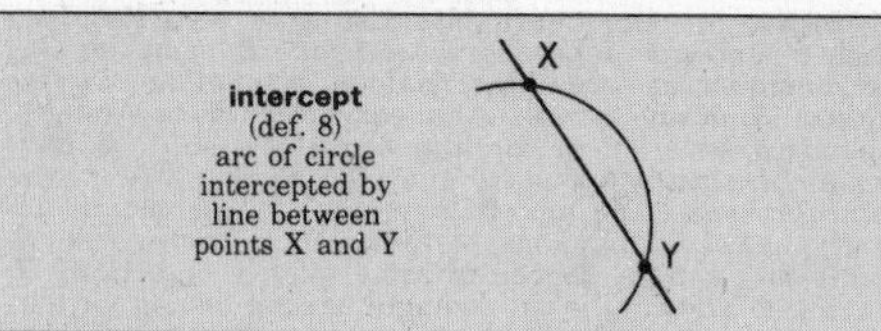

intercept (def. 8) arc of circle intercepted by line between points X and Y

in•ter•cept (*v.* in′tər sept′; *n.* in′tər sept′), *v.t.* **1.** to take, seize, or halt (someone or something on the way from one place to another); cut off from an intended destination: *to intercept a messenger.* **2.** to see or overhear (a message, transmission, etc., meant for another): *We intercepted the enemy's battle plan.* **3.** to stop or check (passage, travel, etc.): *to intercept the traitor's escape.* **4.** *Sports.* to take possession of (a ball or puck) during an attempted pass by an opposing team. **5.** to stop or interrupt the course, progress, or transmission of. **6.** to destroy or disperse (enemy aircraft or a missile or missiles) in the air on the way to a target. **7.** to stop the natural course of (light, water, etc.). **8.** *Math.* to mark off or include, as between two points or lines. **9.** to intersect. **10.** *Obs.* to prevent or cut off the operation or effect of. **11.** *Obs.* to cut off from access, sight, etc. —*n.* **12.** an interception. **13.** *Math.* **a.** an intercepted segment of a line. **b.** (in a coordinate system) the distance from the origin to the point at which a curve or line intersects an axis. [1535–45; < L *interceptus* ptp. of *intercipere,* equiv. to *inter-* INTER- + *-cep-* (comb. form of *cap-,* s. of *capere* to take) + *-tus* ptp. suffix; cf. INCIPIENT] —**in′ter•cep′•tive,** *adj.*

in•ter•cep•tion (in′tər sep′shən), *n.* **1.** an act or instance of intercepting. **2.** the state or fact of being intercepted. **3.** *Mil.* **a.** the engaging of an enemy force in an attempt to hinder or prevent it from carrying out its mission. **b.** the monitoring of enemy radio transmission to obtain information. [1590–1600; < L *interceptiōn-* (s. of *interceptiō*). See INTERCEPT, -ION]

in•ter•cep•tor (in′tər sep′tər), *n.* **1.** a person or thing that intercepts. **2.** *Mil.* a fighter aircraft with fast-reaction capabilities, used to identify and, if appropriate, engage other aircraft in combat. Also, **in′ter•cept′er.** [1590–1600; < L, equiv. to *intercep-* (see INTERCEPT) + *-tor* -TOR²]

in•ter•ces•sion (in′tər sesh′ən), *n.* **1.** an act or instance of interceding. **2.** an interposing or pleading on behalf of another person. **3.** a prayer to God on behalf of another. **4.** *Rom. Hist.* the interposing of a veto, as by a tribune. [1400–50; late ME < L *intercessiōn-* (s. of *intercessiō*), equiv. to *intercess(us)* ptp. of *intercēdere* to INTERCEDE (equiv. to *interced-* var. s. + *-tus* ptp. suffix, with *-dt-* > *-ss-*) + *-iōn-* -ION] —**in′ter•ces′sion•al,** *adj.*

in•ter•ces•sor (in′tər ses′ər, in′tər ses′ər), *n.* a person who intercedes. [1475–85; < L, equiv. to *interced-* (see INTERCESSION) + *-tor* -TOR, with *dt* > *ss*]

in•ter•ces•so•ry (in′tər ses′ə rē), *adj.* having the function of interceding: *an intercessory prayer.* [1570–80; < ML *intercessōrius,* equiv. to L *interced-* (see INTERCESSION) + *-tōrius* -TORY¹, with *dt* > *ss*]

in•ter•change (*v.* in′tər chānj′; *n.* in′tər chānj′), *v.,* **-changed, -chang•ing,** *n.* —*v.t.* **1.** to put each in the place of the other: *to interchange pieces of modular furniture.* **2.** to cause (one thing) to change places with another; transpose. **3.** to give and receive (things) reciprocally; exchange: *The twins interchanged clothes frequently.* **4.** to cause to follow one another alternately; alternate: *to interchange business cares with pleasures.* —*v.i.* **5.** to occur by turns or in succession; alternate. **6.** to change places, as two persons or things, or as one with another. —*n.* **7.** an act or instance of interchanging; reciprocal exchange: *the interchange of commodities.* **8.** a changing of places, as between two persons or things, or of one with another. **9.** alternation; alternate succession. **10.** a highway intersection consisting of a system of several different road levels arranged so that vehicles may move from one road to another without crossing the streams of traffic. [1325–75; INTER- + CHANGE; r. ME *entrechaungen* < MF *entrechangier*] —**in′ter•chang′•er,** *n.*

in•ter•change•a•ble (in′tər chān′jə bəl), *adj.* **1.** (of two things) capable of being put or used in the place of each other: *interchangeable symbols.* **2.** (of one thing) capable of replacing or changing places with something else: *an interchangeable part.* [1400–50; INTERCHANGE + -ABLE; r. late ME *entrechaungeable* < MF *entrechangeable*] —**in′ter•change′a•bil′i•ty, in′ter•change′a•ble•ness,** *n.* —**in′ter•change′a•bly,** *adv.*
—**Syn. 2.** See **exchangeable.**

in•ter•church (in′tər chûrch′), *adj.* interdenominational. [1900–05; INTER- + CHURCH]

in•ter•class (in′tər klas′, -kläs′), *adj.* between classes; involving different classes. [1905–10; INTER- + CLASS]

in•ter•clav•i•cle (in′tər klav′i kəl), *n. Zool.* a median membrane bone developed between the collarbones, or in front of the breastbone, in many vertebrates. [1865–70; INTER- + CLAVICLE] —**in•ter•cla•vic•u•lar** (in′tər klə vik′yə lər), *adj.*

in•ter•coast•al (in′tər kōs′tl), *adj.* existing or done between seacoasts; involving two or more seacoasts. [1925–30; INTER- + COASTAL]

in•ter•col•lege (in′tər kol′ij), *adj.* intercollegiate. [INTER- + COLLEGE]

in•ter•col•le•giate (in′tər kə lē′jit, -jē it), *adj.* **1.** taking place between or participating in activities between different colleges: *intercollegiate athletics.* **2.** of, pertaining to, or representative of two or more colleges. [1870–75; INTER- + COLLEGIATE]

in•ter•co•lo•ni•al (in′tər kə lō′nē əl), *adj.* **1.** between colonies, as of one country. **2.** of or pertaining to two or more colonies. [1850–55; INTER- + COLONIAL] —**in′ter•co•lo′ni•al•ly,** *adv.*

in•ter•co•lum•ni•a•tion (in′tər kə lum′nē ā′shən), *n. Archit.* **1.** the space between two adjacent columns, usually the clear space between the lower parts of the shafts. **2.** the system of spacing between columns. [1655–65; < L *intercolumni(um)* space between columns (see INTER-, COLUMN, -IUM) + -ATION] —**in′ter•co•lum′nal, in′ter•co•lum′nar,** *adj.*

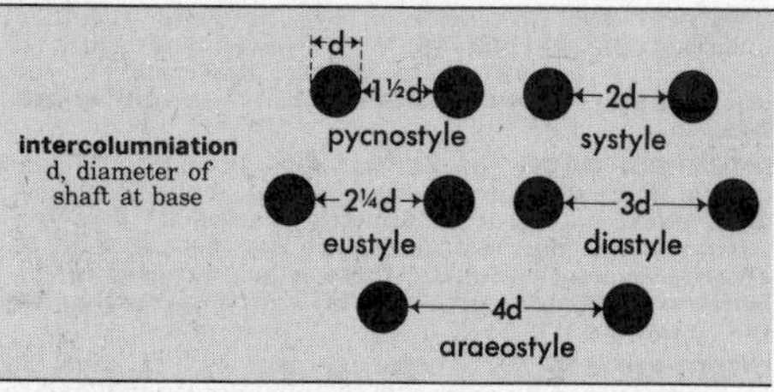

intercolumniation d, diameter of shaft at base

in•ter•com (in′tər kom′), *n. Informal.* **1.** an intercommunication system. **2.** a microphone or receiver of an intercommunication system. [1935–40; by shortening]

in•ter•com•mon (in′tər kom′ən), *v.i. Eng. Law.* to share in the use of a common. [1400–50; INTER- + obs. *common* (v.) (var. of COMMUNE); r. late ME *entrecomo(u)nen* < AF *entrecomuner*] —**in′ter•com′•mon•age,** *n.* —**in′ter•com′mon•er,** *n.*

in•ter•com•mu•ni•cate (in′tər kə myōō′ni kāt′), *v.,* **-cat•ed, -cat•ing.** —*v.i.* **1.** to communicate mutually, as people. **2.** to afford passage from one to another, as rooms. —*v.t.* **3.** to exchange (messages or communications) with one another. [1580–90; < ML *intercommūnicātus* (ptp.). See INTER-, COMMUNICATE] —**in′ter•com•mu′ni•ca•ble,** *adj.* —**in′ter•com•mu′ni•ca•bil′i•ty,** *n.* —**in′ter•com•mu′ni•ca′tion,** *n.* —**in′ter•com•mu′ni•ca′tive,** *adj.* —**in′ter•com•mu′ni•ca′tor,** *n.*

intercommunica′tion sys′tem, a communication system within a building, ship, airplane, local area, etc., with a loudspeaker or receiver for listening and a microphone for speaking at each of two or more points. [1910–15]

in•ter•com•mun•ion (in′tər kə myōōn′yən), *n.* **1.** mutual communion, association, or relations. **2.** *Eccles.* a communion service among members of different denominations. Cf. **close communion, open communion.** [1755–65; INTER- + COMMUNION]

in′ter•bra′chi•al, *adj.*
in′ter•branch′, *adj.*
in′ter•bran′chi•al, *adj.*
in′ter•breath′, *adj.*
in′ter•bri•gade′, *adj.*
in′ter•bron′chi•al, *adj.*
in′ter•busi′ness, *adj.*
in′ter•cal′i•bra′tion, *n.*
in′ter•cam′pus, *adj.*
in′ter•cap′il•lar′y, *adj.*
in′ter•car′di•nal, *adj.*
in′ter-Car′ib•be′an, *adj.*
in′ter•car′pal, *adj.*
in′ter•car′pel•lar′y, *adj.*
in′ter•ca•rot′id, *adj.*
in′ter•car′ri•er, *n.*
in′ter•car′ti•lag′i•nous, *adj.*
in′ter•caste′, *adj.*
in′ter•cat′e•nat′ed, *adj.*
in′ter•caus′a•tive, *adj.*
in′ter•cav′ern•ous, *adj.*
in′ter•cel′e•bra′tion, *n.*
in′ter•cell′, *adj.*
in′ter•cen′tral, *adj.*
in′ter•cer′e•bral, *adj.*
in′ter•chaff′, *v.*
in′ter•chain′, *v.t.*
in′ter•chan′nel, *adj.*
in′ter•charge′, *v.t.,* **-charged, -charg•ing,** *n.*
in′ter•chase′, *v.t.,* **-chased, -chas•ing.**
in′ter•check′, *v.t.*
in′ter•choke′, *v.t.,* **-choked, -chok•ing.**
in′ter•chon′dral, *adj.*
in′ter•chro′mo•so′mal, *adj.;* **-ly,** *adv.*
in′ter•cil′i•ar′y, *adj.*
in′ter•cir′cle, *v.t.,* **-cled, -cling.**
in′ter•cir′cu•late′, *v.,* **-lat•ed, -lat•ing.**
in′ter•cir′cu•la′tion, *n.*
in′ter•cit′y, *adj.*
in′ter•civ′ic, *adj.*
in′ter•civ′i•li•za′tion, *n.*
in′ter•clan′, *adj.*
in′ter•clash′, *n., v.*
in′ter•clasp′, *v.t.*
in′ter•cler′i•cal, *adj.*
in′ter•cloud′, *v.t.*
in′ter•club′, *adj.*
in′ter•clus′ter, *adj.*
in′ter•coc•cyg′e•al, *adj.*
in′ter•co•he′sion, *n.*
in′ter•col′o•ni•za′tion, *n.*
in′ter•col′o•nize, *v.,* **-nized, -niz•ing.**
in′ter•com′bat, *n.*
in′ter•com′bi•na′tion, *n.*
in′ter•com•bine′, *v.t.,* **-bined, -bin•ing.**
in′ter•com•mis′sion, *n.*
in′ter•com•mis′sur•al, *adj.*
in′ter•com•mu′nal, *adj.*

in•ter•com•mu•ni•ty (in′tər kə myo͞o′ni tē), *n., pl.* **-ties,** *adj.* —*n.* **1.** common ownership, use, participation, etc. —*adj.* **2.** of, pertaining to, or between communities: *intercommunity projects.* [1580–90; INTER- + COMMUNITY]

in•ter•con•fes•sion•al (in′tər kən fesh′ə nl), *adj.* common to or occurring between churches having different confessions. [1890–95; INTER- + CONFESSIONAL]

in•ter•con•nect (in′tər kə nekt′), *v.t.* **1.** to connect with one another. —*v.i.* **2.** to be or become connected or interrelated. —*adj.* **3.** *Telecommunications.* **a.** pertaining to customer-owned equipment that is connected to or has access to the public telephone network. **b.** pertaining to companies that supply equipment to customers: *a leading interconnect company.* [1860–65; INTER- + CONNECT] —**in′ter•con•nec′tion,** *n.*

in•ter•con•nect•ed•ness (in′tər kə nek′tid nis), *n.* the quality or condition of being interconnected; interrelatedness: *the interconnectedness of all nations working toward world peace.* [1920–25; INTERCONNECT + -ED² + -NESS]

in•ter•con•so•nan•tal (in′tər kon′sə nan′tl), *adj. Phonet.* (usually of a vowel) immediately following a consonant and preceding a consonant, as the *a* in *pat.* [1930–35; INTER- + CONSONANTAL]

in•ter•con•ti•nen•tal (in′tər kon′tn en′tl), *adj.* **1.** between or among continents; involving two or more continents: *intercontinental trade.* **2.** traveling or capable of traveling between continents: *intercontinental airplanes.* [1850–55; INTER- + CONTINENTAL]

intercontinen′tal ballis′tic mis′sile, any supersonic missile that has a range of at least 3500 nautical mi. (6500 km) and follows a ballistic trajectory after a powered, guided launching. *Abbr.:* ICBM, I.C.B.M. [1955–60]

in•ter•con•ver•sion (in′tər kən vûr′zhən, -shən), *n.* conversion of each of two things into the other; reciprocal conversion. [1860–65; INTER- + CONVERSION]

in•ter•con•vert (in′tər kən vûrt′), *v.t.* to subject to interconversion; interchange. [1950–55; INTER- + CONVERT] —**in′ter•con•vert′i•ble,** *adj.* —**in′ter•con•vert′i•bil′i•ty,** *n.* —**in′ter•con•vert′i•bly,** *adv.*

in•ter•cool•er (in′tər ko͞o′lər), *n.* any device for cooling a fluid between successive heating processes, esp. for cooling a gas between successive compressions. [1895–1900; INTER- + COOLER]

in•ter•cos•tal (in′tər kos′tl, -kô′stl), *adj.* **1.** pertaining to muscles, parts, or intervals between the ribs. **2.** situated between the ribs. **3.** *Shipbuilding.* noting a structural member situated between or divided by continuous members, as frames or keelsons. —*n.* **4.** an intercostal muscle, member, or space. [1590–1600; < NL *intercostālis.* See INTER-, COSTAL] —**in′ter•cos′tal•ly,** *adv.*

in•ter•course (in′tər kôrs′, -kōrs′), *n.* **1.** dealings or communication between individuals, groups, countries, etc. **2.** interchange of thoughts, feelings, etc. **3.** sexual relations or a sexual coupling, esp. coitus. [1425–75; late ME *intercurse* < ML *intercursus* communication, trading, L: a running between. See INTER-, COURSE]
—**Syn. 1.** trade, traffic, relations.

in•ter•crop (*v.* in′tər krop′; *n.* in′tər krop′), *v.,* **-cropped, -crop•ping,** *n. Agric.* —*v.i.* **1.** to grow one crop between the rows of another, as in an orchard or field. —*v.t.* **2.** to grow a crop between the rows of. —*n.* **3.** a crop plant growing between plants of a different crop. Also, **interplant.** [1895–1900; INTER- + CROP]

in•ter•cross (*v.* in′tər krôs′, -kros′; *n.* in′tər krôs′, -kros′), *v.t.* **1.** to cross one with another; place across each other. **2.** to cross (each other), as streets; intersect. **3.** to cross in interbreeding. —*v.i.* **4.** to cross each other; intersect. **5.** to interbreed. —*n.* **6.** an instance of cross-fertilization. [1705–15; INTER- + CROSS]

in•ter•crys•tal•line (in′tər kris′tl in, -īn′, -ēn′), *adj. Crystall.* situated or passing between the crystals of a substance. Cf. **transcrystalline.** [1900–05; INTER- + CRYSTALLINE]

in•ter•cul•tur•al (in′tər kul′chər əl), *adj.* pertaining to or taking place between two or more cultures: *intercultural exchanges in music and art.* [1935–40; INTER- + CULTURAL] —**in′ter•cul′tur•al•ly,** *adv.*

in•ter•cu•po•la (in′tər kyo͞o′pə lə), *n. Archit.* **1.** the space between an inner and an outer dome. **2.** a space between two cupolas. [INTER- + CUPOLA]

in•ter•cur•rent (in′tər kûr′ənt, -kur′-), *adj.* **1.** intervening, as of time or events. **2.** *Pathol.* (of a disease) occurring while another disease is in progress. [1605–15; < L *intercurrent-* (s. of *intercurrēns*) prp. of *intercurrere* to run between. See INTER-, CURRENT] —**in′ter•cur′rence,** *n.* —**in′ter•cur′rent•ly,** *adv.*

in•ter•cut (*v.* in′tər kut′, in′tər kut′; *n.* in′tər kut′), *v.,* **-cut, -cut•ting,** *n. Motion Pictures, Television.* —*v.i.* **1.** to cut from one type of shot to another, as from a long shot to a closeup. —*v.t.* **2.** to insert (shots from other scenes, flashbacks, etc.) into the narrative of a film. **3.** to interrupt the narrative of (a film) with shots from other scenes, flashbacks, etc. Cf. **crosscut.** —*n.* **4.** a film sequence or scene produced by intercutting. [1605–15; INTER- + CUT]

in•ter•de•nom•i•na•tion•al (in′tər di nom′ə nā′shə nl), *adj.* occurring between, involving, or common to different religious denominations. Also called **interchurch.** [1890–95; INTER- + DENOMINATIONAL] —**in′ter•de•nom′i•na′tion•al•ism,** *n.*

in•ter•den•tal (in′tər den′tl), *adj.* **1.** between teeth. **2.** *Phonet.* articulated with the tip of the tongue between the upper and lower front teeth, as the fricatives (th̶) and (th) of *thy* and *thigh.* [1870–75; INTER- + DENTAL] —**in′ter•den′tal•ly,** *adv.*

in•ter•den•til (in′tər den′tl, -til), *n. Archit.* a space between dentils. [1815–25; INTER- + DENTIL]

in•ter•de•part•men•tal (in′tər dē′pärt men′tl, -di pärt-), *adj.* involving or existing between two or more departments: *interdepartmental rivalry.* [1890–95; INTER- + DEPARTMENTAL] —**in′ter•de′part•men′tal•ly,** *adv.*

in•ter•de•pend•ent (in′tər di pen′dənt), *adj.* mutually dependent; depending on each other. [1810–20; INTER- + DEPENDENT] —**in′ter•de•pend′ence, in′ter•de•pend′en•cy,** *n.* —**in′ter•de•pend′ent•ly,** *adv.*

in•ter•dict (*n.* in′tər dikt′; *v.* in′tər dikt′), *n.* **1.** *Civil Law.* any prohibitory act or decree of a court or an administrative officer. **2.** *Rom. Cath. Ch.* a punishment by which the faithful, remaining in communion with the church, are forbidden certain sacraments and prohibited from participation in certain sacred acts. **3.** *Roman Law.* a general or special order of the Roman praetor forbidding or commanding an act, esp. in cases involving disputed possession. —*v.t.* **4.** to forbid; prohibit. **5.** *Eccles.* to cut off authoritatively from certain ecclesiastical functions and privileges. **6.** to impede by steady bombardment: *Constant air attacks interdicted the enemy's advance.* [1250–1300; (n.) < L *interdictum* prohibition, n. use of neut. of *interdictus* ptp. of *interdīcere* to forbid, equiv. to *inter-* INTER- + *-dic-* (var. s. of *dīcere* to speak) + *-tus* ptp. suffix; r. ME *enterdit* < OF < L, as above; (v.) < L *interdictus;* r. ME *enterditen* < OF *entredire* (ptp. *entredit*) < L, as above] —**in′ter•dic′tor,** *n.*

in•ter•dic•tion (in′tər dik′shən), *n.* **1.** an act or instance of interdicting. **2.** the state of being interdicted. **3.** an interdict. **4.** steady bombardment of enemy positions and communications lines for the purpose of delaying and disorganizing progress. [1485–95; < L *interdictiōn-* (s. of *interdictiō*). See INTERDICT, -ION]

in•ter•dic•to•ry (in′tər dik′tə rē), *adj.* of, pertaining to, or noting interdiction. [1745–55; < LL *interdictōrius.* See INTERDICT, -TORY¹]

in•ter•dig•i•tate (in′tər dij′i tāt′), *v.i., v.t.,* **-tat•ed, -tat•ing.** to interlock, as or like the fingers of both hands. [1840–50; INTER- + DIGITATE] —**in′ter•dig′i•ta′tion,** *n.*

in•ter•dis•ci•pli•nar•y (in′tər dis′ə plə ner′ē), *adj.* **1.** combining or involving two or more academic disciplines or fields of study: *The economics and history departments are offering an interdisciplinary seminar on Asia.* **2.** combining or involving two or more professions, technologies, departments, or the like, as in business or industry. [1935–40; INTER- + DISCIPLINARY]

in•ter•est (in′tər ist, -trist), *n.* **1.** the feeling of a person whose attention, concern, or curiosity is particularly engaged by something: *She has a great interest in the poetry of Donne.* **2.** something that concerns, involves, draws the attention of, or arouses the curiosity of a person: *His interests are philosophy and chess.* **3.** power of exciting such concern, involvement, etc.; quality of being interesting: *political issues of great interest.* **4.** concern; importance: *a matter of primary interest.* **5.** a business, cause, or the like in which a person has a share, concern, responsibility, etc. **6.** a share, right, or title in the ownership of property, in a commercial or financial undertaking, or the like: *He bought half an interest in the store.* **7.** a participation in or concern for a cause, advantage, responsibility, etc. **8.** a number or group of persons, or a party, financially interested in the same business, industry, or enterprise: *the banking interest.* **9. interests,** the group of persons or organizations having extensive financial or business power. **10.** the state of being affected by something in respect to advantage or detriment: *We need an arbiter who is without interest in the outcome.* **11.** benefit; advantage: *to have one's own interest in mind.* **12.** regard for one's own advantage or profit; self-interest: *The partnership dissolved because of their conflicting interests.* **13.** influence from personal importance or capability; power of influencing the action of others. **14.** *Finance.* **a.** a sum paid or charged for the use of money or for borrowing money. **b.** such a sum expressed as a percentage of money borrowed to be paid over a given period, usually one year. **15.** something added or thrown in above an exact equivalent: *Jones paid him back with a left hook and added a right uppercut for interest.* **16. in the interest(s) of,** to the advantage or advancement of; in behalf of: *in the interests of good government.* —*v.t.* **17.** to engage or excite the attention or curiosity of: *Mystery stories interested him greatly.* **18.** to concern (a person, nation, etc.) in something; involve: *The fight for peace interests all nations.* **19.** to cause to take a personal concern or share; induce to participate: *to interest a person in an enterprise.* **20.** to cause to be concerned; affect. [1225–75; (n.) ME < ML, L: it concerns, lit., it is between; r. *interesse* < ML, L: to concern, lit., to be between; (v.) earlier *interess* as v. use of the n.; see INTER-, ESSE]

in•ter•est•ed (in′tər ə stid, -trə stid, -tə res′tid), *adj.* **1.** having an interest in something; concerned: *Interested members will meet at noon.* **2.** having the attention or curiosity engaged: *an interested spectator.* **3.** characterized by a feeling of interest. **4.** influenced by personal or selfish motives: *an interested witness.* **5.** participating; having an interest or share; having money involved. [1655–65; INTEREST + -ED³ or -ED²] —**in′ter•est•ed•ly,** *adv.* —**in′ter•est•ed•ness,** *n.*

in•ter•es•ter•i•fi•ca•tion (in′tər ə ster′ə fi kā′shən), *n. Chem.* transesterification. [1940–45; INTER- + ESTERIFICATION]

in′terest group′, a group of people drawn or acting together in support of a common interest or to voice a common concern: *Political interest groups seek to influence legislation.* [1905–10]

in•ter•est•ing (in′tər ə sting, -trə sting, -tə res′ting), *adj.* **1.** engaging or exciting and holding the attention or curiosity: *an interesting book.* **2.** arousing a feeling of interest: *an interesting face.* **3. in an interesting condition,** (of a woman) pregnant. [1705–15; INTEREST + -ING²] —**in′ter•est•ing•ly,** *adv.* —**in′ter•est•ing•ness,** *n.*
—**Syn. 1.** absorbing, entertaining. INTERESTING, PLEASING, GRATIFYING mean satisfying to the mind. Something that is INTERESTING occupies the mind with no connotation of pleasure or displeasure: *an interesting account of a battle.* Something that is PLEASING engages the mind favorably: *a pleasing account of the wedding.* Something that is GRATIFYING fulfills expectations, requirements, etc.: *a gratifying account of his whereabouts; a book gratifying in its detail.* —**Ant. 1.** dull.

in•ter•face (*n.* in′tər fās′; *v.* in′tər fās′, in′tər fās′), *n., v.,* **-faced, -fac•ing.** —*n.* **1.** a surface regarded as the common boundary of two bodies, spaces, or phases. **2.** the facts, problems, considerations, theories, practices, etc., shared by two or more disciplines, procedures, or fields of study: *the interface between chemistry and physics.* **3.** a common boundary or interconnection between systems, equipment, concepts, or human beings. **4.** communication or interaction: *Interface between the parent company and its subsidiaries has never been better.* **5.** a thing or circumstance that enables separate and sometimes incompatible elements to coordinate effectively: *The organization serves as an interface between the state government and the public.* **6.** *Computers.* **a.** equipment or programs designed to communicate information from one system of computing devices or programs to another. **b.** any arrangement for such communication. —*v.t.* **7.** to bring into an interface. **8.** to bring together; connect or mesh: *The management is interfacing several departments with an information service from overseas.* —*v.i.* **9.** to be in an interface. **10.** to function as an interface. **11.** to meet or communicate directly; interact, coordinate, synchronize, or harmonize (often fol. by *with*): *The two communications systems are able to interface with each other.* [1880–85; INTER- + FACE]

in•ter•fa•cial (in′tər fā′shəl), *adj.* **1.** included between two faces. **2.** of, pertaining to, or of the nature of an interface. [1830–40; INTER- + FACIAL]

in′terfa′cial ten′sion, *Physical Chem.* the surface tension at the interface of two liquids.

in•ter•fac•ing (in′tər fā′sing), *n.* a woven or nonwoven material used between the facing and outer fabric of a garment, as in the collar and lapels of a jacket, to add body and give support and shape to the garment. [INTER- + FACING]

in•ter•faith (in′tər fāth′), *adj.* of, operating, or occurring between persons belonging to different religions: *an interfaith service.* [1965–70; INTER- + FAITH]

in•ter•fen•es•tra•tion (in′tər fen′ə strā′shən), *n.* **1.** a space between two windows. **2.** the art or process of arranging the openings in a wall. [1815–25; INTER- + FENESTRATION] —**in•ter•fe•nes•tral** (in′tər fə nes′trəl), *adj.*

in•ter•fere (in′tər fēr′), *v.i.,* **-fered, -fer•ing.** **1.** to come into opposition, as one thing with another, esp. with the effect of hampering action or procedure (often fol. by *with*): *Constant distractions interfere with work.* **2.** to take part in the affairs of others; meddle (often fol. by *with* or *in*): *to interfere in another's life.* **3.** (of things) to strike against each other, or one against another, so as to hamper or hinder action; come into physical collision. **4.** to interpose or intervene for a particular purpose. **5.** to strike one foot or leg against another in moving, as a horse. **6.** *Sports.* **a.** to obstruct the action of an opposing player in a way barred by the rules. **b.** *Football.* to run interference for a teammate carrying the ball. **7.** *Physics.* to cause interference. **8.** to clash; come in collision; be in opposition: *The claims of two nations may interfere.* **9.** *Law.* to claim earlier invention when several patent requests for the same invention are being filed. **10. interfere with,** *Chiefly Brit.* to molest sexually. [1520–30; INTER- + *-fere* < L *ferīre* to strike; modeled on MF *s'entreferir*] —**in′ter•fer′er,** *n.* —**in′ter•fer′ing•ly,** *adv.*

CONCISE PRONUNCIATION KEY: *act, cāpe, dâre, pärt; set, ēqual; if, īce; ox, ōver, ôrder, oil, bo͝ok, bo͞ot, out; up, ûrge; child; sing; shoe; thin, th̶at;* zh as in *treasure.* ə = *a* as in *alone, e* as in *system, i* as in *easily, o* as in *gallop, u* as in *circus;* ᵊ as in *fire* (fīᵊr), *hour* (ouᵊr). l and n can serve as syllabic consonants, as in *cradle* (krād′l), and *button* (but′n). See the full key inside the front cover.

in′ter•com′pa•ny, *adj.*
in′ter•com′pa•ra•ble, *adj.*
in′ter•com•pare′, *v.t.,* **-pared, -par•ing.**
in′ter•com•par′i•son, *n.*
in′ter•com•plex′i•ty, *n., pl.* **-ties.**
in′ter•com′pli•men′ta•ry, *adj.*
in′ter•com′pre•hen′si•bil′i•ty, *n.*
in′ter•con•cil′i•ar′y, *adj.*
in′ter•con•dens′er, *n.*
in′ter•con′dy•lar, *adj.*
in•ter•con•dyl′ic, *adj.*
in′ter•con′dy•loid′, *adj.*
in′ter•con•found′, *v.t.*
in′ter•con•tort′ed, *adj.*
in′ter•con′tra•dic′tion, *n.*
in′ter•con′tra•dic′to•ry, *adj.*
in′ter•co•or′di•nate, *adj.*
in′ter•co•or′di•nate′, *v.,* **-nat•ed, -nat•ing.**
in′ter•cor′a•coid′, *adj.*
in′ter•cor′po•rate, *adj.*
in′ter•cor•pus′cu•lar, *adj.*
in′ter•cor′re•late′, *v.t.,* **-lat•ed, -lat•ing.**
in′ter•cor′re•la′tion, *n.*
in′ter•cor′ti•cal, *adj.*
in′ter•cos′mic, *adj.*
in′ter•cot′y•lar, *adj.*
in′ter•coun′try, *adj.*
in′ter•coun′ty, *adj.*
in′ter•cou′ple, *adj.*
in′ter•cra′ni•al, *adj.*
in′ter•cra′ter, *adj.*
in′ter•cre•ate′, *v.t.,* **-at•ed, -at•ing.**
in′ter•cri′nal, *adj.*
in′ter•cru′ral, *adj.*
in′ter•crust′, *v.t.*
in′ter•cul′ture, *adj.*
in′ter•cul′ture, *n.*
in′ter•curl′, *v.*
in′ter•cus′pi•dal, *adj.*
in′ter•cys′tic, *adj.*
in′ter•de•bate′, *v.,* **-bat•ed, -bat•ing.**
in′ter•de•ceive′, *v.,* **-ceived, -ceiv•ing.**
in′ter•de•pend′, *v.i.*
in′ter•de•pend′a•bil′i•ty, *n.*
in′ter•de•pend′a•ble, *adj.*
in′ter•de•struc′tive, *adj.;* **-ly,** *adv.;* **-ness,** *n.*
in′ter•de•ter′mi•na′tion, *n.*
in′ter•de•ter′mine, *v.t.,* **-mined, -min•ing.**
in′ter•de•vour′, *v.t.*
in′ter•di′a•lec′tal, *adj.;* **-ly,** *adv.*
in′ter•dif′fer•en′ti•ate′, *v.t.,* **-at•ed, -at•ing.**
in′ter•dif′fer•en′ti•a′tion, *n.*
in′ter•dif•fuse′, *v.,* **-fused, -fus•ing.**
in′ter•dif•fu′sion, *n.*

—**Syn. 2.** pry, intrude, encroach, interlope. **4.** intercede.

in•ter•fer•ence (in′tər fēr′əns), *n.* **1.** an act, fact, or instance of interfering. **2.** something that interferes. **3.** *Physics.* the process in which two or more light, sound, or electromagnetic waves of the same frequency combine to reinforce or cancel each other, the amplitude of the resulting wave being equal to the sum of the amplitudes of the combining waves. **4.** *Radio.* **a.** a jumbling of radio signals, caused by the reception of undesired ones. **b.** the signals or device producing the incoherence. **5.** *Football.* **a.** the act of a teammate or of teammates running ahead of a ball-carrier and blocking prospective tacklers out of the way: *to run interference for the halfback.* **b.** such a teammate or such teammates collectively: *to follow one's interference.* **c.** the act of illegally hindering an opponent from catching a forward pass or a kick. **6.** *Aeron.* the situation that arises when the aerodynamic influence of one surface of an aircraft conflicts with the influence of another surface. **7.** *Ling.* **a.** (in bilingualism and foreign-language learning) the overlapping of two languages. **b.** deviation from the norm of either language in such a situation. **8.** the distorting or inhibiting effect of previously learned behavior on subsequent learning. **9.** *Psychol.* the forgetting of information or an event due to inability to reconcile it with conflicting information obtained subsequently. **10. run interference,** *Informal.* to deal with troublesome or time-consuming matters, as for a colleague or supervisor, esp. to forestall problems. [1775–85; INTERFERE + -ENCE]

interfer′ence drag′, *Aeron.* the drag on an aircraft caused by the interaction of two aerodynamic bodies.

interfer′ence mi′croscope, a microscope that utilizes light interference phenomena to create two superimposed images of an object, making possible the observation of transparent objects without using the staining technique. —**interfer′ence micros′copy.**

interfer′ence pat′tern, *Physics.* a series of alternating dark and bright bands produced as a result of light interference. Cf. **diffraction.** [1930–35]

in•ter•fe•ren•tial (in′tər fə ren′shəl), *adj.* of or pertaining to interference. [1875–80; INTERFERE + (DIFFER)-ENTIAL]

in•ter•fer•o•gram (in′tər fēr′ə gram′), *n.* *Optics.* a photographic record of light interference patterns produced with an interferometer, used for recording shock waves and fluid flow patterns. [1920–25; INTERFERE + -O- + -GRAM[1]]

in•ter•fer•om•e•ter (in′tər fə rom′i tər), *n.* **1.** *Optics.* a device that separates a beam of light into two ray beams, usually by means of reflection, and that brings the rays together to produce interference, used to measure wavelength, index of refraction, and astronomical distances. **2.** *Astron.* an instrument for measuring the angular separation of double stars or the diameter of giant stars by means of the interference phenomena of light emitted by these stars. [1895–1900; INTERFERE + -O- + -METER] —**in•ter•fer•o•met•ric** (in′tər fēr′ə me′trik), *adj.* —**in′ter•fer′o•met′ri•cal•ly,** *adv.* —**in′ter•fer•om′e•try,** *n.*

in•ter•fer•on (in′tər fēr′on), *n.* **1.** *Biochem.* any of various proteins, produced by virus-infected cells, that inhibit reproduction of the invading virus and induce resistance to further infection. **2.** *Pharm.* Also called **alpha-interferon.** an interferon produced by genetically engineered bacteria and harvested for use against hairy cell leukemia. [1957; INTERFERE + -ON[1]]

in•ter•fer•tile (in′tər fûr′tl), *adj.* *Bot., Zool.* able to interbreed. [1915–20; INTER- + FERTILE] —**in′ter•fer•til′i•ty,** *n.*

in•ter•fi•bril•lar (in′tər fī′brə lər), *adj.* situated between fibrils. Also, **in•ter•fi•bril•lar•y** (in′tər fī′brə ler′ē). [1880–85; INTER- + FIBRILLAR]

in•ter•file (in′tər fīl′), *v.t.,* **-filed, -fil•ing.** to combine two or more similarly arranged sets of items, as cards or documents, into a single file. [1945–50; INTER- + FILE[1]]

in•ter•fill•ing (in′tər fil′ing), *n.* *Building Trades.* a filling of materials, as brickwork between studs. [INTER- + FILLING]

in•ter•fin•ger (in′tər fing′gər), *v.i.* *Geol.* (of sedimentary rocks) to change laterally from one type to another in a zone where the two types form interpenetrating wedges. [1970–75; INTER- + FINGER]

in•ter•flow (*v.* in′tər flō′; *n.* in′tər flō′), *v.i.* **1.** to flow into each other; intermingle. —*n.* **2.** an interflowing. [1600–10; INTER- + FLOW]

in•ter•flu•ent (in′tər flōō′ənt), *adj.* flowing into one another; intermingling. [1645–55; < L *interfluent-* (s. of *interfluēns*). See INTER-, FLUENT] —**in′ter•flu′ence,** *n.*

in•ter•fluve (in′tər flōōv′), *n.* the land area separating adjacent stream valleys. [1900–05; back formation from *interfluvial* lying between streams. See INTER-, FLUVIAL] —**in′ter•flu′vi•al,** *adj.*

CONCISE ETYMOLOGY KEY: <, descended or borrowed from; >, whence; b., blend of, blended; c., cognate with; cf., compare; deriv., derivative; equiv., equivalent; imit., imitative; obl., oblique; r., replacing; s., stem; sp., spelling, spelled; resp., respelling, respelled; trans., translation; ?, origin unknown; *, unattested; ‡, probably earlier than. See the full key inside the front cover.

in•ter•fold (in′tər fōld′), *v.t.* to fold one within another; fold together. [1570–80; INTER- + FOLD[1]]

in•ter•fo•li•a•ceous (in′tər fō′lē ā′shəs), *adj.* *Bot.* situated between leaves, esp. opposite leaves. Also, **in•ter•fo•li•ar** (in′tər fō′lē ər). [1750–60; INTER- + FOLIACEOUS]

in•ter•fuse (in′tər fyōōz′), *v.,* **-fused, -fus•ing.** —*v.t.* **1.** to intersperse, intermingle, or permeate with something. **2.** to blend or fuse, one with another. **3.** to pour or pass (something) between, into, or through; infuse. —*v.i.* **4.** to become blended or fused, one with another. [1585–95; < L *interfūsus* ptp. of *interfundere* to pour between. See INTER-, FUSE[2]] —**in′ter•fu′sion,** *n.*

in•ter•ga•lac•tic (in′tər gə lak′tik), *adj.* of, existing, or occurring in the space between galaxies: *The science-fiction movie was about an intergalactic war.* [1925–30; INTER- + GALACTIC]

in•ter•gen•er•a•tion•al (in′tər jen′ə rā′shə nl), *adj.* of, pertaining to, or for individuals in different generations or age categories: *intergenerational housing.* [1970–75; INTER- + GENERATION + -AL[1]]

in•ter•ge•ner•ic (in′tər jə ner′ik), *adj.* occurring between different genera. [1920–25; INTER- + GENERIC]

in•ter•gla•cial (in′tər glā′shəl), *adj.* *Geol.* occurring or formed between times of glacial action. [1865–70; INTER- + GLACIAL]

in•ter•glyph (in′tər glif′), *n.* *Archit.* a surface between two grooves, as on a triglyph. [1870–75; INTER- + GLYPH]

in•ter•gov•ern•men•tal (in′tər guv′ərn men′tl, -ər men′-), *adj.* involving two or more governments or levels of government. [1925–30; INTER- + GOVERNMENTAL]

in•ter•gra•da•tion (in′tər grā dā′shən), *n.* **1.** the act or process of intergrading or the state of being intergraded. **2.** an evolutionary process by which different species of organisms tend to merge through a series of intermediate stages or grades. [1870–75; INTER- + GRADATION] —**in′ter•gra•da′tion•al,** *adj.*

in•ter•grade (*n.* in′tər grād′; *v.* in′tər grād′), *n., v.,* **-grad•ed, -grad•ing.** —*n.* **1.** an intermediate grade, form, stage, etc. —*v.i.* **2.** to merge gradually, one into another, as different species through evolution. [1870–75; INTER- + GRADE]

in•ter•gran•u•lar (in′tər gran′yə lər), *adj.* located or occurring between granules or grains: *intergranular corrosion.* [1930–35; INTER- + GRANULAR]

in•ter•group (in′tər grōōp′), *adj.* *Sociol.* taking place or being between groups: *intergroup relationships.* [1880–85; INTER- + GROUP]

in•ter•growth (in′tər grōth′), *n.* growth or growing together, as of one thing with or into another. [1835–45; INTER- + GROWTH]

in•ter•hem•i•spher•ic (in′tər hem′ə sfer′ik), *adj.* of, pertaining to, or between hemispheres, as of the earth: *interhemispheric cooperation.* [1880–85; INTER- + HEMISPHERIC]

in•ter•im (in′tər əm), *n.* **1.** an intervening time; interval; meantime: *in the interim.* **2.** a temporary or provisional arrangement; stopgap; makeshift. **3.** (*cap.*) *Ch. Hist.* any of three provisional arrangements for the settlement of religious differences between German Protestants and Roman Catholics during the Reformation. —*adj.* **4.** for, during, belonging to, or connected with an intervening period of time; temporary; provisional: *an interim order.* —*adv.* **5.** meantime. [1540–50; < L: in the meantime]

in•ter•in•sur•ance (in′tər in shŏŏr′əns, -shûr′-), *n.* See **reciprocal insurance.** [INTER- + INSURANCE]

in•ter•i•on•ic (in′tər ī on′ik), *adj.* between ions. [1900–05; INTER- + IONIC]

in•te•ri•or (in tēr′ē ər), *adj.* **1.** being within; inside of anything; internal; inner; further toward a center: *the interior rooms of a house.* **2.** of or pertaining to that which is within; inside: *an interior view.* **3.** situated well inland from the coast or border: *the interior towns of a country.* **4.** of or pertaining to the inland. **5.** domestic: *interior trade.* **6.** private or hidden; inner: *interior negotiations of the council.* **7.** pertaining to the mind or soul; mental or spiritual: *the interior life.* —*n.* **8.** the internal or inner part; inside. **9.** *Archit.* **a.** the inside part of a building, considered as a whole from the point of view of artistic design or general effect, convenience, etc. **b.** a single room or apartment so considered. **10.** a pictorial representation of the inside of a room. **11.** the inland parts of a region, country, etc.: *the Alaskan interior.* **12.** the domestic affairs of a country as distinguished from its foreign affairs: *the Department of the Interior.* **13.** the inner or inward nature or character of anything. **14.** *Math.* the largest open set contained in a given set, as the points in a circle not including the boundary. [1480–90; < L, comp. adj. equiv. to *inter-* inward + *-ior* comp. suffix; see EXTERIOR] —**in•te•ri•or•i•ty** (in tēr′ē ôr′i tē, -or′-), *n.* —**in•te′ri•or•ly,** *adv.*
—**Syn. 8.** See **inside.** —**Ant. 1, 8.** exterior.

inte′rior an′gle, *Geom.* **1.** an angle formed between parallel lines by a third line that intersects them. **2.** an angle formed within a polygon by two adjacent sides. [1750–60]

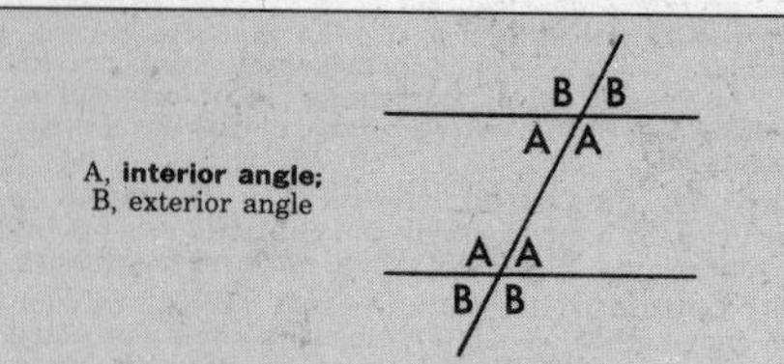

A, **interior angle;**
B, exterior angle

inte′rior decora′tion, 1. See **interior design. 2.** materials used to decorate an interior. [1800–10]

inte′rior design′, 1. the design and coordination of the decorative elements of the interior of a house, apartment, office, or other structural space, including color schemes, fittings, furnishings, and sometimes architectural features. **2.** the art, business, or profession of executing this. Also called **interior decoration.** [1925–30]

inte′rior design′er, a person whose profession is the execution of interior design. Also called **inte′rior dec′orator.** [1935–40]

inte′rior drain′age, *Physical Geog.* a drainage system whose waters do not continue to the ocean either on the surface or underground, but evaporate within the land area.

in•te•ri•or•ism (in tēr′ē ə riz′əm), *n.* *Philos.* a theory that truth is discovered by introspection rather than by examination of the outside world. [INTERIOR + -ISM] —**in•te′ri•or•ist,** *n., adj.*

inte′rior line′man, *Football.* one of the players positioned on the line of scrimmage between the ends.

inte′rior map′ping, *Math.* an open map.

inte′rior mon′ologue, 1. *Literature.* a form of stream-of-consciousness writing that represents the inner thoughts of a character. **2.** *Motion Pictures, Television.* the device of showing a character on screen who does not appear to speak, although the character's voice is heard on the soundtrack to create the illusion that the audience is hearing the character's thoughts. [1920–25]

in•ter•is•land (in′tər ī′lənd), *adj.* being or operating between islands: *interisland transportation.* [1855–60; INTER- + ISLAND]

interj., interjection.

in•ter•ja•cent (in′tər jā′sənt), *adj.* between or among others; intervening; intermediate. [1585–95; < L *interjacent-* (s. of *interjacēns*) prp. of *interjacēre* to lie between. See INTER-, ADJACENT] —**in′ter•ja′cence,** *n.*

in•ter•ject (in′tər jekt′), *v.t.* **1.** to insert between other things: *to interject a clarification of a previous statement.* **2.** *Obs.* to come between. [1570–80; < L *interjectus* ptp. of *interjicere* to throw between, equiv. to *inter-* INTER- + *-jec-* (comb. form of *jac-*, s. of *jacere* to throw) + *-tus* ptp. suffix] —**in′ter•jec′tor,** *n.*
—**Syn. 1.** insinuate, introduce, interpolate, intercalate.

in•ter•jec•tion (in′tər jek′shən), *n.* **1.** the act of interjecting. **2.** something interjected, as a remark. **3.** the utterance of a word or phrase expressive of emotion; the uttering of an exclamation. **4.** *Gram.* **a.** any member of a class of words expressing emotion, distinguished in most languages by their use in grammatical isolation, as *Hey! Oh! Ouch! Ugh!* **b.** any other word or expression so used, as *Good grief! Indeed!* [1400–50; late ME *interjeccio(u)n* < L *interjectiōn-* (s. of *interjectiō*). See INTERJECT, -ION] —**in′ter•jec′tion•al, in•ter•jec•tur•al** (in′tər jek′chər əl), *adj.* —**in′ter•jec′tion•al•ly,** *adv.*

in•ter•jec•tion•al•ize (in′tər jek′shə nl īz′), *v.t.,* **-ized, -iz•ing.** to make into an interjection. Also, *esp. Brit.,* **in′ter•jec′tion•al•ise′.** [1870–75; INTERJECTIONAL + -IZE]

in•ter•jec•to•ry (in′tər jek′tə rē), *adj.* **1.** characterized by interjection; interjectional. **2.** thrust in; interjected: *an interjectory word.* [1855–60; INTERJECT + -ORY[1]] —**in′ter•jec′to•ri•ly,** *adv.*

in•ter•join (in′tər join′), *v.t., v.i.* to join, one with another. [1600–10; INTER- + JOIN]

in•ter•joist (in′tər joist′), *n.* a space between two joists. [1815–25; INTER- + JOIST]

in•ter•ki•ne•sis (in′tər ki nē′sis, -kī-), *n.* *Cell Biol.* interphase. [1905–10; INTER- + KINESIS] —**in•ter•ki•net•ic** (in′tər ki net′ik, -kī-), *adj.*

in•ter•knit (in′tər nit′), *v.t.,* **-knit•ted** or **-knit, -knit•ting.** to knit together, one with another; intertwine. [1795–1805; INTER- + KNIT]

in•ter•knot (in′tər not′), *v.t., v.i.,* **-knot•ted, -knot•ting.** to tie or knot together. [1605–15; INTER- + KNOT[1]]

in•ter•lace (in′tər lās′, in′tər lās′), *v.,* **-laced, -lac•ing.** —*v.i.* **1.** to cross one another, typically passing alternately over and under, as if woven together; intertwine: *Their hands interlaced.* —*v.t.* **2.** to unite or arrange (threads, strips, parts, branches, etc.) so as to intercross one another, passing alternately over and under; intertwine. **3.** to mingle; blend. **4.** to diversify, as with threads woven in. **5.** to intersperse; intermingle: *She interlaced her lecture on Schubert with some of his songs.* [1325–75; INTER- + LACE; r. ME *entrelacen* < MF *en-*

in′ter•dif•fu′sive, *adj.;* **-ness,** *n.*
in′ter•dig′i•tal, *adj.;* **-ly,** *adv.*
in′ter•dis•tin′guish, *v.t.*
in′ter•dis′trict, *adj.*
in′ter•di•vi′sion, *n.*
in′ter•di•vi′sion•al, *adj.;* **-ly,** *adv.*
in′ter•do•min′ion, *adj.*
in′ter•dor′sal, *adj.*
in′ter•ec•cle′si•as′ti•cal, *adj.;* **-ly,** *adv.*
in′ter•e•lec′tion, *adj.*
in′ter•e•lec′trode, *n.*
in′ter•e•lec•tron′ic, *adj.*
in′ter•el′e•ment, *adj., n.*
in′ter•em•brace′, *v.,* **-braced, -brac•ing.**
in′ter•em′pire, *adj.*
in′ter•en•tan′gle, *v.t.,* **-gled, -gling.**
in′ter•en•tan′gle•ment, *n.*
in′ter•en•vi′ron•men′tal, *adj.*
in′ter•ep′i•dem′ic, *adj.*
in′ter•ep′i•the′li•al, *adj.*
in′ter•e′qui•noc′tial, *adj.*
in′ter•es′tu•a•rine′, *adj.*
in′ter•eth′nic, *adj.*
in′ter-Eu′ro•pe′an, *adj.*
in′ter•fac′tion•al, *adj.*
in′ter•fac′ul•ty, *n., pl.* **-ties,** *adj.*
in′ter•fa•mil′ial, *adj.*
in′ter•fam′i•ly, *adj.*
in′ter•fas•cic′u•lar, *adj.*
in′ter•fed′er•a′tion, *n.*
in′ter•fem′o•ral, *adj.*
in′ter•fi′ber, *adj.*
in′ter•fi′brous, *adj.*
in′ter•fil′a•men′ta•ry, *adj.*
in′ter•fil′a•men′tous, *adj.*
in′ter•fi′lar, *adj.*
in′ter•fil′trate, *v.t.,* **-trat•ed, -trat•ing.**
in′ter•fil•tra′tion, *n.*
in′ter•firm′, *adj.*
in′ter•flash′ing, *n.*
in′ter•force′, *n.*
in′ter•fra•ter′nal, *adj.;* **-ly,** *adv.*
in′ter•fra•ter′ni•ty, *adj.*
in′ter•fric′tion, *n.*
in′ter•fron′tal, *adj.*
in′ter•ful′gent, *adj.*
in′ter•func′tion, *adj.*
in′ter•gang′, *adj.*
in′ter•gan′gli•on′ic, *adj.*
in′ter•gen′er•at′ing, *adj.*
in′ter•gen′er•a′tion, *n.*
in′ter•gen′er•a•tive, *adj.*
in′ter•gilt′, *adj.*
in′ter•glan′du•lar, *adj.*
in′ter•glob′u•lar, *adj.*
in′ter•go•nid′i•al, *adj.*
in′ter•gos′sip, *v.,* **-siped** or **-sipped, -sip•ing.**
in′ter•graft′, *v.i.*

trelacer] **—in•ter•lac•ed•ly** (in′tər lā′sid lē), *adv.* **—in′ter•lace′ment,** *n.*

in′terlacing arcade′, an arcade, esp. a blind one, composed of arches **(in′terlacing arch′es)** so arranged and cut that each arch seems to intersect and be intersected by one or more other arches. Also called **intersecting arcade.**

interlacing arcade

In•ter•la•ken (in′tər lä′kən, in′tər lä′kən), *n.* a town in central Switzerland between the lakes of Brienz and Thun: tourist center. 4735.

in•ter•lam•i•nate (in′tər lam′ə nāt′), *v.t.,* **-nat•ed, -nat•ing.** to interlay or lay between laminae. [1810–20; INTER- + LAMINATE] **—in′ter•lam′i•na′tion,** *n.*

in•ter•lan•guage (in′tər lang′gwij), *n.* **1.** a language created or used for international communication. **2.** (in second-language acquisition) the linguistic system characterizing the output of a nonnative speaker at any stage prior to full acquisition of the target language. [1925–30; INTER- + LANGUAGE]

in•ter•lard (in′tər lärd′), *v.t.* **1.** to diversify by adding or interjecting something unique, striking, or contrasting (usually fol. by *with*): *to interlard one's speech with oaths.* **2.** (of things) to be intermixed in. **3.** *Obs.* to mix, as fat with lean meat. [1525–35; INTER- + LARD; r. *enterlard* < MF *entrelarder*] **—in′ter•lar•da′tion, in′ter•lard′ment,** *n.*

in•ter•lay (in′tər lā′), *v.t.,* **-laid, -lay•ing. 1.** to lay between; interpose. **2.** to diversify with something laid between or inserted: *to interlay silver with gold.* [1600–10; INTER- + LAY[1]]

in•ter•leaf (in′tər lēf′), *n., pl.* **-leaves** (-lēvz′). an additional leaf, usually blank, inserted between or bound with the regular printed leaves of a book, as to separate chapters or provide room for a reader's notes. [1735–45; INTER- + LEAF]

in•ter•leave (in′tər lēv′), *v.t.,* **-leaved, -leav•ing. 1.** to provide blank leaves in (a book) for notes or written comments. **2.** to insert blank leaves between (the regular printed leaves). **3.** to insert something alternately and regularly between the pages or parts of: *Interleave the eight-page form with carbon paper.* **4.** to insert (material) alternately and regularly between the pages or parts of something else: *Interleave carbon paper between the pages of the form.* [1660–70; INTER- + LEAVE[3]]

in•ter•leav•ing (in′tər lē′ving), *n. Computers.* a method for making data retrieval more efficient by rearranging or renumbering the sectors on a hard disk or by splitting a computer's main memory into sections so that the sectors or sections can be read in alternating cycles.

in•ter•leu•kin 1 (in′tər lo͞o′kin), *Immunol.* any of several proteins released from certain cells, esp. macrophages, and having various effects on the activity of other cells, as promoting inflammation or enhancing T-cell proliferation. *Abbr.:* IL-1 [1979; INTER- + LEUK(OCYTE) + -IN[2]; so called because such proteins act as agents of communication between different populations of leukocytes]

interleukin 2, 1. *Immunol.* a lymphokine protein, secreted by T cells in response to antigen and interleukin 1, that stimulates the proliferation of T cells. **2.** *Pharm.* a form of this protein produced by genetic engineering and used experimentally in immunotherapy. *Abbr.:* IL-2 Cf. **LAK cell.** [1980–85; see INTERLEUKIN 1]

interleukin 3, *Immunol.* a lymphokine protein, secreted by T cells, that participates in the regulation of blood-cell production. *Abbr.:* IL-3 [1980–85; see INTERLEUKIN 1]

in′terli′brary loan′, 1. a system by which one library obtains a work for a user by borrowing it from another library. **2.** a loan made by this system. [1925–30; INTER- + LIBRARY]

in•ter•line[1] (in′tər līn′), *v.,* **-lined, -lin•ing,** *adj.* —*v.t.* **1.** to write or insert (words, phrases, etc.) between the lines of writing or print. **2.** to mark or inscribe (a document, book, etc.) between the lines. **3.** to transfer (freight) from one carrier to another in the course of shipment. —*v.i.* **4.** to transfer freight from one carrier to another in the course of shipment. —*adj.* **5.** involving or indicating a transfer of passengers or freight from one carrier to another during travel or shipment: *interline flights.* **6.** of or pertaining to transactions between competing carriers, esp. airlines, by which passengers, baggage, and freight are transferred from one carrier to another using only one ticket or one check-in procedure from departure point to destination. [1350–1400; ME < ML *interlineāre.* See INTER-, LINE[1]]

in•ter•line[2] (in′tər līn′), *v.t.,* **-lined, -lin•ing.** to provide (a garment) with an interlining. [1470–80; INTER- + LINE[2]] **—in′ter•lin′er,** *n.*

in•ter•lin•e•al (in′tər lin′ē əl), *adj.* interlinear. [1520–30; INTER- + LINEAL] **—in′ter•lin′e•al•ly,** *adv.*

in•ter•lin•e•ar (in′tər lin′ē ər), *adj.* **1.** situated or inserted between lines, as of the lines of print in a book: *a Latin text with interlinear translation.* **2.** having interpolated lines; interlined. **3.** having the same text in various languages set in alternate lines: *the interlinear Bible.* —*n.* **4.** a book, esp. a textbook, having interlinear matter, as a translation. [1400–50; late ME < ML *interlineāris.* See INTERLINE[1], -AR[1]] **—in′ter•lin′e•ar•ly,** *adv.*

in•ter•lin•e•ate (in′tər lin′ē āt′), *v.t.,* **-at•ed, -at•ing.** interline[1] (defs. 1, 2). [1615–25; < ML *interlineātus,* ptp. of *interlineāre* to INTERLINE[1]; see -ATE[1]] **—in′ter•lin′e•a′tion,** *n.*

in•ter•lin•gua (in′tər ling′gwə), *n.* **1.** an interlanguage. **2.** (*cap.*) an artificial language developed between 1924 and 1951, based primarily upon the Romance languages, and intended mainly as a common international language for scientists. [1920–25; < It. See INTER-, LINGUA]

in•ter•lin•gual (in′tər ling′gwəl), *adj.* pertaining to or using two or more languages: *an interlingual dictionary.* [1850–55; INTER- + LINGUAL] **—in′ter•lin′gual•ism,** *n.*

in•ter•lin•ing[1] (in′tər lī′ning), *n.* **1.** an inner lining placed between the ordinary lining and the outer fabric of a garment. **2.** material, as cotton or wool, for this purpose. **3.** lining and padding quilted together. [1880–85; INTERLINE[2] + -ING[1]]

in•ter•lin•ing[2] (in′tər lī′ning), *n.* **1.** something that is written or inserted between lines of writing or print. **2.** such insertions collectively. [1425–75; late ME; see INTERLINE[1], -ING[1]]

in•ter•link (*v.* in′tər lingk′, in′tər lingk′; *n.* in′tər-lingk′), *v.t.* **1.** to link, one with another. —*n.* **2.** a connecting link. [1580–90; INTER- + LINK[1]]

in•ter•lock (*v.* in′tər lok′, in′tər lok′; *n.* in′tər lok′), *v.i.* **1.** to fit into each other, as parts of machinery, so that all action is synchronized. **2.** to interweave or interlace, one with another: *The branches of the trees interlock to form a natural archway.* **3.** *Railroads.* (of switches, signals, etc.) to operate together in a prearranged order. —*v.t.* **4.** to lock one with another. **5.** to fit (parts) together to ensure coordinated action. **6.** *Railroads.* to arrange (switches, signals, etc.) to effect a predetermined sequence of movement. —*n.* **7.** the fact or condition of interlocking or of being interlocked. **8.** the existence or an instance of an interlocking directorate. **9.** a device for preventing a mechanism from being set in motion when another mechanism is in such a position that the two operating simultaneously might produce undesirable results. **10.** Also called **ignition interlock.** a device or system that prevents an automotive engine from starting until the seat belt for any occupied front seat is fastened. **11.** a stretch fabric made with a circular knitting machine having two alternating sets of long and short needles. **12.** *Motion Pictures.* a device for synchronizing the action of a camera and sound recorder. [1625–35; INTER- + LOCK[1]] **—in′ter•lock′er,** *n.*

interlock′ing direc′torate, a corporate directorate that includes one or more members who serve simultaneously in the directorates of other corporations.

in•ter•lo•cu•tion (in′tər lə kyo͞o′shən), *n.* conversation; dialogue. [1525–35; < L *interlocūtiōn-* (s. of *interlocūtiō*) a speaking between, equiv. to *interlocūt(us)* (see INTERLOCUTOR) + *-iōn-* -ION]

in•ter•loc•u•tor (in′tər lok′yə tər), *n.* **1.** a person who takes part in a conversation or dialogue. **2.** the man in the middle of the line of performers in a minstrel troupe, who acts as the announcer and banters with the end men. **3.** a person who questions; interrogator. [1505–15; < L *interlocū-,* var. s. of *interloquī* to speak between (*inter-* INTER- + *loquī* to speak) + -TOR]

in•ter•loc•u•to•ry (in′tər lok′yə tôr′ē, -tōr′ē), *adj.* **1.** of the nature of, pertaining to, or occurring in conversation: *interlocutory instruction.* **2.** interjected into the main course of speech. **3.** *Law.* **a.** pronounced during the course of an action, as a decision; not finally decisive of a case. **b.** pertaining to an intermediate decision. [1580–90; < ML *interlocūtōrius.* See INTERLOCUTOR, -TORY[1]] **—in′ter•loc′u•to′ri•ly,** *adv.*

in•ter•lope (in′tər lōp′, in′tər lōp′), *v.i.,* **-loped, -lop•ing. 1.** to intrude into some region or field of trade without a proper license. **2.** to thrust oneself into the affairs of others. [1595–1605; prob. back formation from *interloper,* equiv. to INTER- + *-loper* (see LANDLOPER)] **—in′ter•lop′er,** *n.*
—Syn. 1. trespass, poach, encroach. **2.** meddle.

in•ter•lude (in′tər lo͞od′), *n.* **1.** an intervening episode, period, space, etc. **2.** a short dramatic piece, esp. of a light or farcical character, formerly introduced between the parts or acts of miracle and morality plays or given as part of other entertainments. **3.** one of the early English farces or comedies, as those written by John Heywood, which grew out of such pieces. **4.** any intermediate performance or entertainment, as between the acts of a play. **5.** an instrumental passage or a piece of music rendered between the parts of a song, church service, drama, etc. [1275–1325; ME < ML *interlūdium,* equiv. to L *inter-* INTER- + *lūd(us)* play + *-ium* -IUM] **—in′ter•lu′di•al,** *adj.*
—Syn. 1. interval, respite, intermission, pause.

in•ter•lu•nar (in′tər lo͞o′nər), *adj.* pertaining to the moon's monthly period of invisibility between the old moon and the new. [1590–1600; INTER- + LUNAR]

in•ter•lu•na•tion (in′tər lo͞o nā′shən), *n.* the interlunar period. [1805–15; INTER- + LUNATION]

in•ter•mar•riage (in′tər mar′ij, in′tər mar′ij), *n.* **1.** marriage between a man and woman of different races, religions, tribes, castes, or ethnic groups, as between a white and a black or between a Christian and a non-Christian. **2.** marriage between a man and woman of different social classes. **3.** marriage between a man and woman within a specific group, as required by custom or law; endogamy. **4.** marriage between a man and woman belonging to the same small group, esp. if they are close blood relatives. [1570–80; INTER- + MARRIAGE]

in•ter•mar•ry (in′tər mar′ē), *v.i.,* **-ried, -ry•ing. 1.** to become connected by marriage, as two families, tribes, castes, or religions. **2.** to marry within one's family. **3.** to marry outside one's religion, ethnic group, etc. **4.** to marry. [1565–75; INTER- + MARRY[1]]

in•ter•med•dle (in′tər med′l), *v.i.,* **-dled, -dling.** to take part in a matter, esp. officiously; meddle. [1350–1400; INTER- + MEDDLE; r. ME *entremedlen* < AF *entremedler,* OF *entremesler*] **—in′ter•med′dler,** *n.*

in•ter•me•di•a (in′tər mē′dē ə), *adj.* using or involving several media, as dance, slides, electronic music, film, and painting, simultaneously; multimedia. [1965–70; INTER- + MEDIA]

in•ter•me•di•a•cy (in′tər mē′dē ə sē), *n.* the state of being intermediate or of acting intermediately. [1705–15; INTERMEDI(ATE)[1] + -ACY]

in•ter•me•di•ar•y (in′tər mē′dē er′ē), *n., pl.* **-ar•ies,** *adj.* —*n.* **1.** an intermediate agent or agency; a go-between or mediator. **2.** a medium or means. **3.** an intermediate form or stage. —*adj.* **4.** being between; intermediate. **5.** acting between persons, parties, etc.; serving as an intermediate agent or agency: *an intermediary power.* [1785–95; < LL *intermedi(um)* intervening place + -ARY; see INTERMEDIATE[1]]
—Syn. 1. arbitrator, umpire.

in•ter•me•di•ate[1] (in′tər mē′dē it), *adj.* **1.** being, situated, or acting between two points, stages, things, persons, etc.: *the intermediate steps in a procedure.* **2.** of or pertaining to an intermediate school. **3.** *Auto.* mid-size. —*n.* **4.** a person who acts between others; intermediary; mediator. **5.** something intermediate, as a form or class. **6.** *Chem.* a derivative of the initial material formed before the desired product of a chemical process. [1615–25; < ML *intermediātus,* equiv. to L *intermedi(us)* intermediary (*inter-* INTER- + *medius* MIDDLE, in the middle) + *-ātus* -ATE[1]] **—in′ter•me′di•ate•ly,** *adv.* **—in′ter•me′di•ate•ness,** *n.*

in•ter•me•di•ate[2] (in′tər mē′dē āt′), *v.i.,* **-at•ed, -at•ing.** to act as an intermediary; intervene; mediate. [1600–10; < ML *intermediātus,* ptp. of *intermediāre.* See INTER-, MEDIATE] **—in′ter•me′di•a′tor,** *n.* **—in•ter•me•di•a•to•ry** (in′tər mē′dē ə tôr′ē, -tōr′ē), *adj.*

interme′diate card′, *Textiles.* a card used in the carding process to transfer sliver from the breaker card to the finisher card.

in′terme′diate fre′quency, *Radio.* the middle frequency in a superheterodyne receiver, at which most of the amplification takes place. *Abbr.:* if [1920–25]

in′terme′diate host′, *Biol.* the host in which a parasite undergoes development but does not reach sexual maturity. [1875–80]

interme′diate range′ ballis′tic mis′sile, any supersonic missile that has a range of 800 to 1500 nautical mi. (1500 to 2800 km) and follows a ballistic trajectory after a powered, guided launching. *Abbr.:* IRBM, I.R.B.M. [1955–60]

interme′diate school′, 1. a school for pupils in grades 4 through 6. **2.** a junior high school. Cf. **middle school.** [1835–45]

in•ter•me′di•ate-val′ue the′orem (in′tər mē′dē-it val′yo͞o), *Math.* the theorem that a function continuous between two points and having unequal values, *a* and *b,* at the two points takes on all values between *a* and *b.*

interme′diate vec′tor bos′on, *Physics.* one of the three particles that are believed to transmit the weak force: the positively charged W particle, the negatively charged W particle, and the neutral Z^0 particle. [1965–70]

in•ter•me•di•a•tion (in′tər mē′dē ā′shən), *n.* the act of intermediating. [1595–1605; INTERMEDIATE[2] + -ION]

in•ter•ment (in tûr′mənt), *n.* the act or ceremony of interring; burial. [1300–50; INTER + -MENT; r. ME *enter(e)ment* < MF *enterrement*]

CONCISE PRONUNCIATION KEY: act, cāpe, dâre, pärt; set, ēqual; *if,* ice; ox, ōver, ôrder, oil, bo͝ok, bo͞ot, out; up, ûrge; child; sing; shoe; thin, *that;* zh as in *treasure.* ə = *a* as in *alone, e* as in *system, i* as in *easily, o* as in *gallop, u* as in *circus;* ° as in *fire* (fī°r), *hour* (ou°r). l and n can serve as syllabic consonants, as in *cradle* (krād′l), and *button* (but′n). See the full key inside the front cover.

in′ter•grap′ple, *v.,* **-pled, -pling.**
in′ter•gu′lar, *adj.*
in′ter•gy′ral, *adj.*
in′ter•hab′i•ta′tion, *n.*
in′ter•he′mal, *adj.*
in′ter•host′, *v.t.*
in′ter•hos′tile, *adj.*
in′ter•hu′man, *adj.*
in′ter•hy′brid•ize′, *v.i.,* **-ized, -iz•ing.**
in′ter•im•pe′ri•al, *adj.*
in′ter•in•cor′po•ra′tion, *n.*
in′ter•in′de•pend′ence, *n.*
in′ter•in′di•cate′, *v.t.,* **-cat•ed, -cat•ing.**
in′ter•in′di•vid′u•al, *adj.*
in′ter•in′dus•try, *adj.*
in′ter•in′flu•ence, *v.,* **-enced, -enc•ing.**
in′ter•in′hi•bi′tion, *n.*
in′ter•in•hib′i•tive, *adj.*
in′ter•in•sert′, *v.t.*
in′ter•in′sti•tu′tion•al, *adj.;* **-ly,** *adv.*
in′ter•in′su•lar, *adj.*
in′ter•in•volve′, *v.t.,* **-volved, -volv•ing.**
in′ter•jac′u•late′, *v.t.,* **-lat•ed, -lat•ing.**
in′ter•jac′u•la•to′ry, *adj.*
in′ter•judg′ment, *n.*
in′ter•ju′gal, *adj.*
in′ter•jug′u•lar, *adj.*
in′ter•junc′tion, *n.*
in′ter•la′bi•al, *adj.*
in′ter•lab′o•ra•to′ry, *adj.*
in′ter•la•cus′trine, *adj.*
in′ter•la•mel′lar, *adj.*
in′ter•lam′i•nar, *adj.*
in′ter•lap′, *v.i.,* **-lapped, -lap•ping.**
in′ter•lat′i•tu′di•nal, *adj.*
in′ter•lau•da′tion, *n.*
in′ter•lay′er, *n.*
in′ter•lay′er, *v.t.*
in′ter•lend′, *v.,* **-lent, -lend•ing.**
in′ter•lev′el, *adj.*
in′ter•li′bel, *v.t.,* **-beled, -bel•ing** or (*esp. Brit.*) **-belled, -bel•ling.**
in′ter•li′brar•y, *adj.*
in′ter•lie′, *v.i.,* **-lay, -lain, -ly•ing.**
in′ter•lig′a•men′ta•ry, *adj.*
in′ter•lig′a•men′tous, *adj.*
in′ter•light′, *n.*
in′ter•loan′, *adj.*
in′ter•loan′, *n.*
in′ter•lo′bar, *adj.*
in′ter•lo′bate, *adj.*
in′ter•lob′u•lar, *adj.*
in′ter•lo′cal, *adj.;* **-ly,** *adv.*
in′ter•lo′cate, *v.t.,* **-cat•ed, -cat•ing.**

in′ter·me·tal′lic com′pound (in′tər mi tal′ik, in′-), a compound of two or more metals. [1895–1900; INTER- + METALLIC]

in·ter·mez·zo (in′tər met′sō, -med′zō), *n., pl.* **-mez·zos, -mez·zi** (-met′sē, -med′zē), **1.** a short dramatic, musical, or other entertainment of light character, introduced between the acts of a drama or opera. **2.** a short musical composition between main divisions of an extended musical work. **3.** a short, independent musical composition. [1805–15; < It < LL *intermedium;* see INTERMEDIARY]

in·ter·mi·gra·tion (in′tər mī grā′shən), *n.* reciprocal migration; interchange of habitat by migrating groups. [1670–80; INTER- + MIGRATION]

in·ter·mi·na·ble (in tûr′mə nə bəl), *adj.* **1.** incapable of being terminated; unending: *an interminable job.* **2.** monotonously or annoyingly protracted or continued; unceasing; incessant: *I can't stand that interminable clatter.* **3.** having no limits: *an interminable desert.* [1325–75; ME < LL *interminābilis.* See IN-³, TERMINABLE] —**in·ter′mi·na·ble·ness, in·ter′mi·na·bil′i·ty,** *n.* —**in·ter′mi·na·bly,** *adv.*

in·ter·min·gle (in′tər ming′gəl), *v.t., v.i.,* **-gled, -gling.** to mingle, one with another; intermix. [1425–75; late ME; see INTER-, MINGLE] —**in′ter·min′gle·ment,** *n.*

in·ter·mis·sion (in′tər mish′ən), *n.* **1.** a short interval between the acts of a play or parts of a public performance, usually a period of approximately 10 or 15 minutes, allowing the performers and audience a rest. **2.** a period during which action temporarily ceases; an interval between periods of action or activity: *They studied for hours without an intermission.* **3.** the act or fact of intermitting; state of being intermitted: *to work without intermission.* [1400–50; late ME < L *intermissiōn-* (s. of *intermissiō*) interruption, equiv. to *intermiss(us)* (ptp. of *intermittere* to INTERMIT) + *-iōn-* -ION]

in·ter·mis·sive (in′tər mis′iv), *adj.* **1.** of, pertaining to, or characterized by intermission. **2.** intermittent. [1580–90; INTERMISS(ION) + -IVE]

in·ter·mit (in′tər mit′), *v.,* **-mit·ted, -mit·ting.** —*v.t.* **1.** to discontinue temporarily; suspend. —*v.i.* **2.** to stop or pause at intervals; be intermittent. **3.** to cease, stop, or break off operations for a time. [1535–45; < L *intermittere* to leave a space between, drop (for a while), leave off, equiv. to *inter-* INTER- + *mittere* to send, let go] —**in′ter·mit′ter, in′ter·mit′tor,** *n.* —**in′ter·mit′ting·ly,** *adv.*
—**Syn. 1, 3.** interrupt. **3.** desist.

in·ter·mit·tent (in′tər mit′nt), *adj.* **1.** stopping or ceasing for a time; alternately ceasing and beginning again: *an intermittent pain.* **2.** alternately functioning and not functioning or alternately functioning properly and improperly. **3.** (of streams, lakes, or springs) recurrent; showing water only part of the time. [1595–1605; < L *intermittent-* (s. of *intermittēns*) prp. of *intermittere* to INTERMIT; see -ENT] —**in′ter·mit′tence, in′ter·mit′ten·cy,** *n.* —**in′ter·mit′tent·ly,** *adv.*
—**Syn. 1.** interrupted, sporadic.

in′termit′tent cur′rent, *Elect.* a direct current that is interrupted at intervals.

in′termit′tent fe′ver, *Pathol.* **1.** a malarial fever in which feverish periods lasting a few hours alternate with periods in which the temperature is normal. **2.** any fever characterized by intervals of normal temperature. [1615–25]

in·ter·mix (in′tər miks′), *v.t., v.i.* to mix together; intermingle. [1555–65; back formation from *intermixt* (now *intermixed* ptp.) < L *intermixtus* ptp. of *intermiscēre* to mingle together. See INTER-, MIX] —**in′ter·mix′a·ble,** *adj.* —**in′ter·mix′ed·ly,** *adv.*

in·ter·mix·ture (in′tər miks′chər), *n.* **1.** a mass of ingredients mixed together. **2.** something added by intermixing. **3.** the act of intermixing. [1580–90; INTER- + MIXTURE]

in·ter·mod·al (in′tər mōd′l), *adj. Transp.* pertaining to or suitable for transportation involving more than one form of carrier, as truck and rail, or truck, ship, and rail. Also, **multimodal.** Cf. **bimodal** (def. 2). [1960–65; INTER- + MODAL] —**in′ter·mod′al·ism,** *n.*

in·ter·mo·dil·lion (in′tər mō dil′yən, -mə-), *n. Archit.* a space between two modillions. [INTER- + MODILLION]

in·ter·mod·u·la·tion (in′tər moj′ə lā′shən, -mod′yə-), *n.* the production in an electrical device of frequencies that are the sums or differences of frequencies of different inputs or of their harmonics. [1930–35; INTER- + MODULATION]

in·ter·mo·lec·u·lar (in′tər mə lek′yə lər, -mō-), *adj.* existing or occurring between molecules. [1835–45; INTER- + MOLECULAR]

in·ter·mon·tane (in′tər mon′tān), *adj.* located between mountains or mountain ranges: *an intermontane lake.* Also, **in·ter·moun·tain** (in′tər moun′tn). [1800–10, *Amer.;* < L *inter-* INTER- + *montānus,* equiv. to *mont-* (s. of *mōns*) MOUNT² + *-ānus* -ANE]

in·ter·mun·dane (in′tər mun′dān, -mun dān′), *adj.* **1.** existing in the space between worlds or heavenly bodies: *intermundane space.* **2.** of, pertaining to, or between heavenly bodies. [1685–95; INTER- + L *mundānus,* equiv. to *mund(us)* world + *-ānus* -ANE]

in·ter·mu·ral (in′tər myŏŏr′əl), *adj.* **1.** of, pertaining to, or taking place between two or more institutions, cities, etc.: *an intermural track meet.* **2.** occurring or being between walls, as of buildings or cities: *a narrow, intermural forecourt.* [1650–60; < L *intermūrālis* between walls. See INTER-, MURAL]

in·ter·mu·tule (in′tər myōō′chōōl), *n. Archit.* a space between two mutules. [1860–65; INTER- + MUTULE]

in·tern[1] (*v.* in tûrn′; *n.* in′tûrn), *v.t.* **1.** to restrict to or confine within prescribed limits, as prisoners of war, enemy aliens, or combat troops who take refuge in a neutral country. **2.** to impound or hold within a country until the termination of a war, as a ship of a belligerent that has put into a neutral port and remained beyond a limited period. —*n.* **3.** a person who is or has been interned; internee. [1865–70; < F *interner,* v. deriv. of *interne* INTERN³]

in·tern[2] (in′tûrn), *n.* Also, **interne. 1.** a resident member of the medical staff of a hospital, usually a recent medical school graduate serving under supervision. **2.** *Educ.* See **student teacher. 3.** a person who works as an apprentice or trainee in an occupation or profession to gain practical experience, and sometimes also to satisfy legal or other requirements for being licensed or accepted professionally. —*v.i.* **4.** to be or perform the duties of an intern. [1875–80, *Amer.;* < F *interne* < L *internus* INTERN³]

in·tern[3] (in tûrn′), *adj. Archaic.* internal. [1570–80; < L *internus* inward, equiv. to *inter-* INTER- + *-nus* adj. suffix; see EXTERN]

in·ter·nal (in tûr′nl), *adj.* **1.** situated or existing in the interior of something; interior. **2.** of, pertaining to, or noting the inside or inner part. **3.** *Pharm.* oral (def. 4). **4.** existing, occurring, or found within the limits or scope of something; intrinsic: *a theory having internal logic.* **5.** of or pertaining to the domestic affairs of a country: *the internal politics of a nation.* **6.** existing solely within the individual mind: *internal malaise.* **7.** coming from, produced, or motivated by the psyche or inner recesses of the mind; subjective: *an internal response.* **8.** *Anat., Zool.* inner; not superficial; away from the surface or next to the axis of the body or of a part: *the internal carotid artery.* **9.** present or occurring within an organism or one of its parts: *an internal organ.* —*n.* **10.** Usually, **internals.** entrails; innards. **11.** an inner or intrinsic attribute. [1500–10; < ML *internālis,* equiv. to L *intern(us)* INTERN³ + *-ālis* -AL¹] —**in′ter·nal′i·ty, in·ter′nal·ness,** *n.* —**in·ter′nal·ly,** *adv.*

inter′nal au′dit, an audit conducted by company accountants on a regular basis (distinguished from *independent audit*).

inter′nal au′ditory mea′tus, *Anat.* the canal extending through the petrous portion of the temporal bone, through which the glossopharyngeal nerve, the facial nerve, and the auditory nerve and artery pass. See diag. under **ear.**

inter′nal clock′. See **biological clock.** [1955–60]

in·ter·nal-com·bus·tion (in tûr′nl kəm bus′chən), *adj.* of or pertaining to an internal-combustion engine. [1880–85]

inter′nal-combus′tion en′gine, an engine of one or more working cylinders in which the process of combustion takes place within the cylinders. [1880–85]

inter′nal conver′sion, *Physics.* the emission of an electron by an atom with an excited nucleus, occurring as a result of the transfer of energy from the nucleus to the electron. [1925–30]

inter′nal ear′, the inner portion of the ear, involved in hearing and balance, consisting of a bony labyrinth that is composed of a vestibule, semicircular canals, and a cochlea and that encloses a membranous labyrinth. Cf. **ear**¹ (def. 1). See diag. under **ear**¹.

inter′nal en′ergy, *Thermodynam.* a function of thermodynamic variables, as temperature, that represents the internal state of a system that is due to the energies of the molecular constituents of the system. The change in internal energy during a process is equal to the net heat entering the system minus the net work done by the system. *Symbol:* U [1885–90]

inter′nal ex′ile, a state of comparative isolation imposed upon certain political dissidents within the Soviet Union, in which the subject may be forced to live in a remote and often unfamiliar place and in which freedom of movement and personal contact with family, friends, and associates are severely restricted.

inter′nal gear′, *Mach.* a gear having teeth cut on an inner cylindrical surface. Also called **annular gear, ring gear.**

inter′nal hem′orrhoid, *Pathol.* See under **hemorrhoid.**

inter′nal il′iac ar′tery, *Anat.* See **iliac artery** (def. 3). [1835–45]

in·ter·nal·ize (in tûr′nl īz′), *v.t.,* **-ized, -iz·ing. 1.** to incorporate (the cultural values, mores, motives, etc., of another or of a group), as through learning, socialization, or identification. **2.** to make subjective or give a subjective character to. **3.** *Ling.* to acquire (a linguistic rule, structure, etc.) as part of one's language competence. Also, *esp. Brit.,* **in·ter′nal·ise′.** [1940–45; INTERNAL + -IZE] —**in·ter′nal·i·za′tion,** *n.*

inter′nal jug′ular vein′. See under **jugular** (def. 1b).

inter′nal med′icine, the branch of medicine dealing with the diagnosis and nonsurgical treatment of diseases, esp. of internal organ systems. [1900–05]

inter′nal reconstruc′tion, *Historical Ling.* the hypothetical reconstruction of an earlier stage of a language or of some part of it, as its phonology, by deductions from irregularities in its present structure, as the reconstruction of a stage in English when certain instances of *r* were related to *s* in a systematic way by comparing the pair *was:were* to other pairs, as *lose:forlorn.*

inter′nal rela′tion, *Philos.* a relation between two entities such that if they had not been in this relation the nature of each would necessarily have been different. Cf. **external relation.** [1880–85]

inter′nal resist′ance, *Elect.* the resistance within a battery, or other voltage source, that causes a drop in the source voltage when there is a current.

inter′nal rev′enue, the revenue of a government from any domestic source, usually considered to be any source other than customs. [1790–1800, *Amer.*]

Inter′nal Rev′enue Serv′ice, the division of the U.S. Department of the Treasury that collects internal revenue, including income taxes and excise taxes, and that enforces revenue laws. Formerly, **Bureau of Internal Revenue.**

inter′nal rhyme′, *Pros.* **1.** a rhyme created by two or more words in the same line of verse. **2.** a rhyme created by words within two or more lines of a verse. [1900–05]

inter′nal stress′, (in metal or glass pieces, or the like) a stress existing within the material as a result of thermal changes, having been worked, or irregularity of molecular structure. Cf. **micro-stress, residual stress.** [1905–10]

internat., international.

in·ter·na·tion·al (in′tər nash′ə nl), *adj.* **1.** between or among nations; involving two or more nations: *international trade.* **2.** of or pertaining to two or more nations or their citizens: *a matter of international concern.* **3.** pertaining to the relations between nations: *international law.* **4.** having members or activities in several nations: *an international organization.* **5.** transcending national boundaries or viewpoints: *an international benefit; an international reputation.* —*n.* **6.** (*cap.*) any of several international socialist or communist organizations formed in the 19th and 20th centuries. Cf. **First International, Second International, Third International, Fourth International, Labor and Socialist International. 7.** (*sometimes cap.*) a labor union having locals in two or more countries. **8.** an organization, enterprise, or group, esp. a major business concern, having branches, dealings, or members in several countries. **9.** an employee, esp. an executive, assigned to work in a foreign country or countries by a business or organization that has branches or dealings in several countries. [1770–80; INTER- + NATIONAL] —**in′ter·na′tion·al′i·ty,** *n.* —**in′ter·na′tion·al·ly,** *adv.*
—**Syn. 5.** worldwide, cosmopolitan.

in′terna′tional air′ mile′. See **international nautical mile.**

Interna′tional Associa′tion of Li′ons Clubs′, See under **lion.** (def. 7).

interna′tional atom′ic time′, a system of measuring time based on atomic clocks that measure the second as defined as the SI unit of time. *Abbr.:* IAT

Interna′tional Bank′ for Reconstruc′tion and Devel′opment, official name of the **World Bank.**

in′terna′tional can′dle, *Optics.* candle (def. 3b).

In′terna′tional Code′, a code used at sea by the navies of certain nations, using a series of flags representing digits from zero through nine. [1880–85]

Interna′tional Code′ of Sig′nals, a system of maritime signals adopted by many of the maritime nations of the world, using flag, semaphore, and Morse codes in which letters or letter combinations are given arbitrary designations readily understood without requiring translation.

Interna′tional Court′ of Jus′tice, the chief judicial agency of the United Nations, established in 1945 to decide disputes arising between nations. [1905–10]

In′terna′tional Date′ Line′, a theoretical line following approximately the 180th meridian, the regions to the east of which are counted as being one day earlier in their calendar dates than the regions to the west. Also, **date line.** See map on next page.

CONCISE ETYMOLOGY KEY: <, descended or borrowed from; >, whence; b., blend of, blended; c., cognate with; cf., compare; deriv., derivative; equiv., equivalent; imit., imitative; obl., oblique; r., replacing; s., stem; sp., spelling, spelled; resp., respelling, respelled; trans., translation; ?, origin unknown; *, unattested; ‡, probably earlier than. See the full key inside the front cover.

in′ter·lo·ca′tion, *n.*
in′ter·loc′u·lar, *adj.*
in′ter·loc′u·lus, *n., pl.* **-li.**
in′ter·loop′, *n.*
in′ter·loop′, *v.t.*
in′ter·lot′, *v.t.* **-lot·ted, -lot·ting.**
in′ter·lu′cent, *adj.*
in′ter·ma′lar, *adj.*
in′ter·male′, *adj.*
in′ter·mal·le′o·lar, *adj.*
in′ter·mam′ma·ry, *adj.*
in′ter·mam′mil·lar′y, *adj.*
in′ter·man·dib′u·lar, *adj.*
in′ter·ma·no′ri·al, *adj.*
in′ter·mar′gi·nal, *adj.*
in′ter·ma·rine′, *adj.*
in′ter·mar′ket·ing, *adj.*
in′ter·mas′toid, *adj.*
in′ter·mat′, *v.i.,* **-mat·ted, -mat·ting.**
in′ter·match′, *n., v.t.*
in′ter·max′il·lar′y, *adj.*
in′ter·maze′, *v.t.,* **-mazed, -maz·ing.**
in′ter·mean′, *n.*
in′ter·meas′ur·a·ble, *adj.*
in′ter·meas′ure, *v.t.,* **-ured, -ur·ing.**
in′ter·meet′, *v.i.,* **-met, -meet·ing.**
in′ter·melt′, *v.i.*
in′ter·mem′bral, *adj.*
in′ter·mem′brane, *adj.*
in′ter·mem′bra·nous, *adj.*
in′ter·me·nin′ge·al, *adj.*
in′ter·men′stru·al, *adj.*
in′ter·men′tion, *v.*
in′ter·mes′en·ter′ic, *adj.*
in′ter·mesh′, *v.i.*
in′ter·mes′sage, *n.*
in′ter·met′a·car′pal, *adj.*
in′ter·me·tal′lic, *adj.*
in′ter·met′a·mer′ic, *adj.*
in′ter·met′a·tar′sal, *adj.*
in′ter·met′ro·pol′i·tan, *adj.*
in′ter·mi′grate, *v.i.,* **-grat·ed, -grat·ing.**
in′ter·min′is·te′ri·al, *adj.*
in′ter·mi·tot′ic, *adj.*
in′ter·mo·bil′i·ty, *n.*
in′ter·mod′i·fi·ca′tion, *n.*
in′ter·mo′lar, *adj.*
in′ter·mo′men·tar′y, *adj.*
in′ter·mo′tion, *n.*
in′ter·mu·nic′i·pal, *adj.*
in′ter·mu·nic′i·pal′i·ty, *n., pl.* **-ties.**
in′ter·mus′cu·lar, *adj.;* **-ly,** *adv.*
in′ter·mus′cu·lar′i·ty, *n.*
in′ter·mu·se′um, *adj.*
in′ter·nar′i·al, *adj.*
in′ter·na′sal, *adj.*
in′ter·na′tion, *adj.*
in′ter·net′ted, *adj.*
in′ter·neu′ral, *adj.*

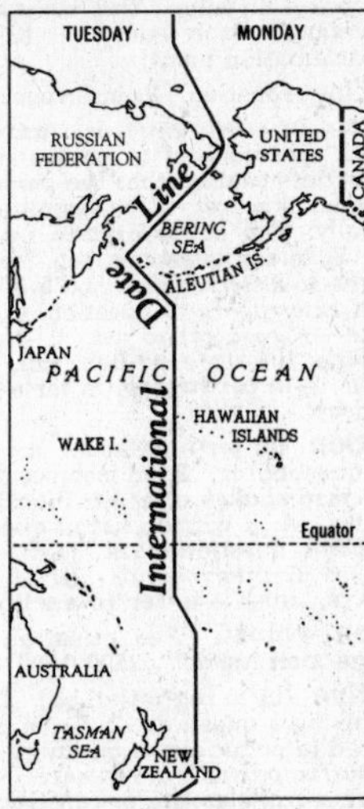

In·ter·na·tio·nale (aN ter na syô nal′), *n.* a revolutionary workers' anthem, first sung in France in 1871. [< F, short for *chanson internationale* international song]

In′terna′tional Goth′ic, a style of Gothic art, esp. painting, developed in Europe in the late 14th and early 15th centuries, chiefly characterized by details carefully delineated in a naturalistic manner, the use of complex perspective, and an emphasis on the decorative or ornamental aspect of drapery, foliage, or setting. Also called **International Style.** [1950–55]

Interna′tional Grand′ Mas′ter, a chess player in the highest class of ability, as determined through specified types of international competitions. Also called **grand master.** Cf. **International Master.**

In′terna′tional Ice′ Patrol′, an annual U.S. Coast Guard patrol of the North Atlantic during the ice season to ascertain the locations of icebergs and to warn ships: undertaken under a 1914 international agreement between 14 maritime countries.

in·ter·na·tion·al·ism (in′tər nash′ə nl iz′əm), *n.* **1.** the principle of cooperation among nations, for the promotion of their common good, sometimes as contrasted with nationalism, or devotion to the interests of a particular nation. **2.** international character, relations, cooperation, or control. **3.** (*cap.*) the principles or methods of a communist or socialist International. [1850–55; INTERNATIONAL + -ISM]

in·ter·na·tion·al·ist (in′tər nash′ə nl ist), *n.* **1.** an advocate of internationalism. **2.** an expert in international law and relations. **3.** (*cap.*) a member or adherent of a communist or socialist International. [1860–65; INTERNATIONAL + -IST]

in·ter·na·tion·al·ize (in′tər nash′ə nl īz′), *v.,* **-ized, -iz·ing.** —*v.t.* **1.** to make international, as in scope or character: *a local conflict that was internationalized into a major war.* **2.** to place or bring under international control. —*v.i.* **3.** to become international: *The automobile company must internationalize in order to meet the competition.* Also, *esp. Brit.,* **in′ter·na′tion·al·ise′.** [1860–65; INTERNATIONAL + -IZE] —**in′ter·na′tion·al·i·za′tion,** *n.*

In′terna′tional La′bor Organiza′tion, a specialized agency of the United Nations working through member nations to improve working conditions throughout the world; originally an affiliate of the League of Nations: Nobel peace prize 1969. *Abbr.:* ILO, I.L.O.

in′terna′tional law′, the body of rules that nations generally recognize as binding in their conduct toward one another. Also called **law of nations.** Cf. **private international law, public international law.** [1830–40]

In′terna′tional Mas′ter, a chess player of high ability but below the level of International Grand Master, as determined through specified types of international competitions.

in′terna′tional match′ point′, (*sometimes caps.*) a unit of scoring in contract bridge tournaments held in Europe. *Abbr.:* IMP

In′terna′tional Mon′etary Fund′, an international organization that promotes the stabilization of the world's currencies and maintains a monetary pool from which member nations can draw in order to correct a deficit in their balance of payments: a specialized agency of the United Nations. *Abbr.:* IMF, I.M.F.

interna′tional Morse′ code′, a form of Morse code used in international radiotelegraphy. Also called **continental code.**

in′terna′tional nau′tical mile′, a unit of distance at sea or in the air equal to 1.852 kilometers. Also called **international air mile.**

In′terna′tional Or′ange, *Naut.* a shade of bright orange, highly visible at a great distance and in murky weather, used to color aircraft, airport towers and hangars, boats, etc., for safety or rescue purposes. [1955–60]

Interna′tional Phonet′ic Al′phabet, the set of symbols and modifiers designed, principally on the basis of articulatory considerations, to provide a consistent and universally understood system for transcribing the speech sounds of any language: devised by the International Phonetic Association. *Abbr.:* IPA, I.P.A. See table under **phonetic alphabet.** [1895–1900]

in′terna′tional pitch′, *Music.* See **diapason normal pitch.** [1900–05]

interna′tional ra′dio si′lence, a radio silence observed on vessels at sea for two three-minute periods each hour to permit distress signals to be heard.

interna′tional rela′tions, a branch of political science dealing with the relations between nations.

Interna′tional Scientif′ic Vocab′ulary, a vocabulary of scientific and technical words, terms, formulas, and symbols that are almost universally understood by scientists and similarly used in at least two languages. *Abbr.:* ISV Cf. **Neo-Latin.**

Interna′tional Stan′dard Book′ Num′ber, a unique, internationally utilized number code assigned to books for the purposes of identification and inventory control. *Abbr.:* ISBN Also called **Standard Book Number.**

Interna′tional Stand′ard Se′rial Num′ber, a unique, internationally agreed upon number code assigned to serial publications, as periodicals and yearbooks, for the purposes of identification and inventory control. *Abbr.:* ISSN

In′terna′tional Style′, **1.** the general form of architecture developed in the 1920's and 1930's by Gropius, Le Corbusier, Mies van der Rohe, and others, characterized by simple geometric forms, large untextured, often white, surfaces, large areas of glass, and general use of steel or reinforced concrete construction. **2.** (*sometimes l.c.*) any of various 20th-century styles in art, as cubism or abstract expressionism, that have gained wide currency in Europe, the Americas, Asia, and elsewhere. **3.** See **International Gothic.** [1930–35]

Interna′tional Sys′tem of U′nits, an internationally accepted coherent system of physical units, derived from the MKSA system, using the meter, kilogram, second, ampere, kelvin, mole, and candela as the basic units **(SI units)** of the fundamental quantities length, mass, time, electric current, temperature, amount of substance, and luminous intensity. *Abbr.:* SI [trans. of the earlier F name *Système Internationale d'Unités*]

In′terna′tional Tel′ecommunica′tions Sat′ellite Organiza′tion. See **Intelsat** (def. 1).

interna′tional tem′perature scale′, a Celsius scale for use in measuring temperatures above −183°C in which specified values are assigned to the ice point, steam point, and melting point of gold, silver, and antimony and the boiling point of sulfur and of oxygen.

interna′tional u′nit, *Pharm.* **1.** an internationally agreed upon standard, as measured by bioassay, to which samples of a substance, as a drug or hormone, are compared to ascertain their relative potency. **2.** the particular quantity of such a substance, which causes a specific biological effect. *Abbr.:* IU [1920–25]

Interna′tional Work′ingmen's Associa′tion, official name of the **First International.**

in·terne (in′tûrn), *n., v.i.,* **-terned, -tern·ing.** intern[2].

in·ter·ne·cine (in′tər nē′sēn, -sin, -nes′ēn, -nes′in), *adj.* **1.** of or pertaining to conflict or struggle within a group: *an internecine feud among proxy holders.* **2.** mutually destructive. **3.** characterized by great slaughter; deadly. Also, **in·ter·ne·cive** (in′ter nē′siv, -nes′iv). [1655–65; < L *internecīnus, internecīvus* murderous, equiv. to *internec(āre)* to kill out, exterminate (*inter-* INTER- + *necāre* to kill) + *-īnus* -INE[1], *-īvus* -IVE]

in·tern·ee (in′tûr nē′), *n.* a person who is or has been interned, as a prisoner of war. [1915–20; INTERN[1] + -EE]

in·ter·neg·a·tive (in′tər neg′ə tiv), *n. Photog.* a color negative of a color transparency, made for purposes of duplication. [INTER- + NEGATIVE]

in·ter·neu·ron (in′tər nŏŏr′on, -nyŏŏr′-), *n. Cell Biol.* any neuron having its cell body, axon, and dendrites entirely within the central nervous system, especially one that conveys impulses between a motor neuron and a sensory neuron. [1935–40; INTER- + NEURON] —**in·ter·neu·ro·nal** (in′tər nŏŏr′ə nl, -nyŏŏr′-, -nŏŏ rōn′l, -nyŏŏ-), *adj.*

in·tern·ist (in′tûr nist, in tûr′nist), *n.* a physician specializing in the diagnosis and nonsurgical treatment of diseases, esp. of adults. [1900–05, *Amer.;* INTERN(AL MEDICINE) + -IST]

in·tern·ment (in tûrn′mənt), *n.* **1.** an act or instance of interning. **2.** the state of being interned; confinement. [1865–70; INTERN[1] + -MENT]

intern′ment camp′, a prison camp for the confinement of enemy aliens, prisoners of war, political prisoners, etc. [1915–20]

in·ter·node (in′tər nōd′), *n.* a part or space between two nodes, knots, or joints, as the portion of a plant stem between two nodes. [1660–70; < L *internōdium.* See INTER-, NODE] —**in′ter·nod′al,** *adj.*

in·tern·ship (in′tûrn ship′), *n.* **1.** the state or condition of being an intern. **2.** the period during which a person serves as an intern. **3.** any official or formal program to provide practical experience for beginners in an occupation or profession: *an internship for management trainees.* **4.** a position as a participant in such a program: *She has accepted an internship in a law firm.* **5.** any period of time during which a beginner acquires experience in an occupation, profession, or pursuit: *She had a long internship before starting her own recording studio.* [1900–05; INTERN[2] + -SHIP]

in·ter·nun·cial (in′tər nun′shəl), *adj.* **1.** serving to announce or connect. **2.** *Anat.* (of a nerve cell or a chain of nerve cells) serving to connect nerve fibers. [1835–45; < L *internūnti(us)* intermediary + -AL[1]]

in·ter·nun·ci·o (in′tər nun′shē ō′, -sē ō′), *n., pl.* **-ci·os.** a papal ambassador ranking next below a nuncio. [1635–45; < It < L *internūntius* an intermediary. See INTER-, NUNCIO]

in·ter·o·ce·an·ic (in′tər ō′shē an′ik), *adj.* connecting or between oceans: *an interoceanic canal.* [1850–55; INTER- + OCEANIC]

in·ter·o·cep·tive (in′tə rō sep′tiv), *adj. Physiol.* pertaining to interoceptors, the stimuli acting upon them, or the nerve impulses initiated by them. [1905–10; INTEROCEPT(OR) + -IVE]

in·ter·o·cep·tor (in′tə rō sep′tər), *n. Physiol.* a receptor, esp. of the viscera, responding to stimuli originating from within the body. [1905–10; INTER(IOR) + -O- + (RE)CEPTOR; cf. EXTEROCEPTOR]

in·ter·oc·u·lar (in′tər ok′yə lər), *adj.* being, or situated, between the eyes. [1820–30; INTER- + OCULAR]

in·ter·of·fice (in′tər ô′fis, -of′is), *adj.* functioning or communicating between the offices of a company or organization; within a company: *an interoffice memo.* [1930–35; INTER- + OFFICE]

in·ter·op·er·a·ble (in′tər op′ər ə bəl, -op′rə bəl), *adj.* capable of being used or operated reciprocally: *interoperable weapons systems.* [1965–70; INTER- + OPERABLE] —**in′ter·op′er·a·bil′i·ty,** *n.* —**in′ter·op′er·a·bly,** *adv.*

in·ter·os·cu·late (in′tər os′kyə lāt′), *v.i.,* **-lat·ed, -lat·ing.** **1.** to interpenetrate; inosculate. **2.** to form a connecting link. [1880–85; INTER- + OSCULATE] —**in′ter·os′cu·la′tion,** *n.*

in·ter·par·ox·ys·mal (in′tər par′ok siz′məl), *adj. Pathol.* occurring in the period or periods between paroxysms. [INTER- + PAROXYSMAL]

in·ter·pel·lant (in′tər pel′ənt), *n.* a person who interpellates; interpellator. [1865–70; < L *interpellant-* (s. of *interpellāns*) prp. of *interpellāre* to interrupt, equiv. to *inter-* INTER- + *-pellant-* speaking; see APPELLANT]

in·ter·pel·late (in′tər pel′āt, in tûr′pə lāt′), *v.t.,* **-lat·ed, -lat·ing.** to call formally upon (a minister or member of a government) in interpellation. [1590–1600; < L *interpellātus* ptp. of *interpellāre* to interrupt, equiv. to *inter-* INTER- + *-pellā(re)* to speak + *-tus* ptp. suffix] —**in·ter·pel·la·tor** (in′tər pə lā′tər, in tûr′pə lā′-), *n.*

in·ter·pel·la·tion (in′tər pə lā′shən, in tûr′pə-), *n.* a procedure in some legislative bodies of asking a government official to explain an act or policy, sometimes leading, in parliamentary government, to a vote of confidence or a change of government. [1520–30; < L *interpellātiōn-* (s. of *interpellātiō*) interruption. See INTERPELLATE, -ION]

in·ter·pen·e·trate (in′tər pen′i trāt′), *v.,* **-trat·ed, -trat·ing.** —*v.t.* **1.** to penetrate thoroughly; permeate. **2.** to penetrate with (something else) mutually or reciprocally. —*v.i.* **3.** to penetrate between things or parts. **4.** to penetrate each other. [1800–10; INTER- + PENETRATE] —**in·ter·pen·e·tra·ble** (in′tər pen′i trə bəl), *adj.* —**in′ter·pen′e·trant,** *adj.* —**in′ter·pen′e·tra′tion,** *n.* —**in′ter·pen′e·tra′tive,** *adj.*

in·ter·per·son·al (in′tər pûr′sə nl), *adj.* **1.** of or pertaining to the relations between persons. **2.** existing or occurring between persons. [1835–45; INTER- + PERSONAL] —**in′ter·per′son·al·ly,** *adv.*

interper′sonal the′ory, *Psychol.* the theory that personality development and behavior disorders are related to and determined by relationships between persons.

in′terper′sonal ther′apy, a type of psychotherapy that focuses on conflicts in one's personal relationships.

in·ter·phase (in′tər fāz′), *n. Cell Biol.* the period of the cell cycle during which the nucleus is not undergoing division, typically occurring between mitotic or meiotic divisions. Also called **interkinesis.** Cf. **G_1 phase, S phase, G_2 phase.** [1920–25; INTER- + PHASE]

CONCISE PRONUNCIATION KEY: act, cāpe, dâre, pärt; set, ēqual; *if,* īce; ox, ōver, ôrder, oil, bŏŏk, bōōt, out; up, ûrge; child; sing; shoe; thin, *th*at; zh as in *treasure.* ə = *a* as in *alone, e* as in *system, i* as in *easily, o* as in *gallop, u* as in *circus;* ᵊ as in *fire* (fīᵊr), *hour* (ouᵊr). l and n can serve as syllabic consonants, as in *cradle* (krād′l), and *button* (but′n). See the full key inside the front cover.

in′ter·nu′cle·ar, *adj.*
in′ter·nu′cle·on′, *adj.*
in′ter·nu′cle·on′ic, *adj.*
in′ter·nu′cle·o·tide′, *adj.*
in′ter·ob·serv′er, *n.*
in′ter·o′cean, *adj.*
in′ter·ol′i·var′y, *adj.*
in′ter·op′er·a·tive, *n., adj.*
in′ter·op′tic, *adj.*
in′ter·or′bi·tal, *adj.;* **-ly,** *adv.*
in′ter·or′gan, *adj.*
in′ter·os′cil·late′, *v.,* **-lat·ed, -lat·ing.**
in′ter·os′se·ous, *adj.*
in′ter·own′er·ship′, *n.*
in′ter·pal′a·tine′, *adj., n.*
in′ter·pal′pe·bral, *adj.*
in′ter·pan·dem′ic, *adj.*
in′ter·pap′il·lar′y, *adj.*
in′ter·pa·ren′chy·mal, *adj.*
in′ter·par·en′tal, *adj.*
in′ter·par′en·thet′ic, *adj.*
in′ter·par′en·thet′i·cal, *adj.;* **-ly,** *adv.*
in′ter·pa·ri′e·tal, *adj.*
in′ter·par′ish, *adj.*
in′ter·par′lia·ment, *adj.*
in′ter·par′lia·men′ta·ry, *adj.*
in′ter·pa·ro′chi·al, *adj.;* **-ly,** *adv.;* **-ness,** *n.*
in′ter·par′ti·cle, *adj.*
in′ter·par′ty, *adj.*
in′ter·pat′tern·ing, *n.*
in′ter·pave′, *v.t.,* **-paved, -pav·ing.**
in′ter·peal′, *v.t.*
in′ter·pec′to·ral, *adj.*
in′ter·pe·dun′cu·lar, *adj.*
in′ter·per·cep′tu·al, *adj.;* **-ly,** *adv.*
in′ter·per′me·ate′, *v.t.,* **-at·ed, -at·ing.**
in′ter·per·vade′, *v.t.,* **-vad·ed, -vad·ing.**
in′ter·per·va′sive, *adj.;* **-ly,** *adv.;* **-ness,** *n.*
in′ter·pet′al·oid′, *adj.*
in′ter·pet′al·ous, *adj.*
in′ter·pet′i·o·lar, *adj.*
in′ter·pha·lan′ge·al, *adj.*
in′ter·pla·cen′tal, *adj.*
in′ter·plait′, *v.t.*
in′ter·pledge′, *v.t.,* **-pledged, -pledg·ing.**
in′ter·pleu′ral, *adj.*
in′ter·plight′, *v.t.*
in′ter·plu′vi·al, *adj.*
in′ter·pol′ish, *v.t.*
in′ter·pol′li·nate′, *v.,* **-nat·ed, -nat·ing.**
in′ter·por′tal, *adj.*
in′ter·pour′, *v.t.*
in′ter·pres′sure, *adj.*
in′ter·pris·mat′ic, *adj.*

in·ter·phone (in′tər fōn′), *n.* **1.** an intercommunication system using telephones to connect offices, stations, etc., as in a building or ship; intercom. **2.** a telephone used in such a system. [1940–45; formerly trademark]

in·ter·plan·e·tar·y (in′tər plan′i ter′ē), *adj.* being or occurring between the planets or between a planet and the sun. [1685–95; INTER- + PLANETARY]

in·ter·plant (*v.* in′tər plant′, -plänt′; *n.* in′tər plant′, -plänt′), *v.i., v.t., n. Agric.* intercrop. [1925–30; INTER- + PLANT]

in·ter·play (*n.* in′tər plā′; *v.* in′tər plā′, in′tər plā′), *n.* **1.** reciprocal relationship, action, or influence: *the interplay of plot and character.* —*v.i.* **2.** to exert influence on each other. [1860–65; INTER- + PLAY]

in·ter·plead (in′tər plēd′), *v.i.,* **-plead·ed** or **-plead** (-pled′) or **-pled, -plead·ing.** *Law.* **1.** to litigate with each other in order to determine which of two parties is the rightful claimant against a third party. **2.** to bring two or more claimants before a court to determine which of them is entitled to a claim that a third party recognizes. [1325–75; INTER- + PLEAD; r. late ME *enterpleden* < AF *enterpleder*]

in·ter·plead·er[1] (in′tər plē′dər), *n. Law.* a judicial proceeding by which, when two parties make the same claim against a third party, the rightful claimant is determined. [1510–20; var. of *enterpleder* < AF (inf. used as n.)]

in·ter·plead·er[2] (in′tər plē′dər), *n. Law.* a party who interpleads. [1840–50; INTERPLEAD + -ER[1]]

In·ter·pol (in′tər pōl′), *n.* an official international agency that coordinates the police activities of more than 100 member nations: organized in 1923 with headquarters in Paris. [*Inter(national Criminal) Pol(ice Organization)*]

in·ter·po·lar (in′tər pō′lər), *adj.* connecting or being between poles: *an interpolar flight.* [1865–70; INTER- + POLAR]

in·ter·po·late (in tûr′pə lāt′), *v.,* **-lat·ed, -lat·ing.** —*v.t.* **1.** to introduce (something additional or extraneous) between other things or parts; interject; interpose; intercalate. **2.** *Math.* to insert, estimate, or find an intermediate term in (a sequence). **3.** to alter (a text) by the insertion of new matter, esp. deceptively or without authorization. **4.** to insert (new or spurious matter) in this manner. —*v.i.* **5.** to make an interpolation. [1605–15; < L *interpolātus* ptp. of *interpolāre* to make new, refurbish, touch up, equiv. to *inter-* INTER- + *-polā-* v. s. (akin to *polire* to POLISH) + *-tus* ptp. suffix] —**in·ter·po·la·ble** (in tûr′pə lə bəl), *adj.* —**in·ter′po·lat′er, in·ter′po·la′tor,** *n.* —**in·ter·po·la·to·ry** (in tûr′pə lə tôr′ē, -tōr′ē), **in·ter′po·la′tive,** *adj.* —**in·ter′po·la′tive·ly,** *adv.*

in·ter·po·la·tion (in tûr′pə lā′shən), *n.* **1.** the act or process of interpolating or the state of being interpolated. **2.** something interpolated, as a passage introduced into a text. **3.** *Math.* **a.** the process of determining the value of a function between two points at which it has prescribed values. **b.** a similar process using more than two points at which the function has prescribed values. **c.** the process of approximating a given function by using its values at a discrete set of points. [1605–15; < L *interpolātiōn-* (s. of *interpolātiō*). See INTERPOLATE, -ION]

in·ter·pose (in′tər pōz′), *v.,* **-posed, -pos·ing.** —*v.t.* **1.** to place between; cause to intervene: *to interpose an opaque body between a light and the eye.* **2.** to put (a barrier, obstacle, etc.) between or in the way of. **3.** to put in (a remark, question, etc.) in the midst of a conversation, discourse, or the like. **4.** to bring (influence, action, etc.) to bear between parties, or on behalf of a party or person. —*v.i.* **5.** to come between other things; assume an intervening position or relation. **6.** to step in between parties at variance; mediate. **7.** to put in or make a remark by way of interruption. [1590–1600; < MF *interposer.* See INTER-, POSE[1]] —**in′ter·pos′a·ble,** *adj.* —**in′ter·pos′al,** *n.* —**in′ter·pos′er,** *n.* —**in′ter·pos′ing·ly,** *adv.*
—**Syn. 1.** introduce, insert, insinuate, inject. **3, 7.** interject. **6.** intervene, intercede.

in·ter·po·si·tion (in′tər pə zish′ən), *n.* **1.** the act or fact of interposing or the condition of being interposed. **2.** something interposed. **3.** the doctrine that an individual state of the U.S. may oppose any federal action it believes encroaches on its sovereignty. [1375–1425; late ME *interposicio(u)n* < L *interpositiōn-* (s. of *interpositiō*), equiv. to *interposit(us)* (ptp. of *interpōnere* to place between) + *-iōn-* -ION]

in·ter·pret (in tûr′prit), *v.t.* **1.** to give or provide the meaning of; explain; explicate; elucidate: *to interpret the hidden meaning of a parable.* **2.** to construe or understand in a particular way: *to interpret a reply as favorable.* **3.** to bring out the meaning of (a dramatic work, music, etc.) by performance or execution. **4.** to perform or render (a song, role in a play, etc.) according to one's own understanding or sensitivity: *The actor interpreted Lear as a weak, pitiful old man.* **5.** to translate orally. **6.** *Computers.* **a.** to transform (a program written in a high-level language) with an interpreter into a sequence of machine actions, one statement at a time, executing each statement immediately before going on to transform the next one. **b.** to read (the patterns of holes in punched cards) with an interpreter, printing the interpreted data on the same cards so that they can be read more conveniently by people. Cf. **interpreter** (def. 3). —*v.i.* **7.** to translate what is said in a foreign language. **8.** to explain something; give an explanation. [1350–1400; ME *interpreten* < L *interpretārī,* deriv. of *interpret-* (s. of *interpres*) explainer] —**in·ter′pret·a·ble,** *adj.* —**in·ter′pret·a·bil′i·ty, in·ter′pret·a·ble·ness,** *n.* —**in·ter′pret·a·bly,** *adv.*
—**Syn. 1.** See **explain.**

CONCISE ETYMOLOGY KEY: <, descended or borrowed from; >, whence; b., blend of, blended; c., cognate with; cf., compare; deriv., derivative; equiv., equivalent; imit., imitative; obl., oblique; r., replacing; s., stem; sp., spelling, spelled; resp., respelling, respelled; trans., translation; ?, origin unknown; *, unattested; ‡, probably earlier than. See the full key inside the front cover.

in·ter·pre·ta·tion (in tûr′pri tā′shən), *n.* **1.** the act of interpreting; elucidation; explication: *This writer's work demands interpretation.* **2.** an explanation of the meaning of another's artistic or creative work; an elucidation: *an interpretation of a poem.* **3.** a conception of another's behavior: *a charitable interpretation of his tactlessness.* **4.** a way of interpreting. **5.** the rendering of a dramatic part, music, etc., so as to bring out the meaning, or to indicate one's particular conception of it. **6.** oral translation. [1250–1300; ME < L *interpretātiōn-* (s. of *interpretātiō*). See INTERPRET, -ATION] —**in·ter′·pre·ta′tion·al,** *adj.*

in·ter·pre·ta·tive (in tûr′pri tā′tiv), *adj.* interpretive. [1560–70; < L *interpretāt(us)* ptp. of *interpretārī* to INTERPRET + -IVE] —**in·ter′pre·ta′tive·ly,** *adv.*

in·ter·pret·er (in tûr′pri tər), *n.* **1.** a person who interprets. **2.** a person who provides an oral translation between speakers who speak different languages. **3.** *Computers.* **a.** hardware or software that transforms one statement at a time of a program written in a high-level language into a sequence of machine actions and executes the statement immediately before going on to transform the next statement. Cf. **compiler** (def. 2). **b.** an electromechanical device that reads the patterns of holes in punched cards and prints the same data on the cards, so that they can be read more conveniently by people. [1350–1400; ME *interpretour* < AF; see INTERPRET, -ER[2]]

in·ter·pre·tive (in tûr′pri tiv), *adj.* **1.** serving to interpret; explanatory. **2.** deduced by interpretation. **3.** made because of interpretation: *an interpretive distortion of language.* **4.** of or pertaining to those arts that require an intermediary, as a performer, for realization, as in music or theater. **5.** offering interpretations, explanations, or guidance, as through lectures, brochures, or films: *the museum's interpretive center.* [1670–80; INTERPRET + -IVE] —**in·ter′pre·tive·ly,** *adv.*

in·ter·pu·pil·lar·y (in′tər pyo͞o′pə ler′ē), *adj. Anat.* between the pupils of the eyes: *interpupillary distance.* [1905–10; INTER- + PUPILLARY[2]]

in·ter·quar′tile range′ (in′tər kwôr′til, -til), *Statistics.* the range of values of a frequency distribution between the first and third quartiles. [1880–85; INTER- + QUARTILE]

in·ter·ra·cial (in′tər rā′shəl), *adj.* of, involving, or for members of different races: *interracial amity.* [1885–90; INTER- + RACIAL] —**in′ter·ra′cial·ly,** *adv.*

in·ter·ra·cial·ism (in′tər rā′shə liz′əm), *n.* action or policy for establishing equality and cooperation between different racial groups. [1930–35; INTERRACIAL + -ISM]

in·ter·ra·di·al (in′tər rā′dē əl), *adj.* situated between the radii or rays: *interradial petals.* [1865–70; INTER- + RADIAL] —**in′ter·ra′di·al·ly,** *adv.*

in′ter·rec′ord gap′ (in′tər rek′ərd), *Computers.* the area or space separating consecutive physical records of data on an external storage medium. Cf. **interblock gap.** [INTER- + RECORD]

in·ter·reg·num (in′tər reg′nəm), *n., pl.* **-nums, -na** (-nə). **1.** an interval of time between the close of a sovereign's reign and the accession of his or her normal or legitimate successor. **2.** any period during which a state has no ruler or only a temporary executive. **3.** any period of freedom from the usual authority. **4.** any pause or interruption in continuity. [1570–80; < L, equiv. to *inter-* INTER- + *rēgnum* REIGN] —**in′ter·reg′nal,** *adj.*

in·ter·re·late (in′tər ri lāt′), *v.t., v.i.,* **-lat·ed, -lat·ing.** to bring or enter into reciprocal relation. [1885–90; back formation from INTERRELATED]

in·ter·re·lat·ed (in′tər ri lā′tid), *adj.* reciprocally or mutually related: *an interrelated series of experiments.* [1820–30; INTER- + RELATED] —**in′ter·re·lat′ed·ly,** *adv.* —**in′ter·re·lat′ed·ness,** *n.*

in·ter·re·la·tion (in′tər ri lā′shən), *n.* reciprocal relation. [1840–50; INTER- + RELATION] —**in′ter·re·la′tion·ship′,** *n.*

in·ter·re·li·gious (in′tər ri lij′əs), *adj.* existing or communicating between different religions. [1890–95; INTER- + RELIGIOUS] —**in′ter·re·li′gious·ly,** *adv.*

in·ter·rex (in′tər reks′), *n., pl.* **in·ter·re·ges** (in′tər-rē′jēz). a person holding supreme authority in a state during an interregnum. [1570–80; < L; see INTER-, REX]

in·ter·ro·bang (in ter′ə bang′), *n.* a printed punctuation mark (‽), available only in some typefaces, designed to combine the question mark (?) and the exclamation point (!), indicating a mixture of query and interjection, as after a rhetorical question. Also, **interabang.** [1965–70, *Amer.;* INTERRO(GATION POINT) + BANG[1], printers' slang for an exclamation point]

interrog., **1.** interrogation. **2.** interrogative.

in·ter·ro·gate (in ter′ə gāt′), *v.,* **-gat·ed, -gat·ing.** —*v.t.* **1.** to ask questions of (a person), sometimes to seek answers or information that the person questioned considers personal or secret. **2.** to examine by questions; question formally: *The police captain interrogated the suspect.* —*v.i.* **3.** to ask questions, esp. formally or officially: *the right to interrogate.* [1475–85; < L *interrogātus* ptp. of *interrogāre* to question, examine, equiv. to *inter-* INTER- + *rogā(re)* to ask + *-tus* ptp. suffix] —**in·ter·ro·ga·ble** (in ter′ə gə bəl), *adj.* —**in·ter′ro·gat′ing·ly,** *adv.* —**in·ter·ro·gee** (in ter′ə gē′), *n.*
—**Syn. 1.** query.

in·ter·ro·ga·tion (in ter′ə gā′shən), *n.* **1.** the act of interrogating; questioning. **2.** an instance of being interrogated: *He seemed shaken after his interrogation.* **3.** a question; inquiry. **4.** a written list of questions. **5.** an interrogation point; question mark. [1350–1400; ME *interrogacio(u)n* < L *interrogātiōn-* (s. of *interrogātiō*). See INTERROGATE, -ION] —**in·ter′ro·ga′tion·al,** *adj.*

interroga′tion point′. See **question mark.** Also called **interroga′tion mark′.** [1590–1600]

in·ter·rog·a·tive (in′tə rog′ə tiv), *adj.* **1.** of, pertaining to, or conveying a question. **2.** *Gram.* forming, constituting, or used in or to form a question: *an interrogative pronoun, suffix, particle, or sentence.* —*n.* **3.** *Gram.* an interrogative word, element, or construction, as *who?* and *what?* [1510–20; < LL *interrogātīvus.* See INTERROGATE, -IVE] —**in′ter·rog′a·tive·ly,** *adv.*

in·ter·ro·ga·tor (in ter′ə gā′tər), *n.* **1.** a person who interrogates. **2.** Also called **challenger.** *Radio.* a transmitter that emits a signal to trigger a transponder. [1745–55; < LL *interrogātor;* see INTERROGATE, -TOR]

in·ter·ro·ga·tor-re·spon·sor (in ter′ə gā′tər ri-spon′sər), *n. Electronics.* a radio or radar transceiver for sending a signal to a transponder and receiving and interpreting the reply. [1945–50]

in·ter·rog·a·to·ry (in′tə rog′ə tôr′ē, -tōr′ē), *adj., n., pl.* **-to·ries.** —*adj.* **1.** conveying or expressing a question; interrogative. —*n.* **2.** a question; inquiry. **3.** *Law.* a formal or written question. [1525–35; < LL *rogātōrius.* See INTERROGATE, -TORY[1]] —**in·ter·rog·a·to·ri·ly** (in′tə rog′ə tôr′ə lē, -tōr′-, -rog′ə tôr′-, -tōr′-), *adv.*

in ter·ro′rem clause′ (in te rôr′em, -rōr′-), *Law.* a clause in a will stating that a beneficiary who contests the will shall lose his or her legacy. [< L *in terrōrem* into terror, i.e., by intimidation, by way of warning]

in·ter·rupt (*v.* in′tə rupt′; *n.* in′tə rupt′), *v.t.* **1.** to cause or make a break in the continuity or uniformity of (a course, process, condition, etc.). **2.** to break off or cause to cease, as in the middle of something: *He interrupted his work to answer the bell.* **3.** to stop (a person) in the midst of doing or saying something, esp. by an interjected remark: *May I interrupt you to comment on your last remark?* —*v.i.* **4.** to cause a break or discontinuance; interfere with action or speech, esp. by interjecting a remark: *Please don't interrupt.* —*n.* **5.** *Computers.* a hardware signal that breaks the flow of program execution and transfers control to a predetermined storage location so that another procedure can be followed or a new operation carried out. [1375–1425; late ME *interrupten* < L *interruptus* ptp. of *interrumpere* to break apart, equiv. to *inter-* INTER- + *rup-,* var. s. of *rumpere* to burst + *-tus* ptp. suffix; see RUPTURE] —**in′ter·rupt′ed·ly,** *adv.* —**in′ter·rupt′ed·ness,** *n.* —**in′ter·rupt′i·ble,** *adj.* —**in′ter·rup′tive,** *adj.*
—**Syn. 1, 3.** intermit. INTERRUPT, DISCONTINUE, SUSPEND imply breaking off something temporarily or permanently. INTERRUPT may have either meaning: *to interrupt a meeting.* To DISCONTINUE is to stop or leave off, often permanently: *to discontinue a building program.* To SUSPEND is to break off relations, operations, proceedings, privileges, etc., for a certain period of time, usually with the stipulation that they will be resumed at a stated time: *to suspend operations during a strike.* —**Ant. 1, 2.** continue.

in·ter·rupt·ed (in′tə rup′tid), *adj. Bot.* having an irregular or discontinuous arrangement, as of leaflets along a stem. [INTERRUPT + -ED[2]]

in′terrupt′ed fern′, a tall fern, *Osmunda claytoniana,* of eastern North America and eastern Asia, having an interruption of growth in the center of some fronds. Also called **Clayton fern.**

in′terrupt′ed screw′, a screw having the thread interrupted in one or more places by longitudinal channels, as in the breech of a cannon or the lead screw of a lathe.

in·ter·rupt·er (in′tə rup′tər), *n.* **1.** a person or thing that interrupts. **2.** *Elect.* a device for interrupting or periodically opening and closing a circuit, as in a doorbell. Also, **in′ter·rup′tor.** [1505–15; INTERRUPT + -ER[1]]

in·ter·rup·tion (in′tə rup′shən), *n.* **1.** an act or instance of interrupting. **2.** the state of being interrupted. **3.** something that interrupts. **4.** cessation; intermission. [1350–1400; ME *interrupcio(u)n* < L *interruptiōn-* (s. of *interruptiō*). See INTERRUPT, -ION]

in·ter·scap·u·lar (in′tər skap′yə lər), *adj. Anat., Zool.*

in′ter·pro·duce′, *v.t.,* **-duced, -duc·ing.**
in′ter·pro·fes′sion·al, *adj.;* **-ly,** *adv.*
in′ter·pro·por′tion·al, *adj.*
in′ter·pro′to·plas′mic, *adj.*
in′ter·pro·vin′cial, *adj.*
in′ter·prox′i·mal, *adj.*
in′ter·psy′chic, *adj.*
in′ter·pter′y·goid′, *adj.*
in′ter·pu′bic, *adj.*
in′ter·pul′mo·nar′y, *adj.*
in′ter·quar′rel, *v.i.,* **-reled, -rel·ing** or (*esp. Brit.*) **-relled, -rel·ling.**
in′ter·quar′ter, *n.*
in′ter·race′, *adj.*
in′ter·ra′di·ate′, *v.i.,* **-at·ed, -at·ing.**
in′ter·ra′di·a′tion, *n.*
in′ter·rail′way′, *adj.*
in′ter·ra′mal, *adj.*
in′ter·re·ceive′, *v.t.,* **-ceived, -ceiv·ing.**
in′ter·re·flect′, *v.*
in′ter·re·flec′tion, *n.*
in′ter·reg′i·men′tal, *adj.*
in′ter·re′gion·al, *adj.;* **-ly,** *adv.*
in′ter·reign′, *v.i.*
in′ter·re′nal, *adj.*
in′ter·re·pel′lent, *adj.*
in′ter·re·pul′sion, *n.*
in′ter·re·sist′, *v.*
in′ter·re·sist′ance, *n.*
in′ter·re·sist′i·bil′i·ty, *n.*
in′ter·re·spon′si·ble, *adj.*
in′ter·re·tic′u·lar, *adj.*
in′ter·re·tic′u·la′tion, *n.*
in′ter·rhyme′, *v.i.,* **-rhymed, -rhym·ing.**
in′ter·road′, *adj.*
in′ter·row′, *adj.*
in′ter·rule′, *v.t.,* **-ruled, -rul·ing.**
in′ter·run′, *v.t.,* **-ran, -run, -run·ning.**
in′ter·sale′, *n.*
in′ter·sa·lute′, *v.i.,* **-lut·ed, -lut·ing.**
in′ter·sam′ple, *n., adj., v.t.,* **-pled, -pling.**
in′ter·scene′, *n.*
in′ter·school′, *n.*
in′ter·sci′ence, *adj.*
in′ter·scribe′, *v.t.,* **-scribed, -scrib·ing.**
in′ter·sea′board′, *adj.*
in′ter·seg′ment, *n., adj.*
in′ter·seg·men′tal, *adj.*
in′ter·sem′i·nal, *adj.*
in′ter·sem′i·nate′, *v.t.,* **-nat·ed, -nat·ing.**
in′ter·sen′so·ry, *adj.*
in′ter·sen′ti·men′tal, *adj.*
in′ter·ses′a·moid′, *adj.*

between the scapulae or shoulder blades. [1715–25; INTER- + SCAPULAR]

in•ter•scho•las•tic (in′tər skə las′tik), *adj.* between schools, or representative of different schools, esp. secondary schools: *interscholastic athletics.* [1895–1900; INTER- + SCHOLASTIC]

in•ter se (in′tər sē′; *Lat.* in′ter se′), **1.** (*italics*) *Latin.* among or between themselves. **2.** *Animal Husb.* the mating of closely related animals to each other. [1885–90; < L *inter sē*]

in•ter•sect (in′tər sekt′), *v.t.* **1.** to cut or divide by passing through or across: *The highway intersects the town.* —*v.i.* **2.** to cross, as lines or wires. **3.** *Geom.* to have one or more points in common: *intersecting lines.* [1605–15; < L *intersectus* ptp. of *intersecāre* to cut through, sever. See INTER-, -SECT]

in•ter•sec•tant (in′tər sek′tənt), *adj.* intersecting: *an intersectant road.* [1860–65; INTERSECT + -ANT]

intersect′ing arcade′. See **interlacing arcade.** [1780–90]

in•ter•sec•tion (in′tər sek′shən), *n.* **1.** a place where two or more roads meet, esp. when at least one is a major highway; junction. **2.** any place of intersection or the act or fact of intersecting. **3.** *Math.* **a.** Also called **meet, product.** the set of elements that two or more sets have in common. *Symbol:* ∩ **b.** the greatest lower bound of two elements in a lattice. [1550–60; < L *intersectiōn-* (s. of *intersectiō*). See INTERSECT, -ION] —**in′ter•sec′tion•al,** *adj.*
—**Syn. 1.** crossroads, crossing, corner.

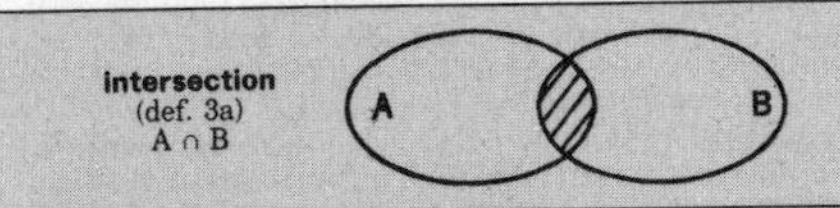

intersection (def. 3a) A ∩ B

in•ter•sep•tal (in′tər sep′tl), *adj.* situated between septa. [1840–50; INTER- + SEPTAL]

in•ter•ses•sion (in′tər sesh′ən), *n.* a period between two academic terms. [1930–35; INTER- + SESSION]

in•ter•sex (in′tər seks′), *n. Biol.* an individual displaying sexual characteristics of both male and female. [1915–20; back formation from INTERSEXUAL]

in•ter•sex•u•al (in′tər sek′sho͞o əl *or, esp. Brit.,* -seks′yo͞o-), *adj.* **1.** existing between the sexes; done or used by both sexes: *intersexual competition.* **2.** *Biol.* pertaining to or having the characteristics of an intersex. [1865–70; INTER- + SEXUAL] —**in′ter•sex′u•al′i•ty, in′ter•sex′u•al•ism,** *n.* —**in′ter•sex′u•al•ly,** *adv.*

in•ter•space (*n.* in′tər spās′; *v.* in′tər spās′), *n., v.,* **-spaced, -spac•ing.** —*n.* **1.** a space between things. **2.** an intervening period of time; interval. —*v.t.* **3.** to put a space between. **4.** to occupy or fill the space between. [1400–50; late ME; see INTER-, SPACE] —**in•ter•spa•tial** (in′tər spā′shəl), *adj.* —**in′ter•spa′tial•ly,** *adv.*

in•ter•spe•cies (in′tər spē′shēz, -sēz), *adj.* existing or occurring between species. Also, **in•ter•spe•cif•ic** (in′tər-spi sif′ik). [1915–20; INTER- + SPECIES]

in•ter•sperse (in′tər spûrs′), *v.t.,* **-spersed, -spers•ing. 1.** to scatter here and there or place at intervals among other things: *to intersperse flowers among shrubs.* **2.** to diversify with something placed or scattered at intervals: *to intersperse a dull speech with interesting anecdotes.* [1560–70; < L *interspersus* (ptp. of *interspergere* to strew here and there), equiv. to *inter-* INTER- + *-spersus,* comb. form of *sparsus,* ptp. of *spargere* to scatter; see DISPERSE] —**in•ter•spers•ed•ly** (in′tər spûr′sid-lē), *adv.* —**in•ter•sper•sion** (in′tər spûr′zhən *or, esp. Brit.,* -shən), **in′ter•sper′sal,** *n.*
—**Syn. 1.** strew, sprinkle.

in•ter•stade (in′tər stād′), *n. Geol.* a period of temporary retreat of ice during a glacial stage; a warming period. Also, **in•ter•sta•di•al** (in′tər stā′dē əl). [INTER- + STADE]

in•ter•state (*adj.* in′tər stāt′; *n.* in′tər stāt′), *adj.* **1.** connecting or involving different states: *interstate commerce.* —*n.* **2.** a highway serving two or more states. **3.** (*sometimes cap.*) a highway that is part of the nationwide U.S. Interstate Highway System. [1835–45, *Amer.*; INTER- + STATE]

In′terstate Com′merce Commis′sion, *U.S. Govt.* a board, consisting of seven members, that supervises and regulates all carriers, except airplanes, engaged in interstate commerce. *Abbr.:* I.C.C., ICC

In′terstate High′way Sys′tem, a network of U.S. highways connecting the 48 contiguous states and most of the cities with populations above 50,000, begun in the 1950's and estimated to carry about a fifth of the nation's traffic.

in•ter•stel•lar (in′tər stel′ər), *adj. Astron.* situated or occurring between the stars: *interstellar dust.* [1620–30; INTER- + STELLAR]

in•ter•stice (in tûr′stis), *n., pl.* **-stic•es** (-stə sēz′, -stə-siz). **1.** an intervening space. **2.** a small or narrow space or interval between things or parts, esp. when one of a series of alternating uniform spaces and parts: *the interstices between the slats of a fence.* **3.** *Rom. Cath. Ch.* the interval of time that must elapse, as required by canon law, before promotion to a higher degree of orders. **4.** an interval of time. [1595–1605; < L *interstitium,* equiv. to *interstit-,* var. s. of *intersistere* to stand or put between + *-ium* -IUM] —**in•ter′sticed,** *adj.*

in•ter•sti•tial (in′tər stish′əl), *adj.* **1.** pertaining to, situated in, or forming interstices. **2.** *Anat.* situated between the cells of a structure or part: *interstitial tissue.* —*n.* **3.** *Crystall.* an imperfection in a crystal caused by the presence of an extra atom in an otherwise complete lattice. Cf. **vacancy** (def. 6). [1640–50; < L *interstiti(um)* INTERSTICE + -AL[1]] —**in′ter•sti′tial•ly,** *adv.*

in′ter•sti′tial-cell′-stim′u•lat•ing hor′mone (in′-tər stish′əl sel′stim′yə lā′ting), *Biochem.* See **ICSH.**

in•ter•stock (in′tər stok′), *n. Hort.* a stock grafted between the understock and the scion. [INTER- + STOCK]

in•ter•strat•i•fy (in′tər strat′ə fī′), *v.,* **-fied, -fy•ing.** —*v.i.* **1.** to lie in interposed or alternate strata. —*v.t.* **2.** to interlay with or interpose between other strata. **3.** to arrange in alternate strata. [1815–25; INTER- + STRATIFY] —**in′ter•strat′i•fi•ca′tion,** *n.*

in•ter•sub•jec•tive (in′tər səb jek′tiv), *adj. Philos.* comprehensible to, relating to, or used by a number of persons, as a concept or language. [1895–1900; INTER- + SUBJECTIVE]

in•ter•ter•ri•to•ri•al (in′tər ter′i tôr′ē əl, -tōr′-), *adj.* existing between territories: *interterritorial laws.* [1885–90, *Amer.*; INTER- + TERRITORIAL]

in•ter•tes•ta•men•tal (in′tər tes′tə men′tl), *adj.* of or pertaining to the period between the close of the Old Testament and the beginning of the New Testament. [1925–30; INTER- + TESTAMENT + -AL[1]]

in•ter•tex•ture (in′tər teks′chər), *n.* **1.** the act of interweaving or the condition of being interwoven. **2.** something formed by interweaving. [1640–50; INTER- + TEXTURE]

in•ter•tid•al (in′tər tīd′l), *adj.* of or pertaining to the littoral region that is above the low-water mark and below the high-water mark. [1880–85; INTER- + TIDAL]

in•ter•till•age (in′tər til′ij), *n. Agric.* tillage between rows of crop plants. [1910–15; INTER- + TILLAGE]

in•ter•trib•al (in′tər trī′bəl), *adj.* occurring between tribes: *intertribal warfare.* [1860–65; INTER- + TRIBAL]

in•ter•tri•glyph (in′tər trī′glif′), *n.* metope. [INTER- + TRIGLYPH]

in•ter•trop•i•cal (in′tər trop′i kəl), *adj.* situated or occurring between the tropic of Cancer and the tropic of Capricorn; tropical. [1785–95; INTER- + TROPICAL]

in•ter•twine (in′tər twīn′), *v.t., v.i.,* **-twined, -twin•ing.** to twine together. [1635–45; INTER- + TWINE[1]] —**in′ter•twine′ment,** *n.* —**in′ter•twin′ing•ly,** *adv.*

in•ter•twist (in′tər twist′), *v.t., v.i.* **1.** to twist together. —*n.* **2.** the act of intertwisting or the condition of being intertwisted. [1650–60; INTER- + TWIST] —**in′ter•twist′ing•ly,** *adv.*

In•ter•type (in′tər tīp′), *Trademark.* a brand of typesetting machine similar to the Linotype.

in•ter•ur•ban (in′tər ûr′bən), *adj.* **1.** of, located in, or operating between two or more cities or towns. —*n.* **2.** a train, bus, etc., or a transportation system operating between cities. [1880–85, *Amer.*; INTER- + URBAN]

in•ter•val (in′tər vəl), *n.* **1.** an intervening period of time: *an interval of 50 years.* **2.** a period of temporary cessation; pause: *intervals between the volleys of gunfire.* **3.** a space between things, points, limits, etc.; interspace: *an interval of ten feet between posts.* **4.** *Math.* **a.** the totality of points on a line between two designated points or endpoints that may or may not be included. **b.** any generalization of this to higher dimensions, as a rectangle with sides parallel to the coordinate axes. **5.** the space between soldiers or units in military formation. **6.** *Music.* the difference in pitch between two tones, as between two tones sounded simultaneously (**harmonic interval**) or between two tones sounded successively (**melodic interval**). **7.** *Chiefly New Eng.* intervale. **8.** *Cards.* a period in a game for placing bets. **9.** *Brit.* an intermission, as between the acts of a play. **10. at intervals, a.** at particular periods of time; now and then: *At intervals, there were formal receptions at the governor's mansion.* **b.** at particular places, with gaps in between: *detour signs at intervals along the highway.* [1250–1300; ME *intervall(e)* < L *intervallum* interval, lit., space between two palisades. See INTER-, WALL] —**in•ter•val•ic, in•ter•val•lic** (in′tər val′ik), *adj.*
—**Syn. 3.** opening, gap, separation, gulf.

in•ter•vale (in′tər vāl′), *n. Chiefly New Eng.* a low-lying tract of land along a river. Also, **interval.** [var. of INTERVAL; by folk etym. taken as INTER- + VALE[1]]

in′terval es′timate, *Statistics.* the interval used as an estimate in interval estimation; a confidence interval.

in′terval estima′tion, *Statistics.* the process of estimating a parameter of a given population by specifying an interval of values and the probability that the true value of the parameter falls within this interval. Cf. **point estimation.**

in′terval of conver′gence, *Math.* an interval associated with a given power series such that the series converges for all values of the variable inside the interval and diverges for all values outside it. Cf. **circle of convergence.**

in•ter•val•om•e•ter (in′tər və lom′i tər), *n.* an automatic device for operating the shutter of a camera at regular intervals, as in making aerial photographs. [1930–35; INTERVAL + -O- + -METER]

in•ter•vene (in′tər vēn′), *v.i.,* **-vened, -ven•ing. 1.** to come between disputing people, groups, etc.; intercede; mediate. **2.** to occur or be between two things. **3.** to occur or happen between other events or periods: *Nothing important intervened between the meetings.* **4.** (of things) to occur incidentally so as to modify or hinder: *We enjoyed the picnic until a thunderstorm intervened.* **5.** to interfere with force or a threat of force: *to intervene in the affairs of another country.* **6.** *Law.* to interpose and become a party to a suit pending between other parties. [1580–90; < L *intervenīre* to come between, equiv. to *inter-* INTER- + *venīre* to COME; see CONVENE]
—**Syn. 1.** arbitrate, interpose.

in•ter•ven•ient (in′tər vēn′yənt), *adj.* **1.** intervening, as in place, time, order, or action. **2.** incidental; extraneous. —*n.* **3.** a person who intervenes. [1595–1605; < L *intervenient-* (s. of *interveniēns*) coming between, prp. of *intervenīre.* See INTERVENE, -ENT]

in′terven′ing se′quence, *Genetics.* intron.

in•ter•ve•nor (in′tər vē′nər), *n.* a person who intervenes, esp. in a lawsuit. Also, **in′ter•ven′er.** [1615–25; INTERVENE + -OR[2]]

in•ter•ven•tion (in′tər ven′shən), *n.* **1.** the act or fact of intervening. **2.** interposition or interference of one state in the affairs of another. [1375–1425; late ME < LL *interventiōn-* (s. of *interventiō*) a coming between. See INTERVENE, -TION] —**in′ter•ven′tion•al, in′ter•ven′tion•ar′y,** *adj.*

in•ter•ven•tion•ism (in′tər ven′shə niz′əm), *n.* the policy or doctrine of intervening, esp. government interference in the affairs of another state or in domestic economic affairs. [1920–25; INTERVENTION + -ISM] —**in′ter•ven′tion•ist,** *n., adj.*

in•ter•ver•te•bral (in′tər vûr′tə brəl), *adj. Anat.* situated between the vertebrae. [1775–85; INTER- + VERTEBRAL] —**in′ter•ver′te•bral•ly,** *adv.*

in′terver′tebral disk′, *Anat.* the plate of fibrocartilage between the bodies of adjacent vertebrae. [1855–60]

in•ter•view (in′tər vyo͞o′), *n.* **1.** a formal meeting in which one or more persons question, consult, or evaluate another person: *a job interview.* **2.** a meeting or conversation in which a writer or reporter asks questions of one or more persons from whom material is sought for a newspaper story, television broadcast, etc. **3.** the report of such a conversation or meeting. —*v.t.* **4.** to have an interview with in order to question, consult, or evaluate: *to interview a job applicant; to interview the president.* —*v.i.* **5.** to have an interview; be interviewed (sometimes fol. by *with*): *She interviewed with eight companies before accepting a job.* **6.** to give or conduct an interview: *to interview to fill job openings.* [1505–15; INTER- + VIEW; r. *enterview* < MF *entrevue,* n. use of fem. of *entrevu,* ptp. of *entrevoir* to glimpse] —**in′ter•view′a•ble,** *adj.*

in•ter•view•ee (in′tər vyo͞o ē′, in′tər vyo͞o ē′), *n.* a person who is interviewed. [1880–85; INTERVIEW + -EE]

in•ter•view•er (in′tər vyo͞o′ər), *n.* **1.** a person who interviews. **2.** a peephole in an entrance door. [1865–70; INTERVIEW + -ER[1]]

in•ter vi•vos (in′tər vī′vōs, vē′-), *Law.* (esp. of a gift or trust) taking effect during the lifetimes of the parties involved; between living persons. [1830–40; < L *inter vīvōs* lit., among the living]

in•ter•vo•cal•ic (in′tər vō kal′ik), *adj. Phonet.* (usually of a consonant) immediately following a vowel and preceding a vowel, as the *v* in *cover.* [1885–90; INTER- + VOCALIC] —**in′ter•vo•cal′i•cal•ly,** *adv.*

in•ter•volve (in′tər volv′), *v.t., v.i.,* **-volved, -volv•ing.** to roll, wind, or involve, one within another. [1660–70; INTER- + L *volvere* to roll; see REVOLVE] —**in•ter•vo•lu•tion** (in′tər və lo͞o′shən), *n.*

in•ter•war (in′tər wôr′), *adj.* occurring during a period of peace between two wars, esp. between World War I and World War II. [1935–40; INTER- + WAR[1]]

in•ter•weave (*v.* in′tər wēv′; *n.* in′tər wēv′), *v.,* **-wove** or **-weaved, -wo•ven** or **-wove** or **-weaved, -weav•ing,** *n.* —*v.t.* **1.** to weave together, as threads, strands, branches, or roots. **2.** to intermingle or combine as if by weaving: *to interweave truth with fiction.* —*v.i.* **3.** to become woven together, interlaced, or intermingled. —*n.* **4.** the act of interweaving or the state of being interwoven; blend: *a perfect interweave of Spanish and American cultures.* [1570–80; INTER- + WEAVE] —**in′ter•weave′ment,** *n.* —**in′ter•weav′er,** *n.* —**in′ter•weav′ing•ly,** *adv.*

in•ter•wind (in′tər wīnd′), *v.t., v.i.,* **-wound** or (*Rare*) **-wind•ed, -wind•ing.** to wind together; intertwine. [1685–95; INTER- + WIND[2]]

CONCISE PRONUNCIATION KEY: *act, cāpe, dâre, pärt; set, ēqual; if, ice; ox, ōver, ôrder, oil, bo͝ok, bo͞ot, out; up, ûrge; child; sing; shoe; thin, that;* zh as in *treasure.* ə = *a* as in *alone, e* as in *system, i* as in *easily, o* as in *gallop, u* as in *circus;* ᵊ as in *fire* (fīᵊr), *hour* (ouᵊr). l and n can serve as syllabic consonants, as in *cradle* (krād′l), and *button* (but′n). See the full key inside the front cover.

in′ter•set′, *v.t.,* **-set, -set•ting.**
in′ter•shade′, *v.t.,* **-shad•ed, -shad•ing.**
in′ter•shift′ing, *adj.*
in′ter•shock′, *v.*
in′ter•shoot′, *v.,* **-shot, -shoot•ing.**
in′ter•shop′, *adj.*
in′ter•site′, *adj.*
in′ter•sit′u•ate′, *v.t.,* **-at•ed, -at•ing.**
in′ter•so′cial, *adj.*
in′ter•so•ci′e•tal, *adj.*
in′ter•so•ci′e•ty, *adj.*
in′ter•soil′, *v.t.*
in′ter•sole′, *v.t.,* **-soled, -sol•ing.**
in′ter•sol′u•bil′i•ty, *n.*
in′ter•sol′u•ble, *adj.*
in′ter•so′nant, *adj.*
in′ter•spe′cial, *adj.*
in′ter•spher′al, *adj.*
in′ter•spic′u•lar, *adj.*
in′ter•spi′nal, *adj.*
in′ter•spi′nous, *adj.*
in′ter•spor′al, *adj.*
in′ter•spous′al, *adj.;* **-ly,** *adv.*
in′ter•sprin′kle, *v.t.,* **-kled, -kling.**
in′ter•squeeze′, *v.t.,* **-squeezed, -squeez•ing.**
in′ter•stage′, *adj.*
in′ter•stam′i•nal, *adj.*
in′ter•sta′tion, *adj.*
in′ter•stim′u•late′, *v.t.,* **-lat•ed, -lat•ing.**
in′ter•stim′u•la′tion, *n.*
in′ter•stim′u•lus, *n., pl.* **-li.**
in′ter•strain′, *n.*
in′ter•strand′, *n., adj.*
in′ter•streak′, *v.t.*
in′ter•stream′, *adj.*
in′ter•street′, *adj.*
in′ter•stri′al, *adj.*
in′ter•stri•a′tion, *n.*
in′ter•strive′, *v.i.,* **-strove, -striv•en, -striv•ing.**
in′ter•struc′ture, *n.*
in′ter•sub•sist′ence, *n.*
in′ter•sub′sti•tut′a•bil′i•ty, *n.*
in′ter•sub′sti•tut′a•ble, *adj.*
in′ter•sub′sti•tu′tion, *n.*
in′ter•sys′tem, *adj.*
in′ter•sys′tem•at′ic, *adj.*
in′ter•sys′tem•at′i•cal, *adj.;* **-ly,** *adv.*
in′ter•talk′, *v.i.*
in′ter•tan′gle, *v.t.,* **-gled, -gling.**
in′ter•tar′sal, *adj.*
in′ter•team′, *adj.*
in′ter•ten•tac′u•lar, *adj.*
in′ter•ter′gal, *adj.*
in′ter•term′, *adj.*
in′ter•ter′mi•nal, *adj.*
in′ter•tex′tu•al, *adj.;* **-ly,** *adv.*
in′ter•thread′ed, *adj.*
in′ter•throng′ing, *adj.*

in•ter•work (in′tər wûrk′), *v.*, **-worked** or **-wrought, -work•ing.** —*v.t.* **1.** to work or weave together; interweave. —*v.i.* **2.** to act one upon the other; interact. [1595–1605; INTER- + WORK]

in•tes•ta•ble (in tes′tə bəl), *adj. Law.* not legally qualified to make a will, as an infant or a lunatic. [1580–90; < L *intestābilis* disqualified from bearing witness, equiv. to *in-* IN-[3] + *testā(ri)* to bear witness + *-bilis* -BLE; see TESTIFY]

in•tes•ta•cy (in tes′tə sē), *n.* the state or fact of being intestate at death. [1760–70; INTEST(ATE) + -ACY]

in•tes•tate (in tes′tāt, -tit), *adj.* **1.** (of a person) not having made a will: *to die intestate.* **2.** (of things) not disposed of by will: *Her property remains intestate.* —*n.* **3.** a person who dies intestate. [1350–1400; ME < L *intestātus,* equiv. to *in-* IN-[3] + *testātus* TESTATE]

in•tes•ti•nal (in tes′tə nl; *Brit.* in′tes tīn′l), *adj.* **1.** occurring in or affecting the intestines. **2.** of, pertaining to, or resembling the intestines. [1590–1600; < NL *intestinālis;* see INTESTINE, -AL[1]] —**in•tes′ti•nal•ly,** *adv.*

intes′tinal amebi′asis, *Pathol.* **1.** See **amebic dysentery. 2.** amebiasis (def. 1).

intes′tinal by′pass, the surgical circumvention, by anastomosis, of a diseased portion of the intestine; also sometimes used to reduce nutrient absorption in morbidly obese patients.

intes′tinal flu′, *Pathol.* influenza with abdominal symptoms, as diarrhea or vomiting.

intes′tinal for′titude, courage; resoluteness; endurance; guts: *to have intestinal fortitude.* [1940–45]

in•tes•tine (in tes′tin), *n.* **1.** Usually, **intestines.** the lower part of the alimentary canal, extending from the pylorus to the anus. **2.** Also called **small intestine.** the narrow, longer part of the intestines, comprising the duodenum, jejunum, and ileum, that serves to digest and absorb nutrients. **3.** Also called **large intestine.** the broad, shorter part of the intestines, comprising the cecum, colon, and rectum, that absorbs water from and eliminates the residues of digestion. —*adj.* **4.** internal; domestic; civil: *intestine strife.* [1525–35; < L *intestīnum,* n. use of neut. of *intestinus* internal, equiv. to *intes-* (var. of *intus* inside) + *-tinus* adj. suffix; cf. VESPERTINE]

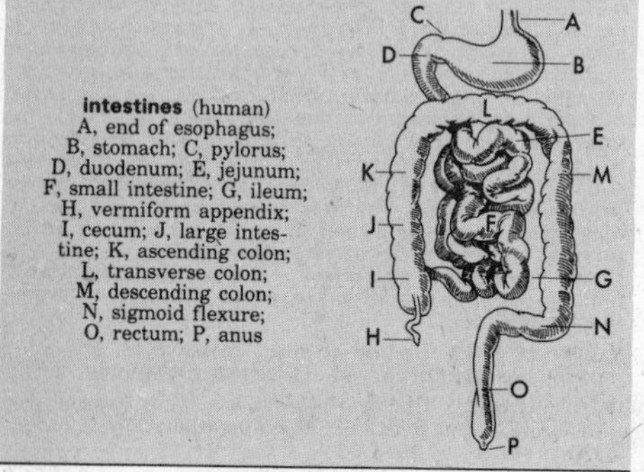

intestines (human)
A, end of esophagus;
B, stomach; C, pylorus;
D, duodenum; E, jejunum;
F, small intestine; G, ileum;
H, vermiform appendix;
I, cecum; J, large intestine; K, ascending colon;
L, transverse colon;
M, descending colon;
N, sigmoid flexure;
O, rectum; P, anus

in•thral (in thrôl′), *v.t.*, **-thralled, -thral•ling.** enthrall. Also, **inthrall.** —**in•thral′ment,** *n.*

in•throne (in thrōn′), *v.t.*, **-throned, -thron•ing.** enthrone.

in•ti•fa•da (in′tə fä′də), *n.* (*sometimes cap.*) a revolt begun in December 1987 by Palestinian Arabs to protest Israel's occupation of the West Bank and Gaza Strip. [1988; < Ar *intifāḍa* lit., a shaking off, der. of *fāḍa* to shake off]

in•ti•ma (in′tə mə), *n., pl.* **-mae** (-mē′). *Anat.* the innermost membrane or lining of some organ or part, esp. that of an artery, vein, or lymphatic. [1870–75; < NL, n. use of fem. of L *intimus, intumus* inmost, equiv. to *in-* IN-[2] + *-timus* superl. suffix; cf. OPTIMAL, ULTIMATE] —**in′ti•mal,** *adj.*

in•ti•ma•cy (in′tə mə sē), *n., pl.* **-cies. 1.** the state of being intimate. **2.** a close, familiar, and usually affectionate or loving personal relationship with another person or group. **3.** a close association with or detailed knowledge or deep understanding of a place, subject, period of history, etc.: *an intimacy with Japan.* **4.** an act or expression serving as a token of familiarity, affection, or the like: *to allow the intimacy of using first names.* **5.** an amorously familiar act; liberty. **6.** sexual intercourse. **7.** the quality of being comfortable, warm, or familiar: *the intimacy of the room.* **8.** privacy, esp. as suitable to the telling of a secret: *in the intimacy of his studio.* [1635–45; INTIM(ATE)[1] + -ACY]
—**Syn. 2.** closeness, familiarity, warmth, affection.

CONCISE ETYMOLOGY KEY: <, descended or borrowed from; >, whence; b., blend of, blended; c., cognate with; cf., compare; deriv., derivative; equiv., equivalent; imit., imitative; obl., oblique; r., replacing; s., stem; sp., spelling, spelled; resp., respelling, respelled; trans., translation; ?, origin unknown; *, unattested; ‡, probably earlier than. See the full key inside the front cover.

in•ti•mate[1] (in′tə mit), *adj.* **1.** associated in close personal relations: *an intimate friend.* **2.** characterized by or involving warm friendship or a personally close or familiar association or feeling: *an intimate greeting.* **3.** very private; closely personal: *one's intimate affairs.* **4.** characterized by or suggesting privacy or intimacy; warmly cozy: *an intimate little café.* **5.** (of an association, knowledge, understanding, etc.) arising from close personal connection or familiar experience. **6.** engaged in or characterized by sexual relations. **7.** (of clothing) worn next to the skin, under street or outer garments: *intimate apparel.* **8.** detailed; deep: *a more intimate analysis.* **9.** showing a close union or combination of particles or elements: *an intimate mixture.* **10.** inmost; deep within. **11.** of, pertaining to, or characteristic of the inmost or essential nature; intrinsic: *the intimate structure of an organism.* **12.** of, pertaining to, or existing in the inmost depths of the mind: *intimate beliefs.* —*n.* **13.** an intimate friend or associate, esp. a confidant. [1600–10; < L *intim(us)* a close friend (n. use of the adj.; see INTIMA) + -ATE[1]] —**in′ti•mate•ly,** *adv.* —**in′ti•mate•ness,** *n.*
—**Syn. 1.** dear. See **familiar. 3.** privy, secret.

in•ti•mate[2] (in′tə māt′), *v.t.*, **-mat•ed, -mat•ing. 1.** to indicate or make known indirectly; hint; imply; suggest. **2.** *Archaic.* to make known; announce. [1530–40; < LL *intimātus,* ptp. of *intimāre* to impress (upon), make known, equiv. to *intim(us)* inmost (see INTIMA) + *-ātus* -ATE[1]] —**in′ti•mat′er,** *n.* —**in′ti•ma′tion,** *n.*
—**Syn. 1.** See **hint.**

in′timate bor′rowing, *Ling.* the borrowing of linguistic forms by one language or dialect from another when both occupy a single geographical or cultural community.

Intima′tions of Immortal′ity, (*Ode: Intimations of Immortality from Recollections of Early Childhood*), a poem (1807) by Wordsworth.

in•time (aN tēm′), *adj. French.* intimate; cozy.

in•tim•i•date (in tim′i dāt′), *v.t.*, **-dat•ed, -dat•ing. 1.** to make timid; fill with fear. **2.** to overawe or cow, as through the force of personality or by superior display of wealth, talent, etc. **3.** to force into or deter from some action by inducing fear: *to intimidate a voter into staying away from the polls.* [1640–50; < ML *intimidātus,* ptp. of *intimidāre* to make afraid, equiv. to L *in-* IN-[2] + *timid(us)* TIMID, afraid + *-ātus* -ATE[1]] —**in•tim′i•da′tion,** *n.* —**in•tim′i•da′tor,** *n.* —**in•tim•i•da•to•ry** (in tim′i də tôr′ē, -tōr′ē), *adj.*
—**Syn. 1.** frighten, subdue, daunt, terrify. See **discourage.** —**Ant. 1.** calm. **3.** encourage.

in•ti•mist (in′tə mist), *adj.* **1.** of or pertaining to the recording of intimate personal and psychological experiences as a basis for art, literature, etc.: *an intimist novel.* —*n.* **2.** an intimist painter, writer, etc. [1900–05; < F *intimiste,* equiv. to *intime* INTIMATE[1] + *-iste* -IST]

in•tinc•tion (in tingk′shən), *n.* (in a communion service) the act of steeping the bread or wafer in the wine in order to enable the communicant to receive the two elements conjointly. [1550–60; < LL *intinctiōn-* (s. of *intinctiō*) a dipping in, equiv. to *intinct(us)* (see IN-[2], TINT[1]) + *-iōn-* -ION]

in•tine (in′tēn, -tīn), *n. Bot.* the inner coat of a spore, esp. a pollen grain. [1825–35; < L *int(us)* within + -INE[2]]

in•ti•tle (in tīt′l), *v.t.*, **-tled, -tling.** entitle.

in•tit•ule (in tit′yo͞ol), *v.t.*, **-uled, -ul•ing.** *Brit.* to give a title to (a legislative act, etc.); entitle. [1375–1425; < LL *intitulāre,* deriv. of *titulus* TITLE (see IN-[2]); r. late ME *entitulen* < MF *entituler* < LL, as above; cf. ENTITLE] —**in•tit′u•la′tion,** *n.*

intl., international. Also, **intnl.**

in•to (in′to͞o; *unstressed* in′to͝o, -tə), *prep.* **1.** to the inside of; in toward: *He walked into the room. The train chugged into the station.* **2.** toward or in the direction of: *going into town.* **3.** to a point of contact with; against: *backed into a parked car.* **4.** (used to indicate insertion or immersion in): *plugged into the socket.* **5.** (used to indicate entry, inclusion, or introduction in a place or condition): *received into the church.* **6.** to the state, condition, or form assumed or brought about: *went into shock; lapsed into disrepair; translated into another language.* **7.** to the occupation, action, possession, circumstance, or acceptance of: *went into banking; coerced into complying.* **8.** (used to indicate a continuing extent in time or space): *lasted into the night; far into the distance.* **9.** (used to indicate the number to be divided by another number): *2 into 20 equals 10.* **10.** *Informal.* interested or absorbed in, esp. obsessively: *She's into yoga.* **11.** *Slang.* in debt to: *I'm into him for ten dollars.* —*adj.* **12.** *Math.* pertaining to a function or map from one set to another set, the range of which is a proper subset of the second set, as the function *f*, from the set of all integers into the set of all perfect squares where $f(x) = x^2$ for every integer. [bef. 1000; ME, OE; see IN, TO]

in•toed (in′tōd′), *adj.* having inwardly turned toes. [1825–35; IN-[1] + TOED]

in•tol•er•a•ble (in tol′ər ə bəl), *adj.* **1.** not tolerable; unendurable; insufferable: *intolerable pain.* **2.** excessive. [1400–50; late ME < L *intolerābilis.* See IN-[3], TOLERABLE] —**in•tol′er•a•bil′i•ty, in•tol′er•a•ble•ness,** *n.* —**in•tol′er•a•bly,** *adv.*
—**Syn. 1.** unbearable, insupportable.

in•tol•er•ance (in tol′ər əns), *n.* **1.** lack of toleration; unwillingness or refusal to tolerate or respect contrary opinions or beliefs, persons of different races or backgrounds, etc. **2.** incapacity or indisposition to bear or endure: *intolerance to heat.* **3.** abnormal sensitivity or allergy to a food, drug, etc. **4.** an intolerant act. [1755–65; < L *intolerantia.* See INTOLERANT, -ANCE]

in•tol•er•ant (in tol′ər ənt), *adj.* **1.** not tolerating or respecting beliefs, opinions, usages, manners, etc., different from one's own, as in political or religious matters; bigoted. **2.** unable or unwilling to tolerate or endure (usually fol. by *of*): *intolerant of very hot weather.* —*n.* **3.** an intolerant person; bigot. [1725–35; < L *intolerant-* (s. of *intolerāns*) impatient. See IN-[3], TOLERANT] —**in•tol′er•ant•ly,** *adv.*
—**Syn. 1.** illiberal, narrow, proscriptive, prejudiced, biased, dictatorial, totalitarian. INTOLERANT, FANATICAL, BIGOTED refer to strongly illiberal attitudes. INTOLERANT refers to an active refusal to allow others to have or put into practice beliefs different from one's own: *intolerant in politics; intolerant of other customs.* BIGOTED is to be so emotionally or subjectively attached to one's own belief as to be hostile to all others: *a bigoted person.* FANATICAL applies to unreasonable or extreme action in maintaining one's beliefs and practices without necessary reference to others: *a fanatical religious sect.*

in•tomb (in to͞om′), *v.t.* entomb. —**in•tomb′ment,** *n.*

in•to•na•co (in ton′ə kō′, -tô′nə-; *It.* ēn tô′nä kô), *n., pl.* **-cos, -ci** (*It.* -chē). (formerly in fresco painting) the last and finest coat of plaster, usually applied in sections and painted while still damp with colors ground in water or a lime-water mixture. Cf. **arriccio.** [1800–10; < It, n. deriv. of *intonacare* to coat, equiv. to *in-* IN-[2] + VL **tunicāre,* by construal of L *tunicātus* "wearing a tunic" as a ptp; see TUNIC, -ATE[1]]

in•to•nate (in′tō nāt′, -tə-), *v.t.*, **-nat•ed, -nat•ing. 1.** to utter with a particular tone or modulation of voice. **2.** to intone; chant. [1785–95; < ML *intonātus,* ptp. of *intonāre* to INTONE. See -ATE[1]]

in•to•na•tion (in′tō nā′shən, -tə-), *n.* **1.** the pattern or melody of pitch changes in connected speech, esp. the pitch pattern of a sentence, which distinguishes kinds of sentences or speakers of different language cultures. **2.** the act or manner of intonating. **3.** the manner of producing musical tones, specifically the relation in pitch of tones to their key or harmony. **4.** something that is intoned or chanted. **5.** the opening phrase in a Gregorian chant, usually sung by one or two voices. [1610–20; < ML *intonātiōn-* (s. of *intonātiō*). See INTONATE, -ION] —**in′to•na′tion•al,** *adj.*

in•tone (in tōn′), *v.*, **-toned, -ton•ing.** —*v.t.* **1.** to utter with a particular tone or voice modulation. **2.** to give tone or variety of tone to; vocalize. **3.** to utter in a singing voice (the first tones of a section in a liturgical service). **4.** to recite or chant in monotone. —*v.i.* **5.** to speak or recite in a singing voice, esp. in monotone; chant. **6.** *Music.* to produce a tone, or a particular series of tones, like a scale, esp. with the voice. [1475–85; < ML *intonāre;* r. earlier *entone* < MF *entoner* < ML; see IN-[2], TONE] —**in•ton′er,** *n.*

in•tor•sion (in tôr′shən), *n.* a twisting about an axis or fixed point, as of the stem of a plant. [1750–60; alter. of LL *intortiōn-* (s. of *intortiō*). See IN[2]-, TORSION]

in•tort•ed (in tôr′tid), *adj.* twisted inwardly about an axis or fixed point; curled; wound: *intorted horns.* [1605–15; < L *intort(us)* (var. ptp. of *intorquēre* to turn or twist in; see IN-[2], TORT) + -ED[2]]

in•tor•tus (in tôr′təs), *adj. Meteorol.* (of a cirrus cloud) having very irregular filaments that often look entangled. [< L: twisted, complicated; see INTORTED]

in to•to (in tō′tō), *Latin.* in all; completely; entirely; wholly.

In•tour•ist (in′to͝or ist), *n.* the official Soviet agency that handles travel arrangements for foreign visitors to the Soviet Union. [< Russ *Inturíst* (acronym from *inostránnyĭ turíst* foreign tourist)]

in•town (in′toun′, in toun′), *adj.* being in the central or metropolitan area of a city or town: *an intown motel.* [1530–40; IN + TOWN]

in•tox•i•cant (in tok′si kənt), *n.* **1.** an intoxicating agent, as alcoholic liquor or certain drugs. —*adj.* **2.** intoxicating or exhilarating: *the clear, intoxicant air of the mountains.* [1860–65; < ML *intoxicant-* (s. of *intoxicāns*), prp. of *intoxicāre* to poison. See IN-[2], TOXICANT]

in•tox•i•cate (*v.* in tok′si kāt′; *adj.* in tok′sə kit, -kāt′), *v.*, **-cat•ed, -cat•ing,** *adj.* —*v.t.* **1.** to affect temporarily with diminished physical and mental control by means of alcoholic liquor, a drug, or another substance, esp. to excite or stupefy with liquor. **2.** to make enthusiastic; elate strongly, as by intoxicants; exhilarate: *The prospect of success intoxicated him.* **3.** *Pathol.* to poison. —*v.i.* **4.** to cause or produce intoxication: *having the power to intoxicate.* —*adj.* **5.** *Archaic.* intoxicated. [1375–1425; late ME < ML *intoxicātus,* ptp. of *intoxicāre* to poison. See IN-[2], TOXIC, -ATE[1]] —**in•tox•i•ca•ble** (in tok′si kə bəl), *adj.* —**in•tox′i•ca′tor,** *n.*

in•tox•i•cat•ed (in tok′si kā′tid), *adj.* **1.** affected by a substance that intoxicates; drunk; inebriated. **2.** mentally or emotionally exhilarated. [1550–60; INTOXICATE + -ED[2]] —**in•tox′i•cat′ed•ly,** *adv.*
—**Syn. 2.** rapt, enthralled.

in′ter•tinge′, *v.t.*, **-tinged, -tinge•ing** or **-ting•ing.**
in′ter•tis′sued, *adj.*
in′ter•touch′, *v.i.*
in′ter•town′, *adj.*
in′ter•tra•bec′u•lar, *adj.*
in′ter•trace′, *v.t.*, **-traced, -trac•ing.**
in′ter•trade′, *n., v.*, **-trad•ed, -trad•ing.**
in′ter•traf′fic, *n., v.*, **-ficked, -fick•ing.**
in′ter•trans•form′a•bil′i•ty, *n.*
in′ter•trans•form′a•ble, *adj.*
in′ter•trans•lat′a•ble, *adj.*
in′ter•trans•ver′sal, *adj.*
in′ter•tri′al, *adj.*
in′ter•troop′, *adj.*
in′ter•tu′ber•al, *adj.*
in′ter•tu•ber′cu•lar, *adj.*
in′ter•tu′bu•lar, *adj.*
in′ter•un′gu•lar, *adj.*
in′ter•un′gu•late, *adj.*
in′ter•un′ion, *n., adj.*
in′ter•u′nit, *adj.*
in′ter•u′ni•ver′si•ty, *adj.*
in′ter•vag′i•nal, *adj.*
in′ter•val′ley, *n.*
in′ter•val′vu•lar, *adj.*
in′ter•va′ri•a′tion, *n.*
in′ter•va•ri′e•tal, *adj.*
in′ter•var′si•ty, *adj.*
in′ter•var′y, *v.i.*, **-var•ied, -var•y•ing.**
in′ter•vas′cu•lar, *adj.*
in′ter•vein′, *v.t.*
in′ter•vein′al, *adj.*
in′ter•vein′ous, *adj.*
in′ter•ven′tral, *adj.*
in′ter•ven•tric′u•lar, *adj.*
in′ter•ven′u•lar, *adj.*
in′ter•ver′bal, *adj.*
in′ter•ve•sic′u•lar, *adj.*
in′ter•vil′lage, *adj.*
in′ter•vil′lous, *adj.*
in′ter•vis′i•bil′i•ty, *n.*
in′ter•vis′it, *v.i.*
in′ter•vis′it•a′tion, *n.*
in′ter•vo•lute′, *adj.*
in′ter•wed′, *v.i.*, **-wed** or **-wed•ded, -wed•ding.**
in′ter•weld′, *v.t.*
in′ter•whiff′, *v.t.*
in′ter•whis′tle, *v.t.*, **-tled, -tling.**
in′ter•wish′, *v.t., n.*
in′ter•word′, *adj.*
in′ter•world′, *n.*
in′ter•wound′, *v.*
in′ter•wrap′, *v.i.*, **-wrapped, -wrap•ping.**
in′ter•wreathe′, *v.*, **-wreathed, -wreath•ing.**
in′ter•wrought′, *adj.*
in′ter•zon′al, *adj.*
in′ter•zone′, *n.*

in·tox·i·cat·ing (in tok′si kā′ting), *adj.* **1.** causing or capable of causing intoxication: *intoxicating beverages.* **2.** exhilarating; exciting: *an intoxicating idea.* [1625–35; INTOXICATE + -ING[2]] —**in·tox′i·cat′ing·ly,** *adv.*

in·tox·i·ca·tion (in tok′si kā′shən), *n.* **1.** inebriation; drunkenness. **2.** an act or instance of intoxicating. **3.** overpowering exhilaration or excitement of the mind or emotions. **4.** *Pathol.* poisoning. [1375–1425; late ME < ML *intoxicātiōn-* (s. of *intoxicātiō*) a poisoning. See INTOXICATE, -ION]

in·tox·i·ca·tive (in tok′si kā′tiv), *adj. Archaic.* **1.** of or pertaining to intoxicants or intoxication. **2.** intoxicating. [1625–35; INTOXICATE + -IVE]

intr., **1.** intransitive. **2.** introduce. **3.** introduced. **4.** introducing. **5.** introduction. **6.** introductory.

intra-, a prefix meaning "within," used in the formation of compound words: *intramural.* Cf. **intro-.** [< LL *intrā-*, repr. L *intrā* (adv. and prep.); akin to INTERIOR, INTER-]

in·tra·ab·dom·i·nal (in′trə ab dom′ə nl), *adj. Anat.* **1.** being within the abdomen. **2.** going into the abdomen, as an injection. [1885–90] —**in′tra·ab·dom′i·nal·ly,** *adv.*

in·tra·a·tom·ic (in′trə ə tom′ik), *adj.* within an atom or atoms. [1900–05]

in·tra·car·di·ac (in′trə kär′dē ak′), *adj.* endocardial (def. 1). [1885–90; INTRA- + CARDIAC]

in·tra·cel·lu·lar (in′trə sel′yə lər), *adj.* within a cell or cells. [1875–80; INTRA- + CELLULAR] —**in′tra·cel′lu·lar·ly,** *adv.*

In′tra·coast′al Wa′terway (in′trə kō′stəl, in′-), a mostly inland water route, partly natural and partly artificial, extending 1550 mi. (2500 km) along the Atlantic coast from Boston to Florida Bay **(Atlantic Intracoastal Waterway)** and 1116 mi. (1800 km) along the Gulf coast from Carrabelle, Fla., to Brownsville, Tex. **(Gulf Intracoastal Waterway):** constructed to protect small craft from the hazards of the open sea.

in·tra·cra·ni·al (in′trə krā′nē əl), *adj.* being or occurring within the skull. [1840–50; INTRA- + CRANIAL]

in·trac·ta·ble (in trak′tə bəl), *adj.* **1.** not easily controlled or directed; not docile or manageable; stubborn; obstinate: *an intractable disposition.* **2.** (of things) hard to shape or work with: *an intractable metal.* **3.** hard to treat, relieve, or cure: *the intractable pain in his leg.* —*n.* **4.** an intractable person. [1535–45; < L *intractābilis.* See IN-[3], TRACTABLE] —**in·trac′ta·bil′i·ty, in·trac′ta·ble·ness,** *n.* —**in·trac′ta·bly,** *adv.*
—**Syn. 1.** perverse, headstrong, dogged, obdurate, stony, willful, froward. **1, 2.** fractious, refractory, unbending, inflexible, adamant, unyielding. See **unruly.** —**Ant. 1.** amiable. **1, 2.** amenable, flexible.

in·tra·cu·ta·ne·ous (in′trə kyōō tā′nē əs), *adj.* **1.** within the skin. **2.** intradermal (def. 2). [1880–85; INTRA- + CUTANEOUS] —**in′tra·cu·ta′ne·ous·ly,** *adv.*

in′tracuta′neous test′, *Immunol.* a test for immunity or allergy to a particular antigen by observing the local reaction following injection of a small amount of the antigen into the skin. Also called **in′trader′mal test′.** Cf. **patch test, scratch test.** [1955–60]

in·tra·day (in′trə dā′), *adj.* occurring during a single day. [1970–75; INTRA- + DAY]

in·tra·der·mal (in′trə dûr′məl), *adj.* **1.** within the dermis. **2.** going between the layers of the skin, as an injection. Also, **in′tra·der′mic.** [1895–1900; INTRA- + DERM(A)[1] + -AL[1]] —**in′tra·der′mal·ly, in′tra·der′mi·cal·ly,** *adv.*

in·tra·dos (in′trə dos′, -dōs′, in trā′dos, -dōs), *n., pl.* **-dos** (-dōz′, -dōz), **-dos·es.** *Archit.* the interior curve or surface of an arch or vault. Cf. **extrados.** See diag. under **arch.** [1765–75; < F, equiv. to *intra-* INTRA- + *dos* back; see DOSSER]

in·tra·ga·lac·tic (in′trə gə lak′tik), *adj. Astron.* existing or occurring within a single galaxy. [1960–65; INTRA- + GALACTIC]

in·tra·mar·gin·al (in′trə mär′jə nl), *adj.* existing or occurring within a margin or limit. [1840–50; INTRA- + MARGINAL]

in·tra·mo·lec·u·lar (in′trə mə lek′yə lər, -mō-), *adj.* existing or occurring within a molecule. [1880–85; INTRA- + MOLECULAR]

in·tra·mun·dane (in′trə mun′dān, -mun dān′), *adj.* existing or occurring within the material world. [1830–40; INTRA- + MUNDANE]

in·tra·mu·ral (in′trə myŏŏr′əl), *adj.* **1.** involving only students at the same school or college: *intramural athletics.* **2.** within the walls, boundaries, or enclosing units, as of a city, institution, or building. Cf. **extramural. 3.** *Anat.* being within the substance of a wall, as of an organ. **4.** involving or understood only by members of a single group, profession, etc.: *an intramural medical conference.* [1840–50; INTRA- + MURAL] —**in′tra·mu′ral·ly,** *adv.*

in·tra mu·ros (in′trä mōō′rōs; *Eng.* in′trə myŏŏr′ōs), *Latin.* within the walls, as of a city.

in·tra·mus·cu·lar (in′trə mus′kyə lər), *adj.* located or occurring within a muscle. [1870–75; INTRA- + MUSCULAR] —**in′tra·mus′cu·lar·ly,** *adv.*

in·tra·na·sal (in′trə nā′zəl), *adj.* occurring within or administered through the nose. [1885–90; INTRA- + NASAL[1]] —**in′tra·na′sal·ly,** *adv.*

in trans., in transit; en route. [< L *in trānsitū*]

intrans., intransitive.

in·tran·si·gent (in tran′si jənt), *adj.* **1.** refusing to agree or compromise; uncompromising; inflexible. —*n.* **2.** a person who refuses to agree or compromise, as in politics. Also, **in·tran′si·geant.** [1875–80; < Sp *intransigente*, equiv. to *in-* IN-[3] + *transigente* (prp. of *transigir* to compromise) < L *trānsigent-* (s. of *trānsigēns*, prp. of *trānsigere* to come to an agreement); see TRANSACT] —**in·tran′si·gence, in·tran′si·gen·cy,** *n.* —**in·tran′si·gent·ly,** *adv.*

in·tran·si·tive (in tran′si tiv), *Gram.* —*adj.* **1.** noting or having the quality of an intransitive verb. —*n.* **2.** See **intransitive verb.** [1605–15; < L *intrānsitīvus.* See IN-[3], TRANSITIVE] —**in·tran′si·tive·ly,** *adv.* —**in·tran′si·tive·ness,** *n.*

intran′sitive verb′, a verb that indicates a complete action without being accompanied by a direct object, as *sit* or *lie*, and, in English, that does not form a passive. [1605–15]

in tran·si·tu (in trän′si tōō′; *Eng.* in tran′si tōō′, -tyōō′), *Latin.* in transit; on the way.

in·trant (in′trənt), *n. Archaic.* a person who enters (a college, association, etc.); entrant. [1550–60; < L *intrant-* (s. of *intrāns*), prp. of *intrāre* to ENTER]

in·tra·nu·cle·ar (in′trə nōō′klē ər, -nyōō′- *or, by metathesis,* -kyə lər), *adj.* existing or taking place within a nucleus. [1885–90; INTRA- + NUCLEAR]
—**Pronunciation.** See **nuclear.**

in·tra·oc·u·lar (in′trə ok′yə lər), *adj.* located or occurring within or administered through the eye. [1820–30; INTRA- + OCULAR] —**in′tra·oc′u·lar·ly,** *adv.*

in′traoc′ular lens′, *Ophthalm.* a plastic lens implanted surgically to replace the eye's natural crystalline lens, usually because the natural lens has developed a cataract. Also called **permanent lens.** Cf. **contact lens.**

in·tra·pre·neur (in′trə prə nûr′, -nŏŏr′, -nyŏŏr′), *n.* an employee of a large corporation who is given freedom and financial support to create new products, services, systems, etc., and does not have to follow the corporation's usual routines or protocols. [1975–80; INTRA- + (ENTRE)PRENEUR] —**in′tra·pre·neur′ship,** *n.*

in·tra·psy·chic (in′trə sī′kik), *adj. Psychol.* from or within the mind or self: *intrapsychic conflict.* [1915–20; INTRA- + PSYCHIC] —**in′tra·psy′chi·cal·ly,** *adv.*

in·tra·spe·cies (in′trə spē′shēz, -sēz), *adj.* existing or occurring within a species. Also, **in·tra·spe·cif·ic** (in′trə spi sif′ik). [1925–30; INTRA- + SPECIES]

in·tra·spi·nal (in′trə spīn′l), *adj. Anat.* **1.** being within the spine. **2.** going into the spinal canal, as an injection. [1830–40; INTRA- + SPINAL] —**in′tra·spi′nal·ly,** *adv.*

in·tra·state (in′trə stāt′), *adj.* existing or occurring within the boundaries of a state, esp. of the United States: *intrastate commerce.* Cf. **interstate.** [1900–05, *Amer.*; INTRA- + STATE]

in·tra·tel·lu·ric (in′trə tə lŏŏr′ik), *adj.* **1.** *Geol.* located in, taking place in, or resulting from action beneath the lithosphere. **2.** *Petrog.* noting or pertaining to crystallization of magma that begins previous to its extrusion on the surface. [1885–90; INTRA- + TELLURIC[1]]

in·tra·u·ter·ine (in′trə yōō′tər in, -tə rīn′), *adj.* located or occurring within the uterus. [1825–35; INTRA- + UTERINE]

intrau′terine device′, any small, mechanical device for semipermanent insertion into the uterus as a contraceptive. *Abbr.:* IUD [1920–25]

in·trav·a·sa·tion (in trav′ə sā′shən), *n. Pathol.* the entrance of foreign matter into a blood vessel of the body. [1665–75; INTRA- + (EXTRA)VASATION]

in·tra·vas·cu·lar (in′trə vas′kyə lər), *adj.* within the blood vessels. [1875–80; INTRA- + VASCULAR]

in·tra·ve·nous (in′trə vē′nəs), *adj.* **1.** within a vein. **2.** of, pertaining to, employed in, or administered by injection into a vein: *an intravenous solution.* —*n.* **3.** an intravenous injection. **4.** intravenous feeding. *Abbr.:* IV [1840–50; INTRA- + VENOUS]

in′trave′nous drip′, *Med.* the continuous, slow introduction of a fluid into a vein of the body. *Abbr.:* IV Also called **drip.**

in·tra·ve·nous·ly (in′trə vē′nəs lē), *adv.* through or within a vein. *Abbr.:* IV [1895–1900; INTRAVENOUS + -LY]

in·tra vi·res (in′trə vī′rēz), *Law.* within the legal power or authority of an individual or corporation (opposed to *ultra vires*). [1875–80; < L *intrā vīrēs* within the powers]

in·tra·vi·tal (in′trə vīt′l), *adj. Biol.* occurring during life. [1885–90; INTRA- + VITAL]

in·tra vi·tam (in′trə vī′tam), *Biol.* during life: *the staining of tissues intra vitam.* [1880–85; < L *intrā vītam*]

in·treat (in trēt′), *v.t., v.i. Archaic.* entreat.

in·trench (in trench′), *v.t., v.i.* entrench.

intrench′ing tool′, a small, collapsible spade used by a soldier in the field for digging foxholes and the like. Also, **entrenching tool.**

in·trep·id (in trep′id), *adj.* resolutely fearless; dauntless: *an intrepid explorer.* [1690–1700; < L *intrepidus,* equiv. to *in-* IN-[3] + *trepidus* anxious; see TREPIDATION] —**in′tre·pid′i·ty, in·trep′id·ness,** *n.* —**in·trep′id·ly,** *adv.*
—**Syn.** brave, courageous, bold. —**Ant.** timid.

Int. Rev., Internal Revenue.

in·tri·ca·cy (in′tri kə sē), *n., pl.* **-cies. 1.** intricate character or state. **2.** an intricate part, action, etc: *intricacies of the law.* [1595–1605; INTRIC(ATE) + -ACY]

in·tri·cate (in′tri kit), *adj.* **1.** having many interrelated parts or facets; entangled or involved: *an intricate maze.* **2.** complex; complicated; hard to understand, work, or make: *an intricate machine.* [1375–1425; late ME < L *intricātus,* ptp. of *intricāre* to entangle, equiv. to *in-* IN-[2] + *tric(ae)* perplexities + *-ātus* -ATE[1]] —**in′tri·cate·ly,** *adv.* —**in′tri·cate·ness,** *n.*
—**Syn. 1.** knotty, tangled, labyrinthine.

in·tri·gant (in′tri gənt; *Fr.* AN TRĒ GÄN′), *n., pl.* **-gants** (-gənts; *Fr.* -GÄN′). a person who engages in intrigue or intrigues. Also, **in′tri·guant.** [1775–85; < F < It *intrigante,* prp. of *intrigare* to INTRIGUE]

in·trigue (*v.* in trēg′; *n.* in trēg′, in′trēg), *v.,* **-trigued, -tri·guing,** *n.* —*v.t.* **1.** to arouse the curiosity or interest of by unusual, new, or otherwise fascinating or compelling qualities; appeal strongly to; captivate: *The plan intrigues me, but I wonder if it will work.* **2.** to achieve or earn by appealing to another's curiosity, fancy, or interest: *to intrigue one's way into another's notice.* **3.** to draw or capture: *Her interest was intrigued by the strange symbol.* **4.** to accomplish or force by crafty plotting or underhand machinations. **5.** *Obs.* to entangle. **6.** *Obs.* to trick or cheat. —*v.i.* **7.** to plot craftily or underhandedly. **8.** to carry on a secret or illicit love affair. —*n.* **9.** the use of underhand machinations or deceitful stratagems. **10.** such a machination or stratagem or a series of them; a plot or crafty dealing: *political intrigues.* **11.** a secret or illicit love affair. **12.** the series of complications forming the plot of a play. [1640–50; < F *intriguer* < It *intrigare* < L *intricāre* to entangle; see INTRICATE] —**in·tri′guer,** *n.* —**in·tri′guing·ly,** *adv.*
—**Syn. 1.** interest, attract, fascinate. **7.** manipulate. **9, 10.** manipulation. **10.** See **conspiracy.**

in·trin·sic (in trin′sik, -zik), *adj.* **1.** belonging to a thing by its very nature: *the intrinsic value of a gold ring.* **2.** *Anat.* (of certain muscles, nerves, etc.) belonging to or lying within a given part. Also, **in·trin′si·cal.** [1480–90; < ML *intrinsecus* inward (adj.), L (adv.), equiv. to *intrin-* (*int(e)r-*, as in INTERIOR + *-im* adv. suffix) + *secus* beside, deriv. of *sequī* to follow] —**in·trin′si·cal·ly,** *adv.*
—**Syn. 1.** native, innate, natural, true, real. See **essential.** —**Ant. 1.** extrinsic.

intrin′sic fac′tor, *Biochem.* a glycoprotein, secreted by the gastric mucosa, that is involved in the intestinal absorption of vitamin B_{12}. [1925–30]

intrin′sic par′ity, *Physics.* parity[1] (def. 4b).

in·tro (in′trō), *n., pl.* **-tros.** *Informal.* **1.** an introduction. **2.** the introductory passage of a piece for a jazz or dance band. [1895–1900; shortening of INTRODUCTION]

intro-, a prefix, meaning "inwardly," "within," occurring in loanwords from Latin (*introspection*); occasionally used in the formation of new words (*introjection*). Cf. **intra-.** [< L, repr. *intrō* (adv.) inwardly, within]

intro., **1.** introduce. **2.** introduced. **3.** introducing. **4.** introduction. **5.** introductory. Also, **introd.**

in·tro·duce (in′trə dōōs′, -dyōōs′), *v.t.,* **-duced, -duc·ing. 1.** to present (a person) to another so as to make acquainted. **2.** to acquaint (two or more persons) with each other personally: *Will you introduce us?* **3.** to present (a person, product, etc.) to a particular group of individuals or to the general public for or as if for the first time by a formal act, announcement, series of recommendations or events, etc.: *to introduce a debutante to society.* **4.** to bring (a person) to first knowledge or experience of something: *to introduce someone to skiing.* **5.** to create, bring into notice, use, etc., for or as if for the first time; institute: *to introduce a new procedure.* **6.** to suggest, propose, or advance for or as if for the first time: *to introduce a theory of geological evolution.* **7.** to present for official consideration or action, as a legislative bill. **8.** to begin; lead into; preface: *to introduce one's speech with an amusing anecdote.* **9.** to put or place into something for the first time; insert: *to introduce a figure into a design.* **10.** to bring in or establish, as something foreign or alien: *Japanese cooking was introduced into America in the 1950's.* **11.** to present (a speaker, performer, etc.) to an audience. **12.** to present (a person) at a royal court. [1425–75; late ME < L *intrōdūcere* to lead inside, equiv. to *intrō-* INTRO- + *dūcere* to lead; see DUKE] —**in′tro·duc′er,** *n.* —**in′tro·duc′i·ble,** *adj.*
—**Syn. 1, 2.** INTRODUCE, PRESENT mean to bring persons into personal acquaintance with each other, as by announcement of names and the like. INTRODUCE is the ordinary term, referring to making persons acquainted who are ostensibly equals: *to introduce a friend to one's sister.* PRESENT, a more formal term, suggests a degree of ceremony in the process, and implies (if only as a matter of compliment) superior dignity, rank, or importance in the person to whom another is presented: *to present a visitor to the president.*

in·tro·duc·tion (in′trə duk′shən), *n.* **1.** the act of introducing or the state of being introduced. **2.** a formal personal presentation of one person to another or others. **3.** a preliminary part, as of a book, musical composition, or the like, leading up to the main part. **4.** an elementary treatise: *an introduction to botany.* **5.** an act or instance of inserting. **6.** something introduced. [1350–1400; ME *introduccion* < L *intrōductiōn-* (s. of *intrōductiō*). See INTRODUCE, -TION]
—**Syn. 3.** INTRODUCTION, FOREWORD, PREFACE refer to material given at the front of a book to explain or introduce it to the reader. A FOREWORD is part of the front matter and is usually written by someone other than the author, often an authority on the subject of the book. A PREFACE is the author's own statement, and often includes acknowledgments. It follows the FOREWORD (if there is one) and is also part of the front matter. The INTRODUCTION is always by the author. It may be extensive and is usually printed as part of the text.

in·tro·duc·to·ry (in′trə duk′tə rē), *adj.* serving or used to introduce; preliminary; beginning: *an introductory course; an introductory paragraph.* Also, **in′tro·duc′tive.** [1350–1400; ME < LL *intrōductōrius,* equiv. to L *intrōduc-*, var. s. of *intrōdūcere* (see INTRODUCE) + *-tōrius* -TORY[1]] —**in′tro·duc′to·ri·ly,** *adv.* —**in′tro·duc′to·ri·ness,** *n.*
—**Syn.** See **preliminary.**

in·tro·gres·sion (in′trə gresh′ən), *n. Genetics.* the introduction of genes from one species into the gene pool of another species, occurring when matings between the two produce fertile hybrids. Also called **in·tro·gres′sive hybridiza′tion** (in′trə gres′iv). [1930–35 (earlier in literal sense of L); < L *intrōgress(us)*, ptp. of *intrōgredī* to go in, enter (*intrō-* INTRO- + *-gred-*, comb. form of *grad(i)* to proceed, walk + *-tus* ptp. suffix, with *-dt-* > *-ss-*) + -ION]

in·tro·it (in′trō it, -troit), *n.* **1.** *Rom. Cath. Ch.* a part of a psalm with antiphon recited by the celebrant of the Mass at the foot of the altar and, at High Mass, sung by the choir when the priest begins the Mass. **2.** *Anglican Ch., Lutheran Ch.* a psalm or anthem sung as the celebrant of the Holy Communion enters the sanctuary. **3.** a choral response sung at the beginning of a religious service. [1475–85; < ML *introitus* (*misse* or *ad missam*), L: entrance, beginning, equiv. to *intro-*, comb. form of *intrō* INTRO- + *-i-*, var. s. of *īre* to go + *-tus* suffix of v. action]

in·tro·ject (in′trə jekt′), *v.t., v.i. Psychoanal.* to incorporate by introjection. [1925; back formation from INTROJECTION]

in·tro·jec·tion (in′trə jek′shən), *n. Psychoanal.* an unconscious psychic process by which a person incorporates into his or her own psychic apparatus the characteristics of another person or object. [1865–70; INTRO- + (IN)JECTION]

in·tro·mit (in′trə mit′), *v.t.,* **-mit·ted, -mit·ting.** to send, put, or let in; introduce; admit. [1375–1425; late ME *intromitten* < L *intrōmittere* to send in, equiv. to *intrō-* INTRO- + *mittere* to send] —**in·tro·mis·si·bil·i·ty** (in′trə mis′ə bil′i tē), *n.* —**in′tro·mis′si·ble,** *adj.* —**in·tro·mis·sion** (in′trə mish′ən), *n.* —**in′tro·mis′sive,** *adj.* —**in′tro·mit′tent,** *adj.* —**in′tro·mit′ter,** *n.*

in·tron (in′tron), *n. Genetics.* a noncoding segment in a length of DNA that interrupts a gene-coding sequence or nontranslated sequence, the corresponding segment being removed from the RNA copy before transcription. Also called **intervening sequence.** Cf. **exon**[2]. [1975–80; perh. INTR(O)- + -ON[1]]

In·tro·pin (in′trə pin), *Pharm., Trademark.* a brand of dopamine hydrochloride.

in·trorse (in trôrs′), *adj. Bot.* turned or facing inward, as anthers that open toward the gynoecium. [1835–45; < L *intrōrsus*, contr. of **intrōversus* toward the inside. See INTRO-, VERSUS] —**in·trorse′ly,** *adv.*

in·tro·spect (in′trə spekt′), *v.i.* **1.** to practice introspection; consider one's own internal state or feelings. —*v.t.* **2.** to look into or examine (one's own mind, feelings, etc.). [1675–85; back formation from INTROSPECTION] —**in′tro·spect′a·ble, in′tro·spect′i·ble,** *adj.* —**in′tro·spec′tive,** *adj.* —**in′tro·spec′tive·ly,** *adv.* —**in′tro·spec′tive·ness,** *n.* —**in′tro·spec′tor,** *n.*

in·tro·spec·tion (in′trə spek′shən), *n.* **1.** observation or examination of one's own mental and emotional state, mental processes, etc.; the act of looking within oneself. **2.** the tendency or disposition to do this. **3.** See **sympathetic introspection.** [1670–80; < L *intrōspect(us)*, ptp. of *intrōspicere* to look within (equiv. to *intrō-* INTRO- + *spec(ere)* to look + *-tus* ptp. suffix) + -ION] —**in′tro·spec′tion·al,** *adj.* —**in′tro·spec′tion·ist,** *n., adj.*
—**Syn. 1.** self-examination, soul-searching.

in·tro·sus·cep·tion (in′trə sə sep′shən), *n.* intussusception. [1785–95; INTRO- + (INTUS)SUSCEPTION]

in·tro·ver·sion (in′trə vûr′zhən, -shən, in′trə vûr′-), *n.* **1.** the act of introverting or the state of being introverted. **2.** the quality, tendency, or disposition of being introverted. **3.** *Psychol.* **a.** the act of directing one's interest inward or to things within the self. **b.** the state of being concerned primarily with one's own thoughts and feelings rather than with the external environment. Cf. **extroversion.** [1645–55; 1910–15 for def. 3; < NL *intrōversiōn-* (s. of *intrōversiō*). See INTRO-, VERSION] —**in·tro·ver·sive** (in′trə vûr′siv), **in·tro·ver·tive** (in′trə vûr′tiv), *adj.*

in·tro·vert (*n., adj.* in′trə vûrt′; *v.* in′trə vûrt′), *n.* **1.** a shy person. **2.** *Psychol.* a person characterized by concern primarily with his or her own thoughts and feelings (opposed to *extrovert*). **3.** *Zool.* a part that is or can be introverted. —*adj.* **4.** *Psychol.* marked by introversion. —*v.t.* **5.** to turn inward: *to introvert one's anger.* **6.** *Psychol.* to direct (the mind, one's interest, etc.) partly to things within the self. **7.** *Anat., Zool.* to turn (a hollow, cylindrical structure) in on itself; invaginate. [1660–70; INTRO- + (IN)VERT]

in·trude (in trōōd′), *v.,* **-trud·ed, -trud·ing.** —*v.t.* **1.** to thrust or bring in without invitation, permission, or welcome. **2.** *Geol.* to thrust or force into. **3.** to install (a cleric) in a church contrary to the wishes of its members. —*v.i.* **4.** to thrust oneself without permission or welcome: *to intrude upon their privacy.* [1525–35; < L *intrūdere* to push in, equiv. to *in-* IN-[2] + *trūdere* to push] —**in·trud′er,** *n.* —**in·trud′ing·ly,** *adv.*
—**Syn. 4.** interfere, interlope. See **trespass.**

Intrud′er in the Dust′, a novel (1948) by William Faulkner.

in·tru·sion (in trōō′zhən), *n.* **1.** an act or instance of intruding. **2.** the state of being intruded. **3.** *Law.* **a.** an illegal act of entering, seizing, or taking possession of another's property. **b.** a wrongful entry after the determination of a particular estate, made before the remainderman or reversioner has entered. **4.** *Geol.* **a.** emplacement of molten rock in preexisting rock. **b.** plutonic rock emplaced in this manner. **c.** a process analogous to magmatic intrusion, as the injection of a plug of salt into sedimentary rocks. **d.** the matter forced in. [1250–1300; ME < ML *intrūsiōn-* (s. of *intrūsiō*), equiv. to L *intrūs(us)*, ptp. of *intrūdere* to INTRUDE (equiv. to *intrūd-* v.s. + *-tus* ptp. suffix, with *dt* < *s*) + *-iōn-* -ION] —**in·tru′sion·al,** *adj.*

in·tru·sive (in trōō′siv), *adj.* **1.** tending or apt to intrude; coming without invitation or welcome: *intrusive memories of a lost love.* **2.** characterized by or involving intrusion. **3.** intruding; thrusting in. **4.** *Geol.* **a.** (of a rock) having been forced between preexisting rocks or rock layers while in a molten or plastic condition. **b.** noting or pertaining to plutonic rocks. **5.** *Phonet.* excrescent (def. 2). [1375–1425; late ME; see INTRUSION, -IVE] —**in·tru′sive·ly,** *adv.* —**in·tru′sive·ness,** *n.*
—**Syn. 1.** annoying, bothersome, interfering, distracting, irksome, worrisome, troublesome, irritating, disturbing.

intrusive r, *Phonet.* See **linking r** (def. 2).

in·trust (in trust′), *v.t.* entrust.

in·tu·bate (in′tōō bāt′, -tyōō-), *v.t.,* **-bat·ed, -bat·ing.** *Med.* **1.** to insert a tube into (the larynx or the like). **2.** to treat by inserting a tube, as into the larynx. [1605–15; IN-[2] + TUBATE] —**in′tu·ba′tion,** *n.*

in·tu·it (in tōō′it, -tyōō′-; in′tōō it, -tyōō-), *v.t., v.i.* to know or receive by intuition. [1770–80; back formation from INTUITION] —**in·tu′it·a·ble,** *adj.*

in·tu·i·tion (in′tōō ish′ən, -tyōō-), *n.* **1.** direct perception of truth, fact, etc., independent of any reasoning process; immediate apprehension. **2.** a fact, truth, etc., perceived in this way. **3.** a keen and quick insight. **4.** the quality or ability of having such direct perception or quick insight. **5.** *Philos.* **a.** an immediate cognition of an object not inferred or determined by a previous cognition of the same object. **b.** any object or truth so discerned. **c.** pure, untaught, noninferential knowledge. **6.** *Ling.* the ability of the native speaker to make linguistic judgments, as of the grammaticality, ambiguity, equivalence, or nonequivalence of sentences, deriving from the speaker's native-language competence. [1400–50; late ME < LL *intuitiōn-* (s. of *intuitiō*) contemplation, equiv. to L *intuit(us)*, ptp. of *intuērī* to gaze at, contemplate + *-iōn-* -ION. See IN-[2], TUITION] —**in′tu·i′tion·less,** *adj.*

in·tu·i·tion·al (in′tōō ish′ə nl, -tyōō-), *adj.* **1.** pertaining to or of the nature of intuition. **2.** characterized by intuition; having intuition. **3.** based on intuition as a principle. [1855–60; INTUITION + -AL[1]] —**in′tu·i′tion·al·ly,** *adv.*

in·tu·i·tion·al·ism (in′tōō ish′ə nl iz′əm, -tyōō-), *n.* intuitionism. [1840–50; INTUITIONAL + -ISM] —**in′tu·i′tion·al·ist,** *n., adj.*

in·tu·i·tion·ism (in′tōō ish′ə niz′əm, -tyōō-), *n.* **1.** *Ethics.* the doctrine that moral values and duties can be discerned directly. **2.** *Metaphys.* **a.** the doctrine that in perception external objects are given immediately, without the intervention of a representative idea. **b.** the doctrine that knowledge rests upon axiomatic truths discerned directly. **3.** *Logic, Math.* the doctrine, propounded by L. E. J. Brouwer, that a mathematical object is considered to exist only if a method for constructing it can be given. [1840–50; INTUITION + -ISM] —**in′tu·i′tion·ist,** *n., adj.*

in·tu·i·tive (in tōō′i tiv, -tyōō′-), *adj.* **1.** perceiving by intuition, as a person or the mind. **2.** perceived by, resulting from, or involving intuition: *intuitive knowledge.* **3.** having or possessing intuition: *an intuitive person.* **4.** capable of being perceived or known by intuition. [1585–95; < ML *intuitīvus.* See INTUITION, -IVE] —**in·tu′i·tive·ly,** *adv.* —**in·tu′i·tive·ness,** *n.*
—**Syn. 2.** innate, inborn, natural.

in·tu·i·tiv·ism (in tōō′i ti viz′əm, -tyōō′-), *n.* **1.** ethical intuitionism. **2.** intuitive perception; insight. [1865–70; INTUITIVE + -ISM] —**in·tu′i·tiv·ist,** *n., adj.*

in·tu·mesce (in′tōō mes′, -tyōō-), *v.i.,* **-mesced, -mesc·ing.** **1.** to swell up, as with heat; become tumid. **2.** to bubble up. [1790–1800; < L *intumēscere* to swell up, equiv. to *in-* IN-[2] + *tumēscere*, equiv. to *tum(ēre)* to swell + *-ēscere* -ESCE]

in·tu·mes·cence (in′tōō mes′əns, -tyōō-), *n.* **1.** a swelling up, as with congestion. **2.** the state of being swollen. **3.** a swollen mass. [1650–60; < F; see INTUMESCE, -ENCE] —**in′tu·mes′cent,** *adj.*

in·turn (in′tûrn′), *n.* an inward turn or curve around an axis or fixed point. [1590–1600; IN-[1] + TURN] —**in′turned′,** *adj.*

in·tus·sus·cept (in′təs sə sept′), *v.t.* to take within, as one part of the intestine into an adjacent part; invaginate. [1825–35; back formation from INTUSSUSCEPTION] —**in′tus·sus·cep′tive,** *adj.*

in·tus·sus·cep·tion (in′təs sə sep′shən), *n.* **1.** a taking within. **2.** *Biol.* growth of a cell wall by the deposition of new particles among the existing particles of the wall. Cf. **apposition** (def. 4). **3.** Also called **invagination.** *Pathol.* the slipping of one part within another, as of the intestine. [1700–10; < L *intus* within + *susceptiōn-* (s. of *susceptiō*) an undertaking, equiv. to *suscept(us)*, ptp. of *suscipere* (see SUSCEPTIBLE) + *-iōn-* -ION]

in·twine (in twīn′), *v.t., v.i.,* **-twined, -twin·ing.** entwine. —**in·twine′ment,** *n.*

in·twist (in twist′), *v.t.* entwist.

In·u·it (in′ōō it, -yōō-), *n., pl.* **-its,** (*esp. collectively*) **-it** for **1.** **1.** a member of the Eskimo peoples inhabiting northernmost North America from northern Alaska to eastern Canada and Greenland. **2.** the language of the Inuit, a member of the Eskimo-Aleut family comprising a variety of dialects. Also, **Innuit.** Also called **Inupik.** [1755–65; < Inuit: people, pl. of *inuk* person]
—**Usage.** See **Eskimo, Indian.**

I·nuk·ti·tut (i nŏŏk′ti tŏŏt′, i nyŏŏk′-), *n.* a dialect of Inuit, spoken in the Canadian Arctic. Also, **I·nuk′ti·tut′.**

in·u·lase (in′yə lās′, -lāz′), *n. Biochem.* an enzyme that converts insulin to levulose. [1890–95; INUL(IN) + -ASE]

in·u·lin (in′yə lin), *n. Chem.* a polysaccharide, $(C_6H_{10}O_5)_n$, obtained from the roots of certain plants, esp. elecampane, dahlia, and Jerusalem artichoke, that undergoes hydrolysis to the dextrorotatory form of fructose: used chiefly as an ingredient in diabetic bread and as a reagent in diagnosing kidney function. Also called **alant starch.** [1805–15; < NL *Inul(a)* a genus of plants (L: elecampane) + -IN[2]]

in·unc·tion (in ungk′shən), *n.* **1.** the act of anointing. **2.** *Med.* the rubbing in of an oil or ointment. **3.** *Pharm.* an unguent. [1595–1605; < L *inunctiōn-* (s. of *inunctiō*), equiv. to *inunct(us)* (ptp. of *inunguere* to ANOINT) + *-iōn-* -ION. See IN-[2], UNCTION]

in·un·dant (in un′dənt), *adj.* **1.** flooding or overflowing. **2.** overwhelming with force, numbers, etc. [1620–30; < L *inundant-* (s. of *inundāns*), prp. of *inundāre*; see INUNDATE]

in·un·date (in′ən dāt′, -un-, in un′dāt), *v.t.,* **-dat·ed, -dat·ing.** **1.** to flood; cover or overspread with water; deluge. **2.** to overwhelm: *inundated with letters of protest.* [1615–25; < L *inundātus*, ptp. of *inundāre* to flood, overflow, equiv. to *in-* IN-[2] + *und(a)* wave + *-ātus* -ATE[1]] —**in′un·da′tion,** *n.* —**in′un·da′tor,** *n.* —**in·un·da·to·ry** (in un′də tôr′ē, -tōr′ē), *adj.*
—**Syn. 2.** glut.

I·nu·pi·aq (i nōō′pē ak′, i nyōō′-), *n., pl.* **-pi·at** (-pē at′). **1.** a member of a group of Eskimos inhabiting northern Alaska along the Bering, Chukchi, and Arctic coasts, and some distance inland. **2.** the Inuit language as spoken by the Inupiaq people. [< Inupiaq *iñupiaq* (pl. *iñupiat*) real person]

I·nu·pik (i nōō′pik), *n.* Inuit.

in·ur·bane (in′ûr bān′), *adj.* not urbane; lacking in courtesy, refinement, etc. [1615–25; IN-[3] + URBANE] —**in·ur·ban·i·ty** (in′ûr ban′i tē), **in′ur·bane′ness,** *n.* —**in′ur·bane′ly,** *adv.*

in·ure (in yŏŏr′, i nŏŏr′), *v.,* **-ured, -ur·ing.** —*v.t.* **1.** to accustom to hardship, difficulty, pain, etc.; toughen or harden; habituate (usually fol. by *to*): *inured to cold.* —*v.i.* **2.** to come into use; take or have effect. **3.** to become beneficial or advantageous. Also, **enure.** [1480–90; v. use of phrase *in ure, en ure* in use, customary < AF *en ure* in use, at work, equiv. to *en* IN + *ure* < L *opera*, pl. of *opus* work; cf. F *oeuvre*] —**in·ur·ed·ness** (in yŏŏr′id nis, i nŏŏr′-, in yŏŏrd′-, i nŏŏrd′-), *n.* —**in·ure′ment,** *n.*

in·urn (in ûrn′), *v.t.* **1.** to put into an urn, esp. ashes after cremation. **2.** to bury; inter. [1595–1605; IN-[2] + URN] —**in·urn′ment,** *n.*

in u·ter·o (in yōō′tə rō′), in the uterus; unborn. [1705–15; < L *in uterō*]

in u′tero sur′gery, surgery performed on a fetus while it is in the womb.

in·u·tile (in yōō′til), *adj.* of no use or service. [1400–50; late ME < L *inūtilis.* See IN-[3], UTILE] —**in·u′tile·ly,** *adv.*

in·u·til·i·ty (in′yōō til′i tē), *n., pl.* **-ties** for **2.** **1.** uselessness. **2.** a useless thing or person. [1590–1600; < L *inūtilitās.* See INUTILE, -ITY]

in·ut·ter·a·ble (in ut′ər ə bəl), *adj.* unutterable. [1595–1605; IN-[3] + UTTERABLE]

inv., 1. invenit. **2.** invented. **3.** invention. **4.** inventor. **5.** inventory. **6.** investment. **7.** invoice.

in va·cu·o (in wä′kōō ō′; *Eng.* in vak′yōō ō′), *Latin.* **1.** in a vacuum. **2.** in isolation.

in·vade (in vād′), *v.,* **-vad·ed, -vad·ing.** —*v.t.* **1.** to enter forcefully as an enemy; go into with hostile intent: *Germany invaded Poland in 1939.* **2.** to enter like an enemy: *Locusts invaded the fields.* **3.** to enter as if to take possession: *to invade a neighbor's home.* **4.** to enter and affect injuriously or destructively, as disease: *viruses that invade the bloodstream.* **5.** to intrude upon: *to invade the privacy of a family.* **6.** to encroach or infringe upon: *to invade the rights of citizens.* **7.** to permeate: *The smell of baking invades the house.* **8.** to penetrate; spread into or over: *The population boom has caused city dwellers to invade the suburbs.* —*v.i.* **9.** to make an invasion: *troops awaiting the signal to invade.* [1485–95; < L *invādere*, equiv. to *in-* IN-[2] + *vādere* to go; see WADE] —**in·vad′a·ble,** *adj.* —**in·vad′er,** *n.*
—**Syn. 1, 2.** penetrate, attack.

in·vag·i·na·ble (in vaj′ə nə bəl), *adj.* capable of being invaginated; susceptible of invagination. [1885–90; INVAGIN(ATE) + -ABLE]

in·vag·i·nate (*v.* in vaj′ə nāt′; *adj.* in vaj′ə nit, -nāt′), *v.,* **-nat·ed, -nat·ing,** *adj.* —*v.t.* **1.** to insert or receive, as into a sheath; sheathe. **2.** to fold or draw (a tubular organ) back within itself; intussuscept. —*v.i.* **3.** to become invaginated; undergo invagination. **4.** to form a pocket by turning in. —*adj.* **5.** folded or turned back upon itself. **6.** sheathed. [1650–60; < ML *invāginātus*, ptp. of *invāgināre* to sheathe. See IN-[2], VAGINATE]

in·vag·i·na·tion (in vaj′ə nā′shən), *n.* **1.** the act or process of invaginating. **2.** *Embryol.* the inward movement of a portion of the wall of a blastula in the formation of a gastrula. **3.** *Pathol.* intussusception (def. 3). **4.** a form or shape resulting from an infolded tissue. [1650–60; INVAGINATE + -ION]

in·va·lid[1] (in′və lid; *Brit.* in′və lēd′), *n.* **1.** an infirm or sickly person. **2.** a person who is too sick or weak to care for himself or herself: *My father was an invalid the last ten years of his life.* **3.** *Archaic.* a member of the armed forces disabled for active service. —*adj.* **4.** unable to care for oneself due to infirmity or disability: *his invalid sister.* **5.** of or for invalids: *invalid diets.* **6.** (of things) in poor or weakened condition: *the invalid state of his rocking chair.* —*v.t.* **7.** to affect with disease; make an invalid: *He was invalided for life.* **8.** to remove from or classify as not able to perform active service, as an invalid. **9.** *Brit.* to remove or evacuate (military personnel) from an active theater of operations because of injury or illness. —*v.i. Archaic.* **10.** to become an invalid. [1635–45; < F *invalide* < L *invalidus* weak. See IN-[3], VALID]

CONCISE ETYMOLOGY KEY: <, descended or borrowed from; >, whence; b., blend of, blended; c., cognate with; cf., compare; deriv., derivative; equiv., equivalent; imit., imitative; obl., oblique; r., replacing; s., stem; sp., spelling, spelled; resp., respelling, respelled; trans., translation; ?, origin unknown; *, unattested; ‡, probably earlier than. See the full key inside the front cover.

in•val•id[2] (in val′id), *adj.* **1.** not valid; without force or foundation; indefensible. **2.** deficient in substance or cogency; weak. **3.** void or without legal force, as a contract. [1625–35; < ML *invalidus,* L: weak; see INVALID[1]] —**in•val′id•ly,** *adv.* —**in•val′id•ness,** *n.*

in•val•i•date (in val′i dāt′), *v.t.,* **-dat•ed, -dat•ing. 1.** to render invalid; discredit. **2.** to deprive of legal force or efficacy; nullify. [1640–50; INVALID[2] + -ATE[1]] —**in•val′i•da′tion,** *n.* —**in•val′i•da′tor,** *n.*
—**Syn. 1.** weaken, impair; disprove, refute, rebut.

in•va•lid•ism (in′və li diz′əm), *n.* prolonged ill health. [1785–95; INVALID[1] + -ISM]

in•va•lid•i•ty[1] (in′və lid′i tē), *n.* lack of validity. [1540–50; < ML *invaliditās.* See INVALID[2], -ITY]

in•va•lid•i•ty[2] (in′və lid′i tē), *n.* invalidism. [1905–10; INVALID[1] + -ITY]

in•val•u•a•ble (in val′yo͞o ə bəl), *adj.* beyond calculable or appraisable value; of inestimable worth; priceless: *an invaluable art collection; her invaluable assistance.* [1570–80; IN-[3] + VALUABLE, in obs. sense "capable of valuation"] —**in•val′u•a•ble•ness,** *n.* —**in•val′u•a•bly,** *adv.*
—**Syn.** precious. —**Ant.** worthless.

In•var (in vär′), *Trademark.* a brand of iron alloy containing 35.5 percent nickel and having a very low coefficient of expansion at atmospheric temperatures.

in•var•i•a•ble (in vâr′ē ə bəl), *adj.* **1.** not variable; not changing or capable of being changed; static or constant. —*n.* **2.** something that is invariable; a constant. [1400–50; late ME; see IN-[3], VARIABLE] —**in•var′i•a•bil′i•ty, in•var′i•a•ble•ness,** *n.* —**in•var′i•a•bly,** *adv.*
—**Syn. 1.** unalterable, unchanging, changeless, invariant, unvarying, immutable. —**Ant. 1.** changing.

in•var•i•ant (in vâr′ē ənt), *adj.* **1.** unvarying; invariable; constant. **2.** *Math.* normal (def. 5e). —*n.* **3.** *Math.* a quantity or expression that is constant throughout a certain range of conditions. [1850–55; IN-[3] + VARIANT] —**in•var′i•ant•ly,** *adv.*

in•va•sion (in vā′zhən), *n.* **1.** an act or instance of invading or entering as an enemy, esp. by an army. **2.** the entrance or advent of anything troublesome or harmful, as disease. **3.** entrance as if to take possession or overrun: *the annual invasion of the resort by tourists.* **4.** infringement by intrusion. [1400–50; late ME < LL *invāsiōn-* (s. of *invāsiō*), equiv. to *invās(us),* ptp. of *invādere* + *-iōn-* -ION; see INVADE]

inva′sion of pri′vacy, an encroachment upon the right to be let alone or to be free from publicity. [1885–90]

in•va•sive (in vā′siv), *adj.* **1.** characterized by or involving invasion; offensive: *invasive war.* **2.** invading, or tending to invade; intrusive. **3.** *Med.* requiring the entry of a needle, catheter, or other instrument into a part of the body, esp. in a diagnostic procedure, as a biopsy. [1400–50; late ME < ML *invāsīvus.* See INVASION, -IVE]

in•vect•ed (in vek′tid), *adj. Heraldry.* **1.** noting an edge of a charge, as an ordinary, consisting of a series of small convex curves. **2.** (of a charge, as an ordinary) having such an edge: *a chevron invected.* Cf. **engrailed.** [1635–45; < L *invect(us)* driven into (see INVECTIVE) + -ED[2]]

in•vec•tive (in vek′tiv), *n.* **1.** vehement or violent denunciation, censure, or reproach. **2.** a railing accusation; vituperation. **3.** an insulting or abusive word or expression. —*adj.* **4.** vituperative; denunciatory; censoriously abusive. [1400–50; late ME < LL *invectīvus* abusive, equiv. to L *invect(us)* (ptp. of *invehī* to attack with words, INVEIGH) + *-īvus* -IVE] —**in•vec′tive•ly,** *adv.* —**in•vec′tive•ness,** *n.*
—**Syn. 1.** contumely, scorn. See **abuse.**

in•veigh (in vā′), *v.i.* to protest strongly or attack vehemently with words; rail (usually fol. by *against*): *to inveigh against isolationism.* [1480–90; < L *invehī* to attack with words, equiv. to *in-* IN-[2] + *vehī* pass. inf. of *vehere* to ride, drive, sail (cf. WAIN)] —**in•veigh′er,** *n.*
—**Syn.** harangue, revile.

in•vei•gle (in vā′gəl, -vē′-), *v.t.,* **-gled, -gling. 1.** to entice, lure, or ensnare by flattery or artful talk or inducements (usually fol. by *into*): *to inveigle a person into playing bridge.* **2.** to acquire, win, or obtain by beguiling talk or methods (usually fol. by *from* or *away*): *to inveigle a theater pass from a person.* [1485–95; var. of *envegle* < AF *enveogler,* equiv. to *en-* EN-[1] + OF *(a)vogler* to blind, deriv. of *avogle* blind < VL **aboculus* eyeless, adj. deriv. of phrase **ab oculis* without eyes. See AB-, OCULAR] —**in•vei′gle•ment,** *n.* —**in•vei′gler,** *n.*
—**Syn. 1.** induce, beguile, persuade. **2.** wheedle.

in•ve•nit (in wā′nit; *Eng.* in vā′nit), *Latin.* he invented it; she invented it. *Abbr.:* inv.

in•vent (in vent′), *v.t.* **1.** to originate or create as a product of one's own ingenuity, experimentation, or contrivance: *to invent the telegraph.* **2.** to produce or create with the imagination: *to invent a story.* **3.** to make up or fabricate (something fictitious or false): *to invent excuses.* **4.** *Archaic.* to come upon; find. [1425–75; late ME *invented* (ptp.) found, discovered (see -ED[2]) < L *inventus,* ptp. of *invenīre* to encounter, come upon, find, equiv. to *in-* IN-[2] + *ven(īre)* to COME + *-tus* ptp. suffix] —**in•vent′i•ble, in•vent′a•ble,** *adj.*
—**Syn. 1.** devise, contrive. See **discover. 2.** imagine, conceive. **3.** concoct.

in•ven•tion (in ven′shən), *n.* **1.** the act of inventing. **2.** *U.S. Patent Law.* a new, useful process, machine, improvement, etc., that did not exist previously and that is recognized as the product of some unique intuition or genius, as distinguished from ordinary mechanical skill or craftsmanship. **3.** anything invented or devised. **4.** the power or faculty of inventing, devising, or originating. **5.** an act or instance of creating or producing by exercise of the imagination, esp. in art, music, etc. **6.** something fabricated, as a false statement. **7.** *Sociol.* the creation of a new culture trait, pattern, etc. **8.** *Music.* a short piece, contrapuntal in nature, generally based on one subject. **9.** *Rhet.* (traditionally) one of the five steps in speech preparation, the process of choosing ideas appropriate to the subject, audience, and occasion. **10.** *Archaic.* the act of finding. [1300–50; ME *invencio(u)n* < L *inventiōn-* (s. of *inventiō*) a finding out, equiv. to *invent(us)* (see INVENT) + *-iōn-* -ION] —**in•ven′tion•al,** *adj.* —**in•ven′tion•less,** *adj.*

in•ven•tive (in ven′tiv), *adj.* **1.** apt at inventing, devising, or contriving. **2.** apt at creating with the imagination. **3.** having the function of inventing. **4.** pertaining to, involving, or showing invention. [1400–50; INVENT + -IVE; r. late ME *inventif* < MF] —**in•ven′tive•ly,** *adv.* —**in•ven′tive•ness,** *n.*

in•ven•tor (in ven′tər), *n.* a person who invents, esp. one who devises some new process, appliance, machine, or article; one who makes inventions. Also, **in•vent′er.** [1500–10; < L; see INVENT, -TOR]

in•ven•to•ry (in′vən tôr′ē, -tōr′ē), *n., pl.* **-to•ries,** *v.,* **-to•ried, -to•ry•ing.** —*n.* **1.** a complete listing of merchandise or stock on hand, work in progress, raw materials, finished goods on hand, etc., made each year by a business concern. **2.** the objects or items represented on such a list, as a merchant's stock of goods. **3.** the aggregate value of a stock of goods. **4.** raw material from the time of its receipt at an industrial plant for manufacturing purposes to the time it is sold. **5.** a detailed, often descriptive, list of articles, giving the code number, quantity, and value of each; catalog. **6.** a formal list of movables, as of a merchant's stock of goods. **7.** a formal list of the property of a person or estate. **8.** a tally of one's personality traits, aptitudes, skills, etc., for use in counseling and guidance. **9.** a catalog of natural resources, esp. a count or estimate of wildlife and game in a particular area. **10.** the act of making a catalog or detailed listing. —*v.t.* **11.** to make an inventory of; enter in an inventory; catalog. **12.** to take stock of; evaluate: *to inventory one's life and accomplishments.* **13.** to summarize: *to inventory the progress in chemistry.* **14.** to keep an available supply of (merchandise); stock. —*v.i.* **15.** to have value as shown by an inventory: *stock that inventories at two million dollars.* [1375–1425; late ME *inventorie* < ML *inventōrium;* see INVENT, -TORY[2]] —**in′ven•to′ri•a•ble,** *adj.* —**in′ven•to′ri•al,** *adj.* —**in′ven•to′ri•al•ly,** *adv.*
—**Syn. 5.** roster, record, register, account. See **list**[1].

in•ve•rac•i•ty (in′və ras′i tē), *n., pl.* **-ties** for 2. **1.** untruthfulness; mendacity. **2.** an untruth; falsehood. [1860–65; IN-[3] + VERACITY]

In•ver•car•gill (in′vər kär′gil), *n.* a city on S South Island, in New Zealand. 53,762.

In′ver Grove′ Heights′ (in′vər), a town in SE Minnesota. 17,171.

In•ver•ness (in′vər nes′, in′vər nes′), *n.* **1.** Also called **In•ver•ness•shire** (in′vər nes′shēr, -shər). a historic county in NW Scotland. **2.** a seaport and administrative district in the Highland region, in N Scotland. 55,045; 1080 sq. mi. (2797 sq. km). **3.** (*often l.c.*) an overcoat with a removable cape. **4.** Also called **Inverness′ cape′.** (*often l.c.*) the cape of this coat or one resembling it, esp. a loose, full, wool or worsted cape in a plaid pattern.

in•verse (*adj., n.* in vûrs′, in′vûrs; *v.* in vûrs′), *adj., n., v.,* **-versed, -vers•ing.** —*adj.* **1.** reversed in position, order, direction, or tendency. **2.** *Math.* **a.** (of a proportion) containing terms of which an increase in one results in a decrease in another. A term is said to be in inverse proportion to another term if it increases (or decreases) as the other decreases (or increases). **b.** of or pertaining to an inverse function. Cf. **direct** (def. 16). **3.** inverted; turned upside down. —*n.* **4.** an inverted state or condition. **5.** something that is inverse; the direct opposite. **6.** *Math.* **a.** an element of an algebraic system, as a group, corresponding to a given element such that its product or sum with the given element is the identity element. **b.** See **inverse function. c.** a point related to a given point so that it is situated on the same radius, extended if necessary, of a given circle or sphere and so that the product of the distances of the two points from the center equals the square of the radius of the circle or sphere. **d.** the set of such inverses of the points of a given set, as the points on a curve. —*v.t.* **7.** to invert. [1605–15; < L *inversus,* ptp. of *invertere* to turn upside down or inside out, REVERSE. See IN-[2], VERSE]

inverse′ cose′cant, *Trig.* See **arc cosecant.** [1905–10]

in′verse co′sine, *Trig.* See **arc cosine.** [1905–10]

inverse′ cotan′gent, *Trig.* See **arc cotangent.** [1905–10]

in′verse func′tion, *Math.* the function that replaces another function when the dependent and independent variables of the first function are interchanged for an appropriate set of values of the dependent variable. In $y = \sin x$ and $x = \arcsin y$, the inverse function of *sin* is *arc sine.* [1810–20]

in′verse im′age, *Math.* the point or set of points in the domain of a function corresponding to a given point or set of points in the range of the function. Also called **counter image.**

in•verse•ly (in vûrs′lē), *adv.* **1.** in an inverse manner. **2.** *Math.* in inverse proportion. [1650–60; INVERSE + -LY]

in′verse se′cant, *Trig.* See **arc secant.**

in′verse sine′, *Trig.* See **arc sine.**

in′verse square′ law′, *Physics, Optics.* one of several laws relating two quantities such that one quantity varies inversely as the square of the other, as the law that the illumination produced on a screen by a point source varies inversely as the square of the distance of the screen from the source.

in′verse tan′gent, *Trig.* See **arc tangent.**

in•ver•sion (in vûr′zhən, -shən), *n.* **1.** an act or instance of inverting. **2.** the state of being inverted. **3.** anything that is inverted. **4.** *Rhet.* reversal of the usual or natural order of words; anastrophe. **5.** *Gram.* any change from a basic word order or syntactic sequence, as in the placement of a subject after an auxiliary verb in a question or after the verb in an exclamation, as "When will you go?" and "How beautiful is the rose!" **6.** *Anat., Pathol.* the turning inward of a part, as the foot. **7.** *Chem.* **a.** a hydrolysis of certain carbohydrates, as cane sugar, that results in a reversal of direction of the rotatory power of the carbohydrate solution, the plane of polarized light being bent from right to left or vice versa. **b.** a reaction in which a starting material of one optical configuration forms a product of the opposite configuration. **8.** *Music.* **a.** the process or result of transposing the tones of an interval or chord so that the original bass becomes an upper voice. **b.** (in counterpoint) the transposition of the upper voice part below the lower, and vice versa. **c.** presentation of a melody in contrary motion to its original form. **9.** *Psychiatry.* assumption of the sexual role of the opposite sex; homosexuality. **10.** *Genetics.* a type of chromosomal aberration in which the position of a segment of the chromosome is changed in such a way that the linear order of the genes is reversed. Cf. **chromosomal aberration. 11.** *Phonet.* retroflexion (def. 3). **12.** Also called **atmospheric inversion, temperature inversion.** *Meteorol.* a reversal in the normal temperature lapse rate, the temperature rising with increased elevation instead of falling. **13.** *Electricity.* a converting of direct current into alternating current. **14.** *Math.* the operation of forming the inverse of a point, curve, function, etc. —*adj.* **15.** pertaining to or associated with inversion therapy or the apparatus used in it: *inversion boots.* [1545–55; < L *inversiōn-* (s. of *inversiō*) a turning in. See INVERSE, -ION]

inver′sion cast′ing, *Metall.* **1.** casting from an electric furnace inverted over the mold. **2.** a process of casting, used esp. for small statuary or the like, in which the mold is inverted after the outer surfaces have hardened so as to drain off the molten metal at the center.

inver′sion cen′ter, *Crystall.* See **center of symmetry.**

inver′sion lay′er, a layer of the atmosphere in which there is a temperature inversion, with the layer tending to prevent the air below it from rising, thus trapping any pollutants that are present.

inver′sion ther′apy, a method used to stretch and align the body, esp. the lower back, by suspending the entire body upside down from an apparatus that grips or supports the feet or knees.

in•ver•sive (in vûr′siv), *adj.* noting, pertaining to, or characterized by inversion. [1870–75; INVERS(ION) + -IVE]

in•vert (*v.* in vûrt′; *adj., n.* in′vûrt), *v.t.* **1.** to turn upside down. **2.** to reverse in position, order, direction, or relationship. **3.** to turn or change to the opposite or contrary, as in nature, bearing, or effect: *to invert a process.* **4.** to turn inward or back upon itself. **5.** to turn inside out. **6.** *Chem.* to subject to inversion. **7.** *Music.* to subject to musical inversion. **8.** *Phonet.* to articulate as a retroflex vowel. —*v.i.* **9.** *Chem.* to become inverted. —*adj.* **10.** *Chem.* subjected to inversion. —*n.* **11.** a person or thing that is inverted. **12.** a homosexual. **13.** (in plumbing) that portion of the interior of a drain or sewer pipe where the liquid is deepest. **14.** an inverted arch or vault. **15.** *Philately.* a two-colored postage stamp with all or part of the central design printed upside down in relation to the inscription. [1525–35; < L *invertere* to turn upside down or inside out, equiv. to *in-* IN-[2] + *vertere* to turn; see VERSE] —**in•vert′i•ble,** *adj.* —**in•vert′i•bil′i•ty,** *n.*
—**Syn. 2.** See **reverse.**

in•vert•ase (in vûr′tās, -tāz), *n. Biochem.* an enzyme, occurring in yeast and in the digestive juices of animals, that causes the inversion of cane sugar into invert sugar. Also, **in•ver•tin** (in vûr′tn). Also called **sucrase.** [1875–80; INVERT + -ASE]

in•ver•te•brate (in vûr′tə brit, -brāt′), *adj.* **1.** *Zool.* **a.** not vertebrate; without a backbone. **b.** of or pertaining to creatures without a backbone. **2.** without strength of character. —*n.* **3.** an invertebrate animal. **4.** a person who lacks strength of character. [1820–30; < NL *invertebrātus.* See IN-[3], VERTEBRATE] —**in•ver′te•bra•cy** (in vûr′tə brə sē), **in•ver′te•brate•ness,** *n.*

invert′ed com′ma, *Brit.* See **quotation mark.** Also called **turned comma.** [1780–90]

invert′ed mor′dent, *Music.* a melodic embellishment consisting of a rapid alternation of a principal tone with an auxiliary tone one degree above it. Also called **pralltriller.**

invert′ed pleat′, a reverse box pleat, having the flat fold turned in. [1910–15]

in•vert•er (in vûr′tər), *n.* **1.** a person or thing that inverts. **2.** *Elect.* a device that converts direct current into alternating current. Cf. **converter.** [1605–15; INVERT + -ER[1]]

invert′ible coun′terpoint, *Music.* counterpoint in which the voices, while retaining their original form, may be interchanged above or below one another in any order.

in•ver•tor (in vûr′tər), *n. Anat.* any muscle that turns a limb or part inward. [1900–05; INVERT + -OR[2]]

in′vert soap′, *Chem.* See **cationic detergent.** [1940–45]

in′vert sug′ar, a mixture of the dextrorotatory forms of glucose and fructose, formed naturally in fruits and produced artificially in syrups or fondants by treating cane sugar with acids. [1875–80]

in•vest (in vest′), *v.t.* **1.** to put (money) to use, by purchase or expenditure, in something offering potential profitable returns, as interest, income, or appreciation in value. **2.** to use (money), as in accumulating something: *to invest large sums in books.* **3.** to use, give, or devote (time, talent, etc.), as for a purpose or to achieve something: *He invested a lot of time in helping retarded children.* **4.** to furnish with power, authority, rank, etc.: *The Constitution invests the president with the power of veto.* **5.** to furnish or endow with a power, right, etc.; vest: *Feudalism invested the lords with absolute authority over their vassals.* **6.** to endow with a quality or characteristic: *to invest a friend with every virtue.* **7.** to infuse or belong to, as a quality or characteristic: *Goodness invests his every action.* **8.** *Metall.* to surround (a pattern) with an investment. **9.** to provide with the insignia of office. **10.** to install in an office or position. **11.** to clothe, attire, or dress. **12.** to cover, adorn, or envelop: *Spring invests the trees with leaves.* **13.** to surround (a place) with military forces or works so as to prevent approach or escape; besiege. —*v.i.* **14.** to invest money; make an investment: *to invest in oil stock.* [1525–35; < ML *investīre* to install, invest (money), surround, clothe in, L: to clothe in, equiv. to *in-* IN-[2] + *vestīre* to clothe, deriv. of *vestis* garment; see VEST] —**in•ves′tor,** *n.*

in•vest•a•ble (in ves′tə bəl), *adj.* **1.** that can be invested. —*n.* **2.** an object suitable as an investment, as a rare coin. Also, **in•vest′i•ble.** [1895–1900; INVEST + -ABLE]

in•ves•ti•ga•ble (in ves′ti gə bəl), *adj.* capable of being investigated. [1585–95; < LL *investīgābilis,* equiv. to L *investīgā(re)* to track down (see INVESTIGATE) + *-bilis* -BLE]

in•ves•ti•gate (in ves′ti gāt′), *v.,* **-gat•ed, -gat•ing.** —*v.t.* **1.** to examine, study, or inquire into systematically; search or examine into the particulars of; examine in detail. **2.** to search out and examine the particulars of in an attempt to learn the facts about something hidden, unique, or complex, esp. in an attempt to find a motive, cause, or culprit: *The police are investigating the murder.* —*v.i.* **3.** to make inquiry, examination, or investigation. [1500–10; < L *investīgātus,* ptp. of *investīgāre* to follow a trail, search out. See IN-[2], VESTIGE, -ATE[1]] —**in•ves′ti•ga′tive, in•ves•ti•ga•to•ry** (in ves′ti gə tôr′ē, -tōr′ē), *adj.* —**in•ves′ti•ga′tor,** *n.*

in•ves•ti•ga•tion (in ves′ti gā′shən), *n.* **1.** the act or process of investigating or the condition of being investigated. **2.** a searching inquiry for ascertaining facts; detailed or careful examination. [1400–50; late ME *investigacio(u)n* < L *investīgātiōn-* (s. of *investīgātiō*). See INVESTIGATE, -ION] —**in•ves′ti•ga′tion•al,** *adj.*

—**Syn. 1, 2.** scrutiny, exploration. INVESTIGATION, EXAMINATION, INQUIRY, RESEARCH express the idea of an active effort to find out something. An INVESTIGATION is a systematic, minute, and thorough attempt to learn the facts about something complex or hidden; it is often formal and official: *an investigation of a bank failure.* An EXAMINATION is an orderly attempt to obtain information about or to make a test of something, often something presented for observation: *a physical examination.* An INQUIRY is an investigation made by asking questions rather than by inspection, or by study of available evidence: *an inquiry into a proposed bond issue.* RESEARCH is careful and sustained investigation.

inves′tigative new′ drug′, *Pharm.* a regulatory classification assigned by the U.S. Food and Drug Administration to an unproven drug, allowing its use in approved studies with human patients. *Abbr.:* IND

in•ves•ti•tive (in ves′ti tiv), *adj.* **1.** of, pertaining to, or empowered to invest: *an investitive act.* **2.** of or pertaining to investiture. [1770–80; < ML *investīt(us)* (see INVESTITURE) + -IVE]

in•ves•ti•ture (in ves′ti chər, -chŏŏr′), *n.* **1.** the act or process of investing. **2.** the formal bestowal, confirmation, or presentation of rank, office, or a possessory or prescriptive right, usually involving the giving of insignia or an official title. **3.** the state of being invested, as with a garment, quality, or office. **4.** something that covers or adorns. **5.** *Archaic.* something that invests. [1350–1400; ME < ML *investītūra,* equiv. to *investīt(us)* (ptp. of *investīre* to install; see INVEST) + *-ūra* -URE]

in•vest•ment (in vest′mənt), *n.* **1.** the investing of money or capital in order to gain profitable returns, as interest, income, or appreciation in value. **2.** a particular instance or mode of investing. **3.** a thing invested in, as a business, a quantity of shares of stock, etc. **4.** something that is invested; sum invested. **5.** the act or fact of investing or state of being invested, as with a garment. **6.** a devoting, using, or giving of time, talent, emotional energy, etc., as for a purpose or to achieve something: *His investment in the project included more time than he cared to remember.* **7.** *Biol.* any covering, coating, outer layer, or integument, as of an animal or vegetable. **8.** the act of investing with a quality, attribute, etc. **9.** investiture with an office, dignity, or right. **10.** a siege or blockade; the surrounding of a place with military forces or works, as in besieging. **11.** Also called **investment compound.** *Metall.* a refractory material applied in a plastic state to a pattern to make a mold. **12.** *Archaic.* a garment or vestment. [1590–1600 for def. 12; 1605–15 for def. 1; INVEST + -MENT]

invest′ment bank′, a financial institution that deals chiefly in the underwriting of new securities. [1920–25] —**invest′ment bank′er.** —**invest′ment bank′ing.**

invest′ment cast′ing, *Metall.* a casting process in which an expendable pattern is surrounded by an investment compound and then baked so that the investment is hardened to form a mold and the pattern material may be melted and run off. Also called **precision casting.** Cf. **lost-wax process.** [1945–50]

invest′ment com′pany, a company that invests its funds in other companies and issues its own securities against these investments. Also called **invest′ment trust′.** [1930–35]

invest′ment com′pound, investment (def. 11).

in•vet•er•a•cy (in vet′ər ə sē), *n.* the quality or state of being inveterate or deeply ingrained: *the inveteracy of people's prejudices.* [1710–20; INVETER(ATE) + -ACY]

in•vet•er•ate (in vet′ər it), *adj.* **1.** settled or confirmed in a habit, practice, feeling, or the like: *an inveterate gambler.* **2.** firmly established by long continuance, as a disease, habit, practice, feeling, etc.; chronic. [1375–1425; late ME < L *inveterātus* (ptp. of *inveterāre* to grow old, allow to grow old, preserve), equiv. to *in-* IN-[2] + *veter-* (s. of *vetus*) old + *-ātus* -ATE[1]; cf. VETERAN] —**in•vet′er•ate•ly,** *adv.* —**in•vet′er•ate•ness,** *n.*

—**Syn. 1.** hardened, constant, habitual. **2.** set, fixed, rooted.

in•vi•a•ble (in vī′ə bəl), *adj. Biol.* (of an organism) incapable of sustaining its own life. [1915–20; IN-[3] + VIABLE] —**in•vi′a•bil′i•ty,** *n.*

in•vid•i•ous (in vid′ē əs), *adj.* **1.** calculated to create ill will or resentment or give offense; hateful: *invidious remarks.* **2.** offensively or unfairly discriminating; injurious: *invidious comparisons.* **3.** causing or tending to cause animosity, resentment, or envy: *an invidious honor.* **4.** *Obs.* envious. [1600–10; < L *invidiōsus* envious, envied, hateful, equiv. to *invidi(a)* ENVY + *-ōsus* -OUS] —**in•vid′i•ous•ly,** *adv.* —**in•vid′i•ous•ness,** *n.*

in•vig•i•late (in vij′ə lāt′), *v.i.,* **-lat•ed, -lat•ing.** **1.** to keep watch. **2.** *Brit.* to keep watch over students at an examination. [1545–55; < L *invigilātus* (ptp. of *invigilāre* to keep watch, stay up late), equiv. to *in-* IN-[2] + *vigilā-* (s. of *vigilāre* to watch; see VIGIL) + *-tus* ptp. suffix] —**in•vig′i•la′tion,** *n.* —**in•vig′i•la′tor,** *n.*

in•vig•or•ant (in vig′ər ənt), *n.* a tonic. [1815–25; INVIGOR(ATE) + -ANT]

in•vig•or•ate (in vig′ə rāt′), *v.t.,* **-at•ed, -at•ing.** to give vigor to; fill with life and energy; energize. [1640–50; IN-[2] + obs. *vigorate* invigorated; see VIGOR, -ATE[1]] —**in•vig′or•at′ing•ly,** *adv.* —**in•vig′or•a′tion,** *n.* —**in•vig′or•a′tive,** *adj.* —**in•vig′or•a′tive•ly,** *adv.* —**in•vig′or•a′tor,** *n.*

—**Syn.** strengthen, vitalize. See **animate.**

in•vin•ci•ble (in vin′sə bəl), *adj.* **1.** incapable of being conquered, defeated, or subdued. **2.** insuperable; insurmountable: *invincible difficulties.* [1375–1425; late ME < LL *invincibilis.* See IN-[3], VINCIBLE] —**in•vin′ci•bil′i•ty, in•vin′ci•ble•ness,** *n.* —**in•vin′ci•bly,** *adv.*

—**Syn. 1.** unyielding. INVINCIBLE, IMPREGNABLE, INDOMITABLE suggest that which cannot be overcome or mastered. INVINCIBLE is applied to that which cannot be conquered in combat or war, or overcome or subdued in any manner: *an invincible army; invincible courage.* IMPREGNABLE is applied to a place or position that cannot be taken by assault or siege, and hence to whatever is proof against attack: *an impregnable fortress; impregnable virtue.* INDOMITABLE implies having an unyielding spirit, or stubborn persistence in the face of opposition or difficulty: *indomitable will.* —**Ant. 1.** conquerable.

Invin′cible Arma′da, Armada.

in vi•no ve•ri•tas (in wē′nō we′ri täs′; *Eng.* in vī′nō ver′i tas′, -täs, vē′nō), *Latin.* in wine there is truth.

in•vi•o•la•ble (in vī′ə lə bəl), *adj.* **1.** prohibiting violation; secure from destruction, violence, infringement, or desecration: *an inviolable sanctuary; an inviolable promise.* **2.** incapable of being violated; incorruptible; unassailable: *inviolable secrecy.* [1400–50; late ME < L *inviolābilis.* See IN-[3], VIOLABLE] —**in•vi′o•la•bil′i•ty, in•vi′o•la•ble•ness,** *n.* —**in•vi′o•la•bly,** *adv.*

in•vi•o•late (in vī′ə lit, -lāt′), *adj.* **1.** free from violation, injury, desecration, or outrage. **2.** undisturbed; untouched. **3.** unbroken. **4.** not infringed. [1375–1425; late ME < L *inviolātus* unhurt, inviolable. See IN-[3], VIOLATE] —**in•vi•o•la•cy** (in vī′ə lə sē), **in•vi′o•late•ness,** *n.* —**in•vi′o•late•ly,** *adv.*

in•vis•cid (in vis′id), *adj.* (of a fluid) having no viscosity. Also, **nonviscous.** [1910–15; IN-[3] + VISCID]

in•vis•i•ble (in viz′ə bəl), *adj.* **1.** not visible; not perceptible by the eye: *invisible fluid.* **2.** withdrawn from or out of sight; hidden: *an invisible seam.* **3.** not perceptible or discernible by the mind: *invisible differences.* **4.** not ordinarily found in financial statements or reflected in statistics or a listing: *Goodwill is an invisible asset to a business.* **5.** concealed from public knowledge. —*n.* **6.** an invisible thing or being. **7. the invisible,** the unseen or spiritual world. [1300–50; ME < L *invīsibilis.* See IN-[3], VISIBLE] —**in•vis′i•bil′i•ty, in•vis′i•ble•ness,** *n.* —**in•vis′i•bly,** *adv.*

—**Syn. 2.** veiled, obscure.

invis′ible glass′, glass that has been curved to eliminate reflections.

invis′ible ink′. See **sympathetic ink.** [1675–85]

invis′ible shad′ow, (in architectural shades and shadows) a three-dimensional space occupied by the shadow projected by a solid and within which a surface is in shadow.

in•vi•ta•tion (in′vi tā′shən), *n.* **1.** the act of inviting. **2.** the written or spoken form with which a person is invited. **3.** something offered as a suggestion: *an invitation to consider a business merger.* **4.** attraction or incentive; allurement. **5.** a provocation: *The speech was an invitation to rebellion.* —*adj.* **6.** invitational. [1590–1600; < L *invītātiōn-* (s. of *invītātiō*), equiv. to *invītā-t(us)* (ptp. of *invītāre* to INVITE) + *-iōn-* -ION]

in•vi•ta•tion•al (in′vi tā′shə nl), *adj.* **1.** restricted to participants who have been invited: *an invitational track meet.* —*n.* **2.** an event, as a sports competition or an art exhibit, restricted to those who have been invited to participate. [1920–25; INVITATION + -AL[1]]

in•vi•ta•to•ry (in vī′tə tôr′ē, -tōr′ē), *adj.* serving to invite; conveying an invitation. [1300–50; ME < LL *invītātōrius,* equiv. to *invītā(re)* to INVITE + *-tōrius* -TORY[1]]

in•vite (*v.* in vīt′; *n.* in′vīt), *v.,* **-vit•ed, -vit•ing,** *n.* —*v.t.* **1.** to request the presence or participation of in a kindly, courteous, or complimentary way, esp. to request to come or go to some place, gathering, entertainment, etc., or to do something: *to invite friends to dinner.* **2.** to request politely or formally: *to invite donations.* **3.** to act so as to bring on or render probable: *to invite accidents by fast driving.* **4.** to call forth or give occasion for: *Those big shoes invite laughter.* **5.** to attract, allure, entice, or tempt. —*v.i.* **6.** to give invitation; offer attractions or allurements. —*n.* **7.** *Informal.* an invitation. [1525–35; < L *invītāre*] —**in•vi•tee** (in′vi tē′, -vī-), *n.* —**in•vit′er, in•vi′tor,** *n.*

—**Syn. 1.** bid. See **call. 2.** solicit. **5.** lure, draw.

in•vit•ing (in vī′ting), *adj.* attractive, alluring, or tempting: *an inviting offer.* [1580–90; INVITE + -ING[2]] —**in•vit′ing•ly,** *adv.* —**in•vit′ing•ness,** *n.*

in vi•tro (in vē′trō), (of a biological process) made to occur in a laboratory vessel or other controlled experimental environment rather than within a living organism or natural setting. Cf. **in vivo.** [1890–95; < L *in vitrō* lit., in glass]

in vi′tro fertiliza′tion, a specialized technique by which an ovum, esp. a human one, is fertilized by sperm outside the body, with the resulting embryo later implanted in the uterus for gestation. [1970–75]

in vi•vo (in vē′vō), (of a biological process) occurring or made to occur within a living organism or natural setting. Cf. **in vitro.** [1900–05; < L *in vīvō* in (something) alive]

in•vo•cate (in′və kāt′), *v.t.,* **-cat•ed, -cat•ing.** *Archaic.* invoke. [1520–30; < L *invocātus* (ptp. of *invocāre* to call upon, INVOKE), equiv. to *in-* IN-[2] + *vocā(re)* to call + *-tus* ptp. suffix] —**in•voc•a•tive** (in vok′ə tiv, in′və-kā′-), *adj.* —**in′vo•ca′tor,** *n.*

in•vo•ca•tion (in′və kā′shən), *n.* **1.** the act of invoking or calling upon a deity, spirit, etc., for aid, protection, inspiration, or the like; supplication. **2.** any petitioning or supplication for help or aid. **3.** a form of prayer invoking God's presence, esp. one said at the beginning of a religious service or public ceremony. **4.** an entreaty for aid and guidance from a Muse, deity, etc., at the beginning of an epic or epiclike poem. **5.** the act of calling upon a spirit by incantation. **6.** the magic formula used to conjure up a spirit; incantation. **7.** the act of calling upon or referring to something, as a concept or document, for support and justification in a particular circumstance. **8.** the enforcing or use of a legal or moral precept or right. [1325–75; ME *invocacio(u)n* < L *invocātiōn-* (s. of *invocātiō*). See INVOCATE, -ION] —**in•voc•a•to•ry** (in vok′ə tôr′ē, -tōr′ē), *adj.*

in•voice (in′vois), *n., v.,* **-voiced, -voic•ing.** —*n.* **1.** an itemized bill for goods sold or services provided, containing individual prices, the total charge, and the terms. **2.** the merchandise or shipment itself. —*v.t.* **3.** to present an invoice to: *The manufacturer invoiced our company for two typewriters.* **4.** to present an invoice for: *five chairs invoiced and shipped last month.* —*v.i.* **5.** to prepare or submit an invoice. **6.** to have a value if or when inventoried: *The merchandise in stock invoiced far more than we expected.* [1550–60; var. of *invoyes,* pl. of obs. *invoy,* var. of ENVOY[1]]

in•voke (in vōk′), *v.t.,* **-voked, -vok•ing.** **1.** to call for with earnest desire; make supplication or pray for: *to invoke God's mercy.* **2.** to call on (a deity, Muse, etc.), as in prayer or supplication. **3.** to declare to be binding or in effect: *to invoke the law; to invoke a veto.* **4.** to appeal to, as for confirmation. **5.** to petition or call on for help or aid. **6.** to call forth or upon (a spirit) by incantation. **7.** to cause, call forth, or bring about. [1480–90; < L *invocāre,* equiv. to *in-* IN-[2] + *vocāre* to call, akin to *vōx* VOICE] —**in•vo′ca•ble,** *adj.* —**in•vok′er,** *n.*

in•vo•lu•cel (in vol′yə sel′), *n. Bot.* a secondary involucre, as in a compound cluster of flowers. See illus. under **involucre.** [1755–65; < NL *involūcellum,* dim. of L *involūcrum* INVOLUCRUM; for formation, see CASTELLUM] —**in•vol•u•cel•late** (in vol′yə sel′it), **in•vol•u•cel•at•ed** (in vol′yə sel′ā tid), *adj.*

in•vo•lu•crate (in′və lōō′krit, -krāt), *adj.* having an involucre. [1820–30; INVOLUCRE + -ATE[1]]

in•vo•lu•cre (in′və lōō′kər), *n.* **1.** *Bot.* a collection or rosette of bracts subtending a flower cluster, umbel, or the like. **2.** a covering, esp. a membranous one. [1570–80; < MF < L *involūcrum* INVOLUCRUM] —**in′vo•lu′cral,** *adj.*

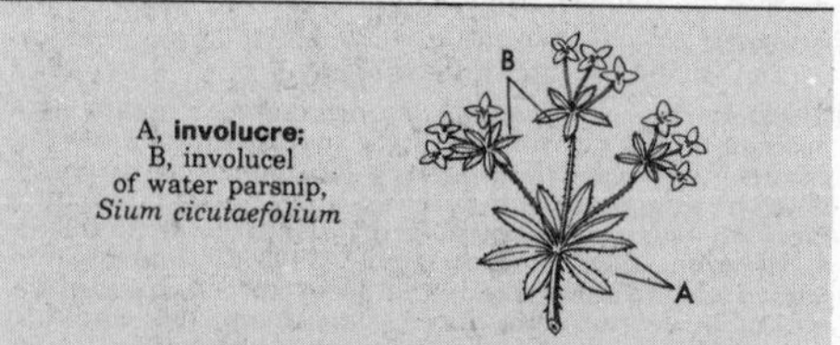

A, **involucre;** B, involucel of water parsnip, *Sium cicutaefolium*

in•vo•lu•crum (in′və lōō′krəm), *n., pl.* **-cra** (-krə). involucre. [1670–80; < NL, L *involūcrum* a wrap, cover, equiv. to *involū-* (var. s. of *involvere* to wrap, cover; see INVOLUTE) + *-crum* instrumental suffix]

in•vol•un•tar•y (in vol′ən ter′ē), *adj.* **1.** not voluntary; independent of one's will; not by one's own choice: *an involuntary listener; involuntary servitude.* **2.** unintentional; unconscious: *an involuntary gesture.* **3.** *Physiol.* acting independently of or done or occurring without volition: *involuntary muscles.* [1525–35; < LL *involuntārius.* See IN-[3], VOLUNTARY] —**in•vol•un•tar•i•ly** (in vol′ən ter′ə lē, -vol′ən târ′-), *adv.* —**in•vol′un•tar′i•ness,** *n.*

—**Syn. 1, 3.** See **automatic. 2.** instinctive. **3.** reflex, uncontrolled. —**Ant. 2.** intentional.

in•vo•lute (*adj., n.* in′və lo͞ot′; *v.* in′və lo͞ot′, in′və-lo͞ot′), *adj., n., v.,* **-lut•ed, -lut•ing.** —*adj.* **1.** intricate; complex. **2.** curled or curved inward or spirally. **3.** *Bot.* rolled inward from the edge, as a leaf. **4.** *Zool.* (of shells) having the whorls closely wound. —*n.* **5.** *Geom.* any curve of which a given curve is the evolute. —*v.i.* **6.** to roll or curl up; become involute. **7.** to return to a normal shape, size, or state. [1655–65; < L *involūtus* (ptp. of *involvere* to roll up, wrap, cover), equiv. to *in-* IN-[2] + *volū-* (var. s. of *volvere* to roll) + *-tus* ptp. suffix; cf. INVOLVE] —**in′vo•lute′ly,** *adv.*

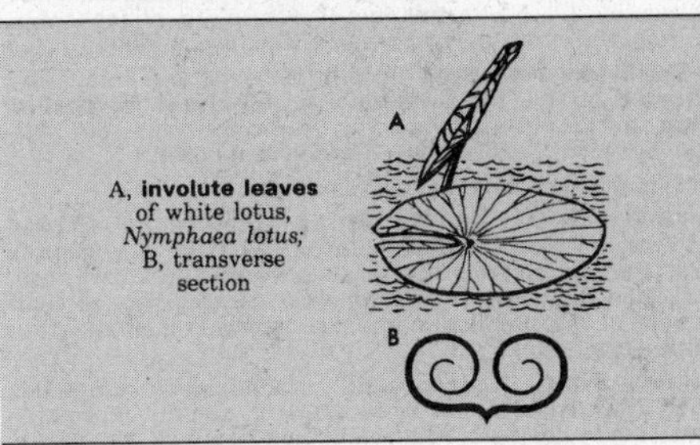

A, **involute leaves** of white lotus, *Nymphaea lotus;* B, transverse section

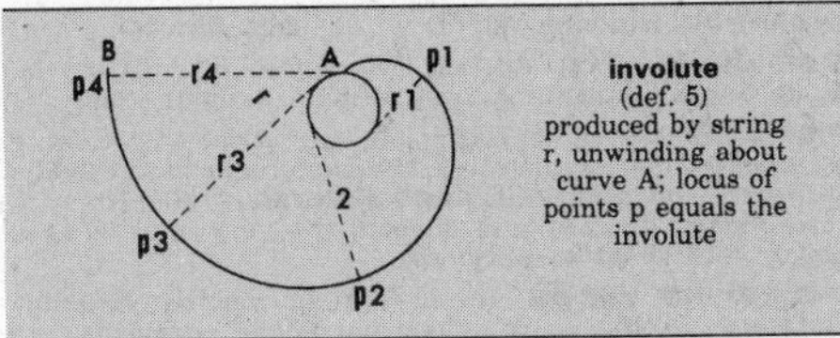

involute (def. 5) produced by string r, unwinding about curve A; locus of points p equals the involute

in•vo•lut•ed (in′və lo͞o′tid, in′və lo͞o′tid), *adj.* **1.** curving or curling inward. **2.** having an involved or complex nature. **3.** having resumed its normal size, shape, or condition. [1810–20; INVOLUTE + -ED[2]]

in′volute teeth′, (in gears) teeth having a profile that is the involute of a circle.

in•vo•lu•tion (in′və lo͞o′shən), *n.* **1.** an act or instance of involving or entangling; involvement. **2.** the state of being involved. **3.** something complicated. **4.** *Bot., Zool.* **a.** a rolling up or folding in upon itself. **b.** a part so formed. **5.** *Biol.* retrograde development; degeneration. **6.** *Physiol.* the regressive changes in the body occurring with old age. **7.** *Gram.* a complex construction in which the subject is separated from its predicate by intervening clauses or phrases. **8.** *Math.* a function that is its own inverse. [1605–15; < ML *involūtiōn-* (s. of *involūtiō*). See INVOLUTE, -ION]

in•vo•lu•tion•al (in′və lo͞o′shə nl), *adj.* **1.** of, pertaining to, or characteristic of involutional melancholia: *involutional symptoms.* —*n.* **2.** a person who suffers from involutional melancholia. [1905–10; INVOLUTION + -AL[1]]

involu′tional melancho′lia, *Psychiatry.* (formerly) extreme depression related to menopause or, less frequently, the male climacteric. [1905–10]

in•volve (in volv′), *v.t.,* **-volved, -volv•ing. 1.** to include as a necessary circumstance, condition, or consequence; imply; entail: *This job involves long hours and hard work.* **2.** to engage or employ. **3.** to affect, as something within the scope of operation. **4.** to include, contain, or comprehend within itself or its scope. **5.** to bring into an intricate or complicated form or condition. **6.** to bring into difficulties (usually fol. by *with*): *a plot to involve one nation in a war with another.* **7.** to cause to be troublesomely associated or concerned, as in something embarrassing or unfavorable: *Don't involve me in your quarrel!* **8.** to combine inextricably (usually fol. by *with*). **9.** to implicate, as in guilt or crime, or in any matter or affair. **10.** to engage the interests or emotions or commitment of: *to become involved in the disarmament movement; to become involved with another woman.* **11.** to preoccupy or absorb fully (usually used passively or reflexively): *You are much too involved with the problem to see it clearly.* **12.** to envelop or enfold, as if with a wrapping. **13.** to swallow up, engulf, or overwhelm. **14. a.** *Archaic.* to roll, surround, or shroud, as in a wrapping. **b.** to roll up on itself; wind spirally; coil; wreathe. [1350–1400; ME *involven* < L *involvere* to roll in or up, equiv. to *in-* IN-[2] + *volvere* to roll; see REVOLVE] —**in•volve′ment,** *n.* —**in•volv′er,** *n.*

—**Syn. 1.** necessitate, require, demand. **6, 7, 9.** INVOLVE, ENTANGLE, IMPLICATE imply getting a person connected or bound up with something from which it is difficult to extricate himself or herself. To INVOLVE is to bring more or less deeply into something, esp. of a complicated, embarrassing, or troublesome nature: *to involve someone in debt.* To ENTANGLE (usually passive or reflexive) is to involve so deeply in a tangle as to confuse and make helpless: *to entangle oneself in a mass of contradictory statements.* To IMPLICATE is to connect a person with something discreditable or wrong: *implicated in a plot.* —**Ant. 7.** extricate.

in•volved (in volvd′), *adj.* **1.** very intricate or complex: *an involved reply.* **2.** implicated: *involved in crime.* **3.** concerned in some affair, esp. in a way likely to cause danger or unpleasantness: *I didn't call the police because I didn't want to get involved.* **4.** committed or engaged, as in a political cause or artistic movement: *The civil rights demonstration attracted the involved young people of the area.* [1600–10; INVOLVE + -ED[2]] —**in•volv•ed•ly** (in vol′vid lē, -volvd′-), *adv.* —**in•volv′ed•ness,** *n.*

—**Syn. 1.** complicated, knotty, tangled, perplexing.

invt., inventory.

in•vul•ner•a•ble (in vul′nər ə bəl), *adj.* **1.** incapable of being wounded, hurt, or damaged. **2.** proof against or immune to attack: *A strong navy made Great Britain invulnerable.* **3.** not open to denial or disproof: *an invulnerable argument.* [1585–95; < L *invulnerābilis.* See IN-[3], VULNERABLE] —**in•vul′ner•a•bil′i•ty, in•vul′ner•a•ble•ness,** *n.* —**in•vul′ner•a•bly,** *adv.*

in•wale (in′wāl′), *n. Naut.* **1.** (in an open boat) a horizontal timber binding together the frames along the top strake. **2.** a strip of reinforcing material within a gunwale. [1870–75; IN + WALE[1]]

in•wall (*v.* in wôl′; *n.* in′wôl′), *v.t.* **1.** to enclose with a wall. —*n.* **2.** an inner wall. **3.** *Metall.* an inwardly sloping wall above the bosh of a blast furnace. [1605–15; IN-[1] + WALL]

in•ward (in′wərd), *adv.* Also, **in′wards. 1.** toward the inside, interior, or center, as of a place, space, or body. **2.** into or toward the mind or soul: *He turned his thoughts inward.* **3.** *Obs.* **a.** on the inside or interior. **b.** in the mind or soul; mentally or spiritually. —*adj.* **4.** proceeding or directed toward the inside or interior. **5.** situated within or in or on the inside; inner; internal: *an inward room.* **6.** pertaining to the inside or inner part. **7.** located within the body: *the inward parts.* **8.** pertaining to the inside of the body: *inward convulsions.* **9.** inland: *inward passage.* **10.** mental or spiritual; inner: *inward peace.* **11.** muffled or indistinct, as the voice. **12.** private or secret. **13.** closely personal; intimate. **14.** *Archaic.* pertaining to the homeland; domestic. —*n.* **15.** the inward or internal part; the inside. **16. inwards,** the inward parts of the body; entrails; innards. [bef. 900; ME; OE *inweard.* See IN, -WARD]

In′ward Light′. See **Inner Light.** [1700–10]

in•ward•ly (in′wərd lē), *adv.* **1.** in or on, or with reference to, the inside or inner part; internally. **2.** privately; secretly: *Inwardly, he disliked his guest.* **3.** within the self; mentally or spiritually: *Look inwardly to discover the truth.* **4.** in low or soft tones; not aloud. **5.** toward the inside, interior, or center. [bef. 1000; ME *inwardli,* OE *inweardlīce.* See INWARD, -LY]

in•ward•ness (in′wərd nis), *n.* **1.** the state of being inward or internal: *the inwardness of the body's organs.* **2.** depth of thought or feeling; concern with one's own affairs and oneself; introspection. **3.** preoccupation with what concerns human inner nature; spirituality. **4.** the fundamental or intrinsic character of something; essence. **5.** inner meaning or significance. **6.** intimacy. [1350–1400; ME; see INWARD, -NESS]

in•weave (in wēv′), *v.t.,* **-wove** or **-weaved, -wo•ven** or **-wove** or **-weaved, -weav•ing. 1.** to weave in or together. **2.** to introduce into or as into a fabric in weaving. **3.** to combine or diversify with something woven in. Also, **enweave.** [1570–80; IN-[1] + WEAVE]

in•wind (in wīnd′), *v.t.,* **-wound, -wind•ing.** enwind.

in•wrap (in rap′), *v.t.,* **-wrapped, -wrap•ping.** enwrap.

in•wreathe (in rēth′), *v.t.,* **-wreathed, -wreath•ing.** enwreathe.

in•wrought (in rôt′), *adj.* **1.** worked in or closely combined with something. **2.** wrought or worked with something by way of decoration. **3.** *Archaic.* wrought or worked in, as a decorative pattern. Also, **enwrought.** [1630–40; IN-[1] + WROUGHT]

in-your-face (in′yo͝or′fās′), *Informal. adj.* involving confrontation; defiant; provocative. [1985–90]

i•o (ē′ō), *n., pl.* **i•os.** a small hawk, *Buteo solitarius,* having two plumage phases and occurring only on the island of Hawaii, where it is a rare species and the only living indigenous bird of prey. Also called **Hawaiian hawk.** [< Hawaiian *ʻio*]

I•o (ī′ō, ē′ō), *n.* **1.** *Class. Myth.* a woman who, being loved by Zeus, was transformed into a white heifer and was, at the wish of Hera, first guarded by Argus and later pursued through the world by a gadfly until she reached Egypt, where she resumed her true shape: identified by the Egyptians with Isis. **2.** *Astron.* a large volcanically active moon of the planet Jupiter.

I•o (ī′ō, ē′ō), *n., pl.* **I•os.** See **Io moth.**

Io, *Symbol, Chem.* ionium.

Io., Iowa.

I/O, 1. inboard-outboard. **2.** *Computers.* input/output.

I.O., indirect object. Also, **IO, i.o.**

Io•an•ni•na (yô ä′nē nä, yä′nē nä), *n.* a city in NW Greece. 39,814. Also, **Io•án′ni•na, Yanina, Yannina.** Serbian, **Janina.**

I•ob•a•tes (ī ob′ə tēz′, ē ob′-), *n. Class. Myth.* a Lycian king commissioned by his son-in-law, Proetus, to kill Bellerophon: after surviving ordeals designed to destroy him, Bellerophon was believed to be divinely protected, and Iobates gave him half his kingdom.

IOC, International Olympic Committee. Also, **I.O.C.**

iod-, var. of **iodo-** before a vowel: *iodic.*

i•o•date (ī′ə dāt′), *n., v.,* **-dat•ed, -dat•ing.** —*n.* **1.** *Chem.* a salt of iodic acid, as sodium iodate, $NaIO_3$. —*v.t.* **2.** Also, **iodinate.** to iodize. [1830–40; IOD(IC ACID) + -ATE[2]] —**i′o•da′tion,** *n.*

i•od•ic (ī od′ik), *adj. Chem.* containing iodine, esp. in the pentavalent state. [1820–30; IOD- + -IC]

iod′ic ac′id, *Chem.* a colorless or white, crystalline, water-soluble solid, HIO_3, used chiefly as a reagent. [1820–30]

i•o•dide (ī′ə did′, -did), *n. Chem.* **1.** a salt of hydriodic acid consisting of two elements, one of which is iodine, as sodium iodide, NaI. **2.** a compound containing iodine, as methyl iodide. [1815–25; IOD- + -IDE]

i•o•dim•e•try (ī′ə dim′i trē), *n. Chem.* iodometry. [1895–1900] —**i•o•di•met•ric** (ī′ō də me′trik), *adj.*

i•o•din•ate (ī′ə dn āt′), *v.t.,* **-at•ed, -at•ing.** *Chem.* to iodize. [IODINE + -ATE[1]] —**i′o•din•a′tion,** *n.*

i•o•dine (ī′ə dīn′, -din; *in Chem. also* ī′ə dēn′), *n. Chem.* a nonmetallic halogen element occurring at ordinary temperatures as a grayish-black crystalline solid that sublimes to a dense violet vapor when heated: used in medicine as an antiseptic. *Symbol:* I; *at. wt.:* 126.904; *at. no.:* 53; *sp. gr.:* (solid) 4.93 at 20°C. Also, **i•o•din** (ī′ə din). [1814; < F *iode* (< Gk *iṓdēs,* orig. rust-colored, but by folk etym. taken as *í(on)* violet + *-ōdēs* -ODE[1]) + -INE[2]; introduced by H. Davy]

iodine 131, *Chem.* a radioactive isotope of iodine having a mass number 131 and a half-life of 8.6 days, used in the diagnosis and treatment of disorders of the thyroid gland. Cf. **radioiodine.**

i•o•dism (ī′ə diz′əm), *n. Pathol.* poisoning caused by sensitivity to or overuse of iodine or its compounds. [1825–35; IOD- + -ISM]

i•o•dize (ī′ə dīz′), *v.t.,* **-dized, -diz•ing.** to treat, impregnate, or affect with iodine or an iodide. Also, *esp. Brit.,* **i′o•dise′.** [1835–45; IOD- + -IZE] —**i′o•di•za′tion,** *n.* —**i′o•diz′er,** *n.*

iodo-, a combining form representing **iodine** in compound words: *iodometry.* Also, *esp. before a vowel,* **iod-.** [comb. form repr. NL *iōdum* IODINE]

i•o•do•form (ī ō′də fôrm′, ī od′ə-), *n. Chem.* a yellowish, crystalline, water-insoluble solid, CHI_3, analogous to chloroform, and having a penetrating odor: used chiefly as an antiseptic. Also called **triiodomethane.** [1830–40; IODO- + -FORM]

i•o•dom•e•try (ī′ə dom′i trē), *n. Chem.* a volumetric analytical procedure for determining iodine or materials that will liberate iodine or react with iodine. Also, **iodimetry.** [1880–85; IODO- + -METRY] —**i•o•do•met•ric** (ī′ō də me′trik), *adj.* —**i′o•do•met′ri•cal•ly,** *adv.*

i•o•do•phor (ī ō′də fôr′, -fōr′), *n. Pharm.* a complex of iodine and a surfactant that releases free iodine in solution, used as an antiseptic and disinfectant. [1950–55; IODO- + *-phor,* var. sp. of -PHORE]

i•o•dop•sin (ī′ə dop′sin), *n. Biochem.* a photosensitive violet pigment that occurs in the cones of the retina and is transformed by light into retinal and an opsin protein. Cf. **rhodopsin.** [1935–40; < Gk *iṓd(ēs)* taken as deriv. of *íon* violet (see IODINE) + OPSIN, on the pattern of RHODOPSIN]

i•o•dous (ī ō′dəs, ī od′əs), *adj. Chem.* **1.** containing iodine, esp. in the trivalent state. **2.** pertaining to or resembling iodine. [1820–30; IOD- + -OUS]

I.O.F., Independent Order of Foresters.

I•o•lan•the (ī′ə lan′thē), *n.* an operetta (1882) by Sir William S. Gilbert and Sir Arthur Sullivan.

i•o•lite (ī′ə līt′), *n. Mineral.* cordierite. [1750–60; < Gk *ío(n)* the violet + -LITE]

I′o moth′, a showy, yellow moth, *Automeris io,* of North America, having a prominent pink and bluish eyespot on each hind wing. [1865–70; named after Io]

i•on (ī′ən, ī′on), *n. Physics, Chem.* **1.** an electrically charged atom or group of atoms formed by the loss or gain of one or more electrons, as a cation **(positive ion),** which is created by electron loss and is attracted to the cathode in electrolysis, or as an anion **(negative ion),** which is created by an electron gain and is attracted to the anode. The valence of an ion is equal to the number of electrons lost or gained and is indicated by a plus sign for cations and a minus sign for anions, thus: Na^+, Cl^-, Ca^{++}, $S^=$. **2.** one of the electrically charged particles formed in a gas by electric discharge or the like. [< Gk *ión* going, neut. prp. of *iénai* to go; term introduced by Michael Faraday in 1834]

I•on (ī′on), *n.* **1.** *Class. Myth.* the eponymous ancestor of the Ionians: a son of Apollo and Creusa who is abandoned by his mother but returns to become an attendant in Apollo's temple at Delphi. **2.** (*italics*) a drama on this subject (415? B.C.) by Euripides.

-ion, a suffix, appearing in words of Latin origin, denoting action or condition, used in Latin and in English to form nouns from stems of Latin adjectives (*communion; union*), verbs (*legion; opinion*), and esp. past participles (*allusion; creation; fusion*). Also, **-ation, -ition, -tion.** Cf. **-cion, -xion.** [< L *-iōn-* (s. of *-iō*) suffix forming nouns, esp. on ptp. stems; r. ME *-ioun* < AF < L *-iōn-*]

Ion., Ionic.

I•o•na (ī ō′nə), *n.* an island in the Hebrides, off the W coast of Scotland: center of early Celtic Christianity.

i′on cham′ber, *Physics.* See **ionization chamber.**

Io•nes•co (yə nes′kō, ē ə-), *n.* **Eu•gène** (*Fr.* œ zhen′; *Eng.* yo͞o jēn′, yo͞o′jēn), 1912–94, French playwright, born in Rumania.

i′on exchange′, the process of reciprocal transfer of ions between a solution and a resin or other suitable solid. [1920–25]

i′on gen′erator, a device for creating negatively charged particles in immediately surrounding air, promoted as a cure for various ills.

I•o•ni•a (ī ō′nē ə), *n.* an ancient region on the W coast of Asia Minor and on adjacent islands in the Aegean: colonized by the ancient Greeks.

I•o•ni•an (ī ō′nē ən), *adj.* **1.** of or pertaining to Ionia. **2.** of or pertaining to the branch of the Greek people named from Ion, their legendary founder. —*n.* **3.** a member of one of the four main divisions of the prehistoric Greeks who invaded the Greek mainland and, after the Dorian invasions, emigrated to the Aegean islands and the coast of Asia Minor. Cf. **Achaean** (def. 5), **Aeolian** (def. 2), **Dorian** (def. 2). **4.** an Ionian Greek. [1555–65; IONI(A) + -AN]

Io′nian Is′lands, a group of Greek islands including Corfu, Levkas, Ithaca, Cephalonia, Paxos, and Zante off the W coast of Greece, and Cerigo off the S coast.

Io′nian mode′, *Music.* an authentic church mode represented on the white keys of a keyboard instrument by an ascending scale from C to C. [1835–45]

Io′nian Sea′, an arm of the Mediterranean between S Italy, E Sicily, and Greece.

i·on·ic (ī on′ik), *adj.* **1.** of or pertaining to ions. **2.** pertaining to or occurring in the form of ions. [1885–90; ION + -IC]

I·on·ic (ī on′ik), *adj.* **1.** *Archit.* noting or pertaining to one of the five classical orders that in ancient Greece consisted of a fluted column with a molded base and a capital composed of four volutes, usually parallel to the architrave with a pulvinus connecting a pair on each side of the column, and an entablature typically consisting of an architrave of three fascias, a richly ornamented frieze, and a cornice corbeled out on egg-and-dart and dentil moldings, with the frieze sometimes omitted. Roman and Renaissance examples are often more elaborate, and usually set the volutes of the capitals at 45° to the architrave. Cf. **composite** (def. 3), **Corinthian** (def. 2), **Doric** (def. 3), **Tuscan** (def. 2). See illus. under **order, volute. 2.** *Pros.* noting or employing a foot consisting either of two long followed by two short syllables **(greater Ionic),** or of two short followed by two long syllables **(lesser Ionic). 3.** noting or pertaining to that variety of the eastern branch of the early Greek alphabet that was used for the writing of the Ionic dialect and that became the variety used for all dialects of Greek from the 4th century B.C. to the present. **4.** of or pertaining to Ionia or the Ionians. **—*n.* 5.** *Pros.* an Ionic foot, verse, or meter. **6.** the dialect of ancient Greek spoken in Euboea, the Cyclades, and on the mainland of Asia Minor at Miletus and elsewhere. **7.** *Trademark.* a style of printing type. [1555–65; < L *Iōnicus* < Gk *Iōnikós* of IONIA; see -IC]

ion′ic bond′, *Chem.* the electrostatic bond between two ions formed through the transfer of one or more electrons. Also called **electrovalence, electrovalent bond.** [1935–40]

i′on implanta′tion, *Electronics.* a method of implanting impurities below the surface of a solid, usually a semiconductor, by bombarding the solid with a beam of ions of the impurity. [1960–65]

i·o·ni·um (ī ō′nē əm), *n. Chem.* a naturally occurring radioactive isotope of thorium. *Symbol:* Io; *at. no.:* 90; *at. wt.:* 230. [1905–10; ION + -IUM]

ioniza′tion cham′ber, *Physics.* an apparatus for detecting and analyzing ionizing radiation, consisting of a vessel filled with a gas at normal or lower than normal pressure and fitted with two electrodes such that the current between the electrodes is a function of the amount of ionization of the gas. Also called **ion chamber.** [1900–05]

ioniza′tion poten′tial, *Physics.* the energy required to remove an electron from an atom. [1910–15]

i·on·ize (ī′ə nīz′), *v.,* **-ized, -iz·ing.** **—*v.t.* 1.** to separate or change into ions. **2.** to produce ions in. **—*v.i.* 3.** to become changed into the form of ions, as by dissolving. Also, *esp. Brit.,* **i′on·ise′.** [1895–1900; ION + -IZE] **—i′on·iz′a·ble,** *adj.* **—i′on·i·za′tion,** *n.* **—i′on·iz′er,** *n.*

i′onizing radia′tion, *Physics.* any radiation, as a stream of alpha particles or x-rays, that produces ionization as it passes through a medium. [1900–05]

iono- a combining form with the meanings "ion," "ionized," "ionosphere," used in the formation of compound words: *ionophore.* [ION + -O-]

i·on·o·gen (ī on′ə jin, -jen′), *n. Physics, Chem.* any substance capable of producing ions, as an electrolyte. [1905–10; ION + -O- + -GEN] **—i·on·o·gen·ic** (ī on′ə-jen′ik), *adj.*

i·on·o·mer (ī on′ə mər), *n. Chem.* any of a class of plastics that because of its ionic bonding action is capable of conducting electric current. [1960–65; IONO- + -MER]

i·o·none (ī′ə nōn′), *n. Chem.* a light-yellow to colorless, slightly water-soluble liquid that is either one or a mixture of two unsaturated ketones having the formula $C_{13}H_{20}O$, used chiefly in perfumery. [1890–95; formerly trademark]

i·on·o·pause (ī on′ə pôz′), *n.* the transitional zone between the ionosphere and the mesosphere. [IONO- + PAUSE]

i·on·o·phore (ī on′ə fôr′, -fōr′), *n. Biochem.* a lipid-soluble substance capable of transporting specific ions through cellular membranes. [1950–55; IONO- + -PHORE]

i·on·o·sonde (ī on′ə sond′), *n.* a pulsed radar device used to measure the height of ionospheric layers. [1950–55; IONO- + SONDE]

i·on·o·sphere (ī on′ə sfēr′), *n.* the region of the earth's atmosphere between the stratosphere and the exosphere, consisting of several ionized layers and extending from about 50 to 250 mi. (80 to 400 km) above the surface of the earth. [1925–30; IONO- + -SPHERE] **—i·on·o·spher·ic** (ī on′ə sfer′ik), *adj.*

i′on propul′sion, *Rocketry.* a projected type of propulsion for vehicles in outer space, the exhaust consisting of positive ions and negative electrons repelled from the vehicle by electrostatic forces, resulting in a very high exhaust velocity.

i·on·to·pho·re·sis (ī on′tə fə rē′sis), *n.* a painless alternative to drug injection in which a weak electrical current is used to stimulate drug-carrying ions to pass through intact skin. [1905–10; < Gk *iont-* (s. of *ión*), prp. of *iénai* to go (cf. ION) + -o- -O- + *phorē-*, verbid s. of *phoreîn* to carry (akin to *phérein;* see BEAR[1]) + *-sis* -SIS] **—i·on·to·pho·ret·ic** (ī on′tə fə ret′ik), *adj.*

CONCISE ETYMOLOGY KEY: <, descended or borrowed from; >, whence; b., blend of, blended; c., cognate with; cf., compare; deriv., derivative; equiv., equivalent; imit., imitative; obl., oblique; r., replacing; s., stem; sp., spelling, spelled; resp., respelling, respelled; trans., translation; ?, origin unknown; *, unattested; ‡, probably earlier than. See the full key inside the front cover.

I.O.O.F., Independent Order of Odd Fellows.

-ior, a suffix of comparatives appearing in words of Latin origin: *superior; ulterior; junior.* [< L *-ior,* masc. and fem. comp. adj. suffix]

Io·shkar-O·la (yu shkär′u lä′), *n.* a city in and the capital of the Mari Autonomous Soviet Socialist Republic, in the RSFSR, in the central Soviet Union in Europe. 227,000. Also, **Yoshkar-Ola.**

i·o·ta (ī ō′tə), *n.* **1.** a very small quantity; jot; whit. **2.** the ninth letter of the Greek alphabet (I, ι). **3.** the vowel sound represented by this letter. [1600–10; < L *iōta* < Gk *iôta* < Sem; cf. Heb *yōdh* YOD]
—Syn. 1. bit, particle, atom, grain, mite.

i·o·ta·cism (ī ō′tə siz′əm), *n.* the conversion of other vowel sounds, esp. in Modern Greek, into (ē), the sound of iota. [1650–60; < LL *iōtacismus* < Gk *iōtakismós.* See IOTA, -AC, -ISM]

IOU, a written acknowledgment of a debt, esp. an informal one consisting only of the letters IOU, the sum owed, and the debtor's signature. Also, **I.O.U.** [1610–20; repr. *I owe you*]

-ious, variant of **-ous,** added to stems of Latin origin, often with corresponding nouns ending in **-ity:** *atrocious; hilarious.* Cf. **-eous.** [ME << L *-iōsus* (see -I-, -OSE[1]) and L *-ius* (masc. sing. adj. ending, as in *varius*)]

I·o·wa (ī′ə wə; *sometimes* ī′ə wā′), *n., pl.* **-was,** *(esp. collectively)* **-wa** for 3. **1.** a state in the central United States: a part of the Midwest. 2,913,387; 56,290 sq. mi. (145,790 sq. km). *Cap.:* Des Moines. *Abbr.:* IA (approved esp. for use with zip code), Ia., Io. **2.** a river flowing SE from N Iowa to the Mississippi River. 291 mi. (470 km) long. **3.** a member of an American Indian people originally of Iowa, Missouri, and Minnesota but now of Oklahoma, Nebraska, and Kansas. **4.** the Siouan language spoken by the Iowa Indians.

I′owa Cit′y, a city in SE Iowa. 50,508.

I·o·wan (ī′ə wən), *adj.* **1.** of or pertaining to Iowa. **—*n.* 2.** a native or inhabitant of Iowa. [1840–50; Iow(A) + -AN]

IPA, 1. See **International Phonetic Alphabet. 2.** International Phonetic Association. **3.** International Press Association. Also, **I.P.A.**

ip·e·cac (ip′i kak′), *n.* **1.** the dried root of a shrubby South American plant, *Cephaelis ipecacuanha,* of the madder family. **2.** the plant itself. **3.** a drug consisting of the dried roots of this plant, used as an emetic, purgative, etc., and as the source of emetine. Also, **ip·e·cac·u·an·ha** (ip′i kak′yōō an′ə). [1780–90, *Amer.;* short for *ipecacuanha* < Pg < Tupi *ipekaaguéne,* equiv. to *ipeh* low + *kaá* leaves + *guéne* vomit]

ip′ecac spurge′, a spurge, *Euphorbia ipecacuanhae,* of the eastern U.S.

ip′ecac syr′up, *Pharm.* a preparation containing ipecac in a syrupy medium, used as an emetic. Also called **syrup of ipecac.**

i.p.h., 1. *Print.* impressions per hour. **2.** inches per hour. Also, **iph**

Iph·i·a·nas·sa (if′ē ə nas′ə), *n.* **1.** (in the *Iliad*) a daughter of Agamemnon, offered to Achilles as a wife if he would return to battle against the Trojans. **2.** a daughter of Proetus and Antia who, with her sisters Iphinoë and Lysippe, was inflicted with madness for her irreverence toward the gods.

Iph·i·cles (if′i klēz′, ī′fi-), *n. Class. Myth.* a son of Alcmene and Amphitryon, the brother of Hercules.

Iph·i·ge·ni·a (if′i jə nī′ə, -nē′ə), *n.* **1.** *Class. Myth.* the daughter of Agamemnon and Clytemnestra and sister of Orestes and Electra: when she was about to be sacrificed to ensure a wind to take the Greek ships to Troy, she was saved by Artemis, whose priestess she became. **2.** a female given name.

Iphigeni′a in Au′lis (ô′lis), **1.** a tragedy (408? B.C.) by Euripides. **2.** an opera (1774) by Christoph Willibald von Gluck.

Iphigeni′a in Tau′ris (tôr′is), **1.** a drama (413? B.C.) by Euripides. **2.** an opera (1779) by Christoph Willibald von Gluck.

I·phin·o·ë (i fin′ō ē′), *n. Class. Myth.* **1.** a daughter of Antia and Proetus who was inflicted with madness for her irreverence toward the gods. Cf. **Iphianassa** (def. 2). **2.** the woman who brought Queen Hypsipyle's message of welcome to Jason and the Argonauts.

I·phi·ti·on (i fish′ē on′), *n.* (in the *Iliad*) a Trojan warrior slain by Achilles.

Iph·i·tus (if′i təs, ī′fi-), *n. Class. Myth.* a son of Eurytus, thrown to his death off the walls of Tiryns by Hercules. Also, **Iph′i·tos.**

I·pia·les (ē pyä′les), *n.* a city in SW Colombia. 42,152.

i·pil-i·pil (ē′pəl ē′pəl), *n.* a fast-growing tropical tree, *Leucaena leucocephala,* of the legume family, that is a source of fertilizer, animal feed, and timber. [< Tagalog *ipil*]

I·pin (ē′bin′), *n. Wade-Giles.* Yibin.

Ip·i·u·tak (ip′ē yōō′tak), *adj.* of, pertaining to, or characteristic of an Eskimo culture of Alaska lasting from A.D. 100 to 600. [1948; after the type site, on the Point Hope peninsula, New Alaska]

IPM, integrated pest management.

ipm, inches per minute. Also, **i.p.m.**

IPO, initial public offering.

I·poh (ē′pō), *n.* a city in and the capital of Perak state, in W Malaysia. 247,969.

ip·o·moe·a (ip′ə mē′ə, ī′pə-), *n.* **1.** any plant belonging to the genus *Ipomoea,* of the morning glory family, certain species of which are cultivated for their large, showy flowers. **2.** the dried root of certain varieties of plants of this genus, yielding a resin sometimes used as a cathartic. [< NL (Linnaeus) < Gk *ip-* (s. of *íps*) worm + *hómoia,* neut. pl. of *hómoios* like; see HOMEO-]

Ip·po·li·tov-I·va·nov (ip′ə lē′tôf ē vä′nôf, -nof, -tof-; *Russ.* ē pu lyē′təf ē vä′nəf), *n.* **Mi·kha·il Mi·khai·lo·vich** (mi kä ēl′ mi kī′lə vich; *Russ.* myi KHU yēl′ myi-KHĪ′lə vyich), 1857–1935, Russian composer.

ipr, inches per revolution. Also, **i.p.r.**

ip·ra·tro′pi·um bro′mide (ip′rə trō′pē əm), *Pharm.* an anticholinergic bronchodilator, $C_{20}H_{30}BrNO_3$, used in the treatment of chronic bronchitis and in airway obstruction diseases. [*i(so)pr(opylnor)atrop(in)ium* a component of the chemical name; see ISOPROPYL, NOR-, ATROPINE, -IUM]

i·pro·ni·a·zid (ī′prə nī′ə zid), *n. Pharm.* a compound, $C_9H_{13}N_3O$, used in the treatment of mental depression and tuberculosis. [1950–55; I(SO)PRO(PYL) + NI(COTINE) + AZ- + -ID[4]]

ips, inches per second. Also, **i.p.s.**

Ip·sam·bul (ip′sam bōōl′), *n.* See **Abu Simbel.**

ip·se dix·it (ip′se dik′sit; *Eng.* ip′sē dik′sit), *Latin.* **1.** he himself said it. **2.** an assertion without proof.

ip·si·lat·er·al (ip′sə lat′ər əl), *adj. Anat.* pertaining to, situated on, or affecting the same side of the body: *ipsilateral paralysis.* Cf. **contralateral.** [1905–10; < L *ipsi-* (comb. form of *ipse* oneself, the very one) + LATERAL] **—ip′si·lat′er·al·ly,** *adv.*

ip·sis·si·ma ver·ba (ip sis′si mä′ wer′bä; *Eng.* ip-sis′ə mə vûr′bə), *Latin.* the very words; verbatim.

ip·so fac·to (ip′sō fak′tō), by the fact itself; by the very nature of the deed: *to be condemned ipso facto.* [1540–50; < L *ipsō factō*]

ip·so ju·re (ip′sō yōō′re; *Eng.* ip′sō jŏŏr′ē), *Latin.* by the law itself; by operation of law.

Ip·sus (ip′səs), *n.* an ancient village in central Asia Minor, in Phrygia: the scene of a battle (301 B.C.) between the successors of Alexander the Great.

Ips·wich (ip′swich), *n.* **1.** a city in SE Suffolk, in E England. 122,600. **2.** a town in NE Massachusetts. 11,158.

IQ, *Psychol.* See **intelligence quotient.** [1960–65]

i.q., the same as. [< L *idem quod*]

Iq·bal (ik bäl′), *n.* **Muhammad,** 1873–1938, Pakistani poet.

I·qui·que (ē kē′ke), *n.* a seaport in N Chile. 64,900.

I·qui·tos (ē kē′tôs), *n.* a city in NE Peru, on the upper Amazon. 110,242.

IR, 1. infrared. **2.** intelligence ratio. **3.** information retrieval.

Ir, Irish (def. 4).

Ir, *Symbol, Chem.* iridium.

ir-[1], var. of **in-[2]** (by assimilation) before *r: irradiate.*

ir-[2], var. of **in-[3]** (by assimilation) before *r: irreducible.*

Ir., 1. Ireland. **2.** Irish.

I.R., 1. immediate reserve. **2.** infantry reserve. **3.** intelligence ratio. **4.** internal revenue.

I·ra (ī′rə), *n.* a male given name: from a Hebrew word meaning "watchful."

IRA, 1. See **individual retirement account. 2.** See **Irish Republican Army.** Also, **I.R.A.**

i·ra·cund (ī′rə kund′), *adj.* prone to anger; irascible. [1815–25; < L *īrācundus,* equiv. to *īrā-* (see IRATE) + *-cundus* inclined to (adj. suffix)] **—i′ra·cun′di·ty,** *n.*

i·ra·de (*Turk.* i Rä′de), *n.* a decree of a Muslim ruler. [1880–85; < Turk < Ar *irādah* will, wish]

I·rak (i rak′, i räk′), *n.* Iraq.

I·ra·ki (i rak′ē, i rä′kē), *n., pl.* **-kis,** *adj.* Iraqi.

I·ran (i ran′, i rän′, ī ran′), *n.* a republic in SW Asia. 34,400,000; ab. 635,000 sq. mi. (1,644,650 sq. km). *Cap.:* Teheran. Formerly (until 1935), **Persia.**

Iran., Iranian.

I·ra·ni·an (i rā′nē ən, i rä′-, ī rā′-), *adj.* **1.** of or pertaining to Iran, its inhabitants, or their language. **2.** of or pertaining to the Iranian languages. —*n.* **3.** a subbranch of the Indo-European family of languages, including esp. Persian, Pashto, Avestan, and Kurdish. **4.** an inhabitant of Iran; Persian. Also, **I·ra·ni** (i ran′ē, i rä′nē, ī rā′-) (for defs. 1, 4). [1835–45; IRAN + -IAN]

Ira′nian Plateau′, a plateau in SW Asia, mostly in Iran, extending from the Tigris to the Indus rivers. 1,000,000 sq. mi. (2,590,000 sq. km).

I·ra·pua·to (ē′rä pwä′tô), *n.* a city in Guanajuato, in central Mexico. 140,342.

I·raq (i rak′, i räk′), *n.* a republic in SW Asia, N of Saudi Arabia and W of Iran, centering in the Tigris-Euphrates basin of Mesopotamia. 11,505,000; 172,000 sq. mi. (445,480 sq. km). *Cap.:* Baghdad. Also, **Irak.**

I·ra·qi (i rak′ē, i rä′kē), *n., pl.* **-qis,** *adj.* —*n.* **1.** a native of Iraq. **2.** Also, **Ira′qi Ar′abic.** the dialect of Arabic spoken in Iraq. —*adj.* **3.** of or pertaining to Iraq, its inhabitants, or their language. Also, **Iraki.** [1770–80; < Ar *ʿIrāqī,* equiv. to *ʿIrāq* IRAQ + *-ī* suffix of appurtenance]

i·ras·ci·ble (i ras′ə bəl), *adj.* **1.** easily provoked to anger; very irritable: *an irascible old man.* **2.** characterized or produced by anger: *an irascible response.* [1350–1400; ME *irascibel* < LL *īrāscibilis,* equiv. to L *īrāsc-* (s. of *īrāscī* to grow angry; equiv. to *īr(a)* IRE + *-ā-* theme vowel + *-sc-* inchoative suffix + *-ī* inf. ending; see -ESCE) + *-ibilis* -IBLE] —**i·ras′ci·bil′i·ty, i·ras′ci·ble·ness,** *n.* —**i·ras′ci·bly,** *adv.*
—**Syn. 1, 2.** testy, touchy, peppery, choleric, short-tempered. See **irritable.** —**Ant. 1, 2.** calm, even-tempered.

i·rate (ī rāt′, ī′rāt), *adj.* **1.** angry; enraged: *an irate customer.* **2.** arising from or characterized by anger: *an irate letter to the editor.* [1830–40; < L *īrātus* ptp. of *īrāscī* to be angry, get angry; see IRASCIBLE, -ATE[1]] —**i·rate′ly,** *adv.* —**i·rate′ness,** *n.*
—**Syn. 1.** furious, irritated, provoked. —**Ant. 1.** calm.

I·ra·zu (ē′rä sōō′), *n.* **Mount,** a volcano in central Costa Rica. 11,200 ft. (3414 m).

IRB, industrial revenue bond.

Ir·bid (ir bid′), *n.* a town in NW Jordan. 125,000.

IRBM, See **intermediate range ballistic missile.** Also, **I.R.B.M.** [1955–60]

IRC, Internal Revenue Code.

ire (īᵊr), *n.* intense anger; wrath. [1250–1300; ME < OF < L *īra* anger] —**ire′less,** *adj.*
—**Syn.** fury, rage, choler, spleen.

Ire., Ireland.

Ire·dell (īᵊr′del), *n.* **James,** 1751–99, associate justice of U.S. Supreme Court, 1790–99.

ire·ful (īᵊr′fəl), *adj.* **1.** full of intense anger; wrathful. **2.** easily roused to anger; irascible. [1250–1300; ME; see IRE, -FUL] —**ire′ful·ly,** *adv.* —**ire′ful·ness,** *n.*

Ire·land (īᵊr′lənd), *n.* **1. John,** 1838–1918, U.S. Roman Catholic clergyman and social reformer, born in Ireland: archbishop of St. Paul, Minn., 1888–1918. **2.** Also called **Emerald Isle.** *Latin,* **Hibernia.** a large western island of the British Isles, comprising Northern Ireland and the Republic of Ireland. 4,991,556; 32,375 sq. mi. (83,850 sq. km). See map in preceding column. **3. Republic of.** Formerly, **Irish Free State** (1922–37), **Eire** (1937–49). a republic occupying most of the island of Ireland. 3,440,427; 27,137 sq. mi. (70,285 sq. km). *Cap.:* Dublin. Irish, **Eire. 4.** *Heraldry.* a coat of arms blazoned as follows: Azure, a harp or stringed argent. —**Ire′land·er,** *n.*

I·re·ne (ī rē′nē *for 1;* ī rēn′ *or, esp. Brit.,* ī rē′nē *for 2*), *n.* **1.** *Class. Myth.* one of the Horae, the personification of peace. **2.** Also, **I·re·na** (ī rē′nə, i rä′nə). A female given name.

i·ren·ic (ī ren′ik, ī rē′nik), *adj.* tending to promote peace or reconciliation; peaceful or conciliatory. Also, **i·ren′i·cal.** [1860–65; < Gk *eirēnikós,* equiv. to *eirḗn(ē)* peace + *-ikos* -IC] —**i·ren′i·cal·ly,** *adv.*

i·ren·ics (ī ren′iks, ī rē′niks), *n.* (*used with a singular v.*) the branch of theology dealing with the promotion of peace and conciliation among Christian churches. Cf. **polemics** (def. 2). [1880–85; see IRENIC, -ICS]

Ir gene (ī′är′), *Immunol.* a gene controlling the magnitude of the immune response to a particular antigen. [1970–75; *i(mmune) r(esponse)*]

Ir·gun (ir gōōn′), *n.* a militant Zionist underground group, active chiefly during the period (1917–48) of British control by mandate of Palestine. —**Ir·gun′ist,** *n.*

I·ri·an Ja·ya (ēr′ē än′ jä′yä), the W part of the island of New Guinea, formerly a Dutch territory: a province of Indonesia since 1963. 957,000; ab. 159,000 sq. mi. (411,810 sq. km). *Cap.:* Jayapura. Formerly, **I′rian Ba′rat** (bär′ät), **West Irian, Netherlands New Guinea, Dutch New Guinea.**

I·ri·cism (ī′rə siz′əm), *n.* Irishism.

I·ri·cize (ī′rə sīz′), *v.t.,* **-cized, -ciz·ing.** (*sometimes l.c.*) Also, *esp. Brit.,* **I′ri·cise′.** Irishize.

i·rid (ī′rid), *n.* any plant belonging to the Iridaceae, the iris family. [1865–70; < NL, L *īrid-,* s. of *īris* IRIS]

irid-, var. of **irido-** before a vowel: *iridectomy.*

i·ri·da·ceous (ir′i dā′shəs, ī′ri-), *adj.* belonging to the Iridaceae family of plants. Cf. **iris family.** [1850–55; < NL *Iridace(ae)* (see IRID, -ACEAE) + -OUS]

ir·i·dec·tome (ir′i dek′tōm, ī′ri-), *n. Surg.* a slender cutting instrument used in performing an iridectomy. [1850–55; IRID- + EC- + -TOME]

ir·i·dec·to·mize (ir′i dek′tə mīz′, ī′ri-), *v.t.,* **-mized, -miz·ing.** *Surg.* to perform an iridectomy on. Also, *esp. Brit.,* **ir′i·dec′to·mise′.** [1875–80; IRIDECTOM(Y) + -IZE]

ir·i·dec·to·my (ir′i dek′tə mē, ī′ri-), *n., pl.* **-mies.** *Surg.* excision of part of the iris. [1850–55; IRID- + -ECTOMY]

ir·i·des (ir′i dēz′, ī′ri-), *n.* a pl. of **iris.**

ir·i·des·cence (ir′i des′əns), *n.* iridescent quality; a play of lustrous, changing colors. [1795–1805; IRID- + -ESCENCE]

ir·i·des·cent (ir′i des′ənt), *adj.* **1.** displaying a play of lustrous colors like those of the rainbow. —*n.* **2.** an iridescent cloth, material, or other substance: *new fall dresses of imported iridescents.* [1790–1800; IRID- + -ESCENT] —**ir′i·des′cent·ly,** *adv.*

ir′ides′cent sea′weed, a red alga, *Irideae cordata,* found on the Pacific coast of North America, having broad, leathery, iridescent blades.

i·rid·ic (i rid′ik, ī rid′-), *adj. Chem.* of or containing iridium, esp. in the tetravalent state. [1835–45; IRID- + -IC]

i·rid·i·um (i rid′ē əm, ī rid′-), *n. Chem.* a precious metallic element resembling platinum: used in platinum alloys and for the points of gold pens. *Symbol:* Ir; *at. wt.:* 192.2; *at. no.:* 77; *sp. gr.:* 22.4 at 20°C. [1804; < L *īrid-,* s. of *īris* rainbow (see IRIS) + -IUM; so named from its iridescence when dissolved in hydrochloric acid]

ir·i·dize (ir′i dīz′, ī′ri-), *v.t.,* **-dized, -diz·ing.** to cover with iridium. Also, *esp. Brit.,* **ir′i·dise′.** [1860–65; IRID- + -IZE] —**ir′i·di·za′tion,** *n.*

irido-, a combining form of Latin origin used, with the meanings "rainbow," "iridescent," "iris (of the eye)," "*Iris* (the genus)," and "iridium," in the formation of compound words: *iridopupillary; iridosmine; iridotomy.* Also, *esp. before a vowel,* **irid-.** [comb. form repr. NL, L, Gk *īrid-* (s. of *îris*) rainbow, iris, etc.; see IRIS]

ir·i·do·cap·su·li·tis (ir′i dō kap′sə lī′tis, -kap′syŏŏ-, ī′ri-), *n. Pathol.* inflammation of the iris and the capsule of the lens. [IRIDO- + CAPSULE + -ITIS]

ir·i·do·cho·roid·i·tis (ir′i dō kôr′oi dī′tis, -kōr′-, ī′ri-), *n. Pathol.* inflammation of the iris and the choroid. [1870–75; < NL; see IRIDO-, CHOROID, -ITIS]

ir·i·dol·o·gy (ir′i dol′ə jē, ī′ri-), *n., pl.* **-gies.** the inspection of the iris of the eye as an aid in determining a person's state of health or in diagnosing a health problem. [1920–25; IRIDO- + -LOGY] —**ir′i·dol′o·gist,** *n.*

ir·i·do·pu·pil·lar·y (ir′i dō pyōō′pə ler′ē, ī′ri-), *adj. Ophthalm.* pertaining to the iris and the pupil. [IRIDO- + PUPILLARY[2]]

ir·i·dos·mine (ir′i doz′min, -dos′-, ī′ri-), *n.* a native alloy of iridium and osmium, usually containing some rhodium, ruthenium, platinum, etc., used esp. for the points of gold pens. Also, **ir·i·dos·mi·um** (ir′i doz′mē əm, -dos′-, ī′ri-). Also called **osmiridium.** [1820–30; IRID- + OSM(IUM) + -INE[2]]

ir·i·dot·o·my (ir′i dot′ə mē, ī′ri-), *n., pl.* **-mies.** *Surg.* incision of the iris, esp. for the formation of an artificial pupil by transverse division of fibers of the iris. [1850–55; IRIDO- + -TOMY]

ir·i·dous (ir′i dəs, ī′ri-), *adj. Chem.* containing trivalent iridium. [IRID- + -OUS]

Ir·i·dum (ir′i dəm), *n.* **Sinus.** See **Sinus Iridum.**

I·ri·na (ī rē′nə), *n.* a female given name.

i·ris (ī′ris), *n., pl.* **i·ris·es, ir·i·des** (ir′i dēz′, ī′ri-), *v.* —*n.* **1.** *Anat.* the contractile, circular diaphragm forming the colored portion of the eye and containing a circular opening, the pupil, in its center. See diag. under **eye. 2.** *Bot.* any plant of the genus *Iris,* having showy flowers and sword-shaped leaves. Cf. **iris family. 3.** a flower of this plant. **4.** (*cap.*) *Class. Myth.* a messenger of the gods, regarded as the goddess of the rainbow. **5.** a rainbow. **6.** any appearance resembling a rainbow. **7.** *Motion Pictures, Television.* an iris-in or iris-out. **8.** *Optics, Photog.* See **iris diaphragm.** —*v.i.* **9.** *Motion Pictures.* to begin or end a take or scene with an iris-in or iris-out, achieved by manipulation of an iris diaphragm on the camera or by editing the film. [1350–1400; ME < L *Īris,* *īris* < Gk *Îris, îris* rainbow, goddess of the rainbow, halo, iris flower or root, iridescent crystal; in some senses < NL < Gk: diaphragm of eye]

iris (bearded), *Iris pallida*

I·ris (ī′ris), *n.* a female given name.

i·ris·a·tion (ī′ri sā′shən), *n.* the effect or quality of being iridescent; iridescence. [1850–55; IRIS + -ATION]

i′ris di′aphragm, *Optics, Photog.* a composite diaphragm with a central aperture readily adjustable for size, used to regulate the amount of light admitted to a lens or optical system. Also called **iris.** [1885–90]

i′ris di′aphragm shut′ter, *Photog.* See **iris shutter.**

i′ris fam′ily, the plant family Iridaceae, characterized by herbaceous plants having bulbs, corms, or rhizomes, sword-shaped grasslike leaves, and usually showy flowers, and including the blackberry lily, crocus, freesia, gladiolus, and iris.

I·rish (ī′rish), *adj.* **1.** of, pertaining to, or characteristic of Ireland, its inhabitants, or their language. —*n.* **2.** the inhabitants of Ireland and their descendants elsewhere. **3.** the aboriginal Celtic-speaking people of Ireland. **4.** Also called **Irish Gaelic.** the Celtic language of Ireland in its historical or modern form. *Abbr.:* Ir, Ir. Cf. **Middle Irish, Old Irish. 5.** See **Irish English. 6.** See **Irish whiskey. 7. get one's Irish up,** *Informal.* to become angry or outraged: *Don't go getting your Irish up over a little matter like that.* [1175–1225; ME *Yrisse, Iris(c)h;* cf. OE *Īras* people of Ireland (c. ON *Īrar*); see -ISH[1]] —**I′rish·ly,** *adv.*

I′rish boat′, a small fishing boat used in the Boston area in the late 19th century, derived from an Irish model and having a cutter rig.

I′rish bridge′, *Brit.* a paved ford. [1920–25]

I′rish bull′, a paradoxical statement that appears at first to make sense. *Example:* He's the kind of guy who looks you right in the eye as he stabs you in the back. [1795–1805]

I′rish Chris′tian Broth′er. See **Brother of the Christian Schools** (def. 2).

I′rish cof′fee, a mixture of hot coffee and Irish whiskey, sweetened and topped with whipped cream. [1945–50]

I′rish elk′, an extinct deerlike mammal of the genus *Megaceros* (*Megaloceros*), of the Pleistocene Epoch, having in the male extremely large, broad antlers. [1815–25]

Irish elk, genus *Megaceros,* height at shoulder about 6 ft. (1.8 m); antlers to 13 ft. (4 m)

I′rish Eng′lish, the English language as spoken in Ireland; Hiberno-English. Also called **Irish.**

I′rish Free′ State′, former name of the Republic of Ireland. Gaelic, **Saorstat Eireann, Saorstat.**

I′rish Gael′ic, Irish (def. 4). [1890–95]

I·rish·ism (ī′ri shiz′əm), *n.* a custom, manner, practice, idiom, etc., characteristic of the Irish. Also, **Iricism.** [1725–35; IRISH + -ISM]

I·rish·ize (ī′ri shīz′), *v.t.,* **-ized, -iz·ing.** (*sometimes l.c.*) to make Irish, as in character or custom; give an Irish character to. Also, **Iricize;** *esp. Brit.,* **I′rish·ise′.** [1825–35; IRISH + -IZE]

I′rish lin′en, a fine, high-count linen handmade in

CONCISE PRONUNCIATION KEY: act, cāpe, dâre, pärt; set, ēqual; *if,* ice; ox, ōver, ôrder, oil, bŏŏk, bōōt, out; up, ûrge; child; sing; shoe; thin, that; zh as in *treasure.* ə = *a* as in *alone, e* as in *system, i* as in *easily, o* as in *gallop, u* as in *circus;* ᵊ as in *fire* (fīᵊr), *hour* (ouᵊr). l and n can serve as syllabic consonants, as in *cradle* (krād′l), and *button* (but′n). See the full key inside the front cover.

Ireland and used for tablecloths, handkerchiefs, doilies, and garment trimmings.

I′rish lord′, any of several marine sculpins of the genus *Hemilepidotus,* found from Alaska to northern California.

I•rish•man (ī′rish mən), *n., pl.* **-men. 1.** a man born in Ireland or of Irish ancestry. **2.** a native or inhabitant of Ireland. [1175–1225; ME; see IRISH, -MAN]

I′rish moss′, a purplish-brown, cartilaginous seaweed, *Chondrus crispus,* of the Atlantic coasts of Europe and North America. Also called **carrageen, carragheen.** [1835–45]

I′rish Pale′, pale² (def. 6).

I′rish pen′nant, *Naut. Slang* (*sometimes offensive*). **1.** an unwhipped rope end. **2.** any strand or rope end left hanging untidily. [1880–85]

I′rish pota′to, potato (def. 1). [1675–85]

I′rish Repub′lican Ar′my, an underground Irish nationalist organization founded to work for Irish independence from Great Britain: declared illegal by the Irish government in 1936, but continues activity aimed at the unification of the Republic of Ireland and Northern Ireland. *Abbr.:* IRA, I.R.A.

I′rish Sea′, a part of the Atlantic between Ireland and England.

I′rish set′ter, one of an Irish breed of setters having a golden-chestnut or mahogany-red coat. [1880–85]

I′rish stew′, a stew usually made of mutton, lamb, or beef, with potatoes, onions, etc. [1805–15]

I′rish ter′rier, one of an Irish breed of terriers having a dense, wiry, reddish coat. [1855–60]

Irish terrier, 18 in. (46 cm) high at shoulder

I′rish tweed′, 1. a sturdy woolen fabric of light warp and dark filling, made in Ireland and used in suits and coats. **2.** any tweed made in Ireland. [1890–95]

I′rish wa′ter span′iel, one of an Irish breed of large water spaniels having a thick, curly, liver-colored coat, a topknot of long, loose curls, and a thin, tapering tail covered with short hair. See illus. under **water spaniel.** [1880–85]

I′rish whis′key, any whiskey made in Ireland, characteristically a product of barley. Also called **Irish.** [1790–1800]

I′rish wolf′hound, one of an Irish breed of large, tall dogs having a rough, wiry coat ranging in color from white to brindle to black. [1660–70]

Irish wolfhound, 32 in. (81 cm) high at shoulder

I•rish•wom•an (ī′rish wo͝om′ən), *n., pl.* **-wom•en. 1.** a woman born in Ireland or of Irish ancestry. **2.** a woman who is a native or inhabitant of Ireland. [1350–1400; ME; see IRISH, WOMAN]

I′rish yew′, a variety of yew, *Taxus baccata stricta,* of Eurasia and northern Africa, having upright branches and dark green foliage with color variations.

i•ris-in (ī′ris in′), *n. Motion Pictures, Television.* the gradual appearance of an image or scene through an expanding circle. [1925–30]

i•ris-out (ī′ris out′), *n. Motion Pictures, Television.* the gradual disappearance of an image or scene through a contracting circle. [1925–30]

i′ris shut′ter, a camera shutter having a group of overlapping blades that open and close at the center when exposing film. Also called **between-the-lens shutter, diaphragm shutter, iris diaphragm shutter.**

i•ri•tis (ī rī′tis), *n. Ophthalm.* inflammation of the iris of the eye. [1810–20; IR(IS) + -ITIS] **—i•rit•ic** (ī rit′ik), *adj.*

irk (ûrk), *v.t.* to irritate, annoy, or exasperate: *It irked him to wait in line.* [1300–50; ME *irken* to grow tired, tire < ON *yrkja* to work, c. OE *wyrcan;* see WORK] **—Syn.** chafe, fret, bother; tire.

irk•some (ûrk′səm), *adj.* **1.** annoying; irritating; exasperating; tiresome: *irksome restrictions.* **2.** *Obs.* causing weariness or disgust. [1400–50; late ME; see IRK, -SOME¹] **—irk′some•ly,** *adv.* **—irk′some•ness,** *n.*

Ir•kutsk (ēʀ ko͞otsk′), *n.* a city in the S Russian Federation in Asia, W of Lake Baikal. 550,000.

Ir•ma (ûr′mə), *n.* a female given name, form of **Erma.**

Ir′min•ger Cur′rent (ûr′ming gər), a branch of the North Atlantic Current, flowing N past the W coast of Iceland and then W.

IRO, International Refugee Organization.

i•ron (ī′ərn), *n.* **1.** *Chem.* a ductile, malleable, silver-white metallic element, scarcely known in a pure condition, but much used in its crude or impure carbon-containing forms for making tools, implements, machinery, etc. *Symbol:* Fe; *at. wt.:* 55.847; *at. no.:* 26; *sp. gr.:* 7.86 at 20°C. Cf. **cast iron, pig iron, steel, wrought iron. 2.** something hard, strong, rigid, unyielding, or the like: *hearts of iron.* **3.** an instrument, utensil, weapon, etc., made of iron. **4.** an appliance with a flat metal bottom, used when heated, as by electricity, to press or smooth clothes, linens, etc. **5.** *Golf.* one of a series of nine iron-headed clubs having progressively sloped-back faces, used for driving or lofting the ball. Cf. **wood**¹ (def. 8). **6.** a branding iron. **7.** any of several tools, structural members, etc., of metals other than iron. **8.** the blade of a carpenter's plane. **9.** *Slang.* a pistol. **10.** a harpoon. **11.** *Med.* a preparation of iron or containing iron, used chiefly in the treatment of anemia, or as a styptic and astringent. **12. irons,** shackles or fetters: *Put him in irons!* **13.** a sword. **14. in irons, a.** *Naut.* (of a sailing vessel) unable to maneuver because of the position of the sails with relation to the direction of the wind. **b.** *Naut.* (of a towing vessel) unable to maneuver because of tension on the towing line. **c.** Also, **into irons.** in shackles or fetters. **15. irons in the fire,** matters with which one is immediately concerned; undertakings; projects: *He had other irons in the fire, so that one failure would not destroy him.* **16. pump iron,** to lift weights as an exercise or in competition. **17. strike while the iron is hot,** to act quickly when an opportunity presents itself. *—adj.* **18.** of, containing, or made of iron: *an iron skillet.* **19.** resembling iron in firmness, strength, color, etc.: *an iron will.* **20.** stern; harsh; cruel. **21.** inflexible; unrelenting. **22.** strong; robust; healthy. **23.** holding or binding strongly: *an iron grip.* **24.** irritating or harsh in tone: *an iron voice.* *—v.t.* **25.** to smooth or press with a heated iron, as clothes or linens. **26.** to furnish, mount, or arm with iron. **27.** to shackle or fetter with irons. **28.** *Metalworking.* to smooth and thin the walls of (an object being deep-drawn). *—v.i.* **29.** to press clothes, linens, etc., with an iron. **30. iron out, a.** to iron or press (an item of clothing or the like). **b.** to remove (wrinkles) from by ironing. **c.** to resolve or clear up (difficulties, disagreements, etc.): *The problem was ironed out months ago.* [bef. 900; ME, OE *iren* (n. and adj.), perh. < **isren,* metathesized from *isern,* var. of *isen;* cf. OS, OHG, ON *īsarn,* Goth *eisarn* < Gmc **isarnam,* perh. < Celtic; cf. Gaulish *Ysarno-, Iserno-* (in place names), OBreton *hoiarn,* Welsh *haearn,* OIr *íarn*] **—i′ron•less,** *adj.* **—i′ron•like′,** *adj.*

I′ron Age′, 1. the period in the history of humankind, following the Stone Age and the Bronze Age, marked by the use of implements and weapons made of iron. **2.** (*l.c.*) *Class. Myth.* the present age, following the bronze age; the last and worst of the four ages of the human race, characterized by danger, corruption, and toil. **3.** (*l.c.*) any age or period of degeneracy or wickedness. [1585–95]

i′ron ammo′nium ox′alate, *Chem.* See **ferric ammonium oxalate.**

i•ron•bark (ī′ərn bärk′), *n.* any of the various Australian eucalyptuses having a hard, solid bark. [1905–10; IRON + BARK²]

i′ron blue′, any of the class of blue pigments having a high tinting strength and ranging in shade and in coloring properties from reddish blue to jet blue: used chiefly in the manufacture of paints and printing inks. [1690–1700]

i•ron•bound (ī′ərn bound′), *adj.* **1.** bound with iron. **2.** rock-bound; rugged. **3.** hard; rigid; unyielding. [1350–1400; ME; see IRON, -BOUND¹]

i′ron brick′, *Masonry.* brick having a sprinkling of dark spots caused by the presence of iron salts.

i•ron•clad (*adj.* ī′ərn klad′; *n.* ī′ərn klad′), *adj.* **1.** covered or cased with iron plates, as a ship for naval warfare; armor-plated. **2.** very rigid or exacting; inflexible; unbreakable: *an ironclad contract.* *—n.* **3.** a wooden warship of the middle or late 19th century having iron or steel armor plating. [1850–55; IRON + CLAD¹]

I′ron Cross′, 1. a German medal awarded for outstanding bravery or service during wartime. **2.** (*l.c.*) *Gymnastics.* an upright, crosslike position held between the rings, with the arms fully extended laterally and the legs held together and pointed downward. [1870–75]

i′ron cur′tain, 1. (*sometimes caps.*) a barrier to understanding and the exchange of information and ideas created by ideological, political, and military hostility of one country toward another, esp. such a barrier between the Soviet Union and its allies and other countries. **2.** an impenetrable barrier to communication or information, esp. as imposed by rigid censorship and secrecy. [used by Winston Churchill in 1946 to describe the line of demarcation between Western Europe and the Soviet zone of influence]

I•ron•de•quoit (i ron′di kwoit′), *n.* a city in W New York. 57,648.

I′ron Duke′, epithet of the first Duke of Wellington.

i•rone (ī rōn′, ī′rōn), *n. Chem.* a colorless liquid of isomeric, unsaturated ketones, $C_{14}H_{22}O$, obtained from orris root: used in perfumery for its odor of violets. [1890–95; IR(IS) + -ONE]

i•ron•er (ī′ər nər), *n.* a person or thing that irons. [1775–85; IRON + -ER]

i•ron•fist•ed (ī′ərn fis′tid), *adj.* **1.** ruthless, harsh, and tyrannical: *an ironfisted dictator.* **2.** stingy; tight-fisted. [1850–55; IRON + FISTED]

i′ron gang′, *Australian.* See **chain gang.** [1830–40]

I′ron Gate′, a gorge cut by the Danube through the Carpathian Mountains, between Yugoslavia and SW Rumania. 2 mi. (3.2 km) long. Also, **I′ron Gates′.**

i′ron gray′, a medium shade of gray, like that of freshly broken iron. [bef. 1000; ME *iren grei,* OE *isengræg*] **—i′ron-gray′,** *adj.*

I′ron Guard′, a Rumanian fascist party that was extremely nationalistic and anti-Semitic, eliminated after World War II. **—I′ron-Guard′,** *adj.*

i′ron hand′, strict or harsh control: *The general governed the country with an iron hand.* [1840–50]

i•ron•hand•ed (ī′ərn han′did), *adj.* having or governing with an iron hand. [1760–70; IRON + HANDED] **—i′ron•hand′ed•ly,** *adv.* **—i′ron•hand′ed•ness,** *n.*

i′ron hat′, *Geol.* gossan.

i•ron-heart•ed (ī′ərn här′tid), *adj.* cruel; heartless; unfeeling. [1610–20] **—i′ron-heart′ed•ly,** *adv.* **—i′ron-heart′ed•ness,** *n.*

i′ron horse′, *Older Use.* a locomotive. [1825–35]

i•ron•ic (ī ron′ik), *adj.* **1.** containing or exemplifying irony: *an ironic novel; an ironic remark.* **2.** ironical. [1620–30; < LL *īrōnicus* < Gk *eirōnikós* dissembling, insincere. See IRONY, -IC]

i•ron•i•cal (ī ron′i kəl), *adj.* **1.** pertaining to, of the nature of, exhibiting, or characterized by irony or mockery: *an ironical compliment; an ironical smile.* **2.** using or prone to irony: *an ironical speaker.* [1570–80; IRONIC + -AL¹] **—i•ron′i•cal•ly,** *adv.* **—i•ron′i•cal•ness,** *n.* **—Syn. 1, 2.** sarcastic, sardonic.

i•ron•ing (ī′ər ning), *n.* **1.** the act or process of smoothing or pressing clothes, linens, etc., with a heated iron. **2.** articles of clothing or the like that have been or are to be ironed. [1700–10; IRON + -ING¹]

i′roning board′, a flat, cloth-covered board or other surface, often foldable and having legs, on which clothing, linens, or similar articles are ironed. [1835–45]

i•ro•nist (ī′rə nist), *n.* a person who uses irony habitually, esp. a writer. [1720–30; IRON(Y)¹ + -IST]

i•ron-jawed (ī′ərn jôd′), *adj.* **1.** having a jaw of or like iron: *an iron-jawed press; an iron-jawed fighter.* **2.** fiercely determined: *an iron-jawed will.* [1880–85]

i′ron law′ of wag′es, *Econ.* the doctrine or theory that wages tend toward a level sufficient only to maintain a subsistence standard of living. Also called **brazen law of wages.** [1895–1900]

i′ron lung′, a chamberlike respirator, formerly used in the treatment of poliomyelitis, that encloses the whole body except the head and in which alternate pulsations of high and low pressure induce normal breathing movements or force air into and out of the lungs. [1930–35]

i′ron maid′en, a medieval instrument of torture fashioned as a box in the shape of a woman, large enough to hold a human being, and studded with sharp spikes on the inside. Also called **i′ron maid′en of Nu′remberg.** [1890–95; trans. of G *eiserne Jungfrau*]

i′ron man′, 1. a person, as a worker or athlete, of great physical endurance who can be depended upon to perform a given task or job tirelessly. **2.** a machine that performs a job formerly done by hand; robot. **3.** *Slang.* a dollar bill or a silver dollar. [1610–20]

i•ron•mas•ter (ī′ərn mas′tər, -mä′stər), *n. Chiefly Brit.* the master of a foundry or ironworks; a manufacturer of iron. [1665–75; IRON + MASTER]

i′ron mold′, a stain on cloth or the like made by rusty iron or by ink pigmented with an iron derivative. [1595–1605]

i•ron•mon•ger (ī′ərn mung′gər, -mong′gər), *n. Chiefly Brit.* a dealer in hardware. [1300–50; ME; see IRON, MONGER]

i•ron•mon•ger•y (ī′ərn mung′gə rē, -mong′-), *n., pl.* **-ger•ies.** *Brit.* **1.** a hardware store or business. **2.** the stock of a hardware store; hardware. [1705–15; IRONMONGER + -Y³]

i′ron monox′ide, *Chem.* See **ferrous oxide.**

i•ron-on (ī′ərn on′, -ôn′), *adj.* **1.** designed to be applied with heat and pressure, as by an iron: *an iron-on patch for pants.* *—n.* **2.** a design, patch, or the like, applied by ironing on. [1955–60; n. use of v. phrase *iron on*]

i′ron ox′ide, *Chem.* See **ferric oxide.**

i′ron perchlo′ride, *Chem.* See **ferric chloride.**

i′ron plant′, aspidistra.

i•ron-pump•er (ī′ərn pum′pər), *n. Informal.* a person who pumps iron; weightlifter. [1975–80] **—i′ron-pump′ing,** *adj., n.*

i′ron put′ty, a compound of iron oxide and boiled linseed oil for caulking pipe joints.

i′ron pyri′tes, 1. pyrite; fool's gold. **2.** marcasite. [1795–1805]

i′ron rust′, rust (def. 1).

i•ron-sick (ī′ərn sik′), *adj. Naut.* noting a wooden hull, fastened with iron, in which chemical interaction between the iron and the wood has resulted in the decay of both; nail-sick. [1620–30] **—i′ron sick′ness.**

i•ron•side (ī′ərn sīd′), *n.* **1.** a strong person with great power of endurance or resistance. **2.** (*cap.*) an epithet or nickname of Edmund II of England. **3.** (*cap.*) Usually, **Ironsides. a.** (*used with a singular v.*) a nickname of Oliver Cromwell. **b.** the soldiers serving under Cromwell. **4. ironsides,** (*usually used with a singular v.*) **a.** an ironclad. **b.** *Eastern U.S.* scup. [1250–1300; ME; see IRON, SIDE[1]]

i•ron•smith (ī′ərn smith′), *n.* a worker in iron; blacksmith. [bef. 1150; ME *irensmith,* OE *isensmith.* See IRON, SMITH]

i′ron so′dium ox′alate, *Chem.* See **ferric sodium oxalate.**

i′ron sponge′, *Metall.* See **sponge iron.** [1875–80]

i•ron•stone (ī′ərn stōn′), *n.* **1.** any iron-bearing mineral or rock with siliceous impurities. **2.** Also called **i′ronstone chi′na.** a hard white stoneware. [1515–25; IRON + STONE]

i′ron sul′fate. See **ferrous sulfate.** [1875–80]

I•ron•ton (ī′ərn tən), *n.* a city in S Ohio, on the Ohio River. 14,290.

i′ron trichlo′ride, *Chem.* See **ferric chloride.**

i′ron vit′riol, *Chem.* See **ferrous sulfate.**

i•ron•ware (ī′ərn wâr′), *n.* articles of iron, as pots, kettles, or tools; hardware. [1400–50; late ME; see IRON, WARE[1]]

i•ron•weed (ī′ərn wēd′), *n.* any of certain North American composite plants of the genus *Vernonia,* having tubular, chiefly purple or red disk flowers. [1810–20; IRON + WEED[1]]

i•ron•wood (ī′ərn wo͝od′), *n.* **1.** any of various trees yielding a hard, heavy wood, as the American hornbeam, *Carpinus caroliniana,* or *Lyonothamnus floribundus,* found on the islands off the coast of S California. **2.** the wood of any of these trees. [1650–60; IRON + WOOD[1]]

i•ron•work (ī′ərn wûrk′), *n.* **1.** work in iron. **2.** objects or parts of objects made of iron: *ornamental ironwork.* [1375–1425; late ME; see IRON, WORK]

i•ron•work•er (ī′ərn wûr′kər), *n.* **1.** a worker in iron. **2.** a person employed in an ironworks. **3.** a person who works with structural steel. [1400–50; late ME; see IRON, WORKER] **—i′ron•work′ing,** *n.*

i•ron•works (ī′ərn wûrks′), *n., pl.* **-works.** (*used with a singular or plural v.*) an establishment where iron is smelted or where it is cast or wrought. [1575–85; IRON + WORKS]

i•ro•ny[1] (ī′rə nē, ī′ər-), *n., pl.* **-nies. 1.** the use of words to convey a meaning that is the opposite of its literal meaning: *the irony of her reply, "How nice!" when I said I had to work all weekend.* **2.** *Literature.* **a.** a technique of indicating, as through character or plot development, an intention or attitude opposite to that which is actually or ostensibly stated. **b.** (esp. in contemporary writing) a manner of organizing a work so as to give full expression to contradictory or complementary impulses, attitudes, etc., esp. as a means of indicating detachment from a subject, theme, or emotion. **3.** See **Socratic irony. 4.** See **dramatic irony. 5.** an outcome of events contrary to what was, or might have been, expected. **6.** the incongruity of this. **7.** an objectively sardonic style of speech or writing. **8.** an objectively or humorously sardonic utterance, disposition, quality, etc. [1495–1505; < L *īrōnia* < Gk *eirōneía* dissimulation, sarcasm, understatement, equiv. to *eírōn* a dissembler + *-eia* -Y[3]]
—Syn. 1, 2. IRONY, SARCASM, SATIRE indicate mockery of something or someone. The essential feature of IRONY is the indirect presentation of a contradiction between an action or expression and the context in which it occurs. In the figure of speech, emphasis is placed on the opposition between the literal and intended meaning of a statement; one thing is said and its opposite implied, as in the comment, "Beautiful weather, isn't it?" made when it is raining or nasty. Ironic literature exploits, in addition to the rhetorical figure, such devices as character development, situation, and plot to stress the paradoxical nature of reality or the contrast between an ideal and actual condition, set of circumstances, etc., frequently in such a way as to stress the absurdity present in the contradiction between substance and form. IRONY differs from SARCASM in greater subtlety and wit. In SARCASM ridicule or mockery is used harshly, often crudely and contemptuously, for destructive purposes. It may be used in an indirect manner, and have the form of irony, as in "What a fine musician you turned out to be!" or it may be used in the form of a direct statement, "You couldn't play one piece correctly if you had two assistants." The distinctive quality of SARCASM is present in the spoken word and manifested chiefly by vocal inflection, whereas SATIRE and IRONY, arising originally as literary and rhetorical forms, are exhibited in the organization or structuring of either language or literary material. SATIRE usually implies the use of irony or sarcasm for censorious or critical purposes and is often directed at public figures or institutions, conventional behavior, political situations, etc.

i•ron•y[2] (ī′ər nē), *adj.* consisting of, containing, or resembling iron. [1350–1400; ME; see IRON, -Y[1]]

Ir•o•quoi•an (ir′ə kwoi′ən), *n.* **1.** a family of North American Indian languages that includes Cherokee, Seneca, Mohawk, and Oneida. **—***adj.* **2.** of, pertaining to, or characteristic of the Iroquois people. **3.** of or belonging to the Iroquoian family of languages. [1690–1700; IROQUOIS + -AN]

Ir•o•quois (ir′ə kwoi′, -kwoiz′), *n., pl.* **-quois,** *adj.* **—***n.* **1.** a member of a North American Indian confederacy, the Five Nations, comprising the Mohawks, Oneidas, Onondagas, Cayugas, and Senecas, and later the Tuscaroras. **—***adj.* **2.** belonging or relating to the Iroquois or their tribes. [1660–70, *Amer.*; < F: adaptation of an unidentified term in an Algonquian language]

Ir•ra (ēr′ä), *n.* the Akkadian god of pestilence.

ir•ra•di•ance (i rā′dē əns), *n. Physics.* incident flux of radiant energy per unit area. Also, **irradiation.** [1660–70; IR-[1] + RADIANCE]

ir•ra•di•ant (i rā′dē ənt), *adj.* irradiating; radiant; shining. [1520–30; < L *irradiant-,* (s. of *irradiāns*), prp. of *irradiāre* to shine upon. See IR-[1], RADIANT]

ir•ra•di•ate (*v.* i rā′dē āt′; *adj.* i rā′dē it, -āt′), *v.,* **-at•ed, -at•ing,** *adj.* **—***v.t.* **1.** to shed rays of light upon; illuminate. **2.** to illumine intellectually or spiritually. **3.** to brighten as if with light. **4.** to radiate (light, illumination, etc.). **5.** to heat with radiant energy. **6.** to treat by exposure to radiation, as of ultraviolet light. **7.** to expose to radiation. **—***v.i.* **8.** *Archaic.* **a.** to emit rays; shine. **b.** to become radiant. **—***adj.* **9.** irradiated; bright. [1595–1605; < L *irradiātus,* ptp. of *irradiāre* to shine upon. See IR-[1], RADIATE] **—ir•ra′di•at′ing•ly,** *adv.* **—ir•ra′di•a′tive,** *adj.* **—ir•ra′di•a′tor,** *n.*

ir•ra•di•a•tion (i rā′dē ā′shən), *n.* **1.** the act of irradiating. **2.** the state of being irradiated. **3.** intellectual or spiritual enlightenment. **4.** a ray of light; beam. **5.** *Optics.* the apparent enlargement of an object when seen against a dark background. **6.** the use of x-rays or other forms of radiation for the treatment of disease, the making of x-ray photographs, the manufacture of vitamin D, etc. **7.** exposure or the process of exposure to x-rays or other radiation. **8.** *Physics.* irradiance. [1580–90; < LL *irradiātiōn-* (s. of *irradiātiō*). See IR-[1], RADIATION]

ir•rad•i•ca•ble (i rad′i kə bəl), *adj.* ineradicable. [1720–30; IR-[2] + L *rādīc(ārī)* to grow roots, take root (taken incorrectly as "to root up") + -ABLE. See ERADICABLE] **—ir•rad′i•ca•bly,** *adv.*

ir•ra•tion•al (i rash′ə nl), *adj.* **1.** without the faculty of reason; deprived of reason. **2.** without or deprived of normal mental clarity or sound judgment. **3.** not in accordance with reason; utterly illogical: *irrational arguments.* **4.** not endowed with the faculty of reason: *irrational animals.* **5.** *Math.* **a.** (of a number) not capable of being expressed exactly as a ratio of two integers. **b.** (of a function) not capable of being expressed exactly as a ratio of two polynomials. **6.** *Algebra.* (of an equation) having an unknown under a radical sign or, alternately, with a fractional exponent. **7.** *Gk. and Lat. Pros.* **a.** of or pertaining to a substitution in the normal metrical pattern, esp. a long syllable for a short one. **b.** noting a foot or meter containing such a substitution. **—***n.* **8.** *Math.* See **irrational number.** [1425–75; late ME < L *irratiōnālis.* See IR-[2], RATIONAL] **—ir•ra′tion•al•ly,** *adv.* **—ir•ra′tion•al•ness,** *n.*
—Syn. 3. unreasonable, ridiculous; insensate.

ir•ra•tion•al•ism (i rash′ə nl iz′əm), *n.* **1.** irrationality in thought or action. **2.** an attitude or belief having a nonrational basis. **3.** a theory that nonrational forces govern the universe. [1805–15; IRRATIONAL + -ISM] **—ir•ra′tion•al•ist,** *adj., n.* **—ir•ra′tion•al•is′tic,** *adj.*

ir•ra•tion•al•i•ty (i rash′ə nal′i tē), *n., pl.* **-ties** for 2. **1.** the quality or condition of being irrational. **2.** an irrational, illogical, or absurd action, thought, etc. [1560–70; IRRATIONAL + -ITY]

ir•ra•tion•al•ize (i rash′ə nl īz′), *v.t.,* **-ized, -iz•ing.** to make or cause to be irrational. Also, *esp. Brit.,* **ir•ra′tion•al•ise′.** [1890–95; IRRATIONAL + -IZE]

irra′tional num′ber, *Math.* a number that cannot be exactly expressed as a ratio of two integers. [1545–55]

Ir•ra•wad•dy (ir′ə wod′ē, -wô′dē), *n.* a river flowing S through Burma (Myanmar) to the Bay of Bengal. 1250 mi. (2015 km) long.

ir•re•al (i rē′əl, i rēl′), *adj.* unreal. [1940–45; IR-[2] + REAL[1]] **—ir•re•al•i•ty** (ir′ē al′i tē), *n.*

ir•re•but•ta•ble (ir′i but′ə bəl), *adj.* not rebuttable; incapable of being rebutted or refuted. [1825–35; IR-[2] + REBUTTABLE]

ir•re•claim•a•ble (ir′i klā′mə bəl), *adj.* not reclaimable; incapable of being reclaimed or rehabilitated: *an irreclaimable swamp; irreclaimable offenders.* [1600–10; IR-[2] + RECLAIMABLE] **—ir′re•claim′a•bil′i•ty, ir′re•claim′a•ble•ness,** *n.* **—ir′re•claim′a•bly,** *adv.*

ir•rec•on•cil•a•ble (i rek′ən sī′lə bəl, i rek′ən sī′-), *adj.* **1.** incapable of being brought into harmony or adjustment; incompatible: *irreconcilable differences.* **2.** incapable of being made to acquiesce or compromise; implacably opposed: *irreconcilable enemies.* **—***n.* **3.** a person or thing that is irreconcilable. **4.** a person who is opposed to agreement or compromise. [1590–1600; IR-[2] + RECONCILABLE] **—ir•rec′on•cil′a•bil′i•ty, ir•rec′on•cil′a•ble•ness,** *n.* **—ir•rec′on•cil′a•bly,** *adv.*

ir•re•cov•er•a•ble (ir′i kuv′ər ə bəl), *adj.* **1.** incapable of being recovered or regained: *an irrecoverable debt.* **2.** unable to be remedied or rectified; irretrievable: *an irrecoverable loss.* [1530–40; IR-[2] + RECOVERABLE] **—ir′re•cov′er•a•ble•ness,** *n.* **—ir′re•cov′er•a•bly,** *adv.*

ir•re•cu•sa•ble (ir′i kyo͞o′zə bəl), *adj.* not to be objected to or rejected. [1770–80; < LL *irrecūsābilis.* See IR-[2], RECUSE, -ABLE] **—ir′re•cu′sa•bly,** *adv.*

ir•re•deem•a•ble (ir′i dē′mə bəl), *adj.* **1.** not redeemable; incapable of being bought back or paid off. **2.** irremediable; irreparable; hopeless. **3.** beyond redemption; irreclaimable. **4.** (of paper money) not convertible into gold or silver. [1600–10; IR-[2] + REDEEMABLE] **—ir′re•deem′a•bil′i•ty, ir′re•deem′a•ble•ness,** *n.* **—ir′re•deem′a•bly,** *adv.*

ir•re•den•ta (ir′i den′tə), *n.* a region that is under the political jurisdiction of one nation but is related to another by reason of cultural, historical, and ethnic ties. [1910–15; < It (*Italia*) *irredenta* (Italy) unredeemed; see IRREDENTIST]

ir•re•den•tist (ir′i den′tist), *n.* **1.** (*usually cap.*) a member of an Italian association that became prominent in 1878, advocating the redemption, or the incorporation into Italy, of certain neighboring regions (**Italia irredenta**) having a primarily Italian population. **2.** a member of a party in any country advocating the acquisition of some region included in another country by reason of cultural, historical, ethnic, racial, or other ties. **—***adj.* **3.** pertaining to or supporting such a party or its doctrine. [1880–85; < It *irredentista,* equiv. to (*Italia*) *irredent(a)* (Italy) unredeemed (fem. of *irredento,* equiv. to *ir-* IR-[2] + *redento* < L *redemptus;* see REDEMPTION) + *-ista* -IST] **—ir′re•den′tism,** *n.*

ir•re•duc•i•ble (ir′i do͞o′sə bəl, -dyo͞o′-), *adj.* **1.** not reducible; incapable of being reduced or of being diminished or simplified further: *the irreducible minimum.* **2.** incapable of being brought into a different condition or form. **3.** *Math.* **a.** of or pertaining to a polynomial that cannot be factored. **b.** of or pertaining to a group that cannot be written as the direct product of two of its subgroups. [1625–35; IR-[2] + REDUCIBLE] **—ir′re•duc′i•bil′i•ty, ir′re•duc′i•ble•ness,** *n.* **—ir′re•duc′i•bly,** *adv.*

ir•re•flex•ive (ir′i flek′siv), *adj.* not reflexive. [1885–90; IR-[2] + REFLEXIVE] **—ir′re•flex′ive•ness, ir′re•flex•iv′i•ty,** *n.*

ir•re•form•a•ble (ir′i fôr′mə bəl), *adj.* **1.** insusceptible to reforming influences; incorrigible. **2.** not subject to improvement; final; perfect: *irreformable doctrine.* [1600–10; IR-[2] + REFORM[1] + -ABLE]

ir•ref•ra•ga•ble (i ref′rə gə bəl), *adj.* not to be disputed or contested. [1525–35; < LL *irrefragābilis,* equiv. to L *ir-* IR-[2] + *refragā(rī)* to resist, oppose + *-bilis* -BLE] **—ir•ref′ra•ga•bil′i•ty, ir•ref′ra•ga•ble•ness,** *n.* **—ir•ref′ra•ga•bly,** *adv.*

ir•re•fran•gi•ble (ir′i fran′jə bəl), *adj.* **1.** not to be broken or violated; inviolable: *an irrefrangible rule of etiquette.* **2.** incapable of being refracted. [1710–20; IR-[2] + REFRANGIBLE] **—ir′re•fran′gi•bil′i•ty, ir′re•fran′gi•ble•ness,** *n.* **—ir′re•fran′gi•bly,** *adv.*

ir•ref•u•ta•ble (i ref′yə tə bəl, ir′i fyo͞o′tə bəl), *adj.* that cannot be refuted or disproved: *irrefutable logic.* [1610–20; < LL *irrefūtābilis.* See IR-[2], REFUTABLE] **—ir•ref′u•ta•bil′i•ty, ir•ref′u•ta•ble•ness,** *n.* **—ir•ref′u•ta•bly,** *adv.*
—Syn. indisputable, incontrovertible, undeniable.

irreg., **1.** irregular. **2.** irregularly.

ir•re•gard•less (ir′i gärd′lis), *adv. Nonstandard.* regardless. [1910–15; IR-[2] (prob. after *irrespective*) + REGARDLESS]
—Usage. IRREGARDLESS is considered nonstandard because of the two negative elements *ir-* and *-less.* It was probably formed on the analogy of such words as *irrespective, irrelevant,* and *irreparable.* Those who use it, including on occasion educated speakers, may do so from a desire to add emphasis. IRREGARDLESS first appeared in the early 20th century and was perhaps popularized by its use in a comic radio program of the 1930's.

ir•reg•u•lar (i reg′yə lər), *adj.* **1.** without symmetry, even shape, formal arrangement, etc.: *an irregular pattern.* **2.** not characterized by any fixed principle, method, continuity, or rate: *irregular intervals.* **3.** not conforming to established rules, customs, etiquette, morality, etc.: *highly irregular behavior.* **4.** not according to rule, or to the accepted principle, method, course, order, etc. **5.** *Gram.* not conforming to the prevalent pattern or patterns of formation, inflection, construction, etc., of a language; having a rule descriptive of a very small number of items: *The English verbs "keep" and "see" are irregular in their inflections.* **6.** *Mil.* (formerly, of troops) not belonging to an organized group of the established forces. **7.** flawed, damaged, or failing to meet a specific standard of manufacture: *a sale of irregular shirts.* **8.** *Bot.* **a.** not uniform. **b.** (of a flower) having the members of some or all of its floral circles or whorls differing from one another in size or shape, or extent of union. **9.** deviating or experiencing deviations from a normally regular or cyclic body function, as bowel habits or menstruation. **10.** (of a stock or commodity market) of mixed market activity; showing no clear up or down trend. **—***n.* **11.** a person or thing that is irregular. **12.** *Com.* a product or material that does not meet specifications or standards of the manufacturer, as one having imperfections in its pattern. **13.** *Mil.* a soldier or combatant not of a regular military force, as a guerrilla or partisan. [1350–1400; < LL *irrēgulāris* (see IR-[2], REGULAR); r. ME *irreguler* < MF] **—ir•reg′u•lar•ly,** *adv.*
—Syn. 1. unsymmetrical, uneven. **2.** unmethodical, unsystematic; disorderly, capricious, erratic, eccentric, lawless. **4.** anomalous, unusual. IRREGULAR, ABNORMAL, EXCEPTIONAL imply a deviation from the regular, the normal, the ordinary, or the usual. IRREGULAR, not according to rule, refers to any deviation, as in form, arrangement, action, and the like; it may imply such deviation as a mere fact, or as regrettable, or even censurable. ABNORMAL means a deviation from the common rule, often implying that this results in an aberrant or regrettably strange form or nature of a thing: *abnormal lack of emotion; A two-headed calf is abnormal.* Ex-

CEPTIONAL means out of the ordinary or unusual; it may refer merely to the rarity of occurrence, or to the superiority of quality: *an exceptional case; an exceptional mind.* Because of the stigma of ABNORMAL, EXCEPTIONAL is today frequently substituted for it in contexts where such a euphemism may be thought to be appropriate: *a school for exceptional children* (children who are abnormal in behavior, mental capacity, or the like).

irreg′ular gal′axy, *Astron.* a galaxy with no specific form and a relatively low mass. [1960–65]

ir•reg•u•lar•i•ty (i reg′yə lar′i tē), *n., pl.* **-ties** for 2, 3. **1.** the quality or state of being irregular. **2.** something irregular. **3.** a breach of rules, customs, etiquette, morality, etc. **4.** occasional mild constipation. [1275–1325; ME *irregularite* < OF < ML *irrēgulāritās.* See IR-², REGULARITY]

irreg′ular var′iable, *Astron.* a variable star whose brightness variation is irregular. Also called **irreg′ular var′iable star′.** [1900–05]

ir•rel•a•tive (i rel′ə tiv), *adj.* **1.** not relative; without relation (usually fol. by *to*). **2.** not pertinent; irrelevant. [1630–40; IR-² + RELATIVE] —**ir•rel′a•tive•ly,** *adv.* —**ir•rel′a•tive•ness,** *n.*

ir•rel•e•vance (i rel′ə vəns), *n.* **1.** the quality or condition of being irrelevant. **2.** an irrelevant thing, act, etc. [1840–50; IR-² + RELEVANCE]

ir•rel•e•van•cy (i rel′ə vən sē), *n., pl.* **-cies.** irrelevance. [1795–1805; IR-² + RELEVANCY]

ir•rel•e•vant (i rel′ə vənt), *adj.* **1.** not relevant; not applicable or pertinent: *His lectures often stray to interesting but irrelevant subjects.* **2.** *Law.* (of evidence) having no probative value upon any issue in the case. [1780–90; IR-² + RELEVANT] —**ir•rel′e•vant•ly,** *adv.*
—**Pronunciation.** The pronunciation of IRRELEVANT (i rel′ə vənt) as (i rev′ə lənt), as if spelled *irrevelant,* is the result of metathesis, the transposition of two sounds, in this case, the (l) and the (v). RELEVANT, the base word, is occasionally subject to the same process. Analogy with words like *prevalent* and *equivalent* may play a role. A similar reordering of the (l) and (v) consonant sounds, although not a strict one-to-one metathesis, can be heard for CALVARY (kal′və rē) when pronounced (kav′əl rē). Here the transposition is reinforced by the existence of the familiar word *cavalry.*

ir•re•liev•a•ble (ir′i lē′və bəl), *adj.* not relievable; incapable of being relieved. [1660–70; IR-² + RELIEVABLE]

ir•re•li•gion (ir′i lij′ən), *n.* **1.** lack of religion. **2.** hostility or indifference to religion; impiety. [1585–95; < L *irreligiōn-* (s. of *irreligiō*). See IR-², RELIGION] —**ir′re•li′gion•ist,** *n.*

ir•re•li•gious (ir′i lij′əs), *adj.* **1.** not religious; not practicing a religion and feeling no religious impulses or emotions. **2.** showing or characterized by a lack of religion. **3.** showing indifference or hostility to religion: *irreligious statements.* [1555–65; < L *irreligiōsus.* See IR-², RELIGIOUS] —**ir′re•li′gious•ly,** *adv.* —**ir′re•li′gious•ness, ir•re•lig•i•os•i•ty** (ir′i lij′ē os′i tē), *n.*
—**Syn. 3.** profane, sacrilegious, ungodly.

ir•rem•e•a•ble (i rem′ē ə bəl, i rē′mē-), *adj. Literary.* permitting no return to the original place or condition; irreversible. [1560–70; < L *irremeābilis,* equiv. to *ir-* IR-² + *remeā(re)* to come back (*re-* RE- + *meāre* to go; cf. PERMEATE) + *-bilis* -BLE] —**ir•rem′e•a•bly,** *adv.*

ir•re•me•di•a•ble (ir′i mē′dē ə bəl), *adj.* not admitting of remedy, cure, or repair: *irremediable conduct.* [1540–50; < L *irremediābilis.* See IR-², REMEDIABLE] —**ir′re•me′di•a•ble•ness,** *n.* —**ir′re•me′di•a•bly,** *adv.*

ir•re•mis•si•ble (ir′i mis′ə bəl), *adj.* **1.** not remissible; unpardonable, as a sin. **2.** unable to be remitted or postponed, as a duty. [1375–1425; late ME < LL *irremissibilis.* See IR-², REMISSIBLE] —**ir′re•mis′si•bil′i•ty, ir′re•mis′si•ble•ness,** *n.* —**ir′re•mis′si•bly,** *adv.*

ir•re•mov•a•ble (ir′i mo͞o′və bəl), *adj.* not removable. [1590–1600; IR-² + REMOVABLE] —**ir′re•mov′a•bil′i•ty, ir′re•mov′a•ble•ness,** *n.* —**ir′re•mov′a•bly,** *adv.*

ir•rep•a•ra•ble (i rep′ər ə bəl), *adj.* not reparable; incapable of being rectified, remedied, or made good: *an irreparable mistake.* [1375–1425; late ME < L *irreparābilis.* See IR-², REPARABLE] —**ir•rep′a•ra•bil′i•ty, ir•rep′a•ra•ble•ness,** *n.* —**ir•rep′a•ra•bly,** *adv.*

ir•re•peal•a•ble (ir′i pē′lə bəl), *adj.* incapable of being repealed or revoked. [1625–35; IR-² + REPEALABLE] —**ir′re•peal′a•bil′i•ty, ir′re•peal′a•ble•ness,** *n.* —**ir′re•peal′a•bly,** *adv.*

ir•re•place•a•ble (ir′i plā′sə bəl), *adj.* incapable of being replaced; unique: *an irreplaceable vase.* [1800–10; IR-² + REPLACEABLE] —**ir′re•place′a•bly,** *adv.*

ir•re•plev•i•sa•ble (ir′i plev′ə sə bəl), *adj. Law.* not replevisable; not capable of being replevied. Also, **ir•re•plev•i•a•ble** (ir′i plev′ē ə bəl). [1615–25; IR-² + REPLEVISABLE]

ir•re•press•i•ble (ir′i pres′ə bəl), *adj.* incapable of being repressed or restrained; uncontrollable: *irrepressible laughter.* [1805–15; IR-² + REPRESSIBLE] —**ir′re•press′i•bil′i•ty, ir′re•press′i•ble•ness,** *n.* —**ir′re•press′i•bly,** *adv.*

ir•re•proach•a•ble (ir′i prō′chə bəl), *adj.* not reproachable; free from blame. [1625–35; IR-² + REPROACHABLE] —**ir′re•proach′a•ble•ness, ir′re•proach′a•bil′i•ty,** *n.* —**ir′re•proach′a•bly,** *adv.*
—**Syn.** blameless, impeccable, unflawed.

ir•re•pro•duc•i•ble (i rē′prə do͞o′sə bəl, -dyo͞o′-), *adj.* not reproducible. [1865–70; IR-² + REPRODUCIBLE] —**ir•re′pro•duc′i•bil′i•ty,** *n.*

ir•re•sist•i•ble (ir′i zis′tə bəl), *adj.* **1.** not resistible; incapable of being resisted or withstood: *an irresistible impulse.* **2.** lovable, esp. calling forth feelings of protective love: *an irresistible puppy.* **3.** enticing; tempting to possess: *an irresistible necklace.* —*n.* **4.** an irresistible person or thing. [1590–1600; < ML *irresistibilis.* See IR-², RESISTIBLE] —**ir′re•sist′i•bil′i•ty, ir′re•sist′i•ble•ness,** *n.* —**ir′re•sist′i•bly,** *adv.*

ir•re•sol•u•ble (ir′i zol′yə bəl, i rez′əl-), *adj.* **1.** incapable of being solved or clarified. **2.** *Archaic.* **a.** incapable of being resolved into component parts; insoluble. **b.** incapable of being relieved. [1640–50; < L *irresolūbilis.* See IR-², RESOLUBLE] —**ir′re•sol′u•bil′i•ty,** *n.*

ir•res•o•lute (i rez′ə lo͞ot′), *adj.* not resolute; doubtful; infirm of purpose; vacillating. [1565–75; IR-² + RESOLUTE] —**ir•res′o•lute′ly,** *adv.* —**ir•res′o•lute′ness,** *n.*

ir•res•o•lu•tion (i rez′ə lo͞o′shən), *n.* lack of resolution; lack of decision or purpose; vacillation. [1585–95; IRRESOLUTE + -ION]

ir•re•solv•a•ble (ir′i zol′və bəl), *adj.* not resolvable; incapable of being resolved, analyzable, or solvable. [1650–60; IR-² + RESOLVABLE] —**ir′re•solv′a•bil′i•ty, ir′re•solv′a•ble•ness,** *n.*

ir•re•spec•tive (ir′i spek′tiv), *adj.* without regard to something else, esp. something specified; ignoring or discounting (usually fol. by *of*): *Irrespective of my wishes, I should go.* [1630–40; IR-² + RESPECTIVE] —**ir′re•spec′tive•ly,** *adv.*

ir•res•pi•ra•ble (i res′pər ə bəl, ir′i spīᵊr′ə bəl), *adj.* not respirable; unfit for breathing. [1815–25; < LL *irrespīrābilis.* See IR-², RESPIRABLE]

ir•re•spon•si•ble (ir′i spon′sə bəl), *adj.* **1.** said, done, or characterized by a lack of a sense of responsibility: *His refusal to work shows him to be completely irresponsible.* **2.** not capable of or qualified for responsibility, as due to age, circumstances, or a mental deficiency. **3.** not responsible, answerable, or accountable to higher authority: *irresponsible as a monarch.* —*n.* **4.** an irresponsible person. [1640–50; IR-² + RESPONSIBLE] —**ir′re•spon′si•bil′i•ty, ir′re•spon′si•ble•ness,** *n.* —**ir′re•spon′si•bly,** *adv.*
—**Syn. 1.** unreliable, undependable, thoughtless.

ir•re•spon•sive (ir′i spon′siv), *adj.* not responsive; not responding, or not responding readily, as in speech, action, or feeling. [1840–50; IR-² + RESPONSIVE] —**ir′re•spon′sive•ness,** *n.*

ir•re•ten•tive (ir′i ten′tiv), *adj.* not retentive; lacking power to retain, esp. mentally. [1740–50; IR-² + RETENTIVE] —**ir′re•ten′tive•ness, ir′re•ten′tion,** *n.*

ir•re•trace•a•ble (ir′i trā′sə bəl), *adj.* not retraceable; unable to be retraced. [1840–50; IR-² + RETRACEABLE] —**ir′re•trace′a•bly,** *adv.*

ir•re•triev•a•ble (ir′i trē′və bəl), *adj.* not retrievable; irrecoverable; irreparable. [1695–1705; IR-² + RETRIEVABLE] —**ir′re•triev′a•bil′i•ty, ir′re•triev′a•ble•ness,** *n.* —**ir′re•triev′a•bly,** *adv.*

ir•rev•er•ence (i rev′ər əns), *n.* **1.** the quality of being irreverent; lack of reverence or respect. **2.** an irreverent act or statement. **3.** the condition of not being reverenced, venerated, respected, etc. [1300–50; ME < L *irreverentia.* See IR-², REVERENCE]

ir•rev•er•ent (i rev′ər ənt), *adj.* not reverent; manifesting or characterized by irreverence; deficient in veneration or respect: *an irreverent reply.* [1485–95; < L *irreverent-* (s. of *irreverēns*) disrespectful. See IR-², REVERENT] —**ir•rev′er•ent•ly,** *adv.*
—**Syn.** irreligious, impious, profane.

ir•re•vers•i•ble (ir′i vûr′sə bəl), *adj.* not reversible; incapable of being changed: *His refusal is irreversible.* [1620–30; IR-² + REVERSIBLE] —**ir′re•vers′i•bil′i•ty, ir′re•vers′i•ble•ness,** *n.* —**ir′re•vers′i•bly,** *adv.*

ir•rev•o•ca•ble (i rev′ə kə bəl), *adj.* not to be revoked or recalled; unable to be repealed or annulled; unalterable: *an irrevocable decree.* [1350–1400; ME < L *irrevocābilis.* See IR-², REVOCABLE] —**ir•rev′o•ca•bil′i•ty, ir•rev′o•ca•ble•ness,** *n.* —**ir•rev′o•ca•bly,** *adv.*

ir•ri•ga•ble (ir′i gə bəl), *adj.* capable of being irrigated. [1835–45; IRRIG(ATE) + -ABLE] —**ir′ri•ga•bly,** *adv.*

ir•ri•gate (ir′i gāt′), *v.t.,* **-gat•ed, -gat•ing. 1.** to supply (land) with water by artificial means, as by diverting streams, flooding, or spraying. **2.** *Med.* to supply or wash (an orifice, wound, etc.) with a spray or a flow of some liquid. **3.** to moisten; wet. [1605–15; < L *irrigātus,* ptp. of *irrigāre* to wet, flood, nourish with water, equiv. to *ir-* IR-¹ + *rigā-* (s. of *rigāre* to provide with water, soak) + *-tus* ptp. suffix] —**ir′ri•ga′tor,** *n.*

ir•ri•ga•tion (ir′i gā′shən), *n.* **1.** the artificial application of water to land to assist in the production of crops. **2.** *Med.* the flushing or washing out of anything with water or other liquid. **3.** the state of being irrigated. [1605–15; < L *irrigātiōn-* (s. of *irrigātiō*). See IRRIGATE, -ION] —**ir′ri•ga′tion•al,** *adj.*

ir•ri•ga•tive (ir′i gā′tiv), *adj.* serving for or pertaining to irrigation. [1860–65; IRRIGATE + -IVE]

ir•rig•u•ous (i rig′yo͞o əs), *adj. Archaic.* well-watered, as land. [1645–55; < L *irriguus,* equiv. to *irrig(āre)* to wet (see IRRIGATE) + *-uus* deverbal adj. suffix]

ir•ri•ta•bil•i•ty (ir′i tə bil′i tē), *n., pl.* **-ties. 1.** the quality or state of being irritable. **2.** *Physiol., Biol.* the ability to be excited to a characteristic action or function by the application of some stimulus: *Protoplasm displays irritability by responding to heat.* [1745–55; < L *irritābilitās.* See IRRITABLE, -ITY]

ir•ri•ta•ble (ir′i tə bəl), *adj.* **1.** easily irritated or annoyed; readily excited to impatience or anger. **2.** *Physiol., Biol.* displaying irritability. **3.** *Pathol.* susceptible to physical irritation. **4.** *Med.* abnormally sensitive to a stimulus. [1655–65; < L *irrītābilis,* equiv. to *irrītā(re)* to IRRITATE + *-bilis* -BLE] —**ir′ri•ta•ble•ness,** *n.* —**ir′ri•ta•bly,** *adv.*
—**Syn. 1.** snappish, petulant, resentful. IRRITABLE, TESTY, TOUCHY, IRASCIBLE are adjectives meaning easily upset, offended, or angered. IRRITABLE means easily annoyed or bothered, and it implies cross and snappish behavior: *an irritable clerk, rude and hostile; Impatient and irritable, he was constantly complaining.* TESTY describes the same kind of behavior or response, particularly to minor annoyances: *always on edge, testy and sharp in response; testy and petulant, resenting any interruption.* TOUCHY emphasizes oversensitivity and readiness to take offense, even when none is intended: *especially touchy about any reference to obesity.* IRASCIBLE means habitually angry or easily aroused to anger: *an irascible tyrant, roaring at employees for the slightest error.*

ir′ritable bow′el syn′drome, *Pathol.* any combination of common disturbances of the bowel, as diarrhea or constipation, occurring with abdominal pain, sometimes accompanied by psychological stress. *Abbr.:* IBS Also called **ir′ritable co′lon, spastic colon.**

ir′ritable heart′, *Pathol.* See **cardiac neurosis.** [1860–65]

ir•ri•tant (ir′i tnt), *adj.* **1.** tending to cause irritation; irritating. —*n.* **2.** anything that irritates. **3.** *Physiol., Pathol.* a biological, chemical, or physical agent that stimulates a characteristic function or elicits a response, esp. an inflammatory response. [1630–40; < L *irritant-* (s. of *irritāns*), prp. of *irritāre* to IRRITATE; see -ANT] —**ir′ri•tan•cy,** *n.*

ir•ri•tate (ir′i tāt′), *v.,* **-tat•ed, -tat•ing.** —*v.t.* **1.** to excite to impatience or anger; annoy. **2.** *Physiol., Biol.* to excite (a living system) to some characteristic action or function. **3.** *Pathol.* to bring (a body part) to an abnormally excited or sensitive condition. —*v.i.* **4.** to cause irritation or become irritated. [1525–35; < L *irritātus,* ptp. of *irritāre* to arouse to anger, excite, aggravate, equiv. to *irritā-* v. stem + *-tus* ptp. suffix] —**ir′ri•ta′tor,** *n.*
—**Syn. 1.** vex, chafe, fret, gall; nettle, ruffle, pique; incense, enrage, infuriate, inflame. IRRITATE, EXASPERATE, PROVOKE mean to annoy or stir to anger. To IRRITATE is to excite to impatience or angry feeling, often of no great depth or duration: *to irritate by refusing to explain an action.* To EXASPERATE is to irritate to a point where self-control is threatened or lost: *to exasperate by continual delays and excuses.* To PROVOKE is to stir to a sudden, strong feeling of resentful anger as by unwarrantable acts or wanton annoyance: *to tease and provoke an animal until it attacks.*

ir•ri•tat•ed (ir′i tā′tid), *adj.* **1.** angered, provoked, or annoyed. **2.** inflamed or made raw, as a part of the body. [1585–95; IRRITATE + -ED²] —**ir′ri•tat′ed•ly,** *adv.*

ir•ri•tat•ing (ir′i tā′ting), *adj.* causing irritation; annoying; provoking: *irritating questions.* [1700–10; IRRITATE + -ING²] —**ir′ri•tat′ing•ly,** *adv.*

ir•ri•ta•tion (ir′i tā′shən), *n.* **1.** the act of irritating or the state of being irritated. **2.** something that irritates. **3.** *Physiol., Pathol.* **a.** the bringing of a bodily part or organ to an abnormally excited or sensitive condition. **b.** the condition itself. [1580–90; < L *irritātiōn-* (s. of *irritātiō*). See IRRITATE, -ION]

ir•ri•ta•tive (ir′i tā′tiv), *adj.* **1.** serving or tending to irritate. **2.** *Pathol.* characterized or produced by irritation of some body part: *an irritative fever.* [1680–90; IRRITATE + -IVE] —**ir′ri•ta′tive•ness,** *n.*

ir•ro•rate (ir′ə rāt′, i rôr′it, i rōr′-), *adj. Zool.* marked with small spots of color; speckled. Also, **ir′ro•rat′ed.** [< L *irrōratus,* ptp. of *irrōrāre* to bedew, equiv. to *ir-* IR-¹ + *rōrā-* (*rōr-,* s. of *rōs* dew + *-ā-* theme vowel) + *-tus* ptp. suffix] —**ir′ro•ra′tion,** *n.*

ir•ro•ta•tion•al (ir′ō tā′shə nl), *adj.* **1.** not having rotation. **2.** *Math.* conservative (def. 7). [1870–75; IR-² + ROTATIONAL] —**ir′ro•ta′tion•al•ly,** *adv.*

ir•rupt (i rupt′), *v.i.* **1.** to break or burst in suddenly. **2.** to manifest violent activity or emotion, as a group of persons. **3.** (of animals) to increase suddenly in numbers through a lessening of the number of deaths. [1850–55; < L *irruptus;* see IRRUPTION]

ir•rup•tion (i rup′shən), *n.* **1.** a breaking or bursting in; a violent incursion or invasion. **2.** *Ecol.* a sudden increase in an animal population. [1570–80; < L *irruptiōn-* (s. of *irruptiō*), equiv. to *irrupt(us),* ptp. of *irrumpere* to burst into (see IR-¹, RUPTURE) + *-iōn-* -ION]

ir•rup•tive (i rup′tiv), *adj.* **1.** of, pertaining to, or characterized by irruption. **2.** irrupting or tending to irrupt. **3.** *Petrol.* intrusive. [1585–95; IRRUPT + -IVE] —**ir•rup′tive•ly,** *adv.*

IRS, Internal Revenue Service.

Ir•tysh (ir tish′), *n.* a river in central Asia, flowing NW from the Altai Mountains in China through NE Kazakhstan and the Russian Federation to the Ob River. ab. 1840 mi. (2960 km) long. Also, **Ir•tish′.**

Ir•vine (ûr′vīn *for 1;* ûr′vin *for 2*), *n.* **1.** a city in SW California. 62,134. **2.** Also, **Ir′vin.** a male given name.

Ir•ving (ûr′ving), *n.* **1. Sir Henry** (*John Henry Brodribb*), 1838–1905, English actor. **2. Washington,** 1783–1859, U.S. essayist, story writer, and historian. **3.** a city in NE Texas, near Dallas. 109,943. **4.** a male given name.

Ir•ving•ite (ûr′ving īt′), *n.* a member of the Catholic Apostolic Church.

Ir•ving•ton (ûr′ving tən), *n.* a town in NE New Jersey, near Newark. 61,493.

Ir•win (ûr′win), *n.* **1. Wallace,** 1875–1959, U.S. journalist and humorist. **2.** his brother **William Henry** (*"Will"*), 1873–1948, U.S. novelist, short-story writer, and journalist. **3.** a male given name.

is (iz), *v.* **1.** 3rd pers. sing. pres. indic. of **be. 2. as is.** See **as**¹ (def. 21). [bef. 900; ME, OE; c. D *is,* ON *es, er,* G, Goth *ist,* L *est,* Gk *estí,* OCS *jestĭ,* Skt *asti*]

is-, var. of **iso-** before a vowel: *isallobar.*

Is., 1. Isaiah. **2.** island. **3.** isle.

is., 1. island. **2.** isle.

Isa., Isaiah.

I•saac (ī′zək), *n.* **1.** a son of Abraham and Sarah, and father of Jacob. Gen. 21:1–4. **2.** a male given name: from a Hebrew word meaning "laughter."

I·saacs (ī′zəks *for 1;* ē säks′ *for 2*), *n.* **1. Sir Isaac Alfred,** 1855–1948, Australian jurist: governor general of Australia 1931–36. **2. Jor·ge** (hôr′hä). 1837–95, Colombian novelist.

Is·a·bel (iz′ə bel′), *n.* a female given name. Also, **Is′a·belle′, Is·a·bel·la** (iz′ə bel′ə).

I·sa·be·la (iz′ə bel′ə; *Sp.* ē′sä ve′lä), *n.* **1.** a city in NW Puerto Rico. 12,087. **2.** former name of **Basilan** (def. 2).

Is·a·bel·la (iz′ə bel′ə), *n.* (*Isabella, or the Pot of Basil*), a narrative poem (1820) by John Keats.

Isabella I, (*"the Catholic"*), 1451–1504, wife of Ferdinand V: queen of Castile 1474–1504; joint ruler of Aragon 1479–1504.

is·ab·nor·mal (ī′sab nôr′məl), *n. Meteorol.* a line on a map or chart connecting points having an equal deviation from the normal value of some meteorological quantity, as temperature. Also, **isoabnormal.** Cf. **isanomal.** [1850–55; IS- + ABNORMAL]

is·a·cous·tic (ī′sə ko͞o′stik *or, esp. Brit.,* ī′sə kou′-), *adj.* of or pertaining to two sounds of equal intensity. [1895–1900; IS- + ACOUSTIC]

Is·a·do·ra (iz′ə dôr′ə, -dōr′ə), *n.* a female given name: derived from Isidor.

Is·a·dore (iz′ə dôr′, -dōr′), *n.* a male given name: from the Greek word meaning "gift of Isis."

is·a·go·ge (ī′sə gō′jē, ī′sə gō′jē), *n.* **1.** an introduction, esp. a scholarly introduction to a field of study or research. **2.** isagogics. [1645–55; < L *isagōga* < Gk *eisagōgḗ,* equiv. to *eiság(ein)* to introduce (*eis-* into + *ágein* to lead) + *-ōgē* verbid n. suffix]

i·sa·gog·ic (ī′sə goj′ik), *adj.* **1.** introductory, esp. to the interpretation of the Bible. —*n.* **2.** isagogics. [1820–30; < L *isagōgicus* < Gk *eisagōgikós.* See ISAGOGE, -IC] —**i′sa·gog′i·cal·ly,** *adv.*

i·sa·gog·ics (ī′sə goj′iks), *n.* (*used with a singular v.*) **1.** introductory studies. **2.** the branch of theology that is introductory to Bible study and exegesis. Also, **isagogic, isagoge.** [1860–65; see ISAGOGIC, -ICS]

I·sai (ī′zī), *n. Douay Bible.* Jesse.

I·sa·iah (ī zā′ə *or, esp. Brit.,* ī zī′ə), *n.* **1.** Also called **Isa′iah of Jeru′salem.** a Major Prophet of the 8th century B.C. **2.** a book of the Bible bearing his name. *Abbr.:* Isa. **3.** a male given name. [< Heb *yəshaʿyāhū* lit., Yahweh's salvation]

I·sa·ian (ī zā′ən *or, esp. Brit.,* ī zī′), *adj.* of, pertaining to, or characteristic of Isaiah or of the book of the Bible bearing his name. Also, **I·sa·ian·ic** (ī′zā an′ik *or, esp. Brit.,* ī′zī-). [1880–85; ISAI(AH) + -AN]

is·al·lo·bar (ī sal′ə bär′), *n. Meteorol.* a line on a weather map or chart connecting points having equal pressure changes. [1910–15; IS- + ALLO- + -BAR]

is·al·lo·therm (ī sal′ə thûrm′), *n. Meteorol.* a line on a weather map or chart connecting points having equal temperature variations within a given period of time. [IS- + ALLO- + -THERM]

is·an·drous (ī san′drəs), *adj. Bot.* having the stamens similar to each other and equal in number to the petals. [IS- + ANDROUS]

is·a·nom·al (ī′sə nom′əl), *n. Meteorol.* a line on a map or chart connecting points having an equal anomaly of a meteorological quantity. Cf. **isabnormal.** [1880–85; IS- + *-anomal,* back formation from ANOMALOUS] —**is′a·nom′a·lous,** *adj.*

is·an·thous (ī san′thəs), *adj. Bot.* having regular flowers. [1850–55; < NL *isanthus.* See IS-, -ANTHOUS]

I·sar (ē′zär), *n.* a river in central Europe, flowing NE from W Austria through S Germany to the Danube River. 215 mi. (345 km) long.

i·sa·rithm (ī′sə riṫh′əm), *n.* isopleth. [IS- + *-arithm,* as in LOGARITHM]

i·sa·tin (ī′sə tin), *n. Chem.* a yellowish-red or orange, crystalline, water-soluble solid, $C_8H_5NO_2$, used chiefly in the synthesis of vat dyes. [1835–45; < Gk *isát(is)* woad + -IN[2]]

-isation, *Chiefly Brit.* var. of **-ization.**

is·aux·e·sis (ī′sôg zē′sis, ī′sôk sē′-), *n. Biol.* growth of a part at the same rate as that of the whole organism. [IS- + AUXESIS] —**is·aux·et·ic** (ī′sôg zet′ik, ī′sôk set′-), *adj.*

is·ba (iz bä′), *n.* izba.

ISBA, International Seabed Authority.

ISBN, See **International Standard Book Number.**

Is·car·i·ot (i skar′ē ət), *n.* **1.** the surname of Judas, the betrayer of Jesus. Mark 3:19; 14:10, 11. **2.** a person who betrays another; traitor. [< L *Iscariōta* < Gk *Iskariṓtēs* < Heb *īsh-qəriyōth* man of Kerioth a village in Palestine] —**Is·car·i·ot·ic** (i skar′ē ot′ik), **Is·car′i·ot′i·cal,** *adj.* —**Is·car′i·ot·ism,** *n.*

is·che·mi·a (i skē′mē ə), *n. Pathol.* local deficiency of blood supply produced by vasoconstriction or local obstacles to the arterial flow. Also, **is·chae′mi·a.** [1855–60; < Gk *ísch(ein)* to suppress, check + -EMIA] —**is·che·mic** (i skē′mik, -skem′ik), *adj.*

Is·chia (ē′skyä), *n.* **1.** an Italian island in the Tyrrhenian Sea, W of Naples: earthquake 1883. 18 sq. mi. (47 sq. km). **2.** a seaport on this island. 14,139.

is·chi·um (is′kē əm), *n., pl.* **-chi·a** (-kē ə). *Anat.* **1.** the lower portion of either innominate bone. See diag. under **pelvis. 2.** either of the bones on which the body rests when sitting. [1640–50; < L < Gk *ischíon* hip-joint] —**is·chi·ad·ic** (is′kē ad′ik), **is·chi·at·ic** (is′kē at′ik), **is′·chi·al,** *adj.*

Is·chys (is′kis), *n. Class. Myth.* a youth who was slain after committing an act of infidelity with Coronis, the beloved of Apollo.

-ise[1], *Chiefly Brit.* var. of **-ize:** *organise.* —**Usage.** See **-ize.**

-ise[2], a noun suffix, occurring in loanwords from French, indicating quality, condition, or function: *franchise; merchandise.* Cf. **-ice.** [ME < OF *-ise,* var. of -ICE]

I′sen·heim Al′tarpiece (ē′zən hīm′), an altarpiece (1510?–15?) painted by Matthias Grünewald.

I·sen·land (ē′sən land′, -lənd, ē′zän-; *Ger.* ē′zən-länt′), *n.* (in the *Nibelungenlied*) the country of Brunhild, usually identified with Iceland.

I·sen·stein (ē′sən stīn′, ē′zən-; *Ger.* ē′zən shtīn′), *n.* (in the *Nibelungenlied*) the home of Brunhild in Isenland. Cf. **Hindfell.**

is·en·thal·pic (ī′sən thal′pik, ī′zən-), *adj. Thermodynam.* pertaining to or characterized by constant enthalpy. [1920–25; IS- + ENTHALPIC]

is·en·trope (ī′sən trōp′, ī′zən-), *n. Thermodynam.* a line on a map or chart joining points having equal entropy. [back formation from ISENTROPIC]

is·en·trop·ic (ī′sən trop′ik, -trō′pik, ī′zən-), *adj. Thermodynam.* **1.** having a constant entropy. **2.** of or pertaining to an isentrope. [1870–75; IS- + ENTROPIC]

I·sère (ē zâr′), *n.* **1.** a river in SE France, flowing from the Alps to the Rhone River. 150 mi. (240 km) long. **2.** a department in SE France. 860,378; 3180 sq. mi. (8235 sq. km). *Cap.:* Grenoble.

I·seult (i so͞olt′), *n.* **1.** Also, **Yseult.** German, **Isolde.** *Arthurian Romance.* **a.** the daughter of a king of Ireland who became the wife of King Mark of Cornwall: she was the beloved of Tristram. **b.** daughter of the king of Brittany, and wife of Tristram. **2.** a female given name.

Is·fa·han (is′fə hän′), *n.* a city in central Iran: the capital of Persia from the 16th into the 18th century. 424,045. Also, **Ispahan.**

-ish[1], **1.** a suffix used to form adjectives from nouns, with the sense of "belonging to" (*British; Danish; English; Spanish*); "after the manner of," "having the characteristics of," "like" (*babyish; girlish; mulish*); "addicted to," "inclined or tending to" (*bookish; freakish*); "near or about" (*fiftyish; sevenish*). **2.** a suffix used to form adjectives from other adjectives, with the sense of "somewhat," "rather" (*oldish; reddish; sweetish*). [ME; OE *-isc;* c. G *-isch,* Goth *-isks,* Gk *-iskos;* akin to -ESQUE]

-ish[2], a suffix occurring in *i*-stem verbs borrowed from French: *ravish.* [< F *-iss-,* extended s. of verbs with infinitives in *-ir* << L *-isc-,* in inceptive verbs]

Ish-bo·sheth (ish bō′shith), *n.* a son and successor of Saul. II Sam. 2–4.

Ish·er·wood (ish′ər wo͝od′), *n.* **Christopher (William Brad·shaw)** (brad′shô), 1904–86, English poet, novelist, and playwright; in the U.S. since 1938.

Ish′erwood fram′ing, *Naval Archit.* a system for framing steel vessels in which light, closely spaced, longitudinal frames are connected by heavy, widely spaced transverse frames with deep webs. Also called **Ish′·erwood sys′tem, longitudinal framing.** [named after B. F. *Isherwood* (1822–1915), American engineer]

Ish·i·ha′ra test′ (ish′ē här′ə), *Ophthalm.* a test for determining color blindness by means of a series of cards each having colored dots that form one pattern to the normal eye and a different pattern to the eye that is color-blind. Also, **Ishiha′ra's test′.** [1920–25; named after S. *Ishihara* (1879–1963), Japanese eye specialist, who devised it]

Ish·ma·el (ish′mē əl, -mā-), *n.* **1.** the son of Abraham and Hagar: both he and Hagar were cast out of Abraham's family by Sarah. Gen. 16:11, 12. **2.** any outcast. **3.** an Arab. [< Heb *Yishmāʿēl* lit., God will hear]

Ish·ma·el·ite (ish′mē ə līt′, -mā ə-, -mə-), *n.* **1.** a descendant of Ishmael, the traditional ancestor of the Arab peoples. **2.** a wanderer or outcast. [1570–80; ISHMAEL + -ITE[1]] —**Ish′ma·el·it′ish,** *adj.*

Ish·tar (ish′tär), *n.* the Assyrian and Babylonian goddess of love and war, identified with the Phoenician Astarte, the Semitic Ashtoreth, and the Sumerian Inanna. Also called **Mylitta.**

Ish′tar Ter′ra (ter′ə), *Astron.* a plateau region in the northern hemisphere of Venus.

I·shum (ē′shəm), *n.* the Akkadian god of fire and the companion of Irra.

Ish·va·ra (ēsh′wər ə), *n. Hinduism.* a personal and supreme god, supposed in dvaita Vedantism to be included with the world and Atman within Brahman.

Is·i·ac (is′ē ak′, iz′-, ī′sē-), *adj.* of or pertaining to Isis or the worship of Isis. Also, **I·si·a·cal** (i sī′ə kəl, ī sī′-). [1700–10; < L *Īsiacus* < Gk *Isiakós.* See ISIS, -AC]

i·sid·i·oid (ī sid′ē oid′), *adj.* of, pertaining to, or resembling an isidium. [1920–25; ISIDI(UM) + -OID]

i·sid·i·um (ī sid′ē əm), *n., pl.* **i·sid·i·a** (ī sid′ē ə). *Bot.* a coralloid outgrowth from the thallus in certain lichens. [1865–70; < NL, deriv. of *Isid-* (s. of *Isis*) ISIS (from the hornlike appearance of the growth); see -IUM]

Is·i·dor (iz′i dôr′, -dōr′), *n.* a male given name. Also, **Is′i·dore′.**

Is·i·do·ra (iz′i dôr′ə, -dōr′ə), *n.* a female given name.

Is′idore of Seville′, Saint (*Isidorus Hispalensis*), A.D. c570–636, Spanish archbishop, historian, and encyclopedist. —**Is′i·do′ri·an, Is′i·do′re·an,** *adj.*

Is·in (is′in), *n.* an ancient Sumerian city in S Iraq: archaeological site.

i·sin·glass (ī′zən glas′, -gläs′, ī′zing-), *n.* **1.** a pure, transparent or translucent form of gelatin, obtained from the air bladders of certain fish, esp. the sturgeon: used in glue and jellies and as a clarifying agent. **2.** mica, esp. in thin, translucent sheets. [1535–45; < MD *huysenblase* (with GLASS for *blase* by folk etym.), lit., sturgeon bladder; c. G *Hausenblase*]

I·sis (ī′sis), *n. Egyptian Relig.* a goddess of fertility, the sister and wife of Osiris and mother of Horus, and usually represented as a woman with a cow's horns with the solar disk between them: later worshiped in the Greek and Roman empires. [< L < Gk *Îsis* < Egyptian *'st*]

Isis

Is·kan·der Bey (is kan′dər bā′), Scanderbeg.

Is·ken·de·run (is ken′də ro͞on′), *n.* **1.** Formerly, **Alexandretta.** a seaport in S Turkey, on the Gulf of Iskenderun. 79,291. **2. Gulf of,** an inlet of the Mediterranean, off the S coast of Turkey. 45 mi. (72 km) long; 28 mi. (45 km) wide.

isl., **1.** island. **2.** isle. Also, **Isl.**

Is·la de Pas·cua (ēz′lä ṫhe päs′kwä), Spanish name of **Easter Island.**

Is·lam (is läm′, iz-, is′ləm, iz′-), *n.* **1.** the religious faith of Muslims, based on the words and religious system founded by the prophet Muhammad and taught by the Koran, the basic principle of which is absolute submission to a unique and personal god, Allah. **2.** the whole body of Muslim believers, their civilization, and the countries in which theirs is the dominant religion. Also called **Muhammadanism.** [1605–15; < Ar *islām* lit., submission (to God)] —**Is·lam·ic** (is lam′ik, -läm′ik, iz-), **Is·lam·it·ic** (is′lə mit′ik, iz′-), *adj.*

Is·lam·a·bad (is lä′mə bäd′, -bad′, -lam′ə bad′), *n.* the capital of Pakistan, in the N part, near Rawalpindi. 77,318.

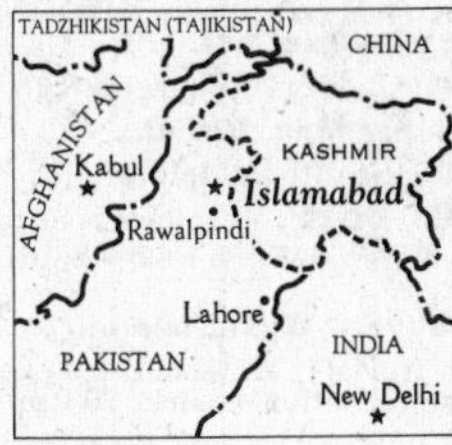

Islam′ic cal′endar, a calendar of 12 lunar months, each beginning with the new moon. See **Muslim Calendar.**

Islam′ic Repub′lic of Maurita′nia, official name of **Mauritania.**

Is·lam·ism (is lä′miz əm, iz-, is′lə miz′-, iz′-), *n.* the religion or culture of Islam. [1740–50; ISLAM + -ISM]

Is·lam·ite (is lä′mīt, iz-, is′lə mīt′, iz′-), *n.* a Muslim. [1790–1800; ISLAM + -ITE[1]]

Is·lam·ize (is′lə mīz′, iz′-, is lä′mīz, iz-), *v.t.,* **-ized, -iz·ing. 1.** to convert to Islam. **2.** to bring into a state of harmony or conformity with the principles and teachings of Islam; give an Islamic character or identity to. Also, *esp. Brit.,* **Is′lam·ise′.** [1840–50; ISLAM + -IZE] —**Is′lam·i·za′tion,** *n.* —**Is′lam·iz′er,** *n.*

is·land (ī′lənd), *n.* **1.** a tract of land completely surrounded by water, and not large enough to be called a continent. See table on next page. **2.** something resembling an island, esp. in being isolated or having little or no direct communication with others. **3.** a raised platform with a counter or other work surface on top situated in the middle area of a room, esp. a kitchen, so as to permit access from all sides. **4.** See **safety island. 5.** a low concrete platform for gasoline pumps at an automotive service station. **6.** a clump of woodland in a prairie. **7.** an isolated hill. **8.** *Anat.* an isolated portion of tissue differing in structure from the surrounding tissue. **9.** *Railroads.* a platform or building between sets of tracks. —*v.t.* **10.** to make into an island. **11.** to dot with islands. **12.** to place on an island; isolate. [bef. 900; ME *iland,* OE *igland, iland,* var. of *iegland,* equiv. to *ieg* island (c. ON *ey*) + *land* LAND; sp. with *-s-* by assoc. with ISLE] —**is′land·ish, is′land·like′,** *adj.* —**is′land·less,** *adj.*

is′land arc′, a curved chain of islands, as the Aleutians or Antilles, usually convex toward the ocean and enclosing a deep-sea basin. [1905–10]

is·land·er (ī′lən dər), *n.* a native or inhabitant of an island. [1540–50; ISLAND + -ER[1]]

is·land-hop (ī′lənd hop′), *v.i.,* **-hopped, -hop·ping.** to travel from island to island, esp. to visit a series of islands in the same chain or area. [1940–45]

is′land of Reil′ (rīl), *Anat.* insula. [named after J. C. *Reil* (d. 1813), German physician]

CONCISE PRONUNCIATION KEY: act, cāpe, dâre, pärt; set, ēqual; if, ice; ox, ōver, ôrder, oil, bo͝ok, bo͞ot, out; up, ûrge; child; sing; shoe; thin, ṫhat; zh as in *treasure.* ə = *a* as in *alone, e* as in *system, i* as in *easily, o* as in *gallop, u* as in *circus;* ᵊ as in *fire* (fīᵊr), *hour* (ouᵊr). l and n can serve as syllabic consonants, as in *cradle* (krād′l), and *button* (but′n). See the full key inside the front cover.

LARGEST ISLANDS OF THE WORLD

Name	Location (Sovereignty)	Area sq. mi.	Area sq. km	Leading City
Greenland	N Atlantic (Danish)	840,000	2,175,000	Godthaab
New Guinea	SW Pacific (Papua New Guinean and Indonesian)	316,000	818,000	Port Moresby; Jayapura
Borneo	SW Pacific (Indonesian, Malaysian, and Bruneian)	290,000	750,000	Banjermasin; Kuching; Bandar Seri Begawan
Madagascar	W Indian Ocean (Malagasy)	227,800	590,000	Antananarivo
Baffin Island	Canadian Arctic (Canadian)	190,000	492,000	Frobisher Bay
Sumatra	E Indian Ocean (Indonesian)	164,147	425,141	Medan
Honshu	NW Pacific (Japanese)	88,851	230,124	Tokyo
Great Britain	NE Atlantic (British)	88,139	228,280	London
Victoria Island	Canadian Arctic (Canadian)	80,340	208,081	—
Ellesmere Island	Canadian Arctic (Canadian)	76,600	198,400	—
Sulawesi	SW Pacific (Indonesian)	72,986	189,034	Ujung Pandang
South Island	SW Pacific (New Zealand)	58,093	150,460	Christchurch
Java	E Indian Ocean (Indonesian)	51,032	132,173	Jakarta
North Island	SW Pacific (New Zealand)	44,281	114,690	Wellington
Cuba	Caribbean (Cuban)	44,218	114,525	Havana
Newfoundland	NW Atlantic (Canadian)	42,734	110,680	St. John's
Luzon	W mid-Pacific (Philippine)	40,420	104,688	Manila
Iceland	N Atlantic (Iceland)	39,698	102,820	Reykjavik
Mindanao	W mid-Pacific (Philippine)	36,537	94,631	Davao
Novaya Zemlya	Russian Arctic (Russian)	35,000	90,650	—

Is′land of the Sun′, *Class. Myth.* Sicily: the island where Helius kept his oxen.

Is′lands of the Blessed′, *Class. Myth.* islands in the ocean at the remotest western end of the world, to which the souls of heroes and worthy persons were said to be transported after death. Also called **Hesperides.**

is′land u′niverse, an external galaxy. [1865–70]

Is•las de la Ba•hí•a (ēz′läz the lä vä ē′ä), Spanish name of **Bay Islands.**

Is•las Mal•vi•nas (ēz′läz mäl vē′näs). See **Falkland Islands.**

isle (īl), *n., v.,* **isled, isl•ing.** —*n.* **1.** a small island. **2.** any island. —*v.t.* **3.** to make into or as if into an isle. **4.** to place on or as if on an isle. [1250–1300; ME *i(s)le* < OF < L *insula*] —**isle′less,** *adj.*

Isle′ of Ca′pri, *Literary.* Capri (def. 1).

Isle′ of Man′. See **Man, Isle of.**

Isle′ of Pines′. See **Pines, Isle of.**

Isle′ of Shoals′ boat′, a sailing boat formerly used in Ipswich Bay, Massachusetts, rigged with two spritsails or gaff sails.

Isle′ of Wight′. See **Wight, Isle of.**

Isle′ Roy′ale (roi′əl), an island in Lake Superior: a part of Michigan; a national park. 208 sq. mi. (540′ sq. km).

is•let (ī′lit), *n.* **1.** a very small island. —*adj.* **2.** *Anat.* situated in or pertaining to the islet of Langerhans: *islet cells.* [1530–40; < MF *islette.* See ISLE, -ET] —**is′let•ed,** *adj.*

is′let cell′ adeno′ma, insulinoma.

is′let of Lang′er•hans (läng′ər häns′, -hänz′, läng′gər-), *Anat.* any of several masses of endocrine cells in the pancreas that secrete insulin, somatostatin, and glucagon. Also called **is′land of Lang′erhans.** [named after Paul *Langerhans* (1847–88), German anatomist, who described them in 1869]

Is•ling•ton (iz′ling tən), *n.* a borough of N London, England. 174,000.

I•slip (ī′slip), *n.* a town on the S shore of Long Island, in SE New York. 13,438.

isls., islands.

ism (iz′əm), *n.* a distinctive doctrine, theory, system, or practice: *This is the age of isms.* [extracted from words with the suffix -ISM]

-ism, a suffix appearing in loanwords from Greek, where it was used to form action nouns from verbs (*baptism*); on this model, used as a productive suffix in the formation of nouns denoting action or practice, state or condition, principles, doctrines, a usage or characteristic, devotion or adherence, etc. (*criticism; barbarism; Darwinism; despotism; plagiarism; realism; witticism; intellectualism*). Cf. **-ist, -ize.** [< Gk *-ismos, -isma* n. suffixes, often directly, often through L *-ismus, -isma,* sometimes through F *-isme,* G *-ismus* (all ult. < Gk)]

Is•ma•el (is′mē əl, -mā-), *n. Douay Bible.* Ishmael (def. 1).

Is•ma•i•li•a (is′mä ə lē′ə, -mī ə-), *n.* a city and seaport at the midpoint of the Suez Canal, in NE Egypt. 189,700. Also, **Isma'iliya.**

Is•ma•'il•i•an (is′mä il′ē ən), *n. Islam.* a member of the Isma'iliya sect. Also, **Is•ma•'il•i** (is′mä il′ē). Also called **Sevener.** [1830–40; < Ar *ismā'īlī* (equiv. to *Ismā'īl* (died A.D. 760), elder son of the imam Ja'far, but disinherited by his father + *-ī* suffix of appurtenance) + -AN]

Is•ma•'i•li•ya (is′mä ə lē′ə, -mī ə-), *n. Islam.* **1.** a branch of Shi'ism, including in its number the Assassins and the Druses, having an esoteric philosophy and asserting Isma'il to be the seventh divinely inspired imam in the succession from Ali. **2.** Ismailia. [< Ar *Ismā'īliyah;* see ISMA'ILIAN]

CONCISE ETYMOLOGY KEY: <, descended or borrowed from; >, whence; b., blend of, blended; c., cognate with; cf., compare; deriv., derivative; equiv., equivalent; imit., imitative; obl., oblique; r., replacing; s., stem; sp., spelling, spelled; resp., respelling, respelled; trans., translation; ?, origin unknown; *, unattested; ‡, probably earlier than. See the full key inside the front cover.

Is•ma•il Pa•sha (is mä′ēl pä′shä), 1830–95, viceroy and khedive of Egypt 1863–79.

Is•me•ne (is mē′nē, -mā′-, iz-), *n. Class. Myth.* a daughter of Oedipus and Jocasta who did not join Antigone in her forbidden burial of their brother Polynices.

is•nad (is näd′), *n. Islam.* the chain of testimony by which a hadith is transmitted. [< Ar *isnād*]

isn't (iz′ənt), contraction of *is not.*
—**Usage.** See **contraction.**
—**Pronunciation.** ISN'T is often pronounced (id′nt) in the South Midland and Southern U.S., with (d), a stop consonant, substituting for (z), a sibilant. This substitution results from an assimilatory process in which the tip of the tongue, in anticipation of the articulatory position for the following (n), touches the upper alveolar ridge. This same process gives (wud′nt) for WASN'T and (bid′nis) for BUSINESS. These pronunciations are heard from speakers on all social levels.

i•so (ī′sō), *n., pl.* **-sos.** *Television Slang.* See **isolated camera.** [by shortening; cf. -O]

ISO, 1. incentive stock option. **2.** International Standardization Organization. **3.** the numerical exposure index of a photographic film under the system adopted by the International Standardization Organization, used to indicate the light sensitivity of the film's emulsion.

iso-, a combining form meaning "equal," used in the formation of compound words: *isochromatic;* in chemistry, used in the names of substances which are isomeric with the substance denoted by the base word: *isocyanic acid.* Also, *esp. before a vowel,* **is-.** [< Gk, comb. form of *ísos* equal]

i•so•ab•nor•mal (ī′sō ab nôr′məl), *n. Meteorol.* isabnormal.

i•so•ag•glu•ti•na•tion (ī′sō ə glōōt′n ā′shən), *n. Med.* the clumping of the red blood cells by a transfusion of the blood or serum of a genetically different individual of the same species. [1905–10; ISO- + AGGLUTINATION] —**i•so•ag•glu•ti′na•tive** (ī′sō ə glōōt′n ā′tiv, -nə-), *adj.*

i•so•ag•glu•ti•nin (ī′sō ə glōōt′n in), *n.* an agglutinin that can effect isoagglutination. [1900–05; ISO- + AGGLUTININ]

i•so•am•yl (ī′sō am′il), *adj. Chem.* containing the isoamyl group; isopentyl. [ISO- + AMYL]

i′soam′yl ac′etate, *Chem.* a colorless liquid, $C_7H_{14}O_2$, used in flavorings, perfumery, and as a solvent. Cf. **banana oil** (def. 1).

i′soam′yl ben′zoate, *Chem.* a colorless liquid, $C_{11}H_{15}O_2$, having a sharp, fruitlike odor: used in cosmetics.

i′soam′yl ben′zyl e′ther, *Chem.* a colorless liquid, $C_{12}H_{18}O$, used in soap perfumes. Also called **benzyl isoamyl ether.**

isoam′yl group′, *Chem.* the univalent group C_5H_{11}. Also called **isoam′yl rad′ical.** Cf. **amyl group, pentyl group.**

i′soam′yl ni′trite, *Pharm.* See **amyl nitrite.**

isoam′yl salic′ylate, *Chem.* a colorless, sometimes slightly yellow, synthetic oil, $C_{12}H_{16}O_3$, having an orchidlike odor: used in perfumery.

i•so•an•ti•bod•y (ī′sō an′ti bod′ē, -an′tē-), *n., pl.* **-bod•ies.** (formerly) an alloantibody. [1915–20; ISO- + ANTIBODY]

i•so•an•ti•gen (ī′sō an′ti jən, -jen′), *n.* (formerly) an alloantigen. [1935–40; ISO- + ANTIGEN]

i•so•bar (ī′sə bär′), *n.* **1.** *Meteorol.* a line drawn on a weather map or chart that connects points at which the barometric pressure is the same. **2.** Also, **i•so•bare** (ī′sə bâr′). *Physics, Chem.* one of two or more atoms having equal atomic weights but different atomic numbers. Cf. **isotope.** [1860–65; < Gk *isobarḗs* of equal weight. See ISO-, BARO-] —**i′so•bar′ism,** *n.*

i•so•bar•ic (ī′sə bar′ik), *adj.* **1.** *Meteorol.* having or showing equal barometric pressure. **2.** *Physics, Chem.* of or pertaining to isobars. [1875–80; ISOBAR + -IC]

i•so•bath (ī′sə bath′), *n.* **1.** an imaginary line or one drawn on a map connecting all points of equal depth below the surface of a body of water. **2.** a similar line for indicating the depth below the surface of the earth of an aquifer or the top of the water table. [1885–90; < Gk *isobathḗs* of equal depth. See ISO-, BATHO-]

i•so•bath•ic (ī′sə bath′ik), *adj.* **1.** having the same depth. **2.** of or pertaining to an isobath. [1890–95; ISOBATH- + -IC]

i•so•bath•y•therm (ī′sə bath′ə thûrm′), *n.* a line on a chart or diagram of a body of water, connecting depths having the same temperature. [1875–80; ISO- + BATHY- + THERM] —**i′so•bath′y•ther′mal, i′so•bath′y•ther′mic,** *adj.*

i•so•bront (ī′sə bront′), *n. Meteorol.* a line on a weather map or chart connecting various points where a given phase of thunderstorm activity occurred simultaneously. [1885–90; ISO- + *-bront* < Gk *brontḗ* thunder]

i•so•bu•tane (ī′sə byōō′tān, -byōō tān′), *n. Chem.* a colorless, flammable gas, C_4H_{10}, used as a fuel, as a refrigerant, and in the manufacture of gasoline by alkylation. [1875–80; ISO- + BUTANE]

i•so•bu•tyl•ene (ī′sə byōōt′l ēn′), *n. Chem.* a colorless, very volatile liquid or flammable gas, C_4H_8, used chiefly in the manufacture of butyl rubber. Also, **i•so•bu•tene** (ī′sə byōō′tēn). [1870–75; ISO- + BUTYLENE]

i′sobu′tyl ni′trite. See **butyl nitrite.** [1975–80; ISO- + BUTYL]

i′so•bu′tyl pro′pionate (ī′sə byōō′til, -byōōt′l, ī′sə-), *Chem.* a colorless liquid, $C_7H_{14}O_2$, used chiefly as a paint, varnish, and lacquer solvent. [ISO- + BUTYL]

i•so•car•box•a•zid (ī′sō kär bok′sə zid), *n. Pharm.* a potent monoamine oxidase inhibitor, $C_{12}H_{13}N_3O_2$, used to treat severe depression. [1955–60; *isocarbox-* contr. and rearrangement of *isoxazolylcarbonyl* a component + (HYDR)AZ(INE) + -ID[3]]

i•so•car•pic (ī′sə kär′pik), *adj. Bot.* having carpels equal in number to the other floral parts. [ISO- + -CARPIC]

i•so•ce•phal•ic (ī′sō sə fal′ik), *adj. Fine Arts.* (of a composition) having the heads of all figures on approximately the same level. Also, **i•so•ceph•a•lous** (ī′sə sef′ə ləs). [ISO- + -CEPHALIC] —**i•so•ceph•a•ly** (ī′sə sef′ə lē), *n.*

i•so•ce•rau•nic (ī′sō si rô′nik), *adj. Meteorol.* representing, having, or indicating equality in the frequency or intensity of thunderstorms: *isoceraunic line; isoceraunic map.* Also, **isokeraunic.** [ISO- + *ceraun-* (< Gk *keraunós* thunderbolt) + -IC]

i•so•chasm (ī′sə kaz′əm), *n. Meteorol.* a line on a map or chart connecting points where auroras are observed with equal frequency. [1880–85; ISO- + CHASM] —**i′so•chas′mic,** *adj.*

i•so•cheim (ī′sə kīm′), *n. Climatol.* a line on a map connecting points that have the same mean winter temperature. Also, **i′so•chime′.** [1860–65; ISO- + *-cheim* < Gk *cheîma* winter cold] —**i′so•chei′mal, i•so•chei•me•nal** (ī′sə kī′mə nl), **i′so•cheim′ic, i′so•chi′mal,** *adj.*

i•so•chor (ī′sə kôr′), *n. Physics.* for a given substance, a curve graphing temperature against pressure, when the volume of the substance is held constant. Also, **i′so•chore′.** Also called **isometric, isometric line.** [ISO- + *-chor* < Gk *chṓra* place, land] —**i•so•chor•ic** (ī′sə kôr′ik, -kor′-), *adj.*

i•so•chro•mat•ic (ī′sə krō mat′ik, ī′sō krə-), *adj.* **1.** *Optics.* having the same color or tint. **2.** *Photog.* orthochromatic. [1820–30; ISO- + CHROMATIC]

i•soch•ro•nal (ī sok′rə nl), *adj.* **1.** equal or uniform in time. **2.** performed in equal intervals of time. **3.** characterized by motions or vibrations of equal duration. [1670–80; < NL *isochron(us)* (< Gk *isóchronos* equal in age or time; see ISO-, CHRON-) + -AL[1]] —**i•soch′ro•nal•ly,** *adv.*

i•so•chrone (ī′sə krōn′), *n.* a line, as on a map, connecting all points having some property simultaneously, as in having the same delay in receiving a radio signal from a given source or requiring the same time to be reached by available transportation from a given center. [1690–1700; back formation from ISOCHRONOUS or ISOCHRONAL]

i•soch•ro•nism (ī sok′rə niz′əm), *n.* an isochronal character or action. [1760–70; ISOCHRONE + -ISM]

i•soch•ro•nize (ī sok′rə nīz′), *v.t.,* **-nized, -niz•ing.** to make isochronal. Also, *esp. Brit.,* **i•soch′ro•nise′.** [ISOCHRONE + -IZE]

i•soch•ro•nous (ī sok′rə nəs), *adj.* isochronal. [1700–10; < NL *isochronus.* See ISOCHRONAL, -OUS] —**i•soch′ro•nous•ly,** *adv.*

i•soch•ro•ny (ī sok′rə nē), *n.* the fact or state of occurrence at the same time; contemporaneity. [1950–55; ISOCHRONE + -Y[3]]

i•soch•ro•ous (ī sok′rō əs), *adj.* having the same color throughout. [1700–10; ISO- + -CHROOUS]

i′so•cit′ric ac′id (ī′sə si′trik, ī′sə-), *Biochem.* a major intermediate in the Krebs cycle, having the formula $C_6H_8O_7$. [1865–70; ISO- + CITRIC ACID]

i•so•cli•nal (ī′sə klīn′l, ī′sō-), *adj.* **1.** of or pertaining to equal direction of inclination; inclining or dipping in the same direction. **2.** noting or pertaining to an isoclinic line. **3.** *Geol.* noting or pertaining to a fold of strata that is of the nature of an isocline. —*n.* **4.** See **isoclinic line.** Also, **i•so•clin•ic** (ī′sə klin′ik, ī′sō-). [1830–40; ISO- + *-clinal* (< Gk *klī́n(ein)* to slope + -AL[1])]

i•so•cline (ī′sə klīn′), *n. Geol.* a fold of strata so tightly compressed that both limbs dip in the same direction. [1885–90; back formation from ISOCLINAL]

i′soclin′ic line′, an imaginary line connecting points on the earth's surface having equal magnetic dip. Also called **isoclinic, isoclinal.** [1890–95]

i•soc•ra•cy (ī sok′rə sē), *n., pl.* **-cies.** a government in which all individuals have equal political power. [1645–55; < Gk *isokratía.* See ISO-, -CRACY] —**i•so•crat** (ī′sə krat′), *n.* —**i′so•crat′ic,** *adj.*

I•soc•ra•tes (ī sok′rə tēz′), *n.* 436–338 B.C., Athenian orator.

i•so•cy•a•nate (ī′sə sī′ə nāt′), *n. Chem.* **1.** a salt or ester of isocyanic acid. **2.** any compound containing the univalent group −NCO. [1870–75; ISOCYAN(IC ACID) + -ATE²]

i′so•cy•an′ic ac′id (ī′sō sī an′ik, ī′sō-), *Chem.* an unstable acid, CHNO, tautomeric with cyanic acid, known only in the form of its salts. [1890–95; ISO- + CYANIC ACID]

i•so•cy•a•nide (ī′sə sī′ə nīd′, -nid), *n. Chem.* a compound containing an isocyano group. Also called **carbylamine.** [1875–80; ISO- + CYANIDE]

i•so•cy•a•nine (ī′sə sī′ə nēn′, -nin), *n. Chem.* a member of the group of cyanine dyes. [ISO- + CYANINE]

i•so•cy•a•no (ī′sə sī′ə nō′), *adj. Chem.* containing an isocyano group. [ISO- + CYANO]

isocy′ano group′, *Chem.* the univalent group −NC. Also called **isocy′ano rad′ical.**

i•so•cy•clic (ī′sə sī′klik, -sik′lik), *adj. Chem.* homocyclic. [1895–1900; ISO- + CYCLIC]

i•so•def (ī′sə def′), *n.* uniform deficiency, esp. a line connecting points of equal deviation from a mean, as on a chart or graph. [ISO- + DEF(ICIENCY)]

i•so•di•a•met•ric (ī′sə dī′ə me′trik), *adj.* **1.** having equal diameters or axes. **2.** having the diameter similar throughout, as a cell. **3.** (of crystals) having two, or three, equal horizontal axes and a third, or fourth, unequal axis at right angles thereto. [1880–85; ISO- + DIAMETRIC]

i•so•di•mor•phism (ī′sō dī môr′fiz əm), *n. Crystall.* isomorphism between the forms of two dimorphous substances. [ISO- + DIMORPHISM] —**i′so•di•mor′phous, i′so•di•mor′phic,** *adj.*

i•so•dom•ic (ī′sə dom′ik), *adj. Archit.* (of ashlar) composed of stones of uniform size. [< Gk *isódom(os)* built in equal courses (see ISO-, DOME) + -IC]

i•so•dose (ī′sə dōs′), *adj.* of or pertaining to points of equal intensity of radiation in a contaminated region: *isodose map; isodose lines.* [1920–25; ISO- + DOSE]

i•so•dros•o•therm (ī′sə dros′ə thûrm′), *n. Meteorol.* a line on a weather map or chart connecting points having an equal dew point. [ISO- + Gk *dróso(s)* dew + -THERM]

i•so•dy•nam•ic (ī′sō dī nam′ik, -di-), *adj.* **1.** pertaining to or characterized by equality of force, intensity, or the like. **2.** noting or pertaining to an imaginary line on the earth's surface connecting points of equal horizontal intensity of the earth's magnetic field. Also, **i′so•dy•nam′i•cal.** [1830–40; ISO- + DYNAMIC]

i•so•e•las•tic (ī′sō i las′tik), *adj. Physics.* noting or pertaining to a substance or system exhibiting uniform elasticity throughout. [ISO- + ELASTIC]

i•so•e•lec•tric (ī′sō i lek′trik), *adj.* of, pertaining to, or having the same electric potential. [1875–80; ISO- + ELECTRIC]

isoelec′tric point′, *Chem.* the pH at which a substance is electrically neutral or at which it is at its minimum ionization. [1895–1900]

i•so•e•lec•tron•ic (ī′sō i lek tron′ik, -ē′lek-), *adj. Physics, Chem.* **1.** noting or pertaining to atoms and ions having an equal number of electrons. **2.** noting or pertaining to atoms, radicals, or ions having either an equal number of electrons or an equal number of valence electrons. [1925–30; ISO- + ELECTRONIC]

i•so•en•zyme (ī′sō en′zīm), *n. Biochem.* isozyme. [1955–60; ISO- + ENZYME]

i•so•flu•rane (ī′sō flo͝or′ān), *n. Pharm.* a volatile, halogenated ether, $C_3H_2ClF_5O$, used as a general anesthetic in surgery. [ISO- + FLU(O)R- + -ANE]

i•so•gam•ete (ī′sə gam′ēt, ī′sō gə mēt′), *n. Cell Biol.* one of a pair of conjugating gametes, exhibiting no differences in form, size, structure, or sex. Cf. **heterogamete.** [1890–95; ISO- + GAMETE] —**i•so•ga•met•ic** (ī′sō-gə met′ik), *adj.*

i•sog•a•mous (ī sog′ə məs), *adj. Biol.* having two similar gametes in which no differentiation can be distinguished, or reproducing by the union of such gametes (opposed to *heterogamous*). [1885–90; ISO- + -GAMOUS]

i•sog•a•my (ī sog′ə mē), *n. Biol.* the fusion of two gametes of similar form, as in certain algae. [1890–95; ISO- + -GAMY]

i•sog•e•nous (ī soj′ə nəs), *adj. Biol.* of the same or similar origin, as parts derived from the same or corresponding tissues of the embryo. [1880–85; ISO- + -GENOUS] —**i•sog′e•ny,** *n.*

i•so•ge•o•therm (ī′sə jē′ə thûrm′), *n.* an imaginary line connecting all points within the earth having the same mean temperature. Also called **geoisotherm.** [1860–65; ISO- + GEO- + THERM] —**i′so•ge′o•ther′mal, i′so•ge′o•ther′mic,** *adj.*

i•so•gloss (ī′sə glos′, -glôs′), *n.* (in the study of the geographical distribution of dialects) a line on a map marking the limits of an area within which a feature of speech occurs, as the use of a particular word or pronunciation. [< G (1892); see ISO-, GLOSS²] —**i′so•glos′sal,** *adj.*

i•so•gon (ī′sə gon′), *n.* a polygon having all angles equal. [1690–1700; ISO- + -GON]

i•sog•o•nal (ī sog′ə nl), *adj.* **1.** equiangular; isogonic. —*n.* **2.** See **isogonal line.** [1855–60; < Gk *isogōn(ios)* equiangular (see ISO-, -GON) + -AL¹] —**i•so•go•nal•i•ty** (ī′sō gə nal′i tē), *n.* —**i•sog′o•nal•ly,** *adv.*

isog′onal line′, an imaginary line, or one drawn on a map, connecting all points of equal magnetic declination. Also called **isogonal, i•so•gone** (ī′sə gōn′), **isogonic.**

i•so•gon•ic (ī′sə gon′ik), *adj.* **1.** having or pertaining to equal angles. **2.** noting or pertaining to an isogonal line. —*n.* **3.** See **isogonal line.** [< Gk *isogṓn(ios)* having equal angles (see ISO-, -GON) + -IC]

i•so•gra•di•ent (ī′sə grā′dē ənt), *n. Meteorol.* a line on a weather map or chart connecting points having the same horizontal gradient of a meteorological quantity, as temperature, pressure, or the like. [ISO- + GRADIENT]

i•so•graft (ī′sə graft′, -gräft′), *n. Surg.* syngraft. [1905–10; ISO- + GRAFT¹]

i•so•gram (ī′sə gram′), *n. Meteorol., Geog.* a line representing equality with respect to a given variable, used to relate points on maps, charts, etc. Also called **isoline.** [1885–90; ISO- + -GRAM¹]

i•so•graph (ī′sə graf′, -gräf′), *n.* (in the study of the geographical distribution of a dialect) a line drawn on a map to indicate areas having common linguistic characteristics. [1935–40; ISO- + -GRAPH] —**i•so•graph•ic** (ī′sə graf′ik), **i′so•graph′i•cal,** *adj.* —**i′so•graph′i•cal•ly,** *adv.*

i•so•griv (ī′sə griv), *n.* a line on a map or chart connecting points of uniform grid variation. [ISO- + GRIV(ATION)]

i•so•ha•line (ī′sə hā′lēn, -līn, -hal′ēn, -īn), *n.* a line on a map of the ocean connecting all points of equal salinity. Also, **i•so•hal•sine** (ī′sə hal′sēn, -sīn). [1900–05; ISO- + *-haline* < Gk *hálinos* salty; see HAL-, -INE¹]

i•so•hel (ī′sə hel′), *n. Meteorol.* a line on a weather map connecting points that receive equal amounts of sunshine. [1900–05; ISO- + *-hel* < Gk *hḗlios* sun]

i•so•hume (ī′sə hyo͞om′), *n. Meteorol.* a line on a weather map or chart connecting points of equal relative humidity. [ISO- + *-hume,* extracted from HUMIDITY]

i•so•hy•et (ī′sə hī′ət), *n. Meteorol.* a line drawn on a map connecting points having equal rainfall at a certain time or for a stated period. [1895–1900; ISO- + *-hyet* < Gk *hyetós* rain] —**i′so•hy′et•al,** *adj.*

i′so•i•on′ic point′ (ī′sō ī on′ik, ī′sō-), *Chem.* the hydrogen ion concentration at which the concentration of the dipolar ion is at a maximum. [1930–35; ISO- + IONIC]

i•so•ke•rau•nic (ī′sō ki rô′nik), *adj.* isoceraunic.

i′so•ki•net′ic ex′ercise (ī′sō ki net′ik, -kī-), **1.** exercise or a program of exercises to increase muscular strength, power, and endurance based on lifting, pulling, or pushing variable weight or resistance at a constant speed. **2.** any specific exercise of this type. [1955–60; ISO- + KINETIC]

i•so•la•ble (ī′sə lə bəl, is′ə-), *adj.* capable of being isolated. [1850–55; ISOL(ATE) + -ABLE] —**i′so•la•bil′i•ty,** *n.*

i•so•lat•a•ble (ī′sə lā′tə bəl, is′ə-), *adj.* isolable. [ISOLATE + -ABLE]

i•so•late (*v.* ī′sə lāt′, is′ə-; *n., adj.* ī′sə lit, -lāt′, is′ə-), *v.,* **-lat•ed, -lat•ing,** *n., adj.* —*v.t.* **1.** to set or place apart; detach or separate so as to be alone. **2.** *Med.* to keep (an infected person) from contact with noninfected persons; quarantine. **3.** *Chem., Bacteriol.* to obtain (a substance or microorganism) in an uncombined or pure state. **4.** *Elect.* to insulate. **5.** *Television.* to single out (a person, action, etc.) for a camera closeup. —*n.* **6.** a person, thing, or group that is set apart or isolated, as for purposes of study. **7.** *Psychol.* a person, often shy or lacking in social skills, who avoids the company of others and has no friends within a group. **8.** *Biol.* an inbreeding population that is isolated from similar populations by physiological, behavioral, or geographic barriers. **9.** *Ling.* a language with no demonstrable genetic relationship, as Basque. **10.** something that has been isolated, as a by-product in a manufacturing process: *an isolate of soy flour.* —*adj.* **11.** isolated; alone. [1800–10; back formation from ISOLATED] —**i′so•la′tor,** *n.*

i•so•lat•ed (ī′sə lā′tid, is′ə-), *adj.* separated from other persons or things; alone; solitary. [1755–65; < F *isolé* isolated (< It; see ISOLATO); see -ATE, -ED²] —**i′so•lat′ed•ly,** *adv.*

i′solated cam′era, a television camera used to isolate a subject, part of a sports play, etc., for instant replay. [1965–70]

i′solated point′, *Math.* a point in a set such that the neighborhood of the point is devoid of any other points belonging to the set.

i′solated set′, *Math.* a set containing none of its accumulation points, consisting, therefore, of only isolated points.

i•so•lat•ing (ī′sə lā′ting, is′ə-), *adj. Ling.* pertaining to or noting a language, as Vietnamese, that uses few or no bound forms and in which grammatical relationships are indicated chiefly through word order. Cf. **agglutinative** (def. 2), **inflectional** (def. 2). [1855–60; ISOLATE + -ING²]

i•so•la•tion (ī′sə lā′shən, is′ə-), *n.* **1.** an act or instance of isolating. **2.** the state of being isolated. **3.** the complete separation from others of a person suffering from contagious or infectious disease; quarantine. **4.** the separation of a nation from other nations by isolationism. **5.** *Psychoanal.* a process whereby an idea or memory is divested of its emotional component. **6.** *Sociol.* See **social isolation.** [1825–35; ISOLATE + -ION] —**Syn. 2.** See **solitude. 3.** segregation.

isola′tion booth′, a soundproof booth located within a television studio, used to prevent the occupant, usually a contestant in a game show, from hearing certain parts of the show.

i•so•la•tion•ism (ī′sə lā′shə niz′əm, is′ə-), *n.* the policy or doctrine of isolating one's country from the affairs of other nations by declining to enter into alliances, foreign economic commitments, international agreements, etc., seeking to devote the entire efforts of one's country to its own advancement and remain at peace by avoiding foreign entanglements and responsibilities. [1920–25, *Amer.*; ISOLATION + -ISM]

i•so•la•tion•ist (ī′sə lā′shə nist, is′ə-), *n.* **1.** a person who favors or works for isolationism. —*adj.* **2.** of, pertaining to, or characteristic of isolationists or isolationism: *to be accused of isolationist sympathies.* [1860–65, *Amer.*; ISOLATION + -IST]

i•so•la•tive (ī′sə lā′tiv, is′ə-), *adj.* noting a change in part of the sound of a word made independently of the phonetic environment of that part. [1885–90; ISOLATE + -IVE]

i•so•la•to (ī′sə lä′tō), *n., pl.* **-toes.** a person who is spiritually isolated from or out of sympathy with his or her times or society. [1850–55; < It < L *insulātus.* See INSULATE]

I•sol•da (i zōl′də, i sōl′-), *n.* a female given name, form of **Iseult.**

I•solde (i sōld′, i sōl′də; *Ger.* ē zôl′də), *n.* German name of **Iseult.**

i•so•lec•i•thal (ī′sə les′ə thəl), *adj. Embryol.* homolecithal. [1925–30; ISO- + LECITHAL]

I•so•lette (ī′sə let′), *Trademark.* a brand of incubator for premature or other newborn infants, providing controlled temperature, humidity, and oxygen levels and having armholes through which the infant can be reached with minimum disturbance to the controlled environment.

i•so•leu•cine (ī′sə lo͞o′sēn, -sin), *n. Biochem.* a crystalline amino acid, $C_6H_{13}O_2$, occurring in proteins, that is essential to the nutrition of humans and animals. *Abbr.:* Ile; *Symbol:* I [1900–05; ISO- + LEUCINE]

i•so•line (ī′sə līn′), *n. Meteorol., Geog.* isogram. [1940–45; ISO- + LINE¹]

i•sol•o•gous (ī sol′ə gəs), *adj. Chem.* (of two or more organic compounds) chemically related but differing in composition other than by nCH_2. [1855–60; ISO- + (HOMO)LOGOUS]

i•so•logue (ī′sə lôg′, -log′), *n. Chem.* one of two or more isologous compounds. Also, **i′so•log′.** [1885–90; back formation from ISOLOGOUS, on the model of *homologue: homologous*]

i•so•mag•net•ic (ī′sō mag net′ik), *adj.* **1.** noting or pertaining to points of equal magnetic force. —*n.* **2.** a line connecting such points. [1895–1900; ISO- + MAGNETIC]

i•so•mer (ī′sə mər), *n.* **1.** *Chem.* a compound displaying isomerism with one or more other compounds. **2.** Also called **nuclear isomer.** *Physics.* a nuclide that exhibits isomerism with one or more other nuclides. [1865–70; back formation from ISOMERIC]

i•som•er•ase (ī som′ə rās′, -rāz′), *n. Biochem.* any of a class of enzymes that catalyze reactions involving intramolecular rearrangements. [1940–45; ISOMER + -ASE]

i•so•mer•ic (ī′sə mer′ik), *adj.* of, pertaining to, or displaying isomerism. [1830–40; < Gk *isomer(ḗs)* having equal parts (see ISO-, -MERE) + -IC] —**i′so•mer′i•cal•ly,** *adv.*

i•som•er•ism (ī som′ə riz′əm), *n.* **1.** *Chem.* the relation of two or more compounds, radicals, or ions that are composed of the same kinds and numbers of atoms but differ from each other in structural arrangement (**structural isomerism**), as CH_3OCH_3 and CH_3CH_2OH, or in the arrangement of their atoms in space and therefore in one or more properties. Cf. **optical isomerism, stereoisomerism. 2.** Also called **nuclear isomerism.** *Physics.* the relation of two or more nuclides that have the same atomic number and mass number but different energy levels and half-lives. **3.** *Chem., Physics.* the phenomenon characterized by such a relation. **4.** the state or condition of being isomerous. [1830–40; ISOMER(IC) + -ISM]

i•som•er•ize (ī som′ə rīz′), *v.i., v.t.,* **-ized, -iz•ing.** *Chem.* to convert into an isomer. Also, *esp. Brit.,* **i•som′er•ise′.** [1890–95; ISOMER + -IZE] —**i•som′er•i•za′tion,** *n.*

i•som•er•ous (ī som′ər əs), *adj.* **1.** having an equal number of parts, markings, etc. **2.** *Bot.* (of a flower) having the same number of members in each whorl. [1855–60; ISO- + -MERE + -OUS]

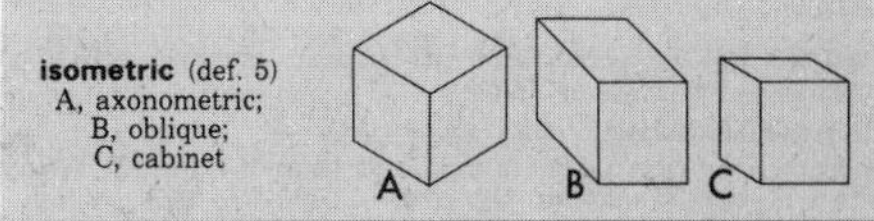

isometric (def. 5)
A, axonometric;
B, oblique;
C, cabinet

i•so•met•ric (ī′sə me′trik), *adj.* Also, **i′so•met′ri•cal. 1.** of, pertaining to, or having equality of measure. **2.** of or pertaining to isometric exercise. **3.** *Crystall.* noting or pertaining to that system of crystallization that is characterized by three equal axes at right angles to one another. Cf. **crystal system. 4.** *Pros.* of equal measure; made up of regular feet. **5.** *Drafting.* designating a method of projection **(isomet′ric projec′tion)** in which a three-dimensional object is represented by a drawing **(i′somet′ric draw′ing)** having the horizontal edges of the object drawn usually at a 30° angle and all verticals projected perpendicularly from a horizontal base, all lines being drawn to scale. Cf. **orthographic projection.** —*n.* **6. isometrics,** isometric exercise (def. 1). **7.** an isometric drawing. **8.** Also called **i′somet′ric line′.** *Physics.* isochor. [1830–40; < Gk *isometr(ía)* ISOMETRY + -IC] —**i′so•met′ri•cal•ly,** *adv.*

i′somet′ric ex′ercise, 1. exercise or a program of exercises to strengthen specific muscles or shape the figure by pitting one muscle or part of the body against another or against an immovable object in a strong but motionless action, as by pressing the fist of one hand against the palm of the other or against a desk. **2.** any specific exercise of this type. [1965–70]

i•so•me•tro•pi•a (ī′sō mi trō′pē ə), *n. Ophthalm.*

CONCISE PRONUNCIATION KEY: *act, cāpe, dâre, pärt; set, ēqual; if, īce; ox, ōver, ôrder, oil, bo͝ok, bo͞ot, out; up, ûrge; child; sing; shoe; thin, that;* zh as in *treasure.* ə = *a* as in *alone, e* as in *system, i* as in *easily, o* as in *gallop, u* as in *circus;* ᵊ as in *fire* (fīᵊr), *hour* (ouᵊr). l and n can serve as syllabic consonants, as in *cradle* (krād′l), and *button* (but′n). See the full key inside the front cover.

equality of refraction in the two eyes of an individual. [< Gk *isómetr(os)* of equal measure (see ISO-, -METER) + -OPIA]

i•som•e•try (ī som′i trē), *n.* **1.** equality of measure. **2.** *Biol.* equal growth rates in two parts of a developing organism. **3.** *Geog.* equality with respect to height above sea level. **4.** *Math.* a function from one metric space onto a second metric space having the property that the distance between two points in the first space is equal to the distance between the image points in the second space. [1940–45; < Gk *isometría.* See ISO-, -METRY]

i•so•morph (ī′sə môrf′), *n.* **1.** an organism that is isomorphic with another or others. **2.** an isomorphous substance. [1860–65; back formation from ISOMORPHOUS]

i•so•mor•phic (ī′sə môr′fik), *adj.* **1.** *Biol.* different in ancestry, but having the same form or appearance. **2.** *Chem., Crystall.* isomorphous. **3.** *Math.* pertaining to two sets related by an isomorphism. [1860–65; ISO- + -MORPHIC]

i•so•mor•phism (ī′sə môr′fiz əm), *n.* **1.** the state or property of being isomorphous or isomorphic. **2.** *Math.* a one-to-one relation onto the map between two sets, which preserves the relations existing between elements in its domain. [1820–30; ISOMORPH(OUS) + -ISM]

i•so•mor•phous (ī′sə môr′fəs), *adj. Chem., Crystall.* (of a compound or mineral) capable of crystallizing in a form similar to that of another compound or mineral, used esp. of substances so closely related that they form end members of a series of solid solutions. [1820–30; ISO- + -MORPHOUS]

i•so•neph (ī′sə nef′), *n. Meteorol.* a line on a weather map or chart connecting points having the same amount of cloudiness. [1840–50; ISO- + *-neph* < Gk *néphos* cloud] —**i•so•ne•phel•ic** (ī′sō nə fel′ik), *adj.*

i•so•ni•a•zid (ī′sə nī′ə zid), *n. Pharm.* a white, crystalline, water-soluble solid, $C_6H_7N_3O$, used in the treatment of tuberculosis. [1950–55; short for ISONICOTINIC ACID HYDRAZIDE]

i′so•nic•o•tin′ic ac′id hy′dra•zide (ī′sə nik′ə-tin′ik; hī′drə zīd′, -zid), *Pharm.* isoniazid. [1950–55; ISO- + NICOTINIC ACID; HYDRAZ(INE) + -IDE]

i•son•o•my (ī son′ə mē), *n.* equality of political rights. [1590–1600; < Gk *isonomía.* See ISO-, -NOMY] —**i•so•nom•ic** (ī′sə nom′ik), **i•son′o•mous,** *adj.*

I•son•zo (ē zôn′tsô), *n.* a river in S Europe, flowing S from the Julian Alps in Yugoslavia to the Gulf of Trieste in Italy. 75 mi. (120 km) long.

i•so•oc•tane (ī′sō ok′tān), *n. Chem.* the octane C_8H_{18}, used as one of the standards in establishing the octane number of a fuel. Cf. **octane number.** [1905–10; ISO- + OCTANE]

i•so•os•mot•ic (ī′sō oz mot′ik, -os-), *adj. Physical Chem.* isotonic (def. 1). [1905–10]

i•so•pach (ī′sə pak′), *n. Geol.* a line drawn on a map connecting all points of equal thickness of a particular geologic formation. [1915–20; ISO- + *-pach* < Gk *páchos* thickness]

i•so•pach•ous (ī′sə pak′əs, ī sop′ə kəs), *adj. Geol.* **1.** having the same thickness. **2.** of or pertaining to an isopach. [1915–20; ISOPACH + -OUS]

i•so•pag (ī′sə pag′), *n.* a line drawn on a map connecting all points where ice exists at approximately the same period during winter. [ISO- + *-pag* < Gk *págos* frost]

i•so•pec•tic (ī′sə pek′tik), *n.* a line drawn on a map connecting all points where ice starts to form at approximately the same period at the onset of winter. [ISO- + *-pectic* < Gk *pēktikós* freezing; see PECTIC]

i•sop•e•din (ī sop′i din, ī′sə pēd′n), *n. Ichthyol.* the underlying layer of a ganoid scale, composed of connective tissue embedded with bone. Also, **i•sop•e•dine** (ī sop′i din, -dēn′, -dīn′). [ISO- + *-pedin* < Gk *pedinós* level]

i•so•pen•tyl (ī′sə pen′til), *adj. Chem.* isoamyl. [1875–80; ISO- + PENT(A)- + -YL]

i•so•pe•rim•e•ter (ī′sō pə rim′i tər), *n. Geom.* a figure whose perimeter is equal to that of another. Also called **i′soperimet′ric fig′ure.** [1665–75; ISO- + PERIMETER]

i•so•pe•rim•e•try (ī′sō pə rim′i trē), *n. Geom.* the study of isoperimeters. [1805–15; ISOPERIMET(E)R + -Y[3]] —**i•so•per•i•met•ric** (ī′sə per′ə me′trik), **i′so•per′i•met′ri•cal,** *adj.*

i′so•phthal′ic ac′id (ī′sə thal′ik, ī′sə-), *Chem.* a colorless, crystalline, slightly water-soluble solid, $C_8H_6O_4$, the meta isomer of phthalic acid: used chiefly in the manufacture of resins and plasticizers. [1865–70; ISO- + PHTHALIC]

i•so•pi•es•tic (ī′sō pī es′tik), *adj.* of or noting equal pressure; isobaric. [1870–75; ISO- + Gk *piest(ós)* compressible (verbid of *piézein* to press) + -IC] —**i′so•pi•es′ti•cal•ly,** *adv.*

i′so•plas′tic graft′ (ī′sə plas′tik, ī′sə-), *Surg.* syngraft. [ISO- + PLASTIC]

i•so•pleth (ī′sə pleth′), *n.* a line drawn on a map through all points having the same numerical value, as of a population figure or geographic measurement. Also called **isarithm.** [1905–10; < Gk *isoplēthḗs* equal in number, equiv. to *iso-* ISO- + *plêth(os)* a great number + *-ēs* adj. suffix]

i•so•pod (ī′sə pod′), *n.* **1.** any freshwater, marine, or terrestrial crustacean of the order or suborder Isopoda, having seven pairs of legs typically adapted for crawling, and a dorsoventrally flattened body, and including wood lice, several aquatic parasites of crabs and shrimps, and numerous swimming or bottom-dwelling species. —*adj.* **2.** of, pertaining to, or characteristic of the Isopoda. **3.** having the feet all alike, or similar in character. [1825–35; < NL *Isopoda.* See ISO-, -POD] —**i•sop•o•dan** (ī sop′-ə dn), *adj., n.* —**i•sop′o•dous,** *adj.*

i•so•pol•i•ty (ī′sə pol′i tē), *n.* equal rights of citizenship, as in different communities; mutual political rights. [1830–40; ISO- + POLITY] —**i•so•po•lit•i•cal** (ī′sō pə lit′i-kəl), *adj.*

i•so•por (ī′sə pôr′), *n.* an imaginary line on the earth's surface connecting points of equal annual change in the declination, inclination, or other components of the earth's magnetic field. Also called **i′sopor′ic line′.** [1930–35; ISO- + *-por* < Gk *póros* path, PORE[2]] —**i′so•por′ic,** *adj.*

i•so•prene (ī′sə prēn′), *n. Chem.* a colorless, volatile, water-insoluble liquid, C_5H_8, of the terpene class, usually obtained from rubber or from oil of turpentine by pyrolysis: used chiefly in the manufacture of synthetic rubber by polymerization. [1855–60; ISO- + *-pr-* (< ?) + -ENE; see TERPENE]

i•so•pren•oid (ī′sə prē′noid), *adj. Chem.* pertaining to, derived from, or similar to isoprene. [1955–60; ISOPRENE + -OID]

i•so•pro•pa•nol (ī′sə prō′pə nôl′, -nol′), *n. Chem.* See **isopropyl alcohol.** [1940–45; ISO- + PROPANE + -OL[1]]

i•so•pro•pyl (ī′sə prō′pil), *adj. Chem.* containing the isopropyl group. [1865–70; ISO- + PROPYL]

i′sopro′pyl al′cohol, *Chem.* a colorless, flammable, water-soluble liquid, C_3H_8O, produced from propylene by the action of sulfuric acid and hydrolysis: used chiefly in the manufacture of antifreeze and rubbing alcohol and as a solvent. Also called **dimethylcarbinol, isopropanol, secondary propyl alcohol.** [1870–75]

i•so•pro•pyl•ben•zene (ī′sə prō′pil ben′zēn, -ben-zēn′), *n. Chem.* cumene. [ISOPROPYL + BENZENE]

i′sopro′pyl e′ther, *Chem.* a colorless, volatile, flammable, slightly water-soluble liquid, $C_6H_{14}O$, used chiefly as a solvent for waxes, fats, and resins.

isopro′pyl group′, *Chem.* the univalent group C_3H_7, an isomer of the propyl group. Also called **isopro′pyl rad′ical.** [1950–55]

i•so•pro•pyl•i•dene•ac•e•tone (ī′sə prō pil′i dēn-as′i tōn′), *n. Chem.* See **mesityl oxide.** [ISOPROPYL + -ID[3] + -ENE + ACETONE]

isopro′pyl mepro′bamate, *Pharm.* carisoprodol.

i•so•pro•ter•e•nol (ī′sə prō ter′ə nôl′, -nol′), *n. Pharm.* a beta-adrenergic receptor agonist, $C_{11}H_{17}NO_3$, used as a bronchodilator. [1955–60; ISOPRO(PYL) + *(Ar)terenol* trade name for a hydrochloride of norepinephrine]

i•sop•ter•ous (ī sop′tər əs), *adj.* belonging or pertaining to social insects of the order Isoptera, comprising the termites. [< NL *Isopter(a)* + -OUS; see ISO-, -PTEROUS]

i•so•pyc•nic (ī′sə pik′nik), *adj.* **1.** Also, **i•so•pyc•nal** (ī′sə pik′nl). having the same density. —*n.* **2.** a line drawn on a map connecting all points having the same density, as of water or air. [1885–90; ISO- + *pycnic,* var. of PYKNIC]

i•so•pyre (ī′sə pī′r′), *n. Mineral.* an impure variety of opal, containing alumina, lime, and iron sesquioxide. [1820–30; ISO- + Gk *pŷr* fire]

i•so•reel (ī′sō rēl′), *n. Television.* the exposed film of one or more isolated cameras that is ready for editing.

i•so•rhythm (ī′sə rith′əm), *n. Music.* a structural feature characteristic of the Ars Nova motet, consisting of a single rhythmic phrase pattern repeated, usually in the tenor, throughout the composition. [1950–55; ISO- + RHYTHM] —**i′so•rhyth′mic,** *adj.* —**i′so•rhyth′mi•cal•ly,** *adv.*

i•sos•ce•les (ī sos′ə lēz′), *adj.* (of a straight-sided plane figure) having two sides equal: *an isosceles triangle; an isosceles trapezoid.* See diag. under **triangle.** [1545–55; < LL < Gk *isoskelḗs* with equal legs, equiv. to *iso-* ISO- + *skél(os)* leg + *-ēs* adj. suffix]

i•so•seis•mic (ī′sə sīz′mik, -sīs′-), *adj. Geol.* **1.** noting or pertaining to equal intensity of earthquake shock. **2.** noting or pertaining to an imaginary line on the earth's surface connecting points characterized by such intensity. —*n.* **3.** an isoseismic line. Also, **i′so•seis′mal.** [ISO- + SEISMIC]

i•sos•mot•ic (ī′soz mot′ik, -sos-), *adj. Physical Chem.* isotonic (def. 1). [1890–95; IS- + OSMOTIC]

i•so•sor•bide di•ni•trate (ī′sə sôr′bīd dī nī′trāt, -sôr′-), *Pharm.* a coronary vasodilator, $C_6H_8N_2O_8$, used in the prophylaxis and treatment of angina. [ISO- + SORB(ITOL) + -IDE; DI-[1] + NITRATE]

i•so•spin (ī′sə spin′), *n. Physics.* See **isotopic spin.** [by shortening]

i•sos•ta•sy (ī sos′tə sē), *n.* **1.** *Geol.* the equilibrium of the earth's crust, a condition in which the forces tending to elevate balance those tending to depress. **2.** the state in which pressures from every side are equal. Also, **i•sos′ta•cy.** [1885–90; ISO- + *-stasy* < Gk *-stasia;* see STASIS, -Y[3]]

i•so•stat•ic (ī′sə stat′ik), *adj.* of, pertaining to, or characterized by isostasy. [1885–90; ISO- + STATIC] —**i′so•stat′i•cal•ly,** *adv.*

i•so•ste•mo•nous (ī′sə stē′mə nəs, -stem′ə-), *adj. Bot.* having stamens equal in number to the sepals or petals. [1825–35; ISO- + Gk *stḗmōn* thread + -OUS] —**i′so•ste′mo•ny,** *n.*

i•so•stere (ī′sə stēr′), *n.* **1.** *Chem.* a compound isosteric with one or more other compounds. **2.** *Meteorol.* a line on a map or chart connecting points of equal atmospheric density. [1895–1900; ISO- + *-stere* < Gk *stereós* solid, hard]

i•so•ster•ic (ī′sə ster′ik), *adj.* **1.** *Chem.* having the same number of valence electrons in the same configuration but differing in the kinds and numbers of atoms. **2.** *Meteorol.* having or showing equal atmospheric density. [1860–65; ISO- + Gk *ster(eós)* solid, hard + -IC]

i•sos•ter•ism (ī sos′tə riz′əm), *n.* **1.** *Chem.* the quality or state of being isosteric. **2.** *Pharm.* the theory that isosteric compounds have identical or similar pharmacological action. [1860–65; ISOSTERE + -ISM]

i•so•struc•tur•al (ī′sə struk′chər əl), *adj. Crystall.* (of two substances) having the same crystal structure but not necessarily a similar chemical composition. [1905–10; ISO- + STRUCTURAL]

i•so•tac (ī′sə tak′), *n.* a line drawn on a map connecting all points where ice starts to melt at approximately the same period in spring. [ISO- + *-tac* < Gk *takênai* to melt or *takerós* melting]

i•so•tach (ī′sə tak′), *n. Meteorol.* a line on a weather map or chart connecting points where winds of equal speeds have been recorded. [1945–50; ISO- + *-tach* < Gk *tachýs* swift; see TACHY-]

i•so•tac•tic (ī′sə tak′tik), *adj. Chem.* (of a polymer) having the same configuration at successive, regularly spaced positions along the chain. Cf. **configuration** (def. 5). [1950–55; ISO- + TACTIC] —**i•so•tac•tic•i•ty** (ī′sō-tak tis′i tē), *n.*

i•so•there (ī′sə thēr′), *n. Climatol.* a line on a weather map or chart connecting points that have the same mean summer temperature. [1850–55; ISO- + *-there* < Gk *théros* summer] —**i•soth•er•al** (ī soth′ər-əl), *adj.*

i•so•therm (ī′sə thûrm′), *n.* **1.** *Meteorol.* a line on a weather map or chart connecting points having equal temperature. **2.** Also called **i′sother′mal line′.** *Physics.* a curve on which every point represents the same temperature. [1855–60; back formation from ISOTHERMAL]

i•so•ther•mal (ī′sə thûr′məl), *adj.* **1.** occurring at constant temperature. **2.** pertaining to an isotherm. —*n.* **3.** *Meteorol.* an isotherm. Also, **i′so•ther′mic.** [1820–30; < F *isotherme* isothermal (< Gk *iso-* ISO- + *thérmē* heat) + -AL[1]] —**i′so•ther′mal•ly,** *adv.*

i′sother′mal proc′ess, *Thermodynam.* a process that takes place without change in temperature.

i•so•ther•mo•bath (ī′sə thûr′mə bath′), *n.* a line drawn on a diagram of a vertical section of the ocean connecting all points having equal temperature. [ISOTHERM + -O- + *-bath* < Gk *báthos* depth] —**i′so•ther′•mo•bath′ic,** *adj.*

i•so•thi•o•cy•a•nate (ī′sə thī′ō sī′ə nāt′), *n.* a chemical compound containing the univalent radical –NCS. [ISO- + THIOCYANATE]

i•so•tim•ic (ī′sə tim′ik), *adj. Meteorol.* (of a line or surface in space) having an equal value of some quantity at a given time. [ISO- + TIME + -IC]

i•so•tone (ī′sə tōn′), *n. Physics.* one of two or more atoms having an equal number of neutrons but different atomic numbers. [1930–35; ISO- + TONE]

i•so•ton•ic (ī′sə ton′ik), *adj.* **1.** Also, **isosmotic.** *Physical Chem.* noting or pertaining to solutions characterized by equal osmotic pressure. Cf. **hypertonic** (def. 2), **hypotonic** (def. 2). **2.** *Physiol.* **a.** noting or pertaining to a solution containing the same salt concentration as mammalian blood. **b.** noting or pertaining to a muscular contraction in which constant tension continues while the length of the muscle decreases, as during mechanical work. **3.** *Music.* of or characterized by equal tones. [1820–30; < Gk *isóton(os)* having equal accent or tone (see ISO-, TONE) + -IC] —**i•so•to•nic•i•ty** (ī′sə tə nis′i-tē), *n.*

i′soton′ic ex′ercise, 1. exercise or a program of exercises to increase muscular strength, power, and endurance based on lifting a constant amount of weight at variable speeds through a range of motion. **2.** any specific exercise of this type.

i′soton′ic so′dium chlo′ride solu′tion, *Pharm.* an aqueous solution of 0.9 percent sodium chloride, isotonic with the blood and tissue fluid, used in medicine chiefly for bathing tissue and, in sterile form, as a solvent for drugs that are to be administered parenterally to replace body fluids. Also called **normal saline solution, physiological salt solution, physiological sodium chloride solution.** Cf. **Ringer's solution.** [1965–70]

i•so•tope (ī′sə tōp′), *n. Chem.* any of two or more forms of a chemical element, having the same number of protons in the nucleus, or the same atomic number, but having different numbers of neutrons in the nucleus, or different atomic weights. There are 275 isotopes of the 81 stable elements, in addition to over 800 radioactive isotopes, and every element has known isotopic forms. Isotopes of a single element possess almost identical properties. [1910–15; ISO- + *-tope* < Gk *tópos* place] —**i•so•top•ic** (ī′sə top′ik), *adj.* —**i′so•top′i•cal•ly,** *adv.*

i′sotop′ic num′ber, *Physics.* the number of neutrons minus the number of protons in an atomic nucleus.

i′sotop′ic spin′, *Physics.* a quantum number that is related to the number of different values of electric charge that a given kind of baryon or meson may have. *Symbol: I* Also called **isospin, i-spin.** [1935–40]

i•sot•o•py (ī sot′ə pē, ī′sə tō′pē), *n. Chem.* the quality or condition of being isotopic; isotopic character. [1915–20; ISOTOPE + -Y[3]]

i•so•tre•tin•o•in (ī′sō tri tin′ō in, -oin), *n. Pharm.* a yellowish-orange to orange crystalline powder, $C_{20}H_{28}O_2$, used in the treatment of cystic acne. [ISO- + *tretinoin* a name for retinoic or Vitamin A acid, equiv. to *t-* (of uncert. derivation) + *retino(ic acid)* (RETIN(OL) + -O- + -IC) + -IN[2]]

i•so•trop•ic (ī′sə trop′ik, -trō′pik), *adj.* **1.** *Physics.* of equal physical properties along all axes. Cf. **anisotropic** (def. 1). **2.** *Zool.* lacking axes that are predetermined, as in some eggs. Also, **i•sot•ro•pous** (ī so′trə pəs). [1860–65; ISO- + -TROPIC] —**i•sot′ro•py,** *n.*

CONCISE ETYMOLOGY KEY: <, descended or borrowed from; >, whence; b., blend of, blended; c., cognate with; cf., compare; deriv., derivative; equiv., equivalent; imit., imitative; obl., oblique; r., replacing; s., stem; sp., spelling, spelled; resp., respelling, respelled; trans., translation; ?, origin unknown; *, unattested; ‡, probably earlier than. See the full key inside the front cover.

i•so•type (ī′sə tīp′), *n.* **1.** a drawing, diagram, or other symbol that represents a specific quantity of or other fact about the thing depicted: *Every isotype of a house on that chart represents a thousand new houses.* **2.** a statistical graph, chart, diagram, etc., that employs such symbols. **3.** *Biol.* any of two or more separate populations of the same or a similar type. **4.** *Immunol.* any antigenic determinant that is common to all individuals in a species. [1880–85; ISO- + TYPE]

i•so•typ•ic (ī′sə tip′ik), *adj.* **1.** of or pertaining to an isotype. **2.** *Crystall.* (of two substances) isostructural and of similar chemical composition. Also, **i′so•typ′i•cal.** [1925–30; ISOTYPE + -IC]

i•sox•su•prine (ī sok′sə prēn′), *n. Pharm.* a sympathomimetic vasodilator, $C_{18}H_{23}NO_3$, used in certain types of peripheral vascular disease. [perh. IS- + OX- + *Supr(ilent)* a trade name for the drug + -INE[2]]

i•so•zyme (ī′sə zīm′), *n. Biochem.* any of the genetically variant forms of certain enzymes that catalyze the same reaction but that may differ in activity, composition, or physical properties. Also called **isoenzyme.** [1955–60; ISO- + (EN)ZYME]

Is•pa•han (is′pə hän′, is′pə hän′), *n.* **1.** Isfahan. **2.** a Persian rug characterized by hand-tied knots and ornamented with floral and animal patterns, usually on a deep red, blue, or green background. [1930–35]

***I*-spin** (ī′spin′), *n. Physics.* See **isotopic spin.**

Isr., **1.** Israel. **2.** Israeli.

Is•ra′ (iz′rə), *n. Islam.* Muhammad's Night Journey from the Ka'ba at Mecca to Jerusalem. Cf. **Mi'raj.** [< Ar *isrā′* night journey]

Is•ra•el (iz′rē əl, -rā-), *n.* **1.** a republic in SW Asia, on the Mediterranean: formed as a Jewish state May 1948. 3,921,700; 7984 sq. mi. (20,679 sq. km). *Cap.:* Jerusalem. **2.** the people traditionally descended from Jacob; the Hebrew or Jewish people. **3.** a name given to Jacob after he had wrestled with the angel. Gen. 32:28. **4.** the northern kingdom of the Hebrews, including 10 of the 12 tribes, sometimes called by the name of the chief tribe, Ephraim. *Cap.:* Samaria. **5.** a group considered by its members or by others as God's chosen people. **6.** a male given name. [bef. 1000; ME, OE < L *Isrāēl* < Gk *Isrāḗl* < Heb *Yisrā′ēl* lit., God perseveres]

Is′rael ben El•i•ez′er (ben el′ē ez′ər, -ā′zər). See **Baal Shem-Tov.**

Is•rae•li (iz rā′lē), *n., pl.* **-lis,** (*esp. collectively*) **-li,** *adj.* —*n.* **1.** a native or inhabitant of modern Israel. —*adj.* **2.** of or pertaining to modern Israel or its inhabitants. [1945–50; < Heb *yisrā′ēlī*, equiv. to *Yisrā′ēl* ISRAEL + -*ī* suffix of appurtenance]

Is•ra•el•ite (iz′rē ə līt′, -rā-), *n.* **1.** a descendant of Jacob, esp. a member of the Hebrew people who inhabited the ancient kingdom of Israel. **2.** one of a group considered by its members or by others as God's chosen people. —*adj.* **3.** of or pertaining to ancient Israel or its people; Hebrew. [1350–1400; ME; see ISRAEL, -ITE[1]]

Is•ra•el•it•ish (iz′rē ə lī′tish, -rā-), *adj.* of or pertaining to the Israelites; Hebrew. Also, **Is•ra•el•it•ic** (iz′rē ə-lit′ik, -rā-). [1525–35; ISRAELITE + -ISH[1]]

Is•ra•fil (iz′rə fēl′), *n. Islamic Myth.* the angel who will sound the trumpet announcing the end of the world.

Is•sa•char (is′ə kär′), *n.* **1.** a son of Jacob and Leah. Gen. 30:18. **2.** one of the 12 tribes of Israel.

Is•sa•char•ite (is′ə kə rīt′), *n.* a member of the tribe of Issachar. [ISSACHAR + -ITE[1]]

Is•sei (ēs′sā′), *n., pl.* **-sei.** **1.** a Japanese who immigrated to the U.S. or Canada after 1907 and was not eligible until 1952 for citizenship. **2.** any Japanese immigrant to the U.S. Also, **is′sei′.** Cf. **Kibei, Nisei, Sansei.** [1935–40; < Japn, equiv. to *is* first + *sei* generation (earlier *it-sei*, *it-seĭ* < MChin, equiv. to Chin *yī* one + *shēng* birth)]

ISSN, International Standard Serial Number.

is•su•a•ble (ish′o͞o ə bəl), *adj.* **1.** able to be issued or to issue. **2.** forthcoming; receivable. **3.** *Law.* admitting of issue being taken. [1560–70; ISSUE + -ABLE] —**is′su•a•bly,** *adv.*

is•su•ance (ish′o͞o əns), *n.* **1.** the act of issuing. **2.** issue. [1860–65, *Amer.*; ISSUE + -ANCE]

is•su•ant (ish′o͞o ənt), *adj. Heraldry.* (of a beast) represented with the body erect and only the forepart visible: *a lion issuant.* [1600–10; ISSUE + -ANT]

is•sue (ish′o͞o or, *esp. Brit.*, is′yo͞o), *n., v.,* **-sued, -su•ing.** —*n.* **1.** the act of sending out or putting forth; promulgation; distribution: *the issue of food and blankets to flood victims.* **2.** something that is printed or published and distributed, esp. a given number of a periodical: *Have you seen the latest issue of the magazine?* **3.** something that is sent out or put forth in any form. **4.** a quantity of something that is officially offered for sale or put into circulation at one time: *a new issue of commemorative stamps; a new bond issue.* **5.** a point in question or a matter that is in dispute, as between contending parties in an action at law. **6.** a point, matter, or dispute, the decision of which is of special or public importance: *the political issues.* **7.** a point the decision of which determines a matter: *The real issue in the strike was the right to bargain collectively.* **8.** a point at which a matter is ready for decision: *to bring a case to an issue.* **9.** something proceeding from any source, as a product, effect, result, or consequence: *His words were the issue of an intelligent man.* **10.** the ultimate result, event, or outcome of a proceeding, affair, etc.: *the issue of a contest.* **11.** a distribution of food rations, clothing, equipment, or ammunition to a number of officers or enlisted soldiers, or to a military unit. **12.** offspring; progeny: *to die without issue.* **13.** a going, coming, passing, or flowing out: *free issue and entry.* **14.** a place or means of egress; outlet or exit. **15.** something that comes out, as an outflowing stream. **16.** *Pathol.* **a.** a discharge of blood, pus, or the like. **b.** an incision, ulcer, or the like, emitting such a discharge. **17.** **issues,** *Eng. Law.* the profits from land or other property. **18.** the printing of copies of a work from the original setting of type with some slight changes: *the third issue of the poem.* **19.** *Obs.* a proceeding or action. **20.** **at issue, a.** being disputed or under discussion. **b.** being at opposite viewpoints; in disagreement: *Medical experts are still at issue over the proper use of tranquilizers.* **21.** **join issue, a.** to enter into controversy or take exception to. **b.** to submit an issue jointly for legal decision. **22.** **take issue,** to disagree; dispute: *He took issue with me on my proposal for a new advertising campaign.*
—*v.t.* **23.** to put out; deliver for use, sale, etc.; put into circulation. **24.** to mint, print, or publish for sale or distribution: *to issue a new coin; to issue a new book.* **25.** to distribute (food, clothing, etc.) to one or more officers or enlisted soldiers or to a military unit. **26.** to send out; discharge; emit.
—*v.i.* **27.** to go, pass, or flow out; come forth; emerge: *to issue forth to battle.* **28.** to be sent, put forth, or distributed authoritatively or publicly, as a legal writ or money. **29.** to be published, as a book. **30.** to originate or proceed from any source. **31.** to arise as a result or consequence; result: *a reaction that issues from the stimulus.* **32.** *Chiefly Law.* to proceed as offspring, or be born or descended. **33.** *Chiefly Law.* to come as a yield or profit, as from land. **34.** *Archaic.* to have the specified outcome, result, etc. (often fol. by *in*). **35.** *Obs.* to end; terminate. [1275–1325; (n.) ME < MF: place or passage out; OF *(e)issue* < VL **exūta*, n. use of fem. of **exūtus*, L *exitus* EXIT; (v.) ME *issuen*, deriv. of the n., or < MF, OF *(e)issu*, ptp. of *issir* to go out (<< L *exīre*); see EXIT] —**is′sue•less,** *adj.* —**is′su•er,** *n.*
—**Syn. 2.** copy, edition, printing. **5-7.** crux. **6, 7.** problem, question. **10.** upshot, conclusion, end. **27.** See **emerge. 30.** flow, emanate, arise, spring. **31.** ensue.
—**Ant. 27.** return.

is′sue par′, *Finance.* See under **par**[1] (def. 4b).

Is•sus (is′əs), *n.* an ancient town in Asia Minor, in Cilicia: victory of Alexander the Great over Darius III 333 B.C.

Is•syk-Kul (is′ik ko͝ol′; *Russ.* ē sik′ko͝ol′), *n.* a mountain lake in NE Kirghizia (Kyrgyzstan). 2250 sq. mi. (5830 sq. km).

-ist, a suffix of nouns, often corresponding to verbs ending in *-ize* or nouns ending in *-ism*, that denote a person who practices or is concerned with something, or holds certain principles, doctrines, etc.: *apologist; dramatist; machinist; novelist; realist; socialist; Thomist.* Cf. **-ism, -istic, -ize.** [ME *-iste* < L *-ista* < Gk *-istēs*; in some words, repr. F *-iste*, G *-ist*, It *-ista*, etc., << L < Gk, as above]

Is•tam•bu•li (is′tam bo͞o′lē, -bo͝ol′ē, -täm-), *n.* a native or inhabitant of Istanbul. [*Istambul* (resp. of ISTANBUL to reflect the assimilation of *n*) + *-i* < Ar *-ī* adj. suffix of appurtenance]

Is•tan•bul (is′tän bo͞ol′, -tan-; is′tän bo͝ol′, -tan-; *Turk.* is täm′bo͝ol), *n.* a port in NW Turkey, on both sides of the Bosporus: built by Constantine I on the site of ancient Byzantium; capital of the Eastern Roman Empire and of the Ottoman Empire; capital removed to Ankara 1923. 5,494,900. Also, **Stambul, Stamboul.** Formerly (A.D. 330–1930), **Constantinople.**

i•stes•so tem•po, l′ (li stes′ō tem′pō; *It.* lē stes′sô tem′pô), *Music.* See **l'istesso tempo.**

Isth., isthmus. Also, **isth.**

isth•mi•an (is′mē ən), *adj.* **1.** of or pertaining to an isthmus. **2.** (*cap.*) of or pertaining to the Isthmus of Corinth or the Isthmus of Panama. —*n.* **3.** a native or inhabitant of an isthmus. [1595–1605; < L *isthmi(us)* (< Gk *ísthmios* of a neck of land, equiv. to *isthm(ós)* neck + *-ios* adj. suffix) + -AN]

Isth′mian Games′, one of the great national festivals of ancient Greece, held every two years on the Isthmus of Corinth. [1595–1605]

isth•mus (is′məs), *n., pl.* **-mus•es, -mi** (-mī). **1.** a narrow strip of land, bordered on both sides by water, connecting two larger bodies of land. **2.** *Anat., Zool.* a connecting, usually narrow, part, organ, or passage, esp. when joining structures or cavities larger than itself. **3.** *Ichthyol.* the narrow fleshy area between the sides of the lower jaw of a fish. [1545–55; < L < Gk *isthmós* neck (of land)] —**isth′moid,** *adj.*

-istic, a suffix of adjectives (and in the plural, of nouns from adjectives) formed from nouns ending in *-ist* and having reference to such nouns, or to associated nouns in *-ism* (*deistic; euphuistic; puristic*). In nouns, it usually has a plural form (*linguistics*). Cf. **-ist, -ic, -ics.** [< L *-isticus* < Gk *-istikos*; in some words, r. *-istique* < F < L, as above]

-istical, a combination of **-istic** and **-al**[1].

-istics, a combination of **-ist** and **-ics.**

is•tle (ist′lē), *n.* a fiber from any of several tropical American plants of the genus *Agave* or *Yucca*, used in making bagging, carpets, etc. Also, **ixtle.** [1880–85; < MexSp *istle, ixtle* < Nahuatl *ichtli*]

Is•to•min (is′tə min), *n.* **Eugene,** born 1925, U.S. concert pianist.

Is•tri•a (is′trē ə; *It.* ēs′trēä), *n.* a peninsula at the N end of the Adriatic, in SW Slovenia and W Croatia. Also called **Is′trian Penin′sula.** —**Is′tri•an,** *adj., n.*

ISV, International Scientific Vocabulary.

it[1] (it), *pron., nom.* **it,** *poss.* **its** or (*Obs. or Dial.*) **it,** *obj.* **it;** *pl. nom.* **they,** *poss.* **their** or **theirs,** *obj.* **them;** *n.* —*pron.* **1.** (used to represent an inanimate thing understood, previously mentioned, about to be mentioned, or present in the immediate context): *It has whitewall tires and red upholstery. You can't tell a book by its cover.* **2.** (used to represent a person or animal understood, previously mentioned, or about to be mentioned whose gender is unknown or disregarded): *It was the largest ever caught off the Florida coast. Who was it? It was John. The horse had its saddle on.* **3.** (used to represent a group understood or previously mentioned): *The judge told the jury it must decide two issues.* **4.** (used to represent a concept or abstract idea understood or previously stated): *It all started with Adam and Eve. He has been taught to believe it all his life.* **5.** (used to represent an action or activity understood, previously mentioned, or about to be mentioned): *Since you don't like it, you don't have to go skiing.* **6.** (used as the impersonal subject of the verb *to be*, esp. to refer to time, distance, or the weather): *It is six o'clock. It is five miles to town. It was foggy.* **7.** (used in statements expressing an action, condition, fact, circumstance, or situation without reference to an agent): *If it weren't for Edna, I wouldn't go.* **8.** (used in referring to something as the origin or cause of pain, pleasure, etc.): *Where does it hurt? It looks bad for the candidate.* **9.** (used in referring to a source not specifically named or described): *It is said that love is blind.* **10.** (used in referring to the general state of affairs; circumstances, fate, or life in general): *How's it going with you?* **11.** (used as an anticipatory subject or object to make a sentence more eloquent or suspenseful or to shift emphasis): *It is necessary that you do your duty. It was a gun that he was carrying.* **12.** *Informal.* (used instead of the pronoun its before a gerund): *It having rained for only one hour didn't help the crops.* —*n.* **13.** (in children's games) the player called upon to perform some task, as, in tag, the one who must catch the other players. **14.** *Slang.* **a.** sex appeal. **b.** sexual intercourse. **15.** **get with it,** *Slang.* to become active or interested: *He was warned to get with it or resign.* **16.** **have it,** *Informal.* **a.** to love someone: *She really has it bad for him.* **b.** to possess the requisite abilities for something; be talented, adept, or proficient: *In this business you either have it or you don't.* **17.** **with it,** *Slang.* **a.** aware of the latest fads, fashions, etc.; up-to-date. **b.** attentive or alert. **c.** understanding or appreciative of something, as jazz. **d.** *Carnival Slang.* being a member of the carnival. [bef. 900; ME, var. of ME, OE *hit*, neut. of HE[1]]
—**Usage.** See **me.**

it[2] (it), *n. Brit. Informal.* sweet vermouth: *gin and it.* [1930–35; *It(alian vermouth)*]

It, Italian (def. 3).

It., **1.** Italian. **2.** Italy.

I.T.A., See **Initial Teaching Alphabet.** Also, **i.t.a.**

I•ta•bu•na (ē′tə bo͞o′nə), *n.* a city in E Brazil. 87,561.

it•a•col•u•mite (it′ə kol′yə mīt′), *n.* a sandstone consisting of interlocking quartz grains and mica scales, found principally in Brazil and North Carolina, and noted for its flexibility in thin slabs. [1860–65; named after *Itacolumi*, mountain in Brazil; see ITE[1]]

it•a•con′ic ac′id (it′ə kon′ik), *Chem.* a colorless crystalline compound, $C_5H_6O_4$, obtained by fermentation, soluble in water, alcohol, and acetone: used as an intermediate in the formation of fibers, resins, etc. [1860–65; rearrangement of the letters of *aconitic* acid, orig. extracted from ACONITE]

I•ta•güí (ē′tä gwē′), *n.* a city in W central Colombia. 123,600.

I•ta•ja•í (ē′tə zhə ē′), *n.* a seaport in S Brazil. 50,669.

Ital., **1.** Italian. **2.** Italic. **3.** Italy.

ital., **1.** italic; italics. **2.** italicized.

I•ta•lia (ē tä′lyä), *n.* Italian name of **Italy.**

Ita′lia ir•re•den′ta (*It.* ēʀ′ʀe den′tä). See under **irredentist** (def. 1).

CONCISE PRONUNCIATION KEY: act, cāpe, dâre, pärt; set, ēqual; *if*, īce; ox, ōver, ôrder, oil, bo͝ok, bo͞ot, out; up, ûrge; child; sing; shoe; thin, *that*; zh as in *treasure*. ə = *a* as in *alone*, *e* as in *system*, *i* as in *easily*, *o* as in *gallop*, *u* as in *circus*; ᵊ as in *fire* (fīᵊr), *hour* (ouᵊr). l and n can serve as syllabic consonants, as in *cradle* (krād′l), and *button* (but′n). See the full key inside the front cover.

I·tal·ian (i tal′yən), *adj.* **1.** of or pertaining to Italy, its people, or their language. —*n.* **2.** a native or inhabitant of Italy, or a person of Italian descent. **3.** a Romance language, the language of Italy, official also in Switzerland. *Abbr.:* It, It., Ital. [1350–1400; ME < ML *Italiānus.* See ITALY, -AN] —**I·tal′ian·esque′,** *adj.*
—**Pronunciation.** The pronunciation of ITALIAN with an initial (ī) sound (pronounced like the word *eye*) and often with level stress on the first and second syllables: (ī′tal′yən) is heard primarily from uneducated speakers. This pronunciation is sometimes facetious or disparaging in purpose and is usually considered offensive.

Ital′ian as′ter, a composite plant, *Aster amellus,* of Eurasia, having clustered, purple flower heads.

I·tal·ian·ate (*adj.* i tal′yə nāt′, -nit; *v.* i tal′yə nāt′), *adj., v.,* **-at·ed, -at·ing.** —*adj.* **1.** Italianized; conforming to the Italian type or style or to Italian customs, manners, etc. **2.** *Art.* in the style of Renaissance or Baroque Italy. **3.** *Archit.* noting or pertaining to a mid-Victorian American style remotely based on Romanesque vernacular residential and castle architecture of the Italian countryside, but sometimes containing Renaissance and Baroque elements. —*v.t.* **4.** to Italianize. [1560–70; < It *italianato.* See ITALIAN, -ATE[1]] —**I·tal′ian·ate′ly,** *adv.* —**I·tal′ian·a′tion,** *n.*

Ital′ian bread′, a crusty, yeast-raised bread made without shortening and unsweetened, usually baked in long, thick loaves with tapered ends.

Ital′ian clo′ver. See **crimson clover.** [1830–40]

Ital′ian corn′ sal′ad, a southern European plant, *Valerianella eriocarpa,* of the valerian family, having edible, spoon-shaped, hairy leaves and dense clusters of pale-blue flowers.

Ital′ian East′ Af′rica, a former Italian territory in E Africa, formed in 1936 by the merging of Eritrea and Italian Somaliland with newly conquered Ethiopia: taken by the British Imperial forces 1941.

Ital′ian grey′hound, one of an Italian breed of toy dogs resembling a greyhound. [1735–45]

Ital′ian hand′, **1.** a medieval script, used in early printing and later considered a standard of fine handwriting. **2.** subtlety, or craftiness: *I sense his fine Italian hand in this matter.*

I·tal·ian·ism (i tal′yə niz′əm), *n.* **1.** an Italian practice, trait, or idiom. **2.** Italian quality or spirit. [1585–95; ITALIAN + -ISM]

I·tal·ian·ist (i tal′yə nist), *n.* a person who specializes in the study of Italy, the Italian people, or the Italian language. [1850–55; ITALIAN + -IST]

I·tal·ian·ize (i tal′yə nīz′), *v.,* **-ized, -iz·ing.** —*v.i.* **1.** to become Italian in manner, character, etc. **2.** to speak Italian. —*v.t.* **3.** to make Italian, esp. in manner, character, etc. Also, *esp. Brit.,* **I·tal′ian·ise′.** [1605–15; ITALIAN + -IZE] —**I·tal′ian·i·za′tion,** *n.*

I·tal·ian·iz·er (i tal′yə nī′zər), *n.* a person or thing that Italianizes: *In matters of food and dress, he is an Italianizer.* [1840–50; ITALIANIZE + -ER[1]]

Ital′ian jas′mine, an evergreen shrub, *Jasminum humile,* of the olive family, having fragrant, golden-yellow flowers.

Ital′ian point′er. See **Spinoni Italiani.**

Ital′ian rye′ grass′, a European grass, *Lolium multiflorum,* naturalized in North America, having flowering spikes and used as a winter turf. Also called **Australian rye grass.** [1855–60]

Ital′ian Soma′liland, a former Italian colony and trust territory in E Africa: now part of the Democratic Somali Republic.

Ital′ian son′net. See **Petrarchan sonnet.** [1875–80]

Ital′ian tur′nip. See **broccoli rabe.**

i·tal·ic (i tal′ik, ī tal′-), *adj.* **1.** designating or pertaining to a style of printing types in which the letters usually slope to the right, patterned upon a compact manuscript hand, and used for emphasis, to separate different kinds of information, etc.: *These words are in italic type.* **2.** (*cap.*) of or pertaining to Italy, esp. ancient Italy or its tribes. —*n.* **3.** Often, **italics.** italic type. **4.** (*cap.*) a branch of the Indo-European family of languages, including ancient Latin, Oscan, Umbrian, and modern Romance. [1555–65; < L *Italicus* < Gk *Italikós,* equiv. to *Ital(ía)* ITALY + *-ikos* -IC]

I·tal·i·cism (i tal′ə siz′əm), *n.* Italianism, esp. an idiom or a characteristic of the Italian language. [1765–75; ITALIC + -ISM]

i·tal·i·cize (i tal′ə sīz′, ī tal′-), *v.,* **-cized, -ciz·ing.** —*v.t.* **1.** to print in italic type. **2.** to underscore with a single line, as in indicating italics. —*v.i.* **3.** to use italics. Also, *esp. Brit.,* **i·tal′i·cise′.** [1785–95; ITALIC + -IZE] —**i·tal′i·ci·za′tion,** *n.*

I·tal·o·phile (i tal′ə fīl′, it′l ə-), *n.* **1.** a person who admires Italian customs, traditions, etc. —*adj.* **2.** Also, **I·tal·o·phil** (i tal′ə fil, it′l ə-). favoring Italian customs, manners, traditions, etc. [1905–10; ITAL(IAN) + -O- + -PHILE]

It·a·ly (it′l ē), *n.* a republic in S Europe, comprising a peninsula S of the Alps, and Sicily, Sardinia, Elba, and other smaller islands: a kingdom 1870–1946. 56,160,000; 116,294 sq. mi. (301,200 sq. km). *Cap.:* Rome. Italian, **Italia.**

I·ta·pe·ti·nin·ga (ē′tə pe′tē nēn′gə), *n.* a city in E Brazil. 56,437.

I·tas·ca (i tas′kə), *n.* **Lake,** a lake in N Minnesota: one of the sources of the Mississippi River.

CONCISE ETYMOLOGY KEY: <, descended or borrowed from; >, whence; b., blend of, blended; c., cognate with; cf., compare; deriv., derivative; equiv., equivalent; imit., imitative; obl., oblique; r., replacing; s., stem; sp., spelling, spelled; resp., respelling, respelled; trans., translation; ?, origin unknown; *, unattested; ‡, probably earlier than. See the full key inside the front cover.

ITC, investment tax credit.

itch (ich), *v.i.* **1.** to have or feel a peculiar tingling or uneasy irritation of the skin that causes a desire to scratch the part affected: *My nose itches.* **2.** to cause such a feeling: *This shirt itches.* **3.** *Informal.* to scratch a part that itches. **4.** to have a desire to do or get something: *to itch after fame.* —*v.t.* **5.** to cause to have an itch: *His wool shirt always itches him.* **6.** *Informal.* to scratch (a part that itches): *to itch a mosquito bite.* **7.** to annoy; vex; irritate: *Her remarks itched me.* —*n.* **8.** the sensation of itching. **9.** an uneasy or restless desire or longing: *an itch for excitement.* **10.** a contagious disease caused by the itch mite, which burrows into the skin (usually prec. by *the*). Cf. **mange, scabies.** [bef. 900; (v.) ME *(y)icchen,* OE *gicc(e)an;* akin to G *jucken,* D *jeuken;* (n.) ME *(y)icche,* OE *gicce,* deriv. of the v.]

itch·ing (ich′ing), *adj.* **1.** of, pertaining to, or characterized by an irritating sensation of the skin. **2.** of, pertaining to, or having a longing or desire to do or have something: *An itching public anxiously awaits her announcement.* **3.** characterized by restlessness or the desire for adventure or activity: *an itching impulse to travel.* **4.** characterized by the desire to grasp; grasping; *an itching palm open for a bribe.* —*n.* **5.** itch. [bef. 1000; ME *(y)ichinge, (y)itchinge* (n., adj.); r. OE *giccende* (adj.). See ITCH, -ING[2], -ING[1]] —**itch′ing·ly,** *adv.*

itch′ mite′, a parasitic mite, *Sarcoptes scabiei,* causing itch or scabies in humans and a form of mange in animals. [1825–35]

itch·y (ich′ē), *adj.,* **itch·i·er, itch·i·est. 1.** having or causing an itching sensation. **2.** characterized by itching. [1520–30; ITCH, + -Y[1]; cf. OE *giccig* (rare) purulent, putrid] —**itch′i·ness,** *n.*

it'd (it′əd), **1.** contraction of *it would.* **2.** contraction of *it had.*
—**Usage.** See **contraction.**

-ite[1], a suffix of nouns denoting esp. persons associated with a place, tribe, leader, doctrine, system, etc. (*Campbellite; Israelite; laborite*); minerals and fossils (*ammonite; anthracite*); explosives (*cordite; dynamite*); chemical compounds, esp. salts of acids whose names end in *-ous* (*phosphite; sulfite*); pharmaceutical and commercial products (*vulcanite*); a member or component of a part of the body (*somite*). Cf. **-itis.** [ME < L *-ita* < Gk *-itēs;* often directly < Gk; in some words repr. F *-ite,* G *-it,* etc. < L < Gk, as above]

-ite[2], a suffix forming adjectives and nouns from adjectives, and from some verbs: *composite; opposite; erudite; requisite.* [< L *-itus* or *-itus* ptp. suffix]

it·e·a (it′ē ə, ī′tē ə), *n.* any tree or shrub belonging to the genus *Itea,* of the saxifrage family, having simple, alternate leaves and clusters of small, greenish-white flowers, as the Virginia willow, *I. virginica.* [< NL (Linnaeus) < Gk *itéa* willow]

I·tel·men (ē′tel men′), *n.* **1.** a member of a small group of Paleo-Asiatic people inhabiting the Kamchatka peninsula in eastern Siberia. **2.** the Chukotian language of the Itelmen people. Also called **Kamchadal.**

i·tem (*n., v.* ī′təm; *adv.* ī′tem), *n.* **1.** a separate article or particular: *50 items on the list.* **2.** a separate piece of information or news, as a short piece in a newspaper or broadcast. **3.** *Slang.* something suitable for a news paragraph or as a topic of gossip, esp. something that is sensational or scandalous: *The bandleader and the new female singer are an item.* **4.** a word formerly used in communications to represent the letter *I.* **5.** an admonition or warning. **6.** *Older Use.* an intimation or hint. —*adv.* **7.** also; likewise (used esp. to introduce each article or statement in a list or series). —*v.t. Archaic.* **8.** to set down or enter as an item, or by or in items. **9.** to make a note of. [1350–1400; ME: likewise (adv.), the same (n.) < L: likewise]
—**Syn. 1.** thing; heading, entry.

i·tem·ize (ī′tə mīz′), *v.,* **-ized, -iz·ing.** —*v.t.* **1.** to state by items; give the particulars of; list the individual units or parts of: *to itemize an account.* **2.** to list as an item or separate part: *to itemize deductions on an income-tax return.* —*v.i.* **3.** to compute an income-tax return by listing separately all assets, credits, allowable deductions, losses, etc. Also, *esp. Brit.,* **i′tem·ise′.** [1855–60, *Amer.;* ITEM + -IZE] —**i′tem·i·za′tion,** *n.* —**i′tem·iz′er,** *n.*

i′tem ve′to. See **line-item veto.**

it·er (it′âr, ī′târ), *n. Anat.* a canal or passage. [1590–1600; < L: journey, route, passage in the body, akin to *ire* to go, Hittite *itar* way, road]

it·er·ance (it′ər əns), *n.* iteration. [1595–1605; ITER(ANT) + -ANCE]

it·er·ant (it′ər ənt), *adj.* characterized by repetition; repeating. [1620–30; < L *iterant-* (s. of *iterāns*), prp. of *iterāre* to repeat. See ITERATE, -ANT]

it·er·ate (it′ə rāt′), *v.,* **-at·ed, -at·ing.** —*v.t.* **1.** to utter again or repeatedly. **2.** to do (something) over again or repeatedly. —*v.i.* **3.** to operate or be applied repeatedly, as a linguistic rule or mathematical formula. [1525–35; < L *iterātus,* ptp. of *iterāre* to repeat, equiv. to *iter-* (s. of *iterum*) again + *-ātus* -ATE[1]]
—**Syn. 1.** reiterate, repeat, rehearse.

it′erated in′tegral, *Math.* **1.** a double integral that is evaluated by first integrating the integrand with respect to one variable with the second variable being held constant and then integrating the resulting function with respect to the second variable. **2.** a multiple integral of three or more variables that is evaluated by an extension of the above method.

it·er·a·tion (it′ə rā′shən), *n.* **1.** the act of repeating; a repetition. **2.** *Math.* **a.** a problem-solving or computational method in which a succession of approximations, each building on the one preceding, is used to achieve a desired degree of accuracy. **b.** an instance of the use of this method. **3.** *Computers.* a repetition of a statement or statements in a program. [1425–75; late ME < L *iterātiōn-,* s. of *iterātiō;* see ITERATE, -ION]

it·er·a·tive (it′ə rā′tiv, -ər ə tiv), *adj.* **1.** repeating; making repetition; repetitious. **2.** *Gram.* frequentative. [1480–90; < LL *iterātīvus.* See ITERATE, -IVE] —**it′er·a′tive·ly,** *adv.* —**it′er·a′tive·ness,** *n.*

Ith·a·ca (ith′ə kə), *n.* **1.** one of the Ionian Islands, off

the W coast of Greece: legendary home of Ulysses. 4156; 37 sq. mi. (96 sq. km). **2.** a city in S New York at the S end of Cayuga Lake. 28,732. —**Ith′a•can,** *adj., n.*

ith•er (ith′ər), *adj., pron., adv. Brit. Dial.* other. —**ith′er•ness,** *n.*

I•tho•me (i thō′mē), *n.* **1. Mount,** a mountain in SW Greece, in SW Peloponnesus. 2630 ft. (802 m). **2.** in ancient geography, a fortress of Messenia on Mount Ithome.

I•thunn (ē′thŏŏn), *n.* Idun. Also, **I′thun.**

ith•y•phal•lic (ith′ə fal′ik), *adj.* **1.** of or pertaining to the phallus carried in ancient festivals of Bacchus. **2.** grossly indecent; obscene. **3.** *Class. Pros.* noting or pertaining to any of several meters employed in hymns sung in Bacchic processions. —*n.* **4.** a poem in ithyphallic meter. **5.** an indecent poem. [1605–15; < LL *ithyphallicus* < Gk *ithyphallikós,* equiv. to *ithý(s)* straight, erect + *phall(ós)* PHALLUS + *-ikos* -IC]

-itic, a combination of **-ite**[1] and **-ic,** used to form adjectives from nouns ending in **-ite:** *Semitic.* [< L *-iticus* < Gk *-itikos,* equiv. to *-it(ēs)* -ITE[1] + *-ikos* -IC; in some words repr. F *-itique* < L < Gk, as above]

i•tin•er•an•cy (ī tin′ər ən sē, i tin′-), *n.* **1.** the act of traveling from place to place. **2.** a going around from place to place in the discharge of duty or the conducting of business. **3.** a body of itinerants, as ministers, judges, or sales representatives. **4.** the state of being itinerant. **5.** the system of rotation governing the ministry of the Methodist Church. Also, **i•tin•er•a•cy** (ī tin′ər ə sē, i tin′-). [1780–90; ITINER(ANT) + -ANCY]

i•tin•er•ant (ī tin′ər ənt, i tin′-), *adj.* **1.** traveling from place to place, esp. on a circuit, as a minister, judge, or sales representative; itinerating; journeying. **2.** characterized by such traveling: *itinerant preaching.* **3.** working in one place for a comparatively short time and then moving on to work in another place, usually as a physical or outdoor laborer; characterized by alternating periods of working and wandering: *an itinerant farm hand.* —*n.* **4.** a person who alternates between working and wandering. **5.** a person who travels from place to place, esp. for duty or business. [1560–70; < LL *itinerant-* (s. of *itinerāns*), prp. of *itinerārī* to journey, equiv. to *itiner-* (s. of *iter*) journey (see ITER) + *-ant-* -ANT] —**i•tin′er•ant•ly,** *adv.*
—**Syn. 1, 3.** wandering, nomadic, migratory, unsettled, roving, roaming; peripatetic. —**Ant. 1.** settled.

i•tin•er•ar•i•um (ī tin′ə râr′ē əm, i tin′-), *n., pl.* **-er•ar•i•a** (-ə râr′ē ə), **-er•ar•i•ums.** *Rom. Cath. Ch.* a prayer in the breviary, used by a priest about to begin a journey. [1700–10; < ML *itinerārium;* see ITINERARY]

i•tin•er•ar•y (ī tin′ə rer′ē, i tin′-), *n., pl.* **-ar•ies,** *adj.* —*n.* **1.** a detailed plan for a journey, esp. a list of places to visit; plan of travel. **2.** a line of travel; route. **3.** an account of a journey; record of travel. **4.** a book describing a route or routes of travel with information helpful to travelers; guidebook for travelers. —*adj.* **5.** of or pertaining to travel or travel routes. **6.** *Obs.* itinerant. [1425–75; late ME < LL *itinerārium,* n. use of neut. of *itinerārius* of a journey, equiv. to *itiner-* (s. of *iter*) journey (see ITER) + *-ārius* -ARY]

i•tin•er•ate (ī tin′ə rāt′, i tin′-), *v.i.,* **-at•ed, -at•ing.** to go from place to place, esp. in a regular circuit, as a preacher or judge. [1590–1600; < LL *itinerātus,* ptp. of *itinerārī* to travel, equiv. to L *itiner-* (s. of *iter*) journey (see ITER) + *-ātus* -ATE[1]] —**i•tin′er•a′tion,** *n.*

-ition, a compound suffix of nouns, being *-tion* with a preceding original or formative vowel, or, in other words, a combination of **-ite**[2] and **-ion:** *expedition; extradition.* [< L *-itiōn-* or *-ītiōn-,* s. of *-itiō* or *-ītiō.* See -ITE[2], -ION]

-itious, a compound suffix occurring in adjectives of Latin origin (*adventitious*) and with adjectives, formed in Latin or English, associated with nouns ending in *-ition* (*ambitious; expeditious*). Cf. **-ite**[2], **-ous.** [< L *-icius* or *-īcius* (as in ADVENTITIOUS); and < L *-itiōsus* or *-ītiōsus* (as in AMBITIOUS)]

-itis, a suffix used in pathological terms that denote inflammation of an organ (*bronchitis; gastritis; neuritis*) and hence, in extended senses, nouns denoting abnormal states or conditions, excesses, tendencies, obsessions, etc. (*telephonitis; baseballitis*). [< NL (or L) *-itis* < Gk]

-itive, a suffix occurring in substantives of Latin origin: *definitive; fugitive.* [< L *-itīvus* or *-ītivus;* see -ITE[2], -IVE]

it'll (it′l), contraction of *it will.*
—**Usage.** See **contraction.**

I•to (ē′tô′), *n.* **Prince Hi•ro•bu•mi** (hē′Rô bŏŏ′mē), 1841–1909, Japanese statesman.

ITO, International Trade Organization.

-itol, *Chem.* a suffix used in names of alcohols containing more than one hydroxyl group: *inositol.* [-ITE[1] + -OL[1]]

its (its), *pron.* the possessive form of **it** (used as an attributive adjective): *The book has lost its jacket. I'm sorry about its being so late.* [1590–1600; earlier *it's,* equiv. to IT[1] + -'S[1]]
—**Usage.** While it is possible to use ITS as a predicate adjective (*The cat is angry because the bowl you're eating out of is its!*) or as a pronoun meaning "that or those belonging to it" (*Your notebook pages are torn. Borrow my notebook—its aren't*), such use is rare and in most circumstances strained. See also **me.**

it's (its), **1.** contraction of *it is: It's starting to rain.* **2.** contraction of *it has: It's been a long time.*
—**Usage.** See **contraction.**

it•self (it self′), *pron.* **1.** a reflexive form of **it:** *The battery recharges itself.* **2.** an emphatic appositive of **it, which, that, this,** or a noun: *which itself is also true; Even without flowers, the bowl itself is beautiful.* **3.** (used as the object of a preposition or as the direct or indirect object of a verb): *The chameleon's ability to change color is a protection for itself.* **4.** its normal or customary self: *After much tender care, the puppy was soon itself again.* [bef. 1000; ME; OE *hit self.* See IT[1], SELF]
—**Usage.** See **myself.**

it•ty-bit•ty (it′ē bit′ē), *adj. Informal.* very small; tiny. Also, **it•sy-bit•sy** (it′sē bit′sē). [1890–95; rhyming compound based on *little bit;* cf. -SY, -Y[1]]

ITU, International Telecommunication Union.

I.T.U., International Typographical Union.

I•tur•bi (i tûr′bē, i tŏŏr′-; *Sp.* ē tōōR′vē), *n.* **José,** 1895–1980, U.S. pianist, conductor, and composer; born in Spain.

I•túr•bi•de (ē tōōR′vē the), *n.* **A•gus•tín de** (ä′gōōs-tēn′ de), 1783–1824, Mexican soldier and revolutionary: as Agustín I, emperor of Mexico 1822–23.

ITV, instructional television.

-ity, a suffix used to form abstract nouns expressing state or condition: *jollity; civility; Latinity.* [var. of *-itie,* ME *-ite* < OF < L *-itāt-* (s. of *-itās*); in many words repr. L *-itās* directly]

IU, 1. immunizing unit. **2.** Also, **I.U.** international unit.

IUD, See **intrauterine device.** [1960–65]

-ium, a suffix found on nouns borrowed from Latin, esp. derivatives of verbs (*odium; tedium; colloquium; delirium*), deverbal compounds with the initial element denoting the object of the verb (*nasturtium*), other types of compounds (*equilibrium; millennium*), and derivatives of personal nouns, often denoting the associated status or office (*collegium; consortium*); **-ium** also occurs in scientific coinages on a Latin model, as in names of metallic elements (*barium; titanium*) and as a Latinization of Gk *-ion* (*pericardium*). [< NL, L, neut. suffix]

IUS, *Rocketry.* See **inertial upper stage.**

IV (ī′vē′), *n., pl.* **IVs, IV's.** an intravenous device for delivering electrolyte solutions, medicines, and nutrients. [1950–55]

IV, 1. intravenous. **2.** intravenous drip. **3.** intravenous injection. **4.** intravenously.

I.V., initial velocity.

i.v., 1. increased value. **2.** initial velocity. **3.** invoice value.

i•va (ī′və, ē′və), *n.* any composite plant of the genus *Iva,* characterized by usually opposite leaves and inconspicuous greenish-yellow flowers. [< NL (Linnaeus); of uncert. orig.]

i•van (ē′vän), *n.* iwan.

I•van (ī′vən; *Russ.* ē vän′), *n.* a male given name, Russian form of **John.**

Ivan III, ("*Ivan the Great*") 1440–1505, grand duke of Muscovy 1462–1505.

Ivan IV, ("*Ivan the Terrible*") 1530–84, first czar of Russia 1547–84.

I•van•hoe (ī′vən hō′), *n.* a novel (1819) by Sir Walter Scott.

I•va•no-Fran•kovsk (ē vä′nə fRun kôfsk′; *Eng.* i vä′nō fräng kôfsk′, -kofsk′), *n.* a city in W Ukraine, S of Lvov. 150,000. Formerly, **Stanislav.** Polish, **Stanisławów.**

I•va•nov (ē vä′nəf), *n.* **Vse•vo•lod Vya•che•sla•vo•vich** (fsye′və lət vyi chyi slä′və vyich), 1895–1963, Russian playwright.

I•va•no•vo (ē vä′nə və), *n.* a city in the W Russian Federation in Europe, NE of Moscow. 465,000. Formerly, **Iva′novo Vo•zne•sensk′** (voz′nə sensk′; *Russ.* və znyi-syensk′).

I•var (ī′vər, ē′vər), *n.* a male or female given name.

I've (īv), contraction of *I have.*
—**Usage.** See **contraction.**

-ive, a suffix of adjectives (and nouns of adjectival origin) expressing tendency, disposition, function, connection, etc.: *active; corrective; destructive; detective; passive; sportive.* Cf. **-ative, -itive.** [< L *-īvus;* in some words, repr. F *-ive,* fem. of *-if*]

Ives (īvz), *n.* **1. Burl (I•cle Ivanhoe)** (bûrl ik′əl), born 1909, U.S. actor and folk singer. **2. Charles Edward,** 1874–1954, U.S. composer. **3. Frederic Eugene,** 1856–1937, U.S. inventor. **4. James Mer•ritt** (mer′it), 1824–95, U.S. lithographer. Cf. **Currier. 5.** a male given name.

IVF, in vitro fertilization.

i•vied (ī′vēd), *adj.* covered or overgrown with ivy: *ivied walls.* [1765–75; IVY + -ED[3]]

I•vi•za (ē vē′sä), *n.* Ibiza.

I•vor (ī′vər, ē′vər), *n.* a male given name.

i•vo•ry (ī′və rē, ī′vrē), *n., pl.* **-ries,** *adj.* —*n.* **1.** the hard white substance, a variety of dentin, composing the main part of the tusks of the elephant, walrus, etc. **2.** this substance when taken from a dead animal and used to make carvings, billiard balls, etc. **3.** some substance resembling this. **4.** an article made of this substance, as a carving or a billiard ball. **5.** a tusk, as of an elephant. **6.** dentin of any kind. **7.** *Slang.* a tooth, or the teeth. **8. ivories,** *Slang.* **a.** the keys of a piano or of a similar keyboard instrument. **b.** dice. **9.** Also called **vegetable ivory.** the hard endosperm of the ivory nut, used for ornamental purposes, for buttons, etc. **10.** a creamy or yellowish white. **11.** a smooth paper finish produced by coating with beeswax before calendering. —*adj.* **12.** consisting or made of ivory. **13.** of the color ivory. [1250–1300; ME < OF *ivurie* < L *eboreus* (adj.), equiv. to *ebor-* (s. of *ebur*) ivory + *-eus* adj. suffix; see -EOUS] —**i′vo•ry•like′,** *adj.*

i′vo•ry-billed wood′pecker (ī′və rē bild′, ī′vrē-), a large, nearly extinct, black and white woodpecker, *Campephilus principalis,* of the southern U.S. and Cuba, having an ivory-colored bill. [1805–15, *Amer.*]

i′vory black′, a fine black pigment made by calcining ivory. [1625–35]

I′vory Coast′, a republic in W Africa: formerly part of French West Africa; gained independence 1960. 12,100,000; 127,520 sq. mi. (330,275 sq. km). *Political Cap.:* Yamoussoukro. *Commercial Cap.:* Abidjan. French, **Côte d'Ivoire.** —**I•vo•ri•an** (ī vôr′ē ən, ī vōr′-), *adj., n.*

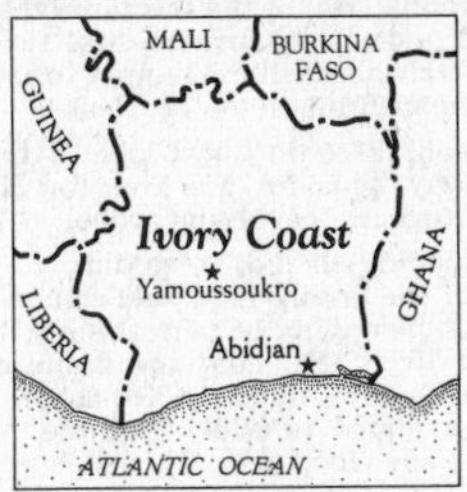

i′vory gull′, a white, arctic gull, *Pagophila eburnea.* [1915–20]

i′vory nut′, 1. the seed of a low, South American palm, *Phytelephas macrocarpa,* yielding vegetable ivory. **2.** a similar seed from other palms. [1915–20]

i′vory palm′, the palm bearing the common ivory nut. [1835–45]

i′vory tow′er, 1. a place or situation remote from worldly or practical affairs: *the university as an ivory tower.* **2.** an attitude of aloofness from or disdain or disregard for worldly or practical affairs: *his ivory tower of complacency.* [trans. of F *tour d'ivoire,* phrase used by C.A. Sainte-Beuve in reference to the isolated life of the poet A. de Vigny (1837)] —**i′vo•ry-tow′ered, i′vo•ry-tow′er•ish,** *adj.* —**i′vo•ry-tow′er•ism, i′vo•ry-tow′er•ish•ness,** *n.* —**i′vo•ry-tow′er•ist, i′vo•ry-tow′•er•ite′,** *n.*

i•vo•ry•type (ī′və rē tīp′, ī′vrē-), *n. Photog.* an antiquated photoprinting technique in which two prints are made of the same image, and the weaker one, made transparent with varnish and colored on the back, is laid over the stronger one. [1855–60, *Amer.;* IVORY + -TYPE]

i•vo•ry-white (ī′və rē hwīt′, -wīt′, ī′vrē-), *adj.* of a creamy or yellowish white in color. [1585–95]

-ivus, a suffix appearing in Latin scientific names: *exfoliativus.* Cf. **-ive.** [< NL, L *-īvus*]

i•vy (ī′vē), *n., pl.* **i•vies,** *adj.* —*n.* **1.** Also called **English ivy.** a climbing vine, *Hedera helix,* having smooth, shiny, evergreen leaves, small, yellowish flowers, and black berries, grown as an ornamental. **2.** any of various other climbing or trailing plants. —*adj.* **3.** (*often cap.*) See **Ivy League** (def. 2). **4.** *New England.* See **mountain laurel.** [bef. 900; ME *ivi;* OE *īfig;* akin to G *Efeu*] —**i′vy•like′,** *adj.*

ivy, *Hedera helix*

I•vy (ī′vē), *n.* a female given name.

i′vy gera′nium, a trailing geranium, *Pelargonium peltatum,* of southern Africa, having a fleshy stem that becomes woody with age, glossy, ivy-shaped leaves, and clusters of flowers ranging from white to deep rose in color. [1890–95]

I′vy League′, 1. a group of colleges and universities in the northeastern U.S., consisting of Yale, Harvard, Princeton, Columbia, Dartmouth, Cornell, the University of Pennsylvania, and Brown, having a reputation for high scholastic achievement and social prestige. **2.** of, pertaining to, or characteristic of Ivy League colleges or their students and graduates. [1935–40] —**I′vy Lea′•guer.**

i′vy vine′. See **Virginia creeper.** [1865–70]

I.W., Isle of Wight.

i.w., 1. inside width. **2.** isotopic weight.

I•wa•ki (ē wä′kē), *n.* a city on NE Honshu, in Japan. 342,076. Formerly, **Taira.**

i•wan (ē′wän), *n.* a vaulted portal opening onto a courtyard: used often in Iranian mosque architecture. Also, **ivan, liwan.** [< Pers *īwān*]

IWC, International Whaling Commission.

i•wis (i wis′), *adv. Obs.* certainly. Also, **ywis.** [bef. 900; ME, adv. use of neut. of OE *gewiss* (adj.) certain; c. D *gewis,* G *gewiss* certain, certainly; akin to WIT[2]; see Y-]

I•wo (ē′wō), *n.* a city in SW Nigeria. 191,684.

I•wo Ji•ma (ē′wə jē′mə, ē′wō; *Japn.* ē′wô jē′mä), one of the Volcano Islands, in the N Pacific, S of Japan: under U.S. administration after 1945; returned to Japan 1968.

I.W.W. See **Industrial Workers of the World.** Also, **IWW**

Ix•elles (ēk sel′), *n.* a city in central Belgium, near Brussels. 86,450. Flemish, **Elsene.**

ix•i•a (ik′sē ə), *n.* any of various southern African plants of the genus *Ixia,* of the iris family, having sword-shaped leaves and showy, ornamental flowers. [< NL (Linnaeus) < Gk *ixía* birdlime, equiv. to *ix(ós)* mistletoe, birdlime (made with mistletoe berries) + *-ia* -IA]

Ix•i•on (ik sī′ən, ik′sē on′), *n. Class. Myth.* a king who was punished by Zeus for his love for Hera by being bound on an eternally revolving wheel in Tartarus.

ix•od•id (ik sod′id, -sō′did, ik′sə did), *n.* **1.** any of numerous ticks of the family Ixodidae, comprising the hard ticks. —*adj.* **2.** belonging or pertaining to the family Ixodidae. [1910–15; < NL *Ixodidae* name of the family, equiv. to *Ixod(es)* genus name (< Gk *ixṓdēs* like birdlime, sticky, clammy, equiv. to *ix(ós)* birdlime + *-ōdēs* -ODE[1]) + *-idae* -IDAE; see -ID[2]]

ix•o•ra (ik′sər ə), *n.* any of numerous tropical shrubs or trees belonging to the genus *Ixora,* of the madder family, having glossy leaves and clusters of showy flowers in a variety of colors. [< NL (Linnaeus) << Skt *īśvara* ISHVARA; the flowers of some species serve as votive offerings in India]

Ix•tac•ci•huatl (ēs′täk sē′wät′l), *n.* Iztaccihuatl. Also, **Ix•ta•ci•huatl** (ēs′tä sē′wät′l).

ix•tle (iks′tlē, ist′lē), *n.* istle.

I•yar (ē yär′, ē′yär), *n.* the eighth month of the Jewish calendar. Also, **Iy•yar′.** Cf. **Jewish calendar.** [1730–40; < Heb *iyyār*]

I•ye•ya•su (ē′ye yä′sōō), *n.* **To•ku•ga•wa** (tô′kōō gä′wä), 1542–1616, Japanese general and public servant. Also, **Ieyasu.**

CONCISE ETYMOLOGY KEY: <, descended or borrowed from; >, whence; b., blend of, blended; c., cognate with; cf., compare; deriv., derivative; equiv., equivalent; imit., imitative; obl., oblique; r., replacing; s., stem; sp., spelling, spelled; resp., respelling, respelled; trans., translation; ?, origin unknown; *, unattested; ‡, probably earlier than. See the full key inside the front cover.

I•za•bal (ē′sä väl′; *Eng.* ē′zə bäl′, -sə-), *n.* **Lake,** a lake in E Guatemala: the largest in the country. ab. 450 sq. mi. (1165 sq. km). Also called **Dulce Gulf.**

I•za•na•gi (ē′zä nä′gē), *n.* the Japanese god who fathered the islands and gods of Japan by a union with his sister Izanami.

I•za•na•mi (ē′zä nä′mē), *n.* a Japanese goddess, the sister of Izanagi.

iz•ar (i zär′), *n.* a long, usually white cotton dress that covers the body completely, worn by women of North Africa and the Middle East. [1830–40; < Ar *izār*]

iz•ard (iz′ərd), *n.* a chamois that inhabits the Pyrenees. [1785–95; < F, var. of *isard* < dial. (Gascon) *isart*]

Iz•ard (iz′ərd), *n.* **Ralph,** 1742–1804, U.S. diplomat and politician.

-ization, a combination of **-ize** and **-ation:** *civilization.*

iz•ba (iz bä′), *n.* the traditional log house of rural Russia, with an unheated entrance room and a single living and sleeping room heated by a clay or brick stove. Also, **isba.** [1775–85; < Russ *izbá* (dim. *istópka*), ORuss *istŭba* house, bath, c. Serbo-Croatian *izba* small room, shack, Czech *jizba* room, Old Czech *jistba, jizdba,* all < Slavic **jĭstŭba* << VL **extūfa,* with short *u* perh. < Gmc **stuba;* see STOVE[1]]

-ize, a verb-forming suffix occurring originally in loanwords from Greek that have entered English through Latin or French (*baptize; barbarize; catechize*); within English, **-ize** is added to adjectives and nouns to form transitive verbs with the general senses "to render, make" (*actualize; fossilize; sterilize; Americanize*), "to convert into, give a specified character or form to" (*computerize; dramatize; itemize; motorize*), "to subject to (as a process, sometimes named after its originator)" (*hospitalize; terrorize; galvanize; oxidize; simonize; winterize*). Also formed with **-ize** are a more heterogeneous group of verbs, usually intransitive, denoting a change of state (*crystallize*), kinds or instances of behavior (*apologize; moralize; tyrannize*), or activities (*economize; philosophize; theorize*). Also, *esp. Brit.,* **-ise**[1]. Cf. **-ism, -ist, -ization.** [< LL *-izāre* < Gk *-izein;* r. ME *-isen* < OF *-iser* < LL, as above]

—Usage. The suffix -IZE has been in common use since the late 16th century; it is one of the most productive suffixes in the language, and scores of words ending in -IZE are in daily use.

Some words ending in -IZE have been widely disapproved in recent years, particularly *finalize* (first attested in the early 1920's) and *prioritize* (around 1970). Such words are most often criticized when they become, as did these two, vogue terms, suddenly heard and seen everywhere, especially in the context of advertising, commerce, education, or government—forces claimed by some to have a corrupting influence upon the language. The criticism has fairly effectively suppressed the use of *finalize* and *prioritize* in belletristic writing, but the words are fully standard and occur regularly in all varieties of speech and writing, especially the more formal types.

The British spelling, -ISE, is becoming less common in British English, especially in technical or formal writing, chiefly because some influential British publishers advocate or have adopted the American form -IZE.

I•zhevsk (ē′zhifsk′), *n.* a city in and the capital of the Udmurt Autonomous Republic, in the Russian Federation in Europe. 549,000.

Iz•mir (iz′mēr), *n.* **1.** Formerly, **Smyrna.** a seaport in W Turkey on the Gulf of Izmir: important city of Asia Minor from ancient times. 636,078. **2. Gulf of.** Formerly, **Gulf of Smyrna.** an arm of the Aegean Sea in W Turkey. 35 mi. (56 km) long; 14 mi. (23 km) wide.

Iz•mit (iz mit′), *n.* a city in NW Turkey, on the E coast of the Sea of Marmara. 141,681. Also, **Kocaeli.**

Iz•tac•ci•huatl (ēs′täk sē′wät′l), *n.* an extinct volcano in S central Mexico, SE of Mexico City. 17,342 ft. Also, **Ixtaccihuatl, Ixtacihuatl.** [< Nahuatl *Iztāccihuātl,* equiv. to *iztāc* white + *cihuātl* woman]

Iz•ves•ti•a (iz ves′tē ə, *Russ.* iz vyes′tyi yə), *n.* (formerly) the official newspaper of the Soviet government. Cf. ***Pravda.***

Iz•zak (ī′zək), *n.* a male given name, form of **Isaac.**

iz•zard (iz′ərd), *n. Chiefly Dial.* the letter Z. [1730–40; var. of ZED]

iz•zat (iz′ət), *n. Anglo-Indian.* **1.** personal dignity or honor. **2.** personal prestige. [1855–60; < Urdu *'izzat* < Pers < Ar *'izzah*]

DEVELOPMENT OF MAJUSCULE						
NORTH SEMITIC	GREEK	ETR	LATIN	MODERN		
				GOTHIC	ITALIC	ROMAN
SEE LETTER I				J	*J*	J

DEVELOPMENT OF MINUSCULE					
ROMAN CURSIVE	ROMAN UNCIAL	CAROL MIN.	MODERN		
			GOTHIC	ITALIC	ROMAN
SEE I	j	SEE I	j	*j*	j

The tenth letter of the English alphabet developed as a variant form of *I* in Medieval Latin, and, except for the preference for the J as an initial letter, the two were used interchangeably, both serving to represent the vowel (i) and the consonant (y). Later, through specialization, it came to be distinguished as a separate sign, acquiring its present phonetic value under the influence of French.

J, j (jā), *n., pl.* **J's** or **Js, j's** or **js.** **1.** the tenth letter of the English alphabet, a consonant. **2.** any spoken sound represented by the letter *J* or *j*, as in *just, major,* or *rajah.* **3.** something having the shape of a J. **4.** a written or printed representation of the letter *J* or *j.* **5.** a device, as a printer's type, for reproducing the letter *J* or *j.*

J, **1.** Jewish. **2.** Also, **j** *Physics.* joule; joules.

J, *Symbol.* **1.** the tenth in order or in a series, or, when *I* is omitted, the ninth. **2.** (*sometimes l.c.*) the medieval Roman numeral for 1. Cf. **Roman numerals.**

j, *Symbol.* **1.** *Math.* a unit vector on the y-axis of a coordinate system. **2.** *Engin.* the imaginary number $\sqrt{-1}$.

J., **1.** *Cards.* Jack. **2.** Journal. **3.** Judge. **4.** Justice.

ja (yä), *adv. German.* yes.

JA, **1.** joint account. **2.** Joint Agent. **3.** Judge Advocate. **4.** Junior Achievement. Also, **J.A.**

Ja., January.

jab (jab), *v.,* **jabbed, jab•bing,** *n.* —*v.t., v.i.* **1.** to poke, or thrust abruptly or sharply, as with the end or point of a stick. **2.** to punch, esp. with a short, quick blow. —*n.* **3.** a poke with the end or point of something; a sharp, quick thrust. **4.** a short, quick punch. [1815–25; var., orig. Scots, of JOB[2]] —**jab′bing•ly,** *adv.*

Ja•bal (jā′bəl), *n.* a son of Lamech, and the progenitor of nomadic shepherds. Gen. 4:20.

Jab•al•pur (jub′əl po͝or′), *n.* a city in central Madhya Pradesh, in central India. 533,751. Also, **Jubbulpore.**

Ja•ba•ri (jä bär′ē), *n.* a male given name: from a Swahili word meaning "brave."

jab•ber (jab′ər), *v.t., v.i.* **1.** to talk or utter rapidly, indistinctly, incoherently, or nonsensically; chatter. —*n.* **2.** rapid, indistinct, or nonsensical talk; gibberish. [1490–1500; appar. imit.; cf. GIBBER, GAB[1]] —**jab′ber•er,** *n.* —**jab′ber•ing•ly,** *adv.*

Jab•ber•wock•y (jab′ər wok′ē), *n., pl.* **-wock•ies,** *adj.* —*n.* **1.** a playful imitation of language consisting of invented, meaningless words; nonsense; gibberish. **2.** an example of writing or speech consisting of or containing meaningless words. —*adj.* **3.** consisting of or comparable to Jabberwocky; meaningless; senseless. Also, **Jab•ber•wock** (jab′ər wok′). [coined by Lewis Carroll in *Jabberwocky,* poem in *Through the Looking Glass* (1871)]

Ja•bir (*Arab.* jä′bir), *n.* Geber.

jab•i•ru (jab′ə ro͞o′, jab′ə ro͞o′), *n.* a large stork, *Jabiru mycteria,* of the warmer regions of the New World. [1640–50; < Pg < Tupi *jabirú*]

Ja•boa•tão (zhä′bwä toun′), *n.* a city in E Brazil, W of Recife. 114,360.

jab•o•ran•di (jab′ə ran′dē, -ran dē′), *n., pl.* **-dis. 1.** any of several South American shrubs belonging to the genus *Pilocarpus,* of the rue family. **2.** the dried leaflets of certain of these plants, esp. *P. jaborandi,* containing the alkaloid pilocarpine, used in medicine. [1870–75; < Pg < Tupi, said to mean "one who makes saliva, one who spits"]

ja•bot (zha bō′, ja- *or, esp. Brit.,* zhab′ō, jab′ō), *n.* a decorative ruffle or other arrangement of lace or cloth attached at the neckline and extending down the front of a woman's blouse or dress or, formerly, of a man's shirt. [1815–25; < F: lit., bird's crop, prob. < Pr (N dials.); see GAVOTTE]

ja•bo•ti•ca•ba (zhə bo͞o′ti kä′bə), *n.* an evergreen tree, *Myrciaria cauliflora,* of the Myrtle family, native to southern Brazil, bearing on the trunk small clusters of edible, grapelike fruit. [1815–25; < Pg *jabuticaba* < Tupi *iauoti kaua*]

Jab•o•tin•sky (yab′ə tin′skē, yä′bə-), *n.* **Vladimir,** 1880–1940, Russian Zionist leader in Palestine.

Ja•brud (jab′ro͝od), *n. Archaeol.* a Paleolithic site in SW Syria, in the Anti-Lebanon mountain range.

jac (jak), *n. Informal.* jacket. [by shortening]

J.A.C., Junior Association of Commerce.

ja•cal (hə käl′, hä-), *n., pl.* **-ca•les** (-kä′lās, -lāz), **-cals.** (in the southwestern U.S. and Mexico) a hut with a thatched roof and walls consisting of thin stakes driven into the ground close together and plastered with mud. [1830–40, *Amer.*; < MexSp < Nahuatl *xahcalli*]

Jac•a•lyn (jak′ə lin), *n.* a female given name.

jac•a•mar (jak′ə mär′), *n.* any tropical American bird of the family Galbulidae, having a long bill and usually metallic green plumage above. [1640–50; < F < Tupi *jacamáciri*]

ja•ça•na (zhä′sə nä′, jä′-), *n.* any of several tropical, ploverlike, aquatic birds of the family Jacanidae, most of them having extremely long toes and claws for walking on floating water plants. Also called **lily-trotter.** [1640–50; < Pg *jaçanã* < Tupi *jasaná*]

jac•a•ran•da (jak′ə ran′də, -ran dä′), *n.* **1.** any of various tropical trees belonging to the genus *Jacaranda,* of the catalpa family, having showy clusters of usually purplish flowers. **2.** any of various related or similar trees. **3.** the often fragrant, ornamental wood of any of these trees. [1745–55; < Pg *jacarandá* < Tupi *yacarandá*]

Ja•car•ta (jə kär′tə), *n.* Jakarta.

ja•cinth (jā′sinth, jas′inth), *n. Mineral.* hyacinth (def. 4). [1200–50; < ML *jacinthus,* L *hyacinthus* HYACINTH; r. ME *jacinct* < OF *jacincte* < ML *jacinctus,* var. of *jacinthus*]

Ja•cinth (jā′sinth, jas′inth), *n.* a female given name, form of **Hyacinth.**

jack[1] (jak), *n.* **1.** any of various portable devices for raising or lifting heavy objects short heights, using various mechanical, pneumatic, or hydraulic methods. **2.** Also called **knave.** *Cards.* a playing card bearing the picture of a soldier or servant. **3.** *Elect.* a connecting device in an electrical circuit designed for the insertion of a plug. **4.** (*cap.*) *Informal.* fellow; buddy; man (usually used in addressing a stranger): *Hey, Jack, which way to Jersey?* **5.** Also called **jackstone.** *Games.* **a.** one of a set of small metal objects having six prongs, used in the game of jacks. **b.** one of any other set of objects, as pebbles, stones, etc., used in the game of jacks. **c. jacks,** (*used with a singular v.*) a children's game in which small metal objects, stones, pebbles, or the like, are tossed, caught, and moved on the ground in a number of prescribed ways, usually while bouncing a rubber ball. **6.** any of several carangid fishes, esp. of the genus *Caranx,* as *C. hippos* (**crevalle jack** or **jack crevalle**), of the western Atlantic Ocean. **7.** *Slang.* money: *He won a lot of jack at the races.* **8.** *Naut.* **a.** a small flag flown at the jack staff of a ship, bearing a distinctive design usually symbolizing the nationality of the vessel. **b.** Also called **jack crosstree.** either of a pair of crosstrees at the head of a topgallant mast, used to hold royal shrouds away from the mast. **9.** (*cap.*) a sailor. **10.** a lumberjack. **11.** applejack. **12.** See **jack rabbit. 13.** a jackass. **14.** jacklight. **15.** a device for turning a spit. **16.** a small wooden rod in the mechanism of a harpsichord, spinet, or virginal that rises when the key is depressed and causes the attached plectrum to strike the string. **17.** *Lawn Bowling.* a small, usually white bowl or ball used as a mark for the bowlers to aim at. **18.** Also called **clock jack.** *Horol.* a mechanical figure that strikes a clock bell. **19.** a premigratory young male salmon. **20.** *Theat.* See **brace jack. 21.** *Falconry.* the male of a kestrel, hobby, or esp. of a merlin. **22. every man jack,** everyone without exception: *They presented a formidable opposition, every man jack of them.* —*v.t.* **23.** to lift or move (something) with or as if with a jack (usually fol. by *up*): *to jack a car up to change a flat tire.* **24.** *Informal.* to increase, raise, or accelerate (prices, wages, speed, etc.) (usually fol. by *up*). **25.** *Informal.* to boost the morale of; encourage (usually fol. by *up*). **26.** to jacklight. —*v.i.* **27.** to jacklight. **28. jack off,** *Slang* (*vulgar*). to masturbate. —*adj.* **29.** *Carpentry.* having a height or length less than that of most of the others in a structure; cripple: *jack rafter; jack truss.* [1350–1400; ME *jakke, Jakke* used in addressing any male, esp. a social inferior, var. of *Jakken,* var. of *Jankin,* equiv. to *Jan* JOHN + *-kin* -KIN; extended in sense to anything male, and as a designation for a variety of inanimate objects]

jack[2] (jak), *n.* jackfruit. [1605–15; < Pg *jaca* < Malayalam *cakka*]

jack[3] (jak), *n.* **1.** a defensive coat, usually of leather, worn in medieval times by foot soldiers and others. **2.** a container for liquor, originally of waxed leather coated with tar. [1325–75; ME *jakke* < MF *jaque(s),* jacket, short, plain upper garment, prob. after *jacques* peasant (see JACQUERIE)]

Jack (jak), *n.* a male given name, form of **Jacob** or **John.**

jack-a-dan•dy (jak′ə dan′dē), *n., pl.* **-dies.** *Older Use.* dandy (def. 1). [1625–35; JACK- + *-a-* (< ?) + DANDY] —**jack′-a-dan′dy•ism,** *n.*

jack•al (jak′əl, -ôl), *n.* **1.** any of several nocturnal wild dogs of the genus *Canis,* esp. *C. aureus,* of Asia and Africa, that scavenge or hunt in packs. **2.** a person who performs dishonest or base deeds as the follower or accomplice of another. **3.** a person who performs menial or degrading tasks for another. [1595–1605; < alter., by assoc. with JACK, of Pers *shag(h)āl*; c. Skt *sṛgāla*]

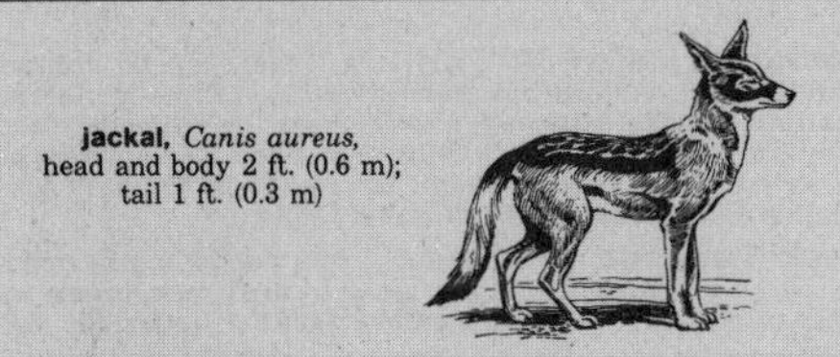

jackal, *Canis aureus,* head and body 2 ft. (0.6 m); tail 1 ft. (0.3 m)

jack•a•napes (jak′ə nāps′), *n.* **1.** an impertinent, presumptuous person, esp. a young man; whippersnapper. **2.** an impudent, mischievous child. **3.** *Archaic.* an ape or monkey. [1400–50; late ME *Jakken-apes,* lit., jack (i.e., man) of the ape, nickname of William de la Pole (1396–1450), Duke of Suffolk, whose badge was an ape's clog and chain]

jack′ arch′, *Archit.* See **flat arch.** [1880–85]

jack•a•roo (jak′ə ro͞o′), *n., pl.* **-roos,** *v.i.,* **-rooed, -roo•ing.** *Australian.* jackeroo.

jack•ass (jak′as′), *n.* **1.** a male donkey. **2.** a contemptibly foolish or stupid person; dolt; blockhead; ass. [1720–30; JACK[1] + ASS[1]] —**jack′ass′er•y,** *n.*

jack′ass bark′, *Naut.* **1.** a barkentine square-rigged on the mainmast above a gaff mainsail. **2.** Also called **four-masted brig.** a sailing ship having four or more masts, the foremast and mainmast being wholly square-rigged, the others being fore-and-aft-rigged. **3.** any sailing ship of three or more masts carrying an otherwise nameless rig. [1860–65]

jack′ass brig′, *Naut.* a two-masted sailing vessel square-rigged on the foremast with a fore-and-aft mainsail; brigantine. [1880–85]

jack′ass gun′ter, *Naut.* a gunter having a wire rope with a traveler in place of the usual upper iron.

jack′ass pen′guin, any of several boldly marked black and white penguins of the genus *Spheniscus,* esp.

CONCISE PRONUNCIATION KEY: act, cāpe, dâre, pärt; set, ēqual; if, īce; ox, ōver, ôrder, oil, bo͝ok, bo͞ot, out; up, ûrge; child; sing; shoe; thin, *th*at; zh as in *treasure.* ə = *a* as in *alone, e* as in *system, i* as in *easily, o* as in *gallop, u* as in *circus;* ə as in *fire* (fīər), *hour* (ouər). l and n can serve as syllabic consonants, as in *cradle* (krād′l), and *button* (but′n). See the full key inside the front cover.

S. demersus, of southern Africa, with a call resembling a donkey's bray. [1860–65]

jack′ass rig′, *Naut.* a rig of sails not conforming to a recognized type. [1880–85]

jack·a·tar (jak′ə tär′), *n. Newfoundland.* a Newfoundland native of mixed French and Amerindian descent. Also, **jackie tar, jacky tar.** [1855–60; perh. JACK-TAR (with *-a-* repr. release of the stop) though the change in sense is unaccounted for]

jack′ bean′, **1.** a bushy tropical plant, *Canavalia ensiformis,* of the legume family, grown esp. for forage. **2.** the white seeds of this plant. [1880–85]

jack′ block′, *Naut.* a block used in raising or lowering a topgallant yard. [1785–95]

jack·boot (jak′bo͞ot′), *n.* **1.** a sturdy leather boot reaching up over the knee, worn esp. by soldiers. **2.** Also called **jack′boot tac′tics.** brutally bullying, militaristic, or authoritarian measures. **3.** a person who uses such measures. [1680–90; JACK[1] + BOOT[1]]

jack·boot·ed (jak′bo͞o′tid), *adj.* **1.** wearing jackboots. **2.** brutally and oppressively bullying: *a jackbooted militarism.* [1840–50; JACKBOOT + -ED[3]]

jack′ chain′, a chain having open links in the form of a figure 8, with one loop at right angles to the other. [1630–40]

jack′ cheese′. See **Monterey Jack.**

jack′ creval′le. See under **jack**[1] (def. 6). [1945–50]

jack′ cross′tree, *Naut.* jack[1] (def. 8b). [1830–40]

jack·daw (jak′dô′), *n.* **1.** a glossy, black, European bird, *Corvus monedula,* of the crow family, that nests in towers, ruins, etc. **2.** See **boat-tailed grackle.** [1535–45; JACK[1] + DAW]

Jack·e·lyn (jak′ə lin), *n.* a female given name.

jack·e·roo (jak′ə ro͞o′), *n., pl.* **-roos,** *v.,* **-rooed, -roo·ing.** *Australian.* —*n.* **1.** an inexperienced person working as an apprentice on a sheep ranch. —*v.i.* **2.** to work as an apprentice on a sheep ranch. Also, **jackaroo.** [1875–80; JACK[1] + (KANG)AROO; cf. -EROO]

jack·et (jak′it), *n.* **1.** a short coat, in any of various forms, usually opening down the front. **2.** something designed to be placed around the upper part of the body for a specific purpose other than use as clothing: *a life jacket.* **3.** a protective outer covering. **4.** the skin of a potato, esp. when it has been cooked. **5.** See **book jacket. 6.** the cover of a paperbound book, usually bearing an illustration. **7.** a paper or cardboard envelope for protecting a phonograph record. **8.** a metal casing, as the steel covering of a cannon, the steel cover around the core of a bullet, or the water jacket on certain types of machine guns. **9.** a folded paper or open envelope containing an official document. —*v.t.* **10.** to put a jacket on (someone or something). [1425–75; late ME *jaket* < MF *ja(c)quet,* equiv. to *jaque* JACK[3] + *-et* -ET] —**jack′et·ed,** *adj.* —**jack′et·less,** *adj.* —**jack′·et·like′,** *adj.*

jack·ey (jak′ē), *n. Brit. Slang.* gin[1]. Also, **jacky.** [1790–1800; prob. *jack* quarter of a pint (perh. development of JACK[3]) + -EY[2]]

jack·fish (jak′fish′), *n., pl.,* (*esp. collectively*) **-fish,** (*esp. referring to two or more kinds or species*) **-fish·es. 1.** any of several pikes, esp. the northern pike. **2.** the sauger. [1735–45; JACK[1] + FISH]

Jack′ Frost′, frost or freezing cold personified. [1815–25]

jack·fruit (jak′fro͞ot′), *n.* **1.** a large, tropical, milky-juiced tree, *Artocarpus heterophyllus,* of the mulberry family, having stiff and glossy green leaves, cultivated for its very large, edible fruit and seeds. **2.** the fruit of this tree, which may weigh up to 70 lb. (32 kg). Also called **jak, jack.** [1810–20; JACK[2] + FRUIT]

jack·ham·mer (jak′ham′ər), *n.* a portable drill operated by compressed air and used to drill rock, break up pavement, etc. [1925–30, *Amer.;* JACK[1] + HAMMER]

Jack·ie (jak′ē), *n.* **1.** a female given name, form of **Jacqueline. 2.** a male given name, form of **Jack.**

jack′ie tar′ (jak′ē), *Newfoundland.* jackatar.

jack′ing en′gine, an engine for moving an idle reciprocating engine or turbine to permit inspection and repairs.

jack-in-the-box (jak′in *th*ə boks′), *n., pl.* **-box·es.** a toy consisting of a box from which an enclosed figure springs up when the lid is opened. Also, **jack′-in-a-box′.** [1545–55]

jack-in-the-pul·pit (jak′in *th*ə po͝ol′pit, -pul′-), *n., pl.* **-pul·pits.** A North American plant, *Arisaema triphyllum,* of the arum family, having an upright spadix arched over by a green or striped purplish-brown spathe. [1840–50, *Amer.*]

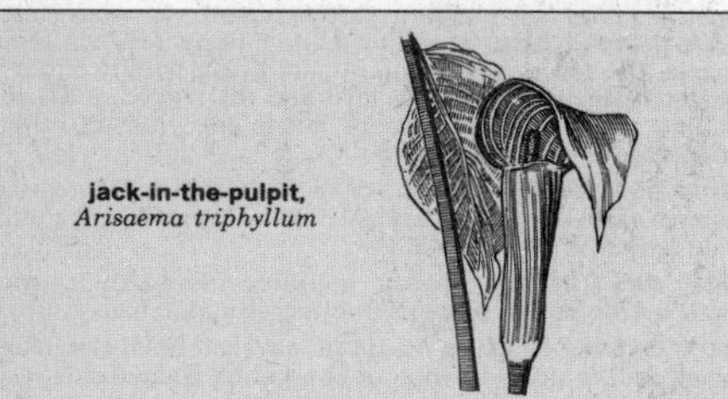

jack-in-the-pulpit, *Arisaema triphyllum*

CONCISE ETYMOLOGY KEY: <, descended or borrowed from; >, whence; b., blend of, blended; c., cognate with; cf., compare; deriv., derivative; equiv., equivalent; imit., imitative; obl., oblique; r., replacing; s., stem; sp., spelling, spelled; resp., respelling, respelled; trans., translation; ?, origin unknown; *, unattested; ‡, probably earlier than. See the full key inside the front cover.

Jack′ Ketch′ (kech), *Brit. Slang.* a public hangman. [1665–75; named after *John Ketch* (1663?–86), English executioner noted for his brutality]

jack·knife (jak′nīf′), *n., pl.* **-knives,** *v.,* **-knifed, -knif·ing,** *adj.* —*n.* **1.** a large pocketknife. **2.** *Fancy Diving.* a dive in which the diver bends in midair to touch the toes, keeping the legs straight, and then straightens out. —*v.i.* **3.** to bend or double over like a jackknife: *The prizefighter jackknifed and fell when he was hit in the stomach.* **4.** (of a trailer truck) to have the cab and trailer swivel at the linkage until they form a V shape, as the result of an abrupt stop or accident. **5.** (in diving) to perform a jackknife. **6.** to move rapidly at an abrupt angle. —*v.t.* **7.** to cause to jackknife: *The blow jackknifed the prizefighter.* **8.** to cut with a jackknife. —*adj.* **9.** resembling a jackknife, as in its shape, function, or manner of opening and folding. [1705–15, *Amer.;* JACK[1] (cf. JOCKTELEG) + KNIFE]

jack′knife clam′. See **razor clam.**

jack·knife-fish (jak′nīf′fish′), *n., pl.* **-fish·es,** (*esp. collectively*) **-fish.** *Ichthyol.* a black and white, American drum, *Equetus lanceolatus,* found in tropical areas of the Atlantic Ocean, having an elongated dorsal fin that is held erect.

jack′ lad′der, 1. *Naut.* See **Jacob's ladder** (def. 2a). **2.** *Lumbering.* See **bull chain.** [1885–90]

jack·leg (jak′leg′), *Chiefly South Midland and Southern U.S.* —*adj.* **1.** unskilled or untrained for one's work; amateur: *a jackleg electrician.* **2.** unscrupulous or without the accepted standards of one's profession: *a jackleg lawyer.* **3.** makeshift; temporary. —*n.* **4.** an unskilled or unscrupulous itinerant worker or practitioner. [1840–50, *Amer.;* perh. JACK[1] + (BLACK)LEG]

jack·light (jak′līt′), *n., v.,* **-light·ed** or **-lit, -light·ing.** —*n.* **1.** a portable cresset, oil-burning lantern, or electric light used as a lure in hunting or fishing at night. —*v.t.* **2.** to hunt or fish for with a jacklight. —*v.i.* **3.** to hunt or fish with the aid of a jacklight. [1785–95; JACK[1] + LIGHT[1]]

jack·light·er (jak′lī′tər), *n.* **1.** a person who hunts or fishes at night with the aid of a jacklight. **2.** a person who illegally hunts deer at night using a jacklight. [1960–65; JACKLIGHT + -ER[1]]

jack′ mack′erel, a mackerellike food fish, *Trachurus symmetricus,* of Pacific coastal waters of the U.S. Also called **horse mackerel.** [1880–85, *Amer.*]

jack′ Mor′mon, 1. a non-Mormon living amicably among Mormons. **2.** a Mormon not active in the church or adhering strictly to Mormon principles. Also, **Jack′ Mor′mon.** [1835–45, *Amer.*]

jack′ oak′, the blackjack, *Quercus marilandica.* [1810–20, *Amer.*]

jack-of-all-trades (jak′əv ôl′trādz′, jak′-), *n., pl.* **jacks-of-all-trades.** a person who is adept at many different kinds of work. [1610–20]

jack-o′-lan·tern (jak′ə lan′tərn), *n.* **1.** a hollowed pumpkin with openings cut to represent human eyes, nose, and mouth and in which a candle or other light may be placed, traditionally made for display at Halloween. **2.** a commercially made lantern resembling this. **3.** any phenomenon of light, as a corona discharge or an ignis fatuus. **4.** a poisonous luminescent orange fungus, *Omphalotus olearius,* often found in clusters at the base of hardwood tree stumps. [1655–65]

jack′ pine′, a scrubby pine, *Pinus banksiana,* growing on tracts of poor, rocky land in Canada and the northern U.S., bearing short needles and curved cones. Also called **gray pine.** [1880–85]

jack′ plane′, *Carpentry.* a plane for rough surfacing. See illus. under **plane**[2]. [1805–15]

jack′ post′, a post for supporting a floor beam, having two telescoping sections, adjustable to any height.

jack·pot (jak′pot′), *n.* **1.** the chief prize or the cumulative stakes in a game or contest, as in bingo, a quiz contest, or a slot machine. **2.** *Poker.* a pot that accumulates until a player opens the betting with a pair of predetermined denomination, usually jacks or better. **3.** an outstanding reward or success. **4. hit the jackpot,** *Informal.* **a.** to achieve a sensational success; have sudden luck: *The firm has hit the jackpot with its new line of computers.* **b.** to win a jackpot. [1880–85, *Amer.;* of uncert. orig.]

whitetail jack rabbit, *Lepus townsendii,* length 22 in. (56 cm); ears 5 in. (13 cm)

jack′ rab′bit, any of various large hares of western North America, having very long hind legs and long ears. [1860–65; JACK(ASS) + RABBIT; so named from the size of its ears]

jack·rab·bit (jak′rab′it), *adj.* **1.** resembling a jack rabbit, as in suddenness or rapidity of movement: *The car made a jackrabbit start when the traffic light turned green.* —*v.i.* **2.** to go or start forward with a rapid, sudden movement. [1925–30; see JACK RABBIT]

jack′ raft′er, a rafter having less than the full length of the roof slope, as one meeting a hip or a valley. [1750–60]

jack′ rod′, *Naut.* a horizontal metal rod or tube to which an awning or other cloth may be seized to support it. Also called **jackstay.**

jack′ rope′, *Naut.* **1.** a rope for bending the foot of a sail to a boom. **2.** a line that is rove through grommets on the reef band of a square sail, and to which lanyards from the jackstay on the yard are toggled to reef the sail.

Jack′ Rose′, a cocktail made with apple brandy, lime or lemon juice, and grenadine. [short for *jacqueminot rose,* named after J. M. *Jacqueminot* (1787–1865), French nobleman and general]

jack′ salm′on, 1. walleye (def. 1). **2.** See **coho salmon.** [1970–75, Amer.]

jack·screw (jak′skro͞o′), *n.* a jack for lifting consisting of a screw steadied by a threaded support and carrying a plate or other part bearing the load. Also called **screw jack.** [1760–70; JACK[1] + SCREW]

jack·shaft (jak′shaft′, -shäft′), *n. Mach.* **1.** Also called **countershaft.** a short shaft, connected by belting, gears, etc., that transmits motion from a motor or engine to a machine or machines being driven (distinguished from *main shaft*). **2.** a shaft on which an idle wheel or fairlead turns. [1895–1900; JACK[1] + SHAFT]

jack·smelt (jak′smelt′), *n., pl.* **-smelts,** (*esp. collectively*) **-smelt.** a large silversides, *Atherinopsis californiensis,* found along the coast of California, that grows to a length of 22 in. (55 cm). [1945–50; JACK[1] + SMELT[2]]

jack·snipe (jak′snīp′), *n., pl.* (*esp. collectively*) **-snipe,** (*esp. referring to two or more kinds or species*) **-snipes. 1.** Also called **half snipe.** a small, short-billed snipe, *Limnocryptes minimus,* of Europe and Asia. **2.** any of several related snipes. **3.** See **pectoral sandpiper.** [1655–65; JACK[1] + SNIPE]

Jack·son (jak′sən), *n.* **1. Andrew** (*"Old Hickory"*), 1767–1845, U.S. general: 7th president of the U.S. 1829–37. **2. Lady Barbara.** See **Ward, Barbara. 3. Helen Hunt** (*Helen Maria Fiske*), 1830–85, U.S. novelist and poet. **4. Jesse L(ouis),** born 1941, U.S. Baptist minister and civil-rights and political activist. **5. Mahalia,** 1911–72, U.S. gospel singer. **6. Robert Hough·wout** (hou′ət), 1892–1954, U.S. jurist: associate justice of the U.S. Supreme Court 1941–54. **7. Thomas Jonathan** (*"Stonewall Jackson"*), 1824–63, Confederate general in the American Civil War. **8.** a city in and the capital of Mississippi, in the central part. 202,895. **9.** a city in W Tennessee. 49,131. **10.** a city in S Michigan. 39,739. **11.** a town in NW Wyoming: resort near Jackson Hole. 4511. **12.** a male given name, meaning "son of Jack."

Jack′son Day′, January 8, a holiday commemorating Andrew Jackson's victory at the Battle of New Orleans in 1815: a legal holiday in Louisiana.

Jack′son Hole′, a valley in NW Wyoming, near the Teton Range: wildlife preserve.

Jack·so·ni·an (jak sō′nē ən), *adj.* **1.** of or pertaining to Andrew Jackson, his ideas, the period of his presidency, or the political principles or social values associated with him: *Jacksonian democracy.* —*n.* **2.** a follower of Andrew Jackson. [1815–25, *Amer.;* JACKSON + -IAN]

Jack·son·ism (jak′sə niz′əm), *n.* the group of political principles or attitudes associated with Andrew Jackson. [1820–30, *Amer.;* JACKSON + -ISM]

Jack·son·ville (jak′sən vil′), *n.* **1.** a seaport in NE Florida, on the St. John's River. 540,898. **2.** a city in central Arkansas. 27,589. **3.** a city in W Illinois. 20,284. **4.** a city in SE North Carolina. 17,056. **5.** a town in E Texas. 12,264.

Jack′sonville Beach′, a city in NE Florida. 15,462.

jack′ staff′, a flagstaff at the bow of a vessel, on which a jack is flown. [1685–95]

jack·stay (jak′stā′), *n. Naut.* **1.** a rod or batten, following a yard, gaff, or boom, to which one edge of a sail is bent. **2.** a rail for guiding the movement of the hanks of a sail. **3.** a transverse stay for stiffening a mast having a gaff sail, coming downward and outward from the head of the mast, passing over a spreader at the level of the gaff, then inclining inward to the mast again near the foot. **4.** See **jack rod.** [1830–40; JACK[1] + STAY[3]]

jack·stone (jak′stōn′), *n.* **1.** jack[1] (def. 5a, b). **2. jackstones,** (*used with a singular v.*) jack[1] (def. 5c). [1805–15; earlier *chackstone,* alter. of *checkstone* pebble, of uncert. orig.]

jack·straw (jak′strô′), *n.* **1.** one of a group of strips of wood or similar objects, as straws or toothpicks, used in the game of jackstraws. **2. jackstraws,** (*used with a singular v.*) a game in which players compete in picking up, one by one, as many jackstraws as possible without disturbing the heap. **3.** *Obs.* **a.** a straw-stuffed figure of a man; scarecrow; straw man. **b.** an insignificant person. [1590–1600; after *Jack Straw,* name or nickname of one of the leaders of the rebellion headed by Wat Tyler in 1381 in England]

jack-tar (jak′tär′), *n.* a sailor. Also, **Jack′ Tar′.** [1775–85]

jack′ tow′el, a long towel with the ends sewed together, for hanging on a roller. [1810–20]

jack′ truss′, any of a number of trapezoidal trusses for supporting those areas of a hip roof not beneath the peak or ridge, parallel to the truss or trusses that meet at the peak or ridge.

jack-up (jak′up′), *n. Informal.* an increase or rise: *a recent jack-up in prices.* [1900–05, *Amer.;* n. use of v. phrase *jack up*]

jack′-up rig′, an offshore drill rig or platform having a floating hull fitted with retractable legs that can be lowered to the seabed to elevate the hull above wave level. Cf. **semisubmersible.** [1965–70]

jack·y (jak′ē), *n.* (*sometimes cap.*) *Brit. Slang.* gin[1]. [see JACKEY]

Jack·y (jak′ē), *n., pl.* **Jack·ies. 1.** (*often l.c.*) a sailor. **2.** a male given name, form of **Jack. 3.** a female given name, form of **Jacqueline.**

jack·yard (jak′yärd′), *n. Naut.* a small, inclined spar upholding the head of a quadrangular gaff topsail similar in form to a lugsail. [1880–85; JACK[1] + YARD[2]]

jack′y tar′ (jak′ē), *Newfoundland.* jackatar.

Jac•mel (*Fr.* zhak mel′), *n.* a seaport in S Haiti. 10,000.

Ja•cob (jā′kəb *for 1, 3; Fr.* zhä kôb′ *for 2*), *n.* **1.** the second son of Isaac, the twin brother of Esau, and father of the 12 patriarchs. Gen. 25:24–34. **2. Fran•çois** (fräɴ swa′), born 1920, French geneticist: Nobel prize for medicine 1965. **3.** a male given name: from a Hebrew word meaning "supplanter."

Ja•cob ben Ash•er (jā′kəb ben ash′ər), c1269–c1340, Hebrew commentator on the Bible and codifier of Jewish law.

Jacobean chair, c1620

Jac•o•be•an (jak′ə bē′ən), *adj.* **1.** of or pertaining to James I of England or to his period. **2.** noting or pertaining to the style of architecture and furnishings prevailing in England in the first half of the 17th century, continuing the Elizabethan style with a gradual introduction of Italian models in architecture and increased elaboration of forms and motifs in furnishings. **3.** of or pertaining to the style of literature and drama produced during the early 17th century. —*n.* **4.** a writer, statesman, or other personage of the Jacobean period. [1750–60; < NL *Jacobae(us)* of *Jacobus* (Latinized form of *James*) + -AN]

Jac′obe′an lil′y, a bulbous plant, *Sprekelia formosissima,* of the amaryllis family, native to Mexico, bearing a large, bright-red flower. Also called **Aztec lily.** [1745–55; allegedly named after St. James (LL *Jacobus*); see JACOBEAN]

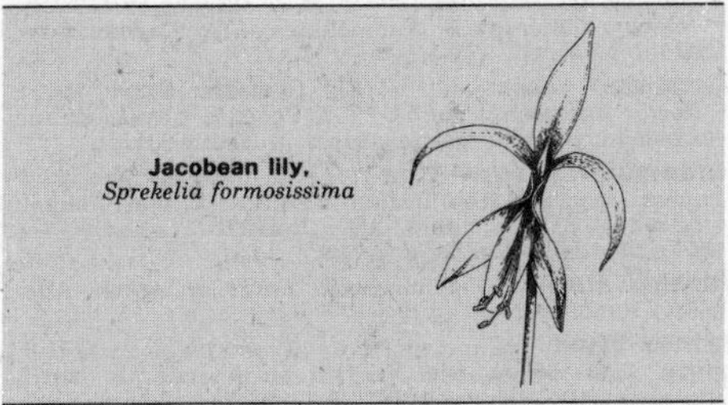
Jacobean lily, *Sprekelia formosissima*

Jac•o•be•than (jak′ə bē′thən), *adj.* noting or pertaining to the architecture of England at the beginning of the 17th century. [1930–35; JACO(BEAN) + (ELIZA)BETHAN]

Ja•co•bi (jə kō′bē; *for 2 also Ger.* yä kō′bē), *n.* **1. Abraham,** 1830–1919, U.S. pediatrician, born in Germany. **2. Karl Gus•tav Ja•kob** (kärl go͝os′täf yä′kôp), 1804–51, German mathematician. **3. Mary Corinna (Putnam),** 1842–1906, U.S. physician (wife of Abraham Jacobi).

Jac•o•bin (jak′ə bin), *n.* **1.** (in the French Revolution) a member of a radical society or club of revolutionaries that promoted the Reign of Terror and other extreme measures, active chiefly from 1789 to 1794: so called from the Dominican convent in Paris, where they originally met. **2.** an extreme radical, esp. in politics. **3.** a Dominican friar. **4.** (*l.c.*) one of a fancy breed of domestic pigeons having neck feathers that hang over the head like a hood. [1275–1325; ME *Jacobin* < OF (*frere*) *jacobin* < ML (*frater*) *Jacōbīnus.* See JACOB, -IN[1]] —**Jac′o•bin′ic, Jac′o•bin′i•cal,** *adj.* —**Jac′o•bin•ism,** *n.*

Ja•co•bi•na (jä′kə bē′nə), *n.* a female given name. Also, **Ja•co•bine** (jä′kə bēn′).

Jac•o•bin•ize (jak′ə bə nīz′), *v.t.,* **-ized, -iz•ing.** to imbue with Jacobinism. Also, *esp. Brit.,* **Jac′o•bin•ise′.** [1785–95; JACOBIN + -IZE] —**Jac′o•bin′i•za′tion,** *n.*

Jac•o•bite (jak′ə bīt′), *n.* **1.** a partisan or adherent of James II of England after his overthrow (1688), or of the Stuarts. **2.** a member of the Syrian Monophysitic church, which was founded in the 6th century A.D. and was governed by the patriarch of Antioch. [1400–50; (in def. 2) late ME (< MF) < ML *Jacōbīta,* after *Jacobus* Baradaeus, bishop of Edessa (d. 578); (in def. 1) cf. JAMES; see ITE[1]] —**Jac•o•bit•ic** (jak′ə bit′ik), **Jac′o•bit′i•cal,** *adj.* —**Jac′o•bit•ism,** *n.*

Jac′obite glass′, an English drinking glass of the late 17th or early 18th century, engraved with Jacobite mottoes and symbols. [1935–40]

Ja•cobs (jā′kəbz), *n.* **1. Helen Hull,** born 1908, U.S. tennis player. **2. Hir•sch(el)** (hûr′shəl), 1904–70, U.S. thoroughbred horse trainer.

Ja•cob•sen (yä′kôp sən), *n.* **Jens Pe•ter** (yens pā′tər), 1847–85, Danish novelist.

ja•cobs•ite (jā′kəb zīt′), *n.* a rare magnetic mineral, manganese iron oxide, $MnFe_2O_4$, similar to magnetite. [1865–70; named after *Jacobsberg* Swedish locality; see -ITE[1]]

Ja′cob's lad′der, 1. a ladder seen by Jacob in a dream, reaching from the earth to heaven. Gen. 28:12. **2.** *Naut.* **a.** Also called **jack ladder, pilot ladder.** a hanging ladder having ropes or chains supporting wooden or metal rungs or steps. **b.** any ladderlike arrangement aloft other than one of rattled shrouds.

Ja•cob's-lad•der (jā′kəbz lad′ər), *n.* any of various plants belonging to the genus *Polemonium,* of the phlox family, esp. *P. caeruleum* (or *P. van-bruntiae*), having blue, cup-shaped flowers and paired leaflets in a ladder-like arrangement. [1725–35]

Ja′cob•son's or′gan (jā′kəb sənz), *Anat., Zool.* either of a pair of blind, tubular, olfactory sacs in the roof of the mouth, vestigial in humans but well-developed in many animals, esp. reptiles. [1870–75; named after L. L. *Jacobson* (d. 1843), Danish anatomist]

Ja′cob's staff′, *pl.* **Jacob's staves. 1.** *Astron.* cross-staff. **2.** *Survey.* a pole providing a firm support for a compass or other instrument. [1540–50]

ja•co•bus (jə kō′bəs), *n., pl.* **-bus•es.** a former gold coin of England issued by James I. [1605–15; Latinized equivalent of JAMES]

jac•o•net (jak′ə net′), *n.* **1.** a cotton fabric of light weight, usually finished as cambric, lawn, organdy, voile, etc., used in the manufacture of clothing and bandages. **2.** a cotton fabric with one glazed surface, used as a lining for the spines of books. [1760–70; < Urdu *jagannāthī,* named after *Jagannāthpūrī* in Orissa, India, where the cloth was first made]

jac•quard (jak′ärd, jə kärd′; *Fr.* zhä kar′), *n.* (*often cap.*) **1.** a fabric with an elaborately woven pattern produced on a Jacquard loom. **2.** See **Jacquard loom.** [1850–55; named after J. M. *Jacquard.* See JACQUARD LOOM]

Jac′quard card′, (in a Jacquard loom) one of a series of perforated cards that control the manipulation of the warp threads and determine the intricate pattern woven on the material.

Jac′quard loom′, a loom for producing elaborate designs in an intricate weave (**Jac′quard weave′**) constructed from a variety of basic weaves. [1850–55; named after J. M. *Jacquard* (1757–1834), French inventor]

Jac•que•line (jak′ə lin, -lēn′, jak′wə-; *Fr.* zhakə lēn′), *n.* a female given name. Also, **Jac′que•lyn.**

Jac•que•rie (zhäk′ rē′), *n.* **1.** the revolt of the peasants of northern France against the nobles in 1358. **2.** (*l.c.*) any peasant revolt. [< F, MF, equiv. to *jaque(s)* peasant (after JACQUES, a name thought to be typical of peasants) + *-rie* -RY]

Jacques (zhäk), *n.* a male given name, French form of **Jacob** or **James.**

Jacques Bon•homme (zhäk bô nôm′), the contemptuous title given by the nobles to the peasants in the revolt of the Jacquerie in 1358 and adopted by the peasants in subsequent revolts. [< F: lit., James goodfellow; see JACK[3]]

jac•ta•tion (jak tā′shən), *n.* **1.** boasting; bragging. **2.** *Pathol.* a restless tossing of the body. [1570–80; < L *jactātiōn-* (s. of *jactātiō*) bragging, equiv. to *jactāt(us)* (ptp. of *jactāre,* freq. of *jacere* to throw) + *-iōn-* -ION]

jac•ti•ta•tion (jak′ti tā′shən), *n.* **1.** *Law.* a false boast or claim that causes injury to another. **2.** *Pathol.* jactation (def. 2). [1625–35; < ML *jactitātiōn-* (s. of *jactitātiō*) tossing, equiv. to L *jactitāt(us)* (ptp. of *jactitāre,* freq. of *jactāre* to throw about; see JACTATION) + *-iōn-* -ION]

jac•u•late (jak′yə lāt′), *v.t.,* **-lat•ed, -lat•ing.** to throw or hurl (a dart, javelin, etc.). [1615–25; < L *jaculātus* (ptp. of *jaculāre* to throw the javelin), equiv. to *jacul(um)* javelin (n. use of neut. of *jaculus* used for hurling, equiv. to *jac-* hurl + *-ulus* adj. suffix) + *-ātus* -ATE[1]] —**jac′u•la′tion,** *n.* —**jac′u•la′tor,** *n.* —**jac•u•la•to•ry** (jak′yə lə tôr′ē, -tōr′ē), *adj.*

jac•u•lif•er•ous (jak′yə lif′ər əs), *adj. Bot., Zool.* having dartlike spines. [1850–55; < NL *jaculifer* dart-bearing (*jaculi-,* comb. form of L *jaculum* dart + *-fer* -FER) + -OUS; see JACULATE]

Ja•cuz•zi (jə ko͞o′zē), *Trademark.* a brand name for a device for a whirlpool bath and related products.

jade[1] (jād), *n.* **1.** either of two minerals, jadeite or nephrite, sometimes green, highly esteemed as an ornamental stone for carvings, jewelry, etc. **2.** an object, as a carving, made from this material. **3.** Also called **jade′ green′.** green, varying from bluish green to yellowish green. [1585–95; < F < It *giada* < obs. Sp (*piedra de*) *ijada* (stone of) colic < VL *īliata,* equiv. to L *īli(a)* flanks (see ILIUM) + *-ata* -ATE[1]; so called because supposed to cure nephritic colic] —**jade′like′,** *adj.*

jade[2] (jād), *n., v.,* **jad•ed, jad•ing.** —*n.* **1.** a worn-out, broken-down, worthless, or vicious horse. **2.** a disreputable or ill-tempered woman. —*v.t., v.i.* **3.** to make or become dull, worn-out, or weary, as from overwork or overuse. [1350–1400; ME; of obscure orig.] —**jad′ish,** *adj.* —**jad′ish•ly,** *adv.* —**jad′ish•ness,** *n.*

jad•ed (jā′did), *adj.* **1.** dulled or satiated by overindulgence: *a jaded appetite.* **2.** worn out or wearied, as by overwork or overuse. **3.** dissipated: *a jaded reprobate.* [1585–95; JADE[2] + -ED[2]] —**jad′ed•ly,** *adv.* —**jad′ed•ness,** *n.*

jade•ite (jā′dīt), *n.* a mineral, essentially sodium aluminum silicate, $NaAlSi_2O_6$, usually fibrous, occurring in compact masses, whitish to dark green: a form of jade. [1860–65; JADE[1] + -ITE[1]]

jade′ plant′, a succulent shrub, *Crassula argentea,* of the stonecrop family, native to southern Africa, having fleshy, oval leaves, often grown as a houseplant.

Ja•dot•ville (*Fr.* zhä dō vēl′), *n.* former name of **Likasi.**

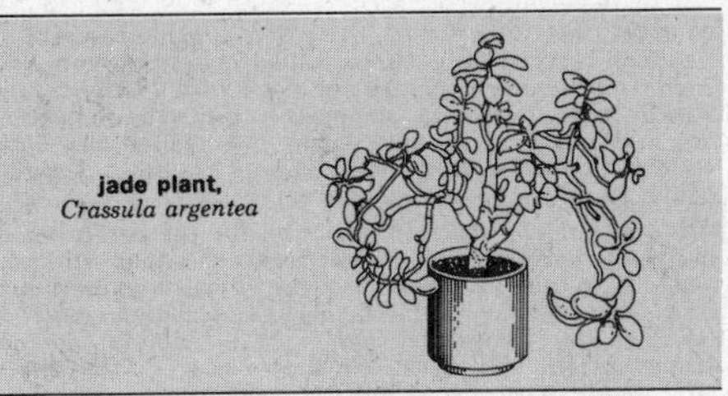
jade plant, *Crassula argentea*

jae•ger (yā′gər; *for 1 also* jā′gər), *n.* **1.** any of several rapacious seabirds of the family Stercorariidae that pursue weaker birds to make them drop their prey. **2.** a hunter. **3.** a member of any of several groups of sharpshooters in the German or Austrian army. Also, **jager, jäger, yager** (for defs. 2, 3). [1770–80; < G *Jäger* hunter, equiv. to *jag(en)* to hunt + *-er* -ER[1]]

Ja•el (jā′əl), *n.* a woman who killed Sisera by hammering a tent pin into his head as he slept. Judges 4:17–22.

Ja•én (hä en′), *n.* a city in S Spain, NNW of Granada. 78,156.

Jaf•fa (jaf′ə, jä′fə; *locally* yä′fä), *n.* a former seaport in W Israel, part of Tel Aviv-Jaffa since 1950: ancient Biblical town. Also, **Yafo.** Ancient, **Joppa.**

Jaf′fa or′ange, a sweet, almost seedless variety of orange grown principally in Israel. [1915–20]

Jaff•na (jäf′nə), *n.* a seaport in N Sri Lanka. 112,000.

jag[1] (jag), *n., v.,* **jagged, jag•ging.** —*n.* **1.** a sharp projection on an edge or surface. —*v.t.* **2.** to cut or slash, esp. in points or pendants along the edge; form notches, teeth, or ragged points in. —*v.i.* **3.** to move with a jerk; jog. [1350–1400; late ME *jagge* (n.), *jaggen* (v.), of obscure orig.] —**jag′less,** *adj.*

jag[2] (jag), *n.* **1.** a period of unrestrained indulgence in an activity; spree; binge: *a crying jag; a talking jag.* **2.** a state of intoxication from liquor. **3.** *Northern, North Midland, and Western U.S.* a load, as of hay or wood. [1590–1600; perh. orig. load of broom or furze (cf. OE *ceacga* broom, furze)]

J.A.G., Judge Advocate General. Also, **JAG**

Jag•an•nath (jug′ə nät′, -nôt′), *n.* **1.** *Hinduism.* a name of Krishna or Vishnu. **2.** Juggernaut (def. 3). Also, **Jag•an•na•tha** (jug′ə nät′hə). [see JUGGERNAUT]

Jag•a•tai (jag′ə tī′), *n.* Chagatai. Also, **Jag′ha•tai′.**

Ja•gel•lo (yä gel′ō), *n., pl.* **-los.** a member of a dynasty ruling in Bohemia, Hungary, Lithuania, and Poland in the 14th to 16th centuries. Also, **Jagiello.** —**Ja•gel•lon** (yä′gə lōn′, yä′gə lōn′), **Ja′gel•lo′ni•an,** *adj.*

ja•ger (yā′gər), *n.* jaeger (defs. 2, 3). Also, **jä′ger.**

jag•ged (jag′id), *adj.* **1.** having ragged notches, points, or teeth; zigzag: *the jagged edge of a saw; a jagged wound.* **2.** having a harsh, rough, or uneven quality. [1400–50; late ME. See JAG[1], -ED[2]] —**jag′ged•ly,** *adv.* —**jag′ged•ness,** *n.*

jag•ger•y (jag′ə rē), *n.* a coarse, dark sugar, esp. that made from the sap of East Indian palm trees. [1590–1600; < Pg (of India) *jágara, jagre* < Malayalam *chakkara* < Skt *śarkarā* SUGAR]

jag•gies (jag′ēz), *n.pl.* a jagged, stairstep effect on curved or diagonal lines that are reproduced in low resolution, as on a printout or computer display.

jag•gy (jag′ē), *adj.,* **-gi•er, -gi•est.** jagged; notched. [1710–20; JAG[1] + -Y[1]]

Ja•giel•lo (yä gyel′ō), *n., pl.* **-los.** Jagello. —**Ja•giel•on** (yä′gyə lōn′, yä′gyə lōn′), **Ja′giel•lo′ni•an,** *adj.*

jag•uar (jag′wär, -yo͞o är′; *esp. Brit.* jag′yo͞o ər), *n.* a large spotted feline, *Panthera onca,* of tropical America, having a tawny coat with black rosettes: now greatly reduced in number and endangered in some areas. [1595–1605; < Pg < Tupi *jaguara*]

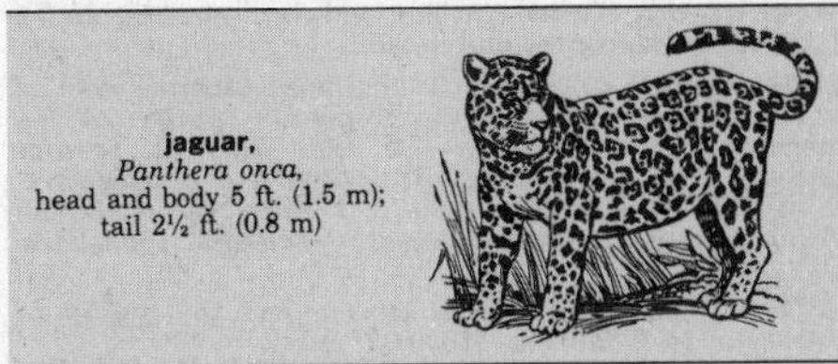
jaguar, *Panthera onca,* head and body 5 ft. (1.5 m); tail 2½ ft. (0.8 m)

ja•gua•run•di (jä′gwə run′dē, -gyo͞o ə-, jag′wə-, -yo͞o ə-), *n., pl.* **-dis.** a long-bodied and long-tailed tropical wildcat, *Felis yagouaroundi,* having a brownish-gray coat and a second color phase of reddish-brown: now reduced in number and endangered in some areas. [1880–85; < Pg < Guarani *jaguarundy* wildcat]

Ja•han•gir (jə hän′gēr, yə-), *n.* 1569–1627, 4th Mogul emperor in India 1605–27 (son of Akbar). Also, **Jehangir.**

Ja•hel (jä′əl), *n. Douay Bible.* Jael.

Jahr•zeit (yär′tsīt, yôr′-), *n. Judaism.* Yahrzeit.

Jah•veh (yä′ve), *n.* Yahweh. Also, **Jah′ve, Jah•weh, Jah•we** (yä′we).

Jah•vism (yä′viz əm), *n.* Yahwism. Also, **Jah•wism** (yä′wiz əm).

Jah•vist (yä′vist), *n.* Yahwist. Also, **Jah•wist** (yä′-wist). —**Jah•vis′tic, Jah•wis′tic,** *adj.*

CONCISE PRONUNCIATION KEY: act, cāpe, dâre, pärt; set, ēqual; *if,* īce; ox, ōver, ôrder, oil, bo͝ok, bo͞ot, out; up, ûrge; child; sing; shoe; thin, *th*at; zh as in *treasure.* ə = *a* as in *alone, e* as in *system, i* as in *easily, o* as in *gallop, u* as in *circus;* ə as in *fire* (fīər), *hour* (ouər). l and n can serve as syllabic consonants, as in *cradle* (krād′l), and *button* (but′n). See the full key inside the front cover.

jai a·lai (hī′ lī′, hī′ ə lī′, hī′ ə lī′), a game resembling handball, played on a three-walled court between two, four, or six players who are equipped with a long, curved wicker basket, or cesta, strapped to the wrist for catching and throwing a small, hard ball against the front wall. Cf. **cancha, fronton.** [1905–10; < Sp < Basque, equiv. to *jai* game + *alai* merry]

jail (jāl), *n.* **1.** a prison, esp. one for the detention of persons awaiting trial or convicted of minor offenses. —*v.t.* **2.** to take into or hold in lawful custody; imprison. Also, *Brit.,* **gaol.** [1225–75; ME *gaiole, jaiole, jaile* < ONF *gaiole,* OF *jaiole* cage < VL **gaviola,* var. of **caveola,* dim. of L *cavea* CAGE; see -OLE[1]] —**jail′a·ble,** *adj.* —**jail′less,** *adj.* —**jail′like′,** *adj.*

jail·bait (jāl′bāt′), *n. Slang.* a girl with whom sexual intercourse is punishable as statutory rape because she is under the legal age of consent. [1930–35, *Amer.;* JAIL + BAIT]

jail·bird (jāl′bûrd′), *n.* a person who is or has been confined in jail; convict or ex-convict. [1595–1605; JAIL + BIRD]

jail·break (jāl′brāk′), *n.* an escape from prison, esp. by forcible means. [1905–10, *Amer.;* JAIL + BREAK]

jail′ deliv′ery, **1.** a liberation of persons from prison, esp. by force. **2.** the act of clearing a jail of prisoners by bringing them to trial, as at the assizes in England. [1425–75; late ME]

jail·er (jā′lər), *n.* **1.** a person who is in charge of a jail or section of a jail. **2.** a person who forcibly confines another. Also, **jail′or.** [1250–1300; ME *gaioler, jaioler, jailer* < OF *jaiolier.* See JAIL, -ER[2]]

jail·house (jāl′hous′), *n., pl.* **-hous·es** (-hou′ziz). a jail or building used as a jail. [1805–15, *Amer.;* JAIL + HOUSE]

jail′house law′yer, a prisoner who has taught himself or herself law while serving time, is knowledgeable about technical legal matters, and gives legal advice, esp. to fellow prisoners. [1965–70; *Amer.*]

Jain (jīn), *n.* **1.** an adherent of Jainism. —*adj.* **2.** of or pertaining to the Jains or Jainism. Also, **Jai·na** (jī′nə), **Jain′ist.** [1795–1805; << Skt *jaina*]

Jain·ism (jī′niz əm), *n.* a dualistic religion founded in the 6th century B.C. as a revolt against current Hinduism and emphasizing the perfectibility of human nature and liberation of the soul, esp. through asceticism and nonviolence toward all living creatures. [1855–60; JAIN + -ISM]

Jai·pur (jī′po͝or), *n.* **1.** a former state in NW India, now part of Rajasthan. **2.** a city in and the capital of Rajasthan, in NW India: known as the "pink city" because of its buildings of that color. 613,144.

Ja·ja·pu·ra (jä′yə po͝or′ə), *n.* Jayapura. Also, **Djajapura.**

jak (jak), *n.* jackfruit.

Ja·kar·ta (jə kär′tə), *n.* a seaport in and the capital of Indonesia, on the NW coast of Java. 4,576,009. Also, **Djakarta, Jacarta.** Formerly, **Batavia.**

jake[1] (jāk), *adj. Slang.* satisfactory; OK; fine: *Everything's jake with me.* [1895–1900; orig. uncert.]

jake[2] (jāk), *n. Slang.* **1.** a homemade or bootleg liquor made from or infused with Jamaica ginger, esp. during Prohibition in the U.S. **2.** Also called **jake′ leg′, jake′-leg paral′ysis.** paralysis caused by drinking this or other liquor made with denatured alcohol. [1925–30, *Amer.;* appar. alter. of JAMAICA (GINGER)]

Jake (jāk), *n.* a male given name, form of **Jacob.**

jakes (jāks), *n, (usually used with a plural v.) Chiefly Dial.* **1.** an outdoor privy; outhouse. **2.** a toilet or bedpan. [1525–35; < F *Jacques,* proper name; cf. JOHN]

Ja′kob-Creutz′feldt disease′ (yä′kəb kroits′felt). See **Creutzfeldt-Jakob disease.**

Ja·kob·son (yä′kəb sən), *n.* **Ro·man** (rō′män, -mən), 1896–1982, U.S. linguist and scholar, born in Russia.

Ja·lal ud-din Ru·mi (ja läl′ o͞od dēn′ ro͞o′mē, o͝od-), 1207–73, Persian poet and mystic.

jal·ap (jal′əp, jä′ləp), *n.* **1.** the dried tuberous root of any of several plants, esp. *Exogonium purga,* of the morning glory family, or the light yellowish powder derived from it, used in medicine chiefly as a purgative. **2.** any of these plants. [1665–75; < MF < Sp *(purga de) Jalapa* purgative from JALAPA] —**ja·lap·ic** (ja lap′ik, jä-), *adj.*

Ja·la·pa (hä lä′pä), *n.* a city in and the capital of Veracruz, in E Mexico. 183,216.

ja·la·pe·ño (hä′lə pān′yō; *Sp.* hä′lä pe′nyô), *n., pl.* **-pe·ños** (-pān′yōz; *Sp.* -pe′nyôs). a hot green or orange-red pepper, the fruit of a variety of *Capsicum annuum,* used esp. in Mexican cooking. Also, **ja′la·pe′ño.** Also called **ja′lape′ño pep′per.** [1935–40; < MexSp *(chile) jalapeño* (chile of) JALAPA]

jal·a·pin (jal′ə pin, jä′lə-), *n.* a resin that is one of the purgative principles of jalap. [1825–35; < NL *jalāp(a)* JALAP + -IN[2]]

ja·lee (jä′lē), *n.* (in Indian architecture) decorated and pierced slabs of marble used as a screen. [1895–1900; < Hindi *jālī* network]

Ja·lis·co (hä lēs′kô), *n.* a state in W Mexico, 4,157,000; 31,152 sq. mi. (80,685 sq. km). *Cap.:* Guadalajara.

ja·lop·y (jə lop′ē), *n., pl.* **-lop·ies.** *Informal.* an old, decrepit, or unpretentious automobile. [1925–30, *Amer.;* orig. uncert.]

CONCISE ETYMOLOGY KEY: <, descended or borrowed from; >, whence; b., blend of, blended; c., cognate with; cf., compare; deriv., derivative; equiv., equivalent; imit., imitative; obl., oblique; r., replacing; s., stem; sp., spelling, spelled; resp., respelling, respelled; trans., translation; ?, origin unknown; *, unattested; ‡, probably earlier than. See the full key inside the front cover.

ja·lor (jä′lər), *n.* any of a wide variety of East Indian rowing and sailing ships. Also, **ja′lur.** [orig. uncert.]

jal·ou·sie (jal′ə sē′ *or, esp. Brit.,* zhal′o͝o zē′), *n.* **1.** a blind or shutter made with horizontal slats that can be adjusted to admit light and air but exclude rain and the rays of the sun. **2.** a window made of glass slats or louvers of a similar nature. [1585–95; < F < It *gelosia* JEALOUSY; so called because such blinds afford a view while hiding the viewer] —**jal′ou·sied′,** *adj.*

jam[1] (jam), *v.,* **jammed, jam·ming,** *n.* —*v.t.* **1.** to press, squeeze, or wedge tightly between bodies or surfaces, so that motion or extrication is made difficult or impossible: *The ship was jammed between two rocks.* **2.** to bruise or crush by squeezing: *She jammed her hand in the door.* **3.** to fill too tightly; cram: *He jammed the suitcase with clothing.* **4.** to press, push, or thrust violently, as into a confined space or against some object: *She jammed her foot on the brake.* **5.** to fill or block up by crowding; pack or obstruct: *Crowds jammed the doors.* **6.** to put or place in position with a violent gesture (often fol. by *on*): *He jammed his hat on and stalked out of the room.* **7.** to make (something) unworkable by causing parts to become stuck, blocked, caught, displaced, etc.: *to jam a lock.* **8.** *Radio.* **a.** to interfere with (radio signals or the like) by sending out other signals of approximately the same frequency. **b.** (of radio signals or the like) to interfere with (other signals). **9.** to play (a piece) in a freely improvised, swinging way; jazz up: *to jam both standard tunes and the classics.* **10.** *Naut.* to head (a sailing ship) as nearly as possible into the wind without putting it in stays or putting it wholly aback. —*v.i.* **11.** to become stuck, wedged, fixed, blocked, etc.: *This door jams easily.* **12.** to press or push, often violently, as into a confined space or against one another: *They jammed into the elevator.* **13.** (of a machine, part, etc.) to become unworkable, as through the wedging or displacement of a part. **14.** *Jazz.* to participate in a jam session. —*n.* **15.** the act of jamming or the state of being jammed. **16.** a mass of objects, vehicles, etc., jammed together or otherwise unable to move except slowly: *a log jam; a traffic jam.* **17.** *Informal.* a difficult or embarrassing situation; fix: *He got himself into a jam with his boss.* **18.** See **jam session.** [1700–10; appar. imit.; cf. CHAMP[1], DAM[1]]

jam[2] (jam), *n.* **1.** a preserve of whole fruit, slightly crushed, boiled with sugar: *strawberry jam.* **2.** **put on jam,** *Australian Slang.* to adopt a self-important manner or use affected speech. [1720–30; perh. special use of JAM[1]] —**jam′like′, jam′my,** *adj.*

Jam., Jamaica.

Ja·mai·ca (jə mā′kə), *n.* **1.** an island in the West Indies, S of Cuba. 4413 sq. mi. (11,430 sq. km). **2.** a republic coextensive with this island: formerly a British colony; became independent in 1962, retaining membership in the Commonwealth of Nations. 2,060,000. *Cap.:* Kingston.

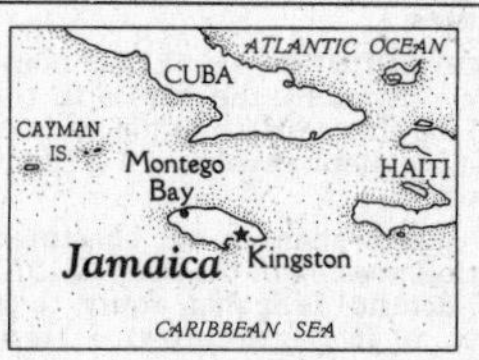

Jamai′ca gin′ger, **1.** an alcoholic extract of ginger used as a flavoring. **2.** powdered ginger root used for medicinal purposes. [1810–20]

Jamai′ca hon′eysuckle. See **yellow granadilla.**

Ja·mai·can (jə mā′kən), *adj.* **1.** of or pertaining to the island of Jamaica or its inhabitants. —*n.* **2.** a native or inhabitant of Jamaica. [1685–95; JAMAIC(A) + -AN]

Jamai′ca rum′, a heavy, pungent, slowly fermented rum made in Jamaica. [1765–75]

Jamai′ca shorts′, shorts extending to the middle of the thigh. [1955–60]

Ja·mal (jə mäl′), *n.* a male given name: from an Arabic word meaning "beauty." Also, **Ja·maal′.**

Ja·mal·pur (jə mäl′po͝or), *n.* a city in N Bangladesh. 60,000.

Ja·mal ud-Din (ja mäl′ o͞od dēn′, o͝od-), (*Jamal ud-Din al-Afghani*), 1838–97, Muslim educator and political leader, born in Persia: founder of modern Pan-Islamism.

jamb[1] (jam), *n.* **1.** *Archit., Building Trades.* **a.** either of the vertical sides of a doorway, arch, window, or other opening. **b.** either of two stones, timbers, etc., forming the sidepieces for the frame of an opening. **2.** *Armor.* greave. Also, **jambe.** [1350–1400; ME *jambe* < MF: leg, jamb < LL *gamba,* var. of *camba* pastern, leg < Gk *kampē* bend of a limb]

jamb[2] (jam), *v.t., v.i. Obs.* jam[1].

jam·ba·lay·a (jum′bə lī′ə), *n.* a dish of Creole origin, consisting of rice cooked with ham, sausage, chicken, or shellfish, herbs, spices, and vegetables, esp. tomatoes, onions, and peppers. [1740–50; < LaF < Pr *jambalaia,* of uncert. orig.]

jam·beau (jam′bō), *n., pl.* **-beaux** (-bōz). **1.** *Armor.* greave. **2.** a spikefish, *Parahollardia lineata,* found in the deep waters of the Atlantic Ocean. [1350–1400; ME < AF, equiv. to *jambe* leg (see JAMB[1]) + *-eau* < L *-ellus* dim. suffix; see -ELLE]

Jam·bi (jäm′bē), *n.* **1.** a province on SE Sumatra, in W Indonesia. **2.** Formerly, **Telanaipura.** a river port in and the capital of this province. 158,559. Also, **Djambi.**

jam·bi·ya (jam bē′yə), *n.* an Arabian knife having a curved, double-edged blade, usually with a central rib. [< Ar *janbīyah*]

jam·bo·ree (jam′bə rē′), *n.* **1.** a carousal; any noisy merrymaking. **2.** a large gathering, as of a political party or the teams of a sporting league, often including a program of speeches and entertainment. **3.** a large gathering of members of the Boy Scouts or Girl Scouts, usually nationwide or international in scope (distinguished from *camporee*). [1860–65, *Amer.;* appar. b. JABBER and SHIVAREE, with *m* from JAM[1] crowd]

jam·bos (jam′bos, -bōs), *n.* See **rose apple.** [< NL, var. of *jambosa* < E *jamb(o)* rose apple (< Hindi *jambu, jambū* < Skt) + L *(r)osa* ROSE[1]]

jamb·stone (jam′stōn′), *n. Masonry.* a stone, or one of the stones, forming one jamb of an opening. [1815–25; JAMB[1] + STONE]

James (jāmz), *n.* **1.** Also called **James′ the Great′.** one of the 12 apostles, the son of Zebedee and brother of the apostle John. Matt. 4:21. **2.** the person identified in Gal. 1:19 as a brother of Jesus: probably the author of the Epistle of St. James. **3.** Also called **James′ the Less′.** (*"James the son of Alphaeus"*) one of the 12 apostles. Matt. 10:3; Mark 3:18; Luke 6:15. **4. Daniel, Jr.** (*"Chappie"*), 1920–78, U.S. Air Force officer: first black general. **5. Henry,** 1811–82, U.S. philosopher and author (father of Henry and William James). **6. Henry,** 1843–1916, U.S. novelist and critic in England (brother of William James). **7. Jesse (Wood·son)** (wo͝od′sən), 1847–82, U.S. outlaw and legendary figure. **8. Will,** 1892–1942, U.S. author and illustrator. **9. William,** 1842–1910, U.S. psychologist and pragmatist philosopher (brother of Henry James). **10.** a river flowing E from the W part of Virginia to Chesapeake Bay. 340 mi. (547 km) long. **11.** a river flowing S from central North Dakota through South Dakota to the Missouri River. 710 mi. (1143 km) long. **12.** one of the books of the New Testament. *Abbr.:* Jas. **13.** a male given name. [ME *Jame(s)* < OF < VL **Jacomus,* for **Jacobus,* alter. of LL *Jacōbus* JACOB; cf. Sp *Jaime,* It *Giacomo*]

James I, 1566–1625, king of England and Ireland 1603–25; as James VI, king of Scotland 1567–1625 (son of Mary Stuart).

James II, 1633–1701, king of England, Ireland, and Scotland 1685–88 (son of Charles I of England).

James III. See **Stuart, James Francis Edward.**

James VI. See **James I.**

James′ Bay′, the S arm of Hudson Bay, in E Canada between Ontario and Quebec provinces. 300 mi. (483 km) long; 160 mi. (258 km) wide.

James′ Ed′ward. See **Stuart, James Francis Edward.**

James·i·an (jām′zē ən), *adj.* **1.** of, pertaining to, or characteristic of the novelist Henry James or his writings. **2.** of, pertaining to, or characteristic of William James or his philosophy. —*n.* **3.** a student or follower of Henry James or William James. Also, **James′e·an.** [1870–75; JAMES + -IAN]

Jame·son (jām′sən), *n.* **Sir Leander Starr** (stär), (*"Doctor Jameson"*), 1853–1917, Scottish physician and statesman: colonial administrator in South Africa.

jame·son·ite (jām′sə nīt′), *n.* a metallic, dark-gray mineral, lead and iron antimony sulfide: formerly mined for lead. [1815–25; named after Robert *Jameson* (1774–1854), Scottish scientist; see -ITE[1]]

James′ Range′, a mountain range in central Australia.

James·town (jāmz′toun′), *n.* **1.** a village in E Virginia: first permanent English settlement in North America 1607; restored 1957. **2.** a city in SW New York. 35,775. **3.** a city in central North Dakota. 16,280. **4.** a seaport in and the capital of St. Helena, in the S Atlantic Ocean. 1475.

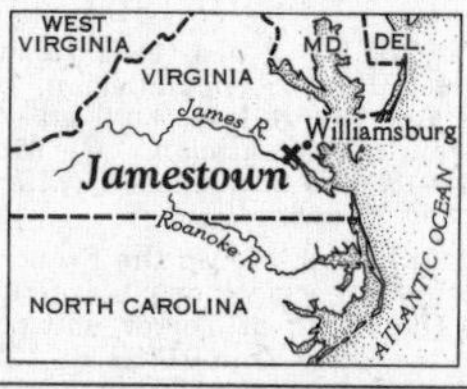

Ja·mie (jā′mē), *n.* **1.** a male given name, form of **James.** **2.** a female given name.

Ja·mi·la (jä mē′lə), *n.* a female given name: from a Swahili word meaning "beautiful."

jam·mies (jam′ēz), *n. (used with a plural v.) Baby Talk.* pajamas. [*jam-* (by aphesis and shortening from PAJAMA) + -Y[2] + -S[3]]

Jam·mu (jum′o͞o), *n.* a city in and the capital of Jammu and Kashmir, in the SW part, in N India. 155,249.

Jam′mu and Kash′mir (jum′o͞o), official name of **Kashmir** (def. 2).

jam·my (jam′ē), *adj.,* **-mi·er, -mi·est.** *Brit. Informal.* **1.** very lucky. **2.** pleasant; easy; desirable: *He has a jammy job.* [1850–55; appar. JAM[2] + -Y[1]; cf. the idioms *to have jam on it* to have something easy; *real jam, pure jam* something easy or pleasant]

Jam·na·gar (jäm nug′ər), *n.* a city in W Gujarat, in W central India. 227,640.

jam′ nut′. See **lock nut** (def. 2). [1860–65]

ja·moke (jə mōk′), *n. Slang.* coffee; a cup of coffee. [1910–15, *Amer.;* prob. JA(VA) + MOCH(A), respelled]

jam-pack (jam′pak′), *v.t.* to fill or pack as tightly or fully as possible: *We jam-packed the basket with all kinds of fruit.* [1920–25]

jam·proof (jam′pro͞of′), *adj.* built so as to prevent jamming: *a jamproof copying machine.* [JAM[1] + -PROOF]

jams (jamz), *n. (used with a plural v.)* **1.** *Informal.* pajamas. **2.** brightly patterned, knee-length drawstring swim trunks. [1965–70; by shortening]

jam′ ses′sion, **1.** a meeting of a group of musicians, esp. jazz musicians, to play for their own enjoyment. **2.** an impromptu jazz performance or special performance by jazz musicians who do not regularly play together. Also called **jam.** [1930–35; perh. JAM[1], or by shortening of JAMBOREE]

Jam•shed•pur (jäm′shed po͝or′), *n.* a city in SE Bihar, in NE India. 465,200.

Jam•shid (jam shēd′), *n. Persian Myth.* the king of the peris who, given a human form as punishment for his boast of immortality, became a powerful and wonder-working Persian king. Also, **Jam•shyd′.**

jam-up (jam′up′), *n.* a stoppage or slowing of motion, work, or the like, due to obstruction, overloading, malfunction, or inefficiency; jam: *Your letters didn't go out yesterday because there was a jam-up in the mail room.* [1940–45; n. use of v. phrase *jam up*]

Jan (jan; *for 1 also Du., Ger.* yän), *n.* **1.** a male given name, form of **John. 2.** a female given name, form of **Janet.**

Jan., January.

Ja•ná•ček (yä′nä chek′), *n.* **Le•oš** (le′ôsh), 1854–1928, Czech composer.

jane (jān), *n. Slang.* a girl or woman. [1905–10, *Amer.*; generic use of the proper name]

Jane (jān), *n.* a female given name: derived from *John.*

Jane′ Doe′ (dō), a fictitious name used in legal proceedings for a female party whose true name is not known. [1935–40; fem. of JOHN DOE]

Jane Eyre (jān′ âr′), a novel (1847) by Charlotte Brontë.

Janes•ville (jānz′vil), *n.* a city in S Wisconsin. 51,071.

Ja•net (zhA ne′ *for 1;* jan′it *for 2*), *n.* **1. Pierre Ma•rie Fé•lix** (pyer mA rē′ fā lēks′), 1859–1947, French psychologist and neurologist. **2.** Also, **Ja•net•ta** (jə net′ə). a female given name, form of **Jane.**

jan•gle (jang′gəl), *v.,* **-gled, -gling,** *n.* —*v.i.* **1.** to produce a harsh, discordant sound, as two comparatively small, thin, or hollow pieces of metal hitting together: *The charms on her bracelet jangle as she moves.* **2.** to speak angrily; wrangle. —*v.t.* **3.** to cause to make a harsh, discordant, usually metallic sound: *He jangled the pots and pans.* **4.** to cause to become irritated or upset: *The loud noise of the motors jangled his nerves.* —*n.* **5.** a harsh or discordant sound. **6.** an argument, dispute, or quarrel. [1250–1300; ME *janglen* < OF *jangler* < Gmc; cf. MD *jangelen* to haggle, whine] —**jan′gler,** *n.* —**jan′gly,** *adj.*

Jan•ice (jan′is), *n.* a female given name, form of **Jane.** Also, **Jan′is.**

Ja•nic•u•lum (jə nik′yə ləm), *n.* a ridge near the Tiber in Rome, Italy. —**Ja•nic′u•lan,** *adj.*

Ja•nie (jā′nē), *n.* a female given name, form of **Jane.** Also, **Ja′ney.**

jan•i•form (jan′ə fôrm′), *adj.* Janus-faced. [1805–15; JAN(US) + -I- + -FORM]

Ja•ni•na (yä′nē nä), *n.* Serbian name of **Ioannina.**

Ja•nine (jə nēn′), *n.* a female given name.

jan•is•sar•y (jan′ə ser′ē), *n., pl.* **-sar•ies. 1.** (*often cap.*) a member of an elite military unit of the Turkish army organized in the 14th century and abolished in 1826 after it revolted against the Sultan. **2.** (*often cap.*) any soldier in the Turkish army. **3.** a member of any group of loyal guards, soldiers, or supporters. Also, **jan•i•zar•y** (jan′ə zer′ē). [1520–30; < F *janissaire* < It *gian(n)izzero* < Turk *yeniçeri,* equiv. to *yeni* new + *çeri* soldiery, militia]

Jan′issary mu′sic, music characteristic of or imitative of that played by a Turkish military band, typically employing cymbals, triangles, bass drum, and Turkish crescents. [1885–90]

jan•i•tor (jan′i tər), *n.* **1.** a person employed in an apartment house, office building, school, etc., to clean the public areas, remove garbage, and do minor repairs; caretaker. **2.** *Archaic.* a doorkeeper or porter. —*v.i.* **3.** to be employed as a janitor. [1575–85; < L *jānitor* doorkeeper, equiv. to *jāni-* (comb. form of *jānus* doorway, covered passage) + *-tor* -TOR] —**jan•i•to•ri•al** (jan′i-tôr′ē əl, -tōr′-), *adj.*

jan•i•tress (jan′i tris), *n.* a woman who is a janitor. [1885–90, *Amer.*; JANIT(O)R + -ESS]
—**Usage.** See **-ess.**

Jan May•en (yän′ mī′ən), a volcanic island in the Arctic Ocean between Greenland and Norway: a possession of Norway. 144 sq. mi. (373 sq. km).

Jan•nings (jan′ingz; *Ger.* yän′ings), *n.* **Emil** (*Theodor Emil Janenz*), 1886–1950, German film actor.

jan•nock (jan′ək), *adj. Brit., Australian Informal.* honest; fair; straightforward. Also, **jonnick.** [1810–20; orig. uncert.]

Jan•sen (jan′sən; *Du.* yän′sən), *n.* **Cor•ne•lis Ot•to** (kôr nā′lis ot′ō), (*Cornelius Jansenius*), 1585–1638, Dutch Roman Catholic theologian.

Jan•sen•ism (jan′sə niz′əm), *n.* the doctrinal system of Cornelis Jansen and his followers, denying free will and maintaining that human nature is corrupt and that Christ died for the elect and not for all humanity. [1650–60; < F *jansénisme.* See JANSEN, -ISM] —**Jan′•sen•ist,** *n.* —**Jan′sen•is′tic, Jan′sen•is′ti•cal,** *adj.*

jan•sky (jan′skē), *n., pl.* **-skies.** a unit of flux density for electromagnetic radiation, used chiefly in radio astronomy. *Abbr.:* Jy [after K. JANSKY]

Jan•sky (jan′skē), *n.* **Karl Guthe,** 1905–50, U.S. engineer: pioneer in radio astronomy.

Jan•u•ar•i•us (jan′yo͞o âr′ē əs), *n.* **Saint,** A.D. 272?–305?, Italian ecclesiastic and martyr: patron saint of Naples. Italian, **San Gennaro.**

Jan•u•ar•y (jan′yo͞o er′ē), *n., pl.* **-ar•ies.** the first month of the year, containing 31 days. *Abbr.:* Jan. [bef. 1000; ME < L, n. use of *Jānuārius,* equiv. to *Jānu(s)* JANUS + *-ārius* -ARY; r. ME *Genever, Jeniver* < AF, OF *Genever, Jenever* < L, as above; r. OE *Januarius* < L]

Ja•nus (jā′nəs), *n.* **1.** an ancient Roman god of doorways, of beginnings, and of the rising and setting of the sun, usually represented as having one head with two bearded faces back to back, looking in opposite directions. **2.** *Astron.* a moon of the planet Saturn, located just outside the rings. [< L, special use of *jānus* doorway, archway, arcade]

Ja′nus cloth′, a worsted fabric, each side of which has a different color. [1875–80]

Ja•nus-faced (jā′nəs fāst′), *adj.* **1.** having two faces, one looking forward, one looking backward, as the Roman deity Janus. **2.** having two contrasting aspects, as the alternation of mood in a capricious person. **3.** two-faced; deceitful. **4.** aware of or concerned with polarities; seeing different and contrasting aspects: *a Janus-faced view of history.* **5.** having or containing contrasting characteristics: *a Janus-faced policy.* [1675–85]

Jap (jap), *adj., n. Slang (disparaging and offensive).* Japanese. [1885–90; shortened form]

JAP (jap), *n. Slang (disparaging and offensive).* a pampered young Jewish woman, esp. one who takes material advantages for granted. [*J(ewish) A(merican) P(rincess)*]

Jap., **1.** Japan. **2.** Japanese.

ja•pan (jə pan′), *n., adj., v.,* **-panned, -pan•ning.** —*n.* **1.** any of various hard, durable, black varnishes, originally from Japan, for coating wood, metal, or other surfaces. **2.** work varnished and figured in the Japanese manner. **3. Japans,** a variety of decorative motifs or patterns derived from Oriental sources, used on English porcelain of the 18th and 19th centuries. —*adj.* **4.** of or pertaining to japan. —*v.t.* **5.** to varnish with japan; lacquer. **6.** to coat with any material that gives a hard, black gloss. [1605–15; special use of JAPAN] —**ja•pan′•ner,** *n.*

Ja•pan (jə pan′), *n.* **1.** a constitutional monarchy on a chain of islands off the E coast of Asia: main islands, Hokkaido, Honshu, Kyushu, and Shikoku. 120,020,000; 141,529 sq. mi. (366,560 sq. km). *Cap.:* Tokyo. Japanese, **Nihon, Nippon. 2. Sea of,** the part of the Pacific Ocean between Japan and mainland Asia.

Japan., Japanese.

Japan′ ce′dar, an evergreen tree, *Cryptomeria japonica,* of Japan, characterized by the pyramidal manner of growth of its branches. Also called **Japanese cedar, sugi.** [1850–55]

Japan′ clo′ver, a drought-resistant bush clover, *Lespedeza striata,* of the legume family, introduced to the southern Atlantic states from Asia, having numerous tiny trifoliate leaves valued for pasturage and hay. [1865–70, *Amer.*]

Japan′ Cur′rent, a warm ocean current in the Pacific, flowing N along the E coast of Taiwan, NE along the E coast of Japan, and continuing in an easterly direction into the open Pacific. Also called **Japan Stream, Kuroshio, Black Stream.**

Jap•a•nese (jap′ə nēz′, -nēs′), *adj., n., pl.* **-nese.** —*adj.* **1.** of, pertaining to, or characteristic of Japan, its people, or their language. —*n.* **2.** a native or inhabitant of Japan. **3.** a person of Japanese ancestry. **4.** the language of Japan. *Abbr.:* Japn., Japn [1580–90; JAPAN + -ESE]

Jap′anese′ androm′eda, an Asian evergreen shrub, *Pieris japonica,* of the heath family, having broad, glossy leaves and drooping clusters of whitish blossoms. Also called **andromeda.** [1945–50]

Jap′anese′ anem′one, an eastern Asian plant, *Anemone hupehensis,* of the buttercup family, having purplish or reddish flowers and grown widely in gardens. [1880–85]

Japanese′ arborvi′tae, a Japanese evergreen tree, *Thuja standishii,* having spreading branches with bright-green leaves.

Jap′anese ar′tichoke. See **Chinese artichoke.** [1900–05]

Jap′anese bar′berry, a thorny barberry, *Berberis thunbergii,* of Japan, having yellow flowers and bearing bright-red fruit, grown as a hedge plant.

Jap′anese bee′tle, a small beetle, *Popillia japonica,* of the scarab family, introduced into the eastern U.S. from Japan, the adult of which feeds on the foliage of fruit and other trees, and the larva of which feeds on plant roots. [1915–20]

Jap′anese black′ pine′, a pine, *Pinus thunbergiana,* of Japan, grown as a seaside ornamental in the U.S.

Jap′anese ce′dar. See **Japan cedar.** [1875–80]

Jap′anese chest′nut. See under **chestnut** (def. 1).

Jap′anese Chin′ (chin), one of a Japanese breed of toy dogs having a long, silky, black and white or red and white coat and a tail carried over the back.

Jap′anese clem′atis, a Japanese woody vine, *Clematis paniculata,* of the buttercup family, having dense clusters of fragrant, white flowers and plumed fruit.

Jap′anese flow′ering cher′ry, any of various ornamental hybrid cherry trees developed in Japan, having white or pink blossoms and inedible fruit. Also called **Jap′anese cher′ry.**

Jap′anese gel′atin, agar (def. 1). Also called **Jap′•anese i′singlass.**

Jap′anese hol′ly, an evergreen shrub, *Ilex crenata,* of Japan, having black fruit and box-shaped foliage, widely grown as an ornamental.

Jap′anese hon′eysuckle, a climbing honeysuckle, *Lonicera japonica,* introduced into the eastern U.S. from Asia, having fragrant, white flowers that fade to yellow.

Jap′anese i′ris, a plant, *Iris kaempferi,* native to Japan, having broad, showy flowers in a variety of colors. [1880–85]

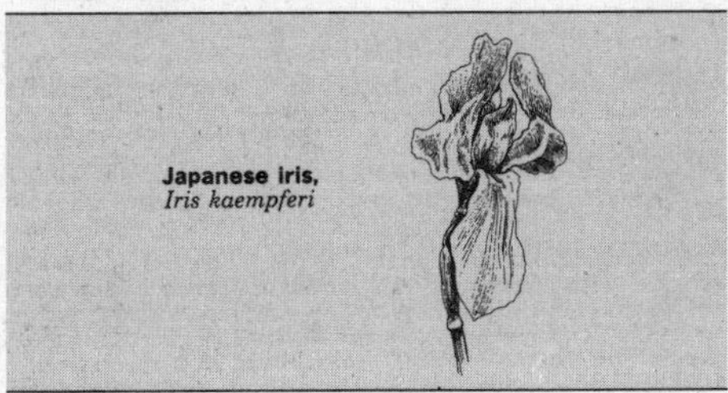
Japanese iris,
Iris kaempferi

Jap′anese i′vy. See **Boston ivy.**

Jap′anese knot′weed. See **Mexican bamboo.**

Jap′anese lac′quer, lacquer (def. 2). [1895–1900]

Jap′anese lan′tern. See **Chinese lantern.** [1890–95]

Jap′anese larch′, a tree, *Larix kaempferi,* of Japan, having bluish-green leaves and egg-shaped cones. [1860–65]

Jap′anese lau′rel, an eastern Asian evergreen shrub, *Aucuba japonica,* of the dogwood family, having dark-green, glossy leaves and scarlet berries.

Jap′anese lawn′ grass′. See **Korean lawn grass.**

Jap′anese ma′ple, a small, graceful maple tree, *Acer palmatum,* of Korea and Japan, having small, purple flowers, the foliage turning bright red in autumn. Also called **full-moon maple.** [1895–1900]

Jap′anese mink′, **1.** a dark-brown arboreal marten, *Martes melampus,* native to Japan, having a long body and bushy tail. **2.** a pale-brown northern Asian weasel, *Mustela siberica.*

Jap′anese oys′ter, a commercial oyster, *Ostrea gigas,* of the Pacific coast of North America, introduced from Japan.

Jap′anese′ pago′da tree′. See **pagoda tree.** [1920–25]

Jap′anese pa′per, paper of a high rag content, used for woodcuts, engravings, etc. [1720–30]

Jap′anese pear′, a tree, *Pyrus pyrifolia,* of China, having bristly toothed leaves and apple-shaped, brownish, hard-fleshed fruit. Also called **sand pear.**

Jap′anese′ persim′mon, **1.** the soft, orange or reddish, edible fruit of an Asian tree, *Diospyros kaki.* **2.** the tree itself. [1905–10]

Jap′anese plum′, **1.** a small tree, *Prunus salicina,* native to China, bearing edible yellowish fruit. **2.** a related shrub, *P. japonica,* native to China and Korea, having pink flowers and edible red fruit. **3.** the fruit of either of these. **4.** loquat. [1900–05]

Jap′anese quail′. See under **coturnix.**

Jap′anese quince′, a flowering quince, *Chaenomeles speciosa,* of Japan, having scarlet flowers and pear-shaped fruit. [1895–1900]

Jap′anese riv′er fe′ver. See **scrub typhus.**

Jap′anese silk′, raw silk of usually high quality produced in Japan, used in the manufacture of such fabrics as shantung and habutai. [1870–75]

Jap′anese span′iel, former name of **Japanese Chin.** [1875–80]

Jap′anese spurge′, a low Japanese plant, *Pachysandra terminalis,* having evergreen leaves and spikes of white flowers, grown as a ground cover. [1920–25]

Jap′anese′ wiste′ria, a wisteria, *Wisteria floribunda,* of Japan, having violet, violet-blue, pink, red, or white flowers, grown in the U.S. as an ornamental.

Jap′anese wolf′, a wolf, *Canis lupus hodophylax,* of Japan. [1875–80]

Jap′anese yew′, a yew, *Taxus cuspidata,* of Japan, grown as an ornamental.

Jap•a•nesque (jap′ə nesk′), *adj.* having a Japanese style. [1880–85; JAPAN + -ESQUE]

Ja•pan•ism (jə pan′iz əm), *n.* **1.** a custom, trait, or other feature peculiar to or characteristic of Japan or its people. **2.** devotion to or preference for Japan and its institutions. [1885–90; < F *japonisme;* see JAPAN, -ISM]

Japan′ Stream′, *Oceanog.* See **Japan Current.**

Japan′ wax′, a pale-yellow, waxy, water-insoluble solid obtained from the fruit of certain sumacs, esp. *Rhus succedanea,* native to Japan and China: used chiefly in the manufacture of candles, furniture polishes, and floor waxes. Also called **Japan′ tal′low, sumac wax.** [1855–60]

jape (jāp), *v.,* **japed, jap•ing,** *n.* —*v.i.* **1.** to jest; joke; gibe. —*v.t.* **2.** to mock or make fun of. —*n.* **3.** a joke; jest; quip. **4.** a trick or practical joke. [1300–50; ME *japen,* perh. < OF *jap(p)er* to bark, of imit. orig.] —**jap′er,** *n.* —**jap′er•y,** *n.* —**jap′ing•ly,** *adv.*

CONCISE PRONUNCIATION KEY: act, cāpe, dâre, pärt; set, ēqual; *if,* īce; ox, ōver, ôrder, oil, bo͝ok, bo͞ot, out; up, ûrge; child; sing; shoe; thin, that; zh as in *treasure.* ə = *a* as in *alone, e* as in *system, i* as in *easily, o* as in *gallop, u* as in *circus;* ᵊ as in *fire* (fīᵊr), *hour* (ouᵊr). l and n can serve as syllabic consonants, as in *cradle* (krād′l), and *button* (but′n). See the full key inside the front cover.

Ja·pheth (jā′fith), *n.* a son of Noah. Gen. 5:32. [< LL < Gk *Iapheth* < Heb *Yepheth*]

Ja·phet·ic (jə fet′ik), *adj.* **1.** of or pertaining to Japheth. **2.** of or pertaining to a hypothesized group of languages of the Caucasus, Mesopotamia, Asia Minor, and southern Europe, including the Caucasian languages, Sumerian, Basque, and Etruscan, formerly thought by some to represent a stage in language development that preceded the development of Indo-European and Semitic. [1820–30; JAPHET(H) + -IC, on the model of HAMITIC, SEMITIC]

Jap·lish (jap′lish), *n.* **1.** Japanese spoken or written with a large admixture of English words and expressions. **2.** English spoken or written with features characteristic of Japanese. [1955–1960; JAP(ANESE) + (ENG)LISH]

Japn., **1.** Japan. **2.** Japanese. Also, **Japn**

ja·po·nai·se·rie (jap′ə nez′ə rē′, -nez′ə rē; *Fr.* zhA-pô nez° RĒ′), *n.* **1.** stylistic characteristics, as in art, decor, or film, influenced by or reflective of Japanese culture and tradition. **2.** something, as an art object, displaying these characteristics. [1895–1900; < F, equiv. to *japonais* Japanese (*Japon* JAPAN + *-ais* < L *-ēnsis* -ENSIS; cf. -ESE) + *-erie* -ERY]

ja·pon·i·ca (jə pon′i kə), *n.* the camellia, *Camellia japonica,* having waxy flowers in a variety of colors. [1810–20; < NL, equiv. to *Japon(ia)* JAPAN + *-ica,* fem. of *-icus* -IC]

Ja·pu·rá (*Port.* zhä′po͞o RÄ′), *n.* a river flowing E from the Andes in SW Colombia through NW Brazil to the Amazon. 1750 mi. (2820 km) long.

ja·pyg·id (jə pij′id), *n.* any eyeless, wingless, primitive insect of the family Japygidae, having a pair of pincers at the rear of its abdomen. [< NL *Japygidae,* equiv. to *Japyg-,* s. of *Japyx* a genus (appar. L *Jāpyx* the eponymous founder of *Jāpygia* < Gk *Iāpygía* a region of S Italy) + *-idae* -IDAE; see -ID[2]]

Ja·ques (jā′kwēz, -kwiz, jāks), *n.* a disillusioned and satirical observer of life, in Shakespeare's *As You Like It.* —**Ja·que·si·an** (jə kwē′zē ən), *adj.*

Jaques-Dal·croze (*Fr.* zhäk′dAl kRōz′), *n.* **É·mile** (*Fr.* ā mēl′), 1865–1950, Swiss composer and teacher: created eurythmics.

jar[1] (jär), *n.* **1.** a broad-mouthed container, usually cylindrical and of glass or earthenware: *a cookie jar.* **2.** the quantity such a container can or does hold. [1585–95; < MF *jarre* < OPr *jarra* < Ar *jarrah* earthen water vessel] —**jar′less,** *adj.*

jar[2] (jär), *v.,* **jarred, jar·ring,** *n.* —*v.i.* **1.** to have a harshly unpleasant or perturbing effect on one's nerves, feelings, thoughts, etc.: *The sound of the alarm jarred.* **2.** to produce a harsh, grating sound; sound discordantly. **3.** to vibrate audibly; rattle: *The window jarred in the frame.* **4.** to vibrate or shake. **5.** to conflict, clash, or disagree. —*v.t.* **6.** to cause to rattle or shake. **7.** to have a sudden and unpleasant effect upon (the feelings, nerves, etc.): *The burglary violently jarred their sense of security.* **8.** to cause to sound harshly or discordantly. —*n.* **9.** a jolt or shake; a vibrating movement, as from concussion. **10.** a sudden unpleasant effect upon the mind or feelings; shock. **11.** a harsh, grating sound. **12.** a discordant sound or combination of sounds. **13.** a quarrel or disagreement, esp. a minor one. [1520–30; prob. imit.; cf. CHIRR] —**jar′ring·ly,** *adv.*

jar[3] (jär), *n.* **1.** *Archaic.* a turn or turning. **2. on the jar,** partly opened; ajar: *The window was on the jar.* [1665–75; var. of CHAR[3], CHARE; cf. AJAR[2]]

ja·ra·be ta·pa·tí·o (*Sp.* hä RÄ′ve tä′pä tē′ô), a dance of Mexican origin, performed by a couple and consisting of nine figures and melodies, in which the partners often dance facing each other but not touching. [< MexSp; Sp *jarabe* lit., sweetened drink, SYRUP; *tapatío* pertaining to Guadalajara (allegedly a word used in this region of Mexico for a serving of three tortillas, orig. a unit of cacao bean currency < Nahuatl *tlapatiotl* price, value)]

Ja·rash (jar′äsh), *n.* Jerash.

jar·din an·glais (zhAR dAN näN gle′), *pl.* ***jar·dins an·glais*** (zhAR dAN zäN gle′). *French.* a landscape garden having winding paths and irregular planting. [lit., English garden]

jar·di·niere (jär′dn ēr′, zhär′dn yâr′), *n.* **1.** an ornamental receptacle or stand for holding plants, flowers, etc. **2.** various vegetables diced and boiled or glazed, used for garnishing meat or poultry. [1835–45; < F, fem. of *jardinier* gardener, equiv. to OF *jardin* GARDEN + *-ier* -IER[2]]

Jar·ed (jar′id), *n.* **1.** (in the *Book of Mormon*) the eponymous ancestor of the Jaredites. **2.** a male given name.

Jar·ed·ite (jar′i dīt′), *n.* (in Mormon belief) a member of a tribe of people who settled America after the dispersal at Babel. [JARED + -ITE[1]]

jar·ful (jär′fo͝ol), *n., pl.* **-fuls.** the amount that a jar can hold. [1865–70; JAR[1] + -FUL]
—**Usage.** See **-ful.**

jar·gon[1] (jär′gən, -gon), *n.* **1.** the language, esp. the vocabulary, peculiar to a particular trade, profession, or group: *medical jargon.* **2.** unintelligible or meaningless talk or writing; gibberish. **3.** any talk or writing that one does not understand. **4.** pidgin. **5.** language that is characterized by uncommon or pretentious vocabulary and convoluted syntax and is often vague in meaning. —*v.i.* **6.** to speak in or write jargon; jargonize. [1300–50; ME *jargoun* < MF; OF *jargon, gargun,* deriv. of an expressive base *garg-; see GARGLE, GARGOYLE] —**jar′gon·y, jar′gon·is′tic,** *adj.* —**jar′gon·ist, jar′·gon·eer′,** *n.*
—**Syn. 1.** See **language. 2.** babble, gabble, twaddle.

jar·gon[2] (jär′gon), *n.* a colorless to smoky gem variety of zircon. Also, **jar·goon** (jär go͞on′). [1760–70; < F < It *giargone* << Pers *zargūn* gold-colored]

jar·gon·ize (jär′gə nīz′), *v.,* **-ized, -iz·ing.** —*v.i.* **1.** to talk jargon or a jargon. —*v.t.* **2.** to translate into jargon. Also, *esp. Brit.,* **jar′gon·ise′.** [1795–1805; JARGON[1] + -IZE] —**jar′gon·i·za′tion,** *n.*

jar·head (jär′hed′), *n. Slang (disparaging).* a U.S. Marine. [JAR[1] + HEAD]

jarl (yärl), *n. Scand. Hist.* a chieftain; earl. [1810–20; < ON *jarl;* see EARL] —**jarl′dom,** *n.*

Jarls·berg (yärlz′bûrg), *Trademark.* a Norwegian hard cheese, similar to Swiss cheese, with a buttery flavor and large holes.

Jar·mo (jär′mō), *n.* a Neolithic village site in northeastern Iraq, dated c6500 B.C. and noted as one of the world's earliest food-producing settlements.

Jar·mo·ite (jär′mō īt′), *n. Archaeol.* a member of the prehistoric people of northeastern Iraq in and around the settlement at Jarmo. [JARMO + -ITE[1]]

jar·o·site (jar′ə sīt′, jə rō′sīt), *n.* a yellowish or brownish mineral, a hydrous sulfate of potassium and iron, $KFe_3(SO_4)_2(OH)_6$, occurring in small crystals or large masses. [1850–55; named after Barranco *Jaroso* (in Almería, Spain); see -ITE[1]]

jar·o·vize (yär′ə vīz′), *v.t.,* **-vized, -viz·ing.** to vernalize. Also, **iarovize, yarovize.** Also *esp. Brit.,* **jar′o·vise′.** [back formation from *jarovization* < Russ *yarovizátsiya,* equiv. to *yarov(ói)* spring (of crops) + *-atsiya* << L *-ātiō* -ATION] —**jar′o·vi·za′tion,** *n.*

jar·rah (jar′ə), *n.* **1.** a hardwood tree, *Eucalyptus marginata,* of western Australia. **2.** the heavy, often attractively grained wood of this tree. [1865–70; < Nyungar *jaril*]

Jar·rell (jar′əl, jə rel′), *n.* **Randall,** 1914–65, U.S. poet and critic.

Jar·row (jar′ō), *n.* a seaport in Tyne and Wear, in NE England, near the mouth of the Tyne River. 28,779.

Jar·ry (zhA RĒ′), *n.* **Al·fred** (Al fRed′), 1873–1907, French poet and playwright.

Ja·ru·zel·ski (yä′Ro͞o zel′skē), *n.* **Woj·ciech (Wi·told)** (voi′cheKH vē′tôld), born 1923, Polish general and political leader: prime minister 1981–85; president 1989–90.

jar·vey (jär′vē), *n., pl.* **-veys.** *Irish Eng.* **1.** a hackney coachman. **2.** a hackney coach. [1790–1800; special use of *Jarvey,* var. of *Jarvis* proper name]

Jar·vik–7 (jär′vik sev′ən), *Med., Trademark.* a four-valved artificial heart for implantation in the human body, replacing the natural heart's ventricles and attaching to its atria: air is pumped into the ventricles from an external air compressor through two connecting hoses that enter the body through the abdominal wall.

Jas., *Bible.* James.

Ja·scha (yä′shə), *n.* a male given name, Russian form of **Jacob** or **James.**

ja·sey (jā′zē), *n., pl.* **-seys.** *Brit. Informal.* a wig, esp. one made of worsted. [1770–80; perh. var. of JERSEY] —**ja′seyed,** *adj.*

jas·mine (jaz′min, jas′-), *n.* **1.** any of numerous shrubs or vines belonging to the genus *Jasminum,* of the olive family, having fragrant flowers and used in perfumery. **2.** any of several other plants having similar fragrant flowers, as the Carolina jessamine. **3.** a pale-yellow color. Also, **jessamine.** [1555–65; < MF *jasmin,* var. of *jassemin* < Ar *yās(a)min* < Pers *yāsman, yāsmin*] —**jas′mined,** *adj.* —**jas′mine·like′,** *adj.*

Jas·mine (jaz′min, jas′-), *n.* a female given name. Also, **Jas′min, Jas·mi·na** (jaz′mə nə, jas′-).

jas′mine tea′, tea scented with jasmine blossoms.

Ja·son (jā′sən), *n.* **1.** *Class. Myth.* a hero, the leader of the Argonauts, who at the request of his uncle Pelias retrieved the Golden Fleece from King Aeëtes of Colchis with the help of Medea. **2.** a male given name: from a Greek word meaning "healer."

jas·pé (ja spā′; *Fr.* zhA spā′), *adj.* given a veined and spotted appearance imitating jasper. [1850–55; < F: ptp. of *jasper* to mottle, deriv. of *jaspe* JASPER[1]]

jas·per[1] (jas′pər), *n.* **1.** a compact, opaque, cryptocrystalline variety of quartz, usually colored red: often used in decorative carvings. **2.** Also called **cameo ware, jas′per·ware′.** a fine, hard stoneware introduced c1775 by Wedgwood, stained various colors by metallic oxides, with raised designs in white. [1300–50; ME *jaspe, jaspre* < MF; OF *jaspe* < L *iaspis* < Gk *iáspis* < Sem; cf. Ar *yashb*]

jas·per[2] (jas′pər), *n. Older Slang.* a fellow; guy. [1895–1900, *Amer.;* special use of proper name *Jasper*]

Jas·per (jas′pər), *n.* **1.** a city in NW Alabama. 11,894. **2.** a resort town in SW Alberta, in SW Canada, on the Athabaska River: headquarters for Jasper National Park. 3060. **3.** a male given name, form of **Caspar.**

Jas′per Na′tional Park′, a national park in the Canadian Rockies in W Alberta, in SW Canada.

Jas·pers (yäs′pərs), *n.* **Karl** (kärl), 1883–1969, German philosopher.

jas·per·y (jas′pə rē), *adj.* **1.** containing or composed of jasper. **2.** resembling jasper. [1825–35; JASPER[1] + -Y[1]]

jass (yäs), *n.* **1.** a card game for two persons that is played with a 36-card pack made by removing all cards below the sixes from a regular 52-card pack, in which point values are assigned to certain melds and to certain cards taken in tricks. **2.** Also, **jasz.** the jack of trumps in klaberjass. [see KLABERJASS]

jas·sid (jas′id), *n.* leafhopper. [1890–95; < NL *Jassidae,* equiv. to *Jass(us)* a genus (appar. L *Jāsus* a town on the coast of Caria < Gk *Iāsós*) + *-idae* -IDAE; see -ID[2]]

Jas·sy (yä′sē; *Rum.* yäsh), *n.* a city in NE Rumania. 262,493. Also, **Yassy.** Rumanian, **Iaşi.**

Jat (jät, jôt), *n.* a member of an Indo-Aryan people living mainly in northwestern India. In early times they offered vigorous resistance to the Muslim invaders of India.

Ja·ta·ka (jä′tə kə), *n. Buddhism.* a collection of fables, many concerning former lives of the Buddha.

ja·ti (jä′tē), *n. Hinduism.* caste (def. 2). Cf. **varna.** [< Skt *jāti*]

ja·to (jā′tō), *n., pl.* **-tos.** a jet-assisted takeoff, esp. one using auxiliary rocket motors that are jettisoned at the completion of the takeoff. [1940–45; *Amer.; j(et) a(ssisted) t(ake)o(ff)*]

jauk (jäk, jôk), *v.i. Scot.* to dally; dawdle. [1560–70; orig. uncert.]

jaun·dice (jôn′dis, jän′-), *n., v.,* **-diced, -dic·ing.** —*n.* **1.** Also called **icterus.** *Pathol.* yellow discoloration of the skin, whites of the eyes, etc., due to an increase of bile pigments in the blood, often symptomatic of certain diseases, as hepatitis. Cf. **physiologic jaundice. 2.** grasserie. **3.** a state of feeling in which views are prejudiced or judgment is distorted, as by envy or resentment. —*v.t.* **4.** to distort or prejudice, as by envy or resentment: *His social position jaundiced his view of things.* [1275–1325; ME *jaundis* < OF *jaunisse,* equiv. to *jaune* yellow (< L *galbinus* greenish-yellow) + *-isse* -ICE]

jaun·diced (jôn′dist, jän′-), *adj.* **1.** affected with or colored by or as if by jaundice: *jaundiced skin.* **2.** affected with or exhibiting prejudice, as from envy or resentment: *a jaundiced viewpoint.* [1630–40; JAUNDICE + -ED[3]]
—**Syn.** **2.** resentful, envious, jealous, embittered.

jaunt (jônt, jänt), *n.* **1.** a short journey, esp. one taken for pleasure. —*v.i.* **2.** to make a short journey. [1560–70; orig. uncert.] —**jaunt′ing·ly,** *adv.*

jaunt′ing car′, a light, two-wheeled, one-horse cart, once common in Ireland, having two seats set back to back, with a perch in front for the driver. [1795–1805]

jaun·ty (jôn′tē, jän′-), *adj.,* **-ti·er, -ti·est. 1.** easy and sprightly in manner or bearing: *to walk with a jaunty step.* **2.** smartly trim, as clothing: *a jaunty hat.* [1655–65; earlier *jentee, juntee* < F *gentil* noble, gentle, GENTEEL with ending taken as -Y[1]] —**jaun′ti·ly,** *adv.* —**jaun′ti·ness,** *n.*

jaup (jôp, jäp), *n. Scot. and North Eng.* **1.** a splash, spurt, or drop of water. **2.** a spot or stain, as from a splash of water or mud. Also, **jawp.** [1505–15; perh. akin to JAW[2]]

Jau·rès (zhô Res′), *n.* **Jean Lé·on** (zhäN lā ôN′), 1859–1914, French socialist and writer.

Jav., Javanese.

Ja·va (jä′və *or, esp. for 2,* jav′ə), *n.* **1.** the main island of Indonesia. 76,100,000 (with Madura); 51,032 sq. mi. (132,173 sq. km). **2.** (*usually l.c.*) *Slang.* coffee: *a cup of java.*

Ja′va black′ rot′, *Plant Pathol.* a disease of stored sweet potatoes, characterized by dry rot of and black protuberances on the tubers, caused by a fungus, *Diplodia tubericola.*

Ja′va cot′ton, kapok.

Ja′va fig′. See **weeping fig.**

Ja′va finch′. See **Java sparrow.**

Ja′va man′, the fossil remains of *Homo erectus* found in Java. [1930–35]

Jav·a·nese (jav′ə nēz′, -nēs′, jä′və-), *adj., n., pl.* **-nese.** —*adj.* **1.** of or pertaining to the island of Java, its people, or their language. —*n.* **2.** a member of the native Malayan people of Java, esp. of that branch of it in the central part of the island. **3.** the Austronesian language of central Java. [1695–1705; *Javan* (JAV(A) + -AN) + -ESE]

Ja·va·ri (zhä′və rē′), *n.* a river in E South America, flowing NE from Peru to the upper Amazon, forming part of the boundary between Peru and Brazil. 650 mi. (1045 km) long. Also, **Ja′va·ry′.** Spanish, **Yavarí.**

Ja′va Sea′, a sea between Java and Borneo.

Ja′va spar′row, a finchlike weaverbird, *Padda oryzivora,* of southeastern Asia, having gray plumage tinged with pink on the belly, often kept as a cage bird. Also called **Java finch.** [1860–65]

Ja′va Trench′, a trench in the Indian Ocean, S of Java: deepest known part of Indian Ocean. 25,344 ft. (7725 m) deep. Formerly, **Ja′va Trough′.**

jave·lin (jav′lin, jav′ə-), *n.* **1.** a light spear, usually thrown by hand. **2.** *Track.* **a.** a spearlike shaft about 8½ ft. (2.7 m) long and usually made of wood, used in throwing for distance. **b.** Also called **jave′lin throw′.** a competitive field event in which the javelin is thrown for distance. —*v.t.* **3.** to strike or pierce with or as if with a javelin. [1505–15; < MF *javeline,* by suffix alter. from *javelot*, AF *gavelot, gaveloc*, prob. < OE *gafeluc*, **gafeloc* << British Celtic **gablākos* presumably, a spear with a forklike head; cf. MIr *gablach* forked branch, javelin, MWelsh *gaflach* (appar. < OIr), deriv. of OIr *gabul* fork, forked branch, c. Old Breton *gabl*, Welsh *gafl*]

ja•ve•li•na (hä′və lē′nə), *n.* See under **peccary.** [1815–25, *Amer.* < AmerSp *jabalina*, Sp: fem of *jabalín* wild boar, dial. var. of *jabalí* < Ar (*khinzīr*) *jabalī* mountain (boar)]

Ja•vel′ wa′ter (zhə vel′, zha-), sodium hypochlorite, NaOCl, dissolved in water, used as a bleach, antiseptic, etc. Also, **Ja•velle′ wa′ter.** [1870–75; trans. of F *eau de Javel*, after *Javel* former town, now in the city of Paris]

Jav•its (jav′its), *n.* **Jacob K(op•pel)** (kō pel′), 1904–86, U.S. politician: senator 1957–81.

jaw[1] (jô), *n.* **1.** either of two bones, the mandible or maxilla, forming the framework of the mouth. **2.** the part of the face covering these bones, the mouth, or the mouth parts collectively: *My jaw is swollen.* **3. jaws,** anything resembling a pair of jaws or evoking the concept of grasping and holding: *the jaws of a gorge; the jaws of death.* **4.** *Mach.* **a.** one of two or more parts, as of a machine, that grasp or hold something: *the jaws of a vise.* **b.** any of two or more protruding parts for attaching to or meshing with similar parts. **5.** Often, **jaws.** Also called **throat.** *Naut.* a forked piece at the end of a gaff, fitting halfway around the mast. **6.** *Slang.* **a.** idle talk; chatter. **b.** impertinent talk. —*v.i.* **7.** *Slang.* **a.** to talk; chat; gossip. **b.** to scold or use abusive language. —*v.t.* **8.** *Slang.* to scold. [1325–75; ME *jawe, jowe* < OF *joue;* orig. uncert.] —**jaw′less,** *adj.*

jaw[2] (jô), *Scot. and North Eng.* —*n.* **1.** a swelling wave of water; billow. —*v.i.* **2.** (of liquid) to surge, splash, or dash forward, as in waves. —*v.t.* **3.** to pour or splash (liquid). [1505–15; perh. akin to JAUP]

ja•wan (jə wän′), *n.* a soldier in the Indian army. [1830–40; < Urdu *javān*]

jaw•bone (jô′bōn′), *n., v.,* **-boned, -bon•ing,** *adj.* —*n.* **1.** a bone of either jaw; a maxilla or mandible. **2.** the bone of the lower jaw; mandible. —*v.t., v.i.* **3.** *Informal.* to attempt to influence or pressure by persuasion rather than by the exertion of force or one's authority, as in urging voluntary compliance with economic guidelines: *The President jawboned the steel industry into postponing price increases.* —*adj.* **4.** *Informal.* obtained by or resorting to such a practice: *jawbone controls.* [1480–90; JAW[1] + BONE] —**jaw′bon′ing,** *n., adj.*

jaw•break•er (jô′brā′kər), *n.* **1.** *Informal.* a word that is hard to pronounce. **2.** a very hard, usually round, candy. **3.** Also called **jaw′ crush′er.** *Mining.* a machine used to break up ore, consisting of a fixed plate and a hinged jaw moved by a toggle joint. [1830–40; JAW[1] + BREAKER[1]] —**jaw′break′ing,** *adj.* —**jaw′•break′ing•ly,** *adv.*

jawed (jôd), *adj.* having a jaw or jaws, esp. of a specified kind (often used in combination): *heavy-jawed; square-jawed.* [1520–30; JAW[1] + -ED[3]]

jaw•fish (jô′fish′), *n., pl.* (*esp. collectively*) **-fish,** (*esp. referring to two or more kinds or species*) **-fish•es.** any of several large-mouthed fishes of the family Opisthognathidae, common along sandy bottoms of warm seas. [JAW[1] + FISH]

Jaw•len•sky (you len′skē), *n.* **A•le•xej von** (ä′le ksā′ fən), 1864?–1941, German painter, born in Russia.

jaw′less fish′, cyclostome. [1965–70; JAW[1] + -LESS]

jaw•like (jô′līk′), *adj.* resembling a jaw or pair of jaws. [JAW[1] + -LIKE]

jawp (jôp, jäp), *n. Scot. and North Eng.* jaup.

jaw•rope (jô′rōp′), *n. Naut.* a rope tied across the jaw of a gaff to hold it to the mast. [1825–35; JAW[1] + ROPE]

jaw's-harp (jôz′härp′), *n.* jew's-harp.

Jaws′ of Life′, *Trademark.* a heavy-duty tool that can cut through metal or pry sections of it apart: used esp. to free people trapped in wrecked vehicles.

Jax•ar•tes (jak sär′tēz), *n.* ancient name of **Syr Darya.**

jay[1] (jā), *n.* **1.** any of several noisy, vivacious birds of the crow family, subfamily Garrulinae, as the crested *Garrulus glandarius*, of the Old World, having brownish plumage with blue, black, and white barring on the wings. Cf. **blue jay, gray jay. 2.** *Informal.* a simpleminded or gullible person. [1275–35; ME *jai* < MF < LL *gāius, gāia*, perh. after L *Gāius* man's name]

jay[2] (jā), *n. Slang.* a marijuana cigarette. [1970–75; prob. sp. of initial consonant of JOINT, perh. suggested by Pig Latin version *ointjay*]

Jay (jā), *n.* **1. John,** 1745–1829, U.S. statesman and jurist: first Chief Justice of the U.S. 1789–95. **2.** a male given name.

Ja•ya•pu•ra (jä′yə pŏŏr′ə), *n.* a city in and the capital of Irian Jaya, on the NE coast, in Indonesia. 45,786. Also, **Jajapura, Djajapura.** Formerly, **Hollandia.**

Ja•ya•wi•ja•ya (jä′yä wē jä′yä), *n.* a range in E central Irian Jaya, on New Guinea. Highest peak, Trikora, 15,584 ft. (4750 m). Formerly, **Orange Mountains.**

jay•bird (jā′bûrd′), *n.* jay[1]. [1655–65, *Amer.*; JAY[1] + BIRD]

Jay•cee (jā′sē′), *n.* a member of a civic group for young business and community leaders. [1945–50, *Amer.*; sp. forms of the letters *JC*, abbr. of *Junior Chamber* in its original name *United States Junior Chamber of Commerce*]

Jay•hawk•er (jā′hô′kər), *n.* **1.** a native or inhabitant of Kansas (used as a nickname). **2.** (*sometimes l.c.*) a plundering marauder, esp. one of the antislavery guerrillas in Kansas, Missouri, and other border states before and during the Civil War. [1855–60, *Amer.*; of uncert. orig.]

Jay′hawker State′, Kansas (used as a nickname).

Jayne (jān), *n.* a female given name.

Jay's′ Trea′ty, *U.S. Hist.* the agreement in 1794 between England and the U.S. by which limited trade relations were established, England agreed to give up its forts in the northwestern frontier, and a joint commission was set up to settle border disputes. Also, **Jay′ Trea′ty.** [named after John JAY]

jay•vee (jā′vē′), *n. Sports.* **1.** a player on a junior varsity team. **2.** See **junior varsity.** [1935–40; sp. form of *JV*, abbr. for *junior varsity*]

jay•walk (jā′wôk′), *v.i.* to cross a street at a place other than a regular crossing or in a heedless manner, as diagonally or against a traffic light. [1915–20, *Amer.*; JAY + WALK] —**jay′walk′er,** *n.*

jazz (jaz), *n.* **1.** music originating in New Orleans around the beginning of the 20th century and subsequently developing through various increasingly complex styles, generally marked by intricate, propulsive rhythms, polyphonic ensemble playing, improvisatory, virtuosic solos, melodic freedom, and a harmonic idiom ranging from simple diatonicism through chromaticism to atonality. **2.** a style of dance music, popular esp. in the 1920's, arranged for a large band and marked by some of the features of jazz. **3.** dancing or a dance performed to such music, as with violent bodily motions and gestures. **4.** *Slang.* liveliness; spirit; excitement. **5.** *Slang.* insincere, exaggerated, or pretentious talk: *Don't give me any of that jazz about your great job!* **6.** *Slang.* similar or related but unspecified things, activities, etc.: *He goes for fishing and all that jazz.* —*adj.* **7.** of, pertaining to, or characteristic of jazz. —*v.t.* **8.** to play (music) in the manner of jazz. **9.** *Informal.* **a.** to excite or enliven. **b.** to accelerate. **10.** *Slang* (*vulgar*). to copulate with. —*v.i.* **11.** to dance to jazz music. **12.** to play or perform jazz music. **13.** *Informal.* to act or proceed with great energy or liveliness. **14.** *Slang* (*vulgar*). to copulate. **15. jazz up,** *Informal.* **a.** to add liveliness, vigor, or excitement to. **b.** to add ornamentation, color, or extra features to, in order to increase appeal or interest; embellish. **c.** to accelerate. [1905–10, *Amer.*; 1915–20 for def. 5; orig. uncert.] —**jazz′er,** *n.*

Jazz′ Age′, the period that in the U.S. extended roughly from the Armistice of 1918 to the stock-market crash of 1929 and was notable for increased prosperity, liberated or hedonistic social behavior, Prohibition and the concomitant rise in production and consumption of bootleg liquor, and the development and dissemination of jazz and ragtime and associated ballroom dances. [1920–25, *Amer.*]

jazz′ band′, a band specializing in jazz, and consisting typically of trumpet, trombone, clarinet, saxophone, piano, double bass, and percussion. [1915–20, *Amer.*]

jazz•er•cise (jaz′ər sīz′), *n.* vigorous dancing done to jazz dance music as an exercise for physical fitness. [1985–90; JAZZ + (EX)ERCISE]

jazz•man (jaz′man′, -mən), *n., pl.* **-men** (-men′, -mən). a musician who plays jazz. [1925–30; JAZZ + MAN[1]]

jazz-rock (jaz′rok′), *n.* music that combines elements of both jazz and rock and is usually performed on amplified electric instruments. [1965–70]

jazz′ shoe′, 1. a man's plain, close-fitting, low-heeled oxford made of soft leather or other material and having a thin, flexible sole, worn for jazz dancing. **2.** any casual shoe resembling this, worn by adults and children. Also called **jazz′ ox′ford.**

jazz′ sing′er, a singer whose vocal technique is similar to that of a musical instrument, and whose singing has a strong jazz feeling, chiefly imparted through phrasing, melodic improvisation, and rhythmic subtlety. [1925–30]

jazz•wom•an (jaz′wŏŏm′ən), *n., pl.* **-wom•en.** a female jazz musician. [JAZZ(MAN) + -WOMAN]

jazz•y (jaz′ē), *adj.,* **jazz•i•er, jazz•i•est. 1.** pertaining to or suggestive of jazz music. **2.** *Informal.* active or lively. **3.** *Informal.* fancy or flashy: *a jazzy sweater.* [1915–20, *Amer.*; JAZZ + -Y[1]] —**jazz′i•ly,** *adv.* —**jazz′i•ness,** *n.*

J-bar lift (jā′bär′), a ski lift having a J-shaped bar against which a skier leans in an upright position while being pulled up the slope. Also called **J-bar.** [1950–55]

JC, junior college.

J.C., 1. Jesus Christ. **2.** Julius Caesar. **3.** jurisconsult. [< L *jūris cōnsultus*]

J.C.B., 1. Bachelor of Canon Law. [< NL *Jūris Canonicī Baccalaureus*] **2.** Bachelor of Civil Law. [< NL *Jūris Civilis Baccalaureus*]

J.C.C., Junior Chamber of Commerce.

J.C.D., 1. Doctor of Canon Law. [< NL *Jūris Canonici Doctor*] **2.** Doctor of Civil Law. [< L *Jūris Civilis Doctor*]

JCI, Jaycees International.

JCL, *Computers.* **1.** See **job control language. 2.** *Informal.* the total specifications made for a job using job control language.

J.C.L., Licentiate in Canon Law. [< L *Jūris Canonici Licentiātus*]

J.C.S., Joint Chiefs of Staff. Also, **JCS**

jct., junction. Also, **jctn.**

JD, *Informal.* **1.** juvenile delinquency. **2.** juvenile delinquent.

JD., (in Jordan) dinar; dinars.

J.D., 1. See **Julian Day. 2.** Doctor of Jurisprudence; Doctor of Law. [< NL *Jūris Doctor*] **3.** Doctor of Laws. [< NL *Jūrum Doctor*] **4.** Justice Department. **5.** *Informal.* **a.** juvenile delinquency. **b.** juvenile delinquent.

JDL, See **Jewish Defense League.**

Je., June.

jeal•ous (jel′əs), *adj.* **1.** feeling resentment against someone because of that person's rivalry, success, or advantages (often fol. by *of*): *He was jealous of his rich brother.* **2.** feeling resentment because of another's success, advantage, etc. (often fol. by *of*): *He was jealous of his brother's wealth.* **3.** characterized by or proceeding from suspicious fears or envious resentment: *a jealous rage; jealous intrigues.* **4.** inclined to or troubled by suspicions or fears of rivalry, unfaithfulness, etc., as in love or aims: *a jealous husband.* **5.** solicitous or vigilant in maintaining or guarding something: *The American people are jealous of their freedom.* **6.** *Bible.* intolerant of unfaithfulness or rivalry: *The Lord is a jealous God.* [1175–1225; ME *jelous, gelos* < OF *gelos* (F *jaloux*) < VL **zēlōsus*, equiv. to LL *zēl(us)* ZEAL + *-ōsus* -OSE[1]] —**jeal′ous•ly,** *adv.* —**jeal′ous•ness,** *n.*

jeal•ous•y (jel′ə sē), *n., pl.* **-ous•ies** for 4. **1.** jealous resentment against a rival, a person enjoying success or advantage, etc., or against another's success or advantage itself. **2.** mental uneasiness from suspicion or fear of rivalry, unfaithfulness, etc., as in love or aims. **3.** vigilance in maintaining or guarding something. **4.** a jealous feeling, disposition, state, or mood. [1175–1225; ME *gelusie, jelosie* < OF *gelosie*, equiv. to *gelos* JEALOUS + *-ie* -Y[3]]

—**Syn. 1.** See **envy.**

jean (jēn *or, for 1, Brit. formerly* jān), *n.* **1.** Sometimes, **jeans.** a sturdy twilled fabric, usually of cotton. **2. jeans,** (*used with a plural v.*) **a.** See **blue jeans. b.** pants of various fabrics, styled or constructed like blue jeans. Cf. **Levi's.** [1485–95; short for *jean fustian*, earlier *Gene(s) fustian* GENOESE or GENOA fustian] —**jeaned,** *adj.*

Jean (*Fr.* zhäN *for 1, 2;* jēn *for 3*), *n.* **1.** born 1921, Grand Duke of Luxembourg since 1964. **2.** a male given name, form of **John. 3.** a female given name.

Jean•ine (jə nēn′), *n.* a female given name. Also, **Jean•nine′.**

Jeanne d'Arc (zhän dARK′), French name of **Joan of Arc.**

Jean•nette (jə net′; *for 2 also Fr.* zhä net′), *n.* **1.** a city in W Pennsylvania, near Pittsburgh. 13,106. **2.** Also, **Jean•net•ta** (jə net′ə), **Jean•ette′.** a female given name, form of **Jean.**

Jean•nie (jē′nē), *n.* a female given name, form of **Jean.** Also, **Jean′ie, Jeanne** (jēn; *Fr.* zhän).

Jeans (jēnz), *n.* **Sir James (Hop•wood)** (hop′wŏŏd), 1877–1946, English astrophysicist and author.

Jebb (jeb), *n.* **Sir Richard Clav•er•house** (klav′ər-hous′), 1841–1905, Scottish scholar of classical Greek.

jeb•el (jeb′əl), *n.* djebel.

Jeb•el ed Druz (jeb′əl ed drŏŏz′), a mountainous region in S Syria: inhabited by Druses. ab. 2700 sq. mi. (6995 sq. km). Also, **Jeb′el el Druz′** (el), **Jeb′el Druze′** (drŏŏz′), **Djebel Druze.**

Jeb•el Mu•sa (jeb′əl mōō′sä), a mountain in NW Morocco, opposite Gibraltar: one of the Pillars of Hercules. 2775 ft. (846 m). Ancient, **Abyla.**

Je•bus (jē′bəs), *n.* an ancient Canaanite city taken by David: it later became Jerusalem.

Jeb•us•ite (jeb′yə sīt′), *n.* a member of an ancient Canaanite people that lived in Jebus. [1525–35; JEBUS + -ITE[1]] —**Jeb•u•sit•ic** (jeb′yə sit′ik), **Jeb′u•sit′i•cal,** *adj.*

Jed•burgh (jed′bûr ō, -bur ō *or, esp. Brit.,* -brə), *n.* a border town in the Borders region, in SE Scotland: ruins of an abbey. 3874.

Jed•da (jed′ə), *n.* Jidda.

jed′ding ax′ (jed′ing), a stonemason's ax, similar to a kevel, having a head with one flat and one pointed face. [1895–1900; *jedding*, var. of *jadding* (*jad* cutting in a quarry (< ?) + -ING[1])]

jee (jē), *interj., v.i., v.t.,* **jeed, jee•ing.** gee[1].

Jeep (jēp), *Trademark.* **1.** a small, rugged military motor vehicle having four-wheel drive and a ¼-ton capacity: widely used by the U.S. Army during and after World War II. **2.** a similar vehicle used by civilians. —*v.i.* **3.** (*l.c.*) to ride or travel in a jeep. [1935–40, *Amer.*; alter. of G.P. (for General Purpose) Vehicle, or special use of Eugene the Jeep, name of fabulous animal in comic strip "Popeye" by E. C. Segar]

jeep′ car′rier, *U.S. Navy.* an antisubmarine escort carrier.

jee•pers (jē′pərz), *interj.* (used as a mild exclamation of surprise or emotion.) Also, **jee′pers cree′pers** (krē′-pərz). [1925–30, *Amer.*; euphemistic alter. of *Jesus*]

jeep•ney (jēp′nē), *n., pl.* **-neys.** a Philippine twin-benched jitney bus, seating about a dozen passengers. [1945–50; JEEP + (JIT)NEY]

jeer[1] (jēr), *v.i.* **1.** to speak or shout derisively; scoff or gibe rudely: *Don't jeer unless you can do better.* —*v.t.* **2.** to shout derisively at; taunt. **3.** to treat with scoffs or derision; mock. **4.** to drive away by derisive shouts (fol. by *out of, off,* etc.): *They jeered the speaker off the stage.* —*n.* **5.** a jeering utterance; derisive or rude gibe. [1555–65; orig. uncert.; cf. OE *cēir* clamor, akin to *cēgan* to call out] —**jeer′er,** *n.* —**jeer′ing•ly,** *adv.*

—**Syn. 1.** sneer; jest. See **scoff**[1]. **2, 3.** deride, ridicule, flout, fleer.

jeer[2] (jēr), *n.* Often, **jeers.** *Naut.* any of various combinations of tackles for raising or lowering heavy yards. [1485–95; JEE + -ER[1]]

jeez (jēz), *interj.* (used as a mild expression of surprise, disappointment, astonishment, etc.) [1920–25, *Amer.*; euphemistic shortening of *Jesus*]

je•fe (he′fe; *Eng.* hā′fā), *n., pl.* **-fes** (-fes; *Eng.* -fāz). *Spanish.* leader; chief; boss.

Jeff (jef), *n.* a male given name, form of **Jeffrey.**

Jeff′ Da′vis pie′, *Southern Cookery.* a custard pie

baked in a pastry shell and containing spices, raisins, pecans, etc. [after Jefferson DAVIS]

Jef•fers (jef′ərz), *n.* **(John) Robinson,** 1887–1962, U.S. poet.

Jef•fer•son (jef′ər sən), *n.* **1. Joseph,** 1829–1905, U.S. actor. **2. Thomas,** 1743–1826, U.S. statesman, diplomat, architect, and author: third president of the U.S. 1801–09. **3.** a male given name.

Jef′ferson Cit′y, a city in and the capital of Missouri, in the central part, on the Missouri River. 33,619.

Jef′ferson Da′vis's Birth′day, June 3 or the first Monday in June, observed as a legal holiday in some Southern states.

Jef′ferson Day′, April 13, Thomas Jefferson's birthday, a legal holiday in Alabama, sometimes celebrated by the Democratic party by the holding of fund-raising dinners.

Jef•fer•so•ni•an (jef′ər sō′nē ən), *adj.* **1.** pertaining to or advocating the political principles and doctrines of Thomas Jefferson, esp. those stressing minimum control by the central government, the inalienable rights of the individual, and the superiority of an agrarian economy and rural society. **—***n.* **2.** a supporter of Thomas Jefferson or Jeffersonianism. [1790–1800, *Amer.*; JEFFERSON + -IAN] **—Jef′fer•so′ni•an•ism,** *n.*

Jef•fer•son•town (jef′ər sən toun′), *n.* a town in N Kentucky. 15,795.

Jef•fer•son•ville (jef′ər sən vil′), *n.* a city in S Indiana, on the Ohio River. 21,220.

Jef•frey (jef′rē), *n.* **1. Francis** (*"Lord Jeffrey"*), 1773–1850, Scottish jurist, editor, and critic. **2.** a male given name: from a Germanic word meaning "divine peace."

Jef′frey pine′, a conifer, *Pinus jeffreyi,* of high mountains in the western U.S., having long needles, large cones, and aromatic bark. [1855–60, *Amer.*; after John *Jeffrey* (1826–54), Scottish gardener, who collected plants in the Pacific Northwest, 1850–54]

Jef•freys (jef′rēz), *n.* **1. George** (*1st Baron Jeffreys of Wem*), 1648–89, English jurist. **2. Sir Harold,** born 1891, British geophysicist and astronomer.

Jef•fries (jef′rēz), *n.* **James J.,** 1875–1953, U.S. boxer: world heavyweight champion 1899–1905.

Jeh (jä), *n. Zoroastrianism.* a female demon who was the companion of Angra Mainyu and was believed to have corrupted the female sex: sometimes considered the first woman.

je•had (ji häd′), *n.* jihad.

Je•han•gir (jə hän′gēr, yə-), *n.* Jahangir.

Je•hoi•a•da (ji hoi′ə də), *n.* a priest of Judah who led the revolt against Athalia. II Kings 11:1–16.

Je•hol (jə hōl′; *Chin.* zhu′hō′, RU′-), *n.* **1.** a region and former province in NE China: incorporated into Manchukuo by the Japanese 1932–45. 74,297 sq. mi. (192,429 sq. km). **2.** former name of **Chengde.**

Je•hosh•a•phat (ji hosh′ə fat′, -hos′-), *n.* a king of Judah, son of Asa, who reigned in the 9th century B.C. I Kings 22:41–50.

Je•ho•vah (ji hō′və), *n.* **1.** a name of God in the Old Testament, an erroneous rendering of the ineffable name, JHVH, in the Hebrew Scriptures. **2.** (in modern Christian use) God. **—Je•ho•vic** (ji hō′vik), *adj.*

Jeho′vah God′, (among the Jehovah's Witnesses) God.

Jeho′vah's Wit′nesses, a Christian sect, founded in the U.S. in the late 19th century, that believes in the imminent destruction of the world's wickedness and the establishment of a theocracy under God's rule.

Je•ho•vist (ji hō′vist), *n.* Yahwist. [1745–55; JEHOV(AH) + -IST] **—Je•ho′vism,** *n.* **—Je•ho•vis•tic** (jē′hō-vis′tik, ji hō-), *adj.*

Je•hu (jē′hyoo͞ *or, often,* -hoo͞), *n.* **1.** a king of Israel noted for his furious chariot attacks. II Kings 9. **2.** (*l.c.*) a fast driver. **3.** (*l.c.*) the driver of a cab or coach.

jejun-, var. of **jejuno-** before a vowel: *jejunectomy.*

je•june (ji joo͞n′), *adj.* **1.** without interest or significance; dull; insipid: *a jejune novel.* **2.** juvenile; immature; childish: *jejune behavior.* **3.** lacking knowledge or experience; uninformed: *jejune attempts to design a house.* **4.** deficient or lacking in nutritive value: *a jejune diet.* [1605–15; < L *jējūnus* empty, poor, mean] **—je•june′ly,** *adv.* **—je•june′ness, je•ju′ni•ty,** *n.*

je•ju•nec•to•my (ji joo͞ nek′tə mē, jē′joo͞-), *n., pl.* **-mies.** *Surg.* excision of part or all of the jejunum. [JEJUN- + -ECTOMY]

jejuno-, a combining form representing **jejunum** in compound words: *jejunostomy.*

je•ju•nos•to•my (ji joo͞ nos′tə mē, jē′joo͞-), *n., pl.* **-mies.** *Surg.* an artificial opening from the jejunum through the abdominal wall, created for the drainage of jejunal contents or for feeding. [1880–85; JEJUNO- + -STOMY]

je•ju•num (ji joo͞′nəm), *n. Anat.* the middle portion of the small intestine, between the duodenum and the ileum. See diag. under **intestine.** [1350–1400; ME < L *jējūnum,* n. use of neut. of *jējūnus* empty, poor, mean; so called because thought to be empty after death] **—je•ju′nal,** *adj.*

Jek′yll and Hyde′ (jek′əl, jē′kəl), a person marked by dual personality, one aspect of which is good and the other bad. [after the protagonist of Robert Louis Stevenson's *The Strange Case of Dr. Jekyll and Mr. Hyde* (1886)]

CONCISE ETYMOLOGY KEY: <, descended or borrowed from; >, whence; b., blend of, blended; c., cognate with; cf., compare; deriv., derivative; equiv., equivalent; imit., imitative; obl., oblique; r., replacing; s., stem; sp., spelling, spelled; resp., respelling, respelled; trans., translation; ?, origin unknown; *, unattested; ‡, probably earlier than. See the full key inside the front cover.

jell (jel), *v.i.* **1.** to congeal; become jellylike in consistency. **2.** to become clear, substantial, or definite; crystallize: *The plan began to jell once we all met to discuss it.* **—***v.t.* **3.** to cause to jell. [1820–30; back formation from JELLY]

jel•la•ba (jə lä′bə), *n.* djellabah.

Jel•li•coe (jel′i kō′), *n.* **John Rush•worth** (rush′-wûrth), **1st Earl,** 1859–1935, British admiral.

jel•lied (jel′ēd), *adj.* **1.** congealed or brought to the consistency of jelly: *jellied consommé.* **2.** containing or spread over with jelly or syrup. [1585–95; JELLY + -ED[2]]

jel•li•fy (jel′ə fī′), *v.,* **-fied, -fy•ing.** **—***v.t.* **1.** to make into a jelly; reduce to a gelatinous state. **—***v.i.* **2.** to turn into jelly; become gelatinous. [1800–10; JELLY + -FY] **—jel′li•fi•ca′tion,** *n.*

Jell-O (jel′ō), *Trademark.* a brand of dessert made from a mixture of gelatin, sugar, and fruit flavoring, dissolved in hot water and chilled until firm.

jel•ly (jel′ē), *n., pl.* **-lies,** *v.,* **-lied, -ly•ing,** *adj.* **—***n.* **1.** a food preparation of a soft, elastic consistency due to the presence of gelatin, pectin, etc., esp. fruit juice boiled down with sugar and used as a sweet spread for bread and toast, as a filling for cakes or doughnuts, etc. **2.** any substance having the consistency of jelly. **3.** *Chiefly Brit.* a fruit-flavored gelatin dessert. **4.** a plastic sandal or shoe. **—***v.t., v.i.* **5.** to bring or come to the consistency of jelly. **—***adj.* **6.** containing or made, spread, or topped with jelly or syrup; jellied: *jelly apples.* [1350–1400; ME *gely* < OF *gelee* frozen jelly < ML *gelāta* frozen, equiv. to L *gel-* freeze + *-āta* -ATE[1]; cf. GEL, COLD] **—jel′ly•like′,** *adj.*

jel•ly•bean (jel′ē bēn′), *n.* a small, bean-shaped, usually brightly colored candy with a hard sugar coating and a firm gelatinous filling. [1900–05, *Amer.*; JELLY + BEAN]

jel′ly coat′, *Biochem.* an ovum-produced glycoprotein that causes adhesion of sperm to the ovum; fertilizin.

jel′ly dough′nut, a raised doughnut filled with jelly or jam and sometimes sprinkled with powdered sugar.

jel•ly•fish (jel′ē fish′), *n., pl.* (*esp. collectively*) **-fish,** (*esp. referring to two or more kinds or species*) **-fish•es.** **1.** any of various marine coelenterates of a soft, gelatinous structure, esp. one with an umbrellalike body and long, trailing tentacles; medusa. **2.** *Informal.* a person without strong resolve or stamina; an indecisive or weak person. [1700–10; 1910–15 for def. 2; JELLY + FISH]

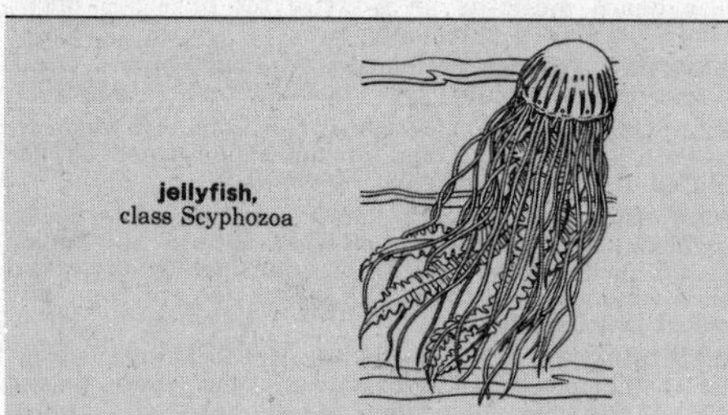

jellyfish, class Scyphozoa

jel′ly fun′gus, any of various fungi of the order Tremellales, distinguished by gelatinous basidiocarp.

jel′ly roll′, **1.** a thin, rectangular layer of sponge cake, spread with fruit jelly and rolled up. **2.** *Slang* (*vulgar*). **a.** the vagina. **b.** sexual intercourse. [1890–95, *Amer.*]

jel•u•tong (jel′ə tông′, -tong′), *n.* **1.** a tree, *Dyera costulata,* of the Malay Peninsula, from which a resinous latex is obtained. **2.** Also called **pontianak.** the latex of these trees, used as a substitute for chicle. **3.** Also called **devil tree.** a tropical Old World tree, *Alstonia scholaris,* of the dogbane family, of which the bark is used in medicine. [1830–40; < Malay]

jem•a•dar (jem′ə där′), *n.* (in India) **1.** any of various government officials. **2.** the supervisor of a staff of servants. **3.** an officer in a sepoy regiment, corresponding in rank to a lieutenant. [1755–65; < Urdu *jamadar,* var. of *jamdar* < Pers < Ar *jam'* aggregation + Pers *dār* holding, leader of]

Je•mappes (*Fr.* zhə MAP′), *n.* a town in SW Belgium, near Mons: French victory over Austrians 1792. 12,455.

Je•mi•ma (jə mī′mə), *n.* a female given name: from a Hebrew word meaning "dove."

jem•my (jem′ē), *v.,* **-mied, -my•ing,** *n., pl.* **-mies.** *Brit.* **—***v.t.* **1.** jimmy[1]. **—***n.* **2.** jimmy[1]. **3.** *Slang.* an overcoat. **4.** the baked head of a sheep. [1745–55]

jen (zhun, RUN), *n.* (in Chinese philosophy) a compassionate love for humanity or for the world as a whole. [< Chin (Wade-Giles) *jên²*, (pinyin) *rén*]

Je•na (yā′nä), *n.* a city in central Germany: Napoleon decisively defeated the Prussians here in 1806. 103,000.

je ne sais quoi (zhən° se KWA′), *French.* an indefinable, elusive quality, esp. a pleasing one: *She has a certain* je ne sais quoi *that charms everybody.* [lit., I don't know what]

Jen•ghis Khan (jeng′gis kän′, -giz, jen′-). See **Genghis Khan.** Also, **Jen′ghiz Khan′.**

Jen•kin•son (jeng′kin sən), *n.* **Robert Banks, 2nd Earl of Liverpool,** 1770–1828, British statesman: prime minister 1812–27.

Jen•ner (jen′ər), *n.* **1. Edward,** 1749–1823, English physician: discoverer of smallpox vaccine. **2. Sir William,** 1815–98, English physician and pathologist.

jen•net (jen′it), *n.* **1.** a female donkey. **2.** a small Spanish horse. Also, **genet.** [1425–75; late ME < MF *genet* < Catalan, var. of *ginet* horse of the Zenete kind < SpAr *zinētī,* dial. var. of *zanātī* pertaining to the Zenete tribe (of Berbers), after *Zanātah* the Zenetes]

Jen•ney (jen′ē), *n.* **William Le Bar•on** (lə bar′ən), 1832–1907, U.S. engineer and architect: pioneer in skyscraper construction.

Jen•nie (jen′ē), *n.* a female given name, form of **Jennifer.** Also, **Jen′ny.**

Jen•ni•fer (jen′ə fər), *n.* a female given name, form of **Guinevere.**

Jen•nings (jen′ingz), *n.* **1.** a city in E Missouri, near St. Louis. 17,026. **2.** a city in SW Louisiana. 12,401.

jen•ny[1] (jen′ē), *n., pl.* **-nies.** **1.** See **spinning jenny.** **2.** the female of certain animals, esp. a female donkey or a female bird: *a jenny wren.* [1590–1600; generic use of *Jenny,* proper name]

jen•ny[2] (jen′ē), *n., pl.* **-nies.** *Naut. Slang.* genoa. Also, **jen′nie.** [shortening and alter. of GENOA]

Jen•sen (yen′zən *for 1;* yen′sən *for 2*), *n.* **1. J. Hans D.** (häns), 1907–73, German physicist: Nobel prize 1963. **2. Jo•han•nes Vil•helm** (yō hä′nəs vil′helm), 1873–1950, Danish poet and novelist: Nobel prize 1944.

Jen•sen•ism (jen′sə niz′əm), *n.* the theory that an individual's IQ is largely due to heredity, including racial heritage. [1965–70; after Arthur R. *Jensen* (born 1923), U.S. educational psychologist, who proposed such a theory; see -ISM] **—Jen′sen•ist, Jen′sen•ite′,** *n., adj.*

jeon (chun), *n., pl.* **jeon.** chon (def. 2).

jeop•ard (jep′ərd), *v.t.* to jeopardize. [1325–75; ME *juparten,* back formation from *jupartie* JEOPARDY, repr. MF *jeu partir* to divide play, play, hence, take a chance]

jeop•ard•ize (jep′ər dīz′), *v.t.,* **-ized, -iz•ing.** to put in jeopardy; hazard; risk; imperil: *He jeopardized his life every time he dived from the tower.* Also, *esp. Brit.,* **jeop′ard•ise′.** [1640–50; JEOPARD(Y) + -IZE]

jeop•ard•ous (jep′ər dəs), *adj.* perilous; dangerous; hazardous; risky. [1425–75; late ME *j(e)upartous,* equiv. to *j(e)upart(i)* JEOPARDY + *-ous* -OUS]

jeop•ard•y (jep′ər dē), *n., pl.* **-dies.** **1.** hazard or risk of or exposure to loss, harm, death, or injury: *For a moment his life was in jeopardy.* **2.** peril or danger: *The spy was in constant jeopardy of being discovered.* **3.** *Law.* the danger or hazard of being found guilty, and of consequent punishment, undergone by criminal defendants on trial. [1200–50; ME *j(e)uparti, joupardi(e), j(e)upardi(e)* < AF, OF: lit., divided game or play, hence, uncertain chance, problem (in chess or love), equiv. to *j(e)u* play, game (< L *jocus* JOKE) + *parti,* ptp. of *partir* to divide; see PARTY]
—Syn. 1, 2. See **danger.** **—Ant. 1, 2.** security.

Jeph•thah (jef′thə), *n.* a judge of Israel. Judges 11, 12.

Je•quié (zhə kye′), *n.* a city in E Brazil. 84,430.

je•quir•i•ty (jə kwir′i tē), *n., pl.* **-ties.** **1.** the Indian licorice, *Abrus precatorius,* of the legume family. **2.** Also called **jequir′ity beans′.** the poisonous scarlet seeds of this plant, used for making necklaces and rosaries. [1880–85; < Pg *jequiriti* < Tupi-Guarani *jekiriti*]

jer (yer), *n.* **1.** *Slavic Ling.* either of two letters (Ъ, Ь) of the Cyrillic alphabet used, as in Old Church Slavonic, to indicate two short vowels, or, as in Russian, to indicate that the preceding consonant is hard or soft. Cf. **hard sign, soft sign.** **2.** either of the short, lax vowels of Old Church Slavonic represented by these signs, front jer (Ь, usually transcribed as ĭ) and back jer (Ъ, usually transcribed as ŭ). [1755–65]

Jer., **1.** *Bible.* Jeremiah. **2.** Jersey.

Je•rash (jer′äsh), *n.* a town in N Jordan, N of Amman: Roman ruins. 29,000. Also, **Jarash.**

Jer•ba (jer′bə), *n.* Djerba.

jer•bo•a (jər bō′ə, jer-), *n.* any of various mouselike rodents of North Africa and Asia, as of the genera *Jaculus* and *Dipus,* with long hind legs used for jumping. [1655–65; < NL < Ar *yarbū'*; see GERBIL]

jerboa, *Jaculus jaculus,* head and body 5 in. (13 cm); tail 8 in. (20 cm)

je•reed (jə rēd′), *n.* a blunt wooden javelin used in games played on horseback in certain Muslim countries in the Middle East. Also, **je•rid′, jerreed, jerrid.** [1655–65; < Ar *jarīd*]

jer•e•mi•ad (jer′ə mī′əd, -ad), *n.* a prolonged lamentation or mournful complaint. [1770–80; JEREMI(AH) + -AD, in reference to Jeremiah's *Lamentations*]

Jer•e•mi•ah (jer′ə mī′ə), *n.* **1.** a Major Prophet of the 6th and 7th centuries B.C. **2.** a book of the Bible bearing his name. *Abbr.:* Jer. **3.** a male given name: from a Hebrew word meaning "God is high." **—Jer′e•mi′an, Jer•e•mi•an•ic** (jer′ə mī an′ik), *adj.*

Jé•ré•mie (zhā RA mē′), *n.* a seaport in SW Haiti. 12,000.

Jer•e•my (jer′ə mē), *n.* a male given name, form of **Jeremiah.**

Je•rez (he RETH′, -RES′), *n.* **1.** Also called **Jerez′ de la Fron•te′ra** (the lä fRôn te′Rä). Formerly, **Xeres.** a city in SW Spain: noted for its sherry. 149,867. **—***adj.* **2.** pertaining to, characteristic of, or resembling sherry from Jerez.

Jer•i (jer′ē), *n.* a female given name, form of **Geraldine.**

Jer•i•cho (jer′i kō′), *n.* **1.** an ancient city of Palestine, N of the Dead Sea, formerly in W Jordan; occupied by Israel 1967–94; since 1994 under Palestinian self-rule. **2.** a town on W Long Island, in SE New York. 12,739.

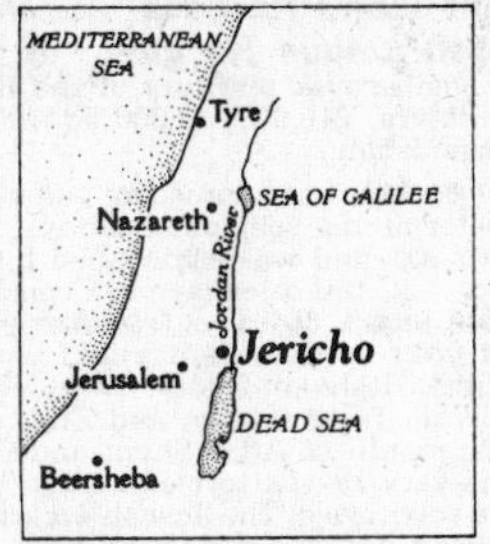

Je•ri•tza (ye′RE tsä′), *n.* **Ma•ri•a** (mä RE′ä), 1887–1982, Austrian operatic soprano.

jerk[1] (jûrk), *n.* **1.** a quick, sharp pull, thrust, twist, throw, or the like; a sudden movement: *The train started with a jerk.* **2.** a spasmodic, usually involuntary, muscular movement, as the reflex action of pulling the hand away from a flame. **3.** any sudden, quick movement of the body, as in dodging something. **4.** *Slang.* a contemptibly naive, fatuous, foolish, or inconsequential person. **5.** (in weightlifting) the raising of a weight from shoulder height to above the head by straightening the arms. **6. jerks,** *Brit. Informal.* See **physical jerks. 7.** a dance, deriving from the twist, in which the dancers alternately thrust out their pelvises and their shoulders. **8. the jerks,** paroxysms or violent spasmodic muscular movements, as resulting from excitement evoked by some religious services. —*v.t.* **9.** to pull, twist, move, thrust, or throw with a quick, suddenly arrested motion: *She jerked the child by the hand.* **10.** to utter in a broken, spasmodic way. **11.** *Informal.* to prepare, dispense, and serve (sodas, ice cream, etc.) at a soda fountain. —*v.i.* **12.** to give a jerk or jerks. **13.** to move with a quick, sharp motion; move spasmodically. **14.** to talk in a broken, spasmodic way. **15.** *Informal.* to work as a soda jerk. **16.** to dance the jerk. **17. jerk off,** *Slang (vulgar).* to masturbate. [1540–50; 1935–40 for def. 4; perh. dial. var. of *yerk* to draw stitches tight (shoemaker's term), thus making the shoe ready to wear, OE *gearcian* to prepare, make ready] —**jerk′er,** *n.*

jerk[2] (jûrk), *v.t.* **1.** to preserve (meat, esp. beef) by cutting in strips and curing by drying in the sun. —*n.* **2.** jerky[2]. [1700–10; back formation from JERKY[2]]

jer•kin (jûr′kin), *n.* a close-fitting jacket or short coat, usually sleeveless, as one of leather worn in the 16th and 17th centuries. [1510–20; orig. uncert.]

jer•kin•head (jûr′kin hed′), *n.* a roof having a hipped end truncating a gable. Also called **shreadhead.** [1835–45; orig. uncert.]

jerk-off (jûrk′ôf′, -of′), *n. Slang (offensive).* a stupid, bumbling, foolish, or lazy person; jerk. [1965–70; *n.* use of v. phrase *jerk off*]

jerk•wa•ter (jûrk′wô′tər, -wot′ər), *adj.* **1.** *Informal.* insignificant and out-of-the-way: *a jerkwater town.* **2.** (formerly) off the main line: *a jerkwater train.* —*n.* **3.** (formerly) a train not running on the main line. [1875–80, *Amer.*; JERK[1] + WATER; so called from the jerking (i.e., drawing) of water to fill buckets for supplying a steam locomotive]

jerk•y[1] (jûr′kē), *adj.,* **jerk•i•er, jerk•i•est. 1.** characterized by jerks or sudden starts; spasmodic. **2.** *Slang.* silly; foolish; stupid; ridiculous. [1855–60; JERK[1] + -Y[1]] —**jerk′i•ly,** *adv.* —**jerk′i•ness,** *n.*

jer•ky[2] (jûr′kē), *n.* meat, esp. beef, that has been cut in strips and preserved by drying in the sun; jerked meat. Also, **jerk.** [1840–50, *Amer.*; alter. of CHARQUI]

Jer•o•bo•am (jer′ə bō′əm), *n.* **1.** the first king of the Biblical kingdom of the Hebrews in N Palestine. **2.** (*l.c.*) a large wine bottle having a capacity of about four ordinary bottles or 3 liters (3.3 qt.).

Jer•old (jer′əld), *n.* a male given name, form of **Gerald.** Also, **Jer′rold.**

Je•rome (jə rōm′; *for 2, 3 also Brit.* jer′əm), *n.* **1. Saint** (*Eusebius Hieronymus*), A.D. c340–420, Christian ascetic and Biblical scholar: chief preparer of the Vulgate version of the Bible. **2. Jerome K(lap•ka)** (klap′kə), 1859–1927, English humorist and playwright. **3.** a male given name: from a Greek word meaning "sacred name."

jer•reed (jə rēd′), *n.* jereed. Also, **jer•rid′.**

jer•ry[1] (jer′ē), *adj. Building Trades Slang.* of inferior materials or workmanship. [1875–80; short for JERRY-BUILT]

jer•ry[2] (jer′ē), *n., pl.* **-ries.** *Chiefly Brit. Slang.* a chamber pot. [1820–30; short for JEROBOAM]

Jer•ry (jer′ē), *n., pl.* **-ries.** *Chiefly Brit. Informal.* **1.** a German. **2.** Germans collectively. [1910–15; GER(MAN) + -Y[1]]

Jer•ry (jer′ē), *n.* **1.** a male given name, form of **Gerald, Gerard, Jeremiah,** and **Jerome. 2.** a female given name, form of **Geraldine.**

jer•ry-build (jer′ē bild′), *v.t.,* **-built, -build•ing.** to build cheaply and flimsily. [1880–85; back formation from *jerry-builder.* See JERRY[2], BUILD] —**jer′ry-build′•er,** *n.*

jer•ry-built (jer′ē bilt′), *adj.* **1.** built cheaply and flimsily. **2.** contrived or developed in a haphazard, unsubstantial fashion, as a project or organization. [1865–70; *jerry* (as in JERRY-BUILD) + BUILT]
—**Syn. 1.** ramshackle, rickety, shoddy, slipshod.

jer′ry can′, 1. Also called **blitz can.** *Mil.* a narrow, flat-sided, five-gallon (19-liter) container for fluids, as fuel. **2.** *Brit.* a can with a capacity of 4½ imperial gallons (5.4 U.S. gallons or 20.4 liters). Also, **jer′ry•can′, jer′ri•can′.** [1940–45; appar. JERRY "German"; the British supposedly manufactured the can after a German prototype]

jer•sey (jûr′zē), *n., pl.* **-seys. 1.** a close-fitting, knitted sweater or shirt. **2.** a plain-knit, machine-made fabric of wool, silk, nylon, rayon, etc., characteristically soft and elastic, used for garments. **3.** (*cap.*) one of a breed of dairy cattle, raised originally on the island of Jersey, producing milk with a high butterfat content. [1575–85; after JERSEY] —**jer′seyed,** *adj.*

Jer•sey (jûr′zē), *n.* **1.** a British island in the English Channel: the largest of the Channel Islands. 79,342; 44 sq. mi. (116 sq. km). *Cap.:* St. Helier. **2.** *Informal.* New Jersey. —**Jer′sey•an,** *n., adj.* —**Jer′sey•ite′,** *n.*

Jer′sey Cit′y, a seaport in NE New Jersey, opposite New York City. 223,532.

Jer′sey Gi′ant, one of a breed of large domestic chickens raised primarily for their meat, originally black but now with a white variety, developed in New Jersey by interbreeding Langshans and large Asiatic fowl.

Jer•sey•man (jûr′zē mən), *n.* **1.** a native or inhabitant of the island of Jersey. **2.** a native or inhabitant of New Jersey. [1815–25; (NEW) JERSEY + -MAN]

Jer′sey pine′. See **Virginia pine.** [1735–45, *Amer.*]

Jer•ub•baal (jer′ə bāl′, jer′ə bā′əl, -bāl′), *n.* Gideon (def. 1).

Je•ru•sa•lem (ji rōō′sə ləm, -zə-), *n.* a city in and the capital of Israel: an ancient holy city and a center of pilgrimage for Jews, Christians, and Muslims; divided between Israel and Jordan 1948–67; Jordanian sector annexed by Israel 1967; capital of Israel since 1950. 407,100. —**Je•ru′sa•lem•ite′,** *adj., n.*

Jeru′salem ar′tichoke, 1. Also called **girasol.** a sunflower, *Helianthus tuberosus,* having edible, tuberous, underground stems or rootstocks. **2.** Also called **sunchoke.** the tuber itself. [1635–45; alter. of It *girasole articiocco* edible sunflower. See GIRASOL, ARTICHOKE]

Jeru′salem cher′ry, an Old World plant, *Solanum pseudocapsicum,* of the nightshade family, having white flowers and bearing cherrylike scarlet or yellow fruits, cultivated as an ornamental. [1780–90, *Amer.*]

Jeru′salem crick′et, a large, nocturnal, wingless, long-horned grasshopper, *Stenopelmatus fuscus,* occurring chiefly in loose soil and sand along the Pacific coast of the U.S. Also called **sand cricket.** [1945–50, *Amer.*]

Jeru′salem cross′, 1. a cross whose four arms are each capped with a crossbar and often with a small Greek cross centered in each quadrant. **2.** See **scarlet lychnis.** [1605–15]

Jeru′salem date′. See **butterfly flower.**

Jeru′salem oak′. See **feather geranium.** [1750–60]

Jeru′salem thorn′, 1. See under **Christ's-thorn. 2.** a spiny tropical American tree, *Parkinsonia aculeata,* of the legume family, having long clusters of large yellow flowers. [1865–70]

Jes•per•sen (yes′pər sən, jes′-), *n.* **(Jens) Ot•to (Har•ry)** (yens ot′ō här′ē), 1860–1943, Danish philologist.

jess (jes), *Falconry.* —*n.* **1.** a short strap fastened around the leg of a hawk and attached to the leash. —*v.t.* **2.** to put jesses on (a hawk). [1300–50; ME *ges* < OF *ges, gez, getz* (nom.) (*get* obl. > F *jet*; cf. JET[1]) << L *jactus* a throwing, equiv. to *jac(ere)* to throw + *-tus* suffix of v. action]

Jess (jes), *n.* a male or female given name, form of **Jesse, Jessie,** or **Jessica.**

jes•sa•mine (jes′ə min), *n.* jasmine.

Jes•sa•myn (jes′ə min), *n.* a female given name, form of **Jasmine.** Also, **Jes′sa•mine.**

jes•sant (jes′ənt), *adj. Heraldry.* **1.** shooting up, as a plant. **2.** coming forth; issuant. [1600–10; perh. alter. of obs. *issant* ISSUANT, by assoc. with obs. *jessant* (of a charge) lying on top of another charge < MF *gesant* (prp. of *gesir* << L *jacēre* to lie), equiv. to *ges-* lie + *-ant* -ANT]

Jes•se (jes′ē), *n.* **1.** the father of David. I Sam. 16. **2.** a male given name: from a Hebrew word meaning "God exists."

Jes•sel•ton (jes′əl tən), *n.* former name of **Kota Kinabalu.**

Jes′se tree′. See **tree of Jesse.**

Jes′se win′dow, a church window having a representation of the tree of Jesse. [1840–50]

Jes•si•ca (jes′i kə), *n.* a female given name, form of **Jesse.**

Jes•sie (jes′ē), *n.* a female given name, form of **Jessica.**

jest (jest), *n.* **1.** a joke or witty remark; witticism. **2.** a bantering remark; a piece of good-natured ridicule; taunt. **3.** sport or fun: *to speak half in jest, half in earnest.* **4.** the object of laughter, sport, or mockery; laughing-stock. **5.** *Obs.* an exploit. Cf. **gest.** —*v.i.* **6.** to speak in a playful, humorous, or facetious way; joke. **7.** to speak or act in mere sport, rather than in earnest; trifle (often fol. by *with*): *Please don't jest with me.* **8.** to utter derisive speeches; gibe or scoff. —*v.t.* **9.** to deride or joke at; banter. [1250–1300; ME; var. sp. of GEST] —**jest′ful,** *adj.* —**jest′ing•ly,** *adv.*
—**Syn. 1.** quip. See **joke. 2.** jape, gibe. **4.** butt.

jest•book (jest′bŏŏk′), *n.* a book of jests or jokes. [1740–50]

jest•er (jes′tər), *n.* **1.** a person who is given to witticisms, jokes, and pranks. **2.** a professional fool or clown, esp. at a medieval court. [1325–75; ME *gester.* See GEST, -ER[1]]

Je•su (jē′zōō, -sōō, jā′-, yā′-), *n. Literary.* Jesus. [1150–1200; ME < LL *Iēsu,* obl. (orig. voc.) form of *Iēsus* < Gk *Iēsoû;* see JESUS]

Jes•u•it (jezh′ōō it, jez′ōō-, jez′yōō-), *n.* **1.** a member of a Roman Catholic religious order **(Society of Jesus)** founded by Ignatius of Loyola in 1534. **2.** (*often l.c.*) a crafty, intriguing, or equivocating person: so called in allusion to the methods ascribed to the order by its opponents. —*adj.* **3.** of or pertaining to Jesuits or Jesuitism. [1550–60; < NL *Jēsuita,* equiv. to L *Jēsu(s)* + *-ita* -ITE[1]]

Jes•u•it•i•cal (jezh′ōō it′i kəl, jez′ōō-, jez′yōō-), *adj.* **1.** of or pertaining to Jesuits or Jesuitism. **2.** (*often l.c.*) practicing casuistry or equivocation; using subtle or oversubtle reasoning; crafty; sly; intriguing. Also, **Jes′u•it′ic.** [1590–1600; JESUIT + -ICAL] —**Jes′u•it′i•cal•ly,** *adv.*

Jes•u•it•ism (jezh′ōō i tiz′əm, jez′ōō-, jez′yōō-), *n.* **1.** the system, principles, or practices of the Jesuits. **2.** (*often l.c.*) a principle or practice, as casuistry, equivocation, or craft, ascribed to the Jesuits by their opponents. Also, **Jes′u•it•ry.** [1600–10; JESUIT + -ISM]

Jes•u•it•ize (jezh′ōō i tiz′, jez′ōō-, jez′yōō-), *v.t., v.i.,* **-ized, -iz•ing.** to make Jesuit or to become a Jesuit. Also, *esp. Brit.,* **Jes′u•it•ise′.** [1635–45; JESUIT + -IZE] —**Jes′u•it•i•za′tion,** *n.*

Jes′uit's bark′, cinchona (def. 2). [1685–95; introduced into Europe from the Jesuit missions in South America]

Jes′uits' res′in, copaiba.

Jes′uit ware′, Chinese porcelain of the early 18th century, decorated with Christian motifs, usually in black and gold on a white background.

Je•sus (jē′zəs, -zəz), *n.* **1.** Also called **Jesus Christ, Christ Jesus, Je′sus of Naz′areth.** born 4? B.C., crucified A.D. 29?, the source of the Christian religion. **2.** (*"the Son of Sirach"*) the author of the Apocryphal book of Ecclesiasticus, who lived in the 3rd century B.C. **3.** *Christian Science.* the supreme example of God's nature expressed through human beings. **4.** Also, **Je•sús** (*Sp.* he sōōs′). a male given name. —*interj.* **5.** (used as an oath or strong expression of disbelief, dismay, awe, disappointment, pain, etc.) [1200–50; ME < LL *Iēsus* < Gk *Iēsoûs* < Heb *Yēshūaʿ,* syncopated var. of *Yəhōshūaʿ* God is help; in Early Modern E, the distinction (lost in ME) between *Jesus* (nom.) and *Jesu* (obl., especially voc.; see JESU) was revived on the model of L and Gk sources; *Jesus* gradually supplanted the older form in both nom. and obl.]

Je′sus Christ′, 1. Jesus (def. 1). **2.** Jesus (def. 5).

Je′sus freak′, *Informal.* a member of any of several fundamentalist groups of chiefly young people **(Je′sus peo′ple)** originating in the early 1970's and emphasizing intense personal devotion to and study of Jesus Christ and his teachings. [1970–75]

jet[1] (jet), *n., v.,* **jet•ted, jet•ting,** *adj.* —*n.* **1.** a stream of a liquid, gas, or small solid particles forcefully shooting forth from a nozzle, orifice, etc. **2.** something that issues in such a stream, as water or gas. **3.** a spout or nozzle for emitting liquid or gas: *a gas jet.* **4.** See **jet plane. 5.** See **jet engine.** —*v.i.* **6.** to travel by jet plane: *to jet to Las Vegas for the weekend.* **7.** to move or travel by means of jet propulsion: *The octopus jetted away from danger.* **8.** to be shot forth in a stream. **9.** to move or travel rapidly: *The star halfback jetted toward*

CONCISE PRONUNCIATION KEY: act, cāpe, dâre, pärt; set, ēqual; *if,* ice; ox, ōver, ôrder, oil, bŏŏk, bōōt, out; up, ûrge; child; sing; shoe; thin, *th*at; zh as in *treasure.* ə = *a* as in *alone, e* as in *system, i* as in *easily, o* as in *gallop, u* as in *circus;* ə as in *fire* (fīər), *hour* (ouər). l and n can serve as syllabic consonants, as in *cradle* (krād′l), and *button* (but′n). See the full key inside the front cover.

the goal line. —*v.t.* **10.** to transport by jet plane: *The nonstop service from New York will jet you to Tokyo in 13 hours.* **11.** to shoot (something) forth in a stream; spout. **12.** to place (a pile or the like) by eroding the ground beneath it with a jet of water or of water and compressed air. —*adj.* **13.** of, pertaining to, or associated with a jet, jet engine, or jet plane: *jet pilot; jet exhaust.* **14.** in the form of or producing a jet or jet propulsion: *jet nozzle.* **15.** by means of a jet airplane: *a jet trip; jet transportation.* [1580–90; 1940–45 for def. 4; < MF *jeter* to throw < VL **jectāre,* alter. of L *jactāre,* equiv. to *jac-* throw + *-t-* freq. suffix + *-āre* inf. suffix]

jet[2] (jet), *n.* **1.** a compact black coal, susceptible of a high polish, used for making beads, jewelry, buttons, etc. **2.** a deep black. **3.** *Obs.* black marble. —*adj.* **4.** consisting or made of jet. **5.** of the color jet; black as jet. [1350–1400; ME *jet, get* < OF *jaiet* << L *gagātēs* < Gk (*líthos*) *gagátēs* Gagatic (stone), named after *Gágai,* town in Lycia; cf. obs. *gagate,* ME, OE *gagātes* < L, as above]

jet′ air′plane. See **jet plane.** [1940–45]

jet·a·va·tor (jet′ə vā′tər), *n. Rocketry.* an extension of the exhaust nozzle of a rocket, for controlling the direction of the exhaust gases. [1955–60; JET[1] + (EL)EVATOR]

jet·bead (jet′bēd′), *n.* a shrub, *Rhodotypos scandens,* of the rose family, having white flowers and glossy black fruit, cultivated as an ornamental. Also called **white kerria.** [1925–30; JET[2] + BEAD]

jet-black (jet′blak′), *adj.* deep-black: *jet-black hair.* [1475–85]

jet′ boat′, a small, propellerless boat powered by an engine that ejects water for its thrust. Also, **jet′boat′.** [1960–65] —**jet′ boat′ing.**

jet·borne (jet′bôrn′, -bōrn′), *adj.* **1.** carried by jet aircraft. **2.** carried by the westerly jet stream. [1965–70; JET[1] + (AIR)BORNE]

jet′ condens′er, a steam condenser in which a jet of water is sprayed into the condenser chamber.

je·té (zhə tā′), *n., pl.* **-tés** (-tāz′; *Fr.* -tā′). *Ballet.* a jump forward, backward, or to the side, from one foot to the other. [1820–30; < F: lit., thrown, ptp. of *jeter* to throw; see JET[1]]

jet′-e·nam·elled ware′ (jet′i nam′əld), English Worcester porcelain ware of the 18th century, transfer-printed in black.

jet′ en′gine, an engine, as an aircraft engine, that produces forward motion by the rearward exhaust of a jet of fluid or heated air and gases. Also called **jet, jet′ mo′tor.** [1940–45]

jet′ gun′, a small, pressurized device that injects a drug at sufficient velocity to penetrate the skin, used esp. for immunizations. Also called **jet′ injec′tor.**

jet-hop (jet′hop′), *v.i.,* **-hopped, -hop·ping.** to travel by jet plane, esp. to travel to a series of destinations on one trip. [1965–70]

Jeth·ro (jeth′rō), *n.* **1.** the father-in-law of Moses. Ex. 3:1. **2.** a male given name.

jet′ lag′, a temporary disruption of the body's normal biological rhythms after high-speed air travel through several time zones. Also, **jet′lag′.** [1965–70] —**jet′-lagged′,** *adj.*

jet·lin·er (jet′lī′nər), *n.* a commercial jet plane for carrying passengers. [1945–50; JET[1] + (AIR)LINER]

jet′ plane′, an airplane moved by jet propulsion. Also called **jet, jet airplane.** [1940–45]

jet·port (jet′pôrt′, -pōrt′), *n.* an airport designed to handle commercial jet planes. [1960–65; JET[1] + PORT[1]]

jet′ print′ing. See **ink-jet printing.**

jet-pro·pelled (jet′prə peld′), *adj.* **1.** propelled by a jet engine or engines. **2.** *Informal.* having a force or speed suggesting something propelled by a jet engine; fast or powerful. [1875–80]

jet′ propul′sion, the propulsion of a body by its reaction to a force ejecting a gas or a liquid from it.

jet·sam (jet′səm), *n.* goods cast overboard deliberately, as to lighten a vessel or improve its stability in an emergency, which sink where jettisoned or are washed ashore. Also, **jet′som.** Cf. **flotsam, lagan.** [1560–70; alter. of *jetson,* syncopated var. of JETTISON]

jet′ set′, a fashionable social set composed of wealthy people who travel frequently by jetliner to parties and resorts. [1950–55] —**jet′-set′ter,** *n.*

jet′ stream′, **1.** strong, generally westerly winds concentrated in a relatively narrow and shallow stream in the upper troposphere of the earth. **2.** similar strong winds in the atmosphere of another planet: *jet streams on Jupiter.* **3.** the exhaust of a jet or rocket engine. [1945–50]

jet·ti·son (jet′ə sən, -zən), *v.t.* **1.** to cast (goods) overboard in order to lighten a vessel or aircraft or to improve its stability in an emergency. **2.** to throw off (something) as an obstacle or burden; discard. **3.** *Cards.* to discard (an unwanted card or cards). —*n.* **4.** the act of casting goods from a vessel or aircraft to lighten or stabilize it. **5.** jetsam. [1375–1425; late ME *jetteson* < AF; OF *getaison* << L *jactātiōn-* (s. of *jactātiō*) JACTATION] —**jet′ti·son·a·ble,** *adj.*

jet·ton (jet′n), *n.* an inscribed counter or token. [1755–65; < F *jeton,* equiv. to *jet(er)* to throw, cast up (accounts), reckon (see JET[1]) + *-on* n. suffix]

jet·ty[1] (jet′ē), *n., pl.* **-ties,** *v.,* **-tied, -ty·ing.** —*n.* **1.** a pier or structure of stones, piles, or the like, projecting into the sea or other body of water to protect a harbor, deflect the current, etc. **2.** a wharf or landing pier. **3.** the piles or wooden structure protecting a pier. **4.** Also, **jutty.** an overhang, as of an upper story beyond a lower. —*v.t.* **5.** to construct (part of a building) so that it projects beyond lower construction; jutty. [1375–1425; late ME *get(t)ey* < OF *jetee,* lit., something thrown out, a projection, n. use of *jetee,* fem. ptp. of *jeter* to throw; see JET[1]]

jet·ty[2] (jet′ē), *adj.* **1.** made of jet. **2.** resembling jet, esp. in color; of a deep black. [1475–85; JET[2] + -Y[1]] —**jet′ti·ness,** *n.*

jet′ wash′, *Aeron.* the backwash caused by a jet engine.

Jet·way (jet′wā′), *Trademark.* an enclosed, telescoping, movable ramplike bridge connecting an airport terminal and an aircraft, for use by passengers in boarding and disembarking.

jeu (zhœ), *n., pl.* ***jeux*** (zhœ). *French.* a game.

jeu de mots (zhœdᵊ mō′), *pl.* ***jeux de mots*** (zhœdᵊ mō′). *French.* a pun. [lit., play of words]

jeu d'es·prit (zhœ des prē′), *pl.* ***jeux d'es·prit*** (zhœ des prē′). *French.* **1.** a witticism. **2.** a literary work showing keen wit or intelligence rather than profundity. [lit., play of spirit]

jeune fille (zhœn fē′yᵊ), *pl.* ***jeunes filles*** (zhœn fē′yᵊ). *French.* a girl or young woman.

jeune pre·mier (*Fr.* zhœn prə myā′), *pl.* **jeunes pre·miers** (*Fr.* zhœn prə myā′). **1.** the male juvenile lead in a play or movie. **2.** a young actor who plays such a role. [1850–55; < F: lit., young first (actor)]

jeune pre·mière (*Fr.* zhœn prə myer′), *pl.* **jeunes pre·mières** (*Fr.* zhœn prə myer′). **1.** the female juvenile lead in a play or movie. **2.** a young actress who plays such a role. [1920–25; < F: lit., young first (actress)]

jeu·nesse do·rée (zhœ nes dô rā′), *French.* wealthy, stylish, sophisticated young people. [lit., gilded youth]

Jev·ons (jev′ənz), *n.* **William Stanley,** 1835–82, English economist and logician.

Jew (jōō), *n.* **1.** one of a scattered group of people that traces its descent from the Biblical Hebrews or from postexilic adherents of Judaism; Israelite. **2.** a person whose religion is Judaism. **3.** a subject of the ancient kingdom of Judah. —*adj.* **4.** *Offensive.* of Jews; Jewish. —*v.t.* **5.** (*l.c.*) *Offensive.* to bargain sharply with; beat down in price (often fol. by *down*). [1125–75; ME *jewe, giu, gyu, ju* < OF *juiu, juieu, gyu* < LL *jūdēus,* L *jūdaeus* < Gk *ioudaîos* < Aram *yehūdāi* < Heb *Yəhūdhī,* deriv. of *Yəhūdhāh* JUDAH; r. OE *iūdēas* Jews < LL *jūdē(us)* + OE *-as* pl. ending]

Jew., Jewish.

Jew-bait·ing (jōō′bā′ting), *n.* active anti-Semitism. [1890–95] —**Jew′-bait′er,** *n.*

jew·el (jōō′əl), *n., v.,* **-eled, -el·ing** or (*esp. Brit.*) **-elled, -el·ling.** —*n.* **1.** a cut and polished precious stone; gem. **2.** a fashioned ornament for personal adornment, esp. of a precious metal set with gems. **3.** a precious possession. **4.** a person or thing that is treasured, esteemed, or indispensable. **5.** a durable bearing used in fine timepieces and other delicate instruments, made of natural or synthetic precious stone or other very hard material. **6.** an ornamental boss of glass, sometimes cut with facets, in stained-glass work. **7.** something resembling a jewel in appearance, ornamental effect, or the like, as a star. —*v.t.* **8.** to set or adorn with jewels. [1250–1300; ME *jouel juel* < AF *jeul,* OF *jouel, joel* < VL **jocāle* plaything, n. use of neut. of **jocālis* (adj.) of play, equiv. to L *joc(us)* JOKE + *-ālis* -AL[1]] —**jew′el·like′,** *adj.*

Jew·el (jōō′əl), *n.* a female given name.

jew′el block′, *Naut.* a block at the end of a yard or gaff for supporting a signal or ensign halyard. Also called **dasher block.** [1760–70]

jew′el box′, **1.** See **jewel case.** **2.** a hinged plastic case for the storage of a compact disc. [1825–35]

jew′el case′, a small box or chest, often lined in a soft fabric and fitted with compartments, designed to hold jewelry. [1855–60]

jew·el·er (jōō′ə lər), *n.* a person who designs, makes, sells, or repairs jewelry, watches, etc.; a person who deals in jewels. Also, *esp. Brit.,* **jew′el·ler.** [1300–50; ME *jueler* < AF *jueler,* MF *juelier.* See JEWEL, -ER[2]]

jew′elers' put′ty. See **putty powder.**

jew′elers' rouge′, colcothar.

jew′eler's saw′ frame′, a U-shaped steel frame with a handle and clamps that hold a piercing saw.

jew·el·fish (jōō′əl fish′), *n., pl.* **-fish·es,** (*esp. collectively*) **-fish.** a brightly colored cichlid fish, *Hemichromis bimaculatus,* native to Africa: popular in home aquariums. [JEWEL + FISH]

jew·el·ry (jōō′əl rē), *n.* **1.** articles of gold, silver, precious stones, etc., for personal adornment. **2.** any ornaments for personal adornment, as necklaces or cuff links, including those of base metals, glass, plastic, or the like. Also, *esp. Brit.,* **jew′el·ler·y.** [1300–50; ME *juelrie* < AF *juelerie,* equiv. to *juel* JEWEL + *-erie* -ERY]

jew·el·weed (jōō′əl wēd′), *n.* any of several plants of the genus *Impatiens,* esp. *I. capensis,* having orange-yellow flowers spotted with reddish brown, or *I. pallida,* having yellow flowers sometimes spotted with brownish red. Cf. **touch-me-not.** [1810–20, *Amer.*; JEWEL + WEED[1]]

Jew·ess (jōō′is), *n. Usually Offensive.* a Jewish girl or woman. [1350–1400; ME *jewesse.* See JEW, -ESS] —**Usage.** See **-ess.**

Jew·ett (jōō′it), *n.* **Sarah Orne** (ôrn), 1849–1909, U.S. short-story writer and novelist.

jew·fish (jōō′fish′), *n., pl.* (*esp. collectively*) **-fish,** (*esp. referring to two or more kinds or species*) **-fish·es.** any of several very large fishes, esp. of the family Serranidae, as the giant sea bass and the groupers *Epinephelus itajara* and *E. nigritus,* found in the tropical Atlantic Ocean. [1690–1700; appar. JEW + FISH]

Jew·ish (jōō′ish), *adj.* **1.** of, pertaining to, or characteristic of the Jews or Judaism: *Jewish customs.* **2.** *Informal.* Yiddish. —*n.* **3.** *Informal.* Yiddish. [1540–50; JEW + -ISH[1]; cf. OE *iudēisc* < LL *iudē(us)* Jew + OE *-isc* -ISH[1]] —**Jew′ish·ly,** *adv.*

Jew′ish Amer′ican Prin′cess. See **JAP.**

Jew′ish Auton′omous Re′gion, an autonomous region in the Khabarovsk territory of the Russian Federation in E Siberia. 216,000; 13,900 sq. mi. (36,000 sq. km). *Cap.:* Birobidzhan.

Jew′ish cal′endar, the lunisolar calendar used by Jews, as for determining religious holidays, that is reckoned from 3761 B.C. and was established by Hillel II in the 4th century A.D., the calendar year consisting of 353 days **(defective year),** 354 days **(regular year),** or 355 days **(perfect year** or **abundant year)** and containing 12 months: Tishri, Heshvan, Kislev, Tevet, Shevat, Adar, Nisan, Iyar, Sivan, Tammuz, Av, and Elul, with the 29-day intercalary month of Adar Sheni added after Adar seven times in every 19-year cycle in order to adjust the calendar to the solar cycle. The Jewish ecclesiastical year begins with Nisan and the civil year with Tishri. Also called **Hebrew calendar.** See table under **calendar.**

Jew′ish Defense′ League′, an organization of militant Jewish activists, founded in 1968 in the U.S. to combat anti-Semitism and defend Jewish interests worldwide. Abbr.: JDL

Jew·ish·ness (jōō′ish nis), *n.* the state or quality of being Jewish. [1540–50; JEWISH + -NESS]

Jew′ish Prin′cess. See **JAP.** [1970–75, *Amer.*]

Jew·ry (jōō′rē), *n., pl.* **-ries.** **1.** the Jewish people collectively. **2.** a district inhabited mainly by Jews; ghetto. **3.** *Archaic.* Judea. [1175–1225; ME *jewerie* < AF *juerie* (OF *juierie*), equiv. to *ju* JEW + *-erie* -ERY]

Jew's′ harp′, (*sometimes l.c.*) a small, simple musical instrument consisting of a lyre-shaped metal frame containing a metal tongue, which is plucked while the frame is held in the teeth, the vibrations causing twanging tones. Also, **Jews′ harp′.** [1585–95; perh. jocular; earlier called *Jew's trump*]

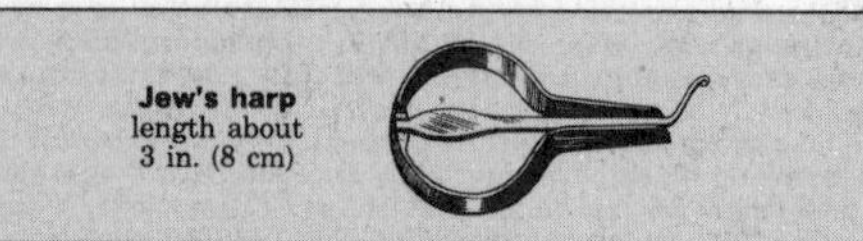
Jew's harp
length about
3 in. (8 cm)

Jez·e·bel (jez′ə bel′, -bəl), *n.* **1.** Also, *Douay Bible,* **Jez′a·bel′.** the wife of Ahab, king of Israel. I Kings 16:31. **2.** (*often l.c.*) a wicked, shameless woman. —**Jez·e·be·li·an** (jez′ə bē′lē ən, -bēl′yən), **Jez·e·bel·ish** (jez′ə bel′ish), *adj.*

Jez·re·el (jez′rē əl, -el′, jez rēl′), *n.* **Plain of,** Esdraelon. —**Jez′re·el·ite′,** *n.*

JFK, John Fitzgerald Kennedy.

jg, junior grade. Also, **j.g.**

jhā·na (jä′nə), *n. Buddhism.* any of four elevated states of mind possible as a result of meditation. [< Pali]

Jhan·si (jän′sē), *n.* a city in SW Uttar Pradesh, in central India. 198,101.

Jhe·lum (jā′ləm), *n.* a river in S Asia, flowing from S Kashmir into the Chenab River in Pakistan. 450 mi. (725 km) long.

JHS, IHS (defs. 1, 2).

J.H.S., junior high school.

JHVH, YHVH. Also, **JHWH**

Jia·mu·si (jyä′mʏ′sē′), *n. Pinyin.* a city in E Heilongjiang province, in NE China. 275,000. Also, **Chiamussu, Kiamusze.**

Jiang·ling (jyäng′ling′), *n. Pinyin.* a city in S Hubei province, in central China, on the Chang Jiang. 15,000. Also, **Chiangling, Kiangling.** Formerly, **Kingchow.**

Jiang Qing (*Chin.* jyäng′ ching′), 1914–91, wife of Mao Zedong: leader of the Gang of Four, arrested 1976, convicted and jailed 1981.

Jiang·su (jyäng′sʏ′), *n. Pinyin.* a maritime province in E China. 44,500,000; 40,927 sq. mi. (106,001 sq. km). *Cap.:* Nanjing. Also, **Kiangsu.**

Jiang·xi (jyäng′shē′), *n. Pinyin.* a province in SE China. 21,070,000; 63,629 sq. mi. (164,799 sq. km). *Cap.:* Nanchang. Also, **Kiangsi.**

jiao (jyou), *n., pl.* **jiao.** a copper-zinc coin and monetary unit of the People's Republic of China, the 10th part of a yuan, equal to 10 fen. Also, **chiao.** [1970–75; < Chin *jiǎo*]

Jiao·zhou (jyou′jō′), *n. Pinyin.* a former German-leased territory (1898–1914) on the Shandong peninsula, in E China, around Jiaozhou Bay. 200 sq. mi. (518 sq. km). Chief city, Tsingtao. Also, **Chiaochou, Kiaochow.**

Jiao′zhou′ Bay′, an inlet of the Yellow Sea, in E China, in Shandong province. 20 mi. (32 km) long; 15 mi. (24 km) wide. Also, **Chiaochou Bay, Kiaochow Bay.**

Jia·yi (jyä′ē′), *n. Pinyin.* Chiai.

jib[1] (jib), *n. Naut.* **1.** any of various triangular sails set forward of a forestaysail or fore-topmast staysail. Cf. **flying jib, inner jib.** See diag. under **ship.** **2.** the inner one of two such sails, set inward from a flying jib. **3.** **cut of one's jib,** one's general appearance, mien, or manner: *I could tell by the cut of his jib that he wasn't the kind of person I'd want to deal with.* —*adj.* **4.** of or pertaining to a jib: *jib clew.* [1655–65; orig. uncert.]

jib[2] (jib), *v.i., v.t.,* **jibbed, jib·bing,** *n. Naut.* jibe[1]. Also, **jibb.**

jib[3] (jib), *v.,* **jibbed, jib·bing,** *n. Chiefly Brit.* —*v.i.* **1.**

CONCISE ETYMOLOGY KEY: <, descended or borrowed from; >, whence; b., blend of, blended; c., cognate with; cf., compare; deriv., derivative; equiv., equivalent; imit., imitative; obl., oblique; r., replacing; s., stem; sp., spelling, spelled; resp., respelling, respelled; trans., translation; ?, origin unknown; *, unattested; ‡, probably earlier than. See the full key inside the front cover.

to move restively sidewise or backward instead of forward, as an animal in harness; balk. **2.** to balk at doing something; defer action; procrastinate. —*n.* **3.** a horse or other animal that jibs. [1805–15; perh. special use of JIB[2]] —**jib′ber,** *n.*

jib[4] (jib), *n.* **1.** the projecting arm of a crane. **2.** the boom of a derrick. [1755–65; appar. short for GIBBET]

ji•ba•ro (hē′vä rô′; *Eng.* hē′bə rō′), *n., pl.* **-ros** (-rôs′; *Eng.* -rōz′). *Spanish.* a worker from the rural regions of Puerto Rico.

jib•ba (jib′ə), *n.* a long, collarless coat or smock worn by Muslims. Also, **djibbah, jib′bah.** [1840–50; < Ar *jibbah,* var. of *jubbah*]

jib′ boom′, *Naut.* a spar forming a continuation of a bowsprit. Also, **jib′boom′.** [1740–50]

jib′ crane′, a crane having an arm guyed at a fixed angle to the head of a rotating mast. [1875–80]

jibe[1] (jīb), *v.,* **jibed, jib•ing,** *n. Naut.* —*v.i.* **1.** to shift from one side to the other when running before the wind, as a fore-and-aft sail or its boom. **2.** to alter course so that a fore-and-aft sail shifts in this manner. —*v.t.* **3.** to cause to jibe. —*n.* **4.** the act of jibing. Also, **gibe, gybe, jib, jibb.** [1685–95; var. of *gybe* < D *gijben,* more commonly *gijpen*]

jibe[2] (jīb), *v.i., v.t.,* **jibed, jib•ing,** *n.* gibe[1].

jibe[3] (jīb), *v.i.,* **jibed, jib•ing.** to be in harmony or accord; agree: *The report does not quite jibe with the commissioner's observations.* [1805–15, *Amer.*; orig. uncert.] —**Syn.** conform, accord, fit.

Ji•bu•ti (ji bo͞o′tē), *n.* Djibouti.

ji•ca•ma (hē′kə mə, hik′ə-), *n.* the large, edible, tuberous root of a tropical American plant, *Pachyrhizus erosus,* of the legume family, eaten as a vegetable either raw or boiled. [1900–05; < MexSp < Nahuatl *xīcama, xīcamatl*]

Ji•ca•ril•la (hē′kə rē′ə), *n., pl.* **-ril•las,** (*esp. collectively*) **-ril•la** for 1. **1.** a member of a group of North American Indians who once inhabited primarily northern New Mexico and southeastern Colorado and are situated in northwestern New Mexico. **2.** the Athabaskan language of the Jicarilla.

Jid•da (jid′də), *n.* the seaport of Mecca, in W Saudi Arabia, on the Red Sea. 561,000. Also, **Jedda.**

jif•fy (jif′ē), *n., pl.* **-fies.** *Informal.* a very short time; moment: *to get dressed in a jiffy.* Also, **jiff** (jif). [1770–80; orig. uncert.] —**Syn.** instant, flash, second, trice.

jig[1] (jig), *n., v.,* **jigged, jig•ging.** —*n.* **1.** *Mach.* a plate, box, or open frame for holding work and for guiding a machine tool to the work, used esp. for locating and spacing drilled holes; fixture. **2.** *Angling.* any of several devices or lures, esp. a hook or gang of hooks weighted with metal and dressed with hair, feathers, etc., for jerking up and down in or drawing through the water to attract fish. **3.** *Mining.* an apparatus for washing coal or separating ore from gangue by shaking and washing. **4.** a cloth-dyeing machine in which the material, guided by rollers, is passed at full width through a dye solution in an open vat. —*v.t.* **5.** to treat, cut, produce, etc., with a jig. —*v.i.* **6.** to use a jig. **7.** to fish with a jig. [1855–60; prob. akin to JIG[2], in sense "jerk to and fro"; orig. and interrelationship of this group of words uncert.]

jig[2] (jig), *n., v.,* **jigged, jig•ging,** *adj.* —*n.* **1.** a rapid, lively, springy, irregular dance for one or more persons, usually in triple meter. **2.** a piece of music for or in the rhythm of such a dance. **3.** *Obs.* prank; trick. **4. the jig is up,** *Slang.* it is hopeless; no chance remains: *When the burglar heard the police siren, he knew the jig was up.* —*v.t.* **5.** to dance (a jig or any lively dance). **6.** to sing or play in the time or rhythm of a jig: *to jig a tune.* **7.** to move with a jerky or bobbing motion; jerk up and down or to and fro. —*v.i.* **8.** to dance or play a jig. **9.** to move with a quick, jerky motion; hop; bob. —*adj.* **10. in jig time,** *Informal.* with dispatch; rapidly: *We sorted the mail in jig time.* [1550–60; in earliest sense "kind of dance" perh. < MF *giguer* to frolic, gambol, prob. < an unattested WGmc verb (cf. GIG[1]); semantic development of other senses unclear] —**jig′like′, jig′gish,** *adj.*

jig[3] (jig), *n.* (formerly used in communications to represent the letter *J.*)

jig[4] (jig), *n. Slang* (*disparaging and offensive*). a black person. [1920–25, *Amer.*; of uncert. orig.; cf. JIGABOO]

jig•a•boo (jig′ə bo͞o′), *n., pl.* **-boos.** *Slang* (*disparaging and offensive*). a black person. [1905–10, *Amer.*; perh. b. *jijiboo* (with same sense, orig. uncert.) or JIG[4] and BUGABOO]

jig′ back′, an inclined cable tramway with two cars that are connected in such a way that as one goes up the other comes down. —**jig′-back′,** *adj.*

jig•ger[1] (jig′ər), *n.* **1.** a person or thing that jigs. **2.** *Naut.* **a.** the lowermost sail set on a jiggermast. **b.** jiggermast. **c.** a light tackle, as a gun tackle. **3.** any of various mechanical devices, many of which have a jerky or jolting motion. **4.** *Informal.* some contrivance, article, or part that one cannot or does not name more precisely: *What is that little jigger on the pistol?* **5.** *Ceram.* a machine for forming plates or the like in a plaster mold rotating beneath a template. **6.** *Mining.* a jig for separating ore. **7.** a jig for fishing. **8.** *Golf.* a club with an iron head intermediate between a mashie and a midiron, now rarely used. **9.** *Billiards, Pool.* a bridge. **10. a.** a 1½-oz. (45-ml) measure used in cocktail recipes. **b.** a small whiskey glass holding 1½ oz. (45 ml). [1665–75; JIG[1] + -ER[1]]

jig•ger[2] (jig′ər), *n.* **1.** Also called **jig′ger flea′.** chigoe. **2.** *Chiefly South Midland and Southern U.S.* chigger. [1750–60; var. of CHIGGER]

jig•ger[3] (jig′ər), *v.t.* **1.** to interfere with. **2.** to manipulate or alter, esp. in order to get something done illegally or unethically: *to jigger company records to conceal a loss.* [1865–70; JIG[2] (in verbal sense) + -ER[6]]

jig•gered (jig′ərd), *adj. Informal.* confounded; damned: *I'm jiggered if I know what that sign means.* [1830–40; perh. JIGGER[3] + -ED[2]]

jig•ger•mast (jig′ər mast′, -mäst′; *Naut.* jig′ər məst), *n. Naut.* **1.** a small mast set well aft in a boat or ship; mizzenmast. **2.** the fourth mast from forward in a ship having five or more masts. Also, **jig′ger mast′.** Also called **jigger.** [1825–35; JIGGER[1] + MAST[1]]

jig•gers (jig′ərz), *interj. Slang.* watch out: *Jiggers! the cops are coming!* [perh. *jigger,* as in JIGGERED + -S[3]]

jig•ger•y-pok•er•y (jig′ə rē pō′kə rē), *n. Chiefly Brit.* **1.** trickery, hocus-pocus; fraud; humbug. **2.** sly, underhanded action. **3.** manipulation: *After a little jiggery-pokery, the engine started.* [1890–95; alter. of *joukery-pawkery.* See JOUK, PAWKY, -ERY]

jig•gle (jig′əl), *v.,* **-gled, -gling,** *n.* —*v.t., v.i.* **1.** to move up and down or to and fro with short, quick jerks. —*n.* **2.** a jiggling movement. [1835–40; JIG[2] + -LE] —**jig′gler,** *n.*

jig•gly (jig′lē), *adj.,* **-gli•er, -gli•est.** **1.** tending to jiggle or marked by a jiggling movement. **2.** *Informal.* featuring women in clothing designed to be sexually suggestive by accentuating the breasts: *jiggly TV shows.* [JIGGLE + -Y[1]]

jig•saw (jig′sô′), *n., v.,* **-sawed, -sawed** or **-sawn, -saw•ing,** *adj.* —*n.* **1.** Also, **jig′ saw′.** an electric machine saw with a narrow blade mounted vertically in a frame, for cutting curves or other difficult lines or patterns. —*v.t.* **2.** to cut or form with a jigsaw. —*adj.* **3.** formed by or as if by a jigsaw: *jigsaw ornamentation.* [1870–75; JIG[2] + SAW[1]]

jig′saw puz′zle, **1.** Also called **picture puzzle.** a set of irregularly cut pieces of pasteboard, wood, or the like that form a picture or design when fitted together. **2.** any complex, confusing situation, condition, or item, as one composed of seemingly diverse or unrelated elements. [1905–10]

ji•had (ji häd′), *n.* **1.** a holy war undertaken as a sacred duty by Muslims. **2.** any vigorous, emotional crusade for an idea or principle. Also, **jehad.** [1865–70; < Ar *jihād* struggle, strife]

Ji•hla•va (yi′hlä vä), *n.* a city in W Moravia, in the S central Czech Republic: former silver-mining center. 51,144. German, **Iglau.**

Ji•lin (jē′lin′), *n. Pinyin.* **1.** a province in NE China, N of the Yalu River. 17,890,000; 72,201 sq. mi. (187,001 sq. km). *Cap.:* Changchun. **2.** a port city in this province, on the Songhua River: a former provincial capital. 720,000. Also, **Chilin, Kirin.**

jill (jil), *n.* (*sometimes cap.*) *Slang.* **1.** a girl or young woman. **2.** a sweetheart. [generic use of JILL]

Jill (jil), *n.* a female given name, form of **Juliana.**

jill•et (jil′it), *n. Scot.* a giddy or flirtatious girl or young woman. [1745–55; earlier *gillot,* equiv. to *Gill* JILL + *-ot* (< F *-otte* as in *Charlotte*)]

jil•lion (jil′yən), *Informal.* —*n.* **1.** an indefinitely vast number; zillion. —*adj.* **2.** of or noting such a quantity: *a jillion problems.* [1940–45; expressive formation based on *million, billion,* etc.] —**jil′lionth,** *n., adj.*

Ji•lo•lo (jī lō′lō), *n.* Halmahera.

Ji•long (jē′lông′), *n. Pinyin.* Chilung.

jilt (jilt), *v.t.* **1.** to reject or cast aside (a lover or sweetheart), esp. abruptly or unfeelingly. —*n.* **2.** a woman who jilts a lover. [1650–60; earlier *jilt* harlot, syncopated var. of JILLET] —**jilt′er,** *n.*

jīm (jēm), *n.* the fifth letter of the Arabic alphabet. [< Ar]

Jim (jim), *n.* a male given name, form of **James.**

Jim′ Crow′, **1.** a practice or policy of segregating or discriminating against blacks, as in public places, public vehicles, or employment. **2.** *Disparaging and Offensive.* a black person. Also, **jim′ crow′.** [1830–40, *Amer.*; so called from the name of a song sung by Thomas Rice (1808–60) in a minstrel show]

Jim-Crow (jim′krō′), *adj.* **1.** favoring or supporting Jim Crow. **2.** for blacks only: *a Jim-Crow school.* Also, **jim′-crow′.**

Jim′ Crow′ism (krō′iz əm), **1.** See **Jim Crow** (def. 1). **2.** any policy of racial segregation. **3.** advocacy of such a policy. Also, **jim′ crow′ism.** [1830–40, *Amer.*; JIM CROW + -ISM]

Jim′ Crow′ law′, *U.S. Hist.* any state law discriminating against black persons. Cf. **Black Code.** [1890–95, *Amer.*]

jim-dan•dy (jim′dan′dē), *adj., n., pl.* **-dies.** *Informal.* —*adj.* **1.** of superior quality; excellent: *a jim-dandy sports car.* —*n.* **2.** something of superior quality or that is an excellent example of its kind: *The new infirmary is a real jim-dandy.* [1875–80; special use of *Jim* proper name + DANDY[1]]

jim′ dash′ (jim), *Print., Journalism.* a dash, often three ems long, used within a headline, between the headline and the main body of printed matter, between items in a single column, or between related but different material within a story. [*jim,* prob. special use of *Jim* proper name]

Ji•mé•nez (hē me′neth), *n.* **Juan Ra•món** (hwän rä-môn′), 1881–1958, Spanish poet: Nobel prize 1956.

Ji•mé•nez de Cis•ne•ros (hē me′neth the thēs ne′-rôs), **Fran•cis•co** (frän thēs′kô), 1436–1517, Spanish cardinal and statesman. Also called **Ximenes.**

Ji•mé•nez de Que•sa•da (hē me′neth the ke sä′-thä, -me′nes), **Gon•za•lo** (gôn thä′lô, -sä′-), 1497?–1579, Spanish explorer and conqueror in South America.

jim•i•ny (jim′ə nē), *interj.* (a mild exclamation of surprise, emotion, or awe.) Also, **jim′mi•ny.** [1810–20; perh. alter. of L *Jēsu Domine* Lord Jesus!]

jim•jams (jim′jamz′), *n.* (*used with a plural v.*) *Slang.* **1.** extreme nervousness; jitters. **2.** See **delirium tremens.** [1540–50; gradational compound based on JAM[1]. Cf. FLIM-FLAM, *jingle-jangle,* etc.]

jim•mie (jim′ē), *n.* Usually, **jimmies.** sprinkle (def. 10). [orig. uncert.]

jim•my[1] (jim′ē), *n., pl.* **-mies,** *v.,* **-mied, -my•ing.** —*n.* **1.** a short crowbar. **2.** a large male crab, esp. of Chesapeake Bay. —*v.t.* **3.** to force open (a door, window, etc.) with a jimmy: *The burglar got in by jimmying the back door.* Also, *esp. Brit.,* **jemmy.** [1840–50; generic use of JIMMY; cf. JACK[1]]

jim•my[2] (jim′ē), *n., pl.* **-mies.** *Australian Slang.* an immigrant. [1835–45; rhyming slang; *Jimmy* (Grant), for *immigrant*]

Jim•my (jim′ē), *n.* a male given name, form of **James.** Also, **Jim′mie.**

jimp (jimp), *adj. Scot. and North Eng.* **1.** slender; trim; delicate. **2.** scant; barely sufficient. Also, **gimp.** [1500–10; orig. uncert.] —**jimp′ly,** *adv.* —**jimp′ness,** *n.*

jim′son weed′ (jim′sən), a coarse, rank-smelling weed, *Datura stramonium,* of the nightshade family, having oaklike, poisonous leaves and tubular white or lavender flowers. Also, **jimp′son weed′** (jimp′sən), **Jim′son weed′.** [1805–15, *Amer.*; var. of *Jamestown weed,* after JAMESTOWN, Virginia]

jin[1] (jin), *n., pl.* **jins,** (*esp. collectively*) **jin.** *Islamic Myth.* jinn.

jin[2] (jin) *Australian Informal.* gin[6].

Jin (jin), *n. Pinyin.* Chin.

Ji•nan (jē′nän′), *n. Pinyin.* a city in and the capital of Shandong province, in E China. 1,100,000. Also, **Chinan, Tsinan.**

jin•gal (jin′gôl), *n.* a large musket fired from a rest, often mounted on a carriage: formerly used in India, China, etc. Also, **gingal, gingall.** [1810–20; < Hindi *janjāl,* var. of *janjār*]

Jing•de•zhen (jing′dœ′jœn′), *n. Pinyin.* a city in E Jiangxi province, in E China: known for its fine porcelain. Also, **Chingtechen, Kingtehchen.** Formerly, **Fowliang.**

jin•gle (jing′gəl), *v.,* **-gled, -gling,** *n.* —*v.i.* **1.** to make clinking or tinkling sounds, as do coins, keys, or other light, resonant metal objects when coming into contact or being struck together repeatedly: *The keys on his belt jingled as he walked.* **2.** to move or proceed with such sounds: *The sleigh, decorated with bells, jingled along the snowy road.* **3.** to sound in a light, repetitious manner suggestive of this, as verse, a sequence of words, or piece of music. **4.** to make rhymes. —*v.t.* **5.** to cause to jingle: *He jingled the coins in his pocket.* —*n.* **6.** a tinkling or clinking sound, as of small bells or of small pieces of resonant metal repeatedly struck one against another. **7.** something that makes such a sound, as a small bell or a metal pendant. **8.** a catchy succession of like or repetitious sounds, as in music or verse. **9.** a piece of verse or a short song having such a catchy succession of sounds, usually of a light or humorous character: *an advertising jingle.* **10.** *Irish Eng. and Australian.* a loosely sprung, two-wheeled, roofed carriage, usually used as a hackney coach. [1350–1400; ME *gynglen,* appar. imit.; cf. D *jengelen;* see -LE] —**jin′gler,** *n.* —**jin′gling•ly,** *adv.* —**jin′gly,** *adj.*

jin′gle bell′, a sleigh bell. [1885–90]

jin′gle shell′, **1.** any of several marine, bivalve mollusks of the genus *Anomia,* having a thin, pearly shell with a conspicuous hole or notch near the hinge of the lower valve. **2.** the shell itself.

jing′ling John′ny, *Music.* crescent (def. 6). [1900–05]

jin•go (jing′gō), *n., pl.* **-goes,** *adj.* —*n.* **1.** a person who professes his or her patriotism loudly and excessively, favoring vigilant preparedness for war and an aggressive foreign policy; bellicose chauvinist. **2.** *Eng. Hist.* a Conservative supporter of Disraeli's policy in the Near East during the period 1877–78. **3. by jingo!** *Informal.* (an exclamation used to emphasize the truth or importance of a foregoing statement, or to express astonishment, approval, etc.): *I know you can do it, by jingo!* —*adj.* **4.** of jingoes. **5.** characterized by jingoism. [1660–70; orig. conjurer's call *hey jingo* appear! come forth! (opposed to *hey presto* hasten away!), taken into general use in the phrase *by Jingo,* euphemism for *by God;* chauvinistic sense from *by Jingo* in political song supporting use of British forces against Russia in 1878]

jin•go•ism (jing′gō iz′əm), *n.* the spirit, policy, or practice of jingoes; bellicose chauvinism. [1875–80; JINGO + -ISM] —**jin′go•ish,** *adj.* —**jin′go•ist,** *n., adj.* —**jin′go•is′tic,** *adj.* —**jin′go•is′ti•cal•ly,** *adv.*

Jin•ja (jin′jä), *n.* a city in SE Uganda, on Lake Victoria. 47,300.

Jin•ju (jin′jo͞o′), *n.* a city in S central South Korea, W of Pusan. 119,371. Also, **Chinju.**

jink (jingk), *n.* **1. jinks,** prankish or frolicsome activities. **2.** *Brit. Dial.* chink. [1690–1700; var. of dial. *chink* to gasp violently; cf. OE *cincung* boisterous laughter]

jin•ker (jing′kər), *n. Australian.* **1.** a sulky. **2.** any of various carts or trailers used to transport logs and timber. [1870–75; var. of *janker* (Scots), of uncert. orig.]

Jin•men (*Chin.* jin′mœn′), *n. Pinyin.* Quemoy.

jinn (jin), *n., pl.* **jinns,** (*esp. collectively*) **jinn.** *Islamic Myth.* any of a class of spirits, lower than the angels, capable of appearing in human and animal forms and influencing humankind for either good or evil. Also, **jin•ni** (ji nē′, jin′ē), **djin, djinn, djinni, jin.** [1675–85; pl. of Ar *jinnī* demon]

Jin•nah (jin′ə), *n.* **Mohammed Ali** (*"Quaid-i-Azam"*), 1876–1948, Muslim leader in India: first governor general of Pakistan 1947–48.

CONCISE PRONUNCIATION KEY: *act, cāpe, dâre, pärt; set, ēqual; if, īce; ox, ōver, ôrder, oil, bo͝ok, bo͞ot, out; up, ûrge; child; sing; shoe; thin,* t͟h*at;* zh as in *treasure.* ə = *a* as in *alone, e* as in *system, i* as in *easily, o* as in *gallop, u* as in *circus;* ° as in *fire* (fī°r), *hour* (ou°r). l and n can serve as syllabic consonants, as in *cradle* (krād′l), and *button* (but′n). See the full key inside the front cover.

jin·rik·i·sha (jin rik′shô, -shä), *n.* a small, two-wheeled, cartlike passenger vehicle with a fold-down top, pulled by one person, formerly used widely in Japan and China. Also, **jin·rick′sha, jin·rick′shaw, jin·rik′·sha.** Also called **rickshaw, ricksha.** [1870–75; < Japn, equiv. to *jin* person + *-riki* power + *-sha* vehicle (< MChin, equiv. to Chin *rénlì shē*)]

jinx (jingks), *n.* **1.** a person, thing, or influence supposed to bring bad luck. —*v.t.* **2.** to bring bad luck to; place a jinx on: *The strike has jinxed my plans to go to Milwaukee for the weekend.* **3.** to destroy the point of: *His sudden laugh jinxed the host's joke.* [1910–15, *Amer.*; perh. < L *jynx* wryneck (bird used in divination and magic) < Gk *iynx*]

Jin·zhou (jin′jō′), *n. Pinyin.* a city in S Liaoning province, in NE China. 750,000. Also, **Chinchow.**

ji·pi·ja·pa (hē′pē hä′pä, -pə), *n.* **1.** Also called **Panama-hat plant.** a tropical American, palmlike plant, *Carludovica palmata.* **2.** a Panama hat made from the young leaves of this plant. [1855–60; < AmerSp, after *Jipijapa,* town in Ecuador]

jird (jērd), *n.* **1.** any of several species of small, burrowing rodents of the genus *Meriones,* subfamily Gerbillinae, inhabiting dry regions of Asia and northern Africa. **2.** gerbil (def. 2). [said to be < Berber]

jit·ney (jit′nē), *n., pl.* **-neys,** *v.,* **-neyed, -ney·ing.** —*n.* **1.** a small bus or car following a regular route along which it picks up and discharges passengers, originally charging each passenger five cents. **2.** *Older Slang.* a nickel; five-cent piece. —*v.t., v.i.* **3.** to carry or ride in a jitney. [1900–05, *Amer.*; of obscure orig.; F *jeton* JETTON is a phonetically implausible source]

jit·ter (jit′ər), *n.* **1. jitters,** nervousness; a feeling of fright or uneasiness (usually prec. by *the*): *Every time I have to make a speech, I get the jitters.* **2.** fluctuations in the image on a television screen or in copy received by facsimile transmission, caused by interference or by momentary failures of synchronization. —*v.i.* **3.** to behave nervously. [1920–25; var. of *chitter* to shiver (ME *chiteren*), gradational var. of CHATTER]

jit·ter·bug (jit′ər bug′), *n., v.,* **-bugged, -bug·ging.** —*n.* **1.** a strenuously acrobatic dance consisting of a few standardized steps augmented by twirls, splits, somersaults, etc., popular esp. in the early 1940's and performed chiefly to boogie-woogie and swing. **2.** a person who dances the jitterbug. —*v.i.* **3.** to dance the jitterbug. [1930–35, *Amer.*; JITTER + BUG[1]] —**jit′ter·bug′·ger,** *n.*

jit·ter·y (jit′ə rē), *adj.,* **-ter·i·er, -ter·i·est.** extremely tense and nervous; jumpy: *He's very jittery about the medical checkup.* [1930–35, *Amer.*; JITTER + -Y[1]] —**jit′·ter·i·ness,** *n.*

jiu·jit·su (jo͞o jit′so͞o), *n.* jujitsu. Also, **jiu·jut·su** (jo͞o-jut′so͞o, -jo͞ot′-).

Jiu·long (*Chin.* jyʏ′lông′), *n. Pinyin.* Kowloon.

ji·va (jē′və), *n.* **1.** *Hinduism.* the individual soul, regarded as a particular manifestation of Atman. **2.** *Jainism.* **a.** the individual soul or life monad, compared to a transparent crystal stained by karmic matter with colors, or lesyas, of varying hues. **b.** all such monads collectively, regarded as the animating principle of the universe. Also called **ji·vat·ma** (jē vät′mə). [1800–10; < Skt: lit., living]

Jí·va·ro (hē′və rō′), *n., pl.* **-ros,** (*esp. collectively*) **-ro** for 1. —*n.* **1.** a member of a group of American Indian peoples of eastern Ecuador and northern Peru, formerly renowned for their custom of preserving the hair and shrunken skin from the severed heads of enemies. **2.** any of the four extant languages of the Jivaro.

jive (jīv), *n., v.,* **jived, jiv·ing,** *adj.* —*n.* **1.** swing music or early jazz. **2.** the jargon associated with swing music and early jazz. **3.** *Slang.* deceptive, exaggerated, or meaningless talk: *Don't give me any of that jive!* —*v.i.* **4.** to play jive. **5.** to dance to jive; jitterbug. **6.** *Slang.* to engage in kidding, teasing, or exaggeration. —*v.t.* **7.** *Slang.* to tease; fool; kid: *Stop jiving me!* —*adj.* **8.** *Slang.* insincere, pretentious, or deceptive. [1920–25; orig. obscure; alleged to be an alter. of GIBE, though the shift in sense and phonetic change are unexplained] —**jiv′er,** *n.*

jiv·ey (jī′vē), *adj.,* **jiv·i·er, jiv·i·est.** *Slang.* resembling, suggesting, or characteristic of jive; lively. [1940–45; JIVE + -EY[1]]

jiv·y (jī′vē), *adj.,* **jiv·i·er, jiv·i·est.** *Slang.* jivey. [JIVE + -Y[1]]

jiz·yah (jiz′yə), *n. Islam.* the poll tax formerly paid by minority religious groups within the Muslim empire. Also, **jiz′ya.** [< Ar]

JJ., **1.** Judges. **2.** Justices.

Jl., July.

jna·na (jə nä′nə), *n. Hinduism.* knowledge acquired through meditation and study as a means of reaching Brahman. Also called **Brahmajnana.** Cf. **bhakti** (def. 1), **karma** (def. 1). [1820–30; < Skt *jñāna*]

jna·na-mar·ga (jə nä′nə mär′gə), *n. Hinduism.* See under **marga.** [1875–80]

Jno., John.

jnt., joint.

jo (jō), *n., pl.* **joes.** *Scot.* beloved one; darling; sweetheart. Also, **joe.** [1520–30; var. of JOY]

Jo (jō), *n.* **1.** a female given name, form of **Josephine. 2.** a male given name, form of **Joseph.**

Jo·ab (jō′ab), *n.* a commander of David's army and the slayer of Abner and Absalom. II Sam. 3:27; 18:14.

CONCISE ETYMOLOGY KEY: <, descended or borrowed from; >, whence; b., blend of, blended; c., cognate with; cf., compare; deriv., derivative; equiv., equivalent; imit., imitative; obl., oblique; r., replacing; s., stem; sp., spelling, spelled; resp., respelling, respelled; trans., translation; ?, origin unknown; *, unattested; ‡, probably earlier than. See the full key inside the front cover.

Jo·a·chim (yō′ä ᴋʜim, yō ä′-), *n.* **1. Jo·seph** (yō′-zef), 1831–1907, Hungarian violinist and composer. **2.** a male given name.

Joan (jōn), *n.* **1.** (*"Fair Maid of Kent"*) 1328–85, wife of Edward, the Black Prince, and mother of Richard II. **2.** a fictitious female pope about A.D. 855–858. **3.** a female given name.

Jo·anne (jō an′), *n.* a female given name. Also, **Jo·ann′, Jo Ann′, Jo·an·na** (jō an′ə).

jo·an·nes (jō an′ēz, -is), *n., pl.* **-nes.** johannes.

Joan′ of Arc′ (ärk), **Saint** (*"the Maid of Orléans"*), 1412?–31, French national heroine and martyr who raised the siege of Orléans. French, **Jeanne d'Arc.**

Jo·ão Pes·so·a (zho͞o ouɴ′ pe sô′ə), a seaport in NE Brazil. 338,629.

Jo·ash (jō′ash), *n.* a king of Judah, reigned 837?–800? B.C., successor of Athaliah. II Kings 13:10–13. Also, *Douay Bible,* **Jo·as** (jō′as).

job[1] (job), *n., v.,* **jobbed, job·bing,** *adj.* —*n.* **1.** a piece of work, esp. a specific task done as part of the routine of one's occupation or for an agreed price: *She gave him the job of mowing the lawn.* **2.** a post of employment; full-time or part-time position: *She was seeking a job as an editor.* **3.** anything a person is expected or obliged to do; duty; responsibility: *It is your job to be on time.* **4.** an affair, matter, occurrence, or state of affairs: *to make the best of a bad job.* **5.** the material, project, assignment, etc., being worked upon: *The housing project was a long and costly job.* **6.** the process or requirements, details, etc., of working: *It was a tedious job.* **7.** the execution or performance of a task: *She did a good job.* **8.** *Slang.* a theft or similar criminal action: *The police caught the gang that pulled that bank job.* **9.** a public or official act or decision carried through for the sake of improper private gain. **10.** *Slang.* an example of a specific or distinctive type: *That little six-cylinder job was the best car I ever owned.* **11.** *Computers.* a unit of work for a computer, generally comprising an application program or group of related programs and the data, linkages, and instructions to the operating system needed for running the programs. **12. do a job on,** *Slang.* **a.** to destroy, defeat, damage, or confound thoroughly: *The thugs did a job on him—he'll be in the hospital for a month.* **b.** to deceive, persuade, or charm glibly; snow. **13. on the job,** alert; observant: *The cops were on the job and caught them red-handed.* —*v.i.* **14.** to work at jobs or odd pieces of work; work by the piece. **15.** to do business as a jobber. **16.** to turn public business, planning, etc., improperly to private gain. —*v.t.* **17.** to assign or give (work, a contract for work, etc.) in separate portions, as among different contractors or workers (often fol. by *out*): *He jobbed out the contract to a number of small outfits.* **18.** to buy in large quantities, as from wholesalers or manufacturers, and sell to dealers in smaller quantities: *He jobs shoes in Ohio and Indiana.* **19.** to get rid of or dispose of: *His party jobbed him when he sought a second term in office.* **20.** to swindle or trick (someone): *They jobbed him out of his property.* **21.** to carry on (public or official business) for improper private gain. —*adj.* **22.** of or for a particular job or transaction. **23.** bought, sold, or handled together: *He's too big a customer to buy in less than job quantities.* [1620–30; 1935–40 for def. 16; orig. uncert.]
—**Syn. 1.** See **task. 2.** See **position.**

job[2] (job), *v.t., v.i.,* **jobbed, job·bing,** *n.* jab. [1480–90; ME *jobben,* of uncert. orig.]

Job (jōb), *n.* **1.** the central figure in an Old Testament parable of the righteous sufferer. **2.** a book of the Bible bearing his name. **3.** a male given name: from a Hebrew word meaning "persecuted."

job′ ac′tion, any means, as a work slowdown, of organized protest or pressure by employees to win some goal or gain from their employers. [1965–70, *Amer.*]

job′ anal′ysis, a detailed study of the requirements necessary to complete a job, taking into consideration chiefly the order of operation, material and machinery needed, and the necessary qualifications of workers. [1920–25]

Jo. Bapt., John the Baptist.

job′ bank′, a data file or agency for matching persons seeking work with suitable job openings. [1970–75]

job·ber (job′ər), *n.* **1.** a wholesale merchant, esp. one selling to retailers. **2.** a pieceworker. **3.** (formerly) a merchant who deals in special, odd, or job lots. **4.** a person who practices jobbery. [1660–70; JOB[1] + -ER[1]]

job·ber·y (job′ə rē), *n.* the conduct of public or official business for the sake of improper private gain. [1825–35; JOBBER + -Y[3]]

job′ case′, *Print.* any of various cases for holding type, esp. one of several that accommodate both upper-case and lowercase letters. Cf. **California job case, case**[2] (def. 8). [1890–95]

job′ classifica′tion, an arrangement of different types of employment within a company or industry, according to the skill, experience, or training required.

job′ control′ lan′guage, *Computers.* a language used to construct statements that identify a particular job to be run and specify the job's requirements to the operating system under which it will run. *Abbr.:* JCL

Job′ Corps′ (job), *U.S. Govt.* an organization within the Department of Labor that operates rural conservation camps and urban training centers for poor youths.

job′ cost′ing. See **job-order costing.**

job′ descrip′tion, an abstract of a job analysis containing the classification of and requirements for a job, used in hiring and placing prospective employees. [1955–60]

job·hold·er (job′hōl′dər), *n.* **1.** a person who has a regular or steady job. **2.** a government employee. [1900–05, *Amer.*; JOB[1] + HOLDER]

job-hop (job′hop′), *v.i.,* **-hopped, -hop·ping.** to change jobs frequently. [1950–55] —**job′-hop′per,** *n.*

job-hunt (job′hunt′), *v.i.* to seek employment; look for a job. [1945–50] —**job′-hunt′er,** *n.*

job·less (job′lis), *adj.* **1.** without a job. **2.** noting or pertaining to persons without jobs, esp. to those who are seeking employment. —*n.* **3.** (*used with a plural v.*) unemployed people collectively, esp. those who are seeking a job (usually prec. by *the*). [1800–10; JOB[1] + -LESS] —**job′less·ness,** *n.*

job′ lot′, **1.** a large, often assorted quantity of goods sold or handled as a single transaction. **2.** a miscellaneous quantity; a quantity of odds and ends. [1850–55]

job′ mar′ket, **1.** the total number of vacant jobs open to those seeking employment. **2.** the aggregate of those persons seeking employment: *Thousands of June graduates entered the job market.*

job′ or′der, a written order to a worker or group of workers to perform a certain job.

job′-order cost′ing (job′ôr′dər), a method of cost accounting by which the total cost of a given unit or quantity is determined by computing the costs that go into making a product as it moves through the manufacturing process. Also called **job costing.** Cf. **process costing.**

job′ print′er, a printer who does letterheads, invoices, announcements, and other miscellaneous work, as distinguished from one who works solely on books, periodicals, etc. —**job′ print′ing.** [1830–40, *Amer.*]

Job's′ com′forter (jōbz), a person who unwittingly or maliciously depresses or discourages someone while attempting to be consoling. [1730–40]

job′ set′ter, a worker who readies or adjusts machinery for tooling on the production line.

job′ shop′, an agency or plant that supplies technical personnel or performs a specific function in a manufacturing process, usually on short-term temporary contracts. —**job′ shop′per.**

Job's-tears (jōbz′tērz′), *n.* **1.** (*used with a plural v.*) the hard, nearly spherical bracts that surround the female flowers of an Asian grass, *Coix lacryma-jobi,* and which when ripe are used as beads. **2.** (*used with a singular v.*) the grass itself. [1590–1600]

job′ stick′, *Print.* See **composing stick.**

job′ tick′et, **1.** a slip or card accompanying a job order and used for giving instructions or for recording time spent on the work. **2.** See **job order.**

job′ work′, **1.** miscellaneous printing work, as distinguished from books, periodicals, etc. **2.** work done by the job. [1795–1805]

Jo·cas·ta (jō kas′tə), *n.* **1.** *Class. Myth.* a queen of Thebes, the wife of Laius and the mother, later the wife, of Oedipus, by whom she bore Eteocles, Polynices, and Antigone: called Epicaste by Homer. **2.** a female given name. Also, **Jo·cas′te.**

Joc·e·lyn (jos′ə lin, jos′lin), *n.* a female given name, form of **Joyce.** Also, **Joc′e·lin, Joc′e·line, Joc′e·lynne.**

Joch·e·bed (jok′ə bed′), *n.* the mother of Aaron and Moses. Ex. 6:20. Also, *Douay Bible,* **Joch′a·bed′.**

jock[1] (jok), *n. Informal.* **1.** jockey. **2.** See **disc jockey.** [1820–30; shortened form of JOCKEY]

jock[2] (jok), *n.* **1.** a jockstrap. **2.** *Informal.* an athlete. **3.** *Informal.* an enthusiast: *a computer jock.* [1950–55; by shortening from JOCKSTRAP]

Jock (jok), *n.* **1.** *Scot. and Irish Eng.* **a.** a nickname for **John. b.** an innocent lad; country boy. **2.** *Brit. Informal.* **a.** a Scottish soldier or a soldier in a Scottish regiment. **b.** any Scot. **3.** a male given name. [1500–10]

jock·ey (jok′ē), *n., pl.* **-eys,** *v.,* **-eyed, -ey·ing.** —*n.* **1.** a person who rides horses professionally in races. **2.** *Informal.* a person who pilots, operates, or guides the movement of something, as an airplane or automobile. —*v.t.* **3.** to ride (a horse) as a jockey. **4.** *Informal.* to operate or guide the movement of; pilot; drive. **5.** to move, bring, put, etc., by skillful maneuvering: *The movers jockeyed the sofa through the door.* **6.** to trick or cheat: *The salesman jockeyed them into buying an expensive car.* **7.** to manipulate cleverly or trickily: *He jockeyed himself into office.* —*v.i.* **8.** to aim at an advantage by skillful maneuvering. **9.** to act trickily; seek an advantage by trickery. [1520–30; special use of JOCK + -EY[2]] —**jock′ey·like′, jock′ey·ish,** *adj.* —**jock′ey·ship′,** *n.*

jock′ey box′, *Chiefly Northwestern U.S.* a glove compartment, esp. in a truck.

jock′ey cap′, a cap with a long visor, worn by jockeys. [1740–50]

jock′ey club′, **1.** an association for the regulation and promotion of thoroughbred horse racing, usually composed of racing officials and thoroughbred owners at a specific racetrack or in a particular region. **2.** a section at a racetrack reserved for members of such an association, containing box seats, a restaurant, and sometimes rooms for social gatherings. [1765–75]

Jock′ey shorts′, *Trademark.* a brand of short, close-fitting underpants with an elastic band around the waist; briefs.

jock′ itch′, *Pathol.* a fungal infection of the skin in the groin area, occurring most commonly in males, esp. in warm climates, characterized by itchy and often scaly lesions; tinea cruris. [1945–50]

jock·o (jok′ō), *n., pl.* **jock·os. 1.** a chimpanzee. **2.** any monkey. [1840–50; < F, Buffon's shortening of *engeko* (taking *en-* as an article) < a word in Mpongwe, Bantu language of Gabon]

Jock·o (jok′ō), *n.* a male given name, form of **Jock.**

Jock′ Scot′, *Angling.* an artificial fly having a yellow floss body, black silk tag, scarlet and yellow tail, wings of scarlet and of jungle cock feathers spotted with yellow and gray, and hackle of guinea fowl and grouse feathers. Also, **Jock′ Scott′.** [generic use of JOCK + *Scot,* a regional allusion]

jock•strap (jok′strap′), *n.* an elasticized belt, a men's undergarment, with a pouch for supporting and protecting the genitals, worn esp. while participating in athletics. Also called **athletic supporter.** [1895–1900; *jock* male organ (var. of JACK¹ male; see JOCK) + STRAP]

jock•te•leg (jok′tə leg′), *n. Brit. Dial.* a large clasp knife or pocketknife; jackknife. Also, **joktaleg.** [1665–75; orig. Scots; first attested as *jackteleg,* perh. with JACK, JOCK and LEG, alluding to knife handles carved in the form of a leg]

jo•cose (jō kōs′, jə-), *adj.* given to or characterized by joking; jesting; humorous; playful: *a jocose and amusing manner.* [1665–75; < L *jocōsus,* equiv. to *joc(us)* JOKE + *-ōsus* -OSE¹] **—jo•cose′ly,** *adv.* **—jo•cose′ness,** *n.*
—Syn. facetious, waggish, witty, funny, droll, comical, sportive, merry. See **jovial.**

jo•cos•i•ty (jō kos′i tē, jə-), *n., pl.* **-ties. 1.** the state or quality of being jocose. **2.** joking or jesting. **3.** a joke or jest. [1640–50; JOCOSE + -ITY]

joc•u•lar (jok′yə lər), *adj.* given to, characterized by, intended for, or suited to joking or jesting; waggish; facetious: *jocular remarks about opera stars.* [1620–30; < L *joculāris,* equiv. to *jocul(us)* little joke (*joc(us)* JOKE + *-ulus* -ULE) + *-āris* -AR¹] **—joc′u•lar•ly,** *adv.*
—Syn. See **jovial.**

joc•u•lar•i•ty (jok′yə lar′i tē), *n., pl.* **-ties. 1.** the state or quality of being jocular. **2.** jocular speech or behavior. **3.** a jocular remark or act. [1640–50; JOCULAR + -ITY]

joc•und (jok′ənd, jō′kənd), *adj.* cheerful; merry; gay; blithe; glad: *a witty and jocund group.* [1350–1400; ME *jocound* < LL *jocundus,* alter. of L *jūcundus* pleasant, equiv. to *ju(vāre)* to help, benefit, please, delight + *-cundus* adj. suffix] **—joc′und•ly,** *adv.*
—Syn. joyous, joyful, blithesome, jolly. See **jovial.**

jo•cun•di•ty (jō kun′di tē), *n., pl.* **-ties** for 2. **1.** the state or an instance of being jocund; gaiety. **2.** a jocund remark or act. [1375–1425; late ME *jocundite;* see JOCUND, -ITY]

jodh•pur (jod′pər), *n.* **1. jodhpurs,** (*used with a plural v.*) riding breeches cut very full over the hips and tapering at the knees to become tightfitting from the knees to the ankles. **2.** Also called **jodh′pur shoe′, jodh′pur boot′.** an ankle-high shoe for wearing with such breeches, having a strap that encircles the ankle and buckles on the side. Cf. **chukka boot.** [1895–1900; after JODHPUR]

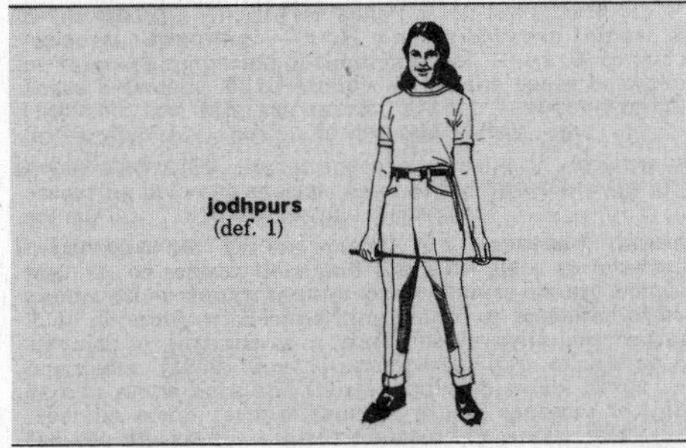
jodhpurs (def. 1)

Jodh•pur (jod′pər; *locally* jōd′po͝or), *n.* **1.** Also called **Marwar.** a former state in NW India, now in Rajasthan. **2.** a city in central Rajasthan, in NW India. 318,894.

Jo•di (jō′dē), *n.* a female given name. Also, **Jo′die.**

Jo. Div., John the Divine.

Jodl (yōd′l), *n.* **Al•fred** (äl′frāt), 1892?–1946, German general: signed the surrender of Germany on behalf of the German high command in World War II.

Jo•do (jō′dō), *n. Japanese.* See **Pure Land.**

Jo•do Shin•shu (jō′dō shin′sho͞o), *Buddhism.* the largest sect of Jodo, stressing simple trust rather than ritual as the means to salvation. [< Japn *Jōdo* Pure Land + *shinshū* true faith (< MChin, equiv. to Chin *jìngtǔ zhēnzōng*)]

Jod′rell Bank′ (jod′rəl), site of a radio astronomy observatory **(Nuffield Radio Astronomy Laboratories)** in NE Cheshire, England, that operates a 250-ft. (76-m) radio telescope.

Jo•dy (jō′dē), *n.* a male or female given name.

joe¹ (jō), *n. Scot.* jo.

joe² (jō), *n. Slang.* coffee. [1840–50; of uncert. orig.]

Joe (jō), *n.* **1.** (*sometimes l.c.*) *Informal.* fellow; guy: *the average Joe who works for a living.* **2.** *Informal.* a personification of a typical, often unprepossessing representative of an occupation, personality trait, state of being, etc., that is expressed, sometimes metonymically, as a mock surname: *Joe Lunchbucket working hard at some factory and paying his taxes year after year; political con artists relying on the gullibility of Joe Schmo.* **3.** a male given name, form of **Joseph.**

Joe′ Blow′, *Slang.* an average citizen; man in the street. Also called **Joe Doakes.** [1935–40, *Amer.;* rhyming phrase. See JOE, BLOW²]

Joe′ Col′lege, a personification of a typical male U.S. college student, esp. in the 1930's. [1935–40; modeled on JOE BLOW]

Joe′ Doakes′ (dōks), *pl.* **Joe Doakes.** *Slang.* See **Joe Blow.** [1940–45]

Jo•el (jō′əl), *n.* **1.** a Minor Prophet of the postexilic period. **2.** a book of the Bible bearing his name. **3.** a male given name: from a Hebrew word meaning "the Lord is God."

Joe′ Mil′ler, 1. a book of jokes. **2.** an old, familiar joke; chestnut. [1780–90; after *Joe Miller's Jestbook* (1739) by John Mottley]

Jo•en•suu (yô′en so͞o′), *n.* a city in SE Finland. 44,318.

joe-pye′ weed′ (jō′pī′), **1.** Also called **purple boneset.** a tall composite weed, *Eupatorium purpureum,* of North America, having clusters of pinkish or purple flowers. **2.** Also called **spotted joe-pye weed.** a related plant, *E. maculatum,* having similar flowers and stems that are often spotted with purple. [1810–20, *Amer.;* orig. uncert.]

Jo. Evang., John the Evangelist.

jo•ey¹ (jō′ē), *n., pl.* **-eys.** *Australian.* **1.** any young animal, esp. a kangaroo. **2.** a young child. [1830–40; orig. uncert.]

jo•ey² (jō′ē), *n., pl.* **-eys.** *Brit. Slang.* **1.** a threepenny piece. **2.** (formerly) a fourpenny piece. [1860–65; named after *Joseph* Hume (1777–1855), English politician who favored the coinage of the fourpenny piece]

Jo•ey (jō′ē), *n., pl.* **Jo•eys.** a clown, esp. in the circus or pantomime and puppet theater. [1895–1900; dim. of *Joseph,* after Joseph Grimaldi]

Jo•ey (jō′ē), *n.* a male given name, form of **Joe** or **Joseph.**

jo′ey glass′, a small tumbler of the 17th century; dram glass.

Jof•fre (zhôf′rᵊ), *n.* **Jo•seph Jacques Cé•saire** (zhô zef′ zhäk sā zer′), 1852–1931, French general in World War I.

Jof•frey (jof′rē), *n.* **Robert** (*Abdullah Jaffa Bey Khan*), 1930–88, U.S. ballet dancer, choreographer, and dance company director.

jog¹ (jog), *v.,* **jogged, jog•ging,** *n.* **—***v.t.* **1.** to move or shake with a push or jerk: *The horseman jogged the reins lightly.* **2.** to cause to function with a jolt for a moment or in a series of disconnected motions: *He jogged the motor and started the machine.* **3.** to push slightly, as to arouse the attention; nudge: *She jogged his elbow when she wanted to be introduced to one of his friends.* **4.** to stir or jolt into activity or alertness, as by a hint or reminder: *to jog a person's memory.* **5.** to cause (a horse) to go at a steady trot. **6.** *Print.* to align the edges of (a stack of sheets of paper of the same size) by gently tapping. **—***v.i.* **7.** to run at a leisurely, slow pace, esp. as an outdoor exercise: *He jogs two miles every morning to keep in shape.* **8.** to run or ride at a steady trot: *They jogged to the stable.* **9.** to move with a jolt or jerk: *Her briefcase jogged against her leg as she walked.* **10.** to or travel with a jolting pace or motion: *The clumsy ca jogged down the bumpy road.* **11.** to go in a desultory or humdrum fashion (usually fol. by *on* or *along*): *He just jogged along, getting by however he could.* **—***n.* **12.** a shake; slight push; nudge. **13.** a steady trot, as of a horse. **14.** an act, instance, or period of jogging: *to go for a jog before breakfast.* **15.** a jogging pace: *He approached us at a jog.* [1540–50; b. *jot* to jog (now dial.) and *shog* to shake, jog (late ME *shoggen*)] **—jog′ger,** *n.*

jog² (jog), *n., v.,* **jogged, jog•ging. —***n.* **1.** an irregularity of line or surface; projection; notch. **2.** a bend or turn: *a country road full of sudden jogs.* **3.** *Theat.* a narrow flat placed at right angles to another flat to make a corner, used esp. in sets representing an interior. **—***v.i.* **4.** to bend or turn: *The road jogs to the right beyond those trees.* [1705–15; var. of JAG¹]

jog′ging pants′, sweatpants, esp. those used for jogging. [1970–75]

jog′ging shoe′, an athletic shoe designed to be worn while jogging. [1975–80]

jog′ging suit′, an outfit consisting of sweatpants and a sweatshirt, used while exercising or as sportswear.

jog•gle (jog′əl), *v.,* **-gled, -gling,** *n.* **—***v.t.* **1.** to shake slightly; move to and fro, as by repeated jerks; jiggle: *She joggled the key in the lock a couple of times before getting the door open.* **2.** to cause to shake or totter as by a sudden, slight push; jostle. **3.** to join or fasten by fitting a projection into a recess. **4.** to fit or fasten with dowels. **—***v.i.* **5.** to move irregularly; have a jogging or jolting motion; shake. **—***n.* **6.** the act of joggling. **7.** a slight shake or jolt. **8.** a moving with jolts or jerks. **9.** a projection on one of two joining objects fitting into a corresponding recess in the other to prevent slipping. **10.** *Carpentry.* an enlarged area, as of a post or king post, for supporting the foot of a strut, brace, etc. [1505–15; JOG¹ + -LE] **—jog′gler,** *n.*

jog′gle post′, 1. a wooden king post having notches or raised areas for receiving and supporting the feet of struts. **2.** a post formed of timbers joggled together. Also called **jog′gle piece′.**

Jog•ja•kar•ta (jog′yə kär′tə, jôg′-), *n.* a city in central Java, in S Indonesia. 342,267. Also, **Jokjakarta.** Dutch, **Djokjakarta.**

jog′ trot′, 1. a slow, regular, jolting pace, as of a horse. **2.** an uneventful, humdrum way of living, doing something, etc.: *a sleepy little town where life proceeded at a jog trot.* [1700–10]

Jo•han•an ben Zak•ka•i (jō han′ən ben zak′ā ī′; *Seph. Heb.* yô′KHä nän′ ben zä kī′), died A.D. c80, Palestinian rabbi who was a leading Pharisaic teacher: disciple of Hillel.

Jo•hann (yō′hän), *n.* a male given name, Germanic form of **John.**

Jo•han•na (jō han′ə, -an′ə), *n.* a female given name.

jo•han•nes (jō han′ēz, -is), *n., pl.* **-nes.** a gold coin formerly used as currency in Portugal, first issued in the early 18th century. Also, **joannes.** [1750–60, *Amer.;* after the name *Joannes* (John V, of Portugal) in the coin's legend. See JOHN]

Jo•han•nes (yō hä′nis, -han′is), *n.* a male given name, form of **John.**

Jo•han•nes•burg (jō han′is bûrg′, -hä′nis-; *Du.* yō hän′əs bœrkh′), *n.* a city in S Transvaal, in the NE Republic of South Africa. 1,441,000.

Johan′nes Dam•a•sce′nus (dam′ə sē′nəs). See **John of Damascus.**

Jo•han•nine (jō han′in, -īn), *adj.* of or pertaining to the apostle John or to the books in the New Testament attributed to him. [1860–65; JOHANN(ES) + -INE¹]

john (jon), *n. Slang.* **1.** a toilet or bathroom. **2.** (*sometimes cap.*) a fellow; guy. **3.** (*sometimes cap.*) a prostitute's customer. [generic use of the proper name]

John (jon), *n.* **1.** the apostle John, believed to be the author of the fourth Gospel, three Epistles, and the book of Revelation. **2.** See **John the Baptist. 3.** (*John Lackland*) 1167?–1216, king of England 1199–1216; signer of the Magna Carta 1215 (son of Henry II of England). **4. Augustus Edwin,** 1878–1961, British painter and etcher. **5.** the fourth Gospel. **6.** any of the three Epistles of John: I, II, or III John. **7.** a male given name. [ME *John, Johan, Jon* < ML *Jō(h)annēs* < Gk *Iōánnēs* < Heb *Yōḥānān,* deriv. of *Yehōḥānān* God has been gracious]

John I, 1. Saint, died A.D. 526, Italian ecclesiastic: pope 523–526. **2.** (*"the Great"*) 1357–1433, king of Portugal 1385–1433.

John II, (*Mercurius*) died A.D. 535, Italian ecclesiastic: pope 533–535.

John III, 1. (*Catelinus*) died A.D. 574, Italian ecclesiastic: pope 561–574. **2.** (*John Sobieski*) 1624–96, king of Poland 1674–96.

John IV, died A.D. 642, pope 640–642.

John V, died A.D. 686, pope 685–686.

John VI, died A.D. 705, Greek ecclesiastic: pope 701–705.

John VII, died A.D. 707, Greek ecclesiastic: pope 705–707.

John VIII, died A.D. 882, Italian ecclesiastic: pope 872–882.

John IX, died A.D. 900, Italian ecclesiastic: pope 898–900.

John X, died A.D. 929?, Italian ecclesiastic: pope 914–928.

John XI, died A.D. 936, Italian ecclesiastic: pope 931–936.

John XII, (*Octavian*) died A.D. 964, Italian ecclesiastic: pope 955–964.

John XIII, died A.D. 972, Italian ecclesiastic: pope 965–972.

John XIV, died A.D. 984, pope 983–984.

John XV, died A.D. 996, Italian ecclesiastic: pope 985–996.

John XVII, (*Sicco*) died 1003, pope 1003.

John XVIII, (*Fasanus*) died 1009, Italian ecclesiastic: pope 1003–09.

John XIX, died 1032, pope 1024–32.

John XXI, (*Petrus Hispanus*) died 1277, Portuguese ecclesiastic: pope 1276–77.

John XXII, (*Jacques Duèse*) c1244–1334, French ecclesiastic: pope 1316–34.

John XXIII, (*Angelo Giuseppe Roncalli*) 1881–1963, Italian ecclesiastic: pope 1958–63.

John′ Bar′leycorn, a personification of barley as used in malt liquor, of malt liquor itself, or of any intoxicating liquor. [1610–20]

John′ Birch′er, Bircher. [1960–65; JOHN BIRCH (SOCIETY) + -ER¹]

John′ Birch′ Soci′ety, an ultraconservative organization, founded in December 1958 by Robert Welch, Jr., chiefly to combat alleged Communist activities in the U.S.

john•boat (jon′bōt′), *n.* a light, square-ended, flat-bottomed skiff. Also, **john′ boat′.** [1900–05, *Amer.;* prob. JOHN (the given name) + BOAT; cf. *joeboat* name for the same type of craft]

John′ Brown's′ Bod′y, a long narrative poem (1928) by Stephen Vincent Benét, about the U.S. Civil War.

John′ Bull′, 1. England; the English people. **2.** the typical Englishman. [1705–15; named after *John Bull,* chief character in Arbuthnot's allegory *The History of John Bull* (1712)] **—John′ Bull′ish. —John′ Bull′•ishness. —John′ Bull′ism.**

John′ Doe′, 1. an anonymous, average man. **2.** a fictitious name used in legal proceedings for a male party whose true name is not known. Cf. **Jane Doe, Richard Roe. 3.** of or for an unknown person; using the name *John Doe* to stand for an unknown person: *The judge issued a John Doe warrant so the police could arrest the culprit when they identified him.*

John′ Do′ry (dôr′ē, dōr′ē), *pl.* **John Dories.** any fish of the family Zeidae, esp. *Zeus faber,* of European seas, having a vertically compressed body and long spines in the dorsal fin. [1600–10; see DORY²; jocular formation]

Joh′ne's disease′ (yō′nəz), *Vet. Pathol.* a chronic diarrheal disease of cattle and sheep caused by infection with *Mycobacterium paratuberculosis,* an organism related to the tubercle bacillus. [1905–10; named after H. A. *Johne* (1839–1910), German scientist]

John F. Kennedy International Airport, international airport in New York City, on SW Long Island. Formerly, **Idlewild.**

John′ Han′cock, 1. See **Hancock, John. 2.** *Informal.* a person's signature: *Put your John Hancock on* *this check.* [1840–50, *Amer.*; named after John HANCOCK, from the boldness and legibility of his signature]

John′ Hen′ry, *pl.* **John Henries** for 1. **1.** *Informal.* a person's signature. **2.** *U.S. Folklore.* a legendary black man of exceptional strength and stamina. [1910–15, *Amer.*; from the proper name]

joh•nin (yō′nin), *n. Vet. Med.* a sterile solution prepared from the growth products of the bacillus *Mycobacterium paratuberculosis,* used chiefly in the diagnosis of Johne's disease. [*john-* (see JOHNE'S DISEASE) + -IN[2]]

John•na (jon′ə), *n.* a female given name.

John•ny (jon′ē), *n., pl.* **-nies** for 1–3. **1.** (*sometimes l.c.*) a familiar term of address for a man or boy. **2.** (*sometimes l.c.*) *Slang.* a short, collarless gown that is fastened in back and is worn by hospital patients, persons being examined in a doctor's office, etc. **3.** (*l.c.*) *Slang.* toilet; bathroom. **4.** a male given name, form of **John.** Also, **John′nie.** [1665–75; JOHN + -Y[2]]

john•ny•cake (jon′ē kāk′), *n. Northern U.S.* a cake or bread made of corn meal and water or milk, usually cooked on a griddle. Also, **john′ny cake′.** [1730–40, *Amer.*; prob. by folk etym. from earlier *jonakin,* of obscure orig.]
—Regional Variation. See **pancake.**

John′ny col′lar, (*often l.c.*) a small, pointed collar on a shirt, dress bodice, or the like, with close-fitting neckline.

John•ny-come-late•ly (jon′ē kum′lāt′lē), *n., pl.* **John•ny-come-late•lies, John•nies-come-late•ly.** a late arrival or participant; newcomer: *the Johnny-come-latelies producing space-war films after the trend had ended.* Also, **John′nie-come-late′ly.** [1825–35; from the proper name JOHNNY]

john′ny house′ (jon′ē), *South Midland and Southern U.S.* See **Johnny** (def. 3).

John•ny-jump-up (jon′ē jump′up′), *n.* **1.** any of certain violets, esp. *Viola pedunculata,* having variously colored flowers. **2.** a small form of the pansy, *V. tricolor.* [1835–45, *Amer.*; so called from its rapid rate of growth; see JOHNNY]

John•ny-on-the-spot (jon′ē on *th*ə spot′, -ôn-), *n. Informal.* a person who is on hand to perform a service, seize an opportunity, deal with an emergency, etc. [1860–65]

John′ny Reb′ (reb), *Informal.* **1.** *U.S. Hist.* a Confederate soldier. **2.** a native or inhabitant of the southern U.S., esp. of one of the former Confederate states; southerner. [1860–65, *Amer.*]

John′ny smok′ers. See **prairie smoke.**

John′ of Aus′tria, (*"Don John"*) 1547?–78, Spanish naval commander and general: victor at the battle of Lepanto.

John′ of Damas′cus, Saint, A.D. c675–749, priest, theologian, and scholar of the Eastern Church, born in Damascus. Also called **Johannes Damascenus.**

John′ of Gaunt′, (*Duke of Lancaster*) 1340–99, English soldier and statesman: fourth son of Edward III; founder of the royal house of Lancaster (father of Henry IV of England).

John′ of Ley′den, (*Jan Beuckelszoon* or *Bockhold*) 1509–36, Dutch Anabaptist.

John′ of Salis′bury, c1115–80, English prelate and scholar.

John′ of the Cross′, Saint (*Juan de Yepis y Álvarez*), 1542–91, Spanish mystic, writer, and theologian: cofounder with Saint Theresa of the order of Discalced Carmelites. Spanish, **San Juan de la Cruz.**

John′ o'Groat's′ House′ (ə grōts′), the northern tip of Scotland, near Duncansby Head, NE Caithness, traditionally thought of as the northernmost point of Britain: *from Land's End to John o'Groat's House.* Also called **John′ o'Groat's′.**

John Paul I, (*Albino Luciani*) 1912–78, Italian ecclesiastic: pope 1978.

John Paul II, (*Karol Wojtyla*) born 1920, Polish ecclesiastic: pope since 1978.

John Q. Public, the average or typical U.S. citizen: *an entertainment aimed at Mr. and Mrs. John Q. Public.* [1935–40, *Amer.*]

Johns (jonz), *n.* **Jasper,** born 1930, U.S. painter.

John•son (jon′sən; *for 3 also Sw.* yŏŏn′sôn), *n.* **1. Andrew,** 1808–75, seventeenth president of the U.S. 1865–69. **2. Charles Spur•geon** (spûr′jən), 1893–1956, U.S. educator and sociologist. **3. Ey•vind** (ā′vin), 1900–76, Swedish writer: Nobel prize 1974. **4. Gerald White,** 1890–1980, U.S. writer. **5. Howard (Deer•ing)** (dēr′ing), 1896?–1972, U.S. businessman: founder of restaurant and motel chain. **6. Jack** (*John Arthur*), 1878–1946, U.S. heavyweight prizefighter: world champion 1908–15. **7. James Wel•don** (wel′dən), 1871–1938, U.S. poet and essayist. **8. Lyn•don Baines** (lin′dən bānz), 1908–73, thirty-sixth president of the U.S. 1963–69. **9. Philip C(ortelyou),** born 1906, U.S. architect and author. **10. Rev•er•dy** (rev′ər dē), 1796–1876, U.S. lawyer and politician: senator 1845–49, 1863–68. **11. Richard Men•tor** (men′tər, -tôr), 1780–1850, vice president of the U.S. 1837–41. **12. Samuel** (*"Dr. Johnson"*), 1709–84, English lexicographer, critic, poet, and conversationalist. **13. Virginia E(sh•el•man)** (esh′əl mən), born 1925, U.S. psychologist: researcher on human sexual behavior (wife of William H. Masters). **14. Walter Perry** (*"Big Train"*), 1887–1946, U.S. baseball player. **15. Sir William,** 1715–74, British colonial administrator in America, born in Ireland.

John′son Cit′y, 1. a city in NE Tennessee. 39,753. **2.** a city in S New York. 17,126.

John•son•ese (jon′sə nēz′, -nēs′), *n.* a literary style characterized by rhetorically balanced, often pompous phraseology and an excessively Latinate vocabulary: so called from the style of writing practiced by Samuel Johnson. [1835–45; JOHNSON + -ESE]

John′son grass′, a sorghum, *Sorghum halepense,* that spreads by creeping rhizomes, grown for fodder. Also called **Aleppo grass, Means grass.** [1880–85, *Amer.*; named after William *Johnson,* American agriculturist who first planted it in 1840]

John•so•ni•an (jon sō′nē ən), *adj.* **1.** of, pertaining to, or characteristic of Samuel Johnson or his works. **2.** having the quality of Johnsonese. **—*n.* 3.** a person who writes in the Johnsonian style. **4.** a teacher or critic who specializes in the works of Samuel Johnson. [1785–95; JOHNSON + -IAN] **—John•so′ni•an•ism,** *n.* **—John•so′ni•an•ly,** *adv.*

John•ston (jon′stən, -sən), *n.* **1. Albert Sidney,** 1803–62, Confederate general in the U.S. Civil War. **2. Joseph Eggleston,** 1807–91, Confederate general in the U.S. Civil War. **3. Mary,** 1870–1936, U.S. writer. **4.** a town in E central Rhode Island. 24,907.

John′ston's or′gan (jon′stənz), *Entomol.* a sense organ in the second segment of the antenna of an insect, sensitive to movements of the antenna's flagellum, as when the insect is in flight. [named after Christopher *Johnston* (d. 1891), American physician]

Johns•town (jonz′toun′), *n.* a city in SW Pennsylvania: disastrous flood 1889. 35,496.

John′ the Bap′tist, the forerunner and baptizer of Jesus. Matt. 3.

Jo•hore (jə hôr′, -hōr′), *n.* a state in Malaysia, on S Malay Peninsula. 1,277,180; 7330 sq. mi. (18,985 sq. km). Also, **Jo•hor′.**

Johore′ Bah′ru (bä′rōō), a city in and the capital of Johore state, Malaysia, in the S part. 136,229.

Joi•a•da (joi′ə də), *n. Douay Bible.* Jehoiada.

joie de vi•vre (zhwAdᵊ vē′vRᵊ), *French.* a delight in being alive; keen, carefree enjoyment of living. [lit., joy of living]

join (join), *v.t.* **1.** to bring in contact, connect, or bring or put together: *to join hands; to join pages with a staple.* **2.** to come into contact or union with: *The brook joins the river.* **3.** to bring together in a particular relation or for a specific purpose, action, etc.; unite: *to join forces against the smugglers.* **4.** to become a member of (an organization, party, etc.): *to join a club.* **5.** to enlist in (one of the armed forces): *to join the Navy.* **6.** to come into the company of; meet or accompany: *I'll join you later.* **7.** to participate with (someone) in some act or activity: *My wife joins me in thanking you for the gift.* **8.** to unite in marriage. **9.** to meet or engage in (battle, conflict, etc.): *The opposing armies joined battle.* **10.** to adjoin; meet: *His land joins mine.* **11.** to draw a curve or straight line between: *to join two points on a graph.* **—*v.i.* 12.** to come into or be in contact or connection: *a place where cliffs and sea join.* **13.** to become united, associated, or combined; associate or ally oneself; participate (usually fol. by *with*): *Please join with us in our campaign.* **14.** to take part with others (often fol. by *in*): *Let's all join in.* **15.** to be contiguous or close; lie or come together; form a junction: *Our farms join along the river.* **16.** to enlist in one of the armed forces (often fol. by *up*): *He joined up to fight for his country.* **17.** to meet in battle or conflict. **—*n.* 18.** a joining. **19.** a place or line of joining; seam. **20.** *Math.* union (def. 10a). [1250–1300; ME *joinen* < OF *joign-* (s. of *joindre* to join) < L *jungere* to YOKE, join] **—join′a•ble,** *adj.*
—Syn. 1. link, couple, fasten, attach; conjoin, combine; associate, consolidate, amalgamate. JOIN, CONNECT, UNITE all imply bringing two or more things together more or less closely. JOIN may refer to a connection or association of any degree of closeness, but often implies direct contact: *One joins the corners of a mortise together.* CONNECT implies a joining as by a tie, link, or wire: *One connects two batteries.* UNITE implies a close joining of two or more things, so as to form one: *One unites layers of veneer sheets to form plywood.* **10.** abut, border. **—Ant. 1, 12.** separate, divide.

join•der (join′dər), *n.* **1.** the act of joining. **2.** *Law.* **a.** the joining of causes of action in a suit. **b.** the joining of parties in a suit. **c.** the acceptance by a party to an action of an issue tendered. [1595–1605; < F *joindre.* See JOIN, -ER[3]]

join•er (joi′nər), *n.* **1.** a person or thing that joins. **2.** a carpenter, esp. one who constructs doors, window sashes, paneling, and other permanent woodwork. **3.** a person who belongs to many clubs, associations, societies, etc., often from indiscriminate enthusiasm, for increased status, to make business or social contacts, or the like. [1350–1400; JOIN + -ER[1]; r. ME *joinour* < AF *joignour,* equiv. to *joign-* (see JOIN) + *-our* -OR[2]]

join′er door′, *Shipbuilding.* a door of wood or light metal set in a nonwatertight bulkhead.

join•er•y (joi′nə rē), *n.* **1.** the craft or trade of a joiner. **2.** woodwork made by a joiner. [1670–80; JOINER + -Y[3]]

joint (joint), *n.* **1.** the place at which two things, or separate parts of one thing, are joined or united, either rigidly or in such a way as to permit motion; juncture. **2.** a connection between pieces of wood, metal, or the like, often reinforced with nails, screws, or glue. **3.** *Anat., Zool.* **a.** the movable or fixed place or part where two bones or elements of a skeleton join. **b.** the form or structure of such a part, as a ball-and-socket, hinge, pivot, etc. **4.** one of the large portions into which a section of meat is divided by a butcher, as the shoulder or leg, esp. as served at table. **5.** *Slang.* a marijuana cigarette. **6.** *Slang.* **a.** a dirty, cheap, or disreputable place of public accommodation or entertainment, esp. a restaurant or nightclub. **b.** a place or establishment, as a hotel, restaurant, etc.: *We stayed in a very classy joint near the ocean.* **7.** *Biol.* **a.** a part, esp. of a plant, insect, etc., connected with another part by an articulation, node, or the like. **b.** a portion between two articulations, nodes, or the like. **8.** *Bot.* the part of a stem from which a branch or leaf grows; node. **9.** *Geol.* a fracture plane in rocks, generally at right angles to the bedding of sedimentary rocks and variously oriented in igneous and metamorphic rocks, commonly arranged in two or more sets of parallel intersecting systems. **10.** *Math.* knot (def. 12). **11. the joint,** *Slang.* prison: *He got out of the joint just before Christmas.* **12.** *Slang* (*vulgar*). penis. **13. out of joint, a.** dislocated, as a bone. **b.** in an unfavorable state; inauspicious: *The time is out of joint.* **c.** out of keeping; inappropriate: *Such behavior seems wholly out of joint with their fine upbringing.* **—*adj.* 14.** shared by or common to two or more: *a joint obligation.* **15.** undertaken or produced by two or more in conjunction or in common: *a joint reply; a joint effort.* **16.** sharing or acting in common: *joint members of a committee.* **17.** joined or associated, as in relation, interest, or action: *joint owners.* **18.** *Law.* joined together in obligation or ownership: *joint heirs.* **19.** of or pertaining to both branches of a bicameral legislature. **20.** pertaining to or noting diplomatic action in which two or more governments are formally united. **—*v.t.* 21.** to unite by a joint or joints. **22.** to form or provide with a joint or joints. **23.** to cut (a fowl, piece of meat, etc.) at the joint; divide at a joint; separate into pieces at the joints: *to joint a chicken.* **24.** *Carpentry.* **a.** to prepare (a board or the like) for fitting in a joint. **b.** to true the bottom of (a wooden plane body) to allow even movement along the surface of the work. **25.** to file the teeth of (a saw) to uniform height. **26.** *Masonry.* to finish (a mortar joint), as by striking. **—*v.i.* 27.** to fit together by or as if by joints: *The cinder blocks jointed neatly.* [1250–1300; 1900–05 for def. 6; ME < OF *joint, jointe* < L *junctum, juncta,* neut. and fem. of *junctus* (ptp. of *jungere* to join), equiv. to *jung-* JOIN + *-tus* ptp. suffix]
—Syn. 15. united, combined, collaborative.

joint′ account′, a bank account in the names of two or more persons or parties and subject to withdrawals by each.

joint′ and last′ survi′vor annu′ity, *Insurance.* an annuity payable until the death of the last of two or more designated persons, though sometimes with reduced amounts after the first such person dies.

joint′ bar′, one of a pair of bars used to join two rails longitudinally.

Joint′ Chiefs′ of Staff′, *U.S. Mil.* the Chiefs of Staff of the Army and the Air Force, the commandant of the Marine Corps, and the Chief of Naval Operations, together with a chairman selected from one of the branches of the armed forces, serving as the principal military advisory body to the President, the National Security Council, and the Secretary of Defense. Also called **Joint′ Chiefs′.**

joint′ commit′tee, *Govt.* a committee appointed from both houses of a bicameral legislature in order to reach a compromise on their differences concerning a particular issue. [1770–80, *Amer.*]

joint′ cus′tody, custody, as of a child whose parents are separated, in which two or more people share responsibility. Cf. **sole custody.** [1975–80]

joint•ed (join′tid), *adj.* **1.** having or provided with joints. **2.** formed with knots or nodes. [1375–1425; late ME; see JOINT, -ED[3]] **—joint′ed•ly,** *adv.* **—joint′ed•ness,** *n.*

joint•er (join′tər), *n.* **1.** a person or thing that joints. **2.** a tool or machine used in making joints. **3.** *Agric.* a device with a triangular head, used with a plow to bury trash. **4.** *Law Obs.* a man who holds a jointure. [1645–55; JOINT + -ER[1]]

joint′er plane′, *Carpentry.* a plane for truing the edges of boards, planing large surfaces, etc. [1815–25]

joint′ fam′ily, a type of extended family composed of parents, their children, and the children's spouses and offspring in one household. Also called **joint′ house′hold.** [1875–80]

joint′ ill′, *Vet. Pathol.* an infectious disease of newborn foals characterized by swollen inflamed joints and high fever, usually fatal. Also called **navel ill.** [1890–95]

joint′ is′sue, *Philately.* one of two or more stamps that are issued jointly by two governments to commemorate an event of common historical interest.

joint•less (joint′lis), *adj.* **1.** without a joint; lacking a joint. **2.** formed as a single piece, without jointing. [1550–60; JOINT + -LESS]

joint′ life′ annu′ity, *Insurance.* an annuity, the payments of which cease at the death of the first of two or more specified persons.

joint′ life′ insur′ance, life insurance covering two or more persons, the benefits of which are paid after the first person dies.

joint•ly (joint′lē), *adv.* together; in combination or partnership; in common: *My brother and I own the farm jointly.* [1300–50; ME; see JOINT, -LY]

joint′ resolu′tion, a resolution adopted by both branches of a bicameral legislative assembly and requiring the signature of the chief executive to become law. [1830–40, *Amer.*]

joint•ress (join′tris), *n. Law.* a woman on whom a jointure has been settled. [1595–1605; JOINT(E)R + -ESS]
—Usage. See **-ess.**

joint′ return′, a U.S. income-tax return reporting the combined income of a married couple.

joint′ run′ner, (in plumbing) incombustible materials for packing a joint to be caulked with lead.

joint′ ses′sion, a joint meeting, as of both houses of a bicameral legislature: *The president addressed a joint session of Congress on the crisis in Central America.* [1860–65, *Amer.*]

joint′ stock′, **1.** stock or capital divided into a number of shares. **2.** a pool of stock held in common. [1605–15]

joint′-stock′ com′pany (joint′stok′), **1.** an association of individuals in a business enterprise with transferable shares of stock, much like a corporation except that stockholders are liable for the debts of the business. **2.** *Brit.* an incorporated business with transferable shares and with shareholders having either limited or unlimited liability for debts of the business. [1800–10]

joint′ stool′, a low wood stool having turned legs with all parts joined by a mortise joint. [1400–50; late ME]

joint′ ten′ancy, *Law.* a holding of property, either real or personal, by two or more persons with each sharing the undivided interest, the entire tenancy passing to the survivor or survivors. Cf. **tenancy in common.**

joint′ ten′ant, *Law.* one of two or more persons who hold property in joint tenancy. Cf. **tenant in common.**

join•ture (join′chər), *n. Law.* **1.** an estate or property settled on a woman in consideration of marriage, to be owned by her after her husband's death. **2.** *Obs.* a joint tenancy limited in favor of a husband and wife. [1325–75; ME < OF < L *junctūra*, equiv. to *junct-* (see JOINT) + *-ūra* -URE] —**join′tured,** *adj.* —**join′ture•less,** *adj.*

joint′ ven′ture, a business enterprise in which two or more companies enter a temporary partnership. *Abbr.:* JV, J.V. —**joint′ ven′turer.** —**joint′ ven′turing.**

joint-ven•ture (joint′ven′chər), *v.*, **-tured, -tur•ing.** *Informal.* —*v.i.* **1.** to establish or enter a joint venture or partnership. —*v.t.* **2.** to establish or run as a joint venture.

joint•worm (joint′wûrm′), *n.* the larva of any of several chalcid flies of the family Eurytomidae, esp. of the genus *Harmolita*, that feeds within the stems of grasses, often causing a gall near the first joint. Also called **strawworm.** [1700–10; JOINT + WORM]

Join•vi•le (zhoiɴ vē′li), *n.* a seaport in S Brazil. 88,647. Also, **Joinville.**

Join•ville (*Fr.* zhwaɴ vēl′ *for 1; Port.* zhoiɴ vē′li *for 2*), *n.* **1. Jean de** (zhäɴ də), 1224?–1317, French chronicler. **2.** Joinvile.

joist (joist), *n.* **1.** any of a number of small, parallel beams of timber, steel, reinforced concrete, etc., for supporting floors, ceilings, or the like. —*v.t.* **2.** to furnish with or fix on joists. [1325–75; ME *giste* < OF < L **jacitum* support, n. use of neut. of L *jacitus* (ptp. of *jacēre* to lie), equiv. to *jaci-* var. s. + *-tus* ptp. suffix] —**joist′less,** *adj.*

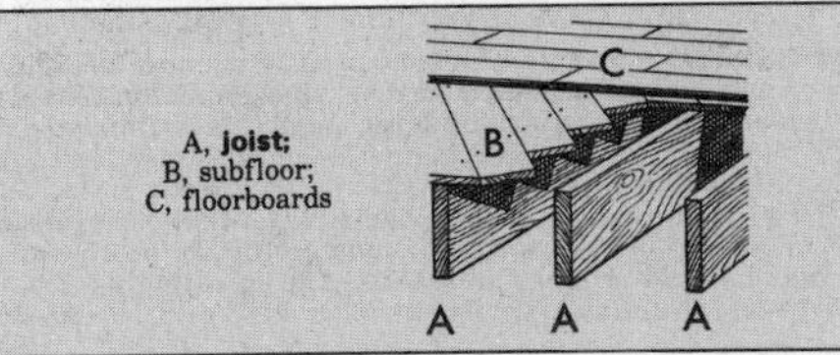

A, **joist;** B, subfloor; C, floorboards

jo•jo•ba (hō hō′bə), *n.* a shrub, *Simmondsia chinensis* (or *S. californica*), of the southwestern U.S. and Mexico, bearing seeds that are the source of an oil **(jojo′ba oil′)** used in cosmetics and as a lubricant. [1920–25; < MexSp]

Jó•kai (yô′koi), *n.* **Mau•rus** (mou′ro͝os) or **Mór** (môr), 1825–1904, Hungarian novelist.

joke (jōk), *n., v.,* **joked, jok•ing.** —*n.* **1.** something said or done to provoke laughter or cause amusement, as a witticism, a short and amusing anecdote, or a prankish act: *He tells very funny jokes. She played a joke on him.* **2.** something that is amusing or ridiculous, esp. because of being ludicrously inadequate or a sham; a thing, situation, or person laughed at rather than taken seriously; farce: *Their pretense of generosity is a joke. An officer with no ability to command is a joke.* **3.** a matter that need not be taken very seriously; trifling matter: *The loss was no joke.* **4.** something that does not present the expected challenge; something very easy: *The test was a joke for the whole class.* **5.** See **practical joke.** —*v.i.* **6.** to speak or act in a playful or merry way: *He was always joking with us.* **7.** to say something in fun or teasing rather than in earnest; be facetious: *He didn't really mean it, he was only joking.* —*v.t.* **8.** to subject to jokes; make fun of; tease. **9.** to obtain by joking: *The comedian joked coins from the audience.* [1660–70; < L *jocus* jest] —**joke′less,** *adj.* —**jok′ing•ly,** *adv.*
—**Syn. 1.** wisecrack, gag, jape, prank, quip, quirk, sally, raillery. JOKE, JEST refer to something said (or done) in sport, or to cause amusement. A JOKE is something said or done for the sake of exciting laughter; it may be raillery, a witty remark, or a prank or trick: *to tell a joke.* JEST, today a more formal word, nearly always refers to joking language and is more suggestive of scoffing or ridicule than is JOKE: *to speak in jest.*

joke•book (jōk′bo͝ok′), *n.* a book of jokes. [1950–55; JOKE + BOOK]

jok•er (jō′kər), *n.* **1.** a person who jokes. **2.** one of two extra playing cards in a pack, usually imprinted with the figure of a jester, used in some games as the highest card or as a wild card. **3.** *U.S. Politics.* a clause or expression inserted in a legislative bill with the unavowed object of defeating the ostensible purpose of the bill if passed. **4.** a seemingly minor, unsuspected clause or wording that is put into an agreement, legal document, etc., to change its effect. **5.** an unexpected or final fact, factor, or condition that changes or reverses a situation or result completely: *He gave her a beautiful diamond engagement ring, but the joker was that it was stolen!* **6.** any method, trick, or expedient for getting the better of another: *They pulled a joker on us to get better seats.* **7.** *Informal.* a man; fellow; chap: *That joker is earning twice as much as I am.* **8.** a person who thinks he or she is very funny; prankster: *Who's the joker who frosted the cake with shaving cream?* **9.** *Informal.* a wise guy; wiseacre; smart aleck: *Tell that joker to stop using my parking space.* [1720–30; JOKE + -ER[1]]

joke•ster (jōk′stər), *n.* a joker, esp. a practical joker. [1875–80; JOKE + -STER]

jok•ey (jō′kē), *adj.,* **jok•i•er, jok•i•est.** lacking in seriousness; frivolous: *The editorial had an offensively jokey tone for such an important subject.* [1815–25; JOKE + -EY[1]] —**jok′i•ly,** *adv.* —**jok′i•ness,** *n.*

Jok•ja•kar•ta (jok′jə kär′tə, jōk′-), *n.* Jogjakarta.

jok•ta•leg (jok′tə leg′), *n. Brit. Dial.* jockteleg.

jok•y (jō′kē), *adj.,* **jok•i•er, jok•i•est.** jokey. [JOKE + -Y[1]]

jole (jōl), *n.* jowl[2].

Jo•li•et (jō′lē et′; *for 1 also Fr.* zhô lye′), *n.* **1. Louis** (lwē), 1645–1700, French explorer of the Mississippi, born in Canada. **2.** a city in NE Illinois. 77,956.

Jo•liette (*Fr.* zhô lyet′), *n.* a city in S Quebec, in E Canada. 16,987.

Jo•liot-Cu•rie (zhô lyō′kʏ rē′), *n.* **1. I•rène** (ē ren′), (*Irène Curie*), 1897–1956, French nuclear physicist: Nobel prize for chemistry 1935 (daughter of Pierre and Marie Curie). **2.** her husband, **(Jean) Fré•dé•ric** (zhäɴ frā dā rēk′), (*Jean Frédéric Joliot*), 1900–58, French nuclear physicist: Nobel prize for chemistry 1935.

Jo•li•vet (zhô lē ve′), *n.* **An•dré** (äɴ drā′), 1905–74, French composer.

jol•li•er (jol′ē ər), *n.* a person who jollies, esp. a person who uses teasing flattery in order to gain a desired aim. [1895–1900, *Amer.*; JOLLY + -ER[1]]

jol•li•fi•ca•tion (jol′ə fi kā′shən), *n.* jolly merrymaking; jolly festivity. [1800–10; JOLLY + -FICATION]

jol•li•fy (jol′ə fī′), *v.t., v.i.,* **-fied, -fy•ing.** to make or become jolly or merry. [1815–25; JOLLY + -FY]

jol•li•ty (jol′i tē), *n., pl.* **-ties. 1.** jolly or merry mood, condition, or activity; gaiety. **2. jollities,** jolly festivities. [1250–1300; ME *jolite* < OF, equiv. to *joli(f)* gay (see JOLLY) + *-te* -TY[2]]
—**Syn. 1.** See **mirth.**

jol•ly (jol′ē), *adj.,* **-li•er, -li•est,** *v.,* **-lied, -ly•ing,** *n., pl.* **-lies,** *adv.* —*adj.* **1.** in good spirits; gay; merry: *In a moment he was as jolly as ever.* **2.** cheerfully festive or convivial: *a jolly party.* **3.** joyous; happy: *Christmas is a jolly season.* **4.** *Chiefly Brit. Informal.* delightful; charming. **5.** *Brit.* **a.** *Informal.* great; thorough: *a jolly blunderer.* **b.** *Slang.* slightly drunk; tipsy. —*v.t.* **6.** *Informal.* to talk or act agreeably to (a person) in order to keep that person in good humor, esp. in the hope of gaining something (usually followed by *along*): *They jollied him along until the job was done.* —*v.i.* **7.** *Informal.* to jolly a person; josh; kid. —*n.* **8.** *Informal.* the practice or an instance of jollying a person. **9.** Usually, **jollies.** *Informal.* pleasurable excitement, esp. from or as if from something forbidden or improper; thrills; kicks: *He gets his jollies from watching horror movies.* —*adv.* **10.** *Brit. Informal.* extremely; very: *He'll jolly well do as he's told.* [1275–1325; ME *joli, jolif* < OF, equiv. to *jol-* (prob. < ON *jōl* YULE) + *-if* -IVE] —**jol′li•ly,** *adv.* —**jol′li•ness,** *n.*
—**Syn. 1–3.** glad, spirited, jovial, sportive, playful. See **gay.** —**Ant. 1–3.** gloomy, melancholy.

Jol′ly bal′ance (jol′ē, yol′ē), a spring balance used for determining the density of a sample by comparison of its weight in air and water. [named after Philipp von *Jolly* (d. 1884), German physicist]

jol′ly boat′, **1.** a light boat carried at the stern of a sailing vessel. **2.** a small pleasure sailboat for use in sheltered waters. [1720–30; *jolly* < Dan *jolle* YAWL]

jol′ly jump′er, *Naut.* any light sail set above a skysail; flying kite. [1880–85]

Jol′ly Rog′er (roj′ər), a flag flown by pirates, having the device of a white skull and crossbones on a black field. [1775–85]

Jolly Roger

Jo•lo (hô lô′), *n.* **1.** an island in the SW Philippines: the main island of the Sulu Archipelago. 237,683; 345 sq. mi. (894 sq. km). **2.** a seaport on this island. 52,429.

Jol•son (jōl′sən), *n.* **Al** (*Asa Yoelson*), 1886–1950, U.S. singer and entertainer, born in Russia.

jolt (jōlt), *v.t.* **1.** to jar, shake, or cause to move by or as if by a sudden rough thrust; shake up roughly: *The bus jolted its passengers as it went down the rocky road.* **2.** to knock sharply so as to dislodge: *He jolted the nail free with a stone.* **3.** to stun with a blow, esp. in boxing. **4.** to shock emotionally or psychologically: *His sudden death jolted us all.* **5.** to bring to a desired state sharply or abruptly: *to jolt a person into awareness.* **6.** to make active or alert, as by using an abrupt, sharp, or rough manner: *to jolt someone's memory.* **7.** to interfere with or intrude upon, esp. in a rough or crude manner; interrupt disturbingly. —*v.i.* **8.** to move with a sharp jerk or a series of sharp jerks: *The car jolted to a halt.* —*n.* **9.** a jolting shock, movement, or blow: *The automobile gave a sudden jolt.* **10.** an emotional or psychological shock: *The news of his arrest gave me quite a jolt.* **11.** something that causes such a shock: *The news was a jolt to me.* **12.** a sudden, unexpected rejection or defeat: *Their policy got a rude jolt from the widespread opposition.* **13.** *Slang.* a prison sentence. **14.** *Slang.* an injection of a narcotic. **15.** a bracing dose of something: *a jolt of whiskey; a jolt of fresh air.* [1590–1600; b. *jot* to jolt and *joll* to bump, both now dial.] —**jolt′er,** *n.* —**jolt′ing•ly,** *adv.* —**jolt′less,** *adj.*

jolt•y (jōl′tē), *adj.,* **jolt•i•er, jolt•i•est.** full of jolts; bumpy. [1825–35; JOLT + -Y[1]] —**jolt′i•ness,** *n.*

Jo•mon (jô′môn), *adj.* of or pertaining to the period of Japanese culture, c8000–300 B.C., corresponding to Mesolithic or early Neolithic, characterized by sunken-pit dwellings and heavy handmade pottery formed with a rope pattern of clay coils. [< Japn *jōmon* rope-pattern]

Jon (jon), *n.* a male given name, form of **John.**

Jo•nah (jō′nə), *n.* **1.** a Minor Prophet who, for his impiety, was thrown overboard from his ship and swallowed by a large fish, remaining in its belly for three days before being cast up onto the shore unharmed. **2.** a book of the Bible bearing his name. **3.** any person or thing regarded as bringing bad luck. **4.** Also, **Jo•nas** (jō′nəs). a male given name: from a Hebrew word meaning "dove." —**Jo′nah•esque′,** *adj.*

Jo′nah crab′, a large, red, deepwater crab, *Cancer borealis*, of the east coast of North America. [1880–85, *Amer.*]

Jon•a•than (jon′ə thən), *n.* **1.** a son of Saul and friend of David. I Sam. 18–20. **2.** *Archaic.* an American, esp. a New Englander. Cf. **Brother Jonathan. 3.** a male given name: from a Hebrew word meaning "God gave."

Jon•a•than (jon′ə thən), *n.* a variety of red apple that matures in early autumn. [1875–80; named after *Jonathan* Hasbrouck (d. 1846), American jurist]

Jon′athan spot′, *Plant Pathol.* a disease of stored apples, esp. the Jonathan, characterized by circular lesions on the fruit.

jones (jōnz), *n.* (*sometimes cap.*) *Slang.* **1.** heroin. **2.** an addiction, esp. to heroin. [1965–70; orig. uncert.]

Jones (jōnz), *n.* **1. An•son** (an′sən), 1798–1858, president of the Republic of Texas. **2. Ca•sey** (kā′sē), (*John Luther Jones*), 1864–1900, U.S. locomotive engineer: folk hero of ballads, stories, and plays. **3. Daniel,** 1881–1967, English phonetician. **4. Ernest,** 1879–1958, Welsh psychoanalyst. **5. (Everett) Le•Roi** (lə roi′, lē′roi), original name of Imamu Amiri Baraka. **6. Henry Arthur,** 1851–1929, English dramatist. **7. Howard Mum•ford** (mum′fərd), 1892–1980, U.S. educator and critic. **8. In•i•go** (in′i gō′), 1573–1652, English architect. **9. John Paul** (*John Paul*), 1747–92, American naval commander in the Revolutionary War, born in Scotland. **10. John Win•ston** (win′stən), 1791–1848, U.S. politician: Speaker of the House 1843–45. **11. Mary Harris** ("*Mother Jones*"), 1830–1930, U.S. labor leader, born in Ireland. **12. Robert Edmond,** 1887–1954, U.S. set designer. **13. Robert Tyre** (tīᵊr), ("*Bobby*"), 1902–71, U.S. golfer. **14. Rufus Matthew,** 1863–1948, U.S. Quaker, teacher, author, and humanitarian. **15. Sir William,** 1746–94, English jurist, linguist, and Sanskrit scholar.

Jones•bor•o (jōnz′bûr ō, -bur ō), *n.* **1.** a city in NE Arkansas. 31,530. **2.** a town in NE Tennessee: oldest town in Tennessee. 2829.

Jones•es (jōn′ziz), *n.pl.* one's neighbors, friends, business associates, etc.: *Keeping up with the Joneses has put him in debt.* [1925–30]

Jones•town (jōnz′toun′), *n.* a former settlement in N Guyana, NW of Georgetown: site of agricultural commune of an American religious cult called the People's Temple; mass suicide and murder 1978.

jon•gleur (jong′glər; *Fr.* zhôɴ glœr′), *n., pl.* **-gleurs** (-glərz; *Fr.* -glœr′). (in medieval France and Norman England) an itinerant minstrel or entertainer who sang songs, often of his own composition, and told stories. Cf. **goliard.** [1755–65; < F; MF *jougleur* (perh. by misreading, *ou* being read *on*), OF *jogleor* < L *joculātor* joker, equiv. to *joculā(rī)* to JOKE + *-tor* -TOR]

Jon′ker di′amond (jong′kər), a noted diamond weighing 726 carats, discovered in the Transvaal in 1934 and cut into 12 pieces.

Jön•kö•ping (yœn′chœ ping), *n.* a city in S Sweden. 107,561.

jon•nick (jon′ik), *adj. Brit., Australian Informal.* jannock.

Jon•quière (*Fr.* zhôɴ kyer′), *n.* a city in S Quebec, in E Canada. 60,354.

jon•quil (jong′kwil, jon′-), *n.* a narcissus, *Narcissus jonquilla*, having long, narrow, rushlike leaves and fragrant, yellow or white flowers. [1620–30; < F *jonquille* < Sp *junquillo*, equiv. to *junc(o)* rush, reed (< L *juncus*) + *-illo* dim. suffix]

Jon•son (jon′sən), *n.* **Ben,** 1573?–1637, English dramatist and poet. —**Jon•so•ni•an** (jon sō′nē ən), *adj.*

jook[1] (jo͝ok, jo͞ok), *n. Slang.* See **juke joint.** Also called **jook′ joint′.**

jook[2] (jo͝ok), *n., v.t., v.i. Scot.* jouk.

Jooss (yōs), *n.* **Kurt** (ko͝ort), 1901–79, German ballet dancer and choreographer.

Jop•lin (jop′lin), *n.* **1. Scott,** 1868–1917, U.S. ragtime pianist and composer. **2.** a city in SW Missouri. 38,893.

Jop•pa (jop′ə), *n.* ancient name of **Jaffa.**

CONCISE PRONUNCIATION KEY: act, cāpe, dâre, pärt; set, ēqual; *if,* ice; ox, ōver, ôrder, oil, bo͝ok, bo͞ot, out; up, ûrge; child; sing; shoe; thin, *that;* zh as in *treasure.* ə = *a* as in *alone*, *e* as in *system*, *i* as in *easily*, *o* as in *gallop*, *u* as in *circus*; ᵊ as in *fire* (fīᵊr), *hour* (ouᵊr). l and n can serve as syllabic consonants, as in *cradle* (krād′l), and *button* (but′n). See the full key inside the front cover.

Jor·daens (yôʀ′däns), *n.* **Ja·cob** (yä′kôp), 1593–1678, Flemish painter.

jor·dan (jôr′dn), *n. Brit. Dial.* See **chamber pot.** [1350–1400; ME *jurdan* urinal, perh. after JORDAN, the river, by coarse jesting]

Jor·dan (jôr′dn; *for 2 also Fr.* zhôʀ däɴ′), *n.* **1. David Starr** (stär), 1851–1931, U.S. biologist and educator. **2. Ma·rie En·ne·mond Ca·mille** (ma ʀē′ enᵊ mônʹ ka-mē′yᵊ), 1838–1922, French mathematician. **3.** Official name, **Hashemite Kingdom of Jordan.** a kingdom in SW Asia, consisting of the former Transjordan and a part of Palestine that, since 1967, has been occupied by Israel. 2,751,968; 37,264 sq. mi. (96,514 sq. km). *Cap.:* Amman. **4.** a river in SW Asia, flowing from S Lebanon through the Sea of Galilee, then S between Israel and Jordan through W Jordan into the Dead Sea. 200 mi. (320 km) long. **5.** a male given name. —**Jor·da·ni·an** (jôr dā′nē ən), *n., adj.*

Jor′dan al′mond, **1.** a large, hard-shelled, Spanish almond used esp. in confectionery. **2.** an almond with a hard, colored coating of sugar. [1400–50; alter. of late ME *jardyne almaund* garden almond; see JARDINIERE]

Jor′dan arc′, *Math.* See **simple arc.** [named after M. E. C. JORDAN]

Jor′dan curve′, *Math.* See **simple closed curve.** [1895–1900; named after M. E. C. JORDAN]

Jor′dan curve′ the′orem, *Math.* the theorem that the complement of a simple closed curve can be expressed as the union of two disjoint sets, each having as boundary the given curve. Cf. **simple closed curve.** [1915–20; named after M. E. C. JORDAN]

Jor′dan en′gine, a machine for beating and refining pulp, used in manufacturing certain grades of paper. [named after Joseph *Jordan,* American inventor, who developed it]

Jor′dan-Höl′der the′orem (jôr′dn hel′dər), *Math.* the theorem that for any two composition series of a group, an isomorphism exists between the corresponding quotient groups of each series, taken in some specified order. [after M.E.C. JORDAN and German mathematician Ludwig Otto *Hölder* (1859–1937)]

Jor·mun·gand (yôr′mo͝on gänd′), *n. Scand. Myth.* See **Midgard serpent.** [< ON *Jǫrmungandr,* equiv. to *jǫrmun-* mighty, great + *gandr* wand, magical staff, magic]

Jor·mun·rek (yôr′mo͝on rek′), *n. Scand. Myth.* (in the *Poetic Edda* and the *Volsunga Saga*) king of the Goths, murderer of Svanhild, the daughter of Sigurd: killed by the Gjukungs; probably identical with Ermanaric (4th century A.D.), the Ostrogothic leader. [< ON *Jǫrmunrek,* equiv. to *jǫrmun-* great + *-rek(r),* earlier *-rikr* (cf. *rikr* powerful, RICH); c. OE *Eormenric*]

jor·na·da (hôr nä′də; *Sp.* hôr nä′thä), *n., pl.* **-das** (-dəz; *Sp.* -thäs). *Southwestern U.S.* a full day's travel across a desert without a stop for taking on water. [1650–60; < Sp < OPr < VL **diurnāta;* see JOURNEY]

jo·ro·po (hə rō′pō; *Sp.* hô ʀô′pô), *n., pl.* **-pos** (-pōz; *Sp.* -pôs). a Venezuelan ballroom dance in quick triple meter. [< AmerSp]

jo·rum (jôr′əm, jōr′-), *n.* **1.** a large bowl or container for holding drink. **2.** the contents of such a container: *a jorum of punch.* **3.** a great quantity. [1720–30; said to be named after *Joram,* who brought silver, gold, and brass bowls to David (2 Samuel 8:10)]

Jos (jôs), *n.* a city in central Nigeria. 105,000.

Jos·e·lyn (jos′ə lin, jos′lin), *n.* a female given name.

Jo·sep (jō′zəp, -səp), *n.* a male given name, form of **Joseph.**

Jo·seph (jō′zəf, -səf), *n.* **1.** Jacob's eleventh son, the first of Jacob and his second wife, Rachel: sold into slavery by his brothers. Gen. 30:22–24; 37. **2.** the husband of Mary who was the mother of Jesus. Matt. 1:16–25. **3.** (*Hinmaton-yalaktit*), c1840–1904, leader of the Nez Percé: led 1000-mi. (1600-km) retreat from U.S. forces in an attempt to reach Canada 1877. **4.** (*l.c.*) a long coat buttoning in the front, worn esp. by women as part of their riding habit in colonial America. **5.** a male given name: from a Hebrew word meaning "increaser."

Joseph I, 1678–1711, king of Hungary 1687–1711; king of Germany 1690–1711; emperor of the Holy Roman Empire 1705–11 (son of Leopold I).

Joseph II, 1741–90, emperor of the Holy Roman Empire 1765–90 (son of Francis I; brother of Leopold II and Marie Antoinette).

Jo·se·phine (jō′zə fēn′, -sə-), *n.* **1. Empress** (*Marie Joséphine Rose Tascher de la Pagerie*). See **Beauharnais, Joséphine de. 2.** a female given name: derived from *Joseph.*

CONCISE ETYMOLOGY KEY: <, descended or borrowed from; >, whence; b., blend of, blended; c., cognate with; cf., compare; deriv., derivative; equiv., equivalent; imit., imitative; obl., oblique; r., replacing; s., stem; sp., spelling, spelled; resp., respelling, respelled; trans., translation; ?, origin unknown; *, unattested; ‡, probably earlier than. See the full key inside the front cover.

Jo′seph of Ar·i·ma·thae′a (ar′ə mə thē′ə), a member of the Sanhedrin who placed the body of Jesus in the tomb. Matt. 27:57–60; Mark 15:43.

Jo·seph's-coat (jō′zəfs kōt′, -səfs-), *n.* a cultivated form of *Amaranthus tricolor,* having headlike clusters of small flowers and blotched and colored leaves. Cf. **tampala.** [1865–70, *Amer.*; named after JOSEPH (def. 1) and his coat of many colors]

Jo·seph·son (jō′zəf sən, -səf-), *n.* **Brian David,** born 1940, British physicist: Nobel prize 1973.

Jo′seph·son junc′tion (jō′zəf sən, -səf-), *Electronics.* a high-speed switch, used in experimental computers, that operates on the basis of a radiative phenomenon (**Jo′sephson effect′**) exhibited by a pair of superconductors separated by a thin insulator. [1965–70; after B. D. JOSEPHSON, who predicted the existence of the effect]

Jo·se·phus (jō sē′fəs), *n.* **Fla·vi·us** (flā′vē əs), (*Joseph ben Matthias*), A.D. 37?–c100, Jewish historian and general.

josh (josh), *v.t., v.i.* **1.** to chaff; banter in a teasing way. —*n.* **2.** good-natured banter. [1835–45, *Amer.*; of obscure orig.] —**josh′er,** *n.*

Josh (josh), *n.* a male given name, form of **Joshua.**

Josh., Joshua.

Josh·u·a (josh′o͞o ə), *n.* **1.** the successor of Moses as leader of the Israelites. Deut. 31:14, 23; 34:9. **2.** a book of the Bible bearing his name. *Abbr.:* Josh. **3.** a male given name: from a Hebrew word meaning "God is salvation."

Josh′ua tree′, an evergreen tree, *Yucca brevifolia,* growing in arid or desert regions of the southwestern U.S., having long, twisted branches. Also called **tree yucca.** [1895–1900]

Jo·si·ah (jō sī′ə), *n.* **1.** Also, *Douay Bible,* **Jo·si·as** (jō-sī′əs). a king of Judah, reigned 640?–609? B.C. II Kings 22. **2.** a male given name. [<< Heb *Yōshīyāh* God upholds]

Jo·sie (jō′zē, -sē), *n.* a female given name, form of **Josephine.**

jos·kin (jos′kin), *n. Chiefly Brit. Slang.* a bumpkin. [1805–15; perh. b. BUMPKIN and dial. *joss* to jostle, bump]

Jos·quin des Prés (zhus′kan də prā′; *Fr.* zhôs kaɴ dā prā′). See **Des Prés, Josquin.**

joss[1] (jos), *n.* a Chinese house idol or cult image. [1705–15; < Chin Pidgin E < Pg *deos* < L *deus* god]

joss[2] (jos), *n. Brit., Australian Informal.* a foreman or boss. [1855–60; orig. uncert.]

jos·ser (jos′ər), *n. Brit. Slang.* fellow, esp. one who is or is made to appear foolish or simpleminded. [1885–90; orig. uncert.]

joss′ house′, a Chinese temple for idol worship. [1765–75]

joss′ stick′, a slender stick of a dried, fragrant paste, burned by the Chinese as incense before a joss. [1880–85]

jos·tle (jos′əl), *v.,* **-tled, -tling,** *n.* —*v.t.* **1.** to bump, push, shove, brush against, or elbow roughly or rudely. **2.** to drive or force by, or as if by, pushing or shoving: *The crowd jostled him into the subway.* **3.** to exist in close contact or proximity with: *The three families jostle each other in the small house.* **4.** to contend with: *rival gangs continually jostling each other.* **5.** to unsettle; disturb: *The thought jostled her complacency.* **6.** *Slang.* to pick the pocket of. —*v.i.* **7.** to bump or brush against someone or something, as in passing or in a crowd; push or shove (often fol. by *with, for,* or *against*): *He jostled for position.* **8.** to exist in close contact or proximity with someone or something. **9.** to compete; contend. **10.** *Slang.* to pick pockets. —*n.* **11.** a shock, push, bump, or brush against someone or something. Also, **justle.** [1350–1400; var. (in ME, var. sp.) of *justle,* equiv. to *just(en)* to JOUST + -LE] —**jos′tle·ment,** *n.* —**jos′tler,** *n.*

Jos·u·e (jos′yo͞o ē), *n. Douay Bible.* Joshua (defs. 1, 2).

jot (jot), *v.,* **jot·ted, jot·ting,** *n.* —*v.t.* **1.** to write or mark down quickly or briefly (usually fol. by *down*): *Jot down his license number.* —*n.* **2.** the least part of something; a little bit: *I don't care a jot.* **3. not a jot or tittle,** not a bit; not at all: *The world situation matters not a jot or tittle to him.* [1520–30; earlier *iot, iote* < L *iōta* < Gk *iôta* IOTA]

jo·ta (hō′tə; *Sp.* hô′tä), *n., pl.* **-tas** (-təz; *Sp.* -täs). **1.** a Spanish dance in triple meter, performed by a couple and marked by complex rhythms executed with the heels and castanets. **2.** the music for this dance. [1840–50; < Sp, prob. OSp *sota* dance, deriv. of *sotar* to dance < L *saltāre*]

jot·ter (jot′ər), *n.* **1.** a person who jots things down. **2.** a small notebook. [1880–85; JOT + -ER[1]]

jot·ting (jot′ing), *n.* **1.** the act of a person who jots. **2.** a quickly written or brief note; memorandum. [1800–10; JOT + -ING[1]] —**jot′ty,** *adj.*

Jo·tun (yô′to͝on), *n. Scand. Myth.* any of a race of giants frequently in conflict with the gods. Also, **Jo′tunn, Jö·tunn** (yœ′to͝on). [1835–45; < ON *jǫtunn* giant; c. OE *ēoten;* akin to EAT]

Jo·tun·heim (yô′to͝on hām′), *n. Scand. Myth.* the outer world, or realm of giants; Utgard. Also, **Jo′tunn·heim′, Jö·tun·heim, Jö·tunn·heim** (yœ′to͝on hām′). [< ON, equiv. to *jǫtunn* giant + *heimr* world, HOME]

jou·al (zho͞o al′, -äl′), *n.* any of the nonstandard dialects of Canadian French, characterized by deviations from the standard phonology, morphology, syntax, and vocabulary, and often containing many borrowings from English. [1960–65; repr. a non-standard pron. of F *cheval* horse]

Jou·bert (zho͞o beʀ′), *n.* **Jo·seph** (zhô zef′), 1754–1824, French moralist and essayist.

Jou·haux (zho͞o ō′), *n.* **Lé·on** (lā ôɴ′), 1879–1954, French labor leader and politician: Nobel peace prize 1951.

jouk (jo͞ok), *Scot.* *n.* **1.** a sudden, elusive movement. —*v.t., v.i.* **2.** to dodge or duck. Also, **jook.** [1510–20; appar. var. of DUCK[2]]

Jou·ka·hai·nen (yō′kə hī′nen), *n. Finnish Legend.* a Lapp magician who tried to kill Väinämöinen.

joule (jo͞ol, joul), *n. Physics.* the SI unit of work or energy, equal to the work done by a force of one newton when its point of application moves through a distance of one meter in the direction of the force: equivalent to 10^7 ergs and one watt-second. *Abbr.:* J, j Also called **newton-meter.** [1885–90; named after J. P. JOULE]

Joule (jo͞ol, joul), *n.* **James Prescott,** 1818–89, English physicist.

Joule′ effect′, *Physics.* the generation of heat by the passage of electricity through a resistance. [1875–80; named after J. P. JOULE]

Joule's′ law′, *Physics.* **1.** the principle that the rate of production of heat by a constant direct current is directly proportional to the resistance of the circuit and to the square of the current. **2.** the principle that the internal energy of a given mass of an ideal gas is solely a function of its temperature. [1850–55; named after J. P. JOULE]

Joule′-Thom′son effect′ (jo͞ol′tom′sən, joul′-), *Thermodynam.* the change of temperature that a gas exhibits during a throttling process, shown by passing the gas through a small aperture or porous plug into a region of low pressure. Cf. **free expansion.** [1895–1900; named after J. P. JOULE and Sir W. THOMSON]

jounce (jouns), *v.,* **jounced, jounc·ing,** *n.* —*v.t., v.i.* **1.** to move joltingly or roughly up and down; bounce. —*n.* **2.** a jouncing movement. [1400–50; late ME; appar. b. *joll* to bump (now obs.) and BOUNCE]

jour., 1. journal. **2.** journeyman.

Jour·dan (zho͞oʀ däɴ′), *n.* **Jean Bap·tiste** (zhäɴ ba-tēst′), **Count,** 1762–1833, French marshal.

journ., journalism.

jour·nal (jûr′nl), *n.* **1.** a daily record, as of occurrences, experiences, or observations: *She kept a journal during her European trip.* **2.** a newspaper, esp. a daily one. **3.** a periodical or magazine, esp. one published for a special group, learned society, or profession: *the October issue of* The English Journal. **4.** a record, usually daily, of the proceedings and transactions of a legislative body, an organization, etc. **5.** *Bookkeeping.* **a.** a daybook. **b.** (in the double-entry method) a book into which all transactions are entered from the daybook or blotter to facilitate posting into the ledger. **6.** *Naut.* a log or logbook. **7.** *Mach.* the portion of a shaft or axle contained by a plain bearing. [1325–75; ME < OF *journal* daily (adj. and n.) < LL *diurnālis* DIURNAL] —**jour′nal·ar′y,** *adj.* —**jour′nal·ish,** *adj.*

jour′nal box′, *Mach.* a box or housing for a journal and its bearing. [1870–75]

jour′nal bronze′, an alloy of about 83 percent copper, 13 percent tin, 3 percent zinc, and 1 percent lead.

jour·nal·ese (jûr′nl ēz′, -ēs′), *n.* **1.** a manner of writing or speaking characterized by clichés, occasional neologism, archness, sensationalizing adjectives, unusual or faulty syntax, etc., used by some journalists, esp. certain columnists, and regarded as typical journalistic style. **2.** writing or expression in this manner: *Get that journalese out of your copy!* —*adj.* **3.** of, pertaining to, or characterized by this manner (often used predicatively): *That word's not English, it's journalese.* [1880–85; JOURNAL + -ESE]

jour·nal in·time (zho͞oʀ na laɴ tēm′), *pl.* ***jour·naux in·times*** (zho͞oʀ nō zaɴ tēm′). *French.* a personal or private diary.

jour·nal·ism (jûr′nl iz′əm), *n.* **1.** the occupation of reporting, writing, editing, photographing, or broadcasting news or of conducting any news organization as a business. **2.** press[1] (def. 32). **3.** a course of study preparing students for careers in reporting, writing, and editing for newspapers and magazines. **4.** writing that reflects superficial thought and research, a popular slant, and hurried composition, conceived of as exemplifying topical newspaper or popular magazine writing as distinguished from scholarly writing: *He calls himself a historian, but his books are mere journalism.* [1825–35; < F *journalisme.* See JOURNAL, -ISM]

jour·nal·ist (jûr′nl ist), *n.* **1.** a person who practices the occupation or profession of journalism. **2.** a person who keeps a journal, diary, or other record of daily events. [1685–95; JOURNAL + -IST]

jour·nal·is·tic (jûr′nl is′tik), *adj.* of, pertaining to, or characteristic of journalists or journalism. [1825–35; JOURNALIST + -IC] —**jour′nal·is′ti·cal·ly,** *adv.*

jour·nal·ize (jûr′nl īz′), *v.,* **-ized, -iz·ing.** —*v.t.* **1.** to tell or relate as one would in keeping a journal. **2.** to enter or record in a journal. **3.** (in double-entry bookkeeping) to enter in a journal, preparatory to posting to the ledger. —*v.i.* **4.** to keep or make entries in a journal. Also, *esp. Brit.,* **jour′nal·ise′.** [1760–70; JOURNAL + -IZE] —**jour′nal·i·za′tion,** *n.* —**jour′nal·iz′er,** *n.*

jour·ney (jûr′nē), *n., pl.* **-neys,** *v.,* **-neyed, -ney·ing.** —*n.* **1.** a traveling from one place to another, usually taking a rather long time; trip: *a six-day journey across the desert.* **2.** a distance, course, or area traveled or suitable for traveling: *a desert journey.* **3.** a period of travel: *a week's journey.* **4.** passage or progress from one stage to another: *the journey to success.* —*v.i.* **5.** to make a journey; travel. [1175–1225; ME *journee* day < OF < VL **diurnāta* a day's time, day's work, etc., equiv. to L *diurn(us)* daily + *-āta,* fem. of *-ātus* -ATE[1]; see -ADE[1]] —**jour′ney·er,** *n.*
—**Syn. 1.** excursion, jaunt, tour. See **trip. 5.** roam, rove; peregrinate.

jour·ney·man (jûr′nē mən), *n., pl.* **-men. 1.** a person who has served an apprenticeship at a trade or handicraft and is certified to work at it assisting or under another person. **2.** any experienced, competent but routine worker or performer. **3.** a person hired to do work for another, usually for a day at a time. [1425–75; late ME *journeman,* equiv. to *journee* a day's work (see JOURNEY) + *man* MAN[1]]

jour•ney•work (jûr′nē wûrk′), *n.* **1.** the work of a journeyman. **2.** necessary, routine, or servile work. [1595–1605; JOURNEY a day's work (obs.) + WORK]

joust (joust, just, jōōst), *n.* **1.** a combat in which two knights on horseback attempted to unhorse each other with blunted lances. **2.** this type of combat fought in a highly formalized manner as part of a tournament. **3. jousts,** tournament. **4.** a personal competition or struggle. —*v.i.* **5.** to contend in a joust or tournament. **6.** to contend, compete, or struggle: *The candidates will joust in a television debate.* Also, **just.** [1250–1300; (v.) ME *justen, jousten* < OF *juster, joster, jouster* to tilt in the lists < VL **juxtāre* to approach, clash, deriv. of L *juxtā* approaching, bordering; (n.) ME *juste, jouste* < OF *juste,* etc., deriv. of *juster*] —**joust′er,** *n.*

Jouve (zhōōv), *n.* **Pierre Jean** (pyeʀ zhäɴ), 1887–1976, French writer.

Jouy′ print′ (zhwē). See **toile de Jouy.**

Jove (jōv), *n.* **1.** Jupiter (def. 1). **2.** *Archaic.* the planet Jupiter. **3. by Jove!** (an exclamation used to emphasize an accompanying remark or to express surprise, approval, etc.): *It was a good fight, by Jove!* [1325–75; ME < L *Jov-* (obl. s. of compound nom. *Juppiter* FATHER Jove), akin. to *deus* god; c. Gk *Zeús* (gen. *Diós*) Zeus]

jo•vi•al (jō′vē əl), *adj.* **1.** endowed with or characterized by a hearty, joyous humor or a spirit of good-fellowship: *a wonderfully jovial host.* **2.** (*cap.*) of or pertaining to the god Jove, or Jupiter. [1580–90; < ML *joviālis* of Jupiter (the planet, supposed to exert a happy influence), equiv. to L *jovi-* (see JOVIAN) + *-ālis* -AL[1]] —**jo′vi•al•ly,** *adv.* —**jo′vi•al•ness,** *n.*
—**Syn. 1.** merry, jolly, convivial, gay, joyful, mirthful. JOVIAL, JOCOSE, JOCULAR, JOCUND agree in referring to someone who is in a good humor. JOVIAL suggests a hearty, joyous humor: *a jovial person.* JOCOSE refers to that which causes laughter; it suggests someone who is playful and given to jesting: *with jocose and comical airs.* JOCULAR means humorous, facetious, mirthful, and waggish: *jocular enough to keep up the spirits of all around him.* JOCUND, now a literary word, suggests a cheerful, light-hearted, and sprightly gaiety: *glad and jocund company.* —**Ant. 1.** gloomy.

jo•vi•al•i•ty (jō′vē al′i tē), *n.* the state or quality of being jovial; merriment; jollity. [1620–30; JOVIAL + -ITY; cf. F *jovialité*]
—**Syn.** See **mirth.**

Jo•vi•an (jō′vē ən), *adj.* **1.** of or pertaining to the Roman god Jupiter. **2.** of or pertaining to the planet Jupiter. [1520–30; < L *Jov-* (see JOVE) + -IAN] —**Jo′vi•an•ly,** *adv.*

Jo•vi•an (jō′vē ən), *n.* (*Flavius Claudius Jovianus*) A.D. 331?–364, Roman emperor 363–364.

Jo′vian plan′et, *Astron.* any of the four large outer planets: Jupiter, Saturn, Uranus, and Neptune.

jow (jou, jō), *Scot.* —*n.* **1.** the ringing, tolling, or sound of a bell. —*v.t.* **2.** to ring or toll (a bell). **3.** to hit or strike (esp. the head). —*v.i.* **4.** to rock from side to side. [1510–20; var. of *joll* (now dial.), ME *jollen* to strike < ?]

Jow•ett (jou′it), *n.* **Benjamin,** 1817–93, English educator and Greek scholar.

jowl[1] (joul, jōl), *n.* **1.** a jaw, esp. the lower jaw. **2.** the cheek. [bef. 1000; ME *chawl, chavell,* OE *ceafl* jaw; c. D *kevel,* G *Kiefer,* ON *kjaptr*] —**jowled,** *adj.*

jowl[2] (joul, jōl), *n.* **1.** a fold of flesh hanging from the jaw, as of a very fat person. **2.** the meat of the cheek of a hog. **3.** the dewlap of cattle. **4.** the wattle of fowls. Also, **jole.** [1275–1325; ME *cholle,* OE *ceole* throat; c. G *Kehle* throat]

jowl•y (jou′lē, jō′-), *adj.,* **jowl•i•er, jowl•i•est.** having prominent jowls. [1870–75; JOWL[1] + -Y[1]]

joy (joi), *n.* **1.** the emotion of great delight or happiness caused by something exceptionally good or satisfying; keen pleasure; elation: *She felt the joy of seeing her son's success.* **2.** a source or cause of keen pleasure or delight; something or someone greatly valued or appreciated: *Her prose style is a pure joy.* **3.** the expression or display of glad feeling; festive gaiety. **4.** a state of happiness or felicity. —*v.i.* **5.** to feel joy; be glad; rejoice. —*v.t.* **6.** *Obs.* to gladden. [1175–1225; ME *joy(e)* < OF *joie, joye* < LL *gaudia,* neut. pl. (taken as fem. sing.) of L *gaudium* joy, equiv. to *gaud-* (base of *gaudēre* to be glad) + *-ium* -IUM]
—**Syn. 1.** rapture. **4.** bliss. See **pleasure.** —**Ant. 1.** misery, unhappiness, sorrow, grief.

Joy (joi), *n.* a female given name. Also, **Joye.**

joy•ance (joi′əns), *n. Archaic.* joyous feeling; gladness. [1580–90; JOY + -ANCE (coined by Spenser)]

joy′ buzz′er, a device used for a practical joke with a handshake, concealed in the palm of the hand and producing a buzzing sound and an unpleasant vibrating sensation when it is pressed against the victim's hand.

Joyce (jois), *n.* **1. James (Augustine Aloysius),** 1882–1941, Irish novelist. **2. William** (*"Lord Haw-Haw"*), 1906–46, U.S. and English Nazi propagandist in Germany. **3.** a female or male given name: from a French word meaning "joy."

Joyc•e•an (joi′sē ən), *adj.* **1.** of, pertaining to, or characteristic of James Joyce or his work. —*n.* **2.** a student of the life and work of James Joyce. **3.** a person who favors or advocates the work, style, or methods of James Joyce. **4.** an imitator of James Joyce. [1925–30; JOYCE + -AN]

joy•ful (joi′fəl), *adj.* **1.** full of joy, as a person or one's heart; glad; delighted. **2.** showing or expressing joy, as looks, actions, or speech. **3.** causing or bringing joy, as an event, a sight, or news; delightful: *the joyful announcement of their marriage.* [1250–1300; ME; see JOY, -FUL] —**joy′ful•ly,** *adv.* —**joy′ful•ness,** *n.*
—**Syn. 1.** joyous, happy, blithe; buoyant, elated, jubilant. See **gay.** —**Ant. 1.** melancholy.

joy•less (joi′lis), *adj.* **1.** without joy or gladness; unhappy: *the joyless days of the war.* **2.** causing no joy or pleasure. [1300–50; ME *joyles.* See JOY, -LESS] —**joy′less•ly,** *adv.* —**joy′less•ness,** *n.*
—**Syn. 1.** sad, cheerless, gloomy, dismal, miserable. —**Ant. 1.** joyous.

joy•ous (joi′əs), *adj.* joyful; happy; jubilant: *the joyous sounds of children at play.* [1275–1325; ME < AF; OF *joios.* See JOY, -OUS] —**joy′ous•ly,** *adv.* —**joy′ous•ness,** *n.*

joy•pop (joi′pop′), *v.i.,* **-popped, -pop•ping.** *Slang.* to take a narcotic drug occasionally, but without being an addict. [1950–55, *Amer.*; JOY + POP[1]] —**joy′pop′per,** *n.*

joy•ride (joi′rīd′), *n., v.,* **-rode, -rid•den, -rid•ing.** —*n.* **1.** a pleasure ride in an automobile, esp. when the vehicle is driven recklessly or used without the owner's permission. **2.** a brief, emotionally exciting interlude. —*v.i.* **3.** to go on a joyride. [1905–10, *Amer.*; JOY + RIDE] —**joy′rid′er,** *n.*

joy•stick (joi′stik′), *n.* **1.** *Informal.* the control stick of an airplane, tank, or other vehicle. **2.** *Computers.* a lever resembling this, used to control movement of a cursor or other graphic element for video games and computer graphics. **3.** any leverlike switch for controlling, manipulating, guiding, or the like. Also, **joy′ stick′.** [1905–10; JOY + STICK[1]]

JP, 1. jet propulsion. **2.** Justice of the Peace.

J.P., Justice of the Peace. Also, **j.p.**

J particle, *Physics.* an early name for the J/psi particle. [1970–75; named by S.C.C. Ting, allegedly from the resemblance of the letter *J* to the Chinese character for *Ting*]

Jpn., 1. Japan. **2.** Japanese. Also, **Jpn**

J/psi particle, (jā′sī′, -psī′), *Physics.* the lightest of the psi particles, the first particle to be discovered that contains a charmed quark. [1975–80; see J PARTICLE, PSI PARTICLE]

Jr., 1. Journal. **2.** Junior.

jr., junior.

JRC, Junior Red Cross.

J.S.D., Doctor of the Science of Law; Doctor of Juristic Science.

J-stroke (jā′strōk′), *n.* (in canoeing) a stroke, made in the shape of the letter *J,* used to alter the course of the canoe, usually to compensate for drifting sideways.

Ju (ʀōō, zhōō), *n.* **1.** Confucian (def. 2). **2.** one of the tutors of aristocratic origin working during the Chou dynasty.

Ju., June.

Juan (wän; *Sp.* hwän), *n.* a male given name, Spanish form of **John.**

Jua•na (wä′nə; *Sp.* hwä′nä), *n.* a female given name.

Jua•na Dí•az (wä′nə dē′äs; *Sp.* hwä′nä thē′äs), a city in S Puerto Rico, NE of Ponce. 10,469.

Juan Car•los I (hwän kär′lôs), **King** (*Juan Carlos Alfonso Victor María de Borbón y Borbón*), born 1938, Spanish monarch, born in Italy: king since 1975.

Juan de Fu•ca (wän′ di fyōō′kə, fōō′-, jōō′ən), a strait between Vancouver Island and NW Washington. 100 mi. (160 km) long; 15–20 mi. (24–32 km) wide. Also called **Juan′ de Fu′ca Strait′.**

Juan de la Cruz (*Sp.* hwän′ de lä kʀōōth′, kʀōōs′), **San** (sän). See **John of the Cross, Saint.**

Juan Fer•nán•dez (wän fər nan′dez, jōō′ən; *Sp.* hwän′ feʀ nän′des), a group of three islands in the S Pacific, 400 mi. (645 km) W of and belonging to Chile: Alexander Selkirk, the alleged prototype of Robinson Crusoe, was marooned here 1704.

Jua•ni•ta (wä nē′tə; *Sp.* hwä nē′tä), *n.* a female given name.

Juá•rez (wär′ez; *Sp.* hwä′ʀes), *n.* **1. Be•ni•to (Pa•blo)** (be nē′tô pä′vlô), 1806–72, president of Mexico 1857–72. **2. Ciudad.** See **Ciudad Juárez.**

ju•ba (jōō′bə), *n.* a lively dance accompanied by rhythmic hand clapping, developed by plantation slaves of the U.S. [1825–35, *Amer.*; of obscure orig.]

Ju•ba (jōō′bä), *n.* **1.** a river in E Africa, flowing S from S Ethiopia through Somalia to the Indian Ocean. 1000 mi. (1609 km) long. Italian, **Giuba. 2.** a city in S Sudan, on the White Nile. 44,000.

Ju•ba (jōō′bä), *n.* a female day name for Monday. See under **day name.**

Ju•bal (jōō′bəl), *n.* son of Lamech and Adah: the progenitor of musicians and those who produce musical instruments. Gen. 4:21.

ju•bate (jōō′bāt), *adj. Zool.* covered with long hairs resembling a mane. [1820–30; < NL *jubātus* maned, equiv. to L *jub(a)* mane + *-ātus* -ATE[1]]

jub•bah (jŏŏb′ə), *n.* a long outer garment with long sleeves, worn in Muslim countries. [1540–50; < Ar]

Jub•bul•pore (jub′əl pôr′, -pōr′, -pŏŏr′), *n.* Jabalpur.

ju•be (jōō′bē, yōō′bā), *n. Archit.* **1.** a screen with an upper platform, separating the choir of a church from the nave and often supporting a rood. **2.** a rood loft. [1715–25; < L *jubē,* first word of prayer beginning *Jubē, Domine, benedicere* consent, O Lord, to bless; said at or near this screen]

ju•bi•lant (jōō′bə lənt), *adj.* showing great joy, satisfaction, or triumph; rejoicing; exultant: *the cheers of the jubilant victors; the jubilant climax of his symphony.* [1660–70; < L *jūbilant-* (s. of *jūbilāns,* prp. of *jūbilāre* to shout, whoop), equiv. to *jūbil-* shout + *-ant-* -ANT] —**ju′bi•lance, ju′bi•lan•cy,** *n.* —**ju′bi•lant•ly,** *adv.*

ju•bi•lar•i•an (jōō′bə lâr′ē ən), *n.* a person who celebrates or has celebrated a jubilee, as a nun observing 25 or more years of religious life. [1775–85; < ML *jūbilāri(us)* (equiv. to *jūbil-* (see JUBILEE) + *-ārius* -ARY) + -AN]

ju•bi•late (jōō′bə lāt′), *v.i.,* **-lat•ed, -lat•ing. 1.** to show or feel great joy; rejoice; exult. **2.** to celebrate a jubilee or joyful occasion. [1595–1605; < L *jūbilātus* (ptp. of *jūbilāre* to shout for joy), equiv. to *jūbil-* shout + *-ātus* -ATE[1]] —**ju•bi•la•to•ry** (jōō′bə lə tôr′ē, -tōr′ē), *adj.*

Ju•bi•la•te (jōō′bə lä′tē; yōō′bə lä′tā, -tē, jōō′-), *n.* **1.** Also called **Ju′bila′te Sun′day.** the third Sunday after Easter: so called from the first word of the 65th Psalm in the Vulgate, which is used as the introit. **2.** a musical setting of this psalm. [1700–10; < L *jūbilāte* shout ye for joy]

ju•bi•la•ti•o (jōō′bə lä′shē ō′, yōō′bə lä′-), *n.* jubilus. [< L: JUBILATION]

ju•bi•la•tion (jōō′bə lā′shən), *n.* **1.** a feeling of or the expression of joy or exultation: *Their jubilation subsided when they lost the second game.* **2.** a joyful or festive celebration. [1350–1400; ME *jubilacioun* (< AF) < L *jūbilātiōn-* (s. of *jūbilātiō*) a shouting for joy, equiv. to *jūbilāt-* (see JUBILATE) + *-iōn-* -ION]

ju•bi•lee (jōō′bə lē′, jōō′bə lē′), *n.* **1.** the celebration of any of certain anniversaries, as the twenty-fifth **(silver jubilee),** fiftieth **(golden jubilee),** or sixtieth or seventy-fifth **(diamond jubilee). 2.** the completion of 50 years of existence, activity, or the like, or its celebration: *Our college will celebrate its jubilee next year.* **3.** any season or occasion of rejoicing or festivity. **4.** rejoicing or jubilation. **5.** *Rom. Cath. Ch.* **a.** an appointed year or other period, ordinarily every 25 years **(ordinary jubilee),** in which a plenary indulgence is granted upon repentance and the performance of certain religious acts. **b.** a period of time **(extraordinary jubilee)** declared by the pope as a time of rejoicing, as for an anniversary, when a plenary indulgence is granted upon repentance and the performance of certain religious acts. **c.** Also called **ju′bilee indul′gence.** the plenary indulgence granted during such a period. **6.** Also, **Ju′bi•le′.** *Chiefly Biblical.* a yearlong period to be observed by Jews once every 50 years, during which Jewish slaves were to be freed, alienated lands were to be restored to the original owner or an heir, the fields were to be left untilled, and all agricultural labors were to be suspended. Lev. 25. Cf. **sabbatical year** (def. 2). **7.** a black American folk song concerned with future happiness or deliverance from tribulation. —*adj.* **8.** flambé (def. 1): *cherries jubilee for dessert.* [1350–1400; ME < MF *jubile* < LL < *jūbilaeus* < LGk *iōbēlaios* (with *ō* and *ē* > *u* and *i* by assimilation to L *jūbilāre* to shout for joy) < Heb *yōbhēl* ram's horn, jubilee]

ju′bilee year′, jubilee (def. 5a). [1350–1400; ME]

ju•bi•lus (jōō′bə ləs), *n., pl.* **-li** (-lī′). *Liturgy.* (in Roman Catholic music) a rejoicing, melodic group of tones to which is chanted the last *"a"* of the second and third alleluias, often following the gradual of the Mass. Also, **jubilatio.** [< ML: shout of joy, L *jūbilum* a wild cry, shepherd's song; see JUBILATE]

Jud., 1. Judges. **2.** Judith (Apocrypha).

jud., 1. judge. **2.** judgment. **3.** judicial. **4.** judiciary.

Ju•dae•a (jōō dē′ə), *n.* Judea. —**Ju•dae′an,** *adj., n.*

Judaeo-, var. of **Judeo-.**

Ju•dae•o-Chris•tian (jōō dā′ō kris′chən, -dē′-), *adj.* Judeo-Christian.

Ju•dah (jōō′də), *n.* **1.** the fourth son of Jacob and Leah. Gen. 29:35. **2.** one of the 12 tribes of Israel traditionally descended from him. **3.** the Biblical kingdom of the Hebrews in S Palestine, including the tribes of Judah and Benjamin. Cf. **Ephraim** (def. 3). **4.** a male given name: from a Hebrew word meaning "praised." Also, *Douay Bible,* **Ju′da** (for defs. 1–3).

Ju′dah ha-Le′vi (hä lē′vī, -lā′vē), (*Judah ben Samuel Halevi*) 1085–1140, Spanish rabbi, physician, poet, and philosopher. Also, **Ju′dah Ha•le′vi.**

Ju′dah ha-Na•si′ (hä nä sē′), A.D. c135–c210, Jewish rabbi and scholar. Also, **Ju′dah Ha•na•si′.** Also called **Judah I.**

Ju•dah•ite (jōō′də īt′), *n.* **1.** a member of the tribe of Judah or of the kingdom of Judah. —*adj.* **2.** of or pertaining to the tribe or kingdom of Judah. [1895–1900; JUDAH + -ITE[1]]

Ju•da•ic (jōō dā′ik), *adj.* **1.** of or pertaining to Judaism: *the Judaic idea of justice.* **2.** of or pertaining to the Jews; Jewish. Also, **Ju•da′i•cal.** [1605–15; < L *jūdaicus* < Gk *ioudaikós,* equiv. to *Ioudaî(os)* JEW + *-ikos* -IC] —**Ju•da′i•cal•ly,** *adv.*

Ju•da•i•ca (jōō dā′i kə), *n.pl.* things pertaining to Jewish life and customs, esp. when of a historical, literary, or artistic nature, as books or ritual objects. [1920–25; < L, n. use of neut. pl. of *jūdaicus* JUDAIC]

Ju•da•ism (jōō′dē iz′əm, -dā-, -də-), *n.* **1.** the monotheistic religion of the Jews, having its ethical, ceremonial, and legal foundation in the precepts of the Old Testament and in the teachings and commentaries of the rabbis as found chiefly in the Talmud. Cf. **Conservative Jew, Orthodox Jew, Reform Jew. 2.** belief in and conformity to this religion, its practices, and ceremonies. **3.** this religion considered as forming the basis of the cultural and social identity of the Jews: *He called assimilation a threat to American Judaism.* **4.** Jews collectively; Jewry. [1485–95; < LL *jūdaismus* < Gk *ioudaismós,* equiv. to *Ioudaî(os)* JEW + *-ismos* -ISM]

Ju•da•ist (jōō′dē ist, -dā-, -də-, jōō dā′-), *n.* **1.** an adherent or supporter of Judaism. **2.** (in the early Christian church) a convert from Judaism who followed or advocated Jewish rites or practices. [1840–50; JUDA(ISM) + -IST] —**Ju′da•is′tic,** *adj.* —**Ju′da•is′ti•cal•ly,** *adv.*

CONCISE PRONUNCIATION KEY: *act, cāpe, dâre, pärt; set, ēqual; if, īce; ox, ōver, ôrder, oil, bŏŏk, bōōt, out; up, ûrge; child; sing; shoe; thin, t͟hat;* zh as in *treasure.* ə = *a* as in *alone, e* as in *system, i* as in *easily, o* as in *gallop, u* as in *circus;* ə as in *fire* (fīər), *hour* (ouər). l and n can serve as syllabic consonants, as in *cradle* (krād′l), and *button* (but′n). See the full key inside the front cover.

Ju•da•ize (jo͞o′dē īz′, -dā-, -də-), *v.*, **-ized, -iz•ing.** —*v.i.* **1.** to conform to the spirit, character, principles, or practices of Judaism. —*v.t.* **2.** to bring into conformity with Judaism. Also, *esp. Brit.*, **Ju′da•ise′.** [1575–85; < LL *jūdaizāre* < Gk *ioudaḯzein*, equiv. to *Ioudaî(os)* JEW + *-izein* -IZE] —**Ju′da•i•za′tion,** *n.* —**Ju′da•iz′er,** *n.*

Ju•das (jo͞o′dəs), *n.* **1.** Also called **Ju′das Iscar′iot.** the disciple who betrayed Jesus. Mark 3:19. **2.** a person treacherous enough to betray a friend; traitor. **3.** Also called **Saint Judas** or **Saint Jude.** one of the 12 apostles (not Judas Iscariot). Luke 6:16; Acts 1:13; John 14:22. **4.** a brother of James (and possibly of Jesus). Matt. 13:55; Mark 6:3. **5.** (*usually l.c.*) Also called **ju′das hole′.** a peephole, as in an entrance door or the door of a prison cell. —*adj.* **6.** (of an animal) used as a decoy to lead other animals to slaughter: *A Judas goat led sheep into the abattoir.* —**Ju′das•like′,** *adj.*

Ju′das Maccabae′us. See **Maccabaeus, Judas.**

Ju′das Priest′, (an exclamation of exasperation or disgust.) [1910–15; euphemism for *Jesus Christ*]

Ju′das tree′, **1.** a purple-flowered Eurasian tree, *Cercis siliquastrum*, of the legume family, supposed to be the kind upon which Judas hanged himself. **2.** any of various other trees of the same genus, as the redbud. [1660–70]

Judd (jud), *n.* a male given name.

jud•der (jud′ər), *Chiefly Brit.* —*v.i.* **1.** to vibrate violently: *an old automobile with a clutch that judders.* —*n.* **2.** a state or instance of juddering. [1930–35; perh. J(OLT) + (SH)UDDER]

Jude (jo͞od), *n.* **1.** a book of the New Testament. **2.** the author of this book, sometimes identified with Judas, the brother of James. **3.** See **Judas** (def. 3). **4.** a male given name, form of **Judd** or **Judah.**

Ju•de•a (jo͞o dē′ə), *n.* the S region of ancient Palestine: existed under Persian, Greek, and Roman rule; divided between Israel and Jordan in 1948; since 1967 completely occupied by Israel. Also, **Judaea.**

Ju•de•an (jo͞o dē′ən), *adj.* **1.** of or pertaining to Judea. —*n.* **2.** a native or inhabitant of Judea. Also, **Judaean.** [1645–55; JUDE(A) + -AN]

Judeo-, a combining form representing **Judaic** or **Judaism** in compound words: *Judeo-Christian.* Also, **Judaeo-.**

Ju•de•o-Chris•tian (jo͞o dā′ō kris′chən, -dē′-), *adj.* of or pertaining to the religious writings, beliefs, values, or traditions held in common by Judaism and Christianity. Also, **Judaeo-Christian.** [1895–1900]

Ju•de•o-Span•ish (jo͞o dā′ō span′ish, -dē′-), *n.* Ladino (def. 1). [1850–55]

Jude′ the Obscure′, a novel (1895) by Thomas Hardy.

Ju•dez•mo (jo͞o dez′mō), *n.* Ladino (def. 1).

Judg., Judges.

judge (juj), *n.*, *v.*, **judged, judg•ing.** —*n.* **1.** a public officer authorized to hear and decide cases in a court of law; a magistrate charged with the administration of justice. **2.** a person appointed to decide in any competition, contest, or matter at issue; authorized arbiter: *the judges of a beauty contest.* **3.** a person qualified to pass a critical judgment: *a good judge of horses.* **4.** an administrative head of Israel in the period between the death of Joshua and the accession to the throne by Saul. **5.** (esp. in rural areas) a county official with supervisory duties, often employed part-time or on an honorary basis. —*v.t.* **6.** to pass legal judgment on; pass sentence on (a person): *The court judged him guilty.* **7.** to hear evidence or legal arguments in (a case) in order to pass judgment; adjudicate; try: *The Supreme Court is judging that case.* **8.** to form a judgment or opinion of; decide upon critically: *You can't judge a book by its cover.* **9.** to decide or settle authoritatively; adjudge: *The censor judged the book obscene and forbade its sale.* **10.** to infer, think, or hold as an opinion; conclude about or assess: *He judged her to be correct.* **11.** to make a careful guess about; estimate: *We judged the distance to be about four miles.* **12.** (of the ancient Hebrew judges) to govern. —*v.i.* **13.** to act as a judge; pass judgment: *No one would judge between us.* **14.** to form an opinion or estimate: *I have heard the evidence and will judge accordingly.* **15.** to make a mental judgment. [1175–1225; (v.) ME *jugen* < AF *juger*, OF *jugier* < L *jūdicāre* to judge, equiv. to *jūdic-* (s. of *jūdex*) a judge + *-āre* inf. suffix; (n.) ME *juge* < OF < L *jūdicem*, acc. of *jūdex*] —**judge′a•ble,** *adj.* —**judg′er,** *n.* —**judge′less,** *adj.* —**judge′like′,** *adj.* —**judge′ship,** *n.* —**judg′ing•ly,** *adv.*

—**Syn. 1.** justice. **2.** arbitrator. JUDGE, REFEREE, UMPIRE refer to one who is entrusted with decisions affecting others. JUDGE, in its legal and other uses, implies particularly that one has qualifications and authority for giving decisions in matters at issue: *a judge appointed to the Supreme Court; a judge in the pie competition.* A REFEREE usually examines and reports on the merits of a case as an aid to a court. An UMPIRE gives the final ruling when arbitrators of a case disagree. **3.** connoisseur, critic. **10.** determine, consider, regard. **13.** adjudge, adjudicate.

judge′ ad′vocate, *pl.* **judge advocates.** *Mil.* a staff officer designated as legal adviser to a commander and charged with the administration of military justice. [1740–50]

judge′ ad′vocate gen′eral, *pl.* **judge advocates general, judge advocate generals.** *Mil.* the chief legal officer of an army, navy, or air force. [1860–65]

Judge′ Lynch′, the personification of lynch law. [1830–40, *Amer.*]

CONCISE ETYMOLOGY KEY: <, descended or borrowed from; >, whence; b., blend of, blended; c., cognate with; cf., compare; deriv., derivative; equiv., equivalent; imit., imitative; obl., oblique; r., replacing; s., stem; sp., spelling, spelled; resp., respelling, respelled; trans., translation; ?, origin unknown; *, unattested; ‡, probably earlier than. See the full key inside the front cover.

judge-made (juj′mād′), *adj.* established by a court, as by an application or interpretation of a law that is allegedly contrary to the intentions of the enacting body or by a decision that does not rest on legislation.

Judg•es (juj′iz), *n.* (*used with a singular v.*) a book of the Bible containing the history of Israel under the judges and covering the period between the death of Joshua and the accession to the throne by Saul. *Abbr.:* Jud.

judg•mat•ic (juj mat′ik), *adj.* judicious. Also, **judg•mat′i•cal.** [1820–30; JUDG(MENT) + (DOG)MATIC] —**judg•mat′i•cal•ly,** *adv.*

judg•ment (juj′mənt), *n.* **1.** an act or instance of judging. **2.** the ability to judge, make a decision, or form an opinion objectively, authoritatively, and wisely, esp. in matters affecting action; good sense; discretion: *a man of sound judgment.* **3.** the demonstration or exercise of such ability or capacity: *The major was decorated for the judgment he showed under fire.* **4.** the forming of an opinion, estimate, notion, or conclusion, as from circumstances presented to the mind: *Our judgment as to the cause of his failure must rest on the evidence.* **5.** the opinion formed: *He regretted his hasty judgment.* **6.** *Law.* **a.** a judicial decision given by a judge or court. **b.** the obligation, esp. a debt, arising from a judicial decision. **c.** the certificate embodying such a decision and issued against the obligor, esp. a debtor. **7.** a misfortune regarded as inflicted by divine sentence, as for sin. **8.** (*usually cap.*) Also called **Last Judgment, Final Judgment.** the final trial of all people, both the living and dead, at the end of the world. Also, *esp. Brit.*, **judge′•ment.** [1250–1300; ME *jug(g)ement* < OF *jugement*, equiv. to *juge-* (s. of *jugier* to JUDGE) + *-ment* -MENT]

—**Syn. 1.** determination. **2.** discrimination, discernment, perspicacity; sagacity, wisdom, intelligence, prudence. **6a.** verdict, decree.

judg•men•tal (juj men′tl), *adj.* **1.** involving the use or exercise of judgment. **2.** tending to make moral judgments: *to avoid a judgmental approach in dealing with divorced couples.* [1905–10; JUDGMENT + -AL[1]]

Judg′ment Book′, *Theol.* the book from which all persons will be judged at the Last Judgment, containing a full record of their acts.

judg′ment call′, **1.** *Sports.* an observational ruling by a referee or umpire that is necessarily subjective because of the disputable nature of the play in question, and one that may be appealed but not protested, as opposed to a matter of official rule interpretation: *Balks and close plays at first are of course judgment calls, and umpires are human.* **2.** any subjective or debatable determination; personal opinion or interpretation. [1840–50]

Judg′ment Day′, the day of the Last Judgment; doomsday. [1585–95]

judg′ment debt′, *Law.* a debt established or confirmed by decree of a court of law. [1830–40]

judg′ment note′, *Law.* a note that expressly authorizes a creditor, in case of default, to seek a judgment in court without notifying the debtor.

Judg′ment of Par′is, *Class. Myth.* the decision by Paris to award Aphrodite the golden apple of discord competed for by Aphrodite, Athena, and Hera.

ju•di•ca•ble (jo͞o′di kə bəl), *adj.* capable of being or liable to be judged or tried. [1640–50; < LL *jūdicābilis*, equiv. to *jūdic(āre)* to JUDGE + *-ābilis* -ABLE]

ju•di•care (jo͞o′di kâr′), *n.* (*often cap.*) a federally funded program providing free or low-cost legal services to the poor. [1965–70; JUDI(CIAL) + CARE, on the model of MEDICARE]

ju•di•ca•tive (jo͞o′di kā′tiv), *adj.* having ability to judge; judging: *the judicative faculty.* [1635–45; < ML *jūdicātīvus*, equiv. to L *jūdic-* (see JUDGE) + *-ātīvus* -ATIVE]

ju•di•ca•tor (jo͞o′di kā′tər), *n.* a person who acts as judge or sits in judgment. [1750–60; < LL, equiv. to L *judicā(re)* to JUDGE + *-tor* -TOR] —**ju•di•ca•to•ri•al** (jo͞o′di kə tôr′ē əl, -tōr′-), *adj.*

ju•di•ca•to•ry (jo͞o′di kə tôr′ē, -tōr′ē), *adj., n., pl.* **-to•ries.** —*adj.* **1.** of or pertaining to judgment or the administration of justice; judiciary: *judicatory power.* —*n.* **2.** a court of law and justice; tribunal; judiciary. **3.** the administration of justice. [1565–75; (n.) < ML *jūdicātōrium* law court, equiv. to *jūdicā(re)* to JUDGE + *-tōrium* -TORY[2]; (adj.) < LL *jūdicātōrius*, equiv. to *jūdicā(re)* + *-tōrius* -TORY[1]]

ju•di•ca•ture (jo͞o′di kā′chər, -kə cho͝or′), *n.* **1.** the administration of justice, as by judges or courts. **2.** the office, function, or authority of a judge. **3.** the jurisdiction of a judge or court. **4.** a body of judges. **5.** the power of administering justice by legal trial and determination. [1520–30; < ML *jūdicātūra*, equiv. to L *jūdic-* (see JUDGE) + *-āt(us)* -ATE[1] + *-ūra* -URE]

ju•di•ci•a•ble (jo͞o dish′ē ə bəl), *adj. Archaic.* judicable. [< L *jūdici(um)* judgment (see JUDGE, -IUM) + -ABLE]

ju•di•cial (jo͞o dish′əl), *adj.* **1.** pertaining to judgment in courts of justice or to the administration of justice: *judicial proceedings; the judicial system.* **2.** pertaining to courts of law or to judges; judiciary: *judicial functions.* **3.** of or pertaining to a judge; proper to the character of a judge; judgelike: *judicial gravity.* **4.** inclined to make or give judgments; critical; discriminating: *a judicial mind.* **5.** decreed, sanctioned, or enforced by a court: *a judicial decision.* **6.** giving or seeking judgment, as in a dispute or contest; determinative: *a judicial duel over lands.* **7.** inflicted by God as a judgment or punishment. [1350–1400; ME < L *jūdiciālis* of the law courts, equiv. to *jūdici(um)* judgment (see JUDGE, -IUM) + *-ālis* -AL[1]] —**ju•di′cial•ly,** *adv.* —**ju•di′cial•ness,** *n.*

—**Syn. 1, 2.** juridical. **2.** forensic. **4.** See **judicious.**

judi′cial con′ference, *Law.* a conference of judges held to discuss improvements in methods or judicial procedure through court rules or otherwise.

judi′cial review′, the power of a court to adjudicate the constitutionality of the laws of a government or the acts of a government official. [1920–25]

judi′cial separa′tion, *Law.* a decree of legal separation of husband and wife that does not dissolve the marriage bond. Also called **limited divorce.**

ju•di•ci•ar•y (jo͞o dish′ē er′ē, -dish′ə rē), *n., pl.* **-ar•ies,** *adj.* —*n.* **1.** the judicial branch of government. **2.** the system of courts of justice in a country. **3.** judges collectively. —*adj.* **4.** pertaining to the judicial branch or system or to judges. [1580–90; orig. adj. < L *jūdiciārius* of the law courts, equiv. to *jūdici(um)* judgment (see JUDGE) + *-ārius* -ARY] —**ju•di′ci•ar′i•ly,** *adv.*

ju•di•cious (jo͞o dish′əs), *adj.* **1.** using or showing judgment as to action or practical expediency; discreet, prudent, or politic: *judicious use of one's money.* **2.** having, exercising, or characterized by good or discriminating judgment; wise, sensible, or well-advised: *a judicious selection of documents.* [1590–1600; < L *jūdici(um)* judgment (see JUDGE, -IUM) + -OUS; cf. It *giudizioso*, F *judicieux*] —**ju•di′cious•ly,** *adv.* —**ju•di′cious•ness,** *n.*

—**Syn. 1.** See **practical. 1, 2.** See **moderate. 2.** rational, reasonable, sober, sound, sagacious, enlightened, considered. JUDICIOUS, JUDICIAL both refer to a balanced and wise judgment. JUDICIOUS implies the possession and use of discerning and discriminating judgment: *a judicious use of one's time.* JUDICIAL has connotations of judgments made in a courtroom and refers to a fair and impartial kind of judgment: *cool and judicial in examining the facts.* —**Ant. 1.** imprudent. **2.** silly, unreasonable.

Ju•dith (jo͞o′dith), *n.* **1.** a devoutly religious woman of the ancient Jews who saved her town from conquest by entering the camp of the besieging Assyrian army and cutting off the head of its commander, Holofernes, while he slept. **2.** a book of the Apocrypha and Douay Bible bearing her name. *Abbr.:* Jud. **3.** a female given name. [< < Heb *yəhūdhith* Jew (fem.)]

ju•do (jo͞o′dō), *n.* **1.** a method of defending oneself or fighting without the use of weapons, based on jujitsu but differing from it in banning dangerous throws and blows and stressing the athletic or sport element. **2.** the sport of fighting by this method. Cf. **jujitsu, karate.** —*adj.* **3.** of or pertaining to this fighting method or sport. [1885–90; < Japn *jūdō* < MChin, equiv. to Chin *róu* soft + *dào* way] —**ju′do•ist,** *n.*

ju•do•ka (jo͞o′dō kä′, jo͞o′dō kä′), *n., pl.* **-kas, -ka. 1.** a contestant in a judo match. **2.** a judo expert. [< Japn, equiv. to *jūdō* JUDO + *ka* person (< MChin, equiv. to Chin *jiā*)]

Ju•dy (jo͞o′dē), *n.* **1.** the wife of Punch in the puppet show called *Punch and Judy.* **2.** Also, **Ju′die.** a female given name, form of **Judith.**

jug[1] (jug), *n., v.,* **jugged, jug•ging.** —*n.* **1.** a large container usually made of earthenware, metal, or glass, commonly having a handle, a narrow neck, and sometimes a cap or cork. **2.** the contents of such a container; jugful: *a jug of wine.* **3.** *Slang.* jail; prison. **4.** **jugs,** *Slang* (*vulgar*). a woman's breasts. —*v.t.* **5.** to put into a jug. **6.** to stew (meat) in an earthenware jug. **7.** *Slang.* to put in jail; imprison. [1530–40; perh. special use of *Jug* hypocoristic form of *Joan*, woman's name]

jug[2] (jug), *n., v.,* **jugged, jug•ging.** —*n.* **1.** a sound made by a bird, esp. a nightingale. —*v.i.* **2.** to make such a sound. [1515–25; imit.]

ju•gal (jo͞o′gəl), *adj.* **1.** of or pertaining to the cheek or the cheekbone. **2.** *Entomol.* pertaining to, involving, or situated near the jugum. [1590–1600; < L *jugālis*, equiv. to *jug(um)* YOKE + *-ālis* -AL[1]]

ju′gal bone′, **1.** (in humans) cheekbone (def. 1). **2.** the corresponding bone in other animals. [1760–70]

ju′gal fur′row, (in certain insects) the crease, between the anal and jugal veins, along which the wing folds.

ju•gate (jo͞o′gāt, -git), *adj.* **1.** *Bot.* having the leaflets in pairs, as a pinnate leaf. **2.** *Entomol.* having a jugum. **3.** (of two or more portraits on a coin, medal, or escutcheon) overlapping. [1885–90; < L *jug(um)* YOKE + -ATE[1]]

jug′ band′, a small group of performers who play chiefly blues or folk music on makeshift or very simple instruments, as washboards, harmonicas, kazoos, and empty jugs, the latter being played by blowing across the openings. Cf. **spasm band.** [1930–35, *Amer.*]

Ju•gend•stil (yo͞o′gənt shtēl′), *n.* (*sometimes l.c.*) art nouveau as practiced in German-speaking countries. [1925–30; < G, equiv. to *Jugend* youth + *Stil* style]

jug•ful (jug′fo͝ol), *n., pl.* **-fuls.** enough to fill a jug. [1825–35; JUG[1] + -FUL]

—**Usage.** See **-ful.**

jugged′ hare′, a stew made of wild rabbit, usually cooked in an earthenware jug or stone pot.

Jug•ger•naut (jug′ər nôt′, -not′), *n.* **1.** (*often l.c.*) any large, overpowering, destructive force or object, as war, a giant battleship, or a powerful football team. **2.** (*often l.c.*) anything requiring blind devotion or cruel sacrifice. **3.** Also called **Jagannath.** an idol of Krishna, at Puri in Orissa, India, annually drawn on an enormous cart under whose wheels devotees are said to have thrown themselves to be crushed. [1630–40; < Hindi *Jagannāth* < Skt *Jagannātha* lord of the world (i.e., the god Vishnu or Krishna), equiv. to *jagat* world + *nātha* lord] —**Jug′ger•naut′ish,** *adj.*

jug•gins (jug′inz), *n., pl.* **-gins•es.** *Chiefly Brit.* a simpleton. [1835–45; orig. uncert.]

jug•gle (jug′əl), *v.,* **-gled, -gling,** *n.* —*v.t.* **1.** to keep (several objects, as balls, plates, tenpins, or knives) in continuous motion in the air simultaneously by tossing and catching. **2.** to hold, catch, carry, or balance precariously; almost drop and then catch hold again: *The center fielder juggled the ball but finally made the catch.* **3.** to alter or manipulate in order to deceive, as by subterfuge or trickery: *to juggle the business accounts; to juggle the facts.* **4.** to manage or alternate the requirements of (two or more tasks, responsibilities, activities, etc.) so as to handle each adequately: *to juggle the obligations of job and school.* —*v.i.* **5.** to perform feats of manual or bodily dexterity, as tossing up and keeping in continuous motion a number of balls, plates, knives, etc. **6.** to use artifice or trickery. —*n.* **7.** the act or fact of juggling. [1350–1400; ME *jog(e)len* < OF *jogler* to serve as buffoon or jester < LL *joculāre* to joke (r. L *joculārī*), equiv. to L *jocul(us)* (*joc(us)* JOKE + *-ulus* -ULE) + *-āre* inf. suffix] —**jug′gling·ly,** *adv.*

jug·gler (jug′lər), *n.* **1.** a person who performs juggling feats, as with balls or knives. **2.** a person who deceives by trickery; trickster. [bef. 1100; ME *jogelour, jogeler, jugelour* < AF *jogelour, jugelur,* OF *jogleor, jougleor* (see JONGLEUR) << L *joculātor* joker, equiv. to *joculā(rī)* (see JUGGLE) + *-tor* -TOR; r. OE *gēogelere* magician, c. G *Gaukler,* both directly < L, as above]

jug·gler·y (jug′lə rē), *n., pl.* **-gler·ies.** **1.** the art or practice of a juggler, esp. sleight of hand. **2.** the performance of juggling feats. **3.** any trickery or deception. [1250–1300; ME *jogel(e)rie* < OF *joglerie,* equiv. to *jogler* JUGGLER + *-ie* -Y[3]]

jug·head (jug′hed′), *n. Slang.* a stupid or foolish person. [1925–30; JUG[1] + HEAD]

ju·glan·da·ceous (jo͞o′glan dā′shəs), *adj.* belonging to the plant family Juglandaceae. Cf. **walnut family.** [< NL *Juglandac(eae)* walnut family (*Jugland-,* s. of *Juglans* the type genus (L (*nux*) *jūglāns* a walnut, equiv. to *jū-,* contr. of *Jov-* JOVE (cf. JUPITER) + *glāns* acorn; see GLAND[1]) + *-aceae* -ACEAE) + -OUS]

Ju·go·slav (yo͞o′gō släv′, -slav′), *n., adj.* Yugoslav. —**Ju′go·slav′ic,** *adj.*

Ju·go·sla·vi·a (yo͞o′gō slä′vē ə), *n.* Yugoslavia. —**Ju′go·sla′vi·an,** *adj., n.*

jug·u·lar (jug′yə lər, jo͞o′gyə-), *adj.* **1.** *Anat.* **a.** of or pertaining to the throat or neck. **b.** noting or pertaining to any of certain large veins of the neck, esp. one (**external jugular vein**) collecting blood from the superficial parts of the head or one (**internal jugular vein**) collecting blood from within the skull. **2.** (of a fish) having the pelvic fins at the throat, before the pectoral fins. —*n.* **3.** *Anat.* a jugular vein. **4. go for the jugular,** to attack a vital and vulnerable trait, feature, element, etc., in an attempt to overcome somebody or something swiftly and totally: *The defense attorney went right for the jugular by attempting to destroy the witness's credibility.* [1590–1600; < LL *jugulāris,* equiv. to L *jugul(um)* throat (see JUGULATE) + *-āris* -AR[1]]

ju·gu·late (jo͞o′gyə lāt′, jug′yə-), *v.t.,* **-lat·ed, -lat·ing.** **1.** to check or suppress (disease) by extreme measures. **2.** to cut the throat of; kill. [1615–25; < L *jugulātus* (ptp. of *jugulāre* to cut the throat of), equiv. to *jugul(um)* throat (*jug(um)* YOKE + *-ulum* -ULE) + *-ā-* theme vowel + *-tus* ptp. suffix] —**ju′gu·la′tion,** *n.*

ju·gum (jo͞o′gəm), *n. Entomol.* the posterior basal area or lobe in the forewing of certain insects, sometimes serving to couple the forewings and hind wings in flight. [1855–60; < NL, L: YOKE]

Ju·gur·tha (jo͞o gûr′thə), *n.* died 104 B.C., king of Numidia 113–104. —**Ju·gur′thine** (jo͞o gûr′thin, -thīn), *adj.*

jug′ wine′, any inexpensive wine sold in large bottles, esp. a bottle containing 1.5 liters (1.6 qt.) or more. [1970–75]

juice (jo͞os), *n., v.,* **juiced, juic·ing.** —*n.* **1.** the natural fluid, fluid content, or liquid part that can be extracted from a plant or one of its parts, esp. of a fruit: *orange juice.* **2.** the liquid part or contents of plant or animal substance. **3.** the natural fluids of an animal body: *gastric juices.* **4.** essence, strength, or vitality: *He's still full of the juice of life.* **5.** any extracted liquid. **6.** *Slang.* **a.** electricity or electric power. **b.** gasoline, fuel oil, etc., used to run an engine. **7.** *Slang.* alcoholic liquor. **8.** *Slang.* **a.** money obtained by extortion. **b.** money loaned at excessive and usually illegal interest rates. **c.** the interest rate itself. **9.** *Slang.* **a.** influence in the right or convenient place, esp. as exerted for selfish or illegal gain. **b.** gossip or scandal. **10. stew in one's own juice.** See **stew** (def. 5). —*v.t.* **11.** to extract juice from. —*v.i.* **12.** *Slang.* to drink alcohol heavily: *to go out juicing on Saturday night.* **13. juice up, a.** to add more power, energy, or speed to; accelerate. **b.** to make exciting or spectacular: *They juiced up the movie by adding some battle scenes.* **c.** to strengthen; increase the effectiveness of: *to juice up the nation's economy.* [1250–1300; ME *ju(i)s* < OF *jus* < L *jūs* broth, soup, sauce, juice] —**juice′less,** *adj.*

juiced (jo͞ost), *adj. Slang.* intoxicated from alcohol; drunk: *When arrested he was definitely juiced.* Also, **juiced′-up′.** [1945–50; JUICE (def. 7) + -ED[3]]

juice·head (jo͞os′hed′), *n. Slang.* a heavy drinker of alcoholic liquor. Also, **juice′-head′.** [1950–55; JUICE (def. 7) + HEAD (def. 21)]

juice′ man′, *Slang.* **1.** an extortionist. **2.** See **loan shark.** [1960–65, *Amer.*]

juic·er (jo͞o′sər), *n.* **1.** a kitchen appliance for extracting juice from fruits and vegetables. **2.** *Theat. Slang.* a stage electrician who works on the lighting of motion-picture, television, and theatrical sets. **3.** *Slang.* a person who drinks alcohol heavily and usually habitually. [1925–30; JUICE + -ER[1]]

juic·y (jo͞o′sē), *adj.,* **juic·i·er, juic·i·est.** **1.** full of juice; succulent: *a juicy pear.* **2.** very profitable, appealing, interesting, satisfying, or substantive: *a juicy contract; a juicy part in a movie.* **3.** very interesting or colorful, esp. when slightly scandalous or improper: *a juicy bit of gossip.* [1400–50; late ME *j(o)usy* full of liquor. See JUICE, -Y[1]] —**juic′i·ly,** *adv.* —**juic′i·ness,** *n.*
—**Syn. 3.** racy, risqué, titillating, sensational, lurid.

Juiz de Fo·ra (zhwēz′ di fô′rä), a city in SE Brazil, N of Rio de Janeiro. 284,069.

ju·jit·su (jo͞o jit′so͞o), *n.* a method developed in Japan of defending oneself without the use of weapons by using the strength and weight of an adversary to disable him. Also, **jiujitsu, jiujutsu, jujutsu.** Cf. **judo, karate.** [1870–75; < Japn *jūjitsu,* earlier *jūjutsu,* equiv. to *jū* soft (see JUDO) + *-jut(u)* technique < MChin, equiv. to Chin *shù*]

ju·ju (jo͞o′jo͞o), *n.* **1.** an object venerated superstitiously and used as a fetish or amulet by tribal peoples of West Africa. **2.** the magical power attributed to such an object. **3.** a ban or interdiction effected by it. [1890–95; allegedly < Hausa *jūjū* fetish] —**ju′ju·ism,** *n.* —**ju′ju·ist,** *n.*

ju·jube (jo͞o′jo͞ob), *n.* **1.** a small candy or lozenge of gum arabic, gelatin, or the like and fruit flavoring. **2.** See **Chinese date.** [1350–1400; ME < ML *jujuba* < L *zīziphum* < Gk *zízyphon* jujube tree]

ju·jut·su (jo͞o jut′so͞o, -jo͞ot′-), *n.* jujitsu.

Ju·juy (ho͞o hwē′), *n.* a city in NW Argentina. 124,487.

juke[1] (jo͞ok), *v.,* **juked, juk·ing,** *n. Football.* —*v.t.* **1.** to make a move intended to deceive (an opponent). —*n.* **2.** a fake or feint, usually intended to deceive a defensive player. [sp. var. of JOUK]

juke[2] (jo͞ok), *n.* jukebox. [by shortening]

juke·box (jo͞ok′boks′), *n.* a coin-operated phonograph, typically in a gaudy, illuminated cabinet, having a variety of records that can be selected by push button. Also called **juke.** [1915–20; JUKE (JOINT) + BOX[1]]

juke′ house′, *Southern U.S.* **1.** a cheap roadhouse. **2.** a brothel. [1940–45; cf. Gullah *juke house* brothel, Bambara *dzugu* wicked]

juke′ joint′, an establishment where one can eat, drink, and, usually, dance to music provided by a jukebox. Also, **jook joint.** Also called **jook.** [1935–40; see JUKE HOUSE]

Jukes (jo͞oks), *n.* the fictitious name of an actual family that was the focus of a 19th-century sociological study of the inheritance of feeble-mindedness and its correlation with social degeneracy. Cf. **Kallikak.**

Jul., July.

ju·lep (jo͞o′lip), *n.* **1.** See **mint julep. 2.** a sweet drink, variously prepared and sometimes medicated. [1350–1400; ME < MF < Ar *julāb* < Pers *gulāb,* equiv. to *gul* rose + *āb* water]

Jules (jo͞olz; *Fr.* zhyl), *n.* a male given name, French form of **Julius.**

Jul·ia (jo͞ol′yə), *n.* a female given name: derived from *Julius.*

Jul·ian (jo͞ol′yən), *n.* **1.** (*Flavius Claudius Julianus*) ("*the Apostate*") A.D. 331–363, Roman emperor 361–363. **2.** a male given name, form of **Julius.**

Jul·ian (jo͞ol′yən), *adj.* of, pertaining to, or characteristic of Julius Caesar. [1585–95; < L *Jūliānus,* equiv. to *Jūli(us)* JULIUS + *-ānus* -AN]

Ju·li·an·a (jo͞o′lē an′ə; *for 1 also Du.* yʏ′lē ä′nä), *n.* **1.** (*Juliana Louise Emma Marie Wilhelmina*) born 1909, queen of the Netherlands 1948–80 (daughter of Wilhelmina I). **2.** Also, **Ju′li·an′na, Ju·li·anne** (jo͞o′lē an′). a female given name, form of **Julia.**

Jul′ian Alps′, a range of the Alps in NW Slovenia. Highest peak, Mt. Triglav, 9394 ft. (2863 m).

Jul′ian cal′endar, the calendar established by Julius Caesar in 46 B.C., fixing the length of the year at 365 days and at 366 days every fourth year. There are 12 months of 30 or 31 days, except for February (which has 28 days with the exception of every fourth year, or leap year, when it has 29 days). Cf. **Gregorian calendar.**

Jul′ian Day′, *Astron.* a serial number equal to the number of days elapsed since January 1, 4713 B.C., proposed by Joseph Scaliger in 1582 and used in astronomical calculations: *January 1, 1965, at noon, Greenwich Civil Time, was Julian Day 2,438,762.0. Abbr.:* J.D.

Ju·lie (jo͞o′lē), *n.* a female given name, form of **Julia.**

ju·li·enne (jo͞o′lē en′; *Fr.* zhʏ lyen′), *adj.* **1.** (of food, esp. vegetables) cut into thin strips or small, matchlike pieces. —*n.* **2.** a clear soup garnished, before serving, with julienne vegetables. [1835–45; < F, generic use of *Julienne* woman's name]

Ju·li·et (jo͞o′lē ət, -et′, jo͞o′lē et′; *esp. for 1* jo͞ol′yət), *n.* **1.** the heroine of Shakespeare's *Romeo and Juliet.* **2.** (used in communications to represent the letter *J*). **3.** Also, **Ju′li·ette′.** a female given name, form of **Julia.**

Ju′liet cap′, a skullcap, often set with pearls or other gems, worn by women for semiformal or bridal wear. [1905–10; named after JULIET (def. 1)]

Jul·ius (jo͞ol′yəs), *n.* a male given name: a Roman family name.

Julius I, Saint, died A.D. 352, Italian ecclesiastic: pope 337–352.

Julius II, (*Giuliano della Rovere*) 1443–1513, Italian ecclesiastic: pope 1503–13.

Julius III, (*Giammaria Ciocchi del Monte* or *Giovanni Maria del Monte*) 1487–1555, Italian ecclesiastic: pope 1550–55.

Jul′ius Cae′sar, 1. See **Caesar, Gaius Julius. 2.** (*italics*) a tragedy (1600?) by Shakespeare. **3.** a walled plain in the first quadrant of the face of the moon: about 55 miles (88 km) in diameter.

Jul·lun·dur (jul′ən dər), *n.* a city in N Punjab, in NW India. 296,103.

Ju·ly (jo͞o lī′, jə lī′), *n., pl.* **-lies.** the seventh month of the year, containing 31 days. *Abbr.:* Jul. [bef. 1050; ME *julie* < AF < L *Jūlius* (CAESAR), after whom it was named; r. OE *Julius* < L; ME *ju(i)l* < OF < L]

Ju·ma·da (jo͞o mä′dä), *n.* either of two successive months of the Muslim year, the fifth (**Jumada I**) or the sixth (**Jumada II**). Cf. **Muslim calendar.** [1760–70; < Ar *jumādā*]

jum·ble (jum′bəl), *v.,* **-bled, -bling,** *n.* —*v.t.* **1.** to mix in a confused mass; put or throw together without order: *You've jumbled up all the cards.* **2.** to confuse mentally; muddle. —*v.i.* **3.** to be mixed together in a disorderly heap or mass. **4.** to meet or come together confusedly. —*n.* **5.** a mixed or disordered heap or mass: *a jumble of paper clips, rubber bands, and string.* **6.** a confused mixture; medley. **7.** a state of confusion or disorder. **8.** Also, **jum′bal.** a small, round, flat cake or cookie with a hole in the middle. [1520–30; perh. b. *joll* to bump (now dial.) and TUMBLE] —**jum′ble·ment,** *n.* —**jum′bler,** *n.* —**jum′bling·ly,** *adv.*
—**Syn. 7.** muddle, hodgepodge; farrago, gallimaufry; mess; chaos. —**Ant. 1.** separate. **7.** order.

jum′ble sale′, *Brit.* See **rummage sale.** [1895–1900]

jum·bo (jum′bō), *n., pl.* **-bos,** *adj. Informal.* —*n.* **1.** a very large person, animal, or thing. **2.** See **jumbo jet. 3.** *U.S. Naut.* **a.** a forestaysail having a boom (**jum′bo boom′**) along its foot, used esp. on schooners. **b.** a sail used in place of a course on a square-rigged ship, having the form of an isosceles triangle set apex downward. **c.** a narrow triangular sail set point downward in place of a foresail on a topsail schooner. —*adj.* **4.** very large: *the jumbo box of cereal.* [1800–10; orig. uncert.; popularized as the name of a large elephant purchased and exhibited by P.T. Barnum in 1882]

jum′bo jet′, a widebody jet airliner. Also, **jumbo.** [1960–65]

jum·buck (jum′buk), *n. Australian.* a sheep. [1815–25; perh. ult. < Kamilaroi *dimba* (meaning unknown), altered by assoc. with BUCK[1]; borrowed into Australian Pidgin E and thence into other Aboriginal languages]

Jum·na (jum′nə), *n.* a river in N India, flowing SE from the Himalayas to the Ganges at Allahabad. 860 mi. (1385 m) long.

jump (jump), *v.i.* **1.** to spring clear of the ground or other support by a sudden muscular effort; leap: *to jump into the air; to jump out a window.* **2.** to rise suddenly or quickly: *He jumped from his seat when she entered.* **3.** to move or jerk suddenly, as from surprise or shock: *He jumped when the firecracker exploded.* **4.** to obey quickly and energetically; hustle: *The waiter was told to jump when the captain signaled.* **5.** *Informal.* to be full of activity; bustle: *The whole town is jumping with excitement.* **6.** to start a campaign, program, military attack, etc.; launch an activity, esp. of major proportions (usually fol. by *off*): *The march jumped off early in the morning.* **7.** *Checkers.* to move from one side of an opponent's piece to a vacant square on the opposite side, thus capturing the opponent's piece. **8.** to rise suddenly in amount, price, etc.: *Costs jumped again this quarter.* **9.** to pass abruptly, ignoring intervening steps or deliberation: *to jump to a conclusion.* **10.** to change abruptly: *The traffic light jumped from green to red.* **11.** to move or change suddenly, haphazardly, aimlessly, or after a short period: *He jumped from job to job.* **12.** to pass or go aimlessly: *He jumped from one thing to another without being able to concentrate on anything.* **13.** to omit letters, numbers, etc.; skip: *This typewriter jumps and needs repairing.* **14.** to parachute from an airplane. **15.** to take eagerly; seize (often fol. by *at*): *He jumped at the offer of a free trip.* **16.** to enter into something with vigor (usually fol. by *in* or *into*): *She jumped into the discussion right away.* **17.** to advance rapidly from one level to another, esp. in rank; pass through or skip intermediate stages in a forward or upward progression: *He jumped from clerk to general manager in a year.* **18.** *Motion Pictures.* (of a shot or frame) to fail to line up properly with the preceding or following frames because of a mechanical fault in the camera or projector. **19.** *Bridge.* to make a jump bid: *She jumped from three clubs to four spades.* **20.** *Journalism.* (of newspaper copy) to continue on a subsequent page, following intervening copy (opposed to *turn*).
—*v.t.* **21.** to leap or spring over: *to jump a narrow stream.* **22.** to cause to leap: *She jumped the horse over the fence.* **23.** to skip or pass over; bypass: *to jump the third grade in school.* **24.** to elevate or advance, esp. in rank, by causing to skip or pass rapidly through intermediate stages: *The boss jumped his son from mail clerk to plant manager.* **25.** to move past or start before (a signal); anticipate: *One car jumped the red light and collided with a truck.* **26.** to increase sharply: *The store jumped its prices.* **27.** *Checkers.* to capture (an opponent's piece) by leaping over. **28.** to attack or pounce upon without warning, as from ambush: *The thugs jumped him in a dark alley.* **29.** *Bridge.* to raise (the bid) by more than necessary to reach the next bidding level, esp. as a signal to one's partner. **30.** *Informal.* **a.** to abscond from; leave: *The robbers jumped town.* **b.** to flee or escape from. **31.** to seize or occupy illegally or forcibly (a mining claim or the like), as on the ground of some flaw in the holder's title. **32.** (of trains, trolleys, etc.) to spring off or leave (the track). **33.** to get on board (a train, bus, etc.) quickly or with little planning or preparation for the trip: *He jumped a plane for Chicago.* **34.** *Journalism.* to continue (a story) from one page to another over intervening copy. **35.** *Metalworking.* to thicken (a bar or the like) by striking the end; upset (often fol. by *up*). **36.** *Slang* (*vulgar*). to engage in an act of coitus with. **37.** to connect (a dead battery) to a live battery by attaching booster cables between the respective terminals. **38. jump aboard** or **on board,** to join a group, activity, etc., esp. one that has been operating or functioning for some time: *After some hesitation, he jumped aboard and contributed heavily to the campaign.* **39. jump all over someone,** to reprimand; criticize: *You don't have to jump all over me just because I'm a little late.* **40. jump bail.** See **bail**[1] (def. 5). **41. jump down someone's throat.** See **throat** (def. 10). **42. jump in** or **into with both feet,** to join or enter into exuberantly, eagerly, hastily, etc. **43. jump on,** to blame or rebuke; reprimand: *He'll jump on anyone who contradicts him.* **44. jump ship.** See **ship** (def. 5). **45. jump the gun.** See **gun**[1] (def. 9).
—*n.* **46.** an act or instance of jumping; leap. **47.** a space, obstacle, apparatus, or the like, cleared or to be cleared in a leap. **48.** a short or hurried journey. **49.** a

CONCISE PRONUNCIATION KEY: act, cāpe, dâre, pärt; set, ēqual; if, īce; ox, ōver, ôrder, oil, bo͝ok, bo͞ot, out; up, ûrge; child; sing; shoe; thin, *th*at; zh as in *treasure.* ə = *a* as in *alone, e* as in *system, i* as in *easily, o* as in *gallop, u* as in *circus;* ə as in *fire* (fīər), *hour* (ouər). l and n can serve as syllabic consonants, as in *cradle* (krād′l), and *button* (but′n). See the full key inside the front cover.

descent by parachute from an airplane. **50.** a sudden rise in amount, price, etc.: *a considerable jump in the stock market.* **51.** a sudden upward or other movement of an inanimate object. **52.** an abrupt transition from one point or thing to another, with omission of what intervenes: *The speaker made an unexplained jump in topic.* **53.** a move or one of a series of moves: *The gangster stayed one jump ahead of the police.* **54.** *Sports.* any of several contests that feature a leap or jump. Cf. **broad jump, high jump.** **55.** *Motion Pictures.* a break in the continuity of action due to a failure to match the action of one frame with the following one of the same scene. **56.** a sudden start as from nervous excitement: *He gave a jump when the firecracker went off.* **57.** *Checkers.* the act of taking an opponent's piece by leaping over it to an unoccupied square. **58. the jumps,** *Informal.* restlessness; nervousness; anxiety. **59.** Also called **breakover.** *Journalism.* the part of a story continued on another page. **60.** *Math.* the difference in limit values at a jump discontinuity of a given function. **61.** *Auto.* jump-start (def. 1). **62. get** or **have the jump on,** to get or have a head start or an initial advantage over: *They got the jump on us in selling the item, but we finally caught up.* **63. on the jump,** in a hurry; running about: *Lively youngsters keep their parents on the jump.*
—*adj.* **64.** *Jazz.* **a.** of, pertaining to, or characteristic of swing. **b.** of, pertaining to, or characteristic of jazz; played at a bright tempo.
—*adv.* **65.** *Obs.* exactly; precisely. [1505–15; cf. Dan *gumpe* to jolt, *gimpe* to move up and down, Sw *gumpa,* LG *gumpen* to jump] —**jump′a·ble,** *adj.* —**jump′ing·ly,** *adv.*
—**Syn. 1.** JUMP, LEAP, VAULT imply propelling oneself by a muscular effort, either into the air or from one position or place to another. JUMP and LEAP are often used interchangeably, but JUMP indicates more particularly the springing movement of the feet in leaving the ground or support: *to jump up and down.* LEAP (which formerly also meant to run) indicates the passage, by a springing movement of the legs, from one point or position to another: *to leap across a brook.* VAULT implies leaping, esp. with the aid of the hands or some instrument, over or upon something: *to vault (over) a fence.*

jump′ ball′, *Basketball.* a ball tossed into the air above and between two opposing players by the referee in putting the ball into play. [1920–25]

jump′ bid′, *Bridge.* a bid higher than necessary to reach the next bidding level, usually to indicate exceptional strength.

jump′ boot′, a heavy leather boot originally designed for wear by paratroopers. [1945–50]

jump′ cut′, *Motion Pictures.* an abrupt break in the continuity of a scene created by editing out part of a shot or scene. [1950–55]

jump′ di′al, a timepiece dial in which the numbers are seen through apertures.

jump′ discontinu′ity, *Math.* a discontinuity of a function at a point where the function has finite, but unequal, limits as the independent variable approaches the point from the left and from the right. Cf. **jump** (def. 60).

jumped-up (jumpt′up′), *adj. Chiefly Brit.* having recently gained prominence or fame and appearing arrogant. [1825–35]

jump·er[1] (jum′pər), *n.* **1.** a person or thing that jumps. **2.** *Basketball.* See **jump shot. 3.** *Sports.* a participant in a jumping event, as in track or skiing. **4.** *Manège.* a horse specially trained to jump obstacles. **5.** a boring tool or device worked with a jumping motion. **6.** Also called **jump wire.** *Elect.* a short length of conductor used to make a connection, usually temporary, between terminals of a circuit or to bypass a circuit. **7.** Also called **jump′er ca′ble.** See **booster cable. 8.** a kind of sled. **9.** Also called **jump′er stay′.** *Naut.* a line preventing the end of a spar or boom from being lifted out of place. **10.** any of various fishes that leap from the water, as the striped mullet or jumprock. [1605–15; JUMP + -ER[1]]

jump·er[2] (jum′pər), *n.* **1.** a one-piece, sleeveless dress, or a skirt with straps and a complete or partial bodice, usually worn over a blouse by women and children. **2.** a loose outer jacket worn esp. by workers and sailors. **3.** *Brit.* a pullover sweater. **4. jumpers,** rompers. [1850–55; obs. *jump* short coat (orig. uncert.) + -ER[1]]

jump′er ant′. See **bulldog ant.** [1905–10]

jump′ head′, *Journalism.* the headline printed over the continued portion of a story in a newspaper, magazine, etc., usually condensed from the main headline.

jump′ing bean′, the seed of any of certain Mexican plants of the genera *Sebastiania* and *Sapium,* of the spurge family: the movements of a moth larva inside the seed cause it to move about or jump. Also called **Mexican jumping bean.** [1885–90, *Amer.*]

jump′ing bris′tletail, any of several thysanuran insects that live in dark, warm, moist places, as under leaves, bark, and dead tree trunks and along rocky seacoasts, and are active jumpers, making erratic leaps when disturbed. Also called **machilid.**

jump′ing gene′, *Informal.* transposon.

jump′ing hare′, *n.* springhare. [1830–40]

jump′ing jack′, **1.** a toy consisting of a jointed figure that is made to jump, move, or dance by pulling a string or stick attached to it. **2.** a conditioning exercise performed by starting from a standing position with legs together and arms resting at the sides and then jumping to a position with the legs spread apart and out to the sides while simultaneously extending the arms out from the sides to an overhead position with the hands touching and finishing by reversing these movements to return to the starting position. [1860–65, *Amer.*]

jump′ing mouse′, any of several primitive, mouselike rodents of the family Zapodidae, having long hind legs, common in the woodlands of Europe, Asia, and North America. [1820–30]

jump′ing-off′ place′ (jum′ping ôf′, -of′), **1.** a place for use as a starting point: *Paris was the jumping-off place for our tour of Europe.* **2.** an out-of-the-way place; the farthest limit of anything settled or civilized. [1820–30, *Amer.*]

jump′ing plant′ louse′, any of numerous lice, of the family Psyllidae, that feed on plant juices and are sometimes pests of fruits and vegetables. Also called **psylla, psyllid.** [1900–05]

jump′ing spi′der, any of several small, hairy spiders, of the family Salticidae, that stalk and jump upon their prey instead of snaring it in a web. [1805–15]

jump′ jet′, a jet airplane capable of taking off and landing vertically or on an extremely short runway or flight deck. Also, **jump′-jet′.** Cf. **STOL, VTOL.** [1960–65]

jump′ line′, *Journalism.* a line of type identifying the page on or from which a newspaper story is continued.

jump·mas·ter (jump′mas′tər, -mä′stər), *n.* a person who supervises the jumping of paratroopers or other parachutists. [1940–45; JUMP + MASTER]

jump-off (jump′ôf′, -of′), *n.* **1.** a place for jumping off. **2.** a point of departure, as of a race or a military attack. **3.** the start of such a departure. **4.** a supplementary contest among horses tied for first place in a jumping contest. [1870–75, *Amer.*; n. use of v. phrase]

jump′ pass′, *Football, Basketball.* a pass in which a player leaps into the air and throws the ball to a teammate before returning to the ground. [1945–50]

jump·rock (jump′rok′), *n.* any of several freshwater suckers of the genus *Moxostoma,* of the southeastern U.S. [1885–90, *Amer.*; perh. JUMP + ROCK[1]]

jump′ rope′, **1.** Also, **jump′ rop′ing.** a children's game or an exercise for children and adults in which a rope is swung over and under the standing jumper, who must leap over it each time it reaches the feet. **2.** the rope used. **3.** to play this game or do this exercise. Also called **skip rope.** [1795–1805]

jump′ seat′, a movable or folding seat, as in a carriage, taxicab, or limousine, used as an extra seat. [1860–65, *Amer.*]

jump-shift (jump′shift′), *n. Bridge.* a jump bid in a suit different from the suit just bid by one's partner.

jump′ shot′, *Basketball.* a shot with one or both hands in which a player leaps into the air and shoots the ball at the basket at the moment of reaching the highest point of the leap. [1905–10]

jump′ spark′, *Elect.* spark[1] (def. 2). [1905–10]

jump-start (jump′stärt′), *n.* **1.** Also, **jump.** *Auto.* the starting of an internal-combustion engine that has a discharged or weak battery by means of booster cables. —*v.t.* **2.** to give a jump-start to: *to jump-start an engine.* **3.** to enliven or revive: *to jump-start a sluggish economy.*

jump·suit (jump′so͞ot′), *n.* **1.** a one-piece suit worn by parachutists for jumping. **2.** a garment fashioned after this, usually combining a shirt or bodice with shorts or trousers in one piece. Also, **jump′ suit′.** [1940–45; JUMP + SUIT]

jump′ turn′, *Skiing.* a turn in which a skier plants one or both poles in the snow in advance of the forward ski, bends close to the ground, and pivots in the air around the pole or poles. [1920–25]

jump′ wire′, *Elect.* jumper[1] (def. 6).

jump·y (jum′pē), *adj.,* **jump·i·er, jump·i·est. 1.** subject to sudden, involuntary starts, esp. from nervousness, fear, excitement, etc. **2.** characterized by sudden starts, jerks, or jumps: *a jumpy narrative.* [1865–70; JUMP + -Y[1]] —**jump′i·ly,** *adv.* —**jump′i·ness,** *n.*
—**Syn. 1.** jittery, skittish, fidgety.

jun (chun), *n., pl.* **jun.** chon (def. 1).

Jun., 1. June. **2.** Junior.

Junc., Junction.

jun·ca·ceous (jung kā′shəs), *adj.* belonging to the plant family Juncaceae. Cf. **rush family.** [1850–55; < NL *Juncace(ae)* rush family (*Junc(us)* the type genus (L: rush) + *-aceae* -ACEAE) + -OUS]

jun·co (jung′kō), *n., pl.* **-cos.** any of several small North American finches of the genus *Junco.* Also called **snowbird.** Cf. **dark-eyed junco, slate-colored junco.** [1700–10; < Sp: rush, bird found in rush beds < L *juncus* rush]

junc·tion (jungk′shən), *n.* **1.** an act of joining; combining. **2.** the state of being joined; union. **3.** a place or point where two or more things are joined, as a seam or joint. **4.** a place or point where two or more things meet or converge. **5.** a place or station where railroad lines meet, cross, or diverge. **6.** an intersection of streets, highways, or roads. **7.** something that joins other things together: *He used the device as a junction between the branch circuit and the main power lines.* [1705–15; < L *junctiōn-* (s. of *junctiō*), equiv. to *junct(us),* ptp. of *jungere* to join (*jung-* JOIN + *-tus* ptp. suffix) + *-iōn-* -ION] —**junc′tion·al,** *adj.*
—**Syn. 3.** union, linkage, coupling; welt. **7.** connection. JUNCTION, JUNCTURE refer to a place, line, or point at which two or more things join. A JUNCTION is also a place where things come together: *the junction of two rivers.* A JUNCTURE is a line or point at which two bodies are joined, or a point of exigency or crisis in time: *the juncture of the head and neck; a critical juncture in a struggle.*

junc′tion box′, *Elect.* an enclosure that houses electric wires or cables that are joined together and protects the connections. [1895–1900]

Junc′tion Cit′y, a city in NE Kansas. 19,305.

junc·tur·al (jungk′chər əl), *adj.* of or pertaining to phonological juncture. [1940–45; JUNCTURE + -AL[1]] —**junc′tur·al·ly,** *adv.*

junc·ture (jungk′chər), *n.* **1.** a point of time, esp. one made critical or important by a concurrence of circumstances: *At this juncture, we must decide whether to stay or to walk out.* **2.** a serious state of affairs; crisis: *The matter has reached a juncture and a decision must be made.* **3.** the line or point at which two bodies are joined; joint or articulation; seam. **4.** the act of joining. **5.** the state of being joined. **6.** something by which two things are joined. **7.** *Phonet.* **a.** a pause or other phonological feature or modification of a feature, as the lengthening of a preceding phoneme or the strengthening of a following one, marking a transition or break between sounds, esp. marking the phonological boundary of a word, clause, or sentence: it is present in such words as *night-rate* and *re-seed* and absent in such words as *nitrate* and *recede.* Cf. **close juncture, open juncture, terminal juncture. b.** the point in a word or group of words at which such a pause or other junctural marker occurs. [1350–1400; ME < L *junctūra,* equiv. to *junct(us)* (see JUNCTION) + *-ūra* -URE]
—**Syn. 1, 3.** See **junction.**

Jun·di·a·í (zho͞on′dyä ē′), *n.* a city in SE Brazil, NW of São Paulo. 145,785.

June (jo͞on), *n.* **1.** the sixth month of the year, containing 30 days. *Abbr.:* Jun. **2.** a female given name. [bef. 1050; ME *jun(e),* OE *iunius* < L *(mēnsis) Jūnius,* after the name of a gens; r. ME *juyng* < OF *juin(g)* < L, as above]

Ju·neau (jo͞o′nō), *n.* a seaport in and the capital of Alaska, in the SE part. 19,528.

June·ber·ry (jo͞on′ber′ē, -bə rē), *n., pl.* **-ries.** the American serviceberry, *Amelanchier canadensis.* [1800–10, *Amer.*; JUNE + BERRY]

June′ bug′, **1.** Also called **May beetle.** any of several large, brown beetles of the genus *Phyllophaga,* of the scarab family, appearing in late spring and early summer. **2.** See **green June beetle. 3.** *Chiefly Northern and North Midland U.S.* a firefly. Also, **June′bug′.** [1825–35]

June bug, *Phyllophaga fusca,* length 1 in. (2.5 cm)

June′ grass′. See **Kentucky bluegrass.** [1850–55, *Amer.*]

Jung (yo͝ong), *n.* **Carl Gus·tav** (kärl go͝os′täf), 1875–1961, Swiss psychiatrist and psychologist.

Jün·ger (yo͝ong′ər; *Ger.* yyng′ər), *n.* **Ernst** (ûrnst; *Ger.* ernst), born 1895, German author.

Jung·frau (yo͝ong′frou′), *n.* a mountain in S Switzerland, in the Bernese Alps. 13,668 ft. (4166 m).

Jung·gram·ma·ti·ker (yo͝ong′grä mä′tē kər), *n. Ling., German.* a group of linguists of the late 19th century who held that phonetic laws are universally valid and allow of no exceptions; neo-grammarians. [lit., young grammarians]

Jung·i·an (yo͝ong′ē ən), *adj.* **1.** of or pertaining to Carl G. Jung or his theories, esp. of archetypes and the collective unconscious. —*n.* **2.** an advocate or follower of Jung's theories. [1930–35; JUNG + -IAN]

jun·gle (jung′gəl), *n.* **1.** a wild land overgrown with dense vegetation, often nearly impenetrable, esp. tropical vegetation or a tropical rain forest. **2.** a tract of such land. **3.** a wilderness of dense overgrowth; a piece of swampy, thickset forestland. **4.** any confused mass or agglomeration of objects; jumble: *a jungle of wrecked automobiles.* **5.** something that baffles or perplexes; maze: *a jungle of legal double-talk.* **6.** a scene of violence and struggle for survival: *The neglected prison was a jungle for its inmates.* **7.** a place or situation of ruthless competition: *the advertising jungle.* **8.** *Slang.* a hobo camp. [1770–80; < Hindi *jaṅgal* < Pali, Prakrit *jaṅgala* rough, waterless place] —**jun′gled,** *adj.*

Jungle, The, a novel (1906) by Upton Sinclair.

Jun′gle Books′, The, a series of jungle stories in two volumes (1894, 1895) by Rudyard Kipling.

jun′gle bun′ny, *Slang (disparaging and offensive).* a black person. [1965–70, *Amer.*]

jun′gle cock′, the male of the jungle fowl.

jun′gle fe′ver, *Pathol.* a severe variety of malarial fever occurring in the East Indies and the tropics. [1795–1805]

jun′gle fowl′, any of several East Indian, gallinaceous birds of the genus *Gallus,* as *G. gallus* **(red jungle fowl)** believed to be the ancestor of the domestic fowl. [1815–25]

jun′gle gera′nium, flame-of-the-woods.

jun·gle·gym (jung′gəl jim′), a playground apparatus consisting of a framework of horizontal and vertical bars on which children can climb. [formerly a trademark]

jun′gle rot′, *Pathol.* any cutaneous disease or condition caused or induced by a tropical climate. [1940–45]

jun·gly (jung′glē), *adj.* resembling or suggesting a jungle. [1790–1800; JUNGLE + -Y[1]]

jun·ior (jo͞on′yər), *adj.* **1.** younger (usually designating the younger of two men bearing the same full name, as a son named after his father; often written as *Jr.* or *jr.* following the name): *May I speak with the junior Mr. Hansen? Mr. Edward Andrew Hansen, Jr.* Cf. **senior** (def. 1). **2.** of more recent appointment or admission, as to an office or status; of lower rank or standing: *a junior partner.* **3.** (in American universities, colleges, and schools)

CONCISE ETYMOLOGY KEY: <, descended or borrowed from; >, whence; b., blend of, blended; c., cognate with; cf., compare; deriv., derivative; equiv., equivalent; imit., imitative; obl., oblique; r., replacing; s., stem; sp., spelling, spelled; resp., respelling, respelled; trans., translation; ?, origin unknown; *, unattested; ‡, probably earlier than. See the full key inside the front cover.

noting or pertaining to the class or year next below that of the senior. **4.** *Finance.* subordinate to preferred creditors, mortgagees, and the like. **5.** of later date; subsequent to: *His appointment is junior to mine by six months.* **6.** composed of younger members: *The junior division of the camp went on the hike.* **7.** being smaller than the usual size: *The hotel has special weekend rates on junior suites.* **8.** (of an iron or steel shape) relatively small, but rolled to a standard form. **9.** of, for, or designating clothing in sizes 3–15 or those who wear it: *a junior dress; junior measurements; the junior department.* —*n.* **10.** a person who is younger than another. **11.** a person who is newer or of lower rank in an office, class, profession, etc.; subordinate. **12.** a student who is in the next to the final year of a course of study. **13.** Often, **juniors. a.** a range of odd-numbered sizes, chiefly from 3 to 15, for garments that fit women and girls with shorter waists, narrower shoulders, and smaller bustlines than those of average build. **b.** the department or section of a store where garments in these sizes are sold. **14.** a garment in this size range. **15.** a woman or girl who wears garments in this size range. **16.** (*cap.*) a member of the Girl Scouts from 9 through 11 years old. **17.** *Informal.* (*often cap.*) a boy; youth; son: *Ask junior to give you a hand with the packing.* [1520–30; < L *jūnior* younger]

jun•ior•ate (jo͞on′yə rāt′, -yər it), *n.* **1.** a two-year course of study for a Jesuit novice in preparation for the course in philosophy. **2.** a seminary for this course. [1835–45; JUNIOR + -ATE[3]]

jun′ior col′lege, 1. a collegiate institution offering courses only through the first one or two years of college instruction and granting a certificate of title instead of a degree. **2.** a division of a college, university, or university system offering general courses during the first two years of instruction or fulfilling administrative duties applicable to freshmen and sophomores. [1895–1900, *Amer.*]

jun′ior coun′sel, *Eng. Law.* **1.** a body of barristers who are lower in rank than the King's Counsel or Queen's Counsel, and who plead outside the bar in the court. **2.** a member of this body of barristers.

jun′ior high′ school′, a school attended after elementary school and usually consisting of grades seven through nine. [1905–10, *Amer.*]

jun•ior•i•ty (jo͞on yôr′i tē, -yor′-), *n.* the state or fact of being junior in age, rank, standing, etc. [1590–1600; JUNIOR + -ITY]

Jun′ior League′, any local branch of a women's organization, the Association of the Junior Leagues of America, Inc., the members of which are engaged in volunteer welfare work, civic affairs, etc. —**Jun′ior Lea′guer.**

jun′ior miss′, 1. a teenage girl, esp. a subdebutante. **2.** See **junior** (def. 13). [1925–30]

jun′ior school′, *Brit.* a school for children aged seven to eleven, similar to a U.S. elementary school. [1870–75]

jun′ior var′sity, *Sports.* a university, college, or school team that consists of players who lack the qualifications or skill necessary for the varsity and compete against other teams of similar composition or ability. [1945–50]

ju•ni•per (jo͞o′nə pər), *n.* **1.** any evergreen, coniferous shrub or tree of the genus *Juniperus,* esp. *J. communis,* having cones that resemble dark-blue or blackish berries used in flavoring gin and in medicine as a diuretic. **2.** a tree mentioned in the Old Testament, said to be the retem. [1350–1400; ME *junipere* < L *jūniperus*]

ju′niper ber′ry, the berrylike cone of a juniper. [1715–25]

ju′niper oil′, an oil obtained from the berries or wood of the common juniper, *Juniperus communis.* [1540–50]

ju′niper tar′, *Pharm.* a medicinal tar derived from the European juniper *Juniperus oxycedrus:* used topically in the treatment of certain skin diseases. Cf. **cade.** [1880–85]

Ju•nius (jo͞on′yəs), *n.* **1.** the pen name of the unknown author of a series of letters published in a London newspaper (1769–72), attacking the British king and his ministers' abuse of royal prerogative in denying John Wilkes his seat in Parliament. **2. Franciscus,** 1589–1677, English philologist, born in Germany.

junk[1] (jungk), *n.* **1.** any old or discarded material, as metal, paper, or rags. **2.** anything that is regarded as worthless, meaningless, or contemptible; trash. **3.** old cable or cordage used when untwisted for making gaskets, swabs, oakum, etc. **4.** *Naut. Slang.* See **salt junk. 5.** *Baseball Slang.* relatively slow, unorthodox pitches that are deceptive to the batter in movement or pace, as knuckleballs or forkballs. —*v.t.* **6.** to cast aside as junk; discard as no longer of use; scrap. —*adj.* **7.** cheap, worthless, unwanted, or trashy. [1480–90; earlier *jonke,* of uncert. orig.]
—**Syn. 1, 2.** rubbish, litter, debris, refuse.

junk[2] (jungk), *n.* a seagoing ship with a traditional Chinese design and used primarily in Chinese waters, having square sails spread by battens, a high stern, and usually a flat bottom. [1545–55; < Pg *junco* a kind of sailing vessel < Malay *jong,* said to be < dial. Chin (Xiamen) *chûn;* cf. Guangdong dial. *syùhn,* Chin *chuán*]

junk[2]

junk[3] (jungk), *n. Slang.* narcotics, esp. heroin. [1920–25; perh. special use of JUNK[1]]

junk′ art′, sculptural assemblage constructed from discarded materials, as glass, scrap metal, plastic, and wood. [1965–70] —**junk′ art′ist.**

junk′ bond′, *Finance.* any corporate bond with a low rating and a high yield, often involving high risk. [1975–80]

junk′ call′, a telephone call soliciting a donation or selling a product or service by a caller making many such calls to a list of prospects. [by analogy with JUNK MAIL]

junk•er (jung′kər), *n. Slang.* a car that is old, worn out, or in bad enough repair to be scrapped. [1880–85, *Amer.,* for an earlier sense; JUNK[1] + -ER[1]]

Jun•ker (yo͝ong′kər), *n.* **1.** a member of a class of aristocratic landholders, esp. in East Prussia, strongly devoted to militarism and authoritarianism, from among whom the German military forces recruited a large number of its officers. **2.** a young German, esp. Prussian, nobleman. **3.** a German official or military officer who is narrow-minded, haughty, and overbearing. [1545–55; < G; OHG *junchērro,* equiv. to *junc* YOUNG + *hērro* HERR]

Jun•ker•dom (yo͝ong′kər dəm), *n.* **1.** the Junkers as a group. **2.** (*sometimes l.c.*) the condition or character of a Junker. **3.** (*sometimes l.c.*) the spirit or policy of the Junkers; Junkerism. [1865–70; JUNKER + -DOM]

Jun•ker•ism (yo͝ong′kə riz′əm), *n.* (*sometimes l.c.*) the spirit or policy of the Junkers. [1865–70; JUNKER + -ISM]

Jun•kers (yo͝ong′kərs), *n.* **Hu•go** (ho͞o′gô), 1859–1935, German aircraft designer and builder.

jun•ket (jung′kit), *n.* **1.** a sweet, custardlike food of flavored milk curded with rennet. **2.** a pleasure excursion, as a picnic or outing. **3.** a trip, as by an official or legislative committee, paid out of public funds and ostensibly to obtain information. —*v.i.* **4.** to go on a junket. —*v.t.* **5.** to entertain; feast; regale. [1350–1400; ME *jonket* < OF (dial.) *jonquette* rush basket, equiv. to *jonc* (< L *juncus* reed) + *-ette* -ETTE] —**jun′ket•er,** *n.*

jun•ke•teer (jung′ki tēr′), *n.* **1.** a person who goes on junkets, esp. regularly or habitually: *weekend junketeers to Las Vegas.* —*v.i.* **2.** to go on a junket, esp. at government or another's expense: *congressmen who regularly junketeer to Europe and the Far East.* [1815–25; JUNKET + -EER, on the model of coinages with *-teer,* often derogatory, as PROFITEER, RACKETEER]

junk′ food′, 1. food, as potato chips or candy, that is high in calories but of little nutritional value. **2.** anything that is attractive and diverting but of negligible substance: *the junk food offered by daytime television.* [1970–75, *Amer.*] —**junk′-food′,** *adj.*

junk•ie (jung′kē), *n. Informal.* **1.** a drug addict, esp. one addicted to heroin. **2.** a person with an insatiable craving for something: *a chocolate junkie.* **3.** an enthusiastic follower; fan; devotee: *a baseball junkie.* Also, **junky.** [1920–25; JUNK[3] + -IE]

junk′ jew′elry, cheap costume jewelry. [1935–40]

junk′ mail′, unsolicited commercial mail. [1950–55]

junk′ mail′er, 1. an organization that sends junk mail in bulk, esp. to solicit business or charitable contributions. **2.** a business that specializes in preparing and distributing junk mail for others. [JUNK MAIL + -ER[1]]

junk•man[1] (jungk′man′), *n., pl.* **-men.** a dealer in resalable used metal, paper, rags, and other junk. [1870–75, *Amer.;* JUNK[1] + MAN[1]]

junk•man[2] (jungk′mən, -man′), *n., pl.* **-men** (-mən, -men′). a member of the crew of a junk. [1860–65; JUNK[2] + MAN[1]]

junk•y[1] (jung′kē), *adj.,* **junk•i•er, junk•i•est.** of the nature of junk; trashy. [1945–50; JUNK[1] + -Y[2]]

junk•y[2] (jung′kē), *n., pl.* **junk•ies.** junkie. [JUNK[3] + -Y[2]]

junk•yard (jungk′yärd′), *n.* a yard for the collection, storage, and resale of junk. [1875–80, *Amer.;* JUNK[1] + YARD[2]]

Ju•no (jo͞o′nō), *n., pl.* **-nos** for 3. **1.** the ancient Roman queen of heaven, a daughter of Saturn and the wife and sister of Jupiter: the protector of women and marriage. Cf. **Hera. 2.** *Astron.* the fourth largest and one of the four brightest asteroids. **3.** a woman of regal appearance or bearing. **4.** *Mil.* the code name for a beach on France's Normandy coast, attacked by Canadian forces as part of the Allies' D-day invasion on June 6, 1944. **5.** a female given name.

Ju′no and the Pay′cock (pā′kok), a play (1924) by Sean O'Casey.

Ju•no•esque (jo͞o′nō esk′), *adj.* (of a woman) stately; regal. [1885–90; JUNO + -ESQUE]

Ju•not (zhy nō′), *n.* **An•doche** (än dôsh′), (*Duc d'Abrantès*), 1771–1813, French marshal.

jun•ta (ho͝on′tə, jun′-, hun′-), *n.* **1.** a small group ruling a country, esp. immediately after a coup d'état and before a legally constituted government has been instituted. **2.** a council. **3.** a deliberative or administrative council, esp. in Spain and Latin America. **4.** junto. [1615–25; < Sp: a meeting, n. use of fem. of L *junctus* (ptp. of *jungere* to JOIN); see JUNCTION]
—**Pronunciation.** When the word JUNTA was borrowed into English from Spanish in the early 17th century, its pronunciation was thoroughly Anglicized to (jun′tə). The 20th century has seen the emergence and, especially in North America, the gradual predominance of the pronunciation (ho͝on′tə), derived from Spanish (ho͞on′tä) through reassociation with the word's Spanish origins. A hybrid form (hun′tə) is also heard.

jun•to (jun′tō), *n., pl.* **-tos.** a self-appointed committee, esp. with political aims; cabal. [1635–45; alter. of JUNTA]

Ju•pi•ter (jo͞o′pi tər), *n.* **1.** Also called **Jove.** the supreme deity of the ancient Romans: the god of the heavens and of weather. Cf. **Zeus. 2.** *Astron.* the planet fifth in order from the sun, having an equatorial diameter of 88,729 mi. (142,796 km), a mean distance from the sun of 483.6 million mi. (778.3 million km), a period of revolution of 11.86 years, and at least 14 moons. It is the largest planet in the solar system. See table under **planet. 3.** *Mil.* a medium-range U.S. ballistic missile of the 1950's, powered by a single liquid-fueled rocket engine.

Ju•pi•ter's-beard (jo͞o′pi tərz bērd′), *n.* See **red valerian.** [1560–70]

ju•pon (jo͞o′pon, jo͞o pon′; *Fr.* zhy pôN′), *n., pl.* **-pons** (-ponz, -ponz′; *Fr.* -pôN′). a close-fitting tunic, usually padded and bearing heraldic arms, worn over armor. Also, **gipon.** [1350–1400; ME *jopo(u)n* < MF *jupon,* equiv. to OF *jupe* a kind of jacket + *-on* n. suffix]

ju•ra (jo͝or′ə; *Lat.* yo͞o′rä), *n.* pl. of **jus.**

Ju•ra (jo͝or′ə; Fr. zhy RA′), *n.* **1.** a department in E France. 238,856; 1952 sq. mi. (5055 sq. km). *Cap.:* Lons-le-Saunier. **2.** See **Jura Mountains.**

ju•ral (jo͝or′əl), *adj.* **1.** pertaining to law; legal. **2.** of or pertaining to rights and obligations. [1625–35; < L *jūr-* (s. of *jūs*) law + -AL[1]] —**ju′ral•ly,** *adv.*

ju•ra•men•ta•do (*Sp.* ho͞o′rä men tä′thô), *n., pl.* **-dos** (-thôs). (formerly) a Muslim, esp. a Moro, bound by an oath to be killed fighting against Christians and other infidels. [< Sp: lit., (one) sworn (ptp. of *juramentar* to swear), equiv. to *jurament-* (< LL *jūrāmentum* oath, equiv. to *jūrā(re)* to swear + *-mentum* -MENT) + *-ado* -ATE[1]]

Ju′ra Moun′tains (jo͝or′ə; *Fr.* zhy RA′), a mountain range in W central Europe, between France and Switzerland, extending from the Rhine to the Rhone. Highest peak, Crêt de la Neige, 5654 ft. (1723 m). Also called **Jura.**

Ju•ras•sic (jo͝o ras′ik), *Geol.* —*adj.* **1.** noting or pertaining to a period of the Mesozoic Epoch, occurring from 190 to 140 million years ago and characterized by an abundance of dinosaurs and the advent of birds and mammals. See table under **geologic time.** —*n.* **2.** the Jurassic Period or System. [1825–35; JUR(A) + *-assic,* suffix extracted from TRIASSIC; cf. F *jurassique*]

ju•rat (jo͝or′at), *n.* **1.** *Law.* a certificate on an affidavit, by the officer, showing by whom, when, and before whom it was sworn to. **2.** a sworn officer; a magistrate; a member of a permanent jury. [1400–50; late ME < ML *jūrātus* sworn man, n. use of L ptp. of *jūrāre* to swear, equiv. to *jūrā-* v. s. + *-tus* ptp. suffix]

ju•ra•tion (jo͝o rā′shən), *n.* an act of taking or administering an oath. [1650–60; < LL *jūrātiōn-* (s. of *jūrātiō*), equiv. to *jūrāt(us)* (see JURAT) + *-iōn-* -ION]

ju•ra•to•ry (jo͝or′ə tôr′ē, -tōr′ē), *adj.* pertaining to, constituting, or expressed in an oath. [1545–55; < LL *jūrātōrius* on oath, equiv. to L *jūrā(re)* to swear + *-tōrius* -TORY[1]]

Jur. D., Doctor of Law. [< L *Jūris Doctor*]

ju•re di•vi•no (yo͞o′Re di wē′nō; *Eng.* jo͝or′ē di vī′nō, -vē′-), *Latin.* by divine law.

ju•re hu•ma•no (yo͞o′Re o͞o mä′nō; *Eng.* jo͝or′ē hyo͞o-mā′nō, -mä′-), *Latin.* by human law.

ju•rel (ho͞o rel′), *n.* any of several carangid food fishes, esp. of the genus *Caranx,* found in warm seas. [1750–60; < Sp < Catalan *sorell,* prob. < L *saurus* < Gk *saûros* lizard]

ju•rid•i•cal (jo͝o rid′i kəl), *adj.* **1.** of or pertaining to the administration of justice. **2.** of or pertaining to law or jurisprudence; legal. Also, **ju•rid′ic.** [1495–1505; < L *jūridic(us)* (*jūri-,* comb. form of *jūs* law + *dic-,* base of *dicere* to say, DICTATE) + -AL[1]] —**ju•rid′i•cal•ly,** *adv.*

jurid′ical days′, days in court on which law is administered; days on which the court can lawfully sit.

ju•ried (jo͝or′ēd), *adj.* having the contents selected for exhibition by a jury: *a juried art show.* [JURY[1] + -ED[3]]

ju•ris•con•sult (jo͝or′is kən sult′, -kon′sult), *n.* **1.** *Roman and Civil Law.* a person authorized to give legal advice. **2.** *Civil Law.* a master of the civil law. *Abbr.:* J.C. [1595–1605; < L *jūris consultus* one skilled in the law. See JUS, CONSULT]

ju•ris•dic•tion (jo͝or′is dik′shən), *n.* **1.** the right, power, or authority to administer justice by hearing and determining controversies. **2.** power; authority; control: *He has jurisdiction over all American soldiers in the area.* **3.** the extent or range of judicial, law enforcement, or other authority: *This case comes under the jurisdiction of the local police.* **4.** the territory over which authority is exercised: *All islands to the northwest are his jurisdiction.* [1250–1300; ME < L *jūris dictiōn-* s. of *jūris dictiō* (see JUS, DICTION); r. ME *jurediccioun* < OF *juredicion* < L, as above] —**ju′ris•dic′tion•al,** *adj.* —**ju′ris•dic′tive,** *adj.* —**ju′ris•dic′tion•al•ly,** *adv.*

jurisp., jurisprudence.

ju•ris•pru•dence (jo͝or′is pro͞od′ns, jo͝or′is pro͞od′-), *n.* **1.** the science or philosophy of law. **2.** a body or system of laws. **3.** a department of law: *medical jurisprudence.* **4.** *Civil Law.* decisions of courts, esp. of reviewing tribunals. [1620–30; < L *jūris prūdentia* knowledge of the law. See JUS, PRUDENCE] —**ju•ris•pru•den•tial** (jo͝or′is pro͞o den′shəl), *adj.* —**ju′ris•pru•den′tial•ly,** *adv.*

ju•ris•pru•dent (jo͝or′is pro͞od′nt), *adj.* **1.** versed in jurisprudence. —*n.* **2.** a person versed in jurisprudence. [1620–30; JURISPRUD(ENCE) + -ENT]

ju•rist (jo͝or′ist), *n.* a person versed in the law, as a judge, lawyer, or scholar. [1475–85; < F *juriste* < ML *jūrist(a).* See JUS, -IST]

ju•ris•tic (jo͝o ris′tik), *adj.* of or pertaining to a jurist

CONCISE PRONUNCIATION KEY: act, cāpe, dâre, pärt; set, ēqual; *if,* īce; ox, ōver, ôrder, oil, bo͝ok, bo͞ot, out; up, ûrge; child; sing; shoe; thin, *th*at; zh as in *treasure.* ə = *a* as in *alone,* e as in *system,* i as in *easily,* o as in *gallop,* u as in *circus;* ə as in *fire* (fīər), *hour* (ouər). l and n can serve as syllabic consonants, as in *cradle* (krād′l), and *button* (but′n). See the full key inside the front cover.

or to jurisprudence; juridical. Also, **ju·ris′ti·cal.** [1825–35; JURIST + -IC] —**ju·ris′ti·cal·ly,** *adv.*

juris′tic per′son, *Law.* See under **person** (def. 11). [1870–75]

Jur. M., Master of Jurisprudence.

ju·ror (jo͝or′ər, -ôr), *n.* **1.** one of a group of persons sworn to deliver a verdict in a case submitted to them; member of a jury. **2.** one of the panel from which a jury is selected. **3.** one of a group of people who judge a competition. **4.** a person who has taken an oath or sworn allegiance. [1250–1300; ME *jurour* < AF (cf. OF *jureur*), equiv. to OF *jur(er)* to swear (< L *jūrāre*) + *-our* -OR[2]]

Ju·ru·á (*Port.* zho͞o′Ro͞o ä′), *n.* a river in E and W South America, flowing NE from E Peru through W Brazil to the Amazon. 1200 mi. (1930 km) long.

ju·ry[1] (jo͝or′ē), *n., pl.* **-ries,** *v.,* **-ried, -ry·ing.** —*n.* **1.** a group of persons sworn to render a verdict or true answer on a question or questions officially submitted to them. **2.** such a group selected according to law and sworn to inquire into or determine the facts concerning a cause or an accusation submitted to them and to render a verdict to a court. Cf. **grand jury, petty jury. 3.** a group of persons chosen to adjudge prizes, awards, etc., as in a competition. —*v.t.* **4.** to judge or evaluate by means of a jury: *All entries will be juried by a panel of professionals.* [1250–1300; ME *jurie, juree,* < OF *juree* oath, juridical inquiry, n. use of *juree,* fem. ptp. of *jurer* to swear; cf. JURAT] —**ju′ry·less,** *adj.*
—**Usage.** See **collective noun.**

ju·ry[2] (jo͝or′ē), *adj. Naut.* makeshift or temporary, as for an emergency: *a jury mast.* [1610–20; cf. *jury mast* (early 17th century), of obscure orig.; perh. to be identified with late ME *i(u)were* help, aid, aph. form of OF *ajurie,* deriv. of *aidier* to AID, with *-rie* -RY]

ju·ry·man (jo͝or′ē mən), *n., pl.* **-men.** a juror. [1570–80; JURY[1] + MAN[1]]
—**Usage.** See **-man.**

ju·ry-pack·ing (jo͝or′ē pak′ing), *n.* the practice of contriving that the majority of those chosen for a jury will be persons likely to have partialities affecting a particular case. [1865–70]

ju·ry-rig (jo͝or′ē rig′), *n., v.,* **-rigged, -rig·ging.** —*n.* **1.** *Naut.* a temporary rig to replace a permanent rig that has been disabled, lost overboard, etc. **2.** any makeshift arrangement of machinery or the like. —*v.t.* **3.** to assemble quickly or from whatever is at hand, esp. for temporary use: *to jury-rig stage lights using automobile headlights.* **4.** *Naut.* to replace (a rudder, mast, etc.) with a jury-rig: *We jury-rigged a fore-topmast after the storm had snapped ours off.* [1780–90]

ju′ry room′, a private room, adjacent to a courtroom, where a trial jury discusses a case and reaches its verdict. [1760–70]

ju′ry wheel′, *Law.* a device, containing slips with the names of prospective jurors, that when spun mixes the names for random selection. [1880–85, *Amer.*]

ju·ry·wom·an (jo͝or′ē wo͝om′ən), *n., pl.* **-wom·en.** a female juror. [1795–1805; JURY[1] + WOMAN]
—**Usage.** See **-woman.**

jus (jus; *Lat.* yo͞os), *n., pl.* **ju·ra** (jo͝or′ə; *Lat.* yo͞o′Rä). *Law.* **1.** a right. **2.** law as a system or in the abstract. [< L *jūs* law, right]

jus (zhʏ; *Eng.* zho͞os, jo͞os), *n. French.* juice; gravy. Cf. **au jus.**

jus ca·no·ni·cum (yo͞os′ kä nō′ni ko͝om′; *Eng.* jus′ kə non′i kəm), *Latin.* See **canon law.**

jus ci·vi·le (jus′ si vī′lē, -vē′-), *Roman Law.* the rules and principles of law derived from the customs and legislation of Rome, as opposed to those derived from the customs of all nations (**jus gentium**) or from fundamental ideas of right and wrong implicit in the human mind (**jus naturale**). [< L: civil law]

jus di·vi·num (yo͞os′ di wē′no͞om; *Eng.* jus′ di vī′nəm), *Latin.* divine law.

jus gen·ti·um (jus′ jen′shē əm), *Roman Law.* See under **jus civile.** [1540–50; < L: law of the nations]

jus na·tu·ra·le (jus′ nach′ə rā′lē, nat′yo͞o-), *Roman Law.* See under **jus civile.** Also, **jus na·tu·rae** (jus′ nach′ə rē′, nat′yo͞o-). [< L: natural law]

jus post·li·mi·ni·i (jus′ pōst′lə min′ē ī′), *Internat. Law.* postliminy. [< L: right of postliminy]

jus pri·mae noc·tis (jus′ prī′mē nok′tis). See **droit du seigneur.** [1885–90]

jus san·gui·nis (jus′ sang′gwə nis), *Law.* the principle that the country of nationality of a child is that of the country of nationality of the parents. [1900–05; < L: right of blood]

Jus·se·rand (zhʏsə RäN′), *n.* **Jean (A·dri·en An·toine) Jules** (zhäN A drē äN′ än twAN′ zhʏl), 1855–1932, French diplomat, historian, and essayist.

jus·sive (jus′iv), *Gram.* —*adj.* **1.** (esp. in Semitic languages) expressing a mild command. —*n.* **2.** a jussive form, mood, case, construction, or word. [1840–50; < L *juss(us)* (ptp. of *jubēre* to command) + -IVE]

jus so·li (jus′ sō′lī, -lē), *Law.* the principle that the country of citizenship of a child is determined by its country of birth. Cf. **jus sanguinis.** [1900–05; < L: right of soil (land)]

just[1] (just), *adj.* **1.** guided by truth, reason, justice, and fairness: *We hope to be just in our understanding of such difficult situations.* **2.** done or made according to principle; equitable; proper: *a just reply.* **3.** based on right; rightful; lawful: *a just claim.* **4.** in keeping with truth or fact; true; correct: *a just analysis.* **5.** given or awarded rightly; deserved, as a sentence, punishment, or reward: *a just penalty.* **6.** in accordance with standards or requirements; proper or right: *just proportions.* **7.** (esp. in Biblical use) righteous. **8.** actual, real, or genuine. —*adv.* **9.** within a brief preceding time; but a moment before: *The sun just came out.* **10.** exactly or precisely: *This is just what I mean.* **11.** by a narrow margin; barely: *The arrow just missed the mark.* **12.** only or merely: *He was just a clerk until he became ambitious.* **13.** actually; really; positively: *The weather is just glorious.* [1325–75; ME < L *jūstus* righteous, equiv. to *jūs* law, right + *-tus* adj. suffix]
—**Syn. 1.** upright; equitable, fair, impartial. **3.** legitimate, legal. **4.** accurate, exact; honest. **5.** merited, appropriate, condign, suited, apt, due. —**Ant. 1.** biased. **4.** untrue. **5.** unjustified.

just[2] (just), *n., v.i.* joust. —**just′er,** *n.*

just·au·corps (zho͞o′stə kôr′, -kōr′; *Fr.* zhʏst ō kôR′), *n., pl.* **-corps** (-kôr′, -kōr′; *Fr.* -kôR′). a fitted, knee-length coat, characterized by wide turned-back cuffs and stiff flared skirts, worn esp. by men in the 17th and 18th centuries. Also called **justicoat.** [1650–60; < F *juste au corps* fitting to the body]

juste-mi·lieu (zhʏst mē lyœ′), *n., pl.* ***juste-mi·lieux*** (zhʏst mē lyœ′). *French.* a point between two extremes; the golden mean. [lit., exact middle]

jus·tice (jus′tis), *n.* **1.** the quality of being just; righteousness, equitableness, or moral rightness: *to uphold the justice of a cause.* **2.** rightfulness or lawfulness, as of a claim or title; justness of ground or reason: *to complain with justice.* **3.** the moral principle determining just conduct. **4.** conformity to this principle, as manifested in conduct; just conduct, dealing, or treatment. **5.** the administering of deserved punishment or reward. **6.** the maintenance or administration of what is just by law, as by judicial or other proceedings: *a court of justice.* **7.** judgment of persons or causes by judicial process: *to administer justice in a community.* **8.** a judicial officer; a judge or magistrate. **9.** (*cap.*) Also called **Jus′tice Depart′ment.** the Department of Justice. **10. bring to justice,** to cause to come before a court for trial or to receive punishment for one's misdeeds: *The murderer was brought to justice.* **11. do justice, a.** to act or treat justly or fairly. **b.** to appreciate properly: *We must see this play again to do it justice.* **c.** to acquit in accordance with one's abilities or potentialities: *He finally got a role in which he could do himself justice as an actor.* [1150–1200; ME < OF < L *jūstitia,* equiv. to *jūst(us)* JUST[1] + *-itia* -ICE] —**jus′tice·less,** *adj.*

Jus·tice (jus′tis), *n.* a town in NE Illinois. 10,552.

jus′tice in eyre′, *Old Eng. Law.* See under **eyre** (def. 2a). [1480–90]

jus′tice of the peace′, a local public officer, usually having jurisdiction to try and determine minor civil and criminal cases and to hold preliminary examinations of persons accused of more serious crimes, and having authority to administer oaths, solemnize marriages, etc. [1325–75; ME]

jus·tic·er (jus′tə sər), *n. Archaic.* a judge or magistrate. [1300–50; ME < AF (cf. OF *justicier*); see JUSTICE, -ER[2]]

jus′tice's court′, *Law.* an inferior tribunal, not of record, having limited jurisdiction, both civil and criminal, and presided over by a justice of the peace. Also, **jus′tice court′.** [1520–30]

jus·tice·ship (jus′tis ship′), *n.* the office of a justice. [1535–45; JUSTICE + -SHIP]

jus·ti·ci·a (ju stish′ē ə), *n.* any of numerous plants and shrubs of the genus *Justicia,* which includes the shrimp plant and water willow. [< NL, after James *Justice* (1698–1763), Scottish horticulturist; see -IA]

jus·ti·ci·a·ble (ju stish′ē ə bəl, -stish′ə bəl), *adj. Law.* capable of being settled by law or by the action of a court: *a justiciable dispute.* [1400–50; late ME < AF < ML *jūstitiābilis.* See JUSTICE, -ABLE] —**jus·ti′ci·a·bil′i·ty,** *n.*

jus·ti·ci·ar (ju stish′ē ər), *n.* **1.** a high judicial officer in medieval England. **2.** the chief political and judicial officer in England from the reign of William I to that of Henry III. **3.** justiciary (def. 2). [1475–85; < ML *jūsticiārius* JUSTICIARY] —**jus·ti′ci·ar·ship′,** *n.*

jus·ti·ci·ar·y (ju stish′ē er′ē), *adj., n., pl.* **-ar·ies.** —*adj.* **1.** of or pertaining to the administration of justice. —*n.* **2.** the office or jurisdiction of a justiciar. **3.** justiciar (defs. 1 and 2). [1470–80; < ML *jūsticiārius.* See JUSTICE, -ARY]

jus·ti·coat (jus′ti kōt′), *n.* justaucorps. [alter. by folk etym.]

jus·ti·fi·a·ble (jus′tə fī′ə bəl, jus′tə fī′-), *adj.* capable of being justified; that can be shown to be or can be defended as being just, right, or warranted; defensible: *justifiable homicide.* [1515–25; < MF; see JUSTIFY, -ABLE] —**jus′ti·fi′a·bil′i·ty, jus′ti·fi′a·ble·ness,** *n.* —**jus′ti·fi′a·bly,** *adv.*

jus·ti·fi·ca·tion (jus′tə fi kā′shən), *n.* **1.** a reason, fact, circumstance, or explanation that justifies or defends: *His insulting you was ample justification for you to leave the party.* **2.** an act of justifying: *The painter's justification of his failure to finish on time didn't impress me.* **3.** the state of being justified. **4.** Also called **justifica′tion by faith′.** *Theol.* the act of God whereby humankind is made or accounted just, or free from guilt or penalty of sin. **5.** *Print.* the spacing of words and letters within a line of type so that all full lines in a column have even margins both on the left and on the right. [1350–1400; ME < LL *jūstificātiōn-* (s. of *jūstificātiō*), equiv. to *jūstificāt(us)* ptp. of *jūstificāre* to JUSTIFY (see JUSTIFICATORY) + *-iōn-* -ION-]

justifica′tion by works′, *Theol.* the belief that a person becomes just before God by the performance of good works: the doctrine against which Luther protested in inaugurating the Protestant Reformation.

jus·tif·i·ca·to·ry (ju stif′i kə tôr′ē, -tōr′ē, jus′tə fi-kā′tə rē), *adj.* serving to justify; providing justification. Also, **jus·ti·fi·ca·tive** (jus′tə fi kā′tiv). [1570–80; < LL *justificā(re)* to JUSTIFY + -TORY[1]]

jus·ti·fy (jus′tə fī′), *v.,* **-fied, -fy·ing.** —*v.t.* **1.** to show (an act, claim, statement, etc.) to be just or right: *The end does not always justify the means.* **2.** to defend or uphold as warranted or well-grounded: *Don't try to justify his rudeness.* **3.** *Theol.* to declare innocent or guiltless; absolve; acquit. **4.** *Print.* **a.** to make (a line of type) a desired length by spacing the words and letters, esp. so that full lines in a column have even margins both on the left and on the right. **b.** to level and square (a strike). —*v.i.* **5.** *Law.* **a.** to show a satisfactory reason or excuse for something done. **b.** to qualify as bail or surety. **6.** *Print.* (of a line of type) to fit exactly into a desired length. [1250–1300; ME *justifien* < OF *justifier* < LL *jūstificāre,* equiv. to L *jūsti-* (comb. form of *jūstus* JUST[1]) + *-ficāre* -FY] —**jus′ti·fi′er,** *n.* —**jus′ti·fy′ing·ly,** *adv.*
—**Syn. 1.** vindicate; validate. **2.** excuse.

Jus·tin (jus′tin; *Fr.* zhʏs taN′; *Ger.* yo͞os tēn′), *n.* a male given name: from a Latin word meaning "just."

Jus·tine (ju stēn′; *Fr.* zhʏs tēn′), *n.* a female given name: derived from *Justin.*

Jus·tin·i·an I (ju stin′ē ən), (*Flavius Anicius Justinianus*) ("*Justinian the Great*") A.D. 483–565, Byzantine emperor 527–565.

Justin′ian Code′, the body of Roman law that was codified and promulgated under Justinian I.

Jus·tin·i·a·ni·an (ju stin′ē ā′nē ən), *adj.* of or pertaining to Justinian I or the Byzantine dynasty (A.D. 518–610) named after him. Also, **Jus·tin′i·a′ne·an.** [1820–30; JUSTINIAN + -IAN]

Jus′tin Mar′tyr (jus′tin mär′tər), **Saint,** A.D. c100–163?, early church historian and philosopher.

just′ intona′tion, *Music.* a system of tuning based on the pure perfect fifth and major third. [1840–50]

Jus·ti·ti·a (ju stish′ē ə), *n.* the ancient Roman personification of justice.

jus·ti·ti·a om·ni·bus (yo͞o stit′ē ä′ ôm′ni bo͝os′; *Eng.* ju stish′ē ə om′nə bəs), *Latin.* justice to all: motto of the District of Columbia.

jus·tle (jus′əl), *v.t., v.i.,* **-tled, -tling,** *n.* jostle.

just·ly (just′lē), *adv.* **1.** in a just manner; honestly; fairly: *Deal justly with the prisoners.* **2.** in conformity to fact or rule; accurately. **3.** deservedly; as deserved. [1300–50; ME; see JUST[1], -LY]

just·ness (just′nis), *n.* **1.** the quality or state of being just, equitable, or right: *His justness was never doubted.* **2.** conformity to fact or rule; correctness; exactness. [1400–50; late ME *justnesse.* See JUST[1], -NESS]

jut (jut), *v.,* **jut·ted, jut·ting,** *n.* —*v.i.* **1.** to extend beyond the main body or line; project; protrude (often fol. by *out*): *The narrow strip of land juts out into the bay.* —*n.* **2.** something that juts out; a projecting or protruding point. [1555–65; var. of JET[1]] —**jut′ting·ly,** *adv.*

jute (jo͞ot), *n.* **1.** a strong, coarse fiber used for making burlap, gunny, cordage, etc., obtained from two East Indian plants, *Corchorus capsularis* and *C. olitorius,* of the linden family. **2.** either of these plants. **3.** any plant of the same genus. [1740–50; < Bengali *jhuṭo*] —**jute′like′,** *adj.*

Jute (jo͞ot), *n.* a member of a continental Germanic tribe, probably from Jutland, that invaded Britain in the 5th century A.D. and settled in Kent. —**Jut′ish,** *adj.*

jute′ board′, a strong, bendable cardboard made from rags and sulfite, used chiefly in the manufacture of shipping cartons.

Jut·land (jut′lənd), *n.* a peninsula comprising the continental portion of Denmark: naval battle between the British and German fleets was fought west of this peninsula 1916. 11,441 sq. mi. (29,630 sq. km). Danish, **Jylland.** —**Jut′land·er,** *n.* —**Jut′land·ish,** *adj.*

jut·ty (jut′ē), *n., pl.* **-ties,** *v.,* **-tied, -ty·ing.** —*n.* **1.** *Archit.* jetty[1] (def. 4). —*v.i., v.t.* **2.** *Obs.* to project beyond. [var. of JETTY]

juv., juvenile.

Ju·var·ra (yo͞o vär′Rä), *n.* **Fi·lip·po** (fē lēp′pô), 1678–1736, Italian architect. Also, **Ju·va·ra** (yo͞o vä′Rä).

Ju·ve·nal (jo͞o′və nl), *n.* (*Decimus Junius Juvenalis*) A.D. c60–140, Roman poet. —**Ju·ve·na·li·an** (jo͞o′və nā′lē ən), *adj.*

ju′ve·nal plum′age (jo͞o′və nl), *Ornith.* the first plumage of birds, composed of contour feathers, which in certain species follows the naked nestling stage and in other species follows the molt of natal down. [< L *juvenālis* youthful, equiv. to *juven(is)* young man or woman + *-ālis* -AL[1]]

ju·ve·nes·cent (jo͞o′və nes′ənt), *adj.* **1.** being or becoming youthful; young. **2.** young in appearance. **3.** having the power to make young or youthful: *a juvenescent elixir.* [1815–25; < L *juvenēscent-* (s. of *juvenēscēns,* prp. of *juvenēscere* to become youthful), equiv. to *juven-* young (see JUVENILE) + *-ēscent-* -ESCENT] —**ju′ve·nes′cence,** *n.*

ju•ve•nile (jo͞o′və nl, -nīl′), *adj.* **1.** of, pertaining to, characteristic of, or suitable or intended for young persons: *juvenile books.* **2.** young; youthful: *juvenile years.* **3.** immature; childish; infantile: *His juvenile tantrums are not in keeping with his age.* —*n.* **4.** a young person; youth. **5.** *Theat.* **a.** a youthful male or female role. **b.** an actor or actress who plays such parts. **6.** a book for children. **7.** *Ornith.* a young bird in the stage when it has fledged, if altricial, or has replaced down of hatching, if precocial. **8.** a two-year-old racehorse. [1615–25; < L *juvenīlis* youthful, equiv. to *juven(is)* youthful + *-īlis* -ILE] —**ju′ve•nile•ly,** *adv.*
—**Syn. 1.** See **young.**

ju′venile court′, a law court having jurisdiction over youths, generally of less than 18 years. [1895–1900, *Amer.*]

ju′venile delin′quency, behavior of a child or youth that is so marked by violation of law, persistent mischievousness, antisocial behavior, disobedience, or intractability as to thwart correction by parents and to constitute a matter for action by the juvenile courts. [1810–20]

ju′venile delin′quent, 1. a minor who cannot be controlled by parental authority and commits antisocial or criminal acts, as vandalism or violence. **2.** a child or youth characterized by juvenile delinquency. [1810–20]

ju′venile hor′mone, *Biochem.* any of a class of insect and plant hormones acting to inhibit the molting of a juvenile insect into its adult form. [1935–40]

ju′venile of′ficer, a police officer concerned with juvenile delinquents. [1950–55]

ju′ve•nile-on′set diabe′tes (jo͞o′və nl on′set′, -ôn′-, -nīl′-), *Pathol.* diabetes (def. 3). [1975–80]

ju′venile rheu′matoid arthri′tis, *Pathol.* rheumatoid arthritis that begins before puberty, often preceded by such symptoms as fever, patchy rash, and weight loss. [1965–70]

ju•ve•nil•i•a (jo͞o′və nil′ē ə, -nil′yə), *n.pl.* **1.** works, esp. writings, produced in one's youth: *His juvenilia were more successful than his mature writings.* **2.** literary or artistic productions suitable or designed for the young: *publishers of juvenilia.* [1615–25; < L, n. use of neut. pl. of *juvenīlis* JUVENILE]

ju•ve•nil•i•ty (jo͞o′və nil′i tē), *n., pl.* **-ties. 1.** juvenile state, character, or manner. **2. juvenilities,** youthful qualities or acts. **3.** an instance of being juvenile. [1615–25; JUVENILE + -ITY]

ju•ve•nil•ize (jo͞o′və nl īz′), *v.t.,* **-ized, -iz•ing. 1.** to make juvenile or immature: *to juvenilize the classics for quick reading.* **2.** to make suitable for or more appealing to children. Also, *esp. Brit.,* **ju′ve•nil•ise′.** [1825–35; JUVENILE + -IZE] —**ju′ve•nil•i•za′tion,** *n.*

Ju•ven•ta Fons (yo͞o ven′tä fons′), an area in the southern hemisphere of Mars, appearing as a dark region when viewed through a telescope.

jux•ta•pose (juk′stə pōz′, juk′stə pōz′), *v.t.,* **-posed, -pos•ing.** to place close together or side by side, esp. for comparison or contrast. [1850–55; back formation from JUXTAPOSITION]

jux•ta•po•si•tion (juk′stə pə zish′ən), *n.* **1.** an act or instance of placing close together or side by side, esp. for comparison or contrast. **2.** the state of being close together or side by side. [1655–65; < F < L *juxtā* side by side + F *position* POSITION] —**jux′ta•po•si′tion•al,** *adj.*

JV, 1. See **joint venture. 2.** junior varsity. Also, **J.V.**

jwlr., jeweler.

J.W.V., Jewish War Veterans.

Jy, jansky; janskies.

Jy., July.

Jyl•land (yʏl′län), *n.* Danish name of **Jutland.**

Jy•väs•ky•lä (yʏ′vas kʏ′la), *n.* a city in S central Finland. 64,500.

CONCISE PRONUNCIATION KEY: act, cāpe, dâre, pärt; set, ēqual; if, īce; ox, ōver, ôrder, oil, bo͝ok, bo͞ot, out; up, ûrge; child; sing; shoe; thin, *th*at; zh as in *treasure.* ə = *a* as in *alone, e* as in *system, i* as in *easily, o* as in *gallop, u* as in *circus;* ᵊ as in *fire* (fīᵊr), *hour* (ouᵊr). l and n can serve as syllabic consonants, as in *cradle* (krād′l), and *button* (but′n). See the full key inside the front cover.

DEVELOPMENT OF MAJUSCULE								
NORTH SEMITIC	GREEK		ETR.	LATIN		MODERN		
						GOTHIC	ITALIC	ROMAN
↓	ƚ	K	ʞ	ʞ	K	𝔎	*K*	K

DEVELOPMENT OF MINUSCULE					
ROMAN CURSIVE	ROMAN UNCIAL	CAROL. MIN.	MODERN		
			GOTHIC	ITALIC	ROMAN
—	K	—	𝔨	*k*	k

The eleventh letter of the English alphabet corresponds to North Semitic *kaph* and Greek *kappa*. The Romans, adopting the alphabet from the Etruscans, at first had three symbols, C, K, and Q, for the *k*-sound. K fell into disuse. It did not appear in English until after the Norman conquest, when, under Norman French influence, it came into use in place of C to distinguish the pronunciation of words of native origin: for example, *cyng* became *king*; *cene*, *keen*; *cynn-*, *kin*; *cnif*, *knife*; and *cnotta*, *knot*. Under other influences, often through loanwords, the symbol entered into more general use.

K, k (kā), *n., pl.* **K's** or **Ks, k's** or **ks. 1.** the eleventh letter of the English alphabet, a consonant. **2.** any sound represented by the letter *K* or *k*, as in *bilk*, *kit*, or *sick*. **3.** something having the shape of a K. **4.** a written or printed representation of the letter *K* or *k*. **5.** a device, as a printer's type, for reproducing the letter *K* or *k*.

K, 1. *Chess.* king. **2.** *Physics.* Kelvin. **3.** the number 1000: *The salary offered is $20K.* [abbr. of KILO-]. **4.** *Music.* See **Köchel listing. 5.** kindergarten: *a K–12 boarding school.* **6.** *Real Estate.* kitchen.

K, *Symbol.* **1.** the eleventh in order or in a series, or, when *I* is omitted, the tenth. **2.** *Chem.* potassium. [< NL *kalium*] **3.** *Computers.* **a.** the number 1024 or 2^{10}: *A binary 32K memory has 32,768 positions.* **b.** kilobyte. **4.** *Baseball.* strikeout; strikeouts. **5.** *Physics.* kaon. **6.** *Biochem.* lysine.

K, *Ecol.* carrying capacity.

k, *Symbol.* **1.** *Math.* a vector on the z-axis, having length 1 unit. **2.** See **Boltzmann constant.**

K., 1. kip; kips. **2.** Knight. **3.** kwacha.

k., 1. *Elect.* capacity. **2.** karat. **3.** kilogram; kilograms. **4.** *Chess.* king. **5.** knight. **6.** knot. **7.** kopeck.

K2 (kā′to͞o′), *n.* a mountain in N Kashmir, in the Karakoram range: second highest peak in the world. 28,250 ft. (8611 m). Also called **Godwin Austen, Dapsang.**

kA, kiloampere; kiloamperes.

ka (kä), *n. Egyptian Relig.* a spiritual entity, an aspect of the individual, believed to live within the body during life and to survive it after death. [1890–95; < Egyptian *k'*]

ka-, var. of **ker-.**

Kaap•stad (käp′stät), *n.* Afrikaans name of **Cape Town.**

kab (kab), *n.* cab².

Ka•'ba (kä′bə, kä′ə bə), *n.* **1.** a small, cubical building in the courtyard of the Great Mosque at Mecca containing a sacred black stone: regarded by Muslims as the House of God and the objective of their pilgrimages. **2.** one of several replicas of this building, sacred to pre-Islamic Arabs. Also, **Ka′bah, Ka'a′bah.** [1895–1900; < Ar *ka'bah*]

ka•bab (kə bob′), *n.* kabob.

ka•ba•ka (kə bä′kə), *n.* the traditional king of Buganda, a region and former kingdom of southern Uganda. [1875–80; < Luganda]

kab•a•la (kab′ə lə, kə bä′-), *n.* cabala. Also, **kab′ba•la.**

Ka•ba•lev•sky (kä′bə lef′skē; *Russ.* kə bu lyef′skyē), *n.* **Dmi•tri** (də mē′trē; *Russ.* dmyē′TRyē), born 1904, Russian composer.

kab•a•lis•tic (kab′ə lis′tik), *adj.* cabalistic. Also, **kab′ba•lis′tic.**

Ka•bar•di•an (kə bär′dē ən), *n.* a Circassian language of the Kabardino-Balkar Autonomous Republic.

Kab•ar•di′no-Bal•kar′ Auton′omous Repub′lic (kab′ər dē′nō bôl kär′, -bal-, -bôl′kär, -bal′-; *Russ.* kə bur dyē′nə bul kär′), an autonomous republic in the Russian Federation in N Caucasia, N of the Georgian Republic. 675,000; 4747 sq. mi. (12,295 sq. km). *Cap.:* Nalchik.

Ka•bei•ri (kə bī′rī, -rē), *n.pl.* Cabiri.

CONCISE ETYMOLOGY KEY: <, descended or borrowed from; >, whence; b., blend of, blended; c., cognate with; cf., compare; deriv., derivative; equiv., equivalent; imit., imitative; obl., oblique; r., replacing; s., stem; sp., spelling, spelled; resp., respelling, respelled; trans., translation; ?, origin unknown; *, unattested; ‡, probably earlier than. See the full key inside the front cover.

Ka•bi•nett (kä′bi net′), *n. German.* cabinet (def. 10). Also called ***Ka•bi•nett•wein*** (kä′bi net′vīn′).

Ka•bir (kə bēr′), *n.* fl. late 15th century, Hindu religious reformer.

kab•loo•na (kab lo͞o′nə), *n. Canadian (chiefly Arctic).* a white man; a European. [1765–75; < Inuit *qablunaaq*, prob. deriv. of *qava* the South; assoc. with *qablu* "eyebrow" has given rise to the spurious trans. "person with big eyebrows"]

ka•bob (kə bob′), *n.* **1.** Usually, **kabobs.** small pieces of meat or seafood seasoned or marinated and broiled, often with tomatoes, green peppers, onions, or other vegetables, usually on a skewer. **2.** (in Anglo-Indian use) roast meat. Also, **cabob, kebab, kebob, kabab.** [1665–75; < Ar, Hindi *kabāb* < Turk *kebap* roast meat. See SHISH KEBAB]

ka-boom (kə bo͞om′), *interj.* (used to represent a sudden and loud sound, as of an explosion or a bass drum). [see KA-, BOOM¹]

ka•bu•ki (kä bo͞o′kē, kə-, kä′bo͞o kē), *n.* **1.** popular drama of Japan, developed chiefly in the 17th century, characterized by elaborate costuming, rhythmic dialogue, stylized acting, music, and dancing, and the performance of both male and female roles by male actors. Cf. **Nō. 2.** *(cap.)* Also called **Grand Kabuki.** public performances of this type of drama. [1895–1900; < Japn: orig., as v., to act dissolutely; usually written with phonograms that carry the meanings "song-dance-skill"]

Ka•bul (kä′bo͝ol, -bəl, kə bo͞ol′), *n.* **1.** a city in and the capital of Afghanistan, in the NE part. 377,715. **2.** a river flowing E from NE Afghanistan to the Indus River in Pakistan. 360 mi. (580 km) long.

Kab•we (käb′wā), *n.* a city in central Zambia: oldest mining town; cave site where the fossil skull of Rhodesian man was found. 143,635. Formerly, **Broken Hill.**

Ka•byle (kə bīl′), *n.* **1.** a member of a branch of the Berber people dwelling in NE Algeria. **2.** the Berber language spoken by the Kabyles. [1730–40; < Ar *qabā'il*, pl. of *qabīlah* tribe]

ka•cha (kuch′ə), *adj.* kutcha. Also, **kach•cha** (kuch′chə).

ka•chi•na (kə chē′nə), *n.* **1.** any of various ancestral spirits deified by the Hopi Indians and impersonated in religious rituals by masked dancers. **2.** a Hopi religious ritual at which such masked dancers perform. **3.** a masked dancer impersonating such a spirit at a Hopi religious ritual. **4.** See **kachina doll.** Also, **katcina, katchina.** [1885–90; < Hopi *ķacina* < Keresan (Santa Ana) *ķâ·cina* (or a cognate word)]

kachi′na doll′, a Hopi Indian doll carved from cottonwood root in representation of a kachina and given as a gift to a child or used as a household decoration. [1945–50, *Amer.*]

Ka•dai (kä′dī), *n.* **1.** a group of languages related to the Thai group and spoken by a small population in southern China and northern Vietnam. **2.** a language family consisting of this group and the Thai group. —*adj.* **3.** of or pertaining to Kadai.

Ká•dár (kä′där), *n.* **Já•nos** (yä′nôsh), 1912–89, Hungarian political leader: general secretary of the Communist party 1956–88.

Kad•da•fi (kə dä′fē), *n.* **Mu•am•mar (Muhammad) al-** or **el-** (mo͞o ä′mär, al, el), Qadhafi.

Kad•dish (*Ashk. Heb.* kä′dish; *Seph. Heb.* kä dēsh′), *n., pl.* **Kad•di•shim** (*Ashk. Heb.* kä dish′im; *Seph. Heb.* kä dē shēm′). *Judaism.* **1.** *(italics)* a liturgical prayer, consisting of three or six verses, recited at specified points during each of the three daily services and on certain other occasions. **2.** *(italics)* Also called ***Mourner's Kaddish.*** the five-verse form of this prayer that is recited at specified points during each of the three daily services by one observing the mourning period of 11 months, beginning on the day of burial, for a deceased parent, sibling, child, or spouse, and by one observing the anniversary of such a death. **3. Kaddishim,** persons who recite this prayer. [1605–15; < Aram *qaddish* holy (one)]

ka•di (kä′dē, kā′-), *n., pl.* **-dis.** qadi.

Ka•di•yev•ka (kə dē′yəf kə; *Russ.* ku dyē′yif kə), *n.* former name of **Stakhanov.**

Ka•du•na (kə do͞o′nə), *n.* a city in central Nigeria. 186,000.

kaf (käf), *n.* the twenty-second letter of the Arabic alphabet, representing a velar stop consonant sound. [< Ar *kāf*]

kaf•fee klatsch (kä′fē kläch′, klach′, kô′-). See **coffee klatsch.** Also, **kaf′fee•klatch′.**

kaf•fee•klatsch•er (kä′fē klä′chər, -klach′ər, kô′-), *n.* a person who participates, esp. regularly, in a kaffee klatsch. [1935–40; KAFFEE KLATSCH + -ER¹]

Kaf•fir (kaf′ər, kä′fər), *n., pl.* **-firs,** *(esp. collectively)* **-fir. 1.** *Disparaging and Offensive.* (in South Africa) a black person: originally used of the Xhosa people only. **2.** *(l.c.)* kafir (def. 4). **3.** *(l.c.) Islam.* kafir (def. 2). [1780–90; < Ar *kāfir* unbeliever, infidel, skeptic]

Kaf′fir lil′y, 1. clivia. **2.** See **crimson flag.** Also, **Kaf′ir lil′y.** [1895–1900]

kaf•fi•yeh (kə fē′ə), *n.* an Arab headdress for men; made from a diagonally folded square of cloth held in place by an agal wound around the head. Also, **keffiyeh, kufiyeh, kuffieh.** [< Ar *kaffiyah*, var. of *kuffiyeh*]

kaffiyeh

Kaf•frar•i•a (kə frâr′ē ə), *n.* a region in the S Republic of South Africa: inhabited mostly by the Xhosa. —**Kaf•frar′i•an,** *adj., n.*

Kaf•ir (kaf′ər, kä′fər, kä′-), *n., pl.* **-irs,** *(esp. collectively)* **-ir. 1.** Also called **Nuristani.** a member of an Indo-European people of Nuristan. **2.** *(l.c.) Islam.* an infidel or unbeliever. **3.** Kaffir (def. 1). **4.** *(l.c.)* Also, **kaffir.** Also called **kaf′ir corn′.** a grain sorghum, *Sorghum bicolor caffrorum*, having stout, short-jointed, leafy stalks, introduced into the U.S. from southern Africa. [1795–1805; < Ar; see KAFFIR]

Kaf•i•ri (kaf′ə rē, kə fēr′ē), *n.* an Indo-Iranian language, or small group of languages, of Nuristan, closely related to but not a part of the Indic subbranch. Also called **Nuristani.**

Ka•fi•ri•stan (kä′fi ri stän′, kaf′ər ə stan′), *n.* former name of **Nuristan.**

Kaf•ka (käf′kä, -kə), *n.* **Franz** (fränts), 1883–1924, Austrian novelist and short-story writer, born in Prague.

Kaf•ka•esque (käf′kə esk′), *adj.* **1.** of, pertaining to, characteristic of, or resembling the literary work of Franz Kafka: *the Kafkaesque terror of the endless interrogations.* **2.** marked by a senseless, disorienting, often menacing complexity: *Kafkaesque bureaucracies.* [1945–50; KAFKA + -ESQUE]

Kaf•re (kaf′rā, käf′-), *n.* Khafre.

kaf•tan (kaf′tan, -tən, kaf tan′), *n.* caftan.

Ka•fu•e (kə fo͞o′ā, kä-), *n.* a river in S central Africa, flowing SE along the Zaire-Zambia border and then SW and E through Zambia to the Zambezi River above Kariba Lake. ab. 600 mi. (965 km) long.

Ka•ga•wa (kä′gä wä′), *n.* **To•yo•hi•ko** (tô′yô hē′kô), 1888–1960, Japanese social reformer and religious leader.

Ka•ge•ra (kä gâr′ə), *n.* a river in equatorial Africa flowing into Lake Victoria from the west: the most remote headstream of the Nile. 430 mi. (690 km) long.

ka•go (kä′gō), *n., pl.* **-gos.** (in Japan) a small basketwork palanquin strung from a pole each end of which rests on the shoulder of a bearer. [1855–60; < Japn: basket, cage]

Ka•go•shi•ma (kä′gô shē′mä), *n.* a seaport on S Kyushu, in SW Japan. 505,077.

ka•gu (kä′go͞o), *n.* a raillike bird, *Rhinochetus jubatus,* of the island of New Caledonia, having a gray body, black-and-white wings, and a long, shaggy crest: an endangered species. [1860–65; < a language of New Caledonia]

Ka•ha•na•mo•ku (kä hä′nä mō′ko͞o), *n.* **Duke Pa•o•a** (pä ō′ä), 1890–1968, U.S. swimmer and surfer.

Kah•lú•a (kä lo͞o′ä, kə lo͞o′ə), *Trademark.* a brand of coffee-flavored liqueur, made in Mexico.

Kahn (kän), *n.* **Louis Isadore,** 1901–74, U.S. architect, born in Estonia.

Kahn′ test′, *Med.* a test for syphilis based on the formation of a precipitate in a mixture of serum and antigen. Cf. **Kline test.** [1960–65; named after R. L. *Kahn* (born 1887), American bacteriologist, its originator]

Ka•ho•o•la•we (kä hō′ō lä′wä, -vä), *n.* an island in central Hawaii, S of Maui: uninhabited. 45 sq. mi. (117 sq. km).

Ka•hu•lu•i (kä′ho͞o lo͞o′ē), *n.* a town on N Maui, in central Hawaii. 12,978.

ka•hu•na (kə ho͞o′nə), *n.* (in Hawaii) a native medicine man or priest. [1885–90; < Hawaiian]

kai•ak (kī′ak), *n.* kayak.

kai′bab squir′rel (kī′bab), a nearly extinct tree squirrel, *Sciurus kaibabensis,* found only in a small area north of the Grand Canyon. [after the *Kaibab* Plateau of N Arizona]

Kai•e•teur (kī′i to͝or′), *n.* a waterfall in central Guyana, on a tributary of the Essequibo River. 741 ft. (226 m) high. Also called **Kaieteur′ Falls′.**

Kai•feng (kī′fung′), *n. Pinyin, Wade-Giles.* a city in NE Henan province, in E China: a former provincial capital. 330,000.

kail (kāl), *n.* kale.

Kai•las•a (kī lä′sə), *n.* a Brahmanical temple dedicated to Shiva, at Ellora, India: architecturally one of the finest of ancient cave temples.

Kai•lu•a (kī lo͞o′ä, -lo͞o′ə), *n.* a city on SE Oahu, in Hawaii. With Lanikai, 35,812.

kail•yard (kāl′yärd′), *n. Scot.* kaleyard.

kail′yard school′. See **kaleyard school.** —**kail′•yard′er,** *n.* —**kail′yard′ism,** *n.*

kain[1] (kān), *n. Scot.* cain.

kain[2] (kīn), *n.* sarong. [1915–20; < Malay: cloth, sarong]

Kain•gang (kīn′gang′), *n., pl.* **-gangs,** (*esp. collectively*) **-gang.** Caingang.

kai′nic ac′id (kī′nik), *Pharm.* an analogue of glutamate, $C_{10}H_{15}NO_4$, derived from the red alga *Digenia simplex,* used experimentally to stimulate certain neurons in the brain. [1953; < Japn *kain(in-sō)* the name of the alga + -IC]

kai•nite (kī′nīt, kā′-), *n.* a mineral, hydrous sulfate of magnesium and potassium chloride, occurring in granular crystalline masses, used as a fertilizer and as a source of potassium salts. [1865–70; < G *Kainit.* See CAINO-, -ITE[1]]

Kair•ouan (*Fr.* keʀ wän′), *n.* a city in NE Tunisia: a holy city of Islam. 54,000. Also, **Kair•wan** (kīᵊr wän′).

kai•ser (kī′zər), *n.* **1.** a German emperor. **2.** an Austrian emperor. **3.** *Hist.* a ruler of the Holy Roman Empire. **4.** a person who exercises or tries to exercise absolute authority; autocrat. [1150–1200; < G << L *Caesar* emperor, special use of proper name (see CAESAR); r. ME *keisere,* (north) *caisere* < ON *keisari* << L as above; cf. OE *cāsere*] —**kai′ser•dom,** *n.*

Kai•ser (kī′zər), *n.* **Henry J(ohn),** 1882–1967, U.S. industrialist.

kai•ser•ism (kī′zə riz′əm), *n.* autocratic rule, like that of a German kaiser. [1910–15; KAISER + -ISM]

kai′ser roll′, a rounded, unsweetened roll, formed by folding the corners of a square of dough toward the center, often sprinkled with poppy seeds before baking.

kai•ser•ship (kī′zər ship′), *n.* the office of kaiser. [1885–90; KAISER + -SHIP]

Kai•sers•lau•tern (kī′zərz lou′tərn; *Ger.* kī′zəʀs lou′-təʀn), *n.* a city in S Rhineland-Palatinate, in SW Germany. 100,300.

k'ai shu (kī′ sho͞o′), a variety of Chinese script developed in the 4th century A.D. and considered standard since that time. Also, *Pinyin,* **kai′shu′.** [< Chin *kǎishū* formal (i.e., square-style, printed-style) writing]

Ka•jaa•ni (kä′yä nē), *n.* a city in central Finland. 34,092.

Ka•jar (kä jär′, kə-), *n.* a dynasty that ruled Persia 1794–1925.

ka•ka (kä′kə), *n.* any of several New Zealand parrots of the genus *Nestor,* esp. *N. meridionalis,* having chiefly greenish and olive-brown plumage. [1765–75; < Maori *kākā,* perh. akin to *kā* to screech]

ka•ka•po (kä′kə pō′), *n., pl.* **-pos** (-pōz′). a large, almost flightless nocturnal parrot, *Strigops habroptilus,* of New Zealand: an endangered species. [1835–45; < Maori *kākāpō* (*kākā* KAKA + *pō* night)]

ka•ke•bu•ton (kä′kə bo͞o′ton), *n.* a thin quilt or coverlet traditionally used when sleeping on a futon. [< Japn, equiv. to *kake(y)* to hang (transit.) (< *kaka-i) + *-buton,* comb. form of *futon* FUTON]

ka•ke•mo•no (kä′kə mō′nō; *Japn.* kä′ke mô′nô), *n., pl.* **-nos, -no.** a vertical hanging scroll containing either text or a painting, intended to be viewed on a wall and rolled when not in use. Cf. **makimono.** [1885–90; < Japn, equiv. to *kake(y)* to hang (see KAKEBUTON) + *mono* thing]

ka•ki (kä′kē), *n., pl.* **-kis. 1.** the Japanese persimmon tree. **2.** the fruit of this tree. [1720–30; < Japn]

kak•is•toc•ra•cy (kak′ə stok′rə sē), *n., pl.* **-cies.** government by the worst persons; a form of government in which the worst persons are in power. [1820–30; < Gk *kákisto(s),* superl. of *kakós* bad + -CRACY] —**ka•kis•to•crat•i•cal** (kə kis′tə krat′i kəl), *adj.*

kal., kalends.

ka•la-a•zar (kä′lä ä zär′, kä′lə az′ər), *n. Pathol.* a chronic, usually fatal disease occurring in tropical areas of Asia and the Western Hemisphere, characterized by irregular fever, enlargement of the spleen, anemia, and emaciation, caused by the protozoan *Leishmania donovani.* Also called **Dumdum fever, visceral leishmaniasis.** [1880–85; < Hindi, equiv. to *kālā* black + Pers *āzār* disease]

Ka•la•ha•ri (kä′lə här′ē, kal′ə-), *n.* a desert region in SW Africa, largely in Botswana. 100,000 sq. mi. (259,000 sq. km).

Ka•la•is (kə lā′is), *n. Class. Myth.* Calais.

Ka•lakh (kä′läkʜ), *n.* an ancient Assyrian city on the Tigris River, founded 1274 B.C. and destroyed by the Medes 612 B.C.: its ruins are at Nimrud near Mosul in northern Iraq. Biblical name, **Calah.**

Ka•lam (kə läm′), *n. Islam.* **1.** (*sometimes l.c.*) a school of philosophical theology originating in the 9th century A.D., asserting the existence of God as a prime mover and the freedom of the will. **2.** the word of Allah. [< Ar *kalām* lit., talk] —**Ka•lam′ist,** *n.*

Kal•a•ma•zoo (kal′ə mə zo͞o′), *n.* a city in SW Michigan. 79,722.

Ka•lam′bo Falls′ (kə läm′bō), an archaeological site at the southeastern end of Lake Tanganyika, on the Zambia-Tanzania border, that has yielded one of the longest continuous cultural sequences in sub-Saharan Africa, beginning more than 100,000 years B.P. and characterized in the earliest levels by evidence of fire use and some simple wooden implements of Lower Paleolithic, or Acheulean, humans.

kal•an•cho•e (kal′ən kō′ē, kə lang′kō ē, kal′ən chō′, kə lan′chō), *n.* any of several chiefly African and Asian succulent plants or shrubs belonging to the genus *Kalanchoe,* of the stonecrop family, having mostly opposite leaves and branching clusters of flowers. [1820–30; < NL]

Ka•lat (kə lät′), *n.* a region in S Baluchistan, in SW Pakistan. Also, **Khelat.**

kal•a•thos (kal′ə thos′), *n., pl.* **-thoi** (-thoi′). *Gk. and Rom. Antiq.* a fruit basket having a conventionalized shape of a lily, often used in ancient art as a symbol of fertility. Also, **calathus.** [1895–1900; < Gk *kálathos*]

Kalb (kalb; *Ger.* kälp), *n.* **Jo•hann** (yō′hän), (*"Baron de Kalb"*), 1721–80, German general in the American Revolutionary Army.

kale (kāl), *n.* **1.** Also called **borecole.** a cabbagelike cultivated plant, *Brassica oleracea acephala,* of the mustard family, having curled or wrinkled leaves: used as a vegetable. **2.** *Scot.* cabbage. **3.** *Slang.* money. Also, **kail.** [1250–1300; ME *cale,* northern var. of COLE]

ka•lei•do•scope (kə lī′də skōp′), *n.* **1.** an optical instrument in which bits of glass, held loosely at the end of a rotating tube, are shown in continually changing symmetrical forms by reflection in two or more mirrors set at angles to each other. **2.** a continually changing pattern of shapes and colors. **3.** a continually shifting pattern, scene, or the like: *The 1920's were a kaleidoscope of fads and fashions.* [1817; < Gk *kal(ós)* beautiful + *eîdo(s)* shape + -SCOPE]

ka•lei•do•scop•ic (kə lī′də skop′ik), *adj.* **1.** of, pertaining to, or created by a kaleidoscope. **2.** changing form, pattern, color, etc., in a manner suggesting a kaleidoscope. **3.** continually shifting from one set of relations to another; rapidly changing: *the kaleidoscopic events of the past year.* Also, **ka•lei′do•scop′i•cal.** [1840–50; KALEIDOSCOPE + -IC] —**ka•lei′do•scop′i•cal•ly,** *adv.* —**Syn. 3.** changeable, fluctuating, protean, variable.

Ka•le•mie (kə lā′mē), *n.* a city in E Zaire, on Lake Tanganyika. 87,000. Formerly, **Albertville.**

kal•en•dar (kal′ən dər), *n.* calendar.

kal•ends (kal′əndz), *n.* (*usually used with a plural v.*) calends.

Ka•le•va (kä′le və), *n.* a hero and progenitor of heroes in Finnish and Estonian folk epics.

Ka•le•va•la (kä′lə vä′lə; *Fin.* kä′le vä′lä), *n.* **1.** (*italics*) the national epic of Finland (1835, enlarged 1849), compiled and arranged by Elias Lönnrot from popular lays of the Middle Ages. **2.** the home or land of Kaleva; Finland. [< Finnish]

kale•yard (kāl′yärd′), *n. Scot.* a kitchen garden. Also, **kailyard.** [1715–25; KALE + YARD[2]]

kale′yard school′, a school of writers describing homely life in Scotland, with much use of Scottish dialect: in vogue toward the close of the 19th century. Also, **kailyard school.** [1895–1900]

Kal•gan (käl′gän′), *n.* Zhangjiakou.

Kal•goor•lie (kal go͝or′lē), *n.* a city in SW Australia: chief center of gold-mining industry in Australia. 9201, with suburbs 19,848.

Kālī

Kā•lī (kä′lē), *n. Hinduism.* the wife of Shiva and the malevolent form of the Mother Goddess. Cf. **Pārvatī.**

kal•ian (käl yän′), *n.* a Persian tobacco pipe in which the smoke is drawn through water; hookah. [1825–35; < Pers *qalyān*]

Ka•li•da•sa (kä′li dä′sə), *n.* fl. 5th century A.D., Hindu dramatist and poet. Also, **Kā′li•dā′sa.**

ka•lif (kā′lif, kal′if), *n.* caliph.

kal•i•fate (kal′ə fāt′, -fit, kā′lə-), *n.* caliphate.

Ka•li•man•tan (kä′lē män′tän), *n.* Indonesian name of Borneo, esp. referring to the southern, or Indonesian, part.

ka•lim•ba (kə lim′bə), *n.* mbira. [1950–55; the instrument's name in a number of Bantu languages of East Africa, e.g., Bisa, Lala (Zambia), Tumbuka, Nyanja (Malawi); cf. MARIMBA]

Ka•li•nin (kə lē′nin; *Russ.* ku lye′nyin), *n.* **1. Mi•kha•il I•va•no•vich** (myi ᴋʜu yēl′ ē vä′nə vyich), 1875–1946, Russian revolutionary: president of the U.S.S.R. 1923–46. **2.** former name (1934–90) of **Tver.**

Ka•li•nin•grad (kə lē′nin grad′, -gräd′, kä-; *Russ.* kə lyi nyin grät′), *n.* a seaport in the W Russian Federation in Europe, on the Bay of Danzig. 380,000. German, **Königsberg.**

kal•i•nite (kal′ə nīt′, kā′lə-), *n.* a mineral, hydrous sulfate of potassium and aluminum, chemically similar to alum. [1865–70; < NL *kali(um)* potassium (see ALKALI, -IUM) + intrusive *-n-* (perh. by assoc. with ALKALINE) + -ITE[1]]

ka•liph (kā′lif, kal′if), *n.* caliph.

Kal•i•spel (kal′ə spel′, kal′ə spel′), *n.* a Salishan language used by the Flathead Indians of Montana and by some neighboring tribes in Idaho and the western part of Washington.

Kal•i•spell (kal′ə spel′, kal′ə spel′), *n.* a city in NW Montana. 10,648.

Ka•lisz (kä′lish), *n.* a city in central Poland. 81,200. German, **Ka•lisch** (kä′lish).

Ka•li Yu•ga (kul′ē yo͝og′ə), *Hinduism.* the fourth and present age of the world, full of conflict and sin. [< Skt]

Kal•li•kak (kal′i kak′), *n.* the fictitious name of an actual family that was the focus of a sociological study: one branch of feeble-minded descendants were mostly social degenerates, while another branch with descendants of normal intelligence were mostly successful. Cf. **Jukes.** [< Gk *kalli-* CALLI- + *kak-* (see CACO-)]

Kal•li•o•pe (kə lī′ə pē), *n. Class. Myth.* calliope (def. 2).

Kal•lis•to (kə lis′tō), *n. Class. Myth.* Callisto (def. 1).

Kal•mar (käl′mär), *n.* a seaport in SE Sweden, on Kalmar Sound. 52,846. —**Kal•mar•i•an** (kal mâr′ē ən), *adj.*

Kal′mar Sound′, a strait between SE Sweden and Öland Island. 85 mi. (137 km) long; 14 mi. (23 km) wide.

kal•mi•a (kal′mē ə), *n.* any North American evergreen shrub belonging to the genus *Kalmia,* of the heath family, having showy flowers, as the mountain laurel. [< NL (Linnaeus), after Peter *Kalm* (1715–79), Swedish botanist; see -IA]

Kal•muck (kal′muk, kal muk′), *n.* **1.** a member of any of a group of Buddhistic Mongol tribes of a region extending from western China to the valley of the lower Volga River. **2.** a Mongolian language used by the part of the Kalmuck people that was formerly powerful in northwest China, specifically in Dzungaria, and is now relocated northwest of the Caspian Sea. Also, **Kal′•muk.**

Kal•myk•i•a (kal mik′ē ə; *Russ.* kul mi′kyə), *n.* an autonomous republic in the Russian Federation in Europe, on the NW shore of the Caspian Sea. 293,000; 75,900 sq. mi. (196,581 sq. km). *Cap.:* Elista. Also, **Kal•myk′i•ya.** Official name, **Kal•myk′ Auton′omous Repub′lic** (kal mik′).

ka•long (kä′lông, -long), *n.* a large flying fox of Southeast Asia. [1815–25; < Javanese]

kal•pa (kul′pə), *n. Hinduism.* a thousand cycles of Maha Yugas. [1785–95; < Skt]

kal•pak (kal′pak), *n.* calpac.

CONCISE PRONUNCIATION KEY: act, cāpe, dâre, pärt; set, ēqual; if, īce; ox, ōver, ôrder, oil, bo͝ok, bo͞ot, out; up, ûrge; child; sing; shoe; thin, *th*at; zh as in *treasure.* ə = a as in *alone,* e as in *system,* i as in *easily,* o as in *gallop,* u as in *circus;* ᵊ as in *fire* (fīᵊr), *hour* (ouᵊr). l and n can serve as syllabic consonants, as in *cradle* (krād′l), and *button* (but′n). See the full key inside the front cover.

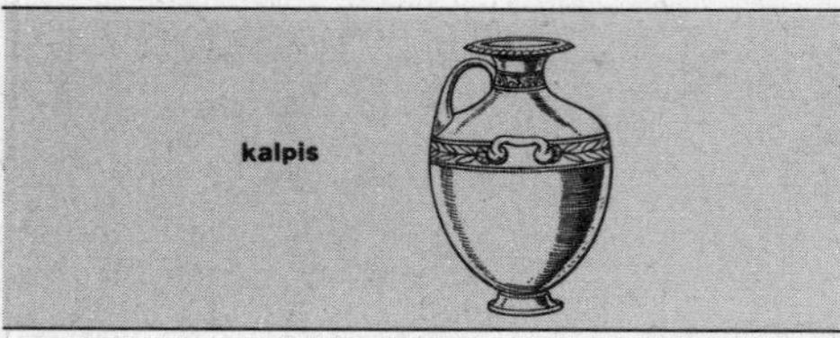
kalpis

kal•pis (kal′pis), *n.* a form of the hydria. [< Gk *kálpis* pitcher]

kal•so•mine (kal′sə mīn′, -min), *n., v.t.,* **-mined, -min•ing.** calcimine.

Ka•lu•ga (ku lo͞o′gə), *n.* a city in the W Russian Federation in Europe, SW of Moscow. 291,000.

Ka•lyp•so (kə lip′sō), *n. Class. Myth.* Calypso (def. 1).

Kam (käm), *n.* a Kam-Tai language spoken in southern China.

Ka•ma (kä′mə), *n.* a river in the E Russian Federation in Europe, flowing from the central Ural Mountains region into the Volga River S of Kazan. 1200 mi. (1930 km) long.

Ka•ma (kä′mə), *n.* **1.** *Hindu Myth.* the god of erotic desire, sometimes seen as an aspect of the god whose other aspect is Mara, or death. **2.** (*l.c.*) the attachment to temporal things personified by this god. [< Skt, special use of *kāma* love, desire, god of love]

ka•ma•ai•na (kä′mə ī′nə), *n.* a longtime resident of Hawaii. [1900–05; < Hawaiian *kama'āina* native born, equiv. to *kama* child, person + *'āina* land, earth]

kam•a•cite (kam′ə sīt′), *n.* a nickel-iron alloy found in meteorites. [1885–90; < G (obs.) *Kamacit* < Gk *kamak-* (s. of *kámax*) pole + G *-it* -ITE[1]]

Ka•ma•dhe•nu (kä′mə dā′no͞o), *n. Hindu Myth.* a celestial cow whose milk is life, and one of whose milkings is the visible world. [< Skt *kāmadhenu,* equiv. to *kāma* love + *dhenu* cow]

Ka•ma•ku•ra (kä′mä ko͞o′RÄ), *n.* **1.** a city on S Honshu, in central Japan, on Sagami Bay: great bronze statue of Buddha. 172,612. **2.** the first period, 1185–1333, during which Japan was ruled by a feudal regime.

ka•ma•la (kə mā′lə, kam′ə lə, kum′-), *n.* a powder from the capsules of an East Indian tree, *Mallotus philippinensis,* of the spurge family, used as a yellow dye and in medicine as an anthelmintic. [1810–20; < Skt]

Kam•ba (käm′bə), *n.* **1.** an agricultural people of central Kenya, renowned as traders and woodcarvers. **2.** the Bantu language of the Kamba.

kam•bal (kum′bəl), *n.* (in India) a blanket or shawl made of coarse wool. [< Hindi < Skt *kambala*]

Kam•cha•dal (käm′chə däl′, käm′chə däl′), *n., pl.* **-dals,** (*esp. collectively*) **-dal.** Itelmen.

Kam•chat•ka (kam chät′kə, -chat′-; *Russ.* kum-chyät′kə), *n.* a peninsula in the NE Russian Federation in Asia, extending S between the Bering Sea and the Sea of Okhotsk. 750 mi. (1210 km) long; 104,200 sq. mi. (269,880 sq. km) wide. —**Kam•chat′kan,** *adj., n.*

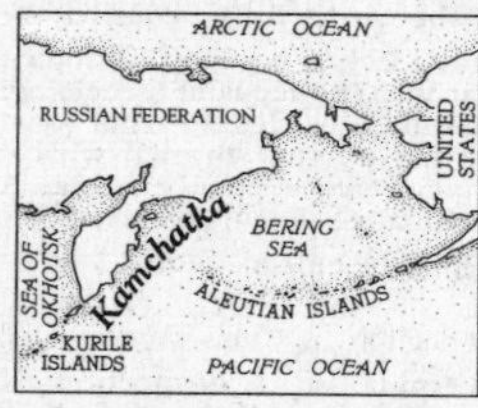

kame[1] (kām), *n. Physical Geog.* a ridge or mound of stratified drift left by a retreating ice sheet. [1860–65 for this sense; special use of Scots, N dial. *kame* comb (ME (dial.) *camb, kambe,* OE *camb, comb*); see COMB[1]]

kame[2] (kām), *n. Scot.* combe. [dial. var. of COMB[2]]

Ka•me•ha•me•ha I (kä mā′hä mā′hä, kə mā′ə-mā′ə), ("*the Great*") 1737?–1819, king of the Hawaiian Islands 1810–19.

Kame′hame′ha Day′, June 11, observed in Hawaii as a holiday in celebration of the birth of Kamehameha I.

ka•me•lau•ki•on (kä mē läf′kē ôn; *Eng.* kam′ə lô′kē-on′, kä′mə lou′-), *n., pl.* **-ki•a** (-kē ä; *Eng.* -kē ə), **-ki•ons.** *Gk. Orth. Ch.* a tall, black, brimless, flat-topped hat, worn by the clergy of the Eastern Church. [< MGk *kamēlaúkion,* alter. of *kalymmaúchion* (deriv. of *kálymma* veil, covering; see CALYPTRA), perh. by assoc. with *kámēlos* CAMEL, but sense relation unclear]

Ka•mensk-U•ral•ski (kä′mənsk yo͝o ral′skē; *Russ.* kä′myinsk o͞o RÄL′skyə), *n.* a city in the W Russian Federation in Asia, near the Ural Mountains. 198,000. Also, **Ka′mensk U•ral′skiy.**

Ka•mer•lingh On•nes (kä′mər ling ô′nəs), **Hei•ke** (hī′kə), 1853–1926, Dutch physicist: Nobel prize 1913.

Ka•me•run (kä′mə Ro͞on′), *n.* German name of **Cameroons.**

ka•mik (kä′mik), *n. Canadian* (*chiefly Eastern Arctic*). a mukluk made of sealskin. [1860–65; < Inuit]

ka•mi•ka•ze (kä′mi kä′zē), *n.* **1.** (during World War II) a member of a special corps in the Japanese air force charged with the suicidal mission of crashing an aircraft laden with explosives into an enemy target, esp. a warship. **2.** an airplane used for this purpose. **3.** a person or thing that behaves in a wildly reckless or destructive manner: *We were nearly run down by a kamikaze on a motorcycle.* —*adj.* **4.** of, pertaining to, undertaken by, or characteristic of a kamikaze: *a kamikaze pilot; a kamikaze attack.* [1940–45; < Japn, equiv. to *kami(y)* god (earlier **kamui*) + *kaze* wind (earlier **kanzai*]

Ka•mi•la•roi (kä′mē lä′roi), *n.* an Australian aboriginal language spoken in northern New South Wales. Also called **Gamilaraay.**

Ka•mi•na (kä mē′nä), *n.* a city in S Zaire. 115,000.

Kam•loops (kam′lo͞ops), *n.* a city in S British Columbia, in SW Canada. 58,311.

Kam•pa•la (käm pä′lə, kam-), *n.* a city in and the capital of Uganda, in the S part. 331,900.

kam•pong (käm′pông, -pong, käm pông′, -pong′), *n.* a small village or community of houses in Malay-speaking lands. Also, **campong.** [1835–45; < Malay *kampung, kampong* grouping or gathering together, esp. a village; cf. COMPOUND[2]]

Kam•pu•che•a (kam′po͞o chē′ə), *n.* **People's Republic of,** a former official name of **Cambodia.** —**Kam′pu•che′an,** *adj., n.*

Kam-Tai (käm′tī′), *n.* a linguistic family including Kam and related languages as well as the Tai and Kadai groups.

Ka•my•shin (kə mish′ən; *Russ.* ku mi′shin), *n.* a city in the SW Russian Federation in Europe, NE of Volgograd, on the Volga River. 112,000.

Kan., Kansas.

ka•na (kä′nə; *Japn.* kä′nä), *n.* a Japanese syllabic script consisting of 71 symbols and having two written varieties. Cf. **hiragana, katakana.** [1720–30; < Japn; earlier *kanna, kari-na* makeshift names (i.e., characters) as opposed to *ma-na* true characters, i.e., KANJI]

ka•nak•a (kə nak′ə, -nä′kə, kan′ə kə), *n.* (*sometimes cap.*) **1.** a native Hawaiian. **2.** a South Sea islander. [< Hawaiian: person]

ka•na•ma•ji•ri (kä′nə mä′jə rē; *Japn.* kä′nä mä′jē-RĒ′), *n.* the standard script of modern Japanese, in which kanji are used for root elements, supplemented by kana for inflections and particles and sometimes for indication of the Japanese pronunciation of kanji. [< Japn, equiv. to *kana* KANA + *majiri* mixing]

Ka•nan•ga (kə näng′gə), *n.* a city in central Zaire. 595,954. Formerly, **Luluabourg.**

Ka•na•nur (kun′ə no͝or′), *n.* Cannanore.

Ka•na•ra (kə när′ə, kä′nər ə), *n.* a region in SW India, on the Deccan Plateau. ab. 60,000 sq. mi. (155,400 sq. km). Also, **Canara.**

Ka•na•rak (kə när′ək), *n.* Konarak.

Ka•na•rese (kä′nə rēz′, -rēs′, kan′ə-), *adj., n., pl.* **-rese.** —*adj.* **1.** of or pertaining to Kanara, a part of the Maharashtra province in W India. —*n.* **2.** one of a Dravidian people living mainly in the state of Karnataka, in southwest India. **3.** Kannada. Also, **Canarese.** [1830–40; KANAR(A) + -ESE]

Ka•na•za•wa (kä′nä zä′wä), *n.* a seaport on W Honshu, in central Japan. 417,681.

kan•ban (kän′bän′), *n.* a method of inventory control, originally developed in Japanese automobile factories, that keeps inventories low by scheduling needed goods and equipment to arrive a short time before a production run begins. [< Japn *kamban* lit., signboard, shopkeeper's in-business sign, prob. alluding to the shop or tavern keeper's final call for orders before taking the sign down, hence "last-minute, just in time" in the context of inventory control < MChin, equiv. to Chin *kàn* look + *bǎn* printing block]

Kan•chen•jun•ga (kän′chən jo͝ong′gə), *n.* a mountain in S Asia, between NE India and Nepal, in the E Himalayas: third highest in the world. 28,146 ft. (8579 m). Also, **Kan•chan•jan•ga** (kän′chən jäng′gə).

Kan•da•har (kun′də här′), *n.* a city in S Afghanistan. 115,000.

Kan•din•sky (kan din′skē; *Russ.* kun dyēn′skyə), *n.* **Was•si•ly** (vas′ə lē) or **Va•si•li** (vas′ə lē, və sil′ē; *Russ.* vu syē′lyə), 1866–1944, Russian painter.

Kan•dy (kan′dē, kän′-), *n.* a city in central Sri Lanka: famous Buddhist temples. 93,602.

kane (kān), *n. Scot.* cain.

Ka•ne•o•he (kä′nā ō′hā), *n.* a town on E Oahu, in Hawaii. 29,919.

kang (käng), *n.* (esp. in northern Chinese houses) a masonry or earthen platform at one end of a room, heated in winter by fires underneath and spread with mats for sleeping. [< Chin *kàng*]

kan•ga•roo (kang′gə ro͞o′), *n., pl.* **-roos,** (*esp. collectively*) **-roo.** any herbivorous marsupial of the family Macropodidae, of Australia and adjacent islands, having a small head, short forelimbs, powerful hind legs used for leaping, and a long, thick tail: several species are threatened or endangered. [1760–70; < Guugu Yimidhirr (Australian Aboriginal language spoken around Cooktown, N Queensland) *gaŋ-urru* large black or gray species of kangaroo] —**kan′ga•roo′like′,** *adj.*

great gray kangaroo, *Macropus giganteus,* head and body 4 ft. (1.2 m); tail 3½ ft. (1 m)

kan′garoo court′, **1.** a self-appointed or mob-operated tribunal that disregards or parodies existing principles of law or human rights, esp. one in a frontier area or among criminals in prison. **2.** any crudely or irregularly operated court, esp. one so controlled as to render a fair trial impossible. [1850–55, *Amer.*]

kangaroo′ rat′, **1.** any of various small jumping rodents of the family Heteromyidae, of Mexico and the western U.S. **2.** an Australian desert rodent of the genus *Notomys.* [1780–90]

kangaroo rat, *Dipodomys phillipsii,* head and body 6 in. (15 cm); tail 7 in. (18 cm)

kangaroo′ vine′, an Australian vine, *Cissus antarctica,* of the grape family, having shiny, leathery leaves.

K'ang Hsi (käng′ shē′), (*Shêng-tsu*) 1654?–1722, Chinese emperor of the Ch'ing dynasty 1662–1722. Also, *Pinyin,* **Kang Xi** (käng′ shē′).

K'ang Tê (käng′ du′). See **Pu-yi, Henry.** Also, **Kang′ Teh′;** *Pinyin,* **Kang′ De′.**

K'ang Yu-wei (käng′ yo͞o′wā′), 1858–1927, Chinese scholar and reformer. Also, *Pinyin,* **Kang You•wei** (käng′ yō′wā′).

kan•ji (kän′jē), *n., pl.* **-ji, -jis.** **1.** a system of Japanese writing using Chinese-derived characters. **2.** a character in this system. [1915–20; < Japn < MChin, equiv. to Chin *hàn* Han (i.e., China) + *zì* characters]

Kan•ka•kee (kang′kə kē′), *n.* a city in NE Illinois. 30,141.

Kan•kan (*Fr.* käN käN′), *n.* a city in E Guinea. 265,000.

Kan•na•da (kä′nə də, kan′ə-), *n.* a Dravidian language spoken mainly in the state of Karnataka, in southwest India. Also called **Kanarese.**

Kan•nap•o•lis (kə nap′ə lis), *n.* a town in W North Carolina. 34,564.

Ka•no (kä′nō), *n.* a city in N Nigeria. 300,000.

ka•no•ne (kə nō′nə), *n., pl.* **-nen** (-nən). a person who is an expert skier. [< G: lit., cannon < It *cannone;* see CANNON]

Kan•pur (kän′po͝or), *n.* a city in S Uttar Pradesh, in N India, on the Ganges River. 1,275,242. Formerly, **Cawnpore, Cawnpur.**

kans (käns), *n.* an Indian grass of the genus *Saccharum,* used in some areas for fodder, thatching, etc., and being in other areas a troublesome weed. [1870–75; < Hindi *kās* < Skt *kāśa;* cf. Pali, Prakrit *kāsa*]

Kans., Kansas.

Kan•sa (kan′zə, -sə), *n., pl.* **-sas,** (*esp. collectively*) **-sa** for 1. **1.** a member of a North American Indian people formerly of eastern Kansas, now living mostly in northern Oklahoma. **2.** the Siouan language of the Kansa. Also called **Kaw.**

Kan•sa (kän′sə), *n. Hindu Legend.* a tyrannical king killed by Krishna.

Kan•san (kan′zən), *n.* **1.** a native or inhabitant of Kansas. **2.** *Geol.* the Kansan Stage. —*adj.* **3.** of or pertaining to the state of Kansas. **4.** *Geol.* of or pertaining to the second stage of the Pleistocene glaciation of North America. [1865–70, *Amer.;* KANS(AS) + -AN]

Kan•sas (kan′zəs), *n.* **1.** a state in the central United States: a part of the Midwest. 2,363,208. 82,276 sq. mi. (213,094 sq. km). *Cap.:* Topeka. *Abbr.:* KS (for use with zip code), Kans., Kan., Kas. **2.** a river in NE Kansas, flowing E to the Missouri River. 169 mi. (270 km) long.

Kan′sas Cit′y, **1.** a city in W Missouri, at the confluence of the Kansas and Missouri rivers. 448,159. **2.** a city in NE Kansas, adjacent to Kansas City, Mo. 161,087.

Kan′sas Cit′y steak′, **1.** See **strip steak.** **2.** See **shell steak.** Also called **Kan′sas Cit′y cut′.**

Kan′sas Cit′y style′, a style of jazz developed in Kansas City, Mo., in the early 1930's, marked by a strong blues influence, the use of riffs as a characteristic formal device, and a less pronounced beat than that of the New Orleans or Chicago style of jazz. [1955–60]

Kan′sas gay′-feath•er (gā′feth′ər). See **prairie button snakeroot.**

Kan′sas-Ne•bras′ka Act′ (kan′zəs nə bras′kə), *U.S. Hist.* the act of Congress in 1854 annulling the Missouri Compromise, providing for the organization of the territories of Kansas and Nebraska, and permitting these territories self-determination on the question of slavery.

kans′ grass′, kans. [1880–85]

Kan•su (kan′so͞o′; *Chin.* gän′so͞o′), *n.* *Wade-Giles.* Gansu.

CONCISE ETYMOLOGY KEY: <, descended or borrowed from; >, whence; b., blend of, blended; c., cognate with; cf., compare; deriv., derivative; equiv., equivalent; imit., imitative; obl., oblique; r., replacing; s., stem; sp., spelling, spelled; resp., respelling, respelled; trans., translation; ?, origin unknown; *, unattested; ‡, probably earlier than. See the full key inside the front cover.

Kant (kant; *Ger.* känt), *n.* **Im·man·u·el** (i man′yo͞o əl; *Ger.* i mä′no͞o el′), 1724–1804, German philosopher.

kan·tar (kän tär′), *n.* (in some Middle Eastern countries) a unit of weight corresponding to the hundredweight, but varying in different localities. [1545–55; < Ar *qinṭar* << L *centenārium;* see QUINTAL]

kan·tha·ros (kan′thər əs), *n., pl.* **-tha·roi** (-thə roi′). *Gk. and Rom. Antiq.* a deep bowl set upon a stem terminating in a foot and having two handles rising from the brim and curving downward to join the body. Also, **cantharus.** [1895–1900; < Gk *kántharos*]

kantharos

Kant·i·an (kan′tē ən, kän′-), *adj.* **1.** of, pertaining to, or resembling the philosophy of Kant. —*n.* **2.** an adherent of the philosophy of Immanuel Kant. [1810–20; KANT + -IAN]

Kan·tor (kan′tər), *n.* **Mac·Kin·lay** (mə kin′lē), 1904–77, U.S. novelist.

Kan·tô·ro·vich (kan tôr′ə vich, kan′tə rō′vich; *Russ.* kun tô′RƏ vyich), *n.* **Le·o·nid Vi·ta·lye·vich** (lā′ə nid vi tal′yə vich; *Russ.* lyi u nyĕt′ vyi tä′lyə vyich), 1912–86, Soviet mathematician and economist: Nobel prize for economics 1975.

Ka·nu·ri (kə no͝or′ē), *n., pl.* **-ris,** (*esp. collectively*) **-ri** for 1. **1.** a member of a people living in northeast Nigeria and in Niger. **2.** the Nilo-Saharan language of the Kanuri people.

kan·zu (kan′zo͞o), *n.* a long, usually white robe worn esp. by men in central and eastern Africa. [1900–05; < Swahili]

Kao·hsiung (gou′shyo͝ong′), *n. Wade-Giles.* a seaport on SW Taiwan. 1,000,000. Also, **Gaoxiong.**

Ka·o·lack (kä′ō lak, kou′lak), *n.* a city in W Senegal. 96,000. Also, **Ka′o·lak.**

kao·li·ang (kou′lē ang′), *n.* **1.** a variety of grain sorghum. **2.** a liquor made from kaoliang stalks. [< Chin (Wade-Giles) *kao¹liang²*, (pinyin) *gāoliang* (*gāo* high + *liáng* millet)]

ka·o·lin (kā′ə lin), *n.* a fine white clay used in the manufacture of porcelain. Also, **ka′o·line.** [1720–30; < F < Chin (Wade-Giles) *Kao¹ling³*, (pinyin) *Gāolǐng* mountain in Jiangxi province that yielded the first kaolin sent to Europe (*gāo* high + *lǐng* hill)] —**ka′o·lin′ic,** *adj.*

ka·o·lin·ite (kā′ə lə nīt′), *n.* a very common mineral, hydrated aluminum disilicate, $Al_2Si_2O_5(OH)_4$, formed by the alteration of other minerals, esp. feldspar: the most common constituent of kaolin. [1865–70; KAOLIN + -ITE¹]

ka·o·lin·ize (kā′ə lə nīz′), *v.t.,* **-ized, -iz·ing.** to convert (minerals containing kaolinite) into kaolin by weathering. Also, *esp. Brit.,* **ka′o·lin·ise′.** [1870–75; KAOLIN + -IZE] —**ka′o·lin·i·za′tion,** *n.*

ka·on (kā′on), *n. Physics.* a meson with strangeness +1 and either positive or zero electric charge, or its antiparticle, with strangeness −1 and either negative or zero electric charge. *Symbol:* K Also called **K meson, K-meson.** [1955–60; *ka-* (sp. of name of letter *k*) + (ME-S)ON] —**ka·on′ic,** *adj.*

Kao Tsu (*Chin.* gou′ dzo͞o′). See **Li Yüan.**

Ka·pell (kə pel′), *n.* **William,** 1922–53, U.S. pianist.

Ka·pell·meis·ter (kä pel′mī′stər, kə-), *n., pl.* **-ter. 1.** a choirmaster. **2.** a conductor of an orchestra. **3.** a bandmaster. [1830–40; < G; see CHAPEL, MASTER]

kaph (käf, kôf), *n.* **1.** the eleventh letter of the Hebrew alphabet. **2.** the consonant sound represented by this letter. Also, **caph.** [1875–80; < Heb: lit., palm (of the hand), sole (of the foot)]

Ka·pi·la (kä′pi lə), *n.* fl. early 6th century B.C., Hindu philosopher: reputed founder of the Sankhya system of Hindu philosophy.

Ka·pi·tsa (kä′pyi tsə), *n.* **Pyotr L(e·o·ni·do·vich)** (pyôtR lyi u nyē′də vyich), 1894–1984, Russian physicist: Nobel prize 1978. Also, **Ka′pi·tza.**

Kap·lan (kap′lən), *n.* **Mor·de·cai Me·na·hem** (môr′di kī′ mä′nə hem′, mə nä′hem), 1881–1983, U.S. religious leader and educator, born in Lithuania: founder of the Reconstructionist movement in Judaism.

Ka·po (kä′pō), *n.* a Nazi concentration camp prisoner who was given privileges in return for supervising prisoner work gangs: often a common criminal and frequently brutal to fellow inmates. Also, **ka′po.** [< G, perh. shortening of F *caporal* CORPORAL²]

ka·pok (kā′pok), *n.* the silky down that invests the seeds of a silk-cotton tree (**ka′pok tree′**), *Ceiba pentandra,* of the East Indies, Africa, and tropical America: used for stuffing pillows, life jackets, etc., and for acoustical insulation. Also called **Java cotton.** [1740–50; < Javanese (or Malay of Java and Sumatra) *kapuk* the name of the tree]

ka′pok oil′, a yellowish-green oil expressed from the seeds of the kapok tree, used esp. in foods and in the manufacture of soap.

Ka·po′si's sarco′ma (kə pō′sēz, kap′ə-), *Pathol.* a cancer of connective tissue characterized by painless, purplish-red to brown plaquelike or pimply lesions on the extremities, trunk, or head, and sometimes involving the lungs, viscera, etc., occurring in a mild form among older men of certain Mediterranean and central African populations and in a more virulent form among persons with AIDS. [after Hungarian dermatologist Moritz *Kaposi,* or Moriz Kohn (1837–1902), who described it in 1872]

ka·po·te (kə pô′tə), *n.* a long coat formerly worn by male Jews of eastern Europe and now worn chiefly by very Orthodox or Hasidic Jews. [< Yiddish < F *capote* CAPOTE]

kap·pa (kap′ə), *n.* **1.** the tenth letter of the Greek alphabet (K, κ). **2.** the consonant sound represented by this letter. [< Gk *káppa* < Sem; see KAPH]

kap·pa·rah (*Seph.* kä pä RÄ′; *Ashk.* kä pô′RƏ), *n., pl.* ***-roth, -rot*** (*Seph.* -RÔT′), ***-ros*** (*Ashk.* -RŌS). *Hebrew.* a ritual performed by some Orthodox Jews before Yom Kippur that consists of swinging a fowl around the head and reciting prayers that symbolically transfer the person's sins to the fowl. [*kappārāh* lit., atonement]

Kap·teyn (käp tīn′), *n.* **Ja·co·bus Cor·ne·lis** (yä kō′bys kôr nā′lis), 1851–1922, Dutch astronomer.

ka·pu·ka (kä′pə kə), *n.* a New Zealand tree, *Griselinia littoralis,* of the dogwood family, having brown, hairy twigs and small, greenish flowers, grown as an ornamental. [< Maori]

Kap·us·ka·sing (kap′ə skā′sing), *n.* a town in central Ontario, in S Canada. 12,014.

ka·put (kä po͝ot′, -po͞ot′, kə-), *adj. Slang.* **1.** ruined; done for; demolished. **2.** unable to operate or continue: *The washing machine is suddenly kaput.* **3. go kaput,** to cease functioning; break down: *The old car finally went kaput.* [1890–95; < G: orig. trickless (in game of piquet) < F (*être*) *capot* (to be) without tricks, i.e., make zero score]

kar·a·bi·ner (kar′ə bē′nər), *n.* carabiner.

Ka·ra·chai (kar′ə chī′), *n., pl.* **-chais,** (*esp. collectively*) **-chai** for 1. **1.** a member of a people living mainly in the Karachai-Cherkessk Autonomous Region, closely related to the Balkar. **2.** the Turkic language of these people.

Ka·ra·chai′-Cher·kess′ Auton′omous Re′gion (kär′ə chī′chər kes′; *Russ.* kə RU chyi′chyiR kyes′), an autonomous region in the Russian Federation in Europe, in the Caucasus. 369,000; 5442 sq. mi. (14,100 sq. km). *Cap.:* Cherkess.

Ka·ra·chi (kə rä′chē), *n.* a seaport in S Pakistan, near the Indus delta: former national capital; now capital of Sind province. 5,103,000.

Ka·ra·fu·to (*Japn.* kä′Rä fo͞o′tô), *n.* Japanese name of **Sakhalin.**

Ka·ra·gan·da (kar′ə gən dä′; *Russ.* kə RƏ gun dä′), *n.* a city in central Kazakhstan. 608,000.

Kar·a·ite (kar′ə īt′), *n. Judaism.* a member of a sect, founded in Persia in the 8th century A.D. by the religious leader Anan ben David, that rejected the Talmud and the teachings of the rabbis in favor of strict adherence to the Bible as the only source of Jewish law and practice. Cf. **Rabbinite.** [1720–30; < Heb *qarā′(im)* (equiv. to *qarā* Biblical scholar, lit., reader + *īm* pl. suffix) + -ITE¹] —**Kar·a·ism** (kar′ə iz′əm), **Kar·a·it·ism** (kar′ə i tiz′əm), *n.* —**Kar·a·it·ic** (kar′ə it′ik), *adj.*

Ka·ra·jan (kar′ə yən; *Ger.* kä′Rä yän′), *n.* **Her·bert von** (hûr′bərt von; *Ger.* heR′bəRt fən), born 1908, Austrian conductor.

Ka·ra-Kal·pak (kär′rə käl päk′, kar′ə kal pak′; *Russ.* ku Rä′kul päk′), *n.* **1.** one of a people living in the Kara-Kalpak Republic and adjacent areas. **2.** the Turkic language of the Kara-Kalpaks.

Kara-Kalpak′ Auton′omous Repub′lic, an autonomous republic in NW Uzbekistan. 904,000; 63,938 sq. mi. (165,600 sq. km). *Cap.:* Nukas.

Ka·rak·lis (kə räk′lis; *Russ.* kə RU klyēs′), *n.* former name of **Kirovakan.**

Ka·ra·ko·ram (kär′ə kôr′əm, -kōr′-, kar′-), *n.* **1.** Also called **Mustagh.** a mountain range in NW India, in N Kashmir. Highest peak, K2, 28,250 ft. (8611 m). **2.** a pass traversing this range, on the route from NE Kashmir to Sinkiang province in China. 18,300 ft. (5580 m).

Ka·ra·ko·rum (kär′ə kôr′əm, -kōr′-, kar′-), *n.* a ruined city in central Mongolian People's Republic: capital of the Mongol Empire in the 13th century.

Kar·a·kul (kar′ə kəl), *n.* (*sometimes l.c.*) **1.** one of an Asian breed of sheep having curly fleece that is black in the young and brown or gray in the adult: raised esp. for lambskins used in the fur industry. Cf. **broadtail, Persian lamb. 2.** (*sometimes l.c.*) a Karakul lambskin. Also, **caracul.** [1850–55; after *Kara Kul* lake on the Pamir plateau, Tajikistan, near where the sheep were bred]

Ka·ra Kum (kar′ə ko͞om′, ko͝om′, kär′ə), a desert S of the Aral Sea, largely in Turkmenistan. ab. 110,000 sq. mi. (284,900 sq. km). Also, **Qara Qum.**

Ka·ra·mi (kə rä′mē), *n.* **Ra·shid** (ra shēd′), born 1921, Lebanese lawyer and statesman. Also, **Ka·ra·meh** (kə rä′mē, -mā).

ka·ran·da (kə run′də), *n.* an Indian shrub or small tree, *Carissa carandas,* of the dogbane family, having white or pink flowers and reddish-black berries. [< Hindi *karaumdā* < Skt *karamarda, karamardaka;* cf. Pali, Prakrit *karamadda*]

Ka·ran·ka·wa (kə rang′kə wä′, -wô′, -wə), *n., pl.* **-was,** (*esp. collectively*) **-wa** for 1. **1.** a member of an extinct tribe of North American Indians who lived in southeastern Texas until the mid 19th century. **2.** the language of the Karankawa.

kar·a·o·ke (kar′ē ō′kē), *n.* an act of singing along to a music video, esp. one from which the original vocals have been electronically eliminated. [1985–1990; < Japn, = *kara* empty + *oke* orchestra]

Ka′ra Sea′ (kär′ə; *Russ.* kä′RƏ), an arm of the Arctic Ocean between Novaya Zemlya and the N Russian Federation.

kar·at (kar′ət), *n.* a unit for measuring the fineness of gold, pure gold being 24 karats fine. *Abbr.:* k., kt. Also, **carat.** [1550–60; sp. var. of CARAT]

ka·ra·te (kə rä′tē), *n.* **1.** a method developed in Japan of defending oneself without the use of weapons by striking sensitive areas on an attacker's body with the hands, elbows, knees, or feet. Cf. **judo, jujitsu. 2.** a sport based on this method of self-defense. [1950–55; < Japn, equiv. to *kara* empty + *te* (earlier **tai*) hand(s)]

ka·ra·te-chop (kə rä′tē chop′), *n., v.,* **-chopped, -chop·ping.** —*n.* **1.** a sharp blow used in karate, usually delivered by a slanting stroke with the side of the hand. —*v.t.* **2.** to strike with a karate-chop. [1965–70]

ka·ra·te·ka (kə rä′tē kä′), *n., pl.* **-ka, -kas.** an expert in karate. [< Japn, equiv. to *karate* KARATE + *-ka* person (< MChin, equiv. to Chin *jiā*)]

kara′te sticks′, nunchaku.

ka·ra′ya gum′ (kə rī′ə), the dried exudate of an Asian tree, *Sterculia urens,* used for finishing textiles and as a thickening agent in cosmetics and foodstuffs. Also called **sterculia gum.** [1890–95; < Hindi *karāl, karāyal* resin]

Kar·ba·la (kär′bə lə), *n.* Kerbela.

Ka·reem (kə rēm′), *n.* a male given name: from an Arabic word meaning "generous."

Ka·re·lia (kə rēl′yə; *Russ.* ku Rye′lyi yə), *n.* **1.** a region in the NW Russian Federation in Europe, comprising Lake Ladoga and Onega Lake and the adjoining area along the E border of Finland. **2.** See **Karelian Autonomous Republic.**

Ka·re·li·an (kə rē′lē ən, -rēl′yən), *adj.* **1.** of or pertaining to Karelia, its people, or their language. —*n.* **2.** a native or inhabitant of Karelia. **3.** the Uralic language of the Karelians, sometimes regarded as a dialect of Finnish. [1850–55; KARELI(A) + -AN]

Kare′lian Auton′omous Repub′lic, an autonomous republic in the NW Russian Federation in Europe. 769,000; 69,720 sq. mi. (180,575 sq. km). *Cap.:* Petrozavodsk. Also called **Karelia.**

Kare′lian Isth′mus, a narrow strip of land between Lake Ladoga and the Gulf of Finland, in the NW Russian Federation.

Ka·ren (kə ren′), *n., pl.* **-rens,** (*esp. collectively*) **-ren,** *adj.* —*n.* **1.** a group of people of eastern and southern Burma (Myanmar). **2.** one of these people. **3.** the language of the Karen, a Tibeto-Burman language of the Sino-Tibetan family. —*adj.* **4.** of or pertaining to the Karen people or their language.

Ka·ren (kar′ən, kär′-), *n.* a female given name, form of **Katherine.** Also, **Kar′in.**

Ka·ri·ba (kə rē′bə), *n.* an artificial lake in SE Africa on the border of SW Zimbabwe and S Zambia: site of hydroelectric power project. ab. 2000 sq. mi. (5200 sq. km).

Kar·kheh (kär kā′, -KHĀ′), *n.* a river in SW Iran, flowing SW to marshes along the Tigris River. ab. 350 mi. (565 km) long.

Karl (kärl), *n.* a male given name, form of **Charles.**

Kar·la (kär′lə), *n.* a female given name, form of **Caroline.**

Karl·feldt (kärl′felt), *n.* **E·rik Ax·el** (ā′Rik äk′səl), 1864–1931, Swedish poet: Nobel prize posthumously 1931.

Karl-Marx-Stadt (kärl′märks′shtät′), *n.* former name (1953–90) of **Chemnitz.**

Kar·loff (kär′lôf, -lof), *n.* **Boris** (*William Henry Pratt*), 1887–1969, British actor in the U.S.

Kar·lo·vy Va·ry (kär′lə vē vär′ē; *Czech.* kär′lô vi vä′Ri), *n.* a city in the W Czech Republic: mineral springs; Carlsbad Decrees (1819). 60,950. German, **Karlsbad.** Formerly, **Carlsbad.**

Karls·bad (kärls′bät′; *Eng.* kärlz′bad), *n.* German name of **Karlovy Vary.**

Karls·ruh·e (kärls′Ro͞o′ə; *Eng.* kärlz′ro͞o′ə), *n.* a city in SW Germany: capital of the former state of Baden. 278,200.

Karl·stad (kärl′städ, -stä), *n.* a city in S Sweden. 74,068.

kar·ma (kär′mə), *n.* **1.** *Hinduism, Buddhism.* action, seen as bringing upon oneself inevitable results, good or bad, either in this life or in a reincarnation: in Hinduism one of the means of reaching Brahman. Cf. **bhakti** (def. 1), **jnana. 2.** *Theosophy.* the cosmic principle according to which each person is rewarded or punished in one incarnation according to that person's deeds in the previous incarnation. **3.** fate; destiny. **4.** the good or bad

CONCISE PRONUNCIATION KEY: act, cāpe, dâre, pärt; set, ēqual; *if,* ice; ox, ōver, ôrder, oil, bo͝ok, bo͞ot, out; up, ûrge; child; sing; shoe; thin, *th*at; zh as in *treasure.* ə = *a* as in *alone, e* as in *system, i* as in *easily, o* as in *gallop, u* as in *circus;* ᵊ as in *fire* (fīᵊr), *hour* (ouᵊr). l and n can serve as syllabic consonants, as in *cradle* (krād′l), and *button* (but′n). See the full key inside the front cover.

emanations felt to be generated by someone or something. [1820–30; < Skt: nom., acc. sing. of *karman* act, deed] **—kar′mic,** *adj.*

kar•ma•dha•ra•ya (kär′mə där′ē ə), *n. Ling.* a compound of two words in which the first is an adjective and the second a substantive, as *blackbird, gentleman,* or *grandson.* [1840–50; < Skt *karmadhāraya*]

Kar•mal (kär mäl′), *n.* **Ba•brak** (bä bräk′), born 1929, Afghan political leader: president 1979–86.

kar•ma•mar•ga (kär′mə mär′gə), *n. Hinduism.* See under **marga.** [1875–80]

Kár•mán (kär′män, -mən), *n.* **Theodore von.** See **Von Kármán, Theodore.**

Kar•nak (kär′nak), *n.* a village in E Egypt, on the Nile: the northern part of the ruins of ancient Thebes.

Kar•na•ta•ka (kär nät′ə kə), *n.* a state in S India. 29,224,046; 74,326 sq. mi. (192,504 sq. km). *Cap.:* Bangalore. Formerly, **Mysore.**

ka•ro (kär′ō), *n., pl.* **-ros.** a shrub or small tree, *Pittosporum crassifolium,* of New Zealand, having shiny leaves with a white, felty underside, red flowers, and densely hairy fruit. [1780–90; < Maori]

Kar•ol (kar′əl), *n.* a female given name.

Kar•o•line (kar′ə līn′, -lin), *n.* a female given name.

ka•ross (kə ros′), *n.* a cloak or rug of animal skins used in southern Africa. [1725–35; < Afrik *karos,* prob. < Khoikhoi]

kar•pas (*Seph.* kär päs′; *Ashk.* kär′päs), *n. Hebrew.* a piece of parsley, celery, or similar green vegetable that is dipped in salt water and eaten at the Seder meal on Passover.

Kar•pov (kär′pôf, -pof; *Russ.* kär′pəf), *n.* **A•na•to•ly** (an′ə tō′lē; *Russ.* u nu tô′lyē), born 1951, Russian chess player.

Kar•rer (kär′ər), *n.* **Paul,** 1889–1971, Swiss chemist, born in Russia: Nobel prize 1937.

kar•ri (kar′ē), *n.* **1.** an Australian gum tree, *Eucalyptus diversicolor.* **2.** the heavy, tough wood of this tree. Also called **kar′ri gum′.** [1865–70; of obscure orig.]

kar•ri-tree (kar′ē trē′), *n.* See **princess tree.** [orig. uncert.]

Kar•roo (kə ro͞o′), *n., pl.* **-roos** for 2. **1.** a vast plateau in the S Republic of South Africa, in Cape of Good Hope province. 100,000 sq. mi. (260,000 sq. km); 3000–4000 ft. (900–1200 m) above sea level. **2.** (*l.c.*) an arid South African tableland with red clay soil. [< Afrik *kar(r)oo* < Khoikhoi; cf. *Xhaeruh, Phaeruh* place name recorded in 1689, Nama *garo* parched, dry, arid, *!garo-b* desolate waste]

kar•ru•sel (kar′ə sel′, kar′ə sel′), *n. Horol.* a revolving escapement for minimizing positional error. [1890–95; prob. alter. of CARROUSEL]

Kars (kärs), *n.* a city in NE Turkey. 53,473.

Karsh (kärsh), *n.* **You•suf** (yo͞o′səf, yo͞o′-), born 1908, Canadian photographer, born in Turkey.

karst (kärst), *n. Geol.* an area of limestone terrane characterized by sinks, ravines, and underground streams. [1900–05; < G, generic use of *Karst,* name of limestone plateau north of Trieste] **—karst′ic,** *adj.*

kart (kärt), *n.* a small, light, low-slung, four-wheeled vehicle, usually powered by a gasoline engine, capable of speeds up to 60 mph (96 km/h), and used for racing or recreation. Also called **go-cart, go-kart.** [1955–60, *Amer.*; sp. var. of CART]

Kart•ti•ke•ya (kär′ti kā′yə), *n.* the Hindu god of bravery. Also, **Kart′i•ke′ya.** Cf. **Skanda.**

Ka•run (kə ro͞on′, kä-), *n.* a river in SW Iran, flowing SW to the Shatt-al-Arab. ab. 515 mi. (830 km) long.

ka•ru•na (ku′ro͝o nä′), *n. Buddhism.* the universal compassion of a Bodhisattva. [1840–50; < Skt *karuṇā*]

Kar•yn (kar′ən, kär′-), *n.* a female given name. Also, **Kar′ynne.**

karyo-, a combining form meaning "nucleus of a cell," used in the formation of compound words: *karyotin.* Also, **caryo-.** [< Gk, comb. form of *káryon* nut, kernel]

kar•y•og•a•my (kar′ē og′ə mē), *n. Cell Biol.* the fusion of the nuclei of cells, as in fertilization. Cf. **plasmogamy.** [1890–95; KARYO- + -GAMY] **—kar•y•o•gam•ic** (kar′ē ə gam′ik), *adj.*

kar•y•o•ki•ne•sis (kar′ē ō ki nē′sis, -kī-), *n. Cell Biol.* **1.** mitosis. **2.** the series of active changes that take place in the nucleus of a living cell in the process of division. [1880–85; KARYO- + -KINESIS] **—kar•y•o•ki•net•ic** (kar′ē ō ki net′ik, -kī-), *adj.*

kar•y•ol•o•gy (kar′ē ol′ə jē), *n. Cell Biol.* the study of the structure and function of cell nuclei. [1890–95; KARYO- + -LOGY]

kar•y•ol•y•sis (kar′ē ol′ə sis), *n. Cell Biol.* the dissolution of a cell nucleus. [1885–90; KARYO- + -LYSIS] **—kar•y•o•lit•ic** (kar′ē ə lit′ik), *adj.*

kar•y•o•plasm (kar′ē ə plaz′əm), *n. Cell Biol.* nucleoplasm. [KARYO- + -PLASM] **—kar′y•o•plas′mic, kar•y•o•plas•mat•ic** (kar′ē ō plaz mat′ik), *adj.*

kar•y•o•some (kar′ē ə sōm′), *n. Cell Biol.* **1.** Also called **chromocenter.** any of several masses of chromatin in the reticulum of a cell nucleus. **2.** a chromosome. [1885–90; KARYO- + -SOME[3]]

kar•y•o•type (kar′ē ə tīp′), *n. Genetics.* the chromosomes of a cell, usually displayed as a systematized arrangement of chromosome pairs in descending order of size. [1925–30; KARYO- + TYPE] **—kar•y•o•typ•ic** (kar′ē ə tip′ik), **kar′y•o•typ′i•cal,** *adj.*

kar•y•o•typ•ing (kar′ē ə tī′ping), *n.* the analysis of chromosomes. [1960–65; KARYOTYPE + -ING[1]]

kas (käs), *n.* (in the Netherlands and in Dutch colonies) a large cabinet of the 17th and 18th centuries, having two doors and often a number of drawers at the bottom, and usually having an elaborately painted or carved decoration with a heavy cornice. [< D; see CASE[2]]

Kas., Kansas.

Ka•sai (kə sī′, kä-), *n.* a river in S central Africa, flowing from central Angola to and then NW along the Angola-Zaire border and through Zaire to the Congo (Zaire) River. ab. 1100 mi. (1770 km) long.

Kas•a•vu•bu (kas′ə vo͞o′bo͞o, kä′sä-), *n.* **Joseph,** 1917?–69, African political leader: first president of the Democratic Republic of the Congo (now Zaire) 1960–65.

Kas•bah (kaz′bə, -bä, käz′-), *n.* the older, native Arab quarter of a North African city, esp. Algiers. Also, **Casbah.** [< Ar *qaṣabah* citadel]

Kas•bek (käz bek′; *Russ.* kuz byek′), *n.* Kazbek.

ka•sha (kä′shə), *n.* **1.** a soft food prepared from hulled and crushed grain, esp. buckwheat. **2.** such grain before cooking. [1800–10; < Russ *kásha*]

Kash•a (kash′ə), *Trademark.* a brand name for a soft fabric of wool and goat's hair, having a napped surface and a slight crosswise streak.

ka•sher (*adj., n.* kä shâr′; *v.* kä′shər), *adj., n., v.t.* kosher.

Ka•shi (kä′shē′, kash′ē), *n. Pinyin.* a city in W Xinjiang Uygur, in extreme W China. 256,890. Also called **Kash•gar** (kash′gär, käsh′-). Formerly, **Shufu.**

ka•shim (kash′im, kä′shim), *n. Alaska.* a building used by Eskimos as a community gathering place or as a place where men congregate and socialize. [1850–55; < Yupik *qasgiq*]

kash•mir (kazh′mēr, kash′-), *n.* cashmere.

Kash•mir (kash′mēr, kazh′-, kash mēr′, kazh-), *n.* **1.** Also, **Cashmere.** a former princely state in SW Asia, adjacent to India, Pakistan, Sinkiang, and Tibet: sovereignty in dispute between India and Pakistan since 1947. **2.** Official name, **Jammu and Kashmir.** the part of this state occupied by India, forming a state in the Indian union. 5,220,000; ab. 53,500 sq. mi. (138,000 sq. km). *Cap.:* Srinagar (summer); Jammu (winter).

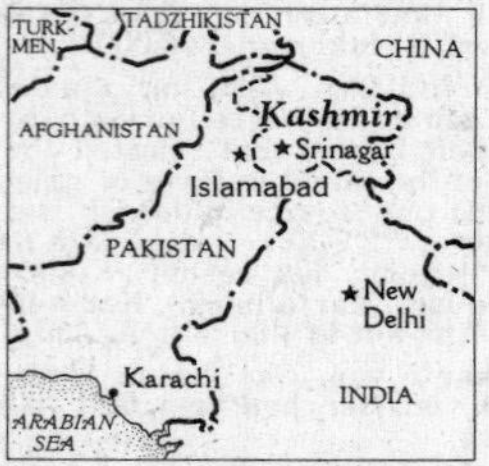

Kash′mir goat′, one of a long-haired breed of goat raised in Tibet and the higher elevations of China, the Indian subcontinent, Afghanistan, and Turkey for its meat, milk, and cashmere wool. Also, **Cashmere goat.**

Kash•mir•i (kash mēr′ē, kazh-), *n., pl.* **-mir•is,** (*esp. collectively*) **-mir•i,** *adj.* —*n.* **1.** a native or inhabitant of Kashmir. **2.** the Indo-Iranian language of the Kashmiri. —*adj.* **3.** of or pertaining to Kashmir or its people.

Kash•mir•i•an (kash mēr′ē ən, kazh-), *adj.* **1.** of, pertaining to, or characteristic of Kashmir or the Kashmiri. —*n.* **2.** a Kashmiri. [1875–80; KASHMIR + -IAN]

Kash′mir rug′, a handmade Oriental rug that is woven flat without pile and covered entirely with embroidered patterns of colored yarns. [1895–1900]

kash•ruth (*Seph. Heb.* käsh ro͞ot′; *Ashk. Heb.* käsh′ro͝ot, -rəs; *Eng.* käsh′rəth), *n.* **1.** the body of dietary laws prescribed for Jews: *an observer of kashruth.* **2.** fitness for use with respect to Jewish law: *the kashruth of a religious object.* Also, **kash•rut′.** [1905–10; < Heb: lit., fitness]

Ka•shu•bi•an (kə sho͞o′bē ən), *n.* a West Slavic language closely related to Polish and spoken in northern Poland near the mouth of the Vistula.

Ka•si (kä′sē), *n.* **Kingdom of,** an ancient kingdom of N India, the capital at present-day Varanasi; flourished in the 8th–6th centuries B.C.

Kas•ka (kas′kə), *n., pl.* **-kas,** (*esp. collectively*) **-ka** for 1. **1.** a member of a group of North American Indians of northern British Columbia and southern Yukon Territory. **2.** the Athabaskan language of the Kaska. [after the Kaska name for McDame Creek in the Cassiar region of N British Columbia]

Ka•spar•ov (kə spär′ôf, -of; *Russ.* ku spär′əf), *n.* **Gary** (*Garry*), born 1963, Armenian chess player.

Kas•per (kas′pər), *n.* a male given name, form of **Caspar.**

Kas•sa (kosh′sho), *n.* Hungarian name of **Košice.**

Kas•sa•la (kä′sä lä′, kas′ə lə), *n.* a city in the E Sudan, near Eritrea. 99,652.

Kas•sa•pa (kä shup′ə), *n.* Kasyapa.

Kas•sel (kas′əl; *Ger.* kä′səl), *n.* a city in central Germany. 203,500. Also, **Cassel.**

Kas•site (kas′īt), *n.* a member of an ancient people related to the Elamites, who ruled Babylonia from c1650 to c1100 B.C. Also, **Cassite.**

Kast•ler (kast ler′), *n.* **Al•fred** (al fred′), 1902–84, French physicist, born in Germany: Nobel prize 1966.

Käst•ner (kast′nər; *Ger.* kest′nər), *n.* **E•rich** (ā′rikh), 1899–1974, German writer.

Kas′tor and Pol′lux (kas′tər, kä′stər), *Class. Myth.* Castor and Pollux.

Kas•tro (*Gk.* käs′trô), *n.* Mytilene (def. 2).

Ka•strop-Rau•xel (*Ger.* käs′trôp rouk′səl), *n.* Castrop-Rauxel.

Kas•ya•pa (käsh yup′ə), *n.* an important disciple of the Buddha who called together a council of Arhats after the death of the Buddha to compose the Pali Canon. Also, **Kassapa.**

kat (kät), *n.* an evergreen shrub, *Catha edulis,* of Arabia and Africa, the leaves of which are used as a narcotic when chewed or made into a beverage. Also, **khat, qat.** [1855–60; < Ar *qāt*]

ka•ta (kä′tə), *n.* an exercise consisting of several of the specific movements of a martial art, esp. a pattern prescribed for defending oneself against several attackers, used in judo and karate training. [1950–55; < Japn: shape, pattern]

kata-, var. of **cata-.** Also, *esp. before a vowel,* **kat-.**

ka•tab•a•sis (kə tab′ə sis), *n., pl.* **-ses** (-sēz′). **1.** a march from the interior of a country to the coast, as that of the 10,000 Greeks after their defeat and the death of Cyrus the Younger at Cunaxa. **2.** a retreat, esp. a military retreat. Cf. **anabasis.** [1830–40; < Gk *katábasis* a going down, descent, equiv. to *kataba-* (s. of *katabainein* to go down) + *-sis* -SIS. See KATA-, BASIS]

kat•a•bat•ic (kat′ə bat′ik), *adj. Meteorol.* (of a wind or air current) moving downward or down a slope. Cf. **anabatic** (def. 1). [1915–20; < Gk *katabatikós* pertaining to going down, equiv. to *kata-* KATA- + *ba-* (s. of *bainein* to go; see BASIS) + *-tikos* -TIC]

Ka•tah•din (kə tä′dn), *n.* **Mount,** the highest peak in Maine, in the central part. 5273 ft. (1607 m).

ka•ta•ka•na (kä′tə kä′nə; *Japn.* kä′tä kä′nä), *n.* the more angular, less commonly used of the two Japanese syllabaries. Cf. **hiragana.** [1720–30; < Japn, equiv. to *kata* part (of kanji) + *kana* KANA]

kat•a•lase (kat′l äs′, -āz′), *n. Biochem.* **1.** catalase. **2.** peroxidase.

ka•tal•y•sis (kə tal′ə sis), *n., pl.* **-ses** (-sēz′). *Chem.* catalysis.

kat•a•lyst (kat′l ist), *n. Chem.* catalyst.

kat•a•lyze (kat′l īz′), *v.t.,* **-lyzed, -lyz•ing.** *Chem.* catalyze. Also, *esp. Brit.,* **kat′a•lyse′. —kat′a•lyz′er,** *n.*

kat•a•mor•phism (kat′ə môr′fiz əm), *n. Geol.* metamorphism at or near the earth's surface: breaks down complex minerals into simpler ones. Cf. **anamorphism.** [1900–05; KATA- + -MORPHISM] **—kat′a•mor′phic,** *adj.*

Ka•tan•ga (kə täng′gə, -tang′-), *n.* former name of **Shaba.**

Kat•ang•ese (kat′äng gēz′, -gēs′, -ang-), *n., pl.* **-ese,** *adj.* —*n.* **1.** a native or inhabitant of Katanga. —*adj.* **2.** of or pertaining to Katanga or its people. Also, **Ka•tan•gan** (kə täng′gən, -tang′-). [KATANG(A) + -ESE]

Ka•tar (kä′tär, kə tär′), *n.* Qatar.

Ka•ta•yev (ku tä′yif), *n.* **Va•len•tin Pe•tro•vich** (və lyin tyēn′ pyi trô′vyich), 1897–1986, Russian writer.

ka•tci•na (kə chē′nə), *n.* kachina. Also, **ka•tchi′na.**

Kate (kāt), *n.* a female given name, form of **Katherine** or **Catherine.**

Ka•tha•re•vu•sa (kä′thə rev′ə sä′, -sə, kath′ə-; *Gk.* kä′thä re′vo͞o sä), *n.* the puristic Modern Greek literary language (distinguished from *Demotic*). Also called **Hellenic.**

Kath•er•ine (kath′ər in, kath′rin), *n.* a female given name: from the Greek word meaning "pure." Also, **Kath′a•rine, Kath•ryn, Kath•rynne** (kath′rin).

Ka•thi•a•war (kä′tē ə wär′), *n.* a peninsula on the W coast of India.

ka•this•ma (*Gk.* kä′thēz mä; *Eng.* ka thiz′mə), *n., pl.* **ka•this•ma•ta** (*Gk.* kä thēz′mä tä; *Eng.* ka thiz′mə tə). one of the 20 divisions of the Psalter in the Greek rite. Also, **cathisma.** [< MGk, Gk *káthisma* seat, equiv. to *kathís(is)* a sitting (equiv. to *kathid-,* s. of *kathízein* to sit down (itself equiv. to *kat-* KAT- + *hízein* to set, sit; see SIT) + *-sis* -SIS, with *-ds-* > *-s-*) + *-ma* agent suffix]

Kath•leen (kath lēn′, kath′lēn), *n.* a female given name, form of **Katherine.** Also, **Kath•lene′, Kath•lyn, Kath•lynne** (kath′lin).

ka•thol•i•kos (kə thol′i kəs, -kos′), *n., pl.* **-kos•es, -koi** (-koi′). catholicos.

Kath•y (kath′ē), *n.* a female given name, form of **Katherine** and **Kathleen.** Also, **Kath′ie.**

Ka•tie (kā′tē), *n.* a female given name, form of **Katherine** or **Catherine.** Also, **Ka′tey.**

kat•i•on (kat′ī′ən, -on), *n. Physical Chem.* cation.

Kat•mai (kat′mī), *n.* **1. Mount,** an active volcano in SW Alaska. 7500 ft. (2286 m). **2.** a national monument including Mt. Katmai and the Valley of Ten Thousand Smokes. 4215 sq. mi. (10,915 sq. km).

Kat•man•du (kät′män do͞o′, kat′man-), *n.* a city in and the capital of Nepal, in the central part. 150,000. Also, **Kath′man•du′.**

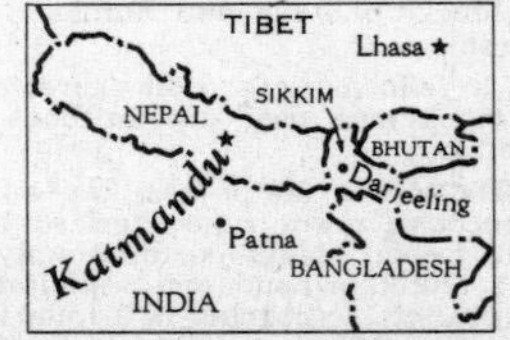

CONCISE ETYMOLOGY KEY: <, descended or borrowed from; >, whence; b., blend of, blended; c., cognate with; cf., compare; deriv., derivative; equiv., equivalent; imit., imitative; obl., oblique; r., replacing; s., stem; sp., spelling, spelled; resp., respelling, respelled; trans., translation; ?, origin unknown; *, unattested; ‡, probably earlier than. See the full key inside the front cover.

Ka•to•wi•ce (kä/tô vē/tse), *n.* a city in S Poland. 344,000. German, **Kat•to•witz** (kä/tô vits).

Ka•tri•na (kə trē/nə), *n.* a female given name, form of **Katherine.** Also, **Ka•try/na.**

Kat•rine (ka/trin), *n.* **Loch,** a lake in central Scotland. 8 mi. (13 km) long.

Kat•te•gat (kat/i gat/, kä/ti gät/), *n.* a strait between Jutland and Sweden. 40–70 mi. (64–113 km) wide. Also, **Cattegat.**

Ka•ty (kā/tē), *n.* a female given name, form of **Katherine** or **Catherine.**

ka•ty•did (kā/tē did), *n.* any of several large, usually green, American long-horned grasshoppers, the males of which produce a characteristic song. [1745–55, *Amer.*; imit.]

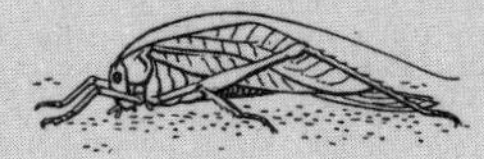
katydid, *Microcentrum rhombifolium,* length 2 in. (5 cm)

Katz (kats), *n.* **Sir Ber•nard** (bûr/nərd), born 1911, British biophysicist, born in Germany: Nobel prize for medicine 1970.

katz•en•jam•mer (kat/sən jam/ər), *n.* **1.** the discomfort and illness experienced as the aftereffects of excessive drinking; hangover. **2.** uneasiness; anguish; distress. **3.** uproar; clamor: *His speech produced a public katzenjammer.* [1840–50; < G, equiv. to *Katzen* (pl. of *Katze* CAT[1]) + *Jammer* discomfort, OHG *jāmar* (n. and adj.); cf. YAMMER]

Ka•u•a•i (kä/o͞o ä/ē, kou/ī), *n.* an island in NW Hawaii. 38,856; 511 sq. mi. (1325 sq. km).

kauch (käkʜ), *n. Scot.* kiaugh.

Kauf•man (kôf/mən), *n.* **George S(imon),** 1889–1961, U.S. dramatist.

Kauf/mann Peak/ (kouf/mən), former name of **Lenin Peak.**

Kau•kau•na (kô kô/nə), *n.* a city in E Wisconsin. 11,310.

Kau•nas (kou/näs), *n.* a city in S central Lithuania. 370,000. Russian, **Kovno.**

Ka•un•da (kä o͞on/dä, -də), *n.* **Kenneth (David),** born 1924, Zambian political leader: president since 1964.

Kau•ra•vas (kou/rə väz/), *n.* (*used with a plural v.*) (in the *Mahabharata*) the cousins and enemies of the Pandavas. Also, **Kurus.**

kau•ri (kou/rē), *n., pl.* **-ris.** **1.** Also, **kau/ri pine/.** a tall, coniferous tree, *Agathis australis,* of New Zealand, yielding a valuable timber and a resin. **2.** the wood of this tree. **3.** any of various other trees of the genus *Agathis.* **4.** See **kauri resin.** [1815–25; < Maori]

kau/ri res/in, a hard resin obtained from the bark of the kauri or found, sometimes in masses of as much as 100 lb. (45 kg), in the soil where the tree has grown: used chiefly in making varnish. Also, **kauri, kau/ri gum/, kau/ri co/pal.** [1855–60]

kau•ry (kou/rē), *n., pl.* **-ries.** kauri.

Kaut•sky (kout/skē), *n.* **Karl Johann** (kärl/ yō/hän), 1854–1938, German socialist writer and editor.

ka•va (kä/və), *n.* **1.** a Polynesian shrub, *Piper methysticum,* of the pepper family, the aromatic roots of which are used to make an intoxicating beverage. **2.** the beverage made from these roots. Also called **ka/va•ka/va, ka/va-ka/va.** [1810–20; < Polynesian (first recorded from Tonga Islands)] **—Ka•va•ic** (kə vä/ik), *adj.*

Ka•va•fis (kä vä/fēs), *n.* **Kon•stan•ti•nos** (kôn/stän dē/nôs), real name of Constantine Cavafy. Also, **Ka•va/•phis.**

Ka•vál•la (kə val/ə; *Gk.* kä vä/lä), *n.* a seaport in E Greece. 46,000.

Ka•ver•i (kô/və rē, kä/-), *n.* Cauvery.

Ka•ve•rin (kə vär/in; *Russ.* ku vye/ʀyin), *n.* **Ve•ni•a•min** (ven/yə mēn/; *Russ.* vyi nyi u myēn/), (*Veniamin Aleksandrovich Zilberg*), born 1902, Russian novelist.

Ka•vir/ Des/ert (kə vēr/), Dasht-i-Kavir.

Kaw (kô), *n.* Kansa.

Ka•wa•ba•ta (kä/wə bä/tə; *Japn.* kä/wä bä/tä), *n.* **Ya•su•na•ri** (yä/so͞o nä/ʀē), 1899–1972, Japanese novelist and short-story writer: Nobel prize 1968.

Ka•wa•gu•chi (kä/wä go͞o/chē), *n.* a city on SE Honshu, in central Japan, N of Tokyo. 379,357.

Ka•wa•sa•ki (kä/wä sä/kē), *n.* a seaport on SE Honshu, in central Japan, SW of Tokyo. 1,040,698.

Kawasa/ki disease/, *Pathol.* an acute illness of unknown cause, occurring primarily in children, characterized by high fever, swollen lymph glands, rash, redness in mouth and throat, and joint pain. [1980–85; after Japanese pediatrician Tomisaku *Kawasaki,* who first described it]

Kay (kā), *n.* **1. Sir,** *Arthurian Romance.* the rude, boastful foster brother and seneschal of Arthur. **2. Ulysses Simp•son** (simp/sən), born 1917, U.S. composer. **3.** a female or male given name: from a Greek word meaning "rejoice."

kayak (def. 2)

kay•ak (kī/ak), *n.* **1.** an Eskimo canoe with a skin cover on a light framework, made watertight by flexible closure around the waist of the occupant and propelled with a double-bladed paddle. **2.** a small boat resembling this, made commercially of a variety of materials and used in sports. **—*v.i.*** **3.** to go or travel by kayak. **—*v.t.*** **4.** to travel on by kayak: *to kayak the Colorado River.* Also, **kaiak, kyak, kyack.** [1750–60; < Inuit *qayaq*] **—kay/ak•er,** *n.*

Kayes (kāz), *n.* a city in W Mali. 34,100.

Ka•yi•ban•da (kä/yi bän/də), *n.* **Gré•goire** (grā gwär/; *Fr.* grā gwaʀ/), 1924–76, president of the Republic of Rwanda 1962–73.

Kay•la (kā/lə), *n.* a female given name.

kay•o (kā/ō/, kā/ō/; *v.* kā/ō/), *n., pl.* **kay•os,** *v.,* **kay•oed, kay•o•ing.** *Slang.* See **KO.** [1920–25, *Amer.*]

Kay/ser-Flei/scher rings/ (kī/zər flī/shər), *Pathol.* deep green pigmentation of the cornea due to copper deposition, seen in Wilson's disease. [1925–30; after German ophthalmologists Bernhard *Kayser* (1869–1954) and Bruno *Fleischer* (1874–1965), who described them]

Kay•se•ri (kī/se rē/, -zə-), *n.* a city in central Turkey. 207,039. Ancient, **Caesarea.**

ka•za•chok (kə zä chôk/), *n., pl.* **-zach•ki** (-zäch kē/). a lively, Slavic folk dance for a solo male dancer, marked esp. by the prisiadka. Also called **kazatsky, kazatske.** [1925–30; < Russ *kazachók* or Ukrainian *kozachók,* equiv. to *kazák, kozák* COSSACK + *-ok* dim. suffix]

Ka•zakh (kə zäk/), *n.* **1.** a member of a nomadic Muslim people living mainly in Kazakhstan. **2.** the Turkic language of the Kazakh people. Also, **Ka•zak/.**

Ka•zakh•stan (kä/zäk stän/; *Russ.* kə zukʜ stän/), *n.* a republic in central Asia, NE of the Caspian Sea and W of China. 14,685,000; 1,064,092 sq. mi. (2,755,998 sq. km). *Cap.:* Alma-Ata. Formerly, **Kazakh/ So/viet So/cialist Repub/lic.**

Ka•zan (kə zan/, -zän/; *for 2 also Russ.* ku zän/), *n.* **1. E•li•a** (i lī/ə, ēl/yə), born 1909, U.S. film and stage director and novelist, born in Turkey. **2.** a city in and capital of the Tatar Autonomous Republic in the SE Russian Federation in Europe, near the Volga River. 993,000.

Ka•zant•za•kis (kaz/ən zak/is, kä/zən zä/kis; *Gk.* kä/zän dzä/kēs), *n.* **Ni•kos** (nē/kôs), 1883–1957, Greek poet and novelist.

ka•zat•sky (kə zät/skē), *n., pl.* **-skies.** kazachok. Also, **ka•zat/ske.** [< Russ *kazátskiĭ* lit., Cossack (adj.)]

Kaz•bek (käz bek/; *Russ.* kuz byek/), *n.* **Mount,** an extinct volcano in the central Caucasus Mountains between the Georgian Republic and the Russian Federation. 16,541 ft. (5042 m). Also, **Kasbek.**

Kaz•da•ği (käz/dä gē/; *Turk.* käz/dä u/), *n.* Turkish name of **Mount Ida** (def. 1).

ka•zoo (kə zo͞o/), *n., pl.* **-zoos.** **1.** a musical toy consisting of a tube that is open at both ends and has a hole in the side covered with parchment or membrane, which produces a buzzing sound when the performer hums into one end. Also called **mirliton.** **2.** *Slang.* **a.** the buttocks. **b.** the anus. [1880–85, *Amer.*; orig. uncert.; alleged to be imit.]

Kaz•vin (kaz vēn/), *n.* Qazvin.

KB, **1.** *Chess.* king's bishop. **2.** *Computers.* kilobyte; kilobytes.

Kb, *Computers.* kilobit; kilobits.

kb, kilobar; kilobars.

K.B., **1.** King's Bench. **2.** Knight Bachelor.

K.B.E., Knight Commander of the British Empire.

KBP, *Chess.* king's bishop's pawn.

kc, **1.** kilocycle; kilocycles. **2.** kilocurie; kilocuries.

K.C., **1.** Kansas City. **2.** King's Counsel. **3.** Knight Commander. **4.** Knights of Columbus.

kcal, kilocalorie; kilocalories.

K.C.B., Knight Commander of the Bath.

kCi, kilocurie; kilocuries.

K.C.M.G., Knight Commander of the Order of St. Michael and St. George.

Kčs., koruna; korunas. [< Czech *k(oruna) č(esko)-s(lovenská)*]

kc/s, kilocycles per second. Also, **kc/sec**

K.C.S.I., Knight Commander of the Order of the Star of India.

K.C.V.O., Knight Commander of the (Royal) Victorian Order.

KD, **1.** kiln-dried. **2.** Also, **k.d.** *Com.* knocked-down.

KD., (in Kuwait) dinar; dinars.

ke•a (kā/ə, kē/ə), *n.* a large, greenish New Zealand parrot, *Nestor notabilis.* [1860–65; < Maori]

Ke•a (*Gk.* ke/ä), *n.* Keos.

Kean (kēn), *n.* **Edmund,** 1787–1833, English actor, esp. known for performance of Shakespearean roles.

Keans•burg (kēnz/bûrg), *n.* a town in E New Jersey. 10,613.

Kear•ney (kär/nē), *n.* a city in S Nebraska, on the Platte. 21,158.

Kearns (kûrnz), *n.* a town in N Utah, near Salt Lake City. 21,353.

Kear•ny (kär/nē), *n.* **1. Philip,** 1814–62, U.S. general. **2.** a city in NE New Jersey, near Newark. 37,735.

keat (kēt), *n. Ornith.* keet.

Kea•ton (kēt/n), *n.* **Buster** (*Joseph Francis Keaton*), 1895–1966, U.S. film comedian and director.

Keats (kēts), *n.* **John,** 1795–1821, English poet. **—Keats/i•an,** *adj.*

Keb (keb), *n. Egyptian Relig.* Geb.

ke•bab (kə bob/), *n.* kabob. Also, **ke•bob/.**

keb•lah (keb/lə), *n.* kiblah.

Ke•ble (kē/bəl), *n.* **John,** 1792–1866, English clergyman and poet.

Kech•ua (kech/wä, -wə), *n., pl.* **-uas,** (*esp. collectively*) **-ua.** Quechua.

Kech•uan (kech/wən), *adj., n., pl.* **-uans,** (*esp. collectively*) **-uan.** **—*adj.*** **1.** Quechuan. **—*n.*** **2.** Quechua.

keck (kek), *v.i.* **1.** to retch; be nauseated. **2.** to feel or show disgust or strong dislike. [1595–1605; perh. akin to CHOKE]

Kecs•ke•mét (kech/ke māt/), *n.* a city in central Hungary. 77,484.

ked (ked), *n.* sheeptick. [1560–70; earlier *cade,* of uncert. orig.]

Ke•dah (kā/dä), *n.* a state in Malaysia, on the W central Malay Peninsula. 954,947; 3660 sq. mi. (9480 sq. km). *Cap.:* Alor Star.

Ke•dar (kē/dər), *n.* the second son of Ishmael. Gen. 25:13.

ked•dah (ked/ə), *n.* kheda.

kedge (kej), *v.,* **kedged, kedg•ing,** *n. Naut.* **—*v.t.*** **1.** to warp or pull (a ship) along by hauling on the cable of an anchor carried out from the ship and dropped. **—*v.i.*** **2.** (of a ship) to move by being kedged. **—*n.*** **3.** Also called **kedge/ an/chor.** a small anchor used in kedging. [1475–85; akin to ME *caggen* to fasten; see CADGE[1]]

ked•ger•ee (kej/ə rē/), *n.* **1.** *East Indian Cookery.* a cooked dish consisting of rice, lentils, and spices. **2.** a cooked dish of rice, fish, hard-boiled eggs, butter, cream, and seasonings. [1655–65; < Hindi *khicṛī, khicaṛī*]

Ke•di•ri (kä dēr/ē), *n.* a city on E Java, in Indonesia. 178,865.

Ke•dron (kē/drən), *n.* Kidron.

Ke•du•shah (*Seph. Heb.* kə do͞o shä/; *Ashk. Heb.* kə do͞o/shô), *n., pl.* **-du•shoth, -du•shot, -du•shos** (*Seph. Heb.* -do͞o shôt/; *Ashk. Heb.* -do͞o/shôs), *Eng.* **-du•shahs.** *Judaism.* a liturgical prayer of varying form that is incorporated into the third blessing of the *Amidah* during the repetition of this prayer by the cantor. [< Heb *qĕdhushshāh* lit., holiness]

ke•ef (kē ef/), *n.* kef (def. 2).

keek (kēk), *v.i. Scot. and North Eng.* to peep; look furtively. [1350–1400; ME *kiken,* c. or < MD, MLG *kiken*]

keel[1] (kēl), *n.* **1.** *Naut.* a central fore-and-aft structural member in the bottom of a hull, extending from the stem to the sternpost and having the floors or frames attached to it, usually at right angles: sometimes projecting from the bottom of the hull to provide stability. **2.** *Literary.* a ship or boat. **3.** a part corresponding to a ship's keel in some other structure, as in a dirigible balloon. **4.** (*cap.*) *Astron.* the constellation Carina. **5.** *Bot., Zool.* a longitudinal ridge, as on a leaf or bone; a carina. **6.** Also called **brace molding.** *Archit.* a projecting molding the profile of which consists of two ogees symmetrically disposed about an arris or fillet. **7. on an even keel,** in a state of balance; steady; steadily: *The affairs of state are seldom on an even keel for long.* **—*v.t., v.i.*** **8.** to turn or upset so as to bring the wrong side or part uppermost. **9. keel over, a.** to capsize or overturn. **b.** to fall as in a faint: *Several cadets keeled over from the heat during the parade.* [1325–75; 1895–1900 for def. 9; ME *kele* < ON *kjǫlr;* c. OE *cēol* keel, ship; see KEEL[2]] **—keeled,** *adj.*

keel[2] (kēl), *n. Brit. Dial.* **1.** keelboat. **2.** a keelboat load of coal; the amount of coal carried by one keelboat. **3.** a measure of coal equivalent to 21 long tons and 4 hundredweight (21.5 metric tons). [1375–1425; late ME *kele* < MD *kiel* ship; c. OE *cēol* ship, G *kiel* ship (obs.), KEEL[1]]

keel[3] (kēl), *v.t. Brit. Dial.* to cool, esp. by stirring. [bef. 900; ME *kelen,* OE *cēlan* to be cool; akin to COOL]

keel[4] (kēl), *n.* a red ocher stain used for marking sheep, lumber, etc.; ruddle. [1475–85; earlier *keyle* (north and Scots dial.); cf. ScotGael *cìl* (itself perh. < E)]

CONCISE PRONUNCIATION KEY: act, cāpe, dâre, pärt; set, ēqual; if, īce; ox, ōver, ôrder, oil, bo͝ok, bo͞ot, out; up, ûrge; child; sing; shoe; thin, *th*at; zh as in *treasure.* ə = a as in *alone,* e as in *system,* i as in *easily,* o as in *gallop,* u as in *circus;* ᵊ as in *fire* (fīᵊr), *hour* (ouᵊr). l and n can serve as syllabic consonants, as in *cradle* (krād/l), and *button* (but/n). See the full key inside the front cover.

keel•age (kē′lij), *n.* a toll on a merchant ship entering a port. [1670–80; KEEL[1] + -AGE]

keel•boat (kēl′bōt′), *n.* a roughly built, shallow freight boat, having a keel to permit sailing into the wind. [1685–95; KEEL[1] or KEEL[2] + BOAT]

keel•boat•man (kēl′bōt′mən), *n., pl.* **-men.** a member of the crew of a keelboat. [1830–40, *Amer.*; KEELBOAT + MAN]

keel′ bone′, carina.

Kee•ler (kē′lər), *n.* **William H.** (*"Wee Willy"*), 1872–1923, U.S. baseball player.

Kee•ley (kē′lē), *n.* **Leslie En•raught** (en′rôt), 1834–1900, U.S. physician.

keel•haul (kēl′hôl′), *v.t.* **1.** *Naut.* to haul (an offender) under the bottom of a ship and up on the other side as a punishment. **2.** to rebuke severely. Also, **keel•hale** (kēl′hāl). Also called **keel•drag** (kēl′drag′), **keel•rake** (kēl′rāk′). [1660–70; < D *kielhalen.* See KEEL[1], HAUL]

Kee′ling Is′lands (kē′ling). See **Cocos Islands.**

keel•less (kēl′lis), *adj.* having no keel, as a ship. [1875–80; KEEL[1] + -LESS]

keel•son (kel′sən, kēl′-), *n. Naut.* any of various fore-and-aft structural members lying above or parallel to the keel in the bottom of a hull. Also, **kelson.** [1605–15; < LG *kielswin* lit., keel swine (sense relation obscure) < Scand; cf. D *kolsvijn,* Dan *kølsvin,* Sw *kölsvin*]

Kee′lung (kē′lo͝ong′), *n. Older Spelling.* Chilung.

keel′ ves′sel, any of various types of sailing vessels in which a fixed, projecting keel gives lateral resistance.

keen[1] (kēn), *adj.,* **-er, -est.** **1.** finely sharpened, as an edge; so shaped as to cut or pierce substances readily: *a keen razor.* **2.** sharp, piercing, or biting: *a keen wind; keen satire.* **3.** characterized by strength and distinctness of perception; extremely sensitive or responsive: *keen eyes; keen ears.* **4.** having or showing great mental penetration or acumen: *keen reasoning; a keen mind.* **5.** animated by or showing strong feeling or desire: *keen competition.* **6.** intense, as feeling or desire: *keen ambition; keen jealousy.* **7.** eager; interested; enthusiastic (often fol. by *about, on,* etc., or an infinitive): *She is really keen on going swimming.* **8.** *Slang.* great; wonderful; marvelous. [bef. 900; 1930–35 for def. 8; ME *kene,* OE *cēne;* c. G *kühn,* OHG *chuoni* bold, ON *kœnn* wise, skillful] —**keen′ly,** *adv.* —**keen′ness,** *n.*
—**Syn. 1, 4.** See **sharp. 2.** cutting, bitter, caustic. **3.** piercing, penetrating, acute. **4.** discerning, acute, astute, sagacious, shrewd, clever. **5.** See **avid. 7.** earnest, fervid. —**Ant. 1, 3, 4.** dull.

keen[2] (kēn), *n.* **1.** a wailing lament for the dead. —*v.i.* **2.** to wail in lamentation for the dead. —*v.t.* **3.** to bewail or lament by or with keening. [1805–15; < Ir *caoine* (n.), *caoin-* (v., s. of *caoinim*) lament] —**keen′er,** *n.*

Keene (kēn), *n.* a city in SW New Hampshire. 21,449.

Keene's′ cement′ (kēnz), *Trademark.* a brand of hard, white finish plaster.

keen•ing (kē′ning), *n.* **1.** the act of a person who keens. **2.** a wailing lament for the dead; keen. [1875–80; KEEN[2] + -ING[1]]

keep (kēp), *v.,* **kept, keep•ing,** *n.* —*v.t.* **1.** to hold or retain in one's possession; hold as one's own: *If you like it, keep it. Keep the change.* **2.** to hold or have the use of for a period of time: *You can keep it for the summer.* **3.** to hold in a given place; store: *You can keep your things in here.* **4.** to maintain (some action), esp. in accordance with specific requirements, a promise, etc.: *to keep watch; to keep step.* **5.** to cause to continue in a given position, state, course, or action: *to keep a light burning; to keep a child happy.* **6.** to maintain in condition or order, as by care and labor: *He keeps his car in good condition.* **7.** to maintain in usable or edible condition; preserve: *If you want to keep meat for a long time, freeze it.* **8.** to hold in custody or under guard, as a prisoner: *They kept him in jail.* **9.** to cause to stay in a particular place; prevent or restrain from departure: *The work kept her at the office.* **10.** to have regularly in stock and for sale: *to keep a large supply of machine parts.* **11.** to maintain in one's service or for one's use or enjoyment: *to keep a car and chauffeur.* **12.** to associate with: *She keeps bad company.* **13.** to have the care, charge, or custody of: *She keeps my dog when I travel.* **14.** to refrain from disclosing; withhold from the knowledge of others: *to keep a secret.* **15.** to withhold from use; reserve; save: *I'll keep this toy until you learn to behave. Keep the good wine for company.* **16.** to hold back or restrain: *They kept the child from talking. Nothing can keep him from doing it.* **17.** to maintain control of; regulate: *to keep the peace; to keep your temper.* **18.** to maintain by writing: *to keep a diary.* **19.** to record (business transactions, daily occurrences, etc.) regularly: *to keep records; to keep a list of visitors.* **20.** to observe; pay obedient regard to (a law, rule, promise, etc.). **21.** to conform to; follow; fulfill: *to keep one's word.* **22.** to observe (a season, festival, etc.) with formalities or rites: *to keep Christmas.* **23.** to maintain or carry on, as an establishment, business, etc.; manage. **24.** to guard; protect: *He kept her from harm.* **25.** to maintain or support: *It costs more each year to keep a house.* **26.** to support or contribute to the support of in return for sexual or other favors. **27.** to take care of; tend: *to keep a vegetable garden.* **28.** to raise (livestock): *These farmers keep goats and cattle.* **29.** to remain in (a place, spot, etc.): *Please keep your seats.* **30.** to maintain one's position in or on: *He kept the job.* **31.** to continue to follow (a path, track, course, etc.). **32.** to maintain in active existence, as an assembly, court, or fair.
—*v.i.* **33.** to continue in an action, course, position, state, etc.: *to keep in sight; to keep going.* **34.** to remain, or continue to be, as specified: *to keep cool.* **35.** to remain or stay in a particular place: *to keep indoors.* **36.** to continue unimpaired or without spoiling: *The food will keep on ice.* **37.** to admit of being reserved for a future occasion: *I have more to tell you, but it will keep.* **38.** to keep oneself or itself as specified (fol. by *away, back, off, out,* etc.): *Keep off the grass.* **39.** to restrain oneself; refrain (usually fol. by *from*): *Try to keep from smiling.* **40. keep at,** to persist in; be steadfast: *You'll never master your French unless you keep at it.* **41. keep back, a.** to hold in check; restrain: *The dikes kept back the floodwaters.* **b.** to stay away from: *The crowds would not keep back from the barrier.* **c.** to refuse to reveal: *The prisoner was keeping back vital information.* **42. keep books,** to maintain financial records. **43. keep down, a.** to hold under control or at a reduced or acceptable level: *to keep your voice down.* **b.** to prevent from going up or increasing: *to keep prices down.* **44. keep in with,** to stay in someone's favor; be on good terms with: *They are social climbers who make certain to keep in with all the right people.* **45. keep on,** to continue; persist: *If you keep on singing they'll ask you to leave.* **46. keep tab** or **tabs on.** See **tab**[1] (def. 11). **47. keep time.** See **time** (def. 40). **48. keep to, a.** to adhere to; conform to: *She keeps to the rules.* **b.** to confine oneself to: *to keep to one's bed.* **49. keep to oneself, a.** to remain aloof from the society of others. **b.** to hold (something) as secret or confidential: *I'll tell you only if you promise to keep it to yourself.* **50. keep track of.** See **track** (def. 22). **51. keep up, a.** to maintain an equal rate of speed, activity, or progress with another or others. **b.** to persevere; continue. **c.** to maintain the good condition of; keep in repair. **d.** Also, **keep up on** or **with.** to stay informed: *to keep up on current events.* **e.** to match one's friends, neighbors, business associates, etc., in success, affluence, etc.
—*n.* **52.** board and lodging; subsistence; support: *to work for one's keep.* **53.** the innermost and strongest structure or central tower of a medieval castle. **54. keeps,** (*used with a singular v.*) a game of marbles in which the players keep the marbles they have won. **55. for keeps,** *Informal.* **a.** under the stipulation that one keeps one's winnings. **b.** with serious intent or purpose. **c.** finally; permanently: *They decided to settle the argument for keeps.* [bef. 1000; ME *kepen,* OE *cēpan* to observe, heed, watch, await, take; perh. akin to OE *gecōp* proper, fitting, *capian* to look, ON *kōpa* to stare] —**keep′a•ble,** *adj.* —**keep′a•bil′i•ty,** *n.*
—**Syn. 1.** KEEP, RESERVE, RETAIN, WITHHOLD refer to having and holding in possession. KEEP (a common word) and RETAIN (a more formal one) agree in meaning to continue to have or hold, as opposed to losing, parting with, or giving up: *to keep a book for a week.* TO RESERVE is to keep for some future use, occasion, or recipient, or to hold back for a time: *to reserve judgment.* TO WITHHOLD is generally to hold back altogether: *to withhold help.* **6.** preserve. **8.** detain, confine. **53.** donjon, dungeon, stronghold. —**Ant. 8.** release.

keep•er (kē′pər), *n.* **1.** a person who guards or watches, as at a prison or gate. **2.** a person who assumes responsibility for another's behavior: *He refused to be his brother's keeper.* **3.** a person who owns or operates a business (usually used in combination): *a hotelkeeper.* **4.** a person who is responsible for the maintenance of something (often used in combination): *a zookeeper; a groundskeeper.* **5.** a person charged with responsibility for the preservation and conservation of something valuable, as a curator or game warden. **6.** a person who conforms to or abides by a requirement: *a keeper of his word.* **7.** a fish that is of sufficient size to be caught and retained without violating the law. **8.** *Football.* a play in which the quarterback retains the ball and runs with it, usually after faking a hand-off or pass. **9.** something that serves to hold in place, retain, etc., as on a door lock. **10.** something that lasts well, as a fruit. **11.** See **guard ring. 12.** an iron or steel bar placed across the poles of a permanent horseshoe magnet for preserving the strength of the magnet during storage. [1250–1300; ME *keper.* See KEEP, -ER[1]] —**keep′er•less,** *adj.* —**keep′er•ship′,** *n.*
—**Syn. 1.** warden, jailer. **2.** custodian, guardian.

keep′er hook′, *Theat.* an S-shaped hook for securing doors, windows, etc., or for fastening a batten to a flat.

keep•ing (kē′ping), *n.* **1.** agreement or conformity in things or elements associated together: *His actions are not in keeping with his words.* **2.** the act of a person or thing that keeps; observance, custody, or care. **3.** maintenance or keep. **4.** holding, reserving, or retaining. [1250–1300; ME *keping.* See KEEP, -ING[1]]
—**Syn. 1.** consistency, congruity, harmony. **2.** protection, charge, guardianship. See **custody.**

keep′ing room′, *Older Use.* hall (def. 11). [1765–75]

keep•sake (kēp′sāk′), *n.* anything kept, or given to be kept, as a token of friendship or affection; remembrance. [1780–90; KEEP (v.) + SAKE[1]]
—**Syn.** souvenir, memento, token.

keeshond,
18 in. (46 cm)
high at shoulder

kees•hond (kās′hond′, kēs′-), *n., pl.* **-hon•den** (-hon′dən). one of a Dutch breed of small dogs having thick, silver-gray hair tipped with black and a tail carried over the back. [1925–30; < D, prob. special use of *Kees* (shortening of proper name *Cornelius*) + *hond* dog; see HOUND[1]]

Kees′ler Air′ Force′ Base′ (kē′slər), a U.S. Air Force installation in S Mississippi, near Biloxi.

kees•ter (kē′stər), *n. Slang.* keister.

keet (kēt), *n.* a young guinea fowl. Also, **keat.** [1855–60, *Amer.*; imit.]

Kee•wa•tin (kē wāt′n), *n.* **1.** a district in the Northwest Territories, in N Canada. 228,160 sq. mi. (590,935 sq. km). **2.** *Geol.* a division of the Archeozoic rocks found in the Canadian Shield.

kef (kāf, kef), *n.* (in the Middle East) **1.** a state of drowsy contentment, esp. from the use of a narcotic. **2.** Also, **keef.** a substance, esp. a smoking preparation of hemp leaves, used to produce this state. Also, **kief, kif.** [1800–10; < Ar *kaif* well-being, pleasure]

Ke•fau•ver (kē′fô vər), *n.* **Es•tes** (es′tis), 1903–63, U.S. political leader: U.S. senator 1949–63.

kef•fi•yeh (kə fē′ə), *n.* kaffiyeh.

ke•fir (kə fēr′), *Middle Eastern Cookery.* a tart-tasting drink originally of the Caucasus, made from cow's or sometimes goat's milk to which the bacteria *Streptococcus* and *Lactobacillus* have been added. [1880–85; < Russ *kefir,* appar. < a Caucasian language; cf. Ossetic *k'æpy, k'æpu* kefir, Mingrelian *kipuri* milk curdled in an animal skin]

Kef•la•vík (kyep′lə vēk′, -vik, kef′-), *n.* a town in SW Iceland, on the S shore of Faxa Bay: site of international airport. 6473.

Kef•lex (kef′leks), *Pharm., Trademark.* a brand of cephalexin.

keg (keg), *n.* **1.** a small cask or barrel, usually holding from 5 to 10 gallons (19 to 38 liters). **2.** a unit of weight, equal to 100 pounds (45 kilograms), used for nails. **3.** Also, **keg′ger.** a keg party; beer bust. [1585–95; earlier *cag* < ON *kaggi*]

keg•ler (keg′lər), *n.* a participant in a bowling game, as candlepins or tenpins. Also, **keg•el•er** (keg′ə lər, keg′lər). [1930–35; < G, equiv. to *Kegel* (nine)pin + *-er* -ER[1]]

keg•ling (keg′ling), *n.* the sport of bowling. Also, **keg•el•ing** (keg′ə ling, keg′ling). [1930–35; KEGL(ER) + -ING[1]]

keg′ par′ty, *Informal.* a beer bust.

ke•hil•lah (*Seph. Heb.* kə hē lä′; *Ashk. Heb.* kə hil′ə), *n., pl.* **-hil•loth, -hil•lot, -hil•los** (*Seph. Heb.* -hē lôt′; *Ashk. Heb.* -hil′ōt, -ōs). the organization of the Jewish population of a community that deals with charities and other communal affairs. [1880–85; < Heb *qəhillāh* community]

kei•ap•ple (kī′ap′əl), *n.* a thorny shrub or small tree, *Dovyalis caffra,* of southern Africa, having round, yellow, juicy-pulped, cranberry-flavored fruit that is edible only when cooked. [1855–60; named after Great *Kei,* river in Cape Province, South Africa]

Kei•fer (kī′fər), *n.* **Joseph Warren,** 1836–1932, U.S. lawyer and politician: Speaker of the House 1881–83.

keir (kēr), *n.* kier.

keis•ter (kē′stər), *n. Slang.* the buttocks; rump. Also, **keester.** [1880–85; earlier, as underworld argot, handbag, suitcase, safe; of obscure orig., but words meaning "chest, box" are frequently adduced as sources, e.g., KIST[1], G *Kiste,* Yiddish *kestl,* etc.]

Kei•ta (kā′tä), *n.* **Mo•di•bo** (mô dē′bô), 1915–77, African statesman: president of Mali 1960–68.

Kei•tel (kīt′l), *n.* **Wil•helm** (vil′helm), 1882–1946, German marshal: chief of the Nazi supreme command 1938–45.

Kei•te•le (kāt′l ā; *Fin.* kā′te le), *n.* **Lake,** a lake in S Finland. ab. 175 sq. mi. (455 sq. km).

Keith (kēth), *n.* **1. Sir Arthur,** 1866–1955, Scottish anthropologist. **2.** a male given name.

keit•lo•a (kīt′lō ə, kāt′-), *n.* a variety of the black rhinoceros having the posterior horn equal to or longer than the anterior horn. [1830–40; said to be < Setswana]

Kei•zer (kī′zər), *n.* a town in NW Oregon. 18,592.

Kek•ko•nen (kek′ə nən; *Fin.* kek′kô nen), *n.* **Ur•ho Ka•le•va** (o͝or′hô kä′le vä), 1900–86, Finnish statesman: president 1956–81.

Ke′ku•lé's for′mula (kā′kə lāz′), *Chem.* the structural formula of benzene represented as a hexagonal ring with alternate single and double bonds between the carbon atoms. See also **benzene ring.** [1935–40; named after F. A. KEKULÉ VON STRADONITZ]

Ke•ku•lé von Stra•do•nitz (kā′ko͞o lā′ fən shträ′-dō nits), **Frie•drich Au•gust** (frē′drikh ou′go͝ost), 1829–96, German chemist.

Ke•lan•tan (kə lan′tan, -län tän′), *n.* a state in Malaysia, on the central Malay Peninsula. 684,738; 5750 sq. mi. (14,893 sq. km). *Cap.:* Kota Bharu.

Kel•cey (kel′sē), *n.* a female given name.

kel•e•be (kel′ə bē), *n. Gk. and Rom. Antiq.* a mixing bowl, characterized by a wide neck and flanged lip from which extend two vertical handles to the shoulder of an oval body, used to mix wine and water. Also called **column krater.** Cf. **krater.** [1855–60; < Gk *kelébē*]

kel•ek (kel′ek), *n.* a raft or float supported on inflated animal skins used in Iraq, parts of Turkey, etc. [1675–85; < Turk]

kel•ep (kel′ep, kə lep′), *n.* a stinging ant, *Ectatomma tuberculatum,* introduced into the U.S. from Guatemala, that preys on the boll weevil. [1900–05; < Kekchi (Mayan language of Guatemala)]

Kel•ler (kel′ər; *for 1 also Ger.* kel′ər), *n.* **1. Gott•fried** (got′frēd; *Ger.* gôt′frēt), 1819–90, Swiss novelist. **2. Helen (Adams),** 1880–1968, U.S. lecturer, author, and

CONCISE ETYMOLOGY KEY: <, descended or borrowed from; >, whence; b., blend of, blended; c., cognate with; cf., compare; deriv., derivative; equiv., equivalent; imit., imitative; obl., oblique; r., replacing; s., stem; sp., spelling, spelled; resp., respelling, respelled; trans., translation; ?, origin unknown; *, unattested; ‡, probably earlier than. See the full key inside the front cover.

educator: blind and deaf from infancy; educated by Annie Sullivan.

kel·li·on (ke lē′on), *n., pl.* **-li·a** (-lē′ə). *Eastern Ch.* **1.** a small community of monks. **2.** a cell in a monastery. [< LGk: little cell, equiv. to L *cell(a)* CELL + Gk *-ion* dim. suffix]

Kell′ner eye′piece (kel′nər), *Optics.* a Ramsden eyepiece having an achromatic lens, used in binoculars. [after Carl *Kellner* (1826–55), German optician and lens maker]

Kel·logg (kel′ôg, -og), *n.* **1. Frank Billings,** 1856–1937, U.S. statesman: Secretary of State 1925–29; Nobel peace prize 1929. **2. W(ill) K(eith),** 1860–1951, U.S. manufacturer of prepared cereals and philanthropist.

Kel′logg-Bri·and′ Pact′ (kel′ôg brē änd′, -BRĒ-ÄN′, -og-), a treaty renouncing war as an instrument of national policy and urging peaceful means for the settlement of international disputes, originally signed in 1928 by 15 nations, later joined by 49 others. Also called **Kel′logg Peace′ Pact′.** [named after F. B. KELLOGG and A. BRIAND]

Kells′, Book′ of (kelz). See ***Book of Kells.***

kel′ly (kel′ē), *n., pl.* **-lies, -lys.** *Slang.* a man's stiff hat, as a derby or straw skimmer. [1910–15; generic use of surname *Kelly,* taken as representative of a stage Irishman wearing such a derby]

Kel·ly (kel′ē), *n.* **1. Ellsworth,** born 1923, U.S. painter and sculptor. **2. Emmett (Leo),** 1898–1979, U.S. circus clown and pantomimist. **3. George (Edward),** 1887–1974, U.S. playwright and actor. **4.** Also, **Kel′lie.** a male or female given name.

kel′ly green′, a strong yellow-green.

ke·loid (kē′loid), *n. Pathol.* an abnormal proliferation of scar tissue, as on the site of a surgical incision. Also, **cheloid.** [1850–55; earlier *kel(is)* keloid (< Gk *kēlís* stain, spot) + -OID] **—ke·loi′dal,** *adj.*

Ke·low·na (ki lō′nə), *n.* a city in S British Columbia, in SW Canada. 59,196.

kelp (kelp), *n.* **1.** any large, brown, cold-water seaweed of the family Laminariaceae, used as food and in various manufacturing processes. See illus. under **stipe. 2.** a bed or mass of such seaweeds. **3.** the ash of these seaweeds. —*v.i.* **4.** to burn these seaweeds for their ash. [1350–1400; appar. dial. var. of ME *culp* < ?]

kelp′ bass′ (bas), a sea bass, *Paralabrax clathratus,* of southern California coastal waters, valued as a food and game fish. [1935–40]

kelp′ crab′, any of several spider crabs common among kelp beds along the Pacific coast of North America. [1885–90, *Amer.*]

kelp·er (kel′pər), *n. Informal.* a native or inhabitant of the Falkland Islands. [1955–60; KELP + -ER[1]]

kelp·fish (kelp′fish′), *n., pl.* (*esp. collectively*) **-fish,** (*esp. referring to two or more kinds or species*) **-fish·es. 1.** any of several blennies that are common among kelp. Cf. **kelp greenling. 2.** any of various other fishes that live among kelp. [1875–80; KELP + FISH]

kelp′ green′ling, a food and game fish, *Hexagrammos decagrammus,* living among the kelp along the Pacific coast of North America. [1955–60]

kel·pie[1] (kel′pē), *n.* (in Scottish legends) a water spirit, usually having the form of a horse, reputed to cause drownings or to warn those in danger of drowning. [1740–50; orig. uncert.]

kel·pie[2] (kel′pē), *n.* See **Australian kelpie.** [1905–10]

kel·py (kel′pē), *n., pl.* **-pies.** kelpie[1].

Kel·sey (kel′sē), *n.* a male or female given name.

Kel·so (kel′sō), *n.* a town in SW Washington. 11,129.

kel·son (kel′sən), *n. Naut.* keelson.

kelt (kelt), *n.* a salmon that has spawned. [1300–50; ME (north) < ?]

Kelt (kelt), *n.* Celt. **—Kelt′ic,** *n., adj.*

kel·ter (kel′tər), *n. Chiefly Brit. Dial.* kilter.

Kel·vin (kel′vin), *n.* **1. William Thomson, 1st Baron,** 1824–1907, English physicist and mathematician. **2.** (*l.c.*) the base SI unit of temperature, defined to be $^1/_{273.16}$ of the triple point of water. *Abbr.:* K —*adj.* **3.** *Thermodynam.* noting or pertaining to an absolute scale of temperature **(Kel′vin scale′)** in which the degree intervals are equal to those of the Celsius scale and in which the triple point of water has the value 273.16 Kelvin. Cf. **absolute temperature scale, Celsius** (def. 2). **4.** Also, **Kel·win** (kel′win). a male given name.

Ke·mal A·ta·türk (ke mäl′ ä′tä TYRK′; *Eng.* kə mäl′ at′ə tûrk′), (*Mustafa* or *Mustapha Kemal*) (*"Kemal Pasha"*) 1881–1938, Turkish general: president of Turkey 1923–38.

Kem·ble (kem′bəl), *n.* **1. Frances Anne** or **Fanny** (*Mrs. Butler*), 1809–93, English actress and author. **2.** her uncle, **John Philip,** 1757–1823, English actor.

Ke·me·ro·vo (kem′ə rō′və; *Russ.* kye′myi RƏ və), *n.* a city in the S Russian Federation in Asia, NE of Novosibirsk. 471,000.

Ke·mi (kem′ē), *n.* a seaport in W Finland, on the Gulf of Bothnia. 27,656.

kemp[1] (kemp), *n.* **1.** *Brit. Dial.* **a.** a strong, brave warrior. **b.** an athlete, esp. a champion. **c.** a professional fighter. **d.** an impetuous or roguish young man. **2.** *Scot. and North Eng.* a contest, as between two athletes or two groups of workers, esp. a reaping contest between farmworkers. —*v.i.* **3.** *Scot. and North Eng.* to contest, fight, or strive, esp. to strive in a reaping contest. [bef. 900; ME *kempe,* OE *cempa;* c. OFris *kempa, kampa,* MD, MLG *kemp(e),* OHG *chemp(i)o;* ult. < WGmc, perh. through L *campiō;* see CHAMPION]

kemp[2] (kemp), *n.* a short, coarse, brittle fiber, used chiefly in the manufacture of carpets. [1350–1400; ME *kempe* coarse (said of hair); akin to OE *cenep* mustache, bristly object, ON *kampr* mustache, cat's whiskers] **—kemp′y,** *adj.*

Kemp (kemp), *n.* **1. Jack F.,** born 1935, U.S. politician: congressman 1970–89. **2.** a male given name.

Kem·pis (kem′pis), *n.* **Thomas à,** 1379?–1471, German ecclesiastic and author.

kempt (kempt), *adj.* **1.** neatly or tidily kept: *a kempt little cottage.* **2.** combed, as hair. [bef. 1050; ME; OE *cemd-* ptp. of *cemban* to COMB[1]; see UNKEMPT]

ken (ken), *n., v.,* **kenned** or **kent, ken·ning.** —*n.* **1.** knowledge, understanding, or cognizance; mental perception: *an idea beyond one's ken.* **2.** range of sight or vision. —*v.t.* **3.** *Chiefly Scot.* **a.** to know, have knowledge of or about, or be acquainted with (a person or thing). **b.** to understand or perceive (an idea or situation). **4.** *Scots Law.* to acknowledge as heir; recognize by a judicial act. **5.** *Archaic.* to see; descry; recognize. **6.** *Brit. Dial. Archaic.* **a.** to declare, acknowledge, or confess (something). **b.** to teach, direct, or guide (someone). —*v.i.* **7.** *Brit. Dial.* **a.** to have knowledge of something. **b.** to understand. [bef. 900; ME *kennen* to make known, see, know, OE *cennan* to make known, declare; c. ON *kenna,* G *kennen;* akin to CAN[1]]

Ken (ken), *n.* a male given name, form of **Kendall** or **Kenneth.**

Ken., Kentucky.

ke·naf (kə naf′), *n.* **1.** a tropical plant, *Hibiscus cannabinus,* of the mallow family, yielding a fiber resembling jute. **2.** the fiber itself, used for cordage and textiles. Also called **deccan hemp, ambary.** [1890–95; < Pers *kanaf,* var. of *kanab;* c. HEMP]

kench (kench), *n.* a deep bin in which animal skins and fish are salted. [1850–55, *Amer.;* orig. uncert.]

Ken′dal green′ (ken′dl), **1.** a coarse woolen cloth, green in color. **2.** a shade of green produced by a dye extracted from the woadwaxen plant. [1505–15; named after *Kendal,* town in Westmoreland, England, where the cloth was originally woven and dyed]

Ken·dall (ken′dl), *n.* **1. Edward Calvin,** 1886–1972, U.S. biochemist: Nobel prize for medicine 1950. **2.** a male given name.

Ken′dal sneck′ bent′, *Angling.* a fishhook having a wide, squarish bend. [prob. named after *Kendal,* England]

ken·do (ken′dō), *n.* a Japanese form of fencing using bamboo staves, with the contestants wearing head guards and protective garments. [1920–25; < Japn *kendō* < MChin, equiv. to Chin *jiàn* sword + *dào* way; cf. BUSHIDO, JUDO, TAO] **—ken′do·ist,** *n.*

Ken·drew (ken′drōō), *n.* **John C(ow·dery)** (kō′drē), born 1917, English scientist: Nobel prize for chemistry 1962.

Ken·il·worth (ken′l wûrth′), *n.* **1.** a town in central Warwickshire, in central England, SE of Birmingham. 20,121. **2.** (*italics*) a novel (1821) by Sir Walter Scott.

Ken′ilworth i′vy, a European climbing vine, *Cymbalaria muralis,* of the figwort family, having irregularly lobed leaves and small, lilac-blue flowers. Also called **coliseum ivy.** [named after KENILWORTH and its castle]

Ke·ni·tra (kə nē′trə), *n.* a port in NW Morocco, NE of Rabat. 135,960.

Ken·more (ken′môr, -mōr), *n.* a city in NW New York, near Buffalo. 18,474.

Ken·nan (ken′ən), *n.* **George Frost,** born 1904, U.S. author and diplomat.

Ken·ne·bec (ken′ə bek′, ken′ə bek′), *n.* a river flowing S through W Maine to the Atlantic. 164 mi. (264 km) long.

Ken·ne·bunk (ken′ə bungk′), *n.* a town in SW Maine, near resorts. 6621.

Ken·ne·bunk·port (ken′ə bungk′pôrt′, -pōrt′), *n.* a town in SW Maine: summer resort. 2952.

Ken·ne·dy (ken′i dē), *n.* **1. Edward Moore** (*Ted*), born 1932, U.S. politician: senator from Massachusetts since 1962. **2. John Fitzgerald,** 1917–63, thirty-fifth president of the U.S. 1961–63. **3. Joseph Patrick,** 1888–1969, U.S. financier and diplomat (father of Edward Moore, John Fitzgerald, and Robert Francis). **4. Robert Francis,** 1925–68, U.S. political leader and government official: attorney general 1961–64; senator from New York 1965–68. **5. Cape,** former name (1963–73) of Cape Canaveral. **6. John F., International Airport.** See **John F. Kennedy International Airport.**

ken·nel[1] (ken′l), *n., v.,* **-neled, -nel·ing** or (*esp. Brit.*) **-nelled, -nel·ling.** —*n.* **1.** a house or shelter for a dog or a cat. **2.** Often, **kennels.** an establishment where dogs or cats are bred, raised, trained, or boarded. **3.** the hole or lair of an animal, esp. a fox. **4.** a wretched abode likened to a doghouse. **5.** a pack of dogs. —*v.t.* **6.** to put into or keep in a kennel: *to kennel a dog for a week.* —*v.i.* **7.** to take shelter or lodge in a kennel. [1300–50; ME *kenel* < AF **kenil* (F *chenil*) < VL **canīle* (L *canis*) dog + *-īle* suffix of place)]

ken·nel[2] (ken′l), *n.* an open drain or sewer; gutter. [1575–85; var. of *cannel,* ME *canel* CHANNEL[1]]

ken′nel club′, an association of dog breeders, usually concerned only with certain breeds of dogs. [1870–75]

Ken′nel·ly-Heav′i·side lay′er (ken′l ē hev′ē sīd′). *Physics.* See **E layer.** [1920–25; named after Arthur Edwin *Kennelly* (1861–1939), U.S. electrical engineer, and O. HEAVISIDE]

Ken·ner (ken′ər), *n.* a city in SE Louisiana, near New Orleans. 66,382.

Ken′ne·saw Moun′tain (ken′ə sô′), a mountain in N Georgia, near Atlanta: battle 1864. 1809 ft. (551 m).

Ken·neth (ken′ith), *n.* a male given name: from an Irish word meaning "handsome."

Ken·nett (ken′it), *n.* a town in SE Missouri. 10,145.

Ken·ne·wick (ken′ə wik), *n.* a city in S Washington, on the Columbia River. 34,397.

ken·ning (ken′ing), *n.* a conventional poetic phrase used for or in addition to the usual name of a person or thing, esp. in Icelandic and Anglo-Saxon verse, as "a wave traveler" for "a boat." [1880–85; < ON; see KEN[1], -ING[1]]

Ken·ny (ken′ē), *n.* **1. Elizabeth** (*"Sister Kenny"*), 1886–1952, Australian nurse: researcher in poliomyelitis therapy. **2.** Also, **Ken′ney, Ken′nie.** a male given name, form of **Kenneth.**

Ken′ny meth′od, *Med.* a method of treating poliomyelitis, in which hot, moist packs are applied to affected muscles to relieve spasms and pain, and a regimen of exercises is prescribed to prevent deformities and to strengthen the muscles. Also called **Ken′ny treat′ment.** [named after E. KENNY]

ke·no (kē′nō), *n.* a game of chance, adapted from lotto for gambling purposes. [1805–15, *Amer.;* < F *quine* five (winning numbers) (< < L *quīnī* five each) + (LOTT)O]

Ke·no·sha (kə nō′shə), *n.* a port in SE Wisconsin, on Lake Michigan. 77,685.

ke·no·sis (ki nō′sis), *n. Theol.* the doctrine that Christ relinquished His divine attributes so as to experience human suffering. [1835–45; < Gk *kénōsis* an emptying (*kenō-,* var. s. of *kenoûn* to empty out, drain + *-sis* -SIS)] **—ke·not·ic** (ki not′ik), *adj.*

Ken·sing·ton (ken′zing tən), *n.* a former borough of Greater London, England: now part of Kensington and Chelsea.

Ken′sington and Chel′sea, a borough of Greater London, England. 161,600.

ken·speck·le (ken′spek′əl), *adj. Scot. and North Eng.* conspicuous; easily seen or recognized. Also, **ken′speck′led.** [1705–15; deriv. (see -LE) of *kenspeck* (< Scand; cf. Norw *kjennespak* quick at recognizing, lit., know-clever); see KEN[1]]

Kent (kent), *n.* **1. James,** 1763–1847, U.S. jurist. **2. Rock·well** (rok′wel′, -wəl), 1882–1971, U.S. illustrator and painter. **3. William,** 1685–1748, English painter, architect, and landscape gardener. **4.** a county in SE England. 1,445,400; 1442 sq. mi. (3735 sq. km). **5.** an ancient English kingdom in SE Great Britain. See map under **Mercia. 6.** a city in NE Ohio. 26,164. **7.** a town in central Washington. 23,152. **8.** a male given name: from the Old English name of a county in England.

ken·te (ken′tā), *n.* a colorful fabric of Ghanaian origin: often worn as a symbol of African-American pride. [1955–60; < Ashanti]

ken′ti·a palm′ (ken′tē ə), a palm, *Howea forsterana,* of Lord Howe Island, Australia, having erect leaves, widely cultivated as an ornamental. Also called **sentry palm.** [1905–10; < NL *Kentia* an earlier genus name, after William *Kent* (died ca. 1828), British plant collector; see -IA]

Kent·ish (ken′tish), *adj.* of or pertaining to Kent or its people. [bef. 950; ME *Kentissh,* OE *Centisc.* See KENT, -ISH[1]]

Kent′ish fire′, *Brit.* prolonged clapping by an audience, esp. in unison, indicating impatience or disapproval. [said to have originated in *Kent,* England, in 1828–29, as an expression of opposition to speakers favoring the Catholic Relief Bill]

Kent·ish·man (ken′tish mən), *n., pl.* **-men.** a native or inhabitant of Kent, England. [KENTISH + MAN[1]]

Kent′ish trac′ery, *Archit.* tracery, originating in Kent in the 14th century, having cusps with split ends.

kent·ledge (kent′lij), *n. Naut.* pig iron used as permanent ballast. [1600–10; orig. uncert.]

Ken·ton (ken′tn), *n.* **Stan(ley Newcomb),** 1912–79, U.S. jazz composer, pianist, and bandleader.

Ken·tuck (kən tuk′), *n. Informal Older Use.* (esp. in the Midwest) **1.** Kentucky. **2.** a native or inhabitant of Kentucky. [by shortening]

Ken·tuck·y (kən tuk′ē), *n.* **1.** a state in the E central United States. 3,661,433; 40,395 sq. mi. (104,625 sq. km). *Cap.:* Frankfort. *Abbr.:* KY (for use with zip code), Ken., Ky. **2.** a river flowing NW from E Kentucky to the Ohio River. 259 mi. (415 km) long. **—Ken·tuck′i·an,** *adj., n.*

Kentuck′y blue′grass, a grass, *Poa pratensis,* of the Mississippi valley, used for pasturage and lawns.

Kentuck′y cof′fee tree′, a tall, North American tree, *Gymnocladus dioica,* of the legume family, the seeds of which **(Kentuck′y cof′fee beans′)** were formerly used as a substitute for coffee beans. [1775–85]

CONCISE PRONUNCIATION KEY: *act, cāpe, dâre, pärt; set, ēqual; if, īce; ox, ōver, ôrder, oil, bŏŏk, bōōt, out; up, ûrge; child; sing; shoe; thin, that;* zh as in *treasure.* ə = *a* as in *alone, e* as in *system, i* as in *easily, o* as in *gallop, u* as in *circus;* ᵊ as in *fire* (fīᵊr), *hour* (ouᵊr). l and n can serve as syllabic consonants, as in *cradle* (krād′l), and *button* (but′n). See the full key inside the front cover.

Kentuck′y Der′by, a horse race for three-year-olds, run annually since 1875, on the first Saturday in May, at Churchill Downs in Louisville, Ky.

Kentuck′y fried′. See **Southern fried.** [1970–75, *Amer.*]

Kentuck′y ri′fle, a long-barreled muzzleloading flintlock rifle developed near Lancaster, Pa., in the early 18th century and widely used on the frontier. Also called **Pennsylvania rifle.** [1825–35]

Kentuck′y war′bler, a wood warbler, *Oporornis formosus,* of the U.S., olive-green above, yellow below, and marked with black on the face. [1805–15, *Amer.*]

Kentuck′y wind′age, *Slang.* a method of correcting for windage, gravity, etc., by aiming a weapon to one side of the target instead of by adjusting the sights.

Kent·wood (kent′wo͝od′), *n.* a city in W Michigan. 30,438.

Ken·ya (ken′yə, kēn′-), *n.* **1.** a republic in E Africa: member of the Commonwealth of Nations; formerly a British crown colony and protectorate. 13,500,000; 223,478 sq. mi. (578,808 sq. km). *Cap.:* Nairobi. **2. Mount,** an extinct volcano in central Kenya. 17,040 ft. (5194 m). **—Ken′yan,** *adj., n.*

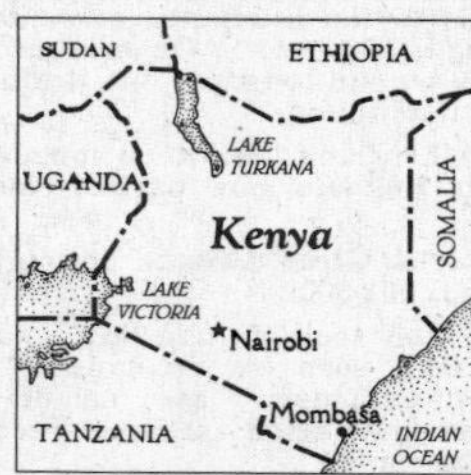

Ken·ya·pith·e·cus (ken′yə pith′i kəs, -pə thē′kəs, kēn′-), *n.* a genus of fossil hominoids of middle Miocene age found in Kenya and having large molars, small incisors, and powerful chewing muscles. [1960–65; < NL, equiv. to *Kenya* KENYA + *pithēcus* ape < Gk *píthēkos*]

Ken·yat·ta (ken yä′tə), *n.* **Jo·mo** (jō′mō), 1893?–1978, Kenyan political leader: president 1964–78.

Ken·yon (ken′yən), *n.* **John Samuel,** 1874–1959, U.S. phonetician and educator.

Ke′ogh plan′ (kē′ō), a pension plan for an unincorporated business entity or self-employed person. Cf. **individual retirement account.** [1970–75, *Amer.*; after Eugene J. *Keogh* (born 1907), N.Y. Congressman]

Ke·o·kuk (kē′ə kuk′), *n.* **1.** c1780–c1848, leader of the Sac tribe. **2.** a city in SE Iowa, on the Mississippi River: large power dam. 13,536.

Ke·os (ke′ôs; *Eng.* kē′os), *n.* a Greek island in the Aegean, off the SE coast of the Greek mainland. 1666; 56 sq. mi. (145 sq. km). Also called **Kea, Zea.**

Ke·phal·le·ni·a (ke fä′lē nē′ä), *n.* Greek name of **Cephalonia.**

Keph·a·los (kef′ə ləs), *n. Class. Myth.* Cephalus.

Ke·phe·us (kē′fē əs, -fyo͞os), *n. Class. Myth.* Cepheus (def. 2).

kep·i (kā′pē, kep′ē), *n., pl.* **kep·is.** a French military cap with a flat circular top and a nearly horizontal visor. [1860–65; < F *képi* < SwissG *Käppi* (*Kapp(e)* CAP + *-i* dim. suffix)]

Kep·ler (kep′lər), *n.* **1. Jo·hann** (yō′hän), 1571–1630, German astronomer. **2.** a crater in the second quadrant of the face of the moon having an extensive ray system: about 22 miles (35 km) in diameter. **—Kep·ler·i·an** (kep lēr′ē ən), *adj.*

Kep′ler's laws′, *Astron.* three laws governing planetary motion: each planet revolves in an ellipse, with the sun at one focus; the line connecting a planet to the sun sweeps out equal areas in equal periods of time **(law of areas);** the square of the period of revolution of each planet is proportional to the cube of the semimajor axis of the planet's orbit **(harmonic law).** [after J. KEPLER]

Kep′ler tel′escope. See **astronomical telescope.** [1905–10; after J. KEPLER]

kept (kept), *v.* **1.** pt. and pp. of **keep.** **—*adj.* 2.** having the expression of principles, ideas, etc., controlled, dominated, or determined by one whose money provides support: *a kept press; a kept writer.* [1670–80 for def. 2]

ker-, an unstressed syllable prefixed to onomatopoeic and other expressive words, usually forming adverbs or interjections: *kerflop; kerplunk; ker-splosh.* Also, **ca-, ka-.** [perh. < Scots dial. *car-, cur-, currie-* (as in *carfuffle, carwhuffle* to disarrange, *carnaptious* irritable, *curriebuction* a confused gathering, etc.), based on *car,* earlier *ker* left (hand or side) < ScotGael *cearr* wrong, awkward, left-handed (cf. MIr *cerr* crooked, maimed); vars. without *r* prob. reflect forms in *r*-less dialects]

Ker·ak (ker′äk, ke räk′), *n.* a town in W Jordan, near the S Dead Sea: ancient citadel of the Moabites. Also, **Krak, El Kerak.** Formerly, **Le Crac.** Ancient, **Kir Moab.**

Ke·ra·la (kā′rə lə, ker′ə-), *n.* a state in SW India: formerly the regions of Travancore and Cochin. 24,380,000; 15,035 sq. mi. (38,940 sq. km). *Cap.:* Trivandrum.

ke·ram·ic (kə ram′ik), *adj.* ceramic.

ke·ram·ics (kə ram′iks), *n.* (*used with a singular or plural v.*) ceramics.

kerat-, var. of **kerato-** before a vowel: *keratitis.*

ker·a·tal·gia (ker′ə tal′jə, -jē ə), *n. Pathol.* pain in the cornea. [KERAT- + -ALGIA]

ker·a·tec·to·my (ker′ə tek′tə mē), *n., pl.* **-mies.** *Surg.* excision of part of the cornea. [1870–75; KERAT- + -ECTOMY]

ker·a·tin (ker′ə tin), *n.* a scleroprotein or albuminoid substance, found in the dead outer skin layer, and in horn, hair, feathers, hoofs, nails, claws, bills, etc. [1840–50; KERAT- + -IN[2]]

ker·a·tin·ize (ker′ə tn īz′), *v.t., v.i.,* **-ized, -iz·ing.** to make or become keratinous. Also, *esp. Brit.,* **ker′a·tin·ise′.** [1895–1900; KERATIN + -IZE] **—ker′a·tin·i·za′·tion,** *n.*

ke·rat·i·nous (kə rat′n əs), *adj.* composed of or resembling keratin; horny. [1895–1900; KERATIN + -OUS]

ker·a·ti·tis (ker′ə tī′tis), *n. Pathol.* inflammation of the cornea. [1855–60; KERAT- + -ITIS]

kerato-, var. of **cerato-:** *keratogenous.* Also, *esp. before a vowel,* **kerat-.**

ker·a·to·con·junc·ti·vi·tis (ker′ə tō kən jungk′tə vī′tis), *n. Ophthalm.* inflammation of the cornea and conjunctiva. [1885–90; KERATO- + CONJUNCTIVITIS]

ker·a·to·co·nus (ker′ə tō kō′nəs), *n., pl.* **-ni** (-nī, -nē). *Pathol.* a degenerative condition characterized by conical protrusion of the cornea and irregular astigmatism. [1855–60; KERATO- + L *cōnus* CONE]

ker·a·tode (ker′ə tōd′), *n.* the horny, fibrous substance forming the skeleton of certain sponges. Also, **keratose.** [1870–75; < Gk *keratṓdēs* hornlike. See KERAT-, -ODE[1]]

ker·a·to·der·ma (ker′ə tō dûr′mə), *n. Pathol.* a disease of the horny layer of the skin, esp. of the soles or palms. Also, **ker·a·to·der·mi·a** (ker′ə tō dûr′mē ə). [1930–35; KERATO- + DERMA]

ker·a·tog·e·nous (ker′ə toj′ə nəs), *adj.* producing horn or a horny substance. [1885–90; KERATO- + -GENOUS]

ker·a·toid (ker′ə toid′), *adj.* **1.** resembling horn; horny. **2.** resembling corneal tissue. [1870–75; < Gk *keratoeidḗs* hornlike. See KERAT-, -OID]

ker·a·tol·y·sis (ker′ə tol′ə sis), *n.* **1.** the loosening or shedding of the horny layer of the epidermis. **2.** *Pathol.* a skin disorder characterized by periodic shedding of the epidermis. [1895–1900; KERATO- + -LYSIS] **—ker·a·to·lyt·ic** (ker′ə tō lit′ik), *adj.*

ker·a·to·ma (ker′ə tō′mə), *n., pl.* **-mas, -ma·ta** (-mə tə). *Pathol.* keratosis. [1885–90; KERAT- + -OMA]

ker·a·tom·e·ter (ker′ə tom′i tər), *n. Ophthalm.* an instrument for measuring the curvature of the cornea. [1885–90; KERATO- + -METER] **—ker·a·to·met·ric** (ker′ə tō me′trik), *adj.* **—ker′a·tom′e·try,** *n.*

ker·a·to·plas·ty (ker′ə tō plas′tē), *n., pl.* **-ties.** plastic surgery performed upon the cornea, esp. a corneal transplantation. [1855–60; KERATO- + -PLASTY] **—ker′·a·to·plas′tic,** *adj.*

ker·a·to·scope (ker′ə tə skōp′), *n. Ophthalm.* an instrument, as Placido's disk, for determining the symmetry of the curvature of the cornea. [1885–90; KERATO- + -SCOPE] **—ker·a·tos·co·py** (ker′ə tos′kə pē), *n.*

ker·a·tose (ker′ə tōs′), *adj.* **1.** having a skeleton formed of horny fibers, as certain sponges. **—*n.* 2.** keratode. [1850–55; KERAT- + -OSE[1]]

ker·a·to·sis (ker′ə tō′sis), *n., pl.* **-ses** (-sēz). *Pathol.* **1.** any skin disease characterized by a horny growth, as a wart. **2.** any horny growth. Also, **keratoma.** [1880–85; KERAT- + -OSIS] **—ker′a·to′sic, ker·a·tot·ic** (ker′ə tot′ik), *adj.*

ker·a·tot·o·my (ker′ə tot′ə mē), *n., pl.* **-mies.** *Surg.* incision of the cornea. [1895–1900; KERATO- + -TOMY]

kerb (kûrb), *n., v.t. Brit.* curb (defs. 1, 15).

Ker·be·la (kûr′bə lə), *n.* a town in central Iraq: holy city of the Shi'ite sect. 107,000. Also, **Karbala.**

Ker·ber·os (kûr′bər əs), *n. Class. Myth.* Cerberus (def. 1).

kerb·ing (kûr′bing), *n. Brit.* curbing.

kerb′ mar′ket, *Brit.* curb (def. 5). Also, **kerb′stone mar′ket.** [1900–05]

kerb·side (kûrb′sīd′), *n. Brit.* curbside.

kerb·stone (kûrb′stōn′), *n. Brit.* curbstone.

Kerch (kerch; *Russ.* kyerch), *n.* **1.** a seaport in E Crimea, in S Ukraine, on Kerch Strait. 157,000. **2.** a strait connecting the Sea of Azov and the Black Sea. 25 mi. (40 km) long.

ker·chief (kûr′chif, -chēf), *n.* **1.** a woman's square scarf worn as a covering for the head or sometimes the shoulders. **2.** a handkerchief. [1250–1300; ME *kerchef,* syncopated var. of *keverchef* < OF *cuevrechef* lit., (it) covers (the) head. See COVER, CHIEF] **—ker′chiefed, ker′chieft,** *adj.*

ker·choo (kər cho͞o′), *interj.* ahchoo. [see KER-, AHCHOO]

Ke·ren·ski (kə ren′skē; *Russ.* kye′ryin skyē), *n.* **A·le·ksan·dr Fe·do·ro·vich** (u lyi ksän′dr fyô′də rəvyich), 1881–1970, Russian revolutionary leader: premier 1917; in the U.S. after 1946. Also, **Ke·ren′sky.**

Ker·e·san (ker′ə sən), *n.* a family of languages spoken by Pueblo tribes of the Rio Grande valley and neighboring areas.

kerf (kûrf), *n.* **1.** a cut or incision made by a saw or the like in a piece of wood. **2.** *Mining.* a deep cut a few inches high, used to undermine a portion of a coal or mineral seam. **3.** the act of cutting or carving. **—*v.t.* 4.** to make a kerf or kerfs in (a piece of wood, a coal seam, etc.). [bef. 1000; ME *kerf, kirf,* OE *cyrf* a cutting (c. OFris *kerf*); akin to CARVE]

ker·floo·ey (kər flo͞o′ē), *adv.* **go kerflooey,** *Informal.* to cease functioning, esp. suddenly and completely; fall apart; fail: *As soon as the storm hit, every light in town went kerflooey.* [see KER-, FLOOEY]

ker·flop (kər flop′), *adv. Informal.* with or as if with a flop: *He fell kerflop.* [1875–80; see KER-, FLOP]

Ker·gue·len (kûr′gə len′, -lən), *n.* an archipelago in the S Indian Ocean: a possession of France. 2700 sq. mi. (7000 sq. km). French, **Ker·gué·len** (keʀ gā len′).

Ker·ki (ker kē′; *Russ.* kyiʀ kyē′), *n.* a city in E Turkmenistan: trade center. 14,300.

Ker·ky·ra (keʀ′kē rä), *n.* Greek name of **Corfu.**

Ker·man (kər män′, ker-), *n.* a city in SE Iran. 88,000.

Ker·man·shah (ker män′shä′, -shô′, kər-, ker′män-, kûr′-), *n.* **1.** a city in W Iran. 190,000. **2.** Kirman.

ker·mes (kûr′mēz), *n.* **1.** a red dye formerly prepared from the dried bodies of the females of a scale insect, *Kermes ilices,* which lives on small, evergreen oaks of the Mediterranean region. **2.** the oak itself, of the genus *Quercus coccifera.* [1590–1600; < F *kermès* < Ar *qirmiz* < Pers; r. earlier *chermez* < It *chermes* < Ar as above; see CRIMSON]

ker·mes·ite (kûr′mē zīt′, -mə sīt′, kûr mes′īt), *n.* a mineral, antimony oxysulfide, Sb_2S_2O, occurring usually in tufts of red capillary crystals. [1835–45; KERMES + -ITE[1]]

ker·mis (kûr′mis), *n.* **1.** (in the Low Countries) a local, annual outdoor fair or festival. **2.** a similar entertainment, usually for charitable purposes. Also, **ker′mess, kirmess.** [1570–80; < D, earlier *ker(c)misse* (*kerc* CHURCH + *misse* MASS); orig. a fair at the dedication of a church]

Ker·mit (kûr′mit), *n.* a male given name.

kern[1] (kûrn), *Print.* **—*n.* 1.** a part of the face of a type projecting beyond the body or shank, as in certain italic letters. **—*v.t.* 2.** to form or furnish with a kern, as a type or letter. **3.** to remove a portion of space between (adjacent letters) in preparation for printing. [1675–85; < F *carne* corner of type << L *cardin-* (s. of *cardō*) hinge]

kern[2] (kûrn), *n. Engin.* the central area of any horizontal section of a wall, column, etc., within which the resultant forces of all compressive loads must pass if there is to be only compression at that point. [< G *Kern* KERNEL; see KERN[4]]

kern[3] (kûrn), *n. Archaic.* **1.** a band of lightly armed foot soldiers of ancient Ireland. **2.** (in Ireland and the Scottish Highlands) a soldier. **3.** an Irish peasant, esp. a crude or boorish one. Also, **kerne.** [1325–75; ME *kerne* < Ir *ceithern* band of foot soldiers; cf. CATERAN]

kern[4] (kûrn), *Brit. Dial.* **—*v.i.* 1.** (of a tree or plant) to produce or form kernels, hard grain, or seed. **—*v.t.* 2.** to cause to granulate, esp. to granulate salt. **3.** to cover with crystalline grains of salt; salt (meat). **—*n.* 4.** *Obs.* a kernel, as of a nut; a grain, as of sand or wheat. [1275–1325; ME *kirnen, kerne* (v.); akin to *kirnelen* to develop into seed; see KERNEL]

kern[5] (kûrn), *v.t., v.i., n. Scot. and North Eng.* churn.

kern[6] (kûrn), *n. Scot. and North Eng.* kirn[2].

Kern (kûrn), *n.* **Jerome (David),** 1885–1945, U.S. composer.

ker·nel (kûr′nl), *n., v.,* **-neled, -nel·ing** or (*esp. Brit.*) **-nelled, -nel·ling.** **—*n.* 1.** the softer, usually edible part contained in the shell of a nut or the stone of a fruit. **2.** the body of a seed within its husk or integuments. **3.** a whole seed grain, as of wheat or corn. **4.** *South Atlantic States.* the pit or seed of a peach, cherry, plum, etc. **5.** the central or most important part of anything; essence; gist; core: *His leadership is the kernel of the organization.* **6.** *Math.* the set of elements that a given function from one set to a second set maps into the identity of the second set. **7.** Also called **rumpf.** *Physical Chem.* the remainder of an atom after the valence electrons have been removed. **—*v.t.* 8.** to enclose as a kernel. [bef. 1000; ME *kirnel,* OE *cyrnel,* dim. of *corn* seed, CORN[1]] **—ker′nel·less,** *adj.* **—ker′nel·ly,** *adj.*

ker′nel sen′tence, a simple, active, declarative sentence containing no modifiers or connectives that may be used in making more elaborate sentences: *The sentence "Good tests are short" is made from two kernel sentences: (1) "Tests are short." (2) "(The) tests are good."*

ker′nel smut′, *Plant Pathol.* a disease of sorghum and other grasses in which the grains are replaced by the black spores of a smut fungus, esp. of the genera *Tilletia* and *Ustilago.*

kern·ing (kûr′ning), *n. Print.* the setting of two letters closer together than is usual by removing space between them. [1675–85; KERN[2] + -ING[1]]

kern·ite (kûr′nīt), *n.* a mineral, hydrated sodium borate, $Na_2B_4O_7 \cdot 4H_2O$, occurring in transparent colorless crystals: the principal source of boron compounds in the U.S. [1925–30; named after *Kern* County, California; see -ITE[1]]

ker·nos (kûr′nos), *n., pl.* **-noi** (-noi). *Gk. Antiq.* a Mycenaean ceramic piece, usually in the form of a ring, to which were attached a number of cups or vases. [1900–05; < Gk *kérnos*]

ker·o (kâr′ō), *n., pl.* **ker·os.** a wooden container, as a beaker, made by the Incas. [< Quechua *qeru*]

ker·o·gen (ker′ə jən, -jen′), *n.* the bituminous matter in oil shale, from which shale oil is obtained by heating and distillation. [1905–10; < Gk *kērό(s)* wax + -GEN]

ker·o·sene (ker′ə sēn′, kar′-, ker′ə sēn′, kar′-), *n.* **1.** a mixture of liquid hydrocarbons obtained by distilling petroleum, bituminous shale, or the like, and widely used as a fuel, cleaning solvent, etc. —*adj.* **2.** using or fueled by kerosene: *a kerosene lamp.* Also, **ker′o·sine′.** [1852; irreg. < Gk *kērós* wax + -ENE; formerly trademark]

Ker·ou·ac (ker′o͞o ak′), *n.* **Jack** (*Jean-Louis Lefris de Kérouac*), 1922–69, U.S. novelist.

ker·plunk (kər plungk′), *adv.* with or as if with a sudden muffled thud: *The huge stone hit the water kerplunk.* [1885–90; see KER-, PLUNK]

Kerr (kûr *or, for 2, 4,* kär), *n.* **1. Clark,** born 1911, U.S. educator: president of the University of California 1958–67. **2. Michael Crawford,** 1827–76, U.S. politician: Speaker of the House 1875–76. **3. Walter F.,** born 1913, U.S. drama critic and author. **4.** a male given name.

Kerr′ cell′ (kär, kûr), *Physics.* a transparent cell filled with a fluid, usually nitrobenzene, and containing two electrodes placed between two polarizing light filters, suitable for demonstrating the Kerr effect and often used as a high-speed camera shutter. [1925–30; see KERR EFFECT]

Kerr′ effect′, *Physics.* the double refraction of light in certain substances, produced by an electric field. [1905–10; named after John Kerr (1824–1907), Scottish physicist]

ker·ri·a (ker′ē ə), *n.* a yellow-flowered shrub, *Kerria japonica,* of the rose family, native to eastern Asia and widely cultivated as an ornamental. Cf. **jetbead.** [1815–25; < NL, named in honor of William *Kerr* (d. 1814), English gardener, who collected plants in South Asia and the Far East; see -IA]

Kerr·ville (kûr′vil), *n.* a town in SW Texas. 15,276.

ker·ry (ker′ē), *n., pl.* **-ries.** one of an Irish breed of small, black dairy cattle. [1875–80; named after KERRY, home of the breed]

Ker·ry (ker′ē), *n.* **1.** a county in W Munster province, in the SW Republic of Ireland. 122,734; 1815 sq. mi. (4700 sq. km). *Co. seat:* Tralee. **2.** a male given name, form of **Kerr.**

Ker′ry blue′ ter′rier, one of an Irish breed of terriers having a soft, wavy, bluish-gray coat. [1920–25]

Kerry blue terrier, 18½ in. (47 cm) high at shoulder

ker·sey (kûr′zē), *n., pl.* **-seys.** **1.** a heavy overcoating of wool or wool and cotton, similar to beaver and melton. **2.** a coarse twilled woolen cloth with a cotton warp, used esp. for work clothes. **3.** a garment made of kersey. [1400–50; late ME; perh. after *Kersey,* in Suffolk, England]

ker·sey·mere (kûr′zē mēr′), *n.* a heavily fulled woolen cloth constructed in twill weave and finished with a fine nap. [1775–85; KERSEY + (CASSI)MERE]

Kerst (kûrst), *n.* **Donald William,** born 1911, U.S. physicist.

Ker·win (kûr′win), *n.* a male given name.

ke·ryg·ma (ki rig′mə), *n., pl.* **-ma·ta** (-mə tə). **1.** the preaching of the gospel of Christ, esp. in the manner of the early church. **2.** the content or message of such preaching. Also, **ke·rug·ma** (ki rug′mə). [1885–90; < Gk *kḗrygma* proclamation, preaching, equiv. to *kēryk-,* s. of *kēryssein* to proclaim + *-ma* resultative n. suffix] —**ker·ig·mat·ic** (ker′ig mat′ik), *adj.*

Kesh·a (kesh′ə), *n.* a female given name: from an African word meaning "favorite."

Kes·i·a (kes′ē ə), *n.* a female given name: from an African word meaning "favorite."

Kes·sel·ring (kes′əl ring), *n.* **Al·bert** (al′bərt; *Ger.* äl′bert), 1885–1960, German field marshal.

kes·trel (kes′trəl), *n.* **1.** a common small falcon, *Falco tinnunculus,* of northern parts of the Eastern Hemisphere, notable for hovering in the air with its head to the wind. **2.** any of several related small falcons, as the American kestrel, *F. sparverius.* [1400–50; late ME *castrell* < MF *quercerelle,* metathetic var. of *crecerelle,* of disputed orig.]

Ket (ket), *n., pl.* **Kets,** (*esp. collectively*) **Ket** for 1. **1.** a member of an indigenous people of central Siberia, living in widely dispersed communities on tributaries of the Yenisei River, between 60° and 67° N latitude. **2.** the Yeniseian language of the Ket, related only to several now extinct languages of the upper Yenisei. Also called **Yenisei Ostyak.** [< Russ < Ket: Ket, man, human being]

ket-, var. of **keto-** before a vowel: *ketene.*

ke·ta (kē′tə), *n.* See **chum salmon.** [1900–05; < Russ *kéta,* earlier *ketá* < Evenki (eastern dials.) *kēta,* or < cognates in other Tungusic languages]

ke·ta·mine (kē′tə mēn′, -min), *n. Pharm.* a synthetic nonbarbiturate general anesthetic, $C_{13}H_{16}ClNO$, used to induce anesthesia, alone or in combination, in surgical or diagnostic procedures of short duration; extensively used in veterinary medicine. [1965–70; KET- + -AMINE]

ketch (kech), *n. Naut.* a sailing vessel rigged fore and aft on two masts, the larger, forward one being the mainmast and the after one, stepped forward of the rudderpost, being the mizzen or jigger. Cf. **yawl**[1] (def. 2). [1475–85; earlier *cache,* appar. n. use of *cache* to CATCH]

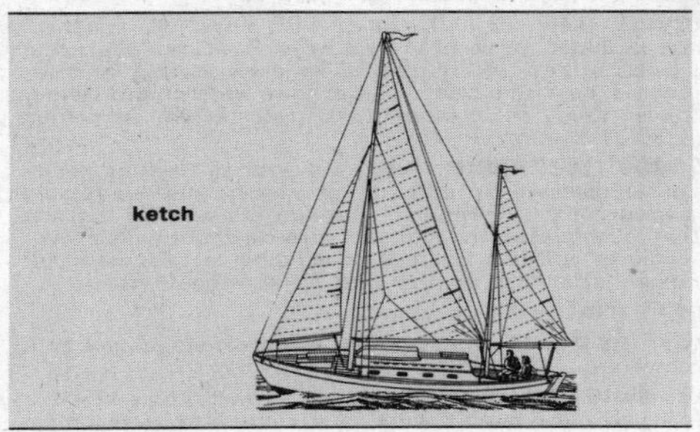
ketch

Ketch·i·kan (kech′i kan′), *n.* a seaport in SE Alaska: transportation and communications center. 7198.

ketch-rigged (kech′rigd′), *adj.* rigged in the manner of a ketch. [1835–45]

ketch·up (kech′əp, kach′-), *n.* **1.** a condiment consisting of puréed tomatoes, onions, vinegar, sugar, spices, etc. **2.** any of various other condiments or sauces for meat, fish, etc.: *mushroom ketchup; walnut ketchup.* Also, **catchup, catsup.** [1705–15; < Malay *kəchap* fish sauce, perh. < dial. Chin *kējāp* (Guangdong) or *ke-tsiap* (Xiamen), akin to Chin *qié* eggplant + *chī* juice]

ke·tene (kē′tēn), *n. Chem.* a colorless, poisonous gas, C_2H_2O, irritating to the lungs, prepared from acetone or acetic acid by pyrolysis: used chiefly in the manufacture of certain commercial chemicals, as acetic anhydride and aspirin. [1905–10; KET- + -ENE]

ke·to (kē′tō), *adj. Chem.* of or derived from a ketone. [1910–15; independent use of KETO-]

keto-, a combining form representing **ketone** in compound words: *ketolysis.* Also, *esp. before a vowel,* **ket-.**

ke·to·co·na·zole (kē′tō kō′nə zōl′, -zôl′), *n. Pharm.* a synthetic substance, $C_{26}H_{28}Cl_2N_4O_4$, used to treat a variety of fungal infections. [KETO- + *-con-* of uncert. derivation + AZOLE]

ke·to·gen·e·sis (kē′tō jen′ə sis), *n. Med.* the production of ketone bodies in the body, as in diabetes mellitus or low-carbohydrate weight-loss diets. [1910–15; KETO- + GENESIS] —**ke′to·gen′ic,** *adj.*

ke·to·hex·ose (kē′tō hek′sōs), *n. Chem.* any of a class of sugars composed of six carbon atoms and a ketone group, as fructose. [1895–1900; KETO- + HEXOSE]

ke·tol·y·sis (ki tol′ə sis), *n., pl.* **-ses** (-sēz′). *Chem.* the breaking down of ketones. [1935–40; KETO- + -LYSIS] —**ke·to·lyt·ic** (kēt′l it′ik), *adj.*

ke·tone (kē′tōn), *n. Chem.* **1.** any of a class of organic compounds containing a carbonyl group, CO, attached to two alkyl groups, as CH_3COCH_3 or $CH_3COC_2H_5$. —*adj.* **2.** containing the ketone group. [1850–55; < G *Keton,* aph. alter. of *Aceton* ACETONE] —**ke·ton·ic** (ki ton′ik), *adj.*

ke′tone bod′y, *Biochem.* any of three compounds, acetoacetic acid, beta-hydroxybutyric acid, or acetone, that are intermediate in the metabolism of fatty acids and that are found in abnormal quantities in the blood and urine during certain pathological conditions, as diabetes mellitus. Also called **acetone body.** [1910–15]

ke′tone group′, *Chem.* the characteristic group occurring in ketones that consists of the carbonyl group attached to two alkyl groups. Also called **ke′tone rad′ical.**

ke·to·ne·mi·a (kē′tō nē′mē ə), *n. Med.* the presence of ketone bodies in the blood. [KETONE + -EMIA]

ke·to·nu·ri·a (kē′tō no͝or′ē ə, -nyo͝or′-), *n. Med.* the presence of ketone bodies in the urine. [1910–15; KETONE + -URIA]

ke·tose (kē′tōs), *n. Biochem.* a monosaccharide that contains a ketone group. [1900–05; KET- + -OSE[2]]

ke·to·sis (ki tō′sis), *n. Pathol.* the accumulation of excessive ketones in the body, as in diabetic acidosis. [1915–20; KET- + -OSIS]

ke·tos·ter·oid (ki tos′tə roid′), *n. Biochem.* any of a group of steroids containing a ketone group. [1935–40; KETO- + STEROID]

Ket·ter·ing (ket′ər ing), *n.* **1. Charles Franklin,** 1876–1958, U.S. engineer and inventor. **2.** a city in SW Ohio. 61,186.

ket·tle (ket′l), *n.* **1.** a metal container in which to boil liquids, cook foods, etc.; pot. **2.** a teakettle. **3.** a kettledrum. **4.** *Geol.* See **kettle hole.** [bef. 900; ME *ketel* < ON *ketill* << L *catillus,* dim. of *catīnus* pot; r. OE *cetel, cietel* << L as above; cf. G *Kessel*]

ket′tle base′, a bombé base to a piece of furniture.

ket·tle-bot·tom (ket′l bot′əm), *adj. Naut.* noting a wide, flat-bottomed hull formerly used for merchant sailing vessels.

ket·tle·drum (ket′l drum′), *n.* a drum consisting of a hollow hemisphere of brass, copper, or fiberglass over which is stretched a skin, the tension of which can be modified by hand screws or foot pedals to vary the pitch. Cf. **timpani.** [1595–1605; KETTLE + DRUM[1]] —**ket′tle·drum′mer,** *n.*

kettledrum

ket′tle hat′, *Armor.* See **chapel de fer.** [1350–1400; ME]

ket′tle hole′, *Geol.* **1.** a deep, kettle-shaped depression in glacial drift. **2.** pothole (def. 3). Also called **kettle.** [1880–85]

ket′tle of fish′, **1.** an awkward, difficult, or bad situation; muddle; mess: *He's managed to get himself into a fine kettle of fish!* **2.** a state of affairs; a matter under consideration: *The new proposal is quite a different kettle of fish from the last one.* [1735–45]

ket′tle stitch′, *Bookbinding.* (in handsewing) a knot tied in the thread that links one section to the next. [1810–20; part trans. of G *Kettelstich,* equiv. to *Kettel* little chain (dim. of *Kette* chain; OHG *ketina* < L *catēna*) + *Stich* STITCH; cf. CHAIN]

ke·tu·bah (*Ashk., Eng.* kə to͞o′bə; *Seph.* kə to͞o bä′), *n., pl.* ***-tu·both, -tu·bot, -tu·bos*** (*Ashk.* -to͞o′bōs; *Seph.* -to͞o bôt′), *Eng.* **-bahs.** *Hebrew.* the formal contract in a Jewish religious marriage that includes specific financial protection for the wife in the event that the husband dies or divorces her. [*kəthubbāh* lit., something written]

Ke·tur·ah (ki to͝or′ə), *n.* the second wife of Abraham. Gen. 25:1.

Ke·tu·vim (*Seph.* kə to͞o vēm′; *Ashk., Eng.* kə to͞o′vim), *n. Hebrew.* the Hagiographa. Also, ***Ke·tu·bim′.*** Cf. ***Tanach.*** [*kəthūbhīm* lit., writings]

keV, See **kiloelectron volt.** Also, **kev**

ke·va·lin (kā′və lin), *n. Jainism.* a person who is free of karmic matter, detached, and omniscient; Tirthankara. [< Skt]

kev·el[1] (kev′əl), *n. Naut.* a sturdy bit, bollard, etc., on which the heavier hawsers of a ship may be secured. [1225–75; ME *kevile* < AF << L *clāvicula* little key (*clāvi(s)* key + *-cula* -CULE[1]); doublet of CLAVICLE]

kev·el[2] (kev′əl), *n.* a hammer for the rough dressing of stone, having one square face and one pyramidal face. [1325–75; ME *kevell,* of uncert. orig.]

Kev·in (kev′in), *n.* a male given name, form of **Kenneth.**

Kev·lar (kev′lär), *Trademark.* a brand of aramid fiber.

Kew (kyo͞o), *n.* a part of Richmond, in Greater London, England: famous botanical gardens **(Kew′ Gar′dens).**

Ke·wa·nee (ki won′ē), *n.* a city in NW Illinois. 14,508.

Kew·pie (kyo͞o′pē), *Trademark.* a brand name for a small, very plump doll with a topknot, usually made of plaster or celluloid.

kex (keks), *n. Brit. Dial.* the dry, usually hollow stem or stalk of various plants, esp. of large plants belonging to the parsley family, as cow parsnip or wild chervil. [1350–1400; ME; of uncert. orig.]

key[1] (kē), *n., pl.* **keys,** *adj., v.,* **keyed, key·ing.** —*n.* **1.** a small metal instrument specially cut to fit into a lock and move its bolt. **2.** any of various devices resembling or functioning as a key: *the key of a clock.* **3.** See **key card.** **4.** something that affords a means of access: *the key to happiness.* **5.** something that secures or controls entrance to a place: *Gibraltar is the key to the Mediterranean.* **6.** something that affords a means of clarifying a problem. **7.** a book, pamphlet, or other text containing the solutions or translations of material given elsewhere, as testing exercises. **8.** a systematic explanation of abbreviations, symbols, etc., used in a dictionary, map, etc.: *pronunciation key.* Cf. **legend** (def. 4). **9.** the system, method, pattern, etc., used to decode or decipher a cryptogram, as a code book, machine setting, or key word. **10.** one of a set of marked parts, designated areas, or levers pressed in operating a typewriter, computer terminal, calculator, etc. **11.** a manually operated lever for opening and closing an electric circuit, used to produce signals in telegraphy. **12.** *Music.* **a.** (in a keyboard instrument) one of the levers that when depressed by the performer sets in motion the playing mechanism. **b.** (on a woodwind instrument) a metal lever that opens and closes a vent. **c.** the relationship perceived between all tones in a given unit of music and a single tone or a keynote; tonality. **d.** the principal tonality of a composition: *a symphony in the key of C minor.* **e.** the keynote or tonic of a scale. **13.** tone or pitch, as of voice: *to speak in a high key.* **14.** mood or characteristic style, as of expression or thought: *He writes in a melancholy key.* **15.** degree of intensity, as of feeling or action. **16.** a pin, bolt, wedge, or other piece inserted in a hole or space to lock or hold parts of a mechanism or structure together; a cotter. **17.** a small piece of steel fitting into matching slots of a hub of a wheel or the like and the shaft on which the wheel is mounted so that torque is transmitted

from one to the other. **18.** a contrivance for grasping and turning a bolt, nut, etc. **19.** *Computers.* a field or group of characters within a record that identifies the record, establishing its position among sorted records, and/or provides information about its contents. **20.** (in a series of advertisements or announcements soliciting replies) a unique code inserted for each medium used, to determine the relative effectiveness of the media. **21.** *Elect.* **a.** a device for opening and closing electrical contacts. **b.** a hand-operated switching device ordinarily formed of concealed spring contacts with an exposed handle or push button, capable of switching one or more parts of a circuit. **22.** *Biol.* a systematic tabular classification of the significant characteristics of the members of a group of organisms to facilitate identification and comparison. **23.** *Masonry.* a keystone. **24.** *Archit.* (in a ribbed vault) a stone, as a boss, at the intersection of two or more ribs. **25.** *Masonry, Carpentry.* a wedge, as for tightening a joint or splitting a stone or timber. **26.** *Carpentry.* a small piece of wood set into a timber across the grain to prevent warping. **27.** *Building Trades.* any grooving or roughness applied to a surface to improve its bond with another surface. **28.** *Basketball.* keyhole (def. 2). **29.** *Photog.* the dominant tonal value of a picture, a high-key picture having light tonal values and minimal contrast and a low-key picture being generally dark with minimal contrast. **30.** *Painting.* the tonal value and intensity of a color or range of colors: *Rembrandt's colors are characterized by their low key.* **31.** *Bot.* a samara. **32.** (*cap.*) a member of the House of Keys. **33. keys,** spiritual authority. **34. power of the keys,** the authority of a pope in ecclesiastical matters, vested in him as successor of St. Peter.
—*adj.* **35.** chief; major; important; essential; fundamental; pivotal: *a key person in the company; key industries.*
—*v.t.* **36.** to regulate or adjust (actions, thoughts, speech, etc.) to a particular state or activity; bring into conformity: *to key one's speech to the intellectual level of the audience.* **37.** *Music.* to regulate the key or pitch of. **38.** *Painting.* **a.** to paint (a picture) in a given key. **b.** to adjust the colors in (a painting) to a particular hue: *He keyed the painting to brown.* **39.** to fasten, secure, or adjust with a key, wedge, or the like, as parts of a mechanism. **40.** to provide with a key. **41.** (in the layout of newspapers, magazines, etc.) to identify, through signs or symbols, the positions of illustrations or pieces of copy in a dummy. **42.** to lock with or as if with a key. **43.** *Masonry.* to provide (an arch or vault) with a keystone. **44.** *Computers.* keyboard (def. 4).
—*v.i.* **45.** to use a key. **46.** *Computers.* keyboard (def. 4). **47. key in,** *Computers.* keyboard (def. 4). **48. key on, a.** *Football.* to watch the position and movements of an opponent in order to anticipate a play: *The defensive backs keyed on the star receiver.* **b.** Also, **key in on.** to single out as of prime importance or interest; be intent on or obsessed with: *a company that is keyed in on growth.* **49. key up, a.** to bring to a particular degree of intensity of feeling, excitement, energy, nervousness, agitation, etc.: *keyed up over the impending test.* **b.** to raise (a piece of masonry) by the insertion of a wedge or wedges. **c.** to raise (the haunches of an arch) by the insertion of a voussoir. [bef. 900; ME *key(e), kay(e),* OE *cǣg, cǣge;* c. OFris *kei, kai*]
—**Syn. 6.** answer, explanation, resolution, clue.

key² (kē), *n., pl.* **keys.** a reef or low island; cay. [1690–1700; < Sp *cayo,* prob. < Arawak]

key³ (kē), *n., pl.* **keys.** *Slang.* a kilogram of marijuana or a narcotic drug. [1965–70, *Amer.*; shortening and resp. of KILOGRAM]

Key (kē), *n.* **Francis Scott,** 1780–1843, U.S. lawyer: author of *The Star-Spangled Banner.*

key·board (kē′bôrd′, -bōrd′), *n.* **1.** the row or set of keys on a piano, organ, or the like. **2.** a set of keys, usually arranged in tiers, for operating a typewriter, typesetting machine, computer terminal, or the like. **3.** any of various musical instruments played by means of a pianolike keyboard, as a piano, electric piano, or organ. —*v.t., v.i.* **4.** Also, **key, key in.** *Computers.* to enter (information) into a computer by means of a keyboard. **5.** to set (text) in type, using a machine that is operated by a keyboard. [1810–20; KEY¹ + BOARD] —**key′board′er, key′board′ist,** *n.*

typewriter keyboard (QWERTY)

typewriter keyboard (Dvorak)

CONCISE ETYMOLOGY KEY: <, descended or borrowed from; >, whence; b., blend of, blended; c., cognate with; cf., compare; deriv., derivative; equiv., equivalent; imit., imitative; obl., oblique; r., replacing; s., stem; sp., spelling, spelled; resp., respelling, respelled; trans., translation; ?, origin unknown; *, unattested; ‡, probably earlier than. See the full key inside the front cover.

key′ card′, a plastic card, similar to a credit card, containing data on an embedded magnetized strip that can electronically unlock a door, activate a machine, etc.

key′ case′, a small case in which keys are carried.

key′ club′, a private nightclub admitting only members and their guests, the members often being given door keys to the club. [1885–90]

Key′ deer′, a race of miniature white-tailed deer, native to the Florida Keys, where the small remaining population is kept in preserves. [1945–50]

keyed (kēd), *adj.* **1.** fitted with keys. **2.** fastened, strengthened, or secured by a key. **3.** *Music.* pitched in a specific key. **4.** reinforced by a keystone. **5.** coordinated, as with a basic color or idea; harmonized (sometimes used in combination): *color-keyed carpeting.* [1790–1800; KEY¹ + -ED³]

Keyes′ technique′ (kīz), a system of treating periodontal diseases by eliminating specific disease-related microorganisms, primarily through nonsurgical therapy that is regulated and adjusted in accordance with microscopic or cultural findings in subgingival plaque specimens. [after U.S. dentist Paul *Keyes,* who devised it]

key′ fruit′, *Bot.* a samara.

key′ grip′, *Motion Pictures.* the chief stagehand on a movie set. [1975–80]

key·hole (kē′hōl′), *n.* **1.** a hole for inserting a key in a lock, esp. one in the shape of a circle with a rectangle having a width smaller than the diameter of the circle projecting from the bottom. **2.** Also called **key.** *Basketball.* the area at each end of the court that is bounded by two lines extending from the end line parallel to and equidistant from the sidelines and terminating in a circle around the foul line. —*adj.* **3.** extremely private or intimate, esp. with reference to information gained as if by peeping through a keyhole. **4.** snooping and intrusive: *a keyhole investigator.* [1585–95; KEY¹ + HOLE]

key′hole saw′, a compass saw for cutting keyholes, etc. [1770–80]

key′ing se′quence, *Cryptography.* a sequence made up of letters or numbers that can encode or decode a polyalphabetic substitution cipher one letter at a time. [1940–45]

Key′ Lar′go (lär′gō), one of the islands in the Florida Keys. 30 mi. (48 km) long; 2 mi. (3.2 km) wide.

key·less (kē′lis), *adj.* **1.** lacking a key or keys. **2.** requiring no key or keys: *a keyless lock operated by a series of push buttons.* [1815–25; KEY¹ + -LESS]

key′ light′, (in photography or motion pictures) the main light that illuminates the subject being photographed or filmed. [1935–40]

Key′ lime′, a yellow lime with a bitter rather than sour taste. [after the Florida Keys]

Key′ lime′ pie′, a custardlike pie made with lime juice, condensed milk, eggs, and flavorings and served in a pastry shell.

key·lock (kē′lok′), *n.* any lock unlocked with a key. [KEY¹ + LOCK¹]

key·man (kē′man′), *n., pl.* **-men.** a person highly important or essential to the functioning of an organization, as the head of a sales force or branch office. [1850–55; KEY¹ + MAN¹]

key′man insur′ance, life insurance taken out by a business firm on an essential or very important employee, with the firm as beneficiary.

key′ mon′ey, **1.** advance rent or security required of a new tenant and given in exchange for the key to the house or apartment. **2.** an amount of money paid, often secretly, to a landlord, superintendent, or current tenant by a person desiring future tenancy. [1895–1900]

Keynes (kānz), *n.* **John Maynard, 1st Baron,** 1883–1946, English economist and writer.

Keynes·i·an (kān′zē ən), *adj.* **1.** of or pertaining to the economic theories, doctrines, or policies of Keynes or his followers, esp. the policy of maintaining high employment and controlling inflation by varying the interest rates, tax rates, and public expenditure. —*n.* **2.** a person who maintains or supports the theories, doctrines, or policies of Keynes. [1935–40; KEYNES + -IAN] —**Keynes·i·an·ism,** *n.*

key·note (kē′nōt′), *n., v.,* **-not·ed, -not·ing.** —*n.* **1.** *Music.* the note or tone on which a key or system of tones is founded; the tonic. **2.** the main idea or central principle of a speech, program, thought, action, etc. **3.** the policy line to be followed, as by a party in a political campaign, that is set forth authoritatively in advance by an address or other formal announcement. **4.** See **keynote address.** —*v.t.* **5.** to announce the policy of (a political party, campaign, assembly, etc.); deliver a keynote address at: *The governor will keynote the convention.* **6.** to serve as the keynote for. **7.** *Music.* to give the keynote of. —*v.i.* **8.** to provide a keynote, esp. a keynote address: *He refused an invitation to keynote.* [1755–65; KEY¹ + NOTE]

key′note address′, a speech, as at a political convention, that presents important issues, principles, policies, etc. Also called **keynote, key′note speech′.** [1905–10]

key·not·er (kē′nō′tər), *n.* a person who delivers a keynote address. Also called **key′note speak′er.** [1925–30, *Amer.*; KEYNOTE + -ER¹]

key·pad (kē′pad′), *n.* **1.** a separate section on some computer keyboards, grouping together numeric keys and those for mathematical or other special functions in an arrangement like that of a calculator. **2.** a panel similarly keyed and used in conjunction with a television set, electronic banking machine, or other electronic device. Also called **numeric keypad.** [1965–70; KEY¹ + PAD¹]

key′ plate′, *Print.* (in color printing) the plate providing the greatest definition of detail, usually the black plate, on which the other plates are registered. [1905–10]

key·punch (kē′punch′), *n.* **1.** Also, **key′ punch′.** Also called **card punch.** a machine, operated by a keyboard, for coding information by punching holes in cards or paper tape in specified patterns. —*v.t.* **2.** to punch holes in (a punch card or paper tape), using a keypunch. **3.** to insert (data) into a computer by means of a keypunch: *to keypunch code numbers.* [1930–35; KEY¹ + PUNCH¹] —**key′punch′er,** *n.*

key′ ring′, a ring, usually of metal, for holding keys. [1885–90]

key′ scarf′, *Shipbuilding.* any of various scarf joints in which the overlapping parts are keyed together.

Key·ser·ling (kī′zəʀ ling), *n.* **Her·mann A·le·xan·der** (heʀ′män ä′le ksän′dəʀ), **Count,** 1880–1946, German philosopher and writer.

key′ sig′nature, *Music.* (in notation) the group of sharps or flats placed after the clef to indicate the tonality of the music following. [1870–75]

key·slot (kē′slot′), *n.* a short, curved slot cut into a shaft for a Woodruff key. Cf. **keyway** (def. 1). [KEY¹ + SLOT¹]

key′ sta′tion, a radio or television station that originates most of a network's broadcasting.

key·stone (kē′stōn′), *n.* **1.** the wedge-shaped piece at the summit of an arch, regarded as holding the other pieces in place. See diag. under **arch. 2.** something on which associated things depend: *the keystone of one's philosophy.* **3.** Also called **key′stone sack′.** *Baseball Slang.* See **second base** (def. 1). [1630–40; KEY¹ + STONE]
—**Syn. 2.** basis, principle, foundation, linchpin.

Key′stone com′edy, 1. a short film of the silent era, often featuring the Keystone Kops. **2.** *Slang.* any situation or incident characterized by farcical bungling, misunderstandings, etc. [1910–15]

key′stone joist′, a reinforced-concrete joist with sloping sides and the top wider than the bottom.

Key′stone Kop′ (kop), **1.** Usually, **Keystone Kops.** (in early silent movies) a team of comic policemen noted for their slapstick routines. **2.** Also, **Key′stone Cop′.** a person noted for bungling inefficiency: *a backfield of Keystone Kops.*

Key·ston·er (kē′stō′nər), *n. Informal.* a native or inhabitant of Pennsylvania (used as a nickname). [KEYSTONE (STATE) + -ER¹]

Key′stone State′, Pennsylvania (used as a nickname).

key·stroke (kē′strōk′), *n.* one stroke of any key on a machine operated by a keyboard, as a typewriter, computer terminal, or Linotype: *I can do 3000 keystrokes an hour.* [1905–10; KEY¹ + STROKE¹]

key·way (kē′wā′), *n.* **1.** *Mach.* a groove in a shaft, the hub of a wheel, etc., for receiving part of a key holding it to another part. **2.** a slot in a lock for receiving and guiding the key. **3.** (in poured-concrete construction) a longitudinal groove in a footing, or in a pour that has set, providing a key for newly poured concrete. **4.** a depression or slot carved into rock to provide a bond or anchorage for a structure, as a dam. [1865–70; KEY¹ + WAY]

Key′ West′, 1. an island off S Florida, in the Gulf of Mexico. 4 mi. (6.4 km) long; 2 mi. (3.2 km) wide. **2.** a seaport on this island: the southernmost city in the U.S.; naval base. 24,292.

key·word (kē′wûrd′), **1.** a word that serves as a key, as to the meaning of another word, a sentence, passage, or the like: *Search the database for the keyword "Ireland."* **2.** a word used to encipher or decipher a cryptogram, as a pattern for a transposition procedure or the basis for a complex substitution. **3.** Also called **catchword.** *Library Science.* a significant or memorable word or term in the title, abstract, or text of an item being indexed, used as the index entry. Also, **key′ word′.** [1855–60; KEY¹ + WORD]

key′word in′dexing, *Library Science.* the process of constructing or compiling an index of published materials using keywords.

kG, kilogauss; kilogausses.

kg, kilogram; kilograms.

kg., **1.** keg; kegs. **2.** kilogram; kilograms.

K.G., **1.** Knight of the Garter. **2.** (in police use) known gambler.

KGB, the intelligence and internal-security agency of the former Soviet Union, organized in 1954 and responsible for enforcement of security regulations, protection of political leaders, the guarding of borders, and clandestine operations abroad. Also, **K.G.B.** Cf. **Cheka.** [< Russ, for *K(omitét) g(osudárstvennoĭ) b(ezopásnosti)* Committee for State Security]

kgf, kilogram-force.

kg-m, kilogram-meter; kilogram-meters.

KGPS, kilograms per second.

khā (ᴋʜä), *n.* the seventh letter of the Arabic alphabet, representing a velar spirant consonant sound. [< Ar]

Kha·ba·rovsk (kə bär′əfsk; *Russ.* ᴋʜu bä′ʀəfsk), *n.* **1.** Formerly, **Far Eastern Region.** a territory of the Russian Federation in NE Asia. 1,565,000; 965,400 sq. mi. (2,500,400 sq. km). **2.** a port in and the capital of this territory, in the SE part, on the Amur River. 568,000.

Kha·bur (*Arab.* ᴋʜä bŏŏr′), *n.* a river in W Asia, flowing S from SE Turkey through NE Syria to the Euphrates. 200 mi. (320 km) long. Also, **Habor.**

Kha·cha·tu·ri·an (kä′chə tŏŏr′ē ən, kach′ə-; *Russ.* ᴋʜə chyə tōō ʀyän′), *n.* **A·ram I·lich** (ar′əm il′yich; *Russ.* u ʀäm′ ē lyēch′), 1903–78, Armenian composer.

Kha·da·fy (kə dä′fē), *n.* **Mu·am·mar (Muhammad) al-** or **el-** (mōō ä′mär, al, el), Qadhafi.

khad·dar (kä′dər), *n.* a handloomed plain-weave cotton fabric produced in India. Also, **kha·di** (kä′dē). [1920–25; < Hindi *khādar*]

Kha·fa·je (KHä′fä yä′, kä′-), *n.* the site of an ancient city in E Iraq: occupied at different times by the Akkadians and the Sumerians. Also, **Kha′fa·jeh.**

Khaf·re (kaf′rā, käf′-), *n.* (*Chephren*) fl. late 26th century B.C., Egyptian king of the fourth dynasty (son of Cheops): builder of second pyramid at El Giza. Also, **Kafre.**

Khai′bar Pass′ (kī′bər). See **Khyber Pass.**

Kha·kass (kə käs′, KHə-), *n., pl.* **-kass·es,** (*esp. collectively*) **-kass** for 1. **1.** a member of a group of peoples living mainly in the Khakass Autonomous Region. **2.** the Turkic language of the Khakass peoples.

Khakass′ Auton′omous Re′gion, an autonomous region in the Russian Federation, in S Siberia. 500,000; 19,161 sq. mi. (49,627 sq. km). *Cap.:* Abakan.

khak·i (kak′ē, kä′kē), *n., pl.* **khak·is,** *adj.* —*n.* **1.** dull yellowish brown. **2.** a stout, twilled cotton cloth of this color, used esp. in making uniforms. **3.** Usually, **khakis.** (*used with a plural v.*) **a.** a uniform made of this cloth, esp. a military uniform. **b.** a garment made of this cloth, esp. trousers. **4.** a similar fabric of wool. —*adj.* **5.** of the color khaki. **6.** made of khaki. [1855–60; < Urdu < Pers *khākī* dusty, equiv. to *khāk* dust + *-ī* suffix of appurtenance] —**khak′i·like′,** *adj.*

Kha·lid (KHä lēd′, kä-, KHal′id, kal′-), *n.* (*Khalid ibn Abdul-Aziz al Saud*) 1913–82, king of Saudi Arabia 1975–82 (son of ibn-Saud and brother of Faisal).

kha·lif (kə lēf′, kä′lif, kal′if), *n.* caliph. Also, **kha·li·fa** (kə lē′fə).

khal·i·fate (kal′ə fāt′, -fit, kä′lə-), *n.* caliphate.

Khal·kha (kal′kə), *n.* a Mongolian language that is the official language of the Mongolian People's Republic and the chief vernacular of the eastern half of the country.

Khal·ki·di·ke (*Gk.* KHäl′ke thē′kē), *n.* Chalcidice.

khal·sa (käl′sə), *n.* a martial fraternity originated in 1699 and remaining as one of the closely knit communities of the Sikhs. [1770–80; < Hindi *khālṣa* lit., pure << Ar *khāliṣah*]

Kha·ma (kä′mə), *n.* **Sir Se·ret·se** (sə ret′sā), 1921–80, Botswanan political leader: president 1966–80.

Kha·me·nei (KHä′mə nā′, kä′-; *Pers.* KHä′me nā′), *n.* **Ayatollah Mohammed Ali,** born 1939, chief Islamic leader of Iran since 1989.

kham·sin (kam sēn′, kam′sin), *n.* a hot southerly wind, varying from southeast to southwest, that blows regularly in Egypt and over the Red Sea for about 50 days, commencing about the middle of March. [1675–85; < Ar *khamsīn* lit., fifty]

khan[1] (kän, kan), *n.* **1.** (in the Altaic group of languages) a title held by hereditary rulers or tribal chiefs. **2.** the supreme ruler of the Tatar tribes, as well as emperor of China, during the Middle Ages: a descendant of Genghis Khan. **3.** a title of respect used in Iran, Afghanistan, Pakistan, India, and other countries of Asia. [1350–1400; ME *Ca(a)n, Chan* << Turkic *Khān,* appar. contr. of *Khāgān,* equiv. to Turk *kağan* ruler]

khan[2] (kän, kan), *n.* an inn or caravansary. [1350–1400; < Ar < Pers; r. ME *alchan* < Ar (*al* the + *khān*)]

khan·ate (kä′nāt, kan′āt), *n.* the area governed by a khan. [1790–1800; KHAN[1] + -ATE[3]]

khan·da (kän′də), *n.* an Indian sword, having a broad, usually single-edged blade and a disklike pommel with a point. [1885–90; < Indo-Aryan; cf. Hindi *khāṛa,* Punjabi *khaṇḍā* sword, Assamese *khāṇḍa* heavy knife (Prakrit *khaṁḍa-*)]

Kha·nia (KHä nyä′), *n.* Greek name of **Canea.**

khan·jar (kän′jär), *n.* a curved dagger of Islamic countries. [1675–85; earlier *canjare, canjer* (< Turk *hançer*) < Pers *khanjar*]

khan·sa·mah (kän′sə mä′), *n. Anglo-Indian.* **1.** a native house steward or butler. **2.** a native male servant. [1635–45; < Hindi *khānsāmā* < Pers *khānsāmān,* equiv. to *khān* master + *sāmān* stores]

Khan·ty (kän′tē, KHän′-), *n., pl.* **-ties,** (*esp. collectively*) **-ty** for 1. **1.** a member of a Uralic people now living in scattered settlements along the river Ob and its tributaries in Siberia, and known from historical records to have lived in northern European Russia. **2.** the Ugric language of the Khanty, consisting of a number of highly divergent dialects. Also called **Ostyak.** [< Russ *khánty* (not declined) < Khanty *xantə, qantə*]

kha′pra bee′tle (kä′prə, kap′rə), a tiny cosmopolitan beetle, *Trogoderma granarium,* that is a pest of stored grain and other dried organic matter. [1925–30; < Hindi *khaprā* lit., destroyer]

kha·rif (kə rēf′), *n.* (in India) a crop sown in early summer for harvesting in the autumn. [1835–45; < Hindi < Ar *kharīf* autumn]

Kha·ri·jite (kär′ə jīt′), *n. Islam.* a member of an ultraconservative, sometimes fanatical, sect emphasizing the importance of strict adherence to Muslim principles of conduct, and advocating the killing of anyone seriously violating those principles. [< Ar *khārij(ī)* dissenter + -ITE[1]]

Khar·kov (kär′kôf, -kof; *Russ.* KHär′kəf), *n.* a city in NE Ukraine: former capital of Ukraine. 1,444,000.

Khar·toum (kär to͞om′), *n.* a city in and the capital of the Sudan, at the junction of the White and Blue Nile rivers: besieged 1885; retaken by the British 1898. 400,000. Also, **Khar·tum′.**

Khartoum′ North′, a city in E central Sudan, on the Blue Nile River, opposite Khartoum. 161,278.

Kha·si (kä′sē), *n.* an Austroasiatic language of Assam, in northeast India.

Khas·ko·vo (KHäs′ko vo), *n.* a city in S Bulgaria. 75,031.

khat (kät), *n.* kat.

kha·tri (ku′trē), *n.* a person who belongs to a Hindu mercantile caste alleged to originate with the Kshatriyas. [1620–30; < Hindi < Skt *kṣatriya* KSHATRIYA]

Khat·ti (KHat′ē), *n.* Hatti. —**Khat′tish,** *adj.*

Khat·tu·sas (KHät′to͝o säs′), *n.* Hattusas.

Khay·yám (kī yäm′, -yam′), *n.* **Omar.** See **Omar Khayyám.**

khed·a (ked′ə), *n.* (in India) an enclosure constructed to ensnare wild elephants. Also, **keddah, khed′ah.** [1790–1800; < Hindi]

khe·dive (kə dēv′), *n.* the title of the Turkish viceroys in Egypt from 1867 to 1914. [< F *khédive* < Turk *hidiv* < Pers *khidīw* prince] —**khe·div′al, khe·div·i·al** (kə dē′vē əl), *adj.* —**khe·div·i·ate** (kə dē′vē it, -āt′), **khe·div·ate** (kə dē′vit, -vāt′), *n.*

Khe·lat (kə lät′), *n.* Kalat.

Kher·son (ker sôn′; *Russ.* KHyir sôn′), *n.* a port in S Ukraine, on the Dnieper River, on the Black Sea. 340,000.

khid·mat·gar (kid′mət gär′), *n.* (in India) a waiter. Also, **khid′mut·gar′, khit·mat·gar, khit·mut·gar** (kit′-mət gär′). [1755–65; < Urdu < Pers, equiv. to *khidmat* service (< Ar *khidmah*) + *-gār* agent suffix]

Khim·ki (kēm′kē; *Russ.* KHyēm′kyi), *n.* a city in the NW RSFSR, in the W Soviet Union in Europe: a suburb NW of Moscow. 118,000.

Khi·os (KHē′ôs), *n.* Greek name of **Chios.**

Khir·bet Qum·ran (kēr′bet ko͝om′rän), an archaeological site in W Jordan, near the NW coast of the Dead Sea: Dead Sea Scrolls found here 1947. Also, **Khir′bet Qûm′ran.**

Khi·va (kē′və; *Russ.* KHyi vä′), *n.* a former Asian khanate along the Amu Darya River, S of the Aral Sea: now divided between Uzbekistan and Turkmenistan.

Khlyst (klist), *n., pl.* **Khlys·ty** (kli stē′), **Khlysts.** a member of a rigorously ascetic Russian sect originating in the 17th century and believing that each successive leader of the sect was an incarnation of Christ. [1855–60; < Russ: lit., whip]

Khmel·nit·sky (kmel nit′skē; *Russ.* KHmyil nyēt′-skyē), *n.* a city in W Ukraine, SW of Kiev. 172,000. Formerly, **Proskurov.**

Khmer (kmâr, kə mâr′), *n.* **1.** a member of a people in Cambodia whose ancestors established an empire about the 5th century A.D. and who reached their zenith during the 9th to the 12th centuries when they dominated most of Indochina. **2.** an Austroasiatic language that is the official language of Cambodia.

Khmer′ Repub′lic, a former official name of **Cambodia.**

Khmer Rouge (kmâr′ ro͞ozh′, kə mâr′), *pl.* **Khmers Rouges** (kmâr′ ro͞ozh′, kə mâr′) for 2. **1.** a Cambodian guerrilla and rebel force and political opposition movement, originally Communist and Communist-backed. **2.** a member or supporter of this force. [< F *Khmer* (or *Khmère*) *rouge* lit., red Khmer]

Khnum (KHno͝om), *n. Egyptian Relig.* a god in the form of a ram who created human beings from clay on a potter's wheel.

Kho·dzhent (kō jent′; *Russ.* KHu jent′), *n.* a city in N Tajikistan on the Syr Darya. 153,000. Formerly (1936–91), **Leninabad.**

Khoi·khoi (koi′koi′), *n., pl.* **-khois,** (*esp. collectively*) **-khoi** for 1. **1.** a member of a pastoral people, physically and linguistically akin to the San, who inhabited Cape Province, South Africa, in the 17th century and now live mainly in Namibia. **2.** the Khoisan language of the Khoikhoi. Also, **Khoe′khoe′.**

Khoi·san (koi′sän), *n.* **1.** a family of languages found chiefly in southern Africa and including the languages of the San and the Khoikhoi. —*adj.* **2.** of or belonging to Khoisan.

kho·ja (kō′jə), *n.* **1.** a teacher in a Muslim school. **2.** (*cap.*) a member of a subsect of the Muslims in India. [1615–25; < Pers *khwāja*]

Kho·mei·ni (KHō mā′nē, KHō-; *Pers.* KHō′mā nē′), *n.* **Ayatollah Ru·hol·lah** (ro͞o hō′lə; *Pers.* ro͞o′hō lä′), 1900?–89, chief Islamic leader of Iran 1979–89.

Khond (kond), *n.* a member of an outcaste Dravidian people of the state of Orissa in eastern India.

Kho·ra·na (kō rä′nə, kō-), *n.* **Har Go·bind** (här gō′-bind), born 1922, U.S. biochemist and researcher in genetics, born in India: Nobel prize for medicine 1968.

Kho·tan (KHō′tän′, kō-), *n. Older Spelling.* Hotan.

khoums (ko͞omz, KHo͞omz), *n., pl.* **khoums.** a coin and monetary unit of Mauritania, the 5th part of an ouguiya. [1970–75; < F < Ar *khums* lit., one fifth]

Khou·rib·ga (ko͞o rēb′gə, ko͝or′ēb gä′), *n.* a city in W central Morocco. 159,000.

Kho·war (kō′wär), *n.* an Indo-Iranian language of northwest Pakistan.

Khru·shchev (kro͞osh′chef, -chôf, kro͞osh′-; *Russ.* KHro͞o shchyôf′), *n.* **Ni·ki·ta S(er·ge·ye·vich)** (ni kē′tə sûr gā′ə vich; *Russ.* nyi kyē′tə syir gye′yə vyich), 1894–1971, Russian political leader: premier of the U.S.S.R. 1958–64.

Khu·fu (ko͞o′fo͞o), *n.* Cheops.

Khul·na (ko͝ol′nä), *n.* a city in S Bangladesh, on the delta of the Ganges. 437,304.

khur·ta (kûr′tə), *n.* kurta.

khus-khus (kus′kəs), *n.* vetiver (def. 2). [1800–10; < Pers, Hindi *khaskhas*]

Khut·bah (KHo͝ot′bə), *n. Islam.* a sermon preached by an imam in a mosque at the time of the Friday noon prayer. [1790–1800; < Ar *khuṭbah*]

Khu·zis·tan (KHo͞o′zi stän′; *Eng.* ko͞o′zə stan′, -stän′), *n.* a province in SW Iran, on the Persian Gulf. 2,187,198; ab. 35,000 sq. mi. (90,650 sq. km). *Cap.:* Ahwaz. Also, **Khu′ze·stan′.**

Khwa·riz·mi (KHwär′iz mē′), *n.* **al-** (al), (*Muhammed ibn-Musa al-Khwarizmi*), A.D. c780–c850, Arab mathematician and astronomer.

Khy′ber knife′ (kī′bər), a long Indian knife having a triangular, single-edged blade with the handle set off center toward the back.

Khy′ber Pass′, the chief mountain pass between Pakistan and Afghanistan, W of Peshawar. 33 mi. (53 km) long; 6825 ft. (2080 m) high. Also, **Khaibar Pass.**

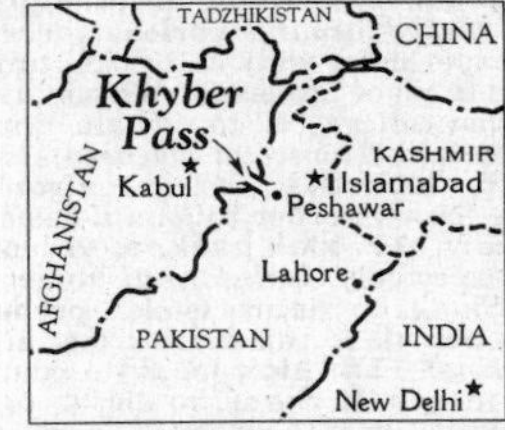

kHz, kilohertz.

Ki (kē), *n.* the Sumerian goddess personifying earth: the counterpart of the Akkadian Aruru.

Ki., *Bible.* Kings.

KIA, 1. Also, **K.I.A.** killed in action. **2.** *pl.* **KIA's, KIAs.** a member of the military services who has been killed in action.

ki·a·boo·ca (kī′ə bo͞o′kə), *n.* padouk. [1825–35; orig. uncert.]

Kia·mu·sze (*Chin.* jyä′mo͞o′su′), *n. Older Spelling.* Jiamusi.

ki·ang (kē äng′), *n.* a wild ass, *Equus kiang,* of Tibet and Mongolia. [1880–85; < Tibetan *kyang* (sp. *rkyang*)]

Kiang·ling (kyang′ling′; *Chin.* gyäng′ling′), *n. Older Spelling.* Jiangling.

Kiang·si (kyang′sē′; *Chin.* gyäng′sē′), *n. Older Spelling.* Jiangxi.

Kiang·su (kyang′so͞o′; *Chin.* gyäng′so͞o′), *n. Older Spelling.* Jiangsu.

Kiao·chow (kyou′chou′; *Chin.* gyou′jō′), *n. Older Spelling.* Jiaozhou.

Kiao′chow′ Bay′. See **Jiaozhou Bay.**

KIAS, knot indicated airspeed.

kiaugh (kyäKH), *n. Scot.* trouble or worry. Also, **kauch.** [1780–90; of uncert. orig.]

ki·a·we (kē ä′vā), *n.* a thorny tree, *Prosopis juliflora,* of the legume family, native to South America and widely naturalized in Hawaii. [< Hawaiian]

kib·ble[1] (kib′əl), *v.,* **-bled, -bling,** *n.* —*v.t.* **1.** to grind or divide into particles or pellets, as coarse-ground meal or prepared dry dog food. —*n.* **2.** grains or pellets resulting from a kibbling process. [1780–90; orig. uncert.]

kib·ble[2] (kib′əl), *n. Brit.* an iron bucket used in mines for hoisting ore. [1665–75; < G *Kübel* pail, vat]

kib·butz (ki bo͝ots′, -bo͞ots′), *n., pl.* **-but·zim** (-bo͝ot-sēm′). (in Israel) a community settlement, usually agricultural, organized under collectivist principles. [1930–35; < ModHeb *kibbuṣ*; cf. Heb *qibbūṣ* gathering]

kib·butz·nik (ki bo͝ots′nik, -bo͞ots′-), *n.* a member of a kibbutz. [1945–50; < Yiddish *kibutsnik,* equiv. to *kibuts* KIBBUTZ + *-nik* -NIK]

kibe (kīb), *n. Med.* a chapped or ulcerated chilblain, esp. on the heel. [1350–1400; ME *kybe,* perh. < Welsh *cibi*]

Ki·bei (kē′bā′), *n., pl.* **-bei.** a person of Japanese descent, born in the U.S. but educated in Japan. Also, **kibei.** Cf. **Issei, Sansei, Nisei.** [< Japn]

kib·itz (kib′its), *Informal.* —*v.i.* **1.** to act as a kibitzer. —*v.t.* **2.** to offer advice or criticism to as a kibitzer: *to kibitz the team from the bleachers.* [1925–30, *Amer.*; < Yiddish *kibetsn,* equiv. to G *kiebitzen* to look on at cards, deriv. of *Kiebitz* busybody, lit., lapwing, plover]

kib·itz·er (kib′it sər), *n. Informal.* **1.** a spectator at a card game who looks at the players' cards over their shoulders, esp. one who gives unsolicited advice. **2.** a giver of uninvited or unwanted advice. **3.** a person who jokes, chitchats, or makes wisecracks, esp. while others are trying to work or to discuss something seriously. [1925–30; < Yiddish; see KIBITZ, -ER[1]] —**Syn. 2.** meddler, busybody, snoop.

kib·lah (kib′lə), *n. Islam.* qibla. Also, **keblah, kib′la.** [1730–40; < Ar *qiblah*]

ki·bosh (kī′bosh, ki bosh′), *n. Informal.* **1.** nonsense. **2. put the kibosh on,** to put an end to; squelch; check: *Another such injury may put the kibosh on her athletic career.* [1830–40; of obscure orig.]

kick (kik), *v.t.* **1.** to strike with the foot or feet: *to kick the ball; to kick someone in the shins.* **2.** to drive, force, make, etc., by or as if by kicks. **3.** *Football.* to score (a field goal or a conversion) by place-kicking or drop-kicking the ball. **4.** *Informal.* to make (a car) increase in speed, esp. in auto racing: *He kicked his car into high gear.* **5.** to strike in recoiling: *The gun kicked his shoulder.* **6.** *Slang.* to give up or break (a drug addiction):

CONCISE PRONUNCIATION KEY: act, cāpe, dâre, pärt; set, ēqual; *if,* ice; ox, ōver, ôrder, oil, bo͝ok, bo͞ot, out; up, ûrge; child; sing; shoe; thin, *that;* zh as in *treasure.* ə = *a* as in *alone, e* as in *system, i* as in *easily, o* as in *gallop, u* as in *circus;* ə as in *fire* (fīər), *hour* (ouər). l and n can serve as syllabic consonants, as in *cradle* (krād′l), and *button* (but′n). See the full key inside the front cover.

Has he kicked the habit? **7.** Poker. raise (def. 24). **8.** Chiefly South Atlantic States. to reject as a suitor; jilt: He courted her for two years—then she kicked him.
—*v.i.* **9.** to make a rapid, forceful thrust with the foot or feet: *He kicked at the ball. You have to kick rapidly when using a crawl stroke.* **10.** to have a tendency to strike with the foot or feet: *That horse kicks when you walk into his stall.* **11.** *Informal.* to resist, object, or complain: *What's he got to kick about?* **12.** to recoil, as a firearm when fired. **13.** to be actively or vigorously involved: *He's still alive and kicking.* **14. kick about,** to move from place to place frequently: *He kicked about a good deal before settling down.* **15. kick around,** *Informal.* **a.** to treat (someone) harshly or inconsiderately. **b.** to consider, discuss, or speculate about (a proposal, project, etc.): *We kicked around various ideas for raising money.* **c.** to experiment with. **d.** to pass time idly; wander from place to place aimlessly: *We just kicked around for a year after college.* **e.** to remain unused, unemployed, or unnoticed: *The script has been kicking around for years.* **16. kick ass,** *Slang (vulgar).* **a.** to act harshly or use force in order to gain a desired result. **b.** to defeat soundly. **17. kick back, a.** to recoil, esp. vigorously or unexpectedly. **b.** *Informal.* to give someone a kickback. **c.** *Slang.* to return (stolen property, money, etc.) to the owner. **d.** to relax: *Let's just kick back and enjoy the weekend.* **18. kick in, a.** to contribute one's share, esp. in money. **b.** *Slang.* to die. **c.** to become operational; activate; go into effect: *The air conditioning kicks in when the temperature reaches 80°F.* **19. kick off, a.** *Football.* to begin play or begin play again by a kickoff: *The Giants won the toss and elected to kick off.* **b.** *Slang.* to die. **c.** to initiate (an undertaking, meeting, etc.); begin: *A rally tomorrow will kick off the campaign.* **20. kick on,** to switch on; turn on: *He kicked on the motor and we began to move.* **21. kick out,** *Informal.* **a.** to oust or eject: *They have been kicked out of the country club.* **b.** to fail; give out: *The power kicked out and the room went black.* **c.** to separate off, as for review or inspection: *The computer kicked out the information in a split second.* **d.** *Surfing.* to turn a surfboard by shifting the weight to the rear, causing the surfboard to come down over the top of a wave, in order to stop a ride. **22. kick over,** *Informal.* (of an internal-combustion engine) to begin ignition; turn over: *The engine kicked over a few times but we couldn't get it started.* **23. kick over the traces.** See **trace**[2] (def. 3). **24. kick the bucket,** *Slang.* See **bucket** (def. 11). **25. kick the tin,** *Australian.* to give a donation; contribute. **26. kick up, a.** to drive or force upward by kicking. **b.** to stir up (trouble); make or cause (a disturbance, scene, etc.): *They kicked up a tremendous row.* **c.** (esp. of a machine part) to move rapidly upward: *The lever kicks up, engaging the gear.* **27. kick upstairs.** See **upstairs** (def. 5).
—*n.* **28.** the act of kicking; a blow or thrust with the foot or feet. **29.** power or disposition to kick. **30.** *Informal.* an objection or complaint. **31.** *Informal.* **a.** thrill; pleasurable excitement: *His biggest kick comes from telling about the victory.* **b.** a strong but temporary interest, often an activity: *Making mobiles is his latest kick.* **32.** *Informal.* **a.** a stimulating or intoxicating quality in alcoholic drink. **b.** vim, vigor, or energy. **33.** *Football.* **a.** an instance of kicking the ball. **b.** any method of kicking the ball: *place kick.* **c.** a kicked ball. **d.** the distance such a ball travels. **e.** a turn at kicking the ball. **34.** a recoil, as of a gun. **35.** *Slang.* a pocket. **36. kicks,** *Slang.* shoes. **37.** *Glassmaking.* **a.** a solid glass base or an indentation at the base of drinking glasses, bottles, etc., that reduces the liquid capacity of the glassware. **b.** Also, **punt.** an indentation at the base of a wine bottle, originally for trapping the sediment. **38. kick in the ass,** *Slang (vulgar).* See **kick** (def. 39a). **39. kick in the pants,** *Informal.* **a.** someone or something that is very exciting, enjoyable, amusing, etc.: *I think you'll like her, she's a real kick in the pants.* **b.** See **kick** (def. 40). **40. kick in the teeth,** an abrupt, often humiliating setback; rebuff: *Her refusal even to talk to me was a kick in the teeth.* [1350–1400; ME *kiken* (v.); orig. uncert.] **—kick′a•ble,** *adj.* **—kick′less,** *adj.*
—Syn. 1. boot. **11.** remonstrate; oppose. **11, 30.** grumble, growl, grouch, moan; protest.

Kick•a•poo (kik′ə po͞o′), *n.* **1.** a member of an Algonquian tribe of North American Indians that originally lived in the upper Midwest and now reside in Coahuila, Mexico, and in Kansas and Oklahoma. **2.** the dialect of the Fox language spoken by the Kickapoo.

kick•back (kik′bak′), *n.* **1.** a percentage of income given to a person in a position of power or influence as payment for having made the income possible: usually considered improper or unethical. **2.** a rebate, usually given secretively by a seller to a buyer or to one who influenced the buyer. **3.** the practice of an employer or a person in a supervisory position of taking back a portion of the wages due workers. **4.** a response, usually vigorous. **5.** a sudden, uncontrolled movement of a machine, tool, or other device, as on starting or in striking an obstruction: *A kickback from a chain saw can be dangerous.* [1930–35, *Amer.*; n. use of v. phrase *kick back*]

kick•ball (kik′bôl′), *n.* a children's game, similar to baseball, in which a large inflated ball, as a soccer ball, is kicked instead of being batted. [1970–75; KICK + BALL[1]]

kick•board (kik′bôrd′, -bōrd′), *n. Swimming.* a buoyant, usually small board that is used to support the arms of a swimmer, used chiefly in practicing kicking movements. [KICK + BOARD]

kick′ box′ing, *n.* a form of boxing in which the gloved combatants may also kick with bare feet.

kick•er (kik′ər), *n.* **1.** a person or thing that kicks. **2.** *Informal.* **a.** a disadvantageous point or circumstance, usually concealed or unnoticed: *The tickets are free, but the kicker is that you have to wait in line for hours to get them.* **b.** a surprising change or turn of events: *The kicker was that their friends knew it before they did.* **3.** something extra, as an additional cost or gain; an added expense or financial incentive. **4.** *Draw Poker.* a card, usually an ace or face card, held with a pair or three of a kind in the hope of drawing a matching card. **5.** (in concrete construction) a low plinth at the base of a column. **6. kickers,** *Slang.* shoes, esp. leisure shoes. **7.** *Naut.* **a.** a small, low-powered outboard motor. **b.** an auxiliary engine on a sailing vessel, river steamer, etc. **8.** *Slang.* the alcoholic liquor in a mixed drink. **9.** Also called **eyebrow, highline, overline, teaser.** *Print., Journalism.* a short line of copy set in a distinctive type above a headline and intended to call attention to it. **10.** *Metall.* a charge of high-carbon iron that produces a vigorous boil when charged into an open-hearth furnace containing slag and molten metal of lower carbon content. **11.** Also called **kick′er light′.** *Photog.* a light source coming from the back and side of a subject and producing a highlight. [1565–75; KICK + -ER[1]]

kick•off (kik′ôf′, -of′), *n.* **1.** *Football.* a place kick or a drop kick from the 40-yd. line of the team kicking at the beginning of the first and third periods or after the team kicking has scored a touchdown or field goal. **2.** *Soccer.* a kick that puts a stationary ball into play from the center line of the field at the start of a quarter or after a goal has been scored. **3.** the initial stage of something; start; beginning: *the campaign kickoff.* Also, **kick′-off′.** [1855–60; n. use of v. phrase *kick off*]

kick′ plate′, a metal plate fastened to the bottom of a door to resist blows and scratches. Also, **kick′plate′.**

kick′ pleat′, an inverted pleat extending upward 6 to 10 in. (15 to 25 cm) from the hemline at the back of a narrow skirt, to allow freedom in walking. [1930–35]

kick′ serve′, *Tennis.* See **American twist.**

kick•shaw (kik′shô′), *n.* **1.** a tidbit or delicacy, esp. one served as an appetizer or hors d'oeuvre. **2.** something showy but without value; trinket; trifle. [1590–1600; back formation from *kickshaws* < F *quelque chose* something (by folk etym.)]

kick•stand (kik′stand′), *n.* a device for supporting a bicycle or motorcycle when not in use, pivoted to the rear axle in such a way that it can be kicked down below the rear wheel. [1945–50; KICK + STAND]

kick-start (kik′stärt′), *v.t.* to start by means of a kick starter: *to kick-start a motorcycle.* Also, **kick′start′.** [1910–15]

kick′ start′er, a starter, as of a motorcycle, that operates by a downward kick on a pedal. Also called **kick′ start′.** [1915–20]

kick′ turn′, *Skiing.* a turn from a stationary position in which a skier lifts one ski to a point where the heel is nearly at right angles to the snow, then faces the ski outward, sets it down in the direction to be turned, and swings the other ski around so that both skis are parallel. [1905–10]

kick•up (kik′up′), *n. Informal.* a fuss; commotion; row. [1785–95; n. use of v. phrase *kick up*]

kick•wheel (kik′hwēl′, -wēl′), *n.* a potter's wheel rotated by kicking. [1890–95; KICK + WHEEL]

kick•y (kik′ē), *adj.,* **kick•i•er, kick•i•est.** *Slang.* pleasurably amusing or exciting: *a kicky tune.* [1780–90; KICK + -Y[1]]

kid[1] (kid), *n., v.,* **kid•ded, kid•ding,** *adj.* —*n.* **1.** *Informal.* a child or young person. **2.** (used as a familiar form of address.) **3.** a young goat. **4.** leather made from the skin of a kid or goat, used in making shoes and gloves. **5.** a glove made from this leather. —*v.i., v.t.* **6.** (of a goat) to give birth to (young). —*adj.* **7.** made of kidskin. **8.** *Informal.* younger: *his kid sister.* [1150–1200; ME *kide* < ON *kith*] **—kid′dish,** *adj.* **—kid′dish•ness,** *n.* **—kid′like′,** *adj.*

kid[2] (kid), *v.,* **kid•ded, kid•ding.** *Informal.* —*v.t.* **1.** to talk or deal jokingly with; banter; jest with: *She is always kidded about her accent.* **2.** to humbug or fool. —*v.i.* **3.** to speak or act deceptively in jest; jest. [1805–15; perh. special use of KID[1]] **—kid′der,** *n.* **—kid′ding•ly,** *adv.*
—Syn. 1. tease, josh, rib.

Kid (kid), *n.* **Thomas.** See **Kyd, Thomas.**

Kidd (kid), *n.* **1. Michael,** born 1919, U.S. dancer and choreographer. **2. William** ("Captain Kidd"), 1645?–1701, Scottish navigator and privateer: hanged for piracy.

Kid•der•min•ster (kid′ər min′stər), *n.* an ingrain carpet 36 in. (91 cm) wide. [1660–70; named after the town in Worcestershire, England, where it was first made]

kid′die car′ (kid′ē), **1.** a toy vehicle for a small child, having three wheels and pushed with the feet. **2.** a small tricycle. Also, **kid′dy car′.** [1915–20, *Amer.*]

kid′die porn′, *Informal.* See **child pornography.** Also, **kid′die•porn′, kid′dy porn′.** [1975–80]

kid•do (kid′ō), *n., pl.* **-dos, -does.** *Informal.* (used as a familiar form of address.) [1880–85; KID[1] + -O]

Kid•dush (*Seph. Heb.* kē do͞osh′; *Ashk. Heb.* kid′əsh), *n. Judaism.* a blessing recited over a cup of wine or over bread on the Sabbath or on a festival. [< Heb *qiddūsh* lit., sanctification]

kid•dy (kid′ē), *n., pl.* **-dies.** *Informal.* a child. Also, **kid′die.** [1570–80; KID[1] + -Y[2]]

kid′ gloves′, 1. gloves made of kid leather. **2. handle with kid gloves,** to treat with extreme tact or gentleness: *He's upset, so handle him with kid gloves today.* [1705–15]

kid•nap (kid′nap), *v.t.,* **-napped** or **-naped, -nap•ping** or **-nap•ing.** to steal, carry off, or abduct by force or fraud, esp. for use as a hostage or to extract ransom. [1675–85; KID[1] + *nap,* var. of NAB] **—kid′nap•pee′, kid′nap•ee′,** *n.* **—kid′nap•per, kid′nap•er,** *n.*
—Syn. seize, bear off, bear away.

Kid•napped (kid′napt), *n.* a novel (1886) by Robert Louis Stevenson.

kid•ney (kid′nē), *n., pl.* **-neys. 1.** *Anat.* either of a pair of bean-shaped organs in the back part of the abdominal cavity that form and excrete urine, regulate fluid and electrolyte balance, and act as endocrine glands. **2.** *Zool.* a corresponding organ in other vertebrate animals or an organ of like function in invertebrates. **3.** the meat of an animal's kidney used as food. **4.** constitution or temperament: *He was a quiet child, of a different kidney from his boisterous brothers.* **5.** kind, sort, or class: *He is only at ease with men of his own kidney.* [1275–1325; ME *kidenei, kidenere* (sing.), *kideneres, kideneren* (pl.); orig. uncert.; perh. a compound based either on *nere* (sing.), *neres* (pl.) kidney (OE **nēore;* cf. OHG *nioro,* ON *nýra*); or *ei* (sing.), *eiren* (pl.) EGG[1], OE *ǣg* (sing.), *ǣgru* (pl.) (by assoc. with the organ's shape); for the first element cf. dial. *kid* pod (akin to COD[2])] **—kid′ney•like′,** *adj.*

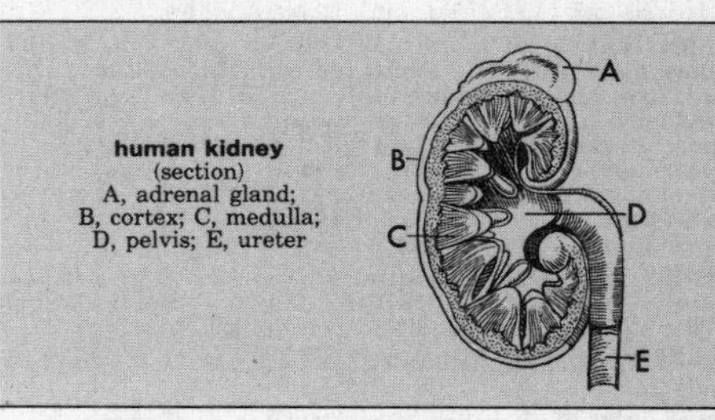

human kidney
(section)
A, adrenal gland;
B, cortex; C, medulla;
D, pelvis; E, ureter

kid′ney bean′, 1. a common bean, *Phaseolus vulgaris,* cultivated in many varieties for its edible seeds and pods. **2.** the mature kidney-shaped seed of this plant. [1540–50]

kid′ney cor′puscle. See **Malpighian corpuscle.**

kid′ney machine′. See **artificial kidney.** [1965–70]

kid•ney-shaped (kid′nē shāpt′), *adj.* having the general shape of a long oval indented at one side; reniform: *a kidney-shaped swimming pool.* [1750–60]

kid′ney stone′, *Pathol.* an abnormal stone, or concretion, composed primarily of oxalates and phosphates, found in the kidney. Also called **renal calculus.** [1970–75]

kid′ney vetch′, an Old World plant, *Anthyllis vulneraria,* of the legume family, formerly used as a remedy for kidney diseases. Also called **woundwort.** [1700–10]

kid′ney worm′, any of various large nematodes parasitic in the kidneys, esp. *Stephanurus dentatus,* found in pigs. [1835–45, *Amer.*]

kid•ney•wort (kid′nē wûrt′, -wôrt′), *n.* the navelwort, *Umbilicus rupestris,* of the stonecrop family, having drooping yellowish-green flowers. [1630–40; KIDNEY + WORT[2], from its use in treating kidney ailments]

kid•porn (kid′pôrn′), *n. Informal.* See **child pornography.** [KID[1] + PORN]

Ki•dron (kē′drən, kid′rən), *n.* a ravine E of Jerusalem, leading to the Mount of Olives: traditionally identified by Jewish, Christian, and Muslim religions as the Valley of Decision, the place of final judgment. Joel 3:2, 12. Also, **Kedron.**

kid•skin (kid′skin′), *n.* **1.** leather made from the skin of a young goat; kid. —*adj.* **2.** made of kidskin: *kidskin gloves.* [1635–45; KID[1] + SKIN]

kid•stakes (kid′stāks′), *n.* (*used with a singular or plural v.*) *Australian Informal.* **1.** pretense or nonsense. **2.** small stakes or a small amount, esp. of money. [1915–20; earlier Brit. slang *kid* nonsense, hoax (appar. n. use of KID[2]) + STAKES (see STAKE[2])]

kid′ stuff′, *Informal.* **1.** something appropriate only for children. **2.** something very easy or simple.

kid•vid (kid′vid′), *n. Slang.* television programs or programming for children. Also, **kid′-vid′.** [1970–75; KID[1] + VID(EO)]

kief (kēf), *n.* kef.

Kief•fer (kē′fər), *n.* a large, brownish-red, hybrid variety of pear. [1875–80; named after Peter *Kieffer* (1812–90), American botanist]

Kiel (kēl), *n.* the capital of Schleswig-Holstein in N Germany, at the Baltic end of the Kiel Canal. 260,900.

kiel•ba•sa (kil bä′sə, kēl-), *n., pl.* **-sas, -sy** (-sē). a smoked sausage of coarsely chopped beef and pork, flavored with garlic and spices. Also called **Polish sausage.** [1950–55; < Pol *kiełbasa,* sausage, c. Czech *klobása,* dial. Serbo-Croatian *klobasa,* Bulg *kŭlbása,* Russ *kolbasá;* ulterior orig. obscure]

Kiel′ Canal′, a canal connecting the North and Baltic seas. 61 mi. (98 km) long. German, **Nord-Ostsee Kanal.**

CONCISE ETYMOLOGY KEY: <, descended or borrowed from; >, whence; b., blend of, blended; c., cognate with; cf., compare; deriv., derivative; equiv., equivalent; imit., imitative; obl., oblique; r., replacing; s., stem; sp., spelling, spelled; resp., respelling, respelled; trans., translation; ?, origin unknown; *, unattested; ‡, probably earlier than. See the full key inside the front cover.

Kiel•ce (kyel′tse), *n.* a city in S Poland. 151,000.

Kien Lung (kyen′ lo͝ong′). See **Ch'ien Lung.**

Kie•pu•ra (kē po͞or′ə), *n.* **Jan (Wik•tor)** (yän vik′tôʀ), 1904?–66, Polish tenor.

kier (kēr), *n.* a large vat in which fibers, yarns, or fabrics are boiled, bleached, or dyed. Also, **keir.** [1565–75; < ON *ker* vessel, vat]

Kier•ke•gaard (kēr′ki gärd′; *Dan.* kēʀ′kə gôʀ′), *n.* **Sö•ren Aa•bye** (sœ′ʀən ô′ʙʏ), 1813–55, Danish philosopher and theologian.

Kier•ke•gaard•i•an (kēr′ki gär′dē ən, kēr′ki gär′-), *adj.* **1.** of, pertaining to, or resembling the philosophy or religious views of Kierkegaard. —*n.* **2.** an adherent of the views of Kierkegaard. [1940–45; KIERKEGAARD + -IAN] —**Kier′ke•gaard′i•an•ism,** *n.*

kie•sel•guhr (kē′zəl go͝or′), *n.* See **diatomaceous earth.** [1870–75; < G, equiv. to *Kiesel* flint + *Gu(h)r* earthy deposit]

kie•ser•ite (kē′zə rīt′), *n.* a mineral, hydrous magnesium sulfate, $MgSO_4 \cdot H_2O$, having a white or yellowish color and found with salt deposits. [1860–65; < G *Kieserit,* named after D. G. *Kieser,* German physician; see -ITE[1]]

Ki•ev (kē′ef, -ev; *Russ.* kyē′yif), *n.* a city in and the capital of Ukraine, on the Dnieper River. 2,144,000.

Ki•ev•an (kē′ef ən, -ev ən), *adj.* **1.** of or pertaining to Kiev. **2.** of or pertaining to the period in Russian history (11th and 12th centuries) when Kiev was the political center of a loose federation of states: *Kievan Russia.* —*n.* **3.** a native or inhabitant of Kiev. [1925–30; KIEV + -AN]

kif (kif), *n.* kef.

Ki•ga•li (kē gä′lē), *n.* a town in and the capital of Rwanda, in the central part. 40,000.

Ki•go•ma-U•ji•ji (ki gō′mə o͞o jē′jē), *n.* a city composed of two merged towns in W Tanzania, on Lake Tanganyika: Stanley found Livingstone in Ujiji 1871. 21,369.

kike (kīk), *n. Slang (disparaging and offensive).* a person of Jewish religion or descent. [1900–05; of obscure orig.; the popular belief that it derives from a Yiddish word for "circle" is dubious]

Ki•kon•go (kē kong′gō), *n.* Kongo (def. 2).

Ki•ku•yu (ki ko͞o′yo͞o), *n., pl.* **-yus,** *(esp. collectively)* **-yu. 1.** a member of an indigenous people of Kenya having an agricultural economy and notable as being the originators of the Mau Mau. **2.** the language of the Kikuyu, a Bantu language. **3.** *(usually l.c.)* Also called **kiku′yu grass′.** a grass, *Pennisetum clandestinum,* native to southern Africa, sometimes used in warm climates for lawns or as pasturage.

Ki•kwit (kē′kwēt), *n.* a city in W Zaire. 150,253.

kil., kilometer; kilometers.

Ki•lau•e•a (kē′lou ā′ä, -ā′ə, kil′ō-), *n.* a crater on Mauna Loa volcano, on SE Hawaii island, in Hawaii. 2 mi. (3.2 km) wide; 4040 ft. (1231 m) high.

Kil•dare (kil dâr′), *n.* a county in Leinster, in the E Republic of Ireland. 104,097; 654 sq. mi. (1695 sq. km). *Co. seat:* Naas.

kil•der•kin (kil′dər kin), *n.* **1.** a unit of capacity, usually equal to half a barrel or two firkins. **2.** an English unit of capacity, equal to 18 imperial gallons (82 liters). [1350–1400; ME, dissimilated var. of *kinderkin* < MD, equiv. to *kinder* (<< Ar *qinṭār* QUINTAL) + *-kin* -KIN]

ki•ley (kī′lē), *n., pl.* **-leys.** *Australian.* kylie.

Kil•gore (kil′gôr, -gōr), *n.* a city in NE Texas. 10,968.

kil•ij (kil′izh), *n.* a Turkish saber with a crescent-shaped blade, sharp on the entire convex edge and sharp on the opposite edge for about 8 in. (20 cm) back from the point. [< Turk *kiliç*]

ki•lim (kē lēm′, kil′im), *n.* a pileless, tapestry-woven rug or other covering made in various parts of the Middle East, eastern Europe, and Turkestan. [1880–85; < Turk < Pers *gilim* coarse-woven blanket]

Kil•i•man•ja•ro (kil′ə mən jär′ō), *n.* a volcanic mountain in N Tanzania: highest peak in Africa. 19,321 ft. (5889 m).

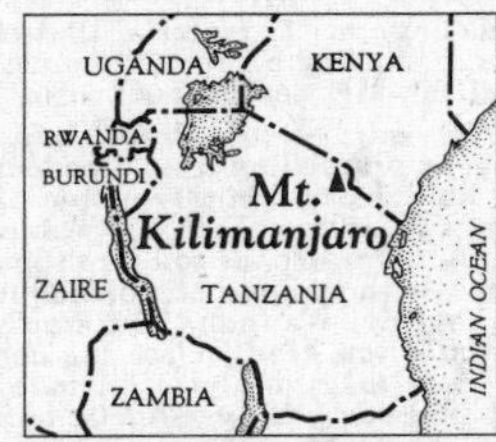

Kil•ken•ny (kil ken′ē), *n.* **1.** a county in Leinster, in the SE Republic of Ireland. 70,806; 796 sq. mi. (2060 sq. km). **2.** its county seat. 9,466.

Kilken′ny cats′, a pair of proverbial cats in Ireland who fought until only their tails were left. [1815–25]

kill[1] (kil), *v.t.* **1.** to deprive of life in any manner; cause the death of; slay. **2.** to destroy; do away with; extinguish: *His response killed our hopes.* **3.** to destroy or neutralize the active qualities of: *to kill an odor.* **4.** to spoil the effect of: *His extra brushwork killed the painting.* **5.** to cause (time) to be consumed with seeming rapidity or with a minimum of boredom, esp. by engaging in some easy activity or amusement of passing interest: *I had to kill three hours before plane time.* **6.** to spend (time) unprofitably: *He killed ten good years on that job.* **7.** *Informal.* to overcome completely or with irresistible effect: *That comedian kills me.* **8.** to muffle or deaden: *This carpet kills the sound of footsteps.* **9.** *Informal.* to cause distress or discomfort to: *These new shoes are killing me.* **10.** *Informal.* to tire completely; exhaust: *The long hike killed us.* **11.** *Informal.* to consume completely: *They killed a bottle of bourbon between them.* **12.** to cancel publication of (a word, paragraph, item, etc.), esp. after it has been set in type. **13.** to defeat or veto (a legislative bill, etc.). **14.** *Elect.* to render (a circuit) dead. **15.** to stop the operation of (machinery, engines, etc.). **16.** *Tennis.* to hit (a ball) with such force that its return is impossible. **17.** *Metall.* **a.** to deoxidize (steel) before teeming into an ingot mold. **b.** to eliminate springiness from (wire or the like). **c.** to cold-roll (sheet metal) after final heat treatment in order to eliminate distortion. **18.** *Ice Hockey.* to prevent the opposing team from scoring in the course of (a penalty being served by a teammate or teammates). —*v.i.* **19.** to inflict or cause death. **20.** to commit murder. **21.** to be killed. **22.** to overcome completely; produce an irresistible effect: *dressed to kill.* **23.** *Slang.* to feel a smarting pain, as from a minor accident; sting: *I stubbed my little toe and that really kills.* **24. kill off, a.** to destroy completely; kill, esp. successively or indiscriminately: *The invaders killed off all the inhabitants of the town.* **b.** *Informal.* to extinguish; eliminate: *The bus ride every day kills off all of my energy.* **25. kill with kindness,** to overdo in one's efforts to be kind. —*n.* **26.** the act of killing, esp. game: *The hounds moved in for the kill.* **27.** an animal or animals killed. **28.** a number or quantity killed. **29.** an act or instance of hitting or destroying a target, esp. an enemy aircraft. **30.** the target so hit or, esp., destroyed. **31.** *Sports.* See **kill shot.** [1175–1225; ME *cullen, killen* to strike, beat, kill, OE **cyllan;* c. dial. G *küllen* (Westphalian). See QUELL] —**kill′a•ble,** *adj.*
—**Syn. 1.** slaughter, massacre, butcher; hang, electrocute, behead, guillotine, strangle, garrote; assassinate. KILL, EXECUTE, MURDER all mean to deprive of life. KILL is the general word, with no implication of the manner of killing, the agent or cause, or the nature of what is killed (whether human being, animal, or plant): *to kill a person.* EXECUTE is used with reference to the putting to death of one in accordance with a legal sentence, no matter what the means are: *to execute a criminal.* MURDER is used of killing a human being unlawfully: *He murdered him for his money.*

kill[2] (kil), *n. Chiefly New York State.* a channel; creek; stream; river: used esp. in place names: *Kill Van Kull.* [1660–70, *Amer.;* < D *kil,* MD *kille* channel]

Kil•lar•ney (ki lär′nē), *n.* **1.** a town in the SW Republic of Ireland. 7,678. **2. Lakes of,** three lakes in SW Ireland.

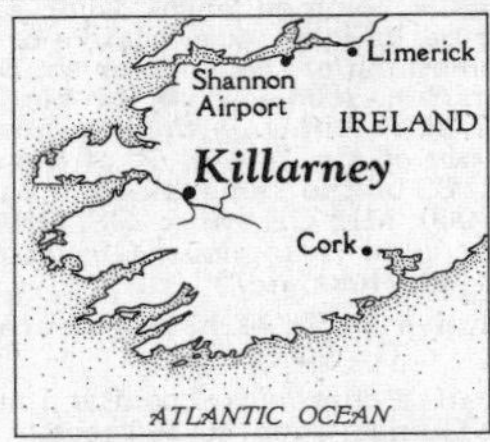

kill•dee (kil′dē), *n. Dial.* killdeer.

kill•deer (kil′dēr′), *n.* an American plover, *Charadrius vociferus,* having two black bands around the upper breast. Also called **kill′deer plov′er.** [1725–35, *Amer.;* imit.]

Kil•leen (ki lēn′), *n.* a city in central Texas. 46,296.

kill•er (kil′ər), *n.* **1.** a person or thing that kills. **2.** See **killer whale. 3.** a device used by a post office for printing cancellations on postage stamps. **4.** a mark of cancellation made on a postage stamp. **5.** *Slang.* something or someone having a formidable impact, devastating effect, etc.: *The math test was a real killer.* —*adj.* **6.** severe; powerful: *a killer cold.* [1525–35; KILL[1] + -ER[1]]

kill′er bars′, an imprint consisting of a series of wavy lines used to cancel postage stamps.

kill′er bee′, 1. a honeybee, *Apis mellifera adansonii,* native to Africa, that is extremely aggressive and attacks in swarms when disturbed: brought to Brazil and accidentally released there in 1956. **2.** an American hybrid of the African and European honeybees produced by the mingling of domesticated European colonies with an expanding and migrating African colony that escaped from an apiary in Brazil. [1975]

kill′er boat′, a boat used for hunting whales and towing them to a factory ship.

kill′er cell′, *Immunol.* any of several types of lymphocyte or leukocyte capable of destroying cells that have acquired foreign characteristics, as a tumor cell.

kill•er-dill•er (kil′ər dil′ər), *n. Older Slang.* killer (def. 5). [1935–40, *Amer.;* rhyming compound]

killer T cell, a killer cell that destroys target cells only when specifically activated by helper T cells. Cf. **natural killer cell.**

kill′er whale′, any of several predatory dolphins, esp. the black-and-white *Orcinus orca,* found in all seas. [1880–85]

kil•lick (kil′ik), *n.* **1.** a small anchor or weight for mooring a boat, sometimes consisting of a stone secured by pieces of wood. **2.** any anchor. [1620–30; orig. uncert.]

kil•lic•kin•nic (kil′i kə nik′), *n.* kinnikinnick. Also, **kil′li•ki•nic′, kil′lic•kin•nick′.**

Kil•lie•cran•kie (kil′ē krang′kē), *n.* a mountain pass in central Scotland, in the Grampians.

kil•li•fish (kil′ē fish′), *n., pl.* *(esp. collectively)* **-fish,** *(esp. referring to two or more kinds or species)* **-fish•es. 1.** any of several small, oviparous cyprinodont fishes, esp. of the genus *Fundulus,* found in salt, brackish, and fresh waters. **2.** any of several livebearers. Cf. **least killifish.** [1805–15, *Amer.;* perh. KILL[2] + *-i-* (unexplained) + FISH]

kill•ing (kil′ing), *n.* **1.** the act of a person or thing that kills. **2.** the total game killed on a hunt. **3.** a quick and unusually large profit or financial gain: *a killing in the stock market.* —*adj.* **4.** that kills. **5.** exhausting: *a killing pace.* **6.** *Informal.* irresistibly funny. [1400–50; late ME (ger.); see KILL[1], -ING[1], -ING[2]] —**kill′ing•ly,** *adv.*

kill′ing frost′, the occurrence of temperatures cold enough to kill all but the hardiest vegetation, esp. the last such occurrence in spring and the first in fall, events that limit the agricultural growing season.

Kil•ling•ly (kil′ing lē), *n.* a town in NE Connecticut. 14,519.

kill-joy (kil′joi′), *n.* a person who spoils the joy or pleasure of others; spoilsport. [1770–80]

Kil•ly (kē lē′), *n.* **Jean-Claude** (zhäɴ klōd′), born 1943, French skier.

kill′ shot′, *Sports.* a decisive smashing or punching of a ball with the hand or a racquet such that it is virtually unreturnable, as in volleyball, handball, or badminton. Also called **kill.**

Kil•mar•nock (kil mär′nək), *n.* **1.** Official name, **Kilmar′nock and Lou′don.** an administrative district in the Strathclyde region, in SW Scotland. 82,520. **2.** a city in this district, SW of Glasgow. 48,992.

Kil•mer (kil′mər), *n.* **(Alfred) Joyce,** 1886–1918, U.S. poet and journalist.

kiln (kil, kiln), *n.* **1.** a furnace or oven for burning, baking, or drying something, esp. one for firing pottery, calcining limestone, or baking bricks. —*v.t.* **2.** to burn, bake, or treat in a kiln. [bef. 900; ME *kiln(e),* OE *cylen* < L *culīna* kitchen]

kiln-dried (kil′drīd′, kiln′-), *adj.* of or pertaining to the reduction of the moisture content in wood by means of artificially controlling the heat, air circulation, and humidity. [1850–55]

kiln-dry (kil′drī′, kiln′-), *v.t.,* **-dried, -dry•ing.** to dry in a kiln. [1530–40]

kiln′ run′ brick′, any of various bricks of sufficient hardness to be exposed to the weather.

ki•lo (kē′lō, kil′ō), *n., pl.* **-los. 1.** kilogram. **2.** kilometer. **3.** (a word used in communications to represent the letter *K.*) [1865–70; shortened form]

kilo-, a Greek combining form meaning "thousand," introduced from French in the nomenclature of the metric system (*kiloliter*); on this model, used in the formation of compound words in other scientific measurements (*kilowatt*). [< F, repr. Gk *chī́lioi* a thousand]

kil•o•bar (kil′ə bär′), *n.* a unit of pressure, equal to 1000 bars (14,500 pounds per square inch; equivalent to 100 megapascals). *Abbr.:* kb [1925–30; KILO- + BAR[3]]

kil•o•bit (kil′ə bit′), *n. Computers.* **1.** 1024 (2^{10}) bits. **2.** (loosely) 1000 bits. *Symbol:* Kb [1960–65; KILO- + BIT[3]]

kil•o•byte (kil′ə bīt′), *n. Computers.* **1.** 1024 (2^{10}) bytes. **2.** (loosely) 1000 bytes. *Symbol:* K, KB [1965–70; KILO- + BYTE]

kil•o•cal•o•rie (kil′ə kal′ə rē), *n. Thermodynam.* one thousand small calories. *Abbr.:* kcal Also called **Calorie, kilogram calorie, large calorie.** Cf. **calorie** (def. 1a). [1890–95; KILO- + CALORIE]

kil•o•cu•rie (kil′ə kyo͝or′ē, -kyo͝o rē′), *n.* a unit of radioactivity, equal to 1000 curies. *Abbr.:* kCi, kc [1945–50; KILO- + CURIE]

kil•o•cy•cle (kil′ə sī′kəl), *n.* a unit equal to 1000 cycles: used esp. in radio as 1000 cycles per second for expressing the frequency of electromagnetic waves; kilohertz. The term *kilohertz* is now preferred in technical use. *Abbr.:* kc [1920–25; KILO- + CYCLE]

kil′o•e•lec′tron volt′ (kil′ō i lek′tron, -i lek′-), 1000 electron-volts. *Abbr.:* keV, kev [1945–50; KILO- + ELECTRON]

kil•o•gauss (kil′ə gous′), *n. Elect.* a unit of magnetic induction, equal to 1000 gauss. *Abbr.:* kG [1890–95; KILO- + GAUSS]

kil•o•gram (kil′ə gram′), *n.* **1.** a unit of mass equal to 1000 grams: the base SI unit of mass, equal to the mass of the international prototype of the kilogram, a platinum-iridium cylinder kept in Sèvres, France. *Abbr.:* kg **2.** a unit of force and weight, equal to the force that produces an acceleration of 9.80665 meters per second per second when acting on a mass of one kilogram. *Abbr.:* kg Also, *esp. Brit.,* **kil′o•gramme′.** [1790–1800; < F *kilogramme.* See KILO-, -GRAM[2]]

kil′ogram cal′orie, *Thermodynam.* kilocalorie. [1895–1900]

kil•o•gram-force (kil′ə gram′fôrs′, -fōrs′), *n. Physics.* a meter-kilogram-second unit of force, equal to the force that produces an acceleration equal to the acceleration of gravity, when acting on a mass of one kilogram. *Abbr.:* kgf Cf. **newton.** [1955–60]

kil•o•gram-me•ter (kil′ə gram′mē′tər), *n. Physics.* a meter-kilogram-second unit of work or energy, equal to the work done by a force of one kilogram when its point of application moves through a distance of one meter in the direction of the force; approximately 7.2 foot-pounds. *Abbr.:* kg-m Cf. **joule.** Also, *esp. Brit.,* **kil′o•gramme′-me′tre.** [1865–70]

kil•o•hertz (kil′ə hûrts′), *n., pl.* **-hertz, -hertz•es.**

CONCISE PRONUNCIATION KEY: *act, cāpe, dâre, pärt; set, ēqual; if, īce; ox, ōver, ôrder, oil, bo͝ok, bo͞ot, out; up, ûrge; child; sing; shoe; thin, that;* zh *as in treasure.* ə = *a* as in *alone, e* as in *system, i* as in *easily, o* as in *gallop, u* as in *circus;* ᵊ as in *fire* (fī^{ə}r), *hour* (ou^{ə}r). l and n can serve as syllabic consonants, as in *cradle* (krād′l), and *button* (but′n). See the full key inside the front cover.

Physics. a unit of frequency, equal to 1000 cycles per second. *Abbr.:* kHz Cf. **kilocycle.** [1925–30; KILO- + HERTZ]

kil•o•li•ter (kil′ə lē′tər), *n.* a unit of volume, equal to 1000 liters; a cubic meter. *Abbr.:* kl Also, *esp. Brit.,* **kil′o•li′tre.** [1800–10; < F *kilolitre.* See KILO-, LITER]

kil•o•meg•a•cy•cle (kil′ə meg′ə sī′kəl), *n.* a unit of frequency, equal to 10^9 cycles per second. *Abbr.:* kMc [KILO- + MEGACYCLE]

kil•o•me•ter (ki lom′i tər, kil′ə mē′-), *n.* a unit of length, the common measure of distances equal to 1000 meters, and equivalent to 3280.8 feet or 0.621 mile. *Abbr.:* km Also, *esp. Brit.,* **kil′o•me′tre.** [1800–10; < F *kilomètre.* See KILO-, METER[1]] **—kil•o•met•ric** (kil′ə-me′trik), **kil′o•met′ri•cal,** *adj.*

—Pronunciation. The usual pronunciation for units of measurement starting with *kilo-,* as *kilocalorie, kiloliter,* and *kilohertz,* as well as for units of length ending in the base word *meter,* as *centimeter, hectometer,* and *millimeter,* gives primary stress to the first syllable and secondary to the third. It would seem logical for KILOMETER to follow this pattern, and in fact the pronunciation (kil′ə mē′tər) has been in use since the early 1800's. A second pronunciation: (ki lom′i tər), with stress on the second syllable only, was first recorded in America before 1830. Although often criticized on the basis of analogy, this pronunciation has persisted in American English, increasing in frequency, and has gained popularity in British English as well. It is reinforced by words for instruments (rather than units) of measurement ending in *-meter,* as *thermometer, barometer,* and *speedometer,* having stress on the *-om* syllable. Both pronunciations are used by educated speakers, including members of the scientific community.

kil•o•par•sec (kil′ə pär′sec′), *n.* a unit of distance, equal to 1000 parsecs. *Abbr.:* kpc [1920–25; KILO- + PARSEC]

kil•o•ton (kil′ə tun′), *n.* **1.** a unit of weight, equal to 1000 tons. **2.** an explosive force equal to that of 1000 tons of TNT. [1945–50; KILO- + TON[1]]

kil•o•volt (kil′ə vōlt′), *n. Elect.* a unit of electromotive force, equal to 1000 volts. *Abbr.:* kV, kv [1860–65; KILO- + VOLT[1]]

kil•o•volt•age (kil′ə vōl′tij), *n. Elect.* electric potential difference or electromotive force, as measured in kilovolts. [1945–50; KILOVOLT + -AGE]

kil•o•volt-am•pere (kil′ə vōlt′am′pēr, -am pēr′), *n.* an electrical unit, equal to 1000 volt-amperes. *Abbr.:* kVA, kva [1905–10]

kil•o•watt (kil′ə wot′), *n.* a unit of power, equal to 1000 watts. *Abbr.:* kW, kw [1880–85; KILO- + WATT]

kil•o•watt-hour (kil′ə wot′ouər′, -ou′ər), *n.* a unit of energy, equivalent to the energy transferred or expended in one hour by one kilowatt of power; approximately 1.34 horsepower-hours. *Abbr.:* kWh, kwhr [1890–95]

Kil•pat•rick (kil pa′trik), *n.* **Hugh Jud•son** (jud′sən), 1836–81, Union general in the U.S. Civil War.

Kil•roy (kil′roi), *n.* a fictitious American male, created by American troops who left the inscription "Kilroy was here" on walls, property, etc., all over the world in the years during and after World War II.

kilt (kilt), *n.* **1.** any short, pleated skirt, esp. a tartan wraparound, as that worn by men in the Scottish Highlands. *—v.t.* **2.** to draw or tuck up, as the skirt, about oneself. **3.** to provide (a skirt) with kilt pleats. [1300–50; ME *kylte,* perh. < Scand; cf. Dan *kilte* to tuck up] **—kilt′like′,** *adj.*

kilt (def. 1)

kilt•ed (kil′tid), *adj.* **1.** wearing a kilt. **2.** gathered in pleats; pleated. [1800–10; KILT + -ED[3]]

kil•ter (kil′tər), *n.* **1.** good condition; order: *The engine was out of kilter.* **2.** *Poker.* skeet[2]. [1630–40; var. of dial. *kelter* < ?]

kilt•ie (kil′tē), *n.* **1.** a person who wears a kilt, esp. a member of a regiment in which the kilt is worn as part of the dress uniform. **2.** a sports shoe with a fringed tongue that flaps over the vamp and conceals all or part of the lacing. **3.** Also called **kilt′ie tongue′, shawl tongue.** the fringed tongue of such a shoe. [1835–45; KILT + -IE]

kilt•ing (kil′ting), *n.* an arrangement of kilt pleats. [1515–25; KILT + -ING[1]]

kilt′ pleat′, a large vertical pleat overlapping one adjoining pleat and being overlapped by the other, as on a kilt.

Kim (kim), *n.* a male or female given name.

CONCISE ETYMOLOGY KEY: <, descended or borrowed from; >, whence; b., blend of, blended; c., cognate with; cf., compare; deriv., derivative; equiv., equivalent; imit., imitative; obl., oblique; r., replacing; s., stem; sp., spelling, spelled; resp., respelling, respelled; trans., translation; ?, origin unknown; *, unattested; ‡, probably earlier than. See the full key inside the front cover.

Kim•ball (kim′bəl), *n.* a male given name.

Kim•ber•ley (kim′bər lē), *n.* **1.** a city in E Cape of Good Hope province, in the central Republic of South Africa: diamond mines. 107,104. **2.** Also, **Kim′ber•ly.** a female given name.

kim•ber•lite (kim′bər līt′), *n. Petrol.* a variety of micaceous peridotite, low in silica content and high in magnesium content, in which diamonds are formed. [1885–90; named after KIMBERLEY, South Africa; see -ITE[1]]

Kim•bun•du (kim bo͝on′do͞o), *n.* a Bantu language of northern Angola. Also called **Mbundu.**

kim•chi (kim′chē), *n. Korean Cookery.* a spicy pickled or fermented mixture containing cabbage, onions, and sometimes fish, variously seasoned, as with garlic, horseradish, red peppers, and ginger. Also, **kim′chee.** [1895–1900; < Korean *kimch′i,* hypercorrection of *cimch′i,* earlier *timchoy* < MChin, equiv. to Chin *chén* steeped + *cài* vegetables]

Kim Il Sung (kim′ il′ so͝ong′, sung′), 1912–94, North Korean political leader: premier 1948–72; president 1972–94.

kim•mer (kim′ər), *n. Scot.* cummer.

ki•mo•no (kə mō′nə, -nō), *n., pl.* **-nos. 1.** a loose, wide-sleeved robe, fastened at the waist with a wide sash, characteristic of Japanese costume. **2.** a woman's loose dressing gown. [1885–90; < Japn: clothing, garb, equiv. to *ki* wear + *mono* thing] **—ki•mo′noed,** *adj.*

kimono (def. 1)

kin (kin), *n.* **1.** a person's relatives collectively; kinfolk. **2.** family relationship or kinship. **3.** a group of persons descended from a common ancestor or constituting a family, clan, tribe, or race. **4.** a relative or kinsman. **5.** someone or something of the same or similar kind: *philosophy and its kin, theology.* **6. of kin,** of the same family; related; akin: *Although their surnames are identical they are not of kin.* *—adj.* **7.** of the same family; related; akin. **8.** of the same kind or nature; having affinity. [bef. 900; ME; OE *cyn;* c. OS, OHG *kunni,* ON *kyn,* Goth *kuni;* akin to L *genus,* Gk *génos,* Skt *jánas.* See GENDER] **—kin′less,** *adj.*

-kin, a diminutive suffix of nouns: *lambkin.* [ME < MD, MLG *-ken;* c. G *-chen*]

ki•na (kē′nə), *n.* a cupronickel coin and monetary unit of Papua New Guinea, equal to 100 toea.

Kin•a•ba•lu (kin′ə bə lo͞o′), *n.* a mountain in N Sabah, in Malaysia: highest peak on the island of Borneo. 13,455 ft. (4101 m). Also, **kin′a•bu•lu′.**

kin•aes•the•sia (kin′əs thē′zhə, -zhē ə, -zē ə), *n.* kinesthesia. Also, **kin′aes•the′sis.**

ki•nase (kī′nās, -nāz, kin′ās, -āz), *n. Biochem.* a transferase that catalyzes the phosphorylation of a substrate by ATP. [1900–05; KIN(ETIC) + -ASE]

Kin•car•dine (kin kär′dn), *n.* a former county in E Scotland. Also called **Kin•car•dine•shire** (kin kär′dn-shēr′, -shər).

kin•chin (kin′chin), *n. Chiefly Brit. Slang.* a child. [1690–1700; < G *Kindchen,* dim. of *Kind* child. See KIND[2], -KIN]

Kin•chin•jun•ga (kin′chin jo͝ong′gə), *n.* Kanchenjunga.

kind[1] (kīnd), *adj.,* **-er, -est. 1.** of a good or benevolent nature or disposition, as a person: *a kind and loving person.* **2.** having, showing, or proceeding from benevolence: *kind words.* **3.** indulgent, considerate, or helpful; humane (often fol. by *to*): *to be kind to animals.* **4.** mild; gentle; clement: *kind weather.* **5.** *Brit. Dial.* loving; affectionate. [bef. 900; ME *kind(e)* natural, well-disposed, OE *gecynde* natural, GENIAL[1]. See KIND[2]]

—Syn. 1. mild, benign, benignant, gentle, tender, compassionate. KIND, GRACIOUS, KINDHEARTED, KINDLY imply a sympathetic attitude toward others, and a willingness to do good or give pleasure. KIND implies a deep-seated characteristic shown either habitually or on occasion by considerate behavior: *a kind father.* GRACIOUS often refers to kindness from a superior or older person to a subordinate, an inferior, a child, etc.: *a gracious monarch.* KINDHEARTED implies an emotionally sympathetic nature, sometimes easily imposed upon: *a kindhearted old woman.* KINDLY, a mild word, refers usually to general disposition, appearance, manner, etc.: *a kindly face.* **—Ant. 1.** cruel.

kind[2] (kīnd), *n.* **1.** a class or group of individual objects, people, animals, etc., of the same nature or character, or classified together because they have traits in common; category: *Our dog is the same kind as theirs.* **2.** nature or character as determining likeness or difference between things: *These differ in degree rather than in kind.* **3.** a person or thing as being of a particular character or class: *He is a strange kind of hero.* **4.** a more or less adequate or inadequate example of something; sort: *The vines formed a kind of roof.* **5.** *Archaic.* **a.** the nature, or natural disposition or character. **b.** manner; form. **6.** *Obs.* gender; sex. **7. in kind, a.** in something of the same kind or in the same way as that received or borne: *They will be repaid in kind for their rudeness.* **b.** in goods, commodities, or services rather than money: *In colonial times, payment was often made in kind.* **8. kind of,** *Informal.* to some extent; somewhat; rather: *The room was kind of dark.* **9. of a kind,** of the same class, nature, character, etc.: *They are two of a kind.* [bef. 900; ME *kinde,* OE *gecynd* nature, race, origin; c. ON *kyndi,* OHG *kikunt,* L *gēns* (gen. *gentis*); see KIN]

—Syn. 1. order, genus, species; race, breed; set.

—Usage. The phrase THESE (or THOSE) KIND OF, followed by a plural noun (*these kind of flowers; those kind of shoes*) is frequently condemned as ungrammatical because it is said to combine a plural demonstrative (*these; those*) with a singular noun, KIND. Historically, KIND is an unchanged or unmarked plural noun like *deer, folk, sheep,* and *swine,* and the construction THESE KIND OF is an old one, occurring in the writings of Shakespeare, Swift, Jane Austen, and, in modern times, Jimmy Carter and Winston Churchill. KIND has also developed the plural KINDS, evidently because of the feeling that the old pattern was incorrect. THESE KIND OF nevertheless persists in use, esp. in less formal speech and writing. In edited, more formal prose, THIS KIND OF and THESE KINDS OF are more common. SORT OF has been influenced by the use of KIND as an unchanged plural: *these sort of books.* This construction too is often considered incorrect and appears mainly in less formal speech and writing.

KIND (or SORT) OF as an adverbial modifier meaning "somewhat" occurs in informal speech and writing: *Sales have been kind* (or *sort*) *of slow these last few weeks.*

kind•a (kīn′də), *adv. Pron. Spelling.* kind of; rather: *The movie was kinda boring.*

kin•der•gar•ten (kin′dər gär′tn, -dn), *n.* a school or class for young children between the ages of four and six years. [1850–55; < G: lit., children's garden, equiv. to *Kinder* children (see KIND[2]) + *Garten* GARDEN]

kin•der•gart•ner (kin′dər gärt′nər, -gärd′-), *n.* **1.** a child who attends a kindergarten. **2.** a kindergarten teacher. Also, **kin′der•gar′ten•er.** [1870–75; < G *Kindergärtner.* See KINDERGARTEN, -ER[1]]

kind•heart•ed (kīnd′här′tid), *adj.* having or showing sympathy or kindness: *a kindhearted woman.* [1525–35; KIND[1] + HEARTED] **—kind′heart′ed•ly,** *adv.* **—kind′•heart′ed•ness,** *n.*

—Syn. See **kind**[1].

kin•jal (kin′jäl), *n.* a double-edged knife of the Caucasus, having a broad blade with edges parallel for most of their length, terminating in a long, sharp point. [< Russ *kinzhál,* prob. < a Turkic language of the Caucasus, ult. < Pers *khanjar* KHANJAR]

kin•dle[1] (kin′dl), *v.,* **-dled, -dling.** *—v.t.* **1.** to start (a fire); cause (a flame, blaze, etc.) to begin burning. **2.** to set fire to or ignite (fuel or any combustible matter). **3.** to excite; stir up or set going; animate; rouse; inflame: *He kindled their hopes of victory.* **4.** to light up, illuminate, or make bright: *Happiness kindled her eyes.* *—v.i.* **5.** to begin to burn, as combustible matter, a light, fire, or flame. **6.** to become aroused or animated. **7.** to become lighted up, bright, or glowing, as the sky at dawn or the eyes with ardor. [1150–1200; ME *kindlen* < ON *kynda;* cf. ON *kindill* torch, candle] **—kin′dler,** *n.*

—Syn. 1–3. fire, light. KINDLE, IGNITE, INFLAME imply setting something on fire. To KINDLE is esp. to cause something gradually to begin burning; it is often used figuratively: *to kindle someone's interest.* To IGNITE is to set something on fire with a sudden burst of flame: *to ignite dangerous hatreds.* INFLAME is now found chiefly in figurative uses, as referring to unnaturally hot, sore, or swollen conditions in the body, or to exciting the mind by strong emotion: *The wound was greatly inflamed.* **3.** arouse, awaken, bestir, incite, stimulate.

kin•dle[2] (kin′dl), *v.,* **-dled, -dling,** *n.* *—v.t.* **1.** (of animals, esp. rabbits) to bear (young); produce (offspring). *—v.i.* **2.** (of animals, esp. rabbits) to give birth, as to a litter. *—n.* **3.** a litter of kittens, rabbits, etc. [1175–1225; ME *kindelen,* v. use of *kindel* offspring, young, equiv. to *kind-* (OE *gecynd* offspring; see KIND[2]) + *-el* -LE]

kind•less (kīnd′lis), *adj.* **1.** lacking kindness; unkind; unsympathetic. **2.** *Obs.* unnatural; inhuman. [1150–1200; ME; see KIND[1], -LESS] **—kind′less•ly,** *adv.*

kind•li•ness (kīnd′lē nis), *n.* **1.** the state or quality of being kindly; benevolence. **2.** a kindly deed. [1400–50; late ME; see KINDLY, -NESS]

kin•dling (kind′ling), *n.* **1.** material that can be readily ignited, used in starting a fire. **2.** the act of one who kindles. [1250–1300; ME; see KINDLE[1], -ING[1]]

kind•ly (kīnd′lē), *adj.,* **-li•er, -li•est,** *adv.* *—adj.* **1.** having, showing, or proceeding from a benevolent disposition or spirit; kindhearted: *kindly people.* **2.** gentle or mild, as rule or laws. **3.** pleasant, agreeable, or benign: *kindly climate.* **4.** favorable, as soil for crops. *—adv.* **5.** in a kind manner; with sympathetic or helpful kindness. **6.** cordially or heartily: *We thank you kindly.* **7.** obligingly; please: *Would you kindly close the door?* **8.** with liking; favorably: *to take kindly to an idea.* [bef. 900; ME *kyndly* (adj. and adv.), OE *gecyndelic* natural, *gecyndelice* naturally; see KIND[1], -LY]

—Syn. 1. See **kind**[1].

kind•ness (kīnd′nis), *n.* **1.** the state or quality of being kind: *kindness to animals.* **2.** a kind act; favor: *his many kindnesses to me.* **3.** kind behavior: *I will never forget your kindness.* **4.** friendly feeling; liking. [1250–1300; ME *kindenes.* See KIND[1], -NESS]

—Syn. 1, 3. benignity, benevolence, humanity, generosity, charity, sympathy, compassion, tenderness. **2.** good turn. **—Ant. 1.** malevolence. **3.** cruelty.

kin•dred (kin′drid), *n.* **1.** a person's relatives collectively; kinfolk; kin. **2.** a group of persons related to another; family, tribe, or race. **3.** relationship by birth or descent, or sometimes by marriage; kinship. **4.** natural relationship; affinity. *—adj.* **5.** associated by origin, nature, qualities, etc.: *kindred languages.* **6.** having the same belief, attitude, or feeling: *We are kindred spirits on the issue of gun control.* **7.** related by birth or descent; having kinship: *kindred tribes.* **8.** belonging to kin or relatives: *kindred blood.* [1125–75; ME, var. (with epenthetic *d*) of *kinrede.* See KIN, -RED] —**kin′dred·less,** *adj.* —**kin′dred·ness,** *n.* —**kin′dred·ship′,** *n.*

Kin·du (kin′do͞o), *n.* a town in E Zaire, on the Lualaba River. Formerly, **Kin·du-Port-Em·pain** (kin′do͞o pôrt′-äm paN′, -pōrt′-).

kine[1] (kīn), *n. Archaic.* a pl. of **cow**[1]. [ME *kyn,* OE *cȳna,* gen. pl. of *cū* cow[1]]

kin·e[2] (kin′ē), *n.* kinescope (def. 1). [shortened form]

kin·e·ma (kin′ə mə), *n. Brit.* cinema.

kin′emat′ic pair′, *Mech.* pair (def. 10). [1875–80]

kin·e·mat·ics (kin′ə mat′iks, kī′nə-), *n.* (*used with a singular v.*) *Physics.* **1.** the branch of mechanics that deals with pure motion, without reference to the masses or forces involved in it. **2.** Also called **applied kinematics.** the theory of mechanical contrivance for converting one kind of motion into another. [1830–40; < Gk *kīnēmat-* (s. of *kīnēma* movement; see CINEMA) + -ICS] —**kin′e·mat′ic, kin′e·mat′i·cal,** *adj.* —**kin′e·mat′i·cal·ly,** *adv.*

kinemat′ic viscos′ity, *Physics.* the coefficient of viscosity of a fluid divided by the density, usually measured in stokes.

kin·e·mat·o·graph (kin′ə mat′ə graf′, -gräf′, kī′nə-), *n.* cinematograph.

kin·e·scope (kin′ə skōp′, kī′nə-), *n., v.,* **-scoped, -scop·ing.** *Television.* —*n.* **1.** Also, **kine.** a cathode-ray tube with a fluorescent screen on which an image is reproduced by a directed beam of electrons. **2.** the motion-picture record of a television program. —*v.t.* **3.** to record (a program) on motion-picture film, using a kinescope. [1930–35; formerly trademark]

Ki·nesh·ma (kē′nish mə; *Russ.* kyē′nyi shmə), *n.* a city in the NW Russian Federation in Europe, NW of Nizhni Novgorod. 101,000.

-kinesia, a combining form with the meaning "movement, muscular activity," used in the formation of compound words: *dyskinesia; hyperkinesia.* Cf. **-kinesis.** [< Gk *-kīnēsia,* equiv. to *kīnēs(is)* (see KINESIS) + *-ia* -IA]

ki·ne·sics (ki nē′siks, -ziks, kī-), *n.* (*used with a singular v.*) the study of body movements, gestures, facial expressions, etc., as a means of communication. [1950–55; < Gk *kīnēs(is)* (see KINESIS) + -ICS] —**ki·ne′sic,** *adj.* —**ki·ne′si·cal·ly,** *adv.*

ki·ne·si·ol·o·gy (ki nē′sē ol′ə jē, -zē-, kī-), *n.* the science dealing with the interrelationship of the physiological processes and anatomy of the human body with respect to movement. [1890–95; < Gk *kīnēsi(s)* movement (see KINESIS) + -O- + -LOGY] —**ki·ne′si·ol′o·gist,** *n.*

ki·ne·sis (ki nē′sis, kī-), *n. Physiol.* the movement of an organism in response to a stimulus, as light. [1900–05; < Gk *kīnēsis* movement, equiv. to *kīnē-,* verbid s. of *kīneîn* to move + *-sis* -SIS]

-kinesis, a combining form with the general sense "movement, activity," used in the formation of compound words, often with the particular senses "reaction to a stimulus" (*photokinesis*), "movement without an apparent physical cause" (*telekinesis*), "activity within a cell" (*karyokinesis*). Cf. **-kinesia.** [< Gk *-kīnēsis;* see KINESIS]

kin·es·the·sia (kin′əs thē′zhə, -zhē ə, -zē ə, kī′nəs-), *n.* the sensation of movement or strain in muscles, tendons, and joints; muscle sense. Also, **kinaesthesia, kin′es·the′sis.** [1875–80; < Gk *kīn(eîn)* to move, set in motion + ESTHESIA] —**kin·es·thet·ic** (kin′əs thet′ik), *adj.*

ki·net·ic (ki net′ik, kī-), *adj.* **1.** pertaining to motion. **2.** caused by motion. **3.** characterized by movement: *Running and dancing are kinetic activities.* [1850–55; < Gk *kīnētikós* moving, equiv. to *kīnē-* (verbid s. of *kīneîn* to move) + *-tikos* -TIC] —**ki·net′i·cal·ly,** *adv.*

-kinetic, a combining form found on adjectives that correspond to nouns ending in **-kinesia** or **-kinesis:** *bradykinetic.* [< Gk *kīnēt(ós)* (see KINETO-) + -IC]

kinet′ic art′, art, as sculptural constructions, having movable parts activated by motor, wind, hand pressure, or other direct means and often having additional variable elements, as shifting lights. [1960–65] —**kinet′ic art′ist.**

kinet′ic en′ergy, *Physics.* the energy of a body or a system with respect to the motion of the body or of the particles in the system. Cf. **potential energy.** [1865–70]

ki·net·i·cism (ki net′ə siz′əm, kī-), *n.* **1.** the quality or state of being kinetic. **2.** See **kinetic art.** [1935–40; KINETIC + -ISM] —**ki·net′i·cist,** *n.*

kinet′ic poten′tial, *Physics.* the kinetic energy minus the potential energy in a system obeying the principle of conservation of energy. *Symbol:* L Also called **Lagrangian function.** [1925–30]

ki·net·ics (ki net′iks, kī-), *n.* (*used with a singular v.*) *Physics.* the branch of mechanics that deals with the actions of forces in producing or changing the motion of masses. [1860–65; see KINETIC, -ICS]

kinet′ic the′ory of gas′es, *Physics.* a theory that the particles in a gas move freely and rapidly along straight lines but often collide, resulting in variations in their velocity and direction. Pressure is interpreted as arising from the impacts of these particles with the walls of a container. [1870–75]

kinet′ic the′ory of heat′, *Physics.* a theory that the temperature of a body is determined by the average kinetic energy of its particles and that an inflow of heat increases this energy. [1860–65]

kinet′ic the′ory of mat′ter, *Physics.* a theory that matter is composed of small particles, all in random motion.

ki·ne·tin (kī′ni tin), *n. Biochem.* a synthetic cytokinin, $C_{10}H_9ON_5$, that retards senescence in plants. [1955; KINET(O)- + -IN[2]]

kineto-, a combining form with the meanings "movement," "movable," "moving," used in the formation of compound words: *kinetograph; kinetosome.* [< Gk *kīnēt(ós)* movable (equiv. to *kīnē-,* verbid s. of *kīneîn* to move + *-tos* adj. suffix) + -O-]

ki·ne·to·chore (ki nē′tə kôr′, -kōr′, -net′ə-, kī-), *n. Biol.* the place on either side of the centromere to which the spindle fibers are attached during cell division. [1930–35; KINETO- + *-chore* < Gk *chōros* place]

ki·ne·to·graph (ki nē′tə graf′, -gräf′, -net′ə-, kī-), *n.* a camera for taking pictures for a kinetoscope. [1890–95, *Amer.;* KINETO- + -GRAPH] —**ki·ne·tog·ra·pher** (kin′i tog′rə fər, kī′ni-), *n.* —**ki·ne·to·graph·ic** (ki nē′tə graf′ik, -net′ə-, kī-), *adj.* —**kin′e·tog′ra·phy,** *n.*

ki·ne·to·scope (ki nē′tə skōp′, -net′ə-, kī-), *n.* an early motion-picture device, invented by Edison, in which the film passed behind a peephole for viewing by a single viewer. [1860–65, *Amer.;* KINETO- + -SCOPE] —**ki·ne·to·scop·ic** (ki nē′tə skop′ik, -net′ə-, kī-), *adj.*

kin·e·to·sis (kin′i tō′sis, kī′nə-), *n. Pathol.* any condition caused by motion of the body, as seasickness. [KINET(O)- + -OSIS]

kin·folk (kin′fōk′), *n.pl. Chiefly South Midland and Southern U.S.* relatives or kindred. Also, **kin′folks′, kinsfolk.** [1425–75; late ME *kinnes-folk;* see KIN, FOLK]

king (king), *n.* **1.** a male sovereign or monarch; a man who holds by life tenure, and usually by hereditary right, the chief authority over a country and people. **2.** (*cap.*) God or Christ. **3.** a person or thing preeminent in its class: *a king of actors.* **4.** a playing card bearing a picture of a king. **5.** *Chess.* the chief piece of each color, whose checkmating is the object of the game; moved one square at a time in any direction. **6.** *Checkers.* a piece that has been moved entirely across the board and has been crowned, thus allowing it to be moved in any direction. **7.** *Entomol.* a fertile male termite. **8.** a word formerly used in communications to represent the letter *K.* —*v.t.* **9.** to make a king of; cause to be or become a king; crown. **10.** *Informal.* to design or make (a product) king-size: *The tobacco company is going to king its cigarettes.* —*v.i.* **11.** to reign as king. **12. king it,** to play the king; behave in an imperious or pretentious manner: *He kinged it over all the other kids on the block.* —*adj.* **13.** *Informal.* king-size. [bef. 900; ME; OE *cyng, cyni(n)g;* c. G *König,* D *koning,* ON *konungr,* Sw *konung,* Dan *konge.* See KIN, -ING[3]] —**king′less,** *adj.* —**king′less·ness,** *n.* —**king′like′,** *adj.*

King (king), *n.* **1. Billie Jean (Mof·fitt)** (mof′it), born 1943, U.S. tennis player. **2. Clarence,** 1842–1901, U.S. geologist and cartographer. **3. Ernest Joseph,** 1878–1956, U.S. naval officer. **4. Martin Luther, Jr.,** 1929–68, U.S. Baptist minister: civil-rights leader; Nobel peace prize 1964. **5. Richard,** 1825–85, U.S. rancher and steamboat operator. **6. Riley B.** ("*B.B.*"), born 1925, U.S. blues singer and guitarist. **7. Rufus,** 1755–1827, U.S. political leader and statesman. **8. William Lyon Mackenzie,** 1874–1950, Canadian statesman: prime minister 1921–26, 1926–30, 1935–48. **9. William Rufus De·Vane** (də vān′), 1786–1853, vice president of the U.S. 1853.

king′ bee′, *South Midland and Southern U.S.* a self-important person. [1890–95, *Amer.;* on the model of QUEEN BEE]

king·bird (king′bûrd′), *n.* any of several American tyrant flycatchers of the genus *Tyrannus,* esp. *T. tyrannus* **(eastern kingbird),** of North America, known for their pugnacious disposition toward predators. Also called **bee martin.** [1770–80, *Amer.;* KING + BIRD]

king·bolt (king′bōlt′), *n.* **1.** a vertical bolt connecting the body of a vehicle with the fore axle, the body of a railroad car with a truck, etc. **2.** (in a roof truss) an iron or steel rod serving as a king post. Also called **king rod.** [1815–25; KING + BOLT[1]]

King′ Charles′ span′iel, a variety of the English toy spaniel having a black-and-tan coat. [1895–1900; named after *Charles* II of England from his liking for this variety]

King·chow (ging′jō′), *n. Older Spelling.* former name of **Jiangling.**

king′ clam′, geoduck.

king′ clos′er (klō′zər), *Masonry.* **1.** a brick of regular length and thickness, used in building corners, having a long bevel from a point on one side to one about halfway across the adjacent end. **2.** a brick of three-quarter length for finishing a course at the end. Also, **king′ clo′sure.** Cf. **queen closer.**

king′ co′bra, a cobra, *Ophiophagus hannah,* of southeastern Asia and the East Indies, that grows to a length of more than 15 ft. (5 m): the largest of the venomous snakes. Also called **hamadryad.** [1890–95]

King′ Cot′ton, *U.S. Hist.* cotton and cotton-growing considered, in the pre-Civil War South, as a vital commodity, the major factor not only in the economy but also in politics. [1850–55, *Amer.*]

king′ crab′, **1.** See **horseshoe crab.** **2.** Also called **Alaskan king crab, Alaska crab.** a large, edible crab, *Paralithodes camtschatica,* of cold North Pacific waters, esp. abundant along the coasts of Alaska and Japan. [1690–1700]

king·craft (king′kraft′, -kräft′), *n.* the art of ruling as king; royal statesmanship. [1635–45; KING + CRAFT]

king·cup (king′kup′), *n.* **1.** any of various common buttercups, as *Ranunculus bulbosus,* having bright-yellow flowers. **2.** *Chiefly Brit.* the marsh marigold. [1530–40; KING + CUP]

king′ dev′il, any of several European hawkweeds introduced into northeastern North America, where they are troublesome weeds. [1890–95]

king·dom (king′dəm), *n.* **1.** a state or government having a king or queen as its head. **2.** anything conceived as constituting a realm or sphere of independent action or control: *the kingdom of thought.* **3.** a realm or province of nature, esp. one of the three broad divisions of natural objects: *the animal, vegetable, and mineral kingdoms.* **4.** *Biol.* a taxonomic category of the highest rank, grouping together all forms of life having certain fundamental characteristics in common: in the five-kingdom classification scheme adopted by many biologists, separate kingdoms are assigned to animals (Animalia), plants (Plantae), fungi (Fungi), protozoa and eucaryotic algae (Protista), and bacteria and blue-green algae (Monera). **5.** the spiritual sovereignty of God or Christ. **6.** the domain over which the spiritual sovereignty of God or Christ extends, whether in heaven or on earth. [bef. 1000; ME; OE *cyningdōm.* See KING, -DOM]
—**Syn. 1.** KINGDOM, MONARCHY, REALM refer to the state or domain ruled by a king or queen. A KINGDOM is a governmental unit ruled by a king or queen: *the kingdom of Norway.* A MONARCHY is primarily a form of government in which a single person is sovereign; it is also the type of power exercised by the monarch: *This kingdom is not an absolute monarchy.* A REALM is the domain, including the subjects, over which the king has jurisdiction; figuratively, a sphere of power or influence: *the laws of the realm.* **2.** dominion, empire, domain.

king′dom come′, **1.** the next world; the hereafter; heaven. **2.** *Informal.* a place or future time seemingly very remote: *You could keep it up till kingdom come.* [1775–85; extracted from the phrase *Thy kingdom come* in the Lord's Prayer]

King′dom Hall′, a meeting place of Jehovah's Witnesses for religious services.

king′dom of ends′, (in Kantian ethics) a metaphorical realm to which belong those persons acting and being acted upon in accordance with moral law.

king·fish (king′fish′), *n., pl.* (*esp. collectively*) **-fish,** (*esp. referring to two or more kinds or species*) **-fish·es.** **1.** any of several marine food fishes of the drum family, esp. of the genus *Menticirrhus,* found off the E coast of the U.S. **2.** Also called **white croaker.** a marine food fish, *Genyonemus lineatus,* found off the Californian coast. **3.** See **king mackerel.** **4.** a large game fish, *Seriola grandis,* found in Australia and New Zealand, closely related to the yellowtail. **5.** any of various other fishes noted esp. for their size. **6.** *Informal.* a person regarded as a leader or authority: *a kingfish in Democratic party circles.* [1740–50; KING + FISH]

king·fish·er (king′fish′ər), *n.* any of numerous fish- or insect-eating birds of the family Alcedinidae that have a large head and a long, stout bill and are usually crested and brilliantly colored. [1400–50; KING + FISHER; r. *king's fisher,* late ME *kinges fisher*]

belted kingfisher, *Megaceryle alcyon,* length 13 in. (33 cm)

king′fisher dai′sy, a bushy southern African plant, *Felicia bergerana,* having grasslike leaves and solitary, bright-blue flowers.

King′ George′'s War′, a war (1744–48) waged by England and its colonies against France, constituting the North American phase of the War of the Austrian Succession.

king-hit (king′hit′), *n. Australian.* a knockout punch. [1920–25]

king·hood (king′ho͝od), *n.* the state of being king; kingship. [1300–50; ME *kinghod.* See KING, -HOOD]

King′ Horn′, the earliest extant verse romance (late 13th century) in the English language.

King′ James′ Ver′sion. See **Authorized Version.** Also called **King′ James′' Bi′ble.**

King′ John′, a drama (1596–97?) by Shakespeare.

King·lake (king′lāk′), *n.* **Alexander William,** 1809–91, English historian.

King′ Lear′ (lēr), a tragedy (1606) by Shakespeare.

king·let (king′lit), *n.* **1.** a king ruling over a small country or territory. **2.** any of several small, greenish, crested birds of the genus *Regulus.* Cf. **goldcrest, golden-crowned kinglet, ruby-crowned kinglet.** [1595–1605; KING + -LET]

king·ly (king′lē), *adj.,* **-li·er, -li·est,** *adv.* —*adj.* **1.** stately or splendid, as resembling, suggesting, or befitting a king; regal: *He strode into the room with a kingly air.* **2.** pertaining or proper to a king: *kingly power.* **3.** having the rank of king. **4.** consisting of kings or others of royal rank: *kingly personages.* —*adv.* **5.** in the manner of a king; regally. [1350–1400; ME; see KING, -LY] —**king′li·ness,** *n.*
—**Syn. 1, 2.** princely, sovereign, majestic, august, magnificent, exalted, grand. KINGLY, REGAL, ROYAL refer to that which is closely associated with a king, or is suitable for one. What is KINGLY may either belong to a king, or be befitting, worthy of, or like a king: *a kingly presence, appearance, graciousness.* REGAL is esp. applied to the office of kingship or the outward manifestations of grandeur and majesty: *regal authority, bearing, splendor, munificence.* ROYAL is applied esp. to what pertains to or is associated with the person of a monarch: *the royal family, word, robes, salute; a royal residence.* —**Ant. 1, 2.** lowly.

king′ mack′erel, a game fish, *Scomberomorus cavalla,* found in the western Atlantic Ocean. Also called **cavalla.** [1935–40]

CONCISE PRONUNCIATION KEY: *act, cāpe, dâre, pärt; set, ēqual; if, īce; ox, ōver, ôrder, oil, bo͝ok, bo͞ot, out; up, ûrge; child; sing; shoe; thin, that;* zh as in *treasure.* ə = *a* as in *alone, e* as in *system, i* as in *easily, o* as in *gallop, u* as in *circus;* ə as in *fire* (fīər), *hour* (ouər). l and n can serve as syllabic consonants, as in *cradle* (krād′l), and *button* (but′n). See the full key inside the front cover.

king·mak·er (king′mā′kər), *n.* a person who has great power and influence in the choice of a ruler, candidate for public office, business leader, or the like. [1590–1600; KING + MAKER] —**king′mak′ing,** *n., adj.*

king-of-arms (king′əv ärmz′), *n., pl.* **kings-of-arms.** a title of certain of the principal heralds of England and certain other kingdoms empowered by their sovereigns to grant armorial bearings. [1400–50; late ME *king of armes.* See KING, ARM²]

king′ of beasts′, the lion. [1350–1400; ME]

king′ of kings′, a king having other kings subject to him. [1350–1400; ME]

King′ of Kings′, **1.** Christ; Jesus. **2.** God; Jehovah. Also, **King′ of Kings′.**

king′ of the for′est, the oak tree.

king′ of the hill′, **1.** a game in which each player attempts to climb to the top of some point, as a mound of earth, and to prevent all others from pushing or pulling him or her off the top. **2.** an undisputed leader or champion. Also called **king′ of the moun′tain.**

king-of-the-salm·on (king′əv *th*ə sam′ən), *n., pl.* **king-of-the-salm·on.** a ribbonfish, *Trachypterus altivelis,* of northern parts of the Pacific Ocean.

king′ pen′guin, a large penguin, *Aptenodytes patagonicus,* found on islands bordering the Antarctic Circle. [1880–85]

King′ Phil′ip's War′, the war (1675–76) between New England colonists and a confederation of Indians under their leader, King Philip.

king·pin (king′pin′), *n.* **1.** *Bowling.* **a.** headpin. **b.** the pin at the center; the number five pin. **2.** *Informal.* the person of chief importance in a corporation, movement, undertaking, etc. **3.** *Informal.* the chief element of any system, plan, or the like. **4.** a kingbolt. **5.** either of the pins that are a part of the mechanism for turning the front wheels in some automotive steering systems. [1795–1805; KING + PIN]

king′ plank′, *Shipbuilding.* a plank running along the center line of a deck, into which all other planks are fitted.

king′ post′, **1.** a structural member running vertically between the apex and base of a triangular roof truss. **2.** *Mach.* a rotating or stationary column for supporting tackle or booms used in lifting. Also, **king′post′, king′-post′.** [1770–80]

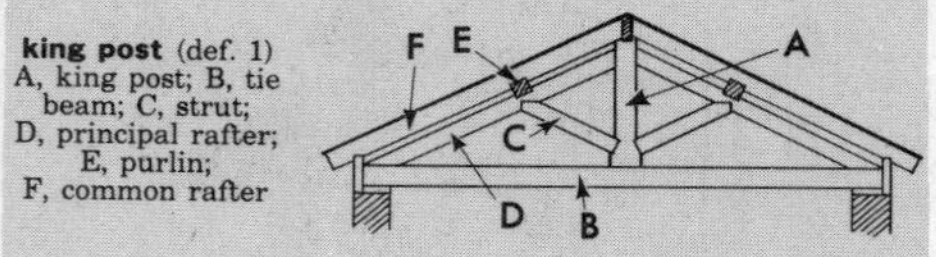

king post (def. 1) A, king post; B, tie beam; C, strut; D, principal rafter; E, purlin; F, common rafter

king′ rail′, a large, long-billed rail, *Rallus elegans,* of North America, having reddish-brown plumage. [1825–35, *Amer.*]

king′ rod′, kingbolt.

Kings (kingz), *n.* (*used with a singular v.*) either of two books of the Bible, I Kings or II Kings, which contain the history of the kings of Israel and Judah. *Abbr.:* Ki.

king′ salm′on. See **chinook salmon.** [1880–85, *Amer.*]

King's′ Bench′, *Brit. Law.* a court, originally the principal court for criminal cases, gradually acquiring a civil jurisdiction concurrent with that of the Court of Common Pleas, and also possessing appellate jurisdiction over the Court of Common Pleas: now a division of the High Court of Justice. Also called, *when a queen is sovereign,* **Queen's Bench.**

king's′ blue′. See **cobalt blue.** [1905–10]

king's′ boun′ty, *Brit.* a grant, given in the royal name, to a mother of triplets. Also called, *when a queen is sovereign,* **queen's bounty.**

Kings′ Can′yon Na′tional Park′, a national park in E California: deep granite gorges; giant sequoias; mountains. 708 sq. mi. (1835 sq. km).

King's′ Cham′pion. See under **Champion of England.**

king's′ col′or, **1.** a white ceremonial ensign with a royal cipher, flown on special occasions by the British Royal Navy. **2.** the union jack as an emblem on the regimental colors of a British military unit. **3. king's colors,** a pair of silk flags with the British royal cipher, announcing the monarch's presence. Also called, *when a queen is sovereign,* **queen's color.**

King's′ Coun′sel, *Brit. Law.* **1.** a body of barristers of a higher status who are specially appointed to be the crown's counsel, and who are permitted to plead inside the bar in the court. **2.** a member of this body of barristers. **3.** an honorary title conferred on a successful barrister when the sovereign is a king, originally for services in representing the crown but now as a mark of professional distinction. Also called, *when a queen is sovereign,* **Queen's Counsel.**

king's′ crown′, a tropical American shrub, *Justicia carnea,* of the acanthus family, bearing clusters of tubular reddish flowers.

king's′ Eng′lish, standard, educated, or correct English speech or usage, esp. of England. Also called, *when a queen is sovereign,* **queen's English.** [1545–55]

CONCISE ETYMOLOGY KEY: <, descended or borrowed from; >, whence; b., blend of, blended; c., cognate with; cf., compare; deriv., derivative; equiv., equivalent; imit., imitative; obl., oblique; r., replacing; s., stem; sp., spelling, spelled; resp., respelling, respelled; trans., translation; ?, origin unknown; *, unattested; ‡, probably earlier than. See the full key inside the front cover.

king's′ ev′idence, *Brit. Law.* evidence for the crown given by an accused person against his or her alleged accomplices. Also called, *when a queen is sovereign,* **queen's evidence.** Cf. **state's evidence.**

king's′ e′vil, scrofula: so called because it was supposed to be curable by the touch of the reigning sovereign. [1350–1400; ME *kynges evel*]

king's′ high′way, *Brit.* a highway built by the national government. Also, **King's′ high′way, King's′ High′way.** Also called, *when a queen is sovereign,* **queen's highway.**

king·ship (king′ship), *n.* **1.** the state, office, or dignity of a king. **2.** rule by a king; monarchy. **3.** aptitude for kingly duties. **4.** (*cap.*) a title used in referring to a king; Majesty (prec. by *His* or *Your*). [1275–1325; ME *kingscip.* See KING, -SHIP]

king-size (king′sīz′), *adj.* **1.** larger or longer than the usual size. **2.** (of a bed) extra large, usually measuring between 76 and 78 in. (193 and 198 cm) wide and between 80 and 84 in. (203 and 213 cm) long. Cf. **full-size, queen-size, twin-size.** **3.** pertaining to or made for a king-size bed: *king-size sheets.* **4.** (of a cigarette) extra long, in contrast to the standard length. **5.** very large, important, or serious; major: *a king-size job.* Also, **king′-sized′.** [1815–25]

Kings·ley (kingz′lē), *n.* **1. Charles,** 1819–75, English clergyman, novelist, and poet. **2. Sidney,** born 1906, U.S. playwright. **3.** a male given name.

King's′ mark′, one of the marks composing a hallmark, consisting of the head of a leopard, formerly a crowned head.

King's′ Men′, an English theatrical company originally called Lord Chamberlain's Men, founded in the late 16th century: William Shakespeare was the company's principal dramatist.

Kings′ Moun′tain, a ridge in N South Carolina: American victory over the British 1780.

king′ snake′, any of several New World constrictors of the genus *Lampropeltis,* that often feed on other snakes. Also, **king′snake′.** [1700–10, *Amer.*; KING + SNAKE]

Kings′ Park′, a town in NW Long Island, in SE New York. 16,131.

king's′ pat′tern, a spoon pattern of the 19th century having a stem decorated with threads, scrolls, and shell motifs.

king's′-pawn′ o′penings (kingz′pôn′), (*used with a singular v.*) a class of chess openings in which the pawn in front of the king is advanced two squares on the first move.

Kings·port (kingz′pôrt′, -pōrt′), *n.* a city in NE Tennessee. 32,027.

King's′ Proc′tor, a British judiciary officer who may intervene in probate, nullity, or divorce actions when collusion, suppression of evidence, or other irregularities are alleged. Also called, *when a queen is sovereign,* **Queen's Proctor.**

king's′ ran′som, an extremely large amount of money: *The painting was sold for a king's ransom.*

King's′ Remem′brancer, (in Great Britain) a judiciary official who collects debts owed to the king. Also called, *when a queen is sovereign,* **Queen's Remembrancer.**

king's′ scout′, (in Great Britain) a boy scout who has achieved the highest level of scouting: similar to the U.S. eagle scout. Also called, *when a queen is sovereign,* **queen's scout.**

king's′ shil′ling, (until 1879) a shilling given a recruit in the British army to bind his enlistment contract. Also called, *when a queen was sovereign,* **queen's shilling.**

King's′ speech′, (in the British Parliament) a speech reviewing domestic conditions and foreign relations, prepared by the ministry in the name of the sovereign, and read at the opening of the Parliament either by the sovereign in person or by commission. Also called, *when a queen is sovereign,* **Queen's speech.**

Kings·ton (kingz′tən, king′stən), *n.* **1.** a seaport in and the capital of Jamaica. 600,000. **2.** a port in SE Ontario, in SE Canada, on Lake Ontario. 56,032. **3.** a city in SE New York, on the Hudson River. 24,481. **4.** a borough in E Pennsylvania, on the Susquehanna River opposite Wilkes-Barre. 15,681.

Kings·ton-up·on-Hull (kingz′tən ə pon′hul′, -ə pôn′-, king′stən-), *n.* official name of **Hull.**

Kings′ton upon′ Thames′ (temz), a borough of Greater London, England. 135,900.

Kings·town (kingz′toun′), *n.* a city in and the capital of St. Vincent and the Grenadines, on SW St. Vincent island. 4308.

Kings·ville (kingz′vil), *n.* a city in S Texas. 28,808.

king's′ weath′er, *Brit. Informal.* fine weather; weather fit for a king.

king's′ yel′low, *Chem.* See under **arsenic trisulfide.**

King·teh·chen (ging′du′jen′), *n. Older Spelling.* Jingdezhen.

king′ truss′, *Building Trades.* a truss having a king post.

Kin·gu (kin′gōō), *n.* (in Akkadian myth) a son of Apsu and Tiamat whose blood Ea and Marduk used in creating the human race.

king′ vul′ture, a large, black-and-white vulture, *Sarcorhamphus papa,* of Central and South America, having colorful wattles and wartlike protuberances on its head and neck. [1880–85]

king-whit·ing (king′hwī′ting, -wī′-), *n., pl.* **-ings,** (*esp. collectively*) **-ing.** See **northern kingfish.**

King′ Wil′liam's War′, the war (1689–97) in which England and its American colonies and Indian allies opposed France and its Indian allies and which constituted the American phase of the War of the Grand Alliance.

king·wood (king′wŏŏd′), *n.* **1.** a Brazilian wood streaked with violet tints, used esp. in cabinetwork. **2.** the tree of the genus *Dalbergia* that yields this wood. [1850–55; KING + WOOD¹]

ki·nin (kī′nin, kin′in), *n. Biochem.* **1.** cytokinin. **2.** any of a group of hormones, formed in body tissues, that cause dilation of blood vessels and influence capillary permeability. [1950–55; independent use of -KININ, or (CYTO)KIN(ESIS) + -IN²]

-kinin, a combining form used in the names of hormones, esp. peptide hormones: *bradykinin; cytokinin.* [< Gk *kin*(*eîn*) to move, set in motion (cf. KINESIS, KINETIC) + -IN²]

kink (kingk), *n.* **1.** a twist or curl, as in a thread, rope, wire, or hair, caused by its doubling or bending upon itself. **2.** a muscular stiffness or soreness, as in the neck or back. **3.** a flaw or imperfection likely to hinder the successful operation of something, as a machine or plan: *There are still a few kinks to be worked out of the plan before we start production.* **4.** a mental twist; notion; whim or crotchet. **5.** *Slang.* **a.** bizarre or unconventional sexual preferences or behavior. **b.** a person characterized by such preferences or behavior. —*v.t., v.i.* **6.** to form, or cause to form, a kink or kinks, as a rope. [1670–80; < D: a twist in a rope]

Kin·kaid (kin kād′), *n.* **Thomas Cas·sin** (kas′in), 1888–1972, U.S. admiral.

Kinkaid′ Act′, *U.S. Hist.* an act of Congress (1904) providing for the granting of 640-acre homesteads to settlers in western Nebraska. [named after Moses *Kinkaid* (1854–1922), American Congressman]

Kin·kaid·er (kin kā′dər), *n. U.S. Hist.* a person who received free land under the provisions of the Kinkaid Act. [KINKAID (ACT) + -ER¹]

kin·ka·jou (king′kə jōō′), *n.* a brownish, arboreal mammal, *Potos flavus,* of Central and South America, having a prehensile tail, related to the raccoon and coati. [1790–1800; < F: wolverine (misapplied by Buffon to *Potos flavus*), earlier *quincajou,* perh. a conflation of *carcajou* CARCAJOU with Ojibwa *kwi·nkwaʔa·ke·* a cognate word]

kinkajou, *Potos flavus,* head and body 1½ ft. (0.5 m); tail 1½ ft. (0.5 m)

kin·kle (king′kəl), *n.* a little kink. [1860–65; KINK + -LE] —**kin′kled, kink′ly,** *adj.*

kink·y (king′kē), *adj.,* **kink·i·er, kink·i·est.** **1.** full of kinks; closely twisted: *a kinky wire.* **2.** (of hair) closely or tightly curled. **3.** *Slang.* marked by unconventional sexual preferences or behavior, as fetishism, sadomasochism, or the like. [1835–45, *Amer.*; KINK + -Y¹] —**kink′i·ly,** *adv.* —**kink′i·ness,** *n.*

Kin·men (*Chin.* kin′mun′), *n. Older Spelling.* Quemoy.

kin·ni·kin·nick (kin′i kə nik′), *n.* **1.** a mixture of bark, dried leaves, and sometimes tobacco, formerly smoked by the Indians and pioneers in the Ohio valley. **2.** any of various plants used in this mixture, esp. the common bearberry, *Arctostaphylos uva-ursi,* of the heath family. Also, **kin′ni·kin·nic′, kin′ni·ki·nick′, kin′·ni·ki·nic′, kin′ni·kin·nik′, killickinnic.** [1790–1800; earlier *killikinnick,* etc., < Unami Delaware *kələk·əni·k·an* lit., admixture, deriv. of Proto-Algonquian **keleken-* mix (it) with something different by hand]

ki·no (kē′nō), *n., pl.* **-nos.** (in Europe) a motion-picture theater; cinema. [< G, shortened form of *Kinematograph* < F *cinématographe* CINEMATOGRAPH]

ki′no gum′ (kē′nō), the reddish or black, catechulike inspissated juice or gum of certain tall trees belonging to the genus *Pterocarpus,* of the legume family, native to India and Sri Lanka, used in medicine, tanning, etc. [1820–30; appar. var. of Malinke *keno* kind of gum]

Kin·ross (kin rôs′, -ros′), *n.* a historic county in E Scotland. Also called **Kin·ross·shire** (kin rôs′shēr, -shər, -ros′-).

kin′ selec′tion, *Biol.* a form of natural selection that favors altruistic behavior toward close relatives resulting in an increase in the altruistic individual's genetic contribution to the next generation.

Kin·sey (kin′zē), *n.* **Alfred Charles,** 1894–1956, U.S. zoologist; directed studies of human sexual behavior.

kins·folk (kinz′fōk′), *n.pl.* kinfolk.

Kin·sha·sa (kin shä′sə, kin′shä sə), *n.* a port in and capital of Zaire, in the NW part, on the Zaire (Congo) River. 1,990,717. Formerly, **Léopoldville.**

kin·ship (kin′ship), *n.* **1.** the state or fact of being of kin; family relationship. **2.** relationship by nature, qualities, etc.; affinity. [1825–35; KIN + -SHIP] —**Syn. 1.** See **relationship. 1, 2.** connection. **2.** bearing.

kins·man (kinz′mən), *n., pl.* **-men. 1.** a blood relative, esp. a male. **2.** a relative by marriage. **3.** a person of the same nationality or ethnic group. [1100–50; late OE *cinnes man.* See KIN, 's¹, MAN¹]

Kin·ston (kin′stən), *n.* a city in E North Carolina. 25,234.

kins·wom·an (kinz′wŏŏm′ən), *n., pl.* **-wom·en. 1.** a female relative. **2.** a woman of the same nationality or ethnic group. [1350–1400; ME; see KIN, 's¹, WOMAN, modeled on *kinsman*]

Kint·pu·ash (kint′po͞o äsh′), *n.* See **Captain Jack.**

Kin·yar·wan·da (kin′yär wän′də), *n.* Ruanda (def. 2).

Kio·ga (kyō′gə), *n.* **Lake.** See **Kyoga, Lake.**

ki·osk (kē′osk, kē osk′), *n.* **1.** a small structure having one or more sides open, used as a newsstand, refreshment stand, bandstand, etc. **2.** a thick, columnlike structure on which notices, advertisements, etc., are posted. **3.** an open pavilion or summerhouse common in Turkey and Iran. **4.** *Brit.* a telephone booth. [1615–25; < F *kiosque* stand in a public park << Turk *köşk* villa < Pers *kūshk* palace, villa]

Kio·to (kē ō′tō; *Japn.* kyô′tô), *n.* Kyoto.

Ki·o·wa (kī′ə wə, -wä′, -wā′), *n., pl.* **-was,** (*esp. collectively*) **-wa** for 1. **1.** a member of a Plains Indian people of the southwestern U.S. **2.** a language that is closely related to Tanoan and is the language of the Kiowa people.

kip[1] (kip), *n.* **1.** the untanned hide of a young or small beast. **2.** a bundle or set of such hides. [1325–75; ME *kipp* < MD, MLG *kip* pack (of hides); akin to ON *kippa* bundle]

kip[2] (kip), *n.* a unit of weight equal to 1000 pounds (453.6 kilograms). [1910–15, *Amer.*; KI(LO) + P(OUND)[2]]

kip[3] (kip), *n.* a paper money and monetary unit of Laos, equal to 100 at. *Abbr.:* K. [1950–55; < Lao *ki:p* currency unit, ingot]

kip[4] (kip), *n., v.,* **kipped, kip·ping.** *Chiefly Brit.* —*n.* **1.** a place to sleep; bed. **2.** sleep. —*v.i.* **3.** to sleep or nap. [1760–70, in sense "brothel"; cf. Dan *kippe* hovel, dive, D *kuf* dive, brothel, MLG *kuffe, küffe, kiffe* hovel; perh. ult. expressive variants of the Gmc base of COVE[1]]

ki·pa (kē pä′), *n., pl.* ***-poth, -pot, -pos*** (*Seph.* -pôt; *Ashk.* -pōs′), *Eng.* **-pas.** *Hebrew.* yarmulke.

kip-ft, one thousand foot-pounds.

Kip·huth (kip′əth), *n.* **Robert J(ohn) H(erman)** (*Bob*), 1890–1967, U.S. swimming coach.

Kip·ling (kip′ling), *n.* **(Joseph) Rud·yard** (rud′yərd), 1865–1936, English author: Nobel prize 1907.

Kip·nis (kip′nis; *Russ.* kyip nyēs′), *n.* **Al·ex·an·der** (al′ig zan′dər, -zän′-; *Russ.* u lyi ksän′dʀ), 1891–1978, Russian singer in the U.S.

kip·per[1] (kip′ər), *n.* **1.** a fish, esp. a herring, that has been cured by splitting, salting, drying, and smoking. **2.** this method of curing fish. **3.** a male salmon during or after the spawning season. —*v.t.* **4.** to cure (herring, salmon, etc.) by splitting, salting, drying and smoking. [bef. 1000; ME *kypre*, OE *cypera* spawning salmon, appar. deriv. of *cyperen* of copper, i.e., copper-colored]

kip·per[2] (kip′ər), *n.* *Australian Informal.* a young male Aborigine, usually 14 to 16 years old, who has recently undergone his tribal initiation rite. [1835–45; < Wiradjuri *gibirr* man]

kip·py (kip′ē), *n., pl.* **-pies.** *Canadian Slang* (*chiefly the Maritime Provinces*). an attractive young woman. [of uncert. orig.]

ki·pu·ka (kē po͞o′kä), *n.* (in Hawaii) a tract of land surrounded by recent lava flows. [< Hawaiian *kipuka*]

Kir (kēr), *n.* an apéritif of white wine or sometimes champagne **(Kir Royale)** flavored with cassis. [< F, after Canon Félix *Kir* (1876–1968), mayor of Dijon, who allegedly created the recipe]

kir·by (kûr′bē), *n., pl.* **-bies.** *Angling.* a fishhook having an even bend. Also called **kir′by hook′.** [1795–1805; after the proper name]

Kir·by (kûr′bē), *n.* a male given name.

Kir·by-Smith (kûr′bē smith′), *n.* **Edmund,** 1824–93, Confederate general in the American Civil War.

Kirch·hoff (kērкн′hôf), *n.* **Gus·tav Ro·bert** (go͝os′täf rō′bert), 1824–87, German physicist.

Kirch′hoff's law′, *Physics, Elect.* **1.** the law that the algebraic sum of the currents flowing toward any point in an electric network is zero. **2.** the law that the algebraic sum of the products of the current and resistance in the conductors forming a closed loop in a network is equal to the algebraic sum of the electromotive forces in the loop. [1865–70; named after G. R. KIRCHHOFF]

Kirch·ner (kērsh′nər, kerk′-; *Ger.* kērкн′nər), *n.* **Ernst Ludwig,** 1880–1938, German expressionist artist.

Kir·ghiz (kir gēz′; *Russ.* kyiʀ gyēs′), *n., pl.* **-ghiz·es,** (*esp. collectively*) **-ghiz** for 1. **1.** a member of a formerly nomadic people dwelling chiefly in Kirghizia (Kyrgyzstan). **2.** the Turkic language of the Kirghiz.

Kir·ghi·zia (kir gē′zhə, -zhē ə, -zē ə; *Russ.* kyiʀ gyē′zyi yə), *n.* a republic in central Asia, S of Kazakhstan and N of Tadzhikistan (Tajikistan). 4,291,000; 76,460 sq. mi. (198,500 sq. km). *Cap.:* Bishkek. Official name, **Kyrgyzstan.** Formerly (1936–91), **Kirghiz′ So′viet So′cialist Repub′lic.**

Kirghiz′ Steppe′, a steppe in Kazakhstan. Also called **The Steppes.**

Ki·ri·ba·ti (kēr′ē bä′tē, kēr′ə bas′), *n.* a republic in the central Pacific Ocean, on the equator, comprising 33 islands. 56,000; 263 sq. mi. (681 sq. km). *Cap.:* Tarawa. Formerly, **Gilbert Islands.**

Ki·ri·len·ko (kyi ʀyi lyen′kə; *Eng.* kir′ə leng′kō), *n.* **An·drei Pa·vlo·vich** (un dʀyā′ pu vlô′vyich; *Eng.* än′drā pav lō′vich), 1906–90, Soviet government official.

Ki·rin (kē′rin′), *n.* *Older Spelling.* Jilin.

kirk (kûrk; *Scot.* kiʀk), *n.* **1.** *Chiefly Scot. and North Eng.* a church. **2. the Kirk,** the Church of Scotland (Presbyterian), as distinguished from the Church of England or the Scottish Episcopal Church. [1150–1200; ME (north and Scots) < ON *kirkja* CHURCH] —**kirk′like′,** *adj.*

Kirk (kûrk), *n.* **1. Grayson (Louis),** born 1903, U.S. educator: president of Columbia University 1953–68. **2.** a male given name.

Kirk·cal·dy (kər kôl′dē, -kô′dē, -kä′-), *n.* a city in SE Fife, in E Scotland, on the Firth of Forth. 142,713.

Kirk·cud·bright (kər ko͞o′brē), *n.* a historic county in SW Scotland. Also called **Kirk·cud·bright·shire** (kər-ko͞o′brē shēr′, -shər).

Kir·ke (kûr′kē), *n.* *Class. Myth.* Circe (def. 1).

Kir·ke·nes (кнēr′kə nes′), *n.* a seaport in NE Norway held by Germans in World War II.

Kirk·land (kûrk′lənd), *n.* **1. Jack,** 1901–69, U.S. writer and playwright. **2.** a town in W Washington, a suburb of Seattle. 18,779.

Kirk′land Lake′, a town in E Ontario, in S Canada: gold-mining center. 12,219.

kirk·man (kûrk′mən; *Scot.* kiʀk′mən), *n., pl.* **-men.** *Scot. and North Eng.* **1.** a member or follower of the Kirk. **2.** a churchman; ecclesiastic. [1300–50; ME; see KIRK, -MAN]

Kirk·pat·rick (kûrk pa′trik), *n.* **1. Jeane (Jordan)** (jēn), born 1926, U.S. diplomat: ambassador to the U.N. 1981–85. **2. Mount,** a mountain in Antarctica, near Ross Ice Shelf. ab. 14,855 ft. (4528 m).

Kirks·ville (kûrks′vil), *n.* a city in N Missouri. 17,167.

Kir·kuk (kir ko͝ok′), *n.* a city in N Iraq. 167,413.

Kirk·wall (kûrk′wôl′, -wəl), *n.* a town on Pomona island, NE of Scotland in the Orkney Islands: administrative center of the Orkney Islands. 4618.

Kirk·wood (kûrk′wo͝od′), *n.* a city in E Missouri, near St. Louis. 27,987.

Kir′li·an photog′raphy (kēr′lē ən), a photographic process that supposedly records electrical discharges naturally emanating from living objects, producing an auralike glow surrounding the object on a photographic plate or film with which the object is in direct contact. [1970–75; after Semyon D. and Valentina K. *Kirlian*, Russian technicians who developed the process]

Kir·man (kir män′, kər-), *n.* a Persian rug marked by ornate flowing designs and light, muted colors. Also called **Kir·man·shah** (kir män′shä′, -shô′, kər-, kir′-män shä′, -shô′, kûr′-), **Kermanshah.** [1875–80; named after KERMAN]

kir·mess (kûr′mis), *n.* kermis.

Kir Mo·ab (kûr mō′ab), ancient name of **Kerak.**

kirn[1] (kûrn; *Scot.* kiʀn), *Scot. and North Eng.* —*v.t., v.i.* **1.** to churn. —*n.* **2.** a churn. Also, **kern.** [1300–50; ME *kirne* (n.) < Scand; cf. ON *kirnuaskr* a churn; c. CHURN]

kirn[2] (kûrn; *Scot.* kiʀn), *n.* *Scot. and North Eng.* **1.** a harvest celebration; a feast or party celebrating a successful harvest. **2.** the harvesting of the last handful of corn, noting either the end of the harvest season or the winning of a race against other reapers. Cf. **kemp**[1] (def. 2). Also, **kern, kurn.** [1770–80; orig. uncert.; perh. akin to CORN[1]]

Ki·rov (kēr′ôf, -of; *Russ.* kyē′ʀəf), *n.* a city in the E Russian Federation in Europe, N of Kazan. 421,000. Formerly, **Vyatka.**

Ki·ro·va·bad (ki rō′və bad′; *Russ.* kyi ʀə vu bät′), *n.* a city in NW Azerbaijan. 232,000. Formerly, **Elisavetpol, Yelizavetpol, Gandzha.**

Ki·ro·va·kan (ki rō′və kän′; *Russ.* kyi ʀə vu kän′), *n.* a city in W Armenia, N of Yerevan. 146,000. Formerly, **Karaklis.**

Ki·ro·vo·grad (ki rō′və grad′; *Russ.* kyi ʀə vu grät′), *n.* a city in S central Ukraine. 237,000. Formerly, **Elisavetgrad, Yelizavetgrad, Zinovievsk.**

kir·pan (kir pän′), *n.* a small dagger worn by orthodox Sikhs. [1900–05; < Punjabi and Hindi < Skt *kṛpāṇa* sword]

Kir′ Royale′. See under **Kir.** [< F: royal Kir]

kirsch (kērsh), *n.* a fragrant, colorless, unaged brandy distilled from a fermented mash of cherries, produced esp. in West Germany, Switzerland, and Alsace, France. Also called **kirsch·was·ser** (kērsh′vä′sər). [1810–20; < G *Kirsch*, shortened form of *Kirschwasser*, equiv. to *Kirsch(e)* CHERRY + *Wasser* WATER]

Kir·sten (kûr′stən, kēr′), *n.* a female given name, Scandinavian form of **Christine.**

Kirt′land's war′bler (kûrt′ləndz), a wood warbler, *Dendroica kirtlandii*, breeding only in north-central Michigan and wintering in the Bahamas, bluish gray above, striped with black and pale yellow below: an endangered species. [1855–60, *Amer.*; named after Jared *Kirtland* (1793–1877), American naturalist]

kir·tle (kûr′tl), *n.* **1.** a woman's loose gown, worn in the Middle Ages. **2.** *Obs.* a man's tunic. [bef. 900; ME *kirtel*, OE *cyrtel*, appar. equiv. to *cyrt(an)* to shorten (<< L *curtus* shortened) + *-el* -LE] —**kir′tled,** *adj.*

Ki·ru·na (kē′ʀʏ nä), *n.* a city in N Sweden: important iron-mining center. 29,705.

Ki·run·di (kē ro͞on′dē), *n.* Rundi (def. 2).

ki·san (kē′sän), *n.* (in India) a peasant. [1930–35; < Hindi *kisān* < Skt *kṛṣāṇa* one who plows]

Ki·san·ga·ni (ki zäng′gä nē, kē′säng gä′-), *n.* a city in N Zaire, on the Zaire (Congo) River. 297,829. Formerly, **Stanleyville.**

Ki·se·levsk (ki sel′yôfsk; *Russ.* kyi syi lyôfsk′), *n.* a city in the S Russian Federation in Asia. 122,000.

Ki·set·la (kē set′lə), *n.* a pidgin language based on Swahili, formerly used for communication between Europeans and Africans. Also, **Ki·set′tla.**

kish (kish), *n.* *Metall.* **1.** a mixture of graphite and slag separated from and floating on the surface of molten pig iron or cast iron as it cools. **2.** dross on the surface of molten lead. [1805–15; < G *Kies* gravel, pyrites; akin to OE *cisel* gravel]

Kish (kish), *n.* an ancient Sumerian and Akkadian city: its site is 8 mi. (13 km) east of the site of Babylon in S Iraq.

Ki·shi (kē′shē), *n.* **No·bu·su·ke** (nô′bo͞o so͞o′ke), born 1896, Japanese statesman: premier 1958–60.

Ki·shi·nev (kish′ə nef′, -nôf′; *Russ.* kyi shi nyôf′), *n.* a city in and the capital of Moldavia (Moldova), in the central part. 503,000. Rumanian, **Chişinău.**

kish·ke (kish′kə), *n.* **1.** Also called **stuffed derma.** *Jewish Cookery.* a beef or fowl intestine stuffed with a mixture, as of flour, fat, onion, and seasonings, and roasted. **2. kishkes,** *Slang.* the innermost parts; guts. Also, **kish′ka.** [1935–40; < Yiddish < Slavic; cf. Pol *kiszka* sausage]

kis·ka·dee (kis′kə dē′), *n.* any of several American flycatchers of the genus *Pitangus*, esp. *P. sulphuratus* **(great kiskadee),** ranging from the southwest U.S. to Argentina and noted for their loud calls and aggressive nature. [1890–95; said to be imit.]

Kis·lev (kis′ləv, kēs lev′), *n.* the third month of the Jewish calendar. Cf. **Jewish calendar.** [< Heb *kislēw*]

kis·met (kiz′mit, -met, kis′-), *n.* fate; destiny. Also, **kis·mat** (kiz′mət, kis′-). [1840–50; < Turk < Pers *qismat* < Ar *qismah* division, portion, lot, fate, akin to *qasama* to divide]

kiss (kis), *v.t.* **1.** to touch or press with the lips slightly pursed, and then often to part them and to emit a smacking sound, in an expression of affection, love, greeting, reverence, etc.: *He kissed his son on the cheek.* **2.** to join lips with in this way: *She kissed him and left.* **3.** to touch gently or lightly: *The breeze kissed her face.* **4.** to put, bring, take, etc., by, or as if by, kissing: *She kissed the baby's tears away.* **5.** *Billiards, Pool.* (of a ball) to make slight contact with or brush (another ball). —*v.i.* **6.** to join lips in respect, affection, love, passion, etc.: *They kissed passionately.* **7.** to express a thought, feeling, etc., by a contact of the lips: *They kissed good-bye at the station.* **8.** to purse and then part the lips, emitting a smacking sound, as in kissing someone. **9.** *Billiards, Pool.* (of a ball) to carom gently off or touch another ball. **10. kiss ass,** *Slang* (*vulgar*). to be obsequious; fawn. **11. kiss off,** *Slang.* **a.** to reject, dismiss, or ignore: *He kissed off their objections with a wave of his hand.* **b.** (used to express contemptuous rejection or dismissal). **c.** to give up, renounce, or dispense with: *Leaving Tulsa meant kissing off a promising job.* —*n.* **12.** an act or instance of kissing. **13.** a slight touch or contact. **14.** *Billiards, Pool.* the slight touch of one ball by another. **15.** a baked confection of egg whites and confectioners' sugar, served as a cookie. **16.** a piece of toffeelike confectionery, sometimes containing nuts, coconut, or the like. **17.** a small, sometimes conical, bite-size piece of chocolate, usually individually wrapped. **18. blow** or **throw a kiss,** to indicate an intended kiss from a distance, usually in bidding farewell, by kissing one's own fingertips and moving the hand toward the person greeted. [bef. 900; ME *kissen* to kiss, OE *cyssan* (c. G *küssen*, ON *kyssa*), deriv. of OE *coss* a kiss; c. ON *koss*, G *Küss*]

KISS (kis), keep it simple, stupid.

kiss·a·ble (kis′ə bəl), *adj.* inviting kissing through being lovable or physically attractive. [1805–15; KISS + -ABLE] —**kiss′a·bil′i·ty, kiss′a·ble·ness,** *n.* —**kiss′a·bly,** *adv.*

kiss·er (kis′ər), *n.* **1.** a person who kisses. **2.** *Slang.* **a.** the face. **b.** the mouth. [1530–40; 1930–35 for def. 2; KISS + -ER[1]]

Kis·sim·mee (ki sim′ē), *n.* a town in central Florida. 15,487.

kiss′ing bridge′, *Canadian* (*chiefly New Brunswick*). a covered bridge. [1775–85]

kiss′ing bug′, **1.** *Informal.* **a.** a person much given to kissing. **b.** an irresistible desire to kiss or be kissed. **2.** any of several assassin bugs that attack humans, sometimes inflicting painful bites. [1895–1900, *Amer.*]

kiss′ing cous′in, **1.** See under **kissing kin. 2.** something closely related or very similar: *a textile that is a kissing cousin to nylon.* [1935–40]

kiss′ing disease′. See **infectious mononucleosis.** [1960–65]

Kis·sin·ger (kis′ən jər), *n.* **Henry A(lfred),** born 1923, U.S. statesman, born in Germany: secretary of state 1973–77; Nobel peace prize 1973.

kiss′ing gate′, *Brit.* a gate hung in a narrow enclosure having the shape of a U or a V, allowing only one person to pass at a time.

kiss′ing gour′ami, a whitish labyrinth fish, *Helostoma temmincki*, found in southeastern Asia, noted for the habit of pressing its fleshy, protrusible lips against those of another: often kept in aquariums. [1930–35]

kiss′ing kin′, any more or less distant kin familiar enough to be greeted with a kiss, as a cousin **(kissing cousin).**

kiss•ing•ly (kis′ing lē), *adv.* lightly; gently. [1830–40; KISS + -ING[2] + -LY]

kiss′ of death′, a fatal or destructive relationship or action: *The support of the outlawed group was the kiss of death to the candidate.* [1945–50]

kiss-off (kis′ôf′, -of′), *n.* **1.** *Slang.* an act or instance of dismissing a person or thing: *The company is about to give you the kiss-off, so you'd better start looking for another job.* **2.** *Billiards, Pool.* kiss (def. 14). [1930–35; n. use of v. phrase *kiss off*]

kiss′ of peace′, **1.** (in certain Christian churches) a ceremonial greeting or embrace given as a token of Christian love and unity. **2.** a ceremonial kiss formerly given, esp. at a baptism or Eucharistic service, as a token of Christian love and unity. Also called **pax.** [1895–1900]

kist[1] (kist), *n. Scot. and North Eng.* **1.** a coffer; a money chest. **2.** any chestlike container; a box, trunk, or basket. **3.** a coffin, esp. a stone one; a sarcophagus. [1300–50; ME *kiste* < ON *kista* CHEST]

kist[2] (kist), *n.* cist[2].

Kist•na (kist′nə), *n.* former name of **Krishna** (def. 2).

kist•vaen (kist′vīn′), *n.* cist[2]. [1705–15; < Welsh *cist faen* stone coffin, equiv. to *cist* coffin (see CIST[2]) + *faen,* lenited form of *maen* stone; see MENHIR]

Ki•su•mu (kē so͞o′mo͞o), *n.* a city in W Kenya. 36,000.

kis•wah (kis′wä), *n. Islam.* a decorative veil draped over the walls of the Ka'ba, now made of black brocade embroidered in gold with inscriptions from the Koran. [1590–1600; < Ar]

Ki•swa•hi•li (kē′swä hē′lē), *n.* Swahili (def. 2). Also, **ki′-Swa•hi′li.**

kit[1] (kit), *n., v.,* **kit•ted, kit•ting.** —*n.* **1.** a set or collection of tools, supplies, instructional matter, etc., for a specific purpose: *a first-aid kit; a sales kit.* **2.** the case for containing these. **3.** such a case and its contents. **4.** a set of materials or parts from which something can be assembled: *a model car made from a kit.* **5.** *Informal.* a set, lot, or collection of things or persons. **6.** a wooden tub, pail, etc., usually circular. **7.** *Chiefly Brit.* a costume or outfit of clothing, esp. for a specific purpose: *ski kit; dancing kit; battle kit.* **8. kit and caboodle** or **boodle,** *Informal.* the whole lot of persons or things; all of something (often prec. by *whole*): *We took along the whole kit and caboodle in the station wagon.* —*v.t.* **9.** to package or make available in a kit: *a new model airplane that has just been kitted for the hobbyist.* **10.** *Chiefly Brit.* to outfit or equip (often fol. by *out* or *up*). [1325–75; ME *kyt, kitt* < MD *kitte* jug, tankard]

kit[2] (kit), *n.* a violin or rebec small enough to be carried in the pocket, used by dancing masters in the 17th and 18th centuries. Also called **pochette, sourdine.** [1510–20; orig. uncert.]

kit[3] (kit), *n.* **1.** kitten. **2.** a young fox, beaver, or other small furbearing animal. [1555–65; shortened form]

Kit (kit), *n.* **1.** a male given name, form of **Christopher.** **2.** a female given name, form of **Catherine** or **Katherine.**

Ki•ta•kyu•shu (kē tä′kyo͞o′sho͞o; *Eng.* ki tä′kē o͞o′-sho͞o), *n.* a seaport on N Kyushu, in S Japan: formed in 1963 by the merger of five cities **(Kokura, Moji, Tobata, Wakamatsu,** and **Yawata).** 1,065,084.

kit•am•bil•la (kit′əm bil′ə), *n.* kitembilla.

Ki•ta•sa•to (kē′tä sä′tô), *n.* **Shi•ba•sa•bu•ro** (shē bä′-sä bo͞o′rô), 1852–1931, Japanese bacteriologist.

kit′ bag′, a small bag or knapsack, as for a soldier. Also, **kit′bag′.** [1895–1900]

kit-cat (kit′kat′), *n.* any of a series of half-length portraits of members of the Kit-Cat Club that were painted by Sir Godfrey Kneller between 1702 and 1717, measure almost uniformly 28 × 36 in. (71 × 91 cm), characteristically portray the head, upper torso, and hands, and are now in the National Gallery, London. Also, **kit-kat.**

Kit′-Cat Club′ (kit′kat′), a club of Whig wits, painters, politicians, and men of letters, including Robert Walpole, John Vanbrugh, William Congreve, Joseph Addison, Richard Steele, and Godfrey Kneller, that flourished in London between 1703 and 1720. Also, **Kit-Kat Club.** [from *Kit* (as short for Christopher) *Cat(ling),* alleged to be the keeper of a pie-house where the club met (with play on *kit-cat,* var. of TIPCAT; see KIT[3], CAT[1])]

kitch•en (kich′ən), *n.* **1.** a room or place equipped for cooking. **2.** culinary department; cuisine: *This restaurant has a fine Italian kitchen.* **3.** the staff or equipment of a kitchen. —*adj.* **4.** of, pertaining to, or designed for use in a kitchen: *kitchen window; kitchen curtains.* **5.** employed in or assigned to a kitchen: *kitchen help.* **6.** of or resembling a pidginized language, esp. one used for communication between employers and servants or other employees who do not speak the same language. [bef. 1000; ME *kichene,* OE *cycene* << L *coquīna,* equiv. to *coqu(ere)* to cook + *-īna* -INE[1]; cf. CUISINE] —**kitch′en•less,** *adj.* —**kitch′en•y,** *adj.*

kitch′en cab′inet, **1.** a cupboard built into a kitchen or a chest of drawers for kitchen use, as for dishes and silverware. **2.** a group of unofficial advisers on whom a head of government appears to rely heavily. [1825–35, *Amer.*]

kitch•en•er (kich′ə nər), *n.* **1.** a person employed in, or in charge of, a kitchen. **2.** an elaborate kitchen stove. [1400–50; late ME; see KITCHEN, -ER[1]]

Kitch•e•ner (kich′ə nər), *n.* **1. Horatio Herbert** (*1st Earl Kitchener of Khartoum and of Broome*), 1850–1916, English field marshal and statesman. **2.** a city in S Ontario, in SE Canada. 131,870.

CONCISE ETYMOLOGY KEY: <, descended or borrowed from; >, whence; b., blend of, blended; c., cognate with; cf., compare; deriv., derivative; equiv., equivalent; imit., imitative; obl., oblique; r., replacing; s., stem; sp., spelling, spelled; resp., respelling, respelled; trans., translation; ?, origin unknown; *, unattested; ‡, probably earlier than. See the full key inside the front cover.

kitch•en•ette (kich′ə net′), *n.* a very small, compact kitchen. Also, **kitch′en•et′.** [1905–10, *Amer.;* KITCHEN + -ETTE]

kitch′en gar′den, a garden where vegetables, herbs, and fruit are grown for one's own use. [1570–80] —**kitch′en gar′dener.**

kitch•en•maid (kich′ən mād′), *n.* a female servant who assists the cook. [1540–50; KITCHEN + MAID]

kitch′en match′, a wooden friction match with a large head, used esp. for igniting gas ovens or burners. [1950–55]

kitch′en mid′den, a mound consisting of shells of edible mollusks and other refuse, marking the site of a prehistoric human habitation. [1860–65; trans. of Dan *kökkenmödding*]

kitch′en police′, *Mil.* **1.** soldiers detailed by roster or as punishment to assist in kitchen duties. **2.** duty as assistant to the cooks. *Abbr.:* K.P. [1915–20]

kitch′en sink′, the final item imaginable on any extensive list of usually disparate items: *He packed everything for his trip except the kitchen sink.* [1870–75, for literal sense]

kitch•en-sink (kich′ən singk′), *adj.* marked by an indiscriminate and omnivorous use of elements: *a kitchen-sink approach to moviemaking.* [1940–45]

kitch′en tea′, *Australian.* a prewedding party to which guests bring an item of kitchenware or other gifts for the bride; shower. Also called **shower tea.** [1945–50]

kitch•en•ware (kich′ən wâr′), *n.* cooking equipment or utensils. [1925–30; KITCHEN + WARE[1]]

kite[1] (kīt), *n., v.,* **kit•ed, kit•ing.** —*n.* **1.** a light frame covered with some thin material, to be flown in the wind at the end of a long string. **2.** any of several small birds of the hawk family Accipitridae that have long, pointed wings, feed on insects, carrion, reptiles, rodents, and birds, and are noted for their graceful, gliding flight. Cf. **black kite, swallow-tailed kite, white-tailed kite.** **3.** *Naut.* See **flying kite.** **4.** *Finance.* **a.** a check drawn against uncollected or insufficient funds, as for redepositing, with the intention of creating a false balance in the account by taking advantage of the time lapse required for collection. **b.** a check whose amount has been raised by forgery before cashing. **5.** a person who preys on others; sharper. —*v.i.* **6.** *Informal.* to fly or move with a rapid or easy motion like that of a kite. **7.** to obtain money or credit through kites. —*v.t.* **8.** to employ (a check or the like) as a kite; to cash or pass (a kite, forged check, etc.). [bef. 900 for def. 2; 1655–65 for def. 1; ME *kyte,* OE *cȳta* kite, bittern; akin to G *Kauz* owl] —**kit′•er,** *n.* —**kite′like′,** *adj.*

kite[2] (kīt), *n. Scot. and North Eng.* kyte.

kite•fly•ing (kīt′flī′ing), *n.* **1.** an act or instance of flying a kite. **2.** the sport or hobby of flying kites. Also called **kiting.** [1795–1805; KITE[1] + FLYING] —**kite′fli′•er, kite′fly′er,** *n.*

kit•em•bil•la (kit′əm bil′ə), *n.* a shrub or small tree, *Dovyalis hebecarpa,* of India and Sri Lanka, having velvety, maroon-purple fruit. Also, **kitambilla.** Also called **Ceylon gooseberry.** [< Sinhalese *kätämbilla*]

kite′ wind′er (wīn′dər), a triangular winder on a staircase.

kit′ fox′, either of two small gray foxes, *Vulpes macrotis* and *V. velox,* found on plains and in open, sandy areas of western North America, commercially valuable for their fur. [1795–1805, *Amer.;* prob. special use of KIT[3]]

kith (kith), *n.* **1.** acquaintances, friends, neighbors, or the like; persons living in the same general locality and forming a more or less cohesive group. **2.** kindred. **3.** a group of people living in the same area and forming a culture with a common language, customs, economy, etc., usually endogamous. [bef. 900; ME; OE *cȳth,* earlier *cȳththu* kinship, knowledge, equiv. to *cūth* COUTH[2] + *-thu* -TH[1]; akin to Goth *kunthi,* G *Kunde* knowledge]

kith′ and kin′, acquaintances and relatives. [1350–1400; ME]

kithara

kith•a•ra (kith′ər ə), *n.* a musical instrument of ancient Greece consisting of an elaborate wooden soundbox having two arms connected by a yoke to which the upper ends of the strings are attached. Also, **cithara.** [1350–1400; ME < Gk *kithára* lyre; cf. GUITAR, ZITHER]

kithe (kīth), *v.t., v.i.,* **kithed, kith•ing.** *Scot. and North Eng.* **1.** to make known by action; show; demonstrate; prove. **2.** *Obs.* to make known by words; announce; declare; proclaim. Also, **kythe.** [bef. 900; ME *kithen,* OE *cȳthan* to make known, deriv. of *cūth* COUTH[2]]

Kit•i•mat (kit′ə mat′), *n.* a seaport on the coast of W British Columbia, in SW Canada. 12,462.

kit•ing (kī′ting), *n.* **1.** kiteflying. **2.** See **hang gliding.** [1860–65; KITE[1] + -ING[1]]

kit-kat (kit′kat′), *n.* kit-cat.

Kit′-Kat Club′ (kit′kat′). See **Kit-Cat Club.**

kit•ling (kit′ling), *n. Brit. Dial.* the young of any animal, esp. a young cat; kitten; kit. [1250–1300; ME *kiteling* < ON *ketlingr.* See CAT[1], -LING[1]]

kitsch (kich), *n.* something of tawdry design, appearance, or content created to appeal to popular or undiscriminating taste. [1925–30; < G, deriv. of *kitschen* to throw together (a work of art)] —**kitsch′y,** *adj.*

Ki Tse (gē′ dzu′), 12th-century B.C., legendary Chinese founder of Korea. Also, **Chi-tsê, Chi-tzŭ.**

kit•tel (kit′l), *n. Yiddish.* a white robe used by Jews, esp. Orthodox Jews, as a ceremonial garment for men and as a burial shroud for both sexes: worn during worship on Rosh Hashanah and Yom Kippur, by a bridegroom during the wedding ceremony, and by the leader of the Seder on Passover. [Yiddish *kitl*]

kit•ten (kit′n), *n.* **1.** a young cat. —*v.t., v.i.* **2.** (of cats) to give birth; bear. [1350–1400; ME *kitoun,* appar. b. *kiteling* KITLING and MF *chitoun,* var. of *chaton* kitten] —**kit′ten•like′,** *adj.*

kit•ten•ish (kit′n ish), *adj.* **1.** coyly playful. **2.** like or in the manner of a kitten. [1745–55; KITTEN + -ISH[1]] —**kit′ten•ish•ly,** *adv.* —**kit′ten•ish•ness,** *n.*

Kit•tie (kit′ē), *n.* a female given name, form of **Katherine** or **Catherine.**

Kit•ti•ka•chorn (kē′tē kä chôrn′), *n.* **Tha•nom** (thä-nôm′), born 1911, Thai army officer and statesman: premier 1963–73.

kit•ti•wake (kit′ē wāk′), *n.* either of two small, pearl-gray gulls of the genus *Rissa,* the black-legged *R. tridactyla* of the North Atlantic and the red-legged and red-billed *R. brevirostris,* of the Bering Sea, both nesting on narrow cliff ledges and having a rudimentary hind toe. [1655–65; imit.]

kit•tle (kit′l), *v.,* **-tled, -tling,** *adj.,* **-tler, -tlest.** *Brit. Dial.* —*v.t.* **1.** to tickle with the fingers; agitate or stir, as with a spoon. **2.** to excite or rouse (a person), esp. by flattery or strong words. —*adj.* **3.** ticklish; fidgety. **4.** requiring skill or caution; precarious. [1475–85; earlier *kytylle, ketil* (cf. ME *kitellinge* (ger.), late OE *kitelung*); c. MHG *kützeln;* akin to ON *kitla,* G *kitzeln* to tickle]

Kitt′ Peak′ Na′tional Observ′atory, the U.S. national astronomical observatory near Tucson, Arizona, having over fifteen telescopes, including a 158-in. (4-m) reflecting telescope.

Kit•tredge (ki′trij), *n.* **George Lyman,** 1860–1941, U.S. literary scholar, philologist, and educator.

kit•ty[1] (kit′ē), *n., pl.* **-ties.** **1.** a kitten. **2.** a pet name for a cat. [1710–20; KITT(EN) + -Y[2]]

kit•ty[2] (kit′ē), *n., pl.* **-ties.** **1.** a pool or reserve of money, often collected from a number of persons or sources and designated for a particular purpose specified by the contributors. **2.** *Cards.* **a.** a pool into which players in a game put a certain amount of their winnings for some special purpose, as to pay for refreshments. **b.** the pot, or a special pot, for the collection of forfeits or payments for certain high hands. **c.** widow (def. 2). [1815–25; KIT[1] + -Y[2]]

Kit•ty (kit′ē), *n.* a female given name, form of **Katherine** or **Catherine.**

kit•ty-cor•nered (kit′ē kôr′nərd), *adj., adv. Chiefly Northern and Western U.S.* cater-cornered. Also, **kit′•ty-cor′ner.** [1885–90]

Kit•ty•hawk (kit′ē hôk′), *n.* a village in NE North Carolina: Wright brothers' airplane flight 1903.

Ki•twe (kē′twä), *n.* a city in N Zambia. 350,000.

Kiung•chow (kyo͝ong′chō′, -chou′; *Chin.* gyo͝ong′jō′), *n. Older Spelling.* Qiongzhou.

Kiung•shan (kyo͝ong′shän′; *Chin.* gyo͝ong′shän′), *n. Older Spelling.* Qiongshan.

Kiu•shu (kē o͞o′sho͞o; *Japn.* kyo͞o′sho͞o), *n.* Kyushu.

ki•va (kē′və), *n.* a large chamber, often wholly or partly underground, in a Pueblo Indian village, used for religious ceremonies and other purposes. [1870–75, *Amer.;* < Hopi *kíva* (*ki-* house + unidentified element)]

kiv•er (kiv′ər), *v.t., v.i., n. New England, Midland, and Southern U.S. Dial.* cover.

Ki•wa•nis (ki wä′nis), *n.* an organization founded in 1915 for the promulgation of higher ideals in business, industrial, and professional life. [allegedly < AmerInd: to make oneself known] —**Ki•wa′ni•an,** *n.*

ki•wi (kē′wē), *n., pl.* **-wis.** **1.** any of several flightless, ratite birds of the genus *Apteryx,* of New Zealand, allied to the extinct moas. **2.** Also called **Chinese gooseberry.** the egg-sized, edible berry of the Chinese gooseberry, having fuzzy brownish skin and slightly tart green flesh. **3.** *Slang.* **a.** a member of an air service, as in World War I, who is confined to ground duty. **b.** a former pilot or member of a flight crew. **4.** *Informal.* a New Zealander. [1825–35; < Maori]

kiwi, *Apteryx australis,* length to 28 in. (71 cm); bill 6 in. (15 cm)

ki•yas (kē yäs′), *n. Islam.* qiyas.

ki•yi (kē′yē), *n.* a small whitefish, *Coregonus kiyi,* found in the deeper waters of the Great Lakes. [1895–1900, *Amer.;* from the specific epithet, alleged to be a local term for the fish, used by Lake Michigan fishermen; < ?]

ki•yoo•dle (kī yo͞od′l), *n. Gulf States.* a worthless dog; mongrel. [see KYOODLE]

Ki•zil Ir•mak (ki zil′ ēr mäk′), a river flowing N through central Turkey to the Black Sea. 600 mi. (965 km) long.

Ki•zil Kum (ki zil′ ko͞om′). See **Kyzyl Kum.**

Kjö·len (chœ′lən), *n.* a mountain range between Norway and Sweden. Highest peak, Mt. Kebnekaise, 7005 ft. (2135 m).

K.J.V., King James Version.

K.K.K., See **Ku Klux Klan.** Also, **KKK**

KKt, *Chess.* king's knight.

KKtP, *Chess.* king's knight's pawn.

kl, kiloliter; kiloliters. Also, **kl.**

kla·ber·jass (klä′bər yäs′), *n.* a card game played with a 32-card pack, made by removing all cards below the sevens from a regular 52-card pack, in which scoring values are assigned to certain cards taken in tricks, to sequences in the same suit, to the king and queen of trumps, and to the last trick. [1890–95; < G *Klaberjass, Klaberjasch* << D *klaverjas,* orig. a trump card, the jack of clubs, in the game of *jas* (*klaver(en)* clubs, lit., CLOVER + *jas,* perh. special use of *Jas,* short for *Jasper* a man's name)]

Kla·bund (klä bo͝ont′), *n.* (*Alfred Henschke*) 1890?–1928, German poet, novelist, and playwright.

Kla·gen·furt (klä′gən fo͝ort′), *n.* a city in S Austria. 86,303.

Klai·pe·da (klī′pe dä; *Eng.* klī′pi də), *n.* **1.** a seaport in NW Lithuania, on the Baltic. 204,000. **2.** a former German territory including this seaport: now a part of Lithuania. 1092 sq. mi. (2828 sq. km). German, **Memel.**

Klam·ath (klam′əth), *n.* a river flowing from SW Oregon through NW California into the Pacific. 250 mi. (405 km) long.

Klam·ath (klam′əth), *n., pl.* **-aths,** (*esp. collectively*) **-ath.** a member of an American Indian people belonging to the Lutuamian group and located in southern Oregon.

Klam′ath Falls′, a city in SW Oregon. 16,661.

Klam′ath Lakes′, two lakes that drain into the Klamath River: one lake **(Upper Klamath Lake)** is in SW Oregon, and the other **(Lower Klamath Lake)** is in N California.

Klam′ath weed′, the St.-John's-wort, *Hypericum perforatum.* [1920–25, *Amer.*; named after the KLAMATH River]

Klan (klan), *n.* **1.** See **Ku Klux Klan. 2.** a chapter of the Ku Klux Klan. —**Klan′ism,** *n.*

Klans·man (klanz′mən), *n., pl.* **-men.** a member of the Ku Klux Klan. [1900–05, *Amer.*; KLAN + 's[1] + MAN[1]]

Klapp·vi·sier (kläp′vi zēr′), *n. Armor.* a visor attached by a hinge at the top: used on basinets of the 14th century. [< G: flap visor]

klatsch (kläch, klach), *n.* a casual gathering of people, esp. for refreshments and informal conversation: *a sewing klatsch.* Also, **klatch.** [1950–55; < G *Klatsch* chitchat, gossip]

Klau·sen·burg (klou′zən bo͝ork′), *n.* German name of **Cluj-Napoca.**

klav·ern (klav′ərn), *n.* **1.** a local branch of the Ku Klux Klan. **2.** a meeting place of the Ku Klux Klan. [1920–25; KL(AN) + (C)AVERN]

kla·vier (klə vēr′, klav′ē ər, klä′vē-), *n.* clavier[2].

klax·on (klak′sən), *n.* a loud electric horn, formerly used on automobiles, trucks, etc., and now often used as a warning signal. Also, **claxon.** [1905–10, *Amer.*; formerly trademark]

klea·gle (klē′gəl), *n.* an official of the Ku Klux Klan. [1920–25, *Amer.*; KL(AN) + EAGLE]

Klé·ber (klā bɛʀ′), *n.* **Jean Bap·tiste** (zhäɴ bᴀ tēst′), 1753–1800, French general.

Klebs (klebz; *Ger.* kläps), *n.* **Ed·win** (ed′win; *Ger.* et′vēn), 1834–1913, German pathologist and bacteriologist.

kleb·si·el·la (kleb′zē el′ə, klep′sē-), *n. Bacteriol.* any of several rod-shaped, aerobic bacteria of the genus *Klebsiella,* certain species of which, as *K. pneumoniae,* are found in the respiratory, intestinal, and genitourinary tracts of humans and animals and are sometimes pathogenic. [< NL (1885), after E. KLEBS; see -ELLA]

Klebs′-Löf′fler bacil′lus (klebz′lef′lər; *Ger.* kläps′lœf′lər), a bacterium, *Corynebacterium diphtheriae,* which causes diphtheria. [1890–95; named after E. KLEBS and F. A. J. LÖFFLER]

Klee (klā), *n.* **Paul** (poul; *Eng.* pôl), 1879–1940, Swiss painter and etcher.

Kleen·ex (klē′neks), *Trademark.* a brand name for a soft, disposable paper tissue, used esp. as a handkerchief.

Klei·ber (klī′bəʀ), *n.* **E·rich** (ā′ʀɪᴋʜ), 1890–1956, Austrian orchestra conductor.

Kleine′-Le·vin′ syn′drome (klīn′lə vin′), *Pathol.* prolonged episodes of excessive sleepiness often accompanied by overeating, hallucinations, and electroencephalogram changes, usually beginning in adolescence. [after German psychologist Willi *Kleine* (fl. 1925) and U.S. psychologist Max *Levin* (born 1901), who independently described it in the 1920's]

Klein (klīn), *n.* **Fe·lix** (fē′liks; *Ger.* fā′liks), 1849–1925, German mathematician.

Klein′ bot′tle, *Geom.* a one-sided figure consisting of a tapered tube the narrow end of which is bent back, run through the side of the tube, and flared to join the wide end, thereby allowing any two points on the figure to be joined by an unbroken line. [1940–45; named after F. KLEIN]

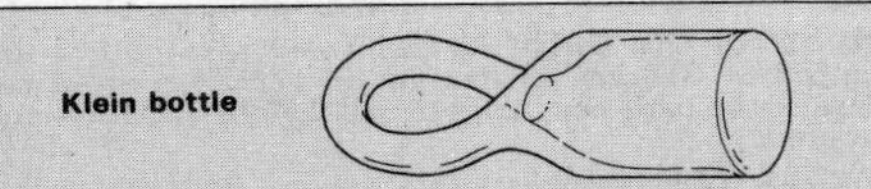

Klein bottle

Klein·i·an (klī′nē ən), *adj.* referring to the theories formulated by Austrian child psychiatrist Melanie Klein (1882–1960). [1950–55; *Klein* + -IAN]

Kleist (klīst), *n.* **(Bernd) Hein·rich (Wil·helm) von** (bɛʀnt hīn′ʀɪᴋʜ vil′helm fən), 1777–1811, German poet, dramatist, and story writer. —**Kleist′i·an,** *adj.*

Klem·pe·rer (klem′pər ər), *n.* **Otto,** 1885–1973, German orchestra conductor.

Kle·o·pa·tra (klē′ə pa′trə, -pä′-, -pā′-), *n.* Cleopatra (def. 2).

klepht (kleft), *n.* a Greek or Albanian brigand, exalted in the war of Greek independence as a patriotic robber; guerrilla. [1810–20; < ModGk *kléphtēs,* var. of ModGk, Gk *kléptēs* thief, rogue; see KLEPTOMANIA] —**kleph′tic,** *adj.*

klep·to (klep′tō), *n., pl.* **-tos,** *adj. Slang.* kleptomaniac. [1955–60; by shortening]

klep·to·ma·ni·a (klep′tə mā′nē ə, -mān′yə), *n. Psychol.* an irresistible impulse to steal, stemming from emotional disturbance rather than economic need. Also, **cleptomania.** [1820–30; *klepto-* (comb. form of Gk *kléptēs* thief) + -MANIA]

klep·to·ma·ni·ac (klep′tə mā′nē ak′), *n. Psychol.* **1.** a person who has kleptomania. —*adj.* **2.** of, pertaining to, or characteristic of kleptomania or a kleptomaniac. Also, **cleptomaniac.** [1860–65; KLEPTOMANI(A) + -AC]

klesh·a (klesh′ə), *n. Yoga.* any of the five hindrances to enlightenment, which are ignorance or avidya, egocentricity, attachments, aversions, and the instinctive will to live. [< Skt *kleśa* lit., suffering, distress]

Kle·ve (klā′və), *n.* German name of **Cleves.**

klez·mer (klez′mər), *n., pl.* **klez·mo·rim** (klez′mə rēm′). **1.** a Jewish folk musician traditionally performing in a small band. **2.** Also, **klez′mer mu′sic.** the type of music performed by such musicians. [< Yiddish]

klick (klik), *n. Slang.* click[2]. Also, **klik.**

klieg′ light′, a powerful type of arc light once widely used in motion-picture studios. [1925–30, *Amer.*; named after the brothers J. H. *Kliegl* (1869–1959) and Anton *Kliegl* (1872–1927), German-born American inventors; final *l* of *Kliegl* prob. taken as initial *l* of *light*]

Klimt (klimt), *n.* **Gus·tav** (go͝os′täf), 1862–1918, Austrian painter.

K-line (kā′līn′), *n. Physics.* one of a series of lines **(K-series)** in the x-ray spectrum of an atom corresponding to radiation **(K-radiation)** produced by the transition of an electron to the K-shell. [1895–1900]

Kline (klīn), *n.* **Franz (Jo·sef)** (jō′zəf, -səf), 1910–62, U.S. painter.

Kline′fel′ter's syn′drome (klīn′fel tərz), *Pathol.* an abnormal condition in which at least one extra X chromosome is present in a male: characterized by reduced or absent sperm production, small testicles, and in some cases enlarged breasts. [named after Harry Fitch *Klinefelter* (born 1912), U.S. physician, co-author of a description of the syndrome]

Kline′ test′, *Med.* a test for syphilis in which the formation of a microscopic precipitate in a mixture of the patient's serum and an antigen indicates a syphilitic condition. Cf. **Kahn test.** [1925–30; named after Benjamin S. *Kline* (1886–1968), American developer of test]

kli·no·tax·is (klī′nə tak′sis), *n. Biol.* a wavering side-to-side motion of the head occurring as an organism moves forward in response to a source of stimulation, caused by the alternating reaction of sensory receptors on either side of the body. Cf. **tropotaxis.** [1935–40; < Gk *klīn(ein)* to cause to lean (cf. CLINO-) + -O- + -TAXIS]

klip·pe (klip′ə), *n.* **1.** *Numis.* a square or lozenge-shaped coin. **2.** *Geol.* an erosional outlier of a nappe. [< G < Sw *klippa* to cut; see CLIP[1]]

klip·spring·er (klip′spring′ər), *n.* a small, agile African antelope, *Oreotragus oreotragus,* of mountainous regions from the Cape of Good Hope to Ethiopia. [1775–85; < Afrik: lit., rock-springer]

klis·mos (kliz′mos), *n., pl.* **-moi** (-moi). an ancient Greek chair, having a deep top rail curving forward from the back, and having legs curving upward and inward: imitated during various classical revivals, esp. in the early 19th century. [< Gk, akin to *klī́nein* to LEAN[1]]

klis·ter (klis′tər), *n.* a sticky wax for use on skis, as for slopes where the snow is excessively wet. [1935–40; < Norw < MLG; c. G *Kleister* paste]

Klon·dike (klon′dīk), *n.* **1.** a region of the Yukon territory in NW Canada: gold rush 1897–98. **2.** a river in this region, flowing into the Yukon. 90 mi. (145 km) long. **3.** (*l.c.*) *Cards.* a variety of solitaire.

klong (klông, klong), *n.* (in Thailand) a canal. [1895–1900; < Thai *khlɔːng* canal, watercourse]

kloof (klo͞of), *n.* (in South Africa) a deep glen; ravine. [1725–35; < Afrik; akin to CLEAVE]

Klop·stock (klôp′shtôk′), *n.* **Frie·drich Gott·lieb** (frē′dʀɪᴋʜ gôt′lēp), 1724–1803, German poet.

klös·se (klā′sə, kläs; *Ger.* klœ′sə), *n.pl. German Cookery.* dumplings. Also, **kloes′se.** [< G, pl. of *Kloss* ball of dough, dumpling]

kluck (kluk), *v.i., v.t., n.* cluck[1].

Kluck (klo͝ok), *n.* **A·le·xan·der von** (ä′le ksän′dəʀ fən), 1846–1934, German general.

Kluck·hohn (kluk′hōn), *n.* **Clyde (Kay Ma·ben)** (mā′bən), 1905–60, American anthropologist.

kludge (klo͞oj), *n. Computers Slang.* a software or hardware configuration that, while inelegant, inefficient, clumsy, or patched together, succeeds in solving a specific problem or performing a particular task. Also, **kluge.** [1960–65; expressive coinage]

klunk·er (klung′kər), *n. Slang.* clunker (def. 2).

klutz (kluts), *n. Slang.* **1.** a clumsy, awkward person. **2.** a stupid or foolish person; blockhead. [1965–70, *Amer.*; < Yiddish *klots* lit., wooden beam < MHG *kloc* (G *Klotz*)]

klutz·y (klut′sē), *adj.,* **klutz·i·er, klutz·i·est.** *Slang.* **1.** clumsy; awkward: *If you weren't so klutzy you wouldn't have dropped it.* **2.** unwieldy; bulky or awkward: *a klutzy pair of boots.* **3.** inept or thoughtless; boneheaded: *a klutzy remark.* [1960–65, *Amer.*; KLUTZ + -Y[1]] —**klutz′i·ness,** *n.*

Klü′ver-Bu′cy syn′drome (klo͞o′vər byo͞o′sē), *Psychiatry.* a syndrome caused by bilateral injury to the temporal lobes and characterized by memory defect, hypersexuality, excessive oral behavior, and diminished fear reactions. [after German-born U.S. neurologist Heinrich *Klüver* (1898–1979) and U.S. neurologist Paul Clancy *Bucy* (born 1904), who jointly described it in 1938]

Kly·don·o·graph (klī don′ə graf′, -gräf′), *Trademark.* a brand name for an instrument that photographically records a surge of voltage, as in a power line.

Klys·tron (klis′tron, klī′stron, -strən), *Trademark.* a brand name for a vacuum tube containing an electron gun, a resonator that changes the velocity of the electron beam in accordance with a signal **(buncher resonator),** a drift tube in which the electron velocity does not change, another resonator that abstracts energy from the electron beam **(catcher resonator),** and an electrode that collects the electrons **(collector electrode).** It has several ultra-high-frequency applications. Cf. **resonator** (def. 4).

km, kilometer; kilometers.

km., **1.** kilometer; kilometers. **2.** kingdom.

kMc, kilomegacycle; kilomegacycles.

K meson, *Physics.* kaon. Also, **K-me·son** (kā′mē′zon, -son, -mez′on, -mes′on). [1950–55]

km/sec, kilometers per second.

KN, *Chess.* king's knight.

kn, knot; knots.

kn., kronen.

knack (nak), *n.* **1.** a special skill, talent, or aptitude: *He had a knack for saying the right thing.* **2.** a clever or adroit way of doing something. **3.** a trick or ruse. **4.** a sharp, cracking sound. **5.** *Archaic.* a knickknack; trinket. [1325–75; ME: trick; perh. same word as *knak* sharp-sounding blow, rap, cracking noise (imit.)] —**Syn. 1.** aptness, facility, dexterity.

knäck·e·bröd (nek′ə bro͞od′, -bred′, knek′-; *Sw.* knek′ə bʀœd′), *n.* flat, thin, brittle unleavened rye bread. [< Sw, equiv. to *knäcke* to break + *bröd* BREAD]

knack·er (nak′ər), *n. Brit.* **1.** a person who buys animal carcasses or slaughters useless livestock for a knackery or rendering works. **2.** a person who buys and dismembers old houses, ships, etc., to salvage usable parts, selling the rest as scrap. **3.** *Dial.* an old, sick, or useless farm animal, esp. a horse. **4.** *Obs.* a harness maker; a saddler. [1565–75; *knack* (< Scand; cf. Icel *hnakkr* nape of the neck, saddle) + -ER[1]]

knack·ered (nak′ərd), *adj. Brit. Slang.* exhausted; very tired: *He is really knackered after work.* [1885–90; *knacker* to tire (attenuation of earlier sense "to kill"; cf. KNACKER def. 1) + -ED[2]]

knack·er·y (nak′ə rē), *n. Brit.* See **rendering works.** [1865–70; KNACK(ER) + -ERY]

knack·wurst (näk′wûrst, -wo͝orst), *n.* a short, thick, highly seasoned sausage. Also, **knockwurst.** [1935–40; < G, equiv. to *knack(en)* to crack, break + *Wurst* sausage. Cf. KNACK]

knag·gy (nag′ē), *adj.,* **-gi·er, -gi·est.** knotty; rough with knots. [1350–1400; ME *knag* spur, projection, peg (c. G *Knagge* knot, peg) + -Y[1]]

knai·del (knād′l), *n., pl.* **knai·dlach** (knād′ləᴋʜ, -läᴋʜ). *Jewish Cookery.* a dumpling, esp. a small ball of matzo meal, eggs, and salt, often mixed with another foodstuff, as ground almonds or grated potato, usually served in soup. [1950–55; < Yiddish *kneydl* dumpling; cf. MHG *knödel* lump, ovary of a flower, G *Knödel* dumpling]

knap[1] (nap), *n. Brit. Dial.* a crest or summit of a small hill. [bef. 1000; ME; OE *cnæpp* top, summit; c. ON *knappr* knob]

knap[2] (nap), *v.i., v.t.,* **knapped, knap·ping.** *Chiefly Brit. Dial.* **1.** to strike smartly; rap. **2.** to break off abruptly. **3.** to chip or become chipped, as a flint or stone. **4.** to bite suddenly or quickly. [1425–75; late ME; c. D *knap* (n.), *knappen* (v.) crack; orig. imit.] —**knap′·per,** *n.*

knap·sack (nap′sak′), *n.* a canvas, nylon, or leather bag for clothes, food, and other supplies, carried on the back by soldiers, hikers, etc. [1595–1605; < LG *knappsack,* equiv. to *knapp* a bite (of food) + *sack* SACK[1]; cf.

CONCISE PRONUNCIATION KEY: *act, cāpe, dâre, pärt; set, ēqual; if, īce; ox, ōver, ôrder, oil, bo͝ok, bo͞ot, out; up, ûrge; child; sing; shoe; thin, that;* zh as in *treasure.* ə = *a* as in *alone, e* as in *system, i* as in *easily, o* as in *gallop, u* as in *circus;* ᵊ as in *fire* (fīᵊr), *hour* (ouᵊr). l and n can serve as syllabic consonants, as in *cradle* (krād′l), and *button* (but′n). See the full key inside the front cover.

dial. E *knap* to snap up, eat greedily] —**knap′sacked′,** *adj.*

knap′sack prob′lem, *Math.* the problem of determining which numbers from a given collection of numbers have been added together to yield a specific sum: used in cryptography to encipher (and sometimes decipher) messages. [so called because the problem is similar to determining what packages are in a closed knapsack when the weights of the individual packages and the filled knapsack are known]

knap•weed (nap′wēd′), *n.* any composite plant of the genus *Centaurea,* esp. the weedy *C. nigra,* having rose-purple flowers set on a dark-colored, knoblike bract. Also called **hardheads, Spanish button.** [1400–50; late ME *knopwed.* See KNOP, WEED[1]]

knar (när), *n.* a knot on a tree or in wood. [1200–50; ME *knarre;* c. D *knar,* LG *knarre*] —**knarred, knar′ry,** *adj.*

knave (nāv), *n.* **1.** an unprincipled, untrustworthy, or dishonest person. **2.** *Cards.* jack[1] (def. 2). **3.** *Archaic.* **a.** a male servant. **b.** a man of humble position. [bef. 1000; ME; OE *cnafa;* c. G *Knabe* boy; akin to ON *knapi* page, boy]
—**Syn. 1.** blackguard, villain, scamp, scapegrace. KNAVE, RASCAL, ROGUE, SCOUNDREL are disparaging terms applied to persons considered base, dishonest, or worthless. KNAVE, which formerly meant merely a boy or servant, in modern use emphasizes baseness of nature and intention: *a dishonest and swindling knave.* RASCAL suggests shrewdness and trickery in dishonesty: *a plausible rascal.* A ROGUE is a worthless fellow who sometimes preys extensively upon the community by fraud: *photographs of criminals in a rogues' gallery.* A SCOUNDREL is a blackguard and rogue of the worst sort: *a thorough scoundrel.* RASCAL and ROGUE are often used affectionately or humorously (*an entertaining rascal; a saucy rogue*), but KNAVE and SCOUNDREL are not. —**Ant.** hero.

knav•er•y (nā′və rē), *n., pl.* **-er•ies. 1.** action or practice characteristic of a knave. **2.** unprincipled, untrustworthy, or dishonest dealing; trickery. **3.** a knavish act or practice. [1520–30; KNAVE + -ERY]

knav•ish (nā′vish), *adj.* **1.** like or befitting a knave; untrustworthy; dishonest. **2.** *Archaic.* waggish; roguish; mischievous. [1350–1400; ME *knavyssh.* See KNAVE, -ISH[1]] —**knav′ish•ly,** *adv.* —**knav′ish•ness,** *n.*

knawel (nôl), *n.* any of several plants belonging to the genus *Scleranthus,* of the pink family, native to Eurasia, esp. *S. annuus,* a common, low-growing weed that forms dense mats. [1570–80; < G *Knauel, Kneuel* knotweed]

knead (nēd), *v.t.* **1.** to work (dough, clay, etc.) into a uniform mixture by pressing, folding, and stretching. **2.** to manipulate by similar movements, as the body in a massage. **3.** to make by kneading: *to knead bread.* **4.** to make kneading movements with: *She kneaded her fist into her palm.* [bef. 950; ME *kneden,* OE *cnedan;* c. G *kneten,* D *kneden*] —**knead′a•ble,** *adj.* —**knead′a•bil′i•ty,** *n.* —**knead′er,** *n.* —**knead′ing•ly,** *adv.*

knead′ed but′ter. See **beurre manié.**

knee (nē), *n., v.,* **kneed, knee•ing.** —*n.* **1.** *Anat.* the joint of the leg that allows for movement between the femur and tibia and is protected by the patella; the central area of the leg between the thigh and the lower leg. See diag. under **skeleton. 2.** *Zool.* the corresponding joint or region in the hind leg of a quadruped; stifle. **3.** a joint or region likened to this but not anatomically homologous with it, as the tarsal joint of a bird, the carpal joint in the forelimb of the horse or cow, etc. **4.** the part of a garment covering the knee. **5.** something resembling a bent knee, esp. a rigid or braced angle between two framing members. **6.** Also called **hip, shoulder.** *Furniture.* the inward curve toward the top of a cabriole leg. **7.** *Building Trades.* **a.** the junction of the top and either of the uprights of a bent. **b.** a curved member for reinforcing the junction of two pieces meeting at an angle. **8.** Also called **kneeler.** a stone cut to follow a sharp return angle. **9. bring someone to his** or **her knees,** to force someone into submission or compliance. **10. cut (someone) off at the knees,** to squelch or humiliate (a person) suddenly and thoroughly: *The speaker cut the heckler off at the knees.* **11. on one's** or **its knees, a.** in a supplicatory position or manner: *I came to him on my knees for the money.* **b.** in a desperate or declining condition: *The country's economy is on its knees.* —*v.t.* **12.** to strike or touch with the knee. **13.** to secure (a structure, as a bent) with a knee. —*v.i.* **14.** *Obs.* to go down on the knees; kneel. [bef. 900; ME *cneo,* OE *cnēo(w);* c. G, D *knie,* ON *knē,* Goth *kniu,* L *genu,* Gk *góny,* Skt *jānu* knee]

knee′ ac′tion, 1. *Auto.* a form of suspension for the front wheels of a vehicle permitting each wheel to rise and fall independently of the other. **2.** limited and temporary bending at a joint provided to relieve a structure or machine part under stress. [1865–70, for an earlier sense]

knee′ bend′, a physical exercise in which a person starts from an erect position, moves to a squatting position, and returns to the original position without using the hands to support the body. [1940–45]

knee′ brace′, *Building Trades.* a diagonal member for bracing the angle between two joined members, as a stud or column and a joist or rafter, being joined to each partway along its length. [1910–15]

knee′ breech′es, breeches (def. 1). [1825–35]

knee•cap (nē′kap′), *n., v.,* **-capped, -cap•ping.** —*n.* **1.** the patella. **2.** a protective covering, usually knitted, for the knee. —*v.t.* **3.** to cripple (a person) by shooting in the knee: *Terrorists were kneecapping prospective jurors.* [1650–60; KNEE + CAP[1]] —**knee′cap′per,** *n.*

knee′ cop′, *Armor.* poleyn.

knee-deep (nē′dēp′), *adj.* **1.** reaching the knees: *knee-deep mud.* **2.** submerged or covered up to the knees: *knee-deep in water.* **3.** deeply embroiled; enmeshed; involved: *knee-deep in trouble.* [1525–35]

knee-high (*adj.* nē′hī′; *n.* nē′hī′), *adj.* **1.** as high as the knees. —*n.* **2. knee-highs.** Also, **knee′ highs′, knee′-hi's′, knee′ his′.** socks, stockings, or boots that cover the lower legs to just below the knees. [1735–45, *Amer.*]

knee•hole (nē′hōl′), *n.* an open space for the knees and legs, as under a desk. [1860–65; KNEE + HOLE]

knee′ jerk′, a reflex extension of the leg, caused by contraction of the quadriceps, resulting from a sharp tap on the patellar tendon; patellar reflex. [1875–80]

knee-jerk (nē′jûrk′), *adj.* **1.** of or pertaining to a knee-jerk. **2.** *Informal.* reacting according to a certain habitual manner; unthinking: *a knee-jerk liberal.* [1895–1900]

kneel (nēl), *v.,* **knelt** or **kneeled, kneel•ing,** *n.* —*v.i.* **1.** to go down or rest on the knees or a knee. —*n.* **2.** the action or position of kneeling. [bef. 1000; ME *knelen,* OE *cnēowlian* (c. LG *knelen,* D *knielen*). See KNEE, -LE] —**kneel′ing•ly,** *adv.*

kneel•er (nē′lər), *n.* **1.** a person or thing that kneels. **2.** a bench, pad, or the like, to kneel on. **3.** a stone for supporting inclined masonry, as coping stones. **4.** knee (def. 8). [1350–1400; ME; see KNEEL, -ER[1]]

kneel′ing bus′, a bus that can lower its body or entrance door to facilitate boarding by the handicapped or elderly. [1975–80]

knee•pad (nē′pad′), *n.* a pad of leather, foam rubber, etc., as one worn by football or basketball players to protect the knee. [KNEE + PAD[1]]

knee•pan (nē′pan′), *n.* the kneecap or patella. [1400–50; late ME. See KNEE, PAN[1]]

knee′ pants′, knee-length pants, esp. those formerly worn by boys considered too young to wear full-length trousers (often used as a term symbolizing youth): *I haven't felt this way since I was in knee pants.* [1865–70]

knee•piece (nē′pēs′), *n.* a piece of armor for protecting the knee, as a poleyn. [1660–70; KNEE + PIECE]

knee′ raft′er, 1. a rafter for maintaining the angle between a principal rafter and a tie or collar beam. **2.** a rafter bent downward at the lower end. Also called **crook rafter.** [1670–80]

knee•sies (nē′zēz), *n.pl.* **play kneesies,** *Informal.* to rub knees with another person, esp. surreptitiously and in an amorous or sexually provocative manner, as while seated at a table. [1950–55; KNEE + -SY + -S[3]]

knee-slap•per (nē′slap′ər), *n. Informal.* a joke evoking boisterous hilarity. [1965–70, *Amer.*]

knee-socks (nē′soks′), *n.pl.* socks reaching to just below the knees. Also, **knee′ socks′, knee′socks′.** [1960–65]

knee-sprung (nē′sprung′), *adj. Vet. Pathol.* (of a horse, mule, etc.) having a forward bowing of the knee caused by shortening of the flexor tendons. [1870–75, *Amer.*]

knees-up (nēz′up′), *n. Brit. Informal.* a party or lively gathering, usually including dancing. [by ellipsis from *Knees up, Mother Brown* a popular dance, orig. a song with the same title (1939)]

knell (nel), *n.* **1.** the sound made by a bell rung slowly, esp. for a death or a funeral. **2.** a sound or sign announcing the death of a person or the end, extinction, failure, etc., of something: *the knell of parting day.* **3.** any mournful sound. —*v.i.* **4.** to sound, as a bell, esp. a funeral bell. **5.** to give forth a mournful, ominous, or warning sound. —*v.t.* **6.** to proclaim or summon by, or as if by, a bell. [bef. 950; (n.) ME *knel,* OE *cynll;* (v.) ME *knellen, knyllen,* OE *cynllan;* c. ON *knylla* to beat, strike; akin to D *knal* bang, *knallen* to bang, G *Knall* explosion, *knallen* to explode]

Knel•ler (nel′ər), *n.* **Sir Godfrey,** 1646–1723, English painter, born in Germany.

knelt (nelt), *v.* a pt. and pp. of **kneel.**

Knes•set (knes′et), *n.* the unicameral parliament of Israel. [1945–50; < ModHeb *kneset,* post-Biblical Heb *kəneseth* gathering]

knew (no͞o, nyo͞o), *v.* pt. of **know.**

Knick•er•bock•er (nik′ər bok′ər), *n.* **1.** a descendant of the Dutch settlers of New York. **2.** any New Yorker. [1800–10, *Amer.;* generalized from Diedrich *Knickerbocker,* fictitious author of Washington Irving's *History of New York*]

knick•ered (nik′ərd), *adj.* wearing knickers. Also, **knick•er•bock•ered** (nik′ər bok′ərd). [1895–1900; KNICKER(S) + -ED[3]]

knick•ers (nik′ərz), *n.* (*used with a plural v.*) **1.** Also, **knick•er•bock•ers** (nik′ər bok′ərz). loose-fitting short trousers gathered in at the knees. **2.** *Chiefly Brit.* **a.** a bloomerslike undergarment worn by women. **b.** panties. **3.** *Brit. Informal.* a woman's or girl's short-legged underpants. **4. to get one's knickers in a twist,** *Brit. Slang.* to get flustered or agitated: *Don't get your knickers in a twist every time the telephone rings.* [1880–85; shortened form of *knickerbockers,* pl. of *knickerbocker,* special use of KNICKERBOCKER]

knick•knack (nik′nak′), *n.* an ornamental trinket or gimcrack; a bit of bric-a-brac. Also, **nick•nack.** [1610–20; gradational compound based on KNACK in obs. sense "toy"] —**knick′knacked′,** *adj.* —**knick′knack′y,** *adj.*

Knies (knēs), *n.* **Karl Gus•tav A•dolf** (kärl go͝os′täf ä′dôlf), 1821–98, German statistician and historical economist.

knife (nīf), *n., pl.* **knives** (nīvz), *v.,* **knifed, knif•ing.** —*n.* **1.** an instrument for cutting, consisting essentially of a thin, sharp-edged, metal blade fitted with a handle. **2.** a knifelike weapon; dagger or short sword. **3.** any blade for cutting, as in a tool or machine. **4. under the knife,** in surgery; undergoing a medical operation: *The patient was under the knife for four hours.* —*v.t.* **5.** to apply a knife to; cut, stab, etc., with a knife. **6.** to attempt to defeat or undermine in a secret or underhanded way. —*v.i.* **7.** to move or cleave through something with or as if with a knife: *The ship knifed through the heavy seas.* [bef. 1100; ME *knif,* OE *cnīf;* c. D *knijf,* G *Kneif,* ON *knīfr*] —**knife′like′,** *adj.* —**knif′er,** *n.*

knife′ box′, a box, often ornamental and sometimes closed with a lid, for containing table knives. [1770–80]

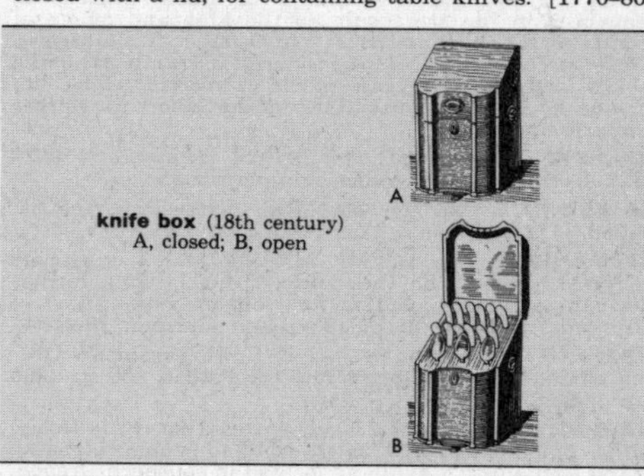

knife box (18th century)
A, closed; B, open

knife′ edge′, 1. the cutting edge of a knife. **2.** anything very sharp. **3.** a wedge on the fine edge of which a scale beam, pendulum, or the like, balances or oscillates. [1810–20]

knife-edged (nīf′ejd′), *adj.* having a thin, sharp edge. [1860–65]

knife′ pleat′, a sharply creased narrow pleat, usually one of a series folded in the same direction. [1890–95]

knife′ rest′, 1. something upon which to rest a knife when it is not being used. **2.** *Mil.* a metal or wood frame strung with barbed wire for use as a movable road barrier or underwater beach obstacle. [1855–60]

knife′ switch′, *Elect.* a form of air switch in which a moving element, usually a hinged blade, is placed between two contact clips. [1905–10]

knight (nīt), *n.* **1.** a mounted soldier serving under a feudal superior in the Middle Ages. **2.** (in Europe in the Middle Ages) a man, usually of noble birth, who after an apprenticeship as page and squire was raised to honorable military rank and bound to chivalrous conduct. **3.** any person of a rank similar to that of the medieval knight. **4.** a man upon whom the nonhereditary dignity of knighthood is conferred by a sovereign because of personal merit or for services rendered to the country. In Great Britain he holds the rank next below that of a baronet, and the title *Sir* is prefixed to the Christian name, as in *Sir John Smith.* **5.** a member of any order or association that designates its members as knights. **6.** *Chess.* a piece shaped like a horse's head, moved one square vertically and then two squares horizontally or one square horizontally and two squares vertically. **7.** *Naut.* **a.** a short vertical timber having on its head a sheave through which running rigging is rove. **b.** any other fitting or erection bearing such a sheave. —*v.t.* **8.** to dub or make (a man) a knight. [bef. 900; ME; OE *cniht* boy, manservant; c. G, D *knecht* servant] —**knight′less,** *adj.*

Knight (nīt), *n.* **1. Eric,** 1897–1943, U.S. novelist, born in England. **2. Frank Hy•ne•man** (hī′nə mən), 1885–1972, U.S. economist.

knight′ bach′elor, *pl.* **knights bachelors, knight bachelors.** bachelor (def. 3). [1600–10]

knight′ banneret′, *pl.* **knights bannerets.** banneret[1] (def. 2). [1875–80]

Knight′, Death′ and the Dev′il, an engraving (1513) by Albrecht Dürer.

knight-er•rant (nīt′er′ənt), *n., pl.* **knights-er•rant.** a wandering knight; a knight who traveled widely in search of adventures, to exhibit military skill, to engage in chivalric deeds, etc. [1300–50; ME]

knight-er•rant•ry (nīt′er′ən trē), *n., pl.* **-er•rant•ries. 1.** the behavior, vocation, or character of a knight-errant. **2.** quixotic conduct or action. [1645–55; KNIGHT-ERRANT + -RY]

knight•head (nīt′hed′), *n. Naut.* **1.** either of a pair of upright members flanking and securing the bowsprit of a ship at the bow, often used as mooring bitts; apostle. **2.** a plate at the fore end of a topgallant forecastle, on an iron or steel sailing ship, through which a spike bowsprit passes. [1705–15; KNIGHT + HEAD]

knight•hood (nīt′ho͝od), *n.* **1.** the rank or dignity of a knight: *to confer knighthood upon him.* **2.** the profession or vocation of a knight. **3.** knightly character or qualities. **4.** the body of knights. [bef. 900; ME *knighthod,* OE *cnihthād.* See KNIGHT, -HOOD]

knight•ly (nīt′lē), *adj.* **1.** characteristic of a knight; noble, courageous, and generous: *knightly deeds.* **2.** being or resembling a knight. **3.** of or belonging to a knight: *knightly duties.* **4.** composed of knights. —*adv.* **5.** in a manner befitting a knight. [bef. 1000; ME; OE *cnihtlic.* See KNIGHT, -LY] —**knight′li•ness,** *n.*

Knight′ of the Bath′, a member of a knightly order founded by George I of England in 1725. [so called because of the bath new knights took before initiation into the order]

Knights, The, a comedy (424 B.C.) by Aristophanes.

Knights′ Hos′pitalers. See under **Hospitaler** (def. 1).

CONCISE ETYMOLOGY KEY: <, descended or borrowed from; >, whence; b., blend of, blended; c., cognate with; cf., compare; deriv., derivative; equiv., equivalent; imit., imitative; obl., oblique; r., replacing; s., stem; sp., spelling, spelled; resp., respelling, respelled; trans., translation; ?, origin unknown; *, unattested; ‡, probably earlier than. See the full key inside the front cover.

Knights′ of Colum′bus, an international fraternal and benevolent organization of Roman Catholic men, founded in New Haven, Connecticut, in 1882.

Knights′ of La′bor, a secret workingmen's organization formed in 1869 to defend the interests of labor.

Knights′ of Mal′ta, the order of Hospitalers.

Knights′ of Pyth′ias, a fraternal order founded in Washington, D.C., in 1864.

Knights′ of St. John′ of Jeru′salem. See under **Hospitaler** (def. 1).

Knights′ of the Ku′ Klux′ Klan′. See **Ku Klux Klan** (def. 2).

Knights′ of the Round′ Ta′ble, a legendary order of knights created by King Arthur.

Knights′ Tem′plars, 1. a Masonic order in the U.S. claiming descent from the medieval order of Templars. **2.** a pl. of **Knight Templar.**

Knight′ Tem′plar, *pl.* **Knights Templars, Knights Templar.** Templar.

knish (knish), *n. Jewish Cookery.* a fried or baked turnover or roll of dough with a filling, as of meat, kasha, or potato, often eaten as an appetizer or snack. [1925–30; < Yiddish < Pol *knysz*]

knit (nit), *v.,* **knit•ted** or **knit, knit•ting,** *n.* —*v.t.* **1.** to make (a garment, fabric, etc.) by interlocking loops of one or more yarns either by hand with knitting needles or by machine. **2.** to join closely and firmly, as members or parts (often fol. by *together*): *The tragedy knitted the family closer together.* **3.** to contract into folds or wrinkles: *to knit the brow.* **4.** to form or create from diverse sources or elements: *She knitted her play from old folk tales and family anecdotes.* —*v.i.* **5.** to become closely and firmly joined together; grow together, as broken bones do. **6.** to contract into folds or wrinkles, as the brow. **7.** to become closely and intimately united. —*n.* **8.** fabric produced by knitting. **9.** a knitted garment. **10.** a style or type of knitting. **11.** the basic stitch in knitting, formed by pulling a loop of the working yarn forward through an existing stitch and then slipping that stitch off the needle. Cf. **purl**[1] (def. 3). [bef. 1000; ME *knitte,* OE *cnyttan* to tie; c. G *knütten;* see KNOT[1]] —**knit′ta•ble,** *adj.* —**knit′ter,** *n.*
—**Syn. 2.** bind, link, unite.

knit•ted (nit′id), *adj.* made by knitting, as a cloth article: *a knitted bedspread.* [1850–55; KNIT + -ED[2]]

knit•ting (nit′ing), *n.* **1.** the act of a person or thing that knits. **2.** the act of forming a fabric by looping a continuous yarn. **3.** knitted work. **4. stick** or **tend to one's knitting, a.** to mind one's own business: *Don't worry about my work—just tend to your knitting.* **b.** to devote oneself to one's assignments or responsibilities: *Years of sticking to his knitting finally paid off.* [1350–1400; ME; see KNIT, -ING[1]]

knit′ting nee′dle, 1. either of two types of instruments used for hand knitting: a straight rod of steel, wood, plastic, etc., pointed at one or both ends, used in pairs, or a single curved, flexible rod with two pointed ends. **2.** any of various needlelike devices used in machine knitting. [1590–1600]

knit•wear (nit′wâr′), *n.* clothing made of knitted fabric. [1920–25; KNIT + WEAR]

knives (nīvz), *n.* pl. of **knife.**

knob (nob), *n., v.,* **knobbed, knob•bing.** —*n.* **1.** a projecting part, usually rounded, forming the handle of a door, drawer, or the like. **2.** a rounded lump or protuberance on the surface or at the end of something, as a knot on a tree trunk. **3.** *Archit.* an ornamental boss, as of carved work. **4.** a rounded hill, mountain, or elevation on a ridge. —*v.t.* **5.** to produce a knob on. **6.** to furnish with a knob. **7.** (in stone cutting) to knock off (excess stone) preparatory to dressing; knobble; skiffle. [1350–1400; ME *knobbe* < MLG] —**knob′like′,** *adj.*

knob•ble (nob′əl), *v.t.,* **-bled, -bling. 1.** to knob (excess stone). **2.** *Metall.* to treat (semirefined puddled iron) on a hearth before shingling to produce wrought iron. [1835–45; KNOB + -LE] —**knob•bler** (nob′lər), *n.*

knob′bling roll′ (nob′ling), *Metalworking.* a roll for a rolling mill, having a series of regularly shaped projections and depressions on its face.

knob•by (nob′ē), *adj.,* **-bi•er, -bi•est. 1.** full of or covered with knobs: *the knobby trunk of a tree.* **2.** shaped like a knob. [1535–45; KNOB + -Y[1]] —**knob′bi•ness,** *n.*

knob′ cel′ery, celeriac.

knob′cone pine′ (nob′kōn′), a pine, *Pinus attenuata,* of the Pacific coast of the U.S., bearing cones with knoblike scales. [1880–85, *Amer.*; KNOB + CONE]

knob•ker•rie (nob′ker′ē), *n.* a short, heavy wooden club with a knob on one end, used esp. by native peoples of South Africa for striking and throwing. [1835–45; < Afrik *knopkierie,* equiv. to *knop* KNOB + *kierie,* said to be < Khoikhoi *kirri, keeri* stick]

knob′ latch′, a latch having a spring bolt controlled by a knob on one or both sides.

knob′ lock′, a lock having a spring bolt moved by a knob or knobs, and a dead bolt moved by a key. [1805–15]

knock (nok), *v.i.* **1.** to strike a sounding blow with the fist, knuckles, or anything hard, esp. on a door, window, or the like, as in seeking admittance, calling attention, or giving a signal: *to knock on the door before entering.* **2.** to strike in collision; bump: *He knocked into a table.* **3.** to make a pounding noise: *The engine of our car is knocking badly.* **4.** *Informal.* to engage in trivial or carping criticism; find fault. **5.** *Cards.* to end a game, as in gin rummy, by laying down a hand in which those cards not included in sets total less than a specific amount.
—*v.t.* **6.** to give a sounding or forcible blow to; hit; strike; beat. **7.** to drive, force, or render by a blow or blows: *to knock a man senseless.* **8.** to make by striking a blow or blows: *to knock a hole in the wall.* **9.** to strike (a thing) against something else. **10.** *Informal.* to criticize, esp. in a carping manner: *He's always knocking everything.* **11.** *Brit. Slang.* to astound; impress greatly. **12. have it knocked,** *Slang.* to be assured of success: *With a government job, he thought he had it knocked.* **13. knock around** or **about,** *Informal.* **a.** to wander aimlessly or idly; loaf. **b.** to mistreat (someone), esp. physically. **c.** to jar; shake up. **14. knock back,** *Slang.* to drink (a beverage), esp. quickly and heartily: *He knocked back two shots of vodka.* **15. knock down, a.** to sell at auction by a blow of the hammer or to a bidder. **b.** to take apart or disassemble, as for facility in handling, storing, shipping, etc. **c.** *Slang.* to receive, as a salary or a scholastic grade; earn: *He knocks down 30 grand a year.* **d.** *Informal.* to lower the price of; reduce: *to knock down end-of-season leftovers.* **e.** *Slang.* to embezzle or steal (money). **f.** to cause (a sailing vessel) to heel, as by a gust of wind, to such a degree that it cannot right itself. **16. knock off, a.** *Informal.* to cease activity, esp. work: *to knock off at five every day.* **b.** to stop doing something; quit: *Knock it off or you'll get into a mess.* **c.** *Slang.* to dispose of; finish. **d.** *Slang.* to murder; kill. **e.** *Slang.* to die. **f.** *Slang.* to get rid of; reduce. **g.** *Slang.* to disable or defeat. **h.** *Slang.* to commit a robbery at; steal from: *The gang knocked off a gas station.* **i.** *Slang. Naut.* to blow the head (of a sailing vessel) off the wind. **j.** to imitate, copy, or plagiarize: *to knock off designer dresses in cheap materials.* **17. knock out, a.** to defeat (an opponent) in a boxing match by striking such a blow that the opponent is unable to rise within the specified time. **b.** to render (a person) unconscious: *Those sleeping pills knocked me out for ten hours.* **c.** to make tired or exhausted: *Christmas shopping always knocks me out.* **d.** *Informal.* to produce quickly, hurriedly, or with ease: *He knocks out two poems a day.* **e.** to damage or destroy: *The explosion knocked out the power for several hours.* **f.** See **knock** (def. 18). **18. knock out of the box,** *Baseball.* to cause a pitcher to be removed from the box because the pitcher has permitted too many hits to be made. Also, **knock out. 19. knock over, a.** to strike (someone or something) from an erect to a prone position: *to knock over a lamp.* **b.** to distress; overcome: *When the announcement came we were completely knocked over.* **c.** *Slang.* to rob, burglarize, or hijack: *He knocked over five banks.* **20. knock the** or **one's socks off,** *Informal.* to have an overwhelming effect on: *The song knocked the socks off the audience.* **21. knock together,** to make or construct in a hurry or with little attention to detail: *He knocked together a couple of tables.* **22. knock up, a.** *Slang.* to make pregnant. **b.** to exhaust; weary; tire. **c.** to damage; mar: *The children knocked up the new table.* **d.** to injure; wound: *He was afraid to come home from school all knocked up again.* **e.** *Brit.* to wake up; rouse; call: *He knocked us up before dawn.*
—*n.* **23.** an act or instance of knocking. **24.** the sound of knocking, esp. a rap, as at a door. **25.** a blow or thump. **26.** *Informal.* an adverse criticism. **27.** the noise resulting from faulty combustion or from incorrect functioning of some part of an internal-combustion engine. **28.** *Cricket.* an innings. **29.** *Brit. Slang.* **a.** one of a combination of dealers who bid together, rather than against each other, at an auction, and later resell the purchases among themselves. **b.** an auction at which this is done. **c.** the sale of merchandise recently obtained by a dealer at an auction. [bef. 1000; 1890–95 for def. 4; ME *knokken, knoken* (v.), OE *cnocian, cnucian;* c. ON *knoka* to thump, knock] —**knock′less,** *adj.*
—**Syn. 1.** See **strike.**

knock•a•bout (nok′ə bout′), *n.* **1.** *Naut.* any of various fore-and-aft-rigged sailing vessels having a single jib bent to a stay from the stemhead, no bowsprit being used: usually rigged as a sloop. **2.** something designed or suitable for rough or casual use, as a sturdy jacket, a secondhand car, etc. **3.** a slapstick comedian or comedy. **4.** *Australian.* an itinerant farm hand or ranch hand; an itinerant handyman. **5.** *Brit. Archaic.* wanderer. —*adj.* **6.** suitable for rough use, as a garment: *a knockabout jacket and jeans.* **7.** characterized by knocking about; rough; boisterous. **8.** slapstick: *knockabout comedy.* **9.** shiftless; aimless: *a knockabout kind of person.* [1875–80; n., adj. use of v. phrase *knock about*]

knock•down (nok′doun′), *adj.* **1.** capable of knocking something down; overwhelming; irresistible: *a knockdown blow.* **2.** constructed in separate parts that can readily be taken apart for easy storage, shipping, etc.: *a knockdown toolshed.* **3.** offered or acquired for less than the prevailing rate: *first-rate goods at knockdown prices.* —*n.* **4.** a knockdown object. **5.** an act or instance of knocking down, esp. by a blow. **6.** something that fells or overwhelms. **7.** reduction or lowering, as in price or number: *The store offered a knockdown of 15 percent to its own employees.* **8.** *Slang.* an introduction, esp. to a person: *He gave me a real knockdown to the company.* **9.** *Naut.* the capsizing of a small boat as a result of a strong gust of wind. [1680–90; adj., n. use of v. phrase *knock down*]

knock-down-drag-out (nok′doun′drag′out′), *adj.* marked by unrelenting violence: *a knock-down-drag-out fight.* Also, **knock′-down′, drag′-out′; knock′-down′-and-drag′-out′.** [1820–30; adj. use of v. phrases *knock down* and *drag out*]

knocked-down (nokt′doun′), *adj.* **1.** composed of parts or units that can be disassembled: *knocked-down furniture.* **2.** *Informal.* condensed, abridged, simplified, unadorned, etc.: *a knocked-down version of a Broadway musical.* [1770–80]

knock•er (nok′ər), *n.* **1.** a person or thing that knocks. **2.** a hinged knob, bar, etc., on a door, for use in knocking. **3.** *Informal.* a persistent and carping critic; faultfinder. **4.** *Slang* (*vulgar*). a female breast. **5. on the knocker,** *Brit. Slang.* canvassing or selling door-to-door. [1350–1400; ME; see KNOCK, -ER[1]]

knock-knee (nok′nē′), *n.* **1.** inward curvature of the legs, causing the knees to knock together in walking. **2. knock-knees,** the knees of a person whose legs have such curvature. [1820–30] —**knock′-kneed′,** *adj.*

knock•off (nok′ôf′, -of′), *n.* **1.** an act or instance of knocking off. **2.** an unlicensed copy of something, esp. fashion clothing, intended to be sold at a lower price than the original. Also, **knock-off.** [1870–75, for an earlier sense; n. use of v. phrase *knock off*]

knock′-on′ effect′ (nok′on′, -ôn′), *Chiefly Brit.* a chain reaction. [adj. use of v. phrase *knock on*]

knock•out (nok′out′), *n.* **1.** an act or instance of knocking out. **2.** the state or fact of being knocked out. **3.** a knockout blow. **4.** *Informal.* a person or thing overwhelmingly attractive, appealing, or successful. **5.** a panel in a casing, can, or box, esp. of metal or plastic, so designed that it can readily be removed, as by punching, hammering, or cutting, to provide an opening into the interior: *a knockout in a junction box.* **6.** *Mach.* a device for knocking something loose, as finished work from a lathe chuck. —*adj.* **7.** that knocks out: *the knockout punch.* [1810–20; 1935–40 for def. 4; n., adj. use of v. phrase *knock out*]

knock′out drops′, chloral hydrate or any similar rapidly acting drug, esp. one put in a drink secretly to make the drinker unconscious. [1890–95]

knock′ rum′my, *Cards.* a variety of rummy for two to six players, in which a player can end a game by laying down a hand with any number of points in cards not included in sets.

knock•wurst (nok′wûrst, -wŏŏrst), *n.* knackwurst.

knoll[1] (nōl), *n.* a small, rounded hill or eminence; hillock. [bef. 900; ME *cnol,* OE *cnoll;* c. Norw *knoll* hillock; akin to D *knol* turnip, Icel *knollur,* G *Knollen,* Dan *knold* tuber] —**knoll′y,** *adj.*

knoll[2] (nōl), *Archaic.* —*v.t.* **1.** to ring or toll a bell for; announce by tolling. **2.** to ring or toll (a bell). —*v.i.* **3.** to sound, as a bell; ring. **4.** to sound a knell. —*n.* **5.** a stroke of a bell in ringing or tolling. [1350–1400; ME (n. and v.); var. of KNELL] —**knoll′er,** *n.*

Knoop′ scale′ (nōōp), a scale of hardness based on the indentation made in the material to be tested by a diamond point. [named after F. *Knoop,* 20th-century American chemist]

knop (nop), *n.* a small knob or similar rounded protuberance, esp. for ornament. [1325–75; ME; OE *cnop;* c. D *knop,* G *Knopf*]

Knopf (knopf), *n.* **Alfred A(braham),** 1892–1984, U.S. publisher.

knosp (nosp), *n.* a budlike ornament. [1800–10; < G *Knospe* bud; akin to KNOP]

Knos•sos (nos′əs), *n.* a ruined city on N central Crete; capital of the ancient Minoan civilization. Also, **Cnossus, Gnossus.** —**Knos′si•an,** *adj.*

knot[1] (not), *n., v.,* **knot•ted, knot•ting.** —*n.* **1.** an interlacing, twining, looping, etc., of a cord, rope, or the like, drawn tight into a knob or lump, for fastening, binding, or connecting two cords together or a cord to something else. **2.** a piece of ribbon or similar material tied or folded upon itself and used or worn as an ornament. **3.** a group or cluster of persons or things: *a knot of spectators.* **4.** the hard, cross-grained mass of wood at the place where a branch joins the trunk of a tree. **5.** a part of this mass showing in a piece of lumber, wood panel, etc. **6.** *Anat., Zool.* a protuberance or swelling on or in a part or process, as in a muscle. **7.** a protuberance in the tissue of a plant; an excrescence on a stem, branch, or root; a node or joint in a stem, esp. when of swollen form. **8.** any of various fungal diseases of trees characterized by the formation of an excrescence, knob, or gnarl. **9.** an involved, intricate, or difficult matter; complicated problem. **10.** *Naut.* **a.** a unit of speed equal to one nautical mile or about 1.15 statute miles per hour. **b.** a unit of 47 feet 3 inches (13.79 meters) on a log line, marked off by knots. **c.** a nautical mile. **11.** a bond or tie: *the knot of matrimony.* **12.** Also called **joint, node.** *Math.* in interpolation, one of the points at which the values of a function are assigned. **13. tie the knot,** *Informal.* to marry: *They will tie the knot in November.* —*v.t.* **14.** to tie in a knot; form a knot in. **15.** to secure or fasten by a knot. **16.** to form protuberances, bosses, or knobs in; make knotty. —*v.i.* **17.** to become tied or tangled in a knot. **18.** to form knots or joints. [bef. 1000; (n.) ME *knot(te),* OE *cnotta;* c. D *knot,* G *knoten* to KNIT; (v.) ME, deriv. of the n.] —**knot′less,** *adj.* —**knot′like′,** *adj.*
—**Syn. 3.** company, band, crew, gang, crowd. **7.** lump, knob, gnarl. **9.** perplexity, puzzle, conundrum.

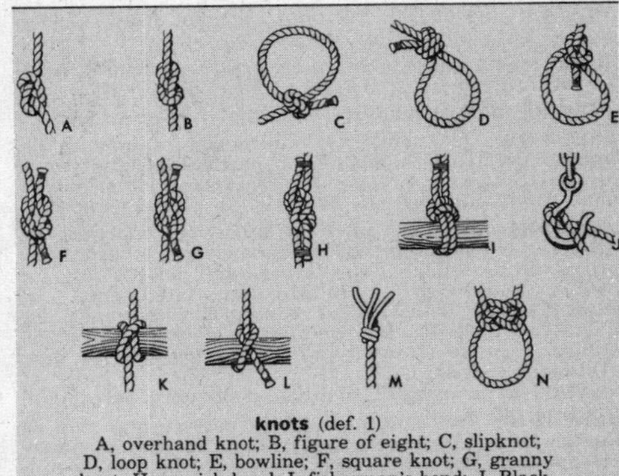

knots (def. 1)
A, overhand knot; B, figure of eight; C, slipknot; D, loop knot; E, bowline; F, square knot; G, granny knot; H, carrick bend; I, fisherman's bend; J, Blackwall hitch; K, clove hitch; L, half hitch; M, Matthew Walker; N, prolonge knot

CONCISE PRONUNCIATION KEY: *act, cāpe, dâre, pärt; set, ēqual; if, īce; ox, ōver, ôrder, oil, bŏŏk, bōōt, out; up, ûrge; child; sing; shoe; thin, that;* zh as in *treasure.* ə = a as in *alone,* e as in *system,* i as in *easily,* o as in *gallop,* u as in *circus;* ᵊ as in *fire* (fīᵊr), *hour* (ouᵊr). l and n can serve as syllabic consonants, as in *cradle* (krād′l), and *button* (but′n). See the full key inside the front cover.

knot[2] (not), *n.* either of two large sandpipers, *Calidris canutus* or *C. tenuirostris,* that breed in the Arctic and winter in the Southern Hemisphere. Also called **gray-back.** [1425–75; late ME; orig. uncert.]

knot′ gar′den, an intricately designed flower or herb garden with plants arranged to create an interlacing pattern, sometimes with fanciful topiary and carefully tended paths. [1510–20]

knot•hole (not′hōl′), *n.* a hole in a board or plank formed by the falling out of a knot or a portion of a knot. [1720–30; KNOT[1] + HOLE]

knot•root (not′ro͞ot′, -ro͝ot′), *n.* See **Chinese artichoke.** [1830–40, *Amer.*; KNOT[1] + ROOT[1]]

knot′ stitch′, a stitch that produces a knot on the fabric surface, made by twining the thread about the needle. [1880–85]

knot•ted (not′id), *adj.* **1.** having knots; knotty. **2.** tied in or fastened with a knot. **3.** made or ornamented with knots. **4.** *Bot.* having many nodes or nodelike swellings; gnarled. **5.** *Zool.* having one or more swellings; nodose. [1125–75; ME *cnotted.* See KNOT[1], -ED[2], -ED[3]]

knot•ter (not′ər), *n.* **1.** a person or thing that ties knots. **2.** a device that ties knots in thread during the manufacture of yarn. **3.** a person or thing that takes out or removes knots. [1705–15; KNOT[1] + -ER[1]]

knot•ting (not′ing), *n.* a decorative pattern produced by interlacing and tying knots in various yarns, as in macramé and tatting. [1605–15; KNOT[1] + -ING[1]]

knot•ty (not′ē), *adj.,* **-ti•er, -ti•est.** **1.** having knots; full of knots: *a knotty piece of wood.* **2.** involved, intricate, or difficult: *a knotty problem.* [1200–50; ME *cnotti.* See KNOT[1], -Y[1]] —**knot′ti•ly,** *adv.* —**knot′ti•ness,** *n.*
—**Syn. 2.** complex, complicated.

knot′ty rhat′any. See under **rhatany** (def. 1).

knot•weed (not′wēd′), *n.* any of several knotty-stemmed plants belonging to the genus *Polygonum,* of the buckwheat family. [1570–80; KNOT[1] + WEED[1]]

knout (nout), *n.* **1.** a whip with a lash of leather thongs, formerly used in Russia for flogging criminals. —*v.t.* **2.** to flog with the knout. [1710–20; < F < Russ *knut,* ORuss < ON *knūtr* knot]

know[1] (nō), *v.,* **knew, known, know•ing,** *n.* —*v.t.* **1.** to perceive or understand as fact or truth; to apprehend clearly and with certainty: *I know the situation fully.* **2.** to have established or fixed in the mind or memory: *to know a poem by heart; Do you know the way to the park from here?* **3.** to be cognizant or aware of: *I know it.* **4.** be acquainted with (a thing, place, person, etc.), as by sight, experience, or report: *to know the mayor.* **5.** to understand from experience or attainment (usually fol. by *how* before an infinitive): *to know how to make gingerbread.* **6.** to be able to distinguish, as one from another: *to know right from wrong.* **7.** *Archaic.* to have sexual intercourse with. —*v.i.* **8.** to have knowledge or clear and certain perception, as of fact or truth. **9.** to be cognizant or aware, as of some fact, circumstance, or occurrence; have information, as about something. **10. know the ropes,** *Informal.* to understand or be familiar with the particulars of a subject or business: *He knew the ropes better than anyone else in politics.* —*n.* **11.** the fact or state of knowing; knowledge. **12. in the know,** possessing inside, secret, or special information. [bef. 900; ME *knowen, knawen,* OE *gecnāwan;* c. OHG *-cnāhan,* ON *knā* to know how, be able to; akin to L *(g)nōvi,* Gk *gignṓskein.* See GNOSTIC, CAN[1]] —**know′er,** *n.*
—**Syn. 1.** KNOW, COMPREHEND, UNDERSTAND imply being aware of meanings. To KNOW is to be aware of something as a fact or truth: *He knows the basic facts of the subject. I know that he agrees with me.* To COMPREHEND is to know something thoroughly and to perceive its relationships to certain other ideas, facts, etc. To UNDERSTAND is to be fully aware not only of the meaning of something but also of its implications: *I could comprehend all he said, but did not understand that he was joking.*

know[2] (nō, nou), *n. Scot. and North Eng.* knoll[1].

know•a•ble (nō′ə bəl), *adj.* capable of being known. [1400–50; late ME; see KNOW[1], -ABLE] —**know′a•ble•ness, know′a•bil′i•ty,** *n.*

know-all (nō′ôl′), *n. Informal.* a know-it-all. [1880–85]

knowe (nou, nō), *n. Scot. and North Eng.* knoll[1]. Also, **know.**

knowed (nōd), *v. Nonstandard.* a pt. and pp. of **know**[1].

know-how (nō′hou′), *n.* knowledge of how to do something; faculty or skill for a particular activity; expertise: *Designing a computer requires a lot of know-how.* [1830–40, *Amer.*; n. use of v. phrase *know how*]

know•ing (nō′ing), *adj.* **1.** affecting, implying, or deliberately revealing shrewd knowledge of secret or private information: *a knowing glance.* **2.** that knows; having knowledge or information; intelligent. **3.** shrewd, sharp, or astute. **4.** conscious; intentional; deliberate. [1325–75; ME *knawynge* (earlier *knowende, knawande*). See KNOW[1], -ING[2]] —**know′ing•ly,** *adv.* —**know′ing•ness,** *n.*
—**Syn. 1.** meaningful, significant, eloquent, perceptive.

know-it-all (nō′it ôl′), *n.* **1.** a person who acts as though he or she knows everything and who dismisses the opinions, comments, or suggestions of others. —*adj.* **2.** of or characteristic of a know-it-all. [1930–35]

knowl•edge (nol′ij), *n.* **1.** acquaintance with facts, truths, or principles, as from study or investigation; general erudition: *knowledge of many things.* **2.** familiarity or conversance, as with a particular subject or branch of learning: *A knowledge of accounting was necessary for the job.* **3.** acquaintance or familiarity gained by sight, experience, or report: *a knowledge of human nature.* **4.** the fact or state of knowing; the perception of fact or truth; clear and certain mental apprehension. **5.** awareness, as of a fact or circumstance: *He had knowledge of her good fortune.* **6.** something that is or may be known; information: *He sought knowledge of her activities.* **7.** the body of truths or facts accumulated in the course of time. **8.** the sum of what is known: *Knowledge of the true situation is limited.* **9.** *Archaic.* sexual intercourse. Cf. **carnal knowledge. 10. to one's knowledge,** according to the information available to one: *To my knowledge he hasn't been here before.* —*adj.* **11.** creating, involving, using, or disseminating special knowledge or information: *A computer expert can always find a good job in the knowledge industry.* [1250–1300; ME *knouleche,* equiv. to *know(en)* to KNOW[1] + *-leche,* perh. akin to OE *-lāc* suffix denoting action or practice, c. ON *(-)leikr;* cf. WEDLOCK] —**know′ledge•less,** *adj.*
—**Syn. 1.** See **information. 4.** understanding, discernment, comprehension; erudition, scholarship.

knowl•edge•a•ble (nol′i jə bəl), *adj.* possessing or exhibiting knowledge, insight, or understanding; intelligent; well-informed; discerning; perceptive. Also, **knowl′edg•a•ble.** [1600–10; KNOWLEDGE + -ABLE] —**knowl′edge•a•bil′i•ty, knowl′edge•a•ble•ness,** *n.* —**knowl′edge•a•bly,** *adv.*

knowl′edge engineer′ing, the practical application of developments in the field of computer science concerned with artificial intelligence.

known (nōn), *v.* **1.** pp. of **know**[1]. —*n.* **2.** a known quantity.

know-noth•ing (nō′nuth′ing), *n.* **1.** an ignorant or totally uninformed person; ignoramus. **2.** an agnostic. **3.** *(caps.) U.S. Hist.* a member of a political party **(American party** or **Know′-Noth′ing par′ty)** prominent from 1853 to 1856, whose aim was to keep control of the government in the hands of native-born citizens: so called because members originally professed ignorance of the party's activities. **4.** a person whose anti-intellectualism, xenophobia, and other political attitudes recall the Know-Nothings. —*adj.* **5.** grossly ignorant; totally uninformed. **6.** agnostic. **7.** *(caps.)* of or pertaining to the Know-Nothings. **8.** of or pertaining to a political know-nothing. [1815–25] —**know′-noth′ing•ism,** *n.*

known′ quan′tity, 1. *Math.* a quantity whose value is given: in algebra, frequently represented by a letter from the first part of the alphabet, as *a, b,* or *c.* **2.** any factor, circumstance, etc., that is already accepted or familiar: *Her honesty is a known quantity.* [1975–80]

Knox (noks), *n.* **1. (William) Frank(lin),** 1874–1944, U.S. publisher and government official. **2. Henry,** 1750–1806, American Revolutionary general: 1st U.S. secretary of war 1785–94. **3. John,** c1510–72, Scottish religious reformer and historian. **4. Phi•lan•der Chase** (fi lan′dər), 1853–1921, U.S. lawyer and politician: secretary of state 1909–13. **5. Fort.** See **Fort Knox.**

Knox•ville (noks′vil), *n.* a city in E Tennessee, on the Tennessee River. 183,139. —**Knox•vil′li•an, Knox′vil•lite′,** *n.*

KNP, *Chess.* king's knight's pawn.

Knt., Knight.

knub (nub), *n.* nub. [in modern use prob. sp. var., influenced by KNOB; cf. NUB]

knub•bly (nub′lē), *adj.,* **-bli•er, -bli•est.** nubbly.

knub•by (nub′ē), *adj.,* **-bi•er, -bi•est.** nubby. Also, **knubbed.**

knuck (nuk), *n.* **1.** *Informal.* knuckle. **2. knucks,** *Slang.* a pair of brass knuckles. [by shortening]

knuck•le (nuk′əl), *n., v.,* **-led, -ling.** —*n.* **1.** a joint of a finger, esp. one of the articulations of a metacarpal with a phalanx. **2.** the rounded prominence of such a joint when the finger is bent. **3.** a joint of meat, consisting of the parts about the carpal or tarsal joint of a quadruped. **4.** an angle or protrusion at the intersection of two members or surfaces, as in the timbers of a ship or in a roof. **5.** See **brass knuckles. 6.** a cylindrical projecting part on a hinge, through which an axis or pin passes; the joint of a hinge. **7.** (in a wire mesh) a bend in a wire crossing another wire. **8.** (on a chair arm) one of the ridges left at the front end by longitudinal flutes carved to accommodate the fingers. **9.** *Naut.* a pronounced edge formed by a change in the form of the shell of a hull. —*v.t.* **10.** to rub or press with the knuckles. **11.** *Marbles.* to shoot (a marble) from the thumb and forefinger. **12. knuckle down, a.** to apply oneself vigorously and earnestly; become serious: *Just knuckle down for an hour or so and finish the work.* **b.** Also, **knuckle under.** to submit; yield. [1325–75; ME *knokel* (akin to D *kneukel,* G *Knöchel*), dim. of a word represented by D *knok,* G *Knochen* bone; see -LE] —**knuck′ly,** *adj.*

knuck′le ball′, *Baseball.* a slow pitch that moves erratically toward home plate, usually delivered by holding the ball between the thumb and the knuckles of the first joints of the first two or three fingers. Also, **knuck′le•ball′.** Also called **knuck•ler** (nuk′lər). [1905–10, *Amer.*]

knuck•le•ball•er (nuk′əl bô′lər), *n. Baseball.* a pitcher who specializes in throwing knuckle balls. [KNUCKLE BALL + -ER[1]]

knuck•le•bone (nuk′əl bōn′), *n.* **1.** (in humans) any of the bones forming a knuckle of a finger. **2.** (in quadrupeds) a bone homologous with a wrist, ankle, or finger bone of humans, or its knobbed end. [1400–50; late ME; see KNUCKLE, BONE]

knuck•le-dust•er (nuk′əl dus′tər), *n.* See **brass knuckles.** [1855–60, *Amer.*]

knuck•le•head (nuk′əl hed′), *n. Informal.* a stupid, bumbling, inept person. [1940–45; KNUCKLE + HEAD] —**knuck′le•head′ed,** *adj.*

knuck′le joint′, 1. a joint forming a knuckle. **2.** *Mach.* a joint between two parts allowing movement in one plane only. [1860–65]

knuck′le sand′wich, *Slang.* a punch in the mouth with a clenched fist. [1970–75]

Knud•sen (no͞od′sən; *Dan.* kno͞o′sən), *n.* **William S.** (*Signius Wilhelm Paul Knudsen*), 1879–1948, U.S. industrialist, born in Denmark.

knull•ing (nul′ing), *n. Archit.* a convex molding having a series of members separated by indentations, as a bead and reel. Also, **knurling, nulling.** [1935–45; var. of KNURLING]

knur (nûr), *n.* a knotty or hard protuberance or growth, as on a tree. [1350–1400; ME *knorre, knor;* c. MLG, MD, MHG *knorre*]

knurl (nûrl), *n.* **1.** a small ridge or bead, esp. one of a series, as on a button for decoration or on the edge of a thumbscrew to assist in obtaining a firm grip. **2.** a knur. —*v.t.* **3.** to make knurls or ridges on. Also, **nurl.** [1600–10; earlier *knurle* (n.). See KNUR, -LE]

knurled (nûrld), *adj.* **1.** having small ridges on the edge or surface; milled. **2.** having knurls or knots; gnarled. [1605–15; KNURL + -ED[3]]

knurl•ing (nûr′ling), *n.* **1.** a series of knurls, as on a knob. **2.** *Archit.* knulling. [1605–15; KNURL + -ING[1]]

knurl′ toe′, *Furniture.* See **French foot** (def. 1).

knurl•y (nûr′lē), *adj.,* **knurl•i•er, knurl•i•est.** having knurls or knots; gnarled. [1595–1605; KNURL + -Y[1]]

Knut (kno͞ot′, knyo͞ot′), *n.* Canute.

KO (*n.* kā′ō′, kā′ō′; *v.* kā′ō′), *n., pl.* **KO's,** *v.,* **KO'd, KO'ing.** *Slang.* —*n.* **1.** a knockout in boxing. —*v.t.* **2.** to knock unconscious, esp. in a boxing match; knock out. Also, **K.O., k.o., kayo.** [1920–25; initial letters of *knock out*]

ko•a (kō′ə), *n.* **1.** a Hawaiian acacia, *Acacia koa,* of the legume family, characterized by spreading branches and gray bark. **2.** the hard, red or golden-brown wood of this tree, used for making furniture. [1840–50; < Hawaiian]

ko•a•la (kō ä′lə), *n.* a sluggish, tailless, gray, furry, arboreal marsupial, *Phascolarctos cinereus,* of Australia. [1800–10; erroneous sp. for earlier *koola(h)* (now obs.) < Dharuk *gú-la*]

koalas, *Phascolarctos cinereus,* length 2½ ft. (0.8 m)

ko•an (kō′än), *n., pl.* **-ans, -an.** *Zen.* a nonsensical or paradoxical question to a student for which an answer is demanded, the stress of meditation on the question often being illuminating. Cf. **mondo.** [1945–50; < Japn *kōan,* earlier *koū-an* < MChin, equiv. to Chin *gōngàn* public proposal]

kob (kob, kōb), *n.* an African antelope, *Kobus kob,* related to the puku and the lechwe. [1765–75; said to be < Wolof *koba*]

Ko•ba•rid (*Serbo-Croatian.* kô′bä ʀēd′; *Eng.* kō′bə-rēd′), *n.* a village in W Slovenia, formerly in Italy: defeat of the Italians by the Germans and Austrians 1917. Italian, **Caporetto.**

Ko•be (kō′bē; *Japn.* kô′bē′), *n.* a seaport on S Honshu, in S Japan. 1,367,392.

Ko′be beef′, meat from the Japanese cattle **(Ko′be cat′tle),** which are specially raised to produce a beef that is highly prized for its extreme tenderness.

Kö•ben•havn (kœ′bən houn′), *n.* Danish name of **Copenhagen.**

Ko•blenz (kō′blents), *n.* Coblenz.

ko•bo (kō′bō), *n., pl.* **-bo, -bos.** a bronze coin and monetary unit of Nigeria, the 100th part of a naira.

ko•bold (kō′bold, -bōld), *n.* (in German folklore) **1.** a spirit or goblin, often mischievous, that haunts houses. **2.** a spirit that haunts mines or other underground places. [1625–35; < G]

Ko•ca•e•li (kō′jä ä′lē, kə ji′lē), *n.* Izmit.

Koch (koch *for 1;* kôᴋʜ *for 2*), *n.* **1. Edward I.,** born 1924, U.S. politician: mayor of New York City since 1977. **2. Ro•bert** (rō′bᴇʀt), 1843–1910, German bacteriologist and physician: Nobel prize 1905.

Kö′chel list′ing (kûr′shəl; *Ger.* kœ′ᴋʜəl), the chronological number of a composition of Mozart as assigned in the catalog of the composer's works compiled in the 19th century by the Austrian musicologist Ludwig von Köchel (1800–1877) and since revised several times. *Abbr.:* K Also called **Kö′chel num′ber.**

Ko•cher (kō′kər; *Ger.* kō′ᴋʜəʀ), *n.* **E•mil The•o•dor** (ā′mēl tā′ō dōʀ′), 1841–1917, Swiss physiologist, pathologist, and surgeon: Nobel prize 1909.

Ko•chi (kō′chē; *Japn.* kô′chē), *n.* a seaport on central Shikoku, in SW Japan. 300,830.

Ko•da•chrome (kō′də krōm′), **1.** *Trademark.* a brand of positive color transparency. —*n.* **2.** *(l.c.)* a positive color transparency.

Ko•dak (kō′dak), *Trademark.* a brand of portable camera introduced by George Eastman in 1888, using a roll of film and intended for taking snapshots.

Ko•dá•ly (kō dī′, -dä′ē; *Hung.* kō′dä yᵊ), *n.* **Zol•tán** (zôl′tän), 1882–1967, Hungarian composer.

CONCISE ETYMOLOGY KEY: <, descended or borrowed from; >, whence; b., blend of, blended; c., cognate with; cf., compare; deriv., derivative; equiv., equivalent; imit., imitative; obl., oblique; r., replacing; s., stem; sp., spelling, spelled; resp., respelling, respelled; trans., translation; ?, origin unknown; *, unattested; ‡, probably earlier than. See the full key inside the front cover.

Ko•del (kō del′), *Trademark.* a brand of polyester fiber, used chiefly in blended cotton and polyester fabrics and as a fiberfill.

Ko•di•ak (kō′dē ak′), *n.* **1.** an island in the N Pacific, near the base of the Alaska Peninsula. 100 mi. (160 km) long. **2.** See **Kodiak bear.**

Ko′diak bear′, a large, brown bear, *Ursus* (*arctos*) *middendorffi,* inhabiting coastal areas of Alaska and British Columbia, that grows to a length of 9 ft. (2.7 m). Also called **Kodiak.** [1895–1900]

Ko•dok (kō′dok), *n.* modern name of **Fashoda.**

ko•el (kō′əl), *n.* any of several cuckoos of the genus *Eudynamys,* of India, the Malay Archipelago, and Australia. [1820–30; < Hindi < Skt *kokila*]

Koest•ler (kest′lər, kes′lər), *n.* **Arthur,** 1905–83, British novelist, critic, and journalist; born in Hungary.

kof (kôf), *n.* koph.

K. of C., Knights of Columbus.

Koff•ka (kôf′kä; *Eng.* kof′kə), *n.* **Kurt** (ko͝ort), 1886–1941, German psychologist in the U.S.

K. of P., Knights of Pythias.

Ko•fu (kō′fo͞o; *Japn.* kô′fo͞o), *n.* a city on S Honshu, in central Japan. 199,272.

Ko•hel•eth (kō hel′eth), *n.* **1.** the book of Ecclesiastes. **2.** its author. Also, **Ko•hel•et, Ko•hel•es** (kō hel′et, -es). [< Heb *qoheleṯ* member of an assembly]

Ko•hen (kō′ən; *Seph. Heb.* kô hen′; *Ashk. Heb.* kō-hän′, kō′hän, koin), *n., pl.* **Ko•ha•nim** (*Seph. Heb.* kô-hä nēm′; *Ashk. Heb.* kō hä nim′, kō hä′nim), *Eng.* **Ko•hens.** Cohen.

Ko•hi•ma (kō′hē mä′), *n.* a town in and the capital of Nagaland, in E India.

Koh•i•noor (kō′ə no͝or′), *n.* an Indian diamond weighing 106 carats; now part of the British crown jewels. Also, **Koh′-i-noor′.** [< Pers *kōhinūr* lit., mountain of light]

kohl (kōl), *n.* a powder, as finely powdered antimony sulfide, used as a cosmetic to darken the eyelids, eyebrows, etc. [1790–1800; < Ar *kohl,* var. of *kuhl.* See ALCOHOL]

Kohl (kōl), *n.* **Hel•mut** (hel′mo͞ot), born 1930, German political leader: chancellor of West Germany 1982–90; Chancellor of Germany since 1990.

Köh•ler (kœ′lər), *n.* **Wolf•gang** (vôlf′gäng), 1887–1967, German psychologist.

kohl•ra•bi (kōl rä′bē, -rab′ē, kōl′rä′bē, -rab′ē), *n., pl.* **-bies.** a cultivated cabbage, *Brassica oleracea gongylodes,* whose stem above ground swells into an edible, bulblike formation. Also called **stem cabbage, turnip cabbage.** [1800–10; < G < It *cavolrape* (pl. of *cavolrapa* lit., stalk or cabbage turnip), with G *Kohl* cabbage for It *cavol-.* See COLE, RAPE[2]]

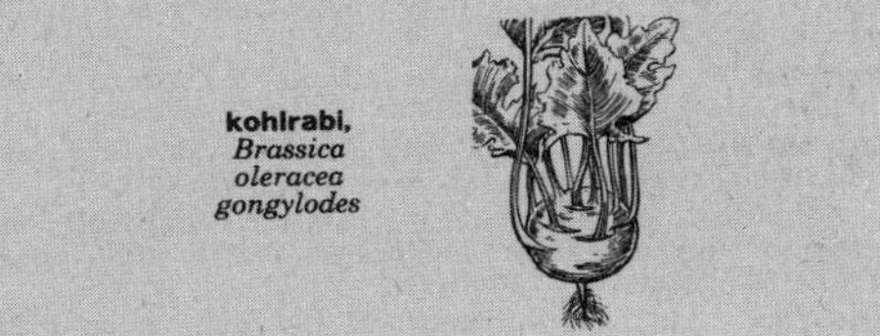
kohlrabi, *Brassica oleracea gongylodes*

Ko•hou•tek (kō hō′tek, kə-), *n. Astron.* a comet that passed around the sun in late 1973 and early 1974 and was barely visible with the naked eye. [named after Luboš *Kohoutek* (b. 1935), Czech astronomer who discovered it in February, 1973]

koi (koi), *n.* any of various colorful cultivated forms of the common carp, *Cyprinus carpio,* apparently originating in Japan and other parts of eastern temperate Asia. [1720–30; < Japn, earlier *kowi* < *kofi,* Old Japn *kwofi* < **kwopi* carp]

koil•o•nych•i•a (koi′lō nik′ē ə), *n. Med.* an abnormal condition in which the outer surfaces of the nails are concave; spoon nail. [1900–05; < Gk *koîl*(*os*) hollow + *onych-* (s. of *ónyx* nail; see ONYX) + -IA]

koi•ne (koi nā′, koi′nā), *n.* **1.** (*usually cap.*) an amalgam of Greek dialects, chiefly Attic and Ionic, that replaced the Classical Greek dialects in the Hellenistic period and flourished under the Roman Empire. **2.** a lingua franca. [1910–15; < Gk *koinē* (*diálektos*) common (dialect); see CENO-[2]]

ko•ji (kō′jē), *n.* a fungus, *Aspergillus oryzae,* used to initiate fermentation of a mixture of soybeans and wheat in the production of soy sauce. [< Japn *kōji* malt, yeast < *kaudi* < *kaūdi* < *kamudati,* prob. equiv. to **kamu* (< **kanpu* mold; cf. *kabu,* a var. outcome of the same etymon) + *-dati,* comb. form of *tati* to rise]

Ko•kand (ko kand′; *Russ.* ku känt′), *n.* a city in NE Uzbekistan, SE of Tashkent: formerly the center of a powerful khanate. 153,000.

ko•kan•ee (kō kan′ē), *n.* any of several lacustrine sockeye salmons. [1870–75; perh. < Shuswap (an Interior Salish language of British Columbia) *kəknǽxʷ*]

Kok•ka (kôk′kä), *adj.* of or pertaining to the branch of Shinto recognized as the official state religion of Japan. Cf. **Shuha.** [< Japn: lit., state < MChin, equiv. to Chin *guójiā*]

Kok•ko•la (kôk′kô lä), *n.* a seaport in E Finland, on the Gulf of Bothnia. 34,000.

ko•ko (kō′kō), *n., pl.* **-kos.** lebbek (def. 2). [1860–65; var. of *kokko,* of uncert. orig.]

Ko•ko (kō′kō), *n.* born 1973, female gorilla, trained to communicate with humans by means of a sign language.

Ko•ko•mo (kō′kə mō′), *n.* a city in central Indiana. 47,808.

Ko•ko Nor (kō′kō′ nôr′), **1.** See **Qing Hai. 2.** former name of **Qinghai.**

Ko•kosch•ka (kō kôsh′kä), *n.* **Os•kar** (ôs′kär), 1886–1980, Austrian painter and dramatist.

kok-sa•ghyz (kōk′sə gēz′), *n.* a central Asian dandelion, *Taraxacum kok-saghyz,* of the composite family, having fleshy roots that yield a rubberlike latex. Also called **Russian dandelion.** [1930–35; < NL < Kazakh *kok-sagïz* lit., root gum]

ko•ku (kō′ko͞o; *Japn.* kô′ko͞o), *n., pl.* **-ku.** a Japanese unit of dry measure equivalent to 5.12 bushels (1.8 hectoliters). [< Japn < MChin, equiv. to Chin *hú* measure]

Ko•ku•ra (kō ko͝or′ə; *Japn.* kô′ko͞o rä′), *n.* See under **Kitakyushu.**

ko•la (kō′lə), *n.* **1.** See **kola nut. 2.** an extract prepared from the kola nut. **3.** the tree producing it. **4.** cola[1]. [1720–30; appar. var. of Malinke *kolo*]

Ko•la (kō′lə; kô′lə), *n.* Also called **Ko′la Penin′sula.** a peninsula in the NW Russian Federation in Europe, between the White and Barents seas.

ko•lac•ky (kə lä′chē, -läch′kē), *n., pl.* **-ky.** a sweet bun filled with jam or pulped fruit. Also, **ko•lach** (kō′-läch), **ko•la•che** (kō lä′chē). [1915–20; < Czech *koláče,* pl. of *koláč* (deriv. of *kolo* WHEEL, circle; cf. KOLO) or *koláčky,* pl. of *koláček,* dim. of *koláč*]

ko′la nut′, a brownish seed, about the size of a chestnut, produced by a tropical tree belonging to the genus *Cola,* containing both caffeine and theobromine: its extract is used in soft drinks. [1865–70]

Ko•lar (kō lär′), *n.* a city in SE Karnataka, in S India: rich mining district. 76,112.

Kol•be (kôl′bə), *n.* **Ge•org** (gā ôrk′), 1877–1947, German sculptor.

Kol•chak (kôl chäk′; *Russ.* kul chyäk′), *n.* **A•le•ksandr Va•si•lye•vich** (u lyi ksändr′ vu syē′lyi vyich), 1874–1920, Russian counterrevolutionary and admiral.

Kol•de•wey (kôl′də vī′), *n.* **Ro•bert** (rob′ərt; *Ger.* rō′-bert), 1855–1925, German archaeologist.

Kolff (kōlf, kolf), *n.* **Wil•lem J(o•han)** (wil′əm yō′hän, -han), born 1911, U.S. physician and inventor, born in the Netherlands: developed the artificial kidney machine.

Kol•ha•pur (kō′lə po͝or′), *n.* a city in S Maharashtra, in SW India. 259,050.

Kol′hapur and Dec′can States′, a group of former princely states in W India: incorporated into Bombay state in 1948; now part of Gujarat and Maharashtra states.

Ko•li (kō′lē), *n., pl.* **-lis,** (*esp. collectively*) **-li.** a people of low caste in northern India.

Ko•li•ma (kə lē′mə; *Russ.* kə li mä′), *n.* Kolyma.

ko•lin•sky (kə lin′skē), *n., pl.* **-skies. 1.** an Asian mink, *Mustela sibirica,* having buff or tawny fur. **2.** the fur of such an animal. [1850–55; perh. alter. of Russ *kolonkí,* pl. of *kolonók* kolinsky << Evenki (NW dials.) *xolongō*]

kol•khoz (kol kôz′; *Russ.* kul khôs′), *n.* (in the U.S.S.R.) a collective farm. [1920–25; < Russ *kolkhóz,* for *kol*(*lektívnoe*) COLLECTIVE + *khoz*(*yáĭstvo*) household, farm, economy]

Koll•witz (kôl′vits), *n.* **Kä•the** (ke′tə), 1867–1945, German graphic artist and sculptor.

Köln (kœln), *n.* German name of **Cologne.**

Kol Ni•dre (*Seph. Heb.* kôl nē drä′; *Ashk. Heb.* kōl′ nid′rə, -rā), *Judaism.* a liturgical prayer for recitation at the beginning of the service on the eve of Yom Kippur asking that all unfulfilled vows to God be nullified and all transgressions forgiven. [< Aram *kōl* all + *nidhrē* vows, promises]

ko•lo (kō′lō), *n., pl.* **-los.** a Serbian folk dance performed by a group arranged in a circle, with the soloists in the center. [1910–15; < Serbo-Croatian *kȍlo* lit., circle, WHEEL]

ko•lo•a (kə lō′ə), *n.* a Hawaiian duck, *Anas wyvilliana,* related to the mallard, having a dusky greenish head and dark chestnut breast. [< Hawaiian: duck]

Ko•lom•na (ku lôm′nə), *n.* a city in the W Russian Federation in Europe, SE of Moscow. 147,000.

Ko•lozs•vár (kô′lôzh vär′), *n.* Hungarian name of **Cluj-Napoca.**

Kol•pi•no (kôl′pyi nə), *n.* a city in the NW Russian Federation in Europe: a suburb SE of St. Petersburg. 114,000.

Kol•we•zi (kōl wez′ē), *n.* a city in S Zaire. 71,000.

Ko•ly•ma (kə lē′mə; *Russ.* kə li mä′), *n.* a river in the NE Russian Federation in Asia, flowing NE to the Arctic Ocean. 1000 mi. (1610 km) long. Also, **Kolima.**

Koly′ma Range′, a mountain range in NE Siberia in the NE Russian Federation.

ko•mat•ik (kō mat′ik), *Chiefly Canadian.* an Eskimo sled made by binding crossbars to wooden runners with rawhide. [1815–25; < Inuit *qamutik*]

Ko•men•ský (*Czech.* kô′men skē), *n.* **Jan A•mos** (*Czech.* yän ä′môs). See **Comenius, John Amos.**

Ko•mi (kō′mē), *n., pl.* **-mis,** (*esp. collectively*) **-mi** for 1. **1.** a member of a Uralic people of northeastern European Russia. **2.** the Permic language of the Komi. Also, **Zyryan, Zyryenian.** [< Russ *kómi* (not declined) < Komi]

Ko′mi Auton′omous Repub′lic, an autonomous republic in the NW Russian Federation in Europe. 1,118,000; 145,221 sq. mi. (376,122 sq. km). *Cap.:* Syktyvkar.

Kom•in•tern (kom′in tûrn′, kom′in tûrn′), *n.* Comintern.

Kom•mu•narsk (kə mo͞o närsk′), *n.* a city in E Ukraine. 123,800.

Ko•mo′do drag′on (kə mō′dō), a monitor lizard, *Varanus komodoensis,* of certain Indonesian islands E of Java, that grows to a length of 10 ft. (3 m): the largest lizard in the world; now rare. Also called **dragon lizard, giant lizard, Komo′do liz′ard.** [1925–30; named after *Komodo,* Indonesian island, its principal range]

Ko•mon•dor (kom′ən dôr′), *n., pl.* **-dors, -dor•ok** (-dôr′ək). one of a Hungarian breed of large dogs having a long, matted, white coat, used for herding sheep and as a watchdog. [1930–35; < Hungarian, allegedly after a Turkic tribal name]

Ko•mos (kō′məs), *n.* Comus.

Kom•so•mol (kom′sə môl′, kom′sə môl′), *n.* (formerly) **1.** a communist organization in the Soviet Union for youths 16 years of age and older. **2.** a member of this organization. Cf. **Octobrist** (def. 2), **Pioneer** (def. 6). Also, **Comsomol.** [< Russ *Komsomól,* for *Kom*(*munistícheskiĭ*) *so*(*yúz*) *mol*(*odëzhi*) Communist Union of Youth]

Kom•so•molsk (kom′sə môlsk′; *Russ.* kəm su-môlsk′), *n.* a city in the E Russian Federation in Asia, on the Amur River. 29,000. Also called **Kom•so•molsk-on-A•mur** (kom′sə môlsk′on ä mo͝or′, -ôn-).

Ko•mu•ra (kô′mo͞o rä′), *n.* **Marquis Ju•ta•ro** (jo͞o′tä-rô′), 1855–1911, Japanese statesman and diplomat.

ko•na (kō′nə), *n.* a southwesterly winter wind in Hawaii, often strong and bringing rain. [1860–65; < Hawaiian]

ko′na cy′clone, a slow-moving cyclone occuring during the winter over the subtropical Pacific Ocean. [1955–60]

ko•nak (kō näk′), *n.* (in Turkey) a large, usually official residence. [< Turk: lit., stopping-place (for the night, on a journey), deriv. of *kon-* camp, make a night's halt]

Ko•na•kri (*Fr.* kô na krē′), *n.* Conakry.

Ko•na•rak (kə när′ək), *n.* a village in E Orissa, in E India: site of the famous Black Pagoda. Also, **Kanarak.**

kon•di•to•rei (kən dit′ə rī′; *Ger.* kôn de′tô rī′), *n.* (*often cap.*) a German pastry and coffee shop. [1930–35; < G, equiv. to *Konditor* confectioner (< L *conditor* one who seasons; *condī*(*re*) to season (cf. CONDIMENT) + *-tor* -TOR) + *-ei* (MHG *-īe* < OF *-ie* -Y[3])]

Kon•dra′tieff wave′ (kən drä′tē ef′, -tyəf), *Econ.* a long business cycle of economic expansion and contraction, postulated to last about 60 years. [named after Nikolaĭ Dmitrievich *Kondrat'ev* (1892–1935?), Russian economist, who postulated it]

Ko•ner (kō′nər), *n.* **Pauline,** born 1912?, U.S. dancer and choreographer.

Ko•nev (kôn′yef; *Russ.* kô′nyif), *n.* **I•van Ste•pa•no•vich** (ē vän′ styi pä′nə vyich), 1897–1973, Russian general and politician.

Kong Fu•zi (kông′ fo͞o′zē′), *Pinyin.* K'ung Fu-tzŭ. Also called **Kong•zi** (kông′zē′).

Kon•go (kong′gō), *n., pl.* **-gos,** (*esp. collectively*) **-go** for 1. **1.** a member of an indigenous people living in west-central Africa along the lower course of the Congo River. **2.** Also called **Kikongo.** the Bantu language of the Kongo people, used as a lingua franca in western Zaire, southern Congo, and northern Angola.

Kong Qiu (*Chin.* kông′ chyo͞o′), *Pinyin.* personal name of **Confucius.**

Kon•ia (kôn′yä, kôn yä′), *n.* Konya.

Kö•nig•grätz (*Ger.* kœ′nikh grets′), *n.* German name of **Hradec Králové.**

Kö•nigs•berg (kœ′nikhs berk′; *Eng.* kā′nigz bûrg′), *n.* German name of **Kaliningrad.**

Kö′nigsberg bridge′ prob′lem, a mathematical problem in graph theory, solved by Leonhard Euler, to show that it is impossible to cross all seven bridges of the Prussian city of Königsberg in a continuous path without recrossing any bridge.

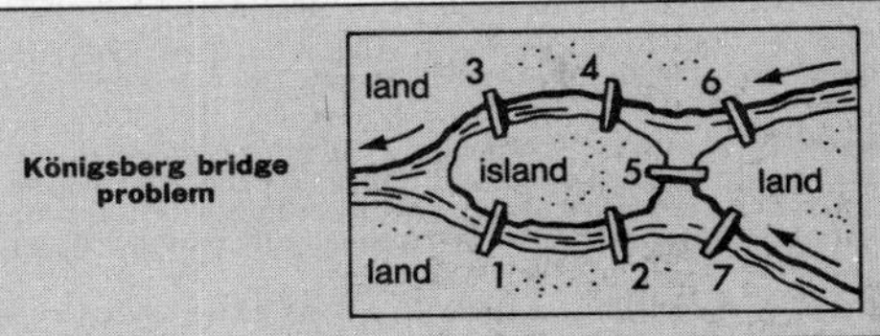

Königsberg bridge problem

Kö•nigs•hüt•te (kœ′nikhs hy′tə), *n.* German name of **Chorzów.**

ko•nim•e•ter (kō nim′i tər), *n.* an instrument for measuring the amount of dust in the air. [1915–20; < Gk *kóni*(*s*) dust + -METER]

Kon•ka•ni (kong′kə nē′, kông′-), *n.* a dialect of Marathi spoken in coastal Maharashtra in western India.

Ko•no•ye (kô′nô ye′), *n.* **Prince Fu•mi•ma•ro** (fo͞o′-mē mä′rô), 1891–1945, Japanese statesman: premier 1937–39, 1940–41.

Kon•rad (kon′rad), *n.* a male given name.

Kon•stan•ti•nov•ka (kon′stən tē′nəf kə; *Russ.* kən-stun tyē′nəf kə), *n.* a city in E Ukraine, NW of Gorlovka. 112,000.

Kon•stanz (kôn′stänts), *n.* German name of **Constance.**

CONCISE PRONUNCIATION KEY: *act, cāpe, dâre, pärt; set, ēqual; if, īce; ox, ōver, ôrder, oil, bo͝ok, bo͞ot, out; up, ûrge; child; sing; shoe; thin, that;* zh as in *treasure.* ə = *a* as in *alone, e* as in *system, i* as in *easily, o* as in *gallop, u* as in *circus;* ᵊ as in *fire* (fīᵊr), *hour* (ouᵊr). l and n can serve as syllabic consonants, as in *cradle* (krād′l), and *button* (but′n). See the full key inside the front cover.

kon•ta•ki•on (kôn tä′kē ôn; *Eng.* kən tä′kē on′), *n., pl.* **-ki•a** (-kē ä; *Eng.* -kē ə). *Gk. Orth. Ch.* a short hymn honoring a saint. Also, **contakion.** [< 1865–70; LGk, special use of *kontákion* scroll, equiv. to *kontak-* (s. of *kóntax*) pole + *-ion* dim. suffix]

Kon•ya (kôn′yä, kôn yä′), *n.* a city in S Turkey, S of Ankara. 246,381. Also, **Konia.** Ancient, **Iconium.**

Koo (ko͞o), *n.* **(Vi Kyuin) Wellington** (wē′ gyin′), (*Ku Wei-chün, Gu Weijun*), 1887–1985, Chinese diplomat and statesman.

Koo•bi Fo•ra (ko͞o′bē fôr′ə), an archaeological locality on the northeastern side of Lake Rudolf, in northern Kenya, yielding important early hominid fossils and some of the oldest hominid areas with stone tools, bone food waste, and possible evidence of fire use, dating from one to two million years ago.

koo•doo (ko͞o′do͞o), *n., pl.* **-doos.** kudu.

kook (ko͞ok), *n. Slang.* **1.** an eccentric, strange, or foolish person. **2.** an insane person. [1955–60; perh. alter. of CUCKOO]

kook•a•bur•ra (ko͝ok′ə bûr′ə, -bur′ə), *n.* an Australian kingfisher, *Dacelo gigas,* having a loud, harsh cry that resembles laughter. Also called **laughing jackass.** [1885–90; < Wiradjuri *gugubarra* (imit.)]

kookaburra, *Dacelo gigas,* length 17 in. (43 cm)

kook•y (ko͞o′kē), *adj.,* **kook•i•er, kook•i•est.** *Slang.* of, like, or pertaining to a kook; eccentric, strange, or foolish. Also, **kook′ie.** [1955–60; KOOK + -Y[1]]

Koop•mans (ko͞op′mənz), *n.* **Tjal•ling Charles** (chä′ling), 1910–85, U.S. economist, born in the Netherlands: Nobel prize 1975.

koo•ra•jong (ko͝or′ə jong′), *n.* kurrajong.

Koord (kûrd, ko͝ord), *n.* a Kurd.

koo•tchar (ko͞o′chər), *n.* any of several small, stingless Australian honeybees of the genus *Trigona.* [1880–85; < Bandjalang (Australian Aboriginal language of NE New South Wales and SE Queensland) *guja*]

Koo•te•nay (ko͞ot′n ā′, -n ē′), *n.* a river flowing from SW Canada through NW Montana and N Idaho, swinging back into Canada to the Columbia River. 400 mi. (645 km) long. Also, **Koo′te•nai′, Kutenay, Kutenai.**

Koo′tenay Lake′, a lake in W Canada, in S British Columbia. 64 mi. (103 km) long.

kop (kop), *n.* (in South Africa) a hill. [1825–35; < Afrik: lit., head, hence high or top part. See COP[3]]

kop., kopeck.

ko•peck (kō′pek), *n.* an aluminum-bronze coin of Russia, the Soviet Union, and its successor states, the 100th part of a ruble. Also, **ko′pek, copeck.** [1690–1700; < Russ *kopéĭka,* equiv. to *kop′ë* lance, spear + *-ka* dim. suffix; so called from the lance with which the figure on the coin was armed]

Ko•peisk (kō päsk′; *Russ.* ku pyäsk′), *n.* a city in the SW Russian Federation in Asia, near the Urals. 146,000. Also, **Ko•peysk′.**

kopf•ring (kôpf′ring′), *n.* a metal ring welded to the nose of a bomb to reduce its penetration in earth or water. [< G, equiv. to *Kopf* head + *Ring* band, RING[1]]

koph (kôf), *n.* **1.** the nineteenth letter of the Hebrew alphabet. **2.** the uvular stop consonant sound represented by this letter. Also, **kof, qoph.** [< Heb *qōph*]

Kop•it (kop′it), *n.* **Arthur,** born 1937, U.S. playwright.

kop•je (kop′ē), *n.* (in South Africa) a small hill. Also, **kop′pie.** [1880–85; < Afrik, equiv. to *kop* KOP + *-je* dim. suffix]

Kop′lik's spots′ (kop′liks), (in measles) small pale spots with reddish rims that appear on the lips and mucous membranes inside the cheeks before the skin eruption takes place. [1895–1900; named after Henry *Koplik* (1858–1927), U.S. pediatrician]

kop•pa (kop′ə), *n.* a letter (Ϙ, ϙ) of some early Greek alphabets, occurring between pi and rho and equivalent to Latin *Q:* later superseded by kappa except for its use as a numeral for 90. [1865–70; < Gk *kóppa* < Sem; akin to Heb *qōph* KOPH]

kor (kôr, kōr), *n.* homer[2]. [< Heb *kōr*]

ko•rad•ji (kə rä′jē), *n. Australian.* boyla. Also, **coraji.** [1793; < Dharuk *ga-rā-ji*]

Ko•rah (kôr′ə, kōr′ə), *n.* a Levite who led a rebellion against Moses and Aaron. Num. 16. Also, **Core.**

Ko•ran (kə rän′, -ran′, kô-, kō-), *n.* the sacred text of Islam, divided into 114 chapters, or suras: revered as the word of God, dictated to Muhammad by the archangel Gabriel, and accepted as the foundation of Islamic law, religion, culture, and politics. Also, **Qur'an.** [1615–25; < Ar *qur'ān* book, reading, akin to *qara'a* to read, recite] —**Ko•ran•ic** (kə ran′ik, kô-, kō-), *adj.*

kor•ban (kôr′bən; *Seph. Heb.* kôʀ bän′; *Ashk. Heb,* kôr′bən), *n.* corban.

CONCISE ETYMOLOGY KEY: <, descended or borrowed from; >, whence; b., blend of, blended; c., cognate with; cf., compare; deriv., derivative; equiv., equivalent; imit., imitative; obl., oblique; r., replacing; s., stem; sp., spelling, spelled; resp., respelling, respelled; trans., translation; ?, origin unknown; *, unattested; ‡, probably earlier than. See the full key inside the front cover.

Kor•but (kôr′bət), *n.* **Olga,** born 1955, Russian gymnast.

Kor•çë (kôr′chə), *n.* a city in SE Albania. 50,900. Italian, **Corizza.**

Kor•da (kôr′də), *n.* **Sir Alexander** (*Sándor Kellner*), 1893–1956, British film producer, born in Hungary.

Kor•do•fan (kôr′dō fän′), *n.* a province in the central Sudan. 3,103,000. ab. 147,000 sq. mi. (380,730 sq. km). *Cap.:* El Obeid.

Kor•do•fan•i•an (kôr′də fan′ē ən), *n.* a subfamily of Niger-Kordofanian that comprises about 30 languages spoken in southern Kordofan. [KORDOFAN + -IAN]

ko•re (kôr′ē, kōr′ē; kôr′ā, kōr′ā), *n., pl.* **ko•rai** (kôr′ī, kōr′ī). **1.** *Gk. Antiq.* a sculptured representation of a young woman, esp. one produced prior to the 5th century B.C. **2.** Also, **Core, Cora.** (*cap.*) *Class. Myth.* Persephone, esp. as a symbol of virginity. [1915–20; < Gk *kórē* girl]

Ko•re•a (kə rē′ə, kô-, kō-), *n.* **1.** a former country in E Asia, on a peninsula SE of Manchuria and between the Sea of Japan and the Yellow Sea: a kingdom prior to 1910; under Japanese rule 1910–45; now divided at 38° N into North Korea and South Korea. Cf. **Korean War. 2. Democratic People's Republic of,** official name of **North Korea. 3. Republic of,** official name of **South Korea.** Cf. **North Korea, South Korea.**

Ko•re•an (kə rē′ən, kô-, kō-), *adj.* **1.** of or pertaining to Korea, its inhabitants, or their language. —*n.* **2.** a native or inhabitant of Korea. **3.** the language of Korea. [1605–15; KORE(A) + -AN]

Kore′an lawn′ grass′, an Asiatic creeping grass, *Zoysia japonica,* used esp. in the southeastern U.S., having purplish spikelets and rootstalks that send up numerous tough, wiry shoots. Also called **Japanese lawn grass.**

Kore′an War′, the war, begun on June 25, 1950, between North Korea, aided by Communist China, and South Korea, aided by the United States and other United Nations members forming a United Nations armed force: truce signed July 27, 1953.

Kore′a Strait′, a strait between Korea and Japan, connecting the Sea of Japan and the East China Sea. 120 mi. (195 km) long.

Ko•ri•ya•ma (kô′ʀē yä′mä), *n.* a city on E central Honshu, in Japan. 286,497.

Korn•berg (kôrn′bûrg), *n.* **Arthur,** born 1918, U.S. biochemist: Nobel prize for medicine 1959.

Korn•gold (kôrn′gōld′; *Ger.* kôʀn′gôlt′), *n.* **E•rich Wolf•gang** (er′ik wo͝olf′gang; *Ger.* ā′ʀɪᴋʜ vôlf′gäng), 1897–1957, Austrian composer, conductor, and pianist in the U.S.

ko•ro (kôr′ō, kōr′ō), *n. Psychiatry.* a culture-specific syndrome, occurring chiefly in China and southeastern Asia, characterized by anxiety and the fear of retraction of the penis or breasts and labia into the body. [< dial. Malay (Kedah) *kɔrɔ* land turtle (standard Malay *kura-kura*]

ko•ro•na (kôr′ə nə, kōr′- *for 1;* kôr′ə nä′ *for 2*), *n.* **1.** Also, **krone.** a former silver coin and monetary unit of Austria, equal to 100 hellers: discontinued after 1923. **2.** koruna. [var. of KRONE[2]]

Kort′ noz′zle (kôrt), *Naut.* a cylindrical fitting around a propeller, tapered inward toward the stern to increase thrust and maneuverability.

Kort•rijk (kôʀᴛ′ʀīk), *n.* Flemish name of **Courtrai.**

ko•ru•na (kôr′ə nä′), *n., pl.* **ko•ru•ny** (kôr′ə nē), **ko•run** (kôr′o͞on), **ko•ru•nas.** an aluminum bronze coin and monetary unit of the Czech Republic, equal to 100 halers. *Abbr.:* Kčs. Also, **korona.** [1925–30; < Czech < L *corōna* a crown, wreath; see CORONA]

Kor•yak (kôr′yak), *n., pl.* **-yaks,** (*esp. collectively*) **-yak** for **1. 1.** a member of a Paleo-Asiatic people of northeastern Siberia. **2.** the Chukotian language of the Koryak people, closely related to Chukchi.

Kor•zyb•ski (kôr zip′skē, -zhip′-; *Pol.* kô zhip′skē), *n.* **Alfred (Hab•dank Skar•bek)** (hab′dangk skär′bek; *Pol.* häp′dängk skär′bek), 1879–1950, U.S. writer on general semantics, born in Poland.

kos (kōs), *n., pl.* **kos.** (in India) a unit of land distance of various lengths from 1 to 3 mi. (1.6 to 4.8 km). Also, **coss.** [< Hindi << Skt *krośa*]

Kos (kos, kôs), *n.* one of the Greek Dodecanese Islands in the SE Aegean Sea, off the SW coast of Turkey. 16,650; 111 sq. mi. (287 sq. km). Also, **Cos.** Italian, **Coo.**

Kos•ci•us•ko (kos′kē us′kō, kos′ē-; *for 1 also Pol.* kôsh cho͞osh′kô), *n.* **1. Thaddeus** (*Tadeusz Andrzej Bonawentura Kościuszko*), 1746–1817, Polish patriot: general in the American Revolutionary army. **2. Mount,** the highest mountain in Australia, in SE New South Wales. 7316 ft. (2230 m).

ko•sha (kō′shə), *n. Hinduism.* any of the five layers of physical and mental being composing the personal self, Atman being within the innermost layer. [< Skt *kośa*]

ko•sher (kō′shər), *adj.* **1.** *Judaism.* **a.** fit or allowed to be eaten or used, according to the dietary or ceremonial laws: *kosher meat; a kosher tallith.* **b.** adhering to the laws governing such fitness: *a kosher restaurant.* **2.** *Informal.* **a.** proper; legitimate. **b.** genuine; authentic. **3. keep kosher,** to adhere to the dietary laws of Judaism. —*n.* **4.** *Informal.* kosher food. —*v.t.* **5.** *Judaism.* to make kosher. Also, **kasher.** [1850–55; 1920–25 for def. 2; < Yiddish < Heb *kāshēr* right, fit]

ko•sher-style (kō′shər stīl′), *adj.* (of a cuisine, restaurant, etc.) featuring traditional Jewish dishes, but not adhering to the dietary laws: *kosher-style cooking.*

Ko•ši•ce (kô′shi tse), *n.* a city in SE Slovakia. 202,368. Hungarian, **Kassa.**

kos•mos (koz′məs, -mōs), *n. Aerospace.* cosmos (def. 5).

Kos•rae (kōs rī′), *n.* an island in the W Pacific: part of the Federated States of Micronesia. 4471; 42 sq. mi. (109 sq. km). Also called **Kusaie.**

Kos•sel (kôs′əl), *n.* **Al•brecht** (äl′bʀᴇᴋʜt), 1853–1927, German chemist: Nobel prize for medicine 1910.

Kos•suth (kos′o͞oth; *Hung.* kô′sho͞ot), *n.* **1. Fer•enc** (feʀ′ents), 1841–1914, Hungarian statesman. **2.** his father, **La•jos** (lo′yôsh), 1802–94, Hungarian patriot, statesman, and writer.

Kos•te•la•netz (kos′tə lä′nits), *n.* **An•dré** (än′drā), 1901–80, U.S. orchestra conductor and pianist, born in Russia.

Kos•ti (kôs′tē), *n.* a city in E central Sudan, on the White Nile. 47,000.

Ko•stro•ma (kos′trə mä′; *Russ.* kə stʀu mä′), *n.* a city in the W Russian Federation in Europe, NE of Moscow, on the Volga. 255,000.

Ko•sy•gin (kə sē′gin; *Russ.* ku si′gyin), *n.* **A•le•ksei Ni•ko•la•ye•vich** (ə lek′sā nik′ə lä′yə vich; *Russ.* u lyi-ksyā′ nyi ku lä′yi vyich), 1904–80, Russian politician: premier of the U.S.S.R. 1964–80.

Ko•ta Bha•ru (kō′tə bär′o͞o), a seaport in and the capital of Kelantan state, in Malaysia, on the E central Malay Peninsula. 55,124. Also, **Ko′ta Bah′ru.**

Ko•ta Ki•na•ba•lu (kō′tə kin′ə bə lo͞o′), a seaport in and the capital of the state of Sabah, in Malaysia, on the NW coast of Borneo. 42,000. Formerly, **Jesselton.**

ko•to (kō′tō; *Japn.* kô′tô′), *n., pl.* **-tos, -to.** a Japanese musical instrument having numerous strings, usually seven or thirteen, that are stretched over a convex wooden sounding board and are plucked with three plectra, worn on the thumb, index finger, and middle finger of one hand. [1785–95; < Japn]

ko•tow (kō′tou′, -tou′), *v.i., n.* kowtow.

Kot•te (kō′tā), *n.* a city in SW Sri Lanka, just E of Colombo. 102,000.

kot•wal (kōt′wäl), *n. Anglo-Indian.* an Indian police officer. Also, **cotwal.** [1575–85; < Hindi *koṭwāl*]

kot•wa•li (kōt′wä lē), *n. Anglo-Indian.* a police station. Also, **kot′wa•lee.** [1835–45; < Hindi *koṭwālī*]

Kot•ze•bue (kôt′sə bo͞o′), *n.* **Au•gust Frie•drich Fer•di•nand von** (ou′go͝ost fʀē′dʀɪᴋʜ feʀ′di nänt′ fən), 1761–1819, German dramatist.

Kou•fax (kō′faks), *n.* **Sanford** (*Sandy*), born 1935, U.S. baseball player.

kou•mis (ko͞o′mis), *n.* kumiss. Also, **kou′miss, kou′myss.**

kou•prey (ko͞o′prā), *n., pl.* **-preys,** (*esp. collectively*) **-prey.** a wild ox, *Bibos* (*Novibos*) *sauveli,* of Laos and Cambodia, having a blackish-brown body with white markings on the back and feet: an endangered species. Also called **gray ox.** [1935–40; (< F) < spoken Khmer *ko:prey* (written *gō brai*) < Pali *gō* cow[1] + Khmer *brai* forest]

kour•bash (ko͝or′bash), *n., v.t.* kurbash.

kou•ros (ko͝or′os), *n., pl.* **kou•roi** (ko͝or′oi). *Gk. Antiq.* a sculptured representation of a young man, esp. one produced prior to the 5th century B.C. [1915–20; < Gk *koûros,* dial. var. of *kóros* boy; cf. KORE]

Kous•se•vitz•ky (ko͞o′sə vit′skē), *n.* **Serge** (sârzh), (*Sergei Alexandrovich Koussevitsky*), 1874–1951, Russian orchestra conductor in the U.S.

Ko•va•lev•sky (kov′ə lef′skē, -lev′-), *n.* **So•nia** (sōn′yə), (*Sofia Vasilievna Kovalevskaya*), 1850–91, Russian mathematician.

Kov•no (kôv′nə), *n.* Russian name of **Kaunas.**

Ko•vrov (kov rôf′, -rof′; *Russ.* ku vʀôf′), *n.* a city in the W Russian Federation in Europe, ENE of Moscow. 143,000.

Ko•weit (kō wāt′), *n.* Kuwait.

ko•whai (kō′wī), *n.* a New Zealand tree, *Sophora tetraptera,* of the legume family, having clusters of golden-yellow flowers. [1825–35; < Maori *kō(w)hai*]

Kow•loon (kou′lo͞on′), *n. Older Spelling.* **1.** a peninsula in SE China, opposite Hong Kong island: a part of the Hong Kong colony. 3 sq. mi. (7.8 sq. km). **2.** a seaport on this peninsula. 715,440. Also called **Jiulong.**

kow•tow (kou′tou′, -tou′, kō′-), *v.i.* **1.** to act in an obsequious manner; show servile deference. **2.** to touch the forehead to the ground while kneeling, as an act of worship, reverence, apology, etc., esp. in former Chinese custom. —*n.* **3.** the act of kowtowing. Also, **kotow.** [1795–1805; < Chin *kòutóu* lit., knock (one's) head] —**kow′tow′er,** *n.*

Ko•yu•kon (koi′yo͞o kon′, kä′-), *n.* **1.** a member of a North American Indian people living in the Yukon River valley in west-central Alaska. **2.** the Athabaskan language of the Koyukon. Also called **Tena.** [resp., after the *Koyukuk* and *Yukon* Rivers, of earlier *Co-Youkon* < Russ *kuyukantsy* (pl.), deriv. of *Kuyukak* the Koyukuk River << Inupiaq *kuiyuk*]

Ko•za•ni (kô zä′nē), *n.* a city in central Greece. 23,240. Also, **Ko•zá′ne.**

Ko•zhi•kode (kō′zhi kōd′), *n.* a city in W Kerala, in SW India. 333,980. Formerly, **Calicut.**

Ko•zlov (koz′lôf, -lof; *Russ.* ku zlôf′), *n.* **1. Frol R(o•ma•no•vich)** (FRÔL RU mä′nə vyich), 1908–65, Russian government official. **2.** former name of **Michurinsk.**

KP, *Chess.* king's pawn.

K.P., **1.** *Mil.* See **kitchen police. 2.** Knight of the Order of St. Patrick. **3.** Knights of Pythias.

kpc, kiloparsec; kiloparsecs.

Kpel•le (kə pel′ə), *n., pl.* **-les,** (*esp. collectively*) **-le** for 1. **1.** a member of an indigenous people living mainly in Liberia. **2.** the Mande language of the Kpelle people.

kph, kilometers per hour. Also, **k.p.h.**

KR, *Chess.* king's rook.

Kr, *Symbol. Chem.* krypton.

Kr., **1.** (in Sweden and the Faeroe Islands) krona; kronor. **2.** (in Iceland) króna; krónur. **3.** (in Denmark and Norway) krone; kroner.

kr., **1.** kreutzer. **2.** krona; kronor. **3.** króna; krónur. **4.** krone; kroner.

Kra (krä), *n.* **Isthmus of,** the narrowest part of the Malay Peninsula, between the Bay of Bengal and the Gulf of Siam. 35 mi. (56 km) wide.

kraal (kräl), *n.* **1.** an enclosure for cattle and other domestic animals in southern Africa. **2.** a village of the native peoples of South Africa, usually surrounded by a stockade or the like and often having a central space for livestock. **3.** such a village as a social unit. **4.** an enclosure where wild animals are exhibited, as in a zoo. —*v.t.* **5.** to shut up in a krall, as cattle. Also, **craal.** [1725–35; < Afrik < Pg *curral* pen; see CORRAL]

K-ra•di•a•tion (kā′rā′dē ā′shən), *n. Physics.* See under **K-line.**

Krae•pe•lin (kRe′pə lēn′), *n.* **E•mil** (ā′mēl), 1856–1926, German psychiatrist.

Krafft-E•bing (kraft′eb′ing, kräft′-; *Ger.* kRäft′ā′-bingk), *n.* **Rich•ard** (rich′ərd; *Ger.* RIKH′ÄRT), **Baron von,** 1840–1902, German neurologist and author of works on sexual pathology.

kraft (kraft, kräft), *n.* a strong, usually brown paper processed from wood pulp, used chiefly for bags and as wrapping paper. [1905–10; < G: lit., strength]

kraft′ proc′ess, *Chem.* See **sulfate process.**

krait (krīt), *n.* any of several large, usually banded, placid but highly venomous snakes constituting the genus *Bungarus,* of the cobra family, common in southeastern Asia and the Malay Archipelago. [1870–75; < Hindi *karait*]

Krak (kräk), *n.* Kerak.

Kra•ka•tau (krak′ə tou′, krä′kə-), *n.* a volcano and small island in Indonesia, between Java and Sumatra: violent eruption 1883. Also, **Kra′ka•tao′, Kra•ka•to•a** (krak′ə tō′ə, krä′kə-).

Kra•kau (*Ger.* krä′kou), *n.* Cracow.

kra•ken (krä′kən), *n.* (*often cap.*) a legendary sea monster causing large whirlpools off the coast of Norway. [< Norw]

Kra•ków (*Pol.* krä′kŏŏf), *n.* Cracow.

kra•ko•wi•ak (krə kō′vē ak′), *n.* a lively Polish folk dance in duple meter with syncopated accents. Also, **cracovienne.** [1885–90; < Pol, deriv. of *Kraków* CRACOW]

Kra•ma•torsk (krä′mə tôrsk′; *Russ.* krə mu tôRSK′), *n.* a city in E Ukraine, in the Donets Basin. 178,000.

Kra•mer (krā′mər), *n.* **John Albert (Jack),** born 1921, U.S. tennis player and promoter.

kran (krän), *n.* a former silver coin of Iran. [1880–85; < Pers *qirān*]

Kra•nach (*Ger.* krä′näkh), *n.* Cranach.

Kra•sno•dar (kras′nə där′; *Russ.* krə snu däR′), *n.* **1.** a territory of the Russian Federation in SE Europe. 4,814,000; 34,200 sq. mi. (88,578 sq. km). **2.** Formerly, **Ekaterinodar, Yekaterinodar.** a city in and the capital of this territory, on the Kuban River, near the Sea of Azov. 560,000.

Kra•sno•yarsk (kras′nə yärsk′; *Russ.* krə snu-yäRsk′), *n.* **1.** a territory of the Russian Federation in N and central Asia. 3,198,000; 827,507 sq. mi. (2,143,243 sq. km). **2.** a town in and the capital of this territory, on the Yenisei River. 796,000.

Kra•sny (kras′nē; *Russ.* krä′snē), *n.* Russian name of **Kyzyl.**

Kra•sny Luch (krä′snē lōōch′), a city in SE Ukraine, E of Donetsk. 106,000.

kra•ter (krā′tər), *n. Gk. and Rom. Antiq.* a mixing bowl characterized by a wide mouth and body with two handles projecting vertically from the juncture of the neck and body, used to mix wine and water. Also, **crater.** Cf. **kelebe.** [1855–60; < Gk *krātḗr;* see CRATER]

K ration, an emergency field ration for U.S. armed forces when other food or rations are not available, consisting of three separate packaged meals of concentrated and dehydrated food. Cf. **C ration.** [1940–45; *K* for Ancel *Keys* (born 1904), American physiologist]

krau•ro•sis (krô rō′sis), *n. Pathol.* atrophy and shrinkage of the skin, esp. of the vulva. [1885–90; < Gk *kraûr(os)* dry, brittle + -OSIS] —**krau•rot•ic** (krô rot′ik), *adj.*

Kraus (krous), *n.* **Karl,** 1874–1936, Austrian writer and editor.

Krause′s cor′puscle (krou′siz), *Anat.* any of numerous encapsulated nerve endings occurring in the skin and mucous membranes, functioning as sensory cold receptors. [after Wilhelm *Krause* (1833–1909), German anatomist, who described them in 1860]

Krauss (krous; *Ger.* kRous), *n.* **Cle•mens** (klā′mens), 1893–1954, Austrian conductor and pianist.

kraut (krout), *n.* **1.** *Informal.* sauerkraut. **2.** (*often cap.*) *Slang (disparaging and offensive).* a German, esp. a German soldier during World War I or World War II. [1915–20; by shortening]

Krebs (kReps; *Eng.* krebz), *n.* **Sir Hans A•dolf** (häns ä′dôlf; *Eng.* hanz ad′olf, ā′dolf), 1900–81, German biochemist in England: Nobel prize for medicine 1953.

Krebs′ cy′cle, *Biochem.* a cycle of enzyme-catalyzed reactions in living cells that is the final series of reactions of aerobic metabolism of carbohydrates, proteins, and fatty acids, and by which carbon dioxide is produced, oxygen is reduced, and ATP is formed. Also called **citric acid cycle, tricarboxylic acid cycle.** [1940–45; after H.A. KREBS]

Krebs′ ure′a cy′cle. See **urea cycle.** [after H.A. KREBS]

Kre•feld (krā′feld; *Ger.* kRā′felt′), *n.* a city in W North Rhine-Westphalia, in W Germany, NW of Cologne. 227,100. Also, **Crefeld.**

Krei•sky (krī′skē), *n.* **Bruno,** 1911–90, Austrian diplomat and political leader: chancellor 1970–83.

Kreis•ler (krīs′lər), *n.* **Fritz** (frits), 1875–1962, Austrian violinist and composer in the U.S.

Kre•men•chug (krem′ən chōōk′, -chōōg′; *Russ.* kRyi-myin chōōk′), *n.* a city in central Ukraine, on the Dnieper River. 210,000.

Krem•lin (krem′lin), *n.* **the Kremlin, 1.** the executive branch of the government of Russia or of the Soviet Union, esp. in regard to its foreign affairs. **2.** the citadel of Moscow, including within its walls the chief offices of the Russian and, formerly, of the Soviet government. [1655–65; earlier *Kremelien* < G (now obs.) < an unattested outcome of ORuss **kremlĭnĭ*, deriv. of *kremlĭ* (Russ *kreml′*, gen *kremlyá*) citadel, akin to ORuss *Kromŭ* the citadel of Pskov, Ukrainian *króma* partition, Russ *kromá, krómka* edge, border]

Krem•lin•ol•o•gy (krem′li nol′ə jē), *n.* the study of the government of the former Soviet Union, esp. the study of those factors governing its foreign affairs. Also called **Sovietology.** [1955–60; KREMLIN + -O- + -LOGY] —**Krem′lin•ol′o•gist,** *n.*

Krems (kRems), *n.* a city in NE Austria, on the Danube. 23,123.

Kře•nek (kər zhen′ek; *Czech.* kRshe′nek), *n.* **Ernst** (eRnst), born 1900, U.S. composer, born in Austria.

Kre•on (krē′on), *n. Class. Myth.* Creon.

krep•lach (krep′ləKH, -läKH), *n.* (*used with a singular or plural v.*) *Jewish Cookery.* turnovers or pockets of noodle dough filled with any of several mixtures, as kasha or chopped chicken livers, usually boiled, and served in soup. Also, **krep′lech** (krep′ləKH). [1890–95; < Yiddish *kreplech,* pl. of *krepl,* akin to dial. G *Kräppel* fritter, G *Krapfen* apple-fritter]

kre•tek (krē′tek), *n. Slang.* a cigarette made of Indonesian tobacco and cloves. [< Javanese *krétèk* such a cigarette, the crackling sound made by the cloves in a lit cigarette]

kreut•zer (kroit′sər), *n.* **1.** any of various former minor coins issued by German states. **2.** a former copper coin of Austria, the 100th part of a florin. [1540–50; < G *Kreuzer,* equiv. to *Kreuz* CROSS (orig. the device on the coin) + *-er* -ER[1]]

Kreut•zer (kroit′sər; *Fr.* kRœ tser′), *n.* **Ro•dolphe** (rô dôlf′), 1766–1831, French violinist.

Kreut′zer Sona′ta, a sonata for violin and piano (1803, Op. 47) by Ludwig van Beethoven.

krewe (krōō), *n.* (esp. in New Orleans) a private social club that sponsors balls, parades, etc., as part of the Mardi Gras festivities. [archaizing or fanciful sp. of CREW[1]; generalized from the *Mistick Krewe of Comus,* the first such club, founded in New Orleans in 1857]

Kreym•borg (krām′bôrg), *n.* **Alfred,** 1883–1966, U.S. poet, playwright, and critic.

Krieg (krēk; *Eng.* krēg), *n., pl.* ***Krie•ge*** (krē′gə), *Eng.* **Kriegs.** *German.* war.

krie•gie (krē′gē), *n. Mil. Slang.* an Allied prisoner of war in a World War II German internment camp. [< G *Krieg(sgefangene)* prisoner of war + -IE]

krieg•spiel (krēg′spēl′, -shpēl′, krēk′-), *n.* **1.** (*sometimes cap.*) a game using small figures and counters that represent troops, ships, etc., played on a map or miniature battlefield, developed for teaching military tactics to officers. **2.** a form of chess in which both players see only their own pieces on a board in front of them and must remember the opponent's moves as told to them by a referee who maintains a third board on which the play of both players is shown. [1805–15; < G *Kriegsspiel,* equiv. to *Krieg(e)s,* gen. of *Krieg* war + *Spiel* game]

Kriem•hild (krēm′hilt), *n.* (in the *Nibelungenlied*) the wife of Siegfried and the sister of Gunther. Cf. **Gudrun.**

krill (kril), *n., pl.* **krill.** any of the small, pelagic, shrimplike crustaceans of the family Euphausiidae, eaten as food by certain whales. [1905–10; < Norw *kril* young fry (of fish)]

krim•mer (krim′ər), *n.* a lambskin from the Crimean region, dressed as a fur, with wool in loose soft curls, usually whitish or pale gray. Also, **crimmer.** [1825–35; < G, equiv. to *Krim* CRIMEA + *-er* -ER[1]]

Kri•o (krē′ō), *n.* an English-based creole of Sierra Leone, a first language of the residents of Freetown and its environs, and a lingua franca elsewhere in the country.

Krips (kRips), *n.* **Jo•sef** (yō′zef), 1902–74, Austrian orchestra conductor.

kris (krēs), *n.* creese. Also, **kriss.**

Krish•na (krish′nə), *n.* **1.** *Hinduism.* an avatar of Vishnu and one of the most popular of Indian deities, who appears in the Bhagavad-Gita as the teacher of Arjuna. **2.** *Informal.* See **Hare Krishna. 3.** Formerly, **Kistna.** a river in S India, flowing E from the Western Ghats to the Bay of Bengal. 800 mi. (1290 km) long. **4.** a male given name. [< Skt *kṛṣṇa*]

Krish′na Men′on (men′ən), **Ven•ga•lil Krish•nan** (ven gä′lēl krish′nən), 1897–1974, Indian politician and statesman.

Kriss Krin•gle (kris′ kring′gəl). See **Santa Claus.** [alter., by folk etym., of G *Christkindl* little Christ child, equiv. to *Christ* CHRIST + *kind* CHILD + *-l* dim. suffix]

Kris•tian•sand (kris′chən sand′; *Norw.* kRis′tyän-sän′), *n.* a seaport in S Norway. 59,477. Formerly, **Christiansand.**

Kris•tin (kris′tən), *n.* a female given name, form of **Christine. Also, Kris′ten.**

Kris•ti•na (kri stē′nə), *n.* a female given name, form of **Christina.**

Kri•ta Yu•ga (krit′ə yŏŏg′ə), *Hinduism.* See **Satya Yuga.** [< Skt *kṛtayuga*]

Kri•voi Rog (kri voi′ rōg′, rôk′; *Russ.* kRyi voi′ Rôk′), a city in SE Ukraine, SW of Dnepropetrovsk. 650,000.

Kroe•ber (krō′bər), *n.* **Alfred Louis,** 1876–1960, U.S. anthropologist.

Krogh (kRôKH), *n.* **(Schack) Au•guste (Steen•berg)** (shäk′ ou′gŏŏst stēn′baRg), 1874–1949, Danish physiologist: Nobel prize for medicine 1920.

Kró•lew•ska Hu•ta (*Pol.* kRŏŏ lef′skä hŏŏ′tä), former name of **Chorzów.**

kro•na (krō′nə), *n., pl.* **-nor** (-nôr). **1.** a silver and cupronickel coin and monetary unit of Sweden, equal to 100 öre. *Abbr.:* Kr., kr. **2.** the monetary unit of the Faeroe Islands, equal to 100 öre. *Abbr.:* Kr., kr. [1870–75; < Sw < ML *corōna;* see KRÓNA]

kró•na (krō′nə), *n., pl.* **-nur** (-nər). a nickel-brass or aluminum coin and monetary unit of Iceland, equal to 100 aurar. *Abbr.:* Kr., kr. [1885–90; < Icel < ML *corōna* gold coin (so called because it bore the imprint of a crown); see CROWN]

Kro•nach (*Ger.* kRō′näKH), *n.* Cranach.

kro•ne[1] (krō′nə), *n., pl.* **-ner** (-nər). **1.** a cupronickel coin and monetary unit of Denmark, equal to 100 öre. *Abbr.:* Kr., kr. **2.** a cupronickel coin and monetary unit of Norway, equal to 100 öre. *Abbr.:* Kr., kr. [1870–75; < Dan, Norw < MLG < ML *corōna;* see KRÓNA]

kro•ne[2] (krō′nə), *n., pl.* **-nen** (-nən). **1.** a former gold coin of Germany, equal to 10 marks. **2.** korona (def. 1). [1870–75; < G; see KRONE[1]]

Kro•neck•er (krō′nek ər; *Ger.* kRō′nek əR), *n.* **Le•o•pold** (lē′ə pōld′; *Ger.* lā′ō pôlt′), 1823–91, German mathematician.

Kro′necker del′ta, *Math.* a function of two variables, i and j, which equals 1 when the variables have the same value, $i = j$, and equals 0 when the variables have different values, $i \neq j$. [1925–30; named after L. KRONECKER]

Kro•nos (krō′nos), *n.* Cronus.

Kron•stadt (kRun shtät′ *for 1;* kRōn′shtät *for 2*), *n.* **1.** a naval base in the NW Russian Federation in Europe, on an island in the Gulf of Finland: fortress founded 1710. **2.** German name of **Brasov.**

kroon (krōōn), *n., pl.* **kroons, kroon•i** (krōō′nē). a former aluminum bronze coin and monetary unit of Estonia, equal to 100 marks or senti. [< Estonian < Sw *krona* KRONA]

Kro•pot•kin (krō pot′kin, krə-; *Russ.* kRu pôt′kyin), *n.* **Prince Pëter A•le•kse•e•vich** (pyôtR′ u lyi ksyā′yi-vyich), 1842–1921, Russian geographer, author, and anarchist.

KRP, *Chess.* king's rook's pawn.

krs, kurus.

Kru•ger (krōō′gər; *Du.* kRY′KHəR), *n.* **Ste•pha•nus Jo•han•nes Paul•us** (ste fä′nœs yō hä′nəs pō′lœs), ("*Oom Paul*"), 1825–1904, South African statesman: president of the Transvaal 1883–1900. —**Kru′ger•ite′,** *n., adj.*

Kru•ger•rand (krōō′gə rand′, -ränd′), *n.* (*sometimes l.c.*) a one-ounce gold coin of the Republic of South Africa, equal to 25 rand: first issued in 1967. [KRUGER + RAND[2]]

Kru•gers•dorp (krōō′gərz dôrp′; *Du.* kRY′KHəRs-dôRp′), *n.* a city in S Transvaal, in the NE Republic of South Africa, NW of Johannesburg. 91,202.

krul•ler (krul′ər), *n.* cruller.

krum•horn (krum′hôrn′), *n.* crumhorn.

krumm•holz (krŏŏm′hōlts), *n., pl.* **-holz.** a forest of stunted trees near the timber line on a mountain. Also called **elfinwood.** [1900–05; < G, equiv. to *krumm* crooked (OHG *krumb;* see CROMORNE) + *Holz* wood; see HOLT]

Krupp (krup; *Ger.* kRŏŏp), *n.* **Al•fred** (al′frid; *Ger.* äl′-fRāt), 1812–87, German industrialist and manufacturer of armaments.

Krup•ska•ya (krŏŏp′skə yə), *n.* **Na•dezh•da Kon•stan•ti•nov•na** (nu dye′zhdə kən stun tyē′nəv nə), 1869–1939, Russian social worker and wife of V.I. Lenin.

Krutch (kro͞och), *n.* **Joseph Wood,** 1893–1970, U.S. critic, biographer, naturalist, and teacher.

Kry·lon (krī′lon), *Trademark.* a brand name for a plastic coating, applied as a liquid, that forms a protective film: used on blueprints, paintings, etc.

kryo-, var. of **cryo-.**

kryp·ton (krip′ton), *n. Chem.* an inert, monatomic gaseous element, present in very small amounts in the atmosphere: used in high-power, tungsten-filament light bulbs. *Symbol:* Kr; *at. wt.:* 83.80; *at. no.:* 36. [1895–1900; < Gk *kryptón,* neut. of *kryptós* hidden, secret; see CRYPT]

KS, Kansas (approved esp. for use with zip code).

***K* selection,** *Ecol.* selection occurring when a population is at or near the carrying capacity of the environment, which is usually stable: tends to favor individuals that successfully compete for resources and produce few, slowly developing young, and results in a stable population of long-lived individuals. Cf. ***r* selection.** Also, ***K*-se·lec·tion** (kā′si lek′shən). **—*K*-se·lect·ed** (kā′si-lek′tid), *adj.*

K-se·ries (kā′sēr′ēz), *n. Physics.* See under **K-line.** [1920–25]

Kshat·ri·ya (ksha′trē ə), *n.* a member of the Hindu royal and warrior class above the Vaisyas and below the Brahmans. Cf. **Shudra.** [1775–85; < Skt *kṣatriya*]

K-shell (kā′shel′), *n. Physics.* the first shell of electrons surrounding the nucleus of an atom and containing, when filled, two electrons having principal quantum number 1. Cf. **L-shell, M-shell, N-shell.** [1965–70]

ksi, one thousand pounds per square inch. [*k,* repr. KILO- + *s(quare) i(nch)*]

K star, *Astron.* a relatively cool, orange-to-red star, as Aldebaran or Arcturus, having a surface temperature between 3500 and 5000 K and an absorption spectrum with strong lines of calcium and many neutral metals. Cf. **spectral type.**

Kt, *Chess.* knight. Also, Kt.

Kt., knight.

kt., 1. karat. **2.** kiloton. **3.** knot.

K.T., 1. Knights Templars. **2.** Knight of the Order of the Thistle.

Kt. Bach., knight bachelor.

K-truss (kā′trus′), *n. Archit.* a truss having in each panel two diagonals running from the ends of one post to the center of the adjacent post, the arrangement being symmetrical about the center of the truss.

Kua·la Lum·pur (kwä′lə lo͝om po͝or′), a city in and the capital of Malaysia, in the SW Malay Peninsula. 937,875.

Kuang·chou (gwäng′jō′), *n. Wade-Giles.* Canton.

Kuan·tan (kwän′tän), *n.* a seaport in and the capital of Pahang state, in Malaysia, on the SE Malay Peninsula. 43,358.

Ku·ban (ko͞o ban′; *Russ.* ko͞o bän′), *n.* a river flowing NW from the Caucasus Mountains to the Black and the Azov seas. 512 mi. (825 km) long. Ancient, **Hypanis.**

Ku·be·lík (ko͝o′be lēk; *Eng.* ko͞ob′ə lik), *n.* **1. Jan** (yän), 1880–1940, Czech violinist and composer in Hungary. **2.** his son, **(Je·ro·nym) Ra·fa·el** (ye′rô nim rä′-fä el), born 1914, Czech conductor.

Ku·blai Khan (ko͞o′blī kän′), 1216–94, khan c1260–94: founder of the Mongol dynasty in China (grandson of Genghis Khan). Also, **Ku′bi·lai Khan′** (ko͞o′bi lī′), **Kubla Khan.**

Ku·bla Khan (ko͞o′blə kän′), **1.** (*italic.*) a poetic fragment (1797) by Coleridge. **2.** See **Kublai Khan.**

ku·chen (ko͞o′KHən), *n.* a yeast-raised coffeecake, often containing fruit. [1850–55; < G *Kuchen* cake]

Ku·ching (ko͞o′ching), *n.* a seaport in and capital of Sarawak state, in E Malaysia: capital of the former colony of Sarawak. 63,491.

ku·do (ko͞o′dō, kyo͞o′-), *n., pl.* **-dos** for 2. **1.** honor; glory; acclaim: *No greater kudo could have been bestowed.* **2.** a statement of praise or approval; accolade; compliment: *one kudo after another.* [1925–30; back formation from KUDOS, construed as a plural]
—Usage. See **kudos**[1].

ku·dos[1] (ko͞o′dōz, -dōs, -dos, kyo͞o′-), *n.* (*used with a singular v.*) honor; glory; acclaim: *He received kudos from everyone on his performance.* [1825–35; irreg. transliteration of Gk *kŷdos*]
—Usage. In the 19th century, KUDOS[1] entered English as a singular noun, a transliteration of a Greek singular noun *kŷdos* meaning "praise or renown." It was at first used largely in academic circles, but it gained wider currency in the 1920's in journalistic use, particularly in headlines: *Playwright receives kudos. Kudos given to track record breakers.* KUDOS is often used, as in these examples, in contexts that do not clearly indicate whether it is singular or plural; and because it ends in *-s,* the marker of regular plurals in English, KUDOS has come to be widely regarded and used as a plural noun meaning "accolades" rather than as a singular mass noun meaning "honor or glory."
The singular form KUDO has been produced from KUDOS by back formation, the same process that gave us the singular *pea* from *pease,* originally both singular and plural, *sherry* from *Xeres* (an earlier spelling of the Spanish city Jerez), and *cherry* from the French singular noun *cherise.* This singular form has developed the meanings "honor" and "statement of praise, accolade."
Both the singular form KUDO and KUDOS as a plural are today most common in journalistic writing. Some usage guides warn against using them.

CONCISE ETYMOLOGY KEY: <, descended or borrowed from; >, whence; b., blend of, blended; c., cognate with; cf., compare; deriv., derivative; equiv., equivalent; imit., imitative; obl., oblique; r., replacing; s., stem; sp., spelling, spelled; resp., respelling, respelled; trans., translation; ?, origin unknown; *, unattested; ‡, probably earlier than. See the full key inside the front cover.

ku·dos[2] (ko͞o′dōz, kyo͞o′-), *n.* pl. of **kudo.**

Kud·run (ko͝od′ro͞on), *n. Germ. Legend.* the heroine of the Middle High German epic of the 13th century.

ku·du (ko͞o′do͞o), *n.* a large African antelope, *Tragelaphus strepsiceros,* the male of which has large corkscrewlike horns. Also, **koodoo.** [1770–80; < Afrik *koedoe* < Khoikhoi ≠*kudu*]

kudu, *Tragelaphus strepsiceros,* 4 ft. (1.2 m) high at shoulder; horns 4 to 5 ft. (1.2 to 1.5 m); length 4½ ft. (1.4 m)

kud′zu vine′ (ko͝od′zo͞o), a fast-growing Chinese and Japanese climbing vine, *Pueraria lobata,* of the legume family, now widespread in the southern U.S., having tuberous, starchy roots and stems: used for fiber, as food and forage, and to prevent soil erosion. Also called **kud′·zu.** [1900–05; < Japn *kuzu,* earlier *kudu,* of uncert. orig.]

Kuen·lun (ko͞on′lo͞on′), *n.* Kunlun.

Ku·fa (ko͞o′fə, -fa), *n.* a town in central Iraq: former seat of Abbassid caliphate; Muslim pilgrimage center. Also called **Al Kufa.**

Ku·fic (ko͞o′fik), *adj.* **1.** of or pertaining to Kufa or its inhabitants. **2.** noting or pertaining to the characters of the Arabic alphabet used in the writing of the original Koran, in the time of Muhammad. **—*n.* 3.** the Kufic alphabet. Also, **Cufic.** [1785–95; KUF(A) + -IC]

ku·fi·yeh (kə fē′ə), *n.* kaffiyeh. Also, **kuf·fi′eh.**

ku·gel (ko͞o′gəl, ko͝og′əl), *n. Jewish Cookery.* a baked casserole resembling a soufflé or pudding. [1840–50; < Yiddish *kugl;* cf. MHG *kugel(e)* ball, sphere (G *Kugel*); perh. akin to CUDGEL]

Ku·gel·hopf (ko͞o′gəl hopf′, -hôpf′), *n. German Cookery.* a sweetened bread, flavored with raisins and almonds, baked in a ring-shaped mold, and usually dusted with powdered sugar before serving. [1885–90; < G *Gugelhopf* (orig. Swiss G), *Gugelhupf* (orig. Austrian, south G dial.), equiv. to *Gugel* a hood with a liripipe and partial covering for the shoulders, worn in the Middle Ages (MHG *gugel,* OHG *chugela, cucula* < LL *cuculla;* see COWL[1]) + *-hopf, -hupf,* n. deriv. of MHG *hopfen* to HOP[1], skip, jump; appar. from the cake's tendency to overflow the pan in a shape likened to the headgear]

Kuhn (ko͞on), *n.* **1. Rich·ard** (rich′ərd; *Ger.* RIKH′ärt), 1900–1967, German chemist, born in Austria: declined 1938 Nobel prize at insistence of Nazi government. **2. Walt,** 1877?–1949, U.S. painter.

Kuh·nau (ko͞o′nou), *n.* **Jo·hann** (yō′hän), 1660–1722, German clavier composer, organist, and author.

Kui·by·shev (kwē′bə shef′, -shev′; *Russ.* ko͞oi′bi-shif), *n.* a port in the Russian Federation in Europe, on the Volga. 1,250,000. Formerly, **Samara.**

Kui·per (kī′pər), *n.* **Gerard Peter,** 1905–73, U.S. astronomer, born in the Netherlands.

Ku Klux·er (ko͞o′ kluk′sər, kyo͞o′), a member of a Ku Klux Klan. Also called **Ku′ Klux′ Klan′ner.** [1875–80, *Amer.;* KU KLUX (KLAN) + -ER[1]]

Ku′ Klux′ism (kluk′siz əm), the doctrines, theories, and practices of the Ku Klux Klan. Also, **Ku′ Klux′er·y** (kluk′sə rē). [1865–70, *Amer.;* KU KLUX (KLAN) + -ISM]

Ku′ Klux′ Klan′ (kluks′ klan′), **1.** a secret organization in the southern U.S., active for several years after the Civil War, which aimed to suppress the newly acquired powers of blacks and to oppose carpetbaggers from the North, and which was responsible for many lawless and violent proceedings. **2.** Official name, **Knights of the Ku Klux Klan.** a secret organization inspired by the former, founded in 1915 and active in the southern and other parts of the U.S., directed against blacks, Catholics, Jews, and the foreign-born. Also called **Ku′ Klux′.** [*Ku Klux* (perh. < Gk *kýklos* circle, assembly) + *Klan,* sp. var. of CLAN]

kuk·ri (ko͝ok′rē), *n.* a large knife having a heavy curved blade that is sharp on the concave side, used by the Nepalese Gurkhas for hunting and combat. [1805–15; < Hindi *kukṛī*]

Kuk·su (ko͝ok′so͞o), *adj.* of, pertaining to, or characteristic of a religious cult among Indians of central California. [< Eastern Pomo *kúksu*]

ku·ku·i (ko͞o ko͞o′ē), *n.* the candlenut tree, *Aleurites moluccana,* of the spurge family, having grayish leaves and clusters of small white flowers: the state tree of Hawaii. [1815–25; < Hawaiian]

ku·lak (ko͝o läk′, -lak′; ko͞o′läk, -lak), *n.* (in Russia) **1.** a comparatively wealthy peasant who employed hired labor or possessed farm machinery and who was viewed and treated by the Communists during the drive to collectivize agriculture in the 1920's and 1930's as an oppressor and class enemy. **2.** (before the revolution of 1917) a prosperous, ruthless, and stingy merchant or village usurer. [1875–80; < Russ *kulák* lit., fist]

ku·le·bya·ka (ko͞o′lə byä′kə; *Russ.* ko͞o lyi byä′kə), *n. Russian Cookery.* coulibiac.

Ku·le·shov (ko͞o′lə shôf′, -shof′; *Russ.* ko͞o lyi shôf′), *n.* **Lev (Vla·di·mi·ro·vich)** (lef vlad′ə mēr′ə vich; *Russ.* lyef vlu dyē′myi rə vyich), 1899–1970, Soviet film director.

ku·le·tuk (ko͞o′lə tuk′), *n. Canadian.* a hip-length overcoat with a hood, usually designed for women; parka. [1895–1900; < Inuit *quliktaq, qulittaq,* deriv. of *quli* the upper part of something]

ku·lich (ko͞o′lich), *n. Russian Cookery.* a sweetened, dome-shaped yeast bread, rich in butter and eggs and also containing raisins and topped with a sugar icing: traditionally made at Easter and served with paskha. [< Russ *kulích* << MGk *ko(u)llíkion,* dim. of Gk *kóllix* circular or oval loaf of bread]

Kul·la (ko͝ol′ä), *n.* the Sumerian and Akkadian god of bricks.

Kul·ler·vo (ko͝ol′lər vô′), *n.* (in the *Kalevala*) a slave who, after a series of tragic misadventures, commits suicide.

Kul·tur (ko͝ol to͝or′), *n. German.* **1.** (in Nazi Germany) native culture, held to be superior to that of other countries and subordinating the individual to national interests. **2.** culture (def. 4). **3.** a civilization characteristic of a time or a people.

Kul·tur·kampf (*Ger.* ko͝ol to͝or′kämpf′), *n.* the conflict between the German imperial government and the Roman Catholic Church from 1872 or 1873 until 1886, chiefly over the control of education and ecclesiastical appointments. [< G: culture struggle, equiv. to *Kultur* CULTURE + *Kampf* battle, struggle (c. OE *camp*); see CAMP[1], KEMP[1]]

Kul·tur·kreis (*Ger.* ko͝ol to͝or′krīs′), *n., pl.* **-krei·se** (-krī′zə). *Anthropol.* formerly, a complex of related cultural traits assumed to diffuse or radiate outward as a unit in concentric waves or circles. [1945–50; < G, equiv. to *Kultur* CULTURE + *Kreis* circle]

Ku·lun (ko͞o′lo͞on′), *n.* Chinese name of **Ulan Bator.**

Ku·ma·mo·to (ko͞o′mə mō′tō; *Japn.* ko͞o′mä mô′tô), *n.* a city on W central Kyushu, in SW Japan. 525,613.

Ku·ma·si (ko͝o mä′sē), *n.* a city in and the capital of Ashanti district, in S Ghana. 275,000.

ku·miss (ko͞o′mis), *n.* **1.** fermented mare's or camel's milk, used as a beverage by Asian nomads. **2.** a similar drink prepared from other milk, esp. that of the cow, and used for dietetic and medicinal purposes. Also, **koumis, koumiss, koumyss.** [1590–1600; < Russ *kumys* < Turkic *kimiz*]

küm·mel (kim′əl; *Ger.* KY′məl), *n.* **1.** a colorless cordial or liqueur flavored with cumin, caraway seeds, etc., made esp. in the Baltic area. **2.** Leyden cheese containing caraway seeds. [1880–85; < G *Kümmel,* OHG *kumil,* appar. dissimilated var. of *kumin* CUMIN]

Kum·mer (ko͝om′ər; *Ger.* ko͝om′ər), *n.* **Ernst E·du·ard** (ûrnst′ ed′wərd; *Ger.* ernst′ ā′do͞o ärt′), 1810–93, German mathematician.

kum·mer·bund (kum′ər bund′), *n.* cummerbund.

kum·quat (kum′kwot), *n.* **1.** a small, round or oblong citrus fruit having a sweet rind and acid pulp, used chiefly for preserves. **2.** any of several citrus shrubs of the genus *Fortunella,* native to China, that bear this fruit. Also, **cumquat.** [1865–70; < dial. Chin (Guangdong) *gāmgwāt* gold citrus fruit, akin to Chin *jīnjú*]

Kun (ko͝on), *n.* **Bé·la** (bā′lo), 1885–1937, Hungarian Communist leader.

kun·da·li·ni (ko͝on′dl ē′nē), *n. Hinduism.* the vital force lying dormant within one until activated by the practice of yoga, which leads one toward spiritual power and eventual salvation. [< Skt *kuṇḍalinī*]

Kundt′ tube′ (ko͝ont), *Physics.* a gas-filled tube used to measure the speed of sound: when a membrane at one end is vibrated at a frequency that produces standing waves, a layer of powder forms lumps at the nodes. [named after August *Kundt* (1839–94), German physicist]

Kung (ko͝ong), *n., pl.* **Kungs,** (*esp. collectively*) **Kung.** a member of a San people of the Kalahari desert basin of southern Africa. Also, **!Kung.**

Kung (ko͝ong, go͝ong), *n.* **1. H. H.** (*K'ung Hsiang-hsi, Kong Xiangxi*), 1881–1967, Chinese financier and statesman. **2. Prince,** 1833–98, Chinese statesman of the late Ch'ing dynasty.

K'ung Ch'iu (ko͝ong′ chyo͞o′), personal name of **Confucius.**

kung fu (kung′ fo͞o′, ko͝ong′), an ancient Chinese method of self-defense by striking blows at vulnerable areas of an attacker's body using fluid movements of the hands and legs. [< Chin *gōngfu* lit., skill]

K'ung Fu-tzŭ (ko͝ong′ fo͞o′dzu′), Chinese name of **Confucius.** Also, **K'ung′ Fu′-tse′.** Also called **K'ung-tzŭ** (ko͝ong′dzu′).

Ku·ni·yo·shi (ko͞o′nē yō′shē; *Japn.* ko͞o′nē yô′shē), *n.* **Ya·su·o** (yä so͞o′ô), 1893–1953, U.S. painter, born in Japan.

Kun·lun (ko͞on′lo͞on′), *n.* a mountain range in China, bordering on the N edge of the Tibetan plateau and extending W across central China: highest peak, 25,000 ft. (7620 m). Also, **Kuenlun.** Also called **Kun′lun Shan′** (shän).

Kun·ming (ko͞on′ming′), *n. Pinyin, Wade-Giles.* a city in and the capital of Yunnan province, in S China: an important transshipment point on the Burma Road in World War II. 1,100,000. Formerly, **Yunnan.**

Kun·san (ko͞on′sän′) *n.* a seaport in W South Korea. 110,140.

Kunst·lied (*Ger.* ko͝onst′lēt′), *n., pl.* **-lie·der** (*Ger.* -lē′-dər). an art song, esp. as distinguished from a folk song. [< G, equiv. to *Kunst* art (OHG: skill, ability) + *Lied* song]

Kun·tse·vo (ko͞on′sə vō′; *Russ.* ko͞on′tsi və), *n.* a former city in the W Russian Federation in Europe, incorporated into Moscow 1962.

kunz·ite (ko͝onts′īt), *n. Mineral.* a transparent lilac-colored variety of spodumene, used as a gem. [1900–05, *Amer.*; named after G. F. *Kunz* (1856–1932), American expert in precious stones; see -ITE[1]]

Kuo·min·tang (kwō′min′tang′, -täng′; *Chin.* gwô′-min′däng′), *n.* the dominant political party of China from 1928 to 1949, founded chiefly by Sun Yat-sen in 1912 and led from 1925 to 1975 by Chiang Kai-shek; the dominant party of the Republic of China (Taiwan) since 1949. [< Chin (Wade-Giles) *kuo*^{2}*min*^{2}*tang*^{3}, (pinyin) *guómín dǎng* national people's party, equiv. to *guó* nation + *mín* people + *dǎng* party; cf. TANG, TONG[2]]

Kuo Mo-jo (*Chin.* gwô′ mô′chô′), *Wade-Giles.* See **Guo Moruo.**

Kuo·pio (kwô′pyô), *n.* a city in central Finland. 73,747.

Kuo-yü (gwô′yʏ′), *n.* Putonghua.

Ku·prin (ko͞o′prin; *Russ.* ko͞o pʀyēn′), *n.* **A·le·xan·der I·va·no·vich** (al′ig zan′dər i vä′nə vich, -zän′-; *Russ.* u lyi ksändʀ′ ē vä′nə vyich), 1870–1938, Russian novelist and short-story writer.

Kur (ko͝or), *n.* (in Sumerian mythology) the world of the dead.

Ku·ra (ko͞o rä′), *n.* a river flowing from NE Turkey, through the Georgian Republic and Azerbaijan, SE to the Caspian Sea. 950 mi. (1530 km) long.

Ku·ra·shi·ki (ko͞o ʀä′shē kē; *Eng.* ko͞o rä′shi kē), *n.* a city on SW Honshu, in Japan. 403,785.

kur·bash (ko͝or′bash), *n.* **1.** a whip with leather thongs, formerly used in Turkey, Egypt, etc. —*v.t.* **2.** to whip with a kurbash. Also, **kourbash.** [1805–15; < Ar *kurbāj* << Turk *kırbaç* whip]

Kur·cha·tov (ko͝or chä′tôf, -tof; *Russ.* ko͞oʀ chä′təf), *n.* **I·gor Va·si·lie·vich** (ē′gəʀ vu syē′lyi vyich), 1903–60, Soviet nuclear physicist.

Kurd (kûrd, ko͝ord; *Pers.* ko͞oʀd), *n.* a member of an Islamic people speaking Kurdish and dwelling chiefly in Kurdistan. [1610–20]

Kurd·ish (kûr′dish, ko͝or′-), *adj.* **1.** of or pertaining to the Kurds or their language. **2.** of or pertaining to Kurdistan, its people, or their language. —*n.* **3.** the language of the Kurds, an Iranian language.

Kur·di·stan (kûr′də stan′; *Pers.* ko͞oʀ′di stän′), *n.* **1.** a mountain and plateau region in SE Turkey, NW Iran, and N Iraq: inhabited largely by Kurds. 74,000 sq. mi. (191,660 sq. km). **2.** any of several types of rugs woven by the Kurds of Turkey or Iran.

Ku·re (ko͞o′ʀe′), *n.* a seaport on SW Honshu, in SW Japan. 234,550.

Kurg (ko͝org), *n.* Coorg.

kur·gan (ko͝or gän′, -gan′), *n.* a circular burial mound constructed over a pit grave and often containing grave vessels, weapons, and the bodies of horses as well as a single human body; originally in use in the Russian Steppes but later spreading into eastern, central, and northern Europe in the third millennium B.C. [1885–90; < Russ *kurgán* burial mound, ORuss, appar. to be identified with *kurganŭ* fortress < Turkic; cf. Turkish, Tatar *kurğan*, Chagatai, Kazakh *korğan* fortress, castle]

Kur·gan (ko͝or gän′; *Russ.* ko͞oʀ gän′), *n.* a city in the S Russian Federation in Asia, near the Ural Mountains. 310,000.

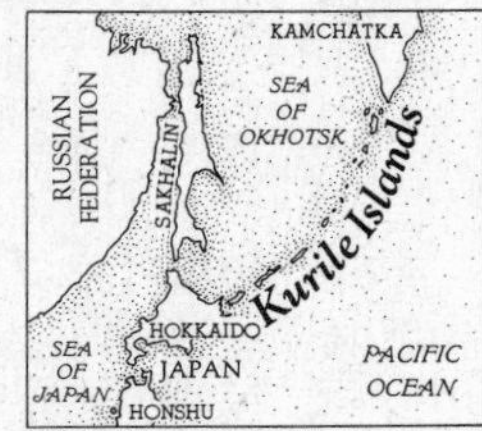

Ku′rile Is′lands (ko͝or′il, ko͞o rēl′), a chain of small islands off the NE coast of Asia, extending from N Japan to the S tip of Kamchatka: renounced by Japan in 1945; under Russian administration. Also, **Ku′ril Is′lands.** Japanese, **Chishima.**

Kur·land (ko͝or′lənd), *n.* Courland.

kur·mi (ko͝or′mē), *n.* a member of a major agricultural caste widespread in northern and central India. [< eastern Hindi *kurmī* or Bengali *kurmi, kuṛmi*; cf. Skt *kuṭumbin-* householder]

kurn (kûʀn), *n. Scot. and North Eng.* kirn[2].

Ku·ro·ki (ko͞o′ʀô kē′), *n.* **Ta·me·mo·to** (tä′me mô′tô), **Count,** 1844–1923, Japanese general.

Ku·ro·pat·kin (ko͝or′ə pat′kin; *Russ.* ko͞o ʀu pät′-kyin), *n.* **A·le·ksei Ni·ko·la·e·vich** (u lyi ksyā′ nyi ku-lä′yi vyich), 1848–1925, Russian general.

Ku·ro·sa·wa (ko͝or′ə sä′wə; *Japn.* ko͞o′ʀô sä′wä), *n.* **A·ki·ra** (ä kē′ʀä), born 1910, Japanese film director.

Ku·ro·shi·o (ko͞o rō′shē ō′; *Japn.* ko͞o ʀô′shē ô′), *n.* See **Japan Current.** [< Japn, equiv. to *kuro* black + *shio* (earlier *shifo*) tide]

kur·ra·jong (kûr′ə jong′), *n.* an Australian bottle tree, *Brachychiton populneus,* having yellowish-white, bell-shaped flowers, grown as an ornamental. Also, **koorajong, currajong, currijong.** [1815–25; < Dharuk *garra-jun* a fishing line, made from the bark of such trees, and perh. misinterpreted as the name of the tree]

Kursk (ko͝orsk; *Russ.* ko͞oʀsk), *n.* a city in the W Russian Federation in Europe. 413,000.

Kurt (kûrt), *n.* a male given name.

kur·ta (kûr′tə), *n.* **1.** a long-sleeved, hip-length shirt worn by men in India. **2.** a sleeveless shirt worn over or under the angiya by Muslim women in India. Also, **khurta.** [1910–15; < Hindi]

kur·to·sis (kûr tō′sis), *n. Statistics.* the state or quality of flatness or peakedness of the curve describing a frequency distribution in the region about its mode. [1900–05; irreg. transliteration of Gk *kýrtōsis* curvature. See CYRTOSIS]

ku·ru (ko͝or′o͞o), *n. Pathol.* a fatal degenerative disease of the central nervous system characterized by progressive lack of coordination and dementia, known only among certain Melanesian peoples, esp. the Fore of New Guinea, and caused by a slow virus: now virtually extinct. [1955–60; < a dialect of Fore, a language of the Eastern Highlands District]

Ku·rukh (ko͝or′ək), *n.* a Dravidian language spoken in central India.

Ku·ru·ne·ga·la (ko͝or′o͞o neg′ə lə, -nā′gə-), *n.* a city in W central Sri Lanka. 28,000.

ku·rus (ko͞o ro͞osh′), *n., pl.* **-rus.** a monetary unit of Turkey, the 100th part of a lira; piaster. [1880–85; < Turk *kuruş*]

Ku·rus (ko͝or′o͞oz), *n.* (*used with a plural v.*) Kauravas.

Ku·ru·su (ko͞o ʀo͞o′so͞o), *n.* **Sa·bu·ro** (sä bo͞o′ʀô), 1888–1954, Japanese diplomat.

Ku·saie (ko͞o sī′), *n.* Kosrae.

Kusch (ko͝osh), *n.* **Po·ly·karp** (pol′i kärp′; *Ger.* pō′ly-kärp′), born 1911, U.S. physicist, born in Germany: Nobel prize 1955.

Kush (ko͝osh, kush), *n.* Cush.

Kush·it·ic (kə shit′ik), *n.* Cushitic.

kus·puk (kus′puk), *n. Alaska, Northern Canada.* **1.** a cloth garment worn by Eskimos over the parka. **2.** a parka of lightweight cloth, worn esp. by Eskimo women and children in summer. [< Yupik *qaspeq*]

Ku·sta·nai (ko͞o stu nī′), *n.* a city in N Kazakhstan, on the Tobol river. 164,000.

Ku·ta·i·si (ko͞o tī′sē; *Russ.* ko͞o tu yē′syi), *n.* a city in the W Georgian Republic in Europe. 194,000. Also, **Ku·ta·is** (ko͞o tīs′; *Russ.* ko͞o tu yēs′).

Ku·ta·ni (ko͞o tä′nē), *n.* Japanese porcelain made in Kaga province in the late 17th century, often with both underglaze and overglaze enamel decoration; imitated in the 19th century. [after *Kutani,* a town in Ishikawa prefecture where it was made]

Kutch (kuch), *n.* **1.** a former state in W India, now part of Gujarat state. **2. Rann of** (run), a salt marsh NE of this area. 9000 sq. mi. (23,310 sq. km). Also, **Cutch.**

kut·cha (kuch′ə), *adj. Anglo-Indian.* crude, imperfect, or temporary. Also, **cutcha, kacha, kachcha.** [< Hindi *kaccā*]

Kutch·in (ko͞och′in), *n., pl.* **-ins,** (esp. collectively) **-in** for 1. **1.** a member of a group of North American Indians who live in the region of the lower Mackenzie River in northwestern Canada and the Yukon and Porcupine rivers of northeastern Alaska. **2.** the Athabaskan language of the Kutchin. [1930–35; < Kutchin *gʷičin* people of, dwellers at (the place specified), occurring as the final element in the names of local bands, and misunderstood as a designation for all Kutchin]

Ku·te·nai (ko͞ot′n ā′, -n ē′), *n.* **1.** a member of a North American Indian people of British Columbia, Montana, and Idaho. **2.** the language of the Kutenai Indians. **3.** Kootenay. Also, **Ku′te·nay′.**

Ku·tu·zov (ko͞o to͞o′zôf, -zof; *Russ.* ko͞o to͞o′zəf), *n.* **Mi·kha·il I·la·ri·o·no·vich** (myi кнu yēl′ ē lə ʀyi ô′nə-vyich), **Prince of Smolensk,** 1745–1813, Russian field marshal and diplomat.

ku·vasz (ko͝ov′äs, ko͞o′väs), *n., pl.* **ku·va·szok** (ko͝ov′-ä sôk′, ko͞o′vä-). one of a Hungarian breed of large dogs having a short, slightly wavy, white coat, used for herding sheep and as watchdogs. [1930–35; < Hungarian < Turk *kavas* guard < Ar *qawwās* bowman]

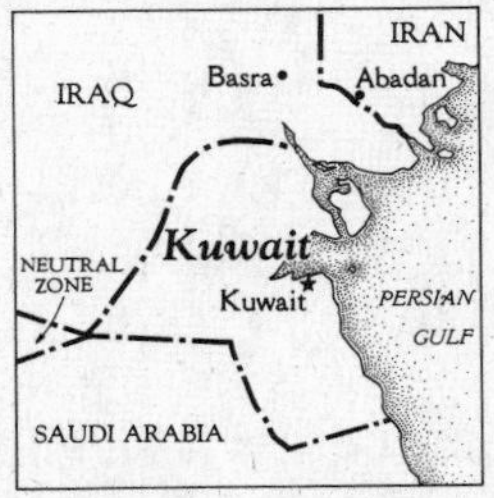

Ku·wait (ko͞o wāt′), *n.* **1.** a sovereign monarchy in NE Arabia, on the NW coast of the Persian Gulf: formerly a British protectorate. 1,100,000; ab. 8000 sq. mi. (20,720 sq. km). **2.** a seaport in and the capital of this monarchy. 800,000. Also, **Koweit.**

Ku·wai·ti (ko͞o wā′tē), *n.* **1.** a native or inhabitant of Kuwait. —*adj.* **2.** of, pertaining to, or characteristic of Kuwait or its inhabitants. [1925–30; < Ar *Kuwayti,* equiv. to *Kuwayt* KUWAIT + *-i* suffix of appurtenance]

Kuyp (*Du.* kœip), *n.* **Aelbert** (*Du.* äl′bəʀt). See **Cuyp, Aelbert.**

Kuz·nets (ko͝oz′nits, ko͞oz′-), *n.* **Simon (Smith),** 1901–85, U.S. economist, born in Russia: Nobel prize 1971.

Ku·znetsk (ko͞oz netsk′; *Russ.* ko͞o znyetsk′), *n.* a city in the W Russian Federation in Europe. 97,000.

Kuznetsk′ Ba′sin, an industrial region in the S Russian Federation in Asia: coal fields.

kV, kilovolt; kilovolts. Also, **kv**

K.V., *Music. Köchel-Verzeichnis,* the chronological listing of Mozart's works (used with a number to identify a specific work).

kVA, kilovolt-ampere; kilovolt-amperes. Also, **kva**

kvass (kväs, kwäs), *n.* a Russian beer made from fermenting rye or barley and having a dark color and sour taste. Also, **quass.** [1545–55; < Russ *kvas*]

kvell (kvel), *v.i. Slang.* to be extraordinarily pleased; esp., to be bursting with pride, as over one's family. [1965–70, *Amer.*; < Yiddish *kveln* be delighted; cf. MHG, G *quellen* well up, gush]

kvetch (kvech), *Slang.* —*v.i.* **1.** to complain, esp. chronically. —*n.* **2.** Also, **kvetch′er.** a person who kvetches. [1960–65, *Amer.*; < Yiddish *kvetshn* lit., to squeeze, pinch; cf. MHG, G *quetschen*]

kW, kilowatt; kilowatts. Also, **kw.**

Kwa (kwä), *adj.* **1.** of, belonging to, or constituting Kwa. —*n.* **2.** a branch of the Niger-Congo subfamily of languages, including Ewe, Ibo, Yoruba, and other languages of coastal West Africa.

kwa·cha (kwä′chə), *n.* **1.** a cupronickel coin, paper money, and monetary unit of Malawi, equal to 100 tambala. *Abbr.:* K. **2.** a cupronickel coin, paper money, and monetary unit of Zambia, equal to 100 ngwee. *Abbr.:* K.

kwai·ken (kwī ken′, kī-), *n., pl.* **-ken.** a curved knife formerly used by Japanese women to commit suicide. [< Japn *k(w)aiken* < MChin, equiv. to Chin *huái* bosom + *jiàn* sword]

Kwa·ja·lein (kwä′jə lān′, -lən), *n.* an atoll in the Marshall Islands, in E Micronesia. 5064. ab. 78 mi. (126 km) long.

Kwa·ki·u·tl (kwä′kē o͞ot′l), *n.* **1.** a member of a North American Indian people of Vancouver Island and the adjacent British Columbian coast. **2.** the language of the Kwakiutl, a Wakashan language.

Kwang·chow (kwäng′chō′, kwang′-; *Chin.* gwäng′-jō′), *n. Older Spelling.* Canton.

Kwang·cho·wan (kwäng′chō′wän′, kwang′-; *Chin.* gwäng′jō′wän′), *n. Older Spelling.* Guangzhouwan.

Kwang·ju (gwäng′jo͞o′), *n.* a city in SW South Korea. 502,753.

Kwang·si Chuang (kwäng′sē′ chwäng′, kwang′sē chwang′; *Chin.* gwäng′sē′ chwäng′), *Older Spelling.* See **Guangxi Zhuang.**

Kwang·tung (kwäng′to͝ong′, kwang′-; *Chin.* gwäng′-do͝ong′), *n. Older Spelling.* Guangdong.

Kwan·tung (kwän′to͝ong′, kwan′-; *Chin.* gwän′-do͝ong′), *n. Older Spelling.* Guandong.

Kwan-yin (kwän′yin′), *n. Buddhism.* one of the Chinese female Boddhisattvas, noted for her kindness: often considered an aspect of Avalokitesvara.

kwan·za (kwän′zə), *n., pl.* **-za, -zas.** a paper money, cupronickel coin, and monetary unit of Angola, equal to 100 lwei: replaced the escudo in 1977.

Kwan·zaa (kwän′zə), *n.* a harvest festival celebrated from Dec. 26th until Jan. 1st among members of some Afro-American organizations. Also, **Kwan·za.** [< Swahili *kwanza* first]

kwar·tje (kwär′chə, -tyə), *n.* a silver 25-cent piece of the Netherlands. [< D < L *quartārius;* see QUARTER]

kwash·i·or·kor (kwä′shē ôr′kôr, -kər), *n. Pathol.* a malnutrition disease, chiefly of children, caused by severe protein and vitamin deficiency and characterized by retarded growth, changes in pigmentation, potbelly, and anemia. [1930–35; < Ga *kwašiɔkɔ* the influence a child is said to be under when his mother becomes pregnant with her next child; sp. with *r*'s is r-less speaker's representation of the vowels]

Kwei·chow (kwā′chou′, -chō′; *Chin.* gwā′jō′), *n. Older Spelling.* Guizhou.

Kwei·lin (kwā′lin′; *Chin.* gwā′lin′), *n. Older Spelling.* Guilin.

Kwei·sui (kwā′swā′; *Chin.* gwā′swā′), *n. Older Spelling.* former name of **Hohhot.** Also, **Kwei·hwa** (gwā′-hwä′).

Kwei·yang (kwā′yäng′, -yang′; *Chin.* gwā′yäng′), *n. Older Spelling.* Guiyang.

kWh, kilowatt-hour. Also, **kwhr, K.W.H.**

KWIC (kwik), *adj.* of or designating an alphabetical concordance of the principal terms in a text showing every occurrence of each term surrounded by a few words of the context. [1955–60; *k(ey)-w(ord)-i(n)-c(ontext)*]

KY, Kentucky (approved esp. for use with zip code).

Ky., Kentucky.

ky·ack[1] (kī′ak), *n.* kayak.

ky·ack[2] (kī′ak), *n.* a type of packsack that consists of two connected sacks and is hung on either side of a packsaddle. [1900–05, *Amer.*; orig. uncert.]

ky·ak (kī′ak), *n.* kayak.

ky·a·nite (kī′ə nīt′), *n.* a mineral, aluminum silicate, Al_2SiO_5, occurring in blue or greenish bladed triclinic

CONCISE PRONUNCIATION KEY: *act, cāpe, dâre, pärt; set, ēqual; if, īce; ox, ōver, ôrder, oil, bo͝ok, bo͞ot, out; up, ûrge; child; sing; shoe; thin, that;* zh as in *treasure.* ə = *a* as in *alone,* e as in *system,* i as in *easily,* o as in *gallop,* u as in *circus;* ᵊ as in *fire* (fīᵊr), *hour* (ouᵊr). l and n can serve as syllabic consonants, as in *cradle* (krād′l), and *button* (but′n). See the full key inside the front cover.

crystals, used as a refractory. Also, **cyanite.** [1785–95; irreg. < Gk *kýan(os)* CYAN + -ITE[1]]

ky•an•ize (kī′ə nīz′), *v.t.*, **-ized, -iz•ing.** to treat (wood) against decay with a solution of mercuric chloride. Also, *esp. Brit.*, **ky′an•ise′.** [1830–40; named after J. H. *Kyan* (1774–1850), Irish developer of the process]

kyat (kyät, kē ät′), *n.* a paper money, cupronickel coin, and monetary unit of Burma (Myanmar), equal to 100 pyas. [1950–55; < Burmese *cʰat* (written *kyap*)]

ky•a•thos (kī′ə thos′, -thəs), *n., pl.* **-thoi** (-thoi′). *Gk. and Rom. Antiq.* a deep bowl set on a foot, used for ladling wine into drinking cups. Also, **cyathus.** [1885–90; < Gk *kýathos*]

Kyd (kid), *n.* **Thomas,** 1558–94, English dramatist. Also, **Kid.**

kye (kā), *n.* a private Korean-American banking club to which members pay contributions and from which they may take out loans, usu. to start small businesses. [1985–90; < Korean]

kyle (kīl), *n. Scot.* a narrow channel of water between two islands or between an island and the mainland; a strait or sound. [1540–50; < ScotGael *caoil* (gen. of *caol*) strait, sound (n. use of *caol* narrow)]

Kyle (kīl), *n.* a male or female given name.

ky•lie (kī′lē), *n., pl.* **-lies.** *Australian.* boomerang. Also, **ki′ley.** [1830–40; < Nyungar *karli*]

ky•lix (kī′liks, kil′iks), *n., pl.* **ky•li•kes** (kī′li kēz′, kil′-i-). *Gk. and Rom. Antiq.* a shallow bowl having two horizontal handles projecting from the sides, often set upon a stem terminating in a foot: used as a drinking cup. Also, **cylix.** [1890–95; < Gk *kýlix* cup]

CONCISE ETYMOLOGY KEY: <, descended or borrowed from; >, whence; b., blend of, blended; c., cognate with; cf., compare; deriv., derivative; equiv., equivalent; imit., imitative; obl., oblique; r., replacing; s., stem; sp., spelling, spelled; resp., respelling, respelled; trans., translation; ?, origin unknown; *, unattested; ‡, probably earlier than. See the full key inside the front cover.

Ky•loe (kī′lō), *n.* See **West Highland.** [1745–55; earlier *Kiley, Kylie* < ScotGael *gaidhealach* Gaelic, Highland, equiv. to *Gaidheal* Highlander, GAEL + *-ach* adj. suffix]

kymo-, var. of **cymo-**: *kymograph.*

ky•mo•gram (kī′mə gram′), *n.* the graphic record produced by a diagnostic kymograph. [1920–25]

ky•mo•graph (kī′mə graf′, -gräf′), *n.* an instrument for measuring and graphically recording variations in fluid pressure, as those of the human pulse. Also, **cymograph.** [1865–70; KYMO- + -GRAPH] —**ky•mo•graph•ic** (kī′mə graf′ik), *adj.*

Kym•ric (kim′rik), *adj., n.* Cymric.

Kym•ry (kim′rē), *n.pl.* Cymry.

Kyo•ga (kyō′gə), *n.* **Lake,** a lake in central Uganda. ab. 1000 sq. mi. (2600 sq. km). Also, **Kioga.**

kyo•gen (kē ō′gen; *Japn.* kyô′gen), *n.* a brief Japanese play performed between Nō plays to provide comic relief. [< Japn *kyōgen*, equiv. to *kyō-* mad + *-gen* talk (< MChin, equiv. to Chin *kuángyán* boast)]

ky•oo•dle (kī o͞od′l), *v.i.*, **-dled, -dling.** to bark or yelp noisily or foolishly; yap. [1920–25, *Amer.*; imit.]

Kyo•to (kē ō′tō; *Japn.* kyô′tô), *n.* a city on S Honshu, in central Japan: the capital of Japan A.D. 794–1868. 1,472,993. Also, **Kioto.**

ky•pho•sco•li•o•sis (kī′fō skō′lē ō′sis, -skol′ē-), *n. Pathol.* a condition in which the spinal column is convex both backward and sideways. [1880–85; < Gk *kȳphó(s)* humpbacked + SCOLIOSIS]

ky•pho•sis (kī fō′sis), *n. Pathol.* an abnormal, convex curvature of the spine, with a resultant bulge at the upper back. Cf. **lordosis, scoliosis.** [1840–50; < Gk *kȳ́phōsis* a hunched state, equiv. to *kȳph(ós)* humpbacked + *-ōsis* -OSIS] —**ky•phot•ic** (kī fot′ik), *adj.*

Kyp•ris (kip′ris), *n.* Cypris.

Ky•ra (kī′rə), *n.* a female given name.

Kyr•gyz•stan (kir′gi stän), *n.* official name of **Kirghizia.**

Kyr•i•a•le (kir′ē ä′lā), *n.* a liturgical book containing the text and musical notations for parts of the ordinary of the Mass. [< NL, equiv. to *Kyri(e)* (see KYRIE ELEISON) + *-āle* -AL[2]]

Kyr•i•e e•le•i•son (*Rom. Cath. Ch., Angl. Ch.* kēr′ē ā′ e lā′ə sôn′, -son′, -sən; *Gk. Orth. Ch.* kē′rē e e le′ē-sôn), **1.** (*italics*) the brief petition "Lord, have mercy," used in various offices of the Greek Orthodox Church and of the Roman Catholic Church. **2.** the brief response or petition in services in the Anglican Church, beginning with the words, "Lord, have mercy upon us." **3.** Also called **Kyr′i•e′.** a musical setting of either of these. [1300–50; ME *kyrieleyson* < ML, LL *Kyrie eleison* < LGk *Kýrie eleēson* Lord, have mercy]

kyte (kīt), *n. Scot. and North Eng.* the paunch; stomach; belly. Also, **kite.** [1530–40; perh. < Scand; cf. Icel *kȳta* stomach of the blenny]

kythe (kīth), *v.t., v.i.*, **kythed, kyth•ing.** *Scot. and North Eng.* kithe.

Ky•the•ra (kē′thē rä), *n.* Greek name of **Cerigo.**

ky•toon (kī to͞on′), *n. Meteorol.* a captive balloon, combining the features of a balloon and a kite, used to maintain meteorological instruments at a fixed height. [var. sp. of KITE + (BALL)OON]

Kyu•shu (kē o͞o′sho͞o; *Japn.* kyo͞o′sho͝o), *n.* an island in SW Japan. 13,600,200; 15,750 sq. mi. (40,793 sq. km). Also, **Kiushu.**

Ky•zyl (ki zil′), *n.* a city in and the capital of the Tuva Autonomous Republic, in the S Russian Federation in Asia. 71,000. Russian, **Krasny.**

Ky•zyl Kum (ki zil′ ko͞om′, ko͝om′), a desert in S Asia, SE of the Aral Sea, in Uzbekistan and Kazakhstan. ab. 90,000 sq. mi. (233,100 sq. km). Also, **Kizil Kum, Qizil Qum.**

Kzyl-Or•da (kə zil′ôr dä′; *Russ.* gzil ur dä′), *n.* a city in S Kazakhstan, on the Syr Darya. 156,000.

DEVELOPMENT OF MAJUSCULE								
NORTH SEMITIC	GREEK		ETR.	LATIN		MODERN		
						GOTHIC	ITALIC	ROMAN
ℓ	˥	ʌ	ɺ	ɺ	L	𝔏	*L*	L

L

DEVELOPMENT OF MINUSCULE					
ROMAN CURSIVE	ROMAN UNCIAL	CAROL. MIN.	MODERN		
			GOTHIC	ITALIC	ROMAN
l	L	l	𝔩	*l*	l

The twelfth letter of the English alphabet derives from North Semitic *lamed,* with its shape exhibiting consistent development. It assumed its present form as a right angle (**L**) in Classical Latin. The minuscule (**l**) is a cursive variant of the capital.

L, l (el), *n., pl.* **L's** or **Ls, l's** or **ls. 1.** the 12th letter of the English alphabet, a consonant. **2.** any spoken sound represented by the letter *L* or *l,* as in *let, dull, cradle.* **3.** something having the shape of an L. **4.** a written or printed representation of the letter *L* or *l.* **5.** a device, as a printer's type, for reproducing the letter *L* or *l.*

L (el), *n., pl.* **L's** or **Ls.** *Informal.* an elevated railroad.

L (el), *n., pl.* **L's** or **Ls.** ell[1].

L, 1. lambert; lamberts. **2.** language. **3.** large. **4.** Latin. **5.** left. **6.** length. **7.** *Brit.* pound; pounds. [< L *libra*] **8.** long: denoting a size longer than regular, esp. for suits and coats made for tall men: *40L.* **9.** longitude. **10.** *Theat.* stage left.

L, *Symbol.* **1.** the 12th in order or in a series, or, if *I* is omitted, the 11th. **2.** (*sometimes l.c.*) the Roman numeral for 50. Cf. **Roman numerals. 3.** *Elect.* inductance. **4.** *Physics.* See **kinetic potential. 5.** *Biochem.* leucine. **6.** *Econ.* a broad measure of total U.S. liquid assets, issued periodically by the Federal Reserve Board. Cf. **M.**

l, 1. large. **2.** liter; liters.

***l*-,** *Symbol, Optics, Chem., Biochem.* levorotatory; levo- (distinguished from *d*-). Cf. **L-.**

L-, *Symbol, Biochem.* (of a molecule) having a configuration resembling the levorotatory isomer of glyceraldehyde: always printed as a small capital, roman character (distinguished from D-). Cf. ***l*-.**

L-, 1. *Chem.* levo-. **2.** *U.S. Mil.* (in designations of light aircraft) liaison: *L-15.*

L., 1. Lady. **2.** Lake. **3.** large. **4.** Latin. **5.** latitude. **6.** law. **7.** left. **8.** lempira; lempiras. **9.** leu; lei. **10.** lev; leva. **11.** book. [< L *liber*] **12.** Liberal. **13.** (in Italy) lira; lire. **14.** place. [< L *locus*] **15.** Lord. **16.** Low. **17.** lumen. **18.** *Theat.* stage left.

l., 1. large. **2.** latitude. **3.** law. **4.** leaf. **5.** league. **6.** left. **7.** length. **8.** *pl.* **ll.,** line. **9.** link. **10.** (in Italy) lira; lire. **11.** liter; liters. **12.** long.

L1, *Ling.* first language; native language.

L2, *Ling.* second language.

la[1] (lä), *n., Music.* **1.** the syllable used for the sixth tone of a diatonic scale. **2.** (in the fixed system of solmization) the tone A. Cf. **sol-fa** (def. 1). [1350–1400; ME; see GAMUT]

la[2] (lô, lä), *interj. Archaic or Dial.* (used as an exclamation of wonder, surprise, etc.): *La, sir, how you do go on!* [bef. 1150; ME, OE; weak var. of *lā* LO]

LA, Louisiana (approved esp. for use with zip code).

La, *Symbol, Chem.* lanthanum.

La., Louisiana.

L.A., 1. Latin America. **2.** Law Agent. **3.** Library Association. **4.** Local Agent. **5.** Los Angeles.

laa·ger (lä′gər), *South African.* —*n.* **1.** a camp or encampment, esp. within a protective circle of wagons. —*v.t., v.i.* **2.** to arrange or encamp in a laager. Also, **lager.** [1840–50; < Afrik *laer,* earlier *lager;* c. G *Lager* camp. See LAIR[1]]

Laa·land (lol′ənd; *Dan.* lô′län), *n.* an island in SE Denmark, S of Zealand. 81,760; 495 sq. mi. (1280 sq. km). Also, **Lolland.**

lab (lab), *n.* laboratory. [by shortening]

Lab (lab), *n. Informal.* See **Labrador retriever.** [by shortening]

Lab., 1. Laborite. **2.** Labrador.

lab., 1. labor. **2.** laboratory. **3.** laborer.

La Baie (lä bā′; *Fr.* lᴀ be′), *n.* a town in S Quebec, in E Canada, near Chicoutimi. 20,935.

La·ban (lā′bən), *n.* the father of Leah and Rachel and the father-in-law of Jacob. Gen. 24:29; 29:16–30.

La′ban dance′ nota′tion sys′tem (lä′bən, lā′-), a system of movement notation, using symbols on a staff, that records the parts of a dancer's body, direction in space, dynamics, and tempo for all kinds of movement: used to record and reconstruct forms of dance and movement. Also called **la·ba·no·ta·tion** (lä′bə nō tā′shən, lā′-). [after dance theorist Rudolf *Laban* (1879–1958), born in Slovakia, who devised it]

lab·a·rum (lab′ər əm), *n., pl.* **-a·ra** (-ər ə). **1.** an ecclesiastical standard or banner, as for carrying in procession. **2.** the military standard of Constantine the Great and later Christian emperors of Rome, bearing Christian symbols. [1650–60; < LL, of obscure orig.]

lab·da·num (lab′də nəm), *n.* a resinous juice that exudes from various rockroses of the genus *Cistus:* used in perfumery, fumigating substances, etc. Also, **ladanum.** [1350–1400; ME *labdanum, lapdanum* < ML, for L *lādanum* < Gk *lḗdanon,* akin to *lêdon* rockrose < Sem]

La·be (lä′be), *n.* Czech name of the **Elbe.**

lab·e·fac·tion (lab′ə fak′shən), *n.* a shaking or weakening; overthrow or downfall. [1610–20; < LL *labefactiōn-* (s. of *labefactiō*), equiv. to *labefact(us)* (ptp. of *labefacere* to loosen) + *-iōn-* -ION]

la·bel (lā′bəl), *n., v.,* **-beled, -bel·ing** or (*esp. Brit.*) **-belled, -bel·ling.** —*n.* **1.** a slip of paper, cloth, or other material, marked or inscribed, for attachment to something to indicate its manufacturer, nature, ownership, destination, etc. **2.** a short word or phrase descriptive of a person, group, intellectual movement, etc. **3.** a word or phrase indicating that what follows belongs in a particular category or classification: *The following definition has the label "Archit."* **4.** *Archit.* a molding or dripstone over a door or window, esp. one that extends horizontally across the top of the opening and vertically downward for a certain distance at the sides. **5.** a brand or trademark, esp. of a manufacturer of phonograph records, tape cassettes, etc.: *She records under a new label.* **6.** the manufacturer using such a label: *a major label that has produced some of the best recordings of the year.* **7.** *Heraldry.* a narrow horizontal strip with a number of downward extensions of rectangular or dovetail form, usually placed in chief as the cadency mark of an eldest son. **8.** *Obs.* a strip or narrow piece of anything. —*v.t.* **9.** to affix a label to; mark with a label. **10.** to designate or describe by or on a label: *The bottle was labeled poison.* **11.** to put in a certain class; classify. **12.** Also, **radiolabel.** *Chem.* to incorporate a radioactive or heavy isotope into (a molecule) in order to make traceable. [1275–1325; ME < MF: ribbon, perh. < Gmc. See LAP[1]] —**la′bel·er,** *n.*

la′beled brack′eting, *Ling.* a representation of the constituent structure of a string, as a word or sentence, comparable to a tree diagram, in which each constituent is shown in brackets and given a subscript grammatical label, with each bracketed item corresponding to a node in a tree diagram.

La Belle Dame Sans Mer·ci (*Fr.* lᴀ bel dᴀm säɴ mer sē′), a ballad (1819) by Keats.

la·bel·lum (lə bel′əm), *n., pl.* **-bel·la** (-bel′ə). *Bot.* the petal of an orchid that differs more or less markedly from the other petals, often forming the most conspicuous part; the lip. [1820–30; < L, dim. of *labrum* lip; for formation see CASTELLUM] —**la·bel′loid,** *adj.*

la·bet·a·lol (lə bet′ə lôl′, -lol′), *n. Pharm.* an alpha- and beta-adrenergic blocking agent, $C_{19}H_{24}N_2O_3$, used in the treatment of hypertension. [prob. *la-,* inversion of *al(pha)* + *beta* + *-l-* of uncert. deriv. + -OL[1]]

la·bi·a (lā′bē ə), *n.* pl. of **labium.**

la·bi·al (lā′bē əl), *adj.* **1.** of, pertaining to, or resembling a labium. **2.** of or pertaining to the lips. **3.** *Phonet.* involving lip articulation, as *p, v, m, w,* or a rounded vowel. **4.** *Music.* having the tones produced by the impact of a stream of air on a sharp liplike edge, as in a flute or the flue pipes of an organ. —*n. Phonet.* **5.** any labial consonant, esp. a bilabial. **6.** any labial sound. [1585–95; < ML *labiālis.* See LABIUM, -AL[1]] —**la′bi·al′i·ty,** *n.* —**la′bi·al·ly,** *adv.*

la·bi·al·ism (lā′bē ə liz′əm), *n.* a tendency, sometimes habitual, to make sounds labial, as in pronouncing the *l* in *love* as a *w*-like sound. [1880–85; LABIAL + -ISM]

la·bi·al·ize (lā′bē ə līz′), *v.t.,* **-ized, -iz·ing.** *Phonet.* to give a labial character to (a sound), for example, to round (a vowel). Also, *esp. Brit.,* **la′bi·al·ise′.** [1865–70; LABIAL + -IZE] —**la′bi·al·i·za′tion,** *n.*

la·bi·al·ized (lā′bē ə līzd′), *adj. Phonet.* pronounced with secondary labial articulation. [1865–70; LABIALIZE + -ED[2]]

la·bi·a ma·jo·ra (lā′bē ə mə jôr′ə, -jōr′ə), *sing.* **la·bi·um ma·jus** (lā′bē əm mā′jəs). *Anat.* the outer folds of skin of the external female genitalia. [1870–75; < NL: greater lips]

la·bi·a mi·no·ra (lā′bē ə mi nôr′ə, -nōr′ə), *sing.* **la·bi·um mi·nus** (lā′bē əm mī′nəs). *Anat.* the inner folds of skin of the external female genitalia. [1830–40; < NL: lesser lips]

la·bi·ate (lā′bē it, -āt′), *adj.* **1.** having parts that are shaped or arranged like lips; lipped. **2.** *Bot.* **a.** belonging to the plant family Labiatae (or Lamiaceae). Cf. **mint family. b.** two-lipped; bilabiate: said of a gamopetalous corolla or gamosepalous calyx. —*n.* **3.** a labiate plant. [1700–10; < NL *labiātus.* See LABIUM, -ATE[1]]

La·biche (lᴀ bēsh′), *n.* **Eu·gène Ma·rin** (œ zhen′ mᴀ raɴ′), 1815–88, French dramatist.

la·bile (lā′bəl, -bīl), *adj.* **1.** apt or likely to change. **2.** *Chem.* (of a compound) capable of changing state or becoming inactive when subjected to heat or radiation. [1400–50; late ME *labyl* < LL *lābilis,* equiv. to L *lāb(ī)* to slip + *-ilis* -ILE] —**la·bil·i·ty** (lə bil′i tē, lā-), *n.*

la·bi·lize (lā′bə līz′), *v.t.,* **-lized, -liz·ing.** to cause to become labile. Also, *esp. Brit.,* **la′bi·lise′.** [1900–05; LABILE + -IZE] —**la′bi·li·za′tion,** *n.*

labio-, a combining form meaning "lip," used in the formation of compound words: *labiodental.* [comb. form repr. L *labium*]

la·bi·o·den·tal (lā′bē ō den′tl), *Phonet.* —*adj.* **1.** articulated with the lower lip touching the upper front teeth, as *f* or *v,* or, rarely, with the upper lip touching the lower front teeth. —*n.* **2.** a labiodental speech sound. [1660–70; LABIO- + DENTAL]

la·bi·o·gres·sion (lā′bē ō gresh′ən), *n. Dentistry.* location of the anterior teeth forward of their natural position. [LABIO- + L *gress(us)* (ptp. of *gradi* to step, walk, go) + -ION]

la·bi·o·na·sal (lā′bē ō nā′zəl), *Phonet.* —*adj.* **1.** articulated with the lips and given resonance in the nasal cavity, as *m.* —*n.* **2.** a labionasal sound. [LABIO- + NASAL[1]]

la·bi·o·ve·lar (lā′bē ō vē′lər), *Phonet.* —*adj.* **1.** pronounced with simultaneous bilabial and velar articulations, as *w.* —*n.* **2.** a labiovelar speech sound. [1890–95; LABIO- + VELAR]

la·bi·o·ve·lar·ize (lā′bē ō vē′lə rīz′), *v.t., v.i.,* **-ized, -iz·ing.** *Phonet.* to make or become labiovelar. Also, *esp. Brit.,* **la′bi·o·ve′lar·ise′.** [1935–40; LABIOVELAR + -IZE] —**la′bi·o·ve′lar·i·za′tion,** *n.*

la·bi·um (lā′bē əm), *n., pl.* **-bi·a** (-bē ə). **1.** a lip or liplike part. **2.** *Anat.* **a.** a lip or lip-shaped structure or part. **b.** any of the folds of skin bordering the vulva. **3.** *Bot.* the lower lip of a bilabiate corolla. **4.** *Entomol.* the posterior, unpaired member of the mouthparts of an insect, formed by the united second maxillae. [1590–1600; < L: lip, akin to *lambere* to lick, LAP[3]. See LABRUM[1], LIP]

lab·lab (lab′lab′), *n.* See **hyacinth bean.** [1815–25; < Ar *lablāb*]

La Bo·hème (lä′ bō em′; *Fr.* lᴀ bô em′), an opera (1896) by Giacomo Puccini.

CONCISE PRONUNCIATION KEY: act, cāpe, dâre, pärt; set, ēqual; if, īce; ox, ōver, ôrder, oil, bo͝ok, bo͞ot, out; up, ûrge; child; sing; shoe; thin, *th*at; zh as in *treasure.* ə = *a* as in *alone, e* as in *system, i* as in *easily, o* as in *gallop, u* as in *circus;* ᵊ as in *fire* (fīᵊr), *hour* (ouᵊr). l and n can serve as syllabic consonants, as in *cradle* (krād′l), and *button* (but′n). See the full key inside the front cover.

la•bor (lā′bər), *n.* **1.** productive activity, esp. for the sake of economic gain. **2.** the body of persons engaged in such activity, esp. those working for wages. **3.** this body of persons considered as a class (distinguished from *management* and *capital*). **4.** physical or mental work, esp. of a hard or fatiguing kind; toil. **5.** a job or task done or to be done. **6.** the physical effort and periodic uterine contractions of childbirth. **7.** the interval from the onset of these contractions to childbirth. **8.** (*cap.*) Also called **Labor Department.** *Informal.* the Department of Labor. —*v.i.* **9.** to perform labor; exert one's powers of body or mind; work; toil. **10.** to strive, as toward a goal; work hard (often fol. by *for*): *to labor for peace.* **11.** to act, behave, or function at a disadvantage (usually fol. by *under*): *to labor under a misapprehension.* **12.** to be in the actual process of giving birth. **13.** to roll or pitch heavily, as a ship. —*v.t.* **14.** to develop or dwell on in excessive detail: *Don't labor the point.* **15.** to burden or tire: *to labor the reader with unnecessary detail.* **16.** *Brit. Dial.* to work or till (soil or the like). —*adj.* **17.** of or pertaining to workers, their associations, or working conditions: *labor reforms.* Also, *esp. Brit.,* **labour.** [1250–1300; ME *labour* < MF < L *labōr-* (s. of *labor*) work] —**la′bor•ing•ly,** *adv.* —**la′•bor•less,** *adj.*
—**Syn. 2.** working people, working class. **4.** exertion. See **work. 6.** parturition, delivery. **9.** drudge. **14.** overdo. —**Ant. 1, 4.** idleness; leisure. **1, 4, 9.** rest.

La′bor and So′cialist Interna′tional, a socialist association, formed in Hamburg in 1923, uniting the Second International and the Vienna International. Cf. **international** (def. 6).

la•bo•ra•re est o•ra•re (lä′bō Rä′Re est ō Rä′Re; *Eng.* lab′ə râr′ē est ə râr′ē). *Latin.* to work is to pray.

lab•o•ra•to•ry (lab′rə tôr′ē, -tōr′ē, lab′ər ə-; *Brit.* lə bor′ə tə rē, -ə trē), *n., pl.* **-ries,** *adj.* —*n.* **1.** a building, part of a building, or other place equipped to conduct scientific experiments, tests, investigations, etc., or to manufacture chemicals, medicines, or the like. **2.** any place, situation, set of conditions, or the like, conducive to experimentation, investigation, observation, etc.; anything suggestive of a scientific laboratory. —*adj.* **3.** serving a function in a laboratory. **4.** relating to techniques of work in a laboratory: *laboratory methods; laboratory research.* [1595–1605; < ML *labōrātōrium* workshop, equiv. to L *labōrā(re)* to LABOR + *-tōrium* -TORY[2]] —**lab′o•ra•to′ri•al,** *adj.* —**lab′o•ra•to′ri•al•ly,** *adv.* —**lab′o•ra•to′ri•an,** *n.*

lab′oratory school′, a school maintained by a college or university for the training of student teachers.

la′bor camp′, 1. Also called **slave labor camp.** a penal colony where inmates are forced to work. **2.** a camp for the shelter of migratory farm workers. [1895–1900]

La′bor Day′, (in the U.S.) a legal holiday, commonly the first Monday in September, in honor of labor. Cf. **Labour Day.** [1885–90]

La′bor Depart′ment, labor (def 8).

la•bored (lā′bərd), *adj.* **1.** done or made with difficulty; heavy: *labored breathing.* **2.** exhibiting a great deal of effort; lacking grace, fluency, or spontaneity: *a labored prose style.* [1525–35; LABOR + -ED[2]] —**la′•bored•ly,** *adv.* —**la′bored•ness,** *n.*
—**Syn. 2.** overdone, ornate, unnatural, stiff. See **elaborate.** —**Ant. 1.** simple, easy. **2.** plain, natural.

la•bor•er (lā′bər ər), *n.* **1.** a person engaged in work that requires bodily strength rather than skill or training: *a laborer in the field.* **2.** any worker. [1275–1325; ME; see LABOR, -ER[1]]

la′bor force′, 1. See **work force. 2.** (in the U.S.) the body of people who are at least 14 years old and are either employed or available for employment. [1880–85]

la•bor-in•ten•sive (lā′bər in ten′siv), *adj.* requiring or using a large supply of labor, relative to capital. [1950–55]

la•bo•ri•ous (lə bôr′ē əs, -bōr′-), *adj.* **1.** requiring much work, exertion, or perseverance: *a laborious undertaking.* **2.** characterized by or requiring extreme care and much attention to detail: *laborious research.* **3.** characterized by or exhibiting excessive effort, dullness, and lack of spontaneity; labored: *a strained, laborious plot.* **4.** given to or diligent in work: *a careful, laborious craftsman.* [1350–1400; ME < L *labōriōsus.* See LABOR, -IOUS] —**la•bo′ri•ous•ly,** *adv.* —**la•bo′ri•ous•ness,** *n.*
—**Syn. 1.** toilsome, arduous, onerous, burdensome, difficult, hard, tiresome, wearisome, fatiguing. **4.** hard-working, industrious, assiduous, sedulous, painstaking.

La•bor•ism (lā′bə riz′əm), *n.* **1.** a political theory favoring the dominance of labor in the economic and political life of a country. **2.** the doctrines and programs of the Labour party. [1900–05; LABOR + -ISM] —**la′bor•is′tic,** *adj.*

La•bor•ite (lā′bə rīt′), *n.* **1.** a member of a political party promoting the interests of labor. **2.** (*l.c.*) an advocate or member of a labor union or movement. [1885–90, *Amer.;* LABOR + -ITE[1]]

La′bor-Man′age•ment Rela′tions Act′ (lā′bər-man′ij mənt). See **Taft-Hartley Act.**

la′bor mar′ket, the available supply of labor considered with reference to the demand for it. [1825–35]

la′bor move′ment, 1. labor unions collectively: *The labor movement supported the bill.* **2.** the complex of organizations and individuals supporting and advocating improved conditions for labor. **3.** the effort of organized labor and its supporters to bring about improved conditions for the worker, as through collective bargaining: *Their activities proved more harmful than helpful to the labor movement.* [1865–70]

CONCISE ETYMOLOGY KEY: <, descended or borrowed from; >, whence; b., blend of, blended; c., cognate with; cf., compare; deriv., derivative; equiv., equivalent; imit., imitative; obl., oblique; r., replacing; s., stem; sp., spelling, spelled; resp., respelling, respelled; trans., translation; ?, origin unknown; *, unattested; ‡, probably earlier than. See the full key inside the front cover.

la′bor of love′, work done for the sake of one's own enjoyment or of benefit to others rather than for material rewards: *He coached amateur baseball teams as a labor of love.* [1665–75]

la•bor om•ni•a vin•cit (lä′bōr ōm′nē ä′ wing′kit; *Eng.* lā′bər om′nē ə vin′sit), *Latin.* work conquers all: motto of Oklahoma.

la′bor pains′, 1. pain encountered during the uterine contractions of childbirth. **2.** difficulties, problems, or setbacks encountered during the initial phase of a business or project. [1745–55]

la′bor rela′tions, the relations between management and labor, esp. with respect to the maintenance of agreements, collective bargaining, etc.: *The firm had excellent labor relations and therefore few work stoppages.* [1940–45]

la•bor•sav•ing (lā′bər sā′ving), *adj.* designed or intended to reduce or replace human labor: *The dishwasher is a laborsaving device.* Also, **la′bor-sav′ing.** [1765–75; LABOR + SAVING]

la′bors of Her′cules, *Class. Myth.* the 12 extraordinary feats performed by Hercules for Eurystheus in order to gain immortality.

la′bor spy′, an employee who is used by management to spy on union activities.

la′bor un′ion, an organization of wage earners or salaried employees for mutual aid and protection and for dealing collectively with employers; trade union. [1865–70]

la′bor un′ionist, unionist (def. 2).

la•bour (lā′bər), *n., v.i., v.t., adj. Chiefly Brit.* labor.
—**Usage.** See **-or**[1].

La′bour Day′, *Brit.* a holiday in honor of labor, celebrated on May 1 in Britain and some parts of the Commonwealth, but on the first Monday in September in Canada, on the fourth Monday in October in New Zealand, and with varying dates in the different states of Australia. Cf. **Labor Day.**

La•bour•ite (lā′bə rīt′), *n.* a member or supporter of the Labour party. Also, **La′bour•ist.** [1900–05; see LABOUR PARTY, -ITE[1]]

La′bour par′ty, a political party in Great Britain, formed in 1900 from various socialist and labor groups and taking its present name in 1906.

Lab•ra•dor (lab′rə dôr′), *n.* **1.** a peninsula in NE North America surrounded by Hudson Bay, the Atlantic, and the Gulf of St. Lawrence, containing the Canadian provinces of Newfoundland and Quebec. 510,000 sq. mi. (1,320,900 sq. km). **2.** the portion of Newfoundland in the E part of the peninsula. 12,012; ab. 120,000 sq. mi. (310,800 sq. km). **3.** (*sometimes l.c.*) See **Labrador retriever.**

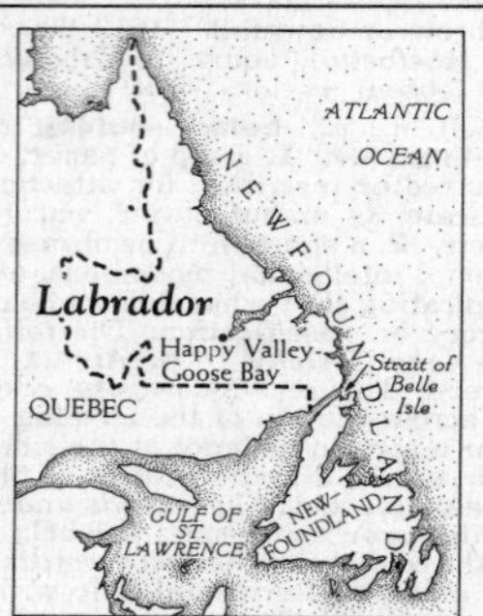

Lab′rador Cur′rent, a cold ocean current flowing S along the Labrador coast through Davis Strait to the Grand Banks where it divides, the E branch joining the North Atlantic Current and the W branch flowing into the Gulf of St. Lawrence. Also called **Arctic Current.**

Lab′rador duck′, an extinct sea duck, *Camptorhynchus labradorius,* of northern North America, having black and white plumage. [1865–70, *Amer.*]

Lab•ra•dor•e•an (lab′rə dôr′ē ən), *adj.* **1.** of or pertaining to Labrador. **2.** noting or pertaining to the Pleistocene ice located mainly E of Hudson Bay. Also, **Lab′ra•dor′i•an.** [1860–65; LABRADOR + *-ean,* var. of -IAN]

lab•ra•dor•ite (lab′rə dô rīt′, lab′rə dôr′īt), *n.* a feldspar mineral of the plagioclase group, often characterized by a brilliant change of colors, with blue and green most common. [1805–15; named after LABRADOR, where first discovered; see -ITE[1]] —**lab•ra•dor•it•ic** (lab′rə dô-rit′ik), *adj.*

Lab′rador retriev′er, one of a breed of retrievers having a short, thick, oily, solid black or yellow coat, raised originally in Newfoundland. See illus. under **retriever.** [1905–10]

Lab′rador tea′, a North American bog shrub, *Ledum groenlandicum,* of the heath family, having evergreen leaves and rounded clusters of white flowers. [1760–70, *Amer.*]

la•bret (lā′bret), *n.* an ornament worn in a pierced hole in the lip. [1855–60; < L *labr(um)* lip + -ET]

la•brid (lā′brid, lab′rid), *n.* **1.** any of numerous fishes of the family Labridae, including the wrasses, the tautog, and the cunner, and characterized chiefly by well-developed teeth and, often, brilliant colors. —*adj.* **2.** belonging or pertaining to the labrids. [< NL *Labridae,* equiv. to *Labr(us)* a genus + *-idae* -ID[2]]

la•brum[1] (lā′brəm, lab′rəm), *n., pl.* **la•bra** (lā′brə, lab′rə). **1.** a lip or liplike part. **2.** *Zool.* **a.** the anterior, unpaired member of the mouthparts of an arthropod, projecting in front of the mouth. **b.** the outer margin of the aperture of a shell of a gastropod. **3.** *Anat.* a ring of cartilage about the edge of a joint surface of a bone. [1810–20; < L: lip; akin to LABIUM]

la•brum[2] (lā′brəm), *n., pl.* **-bra** (-brə). *Archaeol.* an ornamented bathtub of ancient Rome. [< L *lābrum* basin, contr. of *lavābrum* bathtub, equiv. to *lavā(re)* to wash + *-brum* instrumental suffix]

la•bru•sca (lə brus′kə), *adj.* of or derived from the North American fox grape, *Vitis labrusca.* [< NL: the specific epithet, L: a kind of wild grape]

La Bru•yère (lA bRY yeR′), **Jean de** (zhäN də), 1645–96, French moralist and author.

La•bu•an (lä′bo͞o än′), *n.* an island off the W coast of Sabah: part of Sabah state, E Malaysia: a free port. 14,904; 35 sq. mi. (90.65 sq. km).

la•bur•num (lə bûr′nəm), *n.* any of several small trees belonging to the genus *Laburnum,* of the legume family, having elongated clusters of pendulous yellow flowers, esp. *L. alpinum,* the Scotch laburnum. Also called **golden chain.** [1570–80; < NL, L]

labyrinth (def. 1)

lab•y•rinth (lab′ə rinth), *n.* **1.** an intricate combination of paths or passages in which it is difficult to find one's way or to reach the exit. **2.** a maze of paths bordered by high hedges, as in a park or garden, for the amusement of those who search for a way out. **3.** a complicated or tortuous arrangement, as of streets or buildings. **4.** any confusingly intricate state of things or events; a bewildering complex. **5.** (*cap.*) *Class. Myth.* a vast maze built in Crete by Daedalus, at the command of King Minos, to house the Minotaur. **6.** *Anat.* **a.** the internal ear, consisting of a bony portion **(bony labyrinth)** and a membranous portion **(membranous labyrinth). b.** the aggregate of air chambers in the ethmoid bone, between the eye and the upper part of the nose. **7.** a mazelike pattern inlaid in the pavement of a church. **8.** a loudspeaker enclosure with air chambers at the rear for absorbing sound waves radiating in one direction so as to prevent their interference with waves radiated in another direction. [1540–50; < L *labyrinthus* < Gk *labýrinthos;* r. earlier *laborynt* < ML *laborintus,* L, as above]

lab′yrinth fish′, any of several freshwater fishes of the order Labyrinthi, found in southeastern Asia and Africa, having a labyrinthine structure above each gill chamber enabling them to breathe air while out of water.

lab•y•rin•thine (lab′ə rin′thin, -thēn), *adj.* **1.** of, pertaining to, or resembling a labyrinth. **2.** complicated; tortuous: *the labyrinthine byways of modern literature.* Also, **lab•y•rin•thi•an** (lab′ə rin′thē ən), **lab′y•rin′thic.** [1740–50; LABYRINTH + -INE[1]] —**lab′y•rin′thi•cal•ly,** *adv.*

lab•y•rin•thi•tis (lab′ə rin thī′tis), *n. Pathol.* inflammation of the inner ear, or labyrinth, characterized by dizziness, nausea, and visual disturbances. Also called **otitis interna.** [1910–15; < NL; see LABYRINTH, -ITIS]

lab•y•rin•tho•dont (lab′ə rin′thə dont′), *n.* **1.** any member of several orders of small to large lizardlike terrestrial and freshwater amphibians, some ancestral to land vertebrates, forming the extinct subclass Labyrinthodonta that flourished from the Devonian through the Triassic periods, characterized by a solid, flattened skull and conical teeth. —*adj.* **2.** having teeth with complexly infolded enamel surfaces. **3.** belonging to or pertaining to the Labyrinthodonta. [1840–50; < NL *Labyrinthodonta,* equiv. to Gk *labýrinth(os)* LABYRINTH + *-odonta,* neut. pl. of *-odontos* -ODONT]

lac[1] (lak), *n.* a resinous substance deposited on the twigs of various trees in southern Asia by the female of the lac insect: used in the manufacture of varnishes, sealing wax, etc., and in the production of a red coloring matter. Cf. **shellac** (defs. 1, 2). [1545–55; < Hindi *lākh* << Skt *lākṣā*]

lac[2] (läk), *n.* (in India) **1.** the sum of 100,000, esp. of rupees. The usual punctuation for sums of Indian money above a lac is with a comma after the number of lacs: Rs. 30,52,000 (i.e., 30 lacs and 52,000) instead of 3,052,000. **2.** an indefinitely large number. Also, **lakh.** [1605–15; < Hindi *lākh* << Skt *lakṣa*]

lac[3] (lak), *n.* (in prescriptions) milk. [< L]

LAC, leading aircraftsman.

La Ca•na•da-Flint•ridge (lä′ kən yä′də flint′rij′, kə nä′-), a town in SW California. 20,153.

Lac′ca•dive Is′lands (lä′kə dēv′, lak′ə-), a group of islands and coral reefs in the Arabian Sea, off the SW coast of India. ab. 7 sq. mi. (18 sq. km).

Lac′cadive, Min′icoy, and A′mindi′vi Is′lands, former name of **Lakshadweep.**

lac•co•lith (lak′ə lith), *n. Geol.* a mass of igneous rock formed from magma that did not find its way to the surface but spread laterally into a lenticular body, forcing overlying strata to bulge upward. Also, **lac•co•lite** (lak′-

ə lit′). [1875–80; < Gk *lákko(s)* pond + -LITH] —**lac′·co·lith′ic, lac·co·lit·ic** (lak′ə lit′ik), *adj.*

lace (lās), *n., v.,* **laced, lac·ing.** —*n.* **1.** a netlike ornamental fabric made of threads by hand or machine. **2.** a cord or string for holding or drawing together, as when passed through holes in opposite edges. **3.** ornamental cord or braid, esp. of gold or silver, used to decorate uniforms, hats, etc. **4.** a small amount of alcoholic liquor or other substance added to food or drink. —*v.t.* **5.** to fasten, draw together, or compress by or as if by means of a lace. **6.** to pass (a cord, leather strip, etc.), as through holes. **7.** to interlace or intertwine. **8.** to adorn or trim with lace. **9.** to add a small amount of alcoholic liquor or other substance to (food or drink): *He took his coffee laced with brandy.* **10.** to lash, beat, or thrash. **11.** to compress the waist of (a person) by drawing tight the laces of a corset, or the like. **12.** to mark or streak, as with color. —*v.i.* **13.** to be fastened with a lace: *These shoes lace up the side.* **14.** to attack physically or verbally (often fol. by *into*): *The teacher laced into his students.* [1175–1225; (n.) ME *las* < OF *laz, las* << L *laqueus* noose; (v.) ME *lasen* < MF *lacier, lasser, lachier* (F *lacer*) << L *laqueāre* to enclose in a noose, trap] —**lace′like′,** *adj.* —**lac′er,** *n.*

lace′ bug′, any of several bugs of the family Tingidae, characterized by a lacy pattern of ridges on the head, thorax, and wings, and feeding on the leaves of oak, birch, sycamore, etc. [1890–95]

lace-cur·tain (lās′kûr′tn), *adj. Sometimes Offensive.* characteristic of or aspiring to the standards and attributes of the middle class: *Her latest novel traces the rise of a lace-curtain Irish family in Boston.*

Lac·e·dae·mon (las′i dē′mən), *n.* **1.** Sparta. **2.** *Class. Myth.* the son of Zeus and Taÿgete and the founder of the city of Sparta.

Lac·e·dae·mo·ni·an (las′i di mō′nē ən), *adj.* **1.** of or pertaining to ancient Sparta; Spartan. —*n.* **2.** a native or inhabitant of ancient Sparta; a Spartan. [1770–80; LACEDAEMON + -IAN]

lace-fern (lās′fûrn′), *n.* a small, tufted fern, *Cheilanthes gracillima,* having dark-brown stalks and fronds about 4 in. (10.2 cm) long. [1880–85]

lace′ glass′, glass in a filigree pattern. [1880–85]

La Cei·ba (lä sā′vä), *n.* a seaport in N Honduras. 44,057.

lace·leaf (lās′lēf′), *n., pl.* **-leaves.** a submerged aquatic plant, *Aponogeton madagascariensis,* of Madagascar, having tiny white flowers and broad leaves consisting only of veins that float just beneath the surface. Also called **latticeleaf.** [1865–70; LACE + LEAF]

lace·mak·ing (lās′mā′king), *n.* the art, act, or process of making lace. [1825–35; LACE + MAKING]

lace′ pil′low, pillow (def. 3). [1785–95]

lac·er·ate (*v.* las′ə rāt′; *adj.* las′ə rāt′, -ər it), *v.,* **-at·ed, -at·ing,** *adj.* —*v.t.* **1.** to tear roughly; mangle: *The barbed wire lacerated his hands.* **2.** to distress or torture mentally or emotionally; wound deeply; pain greatly: *His bitter criticism lacerated my heart.* —*adj.* **3.** lacerated. [1535–45; < L *lacerātus,* ptp. of *lacerāre* to tear up (deriv. of *lacer* mangled); see -ATE¹] —**lac′er·a·ble,** *adj.* —**lac·er·a·bil·i·ty** (las′ər ə bil′i tē), *n.* —**lac·er·a·tive** (las′ə rā′tiv, -ər ə tiv), *adj.*
—**Syn. 1.** rend. See **maim.**

lac·er·at·ed (las′ə rā′tid), *adj.* **1.** mangled; jagged; torn. **2.** pained; wounded; tortured: *lacerated sensibilities.* **3.** *Bot., Zool.* having the edge variously cut as if torn into irregular segments, as a leaf. [1600–10; LACERATE + -ED²]

lac·er·a·tion (las′ə rā′shən), *n.* **1.** the result of lacerating; a rough, jagged tear. **2.** the act of lacerating. [1590–1600; < L *lacerātiōn-* (s. of *lacerātiō*). See LACERATE, -ION]

La·cer·ta (lə sûr′tə), *n., gen.* **-tae** (-tē). *Astron.* the Lizard, a northern constellation between Cepheus and Pegasus. [< L: LIZARD]

la·cer·tid (lə sûr′tid), *n.* **1.** any of numerous Old World lizards of the family Lacertidae. —*adj.* **2.** belonging or pertaining to the Lacertidae family of lizards. [< NL *Lacertidae.* See LACERTA, -ID²]

lac·er·til·i·an (las′ər til′ē ən, -til′yən), *adj.* **1.** belonging or pertaining to the reptilian suborder Lacertilia, comprising the lizards. —*n.* **2.** a lacertilian reptile. Also, **la·cer·tian** (lə sûr′shən). [1850–55; < NL *Lacertili(a)* (L *Lacert(a)* LACERTA + *-ilia,* neut. pl. of *-ilis* -ILE) + -AN]

lace′ stay′, that part of an Oxford shoe into which eyelets and laces are inserted.

lace-up (lās′up′), *n.* **1.** anything that laces up, esp. a boot with shoelaces that lace up from the vamp to the top of the boot. —*adj.* **2.** having a lace that is laced up as a closure: *a lace-up blouse.* [1830–40; n. and adj. use of v. phrase *lace up*]

lace·wing (lās′wing′), *n.* any of several insects of the family Chrysopidae, having delicate, lacelike wings and golden or copper-colored eyes, the larvae of which are predaceous on aphids and other small insects. [1850–55; LACE + WING]

lace·wood (lās′wo͝od′), *n.* the quartersawed wood of the sycamore tree. [1895–1900; LACE + WOOD¹]

lace·work (lās′wûrk′), *n.* lace (def. 1). [1840–50; LACE + WORK]

Lac·ey (lā′sē), *n.* a town in W Washington. 13,940.

La Chaise (lᴀ shez′), **Père Fran·çois d'Aix de** (fʀäɴ swᴀ′ de də), 1624–1709, French Roman Catholic priest: confessor to Louis XIV.

La·chaise (lə shez′; *Fr.* lᴀ shez′), *n.* **Gas·ton** (gas′tən; *Fr.* gᴀ stôɴ′), 1882–1935, U.S. sculptor, born in France.

lach·es (lach′iz), *n.* (*used with a singular v.*) *Law.* failure to do something at the proper time, esp. such delay as will bar a party from bringing a legal proceeding. [1325–75; ME *lachesse* < AF, var. of MF *laschesse,* deriv. of OF *lasche* slack (< Gmc); see -ICE]

Lach·e·sis (lach′ə sis), *n. Class. Myth.* the Fate who determines the length of the thread of life. [< L < Gk, personification of *láchesis* destiny, equiv. to *lache(în)* to happen or obtain by lot + *-sis* -SIS]

La·chine (lə shēn′; *Fr.* lᴀ shēn′), *n.* a city in S Quebec, in E Canada, near Quebec, on the St. Lawrence. 37,521.

La·chish (lā′kish), *n.* a Canaanite city captured by Joshua: now an archaeological site in Israel.

La Chor·re·ra (lä chôr ʀe′ʀä), *n.* a city in central Panama, just W of the Panama Canal. 26,026.

Lach·ry·ma Chris·ti (lak′rə mə kris′tē), **1.** a table wine produced from grapes grown near Vesuvius, in Italy. **2.** a medium dry, sparkling wine produced in the Piedmont region of Italy. Also, **Lacrima Christi.** [1605–15; < L *lachryma Christī* lit., tear of Christ]

lach·ry·mal (lak′rə məl), *adj.* **1.** of or pertaining to tears. **2.** producing tears. **3.** characterized by tears; indicative of weeping. **4.** *Anat.* lacrimal (def. 2). —*n.* **5.** Also called **lach′rymal bone′.** *Anat.* See **lacrimal bone. 6.** lachrymatory (def. 2). [1535–45; < ML *lachrymālis,* equiv. to L *lachrym(a)* (Hellenized sp. of *lacrima, lacruma* (OL *dacrima*) tear, prob. << Gk *dákryma,* deriv. of *dákry;* see TEAR¹) + *-ālis* -AL¹]

lach·ry·ma·tion (lak′rə mā′shən), *n.* lacrimation. Also, **lach′ri·ma′tion.**

lach·ry·ma·tor (lak′rə mā′tər), *n.* a chemical substance that causes the shedding of tears, as tear gas. Also, **lacrimator.** [1915–20; < ML *lacrimātor,* equiv. to *lacrimā(re)* to shed tears (see LACHRYMATORY) + *-tor* -TOR]

lach·ry·ma·to·ry (lak′rə mə tôr′ē, -tōr′ē), *adj., n., pl.* **-ries.** —*adj.* **1.** of, pertaining to, or causing the shedding of tears. —*n.* **2.** Also called **lachrymal.** a small, narrow-necked vase found in ancient Roman tombs, formerly thought to have been used to catch and keep the tears of bereaved friends. Also, **lacrimatory.** [1650–60; (n.) < ML *lachrymātōrium,* equiv. to *lachrymā(re)* to shed tears + *-tōrium* -TORY²; (adj.) < ML *lachrymātōrius,* equiv. to *lachrymā(re)* + *-tōrius* -TORY¹; see LACHRYMAL]

lach·ry·mose (lak′rə mōs′), *adj.* **1.** suggestive of or tending to cause tears; mournful. **2.** given to shedding tears readily; tearful. [1655–65; < L *lacrimōsus,* equiv. to *lacrim(a)* tear (see LACHRYMAL) + *-ōsus* -OSE¹] —**lach′ry·mose′ly,** *adv.* —**lach·ry·mos·i·ty** (lak′rə mos′i tē), *n.*

La·chute (lə sho͞ot′; *Fr.* lᴀ shʏt′), *n.* a city in S Quebec, in E Canada. 11,729.

lac·ing (lā′sing), *n.* **1.** the act of a person or thing that laces. **2.** a trimming of lace or braid. **3.** a beating or thrashing. **4.** a small amount of alcoholic liquor or any other substance added to food or drink. **5.** a lace used for fastening, as in a shoe or corset. **6.** *Building Trades, Engin.* any member or members, as a batten plate or steel bars, uniting the angles or flanges of a composite girder, column, or strut. **7.** Also called **lac′ing course′.** *Masonry.* **a.** a course of brick in a wall of rubble. **b.** a bond course in a rowlock arch. **8.** *Naut.* any light line for fastening a sail, awning, or other cloth. [1350–1400; ME; see LACE, -ING¹]

la·cin·i·ate (lə sin′ē āt′, -it), *adj. Bot., Zool.* cut into narrow, irregular lobes; slashed; jagged. [1750–60; < NL *lacin(ia)* (special use of L *lacinia* lappet) + -ATE¹]

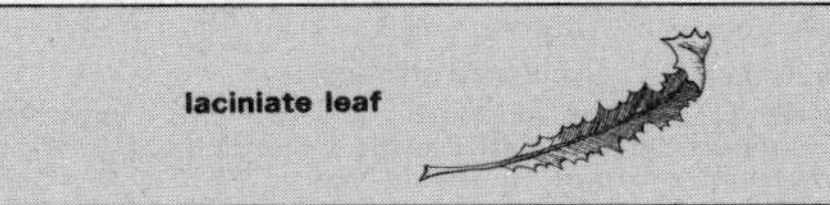
laciniate leaf

lac′ in′sect (lak), a scale insect, *Laccifer lacca,* of southeast Asia, the female of which secretes lac, a substance used in the preparation of shellac, wax, etc.

lack (lak), *n.* **1.** deficiency or absence of something needed, desirable, or customary: *lack of money; lack of skill.* **2.** something missing or needed: *After he left, they really felt the lack.* —*v.t.* **3.** to be without or deficient in: *to lack ability; to lack the necessities of life.* **4.** to fall short in respect of: *He lacks three votes to win.* —*v.i.* **5.** to be absent or missing, as something needed or desirable: *Three votes are lacking to make a majority.* **6. lack in,** to be short of or deficient in: *What he lacks in brains, he makes up for in brawn.* [1125–75; ME *lak;* c. MLG *lak,* MD *lac* deficiency; akin to ON *lakr* deficient]
—**Syn. 1.** dearth, scarcity, paucity, deficit, insufficiency. **1, 3.** want, need. **3.** LACK, WANT, NEED, REQUIRE as verbs all stress the absence of something desirable, important, or necessary. LACK means to be without or to have less than a desirable quantity of something: *to lack courage, sufficient money, enough members to make a quorum.* WANT may imply some urgency in fulfilling a requirement or a desire: *Willing workers are badly wanted. The room wants some final touch to make it homey.* NEED often suggests even more urgency than does WANT stressing the necessity of supplying what is lacking: *to need an operation, better food, a match to light the fire.* REQUIRE, which expresses necessity as strongly as NEED, occurs most frequently in serious or formal contexts: *Your presence at the hearing is required. Successful experimentation requires careful attention to detail.* —**Ant. 1.** surplus.

lack·a·dai·si·cal (lak′ə dā′zi kəl), *adj.* **1.** without interest, vigor, or determination; listless; lethargic: *a lackadaisical attempt.* **2.** lazy; indolent: *a lackadaisical fellow.* [1760–70; *lackadais(y)* (var. of LACKADAY) + -ICAL] —**lack′a·dai′si·cal·ly,** *adv.* —**lack′a·dai′si·cal·ness,** *n.*
—**Syn. 2.** slothful, unambitious, idle.

lack·a·day (lak′ə dā′), *interj. Archaic.* (used as an expression of regret, sorrow, dismay, or disapproval.) [1685–95; alter. of *alack the day*]

Lack·a·wan·na (lak′ə won′ə), *n.* a city in W New York, on Lake Erie, near Buffalo. 22,701.

lack·er (lak′ər), *n., v.t.* lacquer.

lack·ey (lak′ē), *n., pl.* **-eys,** *v.,* **-eyed, -ey·ing.** —*n.* **1.** a servile follower; toady. **2.** a footman or liveried manservant. —*v.t.* **3.** to attend as a lackey does. Also, **lacquey.** [1520–30; < MF *laquais,* perh. < Catalan *lacayo, alacayo* < ?]

lack·ing (lak′ing), *prep.* **1.** being without; not having; wanting; less: *Lacking equipment, the laboratory couldn't undertake the research project.* —*adj.* **2.** wanting; deficient: *He was found lacking in stamina.* [1350–1400; ME; see LACK, -ING²]

Lack′land Air′ Force′ Base′ (lak′lənd), U.S. Air Force installation in SW central Texas, SW of San Antonio.

lack·lus·ter (lak′lus′tər), *adj.* **1.** lacking brilliance or radiance; dull: *lackluster eyes.* **2.** lacking liveliness, vitality, spirit, or enthusiasm: *a lackluster performance.* —*n.* **3.** a lack of brilliance or vitality. Also, *esp. Brit.,* **lack′lus′tre.** [1590–1600; LACK + LUSTER¹]

La·clos (lᴀ klō′), *n.* **Pierre Am·broise Fran·çois Cho·der·los de** (pyeʀ äɴ bʀwaz′ fʀäɴ swa′ shô deʀ lô′ də), 1741–1803, French general and writer.

La·co·ni·a (lə kō′nē ə), *n.* **1.** an ancient country in the S part of Greece. *Cap.:* Sparta. **2.** a city in central New Hampshire. 15,575.

La·co·ni·an (lə kō′nē ən), *adj.* **1.** of or pertaining to ancient Laconia or its people. —*n.* **2.** a native or inhabitant of ancient Laconia. [1820–30; LACONI(A) + -AN]

la·con·ic (lə kon′ik), *adj.* using few words; expressing much in few words; concise: *a laconic reply.* [1580–90; < L *Lacōnicus* < Gk *Lakōnikós* Laconian, equiv. to *Lákōn* a Laconian + *-ikos* -IC] —**la·con′i·cal·ly,** *adv.*
—**Syn.** brief, pithy, terse; succinct. —**Ant.** voluble.

la·con·i·cal (lə kon′i kəl), *adj. Archaic.* laconic. [1570–80; < L *lacōnic(us)* (see LACONIC) + -AL¹]

la·con·i·cum (lə kon′i kəm), *n., pl.* **-ca** (-kə). the sudatorium of an ancient Roman bath. [1690–1700; < L *lacōnicum* sweating room, n. use of neut. of *Lacōnicus* Laconian (see LACONIC); the sweat bath was a Spartan custom]

lac·o·nism (lak′ə niz′əm), *n.* **1.** laconic brevity. **2.** a laconic utterance or sentence. Also, **la·con·i·cism** (lə kon′ə siz′əm). [1560–70; < Gk *lakōnismós,* answering to *lakōnízein* to favor or imitate the Spartans. See LACONIC, -ISM]

La Co·ru·ña (lä′ kô ro͞o′nyä), a seaport in NW Spain. 189,654. Also called **Coruña, Corunna.**

La·coste (lə kôst′, -kost′; *Fr.* lᴀ kôst′), *n.* **Re·né** (rə nā′; *Fr.* ʀə nā′), born 1905, French tennis player.

lac·quer (lak′ər), *n.* **1.** a protective coating consisting of a resin, cellulose ester, or both, dissolved in a volatile solvent, sometimes with pigment added. **2.** any of various resinous varnishes, esp. a resinous varnish obtained from a Japanese tree, *Rhus verniciflua,* used to produce a highly polished, lustrous surface on wood or the like. **3.** Also called **lac′quer ware′, lac′quer·ware′.** ware, esp. of wood, coated with such a varnish, and often inlaid: *They collected fine Oriental lacquers.* **4.** *Slang.* any volatile solvent that produces euphoria when inhaled. —*v.t.* **5.** to coat with lacquer. **6.** to cover, as with facile or fluent words or explanations cleverly worded, etc.; obscure the faults of; gloss (often fol. by *over*): *The speech tended to lacquer over the terrible conditions.* Also, **lacker.** [1570–80; earlier *leckar, laker* < Pg *lacre, lacar,* unexplained var. of *laca* < Ar *lakk* < Pers *lāk* LAC¹] —**lac′quer·er,** *n.*

lac′quer tree′, any of several trees yielding a resin used as lacquer, as *Rhus verniciflua,* of Japan. [1860–65]

lac·quey (lak′ē), *n., pl.* **-queys,** *v.t.,* **-queyed, -quey·ing.** lackey.

La·cre·telle (lᴀ kʀə tel′), *n.* **Jacques de** (zhäk də), 1888–1985, French novelist.

Lac·ri·ma Chris·ti (lak′rə mə kris′tē). See **Lachryma Christi.**

lac·ri·mal (lak′rə məl), *adj.* **1.** lachrymal (defs. 1–3). **2.** Also, **lachrymal.** *Anat.* of, pertaining to, or situated near the organs that secrete tears. —*n.* **3.** See **lacrimal bone.** [1535–45; var. of LACHRYMAL]

lac′rimal bone′, *Anat.* a small, thin, membrane bone forming the front part of the inner wall of each orbit. Also called **lacrimal.** [1850–55]

lac′rimal duct′, *Anat.* either of two small ducts extending from the inner corner of each eyelid to the lacrimal sac. [1790–1800]

lac′rimal gland′, *Anat.* either of two tear-secreting glands situated in the upper outer angle of the orbit. [1780–90]

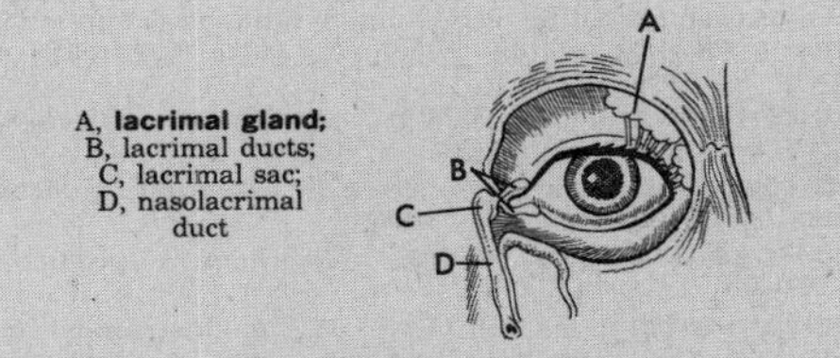

A, **lacrimal gland;** B, lacrimal ducts; C, lacrimal sac; D, nasolacrimal duct

CONCISE PRONUNCIATION KEY: act, cāpe, dâre, pärt; set, ēqual; if, īce; ox, ōver, ôrder, oil, bo͝ok, bo͞ot, out; up, ûrge; child; sing; shoe; thin, *th*at; zh as in *treasure.* ə = *a* as in *alone, e* as in *system, i* as in *easily, o* as in *gallop, u* as in *circus;* ᵊ as in *fire* (fīᵊr), *hour* (ouᵊr). l and n can serve as syllabic consonants, as in *cradle* (krād′l), and *button* (but′n). See the full key inside the front cover.

lac′rimal sac′, *Anat.* the dilated upper portion of the nasolacrimal duct that receives tears from the lacrimal ducts. [1770–80]

lac•ri•ma•tion (lak′rə mā′shən), *n.* the secretion of tears, esp. in abnormal abundance. Also, **lachrymation, lachrimation.** [1565–75; < L *lacrimātiōn-* (s. of *lacrimātiō*) weeping, equiv. to *lacrimāt(us)* ptp. of *lacrimāre* to weep (see LACHRYMAL, -ATE[1]) + *-iōn-* -ION]

lac•ri•ma•tor (lak′rə mā′tər), *n.* lachrymator.

lac•ri•ma•to•ry (lak′rə mə tôr′ē, -tōr′ē), *adj., n., pl.* **-ries.** lachrymatory.

La Crosse (lə krôs′, kros′), a city in W Wisconsin, on the Mississippi River. 48,347.

la•crosse (lə krôs′, -kros′), *n.* a game, originated by Indians of North America, in which two 10-member teams attempt to send a small ball into each other's netted goal, each player being equipped with a crosse or stick at the end of which is a netted pocket for catching, carrying, or throwing the ball. [1710–20, *Amer.*; < CanF: lit., the crook (stick used in the game). See CROSSE]

lact-, var. of **lacto-** before a vowel: *lactalbumin.*

lac•tal•bu•min (lak′təl byo͞o′min), *n. Biochem.* the simple protein of milk, obtained from whey, used in the preparation of certain foods and in adhesives and varnishes. [1880–85; LACT- + ALBUMIN]

lac•tam (lak′tam), *n. Chem.* any of a group of cyclic amides characterized by the NHCO group, derived from aminocarboxylic acids by the intramolecular elimination of water from the amino and carboxylic groups. [1880–85; LACT(ONE) + AM(IDE)]

lac•tar•i•an (lak târ′ē ən), *n.* lactovegetarian (def. 1). [LACT- + -ARIAN, on the model of VEGETARIAN]

lac•ta•ry (lak′tə rē), *adj. Archaic.* of, pertaining to, or of the nature of milk. [1615–25; < L *lactārius* milk-giving. See LACT-, -ARY]

lac•tase (lak′tās, -tāz′), *n. Biochem.* an enzyme capable of hydrolyzing lactose into glucose and galactose. [1890–95; LACT- + -ASE]

lac•tate[1] (lak′tāt), *v.i.,* **-tat•ed, -tat•ing.** to produce milk. [1885–90; < L *lactātus,* ptp. of *lactāre* to suckle. See LACT-, -ATE[1]]

lac•tate[2] (lak′tāt), *n. Chem.* an ester or salt of lactic acid. [1785–95; LACT(IC ACID) + -ATE[2]]

lac′tate dehy′drogenase, *Biochem.* an enzyme that catalyzes the interconversion of pyruvate and lactate, an important step in carbohydrate metabolism: elevated serum levels indicate injury to kidney, skeletal muscle, or heart muscle. *Abbr.:* LDH

lac•ta•tion (lak tā′shən), *n.* **1.** the secretion or formation of milk. **2.** the period of milk production. [1660–70; < LL *lactātiōn-* (s. of *lactātiō*) a giving suck. See LACTATE[1], -ION] **—lac•ta′tion•al,** *adj.* **—lac•ta′tion•al•ly,** *adv.*

lac•te•al (lak′tē əl), *adj.* **1.** pertaining to, consisting of, or resembling milk; milky. **2.** *Anat.* conveying or containing chyle. —*n.* **3.** *Anat.* any of the minute lymphatic vessels that convey chyle from the small intestine to the thoracic duct. [1625–35; < L *lacte(us)* milky (see LACTEOUS) + -AL[1]] **—lac′te•al•ly,** *adv.*

lac•te•ous (lak′tē əs), *adj. Archaic.* milky; of the color of milk. [1640–50; < L *lacteus;* see LACT-, -EOUS]

lac•tes•cent (lak tes′ənt), *adj.* **1.** becoming or being milky. **2.** *Bot., Entomol.* secreting or producing a milky juice. [1660–70; < L *lactēscent-* (s. of *lactēscēns*), prp. of *lactēscere* to turn into milk, produce milk. See LACT-, -ESCENT] **—lac•tes′cence, lac•tes′cen•cy,** *n.*

lacti-, var. of **lacto-:** *lactiferous.*

lac•tic (lak′tik), *adj.* of, pertaining to, or obtained from milk. [1780–90; LACT- + -IC]

lac′tic ac′id, *Biochem.* a colorless or yellowish, syrupy, water-soluble liquid, $C_3H_6O_3$, produced during muscle contraction as a product of anaerobic glucose metabolism, abundant in sour milk, prepared usually by fermentation of cornstarch, molasses, potatoes, etc., or synthesized: used chiefly in dyeing and textile printing, as a flavoring agent in food, and in medicine. [1780–90]

lac•tif•er•ous (lak tif′ər əs), *adj.* **1.** producing or secreting milk: *lactiferous glands.* **2.** conveying milk or a milky fluid: *lactiferous ducts.* [1665–75; < NL *lactifer* that bears milk (see LACTI-, -FER) + -OUS] **—lac•tif′er•ous•ness,** *n.*

lacto-, a combining form meaning "milk," used in the formation of compound words (*lactometer*); specialized in chemical terminology to mean "lactate," or "lactic acid." Also, **lacti-;** *esp. before a vowel,* **lact-.** [< L *lact-* (s. of *lac* milk) + -O-]

lac•to•ba•cil•lus (lak′tō bə sil′əs), *n., pl.* **-cil•li** (-sil′ī). *Bacteriol.* any long, slender, rod-shaped, anaerobic bacterium of the genus *Lactobacillus,* that produces large amounts of lactic acid in the fermentation of carbohydrates, esp. in milk. [< NL (1901); see LACTO-, BACILLUS]

lac•to•fer•rin (lak′tə fer′in), *n. Biochem.* a glycoprotein present in milk, esp. human milk, and supplying iron to suckling infants. [1970–75; LACTO- + FERR(I)- + -IN[2]]

lac•to•fla•vin (lak′tō flā′vin, lak′tō flā′-), *n. Biochem.* riboflavin. [1930–35; LACTO- + -FLAVIN]

lac•to•gen•ic (lak′tə jen′ik), *adj.* stimulating lactation. [1950–55; LACTO- + -GENIC]

lac′togen′ic hor′mone, *Biochem.* prolactin. [1950–55]

lac•tom•e•ter (lak tom′i tər), *n.* an instrument for determining the specific gravity of milk. [1810–20; LACTO- + -METER]

lac•tone (lak′tōn), *n. Chem.* any of a group of internal esters derived from hydroxy acids. [1840–50; LACT- + -ONE] **—lac•ton•ic** (lak ton′ik), *adj.*

lac•to•nize (lak′tō nīz′), *v.t., v.i.,* **-nized, -niz•ing.** to change into a lactone. Also, *esp. Brit.,* **lac′to•nise′.** [1910–15; LACTONE + -IZE] **—lac′to•ni•za′tion,** *n.*

lac•to-o•vo-veg•e•tar•i•an (lak′tō ō′vō vej′i târ′ē ən), *n.* **1.** Also called **lac•to•var•i•an** (lak′tə vâr′ē ən), **ovolactarian, ovo-lacto-vegetarian.** a vegetarian whose diet includes dairy products and eggs. —*adj.* **2.** pertaining to or maintaining a vegetarian diet that includes dairy products and eggs. [1950–55]

lac•to•pro•tein (lak′tō prō′tēn, -prō′tē in), *n.* any protein existing in milk. [1860–65; LACTO- + PROTEIN]

lac•to•scope (lak′tə skōp′), *n.* an optical device for determining the amount of cream in milk. [1855–60; LACTO- + -SCOPE]

lac•tose (lak′tōs), *n.* **1.** *Biochem.* a disaccharide, $C_{12}H_{22}O_{11}$, present in milk, that upon hydrolysis yields glucose and galactose. **2.** a white, crystalline, sweet, water-soluble commercial form of this compound, obtained from whey and used in infant feedings, in confections and other foods, in bacteriological media, and in pharmacology as a diluent and excipient. Also called **milk sugar, sugar of milk.** [1855–60; LACT- + -OSE[2]]

lac•to•veg•e•tar•i•an (lak′tō vej′i târ′ē ən), *n.* **1.** Also called **lactarian.** a vegetarian whose diet includes dairy products. —*adj.* **2.** pertaining to or maintaining a vegetarian diet that includes dairy products. [1905–10; LACTO- + VEGETARIAN]

La Cum•bre (*Sp.* lä ko͞om′bre). See **Uspallata Pass.**

la•cu•na (lə kyo͞o′nə), *n., pl.* **-nae** (-nē), **-nas. 1.** a gap or missing part, as in a manuscript, series, or logical argument; hiatus. **2.** *Anat.* one of the numerous minute cavities in the substance of bone, supposed to contain nucleate cells. **3.** *Bot.* an air space in the cellular tissue of plants. [1655–65; < L *lacūna* ditch, pit, hole, gap, deficiency, akin to *lacus* vat, LAKE[1]. Cf. LAGOON]

la•cu•nal (lə kyo͞on′l), *adj.* **1.** of or pertaining to a lacuna. **2.** having lacunae. Also, **lac•u•nar•y** (lak′yo͝o ner′ē, lə kyo͞o′nə rē). [1840–50; LACUN(A) + -AL[1]]

la•cu•nar (lə kyo͞o′nər), *n., pl.* **la•cu•nars, lac•u•nar•i•a** (lak′yə nâr′ē ə), *adj.* —*n.* **1.** *Archit.* **a.** a coffered vault, ceiling, or soffit. **b.** coffer (def. 4). —*adj.* **2.** lacunal. [1690–1700; LACUN(A) + -AR[1]]

la•cu•nose (lə kyo͞o′nōs), *adj.* full of or having lacunae. Also, **la•cu•nu•lose** (lə kyo͞o′nyə lōs′). [1810–20; < L *lacūnōsus* full of holes or gaps. See LACUNA, -OSE[1]] **—lac•u•nos•i•ty** (lak′yo͝o nos′i tē), *n.*

la•cu•nule (lə kyo͞o′nyo͞ol), *n.* a small lacuna. [1655–65; LACUN(A) + -ULE]

Lac′us So′lis (lak′əs sō′lis), an area in the southern hemisphere of Mars.

la•cus•trine (lə kus′trin), *adj.* **1.** of or pertaining to a lake. **2.** living or growing in lakes, as various organisms. **3.** formed at the bottom or along the shore of lakes, as geological strata. [1820–30; < It *lacustr(e)* of lakes + -INE[1]]

LACW, leading aircraftswoman.

lac•y (lā′sē), *adj.,* **lac•i•er, lac•i•est.** of or resembling lace; lacelike: *a lacy gown; a lacy leaf.* [1795–1805; LACE + -Y[1]] **—lac′i•ly,** *adv.* **—lac′i•ness,** *n.*
—Syn. gossamer, filigree, netlike.

La•cy (lā′sē), *n.* a male given name.

lad (lad), *n.* **1.** a boy or youth. **2.** *Informal.* a familiar or affectionate term of address for a man; chap. **3.** *Brit. Horseracing Informal.* a stable boy. [1250–1300; ME *ladde* < ?; cf. late OE *Ladda* (nickname)] **—lad′dish,** *adj.* **—lad′hood,** *n.*

LAD, See **language acquisition device.**

lad•a•num (lad′nəm), *n.* labdanum.

lad•der (lad′ər), *n.* **1.** a structure of wood, metal, or rope, commonly consisting of two sidepieces between which a series of bars or rungs are set at suitable distances, forming a means of climbing up or down. **2.** something resembling this. **3.** a means of rising, as to eminence: *the ladder of success.* **4.** a graded series of stages or levels in status; a hierarchical order of position or rank: *high on the political ladder.* **5.** *Naut.* companionway (def. 1). **6.** *Chiefly Brit.* a run in a stocking. —*v.t.* **7.** to climb or mount by means of a ladder: *to ladder a wall.* **8.** to furnish with a ladder: *to ladder a water tower.* **9.** *Chiefly Brit.* to cause a run in (a stocking). —*v.i.* **10.** *Chiefly Brit.* to get a run, as in a stocking. **11.** to gain in popularity or importance: *He laddered to the top of his profession.* [bef. 1000; ME *laddre,* OE *hlǣder;* c. G *Leiter,* D *leer* (also *ladder* < Fris); akin to Goth *hleithra* tent; orig., something that slopes. See LEAN[1]] **—lad′der•less,** *adj.* **—lad′der•like′, lad′der•y,** *adj.*

lad′der back′, a chair back having a number of horizontal slats between uprights. [1905–10]

lad′der com′pany. See **hook-and-ladder company.** [1880–85]

lad•der•man (lad′ər mən, -man′), *n., pl.* **-men** (-mən, -men′). a firefighter who is a member of a hook-and-ladder company. [1885–90, *Amer.*; LADDER + MAN[1]]
—Usage. See **-man.**

lad′der pol′ymer, *Chem.* a polymer, as DNA, consisting of double-stranded chains linked by hydrogen bonds or chemical bonds at regular intervals. [1970–75]

lad′der stitch′, an embroidery stitch in which crossbars at equal distances are produced between two solid ridges of raised work. [1880–85]

lad′der tour′nament, *Sports.* a tournament in which the entrants are listed by name and rank, advancement being by means of challenging and defeating an entrant ranked one or two places higher.

lad′der track′, a railroad track linking a series of parallel tracks.

lad′der truck′. See **hook and ladder.** [1885–90, *Amer.*]

lad•der•way (lad′ər wā′), *n. Mining.* a vertical passageway with ladders. [1840–50; LADDER + WAY]

lad•die (lad′ē), *n. Chiefly Scot.* a young lad; boy. [1540–50; LAD + -IE]

lade (lād), *v.,* **lad•ed, lad•en** or **lad•ed, lad•ing.** —*v.t.* **1.** to put (something) on or in, as a burden, load, or cargo; load. **2.** to load oppressively; burden (used chiefly in the passive): *laden with many responsibilities.* **3.** to fill or cover abundantly (used chiefly in the passive): *trees laden with fruit; a man laden with honors.* **4.** to lift or throw in or out, as a fluid, with a ladle or other utensil. —*v.i.* **5.** to take on a load. **6.** to lade a liquid. [bef. 900; ME *laden,* OE *hladan* to load, draw up (water); c. D *laden,* G *laden,* ON *hlatha* to load. Cf. LADLE] **—lad′er,** *n.*

lad•en (lād′n), *adj.* **1.** burdened; loaded down. —*v.t.* **2.** to lade. [1585–95; LADE + -EN[3], -EN[1]]

la-di-da (lä′dē dä′), *Informal.* —*interj.* **1.** (used as an expression of derision directed at affected gentility or pretentious refinement.) —*adj.* **2.** affected; pretentious; foppish: *a la-di-da manner.* —*n.* **3.** an affected or pretentious person. **4.** behavior or speech characterized by affected or exaggerated gentility. Also, **la′-de-da′, lah-di-dah.** [1880–85; derisive imitation of affected, pseudo-elevated speech]

La′dies Aid′, a local organization of women who raise money for their church. [1865–70, *Amer.*]

La′dies Auxil′iary, an association whose members are usually the wives of members of an association with which it is affiliated.

La′dies' Day′, (*often l.c.*) **1.** a special day set aside, either occasionally or regularly, on which women are encouraged to attend or participate in a certain activity at a reduced fee or at no cost: *Friday was Ladies' Day at the ball park.* **2.** a special day on which women are invited or allowed to attend a club meeting or other activity usually restricted to males. [1780–90, *Amer.*]

la•dies'-ear•drops (lā′dēz ēr′drops′), *n., pl.* **-drops.** (*used with a singular or plural v.*) lady's-earrings. [1885–90, *Amer.*]

la•dies'-ear•rings (lā′dēz ēr′ringz′, -ingz), *n., pl.* **-rings.** (*used with a singular or plural v.*) lady's-earrings.

la•dies-in-wait•ing (lā′dēz in wā′ting), *n.* pl. of **lady-in-waiting.**

la′dies' man′, a man who strives especially to please women and to attract their attention and admiration. Also, **lady's man.** [1775–85]

la•dies-of-the-night (lā′dēz əv *th*ə nīt′), *n.* pl. of **lady-of-the-night.**

la′dies' room′, a public lavatory for women. Also called **powder room, women's room.** [1875–80]

la•dies'-to•bac•co (lā′dēz tə bak′ō), *n., pl.* **-cos, -coes.** pussy-toes.

La•din (lə dēn′), *n.* **1.** a Rhaeto-Romanic dialect of the southern Tyrol. **2.** a dialect of Romansh spoken in the Inn River valley of Grisons canton, Switzerland. **3.** a person who speaks Ladin. [1875–80; < Romansh < L *Latīnus* LATIN]

lad•ing (lā′ding), *n.* **1.** the act of lading. **2.** that with which something is laden; load; freight; cargo. [1490–1500; LADE + -ING[1]]

La•di•no (lə dē′nō; *Sp.* lä *th*ē′nô), *n., pl.* **-nos** (-nōz; *Sp.* -nôs) for 2, 3. **1.** Also called **Judeo-Spanish, Judezmo.** a Romance language of Sephardic Jews, based on Old Spanish and written in the Hebrew script. **2.** (in Spanish America) a mestizo. **3.** (*l.c.*) *Southwestern U.S.* a wild, unmanageable, or vicious horse or other ranch animal. [1885–90; < Sp < L *Latīnus* LATIN. Cf. LADIN]

Ladi′no clo′ver, a giant variety of white clover, *Trifolium repens lodigense,* used for pasture and hay. [1920–25]

Lad•is•laus (lad′is lôs′), *n.* **Saint,** c1040–95, king of Hungary 1077–95. Also, **Lad•is•las** (lad′is ləs, -läs′).

la•dle (lād′l), *n., v.,* **-dled, -dling.** —*n.* **1.** a long-handled utensil with a cup-shaped bowl for dipping or conveying liquids. **2.** *Metall.* a bucketlike, refractory-lined container for transferring molten metal. —*v.t.* **3.** to dip or convey with or as if with a ladle: *to ladle soup into bowls.* [bef. 1000; ME *ladel,* OE *hlædel.* See LADE, -LE] **—la′dler,** *n.*

la•dle•ful (lād′l fo͝ol), *n., pl.* **-fuls.** the amount that fills a ladle. [1400–50; late ME. See LADLE, -FUL]
—Usage. See **-ful.**

La•do•ga (lä′də gə), *n.* **Lake,** a lake in the NW Russian Federation in Europe, NE of St. Petersburg: largest lake in Europe. 7000 sq. mi. (18,000 sq. km).

La•don (lād′n), *n. Class. Myth.* a dragon having 100 heads and guarding the garden of the Hesperides: killed by Hercules.

la•drone (lə drōn′), *n. Southwestern U.S.* a thief. Also, **la•dron′.** [1550–60; < Sp *ladrón* < L *latrōn-* (s. of *latrō*) mercenary, bandit]

La•drone′ Is′lands (lə drōn′), former name of **Mariana Islands.** Also called **La•drones** (lə drōnz′; *Sp.* lä *th*rô′nes).

la•dy (lā′dē), *n., pl.* **-dies,** *adj.* —*n.* **1.** a woman who is refined, polite, and well-spoken: *She may be poor and have little education, but she's a real lady.* **2.** a woman of high social position or economic class: *She was born a lady and found it hard to adjust to her reduced circumstances.* **3.** any woman; female (sometimes used in combination): *the lady who answered the phone; a saleslady.* **4.** (Used in direct address: often offensive in the singular): *Ladies and gentlemen, welcome. Lady, out of my way, please.* **5.** wife: *The ambassador and his lady ar-*

rived late. **6.** *Slang.* a female lover or steady companion. **7.** (*cap.*) (in Great Britain) the proper title of any woman whose husband is higher in rank than baronet or knight, or who is the daughter of a nobleman not lower than an earl (although the title is given by courtesy also to the wives of baronets and knights). **8.** a woman who has proprietary rights or authority, as over a manor; female feudal superior. Cf. **lord** (def. 4). **9.** (*cap.*) the Virgin Mary. **10.** a woman who is the object of chivalrous devotion. **11.** (*usually cap.*) **a.** an attribute or abstraction personified as a woman; a designation of an allegorical figure as feminine: *Lady Fortune; Lady Virtue.* **b.** a title prefixed to the name of a goddess: *Lady Venus.* —*adj.* **12.** *Sometimes Offensive.* being a lady; female: *a lady reporter.* **13.** of a lady; ladylike; feminine. [bef. 900; ME *ladi(e),* earlier *lavedi,* OE *hlǣfdige, hlǣfdige,* perh. orig. meaning "loaf-kneader," equiv. to *hlāf* LOAF + *-dige, -dige,* var. of *dǣge* kneader (see DOUGH; cf. ON *deigja* maid); see LORD] —**la′dy·hood′,** *n.* —**la′dy·ish,** *adj.* —**la′dy·ish·ly,** *adv.* —**la′dy·ish·ness,** *n.* —**la′·dy·less,** *adj.*

—**Usage.** In the meanings "refined, polite woman" and "woman of high social position" the noun LADY is the parallel of *gentleman.* As forms of address, both nouns are used in the plural (*Ladies and gentlemen, thank you for your cooperation*), but only LADY occurs in the singular. Except in chivalrous, literary, or similar contexts (*Lady, spurn me not*), this singular is now usually perceived as rude or at least insensitive: *Where do you want the new air conditioner, lady?* Although LADY is still found in phrases or compounds referring to occupation or the like (*cleaning lady; forelady; saleslady*), this use seems to be diminishing. The use of LADY as a modifier (*lady doctor; lady artist*) suggests that it is unusual to find a woman in the role specified. Many women are offended by this use, and it too is becoming less common.

An approach that is increasingly followed is to avoid specifying the sex of the performer or practitioner. *Person* or a sex-neutral term can be substituted for LADY, as *cleaner* for *cleaning lady, supervisor* for *forelady,* and *salesperson* or *salesclerk* for *saleslady.* When circumstances make it relevant to specify sex, *woman* not LADY is used, the parallel term being *man: Men doctors outnumber women doctors on the hospital staff by more than three to one.* See also **-person, -woman.**

—**Syn.** See **woman.**

la′dy ap′ple, a small, yellow apple with a red blush, grown as a specialty variety, and used for eating and in commercial canning. [1810–20]

La′dy Bal′timore cake′, a white layer cake using only the beaten whites of eggs and spread with a fruit-nut filling consisting of raisins, figs, walnuts or pecans, and sometimes candied cherries. Cf. **Lord Baltimore cake.** [1905–10]

la·dy·bee·tle (lā′dē bēt′l), *n.* ladybug. Also, **la′dy bee′tle.** [1875–80; LADY(BUG) + BEETLE[1]]

la′dy·bird bee′tle (lā′dē bûrd′), ladybug. Also called **la′dy·bird′.** [1730–40, *Amer.*; LADY (uninflected possessive case) Virgin Mary + BIRD; i.e. (our) Lady's bird]

La′dy Boun′tiful, *pl.* **Lady Bountifuls, Ladies Bountiful. 1.** a wealthy lady in George Farquhar's *The Beaux' Stratagem,* noted for her kindness and generosity. **2.** (*sometimes l.c.*) a woman of noteworthy generosity or charity.

la·dy·bug (lā′dē bug′), *n.* any of numerous small, round, often brightly colored and spotted beetles of the family Coccinellidae, feeding chiefly on aphids and other small insects, but including several forms that feed on plants. Also called **ladybeetle, lady beetle, ladybird beetle, ladybird.** [1690–1700; LADY + BUG[1]]

ladybug, *Hippodamia convergens,* length ¼ in. (0.6 cm)

La′dy chap′el, a chapel dedicated to the Virgin Mary, attached to a church, and generally behind the high altar at the extremity of the apse. [1400–50; late ME (*oure*) *lady chapell*]

La′dy Chat′ter·ley's Lov′er (chat′ər lēz), a novel (1928) by D. H. Lawrence.

la′dy crab′, a brightly speckled swimming crab, *Ovalipes ocellatus,* of sandy beaches along the Atlantic coast of the U.S. Also called **calico crab.** [1880–85]

La′dy Day′, 1. annunciation (def. 3). **2.** one of various days celebrated in honor of the Virgin Mary. [1250–1300; ME *oure lady day*]

la′dy fern′, a fern, *Athyrium filix-femina,* having delicate, feathery fronds.

la·dy·fin·ger (lā′dē fing′gər), *n.* a small, finger-shaped sponge cake. [1660–70; LADY + FINGER]

la·dy·fish (lā′dē fish′), *n., pl.* (*esp. collectively*) **-fish,** (*esp. referring to two or more kinds or species*) **-fish·es.** a game fish, *Elops saurus,* of warm seas, closely related to but smaller than the tarpon. Also called **tenpounder.** [1705–15; LADY + FISH]

la·dy-in-wait·ing (lā′dē in wā′ting), *n., pl.* **la·dies-in-wait·ing. 1.** a lady who is in attendance upon a queen or princess. **2.** *Facetious.* a woman who is pregnant: *flattering fashions for the lady-in-waiting.* [1860–65]

la·dy-kill·er (lā′dē kil′ər), *n. Informal.* a man who is irresistible to women or has the reputation for being so. —**la′dy-kill′ing,** *n., adj.* [1805–15]

la·dy·kin (lā′dē kin), *n.* (often used as a term of endearment) a little lady. [1850–55; LADY + -KIN]

la·dy·like (lā′dē līk′), *adj.* **1.** like a lady. **2.** befitting a lady: *in a ladylike manner.* [1580–90; LADY + -LIKE] —**la′dy·like′ness,** *n.*

—**Syn. 1, 2.** well-bred, well-mannered, courteous.

la·dy·love (lā′dē luv′), *n.* a beloved woman; sweetheart or mistress. [1725–35; LADY + LOVE]

La′dy Luck′, (*sometimes l.c.*) the personification of luck as a lady bringing good or bad fortune: *Lady Luck was against us and we lost the game.* [1930–35]

la′dy of pleas′ure, a prostitute. [1630–40]

La′dy of the Camel′lias, The, (French, *La Dame aux Camélias*), a novel (1848) and play (1852) by Alexandre Dumas fils.

la′dy of the eve′ning, a prostitute. [1865–70]

la′dy of the house′, the female head of a household (usually prec. by *the*). [1785–95]

La′dy of the Lake′, The, a narrative poem (1810) by Sir Walter Scott.

la·dy-of-the-night (lā′dē əv *th*ə nīt′), *n., pl.* **la·dies-of-the-night.** a tropical American shrub, *Brunfelsia americana,* of the nightshade family, having berrylike yellow fruit and fragrant white flowers. [1865–70]

la′dy palm′, any of several palms of the genus *Rhapis,* native to southeastern Asia and cultivated as houseplants.

la·dy's-ear·rings (lā′dēz ēr′ringz′, -ingz), *n., pl.* **-rings.** (*used with a singular or plural v.*) any of several plants having pendent flowers thought to resemble earrings, as the jewelweed or the fuchsia. Also called **la·dy's-ear·drops** (lā′dēz ēr′drops′), **ladies'-earrings, ladies'-eardrops.**

la·dy·ship (lā′dē ship′), *n.* **1.** (*often cap.*) the form used in speaking of or to a woman having the title of *Lady* (usually prec. by *her* or *your*). **2.** the rank of a lady. [1175–1225; ME; see LADY, -SHIP]

la′dy's maid′, a maid who is a woman's personal attendant, as in dressing. [1800–10]

la′dy's man′. See **ladies' man.** [1775–85]

La·dy·smith (lā′dē smith′), *n.* a city in W Natal, in the E Republic of South Africa: besieged by Boers 1889–1900. 27,000.

La′dy's Not′ for Burn′ing, The, a verse play (1948) by Christopher Fry.

lady's-slipper, *Cypripedium reginae*

la·dy's-slip·per (lā′dēz slip′ər), *n.* **1.** any orchid of the genus *Cypripedium,* the flowers of which have a protruding petal somewhat resembling a slipper: all species are reduced in numbers, some greatly. **2.** any of several other related plants having similar flowers, as of the genera *Paphiopedilum* and *Phragmipedium.* Also, **la′·dy-slip′per.** [1830–40, *Amer.*]

la·dy's-this·tle (lā′dēz this′əl), *n.* a composite plant, *Silybum marianum,* of the Mediterranean region, having glossy, spiny leaves and purplish-red flower heads. Also called **holy thistle, milk thistle.** [1545–55]

la·dy's-thumb (lā′dēz thum′), *n.* a smartweed, *Polygonum persicaria,* of the buckwheat family, having pink or purplish flowers and lance-shaped leaves with a spot resembling a thumbprint. [1830–40, *Amer.*]

la·dy's-tress·es (lā′dēz tres′iz), *n., pl.* **-tress·es.** (*used with a singular or plural v.*) any orchid of the genus *Spiranthes,* having spikes of small flowers. [1540–50]

La′dy Wash′ington gera′nium. See **show geranium.** [named after M. WASHINGTON]

La′dy Win′der·mere's Fan′ (win′dər mērz′), a comedy (1892) by Oscar Wilde.

La·e (lä′ā, lā′ē), *n.* a seaport in E Papua New Guinea: used as a major supply base by the Japanese in World War II. 38,707.

lae·li·a (lē′lē ə), *n.* any of several epiphytic tropical American orchids of the genus *Laelia,* having fleshy leaves and showy flowers. [< NL (1763), perh. after Caius *Laelius,* Roman statesman of the 2d century B.C.; see -A[2]]

Laemm·le (lem′lē), *n.* **Carl,** 1867–1939, U.S. producer of motion pictures, born in Germany.

Laën·nec (lä nek′), *n.* **Re·né Thé·o·phile Hya·cinthe** (rə nā′ tā ô fēl′ yȧ sănt′), 1781–1826, French physician who invented the stethoscope.

lae·o·trop·ic (lē′ə trop′ik, -trō′pik), *adj.* oriented or coiled in a leftward direction, as a left-spiraling snail shell. Cf. **dexiotropic.** [1880–85; < Gk *lai(ós)* left, left side + -O- + -TROPIC]

La·er·tes (lā ûr′tēz, -âr′-), *n. Class. Myth.* the father of Odysseus.

Laes·tryg·o·nes (les trig′ə nēz′), *n.pl., sing.* **Laes·try·gon** (les′tri gon′). *Class. Myth.* giant cannibals encountered by Odysseus on his return to Ithaca. Also, **Laes·try·go·ni·ans** (les′tri gō′nē ənz).

Lae·tar′e Sun′day (lā tär′ē), the fourth Sunday of Lent when the introit begins with "*Laetare Jerusalem*" (Rejoice ye, Jerusalem). Also called **Mid-Lent Sunday.**

Lae·ti·tia (lə tish′ə, -tē′shə), *n.* a female given name.

la·e·trile (lā′i tril), *n.* a controversial drug, purported to cure cancer, prepared from the pits of apricots or peaches and containing about 6 percent cyanide by weight: banned by the FDA. [1950–55; said to be a contr. of *l-mandelonitrile,* equiv. to L- + G *Mandel* almond + -O- + NITRILE]

laevo-, var. of **levo-.**

LaF, Louisiana French.

La Farge (lə färzh′, färj′), **1. John,** 1835–1910, U.S. painter, stained-glass designer, and writer. **2. Oliver Hazard Perry** ("*Oliver II*"), 1901–63, U.S. novelist and anthropologist.

La Fa·yette (laf′ē et′, laf′ā-, lä′fē-, -fā-; *Fr.* lȧ fȧ-yet′), **Ma·rie Ma·de·leine Pioche de la Vergne** (mȧ-rē′ mȧdə len′ pyôsh də lȧ ver′nyə), **Comtesse de,** 1634–93, French novelist.

La·fa·yette (laf′ē et′, laf′ā-, lä′fē-, -fā-; *for 1 also Fr.* lȧ fȧ yet′), *n.* **1. Ma·rie Jo·seph Paul Yves Roch Gil·bert du Mo·tier** (mȧ rē′ zhô zef′ pôl ēv rôk zhēl ber′ dy mô tyā′), **Marquis de.** Also, **La Fayette.** 1757–1834, French soldier, statesman, and liberal leader, who served in the American Revolutionary Army and took a leading part in the French revolutions of 1789 and 1830. **2.** a city in S Louisiana. 81,961. **3.** a city in W Indiana, on the Wabash River. 43,001. **4.** a town in W California. 20,879.

Lafayette′ Escadrille′, a contingent of American aviators who in 1916 served as volunteers (**Escadrille Américaine**) in the French air force and in 1918 became the 103rd Pursuit Squadron of the U.S. Army. [< F *Escadrille Lafayette* lit., Lafayette wing, officially Escadrille No. 124 of the French Army's *Service aéronautique*]

Laf·ca′di·o's Adven′tures (läf kä′dē ōz′), (French, *Les Caves du Vatican*), a novel (1914) by André Gide. Also called ***The Vatican Swindle.***

Laf′fer curve′ (laf′ər), *Econ.* a relationship postulated between tax rates and tax receipts indicating that rates above a certain level actually produce less revenue because they discourage taxable endeavors and vice versa. [1975–80; named after Arthur *Laffer* (born 1940), U.S. economist, who postulated it]

La·fitte (lä fēt′), *n.* **Jean** (zhäN), c1780–c1825, French privateer in the Americas. Also, **La·fite′.**

La Fol·lette (lə fol′it), **Robert Marion,** 1855–1925, U.S. political leader: U.S. senator 1906–25.

La Fon·taine (*Fr.* lȧ fôN ten′), **1. Hen·ri** (*Fr.* äN-rē′), 1854–1943, Belgian statesman: Nobel peace prize 1913. **2. Jean de** (zhäN də), 1621–95, French poet and fabulist.

La Fres·naye (lȧ fre nā′), **Ro·ger de** (rô zhā′ də), 1885–1925, French painter.

lag[1] (lag), *v.,* **lagged, lag·ging,** *n.* —*v.i.* **1.** to fail to maintain a desired pace or to keep up; fall or stay behind: *After five minutes of hard running, some of them began to lag.* **2.** to move or develop slowly, as toward a goal or objective, or in relation to an associated factor (often fol. by *behind*): *to lag behind in production.* **3.** to delay or fail in reaching full development: *The factory lags regularly in making its quota.* **4.** to hang back; linger; delay: *The old friends lagged because they wanted to talk some more.* **5.** to decrease, wane, or flag gradually, as in intensity: *Interest lagged as the meeting went on.* **6.** *Marbles.* to throw one's shooting marble toward a line (**lag line**) on the ground in order to decide on the order of play. **7.** *Billiards, Pool.* string (def. 17b). —*v.t.* **8.** to fail to keep up with: *The industry still lags the national economy.* **9.** *Obs.* to cause to lag. —*n.* **10.** a lagging or falling behind; retardation. **11.** a person who lags behind, is the last to arrive, etc. **12.** an interval or lapse of time: *There was a developmental lag in the diffusion of ideas.* **13.** *Mech.* the amount of retardation of some motion. **14.** *Elect.* the retardation of one alternating quantity, as current, with respect to another related alternating quantity, as voltage, often expressed in degrees. **15.** *Marbles, Billiards.* the act of lagging. [1505–15; < Scand: cf. Norw *lagga* to go slowly]

—**Syn. 1.** loiter, linger. **10.** slowing, slowdown.

—**Ant. 1.** hasten.

lag[2] (lag), *v.,* **lagged, lag·ging,** *n. Chiefly Brit. Slang.* —*v.t.* **1.** to send to penal servitude; imprison. —*n.* **2.** a convict or ex-convict. **3.** a period or term of penal servitude; prison sentence. [1565–75; orig. uncert.]

lag[3] (lag), *n., v.,* **lagged, lag·ging.** —*n.* **1.** one of the staves or strips that form the periphery of a wooden drum, the casing of a steam cylinder, or the like. **2.** *Masonry.* a crosspiece between ribs in a centering. —*v.t.* **3.** to line or cover (an excavation) with lagging. **4.** to cover with insulation, as a steam boiler, to prevent radiation of heat. [1665–75; < Scand; cf. Sw *lagg* stave]

lag·an (lag′ən), *n. Law.* anything sunk in the sea, but attached to a buoy or the like so that it may be recovered. Also, **ligan.** [1525–35; < MF (> ML *laganum*); prob. < Gmc; cf. ON *lǫgn* net laid in the sea]

La·gash (lā′gash), *n.* an ancient Sumerian city between the Tigris and Euphrates rivers, at the modern village of Telloh in SE Iraq: a palace, statuary, and inscribed clay tablets unearthed here.

lag′ bolt′. See **lag screw.**

Lag b'O·mer (läg bō′mər, bə ō′mer), a Jewish festival celebrated on the 18th day of Iyar, being the 33rd day of the Omer, traditionally in commemoration of the end of the plague that killed Rabbi Akiba's students or of the bravery of Bar Kokba. [1900–05; < Heb *lagh bā'ōmer,* equiv. to *lagh* 33rd + *bā,* var. of *bə* in + *'ōmer* OMER]

lag·en (lag′ən), *n. Scot. and North Eng.* laggin.

la·ge·na (lə jē′nə), *n., pl.* **-nae** (-nē). *Zool.* an outpock-

CONCISE PRONUNCIATION KEY: act, cāpe, dâre, pärt; set, ēqual; *if,* ice; ox, ōver, ôrder, oil, bŏŏk, bōōt, out; up, ûrge; child; sing; shoe; thin, *th*at; zh as in *treasure.* ə = *a* as in *alone, e* as in *system, i* as in *easily, o* as in *gallop, u* as in *circus;* ə as in *fire* (fīər), *hour* (ouər). l and n can serve as syllabic consonants, as in *cradle* (krād′l), and *button* (but′n). See the full key inside the front cover.

eting of the saccule of birds, reptiles, and bony fishes corresponding to the cochlear duct of mammals. [< NL, special use of L *lagēna* flask, flagon; c. Gk *lágȳnos*]

la•gen•i•form (lə jen′ə fôrm′), *adj. Bot., Zool.* shaped like a flask; having an enlarged base tapering to a narrow neck. [1820–30; LAGEN(A) + -I- + -FORM]

la•ger[1] (lä′gər, lô′-), *n.* **1.** Also called **la′ger beer′.** a beer stored from six weeks to six months for aging before use. —*v.t.* **2.** to age (beer) usually by storing in tanks at just-below freezing temperatures for several weeks or months. [1835–45; short for *lager beer,* half adoption, half trans. of G *Lagerbier.* See LAIR[1], BEER]

la•ger[2] (lä′gər), *n., v.t., v.i. South African.* laager.

La•ger•kvist (lä′gər kvist′), *n.* **Pär** (pär), 1891–1974, Swedish novelist, poet, and essayist: Nobel prize 1951.

La•ger•löf (lä′gər lœf′), *n.* **Sel•ma (Ot•ti•li•a•na Lo•vi•sa)** (sel′mä ôt′ti lē ä′nä lōō′vi sä′), 1858–1940, Swedish novelist and poet: Nobel prize 1909.

lag•gard (lag′ərd), *n.* **1.** a person or thing that lags; lingerer; loiterer. —*adj.* **2.** moving, developing, or responding slowly; sluggish; dilatory; backward. [1695–1705; LAG[1] + -ARD] —**lag′gard•ness,** *n.*

lag•gard•ly (lag′ərd lē), *adv.* **1.** in the manner of a laggard. —*adj.* **2.** of, pertaining to, characteristic of, or being a laggard: *He behaved in a laggardly fashion.* [1825–35; LAGGARD + -LY]

lag•gen (lag′ən), *n. Scot. and North Eng.* laggin.

lag•gen-gird (lag′ən gûrd′; *Scot.* lag′ən gird′), *n. Scot. and North Eng.* **1.** the bottom hoop securing the staves of a tub or barrel. **2. cast a laggen-gird,** to sire an illegitimate child. [1710–20]

lag•ger[1] (lag′ər), *n.* a laggard. [LAG[1] + -ER[1]]

lag•ger[2] (lag′ər), *n. Chiefly Brit. Slang.* a convict or ex-convict. [1810–20; LAG[2] + -ER[1]]

lag•gin (lag′ən), *n. Scot. and North Eng.* **1.** Usually, **laggins.** the staves at the bottom of a barrel, cask, or other hooped vessel. **2.** the inner angle of a wooden dish, formed by the meeting of the sides and bottom. Also, **lagen, laggen, leglen.** [1580–90; *lagg* (< ON *lǫggr* stave) + *-in,* var. of -ING[3]]

lag•ging[1] (lag′ing), *n.* **1.** the act of falling or staying behind. —*adj.* **2.** lingering; loitering; slow and dragging: *lagging steps.* [1590–1600; LAG[1] + -ING[1], -ING[2]] —**lag′ging•ly,** *adv.*

lag•ging[2] (lag′ing), *n.* **1.** the act of covering a boiler, oil tank, etc., with heat-insulating material. **2.** the covering formed. **3.** the material used. **4.** a number of boards or the like joined together side by side to line an excavation. **5.** *Masonry.* a number of lags, taken as a whole. [1850–55; LAG[3] + -ING[1]]

La•ghouat (lä gwät′), *n.* a city in N Algeria. 26,553.

lag′ line′. See under **lag**[1] (def. 6).

-lagnia, a combining form meaning "coition," used in the formation of compound words: *algolagnia.* [comb. form repr. Gk *lagneía* coition, lust]

la•gniappe (lan yap′, lan′yap), *n.* **1.** *Chiefly Southern Louisiana and Southeast Texas.* a small gift given with a purchase to a customer, by way of compliment or for good measure; bonus. **2.** a gratuity or tip. **3.** an unexpected or indirect benefit. Also, **la•gnappe′.** [1840–50, *Amer.*; < LaF < AmerSp *la ñapa* the addition, equiv. to *la* fem. definite article + *ñapa,* var. of *yapa* < Quechua: that which is added]

La•go de Ni•ca•ra•gua (lä′gô *the* ne′kä rä′gwä), Spanish name of Lake Nicaragua.

lag•o•morph (lag′ə môrf′), *n.* any member of the order Lagomorpha, comprising the hares, rabbits, and pikas, resembling the rodents but having two pairs of upper incisors. [1880–85; < NL *Lagomorpha* name of the order, equiv. to Gk *lagṓ(s)* hare + *morpha,* neut. pl. of *-morphos* -MORPH] —**lag′o•mor′phic, lag′o•mor′phous,** *adj.*

la•goon (lə gōōn′), *n.* **1.** an area of shallow water separated from the sea by low sandy dunes. Cf. **laguna. 2.** Also, **lagune.** any small, pondlike body of water, esp. one connected with a larger body of water. **3.** an artificial pool for storage and treatment of polluted or excessively hot sewage, industrial waste, etc. [1605–15; earlier *laguna* (sing.), *lagune* (pl.) < It < L *lacūna* (sing.), *lacūnae* (pl.) ditch, pool, akin to *lacus* basin, LAKE[1]; see LACUNA] —**la•goon′al,** *adj.*

Lagoon′ Is′lands, a former name of **Tuvalu.**

La•gos (lä′gōs, lā′gos), *n.* a seaport in SW Nigeria: former capital. 1,097,000.

La Grande (lə grand′), a town in NE Oregon. 11,354.

La Grange (lə grānj′), **1.** a city in W Georgia. 24,204. **2.** a city in NE Illinois, near Chicago. 15,681.

La•grange (lə grānj′; *Fr.* lA gräNzh′), *n.* **Jo•seph Louis** (zhô zef′ lwē), **Comte,** 1736–1813, French mathematician and astronomer.

La Grange′ Park′, a city in NE Illinois, near Chicago. 13,359.

Lagrange′'s meth′od, *Math.* a procedure for finding maximum and minimum values of a function of several variables when the variables are restricted by additional conditions. [named after J. L. LAGRANGE]

Lagrange′'s the′orem, *Math.* the theorem that the order of each subgroup of a finite group is a factor of the order of the group. [named after J. L. LAGRANGE]

La•gran′gi•an func′tion (lə grän′jē ən), *Physics.* See **kinetic potential.** [1900–05; named after J. L. LAGRANGE; see -IAN]

CONCISE ETYMOLOGY KEY: <, descended or borrowed from; >, whence; b., blend of, blended; c., cognate with; cf., compare; deriv., derivative; equiv., equivalent; imit., imitative; obl., oblique; r., replacing; s., stem; sp., spelling, spelled; resp., respelling, respelled; trans., translation; ?, origin unknown; *, unattested; ‡, probably earlier than. See the full key inside the front cover.

Lagrang′ian point′, *Astron.* one of five points in the orbital plane of two bodies orbiting about their common center of gravity at which another body of small mass can be in equilibrium. [1960–65; named after J. L. LAGRANGE; see -IAN]

La Gran•ja (*Sp.* lä gräng′hä). See under **San Ildefonso.**

lag′ screw′, a heavy wood screw having a square or hexagonal head driven by a wrench. Also called **coach screw, lag bolt.** See illus. under **screw.** [1870–75]

lag-screw (lag′skrōō′), *v.t.* to fasten with a lag screw.

Lag•ting (läg′ting′), *n.* See under **Storting.** Also, **Lag′thing′.** [1830–40; < Norw; cf. ON *lagthing.* See LAW[1], THING[2]]

La Guai•ra (lä gwī′rä), a seaport in N Venezuela: the port of Caracas. 20,344.

La Guar•di•a (lə gwär′dē ə), **Fi•o•rel•lo H(enry)** (fē′ə-rel′ō), 1882–1947, U.S. lawyer, political reformer, and government administrator: mayor of New York City 1933–45.

La•guerre (lä gâr′; *Fr.* lA ger′), *n.* **Ed•mond-Ni•co•las** (ed môN nē kô lä′), 1834–86, French mathematician.

la•gu•na (lə gōō′nə), *n.* a bay, inlet, or other narrow or shallow body of water (often used in placenames). Cf. **lagoon.** [< Sp or It; see LAGOON]

La•gu•na (lə gōō′nə), *n., pl.* **-nas,** (*esp. collectively*) **-na** for 1. **1.** a Pueblo Indian people of west-central New Mexico. **2.** the Keresan dialect spoken by the Laguna.

Lagu′na Beach′, a town in S California. 17,860.

Lagu′na Hills′, a city in SW California. 33,600.

la•gune (lə gōōn′), *n.* lagoon (def. 2).

La Ha•bra (lə hä′brə), a city in SW California, near Los Angeles. 45,232.

la•har (lä′här), *n. Geol.* **1.** a landslide of wet volcanic debris on the side of a volcano. **2.** the deposit left by such a landslide. [1925–30; < Javanese: lahar, lava]

lah-di-dah (lä′dē dä′), *interj., adj., n.* la-di-da.

La Hogue (lA ôg′), a roadstead off the NW coast of France; naval battle, 1692. Also, **La Houge** (lA ōōg′).

La•hore (lə hôr′, -hōr′), *n.* a city in NE Pakistan: the capital of Punjab province. 2,922,000.

Lahore′ par′ty, *Islam.* See under **Ahmadiya.**

Lah•ti (läKH′tē), *n.* a city in S Finland, NNE of Helsinki. 94,948.

lai (lā), *n.* (in medieval French literature) **1.** a narrative poem written in octosyllabic couplets and dealing with tales of adventure and romance. **2.** a lyric poem, often a love poem, having great metrical variety and designed to be sung to a popular melody. [1200–50; ME < OF. See LAY[4]]

Lai•bach (lī′bäKH), *n.* German name of **Ljubljana.**

la•ic (lā′ik), *adj.* **1.** Also, **la′i•cal.** lay; secular. —*n.* **2.** one of the laity. [1555–65; < LL *lāicus* < Gk *lāïkós* of the people, equiv. to *lā(ós)* people + *-ikos* -IC] —**la′i•cal•ly,** *adv.*

la•i•cism (lā′ə siz′əm), *n.* the nonclerical, or secular, control of political and social institutions in a society (distinguished from *clericalism*). [1930–35; LAIC + -ISM]

la•i•cize (lā′ə sīz′), *v.t.,* **-cized, -ciz•ing.** to remove the clerical character or nature of; secularize: *to laicize a school; to laicize the office of headmaster.* Also, *esp. Brit.,* **la′i•cise′.** [1790–1800; LAIC + -IZE] —**la•i•ci•za•tion** (lā′ə sə zā′shən), *n.*

laid (lād), *v.* pt. and pp. of **lay**[1].

laid-back (lād′bak′), *adj. Slang.* **1.** relaxed or unhurried: *laid-back music rhythms.* **2.** free from stress; easygoing; carefree: *a laid-back way of living.* Also **laid′back′.** [1905–10, for an earlier sense; 1970–75 for current sense]

laid′ deck′, *Shipbuilding.* a wooden deck having planking laid parallel to the sides of the hull so as to follow the curves toward the ends of the vessel.

laid′ pa′per, paper with fine parallel and cross lines produced in manufacturing. Cf. **wove paper.** [1830–40]

laigh (lāKH), *Scot.* —*adj., adv.* **1.** low[1]. —*n.* **2.** a small valley or hollow. [1325–75; ME (Scots). See LOW[1]]

lain (lān), *v.* pp. of **lie**[2].

Laing (lang), *n.* **R(onald) D(avid),** born 1927, British psychiatrist and author, born in Scotland.

lair[1] (lâr), *n.* **1.** a den or resting place of a wild animal: *The cougar retired to its lair.* **2.** a secluded or hidden place, esp. a secret retreat or base of operations; a hideout or hideaway: *a pirate's lair.* **3.** *Brit.* a place in which to lie or rest; a bed. —*v.t.* **4.** to place in a lair. **5.** to serve as a lair for. —*v.i.* **6.** to go to, lie in, or have a lair. [bef. 900; ME *leir,* OE *leger;* c. D, OHG *leger* bed, camp; akin to LIE[2]]

lair[2] (lâr), *n.* **1.** *Brit. Dial.* mud; mire. —*v.i.* **2.** *Scot.* to sink or stick in mud or mire. [1250–1300; v. use of ME *lair* clay, mire < ON *leir* clay, LOAM]

lair[3] (lâr), *n. Chiefly Scot.* lore; learning. [ME (north and Scots) *lare,* OE *lār* LORE]

lair[4] (lâr), *n. Australian Informal.* a man who dresses garishly and is crude or vulgar; showoff. [1930–35; back formation from LAIRY]

laird (lârd; *Scot.* lārd), *n. Scot.* a landed proprietor. [1400–50; late ME *laverd,* northern and Scots form of *loverd* LORD] —**laird′ly,** *adj.* —**laird′ship′,** *n.*

lair•y (lâr′ē), *adj.,* **lair•i•er, lair•i•est.** *Australian Informal.* of, pertaining to, or characteristic of a lair. [1905–10; appar. to be identified with Brit., esp. Cockney slang *lairy* cunning, knowing, conceited, resp. (repr. dial. pron.) of LEERY[1]]

lais•ser-al•ler (le sā A lā′), *n. French.* unchecked freedom or ease; unrestraint; looseness. Also, ***lais•sez-al•ler*** (le sā A lā′). [lit., to allow to go]

lais•sez faire (les′ā fâr′; *Fr.* le sā fer′), **1.** the theory or system of government that upholds the autonomous character of the economic order, believing that government should intervene as little as possible in the direction of economic affairs. **2.** the practice or doctrine of noninterference in the affairs of others, esp. with reference to individual conduct or freedom of action. Also, **lais′ser faire′.** [1815–25; < F: lit., allow to act]

lais•sez-faire (les′ā fâr′; *Fr.* le sā fer′), *adj.* of, pertaining to, or conforming to the principles or practices of laissez faire. Also, **lais′ser-faire′.** [1815–25] —**lais′sez-faire′ism,** *n.*

lais•sez-pas•ser (les′ā pa sā′; *Fr.* le sā pä sā′), *n., pl.* **-ser.** a permit; pass, esp. one issued in lieu of a passport. [< F: lit., allow to pass]

lai•tance (lāt′ns), *n.* a milky deposit on the surface of new cement or concrete, usually caused by too much water. [1905–10; special use of F *laitance* milt, equiv. to *lait* milk (< L *lact-,* s. of *lac*) + *-ance* -ANCE]

lait d'a•mandes (le dA mänd′), *French.* See **almond milk.**

laith (lāth), *Scot.* —*adj.* **1.** loath. —*v.t.* **2.** loathe.

la•i•ty (lā′i tē), *n.* **1.** the body of religious worshipers, as distinguished from the clergy. **2.** the people outside of a particular profession, as distinguished from those belonging to it: *the medical ignorance of the laity.* [1535–45; LAY[3] + -ITY]

La•ius (lā′əs, lī′ əs), *n. Class. Myth.* a king of Thebes, the husband of Jocasta and father of Oedipus: unwittingly killed by Oedipus.

Laj•oi•e (lash′ə wā′), *n.* **Napoleon** ("*Nap*"), 1875–1959, U.S. baseball player.

La Jol•la (lə hoi′ə), a resort area in San Diego, in S California.

LAK cell, *Immunol.* lymphokine-activated killer cell: one of a number of white blood cells removed from a patient's whole blood and cultured with interleukin-2: used experimentally for reinfusion into the body to shrink malignant tumors.

lake[1] (lāk), *n.* **1.** a body of fresh or salt water of considerable size, surrounded by land. See table on next page. **2.** any similar body or pool of other liquid, as oil. [bef. 1000; ME *lak(e), lac(e),* appar. a conflation of OF *lac,* its source, L *lacus* (cf. Gk *lákkos,* OIr *loch,* OE, OS *lagu* sea, water) and OE *lacu* stream, water course (cf. *leccan* to moisten, mod. dial. *lake* stream, channel; see LEACH[1])]

lake[2] (lāk), *n.* **1.** any of various pigments prepared from animal, vegetable, or coal-tar coloring matters by chemical or other union with metallic compounds. **2.** a red pigment prepared from lac or cochineal by combination with a metallic compound. [1610–20; var. of LAC[1]]

Lake (lāk), *n.* **Simon,** 1866–1945, U.S. engineer and naval architect.

Lake′ Ar′al. See **Aral Sea.**

lake′ breeze′, a thermally produced wind blowing during the day from the surface of a large lake to the shore, caused by the difference in the rates of heating of the surfaces of the lake and of the land. Cf. **sea breeze.**

Lake′ Charles′, a city in SW Louisiana. 75,051.

Lake′ Dis′trict, a mountainous region in NW England containing many lakes: tourist center. Also called **Lake′ Coun′try.** Cf. **Lake Poets.**

lake′ dwell′er, an inhabitant of a lake dwelling. [1860–65]

lake′ dwell′ing, a house, esp. of prehistoric times, built on piles or other support over the water of a lake. [1860–65]

Lake′ For′est, a city in NE Illinois, N of Chicago, on Lake Michigan. 15,245.

lake•front (lāk′frunt′), *n.* the land along the edge of a lake: *Property along the lakefront is more expensive every year.* Also called **lakeshore.** [1875–80, *Amer.*; LAKE[1] + FRONT]

Lake′ Hav′a•su Cit′y (hav′ə sōō′), a city in W central Arizona. 15,737.

Lake•head (lāk′hed′), *n.* See **Thunder Bay.**

lake′ her′ring, a cisco or whitefish, esp. *Coregonus artedii,* of the Great Lakes. [1835–45, *Amer.*]

Lake•hurst (lāk′hûrst), *n.* a borough in E New Jersey: naval air station; dirigible hangar. 2908.

Lake′ Isle′ of In′nis•free, The (in′is frē′), a poem (1893) by W. B. Yeats.

Lake′ Jack′son, a town in S Texas. 19,102.

Lake•land (lāk′lənd), *n.* a city in central Florida. 47,406.

Lake′land ter′rier, one of a breed of small, slender terriers, raised originally in northwestern England for hunting foxes. [1925–30]

Lake′ of the Woods′, a lake in S Canada and the N United States, between N Minnesota and Ontario and Manitoba provinces. 1485 sq. mi. (3845 sq. km).

Lake′ Plac′id, a town in NE New York, in the Adirondack Mountains: resort. 2490.

Lake′ Po′ets, the poets Wordsworth, Coleridge, and Southey: so called from their residence in the Lake District. Also called **Lake School.** [1810–20]

lake•port (lāk′pôrt′, -pōrt′), *n.* a port city located on the shore of a lake, esp. one of the Great Lakes. [1870–75, *Amer.*; LAKE[1] + PORT[1]]

lak•er (lā′kər), *n.* **1.** a person associated with a lake, as a resident, visitor, or worker. **2.** a ship designed for navigating on lakes, esp. the Great Lakes. **3.** a fish found in lakes or caught in a lake, esp. the lake trout. **4.** (*cap.*) any one of the Lake Poets. [1790–1800; LAKE[1] + -ER[1]]

lake′ salm′on. See **landlocked salmon.** [1815–25]

Lake′ School′. See **Lake Poets.** [1810–20]

LARGEST LAKES OF THE WORLD

Lake	Country or Countries	Locality	Area sq. mi.	Area sq. km
Caspian Sea	Iran-Azerbaijan-Russian Federation-Kazakhstan-Turkmenistan	W Asia	169,000	438,000
Superior	Canada-United States	Great Lakes, between Ontario and Michigan	31,820	82,415
Victoria	Kenya-Tanzania-Uganda	E central Africa	26,828	69,485
Aral Sea	Kazakhstan-Uzbekistan	Central Asia	26,166	67,770
Huron	Canada-United States	Great Lakes, between Ontario and Michigan	23,010	59,595
Michigan	United States	Great Lakes, between Michigan and Wisconsin	22,400	58,015
Baikal	Russian Federation	S Siberia	13,200	34,188
Tanganyika	Zaire-Tanzania	E central Africa	12,700	32,893
Great Bear Lake	Canada	W Northwest Territories	12,275	31,792
Great Slave Lake	Canada	S Northwest Territories	11,172	28,935
Malawi	Malawi-Mozambique-Tanzania	SE Africa	11,000	28,500
Chad	Chad-Niger-Nigeria	NW central Africa	10,000	26,000
Erie	Canada-United States	Great Lakes, between Ontario and Ohio	9940	25,745
Winnipeg	Canada	S Manitoba	9300	24,085
Ontario	Canada-United States	Great Lakes, between Ontario and New York	7540	19,530
Balkhash	Kazakhstan	SE Kazakhstan	7115	18,430
Ladoga	Russian Federation	NW Russian Federation	7000	18,000
Maracaibo	Venezuela	Along coast of NW Venezuela	6300	16,320
Onega	Russian Federation	NW Russian Federation	3764	9750
Turkana	Kenya-Ethiopia	NW Kenya	3500	9100
Eyre	Australia	NE South Australia	3420	8885
Titicaca	Bolivia-Peru	Altiplano, Andes Mts.	3200	8290
Nicaragua	Nicaragua	SW Nicaragua	3060	7925
Athabaska	Canada	NE Alberta and NW Saskatchewan	3000	7800
Reindeer Lake	Canada	N part of Manitoba-Saskatchewan boundary	2444	6330
Torrens	Australia	E South Australia	2400	6220
Great Salt Lake	United States	NW Utah	2300	5950
Qing Hai	China	NE Qinghai	2300	5950
Issyk-Kul	Kirghizia	NE Kirghizia	2250	5830
Vänern	Sweden	SW Sweden	2141	5545

lake•shore (lāk′shôr′, -shōr′), *n.* lakefront. [1790–1800; LAKE[1] + SHORE[1]]

lake•side (lāk′sīd′), *adj.* **1.** located on the side of a lake: *a lakeside resort.* —*n.* **2.** land bordering a lake: *a summer cottage on the lakeside.* [1550–60; LAKE[1] + SIDE[1]]

Lake•side (lāk′sīd′), *n.* a town in SW California, near San Diego. 23,921.

Lake′ Sta′tion, a town in NW Indiana. 14,294.

lake′ stur′geon, a sturgeon, *Acipenser fulvescens,* of the Great Lakes and Mississippi and St. Lawrence rivers.

Lake′ Success′, a town on Long Island, in SE New York: temporary United Nations headquarters 1946–51. 2396.

lake′ trout′, a large, fork-tailed trout, *Salvelinus namaycush,* of the lakes of Canada and the northern U.S., valued as a food and game fish. [1660–70]

Lake•ville (lāk′vil), *n.* a town in SE Minnesota. 14,790.

lake′ white′fish, a whitefish, *Coregonus clupeaformis,* found in the Great Lakes and north to Alaska, used for food. [1860–65, *Amer.*]

Lake•wood (lāk′wo͝od′), *n.* **1.** a city in central Colorado, near Denver. 112,848. **2.** a city in SW California, near Los Angeles. 74,654. **3.** a city in NE Ohio, on Lake Erie, near Cleveland. 61,963. **4.** a town in E New Jersey. 38,464.

Lake′ Worth′, a city in SE Florida. 27,048.

lakh (lak), *n.* lac[2].

la•kin (lā′kin), *n. Obs.* ladykin. [1490–1500; earlier *laken* for **ladyken* little lady. See LADY, -KIN]

Lak•mé (läk′mā; *Fr.* lak mā′), *n.* an opera (1883) by Léo Delibes.

La•ko•ta (lə kō′tə), *n.* Teton. Also, **La•kho′ta.**

Lak•sha•dweep (luk′shə dwēp′), *n.* a union territory of India comprising a group of islands and coral reefs in the Arabian Sea, off the SW coast of India. 40,237; ab. 12 sq. mi. (31 sq. km). Formerly, **Laccadive, Minicoy, and Amindivi Islands.**

Laksh•mi (luksh′mē), *n.* the Hindu goddess of fortune.

lak•y[1] (lā′kē), *adj.,* **lak•i•er, lak•i•est.** of, pertaining to, or resembling a lake. [1605–15; LAKE[1] + -Y[1]]

lak•y[2] (lā′kē), *adj.* of the color of a lake pigment. [1840–50; LAKE[2] + -Y[1]]

la•la•pa•loo•za (lä′lə pə lo͞o′zə), *n.* lollapalooza. Also, **lal′la•pa•loo′za.**

-lalia, a combining form used in the formation of nouns denoting abnormal or disordered forms of speech, as specified by the initial element: *echolalia; glossolalia.* [< NL < Gk *laliá* talking, chatter, equiv. to *lal(eîn)* to chatter, babble + *-ia* -IA]

La Lí•ne•a (lä lē′ne ä), a seaport in S Spain, near Gibraltar. 52,127.

La•lit•pur (lə lit′po͝or), *n.* a city in E central Nepal, near Katmandu. 135,230. Also called **Patan.**

lall (lal), *v.i. Phonet.* to make imperfect *l-* or *r*-sounds, or both, often by substituting a *w*-like sound for *r* or *l* or a *y*-like sound for *l.* [1875–80; imit.; see LALLATION]

Lal•lan (lal′ən), *adj. Scot.* belonging to the Lowlands of Scotland. [1775–85; var. of LOWLAND]

Lal•lans (lal′ənz), *n.pl.* **1.** the Lowlands of Scotland. **2.** the inhabitants of the Scottish Lowlands. **3.** (*used with a singular v.*) the literary form of the English dialect of the Scottish Lowlands, representing a mixture of the several spoken subdialects.

lal•la•tion (la lā′shən), *n. Phonet.* a speech defect in which *l* is pronounced instead of *r,* or in which an *l*-sound is mispronounced. Cf. **lambdacism.** [1640–50; < L *lallā(re)* to sing *lala* or lullaby + -TION]

L'Al•le•gro (lä lā′grō, la-), *n.* a poem (1632) by John Milton. Cf. ***Il Penseroso.***

Lal′ly col′umn, *Trademark.* a structural steel column, tubular in shape and usu. filled with concrete.

lal•ly•gag (lä′lē gag′, lal′ē-), *v.i.,* **-gagged, -gag•ging.** *Informal.* **1.** to spend time idly; loaf. **2.** to indulge in kisses and caresses; make love; neck. Also, **lollygag.** [1860–65, *Amer.*; orig. uncert.]

La•lo (la lō′), *n.* **(Vic•tor An•toine) E•douard** (vēk tôr′ äɴ twaɴ′ ā dwar′), 1832–92, French composer.

lalo-, a combining form meaning "speech," "speech defect," used in the formation of compound words: *laloplegia.* [< NL, comb. form repr. Gk *lálos* talkative, chattering; see -LALIA]

la•lop•a•thy (la lop′ə thē), *n., pl.* **-thies.** *Pathol.* any defect of speech. [LALO- + -PATHY]

lal•o•ple•gi•a (lal′ə plē′jē ə), *n. Pathol.* paralysis of the speech organs in which the tongue is not affected. [LALO- + -PLEGIA]

La Lou•vière (la lo͞o vyer′), a city in S Belgium, S of Brussels. 23,369.

lam[1] (lam), *v.,* **lammed, lam•ming.** *Slang.* —*v.t.* **1.** to beat; thrash. —*v.i.* **2.** to beat; strike; thrash (usually fol. by *out* or *into*). [1590–1600; < ON *lamdi,* past tense of *lemja* to beat; akin to LAME[1]]

lam[2] (lam), *n., v.,* **lammed, lam•ming.** *Slang.* —*n.* **1.** a hasty escape; flight. **2. on the lam,** escaping, fleeing, or hiding, esp. from the police: *He's been on the lam ever since he escaped from jail.* **3. take it on the lam,** to flee or escape in great haste: *The swindler took it on the lam and was never seen again.* —*v.i.* **4.** to run away quickly; escape; flee: *I'm going to lam out of here as soon as I've finished.* [1885–90; special use of LAM[1]. Cf. *beat it!* be off!]

lām (läm), *n.* the 23rd letter of the Arabic alphabet. [< Ar; see LAMBDA]

Lam (läm, lam), *n.* **Wi•fre•do** (wi frā′dō) or **Wil•fre•do** (wil frā′dō), 1902–82, Cuban painter in Europe.

Lam., Lamentations.

lam., laminated.

la•ma (lä′mə), *n.* a priest or monk in Lamaism. [1645–55; < Tibetan *lama* (sp. *bla ma*) lit., superior one (in Tibetan applied only to monks of high rank)]

La•ma•ism (lä′mə iz′əm), *n.* the Buddhism of Tibet and Mongolia, a Mahayana form including non-Buddhist Indian elements as well as elements of the preexisting Bön shamanism. Cf. **Red Hats, Yellow Hats.** [1810–20; LAMA + -ISM] —**La′ma•ist,** *n.* —**La′ma•is′tic,** *adj.*

La Man•cha (lä män′chä), a plateau region in central Spain: famous as the birthplace of Don Quixote, the hero of Cervantes' novel *Don Quixote de la Mancha.*

La Ma•no Ne•ra (lä mä′nô ne′rä), *Italian.* See **Black Hand** (def. 1a).

La•mar (lə mär′), *n.* **1. Joseph R.,** 1857–1916, U.S. jurist: associate justice of the U.S. Supreme Court 1911–16. **2. Lucius Quin•tus Cin•cin•nat•us** (kwin′təs sin′sə-nat′əs, -nā′təs), 1825–93, U.S. politician and jurist: associate justice of the U.S. Supreme Court 1888–93. **3.** a male given name.

La•marck (lə märk′; *Fr.* la mark′), *n.* **Jean Bap•tiste Pierre An•toine de Mo•net de** (zhäɴ ba tēst′ pyer äɴ-twaɴ′ də mô ne′ də), 1744–1829, French naturalist: pioneer in the field of comparative anatomy.

La•marck•i•an (lə mär′kē ən), *adj.* **1.** of or pertaining to Jean de Lamarck or his theory of organic evolution. —*n.* **2.** a person who holds this theory. [1840–50]

La•marck•ism (lə mär′kiz əm), *n.* the Lamarckian theory that characteristics acquired by habit, use, or disuse may be passed on to future generations through inheritance. [1880–85; LAMARCK + -ISM]

La Marque (lə märk′), a city in SE coastal Texas. 15,372.

La•mar•tine (la mar tēn′), *n.* **Al•phonse Ma•rie Louis de Prat de** (al fôɴs′ ma rē′ lwē də pra də), 1790–1869, French poet, historian, and statesman.

La•mas (lä′mäs), *n.* **Car•los Sa•a•ve•dra** (kär′lôs sä′-ä ve′drä). See **Saavedra Lamas, Carlos.**

la•ma•ser•y (lä′mə ser′ē), *n., pl.* **-ser•ies.** a monastery of lamas. [1865–70; < F *lamaserie*]

La•maze′ meth′od (lə mäz′), *Obstet.* a method by which an expectant mother is prepared for childbirth by education, psychological and physical conditioning, and breathing exercises. Also called **psychoprophylaxis.** [‡1975–80; named after Fernand *Lamaze,* 20th-century French physician, its originator]

lamb (lam), *n.* **1.** a young sheep. **2.** the meat of a young sheep. **3.** a person who is gentle, meek, innocent, etc.: *Their little daughter is such a lamb.* **4.** a person who is easily cheated or outsmarted, esp. an inexperienced speculator. **5. the Lamb,** Christ. —*v.i.* **6.** to give birth to a lamb. [bef. 900; ME, OE; c. D *lam,* G *Lamm,* ON, Goth *lamb;* akin to Gk *élaphos* deer. See ELK]

Lamb (lam), *n.* **1. Charles** ("*Elia*"), 1775–1834, English essayist and critic. **2. Mary Ann,** 1764–1847, English author who wrote in collaboration with her brother Charles Lamb. **3. William, 2nd Viscount Melbourne,** 1779–1848, English statesman: prime minister 1834, 1835–41. **4. Willis E(ugene), Jr.,** born 1913, U.S. physicist: Nobel prize 1955.

lam•ba•da (läm bä′də, -dä), *n., pl.* **-das.** **1.** a Brazilian ballroom dance for couples, with gyrating movements and close interlocking of the partners. **2.** music for this dance. [1985–90; < Brazilian Pg; Pg: a whipping = *lamb(ar)* to whip, lash + *-ada* -ADE[1]]

lam•baste (lam bāst′, -bast′), *v.t.,* **-bast•ed, -bast•ing.** *Informal.* **1.** to beat or whip severely. **2.** to reprimand or berate harshly; censure; excoriate. Also, **lam•bast′.** [1630–40; appar. LAM[1] + BASTE[3]]

lamb•da (lam′də), *n.* **1.** the 11th letter of the Greek alphabet (Λ, λ). **2.** the consonant sound represented by this letter. [< Gk *lá(m)bda* < Sem; see LAMED]

lamb•da•cism (lam′də siz′əm), *n. Phonet.* excessive use of the sound *l,* its misarticulation, or its substitution for the sound *r.* Cf. **lallation.** [1650–60; < L *labdacismus* < Gk *labdakismós*]

lamb′da par′ticle, *Physics.* any of a family of neutral baryons with strangeness −1 or charm +1, and isotopic spin 0. The least massive member of the lambda family was the first strange particle to be discovered. *Symbol:* Λ [1950–55]

lamb•doid (lam′doid), *adj.* having the shape of the Greek capital lambda. Also, **lamb•doi′dal.** [1590–1600; < NL *lambdoīdēs* < Gk *lambdoeidḗs.* See LAMBDA, -OID]

lambdoi′dal su′ture, *Anat.* the lambda-shaped seam or line of joining between the occipital and two parietal bones at the back part of the skull. [1690–1700]

lam•ben•cy (lam′bən sē), *n., pl.* **-cies** for 2. **1.** the quality of being lambent. **2.** something that is lambent. [1810–20; LAMB(ENT) + -ENCY]

lam•bent (lam′bənt), *adj.* **1.** running or moving lightly over a surface: *lambent tongues of flame.* **2.** dealing lightly and gracefully with a subject; brilliantly playful: *lambent wit.* **3.** softly bright or radiant: *a lambent light.* [1640–50; < L *lambent-* (s. of *lambēns*) lapping, prp. of *lambere* to lick] —**lam′bent•ly,** *adv.*

lam•bert (lam′bərt), *n. Optics.* the centimeter-gram-second unit of luminance or brightness, equivalent to 0.32 candles per square centimeter, and equal to the brightness of a perfectly diffusing surface emitting or reflecting one lumen per square centimeter. *Abbr.:* L [1910–15; named after J. H. LAMBERT]

Lam•bert (lam′bərt; *for 2 also Ger.* läm′bert), *n.* **1. Con•stant** (kon′stənt), 1905–51, English composer and conductor. **2. Jo•hann Hein•rich** (yō′hän hīn′rikh), 1728–77, German scientist and mathematician. **3.** a male given name: from Germanic words meaning "land" and "bright."

Lam′bert confor′mal projec′tion, *Cartog.* a conformal projection in which meridians are represented as straight lines converging toward the nearest pole and parallels as arc segments of concentric circles. [1875–80; named after J. H. LAMBERT]

Lam′bert's law′, *Optics.* the law that the luminous intensity of a perfectly diffusing surface in any direction is proportional to the cosine of the angle between that direction and the normal to the surface, for which reason the surface will appear equally bright from all directions. Also called **cosine law.** [after J. H. LAMBERT]

Lam•beth (lam′bith), *n.* a borough of Greater London, England. 296,800.

Lam′beth Con′ference, a convention of the bishops of the Anglican communion, held about every 10 years at Lambeth Palace to confer but not to define doctrine or to legislate on ecclesiastical matters. [1865–70]

Lam′beth degree′, *Anglican Ch.* an honorary degree conferred by the archbishop of Canterbury in divinity, arts, law, medicine, or music. [1855–60]

Lam′beth Pal′ace, the official residence of the archbishop of Canterbury, in Lambeth.

Lam′beth walk′, a spirited ballroom dance popular, esp. in England, in the late 1930's. [1935–40]

lamb•kill (lam′kil′), *n.* See **sheep laurel.** [1805–15,

Amer.; LAMB + KILL[1]; so called because poisonous to sheep]

lamb•kin (lam′kin), *n.* **1.** a little lamb. **2.** a person who is exceptionally sweet, young, and innocent, as a small child. [1570–80; LAMB + -KIN]

lamb•like (lam′līk′), *adj.* like a lamb; gentle; meek. [1590–1600; LAMB + -LIKE]

Lamb′ of God′, Christ. [1350–1400; ME]

lam•boy (lam′boi′), *n.* tonlet. [1540–50; orig. uncert.]

lam•bre•quin (lam′bri kin, lam′bər-), *n.* **1.** a woven fabric covering for a helmet in medieval times to protect it from heat, rust, etc. **2.** a curtain or drapery covering the upper part of an opening, as a door or window, or suspended from a shelf. **3.** *Heraldry.* mantling. **4.** a band of decoration near the top of the body of a vase. [1715–25; < F, MF < MD **lamperken,* equiv. to *lamper* fine translucent cloth + *-ken* -KIN]

lam•bru•sco (lam bro͞o′skō; *It.* läm bro͞o′skô), *n.* a semisweet, lightly effervescent red wine from Italy. [< It < L *labruscum,* fruit of the labrusca vine; see LABRUSCA]

lamb's′ ears′, *pl.* **lamb's ears.** a hardy Middle Eastern plant, *Stachys byzantina,* of the mint family, having white, wooly leaves and small, purple flowers in dense whorls.

lamb•skin (lam′skin′), *n.* **1.** the skin of a lamb, esp. when dressed with its wool, and used for clothing. **2.** leather made from such skin. **3.** parchment made from such skin. [1325–75; ME; see LAMB, SKIN]

lamb's′ let′tuce. See **corn salad.** [1590–1600]

lamb's-quar•ters (lamz′kwôr′tərz), *n., pl.* **-ters.** the pigweed, *Chenopodium album.* [1765–75]

lamb's′ tail′. See **burro's tail.** [1880–85]

lamb's′ tongue′, *Archit.* a molding having a deep, symmetrical profile ending in a narrow edge, as in a sash bar. [1570–80]

lamb's′ wool′, **1.** a soft, virgin wool possessing superior spinning qualities, shorn from a seven-month-old lamb. **2.** a fabric made from this wool. [1545–55]

lame[1] (lām), *adj.,* **lam•er, lam•est,** *v.,* **lamed, lam•ing,** *n.* —*adj.* **1.** crippled or physically disabled, esp. in the foot or leg so as to limp or walk with difficulty. **2.** impaired or disabled through defect or injury: *a lame arm.* **3.** weak; inadequate; unsatisfactory; clumsy: *a lame excuse.* **4.** *Slang.* out of touch with modern fads or trends; unsophisticated. —*v.t.* **5.** to make lame or defective. —*n.* **6.** *Slang.* a person who is out of touch with modern fads or trends, esp. one who is unsophisticated. [bef. 900; ME (adj. and v.); OE *lama* (adj.); c. D *lam,* G *lahm,* ON *lami;* akin to Lith *lúomas*] —**lame′ly,** *adv.* —**lame′ness,** *n.*

lame[2] (lām; *Fr.* lam), *n., pl.* **lames** (lām; *Fr.* lam). *Armor.* any of a number of thin, overlapping plates composing a piece of plate armor, as a fauld, tasset, or gauntlet. [1580–90; < MF < L *lāmina* a thin piece or plate]

la•mé (la mā′; *Fr.* la mā′), *n.* an ornamental fabric in which metallic threads, as of gold or silver, are woven with silk, wool, rayon, or cotton. [1920–25; < F, equiv. to *lame* LAME[2] + *-é* < L *-ātus* -ATE[1]]

lame•brain (lām′brān′), *n. Informal.* a dunce; booby; fool. [1925–30; LAME[1] + BRAIN] —**lame′brained′,** *adj.*

La•mech (lā′mik), *n.* the son of Enoch, and the father of Jabal, Jubal, and Tubal-cain. Gen. 4:18.

la•med (lä′mid, -med), *n.* **1.** the 12th letter of the Hebrew alphabet. **2.** the consonant sound represented by this letter. [1655–65; < Heb *lāmedh;* cf. LAMBDA]

lame′ duck′, **1.** an elected official or group of officials, as a legislator, continuing in office during the period between an election defeat and a successor's assumption of office. **2.** a president who is completing a term of office and chooses not to run or is ineligible to run for reelection. **3.** a person finishing a term of employment after a replacement has been chosen. **4.** anything soon to be supplanted by another that is more efficient, economical, etc. **5.** a person or thing that is disabled, helpless, ineffective, or inefficient. **6.** a person who has lost a great deal of money in speculations on the stock market. [1755–65] —**lame′-duck′,** *adj.*

Lame′ Duck′ Amend′ment. See **Twentieth Amendment.**

lame′-duck′ ses′sion (lām′duk′), (formerly) the December to March session of those members of the U.S. Congress who were defeated for reelection the previous November. [1930–35, *Amer.*]

la•mel•la (lə mel′ə), *n., pl.* **-mel•lae** (-mel′ē), **-mel•las.** **1.** a thin plate, scale, membrane, or layer, as of bone, tissue, or cell walls. **2.** *Bot.* **a.** an erect scale or blade inserted at the junction of the claw and limb in some corollas and forming a part of their corona or crown. **b.** (in mosses) a thin sheet of cells standing up along the midrib of a leaf. **3.** *Mycol.* gill[1] (def. 2). **4.** *Building Trades.* a member of wood, metal, or reinforced concrete, joined in a crisscross pattern with other lamellae to form a vault. **5.** *Ophthalm.* a small disk of gelatin and glycerin mixed with a medicinal substance, used as a medicament for the eyes. [1670–80; < L *lāmella,* dim. of *lāmina* LAME[2]]

la•mel•lar (lə mel′ər, lam′ə lər), *adj.* **1.** referring to a lamella or lamellae. **2.** lamellate. **3.** noting a type of armor composed of small plates or lames laced together. **4.** *Math.* conservative (def. 7). [1785–95; LAMELL(A) + -AR[1]] —**la•mel′lar•ly,** *adv.*

lamel′la roof′, a vaulted roof composed of lamellae.

la•mel•late (lə mel′āt, lam′ə lāt′), *adj.* **1.** composed of or having lamellae. **2.** flat; platelike. Also, **lam′el•lat′ed, la•mel•lose** (lə mel′ōs, lam′ə lōs′). [1820–30; < NL *lāmellātus.* See LAMELLA, -ATE[1]] —**lam′el•late′ly,** *adv.* —**lam•el•los•i•ty** (lam′ə los′i tē), *n.*

lam•el•la•tion (lam′ə lā′shən), *n. Anat.* an arrangement or structure in which there are thin layers, plates, or scales. [1900–05; LAMELL(A) + -ATION]

lamelli-, a combining form representing **lamella** in compound words: *lamelliform.*

la•mel•li•branch (lə mel′ə brangk′), *n.* bivalve. [1850–55; < NL *Lamellibranchia* group name. See LAMELLI-, -BRANCHIA]

la•mel•li•corn (lə mel′i kôrn′), *Entomol.* —*adj.* **1.** having antennae with lamellate terminal segments, as beetles of the group Lamellicornia, including the scarabaeids and stag beetles. **2.** (of an antenna) having lamellate terminal segments. —*n.* **3.** a lamellicorn beetle. [1835–45; < NL *lāmellicornis,* equiv. to *lāmelli-* LAMELLI- + L *-cornis* horned (*corn(ū)* HORN + *-is* adj. suffix)]

la•mel•li•form (lə mel′ə fôrm′), *adj.* shaped like a lamella; platelike; scalelike. [1810–20; LAMELLI- + -FORM]

la•mel•li•ros•tral (lə mel′ə ros′trəl), *adj. Ornith.* having a beak equipped with thin plates or lamellae for straining water and mud from food, as the ducks, geese, swans, and flamingos. Also, **la•mel•li•ros•trate** (lə mel′ə ros′trāt). [1825–35; < NL *lāmellirostr(is)* + -AL[1]. See LAMELLI-, ROSTRAL]

la•ment (lə ment′), *v.t.* **1.** to feel or express sorrow or regret for: *to lament his absence.* **2.** to mourn for or over. —*v.i.* **3.** to feel, show, or express grief, sorrow, or regret. **4.** to mourn deeply. —*n.* **5.** an expression of grief or sorrow. **6.** a formal expression of sorrow or mourning, esp. in verse or song; an elegy or dirge. [1520–30; (n.) < L *lāmentum* plaint; (v.) < L *lāmentārī,* deriv. of *lāmentum*] —**la•ment′er,** *n.* —**la•ment′ing•ly,** *adv.*
—**Syn. 1, 2.** bewail, bemoan, deplore. **3, 4.** grieve, weep. **5.** lamentation, moan. **6.** monody, threnody.

lam•en•ta•ble (lə men′tə bəl, lam′ən tə-), *adj.* **1.** that is to be lamented; regrettable; unfortunate: *a lamentable decision.* **2.** *Rare.* mournful. [1400–50; late ME < L *lāmentābilis,* equiv. to *lāmentā(rī)* (see LAMENT) + *-bilis* -BLE] —**la•men′ta•ble•ness,** *n.* —**la•men′ta•bly,** *adv.*

lam•en•ta•tion (lam′ən tā′shən), *n.* **1.** the act of lamenting or expressing grief. **2.** a lament. **3. Lamentations,** (*used with a singular v.*) a book of the Bible, traditionally ascribed to Jeremiah. *Abbr.:* Lam. [1325–75; < L *lāmentātiōn-* (s. of *lāmentātiō*), equiv. to *lāmentāt(us)* (ptp. of *lāmentārī;* see LAMENT) + *-iōn-* -ION; r. ME *lamentacioun* < AF << L, as above]

la•ment•ed (lə men′tid), *adj.* mourned for, as a person who is dead: *Our late lamented friend.* [1605–15; LAMENT + -ED[2]] —**la•ment′ed•ly,** *adv.*

La Me•sa (lä mā′sə), a city in SW California. 50,342.

La•me•sa (lə mē′sə), *n.* a city in NW Texas. 11,790.

la•mi•a (lā′mē ə), *n., pl.* **-mi•as, -mi•ae** (-mē ē′) for 1, 2. **1.** *Class. Myth.* one of a class of fabulous monsters, commonly represented with the head and breast of a woman and the body of a serpent, said to allure youths and children in order to suck their blood. **2.** a vampire; a female demon. **3.** (*cap., italics.*) a narrative poem (1819) by John Keats. [1350–1400; ME < L < Gk *lámia* a female man-eater]

lam•i•na (lam′ə nə), *n., pl.* **-nae** (-nē′), **-nas.** **1.** a thin plate, scale, or layer. **2.** a layer or coat lying over another, as the plates of minerals or bones. **3.** *Bot.* the blade or expanded portion of a leaf. **4.** *Geol.* a layer of sediment or sedimentary rock only a small fraction of an inch (less than a centimeter) in thickness. [1650–60; < L; see LAME[2]]

lam•i•na•ble (lam′ə nə bəl), *adj.* capable of being laminated. [1790–1800; LAMIN(ATE) + -ABLE]

lam•i•nal[1] (lam′ə nl), *Phonet.* —*adj.* **1.** (of a speech sound) articulated using the blade of the tongue. —*n.* **2.** a laminal speech sound. [< L *lāmin(a)* blade (see LAME[2]) + -AL[1]]

lam•i•nal[2] (lam′ə nl), *adj.* laminar. [LAMIN(A) + -AL[1]]

lam•i•nar (lam′ə nər), *adj.* composed of, or arranged in, laminae. Also, **lam•i•nar•y** (lam′ə ner′ē). [1800–15; LAMIN(A) + -AR[1]]

lam′inar flow′, *Hydraul., Mech.* the flow of a viscous fluid in which particles of the fluid move in parallel layers, each of which has a constant velocity but is in motion relative to its neighboring layers. [1945–50]

lam•i•nar•i•a (lam′ə nâr′ē ə), *n.* any of various often very large kelps of the genus *Laminaria,* some species of which are the source of algins used as thickening or stabilizing agents in foodstuffs and other products. [< NL (1813); see LAMINA, -ARY]

lam•i•nate (*v.* lam′ə nāt′; *adj., n.* lam′ə nāt′, -nit), *v.,* **-nat•ed, -nat•ing,** *adj., n.* —*v.t.* **1.** to separate or split into thin layers. **2.** to form (metal) into a thin plate, as by beating or rolling. **3.** to construct from layers of material bonded together. **4.** to cover or overlay with laminae. —*v.i.* **5.** to split into thin layers. —*adj.* **6.** Also, **laminous.** composed of or having laminae. —*n.* **7.** a laminated product; lamination. [1660–70; < NL *lāminātus.* See LAMINA, -ATE[1]] —**lam′i•na′tor,** *n.*

lam•i•nat•ed (lam′ə nā′tid), *adj.* **1.** formed of or set in thin layers or laminae. **2.** constructed of layers of material bonded together: *laminated wood.* [1660–70; LAMINATE + -ED[2]]

lam•i•na•tion (lam′ə nā′shən), *n.* **1.** act or process of laminating; the state of being laminated. **2.** laminated structure; arrangement in thin layers. **3.** a lamina. [1670–80; LAMINATE + -ION]

lam•i•nec•to•my (lam′ə nek′tə mē), *n., pl.* **-mies.** the surgical removal of part of the posterior arch of a vertebra to provide access to the spinal canal, as for the excision of a ruptured disk. [1890–95; LAMIN(A) + -ECTOMY]

lam•i•ni•tis (lam′ə nī′tis), *n. Vet. Pathol.* inflammation of sensitive laminae in the hoof of a horse, caused by stressful events, as trauma, infection, or parturition. [1835–45; < NL; see LAMINA, -ITIS]

lamino-, a combining form representing **laminal** in compound words.

lam•i•no•al•ve•o•lar (lam′ə nō al vē′ə lər), *adj. Phonet.* **1.** articulated with the blade of the tongue approaching the alveolar ridge. —*n.* **2.** a lamino-alveolar sound, as the Cockney pronunciation of *t* in *tea.*

lam•i•nose (lam′ə nōs′), *adj.* laminate; laminar. [1820–30; LAMIN(A) + -OSE[1]]

lam•i•nous (lam′ə nəs), *adj.* laminate; laminose. [1790–1800; LAMIN(A) + -OUS]

La Mi•ra•da (lä′ mi rä′də), a city in SW California. 40,986.

lam•is•ter (lam′i stər), *n. Slang.* lamster.

la•mi•um (lā′mē əm), *n.* any of several plants belonging to the genus *Lamium,* of the mint family, some species of which have whitish or variegated leaves and are cultivated as ornamentals or ground cover. [< NL (Linnaeus); LL (Pliny): dead nettle, perh. deriv. of *lamia* LAMIA]

Lam•mas (lam′əs), *n.* **1.** a former festival in England, held on August 1, in which bread made from the first harvest of corn was blessed. **2.** a festival **(Feast of St. Peter's Chains)** observed by Roman Catholics on August 1, in memory of St. Peter's imprisonment and his miraculous deliverance. Also called **Lam′mas Day′.** [bef. 900; ME *Lammesse,* OE *hlāmmæsse, hlāfmæsse.* See LOAF, -MAS]

Lam•mas•tide (lam′əs tīd′), *n.* the season of Lammas. [1300–50; ME; see LAMMAS, TIDE[1]]

lam•mer•gei•er (lam′ər gī′ər, -gī^ər), *n.* the largest Eurasian bird of prey, *Gypaëtus barbatus,* ranging in the mountains from southern Europe to China, having a wingspread of 9 to 10 ft. (2.7 to 3 m) and black feathers hanging from below the bill like a mustache. Also, **lam′mer•gey′er, lam′mer•geir′.** Also called **bearded vulture.** [1810–20; < G *Lämmergeier* lit., lambs' vulture (from its preying on lambs), equiv. to *Lämmer,* pl. of *Lamm* LAMB + *Geier* vulture (c. D *gier*)]

La•mont (lə mont′), *n.* a male given name.

La•mou•reux (la mo͞o rœ′), *n.* **Charles** (sharl), 1834–99, French violinist and conductor.

lamp (lamp), *n.* **1.** any of various devices furnishing artificial light, as by electricity or gas. Cf. **fluorescent lamp, incandescent lamp.** **2.** a container for an inflammable liquid, as oil, which is burned at a wick as a means of illumination. **3.** a source of intellectual or spiritual light: *the lamp of learning.* **4.** any of various devices furnishing heat, ultraviolet, or other radiation: *an infrared lamp.* **5.** a celestial body that gives off light, as the moon or a star. **6.** a torch. **7. lamps,** *Slang.* the eyes. **8. smell of the lamp,** to give evidence of laborious study or effort: *His dissertation smells of the lamp.* —*v.t.* **9.** *Slang.* to look at; eye. [1150–1200; ME *lampe* < OF < LL *lampada,* for L *lampas* (s. *lampad-*) < Gk *lampás* lamp; akin to *lámpē* torch, lamp, *lámpein* to shine] —**lamp′less,** *adj.*

lam•pad (lam′pad), *n.* lamp or candlestick. [1790–1800; < Gk *lampad-* (s. of *lampás*) lamp; see LAMP]

lam•pa•daire (lam′pə dâr′, läm′-), *n.* a pedestal of the Empire period for a lamp or candelabrum. [1720–30; < F < ML *lampadārium.* See LAMPAD, -ARY]

Lam•pang (lam′päng′), *n.* a city in NW Thailand. 36,486.

lam•pas (lam′pəs), *n. Vet. Pathol.* congestion of the mucous membrane of the hard palate of horses. Also **lampers.** [1515–25; < MF: disease of horses, OF: disease (of men) with great thirst as symptom]

lamp•black (lamp′blak′), *n.* a fine black pigment consisting of almost pure carbon collected as soot from the smoke of burning oil, gas, etc. [1590–1600; LAMP + BLACK]

Lam•pe•du•sa (lam′pi do͞o′sə, -zə; *It.* läm′pe do͞o′zä), *n.* **1. Giu•sep•pe (To•ma•si) di** (jo͞o zep′pe tô mä′zē dē), 1896–1957, Italian novelist. **2.** an island in the Mediterranean, between Tunisia and Malta: belonging to Italy.

lam′per eel′ (lam′pər), lamprey. [1700–10]

lam•pers (lam′pərz), *n.* (*used with a singular v.*) *Vet. Pathol.* lampas.

lam•pi•on (lam′pē ən), *n.* a small lamp, esp. a small oil lamp with a tinted glass chimney, formerly very popular as a source of illumination on carriages. [1840–50; < F < It *lampione* carriage or street light, aug. of *lampa* LAMP]

lamp•light (lamp′līt′), *n.* the light thrown by a lamp. [1570–80; LAMP + LIGHT[1]]

lamp•light•er (lamp′lī′tər), *n.* **1.** a person employed to light and extinguish street lamps, esp. those burning gas. **2.** a contrivance for lighting lamps. [1740–50; LAMP + LIGHTER]

lamp′ oil′, *South Midland and Southern U.S.* kerosene.

lam•poon (lam po͞on′), *n.* **1.** a sharp, often virulent satire directed against an individual or institution; a work of literature, art, or the like, ridiculing severely the character or behavior of a person, society, etc. —*v.t.* **2.** to mock or ridicule in a lampoon: *to lampoon important leaders in the government.* [1635–45; < F *lampon,* said to be n. use of *lampons* let us guzzle (from a drinking song), impv. of *lamper,* akin to *laper* to lap up < Gmc; see LAP[3]] —**lam•poon′er, lam•poon′ist,** *n.* —**lam•poon′er•y,** *n.*
—**Syn. 1.** See **satire.**

lamp•post (lamp′pōst′), *n.* a post, usually of metal, supporting a lamp that lights a street, park, etc. [1780–90; LAMP + POST[1]]

lam•prey (lam′prē), *n., pl.* **-preys.** any eellike marine

CONCISE ETYMOLOGY KEY: <, descended or borrowed from; >, whence; b., blend of, blended; c., cognate with; cf., compare; deriv., derivative; equiv., equivalent; imit., imitative; obl., oblique; r., replacing; s., stem; sp., spelling, spelled; resp., respelling, respelled; trans., translation; ?, origin unknown; *, unattested; ‡, probably earlier than. See the full key inside the front cover.

or freshwater fish of the order Petromyzoniformes, having a circular, suctorial mouth with horny teeth for boring into the flesh of other fishes to feed on their blood. Also called **lam′prey eel′, lamper eel.** [1250–1300; ME *lampreye* < AF **lampreie* (OF *lamproie*) < LL *lamprēda;* r. OE *lamprede* < ML *lampreda*]

lamprey, *Petromyzon marinus,* length 21 in. (53 cm)

lam·proph·o·ny (lam prof′ə nē), *n. Phonet.* loudness and clarity of voice. Also, **lam·pro·pho·ni·a** (lam′prə fō′nē ə). [1850–55; < Gk *lamprophōnía,* equiv. to *lamprópho̅n(os)* clear of voice (*lampró(s)* clear, distinct + *-phōnos* -PHONOUS) + *-ia* -Y[3]; see -PHONY] —**lam·pro·phon·ic** (lam′prə fon′ik), *adj.*

lam·pro·phyre (lam′prə fīər′), *n. Petrol.* any dark intrusive rock in which dark minerals occur both as phenocrysts and as groundmass. [1885–90; *lampro-* (< Gk *lamprós* clear) + -PHYRE] —**lam·pro·phyr·ic** (lam′prə fir′ik), *adj.*

lamp·shade (lamp′shād′), *n.* a shade, usually translucent or opaque, for shielding the glare of a light source in a lamp or for directing the light to a particular area. [1840–50; LAMP + SHADE]

lamp′ shell′, a mollusklike marine animal; brachiopod. Also, **lamp′shell′.** [1850–55; so called because its shape was thought to resemble that of an ancient Roman oil lamp]

lamp′ trim′mer, a sailor responsible for keeping the oil lamps of a ship burning brightly, esp. the deck and navigation lamps. [1880–85]

lamp·work·ing (lamp′wûr′king), *n.* the method or process of producing articles made of glass tubes or rods formed or shaped while softened by the flame of a lamp or blast lamp. Also, **lamp′work′.** [1655–65; LAMP + WORKING] —**lamp′work′er,** *n.*

lam·py·rid (lam′pə rid), *n.* **1.** any of several beetles of the family Lampyridae, comprising the fireflies. —*adj.* **2.** belonging or pertaining to the lampyrids. [1890–95; < NL *Lampyridae* glowworm family, equiv. to *Lampyr(is)* type genus (< Gk *lampyrís* glowworm; see LAMP) + *-idae* -ID[2]]

lam·ster (lam′stər), *n. Slang.* a fugitive from the law. Also, **lamister.** [1900–05; LAM[2] + -STER]

La·mus (lā′məs), *n. Class. Myth.* **1.** a son of Hercules and Omphale. **2.** the king of a people who attacked 11 ships of Odysseus and devoured their crews.

La·mut (lə mo͞ot′), *n., pl.* **-muts,** (*esp. collectively*) **-mut.** Even. [< Russ < Evenki: those living near the sea (*lamu* sea + *-t* collective n. suffix)]

La·my (lä mē′), *n.* **John Baptist** (*Jean Baptiste l'Amy*), 1814–88, U.S. Roman Catholic clergyman, born in France: archbishop of Santa Fe, New Mexico 1875–88.

LAN (lan), *n.* See **local area network.**

Lan·a (lan′ə, lä′nə), *n.* a female given name, form of **Helen.**

la·na·i (lä nä′ē, lə nī′), *n., pl.* **-na·is.** *Hawaiian.* a veranda, esp. a fully furnished one used as a living room. [1865–70; < Hawaiian *lānai* roofed structure with open sides, porch]

La·na·i (lä nä′ē, lə nī′), *n.* an island in central Hawaii: pineapple plantations. 2204; 141 sq. mi. (365 sq. km).

Lan·ark (lan′ərk), *n.* a historic county in S Scotland. Also called **Lan·ark·shire** (lan′ərk shēr′, -shər).

la·nate (lā′nāt), *adj.* woolly; covered with something resembling wool. Also, **lanose.** [1750–60; < L *lānātus* woolly, equiv. to *lān(a)* wool + *-ātus* -ATE[1]]

Lan·ca·shire (lang′kə shēr′, -shər), *n.* a county in NW England. 1,369,250; 1174 sq. mi. (3040 sq. km). Also called **Lancaster.**

Lan′cashire chair′, *Eng. Furniture.* a chair similar to a Windsor chair, having a rush seat and a back formed of spindles.

Lan·cas·ter (lang′kə stər; *for 4–8 also* lang′kas tər), *n.* **1.** the English royal family that reigned 1399–1461, descended from John of Gaunt (Duke of Lancaster), and that included Henry IV, Henry V, and Henry VI. Cf. **York** (def. 1). **2.** a member of this family. **3.** a city in Lancashire, in NW England. 125,500. **4.** a city in SE Pennsylvania. 54,725. **5.** a town in S California. 48,027. **6.** a city in central Ohio. 34,953. **7.** a town in N Texas. 14,807. **8.** a town in W New York. 13,056. **9.** Lancashire.

Lan·cas·tri·an (lang kas′trē ən), *adj.* **1.** of or pertaining to the royal family of Lancaster. —*n.* **2.** an adherent or member of the house of Lancaster, esp. in the Wars of the Roses. **3.** a native or resident of Lancashire or Lancaster. [1800–10; LANCAST(E)R + -IAN]

lance[1] (lans, läns), *n., v.,* **lanced, lanc·ing.** —*n.* **1.** a long wooden shaft with a pointed metal head, used as a weapon by knights and cavalry soldiers in charging. **2.** a cavalry soldier armed with such a weapon; lancer. **3.** an implement resembling the weapon, as a spear for killing a harpooned whale. **4.** (*cap.*) *Mil.* a U.S. Army surface-to-surface rocket with a range of 47 mi. (75 km) and capable of carrying a tactical nuclear warhead. **5.** a lancet. **6.** See **oxygen lance. 7.** *Mach.* **a.** a tube having a nozzle for cleaning furnace walls and other inaccessible surfaces with air, water, or steam. **b.** a pipe for directing oxygen onto a heated metal object in order to burn a hole in it, the lance also being consumed so as to add to the heat. —*v.t.* **8.** to open with or as if with a lancet. **9.** to pierce with a lance. **10.** to cut through (concrete or the like) with an oxygen lance. [1250–1300; ME *launce* < OF *lance* < L *lancea* (perh. < Celtic)] —**lance′like′,** *adj.*

lance[2] (lans, läns), *n.* See **sand lance.** [perh. special use of LANCE[1], from its shape]

Lance (lans), *n.* a male given name.

lance′ cor′poral, 1. *U.S. Marine Corps.* an enlisted person ranking between private first class and corporal. **2.** *Brit. Mil.* **a.** a corporal of the lowest rank. **b.** (formerly) a private acting as corporal without increased pay. [1780–90; *lance,* shortened form of earlier *lancepesade* < MF *lancepessade* lowest ranking grade of noncommissioned officer < It *lancia spezzata* superior soldier, lit., broken LANCE[1] (from having shivered many lances, i.e., fought well in many battles)]

lance·let (lans′lit, läns′-), *n.* any of several small, lancet-shaped burrowing marine animals of the subphylum Cephalochordata, having a notochord and bearing structural similarities to both vertebrates and invertebrates. Also called **amphioxus.** [1565–75; LANCE[2] + -LET]

Lan·ce·lot (lan′sə lət, -lot′, län′-), *n. Arthurian Romance.* the greatest of Arthur's knights and the lover of Queen Guinevere. Also, **Launcelot.**

lance′ of cour′tesy, a lance having a blunt head to prevent serious injury by a jouster to an opponent.

lanceolate leaf

lan·ce·o·late (lan′sē ə lāt′, -lit), *adj.* **1.** shaped like the head of a lance. **2.** narrow, and tapering toward the apex or sometimes at the base, as a leaf. [1750–60; < L *lanceolātus* armed with a small lance, equiv. to *lanceol(a)* small lance (*lance(a)* LANCE[1] + *-ola* -OLE[1]) + *-ātus* -ATE[1]] —**lan′ce·o·late′ly,** *adv.*

lance·pod (lans′pod′), *n.* any tropical, leguminous tree or shrub of the genus *Lonchocarpus,* the roots of which yield rotenone. [LANCE[1] + POD[1]]

lanc·er (lan′sər, län′-), *n.* a cavalry soldier armed with a lance. [1580–90; < MF *lancier.* See LANCE[1], -ER[2]]

lance′ rest′, a support for a couched lance, fixed to the breastplate of a suit of armor. See diag. under **armor.** [1850–55]

lanc·ers (lan′sərz, län′-), *n.* (*used with a singular v.*) **1.** a set of quadrilles danced in sequence. **2.** music for such a set of dances. [1860–65; pl. of LANCER]

lance′ ser′geant, *Brit. Mil.* **1.** a sergeant of the lowest rank. **2.** (formerly) a corporal appointed to act as sergeant, without increase in pay; an acting sergeant. [1805–15; see LANCE CORPORAL]

lan·cet (lan′sit, län′-), *n.* **1.** a small surgical instrument, usually sharp-pointed and two-edged, for making small incisions, opening abscesses, etc. **2.** *Archit.* **a.** a lancet arch. **b.** a lancet window. [1375–1425; late ME *lancette* < MF. See LANCE[1], -ET]

lan′cet arch′, *Archit.* an arch having a head that is acutely pointed. See illus. under **arch.** [1815–25]

lan′cet clock′, a mantel clock having a case formed like an acutely pointed arch.

lan·cet·ed (lan′si tid, län′-), *adj.* having lancet-headed openings. [1850–55; LANCET + -ED[3]]

lan·cet·fish (lan′sit fish′, län′-), *n., pl.* (*esp. collectively*) **-fish,** (*esp. referring to two or more kinds or species*) **-fish·es.** any large, marine fish of the genus *Alepisaurus,* having daggerlike teeth. [1830–40; LANCET + FISH]

lan′cet win′dow, *Archit.* a high, narrow window terminating in a lancet arch. [1775–85]

lance·wood (lans′wo͝od′, läns′-), *n.* **1.** the tough, elastic wood of any of various trees, esp. *Oxandra lanceolata,* of tropical America, used for carriage shafts, cabinetwork, etc. **2.** a tree that yields this wood. [1690–1700; LANCE[1] + WOOD[1]]

Lan·chow (län′jō′), *n. Older Spelling.* Lanzhou. Also, **Lan′chou′.**

lan·ci·form (lan′sə fôrm′), *adj.* shaped like a lance: *lanciform windows.* [1850–55; LANCE[1] + -I- + -FORM]

lan·ci·nate (lan′sə nāt′), *v.t.,* **-nat·ed, -nat·ing.** to stab or pierce. [1595–1605; < L *lancinātus* ptp. of *lancināre* to tear to pieces, akin to *lanius* butcher, *lacer* torn; see -ATE[1]] —**lan′ci·na′tion,** *n.*

land (land), *n.* **1.** any part of the earth's surface not covered by a body of water; the part of the earth's surface occupied by continents and islands: *Land was sighted from the crow's nest.* **2.** an area of ground with reference to its nature or composition: *arable land.* **3.** an area of ground with specific boundaries: *to buy land on which to build a house.* **4.** rural or farming areas, as contrasted with urban areas: *They left the land for the city.* **5.** *Law.* **a.** any part of the earth's surface that can be owned as property, and everything annexed to it, whether by nature or by the human hand. **b.** any legal interest held in land. **6.** *Econ.* natural resources as a factor of production. **7.** a part of the surface of the earth marked off by natural or political boundaries or the like; a region or country: *They came from many lands.* **8.** the people of a region or country **9.** *Audio.* the flat surface between the grooves of a phonograph record. **10.** a realm or domain: *the land of the living.* **11.** a surface between furrows, as on a millstone or on the interior of a rifle barrel. **12.** *Scot.* a tenement house. **13. see how the land lies,** to investigate in advance; inform oneself of the facts of a situation before acting: *You should see how the land lies before making a formal proposal.* Cf. **lay of the land.** —*v.t.* **14.** to bring to or set on land: *to land passengers or goods from a ship; to land an airplane.* **15.** to bring into or cause to arrive in a particular place, position, or condition: *His behavior will land him in jail.* **16.** *Informal.* to catch or capture; gain; win: *to land a job.* **17.** *Angling.* to bring (a fish) to land, or into a boat, etc., as with a hook or a net. —*v.i.* **18.** to come to land or shore: *The boat lands at Cherbourg.* **19.** to go or come ashore from a ship or boat. **20.** to alight upon a surface, as the ground, a body of water, or the like: *to land on both feet.* **21.** to hit or strike the ground, as from a height: *The ball landed at the far side of the court.* **22.** to strike and come to rest on a surface or in something: *The golf ball landed in the lake.* **23.** to come to rest or arrive in a particular place, position, or condition (sometimes fol. by *up*): *to land in trouble; to land up 40 miles from home.* **24. land on,** *Informal.* to reprimand; criticize: *His mother landed on him for coming home so late.* **25. land on one's feet.** See **foot** (def. 27). [bef. 900; ME (n. and v.), OE (n.); c. D, G, ON, Goth *land;* akin to Ir *lann,* Welsh *llan* church (orig. enclosure), Breton *lann* heath. See LAWN[1]] —**land′like′,** *adj.*

Land (land), *n.* **Edwin Herbert,** 1909–91, U.S. inventor and businessman: created the Polaroid camera.

-land, a combining form of **land:** *hinterland; lowland.*

land′ a′gent, 1. a person or firm engaged at a commission to obtain grants of public lands or to negotiate the buying and selling of private lands between two or more parties. **2.** a government official in charge of the management of public lands. **3.** *Brit.* the steward of an estate. [1820–30, *Amer.*]

land′ art′. See **earth art.** [1965–70]

lan·dau (lan′dô, -dou), *n.* **1.** a four-wheeled, two-seated carriage with a top made in two parts that may be let down or folded back. **2.** a sedanlike automobile with a short convertible back. [1735–45; perh. named after *Landau,* town in Germany where first made]

landau (def. 1)

Lan·dau (län dou′; *Russ.* lun dou′), *n.* **Lev Da·vi·do·vich** (lyef′ du vye′də vyich), 1908–68, Russian scientist: Nobel prize for physics 1962.

lan·dau·let (lan′dô let′), *n.* an automobile having a convertible top for the back seat, with the front seat either roofed or open. Also, **lan′dau·lette′.** [1785–95; LANDAU + -LET]

land′ bank′, 1. a banking association that engages in the financing of transactions in real property, esp. in agricultural land. **2.** a parcel or parcels of land or real estate held in trust, as for future development. [1690–1700] —**land′ bank′ing.**

land′ breeze′, a coastal breeze blowing at night from land to sea, caused by the difference in the rate of cooling of their respective surfaces. Also called **land wind.** Cf. **lake breeze, sea breeze.** [1660–70]

land′ bridge′, 1. *Geol.* an actual or hypothetical strip of land, subject to submergence, that connects adjacent continental landmasses and serves as a route of dispersal for plants and animals: *a prehistoric land bridge between Asia and North America.* **2.** a transcontinental rail route between countries, as those in Europe and the Far East, considered faster and less costly than all-sea routes. Also, **land·bridge** (land′brij′). [1895–1900]

land′ con′tract, 1. a contract for the purchase and sale of land. **2.** a contract in which a purchaser of real estate, upon making an initial payment, agrees to pay the seller stipulated amounts at specified intervals until the total purchase price is paid, the seller retaining legal title to the land as security for the payments.

land′ crab′, any of several crabs, esp. of the family Gecarcinidae, that live chiefly upon land, returning to the sea to breed. [1630–40]

Land′ Day′ak, 1. a member of any of several Dayak tribes of Sarawak and southwestern Borneo. Cf. **Iban. 2.** the Austronesian language of the Land Dayak.

land·ed (lan′did), *adj.* **1.** owning land, esp. an estate: *landed gentry.* **2.** consisting of land: *landed property.* **3.** after shipping; delivered: *a landed price.* [bef. 1000; late ME (see LAND, -ED[3]); r. OE *gelandod* (rare), ptp. of **landian* to endow with land (see -ED[2])]

land·er (lan′dər), *n.* a space probe designed to land on a planet or other solid celestial body. Cf. **orbiter.** [1960–65; LAND + -ER[1]]

Landes (länd), *n.* a department in SW France. 288,323; 3615 sq. mi. (9365 sq. km). *Cap.:* Mont-de-Marsan.

land·fall (land′fôl′), *n.* **1.** an approach to or sighting of land: *The ship will make its landfall at noon tomorrow.* **2.** the land sighted or reached. **3.** a landslide. [1620–30; LAND + FALL]

land·fast (land′fast′, -fäst′), *adj.* attached to or grounded on shore or land: *landfast ice.* [1695–1705; LAND + FAST[1]]

land·fill (land′fil′), *n.* Also called **sanitary landfill. 1.** a low area of land that is built up from deposits of solid refuse in layers covered by soil. **2.** the solid refuse itself. —*v.i.* **3.** to create more usable land by this means. —*v.t.* **4.** to make (an area of land) by means of a landfill. **5.** to use in a landfill: *to landfill millions of tons of garbage each year.* [1940–45, *Amer.;* LAND + FILL]

land·form (land′fôrm′), *n. Geol.* a specific geomorphic feature on the surface of the earth, ranging from large-scale features such as plains, plateaus, and mountains to minor features such as hills, valleys, and alluvial fans. [1890–95; LAND + FORM]

CONCISE PRONUNCIATION KEY: *act, cāpe, dâre, pärt; set, ēqual; if, īce; ox, ōver, ôrder, oil, bo͝ok, bo͞ot, out; up, ûrge; child; sing; shoe; thin, th*at; zh as in *treasure.* ə = *a* as in *alone, e* as in *system, i* as in *easily, o* as in *gallop, u* as in *circus;* ə as in *fire* (fīər), *hour* (ouər). l and n can serve as syllabic consonants, as in *cradle* (krād′l), and *button* (but′n). See the full key inside the front cover.

land′ freeze′, a legal restraint on the sale or transfer of land. [1965–70]

land-grab•ber (land′grab′ər), *n.* a person who seizes land illegally or underhandedly. [1855–60, *Amer.*]

land′ grant′, a tract of land given by the government, as for colleges or railroads. [1850–55]

land′-grant col′lege (land′grant′, -gränt′), a U.S. college or university (**land′-grant univer′sity**) entitled to support from the federal government under the provisions of the Morrill Acts. [1885–90, *Amer.*]

land•grave (land′grāv′), *n.* **1.** (in medieval Germany) a count having jurisdiction over a large territory. **2.** (*usually cap.*) the title of certain German princes. [1510–20; < MLG; see LAND, MARGRAVE]

land•gra•vi•ate (land grā′vē it, -āt′), *n.* the office, jurisdiction, or territory of a landgrave. [1650–60; < ML *landgraviātus.* See LANDGRAVE (ML *landgravius*), -ATE[3]]

land•gra•vine (land′grə vēn′), *n.* **1.** the wife of a landgrave. **2.** a woman of the rank of a landgrave. [1675–85; < D *landgravin,* fem. of *landgraaf* LANDGRAVE]

land•hold•er (land′hōl′dər), *n.* a holder, owner, or occupant of land. [1375–1425; late ME; see LAND, HOLDER] **—land′hold′ing,** *adj., n.*

land•ing (lan′ding), *n.* **1.** the act of a person or thing that lands: *The pilot brought his plane in for a landing.* **2.** a place where persons or goods are landed, as from a ship: *The boat moored at the landing.* **3.** *Archit.* **a.** a platform between flights of stairs. **b.** the floor at the head or foot of a flight of stairs. **4.** *Shipbuilding.* **a.** the overlap of two plates or planks, as in a clinker-built shell. **b.** the distance between the center of a rivet hole and the edge of the plate or shape into which it is cut. [1400–50; late ME; see LAND, -ING[1]]

land′ing card′, **1.** an identification card issued to a traveler for presentation to the immigration authorities. **2.** a card issued to a sailor in a foreign port granting permission to go ashore. [1930–35]

land′ing clerk′, a representative of a shipping line who boards its incoming passenger ships to give passengers information and advice.

land′ing craft′, *Navy.* any of various flat-bottomed vessels designed to move troops and equipment close to shore. [1935–40]

land′ing field′, an area of land large and smooth enough for the landing and takeoff of aircraft. [1920–25]

land′ing flap′, a flap in the undersurface of the trailing edge of an aircraft wing, capable of being moved downward to increase either lift or drag or both, as for landing. Cf. **split flap** (def. 1). [1935–40]

land′ing force′, *Mil.* the ground forces of an amphibious task force that effect the assault landing in an amphibious operation. [1880–85]

land′ing gear′, the wheels, floats, etc., of an aircraft, upon which it lands and moves on ground or water. [1910–15]

land′ing net′, *Angling.* a small, bag-shaped net with a handle at the mouth, for scooping a hooked fish out of the water and bringing it to shore or into a boat. [1645–55]

land′ing par′ty, a component of a ship's company detached for special duty ashore. [1890–95]

land′ing ship′, any of various ships designed for transporting troops and heavy equipment in amphibious warfare, capable of making assault landings directly onto a beach. [1940–45]

land′ing stage′, a floating platform used as a wharf. [1855–60]

land′ing strake′, *Shipbuilding.* the next strake of planking in an open boat below the sheer strake.

land′ing strip′, airstrip. [1925–30]

land′ing tee′, *Aeron.* See **wind tee.**

land•ing-wait•er (lan′ding wā′tər), *n.* landwaiter.

Lan•di•ni (län dē′nē), *n.* **Fran•ces•co** (frän ches′kô), c1325–97, Italian organist and composer. Also, **Lan•di•no** (län dē′nô).

Landi′ni ca′dence, *Music.* a melodic cadential formula, associated esp. with the Ars Nova music of Francesco Landini, progressing from the tonic to the leading tone, then to the submediant and back to the tonic.

Lan•dis (lan′dis), *n.* **Ken•e•saw Mountain** (ken′ə sô′), 1866–1944, U.S. jurist: first commissioner of baseball 1920–44.

land•la•dy (land′lā′dē), *n., pl.* **-dies.** **1.** a woman who owns and leases an apartment, house, land, etc., to others. **2.** a woman who owns or runs an inn, rooming house, or boardinghouse. [1530–40; LAND + LADY]

land′ lane′, *Naut.* (in an ice floe) an opening that leads toward a shore. Also called **land′ lead′** (lēd).

land′ legs′, the ability to adjust one's sense of balance and motion to walking on land, as after a sea journey or flight: *It took the astronauts some time to regain their land legs after the long space mission.* [1870–75; on the model of SEA LEGS]

länd•ler (lent′lər), *n., pl.* **-ler, -lers.** **1.** an Austrian and southern German folk dance in moderately slow triple meter, antecedent to the waltz. **2.** music for this dance. **3.** a piano or orchestral composition patterned after such music. [1875–80; < G: lit., something connected with *Landl* (lit., little land) name for Upper Austria, where the dance first became popular; see -ER[1]]

land•less (land′lis), *adj.* without landed property; not owning land: *a landless noble.* [bef. 1000; ME; OE *landlēas.* See LAND, -LESS] **—land′less•ness,** *n.*

land•line (land′līn′), *n.* **1.** a circuit of wire or cable connecting two ground locations. **2.** *CB Slang.* a telephone. [1860–65; LAND + LINE[1]]

land•locked (land′lokt′), *adj.* **1.** shut in completely, or almost completely, by land: *a landlocked bay.* **2.** having no direct access to the sea: *a landlocked country.* **3.** living in waters shut off from the sea, as some fish. [1615–25; LAND + LOCK[1] + -ED[2]]

land′locked salm′on, a variety of the Atlantic Ocean salmon, *Salmo salar,* confined to the freshwater lakes of New England and adjacent areas of Canada. Also called **lake salmon.** [1865–70, *Amer.*]

land•lop•er (land′lō′pər), *n.* a wanderer, vagrant, or adventurer. Also, **land•loup•er** (land′lou′pər, -lo͞o′pər). [1540–50; < D: lit., land-runner. See LAND, LOPE, -ER[1]]

land•lord (land′lôrd′), *n.* **1.** a person or organization that owns and leases apartments to others. **2.** a person who owns and leases land, buildings, etc. **3.** a person who owns or runs an inn, lodging house, etc. **4.** a landowner. [bef. 1000; ME; OE *landhlāford.* See LAND, LORD] **—land′lord′ly,** *adj.* **—land′lord′ry,** *n.* **—land′lord′ship′,** *n.*

land•lord•ism (land′lôr diz′əm), *n.* the practice under which privately owned property is leased or rented to others for occupancy or cultivation. [1835–45; LANDLORD + -ISM]

land•lub•ber (land′lub′ər), *n.* an unseasoned sailor or someone unfamiliar with the sea. [1690–1700; LAND + LUBBER] **—land′lub′ber•ish,** *adj.* **—land′lub′ber•ly, land′lub′bing,** *adj.*

land•man (land′mən, -man′), *n., pl.* **-men** (-mən, -men′). **1.** landsman (def. 1). **2.** leaseman. **3.** a person who bargains with landowners for the mineral rights to their land, as on behalf of an oil company. [bef. 1000; ME; OE *landmann.* See LAND, MAN[1]]
—Usage. See **-man.**

land•mark (land′märk′), *n.* **1.** a prominent or conspicuous object on land that serves as a guide, esp. to ships at sea or to travelers on a road; a distinguishing landscape feature marking a site or location: *The post office served as a landmark for locating the street to turn down.* **2.** something used to mark the boundary of land. **3.** a building or other place that is of outstanding historical, aesthetic, or cultural importance, often declared as such and given a special status (**land′mark designa′tion**), ordaining its preservation, by some authorizing organization. **4.** a significant or historic event, juncture, achievement, etc.: *The court decision stands as a landmark in constitutional law.* **—***v.t.* **5.** to declare (a building, site, etc.) a landmark: *a movement to landmark New York's older theaters.* [bef. 1000; ME; OE *landmearc.* See LAND, MARK[1]]
—Syn. 4. milestone, watershed, benchmark.

land•mass (land′mas′), *n. Geol.* a part of the continental crust above sea level having a distinct identity, as a continent or large island. [1855–60; LAND + MASS]

land′ meas′ure, **1.** any system of measurement for measuring land. **2.** a unit or a series of units of measurement used in land measure. [1560–70]

land′ mine′, *Mil.* **1.** an explosive charge concealed just under the surface of the ground or of a roadway, designed to be detonated by pressure, proximity of a vehicle or person, etc. **2.** See **aerial mine** (def. 2). [1885–90]

Lan•do (län′dō), *n.* died A.D. 914, Italian ecclesiastic: pope 913–914. Also, **Landus.**

Land′ of Beu′lah, (in Bunyan's *Pilgrim's Progress*) the peaceful land in which the pilgrim awaits the call to the Celestial City.

Land′ of Enchant′ment, New Mexico (used as a nickname).

land′ of′fice, a government office for the transaction of business relating to public lands. [1675–85, *Amer.*]

land′-of•fice busi′ness (land′ô′fis, -of′is), a lively, booming, expanding, or very profitable business. [1830–40, *Amer.*]

land′ of milk′ and hon′ey, **1.** a land of unusual fertility and abundance. **2.** the blessings of heaven. **3.** the Promised Land. Also, **Land′ of Milk′ and Hon′ey.**

land′ of Nod′ (nod), the mythical land of sleep. [1725–35; pun on *Land of Nod* (Gen. 4:16); see NOD]

Land′ of Opportu′nity, Arkansas (used as a nickname).

Land′ of Oz′, an unreal, otherworldly, or magical place. Also called **Oz.** [after the magical place created by L. Frank Baum in *The Wonderful Wizard of Oz* (1900) and other fantasy novels]

Land′ of Prom′ise. See **Promised Land.**

Land′ of the Lit′tle Sticks′, *Canadian.* the part of the north of Canada that lies south of the tree line but contains only stunted evergreens or dwarf deciduous trees.

Land′ of the Mid′night Sun′, **1.** any of those countries containing land within the Arctic Circle where there is a midnight sun in midsummer, esp. Norway, Sweden, or Finland. **2.** Lapland.

Land′ of the Ris′ing Sun′, Japan.

Lan•don (lan′dən), *n.* **Alfred** ("*Alf*") **Moss•man** (môs′mən, mos′-), 1887–1987, U.S. politician.

Lan•dor (lan′dər, -dôr), *n.* **Walter Savage,** 1775–1864, English poet and prose writer.

land•own•er (land′ō′nər), *n.* an owner or proprietor of land. [1725–35; LAND + OWNER] **—land′own′ership′,** *n.* **—land′own′ing,** *n., adj.*

Lan•dow•ska (lan dôf′skə, -dof′-; *Pol.* län dôf′skä), *n.* **Wan•da** (won′də; *Pol.* vän′dä), 1879–1959, Polish harpsichordist, in the U.S. after 1940.

land′ pat′ent, an official document by which title to a portion of public land is conveyed from the government. [1835–45, *Amer.*]

land′ plas′ter, finely ground gypsum, used chiefly as a fertilizer. [1885–90, *Amer.*]

land-poor (land′po͝or′), *adj.* in need of ready money while owning much land. [1870–75, *Amer.*]

land′ pow′er, **1.** a nation having an important and powerful army. **2.** military power on land. [1925–30]

Land•race (land′rās, länd′rä sə), *n.* one of several widely distributed strains of large, white, lop-eared swine of northern European origin. [1930–35; < Dan: lit., country breed, equiv. to *land* country, LAND + *race* breed, stock (< E or F; see RACE[2])]

land′ rail′. See **corn crake.** [1760–70]

land′ rain′, *Pennsylvania.* a steady, heavy rain. [cf. PaG *landrejje,* G *Landregen* lit., country rain]

land′ reform′, any program, esp. when undertaken by a national government, involving the redistribution of agricultural land among the landless. [1840–50, *Amer.*]

Lan′drum-Grif′fin Act′ (lan′drəm grif′in), an act of Congress (1959) outlawing secondary boycotts, requiring public disclosure of the financial records of unions, and guaranteeing the use of secret ballots in union voting.

Land•sat (land′sat′), *n.* a U.S. scientific satellite that studies and photographs the earth's surface by using remote-sensing techniques. [1975–80; LAND (or *land-(sensing)*) + SAT(ELLITE)]

land•scape (land′skāp′), *n., v.,* **-scaped, -scap•ing.** **—***n.* **1.** a section or expanse of rural scenery, usually extensive, that can be seen from a single viewpoint. **2.** a picture representing natural inland or coastal scenery. **3.** *Fine Arts.* the category of aesthetic subject matter in which natural scenery is represented. **4.** *Obs.* a panoramic view of scenery; vista. **—***v.t.* **5.** to improve the appearance of (an area of land, a highway, etc.), as by planting trees, shrubs, or grass, or altering the contours of the ground. **6.** to improve the landscape of. **—***v.i.* **7.** to do landscape gardening as a profession. [1590–1600; 1925–30 for def. 6; < D *landschap;* c. OE *landsceap, landscipe;* akin to G *Landschaft.* See LAND, -SHIP]
—Syn. 1. view, scenery, vista, prospect.

land′scape ar′chitecture, the art of arranging or modifying the features of a landscape, an urban area, etc., for aesthetic or practical reasons. **—land′scape ar′chitect.** [1830–40]

land′scape gar′dening, the art or trade of designing or rearranging large gardens, estates, etc. **—land′scape gar′dener.** [1795–1805]

land•scap•er (land′skā′pər), *n.* a gardener who does landscape gardening. [1960–65; LANDSCAPE + -ER[1]]

land•scap•ist (land′skā′pist), *n.* an artist who paints landscapes. [1835–45; LANDSCAPE + -IST]

Land•seer (land′sēr, -syər), *n.* **Sir Edwin Henry,** 1802–73, English painter, esp. of animals.

Land's′ End′, a cape in Cornwall that forms the SW tip of England.

land•side (land′sīd′), *n.* the part of a plow consisting of a sidepiece opposite the moldboard, for guiding the plow and resisting the side pressure caused by the turning of the furrow. [1525–35; LAND + SIDE[1]]

land•skip (land′skip′), *n. Archaic.* landscape.

lands•knecht (*Ger.* länts′knekht′), *n.* a European mercenary foot soldier of the 16th century, armed with a pike or halberd. Also, **lansquenet.** [< G; see LAND, 's[1], KNIGHT]

land•slide (land′slīd′), *n., v.,* **-slid, -slid** or **-slid•den, -slid•ing.** **—***n.* **1.** the downward falling or sliding of a mass of soil, detritus, or rock on or from a steep slope. **2.** the mass itself. **3.** an election in which a particular victorious candidate or party receives an overwhelming mass or majority of votes: *the 1936 landslide for Roosevelt.* **4.** any overwhelming victory: *She won the contest by a landslide.* **—***v.i.* **5.** to come down in or as in a landslide. **6.** to win an election by an overwhelming majority. Also called, *esp. Brit.,* **land•slip** (land′slip′) (for defs. 1, 2). [1830–40, *Amer.*; LAND + SLIDE]

Lands•mål (länts′môl), *n.* Nynorsk. Formerly, **Lands′maal.** Also, **lands′maal.**

lands•man (landz′mən), *n., pl.* **-men.** **1.** Also, **landman.** a person who lives or works on land. **2.** an inexperienced sailor or one who has not been to sea before.

CONCISE ETYMOLOGY KEY: <, descended or borrowed from; >, whence; b., blend of, blended; c., cognate with; cf., compare; deriv., derivative; equiv., equivalent; imit., imitative; obl., oblique; r., replacing; s., stem; sp., spelling, spelled; resp., respelling, respelled; trans., translation; ?, origin unknown; *, unattested; ‡, probably earlier than. See the full key inside the front cover.

[bef. 1000 for sense "native"; ME *landes man, londes man,* OE *landes mann;* see LAND, 's[1], -MAN]
—Usage. See **-man.**

lands·man (länts′mən), *n., pl.* ***lands·leit*** (länts′līt), *Eng.* **lands·men.** *Yiddish.* a person from the same town, geographical area, region, etc., as another; compatriot.

lands·man·shaft (länts′mən shäft′), *n., pl.* ***-shaf·ten*** (-shäf′tən). *Yiddish.* a fraternal organization made up of immigrants from the same region.

land′ snail′, **1.** any gastropod of the widely distributed order Stylommatophora, containing usually small, brown or mottled hermaphroditic snails: some more colorful species, introduced into North America, are agricultural pests. **2.** any terrestrial snail.

Land·stei·ner (land′stī′nər; *Ger.* länt′shtī′nər), *n.* **Karl** (kärl; *Ger.* käʀl), 1868–1943, Austrian pathologist in the U.S.: Nobel prize 1930.

Lands·ting (läns′ting′), *n.* (formerly) the upper house of the Danish parliament. Also, **Lands·thing** (läns′ting′). Cf. **Rigsdag.** [< Dan, equiv. to *lands,* poss. of *land* LAND + *t(h)ing* THING[2]. See LAGTHING]

land·sturm (*Ger.* länt′shto͝orm′), *n.* (in certain European countries). **1.** a general draft of people in time of war. **2.** the force so drafted or subject to such draft, consisting of all who are capable of bearing arms and not in the army, navy, or Landwehr. [1805–15; < G: lit., land storm]

Land·tag (*Ger.* länt′täkh′), *n. Hist.* the legislature of certain states in Germany. [< G: lit., land parliament. See DAY, DIET[2]]

land-to-land (land′tə land′), *adj.* **1.** designed for launching or traveling from a base on land to a target or destination on land: *land-to-land missile.* **—adv. 2.** from a base on land to a target on land. [1965–70]

Lan·dus (lan′dəs), *n.* Lando.

land·wait·er (land′wā′tər), *n.* a British customs officer who enforces import-export regulations, collects import duties, etc. [1705–15; LAND + WAITER]

land·ward (land′wərd), *adv.* **1.** Also, **land′wards.** toward the land or interior. **—adj. 2.** lying, facing, or tending toward the land or away from the coast. **3.** being in the direction of the land: *a landward breeze.* [1375–1425; late ME; see LAND, -WARD]

land·wash (land′wosh′, -wôsh′), *n. Newfoundland.* the foreshore, esp. that part between high and low tidemarks. [LAND + WASH]

Land·wehr (länt′vār′), *n.* (in Germany, Austria, etc.) the part of the organized military forces of a nation that has completed a certain amount of compulsory training, and whose continuous service is required only in time of war. [1805–15; < G, equiv. to *Land* country, LAND + *Wehr* defense; see WEIR]

land′ wind′ (wind). See **land breeze.** [1590–1600]

Lan·dy (lan′dē), *n.* **John Michael,** born 1930, Australian track-and-field athlete.

land′ yacht′, a wind-driven vehicle with a mast and sails, having three wheels, a single seat, and a steering wheel, used esp. on beaches and other sandy areas. Also called **sand yacht.** [1925–30]

lane[1] (lān), *n.* **1.** a narrow way or passage between hedges, fences, walls, or houses. **2.** any narrow or well-defined passage, track, channel, or course. **3.** a longitudinally marked part of a highway wide enough to accommodate one vehicle, often set off from adjacent lanes by painted lines (often used in combination): *a new six-lane turnpike.* **4.** a fixed route followed by ocean steamers or airplanes. **5.** (in a running or swimming race) the marked-off space or path within which a competitor must remain during the course of a race. **6.** See **bowling alley** (def. 1). [bef. 1000; ME, OE; c. D *laan* avenue, ON *lǫn* oblong hayrick, row of houses]
—Syn. 1. alley. See **path.**

lane[2] (lān), *Scot.* **—adj. 1.** lone. **—n. 2. by one's lane.** See **lonesome** (def. 4).

Lane (lān), *n.* a male given name.

Lan·franc (lan′frangk), *n.* 1005?–89, Italian Roman Catholic prelate and scholar in England: archbishop of Canterbury 1070–89.

lang (lang), *adj., n., adv. Scot. and North Eng.* long[1].

Lang (lang), *n.* **1. Andrew,** 1844–1912, Scottish poet, prose writer, and scholar. **2. Cos·mo Gordon** (koz′mō), 1864–1945, English clergyman: archbishop of Canterbury 1928–42. **3. Fritz,** 1890–1976, U.S. film director, born in Austria. **4. Pearl,** born 1922, U.S. dancer and choreographer.

lang., language.

lang·bein·ite (lang′bī nīt′, läng′-), *n.* a mineral, $K_2Mg_2(SO_4)_3$, occurring in marine salt deposits, used as a fertilizer because of its potassium content. [< G *Langbeinit* (1891), after A. Langbein, 19th-century German chemist; see -ITE[1]]

Lang·e (läng′ə *for 1;* lang *for 2, 3*), *n.* **1. Chris·tian Lou·is** (kʀis′tyän lo͞o′ē, -is), 1869–1938, Norwegian historian: Nobel peace prize 1921. **2. David (Russell),** born 1942, New Zealand political leader: prime minister 1984–89. **3. Dorothea,** 1895–1965, U.S. photographer.

lan·geel (lang′gēl), *n. Australian.* leangle. Also, **lan′·giel.**

Lang·er (lang′ər), *n.* **Susanne (Knauth)** (knout), 1895–1985, U.S. philosopher.

Lang·land (lang′lənd), *n.* **William,** 1332?–c1400, English poet. Also, **Langley.**

lang·lauf (läng′louf′), *n.* **1.** the sport of cross-country skiing. **2.** a cross-country ski run or race. [1925–30; < G: lit., long run. See LONG, LOPE, LEAP]

lang·läuf·er (läng′loi′fər), *n., pl.* **-läuf·er, -läuf·ers.** a participant in cross-country skiing. [1925–30; < G; see LANGLAUF, -ER[1]]

lang′ lay′ (lang), a wire rope in which the lays of the strands and of their component wires are the same. [1885–90; *lang* (var. of ALONG) + LAY[1]]

Lang·ley (lang′lē), *n.* **1. Edmund of.** See **York, Edmund of Langley, 1st Duke of.** **2. Samuel Pier·pont** (pēr′pont), 1834–1906, U.S. astronomer, physicist, and pioneer in aeronautics. **3. William.** See **Langland, William.** **4.** a city in SW British Columbia, in SW Canada, near Vancouver. 15,124.

lang·ley (lang′lē), *n. Physics.* for electromagnetic radiation incident upon a surface, a value of energy per unit area equal to one calorie per square centimeter. [1945–50; after S. P. LANGLEY]

Lang·muir (lang′myo͝or), *n.* **Irving,** 1881–1957, U.S. chemist: Nobel prize 1932.

Lan·go·bard (lang′gə bärd′), *n.* Lombard (def. 2). [< L *Langobardī* (pl.), Latinized form of Germanic tribal name; c. OE *Longbeardan*]

Lan·go·bar·dic (lang′gə bär′dik), *adj.* **1.** Lombard (def. 4). **—n. 2.** a West Germanic language, the language of the ancient Lombards. [1715–25; LANGOBARD + -IC]

lan·gos·ta (läng gôs′tä; *Eng.* lang gos′tə), *n., pl.* ***-tas*** (-täs; *Eng.* -təz). *Spanish.* See **spiny lobster.**

lan·go·sti·no (lang′gə stē′nō), *n., pl.* **-nos.** *Spanish and Creole Cookery.* langoustine. [< Sp; see LANGOUSTINE]

lan·gouste (län go͞ost′; *Eng.* läng go͞ost′), *n., pl.* ***-goustes*** (-go͞ost′; *Eng.* go͞osts′). *French.* See **spiny lobster.**

lan·gous·tine (lang′gə stēn′), *n.* a large prawn, *Nephrops norvegicus,* used for food. [1910–15; < F < Sp *langostino,* equiv. to *langost(a)* crayfish (< VL, for L *locusta* kind of crustacean, LOCUST) + *-ino* -INE[1]]

lan·grage (lang′grij), *n.* a kind of shot consisting of bolts, nails, etc., fastened together or enclosed in a case, formerly used for damaging sails and rigging in sea battles. Also, **lan′gridge.** [1760–70; orig. uncert.]

Lan·gre·nus (lan grē′nəs), *n.* a walled plain in the fourth quadrant of the face of the moon: about 85 miles (135 km) in diameter.

Lan·gre·o (läng gʀe′ô), *n.* a city in N Spain. 58,864.

lang·sat (läng′sät), *n.* **1.** an East Indian tree, *Lansium domesticum,* of the mahogany family. **2.** the yellowish, tart, edible fruit of this tree. Also, **lang·set** (läng′set), **lansa, lansat, lanseh.** [1775–85; < Malay: the name of the tree]

Lang·shan (lang′shan), *n.* one of a breed of large, black or white, white-skinned Asiatic domestic chickens, having a single comb and feathered shanks and producing dark-brown eggs. [1870–75; after *Langshan* (Chin *lángshān*), county and town in N China]

Lang·ston (lang′stən), *n.* **1. John Mercer,** 1829–97, U.S. public official, diplomat, and educator. **2.** a male given name.

lang·syne (lang′zīn′, -sīn′), *Scot.* **—adv. 1.** long since; long ago. **—n. 2.** time long past. Also, **lang′ syne′.** [1490–1500; LANG + SYNE]

Lang·ton (lang′tən), *n.* **Stephen,** c1165–1228, English theologian, historian, and poet: archbishop of Canterbury.

Lang·try (lang′trē), *n.* **Lil·lie** (lil′ē), (*Emily Charlotte Le Breton*) ("the Jersey Lily"), 1852–1929, English actress.

lan·guage (lang′gwij), *n.* **1.** a body of words and the systems for their use common to a people who are of the same community or nation, the same geographical area, or the same cultural tradition: *the two languages of Belgium; a Bantu language; the French language; the Yiddish language.* **2.** communication by voice in the distinctively human manner, using arbitrary sounds in conventional ways with conventional meanings; speech. **3.** the system of linguistic signs or symbols considered in the abstract (opposed to *speech*). **4.** any set or system of such symbols as used in a more or less uniform fashion by a number of people, who are thus enabled to communicate intelligibly with one another. **5.** any system of formalized symbols, signs, sounds, gestures, or the like used or conceived as a means of communicating thought, emotion, etc.: *the language of mathematics; sign language.* **6.** the means of communication used by animals: *the language of birds.* **7.** communication of meaning in any way; medium that is expressive, significant, etc.: *the language of flowers; the language of art.* **8.** linguistics; the study of language. **9.** the speech or phraseology peculiar to a class, profession, etc.; lexis; jargon. **10.** a particular manner of verbal expression: *flowery language.* **11.** choice of words or style of writing; diction: *the language of poetry.* **12.** *Computers.* a set of characters and symbols and syntactic rules for their combination and use, by means of which a computer can be given directions: *The language of many commercial application programs is COBOL.* **13.** a nation or people considered in terms of their speech. **14.** *Archaic.* faculty or power of speech. [1250–1300; ME < AF, var. sp. of *langage,* deriv. of *langue* tongue. See LINGUA, -AGE]
—Syn. 2. See **speech. 4, 9.** tongue; terminology; lingo, lingua franca. LANGUAGE, DIALECT, JARGON, VERNACULAR refer to patterns of vocabulary, syntax, and usage characteristic of communities of various sizes and types. LANGUAGE is applied to the general pattern of a people or race: *the English language.* DIALECT is applied to certain forms or varieties of a language, often those that provincial communities or special groups retain (or develop) even after a standard has been established: *Scottish dialect.* A JARGON is either an artificial pattern used by a particular (usually occupational) group within a community or a special pattern created for communication in business or trade between members of the groups speaking different languages: *the jargon of the theater; the Chinook jargon.* A VERNACULAR is the authentic natural pattern of speech, now usually on the informal level, used by persons indigenous to a certain community, large or small.

lan′guage acquisi′tion device′, *Psycholinguistics.* a hypothesized innate mental faculty present in infants that enables them to construct and internalize the grammar of their native language on the basis of the limited and fragmentary language input to which they are exposed. *Abbr.:* LAD [1960–65]

lan′guage arts′, the skills, including reading, composition, speech, spelling, and dramatics, taught in elementary and secondary schools to give students a thorough proficiency in using the language. [1945–50]

lan′guage death′, *Ling.* the complete displacement of one language by another in a population of speakers.

lan′guage lab′oratory, a special room or rooms with sound-recording and -reproducing equipment for use by students to practice speaking foreign languages, usually with an instructor monitoring the program. [1930–35]

lan′guage plan′ning, the development of policies or programs designed to direct or change language use, as through the establishment of an official language, the standardization or modernization of a language, or the development or alteration of a writing system. [1965–70]

lan′guage trans′fer, transfer (def. 20).

lan′guage univer′sal, *Ling.* a trait or property of language that exists, or has the potential to exist, in all languages. Also called **linguistic universal.** [1965–70]

langue (läng), *n. French.* the linguistic system shared by the members of a community (contrasted with *parole*).

langue de boeuf (*Fr.* läng də bœf′), *pl.* **langues de boeuf** (*Fr.* läng də bœf′). See **ox-tongue partisan.** [1400–50; < F: lit., ox tongue; r. late ME *lange de bef* < MF *langue de boeuf*]

Langue·doc (läng dôk′), *n.* a former province in S France. *Cap.:* Toulouse. **—Langue·do·cian** (lang dō′shən, lang′gwə dō′shən), *adj., n.*

langue d'oc (läng dôk′), the Romance language of medieval southern France: developed into modern Provençal. [1700–10; < F: language of *oc,* yes < L *hōc* (*ille fēcit*) this (he did); cf. OCCITAN]

langue d'oïl (läng dô ēl′, dô′ē, doil′), the Romance language of medieval northern France: developed into modern French. [1695–1705; < F: language of *oïl* (OF; cf. F *oui*), yes < L *hōc ille* (*fēcit*) this he (did)]

lan·guet (lang′gwet), *n.* any of various small tongue-shaped parts, processes, or projections. [1375–1425; late ME < MF *languete,* dim. of *langue* tongue; see -ET]

lan·guette (lang′gwet), *n. Music.* a thin plate fastened to the mouth of certain organ pipes. [1375–1425; late ME; var. of LANGUET]

lan·guid (lang′gwid), *adj.* **1.** lacking in vigor or vitality; slack or slow: *a languid manner.* **2.** lacking in spirit or interest; listless; indifferent. **3.** drooping or flagging from weakness or fatigue; faint. [1590–1600; < L *languidus* faint. See LANGUISH, -ID[4]] **—lan′guid·ly,** *adv.* **—lan′guid·ness,** *n.*
—Syn. 1. inactive, inert, sluggish, torpid. **2.** spiritless. **3.** weak, feeble, weary, exhausted, debilitated. **—Ant. 1.** active, energetic. **3.** vigorous.

lan·guish (lang′gwish), *v.i.* **1.** to be or become weak or feeble; droop; fade. **2.** to lose vigor and vitality. **3.** to undergo neglect or experience prolonged inactivity; suffer hardship and distress: *to languish in prison for ten years.* **4.** to be subjected to delay or disregard; be ignored: *a petition that languished on the warden's desk for a year.* **5.** to pine with desire or longing. **6.** to assume an expression of tender, sentimental melancholy. **—n. 7.** the act or state of languishing. **8.** a tender, melancholy look or expression. [1250–1300; ME < MF *languiss-,* long s. of *languir* << L *languēre* to languish; akin to *laxus* LAX; see -ISH[2]] **—lan′guish·er,** *n.*

lan·guish·ing (lang′gwi shing), *adj.* **1.** becoming languid, in any way. **2.** expressive of languor; indicating tender, sentimental melancholy: *a languishing sigh.* **3.** lingering: *a languishing death.* [1300–50; ME; see LANGUISH, -ING[2]] **—lan′guish·ing·ly,** *adv.*

lan·guish·ment (lang′gwish mənt), *n. Archaic.* **1.** the act or state of languishing. **2.** a languishing expression. [1535–45; LANGUISH + -MENT]

lan·guor (lang′gər), *n.* **1.** lack of energy or vitality; sluggishness. **2.** lack of spirit or interest; listlessness; stagnation. **3.** physical weakness or faintness. **4.** emotional softness or tenderness. [1250–1300; < L (see LANGUISH, -OR[1]); r. ME *langour* sickness, woe < OF < L]

lan·guor·ous (lang′gər əs), *adj.* **1.** characterized by languor; languid. **2.** inducing languor: *languorous fragrance.* [1480–90; LANGUOR + -OUS] **—lan′guor·ous·ly,** *adv.* **—lan′guor·ous·ness,** *n.*

lan·gur (lung go͝or′), *n.* any of various slender, long-tailed monkeys of the genus *Presbytis,* of Asia, feeding on leaves, fruits, and seeds: several species are threatened or endangered. [1820–30; < Hindi *laṅgūr;* akin to Skt *lāṅgūlin* having a tail]

lani-, a combining form meaning "wool," used in the formation of compound words: *laniferous.* [< LL, comb. form of *lāna* WOOL; akin to Gk *lênos* wool]

lan·iard (lan′yərd), *n.* lanyard.

la·ni·ar·y (lā′nē er′ē, lan′ē-), *adj.* **1.** (of teeth) adapted for tearing. **—n. 2.** a laniary tooth; a canine of daggerlike shape. [1820–30; < L *laniārius* of a butcher, equiv. to *lani(us)* butcher + *-ārius* -ARY]

CONCISE PRONUNCIATION KEY: *act, cāpe, dâre, pärt; set, ēqual; if, īce; ox, ōver, ôrder, oil, bo͝ok, bo͞ot, out; up, ûrge; child; sing; shoe; thin, that;* zh as in *treasure.* ə = *a* as in *alone, e* as in *system, i* as in *easily, o* as in *gallop, u* as in *circus;* ᵊ as in *fire* (fīᵊr), *hour* (ouᵊr). l and n can serve as syllabic consonants, as in *cradle* (krād′l), and *button* (but′n). See the full key inside the front cover.

La·nier (lə nēr′), *n.* **Sidney,** 1842–81, U.S. poet and literary scholar.

la·nif·er·ous (lə nif′ər əs), *adj.* wool-bearing: *sheep and other laniferous animals.* [1650–60; < L *lānifer* wool-bearing; see LANI-, -FEROUS]

La·ni·kai (lä′nē kī′), *n.* a town adjoining Kailua, on SE Oahu, in Hawaii. With Kailua, 35,812.

lank (langk), *adj.,* **-er, -est. 1.** (of plants) unduly long and slender: *lank grass; lank, leafless trees.* **2.** (of hair) straight and limp; without spring or curl. **3.** lean; gaunt; thin. [bef. 1000; ME *lanc,* OE *hlanc;* akin to OHG *hlanca* loin, side. Cf. FLANK] **—lank′ly,** *adv.* **—lank′·ness,** *n.*

Lan·kes·ter (lang′kə stər, -kes tər), *n.* **Sir Edwin Ray,** 1847–1929, English zoologist and writer.

lank·y (lang′kē), *adj.,* **lank·i·er, lank·i·est.** ungracefully thin and rawboned; bony; gaunt: *a very tall and lanky man.* [1660–70; LANK + -Y[1]] **—lank′i·ly,** *adv.* **—lank′i·ness,** *n.*

lan·ner (lan′ər), *n.* **1.** a falcon, *Falco biarmicus,* of southern Europe, northern Africa, and southern Asia. **2.** *Falconry.* the female of this bird. [1250–1300; ME *laner* < MF *lanier* kind of falcon, lit., wool weaver (< L *lānārius;*), a term of abuse in the early Middle Ages, applied esp. to laggards and cowards, and so to the lanner, slow in flight and thought to be cowardly]

lan·ner·et (lan′ə ret′), *n. Falconry.* the male lanner, which is smaller than the female. [1400–50; late ME *lanret* < MF *laneret.* See LANNER, -ET]

Lan·ny (lan′ē), *n.* a male given name, form of **Lenny.**

lan·o·lin (lan′l in), *n.* a fatty substance, extracted from wool, used in ointments, cosmetics, waterproof coatings, etc. Also, **lan·o·line** (lan′l in, -l ēn′). Also called **wool fat.** [1880–85; < L *lān(a)* WOOL + -OL[2] + -IN[2]] **—lan·o·lat·ed** (lan′l ā′tid), *adj.*

la·nose (lā′nōs), *adj.* lanate. [1850–55; < L *lānōsus.* See LANI-, -OSE[1]] **—la·nos·i·ty** (lā nos′i tē), *n.*

la·nos·ter·ol (lə nos′tə rôl′, -rol′), *n. Biochem.* a sterol, $C_{30}H_{50}O$, formed from squalene epoxide, that is a precursor in the biosynthesis of cholesterol and is a component of lanolin. [1925–30; LANO(LIN) + STEROL]

La·nox·in (lə nok′sin), *Pharm., Trademark.* a brand of digoxin.

lan·sa (lan′sə), *n.* langsat. Also, **lan·sat** (lan′sət), **lan·seh** (lan′sə).

Lans·berg (lanz′bârg), *n.* a walled plain in the third quadrant of the face of the moon: about 29 miles (46 km) in diameter.

Lans·dale (lanz′dāl), *n.* a city in SE Pennsylvania. 16,526.

Lans·downe (lanz′doun), *n.* **1. Henry Charles Keith Pet·ty-Fitz·mau·rice,** (pet′ē fits môr′is, -mor′-), **5th Marquis of,** 1845–1927, British statesman: viceroy of India 1888–94, foreign secretary 1900–05. **2. William Petty Fitz·mau·rice** (fits môr′is, -mor′-), **2nd Earl of Shelburne, 1st Marquis of,** 1737–1805, British statesman: prime minister 1782–83. **3.** a city in SE Pennsylvania. 11,891.

Lan·sing (lan′sing), *n.* **1. Robert,** 1864–1928, U.S. lawyer and statesman: Secretary of State 1915–20. **2.** a city in and the capital of Michigan, in the S part. 130,414. **3.** a city in NE Illinois, near Chicago. 29,039.

lans·que·net (lans′kə net′), *n.* landsknecht. [< F < G *Landsknecht*]

lan·ta·na (lan tan′ə), *n.* any of numerous chiefly tropical plants belonging to the genus *Lantana,* of the verbena family, certain species of which, as *L. camara,* are cultivated for their aromatic flowers of yellow and orange or blue and violet. [1785–95; < NL < dial. It *lantana* wayfaring tree]

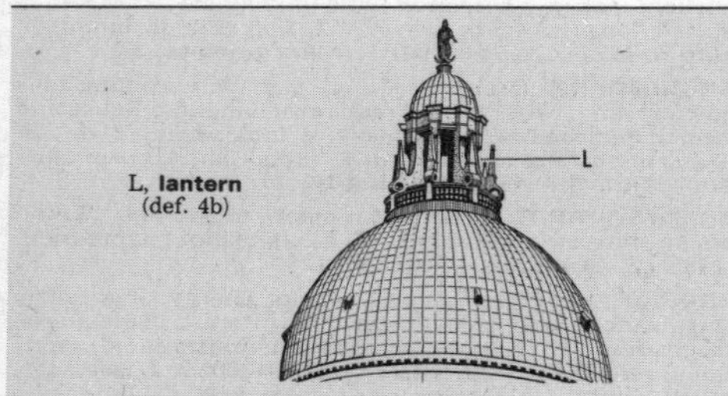

L, **lantern** (def. 4b)

lan·tern (lan′tərn), *n.* **1.** a transparent or translucent, usually portable, case for enclosing a light and protecting it from the wind, rain, etc. **2.** the chamber at the top of a lighthouse, surrounding the light. **3.** See **magic lantern. 4.** *Archit.* **a.** a tall, more or less open construction admitting light to an enclosed area below. **b.** any light, decorative structure of relatively small size crowning a roof, dome, etc. **c.** an open-sided structure on a roof to let out smoke or to assist ventilation. **5.** a light, usually over the entrance to an elevator on each floor of a multistory building, that signals the approach of the elevator. [1250–1300; ME *lanterne* < L *lanterna* (< Etruscan) < Gk *lamptḗr* lamp, light]

lan′tern clock′, an English bracket clock of the late 16th and 17th centuries, having a brass case with corner columns supporting pierced crestings on the sides and front. Also called **birdcage clock.** [1910–15]

CONCISE ETYMOLOGY KEY: <, descended or borrowed from; >, whence; b., blend of, blended; c., cognate with; cf., compare; deriv., derivative; equiv., equivalent; imit., imitative; obl., oblique; r., replacing; s., stem; sp., spelling, spelled; resp., respelling, respelled; trans., translation; ?, origin unknown; *, unattested; ‡, probably earlier than. See the full key inside the front cover.

lan·tern·fish (lan′tərn fish′), *n., pl.* (*esp. collectively*) **-fish,** (*esp. referring to two or more kinds of species*) **-fish·es.** any of several small, deep-sea fishes of the family Myctophidae, having rows of luminous organs along each side, certain species of which migrate to the surface at night. [1745–55; LANTERN + FISH]

lan·tern·fly (lan′tərn flī′), *n., pl.* **-flies.** any of several large tropical insects of the family Fulgoridae, formerly thought to be luminescent. [1745–55; LANTERN + FLY[2]]

lan′tern gear′, a gear mechanism including a lantern wheel.

lan′tern jaw′, 1. a distinctly protruding, often wide lower jaw. **2.** a long, thin jaw. [1690–1700; so called from the fancied resemblance of the face to the shape of a lantern]

lan·tern-jawed (lan′tərn jôd′), *adj.* having a lantern jaw. [1690–1700]

lan′tern ring′, *Mach.* gland[2] (def. 1).

lan′tern slide′, a slide or transparency for projection by a slide projector or magic lantern. [1870–75]

lan′tern wheel′, a wheel, used like a pinion, consisting essentially of two parallel disks or heads whose peripheries are connected by a series of bars that engage with the teeth of another wheel. Also called **lan′tern pin′ion, trundle.** [1785–95]

lan·tha·nide (lan′thə nīd′, -nid), *n. Chem.* any element of the lanthanide series. Also called **lan·tha·non** (lan′thə non′). [1925–30; LANTHAN(UM) + -IDE]

lan′thanide se′ries, *Chem.* the series of rare-earth elements of atomic numbers 57 through 71 (lanthanum through lutetium). [1940–45]

lan·tha·num (lan′thə nəm), *n. Chem.* a rare-earth, trivalent, metallic element, allied to aluminum, found in certain minerals, as monazite. *Symbol:* La; *at. wt.:* 138.91; *at. no.:* 57; *sp. gr.:* 6.15 at 20°C. [< NL (1841), equiv. to *lanthan-* (< Gk *lanthánein* to escape notice; referring to its position on the periodic table) + *-um,* var. of *-ium* -IUM]

lant·horn (lant′hôrn′, lan′tərn), *n. Archaic.* lantern. [1580–90; alter. by folk etym. (lanterns formerly had reflectors made of translucent sheets of horn)]

Lan·tsang (län′tsäng′), *n.* Chinese name of **Mekong.**

la·nu·gi·nose (lə no͞o′jə nōs′, -nyo͞o′-), *adj.* **1.** covered with lanugo, or soft, downy hairs. **2.** of the nature of down; downy. Also, **la·nu·gi·nous** (lə no͞o′jə nəs, -nyo͞o′-). [1685–95; < L *lānūginōsus* downy, woolly, equiv. to *lānūgin-* (s. of *lānūgō;* see LANUGO) + *-ōsus* -OSE[1]] **—la·nu′gi·nous·ness,** *n.*

la·nu·go (lə no͞o′gō, -nyo͞o′-), *n., pl.* **-gos.** *Biol.* a coat of delicate, downy hairs, esp. that with which the human fetus or a newborn infant is covered. [1670–80; < L *lānūgō* woolliness, down, deriv. of *lāna* WOOL]

lan·yard (lan′yərd), *n.* **1.** *Naut.* a short rope or wire rove through deadeyes to hold and tauten standing rigging. **2.** any of various small cords or ropes for securing or suspending something, as a whistle about the neck or a knife from one's belt. **3.** a cord with a small hook at one end, used in firing certain kinds of cannon. **4.** a colored, single-strand cord worn around the left shoulder by a member of a military unit awarded a foreign decoration. **5.** a white cord worn around the right shoulder, as by a military police officer, and secured to the butt of a pistol. Also, **laniard.** [1475–85; b. late ME *lanyer* (< MF *laniere,* OF *lasniere* thong, equiv. to *lasne* noose + *-iere,* fem of *-ier* -IER[2]) and YARD[1]]

Lan·zhou (län′jō′), *n. Pinyin.* a city in and the capital of Gansu province, in N China, on the Huang He. 1,450,000. Also, **Lanchou, Lanchow.**

Lao (lou), *n., pl.* **Laos** (louz), (*esp. collectively*) **Lao** for 1. **1.** a member of a people of Laos and northern Thailand. **2.** the language of these people, belonging to the Thai group of languages.

La·oag (lä wäg′), *n.* a seaport on NW Luzon, in the N Philippines. 69,648.

La·oc·o·ön (lā ok′ō on′), *n.* **1.** *Class. Myth.* a priest of Apollo at Troy who warned the Trojans of the Trojan Horse, and who, with his two sons, was killed by two huge serpents sent by Athena or Apollo. **2.** (*italics*) a late 2nd-century B.C. representation in marble of Laocoön and his sons struggling with the serpents: attributed to Agesander, Athenodorus, and Polydorus of Rhodes. Also, **La·oc′o·on′, Laokoön, Laokoon.**

La·od·a·mas (lā od′ə məs), *n. Class. Myth.* **1.** a son of Eteocles who defended Thebes against the Epigoni, killed Aegialeus, and was killed by Alcmaeon. **2.** (in the *Odyssey*) the son of Alcinous who, not recognizing Odysseus, challenged him to athletic contests when Odysseus landed in Phaeacia.

La·od·a·mi·a (lā od′ə mī′ə), *n. Class Myth.* **1.** a daughter of Acastus who committed suicide so that she could join her husband, Protesilaus, in the underworld. **2.** (in the *Iliad*) the mother, by Zeus, of Sarpedon.

La·od·i·ce (lā od′ə sē′), *n.* (in the *Iliad*) a daughter of Priam and Hecuba who chose to be swallowed up by the earth rather than live as a Greek concubine.

La·od·i·ce·a (lā od′ə sē′ə, lā′ə də-), *n.* ancient name of **Latakia.**

La·od·i·ce·an (lā od′ə sē′ən, lā′ə də-), *adj.* **1.** lukewarm or indifferent, esp. in religion, as were the early Christians of Laodicea. —*n.* **2.** a person who is lukewarm or indifferent, esp. in religion. [1605–15; LAODICE(A) + -AN]

Laoigh·is (lā′ish), *n.* a county in Leinster, in the central Republic of Ireland. 51,169; 623 sq. mi. (1615 sq. km). *County seat:* Port Laoighise. Also called **Leix.**

La·ok·o·ön (lā ok′ō on′), *n.* Laocoön. Also, **La·ok′o·on′.**

La·om·e·don (lā om′i don′), *n. Class. Myth.* a king of Troy and the father of Priam, for whom the walls of Troy were built by Apollo and Poseidon.

Laon (läɴ), *n.* a town in and the capital of Aisne, in N France, E of Paris. 30,168.

La·os (lä′ōs, lous, lā′os; *Fr.* lA ôs′), *n.* a country in SE Asia: formerly part of French Indochina. 2,900,000; 91,500 sq. mi. (236,985 sq. km). *Cap.:* Vientiane.

Lao She (lou′ shu′), *Pinyin, Wade-Giles.* (*Shu Qingchun, Shu Ch'ing-ch'un*) 1899–1966, Chinese novelist.

La·o·tian (lā ō′shən, lou′shən), *n.* **1.** a native or inhabitant of Laos. **2.** Lao. —*adj.* **3.** of or pertaining to Laos, its people, or their language. [< F *laotien;* see LAOS, -IAN]

Lao-tzu (lou′dzu′), *n.* **1.** (*Li Erh, Li Er*) 6th-century B.C. Chinese philosopher: reputed founder of Taoism. **2.** (*italics*) See **Tao Te Ching.** Also, **Lao-tse** (lou′dzu′); *Pinyin,* **Lao·zi** (lou′zœ′).

lap[1] (lap), *n.* **1.** the front part of the human body from the waist to the knees when in a sitting position. **2.** the part of the clothing that lies on the front portion of the body from the waist to the knees when one sits. **3.** a place, environment, or situation of rest or nurture: *the lap of luxury.* **4.** area of responsibility, care, charge, or control: *They dropped the problem right in his lap.* **5.** a hollow place, as a hollow among hills. **6.** the front part of a skirt, esp. as held up to contain something. **7.** a part of a garment that extends over another: *the lap of a coat.* **8.** a loose border or fold. [bef. 900; ME *lappe,* OE *læppa;* c. D *lap;* akin to G *lappen,* ON *leppr* rag, patch]

lap[2] (lap), *v.,* **lapped, lap·ping,** *n.* —*v.t.* **1.** to fold over or around something; wrap or wind around something: *to lap a bandage around one's finger.* **2.** to enwrap in something; wrap up; clothe. **3.** to envelop or enfold: *lapped in luxury.* **4.** to lay (something) partly over something underneath; lay (things) together, one partly over another; overlap. **5.** to lie partly over (something underneath). **6.** to get a lap or more ahead of (a competitor) in racing, as on an oval track. **7.** to cut or polish with a lap. **8.** to join, as by scarfing, to form a single piece with the same dimensions throughout. **9.** to change (cotton, wool, etc.) into a compressed layer or sheet. —*v.i.* **10.** to fold or wind around something. **11.** to lie partly over or alongside of something else. **12.** to lie upon and extend beyond a thing; overlap. **13.** to extend beyond a limit. —*n.* **14.** the act of lapping. **15.** the amount of material required to go around a thing once. **16.** a complete circuit of a course in racing or in walking for exercise: *to run a lap.* **17.** an overlapping part. **18.** the extent or amount of overlapping. **19.** a rotating wheel or disk holding an abrasive or polishing powder on its surface, used for gems, cutlery, etc. **20.** a compressed layer or sheet of cotton, wool, or other fibrous material usually wound on an iron rod or rolled into a cylindrical form for further processing during carding. [1250–1300; ME *lappen* to fold, wrap; c. D *lappen* to patch, mend; akin to LAP[1]]

lap[3] (lap), *v.,* **lapped, lap·ping,** *n.* —*v.t.* **1.** (of water) to wash against or beat upon (something) with a light, slapping or splashing sound: *Waves lapped the shoreline.* **2.** to take in (liquid) with the tongue; lick in: *to lap water from a bowl.* —*v.i.* **3.** to wash or move in small waves with a light, slapping or splashing sound: *The water lapped gently against the mooring.* **4.** to take up liquid with the tongue; lick up a liquid. **5. lap up, a.** *Informal.* to receive enthusiastically: *The audience lapped up his monologue.* **b.** to take in (all of a liquid) with the tongue; drink up: *The cat lapped up her milk and looked for more.* —*n.* **6.** the act of lapping liquid. **7.** the lapping of water against something. **8.** the sound of this: *the quiet lap of the sea on the rocks.* **9.** something lapped up, as liquid food for dogs. [bef. 1000; ME *lappen,* unexplained var. of *lapen,* OE *lapian;* c. MLG *lapen,* OHG *laffan;* akin to L *lambere,* Gk *láptein* to lick, lap]

lap[4] (lap), *v. Archaic.* pt. of **leap.**

la·pac·tic (lə pak′tik), *Med.* —*adj.* **1.** purgative; cathartic. —*n.* **2.** a lapactic agent; purgative. [1745–55; < Gk *lapaktikós* laxative, equiv. to *lapak-* (verbid s. of *lapássein* to evacuate) + *-tikos* -TIC]

La Pal·ma (lə päl′mə), a city in SW California. 15,663.

lapar-, var. of **laparo-** before a vowel: *laparectomy.*

lap·a·rec·to·my (lap′ə rek′tə mē), *n. Surg.* excision of strips of the abdominal wall and suturing of the wounds so as to correct laxity of the abdominal muscles. [1885–90; LAPAR- + -ECTOMY]

laparo-, a combining form borrowed from Greek, where it meant "flank," used with the meaning "abdominal wall" in the formation of compound words: *laparotomy.* Also, *esp. before a vowel,* **lapar-.** [comb. form repr. Gk *lapára* flank (lit., soft part), in use of fem. of *laparós* soft]

lap·a·ro·scope (lap′ər ə skōp′), *n. Surg.* a flexible fiberoptic instrument, passed through a small incision in the abdominal wall and equipped with biopsy forceps, an obturator, scissors or the like, with which to examine the abdominal cavity or perform minor surgery. [1850–55;

LAPARO- + -SCOPE] —**lap·a·ro·scop·ic** (lap′ər ə skop′ik), *adj.* —**lap·a·ros·co·pist** (lap′ə ros′kə pist), *n.*

lap·a·ros·co·py (lap′ə ros′kə pē), *n., pl.* **-pies.** *Surg.* examination of the abdominal cavity or performance of minor abdominal surgery using a laparoscope. [1850–55; LAPARO- + -SCOPY]

lap·ar·o·tome (lap′ər ə tōm′), *n. Surg.* a cutting instrument for performing a laparotomy. [1850–55; LAPARO- + -TOME]

lap·a·rot·o·mize (lap′ə rot′ə mīz′), *v.t.,* **-mized, -miz·ing.** *Surg.* to perform a laparotomy on. [LAPAROTOM(Y) + -IZE] —**lap′a·rot′o·mist,** *n.*

lap·a·rot·o·my (lap′ə rot′ə mē), *n., pl.* **-mies.** *Surg.* **1.** incision through the abdominal wall. **2.** incision into the loin, esp. for access to the abdominal cavity. [1875–80; LAPARO- + -TOMY]

La Paz (lä päs′; *Eng.* lə päz′), **1.** a city in and the administrative capital of Bolivia, in the W part; Sucre is the official capital. 660,700; ab. 12,000 ft. (3660 m) above sea level. **2.** a city in SE Lower California, in NW Mexico. 46,000.

lap′ belt′, (in a motor vehicle) a seat belt secured to the framework of a seat and fastening across the lap of a driver or a passenger. [1950–55]

lap·board (lap′bôrd′, -bōrd′), *n.* a thin, flat board to be held on the lap for use as a table or writing surface. [1830–40; LAP[1] + BOARD]

lap′ child′, *South Midland and Southern U.S.* a child who has not yet begun or has just begun to walk.

lap′ dissolve′, *Motion Pictures.* dissolve (def. 17).

lap′ dog′, a small pet dog that can easily be held in the lap. [1635–45]

lap′ dove′tail joint′. See **half-blind joint.**

la·pel (lə pel′), *n.* either of the two parts of a garment folded back on the chest, esp. a continuation of a coat collar. [1780–90; irreg. dim. of LAP[1]; see -LE] —**la·pelled′,** *adj.* —**la·pel′less,** *adj.*

lapel′ mike′, a small microphone that may be clipped to the speaker's lapel, pocket, or the like. Also called **lap microphone.** [1935–40]

La Pé·rouse (lȧ pā ro͞oz′), **Jean Fran·çois de Ga·laup** (zhäN fräN swȧ′ də gȧ lō′), 1741–88, French naval officer and explorer.

lap·ful (lap′fo͝ol), *n., pl.* **-fuls.** as much as the lap can hold. [1605–15; LAP[1] + -FUL]
—**Usage.** See **-ful.**

lap·i·dar·y (lap′i der′ē), *n., pl.* **-dar·ies,** *adj.* —*n.* **1.** Also, **lap·i·dist** (lap′i dist). a worker who cuts, polishes, and engraves precious stones. **2.** Also, **la·pid·ar·ist** (lə pid′ər ist). an expert in precious stones and the art or techniques used in cutting and engraving them. **3.** the art of cutting, polishing, and engraving precious stones. **4.** an old book on the lore of gems. —*adj.* Also, **lap·i·dar·i·an** (lap′i dâr′ē ən). **5.** of or pertaining to the cutting or engraving of precious stones. **6.** characterized by an exactitude and extreme refinement that suggests gem cutting: *a lapidary style; lapidary verse.* **7.** of, pertaining to, or suggestive of inscriptions on stone monuments. [1325–75; ME *lapidarie* (n.) < L *lapidārius* of stone (adj.), stone-cutter (n.), equiv. to *lapid-* (s. of *lapis*) stone + *-ārius* -ARY]

lap·i·date (lap′i dāt′), *v.t.,* **-dat·ed, -dat·ing. 1.** to pelt with stones. **2.** to stone to death. [1615–25; < L *lapidātus* ptp. of *lapidāre* to stone. See LAPIDARY, -ATE[1]] —**lap′i·da′tion,** *n.*

la·pid·i·fy (lə pid′ə fī′), *v.t., v.i.,* **-fied, -fy·ing.** *Archaic.* to turn into stone. [1650–60; ML *lapidi(ficātiō)* petrifaction (see LAPIDARY, -I-, -FICATION) + -FY] —**lap′·i·dif′i·cal,** *adj.* —**la·pid′i·fi·ca′tion,** *n.*

la·pil·lus (lə pil′əs), *n., pl.* **-pil·li** (-pil′ī). a small stony particle ejected from a volcano. [1740–50; < L: little stone, pebble, dim. of *lapis* stone]

lap·in (lap′in; *Fr.* lȧ paN′), *n., pl.* **lap·ins** (lap′inz; *Fr.* lȧ paN′). **1.** a rabbit. **2.** rabbit fur, esp. when trimmed and dyed. [1900–05; < F, MF, perh., by suffix alteration, from *laperean* rabbit < Ibero-Romance; cf. CONY]

lap·is (lap′is, lā′pis), *n., pl.* **lap·i·des** (lap′i dēz′). **1.** (*ital.*) *Latin.* stone (used in Latin names for minerals, gems, etc.) **2.** See **lapis lazuli.**

lap·is laz·u·li (lap′is laz′o͝o lē, -lī′, lazh′o͝o-, lazh′-o͞o-), **1.** a deep-blue mineral composed mainly of lazurite with smaller quantities of other minerals, used mainly as a gem or as a pigment. **2.** a sky-blue color; azure. Also called **lapis, lazuli.** [1350–1400; ME < ML, equiv. to L *lapis* stone + ML *lazulī*, gen. of *lazulum* lapis lazuli; see AZURE]

lap′ joint′, 1. Also called **plain lap.** a joint, as between two pieces of metal or timber, in which the pieces overlap without any change in form. **2.** any of various joints between two members, as timbers, in which an end or section of one is partly cut away to be overlapped by an end or section of the other, often so that flush surfaces result. —**lap′-joint′ed,** *adj.* [1815–25]

La·place (lȧ plȧs′), *n.* **Pierre Si·mon** (pyer sē mōN′) **Marquis de,** 1749–1827, French astronomer and mathematician.

Laplace′ equa′tion, *Math.* the second-order partial differential equation indicating that the Laplace operator operating on a given function results in zero. Cf. **harmonic** (def. 4c). [1835–45; after P. S. LAPLACE]

Laplace′ trans′form, *Math.* a map of a function, as a signal, defined esp. for positive real values, as a time greater than zero, into another domain where the function is represented as a sum of exponentials. Cf. **Fourier transform.** [1940–45; after P. S. LAPLACE]

Lap·land (lap′land′), *n.* a region in N Norway, N Sweden, N Finland, and the Kola Peninsula of the NW Soviet Union in Europe: inhabited by Lapps.

La Pla·ta (lä plä′tä), **1.** a seaport in E Argentina. 560,341. **2.** See **Plata, Río de la.**

lap′ link′, a chain link for joining two lengths of chain, having a split in one end so that it can be opened to receive other links and then closed again. Also called **monkey link.**

lap′ mi′crophone. See **lapel mike.**

La Porte (lə pôrt′, pōrt′), **1.** a city in NW Indiana. 21,796. **2.** a town in S Texas. 14,062.

Lapp (lap), *n.* **1.** Also called **Lap·land·er** (lap′lan′dər, -lən-). a member of a Finnic people of northern Norway, Sweden, Finland, and adjacent regions. **2.** Also called **Lappish.** any of the languages of the Lapps, closely related to Finnish. Also called **Sami.**

lap·page (lap′ij), *n. Law.* an overlapping of part or all of a piece of land claimed by one person on land claimed by another. [LAP[2] + -AGE]

Lap·peen·ran·ta (läp′pen rän tä), *n.* a city in SE Finland. 54,000.

lap·per[1] (lap′ər), *n.* a person or thing that laps liquid. [1600–10; LAP[3] + -ER[1]]

lap·per[2] (lap′ər), *v.i. Scot. and North Eng.* to clabber; curdle. [1805–15; Scots form of LOPPER[2]]

lap·pet (lap′it), *n.* **1.** a small lap, flap, or loosely hanging part, esp. of a garment or headdress. See illus. under **miter. 2.** a projecting, lobelike structure in certain invertebrate animals. **3.** *Ornith.* a wattle or other fleshy process on a bird's head. **4.** *Textiles.* **a.** a rack or bar containing needles, situated at the front of the reed, and used in the production of figured patterns. **b.** an ornamented fabric produced by lappet weaving. [1565–75; LAP[1] + -ET] —**lap′pet·ed,** *adj.*

lap′pet weav′ing, weaving into which an embroidered pattern produced by additional warp threads has been introduced with the aid of a lappet. [1860–65]

Lap·pish (lap′ish), *n.* **1.** Lapp (def. 2). —*adj.* **2.** Also, **Lap′pic.** of, pertaining to, or characteristic of Lapland or the Lapps. [1870–75; LAPP + -ISH[1]]

L'A·près-mi·di d'un Faune (*Fr.* lȧ pre mē dē dœN fōn′), a poem (1876) by Mallarmé: source of Debussy's musical composition *Prélude à l'Après-midi d'un Faune* (1892–94). English, ***The Afternoon of a Faun.***

lap′ robe′, a blanket, fur covering, or the like, used to cover one's lap or legs, as when sitting outdoors or riding in an open vehicle. [1865–70, *Amer.*]

laps·a·ble (lap′sə bəl), *adj.* liable to lapse. Also, **lapsible.** [1670–80; LAPSE + -ABLE]

Lap·sang (läp′säng′, lap′sang′), *adj.* noting a kind of souchong tea with a strong smoky flavor. [1875–80; orig. uncert.]

lapse (laps), *n., v.,* **lapsed, laps·ing.** —*n.* **1.** an accidental or temporary decline or deviation from an expected or accepted condition or state; a temporary falling or slipping from a previous standard: *a lapse of justice.* **2.** a slip or error, often of a trivial sort; failure: *a lapse of memory.* **3.** an interval or passage of time; elapsed period: *a lapse of ten minutes before the program resumed.* **4.** a moral fall, as from rectitude or virtue. **5.** a fall or decline to a lower grade, condition, or degree; descent; regression: *a lapse into savagery.* **6.** the act of falling, slipping, sliding, etc., slowly or by degrees. **7.** a falling into disuse. **8.** *Insurance.* discontinuance of coverage resulting from nonpayment of a premium; termination of a policy. **9.** *Law.* the termination of a right or privilege through neglect to exercise it or through failure of some contingency. **10.** *Meteorol.* See **lapse rate. 11.** *Archaic.* a gentle, downward flow, as of water. —*v.i.* **12.** to fall or deviate from a previous standard; fail to maintain a normative level: *Toward the end of the book the author lapsed into bad prose.* **13.** to come to an end; stop: *We let our subscription to that magazine lapse.* **14.** to fall, slip, or sink; subside: *to lapse into silence.* **15.** to fall into disuse: *The custom lapsed after a period of time.* **16.** to deviate or abandon principles, beliefs, etc.: *to lapse into heresy.* **17.** to fall spiritually, as an apostate: *to lapse from grace.* **18.** to pass away, as time; elapse. **19.** *Law.* to become void, as a legacy to someone who dies before the testator. **20.** to cease being in force; terminate: *Your insurance policy will lapse after 30 days.* [1520–30; < L *lāpsus* an error, slipping, failing, equiv. to *lāb(ī)* to slide, slip, fall, make a mistake + *-sus*, for *-tus* suffix of v. action] —**laps′er,** *n.*

lapsed (lapst), *adj.* **1.** expired; voided; terminated: *a lapsed insurance policy.* **2.** no longer committed to or following the tenets of a particular belief, obligation, position, etc.: *a lapsed Catholic.* [1610–20; LAPSE + -ED[2]]

lapse′ rate′, *Meteorol.* the rate of decrease of atmospheric temperature with increase of elevation vertically above a given location. [1915–20]

lap·si·ble (lap′sə bəl), *adj.* lapsable. [LAPSE + -IBLE]

lap-size (lap′sīz′), *adj.* of a size to fit the lap: *a lap-size chessboard.* Also, **lap′-sized′.**

lap·strake (lap′strāk′), *adj. Naut.* **1.** clinker-built (def. 2). —*n.* **2.** a vessel with a clinker-built hull. [1765–75, *Amer.*; LAP[2] + STRAKE]

lap·sus (lap′səs; *Lat.* läp′so͞os), *n.* a slip or lapse. [1660–70; < L *lāpsus*; see LAPSE]

lap·sus ca·la·mi (läp′so͞os kä′lä mē′; *Eng.* lap′səs kal′ə mī′, -mē′), *Latin.* a slip of the pen.

lap·sus lin·guae (läp′so͞os ling′gwī; *Eng.* lap′səs ling′gwē), *Latin.* a slip of the tongue.

Lap′tev Sea′ (lap′tef, -tev; *Russ.* lä′ptyif), an arm of the Arctic Ocean N of the Russian Federation in Asia, between Taimyr Peninsula and the New Siberian Islands. Also called **Nordenskjöld Sea.**

lap·top (lap′top′), *n.* a portable, usu. battery-powered microcomputer small enough to rest on the user's lap. [1980–85; LAP[1] + TOP[1]]

La Puen·te (lä pwen′tē, -tā), a city in SW California, E of Los Angeles. 30,882.

La·pu·ta (lə pyo͞o′tə), *n.* an imaginary flying island in Swift's *Gulliver's Travels*, the inhabitants of which engaged in a variety of ridiculous projects and pseudo-scientific experiments. —**La·pu′tan,** *adj., n.*

lap·wing (lap′wing′), *n.* **1.** a large Old World plover, *Vanellus vanellus*, having a long, slender, upcurved crest, an erratic, flapping flight, and a shrill cry. **2.** any of several similar, related plovers. [bef. 1050; ME, var. (by assoc. with WING) of *lapwinke*, OE *hlēapwince* plover. See LEAP, WINK]

la·que·us (lā′kwē əs, lak′wē-), *n., pl.* **la·que·i** (lā′kwē-ī′, -kwē ē′, lak′wē ī′, -wē ē′). *Anat.* lemniscus. [< L: noose]

L'Aq·ui·la (lä′kwē lä), *n.* Aquila.

lar (lär), *n., pl.* **lar·es** (lâr′ēz, lā′rēz) for 1, **lars** for 2. **1.** (*cap.*) *Rom. Religion.* any of the Lares. **2.** *Zool.* See **white-handed gibbon.** [1580–90; < L]

Lar·a·mie (lar′ə mē), *n.* **1.** a city in SE Wyoming. 24,410. **2. Fort.** See **Fort Laramie.**

Lar′amie Range′, a mountain range in N Colorado and SE Wyoming. Highest peak, Laramie Peak, 9020 ft. (2749 m).

la·rar·i·um (lə râr′ē əm), *n., pl.* **-rar·i·a** (-râr′ē ə). (in an ancient Roman home) a shrine for the Lares. [1700–10; < LL *larārium*; see LARES, -ARY]

la ra·za (lä rä′sä), (*sometimes caps.*) *Spanish.* **1.** (*used with a plural v.*) Mexican Americans collectively. **2.** (*used with a singular v.*) Mexican-American culture.

lar·board (lär′bôrd′, -bōrd′; *Naut.* lär′bərd), *Naut.* —*n.* **1.** (formerly) port[2] (def. 1). —*adj.* **2.** (formerly) port[2] (defs. 2, 3). [1300–50; ME *laddeborde* (perh. lit., loading side; see LADE, BOARD); later *larborde* (by analogy with *starboard*)]

lar·ce·ner (lär′sə nər), *n.* a person who commits larceny. Also, **lar′ce·nist.** [1625–35; LARCEN(Y) + -ER[1]]

lar·ce·nous (lär′sə nəs), *adj.* **1.** of, resembling, or characteristic of larceny. **2.** guilty of larceny. [1735–45; LARCEN(Y) + -OUS] —**lar′ce·nous·ly,** *adv.*

lar·ce·ny (lär′sə nē), *n., pl.* **-nies.** *Law.* the wrongful taking and carrying away of the personal goods of another from his or her possession with intent to convert them to the taker's own use. Cf. **grand larceny, petty larceny.** [1425–75; late ME < AF *larcin* theft (< L *latrōcinium* robbery, equiv. to *latrōcin(ārī)* to rob, orig. serve as mercenary soldier (deriv. of *latrō* hired soldier, robber) + *-ium* -IUM) + -Y[3]]

larch (lärch), *n.* **1.** any coniferous tree of the genus *Larix*, yielding a tough durable wood. **2.** the wood of such a tree. [1540–50; earlier *larche* < MHG << L *laric-* (s. of *larix*) larch] —**larch′en,** *adj.*

larch′ saw′fly, a red and black sawfly, *Pristiphora erichsonii*, the larvae of which infest and feed on the leaves of larch.

lard (lärd), *n.* **1.** the rendered fat of hogs, esp. the internal fat of the abdomen. —*v.t.* **2.** to apply lard or grease to. **3.** to prepare or enrich (lean meat, chicken, etc.) with pork or fat, esp. with lardons. **4.** to supplement or enrich with something for improvement or ornamentation: *a literary work larded with mythological allusions.* [1300–50; ME (v.), late ME (n.) < MF *larder* (v.), *lard* (n.) < L *lār(i)dum* bacon fat; akin to Gk *lārinós* fat (adj.)] —**lard′like′,** *adj.*

lar·da·ceous (lär dā′shəs), *adj.* lardlike; fatty. [1815–25; LARD + -ACEOUS]

lard·ass (lärd′as′), *n. Slang* (*vulgar*). **1.** a person having unusually large buttocks. **2.** any very fat person. Also, **lard′-ass′.** [LARD + ASS[2]]

lar·der (lär′dər), *n.* **1.** a room or place where food is kept; pantry. **2.** a supply of food. [1275–1325; ME < AF; OF *lardier*. See LARD, -ER[2]]

lar′der bee′tle, a black beetle, *Dermestes lardarius*, the larvae of which feed on dried meats, hides, furs, etc. [1865–70, *Amer.*]

Lard·ner (lärd′nər), *n.* **Ring(gold Wil·mer)** (ring′gōld′ wil′mər), 1885–1933, U.S. short-story writer and journalist.

lard′ oil′, a colorless or yellowish oil expressed from lard, used chiefly as a lubricant for cutting tools. [1835–45]

lar·don (lär′dn), *n.* a strip of fat used in larding, esp. as drawn through the substance of meat, chicken, etc., with a kind of needle or pin. Also, **lar·doon** (lär do͞on′). [1400–50; late ME *lardun* < MF *lardon* piece of pork, equiv. to *lard* LARD + *-on* n. suffix]

lard·y (lär′dē), *adj.,* **lard·i·er, lard·i·est. 1.** like or consisting of lard: *lardy pastry.* **2.** fat or becoming fat: *a diet designed for the lardy figure.* [1880–85; LARD + -Y[1]]

lar·dy-dar·dy (lär′dē där′dē), *adj. Chiefly Brit. Slang.* characterized by excessive elegance. [1860–65; after LA-DI-DA; for sp. with *r*, cf. ARVO]

CONCISE PRONUNCIATION KEY: act, cāpe, dâre, pärt; set, ēqual; *if*, īce; ox, ōver, ôrder, oil, bo͝ok, bo͞ot, out; up, ûrge; child; sing; shoe; thin, *th*at; zh as in *treasure*. ə = *a* as in *alone*, *e* as in *system*, *i* as in *easily*, *o* as in *gallop*, *u* as in *circus*; ə as in *fire* (fīər), *hour* (ouər). l and n can serve as syllabic consonants, as in *cradle* (krād′l), and *button* (but′n). See the full key inside the front cover.

La•re•do (lə rā′dō), *n.* a city in S Texas, on the Rio Grande. 91,449.

la•ree (lär′ē), *n.* lari.

Lar•es (lâr′ēz, lā′rēz), *n.pl., sing.* **Lar** (lär). *Rom. Religion.* the spirits who, if propitiated, watched over the house or community to which they belonged. Cf. **Penates.** [1590–1600; < L *Larēs*]

lar′es and pena′tes, 1. Lares and Penates, *Rom. Religion.* the benevolent spirits and gods of the household. **2.** the cherished possessions of a family or household. [1765–75; < L *Larēs (et) Penātēs*]

lar•gan•do (lär gän′dō; *It.* läʀ gän′dô), *adj. Music.* allargando. [1890–95; < It, prp. of *largare* < LL *largāre* to make broad; see LARGE]

large (lärj), *adj.,* **larg•er, larg•est,** *n., adv.* —*adj.* **1.** of more than average size, quantity, degree, etc.; exceeding that which is common to a kind or class; big; great: *a large house; a large number; in large measure; to a large extent.* **2.** on a great scale: *a large producer of kitchen equipment.* **3.** of great scope or range; extensive; broad. **4.** grand or pompous: *a man given to large, bombastic talk.* **5.** (of a map, model, etc.) representing the features of the original with features of its own that are relatively large so that great detail may be shown. **6.** famous; successful; important: *He's very large in financial circles.* **7.** *Obs.* generous; bountiful; lavish. **8.** *Obs.* **a.** unrestrained in the use of language; gross; improper. **b.** unrestrained in behavior or manner; uninhibited. **9.** *Naut.* free (def. 33). —*n.* **10.** *Music.* the longest note in mensural notation. **11.** *Obs.* generosity; bounty. **12. at large, a.** free from restraint or confinement; at liberty: *The murderer is still at large.* **b.** to a considerable extent; at length: *to treat a subject at large.* **c.** as a whole; in general: *the country at large.* **d.** Also, **at-large.** representing the whole of a state, district, or body rather than one division or part of it: *a delegate at large.* **13. in large,** on a large scale; from a broad point of view: *a problem seen in large.* Also, **in the large.** —*adv.* **14.** *Naut.* with the wind free or abaft the beam so that all sails draw fully. [1125–75; ME < OF < L *larga,* fem. of *largus* ample, generous] —**large′ness,** *n.*
—**Syn. 1.** huge, enormous, immense, gigantic, colossal; massive; vast. See **great.** —**Ant. 1.** small.

large′ cal′orie, *Thermodynam.* kilocalorie. [1925–30]

large′ cane′. See under **cane** (def. 5).

large′ cran′berry. See under **cranberry** (def. 1).

large•heart•ed (lärj′här′tid), *adj.* having or showing generosity; charitable; understanding. —**large′heart′•ed•ness,** *n.* [1635–45; LARGE + HEARTED]

large′ intes′tine, intestine (def. 3). [1855–60]

large′-leaved cu′cumber tree′ (lärj′lēvd′), a round-headed tree, *Magnolia macrophylla,* of the southeastern U.S., having soft, hairy leaves from 1 to 3 ft. (30 to 90 cm) long, fragrant, cup-shaped, creamy-white flowers with a purplish base which are from 10 to 12 in. (25 to 30 cm) wide, and rose-colored, round fruit. [1880–85, *Amer.*]

large•ly (lärj′lē), *adv.* **1.** to a great extent; in great part; generally; chiefly: *The plan depends largely on his willingness to cooperate. That is largely incorrect.* **2.** in great quantity; much. [1175–1225; ME; see LARGE, -LY]

Large′ Magellan′ic Cloud′, a satellite galaxy of our own Milky Way galaxy, appearing as a hazy cloud in the southern constellations Dorado and Mensa.

large-mind•ed (lärj′mīn′did), *adj.* having tolerant views or liberal ideas; broad-minded. —**large′-mind′•ed•ly,** *adv.* —**large′-mind′ed•ness,** *n.* [1715–25]

large•mouth bass (lärj′mouth′ bas′), a North American freshwater game fish, *Micropterus salmoides,* having an upper jaw extending behind the eye and a broad, dark, irregular stripe along each side of the body. Cf. **smallmouth bass.** See illus. under **bass.** Also, **large′-mouth bass′.** [1875–80, *Amer.*; LARGE + MOUTH]

large-print (lärj′print′), *adj.* set in a type size larger than normal for the benefit of persons with impaired vision: *large-print newspapers.* Also, **large′ print′, large-type** (lärj′tīp′). [1965–70]

larg•er-than-life (lär′jər thən līf′), *adj.* exceedingly imposing, impressive, or memorable, esp. in appearance or forcefulness: *a larger-than-life leader.* [1945–50]

large-scale (lärj′skāl′), *adj.* **1.** very extensive or encompassing; of great scope: *a large-scale business plan.* **2.** made to a large scale: *a large-scale map.* [1885–90]

large′-scale integra′tion, *Electronics.* See **LSI.**

lar•gess (lär jes′, lär′jis), *n.* **1.** generous bestowal of gifts. **2.** the gift or gifts, as of money, so bestowed. **3.** *Obs.* generosity; liberality. Also, **lar•gesse′.** [1175–1225; ME *largesse* < OF; see LARGE, -ICE]

lar•ghet•to (lär get′ō), *adj. adv., n., pl.* **-ghet•tos.** *Music.* —*adj., adv.* **1.** somewhat slow; not so slow as largo, but usually slower than andante. —*n.* **2.** a larghetto movement. [1715–25; < It, dim. of *largo* LARGO]

lar′ gib′bon. See **white-handed gibbon.** [1855–60; after the species name; see LAR]

larg•ish (lär′jish), *adj.* rather large. [1780–90; LARGE + -ISH[1]]

lar•go (lär′gō), *adj., adv., n., pl.* **-gos.** *Music.* —*adj., adv.* **1.** slow; in a broad, dignified style. —*n.* **2.** a largo movement. [1675–85; < It; see LARGE]

Lar•go (lär′gō), *n.* a town in W Florida. 58,977.

la•ri (lär′ē), *n., pl.* **-ri, -ris.** an aluminum coin and monetary unit of the Maldives, the 100th part of a rupee. Also, **laree.**

CONCISE ETYMOLOGY KEY: <, descended or borrowed from; >, whence; b., blend of, blended; c., cognate with; cf., compare; deriv., derivative; equiv., equivalent; imit., imitative; obl., oblique; r., replacing; s., stem; sp., spelling, spelled; resp., respelling, respelled; trans., translation; ?, origin unknown; *, unattested; ‡, probably earlier than. See the full key inside the front cover.

lar•i•at (lar′ē ət), *n.* **1.** a long, noosed rope used to catch horses, cattle, or other livestock; lasso. **2.** a rope used to picket grazing animals. [1825–35; < Sp *la reata* the RIATA]

lar•ine (lar′in), *adj.* **1.** characteristic of or resembling a gull. **2.** of or pertaining to the suborder Lari, family Laridae, comprising the gulls. [< NL *Larinae* name of the subfamily, equiv. to *Lar(us)* genus name (< Gk *láros* a sea bird, a kind of gull) + *-inae* -INE[1]]

La Rio•ja (lä ʀyô′hä), a city in W Argentina. 66,826.

La•ris•sa (lə ris′ə; *Gk.* lä′ʀē sä), *n.* a city in E Thessaly, in E Greece. 72,000. Also, **La′ri•sa.**

la•rith•mics (lə rith′miks), *n.* (*used with a singular v.*) the study of quantitative relations in population aggregates. [< Gk *lā(ós)* people + *(a)rithm(ós)* number + -ICS] —**la•rith′mic,** *adj.*

lar′ix•in′ic ac′id (lâr′ik sin′ik, lâr′-), *Chem.* maltol. [< NL *Larix (decidua)* genus of larch tree + -IN[2] + -IC]

lark[1] (lärk), *n.* **1.** any of numerous, chiefly Old World oscine birds, of the family Alaudidae, characterized by an unusually long, straight hind claw, esp. the skylark, *Alauda arvensis.* **2.** any of various similar birds of other families, as the meadowlark and titlark. [bef. 900; ME *larke,* OE *lāwerce;* c. G *Lerche,* D *leeuwerik,* ON *lǣvirki*]

lark[2] (lärk), *n.* **1.** a merry, carefree adventure; frolic; escapade. **2.** innocent or good-natured mischief; a prank. **3.** something extremely easy to accomplish, succeed in, or to obtain: *That exam was a lark.* —*v.i.* **4.** to have fun; frolic; romp. **5.** to behave mischievously; play pranks. **6.** *Fox Hunting.* (of a rider) to take jumps unnecessarily: *He tired his horse by larking on the way home.* [1805–15; orig. uncert.] —**lark′er,** *n.* —**lark′i•ness, lark′ish•ness,** *n.* —**lark′ing•ly,** *adv.* —**lark′ish, lark′y,** *adj.* —**lark′ish•ly,** *adv.* —**lark′some,** *adj.*

lark′ bun′ting, a finch, *Calamospiza melanocorys,* of the western U.S., the male of which is black with a large, white patch on each wing. [1830–40, *Amer.*]

lark′ spar′row, a North American sparrow, *Chondestes grammacus,* having a distinctive brown-and-white facial pattern. [1885–90, *Amer.*]

lark•spur (lärk′spûr′), *n.* any of several plants belonging to the genera *Delphinium* and *Consolida,* of the buttercup family, characterized by the spur-shaped formation of the calyx and petals. [1570–80; LARK[1] + SPUR]

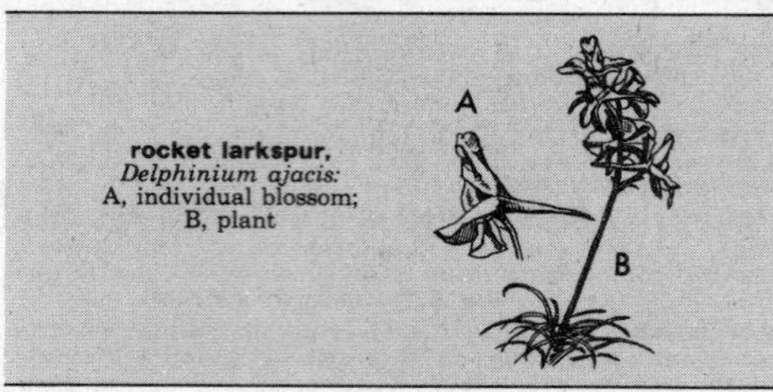

rocket larkspur, *Delphinium ajacis:* A, individual blossom; B, plant

Lark•spur (lärk′spûr′), *n.* a town in W California. 11,064.

lar•men (lär′mən), *n. Japanese Cookery.* ramen. [perh. < Chin *lāmiàn;* see RAMEN]

Lar′mor preces′sion (lär′môr), *Physics.* the precession of charged particles, as electrons, placed in a magnetic field, the frequency of the precession (**Lar′mor fre′quency**) being equal to the electronic charge times the strength of the magnetic field divided by 4π times the mass. [1925–30; named after Sir Joseph *Larmor* (1857–1942), English mathematician]

Lar′mor the′orem, *Physics.* the theorem that an electron subjected only to the force exerted by the nucleus about which it is moving will undergo Larmor precession but no other change in motion when placed in a magnetic field. [1920–25; see LARMOR PRECESSION]

La Roche•fou•cauld (lᴀ rôsh fo͞o kō′), **Fran•çois** (fʀäɴ swᴀ′), **6th Duc de,** 1613–80, French moralist and composer of epigrams and maxims.

La Ro•chelle (lᴀ ʀô shel′), a seaport in and the capital of Charente Maritime, in W France; besieged while a Huguenot stronghold 1627–29. 77,494.

La•Rouche (lə ro͞osh′), *n.* **Lyndon H., Jr.,** born 1922, U.S. economist and politician. —**La•Rouch′i•an,** *n., adj.*

La•rousse (lᴀ ʀo͞os′; *Eng.* lə ro͞os′), *n.* **Pierre A•tha•nase** (pyeʀ ᴀ tᴀ näz′), 1817–75, French grammarian, lexicographer, and encyclopedist.

lar•ri•gan (lar′i gən), *n.* a knee-high boot of oiled leather with a moccasin foot, worn by lumbermen and trappers. [1885–90; orig. uncert.]

lar•ri•kin (lar′i kin), *Australian Slang.* —*n.* **1.** a street rowdy; hoodlum. —*adj.* **2.** disorderly; rowdy. [1865–70; orig. uncert.] —**lar′ri•kin•ism,** *n.*

Lar•ro•cha (läʀ rô′chä), *n.* **A•li•cia de** (ä lē′thyä the, -syä), born 1923, Spanish concert pianist.

lar•rup (lar′əp), *v.t.,* **-ruped, -rup•ing.** to beat or thrash. [1815–25; perh. < D *larpen* to thresh with flails] —**lar′rup•er,** *n.*

lar•rup•ing (lar′ə ping), *adv. Chiefly Western U.S.* very; exceedingly: *That was a larruping good meal.* [1900–05, *Amer.*; LARRUP + -ING[2]]

lar•ry[1] (lar′ē), *n., pl.* **-ries.** a hoe with a perforated blade for mixing mortar or plaster. [1850–55; of obscure orig.]

lar•ry[2] (lar′ē), *n., pl.* **-ries.** See **larry car.**

Lar•ry (lar′ē), *n.* a male given name, form of **Lawrence, Laurence.**

lar′ry car′, *Metall.* a car moving on rails and equipped on its underside with a hopper, used to charge coke ovens from above. Also called **larry.** [akin to LORRY]

Lars (lärz; *Swed., Nor.* läʀs), *n.* a male given name, form of **Lawrence.**

Lar•sa (lär′sə), *n.* an ancient Sumerian city in southern Iraq: archaeological site.

Lar′sen Ice′ Shelf′ (lär′sən), an ice barrier in Antarctica, in the NW Weddell Sea, on the E coast of the Antarctic Peninsula: first explored 1893.

Lar•tigue (lᴀʀ tēg′), *n.* **Jacques Hen•ri** (zhäk äɴ ʀē′), 1894–1986, French photographer and painter.

lar•um (lar′əm), *n.* alarum.

lar•va (lär′və), *n., pl.* **-vae** (-vē). **1.** *Entomol.* the immature, wingless, feeding stage of an insect that undergoes complete metamorphosis. See illus. under **metamorphosis. 2.** any animal in an analogous immature form. **3.** the young of any invertebrate animal. **4. larvae,** *Rom. Antiq.* malignant ghosts, as lemures. [1645–55; < NL; special use of L *larva* a ghost, specter, mask, skeleton; akin to LARES]

lar•val (lär′vəl), *adj.* **1.** of, pertaining to, or in the form of a larva. **2.** Also, **lar•vate** (lär′vāt). (of a disease) masked; not clearly defined. [1650–60; < L *larvālis.* See LARVA, -AL[1]]

lar•vi•cide (lär′və sīd′), *n.* an agent for killing larvae. [1895–1900; LARV(A) + -I- + -CIDE] —**lar′vi•cid′al,** *adj.*

lar•vip•a•rous (lär vip′ər əs), *adj. Zool.* producing larvae, as certain insects and mollusks. [1805–15; LARV(A) + -I- + -PAROUS]

lar•viv•o•rous (lär viv′ər əs), *adj.* larva-eating. [LARV(A) + -I- + -VOROUS]

laryng-, var. of **laryngo-** before a vowel: *laryngectomy.*

la•ryn•ge•al (lə rin′jē əl, lar′ən jē′əl), *adj.* **1.** of, pertaining to, or located in the larynx. **2.** *Phonet.* articulated in the larynx. —*n.* **3.** *Phonet.* a laryngeal sound. **4.** *Historical Ling.* one of several hypothetical phonemes assumed to have existed in Proto-Indo-European and to have been lost in most later Indo-European languages after having modified some contiguous consonants and vowels. Also, **la•ryn•gal** (lə ring′gəl). [1785–95; < NL *larynge(us)* of, pertaining to the larynx (see LARYNG-, -EOUS) + -AL[1]] —**la•ryn′ge•al•ly,** *adv.*

la•ryn•ge•al•ize (lə rin′jē ə līz′, -jə līz′, lar′ən jē′ə-līz′), *v.t.,* **-ized, -iz•ing.** to pronounce with accompanying constriction of the larynx. Also, *esp. Brit.,* **la•ryn′•ge•al•ise′.** [LARYNGEAL + -IZE] —**la•ryn′ge•al•i•za′tion,** *n.*

lar•yn•gec•to•my (lar′ən jek′tə mē), *n., pl.* **-mies.** *Surg.* excision of part or all of the larynx. [1885–90; LARYNG- + -ECTOMY]

lar•yn•gi•tis (lar′ən jī′tis), *n. Pathol.* inflammation of the larynx, often with accompanying sore throat, hoarseness or loss of voice, and dry cough. [1815–25; LARYNG- + -ITIS] —**lar•yn•git•ic** (lar′ən jit′ik), *adj.*

laryngo-, a combining form representing **larynx** in compound words: *laryngotomy.* Also, *esp. before a vowel,* **laryng-.** [comb. form repr. NL *larynx,* Gk *lárynx* (s. *laryng-*) LARYNX; see -O-]

lar•yn•gol•o•gy (lar′ing gol′ə jē), *n.* the branch of medicine dealing with the larynx. [1835–45; LARYNGO- + -LOGY] —**la•ryn•go•log•i•cal** (lə ring′gə loj′i kəl), **la•ryn′go•log′ic,** *adj.* —**lar′yn•gol′o•gist,** *n.*

la•ryn•go•pha•ryn•ge•al (lə ring′gō fə rin′jē əl, -jəl, -far′in jē′əl), *adj.* of, pertaining to, or involving the larynx and pharynx. [1870–75; LARYNGO- + PHARYNGEAL]

la•ryn•go•phar•ynx (lə ring′gō far′ingks), *n., pl.* **-pha•ryn•ges** (-fə rin′jēz), **-phar•ynx•es.** *Anat.* the lower part of the pharynx, above the larynx. [1895–1900; LARYNGO- + PHARYNX]

la•ryn•go•scope (lə ring′gə skōp′), *n. Med.* a rigid or flexible endoscope passed through the mouth and equipped with a source of light and magnification, for examining and performing local diagnostic and surgical procedures on the larynx. [1855–60; LARYNGO- + -SCOPE] —**la•ryn•go•scop•ic** (lə ring′gə skop′ik), *adj.* —**la•ryn•gos•co•pist** (lar′ing gos′kə pist), *n.*

lar•yn•gos•co•py (lar′ing gos′kə pē), *n., pl.* **-pies.** *Med.* an examination by means of a laryngoscope. [1860–65; LARYNGO- + -SCOPY]

lar•yn•got•o•my (lar′ing got′ə mē), *n., pl.* **-mies.** *Surg.* incision of the larynx. [1655–65; LARYNGO- + -TOMY]

la•ryn•go•tra•che•al (lə ring′gō trā′kē əl), *adj.* of, pertaining to, or involving the larynx and trachea. [1875–80; LARYNGO- + TRACHEAL]

lar•ynx (lar′ingks), *n., pl.* **la•ryn•ges** (lə rin′jēz), **lar•ynx•es. 1.** *Anat.* a muscular and cartilaginous structure lined with mucous membrane at the upper part of the trachea in humans, in which the vocal cords are located. **2.** *Zool.* **a.** a similar vocal organ in other mammals. **b.** a corresponding structure in certain lower animals. [1570–80; < NL < Gk *lárynx*]

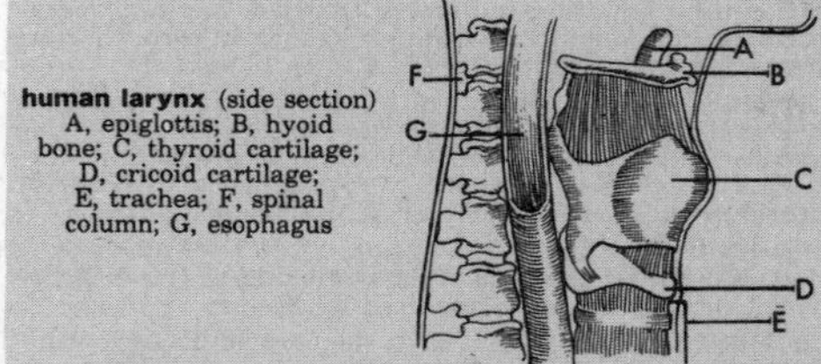

human larynx (side section) A, epiglottis; B, hyoid bone; C, thyroid cartilage; D, cricoid cartilage; E, trachea; F, spinal column; G, esophagus

La•sa (lä′sə, -sä, las′ə), *n. Pinyin, Wade-Giles.* Lhasa.

la•sa•gna (lə zän′yə, lä-), *n.* **1.** large, flat, rectangular strips of pasta. **2.** a baked dish consisting of layers of this pasta, cheese, tomato sauce, and usually meat. Also, **la•sa′gne.** [1840–50; < It < VL **lasania* cooking pot (hence, appar., the contents of the pot), for L *lasanum, lasanus* chamber pot < Gk *lásana* (pl.), orig., trivet or stand for a pot]

La Salle (lə sal′; *for 1, 2 also Fr.* LA SAL′), **1. (Re•né) Ro•bert Ca•ve•lier** (RƏ nā′ RÔ BER′ KA və lyā′), **Sieur de,** 1643–87, French explorer of North America. **2.** a city in S Quebec, in E Canada: suburb of Montreal. 76,299. **3.** a city in N Illinois. 10,347.

las•car (las′kər), *n.* **1.** an East Indian sailor. **2.** *Anglo-Indian.* an artilleryman. Also, **lashkar.** [1615–25; < Pg, short for *lasquarin* soldier < Urdu *lashkarī* < Pers, equiv. to *lashkar* army + *-ī* suffix of appurtenance]

Las Ca•sas (läs kä′säs), **Bar•to•lo•mé de** (bär′tô lô-me′ the), 1474–1566, Spanish Dominican missionary and historian in the Americas.

Las•caux′ Cave′ (LAS kō′), a cave in Lascaux, France, discovered in 1940 and containing exceptionally fine Paleolithic wall paintings and engravings thought to date to Magdalenian times (c13,000–8500 B.C.).

las•civ•i•ous (lə siv′ē əs), *adj.* **1.** inclined to lustfulness; wanton; lewd: *a lascivious, girl-chasing old man.* **2.** arousing sexual desire: *lascivious photographs.* **3.** indicating sexual interest or expressive of lust or lewdness: *a lascivious gesture.* [1400–50; late ME < L *lascīvi(a)* playfulness, wantonness (*lascīv(us)* playful, wanton + *-ia* -IA) + -OUS] **—las•civ′i•ous•ly,** *adv.* **—las•civ′i•ous•ness,** *n.*

Las Cru•ces (läs kro͞o′sis), a city in S New Mexico, on the Rio Grande. 45,086.

lase (lāz), *v.i.,* **lased, las•ing.** *Optics.* to give off coherent light, as in a laser. [1960–65; back formation from LASER]

la•ser (lā′zər), *n. Physics.* a device that produces a nearly parallel, nearly monochromatic, and coherent beam of light by exciting atoms to a higher energy level and causing them to radiate their energy in phase. Also called **optical maser.** [1955–60; *l(ightwave) a(mplification by) s(timulated) e(mission of) r(adiation)*]

la′ser beam′, a beam of radiation produced from a laser, used in surgery, communications, weapons systems, printing, recording and various industrial processes. [1960–65]

la′ser chem′istry, the use of a laser to initiate and control chemical reactions. [1975–80]

la′ser disk′, *Computers, Television.* See **optical disk.** [1980–85]

La Se•re•na (lä se RE′nä), a seaport in central Chile. 71,898.

la′ser print′er, *Computers.* a high-speed printer that uses a laser to form dot-matrix patterns and an electrostatic process to fuse metallic particles to paper a page at a time: capable of producing a variety of character fonts, graphics, and other symbols. **—la′ser print′ing.**

la•ser•scope (lā′zər skōp′), *n.* a surgical instrument that employs a laser beam to destroy diseased tissue or to create small channels; used to open clogged arteries and, in ophthalmology, to treat patients with glaucoma or diabetic retinopathy. [LASER + -SCOPE]

la′ser sur′gery, the surgical use of lasers. [1965–70]

lash[1] (lash), *n.* **1.** the flexible part of a whip; the section of cord or the like forming the extremity of a whip. **2.** a swift stroke or blow, with a whip or the like, given as a punishment: *He received 20 lashes.* **3.** something that goads or pains in a manner compared to that of a whip: *the lash of his sharp tongue.* **4.** a swift dashing or sweeping movement, as of an animal's tail; switch. **5.** a violent beating or impact, as of waves or rain, against something. **6.** an eyelash. **7.** Also called **neck cord.** a cord or a series of cords for lifting the warp in weaving a figured fabric. **—***v.t.* **8.** to strike or beat, as with a whip or something similarly slender and flexible. **9.** to beat violently or sharply against: *The rain lashed the trees.* **10.** to drive by or as if by strokes of a whip: *He lashed them on to greater effort.* **11.** to attack, scold, or punish severely with words: *She lashed the students with harsh criticism.* **12.** to dash, fling, or switch suddenly and swiftly: *The crocodile lashed its tail.* **—***v.i.* **13.** to strike vigorously at someone or something, as with a weapon or whip (often fol. by *out*): *He lashed wildly at his attackers.* **14.** to attack someone or something with harsh words (often fol. by *out*): *to lash out at injustice.* **15.** to move suddenly and swiftly; rush, dash, or flash: *The coiled snake lashed suddenly.* **16.** *Chiefly Brit.* to spend money lavishly or foolishly (usually fol. by *out*). [1300–50; ME *lashe* (n.), *lashen* (v.); perh. of expressive orig.] **—lash′er,** *n.* **—lash′ing•ly,** *adv.* **—lash′less,** *adj.*
—Syn. 14. berate, scold, tongue-lash.

lash[2] (lash), *v.t.* to bind or fasten with a rope, cord, or the like. [1400–50; late ME *lasschyn,* prob. < MD or LG; cf. MD *lasche* patch, gusset, D *laschen* to patch, scarf] **—lash′er,** *n.* **—lash′ing•ly,** *adv.*
—Syn. tie, secure, rope, truss.

LASH (lash), *n.* an ocean-going vessel equipped with special cranes and holds for lifting and stowing cargo-carrying barges that can be sailed up inland waterways or into port facilities from offshore. [1960–65; *l(ighter) a(board) sh(ip)*]

lashed (lasht), *adj.* having lashes or eyelashes, esp. of a specified kind or description (usually used in combination): *long-lashed blue eyes.* [1770–80; LASH[1] + -ED[3]]

lash•ing[1] (lash′ing), *n.* **1.** the act of a person or thing that lashes. **2.** a whipping with or as if with a lash. **3.** a severe scolding; tongue-lashing. [1350–1400; ME; see LASH[1], -ING[1]]

lash•ing[2] (lash′ing), *n.* **1.** a binding or fastening with a rope or the like. **2.** the rope or the like used. [1660–70; LASH[2] + -ING[1]]

lash•ings (lash′ingz), *n.* (*used with a plural v.*) *Chiefly Brit. Informal.* an abundance; plenty (usually fol. by *of*): *strawberries with lashings of cream.* [1820–30; LASH[1] (def. 16) + -ING[1] + -S[3]]

Lash•io (läsh′yō), *n.* a town in N Burma (Myanmar), NE of Mandalay: the SW terminus of the Burma Road.

lash•kar (lash′kər), *n.* lascar.

Lash•kar (lush′kər), *n.* the modern part of Gwalior city in N India: capital of former Gwalior state.

lash′ line′, a rope or cord for lashing together the edges of two flats or other pieces of theatrical scenery. [1930–35]

lash′ rail′, *Naut.* a rail, solidly fixed to the bulwarks of a vessel, to which objects on deck can be lashed.

lash•up (lash′up′), *n. Informal.* **1.** a hastily made or arranged device, organization, etc. **2.** any improvised arrangement. Also, **lash′-up′.** [1895–1900; n. use of v. phrase *lash up*]

las•ing (lā′zing), *n. Optics.* the generation of coherent light by a laser. [LASE + -ING[1]]

Las•ker (läs′kər), *n.* **E•ma•nu•el** (ā mä′no͞o el), 1868–1941, German chess player, mathematician, and author.

Las•ki (las′kē), *n.* **Harold Joseph,** 1893–1950, English political scientist and writer.

Las Pal•mas (läs päl′mäs), a seaport on NE Gran Canaria, in the central Canary Islands. 287,038.

La Spe•zia (lä spe′tsyä), a seaport in NW Italy, on the Ligurian Sea: naval base. 120,717.

lass (las), *n.* **1.** a girl or young woman, esp. one who is unmarried. **2.** a female sweetheart: *a young lad and his lass.* [1250–1300; ME *las, lasse,* of uncert. orig.]

Las•sa (lä′sə, -sä, las′ə), *n. Older Spelling.* Lhasa.

Las′sa fe′ver (lä′sə), *Pathol.* a highly contagious viral disease, largely confined to central West Africa, characterized by fever, difficulty in swallowing, and inflammation of the pharynx, often progressing to infect the lungs, heart, and kidneys, leading to death. [1965–70; after *Lassa,* Nigeria, village where it was first identified]

Las•salle (lə sal′; *Ger.* lä säl′), *n.* **Fer•di•nand** (fûr′dn-and′; *Ger.* feR′di nänt′), 1825–64, German socialist and writer.

Las′sen Peak′ (las′ən), an active volcano in N California, in the S Cascade Range. 10,465 ft. (3190 m). Also called **Mount Lassen.**

Las′sen Volcan′ic Na′tional Park′, a national park in N California, in the S Cascade Range, including Lassen Peak. 163 sq. mi. (422 sq. km).

las•sie (las′ē), *n.* a young girl; lass. [1715–25; LASS + -IE]

las•si•tude (las′i to͞od′, -tyo͞od′), *n.* **1.** weariness of body or mind from strain, oppressive climate, etc.; lack of energy; listlessness; languor. **2.** a condition of indolent indifference: *the pleasant lassitude of the warm summer afternoon.* [1525–35; < L *lassitūdō* weariness, equiv. to *lass(us)* weary + *-i-* -I- + *-tūdō* -TUDE]

las•so (las′ō, la so͞o′), *n., pl.* **-sos, -soes,** *v.,* **-soed, -so•ing.** **—***n.* **1.** a long rope or line of hide or other material with a running noose at one end, used for roping horses, cattle, etc. **—***v.t.* **2.** to catch with or as with a lasso. [1760–70; < Sp *lazo* < L *laqueus* noose, bond; see LACE] **—las′so•er,** *n.*

last[1] (last, läst), *adj. a superl. of* **late** *with* **later** *as compar.* **1.** occurring or coming after all others, as in time, order, or place: *the last line on a page.* **2.** most recent; next before the present; latest: *last week; last Friday.* **3.** being the only one remaining: *my last dollar; the last outpost; a last chance.* **4.** final: *in his last hours.* **5.** ultimate or conclusive; definitive: *the last word in the argument.* **6.** lowest in prestige or importance: *last prize.* **7.** coming after all others in suitability or likelihood; least desirable: *He is the last person we'd want to represent us.* **8.** individual; single: *The lecture won't start until every last person is seated.* **9.** utmost; extreme: *the last degree of delight.* **10.** *Eccles.* (of the sacraments of penance, viaticum, or extreme unction) extreme or final; administered to a person dying or in danger of dying. **—***adv.* **11.** after all others; latest: *He arrived last at the party.* **12.** on the most recent occasion: *When last seen, the suspect was wearing a checked suit.* **13.** in the end; finally; in conclusion. **—***n.* **14.** a person or thing that is last. **15.** a final appearance or mention: *We've seen the last of her. That's the last we'll hear of it.* **16.** the end or conclusion: *We are going on vacation the last of September.* **17. at last,** after a lengthy pause or delay: *He was lost in thought for several minutes, but at last he spoke.* **18. at long last,** after much troublesome or frustrating delay: *The ship docked at long last.* **19. breathe one's last,** to die: *He was nearly 90 when he breathed his last.* [bef. 900; ME *last, latst,* syncopated var. of *latest,* OE *latest, lætest,* superl. of *læt,* LATE]
—Syn. 1. LAST, FINAL, ULTIMATE refer to what comes as an ending. That which is LAST comes or stands after all others in a stated series or succession; LAST may refer to objects or activities: *a seat in the last row; the last game.* That which is FINAL comes at the end, or serves to end or terminate, admitting of nothing further; FINAL is rarely used of objects: *to make a final attempt.* That which is ULTIMATE (literally, most remote) is the last that can be reached, as in progression or regression, experience, or a course of investigation: *ultimate truths.*

last[2] (last, läst), *v.i.* **1.** to go on or continue in time: *The festival lasted three weeks.* **2.** to continue unexpended or unexhausted; be enough: *We'll enjoy ourselves while our money lasts.* **3.** to continue in force, vigor, effectiveness, etc.: *to last for the whole course.* **4.** to continue or remain in usable condition for a reasonable period of time: *They were handsome shoes but they didn't last.* **—***v.t.* **5.** to continue to survive for the duration of (often fol. by *out*): *They lasted the war in Switzerland.* [bef. 900; ME *lasten,* OE *lǣstan* to follow (lit., go in the tracks of), perform, continue, last; c. G *leisten* to follow, Goth *laistjan.* See LAST[3]]
—Syn. 1. See **continue.**

last[3] (last, läst), *n.* **1.** a wooden or metal form in the shape of the human foot on which boots or shoes are shaped or repaired. **2.** the shape or form of a shoe. **3. stick to one's last,** to keep to that work, field, etc., in which one is competent or skilled. **—***v.t.* **4.** to shape on or fit to a last. [bef. 900; ME *lest(e), last(e),* OE *lǣste;* c. G *Leisten;* akin to OE *lāst,* Goth *laists* track] **—last′•er,** *n.*

last[4] (last, läst), *n.* any of various large units of weight or capacity, varying in amount in different localities and for different commodities, often equivalent to 4000 pounds (1814.37 kilograms). [bef. 900; ME; OE *hlæst;* c. D *last,* G *Last* load; akin to LADE]

last-born (last′bôrn′, läst′-), *adj.* **1.** last in order of birth; youngest. **—***n.* **2.** a last-born or youngest child. [1865–70]

last-ditch (last′ditch′, läst′-), *adj.* **1.** done finally in desperation to avoid defeat, failure, disaster, etc.: *a last-ditch attempt to avert war.* **2.** fought with every resource at one's command: *a last-ditch battle for the pennant.* [1905–10; LAST[1] + DITCH] **—last′-ditch′er,** *n.*

Las•tex (las′teks), *Trademark.* a brand of yarn made from a core of latex rubber covered with fabric strands.

Last′ Gos′pel, *Rom. Cath. Ch.* in the order of service for the Mass, the final reading of a Gospel lesson.

last′ hurrah′, **1.** a politician's final campaign. **2.** any final attempt, competition, performance, success, or the like: *his last hurrah as a college football star.* [from *The Last Hurrah,* a novel (1956) by U.S. author Edwin O'Connor (1918–68)]

last-in, first-out (last′in′, fûrst′out′, läst′-), **1.** an inventory plan based on the assumption that materials constituting manufacturing costs should be carried on the books at the market price of the last lot received. *Abbr.:* LIFO Cf. **first-in, first-out. 2.** *Computers.* See **LIFO** (def. 2). [1935–40]

last•ing (las′ting, lä′sting), *adj.* **1.** continuing or enduring a long time; permanent; durable: *a lasting friendship.* **—***n.* **2.** a strong, durable, closely woven fabric for shoe uppers, coverings on buttons, etc. **3.** *Archaic.* the quality of surviving or continuing and maintaining strength, effectiveness, etc. [1125–75 for def. 1; 1775–85 for def. 2; ME (adj.). See LAST[2], -ING[2]] **—last′ing•ly,** *adv.* **—last′ing•ness,** *n.*

Last′ Judg′ment, judgment (def. 8). [1550–60]

last•ly (last′lē, läst′-), *adv.* in conclusion; in the last place; finally. [1325–75; ME *lestely.* See LAST[1], -LY]

last′ mile′, the distance walked by a condemned person from his or her cell to the place of execution.

last′ min′ute (min′it), the time just preceding a deadline or when some decisive action must be taken. [1915–20] **—last′-min′ute,** *adj.*

last′ name′, surname (def. 1). [1895–1900]

Last′ of the Mohi′cans, The, a historical novel (1826) by James Fenimore Cooper. Cf. ***Leather-Stocking Tales.***

last′ post′. See under **post[2]** (def. 7).

last′ quar′ter, *Astron.* the instant, approximately one week after a full moon, when half of the moon's disk is illuminated by the sun. See diag. under **moon.**

last′ rites′, *Rom. Cath. Ch.* See **anointing of the sick.** [1925–30]

last′ straw′, the last of a succession of irritations, incidents, remarks, etc., that leads to a loss of patience, a disaster, etc.: *He has been late before, but this is the last straw.* [1840–50; after the proverb "It is the *last straw* that breaks the camel's back"]

Last′ Sup′per, **1.** the supper of Jesus and His disciples on the eve of His Crucifixion. Cf. **Lord's Supper** (def. 1). **2.** a work of art representing this. **3.** (*italics.*) ***The,*** a mural (1495–98) by Leonardo da Vinci.

Last′ Things′ the subjects of eschatology: the second coming of Christ, the end of history, and the final destiny of the individual and humankind as a whole. [1470–80]

last′ word′, **1.** the closing remark or comment, as in an argument: *By the rules of debate she would have the last word.* **2.** a final or definitive work, statement, etc.: *This report is the last word on the treatment of arthritis.* **3.** the latest, most modern thing: *Casual hairdos are the last word this season.* [1880–85]

Las Ve•gas (läs vā′gəs), **1.** a city in SE Nevada. 164,674. **2.** a city in central New Mexico. 14,322.

Las Ve′gas night′, an evening of casino-style gambling, usually sponsored by a charitable, religious, or other fund-raising organization. [1970–75]

lat[1] (lät), *n., pl.* **lats, la•ti** (lä′tē). a former silver coin of Latvia, equal to 100 santimi. [1920–25; < Latvian *lats,* equiv. to *Lat(vija)* Latvia + *-s* nom. sing. n. ending]

lat[2] (lat), *n. Informal.* See **latissimus dorsi.** [by shortening]

lât (lät), *n. Archit.* (in India) a monolithic stamba. [1790–1800; < Hindi *lāṭ, lāṭh*]

Lat., Latin.

lat., latitude.

la•tah (lä′tə), *n.* a pattern of neurotic behavior, usually induced by a startle, first discovered in Malaya, and characterized by the compulsive imitation of the actions and words of others. Also, **la′ta.** [1880–85; < Malay]

Lat•a•ki•a (lat′ə kē′ə *or, esp. for 1,* lä′tä kē′ä), *n.* **1.** Ancient, **Laodicea.** a seaport in NW Syria, on the Mediterranean. 191,329. **2.** a coastal district in Syria, in the W part. 389,552. **3.** a variety of Turkish tobacco.

latch (lach), *n.* **1.** a device for holding a door, gate, or the like, closed, consisting basically of a bar falling or sliding into a catch, groove, hole, etc. —*v.t.* **2.** to close or fasten with a latch. —*v.i.* **3.** to close tightly so that the latch is secured: *The door won't latch.* **4. latch on, a.** to grab or hold on, as to an object or idea, esp. tightly or tenaciously. **b.** to include or add in; attach: *If we latch the tax on, the bill will come to over $100.* **5. latch onto,** *Informal.* **a.** to take possession of; obtain; get. **b.** to acquire understanding of; comprehend. **c.** to attach oneself to; join in with: *The stray dog latched onto the children and wouldn't go home.* [bef. 950; 1930–35 for def. 5; ME *lacchen,* OE *lǣccan* to take hold of, catch, seize; akin to Gk *lázesthai* to take]

latch·et (lach′it), *n. Archaic.* a strap or lace used to fasten a shoe. [1300–50; ME *lachet* < MF, dial. var. of *lacet.* See LACE, -ET]

latch′ hook′, a hand-held tool similar to a latch needle, used for drawing loops of yarn through canvas or similar material to make rugs and the like.

latch·ing (lach′ing), *n.* any of the loops by which a bonnet is attached to a sail. [1325–75; ME; see LATCH, -ING[1]]

latch·key (lach′kē′), *n., pl.* **-keys.** a key for releasing a latch or springlock, esp. on an outer door. [1815–25; LATCH + KEY[1]]

latch′key child′, a child who must spend at least part of the day alone and unsupervised, as when the parents are away at work. Also called **door-key child.** [1940–45; so called because such a child is provided with a key for getting into the home after school]

latch′ nee′dle, a part of a knitting machine consisting of a thin shaft with a hook on one end and a pivoting latch that closes over the hook so that yarn can be drawn through the developing knitting to make a stitch.

latch·string (lach′string′), *n.* a string passed through a hole in a door, for raising the latch from the outside. [1785–95; LATCH + STRING]

late (lāt), *adj.,* **lat·er** or **lat·ter, lat·est** or **last,** *adv.* **lat·er, lat·est.** —*adj.* **1.** occurring, coming, or being after the usual or proper time: *late frosts; a late spring.* **2.** continued until after the usual time or hour; protracted: *a late business meeting.* **3.** near or at the end of day or well into the night: *a late hour.* **4.** belonging to the time just before the present moment; most recent: *a late news bulletin.* **5.** immediately preceding the present one; former: *the late attorney general.* **6.** recently deceased: *the late Mr. Phipps.* **7.** occurring at an advanced stage in life: *a late marriage.* **8.** belonging to an advanced period or stage in the history or development of something: *the late phase of feudalism.* **9. of late,** lately; recently: *The days have been getting warmer of late.* —*adv.* **10.** after the usual or proper time, or after delay: *to arrive late.* **11.** until after the usual time or hour; until an advanced hour, esp. of the night: *to work late.* **12.** at or to an advanced time, period, or stage: *The flowers keep their blossoms late in warm climates.* **13.** recently but no longer: *a man late of Chicago, now living in Philadelphia.* [bef. 900; ME; OE *læt* slow, late; c. G *lass* slothful, ON *latr,* Goth *lats* slow, lazy, L *lassus* tired] —**late′ness,** *n.*
—**Syn. 1.** tardy; slow, dilatory; delayed, belated. **4.** See **modern.**

late′ blight′, *Plant Pathol.* a disease of plants, esp. potatoes, celery, etc., characterized by spotting, blighting, and withering or decay of the entire plant, caused by any of several fungi, as *Phytophthora infestans* or *Septoria apii.* [1900–05]

late′ bloom′er, a person whose talents or capabilities are slow to develop: *A late bloomer, she wrote her first novel when she was almost 50.*

late-bloom·ing (lāt′blo͞o′ming), *adj.* **1.** of or characteristic of a late bloomer: *late-blooming brilliance.* **2.** late in coming about or showing full development: *the country's late-blooming interest in soccer.* [1965–70]

late′ charge′, a penalty charge in addition to the regularly scheduled payment, as of a loan, if such payment has not been made when due.

late·com·er (lāt′kum′ər), *n.* a person who arrives late: *The latecomers were seated after the overture.* [1865–70; LATE + COMER]

lat·ed (lā′tid), *adj. Literary.* belated. [1585–95; LATE + -ED[2]]

la·teen (la tēn′, lə-), *adj.* pertaining to or having a lateen sail or sails. [1720–30; < F *(voile) latine* Latin (sail)]

la·teen-rigged (la tēn′rigd′, lə-), *adj.* having lateen sails. [1875–80]

lateen′ sail′, a triangular sail set on a long sloping yard, used esp. on the Mediterranean Sea. [1720–30]

lateen sail

CONCISE ETYMOLOGY KEY: <, descended or borrowed from; >, whence; b., blend of, blended; c., cognate with; cf., compare; deriv., derivative; equiv., equivalent; imit., imitative; obl., oblique; r., replacing; s., stem; sp., spelling, spelled; resp., respelling, respelled; trans., translation; ?, origin unknown; *, unattested; ‡, probably earlier than. See the full key inside the front cover.

Late′ Greek′, the Greek of the early Byzantine Empire and of patristic literature, from about A.D. 100 to 700. *Abbr.:* LGk

Late′ Lat′in, the Latin of the late Western Roman Empire and of patristic literature, from about A.D. 150 to 700. *Abbr.:* LL

late·ly (lāt′lē), *adv.* of late; recently; not long since: *He has been very grouchy lately.* [bef. 1000; ME *latli;* OE *lætlice;* see LATE, -LY]

lat·en (lāt′n), *v.t., v.i.* to make or become late. [1875–80; LATE + -EN[1]]

la·ten·cy (lāt′n sē), *n., pl.* **-cies. 1.** the state of being latent. **2.** *Computers.* the time required to locate the first bit or character in a storage location, expressed as access time minus word time. **3.** See **latent period.** [1630–40; LAT(ENT) + -ENCY]

la′tency pe′riod, 1. *Psychoanal.* the stage of personality development, extending from about four or five years of age to the beginning of puberty, during which sexual urges appear to lie dormant. **2.** *Pathol.* See **latent period** (def. 1). [1905–10]

La Tène (*Fr.* la ten′), **1.** *Archaeol.* designating the period or culture of the late Iron Age typified by the structural remains, swords, tools, utensils, etc., found at La Tène. Cf. **Hallstattan. 2.** a shallow area at the E end of the Lake of Neuchâtel, Switzerland, where these remains were found. [1885–90]

late-night (lāt′nīt′), *adj.* of or occurring late at night: *a late-night TV talk show.* [1880–85]

la·ten·si·fy (lā ten′sə fī′), *v.t.,* **-fied, -fy·ing.** *Photog.* to increase the developability of (the latent image on a film or plate) after exposure. [1935–40; LA(TENT) + (IN)TENSIFY, modeled on *latensification,* b. LATENT and INTENSIFICATION] —**la·ten·si·fi·ca·tion** (lā ten′sə fi kā′shən), *n.*

la·tent (lāt′nt), *adj.* **1.** present but not visible, apparent, or actualized; existing as potential: *latent ability.* **2.** *Pathol.* (of an infectious agent or disease) remaining in an inactive or hidden phase; dormant. **3.** *Psychol.* existing in unconscious or dormant form but potentially able to achieve expression: *a latent emotion.* **4.** *Bot.* (of buds that are not externally manifest) dormant or undeveloped. [1610–20; < L *latent-* (s. of *latēns*) prp. of *latēre* to lie hidden; see -ENT] —**la′tent·ly,** *adv.*
—**Syn. 1.** dormant, quiescent, veiled, LATENT, POTENTIAL refer to powers or possibilities existing but hidden or not yet actualized. LATENT emphasizes the hidden character or the dormancy of what is named: *latent qualities, defects, diseases.* That which is POTENTIAL exists in an as yet undeveloped state, but is thought of as capable of coming into full being or activity at some future time: *potential genius, tragedy.* POTENTIAL may be applied also to tangibles: *High-tension wires are a potential source of danger.* —**Ant. 1.** open, active.

la′tent ambigu′ity, *Law.* uncertainty that arises when a seemingly clear written instrument is matched against an extrinsic fact, as when a description of something being sold fits two different items. [1840–50]

la′tent con′tent, *Psychoanal.* the hidden meaning of a fantasy or dream, discoverable by analysis of the content of the dream.

la′tent func′tion, *Sociol.* any function of an institution or other social phenomenon that is unintentional and often unrecognized. Cf. **manifest function.** [1945–50]

la′tent heat′, *Physics.* heat absorbed or radiated during a change of phase at constant temperature and pressure. Cf. **heat of fusion, heat of vaporization.** [1750–60]

la′tent im′age, *Photog.* an invisible image, produced on a sensitized emulsion by exposure to light, that will emerge in development.

la′tent pe′riod, 1. Also, **latency period.** *Pathol.* the interval between exposure to a carcinogen, toxin, or disease-causing organism and development of a consequent disease. **2.** *Physiol.* the interval between stimulus and reaction. Also called **latency.** [1830–40]

la′tent root′, *Math., Now Rare.* See **characteristic root** (def. 2). [1880–85]

la′tent strabis′mus, *Ophthalm.* the tendency, controllable by muscular effort, for one or both eyes to exhibit strabismus.

lat·er·ad (lat′ə rad′), *adv. Anat.* toward the side. [1805–15; < L *later-* (s. of *latus* side) + -AD[3]]

lat·er·al (lat′ər əl), *adj.* **1.** of or pertaining to the side; situated at, proceeding from, or directed to a side: *a lateral view.* **2.** pertaining to or entailing a position, office, etc., that is different but equivalent or roughly equivalent in status, as distinguished from a promotion or demotion: *a lateral move.* **3.** *Phonet.* articulated so that the breath passes on either or both sides of the tongue, as *l.* —*n.* **4.** a lateral part or extension, as a branch or shoot. **5.** *Mining.* a small drift off to the side of a principal one. **6.** *Phonet.* a lateral speech sound. **7.** *Football.* See **lateral pass.** —*v.i.* **8.** *Football.* to throw a lateral pass. **9.** to move laterally or sideways: *migrating birds lateraling down into Cape May.* —*v.t.* **10.** *Football.* to throw (the ball) in a lateral pass. [1590–1600; < L *laterālis* of the side, equiv. to *later-* (s. of *latus*) side + *-ālis* -AL[1]] —**lat′er·al·ly,** *adv.*

lat′eral bud′, *Bot.* See **axillary bud.** [1890–95]

lat′eral canal′, 1. a canal running parallel to a stream that is inconvenient or impossible to navigate. **2.** one of a number of irrigation canals distributing water from a main canal.

lat′eral chain′, *Chem.* See **side chain.**

lat′eral fis′sure, *Anat.* the fissure separating the frontal, temporal, and parietal lobes of the cerebrum. Also called **fissure of Sylvius, Sylvian fissure.**

lat·er·al·i·ty (lat′ə ral′i tē), *n.* **1.** the use of one hand in preference to the other. Cf. **handedness. 2.** the dominance or superior development of one side of the body or brain. [1640–50; LATERAL + -ITY]

lat·er·al·i·za·tion (lat′ər ə lə zā′shən), *n.* functional specialization of the brain, with some skills, as language, occurring primarily in the left hemisphere and others, as the perception of visual and spatial relationships, occurring primarily in the right hemisphere. [1885–90; LATERAL + -IZATION]

lat′eral line′, the line, or system of lines, of sensory structures along the head and sides of fishes and amphibians, by which the animal is believed to detect water current and pressure changes and vibrations. See diag. under **fish.** [1865–70]

lat′eral lisp′, *Phonet.* See under **lisp** (def. 2).

lat′eral magnifica′tion, *Optics.* the ratio of the height of the image to the height of the object in a lens or other optical system. Also called **transverse magnification.**

lat′eral mer′istem, meristem located along the sides of a part, as a stem or root.

lat′eral moraine′, *Geol.* a moraine formed at the side of a glacier.

lat′eral pass′, *Football.* a short pass thrown or tossed parallel to the line of scrimmage or slightly backward from the position of the passer. [1930–35]

lat′eral resist′ance, *Naval Archit.* resistance to sidewise motion caused by wind pressure, supplied by the immersed portion of a hull of a vessel.

lat′eral sys′tem, a system of coding navigational aids by shape, color, and number, according to the side of a channel they occupy and their relative position along that side. Cf. **cardinal system.** [1880–85]

Lat·er·an (lat′ər ən), *n.* the church of St. John Lateran, the cathedral church of the city of Rome; the church of the pope as bishop of Rome.

La′teran Coun′cil, *Rom. Cath. Ch.* any of the five ecumenical councils (1123, 1139, 1179, 1215, 1512–17) held in the Lateran Palace.

Lat′eran Pal′ace, a palace in Rome used as the papal residence from the 4th century A.D. to the removal of the papal court to Avignon, rebuilt in 1586, and now a museum for classical and Christian antiques.

Lat′er Han′, the Han dynasty after the interregnum A.D. 9–25. Cf. **Han** (def. 1), **Earlier Han.**

lat·er·i·grade (lat′ər i grād′), *adj.* having a sideways manner of moving, as a crab. [1750–60; *lateri-* (comb. form of L *latus,* s. *later-*) side, flank (see -I-) + -GRADE]

lat·er·ite (lat′ə rīt′), *n. Geol.* **1.** a reddish ferruginous soil formed in tropical regions by the decomposition of the underlying rocks. **2.** a similar soil formed of materials deposited by water. **3.** any soil produced by the decomposition of the rocks beneath it. [1800–10; < L *later* brick, tile + -ITE[1]] —**lat·er·it·ic** (lat′ə rit′ik), *adj.*

lat·er·i·tious (lat′ə rish′əs), *adj.* of the color of brick; brick-red. Also, **lat′er·i′ceous.** [1650–60; < L *latericius* of brick, equiv. to *later* brick + *-īcius* adj. suffix denoting materials; see -ITIOUS]

lat·est (lā′tist), *adj.* a superl. of **late** with **later** as *compar.* **1.** most recent; current: *latest fashions.* **2.** last. —*adv.* **3. at the latest,** not any later than (a specified time): *Be at the airport by 7 o'clock at the latest.* —*n.* **4. the latest,** the most recent news, development, disclosure, etc.: *This is the latest in personal computers.* [1375–1425; late ME; see LATE, -EST]

late′ wood′, summerwood. [1925–30]

la·tex (lā′teks), *n., pl.* **lat·i·ces** (lat′ə sēz′), **la·tex·es. 1.** a milky liquid in certain plants, as milkweeds, euphorbias, poppies, or the plants yielding India rubber, that coagulates on exposure to air. **2.** *Chem.* any emulsion in water of finely divided particles of synthetic rubber or plastic. [1655–65; < NL, special use of L *latex* water, juice, liquid]

la′tex paint′, paint that has a latex binder and can be removed while it is wet by applying water. Also called **rubber-base paint, water-base paint.** [1950–55]

lath (lath, läth), *n., pl.* **laths** (lat͟hz, laths, lät͟hz, läths), *v.* —*n.* **1.** a thin, narrow strip of wood, used with other strips to form latticework, a backing for plaster or stucco, a support for slates and other roofing materials, etc. **2.** a group or quantity of such strips. **3.** work consisting of such strips. **4.** wire mesh or the like used in place of wooden laths as a backing for plasterwork. **5.** a thin, narrow, flat piece of wood used for any purpose. —*v.t.* **6.** to cover or line with laths. [bef. 1000; ME *la(th)the;* r. ME *latt,* OE *lætt;* c. G *Latte,* D *lat*] —**lath′like′,** *adj.*

lathe (lāt͟h), *n., v.,* **lathed, lath·ing.** —*n.* **1.** a machine for use in working wood, metal, etc., that holds the material and rotates it about a horizontal axis against a tool that shapes it. —*v.t.* **2.** to cut, shape, or otherwise treat on a lathe. [1300–50; ME: frame, stand, lathe; cf. ON *hlath* stack (see LADE), Dan *-lad* in *væverlad* weaver's batten, *savelad* saw bench]

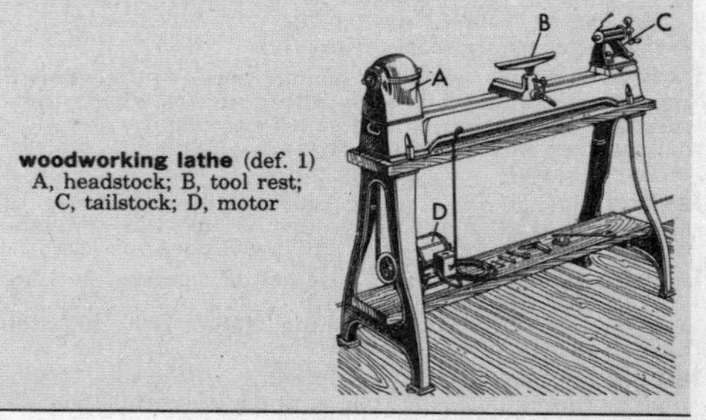

woodworking lathe (def. 1)
A, headstock; B, tool rest; C, tailstock; D, motor

lath·er[1] (lath′ər), *n.* **1.** foam or froth made by a detergent, esp. soap, when stirred or rubbed in water, as by a brush used in shaving or by hands in washing. **2.** foam or froth formed in profuse sweating, as on a horse. **3.** *Informal.* a state of excitement, agitation, nervous tension, or the like: *He was in a lather over my delay.* —*v.i.* **4.** to form a lather: *a soap that lathers well.* **5.** to become covered with lather, as a horse. —*v.t.* **6.** to apply lather to; cover with lather: *He lathered his face before shaving.* **7.** *Informal.* to beat or whip. [bef. 950; ME; OE *lēathor* soap; c. ON *lauthr* (Icel *löthur*) lather, foam] —**lath′er·er,** *n.*

lath·er[2] (lath′ər, lä′thər), *n.* a worker who puts up laths. [LATH + -ER[1]]

lath·er·y (lath′ə rē), *adj.* consisting of, covered with, or capable of producing lather. [1795–1805; LATHER[1] + -Y[1]]

la·thi (lä′tē), *n. Anglo-Indian.* a heavy pole or stick, esp. one used as a club by police. Also, **la′thee.** [1840–50; < Hindi *lāṭhī*]

lath·ing (lath′ing, lä′thing), *n.* **1.** the act or process of applying lath. **2.** a quantity of lath in place. **3.** material used as lath. Also called **lath·work** (lath′wûrk′, läth′-) for defs. 1, 2. [1535–45; LATH + -ING[1]]

lath′ing ham′mer, a hatchet having a small hammer face for trimming and nailing wooden lath. Also called **lath′ing hatch′et.** [1695–1705]

lath·y (lath′ē, lä′thē), *adj.,* **lath·i·er, lath·i·est.** lathlike; long and thin. [1665–75; LATH + -Y[1]]

lath·y·rism (lath′ə riz′əm), *n. Pathol.* a disorder of humans and domestic animals caused by ingestion of the seeds of some legumes of the genus *Lathyrus* and marked by spastic paralysis and pain. [1885–90; < NL *Lathyr(us)* genus name (< Gk *láthyros* a kind of pea) + -ISM]

la·ti (lä′tē), *n.* a pl. of **lat**[1].

lat·i·ces (lat′ə sēz′), *n.* a pl. of **latex.**

la·tic·i·fer (lā tis′ə fər), *n. Bot.* a tubular structure through which latex circulates in a plant. [1925–30; < L *latici-* (s. of *latex;* see LATEX) + -FER]

lat·i·cif·er·ous (lat′ə sif′ər əs), *adj. Bot.* bearing or containing latex. [1825–35; < L *latici-* (s. of *latex;* see LATEX) + -FEROUS]

la·ti·fun·di·o (lat′ə fun′dē ō′, -fo͞on′-; *Sp.* lä′tē fo͞on′dyô), *n., pl.* **-di·os** (-dē ōz′; *Sp.* -dyôs). a great estate of Latin America or Spain. [1920–25; < Sp < L *lātifundium* LATIFUNDIUM]

lat·i·fun·di·um (lat′ə fun′dē əm), *n., pl.* **-di·a** (-dē ə). *Rom. Hist.* a great estate. [1620–30; < L, equiv. to *lāt(us)* wide, broad + *-i-* -I- + *fund(us)* a piece of land, farm, estate + *-ium* -IUM]

lat·i·go (lat′i gō′), *n., pl.* **-gos, -goes.** *n.* a leather strap on the saddletree of a Western saddle used to tighten and secure the cinch. [1870–75, *Amer.;* < Sp *látigo* whip, cinch strap, perh. < Goth **laittug;* cf. OE *lātteh* leading rein, equiv. to *lād-* LEAD[1] + *teh, tēah* TIE]

Lat·i·mer (lat′ə mər), *n.* **Hugh,** c1470–1555, English Protestant Reformation bishop, reformer, and martyr.

Lat·in (lat′n), *n.* **1.** an Italic language spoken in ancient Rome, fixed in the 2nd or 1st century B.C., and established as the official language of the Roman Empire. *Abbr.:* L **2.** one of the forms of literary Latin, as Medieval Latin, Late Latin, Biblical Latin, or Liturgical Latin, or of nonclassical Latin, as Vulgar Latin. **3.** a native or inhabitant of Latium; an ancient Roman. **4.** a member of any of the Latin peoples, or those speaking chiefly Romance languages, esp. a native of or émigré from Latin America. **5.** a member of the Latin Church; a Roman Catholic, as distinguished from a member of the Greek Church. —*adj.* **6.** denoting or pertaining to those peoples, as the Italians, French, Spanish, Portuguese, etc., using languages derived from Latin, esp. the peoples of Central and South America: *a meeting of the Latin republics.* **7.** of or pertaining to the Latin Church. **8.** of or pertaining to Latium, its inhabitants, or their language. **9.** of or pertaining to the Latin alphabet. [bef. 950; ME, OE < L *Latīnus.* See LATIUM, -INE[1]]

La·ti·na (lə tē′nə, la-), *n.* a woman of Latin-American or Spanish-speaking descent. Also, **la·ti′na.** [< Amer Sp, fem. of *latino* LATINO]

Lat′in al′phabet, the alphabetical script derived from the Greek alphabet through Etruscan, used from about the 6th century B.C. for the writing of Latin, and since adopted, with modifications and additions of letters such as *w,* by the languages of Western Europe, including English, as well as many other languages. Also called **Roman alphabet.** [1865–70]

Lat′in Amer′ica, the part of the American continents south of the United States in which Spanish, Portuguese, or French is officially spoken. —**Lat′in Amer′ican.** —**Lat′in-A·mer′i·can,** *n., adj.*

Lat·in·ate (lat′n āt′), *adj.* of, like, pertaining to, or derived from Latin. [1900–05; LATIN + -ATE[1]]

Lat′in Church′, the Roman Catholic Church.

Lat′in cross′, an upright or vertical bar crossed near the top by a shorter horizontal bar. See illus. under **cross.** [1790–1800]

La·tin·i·an (la tin′ē ən), *n.* Latino-Faliscan.

La·tin·ic (lə tin′ik), *adj.* **1.** of or pertaining to the Latin language or the ancient Latin-speaking peoples. **2.** of or pertaining to the modern Latin peoples or nations. [1870–75; LATIN + -IC]

Lat·in·ism (lat′n iz′əm), *n.* a mode of expression derived from or imitative of Latin. [1560–70; < ML *latīnismus.* See LATIN, -ISM]

Lat·in·ist (lat′n ist), *n.* a specialist in Latin. [1530–40; < ML *latīnista.* See LATIN, -IST]

La·tin·i·ty (lə tin′i tē), *n.* **1.** knowledge or use of the Latin language: *He bemoaned the lack of Latinity among today's scholars.* **2.** Latin style or idiom. [1610–20; < L *latīnitās* Latin style. See LATIN, -ITY]

Lat·in·ize (lat′n īz′), *v.,* **-ized, -iz·ing.** —*v.t.* **1.** to cause to conform to the customs, traditions, beliefs, etc., of the Latins or the Latin Church. **2.** to intermix with Latin elements. **3.** to translate into Latin. **4.** to make Latin-American in character: *The influx of Cuban immigrants has Latinized Miami.* **5.** Romanize (def. 3). —*v.i.* **6.** to use words and phrases from Latin: *He Latinizes in his poetry.* Also, *esp. Brit.,* **Lat′in·ise′.** [1580–90; < LL *latīnizāre* to translate into Latin. See LATIN, -IZE] —**Lat′in·i·za′tion,** *n.*

La·ti·no (lə tē′nō, la-), *n., pl.* **-nos.** a person of Latin-American or Spanish-speaking descent. Also, **la·ti′no.** [1945–50, *Amer.;* < Amer Sp, special use of Sp *latino* LATIN, perh. by ellipsis from *latinoamericano* LATIN-AMERICAN]

La·ti·no-Fa·lis·can (lə tē′nō fə lis′kən), *n.* a group of early Italic languages, including Latin and Faliscan. Also, **Lat·in-Fa·lis·can** (lat′n fə lis′kən). Also called **Latinian.** [LATIN + -O-]

Lat′in Quar′ter, the quarter of Paris on the south side of the Seine, especially frequented for centuries by students, writers, and artists.

Lat′in Rite′, **1.** Also called **Roman liturgy, Roman rite.** the forms of worship and liturgy expressed in Liturgical Latin in the Roman Catholic Church in the West. **2.** See **Latin Church.**

Lat′in school′, a secondary school emphasizing instruction in Latin and Greek. [1645–55]

Lat′in square′, *Math.* a square array of numbers, letters, etc., in which each item appears exactly once in each row and column: used in statistical analysis. [1885–90]

La·ti·nus (lə tī′nəs, -tē′-), *n. Rom. Legend.* the father of Lavinia and king of Latium at the time of the arrival of Aeneas.

lat·ish (lā′tish), *adj.* somewhat or rather late. [1605–15; LATE + -ISH[1]]

la·tis·si·mus dor·si (lə tis′ə məs dôr′sī), *pl.* **la·tis·si·mi dor·si** (lə tis′ə mī′ dôr′sī). *Anat.* a broad, flat muscle on each side of the midback, the action of which draws the arm backward and downward and rotates the front of the arm toward the body. [< NL: lit., the broadest (muscle) of the back]

La·ti·tia (lə tish′ə, -tē′shə), *n.* a female given name.

lat·i·tude (lat′i to͞od′, -tyo͞od′), *n.* **1.** *Geog.* **a.** the angular distance north or south from the equator of a point on the earth's surface, measured on the meridian of the point. **b.** a place or region as marked by this distance. **2.** freedom from narrow restrictions; freedom of action, opinion, etc.: *He allowed his children a fair amount of latitude.* **3.** *Astron.* **a.** See **celestial latitude. b.** See **galactic latitude. 4.** *Photog.* the ability of an emulsion to record the brightness values of a subject in their true proportion to one another, expressed as the ratio of the amount of brightness in the darkest possible value to the amount of brightness in the brightest: *a latitude of 1 to 128.* [1350–1400; ME < L *lātitūdō* breadth, equiv. to *lāt(us)* broad + *-i-* -I- + *-tūdō* -TUDE]
—**Syn. 2.** extent, liberty, indulgence. See **range.**

lat·i·tu·di·nal (lat′i to͞od′n l, -tyo͞od′-), *adj.* of or pertaining to latitude. [1535–45; < L *lātitūdin-* (s. of *lātitūdō*) LATITUDE + -AL[1]] —**lat′i·tu′di·nal·ly,** *adv.*

lat·i·tu·di·nar·i·an (lat′i to͞od′n âr′ē ən, -tyo͞od′-), *adj.* **1.** allowing or characterized by latitude in opinion or conduct, esp. in religious views. —*n.* **2.** a person who is latitudinarian in opinion or conduct. **3.** *Anglican Ch.* one of the churchmen in the 17th century who maintained the wisdom of the episcopal form of government and ritual but denied its divine origin and authority. [1655–65; < L *lātitūdin-* (see LATITUDINAL) + -ARIAN] —**lat′i·tu′di·nar′i·an·ism,** *n.*

lat·i·tu·di·nous (lat′i to͞od′n əs, -tyo͞od′-), *adj.* having latitude, scope, range, breadth, etc., esp. of ideas, interests, interpretations, or the like: *a Renaissance man of latitudinous outlook.* [1830–40; < L *lātitūdin-* (see LATITUDINAL) + -OUS]

La·ti·um (lā′shē əm), *n.* a country in ancient Italy, SE of Rome.

lat·ke (lät′kə), *n. Jewish Cookery.* a pancake, esp. one made of grated potato. [1925–30; < Yiddish < East Slavic; cf. Byelorussian *(g)latka,* dial. form of *aladka* kind of pancake, ORuss *oladĭya* (Russ *olád'ya*), prob. < Gk *elá(i)dion,* deriv. of *élaion* OIL]

La·to·na (lə tō′nə), *n.* the goddess Leto as identified in Roman mythology.

La Tor·tue (lᴀ tôr tʏ′). French name of **Tortuga.**

lat·o·sol (lat′ə sôl′, -sol′), *n.* a reddish lateritic soil of the tropics, deeply weathered and infertile, characterized by hydroxides of iron and aluminum. [1945–50; *lat-* (irreg. extracted from L *later;* see LATERITE) + -O- + -SOL]

La Tour (lä to͝or′; *Fr.* lᴀ to͞oʀ′), **Georges de** (zhôrzh də), 1593–1652, French painter.

La Trappe (lᴀ tʀap′), an abbey in Normandy, France, at which the Trappist order was founded.

La Tra·vi·a·ta (lä trä′vē ä′tə; *It.* lä tʀä vyä′tä), an opera (1853) by Giuseppe Verdi.

la·treu·tic (la tro͞o′tik), *adj.* of or pertaining to latria. Also, **la·treu′ti·cal.** [1835–45; < Gk *latreutikós* of divine service, equiv. to *latreú(ein)* to serve (see LATRIA) + *-tikos* -TIC]

la·tri·a (lə trī′ə), *n. Rom. Cath. Theol.* the supreme worship, which may be offered to God only. Cf. **dulia, hyperdulia.** [1350–1400; ME < ML < Gk *latreía* service, worship, akin to *látris* hired servant; see -IA]

la·trine (lə trēn′), *n.* a toilet or something used as a toilet, as a trench in the earth in a camp, or bivouac area. [1635–45; < F < L *lātrīna,* short for *lavātrīna* place for washing, deriv. of *lavāre* to wash]

La·trobe (lə trōb′), *n.* **1. Benjamin Henry,** 1764–1820, U.S. architect and engineer, born in England. **2.** a city in SW Pennsylvania. 10,799.

-latry, a combining form occurring in loanwords from Greek meaning "worship" (*idolatry*); on this model, used in the formation of compound words (*bardolatry*). [< Gk *-latria.* See LATRIA, -Y[3]]

lats (lats), *n.pl. Informal.* latissimus dorsi muscles. [by shortening]

lat·ten (lat′n), *n.* **1.** a brasslike alloy commonly made in thin sheets and formerly much used for church utensils. **2.** tin plate. **3.** any metal in thin sheets. [1300–50; ME *lato(u)n* < MF *laton* copper-zinc alloy << Ar *lāṭūn* < Turkic; cf. Turk *altın* gold]

lat·ter (lat′ər), *adj.* **1.** being the second mentioned of two (distinguished from *former*): *I prefer the latter offer to the former one.* **2.** more advanced in time; later: *in these latter days of human progress.* **3.** near or comparatively near to the end: *the latter part of the century.* **4.** *Obs.* last; final. [bef. 1000; ME *latt(e)re,* OE *lætra,* comp. of *læt* LATE]

lat·ter-day (lat′ər dā′), *adj.* **1.** of a later or following period: *latter-day pioneers.* **2.** of the present period or time; modern: *the latter-day problems of our society.* [1835–45; LATTER + DAY]

Lat′ter-day Saint′, a Mormon. [1825–35, *Amer.*]

lat·ter·ly (lat′ər lē), *adv.* **1.** of late; lately: *He has been latterly finding much to keep himself busy.* **2.** in a later or subsequent part of a period: *Latterly he became a patron of the arts.* [1725–35; LATTER + -LY]

lat·ter·most (lat′ər mōst′, -məst), *adj.* latest; last. [1815–25; LATTER + -MOST]

lat·tice (lat′is), *n., v.,* **-ticed, -tic·ing.** —*n.* **1.** a structure of crossed wooden or metal strips usually arranged to form a diagonal pattern of open spaces between the strips. **2.** a window, gate, or the like consisting of such a structure. **3.** *Physics.* the structure of fissionable and nonfissionable materials geometrically arranged within a nuclear reactor. **4.** Also called **Bravais lattice, crystal lattice, space lattice.** *Crystall.* an arrangement in space of isolated points **(lat′tice points′)** in a regular pattern, showing the positions of atoms, molecules, or ions in the structure of a crystal. **5.** *Math.* a partially ordered set in which every subset containing exactly two elements has a greatest lower bound or intersection and a least upper bound or union. —*v.t.* **6.** to furnish with a lattice or latticework. **7.** to form into or arrange like latticework. [1350–1400; ME *latis* < MF *lattis,* deriv. of *latte* lath < Gmc; see LATH] —**lat′tice·like′,** *adj.*
—**Syn. 1.** trellis, grille, screen, grid.

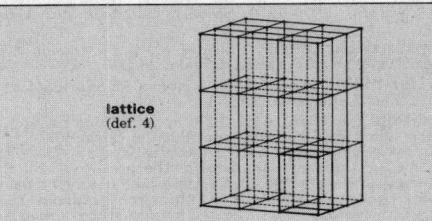

lattice (def. 4)

lat′tice con′stant, *Crystall.* a parameter, either a measure of length or angle, that defines the size and shape of the unit cell of a crystal lattice. Also called **lat′tice param′eter.** [1920–25]

lat·ticed (lat′ist), *adj.* **1.** having a lattice or latticework. **2.** *Biol.* clathrate. [1555–65; LATTICE + -ED[3]]

lat′tice de′fect, *Crystall.* defect (def. 3). [1935–40]

lat′tice gird′er, a trusslike girder having the upper and lower chords connected by latticing. [1850–55]

lat·tice·leaf (lat′is lēf′), *n., pl.* **-leaves.** laceleaf. [1865–70]

lat·tice·work (lat′is wûrk′), *n.* **1.** work consisting of crossed strips usually arranged in a diagonal pattern of open spaces. **2.** a lattice. [1480–90; LATTICE + WORK]

lat·tic·ing (lat′ə sing), *n.* **1.** the act or process of furnishing with or making latticework. **2.** latticework. **3.** (in a composite column, girder, or strut) lacing consisting of crisscross strips of wood, iron, or steel. [1880–85; LATTICE + -ING[1]]

lat·ti·ci·nio (lat′i chēn′yō), *n., pl.* **-ci·ni** (-chē′nē). an opaque, white glass first produced in Venice during the Renaissance, often used in thread form to decorate clear glass pieces. [1850–55; < It < LL *lacticinium* food prepared with milk; see LACT-]

La Tuque (lə to͞ok′, tyo͞ok′; *Fr.* lᴀ tʏk′), a town in S Quebec, in E Canada. 11,556.

la·tus rec·tum (lā′təs rek′təm), *pl.* **la·ter·a rec·ta** (lā′tər ə rek′tə). *Geom.* the chord perpendicular to the principal axis and passing through a focus of an ellipse, parabola, or hyperbola. [1695–1705; < NL: lit., straight side]

Lat·vi·a (lat′vē ə, lät′-), *n.* a republic in N Europe, on the Baltic, S of Estonia, an independent state 1918–40; annexed by the Soviet Union 1940; regained independence 1991. 2,681,000; 25,395 sq. mi. (63,700 sq. km). *Cap.:* Riga. Latvian, **Lat·vi·ja** (lät′vi yä′).

Lat·vi·an (lat′vē ən, lät′-), *adj.* **1.** of or pertaining to Latvia, its inhabitants, or their language. —*n.* **2.** a native or inhabitant of Latvia. **3.** Also, **Lettish, Lett.** the Baltic language of Latvia. [1915–20; LATVI(A) + -AN]

lau·an (lo͞o′än, lo͞o än′, lou-), *n.* See **Philippine mahogany.** [said to be < Tagalog]

laud (lôd), *v.t.* **1.** to praise; extol. —*n.* **2.** a song or hymn of praise. **3. lauds,** (*used with a singular or plural v.*) *Eccles.* a canonical hour, marked esp. by psalms of praise, usually recited with matins. [1300–50; (v.) ME *lauden* < L *laudāre* to praise, deriv. of *laus* (s. *laud-*) praise; (n.) ME *laude,* back formation from *laudes* (pl.) < LL, special use of pl. of L *laus* praise] —**laud′er, lau·da·tor** (lô′dā tər), *n.*
—**Syn. 1.** applaud, honor. —**Ant. 1.** censure.

Laud (lôd), *n.* **William,** 1573–1645, archbishop of Canterbury and opponent of Puritanism: executed for treason.

laud·a·ble (lô′də bəl), *adj.* **1.** deserving praise; praiseworthy; commendable: *Reorganizing the files was a laudable idea.* **2.** *Med. Obs.* healthy; wholesome; not noxious. [1375–1425; late ME < L *laudābilis.* See LAUD, -ABLE] —**laud′a·bil′i·ty, laud′a·ble·ness,** *n.* —**laud′a·bly,** *adv.*

lau·da·num (lôd′n əm, lôd′nəm), *n.* **1.** a tincture of opium. **2.** *Obs.* any preparation in which opium is the chief ingredient. [1595–1605; orig. ML var. of LADANUM; arbitrarily used by Paracelsus to name a remedy based on opium]

lau·da·tion (lô dā′shən), *n.* an act or instance of lauding; encomium; tribute. [1425–75; late ME *laudacion* < L *laudātiōn-* (s. of *laudātiō*) a praising, equiv. to *laudāt(us)* (ptp. of *laudāre* to LAUD) + *-iōn-* -ION]

laud·a·to·ry (lô′də tôr′ē, -tōr′ē), *adj.* containing or expressing praise: *overwhelmed by the speaker's laudatory remarks.* Also, **laud′a·tive.** [1545–55; < LL *laudātōrius,* equiv. to *laudā(re)* to LAUD + *-tōrius* -TORY[1]] —**laud′a·to′ri·ly,** *adv.*
—**Syn.** adulatory, complimentary, commendatory.

Lau·der (lô′dər), *n.* **Sir Harry (Mac·Len·nan)** (mə klen′ən), 1870–1950, Scottish balladeer and composer.

Lau′der·dale Lakes′ (lô′dər dāl′), a city in SE Florida: suburb of Fort Lauderdale. 25,426.

Lau·der·hill (lô′dər hil′), *n.* a city in SE Florida: suburb of Fort Lauderdale. 37,271.

Laud·i·an (lô′dē ən), *adj.* **1.** of or pertaining to Archbishop Laud or his beliefs, esp. that the Church of England preserves more fully than the Roman Catholic Church the faith and practices of the primitive church and that kings rule by divine right. **2.** noting or pertaining to a style of English Gothic architecture of the early 17th century, characterized by a mixture of medieval and Renaissance motifs, attributed to the influence of the policies of Archbishop Laud. —*n.* **3.** a supporter of Archbishop Laud or of Laudianism. [1685–95; LAUD + -IAN]

Laud·i·an·ism (lô′dē ə niz′əm), *n.* the policies and practices of Archbishop Laud or his supporters. [1870–75; LAUDIAN + -ISM]

Lau·e (lou′ə), *n.* **Max The·o·dor Fe·lix von** (mäks tā′ō dōr′ fā′liks fən), 1879–1960, German physicist: Nobel prize 1914.

Lau′e di′agram, *Crystall.* a diffraction pattern used to study crystal structure, consisting of symmetrically arranged spots obtained when a beam of x-rays, electrons, or neutrons is passed through a thin crystal and exposes a photographic plate. Also called **Lau′e pho′tograph.** [after M. von LAUE, who developed it]

Lau·en·burg (lou′ən bûrg′), *n.* a region in Schleswig-Holstein, in NW Germany: duchy under German rulers 1260–1689; later part of Prussia.

laugh (laf, läf), *v.i.* **1.** to express mirth, pleasure, derision, or nervousness with an audible, vocal expulsion of air from the lungs that can range from a loud burst of sound to a series of quiet chuckles and is usually accompanied by characteristic facial and bodily movements. **2.** to experience the emotion so expressed: *He laughed inwardly at the scene.* **3.** to produce a sound resembling human laughter: *A coyote laughed in the dark.* —*v.t.* **4.** to drive, put, bring, etc., by or with laughter (often fol. by *out, away, down,* etc.): *They laughed him out of town. We laughed away our troubles.* **5.** to utter with laughter: *He laughed his consent.* **6. laugh at, a.** to make fun of; deride; ridicule: *They were laughing at him, not along with him.* **b.** to be scornful of; reject: *They stopped laughing at the unusual theory when it was found to be predictive.* **c.** to find sympathetic amusement in; regard with humor: *We can learn to laugh a little at even our most serious foibles.* **7. laugh up one's sleeve.** See **sleeve** (def. 4). **8. laugh off,** to dismiss as ridiculous, trivial, or hollow: *He had received threats but laughed them off as the work of a crank.* **9. laugh out of court,** to dismiss or depreciate by means of ridicule; totally scorn: *His violent protests were laughed out of court by the others.* **10. laugh out of the other side of one's mouth.** to undergo a chastening reversal, as of glee or satisfaction that is premature; be ultimately chagrined, punished, etc.; cry: *She's proud of her promotion, but she'll laugh out of the other side of her mouth when the work piles up.* Also, **laugh on the wrong side of one's mouth** or **face.** —*n.* **11.** the act or sound of laughing; laughter. **12.** an expression of mirth, derision, etc., by laughing. **13.** *Informal.* something that provokes laughter, amusement, or ridicule: *After all the advance publicity, the prizefight turned out to be a laugh.* **14. laughs,** *Informal.* fun; amusement. **15. have the last laugh,** to prove ultimately successful after a seeming defeat or loss: *She smiled slyly, because she knew she would yet have the last laugh on them.* [bef. 900; ME *laughen,* OE *hlæh(h)an* (Anglian); c. D, G *lachen,* ON *hlæja,* Goth *hlahjan*]
—**Syn. 1.** chortle, cackle, cachinnate, guffaw, roar; giggle, snicker, snigger, titter. **11.** LAUGH, CHUCKLE, GRIN, SMILE refer to methods of expressing mirth, appreciation of humor, etc. A LAUGH may be a sudden, voiceless exhalation, but is usually an audible sound, either soft or loud: *a hearty laugh.* CHUCKLE suggests a barely audible series of sounds expressing private amusement or satisfaction: *a delighted chuckle.* A SMILE is a (usually pleasant) lighting up of the face and an upward curving of the corners of the lips (which may or may not be open); it may express amusement or mere recognition, friendliness, etc.: *a courteous smile.* A GRIN, in which the teeth are usually visible, is like an exaggerated smile, less controlled in expressing the feelings: *a friendly grin.*

laugh·a·ble (laf′ə bəl, lä′fə-), *adj.* such as to cause laughter; funny; amusing; ludicrous. [1590–1600; LAUGH + -ABLE] —**laugh′a·ble·ness,** *n.* —**laugh′a·bly,** *adv.*
—**Syn.** humorous, droll, comical, farcical, ridiculous; risible. See **funny.** —**Ant.** sad, melancholy.

laugh·er (laf′ər, lä′fər), *n.* **1.** a person who laughs. **2.** *Informal.* a contest or competition in which one person or team easily overwhelms another; easy victory. [1375–1425; late ME: see LAUGH, -ER[1]]

laugh·ing (laf′ing, lä′fing), *adj.* **1.** that laughs or is given to laughter: *a laughing child.* **2.** uttering sounds like human laughter, as some birds. **3.** suggesting laughter by brightness, color, sound, etc.: *a laughing stream; laughing flowers.* **4.** laughable: *The increase in crime is no laughing matter.* —*n.* **5.** laughter. [1250–1300; ME; see LAUGH, -ING[1], -ING[2]] —**laugh′ing·ly,** *adv.*

laugh′ing gas′. See **nitrous oxide.** [1835–45]

laugh′ing gull′, a North American gull, *Larus atricilla,* having a high, laughlike call. [1780–90, *Amer.*]

laugh′ing hye′na. See **spotted hyena.**

laugh′ing jack′ass, kookaburra. [1780–90; so called because of its loud braying sound]

laugh·ing·stock (laf′ing stok′, lä′fing-), *n.* an object of ridicule; the butt of a joke or the like: *His ineptness as a public official made him the laughingstock of the whole town.* [1525–35; LAUGHING + STOCK]

Laugh′lin Air′ Force′ Base′ (läf′lin), U.S. Air Force installation in SW Texas, SE of Del Rio.

laugh′ line′, *Informal.* crow's-foot (def. 1). [1925–30]

laugh·ter (laf′tər, läf′-), *n.* **1.** the action or sound of laughing. **2.** an inner quality, mood, disposition, etc., suggestive of laughter; mirthfulness: *a man of laughter and goodwill.* **3.** an expression or appearance of merriment or amusement. **4.** *Archaic.* an object of laughter; subject or matter for amusement. [bef. 900; ME; OE *hleahtor;* c. OHG *hlahtar,* ON *hlātr;* see LAUGH] —**laugh′ter·less,** *adj.*

Laugh·ton (lôt′n), *n.* **Charles,** 1899–1962, U.S. actor, born in England.

laugh′ track′, a separate sound track of prerecorded laughter added to the sound track of a radio or television program to enhance or feign audience responses. [1960–65]

lau lau (lou′ lou′), *Polynesian Cookery.* meat and fish wrapped in or covered with leaves and steamed or roasted. Also, **lau′lau′.** [1935–40; < Hawaiian]

lau·mont·ite (lō mon′tīt), *n.* a white zeolite mineral, chiefly hydrated silicate of aluminum and calcium. [1795–1805; named after F. P. N. G. de *Laumont* (1747–1834), French mineralogist who discovered it; see -ITE[1]]

launce (lans, läns), *n.* See **sand lance.** [1615–25; var. of LANCE[2]]

Laun·ce·lot (lan′sə lət, -lot′, län′-), *n. Arthurian Romance.* Lancelot.

Laun·ces·ton (lôn′ses′tən, län′-), *n.* a city on N Tasmania. 38,000, with suburbs 60,000.

launch[1] (lônch, länch), *v.t.* **1.** to set (a boat or ship) in the water. **2.** to float (a newly constructed boat or ship) usually by allowing to slide down inclined ways into the water. **3.** to send forth, catapult, or release, as a self-propelled vehicle or weapon: *Rockets were launched midway in the battle. The submarine launched its torpedoes and dived rapidly.* **4.** to start (a person) on a course, career, etc. **5.** to set going; initiate: *to launch a scheme.* **6.** to throw; hurl: *to launch a spear.* **7.** to start (a new venture) or promote (a new product): *They launched a new breakfast cereal.* —*v.i.* **8.** to burst out or plunge boldly or directly into action, speech, etc. **9.** to start out or forth; push out or put forth on the water. —*n.* **10.** the act of launching. [1300–50; late ME *launche* < AF *lancher* < LL *lanceāre* to wield a lance; see LANCE[1]] —**launch′a·ble,** *adj.*
—**Syn. 5.** inaugurate, institute.

launch[2] (lônch, länch), *n.* **1.** a heavy open or half-decked boat propelled by oars or by an engine. **2.** a large utility boat carried by a warship. [1690–1700; < Sp, Pg *lancha,* earlier Pg *lanchara,* first attested in 1515 in an account of boats encountered near the Strait of Malacca; of unclear orig.; neither Malay *lancar* "swift" nor Rom outcomes of LL *lanceāre* (see LAUNCH[1]) are fully convincing as sources; mod. Malay *lanca* is < Pg]

launch′ control′ cen′ter, any of a number of underground U.S. command facilities prepared to launch land-based missiles in event of war.

launch·er (lôn′chər, län′-), *n.* **1.** a person or thing that launches. **2.** a structural device designed to support and hold a missile in position for firing. [1815–25; LAUNCH[1] + -ER[1]]

launch′ pad′, **1.** the platform on which a missile or launch vehicle undergoes final prelaunch checkout and countdown and from which it is launched from the surface of the earth. **2.** something that serves to launch or initiate: *He used his legal experience as a launch pad for his career in politics.*. Also, **launch′pad′.** Also called **launch′ing pad′, pad.** [1955–60]

launch′ ve′hicle, *Aerospace.* a rocket used to launch a spacecraft or satellite into orbit or a space probe into space. [1955–1960]

launch′ win′dow, a precise time period during which a spacecraft can be launched from a particular site in order to achieve a desired mission, as a rendezvous with another spacecraft. Also called **window.** [1960–65]

laun·der (lôn′dər, län′-), *v.t.* **1.** to wash (clothes, linens, etc.). **2.** to wash and iron (clothes). **3.** *Informal.* **a.** to disguise the source of (illegal or secret funds or profits), usually by transmittal through a foreign bank or a complex network of intermediaries. **b.** to disguise the true nature of (a transaction, operation, or the like) by routing money or goods through one or more intermediaries. **4.** to remove embarrassing or unpleasant characteristics or elements from in order to make more acceptable: *He'll have to launder his image if he wants to run for office.* —*v.i.* **5.** to wash laundry. **6.** to undergo washing and ironing: *The shirt didn't launder well.* —*n.* **7.** (in ore dressing) a passage carrying products of intermediate grade and residue in water suspension. **8.** *Metall.* a channel for conveying molten steel to a ladle. [1300–50; 1970–75 for def. 3; ME: launderer, syncopated var. of *lavandere, lavendere* washer of linen < MF *lavandier(e)* < ML *lavandārius* (masc.), *lavandāria* (fem.), equiv. to L *lavand-* (ger. s. of *lavāre* to wash) + *-ārius, -āria* -ARY; see -ER[2])] —**laun′der·a·ble,** *adj.* —**laun′der·a·bil′i·ty,** *n.* —**laun′der·er,** *n.*

laun·der·ette (lôn′də ret′, län′-, lôn′də ret′, län′-), *n.* a self-service laundry having coin-operated washers, driers, etc. Also, **laun·drette** (lôn dret′, län-). [1945–50; formerly trademark]

laun·dress (lôn′dris, län′-), *n.* a woman whose work is the washing and ironing of clothes, linens, etc. [1540–50; obs. *launder* launderer (see LAUNDER) + -ESS]
—**Usage.** See **-ess.**

Laun·dro·mat (lôn′drə mat′, län′-), *Trademark.* a type of launderette.

laun·dry (lôn′drē, län′-), *n., pl.* **-dries. 1.** articles of clothing, linens, etc., that have been or are to be washed. **2.** a business establishment where clothes, linens, etc., are laundered. **3.** a room or area, as in a home or apartment building, reserved for doing the family wash. [1350–1400; ME *lavendrie* < MF *lavanderie.* See LAUNDER, -Y[3]]

laun′dry list′, *Informal.* a lengthy, esp. random list of items: *a laundry list of hoped-for presents; a laundry list of someone's crimes.* [1955–60]

laun·dry·man (lôn′drē man′, län′-), *n., pl.* **-men. 1.** a person who works in or operates a laundry. **2.** a person who collects and delivers laundry. [1700–10; LAUNDRY + MAN[1]]
—**Usage.** See **-man.**

laun·dry·wom·an (lôn′drē wo͝om′ən, län′-), *n., pl.* **-wom·en. 1.** laundress. **2.** a woman who works in or operates a laundry. **3.** a woman who collects and delivers laundry. [1860–65; LAUNDRY + WOMAN]
—**Usage.** See **-woman.**

lau·ra (läv′rä; *Eng.* lä′vrə), *n. Gk. Orth. Ch.* a monastery consisting formerly of a group of cells or huts for monks who met together for meals and worship. [1720–30; < MGk *laúra* (Gk: lane, passage)]

Lau·ra (lôr′ə), *n.* a female given name: from a Latin word meaning "laurel."

lau·ra·ceous (lô rā′shəs), *adj.* belonging to the plant family Lauraceae. Cf. **laurel family.** [< NL *Lauraceae*) (*Laur(us)* the laurel genus (L: LAUREL) + *-aceae* -ACEAE) + -OUS]

laur·al·de·hyde (lô ral′də hīd′, lo-), *n. Chem.* See **lauric aldehyde.** [LAUR(IC) + ALDEHYDE]

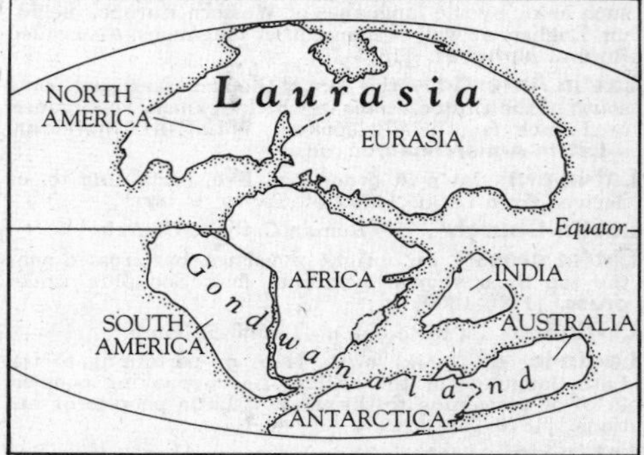

Laur·a·sia (lô rā′zhə, -shə), *n. Geol.* a hypothetical landmass in the Northern Hemisphere near the end of the Paleozoic Era: split apart to form North America and Eurasia. Cf. **Gondwana.** [1930–35; b. LAURENTIAN (def. 2) and EURASIA]

CONCISE ETYMOLOGY KEY: <, descended or borrowed from; >, whence; b., blend of, blended; c., cognate with; cf., compare; deriv., derivative; equiv., equivalent; imit., imitative; obl., oblique; r., replacing; s., stem; sp., spelling, spelled; resp., respelling, respelled; trans., translation; ?, origin unknown; *, unattested; ‡, probably earlier than. See the full key inside the front cover.

lau·rate (lôr′āt, lär′-), *n. Chem.* a salt or ester of lauric acid. [1870–75; LAUR(IC) + -ATE[2]]

lau·re·ate (lôr′ē it, lor′-), *n.* **1.** a person who has been honored for achieving distinction in a particular field or with a particular award: *a Nobel laureate.* **2.** See **poet laureate.** —*adj.* **3.** deserving or having special recognition for achievement, as for poetry (often used immediately after the noun that is modified): *poet laureate; conjurer laureate.* **4.** having special distinction or recognition in a field: *the laureate men of science.* **5.** crowned or decked with laurel as a mark of honor. **6.** consisting of or resembling laurel, as a wreath or crown. [1350–1400; ME; < L *laureātus* crowned with laurel, equiv. to *laure(us)* of laurel (*laur(us)* bay tree + *-eus* -EOUS) + *-ātus* -ATE[1]] —**lau′re·ate·ship′,** *n.*

Lau·reen (lô rēn′), *n.* a female given name, form of **Laura.** Also, **Lau·re·na** (lô rē′nə), **Lau·rene′.**

lau·rel (lôr′əl, lor′-), *n., v.,* **-reled, -rel·ing** or (*esp. Brit.*) **-relled, -rel·ling.** —*n.* **1.** Also called **bay, sweet bay.** a small European evergreen tree, *Laurus nobilis,* of the laurel family, having dark, glossy green leaves. Cf. **laurel family. 2.** any tree of the genus *Laurus.* **3.** any of various similar trees or shrubs, as the mountain laurel or the great rhododendron. **4.** the foliage of the laurel as an emblem of victory or distinction. **5.** a branch or wreath of laurel foliage. **6.** Usually, **laurels.** honor won, as for achievement in a field or activity. **7. look to one's laurels,** to be alert to the possibility of being excelled or surpassed: *New developments in the industry are forcing long-established firms to look to their laurels.* **8. rest on one's laurels,** to be content with one's past or present honors, achievements, etc.: *He retired at the peak of his career and is resting on his laurels.* —*v.t.* **9.** to adorn or wreathe with laurel. **10.** to honor with marks of distinction. [1250–1300; dissimilated var. of ME *laurer,* earlier *lorer* < AF; OF *lorier* bay tree, equiv. to *lor* bay, laurel (< L *laurus*) + *-ier* -IER[2]; see -ER[2]]
—**Syn. 6.** glory, fame, renown, praise.

Lau·rel (lôr′əl, lor′-), *n.* **1. Stan** (*Arthur Stanley Jefferson*), 1890–1965, U.S. motion-picture actor and comedian, born in England. **2.** a city in SE Mississippi. 21,897. **3.** a town in central Maryland. 12,103. **4.** a female given name.

lau′rel cher′ry, a tree, *Prunus caroliniana,* of the rose family, of the southeastern U.S., having small, milky-white flowers and black, shiny fruit. Also called **cherry laurel, mock orange, wild orange.** [1780–90]

lau′rel fam′ily, the plant family Lauraceae, characterized by evergreen or deciduous trees having simple, leathery leaves, aromatic bark and foliage, clusters of small green or yellow flowers, and fruit in the form of a berry or drupe, and including the avocado, bay, laurels of the genera *Laurus* and *Umbellularia,* sassafras, spicebush (*Lindera benzoin*), and the trees that yield camphor and cinnamon.

lau′rel oak′, 1. an oak, *Quercus laurifolia,* of the southeastern U.S., found in moist areas and having shiny dark green leaves. **2.** See **shingle oak.** [1800–10, *Amer.*]

Lau·ren (lôr′ən, lor′-), *n.* a female given name.

lau·rence (lôr′əns, lor′-), *n. Physics.* a shimmering effect seen over a hot surface, such as a pavement or roadway, on a clear and calm day, caused by the irregular refraction of light. Cf. **scintillation** (def. 4). [1790–1800; of unexplained orig.]

Lau·rence (lôr′əns, lor′-), *n.* a male given name, form of **Lawrence.**

Lau·ren·cin (lô RÄN SAN′), *n.* **Ma·rie** (MA RĒ′), 1885–1956, French painter, lithographer, and stage designer.

Lau·rens (lôr′ənz, lor′-), *n.* a town in central South Carolina. 10,587.

Lau·ren·tian (lô ren′shən), *adj.* **1.** of or pertaining to the St. Lawrence River. **2.** *Geol.* noting or pertaining to the granite intrusions and orogeny in Canada around the Great Lakes during Archeozoic time. [1860–65; < LL *Laurenti(us)* Lawrence (orig. adj., equiv. to *Laurent(ēs)* men of *Laurentum* + *-ius* -IOUS) + -AN]

Lauren′tian Moun′tains, a range of low mountains in E Canada, between the St. Lawrence River and Hudson Bay. Also called **Lau·ren′tians.**

Lau′ren·tides Park′ (lôr′ən tīdz′, -tēdz′, lor′-; *Fr.* lô RÄN tēd′), a national park in SE Canada, in Quebec province between the St. Lawrence and Lake St. John.

Lau·ren·ti·us (lô ren′shē əs, -shəs), *n.* **Saint.** See **Lawrence, Saint.**

Laurent′ se′ries (lô rent′; *Fr.* lô RÄN′), *Math.* a power series in which the negative as well as the positive powers appear. [named after Hermann *Laurent* (1841–1908), French mathematician]

Laurent′s′ the′orem, *Math.* the theorem that a function that is analytic on an annulus can be represented by a Laurent series on the annulus. [see LAURENT SERIES]

Lau·ret·ta (lə ret′ə, lô-), *n.* a female given name, form of **Laura.** Also, **Lau·rette** (lô ret′).

lau·ric (lôr′ik, lor′-), *adj. Chem.* of or derived from lauric acid. [1870–75; < L *laur(us)* laurel + -IC]

lau′ric ac′id, *Chem.* a white, crystalline, water-insoluble powder, $C_{12}H_{24}O_2$, a fatty acid occurring as the glyceride in many vegetable fats, esp. coconut oil and laurel oil: used chiefly in the manufacture of soaps, detergents, cosmetics, and lauryl alcohol. Also called **dodecanoic acid.** [1870–75]

lau′ric al′dehyde, *Chem.* a colorless, extremely alcohol-soluble liquid having a strong floral odor, $C_{12}H_{24}O$, used chiefly in perfumery. Also, **lau′ryl al′dehyde.** Also called **lauraldehyde, dodecanal, dodecyl aldehyde.** [1875–80]

Lau·rie (lôr′ē), *n.* **1.** a female given name, form of **Laura. 2.** a male given name, form of **Lawrence.**

Lau·ri·er (lôr′ē ā′; *Fr.* lô RYĀ′), *n.* **Sir Wil·frid** (wil′frid; *Fr.* wēl FRĒD′), 1841–1919, Canadian statesman: prime minister 1896–1911.

Lau·rin·burg (lôr′in bûrg′, lor′in-), *n.* a town in S North Carolina. 11,480.

lau·ro·yl (lôr′ō il, lor′-), *adj. Chem.* containing the lauroyl group. Also, **lau′ryl.** [LAUR(IC) + -O- + -YL]

lau′royl group′, *Chem.* the monovalent organic group $C_{12}H_{23}O$-, derived from lauric acid. Also called **lau′royl rad′ical.**

lau·rus·ti·nus (lôr′ə stī′nəs), *n.* a southern European evergreen shrub, *Viburnum tinus,* of the honeysuckle family, having large clusters of white or pinkish flowers. [1655–65; < NL, formerly *laurus tinus* (L *laurus* laurel + *tinus* a plant, perh. laurustinus)]

lau′ryl al′cohol (lôr′il, lor′-), *Chem.* a compound that, depending upon purity, is either a crystalline solid or colorless liquid, $C_{12}H_{26}O$, obtained by the reduction of fatty acids of coconut oil: used chiefly in the manufacture of synthetic detergents. [1920–25; LAUR(IC) + -YL]

Lau·sanne (lō zan′; *Fr.* lō ZAN′), *n.* a city in and the capital of Vaud, in W Switzerland, on the Lake of Geneva. 134,300.

laut·en·cla·vi·cym·bal (lout′n klä′vē tsĕm′bəl), *n.* a harpsichord with strings of gut rather than metal. [< G: lit., lute-clavichord. See LUTE, CLAVICHORD, CYMBAL]

lau′ter tub′ (lou′tər), *Brewing.* a tank for draining off and filtering the wort from grain mash. [< G *lauter* clear, unmixed]

Lau·tré·a·mont (lō TRĀ A MÔN′), *n.* **Comte de** (*Isidore Lucien Ducasse*), 1846–70, French poet, born in Uruguay.

Lau·trec (lō trek′), *n.* See **Toulouse-Lautrec, Henri.**

Lau·zon (*Fr.* lō zôN′), *n.* a town in S Quebec, in E Canada, across from Quebec City on the St. Lawrence. 13,362.

lav (lav), *n. Informal.* lavatory. [by shortening]

LAV, lymphadenopathy-associated virus. See under **AIDS virus.** [1980–85]

la·va (lä′və, lav′ə), *n.* **1.** the molten, fluid rock that issues from a volcano or volcanic vent. **2.** the rock formed when this solidifies, occurring in many varieties differing greatly in structure and constitution. [1740–50; < It, orig. Neapolitan dial.: avalanche < L *lābēs* a sliding down, falling, akin to *lābī* to slide]

la·va·bo (lə vā′bō, -vä′-), *n., pl.* **-boes. 1.** *Eccles.* **a.** the ritual washing of the celebrant's hands after the offertory in the Mass, accompanied in the Roman rite by the recitation of Psalm 26:6–12. **b.** the passage recited. **c.** the small towel or the basin used. **2.** (in many medieval monasteries) a large stone basin equipped with a number of small orifices through which water flowed, used for the performance of ablutions. **3.** a washbowl with a spigot-equipped water tank above, both mounted on a wall: now often used for decoration or as a planter. [1855–60; < L *lavābō:* I shall wash]

la·vage (lə väzh′, lav′ij), *n.* **1.** a washing. **2.** *Med.* **a.** cleansing by irrigation or the like. **b.** the washing out of the stomach. [1890–95; < F: lit., a washing, equiv. to *lav(er)* to wash (< L *lavāre*) + *-age* -AGE]

La·val (lə val′; *Fr.* LA VAL′), *n.* **1. Pierre** (pyeR), 1883–1945, French lawyer and politician: premier 1931–32, 1935–36; premier of the Vichy government 1942–44; executed for treason 1945. **2.** a city in S Quebec, in E Canada, NW of Montreal, on the St. Lawrence. 268,335. **3.** a city in and the capital of Mayenne, in W France. 54,537.

la·va·la·va (lä′və lä′və), *n.* the principal garment for both sexes in Polynesia, esp. in Samoa, consisting of a piece of printed cloth worn as a loincloth or skirt. Also, **la′va-la′va.** Also called **pareu.** [1890–95; < Samoan: clothing]

lav·a·liere (lav′ə lēr′, lä′və-), *n.* **1.** an ornamental pendant, usually jeweled, worn on a chain around the neck. **2.** See **lavaliere microphone.** Also, **lav′a·lier′, la·val·lière** (*Fr.* LA VA lyeR′). [1915–20; after the Duchesse de *La Vallière* (1644–1710), one of the mistresses of Louis XIV]

lavaliere′ mi′crophone, a small microphone that hangs around the neck of a performer or speaker. Also called **lavaliere.** [1960–65]

La·va·lle·ja (lä′vä ye′hä), *n.* **Juan An·to·nio** (hwän än tō′nyô), 1784–1853, Uruguayan revolutionary: leader in war of independence against Brazil 1825.

lav·a·ret (lav′ə ret′, -ər it), *n.* a whitefish, *Coregonus lavaretus,* found in the lakes of central Europe. [< F < Franco-Provençal << VL **lavaricinus* (cf. LL *levaricinus*); ulterior orig. obscure]

La·va·ter (lä′vä tər, lä vä′tər), *n.* **Jo·hann Kas·par** (yō′hän käs′pär), 1741–1801, Swiss poet, theologian, and physiognomist.

la·va·tion (lā vā′shən), *n.* the process of washing. [1620–30; < L *lavātiōn-* (s. of *lavātiō*) a washing, equiv. to *lavāt(us)* (ptp. of *lavāre* to wash) + *-iōn-* -ION] —**la·va′tion·al,** *adj.*

lav·a·to·ry (lav′ə tôr′ē, -tōr′ē), *n., pl.* **-ries. 1.** a room fitted with equipment for washing the hands and face and usually with flush toilet facilities. **2.** a flush toilet; water closet. **3.** a bowl or basin with running water for washing or bathing purposes; washbowl. **4.** any place where washing is done. [1325–75; ME *lavatorie* < LL *lavātōrium* washing-place, equiv. to L *lavā(re)* to wash + *-tōrium* -TORY[2]]

lave[1] (lāv), *v.,* **laved, lav·ing.** —*v.t.* **1.** to wash; bathe. **2.** (of a river, sea, etc.) to flow along, against, or past; wash. **3.** *Obs.* to ladle; pour or dip with a ladle. —*v.i.* **4.** *Archaic.* to bathe. [bef. 900; ME *laven,* partly < OF *laver* < L *lavāre* to wash; partly repr. OE *lafian* to pour water on, wash, itself perh. < L *lavāre*]

lave[2] (lāv), *n. Scot.* the remainder; the rest. [bef. 1000; ME (Scots); OE *lāf;* c. OHG *leiba,* ON *leif,* Goth *laiba;* akin to LEAVE[1]]

lave[3] (lāv), *adj. Brit.* (of ears) large and drooping. [1350–1400; ME; special use of LAVE[1]]

lav·en·der (lav′ən dər), *n.* **1.** a pale bluish purple. **2.** any Old World plant or shrub belonging to the genus *Lavandula,* of the mint family, esp. *L. angustifolia,* having spikes of fragrant, pale purple flowers. **3.** the dried flowers or other parts of this plant placed among linen, clothes, etc., for scent or as a preservative. **4.** Also called **lav′ender wa′ter.** toilet water, shaving lotion, or the like, made with a solution of oil of lavender. [1225–75; ME *lavendre* < AF < ML *lavendula,* var. of *livendula,* nasalized var. of **lividula* a plant livid in color. See LIVID, -ULE]

lav′ender cot′ton, a silvery-gray, evergreen, woody composite plant, *Santolina chamaecyparissus,* of southern Europe, having yellow flower heads. [1520–30]

la·ver[1] (lā′vər), *n.* **1.** *Old Testament.* a large basin upon a foot or pedestal in the court of the Hebrew tabernacle and subsequently in the temple, containing water for the ablutions of the priests and for the washing of the sacrifices in the temple service. **2.** *Eccles.* the font or water of baptism. **3.** any spiritually cleansing agency. **4.** *Archaic.* **a.** a basin, bowl, or cistern to wash in. **b.** any bowl or pan for water. [1300–50; ME *lavo(u)r* < AF *lavour,* OF *laveoir* < LL *lavātōrium* LAVATORY]

la·ver[2] (lā′vər), *n.* any of several edible seaweeds, esp. of the genus *Porphyra.* [1605–15; < NL, special use of L *laver* a water plant]

La·ver (lā′vər), *n.* **Rod(ney George),** born 1938, Australian tennis player.

La·ve·ran (LAV[ə] RÄN′), *n.* **Charles Louis Al·phonse** (shARl lwē al fôNs′), 1845–1922, French physician and bacteriologist: Nobel prize for medicine 1907.

La Vé·ren·drye (*Fr.* LA vā RÄN dRē′), **Pierre Gaul·tier de Va·renne** (*Fr.* pyeR gō tyā′ də VA Ren′), **Sieur de,** 1685–1749, Canadian explorer of North America.

La·vern (lə vûrn′), *n.* **1.** Also, **La·ver·na** (lə vûr′nə). a female given name, form of **Verna. 2.** a male given name, form of **Vernon.** Also, **La·Vern′, La·verne′.**

La Verne (lə vûrn′), a town in S California. 23,508.

lav·er·ock (lav′ər ək, lāv′rək), *n. Chiefly Scot.* a lark, esp. a skylark. Also, **lav·rock.** (lav′rək). [1275–1325; ME *laverok,* OE *lāwerce* LARK[1]]

La·vin·i·a (lə vin′ē ə), *n.* **1.** *Rom. Legend.* the daughter of Latinus and second wife of Aeneas. **2.** a female given name.

lav·ish (lav′ish), *adj.* **1.** expended, bestowed, or occurring in profusion: *lavish spending.* **2.** using or giving in great amounts; prodigal (often fol. by *of*): *lavish of his time; lavish of affection.* —*v.t.* **3.** to expend or give in great amounts or without limit: *to lavish gifts on a person.* [1425–75; late ME *lavas* profusion (n.), profuse (adj.) < MF *lavasse* downpour of rain, deriv. of *laver* to wash < L *lavāre*] —**lav′ish·er,** *n.* —**lav′ish·ly,** *adv.* —**lav′ish·ness,** *n.*
—**Syn. 1, 2.** unstinted, extravagant, wasteful, improvident; generous, openhanded. LAVISH, PRODIGAL, PROFUSE refer to that which exists in abundance and is poured out copiously. LAVISH suggests (sometimes excessive) generosity and openhandedness: *lavish hospitality; much too lavish.* PRODIGAL suggests wastefulness, improvidence, and reckless impatience of restraint: *a prodigal extravagance.* PROFUSE emphasizes abundance, but may suggest overemotionalism, exaggeration, or the like: *profuse thanks, compliments, apologies.* **3.** heap, pour; waste, squander, dissipate. —**Ant. 1, 2.** niggardly.

La·voi·sier (LA VWA zyā′), *n.* **An·toine Lau·rent** (äN twAN′ lō RÄN′), 1743–94, French scientist: pioneer in the field of chemistry.

law[1] (lô), *n.* **1.** the principles and regulations established in a community by some authority and applicable to its people, whether in the form of legislation or of custom and policies recognized and enforced by judicial decision. **2.** any written or positive rule or collection of rules prescribed under the authority of the state or nation, as by the people in its constitution. Cf. **bylaw, statute law. 3.** the controlling influence of such rules; the condition of society brought about by their observance: *maintaining law and order.* **4.** a system or collection of such rules. **5.** the department of knowledge concerned with these rules; jurisprudence: *to study law.* **6.** the body of such rules concerned with a particular subject or derived from a particular source: *commercial law.* **7.** an act of the supreme legislative body of a state or nation, as distinguished from the constitution. **8.** the principles applied in the courts of common law, as distinguished from equity. **9.** the profession that deals with law and legal procedure: *to practice law.* **10.** legal action; litigation: *to go to law.* **11.** a person, group, or agency acting officially to enforce the law: *The law arrived at the scene soon after the alarm went off.* **12.** any rule or injunction that must be obeyed: *Having a nourishing breakfast was an absolute law in our household.* **13.** a rule or principle of proper conduct sanctioned by conscience, concepts of natural justice, or the will of a deity: *a moral law.* **14.** a rule or manner of behavior that is instinctive or spontaneous: *the law of self-preservation.* **15.** (in philosophy, science, etc.) **a.** a statement of a relation or sequence of phenomena invariable under the same conditions. **b.** a mathematical rule. **16.** a principle based on the predictable consequences of an act, condition, etc.: *the law of supply and demand.* **17.** a rule, principle, or convention regarded as governing the structure or the relationship of an element in the structure of something, as of a language or work of art: *the laws of playwriting; the laws of grammar.* **18.** a commandment or a revelation from God. **19.** (*sometimes cap.*) a divinely appointed order or system. **20. the Law.** See **Law of Moses. 21.** the preceptive part of the Bible, esp. of the

New Testament, in contradistinction to its promises: *the law of Christ.* **22.** *Brit. Sports.* an allowance of time or distance given a quarry or competitor in a race, as the head start given a fox before the hounds are set after it. **23. be a law to** or **unto oneself,** to follow one's own inclinations, rules of behavior, etc.; act independently or unconventionally, esp. without regard for established mores. **24. lay down the law, a.** to state one's views authoritatively. **b.** to give a command in an imperious manner: *The manager laid down the law to the workers.* **25. take the law into one's own hands,** to administer justice as one sees fit without recourse to the usual law enforcement or legal processes: *The townspeople took the law into their own hands before the sheriff took action.* —*v.t.* **26.** *Chiefly Dial.* to sue or prosecute. **27.** *Brit.* (formerly) to expeditate (an animal). [bef. 1000; ME *law(e), lagh(e),* OE *lagu* < ON **lagu,* early pl. of *lag* layer, stratum, a laying in order, fixed tune, (in collective sense) law; akin to LAY[1], LIE[2]] —**law′like′,** *adj.*

law[2] (lô), *adj., adv., n. Obs.* low[1].

law[3] (lô), *v.i., v.t., n. Obs.* low[2].

law[4] (lô), *interj. Older Use.* (used as an exclamation expressing astonishment.) [1580–90; form of LORD]

Law (lô), *n.* **1. Andrew Bon·ar** (bon′ər), 1858–1923, English statesman, born in Canada: prime minister 1922–23. **2. John,** 1671–1729, Scottish financier. **3. William,** 1686–1761, English clergyman and devotional writer.

law-a·bid·ing (lô′ə bī′ding), *adj.* obeying or keeping the law; obedient to law: *law-abiding citizens.* [1830–40] —**law′-a·bid′ing·ness,** *n.*

law′ and or′der, strict control of crime and repression of violence, sometimes involving the possible restriction of civil rights. [1590–1600]

law·book (lô′bo͝ok′), *n.* a book consisting or treating of laws, legal issues, or cases that have been adjudicated. [1150–1200; ME *lagheboc.* See LAW[1], BOOK]

law·break·er (lô′brā′kər), *n.* a person who breaks or violates the law. [bef. 1050; ME *lawbreker;* r. OE *lahbreca.* See LAW[1], BREAKER[1]] —**law′break′ing,** *n., adj.*
—**Syn.** transgressor, criminal offender, perpetrator.

law′ court′. See **court of law.** [1610–20]

Lawes (lôz), *n.* **1. Henry** (*"Harry"*), 1596–1662, English composer. **2. Lewis E(dward),** 1883–1947, U.S. penologist.

law′ French′, Anglo-French as used in legal proceedings and lawbooks in England from the Norman Conquest to the 17th century, some terms of which are still in use. [1635–45]

law·ful (lô′fəl), *adj.* **1.** allowed or permitted by law; not contrary to law: *a lawful enterprise.* **2.** recognized or sanctioned by law; legitimate: *a lawful marriage; a lawful heir.* **3.** appointed or recognized by law; legally qualified: *a lawful king.* **4.** acting or living according to the law; law-abiding: *a lawful man; a lawful community.* [1250–1300; ME *laghful.* See LAW[1], -FUL] —**law′ful·ly,** *adv.* —**law′ful·ness,** *n.*
—**Syn. 1.** legal. **2.** licit.

law·giv·er (lô′giv′ər), *n.* a person who promulgates a law or a code of laws. [1350–1400; ME *lawe givere.* See LAW[1], GIVER] —**law′giv′ing,** *n., adj.*

law-hand (lô′hand′), *n.* a style of handwriting used in old legal documents, esp. in England. [1725–35; LAW[1] + HAND]

law·ing (lô′ing), *n. Scot.* a bill, esp. for food or drink in a tavern. [1525–35; obs. Scots *law* bill, ME (dial.) *lagh* < ON *lag* price, tax, proper place (cf. LAW[1]) + -ING[1]]

law·less (lô′lis), *adj.* **1.** contrary to or without regard for the law: *lawless violence.* **2.** being without law; uncontrolled by a law; unbridled; unruly; unrestrained: *lawless passion.* **3.** illegal: *bootleggers' lawless activity.* [1150–1200; ME *laweles.* See LAW[1], -LESS] —**law′less·ly,** *adv.* —**law′less·ness,** *n.*

law·mak·er (lô′mā′kər), *n.* a person who makes or enacts law; legislator. [1350–1400; ME *lawe maker.* See LAW[1], MAKER] —**law′mak′ing,** *n., adj.*

law·man (lô′man′, -mən), *n., pl.* **-men** (-men′, -mən). an officer of the law, as a sheriff or police officer. [bef. 1000; ME *laweman,* earlier *lageman,* OE *lahmann.* See LAW[1], -MAN]

Law·man (lô′mən), *n.* Layamon.

law′ mer′chant, the principles and rules, drawn chiefly from custom, determining the rights and obligations of commercial transactions; commercial law. [1615–25]

lawn[1] (lôn), *n.* **1.** a stretch of open, grass-covered land, esp. one closely mowed, as near a house, on an estate, or in a park. **2.** *Archaic.* a glade. [1250–1300; ME *launde* < MF *lande* glade < Celtic; cf. Breton *lann* heath. See LAND] —**lawn′y,** *adj.*

lawn[2] (lôn), *n.* a thin or sheer linen or cotton fabric, either plain or printed. [1375–1425; late ME *lawnd, laun,* perh. named after LAON, where linen-making once flourished] —**lawn′y,** *adj.*

lawn′ bowl′ing, a game played with wooden balls on a level, closely mowed green having a slight bias, the object being to roll one's ball as near as possible to a smaller white ball at the other end of the green. Also called **bowls, bowling on the green.** Cf. **bowl**[2] (def. 2), **bowling green, jack**[1] (def. 7), **rink** (def. 5). [1925–30]

lawn′ chair′, a chair or chaise longue designed for use out of doors.

Lawn·dale (lôn′dāl′), *n.* a city in SW California, near Los Angeles. 23,460.

lawn′ mow′er, a hand-operated or motor-driven machine for cutting the grass of a lawn. Also called **mower.** [1865–70]

lawn′ par′ty. See **garden party.** [1850–55]

lawn′ sleeves′, 1. the sleeves of lawn forming part of the dress of an Anglican bishop. **2.** the office of an Anglican bishop. **3.** an Anglican bishop or bishops. [1630–40]

lawn′ ten′nis, tennis, esp. when played on a grass court. [1870–75]

law′ of ac′tion and reac′tion, *Physics.* See under **law of motion.**

law′ of ar′eas, *Astron.* See under **Kepler's laws.**

law′ of av′erages, 1. a statistical principle formulated by Jakob Bernoulli to show a more or less predictable ratio between the number of random trials of an event and its occurrences. **2.** *Informal.* the principle that, in the long run, probability as naively conceived will operate and influence any one occurrence.

law′ of conserva′tion of an′gular momen′tum, *Physics.* See **conservation of angular momentum.**

law′ of conserva′tion of charge′, *Physics.* See **conservation of charge.**

law′ of conserva′tion of en′ergy, *Physics.* See **conservation of energy.**

law′ of conserva′tion of lin′ear momen′tum, *Physics.* See **conservation of linear momentum.**

law′ of conserva′tion of mass′, *Physics.* See **conservation of mass.**

law′ of contradic′tion, *Logic.* the law that a proposition cannot be both true and false or that a thing cannot both have and not have a given property.

law′ of co′sines, *Trigonom.* **1.** a law stating that the square of a side of a plane triangle is equal to the sum of the squares of the other two sides minus twice the product of the other sides multiplied by the cosine of the angle between them. **2.** a law stating that the cosine of an arc of a spherical triangle equals the sum of the product of the cosines of the other two arcs added to the product of the sines of the other two arcs multiplied by the cosine of the angle between them.

law′ of def′inite composi′tion, 1. *Chem.* the statement that in a pure compound the elements are always combined in fixed proportions by weight. **2.** *Logic.* the law that either a proposition or its denial must be true.

law′ of dimin′ishing mar′ginal util′ity, *Econ.* the law that for a single consumer the marginal utility of a commodity diminishes for each additional unit of the commodity consumed.

law′ of dimin′ishing returns′, *Econ.* See **diminishing returns** (def. 2).

law′ of exclud′ed mid′dle, *Logic.* the principle that any proposition must be either true or false.

law′ of expo′nents, *Math.* the theorem stating the elementary properties of exponents, as the property that the product of the same bases, each raised to an exponent, is equal to the base raised to the sum of the exponents: $x^a \cdot x^b = x^{a+b}$.

law′ of gravita′tion, *Physics.* a law stating that any two masses attract each other with a force equal to a constant **(constant of gravitation)** multiplied by the product of the two masses and divided by the square of the distance between them. Also called **law of universal gravitation.** [1755–65]

law′ of iden′tity, *Logic.* the law that any proposition implies itself.

law′ of independ′ent assort′ment, *Genetics.* the principle, originated by Gregor Mendel, stating that when two or more characteristics are inherited, individual hereditary factors assort independently during gamete production, giving different traits an equal opportunity of occurring together. Also called **Mendel's second law, Mendel's law.** [1940–45]

law′ of large′ num′bers, *Math.* the theorem in probability theory that the number of successes increases as the number of experiments increases and approximates the probability times the number of experiments for a large number of experiments. [1935–40]

law′ of Malus′, *Optics.* See **Malus' law.**

law′ of mass′ ac′tion, *Chem.* the statement that the rate of a chemical reaction is proportional to the concentrations of the reacting substances. Also called **mass action law.**

Law′ of Mo′ses, the Pentateuch, containing the Mosaic dispensations, or system of rules and ordinances, and forming the first of the three Jewish divisions of the Old Testament. Cf. **Hagiographa, Prophets.**

law′ of mo′tion, *Physics.* any of three laws of classical mechanics, either the law that a body remains at rest or in motion with a constant velocity unless an external force acts on the body **(first law of motion),** the law that the sum of the forces acting on a body is equal to the product of the mass of the body and the acceleration produced by the forces, with motion in the direction of the resultant of the forces **(second law of motion),** or the law that for every force acting on a body, the body exerts a force having equal magnitude and the opposite direction along the same line of action as the original force **(third law of motion** or **law of action and reaction).** Also called **Newton's law of motion.** [1660–70]

law′ of mul′tiple propor′tion, *Chem.* the statement that where two elements can combine to form more than one compound, the ratio by weight of one element to a given weight of the second is usually a small whole number.

law′ of na′tions. See **international law.** [1540–50]

law′ of par′simony, *Philos.* a principle according to which an explanation of a thing or event is made with the fewest possible assumptions. Cf. **Occam's razor.** [1830–40]

law′ of par′tial pres′sures, *Physics, Chem.* See **Dalton's law.**

law′ of reflec′tion, the principle that when a ray of light, radar pulse, or the like, is reflected from a smooth surface the angle of reflection is equal to the angle of incidence, and the incident ray, the reflected ray, and the normal to the surface at the point of incidence all lie in the same plane.

law′ of refrac′tion, the principle that for a ray, radar pulse, or the like, that is incident on the interface of two media, the ratio of the sine of the angle of incidence to the sine of the angle of refraction is equal to the ratio of the velocity of the ray in the first medium to the velocity in the second medium and the incident ray, refracted ray, and normal to the surface at the point of incidence all lie in the same plane.

law′ of segrega′tion, *Genetics.* the principle, originated by Gregor Mendel, stating that during the production of gametes the two copies of each hereditary factor segregate so that offspring acquire one factor from each parent. Also called **Mendel's first law, Mendel's law.** [1940–45]

law′ of sines′, *Trigonom.* **1.** a law stating that the ratio of a side of a plane triangle to the sine of the opposite angle is the same for all three sides. **2.** a law stating that the ratio of the sine of an arc of a spherical triangle to the sine of the opposite angle is the same for all three arcs.

law′ of superposi′tion, *Geol.* a basic law of geochronology, stating that in any undisturbed sequence of rocks deposited in layers, the youngest layer is on top and the oldest on bottom, each layer being younger than the one beneath it and older than the one above it.

law′ of the jun′gle, a system or mode of action in which the strongest survive, presumably as animals in nature or as human beings whose activity is not regulated by the laws or ethics of civilization. [1890–95]

law′ of the mean′, *Math.* See **mean value theorem.**

Law′ of the Medes′ and the Per′sians, unalterable law. [1350–1400; ME]

law′ of thermodynam′ics, 1. any of three principles variously stated in equivalent forms, being the principle that the change of energy of a thermodynamic system is equal to the heat transferred minus the work done **(first law of thermodynamics),** the principle that no cyclic process is possible in which heat is absorbed from a reservoir at a single temperature and converted completely into mechanical work **(second law of thermodynamics),** and the principle that it is impossible to reduce the temperature of a system to absolute zero in a finite number of operations **(third law of thermodynamics). 2.** See **zeroth law of thermodynamics.**

law′ of thought′, any of the three basic laws of traditional logic: the law of contradiction, the law of excluded middle, and the law of identity.

law′ of trichot′omy, *Math.* See **trichotomy property.**

law′ of univer′sal gravita′tion, *Physics.* See **law of gravitation.**

law′ of war′, rules or a code of rules governing the rights and duties of belligerents in an international war. Cf. **Geneva Convention.** [1945–50]

Law·rence (lôr′əns, lor′-), *n.* **1. D(avid) H(erbert),** 1885–1930, English novelist. **2. Ernest O(rlando),** 1901–58, U.S. physicist: inventor of the cyclotron; Nobel prize 1939. **3. Gertrude,** 1901?–52, English actress. **4. Jacob,** born 1917, U.S. painter and educator. **5. James,** 1781–1813, U.S. naval officer in the War of 1812. **6. Saint.** Also, **Lorenzo.** Latin, **Laurentius.** died A.D. 258?, early church martyr. **7. Sir Thomas,** 1769–1830, English painter. **8. T(homas) E(dward)** (*T. E. Shaw*) (*"Lawrence of Arabia"*), 1888–1935, English archaeologist, adventurer, soldier, and writer. **9.** a city in NE Massachusetts, on the Merrimack River. 63,175. **10.** a city in E Kansas, on the Kansas River. 52,738. **11.** a town in central Indiana. 25,591. **12.** a male given name: from a Latin word meaning "a man of Laurentum."

Law·rence·burg (lôr′əns bûrg′, lor′-), *n.* a town in S Tennessee. 10,175.

Law′rence frame′, a gilded frame for a circular or oval painting, having a rectangular exterior form. [after Sir Thomas LAWRENCE, who alledgedly favored such frames]

law·ren·ci·um (lô ren′sē əm), *n. Chem.* a synthetic, radioactive, metallic element. *Symbol:* Lr; *at. no.:* 103. [1960–65; *Lawrence* Radiation Laboratory, Berkeley, California + -IUM]

Law·ren·tian (lô ren′shən), *adj.* **1.** of, pertaining to, or characteristic of D. H. Lawrence, his works, or his ideas. —*n.* **2.** a person who studies the works of D. H. Lawrence. **3.** an advocate or adherent of the philosophy of D. H. Lawrence. Also, **Law·ren′cian.** [1925–30; LAWRENCE + -IAN; *t* is partial Latinization]

Law·son (lô′sən), *n.* **Robert,** 1892–1957, U.S. illustrator and author, esp. of children's books.

Law·son (lô′sən), *adj.* (*sometimes l.c.*) of or pertaining to a style of overstuffed sofa or chair that is boxy in shape, with square back and seat cushions and broad, square or rounded arms that are lower in height than the back: *a Lawson sofa.* [allegedly from a kind of furniture designed for Thomas W. *Lawson* (1857–1925), U.S. financier]

Law′son crite′rion, *Physics.* (in a hypothetical nuclear fusion reactor) the requirement that in order for the energy produced by fusion to exceed the energy expended in causing the fusion, the product of the density of the fuel and the time during which it is confined at that density **(Law′son prod′uct)** must be greater than a certain number that depends on the kind of fuel used. [after John David *Lawson* (born 1923), English physicist, who formulated it in 1957]

Law′son cy′press. See **Port Orford cedar.** [1855–60; after *Lawson* and Son, a firm of Edinburgh nurserymen, who cultivated the tree from seeds collected in America in 1854]

law·suit (lô′so͞ot′), *n.* a case in a court of law involving a claim, complaint, etc., by one party against another; suit at law. [1615–25; LAW[1] + SUIT]

Law·ton (lôt′n), *n.* a city in SW Oklahoma. 80,054.

law·yer (lô′yər, loi′ər), *n.* **1.** a person whose profession is to represent clients in a court of law or to advise or act for clients in other legal matters. **2.** *New Testament.* an interpreter of the Mosaic Law. Luke 14:3. *—v.i.* **3.** to work as a lawyer; practice law. *—v.t.* **4.** to submit (a case, document, or the like) to a lawyer for examination, advice, clarification, etc. [1350–1400; ME *lawyere.* See LAW[1], -IER[1]] **—law′yer·like′, law′yer·ly,** *adj.*

law·yer·ing (lô′yər ing, loi′ər-), *n. Often Disparaging.* the practice of law; the duties, functions, or skills of a lawyer. [1670–80; LAWYER + -ING[1]]

lax (laks), *adj.,* **-er, -est. 1.** not strict or severe; careless or negligent: *lax morals; a lax attitude toward discipline.* **2.** loose or slack; not tense, rigid, or firm: *a lax rope; a lax handshake.* **3.** not rigidly exact or precise; vague: *lax ideas.* **4.** open, loose, or not retentive, as diarrheal bowels. **5.** (of a person) having the bowels unusually loose or open. **6.** open or not compact; having a loosely cohering structure; porous: *lax tissue; lax texture.* **7.** *Phonet.* (of a vowel) articulated with relatively relaxed tongue muscles. Cf. **tense**[1] (def. 4). [1350–1400; ME < L *laxus* loose, slack, wide; akin to *languēre* to LANGUISH; c. OE *slæc* SLACK[1]] **—lax′ly,** *adv.* **—lax′ness,** *n.*

Lax·alt (lak′sôlt), *n.* **Paul,** born 1922, U.S. politician: senator 1974–87.

lax·a·tion (lak sā′shən), *n.* **1.** a loosening or relaxing. **2.** the state of being loosened or relaxed. **3.** a bowel movement. [1350–1400; ME *laxacion* < L *laxātiōn-* (s. of *laxātiō*) a loosening, equiv. to *laxāt(us)* (ptp. of *laxāre* to loosen, deriv. of *laxus;* see LAX) + *-iōn-* -ION]

lax·a·tive (lak′sə tiv), *n.* **1.** a medicine or agent for relieving constipation. *—adj.* **2.** of, pertaining to, or constituting a laxative; purgative. **3.** *Archaic.* **a.** (of the bowels) subject to looseness. **b.** (of a disease) characterized by looseness of the bowels. [1350–1400; ME *laxatif* (< MF) < ML *laxātīvus* loosening (see LAXATION, -IVE)] **—lax′a·tive·ly,** *adv.* **—lax′a·tive·ness,** *n.*

lax·i·ty (lak′si tē), *n.* the state or quality of being lax; looseness. [1520–30; < L *laxitās* wideness, openness. See LAX, -ITY]

Lax·ness (läks′nes), *n.* **Hall·dór Kil·jan** (häl′dōr kil′yän), born 1902, Icelandic writer: Nobel prize 1955.

lay[1] (lā), *v.,* **laid, lay·ing,** *n. —v.t.* **1.** to put or place in a horizontal position or position of rest; set down: *to lay a book on a desk.* **2.** to knock or beat down, as from an erect position; strike or throw to the ground: *One punch laid him low.* **3.** to put or place in a particular position: *The dog laid its ears back.* **4.** to cause to be in a particular state or condition: *Their motives were laid bare.* **5.** to set, place, or apply (often fol. by *to* or *on*): *to lay hands on a child.* **6.** to dispose or place in proper position or in an orderly fashion: *to lay bricks.* **7.** to place on, along, or under a surface: *to lay a pipeline.* **8.** to establish as a basis; set up: *to lay the foundations for further negotiations.* **9.** to present or submit for notice or consideration: *I laid my case before the commission.* **10.** to present, bring forward, or make, as a claim or charge. **11.** to impute, attribute, or ascribe: *to lay blame on the inspector.* **12.** to bury: *They laid him in the old churchyard.* **13.** to bring forth and deposit (an egg or eggs). **14.** to impose as a burden, duty, penalty, or the like: *to lay an embargo on oil shipments.* **15.** to place dinner service on (a table); set. **16.** to place on or over a surface, as paint; cover or spread with something else. **17.** to devise or arrange, as a plan. **18.** to deposit as a wager; bet: *He laid $10 on the horse.* **19.** to set (a trap). **20.** to place, set, or locate: *The scene is laid in France.* **21.** to smooth down or make even: *to lay the nap of cloth.* **22.** to cause to subside: *laying the clouds of dust with a spray of water.* **23.** *Slang (vulgar).* to have sexual intercourse with. **24.** to bring (a stick, lash, etc.) down, as on a person, in inflicting punishment. **25.** to form by twisting strands together, as a rope. **26.** *Naut.* to move or turn (a sailing vessel) into a certain position or direction. **27.** to aim a cannon in a specified direction at a specified elevation. **28.** to put (dogs) on a scent. *—v.i.* **29.** to lay eggs. **30.** to wager or bet. **31.** to apply oneself vigorously. **32.** to deal or aim blows vigorously (usually fol. by *on, at, about,* etc.). **33.** *Nonstandard.* lie[2]. **34.** *South Midland U.S.* to plan or scheme (often fol. by *out*). **35.** *Midland and Southern U.S.* (of the wind) to diminish; subside: *When the wind lays, it'll rain.* **36.** *Naut.* to take up a specified position, direction, etc.: *to lay aloft; to lay close to the wind.* **37. get laid,** *Slang (vulgar).* to have sexual intercourse. **38. lay aboard,** *Naut.* (formerly, of a fighting ship) to come alongside (another fighting ship) in order to board. **39. lay about one, a.** to strike or aim blows in every direction. **b.** to proceed to do; set about. **40. lay a course, a.** *Naut.* to sail in the desired direction without tacking. **b.** to proceed according to a plan. **41. lay aside, a.** to abandon; reject. **b.** to save for use at a later time; store: *to lay aside some money every month.* **42. lay away, a.** to reserve for later use; save. **b.** to hold merchandise pending final payment or request for delivery: *to lay away a winter coat.* **c.** to bury: *They laid him away in the tomb.* **43. lay back,** *Slang.* to relax. **44. lay by, a.** to put away for future use; store; save: *She had managed to lay by money for college from her earnings as a babysitter.* **b.** *Naut.* (of a sailing vessel) to come to a standstill; heave to; lay to. **c.** *Midland and Southern U.S.* to tend (a crop) for the last time, leaving it to mature without further cultivation. **45. lay close,** *Naut.* (of a sailing vessel) to sail close to the wind. **46. lay down, a.** to give up; yield: *to lay down one's arms.* **b.** to assert firmly; state authoritatively: *to lay down rigid rules of conduct.* **c.** to stock; store: *to lay down wine.* **d.** *Shipbuilding.* to draw at full size (the lines of a hull), as on the floor of a mold loft; lay off; loft. **47. lay for,** *Informal.* to wait for in order to attack or surprise; lie in wait for: *The police are laying for him.* **48. lay in,** to store away for future use: *We laid in a supply of canned goods.* **49. lay into,** *Informal.* to attack physically or verbally; assail: *He laid into the opposition with fiery words.* **50. lay it on,** to exaggerate in one's speech or actions, esp. to engage in exaggerated flattery or reproof: *She was glad to be told what a splendid person she was, but they didn't have to lay it on so much.* Also, **lay it on thick. 51. lay low.** See **low**[1] (defs. 44, 45). **52. lay off, a.** to dismiss (an employee), esp. temporarily because of slack business. **b.** *Informal.* to cease or quit: *He promised to lay off drinking.* **c.** *Slang.* to stop annoying or teasing: *Lay off me, will you?* **d.** *Informal.* to stop work: *They laid off at four and went home.* **e.** to put aside or take off. **f.** to mark off; measure; plot. **g.** *Slang.* to give or hand over; pass on: *They laid off their old sofa on the neighborhood recreation center.* **h.** (of a bookmaker) to transfer all or part of (a wager) to other bookmakers in order to be protected against heavy losses. **i.** to get rid of or transfer (blame, responsibility, etc.): *He tried to lay off the guilt for the crime on his son.* **j.** *Naut.* to sail away from. **k.** *Naut.* to remain stationary at a distance from. **l.** *Shipbuilding.* See **lay**[1] (def. 46d). **53. lay on, a.** to cover with; apply: *to lay on a coat of wax.* **b.** to strike blows; attack violently: *When the mob became unruly, the police began to lay on.* **c.** *Naut.* to sail toward. **d.** *Naut.* to row (an oar) with a full stroke. **e.** *Slang.* to tell, impart, or give to: *Let me lay a little good advice on you.* **f.** *Chiefly Brit. Informal.* to provide as a gift, bonus, or treat; give; treat: *The owners laid on a Christmas dinner for the employees.* **54. lay oneself out,** *Informal.* to try one's best; make a great effort: *They laid themselves out to see that the reception would be a success.* **55. lay open, a.** to cut open: *to lay open an area of tissue with a scalpel.* **b.** to expose; reveal: *Her autobiography lays open shocking facts about her childhood.* **c.** to expose or make vulnerable, as to blame, suspicion, or criticism: *He was careful not to lay himself open to charges of partiality.* **56. lay out, a.** to extend at length. **b.** to spread out in order; arrange; prepare. **c.** to plan; plot; design. **d.** to ready (a corpse) for burial. **e.** *Informal.* to spend or contribute (money). **f.** *Slang.* to knock (someone) down or unconscious. **g.** *Slang.* to scold vehemently; reprimand: *Whenever I come home late from school, my mom really lays me out.* **h.** to make a layout of. **i.** *Chiefly South Midland and Southern U.S.* to absent oneself from school or work without permission or justification; play hooky. **57. lay over, a.** to be postponed until action may be taken: *The vote will have to be laid over until next week.* **b.** to make a stop, as during a trip: *We will have to lay over in Lyons on our way to the Riviera.* **58. lay siege to.** See **siege** (def. 8). **59. lay to, a.** *Naut.* to check the motion of (a ship). **b.** *Naut.* to put (a ship) in a dock or other place of safety. **c.** to attack vigorously. **d.** to put forth effort; apply oneself. **60. lay up, a.** to put away for future use; store up. **b.** to cause to be confined to bed or kept indoors; disable. **c.** *Naut.* to retire (a ship) from active use. **d.** *Naut.* (of a ship) to be retired from active use. **e.** to construct (a masonry structure): *The masons laid the outer walls up in Flemish bond.* **f.** to apply (alternate layers of a material and a binder) to form a bonded material.
—n. **61.** the way or position in which a thing is laid or lies: *the lay of the land.* **62.** *Slang (vulgar).* **a.** a partner in sexual intercourse. **b.** an instance of sexual intercourse. **63.** *Ropemaking.* the quality of a fiber rope characterized by the degree of twist, the angles formed by the strands, and the fibers in the strands. **64.** Also called **lay-up, spread.** (in the garment industry) multiple layers of fabric upon which a pattern or guide is placed for production-line cutting. **65.** batten[3] (defs. 1, 2). **66.** a share of the profits or the catch of a whaling or fishing voyage, distributed to officers and crew. [bef. 900; ME *layen, leggen,* OE *lecgan* (causative of *licgan* to LIE[2]); c. D *leggen,* G *legen,* ON *legja,* Goth *lagjan*]
—Syn. 1. deposit. See **put. 21, 22.** calm, still, quiet.
—Usage. LAY[1] and LIE[2] are often confused. LAY is most commonly a transitive verb and takes an object. Its forms are regular. If "place" or "put" can be substituted in a sentence, a form of LAY is called for: *Lay the folders on the desk. The mason is laying brick. She laid the baby in the crib.* LAY also has many intransitive senses, among them "to lay eggs" (*The hens have stopped laying*), and it forms many phrasal verbs, such as LAY OFF "to dismiss (from employment)" or "to stop annoying or teasing" and LAY OVER "to make a stop."
LIE, with the overall senses "to be in a horizontal position, recline" and "to rest, remain, be situated, etc.," is intransitive and takes no object. Its forms are irregular; its past tense form is identical with the present tense or infinitive form of LAY: *Lie down, children. Abandoned cars were lying along the road. The dog lay in the shade and watched the kittens play. The folders have lain on the desk since yesterday.*
In all but the most careful, formal speech, forms of LAY are commonly heard in senses normally associated with LIE. In edited written English such uses of LAY are rare and are usually considered nonstandard: *Lay down, children. The dog laid in the shade. Abandoned cars were laying along the road. The folders have laid on the desk since yesterday.*

lay[2] (lā), *v.* pt. of **lie**[2].

lay[3] (lā), *adj.* **1.** belonging to, pertaining to, or performed by the people or laity, as distinguished from the clergy: *a lay sermon.* **2.** not belonging to, connected with, or proceeding from a profession, esp. the law or medicine. [1300–50; ME < MF *lai* < ML *lāicus* LAIC]

lay[4] (lā), *n.* **1.** a short narrative or other poem, esp. one to be sung. **2.** a song. [1200–50; ME *lai* < OF, perh. < Celtic; cf. OIr *láed, laíd* metrical composition, poem, lay]

lay[5] (lā), *n.* **1.** (on a loom) a movable frame that contains the shuttles, the race plate, and the reed, and that by its oscillating motion beats the filling yarn into place. **2.** any movable part of a loom. [1780–90; var. of LATHE]

lay·a·bout (lā′ə bout′), *n. Chiefly Brit.* a lazy or idle person; loafer. [1930–35; n. use of v. phrase *lay about,* nonstandard var. of *lie about*]

Lay·a·mon (lā′ə mən, lī′yə-), *n.* fl. c1200, English poet and chronicler. Also called **Lawman.**

lay′ an′alyst, a psychoanalyst who does not have a medical degree. [1925–30]

Layard (lârd, lā′ərd), *n.* **Sir Aus·ten Henry** (ô′stən), 1817–94, English archaeologist, writer, and diplomat.

lay·a·way (lā′ə wā′), *n.* **1.** See **layaway plan. 2.** an article or item purchased through a layaway plan. [1880–85; n. use of v. phrase *lay away*]

lay′away plan′, a method of purchasing by which the purchaser reserves an article with a down payment and claims it only after paying the full balance. Also called **will-call.** [1970–75]

lay′ bap′tism, *Eccles.* baptism administered by a lay-person. [1720–30]

lay′ broth′er, a man who has taken religious vows and habit but is employed by his order chiefly in manual labor. [1670–80]

lay-by (lā′bī′), *n.* **1.** *Brit.* (on a road or railroad) a place beside the main road or track where vehicles may wait. **2.** *Naut.* a mooring place in a narrow river or canal, formed to one side so as to leave the channel free. [1795–1805; n. use of v. phrase *lay by*]

lay′ clerk′. See **lay vicar.** [1805–15]

lay′ day′, 1. *Com.* one of a certain number of days allowed by a charter party for loading or unloading a vessel without demurrage. **2.** *Naut.* a day in which a vessel is delayed in port. [1835–45]

lay·down (lā′doun′), *n. Bridge.* **1.** a hand held by a declarer that is or can be played with all cards exposed because no action by the opponents can prevent the declarer from taking the number of tricks necessary to make the contract. **2.** an unbeatable contract that can so easily be made that a declarer can or does play the hand with all cards exposed. [1905–10; n. use of v. phrase *lay down*]

lay·er (lā′ər), *n.* **1.** a thickness of some material laid on or spread over a surface: *a layer of soot on the window sill; two layers of paint.* **2.** bed; stratum: *alternating layers of basalt and sandstone.* **3.** a person or thing that lays: *a carpet layer.* **4.** a hen kept for egg production. **5.** one of several items of clothing worn one on top of the other. **6.** *Hort.* **a.** a shoot or twig that is induced to root while still attached to the living stock, as by bending and covering with soil. **b.** a plant so propagated. **7.** *Ropemaking.* a machine for laying rope or cable. *—v.t.* **8.** to make a layer of. **9.** to form or arrange in layers. **10.** to arrange or wear (clothing) in layers: *You can layer this vest over a blouse or sweater.* **11.** *Hort.* to propagate by layering. *—v.i.* **12.** to separate into or form layers. **13.** (of a garment) to permit of wearing in layers; be used in layering: *Frilly blouses don't layer well.* [1350–1400; ME *leyer, legger.* See LAY[1], -ER[1]] **—lay′er·a·ble,** *adj.*

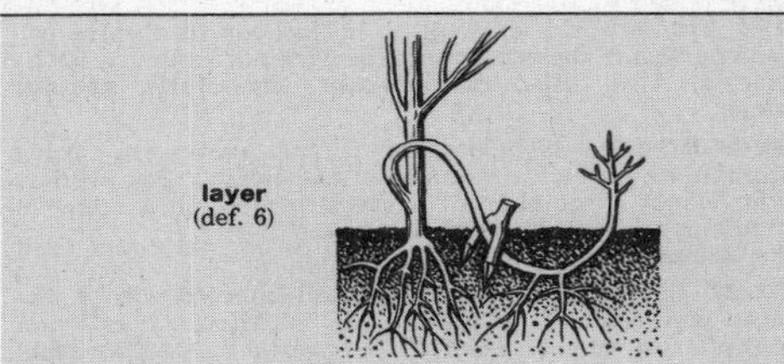
layer (def. 6)

lay′er board′. See **lear board.** [1835–45]

lay′er cake′, a cake made in layers, with a cream, jelly, or other filling between them. [1875–80]

lay·er·ing (lā′ər ing), *n.* **1.** the wearing of lightweight or unconstructed garments one upon the other, as to create a fashionable ensemble or to provide warmth without undue bulkiness or heaviness. **2.** *Tailoring.* the trimming of multiple layers of fabric at the seam allowance of a garment so as to prevent a ridge on the face of the garment when the seam is sewn. **3.** *Hort.* Also, **lay·er·age** (lā′ər ij). a method of propagating plants by causing their shoots to take root while still attached to the parent plant. [LAYER + -ING[1]]

lay·ette (lā et′), *n.* an outfit of clothing, bedding, etc., for a newborn baby. [1830–40; < F; MF *laiete* small coffer, equiv. to *laie* chest (< MD *laeye,* var. of *lade;* akin to LADE) + *-ete* -ETTE]

lay′ fig′ure, 1. a jointed model of the human body, usually of wood, from which artists work in the absence of a living model. **2.** a similar figure used in shops to display costumes. **3.** a person of no importance, individuality, distinction, etc.; nonentity. [1785–95; *lay*, extracted from obs. *layman* < D *leeman*, var. of *ledenman*, equiv. to *leden-* (combining form of *lid* limb, c. OE, ME *lith*) + *man* MAN[1])]

lay′ing on′ of hands′, **1.** *Theol.* a rite in which the cleric's hands are placed on the head of a person being confirmed, ordained, or the like. **2.** (in divine healing) the placing of the hands of the healer upon the person to be cured. [1490–1500]

lay′ interme′diary, *Law.* a layperson who is interposed between a lawyer and client to prevent the existence of a direct relationship between them.

lay·man (lā′mən), *n., pl.* **-men. 1.** a person who is not a member of the clergy; one of the laity. **2.** a person who is not a member of a given profession, as law or medicine. [1150–1200; ME; see LAY[3], MAN[1]]
—Usage. See **-man.**

lay·off (lā′ôf′, -of′), *n.* **1.** the act of dismissing employees, esp. temporarily. **2.** a period of enforced unemployment or inactivity. [1885–90, *Amer.*; n. use of v. phrase *lay off*]

lay′ of the land′, the general state or condition of affairs under consideration; the facts of a situation: *We asked a few questions to get the lay of the land.* Also, *esp. Brit.,* **lie of the land.**

lay·out (lā′out′), *n.* **1.** an arrangement or plan: *We objected to the layout of the house.* **2.** the act of laying or spreading out. **3.** a plan or sketch, as of an advertisement or a page of a newspaper or magazine, indicating the arrangement and relationship of the parts, as of type and artwork. **4.** (in advertising, publishing, etc.) the technique, process, or occupation of making layouts. **5.** *Journalism.* spread (def. 34). **6.** *Informal.* a place, as of residence or business, and the features that go with it; a setup: *a fancy layout with a swimming pool and a tennis court.* **7.** *Informal.* a display or spread, as of dishes at a meal. **8.** a collection or set of tools, implements, or the like. **9.** *Cards.* an arrangement of cards dealt according to a given pattern, as in solitaire. **10.** *Diving, Gymnastics.* a body position in which one is fully extended and arched backward, with the legs together and straight, the head thrown back, and the arms extended sideways. Cf. **pike[7]**, **tuck[1]** (def. 14). [1840–50, *Amer.*; n. use of v. phrase *lay out*]

lay·o·ver (lā′ō′vər), *n.* stopover. [1870–75, *Amer.*; n. use of v. phrase *lay over*]

lay·per·son (lā′pûr′sən), *n.* **1.** a person who is not a member of the clergy; one of the laity. **2.** a person who is not a member of a given profession, as law or medicine. [1970–75; LAY(MAN) + -PERSON]
—Usage. See **-person.**

lay′ read′er, *Anglican Ch.* a layperson authorized by a bishop to conduct certain parts of a service. [1745–55]

Lay·san (lī′sän), *n.* an islet of Hawaii, in the Leeward Islands, NW of Niihau.

lay′ sis′ter, a woman who has taken religious vows and habit but is employed in her order chiefly in manual labor. [1700–10]

Lay·ton (lāt′n), *n.* a town in N Utah. 22,826.

lay·up (lā′up′), *n.* **1.** *Basketball.* a shot with one hand from a point close to the basket, in which a player shoots the ball toward the basket, often off the backboard. **2.** the operation of assembling veneers for pressing into plywood. **3.** the operation of applying alternate layers of material and a binder to form a bonded material. **4.** lay[1] (def. 64). Also, **lay′up′.** [1940–45; n. use of v. phrase *lay up*]

lay′ vic′ar, *Ch. of Eng.* a lay officer in a cathedral who performs those parts of a service not reserved to the priests. Also called **clerk vicar, lay clerk, secular vicar.**

lay·wom·an (lā′wo͝om′ən), *n., pl.* **-wom·en. 1.** a woman who is not a member of the clergy. **2.** a woman who is not a member of a given profession, as law or medicine. [1520–30; LAY[3] + WOMAN]
—Usage. See **-woman.**

laz·ar (laz′ər, lā′zər), *n.* a person infected with a disease, esp. leprosy. [1300–50; ME < ML *lazarus* leper, special use of LL *Lazarus* LAZARUS] **—laz′ar·like′,** *adj.*

laz·a·ret·to (laz′ə ret′ō), *n., pl.* **-tos. 1.** a hospital for those affected with contagious diseases, esp. leprosy. **2.** a building or a ship set apart for quarantine purposes. **3.** Also called **glory hole.** *Naut.* a small storeroom within the hull of a ship, esp. one at the extreme stern. Also, **laz·a·ret, laz·a·rette** (laz′ə ret′). [1540–50; < Upper It (Venetian) *lazareto*, b. *lazzaro* LAZAR and *Nazareto* popular name of a hospital maintained in Venice by the Church of Santa Maria di Nazaret]

Laz·a·rist (laz′ər ist), *n. Rom. Cath. Ch.* Vincentian (def. 1). [1740–50; named after the College of St. *Lazare*, Paris, a former Vincentian center]

Laz·a·rus (laz′ər əs), *n.* **1.** the diseased beggar in the parable of the rich man and the beggar. Luke 16:19–31. **2.** a brother of Mary and Martha whom Jesus raised from the dead. John 11:1–44; 12:1–18. **3. Emma,** 1849–87, U.S. poet. [< LL < Gk *Lázaros* < Heb *El'āzār* Eleazar (one God has helped)]

laze (lāz), *v.,* **lazed, laz·ing,** *n.* —*v.i.* **1.** to idle or lounge lazily (often fol. by *around*): *I was too tired to do anything but laze around this weekend.* —*v.t.* **2.** to pass (time, life, etc.) lazily (usually fol. by *away*). —*n.* **3.** a period of ease or indolence: *a quiet laze in the hammock.* [1585–95; back formation from LAZY]

La·zear (lə zēr′), *n.* **Jesse William,** 1866–1900, U.S. physician and bacteriologist.

laz·u·li (laz′ə lē, -lī′, lazh′ə-), *n.* See **lapis lazuli.** [1780–90]

laz·u·line (laz′ə lēn′, -līn′, lazh′ə-), *adj.* having the color of lapis lazuli. [1875–80; LAZUL(I) + -INE[1]]

laz·u·lite (laz′ə līt′, lazh′ə-), *n.* an azure-blue mineral, hydrous magnesium iron aluminum phosphate, $(FeMg)Al_2P_2O_8(OH)_2$. [1800–10; < ML *lāzul(um)* azure, LAPIS LAZULI + -ITE[1]] **—laz·u·lit·ic** (laz′ə lit′ik, lazh′ə-), *adj.*

laz·u·rite (laz′ə rīt′, lazh′ə-), *n.* a mineral, sodium aluminum silicate and sulfide, $Na_5Al_3Si_3O_{12}S_3$, occurring in deep-blue crystals, used for ornamental purposes. [1890–95; < ML *lāzur* AZURE + -ITE[1]]

la·zy (lā′zē), *adj.,* **-zi·er, -zi·est,** *v.,* **-zied, -zy·ing.** —*adj.* **1.** averse or disinclined to work, activity, or exertion; indolent. **2.** causing idleness or indolence: *a hot, lazy afternoon.* **3.** slow-moving; sluggish: *a lazy stream.* **4.** (of a livestock brand) placed on its side instead of upright. —*v.i.* **5.** to laze. [1540–50; cf. LG *lasich* languid, idle] **—la′zi·ly,** *adv.* **—la′zi·ness,** *n.* **—la′zy·ish,** *adj.*
—Syn. 1. slothful. See **idle. 3.** inert, inactive, torpid.
—Ant. 1. industrious. **3.** quick.

la·zy·bones (lā′zē bōnz′), *n.* (*usually used with a singular v.*) *Informal.* a lazy person. [1580–90]

la′zy eye′, *Informal.* **1.** the deviating eye in strabismus. **2.** an amblyopic eye. **3.** strabismus. **4.** amblyopia. [1935–40]

la′zy guy′, *Naut.* a rope or light tackle for keeping a boom from swinging.

la′zy Su′san, 1. a revolving tray for foods, condiments, etc., placed usually at the center of a dining table. **2.** any similar structure, as a shelf or tabletop, designed to revolve so that whatever it holds can be seen or reached easily. Also, **la′zy su′san, La′zy Su′san.** [1915–20, *Amer.*]

la′zy tongs′, extensible tongs for grasping objects at a distance, consisting of a series of pairs of crossing pieces, each pair pivoted together in the middle and connected with the next pair at the extremities. [1830–40]

lazy tongs

lb., *pl.* **lbs., lb.** pound. [< L *lībra*, pl. *librae*]

L.B., 1. landing barge. **2.** light bomber. **3.** bachelor of letters; bachelor of literature. [< NL *Litterārum Baccalaureus; Literārum Baccalaureus*] **4.** local board.

lb. ap., *Pharm.* pound apothecary's.

L bar. See **angle iron** (def. 2). Also called **L beam.**

lb. av., pound avoirdupois.

lbf, pound-force.

LBJ, Lyndon Baines Johnson.

LBO, leveraged buyout.

lb. t., pound troy.

LC, landing craft.

L.C., Library of Congress.

l.c., 1. left center. **2.** letter of credit. **3.** in the place cited. [< L *locō citātō*] **4.** *Print.* lower case.

L/C, letter of credit. Also, **l/c**

l.c.a., lowercase alphabet.

LCD, liquid-crystal display: a method of displaying readings continuously, as on digital watches, portable computers, and calculators, using a liquid-crystal film, sealed between glass plates, that changes its optical properties when a voltage is applied.

L.C.D., least common denominator; lowest common denominator. Also, **l.c.d.**

L.C.F., lowest common factor. Also, **l.c.f.**

l'cha·im (*Ashk.* lə KHä′yim; *Seph.* lə KHä yēm′), *n. Hebrew.* a toast used in drinking to a person's health or well-being. Also, ***l'cha′yim, lechayim, lehayim.*** [*ləḥayyim* lit., to life]

L chain, *Immunol.* See **light chain.**

LCI, a type of military landing craft used in World War II, designed principally for carrying personnel and landing them on beaches. [*L(anding) C(raft) I(nfantry)*]

L.C.L., *Com.* less than carload lot. Also, **l.c.l.**

L.C.M., least common multiple; lowest common multiple. Also, **l.c.m.**

LCM chair. See **Eames chair** (def. 1). [appar. *L(ounge) C(hair), M(etal)*]

LCT, a type of military landing craft used in World War II, designed for landing tanks and other vehicles on beaches. [*L(anding) C(raft) T(ank)*]

LD, 1. praise (be) to God. [< L *laus Deō*] **2.** learning disability. **3.** learning-disabled. **4.** lethal dose. **5.** long distance (telephone call). **6.** Low Dutch.

LD., (in Libya) dinar; dinars.

Ld., 1. limited. **2.** Lord.

ld., load.

L.D., Low Dutch.

LD_{50}, median lethal dose.

LDC, less developed country. Also, **L.D.C.**

ldg., 1. landing. **2.** loading.

LDH, *Biochem.* lactate dehydrogenase.

LDL, *Biochem.* low-density lipoprotein.

L-do·pa (el′dō′pə), *n. Pharm.* levodopa.

Ldp., 1. ladyship. **2.** lordship.

LDPE, *Chem.* See **low-density polyethylene.**

ldr., leader.

L.D.S., 1. Latter-day Saints. **2.** praise (be) to God forever. [< L *laus Deō semper*] **3.** Licentiate in Dental Surgery.

-le, 1. a suffix of verbs having a frequentative force: *dazzle; twinkle.* **2.** a suffix of adjectives formed originally on verbal stems and having the sense of "apt to": *brittle.* **3.** a noun suffix having originally a diminutive meaning: *bramble.* **4.** a noun suffix indicating agent or instrument: *beadle; bridle; thimble.* [ME *-len*, OE *-lian* (v.); ME *-el*, OE *-ol* (adj.); ME *-el*, OE *-il* (dim.); ME *-el*, OE *-ol*, *-ul* (agent)]

l.e., *Football.* left end.

lea[1] (lē, lā), *n.* **1.** a tract of open ground, esp. grassland; meadow. **2.** land used for a few years for pasture or for growing hay, then plowed over and replaced by another crop. **3.** a crop of hay on tillable land. —*adj.* **4.** untilled; fallow. Also, **ley.** [bef. 900; ME *lege, lei*, OE *lēah*; c. OHG *lōh*, dial. D *loo* (as in *Waterloo*), L *lūcus*]

lea[2] (lē), *n.* **1.** a measure of yarn of varying quantity, for wool usually 80 yards (73 m), cotton and silk 120 yards (110 m), linen 300 yards (274 m). **2.** *Textiles.* **a.** a unit length used to ascertain the linear density of yarns. **b.** a count or number representing units of linear measure per pound in linen or cotton yarn: *a 20-lea yarn.* [1350–1400; perh. back formation from ME *lese*, var. of LEASH]

Le·a (lē *for 1;* lē′ə *for 2*), *n.* **1. Homer,** 1876–1912, U.S. soldier and author: adviser 1911–12 to Sun Yat-sen in China. **2.** a female given name, form of **Leah** or **Lee.**

lea., 1. league. **2.** leather.

leach[1] (lēch), *v.t.* **1.** to dissolve out soluble constituents from (ashes, soil, etc.) by percolation. **2.** to cause (water or other liquid) to percolate through something. —*v.i.* **3.** (of ashes, soil, etc.) to undergo the action of percolating water. **4.** to percolate, as water. —*n.* **5.** the act or process of leaching. **6.** a product or solution obtained by leaching; leachate. **7.** the material leached. **8.** a vessel for use in leaching. [1425–75; late ME *leche* leachate, infusion, prob. OE **læc(e)*, **lec(e)*, akin to *leccan* to wet, moisten, causative of LEAK] **—leach′a·ble,** *adj.* **—leach′a·bil′i·ty,** *n.* **—leach′er,** *n.*

leach[2] (lēch), *n. Naut.* leech[3].

leach·ate (lē′chāt), *n.* a solution resulting from leaching, as of soluble constituents from soil, landfill, etc., by downward percolating ground water: *Leachates in the town's water supply have been traced to a chemical-waste dump.* [1930–35; LEACH[1] + -ATE[2]]

leach·y (lē′chē), *adj.,* **leach·i·er, leach·i·est.** allowing water to percolate through, as sandy or rocky soil; porous. [1840–50, *Amer.*; LEACH[1] + -Y[1]]

Lea·cock (lē′kok), *n.* **Stephen (Butler),** 1869–1944, Canadian humorist and economist.

lead[1] (lēd), *v.,* **led, lead·ing,** *n., adj.* —*v.t.* **1.** to go before or with to show the way; conduct or escort: *to lead a group on a cross-country hike.* **2.** to conduct by holding and guiding: *to lead a horse by a rope.* **3.** to influence or induce; cause: *Subsequent events led him to reconsider his position.* **4.** to guide in direction, course, action, opinion, etc.; bring: *You can lead her around to your point of view if you are persistent.* **5.** to conduct or bring (water, wire, etc.) in a particular course. **6.** (of a road, passage, etc.) to serve to bring (a person) to a place: *The first street on the left will lead you to Andrews Place.* **7.** to take or bring: *The prisoners were led into the warden's office.* **8.** to command or direct (an army or other large organization): *He led the Allied forces during the war.* **9.** to go at the head of or in advance of (a procession, list, body, etc.); proceed first in: *The mayor will lead the parade.* **10.** to be superior to; have the advantage over: *The first baseman leads his teammates in runs batted in.* **11.** to have top position or first place in: *Iowa leads the nation in corn production.* **12.** to have the directing or principal part in: *The minister will now lead us in prayer. He led a peace movement.* **13.** to act as leader of (an orchestra, band, etc.); conduct. **14.** to go through or pass (time, life, etc.): *to lead a full life.* **15.** *Cards.* to begin a round, game, etc., with (a card or suit specified). **16.** to aim and fire a firearm or cannon ahead of (a moving target) in order to allow for the travel of the target while the bullet or shell is reaching it. **17.** *Football.* to throw a lead pass to (an intended receiver): *The quarterback led the left end.*
—*v.i.* **18.** to act as a guide; show the way: *You lead and we'll follow.* **19.** to afford passage to a place: *That path leads directly to the house.* **20.** to go first; be in advance: *The band will lead and the troops will follow.* **21.** to result in; tend toward (usually fol. by *to*): *The incident led to his resignation. One remark often leads to another.* **22.** to take the directing or principal part. **23.** to take the offensive: *The contender led with a right to the body.* **24.** *Cards.* to make the first play. **25.** to be led or submit to being led, as a horse: *A properly trained horse will lead easily.* **26.** *Baseball.* (of a base runner) to leave a base before the delivery of a pitch in order to reach the next base more quickly (often fol. by *away*). **27. lead back,** to play (a card) from a suit that one's partner led. **28. lead off, a.** to take the initiative; begin. **b.** *Baseball.* to be the first player in the batting order or the first batter in an inning. **29. lead on, a.** to induce to follow an unwise course of action; mislead. **b.** to cause or encourage to believe something that is not true. **30. lead out, a.** to make a beginning. **b.** to escort a partner to begin a dance: *He led her out and they began a rumba.* **31. lead someone a chase** or **dance,**

CONCISE ETYMOLOGY KEY: <, descended or borrowed from; >, whence; b., blend of, blended; c., cognate with; cf., compare; deriv., derivative; equiv., equivalent; imit., imitative; obl., oblique; r., replacing; s., stem; sp., spelling, spelled; resp., respelling, respelled; trans., translation; ?, origin unknown; *, unattested; ‡, probably earlier than. See the full key inside the front cover.

to cause someone difficulty by forcing to do irksome or unnecessary things. **32. lead the way.** See **way** (def. 35). **33. lead up to, a.** to prepare the way for. **b.** to approach (a subject, disclosure, etc.) gradually or evasively: *I could tell by her allusions that she was leading up to something.*
—*n.* **34.** the first or foremost place; position in advance of others: *He took the lead in the race.* **35.** the extent of such an advance position: *He had a lead of four lengths.* **36.** a person or thing that leads. **37.** a leash. **38.** a suggestion or piece of information that helps to direct or guide; tip; clue: *I got a lead on a new job. The phone list provided some great sales leads.* **39.** a guide or indication of a road, course, method, etc., to follow. **40.** precedence; example; leadership: *They followed the lead of the capital in their fashions.* **41.** *Theat.* **a.** the principal part in a play. **b.** the person who plays it. **42.** *Cards.* **a.** the act or right of playing first, as in a round. **b.** the card, suit, etc., so played. **43.** *Journalism.* **a.** a short summary serving as an introduction to a news story, article, or other copy. **b.** the main and often most important news story. **44.** *Elect.* an often flexible and insulated single conductor, as a wire, used in connections between pieces of electric apparatus. **45.** the act of taking the offensive. **46.** *Naut.* **a.** the direction of a rope, wire, or chain. **b.** Also called **leader.** any of various devices for guiding a running rope. **47.** *Naval Archit.* the distance between the center of lateral resistance and the center of effort of a sailing ship, usually expressed decimally as a fraction of the water-line length. **48.** an open channel through a field of ice. **49.** *Mining.* **a.** a lode. **b.** an auriferous deposit in an old riverbed. **50.** the act of aiming a gun ahead of a moving target. **51.** the distance ahead of a moving target that a gun must be aimed in order to score a direct hit. **52.** *Baseball.* an act or instance of leading. **53.** *Manège.* (of a horse at a canter or gallop) the foreleg that consistently extends beyond and strikes the ground ahead of the other foreleg: *The horse is cantering on the left lead.*
—*adj.* **54.** most important; principal; leading; first: *lead editorial; lead elephant.* **55.** *Football.* (of a forward pass) thrown ahead of the intended receiver so as to allow him to catch it while running. **56.** *Baseball.* (of a base runner) nearest to scoring: *They forced the lead runner at third base on an attempted sacrifice.* [bef. 900; ME *leden,* OE *lǣdan* (causative of *līthan* to go, travel); c. D *leiden,* G *leiten,* ON *leitha*]
—**Syn. 1.** accompany, precede. See **guide. 3.** persuade, convince. **10.** excel, outstrip, surpass. **34.** head, vanguard. —**Ant. 1.** follow.

lead[2] (led), *n.* **1.** *Chem.* a heavy, comparatively soft, malleable, bluish-gray metal, sometimes found in its natural state but usually combined as a sulfide, esp. in galena. *Symbol:* Pb; *at. wt.:* 207.19; *at. no.:* 82; *sp. gr.:* 11.34 at 20°C. **2.** something made of this metal or of one of its alloys. **3.** a plummet or mass of lead suspended by a line, as for taking soundings. **4.** bullets collectively; shot. **5.** black lead or graphite. **6.** a small stick of graphite, as used in pencils. **7.** Also, **leading.** *Print.* a thin strip of type metal or brass less than type-high, used for increasing the space between lines of type. **8.** a grooved bar of lead or came in which sections of glass are set, as in stained-glass windows. **9. leads,** *Brit.* a roof, esp. one that is shallow or flat, covered with lead. **10.** See **white lead. 11. get the lead out,** *Slang.* to move or work faster; hurry up. **12. heave the lead,** *Naut.* to take a sounding with a lead. —*v.t.* **13.** to cover, line, weight, treat, or impregnate with lead or one of its compounds. **14.** *Print.* to insert leads between the lines of. **15.** to fix (window glass) in position with leads. —*adj.* **16.** made of or containing lead: *a lead pipe; a lead compound.* **17. go over like a lead balloon,** *Slang.* to fail to arouse interest, enthusiasm, or support. [bef. 900; ME *lede,* OE *lēad;* c. D *lood,* OFris *lād* lead, G *Lot* plummet] —**lead′less,** *adj.*
—**Syn. 3.** weight, plumb.

lead′ ac′etate (led), *Chem.* a white, crystalline, water-soluble, poisonous solid, $Pb(C_2H_3O_2)_2 \cdot 3H_2O$, used chiefly as a mordant in dyeing and printing textiles and as a drier in paints and varnishes. Also called **sugar of lead.** [1895–1900]

lead′ ar′senate (led), *Chem.* a white, crystalline, water-insoluble, highly poisonous powder, $PbHAsO_4$, used as an insecticide. [1900–05]

lead′ az′ide (led), *Chem.* a highly toxic, colorless crystalline compound, $Pb(N_3)_2$, that detonates at 660°F (350°C) and is used as a detonator for explosives. [1910–15]

Lead·bel·ly (led′bel′ē), *n.* See **Ledbetter, Huddie.**

lead′ block′ (lēd), *Naut.* any block that alters the direction of a rope; fairlead. Also called **leading block.** [1855–60]

lead′ car′bonate (led), *Chem.* a white crystalline compound, $PbCO_3$, toxic when inhaled, insoluble in water and alcohol: used as an exterior paint pigment. [1870–75]

lead′ chro′mate (led), *Chem.* a yellow crystalline compound, $PbCrO_4$, toxic, insoluble in water: used as an industrial paint pigment. [1900–05]

lead′ col′ic (led), *Pathol.* See **painter's colic.**

lead′ diox′ide (led), *Chem.* a brown crystalline compound, PbO_2, toxic, insoluble in water and alcohol, soluble in glacial acetic acid: used as an oxidizing agent, in lead-acid batteries, and in analytical chemistry. [1900–05]

lead·ed (led′id), *adj.* (of gasoline) containing tetraethyllead. [1935–40; LEAD[2] + -ED[3]]

lead·en (led′n), *adj.* **1.** inertly heavy like lead; hard to lift or move: *a leaden weight; leaden feet.* **2.** dull, spiritless, or gloomy, as in mood or thought: *leaden prose; a leaden atmosphere.* **3.** of a dull gray color: *leaden skies.* **4.** oppressive; heavy: *a leaden silence.* **5.** sluggish; listless: *They moved at a leaden pace.* **6.** of poor quality or little value. **7.** made or consisting of lead. —*v.t.* **8.** to make leaden, sluggish, dull, etc.: *Fatigue had leadened his brain and step.* [bef. 1000; ME *leden,* OE *lēaden.* See LEAD[2], -EN[2]] —**lead′en·ly,** *adv.* —**lead′en·ness,** *n.*

lead·er (lē′dər), *n.* **1.** a person or thing that leads. **2.** a guiding or directing head, as of an army, movement, or political group. **3.** *Music.* **a.** a conductor or director, as of an orchestra, band, or chorus. **b.** the player at the head of the first violins in an orchestra, the principal cornetist in a band, or the principal soprano in a chorus, to whom any incidental solos are usually assigned. **4.** a featured article of trade, esp. one offered at a low price to attract customers. Cf. **loss leader. 5.** *Journalism.* **a.** See **leading article** (def. 1). **b.** Also called **leading article.** *Brit.* the principal editorial in a newspaper. **6.** blank film or tape at the beginning of a length of film or magnetic tape, used for threading a motion-picture camera, tape recorder, etc. Cf. **trailer** (def. 6). **7.** *Angling.* **a.** a length of nylon, silkworm gut, wire, or the like, to which the lure or hook is attached. **b.** the net used to direct fish into a weir, pound, etc. **8.** a pipe for conveying rain water downward, as from a roof; downspout. **9.** a horse harnessed at the front of a team. **10. leaders,** *Print.* a row of dots or a short line to lead the eye across a space. **11.** *Naut.* lead[1] (def. 46b). **12.** a duct for conveying warm air from a hot-air furnace to a register or stack. **13.** *Mining.* a thin vein of ore connected with a large vein. [1250–1300; ME *leder(e).* See LEAD[1], -ER[1]] —**lead′er·less,** *adj.*

lead′er block′, *Naut.* See **lead block.**

lead′er ca′ble, *Naut.* a submarine cable laid along a channel and emitting signals that a vessel can follow when visibility is poor.

lead′er head′, a boxlike head of a downspout connected to a gutter.

lead·er·ship (lē′dər ship′), *n.* **1.** the position or function of a leader: *He managed to maintain his leadership of the party despite heavy opposition.* **2.** ability to lead: *She displayed leadership potential.* **3.** an act or instance of leading; guidance; direction: *They prospered under his leadership.* **4.** the leaders of a group: *The union leadership agreed to arbitrate.* [1815–25; LEADER + -SHIP]

lead·foot (led′fŏŏt′), *n., pl.* **-foots, -feet.** *Informal.* a person who drives a motor vehicle too fast, esp. habitually. [LEAD[2] + FOOT]

lead·foot·ed (led′fŏŏt′id), *adj. Informal.* **1.** awkward; clumsy. **2.** tending to drive too fast. [1955–60; LEAD[2] + FOOTED]

lead-free (led′frē′), *adj.* unleaded. Also, **nonleaded.** [1945–50]

lead′ glass′ (led), glass containing lead oxide. [1855–60]

lead′ glaze′ (led), *Ceram.* a siliceous glaze containing lead oxide as a flux. [1835–45]

lead-in (lēd′in′), *n.* **1.** something that leads in or introduces; introduction; opening. **2.** *Radio, Television.* **a.** the connection between an antenna and a transmitter or receiving set. **b.** the portion of a program or script that precedes or introduces a commercial. —*adj.* **3.** (of a conductor) carrying input to an electric or electronic device or circuit, esp. from an antenna. [1910–15; n., adj. use of v. phrase *lead in*]

lead·ing[1] (lē′ding), *adj.* **1.** chief; principal; most important; foremost: *a leading toy manufacturer.* **2.** coming in advance of others; first: *We rode in the leading car.* **3.** directing, guiding. —*n.* **4.** the act of a person or thing that leads. [1250–1300; ME (n.); see LEAD[1], -ING[2], -ING[1]] —**lead′ing·ly,** *adv.*
—**Syn. 3.** ruling, governing.

lead·ing[2] (led′ing), *n.* **1.** a covering or framing of lead: *the leading of a stained-glass window.* **2.** *Print.* lead[2] (def. 7). [1400–50; late ME; see LEAD[2], -ING[1]]

lead′ing ar′ticle (lē′ding), *Journalism.* **1.** Also called **leader.** the most important or prominent news story in a newspaper. **2.** *Brit.* leader (def. 5b). [1800–10]

lead′ing block′ (lē′ding), *Naut.* See **lead block.** [1855–60]

lead′ing coeffi′cient (lē′ding), *Math.* the coefficient of the term of highest degree in a given polynomial. *5* is the leading coefficient in $5x^3 + 3x^2 - 2x + 1$.

lead′ing edge′ (lē′ding), **1.** *Aeron.* the edge of an airfoil or propeller blade facing the direction of motion. **2.** something that is or represents the most advanced or innovative aspect of a field, activity, profession, etc.; forefront; vanguard: *the leading edge of technology.* [1875–80] —**lead′ing-edge′,** *adj.*

lead′ing in′dicators, *Econ.* data that reflect current economic conditions and can suggest future developments or fluctuations in the nation's economy: issued, usually monthly, by the U.S. Bureau of Economic Analysis in the Commerce Department. Also called **index of leading indicators.**

lead′ing la′dy (lē′ding), an actress who plays the principal female role in a motion picture or play. [1870–75]

lead′ing light′ (lē′ding), an important or influential person: *a leading light of the community.* [1870–75]

lead′ing man′ (lē′ding), an actor who plays the principal male role in a motion picture or play. [1695–1705]

lead′ing mark′ (lē′ding), *Navig.* either of two conspicuous objects regarded as points on a line (**lead′ing line′**) upon which a vessel can sail a safe course. [1795–1805]

lead′ing ques′tion (lē′ding), a question so worded as to suggest the proper or desired answer. [1815–25]

lead′ing strings′ (lē′ding), **1.** strings for leading and supporting a child learning to walk. **2.** excessively restraining guidance: *His parents tried to keep him in leading strings, but he finally married and moved away.* [1670–80]

lead′ing tone′ (lē′ding), *Music.* the seventh degree of a diatonic scale; subtonic. Also called **lead′ing note′.** [1910–15]

lead·ing wind (lē′ding wind′), *Naut.* a wind abeam or on the quarter, esp. one strong enough to be a good sailing wind.

lead′ line′ (led), *Naut.* a line by which a lead is lowered into the water to take soundings: in deep-sea practice, divided into levels one fathom apart, variously treated as marks and deeps. [1475–85]

lead′ monox′ide (led), *Chem.* litharge. [1905–10]

lead-off (lēd′ôf′, -of′), *adj.* leading off or beginning: *the lead-off item on the agenda.* [1885–90; adj. use of v. phrase *lead off*]

lead·off (lēd′ôf′, -of′), *n.* **1.** an act that starts something; start; beginning. **2.** *Baseball.* the player who is first in the batting order or who is first to bat for a team in an inning. [1890–95; n. use of v. phrase *lead off*]

lead′ ox′ide (led), **1.** litharge. **2.** any oxide of lead, as red lead.

lead′ pen′cil (led), a writing or drawing implement made of graphite in a wooden or metal holder. [1680–90]

lead′-pipe cinch′ (led′pīp′), *Slang.* **1.** an absolute certainty: *It's a lead-pipe cinch they'll be there.* **2.** something very easy to accomplish: *Getting him elected will be a lead-pipe cinch.* [1895–1900, *Amer.*]

lead·plant (led′plant′, -plänt′), *n.* a North American shrub, *Amorpha canescens,* of the legume family, the leaves and twigs of which have a gray cast. [1825–35, *Amer.;* LEAD[2] + PLANT]

lead′ poi′soning (led), **1.** *Pathol.* **a.** a toxic condition produced by ingestion, inhalation, or skin absorption of lead or lead compounds, resulting in various dose-related symptoms including anemia, nausea, muscle weakness, confusion, blindness, and coma. **b.** Also called **plumbism, saturnism.** this condition occurring in adults whose work involves contact with lead products. **2.** *Slang.* death or injury inflicted by a bullet or shot. [1875–80]

lead′ screw′ (lēd), (on a lathe) a rotating horizontal screw for moving the tool carriage along the work at a constant rate.

lead′ sheet′ (lēd), a copy of a song containing the melody line, sometimes along with the lyrics and the notations indicating the harmonic structure. [1940–45, *Amer.*]

leads·man (ledz′mən), *n., pl.* **-men.** a sailor who sounds with a lead line. [1500–10; LEAD[2] + 'S[1] + MAN]

lead′ tetraeth′yl (led), *Chem.* tetraethyllead.

lead′ time′ (lēd), the period of time between the initial phase of a process and the emergence of results, as between the planning and completed manufacture of a product. Also, **lead′-time′.** [1940–45, *Amer.*]

lead′ track′ (lēd), a track connecting a railroad yard or facility with a main line or running track.

lead′ tree′ (led), any of several tropical trees or shrubs belonging to the genus *Leucaena,* of the legume family, esp. *L. glauca,* having pinnate leaves and white flowers. [1860–65]

lead-up (lēd′up′), *n.* something that provides an approach to or preparation for an event or situation. [1950–55; n. use of v. phrase *lead up (to)*]

Lead·ville (led′vil), *n.* a town in central Colorado: historic mining boom town. 3879.

lead′ white′ (led), a poisonous pigment used in painting, consisting of white lead and characterized chiefly by a fugitive white color, covering power, and tough, flexible film-forming properties. Also called **Cremnitz white, flake white.**

lead·wort (led′wûrt′, -wôrt′), *n.* any plant or shrub of the genus *Plumbago,* having spikes of blue, white, or red flowers. [1855–60; LEAD[2] + WORT[2]]

lead′wort fam′ily, the plant family Plumbaginaceae, characterized by shrubs and herbaceous plants of seacoasts and semiarid regions, having basal or alternate leaves, spikelike clusters of tubular flowers, and dry, one-seeded fruit, and including leadwort, sea lavender, statice, and thrift.

lead·y (led′ē), *adj.,* **lead·i·er, lead·i·est.** like lead; leaden. [1350–1400; ME *leedy.* See LEAD[2], -Y[1]]

leaf (lēf), *n., pl.* **leaves** (lēvz), *v.* —*n.* **1.** one of the expanded, usually green organs borne by the stem of a plant. See illus. on next page. **2.** any similar or corresponding lateral outgrowth of a stem. **3.** a petal: *a rose leaf.* **4.** leaves collectively; foliage. **5.** *Bibliog.* a unit generally comprising two printed, blank, or illustrated pages of a book, one on each side. **6.** a thin sheet of metal: *silver leaf.* **7.** a lamina or layer. **8.** a sliding, hinged, or detachable flat part, as of a door or tabletop. **9.** a section of a drawbridge. **10.** a single strip of metal in a leaf spring. **11.** a tooth of a small gear wheel, as of a pinion. **12.** See **leaf fat. 13.** *Textiles.* shaft (def. 14). **14. in leaf,** covered with foliage; having leaves: *the pale green tint of the woods newly in leaf.* **15. take a leaf out of** or **from someone's book,** to follow someone's example; imitate: *Some countries that took a leaf out of American industry's book are now doing very well for themselves.* **16. turn over a new leaf,** to begin anew; make a fresh start: *Every New Year's we make resolutions to turn over a new leaf.* —*v.i.* **17.** to put forth leaves. **18.** to turn pages, esp. quickly (usually fol. by *through*): *to leaf through a book.* —*v.t.* **19.** to thumb or turn, as the pages of a book or magazine, in a casual or cursory inspection of the contents. [bef. 900; ME *leef, lef,* OE *lēaf;* c. D *loof,* G *Laub,* ON *lauf,* Goth *laufs*] —**leaf′less,** *adj.* —**leaf′like′,** *adj.*

Common Leaf Shapes and Margins

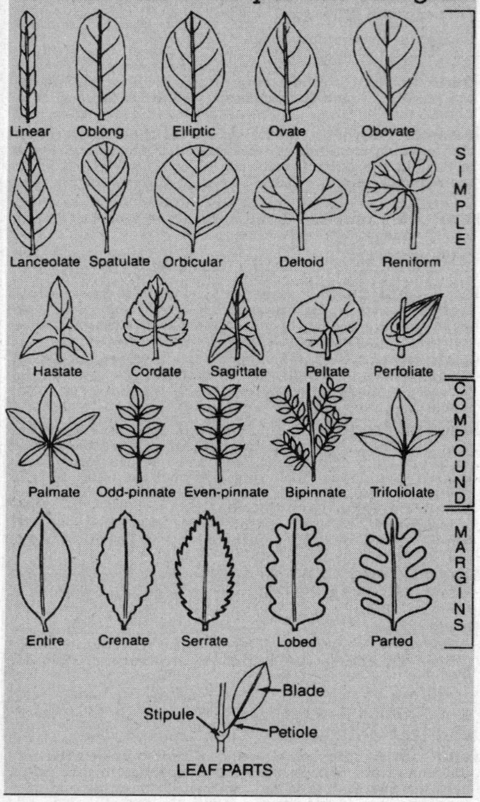

Linear Oblong Elliptic Ovate Obovate
Lanceolate Spatulate Orbicular Deltoid Reniform
Hastate Cordate Sagittate Peltate Perfoliate
SIMPLE
Palmate Odd-pinnate Even-pinnate Bipinnate Trifoliolate
COMPOUND
Entire Crenate Serrate Lobed Parted
MARGINS
Blade
Stipule
Petiole
LEAF PARTS

Leaf (lēf), *n.* **Mun·ro** (mun rō′), 1905–76, U.S. author and illustrator of books for children.

leaf·age (lē′fij), *n.* foliage. [1590–1600; LEAF + -AGE]

leaf′ beet′, chard.

leaf′ bee′tle, any of numerous, often brightly colored beetles of the family Chrysomelidae, that feed on the leaves of plants, the larvae of which infest the roots, stem, and leaves. [1850–55]

leaf·bird (lēf′bûrd′), *n.* any of several greenish, passerine birds of the genus *Chloropsis,* of Asia, related to the bulbuls, and often kept as pets. [LEAF + BIRD]

leaf′ blight′, *Plant Pathol.* **1.** a symptom or phase of many diseases of plants, characterized by necrotic spots or streaks on the leaves, accompanied by seed rot and seedling blight. **2.** any disease so characterized. [1840–50]

leaf′ blotch′, *Plant Pathol.* **1.** a symptom or phase of certain esp. fungal diseases of plants, characterized by necrotic discoloration of the leaves. **2.** any disease so characterized. [1905–10]

leaf′ bud′. See under **bud**[1] (def. 1a). [1655–65]

leaf′ bug′. See **plant bug.**

leaf′ but′terfly, any of various butterflies of the genus *Kallima,* of southern Asia, the East Indies, and Australia, having wings that resemble dead leaves. [1880–85]

leaf′ cor′al, any red algae of the species *Bossea orbigniana,* common as a seaweed along the Pacific coast of the U.S., having calcified, flattened, jointed stems.

leaf′-cut·ting ant′ (lēf′kut′ing), any of several tropical American ants of the genus *Atta* that cut and chew bits of leaves and flowers into a mash that they use to cultivate a fungus garden. [1870–75]

leaf′-cutting bee′, any of the bees of the family Megachilidae that cut circular pieces from leaves or flowers to line their nests. [1795–1805]

leafed (lēft), *adj.* having leaves; leaved. [1545–55; LEAF + -ED[3]]

leaf′ fat′, a layer of fat that surrounds the kidneys, esp. of a hog. [1715–25]

leaf′-foot·ed bug′ (lēf′fo͝ot′id), any of numerous plant-sucking or predaceous bugs of the family Coreidae, typically having leaflike legs: several species are pests of food crops. Also called **coreid bug.**

leaf·hop·per (lēf′hop′ər), *n.* any of numerous leaping, homopterous insects of the family Cicadellidae that suck plant juices, many being serious crop pests. Also called **jassid.** [1850–55, *Amer.;* LEAF + HOPPER]

leaf′ in′sect, any of several orthopterous insects of the family Phillidae, of southern Asia and the East Indies, having a body that resembles a leaf in color and form. Also called **walking leaf.** [1860–65]

leaf′ lard′, lard prepared from the leaf fat of the hog. [1840–50]

leaf·let (lēf′lit), *n., v.,* **-let·ed** or **let·ted, -let·ing** or **-let·ting.** —*n.* **1.** a small flat or folded sheet of printed matter, as an advertisement or notice, usually intended for free distribution. **2.** one of the separate blades or divisions of a compound leaf. **3.** a small leaflike part or structure. **4.** a small or young leaf. —*v.t.* **5.** to distribute leaflets or handbills to or among: *Campaign workers leafleted shoppers at the mall.* —*v.i.* **6.** to distribute leaflets. [1780–90; LEAF + -LET] —**leaf′let·er, leaf′let·ter,** *n.*

leaf·let·eer (lēf′li tēr′), *n.* a person who writes or distributes leaflets. [1890–95; LEAFLET + -EER, on the model of PAMPHLETEER]

leaf′ let′tuce, a type of lettuce having loosely clustered, often curled leaves that are sometimes tinged with red.

leaf′ min′er, any of the larvae of any of numerous insects, as moths of the family Gracilariidae, that live in and feed on the parenchyma of leaves. Also, **leaf′min′·er.** [1820–30]

leaf′ mold′, a compost or layer of soil consisting chiefly of decayed vegetable matter, esp. leaves. Also, **leaf′mold′.** [1835–45]

leaf′ mus′tard. See under **mustard** (def. 2).

leaf′-nosed bat′ (lēf′nōzd′), any of various New and Old World bats, as of the families Phyllostomatidae, Rhinolophidae, and Hipposideridae, having a leaflike flap of skin at the tip of the nose. [1865–70]

leaf′ roll′, *Plant Pathol.* a viral disease of plants, esp. potatoes, characterized by upward rolling of the leaflets, chlorosis, stunting, and necrosis of the phloem. [1925–30]

leaf′ roll′er, any of several insects, esp. moths of the family Tortricidae, the larvae of which form a nest by rolling and tying leaves with spun silk. Also, **leaf′roll′·er.** [1820–30]

leaf′ rust′, *Plant Pathol.* a disease, esp. of cereals and other grasses, characterized by rust-colored pustules of spores on the affected leaf blades and sheaths and caused by any of several rust fungi. [1860–65]

leaf′ scald′, *Plant Pathol.* a bacterial disease of sugarcane, characterized by irregular, bleached streaks on the leaves and defoliation and caused esp. by *Bacterium albilineans.* [1895–1900]

leaf′ spot′, *Plant Pathol.* **1.** a limited, often circular, discolored, diseased area on a leaf, usually including a central region of necrosis. **2.** any disease so characterized. [1900–05]

leaf′ spring′, a long, narrow, multiple spring composed of several layers of spring metal bracketed together: used in some suspension systems of carriages and automobiles. See illus. under **spring.** [1890–95]

leaf·stalk (lēf′stôk′), *n.* petiole (def. 1). [1770–80; LEAF + STALK[1]]

leaf′ war′bler, any of several small, greenish or brownish, Old World warblers of the genus *Phylloscopus* that feed on insects among the leaves of trees. [1925–30]

leaf·y (lē′fē), *adj.,* **leaf·i·er, leaf·i·est.** **1.** having, abounding in, or covered with leaves or foliage: *the leafy woods.* **2.** having broad leaves or consisting mainly of leaves: *leafy vegetables.* **3.** leaflike; foliaceous. [1545–55; LEAF + -Y[1]] —**leaf′i·ness,** *n.*

league[1] (lēg), *n., v.,* **leagued, lea·guing.** —*n.* **1.** a covenant or compact made between persons, parties, states, etc., for the promotion or maintenance of common interests or for mutual assistance or service. **2.** the aggregation of persons, parties, states, etc., associated in such a covenant or compact; confederacy. **3.** an association of individuals having a common goal. **4.** a group of athletic teams organized to promote mutual interests and to compete chiefly among themselves: *a bowling league.* **5.** *Sports.* **a.** See **major league. b.** See **minor league. 6.** group; class; category: *As a pianist he just simply isn't in your league.* **7. in league,** working together, often secretly or for a harmful purpose; united. —*v.t., v.i.* **8.** to unite in a league; combine. [1425–75; earlier *leage* < It *lega,* n. deriv. of *legare* < L *ligāre* to bind; r. late ME *ligg* < MF *ligue* < It *liga,* var. of *lega*]
—**Syn. 1.** See **alliance. 2.** combination, coalition.

league[2] (lēg), *n.* **1.** a unit of distance, varying at different periods and in different countries, in English-speaking countries usually estimated roughly at 3 miles (4.8 kilometers). **2.** a square league, as a unit of land measure. [1350–1400; ME *lege, leuge* < LL *leuga* a Gaulish unit of distance equal to 1.5 Roman miles, appar. < Gaulish; r. OE *lēowe* < LL, as above]

League′ Cit′y, a town in S Texas. 16,578.

League′ of Na′tions, an international organization to promote world peace and cooperation that was created by the Treaty of Versailles (1919): dissolved April 1946.

League′ of Wom′en Vot′ers, a nonpartisan organization that works toward improving the political process: created in 1920 to inform women on public issues. *Abbr.:* LWV

lea·guer[1] (lē′gər), *n.* a member of a league. [1585–95; LEAGUE[1] + -ER[1]]

lea·guer[2] (lē′gər), *Archaic.* —*v.t.* **1.** to besiege. —*n.* **2.** a siege. [1590–1600; < D *leger* army, camp. See LAIR[1]]

Le·ah (lē′ə), *n.* **1.** the first wife of Jacob. Gen. 29:23–26. **2.** a female given name: from a Hebrew word meaning "weary."

Lea·hy (lā′hē), *n.* **William Daniel,** 1875–1959, U.S. admiral and diplomat.

leak (lēk), *n.* **1.** an unintended hole, crack, or the like, through which liquid, gas, light, etc., enters or escapes: *a leak in the roof.* **2.** an act or instance of leaking. **3.** any means of unintended entrance or escape. **4.** *Elect.* the loss of current from a conductor, usually resulting from poor insulation. **5.** a disclosure of secret, esp. official, information, as to the news media, by an unnamed source. **6. take a leak,** *Slang (vulgar).* to urinate. —*v.i.* **7.** to let a liquid, gas, light, etc., enter or escape, as through an unintended hole or crack: *The boat leaks.* **8.** to pass in or out in this manner, as liquid, gas, or light: *gas leaking from a pipe.* **9.** to become known unintentionally (usually fol. by *out*): *The news leaked out.* **10.** to disclose secret, esp. official, information anonymously, as to the news media: *The official revealed that he had leaked to the press in the hope of saving his own reputation.* —*v.t.* **11.** to let (liquid, gas, light, etc.) enter or escape: *This camera leaks light.* **12.** to allow to become known, as information given out covertly: *to leak the news of the ambassador's visit.* [1375–1425; 1955–60 for def. 12; late ME *leken* < ON *leka* to drip, leak; akin to D *lek,* obs. G *lech* leaky. See LEACH[1]] —**leak′er,** *n.* —**leak′less,** *adj.*

leak·age (lē′kij), *n.* **1.** an act of leaking; leak. **2.** something that leaks in or out. **3.** the amount that leaks in or out. **4.** *Com.* an allowance for loss by leaking. **5.** *Physics, Elect.* the loss of all or part of a useful agent, as of the electric current that flows through an insulator **(leak′age cur′rent)** or of the magnetic flux that passes outside useful flux circuits **(leak′age flux′).** [1480–90; LEAK + -AGE]

leak·ance (lē′kəns), *n. Elect.* the reciprocal of the resistance of insulation. [1890–95; LEAK + -ANCE]

Lea·key (lē′kē), *n.* **1. Louis Seymour Baz·ett** (baz′-it), 1903–72, British archaeologist and anthropologist. **2. Mary (Douglas),** 1913–96, British archaeologist (wife of Louis Leakey). **3.** their son, **Richard (Erskine Frere)** (frēr), born 1944, Kenyan paleontologist.

leak·proof (lēk′pro͞of′), *adj.* designed to prevent leaking: *a leakproof bottle.* [1925–30; LEAK + -PROOF]

leak·y (lē′kē), *adj.,* **leak·i·er, leak·i·est.** **1.** allowing liquid, gas, etc., to enter or escape: *a leaky boat; a leaky container.* **2.** *Informal.* unreliable: *a leaky memory; a leaky tongue.* [1600–10; LEAK + -Y[1]] —**leak′i·ness,** *n.*

leal (lēl), *adj. Scot.* loyal; true. [1250–1300; ME *leel* < OF < L *lēgālis* LEGAL; see LOYAL] —**leal′ly,** *adv.* —**le·al·ty** (lē′əl tē), *n.*

Lea·ming·ton (lē′ming tən), *n.* a town in SE Ontario, in S Canada, near Lake Erie. 12,528.

lean[1] (lēn), *v.,* **leaned** or *(esp. Brit.)* **leant; lean·ing;** *n.* —*v.i.* **1.** to incline or bend from a vertical position: *She leaned out the window.* **2.** to incline, as in a particular direction; slant: *The post leans to the left. The building leaned sharply before renovation.* **3.** to incline in feeling, opinion, action, etc.: *to lean toward socialism.* **4.** to rest against or on something for support: *to lean against a wall.* **5.** to depend or rely (usually fol. by *on* or *upon*): *someone he could lean on in an emergency.* —*v.t.* **6.** to incline or bend: *He leaned his head forward.* **7.** to cause to lean or rest; prop: *to lean a chair against the railing.* **8. lean on,** *Informal.* **a.** to exert influence or pressure on in order to gain cooperation, maintain discipline, or the like: *The state is leaning on the company to clean up its industrial wastes.* **b.** to criticize, reprimand, or punish: *I would have enjoyed school more if the teachers hadn't leaned on me so much.* **9. lean over backward(s).** See **bend**[1] (def. 15). —*n.* **10.** the act or state of leaning; inclination: *The tower has a pronounced lean.* [bef. 900; ME *lenen,* OE *hleonian, hlinian;* c. G. *lehnen;* akin to L *clīnāre* to INCLINE, Gk *klīnein*]

lean[2] (lēn), *adj.,* **-er, -est,** *n.* —*adj.* **1.** (of persons or animals) without much flesh or fat; not plump or fat; thin: *lean cattle.* **2.** (of edible meat) containing little or no fat. **3.** lacking in richness, fullness, quantity, etc.; poor: *a lean diet; lean years.* **4.** spare; economical: *a lean prose style.* **5.** *Auto.* (of a mixture in a fuel system) having a relatively low ratio of fuel to air (contrasted with *rich*). **6.** (of paint) having more pigment than oil. Cf. **fat** (def. 12). **7.** *Naut.* (of a bow) having fine lines; sharp. **8.** *Metall.* (of ore) having a low mineral content; low-grade. —*n.* **9.** the part of flesh that consists of muscle rather than fat. **10.** the lean part of anything. **11.** *Typesetting.* matter that is difficult to set because of complexity or intermixed fonts. Cf. **fat** (def. 25). [bef. 1000; ME *lene,* OE *hlǣne*] —**lean′ly,** *adv.* —**lean′·ness,** *n.*
—**Syn. 1.** skinny, lank, lanky. See **thin. 3.** sparse, barren, unfruitful, jejune. —**Ant. 1, 2.** fat. **3.** fruitful.

Lean (lēn), *n.* **David,** 1908–91, British film director.

Le·an·der (lē an′dər), *n. Class. Myth.* a Greek youth, the lover of Hero, who swam the Hellespont every night to visit her until he was drowned in a storm.

lean·er (lē′nər), *n.* **1.** a person or thing that leans. **2.** *Horseshoes.* a thrown horseshoe that leans against the stake. [1530–40; LEAN[1] + -ER[1]]

lean-faced (lēn′fāst′), *adj.* having a thin, narrow face. [1580–90]

lean·gle (ling′gəl, lē ang′gəl), *n. Australian.* an Aboriginal war club or bludgeon. Also, **langeel, langiel.** [1865–70; < Wergaia (Australian Aboriginal language spoken in the vicinity of Wimmera, Victoria) *liengel*]

lean·ing (lē′ning), *n.* inclination; tendency: *strong literary leanings.* [bef. 1000; ME *leninge,* OE *hlining.* See LEAN[1], -ING[1]]
—**Syn.** bent, propensity, proclivity, bias, penchant.

Lean′ing Tow′er of Pi′sa, The, a round, marble campanile in Pisa, Italy, begun in 1174 and now 17 ft. (5.2 m) out of the perpendicular in its height of 179 ft. (54 m).

leant (lent), *v. Chiefly Brit.* a pp. and pt. of **lean**[1].

lean-to (lēn′to͞o′), *n., pl.* **-tos.** **1.** a shack or shed supported at one side by trees or posts and having an inclined roof. **2.** a roof of a single pitch with the higher end abutting a wall or larger building. See illus. under **roof. 3.** a structure with such a roof. [1425–75; late ME; n. use of v. phrase *lean to*]

leap (lēp), *v.,* **leaped** or **leapt, leap·ing,** *n.* —*v.i.* **1.** to spring through the air from one point or position to another; jump: *to leap over a ditch.* **2.** to move or act quickly or suddenly: *to leap aside; She leaped at the opportunity.* **3.** to pass, come, rise, etc., as if with a jump: *to leap to a conclusion; an idea that immediately leaped to mind.* —*v.t.* **4.** to jump over: *to leap a fence.* **5.** to pass over as if by a jump. **6.** to cause to leap: *to leap a horse.* —*n.* **7.** a spring, jump, or bound; a light, springing movement. **8.** the distance covered in a leap; distance jumped. **9.** a place leaped or to be leaped over or from. **10.** a sudden or abrupt transition: *a successful leap from piano class to concert hall.* **11.** a sudden and decisive increase: *a leap in the company's profits.* **12. by leaps and bounds,** very rapidly: *We are progressing by leaps and bounds.* **13. leap in the dark,** an action of which the consequences are unknown: *The experiment was a leap in the dark.* **14. leap of faith,** an act or instance of accepting or trusting in something that cannot readily be seen or proved. [bef. 900; ME *lepen,* OE *hlēapan* to leap, run; c. G *laufen,* ON *hlaupa,* Goth *hlaupan*] —**leap′er,** *n.*
—**Syn. 1.** bound. See **jump.**

leap′ day′, February 29: the extra day added to the Gregorian calendar in leap year. [1590–1600]

leap·frog (lēp′frog′, -frôg′), *n., v.,* **-frogged, -frog·ging.** —*n.* **1.** a game in which players take turns in leaping over another player bent over from the waist. **2.** an advance from one place, position, or situation to another without progressing through all or any of the places or stages in between: *a leapfrog from bank teller to vice president in one short year.* —*v.t.* **3.** to jump over (a person or thing) in or as if in leapfrog: *He leapfrogged the fence to reach the crying child.* **4.** to move or cause to move as if in leapfrog: *Manufacturers are leapfrogging prices because the cost of raw materials has doubled.* —*v.i.* **5.** to move or advance in or as if in leapfrog: *Our tour leapfrogged through six cities in four days.* [1590–1600; LEAP + FROG[1]] —**leap′frog′ger,** *n.*

leap′ sec′ond, an extra second intercalated into the world's timekeeping system about once a year, made necessary by the gradual slowing down of the earth's rotation. [1970–75]

leapt (lept, lēpt), *v.* a pt. and pp. of **leap.**

leap′ year′, 1. (in the Gregorian calendar) a year that contains 366 days, with February 29 as an additional day: occurring in years whose last two digits are evenly divisible by four, except for centenary years not divisible by 400. **2.** a year containing an extra day in any calendar. Cf. **common year.** [1350–1400; ME *lepe yere*]

lear (lēr), *n. Scot. and North Eng.* learning; instruction; lesson. [1350–1400; late ME *lere* lesson, n. use of *lere* to teach, OE *lǣran;* c. D *leren,* G *lehren,* Goth *laisjan;* akin to LORE]

Lear (lēr), *n.* **1. Edward,** 1812–88, English writer of humorous verse and landscape painter. **2.** (*italics*) See ***King Lear.***

lear′ board′, (on a sloping roof) a board laid next to the gutter to receive the turned-up edge of the metal lining. Also called **layer board.** [var. of LAYER]

learn (lûrn), *v.,* **learned** (lûrnd) or **learnt, learn·ing.** —*v.t.* **1.** to acquire knowledge of or skill in by study, instruction, or experience: *to learn French; to learn to ski.* **2.** to become informed of or acquainted with; ascertain: *to learn the truth.* **3.** to memorize: *He learned the poem so he could recite it at the dinner.* **4.** to gain (a habit, mannerism, etc.) by experience, exposure to example, or the like; acquire: *She learned patience from her father.* **5.** (of a device or machine, esp. a computer) to perform an analogue of human learning with artificial intelligence. **6.** *Nonstandard.* to instruct in; teach. —*v.i.* **7.** to acquire knowledge or skill: *to learn rapidly.* **8.** to become informed (usually fol. by *of*): *to learn of an accident.* [bef. 900; ME *lernen,* OE *leornian* to learn, read, ponder (c. G *lernen*); akin to *lesan* to glean (c. G *lesen* to read). See LEAR] —**learn′a·ble,** *adj.*
—**Syn. 1.** LEARN, ASCERTAIN, DETECT, DISCOVER imply adding to one's store of facts. To LEARN is to add to one's knowledge or information: *to learn a language.* To ASCERTAIN is to verify facts by inquiry or analysis: *to ascertain the truth about an event.* To DETECT implies becoming aware of something that had been obscure, secret, or concealed: *to detect a flaw in reasoning.* To DISCOVER is used with objective clauses as a synonym of LEARN in order to suggest that the new information acquired is surprising to the learner: *I discovered that she had been married before.*

learn·ed (lûr′nid *for 1–3;* lûrnd *for 4*), *adj.* **1.** having much knowledge; scholarly; erudite: *learned professors.* **2.** connected or involved with the pursuit of knowledge, esp. of a scholarly nature: *a learned journal.* **3.** of or showing learning or knowledge; well-informed: *learned in the ways of the world.* **4.** acquired by experience, study, etc.: *learned behavior.* [1300–50; ME *lerned.* See LEARN, -ED[2]] —**learn′ed·ly,** *adv.* —**learn′ed·ness,** *n.*

learn′ed bor′rowing (lûr′nid), a word or other linguistic form borrowed from a classical language into a modern language.

learn′ed profes′sion, any of the three vocations of theology, law, and medicine, commonly held to require highly advanced learning. Cf. **profession** (def. 1).

learn′ed soci′ety, an organization devoted to the scholarly study of a particular field or discipline, as modern languages, psychology, or history. [1670–80]

learn·er (lûr′nər), *n.* a person who is learning; student; pupil; apprentice; trainee. [bef. 1000; ME *lerner(e),* OE *leornere;* see LEARN, -ER[1]]

learn·ing (lûr′ning), *n.* **1.** knowledge acquired by systematic study in any field of scholarly application. **2.** the act or process of acquiring knowledge or skill. **3.** *Psychol.* the modification of behavior through practice, training, or experience. [bef. 900; ME *lerning,* OE *leornung.* See LEARN, -ING[1]]
—**Syn. 1.** LEARNING, ERUDITION, LORE, SCHOLARSHIP refer to knowledge existing or acquired. LEARNING is the most general term. It may refer to knowledge obtained by systematic study or by trial and error: *a man of learning; learning in the real world.* ERUDITION suggests a thorough, formal, and profound sort of knowledge obtained by extensive research; it is esp. applied to knowledge in fields other than those of mathematics and physical sciences: *a man of vast erudition in languages.* LORE is accumulated knowledge in a particular field, esp. of a curious, anecdotal, or traditional nature; the word is now somewhat literary: *nature lore; local lore.* SCHOLARSHIP is the formalized learning that is taught in schools, esp. as actively employed by a person trying to master some field of knowledge or extend its bounds: *high standards of scholarship in history.*

learn′ing curve′, *Educ.* a graphic representation of progress in learning measured against the time required to achieve mastery.

learn′ing disabil′ity, a disorder, as dyslexia, usually affecting school-age children of normal or above-normal intelligence, characterized by difficulty in understanding or using spoken or written language, and thought to be related to impairment or slowed development of perceptual motor skills. [1955–60]

learn·ing-dis·a·bled (lûr′ning dis ā′bəld), *adj.* pertaining to or having a learning disability: *a learning-disabled child.* [1970–75]

learn′ing re′sources cen′ter, a library, usually in an educational institution, that includes and encourages the use of audiovisual aids and other special materials for learning in addition to books, periodicals, and the like. [1965–70]

learnt (lûrnt), *v.* a pt. and pp. of **learn.**

lear·y (lēr′ē), *adj.* leery[1].

lease[1] (lēs), *n., v.,* **leased, leas·ing.** —*n.* **1.** a contract renting land, buildings, etc., to another; a contract or instrument conveying property to another for a specified period or for a period determinable at the will of either lessor or lessee in consideration of rent or other compensation. **2.** the property leased. **3.** the period of time for which a lease is made: *a five-year lease.* **4. a new lease on life,** a chance to improve one's situation or to live longer or more happily: *Plastic surgery gave him a new lease on life.* —*v.t.* **5.** to grant the temporary possession or use of (lands, tenements, etc.) to another, usually for compensation at a fixed rate; let: *She plans to lease her apartment to a friend.* **6.** to take or hold by lease: *He leased the farm from the sheriff.* —*v.i.* **7.** to grant a lease; let or rent: *to lease at a lower rental.* [1350–1400; ME *les* < AF (equiv. to OF *lais,* F *legs* legacy), n. deriv. of *lesser* to lease, lit., let go (equiv. to OF *laissier*) < L *laxāre* to RELEASE, let go. See LAX] —**leas′a·ble,** *adj.* —**lease′less,** *adj.* —**leas′er,** *n.*
—**Syn. 6.** rent, charter, hire.

lease[2] (lēs), *n. Textiles.* **1.** a system for keeping the warp in position and under control by alternately crossing the warp yarn over and under the lease rods. **2.** the order of drawing in the warp ends. [1350–1400; ME *lese* length or coil of thread, var. of *lesh* LEASH]

lease·back (lēs′bak′), *n.* the disposal of a building, land, or other property to a buyer under special arrangements for simultaneously leasing it on a long-term basis to the original seller, usually with an option to renew the lease. Also called **sale and leaseback, sale-leaseback.** [1945–50; n. use of v. phrase *lease back*]

lease·hold (lēs′hōld′), *n.* **1.** property acquired under a lease. **2.** a tenure under a lease. —*adj.* **3.** held by lease. [1710–20; LEASE[1] + HOLD[1]]

lease·hold·er (lēs′hōl′dər), *n.* a tenant under a lease. [1855–60; LEASE[1] + HOLDER]

lease·man (lēs′mən), *n., pl.* **-men.** a person who leases land and obtains the rights to its use, esp. oil-drilling rights. Also called **landman.** [LEASE[1] + MAN[1]]

lease-pur·chase (lēs′pûr′chəs), *n.* **1.** the continuing use of property or goods under a lease for a stipulated period with option for the lessee to buy and with part of the rental charges credited toward the purchase price. —*adj.* **2.** of or pertaining to lease-purchase.

lease′ rod′, a rod or bar between the whip roll and the harness on a loom for keeping the warp in place. [1815–25]

leash (lēsh), *n.* **1.** a chain, strap, etc., for controlling or leading a dog or other animal; lead. **2.** check; curb; restraint: *to keep one's temper in leash; a tight leash on one's subordinates.* **3.** *Hunting.* a brace and a half, as of foxes or hounds. —*v.t.* **4.** to secure, control, or restrain by or as if by a leash: *to leash water power for industrial use.* **5.** to bind together by or as if by a leash; connect; link; associate. [1250–1300; ME *lesh,* var. of *lece, lese* < OF *laisse.* See LEASE[1]]

leash′ law′, a local ordinance requiring that dogs be leashed when not on their owners' property. [1715–25]

leas·ing (lē′zing), *n. Archaic.* lying; falsehood. [bef. 950; ME *lesing,* OE *lēasung,* verbal n. of *lēasian* to tell lies, deriv. of *lēas* false. See -LESS, -ING[1]]

least (lēst), *adj., a superl. of* **little** *with* **less** *or* **lesser** *as compar.* **1.** smallest in size, amount, degree, etc.; slightest: *He gave the least amount of money of anyone.* **2.** lowest in consideration, position, or importance. —*n.* **3.** something that is least; the least amount, quantity, degree, etc. **4.** *South Midland U.S.* the youngest in a family or group. **5. at least, a.** at the lowest estimate or figure: *The repairs will cost at least $100.* **b.** at any rate; in any case: *You didn't get a good grade, but at least you passed the course.* Also, **at the least. 6. not in the least,** not in the smallest degree; not at all: *I am not in the least concerned about the outcome of the World Series.* —*adv.* **7.** *superl. of* **little** *with* **less** *as compar.* to the smallest extent, amount, or degree: *That's the least important question of all. He talks least.* [bef. 950; ME *leest(e),* OE *lǣst,* superl. of *lǣssa* LESS]

least′ bit′tern. See under **bittern**[1] (def. 2). [1805–15, *Amer.*]

least′ com′mon denom′inator, *Math.* the smallest number that is a common denominator of a given set of fractions. Also called **lowest common denominator.** [1870–75]

least′ com′mon mul′tiple. *Math.* See **lowest common multiple.** [1815–25]

least′ fly′catcher, a small flycatcher, *Empidonax minimus,* of eastern North America. Also called **chebec.** [1870–75, *Amer.*]

least′ kil′lifish, a fish, *Heterandria formosa,* of coastal swamps from South Carolina to Florida, that feeds on mosquito larvae.

least′ sand′piper, a small, American sandpiper, *Calidris minutilla,* related to the stints of Europe. [1855–60, *Amer.*]

least′ shrew′, a small, brownish shrew, *Cryptotis parva,* of grassy regions of the eastern U.S.

least′ signif′icant dig′it, the digit farthest to the right in a number. *Abbr.:* LSD Cf. **most significant digit.**

least′ squares′, *Statistics.* a method of estimating values from a set of observations by minimizing the sum of the squares of the differences between the observations and the values to be found. Also called **least′-squares′ meth′od, method of least squares.** [1860–65]

least′ up′per bound′, *Math.* an upper bound that is less than or equal to all the upper bounds of a particular set. *3* is the least upper bound of the set consisting of *1, 2, 3. Abbr.:* lub Also called **supremum.**

least·ways (lēst′wāz′), *adv. Dial.* at least; at any rate; leastwise. [1350–1400; ME *leest weye.* See LEAST, -WAYS]

least′ wea′sel, a weasel, *Mustela nivalis,* of northern regions, that grows to a length of about 6 in. (15 cm). Also called **pygmy weasel.**

least·wise (lēst′wīz′), *adv. Informal.* at least; at any rate. [1525–35; LEAST + -WISE]

leath·er (leth′ər), *n.* **1.** the skin of an animal, with the hair removed, prepared for use by tanning or a similar process designed to preserve it against decay and make it pliable or supple when dry. **2.** an article made of this material. **3.** See **stirrup leather.** —*adj.* **4.** pertaining to, made of, or resembling leather: *leather processing; leather upholstery.* **5.** *Slang.* catering to or patronized by customers who typically wear leather clothing, often as a means of signaling interest in or preference for sadomasochistic sexual activity. —*v.t.* **6.** to cover or furnish with leather. **7.** *Informal.* to beat with a leather strap. [bef. 1000; ME *lether,* OE *lether-* (in compounds); c. D, G *leder,* ON *lethr,* MIr *lethar* skin, leather, Welsh *lledr,* Middle Breton *lezr* leather]

leath′er·back tur′tle (leth′ər bak′), a sea turtle, *Dermochelys coriacea,* having the shell embedded in a leathery skin, reaching a length of more than 7 ft. (2.1 m) and a weight of more than 1000 lb. (450 kg): the largest living sea turtle; an endangered species. Also called **leath′er·back′.** [1875–80; LEATHER + BACK[1]]

leath·er·ette (leth′ə ret′), *n.* a material constructed of paper or cloth and finished to simulate the grain, color, and texture of leather. [1875–80; formerly a trademark; see LEATHER, -ETTE]

leath·er·fish (leth′ər fish′), *n., pl.* **-fish·es,** (*esp. collectively*) **-fish.** a filefish. [LEATHER + FISH]

leath·er-hard (leth′ər härd′), *adj.* (of ceramic clay) moist but not sufficiently so to be plastic. [1955–60]

leath·er·jack·et (leth′ər jak′it), *n.* **1.** Also called **leath′er jack′.** any of several carangid fishes having narrow, linear scales embedded in the skin at various angles, esp. *Oligoplites saurus,* found in tropical American waters. **2.** *Australian.* a pancake or other dough fried over a campfire. **3.** the grub of the crane fly. [1760–70; LEATHER + JACKET]

leath·er·leaf (leth′ər lēf′), *n., pl.* **-leaves.** an evergreen shrub, *Chamaedaphne calyculata,* of the heath family, having leathery leaves and one-sided clusters of white, bell-shaped flowers, occurring in bogs in North America. [1810–20, *Amer.;* LEATHER + LEAF]

leath·er-lunged (leth′ər lungd′), *adj.* speaking or capable of speaking in a loud, resonant voice, esp. for prolonged periods: *The leather-lunged senator carried on the filibuster for 18 hours.* [1840–50]

leath·ern (leth′ərn), *adj.* **1.** made of leather. **2.** resembling leather. [bef. 1000; ME, OE *lether(e)n.* See LEATHER, -EN[2]]

leath·er·neck (leth′ər nek′), *n. Slang.* a U.S. marine. [1910–15; from the leather-lined collar which was formerly part of the uniform]

Leath·er·oid (leth′ə roid′), *Trademark.* a brand name for an imitation leather product consisting of chemically treated and vulcanized paper or other vegetable fiber.

leath′er star′, a starfish, *Dermasterias imbricata,* of the western coast of North America, having the body covered by a thick, leathery skin.

Leath′er-Stock·ing Tales′ (leth′ər stok′ing), a series of historical novels by James Fenimore Cooper, comprising *The Pioneers, The Last of the Mohicans, The Prairie, The Pathfinder,* and *The Deerslayer.*

leath·er·wood (leth′ər wo͝od′), *n.* an American shrub, *Dirca palustris,* having a tough bark. Also called **moosewood.** [1735–45, *Amer.;* LEATHER + WOOD[1]]

leath·er·work (leth′ər wûrk′), *n.* **1.** work or decora-

CONCISE PRONUNCIATION KEY: act, cāpe, dâre, pärt; set, ēqual; if, īce; ox, ōver, ôrder, oil, bo͝ok, bo͞ot, out, up, ûrge; child; sing; shoe; thin, *th*at; zh as in *treasure.* ə = *a* as in *alone, e* as in *system, i* as in *easily, o* as in *gallop, u* as in *circus;* ᵊ as in *fire* (fīᵊr), *hour* (ouᵊr). l and n can serve as syllabic consonants, as in *cradle* (krād′l), and *button* (but′n). See the full key inside the front cover.

tion done in leather. **2.** an article or articles made of leather. [1855–60; LEATHER + WORK] **—leath′er·work′er,** *n.*

leath·er·y (leth′ə rē), *adj.* like leather in appearance or texture; tough and flexible. [1545–55; LEATHER + -Y[1]] **—leath′er·i·ness,** *n.*

leave[1] (lēv), *v.,* **left, leav·ing.** *—v.t.* **1.** to go out of or away from, as a place: *to leave the house.* **2.** to depart from permanently; quit: *to leave a job.* **3.** to let remain or have remaining behind after going, disappearing, ceasing, etc.: *I left my wallet home. The wound left a scar.* **4.** to allow to remain in the same place, condition, etc.: *Is there any coffee left?* **5.** to let stay or be as specified: *to leave a door unlocked.* **6.** to let (a person or animal) remain in a position to do something without interference: *We left him to his work.* **7.** to let (a thing) remain for action or decision: *We left the details to the lawyer.* **8.** to give in charge; deposit; entrust: *Leave the package with the receptionist. I left my name and phone number.* **9.** to stop; cease; give up: *He left music to study law.* **10.** to disregard; neglect: *We will leave this for the moment and concentrate on the major problem.* **11.** to give for use after one's death or departure: *to leave all one's money to charity.* **12.** to have remaining after death: *He leaves a wife and three children.* **13.** to have as a remainder after subtraction: *2 from 4 leaves 2.* **14.** *Nonstandard.* let[1] (defs. 1, 2, 6). *—v.i.* **15.** to go away, depart, or set out: *We leave for Europe tomorrow.* **16. leave alone.** See **alone** (def. 4). **17. leave off, a.** to desist from; cease; stop; abandon. **b.** to stop using or wearing: *It had stopped raining, so we left off our coats.* **c.** to omit: *to leave a name off a list.* **18. leave out,** to omit; exclude: *She left out an important detail in her account.* [bef. 900; ME *leven,* OE *lǣfan* (causative formation from base of *lāf* remainder; see LAVE[2]); c. OHG *leiban* (cf. G *bleiben* to remain), ON *leifa,* Goth *-laibjan*] **—leav′er,** *n.*

—Syn. 1, 2. abandon, forsake, desert; relinquish. **9.** forbear, renounce. **10.** ignore, forget. **11.** bequeath, will; devise, transmit. **—Ant. 1, 2.** join.

—Usage. LEAVE is interchangeable with LET when followed by ALONE with the sense "to refrain from annoying or interfering with": *Leave* (or *Let*) *her alone and she will solve the problem easily. When he was left* (or *let*) *alone without interruptions, the boy quickly assembled the apparatus.* The use of LEAVE ALONE for LET ALONE in the sense "not to mention" is nonstandard: *There wasn't any standing room, let* (not *leave*) *alone a seat, so I missed the performance.*

Other substitutions of LEAVE for LET are generally regarded as nonstandard: *Let* (not *Leave*) *us sit down and talk this over. Let* (not *Leave*) *her do it her own way. The police wouldn't let* (not *leave*) *us cross the barriers.* See also **let**[1].

leave[2] (lēv), *n.* **1.** permission to do something: *to beg leave to go elsewhere.* **2.** permission to be absent, as from work or military duty: *The firm offers a maternity leave as part of its benefit program.* **3.** the time this permission lasts: *30 days' leave.* **4.** a parting; departure; farewell: *He took his leave before the formal ceremonies began. We took leave of them after dinner.* **5.** *Metall.* draft (def. 23). **6.** *Bowling.* the pin or pins in upright position after the bowl of the first ball. [bef. 900; ME *leve,* OE *lēaf;* akin to BELIEVE, FURLOUGH, LIEF]

—Syn. 1–3. liberty. **2, 3.** vacation, furlough.

leave[3] (lēv), *v.i.,* **leaved, leav·ing.** to put forth leaves; leaf. [1250–1300; ME *leven,* deriv. of *lef* LEAF]

leaved (lēvd), *adj.* having leaves; leafed. [1200–50; ME *leved.* See LEAVE[3], -ED[2]]

leav·en (lev′ən), *n.* **1.** a substance, as yeast or baking powder, that causes fermentation and expansion of dough or batter. **2.** fermented dough reserved for producing fermentation in a new batch of dough. **3.** an element that produces an altering or transforming influence. *—v.t.* **4.** to add leaven to (dough or batter) and cause to rise. **5.** to permeate with an altering or transforming element. [1300–50; ME *levain* < AF, OF *levain* < VL **levāmen,* equiv. to L *levā(re)* to raise + *-men* deverbal n. suffix (prob. not continuous with L *levāmen* means of alleviating, solace)]

leav·en·ing (lev′ə ning), *n.* **1.** Also called **leav′ening a′gent.** a substance used to produce fermentation in dough or batter; leaven. **2.** the act or process of causing to ferment by leaven. **3.** leaven (def. 3). [1600–10; LEAVEN + -ING[1]]

Leav·en·worth (lev′ən wûrth′, -wərth), *n.* **1.** a city in NE Kansas. 33,656. **2.** a federal and military prison there.

leave′ of ab′sence, **1.** permission to be absent from duty, employment, service, etc.; leave. **2.** the length of time granted in such permission: *a two-year leave of absence.* [1765–75]

leaves (lēvz), *n.* pl. of **leaf.**

Leaves′ of Grass′, a book of poems (first edition, 1855; final edition, 1891–92) by Walt Whitman.

leave-tak·ing (lēv′tā′king), *n.* a saying farewell; a parting or good-bye; departure: *His leave-taking was brief.* [1325–75; ME]

leav·ing (lē′ving), *n.* **1.** something that is left; residue. **2. leavings,** leftovers or remains; refuse. [1300–50; ME *leving.* See LEAVE[1], -ING[1]]

Lea·vis (lē′vis), *n.* **F(rank) R(aymond),** 1895–1978, English critic and teacher.

Leav·itt (lev′it), *n.* **Henrietta,** 1868–1921, U.S. astronomer.

leav·y (lē′vē), *adj.,* **leav·i·er, leav·i·est.** *Archaic.* leafy. [1400–50; late ME *levy.* See LEAF, -Y[1]]

Lea·wood (lē′wo͝od′), *n.* a town in E Kansas. 13,360.

CONCISE ETYMOLOGY KEY: <, descended or borrowed from; >, whence; b., blend of, blended; c., cognate with; cf., compare; deriv., derivative; equiv., equivalent; imit., imitative; obl., oblique; r., replacing; s., stem; sp., spelling, spelled; resp., respelling, respelled; trans., translation; ?, origin unknown; *, unattested; ‡, probably earlier than. See the full key inside the front cover.

Leb·a·nese (leb′ə nēz′, -nēs′), *adj., n., pl.* **-nese.** *—adj.* **1.** of or pertaining to Lebanon or its natives or inhabitants. *—n.* **2.** a native or inhabitant of Lebanon. [1915–20; LEBAN(ON) + -ESE]

Leb·a·non (leb′ə nən *or, esp. for 1,* -non′), *n.* **1.** a republic at the E end of the Mediterranean, N of Israel. 2,780,000; 3927 sq. mi. (10,170 sq. km). *Cap.:* Beirut. **2.** a city in SE Pennsylvania. 25,711. **3.** a city in N central Tennessee. 11,872. **4.** a town in central Indiana. 11,456. **5.** a town in W New Hampshire. 11,134. **6.** a town in W Oregon. 10,413.

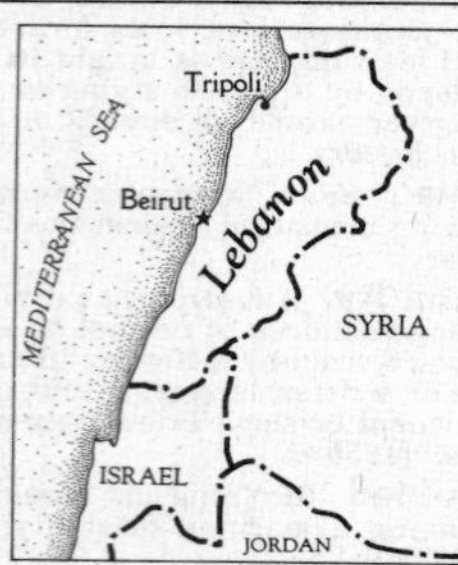

Leb′anon Moun′tains, a mountain range extending the length of Lebanon, in the central part. Highest peak, 10,049 ft. (3063 m).

leb·bek (leb′ek), *n.* **1.** Also called **leb′bek tree′.** a tropical Asian and Australian tree, *Albizzia lebbeck,* of the legume family, having pinnate leaves and greenish-yellow flowers. **2.** Also called **koko.** the hard, durable wood of this tree, used in the construction of buildings. [1760–70; orig. uncert.]

Le·bens·raum (lā′bəns roum′, -bənz-), *n.* (*often l.c.*) **1.** additional territory considered by a nation, esp. Nazi Germany, to be necessary for national survival or for the expansion of trade. **2.** any additional space needed in order to act, function, etc. [1900–05; < G: living space]

le·bes (lē′bēz), *n., pl.* **-bes.** *Gk. and Rom. Antiq.* a wine bowl having an oval body without handles and a rounded base. [1850–55; < L < Gk *lébēs* kettle, cauldron]

Le·besgue (lə beg′), *n.* **Hen·ri Lé·on** (äN rē′ lā ôN′), 1875–1941, French mathematician.

Lebesgue′ in′tegral, *Math.* an integral obtained by application of the theory of measure and more general than the Riemann integral. [named after H. L. LEBESGUE]

leb·ku·chen (lāb′ko͞o kən; *Ger.* lāp′ko͞o′KHən), *n., pl.* **-chen.** a hard, chewy or brittle Christmas cookie, usually flavored with honey and spices and containing nuts and citron. [1905–10, *Amer.;* < G; MHG *lebekuoche.* See LOAF[1], CAKE]

Le Bour·get (lə bo͝or zhā′; *Fr.* lə bo͞oR zhe′), a suburb of Paris: former airport, landing site for Charles A. Lindbergh, May 1927.

Le·brun (lə brœN′), *n.* **1. Al·bert** (al beR′), 1871–1950, president of France 1932–40. **2.** Also, **Le Brun. Charles** (shARl), 1619–90, French painter. **3. Mme. Vigée-.** See **Vigée-Lebrun, Marie Anne Elisabeth.**

le Car·ré (lə ka rā′), **John** (*David John Moore Cornwell*), born 1931, English author of spy novels.

Lec·ce (let′che; *Eng.* lech′ā), *n.* a city in SE Italy: ancient Greek and Roman city; noted for its baroque architecture. 88,693.

lech (lech), *n., v.i.* letch.

le·cha·te·lier·ite (lə shät′l ēr′īt), *n.* a mineral, an amorphous form of silica formed by the fusion by heat of silica and found in fulgurites. [1915–20; < F, after H.-L. *Le Châtelier* (1850–1936), French chemist; see -ITE[1]]

Le Châ′te·lier prin′ciple (lə shät′l yā′), *Physics.* the law that if a constraint is applied to a system in equilibrium, the system adjusts to a new equilibrium that tends to counteract the constraint. [1910–15; see LECHATELIERITE]

le·cha·yim (*Ashk.* lə KHä′yim; *Seph.* lə KHä yēm′), *n. Hebrew.* l'chaim.

lech·er (lech′ər), *n.* **1.** a man given to excessive sexual indulgence; a lascivious or licentious man. *—v.i.* **2.** to engage in lechery. [1125–75; ME *lech(o)ur* < AF; OF *lecheor* glutton, libertine, equiv. to *lech(ier)* to lick (< Gmc; cf. OHG *leccōn* to LICK) + *-eor* -OR[2]]

lech·er·ous (lech′ər əs), *adj.* **1.** given to or characterized by lechery; lustful. **2.** erotically suggestive; inciting to lust: *lecherous photographs.* [1275–1325; ME < MF *lechereus.* See LECHER, -OUS] **—lech′er·ous·ly,** *adv.* **—lech′er·ous·ness,** *n.*

lech′er wires′ (lekH′ər), *Elect.* parallel wires of such length and terminations that the system will resonate, producing standing waves, if the frequency of the excitation is correct. [1925–30; named after E. Lecher (d. 1926), Austrian physicist]

lech·er·y (lech′ə rē), *n., pl.* **-er·ies.** **1.** unrestrained or excessive indulgence of sexual desire. **2.** a lecherous act. [1200–50; ME *lecherie* < OF. See LECHER, -Y[3]]

—Syn. 1. carnality, lust, promiscuity.

lech′o·sos o′pal (lek′ə sōs′), a variety of opal having a deep-green play of color. [*lechosos* < Sp *lechoso* milky, equiv. to *lech(e)* milk (< L *lact-;* see LACT-) + *-oso* (< L *-ōsus* -OUS)]

lech·u·guil·la (lech′ə gē′ə; *Sp.* le′cho͞o gē′yä), *n., pl.* **-guil·las** (-gē′əz; *Sp.* -gē′yäs). a semidesert plant, *Agave lecheguilla,* of Mexico, having a basal rosette of sharply pointed leaves and a very tall flower spike, grown as an ornamental. [1835–45, *Amer.;* < Sp, dim. of *lechuga* LETTUCE]

le·chwe (lēch′wē), *n.* an African antelope, *Kobus leche,* related to the waterbuck, inhabiting wet, grassy plains: a threatened species. [1855–60; prob. < Sesotho *lets'a*]

Le Cid (*Fr.* lə sēd′), a drama (1636) by Corneille.

lec·i·thal (les′ə thəl), *adj. Embryol.* having a yolk, as certain eggs or ova. Also, **lec·i·thic** (les′ə thik). [1890–95; < Gk *lékith(os)* egg yolk + -AL[1]] **—lec′i·thal′i·ty,** *n.*

lec·i·thin (les′ə thin), *n.* **1.** *Biochem.* any of a group of phospholipids, occurring in animal and plant tissues and egg yolk, composed of units of choline, phosphoric acid, fatty acids, and glycerol. **2.** a commercial form of this substance, obtained chiefly from soybeans, corn, and egg yolk, used in foods, cosmetics, and inks. [1860–65; < Gk *lékith(os)* egg yolk + -IN[2]]

Leck·y (lek′ē), *n.* **William Edward Hart·pole** (härt′pōl), 1838–1903, Irish essayist and historian.

Le·conte de Lisle (lə kôNt də lēl′), **Charles Ma·rie** (shARl MA Rē′), 1818–94, French poet.

Le Cor·bu·sier (*Fr.* lə kôR BY zyā′), (*Charles Édouard Jeanneret*), 1887–1965, Swiss architect in France.

Le Crac (lə kräk′), former name of **Kerak.**

Le Creu·sot (lə kRœ zō′), a city in E central France. 33,480.

lect., **1.** lecture. **2.** lecturer.

lec·tern (lek′tərn), *n.* **1.** a reading desk in a church on which the Bible rests and from which the lessons are read during the church service. **2.** a stand with a slanted top, used to hold a book, speech, manuscript, etc., at the proper height for a reader or speaker. [1275–1325; earlier *lectron(e),* late ME *lectryn* < ML *lectrīnum,* deriv. of *lectrum* lectern, equiv. to L *leg(ere)* to read + *-trum* instrumental suffix; r. ME *letroun, lettorne* < MF *letrun* < ML *lectrum,* as above]

lectern (def. 2)

lec·tin (lek′tin), *n. Biochem.* any of a group of proteins that bind to particular carbohydrates in the manner of an antibody and are commonly extracted from plants for use as an agglutinin, as in clumping red blood cells for blood typing. [1954; < L *lēct(us),* ptp. of *legere* to gather, select, read + -IN[2]]

lec·tion (lek′shən), *n.* **1.** a version of a passage in a particular copy or edition of a text; a variant reading. **2.** a portion of sacred writing read in a divine service; lesson; pericope. [1530–40; < L *lēctiōn-* (s. of *lēctiō*) a reading, equiv. to *lēct(us)* (ptp. of *legere* to choose, gather, read; c. Gk *légein* to speak) + *-iōn-* -ION]

lec·tion·ar·y (lek′shə ner′ē), *n., pl.* **-ar·ies.** a book or a list of lections for reading in a divine service. [1770–80; < ML (*liber*) *lēctiōnārius.* See LECTION, -ARY]

lec·tor (lek′tər), *n.* **1.** a lecturer in a college or university. **2.** *Rom. Cath. Ch.* **a.** a member of the next to lowest-ranking of the minor orders. **b.** the order itself. Cf. **acolyte** (def. 2), **exorcist** (def. 2), **ostiary** (def. 1). [1425–75; late ME < L: a reader, equiv. to *leg(ere)* to read + *-tor* -TOR] **—lec·tor·ate** (lek′tər it, -tə rāt′), **lec′tor·ship′,** *n.*

lec·ture (lek′chər), *n., v.,* **-tured, -tur·ing.** *—n.* **1.** a speech read or delivered before an audience or class, esp. for instruction or to set forth some subject: *a lecture on Picasso's paintings.* **2.** a speech of warning or reproof as to conduct; a long, tedious reprimand. *—v.i.* **3.** to give a lecture or series of lectures: *He spent the year lecturing to various student groups.* *—v.t.* **4.** to deliver a lecture to or before; instruct by lectures. **5.** to rebuke or reprimand at some length: *He lectured the child regularly but with little effect.* [1375–1425; late ME < ML *lēctūra* a reading. See LECTION, -URE]

—Syn. 1. address, talk, paper, oration, discourse. **4.** address, teach. **5.** admonish; hector.

lec·tur·er (lek′chər ər), *n.* **1.** a person who lectures. **2.** an academic rank given in colleges and universities to a teacher ranking below assistant professor. [1560–70; LECTURE + -ER[1]]

lec·ture·ship (lek′chər ship′), *n.* the office of lecturer. [1625–35; LECTURE + -SHIP]

Le·cuo·na (lə kwō′nə; *Sp.* le kwô′nä), *n.* **Er·nes·to** (eR nes′tō), 1896–1963, Cuban composer.

led (led), *v.* pt. and pp. of **lead**[1].

LED, light-emitting diode: a semiconductor diode that emits light when conducting current and is used in electronic equipment, esp. for displaying readings on digital watches, calculators, etc.

Le·da (lē′də, lā′-), *n.* **1.** *Class. Myth.* the mother, by her husband Tyndareus, of Castor and Clytemnestra and, by Zeus in the form of a swan, of Pollux and Helen. **2.** *Astron.* a small natural satellite of the planet Jupiter.

Led·bet·ter (led′bet ər), *n.* **Hud·die** (hud′ē), ("*Leadbelly*"), 1885?–1949, U.S. folk singer.

Led·er·berg (led′ər bûrg′), *n.* **Joshua,** born 1925, U.S. geneticist: Nobel prize for medicine 1958.

le·der·ho·sen (lā′dər hō′zən), *n.pl.* leather shorts,

usually with suspenders, worn esp. in Bavaria. [1935–40; < G, equiv. to *Leder* LEATHER + *Hosen* trousers, shorts]

ledge (lej), *n., v.,* **ledged, ledg•ing.** —*n.* **1.** a relatively narrow, projecting part, as a horizontal, shelflike projection on a wall or a raised edge on a tray. **2.** a more or less flat shelf of rock protruding from a cliff or slope. **3.** a reef, ridge, or line of rocks in the sea or other body of water. **4.** *Mining.* **a.** a layer or mass of rock underground. **b.** a lode or vein. **5.** *Carpentry.* a member similar to but larger than a cleat. **6.** *Shipbuilding.* a minor transverse deck beam running between regular deck beams to form part of a coaming. —*v.t.* **7.** to assemble (a door or the like) with ledges. [1300–50; ME *legge,* perh. deriv. of *leggen* to LAY[1]; cf. MHG *legge* layer, edge, OE *lecg* part of a weapon] —**ledge′less,** *adj.*

ledg•er (lej′ər), *n.* **1.** *Bookkeeping.* an account book of final entry, in which business transactions are recorded. **2.** *Building Trades.* **a.** a horizontal timber fastened to the vertical uprights of a scaffold, to support the putlogs. **b.** ribbon (def. 8). **3.** a flat slab of stone laid over a grave or tomb. **4.** Also, **leger.** *Angling.* a lead sinker with a hole in one end through which the line passes, enabling the bait and the sinker to rest on the bottom and allowing the fish to take the bait without detecting the sinker. [1475–85; earlier *legger* book, prob. equiv. to *legg(en)* to LAY[1] + *-er* -ER[1]]

ledg′er beam′, a reinforced-concrete beam having projecting ledges for receiving the ends of joists or the like.

ledg′er board′, **1.** a horizontal board, as in a fence. **2.** *Carpentry.* ribbon (def. 8). [1905–10]

L, ledger lines (def. 1)

ledg′er line′, **1.** Also, **leger line.** Also called **added line.** *Music.* a short line added when necessary above or below the staff to increase the range of the staff. **2.** *Angling.* a line so set that both the bait and sinker rest on the bottom. [1690–1700 for def. 2; 1880–85 for def. 1]

ledg′er pa′per, a foldable paper with a smooth finish.

ledg′er plate′, *Carpentry.* a strip of wood laid flat across the tops of studding as a support for joists.

ledg′er strip′, *Carpentry.* a piece attached to the face of a beam at the bottom as a support for the ends of joists.

ledg•y (lej′ē), *adj.,* **ledg•i•er, ledg•i•est.** having ledges. [1770–80, *Amer.;* LEDGE + -Y[1]]

Le•doux (lə do͞o′), *n.* **Claude-Ni•co•las** (klōd nē kô-lä′), 1736–1806, French architect.

Le Duc Tho (lā′ duk′ tō′), *(Phan Dinh Khai),* 1911–90, Vietnamese politician and statesman: declined 1973 Nobel peace prize.

Led•yard (led′yərd), *n.* a town in SE Connecticut. 13,735.

lee[1] (lē), *n.* **1.** protective shelter: *The lee of the rock gave us some protection against the storm.* **2.** the side or part that is sheltered or turned away from the wind: *We erected our huts under the lee of the mountain.* **3.** *Chiefly Naut.* the quarter or region toward which the wind blows. **4. by the lee,** *Naut.* accidentally against what should be the lee side of a sail: *Careless steering brought the wind by the lee.* **5. under the lee,** *Naut.* to leeward. —*adj.* **6.** pertaining to, situated in, or moving toward the lee. [bef. 900; ME; OE *hlēo(w)* shelter, c. OFris *hli, hly,* OS *hleo,* ON *hlé*]

lee[2] (lē), *n.* Usually, **lees.** the insoluble matter that settles from a liquid, esp. from wine; sediment; dregs. [1350–1400; ME *lie* < MF < ML *lia,* prob. < Gaulish **lig(j)a;* cf. OIr *lige* bed, akin to OE *gelege* bed. See LIE[2]]

Lee (lē), *n.* **1. Ann,** 1736–84, British mystic: founder of Shaker sect in U.S. **2. Charles,** 1731–82, American Revolutionary general, born in England. **3. Doris Em•rick** (em′rik), born 1905, U.S. painter. **4. Fitz•hugh** (fits′hyo͞o′ *or, often,* -yo͞o′; fits hyo͞o′ *or, often,* -yo͞o′), 1835–1905, U.S. general and statesman (grandson of Henry Lee; nephew of Robert E. Lee). **5. Francis Light•foot** (līt′fo͝ot′), 1734–97, American Revolutionary statesman (brother of Richard H. Lee). **6. Gypsy Rose** *(Rose Louise Hovick),* 1914–70, U.S. entertainer. **7. Henry** *("Light-Horse Harry"),* 1756–1818, American Revolutionary general (father of Robert E. Lee). **8. Kuan Yew** (kwän yo͞o), born 1923, Singapore political leader: prime minister since 1959. **9. Richard Henry,** 1732–94, American Revolutionary statesman (brother of Francis L. Lee). **10. Robert E(dward),** 1807–70, U.S. soldier and educator: Confederate general in the American Civil War (son of Henry Lee). **11. Sir Sidney,** 1859–1926, English biographer and critic. **12. Tsung-Dao** (dzo͞ong′dou′), born 1926, Chinese physicist in the U.S.: Nobel prize 1957. **13.** a town in W Massachusetts: resort. 6247. **14.** a male or female given name.

lee•board (lē′bôrd′, -bōrd′), *n. Naut.* either of two broad, flat objects attached to the sides of a sailing ship amidships, the one on the lee side being lowered into the water to prevent the ship from making leeway. [1400–50; late ME: the lee side of a ship; see LEE[1], BOARD]

leech[1] (lēch), *n.* **1.** any bloodsucking or carnivorous aquatic or terrestrial worm of the class Hirudinea, certain freshwater species of which were formerly much used in medicine for bloodletting. **2.** a person who clings to another for personal gain, esp. without giving anything in return, and usually with the implication or effect of exhausting the other's resources; parasite. **3.** *Archaic.* an instrument used for drawing blood. —*v.t.* **4.** to apply leeches to, so as to bleed. **5.** to cling to and feed upon or drain, as a leech: *His relatives leeched him until his entire fortune was exhausted.* **6.** *Archaic.* to cure; heal. —*v.i.* **7.** to hang on to a person in the manner of a leech: *She leeched on to him for dear life.* [bef. 900; ME *leche,* OE *lǣce;* r. (by confusion with LEECH[2]) ME *liche,* OE *lȳce;* c. MD *lieke;* akin to OE *lūcan* to pull out, MHG *liechen* to pull] —**leech′like′,** *adj.*
—**Syn. 2.** bloodsucker; extortioner; sponger.

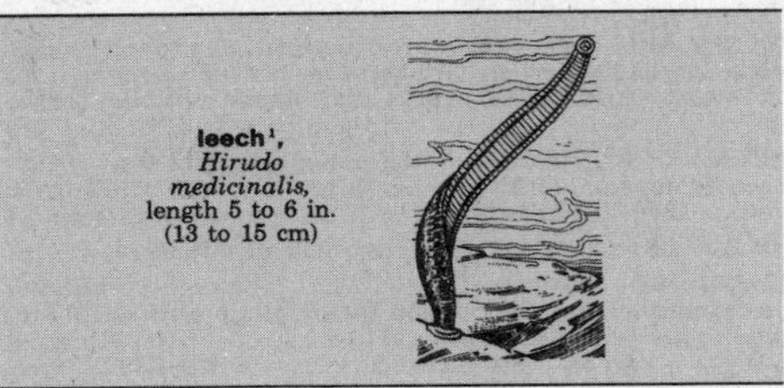
leech[1], *Hirudo medicinalis,* length 5 to 6 in. (13 to 15 cm)

leech[2] (lēch), *n. Archaic.* a physician. [bef. 1150; ME *leche,* OE *lǣce;* c. OS *lāki,* OHG *lāhhi,* Goth *lēkeis;* akin to ON *lǣknir*]

leech[3] (lēch), *n. Naut.* **1.** either of the lateral edges of a square sail. **2.** the after edge of a fore-and-aft sail. See diag. under **sail.** Also, **leach.** [1480–90; earlier *lek, leche, lyche;* akin to D *lijk* leech, ON *lík* nautical term of uncert. meaning]

lee•chee (lē′chē), *n.* litchi.

leech′ line′, *Naut.* a line for hauling the middle of a leech of a square sail up to the yard. Cf. **leech rope.** [1620–30]

leech′ rope′, *Naut.* a boltrope along a leech. [1760–70]

Leeds (lēdz), *n.* a city in West Yorkshire, in N England. 749,000.

lee′ gauge′, *Naut.* See under **gauge** (def. 17).

leek (lēk), *n.* **1.** a plant, *Allium ampeloprasum,* of the amaryllis family, allied to the onion, having a cylindrical bulb and leaves used in cookery. **2.** any of various allied species. [bef. 1000; ME; OE *lēac;* c. G *Lauch,* ON *laukr*]

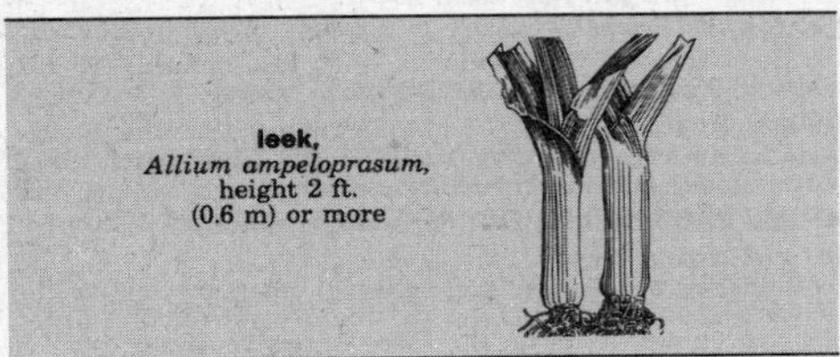
leek, *Allium ampeloprasum,* height 2 ft. (0.6 m) or more

leek-green (lēk′grēn′), *adj.* dull bluish green. [1655–65]

leer[1] (lēr), *v.i.* **1.** to look with a sideways or oblique glance, esp. suggestive of lascivious interest or sly and malicious intention: *I can't concentrate with you leering at me.* —*n.* **2.** a lascivious or sly look. [1520–30; perh. v. use of obs. *leer* cheek (ME *leor,* OE *hlēor;* c. ON *hlȳr* (pl.))] —**leer′ing•ly,** *adv.*

leer[2] (lēr), *adj. Brit. Dial.* **1.** having no burden or load. **2.** faint for lack of food; hungry. [bef. 1050; ME *lere,* OE *gelǣr;* c. G *leer* empty]

leer[3] (lēr), *n.* lehr.

leer•y[1] (lēr′ē), *adj.,* **leer•i•er, leer•i•est.** **1.** wary; suspicious (usually fol. by *of*): *I'm leery of his financial advice.* **2.** *Archaic.* knowing; alert. [1790–1800; LEER[1] + -Y[1]] —**leer′i•ly,** *adv.* —**leer′i•ness,** *n.*

leer•y[2] (lēr′ē), *adj.,* **leer•i•er, leer•i•est.** leer[2]. [LEER[2] + -Y[1]]

lees (lēz), *n.* pl. of **lee**[2].

Lees•burg (lēz′bûrg), *n.* a city in central Florida. 13,191.

lee′ shore′, **1.** a shore toward which the wind blows. **2. on a lee shore,** in difficulty or danger. [1570–80]

Lees′ Sum′mit (lēz), a town in W Missouri. 28,741.

leet (lēt), *n. Brit. Obs.* **1.** a special annual or semiannual court in which the lords of certain manors had jurisdiction over local disputes. **2.** the area over which this jurisdiction extended, including the manor itself and, sometimes, nearby counties or shires. [1400–50; late ME *lete* meeting (of law court) < AF *lete* and AL *leta* (both perh. < OE *gelǣte* meeting of roads; cf. *wætergelǣt* watercourse)]

lee′ tide′, a tidal current running in the direction toward which the wind is blowing. Also, **lee′ward tide′.**

Lee•u•war•den (lā′ʏ wär′dən), *n.* a city in N Netherlands. 85,435.

Lee•u•wen•hoek (lā′vən ho͝ok′; *Du.* lā′ʏ wən ho͝ok′), *n.* **An•ton van** (än′tôn vän), 1632–1723, Dutch naturalist and microscopist.

lee•ward (lē′wərd; *Naut.* lo͞o′ərd), *adj.* **1.** pertaining to, situated in, or moving toward the quarter toward which the wind blows (opposed to *windward*). —*n.* **2.** the lee side; the point or quarter toward which the wind blows. —*adv.* **3.** toward the lee. [1540–50; LEE[1] + -WARD] —**lee′ward•ly,** *adv.*

Lee′ward Is′lands (lē′wərd), a group of islands in the N Lesser Antilles of the West Indies, extending from Puerto Rico SE to Martinique.

lee′ wave′. See **mountain wave.**

lee•way (lē′wā′), *n.* **1.** extra time, space, materials, or the like, within which to operate; margin: *With ten minutes' leeway we can catch the train.* **2.** a degree of freedom of action or thought: *His instructions gave us plenty of leeway.* **3.** Also called **sag.** *Naut.* the amount or angle of the drift of a ship to leeward from its heading. **4.** *Aeron.* the amount a plane is blown off its normal course by cross winds. [1660–70; LEE[1] + WAY]
—**Syn. 2.** latitude, flexibility, cushion.

left[1] (left), *adj.* **1.** of, pertaining to, or located on or near the side of a person or thing that is turned toward the west when the subject is facing north (opposed to *right*). **2.** (*often cap.*) of or belonging to the political Left; having liberal or radical views in politics. **3.** *Math.* pertaining to an element of a set that has a given property when written on the left of an element or set of elements of the set: *a left identity, as 1 in 1 · x = x.* —*n.* **4.** the left side or something that is on the left side. **5.** a turn toward the left: *Make a left at the next corner.* **6. the Left, a.** the complex of individuals or organized groups advocating liberal reform or revolutionary change in the social, political, or economic order. **b.** the position held by these people. Cf. **right** (def. 34a, b). **c.** See **left wing. 7.** (*usually cap.*) *Govt.* **a.** the part of a legislative assembly, esp. in continental Europe, that is situated on the left side of the presiding officer and that is customarily assigned to members of the legislature who hold more radical and socialistic views than the rest of the members. **b.** the members of such an assembly who sit on the left. **8.** *Boxing.* a blow delivered by the left hand. **9.** *Baseball.* See **left field** (def. 1). —*adv.* **10.** toward the left: *She moved left on entering the room.* [1125–75; 1935–40 for def. 6; ME *left, lift, luft,* OE *left* idle, weak, useless, Kentish form of *lyft-* (in *lyftādl* palsy); c. D, LG *lucht;* akin to ME *libbe* (mod. dial. *lib*) to castrate, c. D, LG *lubben*]

left[2] (left), *v.* **1.** pt. and pp. of **leave**[1]. **2. get left, a.** to be left stranded. **b.** to miss an opportunity, objective, etc.

Left′ Bank′, a part of Paris, France, on the S bank of the Seine: frequented by artists, writers, and students. Cf. **Right Bank.**

left′ brain′, the cerebral hemisphere on the left side of the corpus callosum, controlling activity on the right side of the body: in humans, usually showing some degree of specialization for language and calculation. Cf. **right brain.**

left-branch•ing (left′bran′ching, -brän′-), *adj. Ling.* (of a grammatical construction) characterized by greater structural complexity in the position preceding the head, as the phrase *my brother's friend's house;* having most of the constituents on the left in a tree diagram (opposed to *right-branching*). [1960–65]

left′-eyed floun′der (left′īd′), any of several flatfishes of the family Bothidae, having both eyes on the left side of the head. Also, **left′eye floun′der.**

left′ field′, **1.** *Baseball.* **a.** the area of the outfield to the left of center field, as viewed from home plate. **b.** the position of the player covering this area. **2.** *Slang.* a position or circumstance that is remote from an ordinary or general trend. **3. out in left field,** *Slang.* completely mistaken; wrong. [1855–60, *Amer.*]

left′ field′er, *Baseball.* the player whose position is left field. [1865–70, *Amer.*]

left-hand (left′hand′), *adj.* **1.** on or to the left: *a left-hand turn at the intersection.* **2.** of, for, or with the left hand. **3.** *Building Trades.* **a.** (of a door) having the hinges on the left when seen from the exterior of the building, room, closet, etc., to which the doorway leads. **b.** (of a casement sash) having the hinges on the left when seen from inside the window. [1150–1200; ME]

left′-hand bu′oy, *Navig.* a distinctive buoy marking the side of a channel regarded as the left or port side.

left′-hand dag′ger. See **main gauche.**

left-hand•ed (left′han′did), *adj.* **1.** having the left hand more dominant or effective than the right; preferably using the left hand: *a left-handed pitcher.* **2.** adapted to or performed by the left hand: *a left-handed tool; a left-handed tennis serve.* **3.** situated on the side of the left hand. **4.** *Mach.* **a.** rotating counterclockwise. **b.** noting a helical or spiral member, as a gear tooth or screw thread, that twists counterclockwise as it recedes from an observer. **5.** *Building Trades.* left-hand (def. 3). **6.** ambiguous or doubtful and often unfavorable or derogatory by implication: *a left-handed compliment.* **7.** clumsy or awkward. **8.** of, pertaining to, or issuing from a morganatic marriage: so called from the custom, in morganatic marriage ceremonies, of having the bridegroom give his left hand to the bride. —*adv.* **9.** with the left hand: *He writes left-handed.* **10.** toward the left hand; in a counterclockwise direction: *The strands of the rope are laid left-handed.* [1350–1400; ME; see LEFT[1], HANDED] —**left′-hand′ed•ly,** *adv.* —**left′-hand′ed•ness,** *n.*

left-hand•er (left′han′dər, -han′-), *n.* **1.** a person who is left-handed, esp. a baseball pitcher who throws with the left hand. **2.** *Informal.* a slap or punch delivered with the left hand. [1860–65; LEFT-HAND + -ER[1]]

left•ie (lef′tē), *n. Informal.* lefty[1].

left•ist (lef′tist), *n.* **1.** a member of the political Left or a person sympathetic to its views. —*adj.* **2.** of, pertaining to, characteristic of, or advocated by the political Left. Also, **Left′ist.** [1920–25; LEFT[1] + -IST] —**left′ism,** *n.*

left-laid (left′lād′), *adj.* noting a rope, strand, etc., laid in a left-handed, or counterclockwise, direction as one looks away along it (opposed to *right-laid*).

left′-lug′gage of′fice (left′lug′ij), *Brit.* a checkroom for baggage. [1885–90]

left-of-cen•ter (left′əv sen′tər), *adj.* holding liberal views in politics; left-wing. [1940–45]

left•o•ver (left′ō′vər), *n.* **1.** Usually, **leftovers.** food

remaining uneaten at the end of a meal, esp. when saved for later use. **2.** anything left or remaining from a larger amount; remainder. —*adj.* **3.** being left or remaining, as an unused portion or amount: *leftover meat-loaf.* [1890–95; n. use of v. phrase *left over;* see LEFT[2]]
—**Syn. 3.** surplus, excess, extra.

left′ stage′. See **stage left.**

left·ward (left′wərd), *adv.* **1.** Also, **left′wards.** toward or on the left. —*adj.* **2.** situated on the left. **3.** directed toward the left. [1475–85; LEFT[1] + -WARD] —**left′ward·ly,** *adv.*

left′ wing′, **1.** members of a liberal or radical political party, or those favoring extensive political reform. **2.** such a party or a group of such parties. **3.** the part of a political or social organization advocating a liberal or radical position. [1700–10] —**left′-wing′,** *adj.* —**left′-wing′er,** *n.*

left·y[1] (lef′tē), *n., pl.* **left·ies.** *Informal.* **1.** a left-handed person. **2.** a leftist. Also, **leftie.** [1925–30; LEFT[1] + -Y[2]]

left·y[2] (lef′tē), *Informal.* —*adj.* **1.** left-handed. **2.** leftist; left-wing. —*adv.* **3.** with the left hand; in a left-handed manner: *He bats lefty.* [1885–90; LEFT[1] + -Y[1]]

leg (leg), *n., v.,* **legged, leg·ging.** —*n.* **1.** either of the two lower limbs of a biped, as a human being, or any of the paired limbs of an animal, arthropod, etc., that support and move the body. **2.** *Anat.* the lower limb of a human being from the knee to the ankle. **3.** something resembling or suggesting a leg in use, position, or appearance. **4.** the part of a garment that covers the leg: *the leg of a stocking; trouser leg.* **5.** one of usually several, relatively tall, slender supports for a piece of furniture. **6.** one of the sides of a forked object, as of a compass or pair of dividers. **7.** one of the sides of a triangle other than the base or hypotenuse. **8.** a timber, bar, or the like, serving to prop or shore up a structure. **9.** one of the flanges of an angle iron. **10.** one of the distinct sections of any course: *the last leg of a trip.* **11.** *Naut.* **a.** one of the series of straight runs that make up the zigzag course of a sailing ship. **b.** one straight or nearly straight part of a multiple-sided course in a sailing race. **12.** *Sports.* **a.** one of a designated number of contests that must be successfully completed in order to determine the winner. **b.** one of the stretches or sections of a relay race. **13. legs,** (in wine tasting) the rivulets of wine that slowly descend along the inside of a glass after the wine has been swirled, sometimes regarded as an indication that the wine is full-bodied. **14.** *Cricket.* **a.** the part of the field to the left of and behind the batsman as he faces the bowler or to the right of and behind him if he is left-handed. **b.** the fielder playing this part of the field. **c.** the position of this fielder. **15.** *Elect.* a component or branch of a circuit, network, antenna, etc. **16.** *Radio and Television.* a connecting link between stations in a network, as the microwave relays used in transmitting a show from one geographical area to another. **17.** bride[2] (def. 1). **18. leg up, a.** a means of help or encouragement; assist; boost: *Studying the material with a tutor will give you a leg up on passing the exam.* **b.** advantage; edge. **19. not have a leg to stand on,** to lack a valid or logical basis for one's argument or attitude: *Without evidence, the prosecutor doesn't have a leg to stand on.* **20. on one's** or **its last legs,** just short of exhaustion, breakdown, failure, etc.: *The aristocracy was on its last legs.* **21. pull someone's leg, a.** to make fun of someone; tease. **b.** to deceive someone; trick someone. **22. shake a leg,** *Informal.* **a.** to hurry up. **b.** *Older Use.* to dance. **23. stretch one's legs,** to take a walk; get some needed exercise after prolonged sitting: *He got up during the intermission to stretch his legs.* —*v.t.* **24.** to move or propel (a boat) with the legs: *They legged the boat through the tunnel.* **25. leg it,** *Informal.* to walk rapidly or run: *We'd better leg it or we'll be late for class.* **26. leg up,** to help (someone) to mount a horse. [1225–75; 1915–20 for def. 10; ME < ON *leggr*] —**leg′less,** *adj.* —**leg′like′,** *adj.*

leg., **1.** legal. **2.** legate. **3.** legato. **4.** legend. **5.** legislation. **6.** legislative. **7.** legislature.

leg·a·cy (leg′ə sē), *n., pl.* **-cies.** **1.** *Law.* a gift of property, esp. personal property, as money, by will; a bequest. **2.** anything handed down from the past, as from an ancestor or predecessor: *the legacy of ancient Rome.* **3.** *Obs.* the office, function, or commission of a legate. [1325–75; ME *legacie* office of a deputy or legate < ML *lēgātia.* See LEGATE, -ACY]
—**Syn. 1, 2.** inheritance.

le·gal (lē′gəl), *adj.* **1.** permitted by law; lawful: *Such acts are not legal.* **2.** of or pertaining to law; connected with the law or its administration: *the legal profession.* **3.** appointed, established, or authorized by law; deriving authority from law. **4.** recognized by law rather than by equity. **5.** of, pertaining to, or characteristic of the profession of law or of lawyers: *a legal mind.* **6.** *Theol.* **a.** of or pertaining to the Mosaic Law. **b.** of or pertaining to the doctrine that salvation is gained by good works rather than through free grace. —*n.* **7.** a person who acts in a legal manner or with legal authority. **8.** an alien who has entered a country legally. **9.** a person whose status is protected by law. **10.** a fish or game animal, within specified size or weight limitations, that the law allows to be caught and kept during an appropriate season. **11.** a foreigner who conducts espionage against a host country while working there in a legitimate capacity, often in the diplomatic service. **12. legals,** authorized investments that may be made by fiduciaries, as savings banks or trustees. [1490–1500; < L *lēgālis* of the law, equiv. to *lēg-* (s. of *lēx*) law + *-ālis* -AL[1]] —**le′gal·ly,** *adv.*
—**Syn. 3.** licit, legitimate, sanctioned.

le′gal age′, the age at which a person acquires full legal rights and responsibilities, such as the right to make contracts and deeds. [1925–30]

le′gal aid′, free legal service to persons unable to pay for a lawyer. [1885–90]

le′gal aid′ soci′ety, an organization providing free legal guidance and service to persons who cannot afford a lawyer. Also called **le′gal aid′ associa′tion.** [1885–90]

le′gal cap′, ruled writing paper in tablet form, measuring approximately 8½ × 13 to 14 in. (22 × 33 to 36 cm). [1870–75, *Amer.*]

le′gal chem′istry. See **forensic chemistry.**

le·gal·ese (lē′gə lēz′, -lēs′), *n.* language containing an excessive amount of legal terminology or of legal jargon. [1910–15; LEGAL + -ESE]

le′gal hol′iday, a public holiday established by law, during which certain work, government business, etc., is restricted. [1865–70, *Amer.*]

le·gal·ism (lē′gə liz′əm), *n.* **1.** strict adherence, or the principle of strict adherence, to law or prescription, esp. to the letter rather than the spirit. **2.** *Theol.* **a.** the doctrine that salvation is gained through good works. **b.** the judging of conduct in terms of adherence to precise laws. **3.** (*cap.*) (in Chinese philosophy) the principles and practices of a school of political theorists advocating strict legal control over all activities, a system of rewards and punishments uniform for all classes, and an absolute monarchy. [1830–40; LEGAL + -ISM] —**le′gal·ist,** *n.* —**le′gal·is′tic,** *adj.* —**le′gal·is′ti·cal·ly,** *adv.*

le·gal·i·ty (lē gal′i tē), *n., pl.* **-ties.** **1.** the state or quality of being in conformity with the law; lawfulness. **2.** attachment to or observance of law. **3.** Usually, **legalities.** a duty or obligation imposed by law. **4.** *Theol.* reliance on good works for salvation rather than on free grace. [1425–75; late ME *legalite* < ML *lēgālitās.* See LEGAL, -ITY]
—**Syn. 1.** legitimacy, licitness, validity.

le·gal·ize (lē′gə līz′), *v.t.,* **-ized, -iz·ing.** to make legal; authorize. Also, *esp. Brit.,* **le′gal·ise′.** [1710–20; LEGAL + -IZE] —**le′gal·i·za′tion,** *n.*

Le Gal·lienne (lə gal′yən, -gal yen′), **1. Eva,** 1899–91, U.S. actress and producer, born in England. **2.** her father, **Richard,** 1866–1947, English writer.

le′gal list′, *Law.* a list of investments that fiduciaries and certain institutions, such as banks and insurance companies, are legally authorized to make.

le′gal med′icine. See **forensic medicine.**

le′gal mem′ory, *Law.* a period of time, now usually established by statute, during which custom, conduct, or a state of affairs must have existed or continued in order for it to have taken on the force of law or to establish a legal right or title not otherwise provable. [1760–70]

le′gal pad′, a ruled writing tablet, usually yellow and measuring 8½ × 14 in. (22 × 36 cm). [1965–70]

le′gal reserve′, the amount of cash assets that a bank, insurance company, etc., is required by law to set aside as reserves. [1920–25]

le′gal separa′tion. See **judicial separation.**

le·gal-size (lē′gəl sīz′), *adj.* **1.** (of paper) measuring approximately 8½ × 14 in. (22 × 36 cm). **2.** (of office supplies and equipment) made for holding legal-size sheets of paper: *legal-size file folders.* Cf. **letter-size.** Also, **le′gal-sized′.**

le′gal ten′der, currency that may be lawfully tendered in payment of a debt, such as paper money, Federal Reserve notes, or coins. [1730–40]

le′gal weight′, the weight of merchandise itself plus that of its immediate wrapping material but not of the outside shipping container: used esp. in some Latin American countries for the purpose of assessing import duties.

leg′ art′, *Slang.* cheesecake (def. 2).

Le·gas·pi (lə gas′pē; *Sp.* le gäs′pē), *n.* a seaport on SE Luzon, in the Philippines. 99,766. Formerly, **Albay.**

leg·ate (leg′it), *n.* **1.** an ecclesiastic delegated by the pope as his representative. **2.** *Rom. Hist.* **a.** an assistant to a general or to a consul or magistrate, in the government of any army or a province; a commander of a legion. **b.** a provincial governor of senatorial rank appointed by the emperor. **3.** an envoy or emissary. [1125–75; ME *legat* < L *lēgātus* deputy (n. use of masc. ptp. of *lēgāre* to depute), equiv. to *lēgā(re)* + *-tus* ptp. suffix] —**leg′ate·ship′,** *n.*

leg·a·tee (leg′ə tē′), *n.* a person to whom a legacy is bequeathed. [1670–80; < L *lēgāt(us)* (see LEGATE) + -EE]

leg·a·tine (leg′ə tin, -tīn′), *adj.* of, pertaining to, or authorized by a legate. [1605–15; < ML *lēgātinus.* See LEGATE, -INE[1]]

le·ga·tion (li gā′shən), *n.* **1.** a diplomatic minister and staff in a foreign mission. **2.** the official headquarters of a diplomatic minister. **3.** the office or position of a legate; mission. [1425–75; late ME *legacion* < L *lēgātiōn-* (s. of *lēgātiō*) embassy. See LEGATE, -ION] —**le·ga·tion·ar·y** (li gā′shə ner′ē), *adj.*

le·ga·to (lə gä′tō; *It.* le gä′tô), *adj., adv. Music.* smooth and connected; without breaks between the successive tones. Cf. **staccato.** [1805–15; < It, ptp. of *legare* < L *ligāre* to bind]

le·ga·tor (li gā′tər, leg′ə tôr′), *n.* a person who bequeaths; a testator. [1645–55; < L *lēgātor* one who bequeaths, equiv. to *lēgā(re)* to bequeath, depute + *-tor* -TOR] —**leg·a·to·ri·al** (leg′ə tôr′ē əl, -tōr′-), *adj.*

Le·gaz·pi (le gäs′pē), *n.* **Mi·guel Ló·pez de** (mē gel′ lô′peth the, lô′pes). See **López de Legazpi.**

leg-break (leg′brāk′), *n. Cricket.* a ball deviating to the off side from the leg side when bowled. [1885–90]

leg′ bye′, *Cricket.* a run or bye scored on a bowled ball that ricochets off any part of the batsman's body except the hand.

leg′ drop′, *Theat.* a narrow scenery flat or drop, often used in a pair to form an inverted U.

leg·end (lej′ənd), *n.* **1.** a nonhistorical or unverifiable story handed down by tradition from earlier times and popularly accepted as historical. **2.** the body of stories of this kind, esp. as they relate to a particular people, group, or clan: *the winning of the West in American legend.* **3.** an inscription, esp. on a coat of arms, on a monument, under a picture, or the like. **4.** a table on a map, chart, or the like, listing and explaining the symbols used. Cf. **key**[1] (def. 8). **5.** *Numis.* inscription (def. 8). **6.** a collection of stories about an admirable person. **7.** a person who is the center of such stories: *She became a legend in her own lifetime.* **8.** *Archaic.* a story of the life of a saint, esp. one stressing the miraculous or unrecorded deeds of the saint. **9.** *Obs.* a collection of such stories or stories like them. [1300–50; 1900–05 for def. 4; ME *legende* written account of a saint's life < ML *legenda* lit., (lesson) to be read, n. use of fem. of L *legendus,* ger. of *legere* to read; so called because appointed to be read on respective saints' days]
—**Syn. 1.** LEGEND, FABLE, MYTH refer to fictitious stories, usually handed down by tradition (although some fables are modern). LEGEND, originally denoting a story concerning the life of a saint, is applied to any fictitious story, sometimes involving the supernatural, and usually concerned with a real person, place, or other subject: *the legend of the Holy Grail.* A FABLE is specifically a fictitious story (often with animals or inanimate things as speakers or actors) designed to teach a moral: *a fable about industrious bees.* A MYTH is one of a class of stories, usually concerning gods, semidivine heroes, etc., current since primitive times, the purpose of which is to attempt to explain some belief or natural phenomenon: *the Greek myth about Demeter.* —**Ant. 1.** fact.

leg·end·ar·y (lej′ən der′ē), *adj., n., pl.* **-ar·ies.** —*adj.* **1.** of, pertaining to, or of the nature of a legend. **2.** celebrated or described in legend: *a legendary hero.* —*n.* **3.** a collection of legends. [1505–15; < ML *legendārius.* See LEGEND, -ARY] —**leg′end·ar′i·ly,** *adv.*
—**Syn. 1.** heroic, supernatural, strange, superhuman.

leg·end·ist (lej′ən dist), *n.* a person who writes or compiles legends. [1655–65; LEGEND + -IST]

leg·end·ize (lej′ən dīz′), *v.t.,* **-ized, -iz·ing.** to make a legend of: *Devoted followers legendized his honesty.* Also, *esp. Brit.,* **leg′end·ise′.** [1885–90; LEGEND + -IZE]

Le·gen·dre (lə zhän′dər, -zhänd′; *Fr.* lə zhäɴ′drᵊ), *n.* **A·dri·en Ma·rie** (A drē aɴ′ MA rē′), 1752–1833, French mathematician.

Legen′dre equa′tion, *Math.* a differential equation of the form $(1-x^2)d^2y/dx^2 - 2xdy/dx + a(a+1)y = 0$, where *a* is an arbitrary constant. [1880–85; after A. M. LEGENDRE]

leg·end·ry (lej′ən drē), *n.* legends collectively. [1840–50; LEGEND + -RY]

leg·er (lej′ər), *n. Angling.* ledger (def. 4).

Lé·ger (lā zhā′), *n.* **1. A·lex·is Saint-Lé·ger** (A lek sē′ SAN lā zhā′). See **St.-John Perse.** **2. Fer·nand** (fer-näɴ′), 1881–1955, French artist.

leg·er·de·main (lej′ər də mān′), *n.* **1.** sleight of hand. **2.** trickery; deception. **3.** any artful trick. [1400–50; late ME *legerdemeyn, lygarde de mayne* < MF: lit., light of hand] —**leg′er·de·main′ist,** *n.*

le·ger·i·ty (lə jer′i tē), *n.* physical or mental quickness; nimbleness; agility. [1555–65; < MF *legerete,* equiv. to *leger* (< VL **leviārius;* see LEVITY, -ARY) + *-ete* -ITY]
—**Syn.** lightness, grace, alacrity, celerity.

leg′er line′ (lej′ər), *Music.* See **ledger line** (def. 1).

le·ges (lē′jēz; *Lat.* le′ges), *n.* pl. of **lex.**

leg·ged (leg′id, legd), *adj.* **1.** having a specified number or kind of legs (often used in combination): *two-legged; long-legged.* **2.** fitted with legs: *a legged desk.* [1425–75; late ME; see LEG, -ED[3]]

leg·ging (leg′ing), *n.* **1.** a covering for the leg, usually extending from the ankle to the knee but sometimes higher, worn by soldiers, riders, workers, etc. Cf. **chaps, gaiter, puttee.** **2. leggings,** (*used with a plural v.*) **a.** close-fitting trousers, usually with shoulder straps and extending over the instep, worn outdoors in the winter by children, often with a matching coat or jacket. **b.** the pants of a two-piece snowsuit. Also, **leg·gin** (leg′in). [1745–55; LEG + -ING[1]] —**leg′ginged,** *adj.*

leg·gy (leg′ē), *adj.,* **-gi·er, -gi·est.** **1.** having awkwardly long legs. **2.** having long, attractively shaped legs: *a group of tanned, leggy swimmers.* **3.** of, pertaining to, or characterized by showing the legs: *a leggy stage show.* **4.** (of plants) long and thin; spindly. [1780–90; LEG + -Y[1]] —**leg′gi·ness,** *n.*

leg·har·ness (leg′här′nis), *n.* armor for the leg, sometimes including that for the foot. [1350–1400; ME; see LEG, HARNESS]

leg·he·mo·glo·bin (leg hē′mə glō′bin, -hem′ə-), *n. Biochem.* a hemoglobinlike red pigment in the root nodules of leguminous plants, as soybean, that is essential for nitrogen fixation. Also called **legoglobin.** [1965–70; LEG(UME) + HEMOGLOBIN]

leg′ hit′, *Cricket.* a hit made into leg. [1830–40]

Leg·horn (leg′hôrn′ *for 1–3;* leg′ərn, -hôrn′ *for 4*), *n.* **1.** English name of **Livorno.** **2.** (*l.c.*) a fine, smooth, plaited straw. **3.** (*l.c.*) a hat made of such straw, often having a broad, soft brim. **4.** one of a Mediterranean breed of chickens that are prolific layers of white-shelled eggs.

leg·i·bil·i·ty (lej′ə bil′i tē), *n.* **1.** Also, **leg′i·ble·ness.** the state or quality of being legible. **2.** Also called **visibility.** *Typography.* the quality of type that affects the perceptibility of a word, line, or paragraph of printed matter. Cf. **readability** (def. 2). [1670–80; LEGIBLE + -ITY]

leg·i·ble (lej′ə bəl), *adj.* **1.** capable of being read or deciphered, esp. with ease, as writing or printing; easily readable. **2.** capable of being discerned or distinguished: *Anger was legible in his looks and behavior.* [1400–50; late ME < L *legibilis;* equiv. to *leg(ere)* to read + *-ibilis* -IBLE] —**leg′i·bly,** *adv.*

le·gion (lē′jən), *n.* **1.** a division of the Roman army, usually comprising 3000 to 6000 soldiers. **2.** a military or semimilitary unit. **3. the Legion. a.** See **American Legion. b.** See **foreign legion** (def. 2). **4.** any large group of armed men. **5.** any great number of persons or things; multitude. —*adj.* **6.** very great in number: *The holy man's faithful followers were legion.* [1175–1225; ME *legi(o)un* (< OF) < L *legiōn-* (s. of *legiō*) picked body of soldiers, equiv. to *leg(ere)* to gather, choose, read + *-iōn-* -ION]
—**Syn. 5.** throng, mass, host, sea.

le·gion·ar·y (lē′jə ner′ē), *adj., n., pl.* **-ar·ies.** —*adj.* **1.** of, pertaining to, or belonging to a legion. **2.** constituting a legion or legions. —*n.* **3.** *Hist.* a soldier of a Roman legion. **4.** a member of the British Legion. **5.** legionnaire (def. 2). [1570–80; < L *legiōnārius.* See LEGION, -ARY]

le′gionary ant′. See **army ant.**

Le·gion·el·la (lē′jə nel′ə), *n.* a genus of rod- or coccus-shaped aerobic Gram-negative bacteria, certain species of which, as *L. pneumophila,* produce legionnaires' disease. [< NL (1979), after LEGIONNAIRES' DISEASE; see -ELLA]

le·gion·naire (lē′jə nâr′), *n.* **1.** (*often cap.*) a member of the American Legion. **2.** a member of any legion; legionary. [1810–20; < F; see LEGIONARY]

legionnaires′ disease′, *Pathol.* a type of acute pneumonia caused by *Legionella pneumophila* bacterium and characterized by fever, chest pain, cough, and muscle aches. [so called from its first reported occurrence, at an American Legion convention in Philadelphia in 1976]

Le′gion of Hon′or, a French order of distinction instituted in 1802 by Napoleon with membership being granted for meritorious civil or military services. [trans. of F *Légion d'honneur*]

Le′gion of Mer′it, *Mil.* a decoration ranking below the Silver Star and above the Distinguished Flying Cross, awarded to U.S. and foreign military personnel for exceptionally meritorious conduct in the performance of outstanding services to the U.S.

legis., **1.** legislation. **2.** legislative. **3.** legislature.

leg·is·late (lej′is lāt′), *v.,* **-lat·ed, -lat·ing.** —*v.i.* **1.** to exercise the function of legislation; make or enact laws. —*v.t.* **2.** to create, provide, or control by legislation: *attempts to legislate morality.* [1710–20; back formation from LEGISLATION, LEGISLATOR]

leg·is·la·tion (lej′is lā′shən), *n.* **1.** the act of making or enacting laws. **2.** a law or a body of laws enacted. [1645–55; < LL *lēgislātiōn-* (s. of *lēgislātiō*), equiv. to L phrase *lēgis lātiō* the bringing (i.e., proposing) of a law, equiv. to *lēgis* (gen. of *lēx* law) + *lātiō* a bringing; see RELATION]

leg·is·la·tive (lej′is lā′tiv), *adj.* **1.** having the function of making laws: *a legislative body.* **2.** of or pertaining to the enactment of laws: *legislative proceedings; legislative power.* **3.** pertaining to a legislature: *a legislative recess.* **4.** enacted or ordained by legislation or a legislature: *legislative ruling; legislative remedy.* —*n.* **5.** legislature. [1635–45; LEGISLAT(ION) + -IVE] —**leg′is·la′tive·ly,** *adv.*

Leg′islative Assem′bly, *Fr. Hist.* the legislature of France 1791–92.

leg′islative coun′cil, **1.** the upper house of a bicameral legislature. **2.** a unicameral legislature in a British colony consisting of the governor, official members appointed by the governor, and unofficial members representing the indigenous population. **3.** a committee composed of members of both houses of a state legislature that meets between sessions to study particular problems and develop programs for the next session. [1855–60]

leg′islative ve′to, a veto exercised by a legislature nullifying or reversing an action, decision, etc., of the executive branch. [1940–45]

leg·is·la·tor (lej′is lā′tər), *n.* **1.** a person who gives or makes laws. **2.** a member of a legislative body. [1595–1605; < L phrase *lēgis lātor* a law's bringer (i.e., proposer), equiv. to *lēgis* (gen. of *lēx* law) + *lātor* bringer (*lā(tus),* suppletive ptp. of *ferre* to bring + *-tor* -TOR] —**leg′is·la′tor·ship′,** *n.*
—**Syn. 1.** lawmaker, lawgiver.

leg·is·la·to·ri·al (lej′is lə tôr′ē əl, -tōr′-), *adj.* of or pertaining to a legislator, legislature, or legislation; legislative. [1765–75; LEGISLATOR + -IAL]

leg·is·la·trix (lej′is lā′triks), *n., pl.* **leg·is·la·trix·es, leg·is·la·tri·ces** (lej′is lā′tri sēz′, -lə trī′sēz). **1.** a woman who is a member of a legislature. **2.** a woman who makes or promulgates laws. Also, **leg·is·la·tress** (lej′is lā′tris, lej′is lā′-). [1670–80; LEGISLA(TOR) + -TRIX]
—**Usage.** See **-ess, -trix.**

leg·is·la·ture (lej′is lā′chər), *n.* a deliberative body of persons, usually elective, who are empowered to make, change, or repeal the laws of a country or state; the branch of government having the power to make laws, as distinguished from the executive and judicial branches of government. [1670–80; LEGISLAT(OR) + -URE]

le·gist (lē′jist), *n.* an expert in law, esp. ancient law. [1425–75; late ME < ML *lēgista.* See LEGAL, -IST]

le·git (lə jit′), *Informal.* —*adj.* **1.** legitimate. **2.** (of a singing voice) trained in a classical or operatic tradition. **3.** having such a singing voice. **4.** being a singer with such a voice. —*n.* **5.** the legitimate theater or stage. [1905–10; shortened form]

leg·i·tim (lej′i tim), *n. Roman and Civil Law, Scots Law.* the part of an estate that children or other close relatives can claim against the decedent's testament. [1350–1400; ME < L *lēgitima (pars)* the lawful (part), equiv. to *lēgi-* (s. of *lēx* law) + *-tima,* fem. of *-timus* adj. suffix]

le·git·i·ma·cy (li jit′ə mə sē), *n.* the state or quality of being legitimate. [1685–95; LEGITIM(ATE) + -ACY]
—**Syn.** lawfulness, legality, rightfulness.

le·git·i·mate (*adj., n.* li jit′ə mit; *v.* li jit′ə māt′), *adj., v.,* **-mat·ed, -mat·ing,** *n.* —*adj.* **1.** according to law; lawful: *the property's legitimate owner.* **2.** in accordance with established rules, principles, or standards. **3.** born in wedlock or of legally married parents: *legitimate children.* **4.** in accordance with the laws of reasoning; logically inferable; logical: *a legitimate conclusion.* **5.** resting on or ruling by the principle of hereditary right: *a legitimate sovereign.* **6.** not spurious or unjustified; genuine: *It was a legitimate complaint.* **7.** of the normal or regular type or kind. **8.** *Theat.* of or pertaining to professionally produced stage plays, as distinguished from burlesque, vaudeville, television, motion pictures, etc.: *an actor in the legitimate theater.* —*v.t.* **9.** to make lawful or legal; pronounce or state as lawful: *Parliament legitimated his accession to the throne.* **10.** to establish as lawfully born: *His bastard children were afterward legitimated by law.* **11.** to show or declare to be legitimate or proper: *He was under obligation to legitimate his commission.* **12.** to justify; sanction or authorize: *His behavior was legitimated by custom.* —*n.* **13. the legitimate,** the legitimate theater or drama. **14.** a person who is established as being legitimate. [1485–95; < ML *lēgitimātus* (ptp. of *lēgitimāre* to make lawful). See LEGITIM, -ATE[1]] —**le·git′i·mate·ly,** *adv.* —**le·git′i·mate·ness,** *n.* —**le·git′i·ma′tion,** *n.*
—**Syn. 1.** legal, licit. **2.** sanctioned. **4.** valid. **9.** legalize. —**Ant. 1.** illegitimate.

le·git·i·ma·tize (li jit′ə mə tīz′), *v.t.,* **-tized, -tiz·ing.** to make legitimate. Also, *esp. Brit.,* **le·git′i·ma·tise′.** [1785–95; LEGITIMATE + -IZE]

le·git·i·mist (li jit′ə mist), *n.* **1.** a supporter of legitimate authority, esp. of a claim to a throne based on direct descent. —*adj.* **2.** Also, **le·git′i·mis′tic.** of, pertaining to, or supporting legitimate authority. [1835–45; < L *lēgitim(us)* lawful (see LEGITIM) + -IST, modeled on F *légitimiste*] —**le·git′i·mism,** *n.*

le·git·i·mize (li jit′ə mīz′), *v.t.,* **-mized, -miz·ing.** to make legitimate. Also, *esp. Brit.,* **le·git′i·mise′.** [1840–50; < L *lēgitim(us)* (see LEGITIM) + -IZE] —**le·git′i·mi·za′tion,** *n.*

leg·len (leg′lin), *n. Scot. and North Eng.* **1.** laggin. **2.** a milk pail. [1715–25; perh. < Scand; cf. Icel *legillinn* the keg, equiv. to *legill* keg (<< L; see LAGENA) + *-inn* the]

leg·man (leg′man′, -mən), *n., pl.* **-men** (-men′, -mən). **1.** a person employed to transact business outside an office, esp. on behalf of one whose responsibilities require his or her presence in the office. **2.** *Journalism.* a reporter who gathers information by visiting news sources or by being present at news events. Cf. **district man.** [1920–25. *Amer.;* LEG + MAN[1]]

Leg·ni·ca (leg nēt′sə; *Pol.* leg nē′tsä), *n.* a city in SW Poland: formerly in Germany. 75,800. German, **Liegnitz.**

leg-of-mut·ton (leg′ə mut′n, -əv-), *adj.* having the triangular shape of a leg of mutton: *leg-of-mutton sail; a dress with leg-of-mutton sleeves.* Also, **leg′-o′-mut′ton.** [1830–40]

leg·o·glo·bin (leg′ə glō′bin), *n. Biochem.* leghemoglobin.

le·gong (lə gông′, -gong′), *n.* an elegant Balinese dance-pantomime performed by several girls in elaborate costumes. [1925–30; < Balinese *légong*]

leg-pull (leg′pŏŏl′), *n.* an amusing hoax, practical joke, or the like: *The entire story was a hilarious leg-pull.* [1910–15] —**leg′-pull′er,** *n.*

Le·gree (li grē′), *n.* **Simon.** See **Simon Legree.**

leg·room (leg′rōōm′, -rŏŏm′), *n.* space sufficient for keeping one's legs in a comfortable position, as in an automobile. [1925–30; LEG + ROOM]

leg′ stump′, *Cricket.* either of the outside stumps at which the batsman takes his position. Cf. **middle stump, off stump.** [1825–35]

Le·guí·a (le gē′ä), *n.* **Au·gus·to Ber·nar·di·no** (ou-gōōs′tô ber′när thē′nô), 1863–1932, president of Peru 1908–12, 1919–30.

Le·Guin (lə gwin′), *n.* **Ursula K(roeber),** born 1929, U.S. science-fiction writer. Also, **Le Guin′.**

leg·ume (leg′yōōm, li gyōōm′), *n.* **1.** any plant of the legume family, esp. those used for feed, food, or as a soil-improving crop. **2.** the pod or seed vessel of such a plant. **3.** any table vegetable of the legume family. [1670–80; < F *légume* vegetable < L *legūmen* pulse, a leguminous plant, deriv. of *legere* to gather]

leg′ume fam′ily, the large plant family Leguminosae (or Fabaceae), typified by herbaceous plants, shrubs, trees, and vines having usually compound leaves, clusters of irregular, keeled flowers, and fruit in the form of a pod splitting along both sides, and including beans, peas, acacia, alfalfa, clover, indigo, lentil, mesquite, mimosa, and peanut.

le·gu·min (li gyōō′mən), *n. Biochem.* a globulin obtained from the seeds of leguminous and other plants. [1830–40; LEGUME + -IN[2]]

le·gu·mi·nous (li gyōō′mə nəs), *adj.* **1.** pertaining to, of the nature of, or bearing legumes. **2.** belonging to the Leguminosae. Cf. **legume family.** [1650–60; < L *legūmin-* (s. of *legūmen;* see LEGUME) + -OUS]

leg′ warm′ers, a pair of footless, stockinglike knitted coverings for the legs, usually worn over tights, trousers, boots, etc., for warmth, as in a dance class or while exercising, or as a fashion accessory. Also, **leg′warm′ers.** [1970–75]

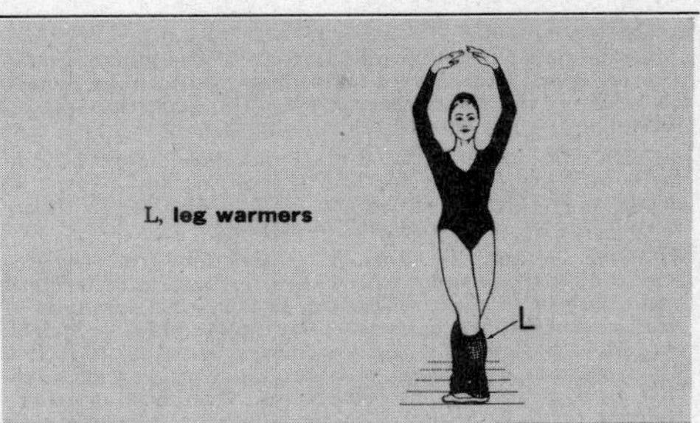

L, **leg warmers**

leg·work (leg′wûrk′), *n.* **1.** work or research involving extensive walking or traveling about, usually away from one's office, as in gathering data for a book, a legal action, etc. **2.** action of the legs as executed by an athlete, dancer, etc. [1890–95, *Amer.;* LEG + WORK]

Le·hár (lā′här; *Hung.* le′här), *n.* **Franz** (fränts), 1870–1948, Hungarian composer of operettas.

Le Ha·vre (lə hä′vrə, -vər; *Fr.* lə A′VRᵊ), a seaport in N France, at the mouth of the Seine. 219,583. Also called **Havre.**

le·ha·yim (*Ashk.* lə KHä′yim; *Seph.* lə KHä yēm′), *n. Hebrew.* l'chaim.

Le·high (lē′hī), *n.* a river in E Pennsylvania, flowing SW and SE into the Delaware River. 103 mi. (165 km) long.

Leh·man (lē′mən, lā′-), *n.* **Herbert H(enry),** 1878–1963, U.S. banker and statesman.

Leh·mann (lā′mən; *Ger.* lā′män), *n.* **1. Lil·li** (lil′ē), 1848–1929, German operatic soprano. **2. Lot·te** (lô′tə), 1888–1976, German operatic soprano in the U.S.

Lehm·bruck (läm′brŏŏk; *Eng.* lem′brŏŏk, läm′-), *n.* **Wil·helm** (vil′helm), 1881–1919, German sculptor.

lehr (lēr, lâr), *n.* an oven used to anneal glass. Also, **leer.** [1905–10; < G *Lehr, Leer* model]

le·hu·a (lā hōō′ä), *n.* **1.** Also called **ohia lehua.** a tree, *Metrosideros villosa,* of the Hawaiian islands, yielding a hard wood. **2.** the bright-red, corymbose flower of this tree. [1885–90; < Hawaiian]

lei[1] (lā, lā′ē), *n., pl.* **leis.** (in the Hawaiian Islands) a wreath of flowers, leaves, etc., for the neck or head. [1835–45; < Hawaiian]

lei[2] (lā), *n.* pl. of **leu.**

Leib·niz (līb′nits; *Ger.* līp′nits), *n.* **Gott·fried Wil·helm von** (*Ger.* gôt′frēt vil′helm fən), 1646–1716, German philosopher, writer, and mathematician. Also, **Leib′nitz.** —**Leib·niz·i·an, Leib·nitz·i·an** (līb nit′sē ən), *adj., n.* —**Leib·niz′i·an·ism, Leib·nitz′i·an·ism,** *n.*

Lei·bo·witz (lē′bə wits), *n.* **Re·né** (rə nā′), born 1913, French conductor and composer, born in Poland.

Leices·ter (les′tər), *n.* **1. 1st Earl of.** See **Dudley, Robert. 2.** a city in Leicestershire, in central England. 290,600. **3.** Leicestershire. **4.** one of an English breed of large sheep, noted for its coarse, long wool and large yield of mutton.

Leices·ter·shire (les′tər shēr′, -shər), *n.* a county in central England. 836,500; 986 sq. mi. (2555 sq. km). Also called **Leicester.**

Lei·chou (lā′jō′), *n. Wade-Giles.* Leizhou.

Lei·den (līd′n), *n.* a city in W Netherlands. 103,246. Also, **Leyden.**

Lei·dy (lī′dē), *n.* **Joseph,** 1823–91, U.S. paleontologist, parasitologist, and anatomist.

Leif (lēf, lāf), *n.* a male given name.

Leif′ Er′icson. See **Ericson, Leif.**

Leigh (lē), *n.* a male or female given name.

Leigh-Mal·lo·ry (lē′mal′ə rē), *n.* **Sir Traf·ford Leigh** (traf′ərd lē), 1892–1944, British Air Force officer.

Leigh·ton (lāt′n), *n.* **Frederick** (*Baron Leighton of Stretton*), 1830–96, English painter and sculptor.

Lei·la (lē′lə, lā′-), *n.* a female given name.

Leins·dorf (līnz′dôrf; *Ger.* līns′dôRf), *n.* **E·rich** (er′ik; *Ger.* ā′RIKH), born 1912, U.S. orchestra conductor, born in Austria.

Lein·ster (len′stər), *n.* a province in the E Republic of Ireland. 1,789,844; 7576 sq. mi. (19,620 sq. km).

lei·o·my·o·ma (lī′ō mī ō′mə), *n., pl.* **-mas, -ma·ta** (-mə tə). *Pathol.* a benign tumor composed of nonstriated muscular tissue. Cf. **rhabdomyoma.** [1885–90; < Gk *leîo(s)* smooth + MYOMA] —**lei·o·my·om·a·tous** (lī′ō mī om′ə təs, -ō′mə təs), *adj.*

lei·po·a (lī pō′ə), *n.* See **mallee fowl.** [< NL (1840), the genus name, equiv. to Gk *leíp(ein)* to leave + *ōi(ón)* egg (see OO-) + NL *-a* -A[2]; alluding to the bird's habit of leaving its eggs in a mound after laying them]

Leip·zig (līp′sig, -sik; *Ger.* līp′tsik), *n.* a city in E central Germany. 563,980. Also, **Leip·sic** (līp′sik).

leish·man·i·a (lēsh man′ē ə, -mā′nē ə, līsh-), *n.* any parasitic flagellate protozoan of the genus *Leishmania,* occurring in vertebrates in an oval or spherical, nonflagellate form, and in invertebrates in an elongated, flagellated form. [< NL (1903), after William Boog *Leishman* (1865–1926), Scottish bacteriologist; see -IA] —**leish·man′i·al, leish·man·ic** (lēsh man′ik, līsh-), **leish·man′i·oid′,** *adj.*

leish·man·i·a·sis (lēsh′mə nī′ə sis, lĭsh′-), *n. Pathol.* any infection caused by a protozoan of the genus *Leishmania.* Also, **leish·man·i·o·sis** (lēsh man′ē ō′sis, -mā′-nē-, lĭsh-). Cf. **kala-azar.** [1910–15; LEISHMAN(IA) + -IASIS]

leis·ter (lē′stər), *n.* **1.** a spearlike implement having three or more prongs, for use in spearing fish. —*v.t.* **2.** to spear (fish) with a leister. [1525–35; < ON *ljóstr* salmon-spear, akin to *ljósta* to strike]

lei·sure (lē′zhər, lezh′ər), *n.* **1.** freedom from the demands of work or duty: *She looked forward to retirement and a life of leisure.* **2.** time free from the demands of work or duty, when one can rest, enjoy hobbies or sports, etc.: *Most evenings he had the leisure in which to follow his interests.* **3.** unhurried ease: *a work written with leisure and grace.* **4. at leisure, a.** with free or unrestricted time. **b.** without haste; slowly. **c.** out of work; unemployed: *Because of the failure of the magazine, many experienced editors are now at leisure.* **5. at one's leisure,** when one has free time; at one's convenience: *Take this book and read it at your leisure.* —*adj.* **6.** free or unoccupied: *leisure hours.* **7.** having leisure: *the leisure class.* **8.** (of clothing) suitable to or adapted for wear during leisure; casual: *a leisure jacket.* **9.** designed or intended for recreational use: *leisure products like bowling balls and video games.* [1250–1300; ME *leisir* < OF, n. use of inf. << L *licēre* to be permitted] —**lei′sur·a·ble,** *adj.* —**lei′sure·less,** *adj.*

lei·sured (lē′zhərd, lezh′ərd), *adj.* **1.** having leisure: *the leisured classes.* **2.** characterized by leisure; leisurely; unhurried: *the leisured manner of his walk.* [1625–35; LEISURE + -ED³]

lei′sure home′, a house for use on weekends, vacations, or the like. —**lei′sure-home′,** *adj.*

lei·sure·ly (lē′zhər lē, lezh′ər-), *adj.* **1.** acting, proceeding, or done without haste; unhurried; deliberate: *a leisurely conversation.* **2.** showing or suggesting ample leisure; unhurried: *a leisurely manner.* —*adv.* **3.** in a leisurely manner; without haste: *to travel leisurely.* [1480–90; earlier *laiserly* (adv.). See LEISURE, -LY] —**lei′sure·li·ness, lei′sure·ness,** *n.*
—**Syn. 1.** See **slow.**

lei′sure suit′, a man's casual suit, consisting of trousers and a matching jacket styled like a shirt, often made in pastel colors. [1970–75, *Amer.*]

lei·sure·wear (lē′zhər wâr′, lezh′ər-), *n.* casual clothes that are designed for wear during leisure time. Also, **lei′sure wear′.** [1960–65; LEISURE + WEAR]

Leith (lēth), *n.* a seaport in SE Scotland, on the Firth of Forth: now part of Edinburgh.

leit·mo·tif (līt′mō tēf′), *n.* a motif or theme associated throughout a music drama with a particular person, situation, or idea. [1875–80; < G: leading motive]

Leix (lāks), *n.* Laoighis.

Lei·zhou (lā′jō′), *n. Pinyin.* a peninsula of SW Guangdong province, in SE China, between the South China Sea and the Gulf of Tonkin. ab. 75 mi. (120 km) long; ab. 30 mi. (48 km) wide. Also, **Leichou, Luichow.**

Le Jeune (*Fr.* lə zhœn′), **Claude** (klōd), (*Claudin*), 1530?–1600?, Flemish composer.

Le·jeune (lə jōōn′, -zhœn′), *n.* **John Ar·cher** (är′-chər), 1867–1942, U.S. Marine Corps general.

lek¹ (lek), *n., v.* **lekked, lek·king.** *Animal Behav.* —*n.* **1.** a traditional place where males assemble during the mating season and engage in competitive displays that attract females. —*v.i.* **2.** (of a male) to assemble in a lek and engage in competitive displays. [1865–70; < Sw: mating ground (perh. elliptically from *lekställe*), mating, game, play, ON *leikr* play, c. OE *lāc* struggle, offering, gift, Goth *laiks* dance, OHG *leih* melody]

lek² (lek), *n.* an aluminum coin and monetary unit of Albania, equal to 100 qintars. [1925–30; < Albanian]

Lek (lek), *n.* a river in the central Netherlands, flowing W to the Meuse River; the N branch of the lower Rhine. 40 mi. (64 km) long.

lek·var (lek′vär), *n. Hungarian Cookery.* a soft, jamlike spread made of sweetened prunes or apricots. [1955–60; < Hungarian *lekvár* jam, marmalade < Slovak, by-form of Czech *lektvar* electuary < MHG *la(c)twārje, latwērge* (G *Latwerge*) < OF *leitüaire, laitüaire* < LL *ēlectuārium* ELECTUARY]

lek·y·thos (lek′ə thos′), *n., pl.* **-thoi** (-thoi′). *Gk. and Rom. Antiq.* an oil jar having an ellipsoidal body, narrow neck, flanged mouth, curved handle extending from below the lip to the shoulder, and a narrow base terminating in a foot: used chiefly for ointments. Also, **lekythus.** Cf. **alabastron, aryballos, askos.** [1850–55; < Gk *lḗkythos*]

lek·y·thus (lek′ə thəs), *n., pl.* **-thi** (-thī′). lekythos.

lekythos

CONCISE ETYMOLOGY KEY: <, descended or borrowed from; >, whence; b., blend of, blended; c., cognate with; cf., compare; deriv., derivative; equiv., equivalent; imit., imitative; obl., oblique; r., replacing; s., stem; sp., spelling, spelled; resp., respelling, respelled; trans., translation; ?, origin unknown; *, unattested; ‡, probably earlier than. See the full key inside the front cover.

Le·la (lē′lə), *n.* a female given name.

Le·land (lē′lənd), *n.* a male given name.

Le·loir (lə lwär′; *Sp.* le lwär′), *n.* **Luis Fe·de·ri·co** (lwēs fe′the re′kô), born 1906, Argentine biochemist, born in France: Nobel prize for chemistry 1970.

Le·ly (lē′lē; *Du.* lā′lē), *n.* **Sir Pe·ter** (pē′tər; *Du.* pā′-tər), (*Pieter van der Faes*), 1618–80, Dutch painter in England.

LEM (lem), *n., pl.* **LEMs, LEM's.** lunar excursion module.

Le·maî·tre (lə me′trᵊ), *n.* **1. Fran·cois É·lie Jules** (fräN swa′ ā lē′ zhyl), 1835–1915, French critic and dramatist. **2. Abbé Georges É·douard** (*Fr.* zhôrzh ā dwar′), 1894–1966, Belgian astrophysicist and priest: formulated big-bang theory.

lem·an (lem′ən, lē′mən), *n. Archaic.* **1.** a sweetheart; lover; beloved. **2.** a mistress. [1175–1225; ME *lemman,* earlier *leofman.* See LIEF, MAN¹]

Le·man (lē′mən), *n.* **Lake.** See **Geneva, Lake of.**

Le Mans (lə mäN′), a city in and the capital of Sarthe, in NW France: auto racing. 155,245.

Le·mass (lə mas′), *n.* **Seán Francis** (shôn), 1899–1971, prime minister of Ireland 1959–66.

Le·May (lə mā′), *n.* **Curtis (Emerson),** 1906–90, U.S. Air Force officer: chief of the Strategic Air Command 1948–61; Chief of Staff of the Air Force 1961–65.

Lem·berg (lem′berk′; *Eng.* lem′bûrg), *n.* German name of **Lvov.**

Le·mes·sus (lə mes′əs), *n.* ancient name of **Limassol.**

Le Mi·san·thrope (*Fr.* lə mē zäN trôp′), a comedy (1666) by Molière.

lem·ma¹ (lem′ə), *n., pl.* **lem·mas, lem·ma·ta** (lem′ə-tə). **1.** a subsidiary proposition introduced in proving some other proposition; a helping theorem. **2.** an argument, theme, or subject, esp. when indicated in a heading. **3.** a word or phrase that is glossed; headword. [1560–70; < L: theme, title, epigram < Gk *lêmma* something received, premise, akin to *lambánein* to take, receive, take for granted]

lem·ma² (lem′ə), *n., pl.* **lem·mas.** *Bot.* a bract in a grass spikelet just below the pistil and stamens. [1745–55; < Gk *lémma* shell, husk, akin to *lépein* to peel]

lem·ma·tize (lem′ə tīz′), *v.t.,* **-tized, -tiz·ing.** to sort (the words in a list or text) in order to determine the headword, under which other words are then listed. Also, *esp. Brit.,* **lem′ma·tise′.** [1965–70; < Gk *lēmmat-* (s. of *lêmma;* see LEMMA¹) + -IZE] —**lem′ma·ti·za′tion,** *n.*

lem·me (lem′ē), *Pron. Spelling.* let me. [reduced form]

brown lemming, *Lemmus trimucronatus,* length to 6½ in. (17 cm)

lem·ming (lem′ing), *n.* any of various small, mouselike rodents of the genera *Lemmus, Myopus,* and *Dicrostonyx,* of far northern regions, as *L. lemmus,* of Norway, Sweden, etc., noted for periodic mass migrations that sometimes result in mass drownings. [1600–10; < Norw; c. Icel *læmingi* lemming, *læmingr* loon; akin to Goth *laian* to revile, Icel *lā* to blame]

Lem·min·käi·nen (lem′in kai′nen), *n.* (in the *Kalevala*) a young, jovial hero who has many adventures in which he is sometimes helped by his mother.

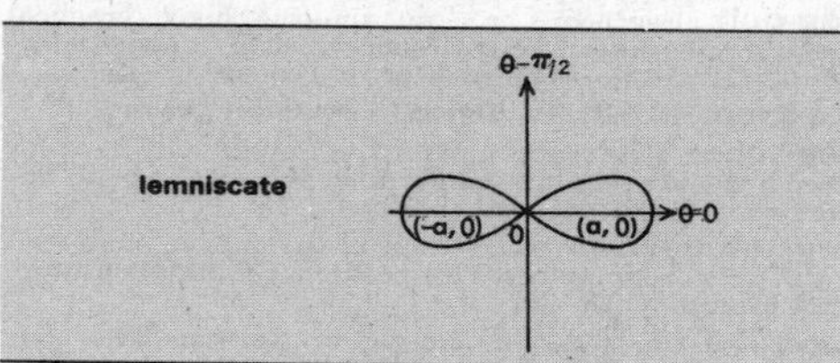

lemniscate

lem·nis·cate (lem nis′kit, lem′nis kāt′, -kit), *n. Analyt. Geom.* a plane curve generated by the locus of the point at which a variable tangent to a rectangular hyperbola intersects a perpendicular from the center to the tangent. Equation: $r^2 = 2a^2\cos\theta$. Also called **Bernoulli's lemniscate.** [1775–85; < L *lēmniscātus* adorned with ribbons. See LEMNISCUS, -ATE¹]

lem·nis·cus (lem nis′kəs), *n., pl.* **-nis·ci** (-nis′ī, -nis′-kē). *Anat.* a band of fibers, esp. of white nerve fibers in the brain. Also called **fillet, laqueus.** [1840–50; < NL, special use of L *lēmniscus* pendent ribbon < Gk *lēmnískos* ribbon]

Lem·ni·tzer (lem′nit sər), *n.* **Ly·man Louis** (lī′mən), 1899–1988, U.S. army officer; chairman Joint Chiefs of Staff 1960–63; supreme allied commander NATO 1963–69.

Lem·nos (lem′nos, -nōs; *Gk.* lēm′nôs), *n.* a Greek island in the NE Aegean. 20,000; 186 sq. mi. (480 sq. km). *Cap.:* Kastro. —**Lem·ni·an** (lem′nē ən), *adj., n.*

lem·on (lem′ən), *n.* **1.** the yellowish, acid fruit of a subtropical citrus tree, *Citrus limon.* **2.** the tree itself. **3.** See **lemon yellow. 4.** *Informal.* a person or thing that proves to be defective, imperfect, or unsatisfactory; dud: *His car turned out to be a lemon.* —*adj.* **5.** made of or with lemon. **6.** having the color, taste, or odor of lemon. [1350–1400; 1905–10 for def. 4; < ML *lemōnium;* r. ME *lymon* < ML *limō,* (s. *limōn-*) < Pers *līmū, līmun*] —**lem′on·ish,** *adj.* —**lem′on·like′, lem′on·y,** *adj.*

lem·on·ade (lem′ə nād′, lem′ə nād′), *n.* a beverage consisting of lemon juice, sweetener, and water, sometimes carbonated. [1655–65; LEMON + -ADE¹, modeled on F *limonade* or Sp *limonada*]

lem′onade ber′ry, a sumac, *Rhus integrifolia,* of southern California, having hairy, dark-red fruits used to make a beverage resembling lemonade. Also called **lem′onade su′mac, sourberry.** [1905–10, *Amer.*]

lem′on balm′. See under **balm** (def. 5). [1885–90]

lem′on drop′, a lemon-flavored lozenge. [1800–10]

lem·on·fish (lem′ən fish′), *n., pl.* **-fish·es,** (*esp. collectively*) **-fish.** *Southern U.S.* the cobia. [LEMON + FISH]

lem′on gera′nium, a garden geranium, *Pelargonium crispum,* having lemon-scented leaves.

lem′on grass′, any of several lemon-scented grasses of the genus *Cymbopogon,* esp. *C. citratus,* of tropical regions, yielding lemon-grass oil. [1830–40]

lem′on-grass oil′ (lem′ən gras′, -gräs′), a yellowish to brownish oil distilled from the leaves of certain lemon grasses, esp. *Cymbopogon citratus,* used chiefly in perfumery. [1885–90]

Lem′on Grove′, a town in SW California, near San Diego. 20,780.

lem′on kal′i (kal′ē, kā′lē), *Brit.* an artificially flavored carbonated lemon drink; lemon soda pop. [1855–60; *kali,* obs. for *kalium;* see ALKALI]

lem′on law′, a law that requires manufacturers to replace, repair, or refund the cost of automobiles that prove to be defective. [1980–85]

lem′on mint′, a plant, *Mentha piperita,* of the central U.S., having white or pinkish flowers and lemon-scented leaves when crushed.

lem′on oil′, a fragrant yellow essential oil obtained from the rinds of lemons or manufactured synthetically, used as a flavoring and in perfumery, furniture polishes, etc. [1895–1900]

lem′on shark′, a common shallow-water shark, *Negaprion brevirostris,* having a yellowish body and inhabiting inshore regions of the Atlantic from North Carolina to Brazil.

lem′on sole′, any of various popular food flatfishes, as *Parophrys vetulus* of the Pacific (**English sole**) and *Pseudopleuronectes americanus* of the Atlantic (**winter flounder** or **blackback flounder**). [1875–80; prob. alter., by folk etym., of F *limande* dab (fish), OF *limande, lime,* of uncert. orig.]

lem′on squash′, *Brit.* lemon soda; a soft drink of lemon juice and soda water. [1875–80]

lem′on verbe′na, a plant, *Aloysia triphylla,* having long, slender leaves with a lemonlike fragrance. Also called **citronalis.** [1865–70]

lem′on vine′. See **Barbados gooseberry** (def. 1).

lem·on·wood (lem′ən wŏŏd′), *n.* **1.** a tropical American tree, *Calycophyllum candidissimum,* of the madder family, having flowers with conspicuous white calyx lobes. **2.** the hard, tough wood of this tree, used for fishing rods and archery bows. Also called **degame.** [1875–80; LEMON + WOOD¹]

lem′on yel′low, a clear, yellowish-green color. [1800–10] —**lem′on-yel′low,** *adj.*

Le Morte d'Ar·thur (lə môrt′ där′thər), a compilation and translation of French Arthurian romances by Sir Thomas Malory, printed by Caxton in 1485. Also, ***Le Morte′ Dar′thur.***

Lem·pa (lem′pä), *n.* a river rising in NW El Salvador, flowing E and then S to the Pacific Ocean. ab. 200 mi. (320 km) long.

Lem′pert opera′tion (lem′pərt), *Surg.* fenestration (def. 3c). [after Julius *Lempert* (1890–1968), U.S. otologist, who devised it]

lem·pi·ra (lem pēr′ə), *n.* a paper money and monetary unit of Honduras, equal to 100 centavos. *Abbr.:* L. [1930–35; < AmerSp, after *Lempira,* Indian chief]

Lem·u·el (lem′yōō əl), *n.* a male given name: from a Hebrew word meaning "devoted to God."

le·mur (lē′mər), *n.* any of various small, arboreal, chiefly nocturnal mammals of the family Lemuridae, of Madagascar and the Comoro Islands, esp. of the genus *Lemur,* usually having large eyes, a foxlike face, and woolly fur: most lemurs are endangered. [1790–1800; < NL, appar. special use of L *lemurēs* (pl.) ghosts, specters] —**le′mur-like′,** *adj.*

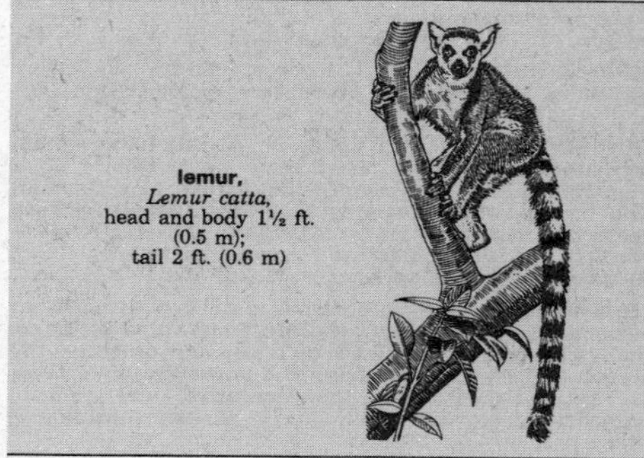
lemur, *Lemur catta,* head and body 1½ ft. (0.5 m); tail 2 ft. (0.6 m)

Le·mu·ra·li·a (lem′yə rā′lē ə, -rāl′yə), *n.* (*sometimes used with a plural v.*) the annual festival in ancient Rome in which the lemures were exorcised from houses. Also, **Le·mu·ri·a** (le myŏŏr′ē ə).

lem·u·res (lem′yə rēz′; *Lat.* lem′ŏŏ res′), *n.pl. Rom. Relig.* the ghosts of the dead of a family, considered as troublesome unless exorcised or propitiated; larvae. [1545–55; < L; see LEMUR]

lem•u•roid (lem′yə roid′), *adj.* **1.** lemurlike; of the lemur kind. —*n.* **2.** a lemur. [1870–75; < NL *Lemuroidea.* See LEMUR, -OID]

Len (len), *n.* a male given name, form of **Leonard.**

Le•na (lē′nə; *Russ.* lye′nə), *n.* **1.** a river in the Russian Federation in Asia, flowing NE from Lake Baikal through the Yakutsk Republic into the Laptev Sea. 2800 mi. (4500 km) long. **2.** a female given name, form of **Helena.**

Le•nae•a (lə nē′ə), *n.* (*sometimes used with a plural v.*) a festival in ancient Athens in honor of Dionysus, celebrated at the beginning of February and comprising a public banquet followed by the performance of comedies. Also, **Le•nai•a** (lə nī′ə).

Le Nain (lə naN′), **An•toine** (äN twaN′), ("*the Elder*"), 1588?–1648, and his two brothers **Louis** (lwē), ("*the Roman*"), 1593?–1648, and **Ma•thieu** (mA tyœ′), 1607–77, French painters.

Len•a•pe (len′ə pē, lə nä′pē), *n., pl.* **-pes,** (*esp. collectively*) **-pe.** Delaware (defs. 5, 6). Also called **Lenni Lenape.** [1720–30, *Amer.*; < Unami Delaware *lənáp•e* (equiv. to Proto-Algonquian **elen-* ordinary + **-a•pe•w* man)]

Le•nard (lā′närt; *Eng.* lā′närd), *n.* **Phi•lipp** (fē′lip), 1862–1947, German physicist, born in Czechoslovakia: Nobel prize 1905.

Le′nard tube′, *Electronics.* an early cathode-ray tube having at the end opposite the cathode a window of thin glass or metal allowing cathode rays (**Le′nard rays′**) to pass out into the atmosphere. [named after P. LENARD]

Len•ca (leng′kə), *n., pl.* **-cas,** (*esp. collectively*) **-ca. 1.** a member of an Indian people of El Salvador and central Honduras. **2.** the language of the Lenca.

Len•clos (läN klō′), *n.* **Anne** (än, An), (*Ninon de Lenclos*), 1620–1705?, French courtesan and wit.

lend (lend), *v.,* **lent, lend•ing.** —*v.t.* **1.** to grant the use of (something) on condition that it or its equivalent will be returned. **2.** to give (money) on condition that it is returned and that interest is paid for its temporary use. **3.** to give or contribute obligingly or helpfully: *to lend one's aid to a cause.* **4.** to adapt (oneself or itself) to something: *The building should lend itself to inexpensive remodeling.* **5.** to furnish or impart: *Distance lends enchantment to the view.* —*v.i.* **6.** to make a loan. **7. lend a hand,** to give help; aid: *If everyone lends a hand, we can have dinner ready in half an hour.* [bef. 900; ME *lenden,* var. (orig. past tense) of *lenen,* OE *lǣnan* (c. D *lenen,* G *lehnen,* ON *lāna*), deriv. of *lǣn* loan; c. G *Lehnen,* ON *lān.* See LOAN[1]] —**lend′er,** *n.*

lend•a•ble (len′də bəl), *adj.* reserved or at hand for purposes of lending: *lendable stock; lendable money.* [1605–15; LEND + -ABLE]

lend′ing li′brary, 1. Also called **circulating library, rental library.** a small library that is maintained by a commercial establishment, as a drugstore, and is composed largely of current books that are lent to customers for a fee. **2.** *Chiefly Brit.* a public library that lends materials or the division or section of it that carries out this function. [1700–10]

lend-lease (lend′lēs′), *n., v.,* **-leased, -leas•ing.** —*n.* **1.** the matériel and services supplied by the U.S. to its allies during World War II under an act of Congress (**Lend′-Lease′ Act′**) passed in 1941: such aid was to be repaid in kind after the war. **2.** the two-way transfer of ideas, styles, etc. —*v.t.* **3.** to supply (matériel or services) as authorized by the Lend-Lease Act. [1935–40]

Le•nex•a (lə nek′sə), *n.* a city in NE Kansas. 18,639.

L'En•fant (läN fäN′), *n.* **Pierre Charles** (pyer sharl), 1754–1825, U.S. engineer, architect, and soldier; born in France: designer of Washington, D.C.

Len•glen (leng′glən, -lən; *Fr.* läN glen′), *n.* **Su•zanne** (so͞o zan′; *Fr.* sy zaN′), 1899–1938, French tennis player.

length (lengkth, length, lenth), *n.* **1.** the longest extent of anything as measured from end to end: *the length of a river.* **2.** the measure of the greatest dimension of a plane or solid figure. **3.** extent from beginning to end of a series, enumeration, account, book, etc.: *a report running 300 pages in length.* **4.** extent in time; duration: *the length of a battle.* **5.** a distance determined by the extent of something specified: *Hold the picture at arm's length.* **6.** a piece or portion of a certain or a known extent: *a length of rope.* **7.** the quality or state of being long rather than short: *a journey remarkable for its length.* **8.** the extent to which a person might or would go in pursuing something: *He went to great lengths to get what he wanted.* **9.** a large extent or expanse of something. **10.** the measure from end to end of a horse, boat, etc., as a unit of distance in racing: *The horse won by two lengths.* **11.** *Clothing.* the extent of a garment related to a point it reaches, as on the wearer's body, the floor, or on a garment used as a standard of measurement (usually used in combination): *an ankle-length gown; a floor-length negligee; a three-quarter-length coat.* **12.** *Pros., Phonet.* **a.** (of a vowel or syllable) quantity, whether long or short. **b.** the quality of vowels. **13.** *Bridge.* the possession of four or more than four cards in a given suit. **14.** *Theat. Archaic.* 42 lines of an acting part. **15. at length, a.** in or to the full extent; completely. **b.** after a time; finally: *At length there was a step forward in the negotiations.* **16. go to any length** or **lengths,** to disregard any impediment that could prevent one from accomplishing one's purpose: *He would go to any lengths to get his own way.* **17. keep at arm's length.** See **arm**[1] (def. 16). [bef. 900; ME *length(e),* OE *lengthu;* c. D *lengte,* ON *lengd.* See LONG[1], -TH[1]]
—**Syn. 1.** span, stretch, reach, scope, measure.

length′ between′ perpendic′ulars, *Naut.* the length of a hull between the forward and after perpendicular. Cf. **perpendicular** (def. 11).

length•en (lengk′thən, leng′-, len′-), *v.t.* **1.** to make longer; make greater in length. —*v.i.* **2.** to become greater in length; grow long or longer. [1490–1500; LENGTH + -EN[1]] —**length′en•er,** *n.*
—**Syn. 1.** elongate, draw out. LENGTHEN, EXTEND, STRETCH, PROLONG, PROTRACT agree in the idea of making longer. To LENGTHEN is to make longer, either in a material or an immaterial sense: *to lengthen a dress.* To EXTEND is to lengthen beyond some original point or so as to reach a certain point: *to extend a railway line by a hundred miles.* To STRETCH is primarily to lengthen by drawing or tension: *to stretch a rubber band.* Both PROLONG and PROTRACT mean esp. to lengthen in time, and therefore apply to intangibles. To PROLONG is to continue beyond the desired, estimated, or allotted time: *to prolong an interview.* To PROTRACT is to draw out to undue length or to be slow in coming to a conclusion: *to protract a discussion.* —**Ant. 1.** shorten.

length′ o′ver all′, *Naut.* the entire length of a vessel, measured from the foremost point of the bow to the aftermost point of the stern.

length•ways (lengkth′wāz′, length′-, lenth′-), *adv., adj.* lengthwise. [1590–1600; LENGTH + -WAYS]

length•wise (lengkth′wīz′, length′-, lenth′-), *adv., adj.* in the direction of the length. [1570–80; LENGTH + -WISE]

length•y (lengk′thē, leng′-, len′-), *adj.,* **length•i•er, length•i•est. 1.** having or being of great length; very long: *a lengthy journey.* **2.** tediously verbose; very long; too long: *a lengthy speech.* [1680–90, *Amer.*; LENGTH + -Y[1]] —**length′i•ly,** *adv.* —**length′i•ness,** *n.*

Len•gua (leng′gwə), *n.* **1.** a member of a group of Indian peoples living in the Gran Chaco area of Paraguay. **2.** any of several languages spoken by these peoples. [1820–25; < Sp; lit., tongue, ref. to their custom of wearing labrets]

le•ni•en•cy (lē′nē ən sē, lēn′yən-), *n., pl.* **-cies. 1.** the quality or state of being lenient. **2.** a lenient act. Also, **le′ni•ence.** [1770–80; LENI(ENT) + -ENCY]

le•ni•ent (lē′nē ənt, lēn′yənt), *adj.* **1.** agreeably tolerant; permissive; indulgent: *He tended to be lenient toward the children. More lenient laws encouraged greater freedom of expression.* **2.** *Archaic.* softening, soothing, or alleviative. [1645–55; < L *lēnient-* (s. of *lēniēns*), prp. of *lēnīre* to soften, alleviate, soothe. See LENIS, -ENT] —**le′ni•ent•ly,** *adv.*

Le•nin (len′in; *Russ.* lye′nyin), *n.* **V(la•di•mir) I(l•yich)** (vlad′ə mēr′ il′yich; *Russ.* vlu dyē′myir ē lyēch′), (*Vladimir Ilyich Ulyanov*) ("*N. Lenin*"), 1870–1924, Russian revolutionary leader: Soviet premier 1918–24.

Le•ni•na•bad (len′i nə bäd′; *Russ.* lyi nyi nu bät′), *n.* former name (1936–91) of **Khodzhent.**

Le•ni•na•kan (len′i nə kän′; *Russ.* lyi nyi nu kän′), *n.* former name of **Gumri.**

Le•nin•grad (len′in grad′; *Russ.* lyi nyin grät′), *n.* former name (1924–91) of **St. Petersburg** (def. 1).

Le•nin•ism (len′ə niz′əm), *n.* the form of Communism as taught by Lenin, with emphasis on the dictatorship of the proletariat. [1915–20; LENIN + -ISM]

Le•nin•ist (len′ə nist), *adj.* **1.** of or pertaining to Lenin or to Leninism. —*n.* **2.** an advocate or supporter of Lenin or Leninism. Also, **Le•nin•ite** (len′ə nīt′). [1915–20; LENIN + -IST]

Le′nin Peak′, a peak in the Trans Alai range, in central Asia, between Kyrgyzstan and Tajikistan. 23,382 ft. (7127 m). Formerly, **Kaufmann Peak.**

Le•ninsk-Kuz•nets•ki (len′insk ko͝oz nets′kē; *Russ.* lye′nyinsk ko͞o znyets′kyē), *n.* a city in the S Russian Federation in Asia. 132,000. Also, **Le′ninsk-Ku•znets′•kiy.**

le•nis (lē′nis, lā′-), *adj., n., pl.* **le•nes** (lē′nēz, lā′-). *Phonet.* —*adj.* **1.** pronounced with relatively weak muscular tension and breath pressure, resulting in weak sound effect: in stressed or unstressed position, (*b, d, g, j, v, th, z,* and *zh*) are lenis in English, as compared with (*p, t, k, ch, f, th, s,* and *sh*), which are fortis. Cf. **fortis** (def. 1). —*n.* **2.** a lenis consonant. [1925–30; < L: soft, mild, gentle]

le•nit•ic (li nit′ik), *adj.* lentic. [1915–20; *lenit-* (as in LENITION, LENITIVE, etc.) + -IC]

le•ni•tion (li nish′ən), *n.* **1.** *Phonet.* a phonological process that weakens consonant articulation at the ends of syllables or between vowels, causing the consonant to become voiced, spirantized, or deleted. **2.** *Ling.* a type of Celtic mutation that derives historically from phonological lenition. [1535–45 for obs. sense "mitigation, assuaging"; 1910–15 for current senses; < L *lēnīt(us)* (ptp. of *lēnīre* to soften; see LENIS, -ITE[2]) + -ION]

len•i•tive (len′i tiv), *adj.* **1.** softening, soothing, or mitigating, as medicines or applications. **2.** mildly laxative. —*n.* **3.** a lenitive medicine or application. **4.** a mild laxative. **5.** *Archaic.* anything that softens or soothes. [1535–45; < ML *lēnītīvus.* See LENITION, -IVE] —**len′i•tive•ly,** *adv.* —**len′i•tive•ness,** *n.*

len•i•ty (len′i tē), *n., pl.* **-ties. 1.** the quality or state of being mild or gentle, as toward others. **2.** a lenient act. [1540–50; < L *lēnitās.* See LENIS, -TY[2]]

Len′ni Len′ape (len′ē), Delaware (defs. 5, 6). Also called **Lenape.**

Len•nox (len′əks), *n.* a town in SW California, near Los Angeles. 18,445.

Len•ny (len′ē), *n.* a male given name, form of **Leonard.** Also, **Len′nie.**

le•no (lē′nō), *n., pl.* **-nos,** *adj.* —*n.* **1.** Also called **le′no weave′, gauze weave.** a weave structure in which paired warp yarns are intertwined in a series of figure eights and filling yarn is passed through each of the interstices so formed, producing a firm, open mesh. **2.** any fabric in this weave. —*adj.* **3.** made in leno weave. [1850–55; perh. Anglicized var. of F *linon* lawn, deriv. of *lin* linen (< L *līnum* flax)]

Le•noir (lə nwar′ *for 1;* lə nôr′, -nōr′ *for 2*), *n.* **1. Jean Jo•seph É•tienne** (zhäN zhō zef′ ā tyen′), 1822–1900, French inventor. **2.** a town in W North Carolina. 13,748.

Le•nore (lə nôr′, -nōr′), *n.* a female given name, form of **Eleanor.** Also, **Le•no•ra** (lə nôr′ə, -nōr′ə).

Le•nô•tre (lə nō′tRᵊ), *n.* **An•dré** (äN drā′), 1613–1700, French architect and landscape designer.

Len•ox (len′əks), *n.* a town in W Massachusetts, in the Berkshire Hills: a former estate (**Tanglewood**) in the area is the site of annual summer music festivals. 6523.

lens (lenz), *n., pl.* **lens•es,** *v.* —*n.* **1.** a piece of transparent substance, usually glass, having two opposite surfaces either both curved or one curved and one plane, used in an optical device in changing the convergence of light rays, as for magnification, or in correcting defects of vision. **2.** a combination of such pieces. **3.** some analogous device, as for affecting sound waves, electromagnetic radiation, or streams of electrons. **4.** *Anat.* See **crystalline lens. 5.** *Geol.* a body of rock or ore that is thick in the middle and thinner toward the edges, similar in shape to a biconvex lens. —*v.t.* **6.** *Motion Pictures.* to film (a motion picture). [1685–95; < NL, special use of L *lēns* a lentil (from its shape); see LENTIL] —**lens′less,** *adj.* —**lens′like′,** *adj.*

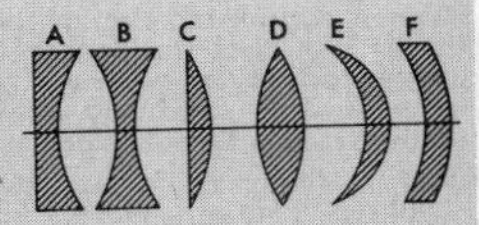

lenses (def. 1) A, plano-concave; B, biconcave (concavo-concave); C, plano-convex; D, biconvex (convexo-convex); E, the meniscus (converging concavo-convex, converging meniscus); F, concavo-convex

lens•board (lenz′bôrd′, -bōrd′), *n. Photog.* the usually removable front panel of a view camera or enlarger on which the lens is mounted. Also, **lens′ board′.** [1890–95; LENS + BOARD]

lens•man (lenz′mən), *n., pl.* **-men.** *Informal.* a photographer. [1950–55; LENS + -MAN]

lens′ tur′ret, *Photog.* a rotating device on a camera for bringing any of several lenses in front of the shutter. [1950–55]

lent (lent), *v.* pt. and pp. of **lend.**

Lent (lent), *n.* (in the Christian religion) an annual season of fasting and penitence in preparation for Easter, beginning on Ash Wednesday and lasting 40 weekdays to Easter, observed by Roman Catholic, Anglican, and certain other churches. [bef. 1000; ME *lente(n),* OE *lencten, lengten* spring, Lent, lit., lengthening (of daylight hours); c. D *lente,* G *Lenz* spring; see LENTEN]

-lent, a suffix occurring in loanwords from Latin, var. of **-ulent:** *pestilent.*

len•ta•men•te (len′tə men′tā; *It.* len′tä men′te), *adv. Music.* slowly. [1755–65; < It, equiv. to *lenta-* (see LENTO) + *-mente* adv. suffix < L: abl. of *mēns* mind, purpose, intention (see MENTAL)]

len•tan•do (len tän′dō; *It.* len tän′dô), *adj. Music.* becoming slower. [1850–55; < It, prp. of *lentare* to make slow; see LENTO]

Lent•en (len′tn), *adj.* **1.** of, pertaining to, or suitable for Lent. **2.** suggesting Lent, as in austerity, frugality, or rigorousness; meager. Also, **lent′en.** [ME, orig. attributive use of *lenten* LENT, later taken as adj. ending in -EN[2]]

len•tic (len′tik), *adj.* pertaining to or living in still water. Also, **lenitic.** [1930–35; < L *lent(us)* slow, motionless + -IC]

len•ti•cel (len′tə sel′), *n. Bot.* a body of cells formed on the periderm of a stem, appearing on the surface of the plant as a lens-shaped spot, and serving as a pore. [1850–55; < NL *lenticella,* dim. of L *lenticula* lentil; see LENTICLE] —**len•ti•cel•late** (len′tə sel′it), *adj.*

len•ti•cle (len′ti kəl), *n.* a window in a clock case revealing the motion of the pendulum bob. [< L *lenticula* lentil, equiv. to *lenti-* (s. of *lēns;* see LENS) + *-cula* -CLE[1]]

len•tic•u•lar (len tik′yə lər), *adj.* **1.** of or pertaining to a lens. **2.** biconvex; convexo-convex. **3.** resembling the seed of a lentil in form; lentil-shaped. [1375–1425; late ME < L *lenticulāris* lentillike, equiv. to *lenticul(a)* (see LENTICLE) + *-āris* -AR[1]] —**len•tic′u•lar•ly,** *adv.*

lentic′ular cloud′, a very smooth, round or oval, lens-shaped cloud that is often seen, singly or stacked in groups, near a mountain ridge.

lentic′ular proc′ess, *Photog.* a method for producing images with a three-dimensional effect by photographing on lenticulated film. [1940–45]

len•tic•u•late (len tik′yə lāt′), *v.t.,* **-lat•ed, -lat•ing.** *Photog.* to impress lenticules on the surface of (film). [1920–25; < L *lenticul(a)* (see LENTICLE) + -ATE[1]]

len•ti•cule (len′ti kyo͞ol′), *n. Photog.* one of many tiny cylindrical or spherical lens segments embossed on the surface of a film used in stereoscopic and color photography. [1880–85; < L *lenticula;* see LENTICLE]

len•ti•form (len′tə fôrm′), *adj.* lenticular. [1700–1710]

len•tig•i•nous (len tij′ə nəs), *adj.* **1.** of or pertaining to a lentigo. **2.** *Bot., Zool.* covered with minute dots; freckled; speckled. Also, **len•tig•i•nose** (len tij′ə nōs′). [1590–1600; < L *lentīginōsus* freckled, equiv. to *lentīgin-* (s. of *lentīgō*) LENTIGO + *-ōsus* -OUS]

len•ti•go (len tī′gō), *n., pl.* **-tig•i•nes** (-tij′ə nēz′). a freckle or other pigmented spot. [1375–1425; late ME (in pl.) < L, equiv. to *lenti-* (var. of *lenti-,* s. of *lēns* LENTIL) + *-gō* n. suffix]

len•til (len′til, -tl), *n.* **1.** a plant, *Lens culinaris,* of the legume family, having flattened, biconvex seeds used as food. **2.** the seed itself. [1200–50; ME < OF *lentille* < VL **lenticula* for L *lenticula.* See LENTICLE]

len′til cut′, *Jewelry.* a cabochon cut in which the upper and lower portions of the stone are identical.

len·tisk (len′tisk), *n.* mastic (def. 1). [1375–1425; late ME *lentiske* < L *lentīscus*]

len·tis·si·mo (len tis′ə mō′; *It.* len tēs′sē mô′), *Music.* —*adj.* **1.** very slow. —*adv.* **2.** very slowly. [1900–05; < It, superl. of *lento* LENTO]

len·ti·vi·rus (len′tə vī′rəs), *n., pl.* **-rus·es.** any slow virus of the genus *Lentivirus,* of the retrovirus family, causing brain disease in sheep and other animals. [LENTI(CULAR) + VIRUS]

len·to (len′tō; *It.* len′tô), *Music.* —*adj.* **1.** slow. —*adv.* **2.** slowly. [1715–25; < It < L *lentus* slow]

len·toid (len′toid), *adj.* **1.** having the shape of a biconvex lens. —*n.* **2.** a lentoid body. [1875–80; < L *lent-* (s. of *lēns*) lentil (see LENS) + -OID]

Len·ya (len′yə, lān′-), *n.* **Lot·te** (lot′ē; *Ger.* lô′tə), (*Karoline Blamauer*), 1900–81, Austrian actress and singer, in the U.S. after 1935 (wife of Kurt Weill).

Le·o (lē′ō), *n., gen.* **Le·o·nis** (lē ō′nis) for 1. **1.** *Astron.* the Lion, a zodiacal constellation between Virgo and Cancer, containing the bright star Regulus. **2.** *Astrol.* **a.** the fifth sign of the zodiac: the fixed fire sign. See illus. under **zodiac. b.** a person born under this sign, usually between July 23rd and August 22nd. **3.** a male given name: from a Greek word meaning "lion."

Le·o I (lē′ō; *It.* le′ô), **Saint,** ("*Leo the Great*"), A.D. c390–461, Italian ecclesiastic: pope 440–461.

Leo II, Saint, died A.D. 683, Sicilian ecclesiastic: pope 682–683.

Leo III, 1. Saint, A.D. c750–816, Italian ecclesiastic: pope 795–816. **2.** ("*the Isaurian*"), A.D. c680–741, Eastern Roman emperor 717–741.

Leo IV, Saint, died A.D. 855, Italian ecclesiastic: pope 847–855.

Leo V, fl. 10th century A.D., Italian ecclesiastic: pope 903.

Leo VI, pope A.D. 928.

Leo VII, died A.D. 939, Italian ecclesiastic: pope 936–939.

Leo VIII, died A.D. 965, Italian ecclesiastic: pope 963–965.

Leo IX, Saint (*Bruno*), 1002–54, German ecclesiastic: pope 1049–54.

Leo X, (*Giovanni de'Medici*), 1475–1521, Italian ecclesiastic: pope 1513–21 (son of Lorenzo de'Medici).

Leo XI, (*Alessandro de'Medici*), 1535–1605, Italian ecclesiastic: pope 1605.

Leo XII, (*Annibale Francesco della Genga*), 1760–1829, Italian ecclesiastic: pope 1823–29.

Leo XIII, (*Giovanni Vincenzo Pecci*), 1810–1903, Italian ecclesiastic: pope 1878–1903.

Le·of·ric (lē of′rik), *n.* died 1057, earl of Mercia c1030–57 (husband of Lady Godiva). Latin, **Leuricus.**

Le·o Mi·nor (lē′ō mī′nər), *gen.* **Le·o·nis Mi·no·ris** (lē ō′nis mī nôr′is, -nōr′-). *Astron.* the Little Lion, a northern constellation between Leo and Ursa Major.

Leom·in·ster (lem′in stər), *n.* a city in N Massachusetts. 34,508.

Le·on (lē′on), *n.* a male given name, form of **Leo.**

Le·ón (lā ōn′; *Sp.* le ôn′), *n.* **1.** a province in NW Spain: formerly a kingdom. 598,721; 5936 sq. mi. (15,375 sq. km). **2.** the capital of this province. 105,235. **3.** a city in W Guanajuato, in central Mexico. 557,000. **4.** a city in W Nicaragua: the former capital. 205,265.

Le·o·na (lē ō′nə), *n.* a female given name. Also, **Le·o·nie** (lē′ə nē, lē ō′nē).

Leon·ard (len′ərd), *n.* **1. William El·ler·y (Channing)** (el′ə rē), 1876–1944, U.S. poet, essayist, and teacher. **2.** a male given name: from Germanic words meaning "lion" and "hardy."

Le·o·nar·desque (lē′ə när desk′, lā′-), *adj.* of, pertaining to, or suggesting Leonardo da Vinci or the style of his paintings. [1860–65; LEONARD(O) + -ESQUE]

Le·o·nar·do da Vin·ci (lē′ə när′dō də vin′chē, lā′-; *It.* le′ô näʀ′dô dä vēn′chē). 1452–1519, Italian painter, sculptor, architect, musician, engineer, mathematician, and scientist.

Le·on·ca·val·lo (le ôn′kä väl′lô), *n.* **Rug·gie·ro** (ʀōōd je′ʀô), 1858–1919, Italian operatic composer and librettist.

le·one (lē ōn′), *n.* a paper money, cupronickel or silver coin, and monetary unit of Sierra Leone, equal to 100 cents. [1960–65; (SIERRA) LEONE]

Le·o·ne (le ô′ne), *n.* **Gio·van·ni** (jô vän′nē), born 1908, Italian political leader: prime minister 1963, 1968; president 1971–78.

Le·o·ni (le ô′nē; *Eng.* lā ō′nē), *n.* **Ra·úl** (rä ōōl′), 1905–72, Venezuelan statesman: president 1964–69.

Le·o·nid (lē′ə nid), *n., pl.* **Le·o·nids, Le·on·i·des** (lē on′i dēz′). *Astron.* any of a shower of meteors occurring around November 15 and appearing to radiate from a point in the constellation Leo. [1875–80; < NL *Leonidēs,* equiv. to L *Leōn-* (s. of *Leō*) LEO + *-idēs* -ID[1]]

Le·on·i·das (lē on′i dəs), *n.* died 480 B.C., Greek hero: king of Sparta 489?–480.

le·o·nine (lē′ə nīn′), *adj.* **1.** of or pertaining to the lion. **2.** resembling or suggestive of a lion. **3.** (*usually cap.*) of or pertaining to Leo, esp. Leo IV or Leo XIII. [1350–1400; ME *leonyn* < L *leōnīnus* lionlike, equiv. to *leōn-* (s. of *leō* LION) + *-īnus* -INE[1]]

CONCISE ETYMOLOGY KEY: <, descended or borrowed from; >, whence; b., blend of, blended; c., cognate with; cf., compare; deriv., derivative; equiv., equivalent; imit., imitative; obl., oblique; r., replacing; s., stem; sp., spelling, spelled; resp., respelling, respelled; trans., translation; ?, origin unknown; *, unattested; ‡, probably earlier than. See the full key inside the front cover.

le′onine verse′, a form of verse, based upon an earlier Latin form, with a rhyme scheme that requires the last word in a line to rhyme with the word just before a caesura or with a word near the middle of the line.

Le·o·no·ra (lē′ə nôr′ə), *n.* a female given name, form of **Eleanor.** Also, **Le·o·nore** (lē′ə nôr′).

Le·o·nov (lē ō′nôf, -nof; *Russ.* lyi ô′nəf), *n.* **1. A·lek·sey Ar·khi·po·vich** (u lyi ksyā′ UR khyē′pə vyich), born 1934, Soviet cosmonaut: first man to walk in space 1965. **2. Le·o·nid Ma·ksi·mo·vich** (lyi u nyēt′ mu-ksyē′mə vyich), born 1899, Russian writer.

le·on·ti·a·sis (lē′ən tī′ə sis), *n. Pathol.* **1.** a lionlike facial distortion. **2.** Also called **le·on·ti′a·sis os′se·a** (os′ē ə). an overgrowth of the cranial and facial bones resulting in a lionlike appearance. [< Gk *leont-,* s. of *léōn* LION + -IASIS]

Le·on·ti·ef (lē on′tē ef′, -əf), *n.* **Was·si·ly** (vä sē′lē), born 1906, U.S. economist, born in Russia: Nobel prize 1973.

Le·on·to·vich (lē on′tə vich), *n.* **Eugenie Kon·stan·tin** (kon′stən tēn′), born 1900, U.S. actress, director, and playwright, born in Russia.

leop·ard (lep′ərd), *n.* **1.** a large, spotted Asian or African carnivore, *Panthera pardus,* of the cat family, usually tawny with black markings; the Old World panther: all leopard populations are threatened or endangered. **2.** the fur or pelt of this animal. **3.** any of various related cats resembling this animal. **4.** *Heraldry.* a lion represented from the side as walking, usually with one forepaw raised, and looking toward the spectator. **5.** *Numis.* **a.** an Anglo-Gallic gold coin issued by Edward III, equal to half a florin, bearing the figure of a leopard. **b.** a silver Anglo-Gallic coin issued by Henry V. **6.** (*cap.*) *Mil.* a 42-ton (38-m ton) West German tank with a 105mm gun. [1250–1300; ME < LL *leōpardus* < Gk *leópardos,* syncopated var. of *leontópardos,* equiv. to *leonto-* (s. of *léōn*) LION + *párdos* PARD[1]]

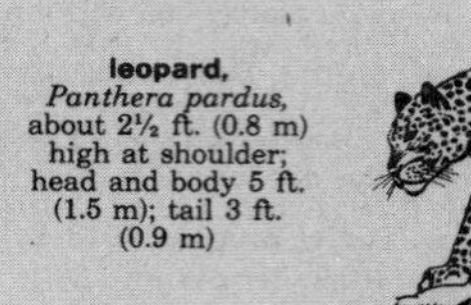

leopard, *Panthera pardus,* about 2½ ft. (0.8 m) high at shoulder; head and body 5 ft. (1.5 m); tail 3 ft. (0.9 m)

leop·ard·ess (lep′ər dis), *n.* a female leopard. [1560–70; LEOPARD + -ESS]
—**Usage.** See **-ess.**

leop′ard frog′, 1. a common North American green frog, *Rana pipiens,* having white-edged, dark oval spots on its back. **2.** any of several similar North American frogs. [1830–40, *Amer.*]

Le·o·par·di (lē′ə pär′dē, lā′-; *It.* le′ô päʀ′dē), *n.* **Count Gia·co·mo** (jä′kə mō′; *It.* jä′kô mô), 1798–1837, Italian poet.

leop′ard lil′y, a tall lily, *Lilium pardalinum,* of California, having drooping, orange-red flowers with purple speckles, a yellow base, and recurved petal tips. [1900–05, *Amer.*]

leop′ard liz′ard, any long-tailed lizard of the genus *Gambelia,* of the western U.S. and northern Mexico, having the body marked with spots and bars of dark or light brown or black.

leop′ard moth′, a moth, *Zeuzera pyrina,* having white wings spotted with black and larvae that bore into the wood of various trees and shrubs. [1810–20]

leop·ard's-bane (lep′ərdz bān′), *n.* any composite plant of the genus *Doronicum,* of Europe and Asia, having alternate, usually clasping leaves and heads of yellow flowers. [1540–50]

leop′ard seal′, a yellowish-gray, spotted seal, *Hydrurga leptonyx,* of the Antarctic. [1890–95]

leop′ard shark′, a small, inshore shark, *Triakis semifasciata,* having distinctive black markings across the back, inhabiting Pacific coastal waters from Oregon through California.

Le·o·pold (lē′ə pōld′), *n.* a male given name: from Germanic words meaning "people" and "bold."

Leopold I, 1. 1640–1705, king of Hungary 1655–1705; emperor of the Holy Roman Empire 1658–1705. **2.** 1790–1865, king of Belgium 1831–65.

Leopold II, 1. 1747–92, emperor of the Holy Roman Empire 1790–92 (son of Francis I; brother of Joseph II and Marie Antoinette). **2.** 1835–1909, king of Belgium 1865–1909 (son of Leopold I of Belgium).

Leopold III, 1901–83, king of Belgium 1934–51 (son of Albert I).

Lé·o·pold·ville (lē′ə pōld vil′, lā′-; *Fr.* lā ô pôld vēl′), *n.* former name of **Kinshasa.** Also, **Le·o·pold·ville** (lē′ə pōld vil′, lā′-).

le·o·tard (lē′ə tärd′), *n.* a skintight, one-piece garment for the torso, having a high or low neck, long or short sleeves, and a lower portion resembling either briefs or tights, worn by acrobats, dancers, etc. Cf. **tights.** [1915–20; named after Jules *Léotard,* 19th-century French aerialist]

Le·o·tine (lē′ə tīn′), *n.* a female given name. Also, **Le′o·tyne′.**

LEP, 1. large electron-positron collider. **2.** limited English proficiency.

Le·pan·to (li pan′tō; *It.* le′pän tô), *n.* **1.** Greek, **Náv·paktos.** a seaport in W Greece, on the Lepanto Strait: Turkish sea power destroyed here 1571. 8170. **2. Gulf of.** See **Corinth, Gulf of. 3. Strait of.** Also called **Rion Strait.** a strait between the Ionian Sea and the Gulf of Corinth. 1 mi. (1.6 km) wide.

Lep·cha (lep′chə), *n., pl.* **-chas,** (*esp. collectively*) **-cha** for 1. **1.** a member of a people of Sikkim and adjacent areas of Nepal, Bhutan, and India. **2.** the Tibeto-Burman language of the Lepcha.

Le·pen·ski Vir (lep′ən skē vēr′; *Serbo-Croatian.* le′-pen skē vēʀ′), the site of an advanced Mesolithic fishing culture on the banks of the Danube in Yugoslavia, characterized by trapezoidal buildings and large stone sculptures of human heads and torsos.

lep·er (lep′ər), *n.* **1.** a person who has leprosy. **2.** a person who has been rejected or ostracized for unacceptable behavior, opinions, character, or the like; anathema; outcast. [1350–1400; ME *lepre* leprosy < L *lepra* < Gk *lépra,* n. use of fem. of *leprós* scaly, akin to *lépos* scale, *lépein* to peel]

lep′er house′, a hospital for lepers; leprosarium. [1850–55]

lepido-, a combining form meaning "scale," used in the formation of compound words: *lepidopteron.* [< Gk, comb. form repr. *lepís* (s. *lepid-*) scale. See LEPER]

lep·i·do·cro·cite (lep′i dō krō′sīt), *n.* a ruby-red to reddish-brown orthorhombic mineral, iron oxyhydroxide, FeO(OH), dimorphous with goethite: an ore of iron, used as a pigment. [1815–25; < G *Lepidokrokit* < Gk *lepido-* LEPIDO- + Gk *krók(ē)* thread, fiber + G *-it* -ITE[1]]

le·pid·o·lite (li pid′l īt′, lep′i dl-), *n.* a mineral of the mica group, potassium lithium aluminum silicate, commonly occurring in lilac, rose-colored, or whitish scaly masses: an ore of lithium. [1790–1800; LEPIDO- + -LITE]

Lep·i·dop·ter·a (lep′i dop′tər ə), *n.* the order comprising the lepidopterous insects. [1725–35; < NL; pl. of LEPIDOPTERON]

lep·i·dop·ter·an (lep′i dop′tər ən), *adj.* **1.** lepidopterous. —*n.* **2.** a lepidopterous insect. [1850–55; LEPIDOPTER(A) + -AN]

lep·i·dop·ter·ol·o·gy (lep′i dop′tə rol′ə jē), *n.* the branch of zoology dealing with butterflies and moths. [1895–1900; LEPIDOPTER(A) + -O- + -LOGY] —**lep·i·dop·ter·o·log·i·cal** (lep′i dop′tər ə loj′i kəl), *adj.* —**lep′i·dop′ter·ist,** *n.*

lep·i·dop·ter·on (lep′i dop′tər ən), *n., pl.* **-ter·a** (-tər ə). any lepidopterous insect. [< NL, equiv. to *lepido-* LEPIDO- + Gk *-pteron,* neut. of *-pteros* -PTEROUS]

lep·i·dop·ter·ous (lep′i dop′tər əs), *adj.* belonging or pertaining to the Lepidoptera, an order of insects comprising the butterflies, moths, and skippers, that in the adult state have four membranous wings more or less covered with small scales. Also, **lep′i·dop′ter·al.** [1790–1800; LEPIDOPTER(A) + -OUS]

lep·i·do·si·ren (lep′i dō sī′rən), *n.* a lungfish, *Lepidosiren paradoxa,* of the Amazon, having an eel-shaped body. [1850–55; < NL; see LEPIDO-, SIREN]

lep·i·dote (lep′i dōt′), *adj. Bot.* covered with scurfy scales or scaly spots. [1830–40; < NL *lepidōtus* < Gk *lepidōtós* scaly, equiv. to *lepidō-* (verbid s. of *lepidoûn* to make scaly; see LEPIDO-) + *-tos* verbid suffix]

Lep·i·dus (lep′i dəs), *n.* **Marcus Ae·mil·i·us** (ē mil′ē əs), died 13 B.C., Roman politician: member of the second triumvirate.

Le·pon′tine Alps′ (li pon′tin), a central range of the Alps in S Switzerland and N Italy. Highest peak, Mt. Leone, 11,684 ft. (3561 m).

lep·o·rid (lep′ə rid), *n., pl.* **le·por·i·dae** (li pôr′i dē′, -por′-), *adj.* —*n.* **1.** an animal of the family Leporidae, comprising the rabbits and hares. —*adj.* **2.** belonging or pertaining to the family Leporidae. [< NL *Leporidae* name of the family, equiv. to *Lepor-,* s. of *Lepus* the type genus (L: hare) + *-idae* -IDAE; see -ID[2]]

lep·o·ride (lep′ə rid, -rīd′, -rēd′), *n.* a Belgian hare formerly believed to be a hybrid of the European rabbit and hare. [1875–80; < F; see LEPORID]

lep·o·rine (lep′ə rin′, -rin), *adj. Zool.* of, pertaining to, or resembling a rabbit or hare. [1650–60; < L *leporīnus,* equiv. to *lepor-* (s. of *lepus*) hare + *-īnus* -INE[1]]

lep·py (lep′ē), *n., pl.* **-pies.** *Western U.S.* an unbranded or motherless calf; maverick. [1935–40; of uncert. orig.]

lep·re·chaun (lep′rə kôn′, -kon′), *n. Irish Folklore.* **1.** a dwarf or sprite. **2.** a conventionalized literary representation of this figure as a little old man who will reveal the location of a hidden crock of gold to anyone who catches him. [1595–1605; < Ir *leipreachán, lucharachán,* MIr *luchrapán, lupra(c)cán,* metathesized forms of OIr *lúchorp(án),* equiv. to *lú-* small + *corp* body (< L *corpus*) + *-án* dim. suffix]

le·pro·ma (le prō′mə), *n., pl.* **-mas, -ma·ta** (-mə tə). *Pathol.* the swollen lesion of leprosy. [1890–95; < NL, L *lepr(a)* leprosy (see LEPER) + -OMA] —**le·prom·a·tous** (le prom′ə təs, -prō′mə-), *adj.*

lep·ro·sar·i·um (lep′rə sâr′ē əm), *n., pl.* **-sar·i·a** (-sâr′ē ə). a hospital for the treatment of lepers. [1840–50; < ML; see LEPROUS, -ARY]

lep·rose (lep′rōs), *adj.* leprous. [< LL *leprōsus* LEPROUS]

lep·ro·sy (lep′rə sē), *n. Pathol.* a chronic, mildly infectious disease caused by *Mycobacterium leprae,* affecting the peripheral nervous system, skin, and nasal mucosa and variously characterized by ulcerations, tubercular nodules, and loss of sensation that sometimes leads to traumatic amputation of the anesthetized part. Also called **Hansen's disease.** [1525–35; perh. < ML *leprōsia* (recorded only as synonym for LEPROSARIUM) < Gk *léprōs(is)* leprosy + *-ia* -Y[3]] —**lep·rot·ic** (le prot′ik), *adj.*

lep·rous (lep′rəs), *adj.* **1.** *Pathol.* affected with leprosy. **2.** of or resembling leprosy. **3.** *Bot., Zool.* covered with scales. [1175–1225; ME < LL *leprōsus.* See LEPER, -OUS] —**lep′rous·ly,** *adv.* —**lep′rous·ness,** *n.*

Lep·si·us (lep′sē ōōs′), *n.* **Karl Rich·ard** (kärl ʀɪᴋʜ′-ärt), 1810–84, German philologist and Egyptologist.

-lepsy, a combining form meaning "seizure," used in the formation of compound words: *epilepsy.* [comb. form repr. NL *-lēpsia* < Gk *-lēpsia,* equiv. to *lēps(is)* a seizure (*lēp-* var. s. of *lambánein* to seize + *-sis* -SIS) + *-ia* -Y[3]]

lep•to (lep′tō), *n. Informal.* leptospirosis. [by shortening]

lepto-, a combining form meaning "thin," "fine," "slight," used in the formation of compound words: *leptophyllous.* [< Gk *lepto-,* comb. form of *leptós* thin, slight, fine, lit., stripped, equiv. to *lép(ein)* to strip + *-tos* adj. suffix]

lep•to•ceph•a•lus (lep′tə sef′ə ləs), *n., pl.* **-li** (-lī′). a colorless, transparent, flattened larva, esp. of certain eels and ocean fishes. [1760–70; < NL; see LEPTO-, -CEPHALOUS]

lep•to•dac•ty•lous (lep′tə dak′tə ləs), *adj.* having slender toes or fingers. [1860–65; LEPTO- + -DACTYLOUS]

lep•to•kurt•ic (lep′tə kûr′tik), *adj. Statistics.* **1.** (of a frequency distribution) being more concentrated about the mean than the corresponding normal distribution. **2.** (of a frequency distribution curve) having a high, narrow concentration about the mode. [1900–05; LEPTO- + irreg. transliteration of Gk *kyrt(ós)* swelling + -IC]

lep•to•kur•to•sis (lep′tō kûr tō′sis), *n. Statistics.* the state of being leptokurtic. [1905–10; < NL; see LEPTOKURTIC, -OSIS]

lep•ton[1] (lep′ton), *n., pl.* **-ta** (-tə). **1.** an aluminum coin of modern Greece, the 100th part of a drachma. **2.** a small copper or bronze coin of ancient Greece. [1715–25; < Gk *leptón* (*nómisma*) a small (coin), n. use of neut. of *leptós* small; see LEPTO-]

lep•ton[2] (lep′ton), *n. Physics.* any of a class of particles with spin of ½ that are not subject to the strong force and that are believed to be truly elementary and not composed of quarks or other subunits. The leptons known or believed to exist are the electron and electron-neutrino, the muon and mu-neutrino, and the tau lepton and tau-neutrino. Cf. **conservation of lepton number.** [1948; < Gk, neut. of *leptós* small, slight; see LEPTO-, -ON[1]] —**lep•ton′ic,** *adj.*

lep′ton num′ber, *Physics.* in a process involving elementary particles, the total number of leptons minus the total number of antileptons. [1955–60]

lep•to•phos (lep′tə fos′), *n. Chem.* a solid compound, $C_{13}H_{10}BrCl_2O_2PS$, used as a nonsystemic insecticide for food crops and lawn grass. [appar. LEPTO- + (*phenyl*)*phos*(*phonothionate*) a chemical component]

lep•to•some (lep′tə sōm′), *n.* a person of asthenic build. [1930–35; LEPTO- + -SOME[3]] —**lep′to•so′mic, lep•to•so•mat•ic** (lep′tō sə mat′ik), *adj.*

lep•to•sper•mum (lep′tə spûr′məm), *n.* any of various shrubs or trees of the genus *Leptospermum,* of the myrtle family, native to Australia and adjacent areas and often cultivated as ornamentals in milder climates. Cf. **tea tree.** [< NL (1776), equiv. to *lepto-* LEPTO- + *-spermum,* neut. of *-spermus* -SPERMOUS]

lep•to•spi•ra (lep′tə spī′rə), *n., pl.* **-rae** (-rē), **-ras.** *Bacteriol.* any of several spirally shaped, aerobic bacteria of the genus *Leptospira,* certain species of which are pathogenic for human beings. [< NL (1917), equiv. to *lepto-* LEPTO- + L *spira* coil; see SPIRE[2]] —**lep′to•spi′•ral,** *adj.*

lep•to•spi•ro•sis (lep′tō spī rō′sis), *n. Pathol., Vet. Pathol.* an infectious disease of humans and of horses, dogs, swine, and other animals, caused by the spirochete *Leptospira interrogans* and characterized by fever, muscle pain, and jaundice, and in severe cases involving the liver and kidney. Cf. **canicola fever, canine leptospirosis, Weil's disease.** [1925–30; < NL; see LEPTOSPIRA, -OSIS]

lep•to•tene (lep′tə tēn′), *n. Cell Biol.* a stage of cell division during the prophase of meiosis, in which the chromosomes are not distinct but appear as a mass of entangled threads. [< F *leptotène* (1900); see LEPTO-, -TENE]

Lep•us (lep′əs, lē′pəs), *n., gen.* **Lep•o•ris** (lep′ər is). *Astron.* the Hare, a small southern constellation south of Orion. [< L]

Le Puy (lə pwē′), a city in and the capital of Haute-Loire, in central France: cathedral. 29,024.

Ler (ler), *n. Irish Myth.* the personification of the sea and the father of Manannan: corresponds to the Welsh Llyr. Also, **Lir.**

Lé•ri•da (le′rē thä), *n.* a city in NE Spain. 90,884.

Ler•mon•tov (lâr′mən tôf′, -tof′; *Russ.* lyer′mən təf), *n.* **Mi•kha•il Yu•rie•vich** (myi khu yēl′ yōō′ryi vyich), 1814–41, Russian poet and novelist.

Ler•na (lûr′nə), *n.* a marshy region near Argos, Greece: the legendary abode of the Hydra slain by Hercules. Also, **Ler•ne** (lûr′nē). —**Ler•nae•an, Ler•ne•an** (lər nē′ən), *adj.*

Ler•ner (lûr′nər), *n.* **Alan Jay,** 1918–86, U.S. lyricist and librettist.

Le•ros (lē′ros, -rōs), *n.* one of the Dodecanese Islands of Greece, off the SW coast of Turkey. 21 sq. mi. (54 sq. km).

Le•roy (lə roi′, lē′roi), *n.* a male given name: from Old French, meaning "the king." Also, **LeRoy′.**

Ler•wick (lûr′wik, ler′-, ler′ik), *n.* a city in and the administrative center of the Shetland Islands, N of Scotland. 6107.

Le Sage (lə sazh′), **A•lain Re•né** (a lan′ rə nā′), 1668–1747, French novelist and dramatist. Also, **Le•sage′.**

Les•bi•an (lez′bē ən), *adj.* **1.** of or pertaining to Lesbos. **2.** (*usually l.c.*) of, pertaining to, or characteristic of female homosexuality. **3.** (*usually l.c.*) erotic; sensual. —*n.* **4.** an inhabitant of Lesbos. **5.** (*usually l.c.*) a female homosexual. [1595–1605; < L *Lesbi(us)* Lesbian (< Gk *Lésbios,* equiv. to *Lésb(os)* LESBOS + *-ios* adj. suffix) + -AN; (defs. 2, 5) alluding to the poet Sappho of Lesbos, whose verse deals largely with her emotional relationships with other women]

Les′bian cyma′tium. See **cyma reversa.** Also, **Les′bian cy′ma.** [1720–30]

les•bi•an•ism (lez′bē ə niz′əm), *n.* homosexual relations between women. [1865–70; LESBIAN + -ISM]

Les′bian leaf′. See **water leaf** (def. 2).

Les′bian ode′, *Pros.* See **Horatian ode.**

les•bo (lez′bō), *n., pl.* **-bos.** *Slang* (*disparaging and offensive*). a lesbian. [1935–40, *Amer.*; LESB(IAN) + -O]

Les•bos (lez′bos, -bōs; *Gk.* lez′vôs), *n.* Mytilene (def. 1).

Les Cayes (lā kā′; *Fr.* lä ka′yə), a seaport on the SW coast of Haiti. 14,000. Also called **Cayes.** Formerly, **Aux Cayes.**

les•che (les′kē), *n.* an arcade or other public place in ancient Greece. [< Gk *léschē* orig., couch, lounging place, place for conversation]

Le•sche•tiz•ky (lesh′ə tit′skē), *n.* **The•o•dor** (tā′ə-dôr′, -dōr′, thē′-), 1830–1915, Polish pianist and composer.

lese′ maj′esty (lēz), **1.** *Law.* **a.** a crime, esp. high treason, committed against the sovereign power. **b.** an offense that violates the dignity of a ruler. **2.** an attack on any custom, institution, belief, etc., held sacred or revered by numbers of people: *Her speech against Mother's Day was criticized as lese majesty.* Also, **lèse′ maj′esty.** [1530–40; < F *lèse-majesté,* after L (*crīmen*) *laesae mājestātis* (the crime) of injured majesty]

Les•ghi•an (lez′gē ən, les′-), *n.* Lezghian.

Les Gueux (lā gœ′), **1.** a league of Dutch and Flemish patriots, composed chiefly of nobles and formed in 1566 to resist the introduction of the Spanish Inquisition into the Netherlands. **2.** (later) any of various Dutch or Flemish partisan groups organized to gain independence for the Netherlands from Spain. [< F: lit., the beggars]

Les Halles (lā al′), (formerly) the large, central, wholesale food market area of Paris, France.

le•sion (lē′zhən), *n.* **1.** an injury; hurt; wound. **2.** *Pathol.* any localized, abnormal structural change in the body. **3.** *Plant Pathol.* any localized, defined area of diseased tissue, as a spot, canker, blister, or scab. —*v.t.* **4.** to cause a lesion or lesions in. [1425–75; late ME < MF < L *laesiōn-* (s. of *laesiō*) injury, equiv. to L *laes(us)* (ptp. of *laedere* to harm, equiv. to *laed-* verb s. + *-tus* ptp. suffix, with *-dt-* > *-s-*) + *-iōn-* -ION]

Les•lie (les′lē, lez′-), *n.* a male or female given name. Also, **Les′ley.**

Les Mi•sé•ra•bles (*Fr.* lā mē zā ra′blə), a novel (1862) by Victor Hugo.

Le•so•tho (lə sōō′tōō, -sō′tō), *n.* a monarchy in S Africa: formerly a British protectorate; gained independence 1966; member of the Commonwealth of Nations. 1,200,000; 11,716 sq. mi. (30,344 sq. km). *Cap.:* Maseru. Formerly, **Basutoland.**

les•pe•de•za (les′pi dē′zə), *n.* any shrub or herb belonging to the genus *Lespedeza,* of the legume family, having trifoliolate leaves and lavender flowers, grown for forage, soil improvement, etc. [< NL (1803), after V. M. de *Zespedez* (misread as *Lespedez*), 18th-century Spanish governor of East Florida]

les•que•rel•la (les′kə rel′ə, lā′kə-), *n.* any of various plants of the genus *Lesquerella,* of the mustard family, having rosettes of simple, hairy leaves, small yellow flowers, and inflated pods, and yielding a seed oil similar to castor oil. Also called **bladderpod.** [< NL, named after Leo *Lesquereux* (d. 1889), Swiss-born U.S. paleobotanist; see -ELLA]

less (les), *adv., a compar. of* **little** *with* **least** *as superl.* **1.** to a smaller extent, amount, or degree: *less exact.* **2.** most certainly not (often prec. by *much* or *still*): *He could barely pay for his own lodging, much less for that of his friend.* **3.** in any way different; other: *He is nothing less than a thief.* **4. less than,** by far short of being; not in the least; hardly at all: *The job is less than perfect.* —*adj., a compar. of* **little** *with* **least** *as superl.* **5.** smaller in size, amount, degree, etc.; not so large, great, or much: *less money; less speed.* **6.** lower in consideration, rank, or importance: *no less a person than the manager.* **7.** fewer: *less than a dozen.* —*n.* **8.** a smaller amount or quantity: *Hundreds of soldiers arrived, but less of them remained.* **9.** something inferior or not as important: *He was tortured for less.* —*prep.* **10.** minus; without: *a year less two days; six dollars less tax.* [bef. 900; ME; OE *lǣs* (adv.), *lǣssa* (adj.); c. OFris *lês* (adv.), *lêssa* (adj.). See LEAST]
—**Syn. 5.** See **small.**
—**Usage.** Even though LESS has been used before plural nouns (*less words; less men*) since the time of King Alfred, many modern usage guides say that only FEWER can be used in such contexts. LESS, they say, should modify singular mass nouns (*less sugar; less money*) and singular abstract nouns (*less honesty; less love*). It should modify plural nouns only when they suggest combination into a unit, group, or aggregation: *less than $50* (a sum of money); *less than three miles* (a unit of distance). With plural nouns specifying individuals or readily distinguishable units, the guides say that FEWER is the only proper choice: *fewer words; fewer men; no fewer than 31 of the 50 states.*
Modern standard English practice does not reflect this distinction. When followed by *than,* LESS occurs at least as often as FEWER in modifying plural nouns that are not units or groups, and the use of LESS in this construction is increasing in all varieties of English: *less than eight million people; no less than 31 of the 50 states.* When not followed by *than,* FEWER is more frequent only in formal written English, and in this construction also the use of LESS is increasing: *This year we have had less crimes, less accidents, and less fires than in any of the last five years.*

-less, an adjective suffix meaning "without" (*childless; peerless*), and in adjectives derived from verbs, indicating failure or inability to perform or be performed (*resistless; tireless*). [ME *-les,* OE *-lēas,* special use of *lēas* free from, without, false; c. ON *lauss,* G *los,* LOOSE]

les•see (le sē′), *n.* a person, group, etc., to whom a lease is granted. [1485–95; < AF. See LEASE[1], -EE] —**les•see′ship,** *n.*

less•en (les′ən), *v.i.* **1.** to become less. —*v.t.* **2.** to make less; reduce. **3.** *Archaic.* to represent as less; depreciate; disparage. [1300–50; late ME *lessenen, lasnen* (see LESS, -EN[1]); r. ME *lessen*]

Les•seps (les′əps; *Fr.* le seps′), *n.* **Fer•di•nand Ma•rie, Vi•comte de** (fer dē nän′ ma rē′, vē kônt də), 1805–94, French engineer and diplomat: promoter of the Suez Canal.

less•er (les′ər), *adj., a compar. of* **little** *with* **least** *as superl.* **1.** smaller, as in size or importance; inferior: *a lesser evil.* —*adv., a compar. of* **little** *with* **least** *as superl.* **2.** less. [1175–1225; ME *lasser, lesser.* See LESS, -ER[4]]

less′er amak′ihi, anianiau.

Less′er Antil′les. See under **Antilles.**

less′er ape′. See under **ape.**

Less′er Bear′, *Astron.* the constellation Ursa Minor.

less′er cel′andine, a Eurasian plant, *Ranunculus ficaria,* of the buttercup family, having heart-shaped leaves and glossy yellow flowers, naturalized in North America. Also called **pilewort.** [1885–90]

less′er corn′stalk bor′er, the larva of a widely distributed pyralid moth, *Elasmopalpus lignosellus,* that damages corn and some other crops by boring into the part of the stalk close to the soil. [1920–25]

Less′er Diony′sia, (in ancient Attica) the wine feasts, processions, and dramatic performances composing one of the festivals honoring Dionysus, held in the middle of December. Also called **Rural Dionysia.**

Less′er Dog′, *Astron.* the constellation Canis Minor.

less′er doxol′ogy. See **Gloria Patri.**

less′er Ion′ic. See under **Ionic** (def. 2).

less′er omen′tum, *Anat.* an omentum attached to the stomach, part of the duodenum, and part of the liver and supporting the hepatic vessels. Also called **gastrohepatic omentum.** Cf. **greater omentum.**

less′er pan′da, panda (def. 2).

less′er peach′ tree′ bor′er, the larva of a clearwing moth, *Synanthedon pictipes,* distributed throughout the eastern U.S. and Canada but most prevalent in the South, that burrows into the injured trunks and branches of stone fruit trees. [1920–25]

less′er pil′grimage, *Islam.* 'umrah.

less′er prai′rie chick′en. See under **prairie chicken** (def. 1).

less′er ror′qual, minke.

Less′er Sanhed′rin, Sanhedrin (def. 2).

Less′er Sun′da Is′lands. See under **Sunda Islands.**

less′er wee′ver. See under **weever** (def. 1).

less′er yel′lowlegs. See under **yellowlegs.**

Les•sing (les′ing), *n.* **1. Doris (May),** born 1919, British novelist. **2. Gott•hold E•phra•im** (gôt′hôlt ā′frä-im), 1729–81, German critic and dramatist.

les•son (les′ən), *n.* **1.** a section into which a course of study is divided, esp. a single, continuous session of formal instruction in a subject: *The manual was broken down into 50 lessons.* **2.** a part of a book, an exercise, etc., that is assigned to a student for study: *The lesson for today is on page 22. He worked assiduously at his music lesson.* **3.** something to be learned or studied: *the lessons of the past.* **4.** a useful piece of practical wisdom acquired by experience or study: *That accident certainly taught him a lesson in careful driving.* **5.** something from which a person learns or should learn; an instructive example: *Her faith should serve as a lesson to all of us.* **6.** a reproof or punishment intended to teach one better ways. **7.** a portion of Scripture or other sacred writing read or appointed to be read at a divine service; lection; pericope. —*v.t.* **8.** to teach; instruct; give a lesson to. **9.** to admonish or reprove. [1175–1225; ME *lesso(u)n* < OF *leçon* < L *lēctiōn-* (s. of *lēctiō*) LECTION]

les•sor (les′ôr, le sôr′), *n.* a person, group, etc., who grants a lease. [1350–1400; ME *lesso(u)r* < AF. See LEASE[1], -OR[2]]

lest (lest), *conj.* **1.** for fear that; so that (one) should not (used negatively to introduce a clause expressive of an action or occurrence requiring caution): *He kept his notes by his side lest faulty memory lead him astray.* **2.** that (used after words expressing fear, danger, etc.): *There was danger lest the plan become known.* [bef. 1000; ME *leste,* contr. of *the lesse the, thi les the;* late OE *the lǣste,* earlier *thȳ lǣs the,* lit., whereby less that (*thȳ* instrumental case of the demonstrative and relative pronoun, *lǣs* LESS, *the* the relative particle)]

Les•ter (les′tər), *n.* a male given name: from the English placename "Leicester."

les•to•bi•o•sis (les′tō bī ō′sis), *n., pl.* **-ses** (-sēz). cleptobiosis characterized by furtive thievery. [< NL < Gk *lēist(és)* robber + *-o-* -O- + *-biosis* -BIOSIS] —**les•to•bi•ot•ic** (les′tō bī ot′ik), *adj.*

le•sya (lesh′yä), *n. Jainism.* any of six possible colors given to the monad, or individual soul, by its karma and being lighter or darker according to the proportion of good or evil included in the karma. [< Skt *leśyā* light]

let[1] (let), *v.,* **let, let•ting,** *n.* —*v.t.* **1.** to allow or permit:

CONCISE PRONUNCIATION KEY: act, cāpe, dâre, pärt; set, ēqual; if, ice; ox, ōver, ôrder, oil, bo͝ok, bo͞ot, out; up, ûrge; child; sing; shoe; thin, that; zh as in *treasure.* ə = *a* as in *alone, e* as in *system, i* as in *easily, o* as in *gallop, u* as in *circus;* ə as in *fire* (fīər), *hour* (ouər). l and n can serve as syllabic consonants, as in *cradle* (krād′l), and *button* (but′n). See the full key inside the front cover.

to let him escape. **2.** to allow to pass, go, or come: *to let us through.* **3.** to grant the occupancy or use of (land, buildings, rooms, space, etc., or movable property) for rent or hire (sometimes fol. by *out*). **4.** to contract or assign for performance, usually under a contract: *to let work to a carpenter.* **5.** to cause to; make: *to let one know the truth.* **6.** (used in the imperative as an auxiliary expressive of a request, command, warning, suggestion, etc.): *Let me see. Let us go. Just let them try it!* —*v.i.* **7.** to admit of being rented or leased: *The apartment lets for $100 per week.* **8. let alone.** See **alone** (def. 5). **9. let be, a.** to refrain from interference. **b.** to refrain from interfering with. **10. let down, a.** to disappoint; fail. **b.** to betray; desert. **c.** to slacken; abate: *We were too near success to let down in our efforts.* **d.** to allow to descend slowly; lower. **e.** *Aeron.* (of an airplane) to descend from a higher to a lower altitude preparatory to making an approach and landing or a similar maneuver. **11. let go.** See **go** (def. 82). **12. let in, a.** to admit. **b.** to involve (a person) in without his or her knowledge or permission: *to let someone in for a loss.* **c.** Also, **let into.** to insert into the surface of (a wall or the like) as a permanent addition: *to let a plaque into a wall.* **d.** Also, **let in on.** to share a secret with; permit to participate in. **13. let off, a.** to release by exploding. **b.** to free from duty or responsibility; excuse. **c.** to allow to go with little or no punishment; pardon: *The judge let off the youthful offender with a reprimand.* **14. let on, a.** to reveal one's true feelings: *She was terrified at the prospect, but didn't let on.* **b.** to pretend: *They let on that they didn't care about not being invited, but I could tell that they were hurt.* **15. let out, a.** to divulge; make known. **b.** to release from confinement, restraint, etc. **c.** to enlarge (a garment). **d.** to terminate; be finished; end: *When does the university let out for the summer?* **e.** to make (a let-out fur or pelt). **16. let someone have it,** *Informal.* to attack or assault, as by striking, shooting, or rebuking: *The gunman threatened to let the teller have it if he didn't move fast.* **17. let up, a.** to slacken; diminish; abate: *This heat wave should let up by the end of the week.* **b.** to cease; stop: *The rain let up for a few hours.* **18. let up on,** to treat less severely; be more lenient with: *He refused to let up on the boy until his grades improved.* —*n.* **19.** *Brit.* a lease. [bef. 900; ME *leten,* OE *lǣtan;* c. D *laten,* G *lassen,* ON *lāta,* Goth *lētan;* akin to Gk *lēdeîn* to be weary, L *lassus* tired. See LATE]
—**Syn. 1.** See **allow. 1.** suffer, grant. **3.** lease, rent, sublet, hire. —**Ant. 1.** prevent.
—**Usage.** LET US is used in all varieties of speech and writing to introduce a suggestion or a request: *Let us consider all the facts before deciding.* The contracted form LET'S occurs mostly in informal speech and writing: *Let's go. Let's not think about that right now.* Perhaps because LET'S has come to be felt as a word in its own right rather than as the contraction of LET US, it is often followed in informal speech and writing by redundant or appositional pronouns: *Let's us plan a picnic. Let's you and I* (or *me*) *get together tomorrow.* Both *Let's you and me* and *Let's you and I* occur in the relaxed speech of educated speakers. The former conforms to the traditional rules of grammar; the latter, nonetheless, occurs more frequently. See also **leave**[1].

let[2] (let), *n., v.,* **let·ted** or **let, let·ting.** —*n.* **1.** (in tennis, badminton, etc.) any play that is voided and must be replayed, esp. a service that hits the net and drops into the proper part of the opponent's court. **2.** *Chiefly Law.* an impediment or obstacle: *to act without let or hindrance.* —*v.t.* **3.** *Archaic.* to hinder, prevent, or obstruct. [bef. 900; ME *letten* (v.), *lette* (n.; deriv. of the v.), OE *lettan* (v.), deriv. of *læt* slow, tardy, LATE; c. ON *letja* to hinder]

-let, a diminutive suffix attached to nouns (*booklet; piglet; ringlet*), and, by extraction from **bracelet,** a suffix denoting a band, piece of jewelry, or article of clothing worn on the part of the body specified by the noun (*anklet; wristlet*). [ME *-let, -lette* < MF *-elet,* equiv. to *-el* (< L *-āle,* neut. of *-ālis* -AL[1] (cf. BRACELET) or < L *-ellus* dim. suffix; cf. -ELLE, CHAPLET) + *-et* -ET]

Le·ta (lē′tə), *n.* a female given name, form of **Latona.**

letch (lech), *Slang.* —*n.* **1.** a lecherous desire or craving. **2.** a lecher. **3.** any strong desire or liking. —*v.i.* **4.** to behave like a lecher (often fol. by *for* or *after*). Also, **lech.** [1790–1800; prob. back formation from LECHER]

let·down (let′doun′), *n.* **1.** a decrease in volume, force, energy, etc.: *a letdown in sales; a general letdown of social barriers.* **2.** disillusionment, discouragement, or disappointment: *The job was a letdown.* **3.** depression; deflation: *He felt a terrible letdown at the end of the play.* **4.** the accelerated movement of milk into the mammary glands of lactating mammals upon stimulation, as by massage or suckling. **5.** *Aeron.* the descent of an aircraft from a higher to a lower altitude preparatory to making an approach and landing or to making a target run or the like. Also, **let′-down′.** [1760–70; n. use of v. phrase *let down*]

Le·tha (lē′thə), *n.* a female given name.

le·thal (lē′thəl), *adj.* **1.** of, pertaining to, or causing death; deadly; fatal: *a lethal weapon; a lethal dose.* **2.** made to cause death: *a lethal chamber; a lethal attack.* **3.** causing great harm or destruction: *The disclosures were lethal to his candidacy.* [1575–85; < L *lētālis,* equiv. to *lēt(um)* death + *-ālis* -AL[1]; sp. (hence pron.) with *-h-* by assoc. with Gk *lḗthē* oblivion] —**le·thal′i·ty, le′thal·ness,** *n.* —**le′thal·ly,** *adv.*
—**Syn. 1.** See **fatal.**

le′thal cham′ber, a room or enclosure where animals may be killed by exposure to a poison gas. [1880–85]

le′thal gene′, *Genetics.* a gene that under certain conditions causes the death of an organism. Also called **le′thal fac′tor, le′thal muta′tion.** [1935–40]

le·thar·gic (lə thär′jik), *adj.* **1.** of, pertaining to, or affected with lethargy; drowsy; sluggish. **2.** producing lethargy. Also, **le·thar′gi·cal.** [1350–1400; < L *lēthargicus* < Gk *lēthargikós;* r. ME *litargik* < ML *litargicus* (see LETHARGY, -IC)] —**le·thar′gi·cal·ly,** *adv.*
—**Syn. 1.** lazy, indolent, torpid.

lethar′gic encephali′tis, *Pathol.* See **sleeping sickness** (def. 2).

leth·ar·gize (leth′ər jīz′), *v.t.,* **-gized, -giz·ing.** to make lethargic; stupefy. Also, *esp. Brit.,* **leth′ar·gise′.** [1605–15; LETHARG(Y) + -IZE]

leth·ar·gy (leth′ər jē), *n., pl.* **-gies. 1.** the quality or state of being drowsy and dull, listless and unenergetic, or indifferent and lazy; apathetic or sluggish inactivity. **2.** *Pathol.* an abnormal state or disorder characterized by overpowering drowsiness or sleep. [1325–75; < LL *lēthargia* < Gk *lēthargía,* equiv. to *lḗtharg(os)* drowsy + *-ia* -Y[3] (see LETHE, -ALGIA); r. ME *litargie* < ML *litargia* < LGk, Gk, as above]

Leth·bridge (leth′brij′), *n.* a city in S Alberta, in SW Canada. 46,752.

Le·the (lē′thē), *n.* **1.** *Class. Myth.* a river in Hades whose water caused forgetfulness of the past in those who drank of it. **2.** (*usually l.c.*) forgetfulness; oblivion. [< L < Gk, special use of *lḗthē* forgetfulness, akin to *lanthánesthai* to forget] —**Le·the·an** (li thē′ən, lē′thē-ən), **Le′thied,** *adj.*

le·thif·er·ous (li thif′ər əs), *adj. Archaic.* lethal. [1645–55; < L *lētifer* (*lēti-,* comb. form of *lētum* death (see LETHAL) + *-fer* bearing) + -OUS; see -FEROUS]

Le·ti·tia (li tish′ə, -tē′shə), *n.* a female given name: from a Latin word meaning "gladness."

Le·to (lē′tō), *n. Class. Myth.* the mother by Zeus of Apollo and Artemis, called Latona by the Romans.

l'é·toile du nord (lā twal dy nôr′), *French.* the star of the north: motto of Minnesota.

Le Tou·quet (lə to͞o kā′), a town in N France, on the English Channel, near Boulogne: seaside summer resort; airport. 4000.

let-out (*adj.* let′out′; *n.* let′out′), *adj.* **1.** (of fur) processed by cutting parallel diagonal slashes into the pelt and sewing the slashed edges together to lengthen the pelt and to improve the appearance of the fur. —*n.* **2.** *Chiefly Brit.* a means of escape; loophole. [1830–40; adj., n. use of v. phrase *let out*]

Le·tronne (li trōn′), *n.* a walled plain in the third quadrant of the face of the moon: about 60 miles (100 km) in diameter.

let's (lets), contraction of *let us.*
—**Usage.** See **contraction, let**[1].

Lett (let), *n.* **1.** a member of a people, the chief inhabitants of Latvia, living on or near the eastern coast of the Baltic Sea; Latvian. **2.** Latvian (def. 3).

Lett., Lettish.

let·ted (let′id), *v.* a pt. and pp. of **let**[2].

let·ter[1] (let′ər), *n.* **1.** a written or printed communication addressed to a person or organization and usually transmitted by mail. **2.** a symbol or character that is conventionally used in writing and printing to represent a speech sound and that is part of an alphabet. **3.** a piece of printing type bearing such a symbol or character. **4.** a particular style of type. **5.** such types collectively. **6.** Often, **letters.** a formal document granting a right or privilege. **7.** actual terms or wording; literal meaning, as distinct from implied meaning or intent (opposed to *spirit*): *the letter of the law.* **8. letters,** (*used with a singular or plural v.*) **a.** literature in general. **b.** the profession of literature. **c.** learning; knowledge, esp. of literature. **9.** an emblem consisting of the initial or monogram of a school, awarded to a student for extracurricular activity, esp. in athletics. **10. to the letter,** to the last particular; precisely: *His orders were carried out to the letter.* —*v.t.* **11.** to mark or write with letters; inscribe. —*v.i.* **12.** to earn a letter in an interscholastic or intercollegiate activity, esp. a sport: *He lettered in track at Harvard.* [1175–1225; ME, var. of *lettre* < OF < L *littera* alphabetic character, in pl., epistle, literature] —**let′ter·er,** *n.* —**let′ter·less,** *adj.*
—**Syn. 8.** See **literature.**

let·ter[2] (let′ər), *n. Chiefly Brit.* a person who lets, esp. one who rents out property. [1375–1425; late ME *letere;* see LET[1], -ER[1]]

let′ter bomb′, an envelope containing an explosive device designed to detonate when the envelope is opened by the recipient. Also called **mail bomb.** [1945–50]

let′ter box′, *Chiefly Brit.* a public or private mailbox. [1765–75]

let·ter-card (let′ər kärd′), *n. Brit.* a large postal card, with gummed edges, that can be folded lengthwise and sealed with the message inside. [1890–95]

let′ter car′rier. See **mail carrier.** [1545–55]

let′ter drop′, (in a door or partition) a slot through which letters can be pushed. [1885–90, *Amer.*]

let·tered (let′ərd), *adj.* **1.** educated or learned. **2.** of, pertaining to, or characterized by learning or literary culture. **3.** marked with or as if with letters. [1275–1325; ME; see LETTER[1], -ED[3]]

let·ter·form (let′ər fôrm′), *n.* **1.** a sheet of stationery used for letters. **2.** the shape of a letter of the alphabet with regard to its design or historical development. [1905–10; LETTER[1] + FORM]

let·ter·head (let′ər hed′), *n.* **1.** a printed heading on stationery, esp. one giving the name and address of a business concern, an institution, etc. **2.** a sheet of paper with such a heading. [1885–90; LETTER[1] + HEAD]

let·ter·ing (let′ər ing), *n.* **1.** the act or process of inscribing with or making letters. **2.** the letters in an inscription; calligraphy. [1635–45; LETTER[1] + -ING[1]]

let·ter·man (let′ər man′, -mən), *n., pl.* **-men** (-men′, -mən). a person who has earned a letter in an interscholastic or intercollegiate activity, esp. a sport. [1715–25; LETTER[1] + MAN[1], -MAN]

let′ter mis′sive, *pl.* **letters missive.** a letter from an official source expressing a command, permission, invitation, etc. [1400–50; late ME < MF *lettre missive* or ML *littera missiva;* see MISSIVE]

let′ter of advice′, 1. a notification from a consignor to a consignee giving specific information as to a shipment, the name of the carrier, the date shipped, etc. **2.** *Com.* a document from the drawer notifying the drawee that a bill of exchange has been drawn. [1675–85]

let′ter of com′fort. See **comfort letter.**

let′ter of cred′it, 1. an order issued by a banker allowing a person named to draw money to a specified amount from correspondents of the issuer. **2.** an instrument issued by a banker authorizing a person named to make drafts upon the issuer up to an amount specified. [1635–45]

let′ter of marque′, license or commission granted by a state to a private citizen to capture and confiscate the merchant ships of another nation. Also, **let′ters of marque′.** Also called **let′ter of marque′ and repris′·al, let′ters of marque′ and repris′al.** [1400–50; late ME]

let·ter-per·fect (let′ər pûr′fikt), *adj.* **1.** knowing one's part, lesson, or the like, perfectly. **2.** precise or exact in every detail; verbatim. [1880–85]

let·ter·press (let′ər pres′), *n.* **1.** the process of printing from letters or type in relief, rather than from intaglio plates or planographically. **2.** matter printed in such a manner. **3.** *Chiefly Brit.* printed text or reading matter, as distinguished from illustrations. —*adv.* **4.** by letterpress: *The circular should be printed letterpress, not offset.* —*adj.* **5.** set in letterpress: *letterpress work.* [1750–60; LETTER[1] + PRESS[1]]

let·ter-qual·i·ty (let′ər kwol′i tē), *adj.* (of computer printers and their output) pertaining to an appearance equal in legibility and resolution to copy typed on an electric typewriter: *A letter-quality printer produces sharper copy than a dot-matrix model.*

let′ter rul′ing, a written ruling sent by the U.S. Internal Revenue Service in response to a query concerning the application of the tax laws to a specific situation.

let·ter·set (let′ər set′), *n.* a process of printing that transfers the image from a letterpress-type relief plate to a roller or blanket from which it is offset. [1960–65; LETTER[1] + SET]

let·ter-size (let′ər sīz′), *adj.* **1.** (of paper) measuring approximately 8½ × 11 in. (22 × 28 cm). **2.** (of office supplies and equipment) made for holding letter-size sheets of paper. Cf. **legal-size.**

let′ters of administra′tion, *Law.* an instrument issued by a court or public official authorizing an administrator to take control of and dispose of the estate of a deceased person. [1490–1500]

let′ters of cre′dence, credentials issued to a diplomat or other governmental representative for presentation to the country to which he or she is sent. Also, **let′·ter of cre′dence.** Also called **let′ters creden′tial.**

let·ter·space (let′ər spās′), *v.t.,* **-spaced, -spac·ing.** *Print.* to space out (the letters of a word or line) for balance or emphasis. [1930–35; LETTER[1] + SPACE]

let′ters pat′ent, *Law.* a written or printed instrument issued by a sovereign power, conferring upon a patentee some right, as the exclusive right to land or the exclusive right to make, use, and sell an invention for a limited time. [1350–1400; ME]

let′ters testamen′tary, *Law.* an instrument issued by a court or public official authorizing an executor to take control of and dispose of the estate of a deceased person.

let′ter stock′, unregistered stock sold privately by a company so as not to have a negative effect on the price of its publicly traded stock.

let·ter·wood (let′ər wo͝od′), *n.* snakewood. [1690–1700, designating another tree; LETTER[1] + WOOD[1], so called from the wood's letterlike markings]

Let·tic (let′ik), *adj.* of or pertaining to the Letts or their language. [1870–75; LETT + -IC]

Let·tie (let′ē), *n.* a female given name, form of **Laetitia.** Also, **Let′ty.**

Let·tish (let′ish), *adj.* **1.** of or pertaining to the Letts or their language. —*n.* **2.** Latvian (def. 3). [1825–35; LETT + -ISH[1]]

let·tre de ca·chet (le trᵊ də KA she′), *pl.* ***let·tres de ca·chet*** (le trᵊ də KA she′). *French.* a letter under the seal of the sovereign, esp. one ordering imprisonment, frequently without trial.

let·tre de change (le trᵊ də shäNzh′), *pl.* ***let·tres de change*** (le trᵊ də shäNzh′). *French.* bill of exchange.

let·tre de cré·ance (le trᵊ də krā äNs′), *pl.* ***let·tres de cré·ance*** (le trᵊ də krā äNs′). *French.* letter of credit.

let·tuce (let′is), *n.* **1.** a cultivated plant, *Lactuca sativa,* occurring in many varieties and having succulent leaves used for salads. **2.** any species of *Lactuca.* **3.** *Slang.* U.S. dollar bills; greenbacks. [1250–1300; 1925–30 for def. 3; ME *letuse,* appar. < OF *laitues,* pl. of *laitue* < L *lactūca* a lettuce, perh. deriv. of *lac,* s. *lact-* milk, with termination as in *erūca* ROCKET[2] (or by assoc. with Gk *galaktoûchos* having milk)]

let·up (let′up′), *n. Informal.* cessation; pause; relief. [1835–45, *Amer.;* n. use of v. phrase *let up*]

Letz·e·burg·esch (let′se bo͝or′gəsh), *n.* a Germanic dialect that is the native language of most of the people of Luxembourg. Also called **Luxembourgian, Luxembourgish.** [the local name for the dialect]

le·u (le′o͞o), *n., pl.* **lei** (lā). a coin and monetary unit of Rumania, equal to 100 bani. *Abbr.:* L. Also, **ley.** [1875–

80; < Rumanian: lit., LION, a designation based on Turk *arslanlı* (*arslan* lion + *-lı* adj. suffix), name given to the Dutch rijksdaalder, which circulated in the later Ottoman Empire and bore the image of a lion]

Leu, *Biochem.* leucine.

leuc-, var. of **leuco-** before a vowel: *leucemia.*

leu•cae•na (lo͞o sē′nə), *n.* any of various tropical trees belonging to the genus *Leucaena,* of the legume family, which includes the lead tree. Cf. **ipil-ipil.** [< NL (1842), appar. < Gk *leukaín(ein)* to become white (deriv. of *leukós* white, bright; see LEUKO-) + NL *-a* -A[2]]

Leu•cas (lo͞o′kəs), *n.* Levkas.

leu•ce•mi•a (lo͞o sē′mē ə), *n. Pathol.* leukemia. —**leu•ce′mic,** *adj.*

leu•cine (lo͞o′sēn, -sin), *n. Biochem.* a white, crystalline, water-soluble amino acid, $C_6H_{13}NO_2$, obtained by the decomposition of proteins and made synthetically: essential in the nutrition of humans and animals. *Abbr.:* Leu; *Symbol:* L [1820–30; LEUC- + -INE[1]]

leu•cite (lo͞o′sīt), *n.* a whitish or grayish mineral, potassium aluminum silicate, $KAlSi_2O_6$, found in alkali volcanic rocks. [1790–1800; < G *Leukit.* See LEUCO-, -ITE[1]] —**leu•cit•ic** (lo͞o sit′ik), *adj.*

leuco-, var. of **leuko-.** Also, *esp. before a vowel,* **leuc-.**

leu′co base′ (lo͞o′kō), *Chem.* a noncolored or slightly colored compound that is produced by reducing a dye and is readily oxidized to regenerate the dye. [1885–90; independent use of LEUCO-]

leu•co•blast (lo͞o′kə blast′), *n.* leukoblast.

leu•co•crat•ic (lo͞o′kə krat′ik), *adj. Geol.* (of a rock) composed mainly of light-colored minerals. [LEUCO- + -CRAT + -IC]

leu•co•cyte (lo͞o′kə sīt′), *n. Immunol.* leukocyte. —**leu′co•cyt′ic,** *adj.*

leu•co•cy•to•sis (lo͞o′kō sī tō′sis), *n. Physiol., Pathol.* leukocytosis. —**leu•co•cy•tot•ic** (lo͞o′kō sī tot′ik), *adj.*

leu•co•der•ma (lo͞o′kə dûr′mə), *n. Pathol.* vitiligo. [1880–85; < NL; see LEUCO-, DERMA]

leu•co•line (lo͞o′kə lēn′, -lin), *n. Chem.* quinoline. [1850–55; LEUC- + -OL[1] + -INE[2]]

leu•co•ma (lo͞o kō′mə), *n. Pathol.* leukoma.

leu•con (lo͞o′kon), *n. Zool.* a type of sponge having a thick body wall with a highly branched canal system leading into the spongocoel. Cf. **ascon, sycon.** [< NL < Gk *leukón,* n. use of neut. of *leukós* white]

leu•co•pe•ni•a (lo͞o′kə pē′nē ə), *n. Med.* leukopenia.

leu•co•pla•ki•a (lo͞o′kə plā′kē ə), *n. Pathol.* leukoplakia. Also called **leu•co•pla•sia** (lo͞o′kə plā′zhə, -zhē ə, -zē ə).

leu•co•plast (lo͞o′kə plast′), *n. Bot.* a colorless plastid in the cells of roots, storage organs, and underground stems, serving as a point around which starch forms. [1885–90; LEUCO- + -PLAST]

leu•co•poi•e•sis (lo͞o′kō poi ē′sis), *n.* leukopoiesis. —**leu•co•poi•et•ic** (lo͞o′kō poi et′ik), *adj.*

leu•co•sis (lo͞o kō′sis), *n. Vet. Pathol.* leukosis. —**leu•cot•ic** (lo͞o kot′ik), *adj.*

Leu•coth•e•a (lo͞o koth′ē ə), *n. Class. Myth.* a sea goddess, the deified Ino, who gave Odysseus a veil as a float after a storm had destroyed his raft. Also, **Leukothea.** [< Gk: lit., the white goddess]

leu•coth•o•e (lo͞o koth′ō ē′), *n.* any of various shrubs of the genus *Leucothoe,* of the heath family, having clusters of white or pinkish flowers. [< NL (1834), after L *Leucothoē* a legendary princess turned into a fragrant bush by Apollo]

leu•co•tome (lo͞o′kə tōm′), *n. Surg.* an instrument for dissecting the white matter of the brain, consisting of a cannula containing a slender rotating blade. [1935–40; LEUCO- + -TOME]

leu•cot•o•my (lo͞o kot′ə mē), *n., pl.* **-mies.** *Chiefly Brit. Surg.* See **prefrontal lobotomy.** [1935–40; LEUCO- + -TOMY]

Leuc•tra (lo͞ok′trə), *n.* a town in ancient Greece, in Boeotia: Thebans defeated Spartans here 371 B.C.

leud (lo͞od), *n., pl.* **leuds, leu•des** (lo͞o′dēz). a vassal or tenant in the early Middle Ages. [1750–60; < ML *leudēs* (pl.) < Gmc; cf. OE *lēode,* G *Leute* people]

Leu′ enkeph′alin (lo͞o), (*sometimes l.c.*) See under **enkephalin.** Also, **Leu′-en•keph′a•lin.** [1975–80]

leuk-, var. of **leuko-** before a vowel.

Leu•kas (lo͞o′kəs), *n.* Levkas.

leu•ke•mi•a (lo͞o kē′mē ə), *n. Pathol.* any of several cancers of the bone marrow that prevent the normal manufacture of red and white blood cells and platelets, resulting in anemia, increased susceptibility to infection, and impaired blood clotting. Also, **leucemia.** [1850–55; earlier *leuchaemia* < G *Leukämie* (1848). See LEUCO-, -EMIA] —**leu•ke′mic,** *adj.*

leuke′mic re•tic′u•lo•en•do•the•li•o′sis (ri tik′yə lō en′dō thē′lē ō′sis), *Pathol.* See **hairy cell leukemia.** [RETICUL(UM) + -O- + ENDOTHELI(UM) + -OSIS]

leu•ke•mid (lo͞o kē′mid), *n.* any cutaneous lesion that occurs in leukemia. [LEUKEM(IA) + -ID[1]]

leuko-, a combining form with the meanings "white," "white blood cell," used in the formation of compound words: *leukopoiesis; leukotomy.* Also, **leuco-;** *esp. before a vowel,* **leuk-.** [< Gk *leuko-,* comb. form of *leukós* white, bright]

leu•ko•blast (lo͞o′kə blast′), *n. Cell Biol.* an immature leukocyte. Also, **leucoblast.** [1900–05; LEUKO- + -BLAST] —**leu′ko•blas′tic,** *adj.*

leu•ko•cyte (lo͞o′kə sīt′), *n. Immunol.* See **white blood cell.** Also, **leucocyte.** [1865–70; LEUKO- + -CYTE] —**leu•ko•cyt•ic** (lo͞o′kə sit′ik), *adj.*

leu•ko•cy•to•sis (lo͞o′kō sī tō′sis), *n. Physiol., Pathol.* an increase in the number of white blood cells in the blood. Also, **leucocytosis.** [1865–70; < NL; see LEUKOCYTE, -OSIS] —**leu•ko•cy•tot•ic** (lo͞o′kō sī tot′ik), *adj.*

leu•ko•der•ma (lo͞o′kə dûr′mə), *n. Pathol.* vitiligo. [1880–85; < NL; see LEUKO-, DERMA]

leu•ko•ma (lo͞o kō′mə), *n. Pathol.* a dense, white opacity of the cornea. Also, **leucoma.** [1700–10; < NL *leucoma.* See LEUKO-, -OMA]

leu•ko•pe•de•sis (lo͞o′kō pi dē′sis), *n.* an outward flow of white blood cells through a blood-vessel wall. [< NL; see LEUKO-, DIAPEDESIS]

leu•ko•pe•ni•a (lo͞o′kə pē′nē ə), *n. Med.* a decrease in the number of white blood cells in the blood. Also, **leucopenia.** Also called **leu•ko•cy•to•pe•ni•a** (lo͞o′kə sī′tə pē′nē ə). [1895–1900; < NL *leucopenia,* equiv. to *leuco-* LEUKO- + Gk *penía* poverty, akin to *pénesthai* to be poor, toil; see -IA] —**leu′ko•pe′nic,** *adj.*

leu•ko•pla•ki•a (lo͞o′kə plā′kē ə), *n. Pathol.* a disorder of a mucous membrane characterized by one or more white patches, occurring most commonly on the cheek, tongue, vulva, or penis: often medically insignificant but sometimes becoming malignant. Also, **leucoplakia.** Also called **leu•ko•pla•sia** (lo͞o′kə plā′zhə, -zhē ə, -zē ə), **leucoplasia.** [1880–85; < NL, equiv. to Gk *leuko-* LEUKO- + *plak-,* s. of *pláx* flat surface, taken as "tongue" + *-ia* -IA]

leu•ko•poi•e•sis (lo͞o′kō poi ē′sis), *n.* the formation and development of white blood cells. Also, **leucopoiesis.** [1910–15; < NL *leucopoiesis.* See LEUKO-, -POIESIS] —**leu•ko•poi•et•ic** (lo͞o′kō poi et′ik), *adj.*

leu•ko•sis (lo͞o kō′sis), *n. Vet. Pathol.* any of several diseases occurring chiefly in chickens, involving proliferation of the leukocytes and characterized by paralysis, blindness, formation of tumors in the internal organs, and bone calcification. Also, **leucosis.** Also called **avian leukosis.** [1700–10; < Gk *leúkōsis* leucoma. See LEUKO-, -OSIS] —**leu•kot•ic** (lo͞o kot′ik), *adj.*

Leu•koth•e•a (lo͞o koth′ē ə), *n.* Leucothea.

leu•kot•o•my (lo͞o kot′ə mē), *n., pl.* **-mies.** *Chiefly Brit. Surg.* See **prefrontal lobotomy.** [1935–40; LEUKO- + -TOMY]

leu•ko•tri•ene (lo͞o′kə trī′ēn), *n. Biochem.* a lipid, $C_{20}H_{30}O_3$, produced by white blood cells in an immune response to antigens, that contributes to allergic asthma and inflammatory reactions. [1975–80; LEUKO- + TRIENE]

Leu•ri•cus (lo͞o rī′kəs, -rē′-), *n.* Leofric.

Leu•tze (loit′sə), *n.* **E•ma•nu•el Gott•lieb** (i man′yo͞o əl got′lēb; *Ger.* ā mä′no͞o el′ gôt′lēp), 1816–68, German painter in the U.S.

lev (lef), *n., pl.* **lev•a** (lev′ə). a coin and monetary unit of Bulgaria, equal to 100 stotinki. *Abbr.:* L., LV. [1900–05; < Bulg: lit., lion, OCS *lĭvŭ,* prob. < OHG *lewo* < L *lēo;* see LEU]

lev-, var. of **levo-** before a vowel: *levulose.*

Lev., Leviticus.

le•vade (lə väd′), *n. Dressage.* a movement in which the horse first lowers its body on increasingly bent hocks, then sits on its hind hooves while keeping its forelegs raised and drawn in. [1940–45; < G < F, equiv. to *lev(er)* to raise + *-ade* -ADE[1]]

Le•val•loi•si•an (lev′ə loi′zē ən, -zhən), *adj.* of, pertaining to, or characteristic of a distinctive late Lower and Middle Paleolithic method of preparing a stone core so that preformed thin, oval or triangular flakes with sharp edges could be struck from it. Also, **Le•val•lois** (lə val′wä). [1930–35; LEVALLOIS(-PERRET) + -IAN]

Le•val•lois-Per•ret (lə val wa pe re′), *n.* a suburb of Paris, in N France, on the Seine. 52,731.

le•vant (li vant′), *v.i. Brit. Slang.* to leave secretly or hurriedly to avoid paying debts. [1750–60; perh. < Sp *levantar* to lift (cf. *levantar el campo* to break camp, leave), freq. of *levar* < L *levāre*] —**le•vant′er,** *n.*

Le•vant (li vant′), *n.* **1.** the lands bordering the E shores of the Mediterranean Sea. **2.** Also called **Levant′ moroc′co.** a superior grade of morocco having a large and prominent grain, originally made in the Levant. [1490–1500; earlier *levaunt* < MF *levant,* n. use (with reference to rising sun) of prp. of *lever* to raise (*se lever* to rise). See LEVER]

Levant′ dol′lar, a silver coin, either a Maria Theresa thaler or an imitation of one, formerly used for trade with Abyssinia, Eritrea, Aden, etc. Imitations bear the date 1780 regardless of the year of minting. Also called **Levant′ tha′ler.**

le•vant•er (li van′tər), *n.* a strong easterly wind in the Mediterranean. [1620–30; LEVANT + -ER[1]]

Le•van•tine (lev′ən tīn′, -tēn′, li van′tin, -tīn), *adj.* **1.** of or pertaining to the Levant. —*n.* **2.** a native of the Levant. [1640–50; LEVANT + -INE[1]] —**Lev′an•tin′ism,** *n.*

Levant′ red′. See **Adrianople red.**

Levant′ sto′rax. See under **storax** (def. 2). [1935–40]

Levant′ worm′seed. See under **wormseed** (def. 1).

le•va•tor (li vā′tər, -tôr), *n., pl.* **lev•a•to•res** (lev′ə tôr′ēz, -tōr′-). **1.** *Anat.* a muscle that raises a part of the body. Cf. **depressor. 2.** *Surg.* an instrument used to raise a depressed part of the skull. [1605–15; < NL, special use of ML *levātor* one who raises (levies) recruits or taxes (L: mitigator), equiv. to L *levā(re)* to raise + *-tor* -TOR]

Le Vau (lə vō′), **Louis** (lwē), 1612–70, French architect.

lev•ee[1] (lev′ē), *n., v.,* **lev•eed, lev•ee•ing.** —*n.* **1.** an embankment designed to prevent the flooding of a river. **2.** *Geol.* See **natural levee. 3.** *Agric.* one of the small continuous ridges surrounding fields that are to be irrigated. **4.** *Hist.* a landing place for ships; quay. —*v.t.* **5.** to furnish with a levee: *to levee a treacherous stream.* [1710–20, *Amer.;* < F *levée* < ML *levāta* embankment, n. use of fem. ptp. of L *levāre* to raise, orig. lighten, akin to *levis* light, not heavy]

lev•ee[2] (lev′ē, le vē′), *n.* **1.** (in Great Britain) a public court assembly, held in the early afternoon, at which men only are received. **2.** a reception, usually in someone's honor: *a presidential levee at the White House.* **3.** *Hist.* a reception of visitors held on rising from bed, as formerly by a royal or other personage. [1665–75; < F *levé,* var. sp. of *lever* rising (n. use of inf.) < L *levāre* to raise; see LEVEE[1]]

lev•el (lev′əl), *adj., n., v.,* **-eled, -el•ing** or (*esp. Brit.*) **-elled, -el•ling,** *adv.* —*adj.* **1.** having no part higher than another; having a flat or even surface. **2.** being in a plane parallel to the plane of the horizon; horizontal. **3.** equal, as one thing with another or two or more things with one another. **4.** even, equable, or uniform. **5.** filled to a height even with the rim of a container: *a level teaspoon of salt.* **6.** mentally well-balanced; sensible; rational: *to keep a level head in a crisis.* **7. one's level best,** one's very best; one's utmost: *We tried our level best to get here on time.*
—*n.* **8.** a device used for determining or adjusting something to a horizontal surface. **9.** *Survey.* **a.** Also called **surveyor's level.** an instrument for observing levels, having a sighting device, usually telescopic, and capable of being made precisely horizontal. **b.** an observation made with this instrument. **c.** See **spirit level. 10.** an imaginary line or surface everywhere at right angles to the plumb line. **11.** the horizontal line or plane in which anything is situated, with regard to its elevation. **12.** a horizontal position or condition. **13.** an extent of land approximately horizontal and unbroken by irregularities. **14.** a level or flat surface. **15.** a position with respect to a given or specified height: *The water rose to a level of 30 feet.* **16.** a position or plane in a graded scale of values; status; rank: *His acting was on the level of an amateur. They associated only with those on their own economic level.* **17.** an extent, measure, or degree of intensity, achievement, etc.: *a high level of sound; an average level of writing skill.* **18.** *Ling.* a major subdivision of linguistic structure, as phonology, morphology, or syntax, often viewed as hierarchically ordered. Cf. **component** (def. 6a), **stratum** (def. 8). **19.** *Mining.* the interconnected horizontal mine workings at a particular elevation or depth: *There had been a cave-in on the 1500-foot level.* **20. find one's** or **one's own level,** to attain the place or position merited by one's abilities or achievements: *He finally found his level as one of the directors of the firm.* **21. on the level,** *Informal.* honest; sincere; reliable: *Is this information on the level?*
—*v.t.* **22.** to make (a surface) level, even, or flat: *to level ground before building.* **23.** to raise or lower to a particular level or position; to make horizontal. **24.** to bring (something) to the level of the ground: *They leveled the trees to make way for the new highway.* **25.** *Informal.* to knock down (a person): *He leveled his opponent with one blow.* **26.** to make equal, as in status or condition. **27.** to make even or uniform, as coloring. **28.** *Historical Ling.* (of the alternative forms of a paradigm) to reduce in number or regularize: *Old English "him" (dative) and "hine" (accusative) have been leveled to Modern English "him."* **29.** to aim or point (a weapon, criticism, etc.) at a mark or objective: *He leveled his criticism at the college as a whole.* **30.** *Survey.* to find the relative elevation of different points in (land), as with a level.
—*v.i.* **31.** to bring things or persons to a common level. **32.** to aim a weapon, criticism, etc., at a mark or objective. **33.** *Survey.* **a.** to take a level. **b.** to use a leveling instrument. **34.** to speak truthfully and openly (often fol. by *with*): *You're not leveling with me about your trip to Chicago.* **35.** *Obs.* to direct the mind, purpose, etc., at something. **36. level off, a.** *Aeron.* to maintain a constant altitude after a climb or descent. **b.** to become stable; reach a constant or limit. **c.** to make even or smooth.
—*adv.* **37.** *Obs.* in a level, direct, or even way or line. [1300–50; ME (n. and v.), var. of *livel* (n.) < MF < VL **lībellum,* for L *lībella* plummet line, level, dim. of *lībra* balance, scales; for formation, see CASTELLUM] —**lev′el•ly,** *adv.* —**lev′el•ness,** *n.*
—**Syn. 1, 2.** flush. LEVEL, EVEN, FLAT, SMOOTH suggest a uniform surface without marked unevenness. That which is LEVEL is parallel to the horizon: *a level surface; A billiard table must be level.* FLAT is applied to any plane surface free from marked irregularities: *a flat roof.* With reference to land or country, FLAT connotes lowness or unattractiveness; LEVEL does not suggest anything derogatory. That which is EVEN is free from irregularities, though not necessarily level or plane: *an even land surface with no hills.* SMOOTH suggests a high degree of evenness in any surface, esp. to the touch and sometimes to the sight: *as smooth as silk.* **22.** smooth, flatten. **24.** raze, demolish, destroy. **26.** equalize. **29.** direct. —**Ant. 1.** uneven. **2.** vertical.

lev′el cross′ing, *Brit.* See **grade crossing.** [1835–45]

lev′el curve′. See **contour line.**

lev•el•er (lev′ə lər), *n.* a person or thing that levels. Also, *esp. Brit.,* **leveller.** [1590–1600; LEVEL + -ER[1]]

lev•el•head•ed (lev′əl hed′id), *adj.* having common sense and sound judgment; sensible. [1875–80, *Amer.;* LEVEL + HEAD + -ED[3]] —**lev′el•head′ed•ly,** *adv.* —**lev′el•head′ed•ness,** *n.*

lev′eling in′strument, *Survey.* an instrument used to establish a horizontal line of sight, usually by means of a spirit level.

lev′eling rod′, *Survey.* rod (def. 19). [1900–05]

Lev•el•land (lev′əl land′), *n.* a city in NW Texas. 13,809.

lev•el•ler (lev′ə lər), *n.* **1.** (*usually cap.*) (during the British Civil War) a member of the Parliamentary army advocating constitutional reforms, equal rights, and religious tolerance. **2.** *Chiefly Brit.* leveler. [1590–1600; LEVEL + -ER[1]]

lev′el line′. See **contour line.** [1660–70]

lev•el-off (lev′əl ôf′, -of′), *n. Aeron.* the maneuver of bringing an aircraft into a horizontal flying position after an ascent or descent. [1925–30; n. use of v. phrase *level off*]

lev′el of signif′icance, See **significance level.**

lev′el play′ing field′, a state of equality; an equal opportunity. [1980–85]

Le•ven (lē′vən), *n.* **Loch,** a lake in E Scotland: ruins of a castle in which Mary Queen of Scots was imprisoned.

lev•er (lev′ər, lē′vər), *n.* **1.** *Mech.* a rigid bar that pivots about one point and that is used to move an object at a second point by a force applied at a third. Cf. **machine** (def. 4b). **2.** a means or agency of persuading or of achieving an end: *Saying that the chairman of the board likes the plan is just a lever to get us to support it.* **3.** *Horol.* the pallet of an escapement. —*v.t., v.i.* **4.** to move with or apply a lever: *to lever a rock; to lever mightily and to no avail.* [1250–1300; ME *levere, levour* for **lever* < AF; OF *levier,* equiv. to *lev(er)* to lift (< L *levāre* to lighten, lift, v. deriv. of *levis* light) + *-ier* -IER[2]]

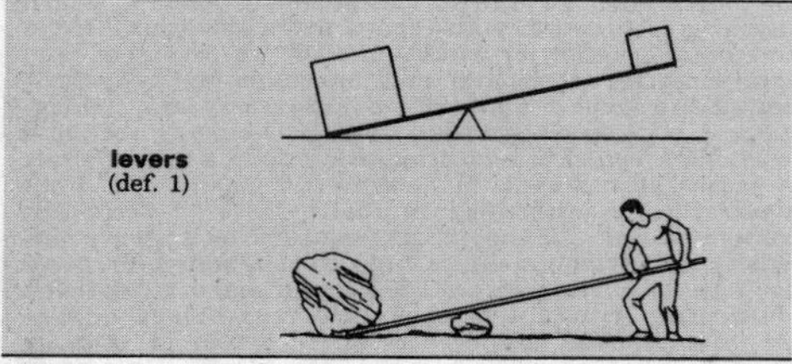

levers (def. 1)

Le•ver (lē′vər), *n.* **Charles James** (*"Cornelius O'Dowd"*), 1806–72, Irish novelist and essayist.

lev′er ac′tion, a rifle action in which the extracting and ejecting of the shell case and the recocking of the weapon are accomplished by a hand-operated lever arm in front of the trigger housing.

lev•er-ac•tion (lev′ər ak′shən, lē′vər-), *adj.* (of a rifle) having a lever action.

lev•er•age (lev′ər ij, lē′vər-), *n., v.,* **-aged, -ag•ing.** —*n.* **1.** the action of a lever. **2.** the mechanical advantage or power gained by using a lever. **3.** power or ability to act or to influence people, events, decisions, etc.; sway: *Being the only industry in town gave the company considerable leverage in its union negotiations.* **4.** the use of a small initial investment, credit, or borrowed funds to gain a very high return in relation to one's investment, to control a much larger investment, or to reduce one's own liability for any loss. —*v.t.* **5.** to exert power or influence on. **6.** to provide with leverage. **7.** to invest or arrange (invested funds) using leverage. [1715–25; LEVER + -AGE]

lev′eraged buy′out, the purchase of a company with borrowed money, using the company's assets as collateral, and often discharging the debt and realizing a profit by liquidating the company. *Abbr.:* LBO

lev′er escape′ment, *Horol.* an escapement in which a pivoted lever, made to oscillate by the escape wheel, engages a balance staff and causes it to oscillate.

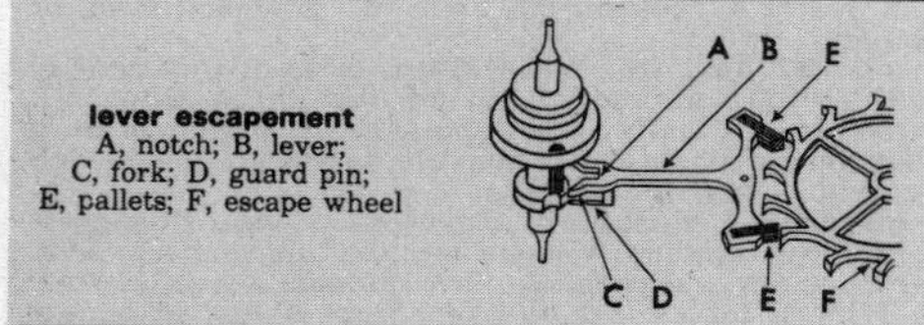

lever escapement
A, notch; B, lever; C, fork; D, guard pin; E, pallets; F, escape wheel

lev•er•et (lev′ər it), *n.* a young hare. [1400–50; late ME < AF, dim. of *levre,* OF *lievre* < L *leporem,* acc. of *lepus* hare; see -ET]

Le•ver•hulme (lē′vər hyōōm′ *or, often,* -yōōm′), *n.* **Viscount** (*William Hesketh Lever*), 1851–1925, English soap manufacturer, originator of an employee profit-sharing plan, and founder of a model industrial town.

Le•ver•ku•sen (lā′vər kōō′zən), *n.* a city in North Rhine-Westphalia, in W Germany, on the Rhine. 154,700.

Le•ver•ri•er (lə ver′ē ā′; *Fr.* lə ve ryā′), *n.* **Ur•bain Jean Jo•seph** (yr baN′ zhäN zhô zef′), 1811–77, French astronomer.

Lev•er•tov (lev′ər tôf′, -tof′), *n.* **Denise,** born 1923, U.S. poet, born in England.

lev′er tum′bler, a flat metal tumbler in a lock.

Lé•vesque (lə vek′; *Fr.* lā vek′), *n.* **Re•né** (rə nā′; *Fr.* rə nā′), born 1922, Canadian political leader: premier of Quebec 1976–85.

Le•vi (lē′vī, lā′vē; *for 5 also* lē′vē), *n.* **1.** a son of Jacob and Leah. Gen. 29:34. **2.** one of the 12 tribes of Israel, traditionally descended from him. **3.** original name of **Matthew** (def. 1). **4.** a Levite. **5.** a male given name: from a Hebrew word meaning "a joining."

CONCISE ETYMOLOGY KEY: <, descended or borrowed from; >, whence; b., blend of, blended; c., cognate with; cf., compare; deriv., derivative; equiv., equivalent; imit., imitative; obl., oblique; r., replacing; s., stem; sp., spelling, spelled; resp., respelling, respelled; trans., translation; ?, origin unknown; *, unattested; ‡, probably earlier than. See the full key inside the front cover.

Le•vi (le′vē), *n.* **Car•lo** (kär′lô), 1902–75, Italian painter and writer.

lev•i•a•ble (lev′ē ə bəl), *adj.* **1.** that may be levied. **2.** liable or subject to a levy. [1475–85; see LEVY, -ABLE]

le•vi•a•than (li vī′ə thən), *n.* **1.** (*often cap.*) *Bible.* a sea monster. **2.** any huge marine animal, as the whale. **3.** anything of immense size and power, as a huge, oceangoing ship. **4.** (*cap., italics*) a philosophical work (1651) by Thomas Hobbes dealing with the political organization of society. [1350–1400; ME *levyathan* < LL *leviathan* << Heb *liwyāthān*]

lev•i•er (lev′ē ər), *n.* a person who levies. [1485–95]

lev•i•gate (*v.* lev′i gāt′; *adj.* lev′i git, -gāt′), *v.,* **-gat•ed, -gat•ing,** *adj.* —*v.t.* **1.** to rub, grind, or reduce to a fine powder, as in a mortar, with or without the addition of a liquid. **2.** *Chem.* to make a homogeneous mixture of, as gels. —*adj.* **3.** *Bot.* having a smooth, glossy surface; glabrous. [1605–15; < L *lēvigātus,* ptp. of *lēvigāre* to smooth, pulverize, equiv. to *lēv(is)* smooth + *-igāre* v. suffix] —**lev′i•ga′tion,** *n.* —**lev′i•ga′tor,** *n.*

lev•in (lev′in), *n. Archaic.* lightning. [1200–50; ME *levene,* obscurely akin to Goth *lauhmuni*]

Le•vine (lə vēn′), *n.* **Jack,** born 1915, U.S. painter.

lev•i•rate (lev′ər it, -ə rāt′, lē′vər it, -və rāt′), *n.* the custom of marriage by a man with his brother's widow, such marriage required in Biblical law if the deceased was childless. Deut. 25:5–10. [1715–25; < L *lēvir* husband's brother (akin to Gk *dāḗr,* Skt *devar,* OE *tācor*) + -ATE[3]] —**lev•i•rat•ic** (lev′ə rat′ik, lē′və-), **lev′i•rat′i•cal,** *adj.*

Le•vi's (lē′vīz), (*used with a plural v.*) *Trademark.* a brand of clothing, esp. blue jeans. Cf. **blue jeans.**

Lé•vis (lē′vis; *Fr.* lā vē′), *n.* a city in S Quebec, in E Canada, across from Montreal, on the St. Lawrence. 17,895.

Lé•vi-Strauss (lā′vē strous′), *n.* **Claude,** born 1908, French anthropologist and educator, born in Belgium: founder of structural anthropology.

lev•i•tate (lev′i tāt′), *v.,* **-tat•ed, -tat•ing.** —*v.i.* **1.** to rise or float in the air, esp. as a result of a supernatural power that overcomes gravity. —*v.t.* **2.** to cause to rise or float in the air. [1665–75; LEVIT(Y) + -ATE[1], modeled on *gravitate*] —**lev′i•ta′tor,** *n.*

lev•i•ta•tion (lev′i tā′shən), *n.* **1.** the act or phenomenon of levitating. **2.** the raising or rising of a body in air by supernatural means. [1660–70; LEVITATE + -ION] —**lev′i•ta′tion•al,** *adj.* —**lev′i•ta′tive,** *adj.*

Le•vite (lē′vīt), *n.* **1.** a member of the tribe of Levi. **2.** a descendant of Levi, esp. one appointed to assist the priests in the temple or tabernacle. [1250–1300; ME < LL *Lēvīta* < Gk *Leuítēs* Levite, equiv. to *Leuí* (< Heb *Lēvī* Levi, Levite) + *-tēs* personal n. suffix]

lev•i•ter (lev′i tər), *adv.* (in prescriptions) lightly. [< L]

Le•vit•i•cal (li vit′i kəl), *adj.* **1.** of or pertaining to the Levites. **2.** of or pertaining to Leviticus or the law (**Levit′ical law′**) contained in Leviticus. [1525–35; < LL *Lēvitic(us)* (see LEVITICUS) + -AL[1]] —**Le•vit′i•cal•ly,** *adv.*

Le•vit•i•cus (li vit′i kəs), *n.* the third book of the Bible, containing laws relating to the priests and Levites and to the forms of Jewish ceremonial observance. *Abbr.:* Lev. [< LL *Lēviticus (liber)* Levitical (book) < Gk *Leuïtikós.* See LEVITE, -IC]

Lev•it•town (lev′it toun′), *n.* a town on W Long Island, in SE New York. 57,045.

lev•i•ty (lev′i tē), *n., pl.* **-ties.** **1.** lightness of mind, character, or behavior; lack of appropriate seriousness or earnestness. **2.** an instance or exhibition of this. **3.** fickleness. **4.** lightness in weight. [1555–65; < L *levitās* lightness, frivolity, equiv. to *levi(s)* light + *-tās* -TY[2]] —**Syn. 1, 2.** frivolity, flippancy, triviality, giddiness.

Lev•kas (lef käs′), *n.* an island in the Ionian group, off the W coast of Greece. 24,581; 114 sq. mi. (295 sq. km). Also, **Leucas, Leukas.** Italian, **Santa Maura.**

le•vo (lē′vō), *adj.* levorotatory. [by shortening]

levo-, a combining form meaning "left," "levorotatory," used in the formation of compound words: *levoglucose; levorotation.* Also, **laevo-;** *esp. before a vowel,* **lev-.** [repr. L *laevus* left, on the left; see -O-]

le•vo•do•pa (lē′və dō′pə), *n. Pharm.* a synthetic substance, $C_9H_{11}NO_4$, that is converted in the brain to dopamine: used chiefly in the treatment of parkinsonism. Also called **L-dopa.** [1965–70; LEVO- + DOPA]

le•vo•glu•cose (lē′və glōō′kōs), *n. Chem.* See under **glucose** (def. 1). [LEVO- + GLUCOSE]

le•vo•ro•ta•to•ry (lē′və rō′tə tôr′ē, -tōr′ē), *adj. Optics, Chem., Biochem.* turning to the left, as the rotation to the left of the plane of polarization of light in certain crystals and compounds. *Symbol: l-* Also, **le•vo•ro•ta•ry** (lē′və rō′tə rē). [1870–75; LEVO- + ROTATORY]

le•vor•pha•nol (lə vôr′fə nôl′, -nol′), *n. Pharm.* a potent synthetic narcotic analgesic, $C_{21}H_{29}NO_7$, as the tartrate, used in the treatment of moderate to severe pain. [LEV- + (*methylm*)*orph(in)an* a chemical component + -OL[1]]

lev′u•lin′ic ac′id (lev′yə lin′ik, lev′-), *Chem.* a white or colorless, water-soluble solid, $C_5H_8O_3$, produced by the hydrolysis of cane sugar, starch, or cellulose; used chiefly in the organic synthesis of nylon, plastics, and pharmaceuticals. [LEVUL(OSE) + -IN[2] + -IC]

lev•u•lose (lev′yə lōs′), *n. Chem.* fructose. [1870–75; LEV- + -ULE + -OSE[2]]

lev•y (lev′ē), *n., pl.* **lev•ies,** *v.,* **lev•ied, lev•y•ing.** —*n.* **1.** an imposing or collecting, as of a tax, by authority or force. **2.** the amount owed or collected. **3.** the conscription of troops. **4.** the troops conscripted. —*v.t.* **5.** to impose (a tax): *to levy a duty on imports.* **6.** to conscript (troops). **7.** to start or wage (war). —*v.i.* **8.** to seize or attach property by judicial order. [1375–1425; late ME *leve(e)* < MF, n. use of fem. ptp. of *lever* to raise < L *levāre,* akin to *levis* light; cf. LEVEE[2]] —**Syn. 6.** draft, enlist, callup.

Le•vy (lē′vē, lev′ē *for 1;* lē′vē, -vī *for 2*), *n.* **1. Uriah Phillips,** 1792–1862, U.S. naval commander. **2.** a male given name.

Lew (lōō), *n.* a male given name, form of **Lewis, Llewellyn,** or **Louis.**

lewd (lōōd), *adj.* **-er, -est.** **1.** inclined to, characterized by, or inciting to lust or lechery; lascivious. **2.** obscene or indecent, as language or songs; salacious. **3.** *Obs.* **a.** low, ignorant, or vulgar. **b.** base, vile, or wicked, esp. of a person. **c.** bad, worthless, or poor, esp. of a thing. [bef. 900; ME *leud, lewed,* OE *lǣwede* lay, unlearned] —**lewd′ly,** *adv.* —**lewd′ness,** *n.*

Lew•es (lōō′is), *n.* **1. George Henry,** 1817–78, English writer and critic. **2.** a city in East Sussex, in SE England: battle 1264. 76,400.

lew•is (lōō′is), *n.* a device for lifting a dressed stone, consisting of a number of pieces fitting together to fill a dovetailed recess cut into the stone. [1730–40; perh. after the surname of the inventor]

lewis

Lew•is (lōō′is), *n.* **1. C(ecil) Day,** 1904–72, British poet: poet laureate after 1968. **2. C(live) S(ta•ples)** (stā′pəlz), (*"Clive Hamilton"*), 1898–1963, English novelist and essayist. **3. Gilbert Newton,** 1875–1946, U.S. chemist. **4. (Harry) Sinclair,** 1885–1951, U.S. novelist, playwright, and journalist: Nobel prize 1930. **5. Isaac Newton,** 1858–1931, U.S. soldier and inventor. **6. Jerry Lee,** born 1935, U.S. country-and-western and rock-'n'-roll singer, musician, and composer. **7. John (Aaron),** born 1920, U.S. jazz pianist, composer, and musical director. **8. John L(ewellyn),** 1880–1969, U.S. labor leader. **9. Matthew Gregory** (*"Monk Lewis"*), 1775–1809, English novelist, dramatist, and poet. **10. Mer•i•weth•er** (mer′i weth′ər), 1774–1809, U.S. explorer: leader of the Lewis and Clark expedition 1804–06. **11. (Percy) Wynd•ham** (win′dəm), 1884–1957, English novelist, essayist, and painter; born in the U.S. **12.** a male given name.

Lew′is ac′id, *Chem.* any substance capable of forming a covalent bond with a base by accepting a pair of electrons from it. [1940–45; named after G. N. LEWIS]

Lew′is and Har′ris, the northernmost island of the Hebrides, in NW Scotland. 825 sq. mi. (2135 sq. km). Also, **Lew′is with Har′ris.**

Lew′is base′, *Chem.* any substance capable of forming a covalent bond with an acid by transferring a pair of electrons to it. [1960–65; named after G. N. LEWIS]

lew′is bolt′, *Building Trades.* an anchor bolt having a conical base around which concrete or lead is poured to hold it. [1870–75]

Lew′is gun′, a light, air-cooled, gas-operated machine gun with a circular magazine, first used in World War I. Also called **Lew′is automat′ic, Lew′is machine′ gun′.** [1910–15; named after I. N. LEWIS]

Lew•i•sham (lōō′ə shəm), *n.* a borough of Greater London, England. 246,600.

lew•is•ite (lōō′ə sīt′), *n.* a pale yellow, odorless compound, $C_2H_2AsCl_3$, used as a blister gas in World War I. [1920–25; named after Winford Lee *Lewis* (1878–1943), American chemist who developed it; see -ITE[1]]

Lew′is Moun′tains, a mountain range in the NW United States and W Canada, in W Montana and Alberta province: part of the Rocky Mountains.

Lew•i•sohn (lōō′ə sən, -zən, -sōn′), *n.* **Lud•wig** (lud′wig), 1882?–1955, U.S. novelist and critic, born in Germany.

Lew•is•ton (lōō′ə stən), *n.* **1.** a city in SW Maine. 40,481. **2.** a city in W Idaho. 27,986.

Lew•is•ville (lōō′is vil′), *n.* a town in N Texas. 24,273.

lex (leks), *n., pl.* **le•ges** (lē′jēz; *Lat.* le′ges). law[1]. [1490–1500; < L *lēx*]

lex., **1.** lexical. **2.** lexicon.

Lex•an (lek′san), *Chem., Trademark.* a brand of hard, practically unbreakable polycarbonate resin, used for shatterproof windows and the like.

Lex•ell (lek′səl), *n. Astron.* a comet that passed closer to the earth than any other comet (1770), but now has an orbit that is too distant from the earth for it to be observed. [after Anders Jean *Lexell* (1740–84), Finnish-born mathematician, who calculated its orbit]

lex•eme (lek′sēm), *n. Ling.* a lexical unit in a language, as a word or base; vocabulary item. [1935–40; LEX(ICAL) or LEX(ICON) + -EME]

lex•i•cal (lek′si kəl), *adj.* **1.** of or pertaining to the words or vocabulary of a language, esp. as distinguished from its grammatical and syntactical aspects. **2.** of, pertaining to, or of the nature of a lexicon. [1830–40; LEXIC(ON) + -AL[1]] —**lex′i•cal′i•ty,** *n.* —**lex′i•cal•ly,** *adv.*

lex•i•cal•ize (lek′si kə līz′), *v.t.,* **-ized, -iz•ing.** *Ling.* **1.** to convert (an affix, a phrase, etc.) into a lexical item, as in using the suffix *-ism* as the noun *ism.* **2.** to represent (a set of semantic features) by a lexical item. Also, *esp. Brit.,* **lex′i•cal•ise′.** [1935–40; LEXICAL + -IZE] —**lex′i•cal•i•za′tion,** *n.*

lex′ical mean′ing, the meaning of a base morpheme. Cf. **grammatical meaning.** [1930–35]

lexicog., **1.** lexicographer. **2.** lexicographical. **3.** lexicography.

lex•i•cog•ra•pher (lek′si kog′rə fər), *n.* a writer, editor, or compiler of a dictionary. [1650–60; < LGk *lexikográph(os)* (see LEXICON, -GRAPH) + -ER[1]]

lex•i•cog•ra•phy (lek′si kog′rə fē), *n.* **1.** the writing, editing, or compiling of dictionaries. **2.** the principles and procedures involved in writing, editing, or compiling dictionaries. [1670–80; LEXIC(ON) + -O- + -GRAPHY] —**lex•i•co•graph•ic** (lek′si kō graf′ik, -si kə-), **lex′i•co•graph′i•cal,** *adj.* —**lex′i•co•graph′i•cal•ly,** *adv.*

lex•i•col•o•gy (lek′si kol′ə jē), *n.* the study of the formation, meaning, and use of words and of idiomatic combinations of words. [1820–30; LEXIC(ON) + -O- + -LOGY] —**lex•i•co•log•i•cal** (lek′si kə loj′i kəl), **lex′i•co•log′ic,** *adj.* —**lex′i•col′o•gist,** *n.*

lex•i•con (lek′si kon′, -kən), *n., pl.* **lex•i•ca** (lek′si kə), **lex•i•cons.** **1.** a wordbook or dictionary, esp. of Greek, Latin, or Hebrew. **2.** the vocabulary of a particular language, field, social class, person, etc. **3.** inventory or record: *unparalleled in the lexicon of human relations.* **4.** *Ling.* **a.** the total inventory of morphemes in a given language. **b.** the inventory of base morphemes plus their combinations with derivational morphemes. [1595–1605; < ML < MGk, Gk *lexikón,* n. use of neut. of *lexikós* of words, equiv. to *léx(is)* speech, word (see LEXIS) + *-ikos* -IC]
—**Syn.** **1.** glossary, thesaurus, gloss, concordance.

lex•i•co•sta•tis•tics (lek′si kō stə tis′tiks), *n.* (*used with a singular v.*) *Ling.* the statistical study of the vocabulary of a language or languages for historical purposes. Cf. **glottochronology.** [1955–60; LEXIC(ON) + -O- + STATISTICS] —**lex′i•co•sta•tis′tic, lex′i•co•sta•tis′ti•cal,** *adj.*

Lex•ing•ton (lek′sing tən), *n.* **1.** a town in E Massachusetts, NW of Boston: first battle of American Revolution fought here April 19, 1775. 29,479. **2.** a city in N Kentucky. 204,165. **3.** a city in central North Carolina. 15,711.

Lex′ington Park′, a town in S Maryland. 10,361.

lex•is (lek′sis), *n. Ling.* the vocabulary of a language, as distinct from its grammar; the total stock of words and idiomatic combinations of them in a language; lexicon. [1955–60; < Gk *léxis* speech, diction, word, text, equiv. to *lég(ein)* to speak, recount (akin to *lógos* account, word, L *legere* to read; see LOGOS, LECTION) + *-sis* -SIS]

lex lo•ci (leks lō′sī, -kē, -kī), *Law.* the law of a place. [1825–35; < L *lēx locī*]

lex non scrip•ta (leks′non skrip′tə, nōn), *Law.* unwritten law; common law. [< L *lēx nōn scrīpta*]

lex scrip•ta (leks skrip′tə), *Law.* written law; statute law. [< L *lēx scrīpta*]

lex ta•li•o•nis (leks′ tal′ē ō′nis), the principle or law of retaliation that a punishment inflicted should correspond in degree and kind to the offense of the wrongdoer, as an eye for an eye, a tooth for a tooth; retributive justice. Also called **talion.** [1590–1600; < L *lēx tāliōnis* law of talion]

ley[1] (lā, lē), *n., adj.* lea[1].

ley[2] (lā), *n.* leu.

ley[3] (lā), *n.* a pewter containing about 80 percent tin and 20 percent lead. [aph. var. of obs. *aley* ALLOY]

Ley•den (līd′n), *n.* **1.** See **Lucas van Leyden.** **2.** **John of.** See **John of Leyden.** **3.** Leiden. **4.** a Dutch cheese similar to Edam, often flavored with caraway seeds, cumin, cinnamon, or cloves.

Ley′den jar′, *Elect.* a device for storing electric charge, consisting essentially of a glass jar lined inside and outside, for about two-thirds of its height, with tinfoil. [1815–25; so called because invented in LEYDEN]

Ley′dig cell′ (lī′dig), *Anat.* any of the interstitial cells of the testes that produce androgens. Also, **Ley′dig's cell′.** [1900–05; named after F. von *Leydig* (1821–1908), German physiologist]

Ley•poldt (lī′pōlt), *n.* **Frederick,** 1835–84, U.S. editor and publisher, born in Germany.

Ley•te (lā′tē; *Sp.* lā′te), *n.* an island in the E central Philippines: focal point of the U.S. invasion of the Philippines 1944. 1,302,648; 3085 sq. mi. (7990 sq. km).

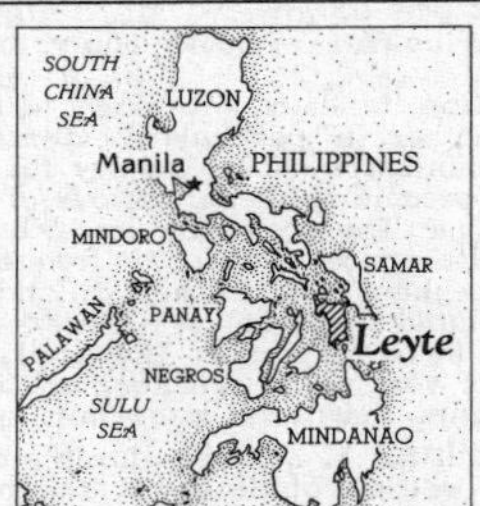

Ley•ton (lāt′n), *n.* a former borough in SE England, near London: now part of Waltham Forest.

lez (lez), *n., pl.* **lez•zes.** *Slang* (*disparaging and offensive*). a lesbian. Also, **lez′zie.** [by shortening and resp.]

leze′ maj′esty (lēz), *Law.* See **lese majesty** (def. 1).

Lez•ghi•an (lez′gē ən), *n.* **1.** a member of a people living mainly in the Dagestan ASSR in the Soviet Union. **2.** a group of Caucasian languages spoken by several peoples, including the Lezghians, in the Dagestan ASSR and adjacent areas in the Soviet Union. Also, **Lesghian, Lez•gin** (lez′gin).

LF, See **low frequency.**

lf, **1.** *Baseball.* left field. **2.** *Baseball.* left fielder. **3.** *Print.* lightface.

lf., **1.** *Baseball.* left field. **2.** *Baseball.* left fielder.

lfb, *Soccer, Field Hockey.* left fullback.

LG, Low German. Also, **L.G.**

lg., **1.** large. **2.** long.

l.g., *Football.* left guard.

lge., large.

L. Ger., **1.** Low German. **2.** Low Germanic.

LGk, Late Greek. Also, **LGk, L.Gk.**

l-glu•cose (el′gloo′kōs), *n. Chem.* See under **glucose** (def. 1). [L(EVOROTATORY) + GLUCOSE]

lgth., length.

lg. tn., long ton.

LH, *Biochem. Physiol.* luteinizing hormone: a hormone produced by the anterior lobe of the pituitary gland that, in the female, stimulates maturation of the ovarian follicle and formation of the corpus luteum: chemically identical to ICSH of the male.

lh, *Sports.* left halfback.

l.h., **1.** left hand. **2.** lower half. Also, **L.H.**

Lha•sa (lä′sə, -sä, las′ə), *n.* a city in and the capital of Tibet, in the SE part: sacred city of Lamaism. 175,000; ab. 12,000 ft. (3650 m) above sea level. Also, **Lasa, Lassa.**

Lha′sa ap′so (ap′sō), *pl.* **Lhasa ap•sos.** one of a breed of small terriers having a long, heavy coat, raised in Tibet as watchdogs. [1930–35; *apso* < Tibetan, written *ab sog*]

l.h.b., *Sports.* left halfback.

L.H.D., **1.** Doctor of Humane Letters. **2.** Doctor of Humanities. [< NL *Litterārum Hūmāniōrum Doctor*]

L-head engine (el′hed′), an internal-combustion engine having the intake and exhaust valves arranged in a chamber along one side of the pistons.

Lhe•vinne (lā vēn′), *n.* **Jo•sef** (jō′zəf), 1874–1944, Russian pianist.

L'Hos•pi•tal (lō pē tal′; *Eng.* lō′pi tal′), *n.* **Guil•laume Fran•çois An•toine de** (gē yōm′ fräN swa′ äN twan′ də), 1661–1704, French mathematician. Also, **L'Hô•pi•tal′.**

L'Hospital's′ rule′, *Math.* the theorem that for the quotient of two functions satisfying certain conditions on a given closed interval, each having infinite limit or zero as limit at a given point, the limit of the quotient at the given point is equal to the limit of the quotient of the derivatives of each function. [named after G. F. A. L'HOSPITAL]

Lho•tse (lōt sä′, hlōt-), *n.* a mountain peak in the Himalayas, on the Nepal-Tibet border: fourth highest peak in the world. 27,890 ft. (8501 m).

LHRH, *Physiol.* luteinizing hormone releasing hormone: a hormone, produced in the hypothalamus, that regulates the release of luteinizing hormone by the pituitary gland.

li[1] (lē), *n. Music.* the solmization syllable used for the semitone between the sixth and seventh degrees of a scale. [alter. of LA[1]]

li[2] (lē), *n., pl.* **li.** a Chinese unit of distance, equivalent to about one-third of a mile (0.5 km). [1580–90; < Chin *lǐ*]

li[3] (lē), *n.* (in Chinese ethical philosophy) the etiquette traditionally prescribed for individuals or groups of people in a given situation. [1910–15; < Chin *lǐ*]

Li (lē), *n.* **1.** a member of an aboriginal people of the island of Hainan in Southeastern China. **2.** the Kadai language of the Li.

Li, *Symbol, Chem.* lithium.

li, link; links.

L.I., **1.** *Brit.* light infantry. **2.** Long Island.

Li•a (lī′ə), *n. Douay Bible.* Leah (def. 1).

li•a•bil•i•ty (lī′ə bil′i tē), *n., pl.* **-ties.** **1.** **liabilities, a.** moneys owed; debts or pecuniary obligations (opposed to *assets*). **b.** *Accounting.* liabilities as detailed on a balance sheet, esp. in relation to assets and capital. **2.** something disadvantageous: *His lack of education is his biggest liability.* **3.** Also, **li′a•ble•ness.** the state or quality of being liable: *liability to disease.* [1785–95; LI(ABLE) + -ABILITY]

liabil′ity insur′ance, insurance covering the insured against losses arising from injury or damage to another person or property.

liabil′ity lim′it, the highest amount that a liability insurer will pay on a single claim.

li•a•ble (lī′ə bəl), *adj.* **1.** legally responsible: *You are liable for the damage caused by your action.* **2.** subject or susceptible: *to be liable to heart disease.* **3.** likely or apt: *He's liable to get angry.* [1535–45; < AF *li(er)* to bind (< L *ligāre*) + -ABLE]
—**Syn.** **1.** obliged, accountable.
—**Usage.** LIABLE is often interchangeable with LIKELY in constructions with a following infinitive where the sense is that of probability: *The Sox are liable* (or *likely*) *to sweep the Series.* Some usage guides, however, say that LIABLE can be used only in contexts in which the outcome is undesirable: *The picnic is liable to be spoiled by rain.* This use occurs often in formal writing but not to the exclusion of use in contexts in which the outcome is desirable: *The drop in unemployment is liable to stimulate the economy.* APT may also be used in place of LIABLE or LIKELY in all the foregoing examples. See also **apt, likely.**

li•aise (lē āz′), *v.i.,* **-aised, -ais•ing.** to form a liaison. [1925–30; back formation from LIAISON]

li•ai•son (lē′ā zôN′, lē′ə zon′, -zən *or, often,* lā′-; lē ā′-zən, -zon; *Fr.* lye zôN′), *n., pl.* **-sons** (-zôNz′, -zonz′, -zənz, -zonz; *Fr.* -zôN′). **1.** the contact or connection maintained by communications between units of the armed forces or of any other organization in order to ensure concerted action, cooperation, etc. **2.** a person who initiates and maintains such a contact or connection. **3.** an illicit sexual relationship. **4.** *Cookery.* the process of thickening sauces, soups, etc., as by the addition of eggs, cream, butter, or flour. **5.** *Phonet.* a speech-sound redistribution, occurring esp. in French, in which an otherwise silent final consonant is articulated as the initial sound of a following syllable that begins with a vowel or with a silent *h,* as the *z-* and *n-*sounds in *Je suis un homme* (zhə swē zœ nôm′). [1640–50; < F, OF < L *ligātiōn-* (s. of *ligātiō*) a binding. See LIGATION]

Lia•kou•ra (*Gk.* lyä′koo rä), *n.* modern name of **Parnassus** (def. 1).

li•a•na (lē ä′nə, -an′ə), *n.* any of various usually woody vines that may climb as high as the tree canopy in a tropical forest. Also, **li•ane** (lē än′). [1790–1800; earlier *liannes* (pl.), appar. misspelling of F *lianes,* pl. of *liane,* deriv. of *lier* to bind; sp. with *-a* is Latinized or pseudo-Sp] —**li•a′noid,** *adj.*

liang (lyäng), *n., pl.* **liang, liangs.** a Chinese unit of weight, equal to $^1/_{16}$ catty, and equivalent to about $1^1/_3$ ounce (37 grams). Also called **tael, haikwan tael.** [1820–30; < Chin *liǎng*]

Liang (lyäng), *n. Wade-Giles, Pinyin.* one of two dynasties that ruled in China, A.D. 502–57, 907–23.

Liang Ch'i-ch'ao (lyäng′ chē′chou′), 1873–1929, Chinese scholar, journalist, and reformer. Also, *Pinyin,* **Liang Qi-chao** (lyäng′ chē′chou′).

Lian•yun•gang (lyän′yœn′gäng′), *n. Pinyin.* a city in NE Jiangsu province, in E China. 207,600. Also, **Lienyünkang.** Formerly, **Xinhailian.**

Liao (lyou), *Wade-Giles, Pinyin.* **1.** a dynasty that ruled in China A.D. 907–1125. **2.** a river in NE China, flowing through S Manchuria into the Gulf of Liaotung. 700 mi. (1125 km) long.

Liao•dong (lyou′dông′), *n. Pinyin.* **1.** a peninsula in NE China, extending S into the Yellow Sea. **2.** **Gulf of,** a gulf W of this peninsula. Also, *Wade-Giles,* **Liao′tung′.**

Liao•ning (lyou′ning′), *n. Pinyin, Wade-Giles.* a province in NE China. 29,500,000; 58,301 sq. mi. (151,000 sq. km). *Cap.:* Shenyang. Formerly, **Fengtien.**

Liao•yang (lyou′yäng′), *n. Pinyin, Wade-Giles.* a city in central Liaoning province, in NE China. 250,000.

Liao•yuan (lyou′ywän′), *n. Pinyin.* a city in SE Jilin province, in NE China. 250,000. Also, *Wade-Giles,* **Liao′yüan′.**

li•ar (lī′ər), *n.* a person who tells lies. [bef. 950; ME *lier,* OE *lēogere.* See LIE[1], -AR[1]]
—**Syn.** falsifier, perjurer, prevaricator.

li•ard (lē är′; *Fr.* lē AR′), *n., pl.* **li•ards** (lē ärz′; *Fr.* lē AR′). a former silver coin of France, the fourth part of a sol, issued from the 15th century to 1793 and made from copper after 1650. [1535–45; named after G. *Liard,* 15th-century French minter]

Li•ard (lē′ärd, lē ärd′, -är′), *n.* a river in W Canada, flowing from S Yukon through N British Columbia and the Northwest Territories into the Mackenzie River. 550 mi. (885 km) long.

li′ar par′adox, a logical paradox that results from consideration of statements of the form "This statement is false." If the statement is true, then it is false, whereas if it is false, then it is true. [1935–40]

li•a•tris (lī a′tris, lī′ə-), *n.* any of various composite plants of the genus *Liatris,* native to North America, having long spikes of purplish flowers. [< NL (1791), of unexplained orig.]

lib (lib), *n. Informal.* **1.** liberation (def. 2): *women's lib; gay lib.* **2.** a libber. [1965–70; by shortening]

Lib., Liberal.

lib., **1.** book. [< L *liber*] **2.** librarian. **3.** library.

li•ba•tion (lī bā′shən), *n.* **1.** a pouring out of wine or other liquid in honor of a deity. **2.** the liquid poured out. **3.** *Often Facetious.* **a.** an intoxicating beverage, as wine, esp. when drunk in ceremonial or celebrative situations. **b.** an act or instance of drinking such a beverage. [1350–1400; ME *libacio(u)n* < L *lībātiōn-* (s. of *lībātiō*) a drink offering, equiv. to *lībāt(us)* (ptp. of *lībāre* to pour; c. Gk *leíbein*) + *-iōn-* -ION] —**li•ba′tion•al, li•ba′tion•ar′y,** *adj.*

Li•ba•tion-bear•ers, The (lī bā′shən bâr′ərz), Choëphori.

Li•bau (lē′bou), *n.* German name of **Liepāja.**

Li•ba•va (lyi bä′və), *n.* Russian name of **Liepāja.**

lib•ber (lib′ər), *n. Informal.* an advocate, follower, or member of a social-reform liberation movement: *a women's libber; a gay libber.* [1970–75, *Amer.;* LIB(ERATION) + -ER[1]]

Lib•by (lib′ē), *n.* **1.** **Willard Frank,** 1908–80, U.S. chemist: Nobel prize 1960. **2.** a female given name, form of **Elizabeth.**

li•bel (lī′bəl), *n., v.,* **-beled, -bel•ing** or (*esp. Brit.*) **-belled, -bel•ling.** —*n.* **1.** *Law.* **a.** defamation by written or printed words, pictures, or in any form other than by spoken words or gestures. **b.** the act or crime of publishing it. **c.** a formal written declaration or statement, as one containing the allegations of a plaintiff or the grounds of a charge. **2.** anything that is defamatory or that maliciously or damagingly misrepresents. —*v.t.* **3.** to publish a libel against. **4.** to misrepresent damagingly. **5.** to institute suit against by a libel, as in an admiralty court. [1250–1300; ME: little book, formal document, esp. plaintiff's statement < L *libellus,* dim. of *liber* book; for formation, see CASTELLUM]

li·bel·ant (lī′bə lənt), *n. Law.* a person who libels, or institutes suit. Also, *esp. Brit.,* **li′bel·lant.** [1720–30; LIBEL + -ANT]

li·bel·ee (lī′bə lē′), *n. Law.* a person against whom a libel has been filed in a court; the respondent. Also, *esp. Brit.,* **li′bel·lee′.** [1855–60; LIBEL + -EE]

li·bel·er (lī′bə lər), *n.* a person who libels; a person who publishes a libel assailing another. Also, *esp. Brit.,* **li′bel·ler.** [1580–90; LIBEL + -ER[1]]

li·bel·ous (lī′bə ləs), *adj.* containing, constituting, or involving a libel; maliciously defamatory. Also, *esp. Brit.,* **li′bel·lous.** [1610–20; LIBEL + -OUS] **—li′bel·ous·ly;** *esp. Brit.,* **li′bel·lous·ly,** *adv.*

li·ber[1] (lī′bər), *n. Bot.* phloem. [1745–55; < L: bark; akin to LEAF]

li·ber[2] (lī′bər; *Lat.* li′ber), *n., pl.* **li·bri** (lī′brī, -brē; *Lat.* li′brē), **li·bers.** a book of public records, as deeds or birth certificates. [< L: book, orig. bark; see LIBER[1]]

Li·ber (lī′bər), *n.* an ancient Italian god of wine and vineyards, in later times identified with Bacchus.

Lib·er·a (lib′ər ə), *n.* an ancient Italian goddess of wine, vineyards, and fertility and the wife of Liber, in later times identified with Persephone.

lib·er·al (lib′ər əl, lib′rəl), *adj.* **1.** favorable to progress or reform, as in political or religious affairs. **2.** (*often cap.*) noting or pertaining to a political party advocating measures of progressive political reform. **3.** of, pertaining to, based on, or advocating liberalism. **4.** favorable to or in accord with concepts of maximum individual freedom possible, esp. as guaranteed by law and secured by governmental protection of civil liberties. **5.** favoring or permitting freedom of action, esp. with respect to matters of personal belief or expression: *a liberal policy toward dissident artists and writers.* **6.** of or pertaining to representational forms of government rather than aristocracies and monarchies. **7.** free from prejudice or bigotry; tolerant: *a liberal attitude toward foreigners.* **8.** open-minded or tolerant, esp. free of or not bound by traditional or conventional ideas, values, etc. **9.** characterized by generosity and willingness to give in large amounts: *a liberal donor.* **10.** given freely or abundantly; generous: *a liberal donation.* **11.** not strict or rigorous; free; not literal: *a liberal interpretation of a rule.* **12.** of, pertaining to, or based on the liberal arts. **13.** of, pertaining to, or befitting a freeman. —*n.* **14.** a person of liberal principles or views, esp. in politics or religion. **15.** (*often cap.*) a member of a liberal party in politics, esp. of the Liberal party in Great Britain. [1325–75; ME < L *līberālis* of freedom, befitting the free, equiv. to *līber* free + *-ālis* -AL[1]] **—lib′er·al·ly,** *adv.* **—lib′er·al·ness,** *n.*
—Syn. 1. progressive. **7.** broad-minded, unprejudiced. **9.** beneficent, charitable, openhanded, munificent, unstinting, lavish. See **generous. 10.** See **ample.**
—Ant. 1. reactionary. **8.** intolerant. **9, 10.** niggardly.

Lib·er·al (lib′ər əl, lib′rəl), *n.* a city in SW Kansas. 14,911.

lib′eral arts′, 1. the academic course of instruction at a college intended to provide general knowledge and comprising the arts, humanities, natural sciences, and social sciences, as opposed to professional or technical subjects. **2.** (during the Middle Ages) studies comprising the quadrivium and trivium, including arithmetic, geometry, astronomy, music, grammar, rhetoric, and logic. [1745–55; trans. of L *artēs līberālēs* works befitting a free man]

lib′eral educa′tion, 1. an education based primarily on the liberal arts, emphasizing the development of intellectual abilities as opposed to the acquisition of professional skills. **2.** wide experience and education: *Foreign travel gave him a liberal education.*

Li·ber·a·li·a (lib′ə rā′lē ə, -rāl′yə), *n.* (*sometimes used with a plural v.*) an ancient Roman festival held annually in honor of Liber and Libera.

lib·er·al·ism (lib′ər ə liz′əm, lib′rə-), *n.* **1.** the quality or state of being liberal, as in behavior or attitude. **2.** a political or social philosophy advocating the freedom of the individual, parliamentary systems of government, nonviolent modification of political, social, or economic institutions to assure unrestricted development in all spheres of human endeavor, and governmental guarantees of individual rights and civil liberties. **3.** (*sometimes cap.*) the principles and practices of a liberal party in politics. **4.** a movement in modern Protestantism that emphasizes freedom from tradition and authority, the adjustment of religious beliefs to scientific conceptions, and the development of spiritual capacities. [1810–20; LIBERAL + -ISM] **—lib′er·al·ist,** *n., adj.* **—lib′er·al·is′tic,** *adj.*

lib·er·al·i·ty (lib′ə ral′i tē), *n., pl.* **-ties. 1.** the quality or condition of being liberal in giving; generosity; bounty. **2.** a liberal gift. **3.** breadth of mind. **4.** broadness or fullness, as of proportions or physical attributes. **5.** liberalism. [1300–50; ME *liberalite* < L *līberālitās.* See LIBERAL, -ITY]

lib·er·al·ize (lib′ər ə līz′, lib′rə-), *v.t., v.i.,* **-ized, -iz·ing.** to make or become liberal. Also, *esp. Brit.,* **lib′er·al·ise′.** [1765–75; LIBERAL + -IZE] **—lib′er·al·i·za′tion,** *n.* **—lib′er·al·iz′er,** *n.*

Lib′eral Ju′daism. See **Reform Judaism.** [1895–1900]

Lib′eral par′ty, a political party in Great Britain, formed about 1830 as a fusion of Whigs and Radicals and constituting one of the dominant British parties in the 19th and early part of the 20th centuries.

lib·er·ate (lib′ə rāt′), *v.t.,* **-at·ed, -at·ing. 1.** to set free, as from imprisonment or bondage. **2.** to free (a nation or area) from control by a foreign or oppressive government. **3.** to free (a group or individual) from social or economic constraints or discrimination, esp. arising from traditional role expectations or bias. **4.** to disengage; set free from combination, as a gas. **5.** *Slang.* to steal or take over illegally: *The soldiers liberated a consignment of cigarettes.* [1615–25; < L *līberātus* (ptp. of *līberāre* to free), equiv. to *līberā-* v. s. + *-tus* ptp. suffix. See LIBERAL, -ATE[1]] **—lib′er·a′tive, lib·er·a·to·ry** (lib′ər ə tôr′ē, -tōr′ē), *adj.* **—lib′er·a′tor,** *n.*
—Syn. 1. deliver, unfetter, disenthrall, loose. See **release. —Ant. 1.** imprison; enthrall.

lib·er·a·tion (lib′ə rā′shən), *n.* **1.** the act of liberating or the state of being liberated. **2.** the act or fact of gaining equal rights or full social or economic opportunities for a particular group. [1400–50; late ME < L *līberātiōn-* (s. of *līberātiō*), equiv. to *līberāt(us)* (see LIBERATE) + *-iōn-* -ION] **—lib′er·a′tion·ist,** *n.*

libera′tion theol′ogy, a 20th-century Christian theology, emphasizing the Biblical and doctrinal theme of liberation from oppression, whether racial, sexual, economic, or political. [1970–75]

Lib·er·a·tor (lib′ə rā′tər), *n.* a four-engined heavy bomber widely used over Europe and the Mediterranean by the U.S. Army Air Force in World War II. *Symbol:* B-24 [< L *līberātor,* equiv. to *līberā(re)* to LIBERATE + *-tor* -TOR]

Li·be·rec (li′be rets), *n.* a city in the NW Czech Republic. 104,000. German, **Reichenberg.**

Li·be·ri·a (lī bēr′ē ə), *n.* a republic in W Africa: founded by freed American slaves 1822. 1,554,000; ab. 43,000 sq. mi. (111,000 sq. km). *Cap.:* Monrovia. **—Li·be′ri·an,** *adj., n.*

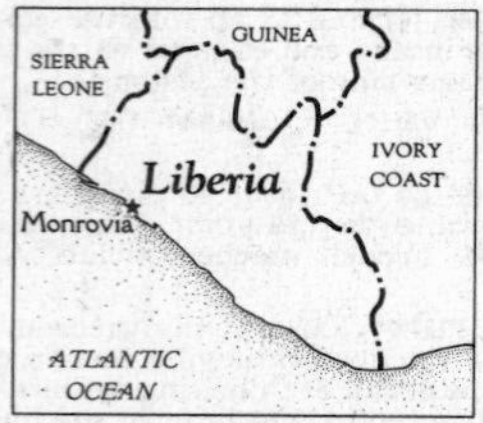

Li·be·ri·us (lī bēr′ē əs), *n.* died A.D. 366, pope 352–366.

lib·er·tar·i·an (lib′ər târ′ē ən), *n.* **1.** a person who advocates liberty, esp. with regard to thought or conduct. **2.** a person who maintains the doctrine of free will (distinguished from *necessitarian*). —*adj.* **3.** advocating liberty or conforming to principles of liberty. **4.** maintaining the doctrine of free will. [1780–90; LIBERT(Y) + -ARIAN] **—lib′er·tar′i·an·ism,** *n.*

Li·ber·tas (li bûr′təs), *n.* the ancient Roman personification of liberty.

li·ber·té, é·ga·li·té, fra·ter·ni·té (lē ber tā′, ā ga lē tā′, fra ter nē tā′), *French.* Liberty, Equality, Fraternity: motto of the French Revolution.

li·ber·ti·cide (li bûr′tə sīd′), *n.* **1.** destruction of liberty. **2.** a person who destroys liberty. [1785–95; LIBERTY + -CIDE] **—li·ber′ti·cid′al,** *adj.*

lib·er·tine (lib′ər tēn′, -tin), *n.* **1.** a person who is morally or sexually unrestrained, esp. a dissolute man; a profligate; rake. **2.** a freethinker in religious matters. **3.** a person freed from slavery in ancient Rome. —*adj.* **4.** free of moral, esp. sexual, restraint; dissolute; licentious. **5.** freethinking in religious matters. **6.** *Archaic.* unrestrained; uncontrolled. [1350–1400; ME *libertyn* < L *lībertīnus* of a freedman (adj.), freedman (n.), equiv. to *lībert(us)* freedman (appar. by reanalysis of *liber-tās* LIBERTY as *libert-ās*) + *-īnus* -INE[1]]
—Syn. 1. roué, debauchee, lecher, sensualist. **4.** amoral, sensual, lascivious, lewd. **—Ant. 1.** prude.

lib·er·tin·ism (lib′ər tē niz′əm, -ti-), *n.* libertine practices or habits of life; disregard of authority or convention in sexual or religious matters. Also, **lib′er·tin′age.** [1605–15; LIBERTINE + -ISM]

lib·er·ty (lib′ər tē), *n., pl.* **-ties. 1.** freedom from arbitrary or despotic government or control. **2.** freedom from external or foreign rule; independence. **3.** freedom from control, interference, obligation, restriction, hampering conditions, etc.; power or right of doing, thinking, speaking, etc., according to choice. **4.** freedom from captivity, confinement, or physical restraint: *The prisoner soon regained his liberty.* **5.** permission granted to a sailor, esp. in the navy, to go ashore. **6.** freedom or right to frequent or use a place: *The visitors were given the liberty of the city.* **7.** unwarranted or impertinent freedom in action or speech, or a form or instance of it: *to take liberties.* **8.** a female figure personifying freedom from despotism. **9. at liberty, a.** free from captivity or restraint. **b.** unemployed; out of work. **c.** free to do or be as specified: *You are at liberty to leave at any time during the meeting.* [1325–75; ME *liberte* < MF < L *lībertās,* equiv. to *līber* free + *-tās* -TY[2]]
—Syn. 4. liberation. See **freedom. 6.** franchise, permission, license, privilege, immunity.

Lib·er·ty (lib′ər tē), *n.* a town in W Missouri. 16,251.

Lib′erty Bell′, the bell of Independence Hall in Philadelphia, rung on July 8, 1776, to announce the adoption of the Declaration of Independence; since then a national symbol of liberty: moved to a special exhibition pavilion behind Independence Hall on January 1, 1976.

Lib′erty bond′, a single Liberty loan bond. [1915–20]

lib′erty cap′, a soft, conical cap given to a freed slave in ancient Rome at manumission of his servitude, used as a symbol of liberty, esp. since the 18th century. Cf. **Phrygian cap.** [1795–1805]

Lib′erty Is′land, a small island in upper New York Bay: site of the Statue of Liberty. Formerly, **Bedloe's Island.**

Lib′erty loan′, any of the five bond issues of the U.S. government floated in World War I.

lib′erty of speech′. See **freedom of speech.**

lib′erty of the press′. See **freedom of the press.** [1760–70]

Lib′erty par′ty, *U.S. Hist.* the first antislavery political party, organized in 1839 and merged with the Free Soil party in 1848.

lib′erty pole′, 1. Also called **lib′erty tree′.** *Amer. Hist.* a pole or tree, often with a liberty cap or a banner at the top, usually located on a village green or in a market square, used by the Sons of Liberty in many colonial towns as a symbol of protest against British rule and around which anti-British rallies were held. **2.** a tall flagpole, traditionally with a liberty cap at the top, serving as a symbol of liberty. [1760–70]

Lib′erty ship′, a slow cargo ship built in large numbers for the U.S. merchant marine during World War II and having a capacity of about 11,000 deadweight tons.

Lib·er·ty·ville (lib′ər tē vil′), *n.* a town in NE Illinois. 16,520.

li′be·rum ve′to (lib′ər əm, lē′bər-), a veto exercised by a single member of a legislative body whose rules require unanimity. [1785–95; < L *līberum,* neut. of *līber* free]

Li·bia (*It.* lē′byä), *n.* Libya.

li·bid·i·nous (li bid′n əs), *adj.* **1.** full of sexual lust; lustful; lewd; lascivious. **2.** of, pertaining to, or characteristic of the libido. [1400–50; late ME *lybydynous* < L *libīdinōsus* willful, lustful, equiv. to *libīdin-* (s. of *libīdō*) LIBIDO + *-ōsus* -OUS] **—li·bid′i·nous·ly,** *adv.* **—li·bid′i·nous·ness,** *n.*

li·bi·do (li bē′dō), *n., pl.* **-dos. 1.** *Psychoanal.* all of the instinctual energies and desires that are derived from the id. **2.** sexual instinct or sexual drive. [1890–95; < L *libīdō* desire, willfulness, lust, akin to *libēre* to be pleasing] **—li·bid·i·nal** (li bid′n l), *adj.* **—li·bid′i·nal·ly,** *adv.*

Li Bo (lē′ bô′), *Pinyin.* See **Li Po.**

li·bra[1] (lī′brə, lē′-), *n., pl.* **-brae** (-brē, -brī). the ancient Roman pound (containing 5053 grains or 327.4 grams). [1350–1400; ME < L *lībra*]

li·bra[2] (lē′vrä), *n., pl.* **-bras** (-vräs). sol[3] (def. 2). [< Sp < L *lībra* LIBRA[1]]

Li·bra (lē′brə, lī′-), *n., gen.* **-brae** (-brī, -brē) for 1. **1.** *Astron.* the Balance, a zodiacal constellation between Virgo and Serpens. **2.** *Astrol.* **a.** the seventh sign of the zodiac: the cardinal air sign. See illus. under **zodiac. b.** Also, **Li′bran.** a person born under this sign, usually between September 23rd and October 22nd. [1350–1400; ME < L *lībra* lit., pair of scales, LIBRA[1]]

li·brar·i·an (lī brâr′ē ən), *n.* **1.** a person trained in library science and engaged in library service. **2.** a person in charge of a library, esp. the chief administrative officer of a library. **3.** a person who is in charge of any specialized body of literature, as a collection of musical scores. [1660–70; LIBR(ARY) + -ARIAN]

li·brar·i·an·ship (lī brâr′ē ən ship′), *n.* **1.** a profession concerned with acquiring and organizing collections of books and related materials in libraries and servicing readers and others with these resources. **2.** the position or duties of a librarian. [1870–75; LIBRARIAN + -SHIP]

li·brar·y (lī′brer′ē, -brə rē, -brē), *n., pl.* **-brar·ies. 1.** a place set apart to contain books, periodicals, and other material for reading, viewing, listening, study, or reference, as a room, set of rooms, or building where books may be read or borrowed. **2.** a public body organizing and maintaining such an establishment. **3.** a collection of manuscripts, publications, and other materials for reading, viewing, listening, study, or reference. **4.** a collection of any materials for study and enjoyment, as films, musical recordings, or maps. **5.** a commercial establishment lending books for a fixed charge; a lending library. **6.** a series of books of similar character or alike in size, binding, etc., issued by a single publishing house. **7.** *Biol.* a collection of standard materials or formulations by which specimens are identified. **8.** canon[1] (def. 9). **9.** *Computers.* a collection of software or data usually reflecting a specific theme or application. [1300–50; ME *libraire* < MF *librairie* < ML *librāria,* n. use of fem. of L *librārius* (adj.) of books, equiv. to *lib(e)r* book + *-ārius* -ARY]
—Pronunciation. LIBRARY, with one *r*-sound following close upon another, is particularly vulnerable to the process of dissimilation—the tendency for neighboring like sounds to become unlike, or for one of them to disappear altogether. The pronunciation (lī′brer ē), therefore, while still the most common, is frequently reduced by educated speakers, both in the U.S. and in England, to the dissimilated (lī′bə rē) or (lī′brē). A third dissimilated form (lī′ber ē) is more likely to be heard from less educated or very young speakers, and is often criticized. See **colonel, February, governor.**

li′brary bind′ing, 1. a tough, durable cloth binding for books. Cf. **edition binding. 2.** the production of books that are bound with library binding. [1900–05]

li′brary card′, a card issued by a library to individuals or organizations entitling them or their representatives to borrow materials. Also called **borrower's card.** [1965–70]

li′brary edi′tion, 1. an edition of a book prepared for library use, esp. with a library binding. **2.** a set of books with common subject matter or authorship and uniform physical characteristics. [1865–70]

Li′brary of Con′gress, one of the major library collections in the world, located in Washington, D.C., and functioning in some ways as the national library of the

U.S. although not officially designated as such: established by Congress in 1800 for service to its members, but now also serving government agencies, other libraries, and the public. Cf. **national library.**

Li′brary of Con′gress classifica′tion, *Library Science.* a system for classifying books and other materials, using for its notation both letters and numerals to allow for expansion: originally developed at the Library of Congress for classifying its books and subsequently adopted by other libraries.

li′brary paste′, a white, smooth paste for paper and lightweight cardboard. [1950–55]

li′brary sci′ence, the study of the organization and administration of a library and of its technical, informational, and reference services. [1900–05]

li′brary steps′, a folding stepladder, esp. one folding into another piece of furniture, as a table or chair. [1755–65]

li′brary ta′ble, a large pedestal writing table or desk. [1735–45]

li•brate (lī′brāt), *v.i.,* **-brat•ed, -brat•ing. 1.** to oscillate or move from side to side or between two points. **2.** to remain poised or balanced. [1615–25; < L *librātus* ptp. of *librāre.* to balance, make level, bring to equilibrium. See LIBRA, -ATE[1]]

li•bra•tion (lī brā′shən), *n. Astron.* a real or apparent oscillatory motion, esp. of the moon. [1595–1605; < L *lībrātiōn-* (s. of *lībrātiō*) a balancing. See LIBRATE, -ION] **—li•bra′tion•al,** *adj.*

li•bra•to•ry (lī′brə tôr′ē, -tōr′ē), *adj.* oscillatory. [1660–70; LIBRATE + -ORY[1]]

li•bret•tist (li bret′ist), *n.* the writer of a libretto. [1860–65; < It *librettista.* See LIBRETTO, -IST]

li•bret•to (li bret′ō), *n., pl.* **-bret•tos, -bret•ti** (-bret′ē). **1.** the text or words of an opera or similar extended musical composition. **2.** a book or booklet containing such a text. [1735–45; < It, dim of *libro* book < L *liber;* see -ET]

Li•bre•ville (*Fr.* lē brə vēl′), *n.* a port in and the capital of Gabon, in the W part, on the Gulf of Guinea. 60,000.

li•bri (lī′brī, -brē; *Lat.* li′brē), *n.* pl. of **liber[2].**

Lib•ri•um (lib′rē əm), *Pharm., Trademark.* a brand of chlordiazepoxide.

Lib•y•a (lib′ē ə), *n.* **1.** *Anc. Geog.* the part of N Africa W of Egypt. **2.** Italian, **Libia.** a republic in N Africa between Tunisia and Egypt: formerly a monarchy 1951–69. 2,800,000; 679,400 sq. mi. (1,759,646 sq. km). *Cap.:* Tripoli.

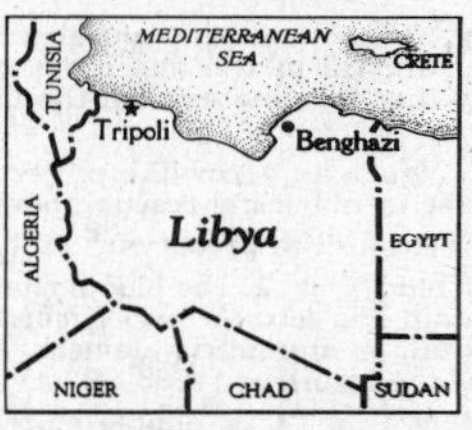

Lib•y•an (lib′ē ən), *adj.* **1.** of or pertaining to Libya or its inhabitants. —*n.* **2.** a native or inhabitant of Libya. **3.** a Berber language of ancient Libya. [1535–45; LIBY(A) + -AN]

Lib′yan Des′ert, a desert in N Africa, in E Libya, W Egypt, and NW Sudan, W of the Nile: part of the Sahara. ab. 650,000 sq. mi. (1,683,500 sq. km).

lice (līs), *n.* pl. of **louse.**

li•cence (lī′səns), *n., v.t.* **-cenced, -cenc•ing.** license.

li•cense (lī′səns), *n., v.,* **-censed, -cens•ing.** —*n.* **1.** formal permission from a governmental or other constituted authority to do something, as to carry on some business or profession. **2.** a certificate, tag, plate, etc., giving proof of such permission; official permit: *a driver's license.* **3.** permission to do or not to do something. **4.** intentional deviation from rule, convention, or fact, as for the sake of literary or artistic effect: *poetic license.* **5.** exceptional freedom allowed in a special situation. **6.** excessive or undue freedom or liberty. **7.** licentiousness. **8.** the legal right to use a patent owned by another. —*v.t.* **9.** to grant authoritative permission or license to. [1325–75; ME *licence* < MF < ML *licentia* authorization, L: freedom, equiv. to *licent-* (s. of *licēns,* prp. of *licēre* to be allowed) + *-ia* -IA; see -ENCE] **—li′cens•a•ble,** *adj.* **—li′cense•less,** *adj.* **—li′cens•er;** *esp. Law,* **li′cen•sor,** *n.*

li′censed prac′tical nurse′, a person who has graduated from an accredited school of nursing and has become licensed to provide basic nursing care under the supervision of a physician or registered nurse. *Abbr.:* LPN [1950–55]

li′censed voca′tional nurse′, a person with specified training who has become licensed to provide vocational assistance to patients. *Abbr.:* LVN

li•cen•see (lī′sən sē′), *n.* a person, company, etc., to whom a license is granted or issued. Also, **li′cen•cee′.** [1865–70; LICENSE + -EE]

li′cense plate′, a plate or tag, usually of metal, bearing evidence of official registration and permission, as for the use of a motor vehicle. [1900–05]

li•cen•sure (lī′sən shər, -shŏŏr′), *n.* the granting of licenses, esp. to engage in professional practice. [1840–50; LICENSE + -URE]

li•cen•ti•ate (lī sen′shē it, -āt′), *n.* **1.** a person who has received a license, as from a university, to practice an art or profession. **2.** the holder of a university degree intermediate between that of bachelor and that of doctor, now confined chiefly to certain continental European universities. [1350–1400; < ML *licentiātus,* n. use of ptp. of *licentiāre* to authorize. See LICENSE, -ATE[1]] **—li•cen′ti•ate•ship′,** *n.* **—li•cen′ti•a′tion,** *n.*

li•cen•tious (lī sen′shəs), *adj.* **1.** sexually unrestrained; lascivious; libertine; lewd. **2.** unrestrained by law or general morality; lawless; immoral. **3.** going beyond customary or proper bounds or limits; disregarding rules. [1525–35; < L *licentiōsus* unrestrained. See LICENSE, -OUS] **—li•cen′tious•ly,** *adv.* **—li•cen′tious•ness,** *n.*
—Syn. 2. abandoned, profligate. **—Ant. 2.** lawful.

li•cet (lē′ket; *Eng.* lī′set), *Latin.* it is allowed.

lich (lich), *n. Brit. Obs.* **1.** the body; the trunk. **2.** a dead body; corpse. Also, **lych.** [bef. 900; ME *liche* body (alive or dead), OE *līc;* c. D *lijk,* G *Leiche,* ON *līk,* Goth *leik.* See LIKE[1]]

li•chee (lē′chē), *n.* litchi.

li•chen (lī′kən), *n.* **1.** any complex organism of the group Lichenes, composed of a fungus in symbiotic union with an alga and having a greenish, gray, yellow, brown, or blackish thallus that grows in leaflike, crustlike, or branching forms on rocks, trees, etc. **2.** *Pathol.* any of various eruptive skin diseases. —*v.t.* **3.** to cover with or as if with lichens. [1595–1605; < L *lichēn* < Gk *leichḗn*] **—li′chen•i•za′tion,** *n.* **—li′chen•like′,** *adj.*

li•chen′ic ac′id (lī ken′ik), *Chem.* See **fumaric acid.** [1830–40; LICHEN + -IC]

li•chen•i•fi•ca•tion (lī ken′ə fi kā′shən), *n. Med.* **1.** a leathery hardening of the skin, usually caused by chronic irritation. **2.** a patch of skin so hardened. [1890–95; LICHEN + -I- + -FICATION]

li•chen•in (lī′kə nin), *n. Chem.* a white, gelatinous, polysaccharide starch, $(C_6H_{10}O_5)_n$, obtained from various lichens. [1830–40; LICHEN + -IN[2]]

li•chen•ous (lī′kə nəs), *adj.* **1.** of, pertaining to, or resembling a lichen. **2.** covered with lichens. [1815–25; LICHEN + -OUS]

Lich•field (lich′fēld′), *n.* a town in SE Staffordshire, in central England, N of Birmingham: birthplace of Samuel Johnson. 87,700.

lich′ gate′, a roofed gate to a churchyard under which a bier is set down during a burial service to await the coming of the clergyman. Also, **lych gate.** Also called **resurrection gate.** [1475–85]

lich′ stone′, a large stone on which to rest a coffin momentarily at the entrance to a cemetery. [1860–65]

licht (liKHt), *n., adj., v.t., v.i., adv. Scot.* light. **—licht′ly,** *adv.*

Lich•ten•stein (lik′tən stēn′), *n.* **Roy,** born 1923, U.S. painter and sculptor.

lic•it (lis′it), *adj.* legal; lawful; legitimate; permissible. [1475–85; < L *licitus* permitted (ptp. of *licēre*); r. earlier *licite* < MF; see -ITE[2]] **—lic′it•ly,** *adv.*

lick (lik), *v.t.* **1.** to pass the tongue over the surface of, as to moisten, taste, or eat (often fol. by *up, off, from,* etc.): *to lick a postage stamp; to lick an ice-cream cone.* **2.** to make, or cause to become, by stroking with the tongue: *to lick a spoon clean.* **3.** (of waves, flames, etc.) to pass or play lightly over: *The flame licked the dry timber.* **4.** *Informal.* **a.** to hit or beat, esp. as a punishment; thrash; whip. **b.** to overcome or defeat, as in a fight, game, or contest. **c.** to outdo or surpass. —*v.i.* **5.** to move quickly or lightly. **6. lick ass,** *Slang* (*vulgar*). See **kiss** (def. 10). **7. lick into shape,** *Informal.* to bring to completion or perfection through discipline, hard work, etc.: *They needed another rehearsal to lick the production into shape.* **8. lick one's chops.** See **chop[3]** (def. 7). **9. lick one's wounds.** See **wound[1]** (def. 4). **10. lick the dust.** See **dust** (def. 16). **11. lick up,** to lap up; devour greedily. —*n.* **12.** a stroke of the tongue over something. **13.** as much as can be taken up by one stroke of the tongue. **14.** See **salt lick. 15.** *Informal.* **a.** a blow. **b.** a brief, brisk burst of activity or energy. **c.** a quick pace or clip; speed. **d.** a small amount: *I haven't done a lick of work all week.* **16.** Usually, **licks.** a critical or complaining remark. **17.** Usually, **licks.** *Jazz Slang.* a musical phrase, as by a soloist in improvising. **18. last licks,** a final turn or opportunity: *We got in our last licks on the tennis court before the vacation ended.* **19. lick and a promise,** a hasty and perfunctory performance in doing something: *I didn't have time to clean thoroughly, so I gave the room a lick and a promise.* [bef. 1000; ME *licken* (v.), OE *liccian;* c. D *likk,* G *lecken;* akin to Goth *bilaigon,* L *lingere,* Gk *leíchein* to lick (up)] **—lick′er,** *n.*
—Syn. 15a. thwack, thump, rap, slap, cuff, buffet.

lick•er-in (lik′ər in′), *n.* a roller on a carding machine, esp. the roller that opens the stock as it is fed into the card and transfers the fibers to the main cylinder. Also called **taker-in.** [1840–50; *lick in* + -ER[1]]

lick•er•ish (lik′ər ish), *adj. Archaic.* **1.** fond of and eager for choice food. **2.** greedy; longing. **3.** lustful; lecherous. Also, **liquorish.** [1300–50; ME *liker(ous)* pleasing to the taste, lit., to a licker (see LICK, -ER[1]) + -ISH[1]] **—lick′er•ish•ly,** *adv.* **—lick′er•ish•ness,** *n.*

lick•e•ty-split (lik′i tē split′), *adv. Informal.* at great speed; rapidly: *to travel lickety-split.* [1835–45, *Amer.;* perh. dial. *licket* rag (for wiping in haste, with one lick) + -Y[1] + SPLIT, as in *split second*]

lick•ing (lik′ing), *n.* **1.** *Informal.* **a.** a beating or thrashing. **b.** a reversal or disappointment; defeat or setback. **2.** the act of a person or thing that licks. [1350–1400; ME; see LICK, -ING[1]]

Lick′ Observ′atory, the astronomical observatory of the University of California, situated on Mount Hamilton, near San Jose, California, and having a 120-in. (3-m) reflecting telescope and a 36-in. (91-cm) refracting telescope.

lick•spit•tle (lik′spit′l), *n.* a contemptible, fawning person; a servile flatterer or toady. Also, **lick′spit′.** [1620–30; LICK + SPITTLE]

lic•o•rice (lik′ər ish, lik′rish, lik′ə ris), *n.* **1.** a Eurasian plant, *Glycyrrhiza glabra,* of the legume family. **2.** the sweet-tasting, dried root of this plant or an extract made from it, used in medicine, confectionery, etc. **3.** a candy flavored with licorice root. **4.** any of various related or similar plants. Also, **liquorice.** [1175–1225; ME *lycorys* < AF < VL **liquiritia* for L *glycyrrhiza* < Gk *glykýrriza* sweetroot (plant), equiv. to *glyký(s)* sweet + *rhiza* ROOT[1]; see -IA]

lic′orice stick′, *Slang.* a clarinet. [1930–35]

lic•tor (lik′tər), *n.* (in ancient Rome) one of a body of attendants on chief magistrates, who preceded them carrying the fasces and whose duties included executing the sentences of criminals. [1580–90; < L; cf. ME *littoures*] **—lic•to•ri•an** (lik tôr′ē ən, -tōr′-), *adj.*

lid (lid), *n., v.,* **lid•ded, lid•ding.** —*n.* **1.** a removable or hinged cover for closing the opening, usually at the top, of a pot, jar, trunk, etc.; a movable cover. **2.** an eyelid. **3.** a restraint, ceiling, or curb, as on prices or news. **4.** *Slang.* a hat, cap, or other head covering. **5.** (in mosses) **a.** the cover of the capsule; operculum. **b.** the upper section of a pyxidium. **6.** *Slang.* one ounce of marijuana. **7. blow the lid off,** *Informal.* to expose to public view, esp. to reveal something scandalous, illegal, etc. **8. blow** or **flip one's lid,** *Slang.* to lose control, esp. to rage hysterically: *He nearly flipped his lid over the way they damaged his car.* Also, **flip one's wig.** —*v.t.* **9.** to supply or cover with a lid. [bef. 1000; ME; OE *hlid;* c. D, G *lid,* ON *hlith* gate, gateway]

li•dar (lī′där), *n. Electronics, Optics.* a device similar to radar in principle and operation but using infrared laser light instead of radio waves and capable of detecting particles and varying physical conditions in the atmosphere. [presumably LI(GHT[1]) + (RA)DAR]

Lid•del Hart (lid′l härt′), **Sir Basil (Henry),** 1895–1970, English military authority and writer.

li•di•a (lid′ē ə; *Sp.* lē′thyä), *n., pl.* **li•dias** (lid′ē əz; *Sp.* lē′thyäs). (in bullfighting) one section of a corrida, comprising the action that takes place from the entrance of the bull to the time it is killed and dragged from the arena by mules. [1890–95; < Sp: bullfight]

Li•di•ce (lid′yi tse; *Eng.* lē′də chā′, lid′ə sē), *n.* a village in the W Czech Republic: suffered a ruthless reprisal by the Nazis in 1942 for the assassination of a high Nazi official. 509.

lid•less (lid′lis), *adj.* **1.** (of objects) without a lid. **2.** (of eyes) without or as if without lids. **3.** watchful, as with unblinking eyes; vigilant. [1515–25; LID + -LESS]

li•do (lē′dō), *n., pl.* **-dos.** *Brit.* **1.** a fashionable beach resort. **2.** a public open-air swimming pool. [1925–30; after the LIDO]

Li•do (lē′dō; *It.* lē′dô), *n.* a chain of sandy islands in NE Italy, between the Lagoon of Venice and the Adriatic: resort.

li•do•caine (lī′də kān′), *n. Pharm.* a synthetic crystalline powder, $C_{14}H_{22}N_2O$, used as a local anesthetic and also in the management of certain arrhythmias. Also called **lignocaine.** [(ACETANI)LID(E) + -O- + *-caine,* extracted from COCAINE (to designate an anesthetic)]

lie[1] (lī), *n., v.,* **lied, ly•ing.** —*n.* **1.** a false statement made with deliberate intent to deceive; an intentional untruth; a falsehood. **2.** something intended or serving to convey a false impression; imposture: *His flashy car was a lie that deceived no one.* **3.** an inaccurate or false statement. **4.** the charge or accusation of lying: *He flung the lie back at his accusers.* **5. give the lie to, a.** to accuse of lying; contradict. **b.** to prove or imply the falsity of; belie: *His poor work gives the lie to his claims of experience.* —*v.i.* **6.** to speak falsely or utter untruth knowingly, as with intent to deceive. **7.** to express what is false; convey a false impression. —*v.t.* **8.** to bring about or affect by lying (often used reflexively): *to lie oneself out of a difficulty; accustomed to lying his way out of difficulties.* **9. lie in one's throat** or **teeth,** to lie grossly or maliciously: *If she told you exactly the opposite of what she told me, she must be lying in her teeth.* Also, **lie through one's teeth.** [bef. 900; (n.) ME; OE *lyge;* c. G *Lüge,* ON *lygi;* akin to Goth *liugn;* (v.) ME *lien,* OE *lēogan* (intransit.); c. G *lügen,* ON *ljúga,* Goth *liugan*]
—Syn. 1. prevarication, falsification. See **falsehood. 6.** prevaricate, fib. **—Ant. 1.** truth.

lie[2] (lī), *v.,* **lay, lain, ly•ing,** *n.* —*v.i.* **1.** to be in a horizontal, recumbent, or prostrate position, as on a bed or the ground; recline. **2.** (of objects) to rest in a horizontal or flat position: *The book lies on the table.* **3.** to be or remain in a position or state of inactivity, subjection, restraint, concealment, etc.: *to lie in ambush.* **4.** to rest, press, or weigh (usually fol. by *on* or *upon*): *These things lie upon my mind.* **5.** to depend (usually fol. by *on* or *upon*). **6.** to be placed or situated: *land lying along the coast.* **7.** to be stretched out or extended: *the broad plain that lies before us.* **8.** to be in or have a specified direction; extend: *The trail from here lies to the west.* **9.** to be found or located in a particular area or place: *The fault lies here.* **10.** to consist or be grounded (usually fol. by *in*): *The real remedy lies in education.* **11.** to be buried in a particular spot: *Their ancestors lie in the family plot.* **12.** *Law.* to be sustainable or admissible, as an action or appeal. **13.** *Archaic.* to lodge; stay the night; sojourn. **14. lie by, a.** to pause for rest; stop activities, work, etc., temporarily. **b.** to lie unused: *Ever since the last member of the family died, the old house has lain by.* **15. lie down,** to assume a horizontal or prostrate position, as for the purpose of resting. **16. lie down on the job,** *Informal.* to do less than one could or should do; shirk one's obligations. **17. lie in,** to be confined to bed in childbirth. **18. lie in state.** See **state**

(def. 14). **19. lie low.** See **low**[1] (def. 45). **20. lie over,** to be postponed for attention or action at some future time: *The other business on the agenda will have to lie over until the next meeting.* **21. lie to,** *Naut.* (of a ship) to lie comparatively stationary, usually with the head as near the wind as possible. **22. lie up, a.** to lie at rest; stay in bed. **b.** (of a ship) to dock or remain in dock. **23. lie with, a.** to be the duty or function of: *The decision in this matter lies with him.* **b.** *Archaic.* to have sexual intercourse with. **24. take lying down,** to hear or yield without protest, contradiction, or resistance: *I refuse to take such an insult lying down.* —*n.* **25.** the manner, relative position, or direction in which something lies. **26.** the haunt or covert of an animal. **27.** *Golf.* the position of the ball relative to how easy or how difficult it is to play. [bef. 900; ME *lien, liggen,* OE *licgan;* c. G *liegen,* D *liggen,* ON *liggja,* Goth *ligan;* akin to Gk *léchesthai* to lie down]
—**Syn. 25.** place, location, site. —**Ant. 1, 2.** stand.
—**Usage.** See **lay**[1].

Lie (lē), *n.* **1. Jonas,** 1880–1940, U.S. painter, born in Norway. **2. (Ma·ri·us) So·phus** (mä′rē o͞os sō′fo͞os), 1842–99, Norwegian mathematician. **3. Tryg·ve Halv·dan** (trig′və hälv′dän; *Nor.* tʀʏg′və hälv′dän), 1896–1968, Norwegian statesman: secretary-general of the United Nations 1946–53.

lie-a-bed (lī′ə bed′), *n.* a person who remains in bed until a relatively late hour; late riser. [1755–65]

Lieb·er·mann (*Ger.* lē′bəʀ män′), *n.* **1. Max** (mäks), 1847–1935, German painter and etcher. **2. Rolf** (rolf), born 1910, Swiss composer.

Lieb·frau·milch (lēb′frou milk′, lēp′-; *Ger.* lēp′frou-milkʜ′), *n.* a white wine produced chiefly in the region of Hesse in West Germany. [1825–35; < G, after *Liebfrauenstift* convent of the Virgin, religious establishment in Worms, where the wine was first made; see MILK (G *Milch*)]

Lie·big (lē′biкн), *n.* **Jus·tus** (yo͝os′to͝os), **Baron von** (fən), 1803–73, German chemist.

Lieb·knecht (lēp′knekнt), *n.* **1. Karl** (käʀl), 1871–1919, German socialist leader. **2.** his father, **Wil·helm** (vil′helm), 1826–1900, German journalist and political leader.

lie-by (lī′bī′), *n., pl.* **-bys.** *Brit.* **1.** a paved section alongside a highway for automobiles in need of emergency repairs. **2.** a railroad siding. [1640–50; n. use of v. phrase *lie by*]

Liech·ten·stein (lik′tən stīn′; *Ger.* likн′tən shtīn′), *n.* a small principality in central Europe between Austria and Switzerland: economically linked with Switzerland. 25,000; 65 sq. mi. (168 sq. km). *Cap.:* Vaduz. —**Liech′·ten·stein′er,** *n.*

lied[1] (līd), *v.* pt. and pp. of **lie**[1].

lied[2] (lēd; *Ger.* lēt), *n., pl.* **lied·er** (lē′dər; *Ger.* lē′dəʀ). a typically 19th-century German art song characterized by the setting of a poetic text in either strophic or through-composed style and the treatment of the piano and voice in equal artistic partnership: *Schubert lieder.* [1850–55; < G]

Lie·der·kranz (lē′dər kränts′, -krants′), **1.** *Trademark.* a brand of strong, soft milk cheese with a creamy center, made in small rectangular blocks. —*n.* **2.** a German choral society or singing club, esp. of men. [1855–60, *Amer.*; < G: garland of songs]

lie′ detec′tor, a polygraph used to determine changes in certain body activities, as blood pressure, pulse, breathing, and perspiration, the results of which may be interpreted to indicate the truth or falsity of a person's answers under questioning. [1905–10, *Amer.*]

lie-down (lī′doun′), *n. Chiefly Brit.* a nap. [1830–40; n. use of v. phrase *lie down*]

lief (lēf), *adv.* **1.** gladly; willingly: *I would as lief go south as not.* —*adj. Archaic.* **2.** willing; desirous. **3.** dear; beloved; treasured. [bef. 900; ME *leef,* OE *lēof;* c. D *lief,* G *lieb,* ON *ljufr,* Goth *liufs;* akin to LOVE]
—**lief′ly,** *adv.*

liege (lēj, lēzh), *n.* **1.** a feudal lord entitled to allegiance and service. **2.** a feudal vassal or subject. —*adj.* **3.** owing primary allegiance and service to a feudal lord. **4.** pertaining to the relation between a feudal vassal and lord. **5.** loyal; faithful: *the liege adherents of a cause.* [1250–1300; ME < OF *li(e)ge* << Gmc **lēt-* vassal + L *-icus* -IC; cf. ML *lēti* barbarians allowed to settle on Roman land (< Gmc; perh. akin to LET[1]), *laeticus* for **lēticus,* deriv. of *lēti*]

Li·ège (lē āzh′; *Fr.* lyezh), *n.* **1.** a city in E Belgium, on the Meuse River: one of the first cities attacked in World War I. 139,333. **2.** a province in E Belgium. 1,019,226; 1521 sq. mi. (3940 sq. km). *Cap.:* Liège. Flemish, **Luik.**

liege·man (lēj′mən, lēzh′-), *n., pl.* **-men. 1.** a vassal; subject. **2.** a faithful follower. [1300–50; ME; see LIEGE, MAN[1]]

Lieg·nitz (lēg′nits), *n.* German name of **Legnica.**

Lie′ group′ (lē), *Math.* a topological group that is a manifold. [1935–40; after M. S. LIE]

lie-in[1] (lī′in′), *n.* a protest demonstration in which participants lie down in a public place against regulations and resist being moved. [1960–65; see LIE[2], -IN[3]]

lie-in[2] (lī′in′), *n. Chiefly Brit.* an act or instance of staying in bed longer than usual, esp. in the morning. [1865–70; n. use of v. phrase *lie in*]

lien[1] (lēn, lē′ən), *n. Law.* the legal claim of one person upon the property of another person to secure the payment of a debt or the satisfaction of an obligation. [1525–35; < AF, OF < L *ligāmen* tie, bandage, equiv. to *ligā(re)* to tie + *-men* n. suffix of result] —**lien′a·ble,** *adj.*

li·en[2] (lī′ən, -en), *n. Anat.* the spleen. [1645–55; < L *liēn* SPLEEN] —**li·e·nal** (lī ēn′l, lī′ə nl), *adj.*

li·en·ec·to·my (lī′ə nek′tə mē), *n., pl.* **-mies.** *Surg.* splenectomy. [LIEN[2] + -ECTOMY]

lien·hold·er (lēn′hōl′dər), *n. Law.* a person who has a lien on particular property. [LIEN + HOLDER]

li·en·i·tis (lī′ə nī′tis), *n. Pathol.* inflammation of the spleen; splenitis. [1835–45; LIEN[2] + -ITIS]

li·en·ter·y (lī′ən ter′ē), *n. Pathol.* a form of diarrhea in which the food is discharged undigested or only partly digested. [1540–50; < ML *lienteria* < Gk *leientería,* equiv. to *leî(os)* smooth + *énter(a)* bowels + *-ia* -Y[3]] —**li′en·ter′ic,** *adj.*

Lien·yün·kang (*Chin.* lyun′yʏn′gäng′), *n. Wade-Giles.* Lianyungang.

lie′ of the land′, *Chiefly Brit.* See **lay of the land.**

Lie·pā·ja (lye′pä yä; *Eng.* lē ep′ə yə), *n.* a seaport in W Latvia, on the Baltic. 114,900. Also, **Lie′pa·ja.** German, **Libau.** Russian, **Libava.**

li·er (lī′ər), *n.* a person or thing that lies, as in wait or in ambush. [1575–85; LIE[2] + -ER[1]]

li·erne (lē ûrn′), *n. Archit.* an ornamental vaulting rib other than one springing from a pier or a ridge rib. [1835–45; < F: binding timber, equiv. to *li(er)* to bind (< L *ligāre*) + *-erne* < ?]

Lies·tal (lēs′täl), *n.* a town in and the capital of Basel-Land, in NW Switzerland. 12,200.

Lie·tu·va (lye′to͞o vä), *n.* Lithuanian name of **Lithuania.**

lieu (lo͞o), *n.* **1.** place; stead. **2. in lieu of,** in place of; instead of: *He gave us an IOU in lieu of cash.* [1250–1300; < MF < L *locus* place; r. ME *liue* < OF *liu* < L; see LOCUS]

Lieut., lieutenant.

Lieut. Col., lieutenant colonel.

Lieut. Comdr., lieutenant commander.

lieu·ten·an·cy (lo͞o ten′ən sē), *n., pl.* **-cies. 1.** the office, authority, incumbency, or jurisdiction of a lieutenant. **2.** lieutenants collectively. [1400–50; late ME *lieutenauncie.* See LIEUTENANT, -ANCY]

lieu·ten·ant (lo͞o ten′ənt; *in Brit. use, except in the navy,* lef ten′ənt), *n.* **1.** *Mil.* **a.** See **first lieutenant. b.** See **second lieutenant. 2.** *U.S. Navy.* a commissioned officer ranking between lieutenant junior grade and lieutenant commander. **3.** a person who holds an office, civil or military, in subordination to a superior for whom he or she acts: *If he can't attend, he will send his lieutenant.* [1325–75; ME < MF, n. use of adj. phrase *lieu tenant* place-holding. See LOCUM TENENS, LIEU, TENANT]

lieuten′ant colo′nel, *U.S. Mil.* a commissioned officer ranking next below a colonel and next above a major. [1590–1600]

lieuten′ant comman′der, *U.S. Navy.* a commissioned officer ranking next below a commander and next above a lieutenant. [1830–40, *Amer.*]

lieuten′ant gen′eral, *U.S. Mil.* a commissioned officer ranking next below a general and next above a major general. [1480–90]

lieuten′ant gov′ernor, 1. a state officer next in rank to a governor, who takes the governor's place in case of the latter's absence, disability, or death. **2.** *Brit.* a deputy governor. **3.** the executive officer of a Canadian province appointed by the governor general. [1585–95] —**lieuten′ant gov′ernorship.**

lieuten′ant jun′ior grade′, *U.S. Navy.* a commissioned officer ranking above an ensign and below a lieutenant. [1905–10]

lieve (lēv), *adv. Dial.* lief.

Li·far (lyi fäʀ′), *n.* **Ser·ge** (syiʀ gyä′; *Fr.* seʀzh), 1905–86, Russian ballet dancer and choreographer, in Paris after 1923.

life (līf), *n., pl.* **lives** (līvz), *adj.* —*n.* **1.** the condition that distinguishes organisms from inorganic objects and dead organisms, being manifested by growth through metabolism, reproduction, and the power of adaptation to environment through changes originating internally. **2.** the sum of the distinguishing phenomena of organisms, esp. metabolism, growth, reproduction, and adaptation to environment. **3.** the animate existence or period of animate existence of an individual: *to risk one's life; a short life and a merry one.* **4.** a corresponding state, existence, or principle of existence conceived of as belonging to the soul: *eternal life.* **5.** the general or universal condition of human existence: *Too bad, but life is like that.* **6.** any specified period of animate existence: *a man in middle life.* **7.** the period of existence, activity, or effectiveness of something inanimate, as a machine, lease, or play: *The life of the car may be ten years.* **8.** a living being: *Several lives were lost.* **9.** living things collectively: *the hope of discovering life on other planets; insect life.* **10.** a particular aspect of existence: *He enjoys an active physical life.* **11.** the course of existence or sum of experiences and actions that constitute a person's existence: *His business has been his entire life.* **12.** a biography: *a newly published life of Willa Cather.* **13.** animation; liveliness; spirit: *a speech full of life.* **14.** resilience; elasticity. **15.** the force that makes or keeps something alive; the vivifying or quickening principle: *The life of the treaty has been an increase of mutual understanding and respect.* **16.** a mode or manner of existence, as in the world of affairs or society: *So far her business life has not overlapped her social life.* **17.** the period or extent of authority, popularity, approval, etc.: *the life of the committee; the life of a bestseller.* **18.** a prison sentence covering the remaining portion of the offender's animate existence: *The judge gave him life.* **19.** anything or anyone considered to be as precious as life: *She was his life.* **20.** a person or thing that enlivens: *the life of the party.* **21.** effervescence or sparkle, as of wines. **22.** pungency or strong, sharp flavor, as of substances when fresh or in good condition. **23.** nature or any of the forms of nature as the model or subject of a work of art: *drawn from life.* **24.** *Baseball.* another opportunity given to a batter to bat because of a misplay by a fielder. **25.** (in English pool) one of a limited number of shots allowed a player: *Each pool player has three lives at the beginning of the game.* **26. as large as life,** actually; indeed: *There he stood, as large as life.* Also, **as big as life. 27. come to life, a.** to recover consciousness. **b.** to become animated and vigorous: *The evening passed, but somehow the party never came to life.* **c.** to appear lifelike: *The characters of the novel came to life on the screen.* **28. for dear life,** with desperate effort, energy, or speed: *We ran for dear life, with the dogs at our heels.* Also, **for one's life. 29. for the life of one,** as hard as one tries; even with the utmost effort: *He can't understand it for the life of him.* **30. not on your life,** *Informal.* absolutely not; under no circumstances; by no means: *Will I stand for such a thing? Not on your life!* **31. take one's life in one's hands,** to risk death knowingly: *We were warned that we were taking our lives in our hands by going through that swampy area.* **32. to the life,** in perfect imitation; exactly: *The portrait characterized him to the life.*
—*adj.* **33.** for or lasting a lifetime; lifelong: *a life membership in a club; life imprisonment.* **34.** of or pertaining to animate existence: *the life force; life functions.* **35.** working from nature or using a living model: *a life drawing; a life class.* [bef. 900; ME *lif(e);* OE *līf;* c. D *lijf,* G *Leib* body, ON *līf* life, body; akin to LIVE[1]]
—**Syn. 13.** vivacity, sprightliness, vigor, verve, activity, energy. —**Ant. 13.** inertia.

life-and-death (līf′ən deth′), *adj.* ending with the death or possible death of one of the participants; crucially important: *The cobra was engaged in a life-and-death struggle with the mongoose.* Also, **life-or-death.** [1680–90]

life′ annu′ity, *Insurance.* any annuity that is contingent upon the survival of the annuitant or annuitants, esp. an annuity that terminates with the death of a single annuitant.

life′ ar′row, *Naut.* an arrowlike projectile for carrying a line for use in maritime rescue operations.

life′ belt′, a beltlike life preserver. [1855–60]

life·blood (līf′blud′), *n.* **1.** the blood, considered as essential to maintain life: *to spill one's lifeblood in war.* **2.** a life-giving, vital, or animating element: *Agriculture is the lifeblood of the country.* [1580–90; LIFE + BLOOD]

life·boat (līf′bōt′), *n.* **1.** a double-ended ship's boat, constructed, mounted, and provisioned so as to be readily able to rescue and maintain persons from a sinking vessel. **2.** a similarly constructed boat used by shore-based rescue services. [1795–1805; LIFE + BOAT]

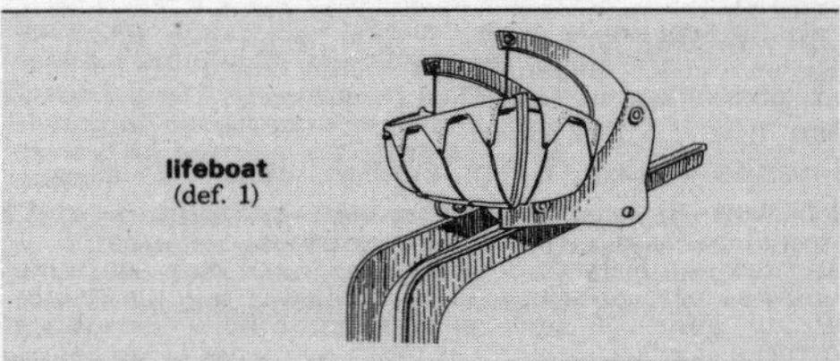

lifeboat (def. 1)

life·boat·man (līf′bōt′mən), *n., pl.* **-men.** a sailor qualified to take charge of a lifeboat or life raft. [1855–60; LIFEBOAT + -MAN]

life′ bu′oy, any of variously formed buoyant devices for supporting a person fallen into the water.

life′ car′, a watertight container used in marine rescue operations, suspended from a hawser and hauled back and forth between a stranded or wrecked vessel and the shore. Also called **ark, safety car.**

life-care (līf′kâr′), *adj.* designed to provide for the basic needs of elderly residents, usu. in return for an initial fee and monthly service payments: *a life-care facility; life-care communities.* Also, **life′ care′.** [1980–85]

life′ cy′cle, 1. *Biol.* the continuous sequence of changes undergone by an organism from one primary form, as a gamete, to the development of the same form again. **2.** a series of stages, as childhood and middle age, that characterize the course of existence of an individual, group, or culture. **3.** any similar series of stages: *the life cycle of a manufactured product.* [1870–75]

life′ expect′ancy, the probable number of years remaining in the life of an individual or class of persons determined statistically, affected by such factors as heredity, physical condition, nutrition, and occupation. Also called **expectancy of life.** [1930–35]

life′ float′, a ring-shaped float of balsa wood or metal tubing, having a grating or network at the center, for rescuing a number of survivors from a foundered vessel.

life′ force′. See **élan vital.** [1895–1900]

CONCISE ETYMOLOGY KEY: <, descended or borrowed from; >, whence; b., blend of, blended; c., cognate with; cf., compare; deriv., derivative; equiv., equivalent; imit., imitative; obl., oblique; r., replacing; s., stem; sp., spelling, spelled; resp., respelling, respelled; trans., translation; ?, origin unknown; *, unattested; ‡, probably earlier than. See the full key inside the front cover.

life•ful (līf′fəl), *adj.* full of life; lively; animated. [1175–1225; ME *lifful.* See LIFE, -FUL]

life•giv•ing (līf′giv′ing), *adj.* imparting, or having the ability to impart, life or vitality; invigorating; vitalizing: *life-giving love and praise.* [1555–65] **—life′-giv′er,** *n.*

life•guard (līf′gärd′), *n.* **1.** an expert swimmer employed, as at a beach or pool, to protect bathers from drowning or other accidents and dangers. **—***v.i.* **2.** to work as a lifeguard. [1640–50; LIFE + GUARD]

Life′ Guards′, (in Britain) a cavalry regiment forming part of the ceremonial guard of the monarch. Cf. **household cavalry.** [1640–50]

life′ his′tory, *Biol.* **1.** the series of living phenomena exhibited by an organism in the course of its development from inception to death. **2.** See **life cycle** (def. 1). [1865–70]

life′ in′stinct. See under **death instinct.** [1905–10]

life′ insur′ance, insurance providing for payment of a sum of money to a named beneficiary upon the death of the policyholder or to the policyholder if still living after reaching a specified age. [1800–10]

life′ in′terest, interest on property that is payable during the owner's lifetime but cannot be passed on to another or others after his or her death.

life′ jack′et, a sleeveless jacket of buoyant or inflatable construction, for supporting the wearer in deep water and preventing drowning. Also called **life vest;** *Brit.,* **air jacket.** [1865–70]

life•less (līf′lis), *adj.* **1.** not endowed with life; having no life; inanimate: *lifeless matter.* **2.** destitute of living things: *a lifeless planet.* **3.** deprived of life; dead: *a battlefield strewn with lifeless bodies.* **4.** without animation, liveliness, or spirit; dull; colorless; torpid: *a lifeless performance of a play.* **5.** insensible, as a person who has fainted. [bef. 1000; ME *lifles,* OE *līflēas.* See LIFE, -LESS] **—life′less•ly,** *adv.* **—life′less•ness,** *n.*
—Syn. 1. inorganic. **3.** defunct. See **dead. 4.** inactive, inert, passive; sluggish; spiritless. **—Ant. 1, 3.** living. **4.** lively.

life•like (līf′līk′), *adj.* resembling or simulating real life: *a lifelike portrait.* [1605–15; LIFE + -LIKE] **—life′like′ness,** *n.*

life•line (līf′līn′), *n.* **1.** a line, fired across a ship or boat, by means of which a hawser for a breeches buoy may be hauled aboard. **2.** a line or rope for saving life, as one attached to a lifeboat. **3.** any of various lines running above the decks, spars, etc., of a ship or boat to give sailors something to grasp when there is danger of falling or being washed away. **4.** a wire safety rope supported by stanchions along the edge of the deck of a yacht. **5.** the line by which a diver is lowered and raised. **6.** any of several anchored lines used by swimmers for support. **7.** a route or means of transportation or communication for receiving or delivering food, medicine, or assistance: *This road is the town's lifeline and must be kept open despite the snow.* **8.** assistance at a critical time. [1690–1700; LIFE + LINE[1]]

life•long (līf′lông′, -long′), *adj.* lasting or continuing through all or much of one's life: *lifelong regret.* [1750–60; LIFE + LONG[1] (adv.)]

life•man•ship (līf′mən ship′), *n.* **1.** the ability to conduct one's life, career, personal relationships, etc., in a successful manner. **2.** the skill or practice of conveying to others a real or apparent sense of one's superiority. [1945–50; LIFE + -MANSHIP; popularized, esp. in sense of def. 2, by the book *Some Notes on Lifemanship* (1950) by British author Stephen Potter (1900–69)]

life′ mask′, a cast of the face of a living person. Cf. **death mask.**

life′ net′, a strong net or the like held by firefighters or others to catch persons jumping from a burning building. [1905–10, *Amer.*]

life′ of Ri′ley, *Informal.* a carefree, comfortable, and thoroughly enjoyable way of living: *Since winning the lottery, he's led the life of Riley.* [1920–25; perh. after the *Reilly* mentioned in various songs popular around 1900, as "The Best of the House Is None Too Good for Reilly"]

Life′ of Sam′uel John′son, The, a biography (1791) by James Boswell.

Life′ on the Mississip′pi, an autobiographical narrative (1883) by Mark Twain.

life-or-death (līf′ər deth′), *adj.* life-and-death. [1680–90]

life′ peer′, *Brit.* a peer whose title ceases at death; nonhereditary peer. [1865–70]

life′ plant′. See **air plant** (def. 2). [1850–55]

life′ preserv′er, **1.** a buoyant jacket, belt, or other like device for keeping a person afloat. **2.** *Brit. Slang.* a weapon, esp. a short stick with a weighted head; blackjack. [1630–40]

lif•er (lī′fər), *n. Slang.* **1.** a person sentenced to or serving a term of life imprisonment. **2.** a person committed to a professional lifetime career in the military. **3.** a person who has devoted a lifetime to a profession, occupation, or pursuit. [1820–30; LIFE + -ER[1]]

life′ raft′, a raft, often inflatable, for use in emergencies, as when a ship must be abandoned or when a plane is downed at sea. [1810–20]

life•sav•er (līf′sā′vər), *n.* **1.** a person who rescues another from danger of death, esp. from drowning. **2.** a person or thing that saves a person, as from a difficult situation or critical moment: *That money was a lifesaver.* **3.** *Chiefly Brit.* a lifeguard. [1880–85; LIFE + SAVER] **—life′sav′ing,** *adj., n.*

Life′saving Serv′ice, a private organization or government agency for general marine rescue operations.

life′ sci′ence, any science that deals with living organisms, their life processes, and their interrelationships, as biology, medicine, or ecology. [1940–45] **—life′ sci′entist.**

life′ sen′tence, a sentence condemning a convicted felon to spend the rest of his or her life in prison. Cf. **death sentence.**

life′ signs′. See **vital signs.**

life-size (līf′sīz′), *adj.* of the natural size of an object, person, etc., in life; of the actual size of a living original: *a life-size statue.* Also, **life′-sized′.** [1835–45]

life′ span′, **1.** the longest period over which the life of any organism or species may extend, according to the available biological knowledge concerning it. **2.** the longevity of an individual. [1915–20]

life•style (līf′stīl′), *n.* the habits, attitudes, tastes, moral standards, economic level, etc., that together constitute the mode of living of an individual or group. Also, **life′ style′, life′-style′.** [1925–30; LIFE + STYLE]

life-sup•port (līf′sə pôrt′, -pōrt′), *adj.* **1.** of or pertaining to equipment or measures that sustain or artificially substitute for essential body functions, as breathing or disposal of body wastes: *Without life-support equipment, the patient might die.* **2.** of or pertaining to equipment or measures that provide, within a surrounding hostile environment, as outer space or ocean depths, a life-sustaining environment similar to that found on the earth's surface: *the life-support system of a spacecraft or submarine.* **3.** of or pertaining to anything that fosters or sustains life, success, or continued existence, as of a person, thing, or nation: *the life-support system of the economy.* [1955–60]

life′ ta′ble, *Insurance.* See **mortality table.** [1860–65]

life-threat•en•ing (līf′thret′ning, -thret′n ing), *adj.* endangering life: *a life-threatening illness.*

life•time (līf′tīm′), *n.* **1.** the time that the life of someone or something continues; the term of a life: *peace within our lifetime.* **2.** *Physics.* See **mean life. —***adj.* **3.** for the duration of a person's life: *He has a lifetime membership in the organization.* [1175–1225; ME *liftime.* See LIFE, TIME]

life′ vest′. See **life jacket.** [1910–15, *Amer.*]

life•work (līf′wûrk′), *n.* the complete or principal work, labor, or task of a lifetime. [1870–75; LIFE + WORK]

Lif•fey (lif′ē), *n.* a river in the E Republic of Ireland, flowing NW and NE from County Wicklow into Dublin Bay. 50 mi. (81 km) long.

LIFO (lī′fō), *n.* **1.** See **last-in, first-out** (def. 1). **2.** *Computers.* a data storage and retrieval technique, usually implemented using a queue, in which the last item stored is the first item retrieved. [*l(ast) i(n,) f(irst) o(ut)*]

lift (lift), *v.t.* **1.** to move or bring (something) upward from the ground or other support to a higher position; hoist. **2.** to raise or direct upward: *He lifted his arm in a gesture of farewell; to lift one's head.* **3.** to remove or rescind by an official act, as a ban, curfew, or tax: *a court decision to lift the ban on strikes by teachers.* **4.** to stop or put an end to (a boycott, blockade, etc.): *The citizenry will have to conserve food and water until the siege against the city is lifted.* **5.** to hold up or display on high. **6.** to raise in rank, condition, estimation, etc.; elevate or exalt (sometimes used reflexively): *His first book lifted him from obscurity. By hard work they lifted themselves from poverty.* **7.** to make audible or louder, as the voice or something voiced: *The congregation lifted their voices in song.* **8.** to transfer from one setting to another: *For the protagonist of the new play, the author has lifted a character from an early novel.* **9.** *Informal.* to plagiarize: *Whole passages had been lifted from another book.* **10.** *Informal.* to steal: *His wallet was lifted on the crowded subway.* **11.** airlift (def. 5). **12.** to remove (plants and tubers) from the ground, as after harvest or for transplanting. **13.** *Horol.* (of an escape wheel) to move (a pallet) by moving along the outer, oblique face. **14.** to pay off (a mortgage, promissory note, etc.). **15.** *Golf.* to pick up (the ball), as to move it from an unplayable lie. **16.** to perform a surgical face lifting on. **17.** *Shipbuilding.* **a.** to transfer (measurements and the like) from a drawing, model, etc., to a piece being built. **b.** to form (a template) according to a drawing, model, etc. **18.** to cease temporarily from directing (fire or bombardment) on an objective or area: *They lifted the fire when the infantry began to advance.* **19.** *Fox Hunting.* to take (hounds) from the line of a fox to where it has just been seen.
—*v.i.* **20.** to go up; yield to upward pressure: *The box is too heavy to lift. The lid won't lift.* **21.** to pull or strain upward in the effort to raise something: *to lift at a heavy weight.* **22.** to move upward or rise; rise and disperse, as clouds or fog. **23.** (of rain) to stop temporarily. **24.** to rise to view above the horizon when approached, as land seen from the sea.
—*n.* **25.** the act of lifting, raising, or rising: *the lift of a hand.* **26.** the distance that anything rises or is raised: *a lift of 20 feet between canal locks.* **27.** a lifting or raising force: *A kite depends on the wind to act as its lift.* **28.** the weight, load, or quantity lifted. **29.** an act or instance of helping to climb or mount: *He gave her a lift onto the wagon.* **30.** a ride in a vehicle, esp. one given to a pedestrian: *Can you give me a lift across town?* **31.** a feeling of exaltation or uplift: *Their visit gave me quite a lift.* **32.** assistance or aid: *The fund-raiser's successful efforts proved a great lift for the organization.* **33.** a device or apparatus for lifting: *a hydraulic lift.* **34.** a movement in which a dancer, skater, etc., lifts up his partner. **35.** *Skiing.* **a.** See **ski lift. b.** See **chair lift. 36.** *Brit.* **a.** elevator (def. 2). **b.** any device used to lift or elevate, as a dumbwaiter or hoist. **37.** *Informal.* a theft. **38.** a rise or elevation of ground. **39.** *Aeron.* the component of the aerodynamic force exerted by the air on an airfoil, having a direction perpendicular to the direction of motion and causing an aircraft to stay aloft. **40.** *Naut.* **a.** the capacity of a cargo ship measured in deadweight tons. **b.** See **topping lift. 41.** one of the layers of leather forming the heel of a boot or shoe. **42.** a special arch support built or inserted into footwear. **43.** *Mining.* the slice or thickness of ore mined in one operation. **44.** *Building Trades.* the height of the quantity of concrete poured into a form at one time. **45.** *Naval Archit.* any of the horizontal planks forming a type of half model (**lift′ mod′el**), able to be removed and measured as a guide to laying out the water lines of the vessel at full scale. **46.** *Typesetting.* fat (def. 25). **47.** *Print.* the quantity of paper loaded into or removed from a press or other printing machine at one time. **48.** *Horol.* **a.** the displacement of a pallet by an escape wheel that has been unlocked. **b.** the angle through which the pallet passes when so displaced. **49.** airlift (defs. 1–3). [1250–1300; 1955–60 for def. 10; ME *liften* < ON *lypta,* deriv. of *lopt* air, c. G *lüften* lit., to take aloft; see LOFT] **—lift′a•ble,** *adj.* **—lift′er,** *n.*
—Syn. 1. elevate. See **raise. —Ant. 1.** lower.

lift•back (lift′bak′), *n. Auto.* hatchback. [1975–80; LIFT + (HATCH)BACK]

lift′ bolt′, *Naut.* an eyebolt, as on a yardarm, to which a topping lift is secured.

lift′ bridge′, a bridge having a section that can be lifted vertically to permit passage of boats beneath it. Also called **vertical lift bridge.** [1840–50]

lift′-drag′ ra′tio (lift′drag′), *Aeron.* the ratio of the lift to the drag of an airfoil. [1915–20]

lift•er (lif′tər), *n.* **1.** a person or thing that lifts. **2.** *Mach.* a device or machine part used for lifting another part, as a cam used for lifting a valve in an engine. [1525–35; LIFT + -ER[1]]

lift•gate (lift′gāt′), *n. Auto.* hatch[2] (def. 9b). [1945–50; LIFT + (TAIL)GATE[1]]

lift′ing sail′, *Naut.* a sail that when filled tends to raise the hull of a ship or boat (opposed to *driving sail*). [1880–85]

lift•off (lift′ôf′, -of′), *n.* **1.** *Aeron., Rocketry.* **a.** the action of an aircraft in becoming airborne or of a rocket in rising from its launching site under its own power. **b.** the instant when such action occurs. **2.** *Informal.* the launching or commencement of a project, plan, etc.: *The liftoff of the sales campaign will be next month.* **—***adj.* **3.** that removes by lifting off; capable of being lifted off: *a liftoff correction tape for typewriters; magnetized, liftoff nameplates.* Also, **lift′-off′.** [1955–60; n., adj. use of v. phrase *lift off*]

lift′off hinge′. See **loose-joint hinge.**

lift′ pump′, a pump in which a liquid is lifted rather than forced up from below. Cf. **force pump.** [1855–60]

lift-slab (lift′slab′), *adj.* noting or pertaining to a technique of constructing multistory buildings in which all horizontal slabs are cast at ground level and, when ready, are raised into position by hydraulic jacks. [1950–55]

lift′ truck′, a dolly or truck for lifting and moving, esp. palletized loads. [1960–65]

lig•a•ment (lig′ə mənt), *n.* **1.** *Anat., Zool.* a band of tissue, usually white and fibrous, serving to connect bones, hold organs in place, etc. **2.** a tie or bond: *The desire for personal freedom is a ligament uniting all peoples.* [1375–1425; late ME < ML *ligāmentum,* L: bandage, equiv. to *ligā(re)* to tie + *-mentum* -MENT]

lig•a•men•tous (lig′ə men′təs), *adj.* pertaining to, of the nature of, or forming a ligament. Also, **lig•a•men′tal, lig′a•men′ta•ry.** [1675–85; LIGAMENT + -OUS] **—lig′a•men′tous•ly,** *adv.*

lig•a•men•tum (lig′ə men′təm), *n., pl.* **-ta** (-tə). *Anat.* ligament. [< ML; see LIGAMENT]

li•gan (lī′gən), *n. Law.* lagan.

li•gand (lī′gənd, lig′ənd), *n.* **1.** *Biochem.* a molecule, as an antibody, hormone, or drug, that binds to a receptor. **2.** *Chem.* a molecule, ion, or atom that is bonded to the central metal atom of a coordination compound. Cf. **complexing agent.** [1945–50; < L *ligandus,* ger. of *ligāre* to bind, tie]

li•gase (lī′gās, -gāz), *n. Biochem.* any of a class of enzymes that catalyze the joining of two molecules by formation of a covalent bond accompanied by the hydrolysis of ATP. [1961; < L *lig(āre)* to tie, bind + -ASE]

li•gate (lī′gāt), *v.t.,* **-gat•ed, -gat•ing.** to bind with or as if with a ligature; tie up (a bleeding artery or the like). [1590–1600; < L *ligātus* (ptp. of *ligāre* to tie, bind); see -ATE[1]]

li•ga•tion (lī gā′shən), *n.* **1.** the act of ligating, esp. of surgically tying up a bleeding artery. **2.** anything that binds or ties up; ligature. [1590–1600; < LL *ligātiōn-* (s. of *ligātiō*), equiv. to L *ligāt(us)* (see LIGATE) + *-iōn-* -ION] **—lig•a•tive** (lig′ə tiv), *adj.*

lig•a•ture (lig′ə chər, -cho͝or′), *n., v.,* **-tured, -tur•ing.** **—***n.* **1.** the act of binding or tying up: *The ligature of the artery was done with skill.* **2.** anything that serves for binding or tying up, as a band, bandage, or cord. **3.** a tie or bond: *the ligature of mutual need that bound them together.* **4.** *Print., Orthography.* a stroke or bar connecting two letters. **5.** *Print.* a character or type combining two or more letters, as *fi* and *ffl.* **6.** *Music.* **a.** slur. **b.** a group of notes connected by a slur. **c.** a metal band for securing the reed of a clarinet or saxophone to the mouthpiece. **7.** *Surg.* a thread or wire for constriction of blood vessels or for removing tumors by strangulation. **—***v.t.* **8.** to bind with a ligature; tie up; ligate. [1350–1400; ME < LL *ligātūra.* See LIGATE, -URE]

li•geance (lī′jəns, lē′-), *n.* **1.** *Chiefly Law.* the territory subject to a sovereign or liege lord. **2.** *Archaic.* allegiance. [1350–1400; ME < MF; see LIEGE, -ANCE]

li•ger (līʹgər), *n.* the offspring of a male lion and a female tiger. Cf. **tiglon.** [1935–40; LI(ON) + (TI)GER]

light[1] (līt), *n., adj.,* **-er, -est,** *v.,* **light•ed** or **lit, light•ing.** —*n.* **1.** something that makes things visible or affords illumination: *All colors depend on light.* **2.** *Physics.* **a.** Also called **luminous energy, radiant energy.** electromagnetic radiation to which the organs of sight react, ranging in wavelength from about 400 to 700 nm and propagated at a speed of 186,282 mi./sec (299,972 km/sec), considered variously as a wave, corpuscular, or quantum phenomenon. **b.** a similar form of radiant energy that does not affect the retina, as ultraviolet or infrared rays. **3.** the sensation produced by stimulation of the organs of sight. **4.** an illuminating agent or source, as the sun, a lamp, or a beacon. **5.** the radiance or illumination from a particular source: *the light of a candle.* **6.** the illumination from the sun; daylight: *We awoke at the first light.* **7.** daybreak or dawn: *when light appeared in the east.* **8.** daytime: *Summer has more hours of light.* **9.** a particular light or illumination in which an object seen takes on a certain appearance: *viewing the portrait in dim light.* **10.** a device for or means of igniting, as a spark, flame, or match: *Could you give me a light?* **11.** a traffic light: *Don't cross till the light changes.* **12.** the aspect in which a thing appears or is regarded: *Try to look at the situation in a more cheerful light.* **13.** the state of being visible, exposed to view, or revealed to public notice or knowledge; limelight: *Stardom has placed her in the light.* **14.** a person who is an outstanding leader, celebrity, or example; luminary: *He became one of the leading lights of Restoration drama.* **15.** *Art.* **a.** the effect of light falling on an object or scene as represented in a picture. **b.** one of the brightest parts of a picture. **16.** a gleam or sparkle, as in the eyes. **17.** a measure or supply of light; illumination: *The wall cuts off our light.* **18.** spiritual illumination or awareness; enlightenment. **19.** *Archit.* **a.** Also called **day.** one compartment of a window or window sash. **b.** a window, esp. a small one. **20.** mental insight; understanding. **21. lights,** the information, ideas, or mental capacities possessed: *to act according to one's lights.* **22.** a lighthouse. **23.** *Archaic.* the eyesight. **24. bring to light,** to discover or reveal: *The excavations brought to light the remnants of an ancient civilization.* **25. come to light,** to be discovered or revealed: *Some previously undiscovered letters have lately come to light.* **26. hide one's light under a bushel,** to conceal or suppress one's talents or successes. **27. in a good** (or **bad**) **light,** under favorable (or unfavorable) circumstances: *She worshiped him, but then she'd only seen him in a good light.* **28. in (the) light of,** taking into account; because of; considering: *It was necessary to review the decision in the light of recent developments.* **29. light at the end of the tunnel,** a prospect of success, relief, or redemption: *We haven't solved the problem yet, but we're beginning to see light at the end of the tunnel.* **30. see the light, a.** to come into existence or being. **b.** to be made public. **c.** to begin to accept or understand a point of view one formerly opposed: *Her father was opposed to her attending an out-of-town college, but he finally saw the light.* **31. shed** or **throw light on,** to clarify; clear up: *His deathbed confession threw light on a mystery of long standing.*
—*adj.* **32.** having light or illumination; bright; well-lighted: *the lightest room in the entire house.* **33.** pale, whitish, or not deep or dark in color: *a light blue.* **34.** (of coffee or tea) containing enough milk or cream to produce a light color.
—*v.t.* **35.** to set burning, as a candle, lamp, fire, match, or cigarette; kindle; ignite. **36.** to turn or switch on (an electric light): *One flick of the master switch lights all the lamps in the room.* **37.** to give light to; furnish with light or illumination: *The room is lighted by two large chandeliers.* **38.** to make (an area or object) bright with or as if with light (often fol. by *up*): *Hundreds of candles lighted up the ballroom.* **39.** to cause (the face, surroundings, etc.) to brighten, esp. with joy, animation, or the like (often fol. by *up*): *A smile lit up her face. Her presence lighted up the room.* **40.** to guide or conduct with a light: *a candle to light you to bed.*
—*v.i.* **41.** to take fire or become kindled: *The damp wood refused to light.* **42.** to ignite a cigar, cigarette, or pipe for purposes of smoking (usually fol. by *up*): *He took out a pipe and lighted up before speaking.* **43.** to become illuminated when switched on: *This table lamp won't light.* **44.** to become bright, as with light or color (often fol. by *up*): *The sky lights up at sunset.* **45.** to brighten with animation or joy, as the face or eyes (often fol. by *up*). [bef. 900; (n. and adj.) ME; OE *lēoht;* c. OS *lioht,* OFris *liacht,* D, G *licht,* Goth *liuhath* (n.); akin to ON *ljōs* (n.), *ljōss* (adj.), L *lūx* (n.), Gk *leukós* bright, white; (v.) ME *lighten,* OE *līhtan,* c. OS *liuhtian,* OHG *liuhten* (G *leuchten*), Goth *liuhtjan*] —**lightʹful,** *adj.* —**lightʹful•ly,** *adv.*

light[2] (līt), *adj.,* **-er, -est,** *adv.,* **-er, -est,** *n.* —*adj.* **1.** of little weight; not heavy: *a light load.* **2.** of little weight in proportion to bulk; of low specific gravity: *a light metal.* **3.** of less than the usual or average weight: *light clothing.* **4.** weighing less than the proper or standard amount: *to be caught using light weights in trade.* **5.** of small amount, force, intensity, etc.: *light trading on the stock market; a light rain; light sleep.* **6.** using or applying little or slight pressure or force: *The child petted the puppy with light, gentle strokes.* **7.** not distinct; faint: *The writing on the page had become light and hard to read.* **8.** easy to endure, deal with, or perform; not difficult or burdensome: *light duties.* **9.** not very profound or serious; amusing or entertaining: *light reading.* **10.** of little importance or consequence; trivial: *The loss of his job was no light matter.* **11.** easily digested: *light food.* **12.** low in any substance, as sugar, starch, or tars, that is considered harmful or undesirable: *light cigarettes.* **13.** (of alcoholic beverages) **a.** not heavy or strong: *a light apéritif.* **b.** (esp. of beer and wine) having fewer calories and usually a lower alcohol content than the standard product. **14.** spongy or well-leavened, as cake. **15.** (of soil) containing much sand; porous or crumbly. **16.** slender or delicate in form or appearance: *a light, graceful figure.* **17.** airy or buoyant in movement: *When she dances, she's as light as a feather.* **18.** nimble or agile: *light on one's feet.* **19.** free from trouble, sorrow, or worry; carefree: *a light heart.* **20.** cheerful; gay: *a light laugh.* **21.** characterized by lack of proper seriousness; frivolous: *light conduct.* **22.** sexually promiscuous; loose. **23.** easily swayed; changeable; volatile: *a heart light of love; His is a life of a man light of purpose.* **24.** dizzy; slightly delirious: *I get light on one martini.* **25.** *Mil.* lightly armed or equipped: *light cavalry.* **26.** having little or no cargo, encumbrance, or the like; not burdened: *a light freighter drawing little water.* **27.** adapted by small weight or slight build for small loads or swift movement: *The grocer bought a light truck for deliveries.* **28.** using small-scale machinery primarily for the production of consumer goods: *light industry.* **29.** *Naut.* noting any sail of light canvas set only in moderate or calm weather, as a royal, skysail, studdingsail, gaff topsail, or spinnaker. **30.** *Meteorol.* (of wind) having a speed up to 7 mph (3 m/sec). Cf. **light air, light breeze.** **31.** *Phonet.* (of *l*-sounds) resembling a front vowel in quality; clear: *French* l *is lighter than English* l. **32.** *Pros.* (of a syllable) **a.** unstressed. **b.** short. **33.** *Poker.* being in debt to the pot: *He's a dollar light.* **34. make light of,** to treat as unimportant or trivial: *They made light of our hard-won victory.* —*adv.* **35.** lightly: *to travel light.* **36.** with no load or cargo hauled or carried: *a locomotive running light to its roundhouse.* —*n.* **37.** a light product, as a beer or cigarette. [bef. 900; ME; OE *lēoht, līht;* c. OFris *li(u)cht,* OS *-līht,* D *licht,* G *leicht,* ON *lēttr,* Goth *leihts*]
—**Syn. 7.** indistinct; faded. **10.** trifling, inconsiderable. **19.** cheery, happy. **21.** flighty. —**Ant. 1.** heavy.

light[3] (līt), *v.i.,* **light•ed** or **lit, light•ing. 1.** to get down or descend, as from a horse or a vehicle. **2.** to come to rest, as on a spot or thing; fall or settle upon; land: *The bird lighted on the branch. My eye lighted on some friends in the crowd.* **3.** to come by chance; happen; hit (usually fol. by *on* or *upon*): *to light on a clue; to light on an ideal picnic spot.* **4.** to fall, as a stroke, weapon, vengeance, or choice, on a place or person: *The choice lighted upon our candidate.* **5. light into,** *Informal.* to make a vigorous physical or verbal attack on: *He would light into anyone with the slightest provocation.* **6. light out,** *Slang.* to leave quickly; depart hurriedly: *He lit out of here as fast as his legs would carry him.* [bef. 900; ME *lihten,* OE *līhtan* to make light, relieve of a weight; see LIGHT[2]]

lightʹ adaptaʹtion, *Ophthalm.* the reflex adaptation of the eye to bright light, consisting of an increase in the number of functioning cones, accompanied by a decrease in the number of functioning rods (opposed to *dark adaptation*). [1895–1900] —**lightʹ-a•daptʹed,** *adj.*

lightʹ airʹ, *Meteorol.* a wind of 1–3 mph (0.5–1.3 m/sec). [1795–1805]

lightʹ and shadeʹ surʹface. See **surface of light and shade.**

light-armed (lītʹärmdʹ), *adj.* carrying light weapons: *light-armed troops.* [1610–20]

Lightʹ Arʹmored Veʹhicle, an eight-wheeled armored reconnaissance car with a 25mm cannon, in service with the U.S. Army and Marine Corps in the 1980's.

lightʹ artilʹlery, *Mil.* **1.** guns and howitzers of small caliber. **2.** (in the U.S.) guns and howitzers of a caliber up to and including 105 mm. Cf. **heavy artillery** (def. 2), **medium artillery.**

light•board (lītʹbôrdʹ, -bōrdʹ), *n.* switchboard (def. 2). [LIGHT[1] + BOARD]

light•boat (lītʹbōtʹ), *n.* a small lightship. [1825–35, *Amer.;* LIGHT[1] + BOAT]

lightʹ bombʹer, *Mil.* a small airplane designed to carry light bomb loads relatively short distances, esp. one having a gross loaded weight of less than 100,000 lb. (45,000 kg). Cf. **heavy bomber, medium bomber.**

lightʹ boxʹ, a boxlike object having a uniformly lighted surface, as of ground glass, against which films or transparencies can be held for examination. [1840–50]

lightʹ breadʹ, *Midland and Southern U.S.* **1.** See **white bread. 2.** any bread leavened with yeast. [1815–25]

lightʹ breezeʹ, *Meteorol.* a wind of 4–7 mph (2–3 m/sec). Cf. **breeze**[1] (def. 2). [1795–1805]

lightʹ bridgeʹ, *Theat.* See under **bridge**[1] (def. 16a).

lightʹ bulbʹ, an electric light. [1880–85]

lightʹ chainʹ, *Immunol.* either of an identical pair of polypeptides in the antibody molecule that lie parallel to the upper parts of the heavy chain pair and are half the molecular weight. Also called **L chain.** [1960–65]

lightʹ coloʹnel, *U.S. Mil. Slang.* a lieutenant colonel.

lightʹ creamʹ, sweet cream with less butterfat than heavy cream.

lightʹ cruisʹer, a naval cruiser having 6-in. (15-cm) guns as its main armament. Cf. **heavy cruiser.**

lightʹ curveʹ, *Astron.* a graph showing variations in brightness of celestial objects over time. [1885–90]

lightʹ displaceʹment, *Naut.* the weight of a ship with all its permanent equipment, excluding the weight of cargo, persons, ballast, dunnage, and fuel, but usually including the weight of permanent ballast and water used to operate steam machinery. Also called **light weight.**

lightʹ draftʹ, *Naut.* the draft of a vessel at its light displacement. [1865–70]

light-du•ty (lītʹdo͞oʹtē, -dyo͞oʹ-), *adj.* made or designed to withstand comparatively moderate loads, use, or stress: *light-duty trucks.* Cf. **heavy-duty.**

lightʹ-e•mit•ting diʹode (lītʹi mitʹing). See **LED.** [1965–70]

light•en[1] (lītʹn), *v.i.* **1.** to become lighter or less dark; brighten: *The sky lightened after the storm.* **2.** to brighten or light up, as the eyes or features: *Her face lightened when she heard the good news.* **3.** to flash as or like lightning (often used impersonally with *it* as subject): *It thundered and lightened for hours.* **4.** *Archaic.* to shine, gleam, or be bright: *steel blades lightening in the sun.* —*v.t.* **5.** to give light to; illuminate: *A full moon lightened the road.* **6.** to brighten (the eyes, features, etc.): *A large smile lightened his face.* **7.** to make lighter or less dark: *Add white to lighten the paint.* **8.** *Obs.* enlighten. **9.** *Obs.* to flash or emit like lightning (usually fol. by *out, forth,* or *down*): *eyes that lightened forth implacable hatred.* [1300–50; ME *lightnen;* see LIGHT[1], -EN[1]] —**lightʹen•er,** *n.*

light•en[2] (lītʹn), *v.t.* **1.** to make lighter in weight: *to lighten the load on a truck.* **2.** to lessen the load of or upon: *to lighten a cargo ship.* **3.** to make less burdensome or oppressive; alleviate; mitigate: *to lighten taxes; to lighten someone's cares.* **4.** to cheer or gladden: *Such news lightens my heart.* —*v.i.* **5.** to become less severe, stringent, or harsh; ease up: *Border inspections have lightened recently.* **6.** to become less heavy, cumbersome, burdensome, oppressive, etc.: *His worries seem to have lightened somewhat.* **7.** to become less gloomy; perk up: *People's spirits usually lighten when spring arrives.* [1350–1400; ME *lightnen;* see LIGHT[2], -EN[1]]
—**Syn. 3.** ease, lessen, reduce. —**Ant. 3.** aggravate.

light•en•ing (lītʹn ing), *n. Med.* the descent of the uterus into the pelvic cavity, occurring toward the end of pregnancy, changing the contour of the abdomen and facilitating breathing by lessening pressure under the diaphragm. [1520–30; LIGHTEN[2] + -ING[1]]

light•er[1] (līʹtər), *n.* **1.** a person or thing that lights or ignites. **2.** a mechanical device used in lighting cigarettes, cigars, or pipes for smoking. [1545–55; LIGHT[1] + -ER[1]]

light•er[2] (līʹtər), *n.* **1.** a large, open, flat-bottomed barge, used in unloading and loading ships offshore or in transporting goods for short distances in shallow waters. —*v.t.* **2.** to convey in or as if in a lighter. [1350–1400; ME; see LIGHT[3], -ER[1]]

light•er•age (līʹtər ij), *n.* **1.** the use of lighters in loading and unloading ships and in transporting goods for short distances. **2.** a fee paid for lighter service. [1475–85; LIGHTER[2] + -AGE]

lightʹer fluʹid, a combustible fluid used in cigarette, cigar, and pipe lighters. [1950–55]

light•er•man (līʹtər mən), *n., pl.* **-men.** a person who navigates a lighter. [1550–60; LIGHTER[2] + -MAN]

light•er-than-air (līʹtər thən ârʹ), *adj. Aeron.* **1.** (of an aircraft) weighing less than the air it displaces, hence obtaining lift from aerostatic buoyancy. **2.** of or pertaining to lighter-than-air craft. [1900–05]

light•face (lītʹfāsʹ), *Print.* —*n.* **1.** a type characterized by thin, light lines.

This is a sample of lightface.

—*adj.* **2.** Also, **lightʹ-facedʹ.** (of printed matter) set in lightface. Cf. **boldface.** [1870–75; LIGHT[2] + FACE]

light•fast (lītʹfastʹ, -fästʹ), *adj.* not affected or faded by light, esp. sunlight; colorfast when exposed to light. [1955–60; LIGHT[1] + FAST[1]] —**lightʹfastʹness,** *n.*

light-fin•gered (lītʹfingʹgərd), *adj.* **1.** skillful at or given to pilfering, esp. by picking pockets; thievish. **2.** having light and nimble fingers. [1540–50] —**lightʹ-finʹgered•ness,** *n.*

light-foot•ed (lītʹfo͝otʹid), *adj.* stepping lightly or nimbly; light of foot; nimble. [1375–1425; late ME] —**lightʹ-footʹed•ly,** *adv.* —**lightʹ-footʹed•ness,** *n.*

lightʹ guideʹ. See **optical fiber.** [1950–55]

light-hand•ed (lītʹhanʹdid), *adj.* **1.** short-handed. **2.** having the hands lightly or only slightly encumbered, as with parcels or bundles. **3.** having a light touch; handling things delicately and deftly. [1400–50; late ME] —**lightʹ-handʹed•ly,** *adv.* —**lightʹ-handʹed•ness,** *n.*

light•head•ed (lītʹhedʹid), *adj.* **1.** giddy, dizzy, or delirious: *After two drinks Pat began to feel lightheaded.* **2.** having or showing a frivolous or volatile disposition; thoughtless: *lightheaded persons.* [1530–40; LIGHT[2] + HEAD + -ED[3]] —**lightʹheadʹed•ly,** *adv.* —**lightʹheadʹed•ness,** *n.*

light•heart•ed (lītʹhärʹtid), *adj.* carefree; cheerful; gay: *a lighthearted laugh.* [1375–1425; late ME *lightherted;* see LIGHT[2], HEART, -ED[3]] —**lightʹheartʹed•ly,** *adv.* —**lightʹheartʹed•ness,** *n.*
—**Syn.** cheery, joyful, blithe, happy, glad, merry, jovial, jocund. —**Ant.** cheerless, melancholy, gloomy.

lightʹ heavʹyweight, a boxer or other contestant intermediate in weight between a middleweight and a heavyweight, esp. a professional boxer weighing up to 175 lb. (80 kg). [1900–05]

lightʹ horseʹ, cavalry carrying light arms and equipment. [1525–35]

light-horse•man (lītʹhôrsʹmən), *n., pl.* **-men.** a light-armed cavalry soldier. [1540–50; LIGHT HORSE + MAN[1]]

light•house (lītʹhousʹ), *n., pl.* **-hous•es** (-houʹziz). **1.** a tower or other structure displaying or flashing a very bright light for the guidance of ships in avoiding dangerous areas, in following certain routes, etc. See illus. on next page. **2.** either of two cylindrical metal towers placed forward on the forecastle of the main deck of a sailing ship, to house the port and starboard running lights. [1655–65; LIGHT[1] + HOUSE]

CONCISE ETYMOLOGY KEY: <, descended or borrowed from; >, whence; b., blend of, blended; c., cognate with; cf., compare; deriv., derivative; equiv., equivalent; imit., imitative; obl., oblique; r., replacing; s., stem; sp., spelling, spelled; resp., respelling, respelled; trans., translation; ?, origin unknown; *, unattested; ‡, probably earlier than. See the full key inside the front cover.

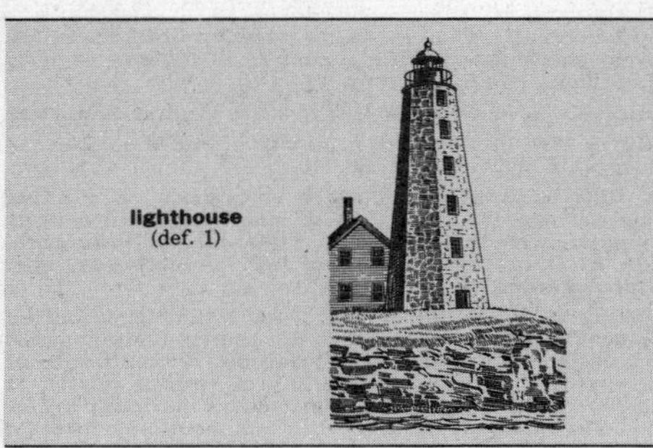
lighthouse (def. 1)

light′house clock′, an American mantel clock of the early 19th century, having the dial and works exposed beneath a glass dome on a tapered, cylindrical body.

light′house cof′feepot, a coffeepot of the late 17th and 18th centuries, having a tapering, circular body with a domed lid.

Light′house Point′, a city in SE Florida. 11,488.

light′house tube′, *Electronics.* a vacuum tube with the electrodes arranged in parallel layers closely spaced, giving a relatively high-power output at high frequencies.

Light′ in Au′gust, a novel (1932) by William Faulkner.

light′ in′fantry, 1. foot soldiers with lightweight weapons and minimal field equipment. **2.** infantry units with a minimal number of crew-served weapons and other supporting equipment. [1840–50]

light·ing (lī′ting), *n.* **1.** the act of igniting or illuminating: *the lighting of many candles; the annual lighting of the Christmas tree.* **2.** the arrangement of lights to achieve particular effects: *to work out the lighting for one's living room.* **3.** an effect achieved by the arrangement of lights: *Several critics praised the lighting of the play.* **4.** the science, theory, or method of achieving particular effects by the use of lights. **5.** the way light falls upon a face, object, etc., esp. in a picture. [bef. 1000; ME *lightinge,* OE *līhting.* See LIGHT[1], -ING[1]]

light·ish[1] (lī′tish), *adj.* rather light in color. [1650–60; LIGHT[1] + -ISH[1]]

light·ish[2] (lī′tish), *adj.* rather light in weight. [LIGHT[2] + -ISH[1]]

light·less (līt′lis), *adj.* **1.** without light or lights; receiving no light; dark. **2.** giving no light. [bef. 1000; ME *lihtles,* OE *lēohtlēas.* See LIGHT[1], -LESS] —**light′less·ness,** *n.*

light′ line′, *Naut.* the line or level to which a ship or boat sinks when fully supplied with fuel and ballast but without cargo. Also called **light′ load′ line′.** [1890–95]

light·ly (līt′lē), *adv.* **1.** with little weight, force, intensity, etc.; gently: *to press lightly on a door bell.* **2.** to only a small amount or degree; slightly: *lightly fried eggs.* **3.** nimbly; quickly: *to leap lightly aside.* **4.** with a lack of concern; indifferently; slightly: *to think lightly of one's achievements.* **5.** cheerfully; without complaining: *to take bad news lightly.* **6.** without due consideration or reason (often used negatively): *an offer not to be refused lightly.* **7.** easily; without trouble or effort: *Lightly come, lightly go.* **8.** frivolously; flippantly: *to behave lightly.* **9.** airily; buoyantly: *flags floating lightly.* [bef. 900; ME *lightli,* OE *lēohtlīce.* See LIGHT[2], -LY]

light′ machine′ gun′, *Mil.* any air-cooled machine gun having a caliber not greater than 0.30 in. (7.6 mm). [1920–25]

light′ meat′. See **white meat** (defs. 1, 2).

light′ me′ter. See **exposure meter.** [1920–25]

light′ mi′croscope, microscope (def. 1). [1940–45]

light-mind·ed (līt′mīn′did), *adj.* having or showing a lack of serious purpose, attitude, etc.; frivolous; trifling: *to be in a light-minded mood.* [1605–15] —**light′-mind′ed·ly,** *adv.* —**light′-mind′ed·ness,** *n.*

light′ min′eral, *Geol.* any rock-forming mineral that has a specific gravity of less than 2.8 and is generally light in color. Cf. **dark mineral.**

light′ min′eral oil′, *Chem.* See under **mineral oil.**

light·ness[1] (līt′nis), *n.* **1.** the state or quality of being light in weight: *the amazing lightness of the new metal.* **2.** the quality of being agile, nimble, or graceful. **3.** lack of pressure or burdensomeness. **4.** lack of seriousness; levity in actions, thoughts, or speech: *That kind of lightness seemed out of place.* **5.** gaiety of manner, speech, style, etc.; cheerfulness: *His lightness was just what the party needed.* [1175–1225; ME. See LIGHT[2], -NESS]
—**Syn. 2.** agility, grace, nimbleness, sprightliness.

light·ness[2] (līt′nis), *n.* **1.** the state or quality of being light or illuminated. **2.** thin or pale coloration. **3.** the relative degree to which an object reflects light, esp. light of complementary or nearly complementary colors. [bef. 1050; ME; OE *līhtness.* See LIGHT[1], -NESS]

light·ning (līt′ning), *n., v.,* **-ninged, -ning,** *adj.* —*n.* **1.** a brilliant electric spark discharge in the atmosphere, occurring within a thundercloud, between clouds, or between a cloud and the ground. —*v.i.* **2.** to emit a flash or flashes of lightning (often used impersonally with *it* as subject): *If it starts to lightning, we'd better go inside.* —*adj.* **3.** of, pertaining to, or resembling lightning, esp. in regard to speed of movement: *lightning flashes; lightning speed.* [1350–1400; ME, var. of *lightening.* See LIGHTEN[1], -ING[1]]

light′ning arrest′er, a device for preventing damage to radio, telephonic, or other electric equipment from lightning or other high-voltage currents, using spark gaps to carry the current to the ground without passing through the device. Also called **arrester.** [1855–60]

light′ning bug′, firefly. [1770–80, *Amer.*]

light′ning rod′, 1. a rodlike conductor installed to divert lightning away from a structure by providing a direct path to the ground. **2.** a person or thing that attracts and absorbs powerful and esp. negative or hostile feelings, opinions, etc., thereby diverting such feelings from other targets: *The unpopular supervisor served as a lightning rod for the criticism that should have been aimed at management.* [1780–90, *Amer.*]

light-o′-love (līt′ə luv′), *n.* **1.** a lover. **2.** a prostitute. Also, **light-of-love** (līt′əv luv′). [1570–80]

light′ op′era, operetta. [1880–85, *Amer.*]

light′ pen′, *Computers.* a hand-held light-sensitive device used for pointing at characters or objects on a CRT in order to make or modify drawings or to indicate functions to be performed. Also called **light′ pen′cil.** [1955–60]

light′ pipe′, *Optics.* an elongated transparent medium, such as an optical fiber, for transmitting light. [1945–50]

light·plane (līt′plān′), *n.* a lightweight passenger airplane with relatively limited performance capability. [1920–25; LIGHT[2] + (AIR)PLANE]

light′ pollu′tion, 1. unwanted or harmful light, as from bright street lights or neon signs. **2.** *Astron.* artificial illumination of the sky that sets a limit on the faintness of stars that can be observed or photographed. [1970–75]

light·proof (līt′prōōf′), *adj.* impervious to light: *a lightproof film cartridge.* [1920–25; LIGHT[1] + -PROOF]

light′ quan′tum, *Physics.* photon. [1920–25]

light-rail (līt′rāl′), *adj.* of or pertaining to a local rail rapid-transit system using large, single passenger cars, railroad-type signals, and, usually, private rights-of-way. [1975–80]

lights (līts), *n.pl.* the lungs, esp. of sheep, pigs, etc. [1150–1200; ME *lihte, lightes,* n. use of *liht* LIGHT[2]; cf. LUNG]

light·ship (līt′ship′), *n.* a ship anchored in a specific location and displaying or flashing a very bright light for the guidance of ships, as in avoiding dangerous areas. *Abbr.:* LS [1830–40; LIGHT[1] + SHIP]

light′ show′, a form of entertainment consisting chiefly of constantly changing patterns of light and color, usually accompanied by music and sound effects. [1965–70]

light·some[1] (līt′səm), *adj.* **1.** light, esp. in form, appearance, or movement; airy; buoyant; agile; nimble; graceful. **2.** cheerful; gay; lighthearted. **3.** frivolous; changeable. [1350–1400; ME *lyghtesum* (c. MHG *lihtsam*). See LIGHT[2], -SOME[1]] —**light′some·ly,** *adv.* —**light′some·ness,** *n.*

light·some[2] (līt′səm), *adj.* **1.** emitting or reflecting light; luminous. **2.** well-lighted; illuminated; bright. [1400–50; late ME *lyghtesum.* See LIGHT[1], -SOME[1]] —**light′some·ly,** *adv.* —**light′some·ness,** *n.*

lights′ out′, 1. *Chiefly Mil.* a signal, usually by drum or bugle, that all or certain camp or barracks lights are to be extinguished for the night. **2.** bedtime. [1865–70]

light-struck (līt′struk′), *adj. Photog.* (of a film or the like) damaged by accidental exposure to light. [1880–85]

light′ ta′ble, a table that has a translucent top illuminated from below and is used typically for making tracings or examining color transparencies.

light′ ther′apy, *Med.* therapeutic exposure to full-spectrum artificial light that simulates sunlight, used to treat various conditions, as seasonal affective disorder. Also called **phototherapy.**

light·tight (līt′tīt′), *adj. Chiefly Brit.* lightproof. [1880–85; LIGHT[1] + TIGHT, on the model of WATERTIGHT, AIRTIGHT, etc.]

light′ valve′, *Elect.* a light-transmitting device having transmissions that vary in accordance with an electric input, as voltage, current, or an electron beam, used chiefly for recording sound on motion-picture film. [1925–30]

light′ verse′, verse that is written to entertain, amuse, or please, often by the subtlety of its form rather than by its literary quality.

light′ weight′, *Naut.* See **light displacement.** [1765–75]

light·weight (līt′wāt′), *adj.* **1.** light in weight. **2.** being lighter in weight, texture, etc., than another item or object of identical use, quality, or function: *a lightweight topcoat; a lightweight alloy for ship construction.* **3.** without seriousness of purpose; trivial or trifling: *lightweight reading.* **4.** of or pertaining to a lightweight: *He's the new lightweight contender.* **5.** (of a horse, esp. a hunter) able to carry up to 165 lb. (75 kg). —*n.* **6.** a person of less than average weight. **7.** *Informal.* a person who is of little influence, importance, or effect. **8.** a boxer or other contestant intermediate in weight between a featherweight and a welterweight, esp. a professional boxer weighing between 126 and 135 lb. (56.7–61 kg). [1765–75; LIGHT[2] + WEIGHT]

light·wood (līt′wŏŏd′, -ŏŏd), *n. Southern U.S.* **1.** Also called **fatwood.** kindling. **2.** resinous pine wood used for kindling. [1675–85; LIGHT[1] + WOOD[1]]

light-year (līt′yēr′, -yēr′), *n.* **1.** *Astron.* the distance traversed by light in one mean solar year, about 5.88 trillion mi. (9.46 trillion km): used as a unit in measuring stellar distances. *Abbr.:* lt-yr **2. light-years, a.** a very great distance, esp. in development or progress: *The new computer is light-years ahead of the old one.* **b.** a very long time: *It's been light-years since I've seen my childhood friends.* [1885–90]

lign-, var. of **ligni-** before a vowel: *lignite.*

lign·al·oes (lī nal′ōz, lig-), *n.* (*used with a singular v.*) agalloch. [1325–75; ME *ligne aloes* < ML *lignum aloēs* wood of the aloe. See LIGN-, ALOE]

ligne (lēn; *Fr.* lēn′yᵊ), *n., pl.* **lignes** (lēnz; *Fr.* lēn′yᵊ). **1.** (in Swiss watchmaking) a unit equal to 0.0888 inch or 2.2558 millimeters, divided into 12 douziemes: used mainly to gauge the thickness of a movement. **2.** line[1] (def. 44). [< F: LINE[1]]

lig·ne·ous (lig′nē əs), *adj.* of the nature of or resembling wood; woody. [1620–30; < L *ligneus* of wood. See LIGN-, -EOUS]

ligni-, a combining form meaning "wood," used in the formation of compound words: *ligniform.* Also, **ligno-;** *esp. before a vowel,* **lign-.** [< L, comb. form repr. *lignum* wood]

lig·ni·form (lig′nə fôrm′), *adj.* having the form of wood; resembling wood, as a variety of asbestos. [1790–1800; LIGNI- + -FORM]

lig·ni·fy (lig′nə fī′), *v.,* **-fied, -fy·ing.** —*v.t.* **1.** to convert into wood; cause to become woody. —*v.i.* **2.** to become wood or woody. [1820–30; LIGNI- + -FY] —**lig′ni·fi·ca′tion,** *n.*

lig·nin (lig′nin), *n.* **1.** *Bot.* an organic substance that, with cellulose, forms the chief part of woody tissue. **2.** *Papermaking.* impure matter found in wood pulp. [1815–25; LIGN- + -IN[2]]

lig′nin sul′fonate, *Chem.* a brown powder consisting of a sulfonate salt made from waste liquor of the sulfate pulping process of soft wood: used in concrete, leather tanning, as an additive in oil-well drilling mud, and as a source of vanillin. Also called **lig·no·sul·fo·nate** (lig′nō sul′fə nāt′).

lig·nite (lig′nīt), *n.* a soft coal, usually dark brown, often having a distinct woodlike texture, and intermediate in density and carbon content between peat and bituminous coal. [1800–10; LIGN- + -ITE[1]] —**lig·nit·ic** (lig-nit′ik), *adj.*

lig′nite wax′. See **montan wax.**

lig·niv·or·ous (lig niv′ər əs), *adj.* xylophagous. [1820–30; LIGNI- + -VOROUS]

ligno-, var. of **ligni-:** *lignocellulose.*

lig·no·caine (lig′nə kān′), *n. Pharm.* lidocaine. [1950–55; LIGNO- + (*xylo*)*caine* an earlier name (LIGNO- being the L version of XYLO-); for *-caine,* see LIDOCAINE]

lig·no·cel·lu·lose (lig′nō sel′yə lōs′), *n. Bot.* any of various compounds of lignin and cellulose comprising the essential part of woody cell walls. [1895–1900; LIGNO- + CELLULOSE] —**lig·no·cel·lu·los·ic** (lig′nō sel′yə los′ik), *adj.*

lig·num vi·tae (lig′nəm vī′tē, vē′tī), **1.** either of two tropical American trees, *Guaiacum officinale* or *G. sanctum,* of the caltrop family, having very hard, heavy wood. **2.** the wood of such a tree, used for making pulley blocks, mallet heads, bearings, etc. **3.** any of several other trees yielding a similar hard wood. [1585–95; < NL, LL, name of the tree, lit., wood of life]

lig·ro·in (lig′rō in), *n.* a flammable mixture of hydrocarbons that boils at from 20°C to 135°C, obtained from petroleum by distillation and used as a solvent. Also, **lig′ro·ine.** [1880–85; orig. obscure]

lig′ snail′ (lig). See **banded Florida tree snail.**

lig·u·la (lig′yə lə), *n., pl.* **-lae** (-lē′), **-las. 1.** *Bot., Zool.* a tonguelike or strap-shaped part or organ. **2.** *Bot.* ligule. [1750–60; < NL, special use of L *li(n)gula* spoon, shoe-strap, equiv. to *lig-,* var. s. of *lingere* to LICK + *-ula* -ULE] —**lig′u·lar,** *adj.* —**lig′u·loid′,** *adj.*

lig·u·late (lig′yə lit, -lāt′), *adj.* **1.** having or forming a ligula. **2.** having the shape of a strap. Also, **lig·u·la·ted** (lig′yə lā′tid). [1745–55; LIGUL(A) + -ATE[1]]

lig·ule (lig′yōōl), *n. Bot.* **1.** a thin, membranous outgrowth from the base of the blade of most grasses. **2.** a strap-shaped corolla, as in the ray flowers of the head of certain composite plants. [1595–1605; < L *ligula;* see LIGULA]

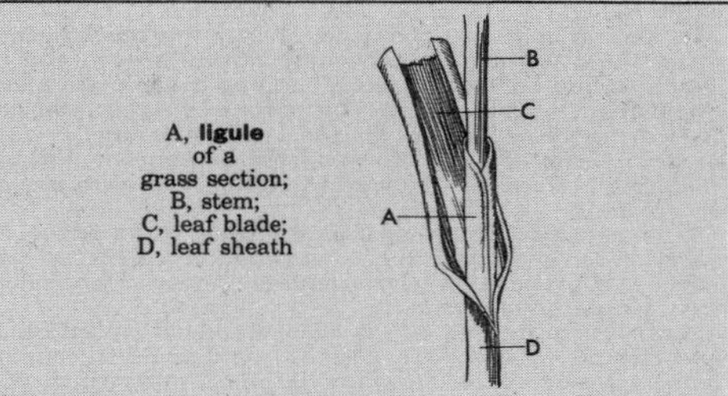

A, ligule of a grass section; B, stem; C, leaf blade; D, leaf sheath

lig·ure (lig′yŏŏr), *n.* a precious stone, probably the jacinth. Ex. 28:19. [1275–1325; ME *ligury* < LL *ligūrius* < LGk *ligýrion* a kind of precious stone]

Li·gu·ri·a (li gyŏŏr′ē ə), *n.* a region in NW Italy. 1,881,982; 2099 sq. mi. (5435 sq. km).

Li·gu·ri·an (li gyŏŏr′ē ən), *n.* **1.** an apparently Indo-European language used in ancient times along the NW coast of the Ligurian Sea. —*adj.* **2.** of or pertaining to Liguria or its inhabitants. [1595–1605; LIGURI(A) + -AN]

Ligu′rian Repub′lic, the republic in NW Italy set up by Napoleon in 1797, incorporated into France in 1805, and united with the Kingdom of Sardinia in 1814.

Ligu′rian Sea′, a part of the Mediterranean between Corsica and the NW coast of Italy.

CONCISE PRONUNCIATION KEY: act, cāpe, dâre, pärt; set, ēqual; if, īce; ox, ōver, ôrder, oil, bŏŏk, bōōt, out; up, ûrge; child; sing; shoe; thin, *th*at; zh as in *treasure.* ə = *a* as in *alone, e* as in *system, i* as in *easily, o* as in *gallop, u* as in *circus;* ᵊ as in *fire* (fīᵊr), *hour* (ouᵊr). l and n can serve as syllabic consonants, as in *cradle* (krād′l), and *button* (but′n). See the full key inside the front cover.

li•gus•trum (li gus′trəm), *n.* any of various shrubs or trees belonging to the genus *Ligustrum,* of the olive family, comprising the privets. [< NL (Linnaeus); L: privet]

Li Hsien-nien (*Chin.* lē′ shyun′nyun′), *Wade-Giles.* See **Li Xiannian.**

Li Hsüeh (lē′ shyœ′), *Chinese.* See **School of Law.**

Li Hung-chang (lē′ hŏŏng′jäng′), 1823–1901, Chinese statesman. Also, *Pinyin,* **Li Hong•zhang** (lē′ hông′-zhäng′).

lik•a•ble (lī′kə bəl), *adj.* readily or easily liked; pleasing: *a likable young man.* Also, **likeable.** [1720–30; LIKE[2] + -ABLE] —**lik′a•ble•ness, lik′a•bil′i•ty,** *n.*
—**Syn.** genial, attractive, winsome, engaging.

Li•ka•si (li kä′sē), *n.* a city in S Zaire. 150,000. Formerly, **Jadotville.**

like[1] (līk), *adj.,* (*Poetic*) **lik•er, lik•est,** *prep., adv., conj., n., v.,* **liked, lik•ing,** *interj.* —*adj.* **1.** of the same form, appearance, kind, character, amount, etc.: *I cannot remember a like instance.* **2.** corresponding or agreeing in general or in some noticeable respect; similar; analogous: *drawing, painting, and like arts.* **3.** bearing resemblance. **4.** *Dial.* likely: *'Tis like that he's gone mad.* **5.** *Dial.* about: *The poor chap seemed like to run away.* **6.** **something like,** *Informal.* something approaching or approximating: *It looked something like this.* —*prep.* **7.** in like manner with; similarly to; in the manner characteristic of: *He works like a beaver.* **8.** resembling (someone or something): *He is just like his father. Your necklace is just like mine.* **9.** characteristic of: *It would be like him to forget our appointment.* **10.** as if there is promise of; indicative of: *It looks like rain.* **11.** as if someone or something gives promise of being: *She looks like a good prospect for the job.* **12.** disposed or inclined to (usually prec. by *feel*): *to feel like going to bed.* **13.** similar or comparable to: *There is nothing like a cold drink of water when one is thirsty. What was he like?* **14.** (used correlatively to indicate similarity through relationship): *like father, like son.* **15.** (used to establish an intensifying, often facetious, comparison): *sleeping like a log.* **16.** as; such as: *There are numerous hobbies you might enjoy, like photography or painting.* **17.** **like anything,** *Informal.* very much; extremely; with great intensity: *He wanted like anything to win.* —*adv.* **18.** nearly; closely; approximately: *The house is more like 40 than 20 years old.* **19.** *Informal.* likely or probably: *Like enough he'll come with us. Like as not her leg is broken.* **20.** *Nonstandard.* **a.** as it were; in a way; somehow. **b.** to a degree; more or less: *standing against the wall, looking very tough like.* —*conj.* **21.** in the same way as; just as; as: *It happened like you might expect it would.* **22.** as if: *He acted like he was afraid. The car runs like new.* —*n.* **23.** a similar or comparable person or thing, or like persons or things; counterpart, match, or equal (usually prec. by a possessive adjective or *the*): *No one has seen his like in a long time. Like attracts like.* **24.** kind; sort; type; ilk (usually prec. by a possessive adjective): *I despise moochers and their like.* **25.** **the like,** something of a similar nature: *They grow oranges, lemons, and the like.* **26.** **the like** or **likes of,** someone or something similar to; the equal of: *I've never seen the like of it anywhere.* —*v.i.* **27.** **like to** or **liked to,** *South Midland and Southern U.S.* was on the verge of or came close to (doing something): *The poor kid like to froze.* —*interj.* **28.** *Informal.* (used esp. in speech, often nonvolitionally or habitually, to preface a sentence, to fill a pause, to express uncertainty, or to intensify or neutralize a following adjective): *Like, why didn't you write to me? The music was, like, really great, you know?* [1150–1200; ME *lic, lik* < ON *līkr;* r. OE *gelic,* c. D *gelijk,* G *gleich,* ON *glīkr,* Goth *galeiks* like, lit., of the same body or form. See Y-, LICH] —**lik′er,** *n.*
—**Usage.** LIKE[1] as a conjunction meaning "as, in the same way as" (*Many shoppers study the food ads like brokers study market reports*) or "as if" (*It looks like it will rain*) has been used for nearly 500 years and by many distinguished literary and intellectual figures. Since the mid-19th century there have been objections, often vehement, to these uses. Nevertheless, such uses are almost universal today in all but the most formal speech and writing. In extremely careful speech and in much formal writing, *as, as if,* and *as though* are more commonly used than LIKE: *The commanding general accepted full responsibility for the incident, as any professional soldier would. Many of the Greenwich Village bohemians lived as if* (or *as though*) *there were no tomorrow.*
The strong strictures against the use of LIKE as a conjunction have resulted in the occasional hypercorrect use of *as* as a preposition where LIKE is idiomatic: *She looks as a sympathetic person.*
LIKE meaning "as if" is also standard in informal speech and writing with a small number of adjectives: *The crew worked like crazy* (or *like mad*) *to finish the job on time.* See also **as.**

like[2] (līk), *v.,* **liked, lik•ing,** *n.* —*v.t.* **1.** to take pleasure in; find agreeable or congenial: *We all liked the concert.* **2.** to regard with favor; have a kindly or friendly feeling for (a person, group, etc.); find attractive: *His parents like me and I like them.* **3.** to wish or prefer: *You can do exactly as you like while you are a guest here.* —*v.i.* **4.** to feel inclined; wish: *We'll have lunch whenever you like.* **5.** *Archaic.* to suit the tastes or wishes; please. **6.** **would like.** See **would** (def. 10). —*n.* **7.** Usually, **likes.** the things a person likes: *a long list of likes and dislikes.* [bef. 900; ME *liken,* OE *līcian;* c. D *lijken,* ON *līka;* see LIKE[1]]

-like, a suffixal use of **like**[1] in the formation of adjectives (*childlike; lifelike*), sometimes hyphenated.

like•a•ble (lī′kə bəl), *adj.* likable.

CONCISE ETYMOLOGY KEY: <, descended or borrowed from; >, whence; b., blend of, blended; c., cognate with; cf., compare; deriv., derivative; equiv., equivalent; imit., imitative; obl., oblique; r., replacing; s., stem; sp., spelling, spelled; resp., respelling, respelled; trans., translation; ?, origin unknown; *, unattested; ‡, probably earlier than. See the full key inside the front cover.

like•li•hood (līk′lē ho͝od′), *n.* **1.** the state of being likely or probable; probability. **2.** a probability or chance of something: *There is a strong likelihood of his being elected.* **3.** *Archaic.* indication of a favorable end; promise. Also, **like′li•ness.** [1350–1400; ME *liklihood.* See LIKELY, -HOOD]

like•ly (līk′lē), *adj.,* **-li•er, -li•est,** *adv.* —*adj.* **1.** probably or apparently destined (usually fol. by an infinitive): *something not likely to happen.* **2.** seeming like truth, fact, or certainty; reasonably to be believed or expected; believable: *a likely story.* **3.** seeming to fulfill requirements or expectations; apparently suitable: *a likely place for a restaurant.* **4.** showing promise of achievement or excellence; promising: *a fine, likely young man.* —*adv.* **5.** probably: *We will likely stay home this evening.* [1250–1300; ME *likli* < ON *līkligr.* See LIKE[1], -LY]
—**Syn. 3.** appropriate.
—**Usage.** LIKELY in the senses "probably destined" and "probably" is often preceded by a qualifying word like *very, more,* or *quite: The board is very likely to turn down the request. The new system will quite likely increase profits.* However, despite statements to the contrary in some usage guides, LIKELY in these senses is standard without such a qualifier in all varieties of English: *It will likely be a bitter debate. The shipment will likely arrive on Thursday.* See also **apt, liable.**

like-mind•ed (līk′mīn′did), *adj.* having a similar or identical opinion, disposition, etc.: *a like-minded friend.* [1520–30; LIKE[1] + -MINDED] —**like′-mind′ed•ly,** *adv.* —**like′-mind′ed•ness,** *n.*

lik•en (lī′kən), *v.t.* to represent as similar or like; compare: *to liken someone to a weasel.* [1275–1325; ME *liknen.* See LIKE[1], -EN[1]]

like•ness (līk′nis), *n.* **1.** a representation, picture, or image, esp. a portrait: *to draw a good likeness of Churchill.* **2.** the state or fact of being like: *I can't get over your likeness to my friend.* **3.** the semblance or appearance of something; guise: *to assume the likeness of a swan.* [bef. 950; ME *liknesse,* OE *līcnes,* var. of *gelīcnes.* See ALIKE, -NESS]
—**Syn. 2.** resemblance, similitude. **3.** shape, form.

like•wise (līk′wīz′), *adv.* **1.** moreover; in addition; also; too: *She is likewise a fine lawyer.* **2.** in like manner; in the same way; similarly: *I'm tempted to do likewise.* [1400–50; late ME; earlier *in like wise* in a like way. See LIKE[1], WISE[2]]

li•kin (lē′kēn′), *n.* (formerly in China) a provincial duty imposed on articles of trade that are in transit. [1875–80; < earlier or dial. Chin, for Chin *líjīn* (*lí* .001 ounce + *jīn* money)]

lik•ing (lī′king), *n.* **1.** preference, inclination, or favor: *to show a liking for privacy.* **2.** pleasure or taste: *much to his liking.* **3.** the state or feeling of a person who likes. [bef. 900; ME; OE *līcung.* See LIKE[2], -ING[1]]
—**Syn. 1.** leaning, propensity, predilection, partiality, fondness, affection. —**Ant. 1.** antipathy.

lik•ker (lik′ər), *n. Eye Dialect.* liquor.

Li•kud (lē′ko͞od, lē ko͞od′), *n.* a conservative political party in Israel, founded in 1973. [< Heb *likkūdh* lit., consolidation]

li•ku•ta (li ko͞o′tə), *n., pl.* **ma•ku•ta** (mä ko͞o′tə). a paper money, aluminum coin, and monetary unit of Zaire, the 100th part of a zaire.

li•la (lē′lä), *n. Hinduism.* creation, seen as the playful activity of a god. [1820–30; < Skt *līlā* play, sport, diversion]

Li•la (lī′lə), *n.* a female given name, form of **Leila.**

li•lac (lī′lək, -läk, -lak), *n.* **1.** any of various shrubs belonging to the genus *Syringa,* of the olive family, as *S. vulgaris,* having large clusters of fragrant purple or white flowers: the state flower of New Hampshire. **2.** pale reddish purple. —*adj.* **3.** having the color lilac. [1615–25; < Sp < Ar *līlak* < Pers, assimilated var. of *nīlak* bluish, equiv. to *nil* blue, indigo (< Skt *nīla*) + *-ak* suffix of appurtenance]

li•la•ceous (lī lā′shəs), *adj.* of or approaching the color lilac. [1850–55; LILAC + -EOUS]

li•lan•ge•ni (li läng′ge nē, lē′läng gen′ē), *n., pl.* **em•a•lan•gen•i** (em′ə läng gen′ē), a cupronickel coin, paper money, and monetary unit of Swaziland, equal to 100 cents.

Lil•i (lil′ē), *n.* a female given name. Also, **Lil′li.**

lil•i•a•ceous (lil′ē ā′shəs), *adj.* **1.** of or like the lily. **2.** belonging to the plant family Liliaceae. Cf. **lily family.** [1725–35; < LL *liliāceus.* See LILY, -ACEOUS]

lil•ied (lil′ēd), *adj.* **1.** abounding in lilies. **2.** *Archaic.* lilylike; white. [1605–15; LILY + -ED[3]]

Lil•i•en•thal (lil′ē ən thôl′; *for 2 also Ger.* lē′lē ən-täl′), *n.* **1. David E(ly),** 1899–1981, U.S. public administrator. **2. Ot•to** (ôt′ō), 1848–96, German aeronautical engineer and inventor.

Lil•ith (lil′ith), *n.* **1.** *Semitic Myth.* a female demon dwelling in deserted places and attacking children. **2.** *Jewish Folklore.* Adam's first wife, before Eve was created.

Li•li•u•o•ka•la•ni (lē lē′o͞o ō kä lä′nē), *n.* **Lydia Ka•me•ke•ha** (kä′me ke′hä), 1838–1917, last queen of the Hawaiian Islands 1891–93.

Lille (lēl), *n.* a city in and the capital of Nord, in N France. 177,218. Formerly, **Lisle.**

Lil•li•an (lil′ē ən), *n.* a female given name. Also, **Lil′i•an.**

Lil•li•bul•le•ro (lil′ē bə lēr′ō), *n.* **1.** a part of the refrain to a song deriding the Irish Roman Catholics, popular in England during and after the revolution of 1688. **2.** the song, or the tune to which it was sung.

Lil•li•put (lil′i put′, -pət), *n.* an imaginary country inhabited by people about 6 in. (15 cm) tall, described in Swift's *Gulliver's Travels.*

Lil•li•pu•tian (lil′i pyo͞o′shən), *adj.* **1.** extremely small; tiny; diminutive. **2.** petty; trivial: *Our worries are Lilliputian when compared with those of people whose nations are at war.* —*n.* **3.** an inhabitant of Lilliput. **4.** a very small person. **5.** a person who is narrow or petty in outlook. [1726; LILLIPUT + -IAN]

Lil•lo (lil′ō), *n.* **George,** 1693?–1739, English dramatist.

Li•long•we (li lông′wā), *n.* a city in and the capital of Malawi, in the SW part. 20,000.

lilt (lilt), *n.* **1.** rhythmic swing or cadence. **2.** a lilting song or tune. —*v.i., v.t.* **3.** to sing or play in a light, tripping, or rhythmic manner. [1300–50; ME *lulte;* perh. akin to D *lul* pipe, *lullen* to lull] —**lilt′ing•ly,** *adv.* —**lilt′ing•ness,** *n.*

lil•y (lil′ē), *n., pl.* **lil•ies,** *adj.* —*n.* **1.** any scaly-bulbed plant of the genus *Lilium,* having showy, funnel-shaped or bell-shaped flowers. Cf. **lily family. 2.** the flower or the bulb of such a plant. **3.** any of various related or similar plants or their flowers, as the mariposa lily or the calla lily. **4.** fleur-de-lis, esp. as the symbol of France. **5.** *Bowling.* a split in which the five, seven, and ten pins remain standing. **6.** **gild the lily.** See **gild**[1] (def. 4). —*adj.* **7.** white as a lily: *her lily hands.* **8.** delicately fair: *a lily maiden.* **9.** pure; unsullied: *the lily truth.* **10.** pale; fragile; weak. [bef. 1000; ME, OE *lilie* < L *līlium;* cf. Gk *leírion*] —**lil′y•like′,** *adj.*

Lil•y (lil′e), *n.* a female given name. Also, **Lil′ly.**

Lil•yan (lil′yən), *n.* a female given name.

lil′y fam′ily, the large plant family Liliaceae, characterized by chiefly herbaceous plants growing from bulbs, corms, rhizomes, or tubers, having narrow, parallel-veined, usually basal leaves, often showy flowers, and fruit in the form of a berry or capsule, and including the aloe, asparagus, aspidistra, hyacinth, numerous species of lily, lily of the valley, trillium, and tulip.

lil′y i′ron, a harpoon whose head may be detached. [1830–40]

lil•y-liv•ered (lil′ē liv′ərd), *adj.* weak or lacking in courage; cowardly; pusillanimous. [1595–1605; LILY + LIVER[1] + -ED[3]]

lily-of-the-Nile (lil′ē əv *th*ə nīl′), *n.* a plant, *Agapanthus africanus,* of the amaryllis family, native to Africa, having large umbels of blue flowers. Also called **African lily.**

lil′y of the val′ley, *pl.* **lilies of the valley.** a plant, *Convallaria majalis,* having an elongated cluster of small, drooping, bell-shaped, fragrant white flowers. [1555–65]

lil′y pad′, the large, floating leaf of a water lily. [1805–15, *Amer.*]

lil•y-trot•ter (lil′ē trot′ər), *n.* jaçana. [1915–20]

lil•y-turf (lil′ē tûrf′), *n.* **1.** liriope. **2.** See **mondo grass.** [LILY + TURF]

lil•y-white (*adj.* lil′ē hwīt′, -wīt′; *n.* lil′ē hwīt′, -wīt′), *adj.* **1.** white as a lily: *soft lily-white skin.* **2.** pure; untouched by corruption or imperfection; above reproach: *He tries to pass himself off as some sort of lily-white saint, but he's not.* **3.** designating or pertaining to any faction, organization, or group opposing the inclusion of blacks, esp. in political or social life. —*n.* **4.** a member of a lily-white organization, esp. a member of a former faction of the Republican party in the South opposed to the inclusion of blacks in the party or in political life in general. [1275–1325; ME *lylie-whyt*]
—**Syn. 3.** segregated, discriminatory, unintegrated.

lim., limit.

Li•ma (lē′mə *or, Sp.,* lē′mä *for 1;* lī′mə *for 2*), *n.* **1.** a city in and the capital of Peru, near the Pacific coast. 3,317,648. **2.** a city in NW Ohio. 47,381.

Li•ma (lē′mə), *n.* a word used in communications to represent the letter *L.* [1950–55]

li′ma bean′ (lī′mə), **1.** a bean, *Phaseolus limensis,* having a broad, flat, edible seed. **2.** the seed, used for food. [1810–20; named after LIMA, Peru]

lim•a•cine (lim′ə sin′, -sin, lī′mə-), *adj.* pertaining to or resembling a slug; sluglike. [1885–90; < L *līmāc-* (s. of *līmāx*) slug, snail + -INE[1]]

lim•a•çon (lim′ə son′), *n. Geom.* a plane curve generated by the locus of a point on a line at a fixed distance from the point of intersection of the line with a fixed circle, as the line revolves about a point on the circumference of the circle. Equation: $r = a\cos\theta + b$. Also called **Pascal's limaçon.** [1575–85; < F: lit., snail, OF, deriv. of *limaz* < L *līmācem,* acc. of *līmāx* snail, slug]

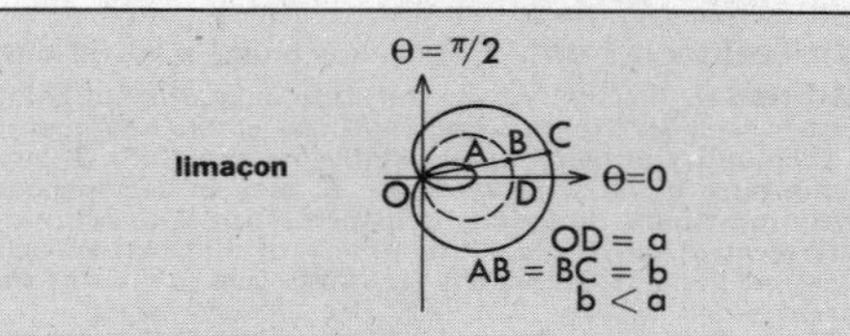

li•man (li män′, -man′), *n. Geol.* **1.** a muddy lagoon, marsh, or lake near the mouth of a river behind part of the delta and more or less protected from open water by a barrier or spit. **2.** an area of mud or silt deposited near the mouth of a river. [1855–60; < Russ *limán* estuary, coastal salt lake < Turk or Crimean Tatar < MGk *liménion, liménas* (cf. Gk *limḗn* harbor)]

Li•mas•sol (lim′ə sôl′), *n.* a seaport in S Cyprus: Phoenician ruins. 48,000. Also, **Limmasol.** Ancient, **Lemessus.**

limb[1] (lim), *n.* **1.** a part or member of an animal body distinct from the head and trunk, as a leg, arm, or wing: *the lower limbs; artificial limbs.* **2.** a large or main branch of a tree. **3.** a projecting part or member: *the four limbs of a cross.* **4.** a person or thing regarded as a part, member, branch, offshoot, or scion of something: *a limb of the central committee.* **5.** *Archery.* the upper or lower part of a bow. **6.** *Informal.* a mischievous child, imp, or young scamp. **7. out on a limb,** in a dangerous or compromising situation; vulnerable: *The company overextended itself financially and was soon out on a limb.* —*v.t.* **8.** to cut the limbs from (a felled tree). [bef. 900; ME, OE *lim;* akin to ON *lim* foliage, *limr* limb, *limi* rod, L *līmus* aslant, *līmen* threshold] —**limb′less,** *adj.* —**Syn. 1.** extremity. **2.** See **branch.**

limb[2] (lim), *n.* **1.** *Astron.* the edge of the disk of the sun, a moon, or a planet. **2.** the graduated edge of a quadrant or similar instrument. **3.** *Bot.* **a.** the upper spreading part of a gamopetalous corolla. **b.** the expanded portion of a petal, sepal, or leaf. [1350–1400; ME < L *limbus;* see LIMBUS[2], LIMBO[1]]

lim•ba (lim′bə), *n.* **1.** an African tree, *Terminalia superba,* having yellowish-brown wood. **2.** the wood of this tree. [1935–40; of uncert. orig.]

lim•bate (lim′bāt), *adj. Bot., Zool.* bordered, as a flower in which one color is surrounded by an edging of another. [1820–30; < LL *limbātus* bordered, edged. See LIMB[2], -ATE[1]]

limbed (limd), *adj.* having a specified number or kind of limbs (often used in combination): *a long-limbed dancer.* [1275–1325; ME; see LIMB[1], -ED[3]]

lim•ber[1] (lim′bər), *adj.* **1.** characterized by ease in bending the body; supple; lithe. **2.** bending readily; flexible; pliant. —*v.i.* **3.** to make oneself limber (usually fol. by *up*): *to limber up before the game.* —*v.t.* **4.** to make (something) limber (usually fol. by *up*): *She tried to limber up her wits before the exam.* [1555–65; perh. akin to LIMB[1]] —**lim′ber•ly,** *adv.* —**lim′ber•ness,** *n.* —**Syn. 2.** pliable. See **flexible.** —**Ant. 1, 2.** stiff. **2.** rigid, unbending.

lim•ber[2] (lim′bər), *Mil.* —*n.* **1.** a two-wheeled vehicle, originally pulled by four or six horses, behind which is towed a field gun or caisson. —*v.t.* **2.** to attach the limber to (a gun) in preparation for moving away (sometimes fol. by *up*). —*v.i.* **3.** to attach a limber to a gun (usually fol. by *up*). [1400–50; late ME *lymo(u)r* pole of a vehicle. See LIMB[1], -ER[1]]

lim•ber[3] (lim′bər), *n.* Usually, **limbers.** *Naut.* a passage or gutter in which seepage collects to be pumped away, located on each side of a central keelson; bilge. [1620–30; perh. < F *lumière* hole, light < LL *lūmināria;* see LUMINARIA]

lim′ber hole′, *Naut.* any of a series of holes pierced through a frame or floor to allow the passage of accumulated moisture. [1620–30]

lim•ber•neck (lim′bər nek′), *n. Vet. Pathol.* a fatal infection of botulism affecting birds, esp. chickens and ducks, characterized by weakness of the neck muscles and inability to eat. [1905–10; LIMBER[1] + NECK]

lim′ber pine′, a pine, *Pinus flexilis,* of western North America, having light, soft wood used locally for railroad ties, poles, fuel, etc.

lim•bic (lim′bik), *adj.* pertaining to or of the nature of a limbus or border; marginal. [1880–85; LIMB(US)[2] + -IC]

lim′bic sys′tem, *Anat.* a ring of interconnected structures in the midline of the brain around the hypothalamus, involved with emotion and memory and with homeostatic regulatory systems. [1950–55]

lim•bo[1] (lim′bō), *n., pl.* **-bos. 1.** (*often cap.*) *Rom. Cath. Theol.* a region on the border of hell or heaven, serving as the abode after death of unbaptized infants (**lim′bo of in′fants**) and of the righteous who died before the coming of Christ (**lim′bo of the fa′thers** or **lim′bo of the pa′triarchs**). **2.** a place or state of oblivion to which persons or things are regarded as being relegated when cast aside, forgotten, past, or out of date: *My youthful hopes are in the limbo of lost dreams.* **3.** an intermediate, transitional, or midway state or place. **4.** a place or state of imprisonment or confinement. [1300–50; ME, from ML phrase *in limbō* on hell's border (L: on the edge), equiv. to *in* on + *limbō,* abl. of *limbus* edge, border (L), place bordering on hell (ML); see LIMBUS[1]]

lim•bo[2] (lim′bō), *n., pl.* **-bos.** a dance from the West Indies, originally for men only, in which the dancer bends backward from the knees and moves with a shuffling step under a horizontal bar that is lowered after each successive pass. [1955–60; cf. Jamaican E *limba* to bend, easily bending; see LIMBER[1]]

Lim•bourg (*Fr.* laɴ bo͞or′), *n.* See under **Limburg.**

Lim•burg (lim′bûrg; *Du.* lim′bœrkh), *n.* a medieval duchy in W Europe: now divided into a province in the SE Netherlands (**Limburg**) and a province in NE Belgium (**Limbourg**).

Lim•burg•er (lim′bûr′gər), *n.* a variety of soft white cheese of strong odor and flavor. Also called **Lim′burger cheese′, Lim′burg cheese′.** [1810–20; named after LIMBURG; see -ER[1]]

lim•bus[1] (lim′bəs), *n., pl.* **-bi** (-bī). limbo[1]. [1400–50; late ME < ML; L: LIMBUS[2]]

lim•bus[2] (lim′bəs), *n., pl.* **-bi** (-bī). *Anat., Zool.* a border, edge, or limb. [1665–75; < NL, L]

lime[1] (līm), *n., v.,* **limed, lim•ing.** —*n.* **1.** Also called **burnt lime, calcium oxide, caustic lime, calx, quicklime.** a white or grayish-white, odorless, lumpy, very slightly water-soluble solid, CaO, that when combined with water forms calcium hydroxide (**slaked lime**), obtained from calcium carbonate, limestone, or oyster shells: used chiefly in mortars, plasters, and cements, in bleaching powder, and in the manufacture of steel, paper, glass, and various chemicals of calcium. **2.** a calcium compound for improving crops grown in soils deficient in lime. **3.** birdlime. —*v.t.* **4.** to treat (soil) with lime or compounds of calcium. **5.** to smear (twigs, branches, etc.) with birdlime. **6.** to catch with or as if with birdlime. **7.** to paint or cover (a surface) with a composition of lime and water; whitewash: *The government buildings were freshly limed.* [bef. 900; ME, OE *līm;* c. D *lijm,* G *Leim,* ON *līm* glue, L *līmus* slime; akin to LOAM] —**lime′less,** *adj.* —**lime′like′,** *adj.*

lime[2] (līm), *n.* **1.** the small, greenish-yellow, acid fruit of a citrus tree, *Citrus aurantifolia,* allied to the lemon. **2.** the tree that bears this fruit. **3.** greenish yellow. —*adj.* **4.** of the color lime. **5.** of or made with limes. [1615–25; < Sp *lima* < Ar *līmah, līm* citrus fruit < Pers *līmū(n);* cf. LEMON] —**lime′less,** *adj.* —**lime′like′,** *adj.*

lime[3] (līm), *n.* the European linden, *Tilia europaea.* [1615–25; unexplained var. of obs. *line, lind,* ME, OE *lind.* See LINDEN]

lime[4] (līm), *n. Informal.* limelight. [shortened form]

lime•ade (līm′ād′, līm′ād′), *n.* a beverage consisting of lime juice, a sweetener, and plain or carbonated water. [1890–95; LIME[2] + -ADE[1]]

lime′ burn′er, a person who makes lime by burning or calcining limestone, shells, etc. [1300–50; ME]

lime′ glass′, inexpensive glass containing a large proportion of lime, used for making cheap glasses, windowpanes, etc. [1905–10]

Lime•house (līm′hous′), *n.* a dock district in the East End of London, England, once notorious for its squalor: formerly a Chinese quarter.

lime′ hy′drate. See **slaked lime.**

lime-juic•er (līm′jo͞o′sər), *n. Slang.* **1.** a British person. **2.** a British sailor. [1855–60; so called because British sailors were required by law to drink lime juice to ward off scurvy]

lime•kiln (līm′kil′, -kiln′), *n.* a kiln or furnace for making lime by calcining limestone or shells. [1250–1300; ME *limkilne.* See LIME[1], KILN]

lime•light (līm′līt′), *n.* **1.** *Theat.* **a.** (formerly) a lighting unit for spotlighting the front of the stage, producing illumination by means of a flame of mixed gases directed at a cylinder of lime and having a special lens for concentrating the light in a strong beam. **b.** the light so produced. **c.** *Chiefly Brit.* a lighting unit, esp. a spotlight. **2.** the center of public attention, interest, observation, or notoriety: *He seems fond of the limelight.* [1820–30; LIME[1] + LIGHT[1]] —**lime′light′er,** *n.*

lime′ lin′iment, *Pharm.* See **carron oil.** [1875–80]

li•men (lī′mən), *n., pl.* **li•mens, lim•i•na** (lim′ə nə). threshold (def. 4). [1890–95; < L *līmen*]

lime•quat (līm′kwot′), *n.* **1.** a hybrid citrus tree produced by crossing the lime and the kumquat. **2.** the tart, pale yellow fruit of this tree. [LIME[2] + (KUM)QUAT]

lim•er•ick (lim′ər ik), *n.* a kind of humorous verse of five lines, in which the first, second, and fifth lines rhyme with each other, and the third and fourth lines, which are shorter, form a rhymed couplet. [1895–1900; after LIMERICK; allegedly from social gatherings where the group sang "Will you come up to Limerick?" after each set of verses, extemporized in turn by the members of the party]

Lim•er•ick (lim′ər ik), *n.* **1.** a county in N Munster, in the SW Republic of Ireland. 100,865; 1037 sq. mi. (2686 sq. km). **2.** its county seat: a seaport at the head of the Shannon estuary. 60,721. **3.** *Angling.* a fishhook having a sharp bend below the barb.

li•mes (lī′mēs), *n., pl.* **lim•i•tes** (lim′i tēz′). **1.** a boundary, esp. the fortified border or frontier of a country. **2.** (*cap.*) See **Siegfried line. 3.** an ancient Roman frontier fortification. [1530–40; < L *līmes;* see LIMIT]

lime•stone (līm′stōn′), *n.* a sedimentary rock consisting predominantly of calcium carbonate, varieties of which are formed from the skeletons of marine microorganisms and coral: used as a building stone and in the manufacture of lime. Cf. **marble.** [1515–25; LIME[1] + STONE]

lime′stone let′tuce, a variety of lettuce derived from Bibb lettuce.

lime′ sul′fur, *Chem.* a mixture of lime and sulfur that has been boiled in water: used in powdered form or in aqueous solution as an insecticide, a fungicide, and a sheep dip. Also, **lime′ sul′phur.** [1905–10]

lime′ tree′, a linden or basswood. [1615–25]

lime′ twig′, 1. a twig smeared with birdlime to catch birds. **2.** a snare or trap. [1400–50; late ME]

lime•wa•ter (līm′wô′tər, -wot′ər), *n.* **1.** an aqueous solution of slaked lime, used in medicine, antacids, and lotions, and to absorb carbon dioxide from the air. **2.** water containing naturally an unusual amount of calcium carbonate or calcium sulfate. [1660–70; LIME[1] + WATER]

lime•wood (līm′wo͝od′), *n.* the wood of a linden. [1725–35; LIME[3] + WOOD[1]]

lim•ey (lī′mē), *n., pl.* **-eys,** *adj. Slang* (*sometimes disparaging and offensive*). —*n.* **1.** a British sailor. **2.** a British person. **3.** a British ship. —*adj.* **4.** British. [1885–90; see LIME-JUICER, -Y[2]]

Lim′ Fjord′ (lēm), a fjord in N Denmark running E from the North Sea to the Kattegat. ab. 110 mi. (175 km) long.

li•mic•o•line (lī mik′ə līn′, -lin), *adj.* shore-inhabiting; of or pertaining to numerous birds of the families Charadriidae, comprising the plovers, and Scolopacidae, comprising the sandpipers. [1870–75; < LL *līmicol(a)* mud-dweller + -INE[1]; see LIME[1], -COLINE]

li•mic•o•lous (lī mik′ə ləs), *adj.* dwelling in mud or muddy regions. [1885–90; < LL *līmicol(a)* mud-dweller + -OUS; see LIME[1], -COLOUS]

lim•i•nal (lim′ə nl, lī′mə-), *adj. Psychol.* of, pertaining to, or situated at the limen. [1880–85; < L *limin-* (s. of *līmen*) threshold + -AL[1]]

lim•i•nal•i•ty (lim′ə nal′i tē), *n. Anthropol.* the transitional period or phase of a rite of passage, during which the participant lacks social status or rank, remains anonymous, shows obedience and humility, and follows prescribed forms of conduct, dress, etc. [< L *limin-* (s. of *līmen*) threshold + -AL[1] + -ITY]

lim•it (lim′it), *n.* **1.** the final, utmost, or furthest boundary or point as to extent, amount, continuance, procedure, etc.: *the limit of his experience; the limit of vision.* **2.** a boundary or bound, as of a country, area, or district. **3.** *Math.* **a.** a number such that the value of a given function remains arbitrarily close to this number when the independent variable is sufficiently close to a specified point or is sufficiently large. The limit of $1/x$ is zero as x approaches infinity; the limit of $(x - 1)^2$ is zero as x approaches 1. **b.** a number such that the absolute value of the difference between terms of a given sequence and the number approaches zero as the index of the terms increases to infinity. **c.** one of two numbers affixed to the integration symbol for a definite integral, indicating the interval or region over which the integration is taking place and substituted in a primitive, if one exists, to evaluate the integral. **4. limits,** the premises or region enclosed within boundaries: *We found them on school limits after hours.* **5.** *Games.* the maximum sum by which a bet may be raised at any one time. **6. the limit,** *Informal.* something or someone that exasperates, delights, etc., to an extreme degree: *You have made errors before, but this is the limit.* —*v.t.* **7.** to restrict by or as if by establishing limits (usually fol. by *to*): *Please limit answers to 25 words.* **8.** to confine or keep within limits: *to limit expenditures.* **9.** *Law.* to fix or assign definitely or specifically. [1325–75; ME *lymyt* < L *līmit-* (s. of *līmes*) boundary, path between fields] —**lim′it•a•ble,** *adj.* —**lim′it•a•ble•ness,** *n.* —**Syn. 2.** confine, frontier, border. **8.** restrain, bound.

lim•i•tar•y (lim′i ter′ē), *adj.* **1.** of, pertaining to, or serving as a limit. **2.** *Archaic.* subject to limits; limited. [1610–20; LIMIT + -ARY]

lim•i•ta•tion (lim′i tā′shən), *n.* **1.** a limiting condition; restrictive weakness; lack of capacity; inability or handicap: *He knows his limitations as a writer.* **2.** something that limits; a limit or bound; restriction: *an arms limitation; a limitation on imports.* **3.** the act of limiting. **4.** the state of being limited. **5.** *Law.* the assignment, as by statute, of a period of time within which an action must be brought, or the period of time assigned: *a statute of limitations.* [1350–1400; ME *lymytacion* < L *līmitātiōn-* (s. of *līmitātiō*) a bounding, equiv. to *līmitāt(us)* (ptp. of *līmitāre* to enclose within boundaries; see LIMIT, -ATE[1]) + *-iōn-* -ION]

lim•i•ta•tive (lim′i tā′tiv), *adj.* limiting; restrictive. [1520–30; < ML *līmitātīvus.* See LIMITATION, -IVE]

lim•it•ed (lim′i tid), *adj.* **1.** confined within limits; restricted or circumscribed: *a limited space; limited resources.* **2.** restricted with reference to governing powers by limitations prescribed in laws and in a constitution: *a limited monarch.* **3.** characterized by an inability to think imaginatively or independently; lacking originality or scope; narrow: *a rather limited intelligence.* **4.** *Chiefly Brit.* **a.** responsible for the debts of a company only to a specified amount proportionate to the percentage of stock held. **b.** (of a business firm) owned by stockholders, each having a restricted liability for the company's debts. **c.** (*usually cap.*) incorporated; Inc. *Abbr.:* Ltd. **5.** (of railroad trains, buses, etc.) making only a limited number of stops en route. —*n.* **6.** a limited train, bus, etc. [1545–55; LIMIT + -ED[2]] —**lim′it•ed•ly,** *adv.* —**lim′it•ed•ness,** *n.*

lim′ited ac′cess high′way, expressway. [1940–45]

lim′ited com′pany, *Brit.* a company in which the shareholders cannot be assessed for debts of the company beyond the sum they still have invested in the company. Also called **lim′it•ed-li•a•bil′i•ty com′pany** (lim′i tid lī′ə bil′i tē). [1850–55]

lim′ited divorce′, *Law.* See **judicial separation.**

lim′ited edi′tion, an edition, as of a book or lithograph, limited to a specified small number of copies. [1900–05] —**lim′it•ed-e•di′tion,** *adj.*

lim′ited liabil′ity, a liability restricted by law or contract, as the liability of owners of shares in a corporation or limited company, or that of a special partner. [1850–55]

lim′ited mon′archy, a monarchy that is limited by laws and a constitution. [1825–35]

lim′ited or′der. See **limit order.**

lim′ited part′ner. See **special partner.** [1905–10]

lim′ited part′nership, a partnership formed by at least one general partner and at least one special partner. Also called **special partnership.** Cf. **general partnership.** [1905–10]

lim′it•ed-pay′ment life′ insur′ance (lim′i tid-pā′mənt), a form of life insurance for which premiums are paid for a designated number of years.

lim′ited pol′icy, *Insurance.* a policy that covers only certain types of losses within an area of risks.

lim′it•ed-slip′ differen′tial (lim′i tid slip′), an automotive differential that can transfer power from a wheel that has lost traction to one that has not.

lim′ited war′, 1. a war conducted with less than a nation's total resources and restricted in aim to less than total defeat of the enemy. **2.** a war restricted to a relatively small area of the world and involving few warring nations. [1935–40]

lim•it•er (lim′i tər), *n.* **1.** a person or thing that limits. **2.** *Electronics.* a device or circuit for limiting the amplitude of a radio, telephone, or recording signal to some predetermined level. [1350–1400; LIMIT + -ER[1]; r. ME *limitour* (see -OR[2])]

lim•i•tes (lim′i tēz′), *n.* pl. of **limes.**

lim•it•ing (lim′i ting), *adj.* **1.** serving to restrict or restrain; restrictive; confining. **2.** *Gram.* of the nature of a limiting adjective or a restrictive clause. [1570–80; LIMIT + -ING[2]]

lim′iting ad′jective, *Gram.* **1.** (in English and some other languages) one of a small group of adjectives that modify the nouns to which they are applied by restricting rather than describing or qualifying. *This, some,* and *certain* are limiting adjectives. **2.** an adjective, as *few* or *other,* that in English follows determiners and precedes descriptive adjectives: *a few red apples.*

lim′iting fac′tor, 1. *Physiol.* the slowest, therefore rate-limiting, step in a process or reaction involving several steps. **2.** *Biol.* an environmental factor that tends to limit population size.

lim•it•less (lim′it lis), *adj.* without limit; boundless: *limitless ambition; limitless space.* [1575–85; LIMIT + -LESS] **—lim′it•less•ly,** *adv.* **—lim′it•less•ness,** *n.* **—Syn.** unbounded, measureless, unending, countless.

lim′it of proportional′ity, *Physics.* See **elastic limit.**

lim′it of resolu′tion, *Optics.* the capacity of an optical system to resolve point objects as separate images.

lim′it or′der, *Stock Market.* an order to buy or sell a specified amount of a security at a specific price. Also called **limited order.** Cf. **stop order, market order.**

lim′it point′, *Math.* See **accumulation point.** [1900–05]

lim′it switch′, a switch that automatically cuts off current to an electric motor when an object moved by it, as an elevator, has passed a given point. [1925–30]

li•miv•o•rous (lī miv′ər əs), *adj. Ecol.* of or pertaining to animals, usually worms or bivalves, that ingest earth or mud to extract the organic matter from it. [< L *līm(us)* slime, mud + -I- + -VOROUS, perh. on the model of LIMICOLOUS]

Lim•ma•sol (lim′ə sôl′), *n.* Limassol.

lim•mer (lim′ər), *n. Scot. and North Eng.* **1.** a woman of loose morals; hussy. **2.** a prostitute or strumpet. **3.** *Obs.* a scoundrel or rogue. [1425–75; late ME (Scots); see LIMB[1] (def. 6; ME *develes lim* limb of Satan), -ER[1]]

limn (lim), *v.t.* **1.** to represent in drawing or painting. **2.** to portray in words; describe. **3.** *Obs.* to illuminate (manuscripts). [1400–50; late ME *lymne,* var. of ME *luminen* to illuminate (manuscripts), aph. var. of *enlumine* < MF *enluminer* < L *inlūmināre* to embellish, lit., light up; see ILLUMINATE]

lim•ner (lim′nər), *n.* **1.** a person who paints or draws. **2.** an itinerant painter of 18th-century America who usually had little formal training. **3.** a person who describes or depicts in words: *an essayist known as a fine limner of prominent people and their careers.* **4.** an illuminator of medieval manuscripts. [1350–1400; ME *lymnour, lymynour;* see LIMN, -OR[2], -ER[1]]

lim•net•ic (lim net′ik), *adj.* pertaining to or living in the open water of a freshwater pond or lake. [1895–1900; < Gk *limnḗt(ēs)* marsh-dwelling (*límn(ē)* pool, marsh + *-ētēs* extended form of *-tēs* agent suffix, from v. stems ending in *-ē-*) + -IC]

lim•nol•o•gy (lim nol′ə jē), *n.* the scientific study of bodies of fresh water, as lakes and ponds, with reference to their physical, geographical, biological, and other features. [1890–95; *limno-* (comb. form repr. Gk *límnē* pool, marsh) + -LOGY] **—lim•no•log•i•cal** (lim′nl oj′i kəl), **lim′no•log′ic,** *adj.* **—lim′no•log′i•cal•ly,** *adv.* **—lim•nol′o•gist,** *n.*

lim•o (lim′ō), *n., pl.* **lim•os.** *Informal.* a limousine. [1965–70 *Amer.;* by shortening; see -O]

Li•moges (li mōzh′; *Fr.* lē mōzh′), *n.* **1.** a city in and the capital of Haute Vienne, in S central France. 147,406. **2.** Also called **Limoges′ ware′.** a type of fine porcelain manufactured at Limoges.

Li•món (lē môn′), *n.* **1. Jo•sé** (hô se′), 1908–72, Mexican dancer and choreographer in the U.S. **2.** Also called **Puerto Limón.** a seaport in E Costa Rica. 27,349.

lim•o•nene (lim′ə nēn′), *n. Chem.* a liquid terpene, $C_{10}H_{16}$, occurring in two optically different forms, the dextrorotatory form being present in the essential oils of lemon, orange, etc., and the levorotatory form in Douglas fir needle oil. [1835–45; < NL *Limon(um)* lemon + -ENE]

li•mo•nite (lī′mə nīt′), *n. Mineral.* an amorphous hydrated ferric oxide, varying in color from dark brown to yellow, used as an ore of iron. [1815–25; < Gk *leimṓn* meadow + -ITE[1]] **—li•mo•nit•ic** (lī′mə nit′ik), *adj.*

Li•mou•sin (lē mōō zaN′), *n.* **1.** a former province in central France. **2.** one of a breed of hardy French beef cattle, now popular in the U.S.

lim•ou•sine (lim′ə zēn′, lim′ə zēn′), *n.* **1.** any large, luxurious automobile, esp. one driven by a chauffeur. **2.** a large sedan or small bus, esp. one for transporting passengers to and from an airport, between train stations, etc. **3.** a former type of automobile having a permanently enclosed compartment for from three to five persons, with a roof projecting forward over the driver's seat in front. [1900–05; < F: kind of motorcar, special use of *limousine* long cloak, so called because worn by the shepherds of LIMOUSIN]

limp[1] (limp), *v.i.* **1.** to walk with a labored, jerky movement, as when lame. **2.** to proceed in a lame, faltering, or labored manner: *His writing limps from one cliché to another. The old car limped along.* **3.** to progress slowly and with great difficulty; make little or no advance: *an economy that limps along at a level just above total bankruptcy.* **—*n.* 4.** a lame movement or gait: *The accident left him with a slight limp.* [1560–70; back formation from obs. *limphault* lame; OE *lemphealt* limping (see HALT[2]); akin to MHG *limpfen* to limp] **—limp′er,** *n.* **—limp′ing•ly,** *adv.*

CONCISE ETYMOLOGY KEY: <, descended or borrowed from; >, whence; b., blend of, blended; c., cognate with; cf., compare; deriv., derivative; equiv., equivalent; imit., imitative; obl., oblique; r., replacing; s., stem; sp., spelling, spelled; resp., respelling, respelled; trans., translation; ?, origin unknown; *, unattested; ‡, probably earlier than. See the full key inside the front cover.

limp[2] (limp), *adj.,* **-er, -est. 1.** lacking stiffness or firmness, as of substance, fiber, structure, or bodily frame: *a limp body.* **2.** lacking vitality; weary; tired; fatigued: *Limp with exhaustion, she dropped into the nearest chair.* **3.** without firmness, force, energy, etc., as of character: *limp, spiritless prose.* **4.** flexible; not stiff or rigid: *a Bible in a limp leather binding.* [1700–10; perh. < Scand; cf. Icel *limpa* slackness, *limpilegur* soft, flabby] **—limp′ly,** *adv.* **—limp′ness,** *n.* **—Syn. 1.** flabby, flaccid, soft. **2, 3.** feeble, weak.

lim•pet (lim′pit), *n.* any of various marine gastropods with a low conical shell open beneath, often browsing on rocks at the shoreline and adhering when disturbed. [bef. 1050; ME *lempet,* OE *lempedu,* nasalized var. of **lepedu* < L *lepada,* acc. of *lepas* < Gk *lepás* limpet]

lim•pid (lim′pid), *adj.* **1.** clear, transparent, or pellucid, as water, crystal, or air: *We could see to the very bottom of the limpid pond.* **2.** free from obscurity; lucid; clear: *a limpid style; limpid prose.* **3.** completely calm; without distress or worry: *a limpid, emotionless existence.* [1605–15; < L *limpidus* clear. See LYMPH, -ID[4]] **—lim•pid′i•ty, lim′pid•ness,** *n.* **—lim′pid•ly,** *adv.*

limp•kin (limp′kin), *n.* a large, loud-voiced, wading bird, *Aramus guarauna,* intermediate in size and character between the cranes and the rails, of the warmer regions of America. [1870–75, *Amer.;* LIMP[1] + -KIN; so called because of its jerky walk]

Lim•po•po (lim pō′pō), *n.* a river in S Africa, flowing from the N Republic of South Africa, through S Mozambique into the Indian Ocean. 1000 mi. (1600 km) long. Also called **Crocodile River.**

limp•sy (limp′sē), *adj. Dial.* flimsy; limp; weak; lazy; flaccid. Also, **limp′sey, lim•sy** (lim′sē). [1815–25, *Amer.;* LIMP[2] + -SY]

limp′ wrist′, *Slang (disparaging and offensive).* a homosexual, esp. a male homosexual. [1960–65]

limp-wrist•ed (limp′ris′tid), *adj. Slang (disparaging and offensive).* **1.** effeminate. **2.** soft; flabby; ineffectual. [1955–60; LIMP[2] + WRIST + -ED[3]]

lim•u•lus (lim′yə ləs), *n., pl.* **-li** (-lī′). a crab of the genus *Limulus;* horseshoe crab. [1830–40; < NL *Limulus* name of the genus, special use of L *līmulus,* dim. of *līmus* sidelong, oblique; see -ULE]

lim•y (lī′mē), *adj.,* **lim•i•er, lim•i•est. 1.** consisting of, containing, or like lime. **2.** smeared with birdlime. [1545–55; LIME[1] + -Y[1]] **—lim′i•ness,** *n.*

lin (lin), *n.* linn.

Lin (lin), *n.* a female given name, form of **Caroline** or **Carolyn.**

lin., 1. lineal. **2.** linear. **3.** liniment.

Li•na (lē′nə), *n.* a female given name.

lin•ac (lin′ak), *n. Physics.* See **linear accelerator.** [1945–50; *lin(ear) ac(celerator)*]

Lin•a•cre (lin′ə kər), *n.* **Thomas,** 1460?–1521, English humanist, translator, scholar, and physician.

lin•age (lī′nij), *n.* **1.** the number of printed lines, esp. agate lines, covered by a magazine article, newspaper advertisement, etc. **2.** the amount charged, paid, or received per printed line, as of a magazine article or short story. **3.** *Archaic.* alignment. Also, **lineage.** [1880–85; LINE[1] + -AGE]

lin•al•o•ol (li nal′ō ôl′, -ol′, lin′ə lōōl′), *n. Chem.* a colorless, unsaturated terpene liquid alcohol, $C_{10}H_{18}O$, having a fragrance similar to that of bergamot oil, obtained from several essential oils: used in perfumery. Also, **lin•a•lol** (lin′ə lôl′, -lol′). [1890–95; < MexSp *lindruáloe* a fragrant Mexican wood (see LIGNALOES) + -OL[1]]

lin′a•lyl ac′etate (lin′ə lil, -lēl′), *Chem.* a colorless, water-insoluble liquid, $C_{12}H_{20}O_2$, having a pleasant odor: used chiefly in perfumes, cosmetics, toilet water, and soap. [1895–1900; LINAL(OOL) + -YL]

Li•na•res (lē nä′Res), *n.* a city in S Spain. 50,516.

li•nar•i•a (lī nâr′ē ə, li-), *n.* any of various plants belonging to the genus *Linaria,* of the figwort family, esp. of the cultivated species, as *L. maroccana* or *L. aeruginea,* having slender clusters of spurred flowers in a variety of colors. [1570–80; < NL; ML *līnāria* toadflax, equiv. to L *lin(um)* flax + *-āria* -ARY]

li•na•rite (lī′nə rīt′, li när′īt), *n.* a mineral, a complex basic sulfate of lead and copper, having a deep-blue color resembling that of azurite. [1835–45; named after LINARES, where found; see -ITE[1]]

Lin Biao (lin′ byou′), 1907–71, Chinese marshal and Communist leader: defense minister 1959–71; leader of abortive coup 1971.

linch•pin (linch′pin′), *n.* **1.** a pin inserted through the end of an axletree to keep the wheel on. **2.** something that holds the various elements of a complicated structure together: *The monarchy was the linchpin of the nation's traditions and society.* Also, **lynchpin.** [1350–1400; unexplained alter. of ME *lynspin,* equiv. to *lyns,* OE *lynis* axle-pin (c. G *Lünse*) + *pin* PIN]

Lin•coln (ling′kən), *n.* **1. Abraham,** 1809–65, 16th president of the U.S. 1861–65. **2. Benjamin,** 1733–1810, American Revolutionary general. **3.** a city in and the capital of Nebraska, in the SE part. 171,932. **4.** a city in Lincolnshire, in E central England. 73,200. **5.** a town in N Rhode Island. 16,949. **6.** a city in central Illinois. 16,327. **7.** a town in S Ontario, in S Canada, on Lake Ontario. 14,196. **8.** Lincolnshire. **9.** one of an English breed of large mutton sheep noted for their heavy fleece of coarse, long wool. **10.** a male given name.

Lin•coln•esque (ling′kə nesk′), *adj.* like or characteristic of Abraham Lincoln: *a Lincolnesque compassion.* [1920–25; LINCOLN + -ESQUE]

Lin′coln green′, 1. an olive-green color. **2.** *Brit. Obs.* a forester's outfit, perhaps of bright green: *clad in Lincoln green.* [1500–10; so called from the color of a fabric originally made in LINCOLN, England]

Lin•coln•i•an (ling kō′nē ən), *adj.* of or pertaining to Abraham Lincoln, his character, or his political principles. [1905–10; *Amer.;* LINCOLN + -IAN]

Lin•coln•i•an•a (ling kō′nē an′ə, -ä′nə, ling′kə-), *n.pl.* materials pertaining to Abraham Lincoln, as objects, writings, or anecdotes. [1920–25; LINCOLN + -IANA]

Lin′coln Park′, a city in SE Michigan. 45,105.

Lin′coln's Birth′day, 1. February 12, a legal holiday in some states of the U.S., in honor of the birth of Abraham Lincoln. **2.** See **Presidents' Day.**

Lin•coln•shire (ling′kən shēr′, -shər), *n.* a county in E England. 521,300; 2272 sq. mi. (5885 sq. km). Also called **Lincoln.**

Lin′coln's Inn′. See under **Inns of Court** (def. 1).

Lin′coln's spar′row, a North American sparrow, *Melospiza lincolnii,* having a buff breast with black streaks. [1825–35, *Amer.;* named (by Audubon) after Thomas *Lincoln* (d. 1883)]

Lin•coln•wood (ling′kən wŏŏd′), *n.* a city in NE Illinois. 11,921.

lin•co•my•cin (ling′kə mī′sin), *n. Pharm.* a toxic antibiotic, $C_{18}H_{34}N_2O_6S$, isolated from *Streptomyces lincolnensis,* used in its hydrochloride form for the treatment of serious Gram-positive penicillin-resistant infections. [1960–65; < NL of the bacteria *linco(lnensis)* specific epithet of the bacteria + -MYCIN]

Lind (lind), *n.* **Jenny** (*Johanna Maria Lind Goldschmidt*) (*"The Swedish Nightingale"*), 1820–87, Swedish soprano.

Lin•da (lin′də), *n.* a female given name: from a Spanish word meaning "pretty."

lin•dane (lin′dān), *n. Chem.* a white, crystalline, water-insoluble powder, $C_6H_6Cl_6$, the gamma isomer of benzene hexachloride: used chiefly as an insecticide, delouser, and weed-killer. [1945–50; named after T. van der *Linden,* 20th-century Dutch chemist; see -ANE]

Lind•bergh (lind′bûrg, lin′-), *n.* **1. Anne (Spencer) Morrow,** born 1906, U.S. writer (wife of Charles Augustus Lindbergh). **2. Charles Augustus,** 1902–74, U.S. aviator: made the first solo, nonstop transatlantic flight 1927.

Lin•de•gren (lin′də gRen), *n.* **E•rik (Jo•han)** (ā′Rik yōō′hän), 1910–68, Swedish poet and literary critic.

Lin′de•löf space′ (lin′də lof′, -lôf′, -lœf′), *Math.* a topological space having the property that every cover consisting of open sets has a subcover consisting of a countable number of subsets. [after Ernst *Lindelöf* (1870–1946), Finnish topologist]

lin•den (lin′dən), *n.* **1.** any tree of the genus *Tilia,* as *T. americana* **(American linden)** or *T. europaea* **(European linden),** having fragrant yellowish-white flowers and heart-shaped leaves, grown as an ornamental or shade tree. Cf. **linden family. 2.** the soft, light, white wood of any of these trees, used for making furniture and in the construction of houses, boxes, etc. [1570–80; n. use of obs. *linden* (adj.) of the lime tree, ME, OE. See LIME[3], -EN[2]]

Lin•den (lin′dən), *n.* a city in NE New Jersey, near Newark. 37,836.

lin′den fam′ily, the plant family Tiliaceae, characterized by deciduous trees or shrubs having simple, usually alternate leaves, fibrous bark, fragrant flowers, and dry, woody fruit, and including the basswood, jute, and linden.

Lin•den•hurst (lin′dən hûrst′), *n.* a village on central Long Island, in SE New York. 26,919.

Lin•den•wold (lin′dən wōld′), *n.* a town in SW New Jersey. 18,196.

Lin•des•nes (lin′dəs nes′), *n.* a cape at the S tip of Norway, on the North Sea. Also called **The Naze.**

Lin•di (lin′dē), *n.* a seaport in SE Tanzania. 13,352.

Lin•dis•farne (lin′dəs färn′), *n.* See **Holy Island** (def. 1).

Lind•ley (lind′lē, lin′-), *n.* **1. John,** 1799–1865, English botanist. **2.** a male or female given name.

Lin•don (lin′dən), *n.* a male given name.

Lind•say (lind′zē, lin′-), *n.* **1. Howard,** 1889–1968, U.S. playwright, producer, and actor. **2. John V(liet)** (vlēt), born 1921, U.S. politician: mayor of New York City 1966–74. **3. (Nicholas) Va•chel** (vā′chəl), 1879–1931, U.S. poet. **4.** a town in SE Ontario, in S Canada. 13,596. **5.** a male or female given name.

Lind•sey (lind′zē, lin′-), *n.* **1. Ben(jamin Barr)** (bär), 1869–1943, U.S. jurist and authority on juvenile delinquency. **2.** a male or female given name.

lin•dy (lin′dē), *n., pl.* **-dies,** *v.,* **-died, -dy•ing. —*n.* 1.** Also called **lin′dy hop′, Lin′dy Hop′.** an energetic jitterbug dance. **—*v.i.* 2.** to dance the lindy. Also, **Lin′dy.** [1930–35; prob. from nickname of Charles A. LINDBERGH]

line[1] (līn), *n., v.,* **lined, lin•ing. —*n.* 1.** a mark or stroke long in proportion to its breadth, made with a pen, pencil, tool, etc., on a surface: *a line down the middle of the page.* **2.** *Math.* a continuous extent of length, straight or curved, without breadth or thickness; the trace of a moving point. **3.** something arranged along a line, esp. a straight line; a row or series: *a line of trees.* **4.** a number of persons standing one behind the other and waiting their turns at or for something; queue. **5.** something resembling a traced line, as a band of color, a seam, or a furrow: *lines of stratification in rock.* **6.** a furrow or wrinkle on the face, neck, etc.: *lines around the eyes.* **7.** an indication of demarcation; boundary; limit: *the county line; a fine line between right and wrong.* **8.** a row of written or printed letters, words, etc.: *a page of 30 lines.* **9.** a verse of poetry: *A line in iambic pentameter contains five feet.* **10.** Usually, **lines.** the words of an actor's part in a drama, musical comedy, etc.: *to rehearse one's lines.* **11.** a short written message: *Drop me a line when you're on vacation.* **12.** a system of public conveyances, as buses or trains, plying regularly over a fixed route: *the northbound line at State Street.* **13.** a trans-

portation or conveyance company: *a steamship line.* **14.** a course of direction; route: *the line of march down Main Street.* **15.** a course of action, procedure, thought, policy, etc.: *That newspaper follows the communist line.* **16.** a piece of pertinent or useful information (usually fol. by *on*): *I've got a line on a good used car.* **17.** a series of generations of persons, animals, or plants descended from a common ancestor: *a line of kings.* **18.** a department of activity; occupation or business: *What line are you in?* **19.** *Informal.* a mode of conversation, esp. one that is glib or exaggerated in order to impress or influence another person: *He really handed her a line about his rich relatives.* **20.** a straight line drawn from an observed object to the fovea of the eye. **21. lines, a.** the outer form or proportions of a ship, building, etc.: *a ship of fine lines.* **b.** a general form, as of an event or something that is made, which may be the basis of comparison, imitation, etc.: *two books written along the same lines.* **c.** a person's lot or portion: *to endure the hard lines of poverty.* **d.** *Chiefly Brit.* a certificate of marriage. **22.** a circle of the terrestrial or celestial sphere: *the equinoctial line.* **23.** banner (def. 7). **24.** *Fine Arts.* **a.** a mark made by a pencil, brush, or the like, that defines the contour of a shape, forms hatching, etc. **b.** the edge of a shape. **25.** *Television.* one scanning line. **26.** *Telecommunications.* **a.** a telephone connection: *Please hold the line.* **b.** a wire circuit connecting two or more pieces of electric apparatus, esp. the wire or wires connecting points or stations in a telegraph or telephone system, or the system itself. **27. the line,** *Geog.* the equator. **28.** a stock of commercial goods of the same general class but having a range of styles, sizes, prices, or quality: *the company's line of shoes.* **29.** an assembly line. **30.** *Law.* a limit defining one estate from another; the outline or boundary of a piece of real estate. **31.** *Bridge.* a line on a score sheet that separates points scored toward game **(below the line)** from points scored by setting a contract, having honors, etc. **(above the line).** **32.** *Music.* any of the straight, horizontal, parallel strokes of the staff, or one placed above or below the staff. **33.** *Mil.* **a.** a defensive position or front. **b.** a series of fortifications: *the Maginot line.* **c.** Usually, **lines.** a distribution of troops, sentries, etc., for the defense of a position or for an attack: *behind the enemy's lines.* **d.** the body of personnel constituting the combatant forces of an army, as distinguished from the supply services and staff corps. **34.** an arrangement of troops of an army or of ships of a fleet as drawn up for battle: *line of battle.* **35.** a body or formation of troops or ships drawn up abreast (distinguished from *column*). **36.** the class of officers serving with combatant units or warships. **37.** the regular forces of an army or navy. **38.** that part of an administrative organization consisting of persons actively engaged on a given project. Cf. **staff**[1] (def. 4). **39.** a thread, string, cord, rope, or the like. **40.** a clothesline: *the wash hanging on the line.* **41.** a cord, wire, or the like, used for measuring or as a guide. **42.** *Naut.* **a.** a pipe or hose: *a steam line.* **b.** a rope or cable used at sea. **43.** *Slang.* a small quantity of cocaine arranged in the form of a slender thread or line, as for sniffing. **44.** Also, **ligne.** a unit, 1/40 inch (0.635 millimeter), for measuring the diameter of buttons. **45.** *Angling.* a length of nylon, silk, linen, cord, or the like, to which are attached the leader, hook, sinker, float, etc. **46.** *Football.* **a.** either of the two front rows of opposing players lined up opposite each other on the line of scrimmage: *a four-man line.* **b.** See **line of scrimmage.** **47.** the betting odds established by bookmakers for events not covered by pari-mutuel betting, esp. sporting events, as football or basketball. **48.** *Ice Hockey.* the two wings and center who make up a team's offensive unit. **49.** *Fencing.* any of the four divisions of the portion of a fencer's body on which a touch can be scored, taken as an area of attack or defense. **50.** *Textiles.* the longer and preferred flax or hemp fibers. Cf. **tow**[2] (def. 2). **51.** *Fox Hunting.* the trail of scent left by a fox. **52.** a unit of length equivalent to 1/12 inch (2.12 millimeters). **53.** *Insurance.* **a.** a class or type of insurance: *casualty line.* **b.** the amount of insurance written for a particular risk. **54.** *Australian Slang.* a girl or woman. **55. bring, come,** or **get into line, a.** to become or cause to become straight, as in a row: *The members of the marching band got into line.* **b.** to conform or cause to conform or agree: *They were persuaded to come into line with the party's policy.* **56. down the line, a.** in all ways; thoroughly; fully: *It's a fine house right down the line—well-built, roomy, attractive.* **b.** in the future. **57. draw the line,** to impose a restriction; limit: *They might exaggerate but would draw the line at outright lying.* **58. go up in one's lines,** *U.S. Theat.* to forget one's part during a performance. Also, *Brit.,* **go up on one's lines. 59. hold the line,** to maintain the status quo, esp. in order to forestall unfavorable developments: *We're trying to hold the line on prices.* **60. in line, a.** in alignment; straight. **b.** in conformity or agreement. **c.** in control (of one's conduct): *to keep one's temper in line.* **d.** prepared; ready. **e.** waiting one behind the other in a queue: *There were eight people in line at the teller's window.* **61. in line with,** in agreement or conformity with: *The action taken was in line with her decision.* **62. in the line of duty,** in the execution of the duties belonging to some occupation, esp. with regard to the responsibility for life and death: *a policeman wounded in the line of duty.* Also, **in line of duty. 63. lay it on the line,** *Informal.* **a.** to give money; pay. **b.** to give the required information; speak directly or frankly: *I'm going to stop being polite and lay it on the line.* **64. off line, a.** occurring or functioning away from an assembly line, work process, etc. **b.** not in operation; not functioning. **65. on a line,** *Baseball.* (of a batted or thrown ball) through the air in an approximately straight line from the point of impact or delivery: *hit on a line between third and short; thrown in on a line from the center fielder.* **66. on line, a.** on or part of an assembly line: *Production will be improved when the new welding equipment is on line.* **b.** in or into operation: *The manufacturing facilities will be on line before November.* **c.** *Computers.* actively linked to a computer: *The printer is not yet on line.* **d.** *Chiefly New York City.* See **line**[1] (def. 60e). **67. on the line,** *Informal.* **a.** being risked or put in jeopardy; in a vulnerable position: *Our prestige and honor are on the line.* **b.** immediately; readily: *paid cash on the line.* **68. out of line, a.** not in a straight line. **b.** in disagreement with what is accepted or practiced. **c.** *Informal.* impertinent; presumptuous: *That last remark was out of line.* **69. read between the lines,** to understand the unexpressed but implied meaning of something said or written: *Her letter sounded cheerful enough, but I read a certain sadness between the lines.* **70. toe the line** or **mark, a.** to conform strictly to a rule, command, etc. **b.** to shoulder responsibilities; do one's duty: *He tried hard to toe the line on the new job.*
—*v.i.* **71.** to take a position in a line; range (often fol. by *up*): *to line up before the start of a parade.* **72.** *Baseball.* **a.** to hit a line drive. **b.** to line out.
—*v.t.* **73.** to bring into a line, or into line with others (often fol. by *up*): *to line up troops.* **74.** to mark with a line or lines: *to line paper for writing.* **75.** to sketch verbally or in writing; outline (often fol. by *out*): *We followed the plan he had lined out.* **76.** to arrange a line along: *to line a coast with colonies.* **77.** to form a line along: *Rocks lined the drive.* **78.** to apply liner to (the eyes). **79.** to delineate with or as if with lines; draw: *to line the silhouette of a person's head.* **80.** *Archaic.* to measure or test with a line. **81. line out, a.** *Baseball.* to be put out by hitting a line drive caught on the fly by a player of the opposing team. **b.** to execute or perform: *He lined out a few songs upon request.* **82. line up,** to secure; make available: *to line up support; to line up a speaker for the banquet.* [bef. 1000; ME *li(g)ne* cord, rope, stroke, series, guiding rule, partly < OF *ligne* << L *līnea,* n. use of fem. of *līneus* flaxen (orig. applied to string), equiv to *līn(um)* flax (see LINE[2]) + *-eus* -EOUS, partly continuing OE *line* string, row, series < L, as above] **—lin′a·ble, line′a·ble,** *adj.* **—line′less,** *adj.* **—line′like′,** *adj.*

line[2] (līn), *v.,* **lined, lin·ing,** *n.* —*v.t.* **1.** to cover the inner side or surface of: *to line the coat with blue silk.* **2.** to serve to cover: *Velvet draperies lined the walls of the room.* **3.** to furnish or fill: *to line shelves with provisions.* **4.** to reinforce the back of a book with glued fabric, paper, vellum, etc. **5. line one's pockets,** to make much money, esp. in an illegal or questionable way. —*n.* **6.** a thickness of glue, as between two veneers in a sheet of plywood. [1350–1400; ME *lynen,* deriv. of *line* linen, flax, OE *līn* < L *līnum* flax]

lin·e·age[1] (lin′ē ij), *n.* **1.** lineal descent from an ancestor; ancestry or extraction: *She could trace her lineage to the early Pilgrims.* **2.** the line of descendants of a particular ancestor; family; race. [1275–1325; LINE(AL) + -AGE; r. ME *linage* < AF; OF *lignage* < VL **lineāticum.* See LINE[1], -AGE]
—Syn. 1. pedigree, parentage, derivation, genealogy. **2.** tribe, clan.

line·age[2] (lī′nij), *n.* linage.

lin·e·al (lin′ē əl), *adj.* **1.** being in the direct line, as a descendant or ancestor, or in a direct line, as descent or succession. **2.** of or transmitted by lineal descent. **3.** linear. [1350–1400; ME < LL *lineālis.* See LINE[1], -AL[1]] **—lin′e·al·ly,** *adv.*

lin·e·a·ment (lin′ē ə mənt), *n.* **1.** Often, **lineaments.** a feature or detail of a face, body, or figure, considered with respect to its outline or contour: *His fine lineaments made him the very image of his father.* **2.** Usually, **lineaments.** distinguishing features; distinctive characteristics: *the lineaments of sincere repentance.* **3.** *Geol.* a linear topographic feature of regional extent that is believed to reflect underlying crustal structure. [1400–50; late ME < L *līneāmentum* a stroke, pl., features, equiv. to *līneā(re)* to draw a line (deriv. of *līnea;* see LINE[1]) + *-mentum* -MENT] **—lin·e·a·men·tal** (lin′ē ə men′tl), *adj.* **—lin′e·a·men·ta′tion,** *n.*

lin·e·ar (lin′ē ər), *adj.* **1.** of, consisting of, or using lines: *linear design.* **2.** pertaining to or represented by lines: *linear dimensions.* **3.** extended or arranged in a line: *a linear series.* **4.** involving measurement in one dimension only; pertaining to length: *linear measure.* **5.** of or pertaining to the characteristics of a work of art in which forms and rhythms are defined chiefly in terms of line. **6.** having the form of or resembling a line: *linear nebulae.* **7.** *Math.* **a.** consisting of, involving, or describable by terms of the first degree. **b.** having the same effect on a sum as on each of the summands: *a linear operation.* **8.** *Electronics.* delivering an output that is directly proportional to the input: *a linear circuit; a linear amplifier.* **9.** threadlike; narrow and elongated: *a linear leaf.* [1635–45; < L *līneāris* of, belonging to lines. See LINE[1], -AR[1]] **—lin′e·ar·ly,** *adv.*

linear leaf

Linear A, an ancient system of writing, not yet deciphered, inscribed on clay tablets, pottery, and other objects found at Minoan sites on Crete and other Greek islands. Cf. **Linear B.** [1905–10]

lin′ear accel′erator, *Physics.* an accelerator in which particles are propelled in straight paths by the use of alternating electric voltages that are timed in such a way that the particles receive increasing increments of energy. Also called **linac.** [1930–35]

lin′ear al′gebra, *Math.* See under **algebra** (def. 2). [1890–95]

Linear B, an ancient system of writing representing a very early form of Greek, deciphered by Michael Ventris chiefly from clay tablets found at Knossos on Crete and at Pylos. Cf. **Linear A.** [1905–10]

lin′ear combina′tion, *Math.* (of mathematical quantities) a sum of products of each quantity times a constant: *The expression* aX + bY + cZ *is a linear combination of* X, Y, *and* Z, *where* a, b, *and* c *are constants.* [1955–60]

lin′ear differen′tial equa′tion, *Math.* an equation involving derivatives in which the dependent variables and all derivatives appearing in the equation are raised to the first power. [1885–90]

lin′ear equa′tion, *Math.* **1.** a first-order equation involving two variables: its graph is a straight line in the Cartesian coordinate system. **2.** any equation such that the sum of two solutions is a solution, and a constant multiple of a solution is a solution. Cf. **linear operator.** [1810–20]

lin′ear frac′tional transforma′tion, *Math.* See **Möbius transformation.**

lin′ear func′tion, *Math.* See **linear transformation.** [1855–60]

lin′ear graph′, *Math.* graph (def. 2b).

lin′ear induc′tion mo′tor, *Elect., Railroads.* an electric motor in which a movable part moves in a straight line, with power being supplied by a varying magnetic field set up by a fixed part of the system, as a metal rail on the ground. Also, **lin′ear-induc′tion mo′tor.** Also called **lin′ear mo′tor.** Cf. **induction motor.** [1965–70]

lin·e·ar·i·ty (lin′ē ar′i tē), *n., pl.* **-ties. 1.** the property, quality, or state of being linear. **2.** *Television.* the accuracy with which the shapes in a televised image are reproduced on the screen of a receiving set. **3.** *Electronics.* the measure of the extent to which a certain response is directly proportional to the applied excitation. [1740–50; LINEAR + -ITY]

lin·e·ar·ize (lin′ē ə rīz′), *v.t.,* **-ized, -iz·ing.** to make linear; give linear form to. Also, *esp. Brit.,* **lin′e·ar·ise′.** [1890–95; LINEAR + -IZE] **—lin′e·ar·i·za′tion,** *n.*

lin′early or′dered set′, *Math.* See **totally ordered set.**

lin′ear mani′fold, *Math.* subspace (def. 2b).

lin′ear meas′ure, 1. any system for measuring length. **2.** any unit used in linear measurement, as the inch, foot, meter, etc. [1885–90]

lin′ear op′erator, *Math.* a mathematical operator with the property that applying it to a linear combination of two objects yields the same linear combination as the result of applying it to the objects separately.

lin′ear perspec′tive, a mathematical system for representing three-dimensional objects and space on a two-dimensional surface by means of intersecting lines that are drawn vertically and horizontally and that radiate from one point **(one-point perspective),** two points **(two-point perspective),** or several points on a horizon line as perceived by a viewer imagined in an arbitrarily fixed position. See diag. under **perspective.** [1835–45]

lin′ear polariza′tion, *Optics.* See **plane polarization.**

lin′ear pro′gramming, *Math.* any of several methods for finding where a given linear function of several nonnegative variables assumes an extreme value and for determining the extreme value, the variable usually being subjected to constraints in the form of linear equalities or inequalities. [1945–50]

lin′ear regres′sion anal′ysis, *Statistics.* regression analysis in which the dependent variable is assumed to be linearly related to the independent variable or variables. Also called **lin′ear regres′sion.**

lin′ear space′, *Math.* See **vector space.** [1890–95]

line′ art′, graphic material that consists of lines or areas of pure black and pure white and requires no screening for reproduction. Cf. **halftone** (def. 2).

lin·e·ar-track·ing (lin′ē ər trak′ing), *adj.* (of a tone arm) designed to move across a phonograph record in a straight line, instead of an arc, so that as the needle tracks the groove, its orientation remains unchanged.

lin′ear transforma′tion, *Math.* a map from one vector space to a vector space having the same field of scalars, with the properties that the map of the sum of two vectors is the sum of the maps of the vectors and the map of a scalar times a vector equals the scalar times the map of the vector. Also called **linear function.** [1885–90]

lin·e·ate (lin′ē it, -āt′), *adj.* marked with lines, esp. parallel lengthwise lines; striped. Also, **lin′e·at′ed.** [1635–45; < L *līneātus* ptp. of *līneāre* to make straight, mark with lines. See LINEAMENT, -ATE[1]]

lin·e·a·tion (lin′ē ā′shən), *n.* **1.** an act or instance of marking with or tracing by lines. **2.** a division into lines. **3.** an outline or delineation. **4.** an arrangement or group of lines. [1350–1400; ME *lyneacion* < LL *līneātiōn-* (s. of *līneātiō*) the drawing of a line, L: direction, line. See LINEATE, -ION]

line·back·er (līn′bak′ər), *n. Football.* **1.** a player on defense who takes a position close behind the linemen. **2.** the position played by this player. [1960–65; LINE[1] + BACKER]

line·bred (līn′bred′), *adj.* produced by linebreeding. [1890–95; LINE[1] + BRED]

line·breed·ing (līn′brē′ding), *n. Genetics.* a form of inbreeding directed toward keeping the offspring closely related to a superior ancestor. [1875–80, *Amer.;* LINE[1] + BREEDING]

line·cast·ing (līn′kas′ting, -kä′sting), *n. Print.* the casting of an entire line of type in a slug. [1910–15] **—line′ cast′er.**

line′ cop′y, *Print.* a document, drawing, or the like, consisting of two tones, as black and white, without intermediate gradations. Cf. **halftone** (def. 1).

line′ cut′, *Print.* an engraving consisting only of lines or areas that are solid black or white. Cf. **halftone** (def. 2). [1900–05]

line′ draw′ing, a drawing done exclusively in line, providing gradations in tone entirely through variations in width and density. [1890–95]

line′ drive′, *Baseball.* a batted ball that travels low, fast, and straight. Also called **liner.** [1930–35]

line′ drop′, *Elect.* the decrease in voltage between two points on an electric line, often caused by resistance or leakage along the line. [1890–95]

line′ engrav′ing, 1. a technique of engraving in which all effects are produced by variations in the width and density of lines incised with a burin. **2.** a metal plate so engraved. **3.** a print or picture made from it. [1800–10] **—line′ engrav′er.**

line′ gale′. See **equinoctial storm.** [1830–40, *Amer.*]

line′ gauge′, a printer's ruler, usually marked off in points, picas, agates, and inches, and sometimes also in centimeters. [1945–50]

line-haul (līn′hôl′), *adj.* noting or pertaining to the transport, usually by truck, of heavy loads of freight for long distances or between cities. Also, **long-haul.**

line-haul·er (līn′hô′lər), *n.* a heavy-duty truck suitable for line-haul transportation. Also, **line′haul′er.** [LINE-HAUL + -ER[1]]

line′ in′tegral, *Math.* the limit, as the norm of the partition of a given curve approaches zero, of the sum of the product of the length of the arcs in the partition times the value of the function at some point on each arc. [1870–75]

line′ i′tem, the distinct title of an entry or account as it appears on a separate line in a bookkeeping ledger or a fiscal budget. **—line′-i′tem,** *adj.*

line′-item ve′to, the power of the executive to veto particular items of a bill without having to veto the entire bill.

line·man (līn′mən), *n., pl.* **-men. 1.** Also, **linesman.** a person who installs or repairs telephone, telegraph, or other wires. **2.** *Football.* one of the players in the line, as a center, guard, tackle, or end. **3.** *Survey.* a person who marks the positions of a survey mark with a range pole or the like. [1855–60; LINE[1] + -MAN]
—Usage. See **-man.**

line′man's pli′ers, pliers with reinforced pincers and insulated handles, used by electricians in working with cable and other heavy wires. See illus. under **plier.**

line′ mark′, a trademark covering all items of a particular product line.

lin·en (lin′ən), *n.* **1.** fabric woven from flax yarns. **2.** Often, **linens.** bedding, tablecloths, shirts, etc., made of linen cloth or a more common substitute, as cotton. **3.** yarn made of flax fiber. **4.** thread made of flax yarns. **5. wash one's dirty linen in public,** to discuss in public one's private scandals, disagreements, or difficulties. *—adj.* **6.** made of linen: *a linen jacket.* [bef. 900; ME *lin(n)en* (n., adj.), OE *linnen, linen* (adj.) made of flax, equiv. to *lin* flax (< L *linum;* see LINE[2]) + *-en* -EN[2]] **—lin′en·y,** *adj.*

lin′en clos′et, a closet in which sheets, towels, table linens, etc., are kept. [1880–85]

lin′en drap′er, *Brit.* a dry-goods merchant. [1540–50]

lin·en·fold (lin′ən fōld′), *n.* an ornamental motif resembling folded linen, carved on paneling. Also called **lin′en pat′tern.** [1890–95; LINEN + FOLD[1]]

lin·en·ized (lin′ə nizd′), *adj.* made or finished to resemble the texture of linen cloth. [LINEN + -IZE + -ED[2]]

lin′en pan′el, a panel carved with a linenfold. [1885–90]

lin′en pa′per, paper, usually superior in quality, made from pure linen or from substitutes that produce a similar paper finish. [1720–30]

line′ of ap′sides, *Astron.* the major axis of an elliptical orbit. Also called **apse line.**

line′ of bat′tle, *Mil., Navy.* a line formed by troops or ships for delivering or receiving an attack.

line′-of-bat′tle ship′ (lin′əv bat′l). See **ship of the line.**

line′ of cred′it. See **credit line** (def. 2). [1955–60]

line′ of′ficer, a military or naval officer serving with combatant units or warships, as distinguished from a staff officer, supply officer, etc. [1840–50, *Amer.*]

line′ of fire′, the straight horizontal line from the muzzle of a weapon in the direction of the axis of the bore, just prior to firing. [1855–60]

line′ of force′, *Physics.* an imaginary line or curve in a field of force, as an electric field, such that the direction of the line at any point is that of the force in the field at that point. Also called **field line.** [1870–75]

line′ of induc′tion, (formerly) a line of force in a magnetic field.

line′ of posi′tion, *Navig.* a line connecting all the possible positions of a ship or aircraft, as determined by a single observation. *Abbr.:* LOP Also called **position line.**

line′ of scrim′mage, *Football.* an imaginary line parallel to the goal lines that passes from one sideline to the other through the point of the football closest to the goal line of each team. [1905–10]

line′ of sight′, 1. Also called **line′ of sight′ing.** an imaginary straight line running through the aligned sights of a firearm, surveying equipment, etc. **2.** *Astron.* an imaginary line from an observer to a celestial body, coincident with the path traveled by light rays received from the body. **3.** *Radio.* a straight line connecting two points sufficiently high and near one another so that the line is entirely above the surface of the earth. **4.** *Ophthalm.* See **line of vision. 5.** sightline. [1550–60]

line′ of site′, *Mil.* a straight line from the muzzle of an artillery gun to its target. [1905–10]

line′ of vi′sion, *Ophthalm.* a straight line that connects the fovea centralis of an eye with the point on which the eye focuses.

lin·e·o·late (lin′ē ə lāt′), *adj. Zool., Bot.* marked with minute lines; finely lineate. Also, **lin′e·o·lat′ed.** [1810–20; < L *lineol(a)* (dim. of *linea* LINE[1]) + -ATE[1]]

line-out (līn′out′), *n. Rugby.* a procedure for putting an out-of-bounds ball back in play, whereby a player outside the touchline tosses the ball high and between two lines of opposing forwards lined up perpendicular to the touchline. [1885–90; n. use of v. phrase *line out* to form a line, line up]

line′ print′er, *Computers.* a printer that produces an entire line of output at a time. [1950–55]

lin·er[1] (lī′nər), *n.* **1.** a ship or airplane operated by a transportation or conveyance company. **2.** eyeliner. **3.** *Baseball.* See **line drive. 4.** a person or thing that traces by or marks with lines. **5.** See **ship of the line.** [1400–50; late ME; see LINE[1], -ER[1]]

lin·er[2] (lī′nər), *n.* **1.** something serving as a lining. **2.** a protective covering, usually of cardboard, for a phonograph record; album; jacket. **3.** a person who fits or provides linings. [1605–15; LINE[2] + -ER[1]]

lin·er·board (lī′nər bôrd′, -bōrd′), *n.* a type of paperboard used esp. for containers, as corrugated boxes. Also, **lin′er board′.** [1945–50; LINER[2] + BOARD]

lin′er note′, Usually, **liner notes.** explanatory or interpretative notes about a record, cassette, etc., printed on the cover or included in the package. [1950–55]

line′ seg′ment, *Geom.* segment (def. 2b).

lines·man (līnz′mən), *n., pl.* **-men. 1.** *Sports.* **a.** an official, as in tennis and soccer, who assists the referee. **b.** *Football.* an official who marks the distances gained and lost in the progress of play and otherwise assists the referee and field judge. **c.** *Ice Hockey.* either of two officials who assist the referee by watching for icing, offside, and substitution violations and fouls and by conducting face-offs. **2.** lineman (def. 1). [1855–60; LINE[1] + 's[1] + -MAN]

line′ space′, (on a typewriter, typesetter, printer, or the like) the horizontal space provided for a line of typing, typesetting, printing, etc. [1950–55]

line′ spec′trum, *Physics.* an electromagnetic spectrum consisting of discrete lines, usually characteristic of excited atoms or molecules. Cf. **band spectrum, continuous spectrum, spectral line.** [1870–75]

line′ squall′, a squall advancing along a front that forms a more or less definite line. [1885–90]

line′ storm′. See **equinoctial storm.** [1840–50]

line′ trim′mer, a gardening device used to trim the edges of lawns by means of a rapidly rotating motor-driven flexible wire or cord. Also called **string trimmer.**

line·up (līn′up′), *n.* **1.** a particular order or disposition of persons or things as arranged or drawn up for action, inspection, etc. **2.** the persons or things themselves. **3.** (in police investigations) a group of persons, including suspects in a crime, lined up to allow inspection and possible identification by the victim or victims of that crime. **4.** *Sports.* the list of the participating players in a game together with their positions: *to announce the starting lineup of a game.* **5.** an organization of people, companies, etc., for some common purpose: *a lineup of support for the new tax bill.* **6.** an overall schedule of programs, events, activities, etc.: *the fall lineup of TV programs.* **7.** a list of products or services offered by a manufacturer or organization: *Does the company's lineup of new cars this year include a convertible?* [1885–90, *Amer.*; n. use of v. phrase *line up*]

line′ vec′tor, *Mech.* See **sliding vector.**

line′ volt′age, *Elect.* the voltage supplied by a power line, measured at the point of use.

line·y (lī′nē), *adj.,* **lin·i·er, lin·i·est.** liny.

lin ft, linear foot.

ling[1] (ling), *n., pl.* (*esp. collectively*) **ling,** (*esp. referring to two or more kinds or species*) **lings. 1.** an elongated, marine, gadid food fish, *Molva molva,* of Greenland and northern Europe. **2.** the burbot. **3.** any of various other elongated food fishes. [1250–1300; ME *ling, lenge;* c. D *leng;* akin to LONG[1], ON *langa*]

ling[2] (ling), *n.* the heather, *Calluna vulgaris.* [1325–75; ME *lyng* < ON *lyng*]

-ling[1], a suffix of nouns, often pejorative, denoting one concerned with (*hireling; underling*), or diminutive (*princeling; duckling*). [ME, OE; c. G *-ling,* ON *-lingr,* Goth *-lings;* see -LE, -ING[1]]

-ling[2], an adverbial suffix expressing direction, position, state, etc.: *darkling; sideling.* [ME, OE; adv. use of gradational var. *lang* LONG[1]]

ling., linguistics.

Lin·ga·la (ling gä′lə), *n.* a Bantu language used as a lingua franca in northern Zaire.

lin·gam (ling′gəm), *n.* **1.** *Sanskrit Gram.* the masculine gender. **2.** (in popular Hinduism) a phallus, symbol of Siva. Also, **lin·ga** (ling′gə). Cf. **yoni.** [< Skt *liṅga* mark, gender, phallus]

Lin·ga·yat (ling gä′yit), *n. Hinduism.* a member of the Lingayata cult. [1665–75; < Kannada *liṅgāyata;* see LINGA]

Lin·ga·ya·ta (ling gä′yə tə), *n. Hinduism.* a Saiva cult emphasizing devotion and faith. Also called **Vira Saiva.** [< Kannada; see LINGAYAT]

Lin′ga·yen′ Gulf′ (ling′gä yen′), a gulf in the Philippines, on the NW coast of Luzon.

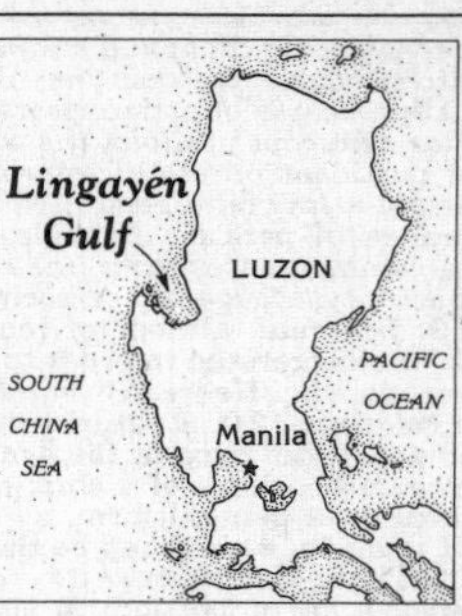

ling·cod (ling′kod′), *n., pl.* **-cods,** (*esp. collectively*) **-cod.** a large-mouthed game fish, *Ophiodon elongatus,* of the North Pacific, related to the greenling. Also, **ling′ cod′.** Also called **cultus.** [1880–85; LING[1] + COD[1]]

lin·ger (ling′gər), *v.i.* **1.** to remain or stay on in a place longer than is usual or expected, as if from reluctance to leave: *We lingered awhile after the party.* **2.** to remain alive; continue or persist, although gradually dying, ceasing, disappearing, etc.: *She lingered a few months after the heart attack. Such practices still linger among the older natives.* **3.** to dwell in contemplation, thought, or enjoyment: *to linger over the beauty of a painting.* **4.** to be tardy in action; delay; dawdle: *to linger in discharging one's duties.* **5.** to walk slowly; saunter along. *—v.t.* **6.** to pass (time, life, etc.) in a leisurely or a tedious manner (usually fol. by *away* or *out*): *We lingered away the whole summer at the beach.* **7.** *Archaic.* to draw out or protract. [1250–1300; ME *lengeren* to dwell, remain (somewhere), freq. of *lengen,* OE *lengan* to delay, prolong, lit., lengthen. See LONG[1], -ER[6]] **—lin′ger·er,** *n.* **—lin′ger·ing·ly,** *adv.*
—Syn. 1, 4. tarry. **1, 5.** loiter.

lin·ge·rie (län′zhə rā′, lan′zhə rē′, -jə-; *Fr.* laNzhə-RĒ′), *n.* **1.** underwear, sleepwear, and other items of intimate apparel worn by women. **2.** *Archaic.* linen goods in general. *—adj.* **3.** having the qualities of lingerie; lacy or frilly. [1825–35; < F, equiv. to MF *linge* linen (< L *lineus* of flax; see LINE[1]) + *-erie* -ERY]

lin·go[1] (ling′gō), *n., pl.* **-goes. 1.** the language and speech, esp. the jargon, slang, or argot, of a particular field, group, or individual: *gamblers' lingo.* **2.** language or speech, esp. if strange or foreign. [1650–60; appar. alter. of LINGUA (FRANCA); cf. Polari *lingo* language]

lin·go[2] (ling′gō), *n., pl.* **-goes.** lingoe.

lin·goe (ling′gō), *n.* **1.** a metal weight attached to the cords of a Jacquard harness, for lowering the warp threads after they have been raised and for keeping the harness cords taut. **2.** the same object attached to a drawloom. Also, **lingo.** [prob. < F *lingot* INGOT]

ling·on·ber·ry (ling′ən ber′ē), *n., pl.* **-ries.** See **mountain cranberry** (def. 1). [1950–55; < Sw *lingon* mountain cranberry + BERRY]

-lings, var. of **-ling**[2]. [ME *-linges.* See -LING[2], -S[1]]

lin·gua (ling′gwə), *n., pl.* **-guae** (-gwē). the tongue or a part like a tongue. [1665–75; < L; akin to TONGUE]

lin′gua fran′ca (frang′kə), *pl.* **lingua francas, lin·guae fran·cae** (ling′gwē fran′sē). **1.** any language that is widely used as a means of communication among speakers of other languages. **2.** (*cap.*) the Italian-Provençal jargon (with elements of Spanish, French, Greek, Arabic, and Turkish) formerly widely used in eastern Mediterranean ports. [1670–80; < It: lit., Frankish tongue]

lin′gua ge·ral′ (zhə räl′), (*often caps.*) a lingua franca based on Tupi and spoken in the Amazon basin of South America. [1855–60; < Pg: general language]

lin·gual (ling′gwəl), *adj.* **1.** of or pertaining to the tongue or some tonguelike part. **2.** pertaining to languages. **3.** *Phonet.* articulated with the aid of the tongue, esp. the tip of the tongue, as *d, n, s,* or *r.* *—n.* **4.** *Phonet.* a lingual sound. [1350–1400; ME: tongue-shaped surgical instrument < ML *linguālis.* See LINGUA, -AL[1]] **—lin′gual·ly,** *adv.*

lin′gual brace′, *Orthodontics.* a specialized dental brace that fits behind the teeth so that it is not visible when the wearer speaks or smiles.

lin′gual protru′sion lisp′, *Phonet.* See under **lisp** (def. 2).

lin·gui·ça (ling gwē′sə; *Port.* liN gwē′sä, -sə), *n.* a highly spiced Portuguese garlic sausage. [< Pg; ulterior orig. uncert.]

lin·gui·form (ling′gwə fôrm′), *adj.* tongue-shaped. [1745–55; < L *lingu(a)* LINGUA + -I- + -FORM]

lin·gui·ne (ling gwē′nē), *n. Italian Cookery.* a type of pasta in long, slender, flat strips. Also, **lin·gui′ni.** [1945–50; < It, pl. of *linguina,* dim. of *lingua* tongue; see -INE[1]]

lin·guist (ling′gwist), *n.* **1.** a specialist in linguistics. **2.** a person who is skilled in several languages; polyglot. [1580–90; < L *lingu(a)* tongue, speech + -IST]

lin·guis·tic (ling gwis′tik), *adj.* **1.** of or belonging to language: *linguistic change.* **2.** of or pertaining to linguistics. [1830–40; LINGUIST + -IC] **—lin·guis′ti·cal·ly,** *adv.*

lin·guis·ti·cal (ling gwis′ti kəl), *adj.* (not in technical use) linguistic. [1815–25; LINGUISTIC + -AL[1]]

linguis′tic anal′ysis, a 20th-century philosophical movement inspired by Ludwig Wittgenstein and marked by close attention paid to the way words are used in order to clarify concepts and to eliminate confusions arising from mystifying preconceptions about language. Also called **ordinary-language philosophy, philosophical analysis.**

CONCISE ETYMOLOGY KEY: <, descended or borrowed from; >, whence; b., blend of, blended; c., cognate with; cf., compare; deriv., derivative; equiv., equivalent; imit., imitative; obl., oblique; r., replacing; s., stem; sp., spelling, spelled; resp., respelling, respelled; trans., translation; ?, origin unknown; *, unattested; ‡, probably earlier than. See the full key inside the front cover.

linguis′tic ar′ea, *Ling.* a geographical area in which several languages sharing common features are spoken.

linguis′tic at′las. See **dialect atlas.** [1920–25]

linguis′tic form′, any meaningful unit of speech, as a sentence, phrase, word, morpheme, or suffix. [1920–25]

linguis′tic geog′raphy. See **dialect geography.** [1925–30] —**linguis′tic geog′rapher.**

lin·guis·ti·cian (ling′gwi stish′ən), *n.* linguist (def. 1). [1890–95; LINGUISTIC + -IAN]

linguis′tic philos′ophy, an approach to philosophical problems used esp. by certain British and American philosophers, inspired by G. E. Moore, and marked by the elucidation of difficult and controversial concepts by resolving them into their elements. [1955–60]

lin·guis·tics (ling gwis′tiks), *n.* (*used with a singular v.*) the science of language, including phonetics, phonology, morphology, syntax, semantics, pragmatics, and historical linguistics. [1850–55; see LINGUISTIC, -ICS]

linguis′tic stock′, **1.** a parent language and all its derived dialects and languages. **2.** the people speaking any of these dialects or languages. [1920–25]

linguis′tic univer′sal. See **language universal.** [1970–75]

lin·gu·la (ling′gyə lə), *n., pl.* **-lae** (-lē′). a tongue-shaped organ, process, or tissue. [1655–65; < NL, L *lingula,* dim of *lingua* tongue; cf. LIGULA] —**lin′gu·lar,** *adj.*

lin·gu·late (ling′gyə lāt′), *adj.* formed like a tongue; ligulate. Also, **lin′gu·lat′ed.** [1790–1800; < L *lingulātus* tongue-shaped; see LINGULA, -ATE[1]]

lin·hay (lin′ē), *n. Newfoundland.* a storage shed or other attachment to the back of a house. [cf. dial. (SW England, Ireland) *linhay* shed, open building; of uncert. orig.]

lin·i·ment (lin′ə mənt), *n.* a liquid or semiliquid preparation for rubbing on or applying to the skin, as for sprains or bruises, usually soothing or counterirritating. [1375–1425; late ME < LL *linimentum* ointment, equiv. to *linī(re)* (for L *linere* to smear) + *-mentum* -MENT]

lin·ing[1] (lī′ning), *n.* **1.** something that is used to line another thing; a layer of material on the inner side or surface of something. **2.** *Bookbinding.* the material used to strengthen the back of a book after the sheets have been folded, backed, and sewed. **3.** the act or process of lining something. [1375–1425; late ME *lynyng.* See LINE[2], -ING[1]]

lin·ing[2] (lī′ning), *n.* **1.** the act of marking or ornamenting a surface with lines. **2.** a design or ornamentation composed of lines. **3.** *Print.* a system of designing type so that all characters of the same point size, regardless of font, will align with one another. [1565–75; LINE[1] + -ING[1]]

link[1] (lingk), *n.* **1.** one of the rings or separate pieces of which a chain is composed. **2.** anything serving to connect one part or thing with another; a bond or tie: *The locket was a link with the past.* **3.** a unit in a communications system, as a radio relay station or a television booster station. **4.** any of a series of sausages in a chain. **5.** a cuff link. **6.** a ring, loop, or the like: *a link of hair.* **7.** *Survey., Civ. Engin.* **a.** (in a surveyor's chain) a unit of length equal to 7.92 inches (20.12 centimeters). **b.** one of 100 rods or loops of equal length forming a surveyor's or engineer's chain. **8.** *Chem.* bond[1] (def. 15). **9.** *Mach.* a rigid, movable piece or rod, connected with other parts by means of pivots or the like, for the purpose of transmitting motion. —*v.t., v.i.* **10.** to join by or as if by a link or links; connect; unite (often fol. by *up*): *The new bridge will link the island to the mainland. The company will soon link up with a hotel chain.* [1375–1425; late ME *link(e)* < ODan *lænkia* chain; c. ON *hlekkr* link (pl., chain), OE *hlence* coat of chain mail, akin to G *Gelenk* joint] —**link′er,** *n.*
—**Syn. 2.** connection, connective, copula. **10.** bond, league, conjoin, fasten, bind, tie, pin.

link[2] (lingk), *n.* a torch, esp. of tow and pitch. [1520–30; perh. special use of LINK[1]; the torches so called may have been made of strands twisted together in chainlike form]

link·age (ling′kij), *n.* **1.** the act of linking; state or manner of being linked. **2.** a system of links. **3.** *Genetics.* an association between two or more genes on a chromosome that tends to cause the characteristics determined by these genes to be inherited as an inseparable unit. **4.** *Mach.* an assembly of four or more rods for transmitting motion, usually in the same plane or in parallel planes. **5.** a factor or relationship that connects or ties one thing to another; link: *Administration officials sought to establish linkage between grain sales and relaxed immigration laws.* **6.** any of various mathematical or drawing devices consisting of a combination of bars or pieces pivoted together so as to turn about one another, usually in parallel planes. **7.** *Elect.* See **flux linkage.** [1870–75; LINK[1] + -AGE]

link′age ed′itor, *Computers.* a system program that combines independently compiled object modules or load modules into a single load module.

link′age group′, *Genetics.* a group of genes in a chromosome that tends to be inherited as a unit. [1935–40]

link′age map′, *Genetics.* See **genetic map.** [1935–40]

linked (lingkt), *adj. Genetics.* (of a gene) exhibiting linkage. [1400–50 for literal sense; late ME; see LINK[1], -ED[2]]

linked′ rhyme′, *Pros.* a rhyme in which the end of one line together with the first sound of the next line forms a rhyme with the end of another line.

linked′ verse′, *Pros.* a Japanese verse form in which stanzas of three lines alternating with stanzas of two lines are composed by two or more poets in alternation. Also called **renga.**

linking r, *Phonet.* **1.** the *r*-sound as reintroduced into an utterance where there is an *r* in the spelling by speakers of an *r*-dropping dialect when a postvocalic *r* they would normally drop, as in the pronunciation of *far* as (fä), becomes intervocalic, as in *far away* pronounced as (fär′ə wā′). **2.** Also called **intrusive r.** the *r*-sound as inserted analogously by speakers of an *r*-dropping dialect between vowels where there is no corresponding *r* in the spelling, as in the pronunciation of *Cuba is* as (kyo͞o′bə riz). [1945–50]

link′ing verb′, copula (def. 2). [1930–35]

Lin·kö·ping (lēn′chœ′pēng), *n.* a city in S Sweden. 112,600.

links (lingks), *n.* (*used with a plural v.*) See **golf course.** [bef. 1100; ME *lynkys* slopes, OE *hlincas,* pl. of *hlinc* rising ground, equiv. to *hlin(ian)* to LEAN[1], bend (akin to Gk *klī́nein* to cause to slope) + *-k* suffix]

links·man (lingks′mən), *n., pl.* **-men.** a person who plays golf; golfer. [1935–40; LINKS + -MAN]

Link′ train′er, *Aeron., Trademark.* a ground training device used in instrument-flight training.

link·up (lingk′up′), *n.* **1.** a contact or linkage established, as between military units or two spacecraft. **2.** something serving as a linking element or system; a connection or hookup. [1940–45; n. use of v. phrase *link up*]

link·work (lingk′wûrk′), *n.* **1.** something composed of links, as a chain. **2.** a linkage. **3.** *Mach.* a mechanism or device in which motion is transmitted by links. [1520–30; LINK[1] + WORK]

Lin·lith·gow (lin lith′gō), *n.* former name of **West Lothian.**

linn (lin), *n. Chiefly Scot.* **1.** a waterfall or torrent of rushing water in a river or stream. **2.** a pool of water, esp. at the foot of a waterfall. **3.** a steep ravine or precipice. Also, **lin.** [bef. 1000; conflation of OE *hlynn* torrent (not recorded in ME), and ScotGael *linne,* c. Ir *linn,* Welsh *llyn*]

Lin·nae·an (li nē′ən), *adj.* **1.** of or pertaining to Linnaeus, who established the binomial system of scientific nomenclature. **2.** noting or pertaining to a system of botanical classification introduced by him, based mainly on the number or characteristics of the stamens and pistils. Also, **Lin·ne′an.** [1745–55; LINNAE(US) + -AN]

Lin·nae·us (li nē′əs), *n.* **Car·o·lus** (kar′ə ləs), (*Carl von Linné*), 1707–78, Swedish botanist.

lin·net (lin′it), *n.* **1.** a small Old World finch, *Carduelis cannabina.* **2.** any of various related birds, as the house finch. [1520–30; earlier *linet* < MF (Walloon, Picard) *linette* (F *linot, linotte*), deriv. of *lin* flax (cf. LINE[1]; so named for its diet of flaxseeds); see -ET]

lin′net hole′, a small hole joining a glassmaking furnace to the arch. [1655–65; *linnet,* prob. < F *lunette;* see LUNETTE]

li·no (lī′nō), *n., pl.* **-nos.** *Chiefly Brit. Informal.* linoleum. [by shortening]

li·no·cut (lī′nə kut′), *n.* **1.** a cut made from a design cut into linoleum mounted on a block of wood. **2.** a print made from such a cut. [1905–10; LINO(LEUM) + CUT]

lin·o·le·ic (lin′l ē′ik, li nō′lē ik), *adj. Chem.* of or derived from linoleic acid. [1855–60; < Gk *lín(on)* flax + OLEIC]

lin′ole′ic ac′id, *Chem.* an unsaturated fatty acid, $C_{18}H_{32}O_2$, occurring as a glyceride in drying oils, as in linseed oil. Also, **li·no′lic ac′id** (lə nō′lik). [1855–60]

li·no·le·um (li nō′lē əm), *n.* **1.** a hard, washable floor covering formed by coating burlap or canvas with linseed oil, powdered cork, and rosin, and adding pigments to create the desired colors and patterns. **2.** any floor covering similar to this. [1863; < L *līn(um)* flax, linen + *oleum* oil; formerly trademark]

lino′leum block′, a piece of thick, soft, cork linoleum often mounted on a block of wood, incised or carved in relief with a design, pattern, or pictorial motif, and used in making prints.

li·no·type (lī′nə tīp′), *v.,* **-typed, -typ·ing.** *Print.* to typeset on a Linotype machine. [see LINOTYPE] —**li′no·typ′er, li′no·typ′ist,** *n.*

Li·no·type (lī′nə tīp′), *Trademark.* a brand of typesetting machine that casts solid lines of type from brass dies, or matrices, selected automatically by actuating a keyboard.

Lin Piao (*Chin.* lin′ byou′), *Wade-Giles.* See **Lin Biao.**

Lins (lēɴs), *n.* a city in E Brazil. 56,601.

lin·sang (lin′sang), *n.* any of several civetlike carnivores of the genera *Prionodon,* of the East Indies, and *Poiana,* of Africa, having retractile claws and a long tail: some East Indies linsangs are endangered. [1880–85; < Javanese *lingsang*]

lin·seed (lin′sēd′), *n.* flaxseed. [bef. 1000; ME *linsed,* OE *līnsǣd.* See LINE[1], SEED]

lin′seed cake′, a cake or a mass made by expressing the oil from linseed, used chiefly as feed for cattle. [1795–1805]

lin′seed meal′, ground linseed cake. [1590–1600]

lin′seed oil′, a drying oil obtained by pressing flaxseed, used in making paints, printing inks, linoleum, etc. [1540–50]

Lin Sen (lin′ sun′), *Wade-Giles, Pinyin.* 1867–1943, Chinese statesman.

lin·sey (lin′zē), *n., pl.* **-seys.** linsey-woolsey.

lin·sey-wool·sey (lin′zē wo͝ol′zē), *n., pl.* **-seys. 1.** a coarse fabric woven from linen warp, or sometimes cotton, and coarse wool filling. **2.** a garment made from this. **3.** *Archaic.* any mixture that is incongruous or of poor quality; jumble: *That last speech was a linsey-woolsey of stale platitudes.* Also called **linsey.** [1425–75; late ME *lynsy wolsye* lit., linen cloth, wool cloth, equiv. to *lyn* (OE *līn;* see LINEN) + *-sy,* var. of *say* cloth (< OF *saie;* akin to ML *sagia* kind of weave, L *sagum* cloak) + *wol* WOOL + *-sye,* var. of *say*]

lin·stock (lin′stok′), *n.* a staff with one end forked to hold a match, formerly used in firing cannon. [1565–75; earlier *lyntstock* < D *lontstock* match-stick, with LINT r. *lont* by assoc. with the material commonly used as tinder]

lint (lint), *n.* **1.** minute shreds or ravelings of yarn; bits of thread. **2.** staple cotton fiber used to make yarn. **3.** cotton waste produced by the ginning process. **4.** a soft material for dressing wounds, procured by scraping or otherwise treating linen cloth. [1325–75; ME, var. of *linnet;* cf. MF *linette* linseed, OE *līnet-* flax (or flax-field) in *līnetwige* LINTWHITE] —**lint′less,** *adj.*

lin·tel (lin′tl), *n.* a horizontal architectural member supporting the weight above an opening, as a window or a door. Also, *Brit.,* **lin′tol.** [1350–1400; ME *lyntel* < MF *lintel,* dissimilated var. of **linter* < L *līmitāris* orig., belonging to or indicating a boundary; later taken as synonym of *līmināris* orig., of the threshold. See LIMIT, -AR[1]]

lint·er (lin′tər), *n.* **1. linters,** short cotton fibers that stick to seeds after a first ginning. **2.** a machine for removing lint from cloth. [1730–40, *Amer.;* LINT + -ER[1]]

Lin·ton (lin′tn), *n.* **1. Ralph,** 1893–1953, U.S. anthropologist. **2.** a male given name.

lint·white (lint′hwīt′, -wīt′), *n. Chiefly Scot.* the linnet, *Carduelis cannabina.* [bef. 900; *lint* (syncopated var. of LINNET) + WHITE; r. ME *lynkwhytte,* alter. (perh. by assoc. with *link* hill (see LINKS) and WHIT) of OE *līnetwige* linnet, lit., flax (or flax-field) trouble-maker, so called because the bird pecks out and eats flaxseed, equiv. to *līnet-* (< ML *līnētum* flax-field) + *-wige,* fem. of *wiga* fighter]

lint·y (lin′tē), *adj.,* **lint·i·er, lint·i·est. 1.** full of or covered with lint: *This blue suit gets linty quickly.* **2.** like lint: *linty bits on his coat.* [1600–10; LINT + -Y[1]]

li·num (lī′nəm), *n.* any of numerous plants of the genus *Linum,* including flax, *L. usitatissimum,* and various other species grown as ornamentals. [< NL (Linnaeus); L *linum* flax]

Li·nus (lī′nəs), *n.* **1.** *Class. Myth.* **a.** a musician and poet, the inventor of melody and rhythm, of whom various stories are told: often identified, through his untimely death, with the harvesting or withering of crops and vegetation. **b.** Also called **Li′nus song′.** a dirge: originally sung in western Asia to mourn the death of crops being harvested, later sung to mourn the death of Linus or that of Adonis. **2.** a male given name.

Li·nus (lī′nəs), *n.* **Saint,** died A.D. 76?, pope 67?–76?.

lin·y (lī′nē), *adj.,* **lin·i·er, lin·i·est. 1.** full of or marked with lines. **2.** resembling lines; linelike. Also, **liney.** [1800–10; LINE[1] + -Y[1]]

Lin·yu (lin′yo͞o′), *n. Pinyin.* former name of **Shanhaiguan.** Also, **Lin′yü′.**

Lin Yu·tang (lin′ yo͞o′täng′), (*Lin Yü-t'ang*) 1895–1976, Chinese author and philologist.

Linz (lints), *n.* a port in N Austria, on the Danube River. 197,962.

Lin·zer torte (lin′zər tôrt′), *pl.* **Lin·zer tortes.** (*sometimes l.c.*) a sweet pastry, often made with powdered nuts, having a filling of red jam and a lattice crust. [1905–10; < G: lit., Linz torte]

li·on (lī′ən), *n.* **1.** a large, usually tawny-yellow cat, *Panthera leo,* native to Africa and southern Asia, having a tufted tail and, in the male, a large mane. **2.** any of various related large wildcats, as the cougar. **3.** a man of great strength, courage, etc. **4.** a person of great importance, influence, charm, etc., who is much admired as a celebrity: *a literary lion.* **5.** the lion as the national emblem of Great Britain. **6.** (*cap.*) *Astron., Astrol.* the constellation or sign of Leo. **7.** (*cap.*) a member of any one of the internationally affiliated service clubs (**International Association of Lions Clubs**) founded in 1917 and dedicated to promoting responsible citizenship, sound government, and community, national, and international welfare. **8.** *Numis.* **a.** a silver, Anglo-Gallic denier, issued during the reign of Henry III, bearing the figure of a lion. **b.** a gold coin of Scotland, issued c1400–1589, bearing the figure of a lion. **c.** any of various other coins bearing the figure of a lion. **d.** hardhead[2]. **9.** *Brit.* an object of interest or note. **10. beard the lion in its den,** to confront or attack someone, esp. a powerful or feared person, in that person's own familiar surroundings. **11. twist the lion's tail,** to tax the patience of or provoke a person, group, nation, or government, esp. that of Great Britain. [bef. 900; ME < OF, var. of *leon* < L *leōn-* (s. of *leō*) < Gk *léōn;* r. ME, OE *lēo* < L, as above] —**li′on·esque′,** *adj.* —**li′on·like′, li′on·ly,** *adj.*

lion and lioness, 3½ ft. (1 m) high at shoulder; head and body 6½ ft. (2 m); tail to 3 ft. (0.9 m)

li·on·cel (lī′ən sel′), *n. Heraldry.* a lion: so called when three or more are displayed on an escutcheon. [1600–10; < MF, dim. of *lion* LION]

Li·o·nel (lī′ə nl), *n.* a male given name, form of **Leon.**

CONCISE PRONUNCIATION KEY: act, cāpe, dâre, pärt; set, ēqual; *if,* īce; ox, ōver, ôrder, oil, bo͝ok, bo͞ot, out; up, ûrge; child; sing; shoe; thin, *th*at; zh as in *treasure.* ə = *a* as in *alone, e* as in *system, i* as in *easily, o* as in *gallop, u* as in *circus;* ə as in *fire* (fīər), *hour* (ouər). l and n can serve as syllabic consonants, as in *cradle* (krād′l), and *button* (but′n). See the full key inside the front cover.

li•on•ess (lī′ə nis), *n.* a female lion. [1250–1300; ME *liones, leonesse* < MF *lion(n)esse.* See LION, -ESS]

li•on•et (lī′ə net′), *n.* a young or small lion. [1580–90; < MF; see LION, -ET]

li•on•fish (lī′ən fish′), *n., pl.* **-fish•es,** (*esp. collectively*) **-fish. 1.** a brightly striped scorpionfish of the genus *Pterois,* esp. *P. volitans,* of the Indo-Pacific region, having long, flamboyant, venomous spiny fins. **2.** an Atlantic scorpionfish, *Scorpaena grandicornis.* [1905–10]

li•on•heart (lī′ən härt′), *n.* a person of exceptional courage and bravery. [1655–65; LION + HEART]

li•on•heart•ed (lī′ən här′tid), *adj.* exceptionally courageous or brave. [1700–10; LION + HEARTED] **—li′on•heart′ed•ly,** *adv.* **—li′on•heart′ed•ness,** *n.*

li•on•ize (lī′ə nīz′), *v.,* **-ized, -iz•ing.** *—v.t.* **1.** to treat (a person) as a celebrity: *to lionize the visiting poet.* **2.** *Brit.* to visit or exhibit the objects of interest of (a place). *—v.i.* **3.** to pursue celebrities or seek their company. **4.** *Brit.* to visit the objects of interest of a place. Also, *esp. Brit.,* **li′on•ise′.** [1800–10; LION + IZE] **—li′on•i•za′•tion,** *n.* **—li′on•iz′er,** *n.*

Li•ons (lī′ənz), *n.* **Gulf of,** a wide bay of the Mediterranean off the coast of S France. French, **Golfe du Lion.**

li′on's share′, the largest part or share, esp. a disproportionate portion: *The eldest son received the lion's share of the estate.* [1780–90; prob. after Aesop's fable in which the lion claimed all the spoils of a hunt]

Liou•ville (lyo͞o vēl′; *Eng.* lē′o͞o vil′), *n.* **Jo•seph** (zhô zef′; *Eng.* jō′zəf, -səf), 1809–82, French mathematician.

Liouville's′ the′orem, *Math.* the theorem that every function of a complex variable, bounded and differentiable for all finite values of the variable, is a constant function. [named after J. LIOUVILLE]

lip (lip), *n., adj., v.,* **lipped, lip•ping.** *—n.* **1.** either of the two fleshy parts or folds forming the margins of the mouth and functioning in speech. **2.** Usually, **lips.** these parts as organs of speech: *I heard it from his own lips.* **3.** a projecting edge on a container or other hollow object: *the lip of a pitcher.* **4.** a liplike part or structure, esp. of anatomy. **5.** any edge or rim. **6.** the edge of an opening or cavity, as of a canyon or a wound: *the lip of the crater.* **7.** *Slang.* impudent talk; back talk: *Don't give me any of your lip.* **8.** *Bot.* either of the two parts into which the corolla or calyx of certain plants, esp. of the mint family, is divided. **9.** *Zool.* **a.** a labium. **b.** the outer or the inner margin of the aperture of a gastropod's shell. **10.** *Music.* the position and arrangement of lips and tongue in playing a wind instrument; embouchure. **11.** the cutting edge of a tool. **12.** the blade, at the end of an auger, which cuts the chip after it has been circumscribed by the spur. **13.** (in a twist drill) the cutting edge at the bottom of each flute. **14. bite one's lip** or **tongue,** to repress one's anger or other emotions: *He wanted to return the insult, but bit his lip.* **15. button one's lip,** *Slang.* to keep silent, esp., to refrain from revealing information: *They told him to button his lip if he didn't want trouble.* Also, **button up. 16. hang on the lips of,** to listen to very attentively: *The members of the club hung on the lips of the visiting lecturer.* **17. keep a stiff upper lip, a.** to face misfortune bravely and resolutely: *Throughout the crisis they kept a stiff upper lip.* **b.** to suppress the display of any emotion. **18. smack one's lips,** to indicate one's keen enjoyment or pleasurable anticipation of: *We smacked our lips over the delicious meal.* *—adj.* **19.** of or pertaining to the lips or a lip: *lip ointment.* **20.** characterized by or made with the lips: *to read lip movements.* **21.** superficial or insincere: *to offer lip praise.* *—v.t.* **22.** to touch with the lips. **23.** *Golf.* to hit the ball over the rim of (the hole). **24.** to utter, esp. softly. **25.** to kiss. *—v.i.* **26.** to use the lips in playing a musical wind instrument. **27. lip off,** *Slang.* to talk impudently or belligerently. [bef. 1000; ME *lip(pe),* OE *lippa;* c. D *lip,* G *Lippe;* akin to Norw *lepe,* L *labium*] **—lip′less,** *adj.* **—lip′like′,** *adj.*

lip-, var. of **lipo-**[1] before a vowel: *lipectomy, lipase, lipemia.*

Li•pan (li pän′), *n., pl.* **-pans,** (*esp. collectively*) **-pan** for 1. **1.** a member of a group of Apache Indians who lived in the U.S. east of the Rio Grande. **2.** the Athabaskan language of the Lipan.

Lip′a•ri Is′lands (lip′ə rē; *It.* lē′pä rē), a group of volcanic islands N of Sicily, belonging to Italy. 10,043; 44 sq. mi. (114 sq. km).

li•pase (lī′pās, lip′ās), *n. Biochem.* any of a class of enzymes that break down fats, produced by the liver, pancreas, and other digestive organs or by certain plants. [1895–1900; LIP- + -ASE]

Lip•chitz (lip′shits), *n.* **Jacques** (zhäk), 1891–1973, U.S. sculptor, born in Lithuania.

lip•ec•to•my (li pek′tə mē, lī-), *n., pl.* **-mies.** *Surg.* the surgical removal of fatty tissue. Cf. **suction lipectomy.** [LIP- + -ECTOMY]

li•pe•mi•a (li pē′mē ə, lī-), *n. Med.* excessive amounts of fat and fatty substances in the blood; hyperlipemia. Also, **li•pae′mi•a.** [1745–55; < NL *lipaemia.* See LIP-, -EMIA] **—li•pe′mic, li•pae′mic,** *adj.*

Li•petsk (lē′petsk; *Russ.* lyē′pyitsk), *n.* a city in the W Russian Federation in Europe, SSE of Moscow. 465,000.

lip′ gloss′, a cosmetic used to give shine, and often a tint, to the lips. Also, **lip′gloss′.** [1935–40]

lip•id (lip′id, lī′pid), *n. Biochem.* any of a group of organic compounds that are greasy to the touch, insoluble in water, and soluble in alcohol and ether: lipids comprise the fats and other esters with analogous properties and constitute, with proteins and carbohydrates, the chief structural components of living cells. Also, **lip•ide** (lip′īd, -id, lī′pīd, -pid). [1920–25; LIP- + -ID[3]]

CONCISE ETYMOLOGY KEY: <, descended or borrowed from; >, whence; b., blend of, blended; c., cognate with; cf., compare; deriv., derivative; equiv., equivalent; imit., imitative; obl., oblique; r., replacing; s., stem; sp., spelling, spelled; resp., respelling, respelled; trans., translation; ?, origin unknown; *, unattested; ‡, probably earlier than. See the full key inside the front cover.

lip′id bi′layer, *Cell Biol.* See **phospholipid bilayer.**

Lip•iz•za•ner (lip′it sä′nər), *n.* Lippizaner.

Lip•mann (lip′mən), *n.* **Fritz Albert,** 1899–1986, U.S. biochemist, born in Germany: Nobel prize for medicine 1953.

lip′ mold′ing, *Furniture.* a bead surrounding the opening of a drawer.

Li Po (lē′ pō′; *Chin:* lē′ bô′), A.D. 701?–762, Chinese poet of the Tang dynasty. Also called **Li Tai Po.**

lipo-[1], a combining form meaning "fat," used in the formation of compound words: *lipolysis.* Also, *esp. before a vowel,* **lip-.** [comb. form repr. Gk *lípos* fat]

lipo-[2], a combining form meaning "lacking," "leaving," used in the formation of compound words: *lipography.* [< Gk, comb. form of *lip-,* weak s. of *leípein* to leave, be lacking; see -O-]

lip•o•chrome (lip′ə krōm′, lī′pə-), *n. Biochem.* any of the naturally occurring pigments that contain a lipid, as carotene. [1885–90; LIPO-[1] + -CHROME] **—lip′o•chro′•mic,** *adj.*

lip•o•cyte (lip′ə sīt′, lī′pə-), *n. Anat.* See **fat cell.** [LIPO-[1] + -CYTE]

lip•o•fill•ing (lip′ə fil′ing, lī′pə-), *n.* the surgical transfer of fat removed by liposuction to areas of the body that need filling out. [1985–90]

lip•o•fus•cin (lip′ə fus′in, lī′pə-), *n. Biochem.* any of several brown pigments similar to melanin that accumulate in animal cells with age and are products of oxidation of lipids and lipoproteins. [1920–25; < G, equiv. to *lipo-* LIPO-[1] + L *fusc(us)* dark, tawny + G *-in* -IN[2]]

lip•o•gram (lip′ə gram′, lī′pə-), *n.* a written work composed of words chosen so as to avoid the use of one or more specific alphabetic characters. [1705–15; < Gk *lipográmmatos* missing a letter. See LIPO-[2], -GRAM[1]] **—lip•o•gram•mat•ic** (lip′ō grə mat′ik, lī′pō-), *adj.*

li•pog•ra•phy (li pog′rə fē, lī-), *n.* unintentional omission in writing, as of a specific letter or syllable. [1885–90; LIPO-[2] + -GRAPHY] **—lip•o•graph•ic** (lip′ə graf′ik, lī′pə-), *adj.*

lip•oid (lip′oid, lī′poid), *adj.* **1.** Also, **lip•oi′dal.** fatty; resembling fat. *—n.* **2.** a fat or fatlike substance, as lecithin or wax. **3.** lipid. [1875–80; LIP- + -OID]

li•pol•y•sis (li pol′ə sis, lī-), *n. Chem.* the hydrolysis of fats into fatty acids and glycerol, as by lipase. [1900–05; < NL; see LIPO-[1], -LYSIS] **—lip•o•lit•ic** (lip′ə lit′ik, lī′pə-), *adj.*

li•po•ma (li pō′mə, lī-), *n., pl.* **-mas, -ma•ta** (-mə tə). *Pathol.* a benign tumor consisting of fat tissue. Also called **fatty tumor.** [1820–30; < NL; see LIP-, -OMA] **—li•pom•a•tous** (li pom′ə təs, -pō′mə-, lī-), *adj.*

lip•o•pex•i•a (lip′ə pek′sē ə, lī′pə-), *n. Biochem.* the storage of fat in the body. Also called **adipopexia, adipopexis.** [< NL; see LIPO-[1], -PEXY] **—lip•o•pec•tic** (lip′ə pek′tik, lī′pə-), *adj.*

lip•o•phil•ic (lip′ə fil′ik, lī′pə), *adj. Physical Chem.* **1.** having a strong affinity for lipids. **2.** promoting the dissolvability or absorbability of lipids. [1945–50; LIPO-[1] + -PHILIC]

lip•o•pol•y•sac•cha•ride (lip′ō pol′ē sak′ə rīd′, -rid, lī′pō-), *n. Biochem.* any of a class of polysaccharides to which lipids are attached. [1950–55; LIPO-[1] + POLYSACCHARIDE]

lip•o•pro•tein (lip′ə prō′tēn, -tē in, lī′pə-), *n. Biochem.* any of the class of proteins that contain a lipid combined with a simple protein. [1905–10; LIPO-[1] + PROTEIN]

lip•o•some (lip′ə sōm′, lī′pə-), *n. Cell. Biol.* a microscopic artificial sac composed of fatty substances and used in experimental research of the cell. [1905–10; LIPO-[1] + -SOME[3]] **—lip′o•so′mal,** *adj.*

lip•o•suc•tion (lip′ə suk′shən, lī′pə-), *n.* the surgical withdrawal of excess fat from local areas under the skin by means of a small incision and vacuum suctioning. [1985–90]

lip•o•trop•ic (lip′ə trop′ik, -trō′pik, lī′pə-), *adj. Chem., Biochem.* having an affinity for lipids and thus preventing or correcting excess accumulation of fat in the liver. [1930–35; LIPO-[1] + -TROPIC] **—li•pot•ro•pism** (li po′trə piz′əm, lī-), *n.*

lip•o•tro•pin (lip′ə trō′pin, lī′pə-), *n. Biochem.* a large polypeptide of the pituitary gland from which endorphins and other endogenous opiates are thought to derive. [1960–65; LIPOTROP(IC) + -IN[2]]

Lip•pe (lip′ə), *n.* a former state in NW Germany: now part of North Rhine-Westphalia.

lipped (lipt), *adj.* **1.** having lips or a lip. **2.** *Bot.* labiate. [1350–1400; ME; see LIP, -ED[3]]

lip•pen (lip′ən), *Chiefly Scot.* *—v.t.* **1.** to trust (a person). **2.** to entrust (something) to a person. *—v.i.* **3.** to have confidence, faith, or trust. [1125–75; ME *lipnen,* earlier *lipnien*]

lip•per (lip′ər), *n. Naut.* **1.** a slightly rough or ripply surface on a body of water. **2.** spray from small waves. [1505–15; n. use of dial. *lipper* to ripple. See LAP[3], -ER[6]]

Lip•pi (lip′ē; *It.* lēp′pē), *n.* **Fi•lip•pi•no** (fil′ə pē′nō; *It.* fē′lēp pē′nô), 1457–1504, and his father, **Fra Fi•lip•po** (frä fi lip′ō; *It.* frä fē lēp′pô) or **Fra Lip•po** (frä lip′ō; *It.* frä lēp′pô), 1406?–69, Italian painters.

Lip•pi•zan•er (lip′it sä′nər), *n.* one of a breed of compact, finely shaped, usually gray or white horses developed at the Austrian Imperial Stud and used generally in dressage exhibitions. Also, **Lipizzaner, Lip•pi•za•na** (lip′it sä′nə), **Lip′piz•zan′er.** [1925–30; < G, equiv. to *Lippizan* of Lippiza (near Trieste, where the Stud was located) + *-er* -ER[1]]

Lipp•mann (lip′mən; *also Fr.* lēp mȧɴ′ *for 1*), *n.* **1. Ga•bri•el** (gȧ brē el′), 1845–1921, French physicist: Nobel prize 1908. **2. Walter,** 1889–1974, U.S. journalist.

Lip•pold (lip′ōld), *n.* **Richard,** born 1915, U.S. sculptor.

lip•py (lip′ē), *adj.,* **-pi•er, -pi•est. 1.** having large or prominent lips. **2.** *Slang.* impudent; fresh. [1870–75; LIP + -Y[1]] **—lip′pi•ness,** *n.*

lip•read (lip′rēd′), *v.,* **-read** (-red′), **-read•ing.** *—v.t.* **1.** to understand spoken words by interpreting the movements of a speaker's lips without hearing the sounds made. *—v.i.* **2.** to use lipreading. Cf. **speechread.** [1890–95; LIP + READ[1]] **—lip′read′er,** *n.*

lip•read•ing (lip′rē′ding), *n.* the reading or understanding, as by a deaf person, of spoken words from the movements of another's lips without hearing the sounds made. Cf. **speechreading.** [1870–75; LIPREAD + -ING[1]]

Lip′schitz condi′tion (lip′shits), *Math.* the property of a function on a closed interval such that the absolute value of the difference in functional values at any two points in the interval is less than a constant times the absolute value of the difference of the points raised to some positive power *m,* called the order. Also called **Hölder condition.** [named after Rudolf *Lipschitz* (1832–1903), German mathematician]

Lips•comb (lip′skəm), *n.* **William Nunn** (nun), **Jr.,** born 1919, U.S. chemist: Nobel prize 1976.

lip′ serv′ice, insincere expression of friendship, admiration, support, etc.; service by words only: *He paid only lip service to the dictator.* [1635–45] **—lip′ serv′er.**

lip•stick (lip′stik′), *n.* a crayonlike oil-based cosmetic used in coloring the lips, usually in a tubular container. [1875–80, *Amer.;* LIP + STICK[1]]

lip′stick plant′, any of several trailing, epiphytic vines of the genus *Aeschynanthus,* of the gesneria family, esp. *A. pulcher* or *A. radicans,* native to southeast Asia, having tubular red or orange flowers.

lip-sync (lip′singk′), *Motion Pictures, Television.* *—v.t., v.i.* **1.** to synchronize (recorded sound) with lip movements, as of an actor in a film. **2.** to match lip movements with (recorded speech or singing): *She did a clumsy job of lip-syncing her big song.* *—n.* **3.** the technical process by which this is done. **4.** the simultaneous recording of voice and picture, esp. the synchronization of lip movements with recorded sound. Also, **lip′synch′, lip′sync′.** [1960–65]

Lip•ton (lip′tən), *n.* **1. Seymour,** born 1903, U.S. sculptor. **2. Sir Thomas John•stone** (jon′stən, -sən), 1850–1931, Scottish merchant and yacht racer.

liq., 1. liquid. **2.** liquor. **3.** (in prescriptions) solution. [< L *liquor*]

li•quate (lī′kwāt), *v.,* **-quat•ed, -quat•ing.** *Metall.* *—v.t.* **1.** to heat (an alloy or mixture) sufficiently to melt the more fusible matter and thus to separate it from the rest, as in the refining of tin. *—v.i.* **2.** to become separated by such a fusion (often fol. by *out*). [1660–70; < L *liquātus,* ptp. of *liquāre* to liquefy, melt. See LIQUID, -ATE[1]] **—li•qua•tion** (lī kwā′shən, -zhən), *n.*

liq•ue•fa•cient (lik′wə fā′shənt), *n.* something that liquefies or promotes liquefaction. [1850–55; < L *liquefacient-* (s. of *liquefaciēns,* prp. of *liquefacere* to LIQUEFY), equiv. to *lique-* (s. of *liquēre* to be liquid) + *-facient* -FACIENT]

liq•ue•fac•tion (lik′wə fak′shən), *n.* **1.** the act or process of liquefying or making liquid. **2.** the state of being liquefied. [1375–1425; late ME < LL *liquefactiōn-* (s. of *liquefactiō*) a melting, equiv. to L *liquefact(us)* (ptp. of *liquefacere* to melt, LIQUEFY) + *-iōn-* -ION] **—liq′ue•fac′tive,** *adj.*

liq′uefied petro′leum gas′, a gas liquefied by compression, consisting of flammable hydrocarbons, as propane and butane, obtained as a by-product from the refining of petroleum or from natural gas: used chiefly as a domestic fuel in rural areas, as an industrial and motor fuel, and in organic synthesis, esp. of synthetic rubber. Also called **bottled gas, compressed petroleum gas, LPG, LP gas.** [1920–25]

liq•ue•fy (lik′wə fī′), *v.t., v.i.,* **-fied, -fy•ing.** to make or become liquid. [1375–1425; late ME *lyquefyen* < OF *liquefier,* trans. of L *liquefacere* to melt (see LIQUEFACIENT); see -FY] **—liq′ue•fi′a•ble,** *adj.* **—liq′ue•fi′er,** *n.*

—Syn. melt, fuse, dissolve, thaw; condense.

li•ques•cent (li kwes′ənt), *adj.* **1.** becoming liquid; melting. **2.** tending toward a liquid state. [1720–30; < L *liquēscent-* (s. of *liquēscēns*), prp. of *liquēscere* to melt. See LIQUID, -ESCENT] **—li•ques′cence,** *n.*

li•queur (li kûr′ *or, esp. Brit.,* -kyo͝or′; *Fr.* lē kœʀ′), *n.* any of a class of alcoholic liquors, usually strong, sweet, and highly flavored, as Chartreuse or curaçao, generally served after dinner; cordial. [1735–45; < F; see LIQUOR]

liq•uid (lik′wid), *adj.* **1.** composed of molecules that move freely among themselves but do not tend to separate like those of gases; neither gaseous nor solid. **2.** of, pertaining to, or consisting of liquids: *a liquid diet.* **3.** flowing like water. **4.** clear, transparent, or bright: *liquid eyes.* **5.** (of sounds, tones, etc.) smooth; agreeable; flowing freely: *the liquid voice of a trained orator.* **6.** in cash or readily convertible into cash without significant loss of principal: *liquid assets.* **7.** *Phonet.* characterizing a frictionless speech sound pronounced with only a partial obstruction of the breath stream and whose utterance can be prolonged as that of a vowel, esp. *l* and *r.* **8.** (of movements, gestures, etc.) graceful; smooth; free and unconstricted: *the ballerina's liquid arabesques.* *—n.* **9.** a liquid substance. **10.** *Phonet.* either *r* or *l,* and sometimes *m, n, ng.* [1350–1400; ME *liquyd* < L *liquidus,* equiv. to *liqu(ēre)* to be liquid + *-idus* -ID[4]] **—liq′•uid•ly,** *adv.* **—liq′uid•ness,** *n.*

—Syn. 1. LIQUID, FLUID agree in referring to matter that is not solid. LIQUID commonly refers to substances, as water, oil, alcohol, and the like, that are neither solids nor gases: *Water ceases to be a liquid when it is frozen or turned to steam.* FLUID is applied to anything that flows, whether liquid or gaseous: *Pipes can carry fluids from place to place.*

liq′uid air′, a pale blue, intensely cold liquid, obtained by the compression and cooling of air: used as a source of oxygen, nitrogen, and inert gases, and as a refrigerant. [1895–1900]

liq•uid•am•bar (lik′wid am′bər, lik′wid am′-), *n.* **1.** any tree of the genus *Liquidambar,* including the sweet gum. **2.** the fragrant, yellowish, balsamic liquid exuded by this tree, used in medicine. Cf. **storax** (def. 2). [1590–1600; < NL: genus name. See LIQUID, AMBER]

liq•ui•date (lik′wi dāt′), *v.,* **-dat•ed, -dat•ing.** —*v.t.* **1.** to settle or pay (a debt): *to liquidate a claim.* **2.** to reduce (accounts) to order; determine the amount of (indebtedness or damages). **3.** to convert (inventory, securities, or other assets) into cash. **4.** to get rid of, esp. by killing: *to liquidate the enemies of the regime.* **5.** to break up or do away with: *to liquidate a partnership.* —*v.i.* **6.** to liquidate debts or accounts; go into liquidation. [1565–75; 1920–25 for def. 4; < LL *liquidātus,* ptp. of *liquidāre* to melt, make clear. See LIQUID, -ATE[1]]
—**Syn. 1.** discharge, clear, erase, cancel.

liq•ui•da•tion (lik′wi dā′shən), *n.* **1.** the process of realizing upon assets and of discharging liabilities in concluding the affairs of a business, estate, etc. **2.** the process of converting securities or commodities into cash. **3.** the state of being liquidated: *an estate in liquidation.* [1565–75; LIQUIDATE + -ION]

liq•ui•da•tor (lik′wi dā′tər), *n.* **1.** a person who liquidates assets, esp. one authorized to do so by a court of law. **2.** an official appointed by a court of law to direct the liquidation of a business. [1855–60; LIQUIDATE + -OR[2]]

liq′uid com′pass, *Navig.* See **wet compass.** [1860–65]

liq′uid crys′tal, a liquid having certain crystalline characteristics, esp. different optical properties in different directions when exposed to an electric field. [1890–95]

liq′uid fire′, flaming petroleum or the like, as employed against an enemy in warfare. [1860–65]

liq′uid glass′. See **sodium silicate.**

liq′uid gold′, a suspension of finely divided gold in a vegetable oil, used chiefly for gilding ceramic ware. [1835–45]

li•quid•i•ty (li kwid′i tē), *n.* **1.** a liquid state or quality. **2.** the ability or ease with which assets can be converted into cash. [1610–20; < L *liquiditās.* See LIQUID, -ITY]

liquid′ity pref′erence, (in Keynesian economics) the degree of individual preference for cash over less liquid assets. [1935–40]

liq•uid•ize (lik′wi dīz′), *v.t.,* **-ized, -iz•ing. 1.** to make liquid; liquefy. **2.** to stimulate; give facility to: *a thought that liquidizes the imagination.* **3.** to cause (a sound) to be full, round, mellifluous, etc. Also, *esp. Brit.,* **liq′uid•ise′.** [1830–40; LIQUID + -IZE]

liq′uid meas′ure, the system of units of capacity ordinarily used in measuring liquid commodities, as milk or oil. English system: 4 gills = 1 pint; 2 pints = 1 quart; 4 quarts = 1 gallon. Metric system: 1000 milliliters = 1 liter; 1000 liters = 1 kiloliter (= 1 cubic meter). [1850–55]

liq′uid ox′ygen, a clear, pale blue liquid obtained by compressing oxygen and then cooling it below its boiling point: used chiefly as an oxidizer in liquid rocket propellants. Also called **lox, LOX** [1875–80]

liq′uid petrola′tum. See **mineral oil.** [1900–05]

liq′uid propel′lant, a rocket propellant in liquid form. Cf. **solid propellant.**

liq′uid pro′tein, *Nutrition.* an amino acid hydrosol used in weight-reduction programs as a substitute for all or some meals: generally regarded as hazardous to health because of low nutritional content and recommended for controlled use only under medical supervision. [1965–70]

liq′uid sto′rax. See under **storax** (def. 2).

liq•ui•dus (lik′wi dəs), *n. Physical Chem.* (on a graph of temperature versus composition) the curve connecting the temperatures at which a liquid solution is in equilibrium with its vapor and with the solid solution. Cf. **solidus[2].** [1900–05; < L; see LIQUID]

liq•uor (lik′ər *or, for 3,* lik′wôr), *n.* **1.** a distilled or spirituous beverage, as brandy or whiskey, as distinguished from a fermented beverage, as wine or beer. **2.** any liquid substance, as broth from cooked meats or vegetables. **3.** *Pharm.* solution (def. 6). **4.** a solution of a substance, esp. a concentrated one used in the industrial arts. —*v.t.* **5.** *Informal.* to furnish or ply with liquor to drink (often fol. by *up*). —*v.i.* **6.** *Informal.* to drink large quantities of liquor (often fol. by *up*). [1175–1225; < L: a liquid, orig. liquidity (*liqu(ēre)* to be liquid + *-or* -OR[1]); r. ME *lic(o)ur* < OF (F *liqueur*) < L *liquōrem,* acc. of *liquor*] —**liq′uor•y,** *adj.*
—**Syn. 2.** juice, drippings.

liq•uo•rice (lik′ə rish, lik′rish, lik′ər is), *n.* licorice.

liq′uorice all′sorts (ôl′sôrts′), *Chiefly Brit.* variously shaped licorice or licorice-centered, sugarcoated candies. [1925–30]

liq•uor•ish (lik′ər ish), *adj. Archaic.* lickerish.

Lir (lēr), *n.* Ler.

li•ra (lēr′ə; *It.* lē′rä), *n., pl.* **li•re** (lēr′ā; *It.* lē′RE), **li•ras. 1.** a coin and monetary unit of Italy, equal to 100 centesimi. *Abbr.:* L., Lit. **2.** a silver, bronze, or chrome steel coin and monetary unit of Turkey, equal to 100 kurus; equal to 100 piasters before 1933; Turkish pound. *Abbr.:* TL. [1610–20; < It < OPr *lieura* < L *lībra* pound]

li•ra da brac•cio (lēr′ə də brä′chō, -chē ō′; *It.* lē′rä dä brät′chô), *pl.* **li•ras da brac•cio,** *It.* **li•re da brac•cio** (lē′RE dä brät′chô). a many-stringed musical instrument of the 15th and 16th centuries, played with a bow and used for polyphonic improvisation. [< It: lyre for the arm]

li•rel•la (li rel′ə, lī-), *n. Bot., Mycol.* the elongated, narrow apothecium of certain lichens. [1830–40; < NL, dim. of L *līra* a ridge, furrow]

li•rel•late (li rel′āt, lī-), *adj.* of, pertaining to, or resembling a lirella. [1885–90; LIRELL(A) + -ATE[1]]

li•ri•o•pe (lə rī′ə pē), *n.* any of several plants belonging to the genus *Liriope,* of the lily family, having tufted, grasslike leaves and clusters of small bluish or white flowers. Also called **lilyturf.** [< NL (1790), prob. < Gk *leíri(on)* LILY + *-ōpē,* fem. deriv. of *-ōpos* having a face or eyes (of the kind specified); cf. L *Līriopē* (Ovid), a fountain nymph]

lir•i•pipe (lir′ē pīp′), *n.* **1.** a hood with a long, hanging peak, worn originally by medieval academics and later adopted for general wear in the 14th and 15th centuries. **2.** a long strip or tail of fabric hanging from a garment or headdress, esp. the peak of this hood or a streamer on a chaperon; tippet. [1540–50; < ML *liripipium,* of obscure orig.]

Li•sa (lē′sə, -zə), *n.* a female given name, form of **Elizabeth.**

Li-sao (*Chin.* lē′sou′), *n. Wade-Giles, Pinyin.* a poem (c320 B.C.) by Ch'ü Yüan.

Lis•bon (liz′bən), *n.* a seaport in and the capital of Portugal, in the SW part, on the Tagus estuary. 760,150. Portuguese, **Lis•bo•a** (lēzh bô′ə).

Li•se (lē′sə, -zə), *n.* a female given name, form of **Elizabeth.**

li•sen•te (li sen′tē), *n.* pl. of **sente.**

Lis•gar (lis′gär), *n.* **Sir John Young,** 1807–76, Canadian political leader: governor general 1869–72.

Li Shih-min (*Chin.* lē′ shœ′mēn′). See **T'ai Tsung.** Also, **Li′ Shi′min′.**

Li•si•chansk (lis′i chänsk′; *Russ.* lyi syi chyänsk′), *n.* a city in the E Ukraine, in the W Soviet Union in Europe, on the Donets River, NE of Donetsk. 120,000.

lisle (līl), *n.* **1.** knit goods, as gloves or hose, made of lisle thread. **2.** See **lisle thread.** —*adj.* **3.** made of lisle thread. [1850–55; named after LISLE, France, where first made]

Lisle (lēl *for 1–3;* līl *for 4*), *n.* **1.** See **Leconte de Lisle. 2.** See **Rouget de Lisle. 3.** former name of **Lille. 4.** a town in NE Illinois. 13,625.

lisle′ thread′, a fine, high-twisted and hard-twisted cotton thread, at least two-ply, used for hosiery, gloves, etc. Also called **lisle.** [1850–55]

lisp (lisp), *n.* **1.** a speech defect consisting in pronouncing *s* and *z* like or nearly like the *th*-sounds of *thin* and *this,* respectively. **2.** *Phonet.* any unconventional articulation of the sibilants, as the pronunciation of *s* and *z* with the tongue between the teeth **(lingual protrusion lisp),** close to or touching the upper front teeth **(dental lisp),** or raised so that the breath is emitted laterally **(lateral lisp). 3.** the act, habit, or sound of lisping. —*v.t., v.i.* **4.** to pronounce or speak with a lisp. **5.** to speak imperfectly, esp. in a childish manner. [bef. 1100; ME *wlispen, lipsen,* OE *āwlyspian;* akin to D *lisp(el)en,* G *lispeln,* Norw *leipsa*] —**lisp′er,** *n.* —**lisp′ing•ly,** *adv.*

LISP (lisp), *n. Computers.* a high-level programming language that processes data in the form of lists: widely used in artificial intelligence applications. [*lis(t) p(rocessing)*]

lis pen•dens (lis pen′denz), *Law.* **1.** a pending suit listed on the court docket. **2.** the rule placing property involved in litigation under the court's jurisdiction. **3.** the principle that the filing of a suit constitutes notice of the claim asserted. [< L *līs pendēns*]

Lis′sa•jous fig′ure (lē′sə zhoo′, lē′sə zhoo′), *Physics.* the series of plane curves traced by an object executing two mutually perpendicular harmonic motions. [1875–80; named after Jules A. *Lissajous* (1822–80), French physicist]

lisse (lēs), *n.* a fine, filmy, lightly crinkled gauze fabric used in strips for making ruching or for finishing garments. [1850–55; < F (*crêpe*) *lisse* smooth (crepe), deriv. of *lisser* to smooth, polish, OF *lischier, licier* < ML *lixāre* to leach, deriv. of LL *lixa* lye; cf. LIXIVIUM]

lis•some (lis′əm), *adj.* **1.** lithesome or lithe, esp. of body; supple; flexible. **2.** agile, nimble, or active. Also, **lis′som.** [1790–1800; var. of LITHESOME] —**lis′some•ly,** *adv.* —**lis′some•ness,** *n.*
—**Ant. 1.** rigid. **2.** clumsy.

lis•sot•ri•chous (li so′tri kəs), *adj.* having straight hair. [1875–80; < Gk *lissó(s)* smooth + *trich-* (s. of *thríx*) hair + -OUS] —**lis•sot′ri•chy,** *n.*

list[1] (list), *n.* **1.** a series of names or other items written or printed together in a meaningful grouping or sequence so as to constitute a record: *a list of members.* **2.** See **list price. 3.** *Computers.* a series of records in a file. **4.** a complete record of stocks handled by a stock exchange. **5.** all of the books of a publisher that are available for sale. —*v.t.* **6.** to set down together in a list; make a list of: *to list the membership of a club.* **7.** to enter in a list, directory, catalog, etc.: *to list him among the members.* **8.** to place on a list of persons to be watched, excluded, restricted, etc. **9.** *Computers.* to print or display in a list: *Let's list the whole program and see where the bug is.* **10.** to register (a security) on a stock exchange so that it may be traded there. **11.** *Archaic.* enlist. —*v.i.* **12.** to be offered for sale, as in a catalog, at a specified price: *This radio lists at $49.95.* **13.** *Archaic.* enlist. [1595–1605; special use of LIST[2] (roll of names, perh. orig. of contestants in the LISTS); cf. F *liste* < It *lista* roll of names, earlier, band, strip (e.g., of paper), border < OHG (G *Leiste*)]
—**Syn. 1.** register. LIST, CATALOG, INVENTORY, ROLL, SCHEDULE imply a definite arrangement of items. LIST denotes a series of names, items, or figures arranged in a row or rows: *a list of groceries.* CATALOG adds the idea of alphabetical or other orderly arrangement, and, often, descriptive particulars and details: *a library catalog.* An INVENTORY is a detailed descriptive list of property, stock, goods, or the like made for legal or business purposes: *a store inventory.* A ROLL is a list of names of members of some defined group often used to ascertain their presence or absence: *a class roll.* A SCHEDULE is a methodical (esp. official) list, often indicating the time or sequence of certain events: *a train schedule.* **6.** record, catalog. **7.** enroll.

list[2] (list), *n.* **1.** a border or bordering strip, usually of cloth. **2.** a selvage. **3.** selvages collectively. **4.** a strip of cloth or other material. **5.** a strip or band of any kind. **6.** a stripe of color. **7.** a division of the hair or beard. **8.** one of the ridges or furrows of earth made by a lister. **9.** a strip of material, as bark or sapwood, to be trimmed from a board. **10.** fillet (def. 6a). —*adj.* **11.** made of selvages or strips of cloth. —*v.t.* **12.** to produce furrows and ridges on (land) with a lister. **13.** to prepare (ground) for planting by making ridges and furrows. **14.** to cut away a narrow strip of wood from the edge of (a stave, plank, etc.). **15.** *Obs.* to apply a border or edge to. [bef. 900; ME *lista,* OE *līst* border; c. D *lijst,* G *Leiste* (OHG *līsta*)]

list[3] (list), *n.* **1.** a careening, or leaning to one side, as of a ship. —*v.i.* **2.** (of a ship or boat) to incline to one side; careen: *The ship listed to starboard.* —*v.t.* **3.** to cause (a vessel) to incline to one side: *The shifting of the cargo listed the ship to starboard.* [1620–30; orig. uncert.]
—**Syn. 2, 3.** tilt, slant, heel.

list[4] (list), *Archaic.* —*v.t.* **1.** to please. **2.** to like or desire. —*v.i.* **3.** to like; wish; choose. [bef. 900; ME *listen, lusten,* OE *(ge)lystan* to please; c. G *gelüsten,* ON *lysta* to desire, akin to Goth *luston* to desire. See LUST]

list[5] (list), *Archaic.* —*v.i.* **1.** to listen. —*v.t.* **2.** to listen to. [bef. 900; ME *listen,* OE *hlystan* to listen, hear, deriv. of *hlyst* ear; c. Sw *lysta;* akin to ON *hlusta* to listen. See LISTEN]

List (list), *n.* **Frie•drich** (frē′drik), 1789–1846, U.S. political economist and journalist, born in Germany.

list•ed (lis′tid), *adj.* **1.** (of a security) admitted to trading privileges on a stock exchange. **2.** (of a telephone number or telephone subscriber) represented in a telephone directory. [1665–75; LIST[1] + -ED[2]]

list•ee (lis tē′), *n.* a person, business, etc., that is included in a list or directory. [LIST[1] + -EE]

lis•tel (lis′tl), *n. Archit.* a narrow list or fillet. [1590–1600; < F < It *listello,* dim. of *lista* band, LIST[2]]

lis•ten (lis′ən), *v.i.* **1.** to give attention with the ear; attend closely for the purpose of hearing; give ear. **2.** to pay attention; heed; obey (often fol. by *to*): *Children don't always listen to their parents.* **3.** to wait attentively for a sound (usually fol. by *for*): *to listen for sounds of their return.* **4.** *Informal.* to convey a particular impression to the hearer; sound: *The new recording doesn't listen as well as the old one.* —*v.t.* **5.** *Archaic.* to give ear to; hear. **6. listen in, a.** to listen to a radio or television broadcast: *Listen in tomorrow for the names of the lottery winners.* **b.** to overhear a conversation or communication, esp. by telephone; eavesdrop: *Someone was listening in to his private calls.* [bef. 950; ME *lis(t)nen,* OE *hlysnan;* c. MHG *lüsenen,* Sw *lyssna;* akin to LIST[5]] —**lis′ten•er,** *n.*
—**Syn. 1.** See **hear.**

lis•ten•a•ble (lis′ə nə bəl), *adj.* pleasant to listen to: *soft, listenable music.* [1915–20; LISTEN + -ABLE] —**lis′ten•a•bil′i•ty,** *n.*

lis•ten•er•ship (lis′ə nər ship′, lis′nər-), *n.* the people or number of people who listen to a radio station, record, type of music, etc.: *The station has a listenership of 200,000.* [1940–45; LISTENER + -SHIP]

lis′tening post′, 1. *Mil.* a post or position, as in advance of a defensive line, established for the purpose of listening to detect the enemy's movements. **2.** any foreign country or city viewed as a source of intelligence about an enemy or rival nation or one that is a potential enemy. **3.** any concealed position maintained to obtain information: *The government had listening posts to keep informed of revolutionary activities.* [1915–20]

list•er[1] (lis′tər), *n.* **1.** Also called **list′er plow′.** a plow with a double moldboard, used to prepare the ground for planting by producing furrows and ridges. **2.** Also called **list′er plant′er, list′er drill′.** a lister plow fitted with attachments for dropping and covering seeds. [1885–90, *Amer.;* LIST[2] + -ER[1]]

list•er[2] (lis′tər), *n.* a person who makes or compiles a list, esp. an appraiser or assessor. [1670–80; LIST[1] + -ER[1]]

Lis•ter (lis′tər), *n.* **Joseph, 1st Baron Lister of Lyme Re•gis** (līm rē′jis), 1827–1912, English surgeon: founder of modern antiseptic surgery.

Lis′ter bag′, a canvas container used esp. for supplying troops in the field with pure water.

lis•ter•el•lo•sis (lis′tər ə lō′sis), *n., pl.* **-ses** (-sēz). *Vet. Pathol.* listeriosis. [1935–40; < NL *listerell(a)* (named after J. LISTER) + -OSIS]

lis•te•ri•a (li stēr′ē ə), *n. Bacteriol.* any of several rod-shaped, aerobic, parasitic bacteria of the genus *Listeria,* pathogenic for humans and animals. [1960–65; < NL, named after J. LISTER; see -IA]

lis•te•ri•o•sis (li stēr′ē ō′sis), *n., pl.* **-ses** (-sēz). *Vet. Pathol.* a disease of wild and domestic mammals, birds, and occasionally of humans, caused by a bacterium, *Listeria monocytogenes,* and characterized by lack of control of movement, paralysis, fever, and monocytosis. Also, **lis•te•ri•a•sis** (lis′tə rē′ə sis). Also called **circling disease.** [1940–45; LISTERI(A) + -OSIS]

Lis•ter•ism (lis′tə riz′əm), *n.* an antiseptic method introduced by Joseph Lister, involving the spraying of the parts under operation with a carbolic acid solution. [1875–80; LISTER + -ISM]

Lis·ter·ize (lis′tə rīz′), *v.t.*, **-ized, -iz·ing.** to treat (a patient, disease, etc.) using the methods of Joseph Lister. Also, *esp. Brit.*, **Lis′ter·ise′.** [1900–05; LISTER + -IZE]

l'i·stes·so tem·po (lē stes′ō tem′pō; *It.* lē stes′sô tem′pô), (of a musical passage or section following a change in time signature) at the same tempo as before. [< It]

list·ing[1] (lis′ting), *n.* **1.** a list; record; catalog. **2.** the act of compiling a list. **3.** something listed or included in a list: *a listing in the telephone directory.* [1635–45; LIST[1] + -ING[1]]

list·ing[2] (lis′ting), *n.* material, as bark or sapwood, that is trimmed from a board. [1400–50; late ME; see LIST[2], -ING[1]]

list·less (list′lis), *adj.* having or showing little or no interest in anything; languid; spiritless; indifferent: *a listless mood; a listless handshake.* [1400–50; late ME *lystles.* See LIST[4], -LESS] **—list′less·ly,** *adv.* **—list′less·ness,** *n.*

list′ price′, the price at which a product is usually sold to the public and from which a trade discount is computed by a wholesaler. [1870–75]

lists (lists), *n.* (*used with a singular or plural v.*) **1.** an enclosed arena for a tilting contest. **2.** the barriers enclosing this arena. **3.** any place or scene of combat, competition, controversy, etc. **4. enter the lists,** to involve oneself in a conflict or contest: *to enter the lists against the protective tariff.* [1350–1400; ME *listes,* pl. of *liste* LIST[2]]

Liszt (list), *n.* **Franz** (fränts), 1811–86, Hungarian composer and pianist. **—Liszt′i·an,** *adj.*

lit[1] (lit), *v.* **1.** a pt. and pp. of **light**[1]. **—***adj.* **2.** *Slang.* under the influence of liquor or narcotics; intoxicated (usually fol. by *up*). [1910–15 for def. 2]

lit[2] (lit), *n.* litas.

lit[3] (lit), *v.* a pt. and pp. of **light**[3].

lit[4] (lit), *n. Informal.* literature: *a college course in English lit.* [by shortening]

Lit., (in Italy) lira; lire.

lit., **1.** liter; liters. **2.** literal. **3.** literally. **4.** literary. **5.** literature.

Li Tai Po (*Chin.* lē′ tī′ bô′). See **Li Po.** Also, **Li′ Tai′bo′.**

lit·a·ny (lit′n ē), *n., pl.* **-nies. 1.** a ceremonial or liturgical form of prayer consisting of a series of invocations or supplications with responses that are the same for a number in succession. **2. the Litany,** the supplication in this form in the *Book of Common Prayer.* **3.** a recitation or recital that resembles a litany. **4.** a prolonged or tedious account: *We heard the whole litany of their complaints.* [bef. 900; < LL *litanīa* < LGk *litaneía* litany, Gk: an entreating, equiv. to *litan-* (s. of *litaínein,* var. of *litaneúein* to pray) + *-eia* -Y[3]; r. ME *letanie,* OE *letania* < ML, LL, as above]
—Syn. 4. list, catalog, enumeration.

li·tas (lē′täs), *n., pl.* **-tai** (-tā), **-tu** (-to͞o). a former silver coin and monetary unit of Lithuania, equal to 100 centai. Also, **lit.** [< Lith]

Lit.B., Bachelor of Letters; Bachelor of Literature. [< L *Lit(t)erārum Baccalaureus*]

li·tchi (lē′chē), *n., pl.* **-tchis. 1.** the fruit of a Chinese tree, *Litchi chinensis,* of the soapberry family, consisting of a thin, brittle shell enclosing a sweet, jellylike pulp and a single seed. **2.** the tree itself. Also, **leechee, lichee.** [1580–90; < NL < Chin *lìzhī* (*lì* scallion + *zhī* branch)]

li′tchi nut′, the brownish, dried litchi fruit. [1875–80]

lit-crit (lit′krit′), *n. Informal.* literary criticism. [by shortening]

Lit.D., Doctor of Letters; Doctor of Literature. [< NL *Lit(t)erārum Doctor*]

lit de jus·tice (lē də zhys tēs′), *French.* **1.** the sofa upon which the king of France sat when holding formal sessions of the parliament. **2.** the session itself. [lit., bed of justice]

lite (lit), *adj.* **1.** an informal, simplified spelling of **light**[2] (defs. 12, 13), used esp. in labeling or advertising commercial products: *lite beer.* **—***n.* **2.** light[2] (def. 37). **—lite′ness,** *n.*

-lite, a combining form used in the names of minerals or fossils: *aerolite; chrysolite.* Also, **-lyte**[2]. Cf. **-lith.** [< F, simplified form of *-lithe* < Gk *líthos* stone; similarly G *-lit,* earlier *-lith*]

li·ter (lē′tər), *n.* a unit of capacity redefined in 1964 by a reduction of 28 parts in a million to be exactly equal to one cubic decimeter. It is equivalent to 1.0567 U.S. liquid quarts and is equal to the volume of one kilogram of distilled water at 4°C. *Abbr.:* l Also, *esp. Brit.,* **litre.** [1800–10; < F *litre,* back formation from *litron* an old measure of capacity, deriv. (with *-on* n. suffix) of ML *litra* < Gk *lítra* pound]

lit·er·a·cy (lit′ər ə sē), *n.* **1.** the quality or state of being literate, esp. the ability to read and write. **2.** possession of education: *to question someone's literacy.* **3.** a person's knowledge of a particular subject or field: *to acquire computer literacy.* [1880–85; LITER(ATE) + -ACY]
—Syn. 2. learning, culture.

lit′eracy test′, an examination to determine whether a person meets the literacy requirements for voting, serving in the armed forces, etc.; a test of one's ability to read and write. [1865–70]

CONCISE ETYMOLOGY KEY: <, descended or borrowed from; >, whence; b., blend of, blended; c., cognate with; cf., compare; deriv., derivative; equiv., equivalent; imit., imitative; obl., oblique; r., replacing; s., stem; sp., spelling, spelled; resp., respelling, respelled; trans., translation; ?, origin unknown; *, unattested; ‡, probably earlier than. See the full key inside the front cover.

lit·er·al (lit′ər əl), *adj.* **1.** in accordance with, involving, or being the primary or strict meaning of the word or words; not figurative or metaphorical: *the literal meaning of a word.* **2.** following the words of the original very closely and exactly: *a literal translation of Goethe.* **3.** true to fact; not exaggerated; actual or factual: *a literal description of conditions.* **4.** being actually such, without exaggeration or inaccuracy: *the literal extermination of a city.* **5.** (of persons) tending to construe words in the strict sense or in an unimaginative way; matter-of-fact; prosaic. **6.** of or pertaining to the letters of the alphabet. **7.** of the nature of letters. **8.** expressed by letters. **9.** affecting a letter or letters: *a literal error.* **—***n.* **10.** a typographical error, esp. involving a single letter. [1350–1400; ME < LL *litterālis* of letters. See LETTER, AL[1]] **—lit′er·al·ness,** *n.*
—Syn. 3. truthful, exact, reliable.

lit·er·al·ism (lit′ər ə liz′əm), *n.* **1.** adherence to the exact letter or the literal sense, as in translation or interpretation: *to interpret the law with uncompromising literalism.* **2.** a peculiarity of expression resulting from this: *The work is studded with these obtuse literalisms.* **3.** exact representation or portrayal, without idealization, as in art or literature: *a literalism more appropriate to journalism than to the novel.* [1635–45; LITERAL + -ISM] **—lit′er·al·ist,** *n.* **—lit′er·al·is′tic,** *adj.* **—lit′er·al·is′ti·cal·ly,** *adv.*

lit·er·al·i·ty (lit′ə ral′i tē), *n., pl.* **-ties. 1.** the quality or state of being literal; literalness. **2.** a literal interpretation. [1640–50; LITERAL + -ITY]

lit·er·al·ize (lit′ər ə liz′), *v.t.,* **-ized, -iz·ing.** to make literal; interpret literally. Also, *esp. Brit.,* **lit′er·al·ise′.** [1820–30; LITERAL + -IZE] **—lit′er·al·i·za′tion,** *n.* **—lit′er·al·iz′er,** *n.*

lit·er·al·ly (lit′ər ə lē), *adv.* **1.** in the literal or strict sense: *What does the word mean literally?* **2.** in a literal manner; word for word: *to translate literally.* **3.** actually; without exaggeration or inaccuracy: *The city was literally destroyed.* **4.** in effect; in substance; very nearly; virtually. [1525–35; LITERAL + -LY]
—Usage. Since the early 20th century, LITERALLY has been widely used as an intensifier meaning "in effect, virtually," a sense that contradicts the earlier meaning "actually, without exaggeration": *The senator was literally buried alive in the Iowa primaries. The parties were literally trading horses in an effort to reach a compromise.* The use is often criticized; nevertheless, it appears in all but the most carefully edited writing. Although this use of LITERALLY irritates some, it probably neither distorts nor enhances the intended meaning of the sentences in which it occurs. The same might often be said of the use of LITERALLY in its earlier sense "actually": *The garrison was literally wiped out: no one survived.*

lit·er·al-mind·ed (lit′ər əl min′did), *adj.* unimaginative; prosaic; matter-of-fact. [1865–70]

lit·er·ar·y (lit′ə rer′ē), *adj.* **1.** pertaining to or of the nature of books and writings, esp. those classed as literature: *literary history.* **2.** pertaining to authorship: *literary style.* **3.** versed in or acquainted with literature; well-read. **4.** engaged in or having the profession of literature or writing: *a literary man.* **5.** characterized by an excessive or affected display of learning; stilted; pedantic. **6.** preferring books to actual experience; bookish. [1640–50; < L *literārius, litterārius* of reading and writing. See LETTER, -ARY] **—lit′er·ar′i·ly,** *adv.* **—lit′·er·ar′i·ness,** *n.*

lit′erary exec′utor, a person entrusted with the publishable works and other papers of a deceased author. [1865–70]

lit·er·ate (lit′ər it), *adj.* **1.** able to read and write. **2.** having or showing knowledge of literature, writing, etc.; literary; well-read. **3.** characterized by skill, lucidity, polish, or the like: *His writing is literate but cold and clinical.* **4.** having knowledge or skill in a specified field: *literate in computer usage.* **5.** having an education; educated. **—***n.* **6.** a person who can read and write. **7.** a learned person. [1400–50; late ME < L *literātus, litterātus* learned, scholarly. See LETTER, -ATE[1]] **—lit′er·ate·ly,** *adv.*
—Syn. 3, 5. well-informed, knowledgeable.

lit·e·ra·ti (lit′ə rä′tē, -rā′-), *n.pl., sing.* **-ra·tus** (-rä′təs, -rā′-). persons of scholarly or literary attainments; intellectuals. [1615–25; < L *līterāti* learned, scholarly people, n. use of pl. of *literātus.* See LITERATE]

lit·e·ra·tim (lit′ə rā′tim), *adv.* letter-for-letter; literally. [1635–45; < ML, a formation based on L *literātus* (see LITERATE), with adv. suffix *-im*]

lit·er·a·tor (lit′ə rā′tər), *n.* littérateur. [1625–35; < L *litterātor* an (inferior) grammarian, orig., one who teaches elementary grammar, equiv. to *litter(a)* LETTER + *-ātor* -ATOR; see LITERATE]

lit·er·a·ture (lit′ər ə chər, -cho͝or′, li′trə-), *n.* **1.** writings in which expression and form, in connection with ideas of permanent and universal interest, are characteristic or essential features, as poetry, novels, history, biography, and essays. **2.** the entire body of writings of a specific language, period, people, etc.: *the literature of England.* **3.** the writings dealing with a particular subject: *the literature of ornithology.* **4.** the profession of a writer or author. **5.** literary work or production. **6.** any kind of printed material, as circulars, leaflets, or handbills: *literature describing company products.* **7.** *Archaic.* polite learning; literary culture; appreciation of letters and books. [1375–1425; late ME *litterature* < L *litterātūra* grammar. See LITERATE, -URE]
—Syn. 1. LITERATURE, BELLES-LETTRES, LETTERS refer to artistic writings worthy of being remembered. In the broadest sense, LITERATURE includes any type of writings on any subject: *the literature of medicine;* usually, however, it means the body of artistic writings of a country or period that are characterized by beauty of expression and form and by universality of intellectual and emotional appeal: *English literature of the 16th century.* BELLES-LETTRES is a more specific term for writings of a light, elegant, or excessively refined character: *His talent is not for scholarship but for belles-lettres.* LETTERS (rare today outside of certain fixed phrases) refers to literature as a domain of study or creation: *a man of letters.*

lit·e·ra·tus (lit′ə rä′təs, -rā′-), *n.* sing. of **literati.**

lith (lith), *n. Brit. Dial.* **1.** an arm or leg; limb. **2.** a joint, as of the finger. **3.** a segment, as of an orange. [bef. 900; ME, OE; c. D, OHG *lid,* ON *lithr,* Goth *lithus* limb, member; akin to G *Glied*]

lith-, var. of **litho-** before a vowel: *lithic.*

-lith, a combining form meaning "stone" (*acrolith; megalith; paleolith*); sometimes occurring in words as a variant form of *-lite* (*batholith; laccolith*). Cf. **-lite.** [see LITHO-]

Lith., **1.** Lithuania. **2.** Also, **Lith** Lithuanian.

lith., **1.** lithograph. **2.** lithographic. **3.** lithography.

lith·arge (lith′ärj, li thärj′), *n.* a yellowish or reddish, odorless, heavy, earthy, water-insoluble, poisonous solid, PbO, used chiefly in the manufacture of storage batteries, pottery, lead glass, paints, enamels, and inks. Also called **lead monoxide, lead oxide, plumbous oxide.** Cf. **red lead.** [1350–1400; earlier *litarge, litharge,* ME *litarge* < MF, apocopated var. of *litargire* < L *lithargyrus* < Gk *lithárgyros* spume of silver, equiv. to *lith-* LITH- + *árgyros* silver]

lithe (lith), *adj.,* **lith·er, lith·est.** bending readily; pliant; limber; supple; flexible: *the lithe body of a ballerina..* Also, **lithe′some.** [bef. 900; ME *lith(e),* OE *lithe;* c. OS *lithi,* G *lind* mild, L *lentus* slow] **—lithe′ly,** *adv.* **—lithe′ness,** *n.*

li·the·mi·a (li thē′mē ə), *n. Med.* the presence of an excessive amount of uric acid in the blood. Also, **li·thae′·mi·a.** Also called **uricacidemia.** [< NL *lithaemia.* See LITH-, -EMIA] **—li·the′mic, li·thae′mic,** *adj.*

lith·i·a (lith′ē ə, lith′yə), *n. Chem.* See **lithium oxide.** [1810–20; < LITHI(UM) + -A[4]]

li·thi·a·sis (li thī′ə sis), *n. Pathol.* the formation or presence of stony concretions, as calculi, in the body. [1650–60; < NL < Gk *lithíāsis;* see LITH-, -IASIS]

lith′ia wa′ter, a mineral water, natural or artificial, containing lithium salts. [1875–80]

lith·ic (lith′ik), *adj.* **1.** pertaining to or consisting of stone. **2.** *Petrol.* pertaining to clastic rocks, either sedimentary or volcanic, containing a large proportion of debris from previously formed rocks: *a lithic sandstone; lithic tuff.* **3.** *Pathol.* pertaining to stony concretions, or calculi, formed within the body, esp. in the bladder. **4.** *Chem.* of, pertaining to, or containing lithium. **—***n.* **5.** *Archaeol.* a stone artifact. [1790–1800; < Gk *lithikós* of stone. See LITH-, -IC] **—lith′i·cal·ly,** *adv.*

-lithic, a combining form used in the names of cultural phases in archaeology characterized by the use of a particular type of tool: *Chalcolithic; Neolithic.* [see LITHIC]

lith·i·fi·ca·tion (lith′ə fi kā′shən), *n. Geol.* the process or processes by which unconsolidated materials are converted into coherent solid rock, as by compaction or cementation. Also called **induration.** [1870–75; LITH- + -I- + -FICATION]

lith·i·fy (lith′ə fī′), *v.,* **-fied, -fy·ing. —***v.t.* **1.** to change (sediment) to stone or rock. **—***v.i.* **2.** to become lithified. [LITH- + -IFY]

lith·i·um (lith′ē əm), *n.* **1.** *Chem.* a soft, silver-white metallic element, the lightest of all metals, occurring combined in certain minerals. *Symbol:* Li; *at. wt.:* 6.939; *at. no.:* 3; *sp. gr.:* 0.53 at 20°C. **2.** *Pharm.* the substance in its carbonate or citrate form used in the treatment or prophylaxis of bipolar disorder or mania. [1810–20; < NL; see LITH-, -IUM]

lith′ium alu′minum hy′dride, *Chem.* a white powder, $LiAlH_4$, used chiefly as a chemical reducing agent, esp. in pharmaceutical and perfume manufacturing.

lith′ium car′bonate, *Chem.* a colorless crystalline compound, Li_2CO_3, slightly soluble in water: used in ceramic and porcelain glazes, pharmaceuticals, and luminescent paints. [1870–75]

lith′ium chlo′ride, *Chem.* a white, water-soluble, deliquescent, crystalline solid, LiCl, used chiefly in the manufacture of mineral water, esp. lithia water, and as a flux in metallurgy.

lith′ium fluor′ide, *Chem.* a fine, white, slightly water-soluble powder, LiF, used chiefly in the manufacture of ceramics. [1940–45]

lith′ium hydrox′ide, *Chem.* a white, crystalline, water-soluble compound, LiOH, used to absorb carbon dioxide, esp. in spacesuits.

lith′ium ox′ide, *Chem.* a white powder, Li_2O, with strong alkaline properties: used in ceramics and glass. Also called **lithia.**

lith′ium ste′arate, *Chem.* a white, crystalline, slightly water-soluble powder, $LiC_{18}H_{35}O_2$, used chiefly in cosmetics, in plastics, and as a lubricant in powder metallurgy.

lith·o (lith′ō), *n., pl.* **lith·os,** *adj., v.,* **lith·oed, lith·o·ing. —***n.* **1.** lithography. **2.** lithograph. **—***adj.* **3.** lithographic. **—***v.t.* **4.** to lithograph. [shortened form]

litho-, a combining form meaning "stone," used in the formation of compound words: *lithography; lithonephrotomy.* Also, *esp. before a vowel,* **lith-.** [< Gk, comb. form of *líthos*]

litho., **1.** lithograph. **2.** lithography. Also, **lithog.**

li·thog·e·nous (li thoj′ə nəs), *adj. Geol.* of or pertaining to organisms, as coral, that secrete stony deposits. [1825–35; LITHO- + -GENOUS]

lith·o·graph (lith′ə graf′, -gräf′), *n.* **1.** a print produced by lithography. **—***v.t.* **2.** to produce or copy by lithography. [1815–25; back formation from LITHOGRAPHY]

li·thog·ra·pher (li thog′rə fər), *n.* a person who works at lithography. [1675–85; LITHOGRAPH(Y) + -ER[1]]

li·thog·ra·phy (li thog′rə fē), *n.* **1.** the art or process of producing a picture, writing, or the like, on a flat, specially prepared stone, with some greasy or oily substance, and of taking ink impressions from this as in ordinary printing. **2.** a similar process in which a substance other than stone, as aluminum or zinc, is used. Cf. **offset** (def. 6). [1700–10; < NL *lithographia.* See LITHO-, -GRAPHY] —**lith′o·graph·ic** (lith′ə graf′ik), **lith′o·graph′i·cal,** *adj.* —**lith′o·graph′i·cal·ly,** *adv.*

lith·oid (lith′oid), *adj.* resembling stone; stonelike. Also, **li·thoi′dal.** [1835–45; < Gk *lithoeidḗs.* See LITH-, -OID]

lithol., lithology.

li·thol·o·gy (li thol′ə jē), *n.* **1.** *Geol.* **a.** (loosely) petrology. **b.** the physical characteristics of a rock or stratigraphic unit. **2.** *Med.* the study of the formation, pathology, and treatment of stones in the human body. [1710–20; LITHO- + -LOGY] —**lith·o·log·ic** (lith′ə loj′ik), **lith′o·log′i·cal,** *adj.* —**lith′o·log′i·cal·ly,** *adv.*

lith·o·marge (lith′ə märj′), *n.* kaolin in compact, massive, usually impure form. [1745–55; < NL *lithomarga* stone marl, equiv. to *litho-* LITHO- + L *marga* marl]

lith·o·me·te·or (lith′ə mē′tē ər), *n. Meteorol.* a mass of dry particles suspended in the atmosphere, as dust or haze. Cf. **hydrometeor.** [1835–45; LITHO- + METEOR]

lith·o·phane (lith′ə fān′), *n.* a transparency made of thin porcelain or bone china having an intaglio design. [1945–50; LITHO- + -PHANE]

lith·o·phile (lith′ə fīl′), *Geol.* —*adj.* **1.** (of a chemical element) concentrated in the earth's crust, rather than in the core or mantle. —*n.* **2.** a lithophile element. [1920–25; LITHO- + -PHILE]

lith·o·phone (lith′ə fōn′), *n.* a Chinese stone chime consisting of 16 stone slabs hung in two rows and struck with a hammer. [1885–90; LITHO- + -PHONE]

lith·o·phyte (lith′ə fīt′), *n.* **1.** *Zool.* a polyp with a hard or stony structure, as a coral. **2.** *Bot.* any plant growing on the surface of rocks. [1765–75; LITHO- + -PHYTE] —**lith·o·phyt·ic** (lith′ə fit′ik), *adj.*

lith·o·pone (lith′ə pōn′), *n.* a white pigment consisting of zinc sulfide, barium sulfate, and some zinc oxide, used as a pigment and filler in the manufacture of paints, inks, leather, paper, linoleum, and face powders. [1880–85; LITHO- + Gk *pónos* a work, structure]

lith·o·print (lith′ə print′), *v.t.* **1.** *Now Rare.* to lithograph. —*n.* **2.** printed matter produced by lithography. [1930–35; LITHO- + PRINT] —**lith′o·print′er,** *n.*

lith·ops (lith′ops), *n.* See **living stones.** [< NL (1922): genus name, equiv. to Gk *lith-* LITH- + *ṓps* eye, face]

lith·o·sere (lith′ə sēr′), *n. Ecol.* a sere originating on rock. [1915–20; LITHO- + SERE[2]]

lith·o·sol (lith′ə sôl′, -sol′), *n.* a group of shallow soils lacking well-defined horizons, esp. an entisol consisting of partially weathered rock fragments, usually on steep slopes. [1935–40; LITHO- + -SOL]

lith·o·sphere (lith′ə sfēr′), *n. Geol.* **1.** the solid portion of the earth (distinguished from *atmosphere, hydrosphere*). **2.** the crust and upper mantle of the earth. [1885–90; LITHO- + -SPHERE] —**lith·o·spher·ic** (lith′ə sfer′ik), *adj.*

lith·o·stra·tig·ra·phy (lith′ō strə tig′rə fē), *n.* the study or character of stratified rocks based solely on their physical and petrographic features. [1955–60; LITHO- + STRATIGRAPHY] —**lith·o·strat·i·graph·ic** (lith′ō strat′i graf′ik), *adj.*

li·thot·o·my (li thot′ə mē), *n., pl.* **-mies.** surgery to remove one or more stones from an organ or duct. [1715–25; < LL *lithotomia* < Gk *lithotomía.* See LITHO-, -TOMY] —**lith·o·tom·ic** (lith′ə tom′ik), **lith′o·tom′i·cal,** *adj.* —**li·thot′o·mist,** *n.*

lith·o·trip·sy (lith′ə trip′sē), *n., pl.* **-sies.** the pulverization and removal of urinary calculi using a lithotripter. Also called **shock wave therapy.** [1825–35; LITHO- + Gk *trîps(is)* rubbing, wear + -Y[3]; see LITHOTRIPTER]

lith·o·trip·ter (lith′ə trip′tər), *n.* a device used for fragmenting kidney stones with ultrasound waves. [1815–25; resp., with -ER[1], of *litho(n)triptor* instrument for crushing kidney stones, pseudo- L deriv. (cf. CAPTOR, RAPTOR) of *litho(n)triptic,* ult. based on the Gk phrase (*phármaka tôn en nephroîs*) *lithōn thryptiká* (drugs) breaking up stones (in the kidneys); *trip-* by assoc. with Gk *tríbein* to rub, knead, pound (v. adj. *triptós*)]

lith·o·trite (lith′ə trīt′), *n. Surg.* an instrument for performing lithotrity. [1830–40; back formation from LITHOTRITY; see -ITE[1]]

li·thot·ri·ty (li tho′tri tē), *n., pl.* **-ties.** *Surg.* the operation of crushing stone in the urinary bladder into particles small enough to be voided. [1820–30; LITHO- + L *trīt(us)* (ptp. of *terere* to rub, grind, crush) + -Y[3]] —**li·thot′ri·tist,** *n.*

Lith·u·a·ni·a (lith′o͞o ā′nē ə), *n.* a republic in N Europe, on the Baltic: an independent state 1918–40; annexed by the Soviet Union 1940; regained independence 1991. 3,690,000; 25,174 sq. mi. (65,200 sq. km). *Cap.:* Vilnius. Lithuanian, **Lietuva.** —**Lith·u·an·ic** (lith′o͞o an′ik), *adj., n.*

Lith·u·a·ni·an (lith′o͞o ā′nē ən), *adj.* **1.** of or pertaining to Lithuania, its inhabitants, or their language. —*n.* **2.** a native or inhabitant of Lithuania. **3.** a Baltic language, the official language of Lithuania. *Abbr.:* Lith. [1600–10; LITHUANI(A) + -AN]

lith·u·re·sis (lith′ə rē′sis), *n. Pathol.* the passage of gravel in the urine. [< NL < Gk *líth(os)* LITH- + *oúrēsis* urination, equiv. to *ourē-* (var. s. of *oureîn* to urinate; see URO-[1]) + *-sis* -SIS]

lith·u·ri·a (lith yo͝or′ē ə), *n. Med.* the presence of an excessive amount of uric acid in the urine. [1875–80; < NL; see LITH-, -URIA]

lith·y (li′thē), *adj. Archaic.* lithe; supple; flexible. [bef. 1000; ME *lethi,* OE *lithig,* akin to D, G *ledig* empty, Icel *lithugu* free, nimble]

lit·i·ga·ble (lit′i gə bəl), *adj.* subject to litigation; actionable by a lawsuit. [1755–65; < L *litigā(re)* to go to law (see LITIGATE) + -BLE]

lit·i·gant (lit′i gənt), *n.* **1.** a person engaged in a lawsuit. —*adj.* **2.** litigating; engaged in a lawsuit. [1630–40; < L *lītigant-* (s. of *lītigāns,* prp. of *lītigāre* to go to law), equiv. to *līt-* (s. of *līs*) a lawsuit + *-ig-* (comb. form of *agere* to carry on) + *-ant-* -ANT]

lit·i·gate (lit′i gāt′), *v.,* **-gat·ed, -gat·ing.** —*v.t.* **1.** to make the subject of a lawsuit; contest at law. **2.** *Archaic.* to dispute (a point, assertion, etc.). —*v.i.* **3.** to carry on a lawsuit. [1605–15; < L *lītigātus* (ptp. of *lītigāre* to go to law). See LITIGANT, -ATE[1]] —**lit′i·ga′tive,** *adj.* —**lit′i·ga′tor,** *n.*

lit·i·ga·tion (lit′i gā′shən), *n.* **1.** the act or process of litigating: *a matter that is still in litigation.* **2.** a lawsuit. [1560–70; < LL *lītigātiōn-* (s. of *lītigātiō*) a dispute. See LITIGATE, -ION]

li·ti·gious (li tij′əs), *adj.* **1.** of or pertaining to litigation. **2.** excessively or readily inclined to litigate: *a litigious person.* **3.** inclined to dispute or disagree; argumentative. [1350–1400; ME < L *lītigiōsus* contentious, equiv. to *lītigi(um)* a quarrel (see LITIGANT, -IUM) + *-ōsus* -OUS] —**li·ti′gious·ly,** *adv.* —**li·ti′gious·ness, li·ti·gi·os·i·ty** (li tij′ē os′i tē), *n.*
—**Syn. 3.** contentious, disputatious, quarrelsome.

lit·mus (lit′məs), *n.* a blue coloring matter obtained from certain lichens, esp. *Roccella tinctoria.* In alkaline solution litmus turns blue, in acid solution, red: widely used as a chemical indicator. [1495–1505; earlier *lytmos* < ON *litmosi* dye-moss, equiv. to *lit-* color, dye + *mosi* moss]

lit′mus pa′per, a strip of paper impregnated with litmus, used as a chemical indicator. [1795–1805]

lit′mus test′, 1. *Chem.* the use of litmus paper or solution to test the acidity or alkalinity of a solution. **2.** a crucial and revealing test in which there is one decisive factor. [1955–60; so called from chemical tests in which litmus or litmus paper is an indicator]

li·to·tes (lī′tə tēz′, lit′ə-, li tō′tēz), *n., pl.* **-tes.** *Rhet.* understatement, esp. that in which an affirmative is expressed by the negative of its contrary, as in "not bad at all." Cf. **hyperbole.** [1650–60; < NL < Gk *lītótēs* orig., plainness, simplicity, deriv. of *lītós* plain, small, meager]

li·tre (lē′tər), *n. Chiefly Brit.* liter.

Litt. B., Bachelor of Letters; Bachelor of Literature. [< L *Lit(t)erārum Baccalaureus*]

Litt. D., Doctor of Letters; Doctor of Literature. [< L *Lit(t)erārum Doctor*]

lit·ten (lit′n), *adj. Archaic.* lighted.

lit·ter (lit′ər), *n.* **1.** objects strewn or scattered about; scattered rubbish. **2.** a condition of disorder or untidiness: *We were appalled at the litter of the room.* **3.** a number of young brought forth by a multiparous animal at one birth: *a litter of six kittens..* **4.** a framework of cloth stretched between two parallel bars, for the transportation of a sick or wounded person; stretcher. **5.** a vehicle carried by people or animals, consisting of a bed or couch, often covered and curtained, suspended between shafts. **6.** straw, hay, or the like, used as bedding for animals or as protection for plants. **7.** the layer of slightly decomposed organic material on the surface of the floor of the forest. **8.** See **cat litter. 9. pick of the litter, a.** the best or choicest of the animals, esp. puppies, in a litter. **b.** the best of any class, group, or available selection. —*v.t.* **10.** to strew (a place) with scattered objects, rubbish, etc.: *to be fined for littering the sidewalk.* **11.** to scatter (objects) in disorder: *They littered their toys from one end of the playroom to the other.* **12.** to be strewn about (a place) in disorder (often fol. by *up*): *Bits of paper littered the floor.* **13.** to give birth to (young), as a multiparous animal. **14.** to supply (an animal) with litter for a bed. **15.** to use (straw, hay, etc.) for litter. **16.** to cover (a floor or other area) with straw, hay, etc., for litter. —*v.i.* **17.** to give birth to a litter: *The cat had littered in the closet.* **18.** to strew objects about: *If you litter, you may be fined.* [1250–1300; ME *litere* bed, litter < AF; OF *litiere* < ML *lectāria,* equiv. to L *lect(us)* bed + *-āria* fem. of *-ārius* -ER[2]] —**lit′ter·er,** *n.*
—**Syn. 2.** clutter. **3.** See **brood. 10.** mess (up). **11.** disarrange, derange.

lit·te·rae hu·ma·ni·o·res (lit′ə rē′ hyo͞o man′ē ôr′ēz, -ōr′ēz), the humanities as a field of study. [1740–50; < ML *litterae hūmāniōrēs* lit., more humane letters]

lit·té·ra·teur (lit′ər ə tûr′; *Fr.* lē tā RA tœR′), *n., pl.* **-teurs** (-tûrz′; *Fr.* -tœR′). a literary person, esp. a writer of literary works. Also, **lit′te·ra·teur′.** [1800–10; < F; see LITERATOR]

lit·te·ra·tim (lit′ə rā′tim), *adv. Obs.* literatim.

lit·ter·bag (lit′ər bag′), *n.* a small paper or plastic bag for trash or rubbish, as one carried in an automobile. [1965–70; LITTER + BAG]

lit·ter·bug (lit′ər bug′), *n.* a person who litters public places with items of refuse: *Litterbugs had thrown beer cans on the picnic grounds.* [1945–50; LITTER + BUG[1]] —**lit′ter·bug′ging,** *n.*

lit·ter·mate (lit′ər māt′), *n.* one of a pair or group of animals born or reared in the same litter. [1920–25; LITTER + MATE[1]]

lit·ter·y (lit′ə rē), *adj.* of, pertaining to, or covered with litter; untidy. [1795–1805; LITTER + -Y[1]]

lit·tle (lit′l), *adj.,* **lit·tler** or **less** or **less·er, lit·tlest** or **least,** *adv.,* **less, least,** *n.* —*adj.* **1.** small in size; not big; not large; tiny: *a little desk in the corner of the room.* **2.** short in duration; not extensive; short; brief: *a little while.* **3.** small in number: *a little group of scientists.* **4.** small in amount or degree; not much: *little hope.* **5.** of a certain amount; appreciable (usually prec. by *a*): *We're having a little difficulty.* **6.** being such on a small scale: *little farmers.* **7.** younger or youngest: *He's my little brother.* **8.** not strong, forceful, or loud; weak: *a little voice.* **9.** small in consideration, importance, position, affluence, etc.: *little discomforts; tax reductions to help the little fellow.* **10.** mean, narrow, or illiberal: *a little mind.* **11.** endearingly small or considered as such: *Bless your little heart!* **12.** amusingly small or so considered: *a funny little way of laughing.* **13.** contemptibly small, petty, mean, etc., or so considered: *filthy little political tricks.* —*adv.* **14.** not at all (used before a verb): *He little knows what awaits him.* **15.** in only a small amount or degree; not much; slightly: *a little known work of art; little better than a previous effort.* **16.** seldom; rarely; infrequently: *We see each other very little.* —*n.* **17.** a small amount, quantity, or degree: *They did little to make him comfortable. If you want some ice cream, there's a little in the refrigerator.* **18.** a short distance: *It's down the road a little.* **19.** a short time: *Stay here for a little.* **20. in little,** on a small scale; in miniature: *a replica in little of Independence Hall.* **21. little by little,** by small degrees; gradually: *The water level rose little by little.* **22. make little of, a.** belittle: *to make little of one's troubles.* **b.** to understand or interpret only slightly: *Scholars made little of the newly discovered text.* **23. not a little,** to a great extent; very much; considerably: *It tired me not a little to stand for three hours.* **24. think little of,** to treat casually; regard as trivial: *They think little of driving 50 miles to see a movie.* [bef. 900; ME, OE *lȳtel* (*lȳt* few, small + *-el* dim. suffix), c. D *luttel,* OHG *luzzil,* ON *litill*] —**lit·tlish** (lit′l ish, lit′lish), *adj.* —**lit′tle·ness,** *n.*
—**Syn. 1–4.** tiny, teeny, wee. LITTLE, DIMINUTIVE, MINUTE, SMALL refer to that which is not large or significant. LITTLE (the opposite of *big*) is very general, covering size, extent, number, quantity, amount, duration, or degree: *a little boy; a little time.* SMALL (the opposite of *large* and of *great*) can many times be used interchangeably with LITTLE, but is especially applied to what is limited or below the average in size: *small oranges.* DIMINUTIVE denotes (usually physical) size that is much less than the average or ordinary; it may suggest delicacy: *the baby's diminutive fingers; diminutive in size but autocratic in manner.* MINUTE suggests that which is so tiny it is difficult to discern, or that which implies attentiveness to the smallest details: *a minute quantity; a minute exam.*

Lit′tle Ab′aco. See under **Abaco.**

Lit′tle Alli′ance, *Europ. Hist.* an economic and military alliance (1920) between Czechoslovakia and Yugoslavia, which were joined the following year by Rumania, formed as a counterbalance to the informal alliance that existed between Austria, Germany, Hungary, and Italy.

Lit′tle Amer′ica, a base in the Antarctic, on the Bay of Whales, S of the Ross Sea: established by Adm. Richard E. Byrd of the U.S. Navy in 1929; used for later Antarctic expeditions.

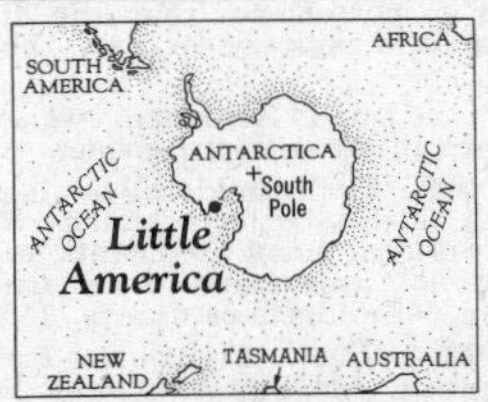

lit′tle auk′, the dovekie, *Alle alle.* [1875–80]

Lit′tle Bear′, *Astron.* the constellation Ursa Minor.

Lit′tle Belt′ Moun′tains, a range of the Rocky Mountains, in central Montana.

Lit′tle Big′horn, a river flowing N from N Wyoming to S Montana into the Bighorn River: General Custer and troops defeated near its juncture by Indians 1876. 80 mi. (130 km) long. Also called **Little Horn.**

lit·tle-bit·ty (lit′l bit′ē), *adj. Informal.* extremely small; tiny. [1900–05, *Amer.; little bit* + -Y[2]]

lit′tle black′ ant′, a widely distributed ant, *Monomorium minimum,* sometimes a household pest.

lit′tle blue′ her′on, a small heron, *Egretta caerulea,* of the warmer parts of the Western Hemisphere, having bluish-gray plumage.

lit′tle blue′stem, a North American forage grass, *Schizachyrium scoparium,* having wide often bluish blades. [1895–1900]

Lit′tle Boy′, the code name for the uranium-fueled atomic bomb dropped by the U.S. on Hiroshima in 1945. Cf. **Fat Man.**

lit′tle brown′ bat′. See under **brown bat.**

lit′tle casi′no, *Casino.* the two of spades.

Lit′tle Colorad′o, a river flowing NW from E Arizona to the E edge of the Grand Canyon, where it flows into the Colorado River. 315 mi. (507 km) long.

Lit′tle Cor′poral, epithet of Napoleon I.

Lit′tle Dae′dala. See under **Daedala.**

Lit′tle Di′omede. See under **Diomede Islands.**

Lit′tle Dip′per, *Astron.* the group of seven bright stars in Ursa Minor resembling a dipper in outline. Also called **Dipper.** [1835–45]

Lit′tle Dog′, *Astron.* the constellation Canis Minor.

lit′tle e′gret. See under **egret** (def. 1).

Lit′tle Eng′lander, an English person who believes the best interests of Britain are served by attention to Britain itself, rather than to the concerns of the empire. [1890–95] **—Lit′tle Eng′landism.**

Lit′tle En′trance, *Eastern Ch.* the solemn procession in which the book of the Gospels is carried through the nave of the church and into the bema. Cf. **Great Entrance.**

Lit′tle Falls′, a township in NE New Jersey. 11,496.

lit′tle fin′ger, the finger farthest from the thumb, the smallest of the five fingers. [1250–1300; ME]

Lit′tle Fox′, *Astron.* the constellation Vulpecula.

Lit′tle Fox′es, The, a play (1939) by Lillian Hellman.

lit′tle grebe′, a small grebe, *Tachybaptus ruficollis,* of the Old World. Cf. **dabchick.**

lit′tle green′ her′on. See **green-backed heron.**

lit′tle gull′, a small, Old World gull, *Larus minutus.*

Lit′tle Horn′. See **Little Bighorn.**

Lit′tle Horse′, *Astron.* the constellation Equuleus.

lit′tle hours′, *Rom. Cath. Ch.* the hours of prime, tierce, sext, and nones, and sometimes also vespers and compline. [1870–75]

lit′tle Joe′, a cast of four in craps. [1885–90]

Lit′tle John′, a large, powerful yeoman who was a member of Robin Hood's band.

Lit′tle League′, a baseball league, founded in 1939 in Williamsport, Pa., consisting of teams whose players are 8 to 12 years of age, usually sponsored by a business, fraternal, or other organization. Cf. **Pony League.** **—Lit′tle Lea′guer.**

Lit′tle Li′on, *Astron.* the constellation Leo Minor.

Lit′tle Lord′ Faunt′le·roy (fônt′lə roi′), **1.** (*italics*) a children's novel (1886) by Frances H. Burnett. **2.** a pampered or excessively well-behaved young boy resembling the hero of this book. **3.** Also called **Lit′tle Lord′ Faunt′leroy suit′.** See **Fauntleroy suit.**

lit′tle magazine′, a magazine, usually small in format and of limited circulation, that publishes literary works. [1895–1900]

lit′tle man′, (*sometimes caps.*) **1.** the common or ordinary person. **2.** *Informal.* the small, ordinary investor, as opposed to big investment institutions. [1930–35]

Lit′tle Men′, a novel (1871) by Louisa May Alcott.

Lit′tle Missour′i, a river in the NW United States, rising in NE Wyoming and flowing NE into the Missouri through N Dakota. 560 mi. (900 km) long.

lit·tle·neck (lit′l nek′), *n.* the quahog clam, *Venus mercenaria,* when young and small. [1850–55, *Amer.*; named after *Little Neck* Bay, N.Y., where it was once plentiful]

lit′tle of′fice, (*sometimes caps.*) *Rom. Cath. Ch.* an office similar to but shorter than the divine office, in honor of a saint, a mystery, or, esp., the Virgin Mary. [1870–75]

lit′tle owl′, a small, European owl, *Athene noctua,* often portrayed in art with the goddess Athena.

lit′tle peo′ple, 1. (in folklore) small, imaginary beings, as elves, fairies, or leprechauns. **2.** the common people, esp. workers, small merchants, or the like, who lead conventional, presumably unremarkable lives. **3.** small children. **4.** midgets or dwarfs. [1720–30]

Lit′tle Prince′, The, (French, *Le Petit Prince*), an allegorical fantasy (1943) by Antoine de Saint-Exupéry.

Lit′tle Rhod′y (rō′dē), Rhode Island (used as a nickname).

Lit′tle Rock′, a city in and the capital of Arkansas, in the central part, on the Arkansas River. 158,461.

Lit′tle Rus′sia, a region in the SW Soviet Union in Europe, consisting mainly of the Ukraine but sometimes considered as including adjacent areas.

Lit′tle Rus′sian, 1. a member of a division of the Russian people dwelling in southern and southwestern Soviet Union in Europe and in adjoining regions. Cf. **Ruthenian. 2.** Ukrainian (def. 3).

lit′tle slam′, *Bridge.* the winning of twelve of the thirteen tricks of a deal. Also called **small slam.** Cf. **grand slam** (def. 1). [1895–1900]

lit′tle spot′ted cat′, a small New World tiger cat, *Felis tigrinus,* ranging from Costa Rica to northern Argentina.

Little St. Bernard. See **St. Bernard, Little.**

lit′tle the′ater, 1. generally noncommercial drama, usually of an experimental nature and directed at a limited audience. **2.** a small theater, producing plays whose effectiveness would be lost in larger houses. **3.** amateur theatricals. [1765–75]

lit′tle toe′, the fifth, outermost, and smallest digit of the foot. [1720–30]

Lit·tle·ton (lit′l tən), *n.* **1. Sir Thomas,** c1407–1481, English jurist and author. **2.** a town in NE Colorado. 28,631.

Lit′tle Tur′tle, (*Michikinikwa*), 1752?–1812, leader of the Miami tribe.

Lit′tle Wom′en, a novel (1868) by Louisa May Alcott.

Litt.M., Master of Letters.

lit·to·ral (lit′ər əl), *adj.* **1.** of or pertaining to the shore of a lake, sea, or ocean. **2.** (on ocean shores) of or pertaining to the biogeographic region between the sublittoral zone and the high-water line and sometimes including the supralittoral zone above the high-water line. **3.** of or pertaining to the region of freshwater lake beds from the sublittoral zone up to and including damp areas on shore. Cf. **intertidal.** **—*n.* 4.** a littoral region. [1650–60; < L *littorālis,* var. of *lītorālis* of the shore, equiv. to *lītor-* (s. of *lītus*) shore + *-ālis* -AL[1]]

lit′toral drift′. See **beach drift.**

Lit·tré (lē trā′), *n.* **Max·i·mi·lien Paul É·mile** (mak sē mē lyaN′ pôl ā mēl′), 1801–88, French lexicographer and philosopher.

li·tu (lē′to͞o), *n.* a pl. of **litas.**

li·tur·gi·cal (li tûr′ji kəl), *adj.* **1.** of or pertaining to formal public worship or liturgies. **2.** of or pertaining to the liturgy or Eucharistic service. **3.** of or pertaining to liturgics. Also, **li·tur′gic.** [1635–45; < ML *litūrgic(us)* < LGk *leitourgikós* ministering (*leitourg(ós)* minister + *-ikos* -IC; see LITURGY) + -AL[1]] **—li·tur′gi·cal·ly,** *adv.*

litur′gical dra′ma, medieval drama, based on incidents in the Bible and performed in churches on holy days, usually in Latin and often chanted.

Litur′gical Lat′in, the Latin characteristic of the liturgies of the Western Church.

li·tur·gics (li tûr′jiks), *n.* (*used with a singular v.*) **1.** the science or art of conducting public worship. **2.** the study of liturgies. [1670–80; pl. of *liturgic* < ML *litūrgicus* liturgical; see -ICS]

li·tur·gi·ol·o·gy (li tûr′jē ol′ə jē), *n.* liturgics. [1860–65; LITURGY + -OLOGY] **—li·tur·gi·o·log·i·cal** (li tûr′jē ə loj′i kəl), *adj.* **—li·tur′gi·ol′o·gist,** *n.*

lit·ur·gist (lit′ər jist), *n.* **1.** an authority on liturgies. **2.** a compiler of a liturgy or liturgies. **3.** a person who uses or favors the use of a liturgy. [1640–50; LITURG(Y) + -IST] **—lit′ur·gism,** *n.* **—lit′ur·gis′tic,** *adj.*

lit·ur·gy (lit′ər jē), *n., pl.* **-gies. 1.** a form of public worship; ritual. **2.** a collection of formularies for public worship. **3.** a particular arrangement of services. **4.** a particular form or type of the Eucharistic service. **5.** the service of the Eucharist, esp. this service (**Divine Liturgy**) in the Eastern Church. [1550–60; < LL *litūrgia* < Gk *leitourgía* public service, eccl. Gk: Eucharist, equiv. to *leitourg(ós)* minister + *-ia* -Y[3]]

lit·u·us (lit′yo͞o əs), *n., pl.* **lit·u·i** (lit′yo͞o ī′). **1.** *Geom.* a polar curve generated by the locus of a point moving so that the square of its radius vector varies inversely as the angle the radius vector makes with the polar axis. Equation: $\theta r^2 = a$. **2.** (in ancient Rome) a crook-shaped staff used by augurs for divination. [1605–15; < L; geometrical sense from the curve's resemblance to such a staff]

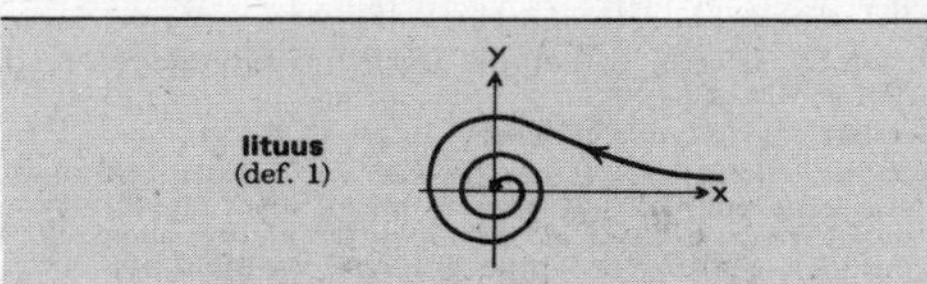

lituus (def. 1)

Lit·vak (lit′väk), *n.* a Jew from Lithuania or a neighboring country or region. [1890–95; < Yiddish *litvak* < Pol *litwak* Lithuanian person (now obs. in this sense), deriv. of *Litwa* Lithuania]

Lit·vi·nov (lit vē′nôf, -nof; *Russ.* lyi tvyē′nəf), *n.* **Maksim Ma·ksi·mo·vich** (mu ksyēm′ mu ksyē′mə vyich), 1876–1951, Russian Communist leader and diplomat.

litz′ wire′ (lits), *Elect.* a wire used as a conductor of alternating current, composed of a number of insulated strands woven together to reduce skin effect. [1925–30; partial trans. of G *Litzendraht* wire made up of strands, equiv. to *Litze* (< L *licium* thread) + *Draht* wire]

Liu Pang (lyo͞o′ bäng′), 247–195 B.C., Chinese emperor: founder of the Han dynasty 202 B.C. Also, *Pinyin,* **Liu′ Bang′.**

Liu Shao·qi (lyo͞o′ shou′chē′), 1898–1973, Chinese Communist leader: head of state 1959–66. Also, *Wade-Giles,* **Liu′ Shao′-ch′i′.**

Liu·zhou (lyo͞o′jō′), *n. Pinyin.* a city in central Guangxi Zhuang region, in S China. 158,800. Also, **Liu′chou′, Liu′chow′.** Formerly, **Maping.**

liv·a·ble (liv′ə bəl), *adj.* **1.** suitable for living in; habitable; comfortable: *It took a lot of work to make the old house livable.* **2.** worth living; endurable: *She needed something to make life more livable.* **3.** that can be lived with; companionable (often used in combination with *with*): *polite and charming but not altogether livable-with.* Also, **liveable.** [1605–15; LIVE[1] + -ABLE] **—liv′a·ble·ness, liv′a·bil′i·ty,** *n.*
—Syn. 2. enjoyable, bearable, worthwhile.

live[1] (liv), *v.,* **lived** (livd), **liv·ing.** **—*v.i.* 1.** to have life, as an organism; be alive; be capable of vital functions: *all things that live.* **2.** to continue to have life; remain alive: *to live to a ripe old age.* **3.** to continue in existence, operation, memory, etc.; last: *a book that lives in my memory.* **4.** to maintain or support one's existence; provide for oneself: *to live on one's income.* **5.** to feed or subsist (usually fol. by *on* or *upon*): *to live on rice and bananas.* **6.** to dwell or reside (usually fol. by *in, at,* etc.): *to live in a cottage.* **7.** to pass life in a specified manner: *They lived happily ever after.* **8.** to direct or regulate one's life: *to live by the golden rule.* **9.** to experience or enjoy life to the full: *At 40 she was just beginning to live.* **10.** to cohabit (usually fol. by *with*). **11.** to escape destruction or remain afloat, as a ship or aircraft. **—*v.t.* 12.** to pass (life): *to live a life of ease.* **13.** to practice, represent, or exhibit in one's life: *to live one's philosophy.* **14. live down,** to live so as to allow (a mistake, disgrace, etc.) to be forgotten or forgiven: *She'll never live that crucial moment of failure down.* **15. live high off** or **on the hog.** See **hog** (def. 10). **16. live in** or **out,** to reside at or away from the place of one's employment, esp. as a domestic servant: *Their butler lives in, but the maids live out.* **17. live it up,** *Informal.* to live in an extravagant or wild manner; pursue pleasure: *He started living it up after he got out of the army.* **18. live up to,** to live in accordance with (expectations or an ideal or standard); measure up to: *He never lived up to his father's vision of him.* **19. live well,** to live comfortably: *They're not wealthy but they live well.* [bef. 900; ME *liven,* OE *lifian, libban;* c. D *leven,* G *leben,* ON *lifa,* Goth *liban*]

live[2] (līv), *adj.,* **liv·er, liv·est** for 4–7, 13–15, *adv.* **—*adj.* 1.** being alive; living; alive: *live animals.* **2.** of, pertaining to, or during the life of a living being: *the animal's live weight.* **3.** characterized by or indicating the presence of living creatures: *the live sounds of the forest.* **4.** *Informal.* (of a person) energetic; alert; lively: *The club members are a really live bunch.* **5.** full of life, energy or activity: *His approach in any business dealing is live and fresh.* **6.** burning or glowing: *live coals in the fireplace.* **7.** having resilience or bounce: *a live tennis ball.* **8.** being in play, as a baseball or football. **9.** loaded or unexploded, as a cartridge or shell: *live ammunition.* **10.** made up of actual persons: *to perform before a live audience.* **11.** (of a radio or television program) broadcast while happening or being performed; not prerecorded or taped: *a live telecast.* **12.** being highly resonant or reverberant, as an auditorium or concert hall. **13.** vivid or bright, as color. **14.** of current interest or importance, as a question or issue; controversial; unsettled. **15.** moving or imparting motion; powered: *the live head on a lathe.* **16.** still in use, or to be used, as type set up or copy for printing. **17.** Also, **alive.** *Elect.* electrically connected to a source of potential difference, or electrically charged so as to have a potential different from that of earth: *a live wire.* **18. live one,** *Slang.* **a.** a person who spends money readily. **b.** a person easily imposed upon or made the dupe of others. **—*adv.* 19.** (of a radio or television program) at the moment of its happening or being performed; not on tape or by prerecording: *a program broadcast live.* [1535–45; 1930–35 for def. 11; aph. var. of ALIVE, used attributively] **—live′ness,** *n.*

live·a·ble (liv′ə bəl), *adj.* livable.

live-ac·tion (līv′ak′shən), *adj.* **1.** *Informal.* live[2] (def. 11). **2.** animated, as distinguished from a single drawing or sketch: *Disney perfected the live-action cartoon.* [1955–60]

live·bear·er (līv′bâr′ər), *n.* any viviparous fish of the family Poeciliidae, often kept in home aquariums. [1930–35; LIVE[2] + BEARER] **—live′bear′ing,** *adj.*

live′ cen′ter (līv). *Mach.* See under **center** (def. 19).

lived (līvd, livd), *adj.* having life, a life, or lives, as specified (usually used in combination): *a many-lived cat.* [1350–1400; ME; see LIFE, -ED[3]]
—Pronunciation. LIVED, meaning "having a certain kind or extent of life," is not derived from the preterit and past participle of the verb *live* (liv), but from the noun *life* (līf), to which the suffix *-ed* has been added. The original pronunciation, therefore, and one still heard, is (līvd), which retains the vowel (ī) of *life.* Since the *f* of *life* changes to *v* with the addition of this suffix, as when *leaf* becomes *leaved,* this LIVED is identical in spelling with the preterit and past participle *lived,* and conflation of the two has led to the increasingly frequent pronunciation of this LIVED as (livd) in such combinations as *long-lived* and *short-lived.* Both pronunciations are considered standard.

live-for·ev·er (liv′fər ev′ər), *n.* a widely cultivated succulent plant, *Sedum telephium,* of the stonecrop family, having fleshy, coarsely toothed leaves and flat clusters of purplish flowers. Also called **orpine.** [1590–1600]

live-in (liv′in′), *adj.* **1.** Also, **sleep-in.** residing at the place of one's employment: *a live-in maid.* **2.** living in a cohabitant relationship. **—*n.* 3.** a live-in person. [1950–55; adj., n. use of v. phrase *live in (a place)*]

live·li·hood (līv′lē ho͝od′), *n.* a means of supporting one's existence, esp. financially or vocationally; living: *to earn a livelihood as a tenant farmer.* [bef. 1000; earlier *liveliod, livelihod,* alter. (by reanalysis as LIVELY + HOOD; cf. obs. *livelihood* liveliness) of ME *livelod,* OE *līflād* conduct of life, way of life (see LIFE, LODE, LOAD)]
—Syn. sustenance, subsistence. See **living.**

live′ load′ (līv). *Engin.* See under **load** (def. 11). [1865–70]

live·long (liv′lông′, -long′), *adj.* (of time) whole or entire, esp. when tediously long, slow in passing, etc.: *We picked apples the livelong day.* [1350–1400; alter. (by assoc. with LIVE[1]) of earlier *leeve long,* ME *leve longe* dear long. See LIEF, LONG[1]]

live·ly (līv′lē), *adj.,* **-li·er, -li·est,** *adv.* **—*adj.* 1.** full or suggestive of life or vital energy; active, vigorous, or brisk: *a lively discussion.* **2.** animated, spirited, vivacious, or sprightly: *a lively tune; a lively wit.* **3.** eventful, stirring, or exciting: *The opposition gave us a lively time.* **4.** bustling with activity; astir: *The marketplace was lively with vendors.* **5.** strong, keen, or distinct; vivid: *a lively recollection.* **6.** striking, telling, or effective, as an expression or instance. **7.** vivid or bright, as color or light: *a lively pink.* **8.** sparkling, as wines. **9.** fresh or invigorating, as air: *a lively breeze.* **10.** rebounding quickly; springing back; resilient: *a lively tennis ball.* **11.** riding the sea buoyantly, as a ship. **—*adv.* 12.** with briskness, vigor, or animation; briskly: *to step lively.* [bef. 1000; ME; OE *līflīc* vital. See LIFE, -LY] **—live′li·ly,** *adv.* **—live′li·ness,** *n.*
—Syn. 1. alert, spry, nimble, agile, quick, pert. **2.**

gay, buoyant. **5.** forceful, clear. **7.** brilliant, clear, glowing. **—Ant. 1.** inactive, torpid. **2.** dull. **5.** weak. **7.** dim.

liv•en (lī′vən), *v.t.* **1.** to put life into; rouse; enliven; cheer (often fol. by *up*): *What can we do to liven up the party?* —*v.i.* **2.** to become more lively; brighten (usually fol. by *up*): *If this party doesn't liven up soon, let's leave.* [1880–85; aph. var. of ENLIVEN] —**liv′en•er,** *n.*

Li•ven•za (lē ven′tsä), *n.* a river in NE Italy, flowing SE to the Adriatic. 70 mi. (113 km) long.

live′ oak′ (līv), **1.** an evergreen oak, *Quercus virginiana,* of the southern U.S., having a short, broad trunk and shiny, oblong leaves: the state tree of Georgia. **2.** any of various related trees. **3.** the hard, durable wood of any of these trees. [1600–10, *Amer.*]

live-out (liv′out′), *adj.* residing away from the place of one's employment: *a live-out cook.* [1965–70; by analogy with LIVE-IN]

liv•er[1] (liv′ər), *n.* **1.** *Anat.* a large, reddish-brown, glandular organ located in the upper right side of the abdominal cavity, divided by fissures into five lobes and functioning in the secretion of bile and various metabolic processes. **2.** an organ in other animals similar to the human liver, often used as food. **3.** a diseased condition of the liver; biliousness: *a touch of liver.* **4.** a reddish-brown color. **5.** a rubberlike, irreversible thickening suspension occurring in paint, ink, etc., due to a chemical reaction between a colloidal pigment and a vehicle or as a result of polymerization of the vehicle. —*adj.* **6.** of the color of liver. —*v.i.* **7.** (of paint, ink, etc.) to undergo irreversible thickening. [bef. 900; ME; OE *lifer,* c. D *lever,* G *Leber,* ON *lifr;* perh. akin to Gk *liparós* fat] —**liv′er•less,** *adj.*

liv•er[2] (liv′ər), *n.* **1.** a person who lives in a manner specified: *an extravagant liver.* **2.** a dweller or resident; inhabitant. [1325–75; ME; see LIVE[1], -ER[1]]

liv•er[3] (lī′vər), *adj.* comparative of **live**[2].

liv′er chest′nut (liv′ər), chestnut (def. 9).

liv′er ex′tract (liv′ər), an extract of mammalian liver, esp. hog or beef, for treating pernicious anemia. [1905–10]

liv′er fluke′ (liv′ər), any of various trematodes, as *Fasciola hepatica,* parasitic in the liver and bile ducts of domestic animals and humans. [1785–95]

liv•er•ied (liv′ə rēd, liv′rēd), *adj.* clad in livery, as servants: *a liveried footman.* [1625–35; LIVERY + -ED[3]]

liv•er•ish (liv′ər ish), *adj.* **1.** resembling liver, esp. in color. **2.** having a liver disorder; bilious. **3.** disagreeable; crabbed; melancholy: *to have a liverish disposition.* [1730–40; LIVER[1] + -ISH[1]] —**liv′er•ish•ness,** *n.*

liv•er•leaf (liv′ər lēf′), *n., pl.* **-leaves.** hepatica. [1810–20, *Amer.;* LIVER[1] + LEAF]

Liv•er•more (liv′ər môr′, -mōr′), *n.* a city in W California. 48,349.

liv′er of sul′fur (liv′ər). See **sulfurated potash.**

Liv•er•pool (liv′ər po͞ol′), *n.* a seaport in Merseyside, in W England, on the Mersey estuary. 548,800. —**Liv•er•pud•li•an** (liv′ər pud′lē ən), *n., adj.*

liv•er-rot (liv′ər rot′), *n. Vet. Pathol.* a disease chiefly of sheep and cattle, characterized by sluggishness, weight loss, and local damage to the liver, caused by infection from the liver fluke. Also called **distomatosis, fascioliasis, liv′er fluke′ disease′.** [1830–40]

liv′er sau′sage (liv′ər), liverwurst. [1850–55]

liv′er spots′ (liv′ər), *Pathol.* a form of chloasma in which irregularly shaped light-brown spots occur on the skin. [1880–85]

liv•er•wort (liv′ər wûrt′, -wôrt′), *n.* any mosslike plant of the class Hepaticae, growing chiefly on damp ground, rocks, or on tree trunks and helping the decay of logs and the disintegration of rocks. [bef. 1100; ME; late OE *liferwyrt.* See LIVER[1], WORT[2]]

liv•er•wurst (liv′ər wûrst′, -wo͝orst′, -wo͝osht′), *n.* a sausage made with a large percentage of liver, esp. one made with pork liver and pork meat. Also called **liver sausage.** [1865–70, *Amer.;* half trans., half adoption of G *Leberwurst*]

liv•er•y[1] (liv′ə rē, liv′rē), *n., pl.* **-er•ies. 1.** a distinctive uniform, badge, or device formerly provided by someone of rank or title for his retainers, as in time of war. **2.** a uniform worn by servants. **3.** distinctive attire worn by an official, a member of a company or guild, etc. **4.** Also called **liv′ery com′pany.** *Brit.* a guild or company of the City of London entitled to wear such livery. **5.** characteristic dress, garb, or outward appearance: *the green livery of summer.* **6.** the care, feeding, stabling, etc., of horses for pay. **7.** See **livery stable. 8.** a company that rents out automobiles, boats, etc. **9.** *Law.* an ancient method of conveying a freehold by formal delivery of possession. [1250–1300; ME *livere* < AF, equiv. to OF *livree* allowance (of food, clothing, etc.), n. use of fem. ptp. of *livrer* to give over < L *līberāre;* see LIBERATE]

liv•er•y[2] (liv′ə rē), *adj.* liverish. [1770–80; LIVER[1] + -Y[1]]

liv′ery col′ors, *Heraldry.* the principal tinctures of a coat of arms, usually one color and one metal, used for liveries, standards, etc.

liv′ery cup′board, a cupboard with pierced doors, formerly used as a storage place for food. Also called **almoner's cupboard.** [1565–75]

liv•er•y•man (liv′ə rē mən, liv′rē-), *n., pl.* **-men. 1.** an owner of or an employee in a livery stable. **2.** *Brit.* a freeman of the City of London, entitled to wear the livery of the ancient guild or city district to which he belongs and to vote in the election of Lord Mayor, chamberlain, and other municipal and honorary officers. **3.** *Obs.* a person in livery, esp. a servant. [1675–85; LIVERY + -MAN]
—Usage. See **-man.**

liv′ery sta′ble, a stable where horses and vehicles are cared for or rented out for pay. [1695–1705]

lives (līvz), *n.* pl. of **life.**

Lives′ of the Po′ets, The, a collection (1779–81), by Samuel Johnson, of biographical and critical essays on 52 English poets.

live′ spin′dle (līv). See under **spindle** (def. 6).

live′ steam′ (līv), **1.** steam direct from the boiler and at full pressure, ready for use in work. **2.** steam that has performed no work or only part of its work. [1870–75, *Amer.*]

live•stock (līv′stok′), *n.* (*used with a singular or plural v.*) the horses, cattle, sheep, and other useful animals kept or raised on a farm or ranch. [1650–60; LIVE[2] + STOCK]

live•trap (līv′trap′), *n., v.,* **-trapped, -trap•ping.** —*n.* **1.** a trap for capturing a wild animal alive and without injury. —*v.t.* **2.** to capture (a wild animal) in a livetrap. [1870–75; LIVE[2] + TRAP[1]]

live′ wire′ (līv), *Informal.* an energetic, keenly alert person. [1900–05, *Amer.*]

live•yer (liv′yər), *n. Canadian* (*chiefly Newfoundland*). a native or resident of Newfoundland or Labrador. Also, **live′yere, liv′ier.** [1900–05; cf. dial. (SW England) *livier* resident, ME; var. of LIVER[2] with -IER[1]]

liv•id (liv′id), *adj.* **1.** having a discolored, bluish appearance caused by a bruise, congestion of blood vessels, strangulation, etc., as the face, flesh, hands, or nails. **2.** dull blue; dark, grayish-blue. **3.** enraged; furiously angry: *Willful stupidity makes me absolutely livid.* **4.** feeling or appearing strangulated because of strong emotion. **5.** reddish or flushed. **6.** deathly pale; pallid; ashen: *Fear turned his cheeks livid for a moment.* [1615–25; < L *lividus* black and blue, equiv. to *līv(ēre)* to be livid (akin to Welsh *lliw* color) + *-idus* -ID[4]] —**liv′id•ly,** *adv.* —**liv′id•ness, li•vid′i•ty,** *n.*

liv•ing (liv′ing), *adj.* **1.** having life; being alive; not dead: *living persons.* **2.** in actual existence or use; extant: *living languages.* **3.** active or thriving; vigorous; strong: *a living faith.* **4.** burning or glowing, as a coal. **5.** flowing freely, as water. **6.** pertaining to, suitable for, or sufficient for existence or subsistence: *living conditions; a living wage.* **7.** of or pertaining to living persons: *within living memory.* **8.** lifelike; true to life, as a picture or narrative. **9.** in its natural state and place; not uprooted, changed, etc.: *living rock.* **10.** very; absolute (used as an intensifier): *to scare the living daylights out of someone.* —*n.* **11.** the act or condition of a person or thing that lives: *Living is very expensive these days.* **12.** the means of maintaining life; livelihood: *to earn one's living.* **13.** a particular manner, state, or status of life: *luxurious living.* **14.** (*used with a plural v.*) living persons collectively (usually prec. by *the*): *glad to be among the living.* **15.** *Brit.* the benefice of a clergyman. [bef. 900; (adj.) ME *lyvyng(e);* r. earlier *liviende,* OE *lifgende* (see LIVE[1], -ING[2]); (n.) ME *living(e)* (see -ING[1])] —**liv′ing•ly,** *adv.* —**liv′ing•ness,** *n.*
—Syn. 1. live, quick. **2.** existing, surviving. **3.** lively, flourishing. **12.** sustenance, subsistence. LIVING, LIVELIHOOD, MAINTENANCE, SUPPORT refer, directly or indirectly, to what is earned or spent for subsistence. LIVING and LIVELIHOOD (a somewhat more formal word), both refer to what one earns to keep (oneself) alive, but are seldom interchangeable within the same phrase: *to earn one's living; to seek one's livelihood.* "To make a living" suggests making just enough to keep alive, and is particularly frequent in the negative: *You cannot make a living out of that.* "To make a livelihood out of something" suggests rather making a business of it: *to make a livelihood out of trapping foxes.* MAINTENANCE and SUPPORT refer usually to what is spent for the living of another: *to provide for the maintenance or support of someone.* MAINTENANCE occasionally refers to the allowance itself provided for livelihood: *They are entitled to a maintenance from this estate.* **—Ant. 1.** dead.

liv′ing bank′, a facility in which donated human organs or tissues are preserved for subsequent transplantation.

liv′ing death′, a completely miserable, joyless existence, experience, situation, etc.; ordeal: *He found the steaming jungle a living death.* [1665–75]

liv′ing fos′sil, an organism that is a living example of an otherwise extinct group and that has remained virtually unchanged in structure and function over a long period of time, as the coelacanth and the horseshoe crab. [1920–25]

liv′ing pic′ture. tableau (def. 3). [1870–75]

liv′ing room′, **1.** a room in a home used, esp. by a family, for leisure activities, entertaining guests, etc.; parlor. **2.** lebensraum. [1815–25]

liv′ing stand′ard. See **standard of living.** [1940–45]

Liv•ing•ston (liv′ing stən), *n.* **1. Robert R.,** 1746–1813, U.S. political figure and jurist. **2.** a township in NE New Jersey. 28,040.

Liv•ing•stone (liv′ing stən), *n.* **1. David,** 1813–73, Scottish missionary and explorer in Africa. **2.** a town in and headquarters of Southern Province, SW Zambia, on the Zambesi River, near Victoria Falls: the former capital. 58,000.

liv′ing stones′, any of various succulent plants of the genus *Lithops,* native to Africa, having solitary yellow or white flowers and thick leaves that resemble stones. Also called **lithops, stoneface, stone plant.**

living stones, genus *Lithops*

liv′ing trust′, a trust that takes effect during the lifetime of the settlor. Also called **trust inter vivos.** Cf. **testamentary trust.**

liv′ing u′nit, a dwelling intended for use by one household. [1935–40]

liv′ing wage′, a wage on which it is possible for a wage earner or an individual and his or her family to live at least according to minimum customary standards. [1885–90]

liv′ing will′, a document instructing physicians, relatives, or others to refrain from the use of extraordinary measures, as life-support equipment, to prolong one's life in the event of a terminal illness. [1970–75]

Li•vo•ni•a (li vō′nē ə), *n.* **1.** a former Russian province on the Baltic: now part of Latvia and Estonia. **2.** a city in SE Michigan, near Detroit. 104,814. —**Li•vo′ni•an,** *adj., n.*

Li•vor•no (lē vôr′nô), *n.* a seaport in W Italy on the Ligurian Sea. 177,526. English, **Leghorn.**

li•vre (lē′vər; *Fr.* lē′vʀ[ə]), *n., pl.* **-vres** (-vərz; *Fr.* -vʀ[ə]). a former money of account and group of coins of France, issued in coin form first in gold, then in silver, finally in copper, and discontinued in 1794. [1545–55; < MF, OF < L *libra* balance, pound]

Liv•y (liv′ē), *n.* (*Titus Livius*) 59 B.C.–A.D. 17, Roman historian.

li•wan (lē′wän), *n.* iwan. [< Ar *līwān* < Pers; see IWAN]

Li Xian•nian (lē′ shyän′nyän′), 1909–92, Chinese Communist leader: president 1983–88.

lix•iv•i•ate (lik siv′ē āt′), *v.t.,* **-at•ed, -at•ing.** to treat with a solvent; leach. [1640–50; LIXIVI(UM) + -ATE[1]] —**lix•iv′i•a′tion,** *n.*

lix•iv•i•um (lik siv′ē əm), *n., pl.* **lix•iv•i•ums, lix•iv•i•a** (lik siv′ē ə). **1.** the solution, containing alkaline salts, obtained by leaching wood ashes with water; lye. **2.** any solution obtained by leaching. [1605–15; < L *lixivium* lye]

Li Xue (lē′ shwœ′), *Pinyin.* See **Li Hsüeh.**

Li Yüan (lē′ yyän′), (*Kao Tsu* or *Gao Zu*), A.D. 565–635, Chinese emperor 618–27: founder of the Tang dynasty. Also, *Pinyin,* **Li′ Yuan′.**

Liz (liz), *n.* a female given name, form of **Elizabeth.**

li•za (lī′zə), *n.* a mullet, *Mugil liza,* found chiefly in the tropical Atlantic Ocean. [1830–40, *Amer.;* < Sp]

Li•za (lī′zə), *n.* a female given name, form of **Elizabeth.**

liz•ard (liz′ərd), *n.* **1.** any of numerous scaly reptiles of the suborder Sauria, order Squamata, typically having a moderately elongate body, a tapering tail, and two pairs of legs held outward from the body, comprising mostly terrestrial and burrowing species. **2.** any of various reptiles resembling a lizard, as a dinosaur or crocodile. **3.** leather made from the skin of the lizard, used for shoes, purses, etc. **4.** (*cap.*) *Astron.* the constellation Lacerta. **5.** See **lounge lizard. 6.** *Naut.* a pennant used as a leader for running rigging, having a thimble or bull's-eye. **7. The Lizard.** See **Lizard Head.** [1350–1400; ME *liserd,* var. of *lesard(e)* < MF *lesarde* < L *lacerta*]

anole lizard, genus *Anolis,* length 4 to 8 in. (10 to 20 cm)

liz•ard•fish (liz′ərd fish′), *n., pl.* (*esp. collectively*) **-fish,** (*esp. referring to two or more kinds or species*) **-fish•es.** any of several large-mouthed fishes of the family Synodontidae, having a lizardlike head. [1745–55; LIZARD + FISH]

Liz′ard Head′, a promontory in SW Cornwall, in SW England: the southernmost point in England. Also called **The Lizard.**

liz•ard's-tail (liz′ərdz tāl′), *n.* either of two marsh herbs of the genus *Saururus,* esp. *S. cernuus,* of North America, having drooping spikes of fragrant, white flowers. [1745–55]

Liz•beth (liz′beth′, -bəth), *n.* a female given name, form of **Elizabeth.**

liz•zie (liz′ē), *n.* See **tin lizzie.** [1910–15]

Liz•zy (liz′ē), *n.* a female given name, form of **Elizabeth.** Also, **Liz′zie.**

Lju•blja•na (lo͞o′blē ä′nə; *Slovene.* lyo͞o′blyä nä), *n.* a city in and the capital of Slovenia, in the central part. 305,211. German, **Laibach.**

Lk., *Bible.* Luke.

'll, 1. a contraction of *will: I'll answer the phone. He'll pay the check. What'll we do?* **2.** contraction of *till*[1] (*used when the preceding word ends in t*): *Wait'll your father comes home!*
—Usage. See **contraction.**

LL, 1. Late Latin. **2.** Low Latin. Also, **L.L.**

ll., lines.

l.l., 1. in the place quoted. [< L *locō laudātō*] **2.** loose-leaf.

lla•ma (lä′mə), *n.* **1.** a woolly-haired South American ruminant of the genus *Lama,* believed to be a domes-

CONCISE PRONUNCIATION KEY: *act, cāpe, dâre, pärt; set, ēqual; if, īce; ox, ōver, ôrder, oil, bo͝ok, bo͞ot, out; up, ûrge; child; sing; shoe; thin, that;* zh as in *treasure.* ə = *a* as in *alone,* *e* as in *system,* *i* as in *easily,* *o* as in *gallop,* *u* as in *circus;* ᵊ as in *fire* (fīᵊr), *hour* (ouᵊr). l and n can serve as syllabic consonants, as in *cradle* (krād′l), and *button* (but′n). See the full key inside the front cover.

ticated variety of the guanaco: often used as a beast of burden. **2.** the fine, soft fleece of the llama, combined with the wool for coating. [1590–1600; < Sp < Quechua *llama* (with palatal *l*)]

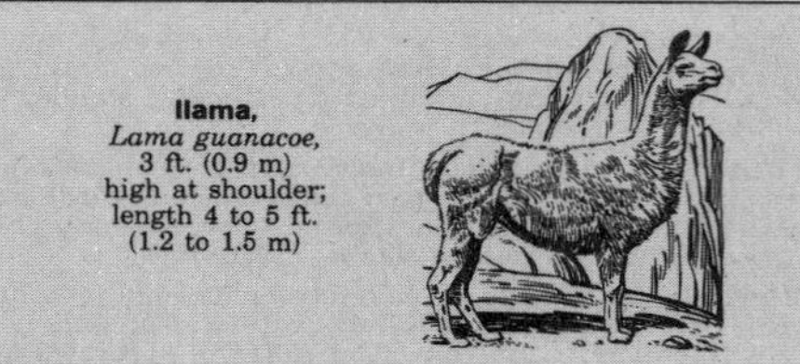

llama, *Lama guanacoe,* 3 ft. (0.9 m) high at shoulder; length 4 to 5 ft. (1.2 to 1.5 m)

Llan•e•lly (la nel′ē; *Welsh.* hla ne′hlē), *n.* a seaport in Dyfed, in S Wales. 76,800.

lla•no (lä′nō; *Sp.* yä′nô), *n., pl.* **-nos** (-nōz; *Sp.* -nôs). (in the southwestern U.S. and Spanish America) an extensive grassy plain with few trees. [1605–15; < Sp: a plain < L *plānus* PLAIN[1]]

Lla•no Es•ta•ca•do (lä′nō es′tə kä′dō, lan′ō), a large plateau in the SW United States, in W Texas and SE New Mexico: cattle-grazing region. 1000–5000 ft. (300–1500 m) above sea level. Also called **Staked Plain.**

L. Lat., **1.** Late Latin. **2.** Low Latin.

LLB, Little League Baseball.

LL.B., Bachelor of Laws. [< L *Lēgum Baccalaureus*]

LL.D., Doctor of Laws. [< L *Lēgum Doctor*]

Lle•ras Ca•mar•go (ye′räs kä mär′gô), **Al•ber•to** (äl ver′tô), 1906–89, Colombian journalist, writer, and political leader: president 1945–46, 1958–62.

Lleu Llaw Gyf•fes (hlī′ hlou′ gu′fes), *Welsh Legend.* the son of Gwydion and Arianhrod, provided with a name, weapons, and a wife through the magic and trickery of Gwydion in spite of the curses of Arianhrod. [< Welsh: lit., lion with the steady hand]

Llew•el•lyn (lo͞o el′in), *n.* **1. Richard** (*Richard David Vivian Llewellyn Lloyd*), 1907?–83, Welsh novelist. **2.** a male given name: associated, by folk etymology, with Welsh *llew* lion or *llyw* leader.

L-line (el′līn′), *n. Physics.* one of a series of lines **(L-series)** in the x-ray spectrum of an atom corresponding to radiation **(L-radiation)** caused by the transition of an electron to the L-shell. [1965–70]

LL.M., Master of Laws. [< L *Lēgum Magister*]

Lloyd (loid), *n.* **1.** *Welsh Legend.* Llwyd. **2. Harold (Clay•ton)** (klāt′n), 1894–1971, U.S. actor. **3. (John) Sel•wyn (Brooke)** (sel′win), 1904–78, British statesman. **4.** a male given name: from a Welsh word meaning "gray."

Lloyd′ George′, David, 1st Earl of Dwy•for (do͞o′-vôr), 1863–1945, British statesman: prime minister 1916–22.

Lloyd's (loidz), *n.* an association of independent English insurance underwriters, founded in London about 1688, originally engaged in underwriting only marine risks but now also issuing policies on almost every type of insurance. [named after Edward *Lloyd,* 17th-century owner of a London coffeehouse that was frequented by insurers against sea risk]

Lloyd's′ Reg′ister, a publication, issued annually by Lloyd's, consisting of a list of all of the world's seagoing vessels and including such information as their age, tonnage, and classification. [1840–50]

Lludd (hlēth), *n. Welsh Legend.* a king of Britain who rid his kingdom of three plagues and was famous for his generosity: sometimes regarded as a god. Also, **Nudd.**

Llwyd (hlo͞o′id; *Eng.* loid), *n. Welsh Legend.* a magician who avenged his friend Gwawl upon Pryderi, the son of Pwyll, by casting various spells upon Pryderi and his estate. Also, **Lloyd.**

Llyr (hlēr), *n. Welsh Legend.* the father of Manawydan: corresponds to the Irish Ler.

LM (*often* lem), lunar module.

lm, *Optics.* lumen; lumens.

L.M., **1.** Licentiate in Medicine. **2.** Licentiate in Midwifery. **3.** Lord Mayor.

lm-hr, *Optics.* lumen-hour; lumen-hours.

LMT, local mean time.

ln, *Symbol, Math.* See **natural logarithm.** [*l*(*ogarithm*) *n*(*atural*)]

lndry rm, *Real Estate.* laundry room.

LNG, liquefied natural gas.

lo[1] (lō), *interj.* look! see! (frequently used in Biblical expressions; now usually used as an expression of surprise in the phrase **lo and behold**). [bef. 900; ME; conflation of *lo* exclamation of surprise, grief, or joy, O! (OE *lā;* see LA[2]) and *lo,* shortened form of *loke* (OE *lōca*), impv. of *loken* to LOOK]

lo[2] (lō), *adj.* an informal, simplified spelling of **low**[1], used esp. in labeling or advertising commercial products: *lo calorie.*

loach (lōch), *n.* any of several slender European and Asian fishes of the family Cobitidae and related families, having several barbels around the mouth. [1325–75; ME *loche* < MF]

CONCISE ETYMOLOGY KEY: <, descended or borrowed from; >, whence; b., blend of, blended; c., cognate with; cf., compare; deriv., derivative; equiv., equivalent; imit., imitative; obl., oblique; r., replacing; s., stem; sp., spelling, spelled; resp., respelling, respelled; trans., translation; ?, origin unknown; *, unattested; ‡, probably earlier than. See the full key inside the front cover.

load (lōd), *n.* **1.** anything put in or on something for conveyance or transportation; freight; cargo: *The truck carried a load of watermelons.* **2.** the quantity that can be or usually is carried at one time, as in a cart. **3.** this quantity taken as a unit of measure or weight or a discrete quantity (usually used in combination): *carload; wagonload.* **4.** the quantity borne or sustained by something; burden: *a tree weighed down by its load of fruit.* **5.** the weight supported by a structure or part. **6.** the amount of work assigned to or to be done by a person, team, department, machine, or mechanical system: *a reasonable load of work.* **7.** something that weighs down or oppresses like a burden; onus: *Supporting her younger brothers has been a heavy load for her.* **8. loads,** *Informal.* a great quantity or number: *loads of fun; loads of people.* **9.** the charge for a firearm. **10.** a commission charged to buyers of mutual-fund shares. **11.** *Engin.* any of the forces that a structure is calculated to oppose, comprising any unmoving and unvarying force **(dead load),** any load from wind or earthquake, and any other moving or temporary force **(live load).** **12.** *Elect.* **a.** the power delivered by a generator, motor, power station, or transformer. **b.** a device that receives power. **13.** *Mech.* the external resistance overcome by an engine, dynamo, or the like, under given conditions, measured and expressed in terms of the power required. **14.** *Geol.* the burden of sediment being carried by a stream or river. Cf. **bed load.** **15.** *Slang.* a sufficient amount of liquor drunk to cause intoxication: *He's got a load on tonight.* **16. get a load of,** *Slang.* **a.** to look at; notice; observe. **b.** to listen to with interest: *Did you get a load of what she said?* —*v.t.* **17.** to put a load on or in; fill: *to load a ship.* **18.** to supply abundantly, lavishly, or excessively with something (often fol. by *down*): *They loaded us down with gifts.* **19.** to weigh down, burden, or oppress (often fol. by *down, with, on,* etc.): *to feel loaded down with responsibilities; to load oneself with obligations.* **20.** to insert a charge, projectile, etc., into (a firearm). **21.** to place (film, tape, etc.) into a camera or other device: *He loaded the film into the camera.* **22.** to place film, tape, etc., into (a camera or other device): *How do you load this camera?* **23.** to take on as a load: *a ship loading coal.* **24.** to add to the weight of, sometimes fraudulently: *The silver candlesticks were loaded with lead.* **25.** *Insurance.* to increase (the net premium) by adding charges, as for expenses. **26.** to add additional or prejudicial meaning to (a statement, question, etc.): *The attorney kept loading his questions in the hope of getting the reply he wanted.* **27.** to overcharge (a word, expression, etc.) with extraneous values of emotion, sentiment, or the like: *emotion that loads any reference to home, flag, and mother.* **28.** to weight (dice) so that they will always come to rest with particular faces upward. **29.** *Baseball.* to have or put runners at (first, second, and third bases): *They loaded the bases with two out in the eighth inning.* **30.** *Fine Arts.* **a.** to place a large amount of pigment on (a brush). **b.** to apply a thick layer of pigment to (a canvas). **31.** *Metalworking.* **a.** (of metal being deep-drawn) to become welded to (the drawing tool). **b.** (of material being ground) to fill the depressions in the surface of (a grinding wheel). **c.** (in powder metallurgy) to fill the cavity of (a die). **32.** *Computers.* **a.** to bring (a program or data) into main storage from external or auxiliary storage. **b.** to place (an input/output medium) into an appropriate device, as by inserting a disk into a disk drive. **33.** *Elect.* to add (a power-absorbing device) to an electric circuit. —*v.i.* **34.** to put on or take on a load, as of passengers or goods: *The bus usually loads at the side door.* **35.** to load a firearm. **36.** to enter a carrier or conveyance (usually fol. by *into*): *The students loaded quickly into the buses.* **37.** to become filled or occupied: *The ship loaded with people in only 15 minutes.* **38. load the dice,** to put someone or something in a advantageous or disadvantageous position; affect or influence the result: *Lack of sufficient education loaded the dice against him as a candidate for the job.* —*adv.* **39. loads,** *Informal.* very much; a great deal: *Thanks loads. It would help loads if you sent some money.* [bef. 1000; ME *lode* (n.); orig. the same word as LODE (OE *lād* way, course, carrying); senses influenced by LADE] —**load′less,** *adj.*
—**Syn. 7.** weight, encumbrance. LOAD, BURDEN referred originally to something placed on a person or animal or put into a vehicle for conveyance. Both LOAD and BURDEN are still used in this literal sense, though BURDEN only infrequently, except in such fixed phrases as *beast of burden* and *a ship of 1500 tons burden* (carrying capacity). Both words have come to be used figuratively to refer to duties, cares, etc., that are oppressively heavy, and this is now the main meaning of BURDEN: *You have taken a load off my mind. Some children are a burden.* **17.** lade. **19.** weight, encumber. —**Ant. 19.** disburden.

load′ displace′ment, *Naut.* the weight, in long tons, of a cargo vessel loaded so that the summer load line touches the surface of the water. [1880–85]

load•ed (lō′did), *adj.* **1.** bearing or having a load; full: *a loaded bus.* **2.** containing ammunition or an explosive charge: *a loaded rifle.* **3.** (of a word, statement, or argument) charged with emotional or associative significance that hinders rational or unprejudiced consideration of the terms involved in a discourse. **4.** *Slang.* **a.** having a great deal of money; rich. **b.** under the influence of alcohol; drunk; intoxicated. **c.** under the influence of drugs. **5.** (of dice) fraudulently weighted so as to increase the chances of certain combinations to appear face up when the dice are thrown. **6.** (of a product, building, etc.) including many extra features, accessories, luxuries, or the like: *The new model sports car is loaded—air conditioning, a tape deck, real leather seats are all included.* **7. loaded for bear,** *Informal.* See **bear**[2] (def. 9). [1655–65; 1940–45 for def. 4; LOAD + -ED[2]]

load•er (lō′dər), *n.* **1.** a person or thing that loads. **2.** a self-propelled machine with a shovel or bucket at the end of articulated arms, used to raise earth or other material and load it into a dump truck. [ME *loder;* see LOAD, -ER[1]]

load′ fac′tor, **1.** the amount or weight of cargo, number of passengers, etc., that an aircraft, vehicle, or vessel can carry. **2.** the percentage of available seats, space, or maximum carrying weight paid for and used by passengers, shippers, etc.: *An airline can't profit on a 40 percent load factor.* **3.** *Elect.* the ratio of the average load over a designated period of time to the peak load occurring in that period. [1890–95]

load′ fund′, a mutual fund that carries transaction charges, usually a percentage of the initial investment.

load•ie (lō′dē), *n. Slang.* loady.

load•ing (lō′ding), *n.* **1.** the act of a person or thing that loads. **2.** that with which something is loaded; load, burden, or charge. **3.** *Elect.* the process of adding reactance to a telephone circuit, radio antenna, etc. **4.** *Aeron.* the ratio of the gross weight of an airplane to engine power **(power loading),** wing span **(span loading),** or wing area **(wing loading).** **5.** *Insurance.* an addition to the net premium, to cover expenses and allow a margin for contingencies and profit. [1425–75; late ME; see LOAD, -ING[1]]

load′ing coil′, *Elect.* an inductance coil used to improve the characteristics of a transmission line. [1900–05]

load′ line′, *Naut.* **1.** Also called **Plimsoll line.** any of various lines marked on the sides of a cargo vessel to indicate the depth to which a vessel may be immersed under certain conditions. Cf. **freeboard** (def. 1a). **2.** the line made by the surface of the water on the hull of a loaded ship. [1880–85]

load line (def. 1) AB, official load line set by American Bureau of Shipping; TF, tropical, fresh water; F, fresh water; T, tropical; S, summer; W, winter; WNA, winter, North Atlantic

load′-line mark′ (lōd′līn′), *Naut.* any of various marks by which the allowable loading and the load line at load displacement are established for a merchant vessel; a load line. Also called **Plimsoll mark.**

load•mas•ter (lōd′mas′tər, -mä′stər), *n.* an aircrew member responsible for the loading and stowage of cargo aboard an aircraft. [1960–65; LOAD + MASTER]

load′ mod′ule, *Computers.* a program or combination of programs in a form ready to be loaded into main storage and executed: generally the output from a linkage editor.

load-shed•ding (lōd′shed′ing), *n.* the deliberate shutdown of electric power in a part or parts of a power-distribution system, generally to prevent the failure of the entire system when the demand strains the capacity of the system. Also, **load′shed′ding.** [1945–50]

load•star (lōd′stär′), *n.* lodestar.

load•stone (lōd′stōn′), *n.* lodestone. [1505–15; earlier *load* LODE + STONE]

load•y (lō′dē), *n., pl.* **load•ies.** *Slang.* a person who is a habitual user of alcohol or drugs. Also, **loadie.** [LOAD (appar. from LOADED intoxicated, or *get a load on* become intoxicated) + -Y[2]]

loaf[1] (lōf), *n., pl.* **loaves** (lōvz). **1.** a portion of bread or cake baked in a mass, usually oblong with a rounded top. **2.** a shaped or molded mass of food, as of sugar or chopped meat: *a veal loaf.* **3.** *Brit.* **a.** the rounded head of a cabbage, lettuce, etc. **b.** *Slang* (*older use*). head or brains: *Use your loaf.* [bef. 950; ME *lo*(*o*)*f,* OE *hlāf* loaf, bread; c. G *Laib,* ON *hleifr,* Goth *hlaifs*]

loaf[2] (lōf), *v.i.* **1.** to idle away time: *He figured the mall was as good a place as any for loafing.* **2.** to lounge or saunter lazily and idly: *We loafed for hours along the water's edge.* —*v.t.* **3.** to pass idly (usually fol. by *away*): *to loaf one's life away.* [1825–35, *Amer.;* back formation from LOAFER]
—**Syn. 2.** loll, idle.

loaf′ bread′, *South Midland and Southern U.S.* commercially baked bread; store-bought bread. [1550–60]

loaf•er (lō′fər), *n.* a person who loafs; lazy person; idler. [1820–30, *Amer.;* perh. short for **landloafer* vagabond; cf. G (obs.) *Landläufer,* D *landloper;* see LANDLOPER] —**loaf′er•ish,** *adj.*

Loaf•er (lō′fər), *Trademark.* a brand name for a moccasinlike slip-on shoe.

loaf′ pan′, a rectangular metal or glass pan for baking cakes, breads, meatloaf, etc. Also, **loaf′pan′.**

lo•a•i•a•sis (lō′ə ī′ə sis), *n. Pathol.* loiasis.

loam (lōm), *n.* **1.** a rich, friable soil containing a relatively equal mixture of sand and silt and a somewhat smaller proportion of clay. **2.** a mixture of clay, sand, straw, etc., used in making molds for founding and in plastering walls, stopping holes, etc. **3.** earth or soil. **4.** *Obs.* clay or clayey earth. —*v.t.* **5.** to cover or stop with loam. [bef. 900; late ME *lome,* earlier *lam*(*e*), OE *lām;* c. D *leem,* G *Lehm* loam, clay; akin to LIME[1]] —**loam′i•ness,** *n.* —**loam′less,** *adj.* —**loam′y,** *adj.*

loan[1] (lōn), *n.* **1.** the act of lending; a grant of the temporary use of something: *the loan of a book.* **2.** something lent or furnished on condition of being returned, esp. a sum of money lent at interest: *a $1000 loan at 10 percent interest.* **3.** loanword. **4. on loan, a.** borrowed for temporary use: *How many books can I have on loan from the library at one time?* **b.** temporarily provided or released by one's regular employer, superior, or owner for use by another: *Our best actor is on loan to another movie studio for two films.* —*v.t.* **5.** to make a loan of; lend: *Will you loan me your umbrella?* **6.** to lend (money) at interest. —*v.i.* **7.** to make a loan or loans; lend. [1150–1200; ME *lon*(*e*), *lan*(*e*) (n.), OE *lān* < ON *lān;* r. its cognate, OE *lǣn* loan, grant, c. D *leen* loan, G *Leh*(*e*)*n* fief; cf. LEND]

—**Usage.** Sometimes mistakenly identified as an Americanism, LOAN[1] as a verb meaning "to lend" has been used in English for nearly 800 years: *Nearby villages loaned clothing and other supplies to the flood-ravaged town.* The occasional objections to LOAN as a verb referring to things other than money, are comparatively recent. LOAN is standard in all contexts but is perhaps most common in financial ones: *The government has loaned money to farmers to purchase seed.*

loan[2] (lōn), *n. Scot.* **1.** a country lane; secondary road. **2.** an uncultivated plot of farmland, usually used for milking cows. Also, **loan·ing** (lō′ning). [1325–75; ME, OE *lone* LANE]

loan·a·ble (lō′nə bəl), *adj.* **1.** that can be loaned. **2.** available for loan for a fee or at interest. —*n.* **3.** something that is loanable. [1840–50; LOAN[1] + -ABLE]

loan·blend (lōn′blend′), *n.* a compound word or expression consisting of both native and foreign elements. [1945–50; LOAN[1] + BLEND]

Lo·an·da (lō an′də, -än′-; *Port.* lo͝o äɴ′də), *n.* Luanda.

loan·er (lō′nər), *n.* **1.** a person or thing that loans. **2.** something, as an automobile or appliance, that is lent esp. to replace an item being serviced or repaired. [1880–85; LOAN[1] + -ER[1]]

loan′ of′fice, **1.** an office for making loans or receiving payments on loans. **2.** a public office for receiving subscriptions to a government loan. **3.** a pawnbroker's shop. [1710–20]

loan′ shark′, *Informal.* a person who lends money at excessively high rates of interest; usurer. [1900–05, *Amer.*]

loan·shark·ing (lōn′shär′king), *n.* the practice of lending money at excessive rates of interest. Also, **loan′-shark′ing.** [1965–70, *Amer.*; LOAN SHARK + -ING[1]]

loan·shift (lōn′shift′), *n. Ling.* **1.** change or extension of the meaning of a word through the influence of a foreign word, as in the application in English of the meaning "profession" to the word *calling* through the influence of Latin *vocātio.* **2.** a word created by loanshift. [1945–50; LOAN[1] + SHIFT]

loan′ transla′tion, **1.** the process whereby a compound word or expression is created by literal translation of each of the elements of a compound word or expression in another language, as *marriage of convenience* from French *mariage de convenance.* **2.** a word or expression so created. Cf. **calque.** [1930–35]

loan′ val′ue, *Insurance.* the highest amount of money that can be borrowed against a life-insurance policy, based on the cash value of the policy.

loan·word, (lōn′wûrd′), *n.* a word in one language that has been borrowed from another language and usually naturalized, as *wine,* taken into Old English from Latin *vinum,* or *macho,* taken into Modern English from Spanish. Also, **loan′ word′.** Also called **loan.** [1870–75; trans. of G *Lehnwort*]

loath (lōth, lōth), *adj.* unwilling; reluctant; disinclined; averse: *to be loath to admit a mistake.* Also, **loth.** [bef. 900; ME *loth, lath,* OE *lāth* hostile, hateful; c. D *leed,* G *leid* sorry, ON *leithr* hateful] —**loath′ness,** *n.*
—**Syn.** See **reluctant.** —**Ant.** eager.

loathe (lōth), *v.t.,* **loathed, loath·ing.** to feel disgust or intense aversion for; abhor: *I loathe people who spread malicious gossip.* [bef. 900; ME *loth(i)en, lath(i)en,* OE *lāthian,* deriv. of *lāth* LOATH] —**loath′er,** *n.*
—**Syn.** detest, abominate, hate. —**Ant.** like.

loath·ful (lōth′fəl), *adj.* **1.** *Scot.* bashful; reluctant. **2.** hateful; loathsome. [1400–50; late ME *lothfull.* See LOATH, -FUL]

loath·ing (lō′thing), *n.* strong dislike or disgust; intense aversion. [1300–50; ME *lathynge.* See LOATHE, -ING[1]] —**loath′ing·ly,** *adv.*
—**Syn.** abhorrence; hatred. See **aversion.**

loath·ly[1] (lōth′lē, lōth′-), *adv.* reluctantly; unwillingly. [bef. 1000; ME *lothliche,* OE *lāthlīce.* See LOATH, -LY (adv. suffix)]

loath·ly[2] (lōth′lē, lōth′-), *adj. Archaic.* loathsome; hideous; repulsive. [bef. 900; ME *lothlic(e),* OE *lāthlic.* See LOATH, -LY (adj. suffix)]

loath·some (lōth′səm, lōth′-), *adj.* causing feelings of loathing; disgusting; revolting; repulsive: *a loathsome skin disease.* [1250–1300; ME *lothsom.* See LOATH, -SOME[1]] —**loath′some·ly,** *adv.* —**loath′some·ness,** *n.*
—**Syn.** offensive, repellent, detestable, abhorrent, abominable. —**Ant.** attractive.

loaves (lōvz), *n.* pl. of **loaf**[1].

lob[1] (lob), *v.,* **lobbed, lob·bing,** *n.* —*v.t.* **1.** *Tennis.* to hit (a ball) in a high arc to the back of the opponent's court. **2.** to fire (a missile, as a shell) in a high trajectory so that it drops onto a target. **3.** *Cricket.* to bowl (the ball) with a slow underhand motion. **4.** to throw (something) slowly in an arc. —*v.i.* **5.** *Tennis.* to lob a ball. —*n.* **6.** *Tennis.* a ball hit in a high arc to the back of the opponent's court. **7.** *Cricket.* a ball bowled with a slow underhand motion. **8.** *Brit. Dial.* a slow, heavy, dull-witted person. [1325–75; in earlier sense, to behave like a *lob* (ME *lobbe, lob* bumpkin, clumsy person, orig. pollack; OE: spider; basic sense, something pendulous); c. MLG, MD *lobbe* dangling part, stockfish, etc.] —**lob′·ber,** *n.*

lob[2] (lob), *n.* lobworm.

Lo·ba·chev·sky (lō′bə chef′skē; *Russ.* lə bu chyef′-skyə), *n.* **Ni·ko·lai I·va·no·vich** (nyi ku lī′ ē vä′nə-vyich), 1793–1856, Russian mathematician.

lo·bar (lō′bər, -bär), *adj.* of or pertaining to a lobe, as of the lungs. [1855–60; < NL *lobāris.* See LOBE, -AR[1]]

lo′bar pneumo′nia, *Pathol.* pneumonia (def. 2). [1855–60]

lo·bate (lō′bāt), *adj.* **1.** having a lobe or lobes; lobed. **2.** having the form of a lobe. **3.** *Ornith.* noting or pertaining to a foot in which the individual toes have membranous flaps along the sides. Also, **lo′bat·ed.** [1750–60; < NL *lobātus.* See LOBE, -ATE[1]] —**lo′bate·ly,** *adv.*

lo·ba·tion (lō bā′shən), *n.* **1.** lobate formation. **2.** a lobe. [1830–40; LOBATE + -ION]

lob·ber (lob′ər), *n. Inland North.* clabber. Also called **lob′bered milk′** (lob′ərd). [b. CLABBER and LOPPER[2]]
—**Regional Variation.** See **clabber.**

lob·by (lob′ē), *n., pl.* **-bies,** *v.,* **-bied, -by·ing.** —*n.* **1.** an entrance hall, corridor, or vestibule, as in a public building, often serving as an anteroom; foyer. **2.** a large public room or hall adjacent to a legislative chamber. **3.** a group of persons who work or conduct a campaign to influence members of a legislature to vote according to the group's special interest. —*v.i.* **4.** to solicit or try to influence the votes of members of a legislative body. —*v.t.* **5.** to try to influence the actions of (public officials, esp. legislators). **6.** to urge or procure the passage of (a bill), by lobbying. [1545–55; < ML *lobia, laubia* covered way < OHG **laubia* (later *lauba*) arbor, deriv. of *laub* LEAF] —**lob′by·er,** *n.*

lob·by·gow (lob′ē gou′), *n. Slang.* an errand boy, as formerly in the Chinatown section of a city. [1905–10, *Amer.*; orig. obscure]

lob·by·ist (lob′ē ist), *n.* a person who tries to influence legislation on behalf of a special interest; a member of a lobby. [1940–45; LOBBY + -IST] —**lob′by·ism,** *n.*

lobe (lōb), *n.* **1.** a roundish projection or division, as of an organ or a leaf. **2.** earlobe. [1515–25; < ML *lobus* (LL: hull, husk, pod) < Gk *lobós,* akin to L *legula* lobe of the ear]

lo·bec·to·my (lō bek′tə mē), *n., pl.* **-mies.** *Surg.* excision of a lobe of an organ or gland. [1910–15; LOBE + -ECTOMY]

lobed (lōbd), *adj.* **1.** having a lobe or lobes; lobate. **2.** *Bot.* (of a leaf) having lobes or divisions extending less than halfway to the middle of the base. [1780–90; LOBE + -ED[3]]

lobe′-finned fish′ (lōb′find′), any fish that has rounded scales and lobed fins, as the coelacanth. Also called **lobe′fin′.**

lo·bel·ia (lō bēl′yə), *n.* any herbaceous or woody plant of the genus *Lobelia,* having long clusters of blue, red, yellow, or white flowers. Cf. **lobelia family.** [1730–40; < NL; named after Matthias de *Lobel* (1538–1616), Flemish botanist, physician to James I of England; see -IA]

lo·be·li·a·ceous (lō bē′lē ā′shəs), *adj.* belonging to the plant family Lobeliaceae. Cf. **lobelia family.** [1820–30; < NL *Lobeliace(ae)* (see LOBELIA, -ACEAE) + -OUS]

lobel′ia fam′ily, the plant family Lobeliaceae (sometimes considered a subfamily, Lobelioideae, of the Campanulaceae, or bellflower family), typified by usually herbaceous plants having milky sap, simple alternate leaves, irregular two-lipped flowers, and fruit in the form of a capsule or berry, and including the cardinal flower, Indian tobacco, and lobelia.

lo·be·line (lō′bə lēn′, -lin), *n. Pharm.* a crystalline, poisonous alkaloid, $C_{22}H_{27}NO_2$, obtained by extraction from lobelia: used chiefly in the form of its sulfate or hydrochloride as a respiratory stimulant and, because of its nicotinelike pharmacological action, as an agent to discourage tobacco smoking. [1835–45; LOBEL(IA) + -INE[2]]

lo·bi (lō′bī), *n.* pl. of **lobus.**

Lo·bi·to (lo͞o bē′to͞o), *n.* a seaport in W Angola. 65,000.

lob·lol·ly (lob′lol′ē), *n., pl.* **-lies.** **1.** *South Midland and Southern U.S.* a mire; mudhole. **2.** a thick gruel. [1590–1600; cf. dial. (Yorkshire) *lob* (of porridge) to bubble while boiling; second element, as in LOBSCOUSE, is obscure]

lob′lolly bay′, an evergreen tree, *Gordonia lasianthus,* of the tea family, having fragrant, long-stalked white flowers and egg-shaped fruit. [1720–30]

lob′lolly boy′, *Obs.* an assistant to the surgeon on board a ship. [1740–50]

lob′lolly pine′, **1.** a coniferous tree, *Pinus taeda,* of the southeastern U.S., having bundles of stout often twisted needles and blackish-gray bark. **2.** the wood of this tree, used for timber and pulpwood. [1750–60, *Amer.*]

lo·bo (lō′bō), *n., pl.* **-bos.** the gray or timber wolf of the western U.S. [1830–40; < Sp < L *lupus* wolf]

lo·bo·lo (lō′bə lə), *n., pl.* **-los.** a bride price, typically of cattle, paid to a bride's father among Bantu-speaking tribes of southern Africa. Also, **lo′bo·la.** [1815–25; < Zulu (*ili*)*lobolo,* (*i*)*lobolo* (with implosive *b*), or a cognate Nguni word]

lo·bose (lō′bōs), *adj. Zool.* having broad, thick pseudopodia, as certain ameboid protozoans. [1880–85; < NL *lobōsus.* See LOBE, -OSE]

lo·bot·o·mize (lə bot′ə mīz′, lō-), *v.t.,* **-mized, -miz·ing.** **1.** to perform a lobotomy on. **2.** to make (someone or something) abnormally tranquil or sluggish. Also, *esp. Brit.,* **lo·bot′o·mise′.** [1940–45; LOBOTOM(Y) + -IZE] —**lo·bot′o·mist,** *n.* —**lo·bot′o·mi·za′tion,** *n.*

lo·bot·o·mized (lə bot′ə mīzd′, lō-), *adj.* **1.** *Surg.* having undergone a lobotomy. **2.** stupefied; benumbed. [1940–45; LOBOTOMIZE + -ED[2]]

lo·bot·o·my (lə bot′ə mē, lō-), *n., pl.* **-mies.** *Surg.* **1.** the operation of cutting into a lobe, as of the brain or the lung. **2.** See **prefrontal lobotomy.**

lob·scouse (lob′skous), *n.* a stew of meat, potatoes, onions, ship biscuit, etc. Also, **lob·scourse** (lob′skôrs, -skōrs). [1700–10; cf. LOBLOLLY; Norw *lapskaus,* Dan *labskovs,* G *labskaus* all ult. < E]

lob·ster (lob′stər), *n., pl.* (*esp. collectively*) **-ster,** (*esp. referring to two or more kinds or species*) **-sters.** **1.** any of various large, edible, marine, usually dull-green, stalk-eyed decapod crustaceans of the family Homaridae, esp. of the genus *Homarus,* having large, asymmetrical pincers on the first pair of legs, one used for crushing and the other for cutting and tearing: the shell turns bright red when cooked. **2.** See **spiny lobster.** **3.** any of various similar crustaceans, as certain crayfishes. **4.** the edible meat of these animals. [bef. 1000; ME *lopster,* OE *loppestre* lit., spidery creature (*loppe* spider (see LOB[1]) + *-stre* -STER); cf. LOP[1]]

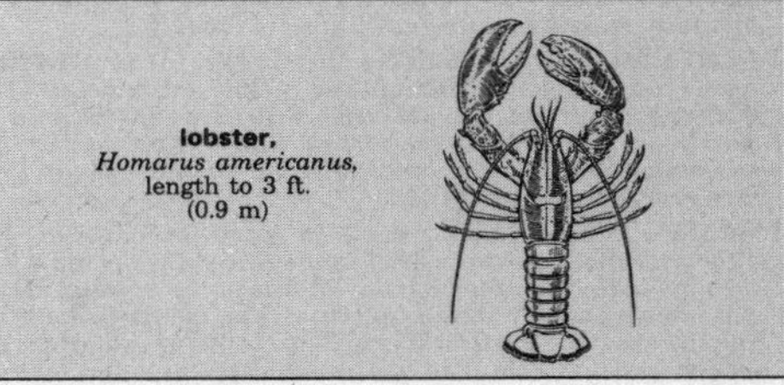
lobster, *Homarus americanus,* length to 3 ft. (0.9 m)

lob·ster·back (lob′stər bak′), *n.* (esp. during the American Revolution) redcoat. [LOBSTER + BACK[1]; in reference to the red color of cooked lobsters]

lob·ster·ing (lob′stər ing), *n.* the act, process, or business of capturing lobsters. [1880–85; LOBSTER + -ING[1]]

lob·ster·man (lob′stər mən), *n., pl.* **-men.** a person who traps lobsters. [1880–85; LOBSTER + -MAN]
—**Usage.** See **-man.**

lob′ster New′burg, (*sometimes l.c.*) lobster cooked in a thick seasoned cream sauce made with sherry or brandy. Also, **lob′ster New′burgh.** Also called **lob′ster à la New′burg, lob′ster à la New′burgh.** [1910–15; *Newburg* is unexplained]

lob′ster pot′, a trap for catching lobsters, typically a box made of wooden slats with a funnellike entrance to the bait. Also called **lob′ster trap′.** [1755–65]

lob′ster roll′, lobster salad served on a frankfurter roll or the like.

lob′ster shift′, *Informal.* **1.** Also called **lob′ster trick′.** dogwatch (def. 2). **2.** See **graveyard shift.**

lob′ster-tail hel′met (lob′stər tāl′), *Armor.* a burgonet fitted with a long, articulated tail of lames for protecting the nape of the neck, worn by cavalry in the 17th century.

lob′ster ther′midor, a dish of cooked lobster meat placed back in the shell with a cream sauce, sprinkled with grated cheese and melted butter, and browned in the oven. Also, **lob′ster Ther′midor.** [1930–35; allegedly named by Napoleon after the month it was first served to him; see THERMIDOR]

lob·stick (lob′stik′), *n. Canadian.* lopstick.

lob·tail (lob′tāl′), *v.i.* (of a whale) to slap the flukes against the surface of the water. [1865–70 (as ger.); appar. LOB[1] in sense "to move heavily" + TAIL[1]]

lob·u·lar (lob′yə lər), *adj.* composed of, having the form of, or pertaining to lobules or small lobes. [1815–25; LOBULE + -AR[1]]

lob′ular pump′, a blower or pump displacing air or liquid by means of rotors having meshing lobes that act as a seal at their place of mesh. Also called **gear pump.**

lob·u·late (lob′yə lit, -lāt′), *adj.* consisting of, divided into, or having lobes. Also, **lob′u·lat′ed.** [1860–65; LOBULE + -ATE[1]] —**lob′u·la′tion,** *n.*

lob·ule (lob′yo͞ol), *n.* **1.** a small lobe. **2.** a subdivision of a lobe. [1675–85; < NL *lobulus.* See LOBE, -ULE]

lob·u·lus (lob′yə ləs), *n., pl.* **-li** (-lī′). *Anat.* a lobule. [1725–35; < NL; see LOBULE]

lo·bus (lō′bəs), *n., pl.* **-bi** (-bī). *Anat.* a lobe. [< NL; see LOBE]

lob·worm (lob′wûrm′), *n.* the lugworm. Also called **lob.** [1645–55; dial. *lob,* earlier *lobbe* orig., something pendulous (see LOB[1]) + WORM]

loc., locative.

lo·ca (lō′kə), *n.* a pl. of **locus.**

lo·cal (lō′kəl), *adj.* **1.** pertaining to or characterized by place or position in space; spatial. **2.** pertaining to, characteristic of, or restricted to a particular place or particular places: *a local custom.* **3.** pertaining to a city, town, or small district rather than an entire state or country: *local transportation.* **4.** stopping at most or all stations: *a local train.* **5.** pertaining to or affecting a particular part or particular parts, as of a physical system or organism: *a local disease.* **6.** *Med.* (of anesthesia or an anesthetic) affecting only a particular part or area of the body, without concomitant loss of consciousness, as distinguished from general anesthesia. —*n.* **7.** a local train, bus, etc. **8.** a newspaper item of local interest. **9.** a local branch of a union, fraternity, etc. **10.** a local anesthetic. **11.** Often, **locals. a.** a local person or resident: *primarily of interest to locals.* **b.** a local athletic team: *the locals versus the state champions.* **12.** stamp (def. 22). **13.** *Brit. Informal.* a neighborhood pub. —*v.i.* **14.** *Informal.* to travel by or take a local train or the like. [1400–50; late ME < LL *locālis.* See LOCUS, -AL[1]] —**lo′cal·ness,** *n.*

lo-cal (lō′kal′, -kal′), *adj.* low-cal.

lo′cal ar′ea net′work, **1.** a system for linking private telecommunications equipment, as in a building or cluster of buildings. **2.** *Computers.* a system for linking

CONCISE PRONUNCIATION KEY: act, cāpe, dâre, pärt; set, ēqual; *if,* īce; ox, ōver, ôrder, oil, bo͝ok, bo͞ot, out; up, ûrge; child; sing; shoe; thin, that; zh as in *treasure.* ə = *a* as in *alone, e* as in *system, i* as in *easily, o* as in *gallop, u* as in *circus;* ᵊ as in *fire* (fīᵊr), *hour* (ouᵊr). l and n can serve as syllabic consonants, as in *cradle* (krād′l), and *button* (but′n). See the full key inside the front cover.

a number of microcomputers, terminals, work stations, etc. with each other or with a mainframe computer in order to share data, printers, information, programs, disks, etc.; usually confined to one office or building. Cf. **network** (def. 6). Also, **LAN.**

lo′cal col′or, **1.** distinctive, sometimes picturesque characteristics or peculiarities of a place or period as represented in literature or drama, or as observed in reality. **2.** *Fine Arts.* the natural color of a particular object as it appears in normal light. [1715–25]

lo•cal-con•tent (lō′kəl kon′tent), *adj.* of or pertaining to the number or percentage of the components of a product, as an automobile, that are manufactured in a specific country: *Local-content laws say 90 percent of the components of the car must be made in the U.S. or import restrictions will apply.*

lo•cale (lō kal′, -käl′), *n.* **1.** a place or locality, esp. with reference to events or circumstances connected with it: *to move to a warmer locale.* **2.** the scene or setting, as of a novel, play, or motion picture: *The locale is a small Kansas town just before World War I.* [1765–75; alter. of earlier *local* < F: n. use of the adj. See LOCAL] —**Syn. 1.** location, site, spot.

lo′cal gov′ernment, **1.** the administration of the civic affairs of a city, town, or district by its inhabitants rather than by the state or country at large. **2.** the governing body of a town or district. [1835–45]

Lo′cal Group′, *Astron.* the group of galaxies, at least 25 of which are known, that includes the Milky Way. [1915–20]

lo•cal•ism (lō′kə liz′əm), *n.* **1.** a word, phrase, pronunciation, or manner of speaking that is peculiar to one locality. **2.** a local custom. **3.** excessive devotion to and promotion of the interests of a particular locality; sectionalism. **4.** attachment to a particular locality. [1815–25; LOCAL + -ISM] —**lo′cal•ist,** *n.* —**lo′cal•is′tic,** *adj.*

lo•cal•ite (lō′kə līt′), *n.* one who lives in a particular locality. [1950–55; LOCAL + -ITE[1]]

lo•cal•i•ty (lō kal′i tē), *n., pl.* **-ties. 1.** a place, spot, or district, with or without reference to things or persons in it or to occurrences there: *They moved to another locality.* **2.** the state or fact of being local or having a location: *the locality that every material object must have.* [1620–30; < LL *locālitās.* See LOCAL, -ITY]

lo•cal•ize (lō′kə līz′), *v.,* **-ized, -iz•ing.** —*v.t.* **1.** to make local; fix in, or assign or restrict to, a particular place, locality, etc. —*v.i.* **2.** to gather, collect, or concentrate in one locality. Also, *esp. Brit.,* **lo′cal•ise′.** [1785–95; LOCAL + -IZE] —**lo′cal•iz′a•ble,** *adj.* —**lo′cal•i•za′tion,** *n.* —**lo′cal•iz′er,** *n.*

lo•cal•ly (lō′kə lē), *adv.* **1.** in a particular place, area, location, etc. **2.** with regard to place. **3.** in a local area; nearby: *Not much interest is taken in the chess tournament locally.* [1400–50; late ME *localliche.* See LOCAL, -LY]

lo′cally com′pact space′, *Math.* a topological space in which each point has a neighborhood that is compact.

lo′cally Euclid′ean space′, *Math.* a topological space in which each point has a neighborhood that is homeomorphic to an open set in a Euclidean space of specified dimension.

lo′cally fi′nite set′, *Math.* a collection of sets in a topological space in which each point of the space has a neighborhood that intersects a finite number of sets of the collection.

lo′cal max′imum, *Math.* maximum (def. 4a).

lo′cal min′imum, *Math.* minimum (def. 5a).

lo′cal op′tion, a right of choice exercised by a minor political division, as a county, esp. as to allowing the sale of liquor. [1875–80]

lo′cal preach′er, **1.** (in early Methodism) a layperson appointed to supervise the congregation and conduct services between visits of a circuit rider. **2.** (in the southern U.S.) a lay preacher. [1765–75]

lo′cal stamp′, stamp (def. 22).

lo′cal stand′ard of rest′, a frame of reference for a portion of the universe in which the mean motion of nearby stars is zero.

lo′cal time′, the time based on the meridian through a specific place, as a city, in contrast to that of the time zone within which the place is located; the time in a specific place as compared to that of another place to the east or west. [1825–35]

lo′cal wind′ (wind), one of a number of winds that are influenced predominantly by the topographic features of a relatively small region.

Lo•car•no (*It.* lô kär′nô), *n.* a town in S Switzerland, on Lake Maggiore: Locarno Pact 1925. 15,300.

CONCISE ETYMOLOGY KEY: <, descended or borrowed from; >, whence; b., blend of, blended; c., cognate with; cf., compare; deriv., derivative; equiv., equivalent; imit., imitative; obl., oblique; r., replacing; s., stem; sp., spelling, spelled; resp., respelling, respelled; trans., translation; ?, origin unknown; *, unattested; ‡, probably earlier than. See the full key inside the front cover.

lo•cate (lō′kāt, lō kāt′), *v.,* **-cat•ed, -cat•ing.** —*v.t.* **1.** to identify or discover the place or location of: *to locate the bullet wound.* **2.** to set, fix, or establish in a position, situation, or locality; place; settle: *to locate our European office in Paris.* **3.** to assign or ascribe a particular location to (something), as by knowledge or opinion: *Some scholars locate the Garden of Eden in Babylonia.* **4.** to survey and enter a claim to a tract of land; take possession of land. —*v.i.* **5.** to establish one's business or residence in a place; settle. [1645–55, *Amer.;* < L *locātus,* ptp. of *locāre* to put in a given position, place; see LOCUS, -ATE[1]] —**lo•cat′a•ble,** *adj.* —**lo′cat•er,** *n.*

lo•ca•tion (lō kā′shən), *n.* **1.** a place of settlement, activity, or residence: *This town is a good location for a young doctor.* **2.** a place or situation occupied: *a house in a fine location.* **3.** a tract of land of designated situation or limits: *a mining location.* **4.** *Motion Pictures.* a place outside of the studio that is used for filming a movie, scene, etc. **5.** *Computers.* any position on a register or memory device capable of storing one machine word. **6.** the act of locating; state of being located. **7.** *Civil Law.* a letting or renting. **8. on location,** *Motion Pictures.* engaged in filming at a place away from the studio, esp. one that is or is like the setting of the screenplay: *on location in Rome.* [1585–95; < L *locātiōn-* (s. of *locātiō*) a placing. See LOCATE, -ION] —**lo•ca′tion•al,** *adj.* —**lo•ca′tion•al•ly,** *adv.*

loc•a•tive (lok′ə tiv), *Gram.* —*adj.* **1.** (in certain inflected languages) noting a case whose distinctive function is to indicate place in or at which, as Latin *domī* "at home." —*n.* **2.** the locative case. **3.** a word in that case. [1795–1805; LOCATE + -IVE, on the model of *vocative*]

lo•ca•tor (lō′kā tər, lō kā′tər), *n.* a person who determines or establishes the boundaries of land or a mining claim. [1600–10; < L *locātor* a contractor, lessor, equiv. to *locā(re)* (see LOCATE) + *-tor* -TOR]

loc. cit. (lok′ sit′), in the place cited. [< L *locō citātō*]

loch (lok, loKH), *n. Scot.* **1.** a lake. **2.** a partially landlocked or protected bay; a narrow arm of the sea. [1350–1400; ME (Scots) *louch, locht* < ScotGael *loch,* OIr *loch* lake, c. L *lacus,* OE *lagu;* see LAKE[1], LOUGH]

Loch•a•ber ax′ (lo KHä′bəR; *Eng.* lo kä′bər), a Scottish battle-ax of the 16th century, having a tall, cleaverlike blade with a hook at its upper end. [1610–20; named after *Lochaber,* Scotland]

loche (lōch), *n.* the North American burbot. [1665–75; < CanF, F: loach]

Loch•earn (lok′ərn), *n.* a city in N Maryland, near Baltimore. 26,908.

lo•chi•a (lō′kē ə, lok′ē ə), *n., pl.* **-chi•a.** *Med.* the liquid discharge from the uterus after childbirth. [1675–85; < NL < Gk, n. use of neut. pl. of *lóchios* of childbirth, equiv. to *lóch(os)* childbirth (akin to *léchesthai* to lie down; see LIE[2]) + *-ios* adj. suffix] —**lo′chi•al,** *adj.*

Loch•in•var (lok′in vär′, loKH′-), *n.* **1.** the hero of a ballad included in the narrative poem *Marmion* (1808) by Sir Walter Scott. **2.** a romantic suitor.

Loch Ness (lok′ nes′, loKH′), a lake in NW Scotland, near Inverness. 23 mi. (37 km) long.

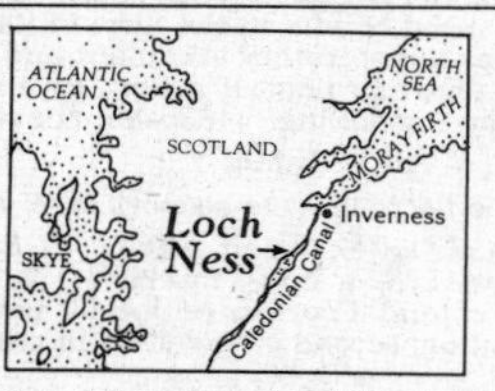

Loch′ Ness′ mon′ster, a large aquatic animal resembling a serpent or a plesiosaurlike reptile, reported to have been seen in the waters of Loch Ness, Scotland, but not proved to exist. [1930–35]

Loch′ Ra′ven (lok), a town in central Maryland, near Baltimore. 25,000.

loch•us (lok′əs), *n., pl.* **loch•i** (lok′ī). (in ancient Greece) a subdivision of an army. [1825–35; < Gk *lóchos* lit., ambush, place for lying in wait, hence, men forming an ambush; cf. LOCHIA]

lo•ci (lō′sī, -kē, -kī), *n.* pl. of **locus.**

lock[1] (lok), *n.* **1.** a device for securing a door, gate, lid, drawer, or the like in position when closed, consisting of a bolt or system of bolts propelled and withdrawn by a mechanism operated by a key, dial, etc. **2.** a contrivance for fastening or securing something. **3.** (in a firearm) **a.** the mechanism that explodes the charge; gunlock. **b.** safety (def. 4). **4.** any device or part for stopping temporarily the motion of a mechanism. **5.** an enclosed chamber in a canal, dam, etc., with gates at each end, for raising or lowering vessels from one level to another by admitting or releasing water. **6.** an air lock or decompression chamber. **7.** complete and unchallenged control; an unbreakable hold: *The congresswoman has a lock on the senatorial nomination.* **8.** *Slang.* someone or something certain of success; sure thing: *He's a lock to win the championship.* **9.** *Wrestling.* any of various holds, esp. a hold secured on the arm, leg, or head: *leg lock.* **10.** *Horol.* (in an escapement) the overlap between a tooth of an escape wheel and the surface of the pallet locking it. **11.** *Metalworking.* a projection or recession in the mating face of a forging die. **12. lock, stock, and barrel,** completely; entirely; including every part, item, or facet, no matter how small or insignificant: *We bought the whole business, lock, stock, and barrel.* **13. under lock and key,** securely locked up: *The documents were under lock and key.* —*v.t.* **14.** to fasten or secure (a door, window, building, etc.) by the operation of a lock or locks. **15.** to shut in a place fastened by a lock or locks, as for security or restraint. **16.** to make fast or immovable by or as if by a lock: *He locked the steering wheel on his car.* **17.** to make fast or immovable, as by engaging parts: *to lock the wheels of a wagon.* **18.** to join or unite firmly by interlinking or intertwining: *to lock arms.* **19.** to hold fast in an embrace: *She was locked in his arms.* **20.** to move (a ship) by means of a lock or locks, as in a canal (often fol. by *through, in, out, down,* or *up*). **21.** to furnish with locks, as a canal. —*v.i.* **22.** to become locked: *This door locks with a key.* **23.** to become fastened, fixed, or interlocked: *gears that lock into place.* **24.** to go or pass by means of a lock or locks, as a vessel. **25.** to construct locks in waterways. **26. lock horns,** to come into conflict; clash: *to lock horns with a political opponent.* **27. lock in, a.** to commit unalterably: *to lock in the nomination of the party's candidates.* **b.** (of an investor) to be unable or unwilling to sell or shift securities. **28. lock off,** to enclose (a waterway) with a lock. **29. lock on,** to track or follow a target or object automatically by radar or other electronic means. **30. lock out, a.** to keep out by or as if by a lock. **b.** to subject (employees) to a lockout. **31. lock up, a.** to imprison for a crime. **b.** *Print.* to make (type) immovable in a chase by securing the quoins. **c.** to fasten or secure with a lock or locks. **d.** to lock the doors of a house, automobile, etc. **e.** to fasten or fix firmly, as by engaging parts. [bef. 900; ME; OE *loc* fastening, bar; c. MLG *lok,* OHG *loh,* ON *lok* a cover, lid, Goth *-luk* in *usluk* opening; akin to OE *lūcan* to shut] —**lock′less,** *adj.*

lock[2] (lok), *n.* **1.** a tress, curl, or ringlet of hair. **2. locks, a.** the hair of the head. **b.** short wool of inferior quality, as that obtained in small clumps from the legs. **3.** a small tuft or portion of wool, cotton, flax, etc. [bef. 900; ME *locke,* OE *locc* lock of hair, c. ON *lokkr,* D *lok* curl, G *Locke*]

lock•a•ble (lok′ə bəl), *adj.* capable of being locked; fitted with a lock: *The car has a lockable glove compartment.* [1890–95; LOCK[1] + -ABLE] —**lock′a•bil′i•ty,** *n.*

lock•age (lok′ij), *n.* **1.** the construction, use, or operation of locks, as in a canal or stream. **2.** passage through a lock or locks. **3.** a toll paid for such passage. [1670–80; LOCK[1] + -AGE]

lock′ bay′, a broadened section of a canal before the gates of a lock. [1870–75]

lock•box (lok′boks′), *n.* **1.** a strongbox. **2.** a rented post-office box equipped with a lock. **3.** Also called **lockout box.** *Television.* a closed box, usually fitted with a lock, containing electronic equipment to unscramble cable television pictures for subscribers only: used esp. to prevent children from watching programs with explicit sexual content. [1870–75, *Amer.;* LOCK[1] + BOX[1]]

lock•down (lok′doun′), *n.* the confining of prisoners to their cells, as following a riot or other disturbance. [1970–75; LOCK[1] + *-down,* prob. extracted from nouns formed from phrasal verbs, such as CRACKDOWN, SHUTDOWN, etc.]

Locke (lok), *n.* **1. Al•ain Le•Roy** (al′in lə roi′, lē′roi), 1886–1954, U.S. educator and author. **2. David Ross** (*"Petroleum V. Nasby"*), 1833–88, U.S. humorist and journalist. **3. John,** 1632–1704, English philosopher.

Locke•an (lok′ē ən), *n.* **1.** an adherent of the philosophy of Locke. —*adj.* **2.** of, pertaining to, or resembling the philosophy of Locke. [J. LOCKE + -AN] —**Lock′e•an•ism, Lock′i•an•ism,** *n.*

locked′ bow′els, *Chiefly South Midland and Southern U.S.* **1.** constipation. **2.** *Older Use.* appendicitis.

lock•er (lok′ər), *n.* **1.** a chest, drawer, compartment, closet, or the like, that may be locked, esp. one at a gymnasium, school, etc. for storage and safekeeping of clothing and valuables. **2.** *Naut.* a chest or compartment in which to stow things. **3.** a refrigerated compartment, as in a locker plant, that may be rented for storing frozen foods. **4.** a person or thing that locks. [1375–1425; late ME *loker.* See LOCK[1], -ER[1]]

Lock•er-Lamp•son (lok′ər lam′sən), *n.* **Frederick** (*Frederick Locker*), 1821–95, English poet.

lock′er plant′, an establishment for storing food under refrigeration, containing lockers for renting to individual users.

lock′er room′, a room containing lockers, as in a gymnasium, factory, or school, for changing clothes and for the storage and safekeeping of personal belongings. [1890–95]

lock•er-room (lok′ər rōōm′, -rŏŏm′), *adj.* of, characteristic of, or suitable to conversation in a locker room; earthy or sexually explicit: *locker-room humor.* [1945–50]

lock•et (lok′it), *n.* **1.** a small case for a miniature portrait, a lock of hair, or other keepsake, usually worn on a necklace. **2.** the uppermost mount of a scabbard. [1325–75; ME *lokat* cross-bar in a framework < AF *loquet,* dim. of *loc* latch < ME. See LOCK[1], -ET]

Lock•hart (lok′härt, lok′ərt), *n.* **John Gibson,** 1794–1854, Scottish biographer and novelist.

lock-in (lok′in′), *n.* **1.** an act or instance of becoming unalterable, unmovable, or rigid. **2.** commitment, binding, or restriction. [1965–70; n. use of v. phrase *lock in*]

lock′ing piece′, *Horol.* (in a striking train) a hooked part, rising and falling on a locking plate and arresting the rotation of the plate after the proper number of strokes. [1810–20]

lock′ing plate′, *Horol.* a narrow wheel geared to a striking train or other mechanism and having a notched rim engaging with another mechanism permitting it to rotate through a specific arc. [1875–80]

lock′ing pli′ers, pliers whose jaws are connected at a sliding pivot, permitting them to be temporarily locked in a fixed position for ease in grasping and turning nuts. See illus. under **plier.**

lock•jaw (lok′jô′), *n. Pathol.* tetanus in which the jaws become firmly locked together; trismus. [1795–1805; LOCK[1] + JAW]

lock′ nut′, *Mach.* **1.** a nut specially constructed to prevent its coming loose, usually having a means of providing extra friction between itself and the screw. **2.**

Also called **jam nut.** a thin supplementary nut screwed down upon a regular nut to prevent its loosening. See illus. under **nut.** Also, **lock′nut′.** [1860–65]

lock•out (lok′out′), *n.* the temporary closing of a business or the refusal by an employer to allow employees to come to work until they accept the employer's terms. [1850–55; n. use of v. phrase *lock out*]

lock′out box′, *Television.* lockbox (def. 3).

Lock•port (lok′pôrt′, -pōrt′), *n.* a city in W New York, on the New York State Barge Canal. 24,844.

lock′ rail′, the rail of a door that meets the shutting stile at the level of the lock. [1815–25]

lock•ram (lok′rəm), *n. Obs.* a rough-textured linen cloth. [1250–1300; ME *lokeram, lokerham,* after *Locronan,* village in Brittany where the cloth was made; perh. conformed to BUCKRAM]

lock′ seam′, a joint between two pieces of sheet metal, made by folding up the overlapping edges against each other, then folding them over in the same direction a number of times. [1955–60]

lock•set (lok′set′), *n.* an assembly of parts making up a complete locking system, esp. one used on a door, including knobs, plates, and a lock mechanism. [LOCK[1] + SET]

lock•smith (lok′smith′), *n.* a person who makes or repairs locks and keys. [1200–50; ME *loksmith* (first attested as surname). See LOCK[1], SMITH] **—lock′smith′er•y,** *n.* **—lock′smith′ing,** *n.*

lock•step (lok′step′), *n.* **1.** a way of marching in very close file, in which the leg of each person moves with and closely behind the corresponding leg of the person ahead. **2.** a rigidly inflexible pattern or process. *—adj.* **3.** rigidly inflexible: *a lockstep educational curriculum.* [1795–1805; LOCK[1] + STEP]

lock′ stitch′, a sewing-machine stitch in which two threads are locked together at small intervals. [1860–65]

lock•up (lok′up′), *n.* **1.** a jail, esp. a local one for temporary detention. **2.** the act of locking up or the state of being locked up. **3.** a temporary imprisonment or detention, as of suspects or prisoners. **4.** a stock that has been held by an individual as a long-term investment, or that a brokerage firm is required by a regulation to hold for a certain period of time before it can be sold. **5.** any investment or credit instrument, as a renewed loan, in which capital is tied up for a long time. **6.** *Print.* **a.** the entire body of type and cuts locked up in a chase preparatory to printing or platemaking. **b.** the act or procedure of locking up type and cuts in a chase. **7.** *Auto.* a sudden stopping of the rotation of a wheel. **8.** *Brit. Informal.* a rented locker, storage space, or garage. [1760–70; n. use of v. phrase *lock up*]

lock′ wash′er, a washer placed under a nut on a bolt or screw, so made as to prevent the nut from shaking loose.

Lock•wood (lok′wo͝od′), *n.* **Bel•va Ann Bennett** (bel′və), 1830–1917, U.S. lawyer and women's-rights activist.

Lock•yer (lok′yər), *n.* **Sir Joseph Norman,** 1836–1920, English astronomer and author.

lo•co (lō′kō), *n., pl.* **-cos,** *v.,* **-coed, -co•ing,** *adj.* *—n.* **1.** locoweed. **2.** *Slang.* an insane person; maniac. **3.** *Vet. Pathol.* locoism. *—v.t.* **4.** to poison with locoweed. **5.** *Slang.* to cause to be insane or crazy. *—adj.* **6.** *Slang.* out of one's mind; insane; crazy. [1835–45, *Amer.*; < Sp: insane]

lo•co ci•ta•to (lō′kō ki tä′tō; *Eng.* lō′kō si tā′tō, si-tä′tō). *Latin.* See **loc. cit.**

lo′co disease′, *Vet. Pathol.* locoism. [1885–90]

Lo•co•fo•co (lō′kō fō′kō), *n.* **1.** (*sometimes l.c.*) a member of the radical faction of the New York City Democrats, organized in 1835 to oppose the conservative members of the party. **2.** (*l.c.*) a friction match or cigar developed in the 19th century, ignited by rubbing against any hard, dry surface. [special use of *locofoco* (cigar), self-lighting, rhyming compound appar. based on LOCO(MOTIVE), taken to mean self-moving; *-foco,* alter. of It *fuoco* fire < L *focus* fireplace]

Lo•co•fo•co•ism (lō′kō fō′kō iz′əm), *n.* (*sometimes l.c.*) the doctrines of the Locofocos. [1830–40, *Amer.*; LOCOFOCO + -ISM]

lo•co•ism (lō′kō iz′əm), *n. Vet. Pathol.* a disease chiefly of sheep, horses, and cattle, caused by the eating of locoweed and characterized by weakness, impaired vision, irregular behavior, and paralysis. Also called **loco, loco disease.** [1895–1900, *Amer.*; LOCO + -ISM]

lo•co•man (lō′kō mən), *n., pl.* **-men.** *Brit. Informal.* a locomotive engine driver. [1940–45; LOCO(MOTIVE) + -MAN]
—Usage. See **-man.**

lo•co•mo•bile (lō′kə mō′bəl, -bēl), *adj.* **1.** automotive; self-propelling. *—n.* **2.** a self-propelled vehicle, traction engine, or the like. [1885–90; see LOCOMOTIVE, MOBILE] **—lo•co•mo•bil•i•ty** (lō′kə mō bil′i tē), *n.*

lo•co•mote (lō′kə mōt′), *v.i.,* **-mot•ed, -mot•ing.** to move about, esp. under one's own power. [1825–35; back formation from LOCOMOTION]

lo•co•mo•tion (lō′kə mō′shən), *n.* the act or power of moving from place to place. [1640–50; see LOCOMOTIVE, MOTION]

lo•co•mo•tive (lō′kə mō′tiv), *n.* **1.** a self-propelled, vehicular engine, powered by steam, a diesel, or electricity, for pulling or, sometimes, pushing a train or individual railroad cars. **2.** an organized group cheer, usually led by a cheerleader, as at a football or basketball game, that begins slowly and progressively increases in speed in such a way as to suggest a steam locomotive. **3.** *Archaic.* any self-propelled vehicle. *—adj.* **4.** of or pertaining to locomotives. **5.** of, pertaining to, or aiding in locomotion or movement from place to place: *the locomotive powers of most animals.* **6.** moving or traveling by means of its own mechanism or powers. **7.** serving to produce such movement; adapted for or used in locomotion: *locomotive organs.* **8.** having the power of locomotion: *an animal that is locomotive at birth.* [1605–15; < L *locō,* abl. of *locus* place + MOTIVE (adj.); cf. ML *in locō movērī* to change position] **—lo′co•mo′tive•ly,** *adv.* **—lo′co•mo′tive•ness, lo′co•mo•tiv′i•ty,** *n.*

locomo′tive engineer′, engineer (def. 3). [1885–90]

lo•co•mo•tor (lō′kə mō′tər), *adj.* **1.** Also, **lo′co•mo′•to•ry.** of, pertaining to, or affecting locomotion. *—n.* **2.** a person or thing that is capable of locomotion. [1815–25; see LOCOMOTIVE, MOTOR]

locomo′tor atax′ia, *Pathol.* See **tabes dorsalis.** [1875–80]

lo•co pri•mo ci•ta•to (lō′kō PRē′mō ki tä′tō; *Eng.* lō′kō prī′mō sī tā′tō, prē′mō si tä′tō). *Latin.* See **loc. primo cit.**

lo•co su•pra ci•ta•to (lō′kō so͞o′PRä ki tä′tō; *Eng.* lō′kō so͞o′prə sī tā′tō, si tä′tō). *Latin.* See **l.s.c.**

lo•co•weed (lō′kō wēd′), *n.* any of various leguminous plants of the genera *Astragalus* and *Oxytropis,* of the southwestern U.S. and Mexico, causing locoism in sheep, horses, etc. [1875–80, *Amer.*; LOCO + WEED[1]]

loc. primo cit. (lok′ prī′mō sit′, prē′mō), in the place first cited. [< L *locō prīmō citātō*]

Lo•cris (lō′kris), *n.* either of two districts in the central part of ancient Greece. **—Lo′cri•an,** *n., adj.*

loc•u•lar (lok′yə lər), *adj. Biol.* having one or more locules. Also, **loc•u•late** (lok′yə lāt′, -lit). [1775–85; < NL *loculāris* kept in boxes. See LOCULUS, -AR[1]]

loc•ule (lok′yo͞ol), *n. Biol.* a small compartment or chamber, as the pollen-containing cavity within an anther. Also called **loculus.** [1885–90; < F < L *loculus;* see LOCULUS]

loc•u•li•cid•al (lok′yə lə sīd′l), *adj. Bot.* (of a capsule) splitting lengthwise so as to divide each locule into two parts. [1810–20; LOCUL(US) + -I- + -CIDAL] **—loc′u•li•cid′al•ly,** *adv.*

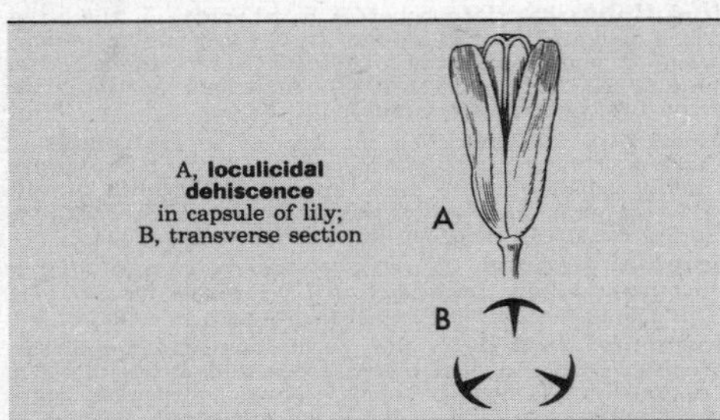

A, **loculicidal dehiscence** in capsule of lily; B, transverse section

loc•u•lus (lok′yə ləs), *n., pl.* **-li** (-lī′, -lē′). **1.** *Biol.* locule. **2.** *Eccles.* a compartment in an altar, in which relics are kept. **3.** a recess in an ancient catacomb or tomb, where a body or cinerary urn was placed. [1855–60; < NL, special use of L *loculus,* dim. of *locus* place; see LOCUS, -ULE]

lo•cum (lō′kəm), *n. Brit.* See **locum tenens.**

lo•cum te•nens (lō′kəm tē′nenz, ten′inz), *pl.* **lo•cum te•nen•tes** (lō′kəm tə nen′tēz). *Chiefly Brit.* a temporary substitute, esp. for a doctor or member of the clergy. Also called **locum.** [1635–45; < ML *locum tenēns* holding the place] **—lo•cum-te•nen•cy** (lō′kəm tē′nən-sē, -ten′ən-), *n.*

lo•cus (lō′kəs), *n., pl.* **-ci** (-sī, -kē, -kī), **-ca** (-kə). **1.** a place; locality. **2.** a center or source, as of activities or power: *locus of control.* **3.** *Math.* the set of all points, lines, or surfaces that satisfy a given requirement. **4.** *Genetics.* the chromosomal position of a gene as determined by its linear order relative to the other genes on that chromosome. [1525–35; < L; OL *stlocus* a place]

lo•cus clas•si•cus (lō′ko͞os kläs′si ko͞os′; *Eng.* lō′kəs klas′i kəs), *pl.* ***lo•ci clas•si•ci*** (lō′kē kläs′si kē′; *Eng.* lō′sī klas′ə sī′, lō′kī klas′i kī′). *Latin.* classical source: a passage commonly cited to illustrate or explain a subject or word.

lo•cus in quo (lō′ko͞os in kwō′; *Eng.* lō′kəs in kwō′), *Latin.* the place in which.

lo•cus si•gil•li (lō′ko͞os sē gēl′lē; *Eng.* lō′kəs si jil′ī), *pl.* ***lo•ci si•gil•li*** (lō′kē sē gēl′lē; *Eng.* lō′sī si jil′ī, lō′-kī). *Latin.* See **L.S.** (def. 3).

lo•cust (lō′kəst), *n.* **1.** Also called **acridid, short-horned grasshopper.** any of several grasshoppers of the family Acrididae, having short antennae and commonly migrating in swarms that strip the vegetation from large areas. **2.** any of various cicadas, as the seventeen-year locust. **3.** any of several North American trees belonging to the genus *Robinia,* of the legume family, esp. *R. pseudoacacia,* having pinnate leaves and clusters of fragrant white flowers. **4.** the durable wood of this tree. **5.** any of various other trees, as the carob and the honey locust. [1150–1200; ME < L *locusta* grasshopper] **—lo′cust•like′,** *adj.*

lo′cust bean′, **1.** carob. **2.** a seed of a carob pod. [1840–50]

lo′cust years′, *Brit.* years of economic hardship. [1948; coined by Winston Churchill (on the basis of the Bible verse Joel 2:25) to describe the years 1931–35 in Britain]

lo•cu•tion (lō kyo͞o′shən), *n.* **1.** a particular form of expression; a word, phrase, expression, or idiom, esp. as used by a particular person, group, etc. **2.** a style of speech or verbal expression; phraseology. [1400–50; late ME < L *locūtiōn-* (s. of *locūtiō*) speech, style of speech, equiv. to *locūt(us)* (ptp. of *loquī* to speak) + *-iōn-* -ION]
—Syn. 1. See **phrase.**

lo•cu•tion•ar•y (lō kyo͞o′shə ner′ē), *adj. Philos., Ling.* pertaining to the act of conveying semantic content in an utterance, considered as independent of the interaction between the speaker and the listener. Cf. **illocutionary, perlocutionary.** [1950–55; LOCUTION + -ARY]

lo•cu•to•ri•um (lō′kyo͞o tôr′ē əm, -tōr′-, lok′yo͞o-), *n., pl.* **-to•ri•a** (-tôr′ē ə, -tōr′-). parlor (def. 4). Also, **locutory.** [1765–75; Latinized form of LOCUTORY]

loc•u•to•ry (lok′yə tôr′ē, -tōr′ē), *n., pl.* **-ries.** locutorium. [1475–85; < ML *locūtōrium,* equiv. to *locū-,* base of *loquī* to speak + *-tōrium* -TORY[2]]

lode (lōd), *n.* **1.** a veinlike deposit, usually metalliferous. **2.** any body of ore set off from adjacent rock formations. **3.** a rich supply or source. **4.** *Brit.* a waterway or channel. [bef. 900; ME; OE *lād* way, course, carrying; c. ON *leith* way, route, OHG *leita* procession. See LOAD, LADE, LEAD[1]]

lo•den (lōd′n), *n.* **1.** a thick, heavily fulled, waterproof fabric, used in coats and jackets for cold climates. **2.** Also called **lo′den green′.** the deep olive-green color of this fabric. [1910–15; < G; OHG *lodo;* cf. OE *lotha* cloak, ON *lothi* fur cloak, *lothinn* shaggy]

lode•star (lōd′stär′), *n.* **1.** a star that shows the way. **2.** Polaris. **3.** something that serves as a guide or on which the attention is fixed. Also, **loadstar.** [1325–75; ME *loode sterre.* See LODE, STAR]

lode•stone (lōd′stōn′), *n.* **1.** a variety of magnetite that possesses magnetic polarity and attracts iron. **2.** a piece of this serving as a magnet. **3.** something that attracts strongly. Also, **loadstone.** [1505–15; LODE (in obs. sense "way, course") + STONE]

lodge (loj), *n., v.,* **lodged, lodg•ing.** *—n.* **1.** a small, makeshift or crude shelter or habitation, as of boughs, poles, skins, earth, or rough boards; cabin or hut. **2.** a house used as a temporary residence, as in the hunting season. **3.** a summer cottage. **4.** a house or cottage, as in a park or on an estate, occupied by a gatekeeper, caretaker, gardener, or other employee. **5.** a resort hotel, motel, or inn. **6.** the main building of a camp, resort hotel, or the like. **7.** the meeting place of a branch of certain fraternal organizations. **8.** the members composing the branch: *The lodge is planning a picnic.* **9.** any of various North American Indian dwellings, as a tepee or long house. Cf. **earth lodge. 10.** the Indians who live in such a dwelling or a family or unit of North American Indians. **11.** the home of a college head at Cambridge University, England. **12.** the den of an animal or group of animals, esp. beavers. *—v.i.* **13.** to have a habitation or quarters, esp. temporarily, as in a hotel, motel, or inn: *We lodged in a guest house.* **14.** to live in rented quarters in another's house: *He lodged with a local family during his college days.* **15.** to be fixed, implanted, or caught in a place or position; come to rest; stick: *The bullet lodged in his leg.* *—v.t.* **16.** to furnish with a habitation or quarters, esp. temporarily; accommodate: *Can you lodge us for the night?* **17.** to furnish with a room or rooms in one's house for payment; have as a lodger: *a boardinghouse that lodges oil workers.* **18.** to serve as a residence, shelter, or dwelling for; shelter: *The château will lodge the ambassador during his stay.* **19.** to put, store, or deposit, as in a place, for storage or keeping; stow: *to lodge one's valuables in a hotel safe.* **20.** to bring or send into a particular place or position. **21.** to house or contain: *The spinal canal lodges and protects the spinal cord.* **22.** to vest (power, authority, etc.). **23.** to put or bring (information, a complaint, etc.) before a court or other authority. **24.** to beat down or lay flat, as vegetation in a storm: *A sudden hail had lodged the crops.* **25.** to track (a deer) to its lair. [1175–1225; ME *logge* < OF *loge* < ML *laubia, lobia;* see LOBBY] **—lodge′a•ble,** *adj.*
—Syn. 8. club, association, society. **16.** house, quarter. **20.** place, set, plant, settle.

Lodge (loj), *n.* **1. Henry Cabot,** 1850–1924, U.S. public servant and author: senator 1893–1924. **2.** his grandson, **Henry Cabot, Jr.,** 1902–85, U.S. journalist, statesman, and diplomat. **3. Sir Oliver Joseph,** 1851–1940, English physicist and writer. **4. Thomas,** 1558?–1625, English poet and dramatist.

lodged (lojd), *adj. Heraldry.* (of a deer or the like) represented as lying down: *a stag lodged.* [1570–80; LODGE + ED[2]]

lodge′pole pine′ (loj′pōl′), **1.** a tall, narrow, slow-growing coniferous tree, *Pinus contorta,* of western North America, having egg-shaped cones that remain closed for years. **2.** the wood of this tree, used as timber. [1855–60, *Amer.*; LODGE + POLE[1]]

lodg•er (loj′ər), *n.* a person who lives in rented quarters in another's house; roomer. [1250–1300; ME *loger* tent-dweller. See LODGE, -ER[1]]

lodg•ing (loj′ing), *n.* **1.** accommodation in a house, esp. in rooms for rent: *to furnish board and lodging.* **2.** a temporary place to stay; temporary quarters. **3. lodgings, a.** a room or rooms rented for residence in another's house. **b.** *Brit.* the rooms of a university student who lives neither on campus nor at home. **4.** the act of lodging. [1350–1400; ME; see LODGE, -ING[1]]

lodg′ing house′, a house in which rooms are rented, esp. a house other than an inn or hotel; rooming house. [1760–70]

lodg′ing knee′, *Shipbuilding.* a knee reinforcing a hull horizontally, as at the ends of deck beams.

lodg•ment (loj′mənt), *n.* **1.** the act of lodging. **2.** the state of being lodged. **3.** something lodged or deposited. **4.** *Mil.* a position or foothold gained from an enemy, or an entrenchment made upon it. **5.** a lodging place; rooming house. **6.** accommodations; lodgings. Also, *esp. Brit.,* **lodge′ment.** [1590–1600; < MF *logement.* See LODGE, -MENT]

Lo•di (lō′dē *for 1;* lō′dī *for 2, 3*), *n.* **1.** a town in N Italy, SE of Milan: Napoleon's defeat of the Austrians

1796. 28,691. **2.** a city in central California, near Sacramento. 35,221. **3.** a city in NE New Jersey. 23,956.

lod·i·cule (lod′i kyo͞ol′), *n. Bot.* one of the specialized scales at the base of the ovary of certain grass flowers. [1860–65; < NL *lōdicula,* dim. of L *lōdix* (s. *lōdic-*) blanket, rug; see -ULE]

Łódź (lo͞oj, lodz; *Pol.* wo͞och), *n.* a city in central Poland, SW of Warsaw. 798,000. Russian, **Lodz** (lôts).

loe (lo͞o), *n., v.t., v.i.,* **loed, loe·ing.** *Scot.* love.

Loeb (lōb; *Ger.* lœb), *n.* **Jacques** (zhäk), 1859–1924, German physiologist and experimental biologist in the U.S.

Loef·fler (lef′lər), *n.* **Charles Martin Tor·nov** (tôr′-nof), 1861–1935, U.S. violinist and composer, born in France.

loel·ling·ite (lel′ing īt′), *n. Mineral.* löllingite.

lo·ess (lō′es, les, lus), *n.* a loamy deposit formed by wind, usually yellowish and calcareous, common in the Mississippi Valley and in Europe and Asia. [1825–35; < G *Löss* < Swiss G *lösch* loose, slack (*sch* taken as a dial. equivalent of G *s*), akin to G *lose* LOOSE] —**lo·ess′i·al, lo·ess′al,** *adj.*

Loes·ser (les′ər), *n.* **Frank (Henry),** 1910–69, U.S. composer and lyricist, esp. of musicals and film songs.

Loewe (lō), *n.* **Frederick,** 1904–88, U.S. composer, born in Austria.

Loe·wi (lō′ē; *Ger.* lœ′vē), *n.* **Ot·to** (ot′ō; *Ger.* ôt′ō), 1873–1961, German pharmacologist in the U.S.: Nobel prize for medicine 1936.

Loe·wy (lō′ē), *n.* **Raymond Fer·nand** (fər nand′), 1893–1986, U.S. industrial designer, born in France.

Löff·ler (lœf′lər), *n.* **Frie·drich Au·gust Jo·han·nes** (frē′drikh ou′go͝ost yō hä′nəs), 1852–1915, German bacteriologist.

Lofn (lô′vən), *n. Scand. Myth.* a goddess who aids those having trouble winning the affections of their beloveds. [< ON; cf. *lofa* to permit, promise]

Lo′fo·ten Is′lands (lō′fo͞ot′n), a group of islands NW of and belonging to Norway: rich fishing grounds. 63,365; 474 sq. mi. (1228 sq. km).

loft (lôft, loft), *n.* **1.** a room, storage area, or the like within a sloping roof; attic; garret. **2.** a gallery or upper level in a church, hall, etc., designed for a special purpose: *a choir loft.* **3.** a hayloft. **4.** an upper story of a business building, warehouse, or factory, typically consisting of open, unpartitioned floor area. **5.** such an upper story converted or adapted to any of various uses, as quarters for living, studios for artists or dancers, exhibition galleries, or theater space. **6.** Also called **loft′ bed′.** a balcony or platform built over a living area and used esp. for sleeping. **7.** *Chiefly Midland and Southern U.S.* an attic. **8.** *Golf.* **a.** the slope of the face of the head of a club backward from the vertical, tending to drive the ball upward. **b.** the act of lofting. **c.** a lofting stroke. **9.** the resiliency of fabric or yarn, esp. wool. **10.** the thickness of a fabric or of insulation used in a garment, as a down-filled jacket. —*v.t.* **11.** to hit or throw aloft: *He lofted a fly ball into center field.* **12.** *Golf.* **a.** to slant the face of (a club). **b.** to hit (a golf ball) into the air or over an obstacle. **c.** to clear (an obstacle) in this manner. **13.** to store in a loft. **14.** *Shipbuilding.* to form or describe (the lines of a hull) at full size, as in a mold loft; lay off. **15.** *Archaic.* to provide (a house, barn, etc.) with a loft. —*v.i.* **16.** to hit or throw something aloft, esp. a ball. **17.** to go high into the air when hit, as a ball. [bef. 1000; ME *lofte* (n.), late OE *loft* < ON *lopt* upper chamber or region, the air, sky. See LIFT] —**loft′less,** *adj.*

loft′ build′ing, a building of several floors with large areas of unobstructed space, originally rented out for light industrial purposes and now frequently converted to residential occupancy.

Loft·ing (lôf′ting, lof′-), *n.* **Hugh,** 1886–1947, U.S. author of books for children, born in England.

loft′ing i′ron, *Golf.* a club whose head has a sloped face, for lofting the ball. Also called **loft′er.** [1885–90]

lofts·man (lôfts′mən, lofts′-), *n., pl.* **-men.** *Shipbuilding.* a person who prepares molds and patterns. [1900–05; LOFT + 's[1] + MAN[1]]
—**Usage.** See **-man.**

loft·y (lôf′tē, lof′-), *adj.,* **loft·i·er, loft·i·est. 1.** extending high in the air; of imposing height; towering: *lofty mountains.* **2.** exalted in rank, dignity, or character; eminent. **3.** elevated in style, tone, or sentiment, as writings or speech. **4.** arrogantly or condescendingly superior in manner; haughty: *to treat someone in a lofty manner.* **5.** *Naut.* noting a rig of a sailing ship having extraordinarily high masts. **6.** (of fabric or yarn) thick and resilient. [1400–50; late ME; see LOFT, -Y[1]] —**loft′i·ly,** *adv.* —**loft′i·ness,** *n.*
—**Syn. 1.** elevated. See **high. 3.** sublime. **4.** supercilious. —**Ant. 2.** lowly. **4.** humble.

log[1] (lôg, log), *n., v.,* **logged, log·ging.** —*n.* **1.** a portion or length of the trunk or of a large limb of a felled tree. **2.** something inert, heavy, or not sentient. **3.** *Naut.* any of various devices for determining the speed of a ship, as a chip log or patent log. **4.** any of various records, made in rough or finished form, concerning a trip made by a ship or aircraft and dealing with particulars of navigation, weather, engine performance, discipline, and other pertinent details; logbook. **5.** *Motion Pictures.* an account describing or denoting each shot as it is taken, written down during production and referred to in editing the film. **6.** a register of the operation of a machine. **7.** Also called **well log.** a record kept during the drilling of a well, esp. of the geological formations penetrated. **8.** *Computers.* any of various chronological records made concerning the use of a computer system, the changes made to data, etc. **9.** *Radio and Television.* a written account of everything transmitted by a station or network. **10.** Also called **log of wood.** *Australian Slang.* a lazy, dull-witted person; fool. —*v.t.* **11.** to cut (trees) into logs: *to log pine trees for fuel.* **12.** to cut down the trees or timber on (land): *We logged the entire area in a week.* **13.** to enter in a log; compile; amass; keep a record of: *to log a day's events.* **14.** to make (a certain speed), as a ship or airplane: *We are logging 18 knots.* **15.** to travel for (a certain distance or a certain amount of time), according to the record of a log: *We logged 30 miles the first day. He has logged 10,000 hours flying time.* —*v.i.* **16.** to cut down trees and get out logs from the forest for timber: *to log for a living.* **17. log in, a.** Also, **log on, sign on.** *Computers.* to enter identifying data, as a name or password, into a multiuser system, so as to be able to do work with the system. **b.** to enter or include any item of information or data in a record, account, etc. **18. log off** or **out,** *Computers.* to terminate a work session using a multiuser system, or a connection to such a system. [1350–1400; ME *logge,* var. of *lugge* pole, limb of tree; cf. obs. *logget* pole; see LUGSAIL, LOGBOOK] —**log′gish,** *adj.*

log[2] (lôg, log), *n. Math.* logarithm.

log-, var. of **logo-** before a vowel: *logarithm.*

-log, var. of **-logue:** *analog.*

log., logic.

lo·gan (lō′gən), *n.* pokelogan.

Lo·gan (lō′gən), *n.* **1. John** or **James** (*Tah-gah-jute*), c1725–80, leader of the Cayuga tribe. **2. Joshua,** born 1908, U.S. playwright, director, and producer. **3. Mount,** a mountain in Canada, in the Mount Elias Mountains: second highest peak in North America. 19,850 ft. (6050 m). **4.** a city in N Utah. 26,844. **5.** a male given name.

lo·gan·ber·ry (lō′gən ber′ē), *n., pl.* **-ries. 1.** the large, dark-red, acid fruit of a plant, *Rubus ursinus loganobaccus.* **2.** the plant itself. [1890–95, *Amer.*; named after James H. *Logan* (1841–1928), American horticulturist who first bred it; see BERRY]

lo·ga·ni·a (lō gā′nē ə), *n.* any of several plants or shrubs of the genus *Logania,* native chiefly to Australia, having small white or pink flowers. Cf. **logania family.** [< NL: genus name, after James Logan (1674–1751), colonial American botanist, born in Ireland; see -IA]

lo·ga·ni·a·ceous (lō gā′nē ā′shəs), *adj.* belonging to the plant family Loganiaceae. Cf. **logania family.** [< NL *Loganiace(ae)* (see LOGANIA, -ACEAE) + -OUS]

loga′nia fam′ily, the plant family Loganiaceae, typified by herbaceous plants, trees, and shrubs of warm regions having usually opposite leaves, clusters of regular flowers, and fruit in the form of a berry, capsule, or fleshy fruit, and including the butterfly bush, Carolina jessamine, logania, and trees of the genus *Strychnos,* which are the source of curare, nux vomica, and strychnine.

Lo·gans·port (lō′gənz pôrt′, -pōrt′), *n.* a city in N Indiana, on the Wabash River. 17,899.

log′an stone′ (log′ən). See **rocking stone.** Also, **loggan stone.** [1750–60; var. of LOGGING STONE]

log·a·oe·dic (log′ə ē′dik, log′ə-), *Pros.* —*adj.* **1.** composed of dactyls and trochees or of anapests and iambs, producing a movement somewhat suggestive of prose. —*n.* **2.** a logaoedic verse. [1835–45; < LL *logaoedicus* < Gk *logaoidikós.* See LOG-, ODE, -IC]

log·a·rithm (lô′gə rith′əm, -rith′-, log′ə-), *n. Math.* the exponent or the power to which a base number must be raised to equal a given number; log: *2 is the logarithm of 100 to the base 10* ($2 = \log_{10} 100$). [1605–15; < NL *logarithmus* < Gk *lóg(os)* LOG- + *arithmós* number; see ARITHMETIC]

log·a·rith·mic (lô′gə rith′mik, -rith′-, log′ə-), *adj. Math.* **1.** pertaining to a logarithm or logarithms. **2.** (of an equation) having a logarithm as one or more of its unknowns. **3.** (of a function) **a.** pertaining to the function $y = \log x$. **b.** expressible by means of logarithms. Also, **log′a·rith′mi·cal.** [1690–1700; LOGARITHM + -IC] —**log′a·rith′mi·cal·ly,** *adv.*

log′arith′mic func′tion, *Math.* a function defined by $y = \log_b x$, esp. when the base, *b,* is equal to *e,* the base of natural logarithms. [1945–50]

log·book (lôg′bo͝ok′, log′-), *n.* a book in which details of a trip made by a ship or aircraft are recorded; log. [1670–80; LOG[1] (def. 3) + BOOK]

log′ chip′, *Naut.* the wooden chip of a chip log, for holding the end of the log line. Also, **log′chip′.** Also called **log ship, logship.** [1840–50]

loge (lōzh), *n.* **1.** (in a theater) the front section of the lowest balcony, separated from the back section by an aisle or railing or both. **2.** a box in a theater or opera house. **3.** any small enclosure; booth. **4.** (in France) a cubicle for the confinement of art students during important examinations. [1740–50; < F; see LODGE]

log′gan stone′ (log′ən). See **rocking stone.** Also, **logan stone.** [var. of LOGGING STONE]

log·ger[1] (lô′gər, log′ər), *n.* **1.** a person whose work is logging; lumberjack. **2.** a tractor used in logging. **3.** a machine for loading logs. [1725–35, *Amer.*; LOG[1] + -ER[1]]

log·ger[2] (lô′gər, log′ər), *adj. Scot.* **1.** heavy or thick. **2.** thick-headed; stupid. [1665–75; back formation from LOGGERHEAD]

log·ger·head (lô′gər hed′, log′ər-), *n.* **1.** a thick-headed or stupid person; blockhead. **2.** See **loggerhead turtle. 3.** See **loggerhead shrike. 4.** a ball or bulb of iron with a long handle, used, after being heated, to melt tar, heat liquids, etc. **5.** a rounded post, in the stern of a whaleboat, around which the harpoon line is passed. **6.** a circular inkwell having a broad, flat base. **7. at loggerheads,** engaged in a disagreement or dispute; quarreling: *They were at loggerheads over the distribution of funds.* [1580–90; *logger* block of wood (first attested alone in 18th century) + HEAD] —**log′ger·head′ed,** *adj.*

log′gerhead shrike′, a common, North American shrike, *Lanius ludovicianus,* gray above and white below with black wings, tail, and facial mask. [1805–15, *Amer.*]

log′gerhead tur′tle, a sea turtle, *Caretta caretta,* having a large head: now greatly reduced in number. Also called **loggerhead.** [1650–60]

log·gets (lô′gits, log′its), *n.* (*used with a singular v.*) a game, formerly played in England, in which players throw pieces of wood at a stake. Also, **log·gats.** [1575–85; pl. of *logget,* equiv. to LOG[1] + -ET]

log·gia (loj′ə, lō′jē ə; *It.* lôd′jä), *n., pl.* **-gias,** *It.* **-gie** (-je). **1.** a gallery or arcade open to the air on at least one side. **2.** a space within the body of a building but open to the air on one side, serving as an open-air room or as an entrance porch. [1735–45; < It; see LODGE]

loggia (def. 2)

log·ging (lô′ging, log′ing), *n.* **1.** the process, work, or business of cutting down trees and transporting the logs to sawmills. **2.** *Naut.* a deduction from the pay of a sailor, made as a fine or forfeit and recorded in the logbook of the ship. [1700–10, *Amer.*; LOG[1] + -ING[1]]

log′ging stone′. See **rocking stone.** [1815–25; dial. *log* to rock + -ING[2]]

Lo·gi (lô′gē, lō′-), *n. Scand. Myth.* a man, a personification of fire, who defeated Loki in an eating contest. [< ON: lit., fire]

lo·gi·a (lō′gē ə, -jē ə, log′ē ə), *n.* a pl. of **logion.**

log·ic (loj′ik), *n.* **1.** the science that investigates the principles governing correct or reliable inference. **2.** a particular method of reasoning or argumentation: *We were unable to follow his logic.* **3.** the system or principles of reasoning applicable to any branch of knowledge or study. **4.** reason or sound judgment, as in utterances or actions: *There wasn't much logic in her move.* **5.** convincing forcefulness; inexorable truth or persuasiveness: *the irresistible logic of the facts.* **6.** *Computers.* See **logic circuit.** [1325–75; ME *logik* < L *logica,* n. use of neut. pl. (in ML taken as fem. sing.) of Gk *logikós* of speech or reason. See LOGO-, -IC] —**log′ic·less,** *adj.*
—**Syn. 4.** sense, cogency.

-logic, a combining form used in the formation of adjectives corresponding to nouns ending in **-logy:** *analogic.* [< Gk *-logikós.* See LOGIC]

log·i·cal (loj′i kəl), *adj.* **1.** according to or agreeing with the principles of logic: *a logical inference.* **2.** reasoning in accordance with the principles of logic, as a person or the mind: *logical thinking.* **3.** reasonable; to be expected: *War was the logical consequence of such threats.* **4.** of or pertaining to logic. [1490–1500; < ML *logicālis.* See LOGIC, -AL[1]] —**log·i·cal·i·ty** (loj′i kal′i tē), **log′i·cal·ness,** *n.* —**log′i·cal·ly,** *adv.*
—**Syn. 1, 3.** valid. —**Ant. 1–3.** unreasonable.

log′ical construc′tion, *Logic, Philos.* anything referred to by an incomplete symbol capable of contextual definition. [1880–85]

log′ical pos′itivism, a philosophical movement that stresses the function of philosophy as a method of criticizing and analyzing science and that rejects all transcendental metaphysics, statements of fact being held to be meaningful only if they have verifiable consequences in experience and in statements of logic, mathematics, or philosophy itself, and with such statements of fact deriving their validity from the rules of language. Also called **log′ical empir′icism.** [1930–35] —**log′ical pos′itivist.**

log′ical sum′, union (def. 10a). [1865–70]

log′ical syn′tax, syntactics. [1920–25]

log′ic array′, *Computers, Electronics.* an arrangement of circuitry on a mass-produced microchip permitting the chip to be easily customized for a specific application. Also called **gate array.** [1970–75]

log′ic cir′cuit, *Computers.* a circuit designed to perform complex functions defined in terms of elementary functions of mathematical logic. Also called **logic.** [1965–70]

log′ic gate′, *Electronics.* gate[1] (def. 16b). [1960–65]

lo·gi·cian (lō jish′ən), *n.* a person who is skilled in logic. [1350–1400; LOGIC + -IAN; r. ME *logicien* < MF]

log·i·cism (loj′ə siz′əm), *n. Logic, Math.* the doctrine, developed chiefly by Gottlob Frege and Bertrand Russell, that mathematics can be reduced to logic. [1935–40; LOGIC + -ISM]

log·i·cize (loj′ə sīz′), *v.,* **-cized, -ciz·ing.** —*v.t.* **1.** to make logical; give logical form to: *to logicize a sequence of events.* —*v.i.* **2.** to employ logic: *One could not logicize about such an occurrence.* Also, *esp. Brit.,* **log′icise′.** [1825–35; LOGIC + -IZE]

lo·gi·on (lō′gē on′, -jē-, log′ē-), *n., pl.* **lo·gi·a** (lō′gē ə, -jē ə, log′ē ə), **lo·gi·ons. 1.** a traditional saying or maxim, as of a religious teacher. **2.** (*sometimes cap.*) *Biblical Criticism.* **a.** a saying of Jesus, esp. one contained in collections supposed to have been among the

CONCISE ETYMOLOGY KEY: <, descended or borrowed from; >, whence; b., blend of, blended; c., cognate with; cf., compare; deriv., derivative; equiv., equivalent; imit., imitative; obl., oblique; r., replacing; s., stem; sp., spelling, spelled; resp., respelling, respelled; trans., translation; ?, origin unknown; *, unattested; ‡, probably earlier than. See the full key inside the front cover.

sources of the present Gospels. **b.** a saying included in the agrapha. [1580–90; < Gk *lógion* saying, oracle, n. use of neut. of *lógios* skilled in words, eloquent. See LOG-, -IOUS]

lo·gis·tic[1] (lō jis′tik, lə-), *adj.* of or pertaining to logistics. Also, **lo·gis′ti·cal.** [1930–35; back formation from LOGISTICS] **—lo·gis′ti·cal·ly,** *adv.*

lo·gis·tic[2] (lō jis′tik, lə-), *n.* Sometimes, **logistics. 1.** symbolic logic. **2.** *Archaic.* mathematical calculation. *—adj.* **3.** of or pertaining to logistic. [1620–30; < F *logistique* < LL *logisticus* of computation < Gk *logistikós* skilled in calculation, rational, equiv. to *logist(ḗs)* calculator, reasoner (**logid-*, base of *logízein* to reckon, v. deriv. of *lógos* word (see LOGOS) + *-tēs* agent suffix, with *dt* > *st*) + *-ikos* -IC]

logis′tic curve′, *Math.* a curve, shaped like a letter S, defined as an exponential function and used to model various forms of growth. [1900–05]

lo·gis·ti·cian[1] (lō′ji stish′ən), *n.* an expert in logistics. [1930–35; LOGISTIC(S) + -IAN]

lo·gis·ti·cian[2] (lō′ji stish′ən), *n.* a person who is skilled in symbolic logic. [1930–35; LOGISTIC[2] + -IAN]

lo·gis·tics (lō jis′tiks, lə-), *n.* (*used with a singular or plural v.*) **1.** the branch of military science and operations dealing with the procurement, supply, and maintenance of equipment, with the movement, evacuation, and hospitalization of personnel, with the provision of facilities and services, and with related matters. **2.** the planning, implementation, and coordination of the details of a business or other operation. [1875–80; < F *logistique* quartermaster's work, equiv. to *log(er)* to LODGE, be quartered (said of troops) + *-istique* -ISTIC; see -ICS]

log·jam (lôg′jam′, log′-), *n.* **1.** an immovable pileup or tangle of logs, as in a river, causing a blockage. **2.** any blockage or massive accumulation: *a logjam of bills before Congress.* [1880–85; LOG[1] + JAM[1]]

log′ line′, *Navig.* the line by which a log or patent log is streamed. [1605–15]

log-log (lôg′lôg′, log′log′), *n.* **1.** the logarithm of a logarithm. *—adj.* **2.** of or pertaining to a device, graph, etc., using log-logs.

log·nor′mal distribu′tion (lôg nôr′məl, log-), *Math.* a distribution of a random variable for which the logarithm of the variable has a normal distribution. [LOG-(ARITHM) + NORMAL]

lo·go (lō′gō),*n., pl.* **-gos. 1.** Also called **logotype.** a graphic representation or symbol of a company name, trademark, abbreviation, etc., often uniquely designed for ready recognition. **2.** *Print.* logotype (def. 1). [by shortening of LOGOTYPE or LOGOGRAM]

LOGO (lō′gō), *n. Computers.* a high-level programming language widely used to teach children how to use computers. [< Gk *lógos* word (see LOGOS), sp. as if an acronym]

logo-, a combining form appearing in loanwords from Greek, where it meant "word," "speech" (*logography*); on this model, used in the formation of new compound words (*logotype*). Also, *esp. before a vowel,* **log-.** Cf. **-logic, -logue, -logy.** [< Gk *logo-*, comb. form of *lógos* LOGOS]

log′ of wood′, log[1] (def. 10).

log·o·gram (lô′gə gram′, log′ə-), *n.* a conventional, abbreviated symbol for a frequently recurring word or phrase, as the symbol & for the word *and.* Also called **log·o·graph** (lô′gə graf′, -gräf′, log′ə-). [1810–20; LOGO- + -GRAM[1]] **—log·o·gram·mat·ic** (lô′gə grə mat′ik, log′ə-), *adj.* **—log′o·gram·mat′i·cal·ly,** *adv.*

log·o·graph·ic (lô′gə graf′ik, log′ə-), *adj.* **1.** of, pertaining to, or using logograms. **2.** of or pertaining to logography. [1775–85; < Gk *logographikós.* See LOGO-, -GRAPHIC] **—log·o·graph′i·cal·ly,** *adv.*

lo·gog·ra·phy (lō gog′rə fē), *n.* **1.** printing with logotypes. **2.** a method of longhand reporting, each of several reporters in succession taking down a few words. [1775–85; < Gk *logographía* speech writing. See LOGO-, -GRAPHY] **—lo·gog′ra·pher,** *n.*

log·o·griph (lô′gə grif, log′ə-), *n.* **1.** an anagram, or a puzzle involving anagrams. **2.** a puzzle in which a certain word, and other words formed from any or all of its letters, must be guessed from indications given in a set of verses. [1590–1600; LOGO- + Gk *grîphos* a fishing basket, riddle] **—log′o·griph′ic,** *adj.*

lo·gom·a·chy (lō gom′ə kē), *n., pl.* **-chies. 1.** a dispute about or concerning words. **2.** an argument or debate marked by the reckless or incorrect use of words; meaningless battle of words. **3.** a game played with cards, each bearing one letter, with which words are formed. [1560–70; < Gk *logomachía.* See LOGO-, -MACHY] **—log·o·mach·ic** (lô′gə mak′ik, log′ə-), **log′o·mach′i·cal,** *adj.* **—lo·gom′a·chist, log′o·mach′,** *n.*

log·o·pe·dics (lô′gə pē′diks, log′ə-), *n.* (*used with a singular v.*) *Med.* the study and treatment of speech defects. Also, **log·o·pe·di·a** (lô′gə pē′dē ə, log′ə-). [1920–25; LOGO- + (ORTHO)PEDICS] **—log′o·pe′dic,** *adj.*

log·o·phile (lô′gə fīl′, log′ə-), *n.* a lover of words. [LOGO- + -PHILE]

log·o·pho·bi·a (lô′gə fō′bē ə, log′ə-), *n.* an obsessive fear of words. [1920–25; LOGO- + -PHOBIA]

log·or·rhe·a (lô′gə rē′ə, log′ə-), *n.* **1.** pathologically incoherent, repetitious speech. **2.** incessant or compulsive talkativeness; wearisome volubility. [1900–05; LOGO- + -RRHEA] **—log′or·rhe′ic,** *adj.*

lo·gos (lō′gos, -gōs, log′os), *n.* **1.** (*often cap.*) *Philos.* the rational principle that governs and develops the universe. **2.** *Theol.* the divine word or reason incarnate in Jesus Christ. John 1:1–14. [1580–90; < Gk *lógos* a word, saying, speech, discourse, thought, proportion, ratio, reckoning, akin to *légein* to choose, gather, recount, tell over, speak; cf. LECTION]

log·o·type (lô′gə tīp′, log′ə-), *n.* **1.** Also called **logo.** a single piece of type bearing two or more uncombined letters, a syllable, or a word. **2.** logo (def. 1). [1810–20; LOGO- + TYPE] **—log′o·typ′y,** *n.*

log·perch (lôg′pûrch′, log′-), *n., pl.* **-perch·es,** (*esp. collectively*) **-perch.** a darter, *Percina caprodes,* of eastern North American lakes and streams, having a piglike snout. [1880–85, *Amer.*; LOG[1] + PERCH[2]]

log′ reel′, *Naut.* a reel from which the line of a log chip runs. [1855–60]

log·roll (lôg′rōl′, log′-), *U.S. Politics.* *—v.t.* **1.** to procure the passage of (a bill) by logrolling. *—v.i.* **2.** to engage in political logrolling. [1825–35, *Amer.*; back formation from LOGROLLING] **—log′roll′er,** *n.*

log·roll·ing (lôg′rō′ling, log′-), *n.* **1.** *U.S. Politics.* the exchange of support or favors, esp. by legislators for mutual political gain as by voting for each other's bills. **2.** cronyism or mutual favoritism among writers, editors, or critics, as in the form of reciprocal flattering reviews; back scratching. **3.** the action of rolling logs to a particular place. **4.** the action of rotating a log rapidly in the water by treading upon it, esp. as a competitive sport; birling. [1785–95, *Amer.*; LOG[1] + ROLLING]

Lo·gro·ño (lô grô′nyô), *n.* a city in N Spain. 84,456.

log′ ship′, *Naut.* See **log chip.** Also, **log′ship′.** [1835–45]

-logue, a combining form used in the names of kinds of discourse, spoken or written: *analogue; monologue; travelogue.* Also, **-log.** [< F < L *-logus* < Gk *-logos.* See LOGOS]

log·way (lôg′wā′, log′-), *n.* gangway (def. 7). [1770–80, *Amer.*; LOG[1] + WAY]

log·wood (lôg′wo͝od′, log′-), *n.* **1.** the heavy, brownish-red heartwood of a West Indian and Central American tree, *Haematoxylon campechianum,* of the legume family, used in dyeing. **2.** the tree itself. [1575–85; LOG[1] + WOOD[1]]

lo·gy (lō′gē), *adj.,* **-gi·er, -gi·est.** lacking physical or mental energy or vitality; sluggish; dull; lethargic. [1840–50, *Amer.*; perh. < D *log* heavy, cumbersome + -Y[1]] **—lo′gi·ly,** *adv.* **—lo′gi·ness,** *n.*

-logy, 1. a combining form used in the names of sciences or bodies of knowledge: *paleontology; theology.* **2.** a termination of nouns referring to writing, discourses, collections, etc.: *trilogy; martyrology.* [ME *-logie* < L *-logia* < Gk. See -LOGUE, -Y[3]]

Lo·hen·grin (lō′ən grin, -grēn′), *n.* **1.** the son of Parzival, and a knight of the Holy Grail. **2.** (*italics*) an opera (composed 1846–48; premiere 1850) by Richard Wagner.

lo·i·a·sis (lō ī′ə sis), *n. Pathol.* infestation with the parasitic eye worm, *Loa loa,* of the subcutaneous tissues and orbit: endemic in West Africa. Also, **loaiasis.** [1910–15; < NL, equiv. to *Lo(a)* a worm genus + *-iasis* -IASIS]

loid (loid), *Slang.* *—v.t.* **1.** to open (a locked door) by sliding a thin piece of celluloid or plastic between the door edge and doorframe to force open a spring lock. *—n.* **2.** a thin piece of celluloid or plastic so used, as by a burglar. [1955–60; shortening of CELLULOID]

loin (loin), *n.* **1.** Usually, **loins.** the part or parts of the human body or of a quadruped animal on either side of the spinal column, between the false ribs and hipbone. **2.** a cut of meat from this region of an animal, esp. a portion including the vertebrae of such parts. See diag. under **beef. 3. loins, a.** the parts of the body between the hips and the lower ribs, esp. regarded as the seat of physical strength and generative power. **b.** the genital and pubic area; genitalia. **4. gird** or **gird up one's loins,** to prepare oneself for something requiring readiness, strength, or endurance: *He girded his loins to face his competitor.* [1275–1325; ME *loyne* < MF *lo(i)gne,* perh. < VL **lumbea,* n. use of fem. of **lumbeus* of the loins, equiv. to L *lumb(us)* loin + *-eus* -EOUS]

loin·cloth (loin′klôth′, -kloth′), *n., pl.* **-cloths** (-klôthz′, -klothz′, -klôths′, -kloths′). a piece of cloth worn around the loins or hips, esp. in tropical regions as the only item of clothing. [1855–60; LOIN + CLOTH]

Loire (lwar), *n.* **1.** a river in France, flowing NW and W into the Atlantic: the longest river in France. 625 mi. (1005 km) long. **2.** a department in central France. 742,396; 1853 sq. mi. (4800 sq. km). *Cap.:* St.-Étienne.

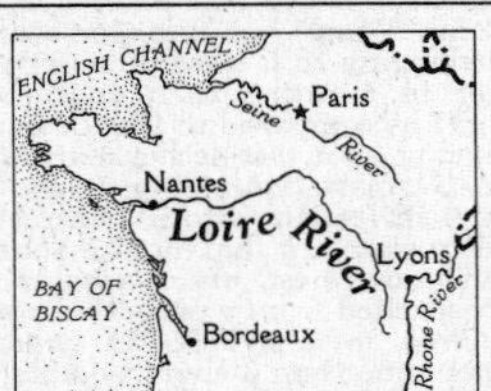

Loire-At·lan·tique (lwar at län tēk′), *n.* a department in NW France. 934,499; 2695 sq. mi. (6980 sq. km). *Cap.:* Nantes. Formerly, **Loire-In·fé·rieure** (lwar an fā ryœr′).

Loi·ret (lwa re′), *n.* a department in central France. 490,189; 2630 sq. mi. (6810 sq. km). *Cap.:* Orléans.

Loir-et-Cher (lwar rā sher′), *n.* a department in central France. 267,896; 2479 sq. mi. (6420 sq. km). *Cap.:* Blois.

Lo·is (lō′is), *n.* a female given name.

loi·ter (loi′tər), *v.i.* **1.** to linger aimlessly or as if aimless in or about a place: *to loiter around the bus terminal.* **2.** to move in a slow, idle manner, making purposeless stops in the course of a trip, journey, errand, etc.: *to loiter on the way to work.* **3.** to waste time or dawdle over work: *He loiters over his homework until one in the morning.* *—v.t.* **4.** to pass (time) in an idle or aimless manner (usually fol. by *away*): *to loiter away the afternoon in daydreaming.* [1300–50; ME *loteren, loytren,* perh. < MD *lotteren* to stagger, totter; cf. D *leuteren* to dawdle] **—loi′ter·er,** *n.* **—loi′ter·ing·ly,** *adv.*

—Syn. 1. LOITER, DALLY, DAWDLE, IDLE imply moving or acting slowly, stopping for unimportant reasons, and in general wasting time. To LOITER is to linger aimlessly: *to loiter outside a building.* To DALLY is to loiter indecisively or to delay as if free from care or responsibility: *to dally on the way home.* To DAWDLE is to saunter, stopping often, and taking a great deal of time, or to fritter away time working in a halfhearted way: *to dawdle over a task.* To IDLE is to move slowly and aimlessly, or to spend a great deal of time doing nothing: *to idle away the hours.* **1–4.** loaf. **2, 3.** delay, tarry.

Lo·ja (lô′hä), *n.* a city in S Ecuador. 46,697.

lo·ka·ca·ra (lō′kä kä′rə), *n. Hinduism.* an action in accordance with socially accepted rules. Cf. **shastracara.** [< Skt *lokācāra* world custom]

Lo·ka·ya·ta (lō kä′yə tə), *n.* a materialistic school of philosophers in India that opposed Hinduism by regarding only matter as real, sense data as the only source of knowledge, and the gratification of the appetites as the only good. [< Skt *lokāyata*]

Lo·ka·ya·ti·ka (lō′kə yä′ti kə), *n.* a member of the Lokayata school. Also called **Charvaka.** [< Skt, equiv. to *lokāyat(a)* LOKAYATA + *-ika* agent suffix]

Lo·ki (lō′kē), *n. Scand. Myth.* a trickster god, born of Jotun ancestry but accepted among the Aesir as Odin's adopted brother: father of the monsters Fenrir, Hel, and the Midgard serpent, and the instigator of Balder's death.

Lok Sab·ha (lôk′ sub′hä), the lower house of parliament in India.

Lo·la (lō′lə), *n.* a female given name, form of **Charlotte** or **Dolores.**

lol·i·gin·id (lol′i jin′id), *n.* any member of the squid family Loliginidae, having an elongated conical body and partially retractable tentacles. [< NL *Loliginidae* family name, equiv. to *loligin-* (s. of *Loligo* the type genus, L *lolligō* squid) + *-idae* -ID[2]]

Lo·li·ta (lō lē′tə), *n.* **1.** (*italics*) a novel (1955) by Vladimir Nabokov. **2.** nymphet (def. 2). **3.** Also, **Lo·le′ta.** a female given name, form of **Charlotte** or **Dolores.** [sense "nymphet" after the novel's title character]

loll (lol), *v.i.* **1.** to recline or lean in a relaxed, lazy, or indolent manner; lounge: *to loll on a sofa.* **2.** to hang loosely; droop; dangle: *The dog stood in the heat with his tongue lolling out of his mouth.* *—v.t.* **3.** to allow to hang, droop, or dangle. *—n. Archaic.* **4.** the act of lolling. **5.** a person or thing that lolls. [1300–50; ME *lollen, lullen* (perh. imit.); cf. MD *lollen* doze, sit over the fire] **—loll′er,** *n.* **—loll′ing·ly,** *adv.*

Lol·land (lol′ənd; *Dan.* lô′län), *n.* Laaland.

lol·la·pa·loo·za (lol′ə pə lo͞o′zə), *n. Slang.* an extraordinary or unusual thing, person, or event; an exceptional example or instance. Also, **lol′la·pa·loo′sa, lalapalooza, lallapalooza.** [1900–05, *Amer.*; orig. uncert.]

Lol·lard (lol′ərd), *n.* an English or Scottish follower of the religious teachings of John Wycliffe from the 14th to the 16th centuries. [1375–1425; late ME < MD *lollaert* mumbler (of prayers), equiv. to *loll(en)* to mumble (see LULL) + *-aert* -ARD] **—Lol′lard·y, Lol′lard·ry, Lol′lard·ism,** *n.*

löl·ling·ite (lel′ing īt′), *n.* a mineral, iron arsenide, $FeAs_2$, occurring in steel-gray prismatic crystals. Also, **loellingite, lol′ling·ite′.** [1840–50; named after *Lölling,* town in Austria where found; see -ITE]

lol·li·pop (lol′ē pop′), *n.* a piece of hard candy attached to the end of a small stick that is held in the hand while the candy is licked. Also, **lol′ly·pop′.** [1785–95; dial. *lolly* tongue + POP[1]]

lol·lop (lol′əp), *v.i.* **1.** *Brit. Dial.* to loll; lounge. **2.** to move forward with a bounding or leaping motion. [1735–45; extended var. of LOLL]

lol·ly (lol′ē), *n., pl.* **-lies. 1.** lollipop. **2.** *Brit. Informal.* **a.** a piece of candy, esp. hard candy. **b.** a treat. **c.** a small bribe or gratuity. **d.** money. **3. do one's lolly,** *Australian Slang.* to lose one's temper. [1765–75; shortening of LOLLYPOP]

lol·ly·gag (lol′ē gag′), *v.i.,* **-gagged, -gag·ging.** lallygag.

lol·ly·wa·ter (lol′ē wô′tər, -wot′ər), *n. Australian Slang.* a sweet soft drink, esp. one brightly colored. [1945–50; LOLLY + WATER]

Lo·lo (lō′lō), *n., pl.* **-los,** (*esp. collectively*) **-lo** for 1. **1.** Also called **Yi.** a member of a people inhabiting the mountainous regions of southwestern China near the eastern borders of Tibet and Burma. **2.** the Sino-Tibetan language or group of languages, related to Burmese, spoken by the Lolo.

lo·ma (lō′mə), *n. Chiefly Southwestern U.S.* a hill or ridge having a broad top. [1840–50, *Amer.*; < Sp, akin to *lomo* back, ridge, LOIN]

Lo′ma Lin′da, a town in SW California. 10,694.

Lo·max (lō′maks), *n.* **John Avery,** 1867–1948, and his son, **Alan,** born 1915, U.S. folklorists.

Lom·bard (lom′bärd, -bərd, lum′-), *n.* **1.** a native or inhabitant of Lombardy. **2.** a member of an ancient Germanic tribe that settled in N Italy. **3.** a banker or moneylender. *—adj.* **4.** Also, **Lom·bar′dic.** of or pertaining to the Lombards or Lombardy.

Lom·bard (lom′bärd, -bərd, lum′-), *n.* **1. Carole** (*Jane Alice Peters*), 1909?–42, U.S. film actress. **2. Peter** (*Petrus Lombardus*), c1100–64?, Italian theologian:

CONCISE PRONUNCIATION KEY: act, cāpe, dâre, pärt; set, ēqual; if, īce; ox, ōver, ôrder, oil, bo͝ok, bo͞ot, out; up, ûrge; child; sing; shoe; thin, *th*at; zh as in *treasure.* ə = *a* as in *alone, e* as in *system, i* as in *easily, o* as in *gallop, u* as in *circus;* ° as in *fire* (fī°r), *hour* (ou°r). l and n can serve as syllabic consonants, as in *cradle* (krād′l), and *button* (but′n). See the full key inside the front cover.

bishop of Paris 1159–64?. **3.** a city in NE Illinois, near Chicago. 37,295.

Lom·bar·di (lom bär′dē, lum-), *n.* **Vince(nt Thomas),** 1913–70, U.S. football coach.

Lom·bar·do (lom bär′dō, lum-), *n.* **Guy (Albert),** 1902–77, U.S. bandleader, born in Canada.

Lom′bard Street′, a street in London, England: a financial center.

Lom·bard·y (lom′bər dē, lum′-), *n.* a region and former kingdom in N Italy. 8,882,366; 9190 sq. mi. (23,800 sq. km).

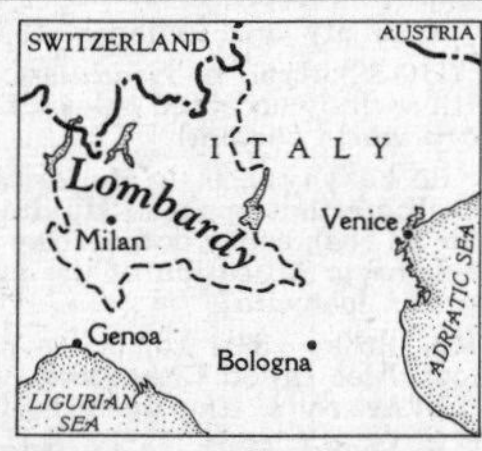

Lom′bardy pop′lar, a poplar, *Populus nigra italica,* having a columnar manner of growth, with branches erect and parallel. [1760–70]

Lom·bok (lom bok′), *n.* an island in Indonesia, E of Bali. 1,300,234; 1826 sq. mi. (4729 sq. km).

Lom·bro′si·an school′ (lom brō′zē ən, -zhən), a school of criminology, promulgating the theories and employing the methods developed by Lombroso. [LOMBROS(O) + -IAN]

Lom·bro·so (lom brō′sō; *It.* lôm brô′sô), *n.* **Ce·sa·re** (che′zä re′), 1836–1909, Italian physician and criminologist.

Lo·mé (lô mā′), *n.* a seaport in and the capital of Togo, on the Gulf of Guinea. 135,000.

lo·ment (lō′ment), *n. Bot.* a pod that is contracted in the spaces between the seeds and that breaks at maturity into one-seeded indehiscent joints. [1375–1425; late ME *lomente* < L *lōmentum* bean meal, face cream made of loment, equiv. to *lō(tus)* (var. of *lautus,* ptp. of *lavāre* to wash; see LAVE[1]) + *-mentum* -MENT] —**lo′ment·like′,** *adj.*

Lo·mi·ta (lō mē′tə), *n.* a town in SW California. 17,191.

Lo·mond (lō′mənd), *n.* **Loch,** a lake in W Scotland. 23 mi. (37 km) long; 27 sq. mi. (70 sq. km).

Lo·mo·no·sov (lom′ə nô′sôf, -sof; *Russ.* lu mu nô′səf), *n.* **Mi·kha·il Va·si·le·vich** (myi KHU yēl′ vu syē′lyi vyich), 1711–65, Russian philosopher, poet, scientist, and grammarian.

Lo·mo·til (lō mōt′l), *Pharm., Trademark.* a brand of diphenoxylate with atropine in its sulfate form, used in the management of diarrhea.

Lom·poc (lom′pok), *n.* a city in SW California. 26,267.

lon., longitude.

Lond., London.

Lon·don (lun′dən), *n.* **1. Jack,** 1876–1916, U.S. short-story writer and novelist. **2.** a metropolis in SE England, on the Thames: capital of the United Kingdom. **3. City of,** an old city in the central part of the former county of London: the ancient nucleus of the modern metropolis. 5400; 1 sq. mi. (3 sq. km). **4. County of,** a former administrative county comprising the City of London and 28 metropolitan boroughs, now part of Greater London. **5. Greater.** Also, **Greater London Council.** an urban area comprising the city of London and 32 metropolitan boroughs. 7,111,500; 609 sq. mi. (1575 sq. km). **6.** a city in S Ontario, in SE Canada. 240,392.

Lon′don broil′, a steak, typically served broiled and crosscut into thin slices. [1965–70, *Amer.*]

Lon′don brown′, carbuncle (def. 3).

Lon′don Com′pany, a company, chartered in England in 1606 to establish colonies in America, that founded Jamestown, Va., in 1607.

Lon·don·der·ry (lun′dən der′ē), *n.* **1.** a county in N Northern Ireland. 130,889; 804 sq. mi. (2082 sq. km). **2.** its county seat: a seaport. 54,000. **3.** a town in SE New Hampshire. 13,598. Also called **Derry** (for defs. 1, 2).

Lon·don·er (lun′də nər), *n.* a native or inhabitant of London. [1350–1400; ME; see LONDON, -ER[1]]

Lon·don·esque (lun′də nesk′), *adj.* **1.** resembling or characteristic of London, England. **2.** resembling or characteristic of the writings of Jack London. [1860–65; LONDON + -ESQUE]

Lon′don forc′es, *Physics, Chem.* forces between atoms or molecules that are related to the physical rather than the chemical properties of the molecules and that are attractive when the particles are in the lowest energy state. [after Fritz Wolfgang *London* (1900–54), U.S. physicist born in Germany]

Lon′don plane′, a tall, hardy, widely spreading plane tree, *Platanus acerifolia,* of North America, having clusters of round, bristly fruit. [1855–60]

Lon·dres (lon′dres), *n.* a cylindrically shaped cigar of medium to large size. [< Sp *londrés* Havana cigar, special use of *Londres* London (cigars for the British market)]

Lon·dri·na (lôN dʀē′nə), *n.* a city in E Brazil. 156,670.

lone (lōn), *adj.* **1.** being alone; without company or accompaniment; solitary; unaccompanied: *a lone traveler.* **2.** standing by itself or apart; isolated: *a lone house in the valley.* **3.** sole; single; only: *That company constitutes our lone competitor in the field.* **4.** unfrequented. **5.** without companionship; lonesome; lonely. **6.** unmarried or widowed. [1325–75; ME; aph. var of ALONE, used attributively] —**lone′ness,** *n.*
—**Syn. 1.** See **alone. 2.** separate, separated, secluded.

lone′ hand′, 1. *Cards.* **a.** a person who holds a hand so strong that he or she can play a deal without the hand of his or her partner. **b.** the hand played by such a person. **2.** a person who by preference conducts his or her affairs without the advice or assistance of others: *a lone hand in investment circles.* **3.** a stand or action taken independently: *a lone hand in the trade negotiations.* [1790–1800]

lone·ly (lōn′lē), *adj.,* **-li·er, -li·est. 1.** affected with, characterized by, or causing a depressing feeling of being alone; lonesome. **2.** destitute of sympathetic or friendly companionship, intercourse, support, etc.: *a lonely exile.* **3.** lone; solitary; without company; companionless. **4.** remote from places of human habitation; desolate; unfrequented; bleak: *a lonely road.* **5.** standing apart; isolated: *a lonely tower.* [1600–10; LONE + -LY] —**lone′li·ly,** *adv.* —**lone′li·ness, lone′li·hood′,** *n.*
—**Syn. 1.** See **alone. 4.** uninhabited, unpopulated. **5.** secluded.

lone·ly-hearts (lōn′lē härts′), *adj.* of or for people seeking counseling or companionship to bring love or romance into their lives: *a lonely-hearts column in the newspaper.* [1930–35]

lon·er (lō′nər), *n.* a person who is or prefers to be alone, esp. one who avoids the company of others: *He was always a loner—no one knew him well.* [1945–50; LONE + -ER[1]]

lone·some (lōn′səm), *adj.* **1.** depressed or sad because of the lack of friends, companionship, etc.; lonely: *to feel lonesome.* **2.** attended with or causing such a state or feeling: *a lonesome evening at home.* **3.** lonely or deserted in situation; remote, desolate, or isolated: *a lonesome road.* —*n.* **4. on** or **by one's lonesome.** Also, *Scot.,* **by one's lane.** *Informal.* alone: *She went walking by her lonesome.* [1640–50; LONE + -SOME[1]] —**lone′some·ly,** *adv.* —**lone′some·ness,** *n.*
—**Syn. 1.** See **alone.**

Lone′ Star′ State′, Texas (used as a nickname).

lone′ wolf′, *Informal.* a person who prefers to live, act, or work alone or independent of others. [1905–10, *Amer.*]

long[1] (lông, long), *adj.* **long·er** (lông′gər, long′-), **long·est** (lông′gist, long′-), *n., adv.* —*adj.* **1.** having considerable linear extent in space: *a long distance; a long handle.* **2.** having considerable duration in time: *a long conversation; a long while.* **3.** extending, lasting, or totaling a number of specified units: *eight miles long; eight hours long.* **4.** containing many items or units: *a long list.* **5.** requiring a considerable time to relate, read, etc.: *a long story.* **6.** extending beyond normal or moderate limits: *a long, boring speech.* **7.** experienced as passing slowly, because of the difficulty, tedium, or unpleasantness involved: *long years of study.* **8.** reaching well into the past: *a long memory.* **9.** the longer of two or the longest of several: *the long way home; a brick with the long side exposed.* **10.** taking a long time; slow: *He's certainly long getting here.* **11.** forward-looking or considering all aspects; broad: *to take a long view of life.* **12.** intense, thorough, or critical; seriously appraising: *a long look at one's past mistakes.* **13.** having an ample supply or endowment of something (often fol. by *on*): *to be long on advice; to be long on brains.* **14.** having a considerable time to run, as a promissory note. **15.** *Chiefly Law.* distant or remote in time: *a long date.* **16.** extending relatively far: *a man with a long reach.* **17.** being higher or taller than usual: *long casement windows.* **18.** being against great odds; unlikely: *a long chance.* **19.** (of beverages) mixed or diluted with a large amount of soda, seltzer, etc.: *highballs, collinses, and other long drinks.* **20.** (of the head or skull) of more than ordinary length from front to back. **21.** *Phonet.* **a.** lasting a relatively long time: *"Feed" has a longer sound than "feet" or "fit."* **b.** belonging to a class of sounds considered as usually longer in duration than another class, as the vowel of *bought* as compared to that of *but,* and in many languages serving as a distinctive feature of phonemes, as the *ah* in German *Bahn* in contrast with the *a* in *Bann,* or the *tt* in Italian *fatto* in contrast with the *t* in *fato* (opposed to *short*). **c.** having the sound of the English vowels in *mate, meet, mite, mote, moot,* and *mute,* historically descended from vowels that were long in duration. **22.** *Pros.* (of a syllable in quantitative verse) lasting a longer time than a short syllable. **23.** *Finance.* holding or accumulating stocks, futures, commodities, etc., with the expectation of a rise in prices: *a long position in chemicals.* **24.** *Gambling.* **a.** marked by a large difference in the numbers of the given betting ratio or in the amounts wagered: *long odds.* **b.** of or pertaining to the larger amount bet. **25.** *Ceram.* (of clay) very plastic; fat.
—*n.* **26.** a comparatively long time: *They haven't been gone for long. Will it take long?* **27.** something that is long: *The signal was two longs and a short.* **28.** a size of garment for men who are taller than average. **29.** a garment, as a suit or overcoat, in this size: *The shorts and the longs are hung separately.* **30.** *Finance.* a person who accumulates or holds stocks or commodities with the expectation of a rise in prices. **31.** *Music.* longa. **32. before long,** soon: *We should have news of her whereabouts before long.* **33. the long and the short of,** the point or gist of; substance of: *The long and the short of it is that they will be forced to sell all their holdings.* Also, **the long and short of.**
—*adv.* **34.** for or through a great extent of space or, esp., time: *a reform long advocated.* **35.** for or throughout a specified extent, esp. of time: *How long did he stay?* **36.** (used elliptically in referring to the length of an absence, delay, etc.): *Will she be long?* **37.** throughout a specified period of time (usually used to emphasize a preceding noun): *It's been muggy all summer long.* **38.** at a point of time far distant from the time indicated: *long before.* **39. as long as, a.** provided that: *As long as you can come by six, I'll be here.* **b.** seeing that; since: *As long as you're going to the grocery anyway, buy me a pint of ice cream.* **c.** Also, **so long as.** during the time that; through the period that: *As long as we were neighbors, they never invited us inside their house.* [bef. 900; (adj.) ME *longe,* OE *lang, long;* c. D, G *lang,* ON *langr,* Goth *langs,* L *longus;* (n.) late ME, deriv. of the adj.; (adv.) ME *long(e),* OE *lange, longe, lange,* c. OS, OHG *lango*] —**long′ly,** *adv.* —**long′ness,** *n.*
—**Syn. 1.** lengthy, extensive. **2.** protracted, prolonged, extended. **6.** overlong, wordy, prolix; tedious, boring.

long[2] (lông, long), *v.i.* to have an earnest or strong desire or craving; yearn: *to long for spring; to long to return home.* [bef. 900; ME *longen,* OE *langian* grow longer, yearn after, summon; see LONG[1]]
—**Syn.** See **yearn.**

long[3] (lông, long), *v.i.* **1.** *Archaic.* to be suitable or fitting. **2.** *Obs.* to be the possession; belong. [1150–1200; ME *longen* to be suitable or proper, BELONG, deriv. of *long* on account (of), attributable (to), dependent (on); OE *gelang* belonging (to), dependent (on); see ALONG]

Long (lông, long), *n.* **1. Crawford Wil·liam·son** (wil′yəm sən), 1815–78, U.S. surgeon. **2. Hu·ey Pierce** (hyōō′ē), 1893–1935, U.S. politician: governor of Louisiana 1928–31; U.S. senator 1931–35. **3. Russell B(il·liu)** (bil′yōō), born 1918, U.S. lawyer and politician: U.S. senator 1948–87 (son of Huey Pierce Long). **4. Stephen Harriman,** 1784–1864, U.S. army officer and explorer.

long., longitude.

lon·ga (long′gə, lông′-), *n. Music.* the second longest note in medieval mensural notation. Also, **long.** [1640–50; < L, fem. of *longus* LONG]

long′ account′, *Finance.* the account of a customer who buys securities or commodities on margin. [1810–20]

long-act·ing (lông′ak′ting, long′-), *adj. Pharm.* sustained-release. [1950–55]

long-a·go (lông′ə gō′, long′-), *adj.* of or pertaining to the distant past or to remote events; ancient: *long-ago exploits remembered only in folk tales.* [1825–35]

lon·gan (long′gən), *n.* **1.** the small, one-seeded, greenish-brown fruit of a large evergreen tree, *Euphoria longana,* of the soapberry family, native to China and allied to the litchi. **2.** the tree itself. Also, **lungan.** [1725–35; < NL *longanum* < Chin *lóngyǎn* lit., dragon's eye]

long′-and-short′ work′ (lông′ən shôrt′, long′-), *Masonry.* an arrangement of rectangular quoins or jambstones set alternately vertically and horizontally. [1860–65]

lon·ga·nim·i·ty (long′gə nim′i tē, lông′-), *n.* patient endurance of hardship, injuries, or offense; forbearance. [1400–50; late ME *longanimyte* < LL *longanimitās* patience, equiv. to *longanimi(s)* patient (*long(us)* LONG[1] + *anim(us)* spirit + *-is* adj. suffix) + *-tās* -TY[2]] —**lon·gan·i·mous** (long gan′ə məs, lông-), *adj.*

long′ arm′, a long pole fitted with any of various devices, as a hook or clamp, for performing tasks otherwise out of reach.

long′ bar′row, *Archaeol.* a funerary barrow having an elongate shape, sometimes constructed over a megalithic chamber tomb and usually containing one or more inhumed corpses along with artifacts: primarily Neolithic but extending into the Bronze Age. Cf. **round barrow.**

Long′ Beach′, 1. a city in SW California, S of Los Angeles: a seaside resort. 361,334. **2.** a city on SW Long Island, in SE New York. 34,073. **3.** (*ital.*) *Mil.* the U.S. Navy's first nuclear-powered surface ship, a guided-missile cruiser launched in 1959.

long·beard (lông′bērd′, long′-), *n.* bellarmine. [1640–50; LONG[1] + BEARD]

long·boat (lông′bōt′, long′-), *n. Naut.* (formerly) the largest boat carried by a sailing ship. [1505–15; LONG[1] + BOAT]

Long′boat Key′, a narrow barrier island in the Gulf of Mexico, SW of Florida, sheltering Sarasota Bay: sports fishing.

long′ bone′, *Anat.* (in vertebrate animals) any of the long, cylindrical, marrow-containing bones of the limbs: *the long bone of the arm.* [1855–60]

long·bow (lông′bō′, long′-), *n.* **1.** a large bow drawn by hand, as that used by English archers from the 12th to the 16th centuries. **2. draw the longbow,** to exaggerate in telling stories; overstate something: *He's sure to draw the longbow on the size of his catch of fish.* [1490–1500; LONG[1] + BOW[2]]

longbow (def. 1)

CONCISE ETYMOLOGY KEY: <, descended or borrowed from; >, whence; b., blend of, blended; c., cognate with; cf., compare; deriv., derivative; equiv., equivalent; imit., imitative; obl., oblique; r., replacing; s., stem; sp., spelling, spelled; resp., respelling, respelled; trans., translation; ?, origin unknown; *, unattested; ‡, probably earlier than. See the full key inside the front cover.

long·bow·man (lông′bō′mən, long′-), *n., pl.* **-men.** an archer who uses a longbow. [1670–80; LONGBOW + -MAN]
—**Usage.** See **-man.**

Long′ Branch′, a city in E New Jersey: seaside resort. 29,819.

long′ card′, *Chiefly Bridge.* a card remaining in a hand after all the opponents' cards in that particular suit have been drawn. [1860–65]

long′-case clock′ (lông′kās′, long′-). See **tall-case clock.**

long-chain (lông′chān′, long′-), *adj. Chem.* pertaining to molecules composed of long chains of atoms, or polymers composed of long chains of monomers. [1925–30]

long′ clam′. See **soft-shell clam.** [1835–45, *Amer.*]

long·cloth (lông′klôth′, long′kloth′), *n.* a fine, white, cotton cloth, of plain weave; high-grade muslin. [1535–45; LONG[1] + CLOTH]

long-day (lông′dā′, long′-), *adj. Bot.* requiring a long photoperiod in order to flower. [1915–20]

Long′ Day's′ Jour′ney Into Night′, a play (1956) by Eugene O'Neill.

Long·den (lông′dən, long′-), *n.* **John Eric** (*Johnny*), born 1907, U.S. jockey and thoroughbred horse trainer.

long′ dis′tance, telephone service between distant places. [1900–05]

long-dis·tance (lông′dis′təns, long′-), *adj.* **1.** of, from, or between distant places: *a long-distance phone call.* **2.** for, over, or covering long distances: *a long-distance runner.* —*adv.* **3.** by long-distance telephone: *to call someone long-distance.* [1880–85]

long′ divi′sion, *Math.* division, usually by a number of two or more digits, in which each step of the process is written down. [1820–30]

long′ doz′en, a dozen plus one; thirteen; baker's dozen. [1860–65]

long-drawn-out (lông′drôn′out′, long′-), *adj.* **1.** lasting a very long time; protracted: *a long-drawn-out story.* **2.** of great length; long: *a long-drawn-out line of soldiers.* Also, **drawn-out, long′-drawn′.** [1900–05]

longe (lunj, lonj), *n., v.,* **longed, longe·ing.** —*n.* **1.** a long rope used to guide a horse during training or exercise. —*v.t.* **2.** to train or exercise (a horse) by use of a longe. Also, **lunge.** [< F, OF: n. use of *longe* (adj.) < L *longa,* fem. of *longus* LONG]

long′-eared owl′ (lông′ērd′, long′-), a mottled-gray owl, *Asio otus,* of the Northern Hemisphere, having a long tuft on each side of the head. [1805–15]

lon·ge·ron (lon′jər ən), *n. Aeron.* a main longitudinal brace or support on an airplane. [1910–15; < F: side-piece, equiv. to *long(er)* to run alongside, skirt (deriv. of *long* LONG[1]) + *-eron* n. suffix]

long′ ess′ (es). See **long s.**

lon·gev·i·ty (lon jev′i tē, lôn-), *n.* **1.** a long individual life; great duration of individual life: *Our family is known for its longevity.* **2.** the length or duration of life: *research in human longevity.* **3.** length of service, tenure, etc.; seniority: *promotions based on longevity.* [1605–15; < L *longaevitās.* See LONGEVOUS, -ITY]

lon·ge·vous (lon jē′vəs, lôn-), *adj. Archaic.* long-lived; living to a great age. [1670–80; < L *longaevus* aged, equiv. to *long(us)* LONG[1] + *aev(um)* time, age, lifetime + *-us* adj. suffix; see -OUS]

long′ face′, an unhappy or gloomy expression: *He's been walking around with a long face ever since he failed the examination.* [1780–90]

long-faced (lông′fāst′, long′-), *adj.* **1.** having an unhappy or gloomy expression; glum. **2.** having a face longer than the usual. [1585–95]

Long·fel·low (lông′fel′ō, long′-), *n.* **Henry Wadsworth** (wodz′wərth), 1807–82, U.S. poet.

Long·ford (lông′fərd, long′-), *n.* a county in Leinster, in the N Republic of Ireland. 31,138; 403 sq. mi. (1044 sq. km). *Co. seat:* Longford.

long′ gal′lery, a large gallery, found esp. in the uppermost stories of Elizabethan and Jacobean manor houses, used as a family room and as a promenade.

long′ game′, **1.** the aspect of golf considered in relation to the ability of a player to hit shots, esp. drives, for distance. Cf. **short game** (def. 1). **2.** a card game in which all cards in the pack are dealt before play. Cf. **short game** (def. 2).

long′ green′, *Slang.* paper money; cash. [1890–95, *Amer.*]

long·hair (lông′hâr′, long′-), *Informal.* —*n.* **1.** *Sometimes Disparaging.* an intellectual. **2.** a person, often gifted, who is very interested in or devoted to the arts, esp. a performer, composer, or lover of classical music. **3.** a person having long hair, esp. a hippie. **4.** a cat having long fur. —*adj.* Also, **long′haired′. 5.** having long hair: *a longhair cat.* **6.** of or characteristic of longhairs or their tastes. [1915–20; LONG[1] + HAIR]

long·hand (lông′hand′, long′-), *n.* **1.** writing of the ordinary kind, in which words are written out in full (distinguished from *shorthand*). —*adj.* **2.** using longhand: *longhand writing.* **3.** written in longhand: *a longhand account of the meeting.* [1660–70; LONG[1] + HAND]

long·han·dles (lông′han′dlz, long′-), *n.* (*used with a plural v.*) *South Midland, Southern, and Western U.S.* long underwear. [LONG[1] + HANDLES]

long′ haul′. See **haul** (def. 21). [1925–30]

long-haul (lông′hôl′, long′-), *adj.* **1.** line-haul. **2.** of or pertaining to a long haul. [1925–30]

long·head (lông′hed′, long′-), *n. Anthropol.* **1.** a dolichocephalic person. **2.** a head with a low cephalic index. [1635–45; LONG[1] + HEAD]

long-head·ed (lông′hed′id, long′-), *adj.* **1.** *Anthropol.* dolichocephalic. **2.** of great discernment or foresight; farseeing or shrewd. Also, **long′head′ed.** [1690–1700] —**long′-head′ed·ly,** *adv.* —**long′-head′ed·ness,** *n.*

long′ horn′, a moist Cheddar of cylindrical shape, weighing about 12 lb. (5.4 kg). [1825–35]

Long·horn (lông′hôrn′, long′-), *n.* **1.** (*l.c.*) See **Texas longhorn. 2.** *Slang.* a Texan. **3.** (*l.c.*) See **long-horned beetle. 4.** one of a nearly extinct English breed of beef cattle having long horns. [1825–35; LONG[1] + HORN]

long′-horned bee′tle (lông′hôrnd′, long′-), any of numerous, often brightly colored beetles of the family Cerambycidae, usually with long antennae, the larva of which bores into the wood of living or decaying trees. Also called **longhorn.** [1830–40]

long′-horned grass′hopper, any of numerous insects of the family Tettigoniidae, having long, threadlike antennae and well-developed stridulating organs on the forewings of the male. Also, **long′horn grass′hopper.** Also called **tettigoniid.** Cf. **katydid.** [1890–95]

long′ horse′, *Gymnastics.* See **vaulting horse.** [1930–35]

long′ house′, a communal dwelling, esp. of the Iroquois and various other North American Indian peoples, consisting of a wooden, bark-covered framework often as much as 100 ft. (30.5 m) in length. [1615–25]

long′ hun′dredweight, a hundredweight of 112 lb. (50.8 kg), the usual hundredweight in Great Britain, but now rare in the U.S. [1930–35]

longi-, a combining form meaning "long," used in the formation of compound words: *longicorn.* [< L, comb. form of *longus* LONG[1]; see -I-]

lon·gi·cau·dal (lon′ji kôd′l), *adj.* having a long tail; macrutous. Also, **lon·gi·cau·date** (lon′ji kô′dāt). [LONGI- + CAUDAL]

lon·gi·corn (lon′ji kôrn′), *Entomol.* —*adj.* **1.** having long antennae. **2.** belonging or pertaining to the Cerambycidae, comprising the long-horned beetles. —*n.* **3.** See **long-horned beetle.** [1840–50; < NL *longicornis* long-horned, equiv. to *longi-* LONGI- + *corn(ū)* HORN + *-is* adj. suffix]

long·ies (lông′ēz, long′-), *n.* (*used with a plural v.*) **1.** long underwear, esp. for winter use. **2.** long pants for boys. [1950–55, *Amer.*; LONG[1] + -IE + -S[3]]

long·ing (lông′ing, long′-), *n.* **1.** strong, persistent desire or craving, esp. for something unattainable or distant: *filled with longing for home.* **2.** an instance of this: *a sudden longing to see old friends.* —*adj.* **3.** having or characterized by persistent or earnest desire: *a longing look.* [bef. 1000; ME; OE *langung;* see LONG[2], -ING[1]] —**long′ing·ly,** *adv.* —**long′ing·ness,** *n.*
—**Syn. 1.** aspiration. See **desire. 3.** desirous, yearning. —**Ant. 1.** apathy.

Lon·gi·nus (lon jī′nəs), *n.* **Dionysius Cas·sius** (kash′-əs), A.D. 213?–273, Greek philosopher and rhetorician. —**Lon·gin·e·an** (lon jin′ē ən), *adj.*

long′ i′ron, *Golf.* a club, as a driving iron, midiron, or mid-mashie, with a long shaft and an iron head the face of which has little slope, for hitting long, low shots. Cf. **short iron.** [1930–35]

long·ish (lông′ish, long′-), *adj.* somewhat long. [1605–15; LONG[1] + -ISH[1]]

Long′ Is′land, an island in SE New York: the boroughs of Brooklyn and Queens of New York City are located at its W end. 118 mi. (190 km) long; 12–20 mi. (19–32 km) wide; 1682 sq. mi. (4356 sq. km).

Long′ Is′land Sound′, an arm of the Atlantic between Connecticut and Long Island. 90 mi. (145 km) long.

lon·gi·tude (lon′ji to͞od′, -tyo͞od′), *n.* **1.** *Geog.* angular distance east or west on the earth's surface, measured by the angle contained between the meridian of a particular place and some prime meridian, as that of Greenwich, England, and expressed either in degrees or by some corresponding difference in time. **2.** *Astron.* **a.** See **celestial longitude. b.** See **galactic longitude.** [1350–1400; ME < L *longitūdō* length. See LONGI-, -TUDE]

lon′gitude by account′, *Navig.* the longitude of the position of a vessel as estimated by dead reckoning.

lon·gi·tu·di·nal (lon′ji to͞od′n l, -tyo͞od′-), *adj.* **1.** of or pertaining to longitude or length: *longitudinal measurement.* **2.** extending in the direction of the length of a thing; running lengthwise: *a thin, longitudinal stripe.* **3.** *Zool.* pertaining to or extending along the long axis of the body, or the direction from front to back, or head to tail. **4.** pertaining to a research design or survey in which the same subjects are observed repeatedly over a period of time. —*n.* **5.** a longitudinal framing member, as in the hull of a ship. [1535–45; < L *longitūdin-* (s. of *longitūdō;* see LONGITUDE) + -AL[1]] —**lon′gi·tu′di·nal·ly,** *adv.*

longitu′dinal coeffi′cient, *Naval Archit.* the ratio of the immersed volume of a hull to the product obtained by multiplying its length on the water line by the immersed area of the midship transverse section, all assuming a given depth of immersion of the hull. Also called **prismatic coefficient.**

longitu′dinal fram′ing, *Naval Archit.* See **Isherwood framing.**

longitu′dinal sec′tion, the representation of an object as it would appear if cut by the vertical plane passing through the longest axis of the object.

longitu′dinal wave′, *Physics.* a wave in which the direction of displacement is the same as the direction of propagation, as a sound wave. Cf. **transverse wave.** [1930–35]

long′ johns′, (*used with a plural v.*) *Informal.* long underwear, esp. for winter use. [1940–45]

long′ jump′, *Track and Field.* **1.** a jump for distance from a running start. **2.** a field event featuring competition in the long jump. Also called **broad jump, running broad jump.** [1880–85]

long-jump (lông′jump′, long′-), *v.i. Track and Field.* to execute a long jump. Also, **broad-jump.**

long′ jump′er, *Track and Field.* a participant in the long jump. Also called **broad jumper.** [1885–90]

long-last·ing (lông′las′ting, -lä′sting, long′-), *adj.* **1.** enduring or existing for a long period of time: *a long-lasting friendship.* **2.** effective for a relatively long period of time: *a long-lasting pain reliever.* **3.** resisting the effects of wear or use over a long period: *a long-lasting fabric used for work clothes.* [1520–30]

long′leaf pine′ (lông′lēf′, long′-), **1.** an American pine, *Pinus palustris,* valued as a source of turpentine and for its timber. **2.** the wood of this tree. Also called **Georgia pine.** [1790–1800, *Amer.*]

long·lin·er (lông′lī′nər, long′-), *n.* a commercial fishing vessel that uses a long line with a large number of hooks attached to it. [1950–55; *long line* + -ER[1]]

long-lived (lông′livd′, -līvd′, long′-), *adj.* **1.** having a long life, existence, or duration: *a long-lived man; long-lived fame.* **2.** (of an object) lasting or functioning a long time: *a long-lived battery.* [1375–1425; late ME; see LONG[1], LIVED] —**long′-lived′ness,** *n.*

Long′ March′, the 6000-mi. (9654-km) retreat of the Chinese Communist party and Red Army from southeastern China (Jiangxi province) to the northwest (Yan-an in Shaanxi province) in 1934–35, during which Mao Zedong became leader of the Communist party. [trans. of Chin *chángzhēng*]

Long·mead·ow (lông′med′ō, -med′ō, long′-), *n.* a town in S Massachusetts. 16,301.

long′ meas′ure, 1. Also called **long′ me′ter.** *Pros.* a four-line stanza in iambic tetrameter, often used in hymns, with the second and fourth lines rhyming and sometimes the first and third lines rhyming as well. **2.** See **linear measure.** [1710–20]

Long·mont (lông′mont, long′-), *n.* a city in N central Colorado. 42,942.

long′ moss′. See **Spanish moss.** [1735–45, *Amer.*]

long·neck (lông′nek′, long′-), *n. Chiefly Texas.* a bottle of beer. [1885–90, for an earlier sense; LONG[1] + NECK]

long′-neck clam′ (lông′nek′, long′-). See **soft-shell clam.** [1900–05, *Amer.*]

Lon·go·bard (long′gō bärd′, -gə-), *n.* Lombard (def. 2).

long′ one′, 1. *Informal.* See **tall one. 2.** *Slang.* a bottle of beer.

Long′ Par′liament, *Eng. Hist.* the Parliament that assembled November 3, 1640, was expelled by Cromwell in 1653, reconvened in 1659, and was dissolved in 1660.

long′ pig′, (among the Maori and Polynesian peoples) human flesh as food for cannibals. [1850–55]

long′ play′, a long-playing phonograph record. [1950–55]

long-play·ing (lông′plā′ing, long′-), *adj.* of or pertaining to microgroove records devised to be played at 33⅓ revolutions per minute. [1945–50]

long′ prim′er, *Print.* a 12-point type. [1590–1600]

long-range (lông′rānj′, long′-), *adj.* **1.** considering or extending into the future: *a long-range outlook; long-range plans.* **2.** designed to cover or operate over a long distance: *long-range rockets.* [1865–70]

long′ ri′fle. See **Kentucky rifle.** [1820–30, *Amer.*]

long-run (lông′run′, long′-), *adj.* happening or presented over a long period of time or having a long course of performances: *a long-run hit play.* [1900–05]

long *s* (es), a style of the letter *s,* suggesting a lowercase *f* in form, formerly common in handwriting and as a type character. Also, **long ess.**

long·ship (lông′ship′, long′-), *n.* a medieval ship used in northern Europe esp. by the Norse, having a long, narrow, open hull, a single square sail, and a large number of oars, which provided most of the propulsion. [1560–70; LONG[1] + SHIP]

long·shore (lông′shôr′, -shōr′, long′-), *adj.* existing, found, or employed along the shore, esp. at or near a seaport: *longshore jobs; longshore current.* [1815–25; aph. var. of *alongshore*]

long′shore drift′. See **beach drift.** [1950–55]

long·shore·man (lông′shôr′mən, -shōr′-, long′-), *n., pl.* **-men.** a person employed on the wharves of a port, as in loading and unloading vessels. [1805–15; LONGSHORE + -MAN]
—**Usage.** See **-man.**

long·shore·wom·an (lông′shôr′wo͝om′ən, -shōr′-, long′-), *n., pl.* **-wom·en.** a woman employed on the wharves of a port, as in loading and unloading vessels. [LONGSHORE(MAN) + -WOMAN]
—**Usage.** See **-woman.**

long·shor·ing (lông′shôr′ing, -shōr′-, long′-), *n.* the work or occupation of a longshoreman. [1925–30; LONGSHORE(MAN) + -ING[1]]

long′ shot′, 1. a horse, team, etc., that has little chance of winning and carries long odds. **2.** an attempt or undertaking that offers much but in which there is little chance for success. **3.** *Motion Pictures, Television.* a camera shot taken at a relatively great distance from the subject and permitting a broad view of a scene. Cf. **closeup** (def. 2), **medium shot. 4. by a long shot,** by any means; by a measurable degree: *They haven't finished by a long shot.* [1785–95]

CONCISE PRONUNCIATION KEY: act, cāpe, dâre, pärt; set, ēqual; if, īce; ox, ōver, ôrder, oil, bo͝ok, bo͞ot, out; up, ûrge; child; sing; shoe; thin, *that;* zh as in *treasure.* ə = *a* as in *alone, e* as in *system, i* as in *easily, o* as in *gallop, u* as in *circus;* ə as in *fire* (fīər), *hour* (ouər). l and n can serve as syllabic consonants, as in *cradle* (krād′l), and *button* (but′n). See the full key inside the front cover.

long-sight·ed (lông′sī′tid, long′-), *adj.* **1.** farsighted; hypermetropic. **2.** having great foresight; foreseeing remote results. [1780–90] —**long′-sight′ed·ness,** *n.*

long·sleev·er (lông′slē′vər, long′-), *n. Australian.* **1.** about 3/4 pint (0.35 liter) of beer. **2.** any tall glass. [1885–90; LONG[1] + SLEEVE + -ER[1]]

long·some (lông′səm, long′-), *adj.* tiresomely long; so protracted as to weary or cause boredom. [bef. 900; ME, OE *longsum, langsum.* See LONG[1], -SOME[1]] —**long′·some·ly,** *adv.* —**long′some·ness,** *n.*

Longs′ Peak′ (lôngz, longz), a peak in N Colorado, in the Rocky Mountain National Park. 14,255 ft. (4345 m).

long′ splice′, a splice for forming a united rope narrow enough to pass through a block, made by unlaying the ends of two ropes for a considerable distance, overlapping the strands so as to make pairs of one strand from each rope, unlaying one of each pair, twisting the other strand into its place in the united rope, and tucking the yarns of the unlaid strand separately into place. Cf. **short splice.** See illus. under **splice.** [1880–85]

long·spur (lông′spûr′, long′-), *n.* any of several fringillid birds of the genus *Calcarius* of tundra or prairie regions of North America, characterized by a long, spurlike hind claw on each foot. [1825–35; LONG[1] + SPUR]

long·stand·ing (lông′stan′ding, long′-), *adj.* existing or occurring for a long time: *a longstanding feud.* [1595–1605; LONG[1] + STANDING]
—**Syn.** enduring, lasting, long-lasting.

long-stemmed (lông′stemd′, long′-), *adj.* **1.** having a long stem or stems: *long-stemmed roses.* **2.** long-legged and slender: *long-stemmed chorus girls.* [1855–60]

Long·street (lông′strēt′, long′-), *n.* **James,** 1821–1904, Confederate general in the U.S. Civil War.

long-suf·fer·ance (lông′suf′ər əns, -suf′rəns, long′-), *n. Archaic.* long-suffering. [1520–30]

long-suf·fer·ing (lông′suf′ər ing, -suf′ring, long′-), *adj.* **1.** enduring injury, trouble, or provocation long and patiently. —*n.* **2.** long and patient endurance of injury, trouble, or provocation: *years of long-suffering and illness.* [1520–30] —**long′-suf′fer·ing·ly,** *adv.*

long′ suit′, **1.** *Cards.* **a.** the suit in which the most cards are held in a hand. **b.** (in bridge) a suit in which four or more cards are held in a hand. **2.** the quality, activity, endeavor, etc., in which one excels: *Diligence is his long suit.* [1875–80]

long′ sweet′ening, *Chiefly Midland and Southern U.S.* liquid sweetening, as maple syrup, molasses, or sorghum. [1705–15, *Amer.*]

long-term (lông′tûrm′, long′-), *adj.* **1.** covering a relatively long period of time: *a long-term lease.* **2.** maturing over or after a relatively long period of time: *a long-term loan; a long-term bond.* **3.** (of a capital gain or loss) derived from the sale or exchange of an asset held for more than a specified time, as six months or one year. [1905–10]

long′-term mem′ory, information stored in the brain and retrievable over a long period of time, often over the entire life span of the individual (contrasted with *short-term memory*). [1965–70]

long·time (lông′tīm′, long′-), *adj.* existing, occurring, or continuing for a long period of time; longstanding: *longtime friends celebrating 50 years of association.* [1575–85; LONG[1] + TIME]

long′ tom′, (*usually caps.*) **1.** a towed 155mm field cannon produced by the U.S. throughout World War II. **2.** a long, heavy cannon formerly carried by small naval vessels. [1825–35]

long′ ton′. See under **ton**[1] (def. 1). *Abbr.:* L.T. [1820–30]

long-tongued (lông′tungd′, long′-), *adj.* talking too much or too openly, esp. of private or confidential matters; chattering; gossipy. [1545–55]

long′ topgal′lant mast′, *Naut.* a single spar fitted above a topmast to carry topgallants, a royal, and all sails above.

Lon·gueuil (lông gāl′, long-; *Fr.* lôɴ gœ′yᵊ), *n.* a city in S Quebec, in E Canada, across from Montreal, on the St. Lawrence. 124,320.

lon·gueur (lông gûr′, long-; *Fr.* lôɴ gœr′), *n., pl.* **-gueurs** (-gûrz′; *Fr.* -gœr′). a long and boring passage in a literary work, drama, musical composition, or the like: *The longueurs in this book make it almost unreadable.* [1815–25; < F: lit., length]

long′ un′derwear, a close-fitting, usually knitted undergarment with legs reaching to the ankles, as a union suit, worn as protection against the cold.

long′ vaca′tion, *Brit.* the summer vacation customary in the law courts and universities. [1685–95]

Long·view (lông′vyo͞o′, long′-), *n.* **1.** a city in NE Texas. 62,762. **2.** a city in SW Washington, on the Columbia. 31,052.

long-waist·ed (lông′wā′stid, long′-), *adj.* of more than average length between the shoulders and waistline; having a low waistline. Cf. **short-waisted.** [1640–50]

long·wall (lông′wôl′, long′-), *adj. Mining.* **1.** noting or pertaining to a means of extracting coal or other minerals in an underground mine from a continuous face, the roof before the face being supported at intervals by temporary or movable artificial supports. Cf. **room-and-pillar.** —*n.* **2.** the continuous face so worked. [1830–40; LONG[1] + WALL]

CONCISE ETYMOLOGY KEY: <, descended or borrowed from; >, whence; b., blend of, blended; c., cognate with; cf., compare; deriv., derivative; equiv., equivalent; imit., imitative; obl., oblique; r., replacing; s., stem; sp., spelling, spelled; resp., respelling, respelled; trans., translation; ?, origin unknown; *, unattested; ‡, probably earlier than. See the full key inside the front cover.

long′ wave′, **1.** *Elect.* an electromagnetic wave over 60 meters in length. **2.** See **L wave.** [1830–40] —**long′-wave′,** *adj.*

long·ways (lông′wāz′, long′-), *adv.* **1.** longwise. **2.** *Dancing.* in two long lines with the couples facing each other: *to perform a country dance longways.* —*adj.* **3.** longwise. [1580–90; LONG[1] + -WAYS]

long-wind·ed (lông′win′did, long′-), *adj.* **1.** talking or writing at tedious length: *long-winded after-dinner speakers.* **2.** continued to a tedious length in speech or writing: *another of his long-winded election speeches.* **3.** able to breathe deeply; not tiring easily. [1580–90] —**long′-wind′ed·ly,** *adv.* —**long′-wind′ed·ness,** *n.*

long·wise (lông′wīz′, long′-), *adj., adv.* lengthwise. [1535–45; LONG[1] + -WISE]

Long·wood (lông′wo͝od′, long′-), *n.* a city in central Florida. 10,029.

Long·worth (lông′wûrth, long′-), *n.* **Nicholas,** 1869–1931, U.S. politician: Speaker of the House 1925–31.

Long·xi (lông′shē′), *n. Pinyin.* former name of **Zhangzhou.** Also, **Lungch′i, Lungki.**

long·yi (long′yē), *n.* lungi.

Lon·i·ten (lon′i tən), *Pharm., Trademark.* a brand name for minoxidil in its pill form, used in the control of high blood pressure.

Lon·nie (lon′ē), *n.* **1.** a male given name, form of **Alonzo.** **2.** Also, **Lon′i.** a female given name. Also, **Lon′ny.**

Lönn·rot (len′rot, -ro͞ot; *Fin.* lœn′rôt), *n.* **E·lias** (e′lyäs), 1802–84, Finnish scholar and editor.

Lons-le-Sau·nier (lôɴ lə sō nyā′), *n.* a city in and the capital of Jura, in E France. 23,292.

loo[1] (lo͞o), *n., pl.* **loos,** *v.,* **looed, loo·ing.** —*n.* **1.** a card game in which forfeits are paid into a pool. **2.** the forfeit or sum paid into the pool. **3.** the fact of being looed. —*v.t.* **4.** to subject to a forfeit at loo. [1665–75; short for *lanterloo* < D *lanterlu* < F *lantur(e)lu,* special use of meaningless refrain of an old song]

loo[2] (lo͞o), *n., pl.* **loos.** *Brit. Informal.* toilet. [1935–40; of uncert. orig.]

loo[3] (lo͞o), *v.i., v.t., n., pl.* **loos.** *Chiefly Northern U.S.* low[2].

loo[4] (lo͞o), *n., pl.* **loos,** *v.t., v.i.,* **looed, loo·ing.** *Scot.* love.

loo·by (lo͞o′bē), *n., pl.* **-bies.** an awkward person, esp. one who is lazy or stupid; lout; lubber. [1350–1400; ME *loby.* See LOB[1], LUBBER]

loof[1] (lo͞of), *n. Scot. and North Eng.* the palm of the hand. [1300–50; ME *lofe* < ON *lōfi,* c. Goth *lōfa*]

loof[2] (lo͞of), *n. Naut.* **1.** the tapering of a hull toward the stern. **2.** *Now Rare.* the broad after part of the bows of a vessel. **3.** *Now Rare.* luff (def. 1). [special uses of LOOF[1]]

loo·fah (lo͞o′fə), *n.* **1.** Also called **dishcloth gourd, rag gourd. a.** any of several tropical vines of the genus *Luffa,* of the gourd family, bearing large, elongated fruit. **b.** the fruit of such a vine. **2.** Also called **vegetable sponge.** the dried, fibrous interior of this fruit, used as a sponge. Also, **loo′fa, luffa.** [1860–65; < NL *Luffa* the genus < Ar *lūf*]

loo·ie (lo͞o′ē), *n. Slang.* a lieutenant of the armed forces. Also, **loo′ey, louie.** [1915–20; resp. of LIEU(TENANT) + -IE]

look (lo͝ok), *v.i.* **1.** to turn one's eyes toward something or in some direction in order to see: *He looked toward the western horizon and saw the returning planes.* **2.** to glance or gaze in a manner specified: *to look questioningly at a person.* **3.** to use one's sight or vision in seeking, searching, examining, watching, etc.: *to look through the papers.* **4.** to tend, as in bearing or significance: *Conditions look toward war.* **5.** to appear or seem to the eye as specified: *to look pale.* **6.** to appear or seem to the mind: *The case looks promising.* **7.** to direct attention or consideration: *to look at the facts.* **8.** to have an outlook or afford a view: *The window looks upon the street.* **9.** to face or front: *The house looks to the east.* —*v.t.* **10.** to give (someone) a look: *He looked me straight in the eye.* **11.** to have an appearance appropriate to or befitting (something): *She looked her age.* **12.** to appear to be; look like: *He looked a perfect fool, coming to the party a day late.* **13.** to express or suggest by looks: *to look one's annoyance at a person.* **14.** *Archaic.* to bring, put, etc., by looks. **15. look after, a.** to follow with the eye, as someone or something moving away: *She looked after him as he walked toward the train station.* **b.** to pay attention to; concern oneself with: *to look after one's own interests.* **c.** to take care of; minister to: *to look after a child.* **16. look back,** to review past events; return in thought: *When I look back on our school days, it seems as if they were a century ago.* **17. look daggers,** to look at someone with a furious, menacing expression: *I could see my partner looking daggers at me.* **18. look down on** or **upon,** to regard with scorn or disdain; have contempt for: *They look down on all foreigners.* **19. look down one's nose at,** to regard with an overbearing attitude of superiority, disdain, or censure: *The more advanced students really looked down their noses at the beginners.* **20. look for, a.** to seek; search for: *Columbus was looking for a shorter route to India when he discovered America.* **b.** to anticipate; expect: *I'll be looking for you at the reception.* **21. look forward to,** to anticipate with eagerness or pleasure: *I always look forward to your visits.* **22. look in, a.** Also, **look into.** to look briefly inside of: *Look in the jar and tell me if any cookies are left.* **b.** Also, **look in on.** to visit (a person, place, etc.) briefly: *I'll look in some day next week.* **23. look into,** to inquire into; investigate; examine: *The auditors are looking into the records to find the cause of the discrepancy.* **24. look on** or **upon, a.** to be a spectator; watch: *The crowd looked on at the street brawl.* **b.** to consider; regard: *They look upon gambling as sinful.* **25. look out, a.** to look to the outside, as from a window or a place of observation: *From her office window, she could look out over the bustling city.* **b.** to be vigilant or on guard: *Look out, there are dangers ahead.* **c.** to afford a view; face: *The room looks out on the garden.* **26. look out for,** to take watchful care of; be concerned about: *He has to look out for his health.* **27. look over,** to examine, esp. briefly: *Will you please look over my report before I submit it?* **28. look sharp, a.** to be alert and quick: *If you want to get ahead, you must look sharp.* **b.** Also, *Brit.,* **look slippy.** to hurry: *You'd better look sharp! It's getting late.* **29. look to, a.** to direct one's glance or gaze to: *If you look to your left, you can see the Empire State Building.* **b.** to pay attention to: *Look to your own affairs and stay out of mine.* **c.** to direct one's expectations or hopes to: *We look to the day when world peace will be a reality.* **d.** to regard with expectation and anticipation: *We look to the future and greater advances in science and technology.* **30. look up, a.** to direct the eyes upward; raise one's glance: *The other guests looked up as she entered the room.* **b.** to become better or more prosperous; improve: *Business is looking up.* **c.** to search for, as an item of information, in a reference book or the like: *Look up the answer in the encyclopedia.* **d.** to seek out, esp. to visit: *to look up an old friend.* **e.** *Naut.* (of a sailing ship) to head more nearly in the direction of its destination after a favoring change of wind. **31. look up to,** to regard with admiration or respect; esteem: *A boy needs a father he can look up to.* —*n.* **32.** the act of looking: *a look of inquiry.* **33.** a visual search or examination. **34.** the way in which a person or thing appears to the eye or to the mind; aspect: *He has the look of an honest man. The tablecloth has a cheap look.* **35.** an expressive glance: *to give someone a sharp look.* **36. looks, a.** general aspect; appearance: *to like the looks of a place.* **b.** attractive, pleasing appearance. [bef. 900; (v.) ME *lōk(i)en,* OE *lōcian;* c. MD *lœken,* akin to dial. G *lugen* to look out; (n.) ME *loke* act of looking, glance, countenance, deriv. of the v.]
—**Syn. 1.** See **watch. 6.** See **seem. 33.** gaze, glance. **34.** appearance, air.

look-a-like (lo͝ok′ə līk′), *n.* **1.** a person or thing that looks like or closely resembles another; double. **2.** a compatible: *The leading brand of computer was expensive so they bought cheap look-alikes.* **3.** a pill or capsule that contains nonprescription stimulants, as caffeine and ephedrine, but is made to appear like one containing illegal or prescription stimulants, as amphetamine or biphetamine. —*adj.* **4.** being or characteristic of a look-alike. Also, **look′a·like′.** [1945–50; n. use of v. phrase *look alike*]

look-down (lo͝ok′doun′), *n.* the appearance of paper when inspected under reflected light. Cf. **look-through.**

look·down (lo͝ok′doun′), *n.* a silvery carangid fish of the genus *Selene,* of the Atlantic Ocean, having a compressed body and eyes placed high on the truncated forehead. [1880–85, *Amer.*; n. use of v. phrase *look down*]

look·ee (lo͝ok′ē), *interj. Older Use.* looky.

look·er (lo͝ok′ər), *n.* **1.** a person who looks. **2.** *Informal.* a very attractive person. [1300–50; ME; 1900–05 for def. 2; see LOOK, -ER[1]]

look·er-on (lo͝ok′ər on′, -ôn′), *n., pl.* **look·ers-on.** a person who looks on; onlooker; witness; spectator. [1530–40; *look on* + -ER[1]]

Look′ Home′ward, An′gel, a novel (1929) by Thomas Wolfe.

look-in (lo͝ok′in′), *n.* **1.** a brief glance. **2.** a short visit. **3.** *Football.* a quick pass play in which the ball is thrown to a receiver running a short diagonal pattern across the center of the field. [1840–50; n. use of v. phrase *look in*]

look′ing glass′, **1.** a mirror made of glass with a metallic or amalgam backing. **2.** the glass used in a mirror. **3.** anything used as a mirror, as highly polished metal or a reflecting surface. [1520–30]

look′ing-glass self′ (lo͝ok′ing glas′, -gläs′), *Sociol.* the self-image an individual forms by imagining what others think of his or her behavior and appearance.

look·ism (lo͝ok′iz əm), *n.* discrimination or prejudice based on a person's physical appearance. [1985–1990]

look·out (lo͝ok′out′), *n.* **1.** the act of looking out or keeping watch. **2.** a watch kept, as for something that may happen. **3.** a person or group keeping a watch. **4.** a station or place from which a watch is kept. **5.** an object of care or concern: *That's not my lookout.* **6.** tailpiece (def. 4). **7.** *Chiefly Brit.* view; prospect; outlook: *The business lookout is far from optimistic.* [1690–1700; n. use of v. phrase *look out*]
—**Syn. 3.** sentinel, sentry, patrol, guard.

Look′out Moun′tain, a mountain ridge in Georgia, Tennessee, and Alabama: a battle of the Civil War fought here, near Chattanooga, Tenn. 1863; highest point, 2126 ft. (648 m).

look-o·ver (lo͝ok′ō′vər), *n.* a brief or superficial examination or reading. [1905–10; n. use of v. phrase *look over*]

look-see (lo͝ok′sē′), *n. Informal.* a visual inspection or survey; look; examination: *have a look-see.* [1880–85]

look-through (lo͝ok′thro͞o′), *n.* the opacity and texture of paper when inspected by transmitted light. Also called **see-through.** Cf. **look-down.** [1935–40]

look·up (lo͝ok′up′), *n.* an act or instance of looking something up, as information in a reference book or an on-line database. Also, **look′-up′.** [1945–50 for an earlier sense; n. use of v. phrase *look up*]

look·y (lo͝ok′ē), *interj. Older Use.* look; look here. Also, **lookee.** [1875–80; alter. of impv. *look ye!*]

loom[1] (lo͞om), *n.* **1.** a hand-operated or power-driven apparatus for weaving fabrics, containing harnesses, lay, reed, shuttles, treadles, etc. See illus. on next page. **2.** the art or the process of weaving. **3.** the part of an oar between the blade and the handle. —*v.t.* **4.** to weave (something) on a loom. [bef. 900; ME *lome,* OE *gelōma* tool, implement. See HEIRLOOM]

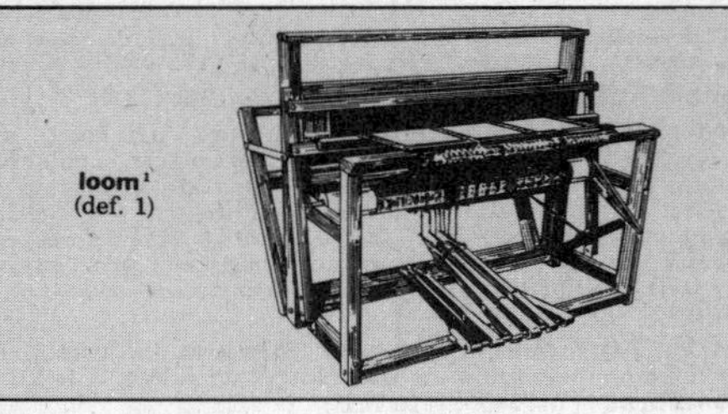
loom[1] (def. 1)

loom[2] (lo͞om), *v.i.* **1.** to appear indistinctly; come into view in indistinct and enlarged form: *The mountainous island loomed on the horizon.* **2.** to rise before the vision with an appearance of great or portentous size: *Suddenly a police officer loomed in front of him.* **3.** to assume form as an impending event: *A battle looms at the convention.* —*n.* **4.** a looming appearance, as of something seen indistinctly at a distance or through a fog: *the loom of a moraine directly in their path.* [1585–95; orig. uncert.]
—**Syn. 2.** rear, tower.

loom[3] (lo͞om), *n. Brit. Dial.* **1.** loon[1]. **2.** a guillemot or murre. [1670–80; < ON *lōmr*]

L.O.O.M., Loyal Order of Moose.

loom·ing (lo͞o′ming), *n.* a mirage in which objects below the horizon seem to be raised above their true positions. [1620–30; LOOM[2] + -ING[1]]

loon[1] (lo͞on), *n.* any of several large, short-tailed, web-footed, fish-eating diving birds of the genus *Gavia,* of the Northern Hemisphere. [1625–35; perh. alter. of LOOM[3]]

loon[2] (lo͞on), *n.* a crazy or simple-minded person. [1400–50; late ME *lowen,* perh. < ON *lūinn* worn, tired; later influenced by LOON[1] and LOONY]

loon·ey (lo͞o′nē), *adj.* **loon·i·er, loon·i·est,** *n., pl.* **loon·eys, loon·ies.** loony.

loon·y (lo͞o′nē), *adj.,* **loon·i·er, loon·i·est,** *n., pl.* **loon·ies.** *Informal.* —*adj.* **1.** lunatic; insane. **2.** extremely or senselessly foolish. —*n.* **3.** a lunatic. Also, **looney, luny.** [1860–65; LUN(ATIC) + -Y[2]] —**loon′i·ness,** *n.*

loon′y bin′, *Informal.* an insane asylum or the psychiatric ward of a hospital. [1880–85]

loon′y tunes′, *Informal.* loony. [1985–90; after *Looney Tunes,* name of a series of animated cartoons]

loop[1] (lo͞op), *n.* **1.** a portion of a cord, ribbon, etc., folded or doubled upon itself so as to leave an opening between the parts. **2.** anything shaped more or less like a loop, as a line drawn on paper, a part of a letter, a part of a path, or a line of motion. **3.** a curved piece or a ring of metal, wood, or the like, used for the insertion of something, as a handle, etc. **4.** See **intrauterine device.** **5.** *Aeron.* a maneuver executed by an airplane in such a manner that the airplane describes a closed curve in a vertical plane. **6.** a circular area at the end of a trolley line, railroad line, etc., where cars turn around. **7.** an arm of a cloverleaf where traffic may turn off or onto a main road or highway. **8.** *Physics.* the part of a vibrating string, column of air or other medium, etc., between two adjacent nodes. **9.** *Elect.* a closed electric or magnetic circuit. **10.** *Computers.* the reiteration of a set of instructions in a routine or program. **11.** a wire, usually of platinum, one end of which is curved to form a loop, used for transferring microorganisms from one medium to another. **12.** a sand bar that encloses or nearly encloses a body of water. **13.** *Figure Skating.* a school figure in which a skater traces a large half circle, a small oval within its arc, and another large half circle to complete the figure while remaining on the same skating edge. **14. the loop,** a group or network of insiders or influential people; inner circle: *to be out of the loop on policy decisions.* **15. the Loop,** the main business district of Chicago. **16. throw** or **knock for a loop,** to astonish or upset: *Her quitting the project really threw me for a loop.* —*v.t.* **17.** to form into a loop. **18.** to make a loop in. **19.** to enfold or encircle in or with something arranged in a loop. **20.** to fasten by forming into a loop, or by means of something formed into a loop (often fol. by *up*): *to loop up the new draperies.* **21.** to cause (a missile or projectile) to trace a looping or looplike trajectory through the air: *to loop a grenade into the building.* **22.** to fly (an airplane) in a loop or series of loops. **23.** to construct a closed electric or magnetic circuit. **24.** *Motion Pictures.* to complete by means of looping: *We still have to loop the final scenes.* —*v.i.* **25.** to make or form a loop: *The river loops around the two counties.* **26.** to move by forming loops, as a measuringworm. **27.** to trace a looping or looplike path through the air: *The fly ball looped high in the air.* **28.** to perform a loop or series of loops in an airplane. **29.** *Motion Pictures.* to record dialogue, sound effects, etc., onto an existing film track or soundtrack. [1350–1400; ME *loupe* loop of cloth, perh. < ScotGael *lub* loop, bend]

loop[2] (lo͞op), *n. Archaic.* a small or narrow opening, as in a wall; loophole. [1300–50; ME *loupe* window; cf. MD *lūpen* peep, peer]

loop[3] (lo͞op), *n. Metalworking.* a hot bloom of pasty consistency, to be worked under a hammer or in rolls. [1665–75; < F *loupe,* special use of *loupe* wen, knob, gnarl << Gmc. See LOUPE]

loop′ back′. See **bow back.**

looped (lo͞opt), *adj.* **1.** having or consisting of loops; loopy. **2.** *Slang.* **a.** drunk; inebriated. **b.** eccentric; loopy. **c.** enthusiastic; keen: *These days he's looped on rodeos.* [1930–35; LOOP[1] + -ED[2], -ED[3]]

loop·er (lo͞o′pər), *n.* **1.** a person or thing that loops something or forms loops. **2.** a measuringworm. **3.** the thread holder in a sewing machine using two threads. **4.** *Baseball.* blooper (def. 3a). [1725–35; LOOP[1] + -ER[1]]

loop·hole (lo͞op′hōl′), *n., v.,* **-holed, -hol·ing.** —*n.* **1.** a small or narrow opening, as in a wall, for looking through, for admitting light and air, or, particularly in a fortification, for the discharge of missiles against an enemy outside. See illus. under **battlement.** **2.** an opening or aperture. **3.** a means of escape or evasion; a means or opportunity of evading a rule, law, etc.: *There are a number of loopholes in the tax laws whereby corporations can save money.* —*v.t.* **4.** to furnish with loopholes. [1585–95; LOOP[2] + HOLE]

loop′hole frame′, a frame in the opening of a wall enclosing a window and some other opening. [1850–55]

loop·ing (lo͞o′ping), *n. Motion Pictures.* the process of fitting speech to film already shot, esp. by making a closed loop of the film for one scene and projecting it repeatedly until a good synchronization of film and recorded speech is achieved. [1475–85 for an earlier sense; LOOP[1] + -ING[1]]

loop′ing mill′, *Metalworking.* a rolling mill for bar stock, wire, and the like, having the successive stands side by side so that the metal forms a loop in passing from stand to stand.

loop′ knot′, a knot made by doubling over a line at its end and tying both thicknesses into a square knot in such a way as to leave a loop. Also called **open hand knot.** See illus. under **knot.** [1785–95]

loop′ of Hen′le (hen′lē), *Anat.* the part of a nephron between the proximal and distal convoluted tubules that extends, in a loop, from the cortex into the medulla of the kidney. Also called **Henle's loop.** [1880–85; named after F. G. J. *Henle* (1809–85), German pathologist]

loop′ stitch′, *Sewing.* any stitch, as the chain stitch, that uses loops in the pattern or process of working.

loop-the-loop (lo͞op′*th*ə lo͞op′), *n.* **1.** an airplane maneuver in which a plane, starting upward, makes one complete vertical loop. **2.** a ride in an amusement park that simulates this maneuver. [1900–05]

loop′ win′dow, a tall, narrow window. [1565–75]

loop·y (lo͞o′pē), *adj.* **loop·i·er, loop·i·est.** **1.** full of loops. **2.** *Slang.* **a.** eccentric; crazy; dotty. **b.** befuddled or confused, esp. due to intoxication. **3.** *Scot.* crafty; sly. [1815–25; LOOP[1] + -Y[1]]

Loos (lōs), *n.* **1. A·dolf** (ä′dolf; *Ger.* ä′dôlf), 1870–1933, Austrian architect and writer. **2. Anita,** 1893–1981, U.S. writer.

loose (lo͞os), *adj.,* **loos·er, loos·est,** *adv., v.* **loosed, loos·ing.** —*adj.* **1.** free or released from fastening or attachment: *a loose end.* **2.** free from anything that binds or restrains; unfettered: *loose cats prowling around in alleyways at night.* **3.** uncombined, as a chemical element. **4.** not bound together: *to wear one's hair loose.* **5.** not put up in a package or other container: *loose mushrooms.* **6.** available for disposal; unused; unappropriated: *loose funds.* **7.** lacking in reticence or power of restraint: *a loose tongue.* **8.** lax, as the bowels. **9.** lacking moral restraint or integrity; *notorious for his loose character.* **10.** sexually promiscuous or immoral; unchaste. **11.** not firm, taut, or rigid: *a loose tooth; a loose rein.* **12.** relaxed or limber in nature: *He runs with a loose, open stride.* **13.** not fitting closely or tightly: *a loose sweater.* **14.** not close or compact in structure or arrangement; having spaces between the parts; open: *a loose weave.* **15.** having few restraining factors between associated constituents and allowing ample freedom for independent action: *a loose federation of city-states.* **16.** not cohering: *loose sand.* **17.** not strict, exact, or precise: *a loose interpretation of the law.* **18.** *Sports.* **a.** having the players on a team positioned at fairly wide intervals, as in a football formation. **b.** (of a ball, hockey puck, etc.) not in the possession of either team; out of player control. **19. hang** or **stay loose,** *Slang.* to remain relaxed and unperturbed. **20. on the loose, a.** free; unconfined, as, esp., an escaped convict or circus animal. **b.** behaving in an unrestrained or dissolute way: *a bachelor on the loose.*
—*adv.* **21.** in a loose manner; loosely (usually used in combination): *loose-flowing.* **22. break loose,** to free oneself; escape: *The convicts broke loose.* **23. cast loose, a.** to loosen or unfasten, as a ship from a mooring. **b.** to send forth; set adrift or free: *He was cast loose at an early age to make his own way in the world.* **24. cut loose, a.** to release from domination or control. **b.** to become free, independent, etc. **c.** to revel without restraint: *After the rodeo they headed into town to cut loose.* **25. let loose, a.** to free or become free. **b.** to yield; give way: *The guardrail let loose and we very nearly plunged over the edge.* **26. turn loose,** to release or free, as from confinement: *The teacher turned the children loose after the class.*
—*v.t.* **27.** to let loose; free from bonds or restraint. **28.** to release, as from constraint, obligation, or penalty. **29.** *Chiefly Naut.* to set free from fastening or attachment: *to loose a boat from its moorings.* **30.** to unfasten, undo, or untie, as a bond, fetter, or knot. **31.** to shoot; discharge; let fly: *to loose missiles at the invaders.* **32.** to make less tight; slacken or relax. **33.** to render less firmly fixed; lessen an attachment; loosen.
—*v.i.* **34.** to let go a hold. **35.** to hoist anchor; get under way. **36.** to shoot or let fly an arrow, bullet, etc. (often fol. by *off*): *to loose off at a flock of ducks.* **37.** *Obs.* to become loose; loosen. [1175–1225; (adj.) ME *los, loos* < ON *lauss* loose, free, empty; c. OE *lēas* (see -LESS), D, G *los* loose, free; (v.) ME *leowsen, lousen,* deriv. of the adj.] —**loose′ly,** *adv.* —**loose′ness,** *n.*
—**Syn. 2.** unbound, untied, unrestricted, unconfined. **10.** libertine, dissolute, licentious. **17.** vague, general, indefinite. **27.** loosen, unbind. **28.** liberate. **32.** ease.

loose′ can′non, a person whose reckless behavior endangers the efforts or welfare of others. [1975–80]

loose′ end′, **1.** a part or piece left hanging, unattached, or unused: *Remind me to tack down that loose end on the stairway carpet.* **2.** an unsettled detail, as of a business matter: *The arrangements have been made, except for a few loose ends.* **3. at loose ends,** in an uncertain or unsettled situation or position: *Ever since leaving the company, he's been at loose ends.* Also, **at a loose end.** [1540–50]

loose-fit·ting (lo͞os′fit′ing), *adj.* (of a garment) fitting loosely; not following the contours of the body closely. Cf. **close-fitting.** [1880–85]

loose-foot·ed (lo͞os′fo͝ot′id), *adj. Naut.* (of a fore-and-aft sail) not having the foot bent to a boom. [1710–20]

loose-joint·ed (lo͞os′join′tid), *adj.* **1.** having or marked by easy, free movement; limber. **2.** having loose joints. **3.** loosely built or framed. [1855–60]

loose′-joint′ hinge′ (lo͞os′joint′), a hinge having a knuckle formed from half of each flap, and with the upper half removable from the pin. Also called **heave-off hinge, liftoff hinge.**

loose-leaf (lo͞os′lēf′), *adj.* **1.** (of a book, notebook, etc.) consisting of individual leaves held in a binder **(loose′-leaf bind′er),** as by rings that open and close, in such a way as to allow their removal, return, or replacement without tearing. **2.** of or for use with a loose-leaf binder: *loose-leaf paper.* [1900–05]

loose-limbed (lo͞os′limd′), *adj.* having supple arms and legs: *a loose-limbed athlete.* [1815–25]

loos·en (lo͞o′sən), *v.t.* **1.** to unfasten or undo, as a bond or fetter. **2.** to make less tight; slacken or relax: *to loosen one's grasp.* **3.** to make less firmly fixed in place: *to loosen a tooth.* **4.** to let loose or set free from bonds, restraint, or constraint. **5.** to make less close or compact in structure or arrangement. **6.** to make less dense or coherent: *to loosen the soil in a garden.* **7.** to relax in strictness or severity, as restraint or discipline: *to loosen restrictions on trade.* **8.** to relieve (the bowels) of their constipated condition. —*v.i.* **9.** to become loose or looser (sometimes fol. by *up*): *His hold loosened. Your shoes will loosen up with wear.* [1350–1400; ME *loosnen.* See LOOSE, -EN[1]] —**loos′en·er,** *n.*

loos′ening of associa′tions, *Psychiatry.* a type of formal thought disorder characterized by shifts from one topic to another in ways that are obliquely related or completely unrelated, occurring as a common symptom of mania and schizophrenia. Also called **derailment.**

loose′ sen′tence, a sentence that does not end with the completion of its main clause, but continues with one or more subordinate clauses or other modifiers. Cf. **periodic sentence.** [1890–95]

loose·strife (lo͞os′strīf′), *n.* **1.** any of various plants belonging to the genus *Lysimachia,* of the primrose family, having clusters of usually yellow flowers, as *L. vulgaris* **(garden loosestrife)** or *L. quadrifolia* **(whorled loosestrife).** **2.** any of several plants belonging to the genus *Lythrum,* of the loosestrife family. Cf. **purple loosestrife.** [1540–50; LOOSE (v.) + STRIFE, mistranslation of L *lysimachia* (< Gk *lysimácheí(os)* + *-a* fem. n. suffix; see LYSI-, -MACHY), plant said to be named after a certain *Lysimachos;* see -IA]

loose′strife fam′ily, the plant family Lythraceae, characterized by herbaceous plants, shrubs, and trees having usually opposite or whorled, simple leaves, clusters of flowers, and fruit in the form of a capsule, and including the crape myrtle, loosestrifes of the genus *Lythrum,* and the henna shrub.

loose-tongued (lo͞os′tungd′), *adj.* unrestrained or irresponsible in speech; given to gossiping. [1640–50; LOOSE + TONGUE + -ED[3]]

loos·ey-goos·ey (lo͞o′sē go͞o′sē), *adj. Slang.* relaxed; calm; unperturbed: *Despite the pressure, he was looseygoosey throughout the game.* [1965–70; rhyming compound (with -Y[1]) based on the idiom *loose as a goose*]

loot[1] (lo͞ot), *n.* **1.** spoils or plunder taken by pillaging, as in war. **2.** anything taken by dishonesty, force, stealth, etc.: *a burglar's loot.* **3.** a collection of valued objects: *The children shouted and laughed as they opened their Christmas loot.* **4.** *Slang.* money: *You'll have a fine time spending all that loot.* **5.** act of looting or plundering: *to take part in the loot of a conquered city.* —*v.t.* **6.** to carry off or take (something) as loot: *to loot a nation's art treasures.* **7.** to despoil by taking loot; plunder or pillage (a city, house, etc.), as in war. **8.** to rob, as by burglary or corrupt activity in public office: *to loot the public treasury.* —*v.i.* **9.** to take loot; plunder: *The conquerors looted and robbed.* [1780–90; < Hindi *lūṭ,* akin to Skt *luṇṭhati* (he) steals] —**loot′er,** *n.*
—**Syn. 1.** booty. **7.** sack, ransack.

loot[2] (lo͞ot), *v. Scot.* pt. of **let**[1].

lop[1] (lop), *v.,* **lopped, lop·ping,** *n.* —*v.t.* **1.** to cut off (branches, twigs, etc.) from a tree or other plant. **2.** to cut off (a limb, part, or the like) from a person, animal, etc. **3.** to cut off the branches, twigs, etc., of (a tree or other plant). **4.** to eliminate as unnecessary or excessive: *We had to lop off whole pages of the report before presenting it to the committee.* **5.** *Archaic.* to cut off the head, limbs, etc., of (a person). —*v.i.* **6.** to cut off branches, twigs, etc., as of a tree. **7.** to remove parts by or as by cutting. —*n.* **8.** parts or a part lopped off. **9.** (of trees) the smaller branches and twigs not useful as timber. [1375–1425; late ME *loppe* part or parts cut off]

lop[2] (lop), *v.,* **lopped, lop·ping,** *adj.* —*v.i.* **1.** to hang loosely or limply; droop. **2.** to sway, move, or go in a drooping or heavy, awkward way. **3.** to move in short, quick leaps: *a rabbit lopping through the garden.* —*v.t.* **4.** to let hang or droop: *He lopped his arms at his sides in utter exhaustion.* —*adj.* **5.** hanging down limply or droopingly: *lop ears.* [1570–80; v. use of obs. *lop* spider or *lop* dangling part of a tree (see LOP[1]); lit., to behave like a *lop,* i.e., to dangle, hang loosely. See LOB[1]]

LOP, *Navig.* See **line of position.**

Lo·pat·ni·kov (lō pat′ni kôf′, -kof′; *Russ.* lu pät′nyi-kəf), *n.* **Ni·co·lai Lvo·vich** (nik′ə lī′ lə vō′vich; *Russ.* nyi ku lī′ lvô′vyich), 1903–76, U.S. composer, born in Russia. Also, **Lo·pat′ni·koff′.**

CONCISE PRONUNCIATION KEY: act, cāpe, dâre, pärt; set, ēqual; *if,* ice; ox, ōver, ôrder, oil, bo͝ok, bo͞ot, out; up, ûrge; child; sing; shoe; thin, *th*at; zh as in *treasure.* ə = a as in *alone,* e as in *system,* i as in *easily,* o as in *gallop,* u as in *circus;* ᵊ as in *fire* (fīᵊr), *hour* (ouᵊr). l and n can serve as syllabic consonants, as in *cradle* (krād′l), and *button* (but′n). See the full key inside the front cover.

lope (lōp), *v.*, **loped, lop·ing,** *n.* —*v.i.* **1.** to move or run with bounding steps, as a quadruped, or with a long, easy stride, as a person. **2.** to canter leisurely with a rather long, easy stride, as a horse. —*v.t.* **3.** to cause to lope, as a horse. —*n.* **4.** the act or the gait of loping. **5.** a long, easy stride. [1375–1425; late ME < D *lopen* to run, c. OE *hlēapan* to LEAP]

lop-eared (lop′ērd′), *adj.* having ears that droop or hang down. [1680–90]

Lo·pe de Ve·ga (lō′pā də vā′gə; *Sp.* lô′pe *th*e ve′gä). See **Vega, Lope de.**

lop·er (lō′pər), *n.* **1.** a person or thing that lopes, as a horse with a loping gait. **2.** Also called **draw runner, draw slip.** *Furniture.* either of two runners coming forward to support a hinged leaf, as the slant front of a desk. [1475–85; LOPE + -ER[1]]

lo·per·a·mide (lō per′ə mīd′), *n. Pharm.* a substance, $C_{29}H_{33}ClN_2O_2$, used in the treatment of diarrhea. [(*ch*)*lo*(*rophenyl*) + (*pi*)*per*(*idine*) + (*butyr*)*amide,* three of its chemical components]

Ló·pez (lō′pez; *Sp.* lô′pes), *n.* **Os·val·do** (ôs väl′dô), (*Osvaldo López Arellano*), born 1921, Honduran air force general: president of Honduras 1963–75.

Ló·pez de A·ya·la (lô′peth *th*e ä yä′lä, lô′pes), **Pe·dro** (pe′*th*rô), 1332–1407, Spanish writer and statesman.

Ló·pez de Le·gaz·pe (lô′peth *th*e le gäth′pe, lô′pes *th*e le gäs′pe), **Mi·guel** (mē gel′), 1510?–72, Spanish conqueror and colonizer of the Philippines 1565: founder of Manila 1571. Also, **Ló′pez de Le·gas′pi** (le gäs′pē).

Ló·pez Ma·te·os (lô′pes mä te′ôs), **A·dol·fo** (ä *th*ôl′fô), 1910–69, Mexican lawyer and politician: president of Mexico 1958–64.

Ló·pez y Fuen·tes (lô′pes ē fwen′tes), **Gre·go·rio** (gʀe gô′ʀyô), 1895–1966, Mexican writer.

loph·o·branch (lof′ə brangk′, lō′fə-), *adj.* **1.** belonging or pertaining to the Lophobranchii, the group of fishes comprising the pipefishes, sea horses, snipefishes, trumpetfishes, etc. —*n.* **2.** a lophobranch fish. [1855–60; < NL *Lophobranchii* name of the group < Gk *lóph*(*os*) crest, tuft + -o- -O- + *branchí*(*a*) BRANCHIA + L -*ī* nom. pl. n. ending] —**loph·o·bran·chi·ate** (lof′ə brang′kē it, -āt′, lō′fə-), *adj., n.*

loph·o·dont (lof′ə dont′, lō′fə-), *adj.* having molar teeth with crowns in the form of transverse ridges. Cf. **bunodont.** [1885–90; < Gk *lóph*(*os*) a crest, tuft + -ODONT]

loph·o·phore (lof′ə fôr′, -fōr′, lō′fə-), *n.* **1.** the ring of ciliated tentacles encircling the mouth of a bryozoan or phoronid. **2.** a similar organ in a brachiopod, composed of two ciliated, spirally coiled tentacles. [1840–50; < Gk *lóph*(*os*) a crest, ridge + -o- -O- + -PHORE] —**lo·phoph·o·ral** (lə fof′ər əl), *adj.*

lop·o·lith (lop′ə lith), *n. Geol.* a mass of igneous rock similar to a laccolith but concave downward rather than upward. [1915–20; < Gk *lop*(*ós*) shell, husk + -o- -O- + -LITH]

lop·per[1] (lop′ər), *n.* a person or thing that lops. [1530–40; LOP[1] + -ER[1]]

lop·per[2] (lop′ər), *v.i., v.t. Scot. and North Central U.S.* (esp. of milk) to curdle or coagulate. [1300–50; ME *loperen,* equiv. to *lop-* (< ON *hlaup* coagulation) + -*er* -ER[6] + -*en* inf. suffix]

lop′ping shears′, long-handled pruning shears. Also called **lop′pers.** [1870–75]

lop·py (lop′ē), *adj.* **-pi·er, pi·est.** hanging limply; lopping: *awkward, loppy arms.* [1850–55; LOP[2] + -Y[1]]
—**Syn.** flabby, flaccid. —**Ant.** erect.

lop·seed (lop′sēd′), *n.* a weedy plant, *Phryma leptostachya,* of Asia and North America, having spikes of whitish paired flowers. [1810–20, *Amer.;* LOP[2] + SEED]

lop·sid·ed (lop′sī′did), *adj.* **1.** heavier, larger, or more developed on one side than on the other; unevenly balanced; unsymmetrical. **2.** leaning to one side. [1705–15; LOP[2] + SIDED] —**lop′sid′ed·ly,** *adv.* —**lop′sid′ed·ness,** *n.*
—**Syn. 1.** uneven, unequal.

lop·stick (lop′stik′), *n. Canadian.* a tree trimmed of all but its topmost branches to serve as a landmark or marker. Also, **lobstick.** [1815–25; LOP[1] + STICK[1]]

loq., loquitur.

lo·qua·cious (lō kwā′shəs), *adj.* **1.** talking or tending to talk much or freely; talkative; chattering; babbling; garrulous: *a loquacious dinner guest.* **2.** characterized by excessive talk; wordy: *easily the most loquacious play of the season.* [1660–70; LOQUACI(TY) + -OUS] —**lo·qua′cious·ly,** *adv.* —**lo·qua′cious·ness,** *n.*
—**Syn. 1.** verbose, voluble. See **talkative.**

lo·quac·i·ty (lō kwas′i tē), *n., pl.* **-ties. 1.** the state of being loquacious; talkativeness; garrulity. **2.** an instance of talkativeness or garrulity; a loquacious flow of talk: *The sherry increased my loquacity.* [1595–1605; < L *loquācitās* talkativeness, equiv. to *loquāci-,* s. of *loquāx* talkative (deriv. of *loquī* to speak; cf. ELOQUENT) + -*tās* -TY[2]]

lo·quat (lō′kwot, -kwat), *n.* **1.** a small evergreen tree, *Eriobotrya japonica,* native to China and Japan, cultivated as an ornamental and for its yellow, plumlike fruit. **2.** the fruit itself. Also called **Japanese plum.** [1810–20; < dial. Chin (Guangdong) *lōkwat,* akin to Chin *lújú*]

lo·qui·tur (lō′kwi to͝oʀ′; *Eng.* lok′wi tər), *Latin.* he speaks; she speaks.

CONCISE ETYMOLOGY KEY: <, descended or borrowed from; >, whence; b., blend of, blended; c., cognate with; cf., compare; deriv., derivative; equiv., equivalent; imit., imitative; obl., oblique; r., replacing; s., stem; sp., spelling, spelled; resp., respelling, respelled; trans., translation; ?, origin unknown; *, unattested; ‡, probably earlier than. See the full key inside the front cover.

Lo·rain (lə rān′, lô-, lō-), *n.* a port in N Ohio, on Lake Erie. 75,416.

Lo·raine (lə rān′, lô-, lō-), *n.* a female given name, form of **Lorraine.**

lo·ral[1] (lôr′əl, lōr′-), *adj.* of or pertaining to lore, knowledge, learning, etc. [LORE[1] + -AL[1]]

lo·ral[2] (lôr′əl, lōr′-), *adj. Zool.* of or pertaining to a lore. [1870–75; LORE[2] + -AL[1]]

lo·ran (lôr′an, lōr′-), *n.* a system of long-range navigation whereby the latitude and longitude of a ship or airplane are determined from the time displacement between radio signals from two or more fixed transmitters. Also, **Lo′ran.** [1940–45, *Amer.; lo*(*ng*) *ra*(*nge*) *n*(*avigation*)]

lor·az·e·pam (lô raz′ə pam′, lə-), *n. Pharm.* a benzodiazepine drug, $C_{15}H_{10}Cl_2N_2O_2$, used chiefly in the management of acute anxiety and for insomnia. [(CH)LOR(O-) + (DI)AZEPAM]

Lor·ca (lôr′kə; *Sp.* lôʀ′kä), *n.* **1.** See **García Lorca. 2.** a city in SE Spain. 60,609.

lord (lôrd), *n.* **1.** a person who has authority, control, or power over others; a master, chief, or ruler. **2.** a person who exercises authority from property rights; an owner of land, houses, etc. **3.** a person who is a leader or has great influence in a chosen profession: *the great lords of banking.* **4.** a feudal superior; the proprietor of a manor. **5.** a titled nobleman or peer; a person whose ordinary appellation contains by courtesy the title *Lord* or some higher title. **6. Lords,** the Lords Spiritual and Lords Temporal comprising the House of Lords. **7.** (*cap.*) (in Britain) **a.** the title of certain high officials (used with some other title, name, or the like): *Lord Mayor of London.* **b.** the formally polite title of a bishop: *Lord Bishop of Durham.* **c.** the title informally substituted for marquis, earl, viscount, etc., as in the use of *Lord Kitchener* for *Earl Kitchener.* **8.** (*cap.*) the Supreme Being; God; Jehovah. **9.** (*cap.*) the Savior, Jesus Christ. **10.** *Astrol.* a planet having dominating influence. —*interj.* **11.** (*often cap.*) (used in exclamatory phrases to express surprise, elation, etc.): *Lord, what a beautiful day!* —*v.* **12. lord it,** to assume airs of importance and authority; behave arrogantly or dictatorially; domineer: *to lord it over the menial workers.* [bef. 900; ME *lord, loverd,* OE *hlāford, hlāfweard* lit., loaf-keeper. See LOAF[1], WARD] —**lord′like′,** *adj.*

Lord′ Bal′timore cake′, a yellow layer cake, using only the yolks of eggs and having a fruit-nut filling consisting of pecans, almonds, maraschino cherries, and macaroon crumbs. Cf. **Lady Baltimore cake.**

Lord′ Chan′cellor, *pl.* **Lords Chancellor.** the highest judicial officer of the British crown: law adviser of the ministry, keeper of the great seal, presiding officer in the House of Lords, etc. Also called **Lord′ High′ Chan′cellor.** [1490–1500]

Lord′ Chief′ Jus′tice, the presiding judge of Britain's High Court of Justice, the superior court of record for both criminal and civil cases.

Lord′ Faun′tleroy suit′. See **Fauntleroy suit.**

Lord′ Haw′-Haw (hô′hô′). See **Joyce, William.**

Lord′ Howe′ Is′land, an island in the S Pacific, E of Australia: a dependency of New South Wales. 287; 5 sq. mi. (13 sq. km).

lord·ing (lôr′ding), *n. Archaic.* **1.** lord. **2.** Often, **lordings.** lords; sirs; gentlemen (often used as a term of address). [1150–1200; ME; OE *hlāfording* prince, lit., offspring of a lord, equiv. to *hlāford* LORD + -*ing* -ING[3]]

lord-in-wait·ing (lôrd′in wā′ting), *n., pl.* **lords-in-wait·ing.** a nobleman in attendance on a British monarch or the Prince of Wales. [1855–60]

Lord′ Jim′, a novel (1900) by Joseph Conrad.

lord·less (lôrd′lis), *adj.* having no lord. [bef. 900; ME *lordles,* OE *hlāfordlēas.* See LORD, -LESS]

Lord′ Lieuten′ant, 1. *Brit.* the title of various high officials holding authority deputed from a sovereign. **2.** (formerly) the viceroy in Ireland. —**Lord′ Lieuten′·ancy.** [1960–65]

lord·ling (lôrd′ling), *n.* a minor, unimportant, or petty lord. [1225–75; ME; see LORD, -LING[1]]

lord·ly (lôrd′lē), *adj.* **-li·er, -li·est,** *adv.* —*adj.* **1.** suitable for a lord, as trappings or ceremonies; grand or magnificent. **2.** insolently imperious; haughty; arrogant; overbearing: *lordly contempt.* **3.** of or pertaining to a lord. **4.** having the character or attributes of a lord. **5.** befitting a lord, as actions: *lordly manners.* —*adv.* **6.** Also, **lord′li·ly.** in the manner of a lord. [bef. 1000; ME; OE *hlāfordlic.* See LORD, -LY] —**lord′li·ness,** *n.*
—**Syn. 1.** majestic, regal, dignified, noble, lofty. **2.** domineering. —**Ant. 2.** meek.

lord′ may′or, (chiefly in Britain and the Commonwealth) the mayor of certain cities or the chief municipal officer of certain boroughs. [1545–55]

Lord′ of hosts′, Jehovah; God. Also, **Lord′ of Hosts′.**

Lord′ of Misrule′, (in England) a person formerly chosen to direct the Christmas revels and sports. [1490–1500]

Lord′ of the Flies′, a novel (1954) by William Golding.

lor·do·sis (lôr dō′sis), *n. Pathol.* an abnormal forward curvature of the spine in the lumbar region, resulting in a swaybacked posture. Cf. **kyphosis, scoliosis.** [1695–1705; < NL < Gk *lórdōsis* lit., a bending back, equiv. to *lord*(*ós*) bent backwards + -*ōsis* -OSIS] —**lor·dot·ic** (lôr dot′ik), *adj.*

Lord′ Priv′y Seal′, (in Britain) a cabinet minister without portfolio. [1550–60]

Lord′ Protec′tor, protector (def. 2b).

Lord′ Pro′vost, the chief magistrate of any of certain large cities in Scotland.

lords-and-la·dies (lôrdz′ən lā′dēz), *n., pl.* **-la·dies.** (*used with a singular v.*) cuckoopint. [1750–60]

Lord's′ day′, the, Sunday. [1175–1225; ME]

lord·ship (lôrd′ship), *n.* **1.** (*often cap.*) a term of respect used when speaking of or to certain noblemen (usually prec. by *his* or *your*). **2.** the state or dignity of a lord. **3.** the authority or power of a lord. **4.** the domain of a lord. **5.** *Brit.* (*often cap.*) a term of respect used when speaking of or to judges (usually prec. by *his* or *your*). [bef. 900; ME; OE *hlāfordscipe.* See LORD, -SHIP]

Lord′ Spir′itual, *pl.* **Lords Spiritual.** a bishop or archbishop belonging to the House of Lords. Cf. **Lord Temporal.** [1400–50; late ME]

Lord's′ Prayer′, the (prâr), the prayer given by Jesus to His disciples, and beginning with the words *Our Father.* Matt. 6:9–13; Luke 11:2–4. [1540–50]

Lord's′ Sup′per, the, 1. the sacrament in commemoration of the Last Supper; communion; Mass; Eucharist. **2.** See **Last Supper.** [1350–1400; ME]

Lord's′ ta′ble, the. See **communion table.** [1525–35]

Lord′ Tem′poral, *pl.* **Lords Temporal.** a member of the House of Lords who is not a member of the clergy. Cf. **Lord Spiritual.** [1400–50; late ME]

lore[1] (lôr, lōr), *n.* **1.** the body of knowledge, esp. of a traditional, anecdotal, or popular nature, on a particular subject: *the lore of herbs.* **2.** learning, knowledge, or erudition. **3.** *Archaic.* **a.** the process or act of teaching; instruction. **b.** something that is taught; lesson. [bef. 950; ME; OE *lār;* c. D *leer,* G *Lehre* teaching. See LEARN] —**lore′less,** *adj.*
—**Syn. 1.** wisdom. See **learning.**

lore[2] (lôr, lōr), *n. Zool.* the space between the eye and the bill of a bird, or a corresponding space in other animals, as snakes. [1615–25; < NL *lōrum,* special use of L *lōrum* thong, strap]

Lor·e·lei (lôr′ə lī′; *Ger.* lō′ʀə lī′), *n.* **1.** a quasilegendary nymph of the Rhine who lured sailors to shipwreck on her rock by singing: a creation of Clemens Brentano in a poem of 1800. **2.** a female given name. [< G, var. of *Lurlei,* cliff overlooking the Rhine, thought to be the abode of a nymph]

Lo·ren (lôr′ən, lōr′-), *n.* a male given name, form of **Lawrence.**

Lo·re·na (lə rē′nə, lô-, lō-), *n.* a female given name.

Lo·rentz (lôr′ənts, lōr′-; *Du.* lō′ʀents), *n.* **Hen·drik An·toon** (hen′dʀik än′tōn), 1853–1928, Dutch physicist: Nobel prize 1902.

Lo′rentz-Fitz·Ger′ald contrac′tion (lôr′ənts fitsjer′əld, lōr′-), *Physics.* See **FitzGerald contraction.** [1920–25]

Lo′rentz force′, *Elect.* the force on a charged particle moving through a region containing both electric and magnetic fields. [1960–65; named after H. A. LORENTZ]

Lo′rentz transforma′tion, *Physics.* the mathematical transformation in the special theory of relativity that describes the way in which measurements of space, time, and other physical quantities differ for two observers in uniform relative motion. [1905–10; named after H. A. LORENTZ]

Lo·renz (lôr′ənz, lōr′-; *Ger.* lō′ʀents), *n.* **A·dolf** (ā′dolf; *Ger.* ä′dôlf), **1.** 1854–1946, Austrian orthopedic surgeon. **2. Kon·rad** (**Za·cha·ri·as**) (kon′rad zak′ə rī′əs; *Ger.* kôn′rät tsä′ĸнä ʀē′äs), born 1903, Austrian ethologist: Nobel prize for medicine 1973.

Lo·ren·zet·ti (lôr′ən zet′ē; *It.* lô′ʀen dzet′tē), *n.* **Am·bro·gio** (äm bʀô′jô), c1319–48, and his brother, **Pie·tro** (pye′tʀô), c1305–48, Italian painters.

Lo·ren·zo (lə ren′zō, lô-, lō-), *n.* **Saint.** See **Lawrence, Saint.**

lo-res (lō′rez′), *adj. Computers Informal.* low-resolution. [by shortening and resp.]

Lo·re·stan (lôr′ə stän′, -stan′, lōr′-), *n.* Luristan.

Lo·ret·ta (lə ret′ə, lô-, lō-), *n.* a female given name, form of **Laura.** Also, **Lo·rette** (lə ret′, lô-, lō-).

Lo·rette·ville (lô ret′vil, lō-; *Fr.* lô ʀet vēl′), *n.* a city in S Quebec, in E Canada: suburb of Quebec. 15,060.

lor·gnette (lôrn yet′), *n.* **1.** a pair of eyeglasses mounted on a handle. **2.** a pair of opera glasses mounted on a handle. [1795–1805; < F, deriv. of *lorgner* to eye furtively; see -ETTE]

lor·gnon (*Fr.* lôʀ nyôɴ′), *n., pl.* **-gnons** (*Fr.* -nyôɴ′). **1.** an eyeglass or a pair of eyeglasses. **2.** See **opera glasses.** [1840–50; < F, equiv. to *lorgn*(*er*) (see LORGNETTE) + -*on* n. suffix]

lo·ri·ca (lə rī′kə, lô-, lō-), *n., pl.* **-cae** (-sē, -kē). **1.** *Zool.* a hard protective case or sheath, as the protective coverings secreted by certain protists. **2.** a cuirass or corselet, originally of leather. [1700–10; (def. 1) < NL, special use of L *lōrīca* corselet (orig. of leather), akin to *lōrum* thong; (def. 2) < L]

lor·i·cate (lôr′i kāt′, -kit, lor′-), *adj. Zool.* covered with a lorica. Also, **lor′i·cat′ed.** [1615–25; < L *lōricātus.* See LORICA, -ATE[1]] —**lor′i·ca′tion,** *n.*

Lo·rient (lô ʀyäɴ′), *n.* a seaport in NW France, on the Bay of Biscay. 71,923.

lor·i·keet (lôr′i kēt′, lor′-, lôr′ə kēt′, lor′-), *n.* any of various small lories. [1765–75; LORY + (PARA)KEET]

lor·i·mer (lôr′ə mər), *n.* a craftsperson who makes hardware for harnesses and riding habits, as bits or spurs. Also, **lor·i·ner** (lôr′ə nər). [1175–1225; ME < AF; OF *lor*(*e*)*mier, lorenier,* deriv. of *lorain* harness strap < VL **lōrāmen,* for L *lōrāmentum* strap, equiv. to *lōr*(*um*) strap, thong + -*ā-* generalized from v. derivatives + -*mentum* -MENT; see -ER[2], -IER[2]]

Lo·rin (lôr′in, lōr′-), *n.* a male given name, form of **Lawrence.**

Lo·ring (lôr′ing, lōr′-), *n.* a male given name.

lo•ris (lôr′is, lōr′-), *n., pl.* **-ris. 1.** Also called **slender loris.** a small, slender, tailless, large-eyed, nocturnal lemur, *Loris gracilis,* of southern India and Sri Lanka. **2.** Also called **slow loris.** a similar but stockier lemur of the genus *Nycticebus,* of southeastern Asia: *N. pygmaeus* is a threatened species. [1765–75; < NL < D *loeris* simpleton, equiv. to *loer* stupid person (< F *lourd* < L *lūridus* LURID) + *-is* -ISH[1]]

lorn (lôrn), *adj.* **1.** forsaken, desolate, bereft, or forlorn. **2.** *Archaic.* lost, ruined, or undone. [1250–1300; ME; OE *loren,* ptp. of *-lēosan* to LOSE (recorded in compounds)] **—lorn′ness,** *n.*

Lor•na (lôr′nə), *n.* a female given name.

Lor•raine (lə rān′, lô-, lō-; *Fr.* lô ren′), *n.* **1.** Also, **Lor•rain′. Claude** (*Claude Gelée*), 1600–82, French painter. **2.** a medieval kingdom in W Europe along the Moselle, Meuse, and Rhine rivers. **3.** a region in NE France, once included in this kingdom: a former province. Cf. **Alsace-Lorraine. 4.** a female given name.

Lorraine′ cross′. See **cross of Lorraine.** [1915–20]

Lor•re (lôr′ē), *n.* **Peter** (*László Loewenstein*), 1904–64, U.S. film actor, born in Hungary.

Lor•rie (lôr′ē), *n.* a female given name, form of **Laura.**

lor•ry (lôr′ē, lor′ē), *n., pl.* **-ries. 1.** *Chiefly Brit.* a motor truck, esp. a large one. **2.** any of various conveyances running on rails, as for transporting material in a mine or factory. **3.** a long, low, horse-drawn wagon without sides. [1830–40; akin to dial. *lurry* to pull, drag, lug]

lo•ry (lôr′ē, lōr′ē), *n., pl.* **-ries.** any of several small, usually brilliantly colored Australasian parrots having the tongue bordered with a brushlike fringe for feeding on nectar and fruit juices. [1685–95; (< D *lori, loeri*) < Malay *lori, luri, nuri* parrot]

los•a•ble (lo͞o′zə bəl), *adj.* susceptible to becoming lost. [1605–15; LOSE + -ABLE] **—los′a•ble•ness,** *n.*

Los Al•a•mi•tos (lôs al′ə mē′tōs, los), a town in S California. 11,529.

Los Al•a•mos (lôs al′ə mōs′, los), a town in central New Mexico: atomic research center. 11,039.

Los Al•tos (lôs al′təs, los), a city in W California. 25,769.

Los An•ge•le•no (lôs an′jə lē′nō, los), Angeleno (def. 1). Also called **Los An•ge•le•an** (lôs an′jə lē′ən, los).

Los An•ge•les (lôs an′jə ləs, -lēz′, los *or, often,* lôs ang′gə ləs, -lēz′, los), a seaport in SW California. 2,966,763; with suburbs 6,997,000; 452 sq. mi. (1170 sq. km).

Los Ba•nos (lôs ban′əs, los), a town in central California. 10,341.

Lo′schmidt's num′ber (lō′shmits), *Chem.* the number of molecules in one cubic centimeter of an ideal gas at standard temperature and pressure, equal to 2.687 × 10^{19}. Cf. **Avogadro's number.** [after Joseph *Loschmidt* (1821–95), Austrian chemist, who calculated it]

lose (lo͞oz), *v.,* **lost, los•ing.** *—v.t.* **1.** to come to be without (something in one's possession or care), through accident, theft, etc., so that there is little or no prospect of recovery: *I'm sure I've merely misplaced my hat, not lost it.* **2.** to fail inadvertently to retain (something) in such a way that it cannot be immediately recovered: *I just lost a dime under this sofa.* **3.** to suffer the deprivation of: *to lose one's job; to lose one's life.* **4.** to be bereaved of by death: *to lose a sister.* **5.** to fail to keep, preserve, or maintain: *to lose one's balance; to lose one's figure.* **6.** (of a clock or watch) to run slower by: *The watch loses three minutes a day.* **7.** to give up; forfeit the possession of: *to lose a fortune at the gaming table.* **8.** to get rid of: *to lose one's fear of the dark; to lose weight.* **9.** to bring to destruction or ruin (usually used passively): *Ship and crew were lost.* **10.** to condemn to hell; damn. **11.** to have slip from sight, hearing, attention, etc.: *to lose him in the crowd.* **12.** to stray from or become ignorant of (one's way, directions, etc.): *to lose one's bearings.* **13.** to leave far behind in a pursuit, race, etc.; outstrip: *She managed to lose the other runners on the final lap of the race.* **14.** to use to no purpose; waste: *to lose time in waiting.* **15.** to fail to have, get, catch, etc.; miss: *to lose a bargain.* **16.** to fail to win (a prize, stake, etc.): *to lose a bet.* **17.** to be defeated in (a game, lawsuit, battle, etc.): *He has lost very few cases in his career as a lawyer.* **18.** to cause the loss of: *The delay lost the battle for them.* **19.** to let (oneself) go astray, miss the way, etc.: *We lost ourselves in the woods.* **20.** to allow (oneself) to become absorbed or engrossed in something and oblivious to all else: *I had lost myself in thought.* **21.** (of a physician) to fail to preserve the life of (a patient). **22.** (of a woman) to fail to be delivered of (a live baby) because of miscarriage, complications in childbirth, etc. *—v.i.* **23.** to suffer loss: *to lose on a contract.* **24.** to suffer defeat or fail to win, as in a contest, race, or game: *We played well, but we lost.* **25.** to depreciate in effectiveness or in some other essential quality: *a classic that loses in translation.* **26.** (of a clock, watch, etc.) to run slow. **27. lose face.** See **face** (def. 30). **28. lose out,** to suffer defeat or loss; fail to obtain something desired: *He got through the preliminaries, but lost out in the finals.* [bef. 900; ME *losen,* OE *-lēosan;* r. ME *lesen,* itself also reflecting OE *-lēosan;* c. G *verlieren,* Goth *fraliusan* to lose. See LOSS]

lo•sel (lō′zəl, lo͞o′-, loz′əl), *Archaic.* *—n.* **1.** a worthless person; scoundrel. *—adj.* **2.** worthless or useless. [1325–75; ME: lit., one who is lost, equiv. to *los-* (ptp. s. of LOSE) + *-el* -LE]

los•er (lo͞o′zər), *n.* **1.** a person, team, nation, etc., that loses: *The visiting team was the loser in the series.* **2.** *Informal.* **a.** a person who has been convicted of a misdemeanor or, esp., a felony: *a two-time loser.* **b.** a person who has failed at a particular activity: *a loser at marriage.* **c.** someone or something that is marked by consistently or thoroughly bad quality, performance, etc.: *Don't bother to see that film, it's a real loser.* **3.** *Slang.* a misfit, esp. someone who has never or seldom been successful at a job, personal relationship, etc. [1300–50; ME *losere* destroyer; see LOSE, -ER[1]]

Los Ga•tos (lôs gat′əs, los), a town in W California. 26,593.

los•ing (lo͞o′zing), *adj.* **1.** causing or suffering loss. *—n.* **2. losings,** losses. [bef. 950; ME, OE; see LOSE, -ING[2], -ING[1]] **—los′ing•ly,** *adv.*

los′ing haz′ard. See under **hazard** (def. 8).

loss (lôs, los), *n.* **1.** detriment, disadvantage, or deprivation from failure to keep, have, or get: *to bear the loss of a robbery.* **2.** something that is lost: *The painting was the greatest loss from the robbery.* **3.** an amount or number lost: *The loss of life increased each day.* **4.** the state of being deprived of or of being without something that one has had: *the loss of old friends.* **5.** death, or the fact of being dead: *to mourn the loss of a grandparent.* **6.** the accidental or inadvertent losing of something dropped, misplaced, stolen, etc.: *to discover the loss of a document.* **7.** a losing by defeat; failure to win: *the loss of a bet.* **8.** failure to make good use of something, as time; waste. **9.** failure to preserve or maintain: *loss of engine speed at high altitudes.* **10.** destruction or ruin: *the loss of a ship by fire.* **11.** a thing or a number of related things that are lost or destroyed to some extent: *Most buildings in the burned district were a total loss.* **12.** *Mil.* **a.** the losing of soldiers by death, capture, etc. **b.** Often, **losses.** the number of soldiers so lost. **13.** *Insurance.* occurrence of an event, as death or damage of property, for which the insurer makes indemnity under the terms of a policy. **14.** *Elect.* a measure of the power lost in a system, as by conversion to heat, expressed as a relation between power input and power output, as the ratio of or difference between the two quantities. **15. at a loss, a.** at less than cost; at a financial loss. **b.** in a state of bewilderment or uncertainty; puzzled; perplexed: *We are completely at a loss for an answer to the problem.* [bef. 900; ME; OE *los* destruction; c. ON *los* looseness, breaking up. See LOSE, LOOSE]
—Syn. 4. privation, deprivation. **—Ant. 1.** gain.

loss′ func′tion, (in decision theory) a function that expresses the loss incurred when a decision is made in terms of various factors.

loss′ lead′er, a popular article that is sold at a very low price or at a loss for the purpose of attracting customers to a retail store. Cf. **leader** (def. 4). [1920–25] **—loss′-lead′ing,** *adj.*

loss•mak•er (lôs′mā′kər, los′-), *n. Chiefly Brit.* a business that consistently operates at a loss. [LOSS + MAKER] **—loss′mak′ing,** *n.*

loss′ ra′tio, *Insurance.* the ratio of the losses paid or accrued by an insurer to premiums earned, usually for a period of one year. [1925–30]

loss•y (lô′sē, los′ē), *adj. Elect.* (of a material or transmission line) causing appreciable loss or dissipation of energy. [1945–50; LOSS + -Y[1]]

lost (lôst, lost), *adj.* **1.** no longer possessed or retained: *lost friends.* **2.** no longer to be found: *lost articles.* **3.** having gone astray or missed the way; bewildered as to place, direction, etc.: *lost children.* **4.** not used to good purpose, as opportunities, time, or labor; wasted: *a lost advantage.* **5.** being something that someone has failed to win: *a lost prize.* **6.** ending in or attended with defeat: *a lost battle.* **7.** destroyed or ruined: *lost ships.* **8.** preoccupied; rapt: *He seems lost in thought.* **9.** distracted; distraught; desperate; hopeless: *the lost look of a man trapped and afraid.* **10. get lost,** *Slang.* **a.** to absent oneself: *I think I'll get lost before an argument starts.* **b.** to stop being a nuisance: *If they call again, tell them to get lost.* **11. lost to, a.** no longer belonging to. **b.** no longer possible or open to: *The opportunity was lost to him.* **c.** insensible to: *lost to all sense of duty.* *—v.t., v.i.* **12.** pt. and pp. of **lose.**
—Syn. 1. forfeited, gone, missing. **3.** confused, perplexed. **4.** squandered. **—Ant. 1.** found.

lost′ cause′, a cause that has been defeated or whose defeat is inevitable. [1860–65]

Lost′ Col′ony, *Amer. Hist.* a settlement of British colonists whom Walter Raleigh sent to Roanoke Island (now part of North Carolina) in 1587 and of whom no trace was found after 1591.

Lost′ Genera′tion, 1. the generation of men and women who came of age during or immediately following World War I: viewed, as a result of their war experiences and the social upheaval of the time, as cynical, disillusioned, and without cultural or emotional stability. **2.** a group of American writers of this generation, including Ernest Hemingway, F. Scott Fitzgerald, and John Dos Passos. [1925–30]

lost′ mo′tion, *Mach.* **1.** motion of a machine or mechanism, esp. a reciprocating one, during which no useful work is performed. **2.** motion between parts in an assembly due to manufacturing tolerances, adjustments, slip, or wear. [1875–80]

Lost′ Ple′iad. See under **Pleiades** (def. 1).

lost′ riv′er, a river that flows into an underground passage or sinkhole. [1835–45, *Amer.*]

lost′ tribes′, the members of the ten tribes of ancient Israel who were taken into captivity in 722 B.C. by Sargon II of Assyria and are believed never to have returned to Palestine. II Kings 17:1–23.

lost′-wax′ proc′ess (lôst′waks′, lost′-), *Metall.* a process of investment casting in which a refractory mold is built up around a pattern of wax and then baked so as to melt and drain off the wax. Also called **cire perdue.** [1930–35; trans. of F *cire perdue*]

lot (lot), *n., v.,* **lot•ted, lot•ting,** *adv.* *—n.* **1.** one of a set of objects, as straws or pebbles, drawn or thrown from a container to decide a question or choice by chance. **2.** the casting or drawing of such objects as a method of deciding something: *to choose a person by lot.* **3.** the decision or choice made by such a method. **4.** allotted share or portion: *to receive one's lot of an inheritance.* **5.** the portion in life assigned by fate or Providence; one's fate, fortune, or destiny: *Her lot had not been a happy one.* **6.** a distinct portion or piece of land: *a building lot.* **7.** a piece of land forming a part of a district, city, or other community. **8.** *South Midland and Southern U.S.* a farmyard or barnyard. **9.** a piece of land having the use specified by the attributive noun or adjective: *a parking lot; a used-car lot.* **10.** *Motion Pictures.* a motion-picture studio and its surrounding property. **11.** a distinct portion or parcel of anything, as of merchandise: *The furniture was to be auctioned off in 20 lots.* **12.** a number of things or persons collectively: *There's one more, and that's the lot.* **13.** kind of person; sort: *He's a bad lot.* **14.** Often, **lots.** a great many or a great deal: *a lot of books; lots of money.* **15.** *Chiefly Brit.* a tax or duty. **16. cast** or **cast in one's lot with,** to ally oneself with; share the life and fortunes of: *She had cast her lot with the bohemian crowd.* **17. draw** or **cast lots,** to settle a question by the use of lots: *They drew lots to see who would go first.* *—v.t.* **18.** to divide or distribute by lot (sometimes fol. by *out*): *to lot furniture for sale; to lot out apples by the basketful.* **19.** to assign to one as his or her lot; allot. **20.** to divide into lots, as land. **21.** *Obs.* to cast or draw lots for. *—v.i.* **22.** to draw lots. *—adv.* **23.** Often, **lots.** a great deal; greatly: *Thanks a lot for the ride. I care lots about my family.* [bef. 950; 1805–15 for def. 14; ME; OE *hlot* portion, choice, decision; c. D *lot,* ON *hlutr;* akin to OE *hlīet,* G *Los,* ON *hlaut,* Goth *hlauts* lot] **—lot′ter,** *n.*
—Syn. 4. part, quota. **7.** plot, parcel. **12.** group, crowd, gang.

Lot (lot), *n.* the nephew of Abraham. His wife was changed into a pillar of salt for looking back during their flight from Sodom. Gen. 13:1–12, 19.

Lot (lôt), *n.* **1.** a river in S France, flowing W to the Garonne. 300 mi. (480 km) long. **2.** a department in S France. 150,725; 2018 sq. mi. (5225 sq. km). *Cap.:* Cahors.

lot., (in prescriptions) a lotion. [< L *lōtiō*]

lo•ta (lō′tə), *n.* (in India) a small container for water, usually of brass or copper and round in shape. Also, **lo′•tah.** [1800–10; < Hindi *lotā*]

lote (lōt), *n. Archaic.* lotus. [1500–10; < L *lōtus*]

Lot-et-Ga•ronne (lô tā ga rôn′), *n.* a department in SW France. 292,616; 2079 sq. mi. (5385 sq. km). *Cap.:* Agen.

loth (lōth, lōth), *adj.* loath.

Lo•thair I (lō thâr′, -târ′), A.D. 795?–855, king of Germany 840–843; emperor of the Holy Roman Empire 840–855 (son of Louis I).

Lothair II, (*"the Saxon"*), c1070–1137, emperor of the Holy Roman Empire and king of the Germans 1125–37.

Lo•thar•i•o (lō thâr′ē ō′), *n., pl.* **-thar•i•os.** (*sometimes l.c.*) a man who obsessively seduces and deceives women. [after the young seducer in Nicholas Rowe's play *The Fair Penitent* (1703)]
—Syn. Don Juan, Romeo, Casanova.

Lo•thi•an (lō′thē ən), *n.* a region in E Scotland. 754,008; 700 sq. mi. (1813 sq. km).

Lo•thi•ans (lō′thē ənz), *n.pl.* **The,** three former counties in SW Scotland: East Lothian, Midlothian, West Lothian.

loth•ly (lōth′lē, lōth′-), *adv. Rare.* loathly[1].

lo•ti (lō′tē), *n., pl.* **ma•lo•ti** (mä lō′tē). a cupronickel coin, paper money, and monetary unit of Lesotho, equal to 100 lisente.

Lo•ti (lô tē′), *n.* **Pierre** (pyer), (*Louis Marie Julien Viaud*), 1850–1923, French novelist.

lo•tic (lō′tik), *adj.* pertaining to or living in flowing water. [1915–20; < L *lōt*(*us*) washed (see LOMENT) + -IC]

lo•tion (lō′shən), *n.* **1.** *Pharm.* a liquid, usually aqueous or sometimes alcoholic preparation containing insoluble material in the form of a suspension or emulsion, intended for external application without rubbing, in such skin conditions as itching, infection, allergy, pain, or the like. **2.** a liquid cosmetic, usually containing agents for soothing or softening the skin, esp. that of the face or hands. [1350–1400; ME *locion* < L *lōtiōn-* (s. of *lōtiō*) a washing. See LOTIC, -ION]

lo•toph•a•gi (lō tof′ə jī′), *n.pl. Class. Myth.* lotus-eaters. [< L *Lōtophagi* < Gk *Lōtophágoi.* See LOTUS-EATER]

Lot•ta (lot′ə), *n.* a female given name, form of **Charlotte.**

lotte (lot; *Fr.* lôt), *n.* angler (def. 3). [< F, MF; cf. ML *lota;* ulterior orig. unknown]

lot•ter•y (lot′ə rē), *n., pl.* **-ter•ies. 1.** a gambling game or method of raising money, as for some public charitable purpose, in which a large number of tickets are sold and a drawing is held for certain prizes. **2.** any scheme for the distribution of prizes by chance. **3.** any happening or process that is or appears to be determined by chance: *to look upon life as a lottery.* [1560–70; < MD *loterie* (whence also F *loterie*). See LOT, -ERY]

Lot·tie (lot′ē), *n.* a female given name, form of **Charlotte.** Also, **Lot′ty.**

lot·to (lot′ō), *n.* **1.** a game of chance in which a leader draws numbered disks at random from a stock and the players cover the corresponding numbers on their cards, the winner being the first to cover a complete row. **2.** a lottery, as one operated by a state government, in which players choose numbers that are matched against those of the official drawing, the winning numbers typically paying large cash prizes. [1770–80; < It < Gmc; see LOT]

lo·tus (lō′təs), *n., pl.* **-tus·es. 1.** a plant believed to be a jujube or elm, referred to in Greek legend as yielding a fruit that induced a state of dreamy and contented forgetfulness in those who ate it. **2.** the fruit itself. **3.** any aquatic plant of the genus *Nelumbo,* of the water lily family, having shieldlike leaves and showy, solitary flowers usually projecting above the water. **4.** any of several water lilies of the genus *Nymphaea.* **5.** a decorative motif derived from such a plant and used widely in ancient art, as on the capitals of Egyptian columns. **6.** any shrubby plant of the genus *Lotus,* of the legume family, having red, pink, yellow, or white flowers. [1530–40; < L *lōtus, lōtos* < Gk *lōtós* the lotus plant, perh of Sem orig.]

lotus (def. 5)

lo·tus-eat·er (lō′təs ē′tər), *n.* **1.** *Class. Myth.* a member of a people whom Odysseus found existing in a state of languorous forgetfulness induced by their eating of the fruit of the legendary lotus; one of the lotophagi. **2.** a person who leads a life of dreamy, indolent ease, indifferent to the busy world; daydreamer. [1825–35; sing. of *lotus-eaters,* trans. of Gk *Lōtophágoi,* n. use of masc. pl. of *lōtophágos* lotus-eating. See LOTUS, -PHAGOUS]

Lo′tus of the Good′ Law′, *Buddhism.* Saddharma-Pundarika. Also called **Lo′tus of the True′ Law′.**

lo′tus posi′tion, a standard seated posture for yoga, with legs intertwined, left foot over right thigh, and right foot over left thigh. [1960–65]

Lo′tus Su′tra, Saddharma-Pundarika.

Lo·tze (lōt′sə; *Ger.* lō′tsə), *n.* **Ru·dolf Her·mann** (ro͞o′dolf hûr′mən; *Ger.* RO͞O′dôlf heR′män), 1817–81, German philosopher.

Lou (lo͞o), *n.* **1.** a male given name, form of **Louis. 2.** a female given name, form of **Louise.**

Louang·phra·bang (lwäng′prä bäng′), *n.* a city in N Laos, on the Mekong River: former royal capital. 44,244. Also, **Luang Prabang.**

louche (lo͞osh), *adj.* dubious; shady; disreputable. [1810–20; < F: lit., cross-eyed; OF *losche,* fem. of *lois* < L *luscus* blind in one eye]

loud (loud), *adj.,* **-er, -est,** *adv.* —*adj.* **1.** (of sound) strongly audible; having exceptional volume or intensity: *loud talking; loud thunder; loud whispers.* **2.** making, emitting, or uttering strongly audible sounds: *a quartet of loud trombones.* **3.** clamorous, vociferous, or blatant; noisy: *a loud party; a loud demonstration.* **4.** emphatic or insistent: *to be loud in one's praises; a loud denial.* **5.** garish, conspicuous, or ostentatious, as colors, dress, or the wearer of garish dress: *loud ties; a loud dresser.* **6.** obtrusively vulgar, as manners or persons. **7.** strong or offensive in smell. —*adv.* **8.** in a loud manner; loudly: *Don't talk so loud.* **9. out loud,** aloud; audibly: *I thought it, but I never said it out loud. Just whisper, don't speak out loud.* [bef. 900; ME; OE *hlūd;* c. OFris, OS *hlūd* (D *luid*), OHG *hlūt* (G *laut*); akin to Gk *klytós* famous] —**loud′ly,** *adv.* —**loud′ness,** *n.*
—**Syn. 1.** resounding; deafening; stentorian. LOUD, NOISY describe a strongly audible sound or sounds. LOUD means characterized by a full, powerful sound or sounds, which make a strong impression on the organs of hearing: *a loud voice, laugh, report.* NOISY refers to a series of sounds, and suggests clamor and discordance, or persistence in making loud sounds that are disturbing and annoying: *a noisy crowd.* **5.** gaudy, flashy, showy. —**Ant. 1.** quiet.

loud·en (loud′n), *v.t., v.i.* to make or become loud. [1795–1805; LOUD + -EN[1]]

loud·ish (lou′dish), *adj.* somewhat loud. [1855–60; LOUD + -ISH[1]]

loud·mouth (loud′mouth′), *n., pl.* **-mouths** (-mouthz′, -mouths′). a loudmouthed person. [1660–70; LOUD + MOUTH]

loud·mouthed (loud′mouthd′, -moutht′), *adj.* loud, gossipy, or indiscreet; vociferous. [1620–30; LOUD + MOUTH + -ED[3]]

loud′ ped′al, *Music.* See **damper pedal.**

loud·speak·er (loud′spē′kər), *n.* **1.** any of various devices, usually electronic, by which speech, music, etc., can be intensified and made audible throughout a room, hall, or the like. **2.** *Audio.* **a.** a device for transforming electric signals into audible sound, most frequently used to reproduce speech and music. **b.** speaker (def. 4). [1880–85; LOUD + SPEAKER]

CONCISE ETYMOLOGY KEY: <, descended or borrowed from; >, whence; b., blend of, blended; c., cognate with; cf., compare; deriv., derivative; equiv., equivalent; imit., imitative; obl., oblique; r., replacing; s., stem; sp., spelling, spelled; resp., respelling, respelled; trans., translation; ?, origin unknown; *, unattested; ‡, probably earlier than. See the full key inside the front cover.

Lou·el·la (lo͞o el′ə), *n.* a female given name.

Lou′ Gehr′ig's disease′, *Pathol.* See **amyotrophic lateral sclerosis.** [1955–60]

lough (lok, loKH), *n. Irish Eng.* **1.** a lake. **2.** a partially landlocked or protected bay; a narrow arm of the sea. Cf. **loch.** [1505–15; Anglo-Irish sp. of Ir *loch* lake; cf. ME *low, lough(e), logh(e),* OE (Northumbrian) *lūh* < British Celtic **lux-* (> Welsh *llwch* (obs.) lake, OBreton *luh,* Breton *louc'h*), appar. < early Ir; see LOCH]

Lough′ Neagh′ (nā), a lake in E central Northern Ireland: largest freshwater lake in the British Isles. ab. 18 mi. (29 km) long and 11 mi. (18 km) wide.

Lou·hi (lō′hi), *n. Finnish Legend.* a sorceress, the mistress of Pohjola and an enemy of the Finns, eventually defeated by Vainamoinen.

lou·ie (lo͞o′ē), *n.* looie.

Lou·ie (lo͞o′ē), *n.* a male given name, form of **Louis.**

lou·is (lo͞o′ē; *Fr.* lwē), *n., pl.* **lou·is** (lo͞o′ēz; *Fr.* lwē). See **louis d'or.** [1680–90]

Lou·is (lo͞o′is *or, for 2,* lo͞o′ē), *n.* **1. Joe** (*Joseph Louis Barrow*), 1914–81, U.S. boxer: world heavyweight champion 1937–49. **2.** a male given name: from a Germanic word meaning "loud battle."

Lou·is I (lo͞o′ē, lo͞o′is; *Fr.* lwē), (*"le Débonaire"; "the Pious"*) A.D. 778–840, king of France and Germany 814–840; emperor of the Holy Roman Empire 814–840 (son of Charlemagne).

Louis II, 1. German, **Ludwig II.** (*"the German"*) A.D. 804?–876, king of Germany 843–876 (son of Louis I). **2.** A.D. 822?–875, king of Italy 844–875; emperor of the Holy Roman Empire 855–875 (son of Lothair I).

Louis II de Bourbon. See **Condé, Prince de.**

Louis IV, (*"the Bavarian"*) 1287?–1347, king of Germany (1314–47); emperor of the Holy Roman Empire 1328–47.

Louis V, (*"le Fainéant"*) A.D. 967?–987, king of France 986–987: last Carolingian to rule France.

Louis VI, (*"the Fat"*) 1081–1137, king of France 1108–37.

Louis VII, (*"the Young"*) 1121?–80, king of France 1137–80 (son of Louis VI).

Louis IX, Saint, 1214?–70, king of France 1226–70.

Louis XI, 1423–83, king of France 1461–83 (son of Charles VII).

Louis XII, (*"the Father of the People"*) 1462–1515, king of France 1498–1515.

Louis XIII, 1601–43, king of France 1610–43 (son of Henry IV of Navarre).

Louis XIV, (*"the Great"; "the Sun King"*) 1638–1715, king of France 1643–1715 (son of Louis XIII).

Louis XV, 1710–74, king of France 1715–74 (great grandson of Louis XIV).

Louis XVI, 1754–93, king of France 1774–92 (grandson of Louis XV and husband of Marie Antoinette).

Louis XVII, (*"Louis Charles of France"*) 1785–95, titular king of France 1793–95 (son of Louis XVI).

Louis XVIII, (*Louis Xavier Stanislas*) 1755–1824, king of France 1814–15, 1815–24 (brother of Louis XVI).

Lou·is·burg (lo͞o′is bûrg′), *n.* a seaport on SE Cape Breton Island, Nova Scotia, in SE Canada: French fortress captured by British 1745, 1758. 1519.

lou·is d'or (lo͞o′ē dôr′; *Fr.* lwē dôR′), *pl.* **lou·is d'or** (lo͞o′ēz dôr′; *Fr.* lwē dôR′). a former gold coin of France, issued from 1640 to 1795; pistole. Also called **louis.** [1680–90; < F: lit., louis of gold; named after LOUIS XIII]

Lou·ise (lo͞o ēz′), *n.* **1. Lake,** a glacial lake in W Canada, in SW Alberta in the Canadian Rockies: resort. 5670 ft. (1728 m) above sea level. **2.** Also, **Lou·i·sa** (lo͞o ē′zə). a female given name: derived from *Louis.*

Lou·ise (lo͞o ēz′), *n.* an opera (1900) by Gustave Charpentier.

Lou′is heel′ (lo͞o′ē), a French heel of medium height, flared out or widened at the base, used on women's shoes. [1905–10; after LOUIS XV]

Lou·i·si·an·a (lo͞o ē′zē an′ə, lo͞o′ə zē-, lo͞o′ē-), *n.* a state in the S United States. 4,203,972; 48,522 sq. mi. (125,672 sq. km). *Cap:* Baton Rouge. *Abbr.:* LA (for use with zip code), La. —**Lou·i′si·an′an, Lou·i′si·an′i·an,** *adj., n.*

Loui′sian′a French′, French as spoken in Louisiana; Cajun. *Abbr.:* LaF

Loui′sian′a her′on. See **tricolored heron.** [1805–15, *Amer.*]

Loui′sian′a Pur′chase, *U.S. Hist.* **1.** a treaty signed with France in 1803 by which the U.S. purchased for $15,000,000 the land extending from the Mississippi River to the Rocky Mountains and from Canada to the Gulf of Mexico. **2.** the land included in this purchase.

Loui′sian′a tan′ager. See **western tanager.** [1805–15, *Amer.*]

Lou′is Napo′leon (lo͞o′ē, lo͞o′is; *Fr.* lwē). See **Napoleon III.**

Lou′is Philippe′, (*"Citizen King"*) 1773–1850, king of France 1830–48.

Lou′is Qua·torze′ (kə tôrz′; *Fr.* KA tôRz′), noting or pertaining to the style of architecture, furnishings, and decoration prevailing in France in the late 17th century, characterized by increasingly classicizing tendencies, and by an emphasis on dignity rather than comfort. Cf. **Régence.** [1850–55; < F: Louis XIV]

Lou′is Quinze′ (kanz; *Fr.* KANz), noting or pertaining to the rococo style of architecture, furnishings, and decoration prevailing in France in the early and mid-18th century, characterized by fantasy, lightness, elegance, and comfort. [1850–55; < F: Louis XV]

Lou′is Seize′ (sez), noting or pertaining to the style of architecture, furnishings, and decoration prevailing in France at the end of the 18th century, continuing the lightness of the Louis Quinze period with a stricter adherence to classical models. [1890–95; < F: Louis XVI]

Lou′is Treize′ (trez; *Fr.* tRez), noting or pertaining to the style of architecture, furnishings, and decoration prevailing in France in the early 17th century, characterized by a gradual transition from the free invention and composition of the renaissance to the classicism of the Louis Quatorze period. [1880–85; < F: Louis XIII]

Lou·is·ville (lo͞o′ē vil′, -ə vəl), *n.* a port in N Kentucky, on the Ohio River: Kentucky Derby. 298,451. —**Lou·is·vill·ian** (lo͞o′ē vil′yən), *n.*

loun (lo͞on), *n. Scot.* loon[2].

lounge (lounj), *v.,* **lounged, loung·ing,** *n.* —*v.i.* **1.** to pass time idly and indolently. **2.** to rest or recline indolently; loll: *We lounged in the sun all afternoon.* **3.** to go or move in a leisurely, indolent manner; saunter (usually fol. by *around, along, off,* etc.). —*v.t.* **4.** to pass (time) in lounging (usually fol. by *away* or *out*): *to lounge away the afternoon.* —*n.* **5.** a sofa for reclining, sometimes backless, having a headrest at one end. **6.** a place for sitting, waiting, smoking, etc., esp. a large public room, as in a hotel, theater, or air terminal, often with adjoining washrooms. **7.** a section on a train, plane, or ship having various club or social facilities. **8.** a cocktail lounge. **9.** *Archaic.* the act or a period of lounging. **10.** *Archaic.* a lounging gait. [1500–10; orig. uncert.] —**loung′y,** *adj.*
—**Syn. 1.** loaf, idle, relax, dally, potter.

lounge′ car′. See **club car.** [1945–50]

lounge′ chair′, a chair designed for lounging, as an easy chair, chaise longue, or recliner. Also called **lounger.** [1900–05]

lounge′ liz′ard, *Older Slang.* **1.** a foppish man who frequents bars, cafés, hotel lounges, etc., with or in search of women. **2.** a sponger; scrounger; parasite. Also called **lizard.** [1910–15]

loung·er (loun′jər), *n.* **1.** a person or thing that lounges. **2.** *Informal.* a lounging robe. **3.** See **lounge chair.** [1500–10; LOUNGE + -ER[1]]

lounge′ suit′, *Chiefly Brit.* a man's suit appropriate for informal occasions. [1900–05]

lounge·wear (lounj′wâr′), *n.* articles of clothing suitable for wear during leisure time, esp. in the home. [1955–60; LOUNGE + WEAR]

loung·ing (loun′jing), *adj.* **1.** (of a garment) worn for leisure, as at home: *lounging robe; lounging jacket.* **2.** lacking energy or vigor; relaxed. [1665–75; LOUNGE + -ING[2]] —**loung′ing·ly,** *adv.*

Louns·bur·y (lounz′ber′ē, -bə rē), *n.* **Thomas Raynes·ford** (rānz′fərd), 1838–1915, U.S. linguist and educator.

loup[1] (lo͞o), *n.* a cloth mask, often of silk or velvet, that covers only half the face. [1825–35; < F: lit., wolf < L *lupus*]

loup[2] (loup, lōp, lo͞op), *Scot.* —*v.i.* **1.** to leap; jump; spring. —*v.t.* **2.** to leap or jump at, over, or into (something). [1325–75; ME *loupe* < ON *hlaupa,* c. OE *hlēapan* to LEAP]

loup-cer·vier (lo͞o′ser vyā′), *n., pl.* **-viers,** (*esp. collectively*) **-vier.** the Canada lynx. [1715–25; < CanF, F: lynx < L *lupus cervārius* wolf that hunts deer (lit.: wolf of or connected with deer). See LUPUS, CERVINE, -IER[2]]

loupe (lo͞op), *n.* any of several varieties of magnifying glasses, used by jewelers and watchmakers, of from 2 to 20 power and intended to fit in the eye socket, to be attached to spectacles, or to be held in the hand. [1905–10; < F, orig. an imperfect gem, a mass of hot metal << Gmc; see LOOP[3], LOB[1]]

loup-ga·rou (lo͞o GA RO͞O′; *Eng.* lo͞o′gə ro͞o′), *n., pl.* ***loups-ga·rous*** (lo͞o GA RO͞O′; *Eng.* lo͞o′gə ro͞oz′). *French.* a werewolf; lycanthrope.

loup′ing ill′ (lou′ping, lō′-, lo͞o′-), *Vet. Pathol.* an acute viral disease of sheep affecting the nervous system, transmitted by a tick. [1810–20; see LOUP[2]]

lour (lou[ə]r, lou′ər), *v.i., n.* lower[2].

Lourdes (lo͝ord, lo͝ordz; *Fr.* lo͞oRd), *n.* a city in SW France: Roman Catholic shrine famed for miraculous cures. 18,096.

Lou·ren·ço Mar·ques (lô ren′sō mär′kes, lō-; *Port.* lô REN′sōō MÄR′kezh), former name of **Maputo.**

lour·ing (louᵊr′ing, lou′ər-), *adj.* lowering.

lour·y (louᵊr′ē, lou′ə rē), *adj.* lowery.

louse (*n.* lous; *v.* lous, louz), *n., pl.* **lice** (līs) for 1–3, **lous·es** for 4, *v.,* **loused, lous·ing.** —*n.* **1.** any small, wingless insect of the order Anoplura **(sucking louse),** parasitic on humans and other mammals and having mouthparts adapted for sucking, as *Pediculus humanus* **(body louse** or **head louse)** and *Phthirius pubis* **(crab louse** or **pubic louse). 2.** any insect of the order Mallophaga **(bird louse, biting louse,** or **chewing louse),** parasitic on birds and mammals, having mouthparts adapted for biting. **3.** See **plant louse. 4.** *Slang.* a contemptible person, esp. an unethical one. —*v.t.* **5.** to delouse. **6. louse up,** *Slang.* to spoil; botch: *Miscasting loused up the movie.* [bef. 900; 1910–15 for def. 4; ME *lous(e), luse,* pl. *lise, lice;* OE *lūs,* pl. *lȳs;* c. D *luis,* G *Laus,* ON *lūs*]

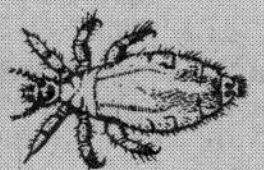

body louse, *Pediculus humanus,* length 1/8 in. (0.4 cm)

louse·wort (lous′wûrt′, -wôrt′), *n.* any plant belonging to the genus *Pedicularis,* of the figwort family, as the wood betony, formerly supposed to cause lice in sheep feeding on it: one species, *P. furbishiae* **(Furbish lousewort),** of parts of Maine and New Brunswick, Canada, having finely toothed leaves and a cluster of yellow flowers, is endangered and was thought to be extinct until specimens were discovered in 1946 and again in 1976. [1570–80; LOUSE + WORT[2]]

lous·y (lou′zē), *adj.,* **lous·i·er, lous·i·est. 1.** infested with lice. **2.** *Informal.* **a.** mean or contemptible: *That was a lousy thing to do.* **b.** wretchedly bad; miserable: *a lousy job; I feel lousy.* **3. lousy with,** *Slang.* well supplied with: *lousy with money.* [1350–1400; ME *lousi.* See LOUSE, -Y[1]] —**lous′i·ly,** *adv.* —**lous′i·ness,** *n.*
—**Syn. 2a.** shabby, nasty, crummy.

lout[1] (lout), *n.* **1.** an awkward, stupid person; clumsy, ill-mannered boor; oaf. —*v.t.* **2.** to flout; treat with contempt; scorn. [1540–50; perh. special use of LOUT[2]]

lout[2] (lout), *v.t., v.i.* to bend, stoop, or bow, esp. in respect or courtesy. [1250–1300; ME *louten,* OE *lūtan;* c. ON *lūta;* akin to LITTLE]

Louth (louth), *n.* a county in Leinster province, in the NE Republic of Ireland. 88,359; 317 sq. mi. (820 sq. km). *Co. seat:* Dunkalk.

lout·ish (lou′tish), *adj.* like or characteristic of a lout; awkward; clumsy; boorish. [1545–55; LOUT[1] + -ISH[1]] —**lout′ish·ly,** *adv.* —**lout′ish·ness,** *n.*
—**Syn.** churlish, uncouth, vulgar, coarse.

lou·troph·o·ros (lōō trof′ə ros′), *n., pl.* **-roi** (-roi′). *Gk. and Rom. Antiq.* a water jar, characterized by an elongated neck and flaring mouth, used to carry water for the marriage bath and set on the tomb of a person who had been unmarried. [1895–1900; < Gk *loutrophóros* lit., bringing water for the bath, equiv. to *loutró(n)* bath (*loú(ein)* to wash + *-phoros* -PHOROUS]

Lou·vain (*Fr.* lōō VAN′), *n.* a city in central Belgium. 29,792.

lou·var (lōō′vär), *n.* a red-finned, deep-sea, tropical fish, *Luvarus imperialis,* having the vent at the base of the pectoral fin. [appar. a pseudo-F sp. of NL *Luvarus* genus name < It (Sicilian) *luvaru*]

lou·ver (lōō′vər), *n.* **1.** any of a series of narrow openings framed at their longer edges with slanting, overlapping fins or slats, adjustable for admitting light and air while shutting out rain. **2.** a fin or slat framing such an opening. **3.** a ventilating turret or lantern, as on the roof of a medieval building. **4.** any of a system of slits formed in the hood of an automobile, the door of a metal locker, etc., used esp. for ventilation. **5.** a door, window, or the like, having adjustable louvers. —*v.t.* **6.** to make a louver in; add louvers to: *to louver a door.* Also, *esp. Brit.,* **louvre.** [1325–75; ME *lover* < MF *lovier* < MD *love* gallery. See LOBBY] —**lou′vered,** *adj.*

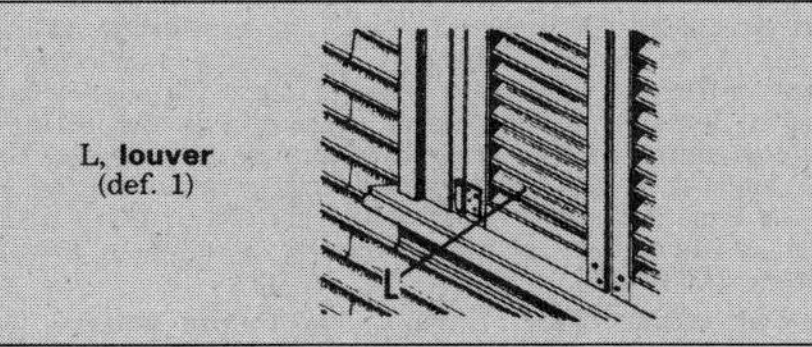

L, louver (def. 1)

lou′ver board′, one of a series of overlapping, sloping boards used as louvers in an opening, so arranged as to admit air but to exclude rain or cut off visibility from the outside. [1400–50; ME]

Lou·ver·tie (lōō′vûr tē), *n.* a female given name.

L'Ou·ver·ture (*Fr.* lōō VER TYR′), *n.* See **Toussaint L'Ouverture.**

lou·vre (lōō′vər), *n., v.t.,* **-vred, -vring.** *Chiefly Brit.* louver.

Lou·vre (lōō′vRᵊ), *n.* a national museum in Paris, France, since 1793: formerly a royal palace.

Louÿs (lwēs), *n.* **Pierre** (pyeR), 1870–1925, French poet and novelist.

lov·a·ble (luv′ə bəl), *adj.* of such a nature as to attract love; deserving love; amiable; endearing. Also, **loveable.** [1300–50; ME *lovable, lufabille.* See LOVE, -ABLE] —**lov′a·bil′i·ty, lov′a·ble·ness,** *n.* —**lov′a·bly,** *adv.*
—**Syn.** dear, tender, warm, affectionate.

lov·age (luv′ij), *n.* a European plant, *Levisticum officinale,* of the parsley family, having coarsely toothed compound leaves, cultivated in gardens. [1350–1400; ME *loveache* < AF *luvesche* (by assoc. with *ache* celery < L *apium*) < OE *lufestice* (by syncope) < ML *levistica,* for LL *levisticum,* alter. of L *ligusticum* lovage, n. use of neut. of *Ligusticus* Ligurian]

lo·va·stat·in (lō′və stat′n), *n.* a drug that reduces the levels of fats in the blood by altering the enzyme activity in the liver that produces lipids. [1985–90; of undetermined orig.]

lov·at (luv′ət), *n.* a grayish blend of colors, esp. of green, used in textiles, as for plaids. [1905–10; prob. after Thomas Alexander Fraser, Lord *Lovat* (1802–75), who popularized tweeds in muted colors as hunters' dress]

love (luv), *n., v.,* **loved, lov·ing.** —*n.* **1.** a profoundly tender, passionate affection for another person. **2.** a feeling of warm personal attachment or deep affection, as for a parent, child, or friend. **3.** sexual passion or desire. **4.** a person toward whom love is felt; beloved person; sweetheart. **5.** (used in direct address as a term of endearment, affection, or the like): *Would you like to see a movie, love?* **6.** a love affair; an intensely amorous incident; amour. **7.** sexual intercourse; copulation. **8.** (*cap.*) a personification of sexual affection, as Eros or Cupid. **9.** affectionate concern for the well-being of others: *the love of one's neighbor.* **10.** strong predilection, enthusiasm, or liking for anything: *her love of books.* **11.** the object or thing so liked: *The theater was her great love.* **12.** the benevolent affection of God for His creatures, or the reverent affection due from them to God. **13.** *Chiefly Tennis.* a score of zero; nothing. **14.** a word formerly used in communications to represent the letter *L.* **15. for love, a.** out of affection or liking; for pleasure. **b.** without compensation; gratuitously: *He took care of the poor for love.* **16. for the love of,** in consideration of; for the sake of: *For the love of mercy, stop that noise.* **17. in love,** infused with or feeling deep affection or passion: *a youth always in love.* **18. in love with,** feeling deep affection or passion for (a person, idea, occupation, etc.); enamored of: *in love with the girl next door; in love with one's work.* **19. make love, a.** to embrace and kiss as lovers. **b.** to engage in sexual activity. **20. no love lost,** dislike; animosity: *There was no love lost between the two brothers.*
—*v.t.* **21.** to have love or affection for: *All her pupils love her.* **22.** to have a profoundly tender, passionate affection for (another person). **23.** to have a strong liking for; take great pleasure in: *to love music.* **24.** to need or require; benefit greatly from: *Plants love sunlight.* **25.** to embrace and kiss (someone), as a lover. **26.** to have sexual intercourse with.
—*v.i.* **27.** to have love or affection for another person; be in love. **28. love up,** to hug and cuddle: *She loves him up every chance she gets.* [bef. 900; (n.) ME; OE *lufu,* c. OFris *luve,* OHG *luba,* Goth *lubō;* (v.) ME *lo-v(i)en,* OE *lufian;* c. OFris *luvia,* OHG *lubōn* to love, L *lubēre* (later *libēre*) to be pleasing; akin to LIEF]
—**Syn. 1.** tenderness, fondness, predilection, warmth, passion, adoration. **1, 2.** LOVE, AFFECTION, DEVOTION all mean a deep and enduring emotional regard, usually for another person. LOVE may apply to various kinds of regard: the charity of the Creator, reverent adoration toward God or toward a person, the relation of parent and child, the regard of friends for each other, romantic feelings for another person, etc. AFFECTION is a fondness for others that is enduring and tender, but calm. DEVOTION is an intense love and steadfast, enduring loyalty to a person; it may also imply consecration to a cause. **2.** liking, inclination, regard, friendliness. **21.** like. **22.** adore, adulate, worship. —**Ant. 1, 2.** hatred, dislike. **21, 22.** detest, hate.

love·a·ble (luv′ə bəl), *adj.* lovable.

love′ affair′, 1. a romantic relationship or episode between lovers; an amour. **2.** an active enthusiasm for something: *my love affair with sailing.* [1585–95]

love′ ap′ple, 1. a tropical, tender plant, *Solanum aculeatissimum,* of the nightshade family, having prickly leaves, clusters of large, star-shaped white flowers, and red, tomatolike fruit. **2.** *Archaic.* the tomato. [1570–80; cf. F *pomme d'amour,* G *Liebesapfel*]

love′ ar′rows, fine needles of rutile crystals embedded in quartz. Also called **flèches d'amour, Cupid's arrows.**

love′ beads′, a necklace of small, often handmade beads, worn as a symbol of peace and goodwill, esp. in the 1960's. [1965–70, *Amer.*]

love·bird (luv′bûrd′), *n.* **1.** any of various small parrots, esp. of the genus *Agapornis,* of Africa, noted for the affection shown one another and often kept as pets. **2. lovebirds,** a pair of lovers, esp. a married couple who show very close mutual love and concern. [1585–95]

love′ child′, a child born out of wedlock. [1795–1805]

Love·craft (luv′kraft′, -kräft′), *n.* **H(oward) P(hillips),** 1890–1937, U.S. horror-story writer.

loved (luvd), *adj.* held in deep affection; cherished: *loved companions; much-loved friends.* [1250–1300; ME]

loved′ one′, a close or cherished relation: *to mourn the loss of our loved ones.* [1860–65]

love-en·tan·gle (luv′en tang′gəl), *n.* the stonecrop, *Sedum acre.* Also, **love′-en·tan′gled.** [1840–50]

love′ feast′, 1. (among the early Christians) a meal eaten in token of brotherly love and charity; agape. **2.** a rite in imitation of this, practiced by a number of modern denominations; a fellowship meal. **3.** a banquet or gathering of persons to promote good feeling, restore friendly relations, honor a special guest, etc. [1570–80]

Love′ for Love′, a comedy (1695) by William Congreve.

love′ game′, *Tennis.* a game in which one's opponent fails to win a point. [1825–35]

love·grass (luv′gras′, -gräs′), *n.* any grass of the genus *Eragrostis,* as *E. curvula* **(weeping lovegrass)** and *E. trichodes* **(sand lovegrass),** cultivated as forage and ground cover. [1695–1705; LOVE + GRASS]

love′ han′dles, *Informal.* bulges of fat at the sides of the waist. [1980–85]

love-in (luv′in′), *n.* a usually organized public gathering of people, held as a demonstration of mutual love or in protest against inhumane policies. [1965–70, *Amer.;* see LOVE, -IN[3]]

love-in-a-mist (luv′in ə mist′), *n.* a plant, *Nigella damascena,* of the buttercup family, having feathery dissected leaves and whitish or blue flowers. [1750–60]

Love·joy (luv′joi′), *n.* **Elijah P(arish),** 1802–37, U.S. abolitionist and newspaper editor.

love′ knot′, a knot of ribbon as a token of love. Also called **lover's knot.** [1350–1400; ME *love knotte*]

Love·lace (luv′lās′), *n.* **Richard,** 1618–56, English poet.

Love·land (luv′lənd), *n.* a city in N Colorado. 30,244.

love·less (luv′lis), *adj.* **1.** without any love: *a loveless marriage.* **2.** feeling no love. **3.** receiving no love; unloved. [1275–1325; ME *loveles.* See LOVE, -LESS] —**love′less·ly,** *adv.* —**love′less·ness,** *n.*

love-lies-bleed·ing (luv′līz′blē′ding), *n.* an amaranth, esp. *Amaranthus caudatus,* having spikes of crimson flowers. [1600–10]

love′ life′, amorous or sexual relations. [1915–20]

Lov·ell (lov′əl), *n.* **1. Sir Alfred Charles Bernard,** born 1931, British astronomer. **2.** a male given name.

love·lock (luv′lok′), *n.* **1.** any lock of hair hanging or worn separately from the rest of the hair. **2.** a long, flowing lock or curl dressed separately from the rest of the hair, worn by courtiers, esp. in the 17th century. [1585–95; LOVE + LOCK[2]]

love·lorn (luv′lôrn′), *adj.* being without love; forsaken by one's lover. [1625–35; LOVE + LORN]

love·ly (luv′lē), *adj.,* **-li·er, -li·est,** *n., pl.* **-lies,** *adv.* —*adj.* **1.** charmingly or exquisitely beautiful: *a lovely flower.* **2.** having a beauty that appeals to the heart or mind as well as to the eye, as a person or a face. **3.** delightful; highly pleasing: *to have a lovely time.* **4.** of a great moral or spiritual beauty: *a lovely character.* —*n.* **5.** *Informal.* a beautiful woman, esp. a show girl. **6.** any person or thing that is pleasing, highly satisfying, or the like: *Every car in the new line is a lovely.* —*adv.* **7.** *Nonstandard.* very well; splendidly. [bef. 900; ME *luvelich,* OE *luflic* amiable. See LOVE, -LY] —**love′li·ly,** *adv.* —**love′li·ness,** *n.*
—**Syn. 1, 2.** See **beautiful.**

love·mak·ing (luv′mā′king), *n.* **1.** the act of courting or wooing. **2.** sexual activity. [1400–50; late ME; see LOVE, MAKING]

love′ match′, a marriage entered into for love alone.

love′ po′tion, a magical potion believed to arouse love or sexual passion toward a specified person, esp. the person offering it. [1640–50]

lov·er (luv′ər), *n.* **1.** a person who is in love with another. **2.** a person who has a sexual or romantic relationship with another. **3.** a person with whom one conducts an extramarital sexual affair. **4.** a person who has a strong enjoyment or liking for something, as specified: *a lover of music.* **5.** a person who loves, esp. a person who has or shows a warm and general affectionate regard for others: *a lover of mankind.* [1175–1225; ME; see LOVE, -ER[1]] —**lov′er·less,** *adj.* —**lov′er·like′,** *adj.*
—**Syn. 4.** devotee, enthusiast, fan.

Lov·er (luv′ər), *n.* **Samuel,** 1797–1868, Irish novelist, painter, and songwriter.

lov·er·ly (luv′ər lē), *adj., adv.* like, characteristic of, or in the manner of a lover; loverlike. [1870–75; LOVER + -LY]

lov′er's knot′. See **love knot.** [1585–95]

lov′ers' lane′, a secluded lane, road, or parking area sought out by lovers for its privacy. [1880–85, *Amer.*]

lov′er's leap′, 1. a high area, as on a cliff, from which frustrated or grieving lovers jump or are reputed to have jumped to their death. **2.** *Backgammon.* a player's move from ace point to twelve point in one roll of the dice. [1800–10]

love′ seat′, a chair or small upholstered sofa for two persons. Also called **courting chair.** [1900–05]

love′ set′, *Tennis.* a set in which one's opponent fails to win a game. [1875–80]

love·sick (luv′sik′), *adj.* **1.** languishing with love: *a lovesick adolescent.* **2.** expressive of such languishing: *a lovesick note.* [1520–30; LOVE + SICK[1]] —**love′sick′·ness,** *n.*

Love's′ La′bour's Lost′, a comedy (1594–95?) by Shakespeare.

love·some (luv′səm), *adj.* **1.** inspiring love; lovely; lovable. **2.** amorous; loving. [bef. 1000; ME *lovesom,* OE *lufsum.* See LOVE, -SOME[1]]

Love Song of J. Alfred Prufrock, The (prōō′frok), a poem (1917) by T. S. Eliot.

Loves′ Park′, a town in N Illinois. 13,192.

love′ vine′, dodder[2]. [1825–35, *Amer.*]

lov·ey (luv′ē), *n. Chiefly Brit. Informal.* sweetheart; dear: used as a term of endearment. [1725–35; LOVE + -EY[2]]

love·y-dove·y (luv′ē duv′ē), *adj. Informal.* amorously affectionate: *a lovey-dovey couple.* [1810–20; orig. affectionate term of address; see LOVE, DOVE[1], -EY[2]]

lov·ing (luv′ing), *adj.* feeling or showing love; warmly affectionate; fond: *loving glances.* [bef. 1000; ME *lovyng;* r. ME *lovende,* OE *lufiende.* See LOVE, -ING[2]] —**lov′ing·ly,** *adv.* —**lov′ing·ness,** *n.*

lov′ing cup′, **1.** a large cup, as of silver, usually with two or more handles, given as a prize, award, token of esteem or affection, etc. **2.** a wine cup, usually of large size with several handles, passed from one person to another, as at a farewell gathering. [1800–10]

lov·ing·est (luv′ing ist), *adj. Informal.* extremely loving and affectionate. [LOVING + -EST[1]]

lov·ing-kind·ness (luv′ing kīnd′nis), *n.* tender kindness motivated by or expressing affection. [1525–35]

low[1] (lō), *adj.,* **-er, -est,** *adv.,* **-er, -est,** *n.* —*adj.* **1.** situated, placed, or occurring not far above the ground, floor, or base: *a low shelf.* **2.** of small extent upward; not high or tall: *A low wall surrounds the property.* **3.** not far above the horizon, as a planet: *The moon was low in the sky.* **4.** lying or being below the general level: *low ground.* **5.** designating or pertaining to regions near sea level, esp. near the sea: *low countries.* **6.** bending or passing far downward; deep: *a low bow.* **7.** (of a garment) low-necked; décolleté: *The dress she wore was fashionably low.* **8.** rising but slightly from a surface: *a low relief on a frieze.* **9.** of less than average or normal height or depth, as a liquid or stream: *The river is low this time of year.* **10.** near the first of a series: *a low number.* **11.** ranked near the beginning or bottom on some scale of measurement: *a low income bracket.* **12.** indicating the bottom or the point farthest down: *the low point in his creative life.* **13.** lacking in strength, energy, or vigor; feeble; weak: *to feel low and listless.* **14.** providing little nourishment or strength, as a diet. **15.** of small number, amount, degree, force, intensity, etc.: *low visibility; a generator with a low output.* **16.** indicated or represented by a low number: *A low latitude is one relatively near the equator.* **17.** soft: subdued; not loud: *a low murmur.* **18.** *Music.* produced by relatively slow vibrations, as sounds; grave in pitch. **19.** assigning or attributing little worth, value, excellence, or the like: *a low estimate of a new book.* **20.** containing a relatively small amount: *a diet low in starches.* **21.** nearing depletion; not adequately supplied: *low on funds; Our stock of towels is low.* **22.** depressed or dejected: *low spirits.* **23.** far down in the scale of rank or estimation; humble: *of low birth.* **24.** of inferior quality or character: *a low grade of fabric; a low type of intellect.* **25.** lacking in dignity or elevation, as of thought or expression. **26.** mean, base, or disreputable: *low tricks; low companions.* **27.** coarse or vulgar: *entertainment of a low sort.* **28.** *Boxing.* struck or delivered below a contestant's belt. **29.** *Biol.* having a relatively simple structure; not complex in organization. **30.** *Phonet.* (of a vowel) articulated with a relatively large opening above the tongue, as the vowels of *hat, hut, hot, ought,* etc. Cf. **high** (def. 23). **31.** *Auto.* of, pertaining to, or operating at the gear transmission ratio at which the drive shaft moves at the lowest speed with relation to the speed of the engine crankshaft, used esp. for temporarily overcoming the weight or inertia of the vehicle; first: *low gear.* **32.** *Baseball.* (of a pitched ball) passing the plate at a level below that of the batter's knees: *a low curve.* **33.** *Cards.* having less value than other cards: *a low card.* **34.** *Metall.* having a relatively small amount of a specified constituent (usually used in combination): *low-carbon steel.* **35.** *Chiefly Brit.* holding to Low Church principles and practices.
—*adv.* **36.** in or to a low position, point, degree, etc.: *The raiders crouched low in the bushes.* **37.** near the ground, floor, or base; not aloft: *The plane flew low.* **38.** in or to a humble or abject state: *Some live low while others live high. She swore she would bring him low.* **39.** in or to a condition of depletion, prostration, or death: *The gas in the tank is running low.* **40.** at comparatively small cost; cheaply: *to buy something low and sell it high.* **41.** at or to a low pitch, volume, intensity, etc.: *to turn the radio low; lights turned down low.* **42.** in a low tone; softly; quietly; *to speak low.* **43.** *Archaic.* far down in time; late. **44.** **lay low, a.** to overpower or kill; defeat: *to lay one's attackers low.* **b.** to knock down; make prostrate. **c.** *Informal.* to lie low. **45.** **lie low, a.** to conceal oneself: *He had to lie low for a while.* **b.** to do nothing until the right opportunity develops; bide one's time: *Until the dispute is settled, you would do best to lie low.*
—*n.* **46.** something that is low, as ground or prices: *numerous marshy lows in the forest; the recent low in the stock market.* **47.** *Auto.* low gear; first gear. **48.** *Meteorol.* an atmospheric low-pressure system; cyclone. Cf. **high** (def. 41). **49.** *Cards.* **a.** the lowest trump card. **b.** a card of small value, or of lower value than other cards. **c.** the lowest score in a game. **d.** a player having such a score. **50.** a point of deepest decline, vulgarity, etc.: *a new low in tastelessness.* **51.** *Slang.* a period of intense depression or discomfort, when the effects of a drug have subsided. [1125–75; ME *lowe, lohe* (adj. and n.), earlier *lāh* < ON *lāgr* (adj.); c. OFris *lēge, lēch,* D *laag,* OHG *laege;* akin to LIE[2]] —**low′ish,** *adj.* —**low′ness,** *n.*
—**Syn. 13.** exhausted, sinking, expiring, dying. **17.** quiet. **18.** deep. **22.** dispirited, unhappy, sad. **23.** lowly, meek, obscure. **26.** ignoble, degraded, servile. **27.** rude, crude. See **mean**[2]. —**Ant. 1–3.** high.

low[2] (lō), *v.i.* **1.** to utter the deep, low sound characteristic of cattle; moo. —*v.t.* **2.** to utter by or as by lowing. —*n.* **3.** the act or the sound of lowing: *the low of a distant herd.* [bef. 1000; ME *lowen,* OE *hlōwan;* c. D *loeien,* OHG *hluoen,* OS *hlōian;* akin to ON *Hlōi* proper name (lit., bellower, shouter), L *clāmāre* to call out]

low[3] (lō), *v.i. Brit. Dial.* **1.** to burn; blaze. **2.** (of a person) to feel strong emotions; glow with excitement. Also, **lowe.** [1300–50; ME < ON *loga* to flame, *log* a flame, akin to G *lohen* (v.), *Lohe* (n.), L *lūcēre* (v.), *lūx* (n.) LIGHT[1]]

CONCISE ETYMOLOGY KEY: <, descended or borrowed from; >, whence; b., blend of, blended; c., cognate with; cf., compare; deriv., derivative; equiv., equivalent; imit., imitative; obl., oblique; r., replacing; s., stem; sp., spelling, spelled; resp., respelling, respelled; trans., translation; ?, origin unknown; *, unattested; ‡, probably earlier than. See the full key inside the front cover.

Low (lō), *n.* **1.** **David,** 1891–1963, English political cartoonist, born in New Zealand. **2.** **Juliette,** 1860–1927, founder of Girl Scouts in the U.S. **3.** **Seth,** 1850–1916, U.S. political reformer, educator, and politician.

low·an (lō′ən), *n.* See **mallee fowl.** [1860–65; < Wemba-Wemba (Australian Aboriginal language spoken around Swan Hill, Victoria) *lauan*]

low′-an′gle shot′ (lō′ang′gəl), (in motion pictures or photography) a shot taken with the camera placed in a position below and pointing upward at the subject.

Low′ Archipel′ago. See **Tuamotu Archipelago.**

low·ball (lō′bôl′), *n.* **1.** *Cards.* a game of draw poker in which the player having the lowest-ranking hand wins the pot. —*v.t.* **2.** to deliberately estimate a lower price for (a service or merchandise) than one intends to charge: *to lowball the cost of a move.* **3.** to give a false estimate or bid for. —*v.i.* **4.** to engage in lowballing. —*adj.* **5.** engaged in or characteristic of lowballing: *a lowball bid.* [LOW[1] + BALL[1]]

low′ beam′, an automobile headlight beam providing short-range illumination of a road and intended chiefly for use in driving on the streets of cities, towns, etc. Cf. **high beam.** [1945–50]

low′ blood′ pres′sure, hypotension. [1920–25]

low′ blow′, **1.** (in boxing) an illegal blow below the waist of an opponent. **2.** an unfair or unsportsmanlike criticism or attack. [1950–55]

low′ board′, a diving board 1 meter (3.2 feet) above the water.

low·born (lō′bôrn′), *adj.* of humble birth. [1175–1225; ME *lohiboren.* See LOW[1], BORN]

low·boy (lō′boi′), *n. U.S. Furniture.* a low chest of drawers on short legs, resembling the lower part of a highboy. [1705–15; LOW[1] + BOY]

lowboy (18th century)

low′ brass′, an alloy of about 80 percent copper and 20 percent zinc, with traces of lead and iron.

low·bred (lō′bred′), *adj.* characterized by or characteristic of low or vulgar breeding; ill-bred; coarse. [1750–60; LOW[1] + BRED]
—**Syn.** unrefined, rude. —**Ant.** noble.

low·brow (*n.* lō′brou′; *adj.* lō′brou′), —*n.* **1.** a person who is uninterested, uninvolved, or uneducated in intellectual activities or pursuits. —*adj.* **2.** being a lowbrow: *that lowbrow idiot.* **3.** of, pertaining to, or proper to a lowbrow: *lowbrow entertainment.* [1905–10, *Amer.;* LOW[1] + BROW] —**low′brow′ism,** *n.*

low-budg·et (lō′buj′it), *adj.* made or done on a small or reduced budget; costing relatively little money: *a low-budget film.* [1955–60]

low′bush blue′berry (lō′bo͝osh′), a shrub, *Vaccinium angustifolium,* of eastern North America, having small, white flowers and blue-black fruit. [1855–60, *Amer.;* LOW[1] + BUSH[1]]

low-cal (lō′kal′, -kal′), *adj. Informal.* containing fewer calories than usual or standard: *a low-cal diet.* [*low cal(orie)*]

Low′ Church′, pertaining to the view or practice in the Anglican Church that emphasizes evangelicalism and lays little stress on the sacraments, church rituals, and church authority. Cf. **High Church, Broad Church.** [1695–1705]

Low′ Church′man, a person who advocates or follows Low Church practices. [1695–1705]

low′ com′edy, comedy that depends on physical action, broadly humorous or farcical situations, and often bawdy or vulgar jokes. Cf. **high comedy.** [1600–10] —**low′ come′dian.**

low-cost (lō′kôst′, -kost′), *adj.* able to be purchased or acquired at relatively little cost: *low-cost life insurance; low-cost housing.* [1930–35]

low-count (lō′kount′), *adj.* (of a woven fabric) having a relatively low number of warp and filling threads per square inch.

Low′ Coun′tries, the lowland region near the North Sea, forming the lower basin of the Rhine, Meuse, and Scheldt rivers, divided in the Middle Ages into numerous small states: corresponding to modern Belgium, Luxembourg, and the Netherlands.

low′ coun′try, a low-lying region or area, as the coastal plains of the Carolinas and Georgia.

low-coun·try (lō′kun′trē), *adj.* **1.** often, **Low-Country.** of or pertaining to the Low Countries. **2.** of or pertaining to a low country. [1790–1800]

low-den·si·ty (lō′den′si tē), *adj.* having a low concentration.

low′-den′sity lipopro′tein, *Biochem.* a plasma protein that is the major carrier of cholesterol in the blood: high levels are associated with atherosclerosis. *Abbr.:* LDL

low′-den′sity polyeth′ylene, *Chem.* highly branched polyethylene with low crystallinity and melting point, and a density of 0.91 to 0.94, prepared at very high pressures, and used mainly for sheeting, films, and packaging materials. *Abbr.:* LDPE Also called **branched polyethylene.** Cf. **high-density polyethylene.**

low·down (*n.* lō′doun′; *adj.* lō′doun′), *Informal.* —*n.* **1.** the real and unadorned facts; the true, secret, or inside information (usually prec. by *the*): *We gave them the lowdown on the new housing project.* —*adj.* **2.** contemptible; base; mean: *a lowdown trick.* **3.** low, esp. socially or morally; degraded. [1540–50; LOW[1] + DOWN[1]]

lowe (lō), *v.i.* **lowed, low·ing.** *Brit. Dial.* low[3].

Low·ell (lō′əl), *n.* **1.** **Ab·bott Lawrence** (ab′ət), 1856–1943, political scientist and educator: president of Harvard University 1909–33. **2.** his sister, **Amy,** 1874–1925, U.S. poet and critic. **3.** **James Russell,** 1819–91, U.S. poet, essayist, and diplomat. **4.** **Percival,** 1855–1916, U.S. astronomer and author (brother of Abbott Lawrence Lowell and Amy Lowell). **5.** **Robert,** 1917–77, U.S. poet. **6.** a city in NE Massachusetts, on the Merrimack River. 92,418. **7.** a male given name: from a Germanic word meaning "little wolf."

Low′ell Observ′atory, the astronomical observatory, situated in Flagstaff, Arizona, at which Pluto was discovered in 1930. [named after P. LOWELL]

low-end (lō′end′), *adj. Informal.* relatively cheap or inexpensive of its kind: *We don't need an expensive car—a low-end model will do.*

low·er[1] (lō′ər), *v.t.* **1.** to cause to descend; let or put down: *to lower a flag.* **2.** to make lower in height or level: *to lower the water in a canal.* **3.** to reduce in amount, price, degree, force, etc. **4.** to make less loud: *Please lower your voice.* **5.** to bring down in rank or estimation; degrade; humble; abase (oneself), as by some sacrifice of self-respect or dignity: *His bad actions lowered him in my eyes.* **6.** *Music.* to make lower in pitch; flatten. **7.** *Phonet.* to alter the articulation of (a vowel) by increasing the distance of the tongue downward from the palate: *The vowel of "clerk" is lowered to (ä) in the British pronunciation.* —*v.i.* **8.** to become lower, grow less, or diminish, as in amount, intensity, or degree: *The brook lowers in early summer. Stock prices rise and lower constantly.* **9.** to descend; sink: *the sun lowering in the west.* —*adj.* **10.** comparative of **low**[1]. **11.** of or pertaining to those portions of a river farthest from the source. **12.** (*often cap.*) *Stratig.* noting an early division of a period, system, or the like: *the Lower Devonian.* —*n.* **13.** a denture for the lower jaw. **14.** a lower berth. [1150–1200; ME, comp. of LOW[1] (adj.)] —**low′er·a·ble,** *adj.*
—**Syn. 1.** drop, depress. **3.** decrease, diminish, lessen. **4.** soften. **5.** humiliate, dishonor, disgrace, debase. —**Ant. 3.** raise, increase. **5.** elevate, honor.

low·er[2] (lou′ər, lou′ᵊr), *v.i.* **1.** to be dark and threatening, as the sky or the weather. **2.** to frown, scowl, or look sullen; glower: *He lowers at people when he's in a bad mood.* —*n.* **3.** a dark, threatening appearance, as of the sky or weather. **4.** a frown or scowl. Also, **lour.** [1250–1300; ME *lour* (n.), *louren* (v.) to frown, LURK; akin to G *lauern,* D *loeren*]
—**Syn. 1.** darken, threaten.

Lower 48 (lō′ər), the states of the continental U.S. exclusive of Alaska; the 48 contiguous states (used esp. by Alaskans).

low′er ap′sis (lō′ər). See under **apsis** (def. 1).

Low′er Aus′tria (lō′ər), a province in NE Austria. 1,439,137; 7092 sq. mi. (18,370 sq. km).

low′er bound′ (lō′ər), *Math.* an element less than or equal to all the elements in a given set: *The numbers 0 and 1 are lower bounds of the set consisting of 1, 2, and 3.*

Low·er Bur·rell (lō′ər bûr′əl, bur′-), a city in SW Pennsylvania. 13,200.

Low′er Califor′nia (lō′ər). See **Baja California.**

Low′er Can′ada (lō′ər), former name of Quebec province 1791–1841.

Low′er Can′ada Rebel′lion (lō′ər), an uprising of 1837, quickly crushed by the British militia, against the British colonial administration in Quebec.

low′er case′ (lō′ər), *Print.* See under **case**[2] (def. 8). [1675–85]

low·er·case (lō′ər kās′), *adj., v.,* **-cased, -cas·ing,** *n.* —*adj.* **1.** (of an alphabetical letter) of a particular form often different from and smaller than its corresponding capital letter, and occurring after the initial letter of a proper name, of the first word in a sentence, etc. *Examples:* a, b, q, r. **2.** *Print.* pertaining to or belonging in the lower case. Cf. **case**[2] (def. 8). —*v.t.* **3.** to print or write with a lowercase letter or letters. —*n.* **4.** a lowercase letter. [1675–85]

low′er cham′ber (lō′ər). See **lower house.** [1880–85]

Low′er Chinook′ (lō′ər), an extinct Chinookan language that was spoken by tribes on both banks of the Columbia River estuary.

low′er class′ (lō′ər), **1.** a class of people below the middle class, having the lowest social rank or standing due to low income, lack of skills or education, and the like. **2.** (broadly) working class. [1765–75]

low·er-class (lō′ər klas′, -kläs′), *adj.* of, pertaining to, or characteristic of the lower class: *lower-class values.* [1890–95]

low·er·class·man (lō′ər klas′mən, -kläs′-), *n., pl.* **-men.** underclassman. [LOWER[1] + CLASS + MAN[1]]
—**Usage.** See **-man.**

low′er crit′icism (lō′ər), a form of Biblical criticism having as its purpose the reconstruction of the original texts of the books of the Bible. Also called **textual criticism.** Cf. **higher criticism.** [1895–1900]

low′er deck′ (lō′ər), *Naut.* **1.** the lowermost deck in a hull having two or three decks. **2.** the deck next above the lowermost, or orlop, deck in a hull having four or more decks. [1700–10]

Low′er Depths′, The (lō′ər), a play (1902) by Maxim Gorki.

Low′er E′gypt (lō′ər). See under **Egypt.**

low′er fun′gus (lō′ər), *Mycol.* any of various fungi that do not produce well-organized fruiting bodies and primarily reproduce asexually, as the chytrids. [1895–1900]

low′er hold′ (lō′ər), *Naut.* the lowermost hold space in a hull having 'tween decks or a shelter deck.

low′er house′ (lō′ər), one of two branches of a legislature, generally more representative and with more members than the upper branch. [1570–80]

low·er·ing (lou′ər ing, lou′ər′ing), *adj.* **1.** dark and threatening, as the sky, clouds, or weather; overcast; gloomy: *lowering skies.* **2.** frowning or sullen, as the face or gaze; scowling; angry. Also, **louring.** [1300–50; ME *louring.* See LOWER², -ING²] —**low′er·ing·ly,** *adv.*

Low′er Klam′ath Lake′ (lō′ər). See under **Klamath Lakes.**

Low′er Lakes′ (lō′ər), (*sometimes l.c.*) *Chiefly Canadian.* Lakes Erie and Ontario, the southernmost Great Lakes.

low′er mast′ (lō′ər), *Naut.* the lowermost spar of a compound mast, stepped in the hull of a vessel and carrying a topmast and any other upper spars.

Low·er Mer·i·on (lō′ər mer′ē ən), a town in SE Pennsylvania, near Philadelphia. 59,651.

Low′er Mich′igan (lō′ər), the southern part of Michigan, S of the Strait of Mackinac. Also called **Low′er Penin′sula.**

low·er·most (lō′ər mōst′ *or, esp. Brit.,* -məst), *adj.* lowest. [1555–65; LOWER¹ + -MOST]

Low′er Palat′inate (lō′ər). See under **Palatinate** (def. 1).

Low′er Paleolith′ic (lō′ər). See under **Paleolithic.**

Low′er Sax′ony (lō′ər), a state in NW Germany. 7,162,000; 18,294 sq. mi. (47,380 sq. km). *Cap.:* Hanover. German, **Niedersachsen.**

low′er school′ (lō′ər), a school that is preparatory to one on a more advanced level. [1855–60]

Low·er Slob·bo·vi·a (lō′ər slə bō′vē ə, slo-), any place considered to be remote, poor, or unenlightened. [after an imaginary country of that name in the comic strip *Li'l Abner* by Al Capp; b. SLOB and Latinized names of remote places, as *Mongolia* and *Siberia*]

low′er world′ (lō′ər), **1.** *Class. Myth.* the regions of the dead, conceived of as lying beneath the surface of the earth; Hades; the underworld. **2.** the earth, as distinguished from the heavenly bodies or from heaven.

low·er·y (lou′ə rē, lou′ər′ē), *adj.* dark and gloomy; threatening: *a lowery sky.* Also, **loury.** [1640–50; earlier *lowry.* See LOWER², -Y¹]

Lowes (lōz), *n.* **John Livingston,** 1867–1945, U.S. scholar, critic, and teacher.

low′est com′mon denom′inator, *Math.* See **least common denominator.** [1935–40]

low′est com′mon mul′tiple, *Math.* the smallest number that is a common multiple of a given set of numbers. Also called **least common multiple.** [1920–25]

Lowes·toft (lōs′tôft, -toft, -təf), *n.* a seaport in NE Suffolk, in E England: famous for a type of china. 51,182.

low′ explo′sive, a relatively slow-burning explosive, usually set off by heat or friction, used for propelling charges in guns or for ordinary blasting.

low′ fre′quency, *Radio.* any frequency between 30 and 300 kilohertz. *Abbr.:* LF [1895–1900] —**low′-fre′·quen·cy,** *adj.*

low′ ful′ham. See under **fulham.**

Low′ Ger′man, 1. the West Germanic languages not included in the High German group, as English, Dutch, Flemish, or Plattdeutsch. *Abbr.:* LG Cf. **High German** (def. 1). **2.** Plattdeutsch. [1835–45]

low-grade (lō′grād′), *adj.* of an inferior quality, worth, value, etc.: *The mine yields low-grade silver ore.* [1875–80; LOW¹ + GRADE]

low′ ground′, Often, **low grounds.** *Southern U.S.* bottom (def. 4). [1650–60]

low′ hur′dles, *Track.* a race in which runners leap over hurdles 2 ft. 6 in. (76 cm) high. Cf. **high hurdles.**

Lo′witz arc′ (lō′vits). See **Arc of Lowitz.**

low-key (lō′kē′), *adj., v.,* **-keyed, -key·ing.** —*adj.* Also, **low′-keyed′. 1.** of reduced intensity; restrained; understated. **2.** (of a photograph) having chiefly dark tones, usually with little tonal contrast (distinguished from *high-key*). —*v.t.* **3.** to make or attempt to make low-key: *to low-key the arms buildup.* [1890–95]

low·land (lō′lənd), *n.* **1.** land that is low or level, in comparison with the adjacent country. **2. the Lowlands,** a low, level region in S, central, and E Scotland. **3. Lowlands,** the speech of those native to the Scottish Lowlands. —*adj.* **4.** of, pertaining to, or characteristic of a lowland or lowlands. **5.** (*cap.*) of, pertaining to, or characteristic of the Lowlands of Scotland or the speech of this area. [1500–10; LOW¹ + LAND]

Low·land·er (lō′lən dər, -lan′-), *n.* **1.** a native of the Lowlands. **2.** (*l.c.*) an inhabitant of a lowland or lowlands. [1685–95; LOWLAND + -ER¹]

low′land fir′. See **grand fir.**

low′land goril′la, the eastern lowland gorilla or western lowland gorilla. See under **gorilla.**

Low′ Lat′in, any form of nonclassical Latin, as Late Latin, Vulgar Latin, or Medieval Latin. [1870–75]

low-lev·el (lō′lev′əl), *adj.* **1.** undertaken by or composed of members having a low status: *a low-level discussion.* **2.** having low status: *low-level personnel.* **3.** undertaken at or from a low altitude: *low-level bombing.* **4.** *Ling.* occurring or operating at the phonetic level of linguistic representation or analysis: *low-level rules governing assimilation.* [1880–85]

low·life (lō′līf′), *n., pl.* **-lifes.** a despicable person, esp. a degenerate or immoral person. [1785–95; LOW¹ + LIFE]

low·li·head (lō′lē hed′), *n. Archaic.* lowly state; lowliness. [1375–1425; late ME *lowliheed.* See LOWLY, -HEAD]

low·ly (lō′lē), *adj.,* **-li·er, -li·est,** *adv.* —*adj.* **1.** humble in station, condition, or nature: *a lowly cottage.* **2.** low in growth or position. **3.** humble in attitude, behavior, or spirit; meek. —*adv.* **4.** in a low position, manner, or degree: *a lowly placed shelf.* **5.** in a lowly manner; humbly. **6.** in a quiet voice; softly: *to converse lowly.* [1300–50; ME; see LOW¹, -LY] —**low′li·ly,** *adv.* —**low′li·ness,** *n.*
—**Syn. 3.** modest, simple, unpretentious.

low-ly·ing (lō′lī′ing), *adj.* **1.** lying near sea level or the ground surface. *low-lying land.* **2.** lying below the usual elevation or altitude. [1855–60]

Low′ Mass′, a Mass that is said, and not sung, by the celebrant, who is assisted by one server, and which has less ceremonial form than a High Mass, using no music or choir. Cf. **High Mass.** [1560–70]

low′ mill′ing, a process for making flour in which the grain is ground once and then bolted. Cf. **high milling.**

low-mind·ed (lō′min′did), *adj.* having or showing a coarse or vulgar taste or interests. [1720–30] —**low′-mind′ed·ly,** *adv.* —**low′-mind′ed·ness,** *n.*

lown¹ (loun), *adj., n., v.t., v.i. South Midland U.S.* calm; quiet. [1375–1425; late ME (Scots) *lownen* (v.), later *lowne* (adj.) < ON *logn* calm (n.), *lugna* to calm]

lown² (lo͞on), *n. Scot.* loon².

Lowndes (loundz), *n.* **William Thomas,** 1798–1843, English bibliographer.

low-necked (lō′nekt′), *adj.* (of a dress or other garment) cut low so as to leave the neck and shoulders exposed; décolleté. [1900–05]

low′ pitch′, *Music.* See **diapason normal pitch.**

low-pitched (lō′picht′), *adj.* **1.** pitched in a low register or key: *a low-pitched aria for the basso.* **2.** produced by slow vibrations; relatively grave in pitch or soft in sound: *a low-pitched whistle.* [1615–25]

low-pow·er (lō′pou′ər), *adj.* (of a radio station) having the power to broadcast to a radius of only 10 to 15 mi. (16 to 24 km). Cf. **full-power.**

low-pres·sure (lō′presh′ər), *adj.* **1.** having or involving a low or below-normal pressure, as steam or water. **2.** without vigor or persistence; not forceful or aggressive: *a low-pressure campaign.* **3.** quietly persuasive; subtle; indirect: *a low-pressure salesman.* [1820–30]

low-priced (lō′prīst′), *adj.* selling at a low price; inexpensive; cheap. [1715–25]

low′ pro′file, a deliberately inconspicuous, modest, or anonymous manner. Also, **low′ pos′ture.** [1970–75] —**low′-pro′file,** *adj.*

low-rate (lō′rāt′), *v.t.,* **-rat·ed, -rat·ing.** to place a low value on: *a policy of low-rating most modern artists.*

low′ relief′, bas-relief. [1705–15]

low-rent (lō′rent′), *adj. Informal.* second-rate; bargain-basement. [1975–80]

low-res·o·lu·tion (lō′rez′ə lo͞o′shən), *adj. Computers.* of or pertaining to CRTs, printers, or other visual output devices that produce images that are not sharply defined (opposed to *high-resolution*).

low·rid·er (lō′rī′dər), *n.* **1.** an individually decorated and customized car fitted with hydraulic jacks that permit lowering of the chassis nearly to the road. **2.** a person, often a teenager, who owns and drives such a car. [1975–80; LOW¹ + RIDER]

low·rid·ing (lō′rī′ding), *n.* the practice of traveling in a lowrider. [1975–80; LOWRID(ER) + -ING¹]

low-rise (lō′rīz′), *adj.* **1.** having a comparatively small number of floors, as a motel or townhouse, and usually no elevator. —*n.* **2.** a low-rise building. [1955–60; on the model of HIGH RISE]

low′ road′, *Slang.* a method, manner, etc., that is underhand, unscrupulous, or otherwise contemptible.

Low·ry (lou′rē), *n.* a male given name, form of **Lawrence.**

lowse (*adj., adv.* lōs; *v.* lōz), *adj.* **lows·er, lows·est,** *adv., v.* **lowsed, lows·ing.** *Brit. Dial.* loose.

low′side win′dow (lō′sīd′), (in medieval English churches) a window set low in the outside wall, permitting the interior to be seen from the outside. Also, **low′side′ win′dow.** Also called **lychnoscope.** [1840–50; LOW¹ + SIDE¹]

low-spir·it·ed (lō′spir′i tid), *adj.* depressed; dejected: *He is feeling rather low-spirited today.* [1580–90] —**low′-spir′it·ed·ly,** *adv.* —**low′-spir′it·ed·ness,** *n.*
—**Syn.** sad, heartsore, dispirited, blue.

Low′ Sun′day, the first Sunday after Easter. Also called **Quasimodo.** [1505–15]

low-tar (*adj.* lō′tär′; *n.* lō′tär′), *adj.* **1.** (of cigarettes or tobacco) containing less tar than usual or standard. —*n.* **2.** a cigarette, blend of tobacco, etc., containing a relatively low amount of tar.

low-tech (lō′tek′), *adj.* low-technology. [by shortening]

low′ technol′ogy, any technology utilizing equipment and production techniques that are relatively unsophisticated (opposed to *high technology*). [1970–75] —**low′-tech·nol′o·gy,** *adj.*

low-ten·sion (lō′ten′shən), *adj. Elect.* subjected to, or capable of operating under, relatively low voltage: *low-tension wire. Abbr.:* lt, L.T. [1895–1900]

low-test (lō′test′), *adj.* (of gasoline) boiling at a comparatively high temperature. [1925–30]

low-tick·et (lō′tik′it), *adj. Informal.* having a relatively low price: *a growing market for low-ticket items.*

low′ tide′, 1. the tide at the point of maximum ebb. **2.** the time of low water. **3.** the lowest point of decline of anything: *His spirits were at low tide.* [1860–65]

low′ wa′ter, water at its lowest level, as in a river. [1520–30] —**low′-wa′ter,** *adj.*

low′-wa′ter mark′, 1. the lowest point reached by a low tide. **2.** something indicating the bottom of a decline. **3.** the lowest or least admirable level: *the low-water mark of political chicanery.* [1520–30]

low′ wine′, Often, **low wines.** *Distilling.* the weak spirits obtained from the first distillation; the result of the first run of the still from the fermented marsh. [1635–45]

lox¹ (loks), *n.* a kind of brine-cured salmon, having either a salt cure **(Scandinavian lox)** or a sugar cure **(Nova Scotia lox),** often eaten with cream cheese on a bagel. [1940–45; < Yiddish *laks* salmon; cf. MHG, OHG *lahs,* c. OE *leax,* ON *lax*]

lox² (loks), *n.* See **liquid oxygen.** Also, **LOX** [1920–25; *l(iquid) ox(ygen)*]

lox·o·dont (lok′sə dont′), *adj.* **1.** having molar teeth with shallow depressions between the ridges. —*n.* **2.** a loxodont animal; an elephant. [< Gk *lox(ós)* slanting, oblique + -ODONT]

lox·o·drome (lok′sə drōm′), *n.* See **rhumb line.** [1875–80; back formation from LOXODROMIC]

lox·o·drom·ic (lok′sə drom′ik), *adj.* **1.** noting, pertaining to, or according to loxodromes or rhumb lines. **2.** noting or pertaining to a map projection, as Mercator's projection, in which rhumb lines appear as straight lines. Also, **lox′o·drom′i·cal.** [1695–1705; < Gk *loxó(s)* slanting, crosswise + *dromikós* of a course; see -DROME, -IC] —**lox′o·drom′i·cal·ly,** *adv.*

lox·o·drom·ics (lok′sə drom′iks), *n.* (*used with a singular v.*) the technique of navigating according to loxodromes or rhumb lines. Also, **lox·od·ro·my** (lok sod′rə mē). [1670–80; see LOXODROMIC, -ICS]

Loy (loi), *n.* a female given name.

loy·al (loi′əl), *adj.* **1.** faithful to one's sovereign, government, or state: *a loyal subject.* **2.** faithful to one's oath, commitments, or obligations: *to be loyal to a vow.* **3.** faithful to any leader, party, or cause, or to any person or thing conceived as deserving fidelity: *a loyal friend.* **4.** characterized by or showing faithfulness to commitments, vows, allegiance, obligations, etc.: *loyal conduct.* [1525–35; < MF, OF *loial, le(i)al* < L *lēgālis* LEGAL] —**loy′al·ly,** *adv.* —**loy′al·ness,** *n.*
—**Syn. 1.** patriotic. **2.** See **faithful.** —**Ant. 1.** faithless, treacherous.

loy·al·ist (loi′ə list), *n.* **1.** a person who is loyal; a supporter of the sovereign or of the existing government, esp. in time of revolt. **2.** (*sometimes cap.*) a person who remained loyal to the British during the American Revolution; Tory. **3.** (*cap.*) an adherent of the republic during the Spanish Civil War, opposed to Franco. [1640–50; LOYAL + -IST] —**loy′al·ism,** *n.*

Loy′al Or′der of Moose′. See under **moose** (def. 2).

loy·al·ty (loi′əl tē), *n., pl.* **-ties. 1.** the state or quality of being loyal; faithfulness to commitments or obligations. **2.** faithful adherence to a sovereign, government, leader, cause, etc. **3.** an example or instance of faithfulness, adherence, or the like: *a man with fierce loyalties.* [1350–1400; ME *loialte* < MF. See LOYAL, -TY²]
—**Syn. 2.** fealty, devotion, constancy. LOYALTY, ALLEGIANCE, FIDELITY all imply a sense of duty or of devoted attachment to something or someone. LOYALTY connotes sentiment and the feeling of devotion that one holds for one's country, creed, family, friends, etc. ALLEGIANCE applies particularly to a citizen's duty to his or her country, or, by extension, one's obligation to support a party, cause, leader, etc. FIDELITY implies unwavering devotion and allegiance to a person, principle, etc. —**Ant. 1, 2.** faithlessness.

Lo·yang (*Chin.* lô′yäng′), *n. Wade-Giles.* Luoyang.

Loy·o·la (loi ō′lə), *n.* **Saint Ignatius of** (*Iñigo López de Loyola*), 1491–1556, Spanish soldier and ecclesiastic: founder of the Society of Jesus.

loz·enge (loz′inj), *n.* **1.** a small, flavored tablet made from sugar or syrup, often medicated, originally diamond-shaped. **2.** *Geom. Now Rare.* diamond (def. 8). **3.** *Heraldry.* **a.** a diamond-shaped charge. **b.** a diamond-shaped shield bearing the arms of a woman. [1300–50; ME *losenge* < MF, OF, perh. < Gaulish **lausa* flat stone + *-enge* < Gmc *-inga* -ING³]

Lo·zère (lô zer′), *n.* a department in S France. 74,825; 2000 sq. mi. (5180 sq. km). *Cap.:* Mende.

Lo·zi (lō′zē), *n.* a Bantu language spoken in Barotseland, in western Zambia.

LP, *pl.* **LPs, LP's.** a phonograph record played at 33⅓ r.p.m.; long-playing record.

L.P., 1. long primer. **2.** low pressure. Also, **l.p.**

LPG, See **liquefied petroleum gas.** Also called **LP gas.**

lpm, *Computers.* lines per minute: a measure of the speed of a printer. Also, **LPM**

LPN, See **licensed practical nurse.**

L.P.S., Lord Privy Seal.

CONCISE PRONUNCIATION KEY: act, cāpe, dâre, pärt; set, ēqual; if, ice; ox, ōver, ôrder, oil, bo͝ok, bo͞ot, out; up, ûrge; child; sing; shoe; thin, *th*at; zh as in *treasure.* ə = *a* as in *alone, e* as in *system, i* as in *easily, o* as in *gallop, u* as in *circus;* ′ as in *fire* (fī′r), *hour* (ou′r). l and n can serve as syllabic consonants, as in *cradle* (krād′l), and *button* (but′n). See the full key inside the front cover.

LR, *Real Estate.* living room.

Lr, *Symbol, Chem.* lawrencium.

L.R., Lloyd's Register.

L-ra·di·a·tion (el′rā′dē ā′shən), *n. Physics.* See under **L-line.**

LRAM, long-range attack missile.

LRBM, long-range ballistic missile.

LRT, light-rail transit.

LS, 1. left side. **2.** letter signed. **3.** library science. **4.** lightship.

L.S., 1. Licentiate in Surgery. **2.** Linnaean Society. **3.** the place of the seal, as on a document. [(def. 3) < L *locus sigillī*]

l.s., See **L.S.** (def. 3).

LSAT, *Trademark.* Law School Admission Test.

l.s.c., in the place mentioned above. [< L *locō suprā citātō*]

LSD, 1. *U.S. Navy.* a seagoing, amphibious ship capable of carrying and launching assault landing craft from a large, inner compartment that can be flooded, and of making emergency repairs at sea to smaller ships. [*l(anding) s(hip) d(eck)*] **2.** *Pharm.* lysergic acid diethylamide: a crystalline solid, $C_{20}H_{25}N_3O$, the diethyl amide of lysergic acid, a powerful psychedelic drug that produces temporary hallucinations and a schizophrenic psychotic state. **3.** See **least significant digit.**

L.S.D., pounds, shillings, and pence. Also, **£.s.d., l.s.d.** [< L *librae, solidī, dēnāriī*]

L-se·ries (el′sēr′ēz), *n. Physics.* See under **L-line.**

L-shell (el′shel′), *n. Physics.* the second shell of electrons surrounding the nucleus of an atom and containing, when filled, eight electrons having principal quantum number 2. Cf. **K-shell, M-shell, N-shell.** [1925–30]

LSI, *Electronics.* large-scale integration: the technology for concentrating several thousand semiconductor devices in an integrated circuit. Cf. **MSI, SSI, VLSI.**

L sill, *Carpentry.* a sill for a building frame composed of a plate resting on the basement wall and a header or joist at the outer edge of the plate. Cf. **box sill.**

LSM, a type of military landing ship slightly more than 200 ft. (60 m) long. [*l(anding) s(hip) m(edium)*]

L.S.S., Lifesaving Service.

LST, an oceangoing military ship, used by amphibious forces for landing troops and heavy equipment on beaches. [*l(anding) s(hip) t(ank)*]

l.s.t., local standard time.

lt, *Elect.* low-tension.

Lt., lieutenant.

lt., light.

L.T., 1. long ton. **2.** *Elect.* low-tension.

l.t., 1. *Football.* left tackle. **2.** local time. **3.** long ton.

LTA, (of an aircraft) lighter-than-air.

Lt. Col., Lieutenant Colonel. Also **LTC**

Lt. Comdr., Lieutenant Commander. Also, **Lt. Com.**

Ltd., limited (def. 4). Also, **ltd.**

Lt. Gen., Lieutenant General. Also, **LTG**

Lt. Gov., Lieutenant Governor.

L.Th., Licentiate in Theology.

Lt. Inf., *Mil.* light infantry.

LTJG, *U.S. Navy.* Lieutenant Junior Grade.

LTL, less-than-truckload lot.

ltr., 1. letter. **2.** lighter.

lt-yr, light-year; light-years.

Lu (lo͞o), *n.* a male or female given name, form of **Lou.**

Lu, *Symbol. Chem.* lutetium.

Lu·a·la·ba (lo͞o′ä lä′bä), *n.* a river in SE Zaire: a headstream of the Zaire (Congo) River. 400 mi. (645 km) long.

Lu·an·da (lo͞o an′də, -än′-), *n.* a seaport in and the capital of Angola, in SW Africa. 475,328. Also, **Loanda.**

Lu·an·da (lo͞o an′də, -än′-), *n.* a female given name: from a Bantu word meaning "melody."

Luang Pra·bang (lwäng′ prä bäng′), Louangphrabang.

Lu·anne (lo͞o an′), *n.* a female given name.

Lu·an·shya (lo͞o än′shä, lwän′-), *n.* a town in central Zambia. 124,000.

Lu·a·pu·la (lo͞o′ə po͞o′lə), *n.* a river in S central Africa, flowing E and N along the Zambia-Zaire border to Lake Mweru. ab. 300 mi. (485 km) long.

lu·au (lo͞o ou′, lo͞o′ou), *n.* **1.** a feast of Hawaiian food, usually held outdoors and usually accompanied by Hawaiian entertainment. **2.** a cooked dish of taro leaves, usually prepared with coconut cream and octopus or chicken. [1835–45; < Hawaiian *lū′au*]

lub, *Math.* See **least upper bound.**

lub., 1. lubricant. **2.** lubricating. **3.** lubrication.

Lu·ba (lo͞o′bə), *n., pl.* **-bas,** (*esp. collectively*) **-ba** for 1. **1.** a member of any of various groups of agricultural and hunting people inhabiting southeastern Zaire, some of whom are famous for their wood carvings. **2.** Also called **Chiluba, Ciluba, Tshiluba.** the Bantu language of the Luba, used as a lingua franca in southern Zaire.

Lu·bang′ Is′lands (lo͞o bäng′), a group of islands in the NW Philippines, located NW of Mindoro. 98 sq. mi. (254 sq. km).

Lu·ba·vitch·er (lo͞o′bə vich′ər, lo͞o bä′vi chər), *n.* **1.** a member of a missionary Hasidic movement founded in the 1700's by Rabbi Shneour Zalman of Lyady. —*adj.* **2.** of or pertaining to the Lubavitchers or their movement. [< Yiddish *lubavitsher,* equiv. to *Lubavitsh* (< Byelorussian *Lyubavichi*) a town which was the center of the movement, 1813–1915 + *-er* -ER[1]]

lub·ber (lub′ər), *n.* **1.** a big, clumsy, stupid person; lout. **2.** an awkward or unskilled sailor; landlubber. —*adj.* **3.** clumsy; stupid; lubberly. —*v.i.* **4.** to behave like a lubber, esp. in the handling of a boat. [1325–75; ME *lobre.* See LOB[1], -ER[1]]

lub′ber grass′hop·per. See **plains grasshopper.** [1875–80]

lub·ber·ly (lub′ər lē), *adj.* **1.** of or resembling a lubber. —*adv.* **2.** in a lubberly manner. [1565–75; LUBBER + -LY] —**lub′ber·li·ness,** *n.*

lub′ber's hole′, *Naut.* (in a top on a mast) an open space through which a sailor may pass instead of climbing out on the futtock shrouds. [1765–75]

lub′ber's knot′, *Naut.* an improperly made reef or square knot, likely to slip loose. Also called **granny, granny knot, granny's knot.**

lub′ber's line′, *Navig.* a vertical line on the forward inner side of the bowl of a fixed compass, used as a reference mark indicating the heading of a vessel. Also, **lub′ber line′.** Also called **lub′ber's mark′, lub′ber's point′.** [1855–65]

Lub·bock (lub′ək), *n.* **1. Sir John, 1st Baron Avebury,** 1834–1913, English author, natural scientist, and statesman. **2.** a city in NW Texas. 173,979.

lube (lo͞ob), *n., v.,* **lubed, lub·ing.** —*n. Informal.* **1.** lubricant. **2.** lubrication, esp. an application of a lubricant to a vehicle. —*v.t.* **3.** to lubricate: *to lube a bicycle chain.* [by shortening]

Lü·beck (ly′bek), *n.* a seaport in N Germany: important Baltic port in the medieval Hanseatic League. 210,500. See map under **Hanseatic League.**

Lu·bitsch (lo͞o′bich), *n.* **Ernst** (ûrnst; *Ger.* ernst), 1892–1947, German film director and producer, in the U.S. after 1922.

Lüb·ke (lyp′kə), *n.* **Hein·rich** (hīn′rikh), 1894–1972, German statesman: president of West Germany 1959–69. Also, **Luebke.**

Lu·blin (lo͞o′blin; *Pol.* lo͞o′blēn), *n.* a city in E Poland. 272,000. Russian, **Lyublin.**

lu·bra (lo͞o′brə), *n. Australian Often Offensive.* an Aborigine girl or woman. [1840–50; prob. < Southeastern language of Tasmania *lubərə*]

lu·bric (lo͞o′brik), *adj. Archaic.* lubricous. [1480–90; < L *lūbricus* slippery, smooth, ML: lewd]

lu·bri·cant (lo͞o′bri kənt), *n.* **1.** a substance, as oil or grease, for lessening friction, esp. in the working parts of a mechanism. —*adj.* **2.** capable of lubricating; used to lubricate. [1815–25; < L *lūbricant-* (s. of *lūbricāns*), prp. of *lūbricāre* to make slippery. See LUBRIC, -ANT]

lu·bri·cate (lo͞o′bri kāt′), *v.,* **-cat·ed, -cat·ing.** —*v.t.* **1.** to apply some oily or greasy substance to (a machine, parts of a mechanism, etc.) in order to diminish friction; oil or grease (something). **2.** to make slippery or smooth; apply a lubricant to: *to lubricate one's hands with a lotion.* **3.** to smooth over, as a difficulty or human relationship; ease: *to lubricate the friction between enemies.* **4.** *Slang.* to provide with intoxicating drinks. **5.** *Slang.* to bribe. —*v.i.* **6.** to act as a lubricant. **7.** to apply a lubricant to something. **8.** *Slang.* to drink or become drunk. [1615–25; < L *lūbricātus,* ptp. of *lūbricāre* to make slippery. See LUBRIC, -ATE[1]] —**lu′bri·ca′tion,** *n.* —**lu′bri·ca′tion·al,** *adj.* —**lu′bri·ca′tive,** *adj.* —**lu·bri·ca·to·ry** (lo͞o′bri kə tôr′ē, -tōr′ē), *adj.*

lu·bri·ca·tor (lo͞o′bri kā′tər), *n.* a person or thing that lubricates. [1750–60; LUBRICATE + -OR[2]]

lu·bri·cious (lo͞o brish′əs), *adj.* **1.** arousing or expressive of sexual desire; lustful; lecherous. **2.** lubricous. [1575–85; LUBRIC + -IOUS] —**lu·bri′cious·ly,** *adv.*
—**Syn. 1.** lascivious, libidinous, pornographic, obscene.

lu·bric·i·ty (lo͞o bris′i tē), *n., pl.* **-ties. 1.** oily smoothness, as of a surface; slipperiness. **2.** ability to lubricate; capacity for lubrication: *the wonderful lubricity of this new oil.* **3.** instability; shiftiness; fleeting nature: *the lubricity of fame and fortune.* **4.** lewdness; lustfulness; lasciviousness; salaciousness. **5.** something that arouses lasciviousness, esp. pornography. [1485–95; earlier *lubrycyte* lewdness < ML *lubricitās* lechery, LL: slipperiness. See LUBRIC, -ITY]

lu·bri·cous (lo͞o′bri kəs), *adj.* **1.** (of a surface, coating, etc.) having an oily smoothness; slippery. **2.** unstable; shifty; fleeting. **3.** lubricious. [1525–35; < L *lūbricus* slippery, LL: unstable]
—**Syn. 2.** unsteady, wavering, undependable.

Lu·bum·ba·shi (lo͞o bo͝om′bä shē), *n.* a city in S Zaire. 451,332. Formerly, **Elisabethville.**

Lu·byan·ka (lo͞o byäng′kə), *n.* a prison and secret-police headquarters in central Moscow. [< Russ *Lyubyán′ka,* named after the adjacent street and square, now Dzerzhinsky Street and Square]

Lu·can (lo͞o′kən), *n.* (*Marcus Annaeus Lucanus*) A.D. 39–65, Roman poet, born in Spain.

Lu·ca·ni·a (lo͞o kā′nē ə), *n.* **1.** an ancient region in S Italy, NW of the Gulf of Taranto. **2.** a modern region in S Italy, comprising most of the ancient region. 617,295; 3856 sq. mi. (9985 sq. km). Italian, **Basilicata.**

lu·carne (lo͞o kärn′), *n.* a dormer window. [1540–50; < F; r. *lucane* < MF; orig. of both F forms obscure]

Lu·cas (lo͞o′kəs), *n.* **1. George,** born 1945, U.S. film director. **2.** a male given name, form of **Luke.**

Lu·cas van Ley·den (lo͞o′käs vän līd′n), (*Lucas Hugensz*) 1494–1533, Dutch painter and engraver.

Luc·ca (lo͞ok′kä), *n.* a city in NW Italy, W of Florence. 91,656.

luce (lo͞os), *n.* a pike, esp. when fully grown. [1350–1400; ME < MF *lus* pike < LL *lūcius*]

Luce (lo͞os), *n.* **1. Clare Boothe,** born 1903, U.S. writer, politician, and diplomat. **2. Henry Robinson,** 1898–1967, U.S. publisher and editor (husband of Clare Boothe Luce).

lu·cent (lo͞o′sənt), *adj.* **1.** shining. **2.** translucent; clear. [1490–1500; < L *lūcent-* (s. of *lūcēns*), prp. of *lūcēre* to shine. See LUCID, -ENT] —**lu′cen·cy;** *Rare,* **lu′cence,** *n.* —**lu′cent·ly,** *adv.*

lu·cerne (lo͞o sûrn′), *n.* alfalfa. Also, **lu·cern′.** [1620–30; alter. (by assoc. with L *lucerna* lamp) of F *luzerne* < Pr *luzerno* glowworm (the plant was so called in allusion to its bright seeds); akin to OPr *luzerna* lamp < VL **lūcerna,* for L *lucerna.* See LUCID]

Lu·cerne (lo͞o sûrn′; *Fr.* ly sern′), *n.* **1.** a canton in central Switzerland. 291,700; 576 sq. mi. (1490 sq. km). **2.** the capital of this canton, on Lake of Lucerne. 65,300. **3. Lake of.** Also called **Lake of the Four Forest Cantons.** a lake in central Switzerland. 24 mi. (39 km) long; 44 sq. mi. (114 sq. km). German, **Luzern.**

lu·ces (lo͞o′sēz), *n.* pl. of **lux.**

Lu·chow (*Chin.* lo͞o′jō′), *n. Older Spelling.* Luzhou. Also, *Wade-Giles,* **Lu′chou′.**

Lu·cia (lo͞o′shə, -shē ə, -sē ə), *n.* a female given name: from a Latin word meaning "light."

Lu·ci·a di Lam·mer·moor (lo͞o chē′ə di lam′ər mo͝or′; *It.* lo͞o chē′ä dē läm′mer mo͝or′), an opera (1835) by Gaetano Donizetti, based on Sir Walter Scott's novel *The Bride of Lammermoor.*

Lu·cian (lo͞o′shən), *n.* **1.** A.D. 117–c180, Greek rhetorician and satirist. **2.** (*"Lucian of Antioch"; "Lucian the Martyr"*) A.D. c240–312, theologian and Biblical critic, born at Samosata, in Syria. **3.** a male given name.

Lu·ci·anne (lo͞o′sē an′), *n.* a female given name.

lu·cid (lo͞o′sid), *adj.* **1.** easily understood; completely intelligible or comprehensible: *a lucid explanation.* **2.** characterized by clear perception or understanding; rational or sane: *a lucid moment in his madness.* **3.** shining or bright. **4.** clear; pellucid; transparent. [1575–85; < L *lūcidus,* equiv. to *lūc-,* s. of *lūx* LIGHT[1] + *-idus* -ID[4]] —**lu·cid′i·ty, lu′cid·ness,** *n.* —**lu′cid·ly,** *adv.*
—**Syn. 1.** plain, understandable, evident, obvious. **2.** sound, reasonable. **3.** radiant, luminous. **4.** limpid.
—**Ant. 1, 4.** obscure. **2.** irrational. **3.** dim.

lu·ci·da (lo͞o′si də), *n., pl.* **-dae** (-dē′). *Astron.* the brightest star in a constellation. [1720–30; < NL, special use of L *lūcida* (*stella*) bright (star), fem. of *lūcidus* LUCID]

Lu·ci·fer (lo͞o′sə fər), *n.* **1.** a proud, rebellious archangel, identified with Satan, who fell from heaven. **2.** the planet Venus when appearing as the morning star. **3.** (*l.c.*) See **friction match.** [bef. 1000; ME, OE < L: morning star, lit., light-bringing, equiv. to *lūci-* (s. of *lūx*) light + *-fer* -FER]

lu·cif·er·in (lo͞o sif′ər in), *n. Biochem.* a pigment occurring in luminescent organisms, as fireflies, that emits light when undergoing oxidation. [1885–90; < L *lūcifer* (see LUCIFER) + -IN[2]]

lu′cifer match′. See **friction match.** [1825–35]

lu·cif·er·ous (lo͞o sif′ər əs), *adj.* **1.** bringing or providing light. **2.** providing insight or enlightenment. [1640–50; < L *lūcifer* (see LUCIFER) + -OUS]

Lu·cil·i·us (lo͞o sil′ē əs), *n.* **Ga·ius** (gā′əs), c180–102? B.C., Roman satirist.

Lu·cille (lo͞o sēl′), *n.* a female given name, form of **Lucia** or **Lucy.** Also, **Lu·cile′.**

Lu·cin·da (lo͞o sin′də), *n.* a female given name, form of **Lucy.**

Lu·cite (lo͞o′sīt), *Trademark.* a transparent or translucent plastic, any of a class of methyl methacrylate ester polymers.

Lu·cius (lo͞o′shəs), *n.* a male given name: from a Latin word meaning "light."

Lu·ci·us I (lo͞o′shē əs, -shəs), **Saint,** died A.D. 254, pope 253–254.

Lucius II, (*Gherardo Caccianemici dell' Orso*) died 1145, Italian ecclesiastic: pope 1144–45.

Lucius III, (*Ubaldo Allucingoli*) died 1185, Italian ecclesiastic: pope 1181–85.

luck (luk), *n.* **1.** the force that seems to operate for good or ill in a person's life, as in shaping circumstances, events, or opportunities: *With my luck I'll probably get pneumonia.* **2.** good fortune; advantage or success, considered as the result of chance: *He had no luck finding work.* **3.** a combination of circumstances, events, etc., operating by chance to bring good or ill to a person: *She's had nothing but bad luck all year.* **4.** some object on which good fortune is supposed to depend: *This rabbit's foot is my luck.* **5. down on one's luck,** in unfortunate circumstances; unlucky: *She hated to see her old friend so down on her luck.* **6. in luck,** lucky; fortunate: *We were in luck, for the bakery was still open.* **7. luck of the draw,** the luck one has in or as if in drawing cards. **8. out of luck,** unlucky; unfortunate: *When it comes to getting World Series tickets, we're usually out of luck.* **9. push one's luck,** *Informal.* to try to make too much of an opportunity; go too far. Also, **crowd one's luck.** —*v. Informal.* **10. luck into** or **onto,** to meet, acquire, become, etc., by good luck: *She lucked into a great job.* **11. luck out,** to have an instance or run of exceptionally good luck: *He lucked out when he made a hole in one during the tournament.* **12. luck upon,** to come across by chance: *to luck upon a profitable investment.* [1400–50; late ME *luk* < MD *luc,* aphetic form of *geluc;* c. G *Glück*]

Łuck (lo͞otsk; *Pol.* wo͞otsk), *n.* Polish name of **Lutsk.**

luck·ie (luk′ē), *n. Scot.* lucky[2].

CONCISE ETYMOLOGY KEY: <, descended or borrowed from; >, whence; b., blend of, blended; c., cognate with; cf., compare; deriv., derivative; equiv., equivalent; imit., imitative; obl., oblique; r., replacing; s., stem; sp., spelling, spelled; resp., respelling, respelled; trans., translation; ?, origin unknown; *, unattested; ‡, probably earlier than. See the full key inside the front cover.

luck·i·ly (luk′ə lē), *adv.* by good luck; fortunately: *Luckily we had enough money.* [1520–30; LUCKY + -LY]

luck·less (luk′lis), *adj.* having no luck; unfortunate; hapless; ill-fated; turning out or ending disastrously: *a luckless venture that ruined many of the investors.* [1555–65; LUCK + -LESS] —**luck′less·ly,** *adv.* —**luck′·less·ness,** *n.*

Luck·now (luk′nou), *n.* a city in and capital of Uttar Pradesh state, in N India: the British besieged it (1857) during Sepoy Rebellion. 826,246.

luck·y[1] (luk′ē), *adj.,* **luck·i·er, luck·i·est.** **1.** having or marked by good luck; fortunate: *That was my lucky day.* **2.** happening fortunately: *a lucky accident.* **3.** bringing or foretelling good luck, or supposed to do so: *a lucky penny.* [1495–1505; LUCK + -Y[1]] —**luck′i·ness,** *n.*
—**Syn. 1.** favored. See **fortunate. 3.** auspicious, propitious, favorable. —**Ant. 1.** unfortunate.

luck·y[2] (luk′ē), *n., pl.* **luck·ies.** *Scot.* **1.** a familiar name applied to an elderly woman, esp. a grandmother; granny. **2.** a familiar name applied to a woman, as one's wife or a barmaid. Also, **luckie.** [1710–20; LUCK + -Y[2]]

lu·cra·tive (lo͞o′krə tiv), *adj.* profitable; moneymaking; remunerative: *a lucrative business.* [1375–1425; late ME *lucratif* (< MF) < L *lucrātīvus* gainful, equiv. to *lucrāt(us)* (ptp. of *lucrārī* to make a profit, gain by economy; see LUCRE) + *-īvus* -IVE] —**lu′cra·tive·ly,** *adv.* —**lu′cra·tive·ness,** *n.*

lu·cre (lo͞o′kər), *n.* monetary reward or gain; money. [1350–1400; ME < L *lucrum* profit; akin to OE *lēan* reward, G *Lohn,* Goth, ON *laun*]

Lu·cre·tia (lo͞o krē′shə, -shē ə), *n.* **1.** Also, **Lu·crece** (lo͞o krēs′). *Rom. Legend.* a Roman woman whose suicide led to the expulsion of the Tarquins and the establishment of the Roman republic. **2.** a female given name.

Lu·cre·tius (lo͞o krē′shəs), *n.* (*Titus Lucretius Carus*) 97?–54 B.C., Roman poet and philosopher. —**Lu·cre′·tian,** *adj.*

Lu·cre·zi·a Bor·gia (lo͞o kret′sē ə bôr′jə, bôr′zhə, -krē′shə; *It.* lo͞o kʀe′tsyä bôʀ′jä), an opera (1833) by Gaetano Donizetti.

lu·cu·brate (lo͞o′kyo͝o brāt′), *v.i.,* **-brat·ed, -brat·ing.** **1.** to work, write, or study laboriously, esp. at night. **2.** to write learnedly. [1615–25; < L *lūcubrātus,* ptp. of *lūcubrāre* to work by artificial light, equiv. to *lūcu-,* var. (before labials) of *lūci-,* comb. form of *lūcere* to shine + *-br(um)* instrumental suffix + *-ā-* theme vowel + *-tus* ptp. suffix] —**lu′cu·bra′tor,** *n.* —**lu·cu·bra·to·ry** (lo͞o-kyo͝o′brə tôr′ē, -tōr′ē), *adj.*

lu·cu·bra·tion (lo͞o′kyo͝o brā′shən), *n.* **1.** laborious work, study, thought, etc., esp. at night. **2.** the result of such activity, as a learned speech or dissertation. **3.** Often, **lucubrations.** any literary effort, esp. of a pretentious or solemn nature. [1585–95; < L *lūcubrātiōn-* (s. of *lūcubrātiō*) night-work. See LUCUBRATE, -ION]

lu·cu·lent (lo͞o′kyo͝o lənt), *adj.* **1.** clear or lucid: *a luculent explanation.* **2.** convincing; cogent. [1375–1425; late ME < L *lūculentus* bright, equiv. to *lūc-* (s. of *lūx*) light + *-ulentus* -ULENT] —**lu′cu·lent·ly,** *adv.*

Lu·cul·lan (lo͞o kul′ən), *adj.* **1.** (esp. of banquets, parties, etc.) marked by lavishness and richness; sumptuous. **2.** of or pertaining to Lucullus or his life style. Also, **Lu·cul·le·an** (lo͞o′kə lē′ən), **Lu·cul′li·an.** [1855–60; < L *Lūcullānus;* see LUCULLUS, -AN]

Lu·cul·lus (lo͞o kul′əs), *n.* **Lucius Li·cin·i·us** (li sin′ē-əs), c110–57? B.C., Roman general and epicure.

Lu·cy (lo͞o′sē), *n.* a female given name. Also, **Lu′ci.**

Lu·cy (lo͞o′sē), *n.* the incomplete skeletal remains of a female hominid found in eastern Ethiopia in 1974 and classified as *Australopithecus afarensis.* [after the Beatles' song "Lucy in the Sky with Diamonds," a tape of which was played in the discoverers' camp during the expedition]

Lu′cy Ston′er (stō′nər), a person who advocates the retention of the maiden name by married women. Cf. **Stone** (def. 5). [1945–50, *Amer.;* Lucy STONE + -ER[1]]

Lü·da (*Chin.* ly′dä′), *n. Pinyin.* former name of **Dalian** (def. 1). Also, **Lüta.**

Ludd (*Welsh.* lyth), *n.* Llud.

Lud·dite (lud′īt), *n.* a member of any of various bands of workers in England (1811–16) organized to destroy manufacturing machinery, under the belief that its use diminished employment. [1805–15; after Ned *Ludd,* 18th-century Leicestershire worker who originated the idea; see -ITE[1]] —**Lud′dism, Lud′dit·ism,** *n.*

lude (lo͞od), *n. Slang.* Quaalude. [1975–80; by shortening]

Lu·den·dorff (lo͞od′n dôrf′), *n.* **E·rich Frie·drich Wil·helm von** (ā′rikh fʀē′dʀikh vil′helm fən), 1865–1937, German general.

Lü·der·itz (ly′dər its), *n.* a seaport in SW Namibia: diamond-mining center. 17,000.

Lu·dhi·a·na (lo͝o′dē ä′nä), *n.* a city in central Punjab, in N India. 401,124.

lu·dic (lo͞o′dik), *adj.* playful in an aimless way: *the ludic behavior of kittens.* [1935–40; < L *lūd-* (s. of *lūdere* to play) + -IC, perh. via F *ludique,* learned formation from same components]

lu·di·crous (lo͞o′di krəs), *adj.* causing laughter because of absurdity; provoking or deserving derision; ridiculous; laughable: *a ludicrous lack of efficiency.* [1610–20; < L *lūdicrus* sportive, equiv. to *lūdicr(um)* a show, public games (*lūdi-,* s. of *lūdere* to play, + *-crum* n. suffix of instrument or result) + *-us* -OUS] —**lu′di·crous·ly,** *adv.* —**lu′di·crous·ness,** *n.*
—**Syn.** farcical. See **funny.**

Lud·low (lud′lō), *n.* **1.** a town in S Salop, in W England: agricultural market center. 23,481. **2.** a town in S Massachusetts. 18,150.

Lud·low (lud′lō), *Typesetting, Trademark.* a brand of machine for casting slugs from matrices handset in a composing stick.

Lud·wig (lud′wig, lo͝od′vig, -wig; *Ger.* lo͞ot′vikh, lo͞od′-), *n.* **1. E·mil** (ā′mēl), (*Emil Cohn*), 1881–1948, German biographer. **2.** a male given name: from a Germanic word meaning "famous warrior."

Ludwig II, German name of **Louis II.**

Lud·wigs·ha·fen (lo͞ot′vikhs hä′fən, lo͞od′-), *n.* a city in SW Germany, on the Rhine opposite Mannheim. 156,700.

Lueb·ke (lyp′kə), *n.* **Hein·rich** (hīn′rikh). See **Lübke, Heinrich.**

Lu·el·la (lo͞o el′ə), *n.* a female given name.

Luen·ing (lo͞o′ning), *n.* **Otto,** born 1900, U.S. composer, conductor, and flutist.

lu·es (lo͞o′ēz), *n. Pathol.* syphilis. [1625–35; < NL, special use of L *luēs* plague, contagion]

lu·et·ic (lo͞o et′ik), *adj. Pathol.* syphilitic. [1895–1900; LUE(S) + -TIC] —**lu·et′i·cal·ly,** *adv.*

luff (luf), *n. Naut.* **1.** the forward edge of a fore-and-aft sail. See diag. under **sail.** —*v.i.* **2.** to bring the head of a sailing ship closer to or directly into the wind, with sails shaking. **3.** (of a sail) to shake from being set too close to the wind: *The sail luffed as we put about for port.* **4.** to raise or lower the outer end of the boom of a crane or derrick so as to move its load horizontally. —*v.t.* **5.** to set (the helm of a ship) in such a way as to bring the head of the ship into the wind. **6.** to raise or lower the outer end of (the boom of a crane or derrick). [1175–1225; ME *lof, loof* steering gear (cf. OF *lof*) < MD (unrecorded), later D *loef* tholepin (of tiller)]

luf·fa (lo͞o′fə, luf′ə), *n.* loofah.

luff′ on luff′, *Naut.* a tackle composed of one luff attached to the fall of another. Also called **luff′ upon luff′.** [1830–40]

luff′ tack′le, *Naut.* a tackle having a double block and a single block, giving a mechanical advantage of three or four, neglecting friction, depending on which is the standing and which is the running block. See diag. under **tackle.** [1690–1700]

Luf·kin (luf′kin), *n.* a city in E Texas. 28,562.

Luft·waf·fe (lo͝oft′väf′ə), *n. German.* air force.

lug[1] (lug), *v.,* **lugged, lug·ging,** *n.* —*v.t.* **1.** to pull or carry with force or effort: *to lug a suitcase upstairs.* **2.** to introduce or interject in an inappropriate or irrelevant manner: *to lug personalities into a discussion of philosophy.* **3.** (of a sailing ship) to carry an excessive amount of (sail) for the conditions prevailing. —*v.i.* **4.** to pull or tug laboriously. **5.** (of an engine or machine) to jerk, hesitate, or strain: *The engine lugs when we climb a steep hill.* —*n.* **6.** an act or instance of lugging; a forcible pull; haul. **7.** a wooden box for transporting fruit or vegetables. **8.** *Slang.* a request for or exaction of money, as for political purposes: *They put the lug on him at the office.* [1300–50; ME *luggen* < Scand; cf. Norw *lugge,* Sw *lugga* to pull by the hair]

lug[2] (lug), *n.* **1.** a projecting piece by which anything is held or supported. **2.** a ridge or welt that helps to provide traction, as on a tire or the sole of a shoe. **3.** *Masonry.* either of the ends of a lug sill. **4.** *Carpentry.* (in a double-hung window) one of a pair of projections extending downward from the ends of the meeting rail of the upper sash. **5.** a leather loop hanging down from a saddle, through which a shaft is passed for support. **6.** *Shipbuilding.* clip[2] (def. 6). **7.** *Slang.* **a.** an awkward, clumsy fellow. **b.** a blockhead. **c.** a man; guy. [1485–95; < Scand; cf. Norw, Sw *lugg* forelock. See LUG[1]]

lug[3] (lug), *n.* lugsail. [by shortening]

lug[4] (lug), *n.* lugworm. [1595–1605; earlier *lugg;* perh. special use of LUG[2]]

Lug (lo͝okh), *n.* an ancient Irish god, probably a solar deity.

Lu·gan·da (lo͞o gan′də, -gän′-), *n.* a Bantu language of Uganda. Also called **Ganda.**

Lu·gansk (lo͞o gänsk′), *n.* a city in E Ukraine, in the Donets Basin. 509,000. Formerly (1935–90), **Voroshilovgrad.**

Lu·gar (lo͞o′gər), *n.* **Richard G(reen),** born 1932, U.S. politician: senator since 1977.

luge (lo͞ozh), *n., v.,* **luged, lug·ing.** —*n.* **1.** a one- or two-person sled for coasting or racing down a chute, used esp. in Europe. —*v.i.* **2.** to go or race on a luge: *to luge at nearly 70 miles per hour.* [1900–05; < dial. F] —**lug′er,** *n.*

Lu·ger (lo͞o′gər), *Trademark.* a brand of automatic pistol of 9-millimeter caliber, made in Germany.

lug′ fore′sail, *Naut.* a gaff foresail having no boom or sometimes a partial boom.

lug·gage (lug′ij), *n.* suitcases, trunks, etc.; baggage. [1590–1600; LUG[1] + -AGE] —**lug′gage·less,** *adj.*

lug·ger (lug′ər), *n. Naut.* a small ship lug-rigged on two or three masts. [1785–95; LUG(SAIL) + -ER[1]]

lug′ger top′sail, *Naut.* a fore-and-aft topsail used above a lugsail.

lug·gie (lug′ē, lo͝og′ē, lo͞o′gē), *n. Scot.* any wooden container with a lug, or handle, as a mug, a pail, or a dish with a handle on the side. [1715–25; LUG[2] + -IE]

lug′ nut′, a large nut fitting on a heavy bolt, used esp. in attaching a wheel to a motor vehicle.

Lu·go (lo͞o′gô), *n.* a city in NW Spain. 63,830.

Lu·go·nes (lo͞o gô′nes), *n.* **Le·o·pol·do** (le′ô pôl′dô), 1874–1938, Argentine poet and diplomat.

Lu·go·si (lo͞o gō′sē), *n.* **Bela,** 1884–1956, U.S. actor, born in Hungary: best known for his roles in horror films.

lug′ pad′, padeye.

lug-rigged (lug′rigd′), *adj. Naut.* rigged with a lugsail or lugsails. [1855–60]

lug·sail (lug′sāl′; *Naut.* lug′səl), *n. Naut.* a quadrilateral sail bent upon a yard that crosses the mast obliquely. See diag. under **sail.** Also called **lug.** [1670–80; ME *lugge* pole (now dial.; cf. LOG[1]) + SAIL]

lug-soled (lug′sōld′), *adj.* (of a shoe, boot, etc.) having lugs on the sole, as to provide secure footing on rugged terrain. Also, **lug′-sole′.** [LUG[2] + SOLE[2] + -ED[3]]

lu·gu·bri·ous (lo͝o go͞o′brē əs, -gyo͞o′-), *adj.* mournful, dismal, or gloomy, esp. in an affected, exaggerated, or unrelieved manner: *lugubrious songs of lost love.* [1595–1605; < L *lūgubri(s)* mournful (akin to *lūgēre* to mourn) + -OUS] —**lu·gu′bri·ous·ly,** *adv.* —**lu·gu′bri·ous·ness, lu·gu·bri·os·i·ty** (lə go͞o′brē os′i tē, -gyo͞o′-), *n.*
—**Syn.** sorrowful, melancholy. —**Ant.** cheerful.

lug·worm (lug′wûrm′), *n.* any burrowing annelid of the genus *Arenicola,* of ocean shores, having tufted gills: used as bait for fishing. Also called **lug.** [1795–1805; LUG[4] + WORM]

lug′ wrench′, a wrench for loosening or tightening lug nuts.

Lu·hsien (*Chin.* lo͞o′shyun′), *n. Wade-Giles.* Luxian.

Lu Hsün (*Chin.* lo͞o′ shyn′), *Wade-Giles.* (*Chou Shu-jen*) See **Lu Xun.** Also, **Lu′ Hsun′.**

Lui·chow (*Chin.* lwē′jō′), *n. Older Spelling.* Leizhou.

Luik (loik, lo͝ok), *n.* Flemish name of **Liège.**

Lu·ing (lo͞o′ing), *n.* one of a breed of beef cattle developed on Luing Island off Scotland by interbreeding Shorthorn bulls and purebred West Highland cows. [1965–70]

Lui·set·ti (lo͞o set′ē), *n.* **Angelo** (*"Hank"*), born 1916, U.S. basketball player.

Lu·kacs (lo͞o′käch), *n.* **George,** 1885–1971, Hungarian literary critic. Hungarian, **Györ·gy Lu·kács** (dyœr′dy[ə] lo͞o′käch).

Lu·kan (lo͞o′kən), *adj.* of or pertaining to the Evangelist Luke or to the Gospel of Luke. [LUKE + -AN]

Lu·kas (lo͞o′kəs), *n.* **Paul,** 1895–1971, U.S. actor, born in Hungary.

Luke (lo͞ok), *n.* **1.** an early Christian disciple and companion of Paul, a physician and probably a gentile: traditionally believed to be the author of the third Gospel and the Acts. **2.** the third Gospel. **3.** a male given name: from the Greek word meaning "man of Lucania."

luke·warm (lo͞ok′wôrm′), *adj.* **1.** moderately warm; tepid. **2.** having or showing little ardor, zeal, or enthusiasm; indifferent: *lukewarm applause.* [1350–1400; ME *lukewarme* tepid, equiv. to *luke* tepid (unexplained alter. of *lew,* OE *gehlēow* tepid) + *warme* WARM] —**luke′·warm′ly,** *adv.* —**luke′warm′ness, luke′warmth′,** *n.*
—**Syn. 2.** halfhearted, cool, apathetic.

Luks (luks), *n.* **George Benjamin,** 1867–1933, U.S. painter.

lu·lab (lo͞o läb′), *n., pl.* **lu·la·bim** (lo͞o lä bēm′), **lu·labs.** *Judaism.* lulav.

LULAC, League of United Latin-American Citizens.

lu·lav (*Seph. Heb.* lo͞o läv′; *Ashk. Heb.* lo͞o′lôv, -ləv), *n., pl.* **lu·la·vim** (*Seph. Heb.* lo͞o lä vēm′; *Ashk. Heb* lo͞o lô′-vim), **lu·lavs.** *Judaism.* a palm branch for use with the etrog during the Sukkoth festival service. Also, **lulab.** [1890–95; < Heb *lūlābh*]

Lu·le·å (lo͞o′le ô′), *n.* a seaport in NE Sweden, on the Gulf of Bothnia. 66,834.

lull (lul), *v.t.* **1.** to put to sleep or rest by soothing means: *to lull a child by singing.* **2.** to soothe or quiet. **3,** to give or lead to feel a false sense of safety; cause to be less alert, aware, or watchful. —*v.i.* **4.** to quiet down, let up, or subside: *furious activity that finally lulled.* —*n.* **5.** a temporary calm, quiet, or stillness: *a lull in a storm.* **6.** a soothing sound: *the lull of falling waters.* **7.** a pacified or stupefied condition: *The drug had put him in a lull.* [1300–50; ME *lullen,* of expressive orig.; cf. Sw *lulla,* G *lullen,* L *lallāre* to sing lullaby] —**lull′·er,** *n.* —**lull′ing·ly,** *adv.*

lull·a·by (lul′ə bī′), *n., pl.* **-bies,** *v.,* **-bied, -by·ing.** —*n.* **1.** a song used to lull a child to sleep; cradlesong. **2.** any lulling song. —*v.t.* **3.** to lull with or as with a lullaby. [1550–60; equiv. to *lulla, lulla(y),* interj. used in cradlesongs (late ME *lullai, lulli*) + *-by,* as in BYE-BYE]

Lul·ly (lo͞o′lē, *Fr.* ly lē′ *for 1;* lul′ē *for 2*), *n.* **1.** Italian, **Lul·li** (lo͞ol′lē). **Jean Bap·tiste** (zhäN bȧ tēst′), 1632–87, French composer, esp. of operas and ballets, born in Italy. **2.** Catalan, **Lull** (lo͞ol). **Raymond** or **Ra·món** (rä-môn′), (*"Doctor Illuminatus"*), 1235?–1315, Spanish theologian, philosopher, and author.

lu·lu[1] (lo͞o′lo͞o), *n.* **1.** *Slang.* any remarkable or outstanding person or thing: *His black eye is a lulu.* **2.** (*cap.*) a female given name, form of **Louise.** [1855–60; in slang sense, perh. generic use of the proper name]

lu·lu[2] (lo͞o′lo͞o), *n. Slang.* a fixed allowance paid to a legislator in lieu of reimbursement for actual expenses. [special use of LULU[1], with play on LIEU, from a facetious remark attributed to New York governor Al Smith]

Lu·lua·bourg (lo͞ol′wä bo͝or′), *n.* former name of **Kananga.**

lumb-, var. of **lumbo-** before a vowel: *lumbar.*

lum·ba·go (lum bā′gō), *n. Pathol.* pain in the lower, or lumbar, region of the back or loins, esp. chronic or recurring pain. [1685–95; < LL, equiv. to L *lumb(us)* LOIN + *-āgō* n. suffix]

lum·bar (lum′bər, -bär), *adj.* **1.** of or pertaining to the loin or loins. —*n.* **2.** a lumbar vertebra, artery, or the

CONCISE PRONUNCIATION KEY: act, cāpe, dâre, pärt; set, ēqual; if, īce; ox, ōver, ôrder, oil, bo͝ok, bo͞ot, out; up, ûrge; child; sing; shoe; thin, *th*at; zh as in *treasure.* ə = *a* as in *alone, e* as in *system, i* as in *easily, o* as in *gallop, u* as in *circus;* [ə] as in *fire* (fī[ə]r), *hour* (ou[ə]r). l and n can serve as syllabic consonants, as in *cradle* (krād′l), and *button* (but′n). See the full key inside the front cover.

like. See illus. under **spinal column.** [1650–60; < NL *lumbāris.* See LUMB-, -AR[1]]

lum′bar plex′us, *Anat.* a network of nerves originating in the spinal nerves of the midback region and innervating the pelvic area, the front of the legs, and part of the feet.

lum′bar punc′ture, *Med.* puncture into the arachnoid membrane of the spinal cord, in the lumbar region, and withdrawal of spinal fluid, performed for diagnosis of the fluid, injection of dye for imaging, or administration of anesthesia or medication. Also called **spinal tap.** [1890–95]

lum•ber[1] (lum′bər), *n.* **1.** timber sawed or split into planks, boards, etc. **2.** miscellaneous useless articles that are stored away. —*v.i.* **3.** to cut timber and prepare it for market. **4.** to become useless or to be stored away as useless. —*v.t.* **5.** to convert (a specified amount, area, etc.) into lumber: *We lumbered more than a million acres last year.* **6.** to heap together in disorder. **7.** to fill up or obstruct with miscellaneous useless articles; encumber. [1545–55; orig. n. use of LUMBER[2]; i.e., useless goods that weigh one down, impede one's movements] **—lum′ber•er,** *n.* **—lum′ber•less,** *adj.*

lum•ber[2] (lum′bər), *v.i.* **1.** to move clumsily or heavily, esp. from great or ponderous bulk: *overloaded wagons lumbering down the dirt road.* **2.** to make a rumbling noise. [1300–50; ME *lomeren;* cf. dial. Sw *lomra* to resound, *loma* to walk heavily] **—lum′ber•ly,** *adj.*
—Syn. 1. trudge, barge, plod.

lum•ber•ing (lum′bər ing), *n.* the trade or business of cutting and preparing lumber. [1765–75; LUMBER[1] + -ING[1]]

lum•ber•jack (lum′bər jak′), *n.* **1.** a person who works at lumbering; logger. **2.** See **lumber jacket. 3.** *Canadian.* the gray jay. [1825–35; LUMBER[1] + JACK[1]]

lum′ber jack′et, a short, straight, wool plaid jacket or coat, for informal wear, usually belted and having patch pockets. Also called **lumberjack.** [1935–45, *Amer.*]

lum•ber•man (lum′bər mən), *n., pl.* **-men. 1.** a person who deals in lumber. **2.** lumberjack. [1810–20, *Amer.*; LUMBER[1] + MAN[1]]
—Usage. See **-man.**

lum•ber•mill (lum′bər mil′), *n.* a mill for dressing logs and lumber. [1820–30, *Amer.*; LUMBER[1] + MILL[1]]

lum′ber room′, *Brit.* a room in a house used for storing odds-and-ends, esp. old furniture. [1735–45]

Lum•ber•ton (lum′bər tən), *n.* a city in S North Carolina. 18,340.

lum•ber•yard (lum′bər yärd′), *n.* a yard where lumber is stored for sale. [1780–90, *Amer.*; LUMBER[1] + YARD[2]]

lumbo-, a combining form meaning "loin," used in the formation of compound words: *lumbosacral.* Also, *esp. before a vowel,* **lumb-.** [comb. form repr. L *lumbus* LOIN; see -O-]

lum•bo•sa•cral (lum′bō sā′krəl), *adj. Anat.* of, pertaining to, or involving the lumbar and sacral regions or parts. [1830–40; LUMBO- + SACRAL]

lum•bri•cal (lum′bri kəl), *n. Anat.* any of four wormlike muscles in the palm of the hand and in the sole of the foot. [1685–95; < NL *lumbricālis,* lit., pertaining to a worm, equiv. to L *lumbrīc(us)* earthworm + *-ālis* -AL[1]]

lum•bri•ca•lis (lum′bri kā′lis), *n., pl.* **-les** (-lēz). *Anat.* lumbrical. [1695–1705; < NL *lumbricālis*]

lum•bri•coid (lum′bri koid′), *adj.* resembling an earthworm. [1840–50; < L *lumbric(us)* earthworm + -OID]

lu•men (lo͞o′mən), *n., pl.* **-mens, -mi•na** (-mə nə). **1.** *Optics.* the unit of luminous flux, equal to the luminous flux emitted in a unit solid angle by a point source of one candle intensity. *Abbr.:* lm **2.** *Anat.* the canal, duct, or cavity of a tubular organ. **3.** *Bot.* (of a cell) the cavity that the cell walls enclose. [1870–75; < NL, special uses of L *lūmen* (s. *lūmin-*) light, window]

lu•men-hour (lo͞o′mən ouᵊr′, -ou′ər), *n. Optics.* a unit of luminous energy, equal to that emitted in 1 hour by a light source emitting a luminous flux of 1 lumen. *Abbr.:* lm-hr [1920–25]

Lum′holtz's kangaroo′ (lo͝om′hōlt siz), boongary. [after Norwegian naturalist Carl S. *Lumholtz* (1851–1922), who first described it]

Lu•mière (lʏ myer′), *n.* **Au•guste Ma•rie Louis Ni•co•las** (ō gʏst′ mᴀ rē′ lwē nē kô lä′), 1862–1954, and his brother, **Louis Jean** (lwē zhäɴ), 1864–1948, French chemists and manufacturers of photographic materials: inventors of a motion-picture camera (1895) and a process of color photography.

Lu•mi•naire (lo͞o′mə nâr′), *Trademark.* a lighting unit consisting of one or more electric lamps with all of the necessary parts and wiring.

Lu•mi•nal (lo͞o′mə nl), *Pharm., Trademark.* a brand of phenobarbital.

lu•mi•nance (lo͞o′mə nəns), *n.* **1.** the state or quality of being luminous. **2.** Also called **luminosity.** the quality or condition of radiating or reflecting light: *the blinding luminance of the sun.* **3.** *Optics.* the quantitative measure of brightness of a light source or an illuminated surface, equal to luminous flux per unit solid angle emitted per unit projected area of the source or surface. [1875–80; < L *lūmin-* (s. of *lūmen*) light + -ANCE]

lu•mi•nar•i•a (lo͞o′mə nâr′ē ə; *Sp.* lo͞o′mē nä′ʀyä), *n., pl.* **-nar•i•as** (-nâr′ē əz; *Sp.* -nä′ʀyäs). (esp. in Mexico) a Christmas lantern consisting of a lighted candle set in sand inside a paper bag. [1945–50; < MexSp, Sp: any lamp or lantern displayed during a festival < ML, LL *lūmināria,* orig. neut. pl. of *lūminaris* lamp; see LUMEN, -AR[1]]

lu•mi•nar•y (lo͞o′mə ner′ē), *n., pl.* **-nar•ies,** *adj.* —*n.* **1.** a celestial body, as the sun or moon. **2.** a body, object, etc., that gives light. **3.** a person who has attained eminence in his or her field or is an inspiration to others: *one of the luminaries in the field of medical science.* —*adj.* **4.** of, pertaining to, or characterized by light. [1400–50; late ME *luminarye* < ML *lūmināria* lamp. See LUMINARIA]

lu•mine (lo͞o′min), *v.t.* **-mined, -min•ing.** *Archaic.* to illumine. [1350–1400; ME *luminen,* aph. var. of *enluminen* to ILLUMINE. See LIMN]

lu•mi•nesce (lo͞o′mə nes′), *v.i.,* **-nesced, -nesc•ing.** to exhibit luminescence. [1895–1900; back formation from LUMINESCENT]

lu•mi•nes•cence (lo͞o′mə nes′əns), *n.* **1.** the emission of light not caused by incandescence and occurring at a temperature below that of incandescent bodies. **2.** the light produced by such an emission. [1885–90; < L *lūmin-* (see LUMEN) + -ESCENCE] **—lu′mi•nes′cent,** *adj.*

lu•mi•nif•er•ous (lo͞o′mə nif′ər əs), *adj.* producing light: *the luminiferous properties of a gas.* [1795–1805; < L *lūmin-* (see LUMEN) + -I- + -FEROUS]

lu•min•ism (lo͞o′mə niz′əm), *n.* a style of landscape painting practiced by some mid-19th-century American artists, esp. of the Hudson River School, that emphasized meticulously crafted realism and a technically precise rendering of atmosphere and of the effects produced by direct and reflected light. [1900–05; < L *lūmin-,* s. of *lūmen* light + -ISM] **—lu′min•ist,** *n., adj.*

lu•mi•no•phore (lo͞o′mə nə fôr′, -fōr′), *n. Physics, Chem.* a molecule or group of molecules that emits light when illuminated. Also, **lu′mi•no•phor′.** [1905–10; < L *lūmin-* (see LUMEN) + -O- + -PHORE]

lu•mi•nos•i•ty (lo͞o′mə nos′i tē), *n., pl.* **-ties. 1.** luminance (def. 2). **2.** the quality of being intellectually brilliant, enlightened, inspired, etc.: *The luminosity of his poetry is unequaled.* **3.** something luminous. **4.** *Astron.* the brightness of a star in comparison with that of the sun: the luminosity of Sirius expressed as 23 indicates an intrinsic brightness 23 times as great as that of the sun. **5.** Also called **luminos′ity fac′tor.** *Optics.* the brightness of a light source of a certain wavelength as it appears to the eye, measured as the ratio of luminous flux to radiant flux at that wavelength. [1625–35; < L *lūminōs(us)* LUMINOUS + -ITY]

luminos′ity class′, *Astron.* a classification of stars of a given spectral type according to their luminosity, breaking them down into dwarfs, giants, and supergiants.

lu•mi•nous (lo͞o′mə nəs), *adj.* **1.** radiating or reflecting light; shining; bright. **2.** lighted up or illuminated; well-lighted: *the luminous ballroom.* **3.** brilliant intellectually; enlightened or enlightening, as a writer or a writer's works: *a luminous concept; luminous prose.* **4.** clear; readily intelligible: *a concise, luminous report.* [1400–50; late ME < L *lūminōsus.* See LUMEN, -OUS] **—lu′mi•nous•ly,** *adv.* **—lu′mi•nous•ness,** *n.*
—Syn. 1. lucid, radiant, resplendent, brilliant. **3.** bright, intelligent. **4.** understandable, perspicuous, lucid. **—Ant. 1, 2.** dark. **3.** stupid. **4.** obscure.

lu′minous emit′tance, *Optics.* luminous flux emitted per unit area.

lu′minous en′ergy, light[1] (def. 2a). [1930–35]

lu′minous flux′, *Optics.* the rate of transmission of luminous energy: expressed in lumens. [1925–30]

lu′minous flux′ den′sity, luminous flux per unit of cross-sectional area.

lu′minous inten′sity, *Optics.* the luminous flux in lumens emitted per unit solid angle by a light source, measured in candles.

lu′minous paint′, paint containing a phosphor that emits visible light when irradiated with ultraviolet light. [1885–90]

lu′minous range′, *Navig.* the distance at which a certain light, as that of a lighthouse, is visible in clear weather, disregarding interference from obstructions and from the curvature of the earth and depending on the power of the light.

lum•mix (lum′iks), *n. Northern and North Midland U.S.* lummox.

lum•mox (lum′əks), *n. Informal.* a clumsy, stupid person. [1815–25; cf. dial. (Midlands) *lommock* large chunk of food, *lommocking* clumsy, awkward; ulterior orig. uncert.]

lump[1] (lump), *n.* **1.** a piece or mass of solid matter without regular shape or of no particular shape: *a lump of coal.* **2.** a protuberance or swelling: *a blow that raised a lump on his head.* **3.** an aggregation, collection, or mass; clump: *All the articles were piled in a great lump.* **4.** Also called **lump of sugar.** a small block of granulated sugar, designed for sweetening hot coffee, tea, etc.: *How many lumps do you take in your coffee?* **5.** majority; plurality; multitude: *The great lump of voters are still undecided.* **6. lumps,** *Informal.* harsh criticism, punishment, or defeat: *The new theory came in for some lumps when other scholars heard of it.* **7.** *Informal.* a heavy, clumsy, and usually stupid person. **8. get** or **take one's lumps,** to receive or endure hardship, punishment, criticism, etc.: *Without its star pitcher, the baseball team will get its lumps today.* —*adj.* **9.** in the form of a lump or lumps: *lump sugar.* **10.** made up of a number of items taken together; not separated or considered separately: *The debts were paid in one lump sum.* —*v.t.* **11.** to unite into one aggregation, collection, or mass (often fol. by *together*): *We lumped the reds and blues together.* **12.** to deal with, handle, consider, etc., in the lump or mass: *to lump unrelated matters indiscriminately.* **13.** to make into a lump or lumps: *to lump dough before shaping it into loaves.* **14.** to raise into or cover with lumps: *a plow lumping the moist earth.* —*v.i.* **15.** to form or raise a lump or lumps: *Stir the gravy so that it doesn't lump.* **16.** to move heavily and awkwardly: *The big oaf lumped along beside me.* [1250–1300; ME *lumpe, lomp(e);* c. early D *lompe* piece, Dan *lump(e)* lump, dial. Norw *lump* block] **—lump′ing•ly,** *adv.*

lump[2] (lump), *v.t. Informal.* to put up with; resign oneself to; accept and endure: *If you don't like it, you can lump it.* [1785–95; *Amer.*; perh. identical with Brit. dial. *lump* to look sullen, of expressive orig.]

lump•ec•to•my (lum pek′tə mē), *n., pl.* **-mies.** the surgical removal of a breast cyst or tumor. [1970–75; LUMP[1] + -ECTOMY]

lum•pen (lum′pən), *adj.* **1.** of or pertaining to disfranchised and uprooted individuals or groups, esp. those who have lost status: *the lumpen bourgeoisie.* —*n.* **2.** a lumpen individual or group. [1945–50; extracted from LUMPENPROLETARIAT]

lum•pen•prole (lum′pən prōl′), *n. Informal.* a member of the lumpenproletariat. [1970–75; see LUMPENPROLETARIAT, PROLE]

lum•pen•pro•le•tar•i•at (lum′pən prō′li târ′ē ət), *n.* (*sometimes cap.*) (esp. in Marxist theory) the lowest level of the proletariat comprising unskilled workers, vagrants, and criminals and characterized by a lack of class identification and solidarity. [1920–25; < G (Marx, 1850), equiv. to *Lumpen* rag or *Lumpen-,* comb. form of *Lump* ragamuffin + *Proletariat* PROLETARIAT]

lump•er (lum′pər), *n.* **1.** a day laborer employed to handle cargo, as fish or timber. **2.** *Biol. Informal.* a taxonomist who believes that classifications should emphasize similarities among organisms and therefore favors large, inclusive taxa (opposed to *splitter*). [1775–85; LUMP[1] (in v. sense) + -ER[1]]

lump•fish (lump′fish′), *n., pl.* (*esp. collectively*) **-fish,** (*esp. referring to two or more kinds or species*) **-fish•es.** any of several thick-bodied, sluggish fishes of the family Cyclopteridae, found in northern seas, having the pelvic fins modified and united into a sucking disk, esp. *Cyclopterus lumpus,* of the North Atlantic. [1735–45; LUMP[1] + FISH]

lump•ish (lum′pish), *adj.* **1.** resembling a lump. **2.** having a heavy appearance; moving clumsily. **3.** having a sluggish mind; unresponsive; dull; stupid. [1400–50; late ME *lumpisch.* See LUMP[1], -ISH[1]] **—lump′ish•ly,** *adv.* **—lump′ish•ness,** *n.*

lump′ of sug′ar, lump[1] (def. 4). [1720–30]

lump•y (lum′pē), *adj.,* **lump•i•er, lump•i•est. 1.** full of lumps: *lumpy gravy.* **2.** covered with lumps, as a surface. **3.** heavy or clumsy, as in movement or style; crude: *a lumpy gait; a lumpy narrative.* **4.** (of water) rough or choppy. [1700–10; LUMP[1] + -Y[1]] **—lump′i•ly,** *adv.* **—lump′i•ness,** *n.*

lump′y jaw′, *Pathol., Vet. Pathol.* actinomycosis. [1885–90, *Amer.*]

Lu•mum•ba (lo͞o mo͝om′bə), *n.* **Pa•trice (Em•er•gy)** (pə trēs′ em′er zhē′), 1925–61, African political leader: premier of the Democratic Republic of the Congo (now Zaire) 1960–61.

Lu•na (lo͞o′nə), *n.* **1.** the ancient Roman goddess personifying the moon, sometimes identified with Diana. **2.** (in alchemy) silver. **3.** (*l.c.*) Also, **lunette.** *Eccles.* the crescent-shaped receptacle within the monstrance, for holding the consecrated Host in an upright position. [< L *lūna* the moon]

lu•na•cy (lo͞o′nə sē), *n., pl.* **-cies. 1.** insanity; mental disorder. **2.** intermittent insanity, formerly believed to be related to phases of the moon. **3.** extreme foolishness or an instance of it: *Her decision to resign was sheer lunacy.* **4.** *Law.* unsoundness of mind sufficient to incapacitate one for civil transactions. [1535–45; LUN(ATIC) + -ACY]
—Syn. 1. derangement, dementia; craziness, madness, mania, aberration. **3.** folly, stupidity. **—Ant. 1, 2.** rationality, sanity.

lu′na moth′, a large, pale-green, American moth, *Actias luna,* having purple-brown markings, lunate spots, and long tails. Also, **Lu′na moth′.** [1850–55, *Amer.*]

lu•nar (lo͞o′nər), *adj.* **1.** of or pertaining to the moon: *the lunar orbit.* **2.** measured by the moon's revolutions: *a lunar month.* **3.** resembling the moon; round or crescent-shaped. **4.** of or pertaining to silver. —*n.* **5.** a lunar observation taken for purposes of navigation or mapping. [1585–95; < L *lūnāris* of the moon. See LUNA, -AR[1]]

lu′nar caus′tic, *Med., Chem.* silver nitrate, $AgNO_3$, esp. in a sticklike mold, used to cauterize tissues. [1790–1800]

lu′nar cy′cle. See **Metonic cycle.** [1695–1705]

lu′nar day′, a division of time that is equal to the elapsed time between two consecutive returns of the same terrestrial meridian to the moon. [1680–90]

lu′nar dis′tance, *Navig.* the observed angle between the moon and another celestial body. [1820–30]

lu′nar eclipse′. See under **eclipse** (def. 1a). [1885–90]

lu′nar excur′sion mod′ule, (*often cap.*) *U.S. Aerospace.* See **lunar module.** *Abbr.:* LEM [1960–65]

lu•nar•i•an (lo͞o nâr′ē ən), *n.* **1.** a being supposedly inhabiting the moon. **2.** a selenographer. [1700–10; < L *lūn(a)* moon + -ARIAN]

lu′nar mod′ule, (*often cap.*) *U.S. Aerospace.* the portion of the Apollo spacecraft in which two astronauts landed on the moon's surface and then returned to the orbiting command module. Also called **lunar excursion module.** *Abbr.:* LM [1965–70]

lu′nar month′, month (def. 5). [1585–95]

Lu′nar Or′biter, *U.S. Aerospace.* one of a series of

space probes that orbited and photographed the moon in 1966 and 1967.

lu′nar rain′bow, moonbow. [1705–15]

lu′nar rov′er, (*often caps.*) *U.S. Aerospace.* a wire-wheeled, battery-powered vehicle used by Apollo astronauts to explore the moon's surface. Also called **lu′nar rov′ing ve′hicle.** [1970–75]

lu′nar year′, year (def. 4a). [1585–95]

lu•nate (lo͞o′nāt), *adj.* **1.** Also, **lu′nat•ed.** crescent-shaped. —*n.* **2.** *Anat.* the second bone from the thumb side of the proximal row of bones of the carpus. **3.** a crescent-shaped, microlithic artifact mounted in a haft to form a composite tool, mostly Mesolithic in origin. [1770–80; < L *lūnātus* crescent-shaped. See LUNA, -ATE[1]] —**lu′nate•ly,** *adv.*

lu•na•tic (lo͞o′nə tik), *n.* **1.** an insane person. **2.** a person whose actions and manner are marked by extreme eccentricity or recklessness. **3.** *Law.* a person legally declared to be of unsound mind and who therefore is not held capable or responsible before the law. —*adj.* **4.** insane; demented; crazy. **5.** characteristic or suggestive of lunacy; wildly or recklessly foolish. **6.** designated for or used by the insane: *a lunatic asylum.* **7.** gaily or lightheartedly mad, frivolous, eccentric, etc.: *She has a lunatic charm that is quite engaging.* Also, **lu•nat•i•cal** (lo͞o nat′i kəl) (for defs. 4, 5, 7). [1250–1300; ME *lunatik* < OF *lunatique* < LL *lūnāticus* moonstruck. See LUNA, -ATIC] —**lu•nat′i•cal•ly,** *adv.*

lu′natic fringe′, members on the periphery of any group, esp. political, social, or religious, who hold extreme or fanatical views. [1910–15, *Amer.*]

lu•na•tion (lo͞o nā′shən), *n.* the period of time from one new moon to the next (about 29½ days); a lunar month. [1350–1400; ME *lunacyon* < ML *lūnātiōn-* (s. of *lūnātiō*). See LUNA, -ATION]

lunch (lunch), *n.* **1.** a light midday meal between breakfast and dinner; luncheon. **2.** any light meal or snack. **3.** a restaurant or lunchroom: *Let's eat at the dairy lunch.* **4. out to lunch,** *Slang.* not paying attention or tending to business; negligent: *You must have been out to lunch when you wrote that weird report.* —*v.i.* **5.** to eat lunch: *We lunched quite late today.* —*v.t.* **6.** to provide lunch for: *They lunched us in regal fashion.* [1585–95; short for LUNCHEON] —**lunch′er,** *n.* —**lunch′less,** *adj.*

lunch•box (lunch′boks′), *n.* a small container, usually of metal or plastic and with a handle, for carrying one's lunch from home to school or work. Also called **lunch-pail, lunch•buck•et** (lunch′buk′it). [1860–65; LUNCH + BOX[1]]

lunch′ count′er, **1.** a counter, as in a store or restaurant, where light meals and snacks are served or are sold to be taken out. **2.** a luncheonette. [1865–70]

lunch•eon (lun′chən), *n.* lunch, esp. a formal lunch held in connection with a meeting or other special occasion: *the alumni luncheon.* [1570–80; dissimilated var. of *nuncheon* (now dial.), ME *none(s)chench* noon drink, equiv. to *none* NOON + *schench*, OE *scenc* a drink, cup, akin to OE *scencan* to pour out, give drink, c. D, G *schenken*] —**lunch′eon•less,** *adj.*

lunch•eon•ette (lun′chə net′), *n.* a small restaurant or lunchroom where light meals are served. [1920–25, *Amer.*; LUNCHEON + -ETTE]

lunch′eon meat′, any of various sausages or molded loaf meats, usually sliced and served cold, as in sandwiches or as garnishes for salads. [1940–45]

lunch•hook (lunch′ho͝ok′), *n. Slang.* **1.** Usually, **lunchhooks.** hands. **2.** a light anchor for mooring a small yacht for a short time. [LUNCH + HOOK]

lunch•meat (lunch′mēt′), *n.* See **luncheon meat.** [LUNCH + MEAT]

lunch•pail (lunch′pāl′), *n.* **1.** lunchbox. **2.** a worker's lunchbox in the shape of a pail, originally for carrying hot food. [1890–95, *Amer.*; LUNCH + PAIL]

lunch•room (lunch′ro͞om′, -ro͝om′), *n.* **1.** a room, as in a school, where light meals or snacks can be bought or where food brought from home may be eaten. **2.** a luncheonette. [1815–25; LUNCH + ROOM]

lunch•time (lunch′tīm′), *n.* a period set aside for eating lunch or the period of an hour or so, beginning roughly at noon, during which lunch is commonly eaten. [1855–60; LUNCH + TIME]

lunch•wag•on (lunch′wag′ən), *n.* a small bus, truck, or other vehicle outfitted for selling or for serving light meals and snacks to the public. [1890–95; LUNCH + WAGON]

lunch•y (lun′chē), *adj.,* **lunch•i•er, lunch•i•est.** *Slang.* **1.** stupid; dull-witted. **2.** carefree or irresponsible. [1960–65; perh. LUNCH (extracted from the idiom *out to lunch* dim-witted, irresponsible) + -Y[1]]

Lund•berg (lund′bərg), *n.* **George A(ndrew),** 1895–1966, U.S. sociologist and author.

Lun′dy's Lane′, (lun′dēz), a road near Niagara Falls, in Ontario, Canada: battle between the British and Americans in 1814.

lune[1] (lo͞on), *n.* **1.** anything shaped like a crescent or a half moon. **2.** a crescent-shaped figure bounded by two arcs of circles, either on a plane or a spherical surface. [1695–1705; < L *lūna* moon]

lune[2] (lo͞on), *n. Falconry.* a line for securing a hawk. [1425–75; late ME, var. of *loyn* < MF *loigne* LONGE]

lunes (lo͞onz), *n.* (*used with a plural v.*) *Archaic.* fits of madness. [1605–15; < F, MF, pl. of *lune* caprice < ML *lūna* fit of lunacy, special use of L *lūna* moon; cf. G *Laune*]

lu•nette (lo͞o net′), *n.* **1.** any of various objects or spaces of crescentlike or semicircular outline or section. **2.** *Archit.* (in the plane of a wall) an area enframed by an arch or vault. **3.** a painting, sculpture, or window filling such an area. **4.** *Fort.* a work consisting of a salient angle with two flanks and an open gorge. **5.** *Ordn.* a towing ring in the trail plate of a towed vehicle, as a gun carriage. **6.** *Eccles.* Luna (def. 3). [1570–80; < F, dim. of *lune* moon < L *lūna*; see -ETTE]

Lu•né•ville (lʏ nā vēl′), *n.* a city in NE France, W of Strasbourg: treaty between France and Austria 1801. 24,700.

lung (lung), *n.* **1.** either of the two saclike respiratory organs in the thorax of humans and the higher vertebrates. **2.** an analogous organ in certain invertebrates, as arachnids or terrestrial gastropods. **3. at the top of one's lungs,** as loudly as possible; with full voice: *The baby cried at the top of his lungs.* [bef. 1000; ME *lungen*, OE; c. G *Lunge*; akin to LIGHT[2], LIGHTS] —**lunged** (lungd), *adj.*

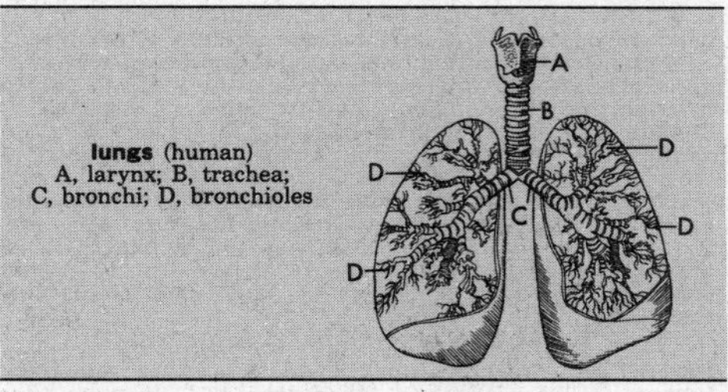

lungs (human)
A, larynx; B, trachea;
C, bronchi; D, bronchioles

lun•gan (lung′gən), *n.* longan.

lung′ book′. See **book lung.** [1880–85]

Lung•ch'i (*Chin.* lo͝ong′chē′), *n. Wade-Giles.* Longxi.

lunge[1] (lunj), *n., v.,* **lunged, lung•ing.** —*n.* **1.** a sudden forward thrust, as with a sword or knife; stab. **2.** any sudden forward movement; plunge. —*v.i.* **3.** to make a lunge or thrust; move with a lunge. —*v.t.* **4.** to thrust (something) forward; cause to move with a lunge: *lunging his finger accusingly.* [1725–35; earlier *longe* for F *allonge* (n.; construed as *a longe*), *allonger* (v.) to lengthen, extend, deliver (blows) < VL **allongāre*, for LL *ēlongāre* to ELONGATE]
—**Syn. 2.** rush, charge, lurch.

lunge[2] (lunj), *n., v.,* **lunged, lung•ing.** longe. [var. of *longe* < F; see LONGE, LUNE[2]]

lun•gee (lo͝ong′gē, lo͝on′jē), *n.* lungi.

lun•geous (lun′jəs), *adj. Brit. Dial.* (of a person) violent; rough. [1675–85; LUNGE[1] + -OUS]

lung•er[1] (lung′ər), *n. Informal.* a person who has chronic lung disease, esp. tuberculosis. [1890–95; LUNG + -ER[1]]

lung•er[2] (lun′jər), *n.* a person or thing that lunges. [1835–45; LUNGE[1] + -ER[1]]

lung•fish (lung′fish′), *n., pl.* (*esp. collectively*) **-fish,** (*esp. referring to two or more kinds or species*) **-fish•es.** any of various slender, air-breathing fishes of the order (or subclass) Dipnoi, of rivers and lakes in Africa, South America, and Australia, having a lunglike air bladder as well as gills and growing to a length of 3 to 6 ft. (0.9 to 1.8 m). [1880–85; LUNG + FISH]

lung′ fluke′, any of various trematodes, as *Paragonimus westermani*, parasitic in the lungs of humans and other mammals. [1895–1900]

lun•gi (lo͝ong′gē, lo͝on′jē), *n.* **1.** a cloth used as a turban, scarf, sarong, etc., in India, Pakistan, and Burma. **2.** a loincloth worn by men in India. Also, **lungee, lungyi, longyi.** [1625–35; < Hindi *lungī* < Pers]

Lung•ki (lo͝ong′kē′), *n. Older Spelling.* Longxi.

lung•worm (lung′wûrm′), *n.* **1.** any nematode worm of the superfamily Metastrongylidae, parasitic in the lungs of various mammals. **2.** a nematode worm of the genus *Rhabdias*, parasitic in the lungs of reptiles and amphibians. [1880–85; LUNG + WORM]

lung•wort (lung′wûrt′, -wôrt′), *n.* **1.** a European plant, *Pulmonaria officinalis*, of the borage family, having blue flowers. **2.** any of various related plants of the genus *Mertensia*, as the North American *M. virginica*, having nodding clusters of blue flowers. [bef. 1000; ME *long-wort, lung-wort* hellebore, OE *lungen-wyrt*; see LUNG, WORT[2]]

lun•gyi (lo͝ong′gē, lo͝on′jē), *n., pl.* **-gyis.** lungi.

luni-, a combining form meaning "moon," used in the formation of compound words: *lunitidal.* [comb. form repr. L *lūna* moon; see -I-]

lu•ni•so•lar (lo͞o′ni sō′lər), *adj.* pertaining to or based upon the relations or joint action of the moon and the sun. [1685–95; LUNI- + SOLAR[1]]

luniso′lar preces′sion, *Astron.* the principal component of the precession of the equinoxes, produced by the gravitational attraction of the sun and the moon on the equatorial bulge of the earth.

lu•ni•tid•al (lo͞o′ni tīd′l), *adj.* pertaining to the part of the tidal movement dependent upon the moon. [1850–55; LUNI- + TIDAL]

lu′nitid′al in′terval, the period of time between the moon's transit and the next high lunar tide. [1850–55]

lun•ker (lung′kər), *n.* **1.** something unusually large for its kind. **2.** *Angling.* a very large game fish, esp. a bass. [1910–15; *lunk-* (see LUNKHEAD) + -ER[1]]

lunk•head (lungk′hed′), *n. Slang.* a dull or stupid person; blockhead. Also called **lunk** (lungk). [1850–55, *Amer.*; *lunk* (perh. b. LUMP[1] and HUNK) + HEAD] —**lunk′head′ed,** *adj.*

lunt (lunt, lo͝ont), *Scot.* —*n.* **1.** a match; the flame used to light a fire. **2.** smoke or steam, esp. smoke from a tobacco pipe. —*v.i.* **3.** to emit smoke or steam. **4.** to smoke a pipe. —*v.t.* **5.** to kindle (a fire). **6.** to light (a pipe, torch, etc.). **7.** to smoke (a pipe). [1540–50; < D *lont* match, fuse; akin to MLG *lunte* match, wick]

Lunt (lunt), *n.* **Alfred,** 1893–1977, U.S. actor (husband of Lynn Fontanne).

lu•nu•la (lo͞o′nyə lə), *n., pl.* **-lae** (-lē′). something shaped like a narrow crescent, as the small, pale area at the base of the fingernail. Also, **lu•nule** (lo͞o′nyo͞ol). [1565–75; < L *lūnula*, equiv. to *lūn(a)* moon + *-ula* -ULE]

lu•nu•lar (lo͞o′nyə lər), *adj.* crescent-shaped: *lunular markings.* [1560–70; LUNUL(A) + -AR[1]]

lu•nu•late (lo͞o′nyə lāt′), *adj.* **1.** having lunular markings. **2.** crescent-shaped. Also, **lu′nu•lat′ed.** [1750–60; LUNUL(A) + -ATE[1]]

lun•y (lo͞o′nē), *adj.,* **lun•i•er, lun•i•est,** *n., pl.* **lun•ies.** loony.

Lu•o (lo͞o ō′, lo͞o′ō), *n., pl.* **Lu•os,** (*esp. collectively*) **Lu•o** for 1. **1.** a member of a people living mainly in southwest Kenya. **2.** the Nilotic language of the Luo people.

Lu•or•a•vet•lan (lo͞o ôr′ə vet′lən, lwôr′-), *n.* Chukotian. Also, **Lu•or•a•wet•lan** (lo͞o ôr′ə wet′lən, lwôr′-). [< Chukchi *ləjʔoravetlʔen* a self-designation, said to mean lit. "proper person" (or < a cognate Koryak word); see -AN]

Luo•yang (lwô′yäng′), *n. Pinyin.* a city in N Henan province, in E China. 750,000. Also, **Loyang.** Formerly, **Henan.**

lu•pa•nar (lo͞o pā′nər, -pä′-), *n.* a brothel; whorehouse. [1860–65; < L *lupānar*, deriv. of *lupa* prostitute, lit., she-wolf]

Lu•pe (lo͞o′pā), *n.* a female given name.

Lu•per•ca•li•a (lo͞o′pər kā′lē ə, -kāl′yə), *n., pl.* **-li•a, -li•as.** a festival held in ancient Rome on the 15th of February to promote fertility and ward off disasters.

Lu•per•cus (lo͞o pûr′kəs), *n.* an ancient Roman fertility god, often identified with Faunus or Pan.

lu•pine[1] (lo͞o′pin), *n.* any of numerous plants belonging to the genus *Lupinus*, of the legume family, as *L. albus* **(white lupine),** of Europe, bearing edible seeds, or *L. perennis*, of the eastern U.S., having tall, dense clusters of blue, pink, or white flowers. [1350–1400; ME < L *lupīnus, lupīnum*, appar. n. use of *lupīnus* LUPINE[2]; cf. G *wolfsbohne* lupine, lit., wolf bean]

lu•pine[2] (lo͞o′pīn), *adj.* **1.** pertaining to or resembling the wolf. **2.** related to the wolf. **3.** savage; ravenous; predatory. [1650–60; < L *lupīnus* of a wolf, equiv. to *lup(us)* wolf + *-īnus* -INE[1]]

lu•po•ma (lo͞o pō′mə), *n. Pathol.* any of the tubercles occurring in lupus vulgaris. [< NL; see LUPUS, -OMA]

lu•pu•lin (lo͞o′pyə lin), *n.* the glandular hairs of the hop, *Humulus lupulus*, formerly used in medicine as a sedative. [1820–30; < NL *lupul(us)* (dim. of L *lupus* the hop plant; see -ULE) + -IN[2]]

lu•pus (lo͞o′pəs), *n. Pathol.* **1.** See **lupus vulgaris. 2.** See **systemic lupus erythematosus.** [1580–90; < ML, special use of L *lupus* wolf] —**lu′pous,** *adj.*

Lu•pus (lo͞o′pəs), *n., gen.* **-pi** (-pī). *Astron.* the Wolf, a southern constellation between Centaurus and Norma. [< L]

lu′pus er•y•the•ma•to′sus (er′ə thē′mə tō′səs, -them′ə-), *Pathol.* any of several autoimmune diseases, esp. systemic lupus erythematosus, characterized by red, scaly skin patches. [1855–60; < NL: erythematous lupus]

lu′pus vul•ga′ris (vul gâr′əs), *Pathol.* a rare form of tuberculosis of the skin, characterized by brownish tubercles that often heal slowly and leave scars. Also called **lupus.** [1855–60; < NL: common lupus]

Lu•ray (lo͞o rā′), *n.* a town in N Virginia: site of Luray Caverns. 3584.

Lur•çat (lʏʀ sa′), *n.* **Jean** (zhäɴ), 1892–1966, French painter and tapestry designer.

lurch[1] (lûrch), *n.* **1.** an act or instance of swaying abruptly. **2.** a sudden tip or roll to one side, as of a ship or a staggering person. **3.** an awkward, swaying or staggering motion or gait. —*v.i.* **4.** (of a ship) to roll or pitch suddenly. **5.** to make a lurch; move with lurches; stagger: *The wounded man lurched across the room.* [1760–70; orig. uncert.] —**lurch′ing•ly,** *adv.*
—**Syn. 5.** lunge, reel, totter.

lurch[2] (lûrch), *n.* **1.** a situation at the close of various games in which the loser scores nothing or is far behind the opponent. **2. leave in the lurch,** to leave in an uncomfortable or desperate situation; desert in time of trouble: *Our best salesperson left us in the lurch at the peak of the busy season.* [1525–35; < MF *lourche* a game, n. use of *lourche* (adj.) discomfited < Gmc; cf. MHG *lurz* left (hand), OE *belyrtan* to deceive]

lurch[3] (lûrch), *v.t.* **1.** *Archaic.* to do out of; defraud; cheat. **2.** *Obs.* to acquire through underhanded means; steal; filch. —*v.i.* **3.** *Brit. Dial.* to lurk near a place; prowl. —*n.* **4.** *Archaic.* the act of lurking or state of watchfulness. [1375–1425; late ME *lorchen*, appar. var. of *lurken* to LURK]

lurch•er (lûr′chər), *n.* **1.** a crossbred dog used esp. by poachers. **2.** *Archaic.* a person who lurks or prowls, as a thief or poacher. [1350–1400; ME; see LURCH[3], -ER[1]]

lur•dan (lûr′dn), *Archaic.* —*n.* **1.** a lazy, stupid, loutish fellow. —*adj.* **2.** lazy; stupid; worthless. [1250–1300; ME < MF *lourdin* dullard, equiv. to *lourd* heavy, dull (< VL **lurdus*, for L *lūridus* LURID) + *-in* < L *-īnus* -INE[1]]

CONCISE PRONUNCIATION KEY: act, cāpe, dâre, pärt; set, ēqual; *if*, īce; ox, ōver, ôrder, oil, bo͝ok, bo͞ot, out; up, ûrge; child; sing; shoe; thin, *th*at; zh as in *treasure*. ə = *a* as in *alone*, *e* as in *system*, *i* as in *easily*, *o* as in *gallop*, *u* as in *circus*; ᵊ as in *fire* (fīᵊr), *hour* (ouᵊr). l and n can serve as syllabic consonants, as in *cradle* (krād′l), and *button* (but′n). See the full key inside the front cover.

lure (lo͝or), *n., v.,* **lured, lur•ing.** —*n.* **1.** anything that attracts, entices, or allures. **2.** the power of attracting or enticing. **3.** a decoy; live or esp. artificial bait used in fishing or trapping. **4.** *Falconry.* a feathered decoy for attracting a hawk, swung at the end of a long line and sometimes baited with raw meat. **5.** a flap or tassel dangling from the dorsal fin of pediculate fishes, as the angler, that attracts prey to the mouth region. **6. in lure,** *Heraldry.* noting a pair of wings joined with the tips downward (opposed to *a vol*). —*v.t.* **7.** to attract, entice, or tempt; allure. **8.** to draw or recall (esp. a falcon), as by a lure or decoy. [1350–1400; ME < AF, OF *luere* (F *leurre*) < Frankish **lothr-,* c. MHG *luoder,* G *Luder* bait] —**lure′ment,** *n.* —**lur′er,** *n.* —**lur′ing•ly,** *adv.*
—**Syn. 1.** temptation. **7.** seduce. —**Ant. 7.** repel.

Lur•ex (lo͝or′eks), *Trademark.* a brand of metallic yarn, made of laminated aluminum foil and transparent film sliced into narrow strips.

Lu•ri•a (lo͝or′ē ə), *n.* **Salvador Edward,** 1912–91, U.S. biologist, born in Italy: Nobel prize for medicine 1969.

lu•rid (lo͝or′id), *adj.* **1.** gruesome; horrible; revolting: *the lurid details of an accident.* **2.** glaringly vivid or sensational; shocking: *the lurid tales of pulp magazines.* **3.** terrible in intensity, fierce passion, or unrestraint: *lurid crimes.* **4.** lighted or shining with an unnatural, fiery glow; wildly or garishly red: *a lurid sunset.* **5.** wan, pallid, or ghastly in hue; livid. [1650–60; < L *lūridus* sallow, ghastly] —**lu′rid•ly,** *adv.* —**lu′rid•ness,** *n.*
—**Syn. 5.** dismal, pale, murky.

Lu•ri•stan (lo͝or′ə stän′, -stan′), *n.* a mountainous region in W Iran. Also, **Lorestan.**

lurk (lûrk), *v.i.* **1.** to lie or wait in concealment, as a person in ambush; remain in or around a place secretly or furtively. **2.** to go furtively; slink; steal. **3.** to exist unperceived or unsuspected. —*n. Australian Informal.* **4.** an underhand scheme; dodge. **5.** an easy, somewhat lazy or unethical way of earning a living, performing a task, etc. **6.** a hideout. [1250–1300; ME *lurken,* freq. of LOWER[2]; cf. Norw *lurka* to sneak away] —**lurk′er,** *n.* —**lurk′ing•ly,** *adv.*
—**Syn. 1.** LURK, SKULK, SNEAK, PROWL suggest avoiding observation, often because of a sinister purpose. To LURK is to lie in wait for someone or to hide about a place, often without motion, for periods of time. SKULK suggests cowardliness and stealth of movement. SNEAK emphasizes the attempt to avoid being seen. It has connotations of slinking and of an abject meanness of manner, whether there exists a sinister intent or the desire to avoid punishment for some misdeed. PROWL implies the definite purpose of seeking for prey; it suggests continuous action in roaming or wandering, slowly and quietly but watchfully, as a cat that is hunting mice.

Lu•sa•ka (lo͞o sä′kə), *n.* a city in and the capital of Zambia, in the S central part. 415,000.

Lu•sa•ti•a (lo͞o sā′shē ə, -shə), *n.* a region in E Germany and SW Poland, between the Elbe and Oder rivers.

Lu•sa•tian (lo͞o sā′shən), *n.* **1.** a native or inhabitant of Lusatia. **2.** Sorbian (def. 2). —*adj.* **3.** of or pertaining to Lusatia, its people, or their language. [1545–55; LUSATI(A) + -AN]

lus•cious (lush′əs), *adj.* **1.** highly pleasing to the taste or smell: *luscious peaches.* **2.** richly satisfying to the senses or the mind: *the luscious style of his poetry.* **3.** richly adorned; luxurious: *luscious furnishings.* **4.** arousing physical, or sexual, desire; voluptuous: *a luscious figure.* **5.** sweet to excess; cloying. [1375–1425; late ME *lucius,* unexplained var. of *licius,* aph. var. of DELICIOUS] —**lus′cious•ly,** *adv.* —**lus′cious•ness,** *n.*
—**Syn. 1.** delectable, palatable. See **delicious.**
—**Ant. 1.** disgusting, unpalatable.

lush[1] (lush), *adj.,* **-er, -est. 1.** (of vegetation, plants, grasses, etc.) luxuriant; succulent; tender and juicy. **2.** characterized by luxuriant vegetation: *a lush valley.* **3.** characterized by luxuriousness, opulence, etc.: *the lush surroundings of his home.* [1400–50; late ME *lusch* slack; akin to OE *lysu* bad, *lēas* lax, MLG *lasch* slack, ON *løskr* weak, Goth *lasiws* weak] —**lush′ly,** *adv.* —**lush′ness,** *n.*
—**Syn. 1.** luxurious, fresh. —**Ant. 1.** withered, stale.

lush[2] (lush), *Slang.* —*n.* **1.** drunkard; alcoholic; sot. **2.** intoxicating liquor. —*v.i.* **3.** to drink liquor. —*v.t.* **4.** to drink (liquor). [1780–90; perh. facetious application of LUSH[1]]

lush•er (lush′ər) *n. Slang.* lush[2] (def. 1). [LUSH[2] (v.) + -ER[1]]

lush•head (lush′hed′), *n. Slang.* lush[2] (def. 1). [1940–45; LUSH[2] + HEAD]

Lü•shun (lʏ′shʏn′), *n. Pinyin, Wade-Giles.* an old city and seaport in S Liaoning province, in NE China, on the Yellow Sea: now part of the urban area of Dalian. 1,650,000. Also called **Port Arthur.** Formerly, *Japanese,* **Ryojunko.**

lush•y[1] (lush′ē), *adj.,* **lush•i•er, lush•i•est.** lush[1]. [1815–25; LUSH[1] + -Y[1]]

lush•y[2] (lush′ē), *adj.,* **lush•i•er, lush•i•est.** *Slang.* drunk; tipsy. [1805–15; LUSH[2] + -Y[1]]

Lu•si•ta•ni•a (lo͞o′si tā′nē ə), *n.* **1.** (*italics*) a British luxury liner sunk by a German submarine in the North Atlantic on May 7, 1915: one of the events leading to U.S. entry into World War I. **2.** an ancient region and Roman province in the Iberian Peninsula, corresponding generally to modern Portugal. —**Lu′si•ta′ni•an,** *adj., n.*

CONCISE ETYMOLOGY KEY: <, descended or borrowed from; >, whence; b., blend of, blended; c., cognate with; cf., compare; deriv., derivative; equiv., equivalent; imit., imitative; obl., oblique; r., replacing; s., stem; sp., spelling, spelled; resp., respelling, respelled; trans., translation; ?, origin unknown; *, unattested; ‡, probably earlier than. See the full key inside the front cover.

lust (lust), *n.* **1.** intense sexual desire or appetite. **2.** uncontrolled or illicit sexual desire or appetite; lecherousness. **3.** a passionate or overmastering desire or craving (usually fol. by *for*): *a lust for power.* **4.** ardent enthusiasm; zest; relish: *an enviable lust for life.* **5.** *Obs.* **a.** pleasure or delight. **b.** desire; inclination; wish. —*v.i.* **6.** to have intense sexual desire. **7.** to have a yearning or desire; have a strong or excessive craving (often fol. by *for* or *after*). [bef. 900; ME *luste,* OE *lust;* c. D, G *lust* pleasure, desire; akin to ON *lyst* desire; see LIST[4]]
—**Syn. 7.** crave, hunger, covet, yearn.

lus•ter[1] (lus′tər), *n.* **1.** the state or quality of shining by reflecting light; glitter, sparkle, sheen, or gloss: *the luster of satin.* **2.** a substance, as a coating or polish, used to impart sheen or gloss. **3.** radiant or luminous brightness; brilliance; radiance. **4.** radiance of beauty, excellence, merit, distinction, or glory: *achievements that add luster to one's name.* **5.** a shining object, esp. one used for decoration, as a cut-glass pendant or ornament. **6.** a chandelier, candleholder, etc., ornamented with cut-glass pendants. **7.** any natural or synthetic fabric with a lustrous finish. **8.** Also called **metallic luster.** an iridescent metallic film produced on the surface of a ceramic glaze. **9.** *Mineral.* the nature of a mineral surface with respect to its reflective qualities: *greasy luster.* —*v.t.* **10.** to finish (fur, cloth, pottery, etc.) with a luster or gloss. —*v.i.* **11.** to be or become lustrous. Also, *esp. Brit.,* **lustre.** [1515–25; < MF *lustre* < It *lustro,* deriv. of *lustrare* to polish, purify < L *lūstrāre* to purify ceremonially, deriv. of *lūstrum* LUSTRUM] —**lus′ter•less,** *adj.*
—**Syn. 1.** See **polish.** —**Ant. 1.** dullness.

lus•ter[2] (lus′tər), *n.* lustrum (def. 1). Also, *esp. Brit.,* **lustre.** [1375–1425; late ME *lustre* < L *lūstrum.* See LUSTRUM]

lus•ter[3] (lus′tər), *n.* a person who lusts: *a luster after power.* [1585–95; LUST + -ER[1]]

lus•tered (lus′tərd), *adj.* having or finished with a luster. [1855–60; LUSTER[1] + -ED[3]]

lus•ter•er (lus′tər ər), *n.* a person who puts a lustrous finish or gloss on textiles. [LUSTER[1] + -ER[1]]

lus•ter•ing (lus′tər ing), *n.* the treatment of fabrics by chemical or mechanical means in order to increase their property to reflect light. [1870–75; LUSTER[1] + -ING[1]]

lus′ter paint′ing, a method of decorating glazed pottery with metallic pigment, originated in Persia, popular from the 9th through the mid-19th centuries.

lus•ter•ware (lus′tər wâr′), *n.* ceramic ware covered with a luster. [1815–25; LUSTER[1] + WARE[1]]

lust•ful (lust′fəl), *adj.* **1.** full of or motivated by lust, greed, or the like: *He was an emperor lustful of power.* **2.** having strong sexual desires; lecherous; libidinous. **3.** *Archaic.* lusty. [bef. 900; ME, OE; see LUST, -FUL] —**lust′ful•ly,** *adv.* —**lust′ful•ness,** *n.*

lust•i•hood (lus′tē ho͝od′), *n.* lustiness; vigor. [1590–1600; LUSTY + -HOOD]

lus•tral (lus′trəl), *adj.* **1.** of, pertaining to, or employed in the lustrum, or rite of purification. **2.** occurring every five years; quinquennial. [1525–35; < L *lūstrālis.* See LUSTRUM, -AL[1]]

lus•trate (lus′trāt), *v.t.,* **-trat•ed, -trat•ing.** to purify by a propitiatory offering or other ceremonial method. [1615–25; < L *lūstrātus,* ptp. of *lūstrāre* to purify, illumine. See LUSTER[1], -ATE[1]] —**lus•tra′tion,** *n.* —**lus•tra•tive** (lus′trə tiv), *adj.*

lus•tre (lus′tər), *n., v.t., v.i.,* **-tred, -tring.** *Chiefly Brit.* luster.

lus•trous (lus′trəs), *adj.* **1.** having luster; shining; luminous: *lustrous eyes.* **2.** brilliant; splendid; resplendent; illustrious: *a lustrous career.* [1595–1605; LUST(E)R[1] + -OUS] —**lus′trous•ly,** *adv.* —**lus′trous•ness,** *n.*
—**Syn. 1.** gleaming, radiant, glowing, shimmering. **2.** refulgent, dazzling, gorgeous.

lus•trum (lus′trəm), *n., pl.* **-trums, -tra** (-trə). **1.** Also, **luster;** *esp. Brit.,* **lustre.** a period of five years. **2.** *Rom. Hist.* a lustration or ceremonial purification of the people, performed every five years, after the taking of the census. [1580–90; < L *lūstrum;* cf. LUSTER[1]]

lust•y (lus′tē), *adj.,* **lust•i•er, lust•i•est. 1.** full of or characterized by healthy vigor. **2.** hearty, as a meal. **3.** spirited; enthusiastic. **4.** lustful; lecherous. [1175–1225; ME: see LUST, -Y[1]] —**lust′i•ly,** *adv.* —**lust′i•ness,** *n.*
—**Syn. 1.** robust, strong, sturdy, stout. —**Ant. 1.** feeble, weak.

lu•sus na•tu•rae (lo͞o′səs nə to͝or′ē, -tyo͝or′ē), a deformed person or thing; freak. [1655–65; < L *lūsus nātūrae* a jest of nature]

Lü•ta (*Chin.* lʏ′dä′), *n. Wade-Giles.* Lüda.

lu•ta•nist (lo͞ot′n ist), *n.* lutenist. [1590–1600]

Lut′ Des′ert (lo͞ot), Dasht-i-Lut.

lute[1] (def. 1)

lute[1] (lo͞ot), *n., v.,* **lut•ed, lut•ing.** —*n.* **1.** a stringed musical instrument having a long, fretted neck and a hollow, typically pear-shaped body with a vaulted back. —*v.i.* **2.** to play a lute. —*v.t.* **3.** to perform (music) on a lute: *a musician skilled at luting Elizabethan ballads.* **4.** to express (a feeling, mood, etc.) by means of a lute: *The minstrel eloquently luted his melancholy.* [1325–75; ME < MF, OF < OPr *laut* < Ar *al ʿūd* lit., the wood]

lute[2] (lo͞ot), *n., v.,* **lut•ed, lut•ing.** —*n.* **1.** luting. —*v.t.* **2.** to seal or cement with luting. [1375–1425; late ME < ML *lutum,* special use of L *lutum* mud, clay]

lute[3] (lo͞ot), *n., v.,* **lut•ed, lut•ing.** —*n.* **1.** a paving tool for spreading and smoothing concrete, consisting of a straightedge mounted transversely on a long handle. —*v.t.* **2.** to spread and smooth (concrete in a pavement) with a lute. [1870–75, *Amer.;* < D *loet*]

lu•te•al (lo͞o′tē əl), *adj.* of, pertaining to, or involving the corpus luteum. [1925–30; (CORPUS) LUTE(UM) + -AL[1]]

lu′teal phase′, *Physiol.* a stage of the menstrual cycle, lasting about two weeks, from ovulation to the beginning of the next menstrual flow. Cf. **follicular phase.**

lu•te•ci•um (lo͞o tē′shē əm), *n. Chem.* lutetium.

lu•te•fisk (lo͞o′tə fisk′), *n. Scandinavian Cookery.* dried cod tenderized by soaking in lye, which is rinsed out before cooking. [< Norw *lutefisk* or Sw *lutfisk,* equiv. to *lut* LYE + *fisk* FISH]

lu•te•in (lo͞o′tē in), *n. Biochem.* **1.** Also called **xanthophyll.** a yellow-red, water-insoluble, crystalline, carotenoid alcohol, $C_{40}H_{56}O_2$, found in the petals of marigold and certain other flowers, egg yolk, algae, and corpora lutea: used chiefly in the biochemical study of the carotenoids. **2.** a preparation consisting of dried and powdered corpora lutea from hogs. [1865–70; < L *lūte(um)* yolk of an egg (n. use of neut. of *lūteus* yellow; see LUTEOUS) + -IN[2]]

lu•te•in•ize (lo͞o′tē ə nīz′), *v.,* **-ized, -iz•ing.** —*v.t.* **1.** to produce corpora lutea in. —*v.i.* **2.** to undergo transformation into corpora lutea. Also, *esp. Brit.,* **lu′te•in•ise′.** [1925–30; LUTEIN + -IZE] —**lu′te•in•i•za′tion,** *n.*

lu′teinizing hor′mone, *Biochem.* See **LH.** [1930–35]

lu•te•nist (lo͞ot′n ist), *n.* a person who plays the lute. Also, **lutanist.** [1590–1600; < ML *lūtānista,* deriv. of *lūtāna* lute; see -IST]

luteo-, a combining form meaning "golden yellow," used in the formation of compound words: *luteotropin.* [comb. form repr. L *lūteus;* see -O-]

lu•te•o•lin (lo͞o′tē ə lin), *n. Chem.* a yellow coloring substance, $C_{15}H_{10}O_6$, obtained from the weed *Reseda luteola:* used in dyeing silk and, formerly, in medicine. [1835–45; < NL (*Reseda*) *luteol(a),* special use of fem. of L *lūteolus* yellowish (dim. of *lūteus* yellow; see LUTEOUS) + -IN[2]]

lu•te•o•trop•ic (lo͞o′tē ə trop′ik, -trō′pik), *adj.* affecting the corpus luteum. Also, **lu•te•o•troph•ic** (lo͞o′tē ə trof′ik, -trō′fik). [1940–45; LUTEO- + -TROPIC]

lu•te•o•tro•pin (lo͞o′tē ə trō′pin), *n.* prolactin. [1940–45; LUTEOTROP(IC) + -IN[2]]

lu•te•ous (lo͞o′tē əs), *adj.* (of yellow) having a light to medium greenish tinge. [1650–60; < L *lūteus* golden-yellow, equiv. to *lūt(um)* yellowweed + *-eus* -EOUS]

lute′ stern′, *Naut.* a transom stern used on small boats, having an open after extension for breaking up seas coming from astern.

lute•string (lo͞ot′string′), *n.* **1.** a silk fabric of high sheen, formerly used in the manufacture of dresses. **2.** a narrow ribbon finished with a high gloss. [1655–65; by folk etymology < F *lustrine* < It *lustrino.* See LUSTER[1], -INE[1]]

lu•te•ti•um (lo͞o tē′shē əm), *n. Chem.* a trivalent rare-earth element. *Symbol:* Lu; *at. wt.:* 174.97; *at. no.:* 71. Also, **lutecium.** [1905–10; < L *Lūtēt(ia)* Paris + -IUM]

Luth., Lutheran.

Lu•ther (lo͞o′thər; *Ger.* lo͞ot′ər), *n.* **1. Mar•tin** (mär′tn; *Ger.* mär′tēn), 1483–1546, German theologian and author: leader, in Germany, of the Protestant Reformation. **2.** a male given name: from Germanic words meaning "famous" and "army."

Lu•ther•an (lo͞o′thər ən), *adj.* **1.** of or pertaining to Luther, adhering to his doctrines, or belonging to one of the Protestant churches that bear his name. —*n.* **2.** a follower of Luther or an adherent of his doctrines; a member of the Lutheran Church. [1515–25; LUTHER + -AN] —**Lu′ther•an•ism, Lu′ther•ism,** *n.*

lu•thern (lo͞o′thərn), *n.* a dormer window. [1660–70; perh. alter. of LUCARNE]

Lu•ther•ville-Ti•mo•ni•um (lo͞o′thər vil′ti mō′nē-əm), *n.* a city in N Maryland, near Baltimore. 17,854.

lu•thi•er (lo͞o′tē ər), *n.* a maker of stringed instruments, as violins. [1875–80; < F, equiv. to *luth* LUTE[1] + *-ier* -IER[2]]

Lu•thu•li (lo͞o to͞o′lē, -tyo͞o′-), *n.* **Albert John,** 1898–1967, African leader in the Republic of South Africa and former Zulu chief: Nobel peace prize 1960.

Lu′tine bell′ (lo͞o′tēn), the salvaged bell from the wrecked British warship *Lutine,* hung in the insurance office of Lloyd's of London and traditionally rung before announcements of ships overdue or lost at sea.

lut•ing (lo͞o′ting), *n.* any of various readily molded substances for sealing joints, cementing objects together, or waterproofing surfaces. [1520–30; LUTE[2] + -ING[1]]

lut•ist (lo͞o′tist), *n.* **1.** a lute player; lutenist. **2.** a maker of lutes. [1620–30; LUTE[1] + -IST]

lu•tose (lo͞o′tōs), *adj.* covered with a powdery substance resembling mud, as certain insects. [1640–50; < L *lutōsus* muddy, equiv. to *lut(um)* mud + *-ōsus* -OSE[1]]

Lutsk (lo͞otsk), *n.* a city in NW Ukraine, in the W Russian Federation in Europe, on the Styr River. 167,000. Polish, **Łuck.**

Lu•tu•am•i•an (lo͞o′to͞o am′ē ən), *n., pl.* **-ans,** (*esp. collectively*) **-an.** a member of a group of American Indian peoples including the Modoc and the Klamath.

Lut•yens (luch′ənz, lut′yənz), *n.* **Sir Edwin Landseer,** 1869–1944, English architect.

Lutz (luts), *n.* (*sometimes l.c.*) *Skating.* a jump in which the skater leaps from the back outer edge of one skate to make one full rotation in the air and lands on the back outer edge of the opposite skate. [1935–40; allegedly after Gustave *Lussi* (born 1898), Swiss figure skater, though the change in form is unexplained]

Löt·zen (lʏ′tsən), *n.* a town in S East Germany, WSW of Leipzig: site of Gustavus Adolphus' victory over Wallenstein in 1632 and Napoleon's victory over the Russians in 1813.

Lüt′zow-Holm Bay′ (lʏ′tsôf hōlm′), an inlet of the Indian Ocean on the coast of Antarctica between Queen Maud Land and Enderby Land.

luv (luv), *n. Eye Dialect.* love.

Lu′-Wang′ school′ (lo͞o′wäng′), *Philos.* See **School of Mind.** [after *Lu* Chin-yüan and *Wang* Shou-jen, two members of the group]

Lu·wi·an (lo͞o′ē ən), *n.* **1.** an extinct ancient Anatolian language written in cuneiform. —*adj.* **2.** of or pertaining to Luwian. [1920–25; *Luwi* nation of ancient Asia Minor + -AN]

lux (luks), *n., pl.* **lu·ces** (lo͞o′sēz). *Optics.* a unit of illumination, equivalent to 0.0929 foot-candle and equal to the illumination produced by luminous flux of one lumen falling perpendicularly on a surface one meter square. *Symbol:* lx Also called **meter-candle.** [1885–90; < L *lūx* LIGHT[1]]

Lux., Luxembourg.

lux·ate (luk′sāt), *v.t.,* **-at·ed, -at·ing.** *Chiefly Med.* to put out of joint; dislocate: *The accident luxated the left shoulder.* [1615–25; < L *luxātus* (ptp. of *luxāre* to put out of joint), equiv. to *lux(us)* dislocated (c. Gk *loxós* oblique) + *-ā-* theme vowel + *-tus* ptp. suffix] —**lux·a′tion,** *n.*

luxe (lo͝oks, luks; *Fr.* lʏks), *n.* **1.** luxury; elegance; sumptuousness: *accommodations providing luxe at low rates.* Cf. **deluxe.** —*adj.* **2.** luxurious; deluxe: *luxe accommodations.* [1550–60; < F < L *luxus* excess]

Lux·em·bourg (luk′səm bûrg′; *Fr.* lʏk sän bo͞or′), *n.* **1.** a grand duchy surrounded by Germany, France, and Belgium. 377,100; 999 sq. mi. (2585 sq. km). **2.** a city in and the capital of this grand duchy. 78,400. **3.** a province in SE Belgium: formerly a part of the grand duchy of Luxembourg. 219,642; 1706 sq. mi. (4420 sq. km). *Cap.:* Arlon. Also, **Luxemburg** (for defs. 1, 2).

Lux·em·bourg·er (luk′səm bûr′gər), *n.* a native or inhabitant of Luxembourg. Also, **Lux′em·burg′er.** [1910–15; < G *Luxemburger;* see LUXEMBOURG, -ER[1]]

Lux·em·bourg·i·an (luk′səm bûr′jē ən, luk′səm-bûr′jē ən), *adj.* **1.** of or pertaining to Luxembourg, its people, or their language. —*n.* **2.** Also, **Lux·em·bourg·ish** (luk′səm bûr′gish). Letzeburgesch. [LUXEMBOURG + -IAN]

Lux·em·burg (luk′səm bûrg′; *Ger.* lo͝ok′səm bo͝ork′), *n.* **1. Ro·sa** (rō′zə; *Ger.* rō′zä), ("*Red Rosa*"), 1870–1919, German socialist agitator, born in Poland. **2.** Luxembourg (defs. 1, 2).

Lu·xian (*Chin.* lʏ′shyän′), *n. Pinyin.* former name of **Luzhou.** Also, **Luhsien.**

Lux·or (luk′sôr), *n.* a town in S (Upper) Egypt, on the Nile: ruins of ancient Thebes. 84,600.

Lu Xun (lo͞o′ shōōn′), (*Zhou Shuren*) 1881–1936, Chinese writer.

lux·u·ri·ance (lug zho͝or′ē əns, luk sho͝or′-), *n.* luxuriant growth or productiveness; rich abundance; lushness. [1720–30; LUXURI(ANT) + -ANCE]

lux·u·ri·ant (lug zho͝or′ē ənt, luk sho͝or′-), *adj.* **1.** abundant or lush in growth, as vegetation. **2.** producing abundantly, as soil; fertile; fruitful; productive: *to settle in luxuriant country.* **3.** richly abundant, profuse, or superabundant. **4.** florid, as imagery or ornamentation; lacking in restraint. [1530–40; < L *luxuriant-* (s. of *luxuriāns*), prp. of *luxuriāre* to be rank or immoderate. See LUXURY, -ANT] —**lux·u′ri·ant·ly,** *adv.*
—**Syn. 1.** teeming. **2.** fruitful, prolific. **3.** copious.

lux·u·ri·ate (lug zho͝or′ē āt′, luk sho͝or′-), *v.i.,* **-at·ed, -at·ing. 1.** to enjoy oneself without stint; revel: *to luxuriate in newly acquired wealth.* **2.** to grow fully or abundantly; thrive: *The plants luxuriated in the new soil.* [1615–25; < L *luxuriātus,* ptp. of *luxuriāre.* See LUXURIANT, -ATE[1]] —**lux·u′ri·a′tion,** *n.*

lux·u·ri·ous (lug zho͝or′ē əs, luk sho͝or′-), *adj.* **1.** characterized by luxury; ministering or conducive to luxury: *a luxurious hotel.* **2.** given to or loving luxury; wanting or requiring what is choice, expensive, or the like: *a person with luxurious tastes.* **3.** given to pleasure, esp. of the senses; voluptuous. **4.** present or occurring in great abundance, rich profusion, etc.; opulent: *a luxurious harvest; music of luxurious beauty.* **5.** excessively ornate; overelaborate: *luxurious prose.* [1300–50; ME < L *luxuriōsus.* See LUXURY, -OUS] —**lux·u′ri·ous·ly,** *adv.* —**lux·u′ri·ous·ness,** *n.*
—**Syn. 1.** rich, sumptuous. **2.** epicurean. **3.** sensual, self-indulgent. —**Ant. 1.** squalid.

lux·u·ry (luk′shə rē, lug′zhə-), *n., pl.* **-ries,** *adj.* —*n.* **1.** a material object, service, etc., conducive to sumptuous living, usually a delicacy, elegance, or refinement of living rather than a necessity: *Gold cufflinks were a luxury not allowed for in his budget.* **2.** free or habitual indulgence in or enjoyment of comforts and pleasures in addition to those necessary for a reasonable standard of well-being: *a life of luxury on the French Riviera.* **3.** a means of ministering to such indulgence or enjoyment: *This travel plan gives you the luxury of choosing which countries you can visit.* **4.** a pleasure out of the ordinary allowed to oneself: *the luxury of an extra piece of the cake.* **5.** a foolish or worthless form of self-indulgence: *the luxury of self-pity.* **6.** *Archaic.* lust; lasciviousness; lechery. —*adj.* **7.** of, pertaining to, or affording luxury: *a luxury hotel.* [1300–50; ME *luxurie* < L *luxuria* rankness, luxuriance, equiv. to *luxur-* (comb. form of *luxus* extravagance) + *-ia* -Y[3]]

lux′ury tax′, a tax on certain goods or services not considered essential and usually relatively high in price. [1900–05]

Lu·zern (*Ger.* lo͞o tsern′), *n.* Lucerne.

Lu·zhou (lʏ′jō′), *n. Pinyin.* a city in S Sichuan province, in central China, on the Chang Jiang. 225,000. Also, **Luchou, Luchow.** Formerly, **Luxian.**

Lu·zon (lo͞o zon′; *Sp.* lo͞o sôn′), *n.* the chief island of the Philippines, in the N part of the group. 26,078,985; 40,420 sq. mi. (104,688 sq. km). *Cap.:* Manila.

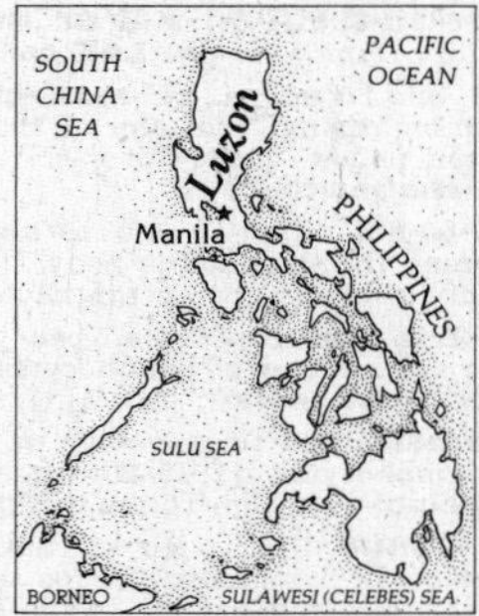

LV., lev; leva.

lv., 1. leave; leaves. **2.** livre; livres.

LVN, See **licensed vocational nurse.**

Lvov (*Russ.* lvôf), *n.* a city in W Ukraine, in the SW Russian Federation in Europe; formerly in Poland. 790,000. German, **Lemberg.** Polish, **Lwów** (lvo͞of). Ukrainian, **Lviv** (lvēf).

LW, low water.

l/w, lumen per watt; lumens per watt.

L wave, an earthquake wave that travels around the earth's surface and is usually the third conspicuous wave to reach a seismograph. Also called **long wave.** Cf. **P wave, S wave.**

lwei (lwā, lə wā′), *n., pl.* **lwei, lweis.** *n.* a monetary unit of Angola, the 100th part of a kwanza.

l.w.m., low water mark.

Lwoff (lwôf), *n.* **An·dré** (äɴ drā′), born 1902, French microbiologist: Nobel prize for medicine 1965.

lwop, leave without pay.

lwp, leave with pay.

LWV, See **League of Women Voters.** Also, **L.W.V.**

lx, *Symbol, Optics.* lux; luces.

LXX, Septuagint.

-ly, 1. a suffix forming adverbs from adjectives: *gladly; gradually; secondly.* **2.** a suffix meaning "every," attached to certain nouns denoting units of time: *hourly; daily.* **3.** an adjective suffix meaning "-like": *saintly; cowardly.* [(adv.) ME *-li, -lich(e),* OE *-lice* (*-lic* adj. suffix + *-e* adv. suffix); (adj.) ME *-li, -ly, -lich(e),* OE *-lic* (c. G *-lich*), suffixal use of *gelic* LIKE[1]]
—**Syn. 3.** See **-ish**[1].

Ly·all·pur (lī′əl po͝or′), *n.* a city in NE Pakistan. 1,092,000.

ly·am-hound (lī′əm hound′), *n. Archaic.* a bloodhound. Also, **lyme-hound.** [1520–30; obs. *lyam* leash (< MF *liem* << L *ligāmen* a band, tie, equiv. to *ligā(re)* to tie + *-men* n. suffix) + HOUND[1]]

ly·ard (lī′ərd), *adj. Chiefly Scot.* streaked or spotted with gray or white. Also, **ly·art** (lī′ərt). [1300–50; ME < MF, OF *liart*]

ly·ase (lī′ās, -āz), *n. Biochem.* any of various enzymes, as decarboxylase, that catalyze reactions involving the formation of or addition to a double bond. [1960–65; < Gk *lý(ein)* to loosen, dissolve (see LYSIS) + -ASE]

Lyau·tey (lyō te′), *n.* **Louis Hu·bert Gon·zalve** (lwē ʏ ber′ gôɴ zalv′), 1854–1934, French marshal: resident general of Morocco 1912–16, 1917–25.

ly·can·thrope (lī′kən thrōp′, lī kan′thrōp), *n.* **1.** a person affected with lycanthropy. **2.** a werewolf or alien spirit in the physical form of a bloodthirsty wolf. [1615–25; < Gk *lykánthrōpos* wolf-man, equiv. to *lýk(os)* WOLF + *ánthrōpos* man]

ly·can·thro·py (lī kan′thrə pē), *n.* **1.** a delusion in which one imagines oneself to be a wolf or other wild animal. **2.** the supposed or fabled assumption of the appearance of a wolf by a human being. [1575–85; < Gk *lykanthrōpía.* See LYCANTHROPE, -Y[3]] —**ly·can·throp·ic** (lī′kən throp′ik), *adj.*

Lyc·a·o·ni·a (lik′ā ō′nē ə, -ōn′yə, lī′kā-), *n.* an ancient country in S Asia Minor: later a Roman province.

ly·cée (lē sā′), *n., pl.* **-cées** (-sāz′; *Fr.* -sā′). a secondary school, esp. in France, maintained by the government. [1860–65; < F < L *lycēum* LYCEUM]

ly·ce·um (lī sē′əm), *n.* **1.** an institution for popular education providing discussions, lectures, concerts, etc. **2.** a building for such activities. **3.** (*cap.*) the gymnasium where Aristotle taught, in ancient Athens. **4.** a lycée. [1570–80; < L *Lycēum, Lycium* < Gk *Lýkeion* place in Athens, so named from the neighboring temple of Apollo; n. use of neut. of *lýkeios,* epithet of Apollo, variously explained]

lych (lich), *n. Brit. Obs.* lich.

lych′ gate′. See **lich gate.**

lych·nis (lik′nis), *n.* any showy-flowered plant belonging to the genus *Lychnis,* of the pink family. Cf. **rose campion, scarlet lychnis.** [1595–1605; < L < Gk *lychnís* red flower, akin to *lýchnos* lamp]

lych·no·scope (lik′nə skōp′), *n.* See **lowside window.** [1835–45; < Gk *lýchn(os)* lamp + -O- + -SCOPE] —**lych·no·scop·ic** (lik′nə skop′ik), *adj.*

Ly·ci·a (lish′ē ə), *n.* an ancient country in SW Asia Minor: later a Roman province.

Ly·ci·an (lish′ē ən), *adj.* **1.** of or pertaining to Lycia. —*n.* **2.** an inhabitant of Lycia. **3.** an Anatolian language of Lycia, written in a form of the Greek alphabet. [1590–1600; LYCI(A) + -AN]

ly·cine (lī′sēn), *n. Chem.* betaine. [1860–65; < Gk *lý-k(ion)* buckthorn + -INE[2]]

ly·co·pene (lī′kə pēn′), *n. Biochem.* a red crystalline substance, $C_{40}H_{56}$, that is the main pigment of certain fruits, as the tomato and paprika, and is a precursor to carotene in plant biosynthesis. [1925–30; earlier *lycop(in)* (< NL *Lycop(ersicon)* tomato genus (< Gk *lýk(os)* WOLF + -o- -O- + *Persikón* PEACH[1]) + -IN[2]) + -ENE]

ly·co·pod (lī′kə pod′), *n.* any erect or creeping, moss-like, evergreen plant of the genus *Lycopodium,* as the club moss or ground pine. Also, **ly·co·po·di·um** (lī′kə-pō′dē əm). [1700–10; < NL *lycopodium,* equiv. to Gk *lýk(os)* wolf + -o- -O- + NL *-podium* -PODIUM; allegedly so named from the claw-like shape of the root]

ly·co·ris (lī′kər is), *n.* any of several bulbous plants belonging to the genus *Lycoris,* of the amaryllis family, native to eastern Asia, bearing clustered, variously colored flowers that appear after the leaves have faded and disappeared. [< NL (1821), appar. after L *Lycōris,* a woman celebrated in the love-elegies of the Roman poet Gallus]

ly·co·sid (lī kō′sid), *n.* **1.** a spider of the family Lycosidae, comprising the wolf spiders. —*adj.* **2.** belonging or pertaining to the family Lycosidae. [< NL *Lycosidae* family name, equiv. to *Lycos(a)* type genus (irreg. < Gk *lýkos* wolf) + *-idae* -ID[2]]

Ly·cra (lī′krə), *Trademark.* a brand of spandex.

Ly·cur·gus (lī kûr′gəs), *n.* fl. 9th century B.C., Spartan lawgiver.

lydd·ite (lid′īt), *n. Chem.* a high explosive consisting chiefly of picric acid. [1885–90; named after *Lydd,* borough in SE England near the site where it was first tested; see -ITE[1]]

Lyd·gate (lid′gāt′, -git), *n.* **John,** c1370–1451?, English monk, poet, and translator.

Lyd·i·a (lid′ē ə), *n.* **1.** an ancient kingdom in W Asia Minor: under Croesus, a wealthy empire including most of Asia Minor. **2.** a female given name.

Lyd·i·an (lid′ē ən), *adj.* **1.** of or pertaining to Lydia. **2.** (of music) softly or sensuously sweet; voluptuous. —*n.* **3.** an inhabitant of Lydia. **4.** an Anatolian language of Lydia, written in a modified Greek alphabet. [1535–45; LYDI(A) + -AN]

Lyd′ian mode′, *Music.* an authentic church mode represented on the white keys of a keyboard instrument by an ascending scale from F to F. [1800–10]

lye (lī), *n. Chem.* **1.** a highly concentrated, aqueous solution of potassium hydroxide or sodium hydroxide. **2.** any solution resulting from leaching, percolation, or the like. [bef. 900; ME *lie, ley,* OE *lēag;* c. D *loog,* G *Lauge* lye, ON *laug* warm bath. See LAVE[1]]

lye·fish (lī′fish′), *n.* lutefisk. [LYE + FISH; see LUTEFISK]

lye′ hom′iny. See under **hominy.** [1815–25, *Amer.*]

Ly·ell (lī′əl), *n.* **Sir Charles,** 1797–1875, English geologist.

ly·gae·id (lī jē′id, lī′jē id), *n.* **1.** Also called **lygae′id bug′, ly′gus bug′** (lī′gəs). any of numerous, often brightly marked bugs of the family Lygaeidae, which feed on the juices of plants in both the larval and adult stages and are important pests of cultivated crops and some fruit trees. —*adj.* **2.** belonging or pertaining to the family Lygaeidae. [< NL *Lygaeidae* family name, equiv. to *Lygae(us)* type genus (< Gk *lȳgaîos* murky) + *-idae* -ID[2]]

ly·ing[1] (lī′ing), *n.* **1.** the telling of lies; untruthfulness. —*adj.* **2.** telling or containing lies; deliberately untruthful; mendacious; false: *a lying report.* [1175–1225; ME; see LIE[1], -ING[1], -ING[2]] —**ly′ing·ly,** *adv.*
—**Syn. 1.** falsehood, falsity, mendacity, prevarication. **2.** deceptive, misleading, fallacious; sham, counterfeit. —**Ant. 1.** truth. **2.** true, candid.

ly·ing[2] (lī′ing), *v.* ppr. of **lie**[2]. —**ly′ing·ly,** *adv.*

ly·ing-in (lī′ing in′), *n., pl.* **lyings-in, lying-ins,** *adj.* —*n.* **1.** the state of being in childbed; confinement. —*adj.* **2.** pertaining to or providing facilities for childbirth: *a lying-in hospital.* [1400–50; late ME *lyynge in.* See LIE[2], -ING[1], IN]

CONCISE PRONUNCIATION KEY: act, cāpe, dâre, pärt; set, ēqual; *if,* īce; ox, ōver, ôrder, oil, bo͝ok, bo͞ot, out; up, ûrge; child; sing; shoe; thin, *th*at; zh as in *treasure.* ə = *a* as in *alone, e* as in *system, i* as in *easily, o* as in *gallop, u* as in *circus;* ˚ as in *fire* (fī˚r), *hour* (ou˚r). l and n can serve as syllabic consonants, as in *cradle* (krād′l), and *button* (but′n). See the full key inside the front cover.

Ly·le (līl), *n.* a male given name.

Lyl·y (lil′ē), *n.* **John,** 1554?–1606, English writer of romances and plays.

Ly·man (lī′mən), *n.* a male given name.

Lyme′ disease′ (līm), *Pathol.* an acute inflammatory disease caused by a tick-borne spirochete, *Borrelia burgdorferi,* characterized by recurrent episodes of decreasing severity in which joint swelling, fever, and rash occur, sometimes with cardiac or nervous system complications. [after *Lyme,* Conn., where it was first described]

lyme-hound (līm′hound′), *n.* lyam-hound.

lymph (limf), *n.* **1.** *Anat., Physiol.* a clear yellowish, slightly alkaline, coagulable fluid, containing white blood cells in a liquid resembling blood plasma, that is derived from the tissues of the body and conveyed to the bloodstream by the lymphatic vessels. **2.** *Archaic.* the sap of a plant. **3.** *Archaic.* a stream or spring of clear, pure water. [1620–30; < L *lympha* water (earlier **limpa;* see LIMPID); pseudo-Gk form, by assoc. with *nympha* < Gk *nýmphē* NYMPH]

lymph-, var. of **lympho-** before a vowel: *lymphoma.*

lym·phad·e·nec·to·my (lim fad′n ek′tə mē, lim′fə dn-), *n., pl.* **-mies.** the excision of one or more lymph nodes, usually as a procedure in the surgical removal or destruction of a cancer. [LYMPH- + ADEN- + -ECTOMY]

lym·phad·e·ni·tis (lim fad′n ī′tis, lim′fə dn-), *n. Pathol.* inflammation of a lymphatic gland. Also called **adenitis.** [1875–80; LYMPH- + ADEN- + -ITIS]

lym·phad·e·no·ma (lim fad′n ō′mə, lim′fə dn-), *n., pl.* **-mas, -ma·ta** (-mə tə). *Pathol.* an enlarged lymph node. [1870–75; LYMPH- + ADEN- + -OMA]

lym·phad·e·nop·a·thy (lim fad′n op′ə thē, lim′fə dn-), *n., pl.* **-thies.** *Pathol.* chronically swollen lymph nodes. [1915–20; LYMPH- + ADENO- + -PATHY]

lym·phad·e·nop′a·thy-as·so·ci·at·ed vi′rus (lim-fad′n op′ə thē ə sō′shē ā′tid, -sē ā′-, lim′fə dn-). See under **AIDS virus.** *Abbr.:* LAV

lymphangi-, a combining form with the meaning "lymph vessel," used in the formation of compound words: *lymphangiography.* [< NL *lymphangion.* See LYMPHO-, ANGIO-]

lym·phan·gi·al (lim fan′jē əl), *adj.* pertaining to the lymphatic vessels. [LYMPHANGI- + -AL[1]]

lym·phan·gi·og·ra·phy (lim fan′jē og′rə fē), *n.* x-ray visualization of lymph vessels and nodes following injection of a contrast medium. Also called **lymphography.** [1940–45; LYMPHANGI- + -O- + -GRAPHY] —**lym·phan·gi·o·gram** (lim fan′jē ə gram′), *n.*

lym·phan·gi·o·ma (lim fan′jē ō′mə), *n., pl.* **-mas, -ma·ta** (-mə tə). *Pathol.* a benign tumor composed of dilated and newly formed lymph vessels. [1875–80; < NL; see LYMPHANGI-, -OMA] —**lym·phan·gi·om·a·tous** (lim fan′jē om′ə təs), *adj.*

lym·phan·gi·tis (lim′fan jī′tis), *n., pl.* **-git·i·des** (-jit′i dēz′). *Pathol.* inflammation of the lymphatic vessels. Also, **lym·phan·gi·i·tis** (lim fan′jē ī′tis). [1835–45; LYMPHANG(I)- + -ITIS]

lym·phat·ic (lim fat′ik), *adj.* **1.** pertaining to, containing, or conveying lymph. **2.** (of persons) having the characteristics, as flabbiness or sluggishness, formerly believed to be due to an excess of lymph in the system. —*n.* **3.** a lymphatic vessel. [1640–50; < NL *lymphāticus.* See LYMPH-, -ATIC] —**lym·phat′i·cal·ly,** *adv.*

lymphat′ic sys′tem, *Anat., Zool.* the system by which lymph is returned from the cells to the blood and by which white blood cells are produced in response to inflammation or presence of antigens; in mammals, the system includes the lymph glands, vessels and sinuses through which lymph is carried, and lymphoid tissues, as bone marrow and the thymus. Also called **lymph system.** [1820–30]

lym·pha·tol·y·sis (lim′fə tol′ə sis), *n. Pathol.* destruction of lymphatic vessels or of lymphoid tissue. [LYMPHAT(IC) + -O- + -LYSIS] —**lym·phat·o·lyt·ic** (lim-fat′l it′ik, lim′fə tl-), *adj.*

lymph·e·de·ma (lim′fi dē′mə), *n. Pathol.* the accumulation of lymph in soft tissue with accompanying swelling, often of the extremities: sometimes caused by inflammation, obstruction, or removal of lymph channels. [1885–90; LYMPH- + EDEMA]

lymph′ node′, any of the glandlike masses of tissue in the lymphatic vessels containing cells that become lymphocytes. Also called **lymph′ gland′.** [1890–95]

lympho-, a combining form representing **lymph** in compound words: *lymphocyte.* Also, *esp. before a vowel,* **lymph-.**

lym·pho·blast (lim′fə blast′), *n. Cell Biol.* a large, metabolically active lymphocyte shortly before it enters into mitosis. [1905–10; LYMPHO- + -BLAST] —**lym′pho·blas′tic,** *adj.*

lym·pho·cyte (lim′fə sīt′), *n. Anat.* a type of white blood cell having a large, spherical nucleus surrounded by a thin layer of nongranular cytoplasm. Cf. **B cell, T cell.** [1885–90; LYMPHO- + -CYTE] —**lym·pho·cyt·ic** (lim′fə sit′ik), *adj.*

lym·pho·cy·to·sis (lim′fə sī tō′sis), *n. Pathol.* an abnormal increase in the number of lymphocytes in the blood. [1895–1900; LYMPHOCYTE + -OSIS] —**lym·pho·cy·tot·ic** (lim′fō sī tot′ik), *adj.*

lym·pho·gran·u·lo·ma (lim′fə gran′yə lō′mə), *n., pl.* **-mas, -ma·ta** (-mə tə). *Pathol.* **1.** any of certain diseases characterized by granulomatous lesions of lymph nodes. **2.** Also called **lym′phogranulo′ma ve·ne′re·um** (və nēr′ē əm), a venereal form of lymphogranuloma, caused by the bacterium *Chlamydia trachomatis* and characterized initially by a lesion on the genitals. **3.** *Obs.* See **Hodgkin's disease.** [1920–25; LYMPHO- + GRANULOMA]

lym·pho·gran·u·lo·ma·to·sis (lim′fə gran′yə lō mə-tō′sis), *n. Pathol.* widespread infectious granuloma of the lymphatic system. [1910–15; LYMPHO- + GRANULOMATOSIS]

lym·phog·ra·phy (lim fog′rə fē), *n.* lymphangiography. [1930–35; LYMPHO- + -GRAPHY]

lym·phoid (lim′foid), *adj.* **1.** of, pertaining to, or resembling lymph. **2.** of or pertaining to the tissue **(lym′phoid tis′sue)** that occurs esp. in the lymph glands, thymus, tonsils, and spleen and produces lymphocytes. [1865–70; LYMPH- + -OID]

lym′phoid cell′, *Anat.* a cell in the lymph glands that produces leukocytes. [1870–75]

lym·pho·kine (lim′fə kīn′), *n. Immunol.* any lymphocyte product, as interferon, that is not an antibody but may participate in the immune response through its effect on the function of other cells, as destroying antigen-coated cells or stimulating macrophages. [1969; LYMPHO(CYTE) + *-kine* < Gk *kineîn* to move; cf. -KININ]

lym′pho·kine-ac·ti·vat·ed kill′er cell′ (lim′fə-kīn ak′tə vā′tid), *Immunol.* See **LAK cell.**

lym·pho·ma (lim fō′mə), *n., pl.* **-mas, -ma·ta** (-mə tə). *Pathol.* a tumor arising from any of the cellular elements of lymph nodes. [1870–75; < NL; see LYMPH-, -OMA] —**lym·pho′ma·toid′,** *adj.*

lym·pho·ma·to·sis (lim′fō mə tō′sis), *n. Pathol.* lymphoma spread throughout the body. [1895–1900; < NL *lymphomat-* (s. of *lymphoma* LYMPHOMA) + -OSIS]

lym·pho·pe·ni·a (lim′fō pē′nē ə, -pēn′yə), *n. Pathol.* a reduction in the number of lymphocytes in the blood. [1905–10; < NL; see LYMPHO-, -PENIA]

lym·pho·poi·e·sis (lim′fō poi ē′sis), *n. Physiol.* the formation of lymphocytes. [1915–20; LYMPHO- + -POIESIS] —**lym·pho·poi·et·ic** (lim′fō poi et′ik), *adj.*

lym·pho·sar·co·ma (lim′fō sär kō′mə), *n. Pathol.* a malignant tumor in lymphatic tissue, caused by the growth of abnormal lymphocytes. [1870–75; < NL; see LYMPHO-, SARCOMA]

lym·pho·tox·in (lim′fə tok′sin), *n. Immunol.* a glycoprotein that is released by antigen-stimulated or mitogen-stimulated T cells and is toxic to various other cells. [1970–75; LYMPHO- + TOXIN]

lym·pho·troph·ic (lim′fə trof′ik, -trō′fik), *adj.* carrying nutrients from the lymph to the tissues. [1980–85]

lymph′ sys′tem, *Anat.* See **lymphatic system.**

Lyn·brook (lin′bro͝ok′), *n.* a village on W Long Island, in SE New York. 20,431.

lyn·ce·an (lin sē′ən), *adj.* **1.** of or pertaining to a lynx; lynxlike. **2.** lynx-eyed; sharp-sighted. [< L *lyncē(us)* sharp-sighted (< Gk *lýnkeios* like a lynx, s. of *lýnx* LYNX + *-eios* adj. suffix) + -AN]

lynch (linch), *v.t.* to put to death, esp. by hanging, by mob action and without legal authority. [1825–35, *Amer.*; v. use of *lynch* in LYNCH LAW] —**lynch′er,** *n.* —**Syn.** See **hang.**

Lynch (linch), *n.* **John** (*Jack*), born 1917, Irish political leader: prime minister 1966–73, 1977–79.

Lynch·burg (linch′bûrg), *n.* a city in central Virginia. 66,743.

lynch′ law′, the administration of summary punishment, esp. death, upon a suspected, accused, or convicted person by a mob acting without legal process or authority. [1805–15, *Amer.*; after the self-instituted tribunals presided over by William *Lynch* (1742–1820) of Pittsylvania, Va., c1776]

lynch·pin (linch′pin′), *n.* linchpin.

Lynd (lind), *n.* **Robert Staugh·ton** (stôt′n), 1892–1970, and his wife **Helen (Mer·rell)** (mer′əl), 1896–1982, U.S. sociologists.

Lyn·da (lin′də), *n.* a female given name.

Lynd·hurst (lind′hûrst), *n.* **1.** a township in NE New Jersey. 20,326. **2.** a city in NE Ohio, near Cleveland. 18,092.

Lyn·don (lin′dən), *n.* a male given name.

Lyn·do·ra (lin dôr′ə, -dōr′-), *n.* a female given name.

Ly·nen (lē′nen), *n.* **Fe·o·dor** (fā ô′dôr), born 1911, German biochemist: Nobel prize in medicine 1964.

Lyn·ette (li net′), *n.* a female given name.

Lyng·vi (ling′vē), *n.* (in the *Volsunga Saga*) a rival of Sigmund for Hjordis who kills Sigmund and is killed by Sigurd.

Lynn (lin), *n.* **1. Janet** (*Janet Lynn Nowicki*), born 1953, U.S. figure-skater. **2.** a seaport in E Massachusetts, on Massachusetts Bay. 78,471. **3.** a male given name, form of **Lincoln, Linton. 4.** Also, **Lynne.** a female given name, form of **Caroline** or **Carolyn.**

Lynn·field (lin′fēld′), *n.* a town in NE Massachusetts. 11,267.

Lynn·wood (lin′wo͝od′), *n.* a city in NW Washington. 21,937.

Lyn·wood (lin′wo͝od′), *n.* a city in SW California. 48,548.

lynx (lingks), *n., pl.* **lynx·es,** (*esp. collectively*) **lynx** for 1, *gen.* **Lyn·cis** (lin′sis) for 2. **1.** any of several wildcats of the genus *Lynx* (or *Felis*), having long limbs, a short tail, and usually tufted ears, esp. *L. lynx* **(Canada lynx),** of Canada and the northern U.S., having grayish-brown fur marked with white. **2.** (*cap.*) *Astron.* a northern constellation between Ursa Major and Auriga. [1300–50; ME < L < Gk *lýnx*] —**lynx′like′,** *adj.*

Canada lynx, *Lynx lynx,* length to 3½ ft. (1 m)

lynx-eyed (lingks′īd′), *adj.* sharp-sighted. [1590–1600]

ly·o·crat·ic (lī′ə krat′ik), *adj. Physical Chem.* noting a colloid owing its stability to the affinity of its particles for the liquid in which they are dispersed. Cf. **electrocratic.** [*lyo-* (see LYOPHILIC) + -CRATIC]

ly·ol·y·sis (lī ol′ə sis), *n. Chem.* solvolysis. [*lyo-* (see LYOPHILIC) + -LYSIS] —**ly·o·lyt·ic** (lī′ə lit′ik), *adj.*

Ly·on (lī′ən *for 1; Fr.* lyôɴ *for 2*), *n.* **1. Mary,** 1797–1849, U.S. pioneer in advocating and providing advanced education for women: founder of Mount Holyoke College. **2.** Lyons.

Ly′on bean′ (lī′ən), a vine, *Mucuna niveum,* of southern Asia and the Philippines, having showy clusters of white flowers and whitish hairy pods, grown widely as a forage crop. [named after W. S. *Lyon* (d. 1916), American botanist]

Ly·on·nais (lē ô ne′), *n.* a former province in E France. Also, **Ly·o·nais′.**

ly·on·naise (lī′ə nāz′; *Fr.* lē ô nez′), *adj.* (of food, esp. fried potatoes) cooked with pieces of onion. [1840–50; < F (*à la*) *lyonnaise* (fem. adj.) in the manner of LYONS]

Ly·on·nesse (lī′ə nes′), *n. Arthurian Romance.* the mythical region where Sir Tristram was born, located near Cornwall in SW England and supposed to have been submerged by the sea.

Ly′on Of′fice of Arms′ (lī′ən), *Scot Heraldry.* See **Heralds' Office.** Also called **Ly′on Of′fice.** [1840–50; obs. *lyon* LION]

Ly·ons (lī′ənz *for 1;* lē ôɴ′ *or, sometimes,* lī′ənz *for 2*), *n.* **1. Joseph Aloysius,** 1879–1939, Australian statesman: prime minister 1932–39. **2.** French, **Lyon.** a city in and the capital of Rhone, in E France at the confluence of the Rhone and Saône rivers. 462,841.

ly·o·phil·ic (lī′ə fil′ik), *adj. Physical Chem.* noting a colloid the particles of which have a strong affinity for the liquid in which they are dispersed. Also, **ly·o·phile** (lī′ə fīl′). [1910–15; *lyo-* (comb. form repr. Gk *lýein* to loose, dissolve, set free; see -O-) + -PHILIC]

ly·oph·i·lize (lī of′ə līz′), *v.t.,* **-lized, -liz·ing.** *Biochem.* (of tissue, blood, serum, or the like) to dry by freezing in a high vacuum. Also, *esp. Brit.,* **ly·oph′i·lise′.** [1935–40; LYOPHIL(IC) + -IZE] —**ly·oph′i·li·za′tion,** *n.*

ly·o·pho·bic (lī′ə fō′bik, -fob′ik), *adj. Physical Chem.* noting a colloid the particles of which have little or no affinity for the liquid in which they are dispersed. [1910–15; *lyo-* (see LYOPHILIC) + -PHOBIC]

ly·o·trop·ic (lī′ə trop′ik, -trō′pik), *adj. Physical Chem.* noting any series of ions, salts, or radicals arranged in descending order relative to the magnitude of their effect on a given solvent. [1920–25; *lyo-* (see LYOPHILIC) + -TROPIC]

Ly·ra (lī′rə), *n., gen.* **-rae** (-rē) for 1. **1.** *Astron.* the Lyre, a northern constellation between Cygnus and Hercules, containing the bright star Vega. **2.** a female given name. **3.** (*l.c.*) glockenspiel.

lyrate leaf

ly·rate (lī′rāt, -rit), *adj.* **1.** *Bot.* (of a pinnate leaf) divided transversely into several lobes, the smallest at the base. **2.** *Zool.* lyre-shaped, as the tail of certain birds. Also, **ly′rat·ed.** [1750–60; < NL *lyrātus.* See LYRE, -ATE[1]] —**ly′rate·ly,** *adv.*

lyre (līᵊr), *n.* **1.** a musical instrument of ancient Greece consisting of a soundbox made typically from a turtle shell, with two curved arms connected by a yoke from which strings are stretched to the body, used esp. to accompany singing and recitation. **2.** (*cap.*) *Astron.* the constellation Lyra. [1175–1225; ME *lire* < L *lyra* < Gk *lýra*]

lyre (def. 1)

lyre′ back′, a back of a chair or the like having a pierced splat in the form of a lyre, often with metal rods representing strings.

lyre·bird (līᵊr′bûrd′), *n.* an Australian passerine bird of the genus *Menura,* the male of which has a long tail that is lyrate when spread. See illus. on next page. [1825–35; LYRE + BIRD]

CONCISE ETYMOLOGY KEY: <, descended or borrowed from; >, whence; b., blend of, blended; c., cognate with; cf., compare; deriv., derivative; equiv., equivalent; imit., imitative; obl., oblique; r., replacing; s., stem; sp., spelling, spelled; resp., respelling, respelled; trans., translation; ?, origin unknown; *, unattested; ‡, probably earlier than. See the full key inside the front cover.

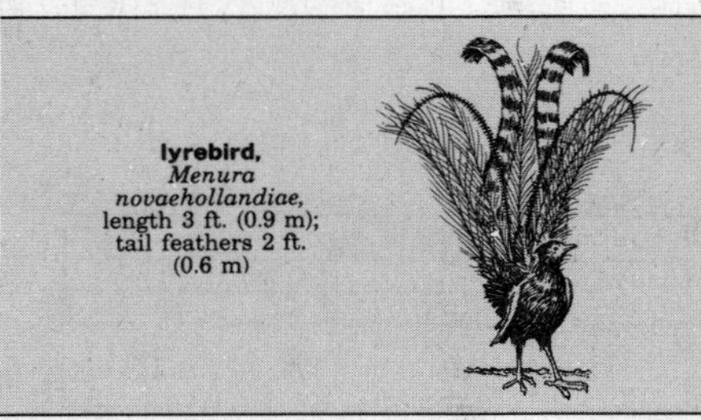

lyrebird, *Menura novaehollandiae,* length 3 ft. (0.9 m); tail feathers 2 ft. (0.6 m)

lyre′-form so′fa (līᵊr′fôrm′), a sofa of the early 19th century having a front rail curving upward and outward at either end to form arms and terminating in a downward scroll.

lyre′ snake′, any of several mildly venomous colubrid snakes of the genus *Trimorphodon,* inhabiting rocky areas from the southwestern U.S. to Central America, having fangs in the rear of the upper jaw and a lyre-shaped marking on the head.

lyr•ic (lir′ik), *adj.* Also, **lyr′i•cal. 1.** (of poetry) having the form and musical quality of a song, and esp. the character of a songlike outpouring of the poet's own thoughts and feelings, as distinguished from epic and dramatic poetry. **2.** pertaining to or writing lyric poetry: *a lyric poet.* **3.** characterized by or expressing spontaneous, direct feeling: *a lyric song; lyric writing.* **4.** pertaining to, rendered by, or employing singing. **5.** (of a voice) relatively light of volume and modest in range: *a lyric soprano.* **6.** pertaining, adapted, or sung to the lyre, or composing poems to be sung to the lyre: *ancient Greek lyric odes.* —*n.* **7.** a lyric poem. **8.** Often, **lyrics.** the words of a song. [1575–85; < L *lyricus* < Gk *lyrikós.* See LYRE, -IC] —**lyr′i•cal•ly,** *adv.* —**lyr′i•cal•ness,** *n.*

lyr•i•cism (lir′ə siz′əm), *n.* **1.** lyric character or style, as in poetry. **2.** lyric feeling; enthusiasm, esp. when unrestrained or exaggerated. [1750–60; LYRIC + -ISM]

lyr•i•cist (lir′ə sist), *n.* **1.** a person who writes the lyrics for songs. **2.** a lyric poet. [1880–85; LYRIC + -IST]

lyr•i•cize (lir′ə sīz′), *v.,* **-cized, -ciz•ing.** —*v.i.* **1.** to write lyrics. **2.** to write lyrically or in a lyric style. —*v.t.* **3.** to put into lyric form; treat in a lyric style. Also, *esp. Brit.,* **lyr′i•cise′.** [1825–35; LYRIC + -IZE] —**lyr′i•ci•za′tion,** *n.*

Ly•rids (lī′ridz), *n.* (*used with a plural v.*) *Astron.* a collection of meteors comprising a meteor shower (**Ly′•rid me′teor show′er**) visible April 22 and having its apparent origin in the constellation Lyra. [LYR(A) + *-ids,* pl. of -ID[1]]

ly•ri•form (lī′rə fôrm′), *adj.* shaped like a lyre. [1855–60; < F *lyriforme.* See LYRE, -I-, -FORM]

lyr•ism (lir′iz əm), *n.* lyricism. [1855–60; < Gk *lyrismós.* See LYRE, -ISM]

lyr•ist (līᵊr′ist *for 1;* lir′ist *for 2*), *n.* **1.** a person who plays the lyre or who sings and accompanies himself or herself on the lyre. **2.** a lyric poet. [1650–60; < L *lyristēs* < Gk *lyristḗs.* See LYRE, -IST]

Lys (lēs), *n.* a river in W Europe, in N France and W Belgium, flowing NE into the Scheldt River at Ghent. 120 mi. (195 km) long.

Lys, *Biochem.* lysine.

lys-, a combining form meaning "lysis," "decomposition," used in the formation of compound words: *lysin.* Also, **lysi-, lyso-.** Cf. **-lysis, -lyze, -lyte.** [< Gk; see LYSIS]

Ly•san•der (lī san′dər), *n.* died 395 B.C., Spartan naval commander and statesman.

Ly•san•dra (li san′drə, lī-), *n.* a female given name.

ly•sate (lī′sāt), *n. Biochem.* the mixture of substances formed by the lysis of cells. [1920–25; LYS(IS) + -ATE[1]]

lyse (lis), *v.,* **lysed, lys•ing.** *Immunol., Biochem.* —*v.t.* **1.** to cause dissolution or destruction of cells by lysins. —*v.i.* **2.** to undergo lysis. [1925–30; back formation from LYSIN or LYSIS]

-lyse, *Chiefly Brit.* var. of **-lyze.**

Ly•sen•ko (li seng′kō; *Russ.* li syen′kə), *n.* **Tro•fim De•ni•so•vich** (tʀu fyĕm′ dyi nyĕ′sə vyich), 1898–1976, Russian biologist and agronomist.

Ly•sen•ko•ism (li seng′kō iz′əm), *n.* a genetic doctrine formulated by Lysenko and asserting that acquired characteristics are inheritable. [1945–50; named after T. D. LYSENKO; see -ISM]

ly•ser′gic ac′id (lī sûr′jik, li-), *Chem.* a crystalline solid, $C_{16}H_{16}N_2O_2$, obtained from ergot or synthesized: used in the synthesis of LSD. [1930–35; LYS- + ERG(OT) + -IC]

lyser′gic ac′id di•eth•yl•am′ide (dī eth′ə lam′īd, -eth′ə lə mīd′), *Pharm.* See **LSD** (def. 2). [1940–45]

lysi-, var. of **lys-:** *lysimeter.*

Lys•i•as (lis′ē əs), *n.* c450–c380 B.C., Athenian orator.

Ly•sim•a•chus (lī sim′ə kəs), *n.* 361?–281 B.C., Macedonian general: king of Thrace 306–281.

ly•sim•e•ter (lī sim′i tər), *n.* an instrument for determining the amount of water-soluble matter in soil. [1875–80; LYSI- + -METER]

ly•sin (lī′sin), *n. Immunol., Biochem.* an antibody causing the disintegration of erythrocytes or bacterial cells. [1895–1900; LYS- + -IN[2]]

ly•sine (lī′sēn, -sin), *n. Biochem.* a crystalline, basic, amino acid, $H_2N(CH_2)_4CH(NH_2)COOH$, produced chiefly from many proteins by hydrolysis, essential in the nutrition of humans and animals. *Abbr.:* Lys; *Symbol:* K [1890–95; LYS- + -INE[2]]

Ly•sip•pus (lī sip′əs), *n.* fl. c360–c320 B.C., Greek sculptor.

ly•sis (lī′sis), *n.* **1.** *Immunol., Biochem.* the dissolution or destruction of cells by lysins. **2.** *Med.* the gradual recession of a disease. Cf. **crisis** (def. 4). [1815–25; < NL < Gk *lýsis* a loosening, releasing, equiv. to *ly-,* var. s. of *lý(ein)* to loosen, release + *-sis* -SIS]

-lysis, a combining form with the meaning "breaking down, loosening, decomposition," used in the formation of compound words: *analysis; electrolysis; paralysis.* [< Gk; see LYSIS]

Ly•sis•tra•ta (lis′ə strä′tə, lī sis′trə tə), *n.* a comedy (411 B.C.) by Aristophanes.

Ly•sith•e•a (lī sith′ē ə), *n. Astron.* a small moon of the planet Jupiter.

lyso-, var. of **lys-.**

ly•so•cline (lī′sə klīn′), *n. Oceanog.* the depth of the ocean at which the solubility of calcium carbonate increases substantially. [1965–70; LYSO- + -CLINE]

ly•so•gen (lī′sə jən, -jen′), *n. Microbiol.* a bacterial cell or strain that has been infected with a temperate virus, one that does not cause destruction of the cell. [1930–35; back formation from LYSOGENIC]

ly•so•gen•e•sis (lī′sə jen′ə sis), *n. Microbiol.* production of a lysogen. [1900–05; LYSO(GEN) + -GENESIS]

ly•so•gen•ic (lī′sə jen′ik), *adj. Microbiol.* harboring a temperate virus as a prophage or plasmid. [1895–1900; LYSO- (repr. LYSIS) + -GENIC]

ly•sog•e•nize (lī soj′ə nīz′), *v.t.,* **-nized, -niz•ing.** *Microbiol.* to make lysogenic. Also, *esp. Brit.,* **ly•sog′e•nise′.** [1950–55; LYSOGEN(IC) + -IZE]

ly•sog•e•ny (lī soj′ə nē), *n. Microbiol.* the state of being lysogenic. [1955–60; LYSO(GENIC) + -GENY]

Ly•sol (lī′sôl, -sol), *Trademark.* a brand of clear, brown, oily solution of cresols in soap, used as a disinfectant and antiseptic.

ly•so•some (lī′sə sōm′), *n. Cell Biol.* a cell organelle containing enzymes that digest particles and that disintegrate the cell after its death. See diag. under **cell.** [1950–55; LYSO- + -SOME[3]] —**ly′so•so′mal,** *adj.*

ly•so•zyme (lī′sə zīm′), *n. Biochem.* an enzyme that is destructive of bacteria and functions as an antiseptic, found in tears, leukocytes, mucus, egg albumin, and certain plants. [1920–25; LYSO- + (EN)ZYME]

lys•so•pho•bi•a (lis′ə fō′bē ə), *n. Psychiatry.* a pathological fear of going insane. [1885–90; < Gk *lýss(a)* rage, rabies, madness + -O- + -PHOBIA]

-lyte[1], a combining form used in the formation of compound words that denote something subjected to a certain process (indicated by a noun ending in **-lysis**): *electrolyte.* [< Gk *lytós* able to be untied or loosened, soluble, verbid of *lýein* to loose, dissolve; c. L *luere* to loose]

-lyte[2], var. of **-lite.**

lyth•ra•ceous (lith rā′shəs, lī thrā′-), *adj.* belonging to the Lythraceae, the loosestrife family of plants. Cf. **loosestrife family.** [< NL *Lythrace(ae)* (*Lythr(um)* the type genus (< Gk *lýthron* gore) + *-aceae* -ACEAE) + -OUS]

lyt•ic (lit′ik), *adj.* of, noting, or pertaining to lysis or a lysin. [1885–90; < Gk *lytikós* able to loosen. See -LYTE[1], -IC]

-lytic, a combining form occurring in adjectives that correspond to nouns ending in **-lysis:** *analytic; paralytic.* [see LYTIC]

lyt•ta (lit′ə), *n., pl.* **lyt•tas, lyt•tae** (lit′ē). a long, worm-shaped cartilage in the tongue of the dog and other carnivorous animals. [1595–1605; < NL < Gk *lýtta,* Attic form of *lýssa* rage, rabies; so named because the cartilage was thought to be a parasite causing rabies]

Lyt•ton (lit′n), *n.* **1. Edward George Earle Lytton Bulwer-, 1st Baron Lytton of Kneb•worth** (neb′wərt), 1803–73. English novelist, dramatist, and politician. **2.** his son, **Edward Robert Bulwer Lytton, 1st Earl Lytton** ("*Owen Meredith*"), 1831–91, English statesman and poet.

Lyu•ber•tsy (lo͞o′bər tsē; *Russ.* lyo͞o′byiʀ tsi), *n.* a city in the W RSFSR, in the central part of the Soviet Union in Europe, SE of Moscow. 160,000.

Lyu•blin (*Russ.* lyo͞o′blyin), *n.* Lublin.

-lyze, a combining form occurring in verbs that correspond to nouns ending in **-lysis:** *catalyze.* Also, *esp. Brit.,* **-lyse.** [LY(SIS) + -(I)ZE]

LZ, landing zone.

CONCISE PRONUNCIATION KEY: *act, cāpe, dâre, pärt; set, ēqual; if, īce; ox, ōver, ôrder, oil, bo͝ok, bo͞ot, out; up, ûrge; child; sing; shoe; thin, that;* zh as in *treasure.* ə = *a* as in *alone, e* as in *system, i* as in *easily, o* as in *gallop, u* as in *circus;* ᵊ as in *fire* (fīᵊr), *hour* (ouᵊr). l and n can serve as syllabic consonants, as in *cradle* (krād′l), and *button* (but′n). See the full key inside the front cover.

DEVELOPMENT OF MAJUSCULE								
NORTH SEMITIC	GREEK		ETR.	LATIN		MODERN		
						GOTHIC	ITALIC	ROMAN
⌇	ᛘ	M	ᛘ	ᛘ	M	𝔐	*M*	M

M

DEVELOPMENT OF MINUSCULE					
ROMAN CURSIVE	ROMAN UNCIAL	CAROL. MIN.	MODERN		
			GOTHIC	ITALIC	ROMAN
∼	ɱ	m	𝔪	*m*	m

The thirteenth letter of the English alphabet developed from North Semitic *mem,* its form changing little through Greek *mu* (μ) to the modern capital and minuscule.

M, m (em), *n., pl.* **M's** or **Ms, m's** or **ms. 1.** the thirteenth letter of the English alphabet, a consonant. **2.** any spoken sound represented by the letter *M* or *m,* as in *my, summer,* or *him.* **3.** something having the shape of an M. **4.** a written or printed representation of the letter *M* or *m.* **5.** a device, as a printer's type, for reproducing the letter *M* or *m.* **6.** *Print.* em.

M, 1. mach. **2.** *Music.* major. **3.** male. **4.** married. **5.** Medieval. **6.** medium. **7.** mega-. **8.** Middle. **9.** modal auxiliary. **10.** modifier. **11.** *Econ.* monetary aggregate: issued periodically by the Federal Reserve Board as various measures of money supply (**M-1, M-1A, M-2,** etc.). Cf. **L. 12.** *Brit.* motorway (used with a road number to designate a major highway): *the M1.*

M, *Symbol.* **1.** the thirteenth in order or in a series, or, when *I* is omitted, the twelfth. **2.** (*sometimes l.c.*) the Roman numeral for 1000. Cf. **Roman numerals. 3.** *Elect.* magnetization. **4.** *Biochem.* methionine.

m, 1. *Physics.* mass. **2.** *Finance.* (of bonds) matured. **3.** medieval. **4.** medium. **5.** meter; meters. **6.** middle. **7.** *Music.* minor.

m, *Symbol, Elect.* magnetic pole strength.

M-, *U.S. Mil.* (used to designate the production model of military equipment, as the M-1 rifle.)

m-, meta-.

M'-, var. of **Mac-.**

M., 1. Majesty. **2.** Manitoba. **3.** markka; markkaa. **4.** Marquis. **5.** *Music.* measure. **6.** medicine. **7.** medium. **8.** meridian. **9.** noon. [< L *merīdiēs*] **10.** Monday. **11.** *pl.* **MM.** Monsieur. **12.** mountain.

m., 1. male. **2.** (in Germany) mark; marks. **3.** married. **4.** masculine. **5.** *Physics.* mass. **6.** medium. **7.** noon. [< L *merīdiēs*] **8.** meter. **9.** middle. **10.** mile. **11.** minute. **12.** (in prescriptions) mix. [< L *misce*] **13.** modification of. **14.** modulus. **15.** molar. **16.** month. **17.** moon. **18.** morning. **19.** mouth.

M-1 (em′wun′), *n., pl.* **M-1's.** a semiautomatic, gas-operated, .30 caliber, clip-fed rifle, with a weight of 8.56 lb. (3.88 kg): the standard U.S. Army rifle in World War II and in the Korean War. See illus. under **rifle.** Also called **Garand rifle, Garand, M-1 rifle.**

M-14 (em′fôr′tēn′, -fōr′-), *n., pl.* **M-14's.** a fully automatic, gas-operated, .30 caliber rifle developed from the M-1: replaced the M-1 as the standard U.S. Army combat rifle.

M-16 (em′siks′tēn′), *n., pl.* **M-16's.** a lightweight, fully automatic rifle shooting a small-caliber bullet at an extremely high velocity: a U.S. Army combat weapon for mobile units and jungle fighting.

ma (mä), *n. Informal.* mother. [shortened var. of MAMA]

MA, 1. Massachusetts (approved esp. for use with zip code). **2.** *Psychol.* mental age.

mA, milliampere; milliamperes.

M.A., 1. See **Master of Arts.** [< L *Magister Artium*] **2.** *Psychol.* mental age. **3.** Military Academy.

MAA, master-at-arms.

ma'am (mam, mäm; *unstressed* məm), *n.* **1.** madam (def. 1). **2.** (in Britain) a term used in addressing the queen or a royal princess. [1660–70; by contr.]

ma-and-pa (mä′ən pä′), *adj.* mom-and-pop.

maar (mär), *n. Geol.* a circular volcanic landform resulting from explosive ash eruptions. [1820–30; < G *Maar* a depression filled with standing water (esp. in the Eifel district)]

CONCISE ETYMOLOGY KEY: <, descended or borrowed from; >, whence; b., blend of, blended; c., cognate with; cf., compare; deriv., derivative; equiv., equivalent; imit., imitative; obl., oblique; r., replacing; s., stem; sp., spelling, spelled; resp., respelling, respelled; trans., translation; ?, origin unknown; *, unattested; ‡, probably earlier than. See the full key inside the front cover.

M.A.Arch., Master of Arts in Architecture.

Ma·a·riv (*Seph.* mä ä rēv′; *Ashk.* mä′riv), *n. Hebrew.* the Jewish religious service conducted every evening. Also, ***Ma·a·rib′.*** Cf. ***Minhah, Shaharith.*** [*ma'ărībh* evening prayer]

Maas (mäs), *n.* Dutch name of the **Meuse.**

Maa·sai (mä sī′, mä′sī), *n., pl.* **-sais,** (*esp. collectively*) **-sai.** Masai.

Maas·tricht (mäs′trikht), *n.* a city in the SE Netherlands, on the Maas River. 110,232. Flemish, **Maestricht.**

Ma·at (mə ät′, mä′ət), *n. Egyptian Relig.* the goddess personifying law and righteousness.

Mab (mab), *n.* See **Queen Mab.**

MAb, *Immunol.* See **monoclonal antibody.**

Ma·bel (mā′bəl), *n.* a female given name. Also, **Ma·belle** (mā bel′, mā′bel), **Ma′ble.**

mabe′ pearl′ (māb, mä′bē), a smooth cultured pearl cultivated in a hemispherical shape so that it has one flat and one convex surface. Also, **mobe pearl.** [orig. uncert.]

Mab·i·no·gi·on, The (mab′ə nō′gē ən), a collection of medieval Welsh romances that were translated (1838–49) by Lady Charlotte Guest.

Ma·ble·ton (mā′bəl tən), *n.* a town in NW Georgia. 25,111.

Ma·buse (*Fr.* ma byz′), *n.* **Jan** (*Flemish.* yän), (*Jan Gossaert* or *Gossart*), 1478?–1533?, Flemish painter.

mac[1] (mak), *n.* (*often cap.*) *Informal.* fellow; bud (a familiar term of address to a man or boy whose name is not known to the speaker). [1650–60; special use of MAC]

mac[2] (mak), *n. Informal.* **1.** a mackintosh. **2.** McIntosh. Also, **mack.** [shortened form]

Mac (mak), *n.* a male given name.

Mac-, a prefix found in many family names of Irish or Scottish Gaelic origin, as *MacBride* and *Macdonald.* Also, **Mc-, Mᶜ-, M'-.** [< Ir, ScotGael *mac* son, OIr *macc;* akin to Welsh, Cornish *mab*]

Mac., Maccabees.

M.Ac., Master of Accountancy.

ma·ca·bre (mə kä′brə, -käb′, -kä′bər), *adj.* **1.** gruesome and horrifying; ghastly; horrible. **2.** of, pertaining to, dealing with, or representing death, esp. its grimmer or uglier aspect. **3.** of or suggestive of the allegorical dance of death. Also, **ma·ca′ber.** [1400–50; < F; cf. late ME *Macabrees daunce* < MF *danse* (*de*) *Macabré,* of uncert. orig.; perh. to be identified with ML *chorēa Machabaeōrum* a representation of the deaths of Judas Maccabaeus and his brothers, but evidence is lacking; the F pron. with mute *e* is a misreading of the MF forms]

ma·ca·co (mə kä′kō, -kā′-), *n., pl.* **-cos. 1.** any of several lemurs, as *Lemur macaco.* **2.** *Obs.* macaque. [1685–95; < Pg: monkey, presumably < a Bantu language of the Atlantic coast; cf. Lingala *makako* ape]

mac·ad·am (mə kad′əm), *n.* **1.** a macadamized road or pavement. **2.** the broken stone used in making such a road. [1815–25; named after J. L. *McAdam* (1756–1836), Scottish engineer who invented it]

mac·a·da·mi·a (mak′ə dā′mē ə), *n.* **1.** any Australian tree of the genus *Macadamia,* esp. *M. ternifolia,* having whorled leaves and elongated clusters of pink flowers. **2.** Also called **macada′mia nut′.** the edible, hard-shelled seed of this tree. Also called **Queensland nut.** [1900–05; < NL, named after John *Macadam* (d. 1865), Australian chemist; see -IA]

mac·ad·am·ize (mə kad′ə mīz′), *v.t.,* **-ized, -iz·ing.** to pave by laying and compacting successive layers of broken stone, often with asphalt or hot tar. Also, *esp. Brit.,* **mac·ad′am·ise′.** [1815–25; MACADAM + -IZE] **—mac·ad′am·i·za′tion,** *n.*

Mac·a·nese (mak′ə nēz′, -nēs′), *n., pl.* **-nese,** *adj.* **—*n.* 1.** a native or inhabitant of Macao. **—*adj.* 2.** of or pertaining to Macao or its inhabitants. Also, **Ma·cao·an** (mə kou′ən). [MACA(O) + *-nese* (-*n*- + -ESE, appar. on the model of BALINESE, JAVANESE, etc.)]

Ma·cao (mə kou′), *n.* **1.** a Portuguese overseas territory in S China, in the delta of the Zhu Jiang River and including two small adjacent islands. 280,000; 6 sq. mi. (16 sq. km). **2.** the seaport and capital of this territory. Portuguese, **Macáu.**

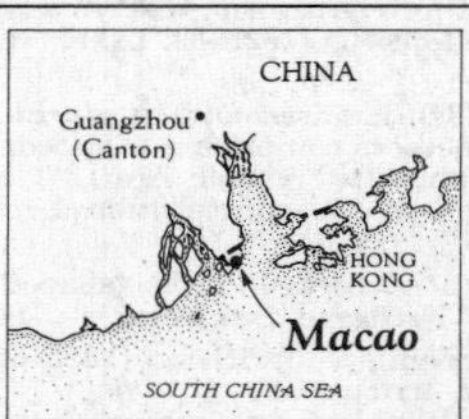

Ma·ca·pá (mə kə pä′), *n.* a city in and the capital of Amapá, in NE Brazil, at the mouth of the Amazon. 140,624.

Ma·ca·pa·gal (mä′kä pä gäl′), *n.* **Di·os·da·do** (dē′ōs dä′dō), born 1910, Philippine statesman: president 1961–65.

ma·caque (mə kak′, -käk′), *n.* any monkey of the genus *Macaca,* chiefly of Asia, characterized by cheek pouches and, usually, a short tail: several species are threatened or endangered. [1690–1700; < F < Pg *macaco* monkey. See MACACO]

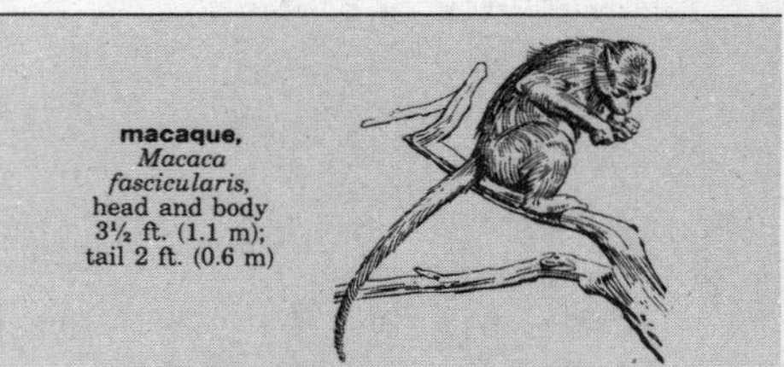

macaque, *Macaca fascicularis,* head and body 3½ ft. (1.1 m); tail 2 ft. (0.6 m)

mac·a·ro·ni (mak′ə rō′nē), *n., pl.* **-nis, -nies** for 2. **1.** small, tubular pasta prepared from wheat flour. **2.** an English dandy of the 18th century who affected Continental mannerisms, clothes, etc. Also, **maccaroni.** [1590–1600; earlier *maccaroni* < dial. It, pl. of *maccarone* (It *maccherone*). See MACAROON]

mac·a·ron·ic (mak′ə ron′ik), *adj.* **1.** composed of or characterized by Latin words mixed with vernacular words or non-Latin words given Latin endings. **2.** composed of a mixture of languages. **3.** mixed; jumbled. **—*n.* 4. macaronics,** macaronic language. **5.** a macaronic verse or other piece of writing. [1605–15; < ML *macarōnicus* < dial. It *maccarone* MACARONI + L *-icus* -IC] **—mac′a·ron′i·cal·ly,** *adv.*

macaro′ni wheat′. See **durum wheat.** [1900–05]

mac·a·roon (mak′ə ro͞on′), *n.* a drop cookie made of egg whites, sugar, usually almond paste or coconut, and sometimes a little flour. [1605–15; < MF *macaron* < dial. It *maccarone* cake or biscuit made of ground almonds; see MACARONI]

Mac·Ar·thur (mək är′thər, mə kär′-), *n.* **Douglas,** 1880–1964, U.S. general: supreme commander of allied forces in SW Pacific during World War II and of UN forces in Korea 1950–51.

Ma·cart′ney rose′ (mə kärt′nē), a trailing or climbing evergreen rose, *Rosa bracteata,* of China, having shiny leaves and large, solitary white flowers. [1805–15; named after George, 1st Earl *Macartney* (1737–1806), British diplomat]

Ma·cas·sar (mə kas′ər), *n.* a former name of **Ujung Pandang.** Also, **Makassar, Makasar.**

Macas′sar oil′, **1.** an oil derived from materials said to be obtained from Macassar, formerly used as a hairdressing. **2.** a similar oil or preparation for the hair.

Macas′sar Strait′. See **Makassar Strait.**

Ma·cáu (mə kou′), *n.* Macao.

Ma·cau·lay (mə kô′lē), *n.* **1. Dame Rose,** c1885–1958, English poet and novelist. **2. Thomas Bab·ing·ton** (bab′ing tən), **1st Baron,** 1800–59, English historian, author, and statesman. —**Ma·cau′lay·an,** *adj.* —**Ma·cau′lay·ism,** *n.*

ma·caw (mə kô′), *n.* any of various large, long-tailed parrots, chiefly of the genus *Ara,* of tropical and subtropical America, noted for their brilliant plumage and harsh voice. [< Pg *macao, macau* < Tupi *mak′o*]

Mac·beth (mək beth′, mak-), *n.* **1.** died 1057, king of Scotland 1040–57. **2.** (*italics*) a tragedy (1606?) by Shakespeare.

Mac·Bride (mək brīd′), *n.* **Seán** (shôn), 1904–88, Irish politician and diplomat, born in France: Nobel peace prize 1974.

Macc., Maccabees.

Mac·ca·bae·us (mak′ə bē′əs), *n.* **Judas** or **Ju·dah** (jo͞o′də), (*"the Hammer"*), died 160 B.C., Judean patriot: military leader 166–160 (son of Mattathias).

Mac·ca·be·an (mak′ə bē′ən), *adj.* of or pertaining to the Maccabees or Judas Maccabaeus. [1815–25; MACCABE(ES) + -AN]

Mac·ca·bees (mak′ə bēz′), *n.* **1.** (*used with a plural v.*) the members of the Hasmonean family of Jewish leaders and rulers comprising the sons of Mattathias and their descendants and reigning in Judea from 167? to 37 B.C., esp. Judas Maccabaeus and his brothers, who defeated the Syrians under Antiochus IV in 165? and rededicated the Temple in Jerusalem. **2.** (*used with a singular v.*) either of two books of the Apocrypha, I Maccabees or II Maccabees, that contain the history of the Maccabees.

mac·ca·boy (mak′ə boi′), *n.* a kind of snuff, usually rose-scented. Also, **mac′co·boy′.** [1730–40; earlier *macabao, macauba, mac(c)ouba* < F *macouba* a kind of aromatic tobacco; special use of *Macouba* place in northern Martinique, where made]

mac·ca·ro·ni (mak′ə rō′nē), *n., pl.* **-nis, -nies.** macaroni.

Mac·don·ald (mək don′əld), *n.* **1. George,** 1824–1905, Scottish novelist and poet. **2. Sir John Alexander,** 1815–91, Canadian statesman, born in Scotland: first prime minister 1867–73, 1878–91.

Mac·Don·ald (mək don′əld), *n.* **James Ramsay,** 1866–1937, British statesman and labor leader: prime minister 1924, 1929–35.

Mac·don·ough (mək don′ə), *n.* **Thomas,** 1783–1825, U.S. naval officer: defeated British on Lake Champlain 1814.

Mac·Dow·ell (mək dou′əl), *n.* **Edward Alexander,** 1861–1908, U.S. composer and pianist.

mace[1] (mās), *n.* **1.** a clublike armor-breaking weapon of war, often with a flanged or spiked metal head, used chiefly in the Middle Ages. **2.** a ceremonial staff carried before or by certain officials as a symbol of office. **3.** macebearer. **4.** *Billiards.* a light stick with a flat head, formerly used at times instead of a cue. [1250–1300; ME < OF (cf. F *masse*) large mallet < VL **mattea*; akin to L *matteola* kind of mallet; cf. Skt *matya* harrow]

mace[2] (mās), *n.* a spice ground from the layer between a nutmeg shell and its outer husk, resembling nutmeg in flavor. [1350–1400; ME, back formation from *macis* (taken as pl.) < MF < L *maccis* a spice]

Mace (mās), *Trademark.* a nonlethal spray containing purified tear gas and chemical solvents that temporarily incapacitate a person mainly by causing eye and skin irritations: used esp. as a means of subduing rioters. Also called **Chemical Mace.**

Mace (mās), *v.t.,* **Maced, Mac·ing.** (*sometimes l.c.*) to attack with Mace spray. [see MACE]

mace·bear·er (mās′bâr′ər), *n.* an official, as of a city or legislative body, who carries a ceremonial mace before dignitaries. [1545–55; MACE[1] + BEARER]

Maced., Macedonia.

mac·é·doine (mas′i dwän′), *n.* **1.** a mixture of fruits or vegetables, often served as a salad. **2.** a medley. [1810–20; < F, after *Macédoine* MACEDONIA, prob. an allusion to the variety of peoples in the region]

Mac·e·do·ni·a (mas′i dō′nē ə, -dōn′yə), *n.* **1.** Also, **Mac·e·don** (mas′i don′). an ancient kingdom in the Balkan Peninsula, in S Europe: now a region in N Greece, SW Bulgaria, and the Republic of Macedonia. **2.** a republic in S Europe: formerly (1945–92) a constituent republic of Yugoslavia. 2,300,000; 9928 sq. mi. (25,713 sq. km). Cap.: Skopje.

Mac·e·do·ni·an (mas′i dō′nē ən), *n.* **1.** a native or inhabitant of Macedonia. **2.** a Slavic language of modern Macedonia. **3.** an extinct language of ancient Macedonia, an Indo-European language of uncertain relationship within the Indo-European language family. —*adj.* **4.** of or pertaining to Macedonia, its inhabitants, or their language. [1550–60; MACEDONI(A) + -AN]

Ma·cei·ó (mä′sä ô′), *n.* a seaport in and the capital of Alagoas, in E Brazil. 409,191.

mac·er (mā′sər), *n.* **1.** macebearer. **2.** (in Scotland) an officer who attends the Court of Session and carries out its orders. [1300–50; ME < AF; MF *massier.* See MACE[1], -ER[2]]

mac·er·ate (mas′ə rāt′), *v.,* **-at·ed, -at·ing.** —*v.t.* **1.** to soften or separate into parts by steeping in a liquid. **2.** to soften or decompose (food) by the action of a solvent. **3.** to cause to grow thin. —*v.i.* **4.** to undergo maceration. **5.** to become thin or emaciated; waste away. [1540–50; < L *mācerātus* (ptp. of *mācerāre* to make soft, weaken, steep); see -ATE[1]] —**mac′er·at′er, mac′er·a′tor,** *n.* —**mac′er·a′tive,** *adj.*
—**Syn. 5.** shrink, shrivel, fade, wither.

mac·er·a·tion (mas′ə rā′shən), *n.* **1.** the act or process of macerating. **2.** a process in winemaking in which the crushed grape skins are left in the juice until they have imparted the desired color or the proper amount of tannins and aroma. [1485–95 < L *mācerātiōn-,* s. of *mācerātiō;* see MACERATE, -ION]

mac·far·lane (mək fär′lin), *n.* an overcoat with an attached cape and two slits in front near the waist. Also, **Mac·far′lane, Mac·Far′lane.** [special use of surname *MacFarlane*]

mach (mäk), *n.* a number indicating the ratio of the speed of an object to the speed of sound in the medium through which the object is moving. *Abbr.:* M Also, **Mach.** Also called **mach number, Mach number.** [named after E. MACH]

Mach (mäk; *Ger.* mäKH), *n.* **Ernst** (ERNSt), 1838–1916, Austrian physicist, psychologist, and philosopher.

mach., **1.** machine. **2.** machinery. **3.** machinist.

Mach·a·bees (mak′ə bēz′), *n.* (*used with a singular v.*) *Douay Bible.* Maccabees (def. 2).

Ma·cha·do de As·siz (mä shä′do͝o di ä sēs′), **Jo·a·quim Ma·ri·a** (zhô′ä kim mä Rē′ä), 1839–1908, Brazilian writer.

Ma·cha·do y Mo·ra·les (mä chä′thô ē mô Rä′les), **Ge·rar·do** (he Rär′thô), 1871–1939, president of Cuba 1925–33.

Ma·cha·do y Ru·iz (mä chä′thô ē Ro͞o ēth′), **An·to·nio** (än tô′nyô), 1875–1939, Spanish writer.

Ma·cha·on (mə kā′on), *n.* (in the *Iliad*) a son of Asclepius who was famed as a healer and who served as physician of the Greeks in the Trojan War.

Ma·chaut (*Fr.* mA shō′), *n.* **Guil·laume de** (*Fr.* gē yōm′ də). See **Guillaume de Machaut.** Also, **Ma·chault′.**

mache (mäsh), *n.* See **corn salad.** Also, **mâche.** [1820–30; < F *mâche,* perh. by apheresis (or by assoc. with *mâcher* to chew) from dial. *pomache,* with same sense, perh. < VL **pōmasca,* deriv. of L *pōmum* fruit]

Ma·chel (mə shel′), *n.* **Sa·mo·ra Moi·sés** (sə môr′ə moi zes′), 1933–86, Mozambique political leader: president 1975–86.

Mach·en (mak′ən), *n.* **Arthur,** 1863–1947, Welsh novelist and essayist.

ma chère (mA sheR′), *French.* (referring to a woman or girl) my dear. Cf. ***mon cher.***

ma·chet·e (mə shet′ē, -chet′ē), *n.* **1.** a large heavy knife used esp. in Latin-American countries in cutting sugarcane and clearing underbrush and as a weapon. **2.** a tarpon, *Elops affinis,* of the eastern Pacific Ocean, having an elongated, compressed body. [1825–35; < Sp, equiv. to *mach(o)* mallet (cf. MACE[1]) + *-ete* n. suffix]

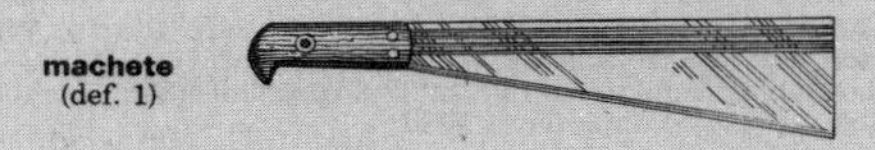
machete (def. 1)

Mach·i·a·vel·li (mak′ē ə vel′ē; *It.* mä′kyä vel′lē), *n.* **Nic·co·lò di Ber·nar·do** (nēk′kô lô′ dē beR när′dô), 1469–1527, Italian statesman, political philosopher, and author.

Mach·i·a·vel·li·an (mak′ē ə vel′ē ən), *adj.* **1.** of, like, or befitting Machiavelli. **2.** being or acting in accordance with the principles of government analyzed in Machiavelli's *The Prince,* in which political expediency is placed above morality and the use of craft and deceit to maintain the authority and carry out the policies of a ruler is described. **3.** characterized by subtle or unscrupulous cunning, deception, expediency, or dishonesty: *He resorted to Machiavellian tactics in order to get ahead.* —*n.* **4.** a follower of the principles analyzed or described in *The Prince,* esp. with reference to techniques of political manipulation. Also, **Mach′i·a·vel′i·an.** [1560–70; MACHIAVELLI + -AN] —**Mach′i·a·vel′li·an·ism, Mach′·i·a·vel′lism,** *n.* —**Mach′i·a·vel′li·an·ly,** *adv.*

ma·chic·o·late (mə chik′ə lāt′), *v.t.,* **-lat·ed, -lat·ing.** to provide with machicolations. [1765–75; < ML *machecoll(um),* a Latinization of MF **machecol* lit., (it) breaks (the) neck (from the use of such openings to drop projectiles on an ascending attacker; *mache,* 3d sing. pres. of *macher* to beat, break, bruise (appar. of expressive orig.) + *col* neck (see COLLAR)) + -ATE[1]; cf. late ME *machecollyd* machicolated]

ma·chic·o·la·tion (mə chik′ə lā′shən), *n. Archit.* **1.** an opening in the floor between the corbels of a projecting gallery or parapet, as on a wall or in the vault of a passage, through which missiles, molten lead, etc., might be cast upon an enemy beneath. **2.** a projecting gallery or parapet with such openings. [1780–90; MACHICOLATE + -ION]

mach·i·lid (mak′ə lid, mə kī′-), *n.* See **jumping bristletail.** [< NL *Machilidae* family name, equiv. to *Machilid-,* s. of *Machilis* a genus + *-idae* -ID[2]]

ma·chin·a·ble (mə shē′nə bəl), *adj.* **1.** (of a material) capable of being cut or shaped with machine tools. Cf. **free-machining. 2.** (of a letter or package) capable of being safely sorted by mail machinery, as a parcel sorter. Also, **ma·chine′a·ble.** [1915–20; MACHINE + -ABLE] —**ma·chin′a·bil′i·ty,** *n.*

mach·i·nate (mak′ə nāt′), *v.i., v.t.,* **-nat·ed, -nat·ing.** to contrive or plot, esp. artfully or with evil purpose: *to machinate the overthrow of the government.* [1590–1600; < L *māchinātus* ptp. of *māchinārī* to invent, contrive, devise artfully. See MACHINE, -ATE[1]] —**mach′i·na′tor,** *n.*

mach·i·na·tion (mak′ə nā′shən), *n.* **1.** an act or instance of machinating. **2.** Usually, **machinations.** crafty schemes; plots; intrigues. [1375–1425; late ME *machinacion* < L *māchinātiōn-* (s. of *māchinātiō*). See MACHINATE, -ION]
—**Syn. 2.** stratagem, device.

ma·chine (mə shēn′), *n., v.,* **-chined, -chin·ing.** —*n.* **1.** an apparatus consisting of interrelated parts with separate functions, used in the performance of some kind of work: *a sewing machine.* **2.** a mechanical apparatus or contrivance; mechanism. **3.** *Mech.* **a.** a device that transmits or modifies force or motion. **b.** Also called **simple machine.** any of six or more elementary mechanisms, as the lever, wheel and axle, pulley, screw, wedge, and inclined plane. **c.** Also called **complex machine.** a combination of simple machines. **4.** *Older Use.* **a.** an automobile or airplane. **b.** a typewriter. **5.** a bicycle or motorcycle. **6.** a vending machine: *a cigarette machine.* **7.** any complex agency or operating system: *the machine of government.* **8.** an organized group of persons that conducts or controls the activities of a political party or organization: *He heads the Democratic machine in our city.* **9.** a person or thing that acts in a mechanical or automatic manner: *Routine work had turned her into a machine.* **10.** any of various contrivances, esp. those formerly used in theater, for producing stage effects **11.** some agency, personage, incident or other feature introduced for effect into a literary composition. —*v.t.* **12.** to make, prepare, or finish with a machine or with machine tools. [1540–50; < F < L *māchina* < Doric Gk *māchanā́* pulley, akin to *mâchos* contrivance; cf. MECHANIC] —**ma·chine′less,** *adj.*

machine′ bolt′, a threaded fastener, used with a nut for connecting metal parts, having a thread diameter of about ¼ in. (6.4 mm) or more and a square or hexagonal head for tightening by a wrench. Cf. **cap screw, machine screw, stove bolt.** See illus. under **bolt**[1].

machine′ gun′, a small arm operated by a mechanism, able to deliver a rapid and continuous fire of bullets as long as the trigger is pressed. [1865–70]

ma·chine-gun (mə shēn′gun′), *v.t.,* **-gunned, -gun·ning.** to shoot at with a machine gun. [1880–85] —**machine′ gun′ner.**

machine′ lan′guage, *Computers.* a coding system built into the hardware of a computer, requiring no translation before being run.

ma·chine·like (mə shēn′līk′), *adj.* like a machine, as in regular movement or uniform pattern of operation: *to conduct business with machinelike efficiency.* [1690–1700; MACHINE + -LIKE]

machine′ pis′tol, a fully automatic pistol; submachine gun. Also called **burp gun.** [1935–40]

ma·chine-read·a·ble (mə shēn′rē′də bəl), *adj. Computers.* of or pertaining to data encoded on an appropriate medium and in a form suitable for processing by computer. [1960–65]

machine′ ri′fle. See **automatic rifle.**

ma·chin·er·y (mə shē′nə rē), *n., pl.* **-er·ies. 1.** an assemblage of machines or mechanical apparatuses: *the machinery of a factory.* **2.** the parts of a machine, collectively: *the machinery of a watch.* **3.** a group of people or a system by which action is maintained or by which some result is obtained: *the machinery of government.* **4.** a group of contrivances for producing stage effects. **5.** the group or aggregate of literary machines, esp. those of supernatural agency **(epic machinery)** in an epic poem. [1680–90; MACHINE + -ERY]
—**Syn. 3.** organization, structure, setup.

machin′ery steel′, low-carbon steel that can be easily machined. Also called **machine′ steel′.**

machine′ screw′, a threaded fastener, either used with a nut or driven into a tapped hole, usually having a diameter of about ¼ in. (6.4 mm) or less and a slotted head for tightening by a screwdriver. Cf. **cap screw, machine bolt.**

machine′ shop′, a workshop in which metal and other substances are cut, shaped, etc., by machine tools. [1820–30, *Amer.*]

ma·chine-stitch (mə shēn′stich′), *v.t.* to sew on a sewing machine. [1895–1900]

machine′ tool′, a power-operated machine, as a lathe, used for general cutting and shaping of metal and other substances. [1860–65] —**ma·chine′-tooled′,** *adj.*

machine′ vi′sion, *Computers.* See **computer vision.**

ma·chine-wash (mə shēn′wosh′, -wôsh′), *v.t., v.i.* to launder by washing machine rather than by hand. [1955–60] —**ma·chine′-wash′a·ble,** *adj.*

machine′ word′, *Computers.* word (def. 9).

CONCISE PRONUNCIATION KEY: *act, cāpe, dâre, pärt; set, ēqual; if, īce; ox, ōver, ôrder, oil, bo͝ok, bo͞ot, out; up, ûrge; child; sing; shoe; thin,* that; zh *as in* treasure. ə = *a as in* alone, *e as in* system, *i as in* easily, *o as in* gallop, *u as in* circus; ᵊ *as in* fire (fīᵊr), hour (ouᵊr). l *and* n *can serve as syllabic consonants, as in* cradle (krād′l), *and* button (but′n). *See the full key inside the front cover.*

ma•chin•ist (mə shē′nist), *n.* **1.** a person who operates machinery, esp. a skilled operator of machine tools. **2.** a person who makes or repairs machines. **3.** *U.S. Navy.* a warrant officer whose duty is to assist the engineering officer in the engine room. [1700–10; MACHINE + -IST]

ma•chis•mo (mä chēz′mō, -chiz′-, mə-), *n.* **1.** a strong or exaggerated sense of manliness; an assumptive attitude that virility, courage, strength, and entitlement to dominate are attributes or concomitants of masculinity. **2.** a strong or exaggerated sense of power or the right to dominate: *The military campaign was an exercise in national machismo.* [1945–50, *Amer.*; < Sp; see MACHO, -ISM]

mach•me•ter (mäk′mē′tər, mak′-), *n. Aeron.* a device that indicates airspeed relative to the speed of sound. [MACH + -METER]

mach′ num′ber, mach. Also, **Mach′ num′ber.** [1935–40]

ma•cho (mä′chō), *adj., n., pl.* **-chos.** —*adj.* **1.** having or characterized by qualities considered manly, esp. when manifested in an assertive, self-conscious, or dominating way. **2.** having a strong or exaggerated sense of power or the right to dominate. —*n.* **3.** assertive or aggressive manliness; machismo. **4.** an assertively virile, dominating, or domineering male. [1925–30, *Amer.*; < Sp: lit., male < L *masculus;* see MASCULINE]

Mach•pe•lah (mak pē′lä), *n.* the site of a cave, probably in the ancient city of Hebron, where Abraham, Sarah, Rebekah, Isaac, Jacob, and Leah were buried. Gen. 23:19; 25:9; 49:30; 50:13.

ma•chree (mə krē′, mə KHRē′), *n. Irish Eng.* my dear. [1820–30; < Ir *mo chroidhe* lit., my heart]

Mach′ scale′ (mak), *Psychol.* a scale that measures how much deceit and manipulation one will approve or condone in order to achieve some end. [1965–70; short for MACHIAVELLI, perh. with play on MACH]

Mach's′ prin′ciple, *Physics.* the proposition that there is no absolute space and that the inertia and acceleration of a body are determined by all of the matter of the universe. [named after E. MACH]

Ma•chu Pic•chu (mä′cho͞o pēk′cho͞o, pē′cho͞o), the site of an ancient Incan and pre-Incan city, about 7000 ft. (2130 m) above sea level in the Andes, in S central Peru.

-machy, a combining form meaning "fighting," used in the formation of compound words: *logomachy.* [< Gk *-machia,* equiv. to *mách(ē)* battle + *-ia* -Y[3]]

mach•zor (*Seph.* mäKH zôr′; *Ashk.* mäKH′zôr, -zôr, -zər), *n., pl.* ***mach•zo•rim*** (*Seph.* mäKH zô rēm′; *Ashk.* mäKH zô′rim), *Eng.* **mach•zors.** *Hebrew.* mahzor.

Ma•cí•as Ngue•ma Bi•yo•go (mə sē′əs əng gwä′mə bē yō′gō), a former name of **Bioko.** Also called **Ma•cí′•as Ngue′ma.**

mac•in•tosh (mak′in tosh′), *n.* mackintosh.

Mac•in•tosh (mak′in tosh′), *n.* **Charles,** 1766–1843, Scottish chemist, inventor, and manufacturer.

Mac•I•ver (mək ī′vər, mə kī′-, mə kē′-), *n.* **1. Loren,** born 1909, U.S. painter. **2. Robert Morrison,** 1882–1970, U.S. sociologist, born in Scotland.

mack[1] (mak), *n. Slang.* a pimp. [1885–90; by shortening of *mackerel* pimp < MF; see MACKEREL]

mack[2] (mak), *n. Informal.* mac[2].

Mack (mak), *n.* **1. Con•nie** (kon′ē), (*Cornelius McGillicuddy*), 1862–1956, U.S. baseball player and manager. **2.** a male given name.

Mac•kay (mə kī′), *n.* a seaport in E Australia. 35,361.

Ma•cke (mä′kə), *n.* **Au•gust** (ou′go͝ost), 1887–1914, German painter.

Mack•en•sen (mä′kən zən), *n.* **Au•gust von** (ou′go͝ost fən), 1849–1945, German field marshal.

Mac•ken•zie (mə ken′zē), *n.* **1. Sir Alexander,** 1764–1820, Scottish explorer in Canada. **2. Alexander,** 1822–92, Canadian statesman, born in Scotland: prime minister 1873–78. **3. William Lyon,** 1795–1861, Canadian political leader and journalist, born in Scotland. **4.** a river in NW Canada, flowing NW from the Great Slave Lake to the Arctic Ocean. 1120 mi. (1800 km) long; with tributaries 2525 mi. (4065 km) long. **5.** a district in the SW Northwest Territories of Canada. 527,490 sq. mi. (1,366,200 sq. km).

Macken′zie Moun′tains, a mountain range in the E Yukon and W Northwest Territories, in NW Canada. Highest peak, Keele Peak, 9750 ft. (2971 m).

mack•er•el (mak′ər əl, mak′rəl), *n., pl.* (*esp. collectively*) **-el,** (*esp. referring to two or more kinds or species*) **-els. 1.** a food fish, *Scomber scombrus,* of the North Atlantic, having wavy cross markings on the back. **2.** See **Spanish mackerel. 3.** any of various similar fishes, as the Atka mackerel. [1250–1300; ME < OF, perh. same word as MF *maquerel* pimp < MD *makelare* broker (by metathesis), equiv. to *makel(en)* to bring together + *-are* -ER[1]]

CONCISE ETYMOLOGY KEY: <, descended or borrowed from; >, whence; b., blend of, blended; c., cognate with; cf., compare; deriv., derivative; equiv., equivalent; imit., imitative; obl., oblique; r., replacing; s., stem; sp., spelling, spelled; resp., respelling, respelled; trans., translation; ?, origin unknown; *, unattested; ‡, probably earlier than. See the full key inside the front cover.

mack′erel gull′, tern[1]. [1790–1800, *Amer.*]

mack′erel shark′, any of several fierce sharks of the family Lamidae, including the great white shark and the mako. [1810–20]

mack′erel sky′, an extensive group of cirrocumulus or altocumulus clouds, esp. when well-marked in their arrangement: so called because of a resemblance to the scales on a mackerel. [1660–70]

Mack•i•nac (mak′ə nô′), *n.* **1. Straits of,** a strait between the peninsulas of Upper Michigan and Lower Michigan, connecting lakes Huron and Michigan. **2.** Also, **Mack′inac Is′land.** an island in Lake Huron at the entrance of this strait. 517; 3 mi. (5 km) long.

Mack′inac Bridge′, a suspension bridge over the Straits of Mackinac, connecting the Upper and Lower peninsulas of Michigan: one of the longest suspension bridges in the world. 3800-ft. (1158-m) center span; 7400 ft. (2256 m) in total length.

mack•i•naw (mak′ə nô′), *n.* a short double-breasted coat of a thick woolen material, commonly plaid. Also called **Mack′inaw coat′, mack′inaw coat′.** [1755–65; sp. var. of MACKINAC] —**mack′i•nawed′,** *adj.*

Mack′inaw blan′ket, a thick woolen blanket, often woven with bars of color, formerly used in the northern and western U.S. by Indians, loggers, etc. [1815–25]

Mack′inaw boat′, a flat-bottomed boat with sharp prow and square stern, propelled by oars and sometimes sails, formerly widely used on the upper Great Lakes.

Mack′inaw trout′. See **lake trout.** [1830–40, *Amer.*]

mack•in•tosh (mak′in tosh′), *n.* **1.** a raincoat made of rubberized cloth. **2.** such cloth. **3.** *Chiefly Brit.* any raincoat. Also, **macintosh.** [1830–40; named after Charles *Macintosh* (1766–1843), its inventor] —**mack′•in•toshed′,** *adj.*

Mack•in•tosh (mak′in tosh′), *n.* **Charles Ren•nie** (ren′ē), 1868–1928, Scottish architect and designer.

mack•le (mak′əl), *n., v.,* **-led, -ling.** —*n.* **1.** a blur in printing, as from a double impression. —*v.t., v.i.* **2.** to blur, as from a double impression in printing. Also, **macule.** [1585–95; var. of earlier *macle, makle;* earlier *macule* MACULE]

Mac•lar•en (mək lar′ən, mə klar′-), *n.* **I•an** (ē′ən, ī′ən). See **Watson, John.**

Mac•lau•rin (mək lôr′in, mə klôr′-), *n.* **Colin,** 1698–1746, Scottish mathematician.

Maclau′rin se′ries, *Math.* a Taylor series in which the reference point is zero. [1905–10; named after C. MACLAURIN]

ma•cle (mak′əl), *n. Mineral.* **1.** chiastolite. **2.** a twinned crystal. [1720–30; < F < L *macula.* See MACULA]

Mac•Leish (mak lēsh′, mə klēsh′), *n.* **Archibald,** 1892–1982, U.S. poet and dramatist.

Mac•Len•nan (mə klen′ən), *n.* **(John) Hugh,** 1907–90, Canadian novelist and essayist.

Mac•leod (mə kloud′), *n.* **1. Fiona.** See **Sharp, William. 2. John James Rick•ard** (rik′ərd), 1876–1935, Scottish physiologist: one of the discoverers of insulin; Nobel prize for medicine 1923.

Mac•Ma•hon (mak ma ôN′), *n.* **Ma•rie Ed•mé Pa•trice Mau•rice** (ma rē′ ed mā pa trēs′ mō rēs′), **Count de** (*Duke of Magenta*), 1808–93, president of France 1873–79.

Mac•Man•us (mək man′əs), *n.* **Seu•mas** (shā′məs), 1869–1960, Irish poet and short-story writer.

Mac•mil•lan (mək mil′ən), *n.* **Harold,** 1894–1986, British statesman: prime minister 1957–63.

Mac•Mil•lan (mək mil′ən), *n.* **Donald Bax•ter** (bak′stər), 1874–1970, U.S. arctic explorer.

Mac•Mon•nies (mək mun′ēz), *n.* **Frederick William,** 1863–1937, U.S. sculptor.

Mac•Neice (mək nēs′), *n.* **Louis,** 1907–63, British poet, born in Northern Ireland.

ma•co (mä′kō), *n.* an Egyptian cotton, used esp. in the manufacture of hosiery and undergarments. [named after *Mako* Bey, 19th-century Egyptian officer]

ma•co•ma (mə kō′mə), *n.* any marine bivalve mollusk of the genus *Macoma,* having a glossy, thin, usually white shell. [< NL]

Ma•comb (mə kōm′), *n.* a city in NW Illinois. 19,632.

Ma•con (mā′kən), *n.* **1. Nathaniel,** 1758–1837, U.S. politician: Speaker of the House 1801–07. **2.** a city in central Georgia. 116,860.

Mâ•con (mä kôN′), *n.* **1.** a city in and the capital of Saône-et-Loire, in E central France. 40,490. **2.** a Burgundy wine, usually white and dry, from the area around Mâcon.

Ma•coun (mə ko͞on′), *n.* a juicy, late-ripening variety of apple that originated in Canada.

Mac•pher•son (mək fûr′sən), *n.* **James,** 1736–96, Scottish author and translator.

MacPher′son strut′, an automobile suspension-system component that consists of a strut combined with a spring and shock absorber and connects the wheel to the frame of the vehicle.

Mac•quar•ie (mə kwôr′ē, -kwor′ē), *n.* a river in SE Australia, in New South Wales, flowing NW to the Darling River. 750 mi. (1210 km) long.

mac•ra•mé (mak′rə mā′), *n., v.t.,* **-méd** or **-méed, -mé•ing.** —*n.* **1.** an elaborately patterned lacelike webbing made of hand-knotted cord, yarn, or the like, and used for wall decorations, hanging baskets, garments, accessories, etc. **2.** the technique or art of producing macramé. —*v.t.* **3.** to make or produce using macramé: *to macramé a wall hanging.* Also, **mac′ra•me′.** [1865–70; < F < It *macramè* kind of fringe on hand towels < Turk *makrama* napkin, face towel < Ar *miqrama* embroidered coverlet]

Mac•read•y (mək rē′dē, mə krē′-), *n.* **William Charles,** 1793–1873, English actor.

mac•ro (mak′rō), *adj., n., pl.* **-ros.** —*adj.* **1.** very large in scale, scope, or capability. **2.** of or pertaining to macroeconomics. —*n.* **3.** anything very large in scale, scope, or capability. **4.** *Photog.* a macro lens. **5.** Also called **macroinstruction.** *Computers.* an instruction that represents a sequence of instructions in abbreviated form. **6.** macroeconomics. [independent use of MACRO-, taken as an adjective, or by shortening of words with MACRO- as initial element]

macro-, a combining form meaning "large," "long," "great," "excessive," used in the formation of compound words, contrasting with *micro-: macrocosm; macrofossil; macrograph; macroscopic.* Also, *esp. before a vowel,* **macr-.** [< Gk *makro-,* comb. form of *makrós* long; c. L *macer* lean; see MEAGER]

mac•ro•bi•o•sis (mak′rō bī ō′sis), *n. Med.* long life. [MACRO- + BIOSIS]

mac•ro•bi•ot•ic (mak′rō bī ot′ik), *adj.* **1.** of or pertaining to macrobiotics or its dietary practices. **2.** of, pertaining to, or serving macrobiotic food: *a macrobiotic restaurant.* **3.** long-lived. **4.** lengthening the life span. —*n.* **5.** a person who adheres to the principles of macrobiotics or who follows its dietary practices. [1790–1800; MACRO- + BIOTIC] —**mac′ro•bi•ot′i•cal•ly,** *adv.*

mac•ro•bi•ot•ics (mak′rō bī ot′iks), *n.* (*used with a singular v.*) a philosophically oriented program incorporating elements from several ancient cultures and emphasizing harmony with nature, esp. through adherence to a diet consisting primarily of whole grains, beans, vegetables, and moderate amounts of seafood and fruit. [1860–65 for general sense "the science of prolonging life"; see MACROBIOTIC, -ICS]

mac•ro•car•pous (mak′rō kär′pəs), *adj.* having large fruit. [MACRO- + -CARPOUS]

mac•ro•ce•phal•ic (mak′rō sə fal′ik), *adj.* **1.** *Cephalom.* being or having a head with a large cranial capacity. **2.** *Craniom.* being or having a skull with a large cranial capacity. Also, **mac•ro•ceph•a•lous** (mak′rō-sef′ə ləs). [1850–55; < Gk *makroképhal(os)* large-headed (see MACRO-, -CEPHALOUS) + -IC] —**mac′ro•ceph′a•ly,** *n.*

mac•ro•cli•mate (mak′rə klī′mit), *n.* the general climate of a large area, as of a continent or country. Cf. **microclimate.** [1935–40; MACRO- + CLIMATE] —**mac•ro•cli•mat•ic** (mak′rō klī mat′ik), *adj.* —**mac′ro•cli•mat′i•cal•ly,** *adv.*

mac•ro•cli•ma•tol•o•gy (mak′rō klī′mə tol′ə jē), *n.* the study of the climatic conditions of a large area. Cf. **macrometeorology, microclimatology.** [MACRO- + CLIMATOLOGY]

mac•ro•cosm (mak′rə koz′əm), *n.* **1.** the great world or universe; the universe considered as a whole (opposed to *microcosm*). **2.** the total or entire complex structure of something: *the macrocosm of war.* **3.** a representation of a smaller unit or entity by a larger one, presumably of a similar structure. [1590–1600; < F *macrocosme* < ML *macrocosmus.* See MACRO-, COSMOS] —**mac′ro•cos′mic,** *adj.* —**mac′ro•cos′mi•cal•ly,** *adv.*

mac•ro•cy•clic (mak′rō sī′klik, -sik′lik), *adj. Chem.* having a ring structure consisting of more than 12 atoms. [1945–50; MACRO- + CYCLIC]

mac•ro•cyst (mak′rə sist′), *n. Mycol.* a large cyst or spore case, esp. the encysted, resting plasmodium of a slime mold. [MACRO- + CYST]

mac•ro•cyte (mak′rə sīt′), *n. Pathol.* an abnormally large red blood cell. [1885–90; MACRO- + -CYTE] —**mac•ro•cyt•ic** (mak′rə sit′ik), *adj.*

mac•ro•dome (mak′rə dōm′), *n. Crystall.* a dome the faces of which are parallel to the greater lateral axis. Cf. **brachydome.** [1880–85; MACRO- + DOME]

mac•ro•don•tia (mak′rə don′shə, -shē ə), *n.* the condition of having abnormally large teeth. Also, **mac•ro•dont•ism** (mak′rə don tiz′əm). Also called **megadontia, megadontism, megadonty.** [< NL; see MACRO-, -ODONT, -IA] —**mac′ro•dont′, mac′ro•don′tic,** *adj.*

mac•ro•ec•o•nom•ics (mak′rō ek′ə nom′iks, -ē′kə-), *n.* (*used with a singular v.*) the branch of economics dealing with the broad and general aspects of an economy, as the relationship between the income and investments of a country as a whole. Cf. **microeconomics.** [1945–50; MACRO- + ECONOMICS] —**mac′ro•ec′o•nom′ic,** *adj.* —**mac•ro•e•con•o•mist** (mak′rō i kon′ə-mist), *n.*

mac•ro•etch (mak′rō ech′), *v.t.* to etch deeply into the surface of (a metal). [MACRO- + ETCH]

mac•ro•ev•o•lu•tion (mak′rō ev′ə lo͞o′shən *or, esp. Brit.,* -ē′və-), *n. Biol.* major evolutionary transition from one type of organism to another occurring at the level of the species and higher taxa. [1935–40; MACRO- + EVOLUTION] —**mac′ro•ev′o•lu′tion•ar′y,** *adj.*

mac•ro•form (mak′rə fôrm′), *n.* an image or reproduction, as of a document, in a size that permits reading or viewing with the naked eye. [1965–70; MACRO- + FORM, on the model of MICROFORM]

mac•ro•fos•sil (mak′rə fos′il), *n.* a fossil large enough to be studied and identified without the use of a microscope. Cf. **microfossil.** [1935–40; MACRO- + FOSSIL]

mac•ro•gam•ete (mak′rō gam′ēt, -gə mēt′), *n. Cell Biol.* (in heterogamous reproduction) the larger and usually female of a pair of conjugating gametes. [1895–1900; MACRO- + GAMETE]

mac•ro•graph (mak′rə graf′, -gräf′), *n.* a representation of an object that is of the same size as or larger than the object. [MACRO- + -GRAPH]

ma•crog•ra•phy (mə krog′rə fē), *n.* **1.** examination or study of an object with the naked eye (opposed to *micrography*). **2.** markedly or excessively large handwriting. [1895–1900; MACRO- + -GRAPHY] —**mac•ro•graph•ic** (mak′rə graf′ik), *adj.*

mac•ro•in•struc•tion (mak′rō in struk′shən), *n. Computers.* macro (def. 5). [1955–60; MACRO- + INSTRUCTION]

mac•ro•lec•i•thal (mak′rō les′ə thəl), *adj. Embryol.* megalecithal. [MACRO- + LECITHAL]

mac′ro lens′ (mak′rō), *Photog.* a lens used to bring into focus objects very close to the camera. [1960–65]

mac•ro•lin•guis•tics (mak′rō ling gwis′tiks), *n.* (*used with a singular v.*) a field of study concerned with language in its broadest sense and including cultural and behavioral features associated with language. [MACRO- + LINGUISTICS] —**mac′ro•lin•guis′tic,** *adj.*

mac•ro•lith (mak′rə lith′), *n. Archaeol.* a stone tool about 1 ft. (30 cm) long. Cf. **microlith, tranchet.** [MACRO- + -LITH]

mac•ro•mere (mak′rə mēr′), *n. Embryol.* one of the large blastomeres that form toward the vegetal pole in embryos undergoing unequal cleavage. [1875–80; MACRO- + -MERE]

mac•ro•me•te•or•ol•o•gy (mak′rō mē′tē ə rol′ə jē), *n.* the study of large-scale atmospheric phenomena, as the general circulation of the air or global weather conditions. Cf. **macroclimatology, mesometeorology, micrometeorology.** [MACRO- + METEOROLOGY] —**mac•ro•me•te•or•o•log•i•cal** (mak′rō mē′tē ər ə loj′i kəl), *adj.*

mac•ro•min•er•al (mak′rō min′ər əl), *n. Nutrition.* any mineral required in the diet in relatively large amounts, esp. calcium, iron, magnesium, phosphorus, potassium, and zinc. [MACRO- + MINERAL]

mac•ro•mol•e•cule (mak′rə mol′ə kyo͞ol′), *n. Chem.* a very large molecule, as a colloidal particle, protein, or esp. a polymer, composed of hundreds or thousands of atoms. [1885–90; MACRO- + MOLECULE] —**mac•ro•mo•lec•u•lar** (mak′rō mə lek′yə lər), *adj.*

mac•ro•mu•tant (mak′rō myo͞ot′nt), *adj.* **1.** undergoing macromutation. **2.** resulting from macromutation. —*n.* **3.** a new type of organism resulting from macromutation. [MACRO- + MUTANT]

mac•ro•mu•ta•tion (mak′rō myo͞o tā′shən), *n. Genetics.* a mutation that has a profound effect on the resulting organism, as a change in a regulatory gene that controls the expression of many structural genes. [MACRO- + MUTATION]

ma•cron (mā′kron, mak′ron), *n.* a horizontal line used as a diacritic over a vowel to indicate that it has a long sound or other specified pronunciation, as (ā) in *fate* (fāt). [1850–55; n. use of Gk *makrón,* neut. of *makrós* long. See MACRO-]

mac•ro•nu•cle•ate (mak′rō no͞o′klē it, -āt′, -nyo͞o′-), *adj.* having a macronucleus. [MACRONUCLE(US) + -ATE[1]]

mac•ro•nu•cle•us (mak′rō no͞o′klē əs, -nyo͞o′-), *n. Biol.* the larger of the two types of nuclei occurring in ciliate protozoans, having a multiple set of chromosomes and functioning in cell metabolism and protein synthesis. Cf. **micronucleus.** [1890–95; < NL; see MACRO-, NUCLEUS] —**mac′ro•nu′cle•ar,** *adj.*

mac•ro•nu•tri•ent (mak′rō no͞o′trē ənt, -nyo͞o′-), *n.* **1.** *Nutrition.* any of the nutritional components of the diet that are required in relatively large amounts: protein, carbohydrate, fat, and the macrominerals. **2.** *Bot.* any of the three chemical elements required by plants in relatively large amounts: nitrogen, phosphorus, and potassium. Cf. **micronutrient.** [1940–45; MACRO- + NUTRIENT]

mac•ro•or•gan•ism (mak′rō ôr′gə niz′əm), *n.* an organism that can be seen with the naked eye. [MACRO- + ORGANISM]

mac•ro•phage (mak′rə fāj′), *n. Cell Biol.* a large white blood cell, occurring principally in connective tissue and in the bloodstream, that ingests foreign particles and infectious microorganisms by phagocytosis. [1885–90; < NL *macrophagus.* See MACRO-, -PHAGE] —**mac•ro•phag•ic** (mak′rə faj′ik), *adj.*

mac•ro•phys•ics (mak′rə fiz′iks), *n.* (*used with a singular v.*) the branch of physics that deals with physical objects large enough to be observed and treated directly. [1905–10; MACRO- + PHYSICS]

mac•ro•phyte (mak′rə fīt′), *n. Bot.* a plant, esp. a marine plant, large enough to be visible to the naked eye. [1905–10; MACRO- + -PHYTE]

mac•ro•plank•ton (mak′rō plangk′tən), *n.* planktonic organisms of about 1 mm in length. [MACRO- + PLANKTON] —**mac•ro•plank•ton•ic** (mak′rō plangk ton′ik), *adj.*

mac•rop•o•dous (mə krop′ə dəs), *adj. Bot.* **1.** (of a leaf) having a long stalk. **2.** (of an embryo) having an enlarged hypocotyl. [1850–55; MACRO- + -PODOUS]

mac•rop•si•a (mə krop′sē ə), *n. Ophthalm.* a defect of vision in which objects appear to be larger than their actual size. Also, **ma•cro•pi•a** (mə krō′pē ə), **mac•rop•sy** (mak′rop sē). Also called **megalopsia, megalopia.** Cf. **micropsia.** [1885–90; < NL; see MACR-, -OPSIA]

mac•ro•scop•ic (mak′rə skop′ik), *adj.* **1.** visible to the naked eye. Cf. **microscopic** (def. 1). **2.** pertaining to large units; comprehensive. Also, **mac′ro•scop′i•cal.** [1870–75; MACRO- + -SCOPE + -IC] —**mac′ro•scop′i•cal•ly,** *adv.*

mac•ro•seg•ment (mak′rō seg′mənt), *n.* a stretch of speech preceded and followed but not interrupted by a pause. Cf. **microsegment.** [1955–60; MACRO- + SEGMENT]

mac•ro•so•ci•ol•o•gy (mak′rō sō′sē ol′ə jē, -sō′shē-), *n.* the sociological study of large-scale social systems and long-term patterns and processes. Cf. **microsociology.** [MACRO- + SOCIOLOGY]

mac•ro•spo•ran•gi•um (mak′rō spə ran′jē əm), *n., pl.* **-gi•a** (-jē ə). *Bot.* megasporangium. [1870–75; MACRO- + SPORANGIUM]

mac•ro•spore (mak′rə spôr′, -spōr′), *n. Bot.* megaspore. [1855–60; MACRO- + -SPORE] —**mac•ro•spor•ic** (mak′rə spôr′ik, -spor′-), *adj.*

mac•ro•struc•ture (mak′rō struk′chər), *n.* **1.** the gross structure of a metal, as made visible to the naked eye by deep etching. **2.** an overall organizational scheme, as of a complex piece of writing. **3.** any overall structure, as a gross anatomical part. [1915–20; MACRO- + STRUCTURE]

ma•cru•ran (mə kro͝or′ən), *adj.* **1.** belonging or pertaining to the suborder Macrura, comprising the lobsters, crayfishes, shrimps, and prawns. —*n.* **2.** a macruran crustacean. [1835–45; < NL *Macrur(a)* (see MACR-, UR-[2]) + -AN]

ma•cru•rous (mə kro͝or′əs), *adj. Zool.* long-tailed, as a lobster (opposed to *brachyurous*). [1820–30; < NL *Macrur(a)* (see MACRURAN) + -OUS]

mac•u•la (mak′yə lə), *n., pl.* **-lae** (-lē′). **1.** a spot or blotch, esp. on one's skin; macule. **2.** *Ophthalm.* **a.** an opaque spot on the cornea. **b.** Also called **macula lutea, yellow spot.** an irregularly oval, yellow-pigmented area on the central retina, containing color-sensitive rods and the central point of sharpest vision. [1350–1400; ME < L: spot, blemish] —**mac′u•lar,** *adj.*

mac•u•la lu•te•a (mak′yə lə lo͞o′tē ə), *pl.* **mac•u•lae lu•te•ae** (mak′yə lē′ lo͞o′tē ē′, mak′yə lī′ lo͞o′tē ī′). macula (def. 2b). [1840–50; < NL: lit., yellow macula; see MACULA, LUTEOUS]

mac′ular degenera′tion, *Ophthalm.* degeneration of the central portion of the retina, resulting in a loss of sharp vision.

mac•u•late (*adj.* mak′yə lit; *v.* mak′yə lāt′), *adj., v.,* **-lat•ed, -lat•ing.** —*adj.* **1.** spotted; stained. **2.** *Archaic.* defiled; impure. —*v.t. Archaic.* **3.** to mark with a spot or spots; stain. **4.** to sully or pollute. [1375–1425; late ME < L *maculātus* (ptp. of *maculāre* to spot, stain). See MACULA, -ATE[1]]

mac•u•la•tion (mak′yə lā′shən), *n.* **1.** the act of spotting. **2.** a spotted condition. **3.** a marking of spots, as on an animal. **4.** a disfiguring spot or stain. [1425–75 for earlier sense "sexual defilement"; late ME < L *maculātiōn-* (s. of *maculātiō*). See MACULATE, -ION]

mac•ule (mak′yo͞ol), *n., v.,* **-uled, -ul•ing.** —*n.* **1.** mackle. **2.** macula. —*v.t., v.i.* **3.** mackle. [1475–85; < L *macula* spot, blemish; cf. MACULA]

ma•cum•ba (mə ko͞om′bə), *n.* a Brazilian cult incorporating the use of fetishes and sorcery and deriving largely from African practices. [1935–40; < Pg]

ma•cush•la (mə ko͝osh′lə), *n. Irish Eng.* darling. [1885–90; < Ir *mo chuisle* lit., my pulse]

Ma•cy (mā′sē), *n.* **R(ow•land) H(us•sey)** (rō′lənd hus′ē), 1823–77, U.S. retail merchant.

mad (mad), *adj.,* **mad•der, mad•dest,** *n., v.,* **mad•ded, mad•ding.** —*adj.* **1.** mentally disturbed; deranged; insane; demented. **2.** enraged; greatly provoked or irritated; angry. **3.** (of animals) **a.** abnormally furious; ferocious: *a mad bull.* **b.** affected with rabies; rabid: *a mad dog.* **4.** extremely foolish or unwise; imprudent; irrational: *a mad scheme to invade France.* **5.** wildly excited or confused: frantic: *mad haste.* **6.** overcome by desire, eagerness, enthusiasm, etc.; excessively or uncontrollably fond; infatuated: *He's mad about the opera.* **7.** wildly gay or merry; enjoyably hilarious: *to have a mad time at the Mardi Gras.* **8.** (of wind, storms, etc.) furious in violence: *A mad gale swept across the channel.* **9.** **like mad,** *Informal.* with great haste, impulsiveness, energy, or enthusiasm: *She ran like mad to catch the bus.* **10.** **mad as a hatter,** completely insane. —*n.* **11.** an angry or ill-tempered period, mood, or spell: *The last time he had a mad on, it lasted for days.* —*v.t.* **12.** *Archaic.* to make mad. —*v.i.* **13.** *Archaic.* to be, become, or act mad. [bef. 900; ME *mad* (adj.), *madden* (intrans. v., deriv. of the adj.); OE *gemǣd(e)d,* ptp. of **gemǣdan* to make mad, akin to *gemād* mad, foolish; c. OS *gemēd,* OHG *gimeit* foolish]
—**Syn. 1.** lunatic, maniacal, crazed, crazy. **2.** furious, exasperated, raging, wrathful, irate. **4.** ill-advised; unsafe, dangerous, perilous. MAD, CRAZY, INSANE are used to characterize wildly impractical or foolish ideas, actions, etc. MAD suggests senselessness and excess: *The scheme of buying the bridge was absolutely mad.* In informal usage, CRAZY suggests recklessness and impracticality: *a crazy young couple.* INSANE is used with some opprobrium to express unsoundness and possible harmfulness: *The new traffic system is simply insane.* **5.** frenzied. —**Ant. 4.** sensible, practical; sound, safe.
—**Usage.** MAD meaning "enraged, angry" has been used since 1300, and this sense is a very common one. Because some teachers and usage critics insist that the only correct meaning of MAD is "mentally disturbed, insane," MAD is often replaced by *angry* in formal contexts: *The President is angry at Congress for overriding his veto.*

MAD (mad), *n.* See **Mutual Assured Destruction.**

mad., madam.

Madag., Madagascar.

Mad•a•gas•car (mad′ə gas′kər), *n.* an island republic in the Indian Ocean, about 240 mi. (385 km) off the SE coast of Africa: formerly a French colony; gained independence 1960. 8,000,000; 227,800 sq. mi. (590,000 sq. km). *Cap.:* Antananarivo. Formerly, **Malagasy Republic.** —**Mad′a•gas′can,** *n., adj.*

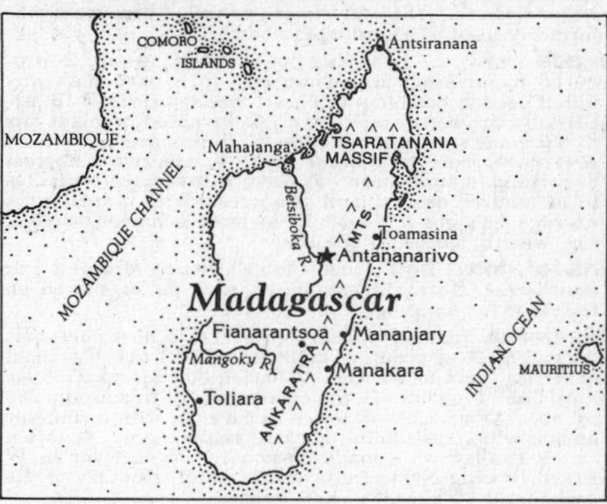

Mad′agas′car jas′mine, a Madagascan twining, woody vine, *Stephanotis floribunda,* of the milkweed family, having waxy-white, fragrant flowers. Also called **wax flower.**

Mad′agas′car per′iwinkle, a plant, *Catharanthus roseus* (or *Vinca rosea*), cultivated for its glossy foliage and pink or white flowers. [1815–25]

Mad•a•lyn (mad′l in), *n.* a female given name, form of **Magdalen.** Also, **Mad′a•lynne.**

mad•am (mad′əm), *n., pl.* **mes•dames** (mā dam′, -däm′) for 1; **mad•ams** for 2, 3. **1.** (*often cap.*) a polite term of address to a woman, originally used only to a woman of rank or authority: *Madam President; May I help you, madam?* **2.** the woman in charge of a household: *Is the madam at home?* **3.** the woman in charge of a house of prostitution. [1250–1300; ME *madame* < OF, orig. *ma dame* my lady; see DAME]

mad•ame (mad′əm; mə dam′, -däm′, ma-; *Fr.* MA-DAM′), *n., pl.* **mes•dames** (mā dam′, -däm′; *Fr.* mā-DAM′). (*often cap.*) **1.** a French title of respect equivalent to "Mrs.", used alone or prefixed to a woman's married name or title: *Madame Curie.* **2.** (in English) a title of respect used in speaking to or of an older woman, esp. one of distinction, who is not of American or British origin. *Abbr.:* Mme. [1590–1600; < F; see MADAM]

Mad′ame Bo′va•ry (bō′və rē), a novel (1857) by Gustave Flaubert.

Mad′ame But′terfly, an opera (1904) by Giacomo Puccini. Also, ***Ma•da′ma But′terfly*** (mə dam′ə, -dä′mə), ***Mad′am But′terfly.***

Ma•dang (mä′däng), *n.* a seaport on the N coast of New Guinea, in Papua New Guinea. 6609.

Ma•da•ria•ga (mä′thä ryä′gä), *n.* **Sal•va•dor de** (säl′vä thôr′ the), (*Salvador de Madariaga y Rojo*), 1886–1978, Spanish diplomat, historian, and writer in England.

mad•cap (mad′kap′), *adj.* **1.** wildly or heedlessly impulsive; reckless; rash: *a madcap scheme.* —*n.* **2.** a madcap person. [1580–90; MAD + CAP[1]]

MADD (mad), *n.* Mothers Against Drunk Driving.

mad•den (mad′n), *v.t.* **1.** to anger or infuriate: *The delays maddened her.* **2.** to make insane. —*v.i.* **3.** to become mad; act as if mad; rage. [1725–35; MAD + -EN[1]]
—**Syn. 1.** provoke, enrage, anger, inflame; exasperate, irritate, vex, annoy. —**Ant. 1.** calm, mollify.

mad•den•ing (mad′n ing), *adj.* **1.** driving to madness or frenzy: *a maddening thirst.* **2.** infuriating or exasperating: *his maddening indifference to my pleas.* **3.** raging; furious: *a maddening wind.* [1735–45; MADDEN + -ING[2]] —**mad′den•ing•ly,** *adv.* —**mad′den•ing•ness,** *n.*

mad•der[1] (mad′ər), *n.* **1.** any plant of the genus *Rubia,* esp. the climbing *R. tinctorum,* of Europe, having open clusters of small, yellowish flowers. Cf. **madder family. 2.** the root of this plant, formerly used in dyeing. **3.** the dye or coloring matter itself. **4.** a color produced by such a dye. [bef. 1000; ME *mad(d)er,* OE *mæd(e)re;* c. ON *mathra,* OHG *matara*]

mad•der[2] (mad′ər), *adj.* comparative of **mad.**

mad′der fam′ily, the large plant family Rubiaceae, characterized by herbaceous plants, trees, and shrubs having simple, opposite, or whorled leaves, usually four- or five-lobed flowers, and fruit in the form of a berry, capsule, or nut, and including the gardenia, madder, partridgeberry, and shrubs and trees that are the source of coffee, ipecac, and quinine.

mad′der lake′, **1.** a strong purple-red color. **2.** a pigment of this color formerly obtained from the madder root, characterized chiefly by lack of permanence. Cf. **rose madder, alizarin.** [1815–25]

mad•dest (mad′ist), *adj.* superlative of **mad.**

mad•ding (mad′ing), *adj.* **1.** acting madly or senselessly; insane; frenzied: *a quiet place far from the mad-*

ding crowd. **2.** making mad: *a madding grief.* [1300–50; ME. See MAD (v.), -ING[2]]

mad·dish (mad′ish), *adj.* somewhat mad. [1565–75; MAD + -ISH[1]]

mad′-dog skull′cap (mad′dôg′, -dog′), *Bot.* a North American skullcap, *Scutellaria lateriflora,* having underground stems and one-sided clusters of blue to white flowers. [1815–25, *Amer.*; so called because it was formerly used as an antispasmodic]

made (mād), *v.* **1.** pt. and pp. of **make.** —*adj.* **2.** produced by making, preparing, etc., in a particular way (often used in combination): *well-made garments.* **3.** artificially produced: *made fur.* **4.** invented or made-up: *to tell made stories about oneself.* **5.** prepared, esp. from several ingredients: *a made dish.* **6.** assured of success or fortune: *a made man.* **7. have it made,** *Informal.* **a.** to be assured or confident of success: *With a straight A average he's got it made.* **b.** to have achieved success, esp. wealth, status, or the like.

made′-down bed′ (mād′doun′), *South Midland and Southern U.S.* a makeshift bed, as a pallet, placed on the floor for sleeping.

Ma·dei·ra (mə dēr′ə, -dâr′ə; *for 1, 2, 5 also Port.* mä-de′ʀə), *n.* **1.** a group of eight islands off the NW coast of Africa, part of Portugal. 270,000; 308 sq. mi. (798 sq. km). *Cap.:* Funchal. **2.** the chief island of this group. 286 sq. mi. (741 sq. km). **3.** (*often l.c.*) a rich, strong white or amber wine, resembling sherry, made there. **4.** (*often l.c.*) a similar wine made elsewhere. **5.** a river in W Brazil flowing NE to the Amazon: chief tributary of the Amazon. 2100 mi. (3380 km) long.

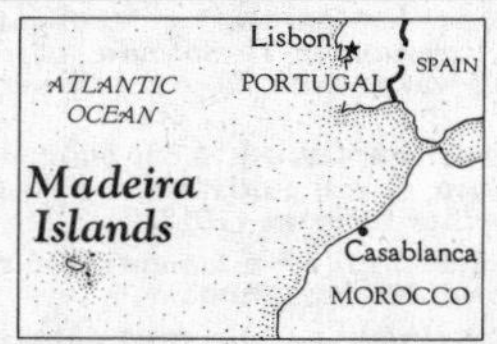

Madei′ra embroi′dery. See **broderie anglaise.** [after the island of MADEIRA, where such embroidery is made in convents]

Madei′ra to′paz, citrine (def. 2).

mad·e·leine (mad′l in, mad′l ān′; *Fr.* mᴀdᵊ len′), *n., pl.* **mad·e·leines** (mad′l inz, mad′l ānz′; *Fr.* mᴀdᵊ len′). *French Cookery.* a small shell-shaped cake made of flour, eggs, sugar, and butter and baked in a mold. [1835–45; < F, earlier *gâteau à la Madeleine,* after the female given name; the attribution of the recipe to an 18th century cook named Madeleine Pau(l)mier is unsubstantiated]

Mad·e·leine (mad′l in, -lin′; *Fr.* mᴀdᵊ len′), *n.* a female given name, form of **Magdalen.** Also, **Mad′e·laine, Mad·e·lene** (mad′l in), **Mad′e·line, Mad′e·lyn.**

made′ mast′, *Naut.* a wooden mast formed of several shaped, longitudinal pieces joined together. Also called **built-up mast.** [1620–30]

mad·e·moi·selle (mad′ə mə zel′, mad′mwə-, mam-zel′; *Fr.* mᴀd mwᴀ zel′), *n., pl.* **mad·e·moi·selles** (mad′ə mə zelz′, mad′mwə-, mam zelz′), **mes·de·moi·selles** (mā′də mə zel′, mād′mwə zel′; *Fr.* mād mwa-zel′). **1.** (*often cap.*) a French title of respect equivalent to "Miss", used in speaking to or of a girl or unmarried woman: *Mademoiselle Lafitte. Abbr.:* Mlle. **2.** a French governess. **3.** See **silver perch** (def. 1). [1635–45; < F; OF *ma damoisele* my noble young lady; see MADAME, DAMSEL]

Ma·de·ra (mə dâr′ə), *n.* a city in central California. 21,732.

Ma·der·no (mä dєʀ′nô), *n.* **Car·lo** (kär′lô), 1556–1629, Italian architect.

Ma·de·ro (mä ᴛʜe′ʀô), *n.* **Fran·cis·co In·da·le·cio** (fṙän sēs′kô ēn′dä le′syô), 1873–1913, Mexican revolutionary and political leader: president 1911–13.

made-to-meas·ure (mād′tə mezh′ər), *adj.* (of a garment, shoes, etc.) made in accordance with a specific individual's measurements. Cf. **ready-to-wear.** [1925–30]

made-to-or·der (mād′to͞o ôr′dər, -tə-), *adj.* **1.** made in accordance with an individual's specifications or requirements: *a made-to-order suit.* Cf. **ready-to-wear.** **2.** perfectly suited. [1905–10]

made-up (mād′up′), *adj.* **1.** concocted; falsely fabricated or invented: *a made-up story.* **2.** being in makeup; wearing facial cosmetics. **3.** put together; finished. [1600–10]

Madge (maj), *n.* a female given name, form of **Margaret.**

mad·house (mad′hous′), *n., pl.* **-hous·es** (-hou′ziz). **1.** a hospital for the confinement and treatment of mentally disturbed persons. **2.** a wild, confused, and often noisy place, set of circumstances, etc.: *The office was a madhouse today.* [1680–90; MAD + HOUSE]
—**Syn. 2.** bedlam, shambles.

Madh·ya Bha·rat (mud′yə bä′rut, -rət), a former state of central India; now included in Madhya Pradesh.

Madh·ya·mi·ka (mäd yu′mi kə), *n. Buddhism.* a school of philosophy, of A.D. c200, that attempted a reconciliation with Hinayana from a Mahayana position. [< Skt]

CONCISE ETYMOLOGY KEY: <, descended or borrowed from; >, whence; b., blend of, blended; c., cognate with; cf., compare; deriv., derivative; equiv., equivalent; imit., imitative; obl., oblique; r., replacing; s., stem; sp., spelling, spelled; resp., respelling, respelled; trans., translation; ?, origin unknown; *, unattested; ‡, probably earlier than. See the full key inside the front cover.

Madh·ya Pra·desh (mud′yə prə dāsh′, prä′desh), a state in central India. 48,230,000; 171,201 sq. mi. (443,411 sq. km). *Cap.:* Bhopal.

Ma·di·an (mā′dē ən), *n. Douay Bible.* Midian.

Mad·i·son (mad′ə sən), *n.* **1. Dol·ly** or **Dol·ley** (dol′ē), (*Dorothea Payne*), 1768–1849, wife of James Madison. **2. James,** 1751–1836, 4th president of the U.S. 1809–17. **3.** a city in and the capital of Wisconsin, in the S part. 170,616. **4.** a city in NE New Jersey. 15,357. **5.** a town in S Connecticut. 14,031. **6.** a city in SE Indiana. 12,472. **7.** a dance in which the participants stand side by side in a line while one person, acting as leader, calls out various steps, each letter of the word "Madison" signaling a specific step.

Mad′ison Av′enue, a street in New York City that is a center of the advertising and public relations industries and that has become a symbol of their attitudes, methods, and practices.

Mad′ison Heights′, a city in SE Michigan: suburb of Detroit. 35,375.

Mad·i·son·ville (mad′ə sən vil′), *n.* a city in W Kentucky. 16,979.

Ma·di·un (mä′dē o͞on′), *n.* a city on E central Java, in Indonesia. 36,147.

mad·ly (mad′lē), *adv.* **1.** insanely or wildly: *The old witch cackled madly.* **2.** with desperate haste or intensity; furiously: *They worked madly to repair the bridge.* **3.** foolishly: *They lived madly, wasting all their money.* **4.** extremely: *They're madly in love.* [1175–1225; ME; see MAD, -LY]

Mad·lyn (mad′lin), *n.* a female given name, form of **Magdalen.** Also, **Mad′lynne.**

madm., madam.

mad·man (mad′man′, -mən), *n., pl.* **-men** (-men′, -mən). a person who is or behaves as if insane; lunatic; maniac. [1300–50; ME *madd man.* See MAD, MAN[1]]

mad′ mon′ey, *Informal.* **1.** a small sum of money carried or kept in reserve for minor expenses, emergencies, or impulse purchases. **2.** a small sum of money carried by a woman on a date to enable her to reach home alone in case she and her escort quarrel and separate. [1915–20]

mad·ness (mad′nis), *n.* **1.** the state of being mad; insanity. **2.** senseless folly: *It is sheer madness to speak as you do.* **3.** frenzy; rage. **4.** intense excitement or enthusiasm. [1350–1400; ME *madnesse.* See MAD, -NESS]

Ma·doe·ra (mä do͞o′ʀä), *n.* Madura.

Ma·don·na (mə don′ə), *n.* **1.** the Virgin Mary (usually prec. by *the*). **2.** a picture or statue representing the Virgin Mary. **3.** (*l.c.*) *Archaic.* an Italian title of formal address to a woman. [1575–85; < It: my lady]

Madon′na and Child′, *Fine Arts.* a representation of the Virgin Mary holding the infant Jesus.

Madon′na lil′y, a lily, *Lilium candidum,* having clusters of pure white, bell-shaped flowers. Also called **Annunciation lily.** [1875–80]

mad·ras (mad′rəs, mə dras′, -dräs′), *n.* **1.** a light cotton fabric of various weaves, esp. one in multicolored plaid or stripes, used for shirts, dresses, jackets, etc. **2.** a thin curtain fabric of a light, gauzelike weave with figures of heavier yarns. **3.** a large, brightly colored kerchief, of silk or cotton, often used for turbans. —*adj.* **4.** made of or resembling madras. [1825–35; named after MADRAS]

Ma·dras (mə dras′, -dräs′), *n.* **1.** a seaport in and the capital of Tamil Nadu state, in SE India, on the Bay of Bengal. 3,169,930. **2.** former name of **Tamil Nadu.**

ma·dra·sah (mə dras′ə), *n. Islam.* a school or college, esp. a school attached to a mosque where young men study theology. Also, **ma·dra′sa.** [< Ar]

Madras′ hemp′, sunn.

Madras′ States′, a former agency of British India, including the Native States of Cochin, Travancore, and Pudukottai.

ma·dre (mä′ᴛʜʀe; *Eng.* mä′drā), *n., pl.* **-dres** (-ᴛʜʀes; *Eng.* -drāz). *Spanish.* mother.

Ma·dre de Di·os (mä′ᴛʜʀe ᴛʜe dyôs′), a river in Peru and Bolivia, flowing E to the Beni River. 900 mi. (1450 km) long.

mad·re·pore (mad′rə pôr′, -pōr′), *n.* any true or stony coral of the order Madreporaria, forming reefs or islands in tropical seas. [1745–55; < F *madrépore* reef-building coral < It *madrepora,* equiv. to *madre* mother (< L *māter*) + *-pora,* for *poro* < Gk *pôros* kind of stone] —**mad·re·por·ic** (mad′rə pôr′ik, -por′-), **mad·re·po·ri·an** (mad′rə pôr′ē ən, -pōr′-), *adj.*

mad·re·por·ite (mad′rə pôr′īt, -pōr′-, mə drep′ə-rīt′), *n.* a sievelike plate in certain echinoderms, through which water passes into the vascular system. [1795–1805; MADREPORE + -ITE[1]]

Ma·drid (mə drid′; *Sp.* mä ᴛʜʀēᴛʜ′), *n.* a city in and the capital of Spain, in the central part. 3,500,000. —**Ma·dri·le·ni·an** (ma′drə lē′nē ən, -lēn′yən), *adj., n.*

mad·ri·gal (mad′ri gəl), *n.* **1.** a secular part song without instrumental accompaniment, usually for four to six voices, making abundant use of contrapuntal imitation, popular esp. in the 16th and 17th centuries. **2.** a lyric poem suitable for being set to music, usually short and often of amatory character, esp. fashionable in the 16th century and later, in Italy, France, England, etc. **3.** any part song. [1580–90; < It *madrigale* < ML *mātricāle* something simple, n. use of neut. of LL *mātricālis* lit., of the womb. See MATRIX, -AL[1]] —**mad′ri·gal·esque′,** *adj.* —**mad·ri·gal·i·an** (mad′rə gal′ē ən, -gal′-yən, -gā′lē ən), *adj.*

mad·ri·gal·ist (mad′ri gə list), *n.* a composer or singer of madrigals. [1780–90; MADRIGAL + -IST]

mad·ri·lène (mad′rə len′, -lān′, mad′rə len′, -lān′), *n.* a consommé flavored with tomato, frequently jelled and served cold. [1930–35; < F (*consommé*) *madrilène* lit., Madrid consommé; see MADRILEÑO]

Ma·dri·le·ño (mad′rə lān′yō; *Sp.* mä′ᴛʜʀē le′nyô), *n., pl.* **-le·nos** (-lān′yōz; *Sp.* -le′nyôs). (*sometimes l.c.*) a native or inhabitant of Madrid, Spain. [1825–35; < Sp *madrileño,* perh. by dissimilation (*d—d* > *d—l*) from **madrideño,* equiv. to *Madrid* MADRID + *-eño* suffix of appurtenance (< L *-ignus, -egnus,* appar. extracted from adjs. formed with *-n-* in which *g* was part of the root, e.g., *larignus* of larch, *salignus* of willow)]

ma·dro·ne (mə drō′nə), *n.* **1.** any of several evergreen trees belonging to the genus *Arbutus,* of the heath family, esp. *A. menziesii* **(Pacific madrone)** of western North America, having red, flaky bark and bearing edible reddish berries. **2.** the pale reddish-brown wood of this tree. Also, **ma·dro′na, ma·dro·ño** (mə drōn′yō). [1835–45, *Amer.*; < AmerSp *madroño;* Sp: strawberry tree (ulterior orig. uncert.)]

mad·tom (mad′tom′), *n.* any of several tadpolelike, freshwater catfishes of the genus *Noturus,* of the central and eastern U.S., having a poisonous pectoral spine: some are threatened or endangered. [1895–1900, *Amer.*; MAD + TOM]

Ma·du·ra (mə do͝or′ə *for 1;* maj′ər ə *for 2*), *n.* **1.** Dutch, **Madoera.** an island in Indonesia, off the NE coast of Java. 76,100,000 with Java; 2112 sq. mi. (5470 sq. km). **2.** Also, **Ma·du·rai** (mad′yo͞o rī′). a city in S Tamil Nadu, in S India. 548,298.

Mad·u·rese (mad′o͞o rēz′, -rēs′), *n.* **1.** a member of a people native to the island of Madura and also inhabiting the northeastern coast of Java. **2.** the Austronesian language spoken by the Madurese.

ma·du·ro (mə do͝or′ō), *adj.* (of cigars) strong and darkly colored. [1885–90; < Sp < L *mātūrus* ripe]

mad·wo·man (mad′wo͝om′ən), *n., pl.* **-wom·en.** a woman who is or behaves as if insane. [1400–50; late ME. See MAD, WOMAN]

Mad′woman of Chail·lot′, The (shä yō′), (French, *La Folle de Chaillot*), a satirical comedy (1945) by Jean Giraudoux.

mad·wort (mad′wûrt′, -wôrt′), *n.* a mat-forming plant, *Aurinia saxatilis* (or *Alyssum saxatille*), of the mustard family, having spatulate leaves and open clusters of pale yellow flowers. [1590–1600; MAD + WORT[2]]

mae (mā), *adj., n., adv. Scot.* more. [bef. 900; ME (north and Scots), OE *mā;* c. G *mehr,* ON *meir,* Goth *mais.* See MORE]

Mae (mā), *n.* a female given name, form of **Mary.**

M.A.E., **1.** Master of Aeronautical Engineering. **2.** Master of Art Education. **3.** Master of Arts in Education.

Mae·an·der (mē an′dər), *n.* ancient name of the **Menderes.**

Ma·e·ba·shi (mä′e bä′shē), *n.* a city in the central part of Honshu, in central Japan. 265,171.

Mae·belle (mā bel′, mā′bel), *n.* a female given name.

Mae·ce·nas (mē sē′nəs, mī-), *n.* **1. Gaius Cil·ni·us** (sil′nē əs), c70–8 B.C., Roman statesman: friend and patron of Horace and Vergil. **2.** a generous patron or supporter, esp. of art, music, or literature.

M.A.Ed., Master of Arts in Education.

Mael (māl), *n. Irish Myth.* a son of Ronan, unjustly killed by him.

mael·strom (māl′strəm), *n.* **1.** a large, powerful, or violent whirlpool. **2.** a restless, disordered, or tumultuous state of affairs: *the maelstrom of early morning traffic.* **3.** (*cap.*) a famous hazardous whirlpool off the NW coast of Norway. [1550–60 for def. 3; < early D *maelstroom,* now sp. *maalstroom,* repr. *mal(en)* to grind + *stroom* stream. See MEAL[2], STREAM]
—**Syn. 2.** tumult, pandemonium, bedlam.

mae·nad (mē′nad), *n.* **1.** bacchante. **2.** a frenzied or raging woman. [1570–80; < L *Maenad-* (s. of *Maenas*) < Gk *Mainás* a bacchante, special use of *mainás* mad-woman] —**mae·nad′ic,** *adj.* —**mae′nad·ism,** *n.*

Mae·ra (mēr′ə), *n. Class. Myth.* Hecuba, after being changed into a dog for blinding Polymestor. Also, **Maira.**

M.Aero.E., Master of Aeronautical Engineering.

ma·es·to·so (mī stō′sō; *It.* mä′es tô′sô), *adj., adv.* with majesty; stately (used as a musical direction). [1715–25; < It: stately, majestic, equiv. to *maest(à)* (< L *mājestās* MAJESTY) + *-oso* -OSE[1]]

Maes·tricht (*Flemish.* mäs′tʀɪᴋʜt), *n.* Maastricht.

maes·tro (mī′strō), *n., pl.* **maes·tros.** **1.** an eminent composer, teacher, or conductor of music: *Toscanini and other great maestros.* **2.** (*cap.*) a title of respect used in addressing or referring to such a person. **3.** a master of any art: *the maestros of poetry.* [1790–1800; < It: master]

Mae·ter·linck (mā′tər lingk′; *Fr.* mᴀ teʀ laɴ′; *Flemish.* mä′teʀ lingk′), *n.* **Comte Mau·rice** (*Fr.* mō ʀēs′), 1862–1947, Belgian poet, dramatist, and essayist: Nobel prize 1911. —**Mae′ter·linck′i·an,** *adj.*

Mae′ West′, an inflatable yellow or orange life jacket for emergency use, esp. by sailors or by airplane pilots in flights over water. [1935–40; named after *Mae* WEST, full-bosomed U.S. comic actress]

Maf·e·king (mä′fi king′), *n.* a town in N Republic of South Africa: former administrative seat of Bechuanaland; besieged for 217 days by Boers 1899–1900. 6900.

ma·fen·ide (mə fen′id), *Pharm.* an antibacterial substance, $C_7H_{10}N_2O_2S$, prepared in cream form and used topically, along with other treatments, on second- to third-degree burns to reduce bacterial growth. [*maf-* (perh. reversed letters from SULFONAMIDE) + (BENZ)EN(E) + -IDE]

maf·fick (maf′ik), *v.i. Brit.* to celebrate with extravagant public demonstrations. [1895–1900; back formation from MAFEKING, taken as v. + -ING[1]; the relief of the besieged city was joyously celebrated in London] —**maf′fick·er,** *n.*

Ma·fi·a (mä′fē ə, maf′ē ə), *n.* **1.** a hierarchically structured secret organization allegedly engaged in smuggling, racketeering, trafficking in narcotics, and other criminal activities in the U.S., Italy, and elsewhere. **2.** (in Sicily) **a.** (*l.c.*) a popular spirit of hostility to legal restraint and to the law, often manifesting itself in criminal acts. **b.** a 19th-century secret society, similar to the Camorra in Naples, that acted in this spirit. **3.** (*often l.c.*) any small powerful or influential group in an organization or field; clique. Also, **Maf′fi·a.** [1870–75; < It < Sicilian: orig., elegance, bravura, courage; of obscure orig.; the word's history prior to the 19th century is unknown, though many fictitious ideas have circulated regarding its age, source, etc., due to the organization's modern notoriety]

maf·ic (maf′ik), *adj. Geol.* of or pertaining to rocks rich in dark, ferromagnesian minerals. Cf. **basic** (def. 4), **ultramafic.** [1910–15; MA(GNESIUM) + L *f(errum)* iron + -IC]

ma·fi·o·so (mä′fē ō′sō), *n., pl.* **-si** (-sē), **-sos.** (*sometimes cap.*) a member of a Mafia or of a mafia. [1870–75; < It, equiv. to *Mafi(a)* MAFIA + *-oso* < L *-ōsus* (see -OUS)]

maf·tir (*Seph.* mäf tēʀ′; *Ashk.* mäf′tēʀ), *n. Hebrew.* **1.** the concluding section of the portion of the Torah chanted or read in a Jewish service on the Sabbath and festivals. **2.** the person who recites the blessings before and after the chanting or reading of this section and who often also chants or reads the Haftarah. [*maphṭīr* lit., dismisser]

mag[1] (mag), *n. Informal.* magazine. [shortened form]

mag[2] (mag), *n., v.,* **magged, mag·ging.** *Brit. Dial.* —*n.* **1.** a magpie. **2.** talk; chatter. —*v.i.* **3.** to talk idly; chatter. [shortened form of MAGPIE]

Mag (mag), *n.* a female given name, form of **Margaret.**

mag., 1. magazine. **2.** magnetism. **3.** magneto. **4.** magnitude. **5.** (in prescriptions) large. [< L *magnus*]

Ma·ga·dan (mä′gə dän′; *Russ.* mə gu dän′), *n.* a city in the NE Russian Federation in Asia, on the Sea of Okhotsk. 138,000.

Ma·ga·lla·nes (*Sp.* mä′gä yä′nes), *n.* See **Punta Arenas.**

Ma·gan·gué (mä′gäng ge′), *n.* a city in NW Colombia. 73,868.

mag·a·zine (mag′ə zēn′, mag′ə zēn′), *n.* **1.** a publication that is issued periodically, usually bound in a paper cover, and typically contains essays, stories, poems, etc., by many writers, and often photographs and drawings, frequently specializing in a particular subject or area, as hobbies, news, or sports. **2.** a room or place for keeping gunpowder and other explosives, as in a fort or on a warship. **3.** a building or place for keeping military stores, as arms, ammunition, or provisions. **4.** a metal receptacle for a number of cartridges, inserted into certain types of automatic weapons and when empty removed and replaced by a full receptacle in order to continue firing. **5.** Also called **magazine′ show′.** *Radio and Television.* **a.** Also called **newsmagazine.** a regularly scheduled news program consisting of several short segments in which various subjects of current interest are examined, usually in greater detail than on a regular newscast. **b.** a program with a varied format that combines interviews, commentary, entertainment, etc. **6.** See **magazine section. 7.** *Photog.* cartridge (def. 4). **8.** a supply chamber, as in a stove. **9.** a storehouse; warehouse. **10.** a collection of war munitions. [1575–85; < F *magasin* < It *magazzino* storehouse < Ar *makhāzin,* pl. of *makhzan* storehouse; used in book titles (from c1640) and periodical titles (in *The Gentleman's Magazine,* 1731)] —**mag′a·zin′ish, mag′a·zin′y,** *adj.*

magazine′ sec′tion, a magazinelike section in the Sunday editions of many newspapers, containing articles rather than news items and often letters, reviews, stories, puzzles, etc. [1955–60]

mag·a·zin·ist (mag′ə zē′nist), *n.* a person who writes for or edits a magazine. [1815–25; MAGAZINE + -IST]

mag′ card′ (mag), **1.** *Computers.* a plastic or paper card with a magnetizable layer on which data can be recorded and from which data can be read. **2.** such a card used in access-control systems, as for automatically unlocking doors. Also called **magnetic card.**

Mag·da (mag′də; *Ger.* mäg′dä), *n.* a female given name, German form of **Magdalen.**

Mag·da·la (mag′də lə), *n.* an ancient town in Palestine, W of the Sea of Galilee: supposed home of Mary Magdalene.

Mag·da·le·na (mag′də lā′nə, -lē′-; *Sp.* mäg′thä le′nä), *n.* **1.** a river in SW Colombia, flowing N to the Caribbean. 1060 mi. (1705 km) long. **2.** a female given name.

Mag′dale′na Bay′, a bay in NW Mexico, on the SW coast of Lower California. 17 mi. (27 km) long; 12 mi. (19 km) wide.

Mag·da·lene (mag′də lēn′, -lən, mag′də lē′nē), *n.* **1. the.** See **Mary Magdalene. 2.** (*l.c.*) a reformed prostitute. **3.** Also, **Mag·da·len** (mag′də lən). a female given name: from a Hebrew word meaning "woman of Magdala."

Mag·da·le·ni·an (mag′də lē′nē ən), *adj.* of or pertaining to the final Paleolithic culture of much of western Europe, dating from c13,000–10,000 B.C. and notable for its artifacts of bone, antler, and ivory and for the cave art of western France and northeastern Spain. [1880–85; < F *magdalénien,* equiv. to *Magdalen-* (Latinization of *La Madeleine,* the type site in SW France) + *-ien* -IAN]

Mag·de·burg (mag′də bûrg′; *Ger.* mäg′də bŏŏʀk′), *n.* the capital of Saxony-Anhalt, in central Germany. 290,579.

Mag′deburg hem′isphere, *Physics.* one of a pair of hemispherical cups from which air can be evacuated when they are placed together: used to demonstrate the force of air pressure. [after MAGDEBURG, where German statesman and physicist Otto von Guericke (1602–86) constructed a pair of such hemispheres]

mage (māj), *n. Archaic.* a magician. [1350–1400; ME < MF < L *magus.* See MAGUS]

M.Ag.Ec., Master of Agricultural Economics.

M.Ag.Ed., Master of Agricultural Education.

Ma·ge·lang (mä′gə läng′), *n.* a city on central Java, in Indonesia. 422,428.

Ma·gel·lan (mə jel′ən), *n.* **1. Ferdinand,** c1480–1521, Portuguese navigator: discoverer of the Straits of Magellan 1520 and the Philippines 1521. **2. Strait of,** a strait near the S tip of South America between the mainland of Chile and Tierra del Fuego and other islands, connecting the Atlantic and the Pacific. 360 mi. (580 km) long; 2½–17 mi. (4–27 km) wide. —**Ma·gel·lan·ic** (maj′ə lan′ik), *adj.*

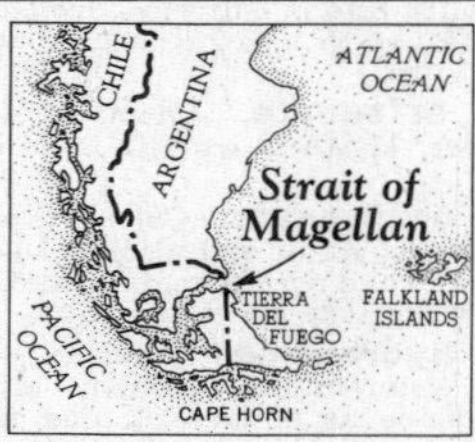

Magel′lan bar′berry, an evergreen shrub, *Berberis buxifolia,* of southern Chile, having prickle-tipped leaves, dark-purple fruit, and orange-yellow flowers, rarely flowering in cultivation.

Mag′ellan′ic cloud′, *Astron.* either of two irregular galactic clusters in the southern heavens that are the nearest independent star system to the Milky Way. [1675–85]

Ma·gen Da·vid (mä′gən dā′vid; *Seph. Heb.* mä gen′ dä vēd′; *Ashk. Heb.* mô′gən dô′vid), *Judaism.* See **Star of David.** [1900–05; < Heb *māghēn dāwīd* lit., shield of David]

Ma·gen·die (mA zhän dē′), *n.* **Fran·çois** (fʀän swA′), 1783–1855, French physiologist.

ma·gen·ta (mə jen′tə), *n.* **1.** fuchsin. **2.** a purplish red. [named after MAGENTA, because the dye was discovered the year of the battle]

Ma·gen·ta (mə jen′tə), *n.* a town in N Italy, W of Milan: the French and Sardinians defeated the Austrians here 1859. 23,690.

mag·film (mag′film′), *n. Motion Pictures.* See under **film** (def. 7b). [MAG(NETIC) + FILM]

mag·gid (*Ashk. Heb., Eng.* mä′gid; *Seph. Heb.* mä-gēd′), *n., pl.* **mag·gi·dim** (*Ashk. Heb.* mä gē′dim; *Seph. Heb.* mä gē dēm′), **mag·gids.** *Judaism.* (esp. in Poland and Russia) a wandering Jewish preacher whose sermons contained religious and moral instruction and words of comfort and hope. [1890–95; < Heb *maggīdh* lit., narrator, messenger]

Mag·gie (mag′ē), *n.* a female given name, form of **Margaret.**

Mag·gio·re (mə jôr′ē, -jōr′ē; *It.* mäd jô′ʀe), *n.* **Lake,** a lake in N Italy and S Switzerland. 83 sq. mi. (215 sq. km).

mag·got (mag′ət), *n.* **1.** a soft-bodied, legless larva of certain flies. **2.** *Archaic.* an odd fancy; whim. [1425–75; late ME *magot, magat,* unexplained var. of *maddock,* ME *mathek* < ON *mathkr;* akin to Dan *maddik* maggot, OE *matha, mathu* grub, maggot, OHG *mado* maggot]

mag·got·y (mag′ə tē), *adj.* **1.** infested with maggots, as food. **2.** *Archaic.* having queer notions; full of whims. **3.** *Australian Slang.* angry; bad-tempered. [1660–70; MAGGOT + -Y[1]]

mag·hem·ite (mag hem′īt, mag′ə mīt′), *n. Mineral.* a strongly magnetic dimorph of hematite. [1925–30; b. MAGNETITE and HEMATITE]

Ma·ghreb (mug′rəb), *n.* the Arabic name for the NW part of Africa, generally including Morocco, Algeria, Tunisia, and sometimes Libya. Also, **Ma′ghrib.**

Ma·ghre·bi (mug′rə bē), *n., pl.* **-bis, -bi** for 1. **1.** a native or inhabitant of the Maghreb. **2.** any of the dialects of Arabic spoken in the Maghreb. —*adj.* **3.** of or pertaining to the Maghreb, its people, or their language. Also, **Ma′ghri·bi.**

Ma·gi (mā′jī), *n. pl., sing.* **-gus** (-gəs). **1.** (*sometimes l.c.*) the wise men, generally assumed to be three in number, who paid homage to the infant Jesus. Matt. 2:1–12. Cf. **Balthazar** (def. 1), **Caspar** (def. 1), **Melchior** (def. 1). **2.** (*sometimes l.c.*) the class of Zoroastrian priests in ancient Media and Persia, reputed to possess supernatural powers. **3.** (*l.c.*) astrologers. —**Ma·gi·an** (mā′jē ən), *adj.* [see MAGUS]

mag·ic (maj′ik), *n.* **1.** the art of producing illusions as entertainment by the use of sleight of hand, deceptive devices, etc.; legerdemain; conjuring: *to pull a rabbit out of a hat by magic.* **2.** the art of producing a desired effect or result through the use of incantation or various other techniques that presumably assure human control of supernatural agencies or the forces of nature. Cf. **contagious magic, imitative magic, sympathetic magic. 3.** the use of this art: *Magic, it was believed, could drive illness from the body.* **4.** the effects produced: *the magic of recovery.* **5.** power or influence exerted through this art: *a wizard of great magic.* **6.** any extraordinary or mystical influence, charm, power, etc.: *the magic in a great name; the magic of music; the magic of spring.* **7.** (*cap.*) the U.S. code name for information from decrypting machine-enciphered Japanese wireless messages before and during World War II. —*adj.* **8.** employed in magic: *magic spells; magic dances; magic rites.* **9.** mysteriously enchanting; magical: *magic beauty.* **10.** of, pertaining to, or due to magic. **11.** producing the effects of magic; magical: *a magic touch.* [1350–1400; ME *magik(e)* witchcraft < LL *magica,* L *magicē* < Gk *magikḗ,* n. use of fem. of *magikós.* See MAGUS, -IC]

—**Syn. 2.** enchantment. MAGIC, NECROMANCY, SORCERY, WITCHCRAFT imply producing results through mysterious influences or unexplained powers. MAGIC may have glamorous and attractive connotations; the other terms suggest the harmful and sinister. MAGIC is an art employing some occult force of nature: *A hundred years ago television would have seemed to be magic.* NECROMANCY is an art of prediction based on alleged communication with the dead (it is called "the black art," because Greek *nekrós,* dead, was confused with Latin *niger,* black): *Necromancy led to violating graves.* SORCERY, originally divination by casting lots, came to mean supernatural knowledge gained through the aid of evil spirits, and often used for evil ends: *spells and charms used in sorcery.* WITCHCRAFT esp. suggests a malign kind of magic, often used against innocent victims: *Those accused of witchcraft were executed.*

mag·i·cal (maj′i kəl), *adj.* **1.** produced by or as if by magic: *The change in the appearance of the room was magical.* **2.** mysteriously enchanting: *a magical night.* **3.** of or pertaining to magic. [1545–55; MAGIC + -AL[1]] —**mag′i·cal·ly,** *adv.*

mag′ical think′ing, a conviction that thinking is equivalent to doing, occurring in dreams, the thought patterns of children, and some types of mental disorders, esp. obsessive-compulsive disorder.

mag′ic bul′let, something that cures or remedies without causing harmful side effects: *So far there is no magic bullet for economic woes.* [1965–70]

Mag′ic Flute′, The, (German, *Die Zauberflöte*), an opera (1791) by Wolfgang Amadeus Mozart.

ma·gi·cian (mə jish′ən), *n.* **1.** an entertainer who is skilled in producing illusion by sleight of hand, deceptive devices, etc.; conjurer. **2.** a person who is skilled in magic; sorcerer. [1350–1400; MAGIC + -IAN; r. ME *magicien* < MF]

—**Syn. 2.** necromancer, enchanter, wizard.

mag′ic lan′tern, a device having an enclosed lamp and a lenslike opening, formerly used for projecting and magnifying images mounted on slides or films. [1690–1700]

Mag′ic Mark′er, *Trademark.* a brand of felt-tip pen.

Mag′ic Moun′tain, The, (German, *Der Zauberberg*), a novel (1924) by Thomas Mann.

mag′ic mush′room, a mushroom, *Psilocybe mexicana,* of Mexico and the southwestern U.S., containing the hallucinogen psilocybin. [1965–70]

mag′ic num′ber, *Physics.* the atomic number or neutron number of an exceptionally stable nuclide. [1945–50]

mag′ic re′alism, a style of painting and literature in which fantastic or imaginary and often unsettling images or events are depicted in a sharply detailed, realistic manner. [1925–30] —**mag′ic re′alist.**

mag′ic square′, a square containing integers arranged in an equal number of rows and columns so that the sum of the integers in any row, column, or diagonal is the same. [1695–1705]

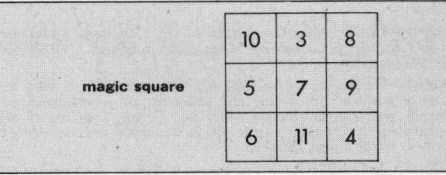

magic square

10	3	8
5	7	9
6	11	4

Ma·gin·da·na·o (mä gēn′dä nä′ō, mə gin′də nou′, mə gin′də nou′), *n., pl.* **-na·os,** (*esp. collectively*) **-na·o. 1.** a member of a Moro people of Mindanao in the Philippines. **2.** the Austronesian language of the Magindanao.

Ma′gi·not line′ (mazh′ə nō′; *Fr.* mA zhē nō′), **1.** a zone of heavy defensive fortifications erected by France along its eastern border in the years preceding World War II, but outflanked in 1940 when the German army attacked through Belgium. **2.** any elaborate line of defense or set of barriers. [1925–30; named after André *Maginot* (1877–1932), French minister of war]

mag·is·te·ri·al (maj′ə stēr′ē əl), *adj.* **1.** of, pertaining to, or befitting a master; authoritative; weighty; of importance or consequence: *a magisterial pronouncement by the director of the board.* **2.** imperious; domineering: *a magisterial tone of command.* **3.** of or befitting a magistrate or the office of a magistrate: *The judge spoke with magisterial gravity.* **4.** of the rank of a magistrate: *magisterial standing.* [1625–35; < ML *magisteriālis* of control, equiv. to L *magisteri(um)* control, mastery (see MAGISTERY) + *-ālis* -AL[1]] —**mag′is·te′ri·al·ly,** *adv.* —**mag′is·te′ri·al·ness,** *n.*

mag·is·te·ri·um (maj′ə stēr′ē əm), *n. Rom. Cath. Ch.* the authority and power of the church to teach religious truth. [1585–95; < L: MAGISTERY]

mag·is·ter·y (maj′ə ster′ē, -stə rē), *n., pl.* **-ter·ies. 1.** an agency or substance, as in alchemy, to which faculties of healing, transformation, etc., are ascribed. **2.** *Obs.*

CONCISE PRONUNCIATION KEY: act, cāpe, dâre, pärt; set, ēqual; if, īce; ox, ōver, ôrder, oil, bŏŏk, bōōt, out; up, ûrge; child; sing; shoe; thin, *th*at; zh as in *treasure.* ə = *a* as in *alone, e* as in *system, i* as in *easily, o* as in *gallop, u* as in *circus;* ə as in *fire* (fīər), *hour* (ouər). l and n can serve as syllabic consonants, as in *cradle* (krād′l), and *button* (but′n). See the full key inside the front cover.

mastership. [1490–1500; < L *magisterium,* equiv. to *magister* MASTER + *-ium* -IUM]

mag·is·tra·cy (maj′ə strə sē), *n., pl.* **-cies. 1.** the office or function of a magistrate. **2.** a body of magistrates. **3.** the district under a magistrate. Also, **mag·is·tra·ture** (maj′ə strā′chər). [1570–80; MAGISTR(ATE) + -ACY]

mag·is·tral (maj′ə strəl), *adj.* **1.** *Pharm.* prescribed or prepared for a particular occasion, as a remedy. Cf. **officinal** (def. 1). **2.** *Fort.* principal; main. **3.** magisterial (def. 1). —*n.* **4.** See **magistral line.** [1565–75; < L *magistrālis* of a master, equiv. to *magist(e)r* MASTER + *-ālis* -AL[1]] —**mag′is·tral′i·ty,** *n.* —**mag′is·tral·ly, mag·is·trat·i·cal·ly** (maj′ə strat′ik lē), *adv.*

mag′istral line′, *Fort.* the line from which the position of the other lines of fieldworks is determined. [1850–55]

mag·is·trate (maj′ə strāt′, -strit), *n.* **1.** a civil officer charged with the administration of the law. **2.** a minor judicial officer, as a justice of the peace or the judge of a police court, having jurisdiction to try minor criminal cases and to conduct preliminary examinations of persons charged with serious crimes. [1350–1400; ME *magistrat* < L *magistrātus* magistracy, magistrate, equiv. to *magist(e)r* MASTER + *-ātus* -ATE[3]] —**mag′is·trate′ship,** *n.*

mag′istrate's court′, 1. a court having limited jurisdiction over minor civil and criminal matters, as matters of contract not exceeding a particular amount of money. **2.** See **police court.** [1865–70]

Mag·le·mo·se·an (mag′lə mō′sē ən, -shən, -zhən), *adj.* of, pertaining to, or characteristic of the first Mesolithic culture of the northern European plain, adapted to forest and waterside habitats and characterized by flint axes, microliths, and bone and antler equipment used in hunting and fishing. Also, **Mag′le·mo′si·an.** [1915–20; *Maglemose* site of Mesolithic station in Denmark + -AN]

mag·lev (mag′lev′), *n.* See **magnetic levitation.** Also, **Mag′lev′.** [1965–70; by shortening]

mag·ma (mag′mə), *n., pl.* **-mas, -ma·ta** (-mə tə). **1.** *Geol.* molten material beneath or within the earth's crust, from which igneous rock is formed. **2.** any crude mixture of finely divided mineral or organic matter. **3.** *Chem., Pharm.* a paste composed of solid and liquid matter. [1400–50; late ME < L: dregs, leavings < Gk *mágma* kneaded mass, salve, equiv. to *mag-* (base of *mássein* to knead, press; see MASS) + *-ma* n. suffix of result] —**mag·mat·ic** (mag mat′ik), *adj.* —**mag′ma·tism,** *n.*

magn-, var. of **magni-** before a vowel: *magnanimous.*

Mag·na (mag′nə), *n.* a town in N Utah. 13,138.

Mag·na Car·ta (mag′nə kär′tə), **1.** the "great charter" of English liberties, forced from King John by the English barons and sealed at Runnymede, June 15, 1215. **2.** any fundamental constitution or law guaranteeing rights and liberties. Also, **Mag′na Char′ta.** [1425–75; late ME < ML]

mag·na cum lau·de (mäg′nə ko͝om lou′dā, -də, -dē; mag′nə kum lô′dē), with great praise: used in diplomas to grant the next-to-highest of three special honors for grades above the average. Cf. **cum laude, summa cum laude.** [1895–1900; < L *magnā cum laude*]

mag·na est ve·ri·tas, et prae·va·le·bit (mäg′nä est we′rī täs′, et prī′wä le′bit; *Eng.* mag′nə est ver′i-tas′, et prē′və lē′bit), *Latin.* truth is great and will prevail.

mag·na·flux (mag′nə fluks′), *v.t.* to test (iron or steel) for defects using the Magnaflux method. [1935–40; see MAGNAFLUX]

Mag·na·flux (mag′nə fluks′), *Trademark.* a test of ferrous metals involving the dusting of a magnetized sample with magnetic powder, or the application of oil containing magnetic particles in suspension, to detect surface cracks and defects.

Mag·na Grae·ci·a (mag′nə grē′shē ə; *Lat.* mäg′nä grī′ki ä′), the ancient colonial cities and settlements of Greece in S Italy.

mag·na·li·um (mag nā′lē əm), *n.* an alloy of magnesium and aluminum, sometimes also containing copper, nickel, tin, and lead. [1895–1900; MAGN(ESIUM) + AL(UMINUM) + -IUM]

Mag·na Ma·ter (mäg′nə mä′ter), *Rom. Relig.* Cybele; Ops; Rhea. [< L *magna māter* great mother]

mag·na·nim·i·ty (mag′nə nim′i tē), *n., pl.* **-ties** for 2. **1.** the quality of being magnanimous. **2.** a magnanimous act. [1300–50; ME *magnanimite* < L *magnanimitās.* See MAGNANIMOUS, -ITY]

mag·nan·i·mous (mag nan′ə məs), *adj.* **1.** generous in forgiving an insult or injury; free from petty resentfulness or vindictiveness: *to be magnanimous toward one's enemies.* **2.** high-minded; noble: *a just and magnanimous ruler.* **3.** proceeding from or revealing generosity or nobility of mind, character, etc.: *a magnanimous gesture of forgiveness.* [1575–85; < L *magnanimus* great-souled, equiv. to *magn(us)* MAGN- + *anim(us)* spirit, soul, mind + *-us* -OUS] —**mag·nan′i·mous·ly,** *adv.* —**mag·nan′i·mous·ness,** *n.*
—**Syn. 1.** big, liberal, unspiteful. **2.** See **noble.**

mag·nate (mag′nāt, -nit), *n.* **1.** a person of great influence, importance, or standing in a particular enterprise, field of business, etc.: *a railroad magnate.* **2.** a person of eminence or distinction in any field: *literary magnates.* **3.** a member of the former upper house in either the Polish or Hungarian parliament. [1400–50; back formation from ME *magnates* (pl.) < LL *magnātēs* leading people, equiv. to L *magn(us)* MAGN- + *-ātēs,* pl. of *-ās* n. suffix] —**mag′nate·ship′,** *n.*

mag·ne·sia (mag nē′zhə, -shə), *n.* a white, tasteless substance, magnesium oxide, MgO, used in medicine as an antacid and laxative. Cf. **milk of magnesia.** [1350–1400; ME: philosophers' stone < ML *magnēsia* < Gk (*hē*) *Magnēsía* (*líthos*) (the stone) of MAGNESIA; sense development obscure] —**mag·ne′sian,** *adj.*

Mag·ne·si·a (mag nē′shē ə, -zhē ə), *n.* ancient name of **Manisa.**

mag·ne·site (mag′nə sīt′), *n.* a mineral, magnesium carbonate, $MgCO_3$, having a characteristic conchoidal fracture and usually occurring in white masses. [1805–15; MAGNES(IA) + -ITE[1]; cf. F *magnésite*]

mag·ne·si·um (mag nē′zē əm, -zhəm, -shē əm), *n.* *Chem.* a light, ductile, silver-white, metallic element that burns with a dazzling white light, used in lightweight alloys, flares, fireworks, in the manufacture of flashbulbs, optical mirrors, and precision instruments, and as a zinc substitute in batteries. *Symbol:* Mg; *at. wt.:* 24.312; *at. no.:* 12; *sp. gr.:* 1.74 at 20°C. [1800–10; < NL; see MAGNESIA, -IUM]

magne′sium ar′senate, *Chem.* a white, water-insoluble powder, $Mg_3(AsO_4)_2 \cdot xH_2O$, used chiefly as an insecticide.

magne′sium car′bonate, *Chem.* a white powder, $MgCO_3$, insoluble in water and alcohol, soluble in acids, used in dentifrices and cosmetics, in medicine as an antacid, and as a refractory material.

magne′sium hydrox′ide, *Chem.* a white, crystalline, slightly water-soluble powder, $Mg(OH)_2$, used chiefly in medicine as an antacid and as a laxative. [1905–10]

magne′sium light′, the strongly actinic white light produced when magnesium is burned: used in photography, signaling, pyrotechnics, etc. [1855–60]

magne′sium ox′ide, *Chem.* magnesia. [1905–10]

magne′sium perox′ide, *Chem.* a white, tasteless, water-insoluble powder, MgO_2, used as an antiseptic and as an oxidizing and bleaching agent. Also called **magne′sium diox′ide.**

magne′sium sil′icate, *Chem.* **1.** a white powder, $3MgSiO_3 \cdot 5H_2O$, with variable hydration, insoluble in water or alcohol, used as a rubber filler, a bleaching agent, an odor absorbent, and in the manufacture of paints and resins. **2.** any silicate containing magnesium, as enstatite, talc, or magnesium trisilicate.

magne′sium sul′fate, *Chem.* a white, water-soluble salt, $MgSO_4$, used chiefly in medicine and in the processing of leather and textiles. Cf. **Epsom salt.** [1885–90]

magne′sium trisil′icate, *Chem.* a white, fine, odorless and tasteless powder, $Mg_2O_8Si_3 \cdot nH_2O$, used industrially to absorb odors and decolorize and pharmaceutically as an antacid.

mag·net (mag′nit), *n.* **1.** a body, as a piece of iron or steel, that possesses the property of attracting certain substances, as iron. **2.** a lodestone. **3.** a thing or person that attracts: *The park was a magnet for pickpockets and muggers.* [1400–50; late ME *magnete* < L *magnēta* < Gk *mágnēta,* acc. of *mágnēs,* short for (*hē*) *Mágnēs* (*líthos*) (the stone) of Magnesia]

magnet-, var. of **magneto-** before some vowels: *magneton.*

mag·net·ic (mag net′ik), *adj.* **1.** of or pertaining to a magnet or magnetism. **2.** having the properties of a magnet. **3.** capable of being magnetized or attracted by a magnet. **4.** pertaining to the magnetic field of the earth: *the magnetic equator.* **5.** exerting a strong attractive power or charm: *a magnetic personality.* **6.** noting or pertaining to various bearings and measurements as indicated by a magnetic compass: *magnetic amplitude; magnetic course; magnetic meridian.* Also, **mag·net′i·cal.** [1625–35; < LL *magnēticus.* See MAGNET, -IC] —**mag·net′i·cal·ly,** *adv.*
—**Syn. 5.** persuasive, charismatic, captivating.

magnet′ic am′plifier, *Elect.* an amplifier that applies the input signal to a primary winding and feeds an alternating current to a secondary winding where this current is modulated by the variations in the primary winding.

magnet′ic anom′aly, *Geol.* a departure from the normal magnetic field of the earth. [1895–1900]

magnet′ic bear′ing, *Navig.* the bearing of a point relative to that of the nearest magnetic pole.

magnet′ic bot′tle, *Physics.* a magnetic field so shaped that it can confine a plasma: used in a proposed design for fusion reactors. [1955–60]

magnet′ic bub′ble, *Computers.* a tiny mobile magnetized area within a magnetic material, the basis of one type of solid-state storage medium **(magnet′ic bub′ble mem′ory).** Cf. **bubble memory.** [1965–70]

magnet′ic card′. See **mag card.**

magnet′ic chart′, *Navig.* a chart showing the magnetic properties of a portion of the earth's surface, as dip, variation, and intensity.

magnet′ic cir′cuit, *Physics.* the closed path described by magnetic flux. It is analogous to the electric circuit with resistance, where flux, reluctance, and magnetomotive force correspond to electric current, resistance, and electromotive force.

magnet′ic coeffi′cient, *Navig.* any of various factors affecting the sensitivity of a ship's magnetic compass as a result of its construction or environment.

magnet′ic com′pass, a compass having a magnetized needle generally in line with the magnetic poles of the earth.

magnet′ic concentra′tion, *Metall.* beneficiation of crushed ore in which a magnetic mineral is separated from gangue by means of a magnetic field.

magnet′ic core′, 1. *Computers.* core[1] (def. 12). **2.** *Elect.* core[1] (def. 3).

magnet′ic course′, *Navig.* a course whose bearing is given relative to the magnetic meridian of the area. Cf. **compass course, true course.**

magnet′ic declina′tion, *Navig.* variation (def. 8).

magnet′ic dip′, dip (def. 32).

magnet′ic disk′, *Computers.* **1.** Also called **disk, hard disk.** a rigid disk coated with magnetic material, on which data and programs can be stored. **2.** See **floppy disk.**

magnet′ic domain′, a portion of a ferromagnetic material where the magnetic moments are aligned with one another because of interactions between molecules or atoms. [1965–70]

magnet′ic drum′, *Computers.* a cylinder coated with magnetic material, on which data and programs can be stored. Also called **drum.** [1945–50]

magnet′ic equa′tor. See **aclinic line.** [1825–35]

magnet′ic field′, 1. a region of space near a magnet, electric current, or moving charged particle in which a magnetic force acts on any other magnet, electric current, or moving charged particle. **2.** See **magnetic intensity.** [1835–45]

magnet′ic field′ strength′. See **magnetic intensity.**

magnet′ic flux′, *Elect.* the total magnetic induction crossing a surface, equal to the integral of the component of magnetic induction perpendicular to the surface over the surface: usually measured in webers or maxwells. [1895–1900]

magnet′ic head′, *Electronics.* head (def. 33). [1945–50]

magnet′ic hystere′sis, *Physics.* hysteresis in a ferromagnetic material; the lag in the response of magnetic induction to changes of magnetic intensity.

magnet′ic induc′tion, *Elect.* **1.** Also called **magnet′ic flux′ den′sity.** a vector quantity used as a measure of a magnetic field. *Symbol:* B **2.** magnetization induced by proximity to a magnetic field. Cf. **electromagnetic induction.** [1850–55]

magnet′ic ink′ char′acter recogni′tion. See **MICR.**

magnet′ic inten′sity, *Elect.* that part of the magnetic induction that is determined at any point in space by the current density and displacement current at that point independently of the magnetic or other physical properties of the surrounding medium. *Symbol:* H Also called **magnetic field, magnetic field strength, magnetizing field, magnetizing force.**

magnet′ic lens′, *Physics.* an electron lens using magnetic fields for focusing an electron beam. [1915–20]

magnet′ic levita′tion, 1. the suspension of an object above or below a second object by means of magnetic repulsion or attraction. **2.** *Railroads.* the suspension of a vehicle above or below a suitable guide rail by such means, often with the vehicle being propelled by a linear induction motor. Also called **maglev.**

magnet′ic merid′ian, a line on the earth's surface, passing in the direction of the horizontal component of the earth's magnetic field.

magnet′ic mine′, *Navy.* an underwater mine set off by any disturbance of its magnetic field, as by the metal hull of a ship. Cf. **acoustic mine, contact mine.** [1935–40]

magnet′ic mir′ror, *Physics.* a region in a magnetic bottle where the magnetic field increases abruptly, causing charged particles that enter it to be reflected. [1890–95]

magnet′ic mo′ment, *Elect.* a vector quantity associated with a given electric current, magnet, or the like, having the property that its vector product with the magnetic induction equals the torque acting on the given object. Also called **dipole moment.** [1860–65]

magnet′ic mon′opole, a hypothetical very heavy particle with an isolated magnetic north pole or magnetic south pole.

magnet′ic nee′dle, a slender magnetized steel rod that, when adjusted to swing in a horizontal plane, as in a compass, indicates the direction of the earth's magnetic fields or the approximate position of north and south. [1840–50]

magnet′ic north′, north as indicated by a magnetic compass, differing in most places from true north. [1805–15]

magnet′ic permeabil′ity, permeability (def. 2).

magnet′ic pick′up, a phonograph pickup in which the vibrations of the stylus cause variations in or motions of a coil in a magnetic field that produces corresponding variations in an electrical voltage. Cf. **crystal pickup.**

magnet′ic pole′, 1. the region of a magnet toward which the lines of magnetic induction converge **(south pole)** or from which the lines of induction diverge **(north pole). 2.** either of the two points on the earth's surface where the dipping needle of a compass stands vertical, one in the arctic, the other in the antarctic. See maps under **North Pole, South Pole.** [1695–1705]

magnet′ic pole′ strength′, *Elect.* a measure of the force exerted by one face of a magnet on a face of another magnet when both magnets are represented by equal and opposite poles. *Symbol:* m

magnet′ic poten′tial, *Elect.* a scalar quantity, analogous to the electric potential, defined at each point in a given magnetic field to be equal to the work done in bringing a unit north pole from infinity to the point. Also called **magnet′ic sca′lar poten′tial.**

magnet′ic pul′ley, *Metall.* a magnetic device for separating metal from sand, refuse, etc.

magnet′ic py′rites, *Mineral.* pyrrhotite.

magnet′ic quan′tum num′ber, *Physics.* the quantum number that designates the component of the orbital angular momentum in a fixed direction and that can assume all integral values between and including the orbital quantum number and the negative of the orbital quantum number. [1920–25]

magnet′ic record′ing, the process of recording sound or other data on magnetic tape, wire, etc. [1940–45] —**magnet′ic record′er.**

magnet′ic res′onance im′aging. See **MRI.**

magnet′ic res′onance scan′. See **MR scan.**

magnet′ic res′onance scan′ner. See **MR scanner.** Also called **magnetic resonance imager.**

magnet′ic roast′ing, *Metall.* roasting of a nonmagnetic ore to render it magnetic so that it can be separated from gangue by means of a magnetic field.

magnet′ic rota′tion, *Optics.* See **Faraday effect.** [1899–1900]

mag•net•ics (mag net′iks), *n.* (*used with a singular v.*) the science of magnetism. [1780–90; see MAGNETIC, -ICS]

magnet′ic star′, *Astron.* a star having a strong magnetic field.

magnet′ic storm′, a temporary disturbance of the earth's magnetic field, induced by radiation and streams of charged particles from the sun. Also called **geomagnetic storm.** [1855–60]

magnet′ic strip′, a strip of magnetic material on which information may be stored, as by an electromagnetic process, for automatic reading, decoding, or recognition by a device that detects magnetic variations on the strip: *a credit card with a magnetic strip to prevent counterfeiting.* Also called **magnetic stripe, stripes.**

magnet′ic stripe′, **1.** See **magnetic strip. 2.** *Motion Pictures.* stripe[1] (def. 8). [1950–55]

magnet′ic susceptibil′ity, *Elect.* the coefficient or set of coefficients of the magnetic intensity in any expression giving the components of magnetization as linear combinations of the components of magnetic intensity. Also called **susceptibility.**

magnet′ic tape′, a ribbon of material, usually with a plastic base, coated on one side **(single tape)** or both sides **(double tape)** with a substance containing iron oxide, to make it sensitive to impulses from an electromagnet: used to record sound, images, data, etc. Also called **electromagnetic tape, tape.** [1935–40]

magnet′ic varia′tion, *Navig.* variation (def. 8).

magnet′ic wire′, a fine wire made from a magnetizable metal and used for wire recording. [1940–45]

mag•net•ism (mag′ni tiz′əm), *n.* **1.** the properties of attraction possessed by magnets; the molecular properties common to magnets. **2.** the agency producing magnetic phenomena. **3.** the science dealing with magnetic phenomena. **4.** strong attractive power or charm: *Everyone succumbed to the magnetism of his smile.* [1610–20; < NL *magnētismus.* See MAGNET, -ISM]

mag•net•ite (mag′ni tīt′), *n.* a very common black iron oxide mineral, Fe_3O_4, that is strongly attracted by magnets: an important iron ore. [1850–55; MAGNET + -ITE[1]; cf. G *Magnetit*]

mag•net•iz•a•ble (mag′ni tī′zə bəl), *adj.* susceptible to magnetization. [1790–1800; MAGNETIZE + -ABLE] —**mag′ne•tiz′a•bil′i•ty,** *n.*

mag•net•i•za•tion (mag′ni tə zā′shən), *n.* **1.** the process of magnetizing or the state of being magnetized. **2.** *Elect.* the magnetic moment per unit volume induced by any external magnetic field: measured in amperes per meter. *Symbol:* M [1885–90; MAGNETIZE + -ATION]

mag•net•ize (mag′ni tīz′), *v.t.,* **-ized, -iz•ing. 1.** to make a magnet of or impart the properties of a magnet to. **2.** to exert an attracting or compelling influence upon: *The evangelist's oratory magnetized his listeners.* **3.** *Archaic.* to mesmerize. Also, *esp. Brit.,* **mag′ne•tise′.** [1775–85; MAGNET + -IZE] —**mag′net•iz′er,** *n.*

mag′netizing field′, *Elect.* See **magnetic intensity.**

mag′netizing force′, *Elect.* See **magnetic intensity.**

mag•ne•to (mag nē′tō), *n., pl.* **-tos.** *Elect.* a small electric generator with an armature that rotates in a magnetic field provided by permanent magnets, as a generator supplying ignition current for certain types of internal combustion engines or a hand-operated generator for telephone signaling. Also called **magne′toelec′tric gen′erator, magnetogenerator.** [1880–85; short for *magnetoelectric generator*]

magneto-, a combining form representing **magnetic** or **magnetism** in compound words: *magnetochemistry.* Also, *esp. before a vowel,* **magnet-.**

mag•ne•to•cal•or′ic effect′ (mag nē′tō kə lôr′ik, -lor′-), *Physics.* an increase or decrease of the temperature of a thermally isolated magnetic substance accompanying an increase or decrease in the intensity of a magnetic field. [1920–25; MAGNETO- + CALORIC]

mag•ne•to•chem•is•try (mag nē′tō kem′ə strē), *n.* the study of magnetic and chemical phenomena in their relation to one another. [1910–15; MAGNETO- + CHEMISTRY] —**mag•ne′to•chem′i•cal,** *adj.*

mag•ne•to•e•las•tic•i•ty (mag nē′tō i la stis′i tē, -ē′la stis′-), *n. Physics.* the phenomenon, consisting of a change in magnetic properties, exhibited by a ferromagnetic material to which stress is applied. Cf. **magnetostriction.** [MAGNETO- + ELASTICITY] —**mag•ne′to•e•las′tic,** *adj.*

mag•ne•to•e•lec•tric (mag nē′tō i lek′trik), *adj.* of or pertaining to the induction of electric current or electromotive force by means of permanent magnets. Also, **mag•ne′to•e•lec′tri•cal.** [1825–35; MAGNETO- + ELECTRIC]

mag•ne•to•e•lec•tric•i•ty (mag nē′tō i lek tris′i tē, -ē′lek-), *n.* electricity developed by the action of magnets. [1825–35; MAGNETO- + ELECTRICITY]

mag•ne•to•en•ceph•a•lo•gram (mag nē′tō en sef′ə lə gram′), *n.* a record of the magnetic field of the brain. *Abbr:* MEG [MAGNETO- + ENCEPHALOGRAM] —**mag•ne•to•en•ceph•a•log•ra•phy** (mag nē′tō en sef′ə log′rə fē), *n.*

mag•ne′to•flu•id dynam′ics (mag nē′tō flo͞o′id), *Physics.* magnetohydrodynamics. [MAGNETO- + FLUID]

mag•ne•to•gas•dy•nam•ics (mag nē′tō gas′dī nam′iks), *n.* (*used with a singular v.*) magnetohydrodynamics. [1965–70; MAGNETO- + GAS + DYNAMICS]

mag•ne•to•gen•er•a•tor (mag nē′tō jen′ə rā′tər), *n.* magneto. [1890–95; MAGNETO- + GENERATOR]

mag•ne•to•gram (mag nē′tə gram′), *n.* the record produced by a magnetograph. [1880–85; MAGNETO- + -GRAM[1]]

mag•ne•to•graph (mag nē′tə graf′, -gräf′), *n.* a recording magnetometer, used esp. for recording variations in the earth's magnetic field. [1840–50; MAGNETO- + -GRAPH] —**mag•ne•to•graph•ic** (mag nē′tə graf′ik), *adj.*

magne′tohy′drodynam′ic genera′tion, *Physics.* the production of electric power without the use of rotating machinery by passing a plasma through a magnetic field. [1955–60; MAGNETO- + HYDRODYNAMIC]

mag•ne•to•hy•dro•dy•nam•ics (mag nē′tō hī′drō dī nam′iks), *n.* (*used with a singular v.*) the branch of physics that deals with the motion of electrically conductive fluids, esp. plasmas, in magnetic fields. *Abbr.:* MHD Also called **hydromagnetics, magnetofluid dynamics, magnetogasdynamics, magnetoplasmadynamics.** [1945–50; MAGNETO- + HYDRODYNAMICS] —**mag•ne′to•hy′dro•dy•nam′ic,** *adj.* —**mag•ne′to•hy′dro•dy•nam′i•cal•ly,** *adv.*

magne′tohy′drodynam′ic wave′, *Physics.* See **Alfvén wave.** [MAGNETO- + HYDRODYNAMIC]

mag•ne′to•me•chan′i•cal ra′tio (mag nē′tō mə kan′i kəl), *Physics.* the ratio of the angular momentum of a rotating charged particle to its magnetic moment; the reciprocal of the gyromagnetic ratio. [MAGNETO- + MECHANICAL]

mag•ne•tom•e•ter (mag′ni tom′i tər), *n.* **1.** an instrument for measuring the intensity of a magnetic field, esp. the earth's magnetic field. **2.** an instrument for detecting the presence of ferrous or magnetic materials, esp. one used to detect concealed weapons at airports. [1820–30; MAGNETO- + -METER] —**mag•ne•to•met•ric** (mag nē′tə me′trik), *adj.* —**mag′ne•tom′e•try,** *n.*

mag•ne′to•mo′tive force′ (mag nē′tə mō′tiv, -nē′-), *Elect.* a scalar quantity that is a measure of the sources of magnetic flux in a magnetic circuit. *Abbr.:* mmf [1883; MAGNETO- + MOTIVE]

mag•ne•ton (mag′ni ton′), *n. Physics.* a unit of magnetic moment, used in measuring the magnetic moment of atomic and subatomic particles. Cf. **Bohr magneton, nuclear magneton.** [1910–15; MAGNET- + -ON[1]]

mag•ne•to•op•tic (mag nē′tō op′tik), *adj.* pertaining to the effect of magnetism upon the propagation of light. [1880–85; MAGNETO- + OPTIC] —**mag•ne′to•op′ti•cal•ly,** *adv.*

mag•ne•to•op•tics (mag nē′tō op′tiks), *n.* (*used with a singular v.*) *Physics.* the branch of physics that deals with magnetooptic phenomena. [1900–05; MAGNETO- + OPTICS]

mag•ne•to•pause (mag nē′tə pôz′), *n. Astron.* **1.** the boundary between the earth's magnetosphere and interplanetary space, ab. 40,000 mi. (65,000 km) above the earth, marked by an abrupt decrease in the earth's magnetic induction. **2.** a similar feature of some other planet. [1960–65; MAGNETO- + PAUSE]

mag•ne•to•plas•ma•dy•nam•ics (mag nē′tō plaz′mə dī nam′iks), *n.* (*used with a singular v.*) magnetohydrodynamics. [MAGNETO- + PLASMA + DYNAMICS]

mag•ne•to•re•sist•ance (mag nē′tō ri zis′təns), *n.* a change in the electrical resistance of a material upon exposure to a magnetic field. [1925–30; MAGNETO- + RESISTANCE] —**mag•ne′to•re•sist′ive,** *adj.*

mag•ne•to•sheath (mag nē′tə shēth′), *n. Astron.* the region between the magnetopause of the earth or of some other planet and the shock front caused by the solar wind. [1965–70; MAGNETO- + SHEATH]

mag•ne•to•sphere (mag nē′tə sfēr′), *n. Astron.* **1.** the outer region of the earth's ionosphere, where the earth's magnetic field controls the motion of charged particles, as in the Van Allen belts. Cf. **magnetopause. 2.** such a region of another planet: *Jupiter's magnetosphere.* [1955–60; MAGNETO- + -SPHERE] —**mag•ne•to•spher•ic** (mag nē′tə sfer′ik), *adj.*

mag•ne•to•stat•ics (mag nē′tō stat′iks), *n.* (*used with a singular v.*) the branch of magnetics that deals with magnetic fields that do not vary with time **(magne′tostat′ic fields′).** [1895–1900; MAGNETO- + STATICS]

mag•ne•to•stric•tion (mag nē′tō strik′shən), *n. Physics.* a change in dimensions exhibited by ferromagnetic materials when subjected to a magnetic field. [1895–1900; MAGNETO- + (CON)STRICTION] —**mag•ne•to•stric•tive** (mag nē′tə strik′tiv), *adj.*

mag•ne•to•tail (mag nē′tə tāl′), *n. Astron.* the narrow and elongated region of the magnetosphere of the earth or of another planet that extends in the direction away from the sun. [1970–75; MAGNETO- + TAIL[1]]

mag•ne•to•tax•is (mag nē′tō tak′sis), *n. Biol.* movement or orientation of an organism in response to a magnetic field. [1960–65; MAGNETO- + -TAXIS] —**mag•ne•to•tac•tic** (mag nē′tō tak′tik), *adj.*

mag•ne•to•ther•mo•e•lec•tric•i•ty (mag nē′tō thûr′mō i lek tris′i tē, -ē′lek-), *n. Physics.* thermoelectricity induced or affected by a magnetic field. [MAGNETO- + THERMOELECTRICITY]

mag•ne•tron (mag′ni tron′), *n. Electronics.* a two-element vacuum tube in which the flow of electrons is under the influence of an external magnetic field, used to generate extremely short radio waves. [1920–25; MAGNE(TO)- + -TRON]

mag′net school′, a public school with special programs and instruction that are not available elsewhere in a school district and that are specially designed to draw students from throughout a district, esp. to aid in desegregation. [1965–70, *Amer.*]

magni-, a combining form appearing in loanwords from Latin, where it meant "large," "great": *magnify.* Also, *esp. before a vowel,* **magn-.** [< L, comb. form of *magnus*]

mag•ni•fic (mag nif′ik), *adj. Archaic.* **1.** magnificent; imposing. **2.** grandiose; pompous. Also, **mag•nif′i•cal.** [1480–90; < L *magnificus* grand (see MAGNI-, -FIC); r. earlier *magnyfyque* < MF < L as above] —**mag•nif′i•cal•ly,** *adv.*

Mag•nif•i•cat (mag nif′i kat′, -kät′; mäg nif′i kät′, män yif′-), *n.* **1.** (*italics*) the hymn of the Virgin Mary in Luke, 1:46–55, beginning "My soul doth magnify the Lord," used as a canticle at evensong or vespers. **2.** a musical setting for this. [1150–1200; ME < L: (it) magnifies (from the first word of the hymn)]

mag•ni•fi•ca•tion (mag′nə fi kā′shən), *n.* **1.** the act of magnifying or the state of being magnified. **2.** the power to magnify. Cf. **power** (def. 20a). **3.** a magnified image, drawing, copy, etc. [1615–25; < LL *magnificātiōn-* (s. of *magnificātiō*). See MAGNIFY, -FICATION]

mag•nif•i•cence (mag nif′ə səns), *n.* **1.** the quality or state of being magnificent; splendor; grandeur; sublimity: *the magnificence of snow-covered mountains; the magnificence of his achievements.* **2.** impressiveness of surroundings: *the magnificence of Versailles.* [1300–50; ME < L *magnificentia,* equiv. to *magnificent-* MAGNIFICENT + *-ia* -Y[3]; see -ENCE]
—**Syn. 1.** majesty, nobility, stateliness. **2.** luxuriousness, opulence, sumptuousness. —**Ant. 2.** squalor, poverty.

mag•nif•i•cent (mag nif′ə sənt), *adj.* **1.** making a splendid appearance or show; of exceptional beauty, size, etc.: *a magnificent cathedral; magnificent scenery.* **2.** extraordinarily fine; superb: *a magnificent opportunity; magnificent weather.* **3.** noble; sublime: *a magnificent poem.* **4.** (*usually cap.*) (formerly used as a title of some rulers) great; grand: *Lorenzo the Magnificent.* **5.** lavishly munificent; extravagant: *a magnificent inheritance.* [1425–75; late ME < MF < L *magnificent-* (s. recorded in comp., superl., and other forms) for *magnificus.* See MAGNIFIC, -ENT] —**mag•nif′i•cent•ly,** *adv.* —**mag•nif′i•cent•ness,** *n.*
—**Syn. 1.** majestic, sumptuous, opulent; exquisite, sublime. MAGNIFICENT, GORGEOUS, SPLENDID, SUPERB are terms of high admiration and all are used informally in weak exaggeration. Something that is MAGNIFICENT is beautiful, princely, grand, or ostentatious: *a magnificent display of paintings; a magnificent view of the harbor.* That which is GORGEOUS moves one to admiration by the richness and (often colorful) variety of its effects: *a gorgeous array of handsome gifts.* That which is SPLENDID is dazzling or impressive in its brilliance, radiance, or excellence: *splendid jewels; a splendid body of scholars.* That which is SUPERB is above others in, or is of the highest degree of, excellence, elegance, or (less often, today) grandeur: *a superb concert; superb wines.* —**Ant. 1.** modest; poor.

mag•nif•i•co (mag nif′i kō′), *n., pl.* **-coes. 1.** a Venetian nobleman. **2.** any person of high rank, major importance, etc. [1565–75; n. use of It *magnifico* (adj.) < L *magnificus.* See MAGNIFIC]

mag•ni•fi•er (mag′nə fī′ər), *n.* **1.** a person or thing that magnifies. **2.** a lens or combination of lenses that magnifies an object; magnifying glass. [1540–50; MAGNIFY + -ER[1]]

mag•ni•fy (mag′nə fī′), *v.,* **-fied, -fy•ing.** —*v.t.* **1.** to increase the apparent size of, as a lens does. **2.** to make greater in actual size; enlarge: *to magnify a drawing in preparing for a fresco.* **3.** to cause to seem greater or more important; attribute too much importance to; exaggerate: *to magnify one's difficulties.* **4.** to make more exciting; intensify; dramatize; heighten: *The playwright magnified the conflict to get her point across.* **5.** *Archaic.* to extol; praise: *to magnify the Lord.* —*v.i.* **6.** to increase or be able to increase the apparent or actual size of an object. [1350–1400; ME *magnifien* < L *magnificāre.* See MAGNI-, -FY] —**mag′ni•fi′a•ble,** *adj.*
—**Syn. 2.** augment, increase, amplify. **3.** overstate. —**Ant. 1, 2.** reduce. **3.** minimize.

mag′nifying glass′, a lens that produces an enlarged image of an object. Cf. **hand lens.** [1655–65]

mag•nil•o•quent (mag nil′ə kwənt), *adj.* speaking or expressed in a lofty or grandiose style; pompous; bombastic; boastful. [1650–60; back formation from L *magniloquentia* elevated language, equiv. to *magniloqu(us)* speaking grandly (*magni-* MAGNI- + *loqu(ī)* to speak + *-us* adj. suffix) + *-entia* -ENCE] —**mag•nil′o•quence,** *n.* —**mag•nil′o•quent•ly,** *adv.*

mag•nis•o•nant (mag nis′ə nənt), *adj. Archaic.* high-sounding. [1835–45; < LL *magnisonant-* (s. of *magnisonāns*). See MAGNI-, SONANT]

Mag•ni•to•gorsk (mag nē′tə gôrsk′; *Russ.* məg nyi-tu gôrsk′), *n.* a city in the W Russian Federation in Asia, on the Ural River, near the boundary between Europe and Asia. 430,000.

mag•ni•tude (mag′ni to͞od′, -tyo͞od′), *n.* **1.** size; extent; dimensions: *to determine the magnitude of an angle.* **2.** great importance or consequence: *affairs of* *magnitude.* **3.** greatness of size or amount. **4.** moral greatness: *magnitude of mind.* **5.** *Astron.* **a.** Also called **visual magnitude, apparent magnitude.** the brightness of a star or other celestial body as viewed by the unaided eye and expressed by a mathematical ratio of 2.512: a star of the first magnitude is approximately 2½ times as bright as one of the second magnitude and 100 times brighter than one of the sixth magnitude. Only stars of the sixth magnitude or brighter can be seen with the unaided eye. **b.** See **absolute magnitude.** **6.** *Math.* a number characteristic of a quantity and forming a basis for comparison with similar quantities, as length. **7. of the first magnitude,** of utmost or major importance: *an artist of the first magnitude.* [1350–1400; ME < L *magnitūdō.* See MAGNI-, -TUDE] **—mag·ni·tu·di·nous** (mag′ni to͞od′n əs, -tyo͞od′-), *adj.*

mag·no·lia (mag nōl′yə, -nō′lē ə), *n.* **1.** any shrub or tree of the genus *Magnolia,* having large, usually fragrant flowers and an aromatic bark, much cultivated for ornament. Cf. **magnolia family. 2.** the blossom of any such shrub or tree, as of the evergreen magnolia tree: the state flower of Louisiana and Mississippi. [< NL (Linnaeus), named after Pierre *Magnol* (1638–1715), French botanist; see -IA]

Mag·no·lia (mag nōl′yə, -nō′lē ə), *n.* a city in SW Arkansas. 11,909.

mag·no·li·a·ceous (mag nō′lē ā′shəs), *adj.* belonging to the plant family Magnoliaceae. Cf. **magnolia family.** [1850–55; < NL *Magnoliace(ae)* (see MAGNOLIA, -ACEAE) + -OUS]

magno′lia fam′ily, the plant family Magnoliaceae, characterized by evergreen or deciduous trees and shrubs having simple, alternate leaves, often showy flowers with a spiral arrangement of their floral parts, and conelike fruit, and including the cucumber tree, magnolia, tulip tree, and umbrella tree.

Magno′lia State′, Mississippi (used as a nickname).

magno′lia war′bler, a black and yellow wood warbler, *Dendroica magnolia,* of North America.

mag·num (mag′nəm), *n.* **1.** a large wine bottle having a capacity of two ordinary bottles or 1.5 liters (1.6 quarts). **2.** a magnum cartridge or firearm. *—adj.* **3.** (of a cartridge) equipped with a larger charge than other cartridges of the same size. **4.** (of a firearm) using such a cartridge. **5.** *Informal.* unusually great in power or size: *a magnum spotlight; a magnum dosage.* [1780–90; < L, neut. of *magnus* large; in reference to firearms, orig. used as a trademark by the Smith and Wesson Co.]

mag′num o′pus, a great work, esp. the chief work of a writer or artist: *Proust's magnum opus is* Remembrance of Things Past. [1785–95; < L]

Mag·nus An·nus (mäg′no͝os än′no͝os), *Latin.* the Great Year: a cycle of years, usually a thousand, that begins with a Golden Age, steadily deteriorates, and ends with a universal catastrophe, either a fire or a flood.

Mag′nus effect′ (mag′nəs), *Mech.* the thrust on a cylinder rotating about its axis while in motion in a fluid, the thrust being perpendicular to the relative motion of the cylinder in the fluid. [1920–25; named after Heinrich G. *Magnus* (1802–70), German scientist]

Mag′nus hitch′, a knot similar to a clove hitch but taking one more turn around the object to which the line is being bent; rolling hitch. [*Magnus,* of unknown orig.]

Ma·gog (mā′gog), *n.* **1.** a people descended from Japheth. Gen. 10:2; Ezek. 38, 39. Cf. **Gog and Magog. 2.** a city in S Quebec, in E Canada. 13,604.

ma·got (ma gō′, mä-, mag′ət), *n.* **1.** See **Barbary ape. 2.** a small, grotesque Japanese or Chinese carved figure. [1600–10; < F, MF, alter. of *Magog,* a people seduced by Satan in Rev. 20:8 (cf. MAGOG); used figuratively in medieval legends of Oriental and hence non-Christian races, and prob. applied derisively to the apes in allusion to the supposed grotesqueness of such races]

mag·pie (mag′pī′), *n.* **1.** either of two corvine birds, *Pica pica* **(black-billed magpie),** of Eurasia and North America, or *P. nuttalli* **(yellow-billed magpie),** of California, having long, graduated tails, black-and-white plumage, and noisy, mischievous habits. **2.** any of several related corvine birds. **3.** any of several black-and-white birds not related to the true magpies, as *Gymnorhina tibicen,* of Australia. **4.** an incessantly talkative person; noisy chatterer; chatterbox. **5.** a person who collects or hoards things, esp. indiscriminately. **6.** *Western U.S.* a black-and-white cow or steer, as a Holstein. [1595–1605; *Mag* Margaret + PIE²]

black-billed magpie,
Pica pica,
length 18 in. (46 cm)

mag′pie goose′, a black-and-white gooselike bird, *Anseranas semipalmatus,* of Australia, believed to be the most primitive waterfowl in existence. [1895–1900]

mag′pie lark′, a black-and-white pied bird, *Grallina cyanoleuca,* inhabiting areas near water in Australia and southern New Guinea. Also, **mag′pie-lark′.** [1885–90]

M. Agr., Master of Agriculture.

Ma·gritte (*Fr.* MA grēt′), *n.* **Re·né** (*Fr.* Rə nā′), 1898–1967, Belgian painter.

Mag·say·say (mäg sī′sī), *n.* **Ra·món** (rä mōn′; *Sp.* rä môn′), 1907–57, Philippine statesman: president 1953–57.

mag′ tape′ (mag), *Computers.* a magnetic tape used for recording data. [*mag,* by shortening of MAGNETIC]

mag·uey (mag′wā, mə gā′; *Sp.* mä gā′), *n.* **1.** any of several plants of the genus *Agave,* of the agave family, esp. the cantala, *A. cantala.* **2.** the fiber from these plants. **3.** a rope made from this or a similar fiber. [1545–55; < Sp < Taino]

Ma·gus (mā′gəs), *n., pl.* **-gi** (-jī). **1.** (*sometimes l.c.*) one of the Magi. **2.** (*l.c.*) a magician, sorcerer, or astrologer. **3.** (*sometimes l.c.*) a Zoroastrian priest. Cf. **Magi** (def. 2). [1615–25; < L < Gk *mágos* < OPers *maguš;* cf. Avestan *moyu*]

mag′ wheel′, *Auto.* a wheel containing magnesium or aluminum generally alloyed with steel, which makes it lighter in weight and shinier than an ordinary steel wheel: used esp. on racing cars and sports cars. [1965–70; *mag,* by shortening of MAGNESIUM]

Mag·yar (mag′yär, mäg′-; *Hung.* mo′dyoR), *n.* **1.** a member of the ethnic group, of the Finno-Ugric stock, that forms the predominant element of the population of Hungary. **2.** Hungarian (def. 3). *—adj.* **3.** of or pertaining to the Magyars or their language; Hungarian.

Ma·gyar·or·szág (mo′dyoR ôR′säg), *n.* Hungarian name of **Hungary.**

Ma·ha·ba·li·pur·am (mə hä′bə lē po͝or′əm), *n.* a village in NE Tamil Nadu, in SE India: Hindu temples; early Dravidian architecture. Also, **Ma·ha′ba·li·pur′, Mamallapuram.**

Ma·ha·bha·ra·ta (mə hä′bär′ə tə), *n.* an epic poem of India dealing mainly with the conflict between the Pandavas and the Kauravas, with many digressions: includes the Bhagavad-Gita. Also, **Ma·ha·bha·ra·tum** (mə hä′bär′ə təm). [< Skt *mahābhārata* great (*mahat*) work relating the story of the descendants of *Bharata*]

Ma·ha·de·va (mə hä′dā′və), *n. Hinduism.* a name of Shiva. [< Skt: great god, equiv. to *mahā-* great + *deva* god. See DEITY]

Ma·ha·la (mə hā′lə), *n.* a female given name.

ma·hal′a mat′ (mə hal′ə), a prostrate evergreen shrub, *Ceanothus prostratus,* of the buckthorn family, native to the Pacific coast of the U.S., having wedge-shaped, spiny-edged leaves and blue flowers. [1905–10, *Amer.; mahala* Indian woman < Yokuts; cf. *mokʰelo* (Chawchila dial.) woman, *moxelo* (Yawelmani dial.) old woman]

ma·ha·leb (mä′hə leb′), *n.* a cherry, *Prunus mahaleb,* introduced into the U.S. from Eurasia, used as a stock in grafting cherries. Also called **ma′haleb cher′ry, St. Lucie cherry.** [1550–60; < Ar *maḥlab*]

Ma·hal·ia (mə hāl′yə), *n.* a female given name, form of **Mahala.**

Ma·hal·la el Ku·bra (mə hal′ə el ko͞o′brə), a city in Egypt, on the Nile delta. 235,000.

Ma·ha·ma·ya (mə hä′mä′yə), *n. Hinduism.* **1.** the mother of the Buddha. **2.** maya (def. 4). [1690–1700; < Skt, equiv. to *mahā-* great + *māyā* MAYA]

Ma·han (mə han′), *n.* **Alfred Thay·er** (thā′ər), 1840–1914, U.S. naval officer and writer on naval history.

ma·ha·ra·jah (mä′hə rä′jə, -zhə), *n.* (formerly) a ruling prince in India, esp. of one of the major states. Also, **ma′ha·ra′ja.** [1690–1700; < Hindi *mahārājā* great king, equiv. to *mahā-* great + *rājā* RAJAH]

ma·ha·ra·nee (mä′hə rä′nē), *n.* **1.** (formerly) the wife of a maharajah. **2.** (formerly) an Indian princess who was sovereign in her own right. Also, **ma′ha·ra′ni.** [1850–55; < Hindi *mahārānī* great queen, equiv. to *mahā-* great + *rānī* RANEE]

Ma·ha·rash·tra (mä′hə räsh′trə), *n.* a state in W central India. 57,430,000; 118,903 sq. mi. (307,959 sq. km). *Cap.:* Bombay.

ma·ha·ri·shi (mä hə rē′shē, mə här′ə-), *n. Hinduism.* **1.** a teacher of spiritual and mystical knowledge; religious sage: often used as an honorary title. **2.** any of the seven great mythological seers of the Vedic and post-Vedic writings: identified with the seven stars of Ursa Major. [< Skt *maharṣi,* equiv. to *maha-* great + *-ṛṣi,* comb. form of *ṛṣi* saint]

Ma·ha·sa·ma·dhi (mə hä′sə mä′dē), *n. Hinduism, Buddhism.* the highest state of samadhi. [< Skt, equiv. to *mahā-* great + *samādhi* SAMADHI]

ma·hat·ma (mə hät′mə, -hat′-), *n.* (*sometimes cap.*) **1.** a Brahman sage. **2.** (esp. in India) a person who is held in the highest esteem for wisdom and saintliness. **3.** (in Theosophy) a great sage who has renounced further spiritual development in order to aid those who are less advanced. [1850–55; < Skt *mahātmā,* nom. sing. of *mahātman* high-souled, magnanimous, equiv. to *mahā-* great + *ātman* ATMAN] **—ma·hat′ma·ism,** *n.*

Mahat′ma Gan′dhi. See **Gandhi, Mohandas Karamchand.**

Ma·ha·vi·ra (mə hä′vēr′ə), *n.* Vardhamana.

Ma·ha·ya·na (mä′hə yä′nə), *n.* the later of the two great schools of Buddhism, chiefly in China, Tibet, and Japan, characterized by eclecticism and a general belief in a common search for salvation, sometimes thought to be attainable through faith alone. Cf. **Hinayana.** [1865–70; < Skt, equiv. to *mahā-* great + *yāna* vehicle] **—Ma·ha·ya·nist** (mä′hə yä′nist), *n.*

Ma·ha Yu·ga (mə hä′ yo͝og′ə), a period of 12,000 years, comprising four Yugas.

Mah·di (mä′dē), *n., pl.* **-dis. 1.** the Muslim messiah, an expected spiritual and temporal ruler destined to establish a reign of righteousness throughout the world. **2.** any of various claimants to this role, esp. Muhammad Ahmed, who established an independent government in the Anglo-Egyptian Sudan that lasted until 1898. [1790–1800; < Ar *mahdīy* he who is guided] **—Mah′dism** (mä′diz əm), *n.* **—Mah′dist,** *n., adj.*

Ma·hen·dra (mä hen drä′), *n.* (*Mahendra Bir Bikram Shah Deva*) 1920–72, king of Nepal 1955–72.

Mah·fouz (mä fo͞oz′), *n.* **Na·guib** (nä gēb′), born 1911, Egyptian author: Nobel prize 1988.

Ma·hi·can (mə hē′kən), *n., pl.* **-cans,** (*esp. collectively*) **-can. 1.** a tribe or confederacy of Algonquian-speaking North American Indians, centralized formerly in the upper Hudson valley. **2.** a member of this tribe or confederacy. Also, **Mohican.** [1605–15; < the Mahican name for themselves: lit., person (people) of the tidal estuary (c. Munsee Delaware *ma·hi·kan;* cf. *-a·hi·kan* in *kihta·hi·kan* ocean, with *kiht-* great)]

ma·hi·ma·hi (mä′hē mä′hē), *n., pl.* **-his.** *Hawaii.* the dolphinfish, esp. when used as a food fish. Also, **ma′·hi·ma′hi.** [1940–45; < Hawaiian]

mah-jongg (mä′jông′, -jong′, -zhông′, -zhong′), *n.* **1.** a game of Chinese origin usually played by four persons with 144 dominolike pieces or tiles marked in suits, counters, and dice, the object being to build a winning combination of pieces. *—v.i.* **2.** to win a game of mah-jongg. Also, **mah′-jong′.** [1920–25; < dial. Chin; cf. Guangdong dial. *màh-jéuk,* Chin *máquè* lit., sparrow (depicted on the first tile of a set)]

Mah·ler (mä′lər), *n.* **Gus·tav** (go͝os′täf), 1860–1911, Austrian composer and conductor, born in Bohemia.

mahl·stick (mäl′stik′, môl′-), *n.* a stick with a padded tip used to support an artist's working hand. Also, **maulstick.** [1875–80; < D *maalstok* lit., painting-stick, equiv. to *mal(en)* to paint + *stok* stick, with *stok* trans. as STICK¹]

Mah·mud II (mä mo͞od′), 1785–1839, sultan of Turkey 1809–39.

Mah·mud′ of Ghaz′ni (mə mo͞od′; guz′nē), A.D. 971?–1030, Muslim Amir of Ghazni 997–1030.

ma·hoe (mə hō′), *n.* **1.** See **hau tree. 2.** a tropical American tree, *Hibiscus elatus,* of the mallow family, having wood used for cabinetwork and gunstocks. **3.** a tree, *Melicytus ramiflora,* of the violet family, native to New Zealand and other Pacific islands, having greenish flowers and blue berries. [1660–70; < F *mahot* < Arawak]

ma·hog·a·ny (mə hog′ə nē), *n., pl.* **-nies,** *adj.* **1.** any of several tropical American trees of the genus *Swietenia,* esp. *S. mahagoni* and *S. macrophylla,* yielding hard, reddish-brown wood used for making furniture. **2.** the wood itself. **3.** any of various similar trees or their wood. Cf. **African mahogany, Philippine mahogany. 4.** a reddish-brown color. *—adj.* **5.** pertaining to or made of mahogany. **6.** of the color mahogany. [1665–75; perh. < some non-Carib language of the West Indies]

mahog′any fam′ily, the plant family Meliaceae, characterized by tropical and subtropical trees and shrubs having alternate, pinnate leaves, usually branched clusters of flowers, and fruit in the form of a berry or leathery capsule, and including the chinaberry, cedars of the genus *Cedrela,* and mahoganies of the genera *Swietenia* and *Khaya.*

Ma·hom·et (mə hom′it), *n.* Muhammad (def. 1).

Ma·hom·e·tan (mə hom′i tn), *n., adj. Archaic.* Muslim (defs. 1, 2). [1520–30; MAHOMET + -AN] **—Ma·hom′et·an·ism,** *n.*

Ma·hón (mä ôn′), *n.* a seaport on E Minorca, in the Balearic Islands. 19,279.

ma·ho·ni·a (mə hō′nē ə), *n.* any of various evergreen shrubs belonging to the genus *Mahonia,* of the barberry family, including the Oregon grape. [< NL (1818), named after Bernard Mc*Mahon* (c1775–1816), U.S. botanist, born in Ireland; see -IA]

Ma·hound (mə hound′, -ho͞ond′), *n. Archaic.* Muhammad. [1350–1400; ME *Mahun, Mahum* < OF, short for MAHOMET; *-d* by assoc. with HOUND¹]

ma·hout (mə hout′), *n.* the keeper or driver of an elephant, esp. in India and the East Indies. [1655–65; < Hindi *mahāut,* var. of *mahāvat;* cf. Prakrit *mahāmatta,* Skt *mahāmatra* elephant driver]

Mah·rat·ta (mə rat′ə), *n.* Maratha.

Mah·rat·ti (mə rat′ē), *n.* Marathi.

Mah′rē and Mah·rā′nē (mä′rə; mä rä′nə), *Zoroastrianism.* See **Mashyē and Mashyānē.**

Mäh·ren (me′Rən), *n.* German name of **Moravia.**

Mäh·risch-Os·trau (me′Rish ôs′tRou), *n.* German name of **Moravská Ostrava.**

ma·hua (mä′hwä), *n.* any of several trees of the genus *Madhuca,* of the sapodilla family, native to India, the Malay Peninsula, and southeastern Asia, esp. *M. latifolia,* the flowers of which are used, fresh or dried, for food or are fermented to prepare an intoxicating drink. Also, **ma′hwa, mohwa, mowra, mowrah.** [1680–90; < Hindi *mahūā* << Skt *madhūka* a tree name]

ma·huang (mä′hwäng′), *n.* a Chinese shrub, *Ephedra sinica,* that is a source of ephedrine. [< Chin *máhuáng* lit., hemp yellow]

mah·zor (*Seph.* mäkh zôr′; *Ashk.* mäkh′zôr, -zôr, -zər), *n., pl.* ***mah·zo·rim*** (*Seph.* mäkh zô rēm′; *Ashk.* mäkh zô′rim), *Eng.* **mah·zors.** *Hebrew.* a Jewish prayer book designed for use on festivals and holy days. Also, ***machzor.*** Cf. ***siddur.***

Ma·ia (mā′yə, mī′ə), *n. Class. Myth.* the eldest of the Pleiades and the mother of Hermes by Zeus.

maid (mād), *n.* **1.** a female servant. **2.** a girl or young unmarried woman. **3.** *Archaic.* a virgin. [1150–1200; ME; apocopated var. of MAIDEN] **—maid′ish,** *adj.* **—maid′ish·ness,** *n.*

mai·dan (mī dän′), *n.* (esp. in India) an open area or space in or near a town, often used as a marketplace or parade ground. [1615–25; < Hindi *maidān* < Pers < Ar *maydān*]

Mai·da·nek (mīd′n ek′, mī dä′nek), *n.* a Nazi concentration camp in eastern Poland, near Lublin.

maid·en (mād′n), *n.* **1.** a girl or young unmarried

CONCISE ETYMOLOGY KEY: <, descended or borrowed from; >, whence; b., blend of, blended; c., cognate with; cf., compare; deriv., derivative; equiv., equivalent; imit., imitative; obl., oblique; r., replacing; s., stem; sp., spelling, spelled; resp., respelling, respelled; trans., translation; ?, origin unknown; *, unattested; ‡, probably earlier than. See the full key inside the front cover.

woman; maid. **2.** a horse that has never won a race. **3.** a race open only to maiden horses. **4.** an instrument resembling the guillotine, formerly used in Scotland for beheading criminals. **5.** *Cricket.* See **maiden over.** —*adj.* **6.** of, pertaining to, or befitting a girl or unmarried woman. **7.** (of a woman) unmarried: *my maiden aunt.* **8.** made, tried, appearing, etc., for the first time: *a maiden flight.* **9.** virgin. **10.** (of a horse) never having won a race or a prize. **11.** (of a prize or a race) offered for or open only to maiden horses. **12.** untried, as a knight, soldier, or weapon. [bef. 1000; ME; OE *mægden,* equiv. to *mægd, mæg(e)th* (c. G *Magd,* Goth *magaths*) + *-en* -EN[5]] —**maid′en·ish,** *adj.* —**maid′en·ship′,** *n.*

Maid′en Cas′tle, an ancient fortification in Dorsetshire, England, first erected c250 B.C. over the remains of Neolithic and Bronze Age settlements of c2000–c1500 B.C.

maidenhair (mād′n hâr′), *n.* any fern of the genus *Adiantum,* the cultivated species of which have fine, glossy stalks and delicate, finely divided fronds. [1325–75; ME; see MAIDEN, HAIR]

maid′enhair spleen′wort, an evergreen fern, *Asplenium trichomanes,* abundant in woody areas of the North Temperate Zone, having thickly clustered fronds. [1830–40]

maidenhair-tree (mād′n hâr′trē′), *n.* ginkgo. [1765–75]

maidenhair-vine (mād′n hâr′vīn′), *n.* See **wire vine.**

maidenhead (mād′n hed′), *n.* **1.** the hymen. **2.** maidenhood; virginity. [1200–50; ME *maidenhed.* See MAIDEN, -HEAD]

maidenhood (mād′n ho͝od′), *n.* the state or time of being a maiden or virgin. Also called **maidhood.** [bef. 900; ME; OE *mægdenhād.* See MAIDEN, -HOOD]

maidenly (mād′n lē), *adj.* pertaining to, characteristic of, or befitting a maiden: *a maidenly blush.* [1400–50; late ME; see MAIDEN, -LY] —**maid′en·li·ness,** *n.*

maid′en name′, a woman's surname before her marriage. Cf. **birth name.** [1680–90]

maid′en o′ver, *Cricket.* an over in which no runs are made. Also called **maiden.** [1850–55]

maid′en pink′, a turf-forming plant, *Dianthus deltoides,* found from western Europe to eastern Asia, having red or pink flowers. [1770–80]

maid′en speech′, the first speech made in a legislature by a newly elected member. [1785–95]

maiden's-tears (mād′nz tērz′, -tėrz′), *n., pl.* **-tears.** See **bladder campion.**

maid′en voy′age, the first voyage of a ship after its acceptance by the owners from the builders. [1900–05]

maidhood (mād′ho͝od′), *n.* maidenhood. [bef. 900; ME; OE *mægthhade,* equiv. to *mægth* (see MAIDEN) + *-hade* -HOOD]

maid-in-waiting (mād′in wā′ting), *n., pl.* **maids-in-wait·ing.** an unmarried woman who serves as an attendant to a queen or princess; lady-in-waiting. [1950–55]

Maid′ Mar′ian, **1.** one of the characters in the old morris dance and May Day festivities; May queen. **2.** Robin Hood's sweetheart.

maid′ of hon′or, **1.** an unmarried woman who is the chief attendant of a bride. Cf. **matron of honor.** **2.** an unmarried woman, usually of noble birth, attendant on a queen or princess. [1580–90]

Maid′ of Or′léans. See **Joan of Arc.**

maidservant (mād′sûr′vənt), *n.* a female servant. [1520–30; MAID + SERVANT]

Maidstone (mād′stōn′, -stən), *n.* a city in Kent, in SE England. 125,300.

Maidu (mī′do͞o), *n., pl.* **-dus,** (*esp. collectively*) **-du** for 1. **1.** a member of a tribe of North American Indians of northeastern California. **2.** the Penutian language of the Maidu.

Maiduguri (mī do͞o′go͞o rē), *n.* a city in NE Nigeria. 179,000.

maieutic (mā yo͞o′tik), *adj.* of or pertaining to the method used by Socrates of eliciting knowledge in the mind of a person by interrogation and insistence on close and logical reasoning. [1645–55; < Gk *maieutikós* of, pertaining to midwifery, equiv. to *maieú(esthai)* to serve as a midwife (akin to *maîa* midwife) + *-tikos* -TIC]

maigre (mā′gər; *Fr.* meʹgrᵊ), *adj.* containing neither flesh nor its juices, as food permissible on days of religious abstinence. [1675–85; < F; see MEAGER]

maihem (mā′hem), *n.* mayhem.

Maikop (mī kôp′), *n.* a city in the SW Russian Federation in Europe, SE of Krasnodar. 149,000.

mail[1] (māl), *n.* **1.** letters, packages, etc., that are sent or delivered by means of the postal system: *Storms delayed delivery of the mail.* **2.** a single collection of such letters, packages, etc., as sent or delivered: *to open one's mail; to find a bill in the mail; The mail for England was put on the noon plane.* **3.** Also, **mails.** the system, usually operated or supervised by the national government, for sending or delivering letters, packages, etc.; postal system: *to buy clothes by mail.* **4.** a train, boat, etc., as a carrier of postal matter. **5. copy the mail,** *CB Slang.* to monitor or listen to a CB transmission. —*adj.* **6.** of or pertaining to mail. —*v.t.* **7.** to send by mail; place in a post office or mailbox for transmission. **8.** to transmit by electronic mail. [1175–1225; ME *male* (n.) < OF *malle* < Gmc; cf. OHG *mal(a)ha* satchel, bag]

mail[2] (māl), *n.* **1.** flexible armor of interlinked rings. **2.** any flexible armor or covering, as one having a protective exterior of scales or small plates. **3.** *Textiles.* an oval piece of metal pierced with a hole through which the warp ends are threaded, serving as an eyelet on a heddle or esp. on the harness cords of a Jacquard loom. —*v.t.* **4.** to clothe or arm with mail. [1250–1300; ME *maille* one of the rings of which armor was composed < OF < L *macula* spot, one of the interstices in a net; cf. MACULA] —**mail′less,** *adj.*

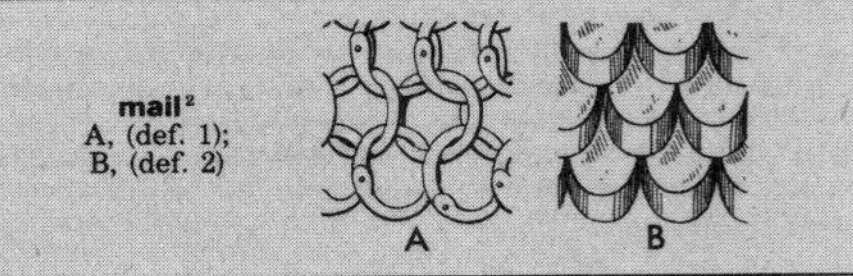

mail[2] A, (def. 1); B, (def. 2)

mail[3] (māl), *n. Scot.* monetary payment or tribute, esp. rent or tax. Also, **maill.** [bef. 1150; ME (north) *mal(e),* late OE *māl* agreement < ON *māl* agreement, speech, c. OE *mæl* speech]

mailable (mā′lə bəl), *adj.* legally acceptable as mail, as in terms of content, size, or weight. [1835–45, *Amer.*; MAIL[1] + -ABLE] —**mail′a·bil′i·ty,** *n.*

mailbag (māl′bag′), *n.* **1.** a large bag used by mail carriers for carrying mail, usually equipped with a shoulder strap. **2.** a large bag or pouch used in transporting mail in bulk from general post offices to branch offices, from city to city, etc. [1805–15; MAIL[1] + BAG]

mailboat (māl′bōt′), *n.* a boat for transporting mail. Also, **mail′ boat′.** [1785–95, *Amer.*; MAIL[1] + BOAT]

mail′ bomb′. See **letter bomb.** [1970–75]

mailbox (māl′boks′), *n.* **1.** a public box in which mail is placed for pickup and delivery by the post office. **2.** a private box, as at a home, into which mail is delivered by the mail carrier. **3.** *Computers.* a file for storing electronic mail. [1800–10; MAIL[1] + BOX[1]]

mail′ car′, a railroad car for carrying mail. [1835–45]

mail′ car′rier, a person, usually employed by the post office, who delivers mail. Also called **letter carrier, postal carrier.** [1780–90, *Amer.*]

mailcatcher (māl′kach′ər), *n. Railroads.* a device on a mail car that, while the train is moving, picks up mailbags suspended beside the track. [1870–75, *Amer.*; MAIL[1] + CATCHER]

mail-cheeked (māl′chēkt′), *adj.* (of certain fishes) having the cheeks crossed with a bony plate. [1825–35]

mail′ drop′, **1.** a receptacle or one of a series of pigeonholelike slots, as in an office, into which incoming mail is placed for pickup. **2.** drop (def. 12). [1970–75]

maile (mī′lā, -lē, mä′ē lā′), *n.* a vine, *Alyxia olivaeformis,* of Hawaii, having small yellowish flowers and fragrant foliage: a traditional lei plant of Hawaii. [1905–10; < Hawaiian]

mailed (māld), *adj.* clad or armed with mail: *a mailed knight.* [1350–1400; ME; see MAIL[2], -ED[3]]

mailed′ fist′, **1.** superior force, esp. military force, when presented as a threat: *The country showed its mailed fist in negotiations.* **2.** brutal or naked power, esp. coercive force: *the mailed fist hidden in the velvet glove.* [1895–1900]

mailer (mā′lər), *n.* **1.** a person who mails or prepares material for mailing. **2.** a container, as a mailing tube or protective envelope, for mailing papers, books, merchandise, etc. **3.** an advertising brochure, form letter, or the like, sent out in the mail. **4.** See **mailing machine.** **5.** *Archaic.* a mailboat. [1880–85, *Amer.*; MAIL[1] + -ER[1]]

Mailer (mā′lər), *n.* **Norman,** born 1923, U.S. writer.

mail′ flag′, *Naut.* **1.** a flag of the International Code of Signals symbolizing the letter *Y,* flown alone by a ship to indicate that it is carrying mail: a square flag with red and yellow diagonal stripes. **2.** any of various other flags indicating that a ship is carrying mail.

Mailgram (māl′gram′), *Trademark.* **1.** a message transmitted electronically to the post office nearest the addressee and then delivered by regular mail. **2.** the service that sends such messages.

mail-in (māl′in′), *adj.* **1.** conducted or responding by mail: *a mail-in referendum.* —*n.* **2.** something conducted or returned by mail, as a questionnaire or vote. [adj., n. use of v. phrase *mail in*]

mailing[1] (mā′ling), *n.* a batch of mail, as of form letters, catalogs, or monthly statements, sent by a mailer at one time: *an enthusiastic response to our latest mailing.* [1945–50; MAIL[1] + -ING[1]]

mailing[2] (mā′ling), *n. Scot.* **1.** a rented farm. **2.** the rent paid by a tenant farmer. [1425–75; late ME; see MAIL[3], -ING[1]]

mail′ing machine′, a machine that prepares mail for sending, as by addressing, stamping, weighing, etc. Also called **mailer.** [1870–75]

mail′ing tube′, an elongated cylinder of cardboard, used for mailing rolled-up papers, magazines, etc.

maill (māl), *n. Scot.* mail[3].

Maillart (mA yAR′), *n.* **Robert** (RÔ beR′), 1872–1940, Swiss engineer.

Maillol (mA yôl′), *n.* **Aristide** (A rēs tēd′), 1861–1944, French sculptor.

maillot (mä yō′, ma-), *n.* **1.** a close-fitting, one-piece bathing suit for women, simply styled and usually having a scoop neck and shoulder straps. **2.** tights worn by dancers, acrobats, etc. **3.** a close-fitting knitted shirt, esp. a pullover. [1885–90; < F: bathing costume, tights, swaddling clothes, var. of earlier *maillol,* deriv. of *maille* MAIL[2]]

mailman (māl′man′), *n., pl.* **-men.** a person employed by the post office to deliver mail; mail carrier. [1860–65; MAIL[1] + MAN[1]]

mail′ or′der, **1.** an order for goods received or shipped through the mail. **2.** the business of selling merchandise through the mail. [1865–70, *Amer.*]

mail-order (māl′ôr′dər), *adj.* **1.** pertaining to or obtained by mail order: *a dozen mail-order rosebushes.* —*v.t.* **2.** to order (merchandise) by mail: *to mail-order fruitcakes for Christmas.* [1865–70]

mail′-order house′, a retail firm that conducts its business by receiving orders and shipping its merchandise through the mail and that supplies its customers with catalogs, circulars, etc. [1905–10, *Amer.*]

mail-out (māl′out′), *n.* **1.** an act or instance of mailing out a quantity of letters, circulars, or the like; mailing. **2.** a form letter, brochure, etc., mailed out. Also, **mail′·out′.** [n. use of v. phrase *mail out*]

mailroom (māl′ro͞om′, -ro͝om′), *n.* **1.** Also, **mail′ room′.** a room used for handling incoming and outgoing mail, as in a large organization. —*adj.* **2.** of or pertaining to a mailroom: *mailroom employees.* [1880–85; MAIL[1] + ROOM]

maim (mām), *v.t.* **1.** to deprive of the use of some part of the body by wounding or the like; cripple: *The explosion maimed him for life.* **2.** to impair; make essentially defective: *The essay was maimed by deletion of important paragraphs.* —*n. Obs.* **3.** a physical injury, esp. a loss of a limb. **4.** an injury or defect; blemish; lack. [1250–1300; ME *mayme,* var. of *mahayme* MAYHEM] —**maimed′ness,** *n.* —**maim′er,** *n.*

—**Syn.** **1.** MAIM, LACERATE, MANGLE, MUTILATE indicate the infliction of painful and severe injuries on the body. To MAIM is to injure by giving a disabling wound, or by depriving a person of one or more members or their use: *maimed in an accident.* To LACERATE is to inflict severe cuts and tears on the flesh or skin: *to lacerate an arm.* To MANGLE is to chop undiscriminatingly or to crush or rend by blows or pressure, as if by machinery: *bodies mangled in a train wreck.* To MUTILATE is to injure the completeness or beauty of a body, esp. by cutting off an important member: *to mutilate a statue, a tree, a person.* **2.** injure, disable, deface, mar.

Maimonides (mī mon′i dēz′), *n.* (*Moses ben Maimon*) ("*RaMBaM*"), 1135–1204, Jewish scholastic philosopher and rabbi, born in Spain: one of the major theologians of Judaism. —**Mai·mon′i·de′an,** *adj., n.*

main[1] (mān), *adj.* **1.** chief in size, extent, or importance; principal; leading: *the company's main office; the main features of a plan.* **2.** sheer; utmost, as strength or force: *to lift a stone by main force.* **3.** of or pertaining to a broad expanse: *main sea.* **4.** *Gram.* syntactically independent; capable of use in isolation. Cf. **dependent** (def. 4), **independent** (def. 14), **main clause.** **5.** *Naut.* **a.** of or pertaining to a mainmast. **b.** noting or pertaining to a sail, yard, boom, etc., or to any rigging belonging to a mainmast. **c.** noting any stay running aft and upward to the head of a mainmast: *main topmast stay.* **6.** *Obs.* **a.** having or exerting great strength or force; mighty. **b.** having momentous or important results; significant. —*n.* **7.** a principal pipe or duct in a system used to distribute water, gas, etc. **8.** physical strength, power, or force: *to struggle with might and main.* **9.** the chief or principal part or point: *The main of their investments was lost during the war.* **10.** *Literary.* the open ocean; high sea: *the bounding main.* **11.** the mainland. **12. in the main,** for the most part; chiefly: *In the main, the novel was dull reading.* —*adv.* **13.** *South Midland U.S.* (*chiefly Appalachian*). very; exceedingly: *The dogs treed a main big coon.* —*v.i., v.t.* **14.** *Slang.* mainline. [bef. 900; (n.) ME *meyn, mayn* strength, power, OE *mægen,* c. ON *megin(n), megn* strength; (adj.) ME *mayn,* partly < ON *megenn, megn* strong, partly independent use of OE *mægen* (n.) taken as an adj. in compounds, as in *mægenweorc,* lit., work of might]

—**Syn.** **1.** cardinal, prime, paramount, primary, capital. **2.** pure, direct. **7.** conduit. **8.** might. —**Ant.** **1.** secondary, least. **8.** weakness.

main[2] (mān), *n.* a cockfighting match. [1560–70; perh. special use of MAIN[1]; cf. *main chance*]

Main (mān; *Ger.* mīn), *n.* a river in central and W Germany, flowing W from the Bohemian Forest in N Bavaria into the Rhine at Mainz. 305 mi. (490 km) long.

Mainbocher (man′bō shā′), *n.* (*Main Rousseau Bocher*), 1891–1976, U.S. fashion designer.

main′ bod′y, *Naut.* the hull, as distinguished from the rest of a ship.

main′ brace′, *Naut.* a brace leading to a main yard. [1480–90]

main′ chance′, an opportunity offering the greatest gain: *Being ambitious, he always had an eye for the main chance.* [1570–80]

main′ clause′, *Gram.* a clause that can stand alone as a sentence, containing a subject and a predicate with a finite verb, as *I was there* in the sentence *I was there when he arrived.* Cf. **subordinate clause.**

main′ course′, *Naut.* a square mainsail. See diag. under **ship.** [1505–15]

main′ deck′, *Naut.* the uppermost weatherproof deck, running the full length of a ship. [1740–50]

main-de-fer (man′ə fer′), *n. Armor.* manifer.

main′ diag′onal, *Math.* See under **diagonal** (def. 9).

main′ drag′, *Slang.* the main street of a city or town; main stem. [1850–55]

Maine (mān), *n.* **1.** a state in the NE United States, on the Atlantic coast. 1,124,660; 33,215 sq. mi. (86,027 sq. km). *Cap.:* Augusta. *Abbr.:* ME (for use with zip code), Me. See map on next page. **2.** a historical region and former province in NW France. **3.** (*italics*) a U.S. battleship blown up in the harbor of Havana, Cuba, on February 15, 1898: this incident stimulated popular support in the U.S. for the Spanish-American War.

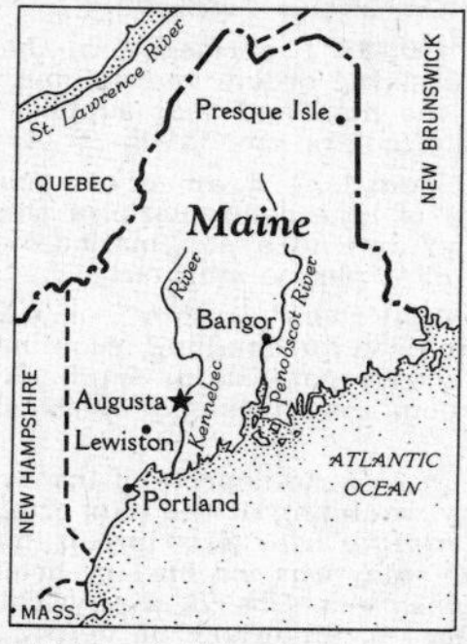

Maine′ coon′ cat′ one of an American breed of large semi-longhaired domestic cats with a shaggy ruff and a long, bushy tail. Also called **Maine′ coon′.**

Maine-et-Loire (me′nā lwAR′), *n.* a department in W France. 629,849; 2787 sq. mi. (7220 sq. km). *Cap.:* Angers.

main′ en′try, **1.** the principal entry of an item in a reference text, often placed in alphabetical order. **2.** *Library Science.* the principal, complete entry of an item in a catalog or bibliography, giving full information on the item, often including its location, and the form by which the item is to be consistently identified and cited. Cf. **added entry.**

Main•er (mā′nər), *n.* a native or inhabitant of the state of Maine. [1875–80, *Amer.*]

main-force (mān′fôrs′, -fōrs′), *adj.* pertaining to regular military units with standard uniforms and equipment.

main•frame (mān′frām′), *n. Computers.* a large computer, often the hub of a system serving many users. Cf. **microcomputer, minicomputer.** [1960–65; MAIN[1] + FRAME]

main gauche (*Fr.* maN gōsh′), a dagger of the 16th and 17th centuries, held in the left hand in dueling and used to parry the sword of an opponent. Also called **left-hand dagger.** [< F: lit., left hand]

main•land (mān′land′, -lənd), *n.* **1.** the principal land of a country, region, etc., as distinguished from adjacent islands or a peninsula: *the mainland of Greece.* **2.** (in Hawaii) the 48 contiguous states of the U.S. [1325–75; ME; see MAIN[1], LAND]

Main•land (mān′land′, -lənd), *n.* **1.** the largest of the Shetland Islands. 18,268; ab. 200 sq. mi. (520 sq. km). **2.** Pomona (def. 3).

main′land Chi′na, the People's Republic of China, as distinguished from Taiwan. **—main′land Chinese′.**

main•land•er (mān′lan′dər, -lən dər), *n.* **1.** a person who lives on a mainland. **2.** (in Hawaii) a person who lives in the continental U.S. [1855–60; MAINLAND + -ER[1]]

main′ line′, **1.** a principal line or route of a railroad, as contrasted with a branch or secondary one. **2.** a principal highway. **3.** *Slang.* **a.** a prominent and readily accessible vein of the body that may be used for a narcotic's injection. **b.** the act of mainlining. [1835–45]

Main′ Line′, **1.** a fashionable residential district west of Philadelphia. **2.** any fashionable district where socially prominent people live. **—Main′-Line′,** *adj.* **—Main′-Lin′er,** *n.*

main•line (mān′līn′, -līn′), *v.,* **-lined, -lin•ing,** *adj.* —*v.i. Slang.* **1.** to inject a narcotic, esp. heroin, directly into a vein. **2.** to use or enjoy something without restriction: *to mainline on TV movies.* —*v.t. Slang.* **3.** to inject (a narcotic, esp. heroin) directly into a vein. **4.** to use, enjoy, or imbibe (something) without restriction: *mainlining coffee all day long.* —*adj.* **5.** having a principal, established, or widely accepted position; major; mainstream: *the membership of mainline churches.* [1935–40, *Amer.*; v., adj. use of MAIN LINE]

main•lin•er (mān′lī′nər, -lī′-), *n.* **1.** *Slang.* a person who mainlines. **2.** a person who belongs to a mainline group. [1930–35, *Amer.*; MAINLINE + -ER[1]]

main•ly (mān′lē), *adv.* **1.** chiefly; principally; for the most part; to the greatest extent: *Our success was due mainly to your efforts. The audience consisted mainly of students.* **2.** *Obs.* greatly; mightily; abundantly. [1225–75; ME *maynliche, maynly.* See MAIN[1], -LY]

main•mast (mān′mast′, -mäst′; *Naut.* mān′məst), *n. Naut.* **1.** the second mast from forward in any ship having two or more masts, except for a yawl, ketch, or dandy. See illus. under **quarterdeck. 2.** the larger forward mast of a yawl, ketch, or dandy. **3.** the sole mast of any of various ships, as sloops or cutters. [1475–85; MAIN[1] + MAST[1]]

main′ mem′ory, *Computers.* See **main storage.**

main•our (mā′nər), *n. Old Eng. Law.* a stolen article found on the person of or near the thief: *to be taken with the mainour.* Also, **manner.** [1225–75; ME < AF *mainoure* (OF *manoeuvre* hand labor); see MANEUVER, INURE]

CONCISE ETYMOLOGY KEY: <, descended or borrowed from; >, whence; b., blend of, blended; c., cognate with; cf., compare; deriv., derivative; equiv., equivalent; imit., imitative; obl., oblique; r., replacing; s., stem; sp., spelling, spelled; resp., respelling, respelled; trans., translation; ?, origin unknown; *, unattested; ‡, probably earlier than. See the full key inside the front cover.

mains (mānz), *n.* (*used with a singular v.*) *Brit. Dial.* the main or home farm of a manor, as where the owner lives; manse. [1425–75; late ME, pl. of *main,* aph. var. of ME *demain, demeine* DEMESNE]

main•sail (mān′sāl′; *Naut.* mān′səl), *n. Naut.* the lowermost sail on a mainmast. See diag. under **ship.** [1425–75; late ME; see MAIN[1], SAIL]

main′ se′quence, *Astron.* a narrow band in the Hertzsprung-Russell diagram in which 90 percent of all observed stars are plotted. [1925–30]

main′ shaft′, *Mach.* the principal shaft of a motor, transmission, etc. (distinguished from *jackshaft*).

main•sheet (mān′shēt′), *n. Naut.* a sheet of a mainsail. [1475–85; see MAIN[1], SHEET[1]]

main•spring (mān′spring′), *n.* **1.** the principal spring in a mechanism, as in a watch. **2.** the chief motive power; the impelling cause. [1585–95; MAIN[1] + SPRING]

main•stay (mān′stā′), *n.* **1.** *Naut.* the stay that secures the mainmast forward. **2.** a person or thing that acts as a chief support or part: *Coffee is the mainstay of the country's economy.* [1475–85; MAIN[1] + STAY[2]] **—Syn. 2.** pillar, bulwark, anchor, prop.

main′ stem′, *Slang.* the main street of a city or town; the main drag. [1825–35, *Amer.*]

main′ stor′age, *Computers.* program-addressable storage that is directly controlled by and generally contained in the CPU; except for cache storage, the fastest type of storage available to any computer system. Also called **main memory, primary memory, real storage.**

main•stream (mān′strēm′), *n.* **1.** the principal or dominant course, tendency, or trend: *the mainstream of American culture.* **2.** a river having tributaries. —*adj.* **3.** belonging to or characteristic of a principal, dominant, or widely accepted group, movement, style, etc.: *mainstream Republicans; a mainstream artist.* **4.** of, pertaining to, or characteristic of jazz falling historically between Dixieland and modern jazz; specifically, swing music. Cf. **traditional** (def. 4). —*v.t.* **5.** to send into the mainstream; cause to join the main force, group, etc.: *to mainstream young people into the labor force.* **6.** to place (handicapped students) in regular school classes. —*v.i.* **7.** to join or be placed in the mainstream. [1660–70; MAIN[1] + STREAM]

main•stream•er (mān′strē′mər), *n.* a member of the mainstream. [1960–65; MAINSTREAM + -ER[1]]

main•stream•ing (mān′strē′ming), *n.* integration of children with special educational problems, as a physical handicap, into conventional classes and school activities. [1975–80; MAINSTREAM + -ING[1]]

main′ street′, **1.** the principal thoroughfare, esp. through the business district, in a small town. **2.** (*caps.*) the outlook, environment, or life of a small town.

Main′ Street′, a novel (1920) by Sinclair Lewis.

main•tain (mān tān′), *v.t.* **1.** to keep in existence or continuance; preserve; retain: *to maintain good relations with neighboring countries.* **2.** to keep in an appropriate condition, operation, or force; keep unimpaired: *to maintain order; to maintain public highways.* **3.** to keep in a specified state, position, etc.: *to maintain a correct posture; to maintain good health.* **4.** to affirm; assert; declare: *He maintained that the country was going downhill.* **5.** to support in speech or argument, as a statement or proposition. **6.** to keep or hold against attack: *to maintain one's ground.* **7.** to provide for the upkeep or support of; carry the expenses of: *to maintain a family.* **8.** to sustain or support: *not enough water to maintain life.* [1200–50; ME *mainteinen* < OF *maintenir* << ML *manūtenēre,* L *manū tenēre* lit., to hold in hand, equiv. to *manū,* abl. of *manus* hand (see MANUAL) + *tenēre* to hold (see TENET)] **—main•tain′a•ble,** *adj.* **—main•tain′a•bil′i•ty,** *n.* **—main•tain′er,** *n.*
—Syn. 1. continue. **1, 2.** keep up. **4.** asseverate. MAINTAIN, ASSERT, AVER, ALLEGE, HOLD, STATE all mean to express an opinion, judgment, or position. MAINTAIN carries the implications of both firmness and persistence in declaring or supporting a conviction: *She maintained her client's innocence even in the face of damaging evidence.* ASSERT suggests assurance, confidence, and sometimes aggressiveness in the effort to persuade others to agree with or accept one's position: *He asserted again and again the government's right to control the waterway.* AVER, like ASSERT, implies confident declaration and sometimes suggests a firmly positive or peremptory tone; in legal use AVER means "to allege as fact": *to aver that the evidence is incontrovertible.* ALLEGE indicates a statement without evidence to support it, and thus can imply doubt as to the validity or accuracy of an assertion: *The official is alleged to have been unaware of the crime.* HOLD means simply to have or express a conviction or belief: *We hold these truths to be self-evident; She held that her rights had been violated.* STATE usually suggests a declaration that is forthright and unambiguous: *He stated his reasons in clear, simple language.* **5.** uphold, defend, vindicate, justify. **7.** See **support.** **—Ant. 1.** discontinue. **5.** contradict.

main•tain•or (mān tā′nər), *n. Law.* a person guilty of maintenance. [1300–50; ME *meyntenour* < AF. See MAINTAIN, -OR[2]]

main•te•nance (mān′tə nəns), *n.* **1.** the act of maintaining. **2.** the state of being maintained: *the maintenance of friendly relations with England.* **3.** care or upkeep, as of machinery or property: *With proper maintenance the car will last for many years.* **4.** means of upkeep, support, or subsistence; livelihood: *to provide a comfortable maintenance.* **5.** alimony or child support. **6.** *Law.* an officious meddling in a suit in which the meddler has no interest, by assisting either party with means to prosecute or defend it. —*adj.* **7.** *Pharm., Psychiatry.* administered to sustain a desired physiological or mental condition: *maintenance dose.* [1275–1325; ME *maintenaunce* < MF *maintenance.* See MAINTAIN, -ANCE]
—Syn. 4. See **living.**

main′tenance and cure′, *Law.* the right of an injured sailor to support and medical treatment.

main•te•nance-free (mān′tə nəns frē′), *adj.* requiring little or no maintenance: *a maintenance-free pool.*

main′tenance of mem′bership, an arrangement or agreement between an employer and a labor union by which employees who are members of the union at the time the agreement is made, or who subsequently join, must either remain members until the agreement expires, or be discharged.

Main•te•non (maNt[ə] nôN′), *n.* **Marquise de** (*Françoise d'Aubigné*), 1635–1719, second wife of Louis XIV.

main•top (mān′top′), *n. Naut.* a platform at the head of the lower mainmast. [1475–85; MAIN[1] + TOP[1]]

main-top•gal•lant (mān′top gal′ənt; *Naut.* mān′tə-gal′ənt), *n.* the main-topgallantmast, its sail, or its yard. See illus. under **ship.** [1620–30]

main-top•gal•lant•mast (mān′top gal′ənt mast′, -mäst′; *Naut.* mān′tə gal′ənt məst), *n. Naut.* the mast next above the main-topmast. [1685–95]

main-top•mast (mān′top′mast′, -mäst′; *Naut.* mān′-top′məst), *n. Naut.* the mast next above the main lower mast. [1485–95]

main-top•sail (mān′top′sāl′; *Naut.* mān′top′səl), *n. Naut.* a topsail set on the mainmast. See diag. under **ship.** [1610–20]

main′-top′sail schoon′er, *Naut.* a two-masted or three-masted schooner having square topsails on the foremast and mainmast: a jackass brig or jackass bark.

main′ verb′, a word used as the final verb in a verb phrase, expressing the lexical meaning of the verb phrase, as *drink* in *I don't drink, going* in *I am going,* or *spoken* in *We have spoken.*

main′ yard′, *Naut.* a yard for a square mainsail. [1475–85]

Mainz (mīnts), *n.* a port in SW central Germany, at the confluence of the Rhine and Main rivers: capital of Rhineland-Palatinate. 172,400. French, **Mayence.**

Mainz′ Psal′ter, a book printed by Johannes Gutenberg: thought by some to be the first book printed from movable type.

ma•iol•i•ca (mə yol′i kə), *n.* majolica.

Mai•que•tí•a (mī′ke tē′ä), *n.* a city in the Federal District, in N Venezuela. 110,400.

mair (mâr), *adj., n., adv. Scot. and North Eng.* more.

Mai•ra (mī′rə), *n. Class. Myth.* Maera.

Mai•sie (mā′zē), *n.* a female given name, Scottish form of **Margaret.**

Mai•son de Mo•lière, La (*Fr.* lA me zôN′ də môlyeR′). See **Comédie Française.**

mai•son•ette (mā′zə net′), *n.* **1.** a small house, esp. one connected to a large apartment building. **2.** an apartment, usually of two floors connected by an internal staircase; duplex apartment. Also, **mai′son•nette′.** [1810–20; < F, OF, equiv. to *maison* house (see MANSION) + *-ette* -ETTE]

maist (māst), *adj., n., adv. Scot. and North Eng.* most.

mai tai (mī′ tī′), a cocktail of rum, curaçao, lemon and pineapple juice, grenadine, and orgeat syrup, poured over crushed ice. [of uncert. orig.]

Mait•land (māt′lənd), *n.* **Frederic William,** 1850–1906, English jurist and legal historian.

maî•tre d′ (mā′tər dē′, mā′trə-), *pl.* **maî•tre d's.** See **maître d'hôtel** (defs. 1–3). [1815–25]

maî•tre de bal•let (*Fr.* me′tR[ə] də bA lā′), *pl.* **maî•tres de bal•let** (*Fr.* me′tR[ə] də bA lā′). See **ballet master.** [1815–25; < F: master of ballet]

maî•tre d'hô•tel (mā′tər dō tel′, mā′trə; *Fr.* me′tR[ə] dō tel′), *pl.* **maî•tres d'hô•tel** (mā′tərz dō tel′, mā′trəz; *Fr.* me′tR[ə] dō tel′). **1.** a headwaiter. **2.** a steward or butler. **3.** the owner or manager of a hotel. **4.** *Cookery.* a sauce of melted butter, minced parsley, and lemon juice or vinegar. [1530–40; < F: master of (the) hotel]

maî•trise (me tRēz′), *n. French.* mastery; skill.

maize (māz), *n.* **1.** (chiefly in British and technical usage) corn[1] (def. 1). **2.** a pale yellow resembling the color of corn. [1545–55; < Sp *maíz* < Hispaniolan Taino *mahís*]

maize′ oil′. See **corn oil.**

Maj., Major.

ma•jes•tic (mə jes′tik), *adj.* characterized by or possessing majesty; of lofty dignity or imposing aspect; stately; grand: *the majestic Alps.* Also, **ma•jes′ti•cal.** [1595–1605; MAJEST(Y) + -IC] **—ma•jes′ti•cal•ly,** *adv.*
—Syn. august, splendid, magnificent, regal, royal, kingly, imperial, noble. **—Ant.** base, mean.

maj•es•ty (maj′ə stē), *n., pl.* **-ties.** **1.** regal, lofty, or stately dignity; imposing character; grandeur: *majesty of bearing; the majesty of Chartres.* **2.** supreme greatness or authority; sovereignty: *All paid tribute to the majesty of Rome.* **3.** (*usually cap.*) a title used when speaking of or to a sovereign (usually prec. by *his, her,* or *your*): *His Majesty's Navy; Will your Majesty hear our petitions?* **4.** a royal personage, or royal personages collectively: *The royal wedding was attended by the majesties of Europe.* **5. Christ in Majesty,** a representation of Christ as ruler of the universe. [1250–1300; ME *majeste* < MF < L *majestāt-* (s. of *majestās*) dignity, grandeur, equiv. to *majes-* (akin to *majus* < *mag-yos, neut. comp. of *magnus* large; cf. MAJOR) + *-tāt-* -TY[2]]

Maj. Gen., Major General.

maj•lis (māj′lis), *n., pl.* **-lis.** (in Islamic countries) **1.** a public audience held by a chieftain, monarch, or other ruler to listen to the requests of petitioners. **2.** a house of parliament, as in Iran. [1815–25; < Ar]

ma•jol•i•ca (mə jol′i kə, mə yol′-), *n.* **1.** Italian earthenware covered with an opaque glaze of tin oxide and usually highly decorated. **2.** any earthenware having an opaque glaze of tin oxide. Also, **maiolica.** [1545–55; earlier *maiolica* < It < ML, var. of LL *Mājorica* MAJORCA, where it was made]

ma•jor (mā′jər), *n.* **1.** a commissioned military officer ranking next below a lieutenant colonel and next above a captain. **2.** one of superior rank, ability, etc., in a specified class. **3.** *Educ.* **a.** a subject or field of study chosen by a student to represent his or her principal interest and upon which a large share of his or her efforts are concentrated: *History was my major at college.* **b.** a student engaged in such study. **4.** a person of full legal age (opposed to *minor*). **5.** *Music.* a major interval, chord, scale, etc. **6.** **the majors, a.** *Sports.* the major leagues: *He coached in the majors as well as in the minors.* **b.** the companies or organizations that lead or control a particular field of activity: *the oil majors.* —*adj.* **7.** greater in size, extent, or importance: *the major part of the town.* **8.** great, as in rank or importance: *a major political issue; a major artist.* **9.** serious or risky: *a major operation.* **10.** of or pertaining to the majority: *the major opinion.* **11.** of full legal age. **12.** *Music.* **a.** (of an interval) being between the tonic and the second, third, sixth, or seventh degrees of a major scale: *a major third; a major sixth.* **b.** (of a chord) having a major third between the root and the note next above it. **13.** pertaining to the subject in which a student takes the most courses: *Her major field is English history.* **14.** (*cap.*) (of one of two male students in an English public school who have the same surname) being the elder or higher in standing: *Hobbes Major is not of a scientific bent.* —*v.i.* **15.** to follow a major course of study: *He is majoring in physics.* [1350–1400; < L, comp. of *magnus* large (cf. MAJESTY); r. ME *majour* < AF < L, as above] —**Syn. 8.** See **capital**[1].

Major (mā′jər), *n.* **John,** born 1943, British political leader: prime minister 1990–97.

ma′jor ax′is, *Math.* the axis of an ellipse that passes through the two foci. [1850–55]

Ma′jor Bar′bara, a comedy (1905) by G. B. Shaw.

Ma•jor•ca (mə jôr′kə, -yôr′-), *n.* a Spanish island in the W Mediterranean: the largest of the Balearic Islands. 460,030; 1405 sq. mi. (3640 sq. km). *Cap.:* Palma. Spanish, **Mallorca.** —**Ma•jor′can,** *adj., n.*

ma•jor-do•mo (mā′jər dō′mō), *n., pl.* **-mos. 1.** a man in charge of a great household, as that of a sovereign; a chief steward. **2.** a steward or butler. **3.** a person who makes arrangements for another. [1580–90; < Sp *mayordomo* < ML *majordomūs* head of the house, equiv. to *major* MAJOR + *domūs,* gen. of *domus* house; see DOME]

ma′jor el′ement, *Geol.* any chemical found in great quantity in the rocks of the earth's crust. Cf. **minor element** (def. 1).

ma•jor•ette (mā′jə ret′), *n.* See **drum majorette.** [1940–45, *Amer.;* (DRUM) MAJOR + -ETTE]

ma′jor gen′eral, a military officer ranking next below a lieutenant general and next above a brigadier general. [1635–45] —**ma′jor-gen′er•al•cy, ma′•jor-gen′er•al•ship′,** *n.*

ma′jor his′tocompatibil′ity com′plex, *Immunol.* See **MHC.**

ma•jor•i•tar•i•an (mə jôr′i târ′ē ən, -jor′-), *adj.* **1.** of, pertaining to, or constituting a majority: *majoritarian democracy.* **2.** supporting or advocating majoritarianism: *majoritarian politics.* —*n.* **3.** a supporter or advocate of majoritarianism. [1915–20; MAJORIT(Y) + -ARIAN]

ma•jor•i•tar•i•an•ism (mə jôr′i târ′ē ə niz′əm, -jor′-), *n.* rule by a majority, esp. the belief that those constituting a simple majority should make the rules for all members of a group, nation, etc. [1960–65; MAJORITARIAN + -ISM]

ma•jor•i•ty (mə jôr′i tē, -jor′-), *n., pl.* **-ties. 1.** the greater part or number; the number larger than half the total (opposed to *minority*): *the majority of the population.* **2.** a number of voters or votes, jurors, or others in agreement, constituting more than half of the total number. **3.** the amount by which the greater number, as of votes, surpasses the remainder (distinguished from *plurality*). **4.** the party or faction with the majority vote: *The Democratic party is the majority.* **5.** the state or time of being of full legal age: *to attain one's majority.* **6.** the military rank or office of a major. **7. join the majority** or **the great majority,** to die. [1545–55; < ML *mājōritās.* See MAJOR, -ITY]
—**Syn. 3.** MAJORITY, PLURALITY, in the context of an election, poll, or other voting situation resulting in a statistically based statement, both denote an amount or number larger than some other. In situations in which only two candidates, options, or positions are concerned, the terms are interchangeable, though MAJORITY is by far the more commonly used: *She beat her opponent by a large majority. The proposal received a large plurality of "Yes" votes.* When three or more choices are available, however, a distinction is made between MAJORITY and PLURALITY. A MAJORITY, then, consists of more than one-half of all the votes cast, while a PLURALITY is merely the number of votes one candidate receives in excess of the votes for the candidate with the next largest number. Thus, in an election in which three candidates receive respectively 500, 300, and 200 votes, the first candidate has a plurality of 200 votes, but not a majority of all the votes cast. If the three candidates receive 600, 300, and 100 votes, the first has a majority of 100 votes (that is 100 votes more than one-half the total of 1000 cast) and a plurality of 300 votes over the nearest opponent.

major′ity lead′er, the leader of the majority party in a legislative body, esp. the party member who directs the activities of the majority party on the floor of either the Senate or the House of Representatives. [1950–55, *Amer.*]

ma′jor key′, *Music.* a key whose essential harmony is based on the major scale. Also called **major mode.**

ma′jor league′, 1. either of the two main professional baseball leagues in the U.S. **2.** a league of corresponding stature in certain other sports, as ice hockey, football, or basketball. [1880–85, *Amer.*]

ma•jor-league (mā′jər lēg′), *adj.* **1.** *Sports.* of, pertaining to, or characteristic of the major leagues. **2.** belonging to or among the best or most important of its kind: *a major-league orchestra.* [1905–10, *Amer.*]

ma•jor-lea•guer (mā′jər lē′gər), *n.* a member of a major-league team. [1880–85, *Amer.;* MAJOR LEAGUE + -ER[1]]

ma′jor med′ical, insurance designed to compensate for particularly large medical expenses due to a severe or prolonged illness, usually by paying a high percentage of medical bills above a certain amount. [1950–55; ellipsis of *major medical expense insurance plan*]

ma′jor mode′, *Music.* **1.** See **major scale. 2.** See **major key.** [1840–50]

ma′jor or′der, *Rom. Cath. Ch.* the degree or grade of priesthood, diaconate, or subdiaconate. Cf. **minor order.** [1720–30]

ma′jor par′ty, a political party with enough electoral strength to periodically gain control of the government or to effectively oppose the party in power. [1945–50]

ma′jor pen′alty, *Ice Hockey.* a penalty consisting of the removal of a player for five minutes from play, no substitute for the player being permitted. Cf. **minor penalty.** [1935–40]

ma′jor piece′, *Chess.* a queen or rook.

ma′jor plan′et, *Astron.* planet (def. 1a).

ma′jor prem′ise, *Logic.* See under **syllogism** (def. 1). [1855–60]

Ma′jor Proph′ets, Isaiah, Jeremiah, and Ezekiel. Cf. **Minor Prophets.**

ma′jor scale′, *Music.* a scale consisting of a series of whole steps except for half steps between the third and fourth and seventh and eighth degrees. Also called **major mode.** [1865–70]

ma′jor sem′inary, a Roman Catholic theological college devoted to training for the priesthood and usually offering a six-year program emphasizing philosophy and theology. [1940–45]

ma′jor suit′, *Bridge.* hearts or spades, esp. with reference to their higher point values. Cf. **minor suit.** [1915–20]

ma′jor ten′ace, *Bridge, Whist.* the ace and queen of a suit held by one player. Cf. **minor tenace, tenace.**

ma′jor term′, *Logic.* See under **syllogism** (def. 1).

ma′jor tran′quilizer, *Pharm.* antipsychotic (def. 2).

ma′jor tri′ad, *Music.* a triad consisting in root position of a root tone with a major third and a perfect fifth above.

Ma•jun•ga (mə jung′gə), *n.* a seaport on NW Madagascar. 76,500.

ma•jus•cule (mə jus′kyo͞ol, maj′ə skyo͞ol′), *adj.* **1.** (of letters) capital. **2.** large, as either capital or uncial letters. **3.** written in such letters (opposed to *minuscule*). —*n.* **4.** a majuscule letter. [1720–30; < L *majuscula* (*littera*) a somewhat bigger (letter), equiv. to *majus-,* s. of *major* MAJOR + *-cula* -CULE[1]] —**ma•jus′cu•lar,** *adj.*

Ma•kah (mə kô′), *n., pl.* **-kahs,** (*esp. collectively*) **-kah** for 1. **1.** a member of an American Indian people of the Olympic Peninsula in northwest Washington. **2.** the Wakashan language of the Makah.

ma•kai (mə kī′), *adv. Hawaii.* toward or by the sea; seaward: *He agreed to purchase the land makai of Diamond Head Road.* Cf. **mauka.** [< Hawaiian, equiv. to *ma* directional particle + *kai* ocean]

Ma•ka•lu (muk′ə lo͞o′), *n.* a mountain in the Himalayas, on the boundary between Nepal and Tibet. 27,790 ft. (8470 m).

Ma•kar•i•os III (mə kar′ē əs, -ōs′; *Gk.* mä kä′rē ôs), (*Michael Christodoulos Mouskos*), 1913–77, Cypriot statesman and Greek Orthodox prelate: archbishop and patriarch of Cyprus 1950–77; president 1960–77 (in exile 1974).

Ma•ka•ro•va (mə kär′ə və; *Russ.* mu kä′rə və), *n.* **Na•ta•lia** (nə tal′yə, -täl′-; *Russ.* nu tä′lyə), born 1940, Soviet ballerina, in the U.S. and England since 1970.

Ma•kas•sar (mə kas′ər), *n.* a former name of **Ujung Pandang.** Also, **Macassar, Ma•kas′ar.**

Ma•kas•sar•ese (mə kas′ə rēz′, -rēs′), *n., pl.* **-ese** for 1. **1.** a member of a Muslim people of southwestern Sulawesi, near Ujung Pandang, closely related to the Buginese. **2.** the Austronesian language of the Makassarese. Also, **Macassarese, Ma•kas′ar•ese′.**

Makas′sar Strait′, a strait between Borneo and Sulawesi (Celebes): naval engagement between the Allied and the Japanese 1942. Also, **Makas′ar Strait′, Macassar Strait.**

make[1] (māk), *v.,* **made, mak•ing,** *n.* —*v.t.* **1.** to bring into existence by shaping or changing material, combining parts, etc.: *to make a dress; to make a channel; to make a work of art.* **2.** to produce; cause to exist or happen; bring about: *to make trouble; to make war.* **3.** to cause to be or become; render: *to make someone happy.* **4.** to appoint or name: *The President made her his special envoy.* **5.** to put in the proper condition or state, as for use; fix; prepare: *to make a bed; to make dinner.* **6.** to bring into a certain form: *to make bricks out of clay.* **7.** to convert from one state, condition, category, etc., to another: *to make a virtue of one's vices.* **8.** to cause, induce, or compel: *to make a horse jump a barrier.* **9.** to give rise to; occasion: *It's not worth making a fuss over such a trifle.* **10.** to produce, earn, or win for oneself: *to make a good salary; to make one's fortune in oil.* **11.** to write or compose: *to make a short poem for the occasion.* **12.** to draw up, as a legal document; draft: *to make a will.* **13.** to do; effect: *to make a bargain.* **14.** to establish or enact; put into existence: *to make laws.* **15.** to become by development; prove to be: *You'll make a good lawyer.* **16.** to form in the mind, as a judgment or estimate: *to make a decision.* **17.** to judge or interpret, as to the truth, nature, meaning, etc. (often fol. by *of*): *What do you make of it?* **18.** to estimate; reckon: *to make the distance at ten miles.* **19.** to bring together separate parts so as to produce a whole; compose; form: *to make a matched set.* **20.** to amount to; bring up the total to: *Two plus two makes four. That makes an even dozen.* **21.** to serve as: *to make good reading.* **22.** to be sufficient to constitute: *One story does not make a writer.* **23.** to be adequate or suitable for: *This wool will make a warm sweater.* **24.** to assure the success or fortune of: *a deal that could make or break him; Seeing her made my day.* **25.** to deliver, utter, or put forth: *to make a stirring speech.* **26.** to go or travel at a particular speed: *to make 60 miles an hour.* **27.** to arrive at or reach; attain: *The ship made port on Friday. Do you think he'll make 80?* **28.** to arrive in time for: *to make the first show.* **29.** to arrive in time to be a passenger on (a plane, boat, bus, train, etc.): *If you hurry, you can make the next flight.* **30.** *Informal.* to gain or acquire a position within: *He made the big time.* **31.** to receive mention or appear in or on: *The robbery made the front page.* **32.** to gain recognition or honor by winning a place or being chosen for inclusion in or on: *The novel made the bestseller list. He made the all-American team three years in a row.* **33.** *Slang.* to have sexual intercourse with. **34.** *Cards.* **a.** to name (the trump). **b.** to take a trick with (a card). **c.** *Bridge.* to fulfill or achieve (a contract or bid). **d.** to shuffle (the cards). **35.** to earn, as a score: *The team made 40 points in the first half.* **36.** *Slang.* (esp. in police and underworld use) **a.** to recognize or identify: *Any cop in town will make you as soon as you walk down the street.* **b.** to charge or cause to be charged with a crime: *The police expect to make a couple of suspects soon.* **37.** to close (an electric circuit). **38.** *South Midland and Southern U.S.* to plant and cultivate or produce (a crop): *He makes some of the best corn in the country.*
—*v.i.* **39.** to cause oneself, or something understood, to be as specified: *to make sure.* **40.** to show oneself to be or seem in action or behavior (usually fol. by an adjective): *to make merry.* **41.** to be made, as specified: *This fabric makes up into beautiful drapes.* **42.** to move or proceed in a particular direction: *They made after the thief.* **43.** to rise, as the tide or water in a ship. **44.** *South Midland and Southern U.S.* (of a crop) to grow, develop, or mature: *It looks like the corn's going to make pretty good this year.* **45. make a play for,** to try to get: *He made a play for his brother's girlfriend. They made a play for control of the company's stock.* **46. make as if** or **as though,** *Informal.* to act as if; pretend: *We will make as if to leave, then come back and surprise him.* **47. make away with, a.** to steal: *The clerk made away with the cash and checks.* **b.** to destroy; kill: *He made away with his enemies.* **c.** to get rid of. **d.** to consume, drink, or eat completely: *The boys made away with the contents of the refrigerator.* **48. make believe,** to pretend; imagine: *The little girl dressed in a sheet and made believe she was a ghost.* **49. make bold** or **so bold,** to have the temerity; be so rash; dare: *May I make so bold as to suggest that you stand when they enter?* **50. make book,** *Slang.* **a.** to take bets and give odds. **b.** to make a business of this. **51. make colors,** *Naut.* to hoist an ensign, as on board a warship. **52. make do,** to function, manage, or operate, usually on a deprivation level with minimal requirements: *During the war we had no butter or coffee, so we had to make do without them.* **53. make down,** *Chiefly Pennsylvania German.* to rain or snow: *It's making down hard.* **54. make fast,** *Chiefly Naut.* to fasten or secure. **55. make for, a.** to go toward; approach: *to make for home.* **b.** to lunge at; attack. **c.** to help to promote or maintain: *This incident will not make for better understanding between the warring factions.* **56. make good, a.** to provide restitution or reparation for: *The bank teller made good the shortage and was given a light sentence.* **b.** to succeed: *Talent and training are necessary to make good in some fields.* **c.** to fulfill: *He made good on his promise.* **d.** *Navig.* to compute (a course) allowing for leeway and compass deviation. **57. make heavy weather, a.** *Naut.* to roll and pitch in heavy seas. **b.** to progress laboriously; struggle, esp. to struggle needlessly: *I am making heavy weather with my income tax return.* **58. make it, a.** *Informal.* to achieve a specific goal: *to make it to the train; to make it through college.* **b.** *Informal.* to succeed in general: *He'll never make it in business.* **c.** *Slang.* to have sexual intercourse. **59. make it so,** *Naut.* strike the ship's bell accordingly: said by the officer of the watch when the hour is announced. **60. make like,** *Informal.* to try or pretend to be like; imitate: *I'm going to go out and make like a gardener.* **61. make off, a.** to run away; depart hastily: *The only witness to the accident made off before the police arrived.* **b.** *Naut.* to stand off from a coast, esp. a lee shore. **62. make off with,** to carry away; steal: *While the family was away, thieves made off with most of their valuables.* **63. make on,** *Chiefly Pennsylvania German.* to turn on, light, or ignite (esp. a light or fire): *Make the light on.* **64. make one's manners,** *Southern U.S.* **a.** to perform an appropriate or expected social courtesy. **b.** *Older Use.* to bow or curtsy. **65. make out, a.** to write out or complete, as a bill or check. **b.** to establish; prove. **c.** to decipher; discern. **d.** to imply, suggest, or impute: *He made me out to be a liar.* **e.** to manage; succeed: *How are you making out in your new job?* **f.** *Slang.* to engage in kissing and caressing; neck. **g.** *Slang.* to have sexual intercourse. **h.** *Chiefly Pennsylvania German.* to turn off or extinguish (esp. a light or fire): *Make the light out.* **66. make over, a.** to remodel; alter: *to make over a dress; to make over a page layout.* **b.** to transfer the title of (property); convey: *After she retired she made over her property to her children and moved to Florida.* **67. make sail,** *Naut.* **a.** to set sails. **b.** to brace the yards of a ship that has been hove to in order to make headway. **68. make shut,** *Chiefly Pennsylvania German.* to close: *Make the door shut.* **69. make time.** See **time** (def. 42). **70. make up, a.** (of parts) to constitute; compose; form. **b.** to put together;

CONCISE PRONUNCIATION KEY: act, cāpe, dâre, pärt; set, ēqual; *if,* ice; ox, ōver, ôrder, oil, bo͝ok, bo͞ot, out; up, ûrge; child; sing; shoe; thin, *that;* zh as in *treasure.* ə = *a* as in *alone, e* as in *system, i* as in *easily, o* as in *gallop, u* as in *circus;* ᵊ as in *fire* (fīᵊr), *hour* (ouᵊr). l and n can serve as syllabic consonants, as in *cradle* (krād′l), and *button* (but′n). See the full key inside the front cover.

construct; compile. **c.** to concoct; invent. **d.** Also, **make up for.** to compensate for; make good. **e.** to complete. **f.** to put in order; arrange: *The maid will make up the room.* **g.** to conclude; decide. **h.** to settle amicably, as differences. **i.** to become reconciled, as after a quarrel. **j.** *Print.* to arrange set type, illustrations, etc., into columns or pages. **k.** to dress in appropriate costume and apply cosmetics for a part on the stage. **l.** to apply cosmetics. **m.** to adjust or balance, as accounts; prepare, as statements. **n.** *Educ.* to repeat (a course or examination that one has failed). **o.** *Educ.* to take an examination that one had been unable to take when first given, usually because of absence. **p.** to specify and indicate the layout or arrangement of (columns, pages, etc., of matter to be printed). **q.** *Atlantic States.* (of the weather or clouds) to develop or gather: *It's making up for a storm.* **r.** *Atlantic States.* (of the sea) to become turbulent: *If the sea makes up, row toward land.* **71. make up to, a.** *Informal.* to try to become friendly with; fawn on. **b.** to make advances to; flirt with: *He makes up to every new woman in the office.* **72. make water, a.** to urinate. **b.** *Naut.* (of a hull) to leak. **73. make with,** *Slang.* **a.** to operate; use: *Let's make with the feet.* **b.** to bring about; provide or produce: *He makes with the big ideas, but can't follow through.*
—*n.* **74.** the style or manner in which something is made; form; build. **75.** production with reference to the maker; brand: *our own make.* **76.** disposition; character; nature. **77.** the act or process of making. **78.** quantity made; output. **79.** *Cards.* the act of naming the trump, or the suit named as trump. **80.** *Elect.* the closing of an electric circuit. **81.** *Jewelry.* the excellence of a polished diamond with regard to proportion, symmetry, and finish. **82.** *Slang.* identifying information about a person or thing from police records: *He radioed headquarters for a make on the car's license plate.* **83. on the make,** *Informal.* **a.** seeking to improve one's social or financial position, usually at the expense of others or of principle. **b.** increasing; advancing. **c.** *Slang.* seeking amorous or sexual relations: *The park was swarming with sailors on the make.* **84. put the make on,** *Slang.* to make sexual overtures to. [bef. 900; ME *maken,* OE *macian;* c. LG, D *maken,* G *machen*] —**mak′a·ble,** *adj.*
—**Syn. 1.** form; build; produce; fabricate, create, fashion, mold. MAKE, CONSTRUCT, MANUFACTURE mean to produce, to put into definite form, or to put parts together to make a whole. MAKE is the general term: *Bees make wax.* CONSTRUCT, more formal, means to put parts together, usually according to a plan or design: *to construct a building.* MANUFACTURE usually refers to producing something from material that requires conversion from one state or condition to another, now almost entirely by means of machinery in a relatively complex process: *to manufacture automobiles by the assembly of different parts.* The term is also often used contemptuously of unimaginative or hackneyed works of art with the implication that the work was produced mechanically, and is used abstractly with the idea of denying genuineness: *to manufacture an excuse.* **7.** transform, change, turn. **8.** force. **10.** get, gain, acquire, obtain, secure, procure. **13.** perform, execute. **18.** judge, gauge. **74.** shape, structure, construction, constitution. —**Ant. 1.** destroy.

make² (māk), *n. Brit. Dial.* **1.** a peer or equal. **2.** a spouse, mate, consort, or lover. **3.** a friend; companion. [bef. 1000; ME *mak, make,* OE *gemaca.* See MATCH²]

make-a·head (māk′ə hed′), *adj.* that can be prepared in advance: *a make-ahead casserole.*

make-and-break (māk′ən brāk′), *adj.* noting or pertaining to a device, operated by an electric current, for automatically opening or closing a circuit once it has been closed or opened by a mechanical springlike device, as in a doorbell. [1855–60]

make·bate (māk′bāt′), *n. Archaic.* a person who causes contention or discord. [1520–30; MAKE¹ + *bate* contention, discord (ME, deriv. of *baten* to fight, strive; see BATE²)]

make-be·lieve (māk′bi lēv′), *n.* **1.** pretense, esp. of an innocent or playful kind; feigning; sham: *the make-believe of children playing.* **2.** a pretender; a person who pretends. —*adj.* **3.** pretended; feigned; imaginary; made-up; unreal: *a make-believe world of fantasy.* [1805–15]

make-do (māk′do͞o′), *n., pl.* **-dos,** *adj.* —*n.* **1.** something that serves as a substitute, esp. of an inferior or expedient nature: *We had to get along with make-dos during the war.* —*adj.* **2.** used as a substitute; makeshift: *make-do curtains.* [1890–95]

Ma·ke·ev·ka (mə kā′əf kə; *Russ.* mu kye′yif kə), *n.* Makeyevka.

make·fast (māk′fast′, -fäst′), *n. Naut.* any structure to which a ship is tied up, as a bollard or buoy. [1895–1900; n. use of v. phrase *make fast*]

make·less (māk′lis), *adj. Archaic.* having no mate or match. [1150–1200; ME; see MAKE², -LESS]

Ma·kem·ie (mə kem′ē, -kā′mē), *n.* **Francis,** 1658?–1708, American Presbyterian clergyman, born in Ireland: founded the first Presbyterian church in America.

make-or-break (māk′ər brāk′), *adj.* either completely successful or utterly disastrous: *a make-or-break marketing policy.* [1915–20]

make·o·ver (māk′ō′vər), *n.* **1.** remodeling; renovation; restoration: *The old house needs a complete makeover.* **2.** a thorough course of beauty and cosmetic treatments: *Assistants spent four hours on the actress's makeover in preparation for the awards ceremony.* [n. use of v. phrase *make over*]

make-peace (māk′pēs′), *n.* a peacemaker. [1510–20; n. use of v. phrase *make peace*]

CONCISE ETYMOLOGY KEY: <, descended or borrowed from; >, whence; b., blend of, blended; c., cognate with; cf., compare; deriv., derivative; equiv., equivalent; imit., imitative; obl., oblique; r., replacing; s., stem; sp., spelling, spelled; resp., respelling, respelled; trans., translation; ?, origin unknown; *, unattested; ‡, probably earlier than. See the full key inside the front cover.

mak·er (mā′kər), *n.* **1.** a person or thing that makes. **2.** a manufacturer (used in combination): *drugmaker; garmentmaker.* **3.** (*cap.*) God. **4.** the party executing a legal instrument, esp. a promissory note. **5.** *Cards.* the player who first names the successful bid. **6.** *Archaic.* a poet. **7. go to** or **meet one's Maker,** to die. [1300–50; ME; see MAKE¹, -ER¹]

make-read·y (māk′red′ē), *n.* **1.** *Print.* the process of preparing a form for printing by overlays or underlays to equalize the impression. **2.** the act or process of making something ready for use: *a charge for make-ready on the new car.* [1820–30; n. use of v. phrase *make ready*]

mak′er's mark′, the personal mark of a goldsmith or silversmith, struck on the completed pieces.

make·shift (māk′shift′), *n.* **1.** a temporary expedient or substitute: *We used boxes as a makeshift while the kitchen chairs were being painted.* —*adj.* **2.** Also, **make′shift′y.** serving as, or of the nature of, a makeshift. [1555–65; n., adj. use of v. phrase *make shift*]
—**Syn. 1.** make-do, contrivance, jury-rig. **2.** emergency, temporary, improvised, jury, ersatz.

make·up (māk′up′), *n.* **1.** facial cosmetics, as eye shadow or lipstick. **2.** cosmetics used on other parts of the body, as to cover birthmarks. **3.** the application of cosmetics. **4.** the ensemble or effect created by such application: *Her makeup was subtle but very effective.* **5.** the total ensemble of cosmetics, wigs, costumes, etc., used by an actor or other performer. **6.** the manner of being made up or put together; composition: *the makeup of a team; the makeup of a situation.* **7.** physical or mental constitution: *the makeup of a criminal.* **8.** the art, technique, or process of arranging or laying out, as pages in a publication. **9.** the appearance of a page, book, newspaper, or the like, resulting from the arrangement and the variation in size and style of the printed elements: *The makeup would be helped by a picture in this corner.* **10.** *Print.* the arrangement of set type, cuts, etc., into columns or pages. **11.** an examination, assignment, or the like, given to offset a student's previous absence or failure. **12.** an amount owed; balance. Also, **make′-up′.** [1805–15; n. use of v. phrase *make up*]

make·weight (māk′wāt′), *n.* **1.** something put in a scale to complete a required weight. **2.** anything added to supply a lack. [1685–95; MAKE¹ + WEIGHT]

make-work (māk′wûrk′), *n.* work, usually of little importance, created to keep a person from being idle or unemployed. [1935–40, *Amer.;* n. use of v. phrase *make work*]

Ma·ke·yev·ka (mə kā′əf kə; *Russ.* mu kye′yif kə), *n.* a city in SE Ukraine, N of the Sea of Azov. 455,000. Also, **Makeevka.**

Ma·khach·ka·la (mə käch′kə lä′; *Russ.* mə кнəch-ku lä′), *n.* a seaport and capital of Dagestan, in the SW Russian Federation in Europe, on the Caspian Sea. 315,000.

Ma·khlouf (mäкн lo͞of′, mä klo͞of′), *n.* **Saint Shar·bel** (shär′bəl), 1828–98, Lebanese monk: canonized 1977.

ma·ki·mo·no (mä′kə mō′nō; *Japn.* mä′kē mô′nô), *n., pl.* **-nos, -no.** a horizontal hand scroll containing either text or a captioned painting, intended to be viewed as it is unrolled from right to left, one segment at a time. Cf. **kakemono.** [1880–85; < Japn, equiv. to *maki* wind + *mono* thing]

mak·ing (mā′king), *n.* **1.** the act of a person or thing that makes: *The making of a violin requires great skill.* **2.** structure; constitution; makeup. **3.** the means or cause of success or advancement: *to be the making of someone.* **4.** Usually, **makings.** capacity or potential: *He has the makings of a first-rate officer.* **5. makings, a.** material of which something may be made: *the makings for a tossed salad.* **b.** *Older Slang.* paper and tobacco with which to make a hand-rolled cigarette. **6.** something made. **7.** the quantity made: *a making of butter.* **8. in the making,** in the process of being made; developing or evolving; growing: *Our space scientists see history in the making.* [bef. 1150; ME; OE *macung.* See MAKE¹, -ING¹]

ma·ki-zu·shi (mä′kē zo͞o′shē), *n.* See under **sushi.** [< Japn]

Mak·kah (mak′kə, -kä), *n.* Mecca (def. 1).

ma·ko (mä′kō, mā′-), *n., pl.* **-kos.** a powerful mackerel shark, *Isurus oxyrinchus,* of the Atlantic and Pacific oceans. Also called **ma′ko shark′.** [1720–30; < Maori]

Ma·kon·de (mə kōn′dā), *n., pl.* **-des,** (*esp. collectively*) **-de** for 1. **1.** a member of a people living in northeastern Mozambique and southeastern Tanzania, renowned as woodcarvers. **2.** the Bantu language of the Makonde people.

mak·soo·rah (mäk so͝or′ə), *n.* (in a mosque) a screen or partition enclosing an area for prayer or a tomb. [< Ar *maqṣūrah*]

Mak′su·tov tel′escope (mak′so͝o tôf′, -tof′), a reflecting telescope in which coma and spherical aberration are reduced to a minimum by a combination of a spherical mirror and a meniscus lens placed inside the radius of curvature of the mirror. [after Russian optician Dmitriĭ Dmitrievich *Maksutov* (1896–1964), who designed such a telescope in 1941]

Ma·kua (mə kwä′), *n.* **1.** a member of a people living in northern Mozambique and adjacent regions of Tanzania and Malawi. **2.** the Bantu language spoken by the Makua.

ma·ku·ta (mä ko͞o′tə), *n.* pl. of **likuta.**

mal-, a combining form meaning "bad," "wrongful," "ill," occurring originally in loanwords from French (*malapert*); on this model, used in the formation of other words (*malfunction; malcontent*). Cf. **male-.** [ME < OF, repr. *mal* adv. (< L *male* badly, ill) and adj. (< L *malus* bad)]

Mal., **1.** Malachi. **2.** Malayan.

Mal′a·bar Coast′ (mal′ə bär′), a region along the entire SW coast of India, extending from the Arabian Sea inland to the Western Ghats. Also called **Malabar.**

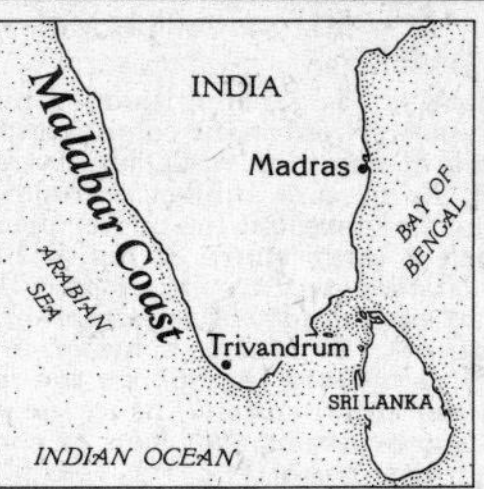

Ma·la·bo (mə lä′bō), *n.* a town in and the capital of Equatorial Guinea, on N Bioko island. 75,000. Formerly, **Santa Isabel.**

mal·ab·sorp·tion (mal′əb sôrp′shən, -zôrp′-), *n. Pathol.* faulty absorption of nutritive material from the intestine. [1930–35; MAL- + ABSORPTION]

Ma·lac·ca (mə lak′ə, -lä′kə), *n.* **1.** a state in Malaysia, on the SW Malay Peninsula: formerly a part of the British Straits Settlements and of the Federation of Malaya. 404,125; 640 sq. mi. (1658 sq. km). **2.** a seaport in and the capital of this state. 87,160. **3. Strait of,** a strait between Sumatra and the Malay Peninsula. 35–185 mi. (56–298 km) wide. Also, **Melaka** (for defs. 1, 2). —**Ma·lac′can,** *adj., n.*

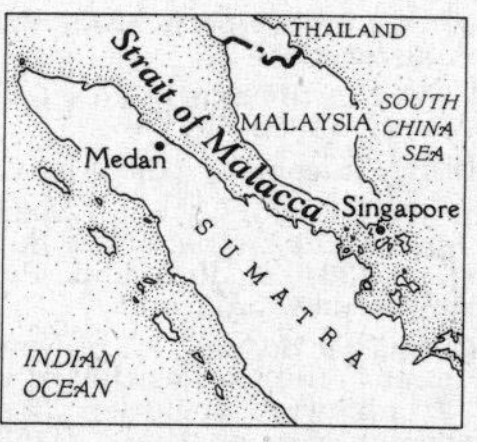

Malac′ca cane′, a cane or walking stick made of the brown, often mottled or clouded stem of an East Indian rattan palm, *Calamus scipionum.* [1835–45]

Mal·a·chi (mal′ə kī′), *n.* **1.** a Minor Prophet of the 5th century B.C. **2.** the book of the Bible bearing his name. *Abbr.:* Mal. Also, *Douay Bible,* **Mal·a·chi·as** (mal′ə kī′əs).

mal·a·chite (mal′ə kīt′), *n.* **1.** a green mineral, basic copper carbonate, $Cu_2CO_3(OH)_2$, an ore of copper, used for making ornamental articles. **2.** a ceramic ware made in imitation of this. [1350–1400; < Gk *malách(ē)* MALLOW + -ITE¹; r. ME *melochites* < MF *melochite,* repr. L *molochītis* < Gk *molochîtis,* deriv. of *molóchē,* var. of *maláchē*]

ma·la·cia (mə lā′shə, -shē ə, -sē ə), *n. Pathol.* **1.** softening, or loss of consistency, of an organ or tissue. **2.** an abnormal craving for highly spiced food. [1650–60; < NL < Gk *malakía* softness, tenderness, weakness. See MALACO-, -IA] —**mal·a·coid** (mal′ə koid′), *adj.* —**mal·a·cot·ic** (mal′ə kot′ik), *adj.*

malaco-, a combining form meaning "soft," used in the formation of compound words: *malacopterygian.* [< Gk *malako-,* comb. form of *malakós*]

mal·a·col·o·gy (mal′ə kol′ə jē), *n.* the science dealing with the study of mollusks. [1830–40; < F *malacologie,* syncopated var. of *malacozoologie.* See MALACO-, ZOOLOGY] —**mal·a·co·log·i·cal** (mal′ə kə loj′i kəl), *adj.* —**mal′a·col′o·gist,** *n.*

mal·a·cop·te·ryg·i·an (mal′ə kop′tə rij′ē ən), *adj.* belonging or pertaining to the Malacopterygii (Malacopteri), a group of soft-finned, teleost fishes. [1825–35; < NL *Malacopterygi(i)* (*malaco-* MALACO- + *-pterygii,* pl. of *-pterygius* finned, winged, adj. deriv. of Gk *pterýgion,* dim. of *ptéryx* wing, fin) + -AN]

mal·a·cos·tra·can (mal′ə kos′trə kən), *adj.* **1.** belonging or pertaining to the crustacean subclass Malacostraca, which includes the lobsters, shrimps, crabs, etc. —*n.* **2.** a malacostracan crustacean. [1825–35; < NL *Malacostrac(a)* order of crustacea (< Gk, neut. pl. of *malakóstrakos* soft-shelled, equiv. to *malak-* MALACO- + *-ostrakos,* adj. deriv. of *óstrakon* shell (of mollusks, etc.); cf. OSTRACIZE) + -AN]

mal·ad·ap·ta·tion (mal′ad əp tā′shən), *n.* incomplete, inadequate, or faulty adaptation. [1875–80; MAL- + ADAPTATION]

mal·a·dapt·ed (mal′ə dap′tid), *adj.* poorly suited or adapted to a particular condition or set of circumstances: *maladapted to the demands of modern society.* [1940–45; MAL- + ADAPTED]

mal·a·dap·tive (mal′ə dap′tiv), *adj.* of, pertaining to, or characterized by maladaptation: *The maladaptive behavior of isolated children was difficult to change.* [1930–35; MAL- + ADAPTIVE]

mal·ad·just·ed (mal′ə jus′tid), *adj.* badly or unsatisfactorily adjusted, esp. in relationship to one's social circumstances, environment, etc. [1880–85; MAL- + ADJUSTED]

mal·ad·just·ment (mal′ə just′mənt), *n.* bad or unsatisfactory adjustment. [1825–35; MAL- + ADJUSTMENT]

mal·ad·min·is·ter (mal′əd min′ə stər), *v.t.* to administer or manage badly or inefficiently: *The mayor was a bungler who maladministered the city budget.* [1695–1705; MAL- + ADMINISTER] —**mal′ad·min′is·tra′tion,** *n.* —**mal′ad·min′is·tra′tor,** *n.*

mal·a·droit (mal′ə droit′), *adj.* lacking in adroitness; unskillful; awkward; bungling; tactless: *to handle a dip-*

lomatic crisis in a very maladroit way. [1665–75; < F, MF; see MAL-, ADROIT] **—mal′a·droit′ly,** *adv.* **—mal′·a·droit′ness,** *n.*
—Syn. clumsy, inept; gauche.

mal·a·dy (mal′ə dē), *n., pl.* **-dies. 1.** any disorder or disease of the body, esp. one that is chronic or deep-seated. **2.** any undesirable or disordered condition: *social maladies; a malady of the spirit.* [1200–50; ME *maladie* < OF, equiv. to *malade* sick (< LL *male habitus* lit., ill-conditioned; see MAL-, HABIT) + *-ie* -Y[3]]
—Syn. 1. illness, sickness, affliction, complaint.

ma·la fi·de (mä′lä fē′de; *Eng.* mā′lə fī′dē), *Latin.* in bad faith; not genuine.

ma·la fi·des (mä′lä fē′des; *Eng.* mā′lə fī′dēz), *Latin.* bad faith; intent to deceive. Cf. **bona fides** (def. 1).

Mal·a·ga (mal′ə gə), *n.* **1.** a strong, sweet dessert wine with a pronounced muscat grape flavor, esp. that produced in Málaga, Spain. **2.** any of the grapes grown in or exported from Málaga. [1600–10]

Má·la·ga (mal′ə gə; *Sp.* mä′lä gä′), *n.* **1.** a province in S Spain, in Andalusia. 867,330; 2813 sq. mi. (7285 sq. km). **2.** a seaport in S Spain, on the Mediterranean. 374,452.

Mal·a·gas·y (mal′ə gas′ē), *n., pl.* **-gas·y, -gas·ies** for 1. **1.** a member of any of various peoples native to the island of Madagascar. **2.** the Austronesian language of Madagascar.

Malagas′y Repub′lic, former name of **Madagascar.**

ma·la·gue·na (mal′ə gān′yə *or, often,* -gwän′-), *n.* a Spanish dance similar to the fandango, originating in Málaga. [1880–85; < Sp *malagueña* (fem.) of MÁLAGA; for suffix, see MADRILENO]

ma·laise (ma lāz′, -me-; *Fr.* MA lez′), *n.* **1.** a condition of general bodily weakness or discomfort, often marking the onset of a disease. **2.** a vague or unfocused feeling of mental uneasiness, lethargy, or discomfort. [1760–70; < F, OF; see MAL-, EASE]

Ma·la·kal (mal′ə kal′, mä′lə käl), *n.* a city in E Sudan, on the White Nile. 30,000.

Mal·a·mud (mal′ə məd, -mo͝od′), *n.* **Bernard,** 1914–86, U.S. novelist and short-story writer.

mal·a·mute (mal′ə myo͞ot′), *n.* (*sometimes cap.*) See **Alaskan malamute.** Also, **malemute.** [1895–1900; < Inupiaq *malimiut* name for local groups of Inupiaq of the Kotzebue Sound region, W Alaska, who bred such dogs]

Ma·lan (mä län′), *n.* **Daniel Fran·çois** (frän swä′), 1874–1959, South African editor and political leader: prime minister 1948–54.

mal·an·ders (mal′ən dərz), *n.* (*used with a singular v.*) *Vet. Pathol.* a dry, scabby or scurfy eruption or scratch behind the knee in a horse's foreleg. Also, **mallanders, mallenders.** Cf. **sallenders.** [1400–50; late ME *malaunder* < MF *malandre* < L *malandria* blister on a horse's neck; see -S[3]]

Ma·lang (mä läng′), *n.* a city on E Java, in S Indonesia. 422,400.

ma·lan·ga (mə lang′gə), *n.* a thick, fleshy-leaved South American plant, *Xanthosoma atrovirens,* of the arum family, having leaves up to 3 ft. (90 cm) long and nearly 2 ft. (60 cm) wide. Also called **West Indian kale.** [< AmerSp]

Ma·lan·je (mə lan′jə), *n.* a city in N Angola. 45,000. Also, **Ma·lan·ge** (mə lan′jə).

mal·a·pert (mal′ə pûrt′), *Archaic.* **—adj. 1.** unbecomingly bold or saucy. **—n. 2.** a malapert person. [1375–1425; late ME: insolent < MF: unskillful. See MAL-, PERT] **—mal′a·pert′ly,** *adv.* **—mal′a·pert′·ness,** *n.*

mal·ap·por·tioned (mal′ə pôr′shənd, -pōr′-), *adj.* (of a state or other political unit) poorly apportioned, esp. divided, organized, or structured in a manner that prevents large sections of a population from having equitable representation in a legislative body. [1960–65; MAL- + APPORTIONED] **—mal′ap·por′tion·ment,** *n.*

mal·a·prop (mal′ə prop′), *n.* malapropism (def. 2). [1815–25; see MALAPROP]

Mal·a·prop (mal′ə prop′), *n.* **Mrs.,** a character in Sheridan's *The Rivals* (1775), noted for her misapplication of words.

mal·a·prop·ism (mal′ə prop iz′əm), *n.* **1.** an act or habit of misusing words ridiculously, esp. by the confusion of words that are similar in sound. **2.** an instance of this, as in "Lead the way and we'll precede." [1840–50; MALAPROP + -ISM] **—mal′a·prop·is′tic,** *adj.*

mal·ap·ro·pos (mal′ap rə pō′), *adj.* **1.** inappropriate; out of place; inopportune; untimely: *a malapropos remark.* **—adv. 2.** inappropriately; inopportunely. [1660–70; < F *mal à propos* badly (suited) to the purpose]

ma·lar (mā′lər), *Anat.* **—adj. 1.** of or pertaining to the cheek or zygomatic bone. **—n. 2.** Also, **ma′lar bone′.** See **zygomatic bone.** [1775–85; < NL *mālāris* of, pertaining to the cheek, equiv. to L *māl(a)* cheek, jaw (see MAXILLA) + *-āris* -AR[1]]

Mä·lar (mā′lər, -lär), *n.* **Lake,** a lake in S Sweden, extending W from Stockholm. 440 sq. mi. (1140 sq. km). Swedish, **Mä·lar·en** (me′lä Rən).

ma·lar·i·a (mə lâr′ē ə), *n.* **1.** *Pathol.* any of a group of diseases, usually intermittent or remittent, characterized by attacks of chills, fever, and sweating: formerly supposed to be due to swamp exhalations but now known to be caused by a parasitic protozoan, which is transferred to the human bloodstream by a mosquito of the genus *Anopheles* and which occupies and destroys red blood cells. **2.** *Archaic.* unwholesome or poisonous air. [1730–40; < It, contr. of *mala aria* bad air] **—ma·lar′i·al, ma·lar′i·an, ma·lar′i·ous,** *adj.*

ma·lar·i·ol·o·gy (mə lâr′ē ol′ə jē), *n.* the study of malaria. [1920–25; MALARI(A) + -O- + -LOGY] **—ma·lar′i·ol′o·gist,** *n.*

ma·lar·key (mə lär′kē), *n. Informal.* speech or writing designed to obscure, mislead, or impress; bunkum: *The claims were just a lot of malarkey.* Also, **ma·lar′ky.** [1925–30, *Amer.*; orig. uncert.]

mal·as·sim·i·la·tion (mal′ə sim′ə lā′shən), *n. Pathol.* imperfect incorporation of nutrients into body tissue. [1860–65; MAL- + ASSIMILATION]

mal·ate (mal′āt, mā′lāt), *n. Chem.* a salt or ester of malic acid. [1785–95; MAL(IC ACID) + -ATE[2]]

mal·a·thi·on (mal′ə thī′on, -ən), *n.* an organic phosphate insecticide, $C_{10}H_{19}O_6S_2P$, of relatively low toxicity for mammals,. [1953]

Ma·la·tya (mä′lä tyä′), *n.* a city in central Turkey. 150,397. Ancient, **Melitene.**

Ma·la·wi (mə lä′wē), *n.* **1.** Formerly, **Nyasaland.** a republic in SE Africa, on the W and S shores of Lake Malawi: formerly a British protectorate and part of the Federation of Rhodesia and Nyasaland; gained independence July 6, 1964; a member of the Commonwealth of Nations. 5,400,000; 49,177 sq. mi. (127,368 sq. km). *Cap.:* Lilongwe. **2. Lake.** Formerly, **Nyasa.** a lake in SE Africa, between Malawi, Tanzania, and Mozambique. 11,000 sq. mi. (28,500 sq. km). **—Ma·la′wi·an,** *adj., n.*

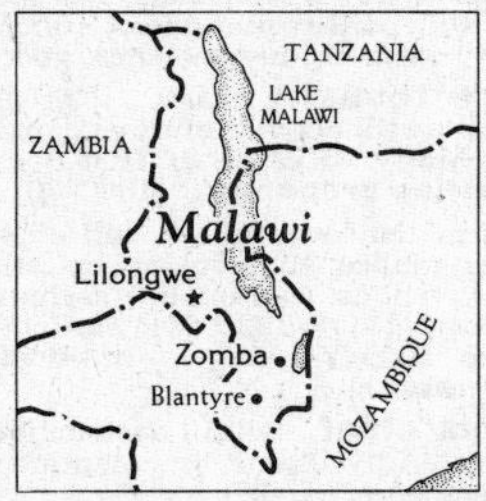

Ma·lay (mā′lā, mə lā′), *adj.* **1.** of, pertaining to, or characteristic of a racially intermixed, generally short-statured people who are the dominant population of the Malay Peninsula and adjacent islands. **2.** of or pertaining to the language or culture of these people. **—n. 3.** a member of the Malay people. **4.** an Austronesian language of Malaysia and Singapore, differing from Indonesian only in orthography.

Ma·lay·a (mə lā′ə), *n.* **1.** See **Malay Peninsula. 2. Federation of.** Formerly, **Malay States, Malay′an Un′ion.** a former federation of 11 states in the S Malay Peninsula: a British protectorate 1948–57; now forms part of Malaysia. 50,690 sq. mi. (131,287 sq. km). *Cap.:* Kuala Lumpur. Cf. **Malaysia** (def. 1).

Mal·a·ya·lam (mal′ə yä′ləm), *n.* a Dravidian language spoken in extreme southwestern India.

Ma·lay·an (mə lā′ən), *adj., n.* Malay. [MALAY + -AN]

Malay′an cam′phor, borneol. [1830–40]

Ma′lay Archipel′ago, an extensive island group in the Indian and Pacific oceans, SE of Asia, including the Greater and Lesser Sunda Islands, the Moluccas, and the Philippines. Also called **Malaysia.**

Ma′lay bear′. See **sun bear.**

Malayo-, a combining form of **Malay.**

Ma·lay·o-Pol·y·ne·sian (mə lā′ō pol′ə nē′zhən, -shən), *n., adj.* Austronesian.

Ma′lay Penin′sula, a peninsula in SE Asia, consisting of W (mainland) Malaysia and the S part of Thailand. Also called **Malaya.**

Ma·lay·sia (mə lā′zhə, -shə), *n.* **1.** a constitutional monarchy in SE Asia: a federation, comprising the former British territories of Malaya, Sabah, and Sarawak: member of the Commonwealth of Nations. 12,100,000; 126,310 sq. mi. (327,143 sq. km). *Cap.:* Kuala Lumpur. **2.** See **Malay Archipelago.**

Ma·lay·sian (mə lā′zhən, -shən), *n.* **1.** a native or inhabitant of Malaysia. **2.** Malay (def. 3). **—adj. 3.** of, pertaining to, or characteristic of Malaysia or its inhabitants. [1880–85; MALAYSI(A) + -AN]

Ma′lay States′, a former name of **Malaya** (def. 2).

Mal·colm (mal′kəm), *n.* a male given name: from a Gaelic word meaning "disciple of Saint Columba."

Malcolm X (eks), (*Malcolm Little*), 1925–65, U.S. black-rights activist and religious leader.

mal·con·tent (mal′kən tent′), *adj.* **1.** not satisfied or content with current conditions or circumstances. **2.** dissatisfied with the existing government, administration, system, etc. **—n. 3.** a malcontent person, esp. one who is chronically discontented or dissatisfied. [1575–85; < MF, OF; see MAL-, CONTENT[2]] **—mal′con·tent′ed·ly,** *adv.* **—mal′con·tent′ed·ness,** *n.*
—Syn. 3. grumbler, complainer, faultfinder.

M.A.L.D., Master of Arts in Law and Diplomacy.

mal de mer (mal də meR′), *French.* seasickness.

Mal·den (môl′dən), *n.* a city in E Massachusetts, near Boston. 53,386.

mal·dis·tri·bu·tion (mal′dis trə byo͞o′shən), *n.* bad or unsatisfactory distribution, as of wealth, among a population or members of a group. [1890–95; MAL- + DISTRIBUTION] **—mal·dis·trib·ut·ed** (mal′di strib′yə-tid), *adj.*

Mal·dives (môl′dēvz, mal′dīvz), a republic in the Indian Ocean, SW of India, consisting of about 2000 islands: British protectorate 1887–1965. 140,000; 115 sq. mi. (298 sq. km). *Cap.:* Male. Also called **Mal′dive Is′·lands. —Mal·div·i·an** (môl div′ē ən, mal-), *adj., n.*

mal du pa·ys (mal dy pā ē′), *French.* homesickness.

male (māl), *n.* **1.** a person bearing an X and Y chromosome pair in the cell nuclei and normally having a penis, scrotum, and testicles, and developing hair on the face at adolescence; a boy or man. **2.** an organism of the sex or sexual phase that normally produces a sperm cell or male gamete. **3.** *Bot.* a staminate plant. **—adj. 4.** of, pertaining to, or being a male animal or plant. **5.** pertaining to or characteristic of a male person; masculine: *a male voice.* **6.** composed of males: *a male choir.* **7.** *Bot.* **a.** designating or pertaining to a plant or its reproductive structure producing or containing microspores. **b.** (of seed plants) staminate. **8.** *Mach.* made to fit into a corresponding open or recessed part: *a male plug.* Cf. **female** (def. 8). [1300–50; ME < MF *ma(s)le* < L *masculus.* See MASCULINE] **—male′ness,** *n.*
—Syn. 1. See **man. 4–7.** MALE, MASCULINE, VIRILE are adjectives that describe men and boys or attributes and conduct culturally ascribed to them. MALE, which is applied to plants and animals as well as to human beings, is a biological or physiological descriptor, classifying individuals on the basis of their potential or actual ability to inseminate in bisexual reproduction. It contrasts with FEMALE in all such uses: *his oldest male relative; the male parts of the flower.* MASCULINE refers essentially to qualities, characteristics, or behaviors deemed by a culture or society to be especially appropriate to or ideally associated with men and boys. In American and Western European culture, these have traditionally included features such as strength, forthrightness, and courage: *a firm, masculine handshake; a masculine impatience at indecision.* VIRILE implies a vigor and muscularity associated with mature manhood and often carries a suggestion of sexual or procreative potency: *his virile good looks; a swaggering, virile walk.* See also **manly. —Ant.** female.

Ma·le (mä′lā, -lē), *n.* a city in and the capital of the Maldives. 17,000.

male-, a combining form meaning "evil," occurring in loanwords from Latin: *malediction.* Cf. **mal-.** [< L; see MAL-]

male′ al′to, countertenor. [1875–80]

mal·e·ate (mal′ē āt′, -it, mā′lē-), *n. Chem.* a salt or ester of maleic acid. [1850–55; MALE(IC ACID) + -ATE[2]]

male·ber·ry (māl′ber′ē, -bə rē), *n., pl.* **-ries.** See **swamp andromeda.** [obs. *male* apple < L *mālus* apple tree + BERRY]

Ma·le′bo Pool′ (mä lā′bō), a lakelike body of water on the boundary between W Zaire and the SE People's Republic of the Congo, formed by the widening of the Zaire (Congo) River about 330 mi. (530 km) from its mouth. ab. 20 mi. (32 km) long; ab. 15 mi. (24 km) wide. Also called **Stanley Pool.**

Male·branche (mal bränsh′), *n.* **Ni·co·las de** (nē kô-lä′ də), 1638–1715, French philosopher.

male′ chau′vinism, the beliefs, attitudes, or behavior of male chauvinists. [1965–70]

male′ chau′vinist, a male who patronizes, disparages, or otherwise denigrates females in the belief that they are inferior to males and thus deserving of less than equal treatment or benefit. [1965–70]

male′ chau′vinist pig′, *Slang (disparaging).* See **male chauvinist.** [1965–70]

Mal·e·cite (mal′ə sīt′), *n., pl.* **-cites,** (*esp. collectively*) **-cite** for 1. **1.** a member of a North American Indian people of southern and western New Brunswick and northern Maine. **2.** the Eastern Algonquian language of the Malecite, mutually intelligible with Passamaquoddy. Also, **Maliseet.**

male′ cow′, *Chiefly South Midland and Southern U.S.* a bull. [1905–10, *Amer.*]

mal·e·dict (mal′i dikt), *Archaic.* **—adj. 1.** accursed. **—v.t. 2.** to put a curse on. [1540–50; < LL *maledictus* accursed, L: ptp. of *maledicere* to speak ill of, abuse, equiv. to *male-* MALE- + *dicere* to say]

mal·e·dic·tion (mal′i dik′shən), *n.* **1.** a curse; imprecation. **2.** the utterance of a curse. **3.** slander. [1400–50; late ME *malediccion* < L *malediction-* (s. of *maledictiō*) slander (LL: curse). See MALE-, DICTION] **—mal′e·dic′tive, mal·e·dic·to·ry** (mal′i dik′tə rē), *adj.*
—Syn. 1. damning, execration. **—Ant. 1.** benediction.

mal·e·fac·tion (mal′ə fak′shən), *n.* an evil deed; crime; wrongdoing. [1375–1425 for an earlier sense; 1595–1605 for current sense; ME *malefaccioun* impotence; see MALEFACT(OR), -ION]

mal·e·fac·tor (mal′ə fak′tər), *n.* **1.** a person who violates the law; criminal. **2.** a person who does harm or evil, esp. toward another. [1400–50; late ME *malefactour* < L *malefactor,* equiv. to *malefac(ere)* to act wickedly, do an evil deed (see MALE-, FACT) + *-tor* -TOR]
—Syn. 1. felon, culprit. **—Ant. 2.** benefactor.

mal·e·fac·tress (mal′ə fak′tris), *n.* a woman who violates the law or does evil. [1640–50; MALEFACT(O)R + -ESS]
—Usage. See **-ess.**

male′ fern′, a bright-green fern, *Dryopteris filix-mas,* of Europe and northeastern North America. [1555–65]

ma•lef•ic (mə lef′ik), *adj.* productive of evil; malign; doing harm; baneful: *a malefic spell.* [1645–55; < L *maleficus* evil-doing, wicked. See MALE-, -FIC]

ma•lef•i•cence (mə lef′ə səns), *n.* **1.** the doing of evil or harm: *the maleficence of thieves.* **2.** the quality or state of being maleficent or harmful. [1590–1600; < L *maleficentia.* See MALEFIC, -ENCE]

ma•lef•i•cent (mə lef′ə sənt), *adj.* doing evil or harm; harmfully malicious: *maleficent destroyers of reputations.* [1670–80; back formation from L *maleficentia* MALEFICENCE; see -ENT]

ma•le′ic ac′id (mə lē′ik), *Chem.* a colorless, crystalline, water-soluble solid, $C_4H_4O_4$, isomeric with fumaric acid, having an astringent, repulsive taste and faint acidulous odor: used in the manufacture of synthetic resins, the dyeing and finishing of textiles, and as a preservative for fats and oils. [1870–75; < F *maléique,* alter. of *malique* MALIC]

male′ic anhy′dride, *Chem.* a colorless crystalline, unsaturated compound, $C_4H_2O_3$, that is soluble in acetone and hydrolyzes in water: used in the production of polyester resins, pesticides, and fumaric and tartaric acids. [1855–60]

male′ic hy′drazide (hī′drə zīd′), *Chem.* a crystalline compound, $C_4N_2H_4O_2$, used as a plant growth inhibitor and weed-killer. [1945–50; HYDR-[2] + AZ- + -IDE (*maleic,* see MALEIC ACID)]

male′ men′opause, a malaise that allegedly affects men in middle age and is said to be responsible for periods of emotional upset and uncharacteristic behavior. [1945–50]

mal•e•mute (mal′ə myo͞ot′), *n.* (*sometimes cap.*) See **Alaskan malamute.**

Ma•len•kov (mä′lən kôf′, -kof′; *Russ.* mə lyin kôf′), *n.* **Ge•or•gi Ma•xi•mi•lia•no•vich** (gyi ôʀ′gyē mə ksyi myilyä′nə vyich), born 1902, Russian political leader: premier of the Soviet Union 1953–55.

mal•en•ten•du (mᴀl än tän dʏ′), *adj., n., pl.* **-dus** (-dʏ′). *French.* —*adj.* **1.** misunderstood; misapprehended. —*n.* **2.** a misunderstanding; mistake.

male-ster•ile (māl′ster′il *or, esp. Brit.,* -īl), *adj. Bot.* producing no pollen or infertile pollen. [1920–25]

ma•lev•o•lence (mə lev′ə ləns), *n.* the quality, state, or feeling of being malevolent; ill will; malice; hatred. [1425–75; < L *malevolentia* (see MALEVOLENT, -ENCE); r. late ME *malivolence* < MF < L as above]
—Syn. maliciousness, spite, spitefulness, grudge, venom. MALEVOLENCE, MALIGNITY, RANCOR suggest the wishing of harm to others. MALEVOLENCE is a smoldering ill will: *a vindictive malevolence in her expression.* MALIGNITY is a deep-seated and virulent disposition to injure; it is more dangerous than MALEVOLENCE, because it is not only more completely concealed but it often instigates harmful acts: *The malignity of his nature was shocking.* RANCOR is a lasting, corrosive, and implacable hatred and resentment.

ma•lev•o•lent (mə lev′ə lənt), *adj.* **1.** wishing evil or harm to another or others; showing ill will; ill-disposed; malicious: *His failures made him malevolent toward those who were successful.* **2.** evil; harmful; injurious: *a malevolent inclination to destroy the happiness of others.* **3.** *Astrol.* evil or malign in influence. [1500–10; < L *malevolent-* (s. of *malevolēns*) ill-disposed, spiteful, equiv. to *male-* MALE- + *volent-* (s. of *volēns*), prp. of *velle* to want, wish for, desire (see WILL[1], -ENT)] **—ma•lev′o•lent•ly,** *adv.*

mal•fea•sance (mal fē′zəns), *n. Law.* the performance by a public official of an act that is legally unjustified, harmful, or contrary to law; wrongdoing (used esp. of an act in violation of a public trust). Cf. **misfeasance** (def. 2), **nonfeasance.** [1690–1700; earlier *malefeasance.* See MALE-, FEASANCE] **—mal•fea′sant,** *adj., n.*

mal•for•ma•tion (mal′fôr mā′shən, -fər-), *n.* faulty or anomalous formation or structure, esp. in a living body: *malformation of the teeth.* [1790–1800; MAL- + FORMATION]

mal•formed (mal fôrmd′), *adj.* faultily or anomalously formed. [1810–20; MAL- + FORMED]
—Syn. misshapen, deformed, distorted, contorted.

mal•func•tion (mal fungk′shən), *n.* **1.** failure to function properly: *a malfunction of the liver; the malfunction of a rocket.* —*v.i.* **2.** to fail to function properly. [1925–30; MAL- + FUNCTION]

Mal•herbe (mᴀl ɛʀb′), *n.* **Fran•çois de** (fʀäɴ swᴀ′ də), 1555–1628, French poet and critic.

Ma•li (mä′lē), *n.* **Republic of,** a republic in W Africa: formerly a territory of France; gained independence 1960. 5,600,000; 463,500 sq. mi. (120,000 sq. km). *Cap.:* Bamako. Formerly, **French Sudan. —Ma′li•an,** *n., adj.*

CONCISE ETYMOLOGY KEY: <, descended or borrowed from; >, whence; b., blend of, blended; c., cognate with; cf., compare; deriv., derivative; equiv., equivalent; imit., imitative; obl., oblique; r., replacing; s., stem; sp., spelling, spelled; resp., respelling, respelled; trans., translation; ?, origin unknown; *, unattested; ‡, probably earlier than. See the full key inside the front cover.

Ma•li•bran (mä′li brän′; *Fr.* mä lē bʀäɴ′; *Sp.* mä′lē-vrän′), *n.* **Ma•ri•a Fe•li•ci•ta** (*Sp.* mä ʀē′ä fe′lē thē′tä), 1808–36, Spanish opera singer, born in France.

Mal′i•bu board′ (mal′ə bo͞o′), a lightweight, fiberglass-covered surfboard, usually about 10 ft. (3 m) long with a rounded nose and tail and a convex bottom for increased maneuverability. [1960–65; after *Malibu* Beach, Los Angeles Co., S California]

mal•ic (mal′ik, mā′lik), *adj.* **1.** pertaining to or derived from apples. **2.** *Chem.* of or derived from malic acid. [1790–1800; < F *malique* < L *māl(um)* apple + F *-ique* -IC]

mal′ic ac′id, *Chem.* a colorless, crystalline, water-soluble solid, $C_4H_6O_5$, occurring in apples and other fruits and as an intermediate in animal metabolism.

mal•ice (mal′is), *n.* **1.** desire to inflict injury, harm, or suffering on another, either because of a hostile impulse or out of deep-seated meanness: *the malice and spite of a lifelong enemy.* **2.** *Law.* evil intent on the part of a person who commits a wrongful act injurious to others. [1250–1300; ME < OF < L *malitia.* See MAL-, -ICE]
—Syn. 1. ill will, spite, spitefulness; animosity, enmity. See **grudge. —Ant. 1.** benevolence, goodwill.

mal′ice afore′thought, *Law.* a predetermination to commit an unlawful act without just cause or provocation (applied chiefly to cases of first-degree murder). Also called **mal′ice prepense′.** [1660–70]

ma•li•cious (mə lish′əs), *adj.* **1.** full of, characterized by, or showing malice; malevolent; spiteful: *malicious gossip.* **2.** *Law.* vicious, wanton, or mischievous in motivation or purpose. [1175–1225; ME *malicius* < OF < L *malitiōsus.* See MALICE, -OUS] **—ma•li′cious•ly,** *adv.* **—ma•li′cious•ness,** *n.*

mali′cious mis′chief, willful destruction of personal property motivated by ill will or resentment toward its owner or possessor. [1760–70]

ma•lign (mə līn′), *v.t.* **1.** to speak harmful untruths about; speak evil of; slander; defame: *to malign an honorable man.* —*adj.* **2.** evil in effect; pernicious; baleful; injurious: *The gloomy house had a malign influence upon her usually good mood.* **3.** having or showing an evil disposition; malevolent; malicious. [1275–1325; ME *maligne* < MF < L *malignus.* See MAL-, BENIGN] **—ma•lign′er,** *n.* **—ma•lign′ly,** *adv.*
—Syn. 1. libel, calumniate; disparage; revile, abuse.

ma•lig•nan•cy (mə lig′nən sē), *n., pl.* **-cies** for 2, 3. **1.** the quality or condition of being malignant. **2.** malignant character, behavior, action, or the like: *the malignancies of war.* **3.** a malignant tumor. Also, **ma•lig′nance** (for defs. 1, 2). [1595–1605; MALIGN(ANT) + -ANCY]

ma•lig•nant (mə lig′nənt), *adj.* **1.** disposed to cause harm, suffering, or distress deliberately; feeling or showing ill will or hatred. **2.** very dangerous or harmful in influence or effect. **3.** *Pathol.* **a.** tending to produce death, as bubonic plague. **b.** (of a tumor) characterized by uncontrolled growth; cancerous, invasive, or metastatic. [1535–45; < LL *malignant-* (s. of *malignāns*), prp. of *malignāre* to act maliciously. See MALIGN, -ANT] **—ma•lig′nant•ly,** *adv.*
—Syn. 1. spiteful, malevolent. **2.** perilous, hurtful, pernicious. **—Ant. 1–3.** benign.

ma•lig•ni•ty (mə lig′ni tē), *n., pl.* **-ties** for 2. **1.** the state or character of being malign; malevolence; intense ill will; spite. **2.** a malignant feeling, action, etc. [1350–1400; ME *malignitee* < L *malignitās.* See MALIGN, -ITY]
—Syn. 1. See **malevolence.**

ma•li•hi•ni (mä′lē hē′nē), *n., pl.* **-hi•nis.** *Hawaiian.* a newcomer to Hawaii.

Ma•lik (mä′lik, mal′ik), *n.* **1. Adam,** 1917–84, Indonesian politician and diplomat. **2.** a male given name: from an Arabic word meaning "king."

Mal•i•ki (mal′i kē), *n. Islam.* one of the four schools of Islamic law, founded by Malik ibn Anas (c715–795). Cf. **Hanafi, Hanbali, Shafi′i.** [< Ar *Mālikī,* deriv. of name of founder, *Mālik* ibn Anas] **—Mal′i•kite′,** *n.*

Ma•lin•da (mə lin′də), *n.* a female given name.

ma•lines (mə lēn′; *Fr.* mᴀ lēn′), *n.* **1.** Also, **ma•line′.** a delicate net resembling tulle, originally made by hand in the town of Mechlin, Belgium. **2.** See **Mechlin lace.** [1840–50; after MALINES]

Ma•lines (mᴀ lēn′; *Eng.* mə lēnz′), *n.* French name of **Mechlin.**

ma•lin•ger (mə ling′gər), *v.i.* to pretend illness, esp. in order to shirk one's duty, avoid work, etc. [1810–20; < F *malingre* sickly, ailing, equiv. to *mal-* MAL- + OF *heingre* haggard (perh. < Gmc)] **—ma•lin′ger•er,** *n.*

Ma•lin•ke (mə ling′kā, -kē), *n., pl.* **-kes,** (*esp. collectively*) **-ke** for 1. **1.** a member of an agricultural people living in Senegal, Gambia, Guinea, Guinea-Bissau, Mali, and Ivory Coast. **2.** the Mande language of the Malinke people. Also, **Ma•lin•ka** (mə ling′kä, -kē). Also called **Mandingo, Mandinka.**

Ma•li•nov•sky (mal′ə nôf′skē, -nof′-, mä′lə-; *Russ.* mə lyi nôf′skyē), *n.* **Ro•di•on Ya•kov•le•vich** (ʀə dyiôn′ yä′kə vlyi vyich), 1898–1967, Russian army officer: minister of defense of the U.S.S.R. 1957–67.

Ma•li•now•ski (mal′ə nôf′skē, -nof′-), *n.* **Bro•ni•slaw Kas•per** (bron′ə släf′ kas′pər; *Pol.* bʀô nē′släf käs′pəʀ), 1884–1942, Polish anthropologist in the U.S.

Ma•li•pie•ro (mä′lē pye′ʀô), *n.* **Gian Fran•ces•co** (jän frän che′skô), 1882–1973, Italian composer.

Mal•i•seet (mal′ə sēt′), *n.* Malecite.

mal•i•son (mal′ə zən, -sən), *n. Archaic.* a curse. [1200–50; ME *maliso(u)n* < OF *maleison* < L *maledictiōn-* (s. of *maledictiō*) MALEDICTION]

mal•kin (mô′kin, môl′-, mal′-), *n. Brit. Dial.* **1.** an untidy woman; slattern. **2.** a scarecrow, ragged puppet, or grotesque effigy. **3.** a mop, esp. one made from a bundle of rags and used to clean out a baker's oven. **4.** a cat. **5.** a hare. Also, **mawkin.** [1200–50; ME: lit., little Molly, equiv. to *Mal,* var. of *Molly* Mary + -KIN]

mall (môl; *Brit. also* mal), *n.* **1.** Also called **shopping mall.** a large retail complex containing a variety of stores and often restaurants and other business establishments housed in a series of connected or adjacent buildings or in a single large building. Cf. **shopping center. 2.** a large area, usually lined with shade trees and shrubbery, used as a public walk or promenade. **3.** *Chiefly Upstate New York.* a strip of land, usually planted or paved, separating lanes of opposite traffic on highways, boulevards, etc. **4.** the game of pall-mall. **5.** the mallet used in the game of pall-mall. **6.** the place or alley where pall-mall was played. [1635–45; by ellipsis from PALL MALL; see MELL[2]]

mal•lan•ders (mal′ən dərz), *n.* (*used with a singular v.*) *Vet. Pathol.* malanders.

mal•lard (mal′ərd), *n., pl.* **-lards,** (*esp. collectively*) **-lard.** a common, almost cosmopolitan, wild duck, *Anas platyrhynchos,* from which the domestic ducks are descended. [1275–1325; ME < MF, OF *mallart* mallard drake, drake; see MALE, -ARD]

mallard, *Anas platyrhynchos,* length 2 ft. (0.6 m)

Mal•lar•mé (mᴀ lᴀʀ mā′), *n.* **Sté•phane** (stā fᴀɴ′), 1842–98, French poet.

mal•le•a•ble (mal′ē ə bəl), *adj.* **1.** capable of being extended or shaped by hammering or by pressure from rollers. **2.** adaptable or tractable: *the malleable mind of a child.* [1350–1400; ME *malliable* < ML *malleābilis,* equiv. to *malle(āre)* to hammer (deriv. of L *malleus* hammer) + *-ābilis* -ABLE] **—mal′le•a•bly,** *adv.* **—mal′le•a•bil′i•ty, mal′le•a•ble•ness,** *n.*
—Syn. 2. impressionable, moldable, flexible, pliable.
—Ant. 2. refractory, intractable.

mal′leable cast′ i′ron, white cast iron that has been malleablized.

mal′leable i′ron, 1. See **malleable cast iron. 2.** See **wrought iron.** [1815–25]

mal•le•a•blize (mal′ē ə blīz′), *v.t.,* **-blized, -bliz•ing.** to make (white cast iron) malleable by annealing it so that the carbon is transformed to graphite or removed completely. Also, *esp. Brit.,* **mal′le•a•blise′.** [1880–85; MALLEABLE + -IZE]

mal•le•ate (mal′ē āt′), *v.t.,* **-at•ed, -at•ing.** to beat or shape with a hammer, as in metalworking. [1590–1600; < L *malleātus* wrought with a hammer, equiv. to L *malle(us)* hammer + *-ātus* -ATE[1]] **—mal′le•a′tion,** *n.*

mal•lee (mal′ē), *n.* **1.** any of various dwarf Australian eucalyptuses, as *Eucalyptus dumosa* and *E. oleosa,* that sometimes form large tracts of brushwood. **2.** the brushwood itself. [1840–50; < Wergaia (Australian Aboriginal language spoken in the Wimmera area, Victoria) *mali*]

mal′lee fowl′, an Australian bird, *Leipoa ocellata,* of variegated gray, brown, white, and black plumage, that lays up to 35 eggs in an incubating mound. Also, **mal′lee-fowl′.** Also called **leipoa, lowan.** [1960–65]

mal•le•muck (mal′ə muk′), *n.* mollymawk. [1685–95]

mal•len•ders (mal′ən dərz), *n.* (*used with a singular v.*) *Vet. Pathol.* malanders.

mal•le•o•lar (mə lē′ə lər), *adj. Anat.* pertaining to a malleolus. [1835–45; MALLEOL(US) + -AR[1]]

mal•le•o•lus (mə lē′ə ləs), *n., pl.* **-li** (-lī′). *Anat.* the bony protuberance on either side of the ankle, at the lower end of the fibula or of the tibia. [1685–95; < L: small hammer, mallet, equiv. to *malle(us)* hammer + *-olus* -OLE[1]]

mal•let (mal′it), *n.* **1.** a hammerlike tool with a head commonly of wood but occasionally of rawhide, plastic, etc., used for driving any tool with a wooden handle, as a chisel, or for striking a surface. **2.** the wooden implement used to strike the balls in croquet. **3.** *Polo.* the long-handled stick, or club, used to drive the ball. [1375–1425; late ME *maillet* < MF, equiv. to *mail* MAUL + *-et* -ET]

mallets (def. 1) A, carpenter's mallet; B, stonecutter's mallet

mal•le•us (mal′ē əs), *n., pl.* **mal•le•i** (mal′ē ī′). *Anat.* the outermost of a chain of three small bones in the middle ear of mammals. Also called **hammer.** Cf. **incus** (def. 1), **stapes.** See diag. under **ear.** [1660–70; < L: hammer]

Mal•lia (mäl yä′), *n.* a town in E Crete: site of an excavated Minoan palace.

mall•ing (mô′ling), *n.* **1.** the overbuilding of shopping malls in a region: *the malling of America.* **2.** the practice of frequenting malls to socialize or shop. [1975–80]

Ma•llor•ca (*Sp.* mä lyôʀ′kä, -yôʀ′-; *Eng.* mä yôr′kə), *n.* Majorca.

Mal·lo·ry (mal′ə rē), *n.* **Stephen Russell,** 1813?–73, U.S. lawyer and politician.

mal·low (mal′ō), *n.* any of various plants of the genus *Malva,* including several popular garden plants, as the musk mallow. [bef. 1000; ME *malue,* OE *mealwe* < L *malva*]

mal′low fam′ily, the plant family Malvaceae, characterized by herbaceous plants, shrubs, and trees having palmately veined, lobed, or compound leaves, sticky juice, often showy five-petaled flowers with stamens united in a column, and fruit in the form of a capsule with several divisions, and including the cotton plant, hibiscus, hollyhock, mallow, okra, and rose of Sharon.

mal′low rose′, a rose mallow of the genus *Hibiscus.* [1830–40]

malm (mäm), *n.* an artificial mixture of chalk and clay for making into bricks. [bef. 900; ME *malme* sand, malm, OE *mealm-* (in *mealmiht* sandy, *mealmstān* sandstone); c. ON *mālmr* metal (in granular form), Goth *malma* sand; akin to OS, OHG *melm* dust. See MEAL[2]]

Mal·mé·dy (mal mā dē′), *n.* See **Eupen and Malmédy.**

Malmes·bur·y (mämz′ber′ē, -bə rē), *n.* **William of.** See **William of Malmesbury.**

Malm·ö (mal′mō; *Swed.* mälm′œ′), *n.* a seaport in S Sweden, on the Sound opposite Copenhagen, Denmark. 229,380.

malm·sey (mäm′zē), *n.* a strong, sweet wine with a strong flavor, originally made in Greece but now made mainly in Madeira. [1325–75; ME *malmesye* < MLG << *Monemvasia* Greek town where it was originally produced]

mal·nour·ished (mal nûr′isht, -nur′-), *adj.* poorly or improperly nourished; suffering from malnutrition: *thin, malnourished victims of the famine.* [1925–30; MAL- + NOURISH + -ED[2]]

mal·nu·tri·tion (mal′nōō trish′ən, -nyōō-), *n.* lack of proper nutrition; inadequate or unbalanced nutrition. [1860–65; MAL- + NUTRITION]

mal·oc·clu·sion (mal′ə klōō′zhən), *n. Dentistry.* faulty occlusion; irregular contact of opposing teeth in the upper and lower jaws. [1885–90; MAL- + OCCLUSION] —**mal′oc·clud′ed,** *adj.*

mal·o·dor (mal ō′dər), *n.* an unpleasant or offensive odor; stench. [1815–25; MAL- + ODOR]

mal·o·dor·ous (mal ō′dər əs), *adj.* having an unpleasant or offensive odor; smelling bad: *a malodorous swamp.* [1840–50; MAL- + ODOROUS] —**mal·o′dor·ous·ly,** *adv.* —**mal·o′dor·ous·ness,** *n.*

Ma·lone (mə lōn′), *n.* **Edmond,** 1741–1812, Irish literary critic and Shakespearean scholar.

ma·lo·nic (mə lō′nik, -lon′ik), *adj. Chem.* of or derived from malonic acid; propanedioic. [1855–60; < F *malonique,* alter. of *malique* MALIC]

malo′nic ac′id, *Chem.* a white, crystalline, water-soluble, dibasic acid, $C_3H_4O_4$, easily decomposed by heat: used chiefly as an intermediate in the synthesis of barbiturates. [1885–90]

mal·o·nyl (mal′ə nil, -nēl′), *adj. Chem.* containing the malonyl group. [1885–90; MALON(IC) + -YL]

mal′onyl group′, *Chem.* the bivalent group $C_3H_2O_2$, derived from malonic acid. Also called **mal′onyl rad′ical.** [1965–70]

mal·o·nyl·u·re·a (mal′ə nil yōō rē′ə, -yōōr′ē ə, -nēl′-), *n. Chem.* See **barbituric acid.** [1885–90; MALONYL + UREA]

Mal·o·ry (mal′ə rē), *n.* **Sir Thomas,** c1400–71, English author.

ma·lo·ti (mä lō′tē), *n.* pl. of **loti.**

mal·pa·is (mäl′pä ēs′), *n. Southwestern U.S.* an extensive area of rough, barren lava flows. [1835–45, *Amer.*; < Sp *mal país* bad country]

Mal·pi·ghi (mäl pē′gē), *n.* **Mar·cel·lo** (mär chel′lô), 1628–94, Italian anatomist. —**Mal·pigh·i·an** (mal pig′ē ən), *adj.*

Malpigh′ian cor′puscle, *Anat.* **1.** Also called **kidney corpuscle, Malpigh′ian bod′y.** the structure at the beginning of a vertebrate nephron, consisting of a glomerulus and its surrounding Bowman's capsule. **2.** a compact aggregation of lymphoid tissue surrounding an arteriole in the spleen. [1840–50]

Malpigh′ian lay′er, *Anat.* the deep, germinative layer of the epidermis. [1875–80]

Malpigh′ian tube′, one of a group of long, slender excretory tubules at the anterior end of the hindgut in insects and other terrestrial arthropods. Also called **Malpigh′ian tu′bule, Malpigh′ian ves′sel.**

Malpigh′ian tuft′, glomerulus (def. 2). [1840–50]

mal·po·si·tion (mal′pə zish′ən), *n. Pathol.* faulty or wrong position, esp. of a part or organ of the body or of a fetus in the uterus. [1830–40; MAL- + POSITION]

mal·prac·tice (mal prak′tis), *n.* **1.** *Law.* failure of a professional person, as a physician or lawyer, to render proper services through reprehensible ignorance or negligence or through criminal intent, esp. when injury or loss follows. **2.** any improper, negligent practice; misconduct or misuse. [1665–75; MAL- + PRACTICE] —**mal·prac·ti·tion·er** (mal′prak tish′ə nər), *n.*

Mal·raux (mal rō′), *n.* **An·dré** (äN drā′), 1901–76, French novelist, critic, and politician.

M.A.L.S., **1.** Master of Arts in Liberal Studies. **2.** Master of Arts in Library Science.

malt (môlt), *n.* **1.** germinated grain, usually barley, used in brewing and distilling. **2.** any alcoholic beverage, as beer, ale, or malt liquor, fermented from malt. **3.** whisky, as Scotch, that is distilled entirely from malted barley. **4.** See **malted milk** (def. 2). —*v.t.* **5.** to convert (grain) into malt by soaking it in water and allowing it to germinate. **6.** to treat or mix with malt, malt extract, etc. **7.** to make (liquor) with malt. —*v.i.* **8.** to become malt. **9.** to produce malt from grain. [bef. 900; ME; OE *mealt;* c. ON *malt,* G *Malz;* akin to MELT]

Mal·ta (môl′tə), *n.* **1.** an island in the Mediterranean between Sicily and Africa. 95 sq. mi. (246 sq. km). **2.** a former British colony consisting of this island and two small adjacent islands: now an independent sovereign state and a member of the Commonwealth of Nations. 297,622; 122 sq. mi. (316 sq. km). *Cap.:* Valletta.

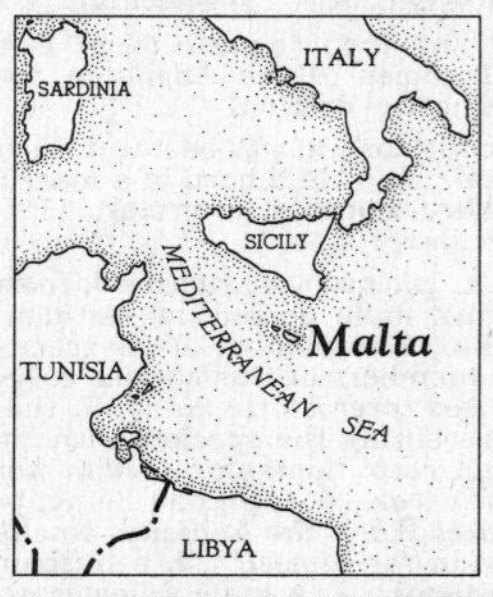

Mal′ta fe′ver, *Pathol.* brucellosis. [1865–70]

malt·ase (môl′tās, -tāz), *n. Biochem.* an enzyme that converts maltose into glucose and causes similar cleavage of many other glucosides. [1885–90; MALT + -ASE]

malt·ed (môl′tid), *n.* See **malted milk.** [1670–80 for sense "made into malt"; MALT + -ED[2]]

malt′ed milk′, **1.** a soluble powder made of dehydrated milk and malted cereals. **2.** a beverage made by dissolving this powder, usually in milk, often with ice cream and flavoring added. [1885–90, *Amer.*]

Mal·tese (môl tēz′, -tēs′), *adj., n., pl.* **-tese.** —*adj.* **1.** of or pertaining to Malta, its people, or their language. —*n.* **2.** a native or inhabitant of Malta. **3.** the Arabic dialect spoken in Malta, using many Italian words. [1605–15; MALT(A) + -ESE]

Mal′tese cat′, a bluish-gray variety of the domestic cat. [1855–60]

Mal′tese cross′, **1.** a cross having four equal arms that expand in width outward. See illus. under **cross. 2.** See **scarlet lychnis.** [1875–80]

Mal′tese dog′, one of a breed of toy dogs having a long, straight, silky white coat. [1790–1800]

malt′ ex′tract, a sweet, gummy substance derived from an infusion of malt. [1830–40]

mal·tha (mal′thə), *n.* **1.** a liquid bitumen used in ancient times as a mortar or waterproofing agent. **2.** any of various natural mixtures of bituminous hydrocarbons. **3.** a viscous mineral liquid or semiliquid bitumen; a mineral tar. [1375–1425; late ME *malthe* < L < Gk *máltha, málthē* mixed wax and pitch]

mal·thene (mal′thēn), *n. Chem.* petrolene. [MALTH(A) + -ENE]

Mal·thus (mal′thəs), *n.* **Thomas Robert,** 1766–1834, English economist and clergyman.

Mal·thu·sian (mal thōō′zhən, -zē ən), *adj.* **1.** of or pertaining to the theories of T. R. Malthus, which state that population tends to increase faster, at a geometrical ratio, than the means of subsistence, which increases at an arithmetical ratio, and that this will result in an inadequate supply of the goods supporting life unless war, famine, or disease reduces the population or the increase of population is checked. —*n.* **2.** a follower of Malthus. [1805–15; MALTHUS + -IAN] —**Mal·thu′sian·ism,** *n.*

Malthu′sian param′eter, *Ecol.* See **r.**

malt′ liq′uor, beer having a relatively high alcohol content, usually 5 to 8 percent. [1685–95]

malt·ol (môl′tôl, -tol), *n. Chem.* a crystalline compound, $C_6H_6O_3$, obtained from larch bark, pine needles, chicory, or roasted malt, used for enhancing flavors and aromas, as in foods, wines, and perfumes. Also called **larixinic acid.** [1890–95; MALT + -OL[1]]

malt·ose (môl′tōs), *n. Chem.* a white, crystalline, water-soluble sugar, $C_{12}H_{22}O_{11}·H_2O$, formed by the action of diastase, esp. from malt, on starch: used chiefly as a nutrient, as a sweetener, and in culture media. Also called **malt′ sug′ar, mal·to·bi·ose** (môl′tō bī′ōs). [1860–65; MALT + -OSE[2]]

mal·treat (mal trēt′), *v.t.* to treat or handle badly, cruelly, or roughly; abuse: *to maltreat a prisoner.* [1700–10; earlier *maltrait* < F *maltraiter.* See MAL-, TREAT] —**mal·treat′er,** *n.* —**mal·treat′ment,** *n.*
—**Syn.** mistreat, injure.

malt′ shop′, a retail establishment specializing in serving ice-cream drinks, as malted milks, milk shakes, and sodas. [1940–45, *Amer.*]

malt·ster (môlt′stər), *n.* a maker of or dealer in malt. [1325–75; ME *malt(e)stere.* See MALT, -STER]

malt·y (môl′tē), *adj.,* **malt·i·er, malt·i·est.** of, like, or containing malt. [1810–20; MALT + -Y[1]] —**malt′i·ness,** *n.*

Ma·lus′ law′ (mə lōōs′; *Fr.* ma lys′), *Optics.* the law stating that the intensity of a beam of plane-polarized light after passing through a rotatable polarizer varies as the square of the cosine of the angle through which the polarizer is rotated from the position that gives maximum intensity. Also called **law of Malus, Malus′ co′sine-squared law′** (kō′sīn skwârd′). [named after E. L. *Malus* (1775–1812), French physicist]

mal·va·ceous (mal vā′shəs), *adj.* belonging to the Malvaceae, the mallow family of plants. Cf. **mallow family.** [1690–1700; < L *malvāceus.* See MALLOW, -ACEOUS]

mal·va·si·a (mal′və sē′ə), *n.* a sweet grape from which malmsey wine is made. [1830–40; < It, for *Monemvasia.* See MALMSEY] —**mal′va·si′an,** *adj.*

Mal·vern (môl′vərn, mô′- *for 1;* mal′vərn *for 2*), *n.* **1.** an urban area in W England, SW of Birmingham: mineral springs; incorporated into Malvern Hills 1974. **2.** a town in central Arkansas. 10,163.

Mal′vern Hill′ (mal′vərn), a plateau in E Virginia, SE of Richmond: battle 1862.

Mal′vern Hills′ (môl′vərn, mô′-), **1.** a range of hills in W England, bisecting Hereford and Worcester: highest point, 1395 ft. (425 m). **2.** a city in Hereford and Worcester, in W England. 80,000.

mal·ver·sa·tion (mal′vər sā′shən), *n. Chiefly Law.* improper or corrupt behavior in office, esp. in public office. [1540–50; < MF, equiv. to *malvers(er)* to embezzle (< L *male versārī* to behave badly, equiv. to *male* badly (see MAL-) + *versārī* to behave, conduct oneself, passive (in middle sense) of *versāre* to turn; see VERSATILE) + *-ation* -ATION]

Mal·vine (mal′vēn, -vīn), *n.* a female given name. Also, **Mal·vi·na** (mal vē′nə, -vī′-).

mal·voi·sie (mal′voi zē, -və-), *n.* **1.** malmsey wine. **2.** the malvasia grape. [1350–1400; < F; r. ME *malvesie* < MF < It *malvasia.* See MALMSEY, MALVASIA]

ma·ma (mä′mə; *for 1 also* mə mä′), *n.* **1.** *Informal.* mother. **2.** *Slang.* **a.** a sexually attractive, usually mature woman. **b.** one's wife. Also, **mamma.** [1545–55; nursery word, with parallels in other European languages, prob. in part inherited or borrowed, in part newly formed; cf. L *mamma,* Gk *mámmē* breast, mama (see MAMMA[2]), F *maman* mama, Welsh *mam* mother (< **mammā*)]

Ma·mal·la·pur·am (mə mä′lə pōōr′əm), *n.* Mahabalipuram.

Ma·mar·o·neck (mə mar′ə nek′), *n.* a city in SE New York. 17,616.

ma′ma's boy′, a boy or man showing excessive attachment to or dependence on his mother. Also called **mother's boy.** [1840–50]

mam·ba (mäm′bä), *n.* any of several long, slender, arboreal snakes of the genus *Dendroaspis,* of central and southern Africa, the bite of which is often fatal. [1860–65; < Nguni; cf. Zulu *imamba, izimamba*]

mam·bo (mäm′bō), *n., pl.* **-bos,** *v.* —*n.* **1.** a fast ballroom dance of Caribbean origin, rhythmically similar to the rumba and cha-cha but having a more complex pattern of steps. —*v.i.* **2.** to dance the mambo. [1945–50; < AmerSp]

Mame (mām), *n.* a female given name.

Mam·e·luke (mam′ə lōōk′), *n.* **1.** a member of a military class, originally composed of slaves, that seized control of the Egyptian sultanate in 1250, ruled until 1517, and remained powerful until massacred or dispersed by Mehemet Ali in 1811. **2.** (*l.c.*) (in Muslim countries) a slave. [1505–15; < Ar *mamlūk* lit., slave, n. use of ptp. of *malaka* to possess]

Ma·mers (mā′mərz), *n. Rom. Legend.* Mars.

Mam·et (mam′it), *n.* **David (Alan),** born 1947, U.S. playwright.

ma·mey (mä mā′, -mē′), *n.* mammee.

Ma·mie (mā′mē), *n.* a female given name, form of **Mary.**

mam·ma[1] (mä′mə, mə mä′), *n.* mama.

mam·ma[2] (mam′ə), *n., pl.* **mam·mae** (mam′ē) for 1; **mam·ma** for 2. **1.** *Anat., Zool.* a structure, characteristic of mammals, that comprises one or more mammary glands with an associated nipple or teat, usually rudimentary unless developed and activated for the secretion of milk in the female after the birth of young. **2.** *Meteorol.* (*used with a plural v.*) hanging, breastlike protuberances on the under surface of a cloud. [bef. 1050; ME < L: breast, teat (whence OE *mamme* teat). See MAMMA[1]]

mam·mal (mam′əl), *n.* any vertebrate of the class Mammalia, having the body more or less covered with hair, nourishing the young with milk from the mammary glands, and, with the exception of the egg-laying monotremes, giving birth to live young. [1820–30; as sing. of NL *Mammalia* neut. pl. of LL *mammālis* of the breast. See MAMMA[2], -AL[1]] —**mam′mal·like′,** *adj.*

mam·ma·li·an (mə mā′lē ən, -māl′yən), *n.* **1.** an animal of the class Mammalia; mammal. —*adj.* **2.** belonging or pertaining to the class Mammalia; characteristic of mammals. [1825–35; < NL *Mammali(a)* (see MAMMAL) + -AN] —**mam·mal·i·ty** (mə mal′i tē), *n.*

mam·mal·o·gy (mə mal′ə jē), *n.* the science dealing with mammals. [1825–35; MAMMA(L) + -LOGY] —**mam·mal′o·gist,** *n.*

mam·ma·ry (mam′ə rē), *adj. Anat., Zool.* of or pertaining to the mamma or breast. [1675–85; MAMM(A)[2] + -ARY]

mam′mary ar′tery. See **thoracic artery.**

mam′mary gland′, any of the compound accessory reproductive organs of female mammals that occur in pairs on the chest or ventral surface and contain milk-producing lobes with ducts that empty into an external nipple, becoming functional when young are born and secreting milk for the duration of suckling. [1825–35]

CONCISE PRONUNCIATION KEY: *act, cāpe, dâre, pärt; set, ēqual; if, īce; ox, ōver, ôrder, oil, bŏŏk, bōōt, out; up, ûrge; child; sing; shoe; thin, that;* zh as in *treasure.* ə = *a* as in *alone, e* as in *system, i* as in *easily, o* as in *gallop, u* as in *circus;* ᵊ as in *fire* (fīᵊr), *hour* (ouᵊr). l and n can serve as syllabic consonants, as in *cradle* (krād′l), and *button* (but′n). See the full key inside the front cover.

mam·mec·to·my (mə mek′tə mē), *n., pl.* **-mies.** *Surg.* mastectomy. [MAMM(A)² + -ECTOMY]

mam·mee (mä mā′, -mē′), *n.* **1.** a tall, tropical American tree, *Mammea americana,* having thick, glossy leaves and fragrant white flowers. **2.** the usually round, edible fruit of this tree, having a russet-colored rind and yellow, juicy flesh. **3.** sapote. Also, **mamey, mammey′.** Also called **mammee′ ap′ple** (for defs. 1, 2). [1565–75; < Sp *mamey,* perh. < Taino]

mam·mer (mam′ər), *v.i. Brit. Dial.* **1.** to stammer or mutter. **2.** to hesitate; be undecided; waver in determination. [1350–1400; ME *mamere.* See MUMBLE, -ER⁶]

mam·met (mam′it), *n.* maumet.

mam·mif·er·ous (ma mif′ər əs), *adj.* having mammae; mammalian. [1795–1805; MAMM(A)² + -I- + -FEROUS]

mam·mil·la (ma mil′ə), *n., pl.* **-mil·lae** (-mil′ē). **1.** *Anat.* the nipple of the mamma, or breast. **2.** any nipplelike process or protuberance. [1685–95; < L: breast, teat, dim. of *mamma* MAMMA²]

mam·mil·lar·i·a (mam′ə lâr′ē ə), *n.* any of various cacti of the genus *Mammillaria,* including the pincushion cactus. [< NL (1824); see MAMMILLA, -ARIA]

mam·mil·lar·y (mam′ə ler′ē), *adj.* of, pertaining to, or resembling a mammilla. [1605–15; MAMMILL(A) + -ARY]

mam·mil·late (mam′ə lāt′), *adj.* having a mammilla or mammillae. Also, **mam′mil·lat′ed.** [1820–30; < LL *mammillātus.* See MAMMILLA, -ATE¹] **—mam′mil·la′tion,** *n.*

mam·mock (mam′ək), *Brit. Dial.* —*n.* **1.** a fragment; scrap. —*v.t.* **2.** to break, tear, or cut into fragments; shred. [1520–30; orig. uncert.]

mam·mo·gram (mam′ə gram′), *n.* an x-ray photograph obtained by mammography. [1935–40; MAMM(A)² + -O- + -GRAM¹]

mam·mog·ra·phy (ma mog′rə fē), *n.* x-ray photography of a breast, esp. for detection of tumors. [1935–40; MAMM(A)² + -O- + -GRAPHY] **—mam·mo·graph·ic** (mam′ə graf′ik), *adj.*

mam·mon (mam′ən), *n.* **1.** *New Testament.* riches or material wealth. Matt. 6:24; Luke 16:9,11,13. **2.** (*often cap.*) a personification of riches as an evil spirit or deity. [1350–1400; ME < LL < Gk *mam(m)ōnâs* < Aram *māmōnā* riches] **—mam′mon·ish,** *adj.*
—Syn. 1. possessions, money, gold.

mam·mon·ism (mam′ə niz′əm), *n.* the greedy pursuit of riches. [1835–45; MAMMON + -ISM] **—mam′mon·ist, mam′mon·ite′,** *n.* **—mam′mon·is′tic,** *adj.*

mam·mo·plas·ty (mam′ə plas′tē), *n. Surg.* reconstruction or alteration in size or contour of the female breast. [1965–70; MAMM(A)² + -O- + -PLASTY]

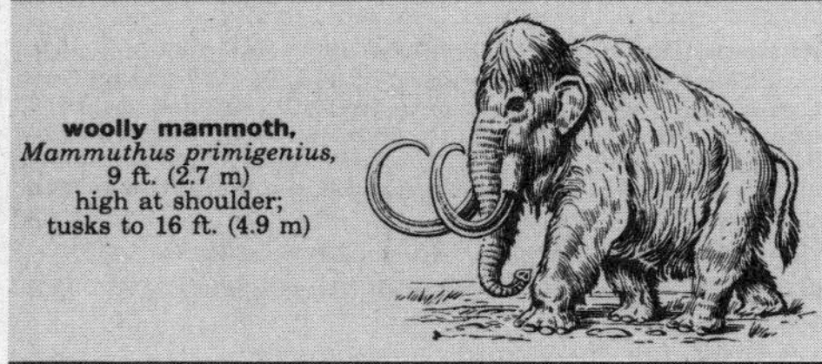

woolly mammoth, *Mammuthus primigenius,* 9 ft. (2.7 m) high at shoulder; tusks to 16 ft. (4.9 m)

mam·moth (mam′əth), *n.* **1.** any large, elephantlike mammal of the extinct genus *Mammuthus,* from the Pleistocene Epoch, having hairy skin and ridged molar teeth. —*adj.* **2.** immensely large; huge; enormous: *a mammoth organization.* [1690–1700; < Russ *mam(m)ot* (now *mámont*), first used in reference to remains of the animal found in Siberia; orig. uncert.]
—Syn. 2. See **gigantic.**

Mam′moth Cave′ Na′tional Park′, a national park in central Kentucky: limestone caverns with onyx formations, stalagmites, and stalactites. 79 sq. mi. (205 sq. km).

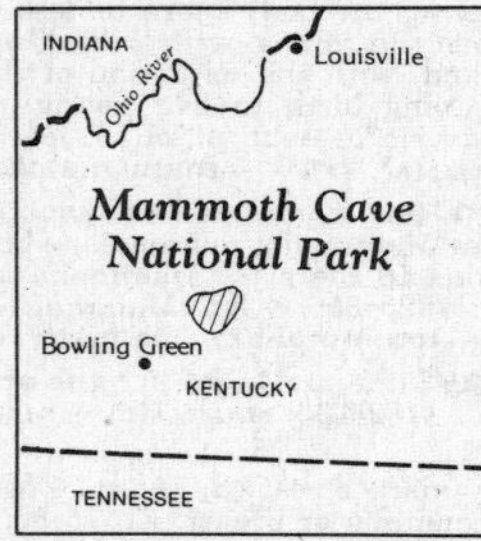

mam·mu·la (mam′yə lə), *n., pl.* **-lae** (-lē′). *Zool.* a small nipplelike process or protuberance. [1810–20; < L: little breast. See MAMMA², -ULE] **—mam′mu·lar,** *adj.*

mam·my (mam′ē), *n., pl.* **-mies. 1.** *Informal.* mother¹. **2.** (formerly in the southern U.S.) a black woman engaged as a nurse to white children or as a servant to a white family. [1515–25; MAMM(A)¹ + -Y²]

CONCISE ETYMOLOGY KEY: <, descended or borrowed from; >, whence; b., blend of, blended; c., cognate with; cf., compare; deriv., derivative; equiv., equivalent; imit., imitative; obl., oblique; r., replacing; s., stem; sp., spelling, spelled; resp., respelling, respelled; trans., translation; ?, origin unknown; *, unattested; ‡, probably earlier than. See the full key inside the front cover.

mam′my chair′, *Naut. Slang.* a slinglike device for raising or lowering passengers to and from ships anchored away from the shore in a heavy swell. [1900–05]

ma·mon·cil·lo (mä′mən sē′ō; *Sp.* mä′môn sē′yô), *n., pl.* **-cil·los** (-sē′ōz; *Sp.* -sē′yôs). the genip, *Melicoccus bijugatus.* [< AmerSp, dim. of *mamón,* of uncert. orig.]

Ma·mo·ré (mä′mô rā′), *n.* a river in Bolivia, flowing N to the Beni River on the border of Brazil to form the Madeira River. 700 mi. (1125 km) long.

Ma′·mun, al- (al′mä mōōn′, -ma-), (*abu-al-'Abbās 'Abdullāh*) A.D. 786–833, caliph of Baghdad 813–833 (son of Harun al-Rashid). Also, **al-Mamoun.**

Ma·mu·ri·us (mə mōōr′ē əs), *n. Rom. Legend.* a smith who made 11 copies of the Ancile to prevent thieves from recognizing the original.

mam·zer (mom′zər), *n.* **1.** bastard; illegitimate child. **2.** *Slang.* rascal. **3.** a child born of a marriage forbidden in Judaism. Also, **momser, momzer.** [1555–65; < Yiddish < Heb *mamzēr*]

man¹ (man), *n., pl.* **men,** *v.,* **manned, man·ning,** *interj.* —*n.* **1.** an adult male person, as distinguished from a boy or a woman. **2.** a member of the species *Homo sapiens* or all the members of this species collectively, without regard to sex: *prehistoric man.* **3.** the human individual as representing the species, without reference to sex; the human race; humankind: *Man hopes for peace, but prepares for war.* **4.** a human being; person: *to give a man a chance; When the audience smelled the smoke, it was every man for himself.* **5.** a husband. **6.** a male lover or sweetheart. **7.** a male follower or subordinate: *the king's men. He's the boss's number one man.* **8.** a male employee or representative, esp. of a company or agency: *a Secret Service man; a man from the phone company.* **9.** a male having qualities considered typical of men or appropriately masculine: *Be a man. The army will make a man of you.* **10.** a male servant. **11.** a valet. **12.** See **enlisted man. 13.** an enthusiast or devotee: *I like jazz, but I'm essentially a classics man.* **14.** *Slang.* male friend; ally: *You're my main man.* **15.** a term of familiar address to a man; fellow: *Now, now, my good man, please calm down.* **16.** *Slang.* a term of familiar address to a man or a woman: *Hey, man, take it easy.* **17.** one of the pieces used in playing certain games, as chess or checkers. **18.** *Hist.* a liegeman; vassal. **19.** *Obs.* manly character or courage. **20. as one man,** in complete agreement or accord; unanimously: *They arose as one man to protest the verdict.* **21. be one's own man, a.** to be free from restrictions, control, or dictatorial influence; be independent: *Now that he has a business he is his own man.* **b.** to be in complete command of one's faculties: *After a refreshing nap he was again his own man.* **22. man and boy,** ever since childhood: *He's been working that farm, man and boy, for more than 50 years.* **23. the man,** *Slang.* **a.** a person or group asserting authority or power over another, esp. in a manner experienced as being oppressive, demeaning, or threatening, as an employer, the police, or a dominating racial group. **b.** a person or group upon whom one is dependent, as the drug supplier for an addict. Also, **the Man. 24. to a man,** with no exception; everyone; all: *To a man, the members of the team did their best.* —*v.t.* **25.** to furnish with men, as for service or defense. **26.** to take one's place for service, as at a gun or post: *to man the ramparts.* **27.** to strengthen, fortify, or brace; steel: *to man oneself for the dangers ahead.* **28.** *Falconry.* to accustom (a hawk) to the presence of men. —*interj.* **29.** *Slang.* an expression of surprise, enthusiasm, dismay, or other strong feeling: *Man, what a ball game!* [bef. 900; (n.) ME; OE *man(n);* c. G *Mann,* D *man,* ON *mathr,* Goth *manna;* (v.) ME *mannen,* OE *mannian* to garrison] **—man′less,** *adj.* **—man′less·ly,** *adv.* **—man′less·ness,** *n.* **—man′·ness,** *n.*
—Syn. MAN, MALE, GENTLEMAN are nouns referring to adult human beings who are biologically male; that is, physiologically equipped to initiate conception but not to bear children. MAN is the most general and most commonly used of the three; it can be neutral, lacking either favorable or unfavorable implication: *a wealthy man; a man of strong character, of unbridled appetites.* It can also signify possession of the most typical or desirable masculine qualities: *to take one's punishment like a man.* MALE emphasizes the physical or sexual characteristics of a man; it may also refer to an animal or plant: *a male in his prime; two males and three females in the pack; a male of the genus* Ilex. In scientific and statistical use, MALE is the neutral contrastive term to FEMALE: *104 females to every 100 males; Among birds, the male is often more colorful than the female.* GENTLEMAN, once used only of men of high social rank, now also specifies a man of courtesy and consideration: *a real gentleman; to behave like a gentleman.* GENTLEMAN is also used as a polite term of reference (*This gentleman is waiting for a table*) or, only in the plural, of address (*Are we ready to begin, gentlemen?*). See also **manly, male.**
—Usage. The use of MAN¹ to mean "human being," both alone and in compounds such as MANKIND, has met with objection in recent years, and the use is declining. The objection is based on the idea that MAN is most commonly used as an exclusive, sex-marked noun meaning "male human being." Critics of the use of MAN as a generic maintain that it is sometimes ambiguous when the wider sense is intended (*Man has built magnificent civilizations in the desert*), but more often flatly discriminatory in that it slights or ignores the membership of women in the human race: *The man in the street wants peace, not war.*
Although some editors and writers reject or disregard these objections to MAN as a generic, many now choose instead to use such terms as *human being(s), human race, humankind, people,* or, when called for by style or context, *women and men* or *men and women.* See also **-man, -person, -woman.**

man² (män, man; *unstressed* mən), *auxiliary v. Scot.* maun.

Man (man), *n.* **Isle of,** an island of the British Isles, in the Irish Sea. 58,773; 227 sq. mi. (588 sq. km). *Cap.:* Douglas.

-man, a combining form of **man:** *layman; postman.*
—Usage. The use of -MAN as the last element in compounds referring to a person of either sex who performs some function (*anchorman; chairman; spokesman*) has declined a great deal in recent years. Only if the reference is to a specific male person are such compounds still widely used: *Roy Johnston, Channel 83 news anchorman.* Sometimes the sex-neutral *-person* is substituted for -MAN when the sex of the individual involved is unknown or irrelevant: *anchorperson; chairperson; spokesperson.* Often when a specific woman is involved, the suffix *-woman* is used: *Doris Powell, Channel 83 news anchorwoman.* And sometimes, when possible, a form with no suffix at all is used: *Roy Johnston, Channel 83 news anchor.*
All terms historically ending in -MAN that designate specific occupations (*foreman; mailman; policeman; repairman;* etc.) were dropped in favor of sex-neutral terms in the *Dictionary of Occupational Titles* (DOT), published by the U.S. Dept. of Labor in 1977. DOT terms for the occupations listed above are *supervisor, mail* or *letter carrier, police officer* (or just *officer*), *repairer* (as in *radio repairer*). Many industries and business firms have adopted similar sex-neutral occupational titles.
One -MAN compound, *freshman,* is still the term generally used in high schools and colleges and in Congress, and it is applied to both sexes. As a modifier, the singular form *freshman* is used with both singular and plural nouns: *a freshman athlete; freshman legislators.* See also **chairperson, man, -person, -woman.**

Man., 1. Manila. **2.** Manitoba.

man., manual.

ma·na (mä′nä), *n. Anthropol.* a generalized, supernatural force or power, which may be concentrated in objects or persons. [1835–45; < Polynesian]

Man·a (man′ā), *n.* Mannai.

man′ about town′, a socially active, sophisticated man who frequents fashionable nightclubs, theaters, restaurants, etc.; playboy; boulevardier. [1775–85]

man·a·cle (man′ə kəl), *n., v.,* **-cled, -cling.** —*n.* **1.** a shackle for the hand; handcuff. **2.** Usually, **manacles.** restraints; checks. —*v.t.* **3.** to handcuff; fetter. **4.** to hamper; restrain: *He was manacled by his inhibitions.* [1275–1325; ME, var. of *manicle* < MF: handcuff < L *manicula* small hand, handle of a plow. See MANUS, -I-, -CLE¹]

ma·na·da (mə nä′də), *n. Southwestern U.S.* a herd of horses. [1835–45; < AmerSp, Sp: herd, flock, crowd, perh. to be identified with OSp *manada* handful, deriv. of *mano* hand < L *manus*]

Ma·na·do (mä nä′dō), *n.* Menado.

man·age (man′ij), *v.,* **-aged, -ag·ing.** —*v.t.* **1.** to bring about or succeed in accomplishing, sometimes despite difficulty or hardship: *She managed to see the governor. How does she manage it on such a small income?* **2.** to take charge or care of: *to manage my investments.* **3.** to dominate or influence (a person) by tact, flattery, or artifice: *He manages the child with exemplary skill.* **4.** to handle, direct, govern, or control in action or use: *She managed the boat efficiently.* **5.** to wield (a weapon, tool, etc.). **6.** to handle or train (a horse) in the exercises of the manège. **7.** *Archaic.* to use sparingly or with judgment, as health or money; husband. —*v.i.* **8.** to conduct business, commercial affairs, etc.; be in charge: *Who will manage while the boss is away?* **9.** to continue to function, progress, or succeed, usually despite hardship or difficulty; get along: *How will he manage with his wife gone? It was a rough time, but we managed.* [1555–65; earlier *manege* < It *maneggiare* to handle, train (horses), deriv. of *mano* < L *manus* hand]
—Syn. 1. arrange, contrive. **4.** guide, conduct, regulate, engineer. See **rule. 5.** handle, manipulate.

man·age·a·ble (man′i jə bəl), *adj.* that can be managed; governable; tractable; contrivable. [1590–1600; MANAGE + -ABLE] **—man′age·a·bil′i·ty, man′·age·a·ble·ness,** *n.* **—man′age·a·bly,** *adv.*

man′aged cur′rency, a currency whose value is established and maintained by deliberate governmental action working through national and international financial institutions, in contrast to the quasi-automatic gold standard. [1920–25]

man·age·ment (man′ij mənt), *n.* **1.** the act or manner of managing; handling, direction, or control. **2.** skill in managing; executive ability: *great management and tact.* **3.** the person or persons controlling and directing the affairs of a business, institution, etc.: *The store is under new management.* **4.** executives collectively, considered as a class (distinguished from *labor*). [1590–1600; MANAGE + -MENT] **—man·age·men·tal** (man′ij-men′tl), *adj.*
—Syn. 1. regulation, administration; superintendence, care, charge, conduct, guidance, treatment.

man′agement informa′tion sys′tem, a computerized information-processing system designed to support the activities and functions of company management. *Abbr.:* MIS

man·ag·er (man′i jər), *n.* **1.** a person who has control or direction of an institution, business, etc., or of a part,

division, or phase of it. **2.** a person who manages: *the manager of our track team.* **3.** a person who controls and manipulates resources and expenditures, as of a household. **4.** *Brit.* (formerly) a theatrical producer. [1580–90; MANAGE + -ER¹] **—man′ag·er·ship′,** *n.*
—Syn. 1. administrator, executive, superintendent, supervisor; boss.

man·ag·er·ess (man′i jər is; *Brit.* man′i jə res′), *n.* a woman who is a manager. [1790–1800; MANAGER + -ESS]
—Usage. See **-ess.**

man·a·ge·ri·al (man′i jēr′ē əl), *adj.* pertaining to management or a manager: *managerial functions; the managerial class of society.* [1760–70; MANAGER + -IAL] **—man′a·ge′ri·al·ly,** *adv.*

man′aging ed′itor, an editor assigned to the supervision and coordination of certain editorial activities of a newspaper, magazine, book publishing company, or the like. *Abbr.:* M.E., m.e. [1860–65, *Amer.*]

Ma·na·gua (mə nä′gwə; *Sp.* mä nä′gwä), *n.* **1. Lake,** a lake in W Nicaragua. 390 sq. mi. (1010 sq. km). **2.** a city in and the capital of Nicaragua, in the W part, on Lake Managua. 556,470.

man·ak (man′ak), *n.* a wooden ball fitted with hooks and attached to a rope, used by Eskimos to secure and haul in seals killed offshore. [< Inuit *manaq*]

man·a·kin (man′ə kin), *n.* any of several small, songless passerine birds of the family Pipridae, of the warmer parts of the Americas, usually having brilliantly colored plumage. [var. of MANIKIN]

Ma·na·la (män′l ə), *n.* Tuonela.

Ma·na·ma (*Pers.* ma na′mə, -ma), *n.* a city in and the capital of Bahrain, on N Bahrain island. 94,697. Also called **Al Manamah.**

ma·ña·na (mä nyä′nä; *Eng.* mə nyä′nə), *Spanish.* —*n.* **1.** tomorrow; the (indefinite) future. —*adv.* **2.** tomorrow; in the (indefinite) future.

Man′ and Su′perman, a comedy (1903) by G. B. Shaw.

Ma·nan·nan (mä′nə nän′, man′ə nan′), *n. Irish Myth.* the god of the sea and son of Ler.

Ma·náos (mä nous′), *n.* a port in and the capital of Amazonas, in N Brazil, on the Río Negro near its confluence with the Amazon: ab. 1000 mi. (1600 km) from the Atlantic but accessible to some ocean trade. 642,582. Also, **Manaus.**

man·as (man′əs, mun′-), *n. Hinduism, Buddhism.* the rational faculty of the mind. [< Skt: mind] **—ma·nas·ic** (mə nas′ik), *adj.*

Ma·nas·sas (mə nas′əs), *n.* a town in NE Virginia: battles of Bull Run 1861, 1862. 15,438.

Ma·nas·seh (mə nas′ə), *n.* **1.** the first son of Joseph. Gen. 41:51. **2.** the tribe of Israel traditionally descended from him. Gen. 48:14–19. **3.** a king of Judah of the 7th century B.C. II Kings 21.

Ma·nas·site (mə nas′it), *n.* a member of the tribe of Manasseh. [MANASS(EH) + -ITE¹]

Ma·nat (mä nät′), *n.* a pre-Islamic Arabian goddess personifying fortune, sometimes considered a daughter of Allah.

man-at-arms (man′ət ärmz′), *n., pl.* **men-at-arms. 1.** a soldier. **2.** a heavily armed soldier on horseback, esp. in medieval times. [1325–75; ME]

man·a·tee (man′ə tē′, man′ə tē′), *n.* any of several plant-eating aquatic mammals of the genus *Trichechus,* of West Indian, Floridian, and Gulf Coast waters, having two flippers in front and a broad, spoon-shaped tail: all species are endangered. [1545–55; < Sp *manatí* < Carib, but associated with L *manātus* provided with hands]

manatee, *Trichechus manatus,* length 8 to 13 ft. (2.4 to 4 m)

Ma·na·tí (mä nä tē′), *n.* a city in N Puerto Rico. 17,347.

Ma·naus (mä nous′), *n.* Manáos.

ma·nav·el·ins (mə nav′ə linz), *n.pl. Naut. Slang.* miscellaneous pieces of gear and material. Also, **ma·nav′il·ins.** [1860–65; orig. uncert.]

Man·a·wy·dan (man′ə wu′dan), *n. Welsh Legend.* a brother of Bran, Efnisien, and Branwen, and the second husband of Rhiannon: he rescued Pryderi from enchantments cast upon him by Llwyd.

man·bote (man′bōt), *n. Old Eng. Law.* a sum of money paid to a lord whose vassal was murdered. [bef. 1000; < OE *manbōt.* See MAN¹, BOOT²]

manche (mänch), *n. Heraldry.* a conventional representation of a sleeve with a flaring end, used as a charge. Also, **maunche, maunch.** [1200–50; ME < MF < L *manicae* (pl.) long sleeves, gloves, handcuffs, deriv. of *manus* hand]

Manche (mänsh), *n.* a department in NW France. 451,662; 2476 sq. mi. (6413 sq. km). *Cap.:* Saint-Lô.

Man·ches·ter (man′ches′tər, -chə stər), *n.* **1.** a city in NW England: connected with the Mersey estuary by a ship canal (35½ mi. [57 km] long). 506,300. **2.** a city in S New Hampshire. 90,936. **3.** a town in central Connecticut. 49,761.

Man′chester School′, a school of economists in England in the first half of the 19th century, devoted to free trade and the repeal of the Corn Law, led by Richard Cobden and John Bright.

Man′chester ter′rier, one of a breed of slender terriers having a short, glossy, black-and-tan coat, raised originally in Manchester, England. [1890–95]

man·chet (man′chit), *n. Archaic.* **1.** a kind of white bread made from the finest flour. **2.** *Chiefly Dial.* a piece or small loaf of such bread. [1375–1425; late ME *mainchet;* orig. uncert.]

man·chette (män shet′), *n.* armpad. [1825–35; < F: dim. of MANCHE; see -ETTE]

man-child (man′chīld′), *n., pl.* **men-chil·dren.** a male child; boy; son. Also, **man′child′.** [1350–1400; ME]

man·chi·neel (man′chə nēl′), *n.* a tropical American tree or shrub, *Hippomane mancinella,* of the spurge family, having a milky, highly caustic, poisonous sap. [1620–30; earlier *mancinell, mançanilla* < F *mancenille* and its source, Sp *manzanilla,* dim. of *manzana* apple, OSp *mazana* < L (*māla*) *Matiāna* (apples) of *Matius* Roman author of a cooking manual (1st century B.C.)]

Man·chu (man chōō′), *n., pl.* **-chus,** (*esp. collectively*) **-chu,** *adj.* —*n.* **1.** a member of a Tungusic people of Manchuria who conquered China in the 17th century and established a dynasty there (**Manchu′ dy′nasty** or **Ch'ing** 1644–1912). **2.** a Tungusic language spoken by the Manchu. —*adj.* **3.** of or pertaining to the Manchu, their country, or their language.

Man·chu·kuo (man′chōō′kwō′; *Chin.* män′jō′kwô′), *n.* a former country (1932–45) in E Asia, under Japanese control: included Manchuria and parts of Inner Mongolia; now a part of China. Also, **Man′chou′kuo′.**

Man·chu·ri·a (man chŏŏr′ē ə), *n.* a historic region in NE China: ancestral home of the Manchu. ab. 413,000 sq. mi. (1,070,000 sq. km). **—Man·chu′ri·an,** *adj., n.*

man·ci·ple (man′sə pəl), *n.* an officer or steward of a monastery, college, etc., authorized to purchase provisions. [1150–1200 in sense "slave"; ME < MF *manciple,* var. of *mancipe* < ML *mancipium,* L: a possession, slave, orig., ownership, equiv. to *mancip-,* s. of *manceps* contractor, agent (*man*(*us*) hand + *-cep-,* comb. form of *capere* to take (see CONCEPT) + *-s* nom. sing. ending) + *-ium* -IUM]

Man·cu·ni·an (man kyōō′nē ən, -kyōōn′yən), *n.* **1.** a native or resident of Manchester, England. —*adj.* **2.** of, pertaining to, or characteristic of Manchester, England, or its natives or residents. [1900–05; < ML *Mancuni*(*um*) MANCHESTER + -AN]

-mancy, a combining form meaning "divination," of the kind specified by the initial element: *necromancy.* [ME *-manci*(*e*), *-mancy*(*e*) < OF *-mancie* < L *-mantia* < Gk *manteía* divination. See MANTIC, -CY]

Man·dae·an (man dē′ən), *n.* **1.** a member of an ancient Gnostic sect extant in Iraq. **2.** the Aramaic language of the Mandaean sacred books. —*adj.* **3.** of or pertaining to the Mandaeans. Also, **Mandean.** [1870–75; < Mandaean *mandayy*(*ā*) Gnostics (lit., the knowing ones) + -AN] **—Man·dae′an·ism,** *n.*

man·da·la (mun′dl ə), *n.* **1.** *Oriental Art.* a schematized representation of the cosmos, chiefly characterized by a concentric configuration of geometric shapes, each of which contains an image of a deity or an attribute of a deity. **2.** (in Jungian psychology) a symbol representing the effort to reunify the self. [1855–60; < Skt *maṇḍala* circle]

Man·da·lay (man′dl ā′, man′dl ā′), *n.* a city in central Burma (Myanmar), on the Irrawaddy River: the former capital of Upper Burma. 532,985.

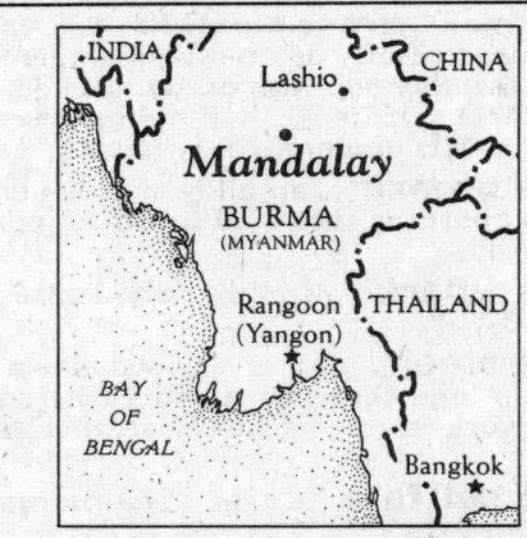

man·da·mus (man dā′məs), *n., pl.* **-mus·es,** *v. Law.* —*n.* **1.** a writ from a superior court to an inferior court or to an officer, corporation, etc., commanding that a specified thing be done. —*v.t.* **2.** to intimidate or serve with such writ. [< L *mandāmus* we command]

Man·dan (man′dan, -dən), *n.* **1.** a member of a Siouan people of North Dakota. **2.** the Siouan language of the Mandan Indians.

Man·dan (man′dən), *n.* a city in S North Dakota, near Bismarck. 15,513.

man·da·rin (man′də rin), *n.* **1.** (in the Chinese Empire) a member of any of the nine ranks of public officials, each distinguished by a particular kind of button worn on the cap. **2.** (*cap.*) the standard Chinese language. **3.** (*cap.*) a northern Chinese dialect, esp. as spoken in and around Beijing. **4.** a small, spiny citrus tree, *Citrus reticulata,* native to China, bearing lance-shaped leaves and flattish, orange-yellow to deep-orange loose-skinned fruit, some varieties of which are called tangerines. **5.** any of several plants belonging to the genus *Disporum* or *Streptopus,* of the lily family, as *S. roseus* (**rose mandarin**) or *D. lanuginosum* (**yellow mandarin**), having drooping flowers and red berries. **6.** an influential or powerful government official or bureaucrat. **7.** a member of an elite or powerful group or class, as in intellectual or cultural milieus: *the mandarins of the art world.* —*adj.* **8.** of or pertaining to a mandarin or mandarins. **9.** elegantly refined, as in language or taste. [1580–90; < Pg *mandarim,* alter. (by assoc. with *mandar* to order) of Malay *məntəri* < Hindi *mantri,* Skt *mantrin* councilor]

man·da·rin·ate (man′dər ə nāt′), *n.* **1.** the status or position of a mandarin. **2.** a group of mandarins or mandarins collectively. **3.** rule or government by mandarins. [1720–30; MANDARIN + -ATE³]

man′darin col′lar, a narrow, stand-up collar, not quite meeting at the front. [1950–55]

man′darin duck′, a crested Asian duck, *Aix galericulata,* having variegated purple, green, chestnut, and white plumage. [1790–1800]

man′darin or′ange, mandarin (def. 4). [1765–75]

man·da·tar·y (man′də ter′ē), *n., pl.* **-tar·ies.** a person or nation holding a mandate. Also, **mandatory.** [1605–15; < LL *mandatārius* one to whom a charge is given. See MANDATE, -ARY]

man·date (man′dāt), *n., v.,* **-dat·ed, -dat·ing.** —*n.* **1.** a command or authorization to act in a particular way on a public issue given by the electorate to its representative: *The president had a clear mandate to end the war.* **2.** a command from a superior court or official to a lower one. **3.** an authoritative order or command: *a royal mandate.* **4.** (in the League of Nations) a commission given to a nation to administer the government and affairs of a former Turkish territory or German colony. **5.** a mandated territory or colony. **6.** *Rom. Cath. Ch.* an order issued by the pope, esp. one commanding the preferment of a certain person to a benefice. **7.** *Roman and Civil Law.* a contract by which one engages gratuitously to perform services for another. **8.** (in modern civil law) any contract by which a person undertakes to perform services for another. **9.** *Roman Law.* an order or decree by the emperor, esp. to governors of provinces. —*v.t.* **10.** to authorize or decree (a particular action), as by the enactment of law. **11.** to order or require; make mandatory: *to mandate sweeping changes in the election process.* **12.** to consign (a territory, colony, etc.) to the charge of a particular nation under a mandate. [1540–50; < L *mandātum,* n. use of neut. of *mandātus,* ptp. of *mandāre* to commission, lit., to give into (someone's) hand. See MANUS, DATE¹]
—Syn. 3. fiat, decree, injunction, edict, ruling.

man·da·tor (man dā′tər), *n.* a person who gives a mandate. [1675–85; < L *mandātor;* see MANDATE, -TOR]

man·da·to·ry (man′də tôr′ē, -tōr′ē), *adj., n., pl.* **-ries.** —*adj.* **1.** authoritatively ordered; obligatory; compulsory: *It is mandatory that all students take two years of math.* **2.** pertaining to, of the nature of, or containing a command. **3.** *Law.* permitting no option; not to be disregarded or modified: *a mandatory clause.* **4.** having received a mandate, as a nation. —*n.* **5.** mandatary. [1655–65; < LL *mandātōrius.* See MANDATE, -TORY¹] **—man′da·to′ri·ly,** *adv.*
—Syn. 1. requisite, exigent.

man-day (man′dā′), *n., pl.* **man-days.** a unit of measurement, esp. in accountancy; based on a standard number of man-hours in a day of work. [1920–25]

Man·de (män′dā), *n.* **1.** a branch of the Niger-Congo subfamily of languages, spoken in western Africa and including Mende, Malinke, Bambara, and Kpelle. **2.** a member of any of the peoples who speak these languages. Also called **Mandingo.**

Man·de·an (man dē′ən), *n., adj.* Mandaean.

Man·del (man′dl, man del′), *n.* a male given name.

Man·de·la (man del′ə), *n.* **Nelson** (**Ro·li·hlah·la**) (rô′-lē lä′lə), born 1918, South African black antiapartheid activist: president of South Africa since 1994.

man·del′ic ac′id (man del′ik, -dē′lik), *Chem.* any of three stereoisomeric acids having the formula $C_8H_8O_3$, esp. dl-mandelic acid, a white, crystalline, slightly water-soluble solid obtainable from amygdalin: used chiefly in medicine as an antiseptic. Also called **amygdalic acid.** [1835–45; < G *Mandel* ALMOND + -IC]

Man·de·ville (man′də vil′), *n.* **1. Bernard de** (də), c1670–1733, English physician and satirist, born in Holland. **2. Sir John,** died 1372, English compiler of a book of travels.

man·di·ble (man′də bəl), *n.* **1.** the bone of the lower jaw. See illus. on next page. **2.** (in birds) **a.** the lower part of the bill. **b. mandibles,** the upper and lower parts of the bill. **3.** (in arthropods) one of the first pair

CONCISE PRONUNCIATION KEY: act, cāpe, dâre, pärt; set, ēqual; if, ice; ox, ōver, ôrder, oil, bŏŏk, bōōt, out; up, ûrge; child; sing; shoe; thin, *th*at; zh as in *treasure.* ə = *a* as in *alone, e* as in *system, i* as in *easily, o* as in *gallop, u* as in *circus;* ˈ as in *fire* (fīˈr), *hour* (ouˈr). l and n can serve as syllabic consonants, as in *cradle* (krād′l), and *button* (but′n). See the full key inside the front cover.

of mouthpart appendages, typically a jawlike biting organ, but styliform or setiform in piercing and sucking species. [1375–1425; late ME < LL *mandibula* jaw, equiv. to *mandi-* (comb. form of L *mandere* to chew) + *-bula* n. suffix of means]

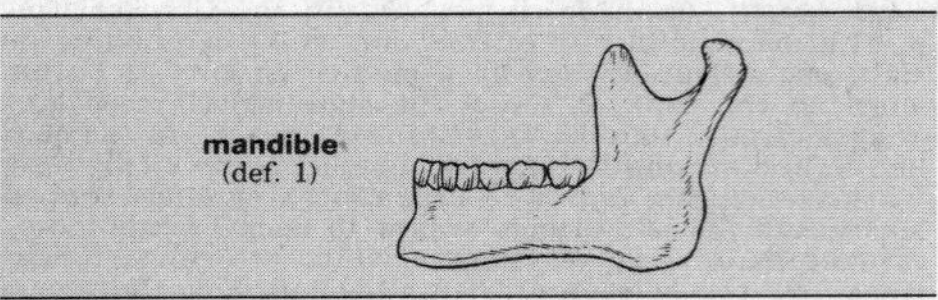
mandible (def. 1)

man·dib·u·lar (man dib′yə lər), *adj.* pertaining to or of the nature of a mandible. [1645–55; < LL *mandibul(a)* MANDIBLE + -AR[1]]

man·dib·u·late (man dib′yə lit, -lāt′), *adj.* **1.** having mandibles. —*n.* **2.** *Entomol.* a mandibulate arthropod of the subphylum Mandibulata, including water fleas, fairy shrimp, millipedes, and centipedes. [1820–30; < NL *mandibulātus* having mandibles. See MANDIBLE, -ATE[1]]

man·dil·ion (man dil′yən), *n.* **1.** a short cloak, with full hanging sleeves, often open or slit under the arms, worn by soldiers in the 16th and 17th centuries. **2.** a similar garment without sleeves, worn by servants in the 16th and 17th centuries. [1570–80; < MF < It *mandiglione,* aug. of *mandiglia* < MF *mandil(le)* << MGk *mandēlion* < L *mantē(i)um* hand towel, napkin]

Man·din·go (man ding′gō), *n., pl.* **-gos, -goes** for 1. **1.** a member of any of a number of peoples forming an extensive linguistic group in western Africa. **2.** Mande. **3.** Malinke.

Man·din·ka (man ding′kə), *n., pl.* **-kas,** (*esp. collectively*) **-ka.** Malinke.

man·di·o·ca (man′dē ō′kə, män′-), *n.* cassava. [< Sp, Pg < Tupi *manioca;* cf. MANIOC]

man·di·ra (mun′dər ə), *n.* a Hindu temple. [1955–60; < Skt: temple]

man·do·la (man dō′lə), *n.* an early lute resembling a large mandolin. [1750–60; < It, var. of *mandora,* alter. of L *pandūra* 3-stringed lute < Gk *pandoûra;* cf. BANDORE]

man·do·lin (man′dl in, man′dl in′), *n.* a musical instrument with a pear-shaped wooden body and a fretted neck. [1700–10; < It *mandolino,* dim. of *mandola,* var. of *mandora,* alter. of *pandora* BANDORE] —**man′do·lin′·ist,** *n.*

mandolin

man·drag·o·ra (man drag′ər ə, man′drə gôr′ə, -gōr′ə), *n.* **1.** mandrake (def. 1). **2.** a mandrake root. [bef. 1000; ME, OE < ML, L *mandragorās* < Gk *mandragóras*]

man·drake (man′drāk, -drik), *n.* **1.** a narcotic, short-stemmed European plant, *Mandragora officinarum,* of the nightshade family, having a fleshy, often forked root somewhat resembling a human form. **2.** the May apple. [1275–1325; ME, var. of *mandrage* (short for MANDRAGORA), taken by folk etymology as MAN[1] + DRAKE[2]]

man·drel (man′drəl), *n. Mach.* **1.** a shaft or bar the end of which is inserted into a workpiece to hold it during machining. **2.** a spindle on which a circular saw or grinding wheel rotates. **3.** the driving spindle in the headstock of a lathe. Also, **man′dril.** [1510–20; perh. akin to F *mandrin*]

man·drill (man′dril), *n.* a large baboon, *Mandrillus* (or *Papio*) *sphinx,* of western Africa, the male of which has a face brightly marked with blue and scarlet and a muzzle that is ribbed: an endangered species. [1735–45; MAN[1] + DRILL[4]]

mandrill, *Mandrillus sphinx,* height 3 ft. (0.9 cm)

CONCISE ETYMOLOGY KEY: <, descended or borrowed from; >, whence; b., blend of, blended; c., cognate with; cf., compare; deriv., derivative; equiv., equivalent; imit., imitative; obl., oblique; r., replacing; s., stem; sp., spelling, spelled; resp., respelling, respelled; trans., translation; ?, origin unknown; *, unattested; ‡, probably earlier than. See the full key inside the front cover.

man·du·cate (man′jŏŏ kāt′), *v.t.,* **-cat·ed, -cat·ing.** *Archaic.* to chew; masticate; eat. [1615–25; < L *mandūcātus,* ptp. of *mandūcāre* to chew, eat, deriv. of *mandūcus* glutton; see -ATE[1]] —**man·du·ca·ble** (man′jŏŏ kə bəl), *adj.* —**man′du·ca′tion,** *n.* —**man·du·ca·to·ry** (man′jŏŏ kə tôr′ē, -tōr′ē), *adj.*

man·dy·as (män dē′äs; *Eng.* man dē′əs, man′dē əs), *n., pl.* **-dy·ai** (-dē′e), *Eng.* **-dy·as·es.** *Gk. Orth. Ch.* **1.** a short, black cloak worn by monks. **2.** a mantle, usually purple, worn by bishops. [< Gk]

mane (mān), *n.* **1.** the long hair growing on the back of or around the neck and neighboring parts of some animals, as the horse or lion. See diag. under **horse. 2.** *Informal.* (on a human being) a head of distinctively long and thick or rough hair. [bef. 900; ME; OE *manu;* c. G *Mähne,* D *manen,* ON *mǫn*] —**maned,** *adj.* —**mane′·less,** *adj.*

man-eat·er (man′ē′tər), *n.* **1.** an animal, esp. a tiger or lion, that eats or is said to eat human flesh. **2.** See **man-eating shark. 3.** a cannibal. **4.** *Slang.* See **femme fatale.** [1590–1600]

man-eat·ing (man′ē′ting), *adj.* feeding on or having an appetite for human flesh: *a man-eating tiger.* [1600–10]

man′-eating shark′, any shark known to attack humans, esp. the great white shark, *Carcharodon carcharias.* Also called **man′-eater shark′, man-eater.** [1885–90]

man·eb (man′eb), *n. Chem.* a carbamate fungicide, $C_4H_6MnN_2S_4$, used for control of numerous crop diseases. [1975–80; prob. *man(ganous) e(thylene) b(is)-,* components of the chemical name; cf. ZINEB]

maned′ wolf′, a South American wild dog, *Chrysocyon jubatus,* having a shaggy, reddish coat and long ears and legs: now reduced in number. [1900–05]

ma·nège (ma nezh′, -nāzh′), *n.* **1.** the art of training and riding horses. **2.** the action, movements, or paces of a trained horse. **3.** a school for training horses and teaching horsemanship. Also, **ma·nege′.** [1635–45; < F < It *maneggio;* see MANAGE]

ma·nes (mā′nēz; *Lat.* mä′nes), *n.* **1.** (*used with a plural v.*) *Rom. Relig.* the souls of the dead; shades. **2.** (*used with a singular v.*) the spirit or shade of a particular dead person. Also, **Ma′nes.** [1350–1400; ME < L *mānēs* (pl.); akin to L *mānis, mānus* good]

Ma·nes (mā′nēz), *n.* A.D. 216?–276?, Persian prophet: founder of Manicheanism. Also called **Manicheus, Mani.**

Ma·net (ma nā′; *Fr.* MA ne′), *n.* **É·douard** (ā dwAR′), 1832–83, French painter.

Man·e·tho (man′ə thō′), *n.* fl. c250 B.C., Egyptian high priest of Heliopolis: author of a history of Egypt.

ma·neu·ver (mə nōō′vər), *n., v.,* **-vered, -ver·ing.** —*n.* **1.** a planned and regulated movement or evolution of troops, warships, etc. **2. maneuvers,** a series of tactical exercises usually carried out in the field by large bodies of troops in simulating the conditions of war. **3.** an act or instance of changing the direction of a moving ship, vehicle, etc., as required. **4.** an adroit move, skillful proceeding, etc., esp. as characterized by craftiness; ploy: *political maneuvers.* —*v.t.* **5.** to change the position of (troops, ships, etc.) by a maneuver. **6.** to bring, put, drive, or make by maneuvers: *He maneuvered his way into the confidence of the enemy.* **7.** to manipulate or manage with skill or adroitness: *to maneuver a conversation.* **8.** to steer in various directions as required. —*v.i.* **9.** to perform a maneuver or maneuvers. **10.** to scheme; intrigue. Also, *esp. Brit.,* **manoeuvre.** [1470–80 for an earlier sense; 1750–60 for current n. sense; < F *manoeuvre,* MF *manuevre* handwork, deriv. of OF *manuvrer* < L *manū operāre* to do handwork, equiv. to *manū* (abl. of *manus* hand) + *operāre* to work (see OPERATE); r. earlier *maanorre* manual labor < MF, as above] —**ma·neu′ver·a·ble,** *adj.* —**ma·neu′ver·a·bil′·i·ty,** *n.* —**ma·neu′ver·er,** *n.*
—**Syn. 4.** stratagem, tactic, ruse, artifice; procedure, scheme, plot, plan. **6.** scheme, contrive, intrigue. **7.** handle, finesse. **10.** plot, plan.

man′ Fri′day, a male assistant to an administrator or executive; right-hand man. [1885–90; after *Friday,* the devoted servant in *Robinson Crusoe*]

man·ful (man′fəl), *adj.* having or showing boldness, courage, or strength; resolute. [1250–1300; ME; see MAN[1], -FUL] —**man′ful·ly,** *adv.* —**man′ful·ness,** *n.*
—**Syn.** See **manly.**

man·ga·bey (mang′gə bā′), *n., pl.* **-beys.** any of several slender, long-tailed monkeys of the genus *Cercocebus,* inhabiting forests of Africa: some species are endangered. [1765–75; after *Mangabey,* a region in Madagascar]

man·ga·nese (mang′gə nēs′, -nēz′), *n. Chem.* a hard, brittle, grayish-white, metallic element, an oxide of which, MnO_2 **(man′ganese diox′ide),** is a valuable oxidizing agent: used chiefly as an alloying agent in steel to give it toughness. *Symbol:* Mn; *at. wt.:* 54.938; *at. no.:* 25; *sp. gr.:* 7.2 at 20°C. [1670–80; < F *manganèse* < It *manganese,* alter. of ML *magnesia* MAGNESIA]

man′ganese bronze′, an alloy that is about 55 percent copper, 40 percent zinc, and up to 3.5 percent manganese. [1830–40]

man′ganese spar′, *Mineral.* rhodonite or rhodochrosite. [1815–25]

man′ganese steel′, any of various steels containing manganese, esp. one that has up to 14 percent manganese, used in work involving heavy strains and impacts. [1890–95]

man′ganese sul′fate, *Chem.* See **manganous sulfate.**

man′ganese vi′olet, 1. a moderate to strong purple color. **2.** a pigment used in painting, consisting of manganese ammonium phosphate and characterized chiefly by its purple color and permanence in oils and tempera. Also called **Nuremberg violet.** [1900–05]

man·gan·ic (man gan′ik, mang-), *adj. Chem.* of or containing manganese, esp. in the trivalent state. [1830–40; MANGAN(ESE) + -IC]

man·ga·nif·er·ous (mang′gə nif′ər əs), *adj. Mineral.* containing manganese. [1850–55; MANGAN(ESE) + -I- + -FEROUS]

Man·ga·nin (mang′gə nin), *Trademark.* a brand name for an alloy of copper, manganese, and nickel, having various electrical applications.

man·ga·nite (mang′gə nīt′), *n.* **1.** a gray to black mineral, hydrous manganese oxide, MnO(OH): gray manganese ore. **2.** *Chem.* any of a series of salts containing tetravalent manganese and derived from either of two acids, H_4MnO_4 or H_2MnO_3. [1820–30; MANGAN(ESE) + -ITE[1]]

man·ga·nous (mang′gə nəs, man gan′əs, mang-), *adj. Chem.* containing bivalent manganese. [1815–25; MANGAN(ESE) + -OUS]

man′ganous sul′fate, *Chem.* a pink, water-soluble, usually tetrahydrate salt, $MnSO_4 \cdot 4H_2O$, used chiefly in fertilizers, paints, and varnishes. Also called **manganese sulfate.**

Mang·be·tu (mäng bā′tōō), *n., pl.* **-tus,** (*esp. collectively*) **-tu** for 1. **1.** a member of a people of northeastern Zaire. **2.** the central Sudanic language of this people.

mange (mānj), *n. Vet. Pathol.* any of various skin diseases caused by parasitic mites, affecting animals and sometimes humans and characterized by loss of hair and scabby eruptions. [1375–1425; late ME *manjewe* < MF *mangeue* an eating, itch, deriv. of *mangier* to eat; see MANGER]

man·gel-wur·zel (mang′gəl wûr′zəl), *n. Chiefly Brit.* a variety of the beet *Beta vulgaris,* cultivated as food for livestock. Also, **mangold-wurzel.** Also called **man′gel, mangold.** [1770–80; < G, var. of *Mangoldwurzel* (*Mangold* beet + *Wurzel* root; cf. WORT[2])]

man·ger (mān′jər), *n.* **1.** a box or trough in a stable or barn from which horses or cattle eat. **2.** *Naut.* **a.** a space at the bow of a ship, having a partition for confining water entering at the hawseholes until it can be drained. **b.** a sunken bottom in a chain locker, covered by a grating and used to collect water from the anchor chain. [1350–1400; ME < MF *maingeure,* deriv. of *mangier* to eat < L *mandūcāre* to chew, eat. See MANDUCATE]

Man·ger (mān′jər), *n. Astron.* Praesepe. [1545–55; as trans. of L *praesēpe*]

man·gey (mān′jē), *adj.,* **-gi·er, -gi·est.** mangy.

man·gle[1] (mang′gəl), *v.t.,* **-gled, -gling. 1.** to injure severely, disfigure, or mutilate by cutting, slashing, or crushing: *The coat sleeve was mangled in the gears of the machine.* **2.** to spoil; ruin; mar badly: *to mangle a text by careless typesetting.* [1350–1400; ME < AF *mangler,* perh. dissimilated var. of OF *mangonner* to mangle; akin to MANGONEL] —**man′gler,** *n.*
—**Syn. 1.** See **maim. 2.** deface; destroy.

man·gle[2] (mang′gəl), *n., v.,* **-gled, -gling.** —*n.* **1.** a machine for smoothing or pressing clothes, household linen, etc., by means of heated rollers. —*v.t.* **2.** to smooth or press with a mangle. **3.** *Metalworking.* to squeeze (metal plates) between rollers. [1765–75; < D *mangel* << LL *manganum.* See MANGONEL]

man·go (mang′gō), *n., pl.* **-goes, -gos. 1.** the oblong, sweet fruit of a tropical tree, *Mangifera indica,* of the cashew family, eaten ripe, or preserved or pickled. **2.** the tree itself. **3.** *Midland U.S.* (*chiefly the Ohio Valley*). a sweet pepper. **4.** *Ornith.* any of several large hummingbirds of the genus *Anthracothorax.* [1575–85; < Pg *manga,* prob. < Malayalam *māṅṅa*]

Man·go·ky (mang gō′kē, mäng-), *n.* a river in S central Madagascar, flowing W and then N to the Mozambique Channel. ab. 350 mi. (565 km) long.

man·gold-wur·zel (mang′gōld wûr′zəl, -gəld-), *n.* mangel-wurzel.

man·go·nel (mang′gə nel′), *n.* (formerly) any of various military engines for throwing large stones, darts, and other missiles. [1250–1300; ME < OF (dim.), deriv. of LL *manganum* < Gk *mánganon* engine of war]

man·go·steen (mang′gə stēn′), *n.* **1.** the juicy, edible fruit of an East Indian tree, *Garcinia mangostana.* **2.** the tree itself. [1590–1600; earlier *mangostan* < D < Malay *manggis(h)utan* (dial. *manggista*) a variety of mangosteen (*manggis* mangosteen + *hutan* forest)]

man·grove (mang′grōv, man′-), *n.* **1.** any tropical tree or shrub of the genus *Rhizophora,* the species of which are mostly low trees growing in marshes or tidal shores, noted for their interlacing above-ground adventitious roots. **2.** any of various similar plants. [1605–15; alter. (by folk etymology) of earlier *mangrow* < Pg *mangue* << Taino]

man′grove snap′per. See **gray snapper.** [1725–35, *Amer.*]

mang′rove swamp′, a coastal marine swamp of tropical or subtropical regions that is dominated by mangrove trees. [1850–55]

Mang·rum (mang′grəm), *n.* **Lloyd,** 1914–73, U.S. golf player.

man·gy (mān′jē), *adj.,* **-gi·er, -gi·est. 1.** having, caused by, or like the mange. **2.** contemptible; mean: *a mangy trick.* **3.** squalid; shabby: *a mangy little suburb.* Also, **mangey.** [1520–30; MANGE + -Y[1]] —**man′gi·ly,** *adv.* —**man′gi·ness,** *n.*

man·han·dle (man′han′dl, man han′dl), *v.t.,* **-dled, -dling. 1.** to handle roughly. **2.** to move by human strength, without the use of mechanical appliances. [1425–75; late ME. See MAN[1], HANDLE]

Man·hat·tan (man hat′n, *or, esp. for 1, 2,* mən-), *n.* **1.** Also called **Man·hat′tan Is′land.** an island in New York City surrounded by the Hudson, East, and Harlem rivers. 13½ mi. (22 km) long; 2½ mi. (4 km) greatest width; 22¼ sq. mi. (58 sq. km). **2.** a borough of New York City approximately coextensive with Manhattan Island: chief business district of the city. 1,427,533. **3.** a city in NE Kansas, on the Kansas River. 32,644. **4.** (*often l.c.*) a cocktail made of whiskey and sweet vermouth, usually with a dash of bitters and a maraschino cherry.

Manhat′tan Beach′, a city in SW California, SW of Los Angeles. 31,542.

Manhat′tan clam′ chow′der, a chowder made from clams, tomatoes, and other vegetables and seasoned with thyme. Cf. **New England clam chowder.** [1930–35, *Amer.*]

Man•hat•tan•ite (man hat′n īt′, mən-), *n.* a native or inhabitant of the borough of Manhattan. [1945–50, *Amer.*; MANHATTAN + -ITE[1]]

Manhat′tan Proj′ect, *U.S. Hist.* the unofficial designation for the U.S. War Department's secret program, organized in 1942, to explore the isolation of radioactive isotopes and the production of an atomic bomb: initial research was conducted at Columbia University in Manhattan. [extracted from U.S. Army Corps of Engineers *Manhattan* District and DSM (Development of Substitute Materials) *Project*]

man•help•er (man′hel′pər), *n.* a long pole for holding a paintbrush, used in painting areas otherwise out of ordinary reach. Also called **striker.** [MAN[1] + HELPER]

man•hole (man′hōl′), *n.* a hole, usually with a cover, through which a person may enter a sewer, drain, steam boiler, etc., esp. one located in a city street. [1785–95; MAN[1] + HOLE]

man•hood (man′ho͝od), *n.* **1.** the state or time of being a man or adult male person; male maturity. **2.** traditional manly qualities. **3.** maleness, as distinguished from femaleness. **4.** virility; potency. **5.** male genitalia. **6.** men collectively. **7.** the state of being human. [1200–50; ME; see MAN[1], -HOOD]

man-hour (man′ou°r′, -ou′ər), *n.* a unit of measurement, esp. in accountancy, based on an ideal amount of work accomplished by one person in an hour. *Abbr.:* man-hr [1915–20]

man•hunt (man′hunt′), *n.* **1.** an intensive search for a criminal, suspect, escaped convict, etc., as by law enforcement agencies. **2.** an intensive search for any person. [1835–45, *Amer.*; MAN[1] + HUNT] **—man′ hunt′er.**

Ma•ni (mä′nē), *n.* Manes.

ma•ni•a (mā′nē ə, mān′yə), *n.* **1.** excessive excitement or enthusiasm; craze: *The country has a mania for soccer.* **2.** *Psychiatry.* See **manic disorder.** [1350–1400; ME < L < Gk *manía* madness; akin to MAENAD, MIND]

Ma•ni•a (mā′nē ə, mān′yə), *n.* an ancient Roman goddess of the dead.

-mania, a combining form of **mania** (*megalomania*); extended to mean "enthusiasm, often of an extreme and transient nature," for that specified by the initial element (*bibliomania*).

ma•ni•ac (mā′nē ak′), *n.* **1.** a raving or violently insane person; lunatic. **2.** any intemperate or overly zealous or enthusiastic person: *a maniac when it comes to details.* —*adj.* **3.** maniacal. [1595–1605; < ML *maniacus* of, pertaining to madness. See MANIA, -AC]

ma•ni•a•cal (mə nī′ə kəl), *adj.* of or pertaining to mania or a maniac. [1670–80; MANIAC + -AL[1]] **—ma•ni′a•cal•ly,** *adv.*

man•ic (man′ik), *adj.* pertaining to or affected by mania. [1900–05; < Gk *manikós* inclined to madness. See MANIA, -IC]
—Syn. frenzied, agitated, frantic.

man•ic-de•pres•sive (man′ik di pres′iv), *Psychiatry.* —*adj.* **1.** suffering from bipolar disorder. —*n.* **2.** a person suffering from this disorder. [1900–05]

man′ic-depres′sive ill′ness. See **bipolar disorder.** Also called **man′ic-de•pres′sion.**

man′ic disor′der, *Psychiatry.* a type of affective disorder characterized by euphoric mood, excessive activity and talkativeness, impaired judgment, and sometimes psychotic symptoms, as grandiose delusions.

Man•i•che•an (man′i kē′ən), *n.* **1.** Also, **Man•i•chee** (man′i kē′). an adherent of the dualistic religious system of Manes, a combination of Gnostic Christianity, Buddhism, Zoroastrianism, and various other elements, with a basic doctrine of a conflict between light and dark, matter being regarded as dark and evil. —*adj.* **2.** of or pertaining to the Manicheans or their doctrines. Also, **Man′i•chae′an.** [1300–50; ME *Maniche* (< LL *Manichaeus* < LGk *Manichaîos* of Manes) + -AN] **—Man′i•che′an•ism, Man′i•che′ism,** *n.*

Man•i•che•us (man′i kē′əs), *n.* Manes.

ma•ni•cot•ti (man′i kot′ē; *It.* mä′nē kôt′tē), *n. Italian Cookery.* a dish consisting of large, tubular noodles stuffed with a mild cheese and baked in a tomato sauce. [1945–50; < It: muffs, pl. of *manicotto,* dim. of *manica* sleeve. See MANCHE]

man•i•cure (man′i kyo͝or′), *n., v.,* **-cured, -cur•ing.** —*n.* **1.** a cosmetic treatment of the hands and fingernails, including trimming and polishing of the nails and removing cuticles. **2.** a manicurist. —*v.t.* **3.** to take care of (the hands and fingernails); apply manicure treatment to. **4.** to trim or cut meticulously: *to manicure a lawn.* —*v.i.* **5.** to give a manicure. [1875–80; < F < L *mani-* (comb. form of *manus* hand) + *cūra* care]

man•i•cur•ist (man′i kyo͝or′ist), *n.* a person who gives manicures. [1885–90; MANICURE + -IST]

man•i•fer (man′ə fer′, -fər), *n. Armor.* a gauntlet for protecting the left hand when holding the reins of a horse. Also, **main-de-fer.** [alter. of MF *main-de-fer* hand of iron]

man•i•fest (man′ə fest′), *adj.* **1.** readily perceived by the eye or the understanding; evident; obvious; apparent; plain: *a manifest error.* **2.** *Psychoanal.* of or pertaining to conscious feelings, ideas, and impulses that contain repressed psychic material: *the manifest content of a dream as opposed to the latent content that it conceals.* —*v.t.* **3.** to make clear or evident to the eye or the understanding; show plainly: *He manifested his approval with a hearty laugh.* **4.** to prove; put beyond doubt or question: *The evidence manifests the guilt of the defendant.* **5.** to record in a ship's manifest. —*n.* **6.** a list of the cargo carried by a ship, made for the use of various agents and officials at the ports of destination. **7.** a list or invoice of goods transported by truck or train. **8.** a list of the cargo or passengers carried on an airplane. [1350–1400; (adj.) ME < L *manifestus, manufestus* detected in the act, evident, visible; (v.) ME *manifesten* < MF *manifester* < L *manifestāre,* deriv. of *manifestus.* See MANUS, INFEST] **—man′i•fest′a•ble,** *adj.* **—man′i•fest′er,** *n.* **—man′i•fest′ly,** *adv.* **—man′i•fest′ness,** *n.*
—Syn. 1. clear, distinct, unmistakable, patent, open, palpable, visible, conspicuous. **3.** reveal, disclose, evince, evidence, demonstrate, declare, express. See **display.** **—Ant. 1.** obscure. **3.** conceal.

man•i•fes•tant (man′ə fes′tənt), *n.* a person who initiates or participates in a public demonstration; demonstrator. [1875–80; < L *manifestant-* (s. of *manifestāns*), prp. of *manifestāre* to MANIFEST; see -ANT]

man•i•fes•ta•tion (man′ə fə stā′shən, -fe-), *n.* **1.** an act of manifesting. **2.** the state of being manifested. **3.** outward or perceptible indication; materialization: *At first there was no manifestation of the disease.* **4.** a public demonstration, as for political effect. **5.** *Spiritualism.* a materialization. [1375–1425; late ME < LL *manifestātiōn-* (s. of *manifestātiō*). See MANIFEST, -ATION]

man•i•fes•ta•tive (man′ə fes′tə tiv), *adj.* manifesting; showing clearly or conclusively. [1635–45; < ML *manifestātīvus,* equiv. to L *manifestāt(us)* (see MANIFEST, -ATE[1]) + *-īvus* -IVE] **—man′i•fes′ta•tive•ly,** *adv.*

Man′ifest Des′tiny, the belief or doctrine, held chiefly in the middle and latter part of the 19th century, that it was the destiny of the U.S. to expand its territory over the whole of North America and to extend and enhance its political, social, and economic influences. [1835–45]

man′ifest func′tion, *Sociol.* any function of an institution or other social phenomenon that is planned and intentional. Cf. **latent function.** [1945–50]

man•i•fes•to (man′ə fes′tō), *n., pl.* **-toes.** a public declaration of intentions, opinions, objectives, or motives, as one issued by a government, sovereign, or organization. [1640–50; < It; see MANIFEST (adj.)]

man•i•fold (man′ə fōld′), *adj.* **1.** of many kinds; numerous and varied: *manifold duties.* **2.** having numerous different parts, elements, features, forms, etc.: *a manifold program for social reform.* **3.** using, functioning with, or operating several similar or identical devices at the same time. **4.** (of paper business forms) made up of a number of sheets interleaved with carbon paper. **5.** being such or so designated for many reasons: *a manifold enemy.* —*n.* **6.** something having many different parts or features. **7.** a copy or facsimile, as of something written, such as is made by manifolding. **8.** any thin, inexpensive paper for making carbon copies on a typewriter. **9.** *Mach.* a chamber having several outlets through which a liquid or gas is distributed or gathered. **10.** *Philos.* (in Kantian epistemology) the totality of discrete items of experience as presented to the mind; the constituents of a sensory experience. **11.** *Math.* a topological space that is connected and locally Euclidean. Cf. **locally Euclidean space.** —*v.t.* **12.** to make copies of, as with carbon paper. [bef. 1000; ME; OE *manigf(e)ald* (adj.). See MANY, -FOLD] **—man′i•fold′ly,** *adv.* **—man′i•fold′ness,** *n.*
—Syn. 1. various, multitudinous, innumerable. See **many.** **2.** varied, divers, multifarious. **—Ant. 1.** simple, single.

man•i•fold•er (man′ə fōl′dər), *n.* a machine for making manifolds or copies, as of writing. [1900–05; MANIFOLD + -ER[1]]

man•i•form (man′ə fôrm′), *adj.* shaped like a hand. [1820–30; < NL *maniformis* hand-shaped. See MANUS, -I-, -FORM]

man•i•kin (man′i kin), *n.* **1.** a little man; dwarf; pygmy. **2.** mannequin. **3.** a model of the human body for teaching anatomy, demonstrating surgical operations, etc. Also, **mannikin.** [1560–70; < D *manneken,* equiv. to *man* MAN[1] + *-ken* -KIN. See MANNEQUIN]

Ma•nil•a (mə nil′ə), *n.* **1.** a seaport in and the capital of the Philippines, on W central Luzon. 1,630,485. *Abbr.:* Man. Cf. **Quezon City.** **2.** See **Manila hemp.** **3.** See **Manila paper.**

Manil′a Bay′, a bay in the Philippines, in W Luzon Island: the American fleet under Admiral Dewey defeated the Spanish fleet 1898.

manil′a grass′, a compact, shade-tolerant, turf-forming grass, *Zoysia matrella,* of southeastern Asia, having stiff leaves and flowering spikelets. [1840–50]

Manil′a hemp′, a fibrous material made from the leafstalks of the abaca, *Musa textilis,* used for making ropes, fabrics, etc. Also called **Manila, manilla.** [1850–55]

Manil′a pa′per, **1.** strong, light-brown or buff paper, originally made from Manila hemp but now also from wood pulp substitutes and various other fibers. **2.** any paper resembling Manila paper. Also called **Manila, manilla.** [1870–75]

Manil′a rope′, rope made from Manila hemp. [1850–55]

ma•nil•la (mə nil′ə), *n.* **1.** See **Manila hemp.** **2.** See **Manila paper.**

ma•nille (mə nil′), *n. Cards.* the second highest trump in certain card games, as the seven of trumps in omber or nine of trumps in klaberjass. Also, **menel.** [1665–75; alter. of Sp *malilla,* dim. of obs. *mala,* n. use of fem. of *malo* bad < L *malus*]

ma•ni•ni (mə nē′nē), *adj. Hawaii.* **1.** small; insignificant. **2.** stingy. [< Hawaiian (slang): stingy]

man′ in the moon′, a fancied semblance of a human face in the disk of the full moon, so perceived because of variations in the moon's topography. [1275–1325; ME]

man′ in the street′, the ordinary person; the average citizen: *the political opinions of the man in the street.* [1825–35]

man•i•oc (man′ē ok′, mā′nē-), *n.* cassava. [1560–70; < Tupi *man(d)ioca;* r. *manihot* < MF < Guarani *man(d)io*]

man•i•ple (man′ə pəl), *n.* **1.** (in ancient Rome) a subdivision of a legion, consisting of 60 or 120 men. **2.** *Eccles.* one of the Eucharistic vestments, consisting of an ornamental band or strip worn on the left arm near the wrist. See illus. under **chasuble.** [1400–50; late ME < ML *manipulus* sudarium, L: military unit, lit., handful, equiv. to *mani-* (comb. form of *manus* hand) + *-pulus* suffix of obscure orig.; perh. akin to *plēnus* FULL]

ma•nip•u•la•ble (mə nip′yə lə bəl), *adj.* capable of or susceptible to being manipulated; manipulatable. [1880–85; MANIPUL(ATE) + -ABLE] **—ma•nip′u•la•bil′i•ty,** *n.*

ma•nip•u•lar (mə nip′yə lər), *adj.* **1.** of or pertaining to the Roman maniple. **2.** of or pertaining to manipulation. —*n.* **3.** a soldier belonging to a maniple. [1615–25; < L *manipulāris.* See MANIPLE, -AR[1]]

ma•nip•u•late (mə nip′yə lāt′), *v.t.,* **-lat•ed, -lat•ing.** **1.** to manage or influence skillfully, esp. in an unfair manner: *to manipulate people's feelings.* **2.** to handle, manage, or use, esp. with skill, in some process of treatment or performance: *to manipulate a large tractor.* **3.** to adapt or change (accounts, figures, etc.) to suit one's purpose or advantage. **4.** *Med.* to examine or treat by skillful use of the hands, as in palpation, reduction of dislocations, or changing the position of a fetus. [1820–30; back formation from MANIPULATION] **—ma•nip′u•lat′a•ble,** *adj.* **—ma•nip′u•la•tive** (mə nip′yə lā′tiv, -yə lə tiv), *adj.* **—ma•nip′u•la′tive•ly,** *adv.* **—ma•nip•u•la•to•ry** (mə nip′yə lə tôr′ē, -tōr′ē), *adj.*
—Syn. 3. juggle, falsify.

ma•nip•u•la•tion (mə nip′yə lā′shən), *n.* **1.** the act of manipulating. **2.** the state or fact of being manipulated. **3.** skillful or artful management. [1720–30; < F, equiv. to *manipule* handful (of grains, etc.; see MANIPLE) + *-ation* -ATION]

ma•nip•u•la•tor (mə nip′yə lā′tər), *n.* **1.** a person who manipulates. **2.** a mechanical device for the remote handling of objects or materials in conditions not permitting the immediate presence of workers. [1850–55; MANIPULATE + -OR[2]]

Ma•ni•pur (mun′i po͝or′), *n.* a state in NE India between Assam and Burma. 1,220,000; 8620 sq. mi. (22,326 sq. km). *Cap.:* Imphal.

Ma•ni•sa (mä′ni sä′), *n.* a city in W Turkey, near the Aegean: Roman defeat of Antiochus the Great 190 B.C. 72,276. Ancient, **Magnesia.**

man•it (man′it), *n.* man-minute. [by syncope and respelling]

Man•i•to•ba (man′i tō′bə), *n.* **1.** a province in central Canada. 1,005,953; 246,512 sq. mi. (638,466 sq. km). *Abbr.:* Man. *Cap.:* Winnipeg. **2. Lake,** a lake in the S part of this province. 120 mi. (195 km) long; 1817 sq. mi. (4705 sq. km). **—Man′i•to′ban,** *adj., n.*

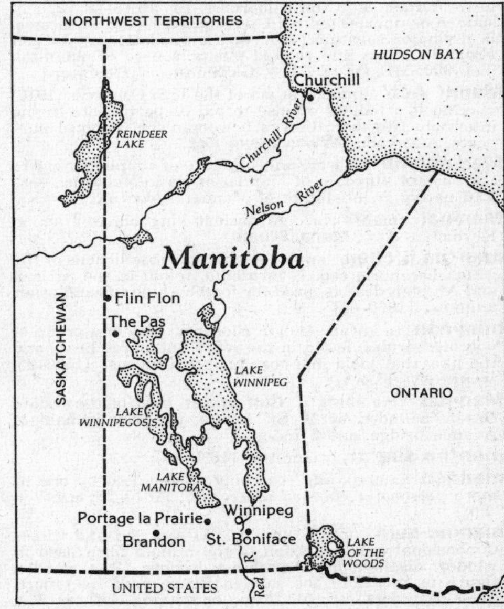

man•i•tou (man′i to͞o′), *n., pl.* **-tous,** (*esp. collectively*) **-tou.** (among the Algonquian Indians) a supernatural being that controls nature; a spirit, deity, or object that possesses supernatural power. Also, **man•i•to** (man′i tō′), **man•i•tu** (man′i to͞o′). [1605–15; < Unami Delaware *monə́t·u,* reinforced by or reborrowed from Ojibwa *manito·* and other cognates (all < Proto-Algonquian **maneto·wa*); sp. influenced by equivalent F word]

CONCISE PRONUNCIATION KEY: act, cāpe, dâre, pärt; set, ēqual; if, īce; ox, ōver, ôrder, oil, bo͝ok, bo͞ot, out; up, ûrge; child; sing; shoe; thin, *th*at; zh as in *treasure.* ə = *a* as in *alone, e* as in *system, i* as in *easily, o* as in *gallop, u* as in *circus;* ° as in *fire* (fī°r), *hour* (ou°r). l and n can serve as syllabic consonants, as in *cradle* (krād′l), and *button* (but′n). See the full key inside the front cover.

Man·i·tou·lin (man′i to͞o′lin), *n.* an island in N Lake Huron belonging to Canada. 80 mi. (130 km) long. Also called **Man′itou′lin Is′land.**

Man·i·to·woc (man′i tə wok′), *n.* a port in E Wisconsin, on Lake Michigan. 32,547.

Ma·ni·za·les (mä′nē sä′les), *n.* a city in W Colombia. 199,904.

Man·ju·sri (mun′jo͝osh rē′), *n. Buddhism.* a Bodhisattva personifying wisdom.

Man·ka·to (man kā′tō), *n.* a city in S Minnesota, on the Minnesota River. 28,651.

Man·kie·wicz (mang′kə wits), *n.* **Joseph L(eo),** born 1909, U.S. motion-picture director, producer, and writer.

man·kind (man′kīnd′ *for 1;* man′kīnd′ *for 2*), *n.* **1.** the human race; human beings collectively without reference to sex; humankind. **2.** men, as distinguished from women. [1250–1300; ME; see MAN[1], KIND[2]] **—Usage.** See **-man.**

man·like (man′līk′), *adj.* **1.** resembling a human being; anthropoid. **2.** belonging or proper to a man; manly: *manlike fortitude.* [1250–1300; ME; see MAN[1], -LIKE] **—man′like′ly,** *adv.* **—man′like′ness,** *n.*

man′ lock′, an air lock serving as a decompression chamber for workers.

man·ly (man′lē), *adj.,* **-li·er, -li·est,** *adv.* **—***adj.* **1.** having qualities traditionally ascribed to men, as strength or bravery. **2.** pertaining to or suitable for males: *manly sports.* **—***adv.* **3.** *Archaic.* in a manly manner. [bef. 900; ME (adj., adv.); OE *manlic* (adj.), *manlice* (adv.). See MAN[1], -LY] **—man′li·ness,** *n.*
—Syn. MANLY, MANFUL, MANNISH mean having the traits or qualities that a culture regards as especially characteristic of or ideally appropriate to adult men. MANLY is usually a term of approval, suggesting traits admired by society, such as determination, decisiveness, and steadiness: *a manly acceptance of the facts; manly firmness of character.* MANFUL, also a term of approval, stresses qualities such as courage, strength, and fortitude: *a manful effort to overcome great odds.* MANNISH is most often used derogatorily in reference to the traits, manners, or accouterments of a woman that are thought to be more appropriate to or typical of a man: *a mannish abruptness in her speech; She wore a severely mannish suit.* See also **male. —Ant. 1.** weak, cowardly.

man-made (man′mād′), *adj.* **1.** produced, formed, or made by humans. **2.** produced artificially; not resulting from natural processes. **3.** *Textiles.* **a.** (of a fiber) manufactured synthetically from a cellulosic or noncellulosic base; produced chemically. **b.** (of a fabric or garment) constructed of synthetically made fibers. [1710–20]

man-min·ute (man′min′it), *n.* a unit of measurement, esp. in accountancy, based on an ideal amount of work accomplished by one person in a minute. [1930–35]

Mann (män, man *for 1, 3;* man *for 2*), *n.* **1. Heinrich** (hīn′rik; *Ger.* hīn′rīKH), 1871–1950, German novelist and dramatist, in the U.S. after 1940 (brother of Thomas Mann). **2. Horace,** 1796–1859, U.S. educational reformer: instrumental in establishing the first normal school in the U.S. 1839. **3. Thom·as** (tom′əs; *Ger.* tō′-mäs), 1875–1955, German novelist and critic, in the U.S. after 1937: Nobel prize 1929.

man·na (man′ə), *n.* **1.** the food miraculously supplied to the Israelites in the wilderness. Ex. 16:14–36. **2.** any sudden or unexpected help, advantage, or aid to success. **3.** divine or spiritual food. **4.** the exudation of the ash *Fraxinus ornus* and related plants: source of mannitol. [bef. 900; ME, OE < LL < Gk *mánna* < Heb *mān*]

Mann′ Act′ (man), an act of the U.S. Congress (1910) making it a federal offense to aid or participate in the interstate transportation of a woman for immoral purposes. Also called **White Slave Act.**

Man·nae·an (ma nē′ən), *adj.* **1.** of or pertaining to the ancient kingdom of Mannai or its inhabitants. **—***n.* **2.** a native or inhabitant of Mannai. [MANNAI + -AN]

Man·nai (man′ä), *n.* an ancient kingdom in Iran, in Kurdistan. Also, **Mana, Minni.**

man′na li′chen, any of several crustose lichens of the genus *Lecanora,* esp. *L. esculenta,* found in the African and Arabian deserts, used for food by humans and other animals. [1860–65]

man·nan (man′an, -ən), *n. Biochem.* any of a group of polysaccharides, found in the ivory nut, carob bean, and the like, that yield mannose upon hydrolysis. [1890–95; MANN(OSE) + -AN]

Man·nar (mə när′), *n.* **Gulf of,** an inlet of the Indian Ocean, bounded by W Sri Lanka, the island chain of Adam's Bridge, and S India.

man′na sug′ar, mannitol. [1830–40]

manned (mand), *adj.* carrying or operated by one or more persons: *a manned spacecraft.* [1610–20; MAN[1] + -ED[2]]

man·ne·quin (man′i kin), *n.* **1.** a styled and three-dimensional representation of the human form used in window displays, as of clothing; dummy. **2.** a wooden figure or model of the human figure used by tailors, dress designers, etc., for fitting or making clothes. **3.** a person employed to wear clothing to be photographed or to be displayed before customers, buyers, etc.; a clothes model. **4.** See **lay figure** (def. 1). Also, **manikin.** [1560–70; < F < D; see MANIKIN]

man·ner[1] (man′ər), *n.* **1.** a way of doing, being done, or happening; mode of action, occurrence, etc.: *I don't like the manner in which he complained.* **2. manners, a.** the prevailing customs, ways of living, and habits of a people, class, period, etc.; mores: *The novels of Jane Austen are concerned with the manners of her time.* **b.** ways of behaving with reference to polite standards; social comportment: *That child has good manners.* **3.** a person's outward bearing; way of speaking to and treating others: *She has a charming manner.* **4.** characteristic or customary way of doing, making, saying, etc.: *houses built in the 19th-century manner.* **5.** air of distinction: *That old gentleman had quite a manner.* **6.** (*used with a singular or plural v.*) kind; sort: *What manner of man is he? All manner of things were happening.* **7.** characteristic style in art, literature, or the like: *verses in the manner of Spenser.* **8.** *Obs.* **a.** nature; character. **b.** guise; fashion. **9. by all manner of means,** by all means; certainly. **10. by no manner of means,** under no circumstances; by no means; certainly not: *She was by no manner of means a frivolous person.* **11. in a manner,** so to speak; after a fashion; somewhat. **12. in a manner of speaking,** in a way; as it were; so to speak: *We were, in a manner of speaking, babes in the woods.* **13. to the manner born, a.** accustomed by birth to a high position: *He was a gentleman to the manner born.* **b.** used to a particular custom, activity, or role from birth. [1125–75; ME *manere* < AF; OF *maniere* << VL **manuāria,* n. use of fem. of *manuārius* handy, convenient (L: of, pertaining to the hand). See MANUS, -ER[2]]
—Syn. 1. method. **3.** demeanor, deportment. MANNER, AIR, BEARING all refer to one's outward aspect or behavior. MANNER applies to a distinctive mode of behavior, or social attitude toward others, etc.: *a gracious manner.* AIR applies to outward appearance insofar as this is distinctive or indicative: *an air of martyrdom.* AIRS imply affectation: *to put on airs.* BEARING applies esp. to carriage: *a noble bearing.* **4.** mode, fashion, style; habit, custom.

man·ner[2] (man′ər), *n. Old Eng. Law.* mainour.

man·nered (man′ərd), *adj.* **1.** having manners as specified (usually used in combination): *ill-mannered people.* **2.** having distinctive mannerisms; affected: *a mannered walk.* [ME *manered.* See MANNER[1], -ED[3]]

Man·ner·heim (mä′nər hām′), *n.* **Baron Carl Gus·taf E·mil von** (kärl go͞os′täf ā′mēl fən), 1867–1951, Finnish soldier and statesman.

Man′nerheim line′, a zone of Finnish fortification erected along part of the border between Finland and Russia before the Finno-Russian War. [named after Baron von MANNERHEIM]

man·ner·ism (man′ə riz′əm), *n.* **1.** a habitual or characteristic manner, mode, or way of doing something; distinctive quality or style, as in behavior or speech: *He has an annoying mannerism of tapping his fingers while he talks. They copied his literary mannerisms but always lacked his ebullience.* **2.** marked or excessive adherence to an unusual or a particular manner, esp. if affected: *Natural courtesy is a world apart from snobbish mannerism.* **3.** (*usually cap.*) a style in the fine arts developed principally in Europe during the 16th century, chiefly characterized by a complex perspectival system, elongation of forms, strained gestures or poses of figures, and intense, often strident color. [1795–1805; MANNER[1] + -ISM] **—man′ner·ist,** *n.* **—man′ner·is′tic,** *adj.* **—man′ner·is′ti·cal·ly,** *adv.*

man·ner·less (man′ər lis), *adj.* without good manners; ill-mannered; discourteous; impolite. [1425–75; late ME *manerles.* See MANNER[1], -LESS] **—man′ner·less·ness,** *n.*

man·ner·ly (man′ər lē), *adj.* **1.** having or showing good manners; courteous; polite. **—***adv.* **2.** with good manners; courteously; politely. [1325–75; ME *manerly.* See MANNER[1], -LY] **—man′ner·li·ness,** *n.*

man′ner of articula′tion, *Phonet.* the degree of obstruction or the type of channel imposed upon the passage of air at a given place of articulation, as denoted by such categories as stop, fricative, nasal, and semivowel.

Man·nes (man′is), *n.* **Leopold Damrosch,** 1899–1964, U.S. composer and chemist.

Mann·heim (man′hīm; *Ger.* män′hīm), *n.* **1. Karl** (kärl; *Ger.* kärl), 1893–1947, German sociologist. **2.** a city in SW Germany at the confluence of the Rhine and Neckar rivers. 295,200.

Mann′heim gold′, a brass alloy used to imitate gold; red brass.

Mann′heim School′, a group of musicians of the mid-18th century in Mannheim, Germany, notable for developing a style of orchestral composition and performance directly antecedent to and influential on the classical style of Haydn and Mozart.

Man·nie (man′ē), *n.* a male given name, form of **Emanuel.**

man·ni·kin (man′i kin), *n.* **1.** manikin. **2.** any of several estrildine finches of the genus *Lonchura,* of Asia, Australia, and the Pacific islands, often kept as cage birds. [var. of MANIKIN]

Man·ning (man′ing), *n.* **Henry Edward,** 1808–92, English prelate and ecclesiastical writer: cardinal 1875–92.

man·nish (man′ish), *adj.* **1.** being typical or suggestive of a man rather than a woman: *mannish clothing styles for women; a mannish voice.* **2.** resembling a man, as in size or manner: *a mannish youth.* [bef. 900; ME; r. ME *mennish,* OE *mennisc;* see MAN[1], -ISH[1]] **—man′nish·ly,** *adv.* **—man′nish·ness,** *n.*
—Syn. 1, 2. See **manly.**

man·nite (man′īt), *n.* mannitol. [1820–30; MANN(OSE) + -ITE[1]]

man·ni·tol (man′i tôl′, -tol′), *n.* **1.** *Chem.* a white, crystalline, sweetish, water-soluble, carbohydrate alcohol, $C_6H_8(OH)_6$, occurring in three optically different forms, the common one being found in the manna of the ash *Fraxinus ornus* and in other plants: used chiefly in the manufacture of resins, electrolytic condensers for radios, plasticizers, and mannitol hexanitrate, and as a pill excipient. **2.** *Pharm.* the substance used as an osmotic diuretic to reduce intraocular and intracranial pressures. [1875–80; MANNITE + -OL[1]]

man′nitol hexani′trate, *Chem., Pharm.* a colorless, crystalline, water-insoluble, explosive solid, $C_6H_8N_6O_{18}$, used as a fulminating agent in percussion caps and in the treatment of hypertension and coronary insufficiency. Also called **nitromannitol, nitromannite.**

man·nose (man′ōs), *n. Chem.* a hexose, $C_6H_{12}O_6$, obtained from the hydrolysis of the ivory nut and yielding mannitol upon reduction. [1885–90; MANN(A) + -OSE[2]]

Man·ny (man′ē), *n.* a male given name, form of **Emanuel.**

ma·no (mä′nō; *Sp.* mä′nô), *n., pl.* **-nos** (-nōz; *Sp.* -nôs). the upper or hand-held stone used when grinding maize or other grains on a metate. [1895–1900, *Amer.;* < Sp: lit., hand < L *manus;* cf. MANUAL]

Ma·no·ah (mə nō′ə), *n.* the father of Samson. Judges 13.

ma·no a ma·no (*Sp.* mä′nô ä mä′nô; *Eng.* mä′nō ə mä′nō), *pl.* **ma·nos a ma·nos** (*Sp.* mä′nôs ä mä′nôs; *Eng.* mä′nō ə mä′nōz, mä′nōz ə mä′nōz) for 1, 2. **1.** (*italics*) *Spanish.* a corrida in which two matadors alternate in fighting two or three bulls each. **2.** a direct confrontation or conflict; head-on competition; duel. **3.** being or resembling such a confrontation: *a mano a mano struggle in the courtroom between two superb criminal lawyers.* **4.** in direct competition or rivalry: *a brash newcomer in tennis taking on the reigning champion mano a mano.* [< Sp: on an equal footing, without advantage (to either of two contestants); lit., hand to hand]

ma·noeu·vre (mə no͞o′vər), *n., v.t., v.i.,* **-vred, -vring.** *Chiefly Brit.* maneuver.

Man′ of Des′tiny, epithet of Napoleon I.

Man′ of Gal′ilee, Jesus.

man′ of God′, **1.** a clergyman. **2.** a holy or devout person, as a saint or prophet. [1350–1400; ME]

man′ of let′ters, **1.** a man engaged in literary pursuits, esp. a professional writer. **2.** a man of great learning; scholar. [1635–45]

Man′ of Sor′rows, (in Christian exegesis) an appellation of Jesus Christ as the suffering Savior. Isa. 53:3.

man′ of straw′. See **straw man.** [1615–25]

man′ of the cloth′, a clergyman or other ecclesiastic.

man-of-the-earth (man′əv thē ûrth′, -ûrth′), *n., pl.* **men-of-the-earth, man-of-the-earths.** a morning glory, *Ipomoea pandurata,* of eastern North America, having white flowers and a very large, tuberous root. Also called **manroot, wild potato, wild sweet potato.** [1825–35, *Amer.*]

man′ of the house′, the male head of a household. [1900–05]

man′ of the world′, a man who is widely experienced in the ways of the world and people; an urbane, sophisticated man. [1300–50; ME]

man-of-war (man′əv wôr′), *n., pl.* **men-of-war. 1.** a warship. **2.** See **Portuguese man-of-war.** [1400–50 in sense "soldier"; late ME]

man′-of-war′ fish′, a small, tropical fish, *Nomeus gronovii,* that lives among the tentacles of the Portuguese man-of-war.

Ma·no·le·te (mä′nô le′te), *n.* (*Manuel Laureano Rodríguez y Sánchez*), 1917–47, Spanish matador.

ma·nom·e·ter (mə nom′i tər), *n.* an instrument for measuring the pressure of a fluid, consisting of a tube filled with a liquid, the level of the liquid being determined by the fluid pressure and the height of the liquid being indicated on a scale. [1700–10; < F *manomètre,* equiv. to *mano-* (< Gk *manós* loose, rare, sparse) + *-mètre* -METER] **—man·o·met·ric** (man′ə me′trik), **man′o·met′ri·cal,** *adj.* **—man′o·met′ri·cal·ly,** *adv.* **—ma·nom′e·try,** *n.*

Ma·non (mä nôN′), *n.* an opera (1884) by Jules Massenet.

Ma·no Ne·ra, La (lä mä′nô ne′rä), *Italian.* See **Black Hand** (def. 1a).

man′ on horse′back, **1.** a military leader who presents himself as the savior of the country during a period of crisis and either assumes or threatens to assume dictatorial powers. **2.** any dictator.

Ma·non Les·caut (*Fr.* mä nôN les kō′), **1.** a novel (1731) by Antoine François Prévost. **2.** an opera (1893) by Giacomo Puccini.

man′ on the street′. See **man in the street.**

man·or (man′ər), *n.* **1.** (in England) a landed estate or territorial unit, originally of the nature of a feudal lordship, consisting of a lord's demesne and of lands within which he has the right to exercise certain privileges, exact certain fees, etc. **2.** any similar territorial unit in medieval Europe, as a feudal estate. **3.** the mansion of a lord with the land belonging to it. **4.** the main house or mansion on an estate, plantation, etc. [1250–1300; ME *maner* < OF *manoir,* n. use of *manoir* to remain, dwell < L *manēre* to remain; see MANSION] **—ma·no·ri·al** (mə nôr′ē əl, -nōr′-), *adj.*

man′or house′, the house of the lord of a manor. Also called **mansion.** [1565–75]

ma·no·ri·al·ism (mə nôr′ē ə liz′əm, -nōr′-), *n.* the manorial organization, or its principles and practices in the Middle Ages. [1895–1900; MANORIAL + -ISM]

ma·no·ri·al·ize (mə nôr′ē ə līz′, -nōr′-), *v.t.,* **-ized, -iz·ing.** to bring under manorialism. Also, *esp. Brit.,* **ma·no′ri·al·ise′.** [1895–1900; MANORIAL + -IZE]

mano′rial sys′tem, manorialism. [1955–60]

man′-o′-war′ bird′ (man′ə wôr′). See **frigate bird.** [1650–60]

man′ pow′er, **1.** the power supplied by human physical exertions: *an ancient building constructed entirely by man power.* **2.** a unit of power, assumed to be equal to the rate at which a person can do mechanical work, and

CONCISE ETYMOLOGY KEY: <, descended or borrowed from; >, whence; b., blend of, blended; c., cognate with; cf., compare; deriv., derivative; equiv., equivalent; imit., imitative; obl., oblique; r., replacing; s., stem; sp., spelling, spelled; resp., respelling, respelled; trans., translation; ?, origin unknown; *, unattested; ‡, probably earlier than. See the full key inside the front cover.

commonly taken as ¹⁄₁₀ horsepower. **3.** rate of work in terms of this unit. **4.** manpower. [1860–65]

man•pow•er (man′pou′ər), *n.* power in terms of people available or required for work or military service: *the manpower of a country.* [1860–65; MAN¹ + POWER]

manque (mäɴk), *n. French.* the numbers 1 to 18 in roulette. Cf. **passe.** [lit., lack]

man•qué (mäng kā′; *Fr.* mäɴ kā′), *adj.* having failed, missed, or fallen short, esp. because of circumstances or a defect of character; unsuccessful; unfulfilled or frustrated (usually used postpositively): *a poet manqué who never produced a single book of verse.* [1770–80; < F, ptp. of *manquer* to lack, be short of < It *mancare,* deriv. of *manco* lacking, defective < ML, LL *mancus* (L: feeble, lit., maimed, having a useless hand, prob. deriv. of *manus* hand)]

man•root (man′ro͞ot′, -ro͝ot′), *n.* man-of-the-earth. [MAN¹ + ROOT¹]

man•rope (man′rōp′), *n. Naut.* a rope placed at the side of a gangway, ladder, or the like, to serve as a rail. [1760–70; MAN¹ + ROPE]

man•sard (man′särd, -sərd), *n.* **1.** Also called **man′•sard roof′.** a hip roof, each face of which has a steeper lower part and a shallower upper part. See illus. under **roof.** Cf. **French roof. 2.** the story under such a roof. [1725–35; < F *mansarde,* named after N. F. MANSART]

Man•sart (mäɴ sar′; *Eng.* man′särt, -sərt), *n.* **1. Jules Har•douin** (zhyl ar dwaɴ′), (*Jules Hardouin*), 1646–1708, French architect: chief architectural director for Louis XIV. **2.** his granduncle, **(Ni•co•las) Fran•çois** (nē kô lä′ fräɴ swa′), 1598–1666, French architect. Also, **Man•sard** (mäɴ sar′; *Eng.* man′särd, -sərd).

man's′ best′ friend′, a dog, esp. as a pet.

manse (mans), *n.* **1.** the house and land occupied by a minister or parson. **2.** the dwelling of a landholder; mansion. [1480–90; earlier *manss, mans* < ML *mānsus* a farm, dwelling, n. use of ptp. of L *manēre* to dwell. See REMAIN]

man•serv•ant (man′sûr′vənt), *n., pl.* **men•serv•ants.** a male servant, esp. a valet. [1545–55; MAN¹ + SERVANT]

Man's′ Fate′, (French, *La Condition Humaine*), a novel (1933) by André Malraux.

Mans•field (manz′fēld′), *n.* **1. Katherine** (*Kathleen Beauchamp Murry*), 1888–1923, English short-story writer. **2. Michael Joseph** (*Mike*), born 1903, U.S. politician: senator 1953–77. **3. Richard,** 1857–1907, U.S. actor, born in Germany. **4. Mount,** a mountain in N Vermont: highest peak of the Green Mountains, 4393 ft. (1339 m). **5.** a city in W Nottinghamshire, in central England. 96,900. **6.** a city in N Ohio. 53,927. **7.** a town in N Connecticut. 20,634. **8.** a town in SE Massachusetts. 13,453.

-manship, a combination of **-man** and **-ship,** used as an independent suffix with the meaning "skill in a particular activity, esp. of a competitive nature": *brinkmanship; grantsmanship; one-upmanship;* sometimes compounded with a plural noun by analogy with *craftsmanship, marksmanship, sportsmanship,* etc.

Man•si (män′sē), *n., pl.* **-sis,** (*esp. collectively*) **-si** for 1. **1.** a member of a Uralic people now living in scattered settlements along western tributaries of the Ob River in Siberia, and known from historical records to have lived in northern European Russia. **2.** the Ugric language of the Mansi, consisting of several highly divergent dialects. Also called **Vogul.**

man•sion (man′shən), *n.* **1.** a very large, impressive, or stately residence. **2.** See **manor house. 3.** Often, **mansions.** *Brit.* a large building with many apartments; apartment house. **4.** *Oriental and Medieval Astron.* each of 28 divisions of the ecliptic occupied by the moon on successive days. **5.** *Archaic.* an abode or dwelling place. [1325–75; ME < L *mānsiōn-* (s. of *mānsiō*) an abiding, abode. See MANSE, -ION]

man-sized (man′sīzd′), *adj. Informal.* **1.** large; big; generous: *a man-sized sandwich.* **2.** formidable: *a man-sized undertaking.* Also, **man′-size′.** [1910–15]

man•slaugh•ter (man′slô′tər), *n.* **1.** *Law.* the unlawful killing of a human being without malice aforethought. **2.** the killing of a human being by another; homicide. [1250–1300; ME; see MAN¹, SLAUGHTER]

man•slay•er (man′slā′ər), *n.* a person who kills another human being. [bef. 1000; ME; *manslaer.* See MAN¹, SLAYER] **—man′slay′ing,** *n., adj.*

man spricht Deutsch (män′ shpʀɪkʜt′ doich′), *German.* German is spoken (here).

man•steal•ing (man′stē′ling), *n.* the act of kidnapping. [1570–80; MAN¹ + STEALING]

man•sue•tude (man′swi to͞od′, -tyo͞od′), *n.* mildness; gentleness: *the mansuetude of Christian love.* [1350–1400; ME < L *mānsuētūdō* tameness, mildness, equiv. to *mānsuē-,* base of *mānsuēscere* to become tame, mild (*man*(*us*) hand + *suēscere* to become accustomed) + *-tūdō* -TUDE]

Man•sur, al- (al′man so͝or′), (*'Abdullāh al-Manṣūr*), A.D. 712?–775, Arab caliph 754–775: founder of Baghdad 764.

Man•sû•ra (man so͝or′ə; *Arab.* mon so͞o′rä), *n.* See **El Mansûra.**

manta, *Manta hamiltoni,* 18 ft. (5.5 m) across "wing tips"; total length 20 ft. (6 m); tail 6 ft. (1.8 m)

man•ta (man′tə; *Sp.* män′tä), *n., pl.* **-tas** (-təz; *Sp.* -täs). **1.** (in Spain and Spanish America) a cloak or wrap. **2.** the type of blanket or cloth used on a horse or mule. **3.** *Mil.* a movable shelter formerly used to protect besiegers, as when attacking a fortress. **4.** *Ichthyol.* Also called **man′ta ray′, devil ray, devilfish.** any of several tropical rays of the small family Mobulidae, esp. of the genus *Manta,* measuring from 2 to 24 ft. (0.6 to 7.3 m) across, including the pectoral fins. See illus. in preceding column. [1690–1700; < Sp < Pr: blanket. See MANTLE]

Man•ta (män′tä, -tə), *n.* a seaport in W Ecuador, on Manta Bay. 64,569.

Man′ta Bay′, an inlet of the Pacific, on the W coast of Ecuador.

man•tai•lored (man′tā′lərd), *adj.* (of women's clothing) tailored in the general style and with the details of men's clothing. Cf. **dressmaker** (def. 2). [1920–25]

man•ta•pa (mun′tə pə), *n.* a porch or vestibule of a Brahman temple. Also, **man′tap•pa.** Also called **chaori.** [< Hindi *maṇḍap* < Skt *maṇḍapa*]

Man•ta•ro (män tä′ʀô; *Eng.* man tär′ō, män-), *n.* a river in central Peru, flowing SE to the Apurímac River. ab. 360 mi. (580 km) long.

man•teau (man′tō, man tō′), *n., pl.* **-teaus, -teaux** (-tōz, -tōz′). *Obs.* a mantle or cloak, esp. one worn by women. [1665–75; < F; see MANTLE]

Man•te•ca (man tē′kə), *n.* a town in central California. 24,925.

Man•te•gna (män te′nyä), *n.* **An•dre•a** (än dʀe′ä), 1431–1506, Italian painter and engraver.

man•tel (man′tl), *n.* **1.** a construction framing the opening of a fireplace and usually covering part of the chimney breast in a more or less decorative manner. **2.** Also called **mantelshelf.** a shelf above a fireplace opening. Also, **mantle.** Also called **man•tel•piece** (man′tl-pēs′), **mantlepiece.** [1480–90; earlier *mantell* mantelet; var. of MANTLE]

man•tel•board (man′tl bôrd′, -bōrd′), *n. Chiefly South Midland U.S.* mantel. [1880–85; MANTEL + BOARD]

man•tel•et (man′tl et′, mant′lit), *n.* **1.** a short mantle. **2.** Also, **mantlet.** *Mil.* **a.** manta (def. 3). **b.** any of various bulletproof shelters or screens. [1350–1400; ME < MF; see MANTLE, -ET]

man•tel•let•ta (man′tl et′ə), *n. Rom. Cath. Ch.* a silk or woolen sleeveless vestment reaching to the knees, worn by cardinals, bishops, and other prelates. [1850–55; < It, prob. < ML *mantelletum,* dim. of L *mantellum* MANTLE]

man•tel•lo•ne (man′tl ō′nē), *n. Rom. Cath. Ch.* a purple mantle extending to the ankles, worn over the cassock by lesser prelates of the papal court. [< It, aug. of *mantello* MANTLE]

man•tel•shelf (man′tl shelf′), *n., pl.* **-shelves.** mantel (def. 2). [1820–30; MANTEL + SHELF]

man•tel•tree (man′tl trē′), *n.* **1.** a wooden or stone lintel over the opening of a fireplace. **2.** a masonry arch used in place of such a lintel. Also, **mantletree.** [1425–75; late ME; see MANTEL, TREE]

Man′ That Corrupt′ed Had′ley•burg, The (had′-lē bûrg′), a short story (1900) by Mark Twain.

man•tic (man′tik), *adj.* **1.** of or pertaining to divination. **2.** having the power of divination. [1580–90; < Gk *mantikós* of a soothsayer, prophetic. See MANTIS, -IC] **—man′ti•cal•ly,** *adv.*

-mantic, a combining form used in the formation of adjectives corresponding to nouns ending in **-mancy:** *necromantic.*

man•ti•core (man′ti kôr′, -kōr′), *n.* a legendary monster with a man's head, horns, a lion's body, and the tail of a dragon or, sometimes, a scorpion. [1300–50; ME < L *manticḥōrās* < Gk, erroneous reading for *martichṓras* < Iranian; cf. Old Persian *martiya-* man, Avestan *xᵛar-* devour, Persian *mardom-khar* < man-eating; prob. ult. alluding to the tiger, once common in the Caspian Sea region]

man•tid (man′tid), *n.* mantis. [MANT(IS) + -ID²]

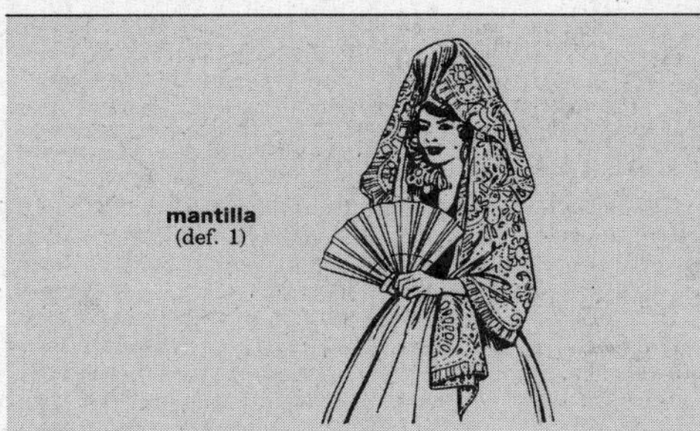

mantilla (def. 1)

man•til•la (man til′ə, -tē′ə), *n.* **1.** a silk or lace head scarf arranged over a high comb and falling over the back and shoulders, worn in Spain, Mexico, etc. **2.** a short mantle or light cape. [1710–20; < Sp; dim. of MANTA]

Man•ti•ne•a (man′tə nē′ə), *n.* an ancient city in S Greece, in Arcadia: battles 362 B.C., 223 B.C.

man•tis (man′tis), *n., pl.* **-tis•es, -tes** (-tēz). any of several predaceous insects of the order Mantidae, having a long prothorax and typically holding the forelegs in an upraised position as if in prayer. Also, **mantid.** Also called **praying mantis.** [1650–60; < NL < Gk *mántis* prophet, kind of insect; akin to MANIA]

mantis, *Mantis religiosa,* length 2 in. (5 cm)

man•tis•pid (man tis′pid), *n.* any neuropterous, mantislike insect of the family Mantispidae, the larvae of which are parasites in the nests of spiders or wasps. [< NL *Mantispidae* family of insects, equiv. to *Mantisp*(*a*) genus name (appar. erroneously for **Mantiopa,* equiv. to *manti*(*s*) MANTIS + Gk *-ōp*(*s*) having a face (of a given sort), resembling (adj. use of *ṓps* face, eye; cf. -OPSIS) + NL *-a* -A²) + *-idae* -ID²]

man•tis•sa (man tis′ə), *n.* **1.** *Math.* the decimal part of a common logarithm. Cf. **characteristic** (def. 3a). **2.** *Obs.* an addition of little or no importance, as to a literary work. [1860–65; < L, var. of *mantisa* addition, makeweight, said to be from Etruscan; logarithmic mantissa so called because it is additional to the characteristic or integral part (term introduced by H. Briggs)]

man′tis shrimp′, any stomatopod crustacean having a pair of appendages modified for grasping prey and resembling those of a mantis. Also called **man′tis crab′.** [1870–75]

man•tle (man′tl), *n., v.,* **-tled, -tling.** **—***n.* **1.** a loose, sleeveless cloak or cape. **2.** something that covers, envelops, or conceals: *the mantle of darkness.* **3.** *Geol.* the portion of the earth, about 1800 mi. (2900 km) thick, between the crust and the core. Cf. **core¹** (def. 10), **crust** (def. 6). **4.** *Zool.* a single or paired outgrowth of the body wall that lines the inner surface of the valves of the shell in mollusks and brachiopods. **5.** a chemically prepared, incombustible network hood for a gas jet, kerosene wick, etc., that, when the jet or wick is lighted, becomes incandescent and gives off a brilliant light. **6.** *Ornith.* the back, scapular, and inner wing plumage, esp. when of the same color and distinct from other plumage. **7.** mantel. **8.** *Metall.* a continuous beam set on a ring of columns and supporting the upper brickwork of a blast furnace in such a way that the brickwork of the hearth and bosh may be readily replaced. **—***v.t.* **9.** to cover with or as if with a mantle; envelop; conceal. **—***v.i.* **10.** to spread or cover a surface, as a blush over the face. **11.** to flush; blush. **12.** (of a hawk) to spread out one wing and then the other over the corresponding outstretched leg. **13.** to be or become covered with a coating, as a liquid; foam: *The champagne mantled in the glass.* [bef. 900; ME *mantel,* OE *mæntel* < L *mantellum*] **—Syn. 2.** veil, cover, blanket, screen, cloak.

Man•tle (man′tl), *n.* **1. Mickey (Charles),** 1931–95, U.S. baseball player. **2. (Robert) Burns,** 1873–1948, U.S. journalist.

man•tle•piece (man′tl pēs′), *n.* mantel. [MANTLE + PIECE]

man′tle plume′, *Geol.* plume (def. 10). [1970–75]

man′tle rock′, *Physical Geog.* the layer of disintegrated and decomposed rock fragments, including soil, just above the solid rock of the earth's crust; regolith. [1890–95]

mant•let (mant′lit), *n. Mil.* mantelet (def. 2).

man•tle•tree (man′tl trē′), *n.* manteltree.

man•tling (mant′ling), *n. Heraldry.* a decorative piece of cloth represented as hanging from a torse so as to cover the sides and rear of a helmet and often so as to frame the escutcheon below. Also called **lambrequin.** See illus. under **coat of arms.** [1500–10; MANTLE + -ING¹]

man-to-man (man′tə man′), *adj.* characterized by directness, openness, etc.; frank and personal: *He had a man-to-man talk with his son about sex.* [1570–80]

man′-to-man′ defense′, *Sports.* a method of defense in team sports, esp. in basketball and football, in which each member of the defensive team is designated to guard a particular member of the offensive team. Cf. **zone defense.** [1955–60]

Man•toux′ test′ (man to͞o′, man′to͞o; *Fr.* mäɴ to͞o′), *Med.* a test for tuberculosis in which a hypersensitive reaction to an intracutaneous injection of tuberculin indicates a previous or current infection. [1930–35; named after C. *Mantoux* (1877–1947), French physician]

man•tra (man′trə, män′-, mun′-), *n. Hinduism.* a word or formula, as from the Veda, chanted or sung as an incantation or prayer. Also, **man•tram** (man′trəm, mun′-). [1800–10; < Skt] **—man′tric,** *adj.*

man-trap (man′trap′), *n.* **1.** an outdoor trap set for humans, as to snare poachers or trespassers. **2.** *Slang.* a woman who is purported to be dangerously seductive or who schemes in her amours; femme fatale. Also **man′•trap′.** [1765–75]

man•tu•a (man′cho͞o ə), *n.* **1.** a woman's loose gown worn as a robe or overdress in the early 18th century. **2.** a mantle. [1670–80; var. of MANTEAU, by assoc. with MANTUA]

Man•tu•a (man′cho͞o ə), *n.* a city in E Lombardy, in N

Italy: birthplace of Vergil. 65,390. Italian, **Man·to·va** (män′tô vä). —**Man′tu·an,** *adj., n.*

Man·u (man′o͞o), *n. Hindu Myth.* the progenitor and lawgiver of the human race.

Ma·nu′a Is′lands (mä no͞o′ä, mə no͞o′ə), a group of three small islands in the E part of American Samoa. 1700; ab. 5 sq. mi. (13 sq. km).

man·u·al (man′yo͞o əl), *adj.* **1.** done, operated, worked, etc., by the hand or hands rather than by an electrical or electronic device: *a manual gearshift.* **2.** involving or using human effort, skill, power, energy, etc.; physical: *manual labor.* **3.** of or pertaining to the hand or hands: *manual deformities.* **4.** of the nature of a manual or handbook: *manual instructions.* —*n.* **5.** a small book, esp. one giving information or instructions: *a manual of mathematical tables.* **6.** a nonelectric or nonelectronic typewriter; a typewriter whose keys and carriage may be powered solely by the typist's hands. **7.** *Mil.* the prescribed drill in handling a rifle: *the manual of arms.* **8.** *Music.* a keyboard, esp. one of several belonging to a pipe organ. **9.** *Auto.* See **manual transmission.** [1375–1425; < L *manuālis* (adj.), *manuāle* (n.) (something) that can be held in the hand (*manu*(*s*) hand + *-ālis, -āle* -AL[1], -AL[2]); r. late ME *manuel* < MF < L, as above] —**man′u·al·ly,** *adv.*

man′ual al′phabet, a set of finger configurations corresponding to the letters of the alphabet, used by the deaf in fingerspelling. See chart below. [1860–65]

man·u·al·ism (man′yo͞o ə liz′əm), *n.* the theory or practice of education for the deaf employing and promoting the use of sign language as the primary means of communication. Cf. **oralism.** [1880–85; MANUAL + -ISM]

man·u·al·ist (man′yo͞o ə list), *n.* **1.** an advocate of manualism. **2.** a person who communicates through sign language. —*adj.* **3.** of or pertaining to manualism. Cf. **oralist.** [1585–95, for an earlier sense; MANUAL + -IST]

man′ual train′ing, training in the various manual arts and crafts, as woodworking. [1875–80, *Amer.*]

man′ual transmis′sion, an automotive transmission in which the driver shifts gears manually. Also called **manual.** [1965–70]

ma·nu′bi·al col′umn (mə no͞o′bē əl, -nyo͞o′-), **1.** a triumphal column decorated with spoils of the enemy. **2.** any triumphal or memorial column. [1840–50; < L *manubiālis,* equiv. to *manubi(ae)* spoils of war + *-ālis* -AL[1]]

ma·nu·bri·um (mə no͞o′brē əm, -nyo͞o′-), *n., pl.* **-bri·a** (-brē ə), **-bri·ums. 1.** *Anat., Zool.* a segment, bone, cell, etc., resembling a handle. **2.** Also called **presternum.** *Anat.* **a.** the uppermost of the three portions of the sternum. Cf. **gladiolus** (def. 2), **xiphisternum. b.** the long process of the malleus. [1650–60; < NL, L: a handle, akin to *manus* hand] —**ma·nu′bri·al,** *adj.*

man·u·code (man′yə kōd′), *n.* any of various birds of paradise of the New Guinea region, having dark, metallic plumage. [1825–35; < F, shortening of NL *Manucodiata* (orig. a genus name) < Malay *manuk dewata* bird of paradise (*manuk* bird + *dewata* gods < an Indo-Aryan word; see DEVA)]

man·u·duc·tion (man′yə duk′shən), *n.* **1.** the act of directing or guiding. **2.** a means of direction, introduction, or guidance. [1495–1505; < ML *manūductiōn-* (s. of *manūductiō*) a leading by the hand. See MANUS, REDUCTION] —**man′u·duc′tive, man′u·duc′to·ry,** *adj.*

Ma·nu·e (mə nyo͞o′ē), *n. Douay Bible.* Manoah.

Man·u·el (man′yo͞o əl), *n.* a male given name.

manuf., **1.** manufacture. **2.** manufacturer. **3.** manufacturing.

man·u·fac·to·ry (man′yə fak′tə rē), *n., pl.* **-ries.** *Archaic.* a factory. [1610–20; obs. *manufact* handmade (< LL *manūfact(us);* see MANUS, FACT) + -ORY[2]]

man·u·fac·ture (man′yə fak′chər), *n., v.,* **-tured, -tur·ing.** —*n.* **1.** the making of goods or wares by manual labor or by machinery, esp. on a large scale: *the manufacture of television sets.* **2.** the making or producing of anything; generation: *the manufacture of body cells.* **3.** the thing or material manufactured; product: *Plastic is an important manufacture.* —*v.t.* **4.** to make or produce by hand or machinery, esp. on a large scale. **5.** to work up (material) into form for use: *to manufacture cotton.* **6.** to invent fictitiously; fabricate; concoct: *to manufacture an account of the incident.* **7.** to produce in a mechanical way without inspiration or originality: *to manufacture a daily quota of poetry.* [1560–70; obs. *manufact* (see MANUFACTORY) + -URE] —**man′u·fac′tur·a·ble,** *adj.* —**man′u·fac′tur·al,** *adj.*
—**Syn. 4.** build. MANUFACTURE, ASSEMBLE, FABRICATE apply to processes in industry. MANUFACTURE, originally to make by hand, now means to make by machine or by industrial process: *to manufacture rubber tires.* To ASSEMBLE is to fit together the manufactured parts of something mechanical: *to assemble an automobile.* To FABRICATE is to construct or build by fitting standardized parts together: *to fabricate houses.* See also **make**[1].

man′ufac′tured home′, **1.** a prefabricated house, assembled in modular sections. **2.** See **mobile home.** Also called **man′ufac′tured hous′ing.**

man·u·fac·tur·er (man′yə fak′chər ər), *n.* **1.** a person, group, or company that owns or runs a manufacturing plant. **2.** a person, group, or company that manufactures. [1710–20; MANUFACTURE + -ER[1]]

manufac′turer's a′gent, an agent representing one or more manufacturers in selling related but noncompeting goods, usually on a commission basis and in a particular territory.

Ma·nu·kau (mä′nə kou′), *n.* a city on N North Island, in New Zealand. 127,800.

man·u·mis·sion (man′yə mish′ən), *n.* the act of manumitting. [1375–1425; late ME < L *manūmissiōn-* (s. of *manūmissiō*). See MANUMIT, MISSION]

man·u·mit (man′yə mit′), *v.t.,* **-mit·ted, -mit·ting.** to release from slavery or servitude. [1375–1425; late ME < L *manūmittere,* earlier *manū ēmittere* to send away from (one's) hand, i.e., to set free. See MANUS, EMIT] —**man′u·mit′ter,** *n.*

ma·nure (mə no͝or′, -nyo͝or′), *n., v.,* **-nured, -nur·ing.** —*n.* **1.** excrement, esp. of animals, or other refuse used as fertilizer. **2.** any natural or artificial substance for fertilizing the soil. —*v.t.* **3.** to treat (land) with fertilizing matter; apply manure to. [1350–1400; ME *manouren* to till, cultivate < MF *manouvrer* to do manual work. See MANEUVER] —**ma·nur′er,** *n.* —**ma·nu′ri·al,** *adj.* —**ma·nu′ri·al·ly,** *adv.*

ma·nus (mā′nəs), *n., pl.* **-nus. 1.** *Anat., Zool.* the distal segment of the forelimb of a vertebrate, including the carpus and the forefoot or hand. **2.** *Roman Law.* power over persons, as that of the husband over the wife. [1510–20; < L: hand]

Ma·nus (mä′no͞os), *n., pl.* **-nus.** a member of a people living on the island of Manus, in the Admiralty Islands.

man·u·script (man′yə skript′), *n.* **1.** the original text of an author's work, handwritten or now usually typed, that is submitted to a publisher. **2.** any text not printed. **3.** a book or document written before the invention of printing. **4.** writing, as distinguished from print. —*adj.* **5.** handwritten or typed, not professionally printed. [1590–1600; < ML *manūscrīptus* written by hand, equiv. to L *manū* by hand (abl. of *manus*) + *scriptus* written; see SCRIPT] —**man′u·script′al,** *adj.*

Ma·nu·ti·us (mə no͞o′shē əs, -nyo͞o′-), *n.* **Al·dus** (ôl′dəs, al′-), (*Teobaldo Mannucci* or *Manuzio*), 1450–1515, Italian printer and classical scholar.

Man·ville (man′vil), *n.* a borough in N central New Jersey. 11,278.

man·ward (man′wərd), *adv.* **1.** Also, **man′wards.** toward humankind: *The church directed its attention manward as well as heavenward.* —*adj.* **2.** directed toward humankind. [1400–50; late ME; see MAN[1], -WARD]

man·way (man′wā′), *n.* a passage in a mine wide enough for a single person. [1880–85, *Amer.*; MAN[1] + WAY]

man·wise (man′wīz′), *adv.* in the manner of a human being: *The dog stood on his hind legs and walked manwise.* [1900–05; MAN[1] + -WISE]

Manx (mangks), *adj.* **1.** of or pertaining to the Isle of Man, its inhabitants, or their language. —*n.* **2.** (*used with a plural v.*) the inhabitants of the Isle of Man. **3.** the Gaelic of the Isle of Man, virtually extinct. [1565–75; syncopated and metathesized form of earlier *Manisk(e)* < ON *manskr* of the Isle of Man, equiv. to *Man* name of the island + *-skr* adj. suffix denoting origin (see -ISH[1])]

manx′ cat′, a tailless variety of the domestic cat. [1855–60]

manx cat

Manx·man (mangks′mən), *n., pl.* **-men.** a native or inhabitant of the Isle of Man. [MANX + -MAN]

man·y (men′ē), *adj.,* **more, most,** *n., pron.* —*adj.* **1.** constituting or forming a large number; numerous: *many people.* **2.** noting each one of a large number (usually fol. by *a* or *an*): *For many a day it rained.* —*n.* **3.** a large or considerable number of persons or things: *A good many of the beggars were blind.* **4. the many,** the greater part of humankind. —*pron.* **5.** many persons or things: *Many of the beggars were blind. Many were unable to attend.* [bef. 900; ME *mani, meni,* OE *manig, menig;* akin to OS, OHG *manag, menig,* Dan *mange,* Goth *managš*]
—**Syn. 1.** multifarious, multitudinous, myriad; divers, sundry, various. MANY, INNUMERABLE, MANIFOLD, NUMEROUS imply the presence or succession of a large number of units. MANY is a popular and common word for this idea: *many times.* NUMEROUS, a more formal word, refers to a great number or to very many units: *letters too numerous to mention.* INNUMERABLE denotes a number that is beyond count or, more loosely, that is extremely difficult to count: *the innumerable stars in the sky.* MANIFOLD implies not only that the number is large but also that there is variety or complexity. —**Ant. 1.** few, single.

man-year (man′yēr′), *n.* a unit of measurement, esp. in accountancy, based on a standard number of man-days in a year of work. [1925–30]

man·y·fold (men′ē fōld′), *adv.* by many times; by multiples: *The state's highway expenses have increased manyfold in the past decade.* [1875–80; MANY + -FOLD]

man·y-one (men′ē wun′; *usually read as* men′ē təwun′), *adj. Logic, Math.* (of a relation) having the property that each element is assigned to one element only but that many elements may be assigned to the same element. [1905–10]

man·y-sid·ed (men′ē sī′did), *adj.* **1.** having many sides. **2.** having many aspects: *a many-sided question.* **3.** having many interests, qualities, accomplishments, etc.; versatile: *The typical person of the Renaissance was many-sided.* [1650–60] —**man′y-sid′ed·ness,** *n.*

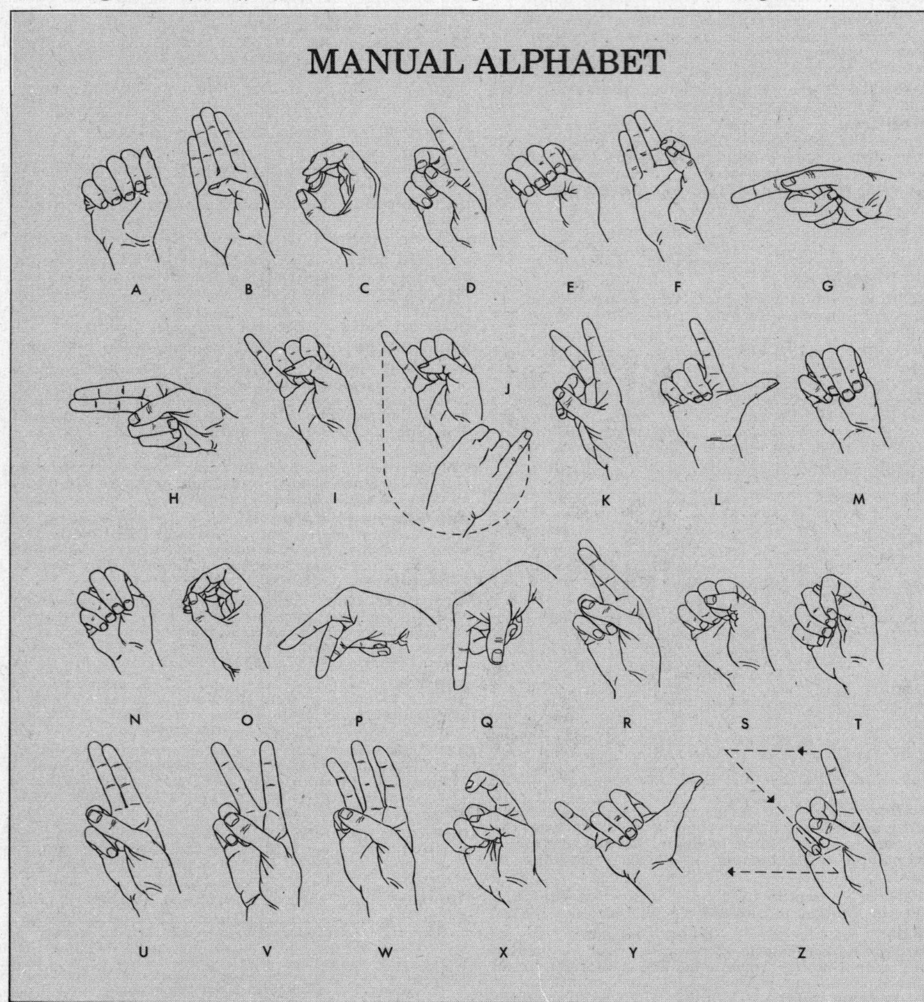

man•y-val•ued (men′ē val′yo͞od), *adj. Math.* (of a function) having the property that some elements in the domain have more than one image point; multiple-valued. Cf. **single-valued.** [1930–35]

man•za•nil•la (man′zə nēl′yə, -nē′ə), *n.* a pale, very dry sherry from Spain. [1835–45; < Sp; see MANCHINEEL]

Man•za•nil•lo (män′sä nē′yô), *n.* a seaport in SE Cuba. 77,880.

man•za•ni•ta (man′zə nē′tə), *n.* **1.** any of several western North American shrubs or small trees belonging to the genus *Arctostaphylos*, of the heath family, having leathery leaves and clusters of white to pink flowers. **2.** the fruit of one of these shrubs. [1840–50, *Amer.*; < Sp, dim. of *manzana* apple; see MANCHINEEL]

Man•zo•ni (män dzô′nē), *n.* **A•les•san•dro (Fran•ces•co Tom•ma•so An•to•nio)** (ä′les sän′drô frän ches′kô tôm mä′zô än tô′nyô), 1785–1873, Italian novelist, poet, and dramatist.

Man•zù (män dzo͞o′), *n.* **Gia•co•mo** (jä′kô mô), 1908–91, Italian sculptor.

MAO, monoamine oxidase.

Mao Dun (mou′ do͞on′), (*Shen Yanbing*), 1896–1981, Chinese writer. Also, *Wade-Giles,* **Mao′ Tun′** (do͞on′).

MAOI, See **monoamine oxidase inhibitor.**

MAO inhibitor. See **monoamine oxidase inhibitor.**

Mao•ism (mou′iz əm), *n.* the political, social, economic, and military theories and policies advocated by Mao Zedong, as those concerning revolutionary movements and guerrilla warfare. [1950–55; MAO (ZEDONG) + -ISM] **—Mao′ist,** *n., adj.*

Mao′ jack′et, a plain, shirtlike jacket, usually blue or gray, with pockets and a high collar, worn by Mao Zedong and universally adopted in the People's Republic of China during his regime. [1965–70]

Mao′ke Moun′tains (mou′kä), a range in the province of Irian Jaya, in Indonesia, on New Guinea. Highest peak, Puncak Jaya, 16,503 ft. (5030 m). Formerly, **Nassau Mountains.**

Ma•o•ri (mä′ô rē, -ō rē, mou′rē, mä′rē), *n., pl.* **-ris,** (*esp. collectively*) **-ri** for 1, *adj.* **—***n.* **1.** a member of the native Polynesian population of New Zealand. **2.** a Polynesian language, the language of the Maoris. **—***adj.* **3.** of or pertaining to the Maoris or their language.

Mao′ suit′, an outfit worn in the People's Republic of China consisting of a Mao jacket and loose trousers.

mao-tai (mou′tī′), *n.* a strong, colorless liquor of China distilled from sorghum and resembling vodka but usually of higher proof. Also, **mao′ tai′.** [< Chin *Máotái,* place in Guizhou province where it was made]

Mao Ze•dong (mou′ zə do͝ong′, dzə-; *Chin.* mou′ zu′dông′), 1893–1976, Chinese Communist leader: chairman of the People's Republic of China 1949–59; chairman of the Chinese Communist party 1943–76. Also, *Wade-Giles,* **Mao Tse-tung** (mou′ tsə to͝ong′, dzə-do͝ong′; *Chin.* mou′ dzu′do͝ong′).

map (map), *n., v.,* **mapped, map•ping.** **—***n.* **1.** a representation, usually on a flat surface, as of the features of an area of the earth or a portion of the heavens, showing them in their respective forms, sizes, and relationships according to some convention of representation: *a map of Canada.* **2.** a maplike delineation, representation, or reflection of anything: *The old man's face is a map of time.* **3.** *Math.* function (def. 4a). **4.** *Slang.* the face: *Wipe that smile off that ugly map of yours.* **5.** *Genetics.* See **genetic map. 6. off the map,** out of existence; into oblivion: *Cities were wiped off the map.* **7. put on the map,** to bring into the public eye; make known, famous, or prominent: *The casino put our town on the map.* **—***v.t.* **8.** to represent or delineate on or as if on a map. **9.** to sketch or plan (often fol. by *out*): *to map out a new career.* [1350–1400; ME *mappe-(mounde)* < ML *mappa mundi* map of the world; special use of L *mappa* napkin, said to be < Punic] **—map′pa•ble,** *adj.* **—map′per,** *n.* **—Syn. 1.** plan, outline, diagram. MAP, CHART, GRAPH refer to representations of surfaces, areas, or facts. MAP most commonly refers to a representation of the surface of the earth or a section of it, or an area of the sky: *a map of England.* A CHART may be an outline map with symbols conveying information superimposed on it, a map designed esp. for navigators on water or in the air, a diagram, or a table giving information in an orderly form: *a chart of the shoals off a coast.* A GRAPH may be a diagram representing a set of interrelated facts by means of dots or lines on a coordinate background; or it may use small figures (people, animals, machines, etc.) appropriate to the facts being represented, each figure standing for a specific number in statistics being given: *a graph of the rise in population from 1900 to 1980.*

Map (map), *n.* **Walter,** c1140–1209?, Welsh ecclesiastic, poet, and satirist. Also, **Mapes** (māps, mā′pēz).

MAP, See **modified American plan.**

Ma•ping (mä′ping′), *n. Pinyin.* former name of **Liuzhou.**

ma•ple (mā′pəl), *n.* **1.** any of numerous trees or shrubs of the genus *Acer*, species of which are grown as shade or ornamental trees, for timber, or for sap. Cf. **maple family. 2.** the wood of any such tree. **3.** the flavor of maple syrup or maple sugar. **4.** *Bowling Slang.* pin (def. 11). [bef. 900; ME *mapel,* OE *mapul-,* in *mapultrēow, mapulder* maple tree, c. OS *mapulder*] **—ma′ple•like′,** *adj.*

ma′ple fam′ily, the plant family Aceraceae, typified by trees and shrubs having sweet sap, simple opposite leaves usually lobed or toothed, clusters of small flowers, and fruit in the form of a double-winged nutlet, and including maples and the box elder.

Ma′ple Grove′, a town in SE Minnesota. 20,525.

Ma′ple Heights′, a city in NE Ohio. 29,735.

ma′ple hon′ey, *Chiefly Northern New England and Eastern Canada.* See **maple syrup.** [1840–50, *Amer.*]

ma′ple leaf′, the national emblem of Canada.

Ma′ple Leaf′, a one-ounce gold coin of Canada showing a maple leaf on the reverse: traded for investment or as a collector's item.

ma′ple-leaved vibur′num (mā′pəl lēvd′), dockmackie.

ma′ple sug′ar, a yellowish-brown sugar produced by boiling down maple syrup. [1710–20, *Amer.*]

ma′ple syr′up, 1. a syrup produced by partially boiling down the sap of the sugar maple or of any of several other maple trees. **2.** a commercial variety of such syrup, often mixed with cane sugar or some other sweetening agent. [1840–50]

Ma•ple•wood (mā′pəl wo͝od′), *n.* **1.** a city in SE Minnesota, near St. Paul. 26,990. **2.** a township in NE New Jersey. 22,950. **3.** a city in E Missouri. 10,960.

map•mak•er (map′mā′kər), *n.* a person who makes maps; cartographer. [1765–75; MAP + MAKER]

Map•pah (mä pä′), *n.* a body of Ashkenazic-oriented commentaries on the *Shulhan Arukh,* written by the Polish Talmudic scholar Moses Isserles (c1520–72) and incorporated by him into the code. Cf. ***Shulhan Arukh.***

map•ping (map′ing), *n.* **1.** the act or operation of making a map or maps. **2.** *Math.* function (def. 4a). [1765–75; MAP + -ING[1]]

map′ tur′tle, any of several aquatic turtles of the genus *Graptemys,* as *G. geographica,* of the eastern and central U.S., usually having yellow stripes on the head and neck.

Ma•pu•to (mə po͞o′tō), *n.* a seaport in and the capital of Mozambique, on Delagoa Bay. 383,775. Formerly, **Lourenço Marques.**

ma•quette (ma ket′, mə-), *n.* a small model or study in three dimensions for either a sculptural or an architectural project. [1900–05; < F < It *macchietta,* dim. of *macchia* a sketch, complex of lines < L *macula* mesh, spot]

ma•qui (mä′kē), *n.* an evergreen shrub, *Aristotelia chilensis,* of Chile, having toothed, oblong leaves, greenish-white flowers, and purple berries, grown as an ornamental in S California. [1695–1705; < Sp < Araucanian]

ma•qui•la•do•ra (mə kē′lə dôr′ə), *n., pl.* **-ras.** a factory run by a U.S. company in Mexico to take advantage of cheap labor and lax regulation. [1985–90; MexSp, perh. < Sp *maquilar* extract a toll]

ma•quil•lage (mak′ē äzh′; *Fr.* mᴀ kē yᴀzh′), *n.* makeup (defs. 1, 2, 5). [1890–95; < F, equiv. to *maquill(er)* to apply makeup (orig. theater argot, perh. to be identified with OF *masquillier* blacken, smear, akin to *mascurer, mascherer,* v. deriv. of VL **mascar-;* see MASQUERADE) + *-age* -AGE]

ma•quis (mä kē′, ma-; *Fr.* mᴀ kē′), *n., pl.* **-quis** (-kēz′; *Fr.* -kē′). **1.** the French underground movement, or Resistance, that combatted the Nazis in World War II. **2.** Also called **maquisard.** a member of this movement. Also, **Ma•quis′.** [1940–45; < F, special use of *maquis, makis* wild, bushy land < It (Corsican dial.) *macchie* (with F *-is* for *-ie*), pl. of *macchia* a thicket < L *macula* spot]

ma•qui•sard (mak′ē zärd′; *Fr.* mᴀ kē zᴀʀ′), *n., pl.* **-sards** (-zärdz′; *Fr.* -zᴀʀ′). maquis (def. 2). [< F; see MAQUIS, -ARD]

mar (mär), *v.t.,* **marred, mar•ring. 1.** to damage or spoil to a certain extent; render less perfect, attractive, useful, etc.; impair or spoil: *That billboard mars the view. The holiday was marred by bad weather.* **2.** to disfigure, deface, or scar: *The scratch marred the table.* [bef. 900; ME *merren,* OE *merran* to hinder, waste; c. OS *merrian,* OHG *merren* to hinder, ON *merja* to bruise, Goth *marzjan* to offend]
—Syn. 1, 2. flaw, injure; blot. MAR, DEFACE, DISFIGURE, DEFORM agree in applying to some form of injury. MAR is general, but usually refers to an external or surface injury, if it is a physical one: *The table was marred by scratches.* DEFACE refers to a surface injury that may be temporary or easily repaired: *a tablecloth defaced by penciled notations.* DISFIGURE applies to external injury of a more permanent and serious kind: *A birthmark disfigured his face.* DEFORM suggests that something has been distorted or internally injured so severely as to change its normal form or qualities, or else that some fault has interfered with its proper development: *deformed by an accident that had crippled him; to deform feet by binding them.* **—Ant. 1, 2.** enhance, adorn.

Mar., March.

mar., **1.** maritime. **2.** married.

M.A.R., Master of Arts in Religion.

Mā•ra (mär′ə), *n.* **1.** *Hindu Myth.* the god of death, sometimes seen as one aspect of a god whose other aspect is Kama, or erotic desire. **2.** *Buddhism.* Satan, who tried to seduce the Buddha at the time of his Enlightenment.

mar•a•bou (mar′ə bo͞o′), *n.* **1.** any of three large storks of the genus *Leptoptilus,* of Africa or the East Indies, having soft, downy feathers under the wings and tail that are used for making a furlike trimming for women's hats and garments. **2.** one of the feathers. **3.** the trimming or material made of the feathers. **4.** thrown silk that can be dyed without being scoured. Also, **marabout.** [1815–25; < F *marabout* lit., MARABOUT]

marabou,
Leptoptilus crumeniferus,
length 5 ft. (1.5 m)

mar•a•bout (mar′ə bo͞ot′, -bo͞o′), *n.* **1.** *Islam.* **a.** a hermit or holy man, esp. in N Africa, often wielding political power and credited with supernatural powers. **b.** the tomb or shrine of such a man. **2.** marabou. [1615–25; < F < Pg *marabuto* < Ar *murābit;* see ALMORAVID, MARAVEDI] **—mar′a•bout′ism,** *n.*

ma•rac•a (mə rä′kə, -rak′ə), *n.* a gourd or a gourd-shaped rattle filled with seeds or pebbles and used, often in a pair, as a rhythm instrument. [1815–25; < Pg < Tupi *marâka*]

Mar•a•cai•bo (mar′ə kī′bō; *Sp.* mä′rä kī′vô), *n.* **1.** a seaport in NW Venezuela. 786,389. **2. Gulf of,** a gulf on the NW coast of Venezuela. **3. Lake,** a lake in NW Venezuela, an extension of the Gulf of Maracaibo: the largest lake in South America. 6300 sq. mi. (16,320 sq. km).

Mar•a•can•da (mar′ə kan′də), *n.* ancient name of **Samarkand.**

Ma•ra•cay (mä′rä kī′), *n.* a city in NE Venezuela, SW of Caracas. 255,134.

mar′ag•ing steel′ (mär′ā′jing), a low-carbon steel that has been heated and quenched to form martensite: contains up to 25 percent nickel. [1960–65; *mar(tensitic) aging*]

ma•rais (mä rā′; *Fr.* mᴀ ʀe′), *n., pl.* **-rais** (-rāz′; *Fr.* -ʀe′). *Gulf States (chiefly Louisiana).* a swamp or bayou. [1785–95; < North American F, F; OF *mareis* < Old Low Franconian **marisk;* see MARSH]

Ma•ra•jó (mä′rä zhô′), *n.* an island in N Brazil, at the mouth of the Amazon. 19,000 sq. mi. (49,000 sq. km).

mar•a•nath•a (mar′ə nath′ə), *interj.* O Lord, come: used as an invocation in I Cor. 16:22. [< Gk *maranathá* < Aramaic *māranā thā*]

Ma•ra•nhão (mä′ʀə nyoun′), *n.* a state in NE Brazil. 4,097,311; 125,312 sq. mi. (324,560 sq. km). *Cap.:* São Luiz.

Ma•ra•ñón (mä′rä nyôn′), *n.* a river in Peru, flowing N and then E, joining the Ucayali to form the Amazon. 1000 mi. (1600 km) long.

ma•ran•ta (mə ran′tə), *n.* any of several tropical American plants of the genus *Maranta,* including arrowroot and several species cultivated as ornamentals for their variegated foliage. [< NL (Linnaeus), after Bartolomeo *Maranta* (1500–71), Italian physician and botanist]

Ma•raş (mə räsh′), *n.* a city in S Turkey, NE of Adana. 149,603.

ma•ras•ca (mə ras′kə), *n.* a wild cherry, *Prunus cerasus marasca,* yielding a small, bitter fruit, from which maraschino is made. [1860–65; < It, aph. var. of *amarasca,* deriv. of *amaro* < L *amārus* bitter]

mar•a•schi•no (mar′ə skē′nō, -shē′-), *n.* a sweet cordial or liqueur distilled from marascas. [1785–95; < It; see MARASCA, -INE[1]]

mar′aschi′no cher′ry, a cherry cooked in colored syrup and flavored with maraschino, used to garnish desserts, cocktails, etc. [1900–05]

ma•ras•mus (mə raz′məs), *n. Pathol.* malnutrition occurring in infants and young children, caused by insufficient intake of calories or protein and characterized by thinness, dry skin, poor muscle development, and irritability. [1650–60; < NL < Gk *marasmós* a wasting away, akin to *maraínein* to weaken, waste away] **—ma•ras′mic,** *adj.* **—ma•ras′moid,** *adj.*

Ma•rat (mᴀ ʀᴀ′), *n.* **Jean Paul** (zhän pôl), 1743–93, French politician and journalist: leader in the French Revolution; assassinated by Charlotte Corday d'Armont.

Ma•ra•tha (mə rä′tə), *n.* a member of a Hindu people inhabiting central and western India. Also, **Mahratta.**

Mara′tha Confed′eracy, a loose league of states in central and western India, c1750–1818.

Ma•ra•thi (mə rä′tē, -rat′ē), *n.* an Indic language of western and central India: the principal language of the state of Maharashtra. Also, **Mahratti.** [1820–30]

mar•a•thon (mar′ə thon′, -thən), *n.* **1.** a foot race over a course measuring 26 mi. 385 yd. (42 km 195 m). **2.** any long-distance race. **3.** any contest, event, or the like, of great, or greater than normal, length or duration or requiring exceptional endurance: *a dance marathon; a sales marathon.* [1895–1900; allusion to Pheidippides' 26-mi. (42-km) run from MARATHON to Athens to carry news of the Greek victory over the Persians in 490 B.C.]

Mar•a•thon (mar′ə thon′), *n.* **1.** a plain in SE Greece, in Attica: the Athenians defeated the Persians here 490 B.C. **2.** an ancient village that is near this plain. **3.** *Class. Myth.* a son of Epopeus and the father of Corinthus.

mar•a•thon•er (mar′ə thon′ər *or, esp. Brit.,* -thə nər),

CONCISE PRONUNCIATION KEY: act, cāpe, dâre, pärt; set, ēqual; if, īce; ox, ōver, ôrder, oil, bo͝ok, bo͞ot, out; up, ûrge; child; sing; shoe; thin, *th*at; zh as in *treasure.* ə = *a* as in *alone, e* as in *system, i* as in *easily, o* as in *gallop, u* as in *circus;* ə as in *fire* (fīər), *hour* (ouər). l and n can serve as syllabic consonants, as in *cradle* (krād′l), and *button* (but′n). See the full key inside the front cover.

n. a runner who competes in a marathon. [1920–25; MARATHON + -ER[1]]

mar′athon group′, *Psychol.* an encounter group that meets for an extended period of time, as eight hours to a week, in the belief that the resultant intensity and intimacy will lead to a more open expression of feelings.

Mar·a·tho·ni·an (mar′ə thō′nē ən), *adj.* **1.** of or pertaining to Marathon. —*n.* **2.** a native or inhabitant of Marathon. [1760–70; MARATHON + -IAN]

Mar′atho′nian bull′, *Class. Myth.* See **Cretan bull.**

ma·raud (mə rôd′), *v.i.* **1.** to roam or go around in quest of plunder; make a raid for booty: *Freebooters were marauding all across the territory.* —*v.t.* **2.** to raid for plunder (often used passively): *At the war's end the country had been marauded by returning bands of soldiers.* —*n.* **3.** *Archaic.* the act of marauding. [1705–15; < F *marauder,* deriv. of *maraud* rogue, vagabond, MF, perh. identical with dial. *maraud* tomcat, of expressive orig.] —**ma·raud′er,** *n.*
—**Syn. 1, 2.** invade, attack; ravage, harry.

ma·raud·ing (mə rô′ding), *adj.* **1.** engaged in raiding for plunder, esp. roaming about and ravaging an area: *marauding bands of outlaws.* **2.** undertaken for plunder: *a marauding raid.* [1745–55; MARAUD + -ING[2]]

mar·a·ve·di (mar′ə vā′dē), *n., pl.* **-dis. 1.** a former gold coin issued by the Moors in Spain. **2.** a former minor copper coin of Spain, discontinued in 1848. [1530–40; < Sp *maravedí* < Ar *Murābiṭīn* the ALMORAVIDS; see MARABOUT]

mar·bel·ize (mär′bə līz′), *v.t.,* **-ized, -iz·ing.** marble. Also, **marbleize;** *esp. Brit.,* **mar′bel·ise′.** [sp. var. of MARBLEIZE] —**mar′bel·i·za′tion,** *n.*

Mar·be·lla (mär ve′lyä, -yä), *n.* a seaport in S Spain, on the Mediterranean: resort center. 33,203.

mar·ble (mär′bəl), *n., adj., v.,* **-bled, -bling.** —*n.* **1.** metamorphosed limestone, consisting chiefly of recrystallized calcite or dolomite, capable of taking a high polish, occurring in a wide range of colors and variegations and used in sculpture and architecture. **2.** any variety of this stone: *Carrara marble.* **3.** an object made of or carved from this stone, esp. a sculpture: *Renaissance marbles.* **4.** a piece of this stone: *the fallen marbles of Roman ruins.* **5.** (not in technical use) any of various breccias or other stones that take a high polish and show a variegated pattern. **6.** a marbled appearance or pattern; marbling: *The woodwork had a greenish marble.* **7.** anything resembling marble in hardness, coldness, smoothness, etc.: *a brow of marble.* **8.** something lacking in warmth or feeling. **9.** a little ball made of stone, baked clay, glass, porcelain, agate, or steel, esp. for use in games. **10. marbles,** (*used with a singular v.*) a game for children in which a marble is propelled by the thumb to hit another marble so as to drive it out of a circle drawn or scratched on the ground. **11. marbles,** *Slang.* normal rational faculties; sanity; wits; common sense: *to have all one's marbles; to lose one's marbles.* —*adj.* **12.** consisting or made of marble. **13.** like marble, as in hardness, coldness, smoothness, etc. **14.** lacking in warmth, compassion, or sympathy: *marble heart.* **15.** of variegated or mottled color. —*v.t.* **16.** to color or stain like variegated marble. **17.** to apply a decorative pattern to (paper, the edges of a book, etc.) by transferring oil pigments floating on water. [1150–1200; ME *marbel,* dissimilated var. of OE *marmel* (in *marmelstān* marble stone) < L *marmor* < Gk *mármaros,* akin to *marmaírein* to sparkle] —**mar′bler,** *n.*

Mar·ble (mär′bəl), *n.* **Alice,** 1913–90, U.S. tennis player.

mar′ble cake′, a cake given a streaked, marblelike appearance by the incomplete mixing of dark, esp. chocolate, and light batters. [1870–75, *Amer.*]

Mar·ble·head (mär′bəl head′, mär′bəl hed′), *n.* a resort in NE Massachusetts: yachting. 20,126.

mar·ble·ize (mär′bə līz′), *v.t.,* **-ized, -iz·ing.** marble. Also, **marbelize;** *esp. Brit.,* **mar′ble·ise′.** [1865–75, *Amer.*; MARBLE + -IZE] —**mar′ble·i·za′tion,** *n.*

mar′ble or′chard, *Northern, North Midland, and Western U.S. Facetious.* cemetery. [1925–30, *Amer.*]

mar·ble·wood (mär′bəl wo͝od′), *n.* **1.** any of several trees having wood somewhat resembling marble in graining or texture, as *Diospyros marmorata,* of southern Asia, or *Olea paniculata,* of Australia. **2.** the wood of any of these trees. [1745–55; MARBLE + WOOD[1]]

mar·bling (mär′bling), *n.* **1.** the act, process, or art of coloring or staining in imitation of variegated marble. **2.** an appearance like that of variegated marble. **3.** the intermixture of fat with lean in a cut of meat, which contributes to flavor and tenderness. **4.** *Bookbinding.* marblelike decoration on the paper edges, lining, or binding boards of a book. [1680–90; MARBLE + -ING[1]]

mar·bly (mär′blē), *adj.* like marble in appearance, hardness, coldness, etc. [1400–50; late ME; see MARBLE, -Y[1]]

Mar·burg (mär′bo͝orк; *Eng.* mär′bûrg), *n.* **1.** a city in central Germany. 75,092. **2.** German name of **Maribor.**

Mar′burg disease′, *Pathol.* a viral disease producing a severe and often fatal illness with fever, rash, diarrhea, vomiting, and gastrointestinal bleeding, transmitted to humans through contact with infected green monkeys. Also called **green monkey disease, Mar′·burg-Eb′o·la disease′** (mär′bûrg eb′ə lə). [after MARBURG, where laboratory workers caught the disease from infected monkeys in 1967; and *Ebola,* river and region in N Zaire, where an outbreak occurred in 1976]

CONCISE ETYMOLOGY KEY: <, descended or borrowed from; >, whence; b., blend of, blended; c., cognate with; cf., compare; deriv., derivative; equiv., equivalent; imit., imitative; obl., oblique; r., replacing; s., stem; sp., spelling, spelled; resp., respelling, respelled; trans., translation; ?, origin unknown; *, unattested; ‡, probably earlier than. See the full key inside the front cover.

marc (märk; *Fr.* MAR), *n.* **1.** the grapes contained in the wine press and the residue, as skins and pips, remaining after the juice is expressed. **2.** (in France) the brandy distilled from this residue. **3.** *Pharm.* the residue that remains following the extraction of active principles from a vegetable drug by means of a solvent. [1595–1605; < MF, akin to *marcher* to tread; see MARCH[1]]

Marc (märk; *for 1 also Ger.* märk), *n.* **1. Franz** (fränts), 1880–1916, German painter. **2.** a male given name, form of **Marcus.**

MARC (märk), *n. Library Science.* a standardized system developed by the Library of Congress for producing and transmitting machine-readable bibliographic records. [*ma(chine) r(eadable) c(atologing)*]

Mar·can (mär′kən), *adj.* of, pertaining to, or characteristic of St. Mark or of the second Gospel. Also, **Markan.** [1900–05; < L *Mārc(us)* MARK + -AN]

Marc·an·ton·i·o (mär′kan tō′nē ō; *It.* mär′kän tô′nyô), *n.* See **Raimondi, Marcantonio.**

Marc′ An′tony (märk). See **Antony, Mark.**

mar·ca·site (mär′kə sīt′), *n.* **1.** a common mineral, iron disulfide, FeS_2, chemically similar to pyrite but crystallizing in the orthorhombic system. **2.** any of the crystallized forms of iron pyrites, much used in the 18th century for ornaments. **3.** a specimen or ornament of this substance. [1375–1425; late ME < ML *marcasīta* < Ar *marqashīṭā* < Aram *marqəshīṭā*] —**mar·ca·sit·i·cal** (mär′kə sit′i kəl), *adj.*

mar·ca·to (mär kä′tō; *It.* mär kä′tô), *adj.* (of notes or chords in a musical score) strongly accented. [1830–40; < It: marked]

Mar·ceau (mär sō′; *Fr.* MAR sō′), *n.* **Mar·cel** (mär-sel′; *Fr.* MAR sel′), born 1923, French actor and pantomimist.

mar·cel (mär sel′), *v.,* **-celled, -cel·ling,** *n.* —*v.t.* **1.** to wave (the hair) by means of special irons, producing the effect of regular, continuous waves **(marcel′ waves′).** —*n.* **2.** a marcelling. **3.** a marcelled condition. [1890–95; named after *Marcel* Grateau (1852–1936), French hairdresser who originated it] —**mar·cel′ler,** *n.*

Mar·cel (mär sel′; *Fr.* MAR sel′), *n.* **1. Ga·bri·el** (GA-brē el′), 1887–1973, French philosopher, dramatist, and critic. **2.** a male given name.

mar·cel·la (mär sel′ə), *n.* a cotton or linen fabric constructed in pique weave, used in the manufacture of vests, mats, etc. [1805–15; alter. of MARSEILLES]

Mar·cel·la (mär sel′ə), *n.* a female given name.

Mar·cel·li·nus (mär′sə lī′nəs), *n.* **Saint,** died A.D. 304, pope 296–304.

Mar·cel·lo (mär chel′lô), *n.* **Be·ne·det·to** (be′ne det′tô), 1686–1739, Italian composer.

Mar·cel·lus (mär sel′əs), *n.* **Marcus Claudius,** 268?–208 B.C., Roman general and consul.

Marcellus I, Saint, died A.D. 309, pope 308–309.

Marcellus II, (*Marcello Cervini*) 1501–55, Italian ecclesiastic: pope 1555.

mar·ces·cent (mär ses′ənt), *adj. Bot.* withering but not falling off, as a part of a plant. [1720–30; < L *marcēscent-,* s. of *marcēscēns* (prp. of *marcēscere* to wither, shrivel), equiv. to *marc(ēre)* to wither + *-ēscent-* -ESCENT] —**mar·ces′cence,** *n.*

march[1] (märch), *v.i.* **1.** to walk with regular and measured tread, as soldiers on parade; advance in step in an organized body. **2.** to walk in a stately, deliberate manner. **3.** to go forward; advance; proceed: *Time marches on.* —*v.t.* **4.** to cause to march. **5. march on,** to march toward, as in protest or in preparation for confrontation or battle: *The angry mob marched on the Bastille.* —*n.* **6.** the act or course of marching. **7.** the distance covered in a single period of marching. **8.** advance; progress; forward movement: *the march of science.* **9.** a piece of music with a rhythm suited to accompany marching. **10. on the march,** moving ahead; progressing; advancing: *Automation is on the march.* **11. steal a march on,** to gain an advantage over, esp. secretly or slyly. [1375–1425; late ME *marchen* < MF *march(i)er,* OF *marchier* to tread, move < Frankish **markōn* presumably, to mark, pace out (a boundary); see MARK[1]]

march[2] (märch), *n.* **1.** a tract of land along a border of a country; frontier. **2. marches,** the border districts between England and Scotland, or England and Wales. —*v.i.* **3.** to touch at the border; border. [1250–1300; ME *marche* < AF, OF < Gmc; cf. OE *gemearc,* Goth *marka* boundary; see MARK[1]]

March (märch), *n.* the third month of the year, containing 31 days. *Abbr.*: Mar. [bef. 1050; ME *March(e)* < AF *Marche;* r. OE *Martius* < L, short for *Mārtius mēnsis* month of Mars (*Mārti-,* s. of *Mārs* + *-us* adj. suffix)]

March (märch *for 1–3;* märкн *for 4*), *n.* **1. Francis Andrew,** 1825–1911, U.S. philologist and lexicographer. **2. Fredric** (*Frederick McIntyre Bickel*), 1897–1975, U.S. actor. **3. Pey·ton Con·way** (pāt′n kon′wā), 1864–1955, U.S. army officer (son of Francis Andrew March). **4.** German name of the **Morava.**

March., Marchioness.

M.Arch., Master of Architecture.

Mar·che (mär′ke), *n.* **Le,** Italian name of **The Marches.**

M.Arch.E., Master of Architectural Engineering.

march·er[1] (mär′chər), *n.* a person who marches on foot: *a line of marchers.* [1605–15; MARCH[1] + -ER[1]]

march·er[2] (mär′chər), *n. Hist.* an inhabitant of, or an officer or lord having jurisdiction over, a march or border territory. [1375–1425; late ME; see MARCH[2], -ER[1]]

March·es (mär′chiz), *n.* **The,** a region in central Italy, bordering the Adriatic. 1,397,892; 3743 sq. mi. (9695 sq. km). Italian, **Le Marche.**

mar·che·sa (mär kā′zə; *It.* mär ke′zä), *n., pl.* **-se** (-zā; *It.* -ze). **1.** an Italian noblewoman, equivalent in rank to a marquise. **2.** the wife or widow of a marchese. [1790–1800; < It; fem. of MARCHESE]

mar·che·se (mär kā′zā; *It.* mär ke′ze), *n., pl.* **-si** (-zē). an Italian nobleman, equivalent in rank to a marquis. [1510–20; < It; see MARQUIS]

Mar·chesh·van (*Seph. Heb.* mär кнesh vän′; *Ashk. Heb.* mär кнesh′vän; *Eng.* mar кнesh′vən, -hesh′-), *n.* Heshvan.

March′ fly′, any of several flies of the family Bibionidae that appear during spring and early summer. [1890–95, *Amer.*]

march′ frac′ture, *Pathol.* See under **stress fracture.**

march′ing or′ders, 1. *Mil.* orders to begin a march or other troop movement. **2.** *Informal.* **a.** orders to start out, move on, proceed, etc.: *We're just sitting by the phone, awaiting our marching orders.* **b.** notice of dismissal from a position or job; walking papers. [1770–80]

mar·chion·ess (mär′shə nis, mär′shə nes′), *n. Brit.* marquise (defs. 1, 2). [1770–80; < ML *marchiōnissa,* equiv. to *marchiōn-* (s. of *marchiō*) MARQUIS + *-issa* -ESS]
—**Usage.** See **-ess.**

march·land (märch′land′, -lənd), *n.* borderland. [1540–50; MARCH[2] + LAND]

march-or·der (märch′ôr′dər), *v.t. Mil.* to prepare (personnel, arms, and equipment) for a march. [1530–40]

march·pane (märch′pān′), *n.* marzipan. [1485–95; < F, dial. var. of *massepain, marcepain* < It *marzapane,* orig. sugar-candy box, perh. < Ar *mawthabān* a seated king]

march-past (märch′past′, -päst′), *n.* a parade or procession, esp. of troops past a reviewing stand. [1875–80; n. use of v. phrase *march past*]

Mar·cia (mär′shə), *n.* a female given name: from a Latin word meaning "warlike."

Mar·cian (mär′shən), *n.* A.D. 392?–457, emperor of the Eastern Roman Empire 450–457. Also, **Mar·ci·a·nus** (mär′shē ā′nəs, mär′sē-).

Mar·ci·a·no (mär′sē ä′nō, -an′ō), *n.* **Rocky** (*Rocco Francis Marchegiano*), 1924–69, U.S. boxer: world heavyweight champion 1952–56.

Mar·cie (mär′sē), *n.* a female given name, form of **Marcia.**

Mar·cion (mär′shən, -shē ən, -sē ən), *n.* A.D. c100–c160, Christian Gnostic.

Mar·cion·ism (mär′shə niz′əm), *n.* the doctrines and principles of the Marcionites. [1880–85; MARCION + -ISM]

Mar·cion·ite (mär′shə nīt′), *n.* **1.** a member of a Gnostic ascetic sect that flourished from the 2nd to 7th century A.D. and that rejected the Old Testament and denied the incarnation of God in Christ. —*adj.* **2.** of or pertaining to the Marcionites or their doctrines. Also, **Mar′cion·ist.** [1530–40; < LL *Marciōnita.* See MARCION, -ITE[1]]

Mar·co·man·ni (mär′kō man′ī), *n.* (*used with a plural v.*) an ancient Germanic people who lived in central Europe. —**Mar·co·man·nic** (mär′kō man′ik), *adj.*

Mar·co·ni (mär kō′nē; *It.* mär kô′nē), *n.* **Gu·gliel·mo** (go͞o lyel′mô), **Marchese,** 1874–1937, Italian electrical engineer and inventor, esp. in the field of wireless telegraphy: Nobel prize for physics 1909.

mar·co·ni·gram (mär kō′ni gram′), *n. Older Use.* a radiogram. Also, **Mar·co′ni·gram′.** [1900–05; MARCONI + -GRAM[1]]

Marco′ni mast′, *Naut.* **1.** an elaborately stayed mast. **2.** *Obs.* a mast for a radio antenna. [after G. MARCONI]

Marco′ni rig′, *Naut.* a rig of triangular sails for a yacht. Also called **Bermuda rig, Bermudan rig, Bermudian rig.** [1915–20; after G. MARCONI] —**Mar·co′·ni-rigged′,** *adj.*

Mar·co Po·lo (mär′kō pō′lō). See **Polo, Marco.**

Mar·cos (mär′kōs), *n.* **Ferdinand E(d·ra·lin)** (ed′rə-lin), born 1917, Philippine political leader: president 1965–86.

Mar·cus (mär′kəs), *n.* **1. Saint.** Also, **Mark.** died A.D. 336, pope 336. **2.** a male given name. [< L *Mārcus* < **māwortkos* pertaining to **Māwort-s* MARS]

Mar′cus Au·re′li·us (ô rē′lē əs, ô rēl′yəs), (*Marcus Annius Verus*) A.D. 121–180, Stoic philosopher and writer: emperor of Rome 161–180. Also called **Mar′cus Aure′lius An·to·ni′nus** (an′tə nī′nəs).

Mar·cu·se (mär ko͞o′zə), *n.* **Herbert,** 1898–1979, U.S. political and social philosopher, born in Germany.

Mar·cy (mär′sē), *n.* **1. Mount,** a mountain in NE New York: highest peak of the Adirondack Mountains, 5344 ft. (1629 m). **2.** a female given name, form of **Marcia.**

Mar del Pla·ta (mär′ ᵺel plä′tä), a city in E Argentina: seaside resort. 407,024.

Mar·di Gras (mär′dē grä′, grä′), **1.** the day before Lent, celebrated in some cities, as New Orleans and Paris, as a day of carnival and merrymaking; Shrove Tuesday. **2.** a pre-Lenten carnival period climaxing on this day. [1690–1700; < F: lit., fat Tuesday]

Mar·duk (mär′do͝ok), *n. Babylonian Relig.* the chief of the Babylonian deities. Also, **Merodach.** Also called **Baal Merodach.**

mare[1] (mâr), *n.* a fully mature female horse or other equine animal. [bef. 900; ME, var. of *mere,* OE *m(i)ere;* c. D *merrie,* G *Mähre,* ON *merr;* akin to OE *mearh,* ON *marr,* Ir *marc* horse. See MARSHAL]

mare[2] (mâr), *n. Obs.* nightmare (def. 3). [bef. 900; ME, OE; c. G *Mahre,* ON *mara.* See NIGHTMARE]

ma·re[3] (mär′ā, mâr′ē), *n., pl.* **ma·ri·a** (mär′ē ə, mâr′-). *Astron.* any of the several large, dark plains on the moon and Mars: Galileo believed that the lunar features were seas when he first saw them through a telescope. [1680–90; < L: sea]

Mar.E., Marine Engineer.

Ma·re Ac·i·dal·i·um (mär′ā as′i dal′ē əm, mâr′ē), (*Sea of Venus*) an area in the northern hemisphere of Mars, appearing as a dark region when viewed telescopically from the earth.

Ma′re Aus·tral′e (ô stral′ē, -strā′lē), (*Southern Sea*) an area near the south pole of Mars, appearing as a dark region when viewed telescopically from the earth.

Ma′re Bo′re·um (bôr′ē əm, bōr′-), (*Northern Sea*) an area near the north pole of Mars, appearing as a dark region when viewed telescopically from the earth.

Ma′re Chro′ni·um (krō′nē əm), an area in the southern hemisphere of Mars, appearing as a dark region when viewed telescopically from the earth.

Ma′re Cim·mer′i·um (si mēr′ē əm), (*Cimmerian Sea*) an area in the southern hemisphere of Mars, appearing as a dark region when viewed telescopically from the earth.

ma·re clau·sum (mâr′ē klô′səm, mär′ā; *Lat.* mä′re klou′so͝om), a body of navigable water under the sole jurisdiction of a nation. Cf. **mare liberum.** [1645–55; < L: closed sea]

Ma·re Cri·si·um (mär′ā krē′sē əm, mâr′ē), (*Sea of Crises*) a dark plain in the first quadrant of the face of the moon: about 66,000 sq. mi. (170,000 sq. km).

Ma′re Er·y·thrae′um (er′i thrē′əm), (*Red Sea*) an area in the southern hemisphere of Mars, appearing as a dark region when viewed telescopically from the earth.

Ma′re Fe·cun·di·ta′tis (fā ko͝on′di tä′tis, fē-), (*Sea of Fertility*) a dark plain in the fourth quadrant and extending into the first quadrant of the face of the moon: about 160,000 sq. mi. (415,000 sq. km).

Ma′re Fri·go′ris (fri gôr′is, -gōr′-), (*Sea of Cold*) a dark plain in the northern hemisphere, in the first and second quadrants of the face of the moon: about 55 mi. (90 km) wide at its narrowest width and 750 mi. (1200 km) long: about 67,000 sq. mi. (174,000 sq. km).

Ma′re Hu′mo·rum (hyo͞o′mər əm, hyo͞o môr′-, -mōr′-), (*Sea of Moisture*) a dark plain in the third quadrant of the face of the moon: about 45,000 sq. mi. (117,000 sq. km).

Ma′re Im′bri·um (im′brē əm), (*Sea of Showers*) a dark plain in the second quadrant of the face of the moon: about 340,000 sq. mi. (880,000 sq. km).

Mare′ Is′land (mâr), an island in the N part of San Francisco Bay, California.

Ma′rek's disease′ (mar′iks, mär′-), *Vet. Pathol.* a contagious cancerous disease of poultry, caused by a herpesvirus and characterized by proliferation of lymphoid cells and paralysis of a limb or the neck. Also called **fowl paralysis, range paralysis.** [after Hungarian veterinarian József *Marek* (1868–1952), who described it in 1907]

ma·re li·be·rum (mâr′ē lib′ər əm, mär′ā; *Lat.* mä′re le′be ro͝om′), a body of navigable water to which all nations have unrestricted access. Cf. **mare clausum.** [1645–55; < L: free sea]

ma·rem·ma (mə rem′ə), *n., pl.* **-rem·me** (-rem′ē). **1.** a marshy region near the seashore, esp. in Italy. **2.** the miasma associated with such a region. [1825–35; < It < L *maritima*, fem. of *maritimus* MARITIME]

Ma·re Nec·ta·ris (mär′ā nek tär′is, mâr′ē), (*Sea of Nectar*) a dark plain in the fourth quadrant of the face of the moon: about 26,000 sq. mi. (67,000 sq. km).

Ma·ren·go (mə reng′gō; *for 1 also It.* mä reng′gô), *n., pl.* **-gos** for 2, *adj.* —*n.* **1.** a village in Piedmont, in NW Italy: Napoleon defeated the Austrians 1800. **2.** a former gold coin of Italy, issued by Napoleon after the battle of Marengo. —*adj.* **3.** (*often l.c.*) (of food) browned in oil and cooked with tomatoes, garlic, wine, and often mushrooms and brandy: *chicken marengo.*

ma·re nos·trum (mä′re nôs′tro͝om; *Eng.* mâr′ē nos′trəm, mär′ā), *Latin.* our sea, esp. the Mediterranean to the ancient Romans.

Ma·re Nu·bi·um (mär′ā no͞o′bē əm, nyo͞o′-, mâr′ē), (*Sea of Clouds*) a dark plain in the third quadrant of the face of the moon: about 95,000 sq. mi. (245,000 sq. km).

mar·e·o·graph (mar′ē ə graf′, -gräf′), *n. Oceanog.* marigraph.

Ma′re Se·ren·i·ta′tis (sə ren′i tä′tis), (*Sea of Serenity*) a dark plain in the first quadrant of the face of the moon: about 120,000 sq. mi. (310,000 sq. km).

Ma′re Si·re′num (si rē′nəm), (*Sea of Sirens*) an area in the southern hemisphere of Mars, appearing as a dark region when viewed telescopically from the earth.

mare's-nest (mârz′nest′), *n.* **1.** something imagined to be an extraordinary discovery but proving to be a delusion or a hoax: *The announced cure for the disease was merely another mare's-nest.* **2.** an extremely confused, entangled, or disordered place, situation, etc.: *We just moved in, and the place is a mare's-nest.* [1610–20]

mares′ of Diome′des (mârz), *Class. Myth.* wild mares owned by Diomedes, a Thracian king, who fed them on human flesh: captured by Hercules in fulfillment of one of his labors.

mare's-tail (mârz′tāl′), *n.* **1.** a long narrow cirrus cloud whose flowing appearance somewhat resembles a horse's tail. **2.** an erect, aquatic, Old World plant, *Hippuris vulgaris*, having crowded whorls of narrow, hairlike leaves. [1755–65]

Ma′re Tran·quil·li·ta′tis (trang kwil′i tä′tis), (*Sea of Tranquillity*) a dark plain in the first quadrant of the face of the moon: about 110,000 sq. mi. (285,000 sq. km).

Ma′re Tyr·rhe′num (ti rē′nəm), (*Tyrrhenian Sea*) an area in the southern hemisphere of Mars, appearing as a dark region when viewed telescopically from the earth.

Ma′re Un·da′rum (un där′əm), (*Sea of Waves*) a dark plain in the first quadrant of the face of the moon: about 4800 sq. mi. (12,000 sq. km).

Ma′re Va·po′rum (vā pôr′əm, -pōr′-), (*Sea of Vapors*) a dark plain in the first quadrant and near the center of the face of the moon: about 39,000 sq. mi. (101,000 sq. km).

ma·rez·zo (mə ret′sō), *n.* an imitation marble composed of Keene's cement, fiber, and coloring matter. [1900–05; < It, deriv. of *marezzare* to marble]

Mar′fan syn′drome (mär′fan, mär fan′), *Pathol.* a hereditary disorder characterized by abnormally elongated bones, esp. in the extremities, hypermotility of the joints, and circulatory and eye abnormalities. [named after Antonin Bernard *Marfan* (1858–1942), French pediatrician, who described it in 1892]

marg., **1.** margin. **2.** marginal.

mar·ga (mär′gə), *n. Hinduism.* any of the three ways to salvation, which are those of devotion to certain gods **(bhakti-marga),** of study **(jnana-marga),** and of actions **(karma-marga).** [< Skt: path]

Mar·ga·ret (mär′gə rit, -grit), *n.* a female given name: from a Greek word meaning "pearl."

Mar′garet of An′jou, 1430–82, queen of Henry VI of England.

Mar′garet of Navarre′, 1492–1549, queen of Navarre 1544–49: patron of literature, author of stories, and poet. Also called **Mar′garet of An·gou·lême′** (äng′go͞o-lem′; *Fr.* än go͞o lem′).

Mar′garet of Valois′, (*"Queen Margot"*) 1533–1615, 1st wife of Henry IV of France: queen of Navarre; patron of science and literature (daughter of Henry II of France and Catherine de' Medici). Also called **Mar′garet of France′.**

Mar′garet Rose′, born 1930, English princess (daughter of George VI; sister of Elizabeth II).

mar·gar′ic ac′id (mär gar′ik, -gär′-), *Chem.* a colorless, crystalline, water-insoluble, fatty acid, $C_{17}H_{34}O_2$, resembling stearic acid, obtained from lichens or synthetically. [1810–20; < Gk *márgar(on)* pearl (prob. back formation from *margarítēs*; see MARGARITE) + -IC]

mar·ga·rine (mär′jər in, -jə rēn′, märj′rin), *n.* a butterlike product made of refined vegetable oils, sometimes blended with animal fats, and emulsified, usually with water or milk. Also called **oleomargarine.** [1870–75; MARGAR(IC) + -INE[2]]

Mar·ga·ri·ta (mär′gə rē′tə), *n.* (*often l.c.*) a cocktail made of tequila, lime or lemon juice, and an orange-flavored liqueur, usually served in a salt-rimmed glass. [1960–65; < AmerSp; appar. special use of Sp *Margarita* MARGARET]

mar·ga·ri·ta·ceous (mär′gər i tā′shəs), *adj.* resembling mother-of-pearl; pearly. [1820–30; < NL *margarītāceus.* See MARGARITE, -ACEOUS]

mar·ga·rite (mär′gə rīt′), *n.* **1.** *Mineral.* **a.** a gray, pink, or yellow mica, occurring in brittle monoclinic crystals. **b.** an aggregate of small, rudimentary crystals resembling minute globules in a row: found in glassy volcanic rocks. **2.** *Obs.* a pearl. [bef. 1000; ME, OE: pearl < L *margarita* < Gk *margarítēs*, perh. < Iranian (cf. Pahlavi *marvārīt* pearl), with final element conformed to Gk *-ītēs* -ITE[1]]

mar·gate (mär′git, -gāt), *n.* a red-mouthed grunt, *Haemulon album*, inhabiting Atlantic waters from Florida to Brazil, valued as a food fish. [1725–35; perh. after MARGATE]

Mar·gate (mär′git, -gāt *for 1;* mär′gāt *for 2*), *n.* **1.** a city in NE Kent, in SE England: seaside resort. 50,145. **2.** a city in SE Florida. 36,044.

mar·gay (mär′gā), *n.* a small tiger cat, *Felis tigrina*, of tropical America: now rare. [1775–85; < F (Buffon), alter. of *maragua* < Pg *maracajá* < Tupi *marakaya*]

marge[1] (märj), *n. Archaic.* margin; edge. [< MF < L *margō*; see MARGIN]

marge[2] (märj), *n. Chiefly Brit. Informal.* margarine. [shortened form]

Marge (märj), *n.* a female given name, form of **Margaret.**

Mar·ge·lan (mär′gə län′; *Russ.* mər gyi län′), *n.* a city in E Uzbekistan, in the S Soviet Union in Asia, NW of Fergana. 111,000.

mar·gent (mär′jənt), *n. Archaic.* margin. [1475–85; alter. of MARGIN]

Mar·ger·y (mär′jə rē), *n.* a female given name, form of **Margaret.**

Mar·ghe·ri·ta (mär′gə rē′tə; *It.* mär′ge rē′tä), *n.* a female given name, Italian form of **Margaret.**

Mar·gie (mär′jē), *n.* a female given name, form of **Margaret.**

mar·gin (mär′jin), *n.* **1.** the space around the printed or written matter on a page. **2.** an amount allowed or available beyond what is actually necessary: *to allow a margin for error.* **3.** a limit in condition, capacity, etc., beyond or below which something ceases to exist, be desirable, or be possible: *the margin of endurance; the margin of sanity.* **4.** a border or edge. **5.** *Philately.* selvage (def. 3). **6.** *Finance.* **a.** security, as a percentage in money, deposited with a broker by a client as a provision against loss on transactions. **b.** the amount representing the customer's investment or equity in such an account. **7.** the difference between the amount of a loan and the market value of the collateral pledged as security for it. **8.** *Com.* the difference between the cost and the selling price. **9.** an amount or degree of difference: *The measure passed by a margin of just three votes.* **10.** *Econ.* the point at which the return from economic activity barely covers the cost of production, and below which production is unprofitable. **11.** *Entomol.* the border of an insect's wing. —*v.t.* **12.** to provide with a margin or border. **13.** to furnish with marginal notes, as a document. **14.** to enter in the margin, as of a book. **15.** *Finance.* to deposit a margin upon. **16.** *Stock Exchange.* to purchase (securities) on margin: *That stock was heavily margined during the last month.* [1300–50; ME < L *margin-* (s. of *margō*) border; akin to MARCH[2]]
—**Syn. 3.** confine, bound. **4.** rim, verge, brink. See **edge.** —**Ant. 4.** center.

mar′gin account′, an account opened by a customer with a brokerage house in which listed securities can be purchased on margin. Cf. **cash account.**

mar·gin·al (mär′jə nl), *adj.* **1.** pertaining to a margin. **2.** situated on the border or edge. **3.** at the outer or lower limits; minimal for requirements; almost insufficient: *marginal subsistence; marginal ability.* **4.** written or printed in the margin of a page: *a marginal note.* **5.** *Sociol.* marked by contact with disparate cultures, and acquiring some but not all the traits or values common to any one of them. **6.** *Econ.* **a.** selling goods at a price that just equals the additional cost of producing the last unit supplied. **b.** of or pertaining to goods produced and marketed at margin: *marginal profits.* [1570–80; < ML *marginālis* of, pertaining to an edge. See MARGIN, -AL[1]] —**mar′gin·al′i·ty,** *n.* —**mar′gin·al·ly,** *adv.*

mar′ginal cost′, *Econ.* the cost of one additional unit of any item produced or bought in quantity. [1925–30]

mar·gi·na·li·a (mär′jə nā′lē ə, -nāl′yə), *n.pl.* marginal notes. [1825–35; < NL, n. use of neut. pl. of ML *marginālis* MARGINAL]

mar·gin·al·ize (mär′jə nl īz′), *v.t.,* **-ized, -iz·ing.** to place in a position of marginal importance, influence, or power: *the government's attempts to marginalize criticism and restore public confidence.* Also, *esp. Brit.,* **mar′gin·al·ise′.** [1825–35 for an earlier sense; MARGINAL + -IZE] —**mar′gin·al·i·za′tion,** *n.*

mar′ginal man′, *Sociol.* a person who participates only slightly in the life of two cultural groups without feeling identified with either group. [1925–30]

mar′ginal sea′, water that lies alongside a state, falls under its authority, and extends about 3½ statute miles (6 kilometers) from the coast.

mar′ginal util′ity, *Econ.* the extra utility or satisfaction derived by a consumer from the consumption of the last unit of a commodity. [1920–25]

mar·gin·ate (mär′jə nāt′), *adj., v.,* **-at·ed, -at·ing.** —*adj.* Also, **mar′gin·at′ed.** **1.** having a margin. **2.** *Entomol.* having the margin of a distinct color: *marginate with purple.* —*v.t.* **3.** to furnish with a margin; border. [1600–10; < L *marginātus*, ptp. of *margināre* to provide with borders or edges. See MARGIN, -ATE[1]] —**mar′gin·a′tion,** *n.*

mar′gin call′, *Stock Exchange.* a demand from a brokerage house to a customer that more money or securities be deposited in his or her margin account when the amount in it falls below that stipulated as necessary to cover the stock purchased. [1960–65]

mar′gin line′, *Naut.* **1.** an imaginary line used in making calculations regarding the flooding of hulls, running fore-and-aft 3 in. (8 cm) below the upper surface of the bulkhead deck at the side. **2.** the line along which the planking on a transom-sterned vessel terminates aft. [1840–50]

mar′gin of safe′ty, *Pharm.* See **therapeutic index.** [1885–90, for an earlier sense]

mar′gin plank′, *Naut.* a plank forming a border for wooden decking. Also called **waterway plank.**

mar·go·sa (mär gō′sə), *n.* neem (def. 2). [1805–15; aph. < Pg *amargosa*, fem. of *amargoso* bitter]

Mar·got (mär′gō, -gət), *n.* a female given name, form of **Margaret.**

mar·gra·vate (mär′grə vāt′), *n.* the province or territory of a margrave. Also, **mar·gra·vi·ate** (mär grā′vē-āt′). [1695–1705; MARGRAVE + -ATE[3]]

mar·grave (mär′grāv), *n.* **1.** (formerly) the hereditary title of the rulers of certain European states. **2.** *Hist.* a hereditary German title, equivalent to marquis. **3.** (originally) a military governor of a German mark, or border province. [1545–55; earlier *marcgrave* < MD, equiv. to *marke* border (c. MARCH[2]) + *grave* count (c. REEVE[1]); cf. G *Markgraf*] —**mar·gra′vi·al,** *adj.*

mar·gra·vine (mär′grə vēn′), *n.* the wife of a margrave. [1685–95; < MD *marcgravinne*, equiv. to *marcgrave* MARGRAVE + *-inne* fem. n. suffix; cf. G *Markgräfin*]

Mar·gre·the II (mär grä′tə), born 1940, queen of Denmark since 1972.

mar·gue·rite (mär′gə rēt′), *n.* **1.** Also called **Paris daisy.** the European daisy, *Bellis perennis.* **2.** any of several daisylike flowers, esp. *Chrysanthemum frutescens*, cultivated for its numerous white-rayed, yellow-centered flowers. [1865–70; < F: daisy, pearl < L *margarita* pearl < Gk; see MARGARITE]

Mar·gue·rite (mär′gə rēt′; *Fr.* mar gə rēt′), *n.* a female given name, French form of **Margaret.**

mar-hawk (mär′hôk′), *n. Falconry.* a falconer who trains or handles the birds badly. [MAR + HAWK[1]]

Mar·hesh·van (*Seph. Heb.* mär khesh vän′; *Ashk. Heb.* mär khesh′vän; *Eng.* mär hesh′vən), *n.* Heshvan.

Ma·ri (mä′rē), *n., pl.* **-ris,** (*esp. collectively*) **-ri** for 1. **1.** a member of a Uralic people living in scattered communities north of Cheboksary and Kazan in European Russia, mainly in the Mari Autonomous Soviet Socialist Republic. **2.** the Finnic language of the Mari. Also called **Cheremis, Cheremiss.** [< Russ *mári* (not declined) < Mari *marij* Mari, man]

Ma•ri•a (mə rē′ə, -rī′ə; *Du., Ger., It., Sp.* mä rē′ä), *n.* a female given name, form of **Mary.**

Ma•ri•a (mə rē′ə), *n.* calaba. [see SANTA MARIA]

ma•ri•a•chi (mär′ē ä′chē; *Sp.* mä ryä′chē), *adj., n., pl.* **-chis** (-chēz; *Sp.* -chēs). —*adj.* **1.** pertaining to traditional Mexican dance music, usually played by a small band of strolling musicians dressed in native costumes. —*n.* **2.** a member of such a band. **3.** the music played by such a band. [1940–45; < MexSp *mariache, mariachi,* perh. < F *mariage* MARRIAGE; the music is said to have been played at weddings in the state of Jalisco, where it originated]

Ma•ri•a de Me•di•ci (*It.* mä rē′ä de me′dē chē). See **Marie de Médicis.**

ma•riage de con•ve•nance (ma ryazh′ də kôn və näns′), *French.* See **marriage of convenience.**

ma•ri•a•lite (mə rē′ə līt′, mar′ē ə-), *n. Mineral.* a member of the scapolite group, rich in sodium and containing no calcium. [1850–55; < G *Marialit;* after *Marie* Rose, wife of Gerhard vom Rath, 19th-century German mineralogist; see -LITE]

Ma•ri•a Lu•i•sa (*Ger.* mä rē′ä lo͞o ē′sä). See **Marie Louise.**

Mar•i•an (mâr′ē ən *or, for 5,* mar′-), *adj.* **1.** of or pertaining to the Virgin Mary. **2.** of or pertaining to some other Mary, as Mary Tudor of England or Mary, Queen of Scots. —*n.* **3.** a person who has a particular devotion to the Virgin Mary. **4.** an adherent or defender of Mary, Queen of Scots. **5.** a female given name, form of **Mary.** [1600–10; MARY + -AN]

Mar′i•an′a Is′lands (mâr′ē an′ə, mar′-, mâr′-, mar′-; *Sp.* mä′rē ä′nä), a group of 15 small islands in the Pacific, E of the Philippines: divided into Guam, a possession of the U.S., and the North Marianas, formally under U.S. trusteeship. 453 sq. mi. (1127 sq. km). Also called **Mar′i•an′as.** Formerly, **Ladrone Islands, Ladrones.** Cf. **North Mariana Islands.**

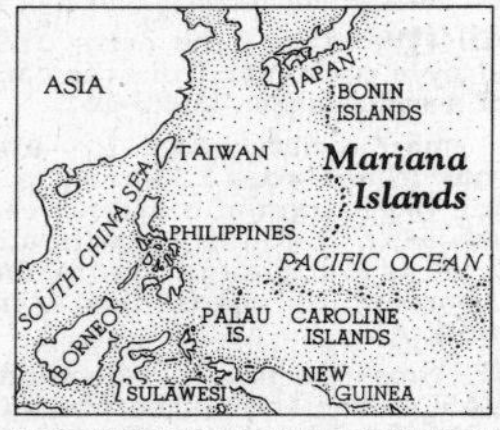

Ma•ri•a•na•o (mä′rē ä nä′ô), *n.* a city in NW Cuba, a suburb of Havana. 368,747.

Mar′ian′a Trench′, a depression in the ocean floor of the Pacific, S and W of the Mariana Islands: site of greatest known depth of any ocean. 36,201 ft. (11,034 m) deep.

Mar•i•an•ism (mâr′ē ə niz′əm), *n.* any religious system emphasizing worship of or devotion to the Virgin Mary. [MARIAN + -ISM]

Mar•i•an•na (mâr′ē an′ə, mar′-), *n.* a female given name.

Mar•i•anne (mâr′ē an′, mar′-), *n.* **1.** the French Republic, personified as a woman. **2.** a female given name.

Ma•rián•ské Láz•ně (mä′ryän ske läz′nye), a spa in W Bohemia, in the W Czech Republic. 18,510. German, **Marienbad.**

Ma•ri•a The•re•sa (mə rē′ə tə rā′sə, -zə), 1717–80, archduchess of Austria; queen of Hungary and Bohemia 1740–80 (wife of Francis II; mother of Joseph II, Leopold II, Marie Antoinette). German, **Ma•ri•a The•re•si•a** (mä-rē′ä te rā′zē ä).

Mari′a There′sa tha′ler, a former silver coin of Austria, issued between 1740 and 1780 and used for trade with Ethiopia and other countries; Levant dollar. Also called **Mari′a There′sa dol′lar.**

Ma′ri Auton′omous Repub′lic (mär′ē; *Russ.* mu-ryē′), an autonomous republic in the Russian Federation in Europe. 750,000; 8994 sq. mi. (23,294 sq. km). *Cap.:* Ioshkar-Ola.

Ma•ri•bor (mär′i bôr′), *n.* a city in N Slovenia, on the Drava River. 185,699. German, **Marburg.**

Mar•i•co•pa (mar′i kō′pə), *n., pl.* **-pas,** (*esp. collectively*) **-pa** for 1. **1.** a member of a North American Indian people of south-central Arizona. **2.** the Yuman language of the Maricopa.

mar•i•cul•ture (mar′i kul′chər), *n.* marine aquaculture. Also called **ocean farming.** [1900–05; < L *mari-,* comb. form of *mare* sea + CULTURE, on the model of AGRICULTURE]

Ma•rie (mə rē′; *for 2 also Fr.* ma rē′), *n.* **1.** (*Marie Alexandra Victoria of Saxe-Coburg*) 1875–1938, queen of Rumania 1914–27. **2.** a female given name, French form of **Mary.**

Ma•rie An•toi•nette (mə rē′ an′twə net′, an′tə-; *Fr.* ma rē′ än twa net′), (*Joséphe Jeanne Marie Antoinette*) 1755–93, queen of France 1774–93: wife of Louis XVI; executed in the French Revolution (daughter of Maria Theresa; sister of Joseph II, Leopold II).

Ma•rie′ Byrd′ Land′ (mə rē′ bûrd′), former name of **Byrd Land.**

CONCISE ETYMOLOGY KEY: <, descended or borrowed from; >, whence; b., blend of, blended; c., cognate with; cf., compare; deriv., derivative; equiv., equivalent; imit., imitative; obl., oblique; r., replacing; s., stem; sp., spelling, spelled; resp., respelling, respelled; trans., translation; ?, origin unknown; *, unattested; ‡, probably earlier than. See the full key inside the front cover.

Ma•rie de France (ma rē′ də fräns′), fl. 12th century, French poet in England.

Ma•rie de Mé•di•cis (ma rē′ də mā dē sēs′), 1573–1642, queen of Henry IV of France: regent 1610–17. Italian, **Maria de Medici.**

Ma•rie Ga•lante (*Fr.* ma rē ga länt′), an island in the E West Indies: a dependency of Guadeloupe. 15,867; 58 sq. mi. (150 sq. km).

Ma•ri•e•hamn (mä rē′ə hä′mən), *n.* a seaport on S Åland Island, in the Baltic. 9538.

Ma•riel (*Sp.* mä ryel′), *n.* a city and seaport of Cuba, on the W coast, SW of Havana. 34,467.

Ma•ri•e•li•to (mär′ē ə lē′tō; *Sp.* mä′rye lē′tô), *n., pl.* **-tos** (-tōz; *Sp.* -tôs). a refugee from Cuba who came to the U.S. in 1980 as part of a mass migration that sailed from Mariel, Cuba. [< AmerSp, equiv. to MARIEL, from which the migration took place + *-ito* n. suffix, usually dim.]

Ma•rie Lou•ise (mə rē′ lo͞o ēz′; *Fr.* ma rē′ lwēz′), 1791–1847, 2nd wife of Napoleon I: empress of France; duchess of Parma 1816–31 (daughter of Francis II of Austria; mother of Napoleon II). German, **Maria Luisa.**

Ma•ri•en•bad (mâr′ē ən bad′, mar′-; *Ger.* mä rē′ən-bät′), *n.* German name of **Mariánské Lázně.**

Mar•i•et•ta (mâr′ē et′ə), *n.* **1.** a city in NW Georgia. 30,805. **2.** a city in SE Ohio, on the Ohio River. 16,467. **3.** a female given name, form of **Mary.**

Ma•riette (ma ryet′), *n.* **Au•guste É•dou•ard** (ō gyst′ ā dwar′), 1821–81, French Egyptologist.

mar•i•gold (mar′i gōld′), *n.* **1.** any of several chiefly golden-flowered composite plants, esp. of the genus *Tagetes,* as *T. erecta,* having strong-scented foliage and yielding an oil that repels root parasites. **2.** any of several unrelated plants, esp. of the genus *Calendula,* as *C. officinalis,* the pot marigold. [1300–50; ME; see MARY (the Virgin), GOLD]

mar′igold win′dow. See **wheel window.** [1730–40]

mar•i•gram (mar′i gram′), *n.* a graphic representation from a marigraph. [< L *mari-* (comb. form of *mare* sea) + -GRAM[1]]

mar•i•graph (mar′i graf′, -gräf′), *n.* a device that automatically registers the rise and fall of the tide. Also, **mareograph.** [1855–60; < L *mari-* (comb. form of *mare* sea) + -GRAPH] —**mar•i•graph•ic** (mar′i graf′ik), *adj.*

ma•ri•jua•na (mar′ə wä′nə), *n.* **1.** hemp (def. 1). **2.** the dried leaves and female flowers of the hemp plant, used in cigarette form as a narcotic or hallucinogen. Also, **ma′ri•hua′na.** [1890–95, *Amer.*; < MexSp *marihuana, mariguana;* traditional assoc. with the personal name *María Juana* is prob. a folk etym.]

Ma•rí•lia (mä rē′lyä), *n.* a city in SE Brazil. 107,305.

Mar•i•lyn (mar′ə lin), *n.* a female given name, form of **Mary.** Also, **Mar′i•lynne.**

ma•rim•ba (mə rim′bə), *n.* a musical instrument, originating in Africa but popularized and modified in Central America, consisting of a set of graduated wooden bars, often with resonators beneath to reinforce the sound, struck with mallets. [1695–1705; < Pg < Kimbundu or a related Bantu language; akin to KALIMBA]

marimba

Mar•in (mär′in), *n.* **John,** 1870–1953, U.S. painter and etcher.

ma•ri•na (mə rē′nə), *n.* a boat basin offering dockage and other service for small craft. [1795–1805; < It, Sp, n. use of fem. of *marino* < L *marinus* MARINE]

Ma•ri•na (mə rē′nə), *n.* **1.** a town in W California. 20,647. **2.** a female given name.

mar•i•nade (*n.* mar′ə nād′; *v.* mar′ə nād′), *n., v.,* **-nad•ed, -nad•ing.** —*n.* **1.** a seasoned liquid, usually of vinegar or wine with oil, herbs, spices, etc., in which meat, fish, vegetables, etc., are steeped before cooking. **2.** meat, fish, vegetables, etc., steeped in it. —*v.t.* **3.** to marinate. [1675–85; < F < Pr *marinado,* n. use of fem. ptp. of *mariná* to cure meat or fish in brine, v. deriv. of *marin* MARINE]

ma•ri•na•ra (mär′ə när′ə, mar′ə nar′ə), *n.* **1.** *Italian Cookery.* a highly seasoned sauce of tomatoes, garlic, and spices. —*adj.* **2.** garnished or served with marinara: *shrimps marinara.* [1945–50; < It (*alla*) *marinara* lit., in sailor's style, fem. of *marinaro* seafaring (adj.), sailor (n.) (dial., for Tuscan *marinaio*), equiv. to *marin(a)* sea, n. use of fem. of *marino* MARINE + *-aro* < L *-ārius* -ARY]

mar•i•nate (mar′ə nāt′), *v.t.,* **-nat•ed, -nat•ing.** to steep (food) in a marinade. [1635–45; prob. < It *marinato,* ptp. of *marinare* to pickle. See MARINE, -ATE[1]] —**mar′i•na′tion,** *n.*

Ma•rin•du•que (*Sp.* mä′rēn do͞o′ke), *n.* an island of the Philippines, between Luzon and Mindoro islands. 173,715. 347 sq. mi. (899 sq. km).

ma•rine (mə rēn′), *adj.* **1.** of or pertaining to the sea; existing in or produced by the sea: *marine vegetation.* **2.** pertaining to navigation or shipping; nautical; naval; maritime. **3.** serving on shipboard, as soldiers. **4.** of or belonging to the marines. **5.** adapted for use at sea: *a marine barometer.* —*n.* **6.** a member of the U.S. Marine Corps. **7.** one of a class of naval troops serving both on shipboard and on land. **8.** seagoing ships collectively, esp. with reference to nationality or class; shipping in general. **9.** a picture with a marine subject; seascape. **10.** naval affairs, or the department of a government, as in France, having to do with such affairs. **11. dead marine,** *Australian Slang.* an empty bottle of beer or spirits. **12. tell it** or **that to the marines!** I don't believe your story; I refuse to be fooled. [1325–75; ME *maryne* < MF *marin* (fem. *marine*) < L *marīnus* of the sea, deriv. of *mare* sea; see -INE[1]]

marine′ archaeol′ogy, the branch of archaeology that deals with the recovery of ancient objects found beneath the sea, as shipwrecks or remains from submerged islands, and with the techniques of underwater exploration, excavation, and retrieval. Also called **nautical archaeology, underwater archaeology.**

marine′ barom′eter, a barometer for use on shipboard, esp. one mounted on gimbals so as to minimize the effects of the motion of the vessel. [1695–1705]

marine′ belt′. See **territorial waters.** [1755–65]

Marine′ Corps′, a branch of the U.S. Armed Forces trained for land, sea, and air combat, typically for land combat in conjunction with an amphibious or airborne landing, and whose commandant is responsible to the secretary of the navy. [1790–1800, *Amer.*]

marine′ engineer′, an officer who operates, maintains, and repairs the machinery of a ship. [1930–35]

marine′ engineer′ing, the branch of mechanical engineering that deals with the design, construction, installation, operation, and repair of the machinery of vessels.

marine′ geol′ogy, the branch of geology dealing with the rocks, sediments, and processes of the floors and margins of the oceans. —**marine′ geol′ogist.**

marine′ glue′, a tarlike composition for coating the seams of a planked deck after caulking. [1840–50]

marine′ insur′ance, 1. See **ocean marine insurance. 2.** See **inland marine insurance.** [1795–1805]

marine′ i′vy, a vine, *Cissus incisa,* of the grape family, native to the southern U.S., having three leaflets or three-lobed leaves and black fruit, grown as a houseplant. [1930–35]

marine′ league′, a unit of 3 nautical miles (5.6 km).

mar•i•ner (mar′ə nər), *n.* **1.** a person who directs or assists in the navigation of a ship; sailor. **2.** (*cap.*) *Aerospace.* one of a series of U.S. space probes that obtained scientific information while flying by or orbiting around the planets Mars, Mercury, and Venus. [1250–1300; ME < AF; OF *marinier.* See MARINE, -ER[2]]
—**Syn. 1.** seafarer. See **sailor.**

marine′ rail′way, a railway having a rolling cradle for hauling ships out of water onto land and returning them. Also called **slipway;** *Brit.,* **patent slip.** [1815–25, *Amer.*]

mar′iner's com′pass, 1. a compass used for navigational purposes, consisting of a pivoted compass card in a gimbal-mounted, nonferrous metal bowl. **2.** (*cap.*) *Astron.* compass (def. 8a). [1620–30]

marine′ superintend′ent, a person who is responsible for the maintenance of the vessels of a shipping line, for their docking and the handling of cargo, and for the hiring of personnel for deck departments. Also called **port captain, port superintendent.**

Mar•i•nette (mar′ə net′), *n.* a city in NE Wisconsin. 11,965.

Ma•ri•net•ti (mar′ə net′ē; *It.* mä′rē net′tē), *n.* **E•mi•lio Fi•lip•po Tom•ma•so** (e mē′lyô fē lēp′pô tôm mä′zô), 1876–1944, Italian writer.

Ma•rin•gá (mä′rēn gä′), *n.* a city in S Brazil. 111,773.

mar•in•gouin (mar′ən gwan′; *Fr.* ma ran gwan′), *n., pl.* **-gouins** (-gwanz′; *Fr.* -gwan′). *Louisiana.* a mosquito, esp. a large swamp mosquito. [< LaF, F; earlier *maringoin, marigon,* said to be < Tupi *marui(m), mbarigui*]

Ma•ri•ni (mə rē′nē; *It.* mä rē′nē), *n.* **1. Giam•bat•tis•ta** (jäm′bät tēs′tä). Also, **Ma•ri•no** (mə rē′nō; *It.* mä-rē′nô). (*"il Cavalier Marino"*) 1569–1625, Italian poet. **2. Ma•ri•no** (mə rē′ nō; *It.* mä rē′nô), 1901–80, Italian sculptor and painter.

Ma•ri•nus I (mə rī′nəs), died A.D. 884, pope 882–884. Also called **Martin II.**

Marinus II, died A.D. 946, pope 942–946. Also called **Martin III.**

Ma•ri•o (mär′ē ō′, mar′-; *It.* mä′ryô), *n.* a male given name: from the Roman family name *Marius.*

Mar•i•ol•a•try (mâr′ē ol′ə trē), *n.* **1.** excessive (and proscribed) veneration of the Virgin Mary, esp. in forms appropriate to God. **2.** veneration of women. [1605–15; MARY + -O- + -LATRY] —**Mar′i•ol′a•ter,** *n.* —**Mar′i•ol′a•trous,** *adj.*

Mar•i•ol•o•gist (mâr′ē ol′ə jist), *n.* a student of Mariology. [MARIOLOG(Y) + -IST]

Mar•i•ol•o•gy (mâr′ē ol′ə jē), *n.* **1.** the body of belief, doctrine, and opinion concerning the Virgin Mary. **2.** the study of the person and nature of the Virgin Mary, esp. in reference to her role in the incarnation of God in Christ. [1855–60; MARY + -O- + -LOGY]

Mar•i•on (mar′ē ən, mâr′-), *n.* **1. Francis,** (*"the Swamp Fox"*), 1732?–95, American Revolutionary general. **2.** a city in central Ohio. 37,040. **3.** a city in central Indiana. 35,874. **4.** a city in E Iowa. 19,474. **5.** a city in S Illinois. 14,031. **6.** a male or female given name.

mar•i•on•ette (mar′ē ə net′), *n.* a puppet manipulated from above by strings attached to its jointed limbs. [1610–20; < F *marionnette,* equiv. to *Marion* (dim. of *Marie* Mary) + *-ette* -ETTE]

Mar•i•otte's′ law′ (mar′ē ots′, mar′ē ots′), *Thermo-*

dynam. See **Boyle's law.** [1895–1900; named after Edme *Mariotte* (d. 1684), French physicist]

mar•i•po/sa lil/y (mar′ə pō′sə, -zə), any lily of the genus *Calochortus,* of the western U.S. and Mexico, having tuliplike flowers of various colors. Also called **mar/i•po/sa, maripo/sa tu/lip.** [1880–85, *Amer.*; < Sp *mariposa* butterfly, moth; so named because blooms were likened to butterflies]

Mar•is (mar′is), *n.* **Roger (Eugene),** 1934–85, U.S. baseball player.

mar•ish (mar′ish), *Archaic.* —*n.* **1.** a marsh. —*adj.* **2.** marshy. [1300–50; ME *mareis* < MF; see MARAIS]

Mar•i•sat (mar′ə sat′), *n.* one of a series of geostationary communications satellites that relay telecommunications between ships at sea and shore stations. [*mari(time) sat(ellite)*]

Mar•i•sol (mar′i sol′), *n.* (*Marisol Escubar*) born 1930, Venezuelan artist, in U.S. since 1950.

Mar•ist (mâr′ist, mar′-), *n. Rom. Cath. Ch.* a member of a religious order founded in Lyons, France, in 1816 for missionary and educational work in the name of the Virgin Mary. [1875–80; < F *Mariste.* See MARY, -IST]

Ma•ri•tain (MA RĒ TAN′), *n.* **Jacques** (zhäk), 1882–1973, French philosopher and diplomat.

mar•i•tal (mar′i tl), **1.** of or pertaining to marriage; conjugal; matrimonial: *marital vows; marital discord.* **2.** *Archaic.* of or pertaining to a husband. [1595–1605; < L *marītālis* of married people, deriv. of *marītus* of marriage. See MARRY[1], -AL[1]] —**mar/i•tal•ly,** *adv.*

mar/ital ther/apy, a psychotherapeutic treatment for married couples, who are seen by a therapist both individually and jointly to assist them in resolving various problems related to their marriage.

mar•i•time (mar′i tīm′), *adj.* **1.** connected with the sea in relation to navigation, shipping, etc. **2.** of or pertaining to the sea: *maritime resources.* **3.** bordering on the sea: *maritime provinces.* **4.** living near or in the sea: *maritime plants.* **5.** characteristic of a sailor; nautical: *maritime clothing.* [1540–50; < L *maritimus* pertaining to the sea, equiv. to *mari-* (s. of *mare* sea) + *-timus* adj. suffix]

Mar/itime Alps/, a range of the Alps in SE France and NW Italy.

mar/itime belt/, *Law.* the part of the sea that is within the jurisdiction of the bordering states.

mar/itime law/, the body of law relating to maritime commerce and navigation, and to maritime matters generally. [1860–65]

Mar/itime Prov/inces, the Canadian provinces of Nova Scotia, New Brunswick, and Prince Edward Island. Also called **Mar/i•times/.** —**Mar/i•tim/er,** *n.*

Ma•ri•tsa (mə rēt′sə), *n.* a river in S Europe, flowing from S Bulgaria along the boundary between Greece and European Turkey and into the Aegean. 300 mi. (485 km) long.

Ma•ri•u•pol (mar′ē ōō′pəl; *Russ.* mə RYi ōō′pəl), *n.* a city in SE Ukraine, on the Sea of Azov. 503,000. Formerly (1948–89), **Zhdanov.**

Mar•i•us (mâr′ē əs, mar′-), *n.* **Gaius,** c155–86 B.C., Roman general and consul: opponent of Lucius Cornelius Sulla.

Ma•ri•vaux (MA RĒ VŌ′), *n.* **Pierre Car•let de Cham•blain de** (pyer KAR le′ də shäN blaN′ də), 1688–1763, French dramatist and novelist.

mar•jo•laine (mär′jə lān′; *Fr.* MAR zhô len′), *n., pl.* **-laines** (-lānz′; *Fr.* -len′) for 2. **1.** (*italics*) *French.* marjoram. **2.** a long, narrow cake with straight sides, usually consisting of layers of meringue and chocolate butter-cream and containing chopped nuts. [< F; OF *majorane* < ML *majorana;* see MARJORAM]

mar•jo•ram (mär′jər əm), *n.* any of several aromatic herbs belonging to the genus *Origanum,* of the mint family, esp. *O. majorana* **(sweet marjoram),** having leaves used as seasoning in cooking. Cf. **oregano.** [1350–1400; ME *majorane* < ML *majorana,* var. of *majoraca,* alter. of L *amāracus* < Gk *amárakos* marjoram]

Mar•jo•ry (mär′jə rē), *n.* a female given name, form of **Margaret.** Also, **Mar/jo•rie.**

mark[1] (märk), *n.* **1.** a visible impression or trace on something, as a line, cut, dent, stain, or bruise: *a small mark on his arm.* **2.** a badge, brand, or other visible sign assumed or imposed: *a mark of his noble rank.* **3.** a symbol used in writing or printing: *a punctuation mark.* **4.** a sign, usually an X or cross, made instead of a signature by someone who does not know how or is unable to write his or her own name. **5.** an affixed or impressed device, symbol, inscription, etc., serving to give information, identify, indicate origin or ownership, attest to character or comparative merit, or the like, as a trademark. **6.** a sign, token, or indication: *to bow as a mark of respect.* **7.** a symbol used in rating conduct, proficiency, attainment, etc., as of pupils in a school: *good marks; bad marks.* **8.** something serving as an indication of position, as a landmark. **9.** a recognized or required standard of quality, accomplishment, etc.; norm: *His dissertation was below the mark.* **10.** distinction or importance; repute; note: *a man of mark.* **11.** a distinctive trait or characteristic: *the usual marks of a gentleman.* **12.** (*usually cap.*) *U.S. Mil.* a designation for an item of military equipment in production, used in combination with a numeral to indicate the order of adoption, and often abbreviated: *a Mark-4 tank; an M-1 rifle.* **13.** an object aimed at; target: *to aim at the mark.* **14.** an object or end desired or striven for; goal. **15.** *Slang.* **a.** an object of derision, scorn, manipulation, or the like: *He was an easy mark for criticism.* **b.** the intended victim of a swindler, hustler, or the like: *The cardsharps picked their marks from among the tourists on the cruise ship.* **16.** *Track.* the starting line. **17.** *Boxing.* the middle of the stomach. **18.** *Lawn Bowling.* jack[1] (def. 17). **19.** *Bowling.* a strike or spare. **20.** *Naut.* any of the distinctively marked points on a deep-sea lead line, occurring at levels of 2, 3, 5, 7, 10, 13, 15, 17, and 20 fathoms above the lead. Cf. **deep** (def. 35). **21.** a tract of land that may have been held in common by a primitive or early medieval community of peasants in Germany. **22.** *Archaic or Hist.* a boundary; frontier. **23. beside the mark,** not pertinent; irrelevant. **24. bless** or **save the mark!** (used as an exclamation of disapproval, contempt, impatience, etc.) Also, **God bless** or **save the mark! 25. make one's mark,** to attain success or fame; achieve one's ambition: *He set out to make his mark as a writer.* **26. on your mark** or **marks!** (in calling the start of a race) take your places: *On your mark! Get set! Go!* Also, **get ready!, ready! 27. wide of the mark,** far from the target or objective; inaccurate or irrelevant: *My first guess was wide of the mark.*
—*v.t.* **28.** to be a distinguishing feature of: *a day marked by rain.* **29.** to put a mark or marks on: *to mark each box with an X.* **30.** to give a grade for; put a grade on: *to mark the final exams.* **31.** scent-mark (def. 2). **32.** to furnish with figures, signs, tags, etc., to indicate price, quality, brand name, or the like: *We marked all the books with prices.* **33.** to trace or form by or as if by marks (often fol. by *out*): *to mark out a plan of attack.* **34.** to indicate or designate by or as if by marks: *to mark passages to be memorized.* **35.** to single out; destine (often fol. by *out*): *to be marked out for promotion.* **36.** to record, as a score. **37.** to make manifest: *to mark approval with a nod.* **38.** to give heed or attention to: *Mark my words!* **39.** to notice or observe: *to mark a change in the weather.*
—*v.i.* **40.** to take notice; give attention; consider. **41.** scent-mark (def. 1). **42. mark down,** to reduce the price of: *These towels have been marked down.* **43. mark off,** to mark the proper dimensions or boundaries of; separate: *We marked off the limits of our lot with stakes.* **44. mark time.** See **time** (def. 45). **45. mark up, a.** to mar or deface with marks. **b.** to mark with notations or symbols. **c.** to fix the selling price of (an article) by adding to the seller's cost an amount to cover expenses and profit: *to mark up dresses 50 percent.* **d.** to increase the selling price of. [bef. 900; (n.) ME; OE *mearc* mark, sign, banner, dividing line, borderland; c. G *Mark* borderland, unit of weight, ON *mǫrk* forest (orig., borderland), unit of weight, Goth *marka* boundary, borderland, L *margō* MARGIN; (v.) ME *marken,* OE *mearcian;* c. OFris *merkia,* OHG *marchōn,* ON *marka* to plan]
—**Syn. 10.** eminence, consequence. **11.** feature, stamp, print. **14.** purpose, objective. **34.** identify, label, tag. **37, 38.** note. **39.** eye, regard, spot.

mark[2] (märk), *n.* **1.** the monetary unit of Germany since 1871: originally a silver coin. Cf. **Deutsche mark, ostmark, reichsmark. 2.** the markka of Finland. **3.** Also, **merk.** a former silver coin of Scotland, equal to 13s. 4d. **4.** a former money of account of England, equal to 13s. 4d. **5.** a former coin of Estonia, the 1/100th part of a kroon: replaced by the sent after 1927. **6.** a former European unit of weight, esp. for gold and silver, generally equal to 8 ounces (249 grams). [bef. 900; ME; OE *marc* unit of weight < ML *marca* < Gmc; see MARK[1]]

Mark (märk), *n.* **1.** one of the four Evangelists: traditionally believed to be the author of the second Gospel. **2.** the second Gospel: *to read aloud from Mark.* **3. King,** *Arthurian Romance.* ruler of Cornwall, husband of Iseult and uncle of Sir Tristram. **4. Saint.** See **Marcus, Saint. 5.** a male given name, form of **Marcus.**

Mar•kan (mär′kən), *adj.* Marcan.

Mark An•to•ny (märk an′tə nē). See **Antony, Mark.**

mark•down (märk′doun′), *n.* **1.** a reduction in price, usually to encourage buying. **2.** the amount by which a price is reduced. [*Amer.*; n. use of v. phrase *mark down*]

marked (märkt), *adj.* **1.** strikingly noticeable; conspicuous: *with marked success.* **2.** watched as an object of suspicion or vengeance: *a marked man.* **3.** having a mark or marks: *beautifully marked birds; to read the marked pages.* **4.** *Ling.* **a.** (of a phoneme) characterized by the presence of a phonological feature that serves to distinguish it from an otherwise similar phoneme lacking that feature, as (d), which, in contrast to (t), is characterized by the presence of voicing. **b.** characterized by the presence of a marker indicating the grammatical function of a construction, as the plural in English, which, in contrast to the singular, is typically indicated by the presence of the marker *-s.* **c.** specifying an additional element of meaning, in contrast to a semantically related item, as *drake* in contrast to *duck,* where *drake* specifies "male" while *duck* does not necessarily specify sex. **d.** occurring less typically than an alternative form, as the word order in *Down he fell* in contrast to the more usual order of *He fell down.* Cf. **unmarked** (def. 2). [ME; OE *gemearcod;* see MARK[1], -ED[2]] —**mark•ed•ly** (mär′kid lē), *adv.* —**mark/ed•ness,** *n.*
—**Syn. 1.** striking, outstanding, obvious, prominent.

mark•er (mär′kər), *n.* **1.** a person or thing that marks. **2.** something used as a mark or indication, as a bookmark or tombstone. **3.** a person who records the scores, points, etc., as in a game or contest. **4.** a counter used in card playing. **5.** *Genetics.* See **genetic marker. 6.** *Psychol.* an object, as a book or topcoat left at a library table, used to establish territorial possession in a public place. **7.** *Ling.* **a.** an element of a construction, as a coordinating conjunction, that is not a part of either immediate constituent. **b.** an element that indicates the grammatical class or function of a construction. **8.** a small radio beacon, automatically operated, used for local navigation of vessels. **9.** mile-marker. **10.** Also called **mark/er pen/, marking pen.** a pen designed for making bold, colorful, or indelible marks, as in making signs. **11.** *Slang.* **a.** a debt, esp. a gambling debt. **b.** a written or signed promise to pay a debt, esp. a gambling debt; a promissory note or IOU. **12.** Also called **mark/er crude/.** *Com.* a grade of oil on which prices of other crude oils are based. **13.** *CB Radio Slang.* one's location while driving on a highway, as determined by the nearest milepost. [1480–90; MARK[1] + -ER[1]]

mark/er gene/, *Genetics.* See **genetic marker.**

mar•ket (mär′kit), *n.* **1.** an open place or a covered building where buyers and sellers convene for the sale of goods; a marketplace: *a farmers' market.* **2.** a store for the sale of food: *a meat market.* **3.** a meeting of people for selling and buying. **4.** the assemblage of people at such a meeting. **5.** trade or traffic, esp. as regards a particular commodity: *the market in cotton.* **6.** a body of persons carrying on extensive transactions in a specified commodity: *the cotton market.* **7.** the field of trade or business: *the best shoes in the market.* **8.** demand for a commodity: *an unprecedented market for leather.* **9.** a body of existing or potential buyers for specific goods or services: *the health-food market.* **10.** a region in which goods and services are bought, sold, or used: *the foreign market; the New England market.* **11.** current price or value: *a rising market for shoes.* **12.** See **stock market. 13. at the market,** at the prevailing price in the open market. **14. in the market for,** ready to buy; interested in buying: *I'm in the market for a new car.* **15. on the market,** for sale; available: *Fresh asparagus will be on the market this week.* —*v.i.* **16.** to buy or sell in a market; deal. **17.** to buy food and provisions for the home. —*v.t.* **18.** to carry or send to market for disposal: *to market produce every week.* **19.** to dispose of in a market; sell. [1100–1150; ME, late OE < VL **marcātus,* L *mercātus* trading, traffic, market] —**mar/ket•er,** *n.*
—**Syn. 19.** vend, merchandise, peddle.

mar•ket•a•ble (mär′ki tə bəl), *adj.* **1.** readily salable. **2.** of or pertaining to selling or buying: *marketable values; marketable areas.* [1590–1600; MARKET + -ABLE] —**mar/ket•a•bil/i•ty, mar/ket•a•ble•ness,** *n.* —**mar/•ket•a•bly,** *adv.*

mar/ketable ti/tle, *Law.* a title to real property that is free from encumbrances, litigation, and other defects and that can readily be sold or mortgaged to a reasonable buyer or mortgagee. Also called **good title, merchantable title, sound title.**

mar/ket anal/ysis, *Com.* the process of determining factors, conditions, and characteristics of a market. —**mar/ket an/alyst.**

mar/ket boat/, 1. a boat that transfers fish from a fishing fleet to a market on shore. **2.** a boat for carrying produce to market. **3.** a boat assigned or used to bring provisions to a ship. [1770–80, *Amer.*]

mar/ket crab/. See **dungeness crab.**

mar•ket•eer (mär′ki tēr′), *n.* a person who sells goods or services in or to a market. [1825–35; MARKET + -EER]

mar/ket gar/den, 1. a garden or farm for growing vegetables to be shipped esp. to local or nearby markets. Cf. **truck farm. 2.** *Brit.* See **truck farm. 3.** (*caps.*) *Mil.* the Allied code name for the unsuccessful invasion of Holland by British and American airborne and infantry forces on September 17, 1944. [1805–15] —**mar/ket gar/dener.** —**mar/ket gar/dening.**

mar•ket•ing (mär′ki ting), *n.* **1.** the act of buying or selling in a market. **2.** the total of activities involved in the transfer of goods from the producer or seller to the consumer or buyer, including advertising, shipping, storing, and selling. [1555–65; MARKET + -ING[1]]

mar/ket let/ter, a publication containing information concerning market conditions, expectations, etc., esp. one produced by a securities brokerage firm or other financial organization.

mar/ket or/der, *Stock Exchange.* an order to buy or sell a specified amount of a security at the best price available. Cf. **limit order, stop order.** [1915–20]

mar•ket•place (mär′kit plās′), *n.* **1.** an open area in a town where a market is held. **2.** the commercial world; the realm of business, trade, and economics. **3.** any sphere considered as a place where ideas, thoughts, artistic creations, etc., compete for recognition. Also, **mar/ket place/.** [1350–1400; ME; see MARKET, PLACE]

mar/ket price/, the price at which a commodity, security, or service is selling in the open market. Also called **market value.** [1400–50; late ME]

mar/ket re/search, the gathering and studying of data relating to consumer preferences, purchasing power, etc., esp. prior to introducing a product on the market. [1925–30]

mar•ket-re•search (mär′kit rē′sûrch, -ri sûrch′), *v.t.* to conduct market research on. [1965–70]

mar/ket share/, *Econ.* the specific percentage of total industry sales of a particular product achieved by a single company in a given period of time.

mar/ket town/, a town where a regularly scheduled market is held. [1400–50; late ME]

mar/ket val/ue, 1. the value of a business, property, etc., in terms of what it can be sold for on the open market; current value (distinguished from *book value*). **2.** See **market price.** [1685–95]

Mar•ke•vich (mär kā′vich; *Russ.* MUR kye′vyich), *n.* **I•gor** (ē′gôR), 1912–83, Russian conductor and composer.

Mark•ham (mär′kəm), *n.* **1. (Charles) Edwin,** 1852–1940, U.S. poet. **2. Mount,** a mountain in Antarctica, SW of the Ross Sea. 15,100 ft. (4600 m). **3.** a town in SE Ontario, in S Canada, near Toronto. 77,037. **4.** a city in NE Illinois, near Chicago. 15,172.

mar•khoor (mär′ko͝or), *n., pl.* **-khoors,** (*esp. collectively*) **-khoor.** markhor.

mar•khor (mär′kôr), *n., pl.* **-khors,** (*esp. collectively*) **-khor.** a wild goat, *Capra falconeri,* of mountainous regions from Afghanistan to India, having compressed, spiral horns and long, shaggy hair: all populations are threatened or endangered. Also, **markhoor.** [1865–70;

CONCISE PRONUNCIATION KEY: *act, cāpe, dâre, pärt; set, ēqual; if, īce; ox, ōver, ôrder, oil, bo͝ok, bo͞ot, out; up, ûrge; child; sing; shoe; thin, that;* zh as in *treasure.* ə = *a* as in *alone, e* as in *system, i* as in *easily, o* as in *gallop, u* as in *circus;* ° as in *fire* (fī°r), *hour* (ou°r). l and n can serve as syllabic consonants, as in *cradle* (krād′l), and *button* (but′n). See the full key inside the front cover.

< Pers mārkhōr lit., serpent-eater, equiv. to *mār* snake + *-khōr* eating; cf. MANTICORE]

mark·ing (mär′king), *n.* **1.** a mark, or a number or pattern of marks: *birds with colorful markings.* **2.** the act of a person or thing that marks: *the marking of papers.* [1275–1325; ME; see MARK[1], -ING[1]]

mark′ing gage′, *Carpentry.* any of various adjustable tools for marking a line parallel to a straight edge against which the tool is moved. [1870–75]

mark′ing pen′, marker (def. 10).

mark·ka (märk′kä), *n., pl.* **-kaa** (-kä). a cupronickel or bronze coin and monetary unit of Finland, equal to 100 pennia; finmark. *Abbr.:* F.Mk., M. [1900–05; < Finnish < G *Mark;* see MARK[2]]

mark′ of the beast′, *Theol.* **1.** the mark put on the forehead of those who worship the beast, the symbol of opposition to God. **2.** the stain of apostasy, regarded as both indelible and inescapable. Rev. 13:16. [1350–1400; ME]

Mar·ko·va (mär kō′və), *n.* **Alicia,** (*Lilian Alicia Marks*), born 1910, English ballet dancer.

Mar′kov chain′ (mär′kôf), *Statistics.* a Markov process restricted to discrete random events or to discontinuous time sequences. Also, **Mar′koff chain′** (mär′kôf). [1940–45; see MARKOV PROCESS]

Mar′kov proc′ess, *Statistics.* a process in which future values of a random variable are statistically determined by present events and dependent only on the event immediately preceding. Also, **Mar′koff proc′ess.** [1935–40; after Russian mathematician Andreĭ Andreevich *Markov* (1856–1922), who developed it]

marks·man (märks′mən), *n., pl.* **-men. 1.** a person who is skilled in shooting at a mark; a person who shoots well. **2.** *Mil.* **a.** the lowest rating in rifle marksmanship, below that of sharpshooter and expert. **b.** a person who has achieved such a rating. [1645–55; MARK[1] + 'S[1] + -MAN] **—marks′man·ship′,** *n.*
—Usage. See **-man.**

marks·wom·an (märks′wo͝om′ən), *n., pl.* **-wom·en.** a woman skilled in shooting at a mark; a woman who shoots well. [1795–1805; MARK[1] + 'S[1] + -WOMAN]
—Usage. See **-woman.**

mark·up (märk′up′), *n.* **1.** *Com.* **a.** the amount added by a seller to the cost of a commodity to cover expenses and profit in fixing the selling price. **b.** the difference between the cost price and the selling price, computed as a percentage of either the selling price or the cost price. **c.** an increase in price, as of a commodity. **d.** the amount by which a price is increased. **2.** the putting of a legislative bill into final form. **3.** a detailed instruction, usually written on a manuscript to be typeset, concerning style of type, makeup of pages, and the like. [1915–20; n. use of v. phrase *mark up*]

marl[1] (märl), *n.* **1.** *Geol.* a friable earthy deposit consisting of clay and calcium carbonate, used esp. as a fertilizer for soils deficient in lime. **2.** *Archaic.* earth. *—v.t.* **3.** to fertilize with marl. [1325–75; ME *marle* < MD < OF < ML *margila,* dim. of L *marga,* said to be < Gaulish] **—mar·la·cious** (mär lā′shəs), **marl′y,** *adj.*

marl[2] (märl), *v.t. Naut.* to wind (a rope) with marline, every turn being secured by a hitch. [1400–50; late ME *marlyn* to ensnare; akin to OE *mǣrels* cable. See MOOR[2]]

Marl·bor·o (märl′bûr ō, -bur ō), *n., pl.* **-bor·os** for 2. **1.** a city in E Massachusetts. 30,617. **2.** (*l.c.*) a twisted, usually iced cruller, combining strands of plain and chocolate dough.

Marl·bor·ough (märl′bûr ō, -bur ō *or, for 1,* -brə, môl′-), *n.* **1. John Churchill, 1st Duke of.** See **Churchill, John, 1st Duke of Marlborough. 2.** Marlboro (def. 1).

Marl′borough leg′, *Furniture.* a tapered leg having a square section.

marled (märld), *adj.* fertilized with marl. [1600–10; MARL[1] + -ED[3]]

Mar·lene (mär lēn′, -lā′nə), *n.* a female given name. Also, **Mar·leen** (mär lēn′), **Mar·le·na** (mär lā′nə).

mar·lin[1] (mär′lin), *n., pl.* (*esp. collectively*) **-lin,** (*esp. referring to two or more kinds or species*) **-lins.** any large, saltwater game fish of the genera *Makaira* and *Tetrapterus,* having the upper jaw elongated into a spearlike structure. [1915–20, *Amer.;* short for MARLINESPIKE]

mar·lin[2] (mär′lin), *n.* marline.

Mar·lin (mär′lin), *n.* a male given name.

mar·line (mär′lin), *n. Naut.* small stuff of two-fiber strands, sometimes tarred, laid up left-handed. Also, **marlin, mar·ling** (mär′ling). [1375–1425; late ME *merlin.* See MARL[2], LINE[1]]

mar·line·spike (mär′lin spīk′), *n. Naut.* a pointed iron implement used in separating the strands of rope in splicing, marling, etc. Also, **mar′lin·spike′, mar·ling·spike** (mär′ling spīk′). [1620–30; orig. *marling spike.* See MARL[2], -ING[1], SPIKE[1]]

Mar·lon (mär′lən), *n.* a male given name.

Mar·lo·vi·an (mär lō′vē ən), *adj.* of, pertaining to, or characteristic of Christopher Marlowe or his writings, esp. his plays. [1585–95; MARLOWE (Latinization with *-v-* substitution) + -IAN]

Mar·lowe (mär′lō), *n.* **1. Christopher,** 1564–93, English dramatist and poet. **2. Julia** (*Sarah Frances Frost Sothern*), 1866–1950, U.S. actress born in England (wife of E. H. Sothern).

CONCISE ETYMOLOGY KEY: <, descended or borrowed from; >, whence; b., blend of, blended; c., cognate with; cf., compare; deriv., derivative; equiv., equivalent; imit., imitative; obl., oblique; r., replacing; s., stem; sp., spelling, spelled; resp., respelling, respelled; trans., translation; ?, origin unknown; *, unattested; ‡, probably earlier than. See the full key inside the front cover.

marl·stone (märl′stōn′), *n.* an indurated marl. Also called **marl·ite** (mär′līt). [1830–40; MARL[1] + STONE]

mar·ma·lade (mär′mə lād′, mär′mə lād′), *n.* a jellylike preserve in which small pieces of fruit and fruit rind, as of oranges or lemons, are suspended. [1515–25; < Pg *marmelada* quince jam, deriv. of *marmelo* quince < L *melimēlum* a kind of apple < Gk *melímēlon* (*méli* honey + *mêlon* a fruit); see -ADE[1]]

mar′malade box′, genipap. [1790–1800]

mar′malade bush′, a shrub, *Streptosolen jamesonii,* of the nightshade family, native to South America, bearing showy trumpet-shaped orange flowers, grown as an ornamental or houseplant.

mar′malade plum′, sapote. [1880–85]

mar′malade tree′, sapote (def. 1). [1865–70]

Mar·ma·ra (mär′mər ə), *n.* **Sea of,** a sea in NW Turkey, between European and Asian Turkey, connected with the Black Sea by the Bosporus, and with the Aegean by the Dardanelles. 4300 sq. mi. (11,135 sq. km). Also, **Mar·mo·ra** (mär′mər ə, mär môr′ə, -mōr′ə).

Mar.Mech.E., Marine Mechanical Engineer.

Mar′mes man′ (mär′məs), the skeletal remains of *Homo sapiens* found in Washington State in 1965 and dating from about 9000 B.C. [after the *Marmes* ranch, where the remains were discovered]

mar·mite (mär′mīt, mär mēt′), *n.* a metal or earthenware cooking pot with a cover, usually large and often having legs. [1795–1805; < F, MF, appar. equiv. to *mar(m)-,* base of *marmotter* to mutter, murmur (see MARMOT) + *mite* expressive word for a cat; prob. orig. a jocular or nursery word, a deep, covered pot being thought of as secretive and hence catlike in comparison to an open pan; cf. OF *marmite* hypocritical]

Mar·mo·la·da (mär′mô lä′dä), *n.* a mountain in N Italy: highest peak of the Dolomites, 11,020 ft. (3360 m).

mar·mo·re·al (mär môr′ē əl, -mōr′-), *adj.* of or like marble: *skin of marmoreal smoothness.* Also, **mar·mo′re·an.** [1790–1800; < L *marmore(us)* made of marble (see MARBLE, -EOUS) + -AL[1]] **—mar·mo′re·al·ly,** *adv.*

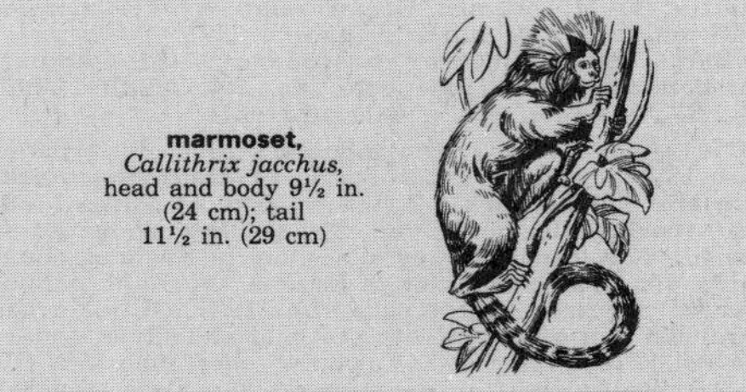

marmoset, *Callithrix jacchus,* head and body 9½ in. (24 cm); tail 11½ in. (29 cm)

mar·mo·set (mär′mə zet′, -set′), *n.* any of several small, squirrellike, South and Central American monkeys of the genera *Callithrix, Leontocebus,* etc., having soft fur and a long, nonprehensile tail: some species are endangered. [1350–1400; ME *marmusette* a kind of monkey, an idol < OF *marmouset,* appar. equiv. to *marmos(er)* to murmur (*marm-* (see MARMOT) + *-oser* v. suffix) + *-et* -ET]

mar·mot (mär′mət), *n.* **1.** any bushy-tailed, stocky rodent of the genus *Marmota,* as the woodchuck. **2.** any of certain related animals, as the prairie dogs. [1600–10; < F *marmotte,* OF, appar. n. deriv. of *marmotter* to mutter, murmur (referring to the whistling noises made by such animals), equiv. to *marm-* imit. base denoting a variety of indistinct, continuous sounds (cf. MURMUR) + *-ot(t)er* suffix of expressive verbs (though v. is attested only in mod. F)]

marmot, *Marmota caligata,* head and body 20 in. (50 cm); tail 10 in. (25 cm)

Marne (märn; *Fr.* MARN), *n.* **1.** a river in NE France, flowing W to the Seine near Paris: battles 1914, 1918, 1944. 325 mi. (525 km) long. **2.** a department in N France. 530,399; 3168 sq. mi. (8205 sq. km). *Cap.:* Châlons-sur-Marne.

Ma·roc (MA RÔK′), *n.* French name of **Morocco.**

mar·o·cain (mar′ə kān′, mar′ə kān′), *n.* a crepe fabric made of silk, wool, or rayon, or a combination of these fibers, and distinguished by a strong rib effect, used in the manufacture of dresses and women's suits; a heavy Canton crepe. Also called **crepe marocain.** [1920–25; < F (*crêpe*) *marocain* Moroccan (crepe)]

Mar·o·nite (mar′ə nīt′), *n.* a member of a body of Uniates living chiefly in Lebanon, who maintain a Syriac liturgy and a married clergy, and who are governed by the patriarch of Antioch. Also called **Mar′onite Chris′tian.** [1505–15; < LL *Marōnīta,* named after St. *Maron,* 4th-century monk, founder of the sect; see -ITE[1]]

ma·roon[1] (mə ro͞on′), *adj.* **1.** dark brownish-red. **2.** *Chiefly Brit.* **a.** a loudly exploding firework consisting of a cardboard container filled with gunpowder. **b.** a similar firework used as a danger or warning signal, as by railway brakemen. [1585–95; < F *marron* lit., chestnut, MF < Upper It (Tuscan *marrone*), perh. ult. deriv. of pre-L *marr-* stone]

ma·roon[2] (mə ro͞on′), *v.t.* **1.** to put ashore and abandon on a desolate island or coast by way of punishment or the like, as was done by buccaneers. **2.** to place in an isolated and often dangerous position: *The rising floodwaters marooned us on top of the house.* **3.** to abandon and leave without aid or resources: *Having lost all his money, he was marooned in the strange city.* —*n.* **4.** (*often cap*) any of a group of blacks, descended from fugitive slaves of the 17th and 18th centuries, living in the West Indies and Guiana, esp. in mountainous areas. **5.** a person who is marooned: *Robinson Crusoe lived for years as a maroon.* [1660–70; < F *mar(r)on,* appar. < AmerSp *cimarrón* wild (see CIMARRON); first used in reference to domestic animals that escaped into the woods, later to fugitive slaves]

ma·ror (*Seph.* mä RÔR′; *Ashk.* mō′RŌR), *n. Hebrew.* a portion of horseradish or other bitter herb that is eaten at the Seder meal on Passover. Also, ***moror.***

Ma·ros (mu′rôsh), *n.* Hungarian name of **Mures.**

ma·rou·flage (mär′ə fläzh′, mär′ə fläzh′), *n.* **1.** a method of attaching a canvas to a wall through adhesion, accomplished by coating the surface with white lead mixed with oil. **2.** a cloth backing for openwork, as on a piece of furniture. [1880–85; < F, equiv. to *maroufl(er)* to attach canvas with strong glue (deriv. of *maroufle* strong glue, appar. a jocular use of *maroufle* rogue, akin to *maraud;* see MARAUD) + *-age* -AGE]

mar·plot (mär′plot′), *n.* a person who mars or defeats a plot, design, or project by meddling. [1700–10; MAR + PLOT]

Marq., 1. Marquess. **2.** Marquis.

Mar·quand (mär kwond′), *n.* **J(ohn) P(hillips),** 1893–1960, U.S. novelist and short-story writer.

marque[1] (märk), *n.* **1.** See **letter of marque. 2.** *Obs.* seizure by way of reprisal or retaliation. [1375–1425; late ME < MF < Pr *marca* seizure by warrant (orig. token) < Gmc; see MARK[1]]

marque[2] (märk), *n.* a product model or type, as of a luxury or racing car. [1905–10; < F: lit., mark, sign, n. deriv. of *marquer* to mark, prob. dial. deriv. of OF *merc, merche* boundary, boundary marker < ON *merki* (from same Gmc base as MARCH[2], MARK[1], MARQUE[1])]

mar·quee (mär kē′), *n.* **1.** a tall rooflike projection above a theater entrance, usually containing the name of a currently featured play or film and its stars. **2.** a rooflike shelter, as of glass, projecting above an outer door and over a sidewalk or a terrace. **3.** Also, **marquess, marquise.** *Brit.* a large tent or tentlike shelter with open sides, esp. one for temporary use in outdoor entertainments, receptions, etc. [1680–90; assumed sing. of MARQUISE, taken as pl.]

marquee (def. 2)

Mar·que·san (mär kā′zən, -sən), *n.* **1.** a Polynesian native of the Marquesas Islands. **2.** the Polynesian language of the Marquesas Islands. —*adj.* **3.** of, pertaining to, or characteristic of the Marquesas Islands, the Marquesans, or their language. [1790–1800; MARQUES(AS ISLANDS) + -AN]

Mar·que′sas Is′lands (mär kā′zəz, -səz, -səs), a group of French islands in the S Pacific. 5593; 480 sq. mi. (1245 sq. km).

mar·quess (mär′kwis), *n. Brit.* **1.** marquee (def. 3). **2.** marquis. [sp. var. of MARQUIS]

mar·que·try (mär′ki trē), *n., pl.* **-tries.** inlaid work of variously colored woods or other materials, esp. in furniture. Also, **mar·que·te·rie** (mär′ki trē). [1555–65; < MF *marqueterie* inlaid work, equiv. to *marquet(er)* to speckle, spot, inlay (lit., make marks < Gmc; see MARK[1]) + *-erie* -ERY]

Mar·quette (mär ket′; *for 1 also Fr.* MAR ket′), *n.* **1. Jacques** (zhäk), ("*Père Marquette*"), 1637–75, French Jesuit missionary and explorer in America. **2.** a city in N Michigan, on Lake Superior. 23,288.

mar·quis (mär′kwis, mär kē′; *Fr.* MAR kē′), *n., pl.* **-quis·es, -quis** (-kēz′; *Fr.* -kē′). a nobleman ranking next below a duke and above an earl or count. Also, *Brit.,* **marquess.** [1250–1300; ME *markis* < MF *marquis* < It *marchese* < ML *(comēs) marc(h)ēnsis* (count) of a borderland. See MARCH[2], -ESE]

Mar·quis (mär′kwis), *n.* **Don(ald Robert Perry),** 1878–1937, U.S. humorist and poet.

mar·quis·ate (mär′kwə zit), *n.* **1.** the rank of a marquis. **2.** the territory ruled by a marquis or a margrave. [1540–50; MARQUIS + -ATE[3], as trans. of F *marquisat,* It *marchesato*]

mar·quise (mär kēz′; *Fr.* MAR kēz′), *n., pl.* **-quis·es** (-kē′ziz; *Fr.* -kēz′). **1.** the wife or widow of a marquis. **2.** a lady holding the rank equal to that of a marquis. **3.** *Jewelry.* **a.** Also called **marquise cut.** a gem cut, esp. for a diamond, yielding a low pointed oval with many facets, usually 58. See illus. on next page. **b.** a gem cut in this style, esp. a diamond. Cf. **navette. 4.** (*often used with a plural v.*) *Brit.* marquee (def. 3). **5.** Also called **marquise′ chair′.** *Fr. Furniture.* a wide bergère. Also, *Brit.,* **marchioness** (for defs. 1, 2). [1700–10; < F; fem. of MARQUIS]

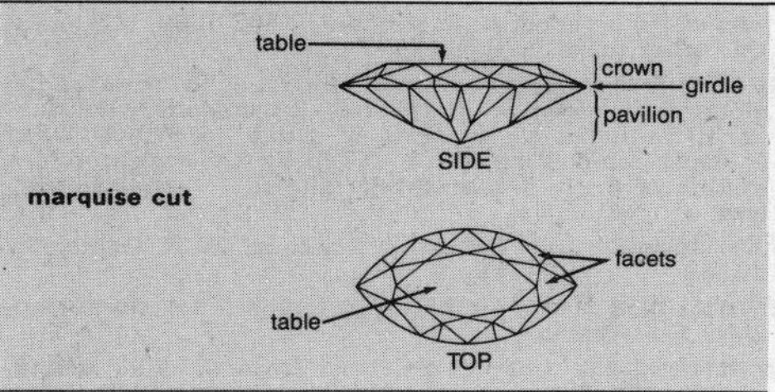

mar•qui•sette (mär′kə zet′, -kwə-), *n.* a lightweight open fabric of leno weave in cotton, rayon, silk, or nylon. [1905–10; < F, dim. of *marquise.* See MARQUISE, -ETTE]

Mar′quis of Queens′ber•ry rules′ (kwēnz′ber′ē, -bə rē), *Boxing.* a set of basic rules for modern boxing, requiring among the main provisions the use of gloves instead of bare knuckles and the 10-second count for a knockout. Also called **Queensberry rules.** [named after Sir John Sholto Douglas (1844–1900), 8th *Marquis of Queensberry,* who supervised the formulation of these rules in 1867]

Mar•ra•kesh (mar′ə kesh′, mar′ə kesh′, mə rä′kesh), *n.* a city in W Morocco. 1,681,700. Also, **Mar′ra•kech′.** Formerly, **Morocco.**

mar′ram grass′ (mar′əm), a grass, *Ammophila arenaria,* having matted, creeping rhizomes, grown on sandy shores of Europe, North America, and Australia to bind the sand. Also called **mar′ram.** [1630–40; orig. East Anglian dial.; < ON *marálmr,* equiv. to *marr* sea (see MERE²) + *hálmr* grass (see HAULM)]

Mar•ran•ism (mə rä′niz əm), *n.* the practices, principles, or condition characteristic of the Marranos. Also, **Mar•ra•no•ism** (mə rä′nō iz′əm). [1730–40; MARRAN(O) + -ISM]

Mar•ra•no (mə rä′nō), *n., pl.* **-nos.** a Spanish or Portuguese Jew who was converted to Christianity during the late Middle Ages, usually under threat of death or persecution, esp. one who continued to adhere to Judaism in secret. [< Sp: lit., pig, from the Jewish law forbidding the eating of pork (prob. < Ar *maḥram* forbidden)]

mar•riage (mar′ij), *n.* **1.** the social institution under which a man and woman establish their decision to live as husband and wife by legal commitments, religious ceremonies, etc. **2.** the state, condition, or relationship of being married; wedlock: *a happy marriage.* **3.** the legal or religious ceremony that formalizes the decision of a man and woman to live as husband and wife, including the accompanying social festivities: *to officiate at a marriage.* **4.** a relationship in which two people have pledged themselves to each other in the manner of a husband and wife, without legal sanction: *trial marriage; homosexual marriage.* **5.** any close or intimate association or union: *the marriage of words and music in a hit song.* **6.** a formal agreement between two companies or enterprises to combine operations, resources, etc., for mutual benefit; merger. **7.** a blending or matching of different elements or components: *The new lipstick is a beautiful marriage of fragrance and texture.* **8.** *Cards.* a meld of the king and queen of a suit, as in pinochle. Cf. **royal marriage.** **9.** a piece of antique furniture assembled from components of two or more authentic pieces. **10.** *Obs.* the formal declaration or contract by which act a man and a woman join in wedlock. [1250–1300; ME *mariage* < OF, equiv. to *mari(er)* to MARRY¹ + *-age* -AGE]
—Syn. 3. matrimony. MARRIAGE, WEDDING, NUPTIALS are terms for the ceremony uniting couples in wedlock. MARRIAGE is the simple and usual term, without implications as to circumstances and without emotional connotations: *to announce the marriage of a daughter.* WEDDING has rather strong emotional, even sentimental, connotations, and suggests the accompanying festivities, whether elaborate or simple: *a beautiful wedding; a reception after the wedding.* NUPTIALS is a formal and lofty word applied to the ceremony and attendant social events; it does not have emotional connotations but strongly implies surroundings characteristic of wealth, rank, pomp, and grandeur: *royal nuptials.* It appears frequently on newspaper society pages chiefly as a result of the attempt to avoid continual repetition of MARRIAGE and WEDDING. **5.** alliance, confederation; weld, junction. **—Ant. 1.** divorce.

mar•riage•a•ble (mar′i jə bəl), *adj.* **1.** suitable or attractive for marriage: *The handsome and successful young man was considered eminently marriageable.* **2.** of an age suitable for marriage: *a marriageable daughter.* [1545–55; MARRIAGE + -ABLE] **—mar′riage•a•bil′i•ty, mar′riage•a•ble•ness,** *n.*

mar′riage bro′ker, a person who arranges marriages, usually between strangers, for a fee. [1675–85]

mar′riage encoun′ter. See under **encounter** (def. 7). [1970–75]

mar′riage of conven′ience, marriage entered into for a personal or family advantage, as for social, political, or economic reasons, usually without love and sometimes without the expectation of sexual relations. [1705–15]

Mar′riage of Fig′a•ro, The (fig′ə rō′), (Italian, *Le nozze di Figaro*), an opera (1786) by Wolfgang Amadeus Mozart.

mar′riage por′tion, dowry. [1760–70]

mar•ried (mar′ēd), *adj.* **1.** united in wedlock; wedded: *married couples.* **2.** of or pertaining to marriage or married persons; connubial; conjugal: *married happiness.* **3.** (of an antique) created from components of two or more authentic pieces. **4.** interconnected or joined; united. **5.** (of a family name) acquired through marriage. —*n.* **6.** Usually, **marrieds.** married couples or married people: *young marrieds moving into their first home.* [1325–75; ME; see MARRY¹, -ED²] **—mar′ried•ly,** *adv.*

mar′ried print′. See **composite print.** [1950–55]

mar•ron (mar′ən, mə rōn′; *Fr.* MA RÔN′), *n.* a large European chestnut, esp. as used in cookery: candied or preserved in syrup. [1970–75; < F; see MAROON¹]

mar•rons gla•cés (*Fr.* MA RÔN′ glA sā′), marrons glazed or coated with sugar, eaten as a confection; candied chestnuts. [1870–75; < F]

mar•row¹ (mar′ō), *n.* **1.** *Anat.* a soft, fatty, vascular tissue in the interior cavities of bones that is a major site of blood cell production. **2.** the inmost or essential part: *to pierce to the marrow of a problem.* **3.** strength or vitality: *Fear took the marrow out of him.* **4.** rich and nutritious food. **5.** *Chiefly Brit.* See **vegetable marrow.** [bef. 900; ME *mar(o)we,* OE *mearg;* c. D *merg,* G *Mark,* ON *mergr*] **—mar′row•ish,** *adj.* **—mar′row•less,** *adj.* **—mar′row•y,** *adj.*

mar•row² (mar′ō; *Scot.* mar′ə), *n. Scot. and North Eng.* **1.** a partner; fellow worker. **2.** a spouse; helpmate. **3.** a companion; close friend. [1400–50; late ME *marwe* fellow worker, partner, perh. < ON *margr* friendly, lit., many]

mar•row•bone (mar′ō bōn′), **1.** a bone containing edible marrow. **2. marrowbones,** *Facetious.* the knees. [1350–1400; ME; see MARROW¹, BONE]

mar•row•fat (mar′ō fat′), *n.* **1.** a large-seeded variety of pea. **2.** the seed itself. [1725–35; MARROW¹ + FAT]

mar′row squash′, any of several squashes having a smooth surface, an oblong shape, and a hard rind. [1860–65, *Amer.*]

Mar•rue•cos (mär RWE′kôs), *n.* Spanish name of **Morocco.**

mar•ry¹ (mar′ē), *v.,* **-ried, -ry•ing.** —*v.t.* **1.** to take as a husband or wife; take in marriage: *Susan married Ed.* **2.** to perform the marriage ceremonies for (two people who wish to be husband and wife); join in wedlock: *The minister married Susan and Ed.* **3.** to give in marriage; arrange the marriage of (often fol. by *off*): *Her father wants to marry her to his friend's son. They want to marry off all their children before selling their big home.* **4.** to unite intimately: *Common economic interests marry the two countries.* **5.** to take as an intimate life partner by a formal exchange of promises in the manner of a traditional marriage ceremony. **6.** to combine, connect, or join so as to make more efficient, attractive, or profitable: *The latest cameras marry automatic and manual features. A recent merger marries two of the nation's largest corporations.* **7.** *Naut.* **a.** to lay together (the unlaid strands of two ropes) to be spliced. **b.** to seize (two ropes) together end to end for use as a single line. **c.** to seize (parallel ropes) together at intervals. **8.** to cause (food, liquor, etc.) to blend with other ingredients: *to marry malt whiskey with grain whiskey.* —*v.i.* **9.** to take a husband or wife; wed. **10.** (of two or more foods, wines, etc.) to combine suitably or agreeably; blend: *This wine and the strong cheese just don't marry.* [1250–1300; ME *marien* < OF *marier* < L *marītāre* to wed, deriv. of *marītus* conjugal, akin to *mās* male (person)] **—mar′ri•er,** *n.*

mar•ry² (mar′ē), *interj. Archaic.* (used as an exclamation of surprise, astonishment, etc.) [1325–75; ME; euphemistic var. of MARY (the Virgin)]

Mar•ry•at (mar′ē ət), *n.* **Frederick,** 1792–1848, English naval officer and novelist.

Mars (märz), *n.* **1.** the ancient Roman god of war and agriculture, identified with the Greek god Ares. **2.** *Astron.* the planet fourth in order from the sun, having a diameter of 4222 miles (6794 km), a mean distance from the sun of 141.6 million miles (227.9 million km), a period of revolution of 686.95 days, and two moons. See table under **planet** (def. 1). —*adj.* **3.** (*often l.c.*) of or pertaining to any of various pigments used in painting that are artificially made from an iron oxide base: *Mars color; Mars pigments.*

Mar•sa•la (mär sä′lə; *It.* mär sä′lä), *n.* **1.** a seaport in W Sicily. 84,280. **2.** a sweet, dark, fortified wine made near Marsala, or a similar wine made elsewhere. —*adj.* **3.** made or flavored with this wine: *veal Marsala.*

Mars′ brown′, **1.** a medium brown color. **2.** a brown pigment used in painting, artificially made from an iron oxide base and characterized by strong film-forming properties and permanence.

marse (märs), *n. Southern U.S.* (used chiefly in representation of southern black speech) master. Also, **mars, massa.** [1870–75]

Mar•seil•laise (mär′sə lāz′, -sā ez′; *Fr.* MAR se yez′), *n.* the French national anthem, written in 1792 by Rouget de Lisle.

mar•seilles (mär sālz′), *n.* a thick cotton fabric woven in figures or stripes with an embossed effect, chiefly for bedspreads and other coverings. [1755–65; after MARSEILLES]

Mar•seilles (mär sā′), *n.* a seaport in and the capital of Bouches-du-Rhône department, in SE France. 914,356. French, **Mar•seille** (MAR se′yᵊ).

marsh (märsh), *n.* a tract of low wet land, often treeless and periodically inundated, generally characterized by a growth of grasses, sedges, cattails, and rushes. [bef. 900; ME *mershe,* OE *mer(i)sc* (c. G *Marsch*). See MERE², -ISH¹; cf. MARAIS, MARISH, MORASS] **—marsh′like′,** *adj.*
—Syn. swamp, bog, fen, marshland, wetland.

Marsh (märsh), *n.* **1. Dame (Edith) Ngai•o** (nī′ō), 1899–1982, New Zealand writer of detective novels. **2. Reginald,** 1898–1954, U.S. painter and illustrator.

Mar•sha (mär′shə), *n.* a female given name.

mar•shal (mär′shəl), *n., v.,* **-shaled, -shal•ing** or (*esp. Brit.*) **-shalled, -shal•ling.** —*n.* **1.** a military officer of the highest rank, as in the French and some other armies. Cf. **field marshal.** **2.** an administrative officer of a U.S. judicial district who performs duties similar to those of a sheriff. **3.** a court officer serving processes, attending court, giving personal service to the judges, etc. **4.** the chief of a police or fire department in some cities. **5.** a police officer in some communities. **6.** See **sky marshal.** **7.** a higher officer of a royal household or court. **8.** an official charged with the arrangement or regulation of ceremonies, parades, etc.: *the marshal of the St. Patrick's Day parade.* —*v.t.* **9.** to arrange in proper order; set out in an orderly manner; arrange clearly: *to marshal facts; to marshal one's arguments.* **10.** to array, as for battle. **11.** to usher or lead ceremoniously: *Their host marshaled them into the room.* **12.** *Heraldry.* to combine (two or more coats of arms) on a single escutcheon. [1225–75; ME *marshal,* syncopated var. of *mareschal* < OF < Gmc; cf. OHG *marahscalh* groom, equiv. to *marah* horse (see MARE¹) + *scalh* servant, c. OE *scealc*] **—mar′shal•cy, mar′shal•ship′,** *n.* **—mar′shal•er;** *esp. Brit.,* **mar′•shal•ler,** *n.*
—Syn. 9. order, dispose; convoke. See **gather.** **—Ant. 9.** scatter.

Mar•shall (mär′shəl), *n.* **1. Alfred,** 1842–1924, English economist. **2. George C(at•lett)** (kat′lit), 1880–1959, U.S. general and statesman: Secretary of State 1947–49; Nobel peace prize 1953. **3. John,** 1755–1835, U.S. jurist and statesman: Chief Justice of the U.S. 1801–35. **4. Thomas Riley,** 1854–1925, vice president of the U.S. 1913–21. **5. Thur•good** (thûr′go͝od), 1908–93, U.S. jurist: associate justice of the U.S. Supreme Court 1967–91. **6.** a city in NE Texas. 24,921. **7.** a town in central Missouri. 12,781. **8.** a town in SW Minnesota. 11,161. **9.** Also, **Mar′shal.** a male given name.

Mar•shall•ese (mär′shə lēz′, -lēs′), *n., pl.* **-ese,** *adj.* —*n.* **1.** a native or inhabitant of the Marshall Islands, esp. a member of a Micronesian people native to the Marshall Islands. **2.** the Polynesian language of the Marshall Islands. —*adj.* **3.** of or pertaining to the Marshall Islands, their inhabitants, or their language. [1940–45; MARSHALL (ISLANDS) + -ESE]

Mar′shall Is′lands, a group of 24 atolls in the N Pacific: formerly mandated to Japan; now under U.S. trusteeship. 27,096; 74 sq. mi. (192 sq. km).

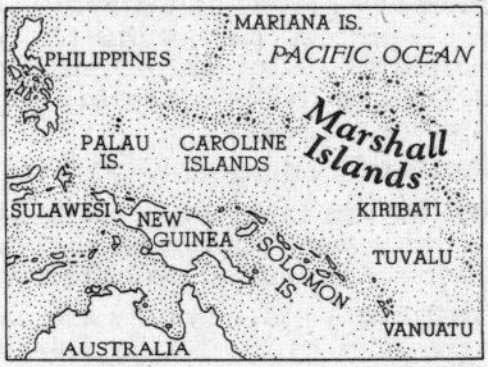

Mar′shall Plan′, **1.** See **European Recovery Program.** **2.** *Informal.* any comprehensive program for federally supported economic assistance, as for urban renewal.

Mar•shall•town (mär′shəl toun′), *n.* a city in central Iowa. 26,938.

Mar•shal•sea (mär′shəl sē′), *n. Brit. Hist.* **1.** the court of the marshal of the royal household. **2.** a debtors' prison in London, abolished in 1842. [1350–1400; ME *marchalsye,* var. of *marschalcie.* See MARSHAL, -CY]

marsh•buck (märsh′buk′), sitatunga. [MARSH + BUCK¹]

marsh′ bug′gy. See **swamp buggy.** [1940–45, *Amer.*]

marsh′ cress′, any cress belonging to the genus *Rorippa,* of the mustard family, esp. *R. islandica,* that grows in marshy areas in North America and Eurasia.

marsh′ deer′, a large South American deer, *Blastocerus dichotomus,* that lives in forests near rivers and swamps: an endangered species. [1890–95]

marsh′ el′der, any of various composite plants of the genus *Iva,* as *I. frutescens,* that grow in salt marshes. [1745–55]

marsh′ fern′, a fern, *Thelypteris palustris,* having pinnatifid fronds and growing in wet places. [1855–60]

Marsh•field (märsh′fēld′), *n.* **1.** a city in SE Massachusetts. 20,916. **2.** a city in central Wisconsin. 18,290.

marsh′ gas′, a gaseous decomposition product of organic matter, consisting primarily of methane. Also called **swamp gas.** [1775–85, *Amer.*]

marsh′ grass′, cordgrass. [1875–85, *Amer.*]

marsh′ hawk′. See **northern harrier.** [1765–75, *Amer.*]

marsh′ hen′, any of various rails or raillike birds. [1700–10, *Amer.*]

marsh•land (märsh′land′), *n.* a region, area, or district characterized by marshes, swamps, bogs, or the like. [bef. 1150; ME *mershland,* OE *merscland.* See MARSH, LAND]

marsh′ mal′low, **1.** an Old World mallow, *Althaea officinalis,* having pink flowers, found in marshy places. **2.** the rose mallow, *Hibiscus moscheutos.* [bef. 1000; ME *marshmalue,* OE *merscmealwe.* See MARSH, MALLOW]

marsh•mal•low (märsh′mel′ō, -mal′ō), *n.* **1.** a sweetened paste or confection made from the mucilaginous root of the marsh mallow. **2.** a similar confection, usually soft and spongy, made from gum arabic or gelatin, sugar, corn syrup, and flavoring. [1905–10; see MARSH MALLOW] **—marsh′mal′low•y,** *adj.*

CONCISE PRONUNCIATION KEY: act, cāpe, dâre, pärt; set, ēqual; if, īce; ox, ōver, ôrder, oil, bo͝ok, bo͞ot, out; up, ûrge; child; sing; shoe; thin, *th*at; zh as in *treasure.* ə = *a* as in *alone, e* as in *system, i* as in *easily, o* as in *gallop, u* as in *circus;* ᵊ as in *fire* (fīᵊr), *hour* (ouᵊr). l and n can serve as syllabic consonants, as in *cradle* (krād′l), and *button* (but′n). See the full key inside the front cover.

marsh′ mar′igold, a yellow-flowered plant, *Caltha palustris,* of the buttercup family, growing in marshes and meadows; cowslip. [1570–80]

marsh′ pink′, any of several eastern North American plants belonging to the genus *Sabatia,* of the gentian family, having rose-pink flowers.

Marsh′'s test′, *Chem.* a test to detect minimal amounts of arsenic. Also, **Marsh′ test′.** [after British chemist James *Marsh* (1794–1846), who described such a test in 1836]

marsh′ tack′y, *South Atlantic States (chiefly South Carolina and Georgia).* **1.** a small, sometimes half-wild horse of the coastal marshes. **2.** *Disparaging.* a poor white living in the marshes. [1830–40]

marsh′ tre′foil. See **buck bean.** [1590–1600]

marsh′ wren′, **1.** Also called **long-billed marsh wren.** a North American wren, *Cistothorus palustris,* that inhabits tall reed beds. **2.** See **sedge wren.** [1785–95, *Amer.*]

marsh•y (mär′shē), *adj.,* **marsh•i•er, marsh•i•est.** **1.** like a marsh; soft and wet; boggy. **2.** pertaining to a marsh. **3.** consisting of or constituting a marsh. [1350–1400; ME *mershi.* See MARSH, -Y[1]] **—marsh′i•ness,** *n.*

Mar•si•lid (mär′sə lid), *Pharm., Trademark.* a brand of iproniazid.

Mar•sil′i•us of Pad′ua (mär sil′ē əs), c1280–1343?, Italian scholar and political theorist. Italian, **Mar•si•glio de•i Mai•nar•di•ni** (mär sē′lyô de′ē mī′när dē′nē).

Mars′ red′, **1.** a deep red-orange color. **2.** a red pigment used in painting, artificially made from an iron oxide base and characterized by strong film-forming properties and permanence. [1890–95]

Mars•ton (mär′stən), *n.* **John,** c1575–1634, English dramatist and satirical poet.

Mars′ton Moor′, a former moor in NE England, west of York: Cromwell's victory over the Royalists 1644.

mar•su•pi•al (mär so͞o′pē əl), *—n.* **1.** any viviparous, nonplacental mammal of the order Marsupialia, comprising the opossums, kangaroos, wombats, and bandicoots, the females of most species having a marsupium containing the mammary glands and serving as a receptacle for the young. *—adj.* **2.** pertaining to, resembling, or having a marsupium. **3.** of or pertaining to the marsupials. [1690–1700; < NL *marsupiālis* pertaining to a pouch. See MARSUPIUM, -AL[1]]

marsu′pial bones′, epipubis.]1810–20]

marsu′pial mole′, a burrowing Australian marsupial of the genus *Notoryctes,* resembling a common mole in form and behavior. Also called **pouched mole.**

marsu′pial mouse′, **1.** any of various mouse-sized to rat-sized marsupials of the family Dasyuridae, occurring in Australia, New Guinea, and Tasmania: some species are rare or endangered. **2.** the mouselike crested-tailed *Dasycercus cristicauda* of Australian deserts. Also called **marsu′pial rat′.**

mar•su•pi•um (mär so͞o′pē əm), *n., pl.* **-pi•a** (-pē ə). the pouch or fold of skin on the abdomen of a female marsupial. [1690–1700; < NL, var. of L *marsuppium* pouch, purse < Gk *marsýppion,* dim. of *mársippos* a bag, pouch]

Mars′ vi′olet, **1.** a dark grayish-purple color. **2.** a purple pigment used in painting, artificially made from an iron oxide base and characterized by strong film-forming properties and permanence.

Mar•sy•as (mär′sē əs), *n. Class. Myth.* a satyr who lost in a flute-playing competition with Apollo and was flayed alive as a penalty.

Mars′ yel′low, **1.** a medium to deep orange-yellow color. **2.** a yellow pigment used in painting, artificially made from an iron hydroxide base and characterized by strong film-forming properties and permanence.

mart[1] (märt), *n.* **1.** market; trading center; trade center. **2.** a building, center, or exposition for the sale of goods by manufacturers and wholesalers to retail merchants. **3.** *Archaic.* a fair. **4.** *Obs.* bargain. [1400–50; late ME < MD *mar(c)t* MARKET]

mart[2] (märt), *n. Scot. and North Eng.* a cow or ox fattened for slaughter. [1300–50; ME < ScotGael; cf. MIr *mart* ox or cow slaughtered for meat, carcass, hence a live ox or cow]

Mar•ta (mär′tə; *It.* mär′tä), *n.* a female given name.

Mar•ta•ban (mär′tə bän′), *n.* **Gulf of,** an inlet of the Bay of Bengal, in Burma.

Mar′ta•gon lil′y (mär′tə gən). See **Turk's-cap lily.** [1835–45; < Turk *martağan* a kind of turban]

mar•tel (mär′tel, mär tel′), *n.* a hammerlike, shafted weapon having a head with a point at one end and a blunt face at the other. Also called **mar•tel-de-fer** (mär′tel də fer′, mär tel′-). [1275–1325; ME < MF < VL **martellus,* dim. of L *martulus, marculus* hammer]

Mar•tel (mär tel′; *Fr.* mar tel′), *n.* **Charles.** See **Charles Martel.**

mar•te•lé (mär′tl ā; *Fr.* mart[e] lā′), *adj. Music.* martellato. [< F: hammered]

mar•tel•la•to (mär′tl ä′tō; *It.* mär′tel lä′tô), *adj.* (of notes or chords in a musical score) heavily accented and detached. [1875–80; < It: hammered, ptp. of *martellare.* See MARTEL, -ATE[1]]

Mar•tel′lo tow′er (mär tel′ō), *Fort.* a circular, towerlike fort with guns on the top. Also, **martel′lo tow′er.** Also called **martel′lo, Martel′lo.** [named after Cape *Mortella,* Corsica, where a tower of this kind was taken by British forces in 1794]

CONCISE ETYMOLOGY KEY: <, descended or borrowed from; >, whence; b., blend of, blended; c., cognate with; cf., compare; deriv., derivative; equiv., equivalent; imit., imitative; obl., oblique; r., replacing; s., stem; sp., spelling, spelled; resp., respelling, respelled; trans., translation; ?, origin unknown; *, unattested; ‡, probably earlier than. See the full key inside the front cover.

mar•tem•per•ing (mär′tem pər ing), *n. Metall.* a quenching process used to harden austenitic steel. [1940–45; MAR(TENSITE) + TEMPER + -ING[1]]

mar•ten (mär′tn), *n., pl.* **-tens,** (*esp. collectively*) **-ten.** **1.** any of several slender, chiefly arboreal carnivores of the genus *Martes,* of northern forests, having a long, glossy coat and bushy tail. **2.** the fur of such an animal, generally a dark brown. [1375–1425; < MLG, equiv. to *mart* marten (c. OE *mearth*) + *-en* -EN[5]; r. late ME *martren* < MF *martrine* marten fur, n. use of fem. of *martrin* pertaining to a marten, equiv. to *martre* marten (< Gmc; cf. G *Marder*) + *-in* -IN[1]]

marten, *Martes americana,* head and body 21 in. (53 cm); tail 9 in. (23 cm)

mar•tens•ite (mär′tn zīt′), *n. Metall.* a metastable microconstituent of any of various forms of carbon steel, produced by undercooling sufficiently below the normal transformation temperature, esp. a hard, brittle product of the decomposition of austenite, produced in this way. [1895–1900; named after Adolf *Martens* (d. 1914), German metallurgist; see -ITE[1]] **—mar•ten•sit•ic** (mär′tn-zit′ik), *adj.*

Mar•tha (mär′thə), *n.* **1.** the sister of Mary and Lazarus. Luke 10:38–42; John 11:1–44. **2.** a female given name: from an Aramaic word meaning "lady."

Mar′tha's Vine′yard, an island off SE Massachusetts: summer resort. 6000; 108¾ sq. mi. (282 sq. km).

Mar′tha Wash′ington chair′, an 18th-century chair having a high upholstered back, a low upholstered seat, and short arms resting on incurvate supports.

Mar′tha Wash′ington mir′ror. See **Constitution mirror.**

Mar′tha Wash′ington ta′ble, a sewing table of the 18th century having an oval top that can be lifted and a central compartment of drawers with semicircular bins at each end.

Mar•tí (mär tē′), *n.* **Jo•sé** (hô se′), 1853–1895, Cuban patriot and writer.

mar•tial (mär′shəl), *adj.* **1.** inclined or disposed to war; warlike: *The ancient Romans were a martial people.* **2.** of, suitable for, or associated with war or the armed forces: *martial music.* **3.** characteristic of or befitting a warrior: *a martial stride.* [1325–75; ME < L *Mārtiālis* of, belonging to Mars, equiv. to *Mārti-* (s. of *Mārs*) + *-ālis* -AL[1]] **—mar′tial•ism,** *n.* **—mar′tial•ist,** *n.* **—mar′tial•ly,** *adv.* **—mar′tial•ness,** *n.*
—Syn. 2. military, soldierly.

Mar•tial (mär′shəl), *n.* (*Marcus Valerius Martialis*) A.D. 43?–104?, Roman epigrammatist, born in Spain.

mar′tial arts′, any of the traditional forms of Oriental self-defense or combat that utilize physical skill and coordination without weapons, as karate, aikido, judo, or kung fu, often practiced as sport. Also, **mar′tial art′.** **—mar′tial art′ist.**

mar′tial law′, **1.** the law temporarily imposed upon an area by state or national military forces when civil authority has broken down or during wartime military operations. **2.** the law imposed upon a defeated country or occupied territory by the military forces of the occupying power. [1525–35]

Mar•tian (mär′shən), *adj.* **1.** of, pertaining to, or like the planet Mars or its hypothetical inhabitants. *—n.* **2.** a supposed inhabitant of the planet Mars: *The science fiction novel was about the invasion of Earth by Martians.* [1350–1400; ME *marcien* < L *Mārti(us)* of, belonging to Mars (see MARCH) + -AN]

mar•tin (mär′tn), *n.* any of several swallows having a deeply forked tail and long, pointed wings. Cf. **house martin, purple martin.** [1425–75; late ME (Scots) *martoune;* presumably generic use of the personal name (< F < LL *Martīnus*), traditionally by assoc. with March (L *Mārtius*), when the bird arrives, and Martinmas, when it leaves; though ME, OF *martinet* has been applied to a variety of birds; cf. F *martin-pêcheur* kingfisher]

Mar•tin (mär′tn), *n.* **1. Ar•cher John Porter** (är′-chər), born 1910, English biochemist: Nobel prize for chemistry 1952. **2. Frank,** 1890–1974, Swiss composer. **3. Glenn Luther,** 1886–1955, U.S. airplane designer and manufacturer. **4. Homer Dodge,** 1836–97, U.S. painter. **5. Joseph W(illiam) Jr.,** 1884–1968, U.S. political leader and publisher: Speaker of the House 1947–49, 1953–55. **6. Saint,** A.D. 316?–397, French prelate: bishop of Tours 370?–397. **7.** a male given name: from the name of the Roman god *Mars.*

Martin I, Saint, died A.D. 655, Italian ecclesiastic: pope 649–655.

Martin II. See **Marinus I.**

Martin III. See **Marinus II.**

Martin IV, (*Simon de Brie* or *Simon de Brion*) c1210–85, French ecclesiastic: pope 1281–85.

Martin V, (*Oddone Colonna*) 1368–1431, Italian ecclesiastic: pope 1417–31.

Mar•ti•na (mär tē′nə), *n.* a female given name. Also, **Mar•tine** (mär tēn′).

Mar•tin du Gard (mar tan dy gar′), **Ro•ger** (rô-zhā′), 1881–1958, French novelist: Nobel prize 1937.

Mar•ti•neau (mär′tn ō′), *n.* **1. Harriet,** 1802–76, English novelist and economist. **2.** her brother, **James,** 1805–1900, English theologian and philosopher.

Mar•ti•nel•li (mär′tn el′ē; *It.* mär′tē nel′lē), *n.* **Gio•van•ni** (jē′ə vä′nē; *It.* jô vän′nē), 1885–1969, U.S. operatic tenor, born in Italy.

mar•ti•net (mär′tn et′, mär′tn et′), *n.* **1.** a strict disciplinarian, esp. a military one. **2.** someone who stubbornly adheres to methods or rules. [1670–80; after General Jean *Martinet* (d. 1672), French inventor of a system of drill] **—mar′ti•net′ish,** *adj.* **—mar′ti•net′•ism,** *n.*

Mar•ti•nez (mär tē′nis), *n.* a town in W California. 22,582.

Mar•ti•nez Ru•iz (mär tē′neth ro͞o ēth′), **Jo•sé** (hô-se′). See **Azorín.**

mar•tin•gale (mär′tn gāl′), *n.* **1.** Also called **standing martingale.** part of the tack or harness of a horse, consisting of a strap that fastens to the girth, passes between the forelegs and through a loop in the neckstrap or hame, and fastens to the noseband: used to steady or hold down the horse's head. See illus. under **harness. 2.** Also called **running martingale.** a similar device that divides at the chest into two branches, each ending in a ring through which the reins pass. **3.** *Naut.* a stay for a jib boom or spike bowsprit. **4.** a system of gambling in which the stakes are doubled or otherwise raised after each loss. [1580–90; < MF: kind of hose fastened at the back, allegedly < Pr *martegalo,* fem. of *martegal,* inhabitant of *Martigue,* town in SE France, though sense appar. influenced by Sp *almártaga* harness < Ar *al-marta'ah* the vein]

mar•ti•ni (mär tē′nē), *n., pl.* **-nis.** a cocktail made with gin or vodka and dry vermouth, usually served with a green olive or a twist of lemon peel. [1885–90; perh. alter. of *Martinez* (an earlier alternate name of the drink, of disputed orig.), by back formation (taking it as pl.), or by assoc. with the vermouth manufacturer Martini, Sola & Co. (later Martini & Rossi)]

Mar•ti•ni (mär tē′nē; *It.* mär tē′nē), *n.* **Si•mo•ne** (sē-mô′ne), 1283–1344, Italian painter.

Mar•ti•ni-Hen•ry (mär tē′nē hen′rē), *n.* a breech-loaded .45 caliber rifle adopted in 1871 as the standard British service weapon, using a center-fire metallic cartridge filled with black powder. [after Swiss inventor Friedrich von *Martini* (1833–97), who designed the breech mechanism, and B. T. *Henry* (see HENRY), who designed the barrel]

Mar•ti•nique (mär′tn ēk′), *n.* an island in the E West Indies; an overseas department of France. 342,000; 425 sq. mi. (1100 sq. km). *Cap.:* Fort-de-France. **—Mar•ti•ni•can** (mär′tn ē′kən), *n.*

Mar′tin Lu′ther King′ Day′, the third Monday in January, a legal holiday in some states of the U.S., commemorating the birthday (Jan. 15) of Martin Luther King, Jr.

Mar•tin•mas (mär′tn məs), *n.* a church festival, November 11, in honor of St. Martin. [1250–1300; ME *Martinmasse.* See Saint MARTIN, -MAS]

Mar•ti•non (mar tē nôn′), *n.* **Jean** (zhän), 1910–76, French violinist, conductor, and composer.

Mar•tins (mär′tnz), *n.* **Peter,** born 1946, U.S. choreographer and ballet master, born in Denmark.

Mar•tins•burg (mär′tnz bûrg′), *n.* a city in NE West Virginia. 13,063.

Mar•tin•son (mär′tn sən; *Sw.* mär′tin sôn′), *n.* **Har•ry Ed•mund** (har′ē ed′mənd; *Sw.* hä′ri ed′mo͝ont), 1904–78, Swedish novelist and poet: Nobel prize 1974.

Mar•tins•ville (mär′tnz vil′), *n.* **1.** a city in S Virginia. 18,149. **2.** a town in central Indiana. 11,311.

Mar•ti•nů (mär′tyi no͞o′), *n.* **Bo•hu•slav** (bô′ho͝o släf′), 1890–1959, Czech composer.

mart•let (märt′lit), *n.* **1.** *Brit. Dial.* a house martin. **2.** *Heraldry.* a representation of a swallow close and without legs, used esp. as the cadency mark of a fourth son. [1530–40; < MF *martelet,* var. of *martinet;* see MARTIN, -ET]

mart•net (märt′net), *n. Naut.* an arrangement of lines formerly used for gathering up a leech of a sail. [1475–85; orig. uncert.]

mar•tyr (mär′tər), *n.* **1.** a person who willingly suffers death rather than renounce his or her religion. **2.** a person who is put to death or endures great suffering on behalf of any belief, principle, or cause: *a martyr to the cause of social justice.* **3.** a person who undergoes severe or constant suffering: *a martyr to severe headaches.* **4.** a person who seeks sympathy or attention by feigning or exaggerating pain, deprivation, etc. *—v.t.* **5.** to make a martyr of, esp. by putting to death. **6.** to torment or torture. [bef. 900; (n.) ME *marter,* OE *martyr* < LL < LGk *mártyr,* var. of Gk *mártys, mártyros* witness; (v.) ME *martiren,* OE *martyrian,* deriv. of n.] **—mar′•tyr•ish,** *adj.* **—mar′tyr•ly,** *adv., adj.*

mar•tyr•dom (mär′tər dəm), *n.* **1.** the condition, sufferings, or death of a martyr. **2.** extreme suffering; torment. [bef. 900; ME *martirdom,* OE *martyrdōm.* See MARTYR, -DOM]

mar•tyr•i•um (mär tir′ē əm), *n., pl.* **-tyr•i•a** (-tir′ē ə). **1.** a place where the relics of a martyr are kept. **2.** a church built above the tomb of a martyr or in honor of a martyr. [1705–15; < LL; see MARTYRY]

mar•tyr•ize (mär′tə rīz′), *v.t.,* **-ized, -iz•ing.** **1.** to make a martyr of: *The ancient Romans martyrized many Christians.* **2.** to torment. Also, *esp. Brit.,* **mar′tyr•ise′.** [1400–50; late ME *martirizen* < ML *martyrizāre.* See MARTYR, -IZE] **—mar′tyr•i•za′tion,** *n.*

mar•tyr•ol•o•gy (mär′tə rol′ə jē), *n., pl.* **-gies.** **1.** the branch of knowledge dealing with the lives of martyrs. **2.** a history of martyrs. **3.** such histories collectively. **4.** a list of martyrs. [1590–1600; < ML *martyrologium* history of martyrs < LGk *martyrológion.* See MARTYR, -O-, -LOGY] **—mar•tyr•o•log•i•cal** (mär′tər ə loj′i kəl), **mar′tyr•o•log′ic,** *adj.* **—mar′tyr•ol′o•gist,** *n.*

mar•tyr•y (mär′tə rē), *n., pl.* **-tyr•ies.** a shrine, chapel, or the like, erected in honor of a martyr. [1250–1300; ME *martirie* suffering, martyrdom < ML *marty-*

rium martyrdom, martyr's grave < LGk *martýrion.* See MARTYR, -Y[3]]

ma•ru′mi kum′quat (mə ro͞o′mē). See **round kumquat.** [*marumi* < Japn, equiv. to *mara* round + *mi(y)* fruit (< **mui*)]

Ma•rut (mə ro͞ot′), *n. Hinduism.* any of a group of storm gods, the offspring of Rudra.

marv (märv), *adj. Slang.* marvelous; wonderful. [by shortening]

Marv (märv), *n.* a male given name, form of **Marvin.**

mar•vel (mär′vəl), *n., v.,* **-veled, -vel•ing** or (*esp. Brit.*) **-velled, -vel•ling.** —*n.* **1.** something that causes wonder, admiration, or astonishment; a wonderful thing; a wonder or prodigy: *The new bridge is an engineering marvel.* **2.** *Archaic.* the feeling of wonder; astonishment. —*v.t.* **3.** to wonder at (usually fol. by a clause as object): *I marvel that you were able to succeed against such odds.* **4.** to wonder or be curious about (usually fol. by a clause as object): *A child marvels that the stars can be.* —*v.i.* **5.** to be filled with wonder, admiration, or astonishment, as at something surprising or extraordinary: *I marvel at your courage.* [1250–1300; ME *mervel* < OF *merveil(l)e* < LL *mīrābilia* marvels, n. use of neut. pl. of L *mīrābilis* marvelous. See ADMIRABLE] —**mar′vel•ment,** *n.*

Mar•vell (mär′vəl), *n.* **Andrew,** 1621–78, English poet and satirist.

mar•vel-of-Pe•ru (mär′vəl əv pə ro͞o′), *n.* the four-o'clock, *Mirabilis jalapa.* [1590–1600]

mar•vel•ous (mär′və ləs), *adj.* **1.** superb; excellent; great: *a marvelous show.* **2.** such as to cause wonder, admiration, or astonishment; surprising; extraordinary. **3.** improbable or incredible: *the marvelous events of Greek myth.* Also, *esp. Brit.,* **mar′vel•lous.** [1300–50; ME *merve(il)lous* < MF *merveilleus.* See MARVEL, -OUS] —**mar′vel•ous•ly,** *adv.* —**mar′vel•ous•ness,** *n.*
—**Syn. 1.** wonderful. **2.** wondrous, amazing, miraculous. **3.** unbelievable. —**Ant. 1.** terrible. **2.** commonplace.

mar•ver (mär′vər), *n.* **1.** a hard, flat surface of stone, wood, or metal, on which a mass of molten glass is rolled and shaped in glassmaking. —*v.t.* **2.** to roll (glass) on a marver. [1825–35; < F *marbre* MARBLE]

Mar•vin (mär′vin), *n.* a male given name.

marv•y (mär′vē), *adj. Slang.* marvelous; delightful. [1965–70; MARV(ELOUS) + -Y[1]]

Mar•wa (mär′wə), *n. Islam.* See **Safa and Marwa.**

Mar•war (mär′wär), *n.* Jodhpur (def. 1).

Marx (märks; *Ger.* märks), *n.* **Karl (Hein•rich)** (kärl hīn′rik; *Ger.* käRl hīn′RIKH), 1818–83, German economist, philosopher, and socialist.

Marx′ Broth′ers, a family of U.S. comedians, including **Julius Henry** (*"Groucho"*), 1890–1977, **Arthur** (*Adolph Marx*) (*"Harpo"*), 1888–1964, **Leonard** (*"Chico"*), 1887–1961, and **Herbert** (*"Zeppo"*), 1901–79.

Marx•i•an (märk′sē ən), *adj.* of or pertaining to Karl Marx or his theories. [1885–90; MARX + -IAN] —**Marx′i•an•ism,** *n.*

Marx•ism (märk′siz əm), *n.* the system of economic and political thought developed by Karl Marx, along with Friedrich Engels, esp. the doctrine that the state throughout history has been a device for the exploitation of the masses by a dominant class, that class struggle has been the main agency of historical change, and that the capitalist system, containing from the first the seeds of its own decay, will inevitably, after the period of the dictatorship of the proletariat, be superseded by a socialist order and a classless society. [1895–1900; MARX + -ISM]

Marx•ist (märk′sist), *n.* **1.** an adherent of Karl Marx or his theories. —*adj.* **2.** of Karl Marx or his theories. [1885–90; MARX + -IST]

Mar•y (mâr′ē), *n.* **1.** Also called **Virgin Mary.** the mother of Jesus. **2.** the sister of Lazarus and Martha. Luke 10:38–42; John 11:1,2. **3.** See **Mary, Queen of Scots. 4.** (*Princess Victoria Mary of Teck*) 1867–1953, Queen of England 1910–36 (wife of George V). **5.** *Slang* (*often offensive*). a male homosexual. **6.** a female given name. [bef. 1000; ME *Marie,* OE *Maria* < LL < Gk < Heb *Miryām*]

Mary I, (*"Bloody Mary"*) 1516–58, queen of England 1553–58 (wife of Philip II of Spain; daughter of Henry VIII). Also called **Mary Tudor.**

Mary II, 1662–94, queen of England 1689–94: joint ruler with her husband William III (daughter of James II).

Mar•ya (mär′yə), *n.* a female given name, form of **Mary.**

Mar•y•ann (mâr′ē an′), *n.* a female given name. Also, **Mar′y•anne′.**

Mar•y•beth (mâr′ē beth′, mâr′ē beth′), *n.* a female given name.

Mar•y•bor•ough (mâr′ē bûr′ō, -bur′ō, -bər e, -brə), *n.* a seaport in E Australia. 20,111.

Mar•y•el•len (mâr′ē el′ən), *n.* a female given name.

Mar′y Jane′, 1. a small, round sponge cake, usually with a circular indentation on top, for topping with fruit, whipped cream, etc., and served as an individual portion. **2. Mary Janes,** *Trademark.* small bits of chocolate, candy, sugar, or the like, for sprinkling on ice cream; sprinkles. **3.** *Trademark.* a brand of young girls' low-heeled shoe of patent leather having across the instep a single strap that fastens at the side.

Mar′y Jane′, *Slang.* marijuana. Also, **mar•y•jane** (mâr′ē jān′, mär′-). [trans. of MexSp *marijuana,* by the popular assumption that it is a compound of Sp *María* and *Juana*]

Mar•y•land (mer′ə lənd), *n.* a state in the E United States, on the Atlantic coast. 4,216,446; 10,577 sq. mi. (27,395 sq. km). *Cap.:* Annapolis. *Abbr.:* MD (for use with zip code), Md. —**Mar′y•land•er,** *n.*

Mar′yland yel′lowthroat, (in former systems of nomenclature) the common yellowthroat, *Geothlypis trichas,* esp. the eastern U.S. subspecies. [1695–1705, *Amer.*]

Mar•y•lou (mâr′ē lo͞o′), *n.* a female given name.

Mar′y Mag′dalene, Mary of Magdala, whom Jesus healed of possession by devils, Luke 8:2: traditionally identified with the repentant woman whom Jesus forgave. Luke 7:37–50.

Mar•y•ol•o•gy (mâr′ē ol′ə jē), *n.* Mariology.

Mar′y, Queen′ of Scots′, (*Mary Stuart*) 1542–87, queen of Scotland 1542–67; beheaded for plotting to assassinate her cousin, Queen Elizabeth I.

Mar′y Tu′dor. See **Mary I.**

Mar•y•ville (mâr′ē vil′), *n.* a city in E Tennessee. 17,480.

mar•zi•pan (mär′zə pan′), *n.* a confection made of almonds reduced to a paste with sugar and often molded into various forms, usually diminutive fruits and vegetables. Also called **marchpane.** [1535–45; < G < It *marzapane.* See MARCHPANE]

mas., masculine.

ma•sa (mä′sə; *Sp.* mä′sä), *n. Mexican Cookery.* flour or dough made of dried, ground corn, used esp. for tortillas. [< Sp: dough < L *massa;* see MASS]

Ma•sac•cio (mä sät′chô; *Eng.* mə sä′chē ō′), *n.* (*Tommaso Guidi*) 1401–28?, Italian painter.

Ma•sa•da (mə sä′də; *Heb.* mə tsä dä′), *n.* a mountain-top fortress in E Israel on the SW shore of the Dead Sea: site of Zealots' last stand against the Romans during revolt of A.D. 66–73.

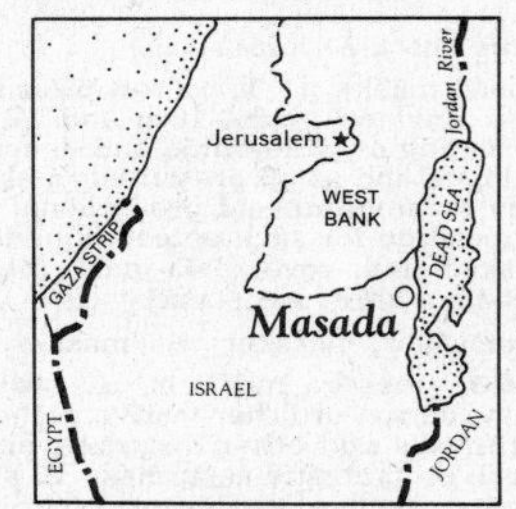

Ma•sai (mə sī′), *n., pl.* **-sais,** (*esp. collectively*) **-sai. 1.** a member of an African people inhabiting the highlands of Kenya and Tanzania and having a largely pastoral economy and a society based on the patrilineal clan. **2.** the Nilotic language of the Masai. Also, **Maasai.**

Ma•san (mä′sän), *n.* a seaport in SE South Korea. 186,890. Formerly, **Ma•sam•po** (mə säm′pō).

Ma•sa•ryk (mas′ə rik; *Czech.* mä′sä RIK), *n.* **1. Jan** (yän), 1886–1948, Czech statesman (son of Tomáš). **2. To•máš Gar•rigue** (tô′mäsh gä′RIK), 1850–1937, Czech statesman: 1st president of Czechoslovakia 1918–35.

Ma•sa•ya (mä sä′yä), *n.* a city in SW Nicaragua. 34,127.

Mas•ba•te (mäs bä′tə), *n.* **1.** one of the central islands of the Philippines. 584,520; 1262 sq. mi. (3269 sq. km). **2.** a city on this island. 52,944.

masc., masculine.

Mas•ca•gni (mäs kä′nyē), *n.* **Pie•tro** (pye′tRô), 1863–1945, Italian operatic composer.

mas•car•a (ma skar′ə; *Brit.* ma skär′ə), *n.* **1.** a substance used as a cosmetic to color the eyelashes and eyebrows. —*v.t.* **2.** to apply mascara to. [1885–90; < Sp: mask; see MASK]

mas•ca•rene′ grass′ (mas′kə rēn′), a creeping grass, *Zoysia tenuifolia,* naturalized in California and Florida, having fine leaves and shoots that make good turf. [1955–60; after the *Mascarene* Islands, east of Madagascar]

mas•ca•ron (mas′kə ron′), *n. Archit.* mask (def. 11). [1655–65; < F < It *mascherone,* aug. of *maschera;* see MASK]

mas•cle (mas′kəl), *n. Heraldry.* a lozenge represented as having a lozenge-shaped hole at the center. [1300–50; ME, deriv. of *mask* (now dial.), var. of MESH; see -LE]

mas•con (mas′kon′), *n. Geol.* a massive concentration of high-density material beneath the surface of the moon. [1965–70; MAS(S) + CON(CENTRATION)]

mas•cot (mas′kot, -kət), *n.* an animal, person, or thing adopted by a group as its representative symbol and supposed to bring good luck: *The U.S. Navy mascot is a goat.* [1880–85; < F *mascotte* < Pr *mascoto* talisman, charm, deriv. of *masco* sorceress. See MASK]

Mas•couche (ma sko͞osh′; *Fr.* mas ko͞osh′), *n.* a town in S Quebec, in E Canada. 20,345.

mas•cu•line (mas′kyə lin), *adj.* **1.** pertaining to or characteristic of a man or men: *masculine attire.* **2.** having qualities traditionally ascribed to men, as strength and boldness. **3.** *Gram.* noting or pertaining to the gender of Latin, Greek, German, French, Spanish, Hebrew, etc., which has among its members most nouns referring to males, as well as other nouns, as Spanish *dedo,* "finger," German *Bleistift,* "pencil." **4.** (of a woman) mannish. —*n. Gram.* **5.** the masculine gender. **6.** a noun or other element in or marking that gender. [1300–50; ME *masculin* < L *masculinus,* equiv. to *masculus* (*mās* male + *-culus* -CULE[1]) + *-īnus* -INE[1]] —**mas′cu•line•ly,** *adv.* —**mas′cu•lin′i•ty, mas′cu•line•ness,** *n.*
—**Syn. 2.** manly. See **male.**

mas′culine caesu′ra, *Pros.* a caesura occurring immediately after a stressed or a long syllable.

mas′culine rhyme′, *Pros.* a rhyme of but a single stressed syllable, as in *disdain, complain.* [1575–85]

mas•cu•lin•ize (mas′kyə lə nīz′), *v.t.,* **-ized, -iz•ing. 1.** *Med.* to produce certain male secondary sex characteristics in (a female). **2.** to make masculine in character, quality, or appearance: *The presence of two large leather sofas seemed to masculinize the whole room.* Also, *esp. Brit.,* **mas′cu•lin•ise′.** [1920–25; MASCULINE + -IZE] —**mas′cu•lin•i•za′tion,** *n.*

Mase•field (mās′fēld′, māz′-), *n.* **John,** 1878–1967, English poet: poet laureate 1930–67.

ma•ser (mā′zər), *n.* a device for amplifying electromagnetic waves by stimulated emission of radiation. Cf. **laser.** [1950–55; *m*(*icrowave*) *a*(*mplification by*) *s*(*timulated*) *e*(*mission of*) *r*(*adiation*)]

Ma•se•ru (mä′sə ro͞o′, maz′ə ro͞o′), *n.* a town in and the capital of Lesotho, in the NW part. 29,000.

mash[1] (mash), *v.t.* **1.** to crush: *He mashed his thumb with a hammer.* **2.** to reduce to a soft, pulpy mass, as by beating or pressure, esp. in the preparation of food. **3.** to mix (crushed malt or meal of grain) with hot water to form wort. —*n.* **4.** a soft, pulpy mass. **5.** a pulpy condition. **6.** a mixture of boiled grain, bran, meal, etc., fed warm to horses and cattle. **7.** crushed malt or meal of grain mixed with hot water to form wort. **8.** *Brit. Slang.* mashed potatoes. [bef. 1000; ME; OE *mǣsc-, masc-* (in compounds); c. G *Maische*]

mash[2] (mash), *Older Slang.* —*n.* **1.** a flirtation or infatuation. **2.** a flirt; sweetheart; lover. —*v.t.* **3.** to flirt with; court the affections of. [1880–85; orig. theatrical argot; of uncert. orig.]

MASH (mash), *n.* mobile army surgical hospital.

Ma•shar•brum (mush′ər bro͝om′), *n.* a mountain in N India, in the Himalayas. 25,660 ft. (7821 m). Also, **Ma′sher•brum′.**

mashed (masht), *n. Informal.* mashed potatoes: *The pork chop comes with string beans and mashed.* [1920–25]

mash•er[1] (mash′ər), *n.* a person or thing that mashes. [1490–1500; MASH[1] + -ER[1]]

mash•er[2] (mash′ər), *n. Slang.* a man who makes advances, esp. to women he does not know, with a view to physical intimacy. [1880–85; MASH[2] + -ER[1]]

mash•gi•ach (mäsh gē′äKH), *n., pl.* ***mash•gi•chim*** (*Seph.* mäsh gē KHēm′; *Ashk.* mäsh gē′KHim). *Hebrew.* mashgiah.

mash•gi•ah (mäsh gē′äKH), *n., pl.* ***mash•gi•him*** (*Seph.* mäsh gē KHēm′; *Ashk.* mäsh gē′KHim). *Hebrew.* an inspector appointed by a board of Orthodox rabbis to guard against any violation of the Jewish dietary laws in food processing plants, meat markets, etc., where food presumed to be kosher is prepared or served for public consumption. Also, ***mashgiach.***

Mash•had (mash had′), *n.* Persian name of **Meshed.**

mash•ie (mash′ē), *n. Golf.* a club with an iron head, the face having more slope than a mashie iron but less slope than a mashie niblick. Also, **mashy.** Also called **number five iron.** [1880–85; perh. < F *massue* club < VL **matteūca,* deriv. of **matte(a)* MACE[1]]

mash′ie i′ron, *Golf.* a club with an iron head, the face having more slope than a mid-mashie but less slope than a mashie. Also called **number four iron.**

mash′ie nib′lick, *Golf.* a club with an iron head whose face has more slope than a mashie but less slope than a pitcher. Also called **number six iron.** [1905–10]

mash•lam (mash′ləm), *n. Brit. Dial.* maslin.

Ma•sho•na (mə shon′ə, -shō′nə), *n., pl.* **-nas,** (*esp. collectively*) **-na.** Shona (def. 1).

ma•shre•bee•yah (mä′shri bē′ə), *n.* meshrebeeyeh. Also, **ma′shre•bee′yeh.**

mash•y (mash′ē), *n., pl.* **mash•ies.** *Golf.* mashie.

Mash•yē and Mash•yā•nē (mash′yə; mäsh yä′nə), *Zoroastrianism.* (in the Avesta) the first couple, man and woman, created by Ahura Mazda from a rhubarb plant grown from the seed of Gayomart. Also called **Mahrē and Mahrānē.**

Mas•i•nis•sa (mas′ə nis′ə), *n.* 238–149 B.C., king of Numidia c210–149. Also, **Massinissa.**

mas•jid (mas′jid), *n. Arabic.* a mosque. Also, ***musjid.***

mask (mask, mäsk), *n.* **1.** a covering for all or part of the face, worn to conceal one's identity. **2.** a grotesque or humorous false face worn at a carnival, masquerade, etc.: *Halloween masks.* **3.** Also called **swim mask.** a device consisting typically of a transparent glass or plastic panel fitted into a flexible rubber gasket that fits snugly around the eyes, over the cheeks, and usually over the nose: used by skin divers. **4.** anything that disguises or conceals; disguise; pretense: *His politeness is a mask for his fundamentally malicious personality.* **5.** a likeness

of a face, as one molded on the face in plaster. Cf. **death mask, life mask. 6.** a covering of wire, gauze, etc., to protect the face, as from splinters, dust, or a pitched ball. **7.** See **gas mask. 8.** any protective covering for the face or head. **9.** any protective covering, as paper, cardboard, plastic, or the like, used for masking an area of something, as of a photograph or window. **10.** the dark shading on the muzzle of certain dogs. **11.** a representation of a face or head, generally grotesque, used as an architectural ornament or as a decorative device in weaponry, furniture, etc. **12.** a person wearing a mask; masker. **13.** masque (defs. 1–3). **14.** Also, **masque.** a cosmetic cream, gel, paste, or the like, that is applied to the face and allowed to remain for a short time before being removed and is used for tightening, cleansing, refreshing, or lubricating the skin. **15.** a piece of cloth, silk, or plastic material covering the face of an actor to symbolize the character being represented: used in Greek and Roman drama and in some modern plays. **16.** the face or head, as of a fox. **17.** *Electronics.* a type of stencil applied to the surface of a semiconductor to permit selective etching or deposition: used in the manufacture of integrated circuits by photolithography. **18.** *Fort.* a screen, as of earth or brush, for concealing or protecting a battery or any military operation. **19.** Also called **braker.** *Shipbuilding.* a sliding timber construction braced against the stern of a hull being launched to keep it from entering the water too rapidly. *—v.t.* **20.** to disguise or conceal; hide; dissemble: *to mask one's intentions.* **21.** to cover or conceal with a mask. **22.** to cover or shield a part of (a design, picture, etc.) in order to prevent reproduction or to protect the surface from the colors used, as in working with an air brush or in painting. **23.** *Fort.* to conceal (a battery or any military operation) from the enemy. **24.** to hinder, as an army, from conducting an operation. *—v.i.* **25.** to put on a mask; disguise oneself. [1525–35; < MF *masque,* perh. directly < It *maschera* mask, disguise < pre-L **maskara,* an extended form of **mask-,* prob. with orig. sense "black" (blackening the face being a simple form of disguise); another development of the same base is early ML *masca* witch, ghost (also, mask); see MASCOT] **—mask′like′,** *adj.*
—Syn. 20. veil, screen, cloak, cover.

mas•ka•longe (mas′kə lonj′), *n., pl.* **-long•es,** (*esp. collectively*) **-longe.** muskellunge.

masked (maskt, mäskt), *adj.* **1.** using or wearing a mask or masks: *a masked burglar; masked actors.* **2.** disguised; concealed; hidden: *masked treachery; masked forces.* **3.** *Bot.* personate[2] (def. 1). **4.** *Zool.* having markings that resemble a mask. [1575–85; MASK + -ED[3]]

masked′ ball′, a ball at which masks are worn. [1770–80]

mask•er (mas′kər, mä′skər), *n.* a person who masks; a person who takes part in a masque. Also, **masquer.** [1540–50; MASK + -ER[1]]

Mas•kil (mäs′kēl), *n., pl.* **Mas•ki•lim** (mäs kē lēm′). *Judaism.* an advocate or supporter of the Haskalah. [< Heb *maśkīl* lit., enlightened] **—Mas•kil•ic** (mä skil′ik), *adj.*

mask•ing (mas′king, mä′sking), *n.* **1.** backing (def. 4). **2.** *Psychol.* obscuring, partially or completely, one sensory process by another, as the dulling of the sense of taste by smoking. [1920–25; MASK + -ING[1], -ING[2]]

mask′ing frame′, *Photog.* easel (def. 2). [1935–40]

mask′ing piece′, *Theat.* a flat, curtain, or other piece of scenery for concealing a part of a stage from the audience.

mask′ing tape′, an easily removed adhesive tape used temporarily for defining margins, protecting surfaces, etc., as when painting, and sometimes also for binding, sealing, or mending. [1935–40]

mas•ki•nonge (mas′kə nonj′), *n., pl.* **-nong•es,** (*esp. collectively*) **-nonge.** muskellunge.

mas•lin (maz′lin), *n. Brit. Dial.* **1.** a mixture of different grains, flours, or meals, esp. rye mixed with wheat. **2.** bread made from such a mixture of grains. **3.** a mixture; medley. Also called **mashlam.** [1275–1325; ME *mastlyoun* < MF *mesteillon,* deriv. of *mesteil* mixture < VL **mi(k)stilium.* See MIXED, -ILE]

mas•och•ism (mas′ə kiz′əm, maz′-), *n.* **1.** *Psychiatry.* the condition in which sexual gratification depends on suffering, physical pain, and humiliation. **2.** gratification gained from pain, deprivation, degradation, etc., inflicted or imposed on oneself, either as a result of one's own actions or the actions of others, esp. the tendency to seek this form of gratification. **3.** the act of turning one's destructive tendencies inward or upon oneself. **4.** the tendency to find pleasure in self-denial, submissiveness, etc. [1890–95; named after L. von SACHER-MASOCH, who described it; see -ISM] **—mas′och•ist,** *n.* **—mas′•och•is′tic,** *adj.* **—mas′och•is′ti•cal•ly,** *adv.*

ma•son (mā′sən), *n.* **1.** a person whose trade is building with units of various natural or artificial mineral products, as stones, bricks, cinder blocks, or tiles, usually with the use of mortar or cement as a bonding agent. **2.** a person who dresses stones or bricks. **3.** (*cap.*) a Freemason. *—v.t.* **4.** to construct of or strengthen with masonry. [1175–1225; ME *machun, mason* < OF *machun, masson* < Frankish **makjon* maker, deriv. of **makōn* to MAKE[1]]

Ma•son (mā′sən), *n.* **1. Charles,** 1730–87, English astronomer and surveyor. Cf. **Mason-Dixon line. 2. George,** 1725–92, American statesman. **3. Lowell,** 1792–1872, U.S. hymnist and educator. **4.** a male given name.

ma′son bee′, any of numerous solitary bees, as of the family Megachilidae, that construct nests of clay. [1765–75]

Ma′son Cit′y, a city in N Iowa. 30,144.

Ma′son-Dix′on line′ (mā′sən dik′sən), the boundary between Pennsylvania and Maryland, partly surveyed by Charles Mason and Jeremiah Dixon between 1763 and 1767, popularly considered before the end of slavery as a line of demarcation between free and slave states. Also, **Ma′son and Dix′on line′.** [1770–80, *Amer.*]

Ma•son•ic (mə son′ik), *adj.* pertaining to or characteristic of Freemasons or Freemasonry. [1790–1800; MASON + -IC] **—Ma•son′i•cal•ly,** *adv.*

Ma•son•ite (mā′sə nīt′), *Trademark.* a brand of hardboard.

Ma′son jar′, a glass jar with a wide mouth and an airtight screw top, much used in home canning. [1880–85, *Amer.*; named after John L. *Mason,* 19th-century American who patented it in 1858]

ma•son•ry (mā′sən rē), *n., pl.* **-ries. 1.** the craft or occupation of a mason. **2.** work constructed by a mason, esp. stonework: *the crumbling masonry of ancient walls.* **3.** (*cap.*) Freemasonry. [1325–75; ME *masonerie* < MF *maçonnerie.* See MASON, -ERY]

ma′son wasp′, any of several solitary wasps, as *Rygchium dorsale,* that construct nests of mud or clay. [1785–95]

Ma•so•rah (mə sôr′ə, -sōr′ə), *n.* a collection of critical and explanatory notes on the Hebrew text of the Old Testament, compiled from the 7th? to 10th centuries A.D. and traditionally accepted as an authoritative exegetic guide, chiefly in matters of pronunciation and grammar. Also, **Ma•so′ra, Massorah, Massora.** [< Heb *māsōrāh*]

Mas•o•rete (mas′ə rēt′), *n.* **1.** one of the writers or compilers of the Masorah. **2.** a person who is versed in the Masorah. Also, **Massorete, Mas•o•rite** (mas′ə rīt′). [1580–90; earlier *mas(s)oreth* < Heb *māsōreth,* with ending conformed to *-ete* (< Gk *-ētēs;* see EXEGETE) or -ITE[1]]

Mas•o•ret•ic (mas′ə ret′ik), *adj.* of or pertaining to the Masorah or the Masoretes. Also, **Mas′o•ret′i•cal, Massoretic, Massoretical.** [1695–1705; MASORETE + -IC]

Mas•pe•ro (mas pə rō′), *n.* **Sir Gas•ton Ca•mille Charles** (gas tôn′ ka mē′y[ə] sharl), 1846–1916, French Egyptologist.

mas. pil., (in prescriptions) a pill mass. [< L *massa pilulāris*]

Mas•qat (mus kat′), *n.* Muscat.

masque (mask, mäsk), *n.* **1.** a form of aristocratic entertainment in England in the 16th and 17th centuries, originally consisting of pantomime and dancing but later including dialogue and song, presented in elaborate productions given by amateur and professional actors. **2.** a dramatic composition for such entertainment. **3.** a masquerade; masked ball; revel. **4.** mask (def. 14). Also, **mask.** [1505–15; < MF; see MASK]

mas•quer (mas′kər, mä′skər), *n.* masker.

mas•quer•ade (mas′kə rād′), *n., v.,* **-ad•ed, -ad•ing.** *—n.* **1.** a party, dance, or other festive gathering of persons wearing masks and other disguises, and often elegant, historical, or fantastic costumes. **2.** a costume or disguise worn at such a gathering. **3.** false outward show; façade; pretense: *a hypocrite's masquerade of virtue.* **4.** activity, existence, etc., under false pretenses: *a rich man's masquerade as a beggar.* *—v.i.* **5.** to go about under false pretenses or a false character; assume the character of; give oneself out to be: *to masquerade as a former Russian count.* **6.** to disguise oneself. **7.** to take part in a masquerade. [1580–90; earlier *masquerada, mascarado,* pseudo-Sp forms of MF *mascarade* < Upper It *mascherada;* see MASK, -ADE[1]] **—mas′quer•ad′er,** *n.*
—Syn. 1. mummery.

mass (mas), *n.* **1.** a body of coherent matter, usually of indefinite shape and often of considerable size: *a mass of dough.* **2.** a collection of incoherent particles, parts, or objects regarded as forming one body: *a mass of sand.* **3.** aggregate; whole (usually prec. by *in the*): *People, in the mass, mean well.* **4.** a considerable assemblage, number, or quantity: *a mass of errors; a mass of troops.* **5.** bulk, size, expanse, or massiveness: *towers of great mass and strength.* **6.** *Fine Arts.* **a.** *Painting.* an expanse of color or tone that defines form or shape in general outline rather than in detail. **b.** a shape or three-dimensional volume that has or gives the illusion of having weight, density, and bulk. **7.** the main body, bulk, or greater part of anything: *the great mass of American films.* **8.** *Physics.* the quantity of matter as determined from its weight or from Newton's second law of motion. *Abbr.:* m Cf. **weight** (def. 2), **relativistic mass, rest mass. 9.** *Pharm.* a preparation of thick, pasty consistency, from which pills are made. **10. the masses,** the ordinary or common people as a whole; the working classes or the lower social classes. *—adj.* **11.** pertaining to, involving, or affecting a large number of people: *mass unemployment; mass migrations; mass murder.* **12.** participated in or performed by a large number of people, esp. together in a group: *mass demonstrations; mass suicide.* **13.** pertaining to, involving, or characteristic of the mass of the people: *the mass mind; a movie designed to appeal to a mass audience.* **14.** reaching or designed to reach a large number of people: *television, newspapers, and other means of mass communication.* **15.** done on a large scale or in large quantities: *mass destruction.* *—v.i.* **16.** to come together in or form a mass or masses: *The clouds are massing in the west.* *—v.t.* **17.** to gather into or dispose in a mass or masses; assemble: *The houses are massed in blocks.* [1350–1400; ME *masse* < L *massa* mass < Gk *mâza* barley cake, akin to *mássein* to knead] **—mass•ed•ly** (mas′id lē, mast′lē), *adv.*
—Syn. 2. assemblage, heap, congeries. **4.** collection, accumulation, pile, conglomeration. **5.** magnitude, dimension. See **size**[1]. **7.** majority. **10.** proletariat, plebeians. **17.** collect, marshal, amass, aggregate. **—Ant. 17.** disperse.

Mass (mas), *n.* **1.** the celebration of the Eucharist. Cf. **High Mass, Low Mass. 2.** (*sometimes l.c.*) a musical setting of certain parts of this service, as the Kyrie eleison, Gloria, Credo, Sanctus, Benedictus, and Agnus Dei. [bef. 900; ME *masse,* OE *mæsse* < VL **messa,* LL *missa,* formerly fem. of L *missus,* ptp. of *mittere* to send, dismiss; perh. extracted from a phrase in the service with *missa est* and a fem. subject]

Mass., Massachusetts.

mas•sa (mas′ə), *n.* marse.

Mas•sa (mäs′sä), *n.* a city in W Italy, near the Ligurian Sea: important marble industry. 65,346.

Mas•sa•chu•sett (mas′ə chōō′sit), *n., pl.* **-setts,** (*esp. collectively*) **-sett** for 1. **1.** a member of an extinct tribe of North American Indians of eastern Massachusetts. **2.** the extinct Algonquian language of the Massachusett and Wampanoag Indians. Also, **Mas′sa•chu′set, Massachusetts.** [1610–20, *Amer.*; the Massachusett name of Great Blue Hill south of Boston, lit., at the big hill]

Mas•sa•chu•setts (mas′ə chōō′sits), *n.* **1.** a state in the NE United States, on the Atlantic coast. 5,737,037; 8257 sq. mi. (21,385 sq. km). *Cap.:* Boston. *Abbr.:* MA (for use with zip code), Mass. **2.** Massachusett.

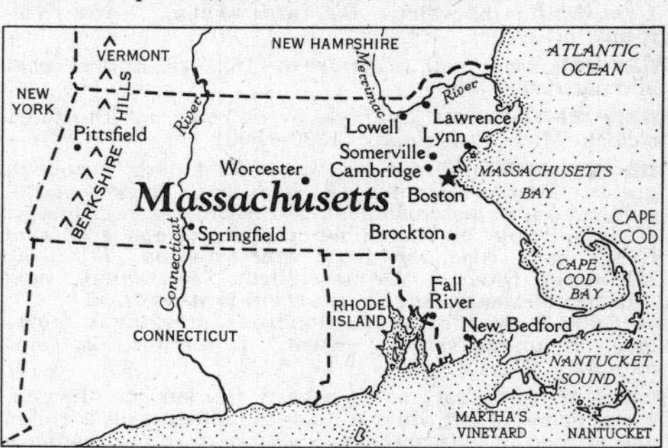

Mas′sachu′setts bal′lot, a ballot on which the candidates, with their party designations, are listed alphabetically in columns under the office for which they were nominated. Cf. **Indiana ballot, office-block ballot.** [1890–95, *Amer.*]

Mas′sachu′setts Bay′, an inlet of the Atlantic, off the E coast of Massachusetts.

Mas′sachu′setts Bay′ Com′pany, a company, chartered in England in 1629 to establish a colony on Massachusetts Bay, that founded Boston in 1630.

mas•sa•cre (mas′ə kər), *n., v.,* **-cred, -cring.** *—n.* **1.** the unnecessary, indiscriminate killing of a large number of human beings or animals, as in barbarous warfare or persecution or for revenge or plunder. **2.** a general slaughter, as of persons or animals: *the massacre of millions during the war.* **3.** *Informal.* a crushing defeat, esp. in sports. *—v.t.* **4.** to kill unnecessarily and indiscriminately, esp. a large number of persons. **5.** *Informal.* to defeat decisively, esp. in sports. [1575–85; (n.) < MF *massacre,* n. deriv. of *massacrer,* OF *maçacrer, macecler,* prob. < VL **matteūcculāre,* v. deriv. of **matteūca* mallet (see MASHIE, MACE[1]); (v.) < MF *massacrer*] **—mas′sa•crer** (mas′ə krər), *n.*
—Syn. 1, 2. carnage, extermination, butchery, genocide. **4.** slay. See **slaughter.**

mass′ ac′tion law′, *Chem.* See **law of mass action.**

mas•sage (mə säzh′, -säj′ *or, esp. Brit.,* mas′äzh), *n., v.,* **-saged, -sag•ing.** *—n.* **1.** the act or art of treating the body by rubbing, kneading, patting, or the like, to stimulate circulation, increase suppleness, relieve tension, etc. **2.** *Slang.* attentive or indulgent treatment; pampering: *ego massage.* *—v.t.* **3.** to treat by massage. **4.** *Slang.* to treat with special care and attention; coddle or pamper: *The store massages its regular customers with gifts and private sales.* **5.** *Informal.* **a.** to manipulate, maneuver, or handle skillfully: *to massage a bill through the Senate.* **b.** to manipulate, organize, or rearrange (data, figures, or the like) to produce a specific result, esp. a favorable one: *The auditors discovered that the company had massaged the books.* [1875–80; < F, equiv. to *mass(er)* to massage (< Ar *massa* to handle) + *-age* -AGE] **—mas•sag′er, mas•sag′ist,** *n.*

massage′ par′lor, 1. a commercial establishment providing massages. **2.** a commercial establishment providing sexual services under the guise of offering massages. [1910–15]

Mas•sa•pe•qua (mas′ə pē′kwə), *n.* a town on SW Long Island, in SE New York. 24,454.

Mas′sape′qua Park′, a town on SW Long Island, in SE New York. 19,779.

mas•sa•sau•ga (mas′ə sô′gə), *n.* a small rattlesnake, *Sistrurus catenatus,* ranging from the Great Lakes to the Mexican border. [1830–40; irreg. after *Missisauga* River, Ontario, Canada]

Mas•sa•soit (mas′ə soit′), *n.* c1580–1661, North American Indian leader: sachem of the Wampanoag tribe; negotiator of peace treaty with the Pilgrims 1621 (father of King Philip).

Mas•sa•ua (mə sä′wə), *n.* a seaport in E Eritrea, in N Ethiopia, on the Red Sea. 18,490. Also, **Mas•sa′wa.**

Mass′ book′, missal (def. 1). [1150–1200; ME]

Mass′ card′, *Rom. Cath. Ch.* a card stating that a Mass will be said, esp. for a deceased person, and sent by the donor, as to the family of the deceased.

mass•cult (mas′kult′), *n.* the forms of culture, as music, drama, and literature, as selected, interpreted, and popularized by the mass media for dissemination to the widest possible audience. [MASS + CULT(URE); coined by U.S. author and social critic Dwight Macdonald (b. 1906) in the essay "Masscult and Midcult" (1960)]

mass′ de′fect, *Physics.* the amount by which the mass of an atomic nucleus differs from the sum of the masses of its constituent particles, being the mass equivalent of the energy released in the formation of the nucleus. Cf. **binding energy.** [1925–30]

mas•sé (ma sā′ *or, esp. Brit.,* mas′ē), *n. Billiards.* a stroke made by hitting the cue ball with the cue held almost or quite perpendicular to the table. Also called **massé′ shot′.** [1870–75; < F: lit., hammered, i.e., struck from above, straight down, equiv. to *masse* sledge hammer (OF *mace;* see MACE[1]) + *-é* -EE]

Mas•se•na (mə sē′nə), *n.* a city in N New York, on the St. Lawrence River. 12,851.

Mas•sé•na (mᴀ sā nᴀ′), *n.* **An•dré** (äɴ drā′), **duc de Ri•vo•li** (*Fr.* rē vô lē′; *It.* rē′vô lē) and **Prince d'Ess•ling** (des′ling), 1758–1817, French marshal under Napoleon I.

mass′-en′er′gy equa′tion (mas′en′ər jē), *Physics.* the equation, $E=mc^2$, formulated by Albert Einstein, expressing the equivalence between mass and energy, where E is energy, m is mass, and c is the velocity of light. [1940–45]

Mas•se•net (mas′ə nā′; *Fr.* mas[ə] ne′), *n.* **Jules É•mile Fré•dé•ric** (zhyl ā mēl′ frā dā rēk′), 1842–1912, French composer.

mas•se•ter (ma sē′tər), *n. Anat.* a short, thick, masticatory muscle, the action of which assists in closing the jaws by raising the mandible or lower jaw. [1660–70; < NL < Gk *massētḗr,* var. of *masētḗr* chewer, masseter, equiv. to *masē-,* var. s. of *masâsthai* to chew + *-tēr* agentive suffix] **—mas•se•ter•ic** (mas′i ter′ik), *adj.*

mas•seur (mə sûr′; *Fr.* mᴀ sœʀ′), *n., pl.* **-seurs** (-sûrz′; *Fr.* -sœʀ′). a man who provides massage as a profession or occupation. [1875–80; < F; see MASSAGE, -EUR]

mas•seuse (mə sōōs′, -sōōz′; *Fr.* mᴀ sœz′). a woman who provides massage as a profession or occupation. [1875–80; < F; see MASSAGE, -EUSE]

Mas•sey (mas′ē), *n.* **1. Vincent,** 1887–1967, Canadian statesman: governor general 1952–59. **2. William Ferguson,** 1856–1925, New Zealand statesman, born in Ireland: prime minister 1912–25.

mass′ hyste′ria, *Psychol.* a condition affecting a group of persons, characterized by excitement or anxiety, irrational behavior or beliefs, or inexplicable symptoms of illness. [1930–35]

mas•si•cot (mas′i kot′), *n.* monoxide of lead, PbO, in the form of a yellow powder, used as a pigment and drier. [1425–75; late ME *masticot* < MF < It *massicotto* < Ar *mashaqūniyā,* perh. < Gk]

mas•sif (ma sēf′, mas′if; *Fr.* mᴀ sēf′), *n.* **1.** a compact portion of a mountain range, containing one or more summits. **2.** a large elevated block of old complex rocks resistant to both erosion and crustal folding. **3.** a band or zone of the earth's crust raised or depressed as a unit and bounded by faults. [1515–25; < F, n. use of *massif* MASSIVE]

Mas•sif Cen•tral (mᴀ sēf säɴ tʀᴀl′), a great plateau and the chief water divide of France, in the central part.

Mas•sil•lon (mas′ə lon′), *n.* a city in NE Ohio. 30,557.

Mas•sine (mä sēn′), *n.* **Lé•o•nide** (lā ô nēd′), 1896–1979, U.S. ballet dancer and choreographer, born in Russia.

Mas•sin•ger (mas′ən jər), *n.* **Philip,** 1583–1640, English dramatist: collaborated with John Fletcher.

Mas•si•nis•a (mas′ə nis′ə), *n.* Masinissa.

mas•sive (mas′iv), *adj.* **1.** consisting of or forming a large mass; bulky and heavy: *massive columns.* **2.** large and heavy-looking: *a massive forehead.* **3.** large in scale, amount, or degree: *a massive breakdown in communications; massive reductions in spending.* **4.** solid or substantial; great or imposing: *massive erudition.* **5.** *Mineral.* having no outward crystal form, although sometimes crystalline in internal structure. [1375–1425; late ME (see MASS, -IVE); r. ME *massif* < MF] **—mas′•sive•ly,** *adv.* **—mas′sive•ness, mas•siv′i•ty,** *n.*

mas′sive retalia′tion, a strategy of military counterattack that involves the use of nuclear weapons. [1950–55, *Amer.*]

mass•less (mas′lis), *adj. Physics.* pertaining to an elementary particle having zero rest mass, as a photon. [1875–80; MASS + -LESS] **—mass′less•ness,** *n.*

mass′ man′, a hypothetical common man, esp. one held to be typical of a mass society, to be characterized by the absence of unique values or distinct personality traits, to lack a sense of personal or social responsibility, and to be readily manipulated by the techniques developed by mass media. [1925–30]

mass′ mar′keting, the production and distribution of a product intended to be sold to a relatively high proportion of the population. [1940–45] **—mass′ mar′•keter.**

mass′ mar′ket pa′perback, a relatively inexpensive paperbound book, typically measuring about 4½ × 7 in. (11 × 18 cm), that is distributed on newsstands, in supermarkets, etc., as well as in bookstores. Also, **mass′-market pa′perback.** Cf. **trade paperback.**

mass′ me′dium, *pl.* **mass media.** any of the means of communication, as television or newspapers, that reach very large numbers of people. [1920–25]

mass′ meet′ing, a large or general assembly to discuss or hear discussed some matter of common interest or concern: *a mass meeting to protest the proliferation of nuclear weapons.* [1725–35, *Amer.*]

mass′ mer′chandiser, a retailer or retail store that seeks to sell large quantities of goods quickly through such means as discounting, customer self-service, or unadorned display and packaging, as in a warehouse. [1955–60] **—mass′ mer′chandising.**

mass′ move′ment, an organized effort by a large number of people, esp. those not forming part of the elite of a given society, to bring about pervasive changes in existing social, economic, or political institutions, frequently characterized by charismatic leadership. [1895–1900]

mass′ noun′, *Gram.* a noun, as *water, electricity,* or *happiness,* that typically refers to an indefinitely divisible substance or an abstract notion, and that in English cannot be used, in such a sense, with the indefinite article or in the plural. [1930–35]

mass′ num′ber, *Physics.* the integer nearest in value to the atomic weight of an atom and equal to the number of nucleons in the nucleus of the atom. *Symbol:* A [1920–25]

Mas′son disk′ (mas′ən), a white disk on which a series of concentric gray circles appear to vanish intermittently when the disk is rotated, used for testing a person's fluctuation of attention and visual threshold.

Mas•so•rah (mə sôr′ə, -sōr′ə), *n.* Masorah. Also, **Mas•so′ra.**

Mas•so•rete (mas′ə rēt′), *n.* Masorete.

Mas•so•ret•ic (mas′ə ret′ik), *adj.* Masoretic. Also, **Mas′so•ret′i•cal.**

mas•so•ther•a•py (mas′ō ther′ə pē), *n. Med.* treatment by massage. [MASS(AGE) + -O- + THERAPY] **—mas′so•ther′a•pist,** *n.*

mass-pro•duce (mas′prə dōōs′, -dyōōs′), *v.t.,* **-duced, -duc•ing.** to produce or manufacture (goods) in large quantities, esp. by machinery. [1920–25] **—mass′-pro•duc′er,** *n.* **—mass′-pro•duc′i•ble,** *adj.*

mass′ produc′tion, the production or manufacture of goods in large quantities, esp. by machinery. [1915–20]

mass′ psychol′ogy, the study of the behavior of large groups of people. [1895–1900]

mass′ soci′ety, *Sociol.* a society whose members are characterized by having segmentalized, impersonal relations, a high degree of physical and social mobility, a spectator relation to events, and a pronounced tendency to conform to external popular norms. [1945–50]

mass′ spec′trograph, *Physics.* a mass spectroscope for recording a mass spectrum on a photographic plate. [1915–20]

mass′ spectrom′eter, *Physics.* a device for identifying the kinds of particles present in a given substance: the particles are ionized and beamed through an electromagnetic field and the manner in which they are deflected is indicative of their mass and, thus, their identity. [1930–35]

mass′ spec′troscope, *Physics.* an instrument used to determine the masses of small, electrically charged particles. [1955–60] **—mass′ spectros′copy.**

mass′ spec′trum, *Physics.* a spectrum of charged particles, arranged in order of mass or mass-to-charge ratios. [1915–20]

mass′ trans′it, a system of large-scale public transportation in a given metropolitan area, typically comprising buses, subways, and elevated trains. Cf. **rapid transit.**

mass′ wast′ing, *Geol.* downhill movement of soil and rock fragments induced by gravity. Also called **wasting.**

mass•y (mas′ē), *adj.,* **mass•i•er, mass•i•est.** massive. [1350–1400; ME; see MASS, -Y[1]] **—mass′i•ness,** *n.*

Mas•sys (mä′sis), *n.* **Quen•tin** (kven′tin; *Eng.* kwen′-tn), 1466?–1530, Flemish painter. Also, **Matsys, Metsys.**

mast[1] (mast, mäst), *n.* **1.** *Naut.* **a.** a spar or structure rising above the hull and upper portions of a ship or boat to hold sails, spars, rigging, booms, signals, etc., at some point on the fore-and-aft line, as a foremast or mainmast. **b.** any of a number of individual spars composing such a structure, as a topmast supported on trestletrees at the head of a lower mast. **c.** any of various portions of a single spar that are beside particular sails, as a topgallant mast and royal mast formed as a single spar. **2.** Also called **pillar.** the upright support of a jib crane. **3.** any upright pole, as a support for an aerial, a post in certain cranes, etc. **4. before the mast,** *Naut.* as an unlicensed sailor: *He served several years before the mast.* —*v.t.* **5.** to provide with a mast or masts. [bef. 900; ME; OE *mæst;* c. G *Mast;* akin to L *mālus* pole] **—mast′less,** *adj.* **—mast′like′,** *adj.*

mast[2] (mast, mäst), *n.* the fruit of the oak and beech or other forest trees, used as food for hogs and other animals. [bef. 900; ME; OE *mæst;* c. G *Mast;* akin to MEAT]

mast-, var. of **masto-** before a vowel: *mastectomy.*

mas•ta•ba (mas′tə bə), *n.* **1.** an ancient Egyptian tomb made of mud brick, rectangular in plan with sloping sides and a flat roof. **2.** (in Islamic countries) a fixed bench, esp. one of stone. Also, **mas′ta•bah.** [1595–1605; < Ar *maṣṭabah*]

mas•tax (mas′taks), *n.* the muscular pharynx of a rotifer, containing a chewing apparatus. [1850–55; < NL < Gk *mástax* mouth, jaws, akin to *masâsthai* to chew]

mast′ ball′, *Naut.* an ornamental ball forming the truck of a mast.

mast′ band′, *Naut.* a hoop of metal around a mast, used as a reinforcement or as an object for attaching stays, tackles, etc.

mast′ bed′, *Naut.* a construction in a wooden deck around the opening for a mast.

mast′ cell′, *Biol.* a large granular cell, common in connective tissue, that produces heparin, histamine, and serotonin. [1885–90; partial trans. of G *Mastzelle,* equiv. to *Mast* fattening of animals for slaughter, MAST[2] + *Zelle* cell]

mast′ clamp′, *Naut.* **1.** a pierced slab of hardwood built into the deck structure of a small ship or boat to receive the force of the mast, which is fitted tightly through it. **2.** Also called **mast hasp.** a metal collar fitted to a thwart of a small boat to steady a mast.

mast′ cloth′, *Naut.* **1.** a partial lining sewed to the back of a square sail to prevent chafing from contact with the mast. **2.** Also called **mast′ cov′er.** a cloth covering part of a mast to protect it against smoke from a funnel. [1635–45]

mas•tec•to•my (ma stek′tə mē), *n., pl.* **-mies.** *Surg.* the operation of removing all or part of the breast or mamma. Also called **mammectomy.** [1920–25; MAST- + -ECTOMY]

mas•ter (mas′tər, mä′stər), *n.* **1.** a person with the ability or power to use, control, or dispose of something: *a master of six languages; to be master of one's fate.* **2.** an owner of a slave, animal, etc. **3.** an employer of workers or servants. **4.** the male head of a household. **5.** a person eminently skilled in something, as an occupation, art, or science: *the great masters of the Impressionist period.* **6.** a person whose teachings others accept or follow: *a Zen master.* **7.** *Chiefly Brit.* a male teacher or schoolmaster. **8.** a worker qualified to teach apprentices and to carry on a trade independently. **9.** a title given to a bridge or chess player who has won or placed in a certain number of officially recognized tournaments. **10.** a person holding this title. **11.** a person who commands a merchant ship; captain. **12.** a victor or conqueror. **13.** a presiding officer. **14.** an officer of the court to whom some or all of the issues in a case may be referred for the purpose of taking testimony and making a report to the court. **15. the Master,** Jesus Christ. **16.** a person who has been awarded a master's degree. **17.** a boy or young man (used chiefly as a term of address). **18.** Also called **matrix.** an original document, drawing, manuscript, etc., from which copies are made. **19.** a device for controlling another device operating in a similar way. Cf. **slave** (def. 5). **20.** *Recording.* **a.** matrix (def. 13). **b.** a tape or disk from which duplicates may be made. **21.** Also called **copy negative.** *Photog.* a film, usually a negative, used primarily for making large quantities of prints. **22.** See **master of foxhounds. 23.** *Archaic.* a work of art produced by a master. —*adj.* **24.** being master; exercising mastery; dominant. **25.** chief or principal: *a master list.* **26.** directing or controlling: *a master switch.* **27.** of or pertaining to a master from which copies are made: *master film; master matrix; master record; master tape.* **28.** dominating or predominant: *a master play.* **29.** being a master of some occupation, art, etc.; eminently skilled: *a master diplomat; a master pianist.* **30.** being a master carrying on one's trade independently, rather than a worker employed by another: *a master plumber.* **31.** characteristic of a master; showing mastery. —*v.t.* **32.** to make oneself master of; become an adept in: *to master a language.* **33.** to conquer or overcome: *to master one's pride.* **34.** to rule or direct as master: *to master a crew.* **35.** *Recording.* to produce a master tape, disk, or record of: *The producer recorded, mixed, and mastered the new album.* [bef. 900; ME *maistre, maister,* OE *magister* < L; akin to *magnus* great] **—mas′ter•less,** *adj.*

—Syn. 1. adept, expert. **26.** main, leading, primary, prime, cardinal. **31.** adept, expert, skillful. **33.** subdue, control. **34.** govern, manage.

mas′ter al′loy, *Metall.* an alloy rich in certain elements, used in small quantities as an additive to melts of alloyed metal.

mas•ter-at-arms (mas′tər ət ärmz′, mä′stər-), *n., pl.* **mas•ters-at-arms. 1.** an officer of a fraternal organization, veterans' society, or the like, empowered to maintain order, exclude unauthorized persons, etc. **2.** *Navy.* a petty officer who has various duties, such as keeping order on the ship, taking charge of prisoners, etc. [1740–50]

mas′ter bath′, a private bathroom adjoining a master bedroom.

mas′ter bed′room, a principal bedroom in a house or apartment, usually the largest, typically occupied by the person or persons who head the household. [1925–30]

mas′ter build′er, 1. a building contractor. **2.** a person skilled in the art of building; architect. [1550–60]

Mas′ter Build′er, The, a play (1892) by Ibsen.

mas′ter class′, a small class for advanced students, esp. a class in performance skills conducted by a distinguished musician. [1950–55]

mas′ter cyl′inder, the hydraulic pump of an automotive braking system that contains a cylinder and one or two pistons, is actuated by the brake pedal, and supplies hydraulic fluid under pressure to the brakes at each wheel.

mas′ter file′, *Computers.* a permanent file, periodically updated, that serves as an authoritative source of data.

mas•ter•ful (mas′tər fəl, mä′stər-), *adj.* **1.** dominating; self-willed; imperious. **2.** having or showing the qualities of a master; authoritative; powerful. **3.** showing mastery or skill; masterly: *a masterful performance.* [1300–50; ME; see MASTER, -FUL] **—mas′ter•ful•ly,** *adv.* **—mas′ter•ful•ness,** *n.*

—Syn. 1. peremptory. **3.** consummate, supreme; adept, expert, skilled, skillful, matchless.

—Usage. At an earlier time, both MASTERFUL and MASTERLY had two senses: "having a commanding or domineering nature or manner" and "possessing the skill of a master." The earliest sense of MASTERLY, "having a commanding nature," has been obsolete since the 18th century. MASTERFUL continues to be used in all varieties of speech and writing in both senses, despite the protests of some who prefer that MASTERFUL be restricted to the sense "dominating or imperious": *The envoy's masterful behavior irritated the citizens. Few painters have produced so many masterful* (or *masterly*) *portraits.*

mas′ter hand′, **1.** an expert: *a master hand at diplomacy.* **2.** great expertness: *to show a master hand.* Also, **mas′ter-hand′.** [1700–10]

mas′ter key′, a key that will open a number of different locks, the proper keys of which are not interchangeable. [1570–80]

mas•ter•ly (mas′tər lē, mä′stər-), *adj.* **1.** like or befitting a master, as in skill or art; worthy of a master; very skillful: *a masterly presentation of the budget.* —*adv.* **2.** in a masterly manner. [1375–1425; late ME *maisterly.* See MASTER, -LY] —**mas′ter•li•ness,** *n.*
—**Usage.** See **masterful.**

mas′ter ma′son, **1.** (*often caps.*) a Freemason who has reached the third degree. **2.** an expert mason. [1325–75; ME *maister masoun*]

mas′ter mechan′ic, a mechanic, esp. one who is thoroughly skilled, in charge of other mechanics. [1830–40]

mas•ter•mind (mas′tər mīnd′, mä′stər-), *v.t.* **1.** to plan and direct (a usually complex project or activity), esp. skillfully: *Two colonels had masterminded the revolt.* —*n.* **2.** a person who originates or is primarily responsible for the execution of a particular idea, project, or the like: *the masterminds of company policy.* [1710–20; MASTER + MIND]

Mas′ter of Arts′, **1.** a master's degree given usually in a specific branch of the humanities or social sciences. **2.** a person who has been awarded this degree. *Abbr.:* M.A., A.M. [1490–1500]

mas′ter of cer′emonies, a person who directs the entertainment at a party, dinner, nightclub, radio or television broadcast, or the like, acting as host and introducing the speakers or performers. [1655–65]

mas′ter of fox′hounds, the person responsible for the conduct of a fox hunt and to whom all members of the hunt and its staff are responsible. *Abbr.:* M.F.H. [1855–60]

Mas′ter of Sci′ence, **1.** a master's degree given usually in a specific branch of the natural sciences, mathematics, or technology. **2.** a person who has been awarded this degree. *Abbr.:* M.S., M.Sc., S.M., Sc.M. [1900–05]

Mas′ter of the Rev′els, an English court official from the late 15th to early 18th centuries responsible to the Lord Chamberlain for overseeing and paying for court entertainments.

mas•ter•piece (mas′tər pēs′, mä′stər-), *n.* **1.** a person's greatest piece of work, as in an art. **2.** anything done with masterly skill: *a masterpiece of improvisation.* **3.** a consummate example of skill or excellence of any kind: *The chef's cake was a masterpiece.* **4.** a piece made by a person aspiring to the rank of master in a guild or other craft organization as a proof of competence. [1570–80; MASTER + PIECE, modeled on D *meesterstuk,* G *Meisterstück*]

mas′ter plan′, a general plan or program for achieving an objective. [1925–30]

mas•ter-plan (mas′tər plan′, mä′stər-), *v.t.,* **-planned, -plan•ning.** **1.** to construct a master plan for: *to master-plan one's career.* **2.** to develop or improve (land, a community, a building complex, or the like) through a long-range plan that balances and harmonizes all elements: *The engineers master-planned the island to provide for increases in the tourist population.*

mas′ter point′, a point awarded to a bridge player who has won or placed in an officially recognized tournament.

mas′ter pol′icy, *Insurance.* a single policy covering a group of people, typically employees of a company, issued to an employer.

mas′ter race′, a race, people, or nation, as the Germans during the Nazi period, whose members consider themselves superior to all others and therefore justified in conquering and ruling them. [1925–30]

Mas•ters (mas′tərz, mä′stərz), *n.* **1. Edgar Lee,** 1869–1950, U.S. poet and novelist. **2. William Howell,** born 1915, U.S. physician: researcher on human sexual behavior (husband of Virginia E. Johnson).

mas′ter's degree′, a degree awarded by a graduate school or department, usually to a person who has completed at least one year of graduate study. Also called **mas′ter's.**

mas′ter ser′geant, **1.** *Army, Air Force, Marine Corps.* a noncommissioned officer ranking next to the highest noncommissioned officer. **2.** *U.S. Air Force.* a noncommissioned officer of one of the three top enlisted grades. [1930–35]

mas•ter•ship (mas′tər ship′, mä′stər-), *n.* **1.** the office, function, or authority of a master. **2.** control; command: *to have mastership over one's desires.* **3.** mastery, as of a subject. **4.** expert skill or knowledge: *He played with the mastership of a devoted musician.* [1375–1425; late ME; see MASTER, -SHIP]

mas•ter•sing•er (mas′tər sing′ər, mä′stər-), *n.* Meistersinger (def. 1). [1800–10]

mas′ter-slave′ manip′ulator (mas′tər slāv′, mä′stər-), any of various devices, guided by the hand of the operator, for imitating the motions and tactile sensitivity of the human hand to a greater or lesser extent: used in situations in which direct handling of the objects or materials involved would be dangerous or impossible. [1950–55]

CONCISE ETYMOLOGY KEY: <, descended or borrowed from; >, whence; b., blend of, blended; c., cognate with; cf., compare; deriv., derivative; equiv., equivalent; imit., imitative; obl., oblique; r., replacing; s., stem; sp., spelling, spelled; resp., respelling, respelled; trans., translation; ?, origin unknown; *, unattested; ‡, probably earlier than. See the full key inside the front cover.

Mas•ter•son (mas′tər sən, mä′stər-), *n.* **William Barclay** ("*Bat*"), 1853–1921, U.S. frontier law officer.

mas•ter•stroke (mas′tər strōk′, mä′stər-), *n.* a masterly action or achievement; an extremely skillful or effective action: *War was avoided by a masterstroke of diplomacy.* Also, **mas′ter stroke′.** [1670–80; MASTER + STROKE[1]]

mas•ter•work (mas′tər wûrk′, mä′stər-), *n.* masterpiece. [1600–10; MASTER + WORK]

mas′ter work′man, **1.** a worker in charge. **2.** a person who is master of a craft. [1425–75; late ME]

mas•ter•wort (mas′tər wûrt′, -wôrt′, mä′stər-), *n.* a European plant, *Astrantia major,* of the parsley family, having pinkish-rose or white flower clusters with purplish bracts beneath. [1540–50; MASTER + WORT[2]]

mas•ter•y (mas′tə rē, mä′stə-), *n., pl.* **-ter•ies** for 1-4. **1.** command or grasp, as of a subject: *a mastery of Italian.* **2.** superiority or victory: *mastery over one's enemies.* **3.** the act of mastering. **4.** expert skill or knowledge. **5.** the state of being master; power of command or control. [1175–1225; MASTER + -Y[3]; r. ME *maistrie* < OF]

mast′ hasp′, *Naut.* See **mast clamp** (def. 2).

mast•head (mast′hed′, mäst′-), *n.* **1.** Also called **flag.** a statement printed in all issues of a newspaper, magazine, or the like, usually on the editorial page, giving the publication's name, the names of the owner and staff, etc. **2.** Also called **nameplate.** a line of type on the front page of a newspaper or the cover of a periodical giving the name of the publication. **3.** *Naut.* **a.** the head of a mast. **b.** the uppermost point of a mast. —*v.t. Naut.* **4.** to hoist a yard to the fullest extent. **5.** to hoist to the truck of a mast, as a flag. **6.** to send to the upper end of a mast as a punishment. —*adj.* **7.** *Naut.* run up to the head of a mast: *masthead rig.* [1740–50; MAST[1] + HEAD]

mast′ house′, *Naut.* **1.** a deckhouse built around a mast as a platform for cargo-handling machinery, gear, and controls. **2.** (formerly) a towerlike crane for stepping and removing masts from ships or boats. **3.** a building in which masts are made. [1760–70]

mas•tic (mas′tik), *n.* **1.** Also called **lentisk.** a small Mediterranean tree, *Pistacia lentiscus,* of the cashew family, that is the source of an aromatic resin used in making varnish and adhesives. **2.** any of several similar or related trees, as a pepper tree, *Schinus molle,* of western South America. **3.** the resin obtained from the mastic. **4.** any similar resin, esp. one yielded by other trees of the same genus. **5.** *Building Trades.* **a.** any of various preparations containing bituminous materials and used as an adhesive or seal. **b.** a pasty form of cement used for filling holes in masonry or plaster. [1350–1400; ME *mastyk* < L *mastichē* < Gk *mastíchē* chewing gum, akin to *mastichân* to gnash the teeth]

mas•ti•cate (mas′ti kāt′), *v.t., v.i.,* **-cat•ed, -cat•ing.** **1.** to chew. **2.** to reduce to a pulp by crushing or kneading, as rubber. [1640–50; < LL *masticātus,* ptp. of *masticāre* to chew. See MASTIC, -ATE[1]] —**mas•ti•ca•ble** (mas′ti kə bəl), *adj.* —**mas′ti•ca′tion,** *n.* —**mas′ti•ca′tor,** *n.*

mas•ti•ca•to•ry (mas′ti kə tôr′ē, -tōr′ē), *adj., n., pl.* **-ries.** —*adj.* **1.** of, pertaining to, or used in or for mastication. —*n.* **2.** *Pharm.* a medicinal substance to be chewed, as to promote the secretion of saliva. [1605–15; < NL *masticātōrius.* See MASTICATE, -TORY[1]]

mas•tiff (mas′tif, mä′stif), *n.* one of a breed of large, powerful, short-haired dogs having an apricot, fawn, or brindled coat. [1300–50; ME *mastif,* perh. extracted from AF *masti(n)s* (taken as **mastifs*), pl. of OF *mastin* < VL (*canis*) **ma(n)suētīnus,* deriv. of L *mansuētus* tame, mild (see MANSUETUDE)]

mastiff,
30 in. (76 cm)
high at shoulder

mas′tiff bat′, any insectivorous bat of the family Molossidae, found in warm areas throughout the world, having a naked tail, folded ears, and small wings and most often seen running along the ground. [1850–55]

mas•tig•i•um (ma stij′ē əm), *n., pl.* **mas•tig•i•a** (ma-stij′ē ə). an extensible, lashlike, anal organ in certain caterpillars. [1895–1900; < NL < Gk *mastígion,* dim. of *mástix* whip]

Mas•ti•goph•o•ra (mas′ti gof′ər ə), *n.* a phylum of protozoans comprising nonphotosynthetic, chiefly free-living flagellates: some species are important pathogens of humans and other animals. [< NL (neut. pl.) < Gk *mastigophóros* whip-bearing, equiv. to *mastig-,* s. of *mástix* whip + -o- -o- + *-phoros* -PHORE. See MASTIGIUM, -PHOROUS]

mas•ti•goph•o•ran (mas′ti gof′ər ən), *n.* **1.** Also, **mas•ti•go•phore** (mas′ti gə fôr′, -fōr′). a protozoan of the phylum Mastigophora. —*adj.* **2.** belonging or pertaining to the Mastigophora. [1905–10; MASTIGOPHOR(A) + -AN]

mast•ing (mas′ting, mä′sting), *n. Naut.* **1.** the masts of a ship, taken as a whole. **2.** the technique, act, or process of placing masts in sailing ships. [1620–30; MAST[1] + -ING[1]]

mas•ti•tis (ma stī′tis), *n.* **1.** *Pathol.* inflammation of the breast. **2.** *Vet. Pathol.* inflammation of the udder, esp. of cows; garget. [1835–45; MAST- + -ITIS] —**mas•tit•ic** (ma stit′ik), *adj.*

masto-, a combining form meaning "breast," used in the formation of compound words: *mastopathy.* Also, *esp. before a vowel,* **mast-.** [comb. form repr. Gk *mastós* breast]

mas•to•car•ci•no•ma (mas′tō kär′sə nō′mə), *n., pl.* **-mas, -ma•ta** (-mə tə). *Pathol.* carcinoma of the breast. [MASTO- + CARCINOMA]

mas•to•cy•to•sis (mas′tō sī tō′sis), *n. Pathol.* an overproduction of mast cells in body tissues. [MAST (CELL) + -O- + -CYTE + -OSIS]

mas•to•don (mas′tə don′), *n.* **1.** a massive, elephant-like mammal of the genus *Mammut* (*Mastodon*), that flourished worldwide from the Miocene through the Pleistocene epochs and, in North America, into recent times, having long, curved upper tusks and, in the male, short lower tusks. **2.** a person of immense size, power, influence, etc. [1805–15; < NL < Gk *mast(ós)* breast + *odṓn* tooth] —**mas′to•don′ic,** *adj.*

mastodon,
Mammut americanum,
7 to 9½ ft.
(2.1 to 2.9 m)
high at shoulder

mas•toid (mas′toid), *adj. Anat.* **1.** of or pertaining to the mastoid process. **2.** resembling a breast or nipple. —*n.* **3.** the mastoid process. [1725–35; < NL *mastoīdēs* < Gk *mastoeidḗs.* See MASTO-, -OID]

mas•toid•ec•to•my (mas′toi dek′tə mē), *n., pl.* **-mies.** *Surg.* the removal of part of a mastoid process, usually for draining an infection. [1895–1900; MASTOID + -ECTOMY]

mas•toid•i•tis (mas′toi dī′tis), *n. Pathol.* inflammation of the mastoid process. [1885–90; MASTOID + -ITIS]

mas′toid proc′ess, a large, bony prominence on the base of the skull behind the ear, containing air spaces that connect with the middle ear cavity. Also called **mastoid, mas′toid bone′.** See diag. under **skull.** [1725–35]

mas•top•a•thy (ma stop′ə thē), *n., pl.* **-thies.** *Pathol.* any disease of the breast. [1855–60; MASTO- + -PATHY]

mas•to•pex•y (mas′tə pek′sē), *n. Surg.* fixation of a pendulous breast. [MASTO- + -PEXY]

mas•tur•bate (mas′tər bāt′), *v.,* **-bat•ed, -bat•ing.** —*v.i.* **1.** to engage in masturbation. —*v.t.* **2.** to practice masturbation upon. [1855–60; < L *masturbātus,* ptp. of *masturbārī* to engage in masturbation] —**mas′tur•ba′tor,** *n.*

mas•tur•ba•tion (mas′tər bā′shən), *n.* **1.** the stimulation or manipulation of one's own genitals, esp. to orgasm; sexual self-gratification. **2.** the stimulation, by manual or other means exclusive of coitus, of another's genitals, esp. to orgasm. [1760–70; MASTURBATE + -ION] —**mas′tur•ba′tion•al,** *adj.* —**mas•tur•ba•to•ry** (mas′tər bə tôr′ē, -tōr′ē), *adj.*

Ma•su•ri•a (mə zo͝or′ē ə), *n.* a region in NE Poland, formerly in East Prussia, Germany: German defeat of Russians 1914–15. German, **Ma•su•ren** (mä zo͞o′rən).

Mas•ving•o (mäz ving′gō), *n.* a city in S central Zimbabwe. 35,000. Formerly, **Fort Victoria, Nyanda.**

mat[1] (mat), *n., v.,* **mat•ted, mat•ting.** —*n.* **1.** a piece of fabric made of plaited or woven rushes, straw, hemp, or similar fiber, or of some other pliant material, as rubber, used as a protective covering on a floor or other surface, to wipe the shoes on, etc. **2.** a smaller piece of material, often ornamental, set under a dish of food, a lamp, vase, etc. **3.** *Sports.* **a.** the padded canvas covering the entire floor of a wrestling ring, for protecting the contestants from injury when thrown. **b.** a thick pad placed on the floor for the protection of tumblers and others engaged in gymnastic sports. **4.** a thickly growing or thick and tangled mass, as of hair or weeds. **5.** a sack made of matting, as for coffee or sugar. **6.** a slablike footing of concrete, esp. one for an entire building. **7.** a heavy mesh reinforcement for a concrete slab. **8. go to the mat,** to contend or struggle in a determined or unyielding way: *The President is going to the mat with Congress over the proposed budget cuts.* —*v.t.* **9.** to cover with or as if with mats or matting. **10.** to form into a mat, as by interweaving. —*v.i.* **11.** to become entangled; form tangled masses. [bef. 900; ME, OE *matte* < LL *matta* mat of rushes < Sem; cf. Heb *mittāh* bed] —**mat′less,** *adj.*

mat[2] (mat), *n., v.,* **mat•ted, mat•ting.** —*n.* **1.** a piece of cardboard or other material placed over or under a drawing, painting, photograph, etc., to serve as a frame or provide a border between the picture and the frame. —*v.t.* **2.** to provide (a picture) with a mat. [1835–40; appar. MAT[1], influenced by MATTE[1]]

mat[3] (mat), *adj., n., v.,* **mat•ted, mat•ting.** matte[1].

mat[4] (mat), *n. Print.* **1.** the intaglio, usually of papier-mâché, impressed from type or a cut, from which a stereotype plate is cast. **2.** matrix (def. 8). [1920–25; shortened form of MATRIX]

mat., **1.** matins. **2.** maturity.

M.A.T., Master of Arts in Teaching.

Ma•ta•be•le (mat′ə bē′lē), *n., pl.* **-les,** (*esp. collectively*) **-le.** Ndebele (def. 1). [1815–25]

Mat•a•cil (mat′ə sil), *Chem., Trademark.* a brand of aminocarb.

Ma•ta•di (mə tä′dē), *n.* a seaport in W Zaire, near the mouth of the Zaire (Congo) River. 142,808.

mat•a•dor (mat′ə dôr′), *n.* **1.** the principal bullfighter in a bullfight who passes the bull with a muleta and then, in many countries, kills it with a sword thrust; a torero. **2.** one of the principal cards in skat and certain other games. **3.** (*cap.*) a jet-powered U.S. surface-to-surface missile. [1665–75; < Sp, equiv. to *mata(r)* to kill (perh. < VL **mattāre,* presumed deriv. of LL *mattus* soft, weak; cf. MATTE[1]) + *-dor* -TOR]

Mat•a•gal•pa (mat′ə gal′pə; *Sp.* mä′tä gäl′pä), *n.* a city in W central Nicaragua. 61,383.

Ma•ta Ha•ri (mä′tə här′ē, mat′ə har′ē), (*Gertrud Margarete Zelle*) 1876–1917, Dutch dancer in France: executed as a spy by the French.

Mat•a•mo•ros (mat′ə môr′əs, -mōr′-; *Sp.* mä′tä mô′rôs), *n.* a seaport in NE Mexico, on the Rio Grande opposite Brownsville, Texas. 187,000.

Ma•tane (mə tan′; *Fr.* MA TAN′), *n.* a city in E Quebec, in SE Canada, on the St. Lawrence River. 12,726.

Mat•a•nus•ka (mat′ə no͞o′skə), *n.* **1.** a river in S Alaska flowing SW to Cook Inlet. 90 mi. (145 km) long. **2.** a village in the valley of this river, NE of Anchorage: site of federal experiment in rural resettlement in 1935.

Ma•tan•zas (mə tan′zəs; *Sp.* mä tän′säs), *n.* a seaport on the NW coast of Cuba. 160,097.

Mat•a•pan (mat′ə pan′), *n.* **Cape,** a cape in S Greece, at the S tip of the Peloponnesus.

Ma′ta•ra dia′mond (mä′tər ə, mat′ər ə). See **Matura diamond.**

match[1] (mach), *n.* **1.** a slender piece of wood, cardboard, or other flammable material tipped with a chemical substance that produces fire when rubbed on a rough or chemically prepared surface. **2.** a wick, cord, or the like, prepared to burn at an even rate, used to fire cannon, gunpowder, etc. [1350–1400; ME *macche* wick < MF *meiche,* OF *mesche* < VL **mesca* lamp wick, metathetic var. of L *myxa* < Gk *mýxa* mucus, nostril, nozzle of a lamp]

match[2] (mach), *n.* **1.** a person or thing that equals or resembles another in some respect. **2.** a person or thing able to cope with another as an equal: *to meet one's match.* **3.** a person or thing that is an exact counterpart of another. **4.** a corresponding, suitably associated, or harmonious pair: *The blue hat and green scarf were not a good match.* **5.** *Sports.* **a.** a game or contest in which two or more contestants or teams oppose each other: *a soccer match.* **b.** a contest consisting of a specific number of sets: *a tennis match.* **6.** any contest or competition that resembles a sports match: *a shouting match.* **7.** a person considered with regard to suitability as a partner in marriage: *a good match.* **8.** a matrimonial union; marriage: *Neither family approved of the match.* —*v.t.* **9.** to equal; be equal to: *My talent does not match his.* **10.** to be the match or counterpart of; harmonize with: *The skirt matches the jacket perfectly.* **11.** to cause to correspond; adapt: *to match one's actions to one's beliefs.* **12.** to fit together, as two things: *to match the pieces of a puzzle.* **13.** to fit (boards) together, side by side or end to end, with a tongue-and-groove or rabbeted joint. **14.** to procure or produce an equal to: *Try though we did, we could not match our first success.* **15.** to place in opposition or conflict: *I matched my wits against his strength.* **16.** to provide with an adversary or competitor of equal power: *The teams were well matched.* **17.** to encounter as an adversary with equal power. **18.** to prove a match for. **19.** to unite in marriage; procure a matrimonial alliance for. **20.** to toss (coins) into the air and then compare the matching or contrasting sides that land facing up, as for determining the winner of a bet. **21.** to match coins with. —*v.i.* **22.** to be equal or suitable: *Our talents match.* **23.** to correspond; be of corresponding size, shape, color, pattern, etc.: *These gloves do not match.* **24.** *Archaic.* to ally oneself in marriage. [bef. 900; ME *macche,* OE *gemæcca* mate, fellow] —**match′a•ble,** *adj.* —**match′er,** *n.*

match•board (mach′bôrd′, -bōrd′), *n.* a board having a tongue formed on one edge and a groove of the same dimensions cut into the other, used with similar boards to compose floors, dados, etc. [1840–50; MATCH[2] + BOARD]

match•board•ing (mach′bôr′ding, -bōr′-), *n.* **1.** a construction of matchboards. **2.** a quantity of matchboards. [1860–65; MATCHBOARD + -ING[1]]

match•book (mach′bo͝ok′), *n.* a small cardboard folder into which several rows of paper matches are stapled or glued. [1810–15; MATCH[1] + BOOK]

match•box (mach′boks′), *n.* a small box, usually of cardboard, for matches. [1780–90; MATCH[1] + BOX[1]]

matched′ or′der, *Stock Exchange.* an order placed with a broker to buy a specified stock at a price above the market price with the intention of immediately selling the stock through another broker at the same price. It is designed to give the appearance of active trading in the stock. [1900–05]

match•less (mach′lis), *adj.* having no equal; peerless; unequaled; incomparable: *matchless courage.* [1520–30; MATCH[2] + -LESS] —**match′less•ly,** *adv.* —**match′less•ness,** *n.*

match•list (mach′list′), *n.* a list of names, telephone numbers, and related information compiled to help people find others who are willing to share a resource or service, as a car pool. [MATCH[2] + LIST[1]]

match•lock (mach′lok′), *n.* **1.** an old form of gunlock in which the priming was ignited by a slow match. **2.** a hand gun, usually a musket, with such a lock. [1630–40; MATCH[1] + LOCK[1]]

match•mak•er[1] (mach′mā′kər), *n.* **1.** a person who arranges or tries to arrange marriages by introducing possible mates. **2.** a person who arranges matches for athletic contests, esp. prizefights and wrestling matches. **3.** any person, organization, etc., that brings two parties together, as to effect a sale or other transaction: *an agent serving as a matchmaker between buyers and sellers.* [1630–40; MATCH[2] + MAKER] —**match′mak′ing,** *n., adj.*

match•mak•er[2] (mach′mā′kər), *n.* a person who makes matches for burning. [1635–45; MATCH[1] + MAKER] —**match′mak′ing,** *n., adj.*

match′ plate′, *Metall.* a plate on which patterns are set to be molded. [1870–75]

match′ play′, *Golf.* play in which the score is reckoned by counting the holes won by each side. Cf. **medal play.** [1885–90] —**match′ play′er.**

match point (mach′ point′ *for 1;* mach′ point′ *for 2*), **1.** (in tennis, squash, handball, etc.) the point that if won would enable the scorer or the scorer's side to win the match. **2.** *Duplicate Bridge.* a scoring unit consisting of one point awarded to a partnership for each opposing partnership whose score they better on a hand and of one-half point for each opposing partnership whose score they equal. [1920–25]

match•stick (mach′stik′), *n.* **1.** a short, slender piece of flammable wood used in making matches. **2.** something that suggests a matchstick, as in thinness or fragility. [1785–95; MATCH[1] + STICK[1]]

match-up (mach′up′), *n.* **1.** a pairing or combining; linkage: *a match-up of federal funds with state aid.* **2.** a direct contest or confrontation, as between two athletes or political candidates. **3.** an investigation of similarities and differences; comparison: *a match-up of property taxes in two counties.* Also, **match′up′.** [1960–65; n. use of v. phrase *match up*]

match•wood (mach′wo͝od′), *n.* **1.** wood suitable for matches. **2.** splinters. [1590–1600; MATCH[1] + WOOD[1]]

mate[1] (māt), *n., v.,* **mat•ed, mat•ing.** —*n.* **1. a.** husband or wife; spouse. **2.** one member of a pair of mated animals. **3.** one of a pair: *I can't find the mate to this glove.* **4.** a counterpart. **5.** an associate; fellow worker; comrade; partner (often used in combination): *classmate; roommate.* **6.** friend; buddy; pal (often used as an informal term of address): *Let me give you a hand with that, mate.* **7.** *Naut.* **a.** See **first mate. b.** any of a number of officers of varying degrees of rank subordinate to the master of a merchant ship. **c.** an assistant to a warrant officer or other functionary on a ship. **8.** an aide or helper, as to an artisan; factotum. **9.** a gear, rack, or worm engaging with another gear or worm. **10.** *Archaic.* an equal in reputation; peer; match. —*v.t.* **11.** to join as a mate or as mates. **12.** to bring (animals) together for breeding purposes. **13.** to match or marry. **14.** to join, fit, or associate suitably: *to mate thought with daring action.* **15.** to connect or link: *a telephone system mated to a computerized information service.* **16.** to treat as comparable. —*v.i.* **17.** to associate as a mate or as mates. **18.** (of animals) to copulate. **19.** (of animals) to pair for the purpose of breeding. **20.** to marry. **21.** (of a gear, rack, or worm) to engage with another gear or worm; mesh. **22.** *Archaic.* to consort; keep company. [1350–1400; ME < MLG; r. ME *mette,* OE *gemetta* messmate, guest. See MEAT] —**mate′less,** *adj.*

mate[2] (māt), *n., v.t.,* **mat•ed, mat•ing,** *interj. Chess.* checkmate (defs. 1, 3, 5). [1175–1225; ME *mat* defeated (adj.), defeat (n.) < OF << Pers; see CHECKMATE]

ma•te[3] (mä′tā, mat′ā), *n.* maté.

ma•té (mä′tā, mat′ā, mä tā′), *n.* **1.** a tealike South American beverage made from the dried leaves of an evergreen tree. **2.** a South American tree, *Ilex paraguariensis,* that is the source of this beverage. **3.** the dried leaves of this tree. Also, **mate.** Also called **Paraguay tea, yerba maté.** [1710–20; < AmerSp *mate,* orig. the vessel in which the herb is steeped < Quechua *mati*]

Mat.E., Materials Engineer.

mat•e•las•sé (mät′lə sā′; *Fr.* MATᵊ lä sā′), *n.* an embossed, compound fabric woven on a dobby or Jacquard loom. Also, **mat′e•las•se′, mat′el•las•se′.** [1880–85; < F, ptp. of *matelasser* to quilt, deriv. of *matelas* MATTRESS]

mate•lot (mat′lō, mat′l ō′), *n. Brit. Slang.* a sailor. Also, **mate′low.** [1910–15; < F << MD *mattenoot* sailor, equiv. to *matte* MAT[1] + *noot* companion (D *genoot*)]

mat•e•lote (mat′l ōt′; *Fr.* MATᵊ lōt′), *n.* a highly seasoned fish stew made with white or red wine. [1720–30; < F, deriv. of *matelot* MATELOT]

ma•ter (mā′tər), *n., pl.* **-ters, -tres** (-trēz). **1.** *Brit. Informal.* mother[1]. **2.** the backing holding the movable parts of an astrolabe. [1585–95; < L *māter*]

ma•ter do•lo•ro•sa (mä′ter dô′lô rō′sä; *Eng.* mā′tər dō′lə rō′sə), *Latin.* **1.** the sorrowful mother. **2.** (*caps.*) the mother of Christ sorrowing for her son.

ma•ter•fa•mil•i•as (mā′tər fə mil′ē əs), *n.* the mother of a family. [1750–60; < L; cf. PATERFAMILIAS]

ma•te•ri•al (mə tēr′ē əl), *n.* **1.** the substance or substances of which a thing is made or composed: *Stone is a durable material.* **2.** anything that serves as crude or raw matter to be used or developed: *Wood pulp is the raw material from which paper is made.* **3.** any constituent element. **4.** a textile fabric: *material for a dress.* **5.** a group of ideas, facts, data, etc., that may provide the basis for or be incorporated into some integrated work: *to gather material for a history of North Carolina; to write material for a comedy show.* **6. materials,** the articles or apparatus needed to make or do something: *writing materials.* **7.** a person considered as having qualities suited to a particular sphere of activity: *The boy's teachers did not think he was college material.* —*adj.* **8.** formed or consisting of matter; physical; corporeal: *the material world.* **9.** relating to, concerned with, or involving matter: *material forces.* **10.** pertaining to the physical rather than the spiritual or intellectual aspect of things: *material comforts.* **11.** pertaining to or characterized by an undue interest in corporeal things; unspiritual. **12.** of substantial import; of much consequence; important: *Your support will make a material difference in the success of our program.* **13.** pertinent or essential (usually fol. by *to*): *a question not material to the subject at hand.* **14.** *Law.* likely to influence the determination of a case: *material evidence.* **15.** *Philos.* of or pertaining to matter as distinguished from form. [1300–50; ME < LL *māteriālis* of, belonging to matter. See MATTER, -AL[1]] —**ma•te′ri•al•ness,** *n.*
—**Syn. 1.** See **matter. 12.** essential, vital. —**Ant. 8.** incorporeal. **12.** unimportant.

mate′rial cause′, *Aristotelianism.* See under **cause** (def. 8b). [1350–1400; ME]

mate′rial cul′ture, *Sociol.* the aggregate of physical objects or artifacts used by a society. Cf. **nonmaterial culture.** [1925–30]

mate′rial equiv′alence, *Logic.* equivalence (def. 4b).

mate′rial implica′tion, *Logic.* equivalence (def. 4a). [1900–05]

ma•te•ri•al•ism (mə tēr′ē ə liz′əm), *n.* **1.** preoccupation with or emphasis on material objects, comforts, and considerations, with a disinterest in or rejection of spiritual, intellectual, or cultural values. **2.** the philosophical theory that regards matter and its motions as constituting the universe, and all phenomena, including those of mind, as due to material agencies. [1740–50; < NL *māteriālismus.* See MATERIAL, -ISM]

ma•te•ri•al•ist (mə tēr′ē ə list), *n.* **1.** a person who is markedly more concerned with material things than with spiritual, intellectual, or cultural values. **2.** an adherent of philosophical materialism. —*adj.* **3.** concerned with material things; materialistic. **4.** of or pertaining to philosophical materialism or its adherents. [1660–70; < NL *māteriālista.* See MATERIAL, -IST] —**ma•te′ri•al•is′tic,** *adj.* —**ma•te′ri•al•is′ti•cal•ly,** *adv.*

ma•te•ri•al•i•ty (mə tēr′ē al′i tē), *n., pl.* **-ties** for 2. **1.** material nature or quality. **2.** something material. [1520–30; < ML *māteriālitās.* See MATERIAL, -ITY]

ma•te•ri•al•ize (mə tēr′ē ə līz′), *v.,* **-ized, -iz•ing.** —*v.i.* **1.** to come into perceptible existence; appear; become actual or real; be realized or carried out: *Our plans never materialized.* **2.** to assume material or bodily form; become corporeal: *The ghost materialized before Hamlet.* —*v.t.* **3.** to give material form to; realize: *to materialize an ambition.* **4.** to invest with material attributes: *to materialize abstract ideas with metaphors.* **5.** to make physically perceptible; cause (a spirit or the like) to appear in bodily form. **6.** to render materialistic. Also, *esp. Brit.,* **ma•te′ri•al•ise′.** [1700–10; MATERIAL + -IZE] —**ma•te′ri•al•i•za′tion,** *n.* —**ma•te′ri•al•iz′er,** *n.*
—**Syn. 1.** emerge, show, rise, issue.

ma•te•ri•al•ly (mə tēr′ē ə lē), *adv.* **1.** to an important degree; considerably: *Their endorsement didn't help materially.* **2.** with reference to matter or material things and conditions; physically. **3.** *Philos.* with regard to matter or substance as distinguished from form. [1350–1400; ME. See MATERIAL, -LY]

mate′rials han′dling, the loading, unloading, and movement of goods, as within a factory or warehouse, esp. by the aid of mechanical devices. [1920–25]

mate′rials sci′ence, the study of the characteristics and uses of various materials, as glass, plastics, and metals. [1960–65]

ma•te•ri•a med•i•ca (mə tēr′ē ə med′i kə), **1.** the remedial substances employed in medicine. **2.** Also called **pharmacognosy.** the science dealing with the sources, physical characteristics, uses, and doses of drugs. [1690–1700; < ML: medical material]

ma•té•ri•el (mə tēr′ē el′), *n.* **1.** the aggregate of things used or needed in any business, undertaking, or operation (distinguished from *personnel*). **2.** *Mil.* arms, ammunition, and equipment in general. Also, **ma•te′ri•el′.** [1805–15; < F; see MATERIAL]

ma•ter•nal (mə tûr′nl), *adj.* **1.** of, pertaining to, having the qualities of, or befitting a mother: *maternal instincts.* **2.** related through a mother: *his maternal aunt.* **3.** derived from a mother: *maternal genes.* [1475–85; < ML *māternālis,* equiv. to L *mātern(us)* (*māter* MOTHER + *-nus* adj. suffix) + *-ālis* -AL[1]] —**ma•ter′nal•ism,** *n.* —**ma•ter′nal•is′tic,** *adj.* —**ma•ter′nal•ly,** *adv.*

ma•ter•nal•ize (mə tûr′nl īz′), *v.t.,* **-ized, -iz•ing.** to make maternal. Also, *esp. Brit.,* **ma•ter′nal•ise′.** [1875–80; MATERNAL + -IZE]

ma•ter•ni•ty (mə tûr′ni tē), *n.* **1.** the state of being a mother; motherhood. **2.** motherly quality; motherliness. **3.** a section of a hospital devoted to the care of women at childbirth and of their newborn infants. —*adj.* **4.** of, pertaining to, or for the period in which a woman is pregnant or has just given birth to a child. **5.** for mothers during and after childbirth or for the care of their newborn babies: *a maternity hospital.* **6.** for wear by pregnant women: *maternity clothes.* [1605–15; < ML *māternitās,* equiv. to L *mātern(us)* (see MATERNAL) + *-itās* -ITY]

mater′nity leave′, a leave of absence for an expectant or new mother for the birth and care of the baby. [1965–70]

Ma′ter Tur•ri′ta (to͝o rē′tə), *Rom. Relig.* Cybele.

mate•ship (māt′ship), *n.* **1.** the state of being a mate. **2.** *Australian.* a mode of conduct among Australian men that stresses equality, friendship, and solidarity. [1585–95; MATE[1] + -SHIP]

mate•y[1] (mā′tē), *n., pl.* **mate•ys.** *Chiefly Brit. Informal.* comrade; chum; buddy. [1825–35; MATE[1] + -Y[2]]

mate•y[2] (mā′tē), *adj. Chiefly Brit. Informal.* sociable; friendly: *a matey chat.* [1910–15; MATE[1] + -Y[1]] —**mate′y•ness, mat′i•ness,** *n.*

math[1] (math), *n.* mathematics. [shortened form]

math[2] (math), *n. Brit. Dial.* **1.** a mowing. **2.** the crop mowed. [1575–85; prob. back formation from AFTERMATH; cf. OE *mæth;* c. G *Mahd*]

math[3] (muth), *n.* an order of Hindu monks. Also, **ma•tha** (muth′ə). [1825–35; < Skt *maṭha* hut]

math., **1.** mathematical. **2.** mathematician. **3.** mathematics.

CONCISE PRONUNCIATION KEY: act, cāpe, dâre, pärt; set, ēqual; *if,* īce; ox, ōver, ôrder, oil, bo͝ok, bo͞ot, out; up, ûrge; child; sing; shoe; thin, *th*at; zh as in *treasure.* ə = a as in *alone,* e as in *system,* i as in *easily,* o as in *gallop,* u as in *circus;* ᵊ as in *fire* (fīᵊr), *hour* (ouᵊr). l and n can serve as syllabic consonants, as in *cradle* (krād′l), and *button* (but′n). See the full key inside the front cover.

math·e·mat·i·cal (math′ə mat′i kəl), *adj.* **1.** of, pertaining to, or of the nature of mathematics: *mathematical truth.* **2.** employed in the operations of mathematics: *mathematical instruments.* **3.** having the exactness, precision, or certainty of mathematics. Also, **math′e·mat′ic.** [1400–50; late ME < L *mathēmatic(us)* pertaining to MATHEMATICS + -AL[1]] **—math′e·mat′i·cal·ly,** *adv.*
—Syn. 3. exact, precise, meticulous, rigorous.

mathemat′ical expecta′tion, 1. *Math.* the product of the probability of the occurrence of an event and the value associated with the occurrence of a given event. **2.** *Statistics.* the summation or integration, over all values of a variate, of the product of the variate and its probability or its probability density. Also called **expectation, expected value.** [1830–40]

mathemat′ical induc′tion, induction (def. 5). [1830–40]

mathemat′ical log′ic. See **symbolic logic.** [1855–60]

math·e·ma·ti·cian (math′ə mə tish′ən), *n.* an expert or specialist in mathematics. [1400–50; late ME *mathematicion.* See MATHEMATICS, -IAN]

math·e·mat·ics (math′ə mat′iks), *n.* **1.** (*used with a singular v.*) the systematic treatment of magnitude, relationships between figures and forms, and relations between quantities expressed symbolically. **2.** (*used with a singular or plural v.*) mathematical procedures, operations, or properties. [1350–1400; ME *mathematic* < L *mathēmatica (ars)* < Gk *mathēmatikḗ (téchnē)* scientific (craft), equiv. to *mathēmat-* (s. of *máthēma*) science, knowledge + *-ikē,* fem. of *-ikos* -IC; see -ICS]

Math·er (math′ər, math′-), *n.* **1. Cotton,** 1663–1728, American clergyman and author. **2.** his father, **Increase** (in′krēs), 1639–1723, American clergyman and author.

Math·ew·son (math′yo͞o sən), *n.* **Christopher** (*"Christy"*), 1880–1925, U.S. baseball player.

Ma·thi·as (mə thī′əs), *n.* **Robert Bruce** (*Bob*), born 1930, U.S. track-and-field athlete.

Ma·thil·de (mə til′də; *Fr.* mA tēld′; *Ger.* mä til′də), *n.* a female given name, French or German form of **Matilda.**

Math·ol·wch (ma thō′lo͝okH), *n.* a legendary king of Ireland and the husband of Branwen.

maths (maths), *n.* (*used with a singular or plural v.*) *Chiefly Brit.* mathematics. [by shortening]

Ma·thu·ra (mut′o͝o rə), *n.* a city in W Uttar Pradesh, in N India: Hindu shrine and holy city; reputed birthplace of Krishna. 140,468. Formerly, **Muttra.**

Ma·thu·sa·la (mə tho͞o′sə lə), *n. Douay Bible.* Methuselah (def. 1).

ma·til·da (mə til′də), *n. Australian.* swag[2] (def. 2). [1890–95; special use of proper name *Matilda*]

Ma·til·da (mə til′də; *for 3 also It.* mä tēl′dä), *n.* **1.** Also called **Maud.** 1102–67, empress of the Holy Roman Empire 1114–25; queen of England 1141 (daughter of Henry I of England). **2.** *Mil.* a 26½-ton British tank of early World War II, having a crew of four and armed with a 40mm gun. **3.** Also, **Ma·til·de** (mə til′də; *Fr.* mA-tēld′; *It.* mä tēl′de). a female given name.

Ma·til′i·ja pop′py (mə til′ə hä′), a tree poppy, *Romneya coulteri,* of California and Mexico, having thin, paperlike leaves and large, solitary, white flowers. [1900–05, *Amer.;* after the *Matilija* Canyon, Ventura County, California]

mat·in (mat′n), *n.* **1.** (*often cap.*) **matins.** Also, *esp. Brit.,* **mattins.** (*usually used with a singular v.*) *Eccles.* **a.** the first of the seven canonical hours. **b.** the service for it, properly beginning at midnight, but sometimes beginning at daybreak. **c.** Also called **Morning Prayer.** the service of public prayer, said in the morning, in the Anglican Church. **2.** *Archaic.* aubade. **—***adj.* **3.** Also, **mat′in·al.** pertaining to the morning or to matins. [1200–50; ME *matyn* (pl. *matines*) < OF *matin* < L *mātūtinus* MATUTINAL]

mat·i·née (mat′n ā′; *esp. Brit.* mat′n ā′), *n.* an entertainment, esp. a dramatic or musical performance, held in the daytime, usually in the afternoon. Also, **mat′i·nee′.** [1840–50; < F: morning. See MATIN]

matinée′ i′dol, a male actor, usually a leading man, idolized esp. by female audiences. [1900–05]

mat′ing ball′, a writhing mass of snakes, usually composed of a single female and 10 or more males attempting to mate with her.

Ma·tisse (mA tēs′), *n.* **Hen·ri** (äN rē′), 1869–1954, French painter.

mat′jes her′ring (mät′yəs), *n.* young herring that have not spawned, often prepared with vinegar, sugar, salt, and spices. Also called **mat′jes.** [partial trans. of D *maatjesharing; matjes-,* earlier *maetgens-, maeghdekins-,* equiv. to *maagd* MAID + *-kin* -KIN + *-s* 'S[1]]

Ma·to Gros·so (mä′to͝o grô′so͝o; *Eng.* mat′ə grō′sō), **1.** a plateau in SW Brazil. **2.** a state in SW Brazil. 1,418,000; 475,378 sq. mi. (1,231,230 sq. km). *Cap.:* Cuiabá. Also, **Matto Grosso.**

Ma·tra·li·a (mə trā′lē ə, -trāl′yə), *n., pl.* **-li·a, -li·as.** (*sometimes used with a plural v.*) an annual festival of ancient Rome celebrated by women in honor of the goddess Matuta. [1895–1900; < L *Mātrālia (festa)* (festival) of *Māter Mātūta* (goddess of dawn); *mātrālia,* neut. pl. of *mātrālis* pertaining to a mother. See MATER, -AL[1]]

mat·rass (ma′trəs), *n. Chem.* a rounded, long-necked glass container, formerly used for distilling and dissolving substances. Also, **mattrass.** [1595–1605; < F *matras,* perh. < Ar *maṭarah* leather bottle < Gk *metrētḗs* a liquid measure]

matri-, a combining form meaning "mother," used in the formation of compound words: *matrilineal.* [< L, comb. form of *māter* MOTHER]

ma·tri·arch (mā′trē ärk′), *n.* **1.** the female head of a family or tribal line. **2.** a woman who is the founder or dominant member of a community or group. **3.** a venerable old woman. [1600–10; MATRI- + -ARCH] **—ma′tri·ar′chal, ma′tri·ar′chic,** *adj.* **—ma′tri·ar′chal·ism,** *n.*

ma·tri·ar·chate (mā′trē är′kit, -kāt), *n.* **1.** a matriarchal system or community. **2.** a social order formerly believed to have preceded patriarchal tribal society in the early period of human communal life, embodying rule by the mothers, or by all adult women. [1880–85; MATRIARCH + -ATE[3]]

ma·tri·ar·chy (mā′trē är′kē), *n., pl.* **-chies. 1.** a family, society, community, or state governed by women. **2.** a form of social organization in which the mother is head of the family, and in which descent is reckoned in the female line, the children belonging to the mother's clan; matriarchal system. [1880–85; MATRI- + -ARCHY]

ma·tri·ces (mā′tri sēz′, ma′tri-), *n.* a pl. of **matrix.**

mat·ri·cide (ma′tri sīd′, mā′-), *n.* **1.** the act of killing one's mother. **2.** a person who kills his or her mother. [1585–95; < L *mātricīdium* (def. 1), *mātricīda* (def. 2); see MATRI-, -CIDE] **—mat′ri·cid′al,** *adj.*

mat·ri·cli·ny (ma′tri klī′nē, mā′-), *n. Genetics.* matrocliny.

ma·tric·u·lant (mə trik′yə lənt), *n.* a person who matriculates; a candidate for matriculation. [1880–85; < LL *mātricul(a)* list (dim. of *mātrix* list; see MATRIX, -ULA) + -ANT]

ma·tric·u·late (*v.* mə trik′yə lāt′; *n.* mə trik′yə lit), *v.,* **-lat·ed, -lat·ing,** *n.* **—***v.t.* **1.** to enroll in a college or university as a candidate for a degree. **2.** to register (a coat of arms), used esp. in Scottish heraldry. **—***v.i.* **3.** to be matriculated. **—***n.* **4.** a person who has been matriculated. [1480–90 for earlier sense; < ML *mātriculātus* (person) listed (for some specific duty), equiv. to *mātrīcul(a)* list (see MATRICULANT) + *-ātus* -ATE[1]] **—ma·tric′u·la′tion,** *n.* **—ma·tric′u·la′tor,** *n.*

mat·ri·fo·cal (ma′trə fō′kəl, mā′-), *adj.* **1.** of, pertaining to, or designating a family unit or structure headed by the mother and lacking a father permanently or for extended periods. **2.** focused or centered on the mother. [1950–55; MATRI- + FOCAL]

mat·ri·lat·er·al (ma′trə lat′ər əl, mā′-), *adj.* related through the mother, as to a maternal uncle. Cf. **patrilateral.** [1950–55; MATRI- + LATERAL] **—mat′ri·lat′er·al·ly,** *adv.*

mat·ri·lin·e·age (ma′trə lin′ē ij, mā′-), *n.* lineal descent traced through the female line. [1945–50; MATRI- + LINEAGE[1]]

mat·ri·lin·e·al (ma′trə lin′ē əl, mā′-), *adj.* inheriting or determining descent through the female line. Also, **mat′ri·lin′e·ar.** Cf. **patrilineal.** [1900–05; MATRI- + LINEAL] **—mat′ri·lin′e·al·ly, mat′ri·lin′e·ar·ly,** *adv.*

mat·ri·lin·y (ma′trə lin′ē, -lī′nē, mā′-), *n., pl.* **-lin·ies.** the tracing of descent through the mother's line of a family. [1905–10; MATRILIN(EAL) + -Y[3]]

mat·ri·lo·cal (ma′trə lō′kəl, mā′-), *adj. Anthropol.* of or pertaining to residence with the wife's family or tribe; uxorilocal: *matrilocal customs.* Cf. **neolocal, virilocal.** [1905–10; MATRI- + LOCAL] **—mat′ri·lo·cal′i·ty,** *n.*

mat·ri·mo·ni·al (ma′trə mō′nē əl), *adj.* of or pertaining to matrimony; marital; nuptial; connubial; conjugal. [1400–50; late ME < LL *mātrimōniālis.* See MATRIMONY, -AL[1]] **—mat′ri·mo′ni·al·ly,** *adv.*

mat·ri·mo·ny (ma′trə mō′nē), *n., pl.* **-nies** for 2. **1.** the state of being married; marriage. **2.** the rite, ceremony, or sacrament of marriage. [1250–1300; ME < L *mātrimōnium* wedlock. See MATRI-, -MONY]

mat′rimony vine′, any plant belonging to the genus *Lycium,* of the nightshade family, species of which are cultivated for their foliage, flowers, and berries. Also called **boxthorn.** [1810–20]

mat·ri·po·tes·tal (ma′trē pō tes′tl, mā′-), *adj. Anthropol.* of or pertaining to the authority exercised by a mother or a mother's blood relatives. [MATRI- + *potestal* < L *potest(ās)* power + -AL[1]]

ma·trix (mā′triks, ma′-), *n., pl.* **ma·tri·ces** (mā′tri-sēz′, ma′-), **ma·trix·es. 1.** something that constitutes the place or point from which something else originates, takes form, or develops: *The Greco-Roman world was the matrix for Western civilization.* **2.** *Anat.* a formative part, as the corium beneath a nail. **3.** *Biol.* **a.** the intercellular substance of a tissue. **b.** See **ground substance. 4.** *Petrol.* the fine-grained portion of a rock in which coarser crystals or rock fragments are embedded. **5.** fine material, as cement, in which lumps of coarser material, as of an aggregate, are embedded. **6.** *Mining.* gangue. **7.** *Metall.* a crystalline phase in an alloy in which other phases are embedded. **8.** *Print.* a mold for casting typefaces. **9.** master (def. 18). **10.** (in a press or stamping machine) a multiple die or perforated block on which the material to be formed is placed. **11.** *Math.* a rectangular array of numbers, algebraic symbols, or mathematical functions, esp. when such arrays are added and multiplied according to certain rules. **12.** *Ling.* a rectangular display of features characterizing a set of linguistic items, esp. phonemes, usually presented as a set of columns of plus or minus signs specifying the presence or absence of each feature for each item. **13.** Also called **master.** a mold made by electroforming from a disk recording, from which other disks may be pressed. **14.** *Archaic.* the womb. [1325–75; ME *matris, matrix* < L *mātrix* female animal kept for breeding (LL: register, orig. of such beasts), parent stem (of plants), deriv. of *māter* mother]

ma·trix·ing (mā′trik sing), *n.* an electronic method of processing quadraphonic sound for recording in a two-channel form, for reconversion to four channels when played back. [1950–55; MATRIX + -ING[1]]

ma′trix mechan′ics, *Physics.* a formulation of nonrelativistic quantum mechanics in which physical quantities are represented by matrices and matrix algebra is used to predict the outcome of physical measurements. Cf. **wave mechanics.**

ma′trix sen′tence, *Ling.* a sentence in which another sentence is embedded: *In "The man who called is waiting," "The man is waiting" is a matrix sentence.* [1960–65]

mat·ro·cli·ny (ma′trə klī′nē, mā′-), *n. Genetics.* inheritance in which the traits of the offspring are derived primarily from the maternal parent (opposed to *patrocliny*). Also, **matriclinу.** [1915–20; *matro-* (var. of MATRI- with -o-) + *-clin-* (< Gk *klínein* to bend, lean, or extracted from INCLINE; cf. CLINE) + -Y[3]] **—mat′ro·cli′nous, mat′ro·clin′al, mat·ro·clin·ic** (ma′trə klin′ik, mā′-), *adj.*

ma·tron (mā′trən), *n.* **1.** a married woman, esp. one who is mature and staid or dignified and has an established social position. **2.** a woman who has charge of the domestic affairs of a hospital, prison, or other institution. **3.** a woman serving as a guard, warden, or attendant for women or girls, as in a prison. [1350–1400; ME *matrone* < L *mātrōna* a married woman, wife, deriv. of *māter* mother] **—ma·tron·al** (mā′trə nl, ma′-), *adj.* **—ma′tron·hood′, ma′tron·ship′,** *n.*

ma·tron·age (mā′trə nij, ma′-), *n.* **1.** the state of being a matron. **2.** guardianship by a matron. **3.** matrons collectively. [1765–75; MATRON + -AGE]

Ma·tron·al·i·a (ma′trə nā′lē ə, -nāl′yə, ma′-), *n., pl.* **-al·i·a, -al·i·as.** (*sometimes used with a plural v.*) an annual festival of ancient Rome held by matrons in honor of Juno. [1700–10; < L *Mātrōnālia (festa),* neut. pl. of *mātrōnālis* of, belonging to a married woman. See MATRON, -AL[1]]

ma·tron·ize (mā′trə nīz′), *v.,* **-ized, -iz·ing.** **—***v.t.* **1.** to cause to become matronly; cause to act as, or fulfill the role of, matron. **2.** to serve as a matron to; chaperon. **—***v.i.* **3.** to become a matron. Also, *esp. Brit.,* **ma′tron·ise′.** [1745–55; MATRON + -IZE]

ma·tron·ly (mā′trən lē), *adj.* **1.** of, pertaining to, or having the characteristics of a matron; maturely dignified; stately. **2.** characteristic of or suitable for a matron. [1650–60; MATRON + -LY] **—ma′tron·li·ness,** *n.*

ma′tron of hon′or, a married woman acting as the principal attendant of the bride at a wedding. Cf. **maid of honor.** [1900–05, *Amer.*]

mat·ro·nym·ic (ma′trə nim′ik), *adj.* metronymic.

MATS (mats), *n.* Military Air Transport Service.

mat·su (mat′so͞o), *n.* a pine, *Pinus massoniana,* of China, yielding a wood used in furniture-making, the construction of houses, etc. [1860–65; < Japn, earlier *matu*]

Ma·tsu (mat so͞o′, mat′so͞o; *Chin.* mä′dzo͞o), *n. Wade-Giles.* an island off the SE coast of China, in the East China Sea: controlled by Taiwan. 11,000; 17 sq. mi. (44 sq. km). Also, **Mazu.** Cf. **Quemoy.**

Ma·tsu·do (mä tso͞o′dô), *n.* a city on E Honshu, in Japan, NE of Tokyo. 400,870.

Ma·tsu·o·ka (mä′tso͞o ô′kä), *n.* **Yo·su·ke** (yô so͞o′ke), 1880–1946, Japanese statesman.

mat·su·ta·ke (mät′so͞o tä′kē, -kā), *n.* an edible fungus, *Armillaria matsutake,* of Japan. Also, **mat′su·ta′ke.** [< Japn, equiv. to *matsu* MATSU (perh. to be taken as "pinecone-shaped") + *take* mushroom; cf. SHIITAKE]

Ma·tsu·ya·ma (mä′tso͞o yä′mä), *n.* a seaport on NW Shikoku, in SW Japan. 401,682.

Mat·sys (mät′sis), *n.* **Quentin.** See **Massys, Quentin.**

matt (mat), *adj., n., v.t.* matte[1].

Matt (mat), *n.* a male given name, form of **Matthew.**

Matt., Matthew.

Mat·ta E·chaur·ren (mä′tä e chour′Ren), **Ro·ber·to An·to·nio Se·bas·tián** (Rô veR′tô än tô′nyô se′väs-tyän′), born 1911, Chilean painter.

Mat·ta·thi·as (mat′ə thī′əs), *n.* died 167? B.C., Jewish priest in Judea (father of Judas Maccabaeus).

matte[1] (mat), *adj., n., v.,* **mat·ted, mat·ting.** **—***adj.* **1.** having a dull or lusterless surface: *matte paint; a matte complexion; a photograph with a matte finish.* **—***n.* **2.** a dull or dead surface, often slightly roughened, as on metals, paint, paper, or glass. **3.** a tool for producing such a surface. **4.** *Metall.* an unfinished metallic product of the smelting of certain sulfide ores, esp. those of copper. **5.** *Motion Pictures.* See **matte shot.** **—***v.t.* **6.** to finish with a matte surface. Also, **mat, matt.** [1640–50; < F *mat* (masc.), *matte* (fem.), OF < LL *mattus* moist, soft, weak, perh. < **maditus,* deriv. of L *madēre* to be wet]

matte[2] (mat), *n. Mining.* a mass of timber caved beneath overburden so as to cushion the fall of the overburden and separate it from mineral to be extracted beneath. [< G; akin to MAT[1]]

mat·ted[1] (mat′id), *adj.* **1.** covered with a dense growth or a tangled mass: *a garden matted with weeds.* **2.** formed into a mat; entangled in a thick mass: *matted hair.* **3.** formed of mats, or of plaited or woven material. **4.** covered with mats or matting. [1600–10; MAT[1] + -ED[2]] **—mat′ted·ly,** *adv.* **—mat′ted·ness,** *n.*

mat·ted[2] (mat′id), *adj.* having a dull finish; matte. [1815–25; MATTE[1] + -ED[2]]

Mat·te·ot·ti (mät′te ôt′tē), *n.* **Gia·co·mo** (jä′kô mô), 1885–1924, Italian socialist leader.

mat·ter (mat′ər), *n.* **1.** the substance or substances of which any physical object consists or is composed: *the matter of which the earth is made.* **2.** physical or corporeal substance in general, whether solid, liquid, or gaseous, esp. as distinguished from incorporeal substance, as spirit or mind, or from qualities, actions, and the like. **3.** something that occupies space. **4.** a particular kind of

CONCISE ETYMOLOGY KEY: <, descended or borrowed from; >, whence; b., blend of, blended; c., cognate with; cf., compare; deriv., derivative; equiv., equivalent; imit., imitative; obl., oblique; r., replacing; s., stem; sp., spelling, spelled; resp., respelling, respelled; trans., translation; ?, origin unknown; *, unattested; ‡, probably earlier than. See the full key inside the front cover.

substance: *coloring matter.* **5.** a situation, state, affair, or business: *a trivial matter.* **6.** an amount or extent reckoned approximately: *a matter of 10 miles.* **7.** something of consequence: *matter for serious thought.* **8.** importance or significance: *decisions of little matter.* **9.** difficulty; trouble (usually prec. by *the*): *There is something the matter.* **10.** ground, reason, or cause: *a matter for complaint.* **11.** the material or substance of a discourse, book, etc., often as distinguished from its form. **12.** things put down in words, esp. printed: *reading matter.* **13.** things sent by mail: *postal matter.* **14.** a substance discharged by a living body, esp. pus. **15.** *Philos.* **a.** that which by integrative organization forms chemical substances and living things. **b.** *Aristotelianism.* that which relates to form as potentiality does to actuality. **16.** *Law.* statement or allegation. **17.** *Print.* **a.** material for work; copy. **b.** type set up. **18.** *Christian Science.* the concept of substance shaped by the limitations of the human mind. **19. a matter of life and death,** something of vital or crucial importance. **20. as a matter of fact,** in reality; actually; in fact: *As a matter of fact, there is no substance to that rumor.* **21. for that matter,** as far as that is concerned; as for that: *For that matter, you are no better qualified to judge than I.* Also, **for the matter of that. 22. no matter, a.** regardless or irrespective of: *We'll never finish on time, no matter how hard we work.* **b.** it is unimportant; it makes no difference: *No matter, this string will do as well as any other.* —*v.i.* **23.** to be of importance; signify: *It matters little.* **24.** *Pathol.* to suppurate. [1175–1225; ME *mater(e), materie* < AF, OF *mat(i)ere, materie* < L *māteria* woody part of a tree, material, substance, deriv. of *māter* MOTHER[1]] —**mat′ter·ful,** *adj.* —**mat′ter·less,** *adj.*

—**Syn. 1.** MATTER, MATERIAL, STUFF, SUBSTANCE refer to that of which physical objects are composed (though all these terms are also used abstractly). MATTER, as distinct from mind and spirit, is a broad word that applies to anything perceived, or known to be occupying space: *solid matter; gaseous matter.* MATERIAL usually means some definite kind, quality, or quantity of matter, esp. as intended for use: *woolen material; a house built of good materials.* STUFF, a less technical word, with approximately the same meanings as MATERIAL, is characterized by being on an informal level when it refers to physical objects (*Dynamite is queer stuff*), and on a literary or poetic one when it is used abstractly (*the stuff that dreams are made on*). SUBSTANCE is the matter that composes a thing, thought of in relation to its essential properties: *a sticky substance.* **5.** question. **7.** concern. **8.** moment. **11.** subject, topic. **23.** count.

mat·ter·ate (mat′ə rāt′), *v.i.*, **-at·ed, -at·ing.** *New England, Upstate New York, and Southern U.S.* to fester; suppurate. [perh. by folk etym. from MATURATE]

Mat·ter·horn (mat′ər hôrn′), *n.* a mountain on the border of Switzerland and Italy, in the Pennine Alps. 14,780 ft. (4505 m). French, **Mont Cervin.**

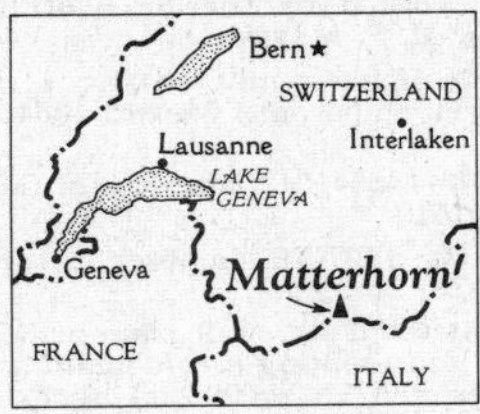

mat′ter in deed′, *Law.* a fact or statement that can be proved or established by a deed or specialty. [1525–35]

mat′ter of course′, something that follows in logical, natural, or customary sequence or that is treated as such: *After such reprisals, war followed as a matter of course.* [1730–40]

mat·ter-of-course (mat′ər əv kôrs′, -kōrs′), *adj.* **1.** occurring or proceeding in or as if in the logical, natural, or customary course of things; expected or inevitable. **2.** accepting things as occurring in their natural course, or characterized by an acceptance of things as such: *to be matter-of-course in confronting the difficulties of existence.* [1830–40]

mat′ter of fact′, 1. something of a factual nature, as an actual occurrence. **2.** *Law.* a statement or allegation to be judged on the basis of the evidence. [1575–85]

mat·ter-of-fact (mat′ər əv fakt′), *adj.* **1.** adhering strictly to fact; not imaginative; prosaic; dry; commonplace: *a matter-of-fact account of the political rally.* **2.** direct or unemotional; straightforward; down-to-earth. [1705–15] —**mat′ter-of-fact′ly,** *adv.* —**mat′ter-of-fact′ness,** *n.*

mat′ter of law′, *Law.* an issue or matter to be determined according to the relevant principles of law.

mat′ter of rec′ord, *Law.* a fact or statement that appears on the record of a court and that can be proved or established by producing such record. [1600–10]

mat′ter wave′. See **de Broglie wave.**

matte′ shot′, *Motion Pictures.* a shot in which parts of the background and sometimes the foreground are masked so that a different background, foreground, image, etc., can be substituted during printing. Also called **matte.**

Matte·son (mat′sən), *n.* a town in NE Illinois. 10,223.

Mat·the·an (ma thē′ən, mə-), *adj.* of or pertaining to the Gospel of Matthew or the traditions contained in it. [1895–1900; < LL *Matthae(us)* MATTHEW + -AN]

Mat·thew (math′yōō), *n.* **1.** one of the four Evangelists, a customs collector from Capernaum, summoned to be one of the 12 apostles: originally called Levi. Matt. 9:9–13. **2.** the first Gospel. *Abbr.:* Matt. **3.** a male given name.

Mat′thew of Par′is, c1200–59, English chronicler. Also called **Mat′thew Par′is.**

Mat·thews (math′yōōz), *n.* **1. (James) Bran·der** (bran′dər), 1852–1929, U.S. writer and educator. **2. Sir Stanley,** born 1915, British soccer player.

Mat′thew Walk′er, a knot formed on the end of a rope by partly unlaying the strands and tying them in a certain way. See illus. under **knot.** [1855–60; after the presumed inventor of the knot]

Mat·thi·as (mə thī′əs), *n.* **1.** a disciple chosen to take the place of Judas Iscariot as one of the apostles. Acts 1:23–26. **2.** 1557–1619, king of Hungary 1608–18; king of Bohemia 1611–17; emperor of the Holy Roman Empire 1612–19 (son of Maximilian II). **3.** Also, **Mat·thy′as.** a male given name, form of **Matthew.**

mat·ting[1] (mat′ing), *n.* **1.** a coarse fabric of rushes, grass, straw, hemp, or the like, used for floor covering, wrapping material, etc. **2.** material for mats. **3.** mats collectively. **4.** the making of mats. [1675–85; MAT[1] + -ING[1]]

mat·ting[2] (mat′ing), *n.* a dull, slightly roughened surface, free from polish, produced by the use of a matte. [1680–90; MATTE[1] + -ING[1]]

mat·tins (mat′nz, -inz), *n.* (*often cap.*) (*usually used with a singular v.*) *Chiefly Brit.* matin (def. 1).

mat·tock (mat′ək), *n.* an instrument for loosening the soil in digging, shaped like a pickax, but having one end broad instead of pointed. [bef. 900; ME *mattok,* OE *mattuc*]

Mat·to Gros·so (mat′ə grō′sō; *Port.* mä′tōō grô′sōō). See **Mato Grosso.**

Mat·toon (mə tōōn′), *n.* a city in E Illinois. 19,787.

mat·trass (ma′trəs), *n. Chem.* matrass.

mat·tress (ma′tris), *n.* **1.** a large pad for supporting the reclining body, used as or on a bed, consisting of a quilted or similarly fastened case, usually of heavy cloth, that contains hair, straw, cotton, foam rubber, etc., or a framework of metal springs. **2.** See **air mattress. 3.** a mat woven of brush, poles, or similar material, used to prevent erosion of the surface of dikes, jetties, embankments, dams, etc. **4.** a layer of concrete placed on bare ground, as to provide a footing; mat. **5.** a layer of any material used to cushion, protect, reinforce, or the like. [1250–1300; ME *materas* < OF < It *materasso* < Ar *maṭraḥ* mat, cushion]

Mat·ty (mat′ē), *n.* a male or female given name. Also, **Mat′tie.**

Ma′tu·ra dia′mond (mä′tər ə, mat′ər ə), *Jewelry.* a zircon heat-treated to render it colorless: not a true diamond. Also, **Matara diamond.** [1875–80; after *Matura,* town in Sri Lanka]

mat·u·rate (mach′ə rāt′), *v.i.*, **-rat·ed, -rat·ing. 1.** *Pathol.* to suppurate. **2.** to mature. [1535–45; < L *mātūrātus,* ptp. of *mātūrāre* to grow ripe, bring to maturity. See MATURE, -ATE[1]] —**ma·tur·a·tive** (mə chŏŏr′ə tiv, mach′ə rā′-), *adj.*

mat·u·ra·tion (mach′ə rā′shən), *n.* the act or process of maturating. [1350–1400; ME: suppuration < ML *mātūrātiōn-* (s. of *mātūrātiō*). See MATURATE, -ION] —**mat′u·ra′tion·al,** *adj.*

matura′tion divi′sion, *Cell Biol.* a stage in meiosis during which the chromosomal number of the reproductive cell is reduced to one chromosome from each original chromosome pair.

ma·ture (mə tŏŏr′, -tyŏŏr′, -chŏŏr′, -chûr′), *adj.*, **-tur·er, -tur·est,** *v.*, **-tured, -tur·ing.** —*adj.* **1.** complete in natural growth or development, as plant and animal forms: *a mature rose bush.* **2.** ripe, as fruit, or fully aged, as cheese or wine. **3.** fully developed in body or mind, as a person: *a mature woman.* **4.** pertaining to or characteristic of full development: *a mature appearance; fruit with a mature softness.* **5.** completed, perfected, or elaborated in full by the mind: *mature plans.* **6.** (of an industry, technology, market, etc.) no longer developing or expanding; having little or no potential for further growth or expansion; exhausted or saturated. **7.** intended for or restricted to adults, esp. by reason of explicit sexual content or the inclusion of violence or obscene language: *mature movies.* **8.** composed of adults, considered as being less susceptible than minors to explicit sexual content, violence, or obscene language, as of a film or stage performance: *for mature audiences only.* **9.** *Finance.* having reached the limit of its time; having become payable or due: *a mature bond.* **10.** *Med.* **a.** having attained definitive form or function, as by maturation of an epithelium from a basal layer. **b.** having attained the end stage of a normal or abnormal biological process: *a mature boil.* **11.** *Geol.* (of a landscape) exhibiting the stage of maximum topographical diversity, as in the cycle of erosion of a land surface. —*v.t.* **12.** to make mature; ripen, as fruit or cheese. **13.** to bring to full development: *His hard experiences in the city matured him.* **14.** to complete or perfect. —*v.i.* **15.** to become mature; ripen, as fruit or cheese. **16.** to come to full development: *Our plans have not yet matured.* **17.** *Finance.* to become due, as a note. [1400–50; late ME < L *mātūrus* ripe, timely, early; akin to MANES, MATUTINAL] —**ma·ture′ly,** *adv.* —**ma·ture′ment,** *n.* —**ma·ture′ness,** *n.* —**ma·tur′er,** *n.*

—**Syn. 1, 3.** aged, grown, adult. **2.** See **ripe. 5.** ready, prepared. **12, 15.** age, develop. —**Ant. 1, 3.** childish, raw, green, young.

Ma·tu·rín (mä′tōō rēn′), *n.* a city in NE Venezuela. 98,188.

ma·tu·ri·ty (mə chŏŏr′i tē, -tŏŏr′-, -tyŏŏr′-, -chûr′-), *n.* **1.** the state of being mature; ripeness: *The fruit will reach maturity in a few days.* **2.** full development; perfected condition: *maturity of judgment; to bring a plan to maturity.* **3.** *Finance.* **a.** the state of being due. **b.** the time when a note or bill of exchange becomes due. [1400–50; late ME *maturite* < L *mātūritās* ripeness. See MATURE, -ITY]

matu′rity-on′set diabe′tes (mə chŏŏr′i tē on′set′, -ôn′-, -tŏŏr′-, -tyŏŏr′-, -chûr′-), *Pathol.* diabetes (def. 4). [1975–80]

matu′rity yield′, *Finance.* See **yield to maturity.**

ma·tu·ti·nal (mə tōōt′n l, -tyōōt′-), *adj.* pertaining to or occurring in the morning; early in the day. [1650–60; < LL *mātūtīnālis* of, belonging to the morning, early, equiv. to L *mātūtīn(us)* of the morning (*Mātūt(a)* goddess of dawn + *-īnus* -INE[1]) + *-ālis* -AL[1]] —**ma·tu′ti·nal·ly,** *adv.*

MATV, master antenna television system.

mat·zah (mät′sə; *Seph. Heb.* mä tsä′; *Ashk. Heb.* mä′tsō), *n.*, *pl.* **mat·zahs** (mät′səz), **mat·zoth, mat·zot, mat·zos** (*Seph. Heb.* mä tsôt′; *Ashk. Heb.* mä′tsōs). matzo.

mat·zo (mät′sə; *Seph. Heb.* mä tsä′; *Ashk. Heb.* mä′tsō), *n.*, *pl.* **mat·zos, mat·zoth, mat·zot** (mät′səz; *Seph. Heb.* mä tsôt′; *Ashk. Heb.* mä′tsōs). **1.** unleavened bread in the form of large crackers, typically square and corrugated, eaten by Jews during Passover. **2.** one of these crackers. Also, **matzah, matzoh.** [1840–50; < Yiddish *matse* < Heb *maṣṣāh*]

mat′zo ball′, a dumpling made from matzo meal, usually served in soup.

mat′zo brei′ (brī), *Jewish Cookery.* small pieces of matzo soaked in water, mixed with beaten eggs, and fried.

mat·zoh (mät′sə; *Seph. Heb.* mä tsä′; *Ashk. Heb.* mä′tsō), *n.*, *pl.* **mat·zohs, mat·zoth, mat·zot** (mät′səz; *Seph. Heb.* mä tsôt′; *Ashk. Heb.* mä′tsōs). matzo.

mat′zo meal′, ground matzos. [1970–75]

Mau·á (mou ä′), *n.* a city in SE Brazil, SE of São Paulo. 101,659.

Mau·beuge (mō bœzh′), *n.* a city in N France, on the Sambre River, near the Belgian border. 35,474.

maud (môd), *n.* **1.** a gray woolen plaid worn by shepherds and others in S Scotland. **2.** a rug or wrap of like material, used as a traveling robe, steamer rug, etc. [1780–90; perh. apocopated var. of obs. *maldy* a coarse gray woolen cloth]

Maud (môd), *n.* **1.** See **Matilda** (def. 1). **2.** Also, **Maude.** a female given name, form of **Matilda.**

maud·lin (môd′lin), *adj.* **1.** tearfully or weakly emotional; foolishly sentimental: *a maudlin story of a little orphan and her lost dog.* **2.** foolishly or mawkishly sentimental because of drunkenness. [1500–10; special use of *Maudlin,* ME *Maudelen* << LL *Magdalēnē* < Gk *Magdalēnḗ* Mary Magdalene, portrayed in art as a weeping penitent] —**maud′lin·ism,** *n.* —**maud′lin·ly,** *adv.* —**maud′lin·ness,** *n.*

Mauds·lay (môdz′lē), *n.* **Henry,** 1771–1831, English mechanical engineer.

Maugham (môm), *n.* **W(illiam) Som·er·set** (sum′ər set′, -sit), 1874–1965, English novelist, dramatist, and short-story writer.

mau·gre (mô′gər), *prep. Archaic.* in spite of; notwithstanding. Also, **mau′ger.** [1225–75; ME < MF: lit., spite, ill-will, equiv. to *mau-* MAL- + *gre* GREE[2]]

Mau·i (mou′ē), *n.* an island in central Hawaii. 54,985; 728 sq. mi. (1886 sq. km).

ma·u·ka (mä ōō′kə), *adv. Hawaii.* toward the mountains; inland. [< Hawaiian, equiv. to *ma-* directional particle + *uka* inland, upland]

maul (môl), *n.* **1.** a heavy hammer, as for driving stakes or wedges. **2.** *Archaic.* a heavy club or mace. —*v.t.* **3.** to handle or use roughly: *The book was badly mauled by its borrowers.* **4.** to injure by a rough beating, shoving, or the like; bruise: *to be mauled by an angry crowd.* **5.** to split with a maul and wedge, as a wooden rail. Also, **mall.** [1200–50; (n.) ME *malle* < OF *mail* mallet, hammer < L *malleus* hammer; (v.) ME *mallen* < OF *maillier,* deriv. of *mail*] —**maul′er,** *n.*

Maul·din (môl′dən), *n.* **William Henry** (*Bill*), born 1921, U.S. political cartoonist.

Mau·lid (mou′lid), *n.* Mawlid. Also, **Mau·lud** (mou′ləd).

Maul·main (mōl mān′, môl-), *n.* Moulmein.

maul·stick (môl′stik′), *n.* mahlstick.

maul·vi (moul′vē), *n.* (in India) an expert in Islamic law: used esp. as a term of respectful address among Muslims. Also, **molvi, moolvee, moolvi, moulvi.** [< Hindi *maulvī* < Ar *mawlawī,* equiv. to *mawlā* master (see MULLAH) + *-ī* suffix of appurtenance]

Ma·u·man (mā ōō′mən), *n. Douay Bible.* Mehuman.

Mau Mau (mou′ mou′), *pl.* **Mau Maus,** (*esp. collectively*) **Mau Mau.** a member of a revolutionary society in Kenya, established in the early 1950's, that consisted chiefly of Kikuyu and engaged in terrorist activities in an attempt to drive out the European settlers and to give government control to the native Kenyans. [< Kikuyu]

Mau·mee (mô mē′, mô′mē), *n.* **1.** a city in NW Ohio. 15,747. **2.** a river in E Indiana and W Ohio, flowing NE to Lake Erie, at Toledo. 175 mi. (280 km) long.

mau·met (mô′mit), *n.* **1.** *Brit. Dial.* **a.** a doll, puppet, scarecrow, or other figure built to resemble a human being. **b.** an empty-headed or mindless person. **2.** *Obs.* an idol; a false god. [1175–1225; ME < OF *mahommet* idol, special use of *Mahommet* MOHAMMED, whose image was thought to be an object of worship] —**mau′met·ry,** *n.*

maun (män, môn), *auxiliary v. Scot.* must. Also, **man.** [1325–75; ME (north and Scots) *man* < ON *man,* earlier *mun* must, shall, will]

CONCISE PRONUNCIATION KEY: act, cāpe, dâre, pärt; set, ēqual; *if,* ice; ox, ōver, ôrder, oil, bŏŏk, bōōt, out; up, ûrge; child; sing; shoe; thin, that; zh as in *treasure.* ə = *a* as in *alone, e* as in *system, i* as in *easily, o* as in *gallop, u* as in *circus;* ˈ as in *fire* (fīˈr), *hour* (ouˈr). l and n can serve as syllabic consonants, as in *cradle* (krād′l), and *button* (but′n). See the full key inside the front cover.

Mau·na Ke·a (mou′nə kā′ə, mô′nə kē′ə), a dormant volcano on the island of Hawaii. 13,784 ft. (4201 m).

Mau′na Ke′a Observ′atory, an astronomical observatory on Mauna Kea, Hawaii, situated at an altitude of 13,600 ft. (4145 m).

mau·na lo·a (mou′nə lō′ə, mô′nə), a vine, *Canavalia microcarpa,* of the legume family, naturalized in Hawaii, having pink or lavender flowers used to make leis. [after MAUNA LOA]

Mau·na Lo·a (mou′nə lō′ə, mô′nə), an active volcano on the island of Hawaii. 13,680 ft. (4170 m).

maunche (mänch), *n. Heraldry.* manche. Also, **maunch.**

maund (mônd), *n.* a unit of weight in India and other parts of Asia, varying greatly according to locality: in India, from about 25 to 82.286 pounds (11 to 37.4 kilograms) (the latter being the government maund). [1575–85; < Hindi *mān* < Skt *māna*]

maun·der (môn′dər), *v.i.* **1.** to talk in a rambling, foolish, or meaningless way. **2.** to move, go, or act in an aimless, confused manner: *He maundered through life without a single ambition.* [1615–25; orig. uncert.] **—maun′der·er,** *n.*

maund·y (môn′dē), *n.* **1.** the ceremony of washing the feet of the poor, esp. commemorating Jesus' washing of His disciples' feet on Maundy Thursday. **2.** Also called **maund′y mon′ey.** money distributed as alms in conjunction with the ceremony of maundy or on Maundy Thursday. [1250–1300; ME *maunde* < OF *mande* < L *mandātum* command, mandate (from the opening phrase *novum mandātum* (Vulgate) of Jesus' words to the disciples after He had washed their feet). See MANDATE]

Maun′dy Thurs′day, the Thursday of Holy Week, commemorating Jesus' Last Supper and His washing of the disciples' feet upon that day. [1400–50; late ME]

Mau·pas·sant (mō′pə sänt′; *Fr.* mō PA SÄN′), *n.* **(Hen·ri Re·né Al·bert) Guy de** (äN RE′ Rə nā′ Al beR′ gē də), 1850–93, French short-story writer and novelist.

Mau·per·tuis (mō peR twē′), *n.* **Pierre Louis Mo·reau de** (pyeR lwē mô RŌ′ də), 1698–1759, French mathematician, astronomer, and biologist.

Mau·ra (môr′ə), *n.* a female given name, Irish form of **Mary.**

Mau·reen (mô rēn′), *n.* a female given name, Irish form of **Mary.** Also, **Mau·rene′, Mau·rine′.**

Mau·re·ta·ni·a (môr′i tā′nē ə), *n.* an ancient kingdom in NW Africa: it included the territory that is modern Morocco and part of Algeria. Also, **Mauritania.** **—Mau′re·ta′ni·an,** *adj., n.*

Mau·riac (mô RYäk′), *n.* **Fran·çois** (fRäN SWA′), 1885–1970, French novelist: Nobel prize 1952.

Mau·rice (môr′is, mor′-, mô rēs′; *for 3 also Fr.* mô-RĒS′), *n.* **1.** German, **Moritz.** 1521–53, German general: elector of Saxony 1547–53. **2. of Nassau,** 1567–1625, Dutch statesman. **3.** a male given name.

Mau·rist (môr′ist), *n.* a member of the Benedictine "Congregation of St. Maur," founded in France in 1618, distinguished for its scholarship and literary works: suppressed during the French Revolution. [1790–1800; St. *Maur* 6th-century French monk and disciple of St. Benedict + -IST]

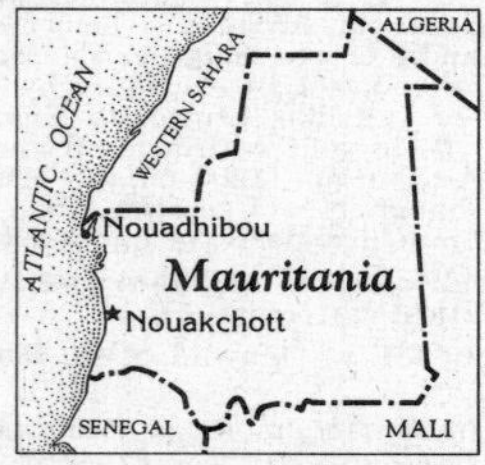

Mau·ri·ta·ni·a (môr′i tā′nē ə), *n.* **1.** Official name, **Islamic Republic of Mauritania.** a republic in W Africa, largely in the Sahara Desert: formerly a French colony; a member of the French Community 1958–66; independent 1960. 1,500,000; 418,120 sq. mi. (1,082,931 sq. km). *Cap.:* Nouakchott. **2.** Mauretania. **—Mau′ri·ta′ni·an,** *adj., n.*

Mau·ri·tius (mô rish′əs, -rish′ē əs), *n.* **1.** an island in the Indian Ocean, E of Madagascar. 880,781; 720 sq. mi. (1865 sq. km). **2.** a republic consisting of this island and dependencies: formerly a British colony. 900,000; 809 sq. mi. (2095 sq. km). *Cap.:* Port Louis. Formerly, **Île de France.** **—Mau·ri′tian,** *adj.*

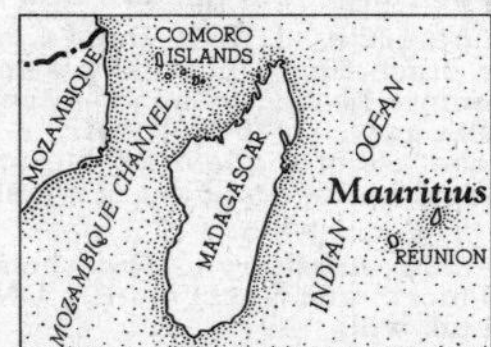

CONCISE ETYMOLOGY KEY: <, descended or borrowed from; >, whence; b., blend of, blended; c., cognate with; cf., compare; deriv., derivative; equiv., equivalent; imit., imitative; obl., oblique; r., replacing; s., stem; sp., spelling, spelled; resp., respelling, respelled; trans., translation; ?, origin unknown; *, unattested; ‡, probably earlier than. See the full key inside the front cover.

Mauri′tius hemp′, a tropical American plant, *Furcraea foetida,* having large, fleshy leaves, cultivated as a source of a hemplike fiber. Also called **cabuya.**

Mau·rois (mô RWA′), *n.* **An·dré** (äN dRā′), (*Émile Salomon Wilhelm Herzog*), 1885–1967, French biographer and novelist.

Mau·ro·ly·cus (môr′ə lī′kəs), *n.* a walled plain in the fourth quadrant of the face of the moon: about 70 miles (110 km) in diameter.

Mau·ry (môr′ē, mor′ē), *n.* **Matthew Fon·taine** (fontān′, fon′tān), 1806–73, U.S. naval officer and scientist.

Mau·ry·a (mour′ē ə), *n.* a member of an ancient Indian people who united northern India and established an empire 322–184 B.C. **—Mau′ry·an,** *adj.*

Mau·ser (mou′zər), *n.* **Peter Paul,** 1838–1914, and his brother, **Wilhelm,** 1834–82, German inventors of firearms.

mau·so·le·um (mô′sə lē′əm, -zə-), *n., pl.* **-le·ums, -le·a** (-lē′ə). **1.** a stately and magnificent tomb. **2.** a burial place for the bodies or remains of many individuals, often of a single family, usually in the form of a small building. **3.** a large, gloomy, depressing building, room, or the like. **4.** (*cap.*) the tomb erected at Halicarnassus in Asia Minor in 350? B.C. Cf. **Seven Wonders of the World.** [1375–1425; late ME < L < Gk *Mausōleîon* the tomb of Mausolus, king of Caria] **—mau′so·le′an,** *adj.*

mauve (mōv), *n.* **1.** a pale bluish purple. **2.** a purple dye obtained from aniline, discovered in 1856: the first of the coal-tar dyes. *—adj.* **3.** of the color of mauve: *a mauve dress.* [1855–60; < F: lit., mallow < L *malva* MALLOW]

mauve′ dec′ade, the 1890's, considered as a social and cultural period characterized by prosperity and complacency.

ma·ven (mā′vən), *n.* an expert or connoisseur. Also, **ma′vin.** [1960–65; < Yiddish < Heb: connoisseur]

mav·er·ick (mav′ər ik, mav′rik), *n.* **1.** *Southwestern U.S.* an unbranded calf, cow, or steer, esp. an unbranded calf that is separated from its mother. **2.** a lone dissenter, as an intellectual, an artist, or a politician, who takes an independent stand apart from his or her associates. **3.** (*cap.*) an electro-optically guided U.S. air-to-ground tactical missile for destroying tanks and other hardened targets at ranges up to 15 mi. (24 km). [1865–70, *Amer.*; after Samuel A. *Maverick* (1803–70), Texas pioneer who left his calves unbranded]
—Syn. 2. nonconformist, independent, loner.

ma·vis (mā′vis), *n. Brit. Chiefly Literary.* a song thrush. [1350–1400; ME *mavys* < AF *mauviz,* prob. equiv. to *ma(u)ve* seagull (< OE *mæw* MEW²) + *-iz* of unclear orig.]

Ma·vis (mā′vis), *n.* a female given name.

Ma·vors (mā′vôrs), *n. Rom. Rel.* Mars.

ma·vour·neen (mə vo͝or′nēn, -vôr′-, -vōr′-), *n. Irish Eng.* darling; dear. Also, **ma·vour′nin.** [1790–1800; < Ir *mo mhuirnín* my darling]

maw¹ (mô), *n.* **1.** the mouth, throat, or gullet of an animal, esp. a carnivorous mammal. **2.** the crop or craw of a fowl. **3.** the stomach, esp. that of an animal. **4.** a cavernous opening that resembles the open jaws of an animal: *the gaping maw of hell.* **5.** the symbolic or theoretical center of a voracious hunger or appetite of any kind: *the ravenous maw of Death.* [bef. 900; ME *mawe,* OE *maga;* c. D *maag,* G *Magen,* ON *magi*]

maw² (mô), *n. Informal.* mother. [var. of MA]

maw·kin (mô′kin), *n.* malkin.

mawk·ish (mô′kish), *adj.* **1.** characterized by sickly sentimentality; weakly emotional; maudlin. **2.** having a mildly sickening flavor; slightly nauseating. [1660–70; obs. *mawk* maggot (late ME < ON *mathkr* maggot) + -ISH¹. See MAGGOT] **—mawk′ish·ly,** *adv.* **—mawk′ish·ness,** *n.*
—Syn. 1. sentimental, teary.

Maw·lid (mou′lid), *n. Islam.* **1.** a Muslim holiday celebrating the birth of Muhammad, occurring on the twelfth day of the month of Rabi' al-awwal, and characterized esp. by the recitation of panegyrical poems honoring Muhammad. **2.** the poems recited on this occasion. Also, **Maulid, Maulud.** [< Ar *mawlid (al-nabi)* birthday (of the Prophet)]

Maw·son (mô′sən), *n.* **Sir Douglas,** 1882–1958, Australian antarctic explorer, born in England.

max (maks), *Slang.* *—n.* **1.** maximum. **2. to the max,** to the greatest or furthest degree; totally: *That book is disgusting to the max.* *—adj.* **3.** maximum. *—adv.* **4.** maximally. *—v.* **5. max out, a.** to reach a point at which no more improvement, profit, or benefit can occur; level off: *In her last job she maxed out at $25,000 a year.* **b.** to reach the limit of one's capacity, endurance, etc.: *The sales department has maxed out and needs more personnel to call on new clients.* [by shortening]

Max (maks), *n.* a male given name, form of **Maximilian.**

max., maximum.

max·i (mak′sē), *n.* **1.** maxiskirt. **2.** a garment having a maxiskirt, as a coat. *—adj.* **3.** of the length of a maxiskirt; having a maxiskirt. [shortening of MAXISKIRT, or independent use of MAXI-]

maxi-, a combining form with the meanings "very large in comparison with others of its kind" (*maxi-taxi; maxibudget*); "of great scope or intensity" (*maxi-service; maxidevaluation*); (of clothing) "long, nearly ankle-length" (*maxicoat; maxiskirt*). [shortening of MAXIMAL or MAXIMUM, by analogy with MINI-]

max·il·la (mak sil′ə), *n., pl.* **max·il·lae** (mak sil′ē). **1.** a jaw or jawbone, esp. the upper. **2.** one of the paired appendages immediately behind the mandibles of arthropods. [1670–80; < NL, special use of L *maxilla* lower jaw, dim. of *māla* (< **maxlā*) upper jaw, cheekbone]

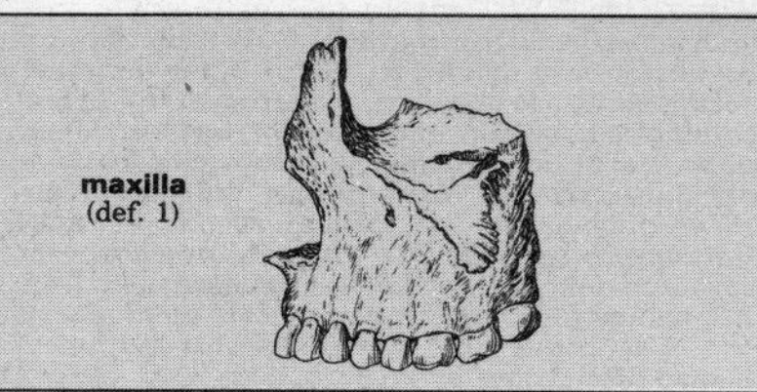
maxilla (def. 1)

max·il·lar·y (mak′sə ler′ē, mak sil′ə rē), *adj., n., pl.* **-lar·ies.** *—adj.* **1.** of or pertaining to a jaw, jawbone, or maxilla. *—n.* **2.** a maxilla or maxillary bone. [1620–30; MAXILL(A) + -ARY]

max·il·li·ped (mak sil′ə ped′), *n.* one member of the three pairs of appendages situated immediately behind the maxillae of crustaceans. [1840–50; MAXILL(A) + -I- + -PED] **—max′il·li·ped′a·ry,** *adj.*

max·il·lo·fa·cial (mak sil′ō fā′shəl), *adj. Anat.* of, pertaining to, or affecting the jaws and the face: *maxillofacial surgery.* [1920–25; MAXILL(A) + -O- + FACIAL]

max·im (mak′sim), *n.* **1.** an expression of a general truth or principle, esp. an aphoristic or sententious one: *the maxims of La Rochefoucauld.* **2.** a principle or rule of conduct. [1400–50; late ME << ML *maxima* (orig. in phrase *maxima prōpositiō* axiom, lit., greatest proposition), n. use of fem. of L *maximus,* superl. of *magnus* great; see MUCH]
—Syn. 1. aphorism, saying, adage, apothegm. See **proverb.**

Max·im (mak′sim; *for 4 also Fr.* mAk sēm′, *Russ.* muksyĕm′), *n.* **1. Hiram Percy,** 1869–1936, U.S. inventor. **2.** his father, **Sir Hiram Stevens,** 1840–1916, English inventor, born in the U.S.: inventor of the Maxim gun. **3. Hudson,** 1853–1927, U.S. inventor and explosives expert (brother of Sir Hiram Stevens Maxim). **4.** a male given name, form of **Maximilian.**

max·i·ma (mak′sə mə), *n.* a pl. of **maximum.**

max·i·mal (mak′sə məl), *adj.* of or being a maximum; greatest possible; highest. [1880–85; MAXIM(UM) + -AL¹] **—max′i·mal·ly,** *adv.*

max′imal ide′al, *Math.* an ideal in a ring that is not included in any other ideal except the ring itself. [1960–65]

max·i·mal·ist (mak′sə mə list), *n.* a person who favors a radical and immediate approach to the achievement of a set of goals or the completion of a program. [< Russ *maksimalíst,* coinage orig. applied in 1906 to an extreme splinter group of the Russian Socialist-Revolutionary party; see MAXIMAL, -IST]

Max′im gun′, an early single-barreled, water-cooled machine gun cocked by the force of its own recoil. [1880–85; after H. S. MAXIM]

Max·i·mil·ian (mak′sə mil′yən), *n.* **1.** 1832–67, archduke of Austria: emperor of Mexico 1864–67. **2.** a male given name.

Maximilian I, 1459–1519, emperor of the Holy Roman Empire 1493–1519.

Maximilian II, 1527–76, emperor of the Holy Roman Empire 1564–76.

Max′imil′ian ar′mor, full plate armor of the early 16th century, representing a combination of Italian and German styles and characterized by extensive use of fluting for lightness and strength.

max·i·min (mak′sə min), *n.* a strategy of game theory employed to maximize a player's minimum possible gain. Cf. **minimax.** [1950–55; MAXI(MUM) + MIN(IMUM)]

max·im·ite (mak′sə mīt′), *n. Chem.* a powerful explosive consisting primarily of picric acid. [1895–1900; named after Hudson MAXIM; see -ITE¹]

max·i·mize (mak′sə mīz′), *v.t.,* **-mized, -miz·ing. 1.** to increase to the greatest possible amount or degree: *to look for ways of maximizing profit.* **2.** to represent at the highest possible estimate; magnify: *He maximized his importance in the program, minimizing the contributions of the other participants.* **3.** to make the greatest or fullest use of: *Maximize your time by planning ahead.* Also, *esp. Brit.,* **max′i·mise′.** [1795–1805; MAXIM(UM) + -IZE] **—max′i·mi·za′tion, max′i·ma′tion,** *n.* **—max′i·miz′er,** *n.*

max·i·mum (mak′sə məm), *n., pl.* **-mums, -ma** (-mə), *adj.* *—n.* **1.** the greatest quantity or amount possible, assignable, allowable, etc. **2.** the highest amount, value, or degree attained or recorded. **3.** an upper limit allowed or allowable by law or regulation. **4.** *Math.* **a.** Also called **relative maximum, local maximum.** the value of a function at a certain point in its domain, which is greater than or equal to the values at all other points in the immediate vicinity of the point. Cf. **absolute maximum. b.** the point in the domain at which a maximum occurs. *—adj.* **5.** that is a maximum; greatest or highest possible or attained: *maximum satisfaction; maximum temperature.* **6.** pertaining to a maximum or maximums. [1730–40; < L, n. use of neut. of *maximus,* superl. of *magnus* great, large] **—max′i·mum·ly,** *adv.*

Max′imum Card′, a picture postcard to which a stamp can be affixed on the picture side, after which it can be cancelled by the appropriate postal service.

max′imum like′lihood estima′tion, *Statistics.* a method of estimating population characteristics from a sample by choosing the values of the parameters that will maximize the probability of getting the particular sample actually obtained from the population.

max′imum prin′ciple, *Math.* the theorem that a function of a complex variable that is analytic in a domain and on its boundary attains its maximum absolute value on the boundary. Also called **max′imum mod′ulus prin′ciple.**

max·i·mum-se·cu·ri·ty (mak′sə məm si kyo͝or′i tē),

adj. (of a correctional facility) designed for or housing prisoners regarded as being very dangerous to society. [1965–70]

max′imum thermom′eter, a thermometer designed to show the highest temperature recorded between resettings. Cf. **minimum thermometer.** [1850–55]

max′imum val′ue the′orem, *Math.* the theorem that for a real-valued function *f* whose domain is a compact set, there is at least one element *x* in the domain of *f* for which *f*(*x*) achieves its largest value.

Max·ine (mak sēn′, mak′sēn), *n.* a female given name.

max·i·skirt (mak′sē skûrt′), *n.* a long skirt or skirt part, as of a coat or dress, ending below the middle of the calf but above the ankle. Also called **maxi.** [MAXI- + SKIRT]

max·ixe (mak sēks′; *Port.* mä shē′shi), *n., pl.* **max·ix·es** (mak sēk′səz; *Port.* mä shē′shis). a ballroom dance originating in Brazil, in moderate duple measure with syncopated rhythms. [1910–15; < Brazilian Pg: lit., West Indian gherkin (allegedly a name given to a Carnival figure, from which the dance took its name), said to be < Kimbundu]

Max Mül·ler (maks′ mul′ər; *Ger.* mäks′ mʏ′lər), **Fried·rich** (frē′drik; *Germ* frē′drikh). See **Müller, Friedrich Max.**

max·well (maks′wel, -wəl), *n. Elect.* the centimeter-gram-second unit of magnetic flux, equal to the magnetic flux through one square centimeter normal to a magnetic field of one gauss. *Abbr.:* Mx [1895–1900; named after J. C. MAXWELL]

Max·well (maks′wel *or, for 2, 3,* -wəl), *n.* **1. Elsa,** 1883–1963, U.S. professional hostess and author. **2. James Clerk** (klärk), 1831–79, Scottish physicist. **3.** a male given name.

Max′well Air′ Force′ Base′, U.S. Air Force installation in SE central Alabama, NW of Montgomery: site of U.S. Air Force Advanced School.

Max′well-Boltz′mann statis′tics (maks′wel bôlts′män, -mən, -wəl), *Physics.* statistics for classical physics, based on the assumption that in a given physical system consisting of indistinguishable particles and regions, all possible arrangements of the particles in the various regions have equal probability. [1965–70; after J. C. MAXWELL and Ludwig BOLTZMANN]

Max′well de′mon, *Physics.* a hypothetical agent or device of arbitrarily small mass that is considered to admit or block selectively the passage of individual molecules from one compartment to another according to their speed, constituting a violation of the second law of thermodynamics. [1875–80; after J. C. MAXWELL]

Max′well Mon′tes, *Astron.* a compact mountain range on Ishtar Terra, one of the regions of highest elevation on Venus.

Max′well's field′ equa′tions, *Elect.* the four fundamental equations that describe the behavior of electric and magnetic fields in time and space and the dependence of these fields on the distribution and behavior of electric charges and currents. Also, **Max′well's equa′tions.** [after J. C. MAXWELL]

may[1] (mā), *auxiliary v., pres. sing. 1st pers.* **may,** *2nd* **may** *or (Archaic)* **may·est** *or* **mayst,** *3rd* **may;** *pres. pl.* **may;** *past* **might. 1.** (used to express possibility): *It may rain.* **2.** (used to express opportunity or permission): *You may enter.* **3.** (used to express contingency, esp. in clauses indicating condition, concession, purpose, result, etc.): *I may be wrong but I think you would be wise to go. Times may change but human nature stays the same.* **4.** (used to express wish or prayer): *May you live to an old age.* **5.** *Archaic.* (used to express ability or power.) Cf. **might**[1]. [bef. 900; ME *mai* 1st and 3rd pers. sing. pres. ind. of *mouen,* OE *mæg* (inf. *magan*); c. G *mögen*]
—Usage. See **can**[1].

may[2] (mā), *n. Archaic.* a maiden. [bef. 900; ME *mai;* OE *mæg*]

May (mā), *n.* **1.** the fifth month of the year, containing 31 days. **2.** the early part of one's life, esp. the prime: *a young woman in her May.* **3.** the festivities of May Day. **4.** (*l.c.*) *Brit.* the hawthorn. **5.** a female given name. *—v.i.* **6.** (*l.c.*) to gather flowers in the spring: *when we were maying.* [bef. 1050; ME, OE *Maius* < L, short for *Maius mēnsis* Maia's month]

May (mā), *n.* **Cape,** a cape at the SE tip of New Jersey, on Delaware Bay.

ma·ya (mä′yä, -yə), *n. Hinduism.* **1.** the power, as of a god, to produce illusions. **2.** the production of an illusion. **3.** (in Vedantic philosophy) the illusion of the reality of sensory experience and of the experienced qualities and attributes of oneself. **4.** (*cap.*) Also called **Mahamaya.** a goddess personifying the power that creates phenomena. [1815–25; < Skt] **—ma′yan,** *adj.*

Ma·ya (mä′yə), *n., pl.* **-yas,** (*esp. collectively*) **-ya,** *adj.* *—n.* **1.** a member of a major pre-Columbian civilization of the Yucatán Peninsula that reached its peak in the 9th century A.D. and produced magnificent ceremonial cities with pyramids, a sophisticated mathematical and calendar system, hieroglyphic writing, and fine sculpture, painting, and ceramics. **2.** a member of a modern American Indian people of southern Mexico, Guatemala, and parts of Honduras who are the descendants of this ancient civilization. **3.** any of the Mayan languages; the historical and modern languages of the Mayas. *—adj.* **4.** Mayan.

Ma·ya·güez (mä′yä gwes′), *n.* a seaport in W Puerto Rico. 82,968.

Ma·ya·kov·ski (mä′yə kôf′skē, -kof′-; *Russ.* mə yukôf′skyē), *n.* **Vla·di·mir Vla·di·mi·ro·vich** (vlad′ə mēr′ vlad′ə mēr′ə vich′; *Russ.* vlu dyĕ′myir vlu dyĕ′myirə vyich), 1893–1930, Russian poet. Also, **Ma′ya·kov′sky.**

Ma·yan (mä′yən), *adj.* **1.** of or pertaining to the Maya, their culture, or their languages. *—n.* **2.** a member of the Mayan tribe. **3.** a group of languages spoken by the Mayas in southern Mexico, Guatemala, and Belize, including Yucatec, Quiché, and Huastec. [1885–90; MAY(A) + -AN]

May′ ap′ple, 1. an American plant, *Podophyllum peltatum,* of the barberry family, bearing an edible, yellowish, egg-shaped fruit. **2.** the fruit itself. Also, **May′ap′·ple.** [1725–35, *Amer.*]

may·be (mā′bē), *adv.* **1.** perhaps; possibly: *Maybe I'll go too.* *—n.* **2.** a possibility or uncertainty. [1375–1425; late ME *may be,* short for *it may be*]

May·beck (mā′bek), *n.* **Bernard,** 1862–1957 U.S. architect.

May′ bee′tle. See **June bug** (def. 1). [1710–20]

May-blob (mā′blob′), *n.* See **marsh marigold.** [1860–65]

May′ Day′, the first day of May, long celebrated with various festivities, as the crowning of the May queen, dancing around the Maypole, and, in recent years, often marked by labor parades and political demonstrations. [1225–75; ME]

May·day (mā′dā′), *n.* the international radiotelephone distress signal, used by ships and aircraft. [1925–30; < F (*venez*) *m'aider* (come) help me!]

Ma·yence (mä yäns′), *n.* French name of **Mainz.**

Ma·yenne (ma yen′), *n.* a department in W France. 252,762; 2012 sq. mi. (5210 sq. km). *Cap.:* Laval.

May·er (mī′ər *or, Ger.,* mī′ər *for 1;* mā′ər *for 2;* mī′ər *for 3*), *n.* **1. Jul·ius Rob·ert von** (jo͞ol′yəs rob′ərt von; *Ger.* yo͞o′lē o͝os rō′bert fən), 1814–78, German physicist. **2. Louis B(urt)** (bûrt), 1885–1957, U.S. motion-picture producer, born in Russia. **3. Maria Goep·pert** (gō′pərt), 1906–72, U.S. physicist, born in Poland: Nobel prize 1963.

may·est (mā′ist), *v. Archaic.* 2nd pers. sing. pres. indic. of **may**[1].

May·fair (mā′fâr′), *n.* a fashionable neighborhood in London, England, E of Hyde Park.

may′fair tan′, suntan (def. 2). [after MAYFAIR]

May·field (mā′fēld′), *n.* a city in SW Kentucky. 10,705.

May′field Heights′, a city in N Ohio, near Cleveland. 21,550.

may·fish (mā′fish′), *n., pl.* **-fish·es,** (*esp. collectively*) **-fish.** See **striped killifish.** [1830–40, *Amer.*; MAY + FISH]

May·flow·er (mā′flou′ər), *n.* **1.** (*italics*) the ship in which the Pilgrims sailed from Southampton to the New World in 1620. **2.** (*l.c.*) any of various plants that blossom in May, as the hepatica or anemone in the U.S., and the hawthorn or cowslip in England. **3.** (*l.c.*) the trailing arbutus, *Epigaea repens:* the state flower of Massachusetts. [1560–70; MAY + FLOWER]

May′flower com′pact, an agreement to establish a government, entered into by the Pilgrims in the cabin of the *Mayflower* on November 11, 1620.

may·fly (mā′flī′), *n., pl.* **-flies. 1.** Also called **shadfly.** any insect of the order Ephemeroptera, having delicate, membranous wings with the front pair much larger than the rear and having an aquatic larval stage usually lasting less than two days. **2.** Also, **May′ fly′.** *Angling.* an artificial fly made to resemble this insect. [1645–55; MAY + FLY[2]]

mayfly,
Hexagenia limbata,
body length
1 in. (2.5 cm)

may·hap (mā′hap′, mā′hap′), *adv. Archaic.* perhaps. [1530–40; short for *it may hap*]

may·hap·pen (mā′hap′ən), *adv. Archaic.* perhaps; mayhap. [1520–30; short for *it may happen*]

may·hem (mā′hem, mā′əm), *n.* **1.** *Law.* the crime of willfully inflicting a bodily injury on another so as to make the victim less capable of self-defense or, under modern statutes, so as to cripple or mutilate the victim. **2.** random or deliberate violence or damage. **3.** a state of rowdy disorder: *Antagonisms between the various factions at the meeting finally boiled over, and mayhem ensued.* [1350–1400; ME *maheym, maim* < AF *mahe(i)m, mahaim* < Gmc; akin to MHG *meidem* gelding, ON *meitha* to injure. See MAIM]

May·hew (mā′hyo͞o), *n.* **1. Jonathan,** 1720–66, American Congregational clergyman. **2. Thomas,** 1593–1682, American colonist, born in England: settler and governor of Martha's Vineyard.

May·ing (mā′ing), *n.* the celebration of May Day. [1350–1400; ME *maiing;* see MAY, -ING[1]]

May·nard (mā′nərd), *n.* a male given name.

may·n't (mā′ənt, mānt), contraction of *may not.*

may·o (mā′ō), *n. Informal.* mayonnaise. [by shortening; cf. -O]

May·o (mā′ō), *n.* **1. Charles Horace,** 1865–1939, and his brother **William James,** 1861–1939, U.S. surgeons. **2.** a county in NW Connaught province, in the NW Republic of Ireland. 114,548; 2084 sq. mi. (5400 sq. km). *Co. seat:* Castlebar.

Ma·yon (mä yôn′), *n.* an active volcano in the Philippines, on SE Luzon Island. 7926 ft. (2415 m).

may·on·naise (mā′ə nāz′, mā′ə nāz′), *n.* a thick dressing of egg yolks, vinegar or lemon juice, oil, and seasonings, used for salads, sandwiches, vegetable dishes, etc. [1835–45; < F, equiv. to *mayon* (perh. var. of *Mahón,* town in Minorca) + *-aise* -ESE]

may·or (mā′ər, mâr), *n.* **1.** the chief executive official, usually elected, of a city, village, or town. **2.** the chief magistrate of a city or borough. [1250–1300; < ML *major* MAJOR; r. ME *mer, mair* < OF *maire*] **—may′or·al,** *adj.* **—may′or·ship′,** *n.*

may·or·al·ty (mā′ər əl tē, mâr′əl-), *n., pl.* **-ties.** the office or tenure of a mayor. [1350–1400; MAYOR + -AL[1] + -TY[2]; r. ME *mairaltee* < MF *mairalte*]

may·or·ess (mā′ər is, mâr′is), *n.* **1.** a woman who is the chief executive official of a city, village, or town. **2.** the wife of a mayor. [1400–50; MAYOR + -ESS; r. late ME *meyresse*]
—Usage. See **-ess.**

May′or of Cas′ter·bridge, The (kas′tər brij′), a novel (1886) by Thomas Hardy.

may′or of the pal′ace, one of a line of hereditary administrative lieutenants to the Merovingian kings who eventually took over royal function and title in the Frankish kingdoms; a palatine. [1520–30; trans. of ML *major domūs;* see MAJOR-DOMO]

may′or's court′, a city court presided over by a mayor. [1800–10]

Ma·yotte (*Fr.* ma yôt′), *n.* one of the Comoro Islands, in the Indian Ocean, NW of Madagascar: an overseas department of France. 52,000; 144 sq. mi. (373 sq. km).

May·pole (mā′pōl′), *n.* (*often l.c.*) a tall pole, decorated with flowers and ribbons, around which people dance or engage in sports during May Day celebrations. [1545–55; MAY + POLE[1]]

may·pop (mā′pop′), *n.* **1.** the edible fruit of the passionflower, *Passiflora incarnata,* of the southern U.S. **2.** the plant itself. **3.** *South Midland and Southern U.S.* May apple. [1850–55, *Amer.*; prob. taboo deformation of earlier *maycock,* earlier *maracock,* perh. < Virginia Algonquian]

May′ queen′, a girl or young woman crowned with flowers and honored as queen in the festivities of May Day.

Mays (māz), *n.* **Willie (Howard),** born 1931, U.S. baseball player.

mayst (māst), *v. Archaic.* 2nd pers. sing. pres. indic. of **may**[1].

may·ten (mī ten′), *n.* a tree, *Maytenus boaria,* native to Chile, having narrow leaves and drooping branches, planted as a street tree in Florida and southern California. [< AmerSp *maitén* < Araucanian *mañtun*]

May·time (mā′tīm′), *n.* the month of May. Also called **May·tide** (mā′tīd′). [1795–1805; MAY + TIME]

may′ tree′, *Brit.* the hawthorn.

may·weed (mā′wēd′), *n.* a composite plant, *Anthemis cotula,* native to Europe and Asia but naturalized in North America, having pungent, rank-smelling foliage and flower heads with a yellow disk and white rays. [1545–55; obs. *mayth* mayweed (ME *maithe,* OE *mægtha*) + WEED[1]]

May′ wine′, a punch consisting typically of Alsatian, Moselle, or Rhine wine, flavored with woodruff.

May·wood (mā′wo͝od′), *n.* **1.** a city in NE Illinois, near Chicago. 27,998. **2.** a city in SW California, near Los Angeles. 21,810.

ma·zal tov (mä′zəl tôv′, tôf′, tōv′). See **mazel tov.**

maz·ard (maz′ərd), *n.* **1.** *Archaic.* **a.** head. **b.** face. **2.** *Obs.* a mazer. [1595–1605; MAZ(ER) + -ARD]

Maz·a·rin (maz′ə rin, maz′ə rēn′; *Fr.* ma za ran′), *n.* **Jules** (jo͞olz; *Fr.* zhyl), (*Giulio Mazarini*), 1602–61, French cardinal and statesman, born in Italy: chief minister of Louis XIV 1642–61.

maz·a·rine (maz′ə rēn′, maz′ə rēn′, -rin), *n.* **1.** a deep, rich blue. **2.** a silver strainer fitting over a meat dish and used for draining the water from boiled fish. [1665–75; < F, perh. named after Cardinal MAZARIN]

Ma·zar-i-Sha·rif (mä zär′ē shä rēf′), *n.* a city in N Afghanistan. 40,000.

Maz·a·tec (maz′ə tek′), *n., pl.* **-tecs,** (*esp. collectively*) **-tec** for 1. **1.** a member of an American Indian people of northern Oaxaca, in Mexico. **2.** the Oto-Manguean language of the Mazatec. **—Maz·a·tec′an,** *adj.*

Ma·za·tlán (mä′sä tlän′), *n.* a seaport in S Sinaloa, in W Mexico. 169,500.

Maz·da (maz′də), *n. Zoroastrianism.* See **Ahura Mazda.**

Maz·da·ism (maz′də iz′əm), *n.* Zoroastrianism. [1870–75; MAZDA + -ISM]

maze (māz), *n., v.,* **mazed, maz·ing.** *—n.* **1.** a confusing network of intercommunicating paths or passages; labyrinth. **2.** any complex system or arrangement that causes bewilderment, confusion, or perplexity: *Her petition was lost in a maze of bureaucratic red tape.* **3.** a state of bewilderment or confusion. **4.** a winding movement, as in dancing. *—v.t.* **5.** *Chiefly Dial.* to daze, perplex, or stupefy. [1250–1300; ME *mase,* n. use of aph. var. of *amasen* to AMAZE] **—maz·ed·ly** (mā′zid lē, māzd′-), *adv.* **—mazed′ness,** *n.* **—maze′like′,** *adj.*

ma·zel tov (mä′zəl tôv′, tôf′, tōv′), an expression of congratulations and best wishes, used chiefly by Jews on an occasion of success or good fortune. Also, **mazal tov.** [1860–65; < Yiddish *mazltov* < Heb *mazzāl ṭōbh* lit., good luck]

ma·zer (mā′zər), *n.* a large metal drinking bowl or cup, formerly of wood. [1150–1200; ME: kind of wood (prob. maple), OE *mæser-* (in adj. *mæseren,* equiv. to *mæser* maple + *-en* -EN[2]); c. ON *mǫsurr* maple, MHG *maser* maple, drinking cup]

ma·zo·path·i·a (mā′zō path′ē ə), *n. Pathol.* any disease of the placenta. Also, **mazopathy.** [1855–60; < NL *maz(a)* placenta (< Gk *mâza* lump, MASS) + -o- + *-pathia* -PATHY]

ma·zop·a·thy (mā zop′ə thē), *n. Pathol.* **1.** mazopathia. **2.** mastopathy.

Ma·zu (*Chin.* mä′zy′), *n. Pinyin.* Matsu.

ma·zu·ma (mə zōō′mə), *n. Slang.* money. [1875–80; < Yiddish *mezumen* < Heb *mezūmān* set, fixed]

ma·zur·ka (mə zûr′kə, -zōōr′-), *n.* **1.** a lively Polish dance in moderately quick triple meter. **2.** music for, or in the rhythm of, this dance. Also, **ma·zour′ka.** [1810–20; < Pol, equiv. to *Mazur* Mazovia (district in northern Poland) + *-ka* n. suffix]

ma·zy (mā′zē), *adj.*, **-zi·er, -zi·est.** full of confusing turns, passages, etc.; like a maze; labyrinthine. [1500–10; MAZE + -Y¹] —**ma′zi·ly,** *adv.* —**ma′zi·ness,** *n.*

maz·zard (maz′ərd), *n.* a wild sweet cherry, *Prunus avium*, used as a rootstock for cultivated varieties of cherries. [1570–80; earlier *mazer;* cf. obs. *mazers* spots, MEASLES; see -ARD]

Maz·zi·ni (mät tsē′nē, mäd dzē′-; *Eng.* mat sē′nē, mad zē′-), *n.* **Giu·sep·pe** (jōō zep′pe), 1805–72, Italian patriot and revolutionary. —**Maz·zi·ni·an** (mat sē′nē ən, mad zē′-), *adj., n.*

MB, *Computers.* megabyte; megabytes.

Mb, *Computers.* megabit; megabits.

mb, *Physics.* **1.** millibar; millibars. **2.** millibarn; millibarns.

M.B., *Chiefly Brit.* Bachelor of Medicine. [< NL *Medicinae Baccalaureus*]

M'Ba (əm bä′), *n.* **Lé·on** (le ôɴ′), 1902–67, African statesman: president of Gabon 1961–67.

M.B.A., Master of Business Administration. Also, **MBA**

Mba·bane (bä bän′, -bä′nē, əm bä′-), *n.* a city in and the capital of Swaziland, in the NW part. 24,000.

Mban·da·ka (bän′dä kä′, əm bän′-), *n.* a city in W Zaire. 134,495. Formerly, **Coquilhatville.**

mbd, (of oil) million barrels per day.

MBE, Multistate Bar Examination.

M.B.E., Member of the Order of the British Empire.

mbi·ra (əm bēr′ə), *n.* a musical instrument of Africa usually made out of a gourd that serves as a resonating box, to which vibrating metal or wooden strips are attached for plucking. [1905–10; < Shona]

Mbm, one thousand feet, board measure.

Mbo·mu (bō′mōō, əm bō′-), *n.* Bomu.

Mboy·a (əm boi′ə), *n.* **Tom** (*Thomas Joseph Mboya*), 1930–69, African political leader in Kenya.

Mbu·ji-Ma·yi (bōō′jē mī′, -mä′yē, əm bōō′-), *n.* a city in S central Zaire. 336,654. Formerly, **Bakwanga.**

Mbun·du (əm bōōn′dōō), *n., pl.* **-dus,** (*esp. collectively*) **-du** for 1. **1.** Also called **Ovimbundu.** a Bantu-speaking people of southern Angola. **2.** Also called **Umbundu.** the Bantu language of the Mbundu people. **3.** Kimbundu.

MC, 1. Marine Corps. **2.** master of ceremonies. **3.** Medical Corps. **4.** Member of Congress.

Mc, 1. megacurie; megacuries. **2.** megacycle.

mC, millicoulomb; millicoulombs.

mc, 1. megacycle. **2.** meter-candle. **3.** millicurie; millicuries.

Mc-, var. of **Mac-.** Also, **Mᶜ-.**

M.C., 1. Master Commandant. **2.** master of ceremonies. **3.** Medical Corps. **4.** Member of Congress. **5.** Member of Council. **6.** *Brit.* Military Cross.

Mc·A·doo (mak′ə dōō′), *n.* **William Gibbs,** 1863–1941, U.S. lawyer and statesman: Secretary of the Treasury 1913–18.

Mc·Al·es·ter (mə kal′i stər), *n.* a city in E Oklahoma. 17,255.

Mc·Al·len (mə kal′ən), *n.* a city in S Texas, on the Rio Grande. 67,042.

MCAT, Medical College Admission Test.

Mc·Au·liffe (mə kô′lif), *n.* **Anthony Clement,** 1898–1975, U.S. Army general.

Mc·Cand·less (mə kand′lis), *n.* a town in SW Pennsylvania. 26,250.

Mc·Car′ran-Wal′ter Act′ (mə kar′ən wôl′tər), the Immigration and Nationality Act enacted by the U.S. Congress in 1952 that removed racial barriers to immigration and empowered the Department of Justice to deport immigrants or naturalized citizens engaging in subversive activities.

Mc·Car·thy (mə kär′thē), *n.* **1. Joseph R(aymond),** 1909–57, U.S. politician. **2. Joseph Vincent,** 1887–1978, U.S. baseball manager. **3. Mary (Therese),** born 1912, U.S. novelist.

Mc·Car·thy·ism (mə kär′thē iz′əm), *n.* **1.** the practice of making accusations of disloyalty, esp. of pro-Communist activity, in many instances unsupported by proof or based on slight, doubtful, or irrelevant evidence. **2.** the practice of making unfair allegations or using unfair investigative techniques, esp. in order to restrict dissent or political criticism. [1945–50; J. R. MCCARTHY + -ISM] —**Mc·Car′thy·ite′,** *n., adj.*

Mc·Cau·ley (mə kô′lē), *n.* **Mary Ludwig Hays,** real name of Molly Pitcher.

Mc·Clel·lan (mə klel′ən), *n.* **George Brin·ton** (brin′tn), 1826–85, Union general in the American Civil War.

CONCISE ETYMOLOGY KEY: <, descended or borrowed from; >, whence; b., blend of, blended; c., cognate with; cf., compare; deriv., derivative; equiv., equivalent; imit., imitative; obl., oblique; r., replacing; s., stem; sp., spelling, spelled; resp., respelling, respelled; trans., translation; ?, origin unknown; *, unattested; ‡, probably earlier than. See the full key inside the front cover.

Mc·Clos·key (mə klos′kē), *n.* **John,** 1810–85, U.S. Roman Catholic clergyman: first U.S. cardinal 1875.

Mc·Cloy (mə kloi′), *n.* **John Jay,** 1895–1989, U.S. lawyer, banker, and government official.

Mc·Clure (mə klŏŏr′), *n.* **Samuel Sidney,** 1857–1949, U.S. editor and publisher, born in Ireland.

Mc·Comb (mə kōm′), *n.* a town in S Mississippi. 12,331.

Mc·Cor·mack (mə kôr′mik), *n.* **1. John,** 1884–1945, U.S. tenor, born in Ireland. **2. John William,** 1891–1980, U.S. politician: Speaker of the House 1962–70.

Mc·Cor·mick (mə kôr′mik), *n.* **1. Cyrus Hall,** 1809–84, U.S. inventor, esp. of harvesting machinery. **2. Robert Rutherford,** 1880–1955, U.S. newspaper publisher.

Mc·Coy (mə koi′), *n.* the genuine thing or person as promised, stated, or implied (usually prec. by *the* or *the real*): *Those other paintings are copies, but this one is the McCoy.* [1880–85; also *Mackay, McKie, the clear McCoy* (of liquor); of uncert. orig.; hypothesized identifications with *Mackay,* a Scottish clan, and *Kid McCoy,* nickname of U.S. boxer Norman Selby (1873–1940), are unsubstantiated]

Mc·Crae (mə krā′), *n.* **John,** 1872–1918, Canadian physician, soldier, and poet.

Mc·Cul·lers (mə kul′ərz), *n.* **Car·son** (kär′sən), 1917–1967, U.S. novelist and short-story writer.

Mc·Don·ald (mək don′ld), *n.* **David John,** 1902–79, U.S. labor leader: president of the United Steelworkers of America 1952–65.

Mc·Doug·all (mək dōō′gəl), *n.* **William,** 1871–1938, U.S. psychologist and writer, born in England.

Mc·Dow·ell (mək dou′əl), *n.* **1. Ephraim,** 1771–1830, U.S. surgeon. **2. Irvin,** 1818–85, Union general in the American Civil War.

M.C.E., Master of Civil Engineering.

Mcf, one thousand cubic feet. Also, **mcf, MCF**

Mcfd, thousands of cubic feet per day.

Mc·Fee (mək fē′), *n.* **William,** 1881–1966, English writer.

mcg, microgram.

Mc·Gov·ern (mə guv′ərn), *n.* **George (Stanley),** born 1922, U.S. politician: Democratic presidential candidate 1972, senator 1963–81.

Mc·Graw (mə grô′), *n.* **John Joseph,** 1873–1934, U.S. baseball player and manager.

Mc·Guf·fey (mə guf′ē), *n.* **William Holmes,** 1800–73, U.S. educator: editor of the *Eclectic Readers,* a series of school readers.

M.Ch.E., Master of Chemical Engineering.

Mc·Hen·ry (mək hen′rē, mə ken′-), *n.* **1.** a town in NE Illinois. 10,908. **2. Fort.** See **Fort McHenry.**

MChin, Middle Chinese.

mCi, millicurie; millicuries.

Mc·In·tire (mak′in tīᵊr′), *n.* **Samuel,** 1757–1811, U.S. architect and woodcarver.

Mc·In·tosh (mak′in tosh′), *n.* a variety of red apple that ripens in early autumn. [1875–80; named after John *McIntosh* of Ontario, Canada, who first cultivated it (1796)]

Mc·In·tyre (mak′in tīᵊr′), *n.* **James Francis Aloysius,** 1886–1979, U.S. Roman Catholic clergyman: cardinal from 1953; archbishop of Los Angeles 1948–70.

M.C.J., Master of Comparative Jurisprudence.

Mc·Kees·port (mə kēz′pôrt′, -pōrt′), *n.* a city in SW Pennsylvania, near Pittsburgh. 31,012.

Mc·Ken·na (mə ken′ə), *n.* **Sio·bhan** (shə vôn′, -von′), 1923–86, Irish actress.

Mc·Ken·zie (mə ken′zē), *n.* **Robert Tait** (tāt), 1867–1938, Canadian physician, educator, and sculptor.

Mc·Kim (mə kim′), *n.* **Charles Fol·len** (fol′ən), 1847–1909, U.S. architect.

Mc·Kin·ley (mə kin′lē), *n.* **1. William,** 1843–1901, 25th president of the U.S. 1897–1901. **2. Mount,** a mountain in central Alaska: highest peak in North America, 20,320 ft. (6194 m).

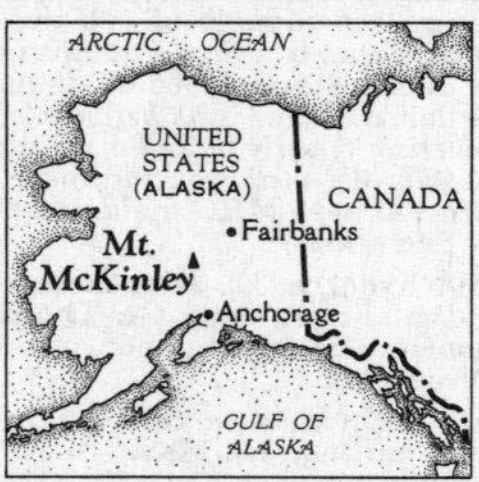

Mc·Kin·ney (mə kin′ē), *n.* a city in NE Texas. 16,249.

Mc·Kis·sick (mə kis′ik), *n.* **Floyd Bix·ler** (biks′lər), 1922–91, U.S. lawyer and civil-rights leader: chairman of Congress of Racial Equality 1963–66, director 1966–68.

M.C.L., 1. Master of Civil Law. **2.** Master of Comparative Law.

Mc·Lar·en (mə klar′ən), *n.* **Norman,** 1914–87, Canadian film director and animator, born in Scotland.

Mc·Leod (mə kloud′), *Trademark.* a brand of garden tool that is a combination of a rake and a hoe. Also called **McLeod′ tool′.**

McLeod′ gauge′, *Physical Chem.* a device for determining very low gas pressures by manometrically measuring the pressure of a sample after its compression to a known fraction of its original volume. [named after Herbert *McLeod* (1841–1932), English chemist]

Mc·Lu·han (mə klōō′ən), *n.* **Marshall,** 1911–80, Canadian cultural historian and mass-communications theorist.

Mc·Mas·ter (mək mas′tər, -mä′stər), *n.* **John Bach,** 1852–1932, U.S. historian and educator.

Mc·Mil·lan (mək mil′ən), *n.* **Edwin Mat·ti·son** (mat′ə sən), 1907–91, U.S. educator and physicist: Nobel prize for chemistry 1951.

Mc·Minn·ville (mək min′vil), *n.* **1.** a town in NW Oregon. 14,080. **2.** a town in central Tennessee. 10,683.

Mc·Mur′do Sound′ (mək mûr′dō), an inlet of Ross Sea, in Antarctica, N of Victoria Land.

Mc·Nair (mək nâr′), *n.* **Lesley James,** 1883–1944, U.S. army officer.

Mc·Na·ma·ra (mak′nə mar′ə), *n.* **Robert Strange,** born 1916, U.S. business executive and government official: Secretary of Defense 1961–68; president of World Bank 1968–81.

Mc·Naugh·ton (mək nôt′n), *n.* **Andrew George Lat·ta** (lat′ə), 1887–1966, Canadian army officer, statesman, diplomat, and scientist.

Mc·Nutt (mək nut′), *n.* **Paul Vo·ries** (vôr′ēz, vōr′-), 1891–1955, U.S. diplomat and government official.

MCP, male chauvinist pig.

M.C.P., Master of City Planning.

Mc·Part·land (mək pärt′lənd), *n.* **Marian,** born 1920, British jazz pianist and composer, in the U.S. since 1946.

Mc·Pher·son (mək fûr′sən, -fėr′-), *n.* **1. Aimee Sem·ple** (sem′pəl), 1890–1944, U.S. evangelist, born in Canada. **2.** a town in central Kansas. 11,753.

M.C.R., Master of Comparative Religion.

Mc·Rey·nolds (mək ren′ldz), *n.* **James Clark,** 1862–1946, U.S. jurist: associate justice of the U.S. Supreme Court 1914–41.

MD, 1. Maryland (approved esp. for use with zip code). **2.** Doctor of Medicine. [< NL *Medicinae Doctor*] **3.** Middle Dutch. **4.** months after date. **5.** muscular dystrophy.

Md, *Music.* right hand. [< It *mano destra* or F *main droite*]

Md, *Symbol, Chem.* mendelevium.

Md., Maryland.

M/D, months after date. Also, **m/d**

M.D., 1. Doctor of Medicine. [< NL *Medicinae Doctor*] **2.** Middle Dutch.

MDA, *Pharm.* methylene dioxyamphetamine: an amphetamine derivative, $C_{10}H_{13}NO_2$, having hallucinogenic and stimulant properties.

MDAP, Mutual Defense Assistance Program.

M-day (em′dā′), *n. Mil.* mobilization day: a day assumed by the Department of Defense as the first day of mobilization, used by the military for planning purposes. [1935–40]

M.Des., Master of Design.

Mde·wa·kan·ton (əm dē wô′kən tōn′, med′ē wô′-), *n.* a member of a North American Indian people belonging to the Santee branch of the Dakota.

m. dict., (in prescriptions) as directed.

Mdlle., *pl.* **Mdlles.** Mademoiselle.

Mdm., *pl.* **Mdms.** Madam.

MDMA, methylene dioxymethamphetamine: an amphetamine derivative, $C_{11}H_{15}NO_2$, that reduces inhibitions and that was used in psychotherapy until it was banned in the U.S. in 1985.

Mdme., *pl.* **Mdmes.** Madame.

mdn, median.

mdnt., midnight.

MDR, minimum daily requirement.

mdse., merchandise.

me (mē), *pron.* **1.** the objective case of **I,** used as a direct or indirect object: *They asked me to the party. Give me your hand.* **2.** *Informal.* (used instead of the pronoun *I* in the predicate after the verb *to be*): *It's me.* **3.** *Informal.* (used instead of the pronoun *my* before a gerund): *Did you hear about me getting promoted?* —*adj.* **4.** of or involving an obsessive interest in one's own satisfaction: *the me decade.* [bef. 900; ME *me,* OE *mē* (dat. and acc. sing.); c. D *mij,* OHG *mir*]

—**Usage. 2.** A traditional rule governing the case of personal pronouns after forms of the verb *to be* is that the nominative or subjective form (*I; she; he; we; they*) must be chosen. Some 400 years ago, owing to the feeling that the postverb position in a sentence is object rather than subject territory, ME and other objective pronouns (*him; her; us; them*) began to replace the subjective forms after *be,* so that *It is I* became *It is me.* Today such constructions—*It's me. That's him. It must be them.*—are almost universal in speech, the context in which they usually occur. In formal speech or edited writing, the subjective forms are used: *It was I who first noticed the problem. My brother was the one who called our attention to the problem, but it wasn't he who solved it. It had been she at the window, not her husband.*

ME and other objective forms have also replaced the subjective forms in speech in constructions like *Me neither; Not us; Who, them?* and in comparisons after *as* or *than: She's no faster than him at getting the answers.* When the pronoun is the subject of a verb that is expressed, the nominative forms are used: *Neither did I. She's no faster than he is at getting the answers.* See also **than.**

3. When a verb form ending in *-ing* functions as a noun, it is traditionally called a gerund: *Walking is good exercise. She enjoys reading biographies.* Usage guides have long insisted that gerunds, being nouns, must be preceded by the possessive form of the pronouns or nouns (*my; your; her; his; its; our; their; child's; author's*) rather than by the objective forms (*me; you; him; her; it; us; them*): *The landlord objected to my* (not *me*) *having guests late at night. Several readers were delighted at the author's* (not *author*) *taking a stand on the issue.* In standard practice, however, both objective and possessive forms appear before gerunds. Possessives are more common in formal edited writing, but the occurrence of objective forms is increasing; in informal writing and speech objective forms are more common: *Many objections have been raised to the government* (or *government's*) *allowing lumbering in national parks. "Does anyone object to me* (or *my*) *reading this report aloud?" the moderator asked.*

ME, 1. Maine (approved esp. for use with zip code). 2. Middle East. 3. Middle English.

Me, *Chem.* methyl.

Me., Maine.

M.E., 1. (*often l.c.*) See **managing editor.** 2. Master of Education. 3. Master of Engineering. 4. Mechanical Engineer. 5. Medical Examiner. 6. Methodist Episcopal. 7. Middle English. 8. Mining Engineer.

M.E.A., Master of Engineering Administration.

mea·con (mē′kən), *v.t.* to give false signals to (electronic navigational equipment), as by means of a radio transmitter. [M(ISLEAD) + (B)EACON]

me·a cul·pa (me′ä kōōl′pä; *Eng.* mā′ə kul′pə, mē′ə), *Latin.* through my fault; my fault (used as an acknowledgment of one's responsibility).

mead[1] (mēd), *n.* 1. an alcoholic liquor made by fermenting honey and water. 2. any of various nonalcoholic beverages. [bef. 900; ME *mede,* OE *medu, meodu;* c. D *mee,* G *Met,* ON *mjǫthr* mead, Skt *madhu* honey, Gk *méthy* wine]

mead[2] (mēd), *n. Archaic.* meadow. [bef. 1000; ME *mede,* OE *mǣd.* See MEADOW]

Mead (mēd), *n.* 1. **George Herbert,** 1863–1931, U.S. philosopher and author. 2. **Margaret,** 1901–78, U.S. anthropologist. 3. **Lake,** a lake in NW Arizona and SE Nevada, formed 1936 by Hoover Dam. 115 mi. (185 km) long; 227 sq. mi. (588 sq. km).

Meade (mēd), *n.* 1. **George Gordon,** 1815–72, Union general in the American Civil War. 2. **James Edward,** born 1907, British economist: Nobel prize 1977.

mead·ow (med′ō), *n.* 1. a tract of grassland used for pasture or serving as a hayfield. 2. a tract of grassland in an upland area near the timberline. [bef. 1000; ME *medwe,* OE *mǣdw-,* obl. s. of *mǣd* MEAD[2]; akin to G *Matte*] —**mead′ow·less,** *adj.* —**mead′ow·y,** *adj.*
—**Syn.** 1. green, range, field.

mead′ow beau′ty, any of several North American plants of the genus *Rhexia,* esp. *R. mariana* or *R. virginica,* having showy rose-pink flowers with eight prominent bright yellow stamens. Also called **deer grass.** [1830–40, *Amer.*]

mead′ow bird′, the bobolink. [1835–45, *Amer.*]

mead′ow fes′cue, a European fescue, *Festuca pratensis,* of the grass family, grown for pasture in North America. [1785–95]

mead′ow grass′, any grass of the genus *Poa,* esp. *P. pratensis,* the Kentucky bluegrass. [1250–1300; ME]

mead·ow·land (med′ō land′), *n.* an area or section of land that is a meadow or is used or kept as a meadow. [1645–55; MEADOW + LAND]

mead·ow·lark (med′ō lärk′), *n.* any of several American songbirds of the genus *Sturnella,* of the family Icteridae, esp. *S. magna* **(eastern meadowlark)** and *S. neglecta* **(western meadowlark),** having a brownish and black back and wings and a yellow breast, noted for their clear, tuneful song. [1605–15; MEADOW + LARK[1]]

western meadowlark, *Sturnella neglecta,* length 9 in. (23 cm)

mead′ow lil′y. See **Canada lily.** [1825–35, *Amer.*]

mead′ow mouse′, any of numerous short-tailed rodents of the genus *Microtus* and allied genera, chiefly of fields and meadows in the temperate Northern Hemisphere. Also called **meadow vole.** [1795–1805]

mead′ow mush′room. See under **mushroom** (def. 2). [1880–85]

mead′ow pars′nip, any North American plant belonging to the genus *Thaspium,* of the parsley family, having yellow or purple flowers. [1825–35, *Amer.*]

mead′ow rue′, any of several plants belonging to the genus *Thalictrum,* of the buttercup family, having leaves resembling those of rue, esp. *T. dioicum,* of North America. [1660–70]

mead′ow saf′fron. See **autumn crocus.** [1570–80]

mead′ow sal′sify, a European weedy, composite plant, *Tragopogon pratensis,* naturalized in North America, having grasslike leaves and yellow flowers. Also called **star-of-Jerusalem.**

mead·ow·sweet (med′ō swēt′), *n.* 1. any plant belonging to the genus *Spiraea,* of the rose family, esp. *S. latifolia,* having white or pink flowers. 2. any plant of the closely related genus *Filipendula* (or *Ulmaria*). [1520–30; MEADOW + SWEET]

mead′ow vole′. See **meadow mouse.** [1860–65]

Mead·ville (mēd′vil), *n.* a city in NW Pennsylvania. 15,544.

mea·ger (mē′gər), *adj.* 1. deficient in quantity or quality; lacking fullness or richness; scanty; inadequate: *a meager salary; meager fare; a meager harvest.* 2. having little flesh; lean; thin: *a body meager with hunger.* 3. maigre. Also, *esp. Brit.,* **mea′gre.** [1300–50; ME *megre* < OF *maigre* < L *macer* lean] —**mea′ger·ly,** *adv.* —**mea′ger·ness,** *n.*
—**Syn.** 1. See **scanty.** 2. gaunt, spare, skinny.

meal[1] (mēl), *n.* 1. the food served and eaten esp. at one of the customary, regular occasions for taking food during the day, as breakfast, lunch, or supper. 2. one of these regular occasions or times for eating food. [bef. 900; ME; OE *mǣl* measure, fixed time, occasion, meal; c. G *Mal* time, *Mahl* meal, ON *māl,* Goth *mēl* time, hour] —**meal′less,** *adj.*

meal[2] (mēl), *n.* 1. a coarse, unsifted powder ground from the edible seeds of any grain: *wheat meal; cornmeal.* 2. any ground or powdery substance, as of nuts or seeds, resembling this. [bef. 900; ME *mele,* OE *melu;* c. G *Mehl,* D *meel,* ON *mjǫl;* akin to Goth *malan,* L *molere* to grind. See MILL[1]] —**meal′less,** *adj.*

-meal, a native English combining form, now unproductive, denoting a fixed measure at a time: *piecemeal.* [ME *-mele,* OE *-mǣlum,* comb. form repr. *mǣl* MEAL[1]]

meal·ie (mē′lē), *n. South African.* 1. Sometimes, **mealies.** corn; maize. 2. an ear of corn. [1850–55; < Afrik *mielie* < Pg *milho* maize, millet < L *milium* MILLET]

meals′ on wheels′, (*sometimes cap.*) a program, usually one supported or subsidized by a charitable, social, or government agency, for delivering hot meals regularly to elderly, disabled, or convalescing persons who are housebound and cannot cook for themselves. [1960–65]

meal′ tick′et, 1. a ticket that entitles the bearer to meals in a specified restaurant, esp. when meals purchased in this manner are offered at reduced rates. 2. *Informal.* someone upon whom one is dependent for one's income or livelihood: *selfish children who look upon their father only as a meal ticket.* 3. *Informal.* something, as an object or ability possessed by a person, that is necessary to that person's livelihood: *The radio announcer's voice was his meal ticket.* [1865–70, *Amer.*]

meal·time (mēl′tīm′), *n.* the usual time for a meal. [1125–75; ME *meeltyme.* See MEAL[1], TIME]

meal·worm (mēl′wûrm′), *n.* the larva of any of several darkling beetles of the genus *Tenebrio,* which infests granaries and is used as food for birds and animals. [1650–60; MEAL[2] + WORM]

meal·y (mē′lē), *adj.,* **meal·i·er, meal·i·est.** 1. having the qualities of meal; powdery; soft, dry, and crumbly: *mealy potatoes; a mealy stone.* 2. of or containing meal; farinaceous: *baked fish with a mealy crust.* 3. covered with or as if with meal or powder: *flowers mealy with their pollen.* 4. flecked as if with meal; spotty: *horses with mealy hides.* 5. pale; sallow: *a mealy complexion.* 6. mealy-mouthed. [1525–35; MEAL[2] + -Y[1]] —**meal′i·ness,** *n.*

meal·y·bug (mē′lē bug′), *n.* any of several scalelike, homopterous insects of the families Pseudococcidae and Eriococcidae that are covered with a powdery wax secretion and feed on plants. [1815–25; MEALY + BUG[1]]

meal·y-mouthed (mē′lē moutht′, -mouthd′), *adj.* avoiding the use of direct and plain language, as from timidity, excessive delicacy, or hypocrisy; inclined to mince words; insincere, devious, or compromising. Also, **meal′y·mouthed′.** [1565–75] —**meal·y-mouth·ed·ly** (mē′lē mou′thid lē, -thid-, -moutht′-, -mouthd′-), *adv.* —**meal′y-mouth′ed·ness,** *n.*

mean[1] (mēn), *v.,* **meant, mean·ing.** —*v.t.* 1. to have in mind as one's purpose or intention; intend: *I meant to compliment you on your work.* 2. to intend for a particular purpose, destination, etc.: *They were meant for each other.* 3. to intend to express or indicate: *What do you mean by "liberal"?* 4. to have as its sense or signification; signify: *The word "freedom" means many things to many people.* 5. to bring, cause, or produce as a result: *This bonus means that we can take a trip to Florida.* 6. to have (certain intentions) toward a person: *He didn't mean you any harm.* 7. to have the value of; assume the importance of: *Money means everything to them. She means the world to him.* —*v.i.* 8. to be minded or disposed; have intentions: *Beware, she means ill, despite her solicitous manner.* 9. **mean well,** to have good intentions; try to be kind or helpful: *Her constant queries about your health must be tiresome, but I'm sure she means well.* [bef. 900; ME *menen,* OE *mǣnan;* c. G *meinen,* D *meenen*]
—**Syn.** 1. contemplate. See **intend.** 2. destine, foreordain. 4. denote, indicate; import, imply, connote.

mean[2] (mēn), *adj.,* **-er, -est.** 1. offensive, selfish, or unaccommodating; nasty; malicious: *a mean remark; He gets mean when he doesn't get his way.* 2. small-minded or ignoble: *mean motives.* 3. penurious, stingy, or miserly: *a person who is mean about money.* 4. inferior in grade, quality, or character: *no mean reward.* 5. low in status, rank, or dignity: *mean servitors.* 6. of little importance or consequence: *mean little details.* 7. unimposing or shabby: *a mean abode.* 8. small, humiliated, or ashamed: *You should feel mean for being so stingy.* 9. *Informal.* in poor physical condition. 10. troublesome or vicious; bad-tempered: *a mean old horse.* 11. *Slang.* skillful or impressive: *He blows a mean trumpet.* [bef. 900; ME *mene,* aph. var. (see Y-) of *imene,* OE *gemǣne;* c. D *gemeen,* G *gemein* common, Goth *gamains* in common; cf. COMMON]
—**Syn.** 2. contemptible, despicable. MEAN, LOW, BASE, SORDID, and VILE all refer to ignoble characteristics worthy of dislike, contempt, or disgust. MEAN suggests pettiness and small-mindedness: *to take a mean advantage.* LOW suggests coarseness and vulgarity: *low company.* BASE suggests selfish cowardice or moral depravity: *base motives.* SORDID suggests a wretched uncleanness, or sometimes an avariciousness without dignity or moral scruples: *a sordid slum; sordid gain.* VILE suggests disgusting foulness or repulsiveness: *vile insinuation; a vile creature.* 3. niggardly, close, tight, parsimonious, illiberal, ungenerous, selfish. See **stingy.** 5. common, humble; undignified, plebeian. 6. inconsequential, insignificant, petty, paltry, little, poor, wretched. 7. squalid, poor.

mean[3] (mēn), *n.* 1. Usually, **means.** (*used with a singular or plural v.*) an agency, instrument, or method used to attain an end: *The telephone is a means of communication. There are several means of solving the problem.* 2. **means, a.** available resources, esp. money: *They lived beyond their means.* **b.** considerable financial resources; riches: *a man of means.* 3. something that is midway between two extremes; something intermediate: *to seek a mean between cynicism and blind faith.* 4. *Math.* **a.** a quantity having a value intermediate between the values of other quantities; an average, esp. the arithmetic mean. **b.** either the second or third term in a proportion of four terms. 5. *Statistics.* expected value. See **mathematical expectation** (def. 2). 6. *Logic.* the middle term in a syllogism. 7. **by all means, a.** (in emphasis) certainly: *Go, by all means.* **b.** at any cost; without fail. 8. **by any means,** in any way; at all: *We were not surprised at the news by any means.* 9. **by means of,** with the help of; by the agency of; through: *We crossed the stream by means of a log.* 10. **by no means,** in no way; not at all: *The prize is by no means certain.* —*adj.* 11. occupying a middle position or an intermediate place, as in kind, quality, degree, or time: *a mean speed; a mean course; the mean annual rainfall.* [1300–50; ME *mene* < MF *meen,* var. of *meien* < L *mediānus;* see MEDIAN]

mean′ anom′aly, *Astron.* the anomaly of a mean planet; the angular distance of the planet from perihelion or aphelion.

me·an·der (mē an′dər), *v.i.* 1. to proceed by or take a winding or indirect course: *The stream meandered through the valley.* 2. to wander aimlessly; ramble: *The talk meandered on.* —*v.t.* 3. *Survey.* to define the margin of (a body of water) with a meander line. —*n.* 4. Usually, **meanders.** turnings or windings; a winding path or course. 5. a circuitous movement or journey. 6. an intricate variety of fret or fretwork. [1570–80; < L *maeander* < Gk *maíandros* a winding, special use of *Maíandros,* the Menderes River, noted for its winding course] —**me·an′der·er,** *n.* —**me·an′der·ing·ly,** *adv.*
—**Syn.** 1. wander, wind, twist, snake, coil.

Me·an·der (mē an′dər), *n.* ancient name of the **Menderes.**

mean′der line′, *Survey.* a zigzag traverse made to define the approximate margin of a natural body of water.

mean′ devia′tion, *Statistics.* a measure of dispersion, computed by taking the arithmetic mean of the absolute values of the deviations of the functional values from some central value, usually the mean or median. Also called **average deviation.** [1890–95]

mean′ dis′tance, *Astron.* the arithmetic mean of the greatest and least distances of a planet from the sun, used in stating the size of an orbit; the semimajor axis. [1885–90]

me·an·drous (mē an′drəs), *adj.* meandering; winding; rambling. [1650–60; MEAND(E)R + -OUS]

mean′ free′ path′, *Physics, Chem.* (in a collection of moving particles) the average distance that a particle travels between successive collisions with other particles.

mean·ie (mē′nē), *n. Informal.* meany.

mean·ing (mē′ning), *n.* 1. what is intended to be, or actually is, expressed or indicated; signification; import: *the three meanings of a word.* 2. the end, purpose, or significance of something: *What is the meaning of life? What is the meaning of this intrusion?* 3. *Ling.* **a.** the nonlinguistic cultural correlate, reference, or denotation of a linguistic form; expression. **b.** linguistic content (opposed to *expression*). —*adj.* 4. intentioned (usually used in combination): *She's a well-meaning person.* 5. full of significance; expressive: *a meaning look.* [1250–1300; ME (n.); see MEAN[1], -ING[1], -ING[2]] —**mean′ing·ly,** *adv.* —**mean′ing·ness,** *n.*
—**Syn.** 1. tenor, gist, drift, trend. MEANING, PURPORT, SENSE, SIGNIFICANCE denote that which is expressed or indicated by something. MEANING is the general word denoting that which is intended to be or actually is expressed or indicated: *the meaning of a word or glance.* SENSE may be used to denote a particular meaning (among others) of a word or phrase: *The word is frequently used in this sense.* SENSE may also be used loosely to refer to intelligible meaning: *There's no sense in what he says.* SIGNIFICANCE refers particularly to a meaning that is implied rather than expressed: *the significance of her glance;* or to a meaning the importance of which may not be easy to perceive immediately: *The real significance of his words was not grasped at the time.* PURPORT is mainly limited to the meaning of a formal document, speech, important conversation, etc., and refers to the gist of something fairly complicated: *the purport of your letter to the editor.*

mean·ing·ful (mē′ning fəl), *adj.* full of meaning, significance, purpose, or value; purposeful; significant: *a meaningful wink; a meaningful choice.* [1850–55; MEANING + -FUL] —**mean′ing·ful·ly,** *adv.* —**mean′ing·ful·ness,** *n.*
—**Syn.** See **expressive.**

mean′ingful rela′tionship, a romantic relationship based upon mutual respect and supportiveness and marked by a sense of commitment and fulfillment.

mean·ing·less (mē′ning lis), *adj.* without meaning, significance, purpose, or value; purposeless; insignificant: *a meaningless reply; a meaningless existence.* [1790–1800; MEANING + -LESS] —**mean′ing·less·ly,** *adv.* —**mean′ing·less·ness,** *n.*

mean′ lat′itude. See **middle latitude.**

CONCISE PRONUNCIATION KEY: act, cāpe, dâre, pärt; set, ēqual; if, īce; ox, ōver, ôrder, oil, bŏŏk, bōōt, out; up, ûrge; child; sing; shoe; thin, *th*at; zh as in *treasure.* ə = *a* as in *alone, e* as in *system, i* as in *easily, o* as in *gallop, u* as in *circus;* ə as in *fire* (fīər), *hour* (ouər). l and n can serve as syllabic consonants, as in *cradle* (krād′l), and *button* (but′n). See the full key inside the front cover.

mean′ length′ of ut′terance, *Psycholinguistics.* the mean number of morphemes produced per sentence, used esp. as a measure of child language development. *Abbr.:* MLU

mean′ life′, *Physics.* **1.** the average time that an unstable particle or nucleus survives before it decays. **2.** See **decay time.** Also called **average life, lifetime.**

mean′ line′, *Print.* an imaginary x-high line. Also called **x-line.**

mean·ly[1] (mēn′lē), *adv.* **1.** in a poor, lowly, or humble manner. **2.** in a base, contemptible, selfish, or shabby manner. **3.** in a stingy or miserly manner. [1350–1400; ME *meneli.* See MEAN[2], -LY]

mean·ly[2] (mēn′lē), *adv. Obs.* moderately. [1350–1400; ME; see MEAN[3], -LY]

mean·ness (mēn′nis), *n.* **1.** the state or quality of being mean. **2.** a mean act: *to answer meannesses with forgiveness.* [1550–60; MEAN[2] + -NESS]

mean′ noon′, *Astron.* the moment when the mean sun's center crosses the meridian.

mean′ plan′et, *Astron.* a hypothetical planet that coincides with a real planet when the real planet is at perihelion and that moves in an orbit at a constant velocity equal to the mean velocity of the real planet.

mean′ propor′tional, *Math.* (between two numbers *a* and *b*) a number *x* for which $a/x = x/b$: *The number 3 is a mean proportional between 1 and 9.* [1565–75]

Means′ grass′ (mēnz). See **Johnson grass.** [1855–60, *Amer.*; after John H. Means (1812–62), governor of South Carolina, 1850–52, who obtained the original seed from Turkey]

mean′ so′lar day′, day (def. 3a).

mean′ so′lar time′, *Astron.* time measured by the hour angle of the mean sun. Also called **mean′ time′.**

mean·spir·it·ed (mēn′spir′i tid), *adj.* petty; small-minded; ungenerous: *a meanspirited man, unwilling to forgive.* [1685–95; MEAN[2] + SPIRITED] —**mean′spir′it·ed·ly,** *adv.* —**mean′spir′it·ed·ness,** *n.*

mean′ square′, *Statistics.* the mean of the squares of a set of numbers. [1835–45]

mean′ square′ devia′tion, *Statistics.* variance (def. 3). [1890–95]

means′ test′, an investigation into the financial position of a person applying for aid from public funds. [1925–30]

mean′ sun′, *Astron.* an imaginary sun moving uniformly in the celestial equator and taking the same time to make its annual circuit as the true sun does in the ecliptic.

meant (ment), *v.* pt. and pp. of **mean**[1].

mean·time (mēn′tīm′), *n.* **1.** the intervening time: *The party is Tuesday, but in the meantime I have to shop and prepare the food.* —*adv.* **2.** meanwhile. [1300–50; ME; see MEAN[3], TIME]

mean′tone sys′tem (mēn′tōn′), *Music.* a system for tuning keyboard instruments, used before the development of tuning by equal temperament and considered practical only for tonalities of not more than two sharps or flats. [1790–1800; MEAN[3] + TONE]

mean′ val′ue, *Math.* the ratio of the integral of a given function over a closed interval to the length of the interval.

mean′ val′ue the′orem, *Math.* the theorem that for a function continuous on a closed interval and differentiable on the corresponding open interval, there is a point in the interval such that the difference in functional values at the endpoints is equal to the derivative evaluated at the particular point and multiplied by the difference in the endpoints. Also called **law of the mean, theorem of the mean.** [1900–05]

mean·while (mēn′hwīl′, -wīl′), *n.* **1.** meantime. —*adv.* **2.** in the intervening time; during the interval. **3.** at the same time: *Meanwhile, the others were back home enjoying themselves.* [1300–50; ME; see MEAN[3], WHILE]

mean·y (mē′nē), *n., pl.* **mean·ies.** *Informal.* a small-minded, petty, or malicious person: *The children said their teacher was a real meany.* Also, **meanie.** [1925–30; MEAN[2] + -Y[2]]

Mean·y (mē′nē), *n.* **George,** 1894–1980, U.S. labor leader: 3rd president of the AFL 1952–55; 1st president of the AFL-CIO 1955–79.

mear (mēr), *n. Brit. Dial.* mere[3].

meas., **1.** measurable. **2.** measure. **3.** measurement.

mea·sle (mē′zəl), *n.* sing. of **measles** (def. 3).

mea·sled (mē′zəld), *adj.* (of swine or other livestock) affected with measles. [1350–1400; ME *meseled.* See MEASLES, -ED[3]]

mea·sles (mē′zəlz), *n.* **1.** (*used with a singular or plural v.*) *Pathol.* **a.** an acute infectious disease occurring mostly in children, characterized by catarrhal and febrile symptoms and an eruption of small red spots; rubeola. **b.** any of certain other eruptive diseases. Cf. **German measles.** **2.** *Vet. Pathol.* a disease in swine and other animals caused by the larvae of certain tapeworms of the genus *Taenia.* **3.** (*used with a plural v.*) the larvae that cause measles in swine and other animals, and that upon maturation produce trichinosis in humans. [1275–1325; ME *mesels,* var. of *maseles* (pl.); c. D *maselen* (pl.), MD *masel;* akin to G *Masern* measles, pl. of *Maser* speck]

mea·sly (mē′zlē), *adj.,* **-sli·er, -sli·est.** **1.** *Informal.* **a.** contemptibly small, meager, or slight: *They paid me a measly fifteen dollars for a day's work.* **b.** wretchedly bad or unsatisfactory: *a measly performance.* **2.** infected with measles, as an animal or its flesh. **3.** pertaining to or resembling measles. [1680–90; MEASL(ES) + -Y[1]]

meas·ur·a·ble (mezh′ər ə bəl), *adj.* capable of being measured. [1300–50; ME *mesurable* < MF < LL *mēnsūrābilis* that can be measured. See MEASURE, -ABLE] —**meas′ur·a·bil′i·ty, meas′ur·a·ble·ness,** *n.* —**meas′ur·a·bly,** *adv.*

meas·ure (mezh′ər), *n., v.,* **-ured, -ur·ing.** —*n.* **1.** a unit or standard of measurement: *weights and measures.* **2.** a system of measurement: *liquid measure.* **3.** an instrument, as a graduated rod or a container of standard capacity, for measuring. **4.** the extent, dimensions, quantity, etc., of something, ascertained esp. by comparison with a standard: *to take the measure of a thing.* **5.** the act or process of ascertaining the extent, dimensions, quantity, etc., of something; measurement. **6.** a definite or known quantity measured out: *to drink a measure of wine.* **7.** any standard of comparison, estimation, or judgment. **8.** a quantity, degree, or proportion: *in large measure.* **9.** a moderate amount: *to live with a measure of enjoyment.* **10.** a limit, or an extent or degree not to be exceeded: *to know no measure.* **11.** reasonable bounds or limits: *no sense of measure.* **12.** a legislative bill or enactment: *The senate passed the new measure.* **13.** Usually, **measures.** actions or procedures intended as a means to an end: *to take measures to avert suspicion.* **14.** a short rhythmical movement or arrangement, as in poetry or music. **15.** a particular kind of such arrangement. **16.** the music contained between two bar lines; bar. **17.** a metrical unit. **18.** an air or melody. **19.** a slow, dignified dance. **20.** *Print.* the width, measured in ems or picas, to which a column or page of printed matter is set. **21. measures,** *Geol.* beds; strata. **22.** *Math.* an abstraction of the property of length; a set function assigning to each set of a collection of sets a value, usually having the properties of sigma finiteness and finite additivity, the functional value of the whole collection being greater than zero. **23. beyond measure,** too much to be reckoned; immeasurably; extremely: *The suffering that they endured was beyond measure.* **24. for good measure,** as an extra: *In addition to dessert, they served chocolates for good measure.* **25. have** or **take one's measure,** to judge or assess someone's character, capabilities, etc.; size up: *During their conversation she was taking his measure as a prospective employee.* **26. in a** or **some measure,** to some extent or degree: *His conclusion is justified in some measure.* —*v.t.* **27.** to ascertain the extent, dimensions, quantity, capacity, etc., of, esp. by comparison with a standard: *to measure boundaries.* **28.** to mark off or deal out by way of measurement (often fol. by *off* or *out*): *to measure out two cups of flour.* **29.** to estimate the relative amount, value, etc., of, by comparison with some standard: *to measure the importance of an issue.* **30.** to judge or appraise by comparison with something or someone else: *to measure Corneille against Racine.* **31.** to serve as the measure of: *Her sacrifices measure the degree of her love.* **32.** to adjust or proportion: *to measure a portion to one's liking.* **33.** to bring into comparison or competition: *to measure one's strength with another's.* **34.** to travel over; traverse: *to measure a room with great strides.* —*v.i.* **35.** to take measurements. **36.** to admit of measurement. **37.** to be of a specified measure. **38. measure one's length,** to fall or be knocked down; fall flat: *He missed a step in the dark and measured his length at the bottom.* **39. measure swords, a.** to test one's preparedness for a contest or encounter. **b.** to battle with swords. **c.** to fight, compete, etc.: *The producer of the poorly reviewed show decided to measure swords with the critics.* **40. measure up, a.** to reach a certain standard: *The exhibition didn't measure up to last year's.* **b.** to be capable or qualified: *As an administrator he couldn't quite measure up.* [1250–1300; ME *mesure* < MF < L *mēnsūra,* equiv. to *mēns(us)* (ptp. of *mētīrī* to measure, mete) + *-ūra* -URE] —**meas′ur·er,** *n.*

M, measure (def. 16)

meas·ured (mezh′ərd), *adj.* **1.** ascertained or apportioned by measure: *The race was over the course of a measured mile.* **2.** accurately regulated or proportioned. **3.** regular or uniform, as in movement; rhythmical: *to walk with measured strides.* **4.** deliberate and restrained; careful; carefully weighed or considered: *measured language; measured terms.* **5.** in the form of meter or verse; metrical. [1350–1400; ME; see MEASURE, -ED[2]] —**meas′ured·ly,** *adv.* —**meas′ured·ness,** *n.*

Meas′ure for Meas′ure, a comedy (1604) by Shakespeare.

meas·ure·less (mezh′ər lis), *adj.* too large or great to be measured; unlimited; immeasurable: *a measureless distance; measureless contempt.* [1350–1400; ME *measureles.* See MEASURE, -LESS] —**meas′ure·less·ly,** *adv.* —**meas′ure·less·ness,** *n.*
—**Syn.** boundless, unbounded, limitless, vast, infinite.

meas·ure·ment (mezh′ər mənt), *n.* **1.** the act of measuring. **2.** a measured dimension. **3.** extent, size, etc., ascertained by measuring. **4.** a system of measuring or measures: *liquid measurement.* [1745–55; MEASURE + -MENT]

meas′urement ton′. See under **ton**[1] (def. 5). [1930–35]

meas′ure of cen′tral tend′ency, *Statistics.* a statistic that in some way specifies the central tendency of a sample of measurements, as the mean, median, or mode.

meas′ure ze′ro, *Math.* the property of a set of points for which, given any small number, there exists a set of intervals such that each point of the given set is contained in at least one of the intervals and such that, essentially, the combined length of the intervals is less than the small number.

meas′uring cup′, a graduated cup used esp. in cooking for measuring ingredients. [1900–05]

meas′uring spoon′, a spoon for measuring amounts, as in cooking, usually part of a set of spoons of different sizes.

meas·ur·ing·worm (mezh′ər ing wûrm′), *n.* the larva of any geometrid moth, which progresses by bringing the rear end of the body forward and then advancing the front end. Also, **meas′uring worm′.** Also called **inchworm, looper, spanworm.** [1835–45, *Amer.*; MEASURING + WORM]

meat (mēt), *n.* **1.** the flesh of animals as used for food. **2.** the edible part of anything, as a fruit or nut: *Crack the walnuts and remove the meats.* **3.** the essential point or part of an argument, literary work, etc.; gist; crux: *The meat of the play is the jealousy between the two brothers.* **4.** solid food: *meat and drink.* **5.** solid or substantial content; pith: *The article was full of meat, with few wasted words.* **6.** a favorite occupation, activity, etc.: *Chess is his meat.* **7.** *Chiefly South Midland and Southern U.S.* pork, esp. bacon. **8.** *Slang* (*vulgar*). penis. **9.** *Archaic.* the principal meal: *to say grace before meat.* **10. piece of meat,** *Slang.* **a.** a person regarded merely as a sex object. **b.** a person, as a prizefighter or laborer, regarded merely as a strong or useful physical specimen. [bef. 900; ME, OE *mete* food, c. OHG *maz,* ON *matr,* Goth *mats*] —**meat′less,** *adj.*

meat′ and pota′toes, *Informal.* the essential or basic part: *Community service is the meat and potatoes of this program.* [‡ 1950–55]

meat-and-po·ta·toes (mēt′n pə tā′tōz, -təz), *adj. Informal.* fundamental; down-to-earth; basic: *What are the meat-and-potatoes issues of the election?* Also, **meat′-and-po·ta′to.** [1945–50]

meat′ ax′, **1.** cleaver (def. 2). **2.** *Informal.* a drastic or ruthless procedure or approach, esp. for reducing or trimming something, as expenditures: *The committee used a meat ax on the recreation budget.* [1825–35]

meat-ax (mēt′aks′), *adj. Informal.* **1.** drastic or severe: *meat-ax defense cuts.* **2.** favoring or advocating drastic reductions: *a meat-ax approach to the budget.*

meat·ball (mēt′bôl′), *n.* **1.** a small ball of ground meat, esp. beef, often mixed with bread crumbs, seasonings, etc., before cooking. **2.** *Slang.* an awkward, clumsy, or ineffectual person. [1830–40; MEAT + BALL[1]]

Meath (mēth, mēth), *n.* a county in Leinster, in the E Republic of Ireland. 95,602; 902 sq. mi. (2335 sq. km). *Co. seat:* Trim.

meat·head (mēt′hed′), *n. Slang.* blockhead; dunce; fool. [1940–45; MEAT + HEAD]

meat′ hooks′, *Slang.* hands or fists. Also **meat′-hooks′.** [1835–45 for literal sense]

meat′ house′, *Chiefly Midland U.S.* a smokehouse.

meat′ loaf′, a dish of ground meat, often mixed with other ingredients, as bread crumbs and seasonings, molded in the shape of a loaf and baked.

meat·man (mēt′man′), *n., pl.* **-men.** a dealer in meat; butcher. [1560–70; MEAT + MAN[1]]
—**Usage.** See **-man.**

meat′ pack′ing, the business or industry of slaughtering cattle and other meat animals and processing the carcasses for sale, sometimes including the packaging of processed meat products. [1870–75, *Amer.*] —**meat′ pack′er.**

meat′ tea′, *Brit.* See **high tea.** [1855–60]

me·a·tus (mē ā′təs), *n., pl.* **-tus·es, -tus.** *Anat.* an opening or foramen, esp. in a bone or bony structure, as the opening of the ear or nose. [1655–65; < L *meātus* course, channel, equiv. to *meā(re)* to go, extend, have a course + *-tus* suffix of v. action] —**me·a′tal,** *adj.*

meat′ wag′on, *Slang.* an ambulance. [1920–25]

meat·y (mē′tē), *adj.,* **meat·i·er, meat·i·est.** **1.** of or like meat. **2.** abounding in meat. **3.** rich in content or thought-provoking matter; full of substance: *a meaty topic for discussion.* [1780–90; MEAT + -Y[1]] —**meat′i·ly,** *adv.* —**meat′i·ness,** *n.*

me·ben·da·zole (mə ben′də zōl′), *n. Pharm.* an anthelmintic substance, $C_{16}H_{13}N_3O_3$, used for treating parasitic worm infestations. [ME(THYL) + *ben(zimi)dazole* a component of its chemical name]

mec (mek), *n. French Slang.* a pimp; mack.

me·ca·te (mə kä′tē), *n. Southwestern U.S.* a rope made of horsehair or sometimes maguey. [1840–50; < MexSp < Nahuatl *mecatl* cord, rope]

Mec·ca (mek′ə), *n.* **1.** Also, **Makkah, Mekka.** a city in and the capital of Hejaz, in W Saudi Arabia: birthplace of Muhammad; spiritual center of Islam. 366,801. **2.** (*often l.c.*) any place that many people visit or hope to visit: *The president's birthplace is a mecca for his admirers.* —**Mec′can,** *adj., n.*

CONCISE ETYMOLOGY KEY: <, descended or borrowed from; >, whence; b., blend of, blended; c., cognate with; cf., compare; deriv., derivative; equiv., equivalent; imit., imitative; obl., oblique; r., replacing; s., stem; sp., spelling, spelled; resp., respelling, respelled; trans., translation; ?, origin unknown; *, unattested; ‡, probably earlier than. See the full key inside the front cover.

Mec′ca bal′sam. See **balm-of-Gilead** (def. 2).

mech., **1.** mechanical. **2.** mechanics. **3.** mechanism.

me·chan·ic (mə kan′ik), *n.* **1.** a person who repairs and maintains machinery, motors, etc.: *an automobile mechanic.* **2.** a worker who is skilled in the use of tools, machines, equipment, etc. **3.** *Slang.* a person skilled in the dishonest handling of cards, dice, or other objects used in games of chance. [1350–1400; ME: mechanical < L *mēchanicus* < Gk *mēchanikós,* equiv. to *mēchan(ḗ)* MACHINE + *-ikos* -IC]

me·chan·i·cal (mə kan′i kəl), *adj.* **1.** having to do with machinery: *a mechanical failure.* **2.** being a machine; operated by machinery: *a mechanical toy.* **3.** caused by or derived from machinery: *mechanical propulsion.* **4.** using machine parts only. **5.** brought about by friction, abrasion, etc.: *a mechanical bond between stones; mechanical erosion.* **6.** pertaining to the design, use, understanding, etc., of tools and machinery: *the mechanical trades; mechanical ability.* **7.** acting or performed without spontaneity, spirit, individuality, etc.: *a mechanical performance.* **8.** habitual; routine; automatic: *Practice that step until it becomes mechanical.* **9.** belonging or pertaining to the subject matter of mechanics. **10.** pertaining to, or controlled or effected by, physical forces. **11.** (of a philosopher or philosophical theory) explaining phenomena as due to mechanical action or the material forces of the universe. **12.** subordinating the spiritual to the material; materialistic. —*n.* **13.** a mechanical object, part, device, etc. **14.** *Print.* a sheet of stiff paper on which has been pasted artwork and type proofs for making a printing plate; paste-up. **15.** *Obs.* a skilled manual laborer, as a carpenter or other artisan. [1375–1425; late ME, equiv. to *mechanic* mechanical + -AL[1]; see MECHANIC] **—me·chan′i·cal·ly,** *adv.* **—me·chan′i·cal·ness, me·chan′i·cal′i·ty,** *n.*

mechan′ical advan′tage, *Mech.* the ratio of output force to the input force applied to a mechanism.

mechan′ical bank′, a toy bank in which a coin is deposited by a mechanical process that is usually activated by pushing a lever.

mechan′ical draw′ing, drawing, as of machinery, done with the aid of rulers, scales, compasses, etc.

mechan′ical engineer′ing, the branch of engineering dealing with the design and production of machinery. **—mechan′ical engineer′.**

mechan′ical equiv′alent of heat′, (in any system of physical units) the number of units of work or energy equal to one unit of heat, as 4.1858 joules, which equals one small calorie. [1835–45]

mechan′ical imped′ance, *Physics.* impedance (def. 2).

mechan′ical met′allurgy, the branch of metallurgy dealing with the response of metals to applied forces.

mechan′ical pen′cil, a pencil for holding lead that can be extended by mechanical means.

mechan′ical pulp′. See **groundwood pulp.**

mechan′ical scan′ning, **1.** *Electronics.* a technique for varying the sector covered by a transmitting or receiving antenna by rotating it. **2.** *Television.* a technique, formerly used in televising, for scanning by means of a scanning disk. Cf. **electrical scanning.**

mechan′ical solidar′ity, *Sociol.* social cohesiveness that is based on shared activities, beliefs, and experiences and is characteristic of simple traditional societies. Cf. **organic solidarity.**

mechan′ical suspen′sion. See under **suspension** (def. 6).

mechan′ical twin′, *Metall.* a crystalline twin formed by the strain set up by an applied force.

mech·a·ni·cian (mek′ə nish′ən), *n.* a person skilled in constructing, working, or repairing machines; mechanic; machinist. [1560–70; MECHANIC + -IAN]

me·chan·ics (mə kan′iks), *n.* **1.** (*used with a singular v.*) the branch of physics that deals with the action of forces on bodies and with motion, comprised of kinetics, statics, and kinematics. **2.** (*used with a singular v.*) the theoretical and practical application of this science to machinery, mechanical appliances, etc. **3.** (*usually used with a plural v.*) the technical aspect or working part; mechanism; structure. **4.** (*usually used with a plural v.*) routine or basic methods, procedures, techniques, or details: *the mechanics of running an office; the mechanics of baseball.* [1640–50; see MECHANIC, -ICS]

mechan′ic's lien′, a lien secured on property, as an automobile, building, or the like, by the contractor who has repaired or built it, in order to ensure payment for labor and materials.

Me·chan·ics·ville (mə kan′iks vil′), *n.* a village in E Virginia, near Richmond: Civil War battle 1862.

mech·an·ism (mek′ə niz′əm), *n.* **1.** an assembly of moving parts performing a complete functional motion, often being part of a large machine; linkage. **2.** the agency or means by which an effect is produced or a purpose is accomplished. **3.** machinery or mechanical appliances in general. **4.** the structure or arrangement of parts of a machine or similar device, or of anything analogous. **5.** the mechanical part of something; any mechanical device: *the mechanism of a clock.* **6.** routine methods or procedures; mechanics: *the mechanism of government.* **7.** mechanical execution, as in painting or music; technique. **8.** the theory that everything in the universe is produced by matter in motion; materialism. Cf. **dynamism** (def. 1), **vitalism** (def. 1). **9.** *Philos.* **a.** the view that all natural processes are explicable in terms of Newtonian mechanics. **b.** the view that all biological processes may be described in physicochemical terms. **10.** *Psychoanal.* the habitual operation and interaction of psychological forces within an individual that assist in interpreting or dealing with the physical or psychological environment. [1655–65; < NL *mēchanismus;* LL *mēchanisma* a contrivance < Gk *mēchan(ḗ)* MACHINE + NL *-ismus,* LL *-isma* -ISM] **—mech′a·nis′·mic,** *adj.*

mech·a·nist (mek′ə nist), *n.* **1.** a person who believes in the theory of mechanism. **2.** a mechanician. [1600–10; MECHAN(IC) + -IST]

mech·a·nis·tic (mek′ə nis′tik), *adj.* **1.** of or pertaining to the theory of mechanism or to mechanists. **2.** of or pertaining to mechanics. **3.** mechanical. [1880–85; MECHANIST + -IC] **—mech′a·nis′ti·cal·ly,** *adv.*

mech·a·nize (mek′ə nīz′), *v.t.,* **-nized, -niz·ing.** **1.** to make mechanical. **2.** to operate or perform by or as if by machinery. **3.** to introduce machinery into (an industry, enterprise, etc.), esp. in order to replace manual labor. **4.** *Mil.* to equip with tanks and other armored vehicles. Also, *esp. Brit.,* **mech′a·nise′.** [1695–1705; MECHAN(IC) + -IZE] **—mech′a·ni·za′tion,** *n.* **—mech′·a·niz′er,** *n.*

mechano- a combining form representing **machine** or **mechanical** in compound words: *mechanoreceptor.* [< Gk *mēchano-,* comb. form repr. *mēchanḗ;* see MACHINE]

mech·a·no·chem·is·try (mek′ə nō kem′ə strē), *n.* the field of chemistry that deals with the direct conversion of chemical into mechanical energy. [1925–30; MECHANO- + CHEMISTRY] **—mech′a·no·chem′i·cal,** *adj.*

mech·a·no·mor·phism (mek′ə nō môr′fiz əm), *n.* *Philos.* the doctrine that the universe is fully explicable in mechanistic terms. [1925–30; MECHANO- + -MORPHISM] **—mech′a·no·mor′phic,** *adj.* **—mech′a·no·mor′phi·cal·ly,** *adv.*

mech·a·no·re·cep·tor (mek′ə nō ri sep′tər), *n.* *Anat.* any of the sense organs that respond to vibration, stretching, pressure, or other mechanical stimuli. [1925–30; MECHANO- + RECEPTOR]

mech·a·no·ther·a·py (mek′ə nō ther′ə pē), *n.* curative treatment by mechanical means. [1885–90; MECHANO + THERAPY] **—mech′a·no·ther′a·pist,** *n.*

Mech·i·tar·ist (mek′i tär′ist), *n.* Mekhitarist.

me·chi·tzah (*Seph.* mə KHē tsä′; *Ashk.* mə KHē′tsə), *n., pl.* ***-chi·tzoth, -chi·tzot, -chi·tzos*** (*Seph.* -KHē tsôt′; *Ashk.* -KHē′tsəz, -KHē′tsōs). *Hebrew.* mehitzah.

Mech·lin (mek′lin), *n.* **1.** French, **Malines.** Flemish, **Mech·e·len** (mekH′ə lən). a city in N Belgium. 64,638. **2.** See **Mechlin lace.**

Mech′lin lace′, **1.** a fine bobbin lace with raised cord, originally made in Mechlin. **2.** a similar lace made by machine. Also called **Mechlin, malines.** [1690–1700; after MECHLIN]

me·chlor·eth·a·mine (me klôr eth′ə mēn′, -klōr-), *n.* *Pharm.* a nitrogen mustard, $C_5H_{11}Cl_2N$, used in combination with other drugs in the treatment of Hodgkin's disease and certain other cancers. [ME(THYL) + CHLOR-[2] + ETH(YL) + AMINE]

Mech·ni·kov (myech′nyi kəf), *n.* **I·lya I·lyich** (ē lyä′ ē lyēch′). See **Metchnikoff, Élie.**

me·cism (mē′siz əm), *n.* *Pathol.* abnormal prolongation of one or more parts of the body. [< Gk *mêk(os)* length + -ISM]

Meck·len·burg (mek′lən bûrg′; *Ger.* mek′lən bŏŏrk′, mä′klən-), *n.* a former state in NE Germany, formed in 1934 from two states (**Mecklenburg-Schwerin** and **Mecklenburg-Strelitz**).

Meck·len·burg-Schwe·rin (mek′lən bûrg′shwer′ən; *Ger.* mek′lən bŏŏrk′shvä rēn′, mä′klən-), *n.* See under **Mecklenburg.**

Meck·len·burg-Stre·litz (mek′lən bûrg′shtrā′lits; *Ger.* mek′lən bŏŏrk′shtrā′lits, mä′klən-), *n.* See under **Mecklenburg.**

Meck·len·burg-Vor·pom·mern (mek′lən bŏŏrk′-fôr′pôm ərn), *n.* German name of **Mecklenburg-Western Pomerania.**

Meck′len·burg-West′ern Pomera′nia (mek′lən-bûrg′), a state in NE Germany. 2,100,000; 8842 sq. mi. (22,900 sq. km). *Cap.:* Schwerin.

mec·li·zine (mek′lə zēn′), *n.* *Pharm.* a compound, $C_{25}H_{27}ClN_2$, used for preventing nausea of motion sickness, pregnancy, etc. [1950–55; ME(THYLBENZENE) + C(H)L(OR)-[2] + -I- + (PIPERA)ZINE]

me·com·e·ter (mi kom′i tər), *n.* *Med.* a caliperlike instrument for measuring the length of newborn infants. [1850–55; < Gk *mêko(s)* length + -METER]

me·co·ni·um (mi kō′nē əm), *n.* **1.** the first fecal excretion of a newborn child, composed chiefly of bile, mucus, and epithelial cells. **2.** fecal mass released at pupation by the larvae of some insects. **3.** the milky sap of the unripe seed pods of the opium poppy; crude opium. [1595–1605; < L < Gk *mēkṓnion,* dim. of *mḗkōn* poppy]

me·cop·ter·an (mi kop′tər ən), *adj.* **1.** mecopterous. —*n.* **2.** Also, **me·cop·ter·on** (mi kop′tə ron′). a mecopterous insect. [see MECOPTEROUS, -AN]

me·cop·ter·ous (mi kop′tər əs), *adj.* belonging or pertaining to the insect order Mecoptera, comprising the scorpionflies and hangingflies. [1888; < NL *Mecopter(a)* (< Gk *mêk(os)* length + *-o-* -O- + *-ptera,* neut. pl. of *-pteros* -PTEROUS) + -OUS; an irregular re-formation of Gk *makrópteros* long-winged]

med (med), *Informal.* —*adj.* **1.** medical: *med school.* —*n.* **2.** medicine. [1890–95; by shortening]

med., **1.** medical. **2.** medicine. **3.** medieval. **4.** medium.

M.Ed., Master of Education.

mé·dail·lon (mā dA yôN′), *n., pl.* ***-dail·lons*** (-dA yôN′). *French.* a portion of food, esp. meat or poultry, cut or served in a round or oval shape.

me·da·ka (mi dak′ə), *n.* a small Japanese fish, *Oryzias latipes,* common in rice fields, often kept in aquariums. [1930–35; < Japn, equiv. to *me(y)* (earlier **mai*) eye + *-daka,* comb. form of *taka* high]

med·al (med′l), *n., v.,* **-aled, -al·ing** or (*esp. Brit.*) **-alled, -al·ling.** —*n.* **1.** a flat piece of metal, often a disk but sometimes a cross, star, or other form, usually bearing an inscription or design, issued to commemorate a person, action, or event, or given as a reward for bravery, merit, or the like: *a gold medal for the best swimmer.* **2.** a similar object bearing a religious image, as of a saint: *a Saint Christopher's medal.* —*v.t.* **3.** to decorate or honor with a medal. [1580–90; earlier *medaille* < MF < It *medaglia* copper coin worth a halfpenny < VL **medālia,* var. (by dissimilation) of LL *mediālia,* n. use of neut. pl. (taken as fem. sing.) of *mediālis* MEDIAL]

med·al·et (med′l et′, med′l it), *n.* a small medal, usually no larger than 1 in. (2.5 cm) in diameter. [1780–90; MEDAL + -ET]

Med′al for Mer′it, a medal awarded by the U.S. to a civilian for distinguished service to the country: discontinued after World War II.

med·al·ist (med′l ist), *n.* **1.** a person to whom a medal has been awarded. **2.** (in a golf tournament) the player having the lowest score in a qualifying round scored by strokes. **3.** a designer, engraver, or maker of medals. Also, *esp. Brit.,* **med′al·list.** [1965–70; < F *médailliste* < It *medaglista.* See MEDAL, -IST]

me·dal·lic (mə dal′ik), *adj.* of or pertaining to medals. [1695–1705; MEDAL + -IC]

me·dal·lion (mə dal′yən), *n.* **1.** a large medal. **2.** anything resembling a medal in form, used as an ornament, in a design, etc. **3.** a permit issued by a governmental agency to operate a taxicab, usually represented by a small metal identification disk displayed on the taxi. **4.** *Archit.* **a.** a tablet, usually rounded, often bearing objects represented in relief. **b.** a member in a decorative design resembling a panel. **5.** médaillon. [1650–60; < F *médaillon* < It *medaglione,* aug. of *medaglia* MEDAL]

Med′al of Free′dom, a former name of the **Presidential Medal of Freedom.** [1940–45, *Amer.*]

Med′al of Hon′or, the highest U.S. military decoration, awarded by Congress to a member of the armed forces for gallantry and bravery in combat, at the risk of life and above and beyond the call of duty. Also called **Congressional Medal of Honor.**

med′al play′, *Golf.* play in which the score is reckoned by counting the strokes taken to complete the round. Also called **stroke play.** Cf. **match play.** [1885–90]

Me·dan (me dän′), *n.* a city in NE Sumatra, in W Indonesia. 635,562.

Med·a·war (med′ə wər), *n.* **Peter Brian,** born 1915, English zoologist and anatomist, born in Brazil: Nobel prize for medicine 1960.

med·dle (med′l), *v.i.,* **-dled, -dling.** to involve oneself in a matter without right or invitation; interfere officiously and unwantedly: *Stop meddling in my personal life!* [1250–1300; ME *medlen* < OF *me(s)dler,* var. of *mesler* (F *mêler*) < VL **misculāre,* freq. of L *miscēre* to mix] **—med′dler,** *n.* **—med′dling·ly,** *adv.*
—Syn. intervene, intrude, pry.

med·dle·some (med′l səm), *adj.* given to meddling; interfering; intrusive. [1605–15; MEDDLE + -SOME[1]] **—med′dle·some·ly,** *adv.* **—med′dle·some·ness,** *n.*
—Syn. See **curious.**

Mede (mēd), *n.* a native or inhabitant of Media. [1350–1400; ME *Medis* (pl.), OE *Mēdas* < L *Mēdī* < Gk *Mêdoi* (pl.), *Mêdos* (sing.) < OPers *Māda*]

Me·de·a (mi dē′ə), *n.* **1.** *Class. Myth.* a sorceress, daughter of Aeëtes and wife of Jason, whom she assisted in obtaining the Golden Fleece: when Jason deserted her, she killed their children. **2.** (*italics*) a tragedy (431 B.C.) by Euripides.

Me·del·lín (me the yēn′), *n.* a city in W Colombia. 1,070,924.

med·e·vac (med′ə vak′), *n., v.,* **-vacked, -vack·ing.** —*n.* **1.** a helicopter for evacuating the wounded from a battlefield. **2.** an ambulance or other vehicle equipped for emergency transport of medical patients. **3.** any of the trained personnel transporting or otherwise tending to the sick or wounded in a medevac. —*v.t.* **4.** to transport (sick or wounded persons) by medevac. Also, **Med′·e·vac′, medivac.** [1965–70, *Amer.*; *med(ical) evac(uation)*; presumably by ellipsis from *medevac helicopter*]

Med·field (med′fēld′), *n.* a city in E Massachusetts. 10,220.

med·fly (med′flī′), *n., pl.* **-flies.** See **Mediterranean fruit fly.** Also, **Med′fly′.** [1930–35; by shortening]

Med·ford (med′fərd), *n.* **1.** a city in E Massachusetts, near Boston. 58,076. **2.** a city in SW Oregon. 39,603.

me·di·a[1] (mē′dē ə), *n.* **1.** a pl. of **medium.** **2.** (*usually used with a plural v.*) the means of communication, as radio and television, newspapers, and magazines, that reach or influence people widely: *The media are covering the speech tonight.* —*adj.* **3.** pertaining to or concerned with such means: *a job in media research.*
—Usage. MEDIA, like *data,* is the plural form of a word borrowed directly from Latin. The singular, MEDIUM, early developed the meaning "an intervening agency, means, or instrument" and was first applied to newspapers two centuries ago. In the 1920's MEDIA began to appear as a singular collective noun, sometimes with the plural MEDIAS. This singular use is now common in the fields of mass communication and advertising, but it is not frequently found outside them: *The media is* (or *are*) *not antibusiness.*

me·di·a[2] (mē′dē ə), *n., pl.* **-di·ae** (-dē ē′). **1.** *Gk. Gram.* a voiced plosive, as β, δ, γ. **2.** *Anat.* the middle layer of an artery or lymphatic vessel. **3.** *Entomol.* a longitudinal vein in the middle portion of the wing of an insect.

CONCISE PRONUNCIATION KEY: act, cāpe, dâre, pärt; set, ēqual; if, īce; ox, ōver, ôrder, oil, bŏŏk, bōōt, out; up, ûrge; child; sing; shoe; thin, *th*at; zh as in *treasure.* ə = *a* as in *alone,* *e* as in *system,* *i* as in *easily,* *o* as in *gallop,* *u* as in *circus;* ᵊ as in *fire* (fīᵊr), *hour* (ouᵊr). l and n can serve as syllabic consonants, as in *cradle* (krād′l), and *button* (but′n). See the full key inside the front cover.

[1835–45; < LL (grammar sense only), n. use of fem. sing. of L *medius* central, MID[1]]

Me·di·a (mē′dē ə), *n.* an ancient country in W Asia, S of the Caspian Sea, corresponding generally to NW Iran. *Cap.:* Ecbatana.

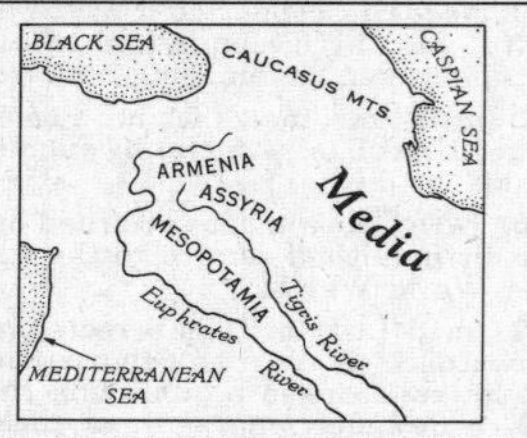

Me′dia Atropate′ne, an ancient region in NW Iran, formerly a part of Media. Also called **Atropatene.**

me′dia cen′ter, a library, usually in school, that contains and encourages the use of audiovisual media and associated equipment as well as books, periodicals, and the like.

me·di·a·cy (mē′dē ə sē), *n.* the state of being mediate. [1375–1425; late ME: intercession; see MEDIATE, -ACY]

me·di·ad (mē′dē ad′), *adv. Anat., Zool.* toward the middle line or plane. [1875–80; MEDI- + L *ad* to, toward]

me·di·ae·val (mē′dē ē′vəl, med′ē-, mid′ē-, mid ē′vəl), *adj.* medieval.

me′dia event′, a celebration, stunt, spectacle, or other activity carefully orchestrated to attract the attention of the news media. [1970–75]

me·di·a·gen·ic (mē′dē ə jen′ik), *adj.* having qualities or characteristics that are especially appealing or attractive when presented in the mass media: *a mediagenic politician.* [1970–75; MEDIA[1] + -GENIC]

me·di·al (mē′dē əl), *adj.* **1.** situated in or pertaining to the middle; median; intermediate. **2.** pertaining to a mean or average; average. **3.** ordinary. **4.** *Phonet.* within a word or syllable; neither initial nor final, as the *t, a,* and *n* in *stand.* **5.** *Entomol.* pertaining to, involving, or situated near the media. —*n.* **6.** *Phonet.* **a.** a medial sound or letter. **b.** media[2] (def. 1). [1560–70; < LL *mediālis* middle. See MEDIUM, -AL[1]] —**me′di·al·ly,** *adv.*

me′dial moraine′, a ridge of glacial drift formed by the junction of two converging valley glaciers.

me·di·an (mē′dē ən), *adj.* **1.** noting or pertaining to a plane dividing something into two equal parts, esp. one dividing an animal into right and left halves. **2.** situated in or pertaining to the middle; medial. —*n.* **3.** *Arith., Statistics.* the middle number in a given sequence of numbers, taken as the average of the two middle numbers when the sequence has an even number of numbers: *4 is the median of 1, 3, 4, 8, 9.* **4.** *Geom.* a straight line from a vertex of a triangle to the midpoint of the opposite side. **5.** Also called **midpoint.** a vertical line that divides a histogram into two equal parts. Cf. **central tendency. 6.** See **median strip.** [1535–45; < L *mediānus* in the middle. See MEDIUM, -AN] —**me′di·an·ly,** *adv.*

Me·di·an (mē′dē ən), *adj.* **1.** of or pertaining to Media, the Medes, or their language. —*n.* **2.** a Mede. **3.** the Iranian language of ancient Media, contemporaneous with Old Persian. [1595–1605; MEDI(A) + -AN]

me′dian le′thal dose′, the quantity of a lethal substance, as a poison or pathogen, or of ionizing radiation that will kill 50 percent of the organisms subjected to it in a specified time period. *Symbol:* LD_{50} [1945–50]

me′dian plane′, *Anat.* a vertical plane that divides an organism into symmetrical halves.

me′dian point′, *Geom.* centroid (def. 2).

me′dian strip′, a paved, planted, or landscaped strip in the center of a highway that separates lanes of traffic going in opposite directions. Also called **me′dial strip′, median.** [1945–50]

me·di·ant (mē′dē ənt), *n.* the third degree of a major or minor musical scale. [1720–30; < It *mediante* < LL *mediant-* (s. of *mediāns*), prp. of *mediāre* to be in the middle. See MEDIUM, -ANT]

me·di·as·ti·num (mē′dē a stī′nəm), *n., pl.* **-as·ti·na** (-a stī′nə). *Anat.* **1.** a median septum or partition between two parts of an organ, or paired cavities of the body. **2.** the partition separating the right and left thoracic cavities, formed of the two inner pleural walls, and, in humans, comprising all the viscera of the thorax except the lungs. [1535–45; < NL; cf. *mediastīnus* of middle class, appar. identical with L *mediast(r)inus* a low-ranking slave, perh. deriv. of *medius* MID[1], though sense and formation unclear] —**me′di·as·ti′nal,** *adj.*

me·di·ate (*v.* mē′dē āt′; *adj.* mē′dē it), *v.,* **-at·ed, -at·ing,** *adj.* —*v.t.* **1.** to settle (disputes, strikes, etc.) as an intermediary between parties; reconcile. **2.** to bring about (an agreement, accord, truce, peace, etc.) as an intermediary between parties by compromise, reconciliation, removal of misunderstanding, etc. **3.** to effect (a result) or convey (a message, gift, etc.) by or as if by an intermediary. —*v.i.* **4.** to act between parties to effect an agreement, compromise, reconciliation, etc. **5.** to occupy an intermediate place or position. —*adj.* **6.** acting through, dependent on, or involving an intermediate agency; not direct or immediate. [1375–1425; late ME < LL *mediātus,* ptp. of *mediāre* to be in the middle, intercede. See MEDIUM, -ATE[1]] —**me′di·ate·ly,** *adv.* —**me′di·ate·ness,** *n.*
—**Syn. 1, 2.** arbitrate. **4.** intercede, interpose.

me′diated generaliza′tion, *Psychol.* generalization (def. 4c).

me·di·a·tion (mē′dē ā′shən), *n.* **1.** action in mediating between parties, as to effect an agreement or reconciliation. **2.** *Internat. Law.* an attempt to effect a peaceful settlement between disputing nations through the friendly good offices of another power. [1350–1400; ME < ML *mediātiōn-* (s. of *mediātiō*). See MEDIATE, -ION]
—**Syn. 1.** MEDIATION, ARBITRATION designate processes for bringing about agreement or reconciliation between opponents in a dispute. MEDIATION implies deliberation that results in solutions that may or may not be accepted by the contending parties. ARBITRATION involves a more formal deliberation, it being understood that the results will be binding on the contending parties.

me·di·a·tive (mē′dē ā′tiv, -ə tiv), *adj.* mediating; mediatory. [1805–15; MEDIATE + -IVE]

me·di·a·tize (mē′dē ə tīz′), *v.t.,* **-tized, -tiz·ing.** to annex (a principality) to another state, while allowing certain rights to its former sovereign. Also, *esp. Brit.,* **me′di·a·tise′.** [1820–30; MEDIATE + -IZE, modeled on G *mediatisieren*] —**me′di·a·ti·za′tion,** *n.*

me·di·a·tor (mē′dē ā′tər), *n.* a person who mediates, esp. between parties at variance. [1250–1300; < LL (see MEDIATE, -TOR); r. ME *mediatour* < AF < LL, as above] —**me′di·a′tor·ship′,** *n.*

me·di·a·to·ri·al (mē′dē ə tôr′ē əl, -tōr′-), *adj.* of, pertaining to, or characteristic of a mediator. [1640–50; MEDIATORY + -AL[1]]

me·di·a·to·ry (mē′dē ə tôr′ē, -tōr′ē), *adj.* **1.** pertaining to mediation. **2.** having the function of mediating. [1610–20; < LL *mediātōrius.* See MEDIATE, -TORY[1]]

me·di·a·trix (mē′dē ā′triks), *n., pl.* **-a·tri·ces** (-ə trī′sēz, -ā′tri sēz′), **-a·trix·es.** a woman who mediates, esp. between parties at variance. Also, **me·di·a·tress, me·di·a·trice** (mē′dē ā′tris). [1425–75; late ME < LL *mediātrix,* fem. of *mediātor* MEDIATOR; see -TRIX]
—**Usage.** See **-ess, -trix.**

Med·i·bank (med′ə bangk′), *n.* the national health-insurance program instituted in Australia. [MEDI(CAL) + BANK[2]]

med·ic[1] (med′ik), *n.* **1.** a member of a military medical corps; corpsman. **2.** a doctor or intern. **3.** a medical student. [1650–60; < L *medicus;* see MEDICAL]

med·ic[2] (med′ik), *n.* any plant belonging to the genus *Medicago,* of the legume family, having trifoliate leaves and grown as a forage crop. Also, **medick.** Cf. **alfalfa, bur clover.** [1400–50; late ME *medike* < L *mēdica* < Gk (*póa*) *Mēdikē* lit., Median (grass)]

med·i·ca·ble (med′i kə bəl), *adj.* responsive to medical treatment; curable. [1610–20; < L *medicābilis* healing, curative. See MEDICAL, -ABLE] —**med′i·ca·bly,** *adv.*

Med·i·caid (med′i kād′), *n.* (*sometimes l.c.*) a U.S. government program, financed by federal, state, and local funds, of hospitalization and medical insurance for persons of all ages within certain income limits. Cf. **Medicare.** [MEDIC(AL) + AID]

med·i·cal (med′i kəl), *adj.* **1.** of or pertaining to the science or practice of medicine: *medical history; medical treatment.* **2.** curative; medicinal; therapeutic: *medical properties.* **3.** pertaining to or requiring treatment by other than surgical means. **4.** pertaining to or giving evidence of the state of one's health: *a medical discharge from the army; a medical examination.* —*n.* **5.** something done or received in regard to the state of one's health, as a medical examination. [1640–50; < ML *medicālis,* equiv. to L *medic(us)* medical (adj.), physician (n.) (deriv. of *medērī* to heal; see -IC) + *-ālis* -AL[1]] —**med′i·cal·ly,** *adv.*

med′ical exam′iner, 1. a physician or other person trained in medicine who is appointed by a city, county, or the like, to perform autopsies on the bodies of persons supposed to have died from unnatural causes and to investigate the cause and circumstances of such deaths. **2.** a physician retained by an insurance company, industrial firm, or the like, to give medical examinations to its clients or employees. [1840–50]

med·i·cal·ize (med′i kə līz′), *v.t.,* **-ized, -iz·ing.** to handle or accept as deserving of or appropriate for medical treatment. Also, *esp. Brit.,* **med′i·cal·ise′.** [MEDICAL + -IZE] —**med′i·cal·i·za′tion,** *n.*

med′ical jurispru′dence. See **forensic medicine.** [1780–90]

me·dic·a·ment (mə dik′ə mənt, med′i kə-), *n.* a healing substance; medicine; remedy. Also called **med·i·cant** (med′i kənt). [1535–45; < L *medicāmentum* remedy, physic, equiv. to *medicā(rī)* to cure + *-mentum* -MENT. See MEDICATE] —**med·i·ca·men·tal** (med′i kə-men′tl), **med′i·ca·men′tous,** *adj.*

Med·i·care (med′i kâr′), *n.* **1.** (*sometimes l.c.*) a U.S. government program of hospitalization insurance and voluntary medical insurance for persons aged 65 and over and for certain disabled persons under 65. Cf. **Medicaid. 2.** (*l.c.*) any of various government-funded programs to provide medical care to a population. [MEDI(CAL) + CARE]

med·i·cate (med′i kāt′), *v.t.,* **-cat·ed, -cat·ing. 1.** to treat with medicine or medicaments. **2.** to impregnate with a medicine: *medicated cough drops; a medicated bandage.* [1615–25; < L *medicātus* medicated (ptp. of *medicāre*), healed (ptp. of *medicārī*). See MEDICAL, -ATE[1]]

med·i·ca·tion (med′i kā′shən), *n.* **1.** the use or application of medicine. **2.** a medicinal substance; medicament. [1375–1425; late ME < L *medicātiōn-* (s. of *medicātiō*). See MEDICATE, -ION]

med·i·ca·tive (med′i kā′tiv), *adj.* medicinal. [1635–45; < ML *medicātīvus.* See MEDICATE, -IVE]

Med·i·ci (med′i chē; *It.* me′dē chē), *n.* **1. Catherine de′.** See **Catherine de Médicis. 2. Cos·mo** or **Co·si·mo de′** (kôz′mô *or* kô′zē mô de), (*"the Elder"*), 1389–1464, Italian banker, statesman, and patron of art and literature. **3. Cosmo** or **Cosimo de′** (*"the Great"*), 1519–74, duke of Florence and first grand duke of Tuscany. **4. Gio·van·ni de′** (jô vän′nē de). See **Leo X. 5. Giu·lio de′** (jōō′lyô de). See **Clement VII. 6. Lo·ren·zo de′** (lô REN′tsô de), (*"Lorenzo the Magnificent"*), 1449–92, poet and patron of the arts and literature: ruler of Florence 1478–92 (father of Leo X). **7. Ma·ri·a de′** (mə rē′ə də; *It.* mä RĒ′ä de). See **Marie de Médicis.** —**Med·i·ce·an** (med′i sē′ən, -chē′ən), *adj.*

me·dic·i·na·ble (mə dis′ə nə bəl), *adj. Archaic.* medicinal. [1350–1400; ME < MF. See MEDICINE, -ABLE]

me·dic·i·nal (mə dis′ə nl), *adj.* **1.** of, pertaining to, or having the properties of a medicine; curative; remedial: *medicinal properties; medicinal substances.* **2.** unpalatable; disagreeable: *a medicinal taste.* [1300–50; ME < L *medicinālis.* See MEDICINE, -AL[1]] —**me·dic′i·nal·ly,** *adv.*

medic′inal leech′, a bloodsucking leech, *Hirudo medicinalis,* of Europe, introduced into the northeastern U.S., usually green with brown stripes, up to 4 in. (10 cm) long: once used by physicians to bleed patients. [1885–90]

med·i·cine (med′ə sin *or, esp. Brit.,* med′sən), *n., v.,* **-cined, -cin·ing.** —*n.* **1.** any substance or substances used in treating disease or illness; medicament; remedy. **2.** the art or science of restoring or preserving health or due physical condition, as by means of drugs, surgical operations or appliances, or manipulations: often divided into medicine proper, surgery, and obstetrics. **3.** the art or science of treating disease with drugs or curative substances, as distinguished from surgery and obstetrics. **4.** the medical profession. **5.** (among North American Indians) any object or practice regarded as having magical powers. **6. give someone a dose** or **taste of his** or **her own medicine,** to repay or punish a person for an injury by use of the offender's own methods. **7. take one's medicine,** to undergo or accept punishment, esp. deserved punishment: *He took his medicine like a man.* —*v.t.* **8.** to administer medicine to. [1175–1225; ME *medicin* < L *medicīna* (*ars*) healing (art), fem. of *medicīnus* pertaining to a physician. See MEDICAL, -INE[1]]
—**Syn. 1.** medication, drug; pharmaceutical; physic.

med′icine ball′, a large, solid, heavy, leather-covered ball, thrown from one person to another for exercise. [1890–95]

Med′icine Bow′ Range′ (bō), a range of the Rocky Mountains, in Wyoming and Colorado. Highest peak, Medicine Bow Peak, 12,014 ft. (3662 m).

med′icine dance′, a ritual dance performed by some North American Indians to invoke supernatural assistance as for driving out disease. [1800–10]

Med′icine Hat′, a city in SE Alberta, in SW Canada. 32,811.

med′icine lodge′, 1. a structure used for various ceremonials of North American Indians. **2.** (*caps.*) the most important religious society among the central Algonquian tribes of North America. [1800–10]

med′icine man′, 1. (among North American Indians and some other aboriginal peoples) a person believed to possess magical or supernatural powers; shaman. **2.** a seller of patent medicine, esp. before 1900, presenting a medicine show to attract customers. [1795–1805]

med′icine show′, a traveling troupe, esp. in the late 1800's, offering entertainment in order to attract customers for the patent medicines or purported cures proffered for sale. [1935–40, *Amer.*]

med·ick (med′ik), *n.* medic[2].

med·i·co (med′i kō′), *n., pl.* **-cos.** *Informal.* **1.** a physician or surgeon; doctor. **2.** a medical student. [1680–90; < Sp *médico,* It *medico* < L *medicus* physician; see MEDICAL]

medico-, a combining form representing **medical** in compound words: *medicolegal.* [comb. form repr. L *medicus* of, pertaining to healing; see MEDICAL]

med·i·co·chi·rur·gi·cal (med′i kō kī rûr′ji kəl), *adj.* **1.** pertaining to medicine and surgery. **2.** *Archaic.* consisting of both physicians and surgeons. [1800–10; MEDICO- + CHIRURGICAL]

med·i·co·le·gal (med′i kō lē′gəl), *adj.* pertaining to medicine and law or to forensic medicine. [1825–35; MEDICO- + LEGAL]

me·di·e·val (mē′dē ē′vəl, med′ē-, mid′ē-, mid ē′vəl), *adj.* **1.** of, pertaining to, characteristic of, or in the style of the Middle Ages: *medieval architecture.* Cf. **Middle Ages. 2.** *Informal.* extremely old-fashioned; primitive. Also, **mediaeval.** [1820–30; < NL *medi(um) aev(um)* the middle age + -AL[1]. See MEDIUM, AGE] —**me′di·e′val·ly,** *adv.*

Me′die′val Greek′, the Greek language of the Middle Ages, usually dated A.D. 700 to 1500. *Abbr.:* MGk, MGk., MGr. Also called **Middle Greek.**

me·di·e·val·ism (mē′dē ē′və liz′əm, med′ē-, mid′ē-, mid ē′və-), *n.* **1.** the spirit, practices, or methods of the Middle Ages. **2.** devotion to or adoption of medieval ideals or practices. **3.** a medieval belief, practice, or the like. Also, **mediaevalism.** [1850–55; MEDIEVAL + -ISM]

me·di·e·val·ist (mē′dē ē′və list, med′ē-, mid′ē-, mid-ē′və-), *n.* **1.** an expert in medieval history, literature, philosophy, etc. **2.** a person who is greatly attracted to the art, culture, spirit, etc., of the Middle Ages. [1850–55; MEDIEVAL + -IST]

Me′die′val Lat′in, the Latin language of the literature of the Middle Ages, usually dated A.D. 700 to 1500, including many Latinized words from other languages. *Abbr.:* ML, M.L. Also called **Middle Latin.** [1880–85]

med·i·gap (med′i gap′), *n.* (*sometimes cap.*) private health insurance that supplements coverage for people already covered by government insurance. [MEDI(CAL) + GAP, on the model of MEDICARE]

Me·dill (mə dil′), *n.* **Joseph,** 1823–99, U.S. journalist.

CONCISE ETYMOLOGY KEY: <, descended or borrowed from; >, whence; b., blend of, blended; c., cognate with; cf., compare; deriv., derivative; equiv., equivalent; imit., imitative; obl., oblique; r., replacing; s., stem; sp., spelling, spelled; resp., respelling, respelled; trans., translation; ?, origin unknown; *, unattested; ‡, probably earlier than. See the full key inside the front cover.

me•di•na (mə dē′nə), *n.* the old Arab quarter of a North African city. [1905–10; < Ar *madīna* city]

Me•di•na (mə dē′nə *for 1;* mə dī′nə *for 2*), *n.* **1.** a city in W Saudi Arabia, where Muhammad was first accepted as the Supreme Prophet from Allah and where his tomb is located. 150,000. **2.** a town in N Ohio. 15,268.

me•di•oc•ra•cy (mē′dē ok′rə sē), *n., pl.* **-cies.** government or rule by a mediocre person or group. [b. MEDIOCRE and -CRACY]

me•di•o•cre (mē′dē ō′kər, mē′dē ō′kər), *adj.* **1.** of only ordinary or moderate quality; neither good nor bad; barely adequate. **2.** rather poor or inferior. [1580–90; < MF < L *mediocris* in a middle state, lit., at middle height, equiv. to *medi(us)* MID[1] + OL *ocris* rugged mountain, c. Gk *ókris,* akin to *ákros* apex; cf. Umbrian *ocar* hill, citadel]
—Syn. 1. average, commonplace. **—Ant. 2.** superior.

me•di•o•cris (mē′dē ō′kris), *adj. Meteorol.* (of a cumulus cloud) of medium height and often lacking a distinctive summit. [< NL: MEDIOCRE]

me•di•oc•ri•ty (mē′dē ok′ri tē), *n., pl.* **-ties. 1.** the state or quality of being mediocre. **2.** mediocre ability or accomplishment. **3.** a mediocre person. [1400–50; late ME *mediocrite* < MF *mediocrite* < L *mediocritāt-* (s. of *mediocritās*) a middle state, moderation. See MEDIOCRE, -ITY]

Medit., Mediterranean.

med•i•tate (med′i tāt′), *v.,* **-tat•ed, -tat•ing.** *—v.i.* **1.** to engage in thought or contemplation; reflect. **2.** to engage in transcendental meditation, devout religious contemplation, or quiescent spiritual introspection. *—v.t.* **3.** to consider as something to be done or effected; intend; purpose: *to meditate revenge.* [1550–60; < L *meditātus,* ptp. of *meditārī* to meditate, contemplate, plan] **—med′i•tat′ing•ly,** *adv.* **—med′i•ta′tor,** *n.*
—Syn. 1. ponder, muse; ruminate; cogitate, study, think. **3.** contemplate, plan, devise, contrive.

med•i•ta•tion (med′i tā′shən), *n.* **1.** the act of meditating. **2.** continued or extended thought; reflection; contemplation. **3.** See **transcendental meditation. 4.** devout religious contemplation or spiritual introspection. [1175–1225; < L *meditātiōn-* (s. of *meditātiō*) a thinking over (see MEDITATE, -ION); r. ME *meditacioun* < AF < L, as above]

med•i•ta•tive (med′i tā′tiv), *adj.* given to, characterized by, or indicative of meditation; contemplative. [1605–15; < LL *meditātīvus.* See MEDITATE, -IVE] **—med′i•ta′tive•ly,** *adv.* **—med′i•ta′tive•ness,** *n.*
—Syn. thoughtful. See **pensive.**

Med•i•ter•ra•ne•an (med′i tə rā′nē ən), *n.* **1.** See **Mediterranean Sea. 2.** a person whose physical characteristics are considered typical of the peoples native to or inhabiting the Mediterranean area. **3. the,** *Informal.* the islands and countries of the Mediterranean Sea collectively. *—adj.* **4.** pertaining to, situated on or near, or dwelling about the Mediterranean Sea. **5.** pertaining to or characteristic of the peoples native to the lands along or near the Mediterranean Sea. **6.** surrounded or nearly surrounded by land. [1585–95; < L *mediterrāne(us)* midland, inland (see MEDIUM, TERRA, -AN, -EOUS) + -AN]

Med′iterra′nean cli′mate, a climate having sunny, hot, dry summers and rainy winters. Also called **etesian climate.** [1895–1900]

Med′iterra′nean fe′ver, *Pathol.* brucellosis. [1810–20]

Med′iterra′nean flour′ moth′, a small cosmopolitan moth, *Anagasta kuehniella,* whose larvae damage stored foodstuffs, as grain and flour. [1890–95, *Amer.*]

Med′iterra′nean fruit′ fly′, a small, black and white, irregularly banded two-winged fly, *Ceratitis capitata,* of many warm regions, that damages citrus and other succulent fruit crops by implanting eggs that hatch into maggots within the fruit. Also called **medfly, Medfly.** [1905–10]

Med′iterra′nean Sea′, a sea surrounded by Africa, Europe, and Asia. 2400 mi. (3865 km) long; 1,145,000 sq. mi. (2,965,550 sq. km); greatest known depth 14,436 ft. (4400 m). Also called **Mediterranean.**

me•di•um (mē′dē əm), *n., pl.* **-di•a** (-dē ə) for 1–9, 11, **-di•ums** for 1–11, 14, *adj.* *—n.* **1.** a middle state or condition; mean. **2.** something intermediate in nature or degree. **3.** an intervening substance, as air, through which a force acts or an effect is produced. **4.** the element that is the natural habitat of an organism. **5.** surrounding objects, conditions, or influences; environment. **6.** an intervening agency, means, or instrument by which something is conveyed or accomplished: *Words are a medium of expression.* **7.** one of the means or channels of general communication, information, or entertainment in society, as newspapers, radio, or television. **8.** *Biol.* the substance in which specimens are displayed or preserved. **9.** Also called **culture medium.** *Bacteriol.* a liquid or solidified nutrient material suitable for the cultivation of microorganisms. **10.** a person through whom the spirits of the dead are alleged to be able to contact the living. **11.** *Fine Arts.* **a.** *Painting.* a liquid with which pigments are mixed. **b.** the material or technique with which an artist works: *the medium of watercolor.* **12.** a size of printing paper, 18½ × 23½ in. (47 × 60 cm) in England, 18 × 23 to 19 × 25 in. (46 × 58 to 48 × 64 cm) in America. **13.** *Chiefly Brit.* a size of drawing or writing paper, 17½ × 22 in. (44 × 56 cm). **14.** Also called **medium strip.** *Midland U.S.* See **median strip. 15. in medium,** *Motion Pictures, Television.* with the principal actors in the middle distance: *The scene was shot in medium.* *—adj.* **16.** about halfway between extremes, as of degree, amount, quality, position, or size: *Cook over medium heat. He is of medium height.* [1575–85; < L: the middle, n. use of neut. of *medius* middle. See MID[1]]
—Syn. 16. average, mean, middling.
—Usage. 7. See **media[1].**

me′dium artil′lery, *U.S. Mil.* guns and howitzers of more than 105mm and less than 155mm caliber, sometimes including the 155mm howitzers. Cf. **heavy artillery** (def. 2), **light artillery** (def. 2).

me′dium bomb′er, *Mil.* a moderately large airplane capable of carrying large bomb loads for moderate distances at medium altitudes, esp. one having a gross loaded weight of 100,000 to 250,000 lb. (45,000 to 113,000 kg). Cf. **heavy bomber, light bomber.** [1930–35]

me′dium fre′quency, *Radio.* any frequency between 300 and 3000 kilohertz. *Abbr.:* MF [1915–20]

me•di•um•is•tic (mē′dē ə mis′tik), *adj.* pertaining to a spiritualistic medium. [1865–70; MEDIUM + -ISTIC]

me′dium octa′vo, a size of book, about 6 × 9½ in. (15 × 24 cm), untrimmed. *Abbr.:* medium 8vo

me′dium of exchange′, anything generally accepted as representing a standard of value and exchangeable for goods or services. [1730–40]

me′dium quar′to, *Chiefly Brit.* a size of book, about 9½ × 12 in. (24 × 30 cm), untrimmed. *Abbr.:* medium 4to

me′di•um-scale integra′tion (mē′dē əm skāl′), *Electronics.* See **MSI.**

me′dium shot′, *Motion Pictures, Television.* a camera shot in which the subject is in the middle distance, permitting some of the background to be seen. Cf. **closeup** (def. 2), **long shot** (def. 3). [1930–35]

me•di•um-sized (mē′dē əm sīzd′), *adj.* neither very large nor very small: *a medium-sized house.* [1880–85]

me′dium strip′, *Midland U.S.* See **median strip.**

me•di•us (mē′dē əs), *n., pl.* **-di•i** (-dē ī′). *Anat.* the middle finger. [1555–65; < L: middle (adj.); see MID[1]]

med•i•vac (med′ə vak′), *n., v.t.,* **-vacked, -vack•ing.** medevac.

med•lar (med′lər), *n.* **1.** a small tree, *Mespilus germanica,* of the rose family, the fruit of which resembles a crab apple and is not edible until the early stages of decay. **2.** any of certain related trees. **3.** the fruit of any of these trees. [1325–75; ME *medler* < AF, equiv. to *medle* (OF *mesle* the fruit < L *mespilum* < Gk *méspilon*) + *-er* -ER[2]]

med•ley (med′lē), *n., pl.* **-leys,** *adj.* *—n.* **1.** a mixture, esp. of heterogeneous elements; hodgepodge; jumble. **2.** a piece of music combining tunes or passages from various sources: *a medley of hit songs from Broadway shows.* *—adj.* **3.** *Archaic.* mixed; mingled. [1300–50; ME *medlee* (n. and adj.) < AF, n. and adj. use of fem. of ptp. of *medler* to mix, fight; see MEDDLE]

med′ley re′lay, 1. *Track.* a relay race in which individual members of a team usually run an unequal portion of the total distance. Cf. **distance medley, sprint medley. 2.** *Swimming.* a relay race in which no member of a team uses the same stroke as another. Cf. **individual medley.** [1945–50]

Mé•doc (mā dok′; *Fr.* mā dôk′), *n.* **1.** a wine-growing region in Gironde, in SW France. **2.** a red Bordeaux wine produced there.

Me•don (mēd′n), *n.* (in the *Odyssey*) a herald who warned Penelope that her suitors were conspiring against Telemachus.

me•drox•y•pro•ges•ter•one (mi drok′sē prō jes′tə rōn′), *n. Pharm.* a progesterone derivative, $C_{24}H_{34}O_4$, used in the treatment of abnormal uterine bleeding and secondary amenorrhea, as a contraceptive of long duration, and in the treatment of certain cancers. [ME(THYL) + (HY)DROXY- + PROGESTERONE]

Med.Sc.D., Doctor of Medical Science.

me•dul•la (mə dul′ə), *n., pl.* **-dul•las, -dul•lae** (-dul′ē). **1.** *Anat.* **a.** the marrow of the bones. **b.** the soft, marrowlike center of an organ, as the kidney or adrenal gland. **c.** See **medulla oblongata. 2.** *Bot.* the pith of plants. [1635–45; < L: marrow, pith]

medul′la oblonga′ta, *pl.* **medulla oblongatas, medullae oblongatae.** *Anat.* the lowest or hindmost part of the brain, continuous with the spinal cord. See diag. under **brain.** [1670–80; < NL: the long medulla]

med•ul•lar•y (med′l er′ē, mej′ə ler′ē, mə dul′ə rē), *adj.* pertaining to, consisting of, or resembling the medulla of an organ or the medulla oblongata. [1610–20; MEDULL(A) + -ARY]

med′ullary ray′, *Bot.* (in the stems of woody plants) one of the vertical bands or plates of unspecialized tissue that radiate between the pith and the bark. Also called **pith ray.** [1820–30]

med′ullary sheath′, 1. *Bot.* a narrow zone made up of the innermost layer of woody tissue immediately surrounding the pith in plants. **2.** *Anat.* See **myelin sheath.** [1840–50]

med•ul•lat•ed (med′l ā′tid, mej′ə lā′-, mə dul′ā tid), *adj. Anat.* myelinated. [1865–70; MEDULL(A) + -ATE[1] + -ED[2]]

med•ul•la•tion (med′l ā′shən, mej′ə lā′-), *n. Biol.* the formation of a medullary sheath about a nerve fiber. [MEDULL(A) + -ATION]

me•du•sa (mə do͞o′sə, -zə, -dyo͞o′-), *n., pl.* **-sas, -sae** (-sē, -zē). *Zool.* a saucer-shaped or dome-shaped, free-swimming jellyfish or hydra. [1750–60; special use of MEDUSA, alluding to the Gorgon's snaky locks] **—me•du•soid** (mə do͞o′soid, -dyo͞o′-), *adj.*

Me•du•sa (mə do͞o′sə, -zə, -dyo͞o′-), *n., pl.* **-sas.** *Class. Myth.* the only mortal of the three Gorgons. She was killed by Perseus, and her head was mounted upon the aegis of Zeus and Athena. [< L < Gk *Médousa,* special use of *médousa,* fem. of *médōn* ruling]

me•du•sa•fish (mə do͞o′sə fish′, -zə-, -dyo͞o′-), *n., pl.* **-fish•es,** (*esp. collectively*) **-fish.** a stromateid fish, *Icichthys lockingtoni,* of deep waters off the coast of California, living as a commensal in and about medusas. [MEDUSA + FISH]

me•du•san (mə do͞o′sən, -zən, -dyo͞o′-), *adj.* **1.** pertaining to a medusa or jellyfish. *—n.* **2.** a medusa or jellyfish. [1840–50; MEDUS(A) + -AN]

meed (mēd), *n. Archaic.* a reward or recompense. [bef. 900; ME *mede,* OE *mēd;* c. G *Miete* hire; akin to OE *meord,* Goth *mizdō,* Gk *misthós* reward]

meek (mēk), *adj.,* **-er, -est. 1.** humbly patient or docile, as under provocation from others. **2.** overly submissive or compliant; spiritless; tame. **3.** *Obs.* gentle; kind. [1150–1200; ME *meke, meoc* < ON *mjūkr* soft, mild, meek] **—meek′ly,** *adv.* **—meek′ness,** *n.*
—Syn. 1. forbearing; yielding; unassuming; pacific, calm, soft. See **gentle.**

Meer (mēr; *Du.* mār), *n.* **Jan van der** (yän vän dər). See **Vermeer, Jan.** Also called **Meer van Delft** (vän delft′).

meer•schaum (mēr′shəm, -shôm), *n.* **1.** a mineral, hydrous magnesium silicate, $H_4Mg_2Si_3O_{10}$, occurring in white, claylike masses, used for ornamental carvings, for pipe bowls, etc.; sepiolite. **2.** a tobacco pipe with a bowl made of this substance. [1775–85; < G *Meerschaum,* equiv. to *Meer* sea (see MERE[2]) + *Schaum* foam]

Mee•rut (mēr′ət), *n.* a city in W Uttar Pradesh, in N India. 367,821.

meet[1] (mēt), *v.,* **met, meet•ing,** *n.* *—v.t.* **1.** to come upon; come into the presence of; encounter: *I would meet him on the street at unexpected moments.* **2.** to become acquainted with; be introduced to: *I've never met your cousin.* **3.** to join at an agreed or designated place or time: *Meet me in St. Louis.* **4.** to be present at the arrival of: *to meet a train.* **5.** to come to or before (one's notice, or a means of noticing, as the eyes or ears): *A peculiar sight met my eyes.* **6.** to come into the company of (a person, group, etc.) in dealings, conference, etc. **7.** to face, eye, etc., directly or without avoidance. **8.** to come into physical contact, juxtaposition, or collision with: *The two cars met each other head-on at high speed.* **9.** to encounter in opposition, conflict, or contest: *Harvard meets Yale next week in football.* **10.** to oppose: *to meet charges with countercharges.* **11.** to cope or deal effectively with (an objection, difficulty, etc.). **12.** to comply with; fulfill; satisfy: *to meet a deadline; to meet a demand.* **13.** to pay in full: *How will you meet expenses?* **14.** to come into conformity with (wishes, expectations, views, etc.). **15.** to encounter in experience: *to meet hostility.* *—v.i.* **16.** to come together, face to face, or into company: *We met on the street.* **17.** to assemble for action, conference, or other common purpose, as a committee, legislature, or class: *The board of directors will meet on Tuesday.* **18.** to become personally acquainted. **19.** to come into contact or form a junction, as lines, planes, or areas: *The two lines meet to form an angle.* **20.** to be conjoined or united. **21.** to concur or agree. **22.** to come together in opposition or conflict, as adversaries or hostile forces. **23. meet halfway, a.** to concede in part, as to the demands of an opposing faction; make concessions, as to another person; compromise: *Despite their differences, the union and the company finally agreed to meet halfway and settle their dispute.* **b.** to anticipate another's actions and conduct oneself accordingly. **24. meet with, a.** to come across; encounter: *to meet with opposition.* **b.** to experience; undergo; receive: *The visitors met with courtesy during their stay.* **c.** to join, as for conference or instruction: *I met with her an hour a day until we solved the problem.* **25. well met,** *Archaic.* welcome. *—n.* **26.** an assembly, as of persons and hounds for a hunt or swimmers or runners for a race or series of races: *a track meet.* **27.** those assembled. **28.** the place of such an assembling. **29.** *Math.* intersection (def. 3a). [bef. 900; ME *meten,* OE *gemētan;* c. ON *mœta,* OS *mōtian.* See MOOT[1]] **—meet′er,** *n.*
—Syn. 7. confront. **8.** join, connect, intersect, cross, converge, unite. **17.** collect. **26.** contest, competition.
—Ant. 17. adjourn, scatter. **19.** diverge.

meet[2] (mēt), *adj.* suitable; fitting; proper. [bef. 1000; ME *mete,* aph. var. (see Y-) of *imete;* repr. OE *gemǣte* suitable, c. G *gemäss* conformable] **—meet′ness,** *n.*
—Syn. apt, appropriate.

meet•ing (mē′ting), *n.* **1.** the act of coming together: *a chance meeting in the park.* **2.** an assembly or conference of persons for a specific purpose: *a ten o'clock business meeting.* **3.** the body of persons present at an assembly or conference: *to read a report to the meeting.* **4.** a hostile encounter; duel. **5.** an assembly for religious worship, esp. of Quakers. **6.** See **meeting house. 7.** a place or point of contact; junction; union: *the meeting of two roads; the meeting of the waters.* **8. take a meeting,** *Informal.* to hold, conduct, or participate in a meeting: *The producer took a meeting with the cast of the film.* [1250–1300; ME; see MEET[1], -ING[1]]
—Syn. 1. encounter; confrontation; rendezvous.

meet′ing house′, 1. a house or building for religious worship. **2.** a house of worship for Quakers. Also, **meet′ing•house′.** [1625–35]

meet′ing post′, a timber with a chamfer at the outer edge of a lock gate that fits against the meeting post of another lock gate. Also called **miter post.** [1870–75]

meet′ing rail′, (in a double-hung window) the rail of each sash that meets a rail of the other when the window is closed. See diag. under **double-hung.**

meet•ly (mēt′lē), *adv.* suitably; fittingly; properly; in a seemly manner. [1350–1400; ME; see MEET[2], -LY]

mef′e•nam′ic ac′id (mef′ə nam′ik, mef′-), *Pharm.* a white powder, $C_{15}H_{15}NO_2$, used as a mild analgesic, anti-inflammatory, and antipyretic in certain types of arthritis and for the relief of moderate short-term pain due to dysmenorrhea. [1960–65; ME(THYL) + *-fen-,* resp. of PHEN(YL) + AM(INOBENZO)IC ACID]

Meg (meg), *n.* a female given name, form of **Margaret.**

MEG, magnetoencephalogram.

meg, *Elect.* megohm; megohms.

CONCISE PRONUNCIATION KEY: act, cāpe, dâre, pärt; set, ēqual; *if,* īce; ox, ōver, ôrder, oil, bo͝ok, bo͞ot, out; up, ûrge; child; sing; shoe; thin, *th*at; zh as in *treasure.* ə = *a* as in *alone, e* as in *system, i* as in *easily, o* as in *gallop, u* as in *circus;* ᵊ as in *fire* (fīᵊr), *hour* (ouᵊr). l and n can serve as syllabic consonants, as in *cradle* (krād′l), and *button* (but′n). See the full key inside the front cover.

mega-, var. of **megalo-** (*megalith*); also the initial element in units of measure that are equal to one million of the units denoted by the base word (*megahertz*). *Symbol:* M Also, *esp. before a vowel,* **meg-.** [comb. form repr. Gk *mégas* large, great]

meg•a•bit (meg′ə bit′), *n. Computers.* **1.** 2^{20} (1,048,576) bits. **2.** (loosely) one million bits. *Abbr.:* Mb [1955–60; MEGA- + BIT[3]]

meg•a•buck (meg′ə buk′), *n. Informal.* **1.** one million dollars. **2. megabucks,** very large sums of money. [1945–50; MEGA- + BUCK[1]]

meg•a•byte (meg′ə bīt′), *n. Computers.* **1.** 2^{20} (1,048,576) bytes. **2.** (loosely) one million bytes. *Abbr.:* MB [1965–70; MEGA- + BYTE]

meg•a•ce•phal•ic (meg′ə sə fal′ik), *adj. Cephalom.* macrocephalic. Also, **meg•a•ceph•a•lous** (meg′ə sef′ə ləs). [MEGA- + CEPHALIC] **—meg′a•ceph′a•ly,** *n.*

meg•a•cit•y (meg′ə sit′ē), *n., pl.* **-cit•ies.** a city having a population of one million or more. [1965–70; MEGA- + CITY]

meg•a•cor•po•ra•tion (meg′ə kôr′pə rā′shən), *n.* a giant company formed from two or more large companies or a number of companies of various sizes. Also called **meg′a•com′pa•ny.** [MEGA- + CORPORATION]

meg•a•cy•cle (meg′ə sī′kəl), *n. Elect.* a unit of frequency, equal to one million cycles per second; megahertz. The term megahertz is now preferred in technical use. *Abbr.:* Mc, mc [1925–30; MEGA- + CYCLE]

meg•a•deal (meg′ə dēl′), *n.* a large business transaction. [1980–85]

meg•a•death (meg′ə deth′), *n.* a unit of one million deaths: used in estimating the fatalities that would occur in a nuclear war. [1950–55; MEGA- + DEATH]

meg•a•dont (meg′ə dont′), *adj.* macrodont. Also, **meg′a•don′tic.** [MEGA- + -(O)DONT]

meg•a•don•tia (meg′ə don′shə, -shē ə), *n.* macrodontia. Also, **meg′a•dont′ism, meg′a•don′ty.** [< NL; see MEGA-, -ODONT, -IA]

meg•a•dose (meg′ə dōs′), *n.* a dose many times the usual amount, as of a vitamin. [1970–75; MEGA- + DOSE]

meg•a•e′lec•tron volt′ (meg′ə i lek′tron), *Physics.* See **million electron volts.** [MEGA- + ELECTRON VOLT]

Me•gae•ra (mə jēr′ə), *n. Class. Myth.* one of the Furies.

meg•a•fau•na (meg′ə fô′nə), *n. Ecol.* land animals of a given area that can be seen with the unaided eye. [MEGA- + FAUNA]

meg•a•flops (meg′ə flops′), *n.* a measure of computer speed, equal to one million floating-point operations per second. [1985–90; see FLOPS]

meg•a•ga•mete (meg′ə gə mēt′, -gam′ēt), *n. Cell Biol.* macrogamete. [1890–95; MEGA- + GAMETE]

meg•a•ga•me•to•phyte (meg′ə gə mē′tə fīt′), *n. Bot.* the female gametophyte in seed plants. [1930–35; MEGA- + GAMETOPHYTE] **—meg•a•ga•me•to•phyt•ic** (meg′ə gə mē′tə fit′ik, -gam′i-), *adj.*

meg•a•hertz (meg′ə hûrts′), *n., pl.* **-hertz, -hertz•es.** *Elect.* a unit of frequency, equal to one million cycles per second. *Abbr.:* MHz [1940–45; MEGA- + HERTZ]

meg•a•hit (meg′ə hit′), *n.* an enterprise, as a movie, that is outstandingly successful. [1980–85]

meg•a•joule (meg′ə joul′, -jo͞ol′), *n. Physics.* a unit of work or energy, equal to one million joules. [MEGA- + JOULE]

meg•a•kar•y•o•blast (meg′ə kar′ē ə blast′), *n. Cell Biol.* a cell that gives rise to a megakaryocyte. [MEGA- + KARYO- + -BLAST]

meg•a•kar•y•o•cyte (meg′ə kar′ē ə sīt′), *n. Cell Biol.* a large bone-marrow cell having a lobulate nucleus, regarded as the source of blood platelets. [1885–90; MEGA- + KARYO- + -CYTE] **—meg•a•kar•y•o•cyt•ic** (meg′ə kar′ē ə sit′ik), *adj.*

megal-, var. of **megalo-** before a vowel: *megalopsia.*

meg•a•lec•i•thal (meg′ə les′ə thəl), *adj. Embryol.* having a large amount of yolk, as certain eggs or ova. [1955–60; MEGA- + LECITHAL]

Meg•a•le•sia (meg′ə lē′zhə, -shə, -sē ə), *n.* (*sometimes used with a plural v.*) an ancient Roman festival in honor of the Magna Mater. Also called **Meg′ale′sian Games′.** [< L, short for *megalēsia* (*lūdī*) Megalesian (games), deriv. of *Megalē* the great (< Gk), surname of the Magna Mater]

-megalia, var. of **-megaly:** *cardiomegalia.*

meg•a•lith (meg′ə lith), *n.* a stone of great size, esp. in ancient construction work, as the Cyclopean masonry, or in prehistoric Neolithic remains, as dolmens or menhirs. [1850–55; MEGA- + -LITH] **—meg′a•lith′ic,** *adj.*

megalith′ic astron′omy, archaeoastronomy.

megalo-, a combining form with the meanings "large, great, grand," "abnormally large," used in the formation of compound words: *megalopolis; megalocardia.* Also, *esp. before a vowel,* **megal-.** Cf. **mega-.** [< Gk, comb. form of *megal-* (s. of *mégas*) great, large]

meg•a•lo•blast (meg′ə lō blast′), *n. Pathol.* an abnormally large, immature, and dysfunctional red blood cell found in the blood of persons with pernicious anemia or certain other disorders. [1895–1900; MEGALO- + -BLAST] **—meg′a•lo•blas′tic,** *adj.*

meg•a•lo•car•di•a (meg′ə lō kär′dē ə), *n. Pathol.* hypertrophy of the heart. [1850–55; MEGALO- + -CARDIA]

meg•a•lo•ce•phal•ic (meg′ə lō sə fal′ik), *adj.* **1.** *Cephalom., Craniom.* macrocephalic. **2.** *Pathol.* afflicted with leontiasis. Also, **meg•a•lo•ceph•a•lous** (meg′ə lō sef′ə ləs). [1875–80; MEGALO- + CEPHALIC] **—meg′a•lo•ceph′a•ly,** *n.*

meg•a•lo•ma•ni•a (meg′ə lō mā′nē ə), *n.* **1.** *Psychiatry.* a symptom of mental illness marked by delusions of greatness, wealth, etc. **2.** an obsession with doing extravagant or grand things. [MEGALO- + -MANIA]

meg•a•lo•ma•ni•ac (meg′ə lō mā′nē ak′), *n.* **1.** a person afflicted with megalomania. *—adj.* **2.** Also, **meg•a•lo•ma•ni•a•cal** (meg′ə lō mə nī′ə kəl), **meg•a•lo•man•ic** (meg′ə lō man′ik). of, pertaining to, or suggesting megalomania or a person who is afflicted with it. [1885–90; MEGALO- + MANIAC]

meg•a•lop•o•lis (meg′ə lop′ə lis), *n.* **1.** a very large city. **2.** an urban region, esp. one consisting of several large cities and suburbs that adjoin each other. Also, **megapolis.** [1825–35; MEGALO- + POLIS]

meg•a•lo•pol•i•tan (meg′ə lō pol′i tn), *adj.* **1.** of, pertaining to, or characteristic of a megalopolis. *—n.* **2.** an inhabitant of a megalopolis. Also, **megapolitan.** [1925–35; from MEGALOPOLIS, modeled after *metropolis: metropolitan*] **—meg′a•lo•pol′i•tan•ism,** *n.*

meg•a•lops (meg′ə lops′), *n. Zool.* the larval stage of marine crabs immediately prior to and resembling the adult stage. [1850–55; < NL, orig. a genus name, equiv. to Gk *megal-* MEGAL- + *ōps* eye, face]

meg•a•lop•si•a (meg′ə lop′sē ə), *n. Ophthalm.* macropsia. Also, **meg•a•lop•i•a** (meg′ə lop′ē ə). [1885–90; MEGAL- + -OPSIA]

meg•a•lo•saur (meg′ə lə sôr′), *n.* any gigantic carnivorous dinosaur of the genus *Megalosaurus,* of the Jurassic and early Cretaceous periods. [1835–45; < NL *Megalosaurus.* See MEGALO-, -SAUR] **—meg′a•lo•sau′ri•an,** *adj., n.*

-megaly, a combining form meaning "irregular enlargement" of the organ of the body specified by the initial element: *cardiomegaly.* Also, **-megalia.** [< NL *-megalia.* See MEGALO-, -Y[3]]

Meg•an (meg′ən), *n.* a female given name.

Me•gan•thro•pus (mə gan′thrə pəs, meg′an thrō′pəs), *n.* a proposed genus of extinct, late lower Pleistocene primates based on two large lower jaws found in Java, and believed to be either Australopithecine or human. [< NL (1942) < Gk *még(as)* large (see MEGA-) + *ánthrōpos* man]

meg•a•phone (meg′ə fōn′), *n., v.,* **-phoned, -phon•ing.** *—n.* **1.** a cone-shaped device for magnifying or directing the voice, chiefly used in addressing a large audience out of doors or in calling to someone at a distance. Cf. **bull horn.** *—v.t., v.i.* **2.** to transmit or speak through or as if through a megaphone. [1875–80, *Amer.;* MEGA- + -PHONE] **—meg•a•phon•ic** (meg′ə fon′ik), *adj.* **—meg′a•phon′i•cal•ly,** *adv.*

meg•a•pode (meg′ə pōd′), *n.* any of several large-footed, short-winged gallinaceous Australasian birds of the family Megapodiidae, typically building a compost-like mound of decaying vegetation as an incubator for their eggs. Also called **brush turkey, moundbird, mound builder, scrub fowl.** [1855–60; < NL *Megapodius* genus name. See MEGA-, -POD]

me•gap•o•lis (mə gap′ə lis), *n.* megalopolis. [1630–40; MEGA- + -POLIS] **—meg•a•pol•i•tan** (meg′ə pol′i tn), *adj., n.*

Meg•a•ra (meg′ər ə), *n.* **1.** a city in ancient Greece: the chief city of Megaris. **2.** *Class. Myth.* a daughter of Creon whose children were slain by her husband, Hercules, in a fit of madness. **—Me•gar•i•an, Me•gar•e•an** (mə gar′ē ən, me-), **Me•gar′ic,** *adj.*

Meg•a•ris (meg′ər is), *n.* a district in ancient Greece, between the Gulf of Corinth and Saronic Gulf.

meg•a•ron (meg′ə ron′), *n., pl.* **-a•ra** (-ər ə), **-a•rons.** (in pre-Hellenic Greek architecture) a building or semi-independent unit of a building, used as a living apartment and typically having a square or rectangular principal chamber and sometimes an antechamber or other small compartments. [1875–80; < Gk *mégaron* (in Homer) the principal living quarters of a palace]

meg•a•spo•ran•gi•um (meg′ə spô ran′jē əm, -spō-), *n., pl.* **-gi•a** (-jē ə). *Bot.* a sporangium containing megaspores. [1885–90; MEGA- + SPORANGIUM]

meg•a•spore (meg′ə spôr′, -spōr′), *n. Bot.* **1.** the larger of the two kinds of spores characteristically produced by seed plants and a few fern allies, developing into a female gametophyte. Cf. **microspore. 2.** the embryo sac of a flowering plant. Also called **macrospore.** [1885–90; MEGA- + SPORE] **—meg•a•spor•ic** (meg′ə-spôr′ik, -spor′-), *adj.*

meg•a•spo•ro•phyll (meg′ə spôr′ə fil, -spōr′-), *n. Bot.* a sporophyll producing megasporangia only. [1895–1900; MEGA- + SPOROPHYLL]

me•gass (mə gas′, -gäs′), *n.* bagasse. Also, **me•gasse′.** [1840–50; unexplained var.]

meg•a•struc•ture (meg′ə struk′chər), *n.* **1.** a very large, usually high-rise building or a complex of such buildings used for many purposes, as for apartments, offices, stores, and athletic facilities. **2.** a very large, complex organization. [1960–65; MEGA- + STRUCTURE]

meg•a•there (meg′ə thēr′), *n.* any of the huge, sloth-like animals of the extinct genus *Megatherium,* or closely related genera, that lived from the Oligocene to the Pleistocene epochs. [1830–40; < NL *Megatherium;* see MEGA-, -THERE]

megathere, genus *Megatherium,* length 20 ft. (6 m)

meg•a•therm (meg′ə thûrm′), *n.* a plant requiring a constant high temperature and abundant moisture for growth. [1875–80; MEGA- + THERM] **—meg′a•ther′mic, meg′a•ther′mal,** *adj.*

meg•a•ton (meg′ə tun′), *n.* **1.** one million tons. **2.** an explosive force equal to that of one million tons of TNT, as that of atomic or hydrogen bombs. *Abbr.:* MT [1950–55; MEGA- + TON[1]] **—meg•a•ton•ic** (meg′ə ton′ik), *adj.*

meg•a•ton•nage (meg′ə tun′ij), *n.* the destructive capacity of nuclear explosives as measured in megatons. [1960–65; MEGATON + -AGE, after TONNAGE]

meg•a•trend (meg′ə trend′), *n.* a major trend or movement. [MEGA- + TREND]

meg•a•vi•ta•min (meg′ə vī′tə min; *Brit. also* meg′ə-vit′ə min), *adj.* **1.** of, pertaining to, or using very large amounts of vitamins: *megavitamin therapy.* Cf. **orthomolecular.** *—n.* **2. megavitamins,** doses of vitamins much larger than the recommended dietary allowances. [1965–70; MEGA- + VITAMIN]

meg•a•volt (meg′ə vōlt′), *n. Elect.* a unit of electromotive force, equal to one million volts. *Abbr.:* MV [1920–25; MEGA- + VOLT]

meg•a•watt (meg′ə wot′), *n. Elect.* a unit of power, equal to one million watts. *Abbr.:* MW [1895–1900; MEGA- + WATT]

Me•ges (mē′jēz), *n.* (in the *Iliad*) a nephew of Odysseus who commanded the Epeans in the Trojan War.

Meg•han (meg′ən), *n.* a female given name.

Me•gid•do (mə gid′ō), *n.* an ancient city in N Israel, on the plain of Esdraelon: site of many battles; often identified with the Biblical Armageddon.

me•gil•lah (mə gil′ə; *for 2 also Seph. Heb.* mə gē lä′), *n., pl.* **-gil•lahs,** *Seph. Heb.* **-gil•loth, -gil•lot** (-gē lôt′). **1.** *Slang.* **a.** a lengthy, detailed explanation or account: *Just give me the facts, not a whole megillah.* **b.** a tediously complicated matter. **2.** (*italics*) *Hebrew.* a scroll, esp. one containing the Book of Esther. Others are the Book of Ecclesiastes, the Song of Solomon, the Book of Ruth, and the Book of Lamentations. Also, **me•gil′la.** [1950–55; < Yiddish *megile* lit., scroll < Heb *məgillāh*]

me•gilp (mə gilp′), *n.* a jellylike vehicle used in oil paints and usually consisting of linseed oil mixed with mastic varnish. [1760–70; orig. obscure]

MEGO (mē′gō), my eyes glaze over.

meg•ohm (meg′ōm′), *n. Elect.* a unit of resistance, equal to one million ohms. *Symbol:* MΩ; *Abbr.:* meg [1865–70; MEG- + OHM]

meg•ohm•me•ter (meg′ōm mē′tər), *n. Elect.* an instrument for measuring large resistances, esp. the resistance of insulation. [MEGOHM + -METER]

me•grim (mē′grim), *n.* **1. megrims,** low spirits; the blues. **2.** a whim or caprice. **3.** migraine. [1350–1400; ME *migrame* a type of headache < MF *migraine* (by misreading, *in* taken as *m*); see MIGRAINE]

Me•hem•et A•li (mi hem′et ä lē′, ä′lē, mä′met), 1769–1849, viceroy of Egypt 1805–48. Also, **Mohammed Ali.**

me•hi•tzah (*Seph.* mə KHē tsä′; *Ashk.* mə KHē′tsə), *n., pl.* **-hit•zoth, hit•zot, -hit•zos** (*Seph.* -KHē tsôt′; *Ashk.* -KHē′tsəz, -KHē′tsōs). *Hebrew.* a curtain or other divider that serves as a partition between the women's and the men's sections in Orthodox Jewish synagogues. Also, ***mechitzah.***

Meh•ta (mā′tə), *n.* **Zu•bin** (zo͞o′bin), born 1936, Indian orchestra conductor, in the U.S. since 1961.

Mé•hul (mā yl′), *n.* **É•tienne Ni•co•las** (ā tyen′ nē kô-lä′) or **Étienne Hen•ri** (äN rē′), 1763–1817, French composer.

Me•hu•man (mi hyo͞o′mən), *n.* one of the seven eunuchs who served in the court of King Ahasuerus. Esther 1:10.

Meigh•en (mē′ən), *n.* **Arthur,** 1874–1960, Canadian statesman: prime minister 1920–21, 1926.

Meigs (megz), *n.* **Fort.** See **Fort Meigs.**

Mei•ji (mā′jē′), *n. Japanese Hist.* the designation of the period of the reign of Emperor Mutsuhito from 1867 to 1912. [1870–75; < Japn *meiji,* earlier *meidi* enlightened peace < MChin, equiv. to Chin *míng* bright + *zhì* pacify]

Meil•hac (me yak′), *n.* **Hen•ri** (äN rē′), 1831–97, French dramatist: collaborator with Ludovic Halévy.

Meil•let (me ye′), *n.* **An•toine** (äN twan′), 1866–1936, French linguist.

Mein Kampf (mīn kämpf′), the autobiography (1925–27) of Adolf Hitler, setting forth his political philosophy and his plan for German conquest.

Mei•nong (mī′nông), *n.* **A•lex•i•us** (ä lek′sē o͝os), 1853–1920, Austrian psychologist and philosopher.

mein•y (mā′nē), *n., pl.* **mein•ies. 1.** *Archaic.* a group or suite of attendants, followers, dependents, etc. **2.** *Scot. Archaic.* a multitude; crowd. Also, **mein′ie.** [1250–1300; ME *meynee* household < OF *meyne, mesnie, mesnede* < VL **mānsiōnāta.* See MANSION, -ATE[1]]

mei•o•nite (mī′ə nīt′), *n. Mineral.* a member of the scapolite group, rich in calcium and containing no sodium. [1800–10; < Gk *meíōn* less + -ITE[1]; cf. F *méionite*]

mei•o•sis (mī ō′sis), *n.* **1.** *Cell Biol.* part of the process of gamete formation, consisting of chromosome conjugation and two cell divisions, in the course of which the diploid chromosome number becomes reduced to the haploid. Cf. **mitosis. 2.** *Rhet.* **a.** belittlement. **b.** expressive understatement, esp. litotes. [1580–90; < Gk *meíōsis* a lessening, equiv. to *meiō-,* var. s. of *meioûn* to lessen (deriv. of *meíōn* less) + *-sis* -SIS] **—mei•ot•ic** (mī ot′ik), *adj.*

Me•ir (mā ēr′, mī′ər), *n.* **Gol•da** (gōl′də), (*Goldie Mabovitch, Goldie Myerson*), 1898–1978, Israeli political leader, born in Russia: prime minister 1969–74.

Meis·sen (mī′sən), *n.* a city in E central Germany, on the Elbe River: famous for fine porcelain. 38,137.

Meis′sen por′celain. See **Dresden china.** [1935–40]

Meiss′ner effect′ (mīs′nər), *Physics.* the loss of magnetism that a superconductor displays when cooled to its transition temperature in a magnetic field. [after German physicist Fritz Walther *Meissner* (1882–1974), who contributed to a description of the effect in 1933]

Meiss′ner's cor′puscle (mīs′nərz). See **tactile corpuscle.** [after German anatomist Georg *Meissner* (1829–1905), who described them in 1853]

Meis·so·nier (me sô nyā′), *n.* **Jean Louis Er·nest** (zhäɴ lwē ᴇʀ nest′), 1815–91, French painter.

Mei·ster·sing·er (mī′stər sing′ər, -zing′-), *n., pl.* **-sing·er, -sing·ers** for 1. **1.** Also, **mastersinger.** a member of one of the guilds, chiefly of workingmen, established during the 14th, 15th, and 16th centuries in the principal cities of Germany, for the cultivation of poetry and music. **2.** (*italics*) ***Die*** (dē), an opera (1867) by Richard Wagner. [1835–45; < G: master singer]

Meit·ner (mīt′nər), *n.* **Li·se** (lē′zə), 1878–1968, Austrian nuclear physicist.

Mé·ji·co (*Sp.* me′hē kô), *n.* Mexico.

MEK, *Chem.* See **methyl ethyl ketone.**

Mek′er burn′er (mek′ər), *Chem.* a gas burner similar to the Bunsen burner but producing a hotter flame by virtue of having at its mouth a metal screen to allow a more intimate mixture of air and gas. [1955–60; named after George *Meker,* 20th-century chemist, its inventor]

Mekh·i·tar·ist (mek′i tär′ist), *n. Rom. Cath. Ch.* a member of an order of Armenian monks founded in Constantinople in the 18th century and following the rule of St. Benedict. Also, **Mechitarist.** [named after Peter M. *Mekhitar* (1676–1749), Armenian religious reformer; see -IST]

Mek·ka (mek′ə), *n.* Mecca (def. 1).

Mek·nès (mek nes′), *n.* a city in N Morocco: former capital of Morocco. 244,520.

Me·kong (mā′kong′; *Thai.* ma kông′), *n.* a river whose source is in SW China, flowing SE along most of the boundary between Thailand and Laos to the South China Sea. 2600 mi. (4200 km) long. Chinese, **Lantsang.**

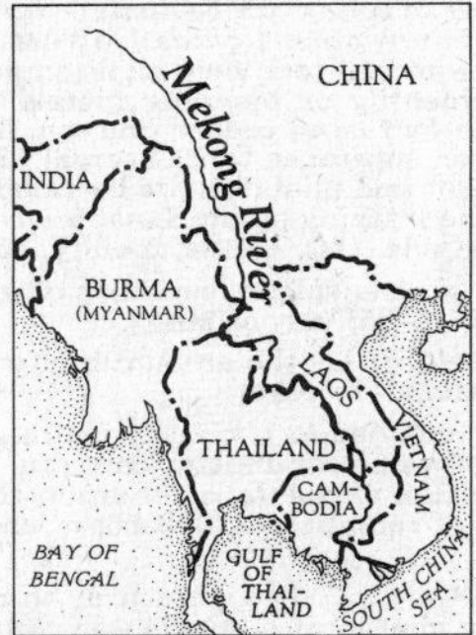

Me′kong Del′ta, the delta of the Mekong River in Vietnam.

mel (mel), *n.* (in prescriptions) honey. [< L]

Mel (mel), *n.* a male given name, form of **Melvin.**

me·la (mā′lä), *n.* (in India) **1.** a religious fair, esp. one held in connection with a festival. **2.** a throng of people. [1790–1800; < Hindi < Skt *melā* assembly, company]

me·lae·na (mi lē′nə), *n. Med.* melena.

Me·la·ka (mə lä′kə), *n.* Malacca (defs. 1, 2).

mel·a·leu·ca (mel′ə lo͞o′kə), *n.* any of various chiefly Australian shrubs or trees belonging to the genus *Melaleuca,* of the myrtle family, including the cajeput and several species of bottlebrush. [< NL (Linnaeus), irreg. coinage from Gk *mélā(s)* black + *leukḗ,* fem. of *leukós* white; so called from its black trunk and white branches]

me·la·med (*Seph.* mə lä med′; *Ashk.* mə lä′mid), *n., pl.* ***-lam·dim*** (*Seph.* -läm dēm′; *Ashk.* -läm′dim). *Hebrew.* a teacher in a Jewish school, esp. a heder. Also, ***melammed.*** [*məlammēd* lit., teacher]

mel·a·mine (mel′ə mēn′, mel′ə mēn′), *n. Chem.* **1.** a white, crystalline, slightly water-soluble solid, $C_3N_3(NH_2)_3$, used chiefly in organic synthesis and in the manufacture of resins, esp. melamine resins. **2.** any of the melamine resins. [1825–35; < G *Melamin,* deriv. of *Melam* distillate of ammonium thiocyanate (arbitrary coinage, but *-am* repr. AMMONIUM); see -INE[2]]

mel′amine res′in, *Chem.* any of the class of thermosetting resins formed by the interaction of melamine and formaldehyde: used chiefly as adhesives for laminated materials and as coatings for paper, plastics, and textiles. [1940–45]

me·lam·med (*Seph.* mə lä med′; *Ashk.* mə lä′mid), *n., pl.* ***-lamm·dim*** (*Seph.* -läm dēm′; *Ashk.* -läm′dim). *Hebrew.* melamed.

Me·lam·pus (mə lam′pəs), *n. Class. Myth.* the first seer and healer: his ears were licked by serpents he had raised, enabling him to understand the speech and wisdom of animals.

melan-, var. of **melano-** before a vowel: *melanism.*

mel·an·cho·li·a (mel′ən kō′lē ə, -kōl′yə), *n.* **1.** a mental condition characterized by great depression of spirits and gloomy forebodings. **2.** *Psychiatry.* See **endogenous depression.** [1685–95; < LL; see MELANCHOLY]

mel·an·cho·li·ac (mel′ən kō′lē ak′), *adj.* **1.** affected with melancholia. —*n.* **2.** a person who is affected with melancholia. [1860–65; MELANCHOLI(A) + -AC]

mel·an·chol·ic (mel′ən kol′ik), *adj.* **1.** disposed to or affected with melancholy; gloomy. **2.** of, pertaining to, or affected with melancholia. [1350–1400; ME *melancolik* < L *melancholicus* < Gk *melancholikós.* See MELANCHOLY, -IC] **—mel′an·chol′i·cal·ly,** *adv.*

mel·an·chol·y (mel′ən kol′ē), *n., pl.* **-chol·ies,** *adj.* —*n.* **1.** a gloomy state of mind, esp. when habitual or prolonged; depression. **2.** sober thoughtfulness; pensiveness. **3.** *Archaic.* **a.** the condition of having too much black bile, considered in ancient and medieval medicine to cause gloominess and depression. **b.** black bile. —*adj.* **4.** affected with, characterized by, or showing melancholy; mournful; depressed: *a melancholy mood.* **5.** causing melancholy or sadness; saddening: *a melancholy occasion.* **6.** soberly thoughtful; pensive. [1275–1325; ME *melancholie* < LL *melancholia* < Gk *melancholía* condition of having black bile, equiv. to *melan-* MELAN- + *cholḗ* bile + *-ia* -IA] **—mel′an·chol′i·ly,** *adv.* **—mel′an·chol′i·ness,** *n.*
—Syn. 1. sadness, dejection, despondency. **2.** seriousness. **4.** gloomy, despondent, blue, dispirited, sorrowful, dismal, doleful, glum, downcast. **6.** serious. **—Ant. 1.** cheer, happiness. **5.** happy.

Me·lanch·thon (mə langk′thən; *Ger.* mā länᴋʜ′tôn), *n.* **Phil·ipp** (fil′ip; *Ger.* fē′lip), (*Philipp Schwarzert*), 1497–1560, German Protestant reformer.

Mel·a·ne·sia (mel′ə nē′zhə, -shə), *n.* one of the three principal divisions of Oceania, comprising the island groups in the S Pacific NE of Australia.

Mel·a·ne·sian (mel′ə nē′zhən, -shən), *adj.* **1.** of or pertaining to Melanesia, its inhabitants, or their languages. —*n.* **2.** a member of any of the native peoples inhabiting Melanesia. **3.** the Austronesian languages of Melanesia, taken collectively. [1840–50; MELANESI(A) + -AN]

Mel′ane′sian Pidg′in Eng′lish, Neo-Melanesian.

mé·lange (mā länzh′, -länj′), *n., pl.* **-langes** (-länzh′, -län′jiz). a mixture; medley. [1645–55; < F; OF *meslance,* equiv. to *mesl(er)* to mix (see MEDDLE) + *-ance* n. suffix << Gmc *-ingō* -ING[1]]

me·lan·ic (mə lan′ik), *adj.* **1.** *Pathol.* melanotic. **2.** of or pertaining to melanism. [1815–25; MELAN- + -IC]

Mel·a·nie (mel′ə nē), *n.* a female given name.

mel·a·nin (mel′ə nin), *n.* any of a class of insoluble pigments, found in all forms of animal life, that account for the dark color of skin, hair, fur, scales, feathers, etc. [1835–45; MELAN- + -IN[2]] **—mel′a·nin·like′,** *adj.*

Me·la·ni·on (mə lā′nē ən), *n. Class. Myth.* a youth of Arcadia, usually identified with Hippomenes as the successful suitor of Atalanta.

Mel·a·nip·pus (mel′ə nip′əs), *n. Class. Myth.* a Theban who killed Tydeus in the battle of the Seven against Thebes and who was, in turn, slain by Amphiaraus. Also, **Mel′a·nip′pos.**

mel·a·nism (mel′ə niz′əm), *n.* **1.** *Ethnol.* the condition in human beings of having a high amount of melanin granules in the skin, hair, and eyes. **2.** *Zool.* the condition in which an unusually high concentration of melanin occurs in the skin, plumage, or pelage of an animal. [1835–45; MELAN- + -ISM] **—mel′a·nis′tic,** *adj.*

mel·a·nite (mel′ə nīt′), *n. Mineral.* a deep black variety of andradite garnet. [1800–10; MELAN- + -ITE[1]] **—mel·a·nit·ic** (mel′ə nit′ik), *adj.*

melano-, a combining form meaning "black," used in the formation of compound words: *melanocyte.* Also, *esp. before a vowel,* **melan-.** [< Gk, comb. form of *mélās*]

me·lan·o·blast (mə lan′ə blast′, mel′ə nə-), *n. Biol.* an undifferentiated cell that develops into a melanophore or melanocyte. [1900–05; MELANO- + -BLAST]

me·lan·o·cyte (mə lan′ə sīt′, mel′ə nə-), *n. Cell Biol.* a cell producing and containing melanin. [1885–90; MELANO- + -CYTE]

me·lan′o·cyte-stim·u·lat·ing hor′mone (mə lan′ə sīt′stim′yə lā′ting, mel′ə nə-), *Biochem.* See **MSH.** [1950–55]

me·lan·o·derm (mə lan′ə dûrm′, mel′ə nə-), *n.* a person with dark pigmentation of the skin. [1920–25; MELANO- + -DERM]

mel·a·noid (mel′ə noid′), *adj.* **1.** of or characterized by melanosis. **2.** resembling melanin; darkish. [1850–55; MELAN- + -OID]

mel·a·no·ma (mel′ə nō′mə), *n., pl.* **-mas, -ma·ta** (-mə tə). *Pathol.* any of several types of skin tumors characterized by the malignant growth of melanocytes. [1825–35; MELAN- + -OMA]

me·lan·o·phore (mə lan′ə fôr′, -fōr′, mel′ə nə-), *n. Biol.* a pigmented connective-tissue cell containing melanin in its cytoplasm, responsible for color changes in many fishes and reptiles. [1900–05; MELANO- + -PHORE]

mel·a·no·sis (mel′ə nō′sis), *n. Pathol.* **1.** abnormal deposition or development of black or dark pigment in the tissues. **2.** a discoloration caused by this. [1815–25; < NL < LGk *melánōsis* a becoming black. See MELAN-, -OSIS]

me·lan·o·some (mə lan′ə sōm′, mel′ə nə-), *n. Cell Biol.* an organelle in melanocytes that synthesizes and stores melanin. [1935–40; MELANO- + -SOME[3]]

me·lan·o·sper·mous (mə lan′ō spûr′məs, mel′ə nō-), *adj.* having dark spores, as certain seaweeds. [1855–60; MELANO- + -SPERM + -OUS]

mel·a·not·ic (mel′ə not′ik), *adj. Pathol.* of or affected with melanosis. Also, **melanic.** [1820–30; MELAN- + -OTIC]

me·lan·o·tro·pin (mə lan′ə trō′pin, mel′ə nə-), *n.* See **MSH.** [MELANO- + -TROPE + -IN[2]]

mel·a·to·nin (mel′ə tō′nin), *n. Physiol.* a hormone secreted by the pineal gland in inverse proportion to the amount of light received by the retina, important in the regulation of biorhythms: in amphibians, it causes a lightening of the skin. [1955–60; < Gk *mélā(s)* black + TONE + -IN[2]]

mel·a·xu·ma (mel′ə ko͞o′mə, -ə zo͞o′-, -ək so͞o′-), *n. Plant Pathol.* a disease of trees, esp. walnuts, characterized by an inky-black liquid oozing from the affected twigs, branches, and trunk, and by bark cankers, caused by any of several fungi, as *Dothiorella gregaria.* [1930–35; < NL, irreg. < Gk *mélā(s)* black + *chýma* fluid (with *x-* repr. Gk *ch-*)]

Mel·ba (mel′bə), *n.* **1. (Dame) Nellie** (*Helen Porter Mitchell Armstrong*), 1861–1931, Australian operatic soprano. **2.** a female given name.

Mel′ba sauce′, a clear raspberry sauce, used esp. as a dessert topping. [1950–55; named after N. MELBA]

Mel′ba toast′, narrow slices of thin, crisp toast. [1920–25; named after N. MELBA]

Mel·bourne (mel′bərn), *n.* **1. 2nd Viscount.** See **Lamb, William. 2.** a seaport in and the capital of Victoria, in SE Australia. 2,864,600. **3.** a city on the E coast of Florida. 44,536. **—Mel·bur·ni·an** (mel bûr′nē ən), *n., adj.*

Mel·chers (mel′chərz), *n.* **Gar·i** (gâr′ē), 1860–1932, U.S. painter.

Mel·chi·a·des (mel kī′ə dēz′), *n.* **Saint,** died A.D. 314, pope 310–314. Also, **Miltiades.**

Mel·chior (mel′kyôr, -kē ôr′), *n.* **1.** one of the three Magi. **2. Lau·ritz (Leb·recht Hom·mel)** (lou′rits, lôr′-its; *Dan.* lou′ʀɪᴛs lib′ʀᴇᴋʜᴛ hom′el), 1890–1973, U.S. operatic tenor, born in Denmark.

Mel·chite (mel′kīt), *n.* **1.** a Christian in Egypt and Syria who accepted the definition of faith adopted by the Council of Chalcedon in A.D. 451. —*adj.* **2.** of or pertaining to the Melchites. Also, **Melkite.** [1610–20; < ML *Melchīta* < MGk *Melchī́tēs* royalist, equiv. to *melch-* < Syriac *malkā* king (or < a deriv. adj. of appurtenance) + *-ītēs* -ITE[1]]

Mel·chiz·e·dek (mel kiz′i dek′), *n.* **1.** a priest and king of Salem. Gen. 14:18. **2.** the higher order of priests in the Mormon Church.

meld[1] (meld), *Cards.* —*v.t., v.i.* **1.** to announce and display (a counting combination of cards in the hand) for a score. —*n.* **2.** the act of melding. **3.** any combination of cards to be melded. [1895–1900; < G *melden* to announce; akin to ME *melden,* OE *meldian* to make known]

meld[2] (meld), *v.t., v.i.* **1.** to merge; blend. —*n.* **2.** a blend. [1935–40; b. MELT[1] and WELD]
—Syn. 1. mix, fuse, combine, consolidate.

meld·er (mel′dər), *n. Scot.* the quantity of meal ground at one time; the yield of meal from a crop or specific amount of grain. [1400–50; late ME *meltyre* < ON *meldr* grain or meal in the mill]

Mel·e·a·ger (mel′ē ā′jər), *n.* **1.** fl. 1st century B.C., Greek epigrammatist. **2.** *Class. Myth.* the heroic son of Althaea, an Argonaut, and the slayer of the Calydonian boar. Cf. **Calydonian hunt.** Also, **Mel·e·a·gros** (mel′ē-ag′ros).

Mel·e·ag·ri·des (mel′ē ag′ri dēz′), *n.pl. Class. Myth.* the sisters of Meleager of Calydon who were changed into guinea hens by Artemis in order to relieve their grief over the death of their brother.

me·lee[1] (mā′lā, mā lā′, mel′ā), *n.* **1.** a confused hand-to-hand fight or struggle among several people. **2.** confusion; turmoil; jumble: *the melee of Christmas shopping.* Also, **mê·lée.** [1640–50; < F *mêlée.* See MEDLEY]

me·lee[2] (mā′lā, mā lā′), *n.* a group of diamonds, each weighing less than 0.25 carat. [1910–15; orig. uncert.]

me·le·na (mə lē′nə), *n. Med.* the discharge of black, tarry, bloody stools, usually resulting from a hemorrhage in the alimentary tract. Also, **melaena.** [< NL < Gk *mélaina,* fem. of *mélās* black]

M.El.Eng., Master of Electrical Engineering.

Mel·e·te (mel′i tē), *n. Class. Myth.* one of the original three Muses, the Muse of meditation. Cf. **Aoede, mneme** (def. 2). [< Gk *melétē* care, attention]

mel·e·tin (mel′i tin), *n. Biochem.* quercetin.

-melia, a combining form occurring in compound words that denote a condition of the limbs, as specified by the initial element: *phocomelia.* [< NL, comb. form repr. Gk *mélos* limb; see -IA]

me·li·a·ceous (mē′lē ā′shəs), *adj.* belonging to the Meliaceae, the mahogany family of plants. Cf. **mahogany family.** [1895–1900; < NL *Meliace(ae)* (equiv. to *Meli(a)* genus name (< Gk *melía* ash tree) + *-aceae* -ACEAE) + -OUS]

Me·li·ae (mē′lē ē′), *n.pl. Class. Myth.* the nymphs born from the blood of Uranus at the time of his mutilation by Cronus; the nymphs of ash trees. [< Gk *melíai,* pl. of *melía* manna, ash tree]

mel·ic (mel′ik), *adj.* **1.** intended to be sung. **2.** noting or pertaining to the more elaborate form of Greek lyric poetry, as distinguished from iambic and elegiac poetry. [1690–1700; < Gk *melikós,* equiv. to *mél(os)* limb, song + *-ikos* -IC]

Mé·liès (mā lyes′), *n.* **Georges** (zhôrzh), 1861–1938, French film director.

mel·i·lite (mel′ə līt′), *n.* a sorosilicate mineral group,

CONCISE PRONUNCIATION KEY: *act, cāpe, dâre, pärt; set, ēqual; if, īce; ox, ōver, ôrder, oil, bo͝ok, bo͞ot, out; up, ûrge; child; sing; shoe; thin, that;* zh as in *treasure.* ə = *a* as in *alone, e* as in *system, i* as in *easily, o* as in *gallop, u* as in *circus;* ᵊ as in *fire* (fīᵊr), *hour* (ouᵊr). l and n can serve as syllabic consonants, as in *cradle* (krād′l), and *button* (but′n). See the full key inside the front cover.

consisting chiefly of sodium, calcium, and aluminum silicates, occurring in igneous rocks. [1790–1800; < NL *melilithus,* equiv. to Gk *méli* honey + *líthos* -LITE]

Me·lil·la (mä lēl′yä), *n.* a seaport belonging to Spain on the NE coast of Morocco, in NW Africa. 60,843.

mel·i·lot (mel′ə lot′), *n.* a cloverlike plant of the genus *Melilotus,* of the legume family, grown as a forage plant. [bef. 1150; ME *mellilot* < L *melilōtos* < Gk *melílōtos* a clover, equiv. to *méli* honey + *lōtós* LOTUS; r. late OE *milotis* < L, as above]

Me·lin·da (mə lin′də), *n.* a female given name.

mel·i·nite (mel′ə nīt′), *n. Chem.* a high explosive containing picric acid. [1885–90; < F *mélinite* < Gk *mḗlin(os)* made of apples (deriv. of *mêlon* apple) + F *-ite* -ITE[1]]

mel·i·oi·do·sis (mel′ē oi dō′sis), *n. Pathol.* a contagious pulmonary disease of rodents that is caused by the bacterium *Pseudomonas pseudomallei* and is frequently transmitted to humans in moist climates of southeastern Asia. [1920–25; < Gk *mēlí(s)* glanders, or a similar distemper affecting asses + -OID + -OSIS]

mel·io·rate (mēl′yə rāt′, mē′lē ə-), *v.t., v.i.,* **-rat·ed, -rat·ing.** ameliorate. [1545–55; < L *meliōrātus* (ptp. of *meliōrāre*) to make better, improve, equiv. to *meliōr-* (s. of *melior*) better + *-ātus* -ATE[1]] **—mel·io·ra·ble** (mēl′yər ə bəl, mē′lē ər ə-), *adj.* **—mel·io·ra·tive** (mēl′yə rā′tiv, -yər ə tiv, mē′lē ə rā′-, -ər ə-), *adj.* **—mel′io·ra′tor,** *n.*

mel·io·ra·tion (mēl′yə rā′shən, mē′lē ə-), *n.* **1.** *Historical Ling.* semantic change in a word to a more approved or more respectable meaning. Cf. **pejoration** (def. 2). **2.** amelioration. [1620–30; < LL *meliōrātiōn-* (s. of *meliōrātiō*), equiv. to *meliōrāt(us)* (see MELIORATE) + *-iōn-* -ION]

mel·io·rism (mēl′yə riz′əm, mē′lē ə-), *n.* the doctrine that the world tends to become better or may be made better by human effort. [1855–60; < L *melior* better + -ISM] **—mel′io·rist,** *n., adj.* **—mel′io·ris′tic,** *adj.*

mel·ior·i·ty (mēl yôr′i tē, -yor′-, mē′lē ôr′-, -or′-), *n.* superiority. [1570–80; < ML *meliōritās,* equiv. to L *meliōr-* (s. of *melior*) better + *-itās* -ITY]

me·lis·ma (mi liz′mə), *n., pl.* **-mas, -ma·ta** (-mə tə). *Music.* an ornamental phrase of several notes sung to one syllable of text, as in plainsong or blues singing. [1605–15; < Gk *mélisma* song, tune. See MELODY, -ISM] **—mel·is·mat·ic** (mel′iz mat′ik), *adj.*

Me·lis·sa (mə lis′ə), *n.* **1.** *Class. Myth.* the sister of Amalthea who nourished the infant Zeus with honey. **2.** Also, **Me·lis·sie, Me·lis·sy** (mə lis′ē). a female given name.

Mel·i·te·ne (mel′i tē′nē), *n.* ancient name of **Malatya.**

Me·li·to·pol (mel′ə tô′pəl; *Russ.* myi lyi tô′pəl), *n.* a city in SE Ukraine, NW of the Sea of Azov: battles 1941, 1943. 174,000.

mel·i·tose (mel′i tōs′), *n. Biochem.* raffinose. [1860–65; < Gk *melit-,* s. of *méli* honey + -OSE[2]]

mel·i·tri·ose (mel′i trī′ōs), *n. Biochem.* raffinose. [MEL[1] + -I- + TRI- + -OSE[2]]

Me·lit·ta (mə lit′ə), *n.* a female given name.

Mel·kite (mel′kīt), *n., adj.* Melchite.

mell[1] (mel), *Brit. Dial.* —*v.t.* **1.** to blend; mix; meld. —*v.i.* **2.** to meddle; concern oneself. [1250–1300; ME *mellen* < MF *meller;* see MEDDLE]

mell[2] (mel), *Scot. and North Eng.* —*n.* **1.** a heavy hammer; mallet. —*v.t.* **2.** to beat with a mallet; hammer. [1250–1300; ME, var. of *mall* hammer < OF *mal, mail* < L *malleus*]

Mel·la·ril (mel′ə ril), *Pharm., Trademark.* a brand of thioridazine.

mel·ler (mel′ər), *n. Theat. Slang.* melodrama (def. 1). [by shortening and alter.]

Mel·lers (mel′ərz), *n.* **Wilfrid Howard,** born 1914, English musicologist and composer.

mel·lif·er·ous (mə lif′ər əs), *adj.* yielding or producing honey. [1650–60; < L *mellifer* honey-bearing (*melli-,* s. of *mel* honey + *-fer* -FER) + -OUS]

mel·lif·lu·ent (mə lif′lo͞o ənt), *adj.* mellifluous. [1595–1605; < LL *mellifluent-* (s. of *mellifluēns*), equiv. to L *melli-* (s. of *mel*) honey + *fluent-* FLUENT] **—mel·lif′lu·ence,** *n.* **—mel·lif′lu·ent·ly,** *adv.*

mel·lif·lu·ous (mə lif′lo͞o əs), *adj.* **1.** sweetly or smoothly flowing; sweet-sounding: *a mellifluous voice; mellifluous tones.* **2.** flowing with honey; sweetened with or as if with honey. [1375–1425; late ME < LL *mellifluus,* equiv. to L *melli-* (s. of *mel*) honey + *-flu(ere)* to flow + *-us* adj. suffix (see -OUS)] **—mel·lif′lu·ous·ly,** *adv.* **—mel·lif′lu·ous·ness,** *n.*
—Syn. 1. melodious, musical, dulcet, harmonious.

mel·lite (mel′īt), *n. Pharm.* a pharmaceutical containing honey. Also, **mellitum.** [1795–1805; < NL *mellītes.* See MEL, -ITE[1]]

mel·li·tum (mə lī′təm), *n., pl.* **-li·ta** (-lī′tə). *Pharm.* mellite. [< NL *mellītum*]

Mel·lon (mel′ən), *n.* **Andrew William,** 1855–1937, U.S. financier: Secretary of the Treasury 1921–32.

mel·lo·phone (mel′ə fōn′), *n.* a marching or military band brass instrument similar in appearance and range to the French horn but slightly smaller and simpler to play. Also called **tenor cor.** [1925–30; MELLO(W) + -PHONE]

Mel·lo·tron (mel′ə tron′), *Trademark.* a brand of synthesizer that simulates the sound of other instruments by using tapes of recorded sounds.

mel·low (mel′ō), *adj.,* **-er, -est,** *v., n.* —*adj.* **1.** soft, sweet, and full-flavored from ripeness, as fruit. **2.** well-matured, as wines. **3.** soft and rich, as sound, tones, color, or light. **4.** made gentle and compassionate by age or maturity; softened. **5.** friable or loamy, as soil. **6.** mildly and pleasantly intoxicated or high. **7.** pleasantly agreeable; free from tension, discord, etc.: *a mellow neighborhood.* **8.** affably relaxed; easygoing; genial: *a mellow teacher who is very popular with her students.* —*v.t., v.i.* **9.** to make or become mellow. **10. mellow out,** *Slang.* **a.** to become detached from worry, strife, stress, etc.; relax: *After final exams let's go down to the beach and mellow out.* **b.** to make more relaxed, agreeable, workable, etc.; soften or smooth: *Chopin really mellows me out when I'm feeling tense.* —*n.* **11.** *Slang.* a state, atmosphere, or mood of ease and gentle relaxation. [1400–50; late ME *mel(o)we,* alter. (perh. by dissimilation, in phrase *meruw fruit*) of ME *meruw,* OE *meru* soft] **—mel′low·ly,** *adv.* **—mel′low·ness,** *n.*
—Syn. 1. See **ripe. 9.** develop, mature, improve.
—Ant. 1. immature, raw, green. **3.** harsh.

Me·lo (mā′lō; *Sp.* me′lô), *n.* a city in NE Uruguay. 38,000.

me·lo·de·on (mə lō′dē ən), *n.* **1.** a small reed organ. **2.** a kind of accordion. Also, **melodion.** [1840–50, *Amer.;* < G, formed on *Melodie* melody; see ACCORDION]

me·lo·di·a (mə lō′dē ə), *n.* an 8 ft. (2.4 m) wooden flue-pipe stop organ resembling the clarabella in tone. [special use of LL *melōdia* MELODY]

me·lod·ic (mə lod′ik), *adj.* **1.** melodious. **2.** of or pertaining to melody, as distinguished from harmony and rhythm. [1815–25; < LL *melōdicus* < Gk *melōidikós.* See MELODY, -IC] **—me·lod′i·cal·ly,** *adv.*

melod′ic in′terval. See under **interval** (def. 6).

melod′ic mi′nor scale′, *Music.* See **minor scale** (def. 2).

me·lod·ics (mə lod′iks), *n.* (*used with a singular v.*) the branch of musical science concerned with the pitch and succession of tones. [1860–65; see MELODIC, -ICS]

Mel·o·die (mel′ə dē), *n.* a female given name.

me·lo·di·on (mə lō′dē ən), *n.* melodeon.

me·lo·di·ous (mə lō′dē əs), *adj.* **1.** of the nature of or characterized by melody; tuneful. **2.** producing melody; sweet-sounding; musical. [1375–1425; late ME < ML *melōdiōsus.* See MELODY, -OUS] **—me·lo′di·ous·ly,** *adv.* **—me·lo′di·ous·ness,** *n.*

mel·o·dist (mel′ə dist), *n.* a composer or a singer of melodies. [1780–90; MELOD(Y) + -IST]

mel·o·dize (mel′ə dīz′), *v.,* **-dized, -diz·ing.** —*v.t.* **1.** to make melodious. —*v.i.* **2.** to make melody. **3.** to blend melodiously. Also, *esp. Brit.,* **mel′o·dise′.** [1655–65; MELOD(Y) + -IZE] **—mel′o·diz′er,** *n.*

mel·o·dra·ma (mel′ə drä′mə, -dram′ə), *n.* **1.** a dramatic form that does not observe the laws of cause and effect and that exaggerates emotion and emphasizes plot or action at the expense of characterization. **2.** melodramatic behavior or events. **3.** (in the 17th, 18th, and early 19th centuries) a romantic dramatic composition with music interspersed. [1800–10; < F *mélodrame,* equiv. to *mélo-* (< Gk *mélos* song) + *drame* DRAMA] **—mel·o·dram·a·tist** (mel′ə dram′ə tist, -drä′mə-), *n.*

mel·o·dra·mat·ic (mel′ə drə mat′ik), *adj.* **1.** of, like, or befitting melodrama. **2.** exaggerated and emotional or sentimental; sensational or sensationalized; overdramatic. —*n.* **3. melodramatics,** melodramatic writing or behavior. [1810–20; MELODRAMA + (DRAMA)TIC] **—mel′o·dra·mat′i·cal·ly,** *adv.*

mel·o·dram·a·tize (mel′ə dram′ə tīz′, -drä′mə-), *v.t.,* **-tized, -tiz·ing. 1.** to make melodramatic. **2.** to turn (a novel, story, etc.) into a melodrama. Also, *esp. Brit.,* **mel′o·dram′a·tise′.** [1810–20; MELODRAMA + (DRAMA)TIZE]

mel·o·dy (mel′ə dē), *n., pl.* **-dies. 1.** musical sounds in agreeable succession or arrangement. **2.** *Music.* **a.** the succession of single tones in musical compositions, as distinguished from harmony and rhythm. **b.** the principal part in a harmonic composition; the air. **c.** a rhythmical succession of single tones producing a distinct musical phrase or idea. **3.** a poem suitable for singing. **4.** intonation, as of a segment of connected speech. [1250–1300; ME *melodie* < ML *melōdia* < Gk *melōidía* (choral) singing, equiv. to *mel-* (see MELIC) + *-ōid-* (see ODE) + *-ia* -Y[3]] **—mel′o·dy·less,** *adj.*
—Syn. 1. See **harmony. 2.** tune, song, descant, theme.

Mel·o·dy (mel′ə dē), *n.* a female given name.

mel·oid (mel′oid), *n.* **1.** a beetle of the family Meloidae, comprising the blister beetles. —*adj.* **2.** belonging or pertaining to the family Meloidae. [1875–80; < NL *Meloidae* name of the family, equiv. to *Melo(ē)* type genus + *-idae* -ID[2]]

mel·on (mel′ən), *n.* **1.** the fruit of any of various plants of the gourd family, as the muskmelon or watermelon. **2.** medium crimson or deep pink. **3.** the visible upper portion of the head of a surfacing whale or dolphin, including the beak, eyes, and blowhole. **4.** *Informal.* **a.** a large extra dividend, often in the form of stock, to be distributed to stockholders: *Profits zoomed so in the last quarter that the corporation cut a nice melon.* **b.** any windfall of money to be divided among specified participants. [1350–1400; ME < LL *mēlōn-* (s. of *mēlō*), short for *mēlopepō* < Gk *mēlopépōn* apple-shaped melon, equiv. to *mêlo(n)* apple + *pépōn* PEPO]

mel·on-bulb (mel′ən bulb′), *n. Furniture.* a large, bulbous turning, sometimes with surface carving, found esp. on the legs and posts of Elizabethan and Jacobean furniture.

mel′on foot′, *Eng. Furniture.* a bun foot having vertical channels.

mel′on pear′, pepino (def. 2).

mel′on seed′, a small, broad, shallow boat for sailing or rowing, formerly used by hunters in various bays and marshes along the coast of New Jersey.

mel′on shrub′, pepino (def. 2).

mel·os (mel′os, -ōs, mē′los, -lōs), *n.* the succession of musical tones constituting a melody. [1730–40; < Gk *mélos* song, tune]

Me·los (mē′los, -lōs, mel′os, -ōs; *Gk.* mē′lôs), *n.* a Greek island in the Cyclades, in the SW Aegean: statue, *Venus de Milo,* found here 1820. 4499; 51 sq. mi. (132 sq. km). Also, **Milo, Milos. —Me·li·an** (mē′lē ən, mēl′yən), *adj., n.*

Mel·pom·e·ne (mel pom′ə nē′), *n. Class. Myth.* the Muse of tragedy. [< L *Melpomenē* < Gk *Melpoménē* special use of fem. of prp. of *mélpesthai* to sing]

Mel·rose (mel′rōz′), *n.* **1.** a city in E Massachusetts, near Boston. 30,055. **2.** a village in SE Scotland, on the Tweed River: ruins of a famous abbey.

Mel′rose Park′, a city in NE Illinois, near Chicago. 20,735.

melt[1] (melt), *v.,* **melt·ed, melt·ed** or **mol·ten, melt·ing,** *n.* —*v.i.* **1.** to become liquefied by warmth or heat, as ice, snow, butter, or metal. **2.** to become liquid; dissolve: *Let the cough drop melt in your mouth.* **3.** to pass, dwindle, or fade gradually (often fol. by *away*): *His fortune slowly melted away.* **4.** to pass, change, or blend gradually (often fol. by *into*): *Night melted into day.* **5.** to become softened in feeling by pity, sympathy, love, or the like: *The tyrant's heart would not melt.* **6.** *Obs.* to be subdued or overwhelmed by sorrow, dismay, etc. —*v.t.* **7.** to reduce to a liquid state by warmth or heat; fuse: *Fire melts ice.* **8.** to cause to pass away or fade. **9.** to cause to pass, change, or blend gradually. **10.** to soften in feeling, as a person or the heart. —*n.* **11.** the act or process of melting; state of being melted. **12.** something that is melted. **13.** a quantity melted at one time. **14.** a sandwich or other dish topped with melted cheese: *a tuna melt.* [bef. 900; ME *melten,* OE *meltan* (intrans.), *m(i)elten* (transit.) to melt, digest; c. ON *melta* to digest, Gk *méldein* to melt] **—melt′a·ble,** *adj.* **—melt′a·bil′i·ty,** *n.* **—melt′ing·ly,** *adv.* **—melt′ing·ness,** *n.*
—Syn. 1. MELT, DISSOLVE, FUSE, THAW imply reducing a solid substance to a liquid state. To MELT is to bring a solid to a liquid condition by the agency of heat: *to melt butter.* DISSOLVE, though sometimes used interchangeably with MELT, applies to a different process, depending upon the fact that certain solids, placed in certain liquids, distribute their particles throughout the liquids: *A greater number of solids can be dissolved in water and in alcohol than in any other liquids.* To FUSE is to subject a solid (usually a metal) to a very high temperature; it applies esp. to melting or blending metals together: *Bell metal is made by fusing copper and tin.* To THAW is to restore a frozen substance to its normal (liquid, semiliquid, or more soft and pliable) state by raising its temperature above the freezing point: *Sunshine will thaw ice in a lake.* **4.** dwindle. **10.** gentle, mollify, relax.

melt[2] (melt), *n.* the spleen, esp. that of a cow, pig, etc. Also, **milt.** [1575–85; var. of MILT]

melt·age (mel′tij), *n.* the amount melted or the result of melting. [MELT[1] + -AGE]

melt·down (melt′doun′), *n.* the melting of a significant portion of a nuclear-reactor core due to inadequate cooling of the fuel elements, a condition that could lead to the escape of radiation. [1960–65; n. use of v. phrase *melt down*]

melt·er (mel′tər), *n.* **1.** a person or thing that melts. **2.** a person in charge of a steelmaking furnace. [1525–35; MELT[1] + -ER[1]]

melt′ing point′, *Physical Chem.* the temperature at which a solid substance melts or fuses. [1835–45]

melt′ing pot′, 1. a pot in which metals or other substances are melted or fused. **2.** a country, locality, or situation in which a blending of races, peoples, or cultures is taking place. [1375–1425; late ME]

mel·ton (mel′tn), *n.* a heavily fulled cloth, often of wool, tightly constructed and finished with a smooth face concealing the weave, used for overcoats, hunting jackets, etc. Also called **mel′ton cloth′.** [1815–25; after *Melton* Mowbray, town in Leicestershire, England]

melt·wa·ter (melt′wô′tər, -wot′ər), *n.* water from melted snow or ice. [1930–35; MELT[1] + WATER]

Me·lun (mə lœN′), *n.* a city in and the capital of Seine-et-Marne, in N France. 38,996.

Me·lun·geon (mə lun′jən), *n.* a member of a people of mixed white, black, and American Indian ancestry living in the southern Appalachians.

Mel·ville (mel′vil), *n.* **1. Herman,** 1819–91, U.S. novelist. **2. Lake,** a saltwater lake on the E coast of Labrador, Newfoundland, in E Canada, separated from the Atlantic Ocean by a narrow inlet: the mouth of the Churchill River is at its W end. ab. 1133 sq. mi. (2935 sq. km). **3.** a male given name. **—Mel·vil′le·an,** *adj., n.*

Mel′ville Is′land, an island in the Arctic Ocean, N of Canada, belonging to Canada. 200 mi. (320 km) long; 130 mi. (210 km) wide.

Mel′ville Penin′sula, a peninsula in N Canada, SE of the Gulf of Boothia. 250 mi. (405 km) long.

Mel·vin (mel′vin), *n.* a male given name. Also, **Mel′·vyn.**

Mel·vin·dale (mel′vin dāl′), *n.* a city in SE Michigan, near Detroit. 12,322.

mem (mem), *n.* **1.** the thirteenth letter of the Hebrew alphabet. **2.** the consonant sound represented by this letter. [1895–1900; < Heb *mēm,* akin to *mayim* water]

mem., 1. member. **2.** memoir. **3.** memorandum. **4.** memorial.

mem·ber (mem′bər), *n.* **1.** a person, animal, plant, group, etc., that is part of a society, party, community, taxon, or other body. **2.** *Govt.* **a.** a member of Congress, esp. of the House of Representatives. **b.** a member of the British Parliament, esp. of the House of Commons. **c.**

any member of a legislative body. **3.** a part or organ of an animal body; a limb, as a leg, arm, or wing. **4.** *Bot.* a structural entity of a plant body. **5.** the penis. **6.** a constituent part of any structural or composite whole, as a subordinate architectural feature of a building. **7.** *Math.* **a.** either side of an equation. **b.** an element of a set. **8.** *Geol.* a stratigraphic unit recognized within a formation, and mapped as such. —*adj.* **9.** being a member of or having membership in an association, organization, etc.: *member countries of the United Nations.* [1250–1300; ME *membre* < OF < L *membrum*] —**mem′ber·less,** *adj.*
—**Syn. 6.** element, portion.

mem·bered (mem′bərd), *adj.* having members, esp. of a specified number or kind (often used in combination): *a four-membered body.* [1375–1425; late ME. See MEMBER, -ED[3]]

Mem′ber of the Wed′ding, The, a novel (1946) and play (1950) by Carson McCullers.

mem·ber·ship (mem′bər ship′), *n.* **1.** the state of being a member, as of a society or club. **2.** the status of a member. **3.** the total number of members belonging to an organization, society, etc. [1640–50; MEMBER + -SHIP]

mem·brane (mem′brān), *n.* **1.** *Anat.* a thin, pliable sheet or layer of animal or vegetable tissue, serving to line an organ, connect parts, etc. **2.** *Cell Biol.* the thin, limiting covering of a cell or cell part. [1375–1425; late ME; ME *membraan* parchment < L *membrāna.* See MEMBER, -AN] —**mem′brane·less,** *adj.*

mem′brane bone′, a bone that develops from membranous tissue. Cf. **cartilage bone.** [1875–80]

mem·bra·no·phone (mem brā′nə fōn′), *n.* any musical instrument, as a drum, in which the sound is produced by striking, rubbing, or blowing against a membrane stretched over a frame. [1935–40; MEMBRANE + -O- + -PHONE] —**mem·bra·no·phon·ic** (mem brā′nə-fon′ik), *adj.*

mem·bra·nous (mem′brə nəs), *adj.* **1.** consisting of, of the nature of, or resembling membrane. **2.** characterized by the formation of a membrane. Also, **mem·bra·na·ceous** (mem′brə nā′shəs). [1590–1600; MEMBRANE + -OUS; cf. F *membraneux*] —**mem′bra·nous·ly,** *adv.*

mem′branous lab′yrinth. See under **labyrinth** (def. 6a). [1865–70]

Me·mel (mā′məl, mem′əl), *n.* **1.** German name of **Klaipeda. 2.** the lower course of the Niemen River. Cf. **Niemen.**

me·men·to (mə men′tō), *n., pl.* **-tos, -toes. 1.** an object or item that serves to remind one of a person, past event, etc.; keepsake; souvenir. **2.** anything serving as a reminder or warning. **3.** (*cap., italics*) *Rom. Cath. Ch.* either of two prayers in the canon of the Mass, one for persons living and the other for persons dead. [1350–1400; ME < L *mementō,* impv. of *meminisse* to remember]
—**Usage.** MEMENTO is sometimes spelled MOMENTO, perhaps by association with *moment.* The word is actually related to *remember.* One of its earliest meanings was "something that serves to warn." The meaning "souvenir" is a recent development: *The stone animal carvings are mementos of our trip to Victoria.* MOMENTO is considered by many to be a misspelling, but it occurs so frequently in edited writing that some regard it as a variant spelling rather than an error.

me·men·to mo·ri (mə men′tō môr′ī, mōr′ī, môr′ē, mōr′ē; *for 1 also Lat.* me men′tō mō′rē), *pl.* **memento mori** for 2. **1.** (*italics*) *Latin.* remember that you must die. **2.** an object, as a skull, serving as a reminder of death or mortality. [1585–95; < L *mementō morī*]

Mem·ling (mem′ling), *n.* **Hans** (häns), c1430–94?, German painter of the Flemish school. Also, **Mem·linc** (mem′lingk).

Mem·non (mem′non), *n.* **1. Colossus of,** (in ancient Egypt) a colossal statue near Thebes said to produce a musical sound when the rays of the early morning sun struck it. Cf. **Vocal Memnon. 2.** *Class. Myth.* an Ethiopian king slain by Achilles in the Trojan War. —**Mem·no·ni·an** (mem nō′nē ən), *adj.*

Mem·no·ni·a (mem nō′nē ə), *n.* an area in the southern hemisphere of Mars, appearing as a light region when viewed telescopically from the earth.

mem·o (mem′ō), *n., pl.* **mem·os.** memorandum. [by shortening; see -O]

mem·oir (mem′wär, -wôr), *n.* **1.** a record of events written by a person having intimate knowledge of them and based on personal observation. **2.** Usually, **memoirs. a.** an account of one's personal life and experiences; autobiography. **b.** the published record of the proceedings of a group or organization, as of a learned society. **3.** a biography or biographical sketch. [1560–70; < F *mémoire* < L *memoria;* see MEMORY]
—**Syn. 2a.** journal, recollections, reminiscences.

mem·oir·ist (mem′wär ist, -wôr-), *n.* a person who writes memoirs. [1760–70; MEMOIR + -IST]

mem·o·ra·bil·i·a (mem′ər ə bil′ē ə, -bil′yə), *n.pl., sing.* **-o·rab·i·le** (-ə rab′ə lē). **1.** mementos; souvenirs. **2.** matters or events worthy to be remembered; points worthy of note. [1800–10; n. use of L *memorābilia* things to be remembered, neut. pl. of *memorābilis* MEMORABLE]

mem·o·ra·bil·i·ast (mem′ər ə bil′ē ast′), *n.* a person who collects mementos or souvenirs, as postcards or playbills. [MEMORABILI(A) + *-ast,* taken as var. of -IST attached to a s. ending in *-i-,* on the model of ENTHUSIAST]

mem·o·ra·ble (mem′ər ə bəl), *adj.* **1.** worth remembering; notable: *a memorable speech.* **2.** easily remembered. [1400–50; late ME < L *memorābilis* worth mentioning, equiv. to *memorā(re)* to mention + *-bilis* -BLE] —**mem′o·ra·bil′i·ty, mem′o·ra·ble·ness,** *n.* —**mem′o·ra·bly,** *adv.*
—**Syn. 1.** noteworthy, impressive, celebrated.

mem·o·ran·dum (mem′ə ran′dəm), *n., pl.* **-dums, -da** (-də). **1.** a short note designating something to be remembered, esp. something to be done or acted upon in the future; reminder. **2.** a record or written statement of something. **3.** an informal message, esp. one sent between two or more employees of the same company, concerning company business: *an interoffice memorandum.* **4.** *Law.* a writing, usually informal, containing the terms of a transaction. **5.** *Diplomacy.* a summary of the state of an issue, the reasons for a decision agreed on, etc. **6.** a document transferring title to goods but authorizing the return of the goods to the seller at the option of the buyer. [1400–50; late ME < L: something to be noted, n. use of neut. of *memorandus,* gerundive of *memorāre* to mention, tell]

me·mo·ri·al (mə môr′ē əl, -mōr′-), *n.* **1.** something designed to preserve the memory of a person, event, etc., as a monument or a holiday. **2.** a written statement of facts presented to a sovereign, a legislative body, etc., as the ground of, or expressed in the form of, a petition or remonstrance. —*adj.* **3.** preserving the memory of a person or thing; commemorative: *memorial services.* **4.** of or pertaining to the memory. [1350–1400; ME < LL *memoriāle,* n. use of neut. of L *memoriālis* for or containing memoranda. See MEMORY, -AL[1]] —**me·mo′ri·al·ly,** *adv.*

Memo′rial Day′, 1. Also called **Decoration Day.** a day, May 30, set aside in most states of the U.S. for observances in memory of dead members of the armed forces of all wars: now officially observed on the last Monday in May. **2.** any of several days, as April 26, May 10, or June 3, similarly observed in various Southern states. [1865–70, *Amer.*]

me·mo·ri·al·ist (mə môr′ē ə list, -mōr′-), *n.* **1.** a person who writes memorials. **2.** a person who writes memoirs. [1700–10; MEMORIAL + -IST]

me·mo·ri·al·ize (mə môr′ē ə līz′, -mōr′-), *v.t.,* **-ized, -iz·ing. 1.** to commemorate. **2.** to present a memorial to. Also, *esp. Brit.,* **me·mo′ri·al·ise′.** [1790–1800; MEMORIAL + -IZE] —**me·mo′ri·al·i·za′tion,** *n.* —**me·mo′ri·al·iz′er,** *n.*

memo′rial park′, cemetery. [1915–20]

mem·o·ried (mem′ə rēd), *adj.* **1.** having a memory (usually used in combination): *short-memoried; long-memoried.* **2.** filled with memories: *a quiet, memoried town.* [1565–75; MEMORY + -ED[3]]

mem·o·rist (mem′ər ist), *n.* a person who has a remarkably retentive memory. [1675–85; MEMOR(Y) + -IST]

me·mo·ri·ter (mə môr′i tər, -ter, -mōr′-), *adv.* **1.** by heart; by memory. —*adj.* **2.** involving or requiring memorization: *the memoriter aspects of a college course.* [1605–15; < L, equiv. to *memori-* (s. of *memor*) mindful of + *-ter* adv. suffix]

mem·o·rize (mem′ə rīz′), *v.,* **-rized, -riz·ing.** —*v.t.* **1.** to commit to memory; learn by heart: *to memorize a poem.* —*v.i.* **2.** to learn by heart: *I've always been able to memorize easily.* Also, *esp. Brit.,* **mem′o·rise′.** [1585–95; MEMOR(Y) + -IZE] —**mem′o·riz′a·ble,** *adj.* —**mem′o·ri·za′tion,** *n.* —**mem′o·riz′er,** *n.*

mem·o·ry (mem′ə rē), *n., pl.* **-ries. 1.** the mental capacity or faculty of retaining and reviving facts, events, impressions, etc., or of recalling or recognizing previous experiences. **2.** this faculty as possessed by a particular individual: *to have a good memory.* **3.** the act or fact of retaining and recalling impressions, facts, etc.; remembrance; recollection: *to draw from memory.* **4.** the length of time over which recollection extends: *a time within the memory of living persons.* **5.** a mental impression retained; a recollection: *one's earliest memories.* **6.** the reputation of a person or thing, esp. after death; fame: *a ruler of beloved memory.* **7.** the state or fact of being remembered. **8.** a person, thing, event, fact, etc., remembered. **9.** commemorative remembrance; commemoration: *a monument in memory of Columbus.* **10.** the ability of certain materials to return to an original shape after deformation. **11.** Also called **computer memory, storage.** *Computers.* **a.** the capacity of a computer to store information subject to recall. **b.** the components of the computer in which such information is stored. **12.** *Rhet.* the step in the classical preparation of a speech in which the wording is memorized. **13.** *Cards.* concentration (def. 7). [1275–1325; ME *memorie* < L *memoria,* equiv. to *memor* mindful, remembering + *-ia* -Y[3]]

mem′ory bank′, 1. the complete records, archives, or the like of an organization, country, etc. **2.** the total of a person's memories or recollections. **3.** See **data bank** (def. 1). [1950–55]

mem′ory cell′, *Immunol.* any small, long-lived lymphocyte that has previously encountered a given antigen and that on reexposure to the same antigen rapidly initiates the immune response **(memory T cell)** or proliferates and produces large amounts of specific antibody **(memory B cell):** the agent of lasting immunity.

mem′ory lane′, the memory of one's past life likened to a road down which one may travel: *The class reunion was a trip down memory lane.* [1950–55]

mem′ory trace′, *Psychol.* engram. [1920–25]

mem′ory verse′, a verse or passage from the Bible to be memorized, esp. by members of a Sunday school.

Mem·phi·an (mem′fē ən), *n.* **1.** a native or inhabitant of the ancient Egyptian city of Memphis. **2.** Egyptian (def. 3). **3.** a native or resident of Memphis, Tennessee. [1585–95; MEMPHI(S) + -AN]

Mem·phis (mem′fis), *n.* **1.** a port in SW Tennessee, on the Mississippi. 646,356. **2.** a ruined city in Lower Egypt, on the Nile, S of Cairo: the ancient capital of Egypt.

Mem·phis (mem′fis), *n.* **1.** a group of international designers and architects, formed in the 1980's and based in Milan, whose work is characterized by the use of bold colors, geometric shapes, and unconventional, often playful, designs. —*adj.* **2.** of or pertaining to this group or its style of design. [the name was allegedly suggested to Ettore Sottsass, one of the group's founders, by the Bob Dylan song "Stuck Inside of Mobile with the Memphis Blues Again" on the evening of December 11, 1980]

Mem·phite (mem′fīt), *adj.* **1.** Also, **Mem·phit·ic** (mem fit′ik). of or pertaining to the ancient Egyptian city of Memphis. —*n.* **2.** Memphian (def. 1). [<< Gk *Memphítēs* inhabitant of Memphis; see -ITE[1]]

Mem·phre·ma·gog (mem′frē mā′gog), *n.* **Lake,** a lake on the boundary between the U.S. and Canada, between N Vermont and S Quebec. 30 mi. (48 km) long.

mem·sa·hib (mem′sä′ib, -ēb), *n.* (formerly, in India) a term of respect for a married European woman. [1855–60; < Hindi, equiv. to *mem* (< E MA'AM) + *sāhib* master (< Ar *ṣāḥib*)]

men (men), *n.* pl. of **man.**

men-, var. of **meno-** before a vowel: *menarche.*

men·ace (men′is), *n., v.,* **-aced, -ac·ing.** —*n.* **1.** something that threatens to cause evil, harm, injury, etc.; a threat: *Air pollution is a menace to health.* **2.** a person whose actions, attitudes, or ideas are considered dangerous or harmful: *When he gets behind the wheel of a car, he's a real menace.* **3.** an extremely annoying person. —*v.t.* **4.** to utter or direct a threat against; threaten. **5.** to serve as a probable threat to; imperil. —*v.i.* **6.** to express or serve as a threat. [1250–1300; ME < MF < L *minācia,* equiv. to *mindruāc-* (s. of *mindruāx*) jutting out, threatening + *-ia* -IA] —**men′ac·er,** *n.* —**men′ac·ing·ly,** *adv.*

men·ac·me (mə nak′mē, mē nak′-), *n. Physiol.* the part of a female's life during which menstruation occurs. [MEN- + ACME]

me·nad (mē′nad), *n.* maenad.

men·a·di·one (men′ə dī′ōn), *n. Pharm.* a synthetic yellow crystalline powder, $C_{11}H_8O_2$, insoluble in water, used as a vitamin K supplement. Also called **vitamin K_3.** [1940–45; ME(THYL) + NA(PHTHALENE) + DI-[1] + -ONE]

Me·na·do (me nä′dō), *n.* a seaport on NE Sulawesi, in NE Indonesia. 169,684. Also, **Manado.**

mé·nage (mā näzh′; *Fr.* mā nazh′), *n., pl.* **-nages** (-nä′zhiz; *Fr.* -nazh′). **1.** a domestic establishment; household. **2.** housekeeping. Also, **me·nage′.** [1250–1300; ME < F << VL **mansiōnāticum.* See MANSION, -AGE]

mé·nage à trois (mā näzh′ ä trwä′; *Fr.* mā nazh A trwa′), a domestic arrangement in which three people having sexual relations occupy the same household. [< F: household of three]

me·nag·er·ie (mə naj′ə rē, -nazh′-), *n.* **1.** a collection of wild or unusual animals, esp. for exhibition. **2.** a place where they are kept or exhibited. **3.** an unusual and varied group of people. [1705–15; < F: lit., housekeeping. See MÉNAGE, -ERY]

Men′ai Strait′ (men′ī), a strait between Anglesey Island and the mainland of NW Wales. 14 mi. (23 km) long.

Me·nam (me näm′), *n.* a former name of **Chao Phraya.**

Me·nan·der (mə nan′dər), *n.* 342?–291 B.C., Greek writer of comedies.

men·ar·che (mə när′kē, me-), *n. Physiol.* the first menstrual period; the establishment of menstruation. [1895–1900; MEN- + *archē* beginning] —**men·ar′che·al, men·ar′chi·al,** *adj.*

Me·nash·a (mə nash′ə), *n.* a city in E Wisconsin. 14,728.

me·nat (mā′nät), *n.* an amulet worn by certain Egyptians in ancient times to secure divine protection and to ensure fertility. [vocalization of Egyptian *mnyt*]

men·a·zon (men′ə zon′), *n. Chem.* a colorless, crystalline compound, $C_6H_{12}N_5O_2PS_2$, used as a systemic insecticide, esp. for control of aphids. [1960–65; ME(THYL) + (AMI)N(O)- + (TRI)AZ(INE) + (THI)ON(ATE)]

men-chil·dren (men′chil′drən, -drin), *n.* pl. of **man-child.** Also, **men′chil′dren.**

Men·ci·us (men′shē əs), *n.* c380–289 B.C., Chinese philosopher. Also called **Mengtzu, Mengtse, Mengtze, Mengzi.**

Menck·en (meng′kən), *n.* **H(enry) L(ouis),** 1880–1956, U.S. writer, editor, and critic. —**Menc·ke·ni·an** (meng kē′nē ən), *adj., n.*

mend (mend), *v.t.* **1.** to make (something broken, worn, torn, or otherwise damaged) whole, sound, or usable by repairing: *to mend old clothes; to mend a broken toy.* **2.** to remove or correct defects or errors in. **3.** to set right; make better; improve: *to mend matters.* —*v.i.* **4.** to progress toward recovery, as a sick person. **5.** (of broken bones) to grow back together; knit. **6.** to improve, as conditions or affairs. **7. mend sail,** *Naut.* to refurl sails that have been badly furled. Also, **mend the furl.** —*n.* **8.** the act of mending; repair or improvement. **9.** a mended place. **10. on the mend, a.** recovering from an illness. **b.** improving in general, as a state of affairs: *The breach between father and son is on the mend.* [1150–1200; ME *menden,* aph. var. of AMEND] —**mend′a·ble,** *adj.*
—**Syn. 1.** fix, restore, retouch. MEND, DARN, PATCH mean to repair something and thus renew its usefulness. MEND is a general expression that emphasizes the idea of making whole something damaged: *to mend a broken dish, a tear in an apron.* DARN and PATCH are more specific, referring particularly to repairing holes or rents. To DARN is to repair by means of stitches interwoven with one another: *to darn stockings.* To PATCH is to cover

a hole or rent (usually) with a piece or pieces of similar material and to secure the edges of these; it implies a more temporary or makeshift repair than the others: *to patch the knees of trousers, a rubber tire.* **2.** rectify, amend, emend. **3.** ameliorate, meliorate. **4.** heal, recover, amend. —**Ant. 1.** ruin, destroy, **4.** die, sicken.

men·da·cious (men dā′shəs), *adj.* **1.** telling lies, esp. habitually; dishonest; lying; untruthful: *a mendacious person.* **2.** false or untrue: *a mendacious report.* [1610–20; < L *mendāci-* (see MENDACITY) + -OUS] —**men·da′cious·ly,** *adv.* —**men·da′cious·ness,** *n.*
—**Ant. 1, 2.** veracious.

men·dac·i·ty (men das′i tē), *n., pl.* **-ties** for 2. **1.** the quality of being mendacious; untruthfulness; tendency to lie. **2.** an instance of lying; falsehood. [1640–50; < LL *mendācitās* falsehood, equiv. to L *mendāci-* (s. of *mendāx*) given to lying, false + *-tās* -TY[2]]
—**Syn. 1, 2.** deception, lie, untruth, deceit.

Men·de (men′dē), *n., pl.* **-des,** (*esp. collectively*) **-de** for 1. **1.** a member of a people living in Sierra Leone and Liberia. **2.** a Niger-Congo language of the Mande branch spoken by the Mende people.

Men·del (men′dl), *n.* **1. Gre·gor Jo·hann** (greg′ər yō′hän; *Ger.* grā′gôr yō′hän), 1822–84, Austrian monk and botanist. **2.** a male given name, form of **Mandel.**

Men·de·le·ev (men′dl ā′əf; *Russ.* myin dyi lye′yef), *n.* **Dmi·tri I·va·no·vich** (dmyē′trē ē vä′nə vyich), 1834–1907, Russian chemist: helped develop the periodic law. Also, **Men′de·ley′ev, Men′de·lej′eff.**

Men′dele′ev's law′, *Chem.* See **periodic law** (def. 2).

men·de·le·vi·um (men′dl ē′vē əm), *n. Chem., Physics.* a transuranic element. *Symbol:* Md, Mv; *at. no.:* 101. [1950–55; named after D. I. MENDELEEV; see -IUM]

Men·de·li·an (men dē′lē ən, -dēl′yən), *adj.* **1.** of or pertaining to Gregor Mendel or to his laws of heredity. —*n.* **2.** a follower of Gregor Mendel; a person who accepts Mendelism. [1900–05; MENDEL + -IAN]

Men·del·ism (men′dl iz′əm), *n.* the theories of heredity advanced by Gregor Mendel. Also, **Men·de·li·an·ism** (men dē′lē ə niz′əm, -dēl′yə-). [1900–05; MENDEL + -ISM]

Men′del's first′ law′, *Genetics.* See **law of segregation.**

Men′del's law′, *Genetics.* **1.** See **law of segregation. 2.** See **law of independent assortment.** [1900–05]

Men·del·sohn (men′dl sən; *Ger.* men′dəl zōn′), *n.* **E·rich** (ā′RIKH), 1887–1953, German architect in England and in the U.S.

Men′del's sec′ond law′, *Genetics.* See **law of independent assortment.**

Men·dels·sohn (men′dl sən; *Ger.* men′dəl zōn′), *n.* **1. Fe·lix** (fē′liks; *Ger.* fā′liks), (*Jacob Ludwig Felix Mendelssohn-Bartholdy*), 1809–47, German composer. **2.** his grandfather, **Mo·ses** (mō′ziz, -zis; *Ger.* mō′zes), 1729–86, German philosopher.

mend·er (men′dər), *n.* **1.** a person or thing that mends. **2.** a piece of sheet metal that has been imperfectly tinned but that may be retinned to an acceptable standard. [1350–1400; ME; see MEND, -ER[1]]

Men·de·res (men′de res′), *n.* **1. Ad·nan** (äd′nän), 1899–1961, Turkish political leader: premier 1950–60. **2.** Ancient, **Maeander, Meander.** a river in W Asia Minor, flowing into the Aegean near Samos. 240 mi. (385 km) long. **3.** Ancient, **Scamander.** a river in NW Asia Minor, flowing across the Trojan plain into the Dardanelles. 60 mi. (97 km) long.

Men·dès-France (men′dis frans′, -fräns′; *Fr.* mäN-des fRäNs′), *n.* **Pierre** (pyeR), 1907–1982, French statesman and economist: premier 1954–55.

men·di·can·cy (men′di kən sē), *n.* **1.** the practice of begging, as for alms. **2.** the state or condition of being a beggar. [1780–90; MENDIC(ANT) + -ANCY]

men·di·cant (men′di kənt), *adj.* **1.** begging; practicing begging; living on alms. **2.** pertaining to or characteristic of a beggar. —*n.* **3.** a person who lives by begging; beggar. **4.** a member of any of several orders of friars that originally forbade ownership of property, subsisting mostly on alms. [1425–75; late ME < L *mendicant-* (s. of *mendicāns*), prp. of *mendicāre* to beg, equiv. to *mendīc(us)* beggarly, needy + *-ant-* -ANT]

men·dic·i·ty (men dis′i tē), *n.* mendicancy. [1350–1400; ME *mendicite* < L *mendicitās* beggary, equiv. to *mendic(us)* needy, beggarly + *-itās* -ITY]

mend·ing (men′ding), *n.* **1.** the act of a person or thing that mends. **2.** articles, esp. clothes, to be mended: *Grandmother always kept her mending in this wicker basket.* [1250–1300; ME; see MEND, -ING[1]]

Men·do·ci·no (men′də sē′nō), *n.* **Cape,** a cape in NW California: the westernmost point in California.

Men·do·ta (men dō′tə), *n.* **Lake,** a lake in S Wisconsin, in N Madison. ab. 15 sq. mi. (39 sq. km).

Men·do·za (men dō′zə; *Sp.* men dô′sä *or, for 1,* -thä), *n.* **1. Pe·dro de** (pe′thRô the), 1487–1537, Spanish soldier and explorer: founder of the first colony of Buenos Aires 1536?. **2.** a city in W central Argentina. 596,796.

me·nel (mə nel′), *n.* manille.

Men·e·la·us (men′l ā′əs), *n. Class. Myth.* a king of Sparta, the husband of Helen and brother of Agamemnon, to whom he appealed for an army against Troy in order to recover Helen from her abductor, Paris.

CONCISE ETYMOLOGY KEY: <, descended or borrowed from; >, whence; b., blend of, blended; c., cognate with; cf., compare; deriv., derivative; equiv., equivalent; imit., imitative; obl., oblique; r., replacing; s., stem; sp., spelling, spelled; resp., respelling, respelled; trans., translation; ?, origin unknown; *, unattested; ‡, probably earlier than. See the full key inside the front cover.

Men·e·lik II (men′l ik), 1844–1913, emperor of Ethiopia 1889–1913.

Me·nem (men′əm), *n.* **Carlos Saul,** born 1931, Argentine political leader: president since 1989.

me·ne, me·ne, tek·el, u·phar·sin (mē′nē, mē′nē, tek′əl, yōō fär′sin), *Aramaic.* numbered, numbered, weighed, divided: the miraculous writing on the wall interpreted by Daniel as foretelling the destruction of Belshazzar and his kingdom. Dan. 5:25–31.

Me·nén·dez de A·vi·lés (me nen′deth the ä′vē-les′), **Pe·dro** (pe′thRô), 1519–74, Spanish admiral and colonizer: founder of St. Augustine, Florida 1565.

Me·ne·ptah (me′nep tä′), *n.* Merneptah.

Me·nes (mē′nēz), *n.* fl. c3200 B.C., traditionally the unifier and 1st king of Egypt: founder of the 1st dynasty. Cf. **Narmer.**

men·folk (men′fōk′), *n.pl.* men, esp. those belonging to a family or community: *The menfolk are all working in the fields.* Also, **men′folks′.** [MEN + FOLK]

M.Eng., Master of Engineering.

Meng·er (meng′ər), *n.* **Karl** (kärl), 1840–1921, Austrian economist.

Men·gis·tu Hai·le Ma·ri·am (meng gis′tōō hī′lē mär′ē əm), born 1937, Ethiopian political leader: head of state 1977–87; president 1987–91.

Meng·zi (mœng′zē′), *n. Pinyin.* **1.** Mencius. **2.** a city in SE Yunnan province, in S China. 50,000. Also, *Older Spellings,* **Meng·tse, Meng·tze** (mung′dzu′); *Wade-Giles,* **Meng·tzu** (mung′dzu′).

men·ha·den (men hād′n), *n., pl.* **-den.** any marine clupeid fish of the genus *Brevoortia,* esp. *B. tyrannus,* resembling a shad but with a more compressed body, common along the eastern coast of the U.S., and used for making oil and fertilizer. [1635–45, *Amer.*; perh. < Narragansett (E sp.) *munnawhatteaûg,* influenced by E dial. *poghaden;* cf. POGY[1]]

men·hir (men′hir), *n. Archaeol.* an upright monumental stone standing either alone or with others, as in an alignment, found chiefly in Cornwall and Brittany. [1830–40; < Breton phrase *men hir,* equiv. to *men* stone + *hir* long]

me·ni·al (mē′nē əl, mēn′yəl), *adj.* **1.** lowly and sometimes degrading: *menial work.* **2.** servile; submissive: *menial attitudes.* **3.** pertaining to or suitable for domestic servants; humble: *menial furnishings.* —*n.* **4.** a domestic servant. **5.** a servile person. [1350–1400; ME *meynyal* < AF *me(i)nial.* See MEINY, -AL[1]] —**me′ni·al·ly,** *adv.* —**Syn. 2.** fawning. See **servile. 4.** attendant, underling, hireling, lackey.

Mé·nière's′ syn′drome (mān yârz′), *Pathol.* a disease of the labyrinth of the ear, characterized by deafness, ringing in the ears, dizziness, and nausea. Also called **Ménière's′ disease′.** [1935–40; named after Prosper *Ménière* (1799–1862), French physician]

me·nin·ges (mi nin′jēz), *n.pl., sing.* **me·ninx** (mē′ningks). *Anat.* the three membranes covering the brain and spinal cord. Cf. **arachnoid** (def. 6), **dura mater, pia mater.** [1610–20; < NL < Gk *mēninges,* pl. of *mēninx* membrane] —**me·nin·ge·al** (mi nin′jē əl), *adj.*

me·nin·gi·o·ma (mə nin′jē ō′mə), *n., pl.* **-mas, -ma·ta** (-mə tə). *Pathol.* a hard, encapsulated tumor that grows slowly along the meninges. [1920–25; shortening of *meningothelioma,* equiv. to MENING(ES) + -O- + (EN-DO)THELIOMA]

men·in·gi·tis (men′in jī′tis), *n. Pathol.* inflammation of the meninges, esp. of the pia mater and arachnoid, caused by a bacterial or viral infection and characterized by high fever, severe headache, and stiff neck or back muscles. [1820–30; < NL; see MENINGES, -ITIS] —**men·in·git·ic** (men′in jit′ik), *adj.*

me·nin·go·cele (mə ning′gə sēl′), *n. Pathol.* a protrusion of the meninges through an opening in the skull or spinal column, forming a bulge or sac filled with cerebrospinal fluid. [1865–70; MENING(ES) + -O- + -CELE[1]]

me·nin·go·coc·cus (mə ning′gō kok′əs), *n., pl.* **-coc·ci** (-kok′sī, -sē). a reniform or spherical bacterium, *Neisseria meningitidis,* that causes cerebrospinal meningitis. [1890–95; < NL; see MENINGES, -O-, COCCUS] —**me·nin′go·coc′cal, me·nin·go·coc·cic** (mə ning′gō-kok′ik, -kok′sik), *adj.*

Me·nip·pe (mə nip′ē), *n. Class. Myth.* a daughter of Orion who, with her sister Metioche, offered herself as a sacrifice to end a plague in Boeotia.

men·is·cec·to·my (men′ə sek′tə mē), *n., pl.* **-mies.** the surgical excision of a meniscus, as of the knee joint. [MENISC(US) + -ECTOMY]

me·nis·co·cy·to·sis (mə nis′kō sī tō′sis), *n. Pathol.* See **sickle cell anemia.** [MENISC(US) + -O- + CYTOSIS]

me·nis·cus (mi nis′kəs), *n., pl.* **-nis·ci** (-nis′ī, -nis′kī, -kē), **-nis·cus·es. 1.** a crescent or a crescent-shaped body. **2.** the convex or concave upper surface of a column of liquid, the curvature of which is caused by surface tension. **3.** *Optics.* a lens with a crescent-shaped section; a concavo-convex or convexo-concave lens. See diag. under **lens. 4.** *Anat.* a disk of cartilage between the articulating ends of the bones in a joint. [1685–95; < NL < Gk *mēnískos* crescent, dim. of *mḗnē* moon] —**me·nis·coid** (mi nis′koid), *adj.*

menisci (def. 2)
A, concave;
B, convex

A B

Men·ku·re (men kōō′re), *n.* Mycerinus.

Men′lo Park′ (men′lō), **1.** a city in W California, near San Francisco. 25,673. **2.** a village in central New Jersey, SE of Plainfield: site of Thomas Edison's laboratory, 1876–87.

Men·ning·er (men′ing ər), *n.* **Charles Frederick,** 1862–1953, and his sons **Karl Augustus,** 1893–1990, and **William Claire,** 1899–1966, U.S. psychiatrists.

Men·non·ite (men′ə nīt′), *n.* a member of an evangelical Protestant sect, originating in Europe in the 16th century, that opposes infant baptism, practices baptism of believers only, restricts marriage to members of the denomination, opposes war and bearing arms, and is noted for simplicity of living and plain dress. [1555–65; < G *Mennonit;* named after *Menno* Simons (1492–1559), Frisian religious leader; see -ITE[1]] —**Men′no·nit·ism,** *n.*

me·no (mā′nō; *It.* me′nô), *adv. Music.* less. [1875–80; < It < L *minus* less]

meno-, a combining form borrowed from Greek, where it meant "month," used with reference to menstruation in the formation of compound words: *menopause.* Also, *esp. before a vowel,* **men-.** [< Gk *mēno-,* comb. form of *mḗn* month; see MOON]

Me·noe·ce·us (mə nē′sē əs, -syōōs), *n. Class. Myth.* **1.** a descendant of the Sparti and the father of Jocasta and Creon, who sacrificed himself to end a plague in Thebes. **2.** the son of Creon of Thebes, who took his own life because of the prophecy that the Seven against Thebes would fail only if a descendant of the Sparti sacrificed himself.

Me·noe·ti·us (mə nē′shē əs), *n. Class. Myth.* **1.** a Titan, the brother of Prometheus, Epimetheus, and Atlas. **2.** one of the Argonauts and the father of Patroclus.

me·nol·o·gy (mi nol′ə jē), *n., pl.* **-gies. 1.** a calendar of the months. **2.** a record or account, as of saints, arranged in the order of a calendar. [1600–10; < NL *mēnologium* < LGk *mēnológion.* See MENO-, -LOGY]

Me·nom·i·nee (mə nom′ə nē), *n., pl.* **-nees,** (*esp. collectively*) **-nee** for 1. **1.** a member of a group of American Indian people of northeastern Wisconsin. **2.** the Eastern Algonquian language of the Menominee. Also, **Menomini.**

Menom′inee white′fish. See **round whitefish.** [1880–85, *Amer.*]

Me·nom·i·ni (mə nom′ə nē), *n., pl.* **-nis,** (*esp. collectively*) **-ni.** Menominee.

Me·nom′o·nee Falls′ (mə nom′ə nē), a city in SE Wisconsin, NW of Milwaukee. 27,845.

Me·nom·o·nie (mə nom′ə nē), *n.* a town in W Wisconsin. 12,769.

me·no mos·so (mā′nō mô′sō; *It.* me′nô môs′sô), *adv. Music.* less rapidly; slower. [1875–80; < It]

men·o·pau·sal (men′ə pô′zəl), *adj.* of, pertaining to, or characteristic of menopause. [1905–10; MENOPAUSE + -AL[1]]

men·o·pause (men′ə pôz′), *n. Physiol.* **1.** the period of permanent cessation of menstruation, usually occurring between the ages of 45 and 55. **2.** See **male menopause.** [1870–75; < F *ménopause.* See MENO-, PAUSE]

men·o·pha·ni·a (men′ə fā′nē ə), *n. Med.* menarche. [1855–60; MENO- + *-phania* appearance < Gk, akin to *phaínein* to appear (see -IA)]

me·nor·ah (mə nôr′ə, -nōr′ə), *n.* **1.** a candelabrum having seven branches (as used in the Biblical tabernacle or the Temple in Jerusalem), or any number of branches (as used in modern synagogues). **2.** a candelabrum having nine branches, for use on the Jewish festival of Hanukkah. [1885–90; < Heb *mənōrāh* lit., lampstand]

menorah (def. 2)

Me·nor·ca (*Sp.* me nôR′kä), *n.* Minorca.

men·or·rha·gi·a (men′ə rā′jē ə, -jə), *n. Pathol.* excessive menstrual discharge. [1770–80; MENO- + -RRHAGIA] —**men·or·rhag·ic** (men′ə raj′ik), *adj.*

men·or·rhe·a (men′ə rē′ə), *n. Physiol.* menstrual flow. Also, **men′or·rhoe′a.** [1855–60; MENO- + -RRHEA] —**men′or·rhe′al, men′or·rhe′ic,** *adj.*

me·nos·che·sis (mə nos′ki sis, men′ə skē′sis), *n. Pathol.* suppression of menstruation. [MENO- + Gk *schésis* checking, retention]

men·o·stax·is (men′ə stak′sis), *n. Pathol.* an abnormally prolonged period of menstruation. [1895–1900; MENO- + Gk *stáxis* dropping, dripping (of blood)]

Me·not·ti (mə not′ē; *It.* me nôt′tē), *n.* **Gian Car·lo** (jän kär′lō; *It.* jän käR′lô), born 1911, U.S. composer, born in Italy.

men's (menz), *n., pl.* **men's. 1.** a range of sizes in even and odd numbers for garments made for men. **2.** a garment in this size range. **3.** the department or section of a store where these garments are sold. Also, **mens.** [MEN + 'S[1]]

men•sa (men′sə), *n., pl.* **-sas, -sae** (-sē) for 1, *gen.* **-sae** for 2. **1.** Also called **altar slab, altar stone.** the flat stone forming the top of the altar in a Roman Catholic church. **2.** (*cap.*) *Astron.* the Table, a southern constellation near Octans. [1685–95; < L *mēnsa* table]

Men•sa (men′sə), *n.* an international fellowship organization for people with IQ's in the top 2 percent of the general population. [< L *mēnsa* table, symbolizing the original conception of the society, "a round table where no one has precedence"] **—Men′san,** *n.*

men•sal[1] (men′səl), *adj.* monthly. [1475–85; < L *mēns(is)* month + -AL[1]]

men•sal[2] (men′səl), *adj.* **1.** of, pertaining to, or used at the table. **2.** *Rom. Cath. Ch.* (of a benefice, church, etc.) set aside for the maintenance of a priest or bishop, esp. for board. [1400–50; late ME < L *mēnsālis* of, pertaining to a table. See MENSA, -AL[1]]

mensch (mench), *n., pl.* **mensch•en** (men′chən), **mensch•es.** *Informal.* a decent, upright, mature, and responsible person. [1950–55; < Yiddish *mentsh* man, human being < MHG *mensch* (G *Mensch*), OHG *mennisco, mannisco;* see MAN[1], -ISH[1]]

mense (mens), *n., v.,* **mensed, mens•ing.** *Brit. Dial.* —*n.* **1.** propriety; discretion. —*v.t.* **2.** to adorn; bring honor to; grace. [1490–1500; var. (north) of *mensk,* ME *menske* courtesy, honor < ON *menska* humanity, c. OE *menniscu* lit., the human state; akin to MENSCH. See MAN[1], -ISH[1]] **—mense′ful,** *adj.* **—mense′less,** *adj.*

men•serv•ants (men′sûr′vənts), *n.* pl. of **manservant.**

men•ses (men′sēz), *n.* (*used with a singular or plural v.*) *Physiol.* the periodic flow of blood and mucosal tissue from the uterus; menstrual flow. [1590–1600; < L *mēnsēs,* pl. of *mēnsis* month]

Men•she•vik (men′shə vik; *Russ.* myin shi vyĕk′), *n., pl.* **-viks, -vik•i** (-vik′ē, -vē′kē; *Russ.* -vyi kyē′). a member of the Russian Social-Democratic Workers' party in opposition to the Bolsheviks: advocated gradual development of full socialism through parliamentary government and cooperation with bourgeois parties; absorbed into the Communist party formed in 1918. Also, **men′she•vik.** [1905–10; < Russ *men'shevík,* equiv. to *mén'sh(iĭ)* lesser (comp. of *málen'kiĭ* small; cf. *men'shinstvó* minority) + *-evik,* var. of *-ovik* n. suffix] **—Men•she•vism** (men′shə viz′əm), *n.* **—Men′she•vist,** *adj.*

mens re•a (menz′ rē′ə), *Law.* a criminal intent. [1860–65; < NL *mēns rea*]

men's′ room′, a public lavatory for men. Also called **men's′ lounge′.** [1925–30, *Amer.*]

mens sa•na in cor•po•re sa•no (mens sä′nä in kôr′pō re′ sä′nō; *Eng.* menz sā′nə in kôr′pə rē′ sā′nō), *Latin.* a sound mind in a sound body.

men•stru•al (men′strōō əl, -strəl), *adj.* **1.** of or pertaining to menstruation or to the menses. **2.** *Archaic.* monthly. [1350–1400; ME *menstruall* < L *mēnstruālis* having monthly courses, equiv. to *mēnstru(a)* monthly courses (n. use of neut. pl. of *mēnstruus* monthly; *mēnstr-* (see SEMESTER) + *-uus* adj. suffix, prob. on the model of *annuus* ANNUAL) + *-ālis* -AL[1]]

men′strual extrac′tion, an abortion procedure involving suction aspiration of the uterine contents early in gestation, before the first missed menstrual period: sometimes performed later. Also called **endometrial aspiration, vacuum aspiration.** [1970–75]

men•stru•ate (men′strōō āt′, -strāt), *v.i.,* **-at•ed, -at•ing.** to undergo menstruation. [1640–50; v. use of earlier *menstruate* menstruous, ME < LL *mēnstruātus,* equiv. to *mēnstru(a)* monthly courses (see MENSTRUAL) + *-ātus* -ATE[1]]

men•stru•a•tion (men′strōō ā′shən, -strā′-), *n.* **1.** the periodic discharge of blood and mucosal tissue from the uterus, occurring approximately monthly from puberty to menopause in nonpregnant women and females of other primate species. **2.** the period of menstruating. [1770–80; MENSTRUATE + -ION]

men•stru•ous (men′strōō əs, -strəs), *adj.* pertaining to menstruation. [1375–1425; late ME: menstruating < L *mēnstruus* monthly; see MENSTRUATE, -OUS]

men•stru•um (men′strōō əm, -strəm), *n., pl.* **-stru•ums, -stru•a** (-strōō ə). a solvent. [1350–1400; special use of ME *menstruum* monthly period < ML (in L only pl. *mēnstrua* occurs). See MENSTRUAL]

men•sur•a•ble (men′shər ə bəl, -sər ə-), *adj.* measurable. [1595–1605; < LL *mēnsūrābilis,* equiv. to *mēnsūrā(re)* to MEASURE + *-bilis* -BLE] **—men′sur•a•bil′i•ty,** *n.*

men•su•ral (men′shər əl, -sər-), *adj.* pertaining to measure. [1600–10; < LL *mēnsūrālis,* equiv. to L *mēnsūr(a)* MEASURE + *-ālis* -AL[1]]

men′sural mu′sic, polyphonic music of the 13th century in which each note has a strictly determined value. [1600–10]

men′sural nota′tion, a system of musical notation of the 13th to the late 16th centuries, marked by the use of note symbols such as the longa and brevis, the absence of bar lines and ties, and the equivalence in value of one note to either two or three of the next smaller degree.

men•su•ra•tion (men′shə rā′shən, -sə-), *n.* **1.** the branch of geometry that deals with the measurement of length, area, or volume. **2.** the act or process of measuring. [1565–75; < LL *mēnsūrātiōn-* (s. of *mēnsūrātiō*) a measuring. See MEASURE, -ATION] **—men′su•ra′tion•al,** *adj.*

men•su•ra•tive (men′shə rā′tiv, -sə-, -shər ə tiv, -sər-), *adj.* adapted for or concerned with measuring. [1825–35; MENSURAT(ION) + -IVE]

men's′ wear′, apparel and accessories for men. Also, **menswear.** [1945–50]

mens•wear (menz′wâr′), *n.* **1.** See **men's wear. 2.** cloth, esp. wool, used in making men's and often women's tailored garments. [1905–10; MEN + 's[1] + WEAR]

-ment, a suffix of nouns, often concrete, denoting an action or resulting state (*abridgment; refreshment*), a product (*fragment*), or means (*ornament*). [< F < L *-mentum,* suffix forming nouns, usually from verbs]

men•tal[1] (men′tl), *adj.* **1.** of or pertaining to the mind: *mental powers; mental suffering.* **2.** of, pertaining to, or affected by a disorder of the mind: *a mental patient; mental illness.* **3.** providing care for persons with disordered minds, emotions, etc.: *a mental hospital.* **4.** performed by or existing in the mind: *mental arithmetic; a mental note.* **5.** pertaining to intellectuals or intellectual activity. **6.** *Informal.* slightly daft; out of one's mind; crazy: *He's mental.* —*n.* **7.** *Informal.* a person with a psychological disorder: *a fascist group made up largely of mentals.* [1375–1425; late ME < LL *mentālis,* equiv. to L *ment-* (s. of *mēns*) MIND + *-ālis* -AL[1]]

men•tal[2] (men′tl), *adj.* of or pertaining to the chin. [1720–30; < L *ment(um)* the chin (see MENTUM) + -AL[1]]

men′tal age′, *Psychol.* the level of native mental ability or capacity of an individual, usually as determined by an intelligence test, in relation to the chronological age of the average individual at this level: *a ten-year-old child with the mental age of a twelve-year-old; a mental age of twelve.* Cf. **achievement age.** [1910–15]

men′tal heal′ing, the healing of a physical ailment or disorder by mental concentration or suggestion. [1885–90] **—men′tal heal′er.**

men′tal health′, 1. psychological well-being and satisfactory adjustment to society and to the ordinary demands of life. **2.** the field of medicine concerned with the maintenance or achievement of such well-being and adjustment. [1825–35]

men′tal ill′ness, any of the various forms of psychosis or severe neurosis. Also called **men′tal disor′der, men′tal disease′.** [1960–65]

men•tal•ism (men′tl iz′əm), *n.* **1.** the doctrine that objects of knowledge have no existence except in the mind of the perceiver. **2.** the doctrine that human conduct reflects the operation of a nonmaterial principle. **3.** any psychological theory that accepts as a proper subject of study the mental basis for human behavior. Cf. **behaviorism.** [1870–75; MENTAL[1] + -ISM] **—men′tal•is′tic,** *adj.* **—men′tal•is′ti•cal•ly,** *adv.*

men•tal•ist (men′tl ist), *n.* **1.** a person who believes in or advocates mentalism. **2.** a person who believes that the mind and its functions are a legitimate area of psychological research. **3.** a mind reader, psychic, or fortuneteller. [1780–90; MENTAL[1] + -IST]

men•tal•i•ty (men tal′i tē), *n., pl.* **-ties. 1.** mental capacity or endowment: *a person of average mentality.* **2.** the set of one's mind; view; outlook: *a liberal mentality.* [1685–95; MENTAL[1] + -ITY]

men•tal•ly (men′tl ē), *adv.* **1.** in or with the mind or intellect; intellectually. **2.** with regard to the mind. [1655–65; MENTAL[1] + -LY]

men′tal reserva′tion, an unexpressed doubt or qualification about a situation, person, etc. [1600–10]

men′tal retarda′tion, a developmental disorder characterized by a subnormal ability to learn and a substantially low IQ. [1900–15]

men′tal telep′athy, telepathy. [1970–75]

men•ta•tion (men tā′shən), *n.* mental activity. [1840–50; < L *ment-* (s. of *mēns*) MIND + -ATION]

men•tee (men tē′), *n.* a person who is guided by a mentor. [MENT(OR) + -EE]

Men•tes (men′tēz), *n.* (in the *Odyssey*) a captain of the Taphians. Athena assumed his form when she urged Telemachus to search for Odysseus.

men•tha•ceous (men thā′shəs), *adj.* belonging to the Menthaceae, a former name for the plant family Labiatae. Cf. **mint family.** [< NL *Menthace(ae)* (*Menth(a)* the type genus (L: MINT[1]) + *-aceae* -ACEAE) + OUS]

men•thene (men′thēn), *n. Chem.* **1.** any of several isomeric, monocyclic terpenes having the formula $C_{10}H_{18}$. **2.** a colorless, liquid terpene, $C_{10}H_{18}$, found in certain essential oils and prepared from menthol. [1830–40; < NL *Menth(a)* (see MINT[1]) + -ENE]

men•thol (men′thôl, -thol), *n.* **1.** Also called **hexahydrothymol, peppermint camphor.** *Chem., Pharm.* a colorless, crystalline, slightly water-soluble alcohol, $C_{10}H_{20}O$, obtained from peppermint oil or synthesized: used chiefly in perfumes, confections, cigarettes, and liqueurs and in medicine for colds and nasal disorders for its cooling effect on mucous membranes. **2.** a mentholated cigarette. —*adj.* **3.** containing menthol; mentholated. [1875–80; < NL *Menth(a)* (see MINT[1]) + -OL[1]]

men•tho•lat•ed (men′thə lā′tid), *adj.* **1.** saturated with or containing menthol: *a mentholated cough drop.* **2.** covered or treated with menthol. [1930–35; MENTHOL + -ATE[1] + -ED[2]]

men•ti•cide (men′tə sīd′), *n.* the systematic effort to undermine and destroy a person's values and beliefs, as by the use of prolonged interrogation, drugs, torture, etc., and to induce radically different ideas. [1950–55; < L *ment-* (s. of *mēns*) MIND + -I- + -CIDE]

men•tion (men′shən), *v.t.* **1.** to refer briefly to; name, specify, or speak of: *Don't forget to mention her contribution to the project.* **2.** to cite formally for a meritorious act or achievement: *He was mentioned in dispatches from the war zone.* **3. not to mention,** in addition to; without mentioning: *We were served a sumptuous entree, not to mention the other courses.* —*n.* **4.** a direct or incidental reference; a mentioning: *to make mention of a place.* **5.** formal recognition for a meritorious act or achievement: *Her entry in the science competition received a special mention.* [1250–1300; < L *mentiōn-* (s. of *mentiō*) a calling to mind, a touching upon (see MENTAL[1]) + -IŌN-; r. ME *mencioun* < AF < L, as above] **—men′tion•a•ble,** *adj.* **—men′tion•er,** *n.*
—Syn. 1. indicate, allude to. **4.** allusion, notice.

Men•ton (men tōn′; *Fr.* mäN tôN′), *n.* a city in SE France, on the Mediterranean: winter resort. 25,314. Italian, **Men•to•ne** (men tô′ne).

men•ton•nière (men′tən yâr′; *Fr.* mäN tô nyeʀ′), *n., pl.* **-ton•nières** (-tən yârz′; *Fr.* -tô nyeʀ′). *Armor.* any of various plate pieces for protecting the lower part of the face, as a beaver. [1815–25; < F, equiv. to *menton* chin + *-ière,* fem. of *-ier* -IER[2]; see BRASSIERE]

men•to•plas•ty (men′tə plas′tē), *n., pl.* **-ties.** plastic surgery to correct a functional or cosmetic deformity of the chin. [< L *ment(um)* chin (see MENTUM) + -O- + -PLASTY]

men•tor (men′tôr, -tər), *n.* **1.** a wise and trusted counselor or teacher. **2.** an influential senior sponsor or supporter. —*v.i.* **3.** to act as a mentor: *She spent years mentoring to junior employees.* —*v.t.* **4.** to act as a mentor to: *The brash young executive did not wish to be mentored by anyone.* [1740–50; after MENTOR (< Gk *Méntōr*)] **—men′tor•ship′,** *n.*
—Syn. 1. adviser, master, guide, preceptor.

Men•tor (men′tôr, -tər), *n.* (in the *Odyssey*) a loyal adviser of Odysseus entrusted with the care and education of Telemachus.

Men•tor (men′tər), *n.* a town in NE Ohio. 42,065.

men•tum (men′təm), *n., pl.* **-ta** (-tə). **1.** *Entomol.* the medial plate of the labium in insects. **2.** *Bot.* a chinlike protuberance formed by the sepals and the base of the column in some orchids. [1685–95; < NL, L *mentum* chin, akin to MOUTH]

men•u (men′yōō, mā′nyōō), *n.* **1.** a list of the dishes served at a meal; bill of fare: *Ask the waiter for a menu.* **2.** the dishes served. **3.** any list or set of items, activities, etc., from which to choose: *What's on the menu this weekend—golf, tennis, swimming?* **4.** *Computers.* a list of options available to a user, as displayed on a CRT or other type of screen. [1650–60; < F: detailed list, n. use of *menu* small, detailed < L *minūtus* MINUTE[2]]

me•nu•do (mə nōō′dō; *Sp.* me nōō′thô), *n.* a spicy Mexican soup made with tripe, onions, tomatoes, chilies, and hominy. [< MexSp; cf. Sp *menudos* giblets, innards, n. use of *menudo* small, insignificant < L *minūtus;* see MINUTE[2], MENU]

men•u-driv•en (men′yōō driv′ən, mān′-), *adj. Computers.* of or pertaining to software that makes extensive use of menus to enable users to choose alternatives and guide program operations.

Men•u•hin (men′yōō in), *n.* **Ye•hu•di** (yə hōō′dē), born 1916, U.S. violinist.

Men•zies (men′zēz), *n.* **Sir Robert Gordon,** 1894–1978, Australian statesman: prime minister 1939–41 and 1949–1966.

Me•o (mē ou′), *n., pl.* **Me•os,** (*esp. collectively*) **Me•o.** Miao (def. 1).

me•ow (mē ou′, myou), *n.* **1.** the characteristic sound a cat makes. **2.** a spiteful or catty remark. —*v.i.* **3.** to make the sound of a cat. **4.** to make a spiteful or catty remark. Also, **miaow, miaou, miaul.** [1870–75; imit.]

M.E.P., Master of Engineering Physics.

m.e.p., mean effective pressure.

M.E.P.A., Master of Engineering and Public Administration.

me•per•i•dine (mə per′i dēn′, -din), *n. Pharm.* a narcotic compound, $C_{15}H_{21}NO_2$, used as an analgesic and sedative. [1945–50; ME(THYL) + (PI)PERIDINE]

Me•phib•o•sheth (mə fib′ə sheth′), *n.* a son of Jonathan, and the grandson of Saul. II Sam 4:4.

Meph•i•stoph•e•les (mef′ə stof′ə lēz′), *n. Medieval Demonology.* one of the seven chief devils and the tempter of Faust. Also, **Me•phis•to** (mə fis′tō). **—Meph•is•to•phe•li•an, Meph•is•to•phe•le•an** (mef′ə stə fē′lē ən, -fēl′yən, mə fis′tə-), *adj.*

me•phit•ic (mə fit′ik), *adj.* **1.** offensive to the smell. **2.** noxious; pestilential; poisonous. [1615–25; < LL *mephiticus.* See MEPHITIS, -IC] **—me•phit′i•cal•ly,** *adv.*

me•phi•tis (mə fī′tis), *n.* **1.** (in nontechnical use) a noxious or pestilential exhalation from the earth, as poison gas. **2.** any noisome or poisonous stench. [1700–10; < L *mephitis, mefītis;* cf. Oscan *Mefit(ei)* the goddess of such exhalations]

me•pro•ba•mate (mə prō′bə māt′, mep′rō bam′āt), *n. Pharm.* a white powder, $C_9H_{18}N_2O_4$, used in medicine chiefly as a tranquilizer for treating anxiety, tension, and skeletal muscle spasm. [1950–55; ME(THYL) + PRO(PYL) + (CAR)BAMATE]

mEq, milliequivalent.

Meq•uon (mek′won), *n.* a town in E Wisconsin. 16,193.

-mer, *Chem.* a combining form meaning "member of a particular group": *isomer.* Cf. **-mere, -merous.** [< Gk *méros* part, portion]

mer., **1.** meridian. **2.** meridional.

mer•bro•min (mər brō′min), *n. Pharm.* an iridescent green, water-soluble powder, $C_{20}H_8Br_2HgNa_2O_6$, that forms a red solution when dissolved in water: used as an antiseptic and as a germicide. [1940–45; MER(CURIC) + BROM(O)- + -IN[2]]

merc (mûrk, mûrs), *n. Slang.* a mercenary soldier. [by shortening]

merc., **1.** mercantile. **2.** mercurial. **3.** mercury.

Mer•ca (mer′kä), *n.* a city in S Somalia. 50,000.

mer•ca•do (meʀ kä′thô), *n., pl.* **-dos** (-thôs). *Spanish.* a market.

Mer•cal′li scale′ (mər käl′ē, mer-; *It.* meʀ käl′lē), *Geol.* a measure of earthquake intensity with 12 divisions ranging from I (felt by very few) to XII (total de-

CONCISE PRONUNCIATION KEY: act, cāpe, dâre, pärt; set, ēqual; *if,* īce; ox, ōver, ôrder, oil, bŏŏk, bōōt, out; up, ûrge; child; sing; shoe; thin, *th*at; zh as in *treasure.* ə = *a* as in *alone, e* as in *system, i* as in *easily, o* as in *gallop, u* as in *circus;* ᵊ as in *fire* (fīᵊr), *hour* (ouᵊr). l and n can serve as syllabic consonants, as in *cradle* (krād′l), and *button* (but′n). See the full key inside the front cover.

struction). [1920–25; named after Giuseppe *Mercalli* (1850–1914), Italian seismologist]

mer•can•tile (mûr′kən tēl′, -tīl′, -til), *adj.* **1.** of or pertaining to merchants or trade; commercial. **2.** engaged in trade or commerce: *a mercantile nation.* **3.** *Econ.* of or pertaining to the mercantile system. [1635–45; < F < It: pertaining to merchants, equiv. to *mercant(e)* merchant (< L *mercant-*, s. of *mercāns* buyer, n. use of prp. of *mercārī* to buy) + *-ile* -ILE]
—Syn. 1. See **commercial.**

mer′cantile a′gency. See **commercial agency.** [1855–60]

mer′cantile pa′per. See **commercial paper.**

mer′cantile sys′tem, *Econ.* a system of political and economic policy, evolving with the modern national state and seeking to secure a nation's political and economic supremacy in its rivalry with other states. According to this system, money was regarded as a store of wealth, and the goal of a state was the accumulation of precious metals, by exporting the largest possible quantity of its products and importing as little as possible, thus establishing a favorable balance of trade. [1770–80]

mer•can•til•ism (mûr′kən ti liz′əm, -tē-, -tī-), *n.* **1.** mercantile practices or spirit; commercialism. **2.** See **mercantile system.** [1870–75; < F *mercantilisme.* See MERCANTILE, -ISM] **—mer′can•til•ist,** *n., adj.* **—mer′•can•til•is′tic,** *adj.*

mer•cap•tan (mər kap′tan), *n. Chem.* any of a class of sulfur-containing compounds having the type formula RSH, in which R represents a radical, and having an extremely offensive, garlicky odor. [1825–35; < L, short for phrase *corpus mercurium captāns* body capturing quicksilver]

mer•cap•tide (mər kap′tīd), *n. Chem.* a metallic salt of a mercaptan. [1825–35; MERCAPT(AN) + -IDE]

mer•cap•to (mər kap′tō), *adj. Chem.* containing the mercapto group; sulfhydryl; thiol. [1970–75; MERCAPT(AN) + -O-]

mercap′to group′, *Chem.* the univalent group –SH. Also called **mercap′to rad′ical.**

mer•cap•to•pu•rine (mər kap′tō pyŏŏr′ēn), *n. Pharm.* a yellow, crystalline, water-insoluble powder, $C_5H_4N_4S$, used in the treatment of leukemia. [1950–55; MERCAPTO + PURINE]

Mer•cast (mûr′kast′, -käst′), *n.* a broadcasting system used by U.S. agencies to deliver messages to government-operated ships. [perh. *Mer(chant Marine broad)cast*]

Mer•ca•tor (mər kā′tər; *for 1 also Flem.* mer kä′tôr), *n.* **1. Ger•har•dus** (jər här′dəs), (*Gerhard Kremer*), 1512–94, Flemish cartographer and geographer. *—adj.* **2.** noting, pertaining to, or according to the principles of a Mercator projection: *a Mercator chart.*

Merca′tor projec′tion, *Cartography.* a conformal projection on which any rhumb line is represented as a straight line, used chiefly in navigation, though the scale varies with latitude and areal size and the shapes of large areas are greatly distorted. Also, **Merca′tor's projec′tion.** [1660–70]

Merca′tor sail′ing, *Navig.* sailing according to rhumb lines, which appear as straight lines on a Mercator chart.

Merca′tor track′, *Navig.* a line appearing straight on a Mercator chart; rhumb line.

Mer•ced (mər sed′), *n.* a city in central California. 36,499.

Mer•ce•des (mer se′thes *for 1;* mər sā′dēz *for 2, 3; for 3 also* mər sē′dēz, mûr′si dēz′), *n.* **1.** a city in SW Uruguay, on the Río Negro. 53,000. **2.** a city in S Texas. 11,851. **3.** a female given name.

mer•ce•nar•y (mûr′sə ner′ē), *adj., n., pl.* **-nar•ies.** *—adj.* **1.** working or acting merely for money or other reward; venal. **2.** hired to serve in a foreign army, guerrilla organization, etc. *—n.* **3.** a professional soldier hired to serve in a foreign army. **4.** any hireling. [1350–1400; ME *mercenarie* < L *mercēnnārius* working for pay, hired worker, mercenary, perh., repr. earlier **mercēd(i)nārius,* equiv. to **mercēdin-,* s. of **mercēdō,* a by-form of *mercēs,* s. *mercēd-* payment, wage (akin to *merx* goods; cf. MERCHANT) + *-ārius* -ARY] **—mer•ce•nar•i•ly** (mûr′sə nâr′ə lē, mûr′sə ner′-), *adv.* **—mer′•ce•nar′i•ness,** *n.*
—Syn. 1. grasping, acquisitive, avaricious, covetous. **—Ant. 1.** altruistic, idealistic, unselfish.

mer•cer (mûr′sər), *n. Chiefly Brit.* a dealer in textile fabrics; dry-goods merchant. [1150–1200; ME < AF; OF *mercier* merchant, equiv. to *merz* merchandise (< L *merx,* acc. *mercem*) + *-ier* -IER[2]; see -ER[2]]

Mer′cer Is′land, a city in W central Washington, on Mercer Island in Lake Washington, east of Seattle. 21,522.

mer•cer•ize (mûr′sə rīz′), *v.t.,* **-ized, -iz•ing.** to treat (cotton yarns or fabric) with caustic alkali under tension, in order to increase strength, luster, and affinity for dye. Also, *esp. Brit.,* **mer′cer•ise′.** [1855–60; named after John *Mercer* (1791–1866), English calico printer, the patentee (1850) of the process; see -IZE] **—mer′cer•i•za′tion,** *n.* **—mer′cer•iz′er,** *n.*

mer•cer•y (mûr′sə rē), *n., pl.* **-cer•ies.** *Brit.* **1.** a mercer's shop. **2.** mercers' wares. [1250–1300; ME *mercerie* < OF. See MERCER, -Y[3]]

mer•chan•dise (*n.* mûr′chən dīz′, -dīs′; *v.* mûr′chən-dīz′), *n., v.,* **-dised, -dis•ing.** *—n.* **1.** the manufactured goods bought and sold in any business. **2.** the stock of goods in a store. **3.** goods, esp. manufactured goods; commodities. *—v.i.* **4.** to carry on trade. *—v.t.* **5.** to buy and sell; deal in; trade. **6.** to plan for and promote the sales of. [1250–1300; ME *marchandise* < OF. See MERCHANT, -ICE] **—mer′chan•dis′a•ble,** *adj.* **—mer′•chan•dis′er,** *n.*

mer•chan•dis•ing (mûr′chən dī′zing), *n.* the planning and promotion of sales by presenting a product to the right market at the proper time, by carrying out organized, skillful advertising, using attractive displays, etc. Also called **mer′chandise plan′ning.** [1350–1400; ME; see MERCHANDISE, -ING[1]]

mer•chan•dize (*n.* mûr′chən dīz′, -dīs′; *v.* mûr′chən-dīz′), *n., v.i., v.t.,* **-dized, -diz•ing.** merchandise.

mer•chant (mûr′chənt), *n.* **1.** a person who buys and sells commodities for profit; dealer; trader. **2.** a storekeeper; retailer: *a local merchant who owns a store on Main Street.* **3.** *Chiefly Brit.* a wholesaler. *—adj.* **4.** pertaining to or used for trade or commerce: *a merchant ship.* **5.** pertaining to the merchant marine. **6.** *Steelmaking.* (of bars and ingots) of standard shape or size. [1250–1300; ME *marchant* < OF *marcheant* < VL **mercātant-* (s. of **mercātāns*), prp. of **mercātāre,* freq. of L *mercārī* to trade, deriv. of *merx* goods] **—mer′chant•like′,** *adj.*

mer•chant•a•ble (mûr′chən tə bəl), *adj. Chiefly Law.* marketable: *merchantable war-surplus goods.* [1475–85; earlier *marchandabull.* See MERCHANT, -ABLE] **—mer′•chant•a•ble•ness,** *n.*

mer′chantable ti′tle, *Law.* See **marketable title.**

mer′chant bank′, *Brit. Finance.* a private banking firm engaged chiefly in investing in new issues of securities and in accepting bills of exchange in foreign trade. [1900–05] **—mer′chant bank′er. —mer′chant bank′•ing.**

mer′chant flag′, the ensign used by all ships engaged in commerce, fishing, etc.

mer′chant guild′, a medieval guild composed of merchants. [1865–70]

mer•chant•man (mûr′chənt mən), *n., pl.* **-men.** a trading ship. Also called **mer′chant ship′, mer′chant ves′sel.** [1520–30; MERCHANT + -MAN]

mer′chant marine′, **1.** the vessels of a nation that are engaged in commerce. **2.** the officers and crews of such vessels. [1850–55, *Amer.*]

mer′chant of death′, a company, nation, or person that sells military arms on the international market, usually to the highest bidder and without scruple or regard for political ramifications. [phrase popularized by the book *Merchants of Death* (1934) by U.S. writers Helmut C. Engelbrecht (1895–1939) and Frank C. Hanighen (1899–1964)]

Mer′chant of Ven′ice, The, a comedy (1596?) by Shakespeare.

mer′chant prince′, a very wealthy or influential merchant. [1835–45]

mer′chant sea′man, a seaman who works on a merchant vessel. [1895–1900]

mer•ci (mer sē′), *interj. French.* thank you.

Mer•ci•a (mûr′shē ə, -shə), *n.* **1.** an early English kingdom in central Britain. **2.** a female given name.

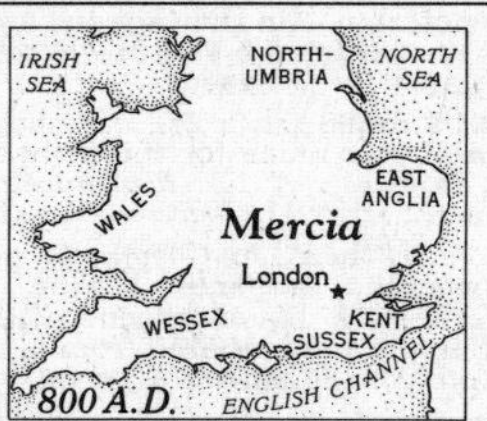

Mer•ci•an (mûr′shē ən, -shən), *adj.* **1.** of or pertaining to Mercia, its inhabitants, or their dialect. *—n.* **2.** a native or inhabitant of Mercia. **3.** the dialect of Old English spoken in Mercia. [1505–15; MERCI(A) + -AN]

mer•ci beau•coup (mer sē′ bō kōō′), *French.* thank you very much.

Mer•cier (*Fr.* mer syā′), *n.* **Dé•si•ré Jo•seph** (dā zē-rā′ zhō zef′), 1851–1926, Belgian cardinal and patriot.

mer•ci•ful (mûr′si fəl), *adj.* full of mercy; characterized by, expressing, or showing mercy; compassionate: *a merciful God.* [1250–1300; ME; see MERCY, -FUL] **—mer′ci•ful•ly,** *adv.* **—mer′ci•ful•ness,** *n.*
—Syn. kind, clement, lenient, forgiving, benignant, tender, sympathetic. **—Ant.** cruel, relentless.

mer•ci•less (mûr′si lis), *adj.* without mercy; having or showing no mercy; pitiless; cruel: *a merciless critic.* [1300–50; ME *mercyles.* See MERCY, -LESS] **—mer′ci•less•ly,** *adv.* **—mer′ci•less•ness,** *n.*
—Syn. hard, relentless, unrelenting, fell, unsympathetic, inexorable. **—Ant.** compassionate.

mer•cu•rate (mûr′kyə rāt′), *n., v.,* **-rat•ed, -rat•ing.** *Chem. —n.* **1.** Also, **mer•cu•ri•ate** (mər kyŏŏr′ē it, -āt′). any salt in which bivalent mercury is part of a complex anion. *—v.t.* **2.** Also, **mercurize.** to introduce mercury into (an organic compound); treat with mercury. [1920–25; MERCURY + -ATE[2]] **—mer′cu•ra′tion,** *n.*

mer•cu•ri•al (mər kyŏŏr′ē əl), *adj.* **1.** changeable; volatile; fickle; flighty; erratic: *a mercurial nature.* **2.** animated; lively; sprightly; quick-witted. **3.** pertaining to, containing, or caused by the metal mercury. **4.** (*cap.*) of or pertaining to the god Mercury. **5.** (*cap.*) of or pertaining to the planet Mercury. *—n.* **6.** *Pharm.* a preparation of mercury used as a drug. [1350–1400; ME < L *mercuriālis* of, pertaining to the god or planet Mercury. See MERCURY, -AL[1]] **—mer•cu′ri•al•ly,** *adv.* **—mer•cu′ri•al•ness, mer•cu′ri•al′i•ty,** *n.*
—Syn. 1. inconstant, indecisive. **2.** spirited. **—Ant. 1.** constant, steady. **2.** phlegmatic.

mercu′rial barom′eter. See **mercury barometer.** [1685–95]

mer•cu•ri•al•ism (mər kyŏŏr′ē ə liz′əm), *n. Pathol.* poisoning by mercury. [1820–30; MERCURIAL + -ISM]

mer•cu•ri•al•ize (mər kyŏŏr′ē ə līz′), *v.t.,* **-ized, -iz•ing.** **1.** to make mercurial, esp. in temperament. **2.** to treat or impregnate with mercury or one of its compounds. Also, *esp. Brit.,* **mer•cu′ri•al•ise′.** [1605–15; MERCURIAL + -IZE] **—mer•cu′ri•al•i•za′tion,** *n.*

mer•cu•ric (mər kyŏŏr′ik), *adj. Chem.* of or containing mercury, esp. in the bivalent state. [1820–30; MERCUR(Y) + -IC]

mercu′ric chlo′ride, *Chem.* a white, crystalline, water-soluble, strongly acrid, highly poisonous solid, $HgCl_2$, prepared by sublimation of chlorine with mercury, and used chiefly as an antiseptic. Also called **bichloride of mercury, mercury bichloride.** [1870–75]

mercu′ric ox′ide, *Chem.* a slightly crystalline, water-soluble, poisonous compound, HgO, occurring as a coarse, orange-red powder **(red mercuric oxide)** or as a fine, orange-yellow powder **(yellow mercuric oxide):** used chiefly as a pigment in paints and as an antiseptic in pharmaceuticals.

mercu′ric sul′fide, *Chem.* a crystalline, water-insoluble, poisonous compound, HgS, occurring as a coarse, black powder **(black mercuric sulfide)** or as a fine, bright-scarlet powder **(red mercuric sulfide):** used chiefly as a pigment and as a source of the free metal. Also, **mercury sulfide.**

mer•cu•ri•fy (mər kyŏŏr′ə fī′), *v.t.,* **-fied, -fy•ing.** to mix with mercury; amalgamate. [1670–80; MERCUR(Y) + -IFY]

mer•cu•rize (mûr′kyə rīz′), *v.t.,* **-rized, -riz•ing.** mercurate (def. 2). Also, *esp. Brit.,* **mer′cu•rise′.** [MERCUR(Y) + -IZE] **—mer′cu•ri•za′tion,** *n.*

Mer•cu•ro•chrome (mər kyŏŏr′ə krōm′), *Pharm., Trademark.* a brand of merbromin.

mer•cu•rous (mər kyŏŏr′əs, mûr′kyər əs), *adj. Chem.* containing univalent mercury, Hg^{+1} or Hg_2^{+2}. [1860–65; MERCUR(Y) + -OUS]

mercu′rous chlo′ride, *Pharm.* calomel. [1880–85]

mer•cu•ry (mûr′kyə rē), *n., pl.* **-ries.** **1.** *Chem.* a heavy, silver-white, highly toxic metallic element, the only one that is liquid at room temperature; quicksilver: used in barometers, thermometers, pesticides, pharmaceutical preparations, reflecting surfaces of mirrors, and dental fillings, in certain switches, lamps, and other electric apparatus, and as a laboratory catalyst. *Symbol:* Hg; *at. wt.:* 200.59; *at. no.:* 80; *sp. gr.:* 13.546 at 20°C; *freezing point:* −38.9°C; *boiling point:* 357°C. **2.** *Pharm.* this metal as used in medicine, in the form of various organic and inorganic compounds, usually for skin infections. **3.** (*cap.*) the ancient Roman god who served as messenger of the gods and was also the god of commerce, thievery, eloquence, and science, identified with the Greek god Hermes. **4.** (*cap.*) *Astron.* the planet nearest the sun, having a diameter of 3031 mi. (4878 km), a mean distance from the sun of 36 million mi. (57.9 million km), and a period of revolution of 87.96 days, and having no satellites: the smallest planet in the solar system. See table under **planet. 5.** a messenger, esp. a carrier of news. **6.** any plant belonging to the genus *Mercurialis,* of the spurge family, esp. the poisonous, weedy *M. perennis* of Europe. **7.** Good-King-Henry. **8.** (*cap.*) *Aerospace.* one of a series of U.S. spacecraft, carrying one astronaut, that achieved the first U.S. suborbital and orbital manned spaceflights. [1300–50; ME *Mercurie* < ML, L *Mercurius,* akin to *merx* goods]

Mercury (def. 3)

mer′cury arc′, *Elect.* a bluish-green electric arc that has passed through a mercury-vapor cathode. [1915–20]

mer′cury barom′eter, a barometer in which the weight of a column of mercury in a glass tube with a sealed top is balanced against that of the atmosphere pressing on an exposed cistern of mercury at the base of the mercury column, the height of the column varying with atmospheric pressure. Also called **mercurial barometer.** Cf. **aneroid barometer.**

mer′cury bichlo′ride, *Chem.* See **mercuric chloride.**

mer′cury ful′minate, *Chem.* a gray, crystalline

CONCISE ETYMOLOGY KEY: <, descended or borrowed from; >, whence; b., blend of, blended; c., cognate with; cf., compare; deriv., derivative; equiv., equivalent; imit., imitative; obl., oblique; r., replacing; s., stem; sp., spelling, spelled; resp., respelling, respelled; trans., translation; ?, origin unknown; *, unattested; ‡, probably earlier than. See the full key inside the front cover.

solid, $Hg(CNO)_2$, used chiefly in the manufacture of commercial and military detonators. Also called **fulminate of mercury.** [1900–05]

mer′cury mass′, *Pharm.* **1.** See **blue mass** (def. 1). **2.** See **blue pill** (def. 1).

mer′cury sul′fide, *Chem.* See **mercuric sulfide.** [1930–35]

mer′cury switch′, *Elect.* an especially quiet switch that opens and closes an electric circuit by shifting a vial containing a pool of mercury so as to cover or uncover the contacts.

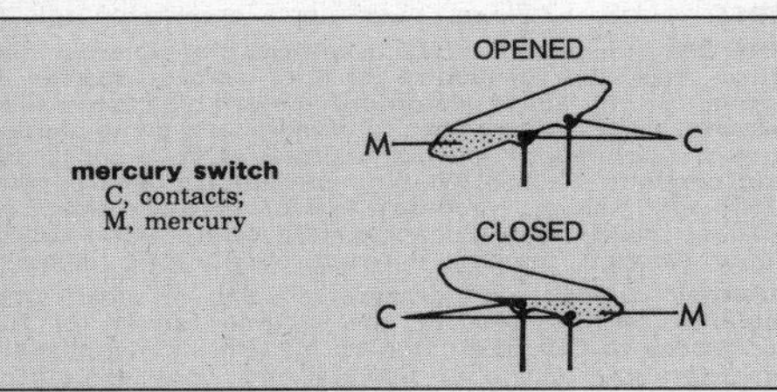

mercury switch C, contacts; M, mercury

mer′cu·ry-va·por lamp′ (mûr′kyə rē vā′pər), *Elect.* a lamp producing a light with a high actinic and ultraviolet content by means of an electric arc in mercury vapor. [1900–05]

mer·cy (mûr′sē), *n., pl.* **-cies** for 4, 5. **1.** compassionate or kindly forbearance shown toward an offender, an enemy, or other person in one's power; compassion, pity, or benevolence: *Have mercy on the poor sinner.* **2.** the disposition to be compassionate or forbearing: *an adversary wholly without mercy.* **3.** the discretionary power of a judge to pardon someone or to mitigate punishment, esp. to send to prison rather than invoke the death penalty. **4.** an act of kindness, compassion, or favor: *She has performed countless small mercies for her friends and neighbors.* **5.** something that gives evidence of divine favor; blessing: *It was just a mercy we had our seat belts on when it happened.* **6. at the mercy of,** entirely in the power of; subject to: *They were at the mercy of their captors.* Also, **at one's mercy.** [1125–75; ME *merci* < OF, earlier *mercit* < L *mercēd-* (s. of *mercēs*) wages (LL, ML: heavenly reward), deriv. of *merx* goods]
—Syn. 1. forgiveness, indulgence, clemency, leniency, lenity, tenderness, mildness. **—Ant. 1.** cruelty.

Mer·cy (mûr′sē), *n.* a female given name.

mer′cy kill′ing, euthanasia (def. 1). [1930–35]

mer′cy seat′, 1. *Bible.* **a.** the gold covering on the ark of the covenant, regarded as the resting place of God. Ex. 25:17–22. **b.** the throne of God. **2.** *South Midland and Southern U.S.* See **mourner's bench.** [1520–30]

mer′cy stroke′. See ***coup de grâce.*** [1695–1705]

merde (meʀd; *Eng.* mârd), *French.* **—n. 1.** excrement. **—interj. 2.** (used as an expletive to express anger, annoyance, disgust, etc.)

mer·div·or·ous (mər div′ər əs), *adj.* coprophagous. [1855–60; < L *merd(a)* dung + -I- + -VOROUS]

mere[1] (mēr), *adj., superl.* **mer·est. 1.** being nothing more nor better than: *a mere pittance; He is still a mere child.* **2.** *Obs.* **a.** pure and unmixed, as wine, a people, or a language. **b.** fully as much as what is specified; completely fulfilled or developed; absolute. [1250–1300; ME < L *merus* pure, unmixed, mere]
—Syn. 1. MERE, BARE imply a scant sufficiency. They are often interchangeable, but MERE frequently means no more than (enough). BARE suggests scarcely as much as (enough). Thus *a mere livelihood* means enough to live on but no more; *a bare livelihood* means scarcely enough to live on.

mere[2] (mēr), *n.* **1.** *Chiefly Brit. Dial.* a lake or pond. **2.** *Obs.* any body of sea water. [bef. 900; ME, OE; c. G *Meer,* ON *marr,* Goth *marei,* OIr *muir,* L *mare*]

mere[3] (mēr), *n. Brit. Dial.* a boundary or boundary marker. Also, **mear.** [bef. 900; ME; OE *(ge)mǣre;* c. ON *mǣri;* akin to L *mūrus* wall, rim]

mère (meʀ; *Eng.* mâr), *n., pl.* ***mères*** (meʀ; *Eng.* mârz). *French.* mother.

-mere, a combining form meaning "part," used in the formation of compound words: *blastomere.* Cf. **-mer, -merous.** [comb. form repr. Gk *méros*]

Mer·e·dith (mer′i dith), *n.* **1. George,** 1828–1909, English novelist and poet. **2. Owen,** pen name of Edward Robert Bulwer Lytton. **3.** Also, **Mer′e·dyth.** a male or female given name.

mere·ly (mēr′lē), *adv.* **1.** only as specified and nothing more; simply: *merely a matter of form.* **2.** *Obs.* **a.** without admixture; purely. **b.** altogether; entirely. [1400–50; late ME *mereli.* See MERE[1], -LY]

me·ren·gue (mə reng′gā), *n., v.,* **-gued, -gu·ing. —n. 1.** a ballroom dance of Dominican and Haitian origin, characterized by a stiff-legged, limping step. **2.** the music for this dance. **—v.i. 3.** to dance the merengue. Also, **méringue.** [1935–40; < AmerSp]

me·rese (mä rēz′, -rēs′), *n.* (on a stemmed glass) a flat, sharp-edged knop joining the stem to the bowl or foot. Also called **collar.** [1920–25; orig. uncert.]

mer·e·tri·cious (mer′i trish′əs), *adj.* **1.** alluring or attractive by a show of flashy or vulgar qualities; tawdry. **2.** based on pretense, deception, or insincerity. **3.** of, pertaining to, or characteristic of a prostitute. [1620–30; < L *meretrīcius* of, pertaining to harlots, equiv. to *meretrīc-* (s. of *meretrīx* harlot, lit., earner, equiv. to *mere-,* s. of *merēre* to earn + *-trix* -TRIX) + *-us* adj. suffix (see -OUS)] **—mer′e·tri′cious·ly,** *adv.* **—mer′e·tri′cious·ness,** *n.*
—Syn. 1. showy, gaudy. **2.** spurious, sham, false.

mer·gan·ser (mər gan′sər), *n., pl.* **-sers,** (*esp. collectively*) **-ser.** any of several fish-eating diving ducks of the subfamily Merginae, having a narrow bill hooked at the tip and serrated at the edges. Also called **fish duck.** [1745–55; < NL, equiv. to L *merg(us)* diver, a kind of water bird + *ānser* GOOSE]

merge (mûrj), *v.,* **merged, merg·ing. —v.t. 1.** to cause to combine or coalesce; unite. **2.** to combine, blend, or unite gradually so as to blur the individuality or individual identity of: *They voted to merge the two branch offices into a single unit.* **—v.i. 3.** to become combined, united, swallowed up, or absorbed; lose identity by uniting or blending (often fol. by *in* or *into*): *This stream merges into the river up ahead.* **4.** to combine or unite into a single enterprise, organization, body, etc.: *The two firms merged last year.* [1630–40; < L *mergere* to dip, immerse, plunge into water] **—mer′gence,** *n.*
—Syn. 1, 2, 3. amalgamate, consolidate.

merg·ee (mûr jē′), *n.* a participant in a merger. [1960–65; MERG(ER) + -EE]

Mer·gen·tha·ler (mûr′gən thô′lər; *Ger.* mer′gən tä′-lər), *n.* **Ott·mar** (ot′mär; *Ger.* ôt′mär), 1854–99, U.S. inventor of the Linotype, born in Germany.

merg·er (mûr′jər), *n.* **1.** a statutory combination of two or more corporations by the transfer of the properties to one surviving corporation. **2.** any combination of two or more business enterprises into a single enterprise. **3.** an act or instance of merging. [1720–30; MERGE + -ER[1]]

Mer·gui (mûr gwē′), *n.* a seaport in S Burma, on the Andaman Sea. 44,000.

mer·i·carp (mer′i kärp′), *n. Bot.* one of the carpels of a schizocarp. [1825–35; *meri-* (comb. form of Gk *merís* part, portion) + -CARP]

mer·i·da (mer′i də), *n.* suntan (def. 2). [appar. after MÉRIDA, Mexico]

Mé·ri·da (me′ʀē thä′), *n.* **1.** a city in and the capital of Yucatán, in SE Mexico. 253,800. **2.** a city in W Venezuela. 74,214.

Mer·i·den (mer′i dn), *n.* a city in central Connecticut. 57,118.

me·rid·i·an (mə rid′ē ən), *n.* **1.** *Geog.* **a.** a great circle of the earth passing through the poles and any given point on the earth's surface. **b.** the half of such a circle included between the poles. **2.** *Astron.* the great circle of the celestial sphere that passes through its poles and the observer's zenith. **3.** a point or period of highest development, greatest prosperity, or the like. **4.** (in acupuncture) any of the pathways in the body along which vital energy flows. **—adj. 5.** of or pertaining to a meridian. **6.** of or pertaining to midday or noon: *the meridian hour.* **7.** of or indicating a period of greatest prosperity, splendor, success, etc. [1350–1400; ME < L *merīdiānus* of noon, equiv. to *merīdi(ēs)* midday (formed from the locative *merīdiē* at midday, by dissimilation < **medī diē; medius* MID[1], *diēs* day) + *-ānus* -AN]

Me·rid·i·an (mə rid′ē ən), *n.* a city in E Mississippi. 46,577.

merid′ian an′gle, *Astron.* the angle, measured eastward or westward through 180°, between the celestial meridian of an observer and the hour circle of a celestial body. Cf. **hour angle.**

merid′ian cir′cle, *Astron.* a transit instrument provided with a graduated vertical scale, used to measure the declinations of heavenly bodies and to determine the time of meridian transits. Also called **circle, transit circle, transit instrument.** [1540–50]

mé·ri·di·enne (mə rid′ē en′, mə rid′ē en′; *Fr.* mā ʀē-dyen′), *n., pl.* **mé·ri·di·ennes** (mə rid′ē enz′, mə rid′ē-enz′; *Fr.* mā ʀē dyen′). *Fr. Furniture.* a short sofa of the Empire period, having arms of unequal height connected by a back with a sloping top. See illus. under **empire.** [< F, special use of fem. of *méridien* MERIDIAN (adj.)]

me·rid·i·o·nal (mə rid′ē ə nl), *adj.* **1.** of, pertaining to, or resembling a meridian. **2.** characteristic of the south or of people inhabiting the south, esp. of France. **3.** southern; southerly. **—n. 4.** an inhabitant of the south, esp. the south of France. [1350–1400; ME < LL *merīdiōnālis* southern, modeled on *septentriōnālis* SEPTENTRIONAL. See MERIDIAN, -AL[1]] **—me·rid′i·o·nal·ly,** *adv.*

Mer·i·lee (mer′i lē′), *n.* a female given name.

Mé·ri·mée (mā ʀē mā′), *n.* **Pros·per** (pʀô speʀ′), 1803–70, French short-story writer, novelist, and essayist.

Me·rín (*Sp.* me ʀēn′), *n.* Mirim.

Me·ri·na (mə rē′nə), *n., pl.* **-nas,** (*esp. collectively*) **-na.** a member of a Malagasy-speaking people who primarily inhabit the interior plateau of Madagascar.

me·ringue (mə rang′), *n.* **1.** a delicate, frothy mixture made with beaten egg whites and sugar or hot syrup, and browned, used as a topping for pies, pastry, etc. **2.** a pastry or pastry shell made by baking such a mixture, sometimes filled with fruit, whipped cream, etc. [1700–10; < F *méringue;* perh. to be identified with dial. (Walloon) *maringue* shepherd's loaf, *marinde* food for an outdoor repast (< L *merenda* light afternoon meal, prob. fem. ger. of *merere* to MERIT, such a meal being part of a laborer's wages), though certain evidence is lacking; assoc. with the town of Meiringen (Bern canton, Switzerland) is solely by folk etym.]

mé·ringue (mā rang′), *n., v.i.,* **-ringued, -ringu·ing.** merengue. [< F < Haitian Creole]

me·ri·no (mə rē′nō), *n., pl.* **-nos,** *adj.* **—n. 1.** (*often cap.*) one of a breed of sheep, raised originally in Spain, valued for their fine wool. **2.** wool from such sheep. **3.** a yarn or fabric made from this wool. **—adj. 4.** made of merino wool, yarn, or cloth. [1775–85; < Sp < Ar (*banū*) *marīn* a Berber tribe known for raising this breed]

Merino, *Ovis aries,* 2 ft. (0.6 m) high at shoulder

Mer·i·on·eth·shire (mer′ē on′ith shēr′, -shər), *n.* a historic county in Gwynedd, in N Wales. Also called **Mer′i·on′eth.**

mer·i·sis (mer′ə sis), *n. Biol.* growth, esp. growth resulting from cell division. Cf. **auxesis.** [1935–40; < Gk *meri-* (comb. form of *merís* part, portion) + -SIS]

mer·i·stem (mer′ə stem′), *n. Bot.* embryonic tissue in plants; undifferentiated, growing, actively dividing cells. [1870–75; < Gk *meristé(ós)* divided, distributed (equiv. to **merid-,* s. of *merízein* to divide into parts (deriv. of *méris* part, share) + *-tos* v. adj. suffix) + *-em* < Gk *-ēma* termination of nouns denoting result of action; cf. -EME]

mer·i·ste·mat·ic (mer′ə stə mat′ik), *adj. Bot.* consisting of or having the properties of meristem. [1880–85; *meristemat-,* base, in derivation, of MERISTEM (see GLOSSEMATICS) + -IC] **—mer′i·ste·mat′i·cal·ly,** *adv.*

me·ris·tic (mə ris′tik), *adj. Biol.* of, pertaining to, or divided into segments or somites. [1890–95; < Gk *meristikós* of division. See MERISTEM, -IC]

mer·it (mer′it), *n.* **1.** claim to respect and praise; excellence; worth. **2.** something that deserves or justifies a reward or commendation; a commendable quality, act, etc.: *The book's only merit is its sincerity.* **3. merits,** the inherent rights and wrongs of a matter, as a lawsuit, unobscured by procedural details, technicalities, personal feelings, etc.: *The case will be decided on its merits alone.* **4.** Often, **merits.** the state or fact of deserving; desert: *to treat people according to their merits.* **5.** *Rom. Cath. Ch.* worthiness of spiritual reward, acquired by righteous acts made under the influence of grace. **6.** *Obs.* something that is deserved, whether good or bad. **—v.t. 7.** to be worthy of; deserve. **—v.i. 8.** *Chiefly Theol.* to acquire merit. **—adj. 9.** based on merit: *a merit raise of $25 a week.* [1175–1225; ME < L *meritum* act worthy of praise (or blame), n. use of neut. of *meritus,* ptp. of *merēre* to earn] **—mer′it·ed·ly,** *adv.* **—mer′it·less,** *adj.*
—Syn. 1. value, credit. MERIT, DESERT, WORTH refer to the quality in a person, action, or thing that entitles recognition, esp. favorable recognition. MERIT is usually the excellence that entitles to praise: *a person of great merit.* DESERT is the quality that entitles one to a just reward: *according to her deserts.* WORTH is always used in a favorable sense and signifies inherent value or goodness: *The worth of your contribution is incalculable.*

mer′it badge′, an insignia or device granted by the Boy Scouts, worn esp. on a uniform to indicate special achievement. Cf. **proficiency badge.**

mer·i·toc·ra·cy (mer′i tok′rə sē), *n., pl.* **-cies. 1.** an elite group of people whose progress is based on ability and talent rather than on class privilege or wealth. **2.** a system in which such persons are rewarded and advanced: *The dean believes the educational system should be a meritocracy.* **3.** leadership by able and talented persons. [1955–60; MERIT + -O- + -CRACY] **—mer·i·to·crat·ic** (mer′i tə krat′ik), *adj.*

mer·i·to·crat (mer′i tə krat′), *n.* a member of a meritocracy. [1955–60; MERITO(CRACY) + -CRAT]

mer·i·to·ri·ous (mer′i tôr′ē əs, -tōr′-), *adj.* deserving praise, reward, esteem, etc.; praiseworthy: *to receive a gift for meritorious service.* [1375–1425; late ME < L *meritōrius* on hire. See MERIT, -TORY[1], -OUS] **—mer′i·to′ri·ous·ly,** *adv.* **—mer′i·to′ri·ous·ness,** *n.*

mer′it pay′, an additional sum paid to an employee, as a schoolteacher, whose work is superior and whose services are valued.

mer′it sys′tem, a system or policy whereby people are promoted or rewarded on the basis of ability and achievement rather than because of seniority, quotas, patronage, or the like. [1895–1900]

merk (merk), *n. Chiefly Scot.* mark[2] (def. 3).

mer·kin (mûr′kən), *n.* false hair for the female pudenda. [1610–20; orig. uncert.]

merle[1] (mûrl), *n. Chiefly Scot.* the blackbird, *Turdus merula.* Also, **merl.** [1350–1400; ME *merule* < MF < L *merulus, merula* ousel, blackbird]

merle[2] (mûrl), *n.* **1.** a bluish gray color mottled with black. **—adj. 2.** being the color merle. [1900–05; orig. uncert.]

Merle (mûrl), *n.* a male or female given name.

mer·lin (mûr′lin), *n.* a small, bold falcon, *Falco columbarius,* of the Northern Hemisphere. Also called **pigeon hawk.** [1350–1400; ME *merlioun, merlone* < AF *merilun,* OF *esmerillon,* dim. of *esmeril* < Gmc; akin to G *Schmerl,* ON *smyrill*]

Mer·lin (mûr′lin), *n.* **1.** *Arthurian Romance.* a venerable magician and seer. **2.** a male given name.

mer·lon (mûr′lən), *n.* (in a battlement) the solid part between two crenels. See illus. under **battlement.** [1695–1705; < F < It *merlone,* aug. of *merlo* (in pl., *merli* battlements) < ?]

CONCISE PRONUNCIATION KEY: act, cāpe, dâre, pärt; set, ēqual; if, īce; ox, ōver, ôrder, oil, bŏŏk, bōōt, out; up, ûrge; child; sing; shoe; thin, *th*at; zh as in *treasure.* ə = *a* as in *alone, e* as in *system, i* as in *easily, o* as in *gallop, u* as in *circus;* ᵊ as in *fire* (fīᵊr), *hour* (ouᵊr). l and n can serve as syllabic consonants, as in *cradle* (krād′l), and *button* (but′n). See the full key inside the front cover.

Mer•lot (mûr′lō; *Fr.* mer lō′), *n.* a dark-blue grape used in winemaking, esp. in the Bordeaux region of France and in areas of Italy, Switzerland, and California. [< F: lit., young blackbird, deriv. of *merle* MERLE[1], prob. alluding to the color of the grape]

mer•maid (mûr′mād′), *n.* **1.** (in folklore) a female marine creature, having the head, torso, and arms of a woman and the tail of a fish. **2.** a highly skilled female swimmer. [1300–50; ME *mermayde.* See MERE[2], MAID]

mer′maid's purse′, the horny or leathery egg case of certain cartilaginous fishes, as skates. [1830–40]

mer′maid's wine′glass, a colony of green algae, *Acetabularia crenulata,* of warm seas, having a cup-shaped cap on a slender stalk.

Mer′maid Tav′ern, an inn formerly located on Bread Street, Cheapside, in the heart of old London: a meeting place and informal club for Elizabethan playwrights and poets.

mer′maid weed′, any of several North American, aquatic plants of the genus *Proserpinaca,* having pinnately dissected leaves either above or below the water. [1810–20, *Amer.*]

mer•man (mûr′man′), *n., pl.* **-men. 1.** (in folklore) a male marine creature, having the head, torso, and arms of a man and the tail of a fish. **2.** a highly skilled male swimmer. [1595–1605; earlier *mere-man;* see MERE[2], MAN[1]]

Mer•nep•tah (mer′nep tä′, mər nep′tä), *n.* king of ancient Egypt c1225–c1215 B.C. (son of Ramses II). Also, **Meneptah.**

mero-, a combining form meaning "part," "partial," used in the formation of compound words: *merogony.* [< Gk *méros* part]

mer•o•blas•tic (mer′ə blas′tik), *adj. Embryol.* (of certain eggs) undergoing partial cleavage, resulting in unequal blastomeres. Cf. **holoblastic.** [1865–70; MERO- + -BLAST + -IC] —**mer′o•blas′ti•cal•ly,** *adv.*

Mer•o•dach (mer′ə däk′), *n.* Marduk.

Mer•o•ë (mer′ō ē′), *n.* a ruined city in Sudan, on the Nile, NE of Khartoum: a capital of ancient Ethiopia that was destroyed A.D c350.

me•rog•o•ny (mə rog′ə nē), *n. Embryol.* the development of an embryo from egg fragments lacking the egg nucleus but having an introduced male nucleus. [1899; MERO- + -GONY] —**mer•o•gon•ic** (mer′ə gon′ik), **me•rog•o•nous,** *adj.*

Mer•o•ite (mer′ō īt′), *n.* an inhabitant of Meroë. [MERO(Ë) + -ITE[1]]

mer•o•mor•phic (mer′ə môr′fik), *adj. Math.* of or pertaining to a function that is analytic, except for poles, in a given domain. [‡1885–90; MERO- + -MORPHIC]

Mer•o•pe (mer′ə pē), *n. Class. Myth.* **1.** a queen of Corinth and the foster mother of Oedipus. **2.** a queen of Messenia, the wife of Cresphontes and mother of Aepytus, who with Aepytus sought revenge upon Polyphontes, the brother and murderer of Cresphontes. **3.** one of the six visible stars in the Pleiades.

me•ro•pi•a (mə rō′pē ə), *n. Ophthalm.* partial blindness. [1855–60; MER(O)- + -OPIA]

mer•o•plank•ton (mer′ə plangk′tən), *n.* a floating mass of eggs and larvae of organisms that are nektonic or benthic in their adult stage; temporary plankton. [1905–10; back formation from *meroplanktonic;* see MERO-, PLANKTONIC]

Me•rops (mē′rops), *n.* (in the *Iliad*) a Percosian augur who foresaw and unsuccessfully tried to prevent the death of his sons in the Trojan War.

me•ros (mē′ros), *n.* (in the Doric order) a flat surface between two channels of a triglyph. [1795–1805; < Gk *mērós* leg-bone, lit., thigh]

-merous, a combining form meaning "having parts" of the kind or number specified by the initial element: *dimerous.* Cf. **-mer, -mere.** [< Gk *-meros,* adj. deriv. of *méros* part, portion, share; see -OUS]

Mer•o•vin•gi•an (mer′ə vin′jē ən, -jən), *adj.* **1.** of or pertaining to the Frankish dynasty established by Clovis, which reigned in Gaul and Germany from A.D. 476 to 751. —*n.* **2.** a member or supporter of the Merovingian dynasty. [1685–95; < F *mérovingien,* equiv. to *méroving-* (< ML < Gmc; cf. OE *Merewīowing* offspring of *Merewig,* grandfather of Clovis) + *-ien* -IAN]

mer•o•zo•ite (mer′ə zō′īt), *n.* (in the asexual reproduction of certain sporozoans) a cell developed from a schizont that parasitizes a red blood cell in the host. [1895–1900; MERO- + ZO- + -ITE[1]]

Mer•ri•am (mer′ē əm), *n.* a town in E Kansas. 10,794.

Mer•rick (mer′ik), *n.* **1. David** (*David Margulies*), born 1912, U.S. theatrical producer. **2.** a town on SW Long Island, in SE New York. 24,478.

Mer•rill (mer′əl), *n.* a male or female given name.

Mer′rill's Maraud′ers, the U.S. soldiers under the command of Brig. Gen. Frank Merrill during World War II, noted esp. for their skill at jungle fighting in the China-Burma-India theater. Also called **Mer′rill's Raid′ers.**

Mer•rill•ville (mer′əl vil′), *n.* a town in NE Indiana. 27,677.

Mer•ri•ly (mer′ə lē), *n.* a female given name, form of **Merry.**

Mer•ri•lyn (mer′ə lin), *n.* a female given name.

Mer•ri•mac (mer′ə mak′), *n.* a warship (originally the Union steamer *Merrimack*) that the Confederates converted into an ironclad, renamed the *Virginia,* and used against the *Monitor* in 1862 in the first battle between ironclads.

Mer•ri•mack (mer′ə mak′), *n.* **1.** a town in S New Hampshire. 15,406. **2.** a river in central New Hampshire and NE Massachusetts, flowing S and NE to the Atlantic. 110 mi. (175 km) long.

mer•ri•ment (mer′i mənt), *n.* **1.** cheerful or joyful gaiety; mirth; hilarity; laughter. **2.** *Obs.* a cause of mirth; a jest, entertainment, etc. [1570–80; MERRY + -MENT]
—**Syn. 1.** See **mirth.** —**Ant. 1.** misery, melancholy.

Mer′ritt Is′land (mer′it), a town in E Florida. 30,708.

mer•ry (mer′ē), *adj.,* **mer•ri•er, mer•ri•est. 1.** full of cheerfulness or gaiety; joyous in disposition or spirit: *a merry little man.* **2.** laughingly happy; mirthful; festively joyous; hilarious: *a merry time at the party.* **3.** *Archaic.* causing happiness; pleasant; delightful. **4. make merry, a.** to be happy or festive: *The New Year's revelers were making merry in the ballroom.* **b.** to make fun of; ridicule: *The unthinking children made merry of the boy who had no shoes.* [bef. 900; ME *meri(e), myrie, murie,* OE *myr(i)ge, mer(i)ge* pleasant, delightful] —**mer′ri•ly,** *adv.* —**mer′ri•ness,** *n.*
—**Syn. 1.** happy, blithe, blithesome, frolicsome, cheery, glad. See **gay. 2.** jolly, jovial, gleeful. —**Ant. 1.** sad. **2.** solemn.

Mer•ry (mer′ē), *n.* a female given name.

mer•ry-an•drew (mer′ē an′drōō), *n.* a clown; buffoon. [1665–75; MERRY + *Andrew,* generic use of the proper name]

mer•ry-bells (mer′ē belz′), *n., pl.* **-bells.** bellwort.

mer•ry-go-round (mer′ē gō round′), *n.* **1.** Also called **carousel, carrousel.** (in amusement parks, carnivals, etc.) a revolving, circular platform with wooden horses or other animals, benches, etc., on which people may sit or ride, usually to the accompaniment of mechanical or recorded music. **2.** a rapid whirl or a busy round, as of social life or business affairs. [1720–30]

mer•ry•mak•er (mer′ē mā′kər), *n.* a person who gaily or enthusiastically takes part in some festive or merry celebration; reveler. [1820–30; MERRY + MAKER]

mer•ry•mak•ing (mer′ē mā′king), *n.* **1.** the act of taking part gaily or enthusiastically in some festive or merry celebration. **2.** a merry festivity; revel. —*adj.* **3.** producing mirth; happy; festive. [1705–15; MERRY + MAKING]

Mer′ry Mount′, *Amer. Hist.* a settlement in Mt. Wollaston (Quincy), Mass., c1625–28, noted for its rejection of Puritan standards of behavior. Also, **Mer′ry•mount′.**

mer•ry•thought (mer′ē thôt′), *n. Chiefly Brit.* the wishbone or furcula of a fowl. [1600–10; so called from the custom of pulling the bone apart until it breaks, the person holding the longer (sometimes shorter) piece supposedly marrying first or being granted a wish at the time]

Mer′ry Wives′ of Wind′sor, The, a comedy (1598–1602?) by Shakespeare.

Mer•senne (mər sen′; *Fr.* mer sen′), *n.* **Ma•rin** (ma-ran′), 1588–1648, French mathematician.

Mersenne′ num′ber, *Math.* a number of the form, $2^p - 1$, where *p* is a prime number. [1890–95; named after M. MERSENNE]

Mer•sey (mûr′zē), *n.* **1.** a river in W England, flowing W from Derbyshire to the Irish Sea. 70 mi. (115 km) long. **2.** a river in SW Nova Scotia, in SE Canada, flowing SE to the Atlantic Ocean. ab. 25 mi. (40 km) long.

Mer•sey•side (mûr′zē sīd′), *n.* a metropolitan county in W England. 1,588,400; 250 sq. mi. (648 sq. km).

Mer•sin (mer sēn′), *n.* a seaport in S Turkey, on the NW coast of the Mediterranean Sea. 130,256.

mer•ten•si•a (mər ten′sē ə, -shē ə, -shə), *n.* any of various plants belonging to the genus *Mertensia,* of the borage family, including the lungworts and the Virginia cowslip. [< NL (1797), after Franz Karl *Mertens* (d. 1831), German botanist; see -IA]

Mer•thi•o•late (mər thī′ə lāt′), *Pharm., Trademark.* a brand of thimerosal.

Mer•thyr Tyd•fil (mûr′thər tid′vil; *Welsh* mer′thir tud′vil), **1.** an administrative district in Mid Glamorgan, in S Wales. 61,500; 43 sq. mi. (113 sq. km). **2.** a city in this district. 55,215.

Mer•ton (mûr′tn), *n.* **1. Robert King,** born 1910, U.S. sociologist. **2. Thomas,** 1915–68, U.S. poet and religious writer, born in France. **3.** a borough of Greater London, England. 173,200.

Mer•vin (mûr′vin), *n.* a male given name. Also, **Mer′•vyn.**

Mer•win (mûr′win), *n.* a male given name. Also, **Mer′wyn.**

Mer•yl (mer′əl), *n.* a female given name, form of **Merle.**

mes-, var. of **meso-** before vowels: *mesencephalon.*

me•sa (mā′sə), *n.* a land formation, less extensive than a plateau, having steep walls and a relatively flat top and common in arid and semiarid parts of the southwestern U.S. and Mexico. [1750–60, *Amer.;* < Sp: table < L *mēnsa*]

Me•sa (mā′sə), *n.* a city in central Arizona, near Phoenix. 152,453.

Me•sa′bi Range′ (mə sä′bē), a range of low hills in NE Minnesota, noted for major iron-ore deposits mined by the open-pit method.

mes•ail (mes′āl), *n. Armor.* a pivoted piece on a helmet between a visor and a beaver. Also, **mezail.** [1865–70; prob. << OF *muçaille* concealment, deriv. of *mucier* to conceal; cf. MICHE]

mé•sal•li•ance (mā′zə lī′əns, mā zal′ē əns; *Fr.* mā-zal yäns′), *n., pl.* **mé•sal•li•anc•es** (mā′zə lī′ən siz, mā-zal′ē ən siz; *Fr.* mā zal yäns′). a marriage with someone who is considered socially inferior; misalliance. [1775–85; < F; see MIS-, ALLIANCE]

mes•arch (mez′ärk, mes′-, mē′zärk, -särk), *adj.* **1.** *Bot.* (of a primary xylem or root) developing from both the periphery and the center; having the older cells surrounded by the younger cells. **2.** *Ecol.* (of a sere) originating in a mesic habitat. [1890–95; MES- + -ARCH]

Me•sa Ver•de (mā′sə vûrd′, vûr′dē), a national park in SW Colorado: ruins of prehistoric cliff dwellings. 80 sq. mi. (207 sq. km).

mesc (mesk), *n. Slang.* mescaline. [by shortening]

mes•cal (me skal′), *n.* **1.** an intoxicating beverage distilled from the fermented juice of certain species of agave. **2.** any agave yielding this spirit. **3.** Also called **peyote.** either of two species of spineless, dome-shaped cactus, *Lophophora williamsii* or *L. diffusa,* of Texas and northern Mexico, yielding the hallucinogen peyote. [1695–1705, *Amer.;* < MexSp *mescal, mezcal, mexcal* < Nahuatl *mexcalli* intoxicant distilled from agave (perh. equiv. to *me(tl)* maguey + *(i)xcalli* something cooked)]

mescal′ bean′, an evergreen shrub or small tree, *Sophora secundiflora,* of the legume family, of the southwestern U.S. and northern Mexico, having clusters of fragrant, violet-blue flowers and pods containing highly poisonous, bright red seeds. [1855–60, *Amer.*]

mescal′ but′ton, one of the dried, buttonlike tops of a mescal of the genus *Lophophora,* used as a hallucinogen, esp. by certain Indians of Mexico and the southwestern U.S. during religious ceremonies; peyote. [1885–90]

Mes•ca•le•ro (mes′kə lâr′ō), *n., pl.* **-ros,** (*esp. collectively*) **-ro.** a member of a group of Apache Indians who originally inhabited northern Mexico and the southwestern U.S. east of the Rio Grande, have intermarried with the Chiricahua and Lipan, and are presently situated in New Mexico.

mes•ca•line (mes′kə lēn′, -lin), *n. Pharm.* a white, water-soluble, crystalline powder, $C_{11}H_{17}NO_3$, obtained from mescal buttons, that produces hallucinations. [1895–1900; MESCAL + -INE[2]]

mes•dames (mā däm′, -dam′; *Fr.* mā dam′), *n.* **1.** a pl. of **madam. 2.** pl. of **madame.**

mes•de•moi•selles (mā′də mə zel′, mād′mwə zel′; *Fr.* mād mwa zel′), *n.* a pl. of **mademoiselle.**

me•seems (mē sēmz′), *v. impers.; pt.* **me•seemed.** *Archaic.* it seems to me. [1350–1400; ME *me semeth;* see ME, SEEM, -S[2]]

me•sem•bry•an•the•mum (mə zem′brē an′thə-məm), *n.* any of various chiefly Old World plants of the genus *Mesembryanthemum,* having thick, fleshy leaves and often showy flowers. [< NL (Linnaeus), irreg. < Gk *mesēmbrí(a)* midday + *ánthemon* flower]

mes•en•ceph•a•lon (mes′en sef′ə lon′, -lən, mez′-), *n., pl.* **-la** (-lə), **-lons.** *Anat.* the midbrain. [1840–50; MES- + ENCEPHALON] —**mes•en•ce•phal•ic** (mes′en sə-fal′ik, mez′-), *adj.*

mes•en•chyme (mes′eng kīm, mez′-), *n. Embryol.* cells of mesodermal origin that are capable of developing into connective tissues, blood, and lymphatic and blood vessels. [1885–90; var. of *mesenchyma* < NL < Gk *mesénchyma,* equiv. to *mes-* MES- + *énchyma* infusion] —**mes•en•chy•mal** (mes eng′kə məl, mez′-), **mes•en•chym•a•tous** (mes′eng kim′ə təs, mez′-), *adj.*

mes•en•ter•i•tis (mes′en tə rī′tis, mez′-, mes en′tə-, mez-), *n. Pathol.* inflammation of the mesentery. [1795–1805; MES- + ENTERITIS]

mes•en•ter•on (mes en′tə ron′, mez-), *n., pl.* **-ter•a** (-tər ə). midgut. [1875–80; MES- + ENTERON] —**mes•en′ter•on′ic,** *adj.*

mes•en•ter•y (mes′ən ter′ē, mez′-), *n., pl.* **-ter•ies.** *Anat.* the membrane, consisting of a double layer of peritoneum, that invests the intestines, attaching them to the posterior wall of the abdomen, maintaining them in position in the abdominal cavity, and supplying them with blood vessels, nerves, and lymphatics, esp. the part of this membrane investing the jejunum and ileum. [1375–1425; late ME < NL *mesenterium* < Gk *mesentérion* (equiv. to *mes-* MES- + *entérion,* neut. of *entérios* of the bowel); see ENTERON] —**mes′en•ter′ic,** *adj.*

mesh (mesh), *n.* **1.** any knit, woven, or knotted fabric of open texture. **2.** an interwoven or intertwined structure; network. **3.** any arrangement of interlocking metal links or wires with evenly spaced, uniform small openings between, as used in jewelry or sieves. **4.** one of the open spaces between the cords or ropes of a net. **5. meshes, a.** the threads that bind such spaces. **b.** the means of catching or holding fast: *to be caught in the meshes of the law.* **6.** *Mach.* the engagement of gear teeth. **7.** *Elect.* a set of branches that forms a closed path in a network so that removal of a branch results in an open path. **8.** *Metall.* a designation of a given fineness of powder used in powder metallurgy in terms of the number of the finest screen through which almost all the particles will pass: *This powder is 200 mesh.* —*v.t.* **9.** to catch or entangle in or as if in a net; enmesh. **10.** to form with meshes, as a net. **11.** *Mach.* to engage, as gear teeth. **12.** to cause to match, coordinate, or interlock: *They tried to mesh their vacation plans.* —*v.i.* **13.** to become enmeshed. **14.** *Mach.* to become or be engaged, as the teeth of one gear with those of another. **15.** to match, coordinate, or interlock: *The two versions of the story don't mesh.* [1375–1425; late ME *mesch,* appar. continuing OE *masc, max;* akin to OHG *māsca,* MD *maesche*]
—**Syn. 2.** web, netting, grill, screen, grid.

Me•shach (mē′shak), *n.* a companion of Daniel. Cf. **Shadrach.**

Me′sha Ste′le (mē′shə). See **Moabite Stone.**

Me•shed (me shed′), *n.* a city in NE Iran: Muslim shrine. 409,616. Persian, **Mashhad.**

mesh′ knot′. See **sheet bend.**

mesh•re•bee•yeh (mesh′rə bē′yə), *n.* (in Islamic countries) an oriel screened by latticework. Also, **mashrebeeyah, mashrebeeyeh.** [< Ar *mashrabīyah*]

CONCISE ETYMOLOGY KEY: <, descended or borrowed from; >, whence; b., blend of, blended; c., cognate with; cf., compare; deriv., derivative; equiv., equivalent; imit., imitative; obl., oblique; r., replacing; s., stem; sp., spelling, spelled; resp., respelling, respelled; trans., translation; ?, origin unknown; *, unattested; ‡, probably earlier than. See the full key inside the front cover.

me·shu·ga (mə shŏŏg′ə), *adj. Slang.* crazy; insane. Also, **me·shug′ga.** [1880–85; < Yiddish *meshuge* < Heb *məshuggā*′]

me·shu·gaas (mish′ə gäs′), *n. Slang.* foolishness; insanity; senselessness. Also, **mishegaas.** [1905–10; < Yiddish *meshugas* < Heb *məshuggā*′]

me·shu·ga·na (mə shŏŏg′ə nə), *n. Slang.* a crazy person. Also, **me·shug′ga·na, me·shug·ge·ner** (mə shŏŏg′ə nər). [1880–85; < Yiddish *meshugener*, equiv. to *meshuga* MESHUGA + epenthetic *n* + *-er* -ER[1]]

mesh·work (mesh′wûrk′), *n.* meshed work; network. [1820–30; MESH + WORK]

mesh·y (mesh′ē), *adj.*, **mesh·i·er, mesh·i·est.** formed with meshes; meshed. [1595–1605; MESH + -Y[1]]

me·si·al (mē′zē əl, -sē-, mez′ē əl, mes′-), *adj.* **1.** medial. **2.** *Dentistry.* directed toward the sagittal plane or midline of the face, along the dental arch. Cf. **buccal** (def. 3), **distal** (def. 2). [1795–1805; MES- + -IAL] **—me′si·al·ly,** *adv.*

mes·ic[1] (mez′ik, mes′-, mē′zik, -sik), *adj.* of, pertaining to, or adapted to an environment having a balanced supply of moisture. [1925–30; MES- + -IC] **—mes′i·cal·ly,** *adv.*

mes·ic[2] (mē′zik, -sik, mez′ik, mes′-); *adj. Physics.* of or pertaining to a meson; mesonic. [1935–40; MES(ON) + -IC]

me·sit·y·lene (mi sit′l ēn′, mes′i tl-), *n. Chem.* a colorless, liquid, aromatic hydrocarbon, C_9H_{12}, occurring naturally in coal tar and prepared from acetone: used chiefly as a chemical intermediate. [1830–40; *mesityl* (see MESITYL OXIDE) + -ENE]

mes′i·tyl ox′ide (mez′i til, mes′-), *Chem.* an oily, colorless liquid, $C_6H_{10}O$, having a honeylike odor: used chiefly as a solvent and in the manufacture of synthetic organic compounds. Also called **isopropylideneacetone, methylisobutenyl ketone.** [1870–75; *mesityl* < NL *mesit(a)* (< Gk *mesítēs* mediator, go-between, equiv. to *mes-* MES- + *-ītēs* -ITE[1]) + -YL]

Mes·mer (mez′mər; *Ger.* mes′mər), *n.* **Franz** (frants, franz; *Ger.* fränts) or **Frie·drich An·ton** (frē′drik an′tn, -ton; *Ger.* frē′drikh än′tōn), 1733–1815, Austrian physician.

mes·mer·ic (mez mer′ik, mes-), *adj.* **1.** produced by mesmerism; hypnotic. **2.** compelling; fascinating. [1820–30; MESMER(ISM) + -IC] **—mes·mer′i·cal·ly,** *adv.*

mes·mer·ism (mez′mə riz′əm, mes′-), *n.* **1.** hypnosis as induced, according to F. A. Mesmer, through animal magnetism. **2.** hypnotism. **3.** a compelling attraction; fascination. [1775–85; MESMER + -ISM] **—mes′mer·ist,** *n.*

mes·mer·ize (mez′mə rīz′, mes′-), *v.t.*, **-ized, -iz·ing.** **1.** to hypnotize. **2.** to spellbind; fascinate. **3.** to compel by fascination. Also, *esp. Brit.*, **mes′mer·ise′.** [1820–30; MESMER(ISM) + -IZE] **—mes′mer·i·za′tion,** *n.* **—mes′mer·iz′er,** *n.*

mesn·al·ty (mēn′l tē), *n. Law.* the estate of a mesne lord. [1535–45; < AF *me(s)nalte*, equiv. to *mesnal* (see MESNE, -AL[1]) + *-te* -TY[2]]

mesne (mēn), *adj. Law.* intermediate or intervening. [1350–1400; ME < AF, sp. var. of *meen* MEAN[3]]

mesne′ lord′, (in old English law) an intermediate feudal lord; the tenant of a chief lord and a lord to his own tenants. [1605–15]

meso-, a combining form meaning "middle," used in the formation of compound words: *mesocephalic.* Also, *esp. before a vowel,* **mes-.** [comb. form repr. Gk *mésos* middle, in the middle; akin to L *medius;* see MID[1]]

Mes·o·a·mer·i·ca (mez′ō ə mer′i kə, mes′-, mē′zō-, -sō-), *n.* **1.** *Anthropol., Archaeol.* the area extending approximately from central Mexico to Honduras and Nicaragua in which diverse pre-Columbian civilizations flourished. **2.** (loosely) Central America. Also, **Mes′o-A·mer′i·ca.** [MESO- + AMERICA] **—Mes′o·a·mer′i·can,** *adj., n.*

mes·o·ap·pen·dix (mez′ō ə pen′diks, mes′-, mē′zō-, -sō-), *n., pl.* **-dix·es, -di·ces** (-di sēz′). *Anat.* the mesentery of the vermiform appendix. [1895–1900; MESO- + APPENDIX] **—mes·o·ap·pen·di·ceal** (mez′ō ap′ən dish′əl, -ə pen′di sē′əl, mes′-, mē′zō-, -sō-), *adj.*

mes·o·blast (mez′ə blast′, mes′-, mē′zə-, -sə-), *n. Embryol.* **1.** the mesoderm. **2.** the primordial middle layer of a young embryo before the segregation of the germ layers, capable of becoming the mesoderm. [1855–60; MESO- + -BLAST] **—mes′o·blas′tic,** *adj.*

mes·o·car·di·um (mez′ə kär′dē əm, mes′-, mē′zə-, -sə-), *n., pl.* **-di·a** (-dē ə). *Embryol.* the double layer of splanchnic mesoderm supporting the embryonic heart. [MESO- + -CARDIUM]

mes·o·carp (mez′ə kärp′, mes′-, mē′zə-, -sə-), *n. Bot.* the middle layer of pericarp, as the fleshy part of certain fruits. See diag. under **pericarp.** [1840–50; MESO- + -CARP]

mes·o·ce·cum (mez′ə sē′kəm, mes′-, mē′zə-, -sə-), *n., pl.* **-ca** (-kə), *Anat.* the mesentery of the cecum. [1895–1900; MESO- + CECUM] **—mes·o·ce·cal** (mez′ə sē′kəl, mes′-, mē′zə-, -sə-), *adj.*

mes·o·ce·phal·ic (mez′ō sə fal′ik, mes′-, mē′zō-, -sō-), *adj. Cephalom.* having a head with a cephalic index between that of dolichocephaly and brachycephaly. [1855–60; MESO- + -CEPHALIC] **—mes′o·ceph′al·y,** *n.*

mes·o·co·lon (mez′ə kō′lən, mes′-, mē′zə-, -sə-), *n., pl.* **-lons, -la** (-lə). *Anat.* the mesentery of the colon. [1685–95; MESO- + COLON[2]]

mes·o·cra·nic (mez′ə krā′nik, mes′-, mē′zə-, -sə-), *adj. Craniom.* having a skull with a cranial index between that of dolichocranic and brachycranic skulls. [MESO- + CRAN(IO)- + -IC]

mes·o·crat·ic (mez′ə krat′ik, mes′-, mē′zə-, -sə-), *adj. Petrol.* (of an igneous rock) composed of light and dark minerals in nearly equal amounts. [1855–60; MESO- + -CRAT + -IC]

mes·o·cy·clone (mez′ə sī′klōn, mes′-, mē′zə-, -sə-), *n. Meteorol.* a small cyclone that arises near a thunderstorm and is sometimes associated with the occurrence of tornadoes. [1970–75; MESO- + CYCLONE]

mes·o·derm (mez′ə dûrm′, mes′-, mē′zə-, -sə-), *n. Embryol.* the middle germ layer of a metazoan embryo. [1870–75; MESO- + -DERM] **—mes′o·der′mal, mes′o·der′mic,** *adj.*

mes·o·dont (mez′ə dont′, mes′-, mē′zə-, -sə-), *adj.* having medium-sized teeth. Also, **mes′o·don′tic.** [1880–85; MES- + -ODONT]

mes·o·dont·ism (mez′ə don′tiz əm, mes′-, mē′zə-, -sə-), *n.* the condition of having medium-sized teeth. Also, **mes′o·don′ty.** [‡1960–65; MESODONT + -ISM]

mes·o·gas·tri·um (mez′ə gas′trē əm, mes′-, mē′zə-, -sə-), *n., pl.* **-tri·a** (-trē ə). *Anat.* the mesentery of the embryonic stomach. [1850–55; < NL, equiv. to *meso-* MESO- + Gk *gastr-,* s. of *gastḗr* belly + NL *-ium* -IUM] **—mes′o·gas′tric,** *adj.*

mes·o·gle·a (mez′ə glē′ə, mes′-, mē′zə-, -sə-), *n.* the noncellular, gelatinous material between the inner and outer body walls of a coelenterate or sponge. Also, **mes′o·gloe′a.** [1885–90; < NL *mesogloea,* equiv. to *meso-* MESO- + Gk *gloía* glue] **—mes′o·gle′al,** *adj.*

me·sog·na·thous (mi zog′nə thəs, -sog′-), *adj. Anthropol.* **1.** having medium, slightly protruding jaws. **2.** having a moderate or intermediate gnathic index of from 98 to 103. Also, **mes·og·nath·ic** (mez′əg nath′ik, mes′-, mē′zəg-, -səg-). [1875–80; MESO- + -GNATHOUS] **—me·sog′na·thism, me·sog′na·thy,** *n.*

mes·o·lec·i·thal (mez′ə les′ə thəl, les′-, mē′zə-, -sə-), *adj. Embryol.* centrolecithal. [MESO- + LECITHAL]

mes·o·lect (mez′ə lekt′, mes′-, mē′zə-, -sə-), *n. Ling.* any variety of language in a creole continuum that is intermediate between the basilect and the acrolect. Cf. **acrolect, basilect.** [MESO- + (DIA)LECT] **—mes′o·lec′tal,** *adj.*

mes·o·lite (mez′ə līt′, mes′-, mē′zə-, -sə-), *n.* a mineral variety of the zeolite group, intermediate in chemical composition between natrolite and scolecite. [1815–25; MESO- + -LITE]

Mes·o·lith·ic (mez′ə lith′ik, mes′-, mē′zə-, -sə-), *adj. Anthropol. (sometimes l.c.)* of, pertaining to, or characteristic of a transitional period of the Stone Age intermediate between the Paleolithic and the Neolithic periods, characterized by adaptation to a hunting, collecting, and fishing economy based on the use of forest, lakeside, and seashore environments; Epipaleolithic. [1865–70; MESO- + -LITHIC]

Me·so·lon·ghi (*Gk.* me′sô lông′gē), *n.* Missolonghi.

mes·o·mere (mez′ə mēr′, mes′-, mē′zə-, -sə-), *n. Embryol.* **1.** a blastomere of intermediate size between a micromere and a macromere. **2.** the intermediate zone of the mesoderm. [1900–05; MESO- + -MERE]

me·som·er·ism (mi zom′ə riz′əm, -som′-), *n. Chem.* resonance (def. 6). [1925–30; MESO- + *-merism,* on the model of ISOMERISM, TAUTOMERISM]

mes·o·me·te·or·ol·o·gy (mez′ō mē′tē ə rol′ə jē, mes′-, mē′zō-, -sō-), *n.* the study of atmospheric phenomena of relatively small size, as thunderstorms or tornadoes, and of the detailed structure of larger disturbances. Cf. **macrometeorology, micrometeorology.** [MESO- + METEOROLOGY] **—mes·o·me·te·or·o·log·i·cal** (mez′ō mē′tē ər ə loj′i kəl, mes′-, mē′zō-, -sō-), *adj.*

mes·o·morph (mez′ə môrf′, mes′-, mē′zə-, -sə-), *n.* a person of the mesomorphic type. [1935–40; MESO- + -MORPH]

mes·o·mor·phic (mez′ə môr′fik, mes′-, mē′zə-, -sə-), *adj.* **1.** pertaining to or having a muscular or sturdy body build characterized by the relative prominence of structures developed from the embryonic mesoderm (contrasted with *ectomorphic, endomorphic*). **2.** *Physical Chem.* pertaining to or existing in an intermediate state, as a liquid crystal in the nematic or smectic state. [1920–25; MESO- + -MORPHIC] **—mes′o·mor′phism,** *n.* **—mes′o·mor′phy,** *n.*

me·son (mē′zon, -son, mez′on, mes′-), *n. Physics.* any hadron, or strongly interacting particle, other than a baryon. Mesons are bosons, having spins of 0, 1, 2, . . . , and, unlike baryons, do not obey a conservation law. Cf. **quark model.** [1935–40; MES- + ON[1]; cf. MESOTRON] **—me·son′ic,** *adj.*

mes·o·neph·ros (mez′ə nef′ros, mes′-, mē′zə-, -sə-), *n., pl.* **-roi** (-roi). *Embryol.* one of the three embryonic excretory organs of vertebrates, becoming the functional kidney of fishes and amphibians and becoming part of the tubules or ductules in the reproductive systems of higher vertebrates. Cf. **metanephros, pronephros.** [1875–80; < NL, equiv. to *meso-* MESO- + Gk *nephrós* kidney] **—mes′o·neph′ric,** *adj.*

mes·o·pause (mez′ə pôz′, mes′-, mē′zə-, -sə-), *n. Meteorol.* **1.** the boundary or transition zone between the mesosphere and the ionosphere. Cf. **mesosphere** (def. 1). **2.** the top of the mesosphere, determined by the appearance of a temperature minimum near an altitude of 50 mi. (80 km). Cf. **mesosphere** (def. 2). [1945–50; MESO- + PAUSE]

mes·o·peak (mez′ə pēk′, mes′-, mē′zə-, -sə-), *n.* the level of maximum temperature in the mesosphere, at an altitude of about 30 mi. (48 km). [MESO- + PEAK[1]]

mes·o·pe·lag·ic (mez′ə pə laj′ik, mes′-, mē′zə-, -sə-), *adj. Oceanog.* of, pertaining to, or living in the ocean at a depth of between 600 ft. (180 m) and 3000 ft. (900 m). [1945–50; MESO- + PELAGIC]

mes·o·phile (mez′ə fīl′, -fil, mes′-, mē′zə-, -sə-), *Bacteriol.* **—***adj.* **1.** mesophilic. **—***n.* **2.** a mesophilic bacterium. [1925–30; MESO- + -PHILE]

mes·o·phil·ic (mez′ə fil′ik, mes′-, mē′zə-, -sə-), *adj.* (of bacteria) growing best at moderate temperatures, between 25°C and 40°C. Also, **mesophile, me·soph·i·lous** (mi zof′ə ləs, -sof′-). [1895–1900; MESO- + -PHILIC]

mes·o·phyll (mez′ə fil, mes′-, mē′zə-, -sə-), *n. Bot.* the parenchyma, usually containing chlorophyll, that forms the interior parts of a leaf. [1830–40; MESO- + -PHYLL] **—mes′o·phyl′lic, mes′o·phyl′lous,** *adj.*

mes·o·phyte (mez′ə fīt′, mes′-, mē′zə-, -sə-), *n.* a plant growing under conditions of well-balanced moisture supply. [1885–90; MESO- + -PHYTE] **—mes·o·phyt·ic** (mez′ə fit′ik, mes′-, mē′zə-, -sə-), *adj.*

mes·o·plank·ton (mez′ə plangk′tən, mes′-, mē′zə-, -sə-), *n.* **1.** plankton that live at middle depths. **2.** planktonic organisms between 0.04 and 0.4 in. (1 mm and 1 cm) in length. [1895–1900; MESO- + PLANKTON]

Mes·o·po·ta·mi·a (mes′ə pə tā′mē ə), *n.* an ancient region in W Asia between the Tigris and Euphrates rivers: now part of Iraq. **—Mes′o·po·ta′mi·an,** *adj., n.*

mes·o·rec·tum (mez′ə rek′təm, mes′-, mē′zə-, -sə-), *n., pl.* **-tums, -ta** (-tə). *Anat.* the mesentery of the rectum. [1825–35; MESO- + RECTUM]

mes·or·rhine (mez′ə rīn′, -rin, mes′-, mē′zə-, -sə-), *adj. Anthropol.* having a moderately broad and high-bridged nose. [1875–80; MESO- + *-rrhine* < Gk *-rhīnos* -nosed, adj. deriv. of *rhī́s* nose] **—mes′or·rhi′ny,** *n.*

mes·o·scale (mez′ə skāl′, mes′-, mē′zə-, -sə-), *adj.* pertaining to meteorological phenomena, such as wind circulation and cloud patterns, that are about 1–100 km (0.6–60 mi.) in horizontal extent. [1955–60; MESO- + SCALE[3]]

mes·o·some (mez′ə sōm′, mes′-, mē′zə-, -sə-), *n.* **1.** the anterior portion of the abdomen in arachnids. **2.** a whorled structure extending inward from the cell membrane in Gram-positive bacteria and containing enzymes for cellular respiration. [1955–60; MESO- + -SOME[3]]

mes·o·sphere (mez′ə sfēr′, mes′-, mē′zə-, -sə-), *n.* **1.** (in the classification of the earth's atmosphere by chemical properties) the region between the ionosphere and the exosphere, extending from about 250–650 mi. (400–1050 km) above the surface of the earth. **2.** (in the classification of the earth's atmosphere by thermal properties) the region between the stratosphere and the thermosphere, extending from about 20–50 mi. (32–80 km) above the surface of the earth. [1945–50; MESO- + -SPHERE] **—mes·o·spher·ic** (mez′ə sfer′ik, mes′-, mē′zə-, -sə-), *adj.*

mes·o·the·li·o·ma (mez′ə thē′lē ō′mə, mes′-, mē′zə-, -sə-), *n., pl.* **-mas, -ma·ta** (-mə tə). *Pathol.* a malignant tumor of the covering of the lung or the lining of the pleural and abdominal cavities, often associated with exposure to asbestos. [1905–10; MESOTHELI(UM) + -OMA]

mes·o·the·li·um (mez′ə thē′lē əm, mes′-, mē′zə-, -sə-), *n., pl.* **-li·a** (-lē ə). *Anat., Embryol.* epithelium of mesodermal origin, which lines the body cavities. [1885–90; MESO- + (EPI)THELIUM] **—mes′o·the′li·al,** *adj.*

mes·o·tho·rax (mez′ə thôr′aks, -thōr′-, mes′-, mē′zə-, -sə-), *n., pl.* **-tho·rax·es, -tho·ra·ces** (-thôr′ə sēz′, -thōr′-). the middle segment of the three divisions of the thorax of an insect, bearing the second pair of legs and the first pair of wings. [1820–30; MESO- + THORAX] **—mes·o·tho·rac·ic** (mez′ə thô ras′ik, -thō-, mes′-, mē′zə-, -sə-), *adj.*

mes·o·tron (mez′ə tron′, mes′-, mē′zə-, -sə-), *n. Physics.* (no longer in technical use) meson. [1935–40; MESO- + (ELEC)TRON] **—mes′o·tron′ic,** *adj.*

mes·o·var·i·um (mez′ə vâr′ē əm, mes′-, mē′zə-, -sə-), *n., pl.* **-var·i·a** (-vâr′ē ə). *Anat.* the mesentery of the ovary. [1885–90; MES- + OVARIUM]

Mes·o·zo·a (mez′ə zō′ə, mes′-, mē′zə-, -sə-), *n. Zool.* the phylum of invertebrates comprising the mesozoans, parasitic wormlike multicellular organisms sometimes considered to be intermediate in complexity between protozoans and metazoans. [1875–80; < NL; see MESO-, -ZOA]

mes·o·zo·an (mez′ə zō′ən, mes′-, mē′zə-, -sə-), *Zool.* **—***n.* **1.** any member of the phylum Mesozoa. **—***adj.* **2.** of or pertaining to the mesozoans. [MESOZO(A) + -AN]

Mes·o·zo·ic (mez′ə zō′ik, mes′-, mē′zə-, -sə-), *Geol.* **—***adj.* **1.** noting or pertaining to an era occurring between 230 and 65 million years ago, characterized by the appearance of flowering plants and by the appearance and extinction of dinosaurs. See table under **geologic time.** **—***n.* **2.** the Mesozoic Era or group of systems. [1830–40; MESO- + ZO- + -IC]

mes·quite (me skēt′, mes′kēt), *n.* **1.** any of several usually spiny trees or shrubs belonging to the genus *Prosopis,* of the legume family, as *P. juliflora* or *P. glandulosa,* of western North America, having bipinnate leaves and beanlike pods and often forming dense thickets. **2.** the wood of such a tree or shrub, used esp. in grilling or barbecuing food. **3.** any of various similar or

CONCISE PRONUNCIATION KEY: act, cāpe, dâre, pärt; set, ēqual; *if,* ice; ox, ōver, ôrder, oil, bŏŏk, bŏŏt, out; up, ûrge; child; sing; shoe; thin, *that;* zh as in *treasure.* ə = *a* as in *alone, e* as in *system, i* as in *easily,* o as in *gallop, u* as in *circus;* ° as in *fire* (fī°r), *hour* (ou°r). l and n can serve as syllabic consonants, as in *cradle* (krād′l), and *button* (but′n). See the full key inside the front cover.

related plants. Also, **mes•quit′.** [1830–40, *Amer.*; < MexSp *mezquite* < Nahuatl *mizquitl*]

Mes•quite (me skēt′, mi-), *n.* a city in NE Texas, E of Dallas. 67,053.

mess (mes), *n.* **1.** a dirty, untidy, or disordered condition: *The room was in a mess.* **2.** a person or thing that is dirty, untidy, or disordered. **3.** a state of embarrassing confusion: *My affairs are in a mess.* **4.** an unpleasant or difficult situation: *She got into a mess driving without a license.* **5.** a dirty or untidy mass, litter, or jumble: *a mess of papers.* **6.** a group regularly taking their meals together. **7.** the meal so taken. **8.** See **mess hall. 9.** *Naval.* messroom. **10.** a quantity of food sufficient for a dish or a single occasion: *to pick a mess of sweet corn for dinner.* **11.** a sloppy or unappetizing preparation of food. **12.** a dish or quantity of soft or liquid food: *to cook up a nice mess of pottage.* **13.** a person whose life or affairs are in a state of confusion, esp. a person with a confused or disorganized moral or psychological outlook. —*v.t.* **14.** to make dirty or untidy (often fol. by *up*): *Don't mess the room.* **15.** to make a mess or muddle of (affairs, responsibilities, etc.) (often fol. by *up*): *They messed the deal.* **16.** to supply with meals, as military personnel. **17.** to treat roughly; beat up (usually followed by *up*): *The gang messed him up.* —*v.i.* **18.** to eat in company, esp. as a member of a mess. **19.** to make a dirty or untidy mess. **20. mess around** or **about, a.** *Informal.* to busy oneself without purpose or plan; work aimlessly or halfheartedly; putter. **b.** *Informal.* to waste time; loaf. **c.** *Informal.* to meddle or interfere. **d.** *Informal.* to involve or associate oneself, esp. for immoral or unethical purposes: *His wife accused him of messing around with gamblers.* **e.** *Slang.* to trifle sexually; philander. **21. mess in** or **with,** to intervene officiously; meddle: *You'll get no thanks for messing in the affairs of others.* **22. mess up, a.** to make dirty, untidy, or disordered. **b.** to make muddled, confused, etc.; make a mess of; spoil; botch. **c.** to perform poorly; bungle: *She messed up on the final exam.* [1250–1300; ME *mes* < OF: a course at a meal < LL *missus* what is sent (i.e., put on the table), n. use of ptp. of L *mittere* to send] —**Syn. 3.** muddle, farrago, hodgepodge. **4.** predicament, plight, muddle, pickle. **15.** confuse, mix up. —**Ant. 1.** tidiness. **3.** order. **15.** arrange.

mes•sage (mes′ij), *n.* **1.** a communication containing some information, news, advice, request, or the like, sent by messenger, radio, telephone, or other means. **2.** an official communication, as from a chief executive to a legislative body: *the President's message to Congress.* **3.** the inspired utterance of a prophet or sage. **4.** *Computers.* one or more words taken as a unit. **5.** the point, moral, or meaning of a gesture, utterance, novel, motion picture, etc. **6. get the message,** *Informal.* to understand or comprehend, esp. to infer the correct meaning from circumstances, hints, etc.: *If we don't invite him to the party, maybe he'll get the message.* [1250–1300; ME < OF < VL *missāticum, equiv. to L *miss(us)* sent (ptp. of *mittere* to send) + *-āticum* -AGE]

mes′sage cen′ter, an office or other area where incoming and outgoing messages, mail, etc., are received and transmitted, as by telephone, computer, or messenger. [1940–45]

mes′sage switch′ing, *Telecommunications.* the process by which data transmissions are stored until a proper circuit is available so that they can be forwarded.

mes′sage u′nit, a measure of the duration of and distance covered by local telephone calls, used by telephone companies as a basis for assessing service charges. [1960–65]

mes•sag•ing (mes′ə jing), *n.* a system or process of transmitting messages, esp. electronically, by computer, telephone, television cable, etc. [MESSAGE + -ING[1]]

Mes•sa•lian (mi sāl′yən, -sā′lē ən), *n.* Euchite. [1585–95; < LGk *Messaliānós* < Syriac *məṣallәyānē* given to prayer]

Mes•sa•li•na (mes′ə lī′nə), *n.* **Valeria,** died A.D. 48, third wife of Claudius I.

mes•sa•line (mes′ə lēn′, mes′ə lēn′), *n.* a thin, soft silk with a twill or satin weave. [1905–10; < F]

mes•san (mes′ən), *n. Scot.* a lap dog; small pet dog. Also, **messin.** [1490–1500; < ScotGael *measàn* pet]

Mes•sa•pic (mə sā′pik, -sap′ik), *n.* an Indo-European language that was spoken in what is now SE Italy and written with an alphabet derived from that of Greek. Also, **Mes•sa•pi•an** (mə sā′pē ən). [1765–75; < L *Mesāp(ius)* pertaining to *Messāpia* the Calabrian peninsula + -IC]

mess′ call′, *Mil.* a bugle call for mess.

Mes•sei•gneurs (*Fr.* mā se nyœr′), *n.* (*sometimes l.c.*) pl. of **Monseigneur.**

Mes•se•ne (me sē′nē), *n.* an ancient city in the SW Peloponnesus; capital of ancient Messenia.

mes•sen•ger (mes′ən jər), *n.* **1.** a person who carries a message or goes on an errand for another, esp. as a matter of duty or business. **2.** a person employed to convey official dispatches or to go on other official or special errands: *a bank messenger.* **3.** *Naut.* **a.** a rope or chain made into an endless belt to pull on an anchor cable or to drive machinery from some power source, as a capstan or winch. **b.** a light line by which a heavier line, as a hawser, can be pulled across a gap between a ship and a pier, a buoy, another ship, etc. **4.** *Oceanog.* a brass weight sent down a line to actuate a Nansen bottle or other oceanographic instrument. **5.** *Archaic.* a herald, forerunner, or harbinger. [1175–1225; ME *messager, messangere* < AF; OF *messagier.* See MESSAGE, -ER[2]] —**Syn. 1.** bearer, courier.

messenger RNA, *Genetics.* a single-stranded molecule of RNA that is synthesized in the nucleus from a DNA template and then enters the cytoplasm, where its genetic code specifies the amino acid sequence for protein synthesis. *Abbr.:* mRNA [1960–65]

Mes•se•ni•a (mə sē′nē ə, -sēn′yə), *n.* a division of ancient Greece, in the SW Peloponnesus: an important center of Mycenaean culture.

Mes•ser•schmitt (mes′ər shmit′), *n.* any of several types of fighter aircraft extensively used by the German air force in World War II, esp. the ME-109. [1935–40; named after Willy *Messerschmitt* (1898–1978), German aircraft designer]

mess′ gear′. See **mess kit.** [1885–90]

mess′ hall′, a place in which a group eats regularly, esp. a dining hall in a military camp, post, etc. [1860–65]

Mes•siaen (mes yäN′), *n.* **O•li•vier Eu•gène Pros•per Charles** (ô lē vyā′ œ zhen′ prô sper′ sharl), 1908–92, French composer and organist.

Mes•si•ah (mi sī′ə), *n.* **1.** the promised and expected deliverer of the Jewish people. **2.** Jesus Christ, regarded by Christians as fulfilling this promise and expectation. John 4:25, 26. **3.** (*usually l.c.*) any expected deliverer. **4.** (*usually l.c.*) a zealous leader of some cause or project. **5.** (*italics*) an oratorio (1742) by George Frideric Handel. Also, *Douay Bible,* **Mes•si•as** (mi sī′əs) (for defs. 1, 2). [< LL (Vulgate) *Messīās* < Gk *Messīās* < Heb *māshīaḥ* lit., anointed] —**Mes•si′ah•ship′,** *n.* —**Mes•si•an•ic** (mes′ē an′ik), *adj.* —**Mes′si•an′i•cal•ly,** *adv.*

mes•si•a•nism (mes′ē ə niz′əm, mə sī′ə-), *n.* **1.** (*often cap.*) the belief in the coming of the Messiah, or a movement based on this belief. **2.** the belief in a leader, cause, or ideology as a savior or deliverer. [1875–80; < LL *Messiān-*, s. of *Messiās* MESSIAH + -ISM] —**mes′si•a•nist, Mes′si•a•nist** *n.*

Mes•si•dor (me sē dôr′), *n.* (in the French Revolutionary calendar) the tenth month of the year, extending from June 19 to July 18.

Mes•sier (mes′ē ā′; *Fr.* me syā′), *n.* **Charles** (sharl), 1730–1817, French astronomer.

Mes′sier cat′alog, *Astron.* a catalog of nonstellar objects compiled by Charles Messier in 1784 and later slightly extended, now known to contain nebulae, galaxies, and star clusters.

Mes′sier num′ber, *Astron.* a number (preceded by M) designating the 109 double stars, clusters, nebulae, and galaxies in the Messier catalog.

mes•sieurs (mās yûrz′, mes′ərz; *Fr.* me syœ′), *n.* pl. of **monsieur.**

mess•i•ly (mes′ə lē), *adv.* in a messy manner. [MESSY + -LY]

mes•sin (mes′ən), *n. Scot.* messan.

Mes•si•na (me sē′nə), *n.* **1.** a seaport in NE Sicily. 265,918. **2. Strait of,** a strait between Sicily and Italy. 2½ mi. (4 km) wide.

Mes•sines (*Fr.* me sēn′), *n.* a village in W Belgium, near Ypres: battles 1914, 1917.

mess′ jack′et, a short, tailless jacket extending to just below the waist, used for semiformal military occasions and now esp. as part of the uniform of waiters, bellhops, etc. [1890–95]

mess′ kit′, a portable set of usually metal cooking and eating utensils, used esp. by soldiers and campers. Also called **mess gear.** [1875–80]

mess•man (mes′mən), *n., pl.* **-men.** *Naval.* an enlisted person who serves in the messroom. [1840–50; MESS + -MAN]

mess•mate (mes′māt′), *n.* a person, esp. a friend, who is a member of a group regularly taking meals together, as in an army camp. [1720–30; MESS + MATE[1]]

mess•room (mes′ro͞om′, -ro͝om′), *n.* a dining room aboard ship or at a naval base. [1805–15; MESS + ROOM]

Messrs. (mes′ərz), pl. of **Mr.**

mes•suage (mes′wij), *n. Law.* a dwelling house with its adjacent buildings and the lands appropriated to the use of the household. [1350–1400; ME < AF, misreading (*n* taken as *u*) of OF *mesnage* MÉNAGE]

mess-up (mes′up′), *n.* a blunder; state of confusion; mix-up. [1900–05; n. use of v. phrase *mess up*]

mess•y (mes′ē), *adj.,* **mess•i•er, mess•i•est. 1.** characterized by a dirty, untidy, or disordered condition: *a messy room.* **2.** causing a mess: *a messy recipe; messy work.* **3.** embarrassing, difficult, or unpleasant: *a messy political situation.* **4.** characterized by moral or psychological confusion. [1835–45; MESS + -Y[1]] —**mess′i•ness,** *n.*

mes•tee (me stē′), *n.* mustee.

mes•ti•za (me stē′zə, mi-), *n.* a woman of racially mixed ancestry, esp., in Latin America, of mixed American Indian and European ancestry or, in the Philippines, of mixed native and foreign ancestry. [< Sp]

mes•ti•zo (me stē′zō, mi-), *n., pl.* **-zos, -zoes.** a person of racially mixed ancestry, esp., in Latin America, of mixed American Indian and European, usually Spanish or Portuguese, ancestry, or, in the Philippines, of mixed native and foreign ancestry. [1580–90; < Sp, n. use of adj. *mestizo* < VL **mixtīcius* mixed]

mes•tra•nol (mes′trə nôl′, -nol′), *n. Pharm.* an estrogen, $C_{21}H_{26}O_2$, used in oral contraceptives in combination with a progestin. [1960–65; contr. and rearrangement of *methoxy-* and *ethynylestradiol,* components of the chemical name]

Meš•tro•vić (mesh′trə vich; *Serbo-Croatian.* mesh′trô vich′), *n.* **I•van** (ī′vən; *Serbo-Croatian.* ē′vän), 1883–1962, Yugoslav sculptor, in the U.S. after 1946.

Mes•u•rol (mez′ə rôl′, -rol′, mes′-), *Chem., Trademark.* a brand of methiocarb.

met (met), *v.* pt. and pp. of **meet**[1].

Met, *Biochem.* methionine.

met-, var. of **meta-** before a vowel: *metempirical.*

met., **1.** metaphor. **2.** metaphysics. **3.** meteorology. **4.** metropolitan.

me•ta[1] (mē′tə), *n., pl.* **-tae** (-tē). (in ancient Rome) a column or post, or a group of columns or posts, placed at each end of a racetrack to mark the turning places. [1570–80; < L *mēta* cone, turning post]

met•a[2] (met′ə), *adj. Chem.* pertaining to or occupying two positions (1, 3) in the benzene ring that are separated by one carbon atom. Cf. **ortho, para**[3]. See diag. under **ortho.** [1875–80; independent use of META-]

Me•ta (mē′tə), *n.* a female given name.

meta-, **1.** a prefix appearing in loanwords from Greek, with the meanings "after," "along with," "beyond," "among," "behind," and productive in English on the Greek model: *metacarpus; metagenesis; metalinguistics.* **2.** *Chem.* **a.** (of acids, salts, or their organic derivatives) a prefix denoting the least hydrated of a series: *metaantimonic,* $HSbO_3$; *meta-antimonous,* $HSbO_2$. Cf. **ortho-, pyro-. b.** a prefix designating the meta position in the benzene ring. *Abbr.:* m-. Cf. **ortho-, para-**[1]. Also, *esp. before a vowel,* **met-.** [< Gk, prefix and prep.; c. OE *mid* with, G *mit,* Goth *mith*]

met•a•bi•o•sis (met′ə bī ō′sis), *n. Biol.* a mode of living in which one organism is dependent on another for preparation of an environment in which it can live. [1895–1900; META- + -BIOSIS] —**met•a•bi•ot•ic** (met′ə bī ot′ik), *adj.* —**met•a•bi•ot′i•cal•ly,** *adv.*

met•a•bol•ic (met′ə bol′ik), *adj.* **1.** of, pertaining to, or affected by metabolism. **2.** undergoing metamorphosis. [1735–45; < Gk *metabolikós* changeable, equiv. to *metabol(ḗ)* (see METABOLISM) + *-ikos* -IC] —**met′a•bol′i•cal•ly,** *adv.*

met′abol′ic heat′, *Physiol.* See **animal heat.**

me•tab•o•lism (mə tab′ə liz′əm), *n.* **1.** *Biol., Physiol.* the sum of the physical and chemical processes in an organism by which its material substance is produced, maintained, and destroyed, and by which energy is made available. Cf. **anabolism, catabolism. 2.** any basic process of organic functioning or operating: *changes in the country's economic metabolism.* [1875–80; < Gk *metabol(ḗ)* change (*meta-* META- + *bolḗ* a throw) + -ISM]

me•tab•o•lite (mə tab′ə līt′), *n. Biol., Physiol.* a product of metabolic action. [1880–85; METABOL(ISM) + -ITE[1]]

me•tab•o•lize (mə tab′ə līz′), *v.t., v.i.,* **-lized, -liz•ing.** to subject to metabolism; change by metabolism. Also, *esp. Brit.,* **me•tab′o•lise′.** [1885–90; METABOL(ISM) + -IZE] —**me•tab′o•liz′a•bil′i•ty,** *n.* —**me•tab′o•liz′a•ble,** *adj.* —**me•tab′o•liz′er,** *n.*

met•a•car•pal (met′ə kär′pəl), *adj. Anat.* **1.** of or pertaining to the metacarpus. —*n.* **2.** a metacarpal bone. [1730–40; META- + CARPAL]

met•a•car•pus (met′ə kär′pəs), *n., pl.* **-pi** (-pī). *Anat.* the part of a hand or forelimb, esp. of its bony structure, included between the wrist, or carpus, and the fingers, or phalanges. See diag. under **skeleton.** [1670–80; < NL (see META-, CARPUS), r. *metacarpium* < Gk *metakárpion*]

met•a•cen•ter (met′ə sen′tər), *n. Naval Archit.* the intersection between two vertical lines, one through the center of buoyancy of a hull in equilibrium, the other through the center of buoyancy when the hull is inclined slightly to one side or toward one end: the distance of this intersection above the center of gravity is an indication of the initial stability of the hull. Also, *esp. Brit.,* **met′a•cen′tre.** [1785–95; < F *métacentre.* See META-, CENTER]

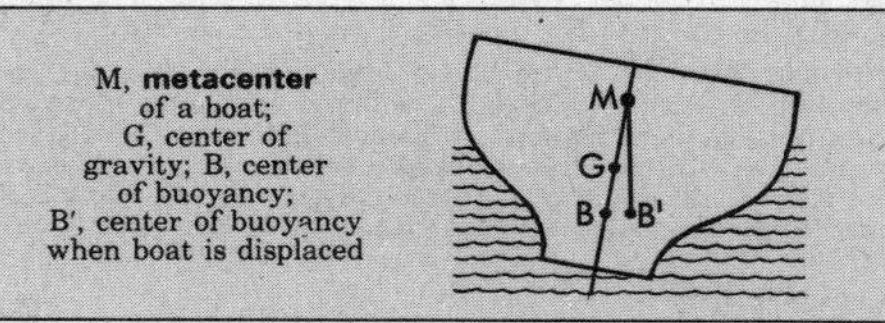

M, **metacenter** of a boat; G, center of gravity; B, center of buoyancy; B′, center of buoyancy when boat is displaced

met•a•cen•tric (met′ə sen′trik), *adj.* **1.** *Naval Archit.* of or pertaining to a metacenter. **2.** *Genetics.* of or pertaining to any chromosome or chromatid whose centromere is centrally located, creating two apparently equal chromosome arms. Cf. **acentric,** (def. 2), **acrocentric, telocentric.** [META- + -CENTRIC] —**met•a•cen•tric•i•ty** (met′ə sen tris′i tē), *n.*

met′acen′tric height′, *Naval Archit.* the distance between the center of gravity and the metacenter of a floating body, as of a vessel.

met•a•cer•car•i•a (met′ə sər kâr′ē ə), *n. pl.* **-car•i•ae** (-kâr′ē ē′). *Zool.* the encysted larva of a trematode, usually found in or on an aquatic intermediate host. Cf. **cercaria.** [1925–30; < NL; see META-, CERCARIA]

met•a•chro•ma•tism (met′ə krō′mə tiz′əm), *n.* change of color, esp. that due to variation in the temperature of a body. [1875–80; META- + CHROMAT- + -ISM] —**met•a•chro•mat•ic** (met′ə krō mat′ik, -krə-), *adj.*

met•a•cin•na•bar (met′ə sin′ə bär′), *n. Mineral.* a polymorph of cinnabar, black mercuric sulfide, HgS. [META- + CINNABAR]

Met•a•com•et (met′ə kom′it), *n.* See **Philip, King.**

met•a•cryst (met′ə krist′), *n. Geol.* a crystal formed by recrystallization of minerals in a metamorphic rock. [1910–15; META- + (PHENO)CRYST]

met•a•di•chlo•ro•ben•zene (met′ə dī klôr′ə ben′-zēn, -ben zēn′, -klōr′-), *n. Chem.* a colorless liquid, $C_6H_4Cl_2$, soluble in alcohol and ether: used as a fumigant and insecticide. Cf. **dichlorobenzene.**

met•a•eth•ics (met′ə eth′iks, met′ə eth′-), *n.* (*usually used with a singular v.*) the philosophy of ethics dealing with the meaning of ethical terms, the nature of moral discourse, and the foundations of moral principles. Also, **met′a•eth′ics.** [1945–50; META- + ETHICS] —**met′a•eth′i•cal,** *adj.*

CONCISE ETYMOLOGY KEY: <, descended or borrowed from; >, whence; b., blend of, blended; c., cognate with; cf., compare; deriv., derivative; equiv., equivalent; imit., imitative; obl., oblique; r., replacing; s., stem; sp., spelling, spelled; resp., respelling, respelled; trans., translation; ?, origin unknown; *, unattested; ‡, probably earlier than. See the full key inside the front cover.

met•a•gal•ax•y (met′ə gal′ək sē), *n., pl.* **-ax•ies.** *Astron.* the complete system of galaxies; the Milky Way and all the surrounding galaxies. [1925–30; META- + GALAXY] —**met•a•ga•lac•tic** (met′ə gə lak′tik), *adj.*

met•age (mē′tij), *n.* **1.** the official measurement of contents or weight. **2.** the charge for such measurement. [1520–30; METE[1] + -AGE]

met•a•gen•e•sis (met′ə jen′ə sis), *n. Biol.* reproduction characterized by the alternation of a sexual generation and a generation that reproduces asexually; alternation of generations. [1885–90; META- + GENESIS] —**met•a•ge•net•ic** (met′ə jə net′ik), **met′a•gen′ic,** *adj.* —**met′a•ge•net′i•cal•ly,** *adv.*

me•tag•na•thous (mə tag′nə thəs), *adj.* **1.** *Ornith.* having the tips of the mandibles crossed, as the crossbills. **2.** *Entomol.* having biting mouthparts in the larval stage and sucking mouthparts in the adult stage. [1870–75; META- + -GNATHOUS] —**me•tag′na•thism,** *n.*

met•al (met′l), *n., v.,* **-aled, -al•ing** or (*esp. Brit.*) **-alled, -al•ling.** —*n.* **1.** any of a class of elementary substances, as gold, silver, or copper, all of which are crystalline when solid and many of which are characterized by opacity, ductility, conductivity, and a unique luster when freshly fractured. **2.** *Chem.* **a.** such a substance in its pure state, as distinguished from alloys. **b.** an element yielding positively charged ions in aqueous solutions of its salts. **3.** an alloy or mixture composed wholly or partly of such substances, as brass. **4.** an object made of metal. **5.** formative material; stuff. **6.** mettle. **7.** *Print.* **a.** See **type metal. b.** the state of being set in type. **8.** molten glass in the pot or melting tank. **9.** *Brit.* See **road metal.** —*v.t.* **10.** to furnish or cover with metal. **11.** *Brit.* to pave or surface (a road) with broken stone. [1250–1300; ME (< OF) < L *metallum* quarry, metal < Gk *métallon* mine, quarry, metal] —**met′al•like′,** *adj.*

metal., **1.** metallurgical. **2.** metallurgy.

met•a•lan•guage (met′ə lang′gwij), *n.* any language or symbolic system used to discuss, describe, or analyze another language or symbolic system. [1935–40; META- + LANGUAGE]

met•al•craft•ing (met′l kraf′ting, -kräf′-), *n.* metalworking. [METAL + CRAFT + -ING[1]]

met′al detec′tor, an electronic device for detecting metal objects, as one used as a portable sweeping unit or one emplaced in an archway at an airport terminal to detect concealed weapons, explosives, etc.

met•a•lep•sis (met′ə lep′sis), *n., pl.* **-ses** (-sēz). *Rhet.* the use of metonymy to replace a word already used figuratively. [1580–90; < L < Gk *metálēpsis,* equiv. to *meta-* META- + *lēp-,* var. s. of *lambánein* to take + *-sis* -SIS] —**met′a•lep′tic, met′a•lep′ti•cal,** *adj.* —**met′a•lep′ti•cal•ly,** *adv.*

met′al-free phthalocy′anine (met′l frē′), *Chem.* phthalocyanine (def. 1).

met•al•head (met′l hed′), *n. Slang.* a fan of heavy metal music; head-banger. [1985–90]

met•a•lin•guis•tic (met′ə ling gwis′tik), *adj.* of or pertaining to metalinguistics or a metalanguage. [1940–45; META- + LINGUISTIC] —**met′a•lin•guis′ti•cal•ly,** *adv.*

met•a•lin•guis•tics (met′ə ling gwis′tiks), *n.* (*used with a singular v.*) the study of the relation between languages and the other cultural systems they refer to. [1945–50; META- + LINGUISTICS]

met•al•ist (met′l ist), *n.* **1.** a person who works with metals. **2.** a person who advocates the use of metallic money exclusively, instead of paper money. Also, **metallist.** [1640–50; METAL + -IST]

met•al•ize (met′l īz′), *v.t.,* **-ized, -iz•ing. 1.** to make metallic; give the characteristics of metal to. **2.** to cover or coat (a metal or nonmetal object or structure) with metal. Also, **metallize.** [1585–95; METAL + -IZE] —**met′al•i•za′tion,** *n.*

metall-, var. of **metallo-** esp. before a vowel: *metallurgy.*

metall., **1.** metallurgical. **2.** metallurgy.

met′al lath′, **1.** any of various meshlike laths of metal for plastering. **2.** nondecorative interior metalwork for supporting lighting fixtures, dropped ceilings, etc. —**met′al lath′er.**

metalli-, var. of **metallo-:** *metalliferous.* [see METALLO-, -I-]

me•tal•lic (mə tal′ik), *adj.* **1.** of, pertaining to, or consisting of metal. **2.** of the nature of or suggesting metal, as in luster, resonance, or hardness: *metallic green; a harsh metallic sound.* **3.** *Chem.* **a.** (of a metal element) being in the free or uncombined state: *metallic iron.* **b.** containing or yielding metal. —*n.* **4.** *Textiles.* **a.** a yarn or fiber made partly or entirely of metal and having a metallic appearance. **b.** a fabric made of such a yarn or fiber. [1560–70; < L *metallicus* < Gk *metallikós* of, for mines. See METAL, -IC] —**me•tal′li•cal•ly,** *adv.* —**met•al•lic•i•ty** (met′l is′i tē), **met•al•le•i•ty** (met′l ē′i tē), *n.*

metal′lic bond′, *Chem.* the type of chemical bond between atoms in a metallic element, formed by the valence electrons moving freely through the metal lattice.

metal′lic glass′. See **glassy alloy.** [1800–10]

me•tal•li•cize (mə tal′ə sīz′), *v.t.,* **-cized, -ciz•ing.** *Elect.* to make (a circuit) thoroughly metallic, as by replacing a ground return with another wire. Also, *esp. Brit.,* **me•tal′li•cise′.** [METALLIC + -IZE]

metal′lic lus′ter, *Ceram.* luster[1] (def. 8). [1785–95]

metal′lic soap′, *Chem.* any usually water-insoluble salt formed by the interaction of a fatty acid and a metal, esp. lead or aluminum: used chiefly as a drier in paints and varnishes and for waterproofing textiles. [1915–20]

metal′lic wood′-boring bee′tle, any of numerous metallic green, blue, copper, or black beetles of the family Buprestidae, the larvae of which bore into the wood of trees.

met•al•lide (met′l īd′), *v.t.,* **-lid•ed, -lid•ing.** to provide (a metal or alloy) with a diffused coating of a metal or metalloid by electrolysis at high temperature in order to impart a particular surface property to the base metal. [1965–70; METALL- + -IDE; perh. orig. a n., var. of METALLOID]

met•al•lif•er•ous (met′l if′ər əs), *adj.* containing or yielding metal. [1650–60; < L *metallifer* (see METALLI-, -FER) + -OUS]

met•al•line (met′l in, -īn′), *adj.* **1.** metallic. **2.** containing one or more metals or metallic salts. [1425–75; late ME *metalline* < ML *metallinus* of metal. See METAL, -INE[1]]

met•al•list (met′l ist), *n.* metalist.

met•al•lize (met′l īz′), *v.t.,* **-lized, -liz•ing.** metalize. Also, *esp. Brit.,* **met′al•lise′.** —**met′al•li•za′tion,** *n.*

metallo-, a combining form representing **metal** in compound words: *metallography.* Also, **metalli-;** *esp. before a vowel,* **metall-.** [< Gk, comb. form of *métallon*]

me•tal•lo•cene (mə tal′ə sēn′), *n. Chem.* an organometallic coordination compound consisting of a metal bonded to one or two rings of cyclopentadiene. Cf. **ferrocene.** [METALLO- + *-cene* < Gk *koinós* shared (see CENO-[2])]

me•tal•lo•graph (mə tal′ə graf′, -gräf′), *n.* a microscope for observing the microstructure of metals. [METALLO- + -GRAPH]

met•al•log•ra•phy (met′l og′rə fē), *n.* the study of the structure of metals and alloys by means of microscopy. [1870–75; < NL *metallographia.* See METALLO-, -GRAPHY] —**met′al•log′ra•pher, met′al•log′ra•phist,** *n.* —**me•tal•lo•graph•ic** (mə tal′ə graf′ik), **me•tal′lo•graph′i•cal,** *adj.*

met•al•loid (met′l oid′), *n.* **1.** a nonmetal that in combination with a metal forms an alloy. **2.** an element that has both metallic and nonmetallic properties, as arsenic, silicon, or boron. —*adj.* **3.** of or pertaining to a metalloid. **4.** resembling both a metal and a nonmetal. [1825–35; METALL- + -OID]

me•tal•lo•or•gan•ic (mə tal′ō ôr gan′ik), *adj. Chem.* organometallic. [1885–90]

me•tal•lo•phone (mə tal′ə fōn′), *n.* any musical instrument consisting of a graduated series of metal bars that may either be struck by hammers operated manually or played with a keyboard. [1885–90; METALLO- + -PHONE]

me•tal•lo•ther•a•py (mə tal′ō ther′ə pē), *n. Med.* therapy by the use of metals or their salts. [1875–80; METALLO- + THERAPY]

Met′al Lum′ber, *Trademark.* a brand of sheet metal pressed and welded together to form joists and studding.

met•al•lur•gy (met′l ûr′jē *or, esp. Brit.,* mə tal′ər jē), *n.* **1.** the technique or science of working or heating metals so as to give them certain desired shapes or properties. **2.** the technique or science of making and compounding alloys. **3.** the technique or science of separating metals from their ores. [1695–1705; < NL *metallurgia* < Gk *metallourg(ós)* working in metals, mining + NL *-ia* -IA. See METALL-, -URGY] —**met′al•lur′gic, met′al•lur′gi•cal,** *adj.* —**met′al•lur′gi•cal•ly,** *adv.* —**met•al•lur•gist** (met′l ûr′jist *or, esp. Brit.,* mə tal′ər jist), *n.*

met•al•mark (met′l märk′), *n.* any of the small, mostly tropical butterflies of the family Riodinidae, often having metallic-colored flecks on the wings. [1905–10; METAL + MARK[1]]

met•a•log•ic (met′ə loj′ik), *n.* the logical analysis of the fundamental concepts of logic. [1835–45; META- + LOGIC]

met′al ox′ide sem′iconductor, *Electronics.* a three-layer sandwich of a metal, an insulator (usually an oxide of the substrate), and a semiconductor substrate, used in integrated circuits. Also, **met′al-ox′ide sem′iconductor.** *Abbr.:* MOS

met′al paste′-up, *Print.* a method for making up a form for printing in which engravings mounted on blocks are positioned on and pasted to a metal base.

met•al•smith (met′l smith′), *n.* a person skilled in making articles of metal. [1350–1400; ME. See METAL, SMITH]

met′al tape′, a high-performance recording tape having a magnetic metal-particle coating that is not an oxide.

met•al•ware (met′l wâr′), *n.* work of metal, esp. utensils, flatware, etc. [1895–1900; METAL + WARE[1]]

met′al wood′, a structural material consisting of a sheet of metal glued between two veneers or of a veneer glued between two sheets of metal.

met•al•work (met′l wûrk′), *n.* objects made of metal. [1840–50; METAL + WORK] —**met′al•work′er,** *n.*

met•al•work•ing (met′l wûr′king), *n.* the act or technique of making metal objects. [1880–85; METAL + WORKING]

met•a•math•e•mat•ics (met′ə math′ə mat′iks), *n.* (*used with a singular v.*) the logical analysis of the fundamental concepts of mathematics, as number, function, etc. [1885–90; META- + MATHEMATICS] —**met′a•math′e•mat′i•cal,** *adj.* —**met•a•math•e•ma•ti•cian** (met′ə math′ə mə tish′ən), *n.*

met•a•mer (met′ə mər), *n. Chem.* a compound exhibiting metamerism with one or more other compounds. [1880–85; META- + -MER]

met•a•mere (met′ə mēr′), *n.* a somite. [1875–80; META- + -MERE]

met•a•mer•ic (met′ə mer′ik), *adj.* **1.** Also, **me•tam•er•al** (mə tam′ər əl). *Zool.* **a.** consisting of metameres. **b.** pertaining to metamerism. **2.** *Chem.* of, pertaining to, or characteristic of metamerism. [1840–50; METAMERE + -IC] —**met′a•mer′i•cal•ly,** *adv.*

me•tam•er•ism (mə tam′ə riz′əm), *n.* **1.** *Zool.* **a.** division into metameres, the developmental process of somite formation. **b.** existence in a metameric state. **2.** *Chem.* isomerism resulting from the attachment of different groups to the same atom, as $C_2H_5NHC_2H_5$ and $CH_3NHC_3H_7$. [1840–50; (in def. 1) METAMERE + -ISM; (in def. 2) META- + (ISO)MERISM]

met•a•mor•phic (met′ə môr′fik), *adj.* **1.** pertaining to or characterized by change of form, or metamorphosis. **2.** *Geol.* pertaining to or exhibiting structural change or metamorphism. [1810–20; META- + -MORPHIC]

met′amor′phic fa′cies, *Geol.* a group of metamorphic rock units characterized by particular mineralogic associations.

met•a•mor•phism (met′ə môr′fiz əm), *n.* **1.** *Geol.* a change in the structure or constitution of a rock due to natural agencies, as pressure and heat, esp. when the rock becomes harder and more completely crystalline. **2.** *Archaic.* metamorphosis. [1835–45; META- + -MORPHISM]

met•a•mor•phose (met′ə môr′fōz, -fōs), *v.,* **-phosed, -phos•ing.** —*v.t.* **1.** to change the form or nature of; transform. **2.** to subject to metamorphosis or metamorphism. —*v.i.* **3.** to undergo or be capable of undergoing a change in form or nature. [1570–80; back formation from METAMORPHOSIS] —**Syn. 1, 3.** mutate, transmute.

Met•a•mor•pho•ses (met′ə môr′fə sēz′), *n.* a series of mythological tales or legends in verse (A.D. 7–8) by Ovid.

met•a•mor•pho•sis (met′ə môr′fə sis), *n., pl.* **-ses** (-sēz′). **1.** *Biol.* a profound change in form from one stage to the next in the life history of an organism, as from the caterpillar to the pupa and from the pupa to the adult butterfly. Cf. **complete metamorphosis. 2.** a complete change of form, structure, or substance, as transformation by magic or witchcraft. **3.** any complete change in appearance, character, circumstances, etc. **4.** a form resulting from any such change. **5.** *Pathol.* **a.** a type of alteration or degeneration in which tissues are changed: *fatty metamorphosis of the liver.* **b.** the resultant form. **6.** *Bot.* the structural or functional modification of a plant organ or structure during its development. [1525–35; < NL *metamorphōsis* < Gk *metamórphōsis* transformation. See META-, -MORPH, -OSIS] —**Syn. 2.** mutation, transmutation. —**Ant. 1, 2.** stasis.

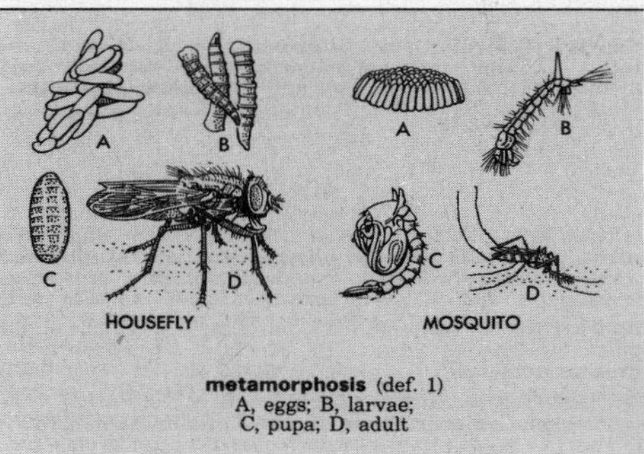

metamorphosis (def. 1)
A, eggs; B, larvae;
C, pupa; D, adult

Metamorphosis, The, (German, *Die Verwandlung*), a short story (1915) by Franz Kafka.

met•a•mor•phous (met′ə môr′fəs), *adj.* metamorphic. [META- + -MORPHOUS]

met•a•neph•ros (met′ə nef′ros), *n., pl.* **-roi** (-roi). *Embryol.* one of the three embryonic excretory organs of higher vertebrates, becoming the permanent and functional kidney. Cf. **mesonephros, pronephros.** [1875–80; < NL < Gk *meta-* META- + *nephrós* kidney] —**met′a•neph′ric,** *adj.*

Met•a•ni•ra (met′ə nī′rə), *n. Class. Myth.* queen of Eleusis, who took Demeter in to nurse her child. Also, **Met′a•nei′ra.**

met•a•ni•tro•phe•nol (met′ə nī′trə fē′nôl, -nol), *n.* See under **nitrophenol** (def. 2). [META- + NITROPHENOL]

met•a•noi•a (met′ə noi′ə), *n.* a profound, usually spiritual, transformation; conversion. [1870–75; < Gk *metánoia* change of mind, repentance; see META-, -NOIA]

me•ta•pe•let (me′tä pe′let), *n., pl.* ***-plot*** (-plôt′). *Hebrew.* a woman who cares for children, esp. on kibbutzim in Israel; foster mother.

metaph., **1.** metaphysical. **2.** metaphysics.

met•a•phase (met′ə fāz′), *n. Cell Biol.* the stage in mitosis or meiosis in which the duplicated chromosomes line up along the equatorial plate of the spindle. [1885–90; META- + PHASE]

met′aphase plate′, *Cell Biol.* a plane in the equatorial region of the spindle in dividing cells, along which the chromosomes become arranged during the metaphase. [1935–40]

Met•a•phen (met′ə fen′), *Pharm., Trademark.* a brand of nitromersol.

met•a•phor (met′ə fôr′, -fər), *n.* **1.** a figure of speech in which a term or phrase is applied to something to which it is not literally applicable in order to suggest a resemblance, as in "A mighty fortress is our God." Cf. **mixed metaphor, simile** (def. 1). **2.** something used, or regarded as being used, to represent something else; emblem; symbol. [1525–35; < L *metaphora* < Gk *metaphorá* a transfer, akin to *metaphérein* to transfer. See META-, -PHORE] —**met·a·phor·i·cal** (met′ə fôr′i kəl, -for′-), **met′a·phor′ic,** *adj.* —**met′a·phor′i·cal·ly,** *adv.* —**met′a·phor′i·cal·ness,** *n.*

met·a·phos·phate (met′ə fos′fāt), *n. Chem.* a salt or ester of metaphosphoric acid. [1825–35; META- + PHOSPHATE]

met′a·phos·phor′ic ac′id (met′ə fos fôr′ik, -for′-), *Chem.* an acid, HPO_3, derived from phosphorous pentoxide, and containing the smallest amount of water of the phosphoric acids. Cf. **phosphoric acid.** [1825–35; META- + PHOSPHORIC]

met·a·phrase (met′ə frāz′), *n., v.,* **-phrased, -phras·ing.** —*n.* **1.** a literal translation. —*v.t.* **2.** to translate, esp. literally. **3.** to change the phrasing or literary form of. [1600–10; < Gk *metáphrasis* a paraphrasing, change of phrasing. See META-, PHRASE]

met·a·phrast (met′ə frast′), *n.* a person who translates or changes a literary work from one form to another, as prose into verse. [1600–10; MGk *metaphrástēs* one who translates, equiv. to **metaphrad-*, base of *metaphrázein* to translate (see META, PHRASE) + *-tēs* agent suffix] —**met′a·phras′tic, met′a·phras′ti·cal,** *adj.* —**met′a·phras′ti·cal·ly,** *adv.*

metaphys., metaphysics.

met·a·phys·ic (met′ə fiz′ik), *n.* **1.** metaphysics. —*adj.* **2.** metaphysical. [1350–1400; ME *metaphisik* < ML *metaphysica* (neut. pl.); see METAPHYSICS]

met·a·phys·i·cal (met′ə fiz′i kəl), *adj.* **1.** pertaining to or of the nature of metaphysics. **2.** *Philos.* **a.** concerned with abstract thought or subjects, as existence, causality, or truth. **b.** concerned with first principles and ultimate grounds, as being, time, or substance. **3.** highly abstract, subtle, or abstruse. **4.** designating or pertaining to the poetry of an early group of 17th-century English poets, notably John Donne, whose characteristic style is highly intellectual and philosophical and features intensive use of ingenious conceits and turns of wit. **5.** *Archaic.* imaginary or fanciful. [1375–1425; late ME *metaphisicalle* < ML *metaphysicālis.* See METAPHYSIC, -AL[1]] —**met′a·phys′i·cal·ly,** *adv.*

met·a·phy·si·cian (met′ə fə zish′ən), *n.* a person who creates or develops metaphysical theories. Also, **met·a·phys·i·cist** (met′ə fiz′ə sist). [1425–75; late ME *metaphisicien,* prob. < MF *metaphysicien,* equiv. to *metaphysique* METAPHYSIC + *-ien* -IAN]

met·a·phys·ics (met′ə fiz′iks), *n.* (*used with a singular v.*) **1.** the branch of philosophy that treats of first principles, includes ontology and cosmology, and is intimately connected with epistemology. **2.** philosophy, esp. in its more abstruse branches. **3.** the underlying theoretical principles of a subject or field of inquiry. **4.** (*cap., italics*) a treatise (4th century B.C.) by Aristotle, dealing with first principles, the relation of universals to particulars, and the teleological doctrine of causation. [1560–70; < ML *metaphysica* < MGk (*tà*) *metaphysiká* (neut. pl.), Gk *tà metà tà physiká* the (works) after the *Physics;* with reference to the arrangement of Aristotle's writings]

met·a·phyte (met′ə fīt′), *n. Bot.* a multicellular plant. [1890–95; META- + -PHYTE] —**met·a·phyt·ic** (met′ə fit′ik), *adj.*

met·a·pla·sia (met′ə plā′zhə, -zhē ə), *n. Pathol.* the transformation of one type of tissue into another. [1885–90; META- + -PLASIA] —**met·a·plas·tic** (met′ə plas′tik), *adj.*

met·a·plasm (met′ə plaz′əm), *n.* **1.** *Cell Biol.* the nonliving matter or inclusions, as starch or pigments, within a cell. **2.** *Gram.* **a.** a change in the structure of a word or sentence made by adding, removing, or transposing the sounds or words of which it is composed or the letters that represent them. **b.** the formation of oblique cases from a stem other than that of the nominative. [1375–1425; late ME *metaplasmus* grammatical change, irregularity < L < Gk *metaplasmós* reforming, remodeling, deriv. of *metaplássein* to mould differently, remodel. See META-, -PLASM] —**met′a·plas′mic,** *adj.*

met·a·pro·tein (met′ə prō′tēn, -tē in), *n. Biochem.* a hydrolytic derivative of protein, insoluble in water but soluble in dilute acids or alkalis. [META- + PROTEIN]

met·a·psy·chol·o·gy (met′ə sī kol′ə jē), *n.* speculative thought dealing systematically with concepts extending beyond the limits of psychology as an empirical science. [1905–10; META- + PSYCHOLOGY] —**met·a·psy·cho·log·i·cal** (met′ə sī′kə loj′i kəl), *adj.*

met·a·scope (met′ə skōp′), *n.* a device for converting infrared radiation into visible light. [META- + -SCOPE]

met·a·se·quoi·a (met′ə si kwoi′ə), *n.* a tall deciduous coniferous tree, *Metasequoia glyptostrobodes,* first known as a fossil and then discovered alive in China. Also called **dawn redwood.** [< NL (1941), the genus name; see META-, SEQUOIA]

met·a·so·ma·tism (met′ə sō′mə tiz′əm), *n. Geol.* **1.** the series of metamorphic processes whereby chemical changes occur in minerals or rocks as a result of the introduction of material, often in hot aqueous solutions, from external sources. **2.** replacement (def. 4). Also, **met·a·so·ma·to·sis** (met′ə sō′mə tō′sis). [1885–90; META- + SOMAT- + -ISM] —**met·a·so·mat·ic** (met′ə sō mat′ik), *adj.*

met·a·sta·ble (met′ə stā′bəl, met′ə stā′-), *adj.* **1.** *Metall.* chemically unstable in the absence of certain conditions that would induce stability, but not liable to spontaneous transformation. **2.** Also, **labile.** *Physics, Chem.* pertaining to a body or system existing at an energy level **(met′asta′ble state′)** above that of a more stable state and requiring the addition of a small amount of energy to induce a transition to the more stable state. [1895–1900; META- + STABLE[2]] —**met·a·sta·bil·i·ty** (met′ə stə bil′i tē), *n.*

Me·ta·sta·sio (me′tä stä′zyô), *n.* (*Pietro Antonio Domenico Bonaventura Trapassi*) 1698–1782, Italian poet and dramatist.

me·tas·ta·sis (mə tas′tə sis), *n., pl.* **-ses** (-sēz′). **1.** *Pathol.* **a.** the transference of disease-producing organisms or of malignant or cancerous cells to other parts of the body by way of the blood or lymphatic vessels or membranous surfaces. **b.** the condition produced by this. **2.** transformation (def. 3). **3.** *Rhet.* a rapid transition, as from one subject to another. **4.** *Physics.* a change in position or orbit of an elementary particle. [1580–90; < Gk *metástasis* a changing. See META-, STASIS] —**met·a·stat·ic** (met′ə stat′ik), *adj.* —**met′a·stat′i·cal·ly,** *adv.*

me·tas·ta·size (mə tas′tə sīz′), *v.i.,* **-sized, -siz·ing.** *Pathol.* (of malignant cells or disease-producing organisms) to spread to other parts of the body by way of the blood or lymphatic vessels or membranous surfaces. Also, *esp. Brit.,* **me·tas′ta·sise′.** [1905–10; METASTAS(IS) + -IZE]

met·a·tar·sal (met′ə tär′səl), *adj.* **1.** of or pertaining to the metatarsus. —*n.* **2.** a bone in the metatarsus. [1730–40; META- + TARSAL] —**met′a·tar′sal·ly,** *adv.*

met′atar′sal arch′, *Anat.* the short lateral arch of the foot formed by the heads of the metatarsal bones.

met·a·tar·sus (met′ə tär′səs), *n., pl.* **-si** (-sī). *Anat., Zool.* the part of a foot or hind limb, esp. its bony structure, included between the tarsus and the toes or phalanges. See diag. under **skeleton.** [1670–80; < NL; see META-, TARSUS]

me·ta·te (mə tä′tē; *Sp.* me tä′te), *n., pl.* **-tes** (-tēz; *Sp.* -tes). a flat stone that has a shallow depression in the upper surface for holding maize or other grains to be ground with a mano. [1825–35, *Amer.;* < MexSp < Nahuatl *metlatl*]

met·a·the·ri·an (met′ə thēr′ē ən), *adj.* **1.** belonging or pertaining to the group Metatheria, comprising the marsupial mammals. —*n.* **2.** a metatherian animal. [1875–80; < NL *Metatheri(a)* name of the group (< Gk *meta-* META- + *thēría,* pl. of *thērion* animal) + -AN]

me·tath·e·sis (mə tath′ə sis), *n., pl.* **-ses** (-sēz′). **1.** the transposition of letters, syllables, or sounds in a word, as in the pronunciation (kumf′tər bəl) for *comfortable* or (aks) for *ask.* **2.** *Chem.* See **double decomposition.** [1600–10; < LL: transposition of letters of a word < Gk *metáthesis* transposition. See META-, THESIS] —**met·a·thet·ic** (met′ə thet′ik), **met′a·thet′i·cal,** *adj.*

me·tath·e·size (mə tath′ə sīz′), *v.t., v.i.,* **-sized, -siz·ing.** to cause to undergo or undergo metathesis. Also, *esp. Brit.,* **me·tath′e·sise′.** [1915–20; METATHES(IS) + -IZE]

met·a·tho·rax (met′ə thôr′aks, -thōr′-), *n., pl.* **-tho·rax·es, -tho·ra·ces** (-thôr′ə sēz′, -thōr′-). the posterior division of the thorax of an insect, bearing the third pair of legs and the second pair of wings. [1810–20; META- + THORAX] —**met·a·tho·rac·ic** (met′ə thô ras′ik, -thō-), *adj.*

met·a·tol·u·i·dine (met′ə tə lo͞o′i dēn′, -din), *n. Chem.* a colorless, slightly water-soluble liquid, C_7H_9N, the meta isomer of toluidine, used in the manufacture of dyes and other organic compounds. [META- + TOLUIDINE]

met·a·troph·ic (met′ə trof′ik, -trō′fik), *adj.* requiring dead organic matter for food. [1895–1900; META- + TROPHIC] —**met·a·troph** (met′ə trof′, -trôf′), *n.* —**me·tat·ro·phy** (mə ta′trə fē), *n.*

Me·tax·as (mə tak′səs; *Gk.* me′tä ksäs′), *n.* **Jo·an·nes** (*Gk.* yô ä′nyes), 1871–1941, Greek general and political leader: dictator 1936–40.

met·a·xy·lem (met′ə zī′ləm, -lem), *n. Bot.* the part of the primary xylem that is the last to be formed, usually having weblike or pitted surfaces. [1900–05; META- + XYLEM]

mé·ta·yage (met′ə yäzh′, mā′tə-), *n.* the system of agriculture based on the use of métayers. [1875–80; < F; see MÉTAYER, -AGE]

mé·ta·yer (met′ə yā′, mā′tə-), *n.* a person who works the land using tools, seed, etc., furnished by the landlord and who receives a share of the harvest in compensation. [1770–80; < F < ML *medietārius,* equiv. to *mediet(ās)* (see MOIETY) + *-ārius* -ARY]

Met·a·zo·a (met′ə zō′ə), *n.* a zoological group comprising the multicellular animals. [1870–75; < NL; see META-, -ZOA] —**met′a·zo′an,** *adj., n.* —**met′a·zo′ic, met′a·zo′al,** *adj.*

Metch·ni·koff (mech′ni kôf′, -kof′; *Russ.* myech′nyi-kəf), *n.* **É·lie** (*Fr.* ā lē′), (*Ilya Ilyich Mechnikov*), 1845–1916, Russian zoologist and bacteriologist in France: Nobel prize for medicine 1908. Russian, **Mechnikov.**

mete[1] (mēt), *v.t.,* **met·ed, met·ing. 1.** to distribute or apportion by measure; allot; dole (usually fol. by *out*): *to mete out punishment.* **2.** *Archaic.* to measure. [bef. 900; ME; OE *metan;* c. D *meten,* ON *meta,* Goth *mitan,* G *messen* to measure, Gk *médesthai* to ponder]
—**Syn. 1.** deal, measure, parcel.

mete[2] (mēt), *n.* **1.** a limiting mark. **2.** a limit or boundary. [1275–1325; ME < MF < L *mēta* goal, turning post]
—**Syn. 2.** bound.

Met.E., metallurgical engineer.

met·em·pir·i·cal (met′em pir′i kəl), *adj.* **1.** beyond or outside the field of experience. **2.** of or pertaining to metempirics. Also, **met′em·pir′ic.** [1874; MET- + EMPIRICAL] —**met′em·pir′i·cal·ly,** *adv.*

met·em·pir·ics (met′em pir′iks), *n.* (*used with a singular v.*) the philosophy dealing with the existence of things outside, or beyond, experience. Also, **met′em·pir′i·cism.** [1874; see METEMPIRIC, -ICS] —**met′em·pir′i·cist,** *n.*

me·tem·psy·cho·sis (mə tem′sə kō′sis, -temp′-, met′əm sī-), *n., pl.* **-ses** (-sēz). the transmigration of the soul, esp. the passage of the soul after death from a human or animal to some other human or animal body. [1580–90; < LL < Gk, equiv. to *metempsȳchō-,* var. s. of *metempsȳchoûsthai* to pass from one body into another (see MET-, EM-[2], PSYCHO-) + *-sis* -SIS] —**met·em·psy·chic** (met′əm sī′kik), **me·tem′psy·cho′sic, me·tem′psy·cho′si·cal,** *adj.*

met·en·ceph·a·lon (met′en sef′ə lon′), *n., pl.* **-lons, -la** (-lə). *Anat.* the anterior section of the hindbrain, comprising the cerebellum and pons. [1870–75; MET- + ENCEPHALON] —**met·en·ce·phal·ic** (met′en sə fal′ik), *adj.*

Met′ enkeph′alin (met), (*sometimes l.c.*) See under **enkephalin.** Also, **Met′-en·keph′a·lin.** [1975–80]

me·te·or (mē′tē ər, -ôr′), *n.* **1.** *Astron.* **a.** a meteoroid that has entered the earth's atmosphere. **b.** a transient fiery streak in the sky produced by a meteoroid passing through the earth's atmosphere; a shooting star or bolide. **2.** any person or object that moves, progresses, becomes famous, etc., with spectacular speed. **3.** (formerly) any atmospheric phenomenon, as hail or a typhoon. **4.** (*cap.*) *Mil.* Britain's first operational jet fighter, a twin-engine aircraft that entered service in 1944. [1570–80; < NL *meteōrum* < Gk *metéōron* meteor, a thing in the air, n. use of neut. of *metéōros* raised in the air, equiv. to *met-* MET- + *eōr-* (var. s. of *aeírein* to raise) + *-os* adj. suffix] —**me′te·or·like′,** *adj.*

meteor., **1.** meteorological. **2.** meteorology.

Me′teor Cra′ter. See **Crater Mound.**

me·te·or·ic (mē′tē ôr′ik, -or′-), *adj.* **1.** of, pertaining to, or consisting of meteors. **2.** resembling a meteor in transient brilliance, suddenness of appearance, swiftness, etc.: *his meteoric rise in politics.* **3.** of or coming from the atmosphere; meteorological. [1625–35; < ML *meteōricus.* See METEOR, -IC] —**me′te·or′i·cal·ly,** *adv.*

me′teor′ic show′er, *Astron.* See **meteor shower.** [1825–35]

me·te·or·ite (mē′tē ə rīt′), *n.* **1.** a mass of stone or metal that has reached the earth from outer space; a fallen meteoroid. **2.** a meteoroid. [1815–25; METEOR + -ITE[1]] —**me·te·or·it·ic** (mē′tē ə rit′ik), **me′te·or·it′i·cal, me·te·or·it·al** (mē′tē ə rīt′l), *adj.*

me′teorite cra′ter, crater (def. 2).

me·te·or·it·ics (mē′tē ə rit′iks), *n.* (*used with a singular v.*) *Astron.* the science that deals with meteors. [1930–35; METEORITE + -ICS] —**me·te·or·it·i·cist** (mē′tē ə rit′ə sist), *n.*

me·te·or·o·gram (mē′tē ôr′ə gram′, -or′-, mē′tē ər ə-), *n. Meteorol.* **1.** a record made by a meteorograph. **2.** a diagram or chart representing the pattern of recurrence of two or more meteorological phenomena over a period of time as observed at a given weather station or group of stations. [1900–05; METEORO(LOGY) + -GRAM[1]]

me·te·or·o·graph (mē′tē ôr′ə graf′, -gräf′, -or′-, mē′tē ər ə-), *n.* an instrument for automatically recording various meteorological conditions, as barometric pressure and temperature, at the same time. [1770–80; METEORO(LOGY) + -GRAPH] —**me·te·or·o·graph·ic** (mē′tē ôr′ə graf′ik, -or′-, mē′tē ər ə-), *adj.* —**me·te·o·rog·ra·phy** (mē′tē ə rog′rə fē), *n.*

me·te·or·oid (mē′tē ə roid′), *n. Astron.* any of the small bodies, often remnants of comets, traveling through space: when such a body enters the earth's atmosphere it is heated to luminosity and becomes a meteor. [1860–65; METEOR + -OID]

meteorol., **1.** meteorological. **2.** meteorology.

me·te·or·o·log·i·cal (mē′tē ər ə loj′i kəl), *adj.* pertaining to meteorology or to phenomena of the atmosphere or weather. Also, **me′te·or·o·log′ic.** [1560–70; < Gk *meteōrologik(ós)* pertaining to celestial phenomena (see METEOROLOGY, -IC) + -AL[1]] —**me′te·or·o·log′i·cal·ly,** *adv.*

me′teorolog′ical sat′ellite, an artificial satellite that gathers data concerning the earth's atmosphere and surface in order to aid meteorologists in understanding weather patterns and producing weather forecasts. Also called **weather satellite.**

me·te·or·ol·o·gy (mē′tē ə rol′ə jē), *n.* **1.** the science dealing with the atmosphere and its phenomena, including weather and climate. **2.** the atmospheric conditions and weather of an area. [1610–20; < Gk *meteōrología* discussion of celestial phenomena. See METEOR, -O-, -LOGY] —**me′te·or·ol′o·gist,** *n.*

me′teor show′er, *Astron.* the profusion of meteors observed when the earth passes through a meteor swarm. Also, **meteoric shower.** [1875–80]

me′teor swarm′, *Astron.* any large number of meteoroids moving in parallel paths. Cf. **meteor shower.**

me·ter[1] (mē′tər), *n.* the fundamental unit of length in the metric system, equivalent to 39.37 U.S. inches, originally intended to be, and being very nearly, equal to one ten-millionth of the distance from the equator to the pole measured on a meridian: defined from 1889 to 1960 as the distance between two lines on a platinum-iridium bar (the "International Prototype Meter") preserved at the International Bureau of Weights and Measures near Paris; from 1960 to 1983 defined as 1,650,763.73 wavelengths of the orange-red radiation of krypton 86 under specified conditions; and now defined as 1/299,792,458 of the distance light travels in a vacuum in one second. *Abbr.:* m Also, *Brit.,* **metre.** [1790–1800; < F *mètre* < Gk *métron* measure]

me·ter[2] (mē′tər), *n.* **1.** *Music.* **a.** the rhythmic element as measured by division into parts of equal time value. **b.** the unit of measurement, in terms of number of beats, adopted for a given piece of music. Cf. **measure** (def. 14). **2.** *Pros.* **a.** poetic measure; arrangement of words in regularly measured, patterned, or rhythmic lines or verses. **b.** a particular form of such arrange-

CONCISE ETYMOLOGY KEY: <, descended or borrowed from; >, whence; b., blend of, blended; c., cognate with; cf., compare; deriv., derivative; equiv., equivalent; imit., imitative; obl., oblique; r., replacing; s., stem; sp., spelling, spelled; resp., respelling, respelled; trans., translation; ?, origin unknown; *, unattested; ‡, probably earlier than. See the full key inside the front cover.

ment, depending on either the kind or the number of feet constituting the verse or both rhythmic kind and number of feet (usually used in combination): *pentameter; dactylic meter; iambic trimeter.* Also, *Brit.,* **metre.** [bef. 900; ME *metir, metur,* OE *meter* < L *metrum* poetic meter, verse < Gk *métron* measure; r. ME *metre* < MF < L as above]

me•ter[3] (mē′tər), *n.* **1.** an instrument for measuring, esp. one that automatically measures and records the quantity of something, as of gas, water, miles, or time, when it is activated. **2.** See **parking meter.** —*v.t.* **3.** to measure by means of a meter. **4.** to process (mail) by means of a postage meter. Also, *Brit.,* **metre.** [1805–15; see METE[1], -ER[1]]

-meter, a combining form meaning "measure," used in the names of instruments measuring quantity, extent, degree, etc.: *altimeter; barometer.* Cf. **-metry.** [< NL *-metrum* < Gk *métron* measure]

me•ter•age (mē′tər ij), *n.* **1.** the practice of measuring; measurement. **2.** a sum or price charged for measurement. [1880–85; METER[3] + -AGE]

me•ter-can•dle (mē′tər kan′dl), *n.* lux. *Abbr.:* mc [1905–10]

me•ter-can•dle-sec•ond (mē′tər kan′dl sek′ənd), *n.* a unit of light-exposure equivalent to one lux for one second.

me′tered mail′, mail on which the postage is printed directly on an envelope or label by a machine licensed by the postal service. [1925–30]

me•ter-kil•o•gram-sec•ond (mē′tər kil′ə gram′-sek′ənd), *adj.* of or pertaining to the system of units in which the meter, kilogram, and second are the principal units of length, mass, and time. *Abbr.:* mks, MKS [1935–40]

me•ter-kil•o•gram-sec•ond-am•pere (mē′tər kil′-ə gram′sek′ənd am′pēr, -am pēr′), *adj.* of or pertaining to the system of units in which the meter, kilogram, second, and ampere are the principal units of length, mass, time, and electric current. *Abbr.:* mksa, MKSA [1935–40]

me′ter maid′, a female member of a police or traffic department responsible for issuing tickets for parking violations. [1955–60, *Amer.*]

metes′ and bounds′ (mēts), the boundaries or limits of a piece of land. [1275–1325; late ME; trans. of AF *metes et boundes.* See METE[2], BOUND[3]]

met•es•trus (met es′trəs), *n.* the luteal phase of the reproductive cycle in mammalian females, occurring after ovulation and characterized by development of the corpus luteum, increased progesterone secretion, and decreased estrogen secretion. Also, **metoestrus.** [1895–1900; MET- + ESTRUS]

meth (meth), *n. Slang.* methamphetamine; Methedrine. [by shortening]

meth-, a combining form representing **methyl** in compound words: *methenamine.*

Meth., Methodist.

meth•a•ce•tin (meth′ə sēt′n), *n. Pharm.* a white, crystalline, water-insoluble powder, $C_9H_{11}NO_2$, used for relieving pain and reducing or preventing fever. Also called **acetanisidine.** [‡1960–65; METH- + ACET- + -IN[2]]

meth•ac•ry•late (meth ak′rə lāt′), *n. Chem.* an ester or salt derived from methacrylic acid. [1860–65; METH- + ACRYL(IC) + -ATE[2]]

methac′rylate res′in, *Chem.* an acrylic resin formed by polymerizing the esters or amides of methacrylic acid.

meth′a•cryl′ic ac′id (meth′ə kril′ik, meth′-), *Chem.* a colorless, liquid acid, $C_4H_6O_2$, produced synthetically, whose methyl ester, methyl methacrylate, polymerizes to yield a clear plastic. Cf. **Lucite, Plexiglas.** [1860–65; METH- + ACRYLIC]

meth•a•done (meth′ə dōn′), *n. Pharm.* a synthetic narcotic, $C_{21}H_{28}ClNO$, similar to morphine but effective orally, used in the relief of pain and as a heroin substitute in the treatment of heroin addiction. Also, **meth•a•don** (meth′ə don′). [1945–50, *Amer.*; METH(YL) + A(MINO) + D(IPHENYL) + (HEPTAN)ONE]

met•hae•mo•glo•bin (met hē′mə glō′bin, -hem′ə-, -hē′mə glō′-, -hem′ə-), *n.* methemoglobin.

meth•am•phet•a•mine (meth′am fet′ə mēn′, -min), *n. Pharm.* a central nervous system stimulant, $C_{10}H_{15}N$, used clinically in the treatment of narcolepsy, hyperkinesia, and for blood pressure maintenance in hypotensive states: also widely used as an illicit drug. [1945–50; METH- + AMPHETAMINE]

meth•a•nal (meth′ə nal′), *n. Chem.* formaldehyde. [METHANE + -AL[3]]

meth•a•na•tion (meth′ə nā′shən), *n. Chem.* the process of converting a mixture, as of hydrogen and carbon monoxide, into methane. [1955–60; METHANE + -ATION]

meth•ane (meth′ān; *Brit.* mē′thān), *n. Chem.* a colorless, odorless, flammable gas, CH_4, the main constituent of marsh gas and the firedamp of coal mines, obtained commercially from natural gas: the first member of the methane, or alkane, series of hydrocarbons. [1865–70; METH- + -ANE]

meth′ane se′ries, *Chem.* See **alkane series.** [1885–90]

meth•an•o•gen (me than′ə jən, -jen′), *n.* any of a diverse group of widely distributed archaebacteria that occur in anaerobic environments, as the intestinal tracts of animals, freshwater and marine sediments, and sewage, and are capable of producing methane from a limited number of substrates, including carbon dioxide and hydrogen, acetate, and methylamines: an important source of natural gas. [1975–80; METHANE- + -O- + -GEN] —**meth•an′o•gen′ic,** *adj.*

meth•a•nol (meth′ə nôl′, -nol′), *n. Chem.* See **methyl alcohol.** [1890–95; METHANE + -OL[1]]

meth•an•the•line (me than′thə lēn′), *n. Pharm.* a compound, $C_{21}H_{26}BrNO_3$, used in the form of its bromide in the treatment of excessive sweating and salivation, peptic ulcer, stomach cramps, and other conditions resulting from nerve dysfunction. [METH- + (X)ANTH- + -E(NE) + (CARBONY)L + -INE[2]]

me•tha•qua•lone (mə thak′wə lōn′, meth′ə kwā′lōn, -kwol′ōn), *n. Pharm.* a nonbarbiturate sedative-hypnotic substance, $C_{16}H_{14}N_2O$, used to induce sleep: also widely used as an illicit drug. [1960–65; METH(YL) + *-a-* ofuncert.derivation + *qu(in)a(zo)l(in)one* (see QUINAZOLINE, -ONE)]

Meth•e•drine (meth′ə drēn′, -drin), *Pharm., Trademark.* a brand of methamphetamine.

me•theg•lin (mə theg′lin), *n.* a variety of spiced mead. [1525–35; < Welsh *meddyglyn,* equiv. to *meddyg* healing (< L *medicus;* see MEDICAL) + *llyn* liquor]

met•he•mo•glo•bin (met hē′mə glō′bin, -hem′ə-, -hē′mə glō′-, -hem′ə-), *n. Biochem.* a brownish compound of oxygen and hemoglobin, formed in the blood, as by the use of certain drugs. Also, **methaemoglobin.** Also called **ferrihemoglobin, hemiglobin.** [1865–70; MET- + HEMOGLOBIN]

me•the•na•mine (me thē′nə mēn′, -min), *n. Chem.* hexamethylenetetramine. [1925–30; METH- + -ENE + AMINE]

meth•i•cil•lin (meth′ə sil′in), *n. Pharm.* a semisynthetic penicillin antibiotic, $C_{17}H_{19}N_2NaO_6S$, used principally in the treatment of severe, penicillin-resistant staphylococci infections. [1960–65; METH(YL) + (PEN)ICILLIN]

meth•im•a•zole (me thim′ə zōl′, -thī′mə-), *n. Pharm.* a white crystalline substance, $C_4H_6N_2S$, that inhibits thyroxin synthesis, used in the treatment of hyperthyroidism. [METH(YL) + IM(ID)AZOLE]

me•thinks (mi thingks′), *v. impers.; pt.* **me•thought.** *Archaic.* it seems to me. [bef. 900; ME *me thinketh,* OE *me thyncth.* See ME, THINK[2], -S[2]]

me•thi•o•carb (me thī′ə kärb′), *n. Chem.* a crystalline compound, $C_{11}H_{15}NO_2S$, used as a nonsystemic insecticide and miticide. [ME(THYL) + THIO- + CARB(AMATE)]

me•thi•o•nine (me thī′ə nēn′, -nin), *n. Biochem.* an amino acid, $CH_3SCH_2CH_2CH(NH_2)COOH$, found in casein, wool, and other proteins or prepared synthetically: used as a supplement to a special diet in the prevention and treatment of certain liver diseases. *Abbr.:* Met; *Symbol:* M [1925–30; b. METHYL and THIONINE]

meth•o•car•ba•mol (meth′ə kär′bə môl′, -mol′), *n. Pharm.* a substance, $C_{11}H_{15}NO_5$, used as a muscle relaxant in combination with other drugs in the treatment of acute, painful musculoskeletal conditions. [METH(YL) + -O- + CARBAM(ATE) + -OL[1]]

meth•od (meth′əd), *n.* **1.** a procedure, technique, or way of doing something, esp. in accordance with a definite plan: *There are three possible methods of repairing this motor.* **2.** a manner or mode of procedure, esp. an orderly, logical, or systematic way of instruction, inquiry, investigation, experiment, presentation, etc.: *the empirical method of inquiry.* **3.** order or system in doing anything: *to work with method.* **4.** orderly or systematic arrangement, sequence, or the like. **5. the Method.** Also called **Stanislavski Method, Stanislavski System.** a theory and technique of acting in which the performer identifies with the character to be portrayed and renders the part in a naturalistic, nondeclamatory, and highly individualized manner. —*adj.* **6.** (*usually cap.*) of, pertaining to, or employing the Method: *a Method actor; Method acting.* [1375–1425; late ME: medical procedure < L *methodus* < Gk *méthodos* systematic course, equiv. to *met-* META- + *hodós* way, road] —**meth′od•less,** *adj.*

—**Syn. 1, 2.** means, technique. METHOD, MODE, WAY imply a manner in which a thing is done or in which it happens. METHOD refers to a settled kind of procedure, usually according to a definite, established, logical, or systematic plan: *the open-hearth method of making steel; one method of solving a problem.* MODE is a more formal word that implies a customary or characteristic fashion of doing something: *Kangaroos have a peculiar mode of carrying their young.* WAY, a word in popular use for the general idea, is equivalent to various more specific words: *someone's way* (manner) *of walking; the best way* (method) *of rapid calculating; the way* (mode) *of holding a pen.* **4.** disposition.

me•thod•i•cal (mə thod′i kəl), *adj.* **1.** performed, disposed, or acting in a systematic way; systematic; orderly: *a methodical person.* **2.** painstaking, esp. slow and careful; deliberate. Also, **me•thod′ic.** [1560–70; *methodic* (< L *methodic(us)* < Gk *methodikós;* see METHOD, -IC) + -AL[1]] —**me•thod′i•cal•ly,** *adv.* —**me•thod′i•cal•ness,** *n.*

—**Syn. 1.** precise. See **orderly.**

Meth•od•ism (meth′ə diz′əm), *n.* **1.** the doctrines, polity, beliefs, and methods of worship of the Methodists. **2.** (*l.c.*) the act or practice of working, proceeding, etc., according to some method or system. **3.** (*l.c.*) an excessive use of or preoccupation with methods, systems, or the like. [1730–40; METHOD + -ISM]

Meth•od•ist (meth′ə dist), *n.* **1.** a member of the largest Christian denomination that grew out of the revival of religion led by John Wesley: stresses both personal and social morality and has an Arminian doctrine and, in the U.S., a modified episcopal polity. **2.** (*l.c.*) a person who relies greatly or excessively on methods or a particular method. —*adj.* **3.** Also, **Meth′od•is′tic, Meth′od•is′ti•cal.** of or pertaining to the Methodists or Methodism. [1585–95; METHOD + -IST] —**Meth′od•is′ti•cal•ly,** *adv.*

Me•tho•di•us (mə thō′dē əs), *n.* **Saint** (*Apostle of the Slavs*), A.D. c825–885, Greek missionary in Moravia (brother of Saint Cyril).

meth•od•ize (meth′ə dīz′), *v.t.,* **-ized, -iz•ing. 1.** to reduce (something) to a method. **2.** to arrange (something) according to a method. Also, *esp. Brit.,* **meth′od•ise′.** [1580–90; METHOD + -IZE] —**meth′od•iz′er,** *n.*

meth′od of least′ squares′, *Statistics.* See **least squares.**

meth•od•ol•o•gy (meth′ə dol′ə jē), *n., pl.* **-gies. 1.** a set or system of methods, principles, and rules for regulating a given discipline, as in the arts or sciences. **2.** *Philos.* **a.** the underlying principles and rules of organization of a philosophical system or inquiry procedure. **b.** the study of the principles underlying the organization of the various sciences and the conduct of scientific inquiry. **3.** *Educ.* a branch of pedagogics dealing with analysis and evaluation of subjects to be taught and of the methods of teaching them. [1790–1800; < NL *methodologia.* See METHOD, -O-, -LOGY] —**meth•od•o•log•i•cal** (meth′-ə dl oj′i kəl), *adj.* —**meth′od•o•log′i•cal•ly,** *adv.* —**meth′od•ol′o•gist,** *n.*

meth•o•hex•i•tal (meth′ō hek′si tal′), *n. Pharm.* a barbiturate anesthetic, used in its sodium form, $C_{14}H_{17}N_2NaO_3$, for induction of general anesthesia or for anesthesia of short duration. [METHO(XY)- + HEX- + (BARB)IT(URIC ACID) + AL(LYL)]

meth•o•prene (meth′ə prēn′), *n. Chem.* a synthetic insect juvenile hormone, $C_{19}H_{34}O_3$, used as a biological pesticide primarily on mosquito and fly larvae to prevent maturing to the adult state. [1970–75; prob. METHO(XY-) + PR(OPYL) + -ENE]

meth•o•trex•ate (meth′ō trek′sāt), *n. Pharm.* a toxic folic acid analogue, $C_{20}H_{22}N_8O_5$, that inhibits cellular reproduction, used primarily in the treatment of psoriasis and certain cancers and as an immunosuppressive agent. [1950–55; METHO(XY)- + *trexate,* of unclear derivation]

me•thought (mi thôt′), *v.* pt. of **methinks.**

meth•ox•ide (meth ok′sid, -sid), *n. Chem.* methylate (def. 1). [METH- + OXIDE]

me•thox•sa•len (me thok′sə lən), *n. Pharm.* a potent compound, $C_{12}H_8O_4$, derived from the seeds of the plant *Ammi majus:* used in combination with certain ultraviolet radiation for the treatment of severe psoriasis. [METHOX(Y)- + (P)S(OR)ALEN]

me•thox•y (mə thok′sē), *adj. Chem.* containing the methoxy group. Also, **meth•ox•yl** (mə thok′sil). [1895–1900; METH- + OXY-[2]]

methoxy-, a combining form occurring in the names of chemical compounds in which the methoxy group is present: *methoxychlor.*

me•thox•y•ben•zene (mə thok′sē ben′zēn, -ben-zēn′), *n. Chem.* anisole. [METHOXY- + BENZENE]

me•thox•y•chlor (mə thok′si klôr′, -klōr′), *n. Chem.* a white, crystalline, water-insoluble solid, $C_{16}H_{15}Cl_3O_2$, used as an insecticide. Also called **DMDT, methoxy DDT.** [1945–50; METHOXY- + CHLOR-[1]]

meth•ox•y•flu•rane (me thok′sē flŏŏr′ān), *n. Pharm.* a potent substance, $C_3H_4Cl_2F_2O$, used as an analgesic in minor surgical procedures and less frequently as a general anesthetic. [1960–65; METHOXY- + FLU(O)R- + (ETH)ANE]

methox′y group′, *Chem.* the univalent group CH_3O-. Also called **methox′y rad′ical.** [1895–1900]

Me•thu•en (mə thōō′ən), *n.* a town in NE Massachusetts, near Lawrence. 36,701.

Me•thu•se•lah (mə thōō′zə lə, -thōōz′lə), *n.* **1.** a patriarch who lived 969 years. Gen. 5:27. **2.** an extremely old man. **3.** a very large wine bottle holding 6½ qt. (6 l).

meth•yl (meth′əl), *adj. Chem.* containing the methyl group. [1835–45; by back formation from METHYLENE] —**me•thyl•ic** (me thil′ik, mə-), *adj.*

methyl-, a combining form occurring in the names of chemical compounds in which the methyl group is present: *methylamine.*

meth′yl ac′etate, *Chem.* a colorless, flammable, volatile liquid, $C_3H_6O_2$, the methyl ester of acetic acid, having a fragrant odor, used chiefly as a solvent. [1900–05]

meth′yl•a•ce′tic ac′id (meth′əl ə sē′tik, -ə set′ik), *Chem.* See **propionic acid.** [1880–85; METHYL- + ACETIC ACID]

meth•yl•al (meth′ə lal′, meth′ə lal′), *n. Chem.* a colorless, flammable, volatile liquid, $C_3H_8O_2$, having a chloroformlike odor, used chiefly as a solvent, in perfumery, and in organic synthesis. Also called **dimethoxymethane, formal.** [1830–40; METHYL- + -AL[3]]

meth′yl al′cohol, *Chem.* a colorless, volatile, water-soluble, poisonous liquid, CH_4O, obtained by the destructive distillation of wood or the incomplete oxidation of natural gas, or produced synthetically from carbon monoxide and hydrogen, used chiefly as a solvent, a fuel, and an automobile antifreeze and in the synthesis of formaldehyde. Also called **methanol, wood alcohol, wood spirit.** [1840–50]

meth•yl•a•mine (meth′ə lə mēn′, -əl am′in), *n. Chem.* any of three derivatives of ammonia in which one or all of the hydrogen atoms are replaced by methyl groups, esp. a gas, CH_5N, with an ammonialike odor, the simplest alkyl derivative of ammonia and, like the latter, forming a series of salts. Also called **monomethylamine.** [1840–50; METHYL- + AMINE]

meth•yl•ate (meth′ə lāt′), *n., v.,* **-at•ed, -at•ing.** *Chem.* —*n.* **1.** Also called **methoxide.** any derivative of methyl alcohol, as sodium methylate, CH_3ONa. **2.** any compound containing the methyl group. —*v.t.* **3.** (in a compound) to replace (one or more hydrogen atoms) with the methyl group. **4.** to mix with methyl alcohol, as in the denaturation of ethyl alcohol. [1825–35; METHYL- + -ATE[1]] —**meth′yl·a′tor,** *n.*

meth′ylated spir′its, ethyl alcohol denatured with methyl alcohol for the purpose of preventing its use as an alcoholic beverage. Also, **meth′ylated spir′it.** [1860–65]

meth·yl·a·tion (meth′ə lā′shən), *n. Chem.* the process of replacing a hydrogen atom with a methyl group. [1875–80; METHYLATE + -ION]

meth·yl·ben·zene (meth′əl ben′zēn, -ben zēn′), *n. Chem.* toluene. [METHYL- + BENZENE]

meth′yl·ben′zyl ac′etate (meth′il ben′zil). See **methylphenylcarbinyl acetate.** [1900–05; METHYL + BENZYL]

meth′yl bro′mide, *Chem.* a colorless, poisonous gas, CH_3Br, used chiefly as a solvent, refrigerant, and fumigant and in organic synthesis. Also called **bromomethane.** [1900–05]

meth·yl·cat·e·chol (meth′əl kat′ə chôl′, -chol′, -shôl′, -shol′, -kôl′, -kol′), *n. Pharm.* guaiacol. [METHYL- + CATECHOL]

meth′yl cel′lulose, *Chem.* a grayish-white powder prepared from cellulose that swells to a highly viscous colloidal solution in water: used as a food additive and in water paints, leather tanning, and cosmetics. [1920–25]

meth′yl chlo′ride, *Chem.* a colorless, poisonous gas, CH_3Cl, used chiefly as a refrigerant, as a local anesthetic, and as a methylating agent in organic synthesis. Also called **chloromethane.** [1875–80]

meth′yl chlo·ro·form′ate (klôr′ə fôr′mit, -māt, klōr′-), *Chem.* a colorless liquid, $C_2H_3ClO_2$, used chiefly in organic synthesis. Also called **meth′yl chlorocar′bonate.** [CHLOROFORM + -ATE[2]]

meth′yl cy′anide, *Chem.* acetonitrile.

meth·yl·cy·clo·hex·a·nol (meth′əl sī′klə hek′sə nōl′, -nol′), *n. Chem.* a colorless, aromatic, viscous liquid mixture, chiefly of the ortho and para forms of $CH_3C_6H_{10}OH$, derived from cresol by hydrogenation: used chiefly as a solvent for rubber, cellulose, esters, and phenols. [1825–35; METHYL- + CYCLOHEXANE + -OL[1]]

meth·yl·do·pa (meth′əl dō′pə), *n. Pharm.* a white powder, $C_{10}H_{13}NO_4$, used in the treatment of hypertension. [1950–55; METHYL- + DOPA]

meth·yl·ene (meth′ə lēn′), *adj. Chem.* containing the methylene group. [< F *méthylène* (coined in 1834), equiv. to Gk *méth(y)* wine (see MEAD[1]) + *hýl(ē)* wood + F *-ène* -ENE, taken to mean "wood-spirits" (*vin ou liqueur spiritueuse du bois*), though elements of the compound are in the wrong order to give this sense]

meth′ylene blue′, *Chem., Pharm.* a dark-green, crystalline compound, $C_{16}H_{18}ClN_3S$, that dissolves in water to form a deep-blue solution: used chiefly as a dye, as a bacteriological and biological stain, and as an antidote for cyanide poisoning. Also called **methylthionine chloride.** [1885–90]

meth′ylene chlo′ride, *Chem.* a colorless, volatile liquid, CH_2Cl_2, used chiefly as a solvent, as a refrigerant, and as a local anesthetic in dentistry. Also called **meth′ylene dichlo′ride, dichloromethane.** [1875–80]

meth′ylene di·ox′y·am·phet′a·mine (dī ok′sē am fet′ə mēn′, -min, -ok′sē-), *Pharm.* See **MDA.** [DI-[1] + OXY- + AMPHETAMINE]

meth′ylene group′, *Chem.* the bivalent organic group $>CH_2$, derived from methane. Also called **meth′ylene rad′ical.**

meth′ylene i′odide, *Chem.* a yellow liquid, CH_2I_2, soluble in alcohol and ether: used for the separation of mixtures of minerals and in organic synthesis. Also called **diiodomethane.**

meth′yl eth′yl ke′tone, *Chem.* a colorless, flammable liquid, C_4H_8O, produced by synthesis or fermentation: used chiefly as a solvent, as a paint remover, and in the manufacture of plastics. *Abbr.:* MEK Also called **butanone.** [1875–80]

meth′yl for′mate, *Chem.* a colorless, water-soluble, flammable liquid, $C_2H_4O_2$, used chiefly in organic synthesis and as a solvent.

meth·yl·gly·ox·al (meth′əl glī ok′sal, -səl), *n. Chem.* See **pyruvic aldehyde.** [1895–1900; METHYL- + *glyoxal,* equiv. to GLY(COL) + OXAL(IC ACID)]

meth′yl group′, *Chem.* the univalent group CH_3-, derived from methane. Also called **meth′yl rad′ical.**

meth·yl·hep·te·none (meth′əl hep′tə nōn′), *n. Chem.* a colorless liquid, $C_8H_{14}O$, occurring in many essential oils and produced by synthesis: used in organic synthesis and in the manufacture of inexpensive perfumes. [METHYL- + HEPTENE + -ONE]

me·thyl·ic (me thil′ik), *adj.* of, pertaining to, or characteristic of the methyl group. [1825–35; METHYL- + -IC]

me·thyl′i·dyne group′ (me thil′i dīn′), *Chem.* the trivalent group $\equiv CH$. Also called **methyl′idyne rad′ical.** [METHYL + -IDE + -INE[2]]

meth′yl·i·so·bu′te·nyl ke′tone (meth′əl ī′sō byōōt′n il, meth′-), *Chem.* See **mesityl oxide.** [METHYL- + ISO- + BUTENE + -YL]

meth′yl isobu′tyl ke′tone, *Chem.* a colorless, slightly water-soluble, flammable liquid, $C_6H_{12}O$, having a pleasant odor: used as a solvent for nitrocellulose, gums, resins, fats, waxes, and oils. Also called **hexone.** [1885–90]

meth′yl isocy′anate, *Chem.* a highly toxic, flammable, colorless liquid, CH_3NCO, used as an intermediate in the manufacture of pesticides: in 1984, the accidental release of a cloud of this gas in Bhopal, India, killed more than 1700 people and injured over 200,000.

meth′yl lac′tate, *Chem.* a colorless liquid, $C_4H_8O_3$, soluble with water and most organic liquids: used chiefly as a solvent for cellulose acetate.

meth·yl·mer·cu·ry (meth′əl mûr′kyə rē), *n. Chem.* any of several extremely toxic organometallic compounds, $Hg(CH_3)_2$, formed from metallic mercury by the action of microorganisms and capable of entering the food chain: used as seed disinfectants. [1915–20; METHYL + MERCURY]

meth′yl methac′rylate, *Chem.* a colorless, volatile, flammable, water-insoluble, liquid, unsaturated ester, $C_5H_8O_2$, that polymerizes readily to a clear plastic. Cf. **Lucite, Plexiglas.** [1930–35]

meth·yl·naph·tha·lene (meth′əl naf′thə lēn′, -nap′-), *n. Chem.* a compound, $C_{11}H_{10}$, whose alpha isomer, a colorless liquid, is used in determining cetane numbers. [1880–85; METHYL- + NAPHTHALENE]

meth′yl o′leate, *Chem.* an oily, clear to amber, water-insoluble liquid, $C_{19}H_{36}O_2$, used chiefly as an intermediate for detergents, wetting agents, and emulsifiers.

meth′yl or′ange, *Chem.* an orange-yellow, slightly water-soluble powder, $C_{14}H_{14}N_3NaO_3S$, used chiefly as an acid-base indicator. Also called **gold orange, helianthine B, orange III, tropaeolin D, tropeolin D.** Cf. **methyl red.** [1880–85]

meth·yl·par·a·ben (meth′əl par′ə ben′), *n. Chem.* a fine, white, needlelike substance, $C_8H_8O_3$, used chiefly as a preservative in foods and pharmaceuticals. [METHYL- + PARA- + BEN(ZOIC ACID)]

meth′yl parathi′on, *Chem.* a synthetic pesticide, $C_8H_{10}NO_5PS$, used in the control of mites and various insects, as aphids, boll weevils, and cutworms. [1955–60]

meth·yl·phen·i·date (meth′əl fen′i dāt′, -fē′ni-), *n. Pharm.* a central nervous system stimulant, $C_{14}H_{19}NO_2$, used in the control of hyperkinetic syndromes and narcolepsy. [1955–60; METHYL + PHEN- + -IDE + -ATE[2]]

meth′yl phe′nol, *Chem.* cresol.

meth′yl·phen·yl·car′bi·nyl ac′etate (meth′əl fen′l kär′bə nil, -fēn′l-, meth′-), *Chem.* a colorless, synthetic liquid, $C_{10}H_{12}O_2$, having a strong floral odor and occurring in oil of gardenia: used chiefly in gardenia and lily perfumes. Also called **methylbenzyl acetate, phenylmethylcarbinyl acetate, styralyl acetate.** [METHYL- + PHENYL + CARB- + -IN[2] + -YL]

meth′yl phen′yl e′ther, *Chem.* anisole.

meth′yl pro′pyl ke′tone, *Chem.* a colorless, slightly water-soluble liquid, $C_5H_{10}O$, used chiefly as a solvent, esp. in lacquers.

meth′yl red′, *Chem.* a water-insoluble solid occurring as a dark-red powder or violet crystals, $C_{15}H_{15}N_3O_2$, used chiefly as an acid-base indicator. Cf. **methyl orange.** [1905–10]

meth′yl·ros·an′i·line chlo′ride (meth′əl rō zan′ə lin, -līn′, meth′-). See **gentian violet.** [METHYL- + ROSANILINE]

meth′yl salic′ylate, *Chem.* a colorless, water-soluble liquid, $C_8H_8O_3$, produced synthetically or by maceration and subsequent distillation from birch or gaultheria: used chiefly in perfumery and flavoring, and in medicine as a counterirritant in external preparations. Also called **sweet birch oil, wintergreen oil.** [1875–80]

meth′yl sty′ryl ke′tone (stī′ril, stir′əl), *Chem.* See **benzylidene acetone.** [STYR(ENE) + -YL]

meth′yl sul′fate, *Chem.* See **dimethyl sulfate.** [1930–35]

meth·yl·tes·tos·ter·one (meth′əl te stos′tə rōn′), *n. Pharm.* a synthetic androgenic steroid drug, $C_{20}H_{30}O_2$, used for its anabolic properties in males in the treatment of hypogonadism and other androgen-deficiency disease states, and in females in the treatment of breast cancer. [1935–40; METHYL + TESTOSTERONE]

meth·yl·the·o·bro·mine (meth′əl thē′ə brō′mēn, -min, meth′-), *n. Chem.* caffeine. [METHYL- + THEOBROMINE]

meth·yl·thi′o·nine chlo′ride (meth′əl thī′ə nēn′, -nin), *Chem.* See **methylene blue.** [METHYL- + THIONINE]

meth′yl trans′ferase, *Biochem.* any of a class of enzymes that catalyze the transfer of methyl groups from one molecule to another.

meth·yl·tri·ni·tro·ben·zene (meth′əl trī nī′trō ben′zēn, -ben zēn′), *n. Chem.* See **TNT.** [METHYL- + TRI- + NITRO- + BENZENE]

meth·y·ser·gide (meth′ə sûr′jīd), *n. Pharm.* an ergot alkaloid derivative, $C_{21}H_{27}N_3O_2$, used in the prophylaxis and treatment of migraine and cluster headaches. [1960–65; METH- + *(l)yserg(ic)* (see LYSERGIC ACID) + -IDE]

met·ic (met′ik), *n.* an alien resident of an ancient Greek city who paid a tax for the right to live there. [1800–10; < LL *metycus,* var. of *metoecus* < Gk *métoikos* emigrant, equiv. to *met-* MET- + *-oikos* dwelling]

me·ti·cal (met′i kal′; *Port.* me ti käl′), *n., pl.* **-cals,** *Port.* **-cais** (-kīsh′). a brass coin and monetary unit of Mozambique, equal to 100 centavos: replaced the escudo in 1980.

me·tic·u·lous (mə tik′yə ləs), *adj.* **1.** taking or showing extreme care about minute details; precise; thorough: *a meticulous craftsman; meticulous personal appearance.* **2.** finicky; fussy: *meticulous adherence to technicalities.* [1525–35; < L *metīculōsus* full of fear, fearful, equiv. to *meti-* for *metū-* (s. of *metus* fear) + *-culōsus,* extracted from *perīculōsus* PERILOUS] —**me·tic′u·lous·ly,** *adv.* —**me·tic′u·lous·ness, me·tic·u·los·i·ty** (mə tik′yə los′i tē), *n.*
—**Syn. 1.** exact, strict, scrupulous. See **painstaking.**
—**Ant. 1, 2.** careless.

mé·tier (mā′tyā, mā tyā′), *n.* **1.** a field of work; occupation, trade, or profession. **2.** a field of work or other activity in which one has special ability or training; forte. [1785–95; < F; OF *mestier* < Gallo-Rom **misterium,* for L *ministerium* MINISTRY]

mé·tis (mā tēs′, -tē′), *n., pl.* **-tis** (-tēs′, -tēz′). **1.** any person of mixed ancestry. **2.** (*cap.*) *Canadian.* the offspring of an American Indian and a white person, esp. one of French ancestry. Also, **me·tis′.** [1810–20; < F, MF < LL *mixtīcius* of mixed blood]

Me·tis (mē′tis), *n. Class. Myth.* a Titaness, the daughter of Oceanus and Tethys and the mother of Athena by Zeus. Zeus swallowed Metis, and Athena was born from his head.

mé·tisse (mā tēs′), *n., pl.* **-tisses** (-tēs′, -tē′siz). **1.** a woman of mixed ancestry. **2.** (*cap.*) *Canadian.* a woman of white, esp. French, and American Indian parentage. Also, **me·tisse′.** [1890–95; < F; fem. of MÉTIS]

met·o·clo·pra·mide (met′ō klō′prə mīd′), *n. Pharm.* a white crystalline substance, $C_{14}H_{22}ClN_3O_2$, used primarily in the symptomatic treatment of certain upper gastrointestinal tract problems, and as an antiemetic. [*met(h)o(benzamide)* a component + C(H)LO(RO)-[2] + *-pr-* of uncert. derivation + AMIDE]

met·oes·trus (met es′trəs, -ē′strəs), *n.* metestrus.

Me·tol (mē′tôl, -tol), *Chem., Trademark.* a brand name for a colorless, water-soluble salt, $C_{14}H_{20}N_2O_6S$, used chiefly as a photographic developer.

me·to·la·zone (me tō′lə zōn′), *n. Pharm.* a thiazide diuretic, $C_{16}H_{16}ClN_3O_3S$, used in the treatment of hypertension and as a diuretic in patients with chronic renal failure. [contr. and rearrangement of METH-, QUINAZOLINE, -ONE components of the chemical name]

Me·ton′ic cy′cle (mi ton′ik), *Astron.* a cycle of 235 synodic months, very nearly equal to 19 years, after which the new moon occurs on the same day of the year as at the beginning of the cycle with perhaps a shift of one day, depending on the number of leap years in the cycle. [1880–85; named after *Meton,* 5th-century B.C. Athenian astronomer; see -IC]

met·o·nym (met′ə nim), *n.* a word used in metonymy. [1830–40; back formation from METONYMY]

met·o·nym·i·cal (met′ə nim′i kəl), *adj.* having the nature of metonymy. Also, **met′o·nym′ic.** [1570–80; < Gk *metōnymik(ós)* (see METONYMY, -IC) + -AL[1]] —**met′o·nym′i·cal·ly,** *adv.*

me·ton·y·my (mi ton′ə mē), *n. Rhet.* a figure of speech that consists of the use of the name of one object or concept for that of another to which it is related, or of which it is a part, as "scepter" for "sovereignty," or "the bottle" for "strong drink," or "count heads (or noses)" for "count people." [1540–50; < LL *metōnymia* < Gk *metōnymía* change of name; see MET-, -ONYM, -Y[3]]

me-too (mē′tōō′), *adj. Slang.* characterized by or involving me-tooism: *a candidate's me-too campaign.* [1925–30; from phrase *me too*]

me-too·ism (mē′tōō′iz əm), *n.* **1.** the adopting of policies, methods, products, etc., similar or identical to those of a peer, rival, or competitor. **2.** the practice of making a product, offering a service, etc., that attempts to duplicate one that is established. [1945–50; ME-TOO + -ISM] —**me′-too′er,** *n.* —**me′-too′ist,** *adj., n.*

met·o·pe (met′ə pē′, -ōp), *n. Archit.* any of the square spaces, either decorated or plain, between triglyphs in the Doric frieze. Also called **intertriglyph.** See diag. under **column.** [1555–65; < Gk *metópē*]

me·top·ic (mi top′ik), *adj. Anat.* of or pertaining to the forehead; frontal. [1875–80; < Gk *métōp(on)* forehead + -IC]

met·o·pro·lol (met′ō prō′lôl, -lol), *n. Pharm.* a beta blocker, $C_{15}H_{25}NO_3$, used in the treatment of hypertension, angina, and cardiac arrhythmias. [contr. of the chemical name]

metr-, var. of **metro-**[2] before a vowel: *metralgia.*

me·tral·gi·a (mi tral′jē ə), *n. Pathol.* pain in the uterus. [1895–1900; METR- + ALGIA]

Met·ra·zol (me′trə zôl′, -zol′), *Pharm., Trademark.* a brand of pentylenetetrazol.

me·tre (mē′tər), *n., v.,* **-tred, -tring.** *Brit.* meter.

met·ric[1] (me′trik), *adj.* pertaining to the meter or to the metric system. [1860–65; < F *métrique,* deriv. of *mètre* METER[1]; see -IC]

met·ric[2] (me′trik), *adj.* **1.** pertaining to distance: *metric geometry.* **2.** metrical. —*n.* **3.** *Math.* a nonnegative real-valued function having properties analogous to those of the distance between points on a real line, as the distance between two points being independent of the order of the points, the distance between two points being zero if, and only if, the two points coincide, and the distance between two points being less than or equal to the sum of the distances from each point to an arbitrary third point. [1750–60; < L *metricus* < Gk *metrikós* of, relating to measuring. See METER[2], -IC]

-metric, a combining form occurring in adjectives that correspond to nouns ending in **-meter** (*barometric*) or **-metry** (*geometric*). [< Gk *-metrikos;* see METER[2], -METRY, -IC]

met·ri·cal (me′tri kəl), *adj.* **1.** pertaining to meter or poetic measure. **2.** composed in meter or verse. **3.** pertaining to measurement. Also, **metric.** [1375–1425; late ME < LL *metric(us)* (see METRIC[2]) + -AL[1]] —**met′ri·cal·ly,** *adv.* —**met·ri·cism** (me′trə siz′əm), **me·tric·i·ty** (me tris′i tē, mi-), *n.*

met′rical mile′, (in track and swimming) a race of 1500 meters, nearly equivalent to a mile.

met·ri·ca·tion (me′tri kā′shən), *n.* the act, process, or result of establishing the metric system as the standard system of measurement. Also called **metrification.** [1960–65; METRIC[1] + -ATION]

met′ric cent′ner, centner (def. 2).

CONCISE ETYMOLOGY KEY: <, descended or borrowed from; >, whence; b., blend of, blended; c., cognate with; cf., compare; deriv., derivative; equiv., equivalent; imit., imitative; obl., oblique; r., replacing; s., stem; sp., spelling, spelled; resp., respelling, respelled; trans., translation; ?, origin unknown; *, unattested; ‡, probably earlier than. See the full key inside the front cover.

met′ric hun′dredweight, a unit of weight equivalent to 50 kilograms.

me•tri•cian (mi trish′ən), *n.* a metrist. [1375–1425; late ME *metricion.* See METRIC^2, -IAN]

met•ri•cize (me′trə sīz′), *v.t.*, **-cized, -ciz•ing. 1.** to express in terms of the metric system. **2.** *Math.* metrize. Also, *esp. Brit.*, **met′ri•cise′.** [1870–75; METRIC^1 + -IZE]

met•rics (me′triks), *n.* (*used with a singular v.*) **1.** the science of meter. **2.** the art of metrical composition. [1895–1900; see METRIC^2, -ICS]

-metrics, a combining form with the meaning "the science of measuring" that specified by the initial element: *biometrics; econometrics.* [see -METRIC, -ICS]

met′ric space′, *Math.* a space with a metric defined on it. [1925–30]

met′ric sys′tem, a decimal system of weights and measures, adopted first in France but now widespread, universally used in science, mandatory for use for all purposes in a large number of countries, and favored for use in most (as in the U.S.). The basic units are the meter (39.37 inches) for length and the gram (15.432 grains) for mass or weight. Derived units are the liter (0.908 U.S. dry quart, or 1.0567 U.S. liquid quart) for capacity, being the volume of 1000 grams of water under specified conditions; the are (119.6 square yards) for area, being the area of a square 10 meters on a side; and the stere (35.315 cubic feet) for volume, being the volume of a cube 1 meter on a side, the term "stere," however, usually being used only in measuring firewood. Names for units larger and smaller than these are formed from the above names by the use of the following prefixes: *kilo-*, 1000; *hecto-*, 100; *deka-*, 10; *deci-*, 0.1; *centi-*, 0.01; *milli-*, 0.001. To these are often added: *tera-*, one trillion; *giga-*, one billion; *mega-*, one million. With the addition of basic physical units it is now officially known by the French name Le Système International d'Unités (abbreviation **SI**) or in English as the International System of Units. See table below. [1860–65]

met′ric ton′, a unit of 1000 kilograms, equivalent to 2204.62 avoirdupois pounds. Also called **tonne.** [1920–25]

met′ric topol′ogy, *Math.* a topology for a space in which open sets are defined in terms of a given metric.

me•trid•i•um (mi trid′ē əm), *n.* any sea anemone of the genus *Metridium,* common in cooler waters of the Northern Hemisphere. [< NL (1815), n. use of neut. of *metridius* having a womb, fruitful < Gk *mētrídios,* deriv. of *mḗtra* womb]

met•ri•fi•ca•tion (me′trə fi kā′shən), *n.* **1.** metrication. **2.** poetic composition in meter or verse form. [METR(IC)^1 or METR(IC)^2 + -I- + -FICATION]

me•trif•on•ate (mi trif′ə nāt′), *n. Pharm.* an organophosphorus compound, $C_4H_8Cl_3O_4P$, used as an insecticide and anthelmintic. Also called **trichlorfon.** [appar. contr. of the chemical name]

met•ri•fy (me′trə fī′), *v.t.*, **-fied, -fy•ing.** to put into meter; compose in verse. [1515–25; < F *métrifier* < ML *metrificāre,* equiv. to *metri-* (comb. form of *metrum* METER^2) + *-ficāre* -FY] **—met′ri•fi′er,** *n.*

met•rist (me′trist, mē′trist), *n.* a person who is skilled in the use of poetic meters. [1525–35; < ML *metrista.* See METER^2, -IST]

me•tri•tis (mi trī′tis), *n. Pathol.* inflammation of the uterus. [1835–45; < NL; see METR-, -ITIS]

met•rize (mi trīz′, me′trīz), *v.t.*, **-rized, -rizing.** *Math.* to find a metric for (a topological space for which the metric topology is the given topology). Also, **metricize;** *esp. Brit.*, **met•rise′.** [METR(IC)^2 + -IZE] **—met•riz′•able,** *adj.* **—met′ri•za′tion,** *n.*

met•ro^1 (me′trō), *n., pl.* **-ros.** (*often cap.*) **1.** the underground electric railway of Paris, France, Montreal, Canada, Washington, D.C., and other cities. **2.** subway (def. 1). [1900–05; < F *métro,* short for *chemin de fer métropolitain* metropolitan railroad]

met•ro^2 (me′trō), *adj., n., pl.* **-ros.** *Informal.* **—adj. 1.** metropolitan (defs. 1, 2). **—n. 2.** metropolis (defs. 1, 2). **3.** (*often cap.*) *Chiefly Canadian.* the government or jurisdiction of a large city. [1900–05; by shortening; or independent use of METRO-^{3}]

metro-^{1}, a combining form meaning "measure," used in the formation of compound words: *metronome.* [comb. form repr. Gk *métron* measure]

metro-^{2}, a combining form meaning "uterus," used in the formation of compound words: *metrorrhagia.* Also, *esp. before a vowel,* **metr-.** [comb. form repr. Gk *mḗtra* womb]

metro-^{3}, a combining form representing **metropolis** or **metropolitan** in compound words: *metroflight; metroland; Metroliner.*

Met•ro•lin•er (me′trō lī′nər), *Trademark.* any of several high-speed, reserved-seat trains run by Amtrak and serving points between Boston, New York City, and Washington, D.C. [METRO- + LINER^1]

me•trol•o•gy (mi trol′ə jē), *n., pl.* **-gies.** the science of weights and measures. [1810–20; METRO-^{1} + -LOGY] **—met•ro•log•i•cal** (me′trə loj′i kəl), *adj.* **—met′ro•log′i•cal•ly,** *adv.* **—me•trol′o•gist,** *n.*

met•ro•ni•da•zole (me′trə ni′də zōl′), *n. Pharm.* a synthetic antimicrobial substance, $C_6H_9N_3O_3$, used chiefly in the treatment of infections, such as *Trichomonas vaginalis* and certain anaerobic bacterial infections. [1960–65; contr. of *2-methyl-5-nitroimidazole* part of the chemical name]

met•ro•nome (me′trə nōm′), *n.* a mechanical or electrical instrument that makes repeated clicking sounds at an adjustable pace, used for marking rhythm, esp. in practicing music. [1810–20; METRO-^{1} + *-nome* < Gk *nómos* rule, law] **—met•ro•nom•ic** (me′trə nom′ik), **met′ro•nom′i•cal,** *adj.* **—met′ro•nom′i•cal•ly,** *adv.*

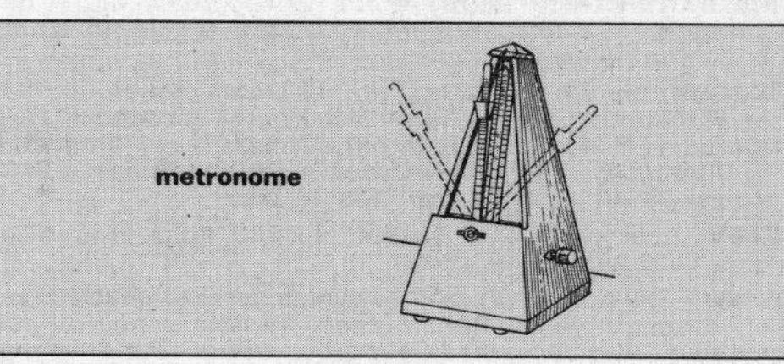
metronome

me•tro•nym•ic (mē′trə nim′ik, me′-), *adj.* **1.** derived from the name of a mother or other female ancestor. **—n. 2.** a metronymic name. Also, **matronymic.** [1865–70; < Gk *mētrōnymikós* named after one's mother]

Met•ro•plex (me′trə pleks′), *n.* (*sometimes l.c.*) a vast metropolitan area that encompasses several cities and their suburbs: *We're moving to the Dallas-Ft. Worth Metroplex.* [prob. METRO-^{3} + (COM)PLEX]

me•trop•o•lis (mi trop′ə lis), *n., pl.* **-lis•es. 1.** any large, busy city. **2.** the chief, and sometimes capital, city of a country, state, or region. **3.** a central or principal place, as of some activity: *the music metropolis of France.* **4.** the mother city or parent state of a colony, esp. of an ancient Greek colony. **5.** the chief see of an ecclesiastical province. [1350–1400; ME < LL *mētropolis* < Gk *mētrópolis* a mother state or city, equiv. to *mētro-,* comb. form of *mḗtēr* MOTHER + *pólis* -POLIS, POLIS]

met•ro•pol•i•tan (me′trə pol′i tn), *adj.* **1.** of, noting, or characteristic of a metropolis or its inhabitants, esp. in culture, sophistication, or in accepting and combining a wide variety of people, ideas, etc. **2.** of or pertaining to a large city, its surrounding suburbs, and other neighboring communities: *the New York metropolitan area.* **3.** pertaining to or constituting a mother country. **4.** pertaining to an ecclesiastical metropolis. **—n. 5.** an inhabitant of a metropolis. **6.** a person who has the sophistication, fashionable taste, or other habits and manners associated with those who live in a metropolis. **7.** *Eastern Ch.* the head of an ecclesiastical province. **8.** an archbishop in the Church of England. **9.** *Rom. Cath. Ch.* an archbishop who has authority over one or more suffragan sees. **10.** (in ancient Greece) a citizen of the mother city or parent state of a colony. [1300–50; ME < LL *mētropolitānus* of, belonging to a metropolis < Gk *mētropolít(ēs)* (see METROPOLIS, -ITE^1) + L *-ānus* -AN] **—met′ro•pol′i•tan•ism,** *n.*

met•ro•pol•i•tan•ize (me′trə pol′i tn īz′), *v.t.*, **-ized, -iz•ing.** to make metropolitan. Also, *esp. Brit.*, **met′ro•pol′i•tan•ise′.** [1850–55; METROPOLITAN + -IZE] **—met′ro•pol′i•tan•i•za′tion,** *n.*

me•tror•rha•gi•a (mē′trə rā′jē ə, -jə, me′-), *n. Pathol.* nonmenstrual discharge of blood from the uterus; uterine hemorrhage. [1770–80; < NL; see METRO-^{2}, -RRHAGIA] **—me•tror•rhag•ic** (mē′trə raj′ik, me′-), *adj.*

met•ro•scope (me′trə skōp′, mē′-), *n. Med.* an instrument for examining the cavity of the uterus. [1835–45, *Amer.*; METRO-^{2} + -SCOPE]

-metry, a combining form with the meaning "the process of measuring" that specified by the initial element: *anthropometry; chronometry.* [< Gk *-metria* action or process of measuring, equiv. to *métr(on)* measure (see METER^2) + *-ia* -Y^3]

Met•sys (met′sis), *n.* **Quen•tin** (*Flemish.* kven′tin; *Eng.* kwen′tn). See **Massys, Quentin.**

Met•ter•nich (met′ər nikh; *Eng.* met′ər nik), *n.* **Prince Kle•mens Wen•zel Ne•po•muk Lo•thar von** (klā′mens ven′tsəl nā′pô mŏŏk lō′tär fən, lō tär′), 1773–1859, Austrian statesman and diplomat. **—Met′•ter•nich′i•an,** *adj.*

met•teur en scène (me tœr än sen′), *pl.* ***met•teurs en scène*** (me tœr än sen′). *French.* a director of a theatrical or cinematic production.

Met•tie (met′ē), *n.* a female given name, form of **Matilda** or **Martha.** Also, **Met′ty.**

met•tle (met′l), *n.* **1.** courage and fortitude: *a man of mettle.* **2.** disposition or temperament: *a man of fine mettle.* **3. on one's mettle,** in the position of being incited to do one's best: *The loss of the first round put him on his mettle to win the match.* [1575–85; var. of METAL] **—Syn. 1.** valor, pluck, vigor, ardor, nerve, fiber.

met•tle•some (met′l səm), *adj.* spirited; courageous. [1655–65; METTLE + -SOME^1]

Me•tuch•en (mi tuch′ən), *n.* a city in NE New Jersey. 13,762.

Metz (mets; *Fr.* mes), *n.* a city in and the capital of Moselle, in NE France: fortress; battles 1870, 1918, 1940, 1944. 117,199.

me•um et tu•um (me′ŏŏm et tōō′ŏŏm; *Eng.* mē′əm et tōō′əm, -tyōō′-), *Latin.* mine and thine.

meu•nière (mən yâr′; *Fr.* mœ nyer′), *adj.* (of food, esp. fish) dipped in flour, sautéed in butter, and sprinkled with lemon juice and chopped parsley. [1840–50; < F, by ellipsis from *à la meunière* lit., in the manner of a miller's wife; fem. of *meunier* miller, OF *molnier* < VL **molinārius,* equiv. to LL *molin(a)* MILL^1 + L *-ārius*

CONCISE PRONUNCIATION KEY: act, cāpe, dâre, pärt; set, ēqual; if, īce; ox, ōver, ôrder, oil, bŏŏk, bōōt, out; up, ûrge; child; sing; shoe; thin, *th*at; zh as in *treasure.* ə = *a* as in *alone, e* as in *system, i* as in *easily, o* as in *gallop, u* as in *circus;* ᵊ as in *fire* (fīᵊr), *hour* (ouᵊr). l and n can serve as syllabic consonants, as in *cradle* (krād′l), and *button* (but′n). See the full key inside the front cover.

METRIC SYSTEM

METRIC UNITS

LINEAR MEASURE	
10 millimeters	=1 centimeter
10 centimeters	=1 decimeter
10 decimeters	=1 meter
10 meters	=1 decameter
10 decameters	=1 hectometer
10 hectometers	=1 kilometer
SQUARE MEASURE	
100 sq. millimeters	=1 sq. centimeter
100 sq. centimeters	=1 sq. decimeter
100 sq. decimeters	=1 sq. meter
100 sq. meters	=1 sq. decameter
100 sq. decameters	=1 sq. hectometer
100 sq. hectometers	=1 sq. kilometer
CUBIC MEASURE	
1000 cu. millimeters	=1 cu. centimeter
1000 cu. centimeters	=1 cu. decimeter
1000 cu. decimeters	=1 cu. meter

LIQUID MEASURE	
10 milliliters	=1 centiliter
10 centiliters	=1 deciliter
10 deciliters	=1 liter
10 liters	=1 decaliter
10 decaliters	=1 hectoliter
10 hectoliters	=1 kiloliter
WEIGHTS	
10 milligrams	=1 centigram
10 centigrams	=1 decigram
10 decigrams	=1 gram
10 grams	=1 decagram
10 decagrams	=1 hectogram
10 hectograms	=1 kilogram
100 kilograms	=1 quintal
10 quintals	=1 ton

METRIC CONVERSION FACTORS

APPROXIMATE CONVERSIONS TO METRIC MEASURES

When You Know	Multiply by	To Find
Length		
inches	2.5	centimeters
feet	30	centimeters
yards	0.9	meters
miles	1.6	kilometers
Area		
square inches	6.5	square centimeters
square feet	0.09	square meters
square yards	0.8	square meters
square miles	2.6	square kilometers
acres	0.4	hectares
Mass (weight)		
ounces	28	grams
pounds	0.45	kilograms
short tons	0.9	metric tons
Volume		
teaspoons	5	milliliters
tablespoons	15	milliliters
cubic inches	16	milliliters
fluid ounces	30	milliliters
cups	0.24	liters
pints	0.47	liters
quarts	0.95	liters
gallons	3.8	liters
cubic feet	0.03	cubic meters
cubic yards	0.76	cubic meters
Temperature (exact)		
degrees Fahrenheit	5/9 (after subtracting 32)	degrees Celsius

APPROXIMATE CONVERSIONS FROM METRIC MEASURES

When You Know	Multiply by	To Find
Length		
millimeters	0.04	inches
centimeters	0.4	inches
meters	3.3	feet
meters	1.1	yards
kilometers	0.6	miles
Area		
square centimeters	0.16	square inches
square meters	1.2	square yards
square kilometers	0.4	square miles
hectares	2.5	acres
Mass (weight)		
grams	0.035	ounces
kilograms	2.2	pounds
metric tons	1.1	short tons
Volume		
milliliters	0.03	fluid ounces
milliliters	0.06	cubic inches
liters	2.1	pints
liters	1.06	quarts
liters	0.26	gallons
cubic meters	35	cubic feet
cubic meters	1.3	cubic yards
Temperature (exact)		
degrees Celsius	9/5 (then add 32)	degrees Fahrenheit

-ARY (*-eu-* from *meule* millstone or *meut* earlier inflected form of *moudre* to grind)]

Meur•sault (mûr sō′; *Fr.* mœʀ sō′), *n.* a dry, white Burgundy wine produced in the district around Meursault in E France. [1825–35]

Meurthe-et-Mo•selle (mœʀ tā mô zel′), *n.* a department in NE France. 722,587; 2038 sq. mi. (5280 sq. km). *Cap.:* Nancy.

Meuse (myo͞oz; *Fr.* mœz), *n.* **1.** Dutch, **Maas.** a river in W Europe, flowing from NE France through E Belgium and S Netherlands into the North Sea. 575 mi. (925 km) long. **2.** a department in NE France. 203,904; 2409 sq. mi. (6240 sq. km). *Cap.:* Bar-le-Duc.

MeV (mev), *Physics.* million electron volts; megaelectron volt. Also, **Mev, mev**

mew[1] (myo͞o), *n.* **1.** the tiny, high-pitched sound a cat or kitten makes. **2.** the characteristic sound a gull makes. *—v.i.* **3.** to make a mew or emit a similar sound. [1275–1325; ME *meuen;* imit.]

mew[2] (myo͞o), *n.* a small gull, *Larus canus,* of Eurasia and northwestern North America. Also called **mew′ gull′.** [bef. 900; ME; OE *mǣwe;* c. G *Müwe*]

mew[3] (myo͞o), *n.* **1.** a cage for hawks, esp. while molting. **2.** a pen in which poultry is fattened. **3.** a place of retirement or concealment. **4. mews,** (*usually used with a singular v.*) *Chiefly Brit.* **a.** (formerly) an area of stables built around a small street. **b.** a street having small apartments converted from such stables. *—v.t.* **5.** *Archaic.* to shut up in or as in a mew; confine; conceal (often fol. by *up*). [1325–75; ME *mue* < MF, akin to *muer* to molt. See MEW[4]]

mew[4] (myo͞o), *v.t., v.i.* to shed (feathers); to molt. [1325–75; ME *mewen* < OF *muer* to molt < L *mūtāre* to change] **—mew′er,** *n.*

Me•war (me wär′), *n.* Udaipur (def. 2).

mewl (myo͞ol), *v.i.* to cry, as a baby, young child, or the like; whimper. [1590–1600; imit.] **—mewl′er,** *n.*

Mex., 1. Mexican. **2.** Mexico.

Mex•i•cal•i (mek′si kal′ē; *Sp.* me′hē kä′lē), *n.* a city in and the capital of Lower California, in NW Mexico, on the Mexican-U.S. border. 390,400.

Mex•i•can (mek′si kən), *adj.* **1.** of or pertaining to Mexico or its people. **2.** of or pertaining to Spanish as used in Mexico. **3.** of or pertaining to the Nahuatl language or its speakers. *—n.* **4.** a native or inhabitant of Mexico, or a person of Mexican descent. **5.** Nahuatl (defs. 1, 2). [1595–1605; < Sp *mexicano.* See MEXICO, -AN]

Mex•i•can-A•mer•i•can (mek′si kən ə mer′i kən), *n.* **1.** Also, **Mex′ican Amer′ican.** a citizen or resident of the U.S. of Mexican birth or descent; Chicano. *—adj.* **2.** of or pertaining to Mexican-Americans or their culture; Chicano. [1950–55]

Mex′ican ap′ple. See **white sapote.**

Mex′ican bamboo′, a hardy plant, *Polygonum cuspidatum,* of the buckwheat family, native to Japan, having small, greenish-white flowers and tending to escape from cultivation.

Mex′ican bead′ed liz′ard. See **beaded lizard.**

Mex′ican bean′ beet′le, a ladybird beetle, *Epilachna varivestis,* introduced into the U.S. from Mexico, that feeds on the foliage of the bean plant. Also called **bean beetle.** [1920–25]

Mex′ican fire′-plant (fīᵊr′plant′, -plänt′), a showy plant, *Euphorbia heterophylla,* of the spurge family, growing in the central U.S. to central South America, having red or mottled red and white bracts. Also called **wild poinsettia.**

Mex′ican free′-tailed bat′, any of several small, insect-eating bats of the genus *Tadarida,* of Mexico and the southwestern U.S., inhabiting limestone caves: residual DDT has reduced most populations.

Mex′ican fruit′fly, a brightly colored fly, *Anastrepha ludens,* whose larvae are a serious pest chiefly of citrus fruits and mangoes in Mexico, Central America, and southern Texas. [1920–25]

Mex′ican ground′ cher′ry, tomatillo.

Mex′ican hair′less, one of a breed of small dogs having no hair except for a tuft on the top of the head and a little fuzz on the lower part of the tail. [1895–1900]

Mex′ican hat′ dance′, 1. a dance performed by couples, consisting of eight measures during which the dancers kick out each foot alternately, followed by eight more measures during which they swing around with interlocking arms. **2.** a folk and courtship dance for a solo male around and on the brim of a Mexican sombrero.

Mex′ican i′vy. See **cup-and-saucer vine.**

Mex•i•can•ize (mek′si kə nīz′), *v.t., v.i.,* **-ized, -iz•ing.** to make or become Mexican or like the Mexican, as in manner, customs, or dress. Also, *esp. Brit.,* **Mex′i•can•ise′.** [1840–50, *Amer.;* MEXICAN + -IZE] **—Mex′i•can•i•za′tion,** *n.*

Mex′ican jade′, Mexican onyx artificially colored green.

Mex′ican jump′ing bean′. See **jumping bean.** [1880–85]

Me•xi•ca•no (me′hē kä′nō; *Sp.* me ʜē kä′nô), *n., pl.* **-nos** (-nōz; *Sp.* -nôs) for 2. **1.** the Nahuatl language. **2.** a Mexican citizen. [< Sp *mexicano* MEXICAN]

Mex′ican on′yx, *Mineral.* a translucent, banded variety of calcite, used for ornamental and decorative pieces. Also called **onyx marble.** [1890–95]

Mex′ican or′ange, an aromatic, evergreen citrus shrub, *Choisya ternata,* of Mexico, having fragrant, white flowers, grown as an ornamental. [1950–55]

Mex′ican pop′py. See under **prickly poppy.** [1840–50, *Amer.*]

Mex′ican Span′ish, Spanish as used in Mexico. *Abbr.:* MexSp

Mex′ican stand′-off, *Informal (sometimes offensive).* a stalemate or impasse; a confrontation that neither side can win. [1890–95]

Mex′ican star′, frostflower (defs. 1 and 2).

Mex′ican sun′flower, tithonia.

Mex′ican tea′, a goosefoot, *Chenopodium ambrosioides,* having strong-smelling leaves sometimes used medicinally or as flavoring. [1820–30]

Mex′ican War′, the war between the U.S. and Mexico, 1846–48.

Mex•i•co (mek′si kō′), *n.* **1.** a republic in S North America. 63,000,000; 761,530 sq. mi. (1,972,363 sq. km). *Cap.:* Mexico City. See map below. **2.** a state in central Mexico. 6,245,000; 8268 sq. mi. (21,415 sq. km). *Cap.:* Toluca. **3. Gulf of,** Mexican, **Gol•fo de Mé•xi•co** (gôl′fô t͟he me′hē kô′). an arm of the Atlantic surrounded by the U.S., Cuba, and Mexico. 700,000 sq. mi. (1,813,000 sq. km); greatest depth 12,714 ft. (3875 m). **4.** a town in NE Missouri. 12,276. Mexican, **Mé•xi•co** (me′hē kô′) (for defs. 1, 2). Spanish, **Méjico** (for defs. 1, 2).

Mex′ico Cit′y, a city in and the capital of Mexico, in the central part. 8,906,000; ab. 7400 ft. (2255 m) above sea level. Official name, **Mé•xi•co, Dis•tri•to Fe•de•ral** (me′hē kô′ dēs trē′tô fe t͟he ʀäl′).

MexSp, Mexican Spanish.

Mey•er (mī′ər), *n.* **1. Adolf,** 1866–1950, U.S. psychiatrist, born in Switzerland. **2. Albert (Gregory),** 1903–65, U.S. Roman Catholic clergyman. **3. Jul•ius Lo•thar** (jo͞ol′yəs lō′thär; *Ger.* yo͞o′lē o͞os lō′tär, lō tär′), 1830–95, German chemist. **4.** a male given name.

Mey•er•beer (mī′ər bēr′; *Ger.* mī′əʀ bāʀ′), *n.* **Gia•co•mo** (jä′kô mô), (*Jakob Liebmann Beer*), 1791–1864, German composer.

Mey•er•hof (mī′ər hof′; *Ger.* mī′əʀ hōf′), *n.* **Ot•to** (ot′ō; *Ger.* ôt′ō), 1884–1951, German physiologist: Nobel prize for medicine 1922.

Meyn•ell (men′l), *n.* **Alice Christiana (Thompson),** 1850–1922, English poet and essayist.

mez•ail (mez′āl), *n. Armor.* mesail.

mé•zair (mā zâr′), *n. Dressage.* a movement in which the horse makes a series of short jumps forward while standing on its hind legs. [1745–55; < F < It *mezzaria* lit., middle gait]

me•ze•re•um (mə zēr′ē əm), *n.* a shrub, *Daphne mezereum,* native to Eurasia, having clusters of fragrant purplish flowers. Also, **me•ze•re•on** (mə zēr′ē on′). Also called **daphne.** [1470–80; (< NL) < ML *mezereon* < Ar *māzaryūn* < Pers]

mez•lo•cil•lin (mez′lə sil′in), *n. Pharm.* a wide-spectrum semisynthetic penicillin, $C_{21}H_{25}N_5O_8S_2$, used parenterally in the treatment of infections due to *Pseudomonas aeruginosa.* [ME(THYL) + (IMIDA)ZOL(E) (rearranged), components of the chemical name + (PENI)CILLIN]

me•zu•zah (mə zo͞oz′ə; *Seph. Heb.* mə zo͞o zä′; *Ashk. Heb.* mə zo͞o′zə), *n., pl.* **-zu•zoth, -zu•zot, -zu•zos** (*Seph. Heb.* -zo͞o zôt′; *Ashk. Heb.* -zo͞o′zōs); *Eng.* **-zu•zahs.** *Judaism.* a parchment scroll inscribed on one side with the Biblical passages Deut. 6:4–9 and 11:13–21 and on the other side with the word *Shaddai* (a name applied to God), inserted in a small case or tube so that *Shaddai* is visible through an aperture in front, and attached by some Jews to the doorpost of the home. Also, **me•zu′za.** [1640–50; < Heb *məzūzāh* lit., doorpost]

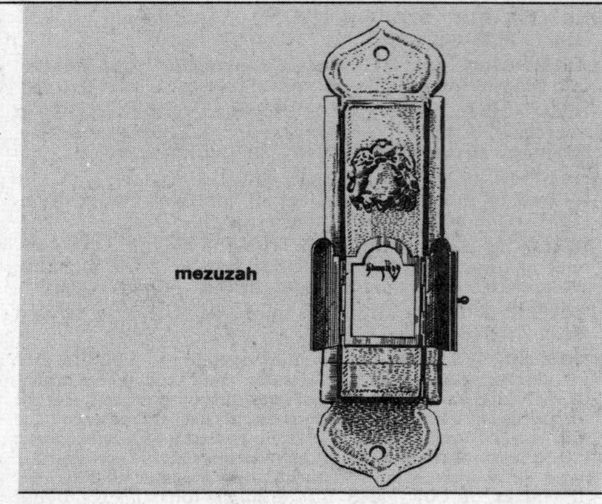

mezuzah

mez•za•nine (mez′ə nēn′, mez′ə nēn′), *n.* **1.** the lowest balcony or forward part of such a balcony in a theater. **2.** a low story between two other stories of greater height in a building, esp. when the low story and the one beneath it form part of one composition; an entresol. [1705–15; < F < It *mezzanino,* equiv. to *mezzan(o)* middle (< L *mediānus* MEDIAN) + *-ino* dim. suffix]

mez•za vo•ce (met′sə vō′chā, med′zə, mez′ə), with half the power of the voice (used as a musical direction). *Abbr.:* m.v. [1765–75; < It]

mez•zo (met′sō, med′zō, mez′ō), *adj., n., pl.* **-zos.** *—adj.* **1.** middle; medium; half. *—n.* **2.** a mezzo-soprano. [1805–15; < It < L *medius* middle]

mez′zo for′te (fôr′tā), *Music.* somewhat softer than forte but louder than piano; moderately loud. [1805–15; < It: lit., half loud]

mez′zo pia′no (pē ä′nō), *Music.* somewhat louder than piano but softer than forte; moderately soft. [1805–15; < It: lit., half soft]

mez•zo-re•lie•vo (met′sō ri lē′vō, med′zō-, mez′ō-), *n., pl.* **-vos** (-vōz). sculptured relief intermediate between high relief and bas-relief. [1590–1600; < It]

mez•zo-so•pran•o (met′sō sə pran′ō, -prä′nō, med′zō-, mez′ō-), *n., pl.* **-pran•os, -pran•i** (-pran′ē, -prä′nē), *adj. Music.* *—n.* **1.** a voice or voice part intermediate in compass between soprano and contralto. **2.** a person having such a voice. *—adj.* **3.** of, pertaining to, characteristic of, or suitable to a mezzo-soprano. [1745–55; < It]

mez′zo-sopran′o clef′, *Music.* a C clef locating middle C on the line next to the lowest line of the staff. [1805–15]

mez•zo•tint (met′sō tint′, med′zō-, mez′ō-), *n.* **1.** a method of engraving on copper or steel by burnishing or scraping away a uniformly roughened surface. **2.** a print produced by this method. *—v.t.* **3.** to engrave in mezzotint. [1730–40; < It *mezzotinto* half-tint. See MEZZO, TINT] **—mez′zo•tint′er,** *n.*

MF, 1. See **medium frequency. 2.** Middle French.

mF, millifarad; millifarads. Also, **mf**

mf, 1. See **medium frequency. 2.** millifarad; millifarads.

mf., 1. *Music.* mezzo forte. **2.** microfarad.

m/f, male or female: used esp. in classified ads. Also, **M/F**

M.F., 1. Master of Forestry. **2.** Middle French.

M.F.A., Master of Fine Arts.

mfd., 1. manufactured. **2.** microfarad.

mfg., manufacturing.

CONCISE ETYMOLOGY KEY: <, descended or borrowed from; >, whence; b., blend of, blended; c., cognate with; cf., compare; deriv., derivative; equiv., equivalent; imit., imitative; obl., oblique; r., replacing; s., stem; sp., spelling, spelled; resp., respelling, respelled; trans., translation; ?, origin unknown; *, unattested; ‡, probably earlier than. See the full key inside the front cover.

m/f/h, male, female, handicapped: used esp. in classified ads. Also, **M/F/H**

M.F.H., See **master of foxhounds.**

MFlem, Middle Flemish.

M.For., Master of Forestry.

mfr., **1.** manufacture. **2.** *pl.* **mfrs.** manufacturer.

M.Fr., Middle French.

M.F.S., **1.** Master of Food Science. **2.** Master of Foreign Service. **3.** Master of Foreign Study.

M.F.T., Master of Foreign Trade.

MG, **1.** machine gun. **2.** major general. **3.** military government. **4.** myasthenia gravis.

Mg, *Music.* left hand. [< F *main gauche*]

Mg, *Symbol, Chem.* magnesium.

mg, milligram; milligrams.

mGal, milligal; milligals.

MGB, the Ministry of State Security in the U.S.S.R. that functioned as the government's secret-police organization from 1946–53. Cf. **KGB.** [< Russ, for *Ministérstvo gosudárstvennoĭ bezopásnosti*]

mgd, millions of gallons per day.

MGk., Medieval Greek. Also, **MGk**

mgmt, management.

MGr., Medieval Greek.

mgr., **1.** manager. **2.** Monseigneur. **3.** Monsignor. Also, **Mgr.**

mgt., management.

MGy Sgt, master gunnery sergeant.

mH, millihenry; millihenries. Also, **mh**

M.H., Medal of Honor.

M.H.A., Master in Hospital Administration; Master of Hospital Administration.

MHC, major histocompatibility complex: (in mammals) a group of genes located next to or near each other on a specific chromosome, the sixth in humans, most of which encode glycoproteins of highly variable shapes that are expressed on almost all cell surfaces: it plays the dominant role in distinguishing one individual's cells from another's and in determining the histocompatibility of any two individuals. Cf. **HLA.**

MHD, *Physics.* magnetohydrodynamics.

M.H.E., Master of Home Economics.

MHG, Middle High German. Also, **M.H.G.**

mho (mō), *n., pl.* **mhos.** *Elect.* See under **siemens.** Also called **reciprocal ohm.**

M.H.R., Member of the House of Representatives.

M.H.W., mean high water. Also, **m.h.w., MHW**

MHz, megahertz.

mHz, millihertz.

mi (mē), *n. Music.* **1.** the syllable used for the third tone of a diatonic scale. **2.** (in the fixed system of solmization) the tone E. Cf. **sol-fa** (def. 1). [1520–30; see GAMUT]

MI, Michigan (approved esp. for use with zip code).

MI, *Pathol.* myocardial infarction.

MI5 (em′ī′fīv′), *n.* (in Great Britain) the government's security and counterespionage service that works in liaison with Scotland Yard's Special Branch. [*M(ilitary) I(ntelligence, Section)* 5]

MI6 (em′ī′siks′), *n.* (in Great Britain) the government's secret intelligence service. [*M(ilitary) I(ntelligence, Section)* 6]

mi, mile; miles.

mi., **1.** mile; miles. **2.** mill; mills.

M.I., **1.** Military Intelligence. **2.** Mounted Infantry.

MIA, *pl.* **MIA's, MIAs** for 2. **1.** missing in action. **2.** a soldier declared missing in action.

M.I.A., **1.** Master of International Affairs. **2.** *Mil.* missing in action.

Mi•am•i (mī am′ē, -am′ə), *n., pl.* **-am•is** (*esp. collectively*) **-am•i.** **1.** a member of a North American Indian tribe of the Algonquian family, formerly located in northern Indiana, southern Michigan, and possibly Illinois, now extinct as a tribe. **2.** their dialect of the Illinois language.

Mi•am•i (mī am′ē, -am′ə), *n.* **1.** a city in SE Florida: seaside resort. 346,931. **2.** Also called **Great Miami.** a river in W Ohio, flowing S into the Ohio River. 160 mi. (260 km) long. **3.** a city in NE Oklahoma. 14,237. **—Mi•am′i•an,** *n.*

mi•a•mi•a (mī′ə mī′ə), *n.* a temporary, hutlike shelter built by Aboriginal tribes in Australia. [1835–45; < Ganay (or Kurnai, Australian Aboriginal language spoken in Gippsland, Victoria), recorded as *mai-mai* camp, hut]

Miam′i Beach′, a city in SE Florida on an island 2½ mi. (4 km) across Biscayne Bay from Miami: seaside resort. 96,298.

Mi•am•is•burg (mī am′ēz bûrg′), *n.* a town in W Ohio. 15,304.

Miam′i Springs′, a town in SE Florida, near Miami. 12,350.

Mi•an•to•no•mo (mī an′tə nō′mō, mē-), *n.* died 1643, leader of the Narragansetts.

Mi•ao (mē ou′), *n., pl.* **Mi•aos,** (*esp. collectively*) **Mi•ao** for 1. **1.** Also, **Meo.** a member of a diverse group of seminomadic farming people of the mountains of southeastern China and adjacent areas of Laos, North Vietnam, and Thailand. **2.** a Miao-Yao language spoken in parts of southern China and Southeast Asia. Also called **Hmong.**

mi•aow (mē ou′, myou), *n., v.i.* meow. Also, **mi•aou′, mi•aul** (mē oul′, mē ôl′).

Miao-Yao (myou′you′), *n.* a family of languages, affiliated with Kam-Tai, spoken in southern China and Southeast Asia.

mi•as•ma (mī az′mə, mē-), *n., pl.* **-mas, -ma•ta** (-mə tə). **1.** noxious exhalations from putrescent organic matter; poisonous effluvia or germs polluting the atmosphere. **2.** a dangerous, foreboding, or deathlike influence or atmosphere. [1655–65; < NL < Gk *míasma* stain, pollution, akin to *miainein* to pollute, stain] **—mi•as′mal, mi•as•mat•ic** (mī′az mat′ik), **mi′as•mat′i•cal, mi•as′mic,** *adj.*

Mi•ass (mē äs′; *Russ.* myi äs′), *n.* a city in the S RSFSR, in the W Soviet Union in Asia, near the Ural Mountains. 150,000.

mi•a•zine (mī′ə zēn′, -zin, mī az′ēn, -in), *n. Chem.* pyrimidine (def. 1). [M(ETA-) + (D)IAZINE]

mib (mib), *n.* **1.** a playing marble, esp. one that is not used as a shooter. **2. mibs,** (*used with a singular v.*) the game of marbles. [1890–95, *Amer.*; shortened var. of MARBLE]

mic (mīk), *n. Informal.* a microphone. [by shortening]

Mic., *Bible.* Micah.

mi•ca (mī′kə), *n.* any member of a group of minerals, hydrous silicates of aluminum with other bases, chiefly potassium, magnesium, iron, and lithium, that separate readily into thin, tough, often transparent, and usually elastic laminae; isinglass. [1700–10; < L *mīca* crumb, morsel, grain] **—mi′ca•like′,** *adj.*

mi•ca•ceous (mī kā′shəs), *adj.* **1.** consisting of, containing, or resembling mica. **2.** of or pertaining to mica. [1765–75; MIC(A) + -ACEOUS]

Mi•cah (mī′kə), *n.* **1.** a Minor Prophet of the 8th century B.C. **2.** a book of the Bible bearing his name. *Abbr.:* Mic. **3.** a male given name.

Mic•co•su•kee (mik′ə so͞o′kē), *n., pl.* **-kis,** (*esp. collectively*) **-ki,** *adj.* Mikasuki.

mice (mīs), *n.* pl. of **mouse.**

mi•celle (mi sel′), *n. Physical Chem.* an electrically charged particle formed by an aggregate of molecules and occurring in certain colloidal electrolyte solutions, as those of soaps and detergents. [1880–85; < NL *mīcella*, equiv. to L *mīc(a)* crumb, grain + *-ella* -ELLE] **—mi•cel′lar,** *adj.* **—mi•cel′lar•ly,** *adv.*

Mich., **1.** Michaelmas. **2.** Michigan.

Mi•chael (mī′kəl), *n.* **1.** a militant archangel. Dan. 10:13. **2.** Rumanian, **Mi•hai** (mē hī′). born 1921, king of Rumania 1927–30, 1940–47 (son of Carol II). **3.** (*italics*) a narrative poem (1800) by Wordsworth. **4.** a male given name.

Michael VIII Pa•lae•ol•o•gus (pā′lē ol′ə gəs, pal′ē-), 1234–1282, Byzantine ruler 1259–82, first of the Palaeologus emperors.

Mich•ael•mas (mik′əl məs), *n. Chiefly Brit.* a festival celebrated on September 29 in honor of the archangel Michael. Also called **Mich′aelmas Day′.** [bef. 1150; ME *Mighelmes*; OE (*Sanct*) *Michaeles masse* (St.) Michael's mass]

Mich′aelmas dai′sy, an aster. [1775–85]

Mi•chal (mī′kəl), *n.* a daughter of Saul, who became the wife of David. I Sam. 14:49; 18:27.

Mi•chaux (mē shō′), *n.* **Hen•ri** (äN rē′), 1899–1984, French poet and painter, born in Belgium.

miche (mich), *v.i.,* **miched, mich•ing.** *Brit. Dial.* to lurk out of sight. [1175–1225; ME *mychen, michen* < OF *muchier* to hide] **—mich′er,** *n.*

Mi•che•as (mī kē′əs), *n. Douay Bible.* Micah (defs. 1, 2).

Mi•chel•an•ge•lo (mī′kəl an′jə lō′, mik′əl-; *It.* mē′kel än′je lô), *n.* (*Michelangelo Buonarroti*) 1475–1564, Italian sculptor, painter, architect, and poet.

Mi•chele (mi shel′), *n.* a female given name. Also, **Mi•chelle′.**

Mi•che•let (mēshᵊ lā′), *n.* **Jules** (zhyl), 1798–1874, French historian.

Mi•chel•son (mī′kəl sən), *n.* **Albert Abraham,** 1852–1931, U.S. physicist, born in Prussia (now Poland): Nobel prize 1907.

Miche•ner (mish′nər *for 1;* mich′ə nər, mich′nər *for 2*), *n.* **1. (Daniel) Roland,** 1900–91, Canadian public official and diplomat: governor general 1967–74. **2. James A(lbert),** born 1907, U.S. novelist.

Mich•i•gan (mish′i gən), *n.* **1.** a state in the N central United States. 9,258,344; 58,216 sq. mi. (150,780 sq. km). *Cap.:* Lansing. *Abbr.:* MI (for use with zip code), Mich. **2. Lake,** a lake in the N central U.S., between Wisconsin and Michigan: one of the five Great Lakes. 22,400 sq. mi. (58,015 sq. km). **3.** a card game of the stops family, for three to eight players.

Mich′igan bank′roll, *Slang.* **1.** a large roll of paper money in small denominations. **2.** a roll of counterfeit paper money or a roll of money-sized paper surrounded by one or more genuine bills. Also called **Mich′igan roll′.** [1930–35]

Mich′igan Cit′y, a port in NW Indiana, on Lake Michigan. 36,850.

Mich•i•gan•der (mish′i gan′dər), *n.* a native or inhabitant of Michigan. Also called **Mich•i•gan•ite** (mish′i gə nīt′). [1825–35, *Amer.*; b. MICHIGAN and GANDER, name first applied to Lewis Cass, governor of the Michigan Territory (1813–31)]

Mich•i•ga•ni•an (mish′i gā′nē ən, -gan′ē-), *adj.* **1.** of, pertaining to, or characteristic of Michigan or its inhabitants. **—***n.* **2.** a Michigander. [1805–15, *Amer.*; MICHIGAN + -IAN]

Mich′igan rum′my, *Cards.* a variety of five hundred rummy in which each player scores his or her melds as played.

Mi•cho•a•cán (mē′chô ä kän′), *n.* a state in SW Mexico. 2,805,000; 23,196 sq. mi. (60,080 sq. km). *Cap.:* Morelia.

Mi•chol (mī′kəl), *n. Douay Bible.* Michal.

Mi•chu•rinsk (mi cho͝or′insk; *Russ.* myi chyo͞o′ryinsk), *n.* a city in the W RSFSR, in central Soviet Union in Europe, S of Ryazan. 102,000. Formerly, **Kozlov.**

Mick (mik), *n.* (*often l.c.*) *Slang* (*usually disparaging and offensive*). a person of Irish birth or descent. [1870–75, *Amer.*; generic use of *Mick,* hypocoristic form of MICHAEL]

Mick•ey (mik′ē), *n., pl.* **-eys,** *adj.* **—***n.* **1.** Also called **Mick′ey Finn′.** *Slang.* a drink, usually alcoholic, to which a drug, purgative, or the like, has been secretly added, that renders the unsuspecting drinker helpless. **2.** (*often l.c.*) Also, **micky.** a potato, esp. a roasted Irish potato. **3.** a male or female given name. **—***adj.* **4.** (*sometimes l.c.*) See **mickey mouse.** [1925–30, *Amer.*; *Mick* (see MICK) + -EY[2]]

mick′ey mouse′, (*often caps.*) *Informal.* **1.** trite and commercially slick in character; corny: *mickey mouse music.* **2.** useless, insignificant, or worthless: *mickey mouse activities just to fill up one's time.* **3.** trivial or petty: *mickey mouse regulations.* [1930–35; after the animated cartoon character created by Walt Disney, orig. with reference to the banal dance-band music played as background to the cartoons]

Mic•kie•wicz (mits kye′vich), *n.* **A•dam** (ä′däm), 1798–1855, Polish poet.

mick•le (mik′əl), *adj. Archaic.* great; large; much. [bef. 900; ME *mikel* < ON *mikill;* r. ME *michel,* OE *micel* (see MUCH); c. OHG *mihhil,* Goth *mikils,* akin to L *magnus,* Gk *mégas*]

mick•y (mik′ē), *n., pl.* **mick•ies.** (*sometimes cap.*) Mickey (def. 2).

Mic•mac (mik′mak), *n., pl.* **-macs,** (*esp. collectively*) **-mac** for 1. **1.** a member of a North American Indian people now living mostly in Quebec, New Brunswick, Nova Scotia, and Prince Edward Island. **2.** the Algonquian language of these people.

MICR, magnetic ink character recognition: a technique for reading and processing data printed with ink that contains magnetic particles: used esp. in sorting bank checks automatically.

mi•cra (mī′krə), *n.* a pl. of **micron.**

mi•cri•fy (mī′krə fī′), *v.t.,* **-fied, -fy•ing.** to make small or insignificant. [1830–40; MICR- + -IFY]

mi•cro (mī′krō), *adj., n., pl.* **-cros.** **—***adj.* **1.** extremely small. **2.** minute in scope or capability. **3.** of or pertaining to microcomputers. **4.** of or pertaining to microeconomics. **—***n.* **5.** anything extremely small in scope or capability. **6.** a microcomputer. **7.** microeconomics. [independent use of MICRO-, or shortening of words with this initial element]

micro-, a combining form with the meanings "small" (*microcosm; microgamete*), "very small in comparison with others of its kind" (*microcassette; microlith*), "too small to be seen by the unaided eye" (*microfossil; microorganism*), "dealing with extremely minute organisms, organic structures, or quantities of a substance" (*microdissection; microscope*), "localized, restricted in scope or area" (*microburst; microhabitat*), "(of a discipline) focusing on a restricted area" (*microeconomics*), "containing or dealing with texts that require enlargement to be read" (*microfilm; microreader*), "one millionth" (*microgram*). Also, *esp. before a vowel,* **micr-.** [< Gk: comb. form repr. *mīkrós* small]

mi•cro•am•me•ter (mī′krō am′mē tər), *n.* an instrument for measuring extremely small electric currents, calibrated in microamperes. [1925–30; MICRO- + AMMETER]

mi•cro•am•pere (mī′krō am′pēr, -am pēr′), *n. Elect.* a unit of electric current, equal to one millionth of an ampere. *Symbol:* μA [1900–05; MICRO- + AMPERE]

mi•cro•a•nal•y•sis (mī′krō ə nal′ə sis), *n., pl.* **-ses** (-sēz′). **1.** *Chem.* the analysis of very small samples of substances. **2.** the detailed analysis of a sphere of behavior, as of human communication. [1855–60; MICRO- + ANALYSIS] **—mi•cro•an•a•lyst** (mī′krō an′l ist), *n.* **—mi•cro•an•a•lyt•i•cal** (mī′krō an′l it′i kəl), **mi′cro•an′a•lyt′ic,** *adj.*

mi•cro•a•nat•o•my (mī′krō ə nat′ə mē), *n.* the branch of anatomy dealing with microscopic structures (distinguished from *gross anatomy*). [1895–1900; MICRO- + ANATOMY] **—mi•cro•an•a•tom•ic** (mī′krō an′ə tom′-

CONCISE PRONUNCIATION KEY: act, cāpe, dâre, pärt; set, ēqual; *if,* ice; ox, ōver, ôrder, oil, bo͝ok, bo͞ot, out; up, ûrge; child; sing; shoe; thin, that; zh as in *treasure.* ə = *a* as in *alone, e* as in *system, i* as in *easily, o* as in *gallop, u* as in *circus;* ᵊ as in *fire* (fīᵊr), *hour* (ouᵊr). l and n can serve as syllabic consonants, as in *cradle* (krād′l), and *button* (but′n). See the full key inside the front cover.

ik), **mi′cro·an′a·tom′i·cal,** *adj.* **—mi′cro·an′a·tom′i·cal·ly,** *adv.* **—mi′cro·a·nat′o·mist,** *n.*

mi·cro·an·gi·op·a·thy (mī′krō an′jē op′ə thē), *n. Pathol.* any disease of the small blood vessels. [MICRO- + ANGIO- + -PATHY]

mi·cro·bac·te·ri·um (mī′krō bak tēr′ē əm), *n., pl.* **-te·ri·a** (-tēr′ē ə). *Bacteriol.* any of several rod-shaped, thermoduric, saprophytic bacteria of the genus *Microbacterium,* found chiefly in dairy products. [< NL; see MICRO-, BACTERIUM]

mi·cro·bal·ance (mī′krə bal′əns), *n. Chem.* a balance for weighing minute quantities of material. [1900–05; MICRO- + BALANCE]

mi·cro·bar (mī′krə bär′), *n.* a centimeter-gram-second unit of pressure, equal to one millionth of a bar; one dyne per square centimeter. Also called **barye.** [1915–20; MICRO- + BAR[3]]

mi·cro·bar·o·gram (mī′krə bär′ə gram′), *n. Meteorol.* a record made by a microbarograph. [MICRO- + BAROGRAM]

mi·cro·bar·o·graph (mī′krə bär′ə graf′, -gräf′), *n. Meteorol.* a barograph for recording minute fluctuations of atmospheric pressure. [MICRO- + BAROGRAPH]

mi·crobe (mī′krōb), *n.* a microorganism, esp. a pathogenic bacterium. [1880–85; < F < Gk *mikro-* MICRO- + *bíos* life] **—mi′crobe·less,** *adj.* **—mi·cro′bi·al, mi·cro′bic, mi·cro′bi·an,** *adj.*

mi·cro·bi·cide (mī krō′bə sīd′), *n.* a substance or preparation for killing microbes. [1880–85; MICROBE + -I- + -CIDE] **—mi·cro′bi·cid′al,** *adj.*

mi·cro·bi·ol·o·gy (mī′krō bī ol′ə jē), *n.* the branch of biology dealing with the structure, function, uses, and modes of existence of microscopic organisms. [1885–90; MICRO- + BIOLOGY] **—mi·cro·bi·o·log·i·cal** (mī′krō bī′ə loj′i kəl), **mi′cro·bi′o·log′ic,** *adj.* **—mi′cro·bi′o·log′i·cal·ly,** *adv.* **—mi′cro·bi·ol′o·gist,** *n.*

mi·cro·blade (mī′krə blād′), *n.* bladelet. Also, **mi′cro-blade′.** [1965–70; MICRO- + BLADE]

mi·cro·brew·er·y (mī′krō brōō′ə rē, -brŏŏr′ē), *n., pl.* **-er·ies.** a brewery producing less than 15,000 barrels per year and usually concentrating on exotic or high quality beer. [1985–90]

mi·cro·burst (mī′krə bûrst′), *n. Meteorol.* an intense, localized downdraft of air that spreads on the ground, causing rapid changes in wind direction and speed; a localized downburst. [1980–85; MICRO- + BURST]

mi·cro·bus (mī′krō bus′), *n.* minibus. [1940–45; MICRO- + BUS[1]]

mi·cro·cap·sule (mī′krō kap′səl, -sōōl, -syōōl), *n. Chem.* a tiny capsule, 20–150 microns in diameter, used for slow-release application of drugs, pesticides, flavors, etc. [1960–65; MICRO- + CAPSULE]

mi·cro·cas·sette (mī′krō kə set′, -ka-), *n.* a very small audio tape cassette smaller than a minicassette, for use with a pocket-size tape recorder. [1975–80; MICRO- + CASSETTE]

mi·cro·ce·phal·ic (mī′krō sə fal′ik), *adj. Cephalom., Pathol.* having a head with a small braincase. Also, **mi·cro·ceph·a·lous** (mī′krə sef′ə ləs). [< NL *microcephalicus.* See MICRO-, CEPHALIC] **—mi′cro·ceph′a·ly,** *n.*

mi·cro·chem·is·try (mī′krō kem′ə strē), *n.* the branch of chemistry dealing with minute quantities of substances. [1885–90; MICRO- + CHEMISTRY] **—mi·cro·chem·i·cal** (mī′krō kem′i kəl), *adj.*

mi·cro·chip (mī′krō chip′), *n. Electronics.* chip[1] (def. 5). [1965–70; MICRO- + CHIP[1]]

Mi·cro·ci·on·a (mī′krə sī′ə nə), *n.* a genus of bright-red sponges of the Atlantic coasts of North America and Europe, used in experiments on the dissociation and reintegration of sponge cells. [< NL < Gk *mikro-* MICRO- + *kīōn* column + NL *-a* -A[2]]

mi·cro·cir·cuit (mī′krō sûr′kit), *n. Electronics.* See **integrated circuit.** [1955–60; MICRO- + CIRCUIT]

mi·cro·cir·cuit·ry (mī′krō sûr′ki trē), *n. Electronics.* **1.** a detailed plan of an integrated circuit or a network of such circuits. **2.** the components of a network of integrated circuits. [1960–65; MICRO- + CIRCUITRY]

mi·cro·cir·cu·la·tion (mī′krō sûr′kyə lā′shən), *n.* the movement of blood through the arterioles, capillaries, and venules. [1955–60; MICRO- + CIRCULATION] **—mi·cro·cir·cu·la·to·ry** (mī′krō sûr′kyə lə tôr′ē), *adj.*

mi·cro·cli·mate (mī′krə klī′mit), *n.* the climate of a small area, as of confined spaces such as caves or houses **(cryptoclimate),** of plant communities, wooded areas, etc. **(phytoclimate),** or of urban communities, which may be different from that in the general region. Cf. **macroclimate.** [1920–25; MICRO- + CLIMATE] **—mi·cro·cli·mat·ic** (mī′krō klī mat′ik), *adj.* **—mi′cro·cli·mat′i·cal·ly,** *adv.*

mi·cro·cli·ma·tol·o·gy (mī′krō klī′mə tol′ə jē), *n.* the study of a microclimate. Cf. **macroclimatology, micrometeorology.** [1930–35; MICRO- + CLIMATOLOGY] **—mi·cro·cli·ma·to·log·ic** (mī′krō klī′mə tl oj′ik), **mi′cro·cli′ma·to·log′i·cal,** *adj.* **—mi′cro·cli′ma·tol′o·gist,** *n.*

mi·cro·cline (mī′krə klīn′), *n.* a mineral of the feldspar group, potassium aluminum silicate, $KAlSi_3O_8$, identical in composition with orthoclase but having triclinic instead of monoclinic crystals, used in making porcelain. [1840–50; MICRO- + *-cline* < Gk *klī́nein* to LEAN[1], referring to the angles between its cleavage planes, which differ slightly from 90°]

mi·cro·coc·cus (mī′krə kok′əs), *n., pl.* **-coc·ci** (-kok′sī, -sē). *Bacteriol.* any spherical bacterium of the genus *Micrococcus,* occurring in irregular masses, many species of which are pigmented and are saprophytic or parasitic. [< NL (1872); see MICRO-, COCCUS] **—mi′cro·coc′cal, mi·cro·coc·cic** (mī′krə kok′sik), *adj.*

mi·cro·code (mī′krə kōd′), *n. Computers.* **1.** one or more microinstructions. **2.** the notation for writing microprograms on a given computer. [MICRO- + CODE]

mi·cro·com·po·nent (mī′krō kəm pō′nənt), *n.* a hi-fi component considerably smaller than a minicomponent and much smaller than a standard-size component. [MICRO- + COMPONENT]

mi·cro·com·put·er (mī′krō kəm pyōō′tər), *n.* a compact and relatively inexpensive computer, with less capacity and capability than a minicomputer, consisting of a microprocessor and other components of a computer, miniaturized where possible: used in small business, by hobbyists, etc. Cf. **home computer, mainframe, personal computer.** [1970–75; MICRO- + COMPUTER]

mi·cro·com·put·ing (mī′krō kəm pyōō′ting), *n. Computers.* the use of microcomputers. [MICRO- + COMPUTING]

mi·cro·con·stit·u·ent (mī′krō kən stich′ōō ənt), *n.* a microscopically small constituent of a metal or alloy. [1900–05; MICRO- + CONSTITUENT]

mi·cro·cop·y (mī′krə kop′ē), *n., pl.* **-cop·ies.** a microphotographic copy of a printed page or the like, as in microfilm or microfiche. [1930–35; MICRO- + COPY]

mi·cro·cosm (mī′krə koz′əm), *n.* **1.** a little world; a world in miniature (opposed to *macrocosm*). **2.** anything that is regarded as a world in miniature. **3.** human beings, humanity, society, or the like, viewed as an epitome or miniature of the world or universe. Also called **mi·cro·cos·mos** (mī′krə koz′məs, -mōs). [1150–1200; ME *microcosme* < ML *micrŏcosmus* < Gk *mikròs kósmos* small world. See MICRO-, COSMOS] **—mi′cro·cos′mic, mi′cro·cos′mi·cal,** *adj.*

mi′crocos′mic salt′, *Chem.* See **sodium ammonium phosphate.** [1775–85]

mi·cro·crys·tal (mī′krə kris′tl), *n.* a microscopic crystal. [1890–95; MICRO- + CRYSTAL]

mi·cro·crys·tal·line (mī′krō kris′tl in, -īn′-), *adj.* minutely crystalline; composed of microscopic crystals. [1875–80; MICRO- + CRYSTALLINE] **—mi·cro·crys·tal·lin·i·ty** (mī′krō kris′tl in′i tē), *n.*

mi·cro·cul·ture (mī′krō kul′chər), *n.* subculture (def. 3b). [MICRO- + CULTURE] **—mi′cro·cul′tur·al,** *adj.*

mi·cro·cu·rie (mī′krə kyŏŏr′ē, mī′krō kyŏŏ rē′), *n. Physics, Chem.* a unit of radioactivity, equal to one millionth of a curie; 3.70×10^4 disintegrations per second. *Symbol:* μCi, μc [1910–15; MICRO- + CURIE]

mi·cro·cyte (mī′krə sīt′), *n. Pathol.* an abnormally small red blood cell. [1875–80; MICRO- + -CYTE] **—mi·cro·cyt·ic** (mī′krə sit′ik), *adj.*

mi·cro·den·si·tom·e·ter (mī′krō den′si tom′i tər), *n. Photog.* a densitometer for measuring the density of minute areas of photographic negatives. [1930–35; MICRO- + DENSITOMETER]

mi·cro·de·tec·tor (mī′krō di tek′tər), *n.* **1.** an instrument measuring small quantities or changes. **2.** *Elect.* an extremely sensitive galvanometer. [MICRO- + DETECTOR]

mi·cro·dis·sec·tion (mī′krō di sek′shən), *n.* dissection performed under a microscope. [1910–15; MICRO- + DISSECTION]

mi·cro·dis·til·la·tion (mī′krō dis′tl ā′shən), *n. Chem.* the distillation of minute quantities of material. [MICRO- + DISTILLATION]

mi·cro·don·tia (mī′krə don′shə, -shē ə), *n.* abnormally small teeth. Also, **mi·cro·dont·ism** (mī′krə dontiz′əm), **mi′cro·don′ty.** [< NL; see MICR-, -ODONT, -IA] **—mi·cro·dont** (mī′krə dont′), **mi′cro·don′tic, mi′cro·don′tous,** *adj.*

mi·cro·dot (mī′krə dot′), *n., v.t.,* **-dot·ted, -dot·ting.** **—***n.* **1.** a photograph reduced to the size of a printed period, used esp. to transmit messages, photographs, drawings, etc. **—***v.t.* **2.** to make a microdot of. [1945–50; MICRO- + DOT[1]]

mi·cro·earth·quake (mī′krō ûrth′kwāk′), *n.* an earthquake of very low intensity (magnitude of 2 or less on the Richter scale). Also called **microtremor.** [1965–70; MICRO- + EARTHQUAKE]

mi·cro·e·col·o·gy (mī′krō i kol′ə jē), *n.* the ecology of a microhabitat. [1960–65; MICRO- + ECOLOGY] **—mi·cro·ec·o·log·i·cal** (mī′krō ek′ə loj′i kəl, -ē′kə-), *adj.*

mi·cro·ec·o·nom·ics (mī′krō ek′ə nom′iks, -ē′kə-), *n.* (*used with a singular v.*) the branch of economics dealing with particular aspects of an economy, as the price-cost relationship of a firm. Cf. **macroeconomics.** [1945–50; MICRO- + ECONOMICS] **—mi′cro·ec′o·nom′ic,** *adj.* **—mi·cro·e·con·o·mist** (mī′krō i kon′ə mist), *n.*

mi·cro·e·lec·tron·ics (mī′krō i lek tron′iks, -ē′lek-), *n.* (*used with a singular v.*) the technology dealing with the design, development, and construction of electronic systems utilizing extremely small elements, esp. solid-state devices employing microminiaturization. [1955–60; MICRO- + ELECTRONICS] **—mi′cro·e·lec·tron′ic,** *adj.*

mi·cro·e·lec·tro·pho·re·sis (mī′krō i lek′trō fə rē′sis), *n. Chem.* any of several techniques for observing, by means of a microscope or an ultramicroscope, the electrophoresis of minute surface particles. [1955–60; MICRO- + ELECTROPHORESIS] **—mi·cro·e·lec·tro·pho·ret·ic** (mī′krō i lek′trō fə ret′ik), *adj.*

mi·cro·en·cap·su·la·tion (mī′krō en kap′sə lā′shən, -syŏŏ-), *n. Chem.* the process of enclosing chemical substances in microcapsules. [1960–65; MICRO- + ENCAPSULATION]

mi·cro·en·vi·ron·ment (mī′krō en vī′ərn mənt, -vī′rən-), *n.* the environment of a small area or of a particular organism; microhabitat. [1950–55; MICRO- + ENVIRONMENT] **—mi·cro·en·vi·ron·men·tal** (mī′krō en-vī′ərn men′tl, -vī′rən-), *adj.*

mi·cro·ev·o·lu·tion (mī′krō ev′ə lōō′shən *or, esp. Brit.,* -ē′və-), *n. Biol.* **1.** evolutionary change involving the gradual accumulation of mutations leading to new varieties within a species. **2.** minor evolutionary change observed over a short period of time. [1935–40; MICRO- + EVOLUTION] **—mi′cro·ev′o·lu′tion·ar′y,** *adj.*

mi·cro·far·ad (mī′krə far′əd, -ad), *n. Elect.* a unit of capacitance, equal to one millionth of a farad. *Abbr.:* mf., mfd. *Symbol:* μF, μf [1870–75; MICRO- + FARAD]

mi·cro·fau·na (mī′krō fô′nə), *n., pl.* **-nas, -nae** (-nē). (*used with a singular or plural v.*) **1.** *Biol.* microscopic animals. **2.** *Ecol.* the fauna of a microhabitat. [1900–05; MICRO- + FAUNA] **—mi′cro·fau′nal,** *adj.*

mi·cro·fi·ber (mī′krō fī′bər), *n.* a very fine polyester fiber, weighing less than one denier per filament, used esp. for clothing. [1985–90]

mi·cro·fi·bril (mī′krō fī′brəl, -fib′rəl), *n. Cell Biol.* a microtubule, microfilament, or other fine threadlike structure of a cell. [1935–40; MICRO- + FIBRIL]

mi·cro·fiche (mī′krə fēsh′), *n., pl.* **-fiche, -fich·es,** *v.,* **-fiched, -fich·ing.** **—***n.* **1.** a flat sheet of microfilm in a form suitable for filing, typically measuring 4 by 6 in. (10 by 15 cm) and containing microreproductions, as of printed or graphic matter, in a grid pattern. **—***v.t.* **2.** to enter or record on a microfiche: *The correspondence was microfiched for easy storage.* Also called **fiche, filmcard.** [1945–50; MICRO- + F *fiche* small card]

mi·cro·fil·a·ment (mī′krə fil′ə mənt), *n. Cell Biol.* a minute, narrow tubelike cell structure composed of a protein similar to actin, occurring singly and in bundles, involved in cytoplasmic movement and changes in cell shape. [1960–65; MICRO- + FILAMENT] **—mi·cro·fil·a·men·tous** (mī′krō fil′ə men′təs), *adj.*

mi·cro·fi·lar·i·a (mī′krō fi lâr′ē ə), *n., pl.* **-lar·i·ae** (-lâr′ē ē′). the embryonic larva of the nematode parasite *Filaria* or of related genera, esp. of those species that cause heartworm in dogs and elephantiasis in humans. [1875–80; < NL; see MICRO-, FILARIA]

mi·cro·film (mī′krə film′), *n.* **1.** a film bearing a miniature photographic copy of printed or other graphic matter, usually of a document, newspaper or book pages, etc., made for a library, archive, or the like. **2.** a film, esp. of motion-picture stock, on which microcopies are made. **—***v.t.* **3.** to make a microfilm of. [1930–35; MICRO- + FILM] **—mi′cro·film′er,** *n.*

mi·cro·flo·ra (mī′krə flôr′ə, -flōr′ə), *n., pl.* **-flo·ras, -flo·rae** (-flôr′ē, -flōr′ē). (*used with a singular or plural v.*) **1.** *Biol.* microscopic plants. **2.** *Ecol.* the flora of a microhabitat. [1900–05; MICRO- + FLORA] **—mi′cro·flo′ral,** *adj.*

mi·cro·form (mī′krə fôrm′), *n.* any form, either film or paper, containing microreproductions. [1955–60; MICRO- + FORM]

mi·cro·fos·sil (mī′krō fos′il), *n.* a fossil so small that it can be studied and identified only with a microscope. Cf. **macrofossil.** [1920–25; MICRO- + FOSSIL]

mi·cro·gam·ete (mī′krō gam′ēt, -gə mēt′), *n. Cell Biol.* (in heterogamous reproduction) the smaller and, usually, the male of two conjugating gametes. [1890–95; MICRO- + GAMETE]

mi·cro·gram[1] (mī′krə gram′), *n.* a unit of mass or weight equal to one millionth of a gram, used chiefly in microchemistry. *Symbol:* μg Also, *esp. Brit.,* **mi′cro·gramme′.** [1885–90; MICRO- + -GRAM[2]]

mi·cro·gram[2] (mī′krə gram′), *n.* micrograph (def. 2). [MICRO- + -GRAM[1]]

mi·cro·graph (mī′krə graf′, -gräf′), *n.* **1.** an instrument for executing extremely minute writing or engraving. **2.** *Optics.* a photograph taken through a microscope or a drawing of an object as seen through a microscope. [1870–75; MICRO- + -GRAPH]

mi·cro·graph·i·a (mī′krə graf′ē ə), *n.* **1.** minute handwriting. **2.** *Pathol.* a neurological condition, usually symptomatic of parkinsonism, in which the handwriting becomes progressively smaller. [< NL; see MICRO-, -GRAPH, -IA]

mi·cro·graph·ics (mī′krə graf′iks), *n.* (*used with a singular v.*) the technique of photographing written or printed pages in reduced form to produce microfilm or microfiche. [1965–70; *micrograph(ic)* (see MICROGRAPHY, -GRAPHIC) + -ICS]

mi·crog·ra·phy (mī krog′rə fē), *n.* **1.** the description or delineation of microscopic objects. **2.** examination or study with the microscope (opposed to *macrography*). **3.** the technique or practice of using the microscope. **4.** the art or practice of writing in very small characters. [1650–60; MICRO- + -GRAPHY] **—mi·crog′ra·pher,** *n.* **—mi·cro·graph·ic** (mī′krə graf′ik), *adj.*

mi·cro·grav·i·ty (mī′krō grav′i tē), *n.* a condition, esp. in space orbit, where the force of gravity is so weak that weightlessness results. [MICRO- + GRAVITY]

mi·cro·groove (mī′krə grōōv′), *n.* a needle groove so narrow that over 200 can be cut in an inch of playing surface on a long-playing record. [MICRO- + GROOVE]

mi·cro·hab·i·tat (mī′krō hab′i tat′), *n.* an extremely localized, small-scale environment, as a tree stump or a dead animal. [1930–35; MICRO- + HABITAT]

mi·cro·im·age (mī′krō im′ij), *n.* a microreproduction. Also, **mi′cro·im′age.** [1945–50]

mi·cro·inch (mī′krō inch′), *n.* a unit of length equal to one millionth of an inch. *Symbol:* μin [1940–45; MICRO- + INCH[1]]

mi·cro·in·ject (mī′krō in jekt′), *v.t. Biol.* to inject into a single cell or cell part. [MICRO- + INJECT]

mi·cro·in·jec·tion (mī′krō in jek′shən), *n. Biol.* injection performed under a microscope, esp. of a solution or gene transplant into a cell or cell part. [1920–25; MICRO- + INJECTION]

mi·cro·in·struc·tion (mī′krō in struk′shən), *n. Computers.* an instruction that defines part of a machine-language instruction in terms of simpler operations. [1955–60; MICRO- + INSTRUCTION]

CONCISE ETYMOLOGY KEY: <, descended or borrowed from; >, whence; b., blend of, blended; c., cognate with; cf., compare; deriv., derivative; equiv., equivalent; imit., imitative; obl., oblique; r., replacing; s., stem; sp., spelling, spelled; resp., respelling, respelled; trans., translation; ?, origin unknown; *, unattested; ‡, probably earlier than. See the full key inside the front cover.

mi•cro•lec•i•thal (mī′krə les′i thəl), *adj. Embryol.* having a small amount of yolk, as certain eggs or ova. [MICRO- + LECITHAL]

mi•cro•lite (mī′krə līt′), *n. Mineral.* **1.** any microscopic crystal. **2.** a mineral, principally calcium pyrotantalate, $Ca_2Ta_2O_7$, occurring in cubic crystals. [1825–35; MICRO- + -LITE]

mi•cro•lith (mī′krə lith), *n. Archaeol.* a tiny stone tool, often of geometric shape, made from a bladelet and mounted singly or in series as the working part of a composite tool or weapon. Cf. **macrolith, tranchet.** [1875–80; MICRO- + -LITH]

mi•cro•lith•ic (mī′krə lith′ik), *adj.* **1.** pertaining to or characterized by the use of microliths, as a people or culture. **2.** of the nature of or resembling a microlith, as a tool. [1870–75; MICROLITH + -IC]

mi•cro•lit•ic (mī′krə lit′ik), *adj. Petrog.* of or pertaining to the texture of a porphyry whose groundmass consists of microlites in a glassy matrix. [1875–80; MICROLITE + -IC]

mi•crol•o•gy (mī krol′ə jē), *n.* excessive attention to petty details or distinctions. [1650–60; < Gk *mikrología* minute discussion, frivolity. See MICRO-, -LOGY] —**mi•cro•log•i•cal** (mī′krə loj′i kəl), **mi′cro•log′ic,** *adj.* —**mi•crol′o•gist,** *n.*

mi•cro•man•age (mī′krō man′ij), *v.t.,* **-aged, -ag•ing.** to manage or control with excessive attention to minor details. [1985–90] —**mi′cro•man′age•ment,** *n.*

mi•cro•ma•nip•u•la•tion (mī′krō mə nip′yə lā′shən), *n.* the technique of performing mechanical operations under high magnification through the use of specialized tools. [1920–25; MICRO- + MANIPULATION]

mi•cro•mere (mī′krə mēr′), *n.* a small blastomere, as one of those that form toward the animal pole in embryos that undergo unequal cleavage or those that occur in the embryo of mammals. [1875–80; MICRO- + -MERE]

mi•cro•me•te•or•ol•o•gy (mī′krō mē′tē ə rol′ə jē), *n.* the study of local and small-scale atmospheric phenomena, usually confined to the physical and dynamic occurrences within a shallow stratum of air adjacent to the ground. Cf. **macrometeorology, mesometeorology, microclimatology.** [1925–30; MICRO- + METEOROLOGY] —**mi•cro•me•te•or•o•log•i•cal** (mī′krō mē′tēr ə loj′i kəl), *adj.*

mi•crom•e•ter[1] (mī krom′i tər), *n.* **1.** any of various devices for measuring minute distances, angles, etc., as in connection with a telescope or microscope. **2.** Also called **mike, microm′eter cal′iper.** a precision instrument with a spindle moved by a finely threaded screw, for the measurement of thicknesses and short lengths, commonly used by machinists for turning shafts or boring holes. Also, *esp. Brit.,* **mi•crom′e•tre.** [1660–70; MICRO- + -METER]

mi•cro•me•ter[2] (mī′krō mē′tər), *n.* micron (def. 1). [MICRO- + METER[1]]

mi•cro•meth•od (mī′krə meth′əd), *n.* **1.** the use of magnification, usually by using a microscope, for study or for performing mechanical operations on a very small scale. **2.** the use of much smaller quantities for achieving test results than is standard for the procedure. [1915–20; MICRO- + METHOD]

mi•crom•e•try (mī krom′i trē), *n.* the act or process of taking measurements with a micrometer. [1850–55; MICRO- + -METRY] —**mi•cro•met•ri•cal** (mī′krə me′tri kəl), **mi′cro•met′ric,** *adj.* —**mi′cro•met′ri•cal•ly,** *adv.*

micromicro-, pico-.

mi•cro•mi•cro•far•ad (mī′krō mī′krō far′əd, -ad), *n. Elect.* picofarad. *Symbol:* μμF [1905–10; MICRO- + MICROFARAD]

mi•cro•min•i (mī′krō min′ē), *adj., n., pl.* **-min•is.** *Informal.* —*adj.* **1.** microminiature. —*n.* **2.** something of a microminiature size: *Among rosebushes, the microminis are just 6 inches tall.* **3.** an extremely short miniskirt. [1965–70; MICRO- + MINI(ATURE) or MINI]

mi•cro•min•i•a•ture (mī′krō min′ē ə chər, -chŏŏr′, -min′ə-), *adj.* built on an extremely small scale, smaller than subminiature, esp. of electronic equipment with small solid-state components in the place of vacuum tubes. [1955–60; MICRO- + MINIATURE]

mi•cro•min•i•a•tur•i•za•tion (mī′krō min′ē ə chər ə zā′shən, -min′ə-), *n.* extreme miniaturization, esp. of electronic equipment, with extensive use of integrated circuits. [1950–55; MICRO- + MINIATURIZATION]

mi•cro•min•i•a•tur•ize (mī′krō min′ē ə chə rīz′, -min′ə-), *v.t.,* **-ized, -iz•ing.** (esp. of electronic equipment) to make extremely small; subject to microminiaturization. Also, *esp. Brit.,* **mi′cro•min′i•a•tur•ise′.** [1955–60; MICRO- + MINIATURIZE]

mi•cro•mo•tion (mī′krə mō′shən), *n.* **1.** a motion, esp. a periodic one, of very short duration or length. **2.** (in time and motion study) the analysis of the time of a work performance in its basic subdivisions with the aid of a timing apparatus, motion-picture equipment, etc. [1910–15; MICRO- + MOTION]

mi•cro•mount (mī′krə mount′), *n.* a mineralogical specimen displayed in such a way as to facilitate viewing it under a binocular microscope. [MICRO- + MOUNT[1]]

mi•cron (mī′kron), *n., pl.* **-crons, -cra** (-krə). **1.** Also called **micrometer.** the millionth part of a meter. *Symbol:* μ, mu **2.** *Physical Chem.* a colloidal particle whose diameter is between 0.2 and 10 microns. **3.** *Physics.* a very small unit of pressure, equal to that exerted by a column of mercury 1μ high. Also, **mikron.** [1880–85; < Gk *mīkrón* a little, n. use of neut. sing. of *mīkrós* small; see -ON[1]]

Mi•cro•ne•sia (mī′krə nē′zhə, -shə), *n.* **1.** one of the three principal divisions of Oceania, comprising the small Pacific islands N of the equator and E of the Philippines, whose main groups are the Mariana Islands, the Caroline Islands, and the Marshall Islands. **2. Federated States of,** a federation comprising the districts of Ponape, Truk, Yap, and Kosrae: part of the Trust Territory of the Pacific Islands.

Mi•cro•ne•sian (mī′krə nē′zhən, -shən), *adj.* **1.** of or pertaining to Micronesia, its inhabitants, or their languages. —*n.* **2.** a native of Micronesia. **3.** the Malayo-Polynesian languages of Micronesia, taken collectively. [MICRONESI(A) + -AN]

mi•cro•nu•cle•ate (mī′krō nōō′klē it, -āt′, -nyōō′-), *adj. Biol.* having a micronucleus. [1955–60; MICRONUCLE(US) + -ATE[1]]

mi•cro•nu•cle•us (mī′krō nōō′klē əs, -nyōō′-), *n., pl.* **-cle•i** (-klē ī′). *Biol.* the smaller of the two types of nuclei occurring in ciliate protozoans. Cf. **macronucleus.** [1890–95; MICRO- + NUCLEUS] —**mi′cro•nu′cle•ar,** *adj.*

mi•cro•nu•tri•ent (mī′krō nōō′trē ənt, -nyōō′-), *n. Biochem.* an essential nutrient, as a trace mineral or vitamin, that is required by an organism in minute amounts. [1935–40; MICRO- + NUTRIENT]

mi•cro•or•gan•ism (mī′krō ôr′gə niz′əm), *n.* any organism too small to be viewed by the unaided eye, as bacteria, protozoa, and some fungi and algae. [1875–80; MICRO- + ORGANISM] —**mi•cro•or•gan•ic** (mī′krō ôr gan′ik), **mi′cro•or′gan•is′mal,** *adj.*

mi•cro•pa•le•on•tol•o•gy (mī′krō pā′lē ən tol′ə jē, -pal′ē-), *n.* the branch of paleontology dealing with the study of microscopic fossils. [1880–85; MICRO- + PALEONTOLOGY] —**mi•cro•pa•le•on•to•log•i•cal** (mī′krō pā′lē on′tl oj′i kəl, -pal′ē-), **mi′cro•pa′le•on′to•log′ic,** *adj.* —**mi′cro•pa′le•on•tol′o•gist,** *n.*

mi•cro•par•a•site (mī′krō par′ə sīt′), *n.* a parasitic microorganism. [1880–85; MICRO- + PARASITE] —**mi•cro•par•a•sit•ic** (mī′krō par′ə sit′ik), *adj.*

mi•cro•pa•thol•o•gy (mī′krō pə thol′ə jē), *n.* the branch of pathology dealing with the microscopic study of changes that occur in tissues and cells during disease. [MICRO- + PATHOLOGY]

mi•cro•phage (mī′krə fāj′), *n. Immunol.* a small phagocytic cell in blood or lymph, esp. a polymorphonuclear leukocyte. [1885–90; MICRO- + -PHAGE]

mi•cro•phone (mī′krə fōn′), *n.* an instrument capable of transforming sound waves into changes in electric currents or voltage, used in recording or transmitting sound. [1875–80; MICRO-, in sense "enlarging" (extracted from MICROSCOPE) + -PHONE]

mi•cro•phon•ic (mī′krə fon′ik), *adj.* **1.** of, pertaining to, or in the nature of a microphone. **2.** *Electronics.* tending to or capable of exhibiting microphonism. [1840–50; MICROPHONE + -IC]

mi•cro•phon•ism (mī′krə fō′niz əm), *n. Electronics.* a usually undesirable property of some electronic circuits or components in which mechanical vibrations of a component affect the signal being transmitted through the circuit. [1945–50; MICROPHONE + -ISM]

mi•cro•pho•to•graph (mī′krə fō′tə graf′, -gräf′), *n.* **1.** microfilm (def. 1). **2.** a small photograph requiring optical enlargement to render it visible in detail. **3.** a photomicrograph. [1855–60; MICRO- + PHOTOGRAPH] —**mi•cro•pho•to•graph•ic** (mī′krə fō′tə graf′ik), *adj.* —**mi•cro•pho•tog•ra•phy** (mī′krō fə tog′rə fē), *n.*

mi•cro•pho•tom•e•ter (mī′krō fō tom′i tər), *n. Optics.* a photometer adapted for measuring the intensity of light emitted, transmitted, or reflected by minute objects. [1895–1900; MICRO- + PHOTOMETER] —**mi•cro•pho•to•met•ric** (mī′krō fō′tə me′trik), *adj.* —**mi′cro•pho′to•met′ri•cal•ly,** *adv.* —**mi′cro•pho•tom′e•try,** *n.*

mi•cro•phys•ics (mī′krə fiz′iks), *n.* (*used with a singular v.*) the branch of physics dealing with physical objects that are not large enough to be observed and treated directly, as elementary particles, atoms, and molecules. Cf. **particle physics.** [1880–85; MICRO- + PHYSICS] —**mi′cro•phys′i•cal,** *adj.*

mi•cro•phyte (mī′krə fīt′), *n.* a microscopic plant. [1860–65; MICRO- + -PHYTE] —**mi•cro•phyt•ic** (mī′krə fit′ik), *adj.*

mi•cro•pi•pette (mī′krō pī pet′, -pi-), *n.* a very slender pipette for transferring or measuring minute amounts of fluid, microorganisms, etc. Also, **mi′cro•pi•pet′.** [1915–20; MICRO- + PIPETTE]

mi•cro•plank•ton (mī′krō plangk′tən), *n.* plankton visible as individual organisms only with the aid of a microscope, which excludes most animal plankton. Cf. **nannoplankton.** [1900–05; MICRO- + PLANKTON]

mi•cro•pore (mī′krə pôr′, -pōr′), *n.* a tiny opening, as in specialized biological filters or in the shells of some animals. [1880–85; MICRO- + PORE[2]]

mi•cro•po•rous (mī′krə pôr′əs, -pōr′-), *adj.* composed of or having extremely small pores. [1885–90; MICRO- + POROUS]

mi•cro•print (mī′krə print′), *n.* a microphotograph reproduced in print for reading by a magnifying device. [1930–35; MICRO- + PRINT]

mi•cro•probe (mī′krə prōb′), *n.* **1.** *Chem., Spectroscopy.* a device used to excite radiation by a material in order to determine chemical or elemental composition from the emission spectrum produced. **2.** *Surg.* a miniature probe for use in microsurgery. [MICRO- + PROBE]

mi•cro•proc•es•sor (mī′krō pros′es ər, -ə sər *or, esp. Brit.,* -prō′ses ər, -sə sər), *n. Computers.* an integrated circuit that performs all the functions of a CPU. [1965–70; MICRO- + PROCESSOR] —**mi′cro•proc′es•sing,** *n.*

mi•cro•pro•gram (mī′krə prō′gram, -grəm), *n. Computers.* a set of microinstructions that defines the individual operations that a computer carries out in response to a machine-language instruction. [1950–55; MICRO- + PROGRAM] —**mi′cro•pro′gram•ma•ble,** *adj.*

mi•cro•pro•gram•ming (mī′krə prō′gram ing, -grə-ming), *n. Computers.* the use or preparation of microprograms. [MICRO- + PROGRAMMING]

mi•cro•pro•jec•tor (mī′krō prə jek′tər), *n.* a microscope equipped with a prism or mirror to project a greatly magnified image of a microscopic slide onto a distant screen. [1930–35; MICRO- + PROJECTOR]

mi•crop•si•a (mī krop′sē ə), *n. Ophthalm.* a defect of vision in which objects appear to be smaller than their actual size. Also, **mi•cro•pi•a** (mī krō′pē ə), **mi•crop•sy** (mī′krop sē). Cf. **macropsia.** [1895–1900; MICR- + -OPSIA] —**mi•crop•tic** (mī krop′tik), *adj.*

mi•cro•pub•lish (mī′krə pub′lish), *v.t.* to publish on microfilm or microfiche. [1970–75; as back formation from *micropublication;* see MICRO-, PUBLISH] —**mi•cro•pub•li•ca•tion** (mī′krə pub′li kā′shən), *n.* —**mi′cro•pub′lish•er,** *n.*

mi•cro•pump (mī′krə pump′), *n.* a tiny pump implanted under the skin for the timed administration of medication. Cf. **solion.** [MICRO- + PUMP[1]]

mi•cro•pyle (mī′krə pīl′), *n.* **1.** *Zool.* any minute opening in an ovum through which a spermatozoon can enter, as in many insects. **2.** *Bot.* the minute orifice or opening in the integuments of an ovule. See diag. under **orthotropous.** [1815–25; MICRO- + Gk *pýlē* gate] —**mi′cro•py′lar,** *adj.*

mi•cro•py•rom•e•ter (mī′krō pī rom′i tər), *n.* an optical pyrometer used to measure the temperature of small glowing bodies. [MICRO- + PYROMETER]

mi•cro•read•er (mī′krō rē′dər), *n.* a device for projecting an enlarged image of a microfilm or microphotograph, esp. on a ground-glass screen. [1945–50; MICRO- + READER]

mi•cro•re•lief (mī′krō ri lēf′), *n.* surface features of the earth of small dimensions, commonly less than 50 ft. (15 m). Also called **microtopography.** [1930–35; MICRO- + RELIEF[2]]

mi•cro•re•pro•duc•tion (mī′krō rē′prə duk′shən), *n.* **1.** a photographic image too small to be read by the unaided eye. **2.** the technique of producing such images. [1935–40; MICRO- + REPRODUCTION]

micros., microscopy.

mi•cro•scope (mī′krə skōp′), *n.* **1.** an optical instrument having a magnifying lens or a combination of lenses for inspecting objects too small to be seen or too small to be seen distinctly and in detail by the unaided eye. **2.** (*cap.*) *Astron.* the constellation Microscopium. [1650–60; < NL *mīcroscopium.* See MICRO-, -SCOPE]

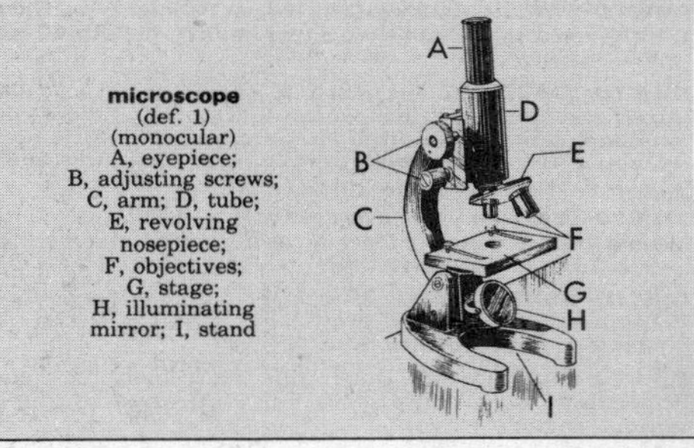

microscope (def. 1) (monocular) A, eyepiece; B, adjusting screws; C, arm; D, tube; E, revolving nosepiece; F, objectives; G, stage; H, illuminating mirror; I, stand

mi•cro•scop•ic (mī′krə skop′ik), *adj.* **1.** so small as to be invisible or indistinct without the use of the microscope: *microscopic organisms.* Cf. **macroscopic. 2.** very small; tiny. **3.** of, pertaining to, or involving a microscope: *microscopic investigation.* **4.** very detailed; meticulous: *a microscopic view of society.* **5.** suggestive of the precise use of the microscope; minute: *microscopic exactness.* Also, **mi′cro•scop′i•cal.** [1670–80; MICROSCOPE + -IC] —**mi′cro•scop′i•cal•ly,** *adv.*

Mi•cro•sco•pi•um (mī′krə skō′pē əm), *n., gen.* **-pi•i** (-pē ī′). *Astron.* the Microscope, a small southern constellation south of Capricorn. [< NL]

mi•cros•co•py (mī kros′kə pē, mī′krə skō′pē), *n.* **1.** the use of the microscope. **2.** microscopic investigation. [1655–65; MICROSCOPE + -Y[3]] —**mi•cros•co•pist** (mī kros′kə pist, mī′krə skō′pist), *n.*

mi•cro•sec•ond (mī′krə sek′ənd), *n.* a unit of time equal to one millionth of a second. *Symbol:* μsec [1905–10; MICRO- + SECOND[2]]

mi•cro•seg•ment (mī′krə seg′mənt), *n.* a stretch of speech preceded and followed but not interrupted by juncture. Cf. **macrosegment.** [1955–60; MICRO- + SEGMENT]

mi•cro•seism (mī′krə sī′zəm, -səm), *n. Geol.* a feeble, recurrent vibration of the ground recorded by seismographs and believed to be due to an earthquake or a storm at sea. [1885–90; MICRO- + SEISM] —**mi′cro•seis′mic, mi′cro•seis′mi•cal,** *adj.*

mi•cro•sleep (mī′krō slēp′), *n. Psychol.* a moment of sleep followed by disorientation, experienced esp. by persons suffering from narcolepsy or sleep deprivation. [1940–45; MICRO- + SLEEP]

mi•cro•so•ci•ol•o•gy (mī′krō sō′sē ol′ə jē, -sō′shē-), *n.* the sociological study of small groups and social units within a larger social system. Cf. **macrosociology.** [1940–45; MICRO- + SOCIOLOGY]

mi•cro•some (mī′krə sōm′), *n. Cell Biol.* a small inclusion, consisting of ribosomes and fragments of the endoplasmic reticulum and mitochondria, in the cytoplasm of a cell. [1880–85; MICRO- + -SOME[3]] —**mi′cro•so′mal, mi′cro•so′mi•al, mi′cro•so′mic,** *adj.*

mi·cro·spec·tro·pho·tom·e·ter (mī′krō spek′trə fō tom′i tər), *n. Optics.* a spectrophotometer for examining light emitted, transmitted, or reflected by minute objects. [1950–55; MICRO- + SPECTROPHOTOMETER] —**mi·cro·spec·tro·pho·to·met·ric** (mī′krō spek′trō fō′tə me′trik), *adj.* —**mi′cro·spec′tro·pho·tom′e·try,** *n.*

mi·cro·spo·ran·gi·um (mī′krō spô ran′jē əm, -spō-), *n., pl.* **-gi·a** (-jē ə). *Bot.* a sporangium containing microspores. [1880–85; MICRO- + SPORANGIUM]

mi·cro·spore (mī′krə spôr′, -spōr′), *n. Bot.* **1.** the smaller of the two kinds of spores characteristically produced by seed plants and some fern allies, developing into a male gametophyte. Cf. **megaspore. 2.** a pollen grain. [1855–60; MICRO- + SPORE] —**mi·cro·spor·ic** (mī′krə spôr′ik, -spor′-), **mi·cro·spor·ous** (mī′krə spôr′əs, -spōr′-, mī kros′pər əs), *adj.*

mi·cro·spo·ro·cyte (mī′krə spôr′ə sīt′, -spōr′-), *n. Bot.* one of the mother cells that produce four microspores by meiosis. [1935–40; MICROSPORE + -O- + -CYTE]

mi·cro·spo·ro·phyll (mī′krə spôr′ə fil, -spōr′-), *n. Bot.* a leaflike organ bearing microsporangia. [1890–95; MICRO- + SPOROPHYLL]

mi·cro·stat (mī′krə stat′), *n.* a negative of a microphotograph made directly from a negative by a copy camera. [MICRO- + -STAT]

mi·cro·state (mī′krō stāt′), *n.* ministate. [1965–70; MICRO- + STATE]

mi·cro·steth·o·scope (mī′krə steth′ə skōp′), *n. Med.* a stethoscope containing an apparatus that greatly amplifies the sounds heard. [MICRO- + STETHOSCOPE]

mi·cro·stress (mī′krə stres′), *n. Metall.* a stress in the microstructure of a metal, as one caused by the distortion of space lattices. [MICRO- + STRESS]

mi·cro·struc·ture (mī′krō struk′chər), *n. Metall.* the structure of a metal or alloy as observed, after etching and polishing, under a high degree of magnification. [1880–85; MICRO- + STRUCTURE]

mi·cro·sur·ger·y (mī′krō sûr′jə rē, mī′krō sûr′-), *n.* any of various surgical procedures performed under magnification and with small specialized instruments, permitting very delicate operations, as the reconnection of severed blood vessels and nerves. [1925–30; MICRO- + SURGERY] —**mi′cro·sur′gi·cal,** *adj.*

mi·cro·switch (mī′krə swich′), *n.* a highly sensitive switch used in automatic-control devices. [1955–60; MICRO- + SWITCH]

mi·cro·teach·ing (mī′krō tē′ching), *n.* a scaled-down teaching procedure with a few students under controlled conditions, often videotaped in order to analyze teaching techniques and develop new teaching skills. [1970–75; MICRO- + TEACHING]

mi·cro·tek·tite (mī′krō tek′tīt), *n. Geol.* a microscopic tektite found in ocean sediments and polar ice. [1965–70; MICRO- + TEKTITE]

mi·cro·therm (mī′krə thûrm′), *n.* a plant requiring a minimum of heat for growth. [1870–75; MICRO- + -THERM] —**mi′cro·ther′mic,** *adj.*

mi·cro·thin (mī′krō thin′), *adj.* extremely or, sometimes, microscopically thin: *a microthin layer of aluminum.* [MICRO- + THIN]

mi·cro·tome (mī′krə tōm′), *n.* an instrument for cutting very thin sections, as of organic tissue, for microscopic examination. [1855–60; MICRO- + -TOME] —**mi·cro·tom·ic** (mī′krə tom′ik), *adj.* —**mi·crot′o·mist,** *n.*

mi·crot·o·my (mī krot′ə mē), *n., pl.* **-mies.** the cutting of very thin sections with the microtome. [MICRO- + -TOMY]

mi·cro·tone (mī′krə tōn′), *n.* any musical interval smaller than a semitone, specifically, a quarter tone. [1915–20; MICRO- + TONE] —**mi′cro·ton′al,** *adj.* —**mi′·cro·to·nal′i·ty,** *n.* —**mi′cro·ton′al·ly,** *adv.*

mi·cro·to·pog·ra·phy (mī′krō tə pog′rə fē), *n.* microrelief. [MICRO- + TOPOGRAPHY]

mi·cro·trem·or (mī′krō trem′ər), *n.* microearthquake. [MICRO- + TREMOR]

mi·cro·tu·bule (mī′krō to͞o′byo͞ol, -tyo͞o′-), *n. Cell Biol.* a hollow cylindrical structure in the cytoplasm of most cells, involved in intracellular shape and transport. See diag. under **cell.** [1960–65; MICRO- + TUBULE]

mi·cro·vas·cu·la·ture (mī′krō vas′kyə lə chər), *n. Anat.* the system of tiny blood vessels, including capillaries, venules, and arterioles, that perfuse the body's tissues. [1955–60; MICRO- + VASCUL(AR) + *-ature,* as in MUSCULATURE] —**mi′cro·vas′cu·lar,** *adj.*

mi·cro·vil·lus (mī′krō vil′əs), *n., pl.* **-vil·li** (-vil′ī). *Cell Biol.* any of the small, fingerlike projections of the surface of an epithelial cell. See diag. under **cell.** [1950–55; MICRO- + VILLUS] —**mi′cro·vil′lar, mi′cro·vil′lous,** *adj.*

mi·cro·volt (mī′krə vōlt′), *n. Elect.* a unit of electromotive force or potential difference equal to one millionth of a volt. *Symbol:* μV, μv [1865–70; MICRO- + VOLT]

mi·cro·watt (mī′krō wot′), *n. Elect.* a unit of power equal to one millionth of a watt. *Symbol:* μW, μw [1910–15; MICRO- + WATT]

mi·cro·wave (mī′krə wāv′), *n., v.,* **-waved, -wav·ing.** —*n.* **1.** an electromagnetic wave of extremely high frequency, 1 GH_3 or more, and having wavelengths of from 1 mm to 30 cm. **2.** See **microwave oven.** —*v.t.* **3.** to use a microwave oven. —*v.t.* **4.** to cook, defrost, or otherwise prepare in a microwave oven. [1930–35; MICRO- + WAVE] —**mi′cro·wave′a·ble,** *adj.*

mi′crowave ov′en, an electrically operated oven using high-frequency electromagnetic waves that penetrate food, causing its molecules to vibrate and generating heat within the food to cook it in a very short time. [1960–65]

mi′crowave spectros′copy, *Physics.* the determination of those frequencies of the microwave spectrum that are selectively absorbed by certain materials, providing information about atomic, molecular, and crystal-line structure. —**mi′crowave spec′troscope.**

mi′crowave spec′trum, *Electronics.* a spectrum of electromagnetic radiations whose wavelengths fall in the microwave range. [1945–50]

mi·cro·zo·on (mī′krə zō′on, -ən), *n., pl.* **-zo·a** (-zō′ə). a microscopic animal, esp. a protozoan. [1860–65; MICRO- + -ZOON]

mic·tu·rate (mik′chə rāt′), *v.i.,* **-rat·ed, -rat·ing.** to pass urine; urinate. [1835–45; < L *mictur(īre)* to desire to urinate (*mict(us),* ptp. of *mingere* to urinate + *-ur-* desiderative suffix + *-ī-* theme vowel + *-re* inf. ending) + -ATE[1]]

mic·tu·ri·tion (mik′chə rish′ən), *n.* the act of passing urine; urination. [1715–25; < L *micturī(re)* to desire to urinate (see MICTURATE) + -TION]

mid[1] (mid), *adj.* **1.** being at or near the middle point of: *in mid autumn.* **2.** being or occupying a middle place or position: *in the mid nineties of the last century.* **3.** *Phonet.* (of a vowel) articulated with an opening above the tongue relatively intermediate between those for high and low: the vowels of *beet, bet,* and *hot* are respectively high, mid, and low. Cf. **high** (def. 23), **low** (def. 30). —*n.* **4.** *Archaic.* the middle. [bef. 900; ME, OE *midd-* (both an adj. and the initial element of a compound; modern spellings such as *mid autumn* are prob. a reanalysis of MID- as an adj.); c. OHG *mitti,* ON *mithr,* Goth *midjis,* OIr *mide,* L *medius,* Gk *mésos,* Skt *madhya* middle, OCS *mežda* limit, border]

mid[2] (mid), *prep.* amid. Also, **'mid.**

mid[3] (mid), *n. Informal.* a midshipman. [by shortening]

mid-, a combining form representing **mid**[1] in compound words: *midday; mid-Victorian.* [ME, OE; see MID[1]]

Mid., Midshipman.

mid., middle.

M.I.D., Master of Industrial Design.

mid·af·ter·noon (mid′af′tər no͞on′, -äf′-), *n.* **1.** the part of the afternoon centering approximately on three o'clock; the period approximately halfway between noon and sunset. —*adj.* **2.** occurring in or pertaining to mid-afternoon: *a midafternoon nap.* [1895–1900; MID- + AFTERNOON]

mid·air (mid âr′), *n.* any point in the air not contiguous with the earth or other solid surface: *to catch a ball in midair.* [1660–70; MID- + AIR[1]]

Mid·a·mer·i·ca (mid′ə mer′i kə), *n.* See **Middle America** (def. 2). [1925–30, *Amer.;* MID- + AMERICA]

Mi·das (mī′dəs), *n.* **1.** *Class. Myth.* a Phrygian king, son of Gordius, who was given by Dionysus the power of turning whatever he touched into gold. **2.** a person of great wealth or great moneymaking ability.

Mi′das touch′, the ability to turn any business venture one is associated with into an extremely profitable one. [1880–85; see MIDAS]

mid-At·lan·tic (mid′at lan′tik), *adj.* using, manifesting, or characterized by a mixture of American and British behavior or speech.

Mid′-At·lan′tic Ridge′ (mid′at lan′tik, mid′at-lan′-), a north-south suboceanic ridge in the Atlantic Ocean from Iceland to Antarctica on whose crest are several groups of islands; shown by plate tectonics to be the axis along which North America has split away from Eurasia, and along which South America has split away from Africa.

mid·band (mid′band′), *n.* **1.** *Electronics.* a band in the middle of a range of frequencies. **2.** (in pewter work) a decorated band reinforcing a tankard at its middle. [MID- + BAND[2]]

mid·brain (mid′brān′), *n. Anat.* the middle of the three primary divisions of the brain in the embryo of a vertebrate or the part of the adult brain derived from this tissue; mesencephalon. [1870–75; MID- + BRAIN]

Mid-Cit·ies (mid′sit′ēz), *n.* (*usually used with a singular v.*) the extensive suburban area developed between Dallas and Fort Worth, Texas.

mid·course (mid′kôrs′, -kōrs′), *n.* **1.** the middle of a course. **2.** *Rocketry.* the portion of a ballistic trajectory between the end of powered flight and the beginning of the reentry phase. **3.** *Aerospace.* the portion of a space trajectory between leaving the earth's vicinity and arrival at the desired destination, as another planet. [1555–65; MID- + COURSE]

mid′course correc′tion, a navigational correction made in the course of a ship, airplane, rocket, or space vehicle at some point between the beginning and end of the journey. [1955–60]

mid·cult (mid′kult′), *n.* **1.** (*sometimes cap.*) the intellectual culture intermediate between highbrow and lowbrow; middlebrow culture. —*adj.* **2.** of, pertaining to, or characteristic of such culture. [1955–60, *Amer.; mid(dlebrow) cult(ure);* see MASSCULT]

mid·day (*n.* mid′dā′, -dā′; *adj.* mid′dā′), *n.* **1.** the middle of the day; noon or the time centering around noon. —*adj.* **2.** of or pertaining to the middle part of the day: *a midday news broadcast.* [bef. 1000; ME; OE *middæg.* See MID-, DAY]

Mid·del·burg (mid′l bûrg′), *n.* a city in the SW Netherlands. 38,854.

mid·den (mid′n), *n.* **1.** a dunghill or refuse heap. **2.** See **kitchen midden.** [1300–50; ME *midding* < ODan *mykdyngja,* equiv. to *myk* manure + *dyngja* pile (Dan *mødding*)]

mid·die (mid′ē), *n. Informal.* a midshipman. [see MIDDY[1]]

mid·dle (mid′l), *adj., n., v.,* **-dled, -dling.** —*adj.* **1.** equally distant from the extremes or outer limits; central: *the middle point of a line; the middle singer in a trio.* **2.** intermediate or intervening: *the middle distance.* **3.** medium or average: *a man of middle size.* **4.** (*cap.*) (in the history of a language) intermediate between periods classified as Old and New or Modern: *Middle English.* **5.** *Gram.* (in some languages) noting a voice of verb inflection in which the subject is represented as acting on or for itself, in contrast to the active voice in which the subject acts, and the passive voice in which the subject is acted upon, as in Greek, *egrapsámēn* "I wrote for myself," *égrapsa* "I wrote," *egráphēn* "I was written." **6.** (*often cap.*) *Stratig.* noting the division intermediate between the upper and lower divisions of a period, system, or the like: *the Middle Devonian.* —*n.* **7.** the point, part, position, etc., equidistant from extremes or limits. **8.** the central part of the human body, esp. the waist: *He gave him a punch in the middle.* **9.** something intermediate; mean. **10.** (in farming) the ground between two rows of plants. —*v.t., v.i.* **11.** *Chiefly Naut.* to fold in half. [bef. 900; ME, OE *middel;* c. G *mittel;* akin to ON *methal* among. See MID[1]]
—**Syn. 1.** equidistant, halfway, medial, midway. **7.** midpoint. MIDDLE, CENTER, MIDST indicate something from which two or more other things are (approximately or exactly) equally distant. MIDDLE denotes, literally or figuratively, the point or part equidistant from or intermediate between extremes or limits in space or in time: *the middle of a road.* CENTER, a more precise word, is ordinarily applied to a point within circular, globular, or regular bodies, or wherever a similar exactness appears to exist: *the center of the earth;* it may also be used metaphorically (still suggesting the core of a sphere): *center of interest.* MIDST usually suggests that a person or thing is closely surrounded or encompassed on all sides, esp. by that which is thick or dense: *the midst of a storm.* —**Ant. 1.** extreme. **7.** extremity.

mid′dle age′, the period of human life between youth and old age, sometimes considered as the years between 45 and 65 or thereabout. [1350–1400; ME]

mid·dle-aged (mid′l ājd′), *adj.* **1.** being of the age intermediate between youth and old age, roughly between 45 and 65. **2.** characteristic of or suitable for persons of this age. [1600–10] —**mid·dle-a·ged·ly** (mid′l-ā′jid lē, -ājd′-), *adv.* —**mid′dle-a′ged·ness,** *n.*

Mid′dle Ag′es, the time in European history between classical antiquity and the Italian Renaissance (from about 500 A.D. to about 1350): sometimes restricted to the later part of this period (after 1100) and sometimes extended to 1450 or 1500. [1715–25; pl. of *Middle Age,* trans. of NL *Medium Aevum*]

mid′dle-age spread′ (mid′l āj′), an increase in bulk, esp. in the waist and buttocks, associated with the onset of middle age and the body's decreasing ability to metabolize calories efficiently. [1935–40]

Mid′dle Amer′ica, 1. average middle-class Americans as a group, as distinguished from the rich or poor or the politically extreme. **2.** the Midwest. **3.** continental North America S of the U.S., comprising Mexico, Central America, and usually the West Indies. 92,000,000; 1,060,118 sq. mi. (2,745,705 sq. km). —**Mid′dle Amer′·ican.** —**Mid′dle-A·mer′i·can,** *adj.*

Mid′dle Atlan′tic States′, New York, New Jersey, and Pennsylvania. Also called **Middle States.**

mid·dle-born (mid′l bôrn′), *adj.* **1.** neither first nor last in order of birth, esp. second in a family of three children. —*n.* **2.** a middle-born child.

Mid·dle·bor·ough (mid′l bûr′ō, -bur′ō), *n.* a town in SE Massachusetts. 16,404.

mid·dle·break·er (mid′l brā′kər), *n.* lister (def. 1). [MIDDLE + BREAKER[1]]

mid·dle·brow (mid′l brou′), *n. Informal.* a person of conventional tastes and interests in matters of culture; a moderately cultivated person. [1920–25; MIDDLE + BROW, on the model of HIGHBROW, LOWBROW] —**mid′·dle·brow′ism,** *n.*

Mid′dle·burg Heights′ (mid′l bûrg′), a town in N Ohio. 16,218.

mid·dle·bust·er (mid′l bus′tər), *n. Southern U.S.* lister (def. 1). [1905–10, *Amer.;* MIDDLE + BUSTER]

middle C, *Music.* the note indicated by the first leger line above the bass staff and the first below the treble staff. [1830–40]

Mid′dle Chinese′, the Chinese language of the 7th and 8th centuries A.D. *Abbr.:* MChin

mid′dle class′, 1. a class of people intermediate between the classes of higher and lower social rank or standing; the social, economic, cultural class, having approximately average status, income, education, tastes, and the like. **2.** the class traditionally intermediate between the aristocratic class and the laboring class. **3.** an intermediate class. [1760–70]

mid·dle-class (mid′l klas′, -kläs′), *adj.* of, pertaining to, or characteristic of the middle class; bourgeois: *middle-class taste; middle-class morality.* [1890–95] —**mid′dle-class′ness,** *n.*

Mid′dle Com′edy, Greek Attic comedy of the 4th century B.C. The few extant fragments are characterized chiefly by a realistic depiction of everyday life. Cf. **New Comedy, Old Comedy.**

Mid′dle Con′go, former name of the People's Republic of the Congo.

mid′dle dis′tance, 1. Also called **middle ground, middle plane.** *Fine Arts.* the represented space between the foreground and background in paintings, drawings, etc. **2.** (in track) a race distance ranging from 400 meters or 440 yards to 1 mile. [1805–15]

Mid′dle Dutch′, the Dutch language of the period c1100–c1500. *Abbr.:* MD

mid′dle ear′, *Anat.* the middle portion of the ear, consisting of the tympanic membrane and an air-filled chamber lined with mucous membrane, that contains the malleus, incus, and stapes. Cf. **ear**[1] (def. 1). See diag. under **ear**[1]. [1885–90]

Mid′dle East′, **1.** Also called **Mideast.** (loosely) the area from Libya E to Afghanistan, usually including Egypt, Sudan, Israel, Jordan, Lebanon, Syria, Turkey, Iraq, Iran, Saudi Arabia, and the other countries of the Arabian peninsula. **2.** (formerly) the area including Iran, Afghanistan, India, Tibet, and Burma. —**Mid′dle East′ern.** —**Mid′dle East′erner.**

Mid′dle Eng′lish, the English language of the period c1150–c1475. *Abbr.:* ME [1830–40]

mid′dle fin′ger, the finger between the forefinger and the third finger. [bef. 1000; ME, OE]

Mid′dle Flem′ish, the Flemish language of the 14th, 15th, and 16th centuries.

Mid′dle French′, the French language of the 14th, 15th, and 16th centuries. *Abbr.:* MF [1885–90]

mid′dle game′, *Chess.* the stage between the opening and the end game, characterized by complicated moves by both opponents with pieces at full strength. [1890–95]

Mid′dle Greek′. See **Medieval Greek.** [1885–90]

mid′dle ground′, **1.** an intermediate position, area, or recourse between two opposites or extremes; a halfway or neutral standpoint. **2.** See **middle distance** (def. 1). **3.** *Naut.* a length of comparatively shallow water having channels on both sides. [1775–85]

mid′dle guard′, *Football.* a defensive lineman positioned opposite the offensive center and between the defensive tackles, as in a three- or five-man line. Also called **nose guard.** [1870–75, for an earlier sense]

mid·dle·hand (mid′l hand′), *n. Cards.* the player on the dealer's right in a game with three players. Cf. **endhand, forehand** (def. 7). [MIDDLE + HAND]

Mid′dle High′ Ger′man, the High German language of the period 1100–1500. *Abbr.:* MHG

Mid′dle I′rish, the Irish language of the 11th, 12th, and 13th centuries.

Mid′dle King′dom, **1.** Also called **Mid′dle Em′pire.** the period in the history of ancient Egypt, c2000–1785 B.C., comprising the 11th to 14th dynasties. Cf. **New Kingdom, Old Kingdom. 2.** *Hist.* **a.** the 18 inner provinces of China, taken collectively. **b.** (loosely) China. **3.** the Chinese Empire: originally so called from its supposed location in the center of the earth. [1655–65]

mid′dle lamel′la, *Bot.* the layer of cementing material, composed of pectates and similar substances, between the walls of adjacent cells. [1920–25]

Mid′dle Lat′in. See **Medieval Latin.**

mid′dle lat′itude, the latitude of the point that is midway between two parallels on the same side of the equator. Also called **mean latitude.** [1700–10]

mid·dle-lev·el (mid′l lev′əl), *adj.* occurring at or having a middle or intermediate position or status: *middle-level management.*

Mid′dle Low′ Ger′man, Low German of the period c1100–c1500. [1885–90]

mid·dle·man (mid′l man′), *n., pl.* **-men. 1.** a person who plays an economic role intermediate between producer and retailer or consumer. **2.** a person who acts as an intermediary. [1400–50; late ME: maker of girdles; see MIDDLE, MAN[1]]

mid′dle man′agement, the middle echelon of administration in business and industry. [1945–50]

Mid·dle·march (mid′l märch′), *n.* a novel (1871–72) by George Eliot.

mid·dle·most (mid′l mōst′), *adj.* midmost. [1275–1325; ME *middelmast.* See MIDDLE, -MOST]

mid′dle name′, the part of a person's name occurring between the first and family names, as a second given name or a maternal surname. [1825–35, *Amer.*]

mid·dle-of-the-road (mid′l əv *th*ə rōd′), *adj.* **1.** favoring, following, or characterized by an intermediate position between two extremes, esp. in politics; moderate. **2.** of, pertaining to, or describing a type of popular music that avoids extremes of style and is catchy and tuneful enough to have broad appeal. —*n.* **3.** Also called **easy listening.** popular music having comparatively conventional, melodic qualities and hence having broad commercial appeal. [1890–95, *Amer.*] —**mid′·dle-of-the-road′er,** *n.* —**mid′dle-of-the-road′ism,** *n.*

Mid′dle Paleolith′ic. See under **Paleolithic.**

mid′dle pas′sage, *Hist.* the part of the Atlantic Ocean between the west coast of Africa and the West Indies: the longest part of the journey formerly made by slave ships. Also, **Mid′dle Pas′sage.** [1780–90]

Mid′dle Path′, *Buddhism.* the conduct of life by a religious person in such a way as to avoid the extremes of luxury and asceticism.

Mid′dle Per′sian, the Persian language at a stage that begins c300 B.C. and includes Pahlavi (attested from the 3rd to the 7th centuries A.D.) as well as the West Iranian literatures (3rd–10th centuries A.D.) of religions carried outside Persia. *Abbr.:* MPers

mid′dle plane′. See **middle distance** (def. 1).

Mid′dle Riv′er, a city in N Maryland: suburb of Baltimore. 26,756.

Mid·dles·bor·ough (mid′lz bûr′ō, -bur′ō), *n.* a city in SE Kentucky. 12,251.

Mid·dles·brough (mid′lz brə), *n.* a seaport in NE England, on the Tees estuary. 153,300.

mid·dl·es·cence (mid′l es′əns), *n.* the middle-age period of life, esp. when considered a difficult time of self-doubt and readjustment. [1960–65; b. MIDDLE and ADOLESCENCE] —**mid′dl·es′cent,** *adj.*

Middle East

mid′dle school′, a school intermediate between elementary school and high school, usually encompassing grades five or six through eight. Cf. **intermediate school.** [1830–40]

Mid·dle·sex (mid′l seks′), *n.* **1.** a former county in SE England, now part of Greater London. **2.** a borough in central New Jersey. 13,480.

mid·dle-sized (mid′l sīzd′), *adj.* medium-sized. [1625–35]

Mid′dle States′. See **Middle Atlantic States.**

mid′dle stump′, *Cricket.* the stump inside of the leg stump and the off stump; the second of the three stumps of a wicket.

Mid′dle Tem′ple, **1.** See under **Inns of Court** (def. 1). **2.** See under **temple**[1] (def. 10). [1595–1605]

mid′dle term′. See under **syllogism** (def. 1). [1595–1605]

Mid·dle·ton (mid′l tən), *n.* **1. Thomas,** c1570–1627, English dramatist. **2.** a town in S Wisconsin. 11,779.

mid·dle·tone (mid′l tōn′), *n.* halftone (def. 1). [1960–65; MIDDLE + TONE]

Mid·dle·town (mid′l toun′), *n.* **1.** a township in E New Jersey. 62,574. **2.** a city in SW Ohio, on the Miami River. 43,719. **3.** a city in central Connecticut, on the Connecticut River. 39,040. **4.** a city in SE New York. 21,454. **5.** a town in SE Rhode Island. 17,216. **6.** a town in E Pennsylvania. 10,122.

Mid·dle·town (mid′l toun′), *n.* (*sometimes l.c.*) a typical American town or small city with traditional values and mores. [after a pseudonymously named town studied in a book with the same title (1929) by U.S. sociologists Robert S. Lynd (1892–1970) and Helen Merrell Lynd (1896–1982); the town actually studied was Muncie, Ind.] —**Mid′dle·town′er,** *n.*

mid′dle watch′, *Naut.* the watch from midnight until 4 A.M. Also called **graveyard watch, midwatch.** [1605–15]

mid·dle·weight (mid′l wāt′), *n.* **1.** a boxer or other contestant intermediate in weight between a welterweight and a light heavyweight, esp. a professional boxer weighing up to 160 pounds (72.5 kg). —*adj.* **2.** *Boxing.* of or pertaining to middleweights: *the middleweight division.* **3.** (of a horse, esp. a hunter) able to carry up to 185 pounds (83.9 kg). [1870–75; MIDDLE + WEIGHT]

Mid′dle West′, the region of the United States bounded on the W by the Rocky Mountains, on the S by the Ohio River and the S extremities of Missouri and Kansas, and on the E, variously, by the Allegheny Mountains, the E border of Ohio, or the E border of Illinois. Also called **Midwest.** —**Mid′dle West′erner.**

Mid′dle West′ern, of or pertaining to the Middle West. Also called **Midwestern.** [1905–10, *Amer.*]

mid′dle years′. See **middle age.**

mid·dling (mid′ling), *adj.* **1.** medium, moderate, or average in size, quantity, or quality: *The returns on such a large investment may be only middling.* **2.** mediocre; ordinary; commonplace; pedestrian: *The restaurant's entrées are no better than middling.* **3.** *Older Use.* in fairly good health. —*adv.* **4.** moderately; fairly. —*n.* **5. middlings,** any of various products or commodities of intermediate quality, grade, size, etc., as the coarser particles of ground wheat mingled with bran. **6.** Often, **middlings.** Also called **mid′dling meat′.** *Chiefly Midland and Southern U.S.* salt pork or smoked side meat. [1375–1425; late ME (north). See MID[1], -LING[2]] —**mid′·dling·ly,** *adv.*

mid·dy[1] (mid′ē), *n., pl.* **-dies. 1.** *Informal.* a midshipman. **2.** See **middy blouse.** [1825–35; MID(SHIPMAN) + -Y[2]]

mid·dy[2] (mid′ē), *n., pl.* **-dies.** *Australian Slang.* a medium-size drinking glass commonly holding half a pint and used for beer. [1940–45; MID[1] + -Y[2]]

mid′dy blouse′, any of various loose blouses with a sailor collar, often extending below the waistline to terminate in a broad band or fold, as worn by sailors, women, or children. [1910–15]

Mid·east (mid′ēst′), *n.* See **Middle East.** [1940–45; MID- + EAST] —**Mid′east′ern,** *adj.*

mid·en·gine (mid′en′jən), *adj. Auto.* of or pertaining to a configuration in which the engine is located behind the driver and between the front and rear wheels: *midengine sports car; midengine design.* [MID- + ENGINE]

mid·field (mid′fēld′, -fēld′), *n.* the middle area of a sports field, esp. the area midway between the two goals. [MID- + FIELD]

mid·field·er (mid′fēl′dər, -fēl′-), *n.* a player active in the midfield, as in soccer, often playing both offensively and defensively. [MIDFIELD + -ER[1]]

Mid·gard (mid′gärd), *n. Scand. Myth.* the middle earth, home of men, lying between Niflheim and Muspelheim, formed from the body of Ymir. [< ON *mithgarthr,* c. OE *middangeard* the earth, the abode of men. See MID-, YARD[2]]

Mid′gard ser′pent, *Scand. Myth.* a serpent, the child of Loki and Angerboda, who lies wrapped around the world, tail in mouth, and is destined to kill and to be killed by Thor at Ragnarok; Jormungand.

midge (mij), *n.* **1.** any of numerous minute dipterous insects, esp. of the family Chironomidae, somewhat resembling a mosquito. Cf. **gnat** (def. 1). **2.** a tiny person. [bef. 900; ME *mygge,* OE *mycg(e)*; c. G *Mücke,* ON *mý*; akin to Gk *myîa,* L *musca* fly]

midg·et (mij′it), *n.* **1.** (not in technical use) an extremely small person having normal physical proportions. **2.** any animal or thing that is very small for its kind. —*adj.* **3.** very small or of a class below the usual

size. **4.** being a miniature replica or model. [1850–55; MIDGE + -ET] **—midg′et·ism,** *n.*
—Syn. 1. See **dwarf.**

midg′et golf′, *Informal.* See **miniature golf.**

Mid′ Gla·mor′gan (glə môr′gən), a county in S Wales. 540,100. 393 sq. mi. (1019 sq. km).

mid·gut (mid′gut′), *n.* **1.** *Zool.* **a.** the middle portion of the vertebrate alimentary canal, posterior to the stomach or gizzard and extending to the cecum, functioning in the digestion and absorption of food; the small intestine. **b.** the anterior portion of the arthropod colon, composed of endodermal tissue. **2.** *Embryol.* the middle part of the embryonic alimentary canal from which the intestines develop. Cf. **foregut, hindgut.** [1870–75; MID- + GUT]

mid·heav·en (mid hev′ən), *n.* *Astrol.* the point of a horoscope corresponding to the zenith: the cusp of the tenth house. [1585–95; MID- + HEAVEN]

mid·i (mid′ē), *n.* **1.** a skirt, dress, or coat, of mid-calf length. —*adj.* **2.** of the length of a midiskirt. [extracted from MIDISKIRT]

Mi·di (mē dē′), *n.* the south of France. [< F: midday, south; OF, equiv. to *mi-* middle, half (< L *medius;* see MID[1]) + *di* day (< L *diem,* acc. of *diēs*)]

MIDI (mid′ē), *n.* Musical Instrument Digital Interface: a standard means of sending digitally encoded information about music between electronic devices, as between synthesizers and computers.

Mid·i·an (mid′ē ən), *n.* a son of Abraham and Keturah. Gen. 25:1–4.

Mid·i·an·ite (mid′ē ə nīt′), *n.* **1.** a member of an ancient desert people of northwest Arabia near the Gulf of Aqaba, believed to have descended from Midian. —*adj.* **2.** of or pertaining to the Midianites. [MIDIAN + -ITE[1]]

mid·i·nette (mid′n et′; *Fr.* mē dē net′), *n., pl.* **-nettes** (-nets′; *Fr.* -net′). a young Parisian saleswoman or seamstress. [1905–10; < F, b. *midi* noon and *dînette* light meal (see DINNER, -ETTE); hence, one who has time for only a light meal at noon, with play on *-ette* as a fem. personal suffix, as in *grisette* GRISETTE]

mid·i·ron (mid′ī′ərn), *n.* *Golf.* a club with an iron head the face of which has more slope than a driving iron but less slope than a mid-mashie. Also called **number two iron.** [1900–05; MID- + IRON]

mid·i·skirt (mid′ē skûrt′), *n.* a skirt or skirt part, as of a dress or coat, ending at the middle of the calf. Also, **midi.** [1965–70; MID- + (MIN)ISKIRT]

mid·land (mid′lənd), *n.* **1.** the middle or interior part of a country. **2.** (*cap.*) the dialect of English spoken in the central part of England. **3.** (*cap.*) the dialect of English spoken in the southern parts of Illinois, Indiana, Ohio, Pennsylvania, and New Jersey, and in West Virginia, Kentucky, and eastern Tennessee, and throughout the southern Appalachians. —*adj.* **4.** in or of the midland; inland. **5.** (*cap.*) of or pertaining to Midland. [1400–50; late ME. See MID-, LAND]

Mid·land (mid′lənd), *n.* **1.** a city in W Texas. 70,525. **2.** a city in central Michigan. 37,250. **3.** a town in S Ontario, in S Canada, on Georgian Bay of Lake Huron. 12,132.

Mid·lands (mid′ləndz), *n.pl.* the central part of England; the midland counties.

mid·leg (*n.* mid′leg′; *adv.* mid′leg′), *n.* **1.** the middle part of the leg. **2.** one of the second pair of legs of an insect. —*adv.* **3.** at the middle of the leg. [1580–90; MID- + LEG]

Mid′-Lent Sun′day (mid′lent′). See **Laetare Sunday.** [1350–1400; ME]

mid·lev·el (mid′lev′əl), *adj.* middle-level.

mid·life (*n.* mid′līf′; *adj.* mid′līf′), *n.* **1.** See **middle age.** —*adj.* **2.** middle-aged. Also, **mid′-life′.** [1895–1900; MID- + LIFE]

mid′life cri′sis, a period of psychological stress occurring in middle age, thought to be triggered by a physical, occupational, or domestic event, as menopause, diminution of physical prowess, job loss, or departure of children from the home. [1970–75]

mid·line (mid′līn′), *n.* *Zool.* the median plane of the body of an animal. [1865–70; MID- + LINE[1]]

Mid·lo·thi·an (mid lō′thē ən *for 1;* mid lō′thē ən *for 2*), *n.* **1.** Formerly, **Edinburgh.** a historic county in SE Scotland. **2.** a town in NE Illinois. 14,274.

mid·mash·ie (mid′mash′ē), *n.* *Golf.* a club with an iron head the face of which has more slope than a midiron but less slope than a mashie iron. Also called **number three iron.** [MID- + MASHIE]

mid·morn·ing (mid′môr′ning), *n.* **1.** the middle of the morning; the time centering around the midpoint between early morning and noon. —*adv.* **2.** in the middle of the morning: *He usually arrives midmorning.* —*adj.* **3.** occurring during, taking place in, or pertaining to the middle of the morning: *our midmorning coffee break.* [1900–05; MID- + MORNING]

mid·most (mid′mōst′), *adj.* **1.** being in the very middle; middlemost; middle. **2.** being or occurring at or near the middle part or point of. **3.** most intimate or private; innermost. —*adv.* **4.** in the midmost part; in the midst. [bef. 1000; MID- + -MOST; r. ME, OE *mid mest*]

MIDN, Midshipman.

Midn., Midshipman.

mid·night (mid′nīt′), *n.* **1.** the middle of the night; twelve o'clock at night. —*adj.* **2.** of or pertaining to midnight. **3.** resembling midnight, as in darkness. **4. burn the midnight oil,** to study or work far into the night: *After months of burning the midnight oil, he really needed a vacation.* [bef. 900; ME; OE *midniht.* See MID-, NIGHT] **—mid′night′ly,** *adj., adv.*

mid′night sun′, the sun visible at midnight in midsummer in arctic and antarctic regions. [1855–60]

mid·noon (mid′nōōn′), *n.* midday. [1570–80; MID- + NOON]

mid′-o·cean ridge′ (mid′ō′shən), any of several seismically active submarine mountain ranges that extend through the Atlantic, Indian, and South Pacific oceans: each is hypothesized to be the locus of seafloor spreading. [1960–65]

mid′ off′, *Cricket.* **1.** the position of a fielder on the off side of the wicket. **2.** the fielder occupying this position. Also, **mid′-off′.** Also called **mid wicket off.** [1880–85]

mid′ on′, *Cricket.* **1.** the position of a fielder on the on side of the wicket. **2.** the fielder occupying this position. Also, **mid′-on′.** Also called **mid wicket on.**

mid·point (mid′point′), *n.* **1.** a point at or near the middle of, or equidistant from, both ends, as of a line: *the midpoint of a boundary.* **2.** a point in time halfway between the beginning and the end, as of a process, event, or situation: *the midpoint of the negotiations.* **3.** *Geom.* the point on a line segment or an arc that is equidistant, when measured along the line or the arc, from both endpoints. **4.** *Statistics.* median (def. 5). **5.** *Astrol.* the point on the arc that is equidistant from two planets: regarded as a sensitive point and used in horoscopic interpretations. Also, **mid′-point′.** [1325–75; ME. See MID-, POINT]

mid·range (mid′rānj′), *adj.* *Audio.* **1.** of, pertaining to, or occupying the middle audio frequencies: *a midrange frequency.* —*n.* **2.** this portion of a range: *this speaker operates best in the midrange.* [1945–50; MID- + RANGE]

mid·rash (*Seph. Heb.* mē drāsh′; *Ashk. Heb.* mi′drāsh), *n., pl.* **mid·ra·shim** (*Seph. Heb.* mē drä shēm′; *Ashk. Heb.* mi drô′shim), **mid·ra·shoth, mid·ra·shot, mid·ra·shos** (*Seph. Heb.* mē drä shôt′; *Ashk. Heb.* midrô′shōs). **1.** an early Jewish interpretation of or commentary on a Biblical text, clarifying or expounding a point of law or developing or illustrating a moral principle. **2.** (*cap.*) a collection of such interpretations or commentaries, esp. those written in the first ten centuries A.D. [1605–15; < Heb *midrāsh* lit., exposition] **—mid·rash·ic** (mid rash′ik), *adj.*

mid·rib (mid′rib′), *n.* *Bot.* the central or middle rib of a leaf. [1690–1700; MID- + RIB[1]]

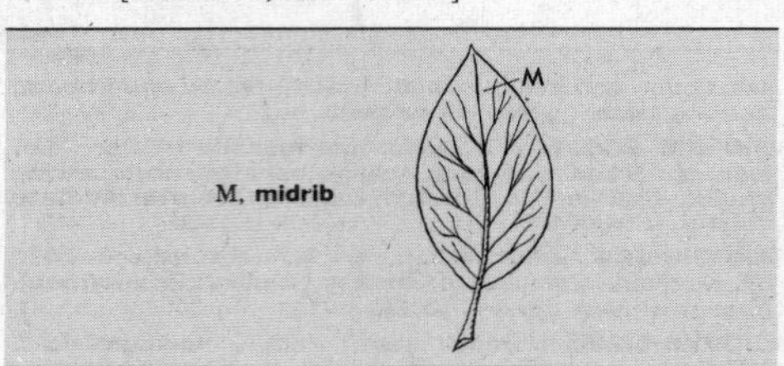

M, midrib

mid·riff (mid′rif), *n.* **1.** diaphragm (def. 1). **2.** the middle part of the body, between the chest and the waist. **3.** the part of a dress or bodice, usually close-fitting, that covers this part of the body. **4.** a garment that exposes this part of the body. —*adj.* **5.** noting or pertaining to the middle part of the human body, the part of a garment that covers it, or a garment that exposes it. [bef. 1000; ME *mydryf,* OE *midhrif,* equiv. to *mid(d)* MID[1] + *hrif* belly]

mid·rise (mid′rīz′), *adj.* **1.** (of a building) having a moderately large number of stories, usually five to ten, and equipped with elevators. —*n.* **2.** a mid-rise apartment or office building. [1965–70; MID- + (HIGH)-RISE]

mid·sag′it·tal plane′ (mid saj′i tl), *Craniom.* a plane passing through the nasion when the skull is oriented in the Frankfurt horizontal. [1955–60; MID- + SAGITTAL]

mid·sec·tion (mid′sek′shən), *n.* **1.** the middle section or part of anything. **2.** the solar plexus; midriff: *a hard right to the midsection.* [1935–40; MID- + SECTION]

mid·ship (mid′ship′), *adj.* in or belonging to the middle part of a ship. [1545–55; MID- + SHIP]

mid·ship·man (mid′ship′mən, mid ship′-) *n., pl.* **-men. 1.** a student, as at the U.S. Naval Academy, in training for commission as ensign in the Navy or second lieutenant in the Marine Corps. Cf. **cadet** (def. 2). **2.** *Brit. Navy.* **a.** an officer of the rank held by young men immediately upon graduating from the government naval schools. **b.** (*cap.*) the title and rank of such a graduate. **c.** (formerly) one of a class of boys or young men who formed the group from which officers were chosen. **3.** Also called **singingfish.** any toadfish of the genus *Porichthys,* having many small luminous organs on the underside and producing a buzzing sound with its air bladder. [1620–30; MIDSHIP + -MAN]

mid·ships (mid′ships′), *adv.* amidships. [1620–30]

mid·size (mid′sīz′), *adj.* **1.** (of an automobile) being between a compact and a large car in size and having a combined passenger and luggage volume of 110–120 cu. ft. (3.1–3.4 m^3). **2.** intermediate. [1965–70]

mid·sole (mid′sōl′), *n.* a layer of material or cushioning between the outsole and the insole of a shoe. [MID- + SOLE[2]]

midst[1] (midst), *n.* **1.** the position of anything surrounded by other things or parts, or occurring in the middle of a period of time, course of action, etc. (usually prec. by *the*): *a familiar face in the midst of the crowd; in the midst of the performance.* **2.** the middle point, part, or stage (usually prec. by *the*): *We arrived in the midst of a storm.* **3. in our, your,** or **their midst,** in the midst of or among us (you, them): *To think there was a spy in our midst!* [1350–1400; ME, equiv. to *middes* (aph. var. of *amiddes* AMIDST) + excrescent *-t*]
—Syn. 1, 2. thick, core, heart. See **middle.** **—Ant. 1, 2.** edge, periphery.

midst[2] (midst), *prep.* amidst.

mid·stream (mid′strēm′), *n.* **1.** the middle of a stream. **2.** the middle period of a process, course, or the like. [1275–1325; ME *myddstreme.* See MID-, STREAM]

mid·sum·mer (mid′sum′ər, -sum′-), *n.* **1.** the middle of summer. **2.** the summer solstice, around June 21. [bef. 900; ME, OE *midsumer.* See MID[1], SUMMER[1]] **—mid′sum′mer·y,** *adj.*

Mid′summer Day′, *Chiefly Brit.* the saint's day of St. John the Baptist, celebrated on June 24, being one of the four quarter days in England. Also called **St. John's Day.** [bef. 1150; ME, OE]

Mid′summer Eve′, *Chiefly Brit.* the evening preceding Midsummer Day: formerly believed to be a time when witches and other supernatural beings caused widespread mischief. Also called **Mid′summer Night′, St. John's Eve, St. John's Night.** [1400–50; late ME]

mid′summer mad′ness, a temporary lapse into foolishness, senseless behavior, folly, etc., esp. during the summer. [1595–1605]

Mid′summer Night's′ Dream′, A, a comedy (1595?) by Shakespeare.

mid-teen (mid′tēn′), *adj.* **1.** of, pertaining to, or characteristic of a person 15–17 years old: *specializing in mid-teen clothes.* —*n.* **2.** a person 15–17 years old: *an ad campaign aimed at mid-teens.* **3. mid-teens,** numbers, amounts, ages, etc., midway between 13 and 19: *He started at a salary in the mid-teens.*

mid·term (mid′tûrm′), *n.* **1.** the middle or halfway point of a term, as a school term or term of office. **2.** Often, **midterms.** *Informal.* an examination or series of examinations at the middle of a school term. —*adj.* **3.** pertaining to or occurring on or about the middle of a term, as a school term or term of office: *a midterm recess; midterm elections.* [1865–70; MID- + TERM]

mid·town (mid′toun′, -toun′), *n.* **1.** the middle part of a city or town between uptown and downtown. —*adj.* **2.** of, pertaining to, or situated in this part: *a midtown restaurant.* —*adv.* **3.** to or in this part: *She works midtown.* [1930–35; MID- + TOWN]

Mid·vale (mid′vāl′), *n.* a town in N Utah. 10,144.

mid-Vic·to·ri·an (mid′vik tôr′ē ən, -tōr′-), *adj.* **1.** of, pertaining to, or characteristic of the middle portion (about 1850 to 1890) of the reign of Queen Victoria (reigned 1837–1901) in England: *mid-Victorian writers.* —*n.* **2.** a person, as a writer, belonging to the mid-Victorian time. **3.** a person of mid-Victorian tastes, standards, ideas, etc. [1900–05] **—mid′-Vic·to′ri·an·ism,** *n.*

mid′wall′ col′umn (mid′wôl′), a column or the like carrying a wall overhanging it on both sides. Also called **mid′wall′ shaft′.** [MID- + WALL]

mid·watch (mid′woch′), *n.* *Naut.* See **middle watch.** [1525–35; MID- + WATCH]

mid·way (*adv., adj.* mid′wā′; *n.* mid′wā′), *adv., adj.* **1.** in the middle of the way or distance; halfway. —*n.* **2.** a place or part situated midway. **3.** (*often cap.*) the place or way, as at a fair or carnival, on or along which sideshows and similar amusements are located. **4.** the amusements, concessions, etc., located on or around this place or way. [bef. 900; ME *midwei,* OE *midweg;* see MID[1], WAY[1]; def. 3 and 4 after the *Midway* Plaisance, the main thoroughfare of the World Columbian Exposition, held in Chicago in 1893]

Mid·way (mid′wā′), *n.* **1.** several U.S. islets in the N Pacific, about 1300 mi. (2095 km) NW of Hawaii: Japanese defeated in a naval battle June, 1942; 2 sq. mi. (5 sq. km). **2.** an airport in Chicago.

mid·week (*n.* mid′wēk′, -wēk′; *adj.* mid′wēk′), *n.* **1.** the middle of the week. **2.** (*cap.*) (among the Quakers) Wednesday. —*adj.* **3.** of, pertaining to, or occurring in the middle of the week. [1700–10; MID- + WEEK]

mid·week·ly (mid′wēk′lē), *adj.* **1.** midweek. —*adv.* **2.** in the middle of the week. [MIDWEEK + -LY]

Mid·west (mid′west′), *n.* **1.** See **Middle West.** —*adj.* **2.** Also, **Mid·west·ern.** See **Middle Western.** [MID- + WEST] **—Mid′west′ern·er,** *n.*

Mid′west Cit′y, a city in central Oklahoma, near Oklahoma City. 49,559.

mid′ wick′et off′, *Cricket.* See **mid off.** [1840–50]

mid′ wick′et on′, *Cricket.* See **mid on.** [1840–50]

mid·wife (mid′wīf′), *n., pl.* **-wives** (-wīvz′), *v.,* **-wifed** or **-wived, -wif·ing** or **wiv·ing.** —*n.* **1.** a person trained to assist women in childbirth. **2.** a person or thing that produces or aids in producing something new or different. —*v.t.* **3.** to assist in the birth of (a baby). **4.** to produce or aid in producing (something new): *to midwife a new generation of computers.* [1250–1300; ME *midwif,* equiv. to *mid* with, accompanying (OE; cf. META-) + *wif* woman (OE *wīf;* see WIFE)]

mid·wife·ry (mid wif′ə rē, -wīf′rē, mid′wī fə rē, -wīf′rē), *n.* the technique or practice of a midwife. [1475–85; see MIDWIFE, -ERY]

mid′wife toad′, a European toad, *Alytes obstetricans* (family Discoglossidae), noted for its unusual breeding habits, in which mating occurs on land and the male broods the egg strings by wrapping them around his legs. [1900–05]

mid·win·ter (*n.* mid′win′tər, -win′-; *adj.* mid′win′tər), *n.* **1.** the middle of winter. **2.** the winter solstice, around December 22. —*adj.* **3.** of, pertaining to, or occurring in the middle of the winter. [bef. 1150; ME, OE; see MID[1], WINTER] **—mid′win′try, mid′win′ter·ly,** *adj.*

mid·year (mid′yēr′, -yēr′ *for 1;* mid′yēr′ *for 2, 3*), *n.* **1.** the middle of the year. **2.** Often, **midyears.** *Infor-*

CONCISE ETYMOLOGY KEY: <, descended or borrowed from; >, whence; b., blend of, blended; c., cognate with; cf., compare; deriv., derivative; equiv., equivalent; imit., imitative; obl., oblique; r., replacing; s., stem; sp., spelling, spelled; resp., respelling, respelled; trans., translation; ?, origin unknown; *, unattested; ‡, probably earlier than. See the full key inside the front cover.

mal. an examination at the middle of a school year. —*adj.* **3.** of, pertaining to, or occurring in midyear: *midyear exams.* [1325–75; ME; see MID-, YEAR]

M.I.E., Master of Industrial Engineering.

Miel·zi·ner (mēl zē′nər, mel-), *n.* **Jo** (jō), 1901–76, U.S. stage designer, born in France.

mien (mēn), *n.* air, bearing, or demeanor, as showing character, feeling, etc.: *a man of noble mien.* [1505–15; prob. aph. var. of obs. *demean* bearing, DEMEAN[2]; spelled with *-ie-* to distinguish it from MEAN[2]]
—**Syn.** appearance, look; carriage.

Mie′ scat′tering (mē), *Optics.* the scattering of light by particles that are large relative to the wavelength of the light. Cf. **Rayleigh scattering.** [named after Gustav *Mie* (1868–1957), German physicist]

Mies van der Ro·he (mēz′ van dər rō′ə, fän, mēs′), **Lud·wig** (lud′wig), 1886–1969, U.S. architect, born in Germany. Also, **Mi·ës van der Ro·he** (mē′əs van dər rō′ə, fän, mēz′, mēs′).

miff (mif), *n.* **1.** petulant displeasure; ill humor. **2.** a petty quarrel. —*v.t.* **3.** to give minor offense to; offend. [1615–25; perh. imit. of exclamation of disgust; cf. G *muffen* to sulk]
—**Syn. 3.** annoy, provoke, irritate, vex.

miffed (mift), *adj.* put into an irritable mood, esp. by an offending incident: *I was miffed when they didn't invite me to the party.* [1815–25; MIFF + -ED[2]]

Miff·lin (mif′lin), *n.* **Thomas,** 1744–1800, American politician and Revolutionary general: president of the Continental Congress 1783–84; governor of Pennsylvania 1790–99.

miff·y (mif′ē), *adj.,* **miff·i·er, miff·i·est.** *Informal.* touchy; inclined to take offense. [1690–1700; MIFF + -Y[1]]

Mi·fu·ne (mi fo͞o′nē; *Japn.* mē fo͞o′ne), *n.* **To·shi·ro** (tə shēr′ō; *Japn.* tô shē′ʀô), born 1920, Japanese film actor, born in China.

mig (mig), *n. Chiefly Northern, North Midland, and Western U.S.* **1.** a playing marble, esp. one that is not used as a shooter. **2. migs,** (*used with a singular v.*) the game of marbles. Also, **migg.** [perh. var. of MIB with *g* from GAME]

MiG (mig), *n.* any of several Russian-built fighter aircraft, as the MiG-15, a jet used in the Korean War. Also, **Mig, MIG** [named after Artem *Mi(koyan)* and Mikhail *G(urevich),* Russian aircraft designers]

mig·gle (mig′əl), *n.* **1.** a playing marble, esp. one that is not used as a shooter. **2. miggles,** (*used with a singular v.*) the game of marbles. [1890–95, *Amer.*; perh. MIG + (MARB)LE]

might[1] (mīt), *auxiliary v.* **1.** pt. of **may**[1]. **2.** (used to express possibility): *They might be at the station.* **3.** (used to express advisability): *You might at least thank me.* **4.** (used in polite requests for permission): *Might I speak to you for a moment?*

might[2] (mīt), *n.* **1.** physical strength: *He swung with all his might.* **2.** superior power or strength; force: *the theory that might makes right.* **3.** power or ability to do or accomplish; capacity: *the might of the ballot box.* **4. with might and main,** with all the vigor, force, or energy at one's command: *They pulled with might and main.* [bef. 900; ME *myghte,* OE *miht, meaht;* c. G *macht,* Goth *mahts;* akin to MAY[1]] —**might′less,** *adj.*
—**Syn. 1–3.** See **strength.** —**Ant. 1–3.** weakness.

might·i·ly (mīt′l ē), *adv.* **1.** in a mighty manner; powerfully or vigorously. **2.** to a great extent or degree; very much: *to desire something mightily.* [bef. 900; ME; OE *mihtiglīce.* See MIGHTY, -LY]

might·n't (mīt′nt), contraction of *might not.*

might·y (mī′tē), *adj.,* **might·i·er, might·i·est,** *adv., n.* —*adj.* **1.** having, characterized by, or showing superior power or strength: *mighty rulers.* **2.** of great size; huge: *a mighty oak.* **3.** great in amount, extent, degree, or importance; exceptional: *a mighty accomplishment.* —*adv.* **4.** *Informal.* very; extremely: *I'm mighty pleased.* —*n.* **5.** (*used with a plural v.*) mighty persons collectively (usually prec. by *the*): *the rich and the mighty.* [bef. 900; ME; OE *mihtig.* See MIGHT[2], -Y[1]] —**might′i·ness,** *n.*
—**Syn. 1.** strong, puissant. See **powerful. 2.** immense, enormous, tremendous, sizable. —**Ant. 1.** feeble. **2.** small.

mi·gnon (min yon′; *Fr.* mē nyôɴ′), *adj.* small and pretty; delicately pretty. [1550–60; < F; see MINION]

Mi·gnon (mē nyôɴ′), *n.* an opera (1866) by Ambroise Thomas.

mi·gnon·ette (min′yə net′), *n.* **1.** a plant, *Reseda odorata,* common in gardens, having racemes of small, fragrant, greenish-white flowers with prominent orange anthers. **2.** a grayish green resembling the color of a reseda plant. [1690–1700; < F; see MIGNON, -ETTE]

mi·gnonne (min yon′; *Fr.* mē nyôɴ′), *adj.* **1.** small and delicate. —*n.* **2.** (*cap.*) Also, **Mi·gnon** (min yon′; *Fr.* mē nyôɴ′). a female given name. [1550–60; < F, fem. of *mignon* MIGNON]

mi·graine (mī′grān *or, Brit.,* mē′-), *n.* an extremely severe paroxysmal headache, usually confined to one side of the head and often associated with nausea; hemicrania. [1325–75; ME < MF < LL *hēmicrānia* HEMICRANIA; cf. MEGRIM] —**mi·grain′oid,** *adj.* —**mi·grain′ous,** *adj.*

mi·grant (mī′grənt), *adj.* **1.** migrating, esp. of people; migratory. —*n.* **2.** a person or animal that migrates. **3.** Also called **mi′grant work′er.** a person who moves from place to place to get work, esp. a farm laborer who harvests crops seasonally. [1665–75; < L *migrant-* (s. of *migrāns*), prp. of *migrāre.* See MIGRATE, -ANT]

mi·grate (mī′grāt), *v.i.,* **-grat·ed, -grat·ing. 1.** to go from one country, region, or place to another. **2.** to pass periodically from one region or climate to another, as certain birds, fishes, and animals: *The birds migrate southward in the winter.* **3.** to shift, as from one system, mode of operation, or enterprise to another. **4.** *Physiol.* (of a cell, tissue, etc.) to move from one region of the body to another, as in embryonic development. **5.** *Chem.* **a.** (of ions) to move toward an electrode during electrolysis. **b.** (of atoms within a molecule) to change position. **6.** (at British universities) to change or transfer from one college to another. [1690–1700; < L *migrātus* (ptp. of *migrāre* to move from place to place, change position or abode), equiv. to *migrā-* v. s. + *-tus* ptp. suffix] —**mi′gra·tor,** *n.*
—**Syn. 1.** move, resettle. MIGRATE, EMIGRATE, IMMIGRATE are used of changing one's abode from one country or part of a country to another. To MIGRATE is to make such a move either once or repeatedly: *to migrate from Ireland to the United States.* To EMIGRATE is to leave a country, usually one's own (and take up residence in another): *Each year many people emigrate from Europe.* To IMMIGRATE is to enter and settle in a country not one's own: *There are many inducements to immigrate to South America.* MIGRATE is applied both to people or to animals that move from one region to another, esp. periodically; the other terms are generally applied to movements of people. —**Ant. 1.** remain.

mi·gra·tion (mī grā′shən), *n.* **1.** the process or act of migrating. **2.** a migratory movement: *preparations for the migration.* **3.** a number or body of persons or animals migrating together. **4.** *Chem.* a movement or change of position of atoms within a molecule. **5.** *Physics.* diffusion (def. 3a). [1605–15; < L *migrātiōn-* (s. of *migrātiō*). See MIGRATE, -ION] —**mi·gra′tion·al,** *adj.*

mi·gra·to·ry (mī′grə tôr′ē, -tōr′ē), *adj.* **1.** migrating. **2.** periodically migrating: *a migratory species; migratory workers.* **3.** pertaining to a migration: *migratory movements of birds.* **4.** roving; nomadic; wandering. Also, **mi′gra·tive.** [1745–55; MIGRATE + -ORY[1]]

mi′gratory lo′cust, any of several locusts that migrate in great swarms, esp. *Locusta migratoria,* of Africa and Asia. Also called **mi′gratory grass′hopper.** [1870–75]

mig·ue·let (mig′ə let′), *n.* miquelet.

Mi·hai·lo·vić (*Serbo-Croatian.* mi hī′lô vich), *n.* **Dra·ža** (*Serbo-Croatian.* dʀä′zhä). See **Mikhailovitch, Draja.**

mih·rab (mēr′əb), *n.* (in a mosque) a niche or decorative panel designating the kiblah. [1810–20; < Ar *miḥrāb*]

mi·ka·do (mi kä′dō), *n., pl.* **-dos. 1.** (*sometimes cap.*) a title of the emperor of Japan. **2.** (*cap., italics*) an operetta (1885) by Sir William S. Gilbert and Sir Arthur Sullivan. **3.** (*cap.*) a steam locomotive having a two-wheeled front truck, eight driving wheels, and a two-wheeled rear truck. See table under **Whyte classification.** [1720–30; < Japn, equiv. to *mi-* exalted + *kado* gate, door (of the imperial palace)]

Mik·a·su·ki (mik′ə so͞o′kē), *n., pl.* **-kis,** (*esp. collectively*) **-ki** for 1. **1.** a member of an American Indian people, formerly part of the Creek Confederacy and surviving chiefly as one of the two branches of the Muskogean family represented among the Florida Seminoles. **2.** the Muskogean language of the Mikasuki. Also, **Miccosukee.** [< a native town name]

mike[1] (mīk), *n., v.,* **miked, mik·ing.** —*n.* **1.** Also, **mic.** *Informal.* a microphone. —*v.t.* **2.** *Informal.* to supply or amplify with one or more microphones; attach a microphone to: *to mike a singer.* —*v.i.* **3.** *Informal.* to use or position a microphone: *to mike properly when recording a singer.* [by shortening and resp.]

mike[2] (mīk), *n.* a forklike support for a light cannon on a sailing ship. [1300–50; ME; perh. < MD *micke* forked instrument]

mike[3] (mīk), *n., v.,* **miked, mik·ing.** *Brit. Slang.* —*n.* **1.** loafing; idling. —*v.i.* **2.** to loaf. [1815–25; orig. uncert.]

mike[4] (mīk), *n., v.,* **miked, mik·ing.** —*n.* **1.** micrometer[1] (def. 2). —*v.t.* **2.** to measure with a micrometer. [by shortening and resp. of MICROMETER]

Mike (mīk), *n.* **1.** a male given name, form of **Michael. 2.** (*l.c.*) a word used in communications to represent the letter *M.*

mike′ fright′, *Informal.* extreme nervousness experienced on speaking into a microphone, as on radio or television. [1935–40; on the model of STAGE FRIGHT]

Mike-Mike (mīk′mīk′), *n. Mil. Slang.* a millimeter.

Mi·khai·lo·vitch (*Serbo-Croatian.* mi hī′lô vich), *n.* **Dra·ja** (dʀä′zhä), 1893–1946, Yugoslav military leader. Also, **Draža Mihailović.**

Mi·ko·nos (mē′kô nôs), *n.* Greek name of **Mykonos.**

Mi·ko·yan (mē′kô yän′; *Russ.* myi ku yän′), *n.* **A·na·stas I·va·no·vich** (u nu stäs′ ē vä′nə vyich), 1895–1978, Soviet official: president of the Soviet Union 1964–65.

mi·kron (mī′kron), *n., pl.* **-krons, -kra** (-krə). micron.

mik·vah (*Seph.* mē kvä′; *Ashk., Eng.* mik′və), *n., pl.* ***-voth, -vot, -vos*** (*Seph.* -vôt′; *Ashk.* -vōs), *Eng.* **-vahs.** *Hebrew.* a ritual bath to which Orthodox Jews are traditionally required to go on certain occasions, as before the Sabbath and after each menstrual period, to cleanse and purify themselves. Also, ***mik′veh.***

mil[1] (mil), *n.* **1.** a unit of length equal to 0.001 of an inch (0.0254 mm), used in measuring the diameter of wires. **2.** a military unit of angular measurement equal to the angle subtended by 1/6400 of a circumference. **3.** (less accurately) the angle subtended by an arc equal to 1/1000 of the radius or distance. **4.** (used formerly in pharmaceutical prescriptions) a milliliter. **5.** a former bronze coin of the mandate of Palestine, the 1000th part of a pound. [1715–25; short for L *millēsimus* thousandth, equiv. to *mill(e)* thousand (see MILE) + *-ēsimus* ordinal suffix]

mil[2] (mil), *n. Slang.* a million. [by shortening]

mil., **1.** military. **2.** militia.

mi·la·dy (mi lā′dē), *n., pl.* **-dies. 1.** an English noblewoman (often used as a term of address). **2.** a woman regarded as having fashionable or expensive tastes: *milady's spring wardrobe.* Also, **mi·la′di.** [1830–40; < F < E *my lady*]

mil·age (mī′lij), *n.* mileage.

Mi·lan (mi lan′, -län′), *n.* an industrial city in central Lombardy, in N Italy: cathedral. 1,710,263. Italian, **Mi·la·no** (mē lä′nô).

mil·a·naise (mil′ə nāz′; *Fr.* mē lᴀ nez′), *adj. French Cookery.* served with macaroni, or sometimes spaghetti, that has been flavored with tomatoes, mushrooms, shredded meat, etc.: *veal cutlets à la milanaise.* [< F *à la milanaise* in the style of Milan]

Mil·an·ese (mil′ə nēz′, -nēs′ *for 1–4;* mil′ə nä′zē *or, It.,* mē′lä ne′ze *for* 5), *n., pl.* **-ese,** *adj.* —*n.* **1.** a native or inhabitant of Milan, Italy. **2.** the Italian dialect spoken in Milan. **3.** (*l.c.*) *Textiles.* **a.** a run-resistant, warp-knitted fabric of silk, rayon, or nylon used in the manufacture of women's apparel. **b.** a warp-knit structure in which two sets of threads are knitted in an interlocking series forming a crossed diagonal or diamond pattern. **c.** the machine that produces this knit structure. —*adj.* **4.** of, pertaining to, or characteristic of Milan, Italy, its inhabitants, or their dialect of Italian. **5.** *Italian Cookery.* **a.** (esp. of meats) coated with flour or bread crumbs and browned in hot oil or butter. **b.** (esp. of pasta) having a sauce of tomatoes, mushrooms, grated cheese, shredded meat, and truffles: *spaghetti Milanese.* [1475–85; < It; see MILAN, -ESE]

Mil′anese chant′. See **Ambrosian chant.**

Mi·la·nov (mil′ə nôf′, -nof′; *Serbo-Croatian.* mē′lä nôf′), *n.* **Zin·ka** (zing′kə; *Serbo-Croatian.* zing′kä) (*Zinka Kunc*), born 1906, Yugoslavian soprano, in the U.S.

Mi·laz·zo (mē lät′tsô), *n.* a seaport in NE Sicily, in Italy. 26,623.

milch (milch), *adj.* (of a domestic animal) yielding milk; kept or suitable for milk production. [1250–1300; ME *milche;* cf. OE *-milce* (in *thrimilce* the month of May, i.e., the month when cows could be milked thrice a day); see MILK]

milch′ cow′. See **milk cow.** [1375–1425; late ME]

milch′ glass′. See **milk glass.**

mil·chig (mil′ᴋʜig, -ᴋʜik), *adj. Judaism.* (in the dietary laws) consisting of, made from, or used only for milk or dairy products. Cf. **fleishig, pareve.** [1925–30; < Yiddish *milkhik,* equiv. to *milkh* MILK + *-ik* -Y[1]]

mild (mīld), *adj.,* **-er, -est,** *n.* —*adj.* **1.** amiably gentle or temperate in feeling or behavior toward others. **2.** characterized by or showing such gentleness, as manners or speech: *a mild voice.* **3.** not cold, severe, or extreme, as air or weather: *mild breezes.* **4.** not sharp, pungent, or strong: *a mild flavor.* **5.** not acute or serious, as disease: *a mild case of flu.* **6.** gentle or moderate in force or effect: *mild penalties.* **7.** soft; pleasant: *mild sunshine.* **8.** moderate in intensity, degree, or character: *mild regret.* **9.** *Brit. Dial.* comparatively soft and easily worked, as soil, wood, or stone. **10.** *Obs.* kind or gracious. —*n.* **11.** *Brit.* beer that has a blander taste than bitter. [bef. 900; ME, OE *milde;* c. G *mild;* akin to Gk *malthakós* soft] —**mild′ly,** *adv.* —**mild′ness,** *n.*
—**Syn. 1.** soft, pleasant. See **gentle. 3.** temperate, moderate, clement. **4.** bland. —**Ant. 1.** forceful. **3.** severe. **6.** harsh.

mild·en (mīl′dn), *v.t., v.i.* to make or become mild or milder. [1595–1605; MILD + -EN[1]]

mil·dew (mil′do͞o′, -dyo͞o′), *n.* **1.** *Plant Pathol.* a disease of plants, characterized by a cottony, usually whitish coating on the surface of affected parts, caused by any of various fungi. **2.** any of these fungi. Cf. **downy mildew, powdery mildew. 3.** any of similar coatings or discolorations, caused by fungi, as that which appears on fabrics, paper, leather, etc., when exposed to moisture. —*v.t., v.i.* **4.** to affect or become affected with mildew. [bef. 1000; ME: honeydew, mildew; OE *mildēaw,* equiv. to *mil-* honey (c. Goth *milith,* akin to L *mel,* Gk *méli*) + *dēaw* DEW] —**mil′dew′y,** *adj.*

mil·dew·cide (mil′do͞o sīd′, -dyo͞o-), *n.* a chemical for destroying mildew. Also, **mil·dew·i·cide** (mil′do͞o ə sīd′, -dyo͞o-). [MILDEW + -CIDE]

mil·dew·proof (mil′do͞o pro͞of′, -dyo͞o-), *adj.* **1.** able to withstand or repel the effect of mildew. —*v.t.* **2.** to enable (fabric, paper, etc.) to withstand or repel the effect of mildew. [MILDEW + -PROOF]

mild′ mercu′rous chlo′ride, *Pharm.* calomel.

Mil·dred (mil′drid), *n.* a female given name: from Old English words meaning "mild" and "strength."

mild′ sil′ver pro′tein, *Pharm.* a compound of silver and a protein, applied to mucous membranes as a mild antiseptic.

mild′ steel′, low-carbon steel, containing no more than 0.25 percent carbon. Also called **soft steel.** [1865–70]

mile (mīl), *n.* **1.** Also called **statute mile.** a unit of distance on land in English-speaking countries equal to 5280 feet, or 1760 yards (1.609 kilometers). **2.** See **nautical mile. 3.** See **international nautical mile. 4.** any of various other units of distance or length at different periods and in different countries. Cf. **Roman mile. 5.** a notable distance or margin: *missed the target by a mile.* *Abbr.:* mi, mi. [bef. 1000; ME; OE *mīl* < L *mīlia* (*passuum*) a thousand (paces)]

mile·age (mī′lij), *n.* **1.** the aggregate number of miles traveled over in a given time. **2.** length, extent, or distance in miles. **3.** the number of miles or the average distance that a vehicle can travel on a specified quantity of fuel: *the car gets good mileage.* **4.** wear, use, advantage, or profit: *She won't get much more mileage out of*

CONCISE PRONUNCIATION KEY: *act, cāpe, dâre, pärt; set, ēqual; if, īce; ox, ōver, ôrder, oil, bo͝ok, bo͞ot, out; up, ûrge; child; sing; shoe; thin, that;* zh as in *treasure.* ə = *a* as in *alone, e* as in *system, i* as in *easily, o* as in *gallop, u* as in *circus;* ′ as in *fire* (fī′r), *hour* (ou′r). l and n can serve as syllabic consonants, as in *cradle* (krād′l), and *button* (but′n). See the full key inside the front cover.

this old coat. **5.** an allowance for traveling expenses at a fixed rate per mile: *His mileage came to $90.* **6.** a fixed charge per mile, as for railroad transportation. **7.** See **mileage ticket.** Also, **milage.** [1745–55, *Amer.*; MILE + -AGE]

mile′age tick′et, **1.** a book **(mile′age book′)** or ticket containing coupons good for a certain number of miles of transportation at a fixed rate per mile. **2.** one of the coupons. [1880–85, *Amer.*]

mile•long (mīl′lông′, -long′), *adj.* extending for a mile: *a milelong beach.* [1825–35; MILE + LONG[1]]

mile-mark•er (mīl′mär′kər), *n.* a numbered milepost along a highway: used as a way of determining the exact location of a vehicle. Also, **mile′mark′er.** Also called **marker.**

mile•post (mīl′pōst′), *n.* **1.** any of a series of posts set up to mark distance by miles, as along a highway, or an individual post showing the distance to or from a place. **2.** a notable point or significant event in the progress or development of something; milestone. [1760–70, *Amer.*; MILE + POST[1]]

mil•er (mī′lər), *n.* **1.** a participant in a one-mile race. **2.** an athlete who specializes in one-mile races. **3.** a racehorse that can compete well in a one-mile race. [1890–95; MILE + -ER[1]]

Miles (mīlz), *n.* **1. Nelson Appleton,** 1839–1925, U.S. army officer. **2.** a male given name: from a Germanic word meaning "merciful."

Mi•le•sian (mi lē′zhən, -shən, mī-), *adj.* **1.** of or pertaining to Miletus. **2.** *Philos.* noting or pertaining to a school of philosophers of the late 7th to early 5th centuries B.C., including Thales, Anaximander, and Anaximenes, which was primarily concerned with the nature of matter and change. —*n.* **3.** a native of Miletus. [1540–50; < L *Milēsi(us)* inhabitant of MILETUS + -AN]

Mi•le•sian (mi lē′zhən, -shən, mī-), *n. Irish Legend.* **1.** any of the race of people from Spain who invaded Ireland and defeated the Tuatha Dé Danann, and who were the ancestors of the present Irish people. **2.** (*sometimes l.c.*) an Irishman. —*adj.* **3.** (*sometimes l.c.*) Irish. [1765–75; *Milēsi(us)* (Latinization of Ir *Miled,* legendary Spanish king) + -AN]

mile•stone (mīl′stōn′), *n.* **1.** a stone functioning as a milepost. **2.** a significant event or stage in the life, progress, development, or the like of a person, nation, etc.: *Her getting the job of supervisor was a milestone in her career.* [1740–50; MILE + STONE]

Mi•le•tus (mī lē′təs), *n.* **1.** *Class. Myth.* a son of Apollo and Aria, and the founder of the city of Miletus. **2.** an ancient city in Asia Minor, on the Aegean.

mil•foil (mil′foil′), *n.* yarrow (def. 1). [1250–1300; ME < OF < L *mīlifolium,* equiv. to *mīli-,* comb. form of *mīlle* thousand + *folium* leaf]

Mil•ford (mil′fərd), *n.* **1.** a city in S Connecticut, on Long Island Sound. 49,101. **2.** a city in central Massachusetts. 23,390. **3.** a male given name.

Mil′ford Ha′ven, **1.** a bay in SW Wales. **2.** a seaport on the N side of this bay, in Dyfed county. 13,745.

Mi•lhaud (mē yō′, mē ō′), *n.* **Da•rius** (dᴀ ʀʏʏs′), 1892–1974, French composer, in U.S. from 1940.

mil•ia•ren•sis (mil′yə ren′sis), *n., pl.* **-ses** (-sēz). a silver coin of ancient Rome, introduced by Constantine I as the 14th part of a solidus. Under Justinian it became the 12th part. [< LL, deriv. of L *mīlle* thousand; see -ESE]

mil•i•ar•i•a (mil′ē âr′ē ə), *n. Pathol.* an inflammatory disease of the skin, located about the sweat glands, marked by the formation of vesicles or papules resembling millet seeds; prickly heat. [1700–10; < NL *miliāria,* L: fem. of *miliārius* MILIARY]

mil•i•ar•y (mil′ē er′ē, mil′yə rē), *adj.* **1.** resembling millet seeds. **2.** *Pathol.* accompanied by papules or vesicles resembling millet seeds: *miliary fever.* [1675–85; < L *miliārius* of millet, equiv. to *mili(um)* MILLET + *-ārius* -ARY]

mil′iary tuberculo′sis, *Pathol.* tuberculosis in which the bacilli are spread by the blood from one point of infection, producing small tubercles in other parts of the body. [1895–1900]

Mil•i•cent (mil′ə sənt), *n.* a female given name.

mi•lieu (mil yōō′, mēl-; *Fr.* mē lyœ′), *n., pl.* **-lieus,** *Fr.* **-lieux** (-lyœ′). surroundings, esp. of a social or cultural nature: *a snobbish milieu.* [1795–1805; < F, equiv. to *mi* (< L *medius* middle; see MEDIUM) + *lieu* LIEU]
—Syn. background, sphere, setting. See **environment.**

milieu′ ther′apy, a type of inpatient therapy, used in psychiatric hospitals, involving prescription of particular activities and social interactions according to a patient's emotional and interpersonal needs. [1935–40]

milit., military.

mil•i•tant (mil′i tənt), *adj.* **1.** vigorously active and aggressive, esp. in support of a cause: *militant reformers.* **2.** engaged in warfare; fighting. —*n.* **3.** a militant person. **4.** a person engaged in warfare or combat. [1375–1425; late ME < L *mīlitant-* (s. of *mīlitāns*), prp. of *mīlitāre* to serve as a soldier. See MILITATE, -ANT] **—mil′i•tan•cy, mil′i•tant•ness,** *n.* **—mil′i•tant•ly,** *adv.*
—Syn. 1. belligerent, combative, contentious. See **fanatic.**

mil•i•tar•i•a (mil′i târ′ē ə), *n.pl.* collected or collectible military objects, as uniforms and firearms, having historical interest. [1960–65; MILITAR(Y) + -IA]

mil•i•ta•rism (mil′i tə riz′əm), *n.* **1.** a strong military spirit or policy. **2.** the principle or policy of maintaining a large military establishment. **3.** the tendency to regard military efficiency as the supreme ideal of the state and to subordinate all other interests to those of the military. [1860–65; < F *militarisme,* equiv. to *militar-* (< L *mīlitār(is)* MILITARY) + *-isme* -ISM]

mil•i•ta•rist (mil′i tər ist), *n.* **1.** a person imbued with militarism. **2.** a person skilled in the conduct of war and military affairs. [1595–1605; MILITAR(Y) + -IST] **—mil′i•ta•ris′tic,** *adj.* **—mil′i•ta•ris′ti•cal•ly,** *adv.*

mil•i•ta•rize (mil′i tə rīz′), *v.t.,* **-rized, -riz•ing. 1.** to equip with armed forces, military supplies, or the like. **2.** to make military. **3.** to imbue with militarism. Also, *esp. Brit.,* **mil′i•ta•rise′.** [1875–80; MILITAR(Y) + -IZE] **—mil′i•ta•ri•za′tion,** *n.*

mil•i•tar•y (mil′i ter′ē), *adj., n., pl.* **-tar•ies, -tar•y.** —*adj.* **1.** of, for, or pertaining to the army or armed forces, often as distinguished from the navy: *from civilian to military life.* **2.** of, for, or pertaining to war: *military preparedness.* **3.** of or pertaining to soldiers. **4.** befitting, characteristic of, or noting a soldier: *a military bearing.* **5.** following the life of a soldier: *a military career.* **6.** performed by soldiers: *military duty.* —*n.* **7. the military, a.** the military establishment of a nation; the armed forces. **b.** military personnel, esp. commissioned officers, taken collectively: *the bar, the press, and the military.* [1575–85; < L *mīlitāri(s),* equiv. to *mīlit-* (s. of *mīles*) soldier + *-āris* -ARY] **—mil•i•tar•i•ly** (mil′i târ′ə lē, mil′i ter′ə lē), *adv.* **—mil′i•tar′i•ness,** *n.*
—Syn. 3. soldierly, soldierlike, martial.

mil′itary acad′emy, **1.** a private school organized somewhat along the lines of and following some of the procedures of military life. **2.** a school that trains men and women for military careers as army officers, usually as part of a college education. Also called **military school.** [1770–80, *Amer.*]

mil′itary attaché′, attaché (def. 2). [1855–60]

mil′itary brush′, one of a pair of matched hairbrushes having no handles, esp. for men and boys. [1925–30]

mil′itary gov′ernment, a government in defeated territory administered by the military commander of a conquering nation.

mil′itary gov′ernor, the military officer in command of a military government. [1860–65, *Amer.*]

mil′i•tar•y-in•dus′tri•al com′plex (mil′i ter′ē in dus′trē əl), a network of a nation's military force together with all of the industries that support it. [1960–65]

mil′itary law′, the body of laws relating to the government of the armed forces; rules and regulations for the conduct of military personnel. [1730–40]

mil′itary march′, a brisk march, esp. one suitable for a military parade.

mil′itary pace′, a pace, equal to a single step, used to coordinate the marching of soldiers, equal in the U.S. to 2½ ft. (76 cm) for quick time and 3 ft. (91 cm) for double time.

mil′itary pentath′lon. See **modern pentathlon.**

mil′itary police′, soldiers who perform police duties within the army. *Abbr.:* MP Cf. **shore patrol.** [1820–30]

mil′itary school′. See **military academy.** [1770–80, *Amer.*]

mil′itary sci′ence, **1.** the study of the causative factors and tactical principles of warfare. **2.** an academic course dealing with these factors and principles. [1820–30]

mil•i•tate (mil′i tāt′), *v.i.,* **-tat•ed, -tat•ing. 1.** to have a substantial effect; weigh heavily: *His prison record militated against him.* **2.** *Obs.* **a.** to be a soldier. **b.** to fight for a belief. [1615–25; < L *mīlitātus* (ptp. of *mīlitāre* to serve as a soldier), equiv. to *mīlit-* (s. of *mīles*) soldier + *-ātus* -ATE[1]] **—mil′i•ta′tion,** *n.*
—Usage. See **mitigate.**

mi•li•tia (mi lish′ə), *n.* **1.** a body of citizens enrolled for military service, and called out periodically for drill but serving full time only in emergencies. **2.** a body of citizen soldiers as distinguished from professional soldiers. **3.** all able-bodied males considered by law eligible for military service. [1580–90; < L *mīlitia* soldiery, equiv. to *mīlit-* (s. of *mīles*) soldier + *-ia* -IA]

mi•li•tia•man (mi lish′ə mən), *n., pl.* **-men.** a person serving in the militia. [1770–80; MILITIA + -MAN]
—Usage. See **-man.**

mil•i•um (mil′ē əm), *n., pl.* **mil•i•a** (mil′ē ə). *Pathol.* a small white or yellowish nodule resembling a millet seed, produced in the skin by the retention of sebaceous secretion. [1350–1400; ME *mylium* < NL, L: millet]

milk (milk), *n.* **1.** an opaque white or bluish-white liquid secreted by the mammary glands of female mammals, serving for the nourishment of their young. **2.** this liquid as secreted by cows, goats, or certain other animals and used by humans for food or as a source of butter, cheeses, yogurt, etc. **3.** any liquid resembling this, as the liquid within a coconut, the juice or sap of certain plants, or various pharmaceutical preparations. **4. cry over spilled milk,** to lament what cannot be changed or corrected; express sorrow for past actions or events: *Crying over spilled milk will do you no good now.* —*v.t.* **5.** to press or draw milk from the udder or breast of. **6.** to extract something from as if by milking. **7.** to get something from; exploit: *The swindler milked her of all her savings.* **8.** to extract; draw out: *He's good at milking laughs from the audience.* —*v.i.* **9.** to yield milk, as a cow. **10.** to milk a cow or other mammal. [bef. 900; ME; OE *meol(o)c,* (Anglian) *milc;* c. G *Milch,* ON *mjǫlk,* Goth *miluks;* akin to L *mulgēre,* Gk *amélgein* to milk] **—milk′less,** *adj.*

milk′ ad′der. See **milk snake.**

milk′ bank′, a place for collection and storage of human milk for dispensing to those who require it, as for infants who are allergic to cows' milk and whose mothers' milk is unavailable. [1945–50]

milk′ bar′, a simple restaurant, often with an open front, or a counter or booth where milk drinks, sandwiches, etc., are sold. [1930–35]

milk′ bench′. See **water bench.**

milk′ choc′olate, **1.** chocolate that has been mixed with milk. **2.** a piece or bar of candy made of or coated with such chocolate. [1715–25]

milk′ cow′, **1.** a cow that is raised for its milk rather than for beef. **2.** *Informal.* a source of easily gained income; profitable venture: *The new subsidiary turns out to be a real milk cow.* [1400–50; late ME]

milk•er (mil′kər), *n.* **1.** a person or thing that milks. **2.** See **milking machine. 3.** a cow or other animal that gives milk. [1490–1500; MILK + -ER[1]]

milk′ fe′ver, **1.** *Pathol.* fever coinciding with the beginning of lactation, formerly believed to be due to lactation but really due to infection. **2.** *Vet. Pathol.* an acute disorder of calcium metabolism affecting dairy cows shortly after calving, causing somnolence and paralysis of the hind legs. [1750–60]

milk•fish (milk′fish′), *n., pl.* **-fish•es,** (*esp. collectively*) **-fish.** a herringlike fish, *Chanos chanos,* of warm ocean waters in southeastern Asia. [1875–80; MILK + FISH, so called from its color]

milk′ float′, *Brit.* a motor vehicle, usually battery powered, in which bottles or cartons of milk and other dairy products are delivered to homes by a daily or regular route. [1885–90]

milk′ glass′, an opaque white glass. [1870–75]

milk′ gra′vy, a gravy or sauce made from cooking fat, milk, flour, and seasonings. [1795–1805, *Amer.*]

milk′ing machine′, an electric machine for milking cows. Also called **milker.** [1890–95]

milk′ing par′lor, a room in or attached to a barn on a modern dairy farm maintained exclusively for the mechanical milking of cows. [1945–50]

milk′ing stool′, a low, usually three-legged stool with a flat seat in the shape of a half circle, used by a person when milking a cow. [1820–30]

milk′ leg′, *Pathol.* a painful swelling of the leg soon after childbirth, due to thrombosis of the large veins. [1895–1900]

milk•maid (milk′mād′), *n.* a woman who milks cows or is employed in a dairy; dairymaid. [1545–55; MILK + MAID]

milk•man (milk′man′), *n., pl.* **-men.** a person who sells or delivers milk. [1580–90; MILK + MAN[1]]
—Usage. See **-man.**

milk′ mush′room, any of the common latex-containing mushrooms of the genus *Lactarius.*

milk′ of al′monds. See **almond milk.** [1400–50; late ME]

milk′ of magne′sia, a milky white suspension in water of magnesium hydroxide, $Mg(OH)_2$, used as an antacid or laxative. [1875–80; formerly trademark]

milk′ pow′der. See **dry milk.** [1825–35]

milk′ punch′, a beverage containing milk and alcoholic liquor with sugar, flavoring, etc. [1695–1705]

milk′ run′, *Slang.* a routine trip or undertaking, esp. one presenting little danger or difficulty: *The flight from New York to Chicago was a milk run for the experienced pilot and crew.* [1940–45]

milk′ shake′, a frothy drink made of cold milk, flavoring, and usually ice cream, shaken together or blended in a mixer. Also, **milk′shake′.** [1885–90, *Amer.*]

milk•shed (milk′shed′), *n.* a region producing milk for a specific community: *the St. Louis milkshed.* [1925–30, *Amer.*; MILK + SHED[2], on the model of WATERSHED]

milk′ sick′ness, *Pathol.* a disease of humans, formerly common in some parts of the Middle West, caused by consuming milk from cattle that have been poisoned by eating certain kinds of snakeroot. [1815–25, *Amer.*]

milk′ snake′, any of numerous, usually brightly marked king snakes of the subspecies *Lampropeltis triangulum (doliata),* of North America. Also called **house snake, milk adder.** [1790–1800, *Amer.*; so called because they were said to suck milk from cows]

milk•sop (milk′sop′), *n.* a weak or ineffectual person. [1350–1400; ME. See MILK, SOP] **—milk′sop′ism,** *n.* **—milk′sop′py, milk′sop′ping,** *adj.*
—Syn. milquetoast, softy, namby-pamby, wimp.

milk′ sug′ar, lactose. [1840–50]

milk′ this′tle, lady's-thistle.

milk′ toast′, toast, usually buttered, served in hot milk with sugar or with salt and pepper. [1850–55, *Amer.*]

milk-toast (milk′tōst′), *adj.* **1.** easily dominated; extremely mild; ineffectual; namby-pamby; wishy-washy. —*n.* **2.** milquetoast. [1815–25]

milk′ tooth′, one of the temporary teeth of a mammal that are replaced by the permanent teeth. Also called **baby tooth, deciduous tooth.** [1720–30]

milk′ train′, *Informal.* a local train running through the early hours of the morning. [1850–55, *Amer.*]

milk′ vetch′, **1.** a European plant, *Astragalus glycyphyllos,* of the legume family, believed to increase the secretion of milk in goats. **2.** any herb of certain allied genera. [1590–1600]

milk•weed (milk′wēd′), *n.* **1.** any of several plants that secrete a milky juice or latex, esp. those of the genus *Asclepias,* as *A. syriaca.* Cf. **milkweed family. 2.** any of various other plants having a milky juice, as certain spurges. [1590–1600; MILK + WEED[1]]

milk′weed bee′tle, any of several small red, black-spotted elongated beetles of the genus *Tetraopes,* common in eastern North America, that inhabit the milkweed. [1835–45]

milk′weed bug′, any of several red and black lygaeid

bugs, as *Oncopeltus fasciatus,* that feed on the juice of the milkweed. [1900–05]

milk′weed but′terfly, See **monarch butterfly.** [1875–80, *Amer.*]

milk′weed fam′ily, the plant family Asclepiadaceae, characterized by herbaceous plants, shrubs, and vines having simple, opposite or whorled leaves, usually milky juice, umbellike clusters of small flowers, and long pods that split open to release tufted, airborne seeds, and including the anglepod, butterfly weed, milkweed, stephanotis, and wax plant.

milk′weed tor′toise bee′tle. See under **tortoise beetle.**

milk-white (milk′hwīt′, -wīt′), *adj.* of a white or slightly blue-white color, as that of milk. [bef. 1000; ME, OE]

milk•wood (milk′wo͝od′), *n.* any of various trees having a milky juice, as *Pseudomedia spuria,* of Jamaica. [1860–65; MILK + WOOD[1]]

milk•wort (milk′wûrt′, -wôrt′), *n.* **1.** any plant or shrub of the genus *Polygala,* formerly supposed to increase the secretion of milk. **2.** See **sea milkwort.** [1570–80; MILK + WORT[2]]

milk•y (mil′kē), *adj.,* **milk•i•er, milk•i•est. 1.** of or like milk, esp. in appearance or consistency. **2.** white or whitish in color. **3.** giving a good supply of milk. **4.** meek, tame, timid, or spiritless. [1350–1400; ME; see MILK, -Y[1]] **—milk′i•ly,** *adv.* **—milk′i•ness,** *n.*

Milk′y Way′, *Astron.* the spiral galaxy containing our solar system. With the naked eye it is observed as a faint luminous band stretching across the heavens, composed of innumerable stars, most of which are too distant to be seen individually. [1350–1400; ME, trans. of L *via lactea;* cf. GALAXY]

mill[1] (mil), *n.* **1.** a factory for certain kinds of manufacture, as paper, steel, or textiles. **2.** a building equipped with machinery for grinding grain into flour and other cereal products. **3.** a machine for grinding, crushing, or pulverizing any solid substance: *a coffee mill.* **4.** any of various machines that modify the shape or size of a workpiece by rotating tools or the work: *rolling mill.* **5.** any of various other apparatuses for shaping materials or performing other mechanical operations. **6.** a business or institution that dispenses products or services in an impersonal or mechanical manner, as if produced in a factory: *a divorce mill; a diploma mill.* **7.** *Mach.* a cutter on a milling machine. **8.** a steel roller for receiving and transferring an impressed design, as to a calico-printing cylinder or a banknote-printing plate. **9.** *Mining.* a place or set of machinery for crushing or concentrating ore. **10.** *Slang.* a boxing match or fistfight. **11. through the mill,** *Informal.* undergoing or having undergone severe difficulties, trials, etc., esp. with an effect on one's health, personality, or character: *He's really been through the mill since his wife's death.* —*v.t.* **12.** to grind, work, treat, or shape in or with a mill. **13.** *Coining.* **a.** to make a raised edge on (a coin or the like). **b.** to make narrow, radial grooves on the raised edge of (a coin or the like). **14.** to beat or stir, as to a froth: *to mill chocolate.* **15.** *Slang.* to beat or strike; fight; overcome. —*v.i.* **16.** to move around aimlessly, slowly, or confusedly, as a herd of cattle (often fol. by *about* or *around*). **17.** *Slang.* to fight or box. [bef. 950; ME *milne, mille* (n.), OE *myl(e)n* < LL *molīna,* n. use of fem. of *molīnus* of a mill, equiv. to L *mol(a)* mill + *-īnus* -INE[1]]
—Syn. 16. crowd, wander, roam, teem.

mill[2] (mil), *n.* a unit of monetary value equal to 0.001 of a U.S. dollar; one tenth of a cent: used at various times and places in the U.S. as a money of account, esp. in certain tax rates. [1785–95, *Amer.;* short for L *millēsimus* thousandth; see MIL]

Mill (mil), *n.* **1. James,** 1773–1836, English philosopher, historian, and economist, born in Scotland. **2.** his son **John Stuart,** 1806–73, English philosopher and economist.

mill., million.

mill•a•ble (mil′ə bəl), *adj.* capable of being milled: *millable wheat.* [1900–05; MILL[1] + -ABLE] **—mill′a•bil′i•ty,** *n.*

mill•age (mil′ij), *n.* the tax rate, as for property, assessed in mills per dollar.

Mil•lais (mi lā′), *n.* **Sir John Everett,** 1829–96, English painter.

Mil•lard (mil′ərd), *n.* a male given name.

Mil•lay (mi lā′), *n.* **Edna St. Vincent** (*Mrs. Eugen Jan Boissevain*), 1892–1950, U.S. poet.

mill•board (mil′bôrd′, -bōrd′), *n. Bookbinding.* a strong, thick pasteboard used to make book covers. [1705–15; MILL(ED) + BOARD]

Mill•brae (mil′brā), *n.* a city in W California, on San Francisco Bay. 20,058.

Mill•burn (mil′bərn), *n.* a township in NE New Jersey. 19,543.

Mill•bur•y (mil′ber′ē, -bə rē), *n.* a city in central Massachusetts. 11,808.

mill•cake (mil′kāk′), *n.* See **linseed cake.** [1830–40; MILL[1] + CAKE]

mill′ chis′el, a woodworking chisel having a blade more than 8 in. (20 cm) long. Also called **millwright chisel.**

mill′ construc′tion, heavy, fire-resistant timber construction within masonry walls, all vertical communication being within masonry towers provided with fire doors.

mill•dam (mil′dam′), *n.* a dam built in a stream to furnish a head of water for turning a mill wheel. [1150–1200; ME; see MILL[1], DAM[1]]

Mil•le•cent (mil′ə sənt), *n.* a female given name.

milled (mild), *v.* **1.** pt. and pp. of **mill**[1]. —*adj.* **2.** (of a coin) struck by a mill or press and usually finished with transverse ribs or grooves: *milled dimes and quarters.* **3.** ground or hulled in a mill: *milled wheat.* **4.** pressed flat by rolling: *milled board.* **5.** *Obs.* (of metal) polished by mechanical means: *a suit of milled armor.* [1615–25; MILL[1] + -ED[2]]

Mil•ledge•ville (mil′ij vil′), *n.* a city in central Georgia: state capital 1807–68. 12,176.

mille-feuille (mēl fœ′y(ə)), *n., pl.* **-feuilles** (-fœ′y(ə)). *French Cookery.* napoleon (def. 1). Also, **mille-feuille′.** [1890–95; < F, equiv. to *mille* thousand (< L; see MILLI-) + *feuille* leaf, sheet (< L *folia,* neut. pl. (taken as fem. sing.) of *folium*)]

mil•le•fi•o•ri (mil′ə fē ôr′ē, -ōr′ē), *n.* decorative glass made by fusing multicolored glass canes together, cutting them crosswise, joining them into new groups, embedding the groups in transparent glass, and blowing the resultant mass into a desired shape. Also, **mil′le•fi•o′re.** [1840–50; < It, equiv. to *mille* thousand (< L) + *fiori,* pl. of *fiore* < L *flōri-* (s. of *flōs*) FLOWER]

mille•fleur (mēl flûr′, -flo͞or′; *Fr.* mēl flœr′), *adj.* having a background sprinkled with representations of flowers, as certain tapestries or pieces of glasswork. [1905–10; < F *mille fleurs* lit., thousand flowers; cf. MILLEFIORI]

mil•le•nar•i•an (mil′ə nâr′ē ən), *adj.* **1.** of or pertaining to a thousand, esp. the thousand years of the prophesied millennium. **2.** of or pertaining to the millennium, esp. of Christian prophecy, or millennialism: *millenarian zeal.* —*n.* **3.** a believer in the coming of the millennium. [1545–55; MILLENARY + -AN]

mil•le•nar•y (mil′ə ner′ē), *adj., n., pl.* **-nar•ies.** —*adj.* **1.** consisting of or pertaining to a thousand, esp. a thousand years. **2.** pertaining to the millennium. —*n.* **3.** an aggregate of a thousand. **4.** millennium. **5.** millenarian. [1540–50; < LL *millēnārius* consisting of a thousand, equiv. to *millēn(ī)* a thousand each (L *mill(e)* thousand + *-ēnī* distributive suffix) + *-ārius* -ARY]

mil•len•ni•al (mi len′ē əl), *adj.* **1.** of or pertaining to a millennium or the millennium. **2.** worthy or suggestive of the millennium. [1655–65; MILLENNI(UM) + -AL[1]] **—mil•len′ni•al•ly,** *adv.*

Millen′nial Church′, the church of the Shakers.

mil•len•ni•al•ism (mi len′ē ə liz′əm), *n.* a belief in the millennium. Also called **mil•le•nar•i•an•ism** (mil′ə nâr′ē ə niz′əm). [1905–10; MILLENNIAL + -ISM] **—mil•len′ni•al•ist,** *n.*

mil•len•ni•um (mi len′ē əm), *n., pl.* **-ni•ums, -ni•a** (-nē ə). **1.** a period of 1000 years. **2. the millennium,** the period of a thousand years during which Christ will reign on earth. Rev. 20:1–7. **3.** a period of general righteousness and happiness, esp. in the indefinite future. **4.** a thousandth anniversary. [1630–40; < NL, equiv. to L *mill(e)* a thousand + *-ennium,* extracted from BIENNIUM, TRIENNIUM, etc.]

mil•le•pede (mil′ə pēd′), *n.* millipede.

mil•le•pore (mil′ə pôr′, -pōr′), *n.* a coralline hydrozoan of the genus *Millepora,* having a smooth calcareous surface with many perforations. [1745–55; < NL *millepora,* equiv. to *mille* thousand + *-pora* passage; see PORE[2]]

mill•er (mil′ər), *n.* **1.** a person who owns or operates a mill, esp. a mill that grinds grain into flour. **2.** See **milling machine. 3.** any moth, esp. of the family Noctuidae, having wings that appear powdery. [1325–75; ME *millere,* assimilated var. of *milnere,* equiv. to *milne* MILL[1] + *-ere* -ER[1]]

Mill•er (mil′ər), *n.* **1. Arthur,** born 1915, U.S. playwright and novelist. **2. Glenn,** 1904–44, U.S. dance bandleader and trombonist. **3. Henry,** 1891–1980, U.S. novelist. **4. Joa•quin** (wä kēn′), (*Cincinnatus Heine Miller*), 1841–1913, U.S. poet. **5. Joe** (*Joseph* or *Josias Miller*), 1684–1738, English actor, after whom *Joe Miller's Jestbook* was named. **6. William,** 1782–1849, U.S. religious leader: founder of the Adventist Church.

Mille•rand (mēl rän′), *n.* **A•le•xan•dre** (A lek sän′drə), 1859–1943, president of France 1920–24.

mill•er•bird (mil′ər bûrd′), *n.* a rare, small, gray-brown, thin-billed warbler, *Acrocephalus familiaris,* occurring only on the Hawaiian islet of Nihoa: the subspecies that inhabited the islet of Laysan is now extinct. [MILLER + BIRD]

Mill′er in′dex, *Crystall.* one of three integers giving the orientation and position of the face of a crystal in terms of the reciprocals, in lowest terms, of the intercepts of the face with each axis of the crystal. [1895–1900; named after W. H. *Miller* (1801–80), British mineralogist]

mill•er•ite (mil′ə rīt′), *n.* a mineral, nickel sulfide, NiS, occurring in slender, bronze-colored crystals: a minor ore of nickel. [1850–55; *Miller* (see MILLER INDEX) + -ITE[1]]

Mill•er•ite (mil′ə rīt′), *n.* a follower of William Miller, a U.S. preacher who taught that the Second Advent of Christ and the beginning of the millennium were to occur in 1843. [1835–45, *Amer.;* W. MILLER + -ITE[1]]

mill•er's-thumb (mil′ərz thum′), *n.* any of several small, freshwater sculpins of the genus *Cottus,* of Europe and North America. [1400–50; late ME *milneres thume;* the fish is so called from its thumblike head]

Mil•les (mil′əs), *n.* **Carl** (*Carl Wilhelm Emil Anderson*), 1875–1955, U.S. sculptor, born in Sweden.

mil•les•i•mal (mi les′ə məl), *adj.* **1.** thousandth. —*n.* **2.** a thousandth part. [1710–20; < L *millēsim(us)* thousandth (*mille* thousand + *-ēsimus* ordinal suffix) + -AL[1]] **—mil•les′i•mal•ly,** *adv.*

mil•let (mil′it), *n.* **1.** a cereal grass, *Setaria italica,* extensively cultivated in the East and in southern Europe for its small seed, or grain, used as food for humans and fowls, but in the U.S. grown chiefly for fodder. **2.** any of various related or similar grasses cultivated as grain plants or forage plants. **3.** the grain of any of these grasses. [1375–1425; late ME *milet* < MF, equiv. to *mil* (< L *milium* millet) + *-et* -ET]

Mil•let (mi lā′; *for 2 also Fr.* mē le′), *n.* **1. Francis Davis,** 1846–1912, U.S. painter, illustrator, and journalist. **2. Jean Fran•çois** (zhän fʀän swa′), 1814–75, French painter.

mill′ hole′, *Mining.* drawhole.

mill•house (mil′hous′), *n., pl.* **-hous•es** (-hou′ziz). a building that houses milling machinery, esp. of flour. [1250–1300; ME *milnehous;* see MILL[1], HOUSE]

milli-, a combining form meaning "thousand" (*millipede*): in the metric system, used in the names of units equal to one thousandth of the given base unit (*millimeter*). [< F < L, comb. form of *mille* thousand]

mil•li•am•me•ter (mil′ē am′mē′tər), *n.* an instrument for measuring small electric currents, calibrated in milliamperes. [1900–05; MILLIAM(PERE) + -METER]

mil•li•am•pere (mil′ē am′pēr, -am pēr′), *n. Elect.* a unit of electric current equal to one thousandth of an ampere. *Abbr.:* mA [1890–95; < F; see MILLI-, AMPERE]

mil•liard (mil′yərd, -yärd), *n. Brit.* one thousand millions; equivalent to U.S. billion. [1785–95; < F; see MILLI-, -ARD]

mil•li•ar•y (mil′ē er′ē), *adj.* **1.** of, pertaining to, or designating the ancient Roman mile of a thousand paces. **2.** marking a mile. [1600–10; < L *milliārius* comprising a thousand, a thousand paces long. See MILLI-, -ARY]

mil•li•bar (mil′ə bär′), *n.* a centimeter-gram-second unit of pressure equal to one thousandth of a bar or 1000 dynes per square centimeter, used to measure air pressure. *Abbr.:* mb [1905–10; MILLI- + BAR[3]]

mil•li•barn (mil′ə bärn′), *n.* one thousandth of a barn. *Abbr.:* mb [1950–55; MILLI- + BARN[2]]

Mil•li•cent (mil′ə sənt), *n.* a female given name: from Germanic words meaning "work" and "strong."

mil•li•cur•ie (mil′i kyo͝or′ē, -kyo͝o rē′), *n. Physics, Chem.* a unit of radioactivity equal to one thousandth of a curie; 3.70×10^7 disintegrations per second. *Abbr.:* mCi, mc [1905–10; MILLI- + CURIE]

mil•li•de•gree (mil′i di grē′), *n.* one thousandth of a degree. [1940–45; MILLI- + DEGREE]

Mil•lie (mil′ē), *n.* a female given name, form of **Millicent** or **Mildred.**

mil•lieme (mēl yem′, mē yem′), *n.* **1.** a cupronickel coin of Egypt and Sudan, the 1000th part of a pound or the 10th part of a piaster. **2.** a former coin and monetary unit of Libya, the 1000th part of a pound: replaced by the dirham. [1900–05; < F *millième* << L *millēsimus* thousandth, equiv. to *mille* thousand + *-ēsimus* ordinal suffix]

mil•li•e•quiv•a•lent (mil′ē i kwiv′ə lənt), *n.* a unit of measure, applied to electrolytes, that expresses the combining power of a substance. *Abbr.:* mEq [1925–30; MILLI- + EQUIVALENT]

mil•lier (mēl yā′), *n.* 1000 kilograms; a metric ton. [< F < L *milliārius.* See MILLI-, -IER[2]]

mil•li•far•ad (mil′ə far′əd, -ad), *n. Elect.* a unit of capacitance, equal to one thousandth of a farad. *Abbr.:* mF, mf [1960–65; MILLI- + FARAD]

mil•li•gal (mil′i gal′), *n.* a unit of acceleration, equal to one thousandth of a gal; one thousandth of a centimeter per second per second. *Abbr.:* mGal [1910–15; MILLI- + GAL[2]]

mil•li•gram (mil′i gram′), *n.* a unit of mass or weight equal to one thousandth of a gram, and equivalent to 0.0154 grain. *Abbr.:* mg Also, *esp. Brit.,* **mil′li•gramme′.** [1800–10; < F *milligramme.* See MILLI-, -GRAM[2]]

mil•li•gram-hour (mil′i gram′ou(ə)r′, -ou′ər), *n. Radiotherapy.* a unit of measure for a dose of radium expressed as the amount of radiation received by exposure to one milligram of radium for one hour.

mil•li•hen•ry (mil′ə hen′rē), *n., pl.* **-ries, -rys.** *Elect.* a unit of inductance equal to one thousandth of a henry. *Abbr.:* mH, mh [1905–10; MILLI- + HENRY]

Mil•li•kan (mil′i kən), *n.* **Robert Andrews,** 1868–1953, U.S. physicist: Nobel prize 1923.

mil•li•lam•bert (mil′ə lam′bərt), *n. Optics.* a unit of luminance equal to one thousandth of a lambert. *Abbr.:* mL [1915–20; MILLI- + LAMBERT]

mil•li•li•ter (mil′ə lē′tər), *n.* a unit of capacity equal to one thousandth of a liter, and equivalent to 0.033815 fluid ounce, or 0.061025 cubic inch. *Abbr.:* ml Also, *esp. Brit.,* **mil′li•li′tre.** [1800–10; < F *millilitre.* See MILLI-, LITER]

mil•li•lux (mil′ə luks′), *n. Optics.* a unit of illumination, equal to one thousandth of a lux. *Abbr.:* mlx [MILLI- + LUX]

mil•lime (mil′im, -ēm), *n.* an aluminum coin of Tunisia, the 1000th part of a dinar. [1970–75; appar. alter. of F *millième* thousandth]

mil•li•me•ter (mil′ə mē′tər), *n.* a unit of length equal to one thousandth of a meter and equivalent to 0.03937 inch. *Abbr.:* mm Also, *esp. Brit.,* **mil′li•me′tre.** [1800–10; < F *millimètre.* See MILLI-, METER[1]] **—mil•li•met•ric** (mil′ə me′trik), *adj.*

mil•li•mi•cron (mil′ə mī′kron), *n., pl.* **-crons, -cra** (-krə). a unit of length equal to one thousandth of a micron; one-billionth of a meter. *Symbol:* mμ Cf. **nanometer.** [1900–05; MILLI- + MICRON]

mil•li•mole (mil′ə mōl′), *n.* one thousandth of a mole. *Abbr.:* mM [1900–05; MILLI- + MOLE[4]]

CONCISE PRONUNCIATION KEY: act, cāpe, dâre, pärt; set, ēqual; *if,* īce; ox, ōver, ôrder, oil, bo͝ok, bo͞ot, out; up, ûrge; child; sing; shoe; thin, *th*at; zh as in *treasure.* ə = *a* as in *alone, e* as in *system, i* as in *easily, o* as in *gallop, u* as in *circus;* (ə) as in *fire* (fī(ə)r), *hour* (ou(ə)r). l and n can serve as syllabic consonants, as in *cradle* (krād′l), and *button* (but′n). See the full key inside the front cover.

mil•line (mil′līn′, mil līn′), *n.* **1.** one agate line of advertising one column in width appearing in one million copies of a periodical. **2.** Also called **mil′line rate′.** the charge or cost per milline. [MIL(LION) + LINE[1]]

mil•li•ner (mil′ə nər), *n.* a person who designs, makes, or sells hats for women. [1520–30; var. of obs. *Milaner* native of Milan, dealer in goods from Milan; see -ER[1]]

mil•li•ner•y (mil′ə ner′ē, -nə rē), *n.* **1.** women's hats and other articles made or sold by milliners. **2.** the business or trade of a milliner. [1670–80; MILLINER + -Y[3]]

mill•ing (mil′ing), *n.* **1.** an act or instance of subjecting something to the operation of a mill. **2.** an act or process of producing plane or shaped surfaces with a milling machine. **3.** *Coining.* **a.** an act or process of making a raised edge on a coin or the like. **b.** an act or process of making narrow, radial grooves on such a raised edge. **c.** a number of grooves so made. **4.** *Slang.* a beating or thrashing. [1425–75; late ME. See MILL[1], -ING[1]]

mill′ing machine′, a machine tool for rotating a cutter **(mill′ing cut′ter)** to produce plane or formed surfaces on a workpiece, usually by moving the work past the cutter. Also called **miller.** [1875–80]

Mil•ling•ton (mil′ing tən), *n.* a town in SW Tennessee. 20,236.

mil•lion (mil′yən), *n., pl.* **-lions,** (*as after a numeral*) **-lion,** *adj.* —*n.* **1.** a cardinal number, a thousand times one thousand. **2.** a symbol for this number, as 1,000,000 or M̄. **3. millions,** a number between 1,000,000 and 999,999,999, as in referring to an amount of money: *His fortune was in the millions of dollars.* **4.** the amount of a thousand thousand units of money, as pounds, dollars, or francs: *The three Dutch paintings fetched a million.* **5.** a very great number of times: *Thanks a million.* **6. the million** or **the millions,** the mass of the common people; the multitude: *poetry for the millions.* —*adj.* **7.** amounting to one million in number. **8.** amounting to a very great number: *a million things to do.* [1350–1400; ME *milioun* < MF < early It *millione,* equiv. to *mille* thousand (< L) + *-one* aug. suffix]

mil•lion•aire (mil′yə nâr′), *n.* **1.** a person whose wealth amounts to a million or more in some unit of currency, as dollars. **2.** any very rich person. Also, **mil′•lion•naire′.** [1820–30; < F *millionnaire,* equiv. to *million* MILLION + *-aire* -ARY] —**mil′lion•aire′dom,** *n.*

mil•lion•air•ess (mil′yə nâr′is), *n.* **1.** a woman who is a millionaire. **2.** the wife of a millionaire. [1880–85; MILLIONAIRE + -ESS]
—**Usage.** See **-ess.**

mil′lion elec′tron volts′, *Physics.* a unit of energy equal to the energy acquired by an electron in falling through a potential of 10^6 volts. *Abbr.:* MeV Also, **megaelectron volt.**

mil•lion•fold (mil′yən fōld′), *adj.* **1.** comprising a million parts or members. **2.** a million times as great or as much: *a millionfold increase.* —*adv.* **3.** in a millionfold measure. [1860–65; MILLION + -FOLD]

mil•lionth (mil′yənth), *adj.* **1.** coming last in a series of a million. **2.** being one of a million equal parts. —*n.* **3.** the millionth member of a series. **4.** a millionth part, esp. of one (1/1,000,000). [1665–75; MILLION + -TH[2]]

mil•li•pede (mil′ə pēd′), *n.* any terrestrial arthropod of the class Diplopoda, having a cylindrical body composed of 20 to more than 100 segments, each with two pairs of legs. Also, **millepede.** [1595–1605; < L *mīlipeda* (Pliny), equiv. to *mīli-* MILLI- + *-peda,* deriv. of *pēs,* s. *ped-* FOOT]

millipede, *Cambala annulata,* length 1 in. (2.5 cm)

mil•li•ra•di•an (mil′ə rā′dē ən), *n.* one thousandth of a radian. [1950–55; MILLI- + RADIAN]

mil•li•rem (mil′ə rem′), *n.* one thousandth of a rem. *Abbr.:* mrem [1950–55; MILLI- + REM]

mil•li•roent•gen (mil′ə rent′gən, -jən, -runt′-), *n.* a unit of radiation equal to one thousandth of a roentgen. *Abbr.:* mR, mr [1950–55; MILLI- + ROENTGEN]

mil•li•sec•ond (mil′ə sek′ənd), *n.* one thousandth of a second. *Abbr.:* msec [1905–10; MILLI- + SECOND[2]]

mil•li•volt (mil′ə vōlt′), *n. Elect.* a unit of electromotive force equal to one thousandth of a volt. *Abbr.:* mV, mv [1885–90; MILLI- + VOLT]

mil•li•watt (mil′ə wot′), *n.* a unit of power equal to one thousandth of a watt. *Abbr.:* mW [1910–15; MILLI- + WATT]

Mill′ on the Floss′, The, a novel (1860) by George Eliot.

mill•pond (mil′pond′), *n.* a pond for supplying water to drive a mill wheel. [1640–50; MILL[1] + POND]

mill•race (mil′rās′), *n.* **1.** the channel in which the current of water driving a mill wheel flows to the mill. **2.** the current itself. [1470–80; MILL[1] + RACE[1]]

mill•rind (mil′rīnd′, -rind), *n.* rind[2]. [1535–45; MILL[1] + RIND[2]]

mill-run (mil′run′), *adj.* coming directly from a mill, esp. without having been sorted: *mill-run carpets.* [1880–85, *Amer.*]

mill•run (mil′run′), *n.* **1.** millrace. **2.** a test of the mineral content or quality of a rock or ore consisting of the actual milling of a sample. **3.** the mineral obtained by means of this test. [1645–55; MILL[1] + RUN]

CONCISE ETYMOLOGY KEY: <, descended or borrowed from; >, whence; b., blend of, blended; c., cognate with; cf., compare; deriv., derivative; equiv., equivalent; imit., imitative; obl., oblique; r., replacing; s., stem; sp., spelling, spelled; resp., respelling, respelled; trans., translation; ?, origin unknown; *, unattested; ‡, probably earlier than. See the full key inside the front cover.

Mills (milz), *n.* **Robert,** 1781–1855, U.S. architect and engineer.

mill′ scale′, scale[1] (def. 6b). [1875–80]

Mills′ cross′, a type of radio telescope consisting of two arrays of antennas perpendicular to each other. [1960–65; after Bernard Y. *Mills* (born 1920), Australian astronomer]

Mills′ grenade′, *Mil.* a type of high-explosive grenade weighing about 1.5 lb. (0.7 kg). Also called **Mills′ bomb′.** [1915–20; named after Sir W. *Mills* (1856–1932), its English inventor]

mill•stone (mil′stōn′), *n.* **1.** either of a pair of circular stones between which grain or another substance is ground, as in a mill. **2.** anything that grinds or crushes. **3.** any heavy mental or emotional burden (often used in the phrase *a millstone around one's neck*). [bef. 1050; ME *milneston,* OE *mylenstān.* See MILL[1], STONE]

mill•stream (mil′strēm′), *n.* **1.** the stream in a millrace. **2.** millrace. [1805–15; MILL[1] + STREAM]

Mill′ Val′ley, a town in W California, NW of San Francisco. 12,967.

Mill•ville (mil′vil), *n.* a city in S New Jersey. 24,815.

mill′ wheel′, a wheel, esp. a waterwheel, for driving a mill. [bef. 1000; ME *myln whele,* OE *mylenhwēol.* See MILL[1], WHEEL]

mill•work (mil′wûrk′), *n.* **1.** ready-made carpentry work from a mill. **2.** work done in a mill. **3.** profiled or finished woodwork, as moldings or lattices. Also, **mill′ work′.** [1760–70; MILL[1] + WORK]

mill•wright (mil′rīt′), *n.* **1.** a person who erects the machinery of a mill. **2.** a person who designs and erects mills and mill machinery. **3.** a person who maintains and repairs machinery in a mill. [1350–1400; ME. See MILL[1], WRIGHT]

mill′wright chis′el. See **mill chisel.**

Mil•ly (mil′ē), *n.* a female given name, form of **Millicent** or **Mildred.**

Milne (miln), *n.* **A(lan) A(lexander),** 1882–1956, English novelist, playwright, and author of prose and verse for children.

Milne-Ed•wards (miln′ed′wərdz; *Fr.* mēl nā dwars′), *n.* **Hen•ri** (äN rē′), 1800–85, French zoologist.

Milne′ meth′od, *Math.* a numerical method, involving Simpson's rule, for solving a linear differential equation. [named after E. A. *Milne* (1896–1950), English astronomer and mathematician]

Mil•ner (mil′nər), *n.* **Alfred, 1st Viscount,** 1854–1925, British statesman and colonial administrator.

mi•lo (mī′lō), *n., pl.* **-los.** a grain sorghum having white, yellow, or pinkish seeds, grown chiefly in Africa, Asia, and the U.S. Also called **mi′lo maize′.** [1880–85, *Amer.*; of uncert. orig.]

Mi•lo (mī′lō; *for 1 also Gk.* mē′lô), *n.* **1.** Also, **Mi•los** (*Gk.* mē′lôs). Melos. **2.** a male given name.

mi•lord (mi lôrd′), *n.* an English nobleman or gentleman (usually used as a term of address). [1590–1600; < F < E phrase *my lord*]

Mi•losz (mē′losh; *Pol.* mē′wôsh), *n.* **Czes•law** (ches′lô; *Pol.* ches′wäf), born 1911, U.S. poet and novelist, born in Poland: Nobel prize 1980.

mil•pa (mil′pə), *n.* (in certain tropical regions) a tract of land cleared from the jungle, usually by burning, farmed for a few seasons, and then abandoned. [1835–45, *Amer.*; < MexSp < Nahuatl *milpan,* equiv. to *mil(li)* cultivated field + *-pan* locative suffix]

Mil•pi•tas (mil pē′təs), *n.* a town in W California. 37,820.

milque•toast (milk′tōst′), *n.* (*sometimes cap.*) a very timid, unassertive, spineless person, esp. one who is easily dominated or intimidated: *a milquetoast who's afraid to ask for a raise.* Also called **Caspar Milquetoast.** [1935–40, *Amer.*; after Caspar *Milquetoast,* a character in *The Timid Soul,* comic strip by H. T. Webster (1885–1952), American cartoonist]

M.I.L.R., Master of Industrial and Labor Relations.

mil•reis (mil′rās′; *Port.* mēl rāis′), *n., pl.* **-reis. 1.** a silver coin and former monetary unit of Brazil, equal to 1000 reis, discontinued in 1942. **2.** a gold coin and former monetary unit of Portugal, equal to 1000 reis, discontinued in 1910. [1580–90; < Pg: a thousand reis. See MILLI-, REIS]

milt (milt), *n.* **1.** the sperm-containing secretion of the testes of fishes. **2.** the testes and sperm ducts when filled with this secretion. **3.** melt[2]. [bef. 900; ME *milte, milt,* OE *milte* spleen; c. G *Milz,* MD *milte* milt, spleen; akin to MELT[2]]

milt•er (mil′tər), *n.* a male fish in breeding time. [1595–1605; MILT + -ER[1]]

Mil•ti•a•des (mil tī′ə dēz′), *n.* **1.** c540–488? B.C., Athenian general. **2.** Melchiades.

Mil•ton (mil′tn), *n.* **1. John,** 1608–74, English poet. **2.** a town in SE Ontario, in S Canada. 28,067. **3.** a town in E Massachusetts, near Boston. 25,860. **4.** a male given name: a family name taken from a placename meaning "mill town."

mil•to•ni•a (mil tō′nē ə), *n.* any of various epiphytic tropical American orchids of the genus *Miltonia,* having sprays of showy, flat, variously colored flowers. Also called **pansy orchid.** [< NL (1837), after Charles W. W. Fitzwilliam, Viscount *Milton* (1786–1857), English statesman and horticulturist; see -IA]

Mil•ton•ic (mil ton′ik), *adj.* **1.** of or pertaining to the poet Milton or his writings. **2.** resembling Milton's majestic style. Also, **Mil•to•ni•an** (mil tō′nē ən). [1700–10; MILTON + -IC]

Mil•town (mil′toun′), *Pharm., Trademark.* a brand of meprobamate.

Mil•wau•kee (mil wô′kē), *n.* a port in SE Wisconsin, on Lake Michigan. 636,212. —**Mil•wau′kee•an,** *n.*

Mil•wau•kie (mil wô′kē), *n.* a town in NW Oregon. 17,931.

Mi•lyu•kov (mil′yə kôf′, -kof′; *Russ.* myi lyōō kôf′), *n.* **Pa•vel Ni•ko•la•e•vich** (pä′vəl nik′ə lä′yə vich; *Russ.* pä′vyil nyi ku lä′yi vyich), 1859–1943, Russian statesman and historian.

mim (mim), *adj. Brit. Dial.* primly modest or demure. [1670–80; perh. b. MUM[1] and PRIM]

mīm (mēm), *n.* the twenty-fourth letter of the Arabic alphabet. [< Ar]

Mi•mam•sa (mē mäm′sä), *n. Hinduism.* a school of philosophy formed originally to explain the Vedas. [1780–90; < Skt *mīmāṃsā* inquiry, examination]

Mi•mas (mī′mas, mē′-), *n.* **1.** *Astron.* one of the moons of Saturn. **2.** *Class. Myth.* one of the Gigantes, killed by Hercules. **3.** *Rom. Legend.* a companion of Aeneas, killed by Mezentius.

Mim•ba (mim′bä), *n.* a female day name for Saturday. See under **day name.**

mim•bar (mim′bär), *n.* a pulpit in a mosque. [1810–20; < Ar *minbar*]

mime (mīm, mēm), *n., v.,* **mimed, mim•ing.** —*n.* **1.** the art or technique of portraying a character, mood, idea, or narration by gestures and bodily movements; pantomime. **2.** an actor who specializes in this art. **3.** an ancient Greek or Roman farce that depended for effect largely upon ludicrous actions and gestures. **4.** a player in such a farce. **5.** mimic (def. 4). **6.** a jester, clown, or comedian. —*v.t.* **7.** to mimic. **8.** to act in mime. —*v.i.* **9.** to play a part by mime or mimicry. [1610–20; < L *mīmus* < Gk *mîmos* imitator, mime, akin to *mimeîsthai* to copy, imitate] —**mim′er,** *n.*

mim•e•o (mim′ē ō′), *n., pl.* **mim•e•os,** *v.t. Informal.* mimeograph. [1940–45; by shortening]

mim•e•o•graph (mim′ē ə graf′, -gräf′), *n.* **1.** a printing machine with an ink-fed drum, around which a cut waxed stencil is placed and which rotates as successive sheets of paper are fed into it. **2.** a copy made from a mimeograph. —*v.t.* **3.** to duplicate (something) by means of a mimeograph. [formerly a trademark]

mi•me•sis (mi mē′sis, mī-), *n.* **1.** *Rhet.* imitation or reproduction of the supposed words of another, as in order to represent his or her character. **2.** *Biol.* imitation. **3.** *Zool.* mimicry. **4.** Also, **mimosis.** *Pathol.* **a.** the simulation, due to hysteria, of the symptoms of a disease. **b.** the simulation of the symptoms of one disease by another. [1640–50; < Gk *mī́mēsis* imitation, equiv. to *mīmē-* (var. s. of *mimeîsthai* to copy) + *-sis* -SIS]

mi•met•ic (mi met′ik, mī-), *adj.* **1.** characterized by, exhibiting, or of the nature of imitation or mimicry: *mimetic gestures.* **2.** mimic or make-believe. [1625–35; < Gk *mīmētikós* imitative, equiv. to *mīmē-* (see MIMESIS) + *-tikos* -TIC] —**mi•met′i•cal•ly,** *adv.*

mim•e•tism (mim′i tiz′əm, mī′mə-), *n.* mimicry (defs. 1, 3). [1880–85; MIMET(IC) + -ISM]

mim•e•tite (mim′i tīt′, mī′mi-), *n.* a mineral, lead chloroarsenate, $Pb_5As_3O_{12}Cl$, occurring in yellow to brown prismatic crystals or globular masses: a minor ore of lead. [1850–55; < Gk *mimēt(és)* imitator (equiv. to *mimē-* (see MIMESIS) + *-tēs* agent suffix) + -ITE[1]]

Mi•mi (mē′mē, mim′ē; *Fr.* mē mē′), *n.* a female given name.

mim•ic (mim′ik), *v.,* **-icked, -ick•ing,** *n., adj.* —*v.t.* **1.** to imitate or copy in action, speech, etc., often playfully or derisively. **2.** to imitate in a servile or unthinking way; ape. **3.** to be an imitation of; simulate; resemble closely. —*n.* **4.** a person who mimics, esp. a performer skilled in mimicking others. **5.** a copy or imitation of something. **6.** a performer in a mime. —*adj.* **7.** imitating or copying something, often on a smaller scale: *a mimic battle.* **8.** apt at or given to imitating; imitative; simulative. [1580–90; < L *mimicus* < Gk *mimikós.* See MIME, -IC] —**mim′ick•er,** *n.*
—**Syn. 1.** follow, mock; impersonate; simulate, counterfeit. **7.** mock, simulated.

mim•i•cal (mim′i kəl), *adj. Archaic.* mimic. [1595–1605; MIMIC + -AL[1]] —**mim′i•cal•ly,** *adv.*

mim•ic•ry (mim′ik rē), *n., pl.* **-ries. 1.** the act, practice, or art of mimicking. **2.** *Biol.* the close external resemblance of an organism, the mimic, to some different organism, the model, such that the mimic benefits from the mistaken identity, as seeming to be unpalatable or harmful. **3.** an instance, performance, or result of mimicking. [1680–90; MIMIC + -RY]

mi•mo•sa (mi mō′sə, -zə), *n.* **1.** any of numerous plants, shrubs, or trees belonging to the genus *Mimosa,* of the legume family, native to tropical or warm regions, having small flowers in globular heads or cylindrical spikes and often sensitive leaves. **2.** any of various similar or related plants, esp. of the genus *Acacia,* as the silver wattle, or *Albizzia,* as the silk tree. **3.** a cocktail of orange juice and champagne, usually in equal parts. [1695–1705; < NL, equiv. to L *mīm(us)* MIME + *-ōsa,* fem. of *-ōsus* -OSE[1]]

mim•o•sa•ceous (mim′ə sā′shəs, mī′mə-), *adj.* belonging to the Mimosaceae, now regarded as a subfamily (Mimosoideae) of the legume family. Cf. **legume family.** [< NL *Mimosac(ae)* name of the family (see MIMOSA, -ACEAE) + -OUS]

mi•mo•sis (mi mō′sis, mī′-), *n. Pathol.* mimesis (def. 4).

Mims (mimz), *n.* **Fort.** See **Fort Mims.**

min, minim; minims.

Min (min), *n.* a group of Chinese languages spoken in southeastern China, including Foochow and Fukienese.

min., 1. mineralogical. **2.** mineralogy. **3.** minim. **4.** minimum. **5.** mining. **6.** minor. **7.** minuscule. **8.** minute; minutes.

mi•na[1] (mī′nə), *n., pl.* **-nae** (-nē), **-nas.** an ancient unit of weight and value equal to the sixtieth part of a talent. [1570–80; < L < Gk *mnâ* < Sem; cf. Heb *māneh* mina]

mi•na[2] (mī′nə), *n.* myna.

min•a•ble (mī′nə bəl), *adj.* capable of being mined, esp. profitably. Also, **mineable.** [1560–70; MINE[2] + -ABLE]

mi•na•cious (mi nā′shəs), *adj.* menacing; threatening. [1650–60; < L *mināci-* (s. of *minax*) overhanging, threatening + -OUS] —**mi•na′cious•ly,** *adv.* —**mi•na′cious•ness, mi•nac•i•ty** (mi nas′i tē), *n.*

mi•nah[1] (mī′nə), *n.* myna.

mi•nah[2] (mē′nä), *n. Indian Archit.* a memorial tower, as a stamba. [< Hindi *minār,* apocopated var. of *minārā;* see MINARET]

Min•a•ma′ta disease′ (min′ə mä′tə), *Pathol.* a severe form of mercury poisoning, characterized by neurological degeneration. [after *Minamata* Bay, Japan, where fish containing alkyl mercury compounds caused the disease in those who ate them during the period 1953–58]

Mi•na•mo•to (mē′nä mô′tô), *n., pl.* **-to.** a member of a powerful family in Japan that ruled as shoguns from 1192 to 1333.

Mi•nang•ka•bau (mē′näng kə bou′), *n.* **1.** a member of an Indonesian people native to west-central Sumatra. **2.** the Austronesian language of these people.

min•a•ret (min′ə ret′, min′ə ret′), *n.* a lofty, often slender, tower or turret attached to a mosque, surrounded by or furnished with one or more balconies, from which the muezzin calls the people to prayer. [1675–85; < F *minaret,* Sp *minarete,* or It *minaretto* << Ar *manārah* lighthouse, perh. akin to *nār* fire] —**min′a•ret′ed,** *adj.*

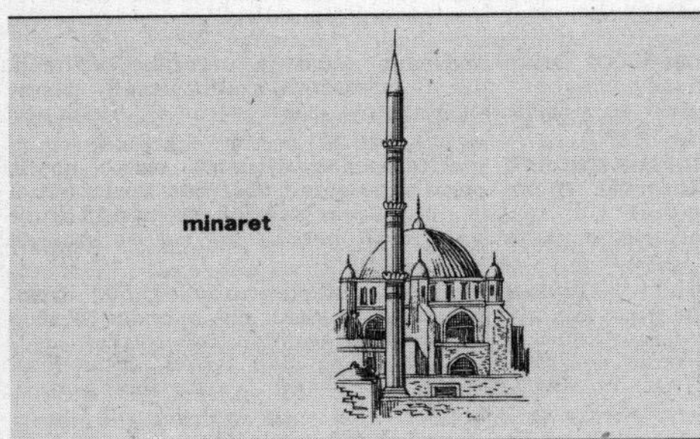

Mi′nas Ba′sin (mī′nəs), a bay in E Canada, the easternmost arm of the Bay of Fundy, in N Nova Scotia: noted for its high tides.

Mi•nas de Ri•o•tin•to (mē′näs the RE′ô tēn′tô), a town in SW Spain: copper mines. 7903.

Mi•nas Ge•rais (mē′nəs zhi RīS′), a state in E Brazil. 13,643,886; 224,701 sq. mi. (581,975 sq. km). *Cap.:* Belo Horizonte.

min•a•to•ry (min′ə tôr′ē, -tōr′ē), *adj.* menacing; threatening. Also, **min′a•to′ri•al.** [1525–35; < LL *minātōrius,* equiv. to L *mināt(ī)* to MENACE + *-tōrius* -TORY[1]] —**min′a•to′ri•ly,** *adv.*

min•au•dière (mē′nō dyâr′; *Fr.* mē nō dyeR′), *n., pl.* **-dieres** (-dyârz′; *Fr.* -dyeR′). a small, sometimes jeweled case for a woman's cosmetics or other personal objects, often carried as a handbag. Also, **min′au•diere′.** [1935–40 (earlier in sense "coquette"); < F *minaudière* orig., coquette, person with affected manners, n. use of fem. of *minaudier* affected, equiv. to *minaud(er)* to have an affected manner (v. deriv., with *-aud* adj. suffix (see RIBALD), of *mine* facial expression, prob. < Breton *min* muzzle) + *-ier* -IER[2]]

mince (mins), *v.,* **minced, minc•ing,** *n.* —*v.t.* **1.** to cut or chop into very small pieces. **2.** to soften, moderate, or weaken (one's words), esp. for the sake of decorum or courtesy. **3.** to perform or utter with affected elegance. **4.** to subdivide minutely, as land or a topic for study. —*v.i.* **5.** to walk or move with short, affectedly dainty steps. **6.** *Archaic.* to act or speak with affected elegance. **7. not mince words** or **matters,** to speak directly and frankly; be blunt or outspoken: *He was angry and didn't mince words.* —*n.* **8.** something cut up very small; mincemeat. [1350–1400; ME *mincen* < MF *minc(i)er* < VL **minūtiāre* to mince; see MINUTE[2]] —**minc′er,** *n.*

mince•meat (mins′mēt′), *n.* **1.** a mixture composed of minced apples, suet, and sometimes meat, together with raisins, currants, candied citron, etc., for filling a pie. **2.** anything cut up very small, esp. meat. **3. make mincemeat of,** to destroy utterly: *He made mincemeat of his opponent's charges.* [1655–65; MINCE + MEAT]

mince′ pie′, a pie filled with mincemeat. Also, **minced′ pie′.** [1590–1600]

Min•chah (*Seph.* mēn KHä′; *Ashk.* min′KHə), *n. Hebrew.* Minhah.

minc•ing (min′sing), *adj.* (of the gait, speech, behavior, etc.) affectedly dainty, nice, or elegant. [1520–30; MINCE + -ING[2]] —**minc′ing•ly,** *adv.*

mind (mīnd), *n.* **1.** (in a human or other conscious being) the element, part, substance, or process that reasons, thinks, feels, wills, perceives, judges, etc.: *the processes of the human mind.* **2.** *Psychol.* the totality of conscious and unconscious mental processes and activities. **3.** intellect or understanding, as distinguished from the faculties of feeling and willing; intelligence. **4.** a particular instance of the intellect or intelligence, as in a person. **5.** a person considered with reference to intellectual power: *the greatest minds of the twentieth century.* **6.** intellectual power or ability. **7.** reason, sanity, or sound mental condition: *to lose one's mind.* **8.** a way of thinking and feeling; disposition; temper: *a liberal mind.* **9.** a state of awareness or remembrance: *The poem puts me in mind of experiences both new and forgotten.* **10.** opinion, view, or sentiments: *to change one's mind.* **11.** inclination or desire: *to be of a mind to listen.* **12.** purpose, intention, or will: *Let me know your mind in this matter before Tuesday.* **13.** psychic or spiritual being, as opposed to matter. **14.** a conscious or intelligent agency or being: *an awareness of a mind ordering the universe.* **15.** remembrance or recollection; memory: *Former days were called to mind.* **16.** attention; thoughts: *He can't keep his mind on his studies.* **17.** *Chiefly South Midland and Southern U.S.* notice; attention: *When he's like that, just pay him no mind.* **18.** *Rom. Cath. Ch.* a commemoration of a person's death, esp. by a Requiem Mass. Cf. **month's mind, year's mind. 19.** (*cap.*) Also called **Divine Mind.** *Christian Science.* God; the incorporeal source of life, substance, and intelligence. Cf. **mortal mind. 20. bear** or **keep in mind,** to remember: *Bear in mind that the newspaper account may be in error.* **21. blow one's mind.** *Slang.* **a.** to change one's perceptions, awareness, etc., as through the use of drugs or narcotics. **b.** to overwhelm a person with intense excitement, pleasure, astonishment, or dismay: *Cool jazz really blows my mind.* **22. cross one's mind,** to occur suddenly to one: *A disturbing thought crossed her mind.* **23. give someone a piece of one's mind,** *Informal.* to rebuke, reprimand, or scold sharply: *I'll give him a piece of my mind for telling such a lie!* **24. have a good mind to,** to feel tempted or inclined to: *I have a good mind to leave you here all alone.* **25. have half a mind to,** to be almost decided to; be inclined to. **26. know one's own mind,** to be firm in one's intentions, opinions, or plans; have assurance: *She may be only a child, but she knows her own mind.* **27. make up one's mind,** to decide; form an opinion or decision; resolve: *He couldn't make up his mind which course to follow.* **28. meeting of minds,** complete agreement; accord: *A meeting of minds between the union and the employer seemed impossible.* **29. on one's mind,** constantly in one's thoughts; of concern to one: *The approaching trial was on his mind.* **30. out of one's mind, a.** mad; insane: *You must be out of your mind to say such a ridiculous thing.* **b.** totally distracted: *He's out of his mind with worry.* **c.** emotionally overwhelmed: *out of her mind with joy.* **31. presence of mind,** ability to think and to remain in control of oneself during a crisis or under stress: *She had enough presence of mind to remember the license plate of the speeding car.*
—*v.t.* **32.** to pay attention to. **33.** to heed or obey (a person, advice, instructions, etc.). **34.** to apply oneself or attend to: *to mind one's own business.* **35.** to look after; take care of; tend: *to mind the baby.* **36.** to be careful, cautious, or wary about: *Mind what you say.* **37.** to feel concern at; care about. **38.** to feel disturbed or inconvenienced by; object to (usually used in negative or interrogative constructions): *Would you mind handing me that book?* **39.** to regard as concerning oneself or as mattering: *Don't mind his bluntness.* **40.** *Dial.* **a.** to perceive or notice. **b.** to remember. **c.** to remind.
—*v.i.* **41.** to pay attention. **42.** to obey. **43.** to take notice, observe, or understand (used chiefly in the imperative): *Mind now, I want you home by twelve.* **44.** to be careful or wary. **45.** to care, feel concern, or object (often used in negative or interrogative constructions): *Mind if I go? Don't mind if I do.* **46.** to regard a thing as concerning oneself or as mattering: *You mustn't mind about their gossiping.* **47. never mind,** don't worry or be troubled; it is of no concern: *Never mind—the broken glass will be easy to replace.* [bef. 900; (n.) ME *mynd(e),* aph. var. (see Y-) of *imynd,* OE *gemynd* memory, remembrance, mind; c. Goth *gamunds;* akin to L *mēns* mind, Gk *manía* madness; (v.) ME *minden,* deriv. of the n.]
—**Syn. 1.** reason. MIND, INTELLECT, INTELLIGENCE refer to mental equipment or qualities. MIND is that part of a human being that thinks, feels, and wills, as contrasted with body: *His mind was capable of grasping the significance of the problem.* INTELLECT is reasoning power as distinguished from feeling; it is often used in a general sense to characterize high mental ability: *to appeal to the intellect, rather than the emotions.* INTELLIGENCE is ability to learn and to understand; it is also mental alertness or quickness of understanding: *A dog has more intelligence than many other animals.* **6.** MIND, BRAIN, BRAINS may refer to mental capacity. MIND is the philosophical and general term for the center of mental activity, and is therefore used of intellectual powers: *a brilliant mind.* BRAIN is properly the physiological term for the organic structure that makes mental activity possible (*The brain is the center of the nervous system.*), but it is often applied, like mind, to intellectual capacity: *a fertile brain.* BRAINS is the anatomical word (*the brains of an animal used for food*), but, in popular usage, it is applied to intelligence (particularly of a shrewd, practical nature): *To run a business takes brains.* **10.** bent, leaning, proclivity, penchant; wish, liking. **11.** intent. **33.** mark.

mind-al•ter•ing (mīnd′ôl′tər ing), *adj.* causing marked changes in patterns of mood and behavior, as a hallucinogenic drug.

Min•da•na•o (min′də nä′ō, -nou′; *Sp.* mēn′dä nou′), *n.* the second largest island of the Philippines, in the S part of the group. 10,908,730; 36,537 sq. mi. (94,631 sq. km).

Min′dana′o Deep′, an area in the Pacific Ocean W of the Philippines: one of deepest points in any ocean. 34,440 ft. (10,497 m).

mind′ bend′er, *Slang.* **1.** mindblower. **2.** a person or thing that radically and suddenly affects one's thinking, perceptions, psyche, etc. [1960–65]

mind-bend•ing (mīnd′ben′ding), *adj. Slang.* mind-blowing. [1960–65] —**mind′-bend′ing•ly,** *adv.*

mind•blow•er (mīnd′blō′ər), *n. Slang.* **1.** a hallucinogenic drug. **2.** something that astounds, excites, or dismays: *The news of the loss of the cargo ships was a real mindblower.* [1965–70; MIND + BLOW[2] + -ER[1]]

mind-blow•ing (mīnd′blō′ing), *adj. Slang.* **1.** overwhelming; astounding: *Spending a week in the jungle was a mind-blowing experience.* **2.** producing a hallucinogenic effect: *a mind-blowing drug.* [1965–70]

mind′-bod′y prob′lem (mīnd′bod′ē), *Philos.* the problem of explaining the relation of the mind to the body. [1920–25]

mind-bog•gling (mīnd′bog′ling), *adj. Slang.* **1.** intellectually overwhelming: *a mind-boggling puzzle.* **2.** emotionally or psychologically overwhelming; mind-blowing. [1960–65] —**mind′-bog′gling•ly,** *adv.*

M.Ind.E., Master of Industrial Engineering.

mind•ed (mīn′did), *adj.* **1.** having a certain kind of mind (usually used in combination): *strong-minded.* **2.** inclined or disposed. [1495–1505; MIND + -ED[3]]

Min•den (min′dən), *n.* a city in NW Louisiana. 15,074.

mind•er (mīn′dər), *n.* **1.** *Chiefly Brit.* a person who looks after something (usually used in combination): *a baby-minder.* **2.** *Brit.* See **foster child.** [1400–50; late ME: one who remembers. See MIND, -ER[1]]

mind-ex•pand•ing (mīnd′ik span′ding), *adj.* heightening perceptions in a hallucinatory way: *mind-expanding drugs.* [1960–65]

mind•ful (mīnd′fəl), *adj.* attentive, aware, or careful (usually fol. by *of*): *mindful of one's responsibilities.* [1375–1425; late ME *mindeful.* See MIND, -FUL] —**mind′ful•ly,** *adv.* —**mind′ful•ness,** *n.*
—**Syn.** heedful, thoughtful, regardful.

mind•less (mīnd′lis), *adj.* **1.** without intelligence; senseless: *a mindless creature.* **2.** unmindful or heedless: *mindless of all dangers.* [bef. 1000; ME *myndles,* OE *gemyndlēas.* See MIND, -LESS] —**mind′less•ly,** *adv.* —**mind′less•ness,** *n.*

Min•do•ro (min dôr′ō, -dōr′ō; *Sp.* mēn dô′Rô), *n.* a central island of the Philippines. 669,369; 3922 sq. mi. (10,158 sq. km).

mind′ read′er, a person professing the ability of mind reading, esp. as a professional entertainer. [1885–90]

mind′ read′ing, **1.** the ability to discern the thoughts of others without the normal means of communication, esp. by means of a preternatural power. **2.** an act or the practice of so discerning the thoughts of another. [1880–85]

mind-set (mīnd′set′), *n.* **1.** an attitude, disposition, or mood. **2.** an intention or inclination. [1925–30]

mind's′ eye′, the hypothetical site of visual recollection or imagination: *In her mind's eye she saw the city as it had been in Caesar's time.* [1375–1425; late ME]

Mind•szen•ty (mind′sen tē), *n.* **Joseph** (*Joseph Pehm*), 1892–1975, Hungarian Roman Catholic clergyman: primate of Hungary 1945–74.

mind-your-own-busi•ness (mīnd′yər ōn biz′nis), *n.* baby's-tears.

mine[1] (mīn), *pron.* **1.** a form of the possessive case of *I* used as a predicate adjective: *The yellow sweater is mine.* **2.** something that belongs to me: *Mine is the red car.* **3.** *Archaic.* my (used before a word beginning with a vowel or a silent *h,* or following a noun): *mine eyes; lady mine.* [bef. 900; ME; OE *mīn* MY; c. ON *mīn,* G *mein,* Goth *meina;* see ME]

mine[2] (mīn), *n., v.,* **mined, min•ing.** —*n.* **1.** an excavation made in the earth for the purpose of extracting ores, coal, precious stones, etc. **2.** a place where such minerals may be obtained, either by excavation or by washing the soil. **3.** a natural deposit of such minerals. **4.** an abundant source; store: *a mine of information.* **5.** a device containing a charge of explosive in a watertight casing, floating on or moored beneath the surface of the water for the purpose of blowing up an enemy ship that strikes it or passes close by it. **6.** a similar device used on land against personnel or vehicles; land mine. **7.** a subterranean passage made to extend under an enemy's works or position, as for the purpose of securing access or of depositing explosives for blowing up a military position. **8.** a passageway in the parenchyma of a leaf, made by certain insects. —*v.i.* **9.** to dig in the earth for the purpose of extracting ores, coal, etc.; make a mine. **10.** to extract coal, ore, or the like, from a mine. **11.** to make subterranean passages. **12.** to place or lay mines, as in military or naval operations. —*v.t.* **13.** to dig in (earth, rock, etc.) in order to obtain ores, coal, etc. **14.** to extract (ore, coal, etc.) from a mine. **15.** to avail oneself of or draw useful or valuable material from: *to mine every reference book available in writing the term paper.* **16.** to use, esp. a natural resource: *to mine the nation's forests.* **17.** to make subterranean passages in or under; burrow. **18.** to make (passages, tunnels, etc.) by digging or burrowing. **19.** to dig away or remove the foundations of. **20.** to place or lay military or naval mines under: *to mine an enemy supply road.* **21.** *Agric.* to grow crops in (soil) over an extended time without fertilizing. **22.** to remove (a natural resource) from its source without attempting to replenish it. [1275–1325; 1875–80 for def. 5; (v.) ME *minen* < OF *miner* (c. Pr, Sp *minar,* It *minare*) < VL **mināre,* prob. < a Celtic base **mein-;* cf. MIr *méin,* Welsh *mwyn* ore, mineral; (n.) ME < MF, perh. n. deriv. of *miner;* cf. ML *mina* mine, mineral]
—**Syn. 4.** supply, stock, fund, hoard.

Min.E., Mineral Engineer.

mine•a•ble (mī′nə bəl), *adj.* minable. [1560–70; MINE[2] + -ABLE]

mine′ detec′tor, an electromagnetic device for locating buried or concealed land mines. [1940–45]

mine′ exam′iner, an official who inspects a mine to ensure compliance with safety requirements. Cf. **fire boss.**

mine•field (mīn′fēld′), *n. Mil., Naval.* an area of land or water throughout which explosive mines have been laid. [1885–90; MINE[2] + FIELD]

mine•lay•er (mīn′lā′ər), *n.* a naval ship equipped for

CONCISE PRONUNCIATION KEY: act, cāpe, dâre, pärt; set, ēqual; *if,* ice; ox, ōver, ôrder, oil, bŏŏk, bōōt; out; up, ûrge; child; sing; shoe; thin, *that;* zh as in *treasure.* ə = a as in *alone,* e as in *system,* i as in *easily,* o as in *gallop,* u as in *circus;* ᵊ as in *fire* (fīᵊr), *hour* (ouᵊr). l and n can serve as syllabic consonants, as in *cradle* (krād′l), and *button* (but′n). See the full key inside the front cover.

laying mines in the water. [1905–10; MINE[2] + LAY[1] + -ER[1]]

Min•e•o•la (min′ē ō′lə), *n.* a village on W Long Island, in SE New York. 20,757.

min•er (mī′nər), *n.* **1.** Also called **mineworker.** a person who works in a mine, esp. a commercial mine producing coal or metallic ores. **2.** a mechanical device used in mining: *a miner for extracting ores from the ocean floor.* **3.** any of several Australian birds of the genus *Manorina,* feeding on honey and typically having a loud call. **4.** any of various insect larvae that create tunnels in the parenchyma of leaves. **5.** (formerly) a person who places or lays military or naval mines. [1225–75; MINE[2] + -ER[1]; r. ME *minour* < AF (see -OR[2])]

min•er•al (min′ər əl, min′rəl), *n.* **1.** any of a class of substances occurring in nature, usually comprising inorganic substances, as quartz or feldspar, of definite chemical composition and usually of definite crystal structure, but sometimes also including rocks formed by these substances as well as certain natural products of organic origin, as asphalt or coal. **2.** a substance obtained by mining, as ore. **3.** (loosely) any substance that is neither animal nor vegetable. **4. minerals,** *Brit.* See **mineral water. 5.** *Nutrition.* any of the inorganic elements, as calcium, iron, magnesium, potassium, or sodium, that are essential to the functioning of the human body and are obtained from foods. **—*adj.* 6.** of the nature of a mineral; pertaining to a mineral or minerals. **7.** containing or impregnated with a mineral or minerals. **8.** neither animal nor vegetable; inorganic: *mineral matter.* [1375–1425; late ME < MF, OF *mineral* < ML *minerāle* (n.), *minerālis* (adj.), equiv. to *miner(a)* mine, ore (< OF *miniere* < VL **mināria; min-* (see MINE[2]) + L *-āria* -ARY) + *-āle, -ālis* -AL[1]]

mineral., **1.** mineralogical. **2.** mineralogy.

min′eral char′coal, a fibrous substance resembling charcoal and having a high carbon content, often occurring in thin layers in bituminous coal. Also called **mother of coal.** [1795–1805]

min•er•al•ize (min′ər ə līz′, min′rə-), *v.,* **-ized, -iz•ing.** **—*v.t.* 1.** to convert into a mineral substance. **2.** to transform (a metal) into an ore. **3.** to impregnate or supply with mineral substances. **—*v.i.* 4.** to study or collect the minerals of a region. Also, *esp. Brit.,* **min′er•al•ise′.** [1645–55; MINERAL + -IZE] **—min′er•al•i•za′•tion,** *n.* **—min′er•al•iz′er,** *n.*

min′eral jel′ly, *Chem.* a gelatinous product made from petroleum, used to stabilize certain explosives. [1900–05]

min′eral king′dom, minerals collectively. Cf. **animal kingdom, plant kingdom.** [1685–95]

min•er•al•o•cor•ti•coid (min′ər ə lō kôr′ti koid′), *n.* **1.** *Biochem.* any of a group of corticosteroid hormones, synthesized by the adrenal cortex, that regulate the excretion or reabsorption of sodium and potassium by the kidneys, salivary glands, and sweat glands. **2.** *Pharm.* any of various natural or synthetic drugs having mineralocorticoid activity. [1945–50; MINERAL + -O- + CORTIC(O)- + -OID]

min•er•al•o•gy (min′ə rol′ə jē, -ral′ə-), *n.* the science or study of minerals. [1680–90; MINERA(L) + -LOGY] **—min•er•al•og•i•cal** (min′ər ə loj′i kəl), **min′er•al•og′ic,** *adj.* **—min′er•al•og′i•cal•ly,** *adv.* **—min′er•al′o•gist,** *n.*

min•er•al•oid (min′ər ə loid′), *n.* a mineral substance that does not have a definite chemical formula or crystal form. [1910–15; MINERAL + -OID]

min′eral oil′, a colorless, oily, almost tasteless, water-insoluble liquid, usually of either a standard light density (**light mineral oil**) or a standard heavy density (**heavy mineral oil**), consisting of mixtures of hydrocarbons obtained from petroleum by distillation: used chiefly as a lubricant, in the manufacture of cosmetics, and in medicine as a laxative. Also called **liquid petrolatum.** [1795–1805]

min′eral pitch′, asphalt. [1790–1800]

min′eral spir′its, a volatile distillation product of petroleum, used as a thinner for paints and varnishes. Cf. **naphtha** (def. 1). [1885–90]

min′eral spring′, a spring of water that contains a significant amount of dissolved minerals. [1775–85]

min′eral tar′, bitumen of the consistency of tar; maltha. [1790–1800]

min′eral wa′ter, **1.** water containing dissolved mineral salts or gases, esp. such water considered healthful to drink. **2. mineral waters,** *Brit.* **a.** carbonated water; soda water. **b.** artificially flavored, bottled soft drinks; soda pop. [1555–65]

min′eral wax′, ozocerite. [1860–65]

Min′eral Wells′, a city in N central Texas. 14,468.

min′eral wool′, a woollike material for heat and sound insulation, made by blowing steam or air through molten slag or rock. Also called **rock wool.** [1880–85]

min′er's ane′mia, *Pathol.* hookworm (def. 2). [1895–1900]

min′er's di′al, *Mining, Survey.* dial (def. 6).

min′er's inch′, a unit of measure of water flow, varying with locality but often a flow equaling 1.5 cu. ft. (0.04 m^3) per minute. [1865–70, *Amer.*]

min′er's let′tuce. See **winter purslane.** [1915–20, *Amer.*]

Mi•ner•va (mi nûr′və), *n.* **1.** the ancient Roman goddess of wisdom and the arts, identified with the Greek goddess Athena. **2.** a woman of great wisdom. **3.** a female given name.

min•e•stro•ne (min′ə strō′nē; *It.* mē′ne strô′ne), *n.* *Italian Cookery.* a thick vegetable soup, often containing herbs, beans, bits of pasta, etc., and served with Parmesan cheese. [1890–95; < It, equiv. to *minestr(a)* kind of soup (lit., something served; see MINISTER) + *-one* aug. suffix]

mine•sweep•er (mīn′swē′pər), *n. Navy.* a specially equipped ship used for dragging a body of water in order to remove or destroy enemy mines. [1900–05; MINE[2] + SWEEPER] **—mine′sweep′ing,** *n.*

mi•nette (mi net′), *n. Petrol.* a syenitic lamprophyre composed chiefly of orthoclase and biotite. [1875–80; < G < F; see MINE[2], -ETTE]

min•e•ver (min′ə vər), *n.* miniver.

mine•work•er (mīn′wûr′kər), *n.* miner. Also, **mine′ work′er.** [1900–05; MINE[2] + WORKER]

Ming (ming), *n. Wade-Giles, Pinyin.* **1.** a dynasty in China, 1368–1644, marked by the restoration of traditional institutions and the development of the arts, esp. in porcelain, textiles, and painting. **—*adj.* 2.** of or pertaining to the Ming dynasty or to the art objects and forms developed during this period. **3.** noting the fine porcelains produced in the Ming dynasty, esp. those produced by the imperial factory before 1620, noted for their brilliant, fine colors, chiefly underglaze or enamel on glaze, on a body of high quality.

min•gle (ming′gəl), *v.,* **-gled, -gling,** *n.* **—*v.i.* 1.** to become mixed, blended, or united. **2.** to associate or mix in company: *She refuses to mingle with bigots.* **3.** to associate or take part with others; participate. **—*v.t.* 4.** to mix or combine; put together in a mixture; blend. **5.** to unite, join, or conjoin. **6.** to associate in company: *a hostess who mingles diplomats with executives.* **7.** to form by mixing; compound; concoct. **—*n.* 8. mingles,** two or more single, unrelated adults who live together. [1425–75; late ME *menglen,* equiv. to *meng(en)* to mix (OE *mengan;* c. D, G *mengen*) + *-(e)len* -LE] **—min′gle•ment,** *n.* **—min′gler,** *n.*
—Syn. 4. commingle, intermingle, intermix. See **mix.**

min•gle-man•gle (ming′gəl mang′gəl), *n.* a jumbled or confused mixture; hodgepodge. [1540–50; gradational compound; see MINGLE, MANGLE[1]]

Min•gre•li•an (min grē′lē ən, ming-), *n.* a South Caucasian language spoken near the extreme eastern end of the Black Sea.

ming′ tree′ (ming), **1.** any of various trees or shrubs used in bonsai arrangements, esp. when shaped to have flat-topped, asymmetrical branches. **2.** an artificial tree created with plant material, wire, etc., to resemble such a bonsai tree. [1945–50; perh. named after MING]

Min•gus (ming′gəs), *n.* **Charles** (*Charlie*), 1922–79, U.S. jazz bass player and composer.

min•gy (min′jē), *adj.,* **-gi•er, -gi•est.** mean and stingy; niggardly. [1885–90; M(EAN[2]) + (ST)INGY[1]]

min•hag (*Seph.* mēn häg′; *Ashk.* min′häg), *n., pl.* ***min•ha•gim*** (*Seph.* mēn hä gēm′; *Ashk.* min hä′gim). *Hebrew.* a custom or procedure among Jews that is so firmly established as to have almost the binding force of law. [*minhāgh* custom] **—min•ha′gic,** *adj.*

Min•hah (Seph. mēn KHä′; *Ashk.* min′KHə), *n. Hebrew.* the daily Jewish religious service conducted in the afternoon. Also, ***Minchah.*** Cf. ***Maariv, Shaharith.*** [*minḥāh*]

Mi•nho (mē′nyo͞o), *n.* a river in SW Europe, flowing SSW from NW Spain along the N boundary of Portugal into the Atlantic. 171 mi. (275 km) long. Spanish, **Miño.**

Min•how (min′hō′), *n. Older Spelling.* former name of **Fuzhou.**

min•i (min′ē), *n.* **1.** miniskirt. **2.** a minicomputer. **3.** anything of a small, reduced, or miniature size. **—*adj.* 4.** of the length of a miniskirt. [independent use of MINI-, or by shortening of words with MINI- as initial element]

mini-, a combining form with the meanings "of a small or reduced size in comparison with others of its kind" (*minicalculator; minicar; minigun*); "limited in scope, intensity, or duration" (*miniboom; minicourse; minirecession*); (of clothing) "short, not reaching the knee" (*minidress; miniskirt*). [by shortening of MINIATURE, MINIMAL, or MINIMUM]
—Note. The list at the bottom of this page provides the spelling, syllabification, and stress for words whose meanings may be easily inferred by combining the meaning of MINI- and an attached base word, or base word plus a suffix. Appropriate parts of speech are also shown. Words prefixed by MINI- that have special meanings or uses are entered in their proper alphabetical places in the main vocabulary or as derived forms run on at the end of a main vocabulary entry.

min•i•ate (min′ē āt′), *v.t.,* **-at•ed, -at•ing.** to illuminate (a manuscript) in red; rubricate. [1650–60; < ML *miniātus* rubricated, illuminated, L: colored red with cinnabar, equiv. to *mini(um)* MINIUM + *-ātus* -ATE[1]] **—min′i•a′tor,** *n.*

min•i•a•ture (min′ē ə chər, -cho͝or′, min′ə chər), *n.* **1.** a representation or image of something on a small or reduced scale. **2.** a greatly reduced or abridged form or copy. **3.** a very small painting, esp. a portrait, on ivory, vellum, or the like. **4.** the art of executing such a painting. **5.** an illumination in an illuminated manuscript or book. **6. in miniature,** in a reduced size; on a small scale: *The zoo exhibition offered a jungle in miniature.* **—*adj.* 7.** being, on, or represented on a small scale; reduced. [1580–90; < It *miniatura* miniature painting < ML *miniātūra,* equiv. to *miniāt(us)* (see MINIATE) + *-ūra* -URE; sense development perh. influenced by L base *min-* (see MINI-, MINOR)]
—Syn. 7. minute, microscopic, diminutive, tiny, minuscule.

min′iature bull′ ter′rier, one of an English breed of small muscular dogs resembling a smaller version of a standard bull terrier, with a short, flat, harsh coat of glossy white or white with brindle patches.

min′iature cam′era, *Photog.* a small camera using film that is 35 millimeters wide or less. Also called **minicam.** [1920–25]

min′iature golf′, a game or amusement modeled on golf and played with a putter and golf ball, in which each very short, grassless "hole" constitutes an obstacle course, consisting of wooden alleys, tunnels, bridges, etc., through which the ball must be driven to hole it. Also called **midget golf.** [1910–15]

min′iature photog′raphy, photography with a camera using film that is 35 millimeters wide or less. [1955–60]

min′iature pin′scher, one of a German breed of toy dogs resembling a smaller version of the Doberman pinscher, having a flat skull, a smooth coat, erect ears, and a docked tail, bred originally as a watchdog. [1925–30]

min′iature schnau′zer, one of a German breed of sturdily built terriers resembling a smaller version of the standard schnauzer, having a wiry, pepper-and-salt, black, or black-and-silver coat, a rectangular head, bushy whiskers, and a docked tail, and originally developed as a farm dog but now raised primarily as a pet. [1925–30]

min•i•a•tur•ist (min′ē ə chər ist, min′ə chər-), *n.* **1.** an artist whose specialty is small, discrete works. **2.** a person who makes, collects, or specializes in miniature objects: *a miniaturist with a collection of dollhouses.* [1850–55; MINIATURE + -IST]

min•i•a•tur•ize (min′ē ə chə rīz′, min′ə-), *v.t.,* **-ized, -iz•ing.** to make in extremely small size in order to keep volume or weight to a minimum: *to miniaturize electronic equipment.* Also, *esp. Brit.,* **min′i•a•tur•ise′.** [1945–50; MINIATURE + -IZE] **—min′i•a•tur•i•za′tion,** *n.*

min•i•bike (min′ē bīk′), *n.* a small, lightweight motorcycle with a low frame and designed generally for off-highway use. Also called **minicycle.** [1960–65; MINI- + BIKE[1]] **—min′i•bik′er,** *n.*

min•i•blind (min′ē blīnd′), *n.* a venetian blind with narrow slats. [MINI- + BLIND]

min•i•bus (min′ē bus′), *n.* a small bus, seating about 15 passengers and typically transporting people short distances. Also called **microbus.** [1840–50; MINI- + BUS[1]; the 19th-century word, meaning "small carriage," perh. MINI(MUM) + (OMNI)BUS]

min•i•cab (min′ē kab′), *n. Chiefly Brit.* a minicar that serves as a taxicab. [1955–60; MINI- + CAB[1]]

min•i•cam (min′ē kam′), *n.* **1.** *Television.* a lightweight, hand-held television camera. **2.** *Photog.* See **miniature camera.** Also, **min•i•cam•er•a** (min′ē kam′ər ə, -kam′rə). [1935–40; MINI(ATURE) or MINI- + CAM(ERA)]

min•i•car (min′ē kär′), *n.* a very small car, esp. a subcompact. [1945–50, in sense "miniature car"; MINI- + CAR[1]]

min•i•cas•sette (min′ē kə set′), *n.* a small cassette enclosing a length of audiotape for use with a pocket-size tape recorder, esp. one used for dictating. Cf. **cassette, microcassette.** [MINI- + CASSETTE]

min•i•coach (min′ē kōch′), *n.* a small bus or buslike van. [MINI- + COACH]

min•i•com•po•nent (min′ē kəm pō′nənt), *n.* a hi-fi component considerably smaller than a standard-size component and larger than a microcomponent. [MINI- + COMPONENT]

min•i•com•put•er (min′ē kəm pyo͞o′tər), *n.* a computer with processing and storage capabilities smaller than those of a mainframe but larger than those of a microcomputer, used by small businesses, in manufacturing processes, in scientific research, etc. [1965–70; MINI- + COMPUTER]

Min•i•con•jou (min′i kon′jo͞o), *n., pl.* **-jous,** (*esp. collectively*) **-jou.** a member of a North American Indian people belonging to the Teton branch of the Dakota Indians and originally inhabiting parts of Wyoming, South Dakota, and Nebraska.

min•i•con•ven•tion (min′ē kən ven′shən), *n.* a small-scale or preliminary convention, esp. a political convention prior to a larger or national convention. [MINI- + CONVENTION]

Min′i•coy Is′land (min′i koi′), a small island in the S Laccadive Islands, off the SW coast of India. 1.25 sq. mi. (3.24 sq. km).

min•i•cy•cle (min′ē sī′kəl), *n.* minibike. [MINI- + (BI)CYCLE]

Min′ié ball′ (min′ē, min′ē ā′; *Fr.* mē nyā′), a conical bullet with a hollow base that expanded when fired, used in the 19th century. [1855–60; named after C. E. *Minié* (1814–79), French officer who invented it]

min•i•fy (min′ə fī′), *v.t.,* **-fied, -fy•ing. 1.** to make

CONCISE ETYMOLOGY KEY: <, descended or borrowed from; >, whence; b., blend of, blended; c., cognate with; cf., compare; deriv., derivative; equiv., equivalent; imit., imitative; obl., oblique; r., replacing; s., stem; sp., spelling, spelled; resp., respelling, respelled; trans., translation; ?, origin unknown; *, unattested; ‡, probably earlier than. See the full key inside the front cover.

min′i•bib′li•og′ra•phy, *n., pl.* **-phies.**
min′i•cal′cu•la′tor, *n.*
min′i•cir′cuit, *n.*
min′i•cit′y, *n., pl.* **-cit•ies.**
min′i•con′do, *n., pl.* **-dos.**
min′i•con′do•min′i•um, *n.*
min′i•con•glom′er•ate, *n.*
min′i•cy′clone, *n.*
min′i•de•pres′sion, *n.*
min′i•de•val′u•a′tion, *n.*
min′i•dra′ma, *n.*
min′i•farm′, *n.*
min′i•home′, *n.*
min′i•hos′pi•tal, *n.*
min′i•in′dus•try, *n., pl.* **-tries.**
min•i-LP, *n., pl.* **-LPs, -LP's.**
min′i•mel′o•dra′ma, *n.*
min′i•na′tion, *n.*
min′i•op′er•a, *n.*
min′i•pool′, *n.*
min′i•rac′er, *n.*
min′i•re•ces′sion, *n.*
min′i•scan′dal, *n.*
min′i•sum′mit, *n.*
min′i•tour′, *n.*
min′i•train′, *n.*
min′i•va•ca′tion, *n.*
min′i•ware′house′, *n.*

less. **2.** to minimize. [1670–80; < L *min(us)* less + -IFY, modeled on *magnify*] **—min′i·fi·ca′tion,** *n.*

Min·i·gun (min′ē gun′), *n.* a U.S. aircraft machine gun consisting of a rotating cluster of six barrels using 7.62mm ammunition and capable of variable rates of fire of up to 6000 rounds per minute.

min·i·kin (min′i kin), *n.* **1.** a person or object that is delicate, dainty, or diminutive. **2.** a printing type (about 3½ point). *—adj.* **3.** delicate, dainty, or mincing. [1535–45; < MD *minneken* friend, lover, equiv. to *minne* love + *-ken* -KIN]

min·i·lab (min′ē lab′), *n.* a small business that develops film and makes prints quickly, often using computerized equipment. Also, **min′i-lab′.** [MINI- + LAB]

min·i·lap·a·rot·o·my (min′ē lap′ə rot′ə mē), *n., pl.* **-mies.** *Surg.* laparotomy with a small incision into the abdomen, often no more than 1 in. (2.5 cm), used esp. for tubal ligation. [MINI- + LAPAROTOMY]

min·im (min′əm), *n.* **1.** the smallest unit of liquid measure, ¹⁄₆₀ of a fluid dram, roughly equivalent to one drop. *Abbr.:* min, min.; *Symbol:* M, ♏ **2.** *Music.* a note, formerly the shortest in use, but now equivalent in time value to one half of a semibreve; half note. See illus. under **note. 3.** the least quantity of anything. **4.** something very small or insignificant. **5.** (*cap.*) a member of a mendicant religious order founded in the 15th century by St. Francis of Paola. *—adj.* **6.** smallest. **7.** very small. [1400–50; late ME < ML, L *minimus*; as musical term, < ML (*nota*) *minima*; see MINIMUM]

min·i·ma (min′ə mə), *n.* a pl. of **minimum.**

min·i·mal (min′ə məl), *adj.* **1.** constituting a minimum: *a minimal mode of transportation.* **2.** barely adequate or the least possible: *minimal care.* [1660–70; MINIM(UM) + -AL[1]] **—min′i·mal·ly,** *adv.*
—Syn. 2. nominal, minimum.

min′imal art′, a chiefly American style in painting and sculpture that developed in the 1960's largely in reaction against abstract expressionism, shunning illusion, decorativeness, and emotional subjectivity in favor of impersonality, simplification of form, and the use of often massive, industrially produced materials for sculpture, and extended its influence to architecture, design, dance, theater, and music. Also, **Min′imal Art′.** Also called **minimalism, rejective art.** [1965]

min·i·mal·ism (min′ə mə liz′əm), *n.* (*sometimes cap.*) **1.** *Music.* a reductive style or school of modern music utilizing only simple sonorities, rhythms, and patterns, with minimal embellishment or orchestrational complexity, and characterized by protracted repetition of figurations, obsessive structural rigor, and often a pulsing, hypnotic effect. **2.** See **minimal art.** [1965–70; MINIMAL + -ISM]

min·i·mal·ist (min′ə mə list), *n.* **1.** a person who favors a moderate approach to the achievement of a set of goals or who holds minimal expectations for the success of a program. **2.** a practitioner of minimalism in music or art. *—adj.* **3.** of, pertaining to, or characteristic of minimalism. **4.** being or offering no more than what is required or essential: *a minimalist program for tax reform.* [1905–10; in political use < F *minimaliste* (see MINIMAL, -IST), trans. of Russ *men'shevík* MENSHEVIK; subsequent uses perh. recoinage with MINIMAL, -IST]

min·i·mal·ize (min′ə mə līz′), *v.t.,* **-ized, -iz·ing.** to make minimal: *to minimalize tax increases.* Also, *esp. Brit.,* **min′i·mal·ise′.** [MINIMAL + -IZE] **—min′i·mal·i·za′tion,** *n.*

min′imal pair′, *Ling.* a pair of words, as *pin* and *bin,* or *bet* and *bed,* differing only by one sound in the same position in each word, esp. when such a pair is taken as evidence for the existence of a phonemic contrast between the two sounds. [1940–45]

min·i·mar·ket (min′ē mär′kit), *n.* a grocery store or delicatessen. [1960–65; MINI- + MARKET]

min·i·mart (min′ē märt′), *n.* a minimarket. [MINI- + MART[1]]

min·i·max (min′ə maks′), *n.* a strategy of game theory employed to minimize a player's maximum possible loss. Cf. **maximin.** [1940–45; MINI(MUM) + MAX(IMUM)]

min·i·mill (min′ē mil′), *n.* a small mill or manufacturing plant, esp. a steel plant that utilizes electric furnaces to melt down scrap for producing its products. [1970–75; MINI- + MILL[1]]

min·i·mize (min′ə mīz′), *v.t.,* **-mized, -miz·ing. 1.** to reduce to the smallest possible amount or degree. **2.** to represent at the lowest possible amount, value, importance, influence, etc., esp. in a disparaging way; belittle. Also, *esp. Brit.,* **min′i·mise′.** [1795–1805; MINIM(UM) + -IZE] **—min′i·mi·za′tion,** *n.* **—min′i·miz′er,** *n.*

min·i·mum (min′ə məm), *n., pl.* **-mums, -ma** (-mə), *adj.* *—n.* **1.** the least quantity or amount possible, assignable, allowable, or the like. **2.** the lowest speed permitted on a highway. **3.** the lowest amount, value, or degree attained or recorded. **4.** an arbitrary amount set by a restaurant, nightclub, etc., as the least amount to be charged each person for food and drink. Cf. **cover charge. 5.** *Math.* **a.** Also called **relative minimum, local minimum.** the value of a function at a certain point in its domain, which is less than or equal to the values at all other points in the immediate vicinity of the point. Cf. **absolute minimum. b.** the point in the domain at which a minimum occurs. *—adj.* **6.** noting or indicating a minimum. **7.** least possible: *minimum risk.* **8.** lowest: *a minimum rate.* **9.** pertaining to a minimum or minimums. [1655–65; < L, neut. of *minimus* smallest, least. See MINOR]

min′i·mum-ac′cess pro′gramming (min′ə məm-ak′ses), *Computers.* a method of programming in which latency is reduced to a minimum. Also called **forced coding, min′i·mum-la′ten·cy pro′gramming** (min′ə-məm lāt′n sē), **optimum programming.**

min′imum lend′ing rate′, the official interest rate charged by the Bank of England and below which it will refrain from lending money.

min·i·mum-se·cu·ri·ty (min′ə məm si kyŏŏr′i tē), *adj.* (of a prison) designed for prisoners regarded as being less dangerous; having fewer restrictions. [1960–65]

min′imum thermom′eter, a thermometer designed to show the lowest temperature recorded between resettings. Cf. **maximum thermometer.** [1855–60]

min′imum till′age, no-tillage. Also, **min′imum-till′, min′imum till′.** [1975–80]

min′imum wage′, the lowest wage payable to employees in general or to designated employees as fixed by law or by union agreement. [1855–60]

min·i·mum-wage (min′ə məm wāj′), *adj.* **1.** of or pertaining to a minimum wage: *minimum-wage demands.* **2.** paid or earning a minimum wage: *a minimum-wage worker.* **3.** paying a minimum wage: *a minimum-wage job.*

min·i·mus (min′ə məs), *n., pl.* **-mi** (-mī′). **1.** a creature or being that is the smallest or least significant. **2.** *Anat.* the little finger or toe. [1580–90; < NL, L: lit., smallest]

min·ing (mī′ning), *n.* **1.** the act, process, or industry of extracting ores, coal, etc., from mines. **2.** the laying of explosive mines. [1250–1300; ME: undermining (walls in an attack); see MINE[2], -ING[1]]

Mining Eng., Mining Engineer.

min′ing engineer′ing, the branch of engineering dealing with the location and appraisal of mineral deposits and the laying out, equipment, and management of mines. **—min′ing engineer′.**

min′ing geol′ogy, geology applied to the exploitation of mineral deposits. [1905–10]

min·i·nuke (min′ē nōōk′, -nyōōk′), *n. Informal.* a low-powered nuclear device. [1970–75; MINI- + NUKE]

min·ion (min′yən), *n.* **1.** a servile follower or subordinate of a person in power. **2.** a favored or highly regarded person. **3.** a minor official. **4.** *Print.* a 7-point type. *—adj.* **5.** dainty; elegant; trim; pretty. [1490–1500; < MF *mignon,* for OF *mignot* dainty < ?]

min′ion of the law′, a policeman.

min·i·park (min′ē pärk′), *n.* See **pocket park.** [1965–70; MINI- + PARK]

min·i·pig (min′ē pig′), *n.* a breed of miniature pig developed for use in research laboratories. [1950–55; MINI- + PIG[1]]

min·i·pill (min′ē pil′), *n. Pharm.* an oral birth control pill that contains only a progestin and is to be taken daily without monthly cessation. [1965–70; MINI- + PILL[1]]

min·i·re·cord·er (min′ē ri kôr′dər), *n.* a small tape recorder, using minicassettes. [MINI- + RECORDER]

min·is·cule (min′ə skyōōl′), *adj.* minuscule.
—Usage. See **minuscule.**

min·i·se·ries (min′ē sēr′ēz), *n., pl.* **-ries. 1.** a short series of events or presentations. **2.** *Television.* a program or film broadcast in parts, as the dramatization of a literary work: *The novel was made into a four-part miniseries.* [1970–75; MINI- + SERIES]

min·ish (min′ish), *v.t., v.i. Archaic.* to diminish or lessen. [1300–50; late ME, var. (assimilated to -ISH[2]) of *menuse* < MF *menu(i)sier* < VL **minūtiāre* to lessen. See MINUTE[2], MINCE]

min·i·ski (min′ē skē′), *n., pl.* **-skis, -ski. 1.** a short ski used by a beginner. **2.** a very short ski worn by a skibobber for balance. Also, **min′i-ski′.** [1965–70; MINI- + SKI]

min·i·skirt (min′ē skûrt′), *n.* a very short skirt or skirt part, as of a coat or dress, ending several inches above the knee. Also called **mini.** [1960–65; MINI(ATURE) + SKIRT] **—min′i·skirt′ed,** *adj.*

min·i·state (min′ē stāt′), *n.* a small, independent nation. Also, **min′i-state′.** Also called **microstate.** [1965–70; MINI- + STATE]

min·is·ter (min′ə stər), *n.* **1.** a person authorized to conduct religious worship; member of the clergy; pastor. **2.** a person authorized to administer sacraments, as at Mass. **3.** a person appointed by or under the authority of a sovereign or head of a government to some high office of state, esp. to that of head of an administrative department: *the minister of finance.* **4.** a diplomatic representative accredited by one government to another and ranking next below an ambassador. Cf. **envoy**[1] (def. 1). **5.** a person acting as the agent or instrument of another. *—v.t.* **6.** to administer or apply: *to minister the last rites.* **7.** *Archaic.* to furnish; supply. *—v.i.* **8.** to perform the functions of a religious minister. **9.** to give service, care, or aid; attend, as to wants or necessities.: *to minister to the needs of the hungry.* **10.** to contribute, as to comfort or happiness. [1250–1300; (n.) ME *ministre, minister* (< OF *ministre*)< L *minister* servant, equiv. to *minis-* (var. of *minus* a lesser amount; akin to *minor* MINOR) + *-ter* n. suffix; r. ME *menistre* < OF < L, as above; (v.) ME *ministren* < OF *ministrer* < L *ministrāre* to act as a servant, attend, deriv. of *minister*]
—Syn. 9. answer, tend, oblige.

min·is·te·ri·al (min′ə stēr′ē əl), *adj.* **1.** pertaining to the ministry of religion, or to a minister or other member of the clergy. **2.** pertaining to a ministry or minister of state. **3.** pertaining to or invested with delegated executive authority. **4.** of ministry or service. **5.** serving as an instrument or means; instrumental. [1555–65; < LL *ministeriālis,* equiv. to L *ministeri(um)* MINISTRY + *-ālis* -AL[1]] **—min′is·te′ri·al·ly,** *adv.*

min·is·te·ri·um (min′ə stēr′ē əm), *n.* (*sometimes cap.*) an organization of local ministers or religious leaders who work with other community leaders on social or educational programs. [1855–60; < L; see MINISTRY]

min′ister plenipoten′tiary, plenipotentiary. [1635–45]

min′ister res′ident, *pl.* **ministers resident.** a diplomatic agent serving in a minor country and ranking next below an ambassador. [1840–50, *Amer.*]

min′ister without′ portfo′lio, *pl.* **ministers without portfolios.** a minister of state who is not appointed to any specific department in a government. [1910–15]

min·is·trant (min′ə strənt), *adj.* **1.** ministering. *—n.* **2.** a person who ministers. [1660–70; < L *ministrant-* (s. of *ministrāns*), prp. of *ministrāre* to serve. See MINISTER, -ANT]

min·is·tra·tion (min′ə strā′shən), *n.* **1.** the act of ministering care, aid, religious service, etc. **2.** an instance of this. [1300–50; ME *ministracioun* < L *ministrātiōn-* (s. of *ministrātiō*) service, equiv. to *ministrāt(us)* (ptp. of *ministrāre* to serve; see MINISTER) + *-iōn* -ION] **—min′is·tra′tive,** *adj.*

min·is·try (min′ə strē), *n., pl.* **-tries. 1.** the service, functions, or profession of a minister of religion. **2.** the body or class of ministers of religion; clergy. **3.** the service, function, or office of a minister of state. **4.** the body of ministers of state. **5.** (*usually cap.*) any of the administrative governmental departments of certain countries usually under the direction of a minister of state. **6.** (*usually cap.*) the building that houses such an administrative department. **7.** the term of office of a minister of state. **8.** an act or instance of ministering; ministration; service. **9.** something that serves as an agency, instrument, or means. [1175–1225; ME < L *ministerium,* equiv. to *minister* MINISTER + *-ium* -IUM]

min·i·sub (min′ē sub′), *n.* a small submarine, holding only one or a few persons, used in naval operations, underwater exploration, or conducting underwater experiments. [1955–60; MINI- + SUB]

min·i·track (min′i trak′), *n.* a system for tracking satellites, space vehicles, or rockets by means of radio waves. [1955–60; MINI(ATURE) + TRACK]

min·i·um (min′ē əm), *n.* See **red lead.** [1350–1400; ME < L: cinnabar, red lead]

Min·i-Vac (min′ē vak′), *Trademark.* a brand of minivacuum. [by shortening]

min·i·vac·u·um (min′ē vak′yōō əm, -yōōm), *n.* a small, hand-held vacuum cleaner, as for vacuuming upholstered furniture or car seats, or other relatively small areas. [MINI- + VACUUM]

min·i·van (min′ē van′), *n.* a small passenger van, somewhat larger than a station wagon, typically with side or rear windows and rear seats that can be removed for hauling small loads. Also, **min′i-van′.** [MINI- + VAN[2]]

min·i·ver (min′ə vər), *n.* **1.** (in the Middle Ages) a fur of white or spotted white and gray used for linings and trimmings. Cf. **vair** (def. 1). **2.** any white fur, particularly that of the ermine, used esp. on robes of state. Also, **minever.** [1250–1300; ME *meniver* < MF *menu vair* small VAIR; see MENU]

min·i·vet (min′ə vet′), *n.* any of several small, long-tailed Asian cuckoo-shrikes of the genus *Pericrocotus,* having in the male black and red and in the female black and orange plumage. [1860–65; orig. uncert.]

mink (mingk), *n., pl.* **minks,** (*esp. collectively*) **mink. 1.** a semiaquatic weasellike animal of the genus *Mustela,* esp. the North American *M. vison.* **2.** the fur of this animal, brownish in the natural state and having lustrous outside hairs and a thick, soft undercoat. **3.** a coat, stole, etc., made of this fur. [1425–75; late ME, of uncert. orig.]

mink, *Mustela vison,* head and body 15 in. (38 cm); tail to 9 in. (23 cm)

min·ke (ming′kē), *n.* a dark-colored baleen whale, *Baleanoptera acutorostrata,* inhabiting temperate and polar seas and growing to a length of 33 ft. (10 m): reduced in numbers. Also called **min′ke whale′, lesser rorqual.** [1930–35; < Norw *minkehval,* allegedly after a crew member of the Norwegian whaling pioneer Svend Foyn (1809–94), named *Meincke,* who mistook a pod of minkes for blue whales]

Min·kow·ski (ming kôf′skē, -kof′-), *n.* **Her·mann** (hûr′mən; *Ger.* hɛʀ′män), 1864–1909, German mathematician.

Minkow′ski world′, *Math.* a four-dimensional space in which the fourth coordinate is time and in which a single event is represented as a point. Also called **Minkow′ski u′niverse.** [named after H. MINKOWSKI]

Minn., Minnesota.

Min·na (min′ə), *n.* a female given name.

Min·ne·ap·o·lis (min′ē ap′ə lis), *n.* a city in SE Minnesota, on the Mississippi. 370,951. **—Min·ne·a·pol·i·tan** (min′ē ə pol′i tn), *n.*

min·ne·o·la (min′ē ō′lə), *n.* a juicy, pear-shaped variety of tangelo.

min·ne·sing·er (min′ə sing′ər), *n.* one of a class of German lyric poets and singers of the 12th, 13th, and 14th centuries. [1815–25; < G, equiv. to *Minne* love + *Singer* singer]

Min·ne·so·ta (min′ə sō′tə), *n.* **1.** a state in the N central United States. 4,077,148; 84,068 sq. mi. (217,735 sq. km). *Cap.:* St. Paul. *Abbr.:* MN (for use with zip code), Minn. **2.** a river flowing SE from the W border of Minnesota into the Mississippi near St. Paul. 332 mi. (535 km) long. **—Min′ne·so′tan,** *adj., n.*

Minneso′ta Multipha′sic Personal′ity In′·ventory, *Psychol.* a widely used test designed to identify configurations of personality traits in normal persons and to study the personality patterns occurring in various types of mental illness. *Abbr.:* MMPI [1940–45; after the University of *Minnesota,* where it was developed]

Min·ne·ton·ka (min′i tong′kə), *n.* a city in E Minnesota, near Minneapolis. 38,688.

Min·ne·wit (min′yoo͞ it, -ə wit), *n.* **Peter.** See **Minuit, Peter.**

Min·ni (min′ē), *n., pl.* **-nis,** (*esp. collectively*) **-ni. 1.** an ancient people of Asia Minor. **2.** Mannai.

min·nie (min′ē), *n. Scot. and North Eng. Informal.* mother; mom. Also, **minny.** [pet var. of MITHER]

Min·nie (min′ē), *n.* a female given name, form of **Mary.**

min·now (min′ō), *n., pl.* (*esp. referring to two or more kinds or species*) **-nows,** (*esp. collectively, Rare*) **-now** for 1, 2, 3. **1.** a small, European cyprinoid fish, *Phoxinus phoxinus.* **2.** any other fish of the family Cyprinidae, including the carps, goldfishes, and daces. **3.** any of various unrelated, small fishes. **4.** a person or thing that is comparatively small or insignificant. [1325–75; ME *minwe,* OE **mynwe* (fem.) for *myne* (masc.); c. OHG *munewa* kind of fish]

min·ny[1] (min′ē), *n., pl.* **-nies.** *Chiefly Inland North and North Midland U.S.* minnow. [perh. **min* (OE *myne* minnow) + -Y[2]]

min·ny[2] (min′ē), *n., pl.* **-nies.** *Scot. and North Eng.* minnie.

Mi·ño (mē′nyô), *n.* Minho.

Mi·no·an (mi nō′ən, mī-), *adj.* **1.** of or pertaining to the ancient civilization of the island of Crete, dating from about 3000 to 1100 B.C. **—*n.* 2.** a native or inhabitant of ancient Crete. [1890–95; MINO(S) + -AN]

min·o·cy·cline (min′ō sī′klēn, -klin) *n. Pharm.* a long-acting, broad-spectrum, semisynthetic antibiotic drug, $C_{23}H_{27}N_3O_7$, derived from tetracycline. [(A)MINO- + (*deoxytetra*)*cycline,* a chemical component; see DEOXY-, TETRACYCLINE]

mi·nor (mī′nər), *adj.* **1.** lesser, as in size, extent, or importance, or being or noting the lesser of two: *a minor share.* **2.** not serious, important, etc.: *a minor wound; a minor role.* **3.** having low rank, status, position, etc.: *a minor official.* **4.** under the legal age of full responsibility. **5.** *Educ.* of or pertaining to a field of study constituting a student's minor. **6.** *Music.* **a.** (of an interval) smaller by a chromatic half step than the corresponding major interval. **b.** (of a chord) having a minor third between the root and the note next above it. **7.** of or pertaining to the minority. **8.** (*cap.*) (of two male students in an English public school who have the same surname) being the younger or lower in standing: *Jackson Minor sits over here.* **—*n.* 9.** a person under the legal age of full responsibility. **10.** a person of inferior rank or importance in a specified group, class, etc. **11.** *Educ.* **a.** a subject or a course of study pursued by a student, esp. a candidate for a degree, subordinately or supplementarily to a major or principal subject or course. **b.** a subject for which less credit than a major is granted in college or, occasionally, in high school. **12.** *Music.* a minor interval, chord, scale, etc. **13.** *Math.* the determinant of the matrix formed by crossing out the row and column containing a given element in a matrix. **14.** (*cap.*) See **Friar Minor. 15. the minors,** *Sports.* the minor leagues. **—*v.i.* 16.** to choose or study as a secondary academic subject or course: *to major in sociology and minor in art history.* [1250–1300; ME < L: smaller, less; akin to OE *min* small, ON *minni* smaller, Goth *minniza* younger, Skt *mīnāti* (he) diminishes, destroys]
—Syn. 1. smaller, inferior, secondary, subordinate. **3.** petty, unimportant, small. **9.** child, adolescent. **—Ant. 1.** major.

Mi·nor (mī′nər), *n.* a male given name.

mi′nor ax′is, *Math.* the axis of an ellipse that is perpendicular to the major axis at a point equidistant from the foci. [1860–65]

Mi·nor·ca (mi nôr′kə), *n.* **1.** Spanish, **Menorca.** one of the Balearic Islands, in the W Mediterranean. 50,217; 271 sq. mi. (700 sq. km). **2.** one of a Mediterranean breed of white-skinned chickens.

CONCISE ETYMOLOGY KEY: <, descended or borrowed from; >, whence; b., blend of, blended; c., cognate with; cf., compare; deriv., derivative; equiv., equivalent; imit., imitative; obl., oblique; r., replacing; s., stem; sp., spelling, spelled; resp., respelling, respelled; trans., translation; ?, origin unknown; *, unattested; ‡, probably earlier than. See the full key inside the front cover.

Mi·nor·can (mi nôr′kən), *adj.* **1.** of or pertaining to Minorca. **—*n.* 2.** a native or inhabitant of Minorca. [1750–60; MINORC(A) + -AN]

mi′nor can′on, a canon attached to a cathedral or collegiate church, though not necessarily a member of the chapter. Cf. **honorary canon.** [1670–80]

mi′nor coin′, a coin made of base metal. Cf. **subsidiary coin.**

mi′nor el′ement, 1. *Geol.* any chemical element found in small quantities in the rocks of the earth's crust. Cf. **major element. 2.** *Biochem.* See **trace element.** [1940–45]

Mi·nor·ite (mī′nə rīt′), *n.* See **Friar Minor.** [1555–65; (FRIARS) MINOR, trans. of ML *frātrēs minōrēs* lit., lesser brothers, a name emphasizing their humility; see -ITE[1]]

mi·nor·i·ty (mi nôr′i tē, -nor′, -mī-), *n., pl.* **-ties,** *adj.* **—*n.* 1.** the smaller part or number; a number, part, or amount forming less than half of the whole. **2.** a smaller party or group opposed to a majority, as in voting or other action. **3.** a group differing, esp. in race, religion, or ethnic background, from the majority of a population: *legislation aimed at providing equal rights for minorities.* **4.** a member of such a group. **5.** the state or period of being under the legal age of full responsibility. **—*adj.* 6.** of or pertaining to a minority. [1525–35; < ML *minōritās.* See MINOR, -ITY]
—Syn. 5. childhood, boyhood, girlhood.

minor′ity group′, minority (def. 3). [1960–65]

minor′ity lead′er, the party member who directs the activities of the minority party on the floor of a legislative body, as of the U.S. Congress. [1945–50, *Amer.*]

mi′nor key′, *Music.* **1.** a key or mode based on a minor scale. **2.** a less jubilant or more restrained mood, atmosphere, or quality: *The conversation shifted to a minor key with news of the defeat.* [1810–20]

mi′nor league′, any association of professional sports teams other than the major leagues, esp. when the member teams are associated with or controlled by major-league teams, which use them as training and proving teams for promising players. [1880–85, *Amer.*]

mi·nor-league (mī′nər lēg′), *adj.* **1.** of or pertaining to a minor league. **2.** of little import or consequence: *a painter with a minor-league talent.* [1945–50, *Amer.*]
—Syn. 2. insignificant, lesser, second-rate.

mi·nor-lea·guer (mī′nər lē′gər), *n.* **1.** a member of a minor-league team. **2.** *Informal.* a person whose skill or ability is suited only to a minor league or to a minor role in life. [1880–85, *Amer.*; MINOR LEAGUE + -ER[1]]

mi′nor mode′, *Music.* a scale or key in which the third degree is a minor third above the tonic. [1770–80]

mi′nor or′der, *Rom. Cath. Ch.* the degree or grade of acolyte, exorcist, lector, or ostiary. Cf. **major order.** [1835–45]

mi′nor par′ty, a political party with so little electoral strength that its chance of gaining control of the government is slight. [1650–60]

mi′nor pen′alty, *Ice Hockey.* a penalty consisting of the removal of a player from play for two minutes, no substitute for the player being permitted. Cf. **major penalty.** [1935–40]

mi′nor piece′, *Chess.* a bishop or knight. [1860–65]

mi′nor plan′et, *Astron.* asteroid (def. 1). [1860–65]

mi′nor prem′ise, *Logic.* See under **syllogism** (def. 1). [1720–30]

Mi′nor Proph′ets, Hosea, Joel, Amos, Obadiah, Jonah, Micah, Nahum, Habakkuk, Zephaniah, Haggai, Zechariah, and Malachi. Cf. **Major Prophets.**

mi′nor scale′, 1. Also called **harmonic minor scale.** a scale having half steps between the second and third, fifth and sixth, and seventh and eighth degrees, with whole steps for the other intervals. **2.** Also called **melodic minor scale.** a scale having the third degree lowered a half step when ascending, and the seventh, sixth, and third degrees lowered a half step when descending. [1885–90]

mi′nor sem′inary, a Roman Catholic preparatory school where persons planning to enter the priesthood follow a course of secondary education.

mi′nor sen′tence, *Gram.* **1.** any sentence that is not a true full sentence; a transformation by deletion from a full sentence. **2.** a sentence not having the usual subject-predicate structure, as *Down with the dictator!*

mi′nor suit′, *Bridge.* diamonds or clubs. Cf. **major suit.** [1925–30]

mi′nor ten′ace, *Bridge, Whist.* the king and jack of a suit held by one player. Cf. **major tenace, tenace.**

mi′nor term′, *Logic.* See under **syllogism** (def. 1). [1835–45]

mi′nor tran′quilizer, *Pharm.* See **antianxiety drug.** [1965–70]

mi′nor tri′ad, *Music.* a triad consisting in root position of a root tone with a minor third and a perfect fifth above.

Mi·nos (mī′nəs, -nos), *n. Class. Myth.* a king of Crete: he ordered Daedalus to build the Labyrinth.

Mi·not (mī′nət), *n.* **1. George Rich·ards** (rich′ərdz), 1885–1950, U.S. physician: Nobel prize 1934. **2.** a city in N North Dakota. 32,843.

Min·o·taur (min′ə tôr′), *n.* **1.** *Class. Myth.* a monster, the offspring of Pasiphaë and the Cretan bull, that had the head of a bull on the body of a man: housed in the Cretan Labyrinth, it was fed on human flesh until Theseus, helped by Ariadne, killed it. **2.** any person or thing that devours or destroys. [< L *Mīnōtaurus* < Gk *Mīnṓtauros,* equiv. to *Mīnō*(s) MINOS + *taûros* bull]

mi·nox·i·dil (mi nok′si dil′), *n. Pharm.* a potent peripheral vasodilator used in the treatment of severe hypertension, also applied topically to promote hair growth in some types of baldness. [(A)MIN(O)- + OX(Y)- + (*piper*)*idi*(*ny*)*l,* a chemical component; see PIPERIDINE, -YL]

Minsk (minsk; *Russ.* myĕnsk), *n.* a city in and the capital of Byelorussia (Belarus), in the central part, on a tributary of the Berezina. 1,589,000.

min·ster (min′stər), *n.* **1.** a church actually or originally connected with a monastic establishment. **2.** any large or important church, as a cathedral. [bef. 900; ME, OE *mynster* (c. G *Münster*) < VL **monisterium,* for LL *monastērium* MONASTERY]

min·strel (min′strəl), *n.* **1.** a medieval poet and musician who sang or recited while accompanying himself on a stringed instrument, either as a member of a noble household or as an itinerant troubadour. **2.** a musician, singer, or poet. **3.** one of a troupe of comedians, usually white men made up as black performers, presenting songs, jokes, etc. [1175–1225; ME *ministrel* < OF < LL *ministeriālis* servant (n. use of adj.); see MINISTERIAL]

min′strel show′, a popular stage entertainment featuring comic dialogue, song, and dance in highly conventionalized patterns, performed by a troupe of actors, traditionally comprising two end men and a chorus in blackface and an interlocutor: developed in the U.S. in the early and mid-19th century. [1865–70, *Amer.*]

min·strel·sy (min′strəl sē), *n.* **1.** the art or practice of a minstrel. **2.** minstrels' songs, ballads, etc.: *a collection of Scottish minstrelsy.* [1275–1325; ME *minstralcie* (< AF *menestralsie*) < AL *ministralcia, menestralcia.* See MINSTREL, -CY]

mint[1] (mint), *n.* **1.** any aromatic herb of the genus *Mentha,* having opposite leaves and small, whorled flowers, as the spearmint and peppermint. Cf. **mint family. 2.** a soft or hard confection, often shaped like a wafer, that is usually flavored with peppermint and often served after lunch or dinner. **3.** any of various flavored hard candies packaged as a roll of small round wafers. **—*adj.* 4.** made or flavored with mint: *mint tea.* [bef. 1000; ME, OE *minte* (c. OHG *minza*) < L *ment*(*h*)*a* < Gk *mínthē*]

mint[2] (mint), *n.* **1.** a place where coins, paper currency, special medals, etc., are produced under government authority. **2.** a place where something is produced or manufactured. **3.** a vast amount, esp. of money: *He made a mint in oil wells.* **—*adj.* 4.** *Philately.* (of a stamp) being in its original, unused condition. **5.** unused or appearing to be newly made and never used: *a book in mint condition.* **—*v.t.* 6.** to make (coins, money, etc.) by stamping metal. **7.** to turn (metal) into coins: *to mint gold into sovereigns.* **8.** to make or fabricate; invent: *to mint words.* [bef. 900; ME *mynt,* OE *mynet* coin < L *monēta* coin, mint, after the temple of Juno *Monēta,* where Roman money was coined] **—mint′er,** *n.*

mint[3] (mint), *Scot. and North Eng.* **—*n.* 1.** intent; purpose. **2.** an attempt; try; effort. **—*v.t.* 3.** to try (something); attempt. **4.** to take aim at (something) with a gun. **5.** to hit or strike at (someone or something). **—*v.i.* 6.** to try; attempt. **7.** to take aim. [bef. 900; (v.) ME *minten,* OE (*ge*)*myntan* to intend; akin to MIND; (n.) ME, deriv. of the v.]

mint·age (min′tij), *n.* **1.** the act or process of minting. **2.** the product or result of minting; coinage. **3.** the charge for or cost of minting or coining. **4.** the output of a mint. **5.** a stamp or character impressed. [1560–70; MINT[2] + -AGE]

mint′ fam′ily, the large plant family Labiatae (or Lamiaceae), characterized by aromatic herbaceous plants having square stems, simple leaves, clusters of two-lipped flowers, and fruit in the form of small nutlets, and including basil, bee balm, catnip, coleus, lavender, marjoram, oregano, peppermint, rosemary, sage, spearmint, and thyme.

mint′ gera′nium, costmary.

Min·the (min′thē), *n. Class. Myth.* a nymph who was changed into a mint plant by Persephone to protect her from Hades.

mint′ ju′lep, an alcoholic drink traditionally made with bourbon, sugar, and finely cracked ice and garnished with sprigs of mint, served in a tall, frosted glass: also made with other kinds of whiskey, brandy, and sometimes rum. [1800–10, *Amer.*]

mint·mark (mint′märk′), *n.* a letter or other symbol on a coin that identifies the mint at which it was struck. [1790–1800; MINT[2] + MARK[1]]

Min·to (min′tō), *n.* **Gilbert John El·li·ot-Mur·ray-Ky·nyn·mond** (el′ē ət mûr′ē ki nin′mənd, -mur′ē-, el′yət-), **4th Earl of,** 1845–1914, British colonial administrator: governor general of Canada 1898–1904; viceroy of India 1905–10.

mint·y[1] (min′tē), *adj.,* **mint·i·er, mint·i·est.** having the flavor or aroma of mint. [1875–80; MINT[1] + -Y[1]]

min·ty[2] (min′tē), *adj.,* **mint·i·er, mint·i·est.** *Slang.* **1.** homosexual. **2.** effeminate. [perh. special use of MINTY[1]]

Mi·nu·ci·us Fe·lix (mi noo͞′shē əs fē′liks, -shəs, -nyoo͞′-), **Marcus,** Roman writer of the 2nd century A.D. whose dialogue *Octavius* is the earliest known work of Latin-Christian literature.

min·u·end (min′yoo͞ end′), *n. Arith.* a number from which another is subtracted. Cf. **subtrahend.** [1700–10; < L *minuendus* (*numerus*) (number) to be diminished or made smaller, (gerundive of *minuere*), equiv. to *minu-* (see MINUS) + *-endus* gerundive suffix]

min·u·et (min′yoo͞ et′), *n.* **1.** a slow, stately dance in triple meter, popular in the 17th and 18th centuries. **2.** a piece of music for such a dance or in its rhythm. [1665–75; < F *menuet,* equiv. to *menu* small (see MENU) + *-et* -ET; so called from the shortness of the dancers' steps]

Min·u·it (min′yoo͞ it), *n.* **Peter,** 1580–1638, Dutch colonial administrator in America: director general of the New Netherlands 1626–31. Also, **Minnewit.**

mi·nus (mī′nəs), *prep.* **1.** less by the subtraction of; decreased by: *Ten minus six is four.* **2.** lacking or without:

a book minus its title page. —*adj.* **3.** involving or noting subtraction. **4.** algebraically negative: *a minus quantity.* **5.** less than; just below in quality: *to get a C minus on a test.* **6.** *Informal.* having negative qualities or characteristics; inferior. **7.** *Mycol.* (in heterothallic fungi) designating, in the absence of morphological differentiation, one of the two strains of mycelia that unite in the sexual process. —*n.* **8.** See **minus sign. 9.** a minus quantity. **10.** a deficiency or loss. **11.** *Informal.* a person or thing with no apparent abilities, usefulness, etc.: *The last applicant was a definite minus.* [1300–50; ME < L, neut. of *minor* less; see MINOR]

mi•nus•cule (min′ə skyo͞ol′, mi nus′kyo͞ol), *adj.* **1.** very small. **2.** (of letters or writing) small; not capital. **3.** written in such letters (opposed to *majuscule*). —*n.* **4.** a minuscule letter. **5.** a small cursive script developed in the 7th century A.D. from the uncial, which it afterward superseded. [1695–1705; < L *minusculus* smallish. See MINUS, -CULE[1]] —**mi•nus′cu•lar,** *adj.*

—**Usage.** MINUSCULE, from Latin *minus* meaning "less," has frequently come to be spelled MINISCULE, perhaps under the influence of the prefix *mini-* in the sense "of a small size." Although this newer spelling is criticized by many, it occurs with such frequency in edited writing that some consider it a variant spelling rather than a misspelling.

mi′nus sight′, *Survey.* a foresight used in leveling.

mi′nus sign′, *Arith.* the symbol (−) denoting subtraction or a negative quantity. [1660–70]

mi′nus tick′, *Stock Exchange.* downtick (def. 2).

min•ute[1] (min′it), *n., v.,* **-ut•ed, -ut•ing,** *adj.* —*n.* **1.** the sixtieth part (1/60) of an hour; sixty seconds. **2.** an indefinitely short space of time: *Wait a minute!* **3.** an exact point in time; instant; moment: *Come here this minute!* **4. minutes,** the official record of the proceedings at a meeting of a society, committee, or other group. **5.** *Chiefly Brit.* a written summary, note, or memorandum. **6.** a rough draft, as of a document. **7.** *Geom.* the sixtieth part of a degree of angular measure, often represented by the sign ′, as in 12° 10′, which is read as 12 degrees and 10 minutes. Cf. **angle**[1] (def. 1c). **8. up to the minute,** modern; up-to-date: *The building design is up to the minute.* —*v.t.* **9.** to time exactly, as movements or speed. **10.** to make a draft of (a document or the like). **11.** to record in a memorandum; note down. **12.** to enter in the minutes of a meeting. —*adj.* **13.** prepared in a very short time: *minute pudding.* [1350–1400; ME < ML *minūta,* n. use of fem. of *minūtus* MINUTE[2]]

—**Syn. 2.** jiffy, second. MINUTE, INSTANT, MOMENT refer to small amounts of time. A MINUTE, properly denoting 60 seconds, is often used loosely for any very short space of time (and may be interchangeable with *second*): *I'll be there in just a minute.* An INSTANT is practically a point in time, with no duration, though it is also used to mean a perceptible amount of time: *not an instant's delay.* MOMENT denotes much the same as INSTANT, though with a somewhat greater sense of duration (but somewhat less than MINUTE): *It will only take a moment.*

mi•nute[2] (mī no͞ot′, -nyo͞ot′, mi-), *adj.* **-nut•er, -nut•est. 1.** extremely small, as in size, amount, extent, or degree: *minute differences.* **2.** of minor importance; insignificant; trifling. **3.** attentive to or concerned with even the smallest details: *a minute examination.* [1425–75; late ME < L *minūtus* (ptp. of *minuere* to make smaller or fewer), equiv. to *minū-* verb s. + *-tus* ptp. suffix. See MINUS, MINOR] —**mi•nute′ness,** *n.*

—**Syn. 1.** tiny, infinitesimal, minuscule. See **little. 3.** detailed, exact, precise. —**Ant. 1.** large. **3.** rough, general.

min′ute gun′ (min′it), a cannon fired at intervals of a minute, esp. as a signal of distress or in a military funeral ceremony. [1720–30]

min′ute hand′ (min′it), the hand that indicates the minutes on a clock or watch, usually longer than the hour hand. [1720–30]

min•ute•ly[1] (min′it lē), *adj.* **1.** occurring every minute. —*adv.* **2.** every minute; minute by minute. [1590–1600; MINUTE[1] + -LY]

mi•nute•ly[2] (mī no͞ot′lē, -nyo͞ot′-, mi-), *adv.* **1.** in a minute manner, form, or degree; in minute detail. **2.** into tiny or very small pieces. [1590–1600; MINUTE[2] + -LY]

Min•ute•man (min′it man′), *n., pl.* **-men. 1.** (*sometimes l.c.*) a member of a group of American militiamen just before and during the Revolutionary War who held themselves in readiness for instant military service. **2.** a U.S. intercontinental ballistic missile with three stages, powered by solid-propellant rocket engines. **3.** a member of a small, secret, ultraconservative organization formed into armed groups for the declared purpose of conducting guerrilla warfare against a communist invasion of the U.S. [1765–75, *Amer.;* MINUTE[1] + MAN[1]]

min′ute steak′ (min′it), a thin slice of beefsteak that is prepared by sautéeing quickly on each side. [1930–35]

mi•nu•ti•a (mi no͞o′shē ə, -shə, -nyo͞o′-), *n., pl.* **-ti•ae** (-shē ē′). Usually, **minutiae.** precise details; small or trifling matters: *the minutiae of his craft.* [1745–55; < L *minūtia* smallness, equiv. to *minūt(us)* MINUTE[2] + *-ia* -IA] —**mi•nu′ti•al,** *adj.*

minx (mingks), *n.* a pert, impudent, or flirtatious girl. [1535–45; perh. < LG *minsk* man, impudent woman; c. G *Mensch;* see MENSCH] —**minx′ish,** *adj.*

Mi•ny•a•des (mə nī′ə dēz′), *n.pl. Class. Myth.* the daughters of Minyas who were driven mad by Dionysus as a punishment for refusing to take part in his revels.

min•yan (*Seph.* mēn yän′; *Ashk., Eng.* min′yən), *n., pl.* ***min•yan•im*** (*Seph.* mēn yä nēm′; *Ashk.* min yô′nim), *Eng.* **min•yans.** *Hebrew.* **1.** the number of persons required by Jewish law to be present to conduct a communal religious service, traditionally a minimum of 10 Jewish males over 13 years of age. **2.** such a group. [*min-yān* lit., number]

Min•yan (min′yən), *Class. Myth.* —*adj.* **1.** descended from Minyas. **2.** being or pertaining to a gray, wheel-thrown pottery produced in ancient Greece during the early part of the Helladic period, c2000 B.C. —*n.* **3. Minyans.** Also, **Min•yae** (min′yē). the descendants of Minyas who inhabited Orchomenus in Boeotia and Iolcus in Thessaly.

Min•y•as (min′ē əs), *n. Class. Myth.* a king of Orchomenus, famed for his wealth.

Mi•o•cene (mī′ə sēn′), *Geol.* —*adj.* **1.** noting or pertaining to an epoch of the Tertiary Period, occurring from 25 to 10 million years ago, when grazing mammals became widespread. See table under **geologic time.** —*n.* **2.** the Miocene Epoch or Series. [1825–35; *mio-* (< Gk *meíōn* less) + -CENE]

mi•o•sis (mī ō′sis), *n., pl.* **-ses** (-sēz). *Med.* excessive constriction of the pupil of the eye, as a result of drugs, disease, or the like. Also, **myosis.** Cf. **mydriasis.** [1810–20; var. of *myosis* < Gk *mý(ein)* to shut (the eyes) + *-ōsis* -OSIS]

mi•ot•ic (mī ot′ik), *adj.* **1.** pertaining to or producing miosis. —*n.* **2.** a miotic drug. Also, **myotic.** [1860–65; MIO(SIS) + -TIC]

MIP, monthly investment plan.

Mi•phib•o•seth (mi fib′ə seth′), *n. Douay Bible.* Mephibosheth.

miq•ue•let (mik′ə let′), *n.* **1.** (in the Peninsular War) a Spanish guerrilla who fought against the French. **2.** a soldier in any of several Spanish infantry regiments. **3.** a flintlock of a type developed in Spain. Also, **miguelet.** [1660–70; < Catalan, equiv. to *Miquel* Michael + *-et* -ET]

Miq•ue•lon (mik′ə lon′; *Fr.* mēkᵊ lôN′), *n.* See **St. Pierre and Miquelon.**

mir (mēr; *Russ.* myēR), *n., pl.* ***mi•ri*** (mēr′ē; *Russ.* myē′-Ri). *Russian.* a village commune of peasant farmers in prerevolutionary Russia.

MIr., Middle Irish. Also, **M.Ir.**

Mi•ra (mī′rə), *n.* **1.** *Astron.* the first long-period pulsating variable star to be discovered, with a period averaging 331 days. It is a red giant and a component of a binary star in the constellation Cetus. **2.** a female given name.

Mi•ra•beau (mir′ə bō′; *Fr.* mē RA bō′), *n.* **Ho•no•ré Ga•bri•el Vic•tor Ri•que•ti** (ô nô RĀ′ GA bRē el′ vēk tôR′ Rēkᵊ tē′), **Count de,** 1749–91, French Revolutionary statesman and orator.

Mi•ra•bel (mir′ə bel′; *Fr.* mē RA bel′), *n.* a town in S Quebec, in E Canada. 14,080.

mir•a•belle (mir′ə bel′, mir′ə bel′), *n.* a dry, white plum brandy from Alsace. [1700–10; < F; MF *mirabolan* MYROBALAN, by folk etym.]

mi•ra•bi•le dic•tu (mē Rä′bi le′ dik′to͞o; *Eng.* mi-rab′ə lē dik′to͞o, -tyo͞o), *Latin.* strange to say; marvelous to relate.

mi•ra•bi•li•a (mē′Rä bil′i ä′; *Eng.* mir′ə bil′ē ə), *n.pl. Latin.* marvels; miracles.

mi•rab•i•lite (mi rab′ə līt′), *n. Mineral.* a decahydrate form of sodium sulfate, $Na_2SO_4 \cdot 10H_2O$. Cf. **Glauber's salt.** [1850–55; < L *(sal) mīrābil(is)* wonderful (salt) + -ITE[1]]

mi•ra•cid•i•um (mī′rə sid′ē əm), *n., pl.* **-cid•i•a** (-sid′-ē ə). the larva that hatches from the egg of a trematode worm or fluke. [1895–1900; < NL, equiv. to *mirac-* (< Gk *meirak-* (s. of *meîrax*) boy, girl) + *-idium* -IDIUM] —**mi′ra•cid′i•al,** *adj.*

mir•a•cle (mir′ə kəl), *n.* **1.** an effect or extraordinary event in the physical world that surpasses all known human or natural powers and is ascribed to a supernatural cause. **2.** such an effect or event manifesting or considered as a work of God. **3.** a wonder; marvel. **4.** a wonderful or surpassing example of some quality: *a miracle of modern acoustics.* **5.** See **miracle play.** [1125–75; ME *miracle, miracul* (< OF *miracle*) < L *mīrāculum,* equiv. to *mīrā(rī)* to wonder at + *-culum* -CLE[2]]

mir′acle drug′. See **wonder drug.** [1950–55]

mir′acle fruit′, 1. the berrylike fruit of either of two African shrubs, *Synsepalum dulcificum* or *Thaumatococcus daniellii,* that, when chewed, causes sour substances to taste sweet. **2.** Also called **serendipity berry.** the similar fruit of an African shrub, *Dioscoreophyllum cumminsii.* Also called **mir′acle ber′ry, miraculous fruit.** [1885–90]

mir′acle man′, 1. a person who performs or appears to perform miracles. **2.** a person who performs or is capable of performing exceptional deeds, as from skill or talent: *He's a miracle man when it comes to repairing engines.* [1565–75]

mir′acle mile′, an extended area of fashionable or expensive shops, restaurants, etc., usually along an urban or suburban thoroughfare.

Miracle of St. Mark, The, a painting (1548) by Tintoretto.

mir′acle play′, a medieval dramatic form dealing with religious subjects such as Biblical stories or saints' lives, usually presented in a series or cycle by the craft guilds. Cf. **morality play, mystery play.** [1850–55]

mi•rac•u•lous (mi rak′yə ləs), *adj.* **1.** performed by or involving a supernatural power or agency: *a miraculous cure.* **2.** of the nature of a miracle; marvelous. **3.** having or seeming to have the power to work miracles: *miraculous drugs.* [1400–50; late ME < ML *mīrāculōsus,* equiv. to L *mīrācul(um)* MIRACLE + *-ōsus* -OUS] —**mi•rac′u•lous•ly,** *adv.* —**mi•rac′u•lous•ness,** *n.*

—**Syn. 2.** extraordinary. MIRACULOUS, PRETERNATURAL, SUPERNATURAL refer to that which seems to transcend the laws of nature. MIRACULOUS refers to something that apparently contravenes known laws governing the universe: *a miraculous success.* PRETERNATURAL suggests the possession of supernormal qualities: *Dogs have a preternatural sense of smell.* It may also mean *supernatural: Elves are preternatural beings.* SUPERNATURAL suggests divine or superhuman properties: *supernatural aid in battle.*

mirac′ulous fruit′. See **miracle fruit.** [1885–90]

mir•a•dor (mir′ə dôr′, -dōr′), *n.* (in Spanish-speaking countries) any architectural feature, as a loggia or balcony, affording a view of the surroundings. [1660–70; < Sp < Catalan, equiv. to *mira(r)* to look at (< L *mīrārī* to wonder at) + *-dor* agent suffix (< L *-tor* -TOR)]

Mi•ra•flo•res (mir′ə flôr′əs, -flōr′-; *Sp.* mē′Rä flô′-Res), *n.pl.* the locks of the Panama Canal, near the Pacific entrance.

mi•rage (mi räzh′), *n.* **1.** an optical phenomenon, esp. in the desert or at sea, by which the image of some object appears displaced above, below, or to one side of its true position as a result of spatial variations of the index of refraction of air. **2.** something illusory, without substance or reality. **3.** (*cap.*) *Mil.* any of a series of supersonic, delta-wing, multirole French fighter-bombers. [1795–1805; < F, equiv. to *(se) mir(er)* to look at (oneself), be reflected (< L *mīrārī* to wonder at) + *-age* -AGE]

—**Syn. 2.** illusion, phantom, fancy.

Mi•'raj (mēr′äj), *n. Islam.* Muhammad's miraculous ascension from Jerusalem, through the seven heavens, to the throne of God. The site from which he ascended is now the shrine of the Dome of the Rock. Cf. **Isra', Night Journey.** [< Ar *mi'rāj* lit., ladder, stairs]

Mir•a•mar (mir′ə mär′), *n.* a town in SE Florida. 32,813.

Mi•ran•da (mi ran′də; *also for 1, 4, Sp.* mē Rän′dä), *n.* **1. Fran•cis•co de** (fRän sēs′kô ᵺe), 1750–1816, Venezuelan revolutionist and patriot. **2.** *Astron.* a moon of the planet Uranus. **3.** daughter of Prospero in Shakespeare's *The Tempest.* **4.** a female given name: from a Latin word meaning "to be admired." —*adj.* **5.** *Law.* of, pertaining to, or being upheld by the Supreme Court ruling (Miranda v. Arizona, 1966) requiring law-enforcement officers to warn a person who has been taken into custody of his or her rights to remain silent and to have legal counsel.

Mi′ra var′iable, *Astron.* any of a group of long-period variable stars having a variability similar to that of the star Mira.

mire (mīᵊr), *n., v.,* **mired, mir•ing.** —*n.* **1.** a tract or area of wet, swampy ground; bog; marsh. **2.** ground of this kind, as wet, slimy soil of some depth or deep mud. —*v.t.* **3.** to plunge and fix in mire; cause to stick fast in mire. **4.** to involve; entangle. **5.** to soil with mire; bespatter with mire. —*v.i.* **6.** to sink in mire or mud; stick. [1300–50; ME < ON *mýrr* bog; c. OE *mēos* MOSS]

mire•poix (mir pwä′), *n.* **1.** a flavoring made from diced vegetables, seasonings, herbs, and sometimes meat, often placed in a pan to cook with meat or fish. **2.** finely chopped vegetables, as onions and carrots, sometimes with meat, often used as a bed for meat that is to be braised. Also, **mire•pois′.** [1875–80; < F; said to have been named after C. P. G. F. de Lévis, duke of *Mirepoix,* 18th-century French diplomat]

Mir•i•am (mir′ē əm), *n.* **1.** the sister of Moses and Aaron. Num. 26:59. **2.** a female given name, form of **Mary.**

Mi•rim (mi rim′; *Port.* mi RēN′), *n.* **Lake,** a lake on the E Uruguay-S Brazil border. ab. 108 mi. (174 km) long. Spanish, **Merín.**

mirk (mûrk), *n., adj.* murk.

mirk•y (mûr′kē), *adj.,* **mirk•i•er, mirk•i•est.** murky.

mir•li•ton (mir′li ton′; *Fr.* mēR lē tôN′), *n., pl.* **mir•li•tons** (mir′li tonz′; *Fr.* mēR lē tôN′). **1.** kazoo. **2.** chayote. [1810–20; < F: lit., reed-pipe]

Mi•ró (mē rō′; *Sp.* mē Rô′), *n.* **1. Ga•bri•el** (gä′vRē-el′), 1879–1930, Spanish novelist, short-story writer, and essayist. **2. Jo•an** (hō än′, hwän), 1893–1983, Spanish painter.

mir•ror (mir′ər), *n.* **1.** a reflecting surface, originally of polished metal but now usually of glass with a silvery, metallic, or amalgam backing. **2.** such a surface set into a frame, attached to a handle, etc., for use in viewing oneself or as an ornament. **3.** any reflecting surface, as the surface of calm water under certain lighting conditions. **4.** *Optics.* a surface that is either plane, concave, or convex and that reflects rays of light. **5.** something that gives a minutely faithful representation, image, or idea of something else: *Gershwin's music was a mirror of its time.* **6.** a pattern for imitation; exemplar: *a man who was the mirror of fashion.* **7.** a glass, crystal, or the like, used by magicians, diviners, etc. **8. with mirrors,** by or as if by magic. —*v.t.* **9.** to reflect in or as if in a mirror. **10.** to reflect as a mirror does. **11.** to mimic or imitate (something) accurately. **12.** to be or give a faithful representation, image, or idea of: *Her views on politics mirror mine completely.* —*adj.* **13.** *Music.* (of a canon or fugue) capable of being played in retrograde or in inversion, as though read in a mirror placed beside or below the music. [1175–1225; ME *mirour* < OF *mireo(u)r,* equiv. to *mir-* (see MIRAGE) + *-eo(u)r* < L *-ātor* -ATOR] —**mir′ror•like′,** *adj.*

—**Syn. 6.** model, epitome, paradigm.

mir′ror im′age, 1. an image of an object, plan, person, etc., as it would appear if viewed in a mirror, with right and left reversed. **2.** an object having a spatial arrangement that corresponds to that of another object except that the right-to-left sense on one object corresponds to the left-to-right sense on the other. [1880–85]

mir′ror plant′, a shrub, *Coprosma repens,* of the madder family, native to New Zealand and cultivated in warm regions, having glossy, often variegated leaves.

mir•ror-writ•ing (mir′ər rī′ting), *n.* backward writing that resembles a mirror image of ordinary script. [1770–80]

mirth (mûrth), *n.* **1.** gaiety or jollity, esp. when accompanied by laughter: *the excitement and mirth of the holiday season.* **2.** amusement or laughter: *He was unable to conceal his mirth.* [bef. 900; ME *mirthe,* OE *myrgth.* See MERRY, -TH[1]] —**mirth′less,** *adj.*

—**Syn. 1, 2.** MIRTH, GLEE, HILARITY, MERRIMENT, JOLLITY, JOVIALITY refer to the gaiety characterizing people who are enjoying the companionship of others. MIRTH suggests spontaneous amusement or gaiety, manifested briefly in laughter: *uncontrolled outbursts of mirth.* GLEE suggests an effervescence of high spirits or exultation, often manifested in playful or ecstatic gestures; it may apply also to a malicious rejoicing over mishaps to others: *glee over the failure of a rival.* HILARITY implies noisy and boisterous mirth, often exceeding the limits of reason or propriety: *hilarity aroused by practical jokes.* MERRIMENT suggests fun, good spirits, and good nature rather than the kind of wit and sometimes artificial funmaking that cause hilarity: *The house resounded with music and sounds of merriment.* JOLLITY and JOVIALITY may refer either to a general atmosphere of mirthful festivity or to the corresponding traits of individuals. JOLLITY implies an atmosphere of easy and convivial gaiety, a more hearty merriment or a less boisterous hilarity: *The holiday was a time of jollity.* JOVIALITY implies a more mellow merriment generated by people who are hearty, generous, benevolent, and high-spirited: *the joviality of warm-hearted friends.* —**Ant. 1.** gloom.

mirth·ful (mûrth′fəl), *adj.* **1.** joyous; gay; jolly: *a mirthful laugh.* **2.** providing mirth; amusing: *a mirthful experience.* [1275–1325; ME; see MIRTH, -FUL] —**mirth′ful·ly,** *adv.* —**mirth′ful·ness,** *n.*

MIRV (mûrv), *n.* See **multiple independently targetable reentry vehicle.** Also, **M.I.R.V.**

mir·y (mīər′ē), *adj.,* **mir·i·er, mir·i·est. 1.** of the nature of mire; swampy: *miry ground.* **2.** abounding in mire; muddy. **3.** covered or bespattered with mire. [1350–1400; ME; see MIRE, -Y[1]] —**mir′i·ness,** *n.*

mir·za (mûr′zə; *Pers.* mēr′zä), *n.* (in Persia, or Iran) **1.** a royal prince (placed after the name when used as a title). **2.** (a title of honor for men, prefixed to the name). [1605–15; < Pers < Ar *amīr* commander (cf. AMIR, EMIR) + *zād* born]

MIS, See **management information system.**

mis-[1], a prefix applied to various parts of speech, meaning "ill," "mistaken," "wrong," "wrongly," "incorrectly," or simply negating: *mistrial; misprint; mistrust.* [ME; OE *mis(se)-;* c. G *miss-,* Goth *missa-* (see MISS[1]); often r. ME *mes-* < OF < WGmc **mis(s)-*]

—**Note.** The lists at the bottom of this and following pages provide the spelling, syllabification, and stress for words whose meanings may be easily inferred by combining the meaning of MIS- and an attached base word, or base word plus a suffix. Appropriate parts of speech are also shown. Words prefixed by MIS- that have special meanings or uses are entered in their proper alphabetical places in the main vocabulary or as derived forms run on at the end of a main vocabulary entry.

mis-[2], var. of **miso-** before some vowels: *misanthrope.*

mis·ad·dress (mis′ə dres′), *v.t.,* **-dressed** or **-drest, -dress·ing.** to address incorrectly or improperly: *to misaddress a letter.* [1640–50; MIS-[1] + ADDRESS]

mis·ad·ven·ture (mis′əd ven′chər), *n.* an instance of bad fortune; mishap. [1250–1300; MIS[1]- + ADVENTURE; r. ME *mesaventure* < OF]

—**Syn. 1.** mischance, accident; disaster, calamity, catastrophe.

mis·ad·vise (mis′əd vīz′), *v.t.,* **-vised, -vis·ing.** to give bad or inappropriate advice to. [1325–75; ME. See MIS-[1], ADVISE] —**mis·ad·vice** (mis′əd vīs′), *n.*

mis·a·ligned (mis′ə līnd′), *adj.* improperly aligned. [1945–50; MISALIGN + -ED[2]] —**mis′a·lign′ment,** *n.*

mis·al·li·ance (mis′ə lī′əns), *n.* an improper or incompatible association, esp. in marriage; mésalliance. [1730–40; MIS-[1] + ALLIANCE, modeled on F *mésalliance*]

mis·al·lo·cate (mis al′ə kāt′), *v.t.,* **-cat·ed, -cat·ing.** to allocate mistakenly or improperly: *to misallocate resources.* [MIS-[1] + ALLOCATE] —**mis′al·lo·ca′tion,** *n.*

mis·al·ly (mis′ə lī′), *v.t.,* **-lied, -ly·ing.** to ally improperly or unsuitably. [1690–1700; MIS-[1] + ALLY]

mis·an·dry (mis′an drē), *n.* hatred of males. Cf. **misogyny.** [1945–50; MIS-[2] + *-andry* (as in POLYANDRY), on the model of MISOGYNY] —**mis′an·drist,** *n.*

mis·an·thrope (mis′ən thrōp′, miz′-), *n.* a hater of humankind. Also, **mis·an·thro·pist** (mis an′thrə pist, miz-). [1555–65; n. use of Gk *mīsánthrōpos* hating humankind, misanthropic. See MIS-[2], ANTHROPO-]

mis·an·throp·ic (mis′ən throp′ik, miz′-), *adj.* **1.** of, pertaining to, or characteristic of a misanthrope. **2.** characterized by misanthropy. Also, **mis′an·throp′i·cal.** [1755–65; MISANTHROPE + -IC] —**mis′an·throp′i·cal·ly,** *adv.*

—**Syn. 1.** antisocial, unfriendly, morose, surly.

CONCISE ETYMOLOGY KEY: <, descended or borrowed from; >, whence; b., blend of, blended; c., cognate with; cf., compare; deriv., derivative; equiv., equivalent; imit., imitative; obl., oblique; r., replacing; s., stem; sp., spelling, spelled; resp., respelling, respelled; trans., translation; ?, origin unknown; *, unattested; ‡, probably earlier than. See the full key inside the front cover.

mis·an·thro·py (mis an′thrə pē, miz-), *n.* hatred, dislike, or distrust of humankind. [1650–60; < Gk *misanthrōpía.* See MISANTHROPE, -Y[3]]

mis·ap·plied (mis′ə plīd′), *adj.* mistakenly applied; used wrongly. [1620–30; MIS-[1] + APPLIED]

mis·ap·ply (mis′ə plī′), *v.t.,* **-plied, -ply·ing.** to make a wrong application or use of. [1565–75; MIS-[1] + APPLY] —**mis·ap·pli·ca·tion** (mis′ap li kā′shən), *n.* —**mis′ap·pli′er,** *n.*

mis·ap·pre·hend (mis′ap ri hend′), *v.t.* to misunderstand. [1645–55; MIS-[1] + APPREHEND] —**mis′ap·pre·hend′ing·ly,** *adv.*

mis·ap·pre·hen·sion (mis′ap ri hen′shən), *n.* misunderstanding. [1620–30; MIS-[1] + APPREHENSION] —**mis′ap·pre·hen′sive,** *adj.* —**mis′ap·pre·hen′sive·ly,** *adv.* —**mis′ap·pre·hen′sive·ness,** *n.*

mis·ap·pro·pri·ate (mis′ə prō′prē āt′), *v.t.,* **-at·ed, -at·ing. 1.** to put to a wrong use. **2.** to apply wrongfully or dishonestly, as funds entrusted to one's care. [1855–60; MIS-[1] + APPROPRIATE] —**mis′ap·pro′pri·a′tion,** *n.*

mis·ar·range (mis′ə rānj′), *v.t.,* **-ranged, -rang·ing.** to arrange incorrectly or improperly: *to misarrange a file.* [MIS-[1] + ARRANGE] —**mis′ar·range′ment,** *n.*

mis·be·come (mis′bi kum′), *v.t.,* **-came, -come, -com·ing.** to be unsuitable, unbecoming, or unfit for. [1520–30; MIS-[1] + BECOME]

mis·be·got·ten (mis′bi got′n), *adj.* **1.** unlawfully or irregularly begotten; illegitimate: *his misbegotten son.* **2.** badly conceived, made, or carried out: *his misbegotten plan.* Also, **mis′be·got′.** [1540–50; MIS-[1] + BEGOTTEN]

mis·be·have (mis′bi hāv′), *v.,* **-haved, -hav·ing.** —*v.i.* **1.** to behave badly or improperly: *The children misbehaved during our visit.* —*v.t.* **2.** to conduct (oneself) without regard for good manners or accepted moral standards: *Several of the guests misbehaved themselves.* [1425–75; late ME; see MIS-[1], BEHAVE] —**mis′be·hav′er,** *n.*

mis·be·hav·ior (mis′bi hāv′yər), *n.* improper, inappropriate, or bad behavior. Also, *esp. Brit.,* **mis′be·hav′iour.** [1480–90; MIS-[1] + BEHAVIOR]

mis·be·lief (mis′bi lēf′), *n.* **1.** erroneous belief; false opinion. **2.** erroneous or unorthodox religious belief. [1175–1225; ME; see MIS-[1], BELIEF]

mis·be·lieve (mis′bi lēv′), *v.,* **-lieved, -liev·ing.** *Obs.* —*v.i.* **1.** to believe wrongly; hold an erroneous belief. —*v.t.* **2.** to disbelieve; doubt. [1250–1300; ME; see MIS-[1], BELIEVE] —**mis′be·liev′er,** *n.* —**mis′be·liev′ing·ly,** *adv.*

mis·brand (mis brand′), *v.t.* **1.** to brand or label erroneously. **2.** to brand illegally, as with another's trademark. [1900–05; MIS-[1] + BRAND]

misc., 1. miscellaneous. **2.** miscellany.

mis·cal·cu·late (mis kal′kyə lāt′), *v.t., v.i.,* **-lat·ed, -lat·ing.** to calculate or judge incorrectly: *to miscalculate the time required.* [1690–1700; MIS-[1] + CALCULATE] —**mis′cal·cu·la′tion,** *n.* —**mis·cal′cu·la′tor,** *n.*

mis·call (mis kôl′), *v.t.* to call by a wrong name. [1400–50; late ME; see MIS-[1], CALL] —**mis·call′er,** *n.*

mis·car·riage (mis kar′ij; *for 1 also* mis′kar′ij), *n.* **1.** the expulsion of a fetus before it is viable, esp. between the third and seventh months of pregnancy; spontaneous abortion. Cf. **abortion** (def. 1). **2.** failure to attain the just, right, or desired result: *a miscarriage of justice.* **3.** failure of something sent, as a letter, to reach its destination. **4.** *Chiefly Brit.* transportation of goods not in accordance with the contract of shipment. [1605–15; MIS-[1] + CARRIAGE]

mis·car·ry (mis kar′ē; *for 1 also* mis′kar′ē), *v.i.,* **-ried, -ry·ing. 1.** to have a miscarriage of a fetus. **2.** to fail to attain the right or desired end; be unsuccessful: *The plan miscarried.* **3.** to go astray or be lost in transit, as a letter. [1275–1325; ME *miscarien.* See MIS-[1], CARRY]

mis·cast (mis kast′, -käst′), *v.t.,* **-cast, -cast·ing. 1.** to assign an unsuitable role to (an actor): *Tom was miscast as Romeo.* **2.** to allot (a role) to an unsuitable actor. **3.** to select unsuitable actors for (a play, motion picture, or the like). [1925–30; MIS-[1] + CAST[1]]

Misc. Doc., miscellaneous document.

mis·ce (mis′ē, mēs), *v.* (in prescriptions) mix. [< L]

mis·ceg·e·na·tion (mi sej′ə nā′shən, mis′i jə-), *n.* **1.** marriage or cohabitation between a man and woman of different races, esp., in the U.S., between a black and a white person. **2.** interbreeding between members of different races. **3.** the mixing or a mixture of races by interbreeding. [irreg. < L *miscē(re)* to mix + *gen(us)* race, stock, species + -ATION; allegedly coined by U.S. journalist David Goodman Croly (1829–89) in a pamphlet published anonymously in 1864] —**mis·ce·ge·net·ic** (mis′i jə net′ik, mi sej′ə-), *adj.*

mis·cel·la·ne·a (mis′ə lā′nē ə), *n.pl.* miscellaneous collected writings, papers, or objects. [1565–75; < L *miscellānea* hash, hodgepodge, n. use of neut. pl. of *miscellāneus* MISCELLANEOUS]

mis·cel·la·ne·ous (mis′ə lā′nē əs), *adj.* **1.** consisting of members or elements of different kinds; of mixed character: *a book of miscellaneous essays on American history.* **2.** having various qualities, aspects, or subjects: *a miscellaneous discussion.* [1630–40; < L *miscellāneus* mixed, of all sorts, equiv. to *miscell(us)* mixed + *-ān(us)* -AN + *-eus* -EOUS] —**mis′cel·la′ne·ous·ly,** *adv.* —**mis′cel·la′ne·ous·ness,** *n.*

—**Syn. 1.** divers, varied, heterogeneous, diversified. MISCELLANEOUS, INDISCRIMINATE, PROMISCUOUS refer to mixture and lack of order, and may imply lack of discernment or taste. MISCELLANEOUS emphasizes the idea of the mixture of things of different kinds or natures: *a miscellaneous assortment of furniture.* INDISCRIMINATE emphasizes lack of discrimination in choice (and consequent confusion): *indiscriminate praise.* PROMISCUOUS is even stronger than INDISCRIMINATE in its emphasis of complete absence of discrimination: *promiscuous in his friendships.*

mis·cel·la·nist (mis′ə lā′nist; *Brit.* mi sel′ə nist), *n.* a person who writes, compiles, or edits miscellanies. [1800–10; MISCELLAN(Y) + -IST]

mis·cel·la·ny (mis′ə lā′nē; *Brit.* mi sel′ə nē), *n., pl.* **-nies. 1.** a miscellaneous collection or group of various or somewhat unrelated items. **2.** a miscellaneous collection of literary compositions or pieces by several authors, dealing with various topics, assembled in a volume or book. **3. miscellanies,** a miscellaneous collection of articles or entries, as in a book. [1590–1600; Anglicized var. of MISCELLANEA]

—**Syn. 2.** anthology.

mis·chance (mis chans′, -chäns′), *n.* a mishap or misfortune. [1250–1300; MIS-[1] + CHANCE; r. ME *mescheance* < OF]

mis·chan·ter (mis chan′tər, mi shan′-), *n. Scot. and North Eng.* mishanter.

mis·chief (mis′chif), *n.* **1.** conduct or activity that playfully causes petty annoyance. **2.** a tendency or disposition to tease, vex, or annoy. **3.** a vexatious or annoying action. **4.** harm or trouble, esp. as a result of an agent or cause. **5.** an injury or evil caused by a person or other agent or cause. **6.** a cause or source of harm, evil, or annoyance. **7.** the devil. [1250–1300; ME *meschef* < OF, n. deriv. of *meschever* to end badly, come to grief. See MIS-[1], ACHIEVE]

—**Syn. 4.** hurt. See **damage.**

mis·chief-mak·er (mis′chif mā′kər), *n.* a person who causes mischief, esp. one who stirs up discord, as by talebearing. [1700–10] —**mis′chief-mak′ing,** *adj., n.*

mis′chief night′, Halloween or, in some areas, the night before Halloween, as an occasion for pranks and minor vandalism by young people. [1860–65]

mis·chie·vous (mis′chə vəs), *adj.* **1.** maliciously or playfully annoying. **2.** causing annoyance, harm, or trouble. **3.** roguishly or slyly teasing, as a glance. **4.** harmful or injurious. [1300–50; ME *mischevous* < AF *meschevous.* See MISCHIEF, -OUS] —**mis′chie·vous·ly,** *adv.* —**mis′chie·vous·ness,** *n.*

—**Pronunciation.** Pronunciations of MISCHIEVOUS with stress on the second syllable: (mis chē′vē əs) or, less commonly, (mis chē′vəs), instead of on the first: (mis′chə vəs), are usually considered nonstandard. The pronunciation (mis chē′vē əs), with the additional syllable, occurs by analogy with such words as *previous* and *devious.*

misch′ met′al (mish), a pyrophoric alloy, containing approximately 50 percent cerium and 45 percent lanthanum, made from a mixture of various rare-earth chlorides by electrolysis. [1920–25; < G *Mischmetall,* equiv. to *misch(en)* to MIX + *Metall* METAL]

mis·choose (mis cho͞oz′), *v.,* **-chose; -cho·sen** or (*Obs.*) **-chose; -choos·ing.** —*v.i.* **1.** to make a wrong or improper choice. —*v.t.* **2.** to choose wrongly or improperly. [1200–50; MIS-[1] + CHOOSE; r. ME *mischesen*]

mis·ci·ble (mis′ə bəl), *adj. Chem., Physics.* capable of being mixed: *miscible ingredients.* [1560–70; < L *misc(ēre)* to mix, mingle + -IBLE] —**mis′ci·bil′i·ty,** *n.*

mis·cite (mis sīt′), *v.t., v.i.,* **-cit·ed, -cit·ing.** to misquote. [1585–95; MIS-[1] + CITE] —**mis′ci·ta′tion,** *n.*

mis·code (mis kōd′), *v.t.,* **-cod·ed, -cod·ing.** to code mistakenly, as in data processing. [1960–65; MIS-[1] + CODE (v.)]

mis·col·or (mis kul′ər), *v.t.* **1.** to give a wrong color to. **2.** to misrepresent: *She miscolored the facts.* [1800–10; MIS-[1] + COLOR]

mis·com·mu·ni·cate (mis′kə myo͞o′ni kāt′), *v.t., v.i.,* **-cat·ed, -cat·ing.** to communicate mistakenly, unclearly, or inadequately. [MIS[1]- + COMMUNICATE] —**mis′com·mu′ni·ca′tion,** *n.*

mis·con·ceive (mis′kən sēv′), *v.t., v.i.,* **-ceived, -ceiv·ing.** to conceive or interpret wrongly; misunderstand. [1350–1400; ME; see MIS-[1], CONCEIVE] —**mis′con·ceiv′er,** *n.*

mis·con·cep·tion (mis′kən sep′shən), *n.* an erroneous conception; mistaken notion. [1655–65; MIS-[1] + CONCEPTION]

mis·con·duct (*n.* mis kon′dukt; *v.* mis′kən dukt′), *n.* **1.** improper conduct; wrong behavior. **2.** unlawful conduct by an official in regard to his or her office, or by a person in the administration of justice, such as a lawyer, witness, or juror; malfeasance. —*v.t.* **3.** to mismanage. **4.** to misbehave (oneself). [1700–10; MIS-[1] + CONDUCT]

—**Syn. 1.** wrongdoing, misbehavior, misdeed, misstep.

mis·con·struc·tion (mis′kən struk′shən), *n.* **1.** wrong construction; misinterpretation: *to put a misconstruction upon an action.* **2.** an act or instance of misconstruing. [1505–15; MIS-[1] + CONSTRUCTION]

---

mis′ac·cused′, *adj.*
mis·act′, *v.i.*
mis′a·dapt′, *v.*
mis′ad·ap·ta′tion, *n.*
mis·add′, *v.*
mis′ad·ju′di·cat′ed, *adj.*
mis′ad·just′, *v.*
mis′ad·just′ed, *adj.*
mis′ad·just′ment, *n.*
mis′ad·min′is·tra′tion, *n.*
mis·aim′, *v., n.*
mis′al·le·ga′tion, *n.*
mis′al·lege′, *v.t.,* **-leged, -leg·ing.**
mis′al·lot′, *v.t.,* **-lot·ted, -lot·ting.**
mis′al·lot′ment, *n.*
mis·al′pha·bet·ize′, *v.t.,* **-ized, -iz·ing.**
mis′a·nal′y·sis, *n., pl.* **-ses.**
mis·an′a·lyze′, *v.t.,* **-lyzed, -lyz·ing.**
mis′ap·pel·la′tion, *n.*
mis′ap·pend′ed, *adj.*
mis′ap·point′, *v.t*
mis′ap·prais′al, *n.*
mis′ap·praise′, *v.t.,* **-praised, -prais·ing.**
mis′ar·tic′u·late′, *v.,* **-lat·ed, -lat·ing.**
mis′ar·tic′u·la′tion, *n.*
mis′as·sem′ble, *v.,* **-bled, -bling.**
mis′as·sert′, *v.t.*
mis′as·ser′tion, *n.*
mis′as·sess′ment, *n.*
mis′as·sign′, *v.*
mis′as·sign′ment, *n.*
mis′as·sump′tion, *n.*
mis′at·trib′ute, *v.,* **-ut·ed, -ut·ing.**
mis′at·tri·bu′tion, *n.*
mis′au·thor·i·za′tion, *n.*
mis·au′thor·ize′, *v.t.,* **-ized, -iz·ing.**
mis′a·ver′, *v.t.,* **-verred, -ver·ring.**
mis′a·ward′, *v.t*
mis·bal′ance, *n., v.,* **-anced, -anc·ing.**
mis′be·stow′, *v.t*
mis·bill′, *v.t.*
mis·bind′, *v.,* **-bound, -bind·ing.**
mis·brew′, *v.t.*
mis·build′, *v.,* **-built, -build·ing.**
mis·but′ton, *v.t.*

mis·con·strue (mis′kən stro͞o′ *or, esp. Brit.,* mis-kon′stro͞o), *v.t.,* **-strued, -stru·ing.** to misunderstand the meaning of; take in a wrong sense; misinterpret. [1350–1400; ME; see MIS-[1], CONSTRUE]
—Syn. misread, misapprehend, misjudge.

mis·cop·y (mis kop′ē), *v.,* **-cop·ied, -cop·y·ing,** *n., pl.* **-cop·ies.** —*v.t.* **1.** to copy incorrectly: *to miscopy an address.* —*n.* **2.** an incorrect copy. [1815–25; MIS-[1] + COPY]

mis·coun·sel (mis koun′səl), *v.t.,* **-seled, -sel·ing** or (*esp. Brit.*) **-selled, -sel·ling.** to advise wrongly. [1350–1400; ME; see MIS-[1], COUNSEL]

mis·count (*v.* mis kount′; *n.* mis′kount′), *v.t., v.i.* **1.** to count or calculate erroneously. —*n.* **2.** an erroneous counting; miscalculation. [1350–1400; MIS-[1] + COUNT[1]; r. ME *mesconten* < MF *mesconter*]

mis·cre·ance (mis′krē əns), *n.* a misbelief or false religious faith. [1350–1400; ME < MF *mescreance,* equiv. to *mes-* MIS-[1] + *creance* < VL **crēdentia* CREDENCE]

mis·cre·an·cy (mis′krē ən sē), *n.* **1.** the state or condition of a miscreant; villainy. **2.** *Archaic.* miscreance. [1605–15; MISCRE(ANT) + -ANCY]

mis·cre·ant (mis′krē ənt), *adj.* **1.** depraved, villainous, or base. **2.** *Archaic.* holding a false or unorthodox religious belief; heretical. —*n.* **3.** a vicious or depraved person; villain. **4.** *Archaic.* a heretic or infidel. [1350–1400; ME < MF *mescreant* unbelieving, equiv. to *mes-* MIS-[1] + *creant* << L *crēdent-* CREDENT]

mis·cre·ate (*v.* mis′krē āt′; *adj.* mis′krē it, -āt′), *v.,* **-at·ed, -at·ing,** *adj. Rare.* —*v.t., v.i.* **1.** to create amiss or deformed. —*adj.* **2.** miscreated. [1580–90; MIS-[1] + CREATE] **—mis′cre·a′tion,** *n.* **—mis′cre·a′tive,** *adj.* **—mis′cre·a′tor,** *n.*

mis·cre·at·ed (mis′krē ā′tid), *adj.* badly or wrongly created; misshapen; monstrous. [1575–85; MIS-[1] + CREATED]

mis·cue[1] (mis kyo͞o′), *n., v.,* **-cued, -cu·ing.** —*n.* **1.** *Sports.* a failure to execute a play, stroke, or maneuver properly; an error. **2.** *Informal.* a mistake. **3.** *Informal.* to make a mistake. **4.** *Theat.* to fail to answer one's cue or to answer another's cue. —*v.t.* **5.** to give the wrong cue to. [1880–85; MIS-[1] + CUE[1]]

mis·cue[2] (mis kyo͞o′), *n., v.,* **-cued, -cu·ing.** *Billiards, Pool.* —*n.* **1.** a stroke in which the cue fails to make solid contact with the cue ball. —*v.i.* **2.** to make a miscue. [1870–75; MIS-[1] + CUE[2]]

mis·date (mis dāt′), *v.,* **-dat·ed, -dat·ing,** *n.* —*v.t.* **1.** to assign or affix a wrong date to. —*n.* **2.** a wrong date. [1580–90; MIS-[1] + DATE[1]]

mis·deal (mis dēl′), *v.,* **-dealt, -deal·ing,** *n.* —*v.t., v.i.* **1.** to deal wrongly or incorrectly, esp. to deal the wrong number at cards. —*n.* **2.** *Cards.* a deal in which the wrong number of cards have been distributed or in which the cards were dealt in the wrong order or manner, necessitating a new deal and the cancellation of any points made on the hand, sometimes with a penalty to the dealer. [1475–85; MIS-[1] + DEAL[1]] **—mis·deal′er,** *n.*

mis·deed (mis dēd′), *n.* an immoral or wicked deed. [bef. 900; ME *misdede,* OE *misdǣd.* See MIS-[1], DEED]
—Syn. offense, transgression, fault.

mis·deem (mis dēm′), *v.t., v.i.* to have a wrong opinion of; misjudge: *to misdeem someone's ability.* [1250–1300; ME *misdemen.* See MIS-[1], DEEM]

mis·de·mean (mis′di mēn′), *v.t. Rare.* to misbehave (oneself). [1350–1400; late ME; see MIS-[1], DEMEAN[2]]

mis·de·mean·ant (mis′di mē′nənt), *n.* **1.** a person who is guilty of misbehavior. **2.** *Law.* a person who has been convicted of a misdemeanor. [1810–20; MISDEMEAN + -ANT]

mis·de·mean·or (mis′di mē′nər), *n.* **1.** *Law.* a criminal offense defined as less serious than a felony. **2.** an instance of misbehavior; misdeed. Also, *esp. Brit.,* **mis′·de·mean′our.** [1480–90; MIS-[1] + DEMEANOR]

mis·de·rive (mis′di rīv′), *v.t., v.i.,* **-rived, -riv·ing.** to derive incorrectly; assign a wrong derivation to. [1640–50; MIS-[1] + DERIVE]

mis·de·scribe (mis′di skrīb′), *v.t., v.i.,* **-scribed, -scrib·ing.** to describe incorrectly or falsely. [1820–30; MIS-[1] + DESCRIBE] **—mis·de·scrip·tion** (mis′di skrip′shən), *n.* **—mis′de·scrip′tive,** *adj.*

mis·di·ag·nose (mis dī′əg nōs′, -nōz′, mis′dī əg nōs′, -nōz′), *v.,* **-nosed, -nos·ing.** —*v.i.* **1.** to make an incorrect diagnosis. —*v.t.* **2.** to diagnose erroneously: *to misdiagnose the nation's ills.* [1925–30; MIS-[1] + DIAGNOSE]

mis·di·ag·no·sis (mis′dī əg nō′sis), *n., pl.* **-ses** (-sēz). *n.* an incorrect diagnosis. [1945–50; MIS-[1] + DIAGNOSIS]

mis·di·al (*v.* mis dī′əl, -dīl′; *n.* mis′dī′əl, -dīl′), *v.* **-di·aled, -di·al·ing** or (*esp. Brit.*) **-di·alled, -di·al·ling,** *n.* —*v.t., v.i.* **1.** to dial incorrectly. —*n.* **2.** an act or instance of misdialing. [1960–65; MIS-[1] + DIAL]

mis·di·rect (mis′di rekt′), *v.t.* to direct or address wrongly or incorrectly: *to misdirect a person; to misdirect a letter.* [1595–1605; MIS-[1] + DIRECT]

mis·di·rec·tion (mis′di rek′shən), *n.* **1.** a wrong or incorrect direction, guidance, or instruction. **2.** *Law.* an erroneous charge to the jury by a judge. [1760–70; MIS-[1] + DIRECTION]

mis·do (mis do͞o′), *v.,* **-did, -done, -do·ing.** —*v.t.* **1.** to do badly or wrongly; botch. —*v.i.* **2.** *Obs.* to behave improperly. [bef. 950; ME *misdon,* OE *misdōn.* See MIS-[1], DO[1]] **—mis·do′er,** *n.*

mis·doubt (mis dout′), *v.t., v.i.* **1.** to doubt or suspect. —*n.* **2.** doubt or suspicion. [1530–40; MIS-[1] + DOUBT]

mise (mēz, mīz), *n.* **1.** a settlement or agreement. **2.** *Law.* the issue in a proceeding instituted on a writ of right. [1400–50; late ME < AF: a putting, setting down (e.g. of expenses), n. use of fem. of *mis* set down < L *missus* ptp. of *mittere* to send, bestow]

mis·ease (mis ēz′), *n.* **1.** *Archaic.* discomfort; distress; suffering. **2.** *Obs.* poverty. [1150–1200; ME *misese* < OF *mesaise.* See MIS-[1], EASE]

mis·ed·u·cate (mis ej′o͝o kāt′), *v.t.,* **-cat·ed, -cat·ing.** to educate improperly. [MIS-[1] + EDUCATE] **—mis′ed·u·ca′tion,** *n.*

mise en scène (mē zäɴ sen′), *French.* **1.** the process of setting a stage, with regard to placement of actors, scenery, properties, etc. **2.** the stage setting or scenery of a play. **3.** surroundings; environment.

mis·em·ploy (mis′em ploi′), *v.t.* to use for the wrong purpose; use wrongly or improperly; misuse. [1600–10; MIS-[1] + EMPLOY] **—mis′em·ploy′ment,** *n.*

mis en bou·teilles (mē zäɴ bo͞o te′yᵊ), *French.* **1.** bottled. **2.** (of a wine) bottled by a specified château, shipper, etc.

Mi·se·no (mē ze′nô), *n.* a cape in SW Italy, on the N shore of the Bay of Naples: ruins of ancient Misenum, a Roman naval station and resort.

Mi·se·nus (mī sē′nəs), *n. Rom. Legend.* a son of Aeolus who challenged the gods to a musical contest and was killed by them for his arrogance.

mi·ser (mī′zər), *n.* **1.** a person who lives in wretched circumstances in order to save and hoard money. **2.** a stingy, avaricious person. **3.** *Obs.* a wretched or unhappy person. [1535–45; < L: wretched]
—Syn. 2. skinflint, tightwad, pinchpenny.

Miser, The, (French, *L'Avare*), a comedy (1668) by Molière.

mis·er·a·ble (miz′ər ə bəl, miz′rə-), *adj.* **1.** wretchedly unhappy, uneasy, or uncomfortable: *miserable victims of war.* **2.** wretchedly poor; needy. **3.** of wretched character or quality; contemptible: *a miserable villain.* **4.** attended with or causing misery: *a miserable existence.* **5.** manifesting misery. **6.** worthy of pity; deplorable: *a miserable failure.* [1375–1425; late ME < L *miserābilis,* equiv. to *miserā(rī)* to pity (deriv. of *miser* wretched) + *-bilis* -BLE] **—mis′er·a·ble·ness,** *n.* **—mis′er·a·bly,** *adv.*
—Syn. 1. forlorn, disconsolate, doleful, distressed. See **wretched. 2.** destitute. **3.** despicable, mean, low, abject. **6.** pitiable, lamentable. **—Ant. 1.** happy. **2.** wealthy. **3.** good.

Mis·e·re·re (miz′ə rãr′ē, -rēr′ē), *n.* **1.** the 51st Psalm, or the 50th in the Douay Bible. **2.** a musical setting for it. **3.** (*l.c.*) a prayer or expression of appeal for mercy. **4.** (*l.c.*) misericord (def. 3). [< L *miserēre* lit., have pity (impv.), first word of the psalm]

mis·er·i·cord (miz′ər i kôrd′, mi zer′i kôrd′), *n.* **1.** a room in a monastery set apart for those monks permitted relaxation of the monastic rule. **2.** Also, **subsellium.** a small projection on the underside of a hinged seat of a church stall, which, when the seat is lifted, gives support to a person standing in the stall. **3.** a medieval dagger, used for the mercy stroke to a wounded foe. Also, **mis′·er·i·corde′.** [1200–50; ME *misericorde* lit., pity, mercy, an act of clemency < MF < L *misericordia* pity, equiv. to *misericord-* (s. of *misericors*) compassionate (*miseri-,* s. of *miserēre* to pity + *cord-* s. of *cor* heart) + *-ia* -Y[3]]

mi·ser·ly (mī′zər lē), *adj.* of, like, or befitting a miser; penurious; stingy; niggardly. [1585–95; MISER + -LY] **—mi′ser·li·ness,** *n.*
—Syn. cheap, parsimonious. See **stingy. —Ant.** generous.

mis·er·y (miz′ə rē), *n., pl.* **-er·ies. 1.** wretchedness of condition or circumstances. **2.** distress or suffering caused by need, privation, or poverty. **3.** great mental or emotional distress; extreme unhappiness. **4.** a cause or source of distress. **5.** *Older Use.* **a.** a pain: *a misery in my left side.* **b.** rheumatism. **c.** Often **miseries.** a case or period of despondency or gloom. [1325–75; ME *miserie* < L *miseria,* equiv. to *miser* wretched + *-ia* -Y[3]]
—Syn. 1. tribulation, trial, suffering. **3.** grief, anguish, woe, torment, desolation. See **sorrow. —Ant. 3.** happiness.

mis′ery in′dex, an unofficial indication of a nation's economic health, derived by adding the percentage rate of inflation to the percentage of unemployed workers: *With inflation running at 15 percent and unemployment at 8 percent, the misery index is 23 percent.* [1975–80]

mis·es·teem (mis′e stēm′), *v.t.* to fail to value or respect properly. [1605–15; MIS-[1] + ESTEEM]

mis·es·ti·mate (*v.* mis es′tə māt′; *n.* mis es′tə mit), *v.,* **-mat·ed, -mat·ing,** *n.* —*v.t.* **1.** to estimate wrongly or inadequately. —*n.* **2.** a wrong or inadequate estimate. [1835–45; MIS-[1] + ESTIMATE] **—mis·es′ti·ma′tion,** *n.*

mis·fea·sance (mis fē′zəns), *n. Law.* **1.** a wrong, actual or alleged, arising from or consisting of affirmative action. **2.** the wrongful performance of a normally lawful act; the wrongful and injurious exercise of lawful authority. Cf. **malfeasance, nonfeasance.** [1590–1600; < AF *mesfesance.* See MIS-[1], FEASANCE]

mis·fea·sor (mis fē′zər), *n. Law.* a person who is guilty of misfeasance. [1625–35; < AF *mesfesor.* See MISFEASANCE, -OR[2]]

mis·fea·ture (mis fē′chər), *n. Archaic.* a distorted feature. [1815–25; MIS-[1] + FEATURE] **—mis·fea′tured,** *adj.*

mis·feed (mis fēd′), *v.i.,* **-fed, -feed·ing.** (of a machine, paper, materials, etc.) to feed incorrectly: *The copying machine will jam if it starts to misfeed.* [MIS-[1] + FEED]

mis·file (mis fīl′), *v.t.,* **-filed, -fil·ing.** to file (papers, documents, records, etc.) incorrectly; file in the wrong place. [MIS-[1] + FILE[1]]

mis·fire (*v.* mis fīᵊr′; *n.* mis′fīᵊr′), *v.,* **-fired, -fir·ing,** *n.* —*v.i.* **1.** (of a rifle or gun or of a bullet or shell) to fail to fire or explode. **2.** (of an internal-combustion engine) to fail to ignite properly or when expected. **3.** to fail to achieve the desired result, effect, etc.: *His criticisms completely misfired.* —*n.* **4.** an act or instance of misfiring. [1745–55; MIS-[1] + FIRE]

mis·fit (mis fit′ *for 1;* mis fit′, mis′fit′ *for 2;* mis′fit′ *for 3*), *v.,* **-fit·ted, -fit·ting,** *n.* —*v.t., v.i.* **1.** to fit badly. —*n.* **2.** something that fits badly, as a garment that is too large or too small. **3.** a person who is not suited or is unable to adjust to the circumstances of his or her particular situation: *a misfit in one's job.* [1815–25; MIS-[1] + FIT[1]]

mis·for·tune (mis fôr′chən), *n.* **1.** adverse fortune; bad luck. **2.** an instance of this; mischance; mishap. [1400–50; late ME. See MIS-[1], FORTUNE]
—Syn. 2. accident; disaster, calamity, catastrophe; reverse; blow. See **affliction.**

mis·func·tion (mis fungk′shən), *n., v.i.* malfunction. [MIS-[1] + FUNCTION]

mis·give (mis giv′), *v.,* **-gave, -giv·en, -giv·ing.** —*v.t.* **1.** (of one's mind, heart, etc.) to give doubt or apprehension to. —*v.i.* **2.** to be apprehensive. [1505–15; MIS-[1] + GIVE]

mis·giv·ing (mis giv′ing), *n.* Often, **misgivings.** a feeling of doubt, distrust, or apprehension. [1595–1605; MISGIVE + -ING[1]] **—mis·giv′ing·ly,** *adv.*
—Syn. suspicion, mistrust, hesitation. See **apprehension.**

mis·gov·ern (mis guv′ərn), *v.t.* to govern or manage badly. [1375–1425; late ME *misgovernen.* See MIS-[1], GOVERN] **—mis·gov′ern·ment, mis·gov′ern·ance,** *n.*

mis·guide (mis gīd′), *v.t.,* **-guid·ed, -guid·ing.** to guide wrongly; misdirect. [1325–75; MIS-[1] + GUIDE; r. ME *misgien;* see GUY[2]] **—mis·guid′ance,** *n.* **—mis·guid′er,** *n.*

mis·guid·ed (mis gī′did), *adj.* misled; mistaken: *Their naive actions were a misguided attempt to help the poor.* [1480–90; MISGUIDE + -ED[2]] **—mis·guid′ed·ly,** *adv.* **—mis·guid′ed·ness,** *n.*

mis·han·dle (mis han′dl), *v.t.,* **-dled, -dling. 1.** to handle badly; maltreat: *to mishandle a dog.* **2.** to manage badly: *to mishandle an estate.* **3.** to lose or misplace: *to mishandle baggage.* [1490–1500; MIS-[1] + HANDLE]

mi·shan·ter (mi shan′tər), *n. Scot. and North Eng.* a misfortune; mishap. Also, **mischanter.** [1745–55; var. of *misaunter,* equiv. to MIS-[1] + *aunter,* var. of obs. *aventure* ADVENTURE]

mis·hap (mis′hap, mis hap′), *n.* an unfortunate accident. [1300–50; ME; see MIS-[1], HAP]
—Syn. misadventure, mischance.

Mish·a·wa·ka (mish′ə wô′kə), *n.* a city in N Indiana, near South Bend. 40,224.

mis·hear (mis hēr′), *v.t.,* **-heard, -hear·ing.** to hear incorrectly or imperfectly: *to mishear a remark.* [bef. 1000; ME *misheren,* OE *mishīeran.* See MIS-[1], HEAR]

mish·e·gaas (mish′i gäs′), *n.* meshugaas.

Mi·shi·ma (mi shē′mə; *Japn.* mē′shē mä′), *n.* **Yu·ki·o** (yo͞o′kē ō′; *Japn.* yo͞o′kē ô′), (*Kimitake Hiraoka*), 1925–70, Japanese novelist and playwright.

mis·hit (*v.* mis hit′; *n., adj.,* mis′hit′), *v.,* **-hit, -hit·ting,** *n., adj.* —*v.t.* **1.** to hit (a ball) badly or incorrectly, as in tennis or cricket. —*n.* **2.** a bad or faulty hit, as in tennis or cricket. —*adj.* **3.** (of a ball) hit badly. [1880–85; MIS-[1] + HIT]

mish·mash (mish′mäsh′, -mash′), *n.* a confused mess; hodgepodge; jumble. Also, **mish·mosh** (mish′mosh′). [1425–75; late ME; gradational formation based on MASH]

Mish·nah (*Eng., Ashk. Heb.* mish′nə; *Seph. Heb.* mēsh-nä′), *n., pl.* **Mish·na·yoth, Mish·na·yot, Mish·na·yos** (*Eng., Ashk. Heb.* mish′nə yōs′; *Seph. Heb.* mēsh nä-yôt′), *Eng.* **Mish·nahs.** *Judaism.* **1.** the collection of oral laws compiled about A.D. 200 by Rabbi Judah ha-

CONCISE PRONUNCIATION KEY: *act, cāpe, dâre, pärt; set, ēqual; if, īce; ox, ōver, ôrder, oil, bo͝ok, bo͞ot, out; up, ûrge; child; sing; shoe; thin, that;* zh as in *treasure.* ə = *a* as in *alone, e* as in *system, i* as in *easily, o* as in *gallop, u* as in *circus;* ᵊ as in *fire* (fīᵊr), *hour* (ouᵊr). l and n can serve as syllabic consonants, as in *cradle* (krād′l), and *button* (but′n). See the full key inside the front cover.

mis·but′toned, *adj.*
mis·cap′tion, *v.t.*
mis·cat′a·log′, *v.t.*
mis·cat′e·go·rize′, *v.t.,* **-rized, -riz·ing.**
mis·cat′e·go·rized′, *adj.*
mis·cen′sure, *v.,* **-sured, -sur·ing.**
mis·chan′nel, *v.,* **-neled, -nel·ing** or (*esp. Brit.*) **-nelled, -nel·ling.**
mis·char′ac·ter·ize′, *v.t.,* **-ized, -iz·ing.**
mis·charge′, *v.,* **-charged, -charg·ing.**
mis·claim′, *v.t.*
mis·class′, *v.*
mis·clas′si·fi·ca′tion, *n.*
mis·clas′si·fy′, *v.t.,* **-fied, -fy·ing.**
mis·coin′, *v.*
mis·coin′age, *n.*
mis′com·pre·hen′sion, *n.*
mis′com·pu·ta′tion, *n.*
mis′com·pute′, *v.,* **-put·ed, -put·ing.**
mis′con·jec′ture, *v.,* **-tured, -tur·ing;** *n.*
mis·con′ju·gate′, *v.,* **-gat·ed, -gat·ing.**
mis′con·nect′, *v.*
mis′con·nec′tion, *n.*
mis′co·or′di·nate′, *v.,***-nat·ed, -nat·ing.**
mis′cor·re·la′tion, *n.*
mis·cul′ti·vat′ed, *adj.*
mis·cut′, *v.,* **-cut, -cut·ting.**
mis′de·clare′, *v.,* **-clared, -clar·ing.**
mis′de·fine′, *v.t.,* **-fined, -fin·ing.**
mis′de·liv′er, *v.t.*
mis′de·liv′er·y, *n., pl.* **-er·ies.**
mis′de·vel′op, *v.*
mis·di′a·grammed′, *adj.*
mis·dic′tat·ed, *adj.*
mis′dis·tri·bu′tion, *n.*
mis′di·vide′, *v.,* **-vid·ed, -vid·ing.**
mis′di·vi′sion, *n.*
mis·draw′, *v.,* **-drew, -drawn, -draw·ing.**
mis·ed′it, *v.t.*
mis·em′pha·sis, *n., pl.* **-ses.**
mis·em′pha·size′, *v.t.,* **-sized, -siz·ing.**
mis′en·code′, *v.t.,***-cod·ed, -cod·ing.**

Nasi and forming the basic part of the Talmud. **2.** an article or section of this collection. Also, **Mish′na.** [1600–10; < Medieval Heb *mishnāh* lit., teaching by oral repetition] **—Mish·na·ic** (mish nā′ik), **Mish′nic, Mish′·ni·cal,** *adj.*

mish·po·cha (mish pô′khə, -po͝okh′ə), *n. Yiddish.* an entire family network comprising relatives by blood and marriage and sometimes including close friends; clan.

mis·i·den·ti·fy (mis′ī den′tə fī′, -i den′-), *v.t.,* **-fied, -fy·ing.** to identify incorrectly. [1890–95; MIS-¹ + IDENTIFY] **—mis′i·den′ti·fi·ca′tion,** *n.*

mis·im·pres·sion (mis′im presh′ən), *n.* a faulty or incorrect impression; a misconception or misapprehension. [1660–70; MIS-¹ + IMPRESSION]

mis·in·form (mis′in fôrm′), *v.t.* to give false or misleading information to. [1350–1400; ME *misenfourmen.* See MIS-¹, INFORM] **—mis′in·form′ant, mis′in·form′·er,** *n.* **—mis′in·form′a·tive,** *adj.* **—mis·in·for·ma·tion** (mis′in fər mā′shən), *n.*
—Syn. mislead, misdirect.

mis·in·ter·pret (mis′in tûr′prit), *v.t., v.i.* to interpret, explain, or understand incorrectly. [1580–90; MIS-¹ + INTERPRET] **—mis′in·ter′pret·a·ble,** *adj.* **—mis′in·ter′pre·ta′tion,** *n.* **—mis′in·ter′pret·er,** *n.*

mis·join·der (mis join′dər), *n. Law.* a joining in one suit or action of causes or of parties not permitted to be so joined. [1850–55; MIS-¹ + JOINDER]

mis·judge (mis juj′), *v.t., v.i.,* **-judged, -judg·ing.** to judge, estimate, or value wrongly or unjustly. [1525–35; MIS-¹ + JUDGE] **—mis·judg′er,** *n.* **—mis·judg′ing·ly,** *adv.* **—mis·judg′ment;** *esp. Brit.,* **mis·judge′ment,** *n.*

Mis·ki·to (mə skē′tō), *n., pl.* **-tos,** (*esp. collectively*) **-to** for 1. **1.** a member of an American Indian people of northeastern Nicaragua and adjacent areas of Honduras. **2.** the language of the Miskito. Also, **Mosquito.**

mis·know (mis nō′), *v.t.,* **-knew, -known, -know·ing.** to fail to understand or recognize; misunderstand: *to misknow the problem.* [1250–1300; ME *misknowen.* See MIS-¹, KNOW¹] **—mis·knowl·edge** (mis nol′ij), *n.*

Mis·kolc (mish′kôlts), *n.* a city in N Hungary. 199,000.

mis·la·bel (mis lā′bəl), *v.t.,* **-beled, -bel·ing** or (*esp. Brit.*) **-belled, -bel·ling.** to label wrongly, incorrectly, or misleadingly. [MIS-¹ + LABEL]

mis·lay (mis lā′), *v.t.,* **-laid, -lay·ing. 1.** to lose temporarily; misplace: *He mislaid his keys.* **2.** to lay or place wrongly; arrange or situate improperly: *to mislay linoleum.* [1350–1400; ME *mysse layen.* See MIS-¹, LAY¹] **—mis·lay′er,** *n.*

mis·lead (mis lēd′), *v.,* **-led, -lead·ing.** *—v.t.* **1.** to lead or guide wrongly; lead astray. **2.** to lead into error of conduct, thought, or judgment. *—v.i.* **3.** to be misleading; tend to deceive: *vague directions that often mislead.* [bef. 1050; ME *misleden,* OE *mislǣdan.* See MIS-¹, LEAD¹] **—mis·lead′er,** *n.*
—Syn. 1. misguide, misdirect. **2.** delude, deceive.

mis·lead·ing (mis lē′ding), *adj.* deceptive; tending to mislead. [1630–40; MISLEAD + -ING²] **—mis·lead′ing·ly,** *adv.* **—mis·lead′ing·ness,** *n.*

mis·leared (mis lērd′), *adj. Scot. and North Eng.* ill-mannered; rude; crude. [1685–95; ptp. of *mislear,* ME *misleren,* OE *mislǣran* to teach amiss. See MIS-¹, LEARN]

mis·like (mis līk′), *v.t.,* **-liked, -lik·ing.** *Archaic.* **1.** to dislike. **2.** to displease. [bef. 900; ME *misliken,* OE *mislīcian.* See MIS-¹, LIKE²] **—mis·lik′er,** *n.*

mis·lo·cate (mis lō′kāt, mis′lō kāt′), *v.t.,* **-cat·ed, -cat·ing. 1.** to misplace. **2.** to specify a wrong location for: *to mislocate the source of the Nile.* [1810–20; MIS-¹ + LOCATE] **—mis′lo·ca′tion,** *n.*

mis·man·age (mis man′ij), *v.t., v.i.,* **-aged, -ag·ing.** to manage incompetently or dishonestly: *to mismanage funds.* [1680–90; MIS-¹ + MANAGE] **—mis·man′age·ment,** *n.* **—mis·man′ag·er,** *n.*
—Syn. mishandle, bungle, botch, maladminister.

mis·mar·riage (mis mar′ij), *n.* an unsuitable or unhappy marriage. [1810–20; MIS-¹ + MARRIAGE]

mis·match (mis mach′; *for 2 also* mis′mach′), *v.t.* **1.** to match badly or unsuitably. *—n.* **2.** a bad or unsatisfactory match. [1590–1600; MIS-¹ + MATCH²]

mis·mate (mis māt′), *v.t., v.i.,* **-mat·ed, -mat·ing.** to mate unsuitably or wrongly. [1890–95; MIS-¹ + MATE¹]

mis·move (mis mo͞ov′), *n.* a wrong or prohibited move, as in a game. [1875–80, *Amer.;* MIS-¹ + MOVE]

mis·name (mis nām′), *v.t.,* **-named, -nam·ing.** to name incorrectly or wrongly; miscall. [1475–85; MIS-¹ + NAME]

mis·no·mer (mis nō′mər), *n.* **1.** a misapplied or inappropriate name or designation. **2.** an error in naming a person or thing. [1425–75; late ME < AF, n. use of MF *mesnomer* to misname, equiv. to *mes-* MIS-¹ + *nomer* < L *nōmināre;* see NOMINATE]

mi·so (mē′sō; *Japn.* mē′sô), *n. Japanese Cookery.* a fermented seasoning paste of soybeans, often with rice or barley added, used to flavor soups and sauces. [1720–30; < Japn, prob. < dial. Korean, equiv. to Korean *meju* soybean malt]

miso-, a combining form meaning "hate," with the object of hatred specified by the following element: *misogyny.* Also, **mis-.** [< Gk, comb. form of *mīseîn* to hate, *mîsos* hatred]

mis·o·cai·ne·a (mis′ō kī′nē ə, -kā′-, mī′sō-), *n.* an abnormal aversion to anything new. [< NL; see MISO-, CAINO-, -IA]

mi·sog·a·my (mi sog′ə mē, mī-), *n.* hatred of marriage. [1650–60; MISO- + -GAMY] **—mis·o·gam·ic** (mis′ə gam′ik, mī′sə-), *adj.* **—mi·sog′a·mist,** *n.*

mi·sog·y·nism (mi soj′ə niz′əm, mī-), *n.* misogyny. [1820–30; see MISOGYNY, -ISM]

mi·sog·y·ny (mi soj′ə nē, mī-), *n.* hatred, dislike, or mistrust of women. Cf. **misandry.** [1650–60; < NL *misogynia.* See MISO-, GYN-, -Y³] **—mi·sog′y·nic, mi·sog′y·nous, mi·sog′y·nis′tic,** *adj.* **—mi·sog′y·nist,** *n.*

mi·sol·o·gy (mi sol′ə jē, mī-), *n.* distrust or hatred of reason or reasoning. [1825–35; MISO- + -LOGY] **—mi·sol′o·gist,** *n.*

mis·o·ne·ism (mis′ō nē′iz əm, mī′sō-), *n.* hatred or dislike of what is new or represents change. [1885–90; < It *misoneismo.* See MISO-, NEO-, -ISM] **—mis′o·ne′ist,** *n.* **—mis′o·ne·is′tic,** *adj.*

mis·o·pe·di·a (mis′ō pē′dē ə, mī′sō-), *n.* hatred of children, esp. one's own. Also, **mis′o·pae′di·a.** [< NL *misopaedia;* see MISO-, PED-¹, -IA] **—mis′o·pe′dist,** *n.*

mis·o·ri·ent (mis ôr′ē ent′, -ōr′-), *v.t.* to orient wrongly or improperly. [1950–55; MIS- + ORIENT (v.)]

mis·o·ri·en·tate (mis ôr′ē ən tāt′, -en-, -ōr′-), *v.t.,* **-tat·ed, -tat·ing.** misorient. [1950–55; MIS-¹ + ORIENTATE] **—mis·o′ri·en·ta′tion,** *n.*

mis·per·ceive (mis′pər sēv′), *v.t.,* **-ceived, -ceiv·ing.** to understand or perceive incorrectly; misunderstand. [1920–25; MIS-¹ + PERCEIVE] **—mis·per·cep·tion** (mis′pər sep′shən), *n.*

mis·pick (mis′pik′), *n.* **1.** a pick or filling yarn that has failed to interlace with the warp as a result of a mechanical defect in the loom. **2.** a defect in a fabric caused by such a pick or filling yarn. [MIS-¹ + PICK³]

mis·pick·el (mis′pik′əl), *n. Mineral.* arsenopyrite. [1675–85; < G *Mispickel*]

mis·place (mis plās′), *v.t.,* **-placed, -plac·ing. 1.** to put in a wrong place. **2.** to put in a place afterward forgotten; lose; mislay. **3.** to place or bestow improperly, unsuitably, or unwisely: *to misplace one's trust.* [1545–55; MIS-¹ + PLACE] **—mis·place′ment,** *n.*
—Syn. 1, 2. See **displace. 3.** misapply.

mis′placed mod′ifier, *Gram.* a word, phrase, or clause that seems to refer to or modify an unintended word because of its placement in a sentence, as *when young* in *When young, circuses appeal to all of us.* Cf. **dangling participle.**
—Usage. Sometimes, as in the example above, a MISPLACED MODIFIER can cause a temporarily puzzling or ludicrous reading of a passage; at other times it can result in ambiguity: *Tall and handsome, the people looked at him with awe and admiration.* Usually some rearrangement of elements, and occasionally an addition, can make relationships clear and unambiguous: *Circuses appeal to all of us when young* (or *when we are young*). *Because he was tall and handsome, the people looked at him with awe and admiration.* See also **dangling participle.**

mis·play (*n.* mis plā′, mis′plā′; *v.* mis plā′), *Sports, Games.* *—n.* **1.** a wrong or bad play. **2.** a play prohibited by the rules. *—v.t.* **3.** to make an error or incorrect play on or with; play wrongly: *The catcher misplayed the ball, allowing the base runner to score.* **4.** to make a play on or with (a card, chess piece, etc.) prohibited by the rules. [1865–70, *Amer.;* MIS-¹ + PLAY]

mis·plead (mis plēd′), *v.i., v.t.,* **-plead·ed** or **-plead** (-pled) or **-pled, -plead·ing.** to plead incorrectly. [1670–80; MIS-¹ + PLEAD]

mis·plead·ing (mis plē′ding), *n. Law.* a mistake in pleading, as a misjoinder of parties or a misstatement of a cause of action. [1525–35; MIS-¹ + PLEADING]

mis·print (*n.* mis′print′, mis print′; *v.* mis print′), *n.* **1.** a mistake in printing, as an instance of printing a letter or word other than that intended. *—v.t.* **2.** to print incorrectly. [1485–95; MIS-¹ + PRINT]

mis·prise (mis prīz′), *v.t.,* **-prised, -pris·ing.** misprize. **—mis·pris′er,** *n.*

mis·pri·sion¹ (mis prizh′ən), *n.* **1.** a neglect or violation of official duty by one in office. **2.** failure by one not an accessory to prevent or notify the authorities of treason or felony. **3.** a contempt against the government, monarch, or courts, as sedition, lese majesty, or a contempt of court. **4.** a mistake; misunderstanding. [1375–1425; late ME < AF, OF *mesprision,* equiv. to *mes-* MIS-¹ + *prision* < L *prēnsiōn-,* var. of *prehēnsiōn-* (s. of *prehēnsiō*) PREHENSION]

mis·pri·sion² (mis prizh′ən), *n.* contempt or scorn. [1580–90; MISPRISE + -ION]

mis·prize (mis prīz′), *v.t.,* **-prized, -priz·ing.** to despise; undervalue; slight; scorn. Also, **misprise.** [1300–50; ME *misprise* < MF *mesprisier,* equiv. to *mes-* MIS-¹ + *prisier* to PRIZE²] **—mis·priz′er,** *n.*

mis·pro·nounce (mis′prə nouns′), *v.t., v.i.,* **-nounced, -nounc·ing.** to pronounce incorrectly. [1585–95; MIS-¹ + PRONOUNCE] **—mis′pro·nounc′er,** *n.* **—mis·pro·nun·ci·a·tion** (mis′prə nun′sē ā′shən), *n.*

mis·proud (mis proud′), *adj. Archaic.* unreasonably proud. [1275–1325; ME; see MIS-¹, PROUD]

mis·punc·tu·ate (mis pungk′cho͞o āt′), *v.t.,* **-at·ed, -at·ing.** to punctuate incorrectly. [1840–50; MIS-¹ + PUNCTUATE] **—mis·punc′tu·a′tion,** *n.*

mis·quo·ta·tion (mis′kwō tā′shən), *n.* **1.** the act of misquoting. **2.** an instance or occasion of misquoting or of being misquoted. [1765–75; MIS-¹ + QUOTATION]

mis·quote (mis kwōt′), *v.,* **-quot·ed, -quot·ing,** *n.* *—v.t., v.i.* **1.** to quote incorrectly. *—n.* **2.** a quotation that is incorrect. [1590–1600; MIS-¹ + QUOTE] **—mis·quot′er,** *n.*

Misr (mis′rə), *n.* Arabic name of **Egypt.**

mis·read (mis rēd′), *v.t., v.i.,* **-read** (red), **-read·ing. 1.** to read wrongly. **2.** to misunderstand or misinterpret. [1800–10; MIS-¹ + READ¹] **—mis·read′er,** *n.*

mis·reck·on (mis rek′ən), *v.t., v.i.* to reckon incorrectly; miscalculate. [1515–25; MIS-¹ + RECKON]

mis·re·demp·tion (mis′ri demp′shən), *n.* illegal or fraudulent traffic in consumer product coupons, including mail theft and counterfeiting. [MIS-¹ + REDEMPTION]

mis·re·mem·ber (mis′ri mem′bər), *v.t., v.i.* **1.** to remember incorrectly. **2.** to fail to remember; forget. [1525–35; MIS-¹ + REMEMBER]

mis·re·port (mis′ri pôrt′, -pōrt′), *v.t.* **1.** to report incorrectly or falsely. *—n.* **2.** an incorrect or false report. [1375–1425; late ME *misreport(e)* (n.), *misreporten* (v.); see MIS-¹, REPORT] **—mis′re·port′er,** *n.*

mis·rep·re·sent (mis′rep ri zent′), *v.t.* **1.** to represent incorrectly, improperly, or falsely. **2.** to represent in an unsatisfactory manner. [1640–50; MIS-¹ + REPRESENT] **—mis′rep·re·sen·ta′tion,** *n.* **—mis′rep·re·sen′ta·tive,** *adj.* **—mis′rep·re·sent′er,** *n.*
—Syn. MISREPRESENT, DISTORT, FALSIFY, BELIE share the sense of presenting information in a way that does not accord with the truth. MISREPRESENT usually involves a deliberate intention to deceive, either for profit or advantage: *The dealer misrepresented the condition of the car.* DISTORT implies a purposeful twisting or emphasizing of certain statements so as to produce an inaccurate or misleading impression: *cleverly distorting the facts to create an impression of his own innocence.* FALSIFY suggests a tampering with or alteration of facts, records, or documents, especially with the intent to cheat or deceive: *He falsified the birth records to conceal his age.* BELIE means to create an impression that is inconsistent with the facts, or that contradicts other evidence but it does not usually suggest intent to deceive: *Her casual, relaxed manner belies her insecurity.*

mis·rule (mis ro͞ol′), *n., v.,* **-ruled, -rul·ing.** *—n.* **1.** bad or unwise rule; misgovernment. **2.** disorder or lawlessness. *—v.t.* **3.** to misgovern. [1300–50; ME *misreulen* (v.), *misreule* (n.). See MIS-¹, RULE] **—mis·rul′er,** *n.*

mis·run (mis run′, mis′run), *n. Metall.* an incomplete casting, the metal of which has solidified prematurely. [MIS-¹ + RUN]

miss¹ (mis), *v.t.* **1.** to fail to hit or strike: *to miss a target.* **2.** to fail to encounter, meet, catch, etc.: *to miss a train.* **3.** to fail to take advantage of: *to miss a chance.* **4.** to fail to be present at or for: *to miss a day of school.* **5.** to notice the absence or loss of: *When did you first miss your wallet?* **6.** to regret the absence or loss of: *I miss you all dreadfully.* **7.** to escape or avoid: *He just missed being caught.* **8.** to fail to perceive or understand: *to miss the point of a remark.* *—v.i.* **9.** to fail to hit something. **10.** to fail of effect or success; be unsuccessful. **11. miss fire.** See **fire** (def. 25). **12. miss out,** *Chiefly Brit.* to omit; leave out. **13. miss out on,** to fail to take advantage of, experience, etc.: *You missed out on a great opportunity.* *—n.* **14.** a failure to hit something. **15.** a failure of any kind. **16.** an omission. **17.** a misfire. [bef. 900; ME *missen,* OE *missan;* c. OFris *missa,* MLG, MD, OHG *missen,* ON *missa* to fail to hit or reach] **—miss′a·ble,** *adj.*

miss² (mis), *n., pl.* **miss·es. 1.** (*cap.*) a title of respect for an unmarried woman, conventionally prefixed to her name or to the name of that which she represents: *Miss Mary Jones; Miss Sweden.* **2.** (used by itself, as a term of address, esp. to a young woman): *Miss, please bring me some ketchup.* **3.** (*cap.*) a title prefixed to a mock surname used to represent a particular attribute of the person, esp. one excessively prominent: *Miss Innocent; Miss Congeniality.* **4.** a young unmarried woman; girl: *a radiant miss of 18 or so.* **5. misses, a.** a range of sizes, chiefly from 6 to 20, for garments that fit women of average height and build. **b.** the department or section of a store where these garments are sold. **c.** a garment in this size range. [1600–10; short for MISTRESS]
—Usage. See **Ms.**

Miss., Mississippi.

miss., 1. mission. **2.** missionary.

mis·sa (mēs′sä; *Eng.* mis′ə), *n. Latin.* Mass.

mis·sa can·ta·ta (mis′ə kən tä′tə), a Mass whose

CONCISE ETYMOLOGY KEY: <, descended or borrowed from; >, whence; b., blend of, blended; c., cognate with; cf., compare; deriv., derivative; equiv., equivalent; imit., imitative; obl., oblique; r., replacing; s., stem; sp., spelling, spelled; resp., respelling, respelled; trans., translation; ?, origin unknown; *, unattested; ‡, probably earlier than. See the full key inside the front cover.

mis′e·val′u·ate′, *v.t.,* **-at·ed, -at·ing.**
mis′e·val′u·a′tion, *n.*
mis′ex·plained′, *adj.*
mis·fash′ion, *n.*
mis·fash′ioned, *adj.*
mis·field′, *v.*
mis·fo′cus, *v.,* **-cused, -cus·ing** or (*esp. Brit.*) **-cussed, -cus·sing.**
mis·fo′cused, *adj.*
mis·fo′cussed, *adj.*
mis·form′, *v.*
mis′for·ma′tion, *n.*
mis·formed′, *adj.*
mis·frame′, *v.,* **-framed, -fram·ing.**
mis·gauge′, *v.t.,* **-gauged, -gaug·ing.**
mis·grade′, *v.,* **-grad·ed, -grad·ing.**
mis·grad′ed, *adj.*
mis·graft′, *v.*
mis′in·fer′, *v.,* **-ferred, -fer·ring.**
mis·in′fer·ence, *n.*
mis′in·struct′, *v.t.*
mis′in·struc′tion, *n.*
mis′in·tend′, *v.*
mis′in·ten′tion, *n.*
mis·i′tem·ized′, *adj.*
mis·join′, *v.*
mis·learn′, *v.,* **-learned** or **-learnt, -learn·ing.**
mis·make′, *v.,* **-made, -mak·ing.**
mis·mark′, *v.*
mis·meas′ure, *v.,* **-ured, -ur·ing.**
mis·meas′ure·ment, *n.*
mis·mesh′, *v.*
mis·mount′, *v.*
mis·nar′rate, *v.,* **-rat·ed, -rat·ing.**
mis·nav′i·gate′, *v.,* **-gat·ed, -gat·ing.**
mis′nav·i·ga′tion, *n.*
mis·num′ber, *v.*
mis·oc′cu·py′, *v.,* **-pied, -py·ing.**
mis′op·er·a′tion, *n.*
mis·or′der, *v.*
mis′or′gan·i·za′tion, *n.*
mis·or′gan·ize′, *v.,* **-ized, -iz·ing.**
mis·pack′age, *v.t.,* **-aged, -ag·ing.**
mis·pack′aged, *adj.*

music is equivalent to that of the High Mass but that is less elaborate in its celebration. Also called **sung Mass.** [1900–05; < LL: lit., sung mass; see MASS, CANTATA]

mis•sal (mis′əl), *n.* **1.** (*sometimes cap.*) *Rom. Cath. Ch.* the book containing the prayers and rites used by the priest in celebrating Mass over the course of the entire year. **2.** any book of prayers or devotions. [1300–50; ME < ML *missāle*, n. use of neut. of *missālis*, equiv. to *miss(a)* MASS + *-ālis* -AL[1]]

mis′sal stand′, a lectern for a missal, esp. one on an altar. Also called **altar stand.**

mis•say (mis sā′), *v.*, **-said, -say•ing.** —*v.t.* **1.** to say or speak ill of; vilify; slander. **2.** to say wrongly. —*v.i.* **3.** to speak wrongly or incorrectly. [1175–1225; ME *mis-seyen.* See MIS-[1], SAY[1]] —**mis•say′er,** *n.*

mis•seem (mis sēm′), *v.t. Archaic.* misbecome. [1300–50; ME *missemen.* See MIS-[1], SEEM]

mis′sel thrush′ (mis′əl). See **mistle thrush.**

mis•send (mis send′), *v.t.*, **-sent, -send•ing.** to send or forward, esp. mail, to a wrong place or person. [1400–50; late ME *missenden.* See MIS-[1], SEND]

mis•shape (mis shāp′, mish-), *v.t.*, **-shaped, -shaped** or **-shap•en, -shap•ing.** to shape badly or wrongly; deform. [1400–50; late ME; see MIS-[1], SHAPE]

mis•shap•en (mis shā′pən, mish-), *adj.* badly shaped; deformed. [1350–1400; ME: ptp. of MISSHAPE; see -EN[3]] —**mis•shap′en•ly,** *adv.* —**mis•shap′en•ness,** *n.*

mis•sile (mis′əl *or, esp. Brit.*, -īl), *n.* **1.** an object or weapon for throwing, hurling, or shooting, as a stone, bullet, or arrow. **2.** See **guided missile. 3.** See **ballistic missile.** —*adj.* **4.** capable of being thrown, hurled, or shot, as from the hand or a gun. **5.** used or designed for discharging missiles. [1600–10; < L, neut. of *missilis*, equiv. to *miss(us)* (ptp. of *mittere* to send, throw) + *-ilis* -ILE]

mis•sil•eer (mis′ə lēr′), *n.* missileman. [MISSILE + -EER]

mis′sile gap′, a lag in one country's missile production relative to the production of another country.

mis•sile•man (mis′əl mən *or, esp. Brit.*, -īl-), *n., pl.* **-men. 1.** a person who builds, designs, launches, or operates guided missiles. **2.** a technician or scientist whose work pertains to missilery. Also called **missileer.** [1950–55; MISSILE + -MAN]

mis•sile•ry (mis′əl rē), *n.* the science of the construction and use of guided missiles. Also, **mis′sil•ry.** [1875–80; MISSILE + -RY]

miss•ing (mis′ing), *adj.* lacking, absent, or not found: *a missing person.* [1520–30; MISS[1] + -ING[2]]

miss′ing link′, 1. a hypothetical form of animal assumed to have constituted a connecting link between the anthropoid apes and humans, sometimes identified as the genus *Australopithecus.* **2.** something lacking for the completion of a series or sequence. [1850–55]

miss′ing mass′, *Astrophysics.* the difference in mass in the universe between that observed to exist and that necessary for the closed universe model. [1975–80]

mis•si•ol•o•gy (mis′ē ol′ə jē), *n. Christianity.* the theological study of the mission of the church, esp. the character and purpose of missionary work. [1920–25; MISSI(ON) + -O- + -LOGY]

mis•sion (mish′ən), *n.* **1.** a group or committee of persons sent to a foreign country to conduct negotiations, establish relations, provide scientific and technical assistance, or the like. **2.** the business with which such a group is charged. **3.** a permanent diplomatic establishment abroad; embassy; legation. **4.** *Mil.* an operational task, usually assigned by a higher headquarters: *a mission to bomb the bridge.* **5.** *Aerospace.* an operation designed to carry out the goals of a specific program: *a space mission.* **6.** a group of persons sent by a church to carry on religious work, esp. evangelization in foreign lands, and often to establish schools, hospitals, etc. **7.** an establishment of missionaries in a foreign land; a missionary church or station. **8.** a similar establishment in any region. **9.** the district assigned to a missionary. **10.** missionary duty or work. **11.** an organization for carrying on missionary work. **12.** Also called **rescue mission.** a shelter operated by a church or other organization offering food, lodging, and other assistance to needy persons. **13. missions,** organized missionary work or activities in any country or region. **14.** a church or a region dependent on a larger church or denomination. **15.** a series of special religious services for increasing religious devotion and converting unbelievers: *to preach a mission.* **16.** an assigned or self-imposed duty or task; calling; vocation. **17.** a sending or being sent for some duty or purpose. **18.** those sent. —*adj.* **19.** of or pertaining to a mission. **20.** (*usually cap.*) noting or pertaining to a style of American furniture of the early 20th century, created in supposed imitation of the furnishings of the Spanish missions of California and characterized by the use of dark, stained wood, by heaviness, and by extreme plainness. Also called **foreign mission** (for defs. 3, 6). [1590–1600; 1925–30 for def. 4; < L *missiōn-* (s. of *missiō*) a sending off, equiv. to *miss(us)* (ptp. of *mittere* to send) + *-iōn-* -ION] —**mis′sion•al,** *adj.*

Mis•sion (mish′ən), *n.* a city in S Texas. 22,589.

mis•sion•ar•y (mish′ə ner′ē), *n., pl.* **-ar•ies,** *adj.* —*n.* Also, **mis′sion•er. 1.** a person sent by a church into an area to carry on evangelism or other activities, as educational or hospital work. **2.** a person strongly in favor of a program, set of principles, etc., who attempts to persuade or convert others. **3.** a person who is sent on a mission. —*adj.* **4.** pertaining to or connected with religious missions. **5.** engaged in such a mission, or devoted to work connected with missions. **6.** reflecting or prompted by the desire to persuade or convert others: *the missionary efforts of political fanatics.* **7.** characteristic of a missionary. [1635–45; < NL *missiōnārius.* See MISSION, -ARY]

mis′sionary apostol′ic, *pl.* **missionaries apostolic.** *Rom. Cath. Ch.* an honorary title conferred by the pope on certain missionaries.

mis′sionary posi′tion, a position for sexual intercourse in which the couple lies face to face with the male on top. [1965–70; so called because it was allegedly favored by Christian missionaries working among indigenous peoples, in preference to positions in which the man approaches the woman from behind]

Mis′sionary Ridge′, a ridge in NW Georgia and SE Tennessee: Civil War battle 1863.

mis′sion control′, *Aerospace.* a command center for the control, monitoring, and support of activities connected with manned space flight. Also called **mis′sion control′ cen′ter.** [1960–65]

mis•sion•ize (mish′ə nīz′), *v.*, **-ized, -iz•ing.** —*v.i.* **1.** to conduct missionary work. —*v.t.* **2.** to conduct missionary work in or among. Also, *esp. Brit.*, **mis′sion•ise′.** [1820–30; MISSION + -IZE]

mis′sion spe′cialist, *U.S. Aerospace.* the crew member of a space shuttle who is assigned primary responsibility for carrying out operations related to the payload of the shuttle. [1975–80]

Mis′sion Vi•e′jo (vē ā′hō), a city in SW California. 50,666.

mis•sis (mis′iz, -is), *n.* **1.** *Older Use.* wife: *I'll have to ask the missis.* **2.** the mistress of a household. Also, **missus.** [1780–90; var. of MISTRESS]

miss•ish (mis′ish), *adj.* prim; affected; prudish. [1785–95; MISS[2] + -ISH[1]] —**miss′ish•ness,** *n.*

Mis•sis•sau•ga (mis′ə sô′gə), *n.* a city in SE Ontario, in S Canada, on the SW shore of Lake Ontario: suburb of Toronto. 315,056.

Mis•sis•sip•pi (mis′ə sip′ē), *n.* **1.** a state in the S United States. 2,520,638; 47,716 sq. mi. (123,585 sq. km). *Cap.:* Jackson. *Abbr.:* MS (for use with zip code), Miss. **2.** a river flowing S from N Minnesota to the Gulf of Mexico: the principal river of the U.S. 2470 mi. (3975 km) long; from the headwaters of the Missouri to the Gulf of Mexico 3988 mi. (6418 km) long.

Mis•sis•sip•pi•an (mis′ə sip′ē ən), *adj.* **1.** of or pertaining to the state of Mississippi or the Mississippi River. **2.** *Geol.* noting or pertaining to a period of the Paleozoic Era, occurring from about 345 million to 310 million years ago and characterized as the age of amphibians. See table under **geologic time.** —*n.* **3.** a native or inhabitant of Mississippi. **4.** *Geol.* the Mississippian Period or System: the former is sometimes considered an epoch of the Carboniferous Period. [1765–75, *Amer.*; MISSISSIPPI + -AN]

mis•sive (mis′iv), *n.* **1.** a written message; letter. —*adj.* **2.** sent or about to be sent, esp. of a letter from an official source. [1400–50; late ME (*letter*) *missive* < ML (*littera*) *missīva* sent (letter), equiv. to L *miss(us)* (ptp. of *mittere* to send) + *-īva*, fem. of *-īvus* -IVE]

Miss′ Ju′lie, a play (1888) by Strindberg.

Mis•so•lon•ghi (mis′ə lông′gē), *n.* a town in W Greece, on the Gulf of Patras: Byron died here 1824. 11,614. Also, **Mesolonghi.**

Mis•sou•la (mi zo͞o′lə), *n.* a city in W Montana. 33,388.

Mis•sour•i (mi zo͝or′ē, -zo͝or′ə), *n., pl.* **-sour•is,** (*esp. collectively*) **-sour•i** for 3. **1.** a state in the central United States. 4,917,444; 69,674 sq. mi. (180,455 sq. km). *Cap.:* Jefferson City. *Abbr.:* MO (for use with zip code), Mo. **2.** a river flowing from SW Montana into the Mississippi N of St. Louis, Mo. 2723 mi. (4382 km) long. **3.** a member of a North American Indian tribe belonging to the Siouan linguistic stock, located on the Missouri River in early historic times and now extinct as a tribe. **4. from Missouri,** *Informal.* unwilling to accept something without proof; skeptical: *I'm from Missouri—you'll have to show me that you're right.* —**Mis•sour′i•an,** *adj., n.*

Missour′i Cit′y, a city in SE Texas. 24,533.

Missour′i Com′promise, *U.S. Hist.* an act of Congress (1820) by which Missouri was admitted as a slave state, Maine as a free state, and slavery was prohibited in the Louisiana Purchase north of latitude 36°30′N, except for Missouri. Cf. **Kansas-Nebraska Act.**

Missour′i gourd′, calabazilla.

Missour′i meer′schaum, corncob (def. 2).

miss•out (mis′out′), *n.* (in the game of craps) a losing throw of the dice. [1925–30; n. use of v. phrase *miss out*]

mis•speak (mis spēk′), *v.t., v.i.*, **-spoke, -spok•en, -speak•ing. 1.** to speak, utter, or pronounce incorrectly. **2.** to speak inaccurately, inappropriately, or too hastily. [1150–1200; ME *misspeken*; see MIS-[1], SPEAK; cf. OE *missprecan* to murmur]

mis•spell (mis spel′), *v.t., v.i.*, **-spelled** or **-spelt, -spell•ing.** to spell incorrectly. [1645–55; MIS-[1] + SPELL[1]]

mis•spell•ing (mis spel′ing), *n.* **1.** the act of spelling incorrectly: *Note his misspelling of that word.* **2.** an incorrectly spelled word: *You have three misspellings in your letter.* [1685–95; MIS-[1] + SPELLING]

mis•spend (mis spend′), *v.t.*, **-spent, -spend•ing.** to spend wrongly or unwisely; squander; waste. [1350–1400; ME. See MIS-[1], SPEND] —**mis•spend′er,** *n.*

mis•spent (mis spent′), **1.** pt. and pp. of **misspend.** —*adj.* **2.** spent wrongly or unwisely; wasted: *misspent youth.*

mis•state (mis stāt′), *v.t.*, **-stat•ed, -stat•ing.** to state wrongly or misleadingly; make a wrong statement about. [1640–50; MIS-[1] + STATE] —**mis•state′ment,** *n.* —**mis•stat′er,** *n.*

—**Syn.** misreport, falsify, alter, distort.

mis•step (mis step′), *n.* **1.** a wrong step. **2.** an error or slip in conduct; faux pas. [1250–1300; ME *missteppen.* See MIS-[1], STEP]

—**Syn. 2.** fault, transgression, lapse, indiscretion.

mis•strike (mis strīk′), *n. Numis.* a coin having the design stamped off center. [1955–60; MIS-[1] + STRIKE]

mis•sus (mis′əz, -əs), *n.* missis.

miss•y (mis′ē), *n., pl.* **miss•ies.** *Informal.* young miss; girl. [1670–80; MISS[2] + -Y[2]]

mist (mist), *n.* **1.** a cloudlike aggregation of minute globules of water suspended in the atmosphere at or near the earth's surface, reducing visibility to a lesser degree than fog. **2.** a cloud of particles resembling this: *She sprayed a mist of perfume onto her handkerchief.* **3.** something that dims, obscures, or blurs: *the mist of ignorance.* **4.** a haze before the eyes that dims the vision: *a mist of tears.* **5.** a suspension of a liquid in a gas. **6.** a drink of liquor served over cracked ice. **7.** a fine spray produced by a vaporizer to add moisture to the air for breathing. —*v.i.* **8.** to become misty. **9.** to rain in very fine drops; drizzle (usually used impersonally with *it* as subject): *It was misting when they went out for lunch.* —*v.t.* **10.** to make misty. **11.** to spray (plants) with a finely diffused jet of water, as a means of replacing lost moisture. [bef. 900; (n.) ME, OE; c. D, LG, Sw *mist;* akin to Gk *omíchlē* fog, Russ *mgla* mist, Skt *megha* cloud; (v.) ME *misten,* OE *mistian,* deriv. of the n.] —**mist′less,** *adj.*

—**Syn. 3, 4.** See **cloud.**

mist., (in prescriptions) a mixture. [< L *mistūra*]

mis•tak•a•ble (mi stā′kə bəl), *adj.* capable of being or liable to be mistaken or misunderstood. [1640–50; MIS-

CONCISE PRONUNCIATION KEY: act, cāpe, dâre, pärt; set, ēqual; *if*, īce; ox, ōver, ôrder, oil, bo͝ok, bo͞ot, out; up, ûrge; child; sing; shoe; thin, *th*at; zh as in *treasure.* ə = *a* as in *alone,* *e* as in *system,* *i* as in *easily,* *o* as in *gallop,* *u* as in *circus;* ᵊ as in *fire* (fīᵊr), *hour* (ouᵊr). l and n can serve as syllabic consonants, as in *cradle* (krād′l), and *button* (but′n). See the full key inside the front cover.

mis•packed′, *adj.*
mis•page′, *v.t.*, **-paged, -pag•ing.**
mis′pag•i•na′tion, *n.*
mis•par′a•phrase′, *v.*, **-phrased, -phras•ing.**
mis•parse′, *v.t.*, **-parsed, -pars•ing.**
mis•patch′, *v.t.*
mis′per•form′, *v.*
mis′per•form′ance, *n.*
mis•phrase′, *v.t.*, **-phrased, -phras•ing.**
mis•pic′ture, *v.t.*, **-tured, -tur•ing.**
mis•plan′, *v.*, **-planned, -plan•ning.**
mis•plant′, *v.t.*
mis′por•tray′al, *n.*
mis′po•si′tion, *v.t.*
mis•prac′tice, *n., v.*, **-ticed, -tic•ing.**
mis•prac′tise, *n., v.*, **-tised, -tis•ing.**
mis′pre•dict′, *v.*
mis′pre•scribe′, *v.*, **-scribed, -scrib•ing.**
mis′pre•sent′, *v.t.*
mis•prin′ci•pled, *adj.*
mis′pro•duce′, *v.*, **-duced, -duc•ing.**
mis′pro•por′tion, *n.*
mis′pro•pos′al, *n.*
mis′pro•pose′, *v.*, **-posed, -pos•ing.**
mis′pro•voke′, *v.t.*, **-voked, -vok•ing.**
mis•pub′li•cized′, *adj.*
mis•pub′lished, *adj.*
mis•pur′chase, *v.t.*, **-chased, -chas•ing.**
mis•qual′i•fy′, *v.*, **-fied, -fy•ing.**
mis•rate′, *v.*, **-rat•ed, -rat•ing.**
mis′rec•ol•lect′, *v.*
mis′rec•ol•lec′tion, *n.*
mis′re•fer′, *v.*, **-ferred, -fer•ring.**
mis•ref′er•ence, *n.*
mis′re•flect′, *v.*
mis′re•form′, *v.*
mis•reg′is•ter, *v.*
mis′reg•is•tra′tion, *n.*
mis•reg′u•late′, *v.t.*, **-lat•ed, -lat•ing.**
mis′re•late′, *v.*, **-lat•ed, -lat•ing.**

TAKE + -ABLE] —**mis·tak′a·ble·ness,** *n.* —**mis·tak′a·bly,** *adv.*

mis·take (mi stāk′), *n., v.,* **-took, -tak·en, -tak·ing.** —*n.* **1.** an error in action, calculation, opinion, or judgment caused by poor reasoning, carelessness, insufficient knowledge, etc. **2.** a misunderstanding or misconception. **3. and no mistake,** for certain; surely: *He's an honorable person, and no mistake.* —*v.t.* **4.** to regard or identify wrongly as something or someone else: *I mistook him for the mayor.* **5.** to understand, interpret, or evaluate wrongly; misunderstand; misinterpret. —*v.i.* **6.** to be in error. [1300–30; ME *mistaken* (v.) < ON *mistaka* to take in error. See MIS-¹, TAKE] —**mis·tak′er,** *n.* —**mis·tak′ing·ly,** *adv.*
—**Syn. 1.** inaccuracy, erratum, fault, oversight. MISTAKE, BLUNDER, ERROR, SLIP refer to deviations from right, accuracy, correctness, or truth. A MISTAKE, grave or trivial, is caused by bad judgment or a disregard of rule or principle: *It was a mistake to argue.* A BLUNDER is a careless, stupid, or gross mistake in action or speech, suggesting awkwardness, heedlessness, or ignorance: *Through his blunder the message was lost.* An ERROR (often interchanged with MISTAKE) is an unintentional wandering or deviation from accuracy, or right conduct: *an error in addition.* A SLIP is usually a minor mistake made through haste or carelessness: *a slip of the tongue.* **5.** misconceive, misjudge, err. —**Ant. 2.** understanding.

mis·tak·en (mi stā′kən), *adj.* **1.** wrongly conceived, held, or done: *a mistaken antagonism.* **2.** erroneous; incorrect; wrong: *a mistaken answer.* **3.** having made a mistake; being in error. [1590–1600; ptp. of MISTAKE; see -EN³] —**mis·tak′en·ly,** *adv.* —**mis·tak′en·ness,** *n.*
—**Syn. 1.** inaccurate, misconceived.

Mis·tas·si·ni (mis′tə sē′nē), *n.* a lake in E Canada, in Quebec province. 840 sq. mi. (2176 sq. km).

mist·bow (mist′bō′), *n.* fogbow. [1895–1900; MIST + BOW²]

mist·coat (mist′kōt′), *n.* (in house painting or interior decoration) a coat of thinner, sometimes pigmented, applied to a finish coat of paint to increase its luster. [MIST + COAT]

mis·teach (mis tēch′), *v.t.,* **-taught, -teach·ing.** to teach wrongly or badly. [bef. 1000; ME *mistechen,* OE *mistǣcan.* See MIS-¹, TEACH] —**mis·teach′er,** *n.*

mis·ter¹ (mis′tər), *n.* **1.** (*cap.*) a conventional title of respect for a man, prefixed to the name and to certain official designations (usually written as the abbreviation *Mr.*). **2.** *Informal.* sir (used in direct address and not followed by the name of the man addressed): *Mister, is this your umbrella?* **3.** (*cap.*) a title prefixed to a mock surname that is used to represent possession of a particular attribute, identity, etc.: *Mister Know-it-all.* **4.** the informal or social title used in addressing a military warrant officer or any naval officer below the rank of commander. **5.** (esp. in military schools and colleges) **a.** a term of respect used by cadets in addressing upperclassmen: used with surname. **b.** a term of disparagement used by upperclassmen in addressing cadets: *Mister, tuck in that shirttail!* **6.** *Older Use.* husband: *You and the mister staying long?* —*v.t.* **7.** to address or speak of as "mister" or "Mr." [1545–55; var. of MASTER]

mist·er² (mis′tər), *n.* a spray, nozzle, or similar device for misting plants. [MIST + -ER¹]

Mis′ter Char′lie, *Slang* (*often disparaging*). **1.** a white man. **2.** white men collectively. [1940–45]

mis·te·ri·o·so (mi stēr′ē ō′sō; *It.* mē′ste ryô′sô), *adj. Music.* mysterious, strange, or weird. [< It, equiv. to *mysteri(o)* MYSTERY¹ + *-oso* -OUS]

mist·flow·er (mist′flou′ər), *n.* a North American composite plant, *Eupatorium coelestinum,* having heads of blue flowers. [1855–60, *Amer.*; MIST + FLOWER]

mis·think (mis thingk′), *v.,* **-thought, -think·ing.** *Archaic.* —*v.i.* **1.** to think incorrectly or unfavorably. —*v.t.* **2.** to think unfavorably or ill of. [1175–1225; ME *misthenken.* See MIS-¹, THINK¹]

Mis·ti (mēs′tē), *n.* See **El Misti.**

mis·time (mis tīm′), *v.t.,* **-timed, -tim·ing.** to time badly; perform, say, propose, etc., at a bad or inappropriate time. [bef. 1000; ME *mistimen,* OE *mistīmian.* See MIS-¹, TIME]

mis′tle thrush′ (mis′əl), a large, European thrush, *Turdus viscivorus,* that feeds on the berries of the mistletoe. Also called **missel thrush.** [1765–75; obs. *mistle* (OE *mistel*) mistletoe]

mis·tle·toe (mis′əl tō′), *n.* **1.** a European plant, *Viscum album,* having yellowish flowers and white berries, growing parasitically on various trees, used in Christmas decorations. **2.** any of several other related, similar plants, as *Phoradendron serotinum,* of the U.S.: the state flower of Oklahoma. [bef. 1000; ME *mistelto,* appar. back formation from OE *misteltān* (*mistel* mistletoe, basil + *tān* twig), the *-n* being taken as pl. ending; c. ON *mistilteinn*]

CONCISE ETYMOLOGY KEY: <, descended or borrowed from; >, whence; b., blend of, blended; c., cognate with; cf., compare; deriv., derivative; equiv., equivalent; imit., imitative; obl., oblique; r., replacing; s., stem; sp., spelling, spelled; resp., respelling, respelled; trans., translation; ?, origin unknown; *, unattested; ‡, probably earlier than. See the full key inside the front cover.

mistletoe, *Phoradendron serotinum*

mis′tletoe cac′tus, a tropical, branched cactus, *Rhipsalis baccifera* (or *cassutha*), having cylindrical stems and mistletoelike fruit. [1885–90]

mis·took (mi stŏŏk′), *v.* pt. of **mistake.**

mis·tral (mis′trəl, mi sträl′), *n.* a cold, dry, northerly wind common in southern France and neighboring regions. [1595–1605; < MF < Pr; OPr *maistral* < L *magistrālis* MAGISTRAL]

Mis·tral (mē STRAL′ *for 1;* mēs TRÄL′ *for 2*), *n.* **1. Fré·dé·ric** (frā dā REK′), 1830–1914, French Provençal poet: Nobel prize 1904. **2. Ga·bri·e·la** (gä′vRē e′lä), (*Lucila Godoy Alcayaga*), 1889–1957, Chilean poet and educator: Nobel prize for literature 1945.

mis·trans·late (mis′trans lāt′, -tranz-, mis trans′lāt, -tranz′-), *v.t., v.i.,* **-lat·ed, -lat·ing.** to translate incorrectly. [1525–35; MIS-¹ + TRANSLATE] —**mis′trans·la′tion,** *n.*

mis·treat (mis trēt′), *v.t.* to treat badly or abusively. [1425–75; late ME *mistreten.* See MIS-¹, TREAT] —**mis·treat′ment,** *n.*
—**Syn.** maltreat, ill-treat, misuse, wrong.

mis·tress (mis′tris), *n.* **1.** a woman who has authority, control, or power, esp. the female head of a household, institution, or other establishment. **2.** a woman employing, or in authority over, servants or attendants. **3.** a female owner of an animal, or formerly, a slave. **4.** a woman who has the power of controlling or disposing of something at her own pleasure: *mistress of a great fortune.* **5.** (*sometimes cap.*) something regarded as feminine that has control or supremacy: *Great Britain, the mistress of the seas.* **6.** a woman who is skilled in something, as an occupation or art. **7.** a woman who has a continuing, extramarital sexual relationship with one man, esp. a man who, in return for an exclusive and continuing liaison, provides her with financial support. **8.** *Brit.* a female schoolteacher; schoolmistress. **9.** (*cap.*) a term of address in former use and corresponding to Mrs., Miss, or Ms. **10.** *Archaic.* sweetheart. [1275–1325; ME *maistresse* < MF, OF, equiv. to *maistre* MASTER + *-esse* -ESS] —**mis′tressed,** *adj.* —**mis′tress·ship′,** *n.*
—**Usage.** See **-ess.**

mis′tress of cer′emonies, a woman who directs the entertainment at a party, dinner, or the like. [1950–55]

mis·tri·al (mis trī′əl, -trīl′), *n. Law.* **1.** a trial terminated without conclusion on the merits of the case because of some error in the proceedings. **2.** an inconclusive trial, as where the jury cannot agree. [1620–30; MIS-¹ + TRIAL]

mis·trust (mis trust′), *n.* **1.** lack of trust or confidence; distrust. —*v.t.* **2.** to regard with mistrust, suspicion, or doubt; distrust. **3.** to surmise. —*v.i.* **4.** to be distrustful. [1350–1400; ME *mistrusten* (v.), *mistrust* (n.). See MIS-¹, TRUST] —**mis·trust′er,** *n.* —**mis·trust′ing·ly,** *adv.*

mis·trust·ful (mis trust′fəl), *adj.* full of mistrust; suspicious. [1520–30; MISTRUST + -FUL] —**mis·trust′ful·ly,** *adv.* —**mis·trust′ful·ness,** *n.*

mis·tryst (mis trīst′), *v.t. Scot. and North Eng.* **1.** to fail to meet or to keep an appointment with (someone). **2.** to be confused or perplexed by (something). [1810–20; MIS-¹ + TRYST]

mist·y (mis′tē), *adj.,* **mist·i·er, mist·i·est.** **1.** abounding in or clouded by mist. **2.** of the nature of or consisting of mist. **3.** appearing as if seen through mist; indistinct or blurred in form or outline. **4.** obscure; vague. [bef. 900; ME; OE *mistig.* See MIST, -Y¹] —**mist′i·ly,** *adv.* —**mist′i·ness,** *n.*

mist·y-eyed (mis′tē īd′), *adj.* **1.** on the verge of tears. **2.** sentimental: *a misty-eyed romantic.* [1955–60]

mis·un·der·stand (mis′un dər stand′), *v.t.,* **-stood, -stand·ing.** **1.** to take (words, statements, etc.) in a wrong sense; understand wrongly. **2.** to fail to understand or interpret rightly the words or behavior of. [1150–1200; ME *misunderstanden.* See MIS-¹, UNDERSTAND] —**mis′un·der·stand′er,** *n.*
—**Syn. 1.** misconstrue, misapprehend, misinterpret.

mis·un·der·stand·ing (mis′un dər stan′ding), *n.* **1.** failure to understand correctly; mistake as to meaning or intent. **2.** a disagreement or quarrel. [1400–50; late ME; see MIS-¹, UNDERSTANDING] —**mis′un·der·stand′ing·ly,** *adv.*
—**Syn. 1.** misapprehension, error, misconception. **2.** discord, difference, difficulty, dissension. —**Ant. 2.** concord.

mis·un·der·stood (mis′un dər stŏŏd′), *adj.* **1.** improperly understood or interpreted. **2.** unappreciated. [1585–95; MIS-¹ + UNDERSTOOD]

mis·us·age (mis yōō′sij, -zij), *n.* **1.** wrong or improper usage, as of words. **2.** bad or abusive treatment. [1525–35; MIS-¹ + USAGE]

mis·use (*n.* mis yōōs′; *v.* mis yōōz′), *n., v.,* **-used, -us·ing.** —*n.* **1.** wrong or improper use; misapplication. **2.** *Obs.* bad or abusive treatment. —*v.t.* **3.** to use wrongly or improperly; misapply. **4.** to treat badly or abusively; maltreat. [1350–1400; ME; see MIS-¹, USE]
—**Syn. 1.** misemployment, misappropriation.

mis·us·er¹ (mis yōō′zər), *n. Law.* abuse of a right; unlawful use of an office, franchise, benefit, etc. [1615–25; n. use of MF *mesuser* to MISUSE]

mis·us·er² (mis yōō′zər), *n.* a person who misuses. [1540–50; MIS-¹ + USER]

mis·ven·ture (mis ven′chər), *n.* an unfortunate undertaking; misadventure. [1555–65; MIS-¹ + VENTURE]

mis·word (mis wûrd′), *v.t.* to word incorrectly. [1880–85; MIS-¹ + WORD]

Mi·tan·ni (mi tan′ē), *n.* the Hurrian kingdom in NW Mesopotamia in the 15th and 14th centuries B.C.

Mi·tan·ni·an (mi tan′ē ən), *n.* **1.** a native or inhabitant of the Mitanni kingdom. —*adj.* **2.** of or pertaining to the Mitannians or the Mitanni kingdom. [1895–1900; MITANNI + -AN]

MITC, mortgage investment tax credit.

Mitch·ell (mich′əl), *n.* **1. Arthur,** born 1934, U.S. ballet dancer, choreographer, and ballet company director. **2. John,** 1870–1919, U.S. labor leader. **3. Margaret,** 1900–49, U.S. novelist. **4. Maria,** 1818–89, U.S. astronomer. **5. Silas Weir** (wēr), 1829–1914, U.S. physician and novelist. **6. William,** 1879–1936, U.S. general: pioneer in the field of aviation. **7. Mount,** a mountain in W North Carolina: highest peak in the E United States, 6684 ft. (2037 m). **8.** a city in SE South Dakota. 13,916. **9.** a male given name, form of **Michael.**

mite¹ (mīt), *n.* any of numerous small to microscopic arachnids of the subclass Acari, including species that are parasitic on animals and plants or that feed on decaying matter and stored foods. Also called **acarid.** [bef. 1000; ME *myte,* OE *mīte;* c. MD *mīte,* OHG *miza* midge]

mite² (mīt), *n.* **1.** a contribution that is small but is all that a person can afford. **2.** a very small sum of money. **3.** a coin of very small value. **4.** a very small object. **5.** a very small creature. —*adv.* **6.** to a small extent; somewhat (often prec. by *a*): *a mite selfish.* [1300–50; ME *myte* < MD *mīte* small copper coin; ult. identical with MITE¹]

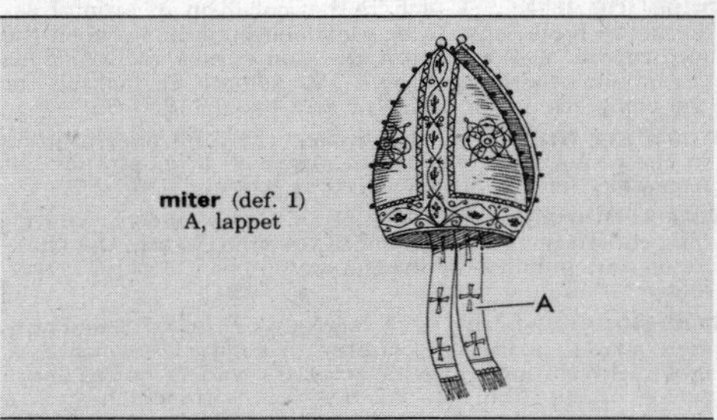

miter (def. 1)
A, lappet

mi·ter (mī′tər), *n.* **1.** the official headdress of a bishop in the Western Church, in its modern form a tall cap with a top deeply cleft crosswise, the outline of the front and back resembling that of a pointed arch. **2.** the office or rank of a bishop; bishopric. **3.** *Judaism.* the official headdress of the ancient high priest, bearing on the front a gold plate engraved with the words *Holiness to the Lord.* Ex. 28:36–38. **4.** a fillet worn by women of ancient Greece. **5.** *Carpentry.* an oblique surface formed on a piece of wood or the like so as to butt against an oblique surface on another piece to be joined with it. **6.** *Naut.* the inclined seam connecting the two cloths of an angulated sail. —*v.t.* **7.** to bestow a miter upon, or raise to a rank entitled to it. **8.** to join with a miter joint. **9.** to cut to a miter. **10.** to join (two edges of fabric) at a corner by various methods of folding, cutting, and stitching. Also, *esp. Brit.,* **mitre.** [1350–1400; ME *mitre* (n.) < L *mitra* < Gk *mítra* turban, headdress]

mi′ter box′, *Carpentry.* any of various fixed or adjustable guides for a saw in making miters or cross cuts, esp. a troughlike box open at the ends and guiding the saw by slots in the opposite sides. [1670–80]

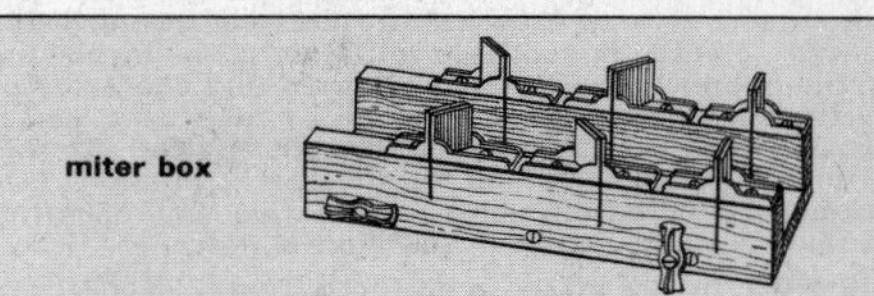

miter box

mis/re·li′ance, *n.*
mis/re·ly′, *v.i.,* **-lied, -ly·ing.**
mis·ren′der, *v.t.*
mis/re·print′, *v.t.*
mis/re·ward′, *v.t.*
mis·rhymed′, *adj.*
mis·route′, *v.t.,* **-rout·ed, -rout·ing.**
mis·sam′ple, *v.,* **-pled, -pling.**
mis·seat′, *v.t.*
mis·set′, *v.,* **-set, -set·ting.**
mis·ship′, *v.,* **-shipped, -ship·ping.**
mis·ship′ment, *n.*
mis·sing′, *v.,* **-sang, -sung, -sing·ing.**
mis·sort′, *v.*
mis·sound′, *v.*
mis·space′, *v.t.,* **-spaced, -spac·ing.**
mis·spec′i·fied′, *adj.*
mis·stamp′, *v.t.*
mis·start′, *v.*
mis·steer′, *v.*
mis·style′, *v.,* **-styled, -styl·ing.**
mis/sup·pose′, *v.,* **-posed, -pos·ing.**
mis/syl·lab/i·fi·ca′tion, *n.*
mis/syl·lab′i·fy′, *v.t.,* **-fied, -fy·ing.**
mis·term′, *v.t.*
mis·thread′, *v.*
mis·throw′, *v.,* **-threw, -thrown, -throw·ing.**
mis·tilled′, *adj.*
mis·ti′tle, *v.t.,* **-tled, -tling.**
mis·trace′, *v.,* **-traced, -trac·ing.**
mis·track′ing, *n.*
mis·train′, *v.*
mis/tran·scribe′, *v.t.,* **-scribed, -scrib·ing.**
mis/tran·scrip′tion, *n.*
mis·truth′, *n.*
mis·tune′, *v.,* **-tuned, -tun·ing.**
mis·tu′tor, *v.*
mis·type′, *v.,* **-typed, -typ·ing.**
mis·typed′, *adj.*
mis·un′ion, *n.*
mis/u′ti·li·za′tion, *n.*
mis·val′ue, *v.t.,* **-ued, -u·ing.**
mis/vo·cal·i·za′tion, *n.*
mis·wire′, *v.,* **-wired, -wir·ing.**
mis·wor′ship, *v.,* **-shiped, -ship·ing** or (*esp. Brit.*) **-shipped, -ship·ping.**
mis·write′, *v.t.,* **-wrote, -writ·ten, -writ·ing.**
mis·zone′, *v.,* **-zoned, -zon·ing.**

mi•tered (mī′tərd), *adj.* **1.** shaped like a bishop's miter or having a miter-shaped apex. **2.** wearing, or entitled or privileged to wear, a miter. [1350–1400; ME; see MITER, -ED[3]]

mi′tered jib′, *Naut.* a diagonal-cut jib. Also called **mi′ter jib′.**

mi•ter•er (mī′tər ər), *n.* a machine or tool for making miters. [MITER + -ER[1]]

mi•ter•gate (mī′tər gāt′), *n.* (in a canal or the like) a lock gate having two leaves so made as to close at an angle pointing upstream. [MITER + GATE[1]]

mi′ter gear′, either of a pair of bevel gears of equal size for driving shafts at right angles to each other. [1905–10]

mi′ter joint′, a joint, esp. a butt joint, between two pieces of wood or the like, meeting at an angle in which each of the butting surfaces is cut to an angle equal to half the angle of junction. [1680–90]

mi′ter post′. See **meeting post.** [1830–40]

mi′ter saw′, a backsaw used for cutting miters.

mi′ter square′, an instrument for laying out miter joints, consisting of two straightedges joined at a 45° angle. [1670–80]

mi•ter•wort (mī′tər wûrt′, -wôrt′), *n.* any of several plants belonging to the genus *Mitella,* of the saxifrage family, having a capsule that resembles a bishop's miter. Also, *esp. Brit.,* **mitrewort.** [1810–20, *Amer.*; MITER + WORT[2]]

Mit•ford (mit′fərd), *n.* **Mary Russell,** 1787–1855, English novelist, poet, playwright, and essayist.

mith•an (mith′ən), *n., pl.* **-an.** gayal. [1835–45; < Assamese *methon*]

mith•er (mith′ər), *n. Scot. and North Eng.* mother.

Mith•rae•um (mi thrē′əm), *n., pl.* **Mith•rae•a** (mi-thrē′ə), **Mith•rae•ums.** a temple of Mithras. [1875–80; < NL < Gk *Mithraîon,* equiv. to *Míthr*(*ās*) MITHRAS + *-aion* suffix of place]

Mith•ra•ism (mith′rə iz′əm), *n.* an ancient Persian religion in which Mithras was worshiped, involving secret rituals to which only men were admitted: a major competitor of Christianity in the Roman empire during the 2nd and 3rd centuries A.D. Also, **Mith•ra•i•cism** (mith rā′ə siz′əm). [MITHRA(S) + -ISM] —**Mith•ra•ic** (mith rā′ik), **Mith′ra•is′tic,** *adj.* —**Mith′ra•ist,** *n.*

Mith•ras (mith′ras), *n. Persian Myth.* the god of light and truth, later of the sun. Also, **Mith•ra** (mith′rə). [< L < Gk *Mithrās* < OPers *Mithra*]

mith•ri•date (mith′ri dāt′), *n. Old Pharm.* a confection believed to contain an antidote to every poison. [1520–30; earlier *mithridatum* < ML, var. of LL *mithridātium,* n. use of neut. of *Mithridātius,* equiv. to *Mithridāt*(*ēs*) MITHRIDATES VI (see MITHRIDATISM) + *-ius* -IOUS]

Mith•ri•da•tes VI (mith′ri dā′tēz), (*"the Great"*) 132?–63 B.C., king of Pontus 120–63. Also called **Mith•ri•da′tes Eu′pa•tor**(yōō′pə tôr′).

mith•ri•da•tism (mith′ri dā′tiz əm), *n.* the production of immunity against the action of a poison by taking the poison in gradually increased doses. [1850–55; after MITHRIDATES VI, said to have so immunized himself; see -ISM] —**mith•ri•dat•ic** (mith′ri dat′ik), *adj.*

mith•ri•da•tize (mith′ri dā′tiz), *v.t.,* **-tized, -tiz•ing.** to induce a state of mithridatism in (a person). Also, *esp. Brit.,* **mith′ri•da′tise.** [1865–70; MITHRIDAT(ISM) + -IZE]

mit•i•cide (mit′ə sīd′), *n. Chem.* a substance or preparation for killing mites. [1945–50; MITE[1] + -I- + -CIDE] —**mit′i•cid′al,** *adj.*

mit•i•gate (mit′i gāt′), *v.,* **-gat•ed, -gat•ing.** —*v.t.* **1.** to lessen in force or intensity, as wrath, grief, harshness, or pain; moderate. **2.** to make less severe: *to mitigate a punishment.* **3.** to make (a person, one's state of mind, disposition, etc.) milder or more gentle; mollify; appease. —*v.i.* **4.** to become milder; lessen in severity. [1375–1425; late ME *mitigaten* < L *mītigātus* (ptp. of *mītigāre* to calm, soften, soothe), equiv. to *mit*(*is*) mild, soft, gentle + *-ig-* (comb. form of *agere* to do, cause to do, make) + *-ātus* -ATE[1]] —**mit•i•ga•ble** (mit′i gə bəl), *adj.* —**mit′i•gat′ed•ly,** *adv.* —**mit′i•ga′tion,** *n.* —**mit′i•ga′tive, mit•i•ga•to•ry** (mit′i gə tôr′ē, -tōr′ē), *adj.* —**mit′i•ga′tor,** *n.*

—**Usage.** MITIGATE, whose central meaning is "to lessen" or "make less severe," is sometimes confused with MILITATE, "to have effect or influence," in the phrase *mitigate against: This criticism in no way militates* (not *mitigates*) *against your going ahead with your research.* Although this use of MITIGATE occasionally occurs in edited writing, it is rare and is widely regarded as an error.

Mi•tla (mēt′lä), *n.* the ruins of a Zapotec Indian city near Oaxaca, Mexico, yielding elaborate remains of temples and other artifacts.

Mit•nag•ged (*Eng., Ashk. Heb.* mis nä′gid; *Seph. Heb.* mēt nä ged′), *n., pl.* **Mit•nag•ge•dim** (*Eng., Ashk. Heb.* mis näg′dim; *Seph. Heb.* mēt näg dēm′). *Judaism.* a member of an Orthodox Jewish movement in central or eastern Europe in the 18th and 19th centuries that advocated an intellectual, legalistic approach to Judaism and opposed the emotional, mystical approach of the Hasidim. Cf. **Hasid** (def. 1). [1900–05; < Medieval Heb *mithnaggēdh,* Yiddish *misnaged* < Heb *mithnaggēdh* opposing, opponent]

mi•to•chon•dri•on (mī′tə kon′drē ən), *n., pl.* **-dri•a** (-drē ə). *Cell Biol.* an organelle in the cytoplasm of cells that functions in energy production. See diag. under **cell.** [1900–05; < Gk *míto*(*s*) thread + *chóndrion* small grain, equiv. to *chóndr*(*os*) grain, corn + *-ion* dim. suffix] —**mi′to•chon′dri•al,** *adj.*

mi•to•gen (mī′tə jən, -jen′), *n. Biol.* any substance or agent that stimulates mitotic cell division. [1950–55; MITO(SIS) + -GEN] —**mi•to•gen•ic** (mī′tə jen′ik), *adj.*

mi•to•sis (mī tō′sis), *n. Cell Biol.* the usual method of cell division, characterized typically by the resolving of the chromatin of the nucleus into a threadlike form, which condenses into chromosomes, each of which separates longitudinally into two parts, one part of each chromosome being retained in each of two new cells resulting from the original cell. Cf. **meiosis.** [1885–90; < Gk *mít*(*os*) a thread + -OSIS] —**mi•tot•ic** (mī tot′ik), *adj.* —**mi•tot′i•cal•ly,** *adv.*

mitot′ic spin′dle, spindle (def. 11).

mi•tra (mī′trə), *n. Bot.* **1.** the mitriform pileus of certain fungi. **2.** a galea. [1630–40; < L: head band; see MITER]

Mi•tra (mē′trə), *n. Hinduism.* the Vedic god of justice.

mi•trail•leuse (mē tʀa yœz′), *n., pl.* ***-trail•leuses*** (-tʀa yœz′). *French.* a machine gun.

mi•tral (mī′trəl), *adj.* **1.** of or resembling a miter. **2.** *Anat.* of, pertaining to, or situated near the mitral valve of the heart. [1600–10; MIT(E)R + -AL[1]]

mi′tral insuffi′ciency, *Pathol.* abnormal closure of the mitral valve resulting in regurgitation of blood into the atrium and leading to reduced heart function or heart failure. Also called **mi′tral incom′petence.** [1875–80]

mi′tral steno′sis, *Pathol.* abnormal narrowing of the mitral valve usually resulting from disease, as rheumatic fever, and obstructing the free flow of blood from the atrium to the ventricle. [1870–75]

mi′tral valve′, *Anat.* the valve between the left atrium and left ventricle of the heart, consisting of two triangular flaps of tissue, that prevents the blood from flowing back into the atrium. Also called **bicuspid valve.** Cf. **tricuspid valve.** [1685–95]

mi•tre (mī′tər), *n., v.t.,* **-tred, -tring.** *Chiefly Brit.* miter.

Mi•tre (mē′trā; *Sp.* me′tʀe), *n.* **Bar•to•lo•mé** (bäʀ′tô-lô me′), 1821–1906, Argentine soldier, statesman, and author: president of Argentina 1862–68.

mi•tre•wort (mī′tər wûrt′, -wôrt′), *n. Chiefly Brit.* miterwort.

mi•tri•form (mī′trə fôrm′), *adj.* shaped like the miter of a bishop. [1820–30; < NL *mitriformis.* See MITER, -I-, -FORM]

Mi•tro•pou•los (mi trop′ə ləs; *Gk.* mē trô′pōō lôs), *n.* **Di•mi•tri** (di mē′trē; *Gk.* thē mē′tʀē), 1897–1960, Greek symphony orchestra conductor in the U.S.

Mit•scher (mich′ər), *n.* **Marc Andrew,** 1887–1947, U.S. naval officer and aviator.

mits•vah (*Seph.* mēts vä′, mits-; *Eng., Ashk.* mits′və), *n., pl.* ***-voth, -vot, -vos*** (*Seph.* -vôt′; *Ashk.* -vōs), *Eng.* **-vahs.** *Hebrew.* mitzvah.

mitt (mit), *n.* **1.** *Baseball.* **a.** a rounded glove with one internal section for the four fingers and another for the thumb and having the side next to the palm of the hand protected by a thick padding, used by catchers. **b.** a somewhat similar glove but with less padding and having sections for the thumb and one or two fingers, used by first basemen. Cf. **baseball glove. 2.** a mitten. **3.** *Slang.* a hand. **4.** a glove that leaves the lower ends of the fingers bare, esp. a long one made of lace or other fancy material and worn by women. [1755–65; short for MITTEN]

mitt., (in prescriptions) send. [< L *mitte*]

Mit•tag-Lef•fler (mit′täg lef′lər), *n.* **Mag•nus Gö•sta** (mäng′nus yœ′stä), 1846–1927, Swedish mathematician.

Mit•tel•eu•ro•pa (mit′l oi rō′pä), *n. German.* Central Europe.

mit•tel•schmerz (mit′l shmärts′), *n.* dull abdominal pain occurring at the time of ovulation, attributed to the presence of free blood in the peritoneal cavity from the ruptured ovarian follicle. [1890–95; < G, equiv. to *mittel-* mid-, MIDDLE + *Schmerz* pain]

mit•ten (mit′n), *n.* **1.** a hand covering enclosing the four fingers together and the thumb separately. **2.** mitt (def. 4). [1350–1400; ME *miteyn* < MF, OF *mitaine,* equiv. to *mite* mitten (< ?) + *-aine* -AN] —**mit′ten•like′,** *adj.*

Mit•ter•rand (mēt[e] ʀäɴ′; *Eng.* mē′tə räɴ′, -rand′, mit′ə-), *n.* **Fran•çois (Mau•rice Ma•rie)** (fʀäɴ swa′ mô-ʀēs′ ma ʀē′), 1916–96, French political leader: president 1981–95.

mit•ti•mus (mit′ə məs), *n., pl.* **-mus•es.** *Law.* **1.** a warrant of commitment to prison. **2.** a writ for removing a suit or a record from one court to another. [1400–50; late ME < L: we send, first word of such a writ; see REMIT]

Mit•ty (mit′ē), *n.* See **Walter Mitty.** —**Mit′ty•esque′, Mit′ty•ish,** *adj.*

Mi•tum′ba Moun′tains (mi tōōm′bə), a mountain range in E Zaire, parallel to the coasts of Lake Tanganyika and Lake Edward.

Mit•zi (mit′sē), *n.* a female given name. Also, **Mit′zie.**

mitz•vah (*Seph.* mēts vä′, mits-; *Eng., Ashk.* mits′və), *n., pl.* ***-voth, -vot, -vos*** (*Seph.* -vôt′; *Ashk.* -vōs), *Eng.* **-vahs.** *Hebrew.* **1.** any of the collection of 613 commandments or precepts in the Bible and additional ones of rabbinic origin that relate chiefly to the religious and moral conduct of Jews. **2.** any good or praiseworthy deed. Also, ***mitsvah.*** [*miṣwāh* commandment]

Mi•wok (mē′wok), *n., pl.* **-woks,** (*esp. collectively*) **-wok** for 1. **1.** a member of an American Indian people formerly living in several noncontiguous areas of California north of San Francisco Bay and eastward from the San Joaquin-Sacramento delta to the Sierras. **2.** any of the Penutian languages spoken by the Miwok.

mix (miks), *v.,* **mixed** or **mixt, mix•ing,** *n.* —*v.t.* **1.** to combine (substances, elements, things, etc.) into one mass, collection, or assemblage, generally with a thorough blending of the constituents. **2.** to put together indiscriminately or confusedly (often fol. by *up*). **3.** to combine, unite, or join: *to mix business and pleasure.* **4.** to add as an element or ingredient: *Mix some salt into the flour.* **5.** to form or make by combining ingredients: *to mix a cake; to mix mortar.* **6.** to crossbreed. **7.** *Motion Pictures.* **a.** to combine, blend, edit, etc. (the various components of a soundtrack): *to mix dialogue and sound effects.* **b.** to complete the mixing process on (a film, soundtrack, etc.): *an important movie that took months to mix.* **8.** to combine (two or more separate recordings or microphone signals) to make a single recording or composite signal. —*v.i.* **9.** to become mixed: *a paint that mixes easily with water.* **10.** to associate or mingle, as in company: *to mix with the other guests at a party.* **11.** to be crossbred, or of mixed breeding. **12.** *Boxing.* to exchange blows vigorously and aggressively: *The crowd jeered as the fighters clinched, refusing to mix.* **13. mix down,** to mix the tracks of an existing recording to make a new recording with fewer tracks: *the four-track tape was mixed down to stereo.* **14. mix it up,** *Slang.* **a.** to engage in a quarrel. **b.** to fight with the fists. Also, **mix it. 15. mix up, a.** to confuse completely, esp. to mistake one person or thing for another: *The teacher was always mixing up the twins.* **b.** to involve or entangle. —*n.* **16.** an act or instance of mixing. **17.** the result of mixing; mixture: *cement mix; an odd mix of gaiety and sadness.* **18.** a commercially prepared blend of ingredients to which usually only a liquid must be added to make up the total of ingredients necessary or obtain the desired consistency: *a cake mix; muffin mix.* **19.** mixer (def. 4). **20.** the proportion of ingredients in a mixture; formula: *a mix of two to one.* **21.** *Informal.* a mess or muddle; mix-up. **22.** *Music.* an electronic blending of tracks or sounds made to produce a recording. [1470–80; back formation from *mixt* MIXED] —**mix′a•ble,** *adj.* —**mix′a•bil′i•ty, mix′a•ble•ness,** *n.*

—**Syn. 1, 9.** commingle, jumble, unite, amalgamate, fuse. MIX, BLEND, COMBINE, MINGLE concern the bringing of two or more things into more or less intimate association. MIX is the general word for such association: *to mix fruit juices.* BLEND implies such a harmonious joining of two or more types of colors, feelings, etc., that the new product formed displays some of the qualities of each: *to blend fragrances or whiskeys.* COMBINE implies such a close or intimate union that distinction between the parts is lost: *to combine forces.* MINGLE usually suggests retained identity of the parts: *to mingle voices.* **9.** coalesce. **17.** concoction; formula.

Mix (miks), *n.* **Thomas Edwin** (*Tom*), 1880–1940, U.S. film actor in westerns.

mix-and-match (miks′ən mach′), *adj.* **1.** made up of complementary elements taken from different sets or sources: *a mix-and-match approach to interior decoration.* —*v.t., v.i.* **2.** to combine in a harmonious or interesting way, as articles of clothing in an ensemble.

mixed (mikst), *adj.* **1.** put together or formed by mixing. **2.** composed of different constituents or elements: *a mixed form of government.* **3.** of different kinds combined: *mixed nuts; mixed emotions.* **4.** involving or comprised of persons of different sex, class, character, belief, religion, or race: *mixed company; a mixed neighborhood.* **5.** *Law.* involving more than one issue or aspect: *a mixed question of law and fact.* **6.** *Phonet.* (of a vowel) central. **7.** *Math.* (of partial derivatives) of second or higher order and involving differentiation with respect to more than one variable. **8.** (of trains) composed of both passenger and freight cars. **9.** *Logic.* containing quantifiers of unlike kind. **10.** (of a stock or commodity market) characterized by uneven price movements, with some prices rising and others falling. [1400–50; late ME *mixt* < L *mixtus,* ptp. of *miscēre* to mingle. Cf. MIX] —**mix•ed•ly** (mik′sid lē, mikst′lē), *adv.* —**mix′ed•ness,** *n.*

mixed′ ac′id, *Chem.* any mixture of nitric acid and sulfuric acid, used as a nitrating agent in the manufacture of explosives, plastics, etc.

mixed′ bag′, *Informal.* an often unexpected assortment of various things, people, or ideas: *The concert was a mixed bag of works from three centuries.* [1935–40]

mixed′ bless′ing, something that, although generally favorable or advantageous, has one or more unfavorable or disadvantageous features. [1930–35]

mixed′ bud′. See under **bud**[1] (def. 1a). [1955–60]

mixed′ dou′bles, (in tennis) a doubles match with a man and a woman on each side.

mixed′ drink′, an alcoholic drink combining two or more ingredients, as liquor, fruit juice, and flavorings. [1940–45]

mixed′ econ′omy, an economy in which there are elements of both public and private enterprise. [1935–40]

mixed′ four′some, a foursome of two teams, each comprised of a man and a woman. [1885–90, *Amer.*]

mixed′ grill′, an assortment of several kinds of broiled or grilled meats, and usually vegetables, served together, as a lamb chop, a pork sausage, a piece of liver, grilled tomatoes, and mushrooms. [1910–15]

mixed′ lay′er, *Oceanog.* the surface layer of water, seasonally varying in thickness, that is at almost uniform temperature owing to agitation by waves and wind.

mixed′ mar′riage, a marriage between persons of different religions or races. [1690–1700]

mixed′ me′dia, **1.** multimedia. **2.** artistic media, as pen and ink, chalk, and graphite, used in combination: *an old master drawing in mixed media.* [1960–65] —**mixed′-me′di·a,** *adj.*

mixed′ met′aphor, the use in the same expression of two or more metaphors that are incongruous or illogical when combined, as in "The president will put the ship of state on its feet." [1790–1800]

mixed′ nerve′, *Anat.* a nerve composed of both sensory and motor fibers. [1875–80]

mixed′ num′ber, *Arith.* a number consisting of a whole number and a fraction or decimal, as 4½ or 4.5. [1535–45]

mixed-up (mikst′up′), *adj.* completely confused or emotionally unstable: *a mixed-up teenager.* [1860–65]

mix·er (mik′sər), *n.* **1.** a person or thing that mixes. **2.** a person, with reference to sociability: *She's a good mixer to have at a large party.* **3.** a kitchen utensil or an electrical appliance having one or more beaters and used in mixing, beating, or blending foods. **4.** Also, **mix.** a beverage, as ginger ale, fruit juice, or soda water that can be combined with liquor to produce a mixed drink, esp. a highball. **5.** *Audio.* an electronic device for blending, fading, substitution, etc., of sounds from various sources, as from microphones or separately recorded soundtracks, for broadcast or recording. **6.** *Radio and Television, Recording.* a technician who operates a mixer in a studio. **7.** the person responsible for the original recording of a movie soundtrack. Cf. **recordist. 8.** a social event, as a party or dance, where people can meet informally. **9.** See **mixing faucet. 10.** *Metall.* a container for blending and storing molten pig iron from several blast furnaces. [1605–15; MIX + -ER[1]]

mix′ing fau′cet, a single outlet for water from separately controlled hot-water and cold-water taps.

mix′ing ra′tio, the ratio of the mass of water vapor in the air to the mass of the dry air, a measure of atmospheric humidity. Cf. **absolute humidity, dew point, relative humidity, specific humidity.**

mix′ing valve′, a valve receiving water from both a hot-water and a cold-water line and controlling the relative amount of water admitted from each. [1900–05]

mix·ol·o·gist (mik sol′ə jist), *n. Usually Facetious.* a person skilled in making mixed drinks; bartender. [1855–60, *Amer.*; MIX + -O- + -LOG(Y) + -IST]

mix·ol·o·gy (mik sol′ə jē), *n. Usually Facetious.* the art or skill of preparing mixed drinks. [1945–50; MIX + -O- + -LOGY]

mix′o·lyd′i·an mode′ (mik′sə lid′ē ən, mik′-), *Music.* an authentic church mode represented on the white keys of a keyboard instrument by an ascending scale from G to G. [1770–80; < Gk *mixolýdi(os)* (*mixo-*, comb. form of *míxis* a mingling + *Lýdios* Lydian) + -AN]

mix·o·ploid (mik′sə ploid′), *n. Genetics.* an organism having an unequal number of chromosome sets in adjacent cells or tissues. [1930–35; *mixo-* (< Gk, comb. form of *míxis* a mingling) + -PLOID] —**mix′o·ploi′dy,** *n.*

mix·o·troph (mik′sə trof′, -trōf′), *n. Biol.* any organism capable of existing as either an autotroph or heterotroph. [back formation from *mixotrophic*, equiv. to Gk *mixo-* (see MIXOPLOID) + -TROPHIC] —**mix′o·troph′ic,** *adj.*

mixt (mikst), *v.* a pt. and pp. of **mix.** [in place of MIXED by phonetic sp. of *-t* for *-ed*]

mixt., mixture.

Mix·tec (mēs′tek), *n., pl.* **-tecs,** (*esp. collectively*) **-tec** for 1. **1.** a member of an Amerindian people of Guerrero, Oaxaca, and Puebla, Mexico. **2.** the Oto-Manguean language of the Mixtecs, consisting of a number of highly divergent dialects. Also, **Mixteco.** [1840–50; < MexSp *mixteco* < Nahuatl *mixtēcah*, pl. of *mixtēcatl* person from *Mixtlān* (*mix(tli)* cloud + *-tlān* locative suffix, *-tēcatl* suffix of personal nouns)] —**Mix·tec′an,** *adj., n.*

Mix·te·co (mēs tek′ō), *n., pl.* **-cos,** (*esp. collectively*) **-co.** Mixtec.

mix·ture (miks′chər), *n.* **1.** a product of mixing. **2.** any combination or blend of different elements, kinds, qualities, etc.: *a mixture of good and bad traits.* **3.** *Chem., Physics.* an aggregate of two or more substances that are not chemically united and that exist in no fixed proportion to each other. **4.** a fabric woven of yarns combining various colors: *a heather mixture.* **5.** the act of mixing or the state of being mixed. **6.** an added element or ingredient; admixture. [1425–75; late ME < L *mixtūra*, equiv. to *mixt(us)* MIXED + *-ūra* -URE]
—**Syn. 1.** blend, combination; compound. **2.** conglomeration, miscellany, jumble; medley; mélange, potpourri, hodgepodge.

mix-up (miks′up′), *n.* **1.** a confused state of things; muddle; tangle. **2.** a fight. [1835–45; n. use of v. phrase *mix up*]

Mi·ya·za·ki (mē′yä zä′kē), *n.* a city on SE Kyushu, in Japan. 264,858.

Mi·zar (mī′zär), *n. Astron.* a double star in the middle of the constellation Ursa Major. [< Ar *mi'zar* lit., apron]

Miz·ra·chi (miz rä′KHē), *n.* **1.** a Zionist movement, founded in 1902, chiefly devoted to furthering the integration of Zionism and religious orthodoxy. —*adj.* **2.** of or pertaining to Mizrachi. Also, **Miz·ra′hi.** [1910–15; < Heb *mizrāḥī*, an acronym from *m(erkā)z r(ū)ḥ(ān)ī* spiritual center, with pun on *mizrāḥī* eastern]

CONCISE ETYMOLOGY KEY: <, descended or borrowed from; >, whence; b., blend of, blended; c., cognate with; cf., compare; deriv., derivative; equiv., equivalent; imit., imitative; obl., oblique; r., replacing; s., stem; sp., spelling, spelled; resp., respelling, respelled; trans., translation; ?, origin unknown; *, unattested; ‡, probably earlier than. See the full key inside the front cover.

miz·rah (*Seph.* mēz RÄKH′; *Ashk.* miz′RÄKH), *n. Hebrew.* **1.** a decorative figure, usually bearing an inscription, that is hung on the eastern wall in Jewish homes or synagogues to indicate the direction to face in prayer. **2.** the eastern wall in a synagogue, which contains the Holy Ark. Also, **miz·rach′.** [*mizrāḥ* lit., east]

miz·zen (miz′ən), *Naut.* —*n.* **1.** a fore-and-aft sail set on a mizzenmast. Cf. **crossjack, spanker** (def. 1a). See diag. under **ship. 2.** mizzenmast. —*adj.* **3.** of or pertaining to a mizzenmast. **4.** noting a sail, yard, boom, etc., or any rigging belonging to a mizzen lower mast or to some upper mast of a mizzenmast. **5.** noting any stay running aft and upward to the head of a mizzen lower mast or some specified upper mast of a mizzenmast: *mizzen topmast stay.* Also, **miz′en.** [1375–1425; late ME *meson, mesan*, prob. < It *mezzana*]

miz·zen·mast (miz′ən mast′, -mäst′; *Naut.* miz′ən-məst), *n. Naut.* **1.** the third mast from forward in a vessel having three or more masts. See illus. under **quarterdeck. 2.** the after and shorter mast of a yawl, ketch, or dandy; jiggermast. Also, **miz′en·mast′.** [1375–1425; late ME *meson mast.* See MIZZEN, MAST[1]]

miz·zle[1] (miz′əl), *v.,* **-zled, -zling,** *n. South Midland and Southern U.S.* —*v.t., v.i.* **1.** to rain in fine drops; drizzle; mist. —*n.* **2.** mist or drizzle. [1475–85; c. dial D *mizzelen*, LG *miseln* to drizzle; akin to MD *misel* mist, dew; see -LE]

miz·zle[2] (miz′əl), *v.i.,* **-zled, -zling.** *Brit. Slang.* to disappear or leave suddenly. [1775–85; orig. uncert.]

miz·zle[3] (miz′əl), *v.t.,* **-zled, -zling.** *South Midland and Southern U.S.* to confuse; muddle. [1575–85; orig. uncert.]

M.J., Master of Journalism.

Mjol·nir (myôl′nir), *n. Scand. Myth.* the hammer of Thor, used as a weapon against the Jotuns, heard as thunder by humans. [< ON *Mjǫllnir*, akin to OCS *mlĭniji*, Russ *mólniya*, OPruss *mealde* lightning, Latvian *milna* hammer of the thunder god]

mk., **1.** *pl.* **mks.** mark[2] (def. 1). **2.** markka.

MKS, meter-kilogram-second. Also, **mks**

MKSA, meter-kilogram-second-ampere. Also, **mksa**

mkt., market.

mktg., marketing.

ML, Medieval Latin. Also, **M.L.**

mL, millilambert; millilamberts.

ml, milliliter; milliliters.

ml., **1.** mail. **2.** milliliter; milliliters.

MLA, Modern Language Association.

M.L.A., **1.** Master of Landscape Architecture. **2.** Modern Language Association.

M.L.Arch., Master of Landscape Architecture.

MLB, Maritime Labor Board.

MLD, **1.** median lethal dose. **2.** minimum lethal dose.

Mlec·cha (mlech′ə, mə lech′ə), *n. Hinduism.* **1.** a non-Indian barbarian of whatever race or color. **2.** a class of untouchables comprising such persons. [< Skt]

MLF, Multilateral Nuclear Force.

MLG., Middle Low German. Also, **M.L.G.**

M-line (em′līn′), *n. Physics.* one of a series of lines (**M-series**) in the x-ray spectrum of an atom corresponding to radiation (**M-radiation**) caused by the transition of an electron to the M-shell. [1920–25]

Mlle., Mademoiselle. Also, **Mlle**

Mlles., Mesdemoiselles.

MLR, minimum lending rate.

MLS, *Real Estate.* Multiple Listing Service.

M.L.S., Master of Library Science.

MLU, See **mean length of utterance.**

MLW, mean low water.

mlx, millilux; millilucis.

mM, millimole; millimoles.

mm, millimeter; millimeters.

MM., Messieurs.

mm., **1.** *Music.* measures. **2.** thousands. [< L *millia*] **3.** millimeter; millimeters.

M.M., **1.** Master Mason. **2.** Master Mechanic. **3.** Master of Music.

Mma·ba·tho (mä bä′tō), *n.* a town in and the capital of Bophuthatswana, W of Johannesburg.

Mme., Madame.

M.M.E., **1.** Master of Mechanical Engineering. **2.** Master of Mining Engineering. **3.** Master of Music Education.

Mmes., Mesdames.

M.Met.E., Master of Metallurgical Engineering.

mmf, *Elect.* magnetomotive force. Also, **m.m.f.**

M.Mgt.E., Master of Management Engineering.

mm Hg, millimeter of mercury. Also, **mmHg**

mmho, millimho; millimhos.

MMPI, Minnesota Multiphasic Personality Inventory.

M.M.Sc., Master of Medical Science.

MMT, **1.** *Astron.* See **Multiple Mirror Telescope. 2.** *Chem.* methylcyclopentadienyl manganese tricarbonyl, $C_9H_7MnO_3$, a lead-free, toxic antiknock gasoline additive.

M.Mus., Master of Music.

M.Mus.Ed., Master of Music Education.

MN, Minnesota (approved esp. for use with zip code).

Mn, *Symbol, Chem.* manganese.

M.N.A., Master of Nursing Administration.

M'Nagh′ten test′ (mək nôt′n), a rule that defines a person as legally insane when that person cannot distinguish right from wrong. [after Daniel *M'Naghten* (d. 1865), defendant in a murder case adjudicated in England in 1843]

M.N.A.S., Member of the National Academy of Sciences.

M.N.E., Master of Nuclear Engineering.

mne·me (nē′mē), *n.* **1.** *Psychol.* the retentive basis or basic principle in a mind or organism accounting for memory. **2.** (*cap.*) *Class. Myth.* the Muse of memory, one of the original three Muses. Cf. **Aoede, Melete.** [1910–15; < Gk *mnḗmē* memory; see MNEMONIC] —**mne·mic** (nē′mik), *adj.*

mne·mon·ic (ni mon′ik), *adj.* **1.** assisting or intended to assist the memory. **2.** pertaining to mnemonics or to memory. —*n.* **3.** something intended to assist the memory, as a verse or formula. **4.** *Computers.* a programming code that is easy to remember, as *STO* for "store." [1745–55; < Gk *mnēmonikós* of, relating to memory, equiv. to *mnḗmon-* (s. of *mnḗmōn*) mindful + *-ikos* -IC] —**mne·mon′i·cal·ly,** *adv.*

mne·mon·ics (ni mon′iks), *n.* (*used with a singular v.*) the process or technique of improving or developing the memory. Also called **mne·mo·tech·nics** (nē′mō tek′-niks). [1700–10; see MNEMONIC, -ICS]

Mne·mos·y·ne (nē mos′ə nē′, -moz′-), *n.* the ancient Greek goddess of memory, a daughter of Uranus and Gaea and the mother by Zeus of the Muses. [< Gk *mnēmosýnē* memory, akin to *mnâsthai* to remember, *mnḗmōn* mindful]

Mnes·i·cles (nes′ə klēz′), *n.* Greek architect of the 5th century B.C.

Mngr., Monsignor.

mngr., manager.

M.N.S., Master of Nutritional Science.

M.Nurs., Master of Nursing.

mo (mō), *n. Informal.* moment (def. 1). [by shortening]

-mo, a suffix occurring in a series of compounds that describe book sizes according to the number of leaves formed by the folding of a single sheet of paper: *sixteenmo.* [comb. form extracted from DUODECIMO]

MO, **1.** method of operation. **2.** Missouri (approved esp. for use with zip code). **3.** mode of operation. **4.** modus operandi.

Mo, *Symbol, Chem.* molybdenum.

Mo., **1.** Missouri. **2.** Monday.

mo., **1.** *pl.* **mos.** month. **2.** months.

M.O., **1.** mail order. **2.** manually operated. **3.** Medical Officer. **4.** method of operation. **5.** mode of operation. **6.** modus operandi. **7.** money order.

m.o., **1.** mail order. **2.** modus operandi. **3.** money order.

mo·a (mō′ə), *n.* any of several flightless birds of the family Dinornithidae, of New Zealand, related to the kiwis but resembling the ostrich: extinct since about the end of the 18th century. [1810–20; < Maori]

moa, *Dinornis maximus,* height 10 ft. (3 m)

Mo·ab (mō′ab), *n.* an ancient kingdom E of the Dead Sea, in what is now Jordan. See map under **Philistia.**

Mo·ab·ite (mō′ə bīt′), *n.* **1.** an inhabitant or native of Moab. **2.** an extinct language of Moab, in the Canaanite group of Semitic languages. —*adj.* **3.** Also, **Mo·a·bit·ic** (mō′ə bit′ik), **Mo·a·bit·ish** (mō′ə bī′tish). of or pertaining to the ancient kingdom of Moab, its people, or their language. [1350–1400; ME < L *Mōabita* < Gk *Mōabítēs*, repr. Heb *mōābī.* See MOAB, -ITE[1]]

Mo′abite Stone′, a slab of black basalt bearing an inscription recording the victory of Mesha, the king of Moab, over the Israelites, about 860 B.C. Also called **Mesha Stele.** [1865–70]

moan (mōn), *n.* **1.** a prolonged, low, inarticulate sound uttered from or as if from physical or mental suffering. **2.** any similar sound: *the moan of the wind.* **3.** complaint or lamentation. —*v.i.* **4.** to utter moans, as of pain or grief. **5.** (of the wind, sea, trees, etc.) to make any sound suggestive of such moans: *The wind moaned through the trees.* —*v.t.* **6.** to utter (something) inarticulately or pitifully, as if in lamentation: *He moaned his response.* **7.** to lament or bemoan: *to moan one's fate.* [1175–1225; ME *mone, man(e)* (n.), OE **mān*, inferred from its deriv. *mǣnan* to mourn] —**moan′ful,** *adj.* —**moan′ful·ly,** *adv.* —**moan′ing·ly,** *adv.*
—**Syn. 1.** See **groan. 4.** grieve. **4, 7.** mourn. **7.** deplore.

moat (mōt), *n.* **1.** a deep, wide trench, usually filled with water, surrounding the rampart of a fortified place, as a town or a castle. **2.** any similar trench, as one used for confining animals in a zoo. [1325–75; ME *mote* < OF: clod, mound, of obscure orig.]

mob (mob), *n., adj., v.,* **mobbed, mob·bing.** —*n.* **1.** a disorderly or riotous crowd of people. **2.** a crowd bent on or engaged in lawless violence. **3.** any group or collection of persons or things. **4.** the common people; the masses; populace or multitude. **5.** a criminal gang, esp. one involved in drug trafficking, extortion, etc. **6. the Mob,** Mafia (def. 1). **7.** *Sociol.* a group of persons stimulating one another to excitement and losing ordinary rational control over their activity. **8.** a flock, herd, or drove of animals: *a mob of sheep.* —*adj.* **9.** of, pertaining to, or characteristic of a lawless, irrational, disorderly, or riotous crowd: *mob rule; mob instincts.* **10.** directed at or reflecting the lowest intellectual level of the common people: *mob appeal; the mob mentality.* —*v.t.* **11.** to crowd around noisily, as from curiosity or hostility: *Spectators mobbed the courtroom.* **12.** to attack in a riotous mob: *The crowd mobbed the consulate.* **13.** *Fox Hunting.* to chop (a fox). [1680–90; short for L *mōbile vulgus* the movable (i.e., changeable, inconstant) common people] —**mob′ber, mob′bist,** *n.* —**mob′bish,** *adj.* —**mob′bish·ly,** *adv.* —**mob′bish·ness,** *n.* —**mob′bism,** *n.*

mob·cap (mob′kap′), *n.* a soft cloth cap with a full crown, fitting down over the ears and frequently tying beneath the chin, formerly worn indoors by women. [1785–95; perh. *mob* slattern (itself perh. var. of *Mab* for *Mabel*) + CAP[1]]

mobe′ pearl′ (mōb′, mō′bē). See **mabe pearl.**

Mo·ber·ly (mō′bər lē), *n.* a city in N central Missouri. 13,418.

mo·bile (mō′bəl, -bēl *or, esp. Brit.,* -bīl *for 1-8, 10, 11;* mō′bēl *or, Brit.,* -bīl *for 9*), *adj.* **1.** capable of moving or being moved readily. **2.** utilizing motor vehicles for ready movement: *a mobile library.* **3.** *Mil.* permanently equipped with vehicles for transport. **4.** flowing freely, as a liquid. **5.** changeable or changing easily in expression, mood, purpose, etc.: *a mobile face.* **6.** quickly responding to impulses, emotions, etc., as the mind. **7.** *Sociol.* **a.** characterized by or permitting the mixing of social groups. **b.** characterized by or permitting relatively free movement from one social class or level to another. **8.** of or pertaining to a mobile. —*n.* **9.** a piece of sculpture having delicately balanced units constructed of rods and sheets of metal or other material suspended in midair by wire or twine so that the individual parts can move independently, as when stirred by a breeze. Cf. **stabile** (def. 3). **10.** *Informal.* a mobile home. **11.** *CB Radio Slang.* a vehicle. [1480–90; < L, neut. of *mōbilis* movable, equiv. to *mō-* (var. s. of *movēre* to MOVE) + *-bilis* -BLE]

Mo·bile (mō bēl′, mō′bēl), *n.* **1.** a seaport in SW Alabama at the mouth of the Mobile River. 200,452. **2.** a river in SW Alabama, formed by the confluence of the Alabama and Tombigbee rivers. 38 mi. (61 km) long.

-mobile, a combining form extracted from **automobile,** occurring as the final element in compounds denoting specialized types of motorized conveyances: *snowmobile;* esp. productive in coinages naming vehicles equipped to procure or deliver objects, provide services, etc., to people without regular access to these: *bloodmobile; bookmobile; clubmobile; jazzmobile.*

Mo′bile Bay′ (mō′bēl), a bay of the Gulf of Mexico, in SW Alabama: Civil War naval battle 1864. 36 mi. (58 km) long; 8–18 mi. (13–29 km) wide.

mo′bile home′, a large house trailer, designed for year-round living in one place. Also, **mo′bile·home′.** Also called **manufactured home.** [1950–55]

mo′bile phone′. See **cellular phone.**

mo′bile u′nit, 1. a vehicle supplied with the basic equipment or materials necessary for a particular purpose, as for televising on location or being used as an x-ray or inoculation clinic. **2.** a transceiver in a vehicle or carried by a person. [1930–35]

mo·bil·i·ty (mō bil′i tē), *n.* **1.** the quality of being mobile. **2.** *Sociol.* the movement of people in a population, as from place to place, from job to job, or from one social class or level to another. Cf. **horizontal mobility, vertical mobility.** [1375–1425; late ME *mobilite* < L *mōbilitās.* See MOBILE, -ITY]

mo·bi·lize (mō′bə līz′), *v.,* **-lized, -liz·ing.** —*v.t.* **1.** to assemble or marshal (armed forces, military reserves, or civilian persons of military age) into readiness for active service. **2.** to organize or adapt (industries, transportation facilities, etc.) for service to the government in time of war. **3.** to marshal, bring together, prepare (power, force, wealth, etc.) for action, esp. of a vigorous nature: *to mobilize one's energy.* **4.** to increase or bring to a full stage of development: *to mobilize one's anger.* —*v.i.* **5.** to be or become assembled, organized, etc., as for war: *to mobilize for action.* Also, *esp. Brit.,* **mo′bi·lise′.** [1830–40; back formation from *mobilization.* See MOBILE, -IZATION] —**mo′bi·liz′a·ble,** *adj.* —**mo′bi·li·za′tion,** *n.* —**mo′bi·liz′er,** *n.*

Mö·bi·us (mœ′bē əs, mā′-, mō′-; *Ger.* mœ′bē o͝os), *n.* **Au·gust Fer·di·nand** (ou′go͝ost fer′di nänt′), 1790–1868, German mathematician. Also, **Moebius.**

Mö′bius strip′, *Geom.* a continuous, one-sided surface formed by twisting one end of a rectangular strip through 180° about the longitudinal axis of the strip and attaching this end to the other. Also called **Mö′bius band′.** [1900–05; named after A. F. MÖBIUS]

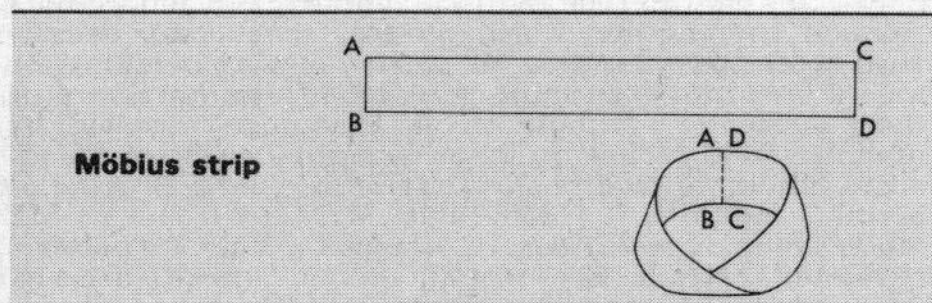

Möbius strip

Mö′bius transforma′tion, *Math.* a map of the complex plane to itself in which a point z is mapped to a point w by $w = (az + b)/(cz + d)$, where a, b, c, and d are complex numbers and $ad - bc$ does not equal zero. Also called **bilinear transformation, linear fractional transformation.** [see MÖBIUS STRIP]

mo·ble (mob′əl), *v.t.,* **-bled, -bling.** *Archaic.* to wrap the head of, as in a hood. [1595–1605; var. of MUFFLE]

mob·oc·ra·cy (mob ok′rə sē), *n., pl.* **-cies. 1.** political control by a mob. **2.** the mob as a ruling class. [1745–55; MOB + -O- + -CRACY] —**mob·o·crat** (mob′ə-krat′), *n.* —**mob′o·crat′ic, mob′o·crat′i·cal,** *adj.*

mob·ster (mob′stər), *n.* a member of a criminal mob. [1915–20, *Amer.;* MOB + -STER]

Mo·bu·tu Se·se Se·ko (mō bo͞o′to͞o ses′ā sek′ō, mə-), **1.** (*Joseph-Désiré Mobutu*), born 1930, Zairian political leader: president since 1965. **2. Lake,** official name of Lake Albert.

Mo·by Dick (mō′bē dik′), a novel (1851) by Herman Melville.

moc (mok), *n. Informal.* moccasin. [shortened form]

Mo·çam·bi·que (*Port.* mo͞o′səm bē′kə), *n.* Mozambique.

moc·ca·sin (mok′ə sin, -zən), *n.* **1.** a heelless shoe made entirely of soft leather, as deerskin, with the sole brought up and attached to a piece of U-shaped leather on top of the foot, worn originally by the American Indians. **2.** a hard-soled shoe or slipper resembling this, often decorated with beads. **3.** any of several North American snakes of the genus *Agkistrodon* (*Ancistrodon*), esp. the cottonmouth. [1605–15, *Amer.;* < Virginia Algonquian < Proto-Algonquian **maxkeseni*]

moc′casin flow′er, 1. the lady's-slipper. **2.** a cypripedium, *Cypripedium acaule,* of the U.S. [1670–80, *Amer.*]

mo·cha (mō′kə), *n.* **1.** (*cap.*) Also, **Mukha.** a seaport in the Republic of Yemen, on the Red Sea. 25,000. **2.** a choice variety of coffee, originally grown in Arabia. **3.** a flavoring obtained from a coffee infusion or a combined infusion of chocolate and coffee. **4.** a brownish chocolate color. **5.** a glove leather, finer and thinner than doeskin, the best grades of which are made from Arabian goatskins. [1765–75 for def. 2]

Mo′cha ware′, a pottery ware of the late 18th through the early 20th centuries, ornamented with colored glaze worked into branchlike patterns by drops of a diffusing agent applied while the glaze is still wet. [1830–40]

Mo·chi·ca (mō chē′kə), *adj.* of, pertaining to, or characteristic of a pre-Inca culture that flourished on the northern coast of Peru from the 3rd century B.C. to the 7th century A.D. and is especially noted for fine pottery vessels with stirrup spouts, some bearing drawings of all aspects of cultural life. Also, **Moc·he** (mō′chā; *Sp.* mô′-che).

mo·chi·la (mō chē′lə), *n.* a flap of leather on the seat of a saddle, used as a covering and sometimes as a base to which saddlebags are attached. [1855–60, *Amer.;* < Sp: lit., knapsack, deriv. of *mochil* errand boy < Basque *motxil,* dim. of *motil, mutil* boy, servant < L *mutilus* mutilated (from the custom of shaving boys' heads)]

mock (mok), *v.t.* **1.** to attack or treat with ridicule, contempt, or derision. **2.** to ridicule by mimicry of action or speech; mimic derisively. **3.** to mimic, imitate, or counterfeit. **4.** to challenge; defy: *His actions mock convention.* **5.** to deceive, delude, or disappoint. —*v.i.* **6.** to use ridicule or derision; scoff; jeer (often fol. by *at*). **7. mock up,** to build a mock-up of. —*n.* **8.** a contemptuous or derisive imitative action or speech; mockery or derision. **9.** something mocked or derided; an object of derision. **10.** an imitation; counterfeit; fake. **11.** *Shipbuilding.* **a.** a hard pattern representing the surface of a plate with a warped form, upon which the plate is beaten to shape after furnacing. **b.** bed (def. 23). —*adj.* **12.** feigned; not real; sham: *a mock battle.* [1400–50; late ME *mokken* < MF *mocquer*] —**mock′a·ble,** *adj.* —**mock′er,** *n.* —**mock′ing·ly,** *adv.*
—**Syn. 1.** deride; taunt, flout, gibe; chaff, tease. See **ridicule. 5.** cheat, dupe, fool, mislead.

mock·a·do (mə kä′dō), *n., pl.* **-does.** a fabric simulating velvet, popular in the 16th and 17th centuries. [1535–45; earlier *mockeado* < It *moccaiardo* (by assoc. with MOCK). See MOHAIR]

mock′ chick′en, minced veal, pork, or other meat, molded onto a stick or skewer so that it somewhat resembles a chicken leg, then breaded and braised. Also called **city chicken.**

mock′ ep′ic, a long, humorous poem written in mock-heroic style.

mock·er·nut (mok′ər nut′), *n.* **1.** a North American hickory, *Carya tomentosa,* bearing a sweet, edible nut. **2.** the nut itself. Also called **mock′ernut hick′ory.** [1795–1805, *Amer.;* appar. MOCKER + NUT]

mock·er·y (mok′ə rē), *n., pl.* **-er·ies. 1.** ridicule, contempt, or derision. **2.** a derisive, imitative action or speech. **3.** a subject or occasion of derision. **4.** an imitation, esp. of a ridiculous or unsatisfactory kind. **5.** a mocking pretense; travesty: *a mockery of justice.* **6.** something absurdly or offensively inadequate or unfitting. [1400–50; late ME *moquerie* < MF. See MOCK, -ERY]
—**Syn. 4.** mimicry.

mock-he·ro·ic (mok′hi rō′ik), *adj.* **1.** imitating or burlesquing that which is heroic, as in manner, character, or action: *mock-heroic dignity.* **2.** of or pertaining to a form of satire in which trivial subjects, characters, and events are treated in the ceremonious manner and with the elevated language and elaborate devices characteristic of the heroic style. —*n.* **3.** an imitation or burlesque of something heroic. [1705–15] —**mock′-he·ro′i·cal·ly,** *adv.*

mock·ing·bird (mok′ing bûrd′), *n.* **1.** any of several gray, black, and white songbirds of the genus *Mimus,* esp. *M. polyglottos,* of the U.S. and Mexico, noted for their ability to mimic the songs of other birds. **2.** any of various related or similar birds, as *Melanotis caerulescens* **(blue mockingbird),** of Mexico. [1670–80, *Amer.;* MOCKING + BIRD]

mock′ mold′, *Shipbuilding.* bed (def. 23).

mock′ moon′, paraselene. [1645–55]

mock′ or′ange, 1. Also called **syringa.** any of various shrubs belonging to the genus *Philadelphus,* of the saxifrage family, esp. *P. coronarius,* a widely cultivated species having fragrant white flowers. **2.** any of various other shrubs or trees having flowers or fruit resembling those of the orange, as the laurel cherry. [1725–35]

mock′ pen′dulum, a false pendulum bob attached to the balances of certain timepieces and visible through a slot in the dial or case.

mock′ pennyroy′al, pennyroyal (def. 2). [1855–60]

mock′ straw′berry. See **Indian strawberry.**

mock′ sun′, parhelion.

mock′ tur′tle soup′, a rich, clear soup prepared to resemble green turtle soup, made with a calf's head or other meat, seasonings, and often with wine. [1775–85]

mock-up (mok′up′), *n.* a model, often full-size, for study, testing, or teaching: *a mock-up of an experimental aircraft.* Also, **mock′up′.** [1915–20; n. use of v. phrase *mock up*]

Moc·te·zu·ma (*Sp.* môk′te so͞o′mä), *n.* See **Montezuma II.**

mod[1] (mod), *adj.* **1.** very modern; up-to-date; being in the vanguard in style, dress, etc. **2.** (*sometimes cap.*) of or pertaining to a style of dress of the 1960's, typified by miniskirts, bell-bottom trousers, boots, and bright colors and patterns. —*n.* **3.** a person who is in the vanguard in style, dress, etc. **4.** (*sometimes cap.*) a British teenager of the 1960's who affected a very neat, sophisticated appearance and wore fancy clothing inspired by Edwardian dress. [1955–60; shortened form of MODERN]

mod[2] (mod), *n. Informal.* modification. [by shortening]

Mod, 1. modal auxiliary. **2.** modifier.

mod., 1. moderate. **2.** *Music.* moderato. **3.** modern.

mod′a·cryl′ic fi′ber (mod′ə kril′ik, mod′-), any of various synthetic copolymer textile fibers, as Dynel, containing less than 85 percent but more than 35 percent of acrylonitrile. Also called **mod′a·cryl′ic.** [1955–60; MOD(IFIED) + ACRYLIC]

mod·al (mōd′l), *adj.* **1.** of or pertaining to mode, manner, or form. **2.** *Music.* **a.** pertaining to mode, as distinguished from key. **b.** based on a scale other than major or minor. **3.** Also, **single modal.** *Transp.* pertaining to or suitable for transportation involving only one form of a carrier, as truck, rail, or ship. Cf. **bimodal** (def. 3), **intermodal. 4.** *Gram.* noting or pertaining to mood. **5.** *Philos.* pertaining to a mode of a thing, as distinguished from one of its basic attributes or from its substance or matter. **6.** *Logic.* exhibiting or expressing some phase of modality. —*n.* **7.** See **modal auxiliary.** [1560–70; < ML *modālis.* See MODE[1], -AL[1]] —**mod′al·ly,** *adv.*

mod′al auxil′iary, *Gram.* any of the group of English auxiliary verbs, including *can, could, may, might, shall, should, will, would,* and *must,* that are used with the base form of another verb to express distinctions of mood. [1930–35]

mo·dal·i·ty (mō dal′i tē), *n., pl.* **-ties. 1.** the quality or state of being modal. **2.** an attribute or circumstance that denotes mode or manner. **3.** Also called **mode.** *Logic.* the classification of propositions according to whether they are contingently true or false, possible, impossible, or necessary. **4.** *Med.* the application of a therapeutic agent, usually a physical therapeutic agent. **5.** one of the primary forms of sensation, as vision or touch. [1610–20; < ML *modālitās.* See MODAL, -ITY]

mode[1] (mōd), *n.* **1.** a manner of acting or doing; method; way: *modern modes of transportation.* **2.** a particular type or form of something: *Heat is a mode of motion.* **3.** a designated condition or status, as for performing a task or responding to a problem: *a machine in the automatic mode.* **4.** *Philos.* **a.** appearance, form, or disposition taken by a thing, or by one of its essential properties or attributes. **b.** (in the philosophy of Spinoza) one of the nonessential qualifications of God, contingent upon other modes. Cf. **attribute** (def. 9). **5.** *Logic.* **a.** modality (def. 3). **b.** mood[2] (def. 2). **6.** *Music.* any of various arrangements of the diatonic tones of an octave, differing from one another in the order of the whole steps and half steps; scale. **7.** *Gram.* mood[2] (def. 1). **8.** *Statistics.* the value of the variate at which a relative or absolute maximum occurs in the frequency distribution of the variate. **9.** *Petrog.* the actual mineral composition of a rock, expressed in percentages by weight. **10.** *Physics.* any of the distinct patterns of oscillation that a given periodically varying system can have. [1250–1300; ME *mod(e)* (< OF) < L *modus* measured amount, limit, manner, kind, tone]
—**Syn. 1.** See **method.**

mode[2] (mōd), *n.* **1.** fashion or style in manners, dress, etc.: *He was much concerned to keep up with the latest mode.* **2.** a light gray or drab color. [1635–45; < F < L *modus;* see MODE[1]]

mod·el (mod′l), *n., adj., v.,* **-eled, -el·ing** or (*esp. Brit.*) **-elled, -el·ling.** —*n.* **1.** a standard or example for imitation or comparison. **2.** a representation, generally in miniature, to show the construction or appearance of something. **3.** an image in clay, wax, or the like, to be reproduced in more durable material. **4.** a person or thing that serves as a subject for an artist, sculptor, writer, etc. **5.** a person whose profession is posing for artists or photographers. **6.** a person employed to wear clothing or pose with a product for purposes of display and advertising. **7.** a style or design of a particular product: *His car is last year's model.* **8.** a pattern or mode of structure or formation. **9.** a typical form or style. **10.** a simplified representation of a system or phenomenon, as in the sciences or economics, with any

CONCISE PRONUNCIATION KEY: act, cāpe, dâre, pärt; set, ēqual; if, īce; ox, ōver, ôrder, oil, bo͝ok, bo͞ot, out; up, ûrge; child; sing; shoe; thin, *th*at; zh as in *treasure.* ə = *a* as in *alone, e* as in *system, i* as in *easily, o* as in *gallop, u* as in *circus;* ° as in *fire* (fī°r), *hour* (ou°r). l and n can serve as syllabic consonants, as in *cradle* (krād′l), and *button* (but′n). See the full key inside the front cover.

hypotheses required to describe the system or explain the phenomenon, often mathematically. **11.** *Zool.* an animal that is mimicked in form or color by another. —*adj.* **12.** serving as an example or model: *a model home open to prospective buyers.* **13.** worthy to serve as a model; exemplary: *a model student.* **14.** being a small or miniature version of something: *He enjoyed building model ships.* —*v.t.* **15.** to form or plan according to a model. **16.** to give shape or form to; fashion. **17.** to make a miniature model of. **18.** to fashion in clay, wax, or the like. **19.** to simulate (a process, concept, or the operation of a system), commonly with the aid of a computer. **20.** to display to other persons or to prospective customers, esp. by wearing: *to model dresses.* **21.** to use or include as an element in a larger construct: *to model new data into the forecast.* —*v.i.* **22.** to make models. **23.** to produce designs in some plastic material. **24.** to assume a typical or natural appearance, as the parts of a drawing in progress. **25.** to serve or be employed as a model. [1565–75; earlier *modell* < MF *modelle* < It *modello* < VL **modellus,* equiv. to L *mod(ulus)* (see MODULE) + *-ellus* -ELLE] —**mod′el·er;** *esp. Brit.,* **mod′el·ler,** *n.*
—**Syn. 1.** paragon; prototype, archetype, mold, original. See **ideal. 16.** design.

mod·el·ing (mod′l ing), *n.* **1.** the act, art, or profession of a person who models. **2.** the process of producing sculptured form with some plastic material, as clay. **3.** the technique of rendering the illusion of volume on a two-dimensional surface by shading. **4.** the treatment of volume, as the turning of a form, in sculpture. **5.** the representation, often mathematical, of a process, concept, or operation of a system, often implemented by a computer program. **6.** Also called **imitation.** *Psychol.* therapy in which a particular behavior is elicited by the observation of similar behavior in others. Also, *esp. Brit.,* **mod′el·ling.** [1575–85; MODEL + -ING[1]]

mod·el·ist (mod′l ist), *n.* a person who makes models, as of airplanes. [1670–80; MODEL + -IST]

Model T, an automobile with a 2.9-liter, 4-cylinder engine, produced by the Ford Motor Company from 1909 through 1927, considered to be the first motor vehicle successfully mass-produced on an assembly line.

mo·dem (mō′dəm, -dem), *Computers.* —*n.* **1.** an electronic device that makes possible the transmission of data to or from a computer via telephone or other communication lines. —*v.t.* **2.** to send or receive (information, data, or the like) via a modem. [*mo(dulator)-demodulator)*]

Mo·de·na (mōd′n ə; *It.* mô′de nä), *n.* a city in N Italy, NW of Bologna. 178,959.

mod·er·ate (*adj., n.* mod′ər it, mod′rit; *v.* mod′ə rāt′), *adj., n., v.,* **-at·ed, -at·ing.** —*adj.* **1.** kept or keeping within reasonable or proper limits; not extreme, excessive, or intense: *a moderate price.* **2.** of medium quantity, extent, or amount: *a moderate income.* **3.** mediocre or fair: *moderate talent.* **4.** calm or mild, as of the weather. **5.** of or pertaining to moderates, as in politics or religion. —*n.* **6.** a person who is moderate in opinion or opposed to extreme views and actions, esp. in politics or religion. **7.** (*usually cap.*) a member of a political party advocating moderate reform. —*v.t.* **8.** to reduce the excessiveness of; make less violent, severe, intense, or rigorous: *to moderate the sharpness of one's words.* **9.** to preside over or at (a public forum, meeting, discussion, etc.). —*v.i.* **10.** to become less violent, severe, intense, or rigorous. **11.** to act as moderator; preside. [1350–1400; ME *moderate* (adj.), *moderaten* (v.) < L *moderātus* (ptp. of *moderārī* to restrain, control), equiv. to *moderā-* v. s. (see MODEST) + *-tus* ptp. suffix] —**mod′er·ate·ly,** *adv.* —**mod′er·ate·ness,** *n.*
—**Syn. 1.** reasonable, temperate, judicious, just, cool, steady, calm. MODERATE, TEMPERATE, JUDICIOUS, REASONABLE all stress the avoidance of excess—emotional, physical, intellectual, or otherwise. MODERATE implies response or behavior that is by nature not excessive: *a moderate drinker, a moderate amount of assistance.* TEMPERATE, interchangeable with MODERATE in some general uses, usually stresses the idea of caution, control, or self-restraint: *a surprisingly temperate response to the angry challenge.* JUDICIOUS emphasizes prudence and the exercise of careful judgment: *a judicious balance between freedom and restraint; judicious care to offend neither side.* REASONABLE suggests the imposition or adoption of limits derived from the application of reason or good sense: *a reasonable price; a reasonable amount of damages allotted to each claimant.* **2.** average. **8.** meliorate, pacify, calm, mitigate, soften, mollify, temper, qualify, appease, abate, lessen, diminish. See **allay.** —**Ant. 5, 6.** radical.

mod′erate breeze′, a wind of 13–18 mph (5.8–8 m/sec). [1795–1805]

mod′erate gale′, a wind of 32–38 mph (14–17 m/sec). [1695–1705]

mod·er·a·tion (mod′ə rā′shən), *n.* **1.** the quality of being moderate; restraint; avoidance of extremes or excesses; temperance. **2.** the act of moderating. **3. moderations,** *Brit.* the first public examinations at Oxford University for the B.A. degree in mathematics or in classics. **4. in moderation,** without excess; moderately; temperately: *to drink in moderation.* [1375–1425; late ME *moderacion* < L *moderātiōn-* (s. of *moderātiō*). See MODERATE, -ION]

mod·er·a·tion·ist (mod′ə rā′shə nist), *n.* a person who favors, supports, or promotes moderation. [1840–50; MODERATION + -IST]

mod·e·ra·to (mod′ə rä′tō), *adj. Music.* moderate; in moderate time. [1715–25; < It < L *moderātus* MODERATE]

CONCISE ETYMOLOGY KEY: <, descended or borrowed from; >, whence; b., blend of, blended; c., cognate with; cf., compare; deriv., derivative; equiv., equivalent; imit., imitative; obl., oblique; r., replacing; s., stem; sp., spelling, spelled; resp., respelling, respelled; trans., translation; ?, origin unknown; *, unattested; ‡, probably earlier than. See the full key inside the front cover.

mod·er·a·tor (mod′ə rā′tər), *n.* **1.** a person or thing that moderates. **2.** a person who presides over a panel discussion on radio or television. **3.** a presiding officer, as at a public forum, a legislative body, or an ecclesiastical body in the Presbyterian Church. **4.** *Physics.* a substance, as graphite or heavy water, used to slow neutrons to speeds at which they are more efficient in causing fission. [1350–1400; ME < L *moderātor,* equiv. to *moderā(rī)* to control (see MODERATE) + *-tor* -TOR] —**mod·er·a·to·ri·al** (mod′ər ə tôr′ē əl, -tōr′-), *adj.* —**mod′er·a′tor·ship′,** *n.*

mod·ern (mod′ərn), *adj.* **1.** of or pertaining to present and recent time; not ancient or remote: *modern city life.* **2.** characteristic of present and recent time; contemporary; not antiquated or obsolete: *modern viewpoints.* **3.** of or pertaining to the historical period following the Middle Ages: *modern European history.* **4.** of, pertaining to, or characteristic of contemporary styles of art, literature, music, etc., that reject traditionally accepted or sanctioned forms and emphasize individual experimentation and sensibility. **5.** (*cap.*) new (def. 12). **6.** *Typography.* noting or descriptive of a font of numerals in which the body aligns on the baseline, as **1234567890.** Cf. **old style** (def. 3). —*n.* **7.** a person of modern times. **8.** a person whose views and tastes are modern. **9.** *Print.* a type style differentiated from old style by heavy vertical strokes and straight serifs. [1490–1500; < MF *moderne* < LL *modernus,* equiv. to L *mod(o), mod(ō)* lately, just now (orig. abl. sing. of *modus* MODE[1]) + *-ernus* adj. suffix of time] —**mod′ern·ly,** *adv.* —**mod′ern·ness,** *n.*
—**Syn. 1.** MODERN, RECENT, LATE apply to that which is near to or characteristic of the present as contrasted with any other time. MODERN is applied to those things that exist in the present age, esp. in contrast to those of a former age or an age long past; hence the word sometimes has the connotation of up-to-date and, thus, good: *modern ideas.* That which is RECENT is separated from the present or the time of action by only a short interval; it is new, fresh, and novel: *recent developments.* LATE may mean nearest to the present moment: *the late reports on the battle.*

mod′ern cut′, *Jewelry.* any of several modifications or combinations of the brilliant cut, step cut, or table cut, having the girdle outline often in some novel form. Also, **mod′erne cut′.**

mod′ern dance′, a form of contemporary theatrical and concert dance employing a special technique for developing the use of the entire body in movements expressive of abstract ideas. [1910–15]

mo·derne (mō dârn′, mə-), *adj.* pretentiously modern; striving to appear modern but lacking style or conviction. [< F: MODERN]

Mod′ern Eng′lish, the English language since c1475. Also called **New English.**

Mod′ern French′, the French language since c1600. [1895–1900]

Mod′ern Greek′, the Greek language since c1500. *Abbr.:* ModGk Also called **New Greek.** [1740–50]

Mod′ern He′brew, the living language of modern Israel, a revived form of ancient Hebrew. *Abbr.:* ModHeb Also called **New Hebrew.** [1970–75]

Mod′ern Icelan′dic, the Icelandic language since c1550. [1925–30]

mod·ern·ism (mod′ər niz′əm), *n.* **1.** modern character, tendencies, or values; adherence to or sympathy with what is modern. **2.** a modern usage or characteristic. **3.** (*cap.*) *Theol.* **a.** the movement in Roman Catholic thought that sought to interpret the teachings of the Church in the light of philosophic and scientific conceptions prevalent in the late 19th and early 20th centuries: condemned by Pope Pius X in 1907. **b.** the liberal theological tendency in Protestantism in the 20th century. **4.** (*sometimes cap.*) a deliberate philosophical and practical estrangement or divergence from the past in the arts and literature occurring esp. in the course of the 20th century and taking form in any of various innovative movements and styles. [1730–40; MODERN + -ISM]

mod·ern·ist (mod′ər nist), *n.* **1.** a person who follows or favors modern ways, tendencies, etc. **2.** a person who advocates the study of modern subjects in preference to ancient classics. **3.** an adherent of modernism in theological questions. —*adj.* **4.** of modernists or modernism. [1580–90; MODERN + -IST]

mod·ern·is·tic (mod′ər nis′tik), *adj.* **1.** modern. **2.** of or pertaining to modernism or modernists. [1905–10; MODERN + -ISTIC] —**mod′ern·is′ti·cal·ly,** *adv.*

mo·der·ni·ty (mo dûr′ni tē, mō-), *n., pl.* **-ties. 1.** the quality of being modern. **2.** something modern. [1620–30; MODERN + -ITY]

mod·ern·ize (mod′ər nīz′), *v.,* **-ized, -iz·ing.** —*v.t.* **1.** to make modern; give a new or modern character or appearance to: *to modernize one's ideas; to modernize a kitchen.* —*v.i.* **2.** to become modern; adopt modern ways, views, etc. Also, *esp. Brit.,* **mod′ern·ise′.** [1740–50; MODERN(ISM) + -IZE] —**mod′ern·i·za′tion,** *n.* —**mod′ern·iz′er,** *n.*
—**Syn. 1.** renovate, refurbish, update.

mod′ern jazz′, any of various styles of jazz that have evolved since the early 1940's and are marked generally by harmonic and rhythmic complexity, emphasis on chord progressions rather than melody, a tendency to draw on classical forms and styles, and eclectic, allusive melodic tags in improvisation. Also called **progressive jazz.** Cf. **bop[1], cool jazz, hard bop.** [1950–55]

mod′ern lan′guage, one of the literary languages currently in use in Europe, as French, Spanish, or German, treated as a departmental course of study in a school, college, or university. [1830–40]

mod′ern pentath′lon, an athletic contest comprising five different events, a 300-meter freestyle swim, a 4000-meter cross-country run, a 5000-meter equestrian steeplechase, épée fencing, and pistol target-shooting at 25 meters, the winner being the contestant with the highest total score. Also called **military pentathlon, pentathlon.** [1940–45]

Mod′ern Per′sian, the Persian language since the Middle Persian stage.

mod′ern syn′thesis, *Biol.* a consolidation of the results of various lines of investigation from the 1920's through the 1950's that supported and reconciled the Darwinian theory of evolution and the Mendelian laws of inheritance in terms of natural selection acting on genetic variation.

Mo·der·sohn-Beck·er (mō′dəʀ zōn bek′əʀ), *n.* **Paula** (pou′lä), 1876–1907, German painter.

mod·est (mod′ist), *adj.* **1.** having or showing a moderate or humble estimate of one's merits, importance, etc.; free from vanity, egotism, boastfulness, or great pretensions. **2.** free from ostentation or showy extravagance: *a modest house.* **3.** having or showing regard for the decencies of behavior, speech, dress, etc.; decent: *a modest neckline on a dress.* **4.** limited or moderate in amount, extent, etc.: *a modest increase in salary.* [1555–65; < L *modestus* restrained, decorous, equiv. to *modes-* (s. of **modus,* an s-stem akin to *modus* MODE[1], perh. < **medos,* with the vowel of *modus;* cf. *moderārī* to MODERATE, from the same n. stem) + *-tus* adj. suffix] —**mod′est·ly,** *adv.*
—**Syn. 1.** retiring, unassuming. **1, 2.** unpretentious, unobtrusive. **3.** pure, virtuous. MODEST, DEMURE, PRUDISH imply conformity to propriety and decorum, and a distaste for anything coarse or loud. MODEST implies a becoming shyness, sobriety, and proper behavior: *a modest, self-respecting person.* DEMURE implies a bashful, quiet simplicity, staidness, and decorum; but can also indicate an assumed or affected modesty: *a demure young chorus girl.* PRUDISH suggests an exaggeratedly self-conscious modesty or propriety in behavior or conversation of one who wishes to be thought of as easily shocked and who often is intolerant: *a prudish objection to a harmless remark.* —**Ant. 3.** bold, coarse.

Mo·des·to (mə des′tō), *n.* a city in central California. 106,105.

mod·es·ty (mod′ə stē), *n., pl.* **-ties. 1.** the quality of being modest; freedom from vanity, boastfulness, etc. **2.** regard for decency of behavior, speech, dress, etc. **3.** simplicity; moderation. [1525–35; < L *modestia.* See MODEST, -Y[3]]

mod′esty pan′el, a panel across the front of a desk, esp. an office desk, designed to conceal the legs of a person seated at it.

MODFET (mod′fet′), *n. Electronics.* modulation-doped field effect transistor.

ModGk, Modern Greek. Also, **Mod. Gk., Mod. Gr.**

ModHeb, Modern Hebrew. Also, **Mod. Heb.**

mod·i·cum (mod′i kəm), *n.* a moderate or small amount: *He hasn't even a modicum of common sense.* [1425–75; late ME < L, n. use of neut. of *modicus* moderate, equiv. to *modi-,* comb. form of *modus* limit (see MODE[1]) + *-cus* adj. suffix]

modif., modification.

mod·i·fi·cand (mod′ə fi kand′), *n. Gram.* a word that is modified, or qualified, by another. In *red books, books* is a modificand. [1825–35; < L *modificandum* (a thing) to be measured or limited, ger. of *modificāre* to MODIFY]

mod·i·fi·ca·tion (mod′ə fi kā′shən), *n.* **1.** an act or instance of modifying. **2.** the state of being modified; partial alteration. **3.** a modified form; variety. **4.** *Biol.* a change in a living organism acquired from its own activity or environment and not transmitted to its descendants. **5.** limitation or qualification. **6.** *Gram.* **a.** the use of a modifier in a construction, or of modifiers in a class of constructions or in a language. **b.** the meaning of a modifier, esp. as it affects the meaning of the word or other form modified: *Limitation is one kind of modification.* **c.** a change in the phonological shape of a morpheme, word, or other form when it functions as an element in a construction, as the change of *not* to *-n't* in *doesn't.* **d.** an adjustment in the form of a word as it passes from one language to another. [1495–1505; < L *modificātiōn-* (s. of *modificātiō*), equiv. to *modificāt(us)* (ptp. of *modificāre;* see MODIFY) + *-iōn-* -ION]

mod·i·fi·ca·to·ry (mod′ə fi kə tôr′ē, -tōr′ē), *adj.* modifying. Also, **mod′i·fi·ca′tive.** [1815–25; < L *modificāt(us)* (see MODIFICATION) + -ORY[1]]

mod′ified Amer′ican plan′, (in hotels) a system of paying a single fixed rate that covers room, breakfast, and one other meal, usually dinner. *Abbr.:* MAP Cf. **American plan, demi-pension, European plan.**

mod·i·fi·er (mod′ə fī′ər), *n.* **1.** a person or thing that modifies. **2.** *Gram.* **a.** a word, phrase, or sentence element that limits or qualifies the sense of another word, phrase, or element in the same construction. **b.** the immediate constituent of an endocentric construction that is not the head. [1575–85; MODIFY + -ER[1]]
—**Usage.** See **dangling participle, misplaced modifier.**

mod·i·fy (mod′ə fī′), *v.,* **-fied, -fy·ing.** —*v.t.* **1.** to change somewhat the form or qualities of; alter partially; amend: *to modify a contract.* **2.** *Gram.* (of a word, phrase, or clause) to stand in a syntactically subordinate relation to (another word, phrase, or clause), usually with descriptive, limiting, or particularizing meaning; be a modifier. In *a good man, good* modifies *man.* **3.** to be the modifier or attribute of. **4.** to change (a vowel) by umlaut. **5.** to reduce or lessen in degree or extent; moderate; soften: *to modify one's demands.* —*v.i.* **6.** to be or become modified. [1350–1400; ME *modifien* < MF *modifier* < L *modificāre* to impose a rule or pattern, regulate, restrain. See MODE[1], -IFY] —**mod′i·fi′a·ble,** *adj.* —**mod′i·fi′a·bil′i·ty, mod′i·fi′a·ble·ness,** *n.*
—**Syn. 1.** vary, adjust, shape, reform. **5.** MODIFY, QUALIFY, TEMPER suggest altering an original statement, condition, or the like, so as to avoid anything excessive or extreme. To MODIFY is to alter in one or more particulars, generally in the direction of leniency or moderation: *to modify demands, rates.* To QUALIFY is to restrict or limit by exceptions or conditions: *to qualify one's praise,*

hopes. To TEMPER is to alter the quality of something, generally so as to diminish its force or harshness: *to temper one's criticism with humor.*

Mo•di•glia•ni (mō dē′lē ä′nē, mō′dēl yä′-; *It.* mô′dē-lyä′nē), *n.* **A•me•de•o** (ä′me de′ô), 1884–1920, Italian painter and sculptor in France.

mo•dil•lion (mō dil′yən, mə-), *n. Archit.* an ornamental cantilever beneath the corona or similar member of a cornice, stringcourse, etc. [1555–65; < It *modiglione* < VL *mutiliōnem, var. of *mūtuliōnem, acc. of *mūtuliō. See MUTULE, -ION]

mo•di•o•lus (mō dī′ə ləs, mə-), *n., pl.* **-li** (-lī′). *Anat.* the central, conical axis of the cochlea of the ear. [1685–95; < NL, L: nave of a wheel bucket, drinking vessel, equiv. to *modi(us)* a dry measure (perh. deriv. of *modus* MODE[1]) + *-olus* -OLE[1]] **—mo•di′o•lar,** *adj.*

mod•ish (mō′dish), *adj.* in the current fashion; stylish. [1650–60; MODE[2] + -ISH[1]] **—mod′ish•ly,** *adv.* **—mod′•ish•ness,** *n.*
—Syn. smart, chic, fashionable, trendy.

mo•diste (mō dēst′; *Fr.* mô dēst′), *n., pl.* **-distes** (-dēsts′; *Fr.* -dēst′). *Older Use.* a female maker of or dealer in women's fashionable attire. [1830–40; < F; see MODE[2], -IST]

Mo•djes•ka (mô jes′kə), *n.* **He•le•na** (hə lā′nə), (*Helena Opid Modrzejewska*), 1840–1909, Polish actress, in U.S. after 1876.

Mo•doc (mō′dok), *n., pl.* **-docs,** (*esp. collectively*) **-doc.** a member of an American Indian people belonging to the Lutuamian group and ranging from southern Oregon to northern California.

mo′dock wool′ (mō′dok). See **territory wool.** [special use of MODOC]

mod. praesc., (in prescriptions) in the manner prescribed; as directed. [< L *modō praescrīptō*]

Mo•dred (mō′drid), *n. Arthurian Romance.* the nephew and treacherous killer of Arthur. Also, **Mordred.**

mod•u•lar (moj′ə lər), *adj.* **1.** of or pertaining to a module or a modulus. **2.** composed of standardized units or sections for easy construction or flexible arrangement: *a modular home; a modular sofa.* **3.** *Math.* (of a lattice) having the property that for any two elements with one less than the other, the union of the smaller element with the intersection of the larger element and any third element of the lattice is equal to the intersection of the larger element with the union of the smaller element and the third element. **4.** *Computers.* composed of software or hardware modules that can be altered or replaced without affecting the remainder of the system. **—*n.* 5.** something, as a house or piece of furniture, built or organized in self-contained units or sections. **6.** a self-contained unit or item, as of furniture, that can be combined or interchanged with others like it to create different shapes or designs. [1790–1800; < NL *modulāris.* See MODULE, -AR[1]]

mod′ular arith′metic, arithmetic in which numbers that are congruent modulo a given number are treated as the same. Cf. **congruence** (def. 2), **modulo, modulus** (def. 2b). [1955–60]

mod•u•lar•i•ty (moj′ə lar′i tē, mod′yə-), *n.* the use of individually distinct functional units, as in assembling an electronic or mechanical system. [1935–40; MODULAR + -ITY]

mod•u•lar•ize (moj′ə lə rīz′), *v.t.,* **-ized, -iz•ing.** to form or organize into modules, as for flexibility. Also, *esp. Brit.,* **mod′u•lar•ise′.** [1955–60; MODULAR + -IZE] **—mod′u•lar•i•za′tion,** *n.*

mod•u•late (moj′ə lāt′), *v.,* **-lat•ed, -lat•ing.** **—*v.t.* 1.** to regulate by or adjust to a certain measure or proportion; soften; tone down. **2.** to alter or adapt (the voice) according to the circumstances, one's listener, etc. **3.** *Music.* **a.** to attune to a certain pitch or key. **b.** to vary the volume of (tone). **4.** *Telecommunications.* to cause the amplitude, frequency, phase, or intensity of (a carrier wave) to vary in accordance with a sound wave or other signal, the frequency of the signal wave usually being very much lower than that of the carrier. **—*v.i.* 5.** *Telecommunications.* **a.** to modulate a carrier wave. **b.** *CB Slang.* to talk; visit: *Enjoyed modulating with you.* **6.** *Music.* to pass from one key to another: *to modulate abruptly from A to B flat.* [1550–60; < L *modulātus* (ptp. of *modulārī* to regulate (sounds), set to music, play an instrument). See MODULE, -ATE[1]] **—mod•u•la•bil•i•ty** (moj′ə lə bil′i tē), *n.* **—mod′u•la′tive, mod•u•la•to•ry** (moj′ə lə tôr′ē, -tōr′ē), *adj.*
—Syn. 2. temper, control.

mod•u•la•tion (moj′ə lā′shən, mod′yə-), *n.* **1.** the act of modulating. **2.** the state of being modulated. **3.** *Music.* transition from one key to another. **4.** *Gram.* **a.** the use of a particular distribution of stress or pitch in a construction, as the use of rising pitch on *here* in *John is here?* **b.** the feature of a construction resulting from such use. [1350–1400; ME < L *modulātiōn-* (s. of *modulātiō*) rhythmical measure. See MODULATE, -ION]

mod•u•la•tor (moj′ə lā′tər), *n.* **1.** a person or thing that modulates. **2.** *Telecommunications.* a device for modulating a carrier wave. [1490–1500; < L *modulātor;* see MODULATE, -TOR]

mod•ule (moj′o͞ol), *n.* **1.** a separable component, frequently one that is interchangeable with others, for assembly into units of differing size, complexity, or function. **2.** any of the individual, self-contained segments of a spacecraft, designed to perform a particular task: *the spacecraft's command module; a lunar module.* **3.** a standard or unit for measuring. **4.** a selected unit of measure, ranging in size from a few inches to several feet, used as a basis for the planning and standardization of building materials. **5.** *Math.* an Abelian group with a set of left or right operators forming a ring such that for any two operators and any group element the result of having the first operator act on the element, giving a second element, and the second operator act on the second element is equal to the result of having a single operator, formed by adding or multiplying the two operators, act on the first element. Cf. **ring**[1] (def. 23). **6.** *Computers.* **a.** part of a program that performs a distinct function. **b.** an interchangeable, plug-in hardware unit. [1555–65; < L *modulus;* see MODULUS]

mod•u•lo (moj′ə lō′), *adv. Math.* with respect to a modulus: *6 is congruent to 11, modulo 5.* [1895–1900; < NL *modulō,* abl. of L *modulus* MODULUS]

mod•u•lus (moj′ə ləs), *n., pl.* **-li** (lī). **1.** *Physics.* a coefficient pertaining to a physical property. **2.** *Math.* **a.** that number by which the logarithms in one system are multiplied to yield the logarithms in another. **b.** a quantity by which two given quantities can be divided to yield the same remainders. **c.** See **absolute value.** [1555–65; < L: a unit of measure; see MODE[1], -ULE]

mod′ulus of elastic′ity, *Physics.* any of several coefficients of elasticity of a body, expressing the ratio between a stress or force per unit area that acts to deform the body and the corresponding fractional deformation caused by the stress. Also called **coefficient of elasticity, elastic modulus.** [1800–10]

mod′ulus of rigid′ity, *Physics.* See **shear modulus.** [1875–80]

mod′ulus of tor′sion, *Physics.* See **shear modulus.**

mo•dus op•e•ran•di (mō′dəs op′ə ran′dē, -dī; *Lat.* mō′do͝os ō′pe rän′dē), *pl.* **mo•di op•e•ran•di** (mō′dē op′ə ran′dē, mō′dī op′ə ran′dī; *Lat.* mō′dē ō′pe rän′dē). mode of operating or working. [1645–55; < L *modus operandī*]

mo•dus vi•ven•di (mō′dəs vi ven′dē, -dī), *pl.* **mo•di vi•ven•di** (mō′dē vi ven′dē, mō′dī vi ven′dī). **1.** manner of living; way of life; lifestyle. **2.** a temporary arrangement between persons or parties pending a settlement of matters in debate. [1875–80 < L *modus vivendī* mode of living]

Moe (mō), *n.* a male given name, form of **Morris** or **Moses.**

Moe•bi•us (mœ′bē əs, mā′-, mō′-), *n.* **August Ferdinand.** See **Möbius, August Ferdinand.**

Moe•rae (mē′rē), *n.pl. Class. Myth.* the Fates.

Moe•si•a (mē′shē ə), *n.* an ancient country in S Europe, S of the Danube and N of ancient Thrace and Macedonia: later a Roman province.

Moe•so•goth (mē′sō goth′, -sə-), *n.* one of the Christianized Goths who settled in Moesia in the 4th century A.D.

Moe•so•goth•ic (mē′sō goth′ik, -sə-), *adj.* of or pertaining to the Moesogoths or their language. [MOESOGOTH + -IC]

mo•fette (mō fet′; *Fr.* mô fet′), *n.* **1.** a noxious emanation, consisting chiefly of carbon dioxide, escaping from the earth in regions of nearly extinct volcanic activity. **2.** one of the openings or fissures from which this emanation issues. Also, **mof•fette′.** [1815–25; < F < It *moffetta* (Neapolitan *mufeta*), equiv. to *muff(a)* (Upper It *mofa*) mould (< Langobardic; cf. G *Muff* mould, late MHG *müffeln* to give off a foul smell) + *-etta* -ETTA]

mog[1] (mog), *v.,* **mogged, mog•ging.** *Dial.* **—*v.i.* 1.** to move on, depart, or decamp (usually fol. by *off* or *on*). **2.** to walk or move along gently, slowly, and steadily. **—*v.t.* 3.** to cause to go from one place to another. [1665–75; M(OVE) + (J)OG[1]]

mog[2] (mog), *n.* moggy. [by shortening]

Mo•ga•di•shu (mô′gä dē′shōō), *n.* a seaport in and the capital of Somalia, in the S part. 400,000. Italian, **Mo•ga•di•scio** (mô′gä dē′shô).

Mog•a•dor (mog′ə dôr′, -dōr′; *Fr.* mô gȧ dôr′), *n.* **1.** former name of **Essaouira. 2.** (*l.c.*) Also, **mog′a•dore′.** a ribbed fabric of silk or rayon warp and cotton or linen filling, used for neckties.

Mo•gen Da•vid (mō′gən dā′vid; *Seph. Heb.* mä gen′ dä vēd′; *Ashk. Heb.* mô′gən dô′vid), *Judaism.* See **Star of David.** [1900–05]

mog•gy (mog′ē), *n., pl.* **-gies.** *Brit. Informal.* a cat. Also, **mog.** [1815–25; said to be orig. Cockney; supposed derivations from dial. (W Midlands) *Moggy* pet name for a calf, or from personal name MAGGIE, are dubious]

Mo•ghul (mō′gəl, -gul, mō gul′), *n., adj.* Mogul (defs. 1, 2, 6).

Mo•gi das Cru•zes (mo͝o zhē′ däs kro͞o′zis), a city in SE Brazil, E of São Paulo. 111,554.

mog•i•la•li•a (moj′ə lā′lē ə, -lāl′yə), *n.* any speech defect, as stuttering or stammering. Also, **molilalia.** [1875–80; < Gk *mogilál(os)* hardly talking (*mógi(s)* with difficulty + *lálos* babbling) + *-ia* -IA]

Mo•gi•lev (mō′gi lef′; *Russ.* mə gyi lyôf′), *n.* a city in E Byelorussia (Belarus), on the Dnieper. 359,000.

mo•go (mō′gō), *n., pl.* **-gos.** *Australian.* a stone hatchet used by the Aborigines. [1815–25; < Dharuk *mu-gu*]

Mo•gol•lon (mō′gə yōn′), *n.* **1.** an extensive plateau or mesa in central Arizona; the southwestern margin of the Colorado Plateau. **2.** a mountain range in W New Mexico. **—*adj.* 3.** *Archaeol.* of or pertaining to an Amerindian culture of southeastern Arizona and southwestern New Mexico 100 B.C.–A.D. 1000, characterized by pit houses also used for burials and a distinctive black-on-white pottery decorated with human and animal figures.

mo•go•te (mə gō′tē), *n.* **1.** a residual hillock of limestone, honeycombed with cavities. **2.** *Southwestern U.S.* a patch of thickly grown brush or dense shrubbery. [1925–30; < AmerSp, Sp: knoll, stack of sheaves]

mo•gul (mō′gəl), *n.* a bump or mound of hard snow on a ski slope. [1960–65; < dial. G; cf. Austrian dial. *Mugel* small hill] **—mo′guled,** *adj.*

Mo•gul (mō′gəl, -gul, mō gul′), *n.* **1.** any of the Mongol conquerors of India who established an empire that lasted from 1526 to 1857, but held only nominal power after 1803. Cf. **Great Mogul. 2.** any of their descendants. **3.** (*l.c.*) an important, powerful, or influential person: *a mogul of the movie industry.* **4.** a Mongol or Mongolian. **5.** *Railroads.* a steam locomotive having a two-wheeled front truck, six driving wheels, and no rear truck. See table under **Whyte classification. —*adj.* 6.** of or pertaining to the Moguls or their empire. Also **Moghul, Mughal** (for defs. 1, 2, 6). [1580–90; < Pers *mughul* MONGOL]

mo•hair (mō′hâr′), *n.* **1.** the coat or fleece of an Angora goat. **2.** a fabric made of yarn from this fleece, in a plain weave for draperies and in a pile weave for upholstery. **3.** a garment made of this fabric. [1560–70; var. (by folk etym.) of earlier *mocayare* < It *moccaiaro* < Ar *mukhayyar* lit., chosen, choice, ptp. of *khayyara* to choose]

Moham., Mohammedan.

Mo•ham•med (mo͝o ham′id, -hä′mid, mō-), *n.* Muhammad (def. 1).

Mohammed II, (*"the Conqueror"*) 1430–81, sultan of Turkey 1451–81: conqueror of Constantinople 1453.

Moham′med A•li′ (ä lē′, ä′lē), **1. Mau•la•na** (mô-lä′nə), 1878–1931, Indian journalist and political leader: advocate of Indian nationalization. **2.** See **Mehemet Ali.**

Mo•ham•med•an (mo͝o ham′i dn, mō-), *adj.* **1.** of or pertaining to Muhammad or Islam; Islamic; Muslim. **—*n.* 2.** an adherent of Islam; Muslim. [1675–85; MOHAMMED + -AN]

Mo•ham•med•an•ism (mo͝o ham′i dn iz′əm, mō-), *n.* Muhammadanism; Islam. [MOHAMMEDAN + -ISM]

Mo•ham•med•an•ize (mo͝o ham′i dn īz′, mō-), *v.t.,* **-ized, -iz•ing.** Islamize. Also, *esp. Brit.,* **Mo•ham′med•an•ise′.** [1820–30; MOHAMMEDAN + -IZE]

Moham′med ibn′-Ka′sim (mo͝o ham′id ib′ən kä′-sim, -hä′mid), fl. early 8th century A.D., Muslim conqueror of the Sind region in India. Also, **Moham′med ibn′-Qa′sim.**

Moham′med of Ghor′ (gôr, gōr), (*Mu'izz-ad-din*), died 1206, Muslim Sultan of Ghazni 1173–1206: established Muslim power in India. Also, **Muhammed Ghori.**

Moham′med Za•hir′ Shah′ (zä hēr′), born 1914, king of Afghanistan 1933–73.

Mo•har•ram (mo͝o har′əm, mō-), *n.* the first month of the Muslim calendar. Also, **Muharram.** Cf. **Muslim calendar.** [1605–15; < Ar *muḥarram* lit., forbidden]

Mo•ha•ve (mō hä′vē), *n., pl.* **-ves,** (*esp. collectively*) **-ve,** *adj.* **—*n.* 1.** a member of a North American Indian tribe belonging to the Yuman linguistic family, formerly located in the Colorado River valley of Arizona and California. **—*adj.* 2.** of or pertaining to the Mohave tribe. Also, **Mojave.**

Moha′ve Des′ert. See **Mojave Desert.**

Mo•hawk (mō′hôk), *n., pl.* **-hawks,** (*esp. collectively*) **-hawk. 1.** a member of a tribe of the most easterly of the Iroquois Five Nations, formerly resident along the Mohawk River, New York. **2.** the Iroquoian language of the Mohawk Indians. **3.** a river flowing E from central New York to the Hudson. 148 mi. (240 km) long. **4.** (*often l.c.*) Also called **Mo′hawk hair′cut.** a hairstyle in which the head is shaved bare except for a strip of hair, usually with blunt, brushlike ends, down the center of the scalp from the forehead to the nape of the neck. **5.** *Mil.* a twin turboprop, two-seat U.S. Army aircraft fitted with cameras, radar, and infrared sensors and designed to monitor enemy operations.

Mo•he•gan (mō hē′gən), *n., pl.* **-gans,** (*esp. collectively*) **-gan.** a member of a group of Pequot Indians that broke with the Pequot and then fought against them in the Pequot War.

mo•hel (*Seph.* mô hel′; *Ashk.* mō′hāl, mō′əl, moi′-; *Eng.* mō′hāl), *n., pl.* ***mo•hal•im*** (*Seph., Ashk.* mô′hä-lēm′), *Eng.* **mo•hels.** *Hebrew.* the person who performs the circumcision in the Jewish rite of circumcising a male child on the eighth day after his birth.

Mo•hen•jo-Da•ro (mō hen′jō där′ō), *n.* an archaeological site in Pakistan, near the Indus River: six successive ancient cities were built here.

Mo•hi•can (mō hē′kən), *n., pl.* **-cans,** (*esp. collectively*) **-can.** Mahican.

Moh•ism (mō′iz əm), *n.* the doctrine of Mo-Tze, stressing universal love, not limited by special affections or obligations, and opposition to Confucianism and traditionalism. [Mo(-TZE) + hiatus-filling *-h-* + -ISM] **—Moh′ist,** *n., adj.*

Mo•hock (mō′hok), *n.* one of a group of aristocratic ruffians who attacked people at night on the streets of London in the early part of the 18th century. [1705–15; var. of MOHAWK] **—Mo′hock•ism,** *n.*

Mo•hole (mō′hōl′), *n.* a hole bored through the earth's crust into the region below the Mohorovičić discontinuity, for geological research. [*Mo(horovičić)* (see MOHOROVIČIĆ DISCONTINUITY) + HOLE]

CONCISE PRONUNCIATION KEY: act, cāpe, dâre, pärt; set, ēqual; *if,* īce; ox, ōver, ôrder, oil, bo͝ok, bo͞ot, out; up, ûrge; child; sing; shoe; thin, *th*at; zh as in *treasure.* ə = *a* as in *alone, e* as in *system, i* as in *easily, o* as in *gallop, u* as in *circus;* ə as in *fire* (fīər), *hour* (ouər). l and n can serve as syllabic consonants, as in *cradle* (krād′l), and *button* (but′n). See the full key inside the front cover.

Mo·holy-Nagy (mə hō′lē noj′; *Hung.* mō′hoi nod′yᵊ), *n.* **Lász·ló** (las′lō; *Hung.* läs′lō) or **La·dis·laus** (lä′dis-lous′), 1895–1946, Hungarian painter, designer, and photographer, in the U.S. after 1936.

Mo·ho·ro′vi·čić discontinu′ity (mō′hô rō′və-chich, -hō-), *Geol.* the discontinuity between the crust and the mantle of the earth, occurring at depths that average about 22 mi. (35 km) beneath the continents and about 6 mi. (10 km) beneath the ocean floor. Also, **Mo′·ho.** [1935–40; named after Andrija *Mohorovičić* (1857–1936), Croatian geophysicist, who discovered it]

Mohs′ scale′ (mōz), a scale of hardness used in mineralogy. Its degrees, in increasing hardness, are: talc 1; gypsum 2; calcite 3; fluorite 4; apatite 5; feldspar 6; quartz 7; topaz 8; sapphire 9; diamond 10. *Abbr.:* MSH [1875–80; named after F. *Mohs* (1773–1839), German mineralogist]

mo·hur (mō′hər), *n.* any of various gold coins of India, introduced in the 16th century by various Mogul princes and later used by the British as the standard gold coin of India. [1690–1700; earlier *muhr* < Urdu < Pers: seal, gold coin; akin to Skt *mudrā*]

moh·wa (mō′wə), *n.* mahua.

M.O.I., *Brit.* **1.** Ministry of Information. **2.** Ministry of the Interior.

moi·dore (moi′dôr, -dōr), *n.* a former gold coin of Portugal and Brazil. [1695–1705; < Pg *moeda de ouro* coin of gold < L *monēta dē aurō.* See MONEY, DE, OR[3]]

moi·e·ty (moi′i tē), *n., pl.* **-ties. 1.** a half. **2.** an indefinite portion, part, or share. **3.** *Anthropol.* one of two units into which a tribe or community is divided on the basis of unilineal descent. [1400–50; late ME *moite* < MF < L *medietāt-* (s. of *medietās*) the middle, equiv. to *medi(us)* mid + *-etāt-*, var., after vowels, of *-itāt-* -ITY]

moil (moil), *v.i.* **1.** to work hard; drudge. **2.** to whirl or churn ceaselessly; twist; eddy. —*v.t.* **3.** *Archaic.* to wet or smear. —*n.* **4.** hard work or drudgery. **5.** confusion, turmoil, or trouble. **6.** *Glassmaking.* a superfluous piece of glass formed during blowing and removed in the finishing operation. **7.** *Mining.* a short hand tool with a polygonal point, used for breaking or prying out rock. [1350–1400; ME *moillen* to make or get wet and muddy < MF *moillier* < VL **molliāre*, deriv. of L *mollis* soft] —**moil′er,** *n.* —**moil′ing·ly,** *adv.*

Moi·ra (moi′rə), *n., pl.* **-rai** (-rī) for 1, 2. **1.** *Class. Myth.* **a.** the personification of fate. **b. Moirai,** the Fates. **2.** (*often l.c.*) (among ancient Greeks) a person's fate or destiny. **3.** a female given name.

moire (mwär, môr, mōr), *n.* any moiré fabric. [1650–60; < F < E MOHAIR]

moi·ré (mwä rā′, môr′ā, mōr′ā; *Fr.* MWA RĀ′), *adj.* **1.** (of silks and other fabrics) presenting a watery or wavelike appearance. —*n.* **2.** a design pressed on silk, rayon, etc., by engraved rollers. **3.** any silk, rayon, etc., fabric with a watery or wavelike appearance. **4.** *Print.* an interference pattern of dots appearing in the print of process color. [1810–20; < F; see MOIRE, -EE]

moiré′ effect′, *n. Optics.* the appearance, when two regularly spaced sets of lines are superimposed, of a new set of lines **(moiré′ pat′tern)** passing through the points where the original lines cross at small angles. [1950–55]

Moi·se·i·vich (moi sā′i vich), *n.* **Ben·no** (ben′ō), 1890–1963, English pianist, born in Russia. Also, **Moi·se′i·witsch.**

Moi·se·yev (moi sā′yev, -yəf; *Russ.* mĭ sye′yif), *n.* **I·gor A·le·xan·dro·vich** (ē′gər u lyi ksän′drə vyich), born 1906, Russian dancer and choreographer.

Mois·san (mwA sän′), *n.* **Hen·ri** (än rē′), 1852–1907, French chemist: Nobel prize 1906.

moist (moist), *adj.* **-er, -est. 1.** moderately or slightly wet; damp. **2.** (of the eyes) tearful. **3.** accompanied by or connected with liquid or moisture. **4.** (of the air) having high humidity. [1325–75; ME *moiste* < MF; connected with L *mūcidus* MUCID] —**moist′ful,** *adj.* —**moist′less,** *adj.* —**moist′ly,** *adv.* —**moist′ness,** *n.* —**Syn. 1.** dank. See **damp.** —**Ant. 1, 2.** dry.

mois·ten (moi′sən), *v.t., v.i.* to make or become moist. [1570–80; MOIST + -EN[1]] —**moist′en·er,** *n.* —**Syn.** dampen, wet, sponge, spray.

mois·ture (mois′chər), *n.* **1.** condensed or diffused liquid, esp. water: *moisture in the air.* **2.** a small quantity of liquid, esp. water; enough liquid to moisten. [1325–75; ME; see MOIST, -URE; cf. MF *moistour*] —**mois′ture·less,** *adj.*

mois·tur·ize (mois′chə rīz′), *v.,* **-ized, -iz·ing.** —*v.t.* **1.** to add or restore moisture to (something): *to moisturize one's skin with lotion; to moisturize air.* —*v.i.* **2.** to make something moist; counteract a dry condition with moisture: *a skin cream that moisturizes while you sleep.* Also, *esp. Brit.,* **mois′tur·ise′.** [1940–45; MOISTURE + -IZE]

mois·tur·iz·er (mois′chə rī′zər), *n.* a cosmetic preparation, as a cream or lotion, used to restore moisture to the skin, esp. of the face and neck. [1955–60; MOISTURIZE + -ER[1]]

moit (moit), *n.* **1.** a foreign particle found in wool, as a burr, twig, or seed. —*v.t.* **2.** to remove moits from (wool). Also, **mote.** [1860–65; orig. sp. var. (N England) of MOTE[1], with silent *-i-*, which served only to mark the *o* long; but by sp. pron. *-oi-* now has its usual value]

moit·y (moi′tē), *adj.,* **moit·i·er, moit·i·est.** full of moits. Also, **motey.** [1875–80; MOIT + -Y[1]]

mo·jar·ra (mō här′ə), *n.* any of several chiefly tropical, silvery fishes of the family Gerridae, having a protrusible mouth and grooves at the bases of the dorsal and anal fins into which the fins can be folded. [< Sp: lit., point of a lance < Ar *muḥarrab* pointed, sharp, ptp. of *ḥarrab* to sharpen]

Mo·ja·ve (mō hä′vē), *n., pl.* **-ves,** (*esp. collectively*) **-ve,** *adj.* Mohave.

Moja′ve Des′ert, a desert in S California: part of the Great Basin. ab. 15,000 sq. mi. (38,850 sq. km). Also, **Mohave Desert.**

Mo·ji (mô′jē), *n.* See under **Kitakyushu.**

mo·jo (mō′jō), *n., pl.* **-jos, -joes. 1.** the art or practice of casting magic spells; magic; voodoo. **2.** an object, as an amulet or charm, that is believed to carry a magic spell. [1925–30, *Amer.*; cf. Gullah *moco* witchcraft, magic, prob. akin to Fulani *moco'o* medicine man (c represents voiced palatal stop)]

Mo·ka·pu (mō kä′po͞o), *n.* a town on E Oahu, in central Hawaii. 11,615.

moke (mōk), *n.* **1.** *Older Slang* (*disparaging and offensive*). a black person. **2.** *Brit. Slang.* a donkey. **3.** *Australian Slang.* a poor-looking, inferior horse. [1840–50; orig. uncert.]

Mo·ki (mō′kē), *n., pl.* **-kis,** (*esp. collectively*) **-ki.** Hopi (def. 1). Also, **Moqui.**

Mok·po (môk′pō), *n.* a seaport in SW South Korea. 177,801.

mo·ksha (mōk′shə), *n. Buddhism, Hinduism, Jainism.* freedom from the differentiated, temporal, and mortal world of ordinary experience. Also, **mo′ksa.** Also called **mukti.** [1775–85; < Skt *mokṣa*]

mol (mōl), *n. Chem.* mole[4].

mol., **1.** molecular. **2.** molecule.

mo·la[1] (mō′lə), *n., pl.* (*esp. collectively*) **-la,** (*esp. referring to two or more kinds or species*) **-las.** any of several thin, silvery fishes of the family Molidae, of tropical and temperate seas. Cf. **ocean sunfish.** [1595–1605; < L: millstone; so called from its shape]

mo·la[2] (mō′lə; *Sp.* mô′lä), *n., pl.* **-las** (-ləz; *Sp.* -läs). a colorfully appliquéd piece of fabric handcrafted by the Cuna Indian women of the islands in the Gulf of San Blas and used for clothing, decoration, etc. [1940–45; < Cuna: clothing, blouse, mola]

mo·lal (mō′ləl), *adj. Chem.* noting or pertaining to a solution containing one mole of solute per kilogram of solvent. [1905–10; MOLE[4] + -AL[1]]

mo·lal·i·ty (mō lal′i tē), *n., pl.* **-ties.** *Chem.* the number of moles of solute per kilogram of solvent. [1920–25; MOLAL + -ITY]

mo·lar[1] (mō′lər), *n.* **1.** Also called **mo′lar tooth′.** a tooth having a broad biting surface adapted for grinding, being one of twelve in humans, with three on each side of the upper and lower jaws. See illus. under **tooth.** —*adj.* **2.** adapted for grinding, as teeth. **3.** pertaining to such teeth. [1535–45; < L *molāris* grinder, short for (*dēns*) *molāris* grinding (tooth), equiv. to *mol(a)* millstone + *-āris* -AR[1]]

mo·lar[2] (mō′lər), *adj. Physics.* pertaining to a body of matter as a whole, as contrasted with molecular and atomic. [1860–65; < L *mōl(ēs)* a mass + -AR[1]]

mo·lar[3] (mō′lər), *adj. Chem.* **1.** pertaining to a solution containing one mole of solute per liter of solution. **2.** noting or pertaining to gram-molecular weight. [1860–65; MOLE[4] + -AR[1]]

mo′lar heat′ capac′ity, *Thermodynam.* the heat capacity of one mole of a substance.

mo·lar·i·ty (mō lar′i tē), *n. Chem.* the number of moles of solute per liter of solution. [1930–35; MOLAR[3] + -ITY]

mo′lar vol′ume, *Chem.* the volume occupied by one mole of a gas, liquid, or solid. Also called **mo′lal vol′·ume, mole volume.** Cf. **Avogadro's law.** [1945–50]

mo·las·ses (mə las′iz), *n.* a thick syrup produced during the refining of sugar or from sorghum, varying from light to dark brown in color. [1575–85; earlier *molassos, molasso(e)s* < Pg *melaços,* pl. of *melaço* (< LL *mellāceum* half-boiled new wine, for **mellāceum,* neut. of **mellāceus* honeylike, equiv. to *mell-*, s. of *mel* honey + *-āceus* -ACEOUS)]

mold[1] (mōld), *n.* **1.** a hollow form or matrix for giving a particular shape to something in a molten or plastic state. **2.** the shape created or imparted to a thing by a mold. **3.** something formed in or on a mold: *a mold of jelly.* **4.** a frame on which something is formed or made. **5.** shape or form. **6.** a prototype, example, or precursor. **7.** a distinctive nature, character, or type: *a person of a simple mold.* **8.** *Shipbuilding.* **a.** a three-dimensional pattern used to shape a plate after it has been softened by heating. **b.** a template for a frame. **9.** *Archit.* **a.** a molding. **b.** a group of moldings. —*v.t.* **10.** to work into a required shape or form; shape. **11.** to shape or form in or on a mold. **12.** *Metall.* to form a mold of or from, in order to make a casting. **13.** to produce by or as if by shaping material; form. **14.** to have influence in determining or forming: *to mold the character of a child.* **15.** to ornament with moldings. Also, *esp. Brit.,* **mould.** [1175–1225; (n.) ME *molde* < OF *modle* < L *modulus* MODULE; (v.) ME, deriv. of the n.] —**mold′a·ble,** *adj.* —**mold′a·bil′i·ty,** *n.*

mold[2] (mōld), *n.* **1.** a growth of minute fungi forming on vegetable or animal matter, commonly as a downy or furry coating, and associated with decay or dampness. **2.** any of the fungi that produce such a growth. —*v.t., v.i.* **3.** to become or cause to become overgrown or covered with mold. Also, *esp. Brit.,* **mould.** [1150–1200; late ME *mowlde,* appar. n. use of var. of earlier *mowled,* ptp. of *moulen, mawlen* to grow moldy, c. dial. Dan *mugle*]

mold[3] (mōld), *n.* **1.** loose, friable earth, esp. when rich in organic matter and favorable to the growth of plants. **2.** *Brit. Dial.* ground; earth. Also, *esp. Brit.,* **mould.** [bef. 900; ME, OE *molde* earth, dust, ground; c. Goth *mulda* dust; akin to MEAL[2], MILL[1]]

Mol·dau (môl′dou, mōl′-), *n.* German name of the **Vltava.**

Mol·da·vi·a (mol dā′vē ə, -vyə), *n.* **1.** a region in NE Rumania: formerly a principality that united with Wallachia to form Rumania. *Cap.:* Jassy. **2.** Official name **Moldova.** Formerly, **Molda′vian So′viet So′cialist Repub′lic.** a republic in SE Europe: formed in 1940 from the former republic of Moldavia and the ceded Rumanian territory of Bessarabia. 4,341,000, 13,100 sq. mi. (33,929 sq. km). *Cap.:* Kishinev.

Mol·da·vi·an (mol dā′vē ən, -dāv′yən), *adj.* **1.** of or pertaining to Moldavia, its people, or their language. —*n.* **2.** a native or inhabitant of Moldavia. **3.** a dialect of Rumanian spoken in Moldavia (Moldova) and written in the Cyrillic alphabet. [MOLDAVI(A) + -AN]

mol·da·vite (môl′də vīt′, mōl-), *n. Mineral.* a green tektite found in Bohemia. [1895–1900; < G *Moldawit,* after the MOLDAU River; see -ITE[1]]

mold-blown (mōld′blōn′), *adj.* blown-molded.

mold·board (mōld′bôrd′, -bōrd′), *n.* **1.** the curved metal plate in a plow that turns over the earth from the furrow. **2.** a large blade mounted on the front of a bulldozer to push loose earth. **3.** a board forming one side or surface of a mold for concrete. [1300–50; r. earlier *moldbred,* ME *mold bred.* See MOLD[3] (defs. 1 and 2), MOLD[1] (def. 3), BOARD]

mold′ed breadth′, *Naval Archit.* the extreme breadth of the framing of a vessel, excluding the thickness of the plating or planking. [1790–1800]

mold′ed depth′, *Naval Archit.* the depth of a vessel at the broadest transverse section from the top of the keel to the upper side of the main deck beam at the side.

mold·er[1] (mōl′dər), *v.i.* **1.** to turn to dust by natural decay; crumble; disintegrate; waste away: *a house that had been left to molder.* —*v.t.* **2.** to cause to molder. [1525–35; obs. *mold* to crumble (v. use of MOLD[3]) + -ER[6]]

mold·er[2] (mōl′dər), *n.* **1.** a person or thing that molds. **2.** a person who makes molds. **3.** *Print.* one of a set of electrotyped plates used only for making duplicate electrotypes. [1400–50; late ME; see MOLD[1], -ER[1]]

mold·ing (mōl′ding), *n.* **1.** the act or process of molding. **2.** something molded. **3.** a strip of contoured wood or other material placed just below the juncture of a wall and a ceiling. **4.** *Archit., Furniture.* **a.** any of various long, narrow, ornamental surfaces that are either continuous or discontinuous, with uniform cross sections for the full length and a strikingly modeled profile that casts strong shadows: used on frames, tables, etc., and certain architectural members, as cornices, stringcourses, or bases. **b.** a strip of wood, stone, etc., having such a surface. [1300–50; ME; see MOLD[1], -ING[1]]

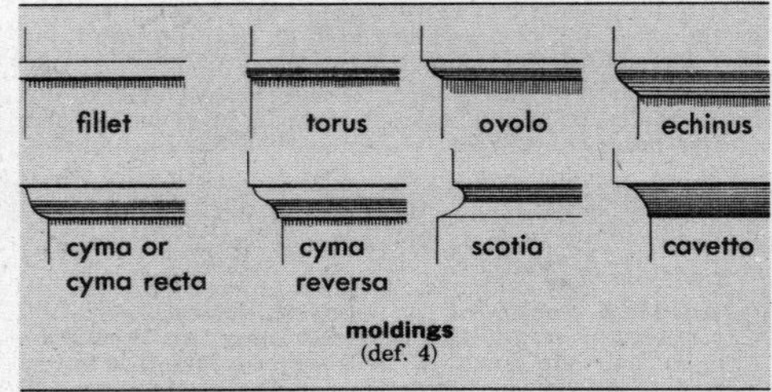

moldings
(def. 4)

mold′ing board′, a board upon which bread is kneaded, cookies prepared, etc. [1300–50; ME]

mold′ing plane′, *Carpentry.* a plane having a blade or a number of blades profiled to form moldings. [1670–80]

mold′ loft′, a broad, roofed area where molds and patterns are prepared for construction of a ship or airplane. [1705–15]

Mol·do·va (môl dō′və), *n.* official name of **Moldavia** (def. 2). —**Mol·do′van,** *adj., n.*

mold·warp (mōld′wôrp′), *n.* the common European mole, *Talpa europaea.* [1275–1325; ME *moldwerp* lit., earth-thrower (see MOLD[3], WARP); c. OS *moldwerp,* MHG *moltwerf*]

mold′ wash′, *Metall.* a coating applied in liquid form to walls of a mold cavity.

mold·y (mōl′dē), *adj.,* **mold·i·er, mold·i·est. 1.** overgrown or covered with mold. **2.** musty, as from decay or age. **3.** *Informal.* old-fashioned; outmoded: *moldy ideas about higher education.* [1350–1400; ME; see MOLD[2], -Y[1]] —**mold′i·ness,** *n.*

mold′y fig′, *Slang.* **1.** a musician or fan who likes traditional jazz or Dixieland rather than modern jazz. **2.** any person or thing that is old-fashioned or conservative. [1945–50, *Amer.*] —**mold′y-fig′,** *adj.*

mole[1] (mōl), *n.* **1.** any of various small insectivorous mammals, esp. of the family Talpidae, living chiefly underground, and having velvety fur, very small eyes, and strong forefeet. **2.** a spy who becomes part of and works from within the ranks of an enemy governmental staff or intelligence agency. Cf. **double agent. 3.** *Mach.* a large, powerful machine for boring through earth or rock, used in the construction of tunnels. [1350–1400; ME *molle;* akin to MD, MLG *mol*]

mole[1], *Scalopus aquaticus,* head and body 6½ in. (16 cm); tail to 1½ in. (3.8 cm)

mole[2] (mōl), *n.* a small, congenital spot or blemish on the human skin, usually of a dark color, slightly elevated, and sometimes hairy; nevus. [bef. 1000; ME; OE *māl;* c. OHG *meil* spot, Goth *mail* wrinkle]

mole[3] (mōl), *n.* **1.** a massive structure, esp. of stone, set up in the water, as for a breakwater or a pier. **2.** an anchorage or harbor protected by such a structure. [1540–50; < L *mōlēs* mass, dam, mole]

mole[4] (mōl), *n. Chem.* the molecular weight of a substance expressed in grams; gram molecule. Also, **mol.** [1900–05; < G *Mol,* short for *Molekül* MOLECULE]

mole[5] (mōl), *n. Pathol.* a fleshy mass in the uterus formed by a hemorrhagic dead ovum. [1605–15; < NL *mola,* special use of *mola* millstone]

mo•le[6] (mō′lā; *Sp.* mô′le), *n. Mexican Cookery.* a spicy sauce flavored with chocolate, usually served with turkey or chicken. [1925–30; < MexSp < Nahuatl *mōlli* sauce; cf. GUACAMOLE]

Mo•lech (mō′lek), *n.* Moloch (defs. 1, 2).

mole′ crab′, a burrowing crustacean of the genus *Emerita,* found on sandy ocean beaches of North America, having a distinctly curved carapace. Also called **sandbug.**

mole′ crick′et, any of several burrowing crickets of the family Gryllotalpidae that have fossorial forelegs and that feed on the roots of plants. [1705–15]

mo•lec•u•lar (mə lek′yə lər), *adj.* of or pertaining to or caused by molecules: *molecular structure.* [1815–25; MOLECULE + -AR[1]] **—mo•lec′u•lar•ly,** *adv.*

molec′ular astron′omy, the branch of astronomy dealing with the study of molecules in space. [1965–70]

molec′ular beam′, *Physics.* a stream of molecules freed from a substance, usually a salt, by evaporation and then passed through a narrow slit for focusing, for investigating the properties of nuclei, atoms, and molecules. Also called **molec′ular ray′.**

molec′ular biol′ogy, the branch of biology that deals with the nature of biological phenomena at the molecular level through the study of DNA and RNA, proteins, and other macromolecules involved in genetic information and cell function, characteristically making use of advanced tools and techniques of separation, manipulation, imaging, and analysis. Also called **new biology.** [1935–40]

molec′ular clock′, the changes in the amino acid sequences of proteins that take place during evolution and speciation, and from which the dates of branchings of taxonomic groups can be deduced.

molec′ular distilla′tion, *Chem.* a vacuum distillation in which the molecules of the distillate reach the condenser before colliding with one another.

molec′ular film′, *Physical Chem.* a film or layer one molecule thick. Also called **monolayer.**

molec′ular for′mula, *Chem.* a chemical formula that indicates the kinds of atoms and the number of each kind in a molecule of a compound. Cf. **empirical formula, structural formula.** [1900–05]

molec′ular genet′ics, a subdivision of genetics concerned with the structure and function of genes at the molecular level. [1965–70]

mo•lec•u•lar•i•ty (mə lek′yə lar′i tē), *n. Chem.* the number of molecules or atoms that participate in an elementary process. [1835–45; MOLECULAR + -ITY]

molec′ular or′bital, *Physics, Chem.* See under **orbital** (def. 2a). [1930–35]

molec′ular sieve′, *Chem.* a compound with molecule-size pores, as some sodium aluminum silicates, that chemically locks molecules in them: used in purification and separation processes. [1925–30]

molec′ular spec′trum, *Spectroscopy.* the spectrum of light emitted or absorbed by a species of molecule.

molec′ular weight′, *Chem.* the average weight of a molecule of an element or compound measured in units once based on the weight of one hydrogen atom taken as the standard or on 1/16 the weight of an oxygen atom, but after 1961 based on 1/12 the weight of the carbon-12 atom; the sum of the atomic weights of all the atoms in a molecule. *Abbr.:* mol. wt. Also called **formula weight.** [1875–80]

mol•e•cule (mol′ə kyōōl′), *n.* **1.** *Chem., Physics.* the smallest physical unit of an element or compound, consisting of one or more like atoms in an element and two or more different atoms in a compound. **2.** *Chem.* a quantity of a substance, the weight of which, measured in any chosen unit, is numerically equal to the molecular weight; gram molecule. **3.** any very small particle. [1785–95; earlier *molecula* < NL, equiv. to L *mōlē(s)* mass + *-cula* -CULE[1]]

mole′ frac′tion, *Chem.* the ratio of the number of moles of a given component of a mixture to the total number of moles of all the components. [1920–25]

mole•hill (mōl′hil′), *n.* **1.** a small mound or ridge of earth raised up by a mole or moles burrowing under the ground. **2. make a mountain out of a molehill,** to exaggerate a minor difficulty. [1400–50; late ME; see MOLE[1], HILL]

mole′ plow′, a plow typically having a pointed shoe at the end of a vertical support, for cutting a hollow drainage channel below the surface. [1790–1800]

mole rat (mōl′rat′), *n.* **1.** any of several eastern European burrowing rodents, esp. those of the genus *Spalax,* having no tail, short limbs, and small eyes with permanently closed lids. **2.** bandicoot (def. 2). Also, **mole′-rat′, mole′rat′.** [1775–85]

mole′ sal′amander, ambystomid.

mole•skin (mōl′skin′), *n.* **1.** the soft, deep-gray, fragile fur of the mole. **2.** a strong and heavy napped, twilled cotton fabric used for sportswear and work clothing. **3. moleskins,** a garment, esp. trousers, of this fabric. **4.** a soft, usually adhesive-backed fabric applied to the feet or other areas of the body to prevent irritation or abrasion. [1660–70; MOLE[1] + SKIN]

mo•lest (mə lest′), *v.t.* **1.** to bother, interfere with, or annoy. **2.** to make indecent sexual advances to. [1325–75; ME *molesten* < L *molestāre* to irk, deriv. of *molestus* irksome; cf. *mōlēs* mass, burden, trouble] **—mo•les•ta•tion** (mō′le stā′shən, mol′e-), *n.* **—mo•lest′er,** *n.* **—mo•lest′ful,** *adj.*
—Syn. 1. harass, harry, trouble, plague, hector, torment. See **attack.**

mol•et (mol′it), *n.* mullet[2].

mole′ vol′ume, *Chem.* See **molar volume.**

Mo•lière (mōl yâr′; *Fr.* mô lyer′), *n.* (*Jean Baptiste Poquelin*) 1622–73, French actor and playwright.

mol•i•la•li•a (mol′ə lā′lē ə, -lāl′yə), *n.* mogilalia.

Mo•li•na (mō lē′nə, mə-; *Sp.* mô lē′nä), *n.* **1. Lu•is** (lōō ēs′), 1535–1600, Spanish Jesuit theologian. **2. Tirso de.** See **Tirso de Molina.**

mo•line (mō′lin, mō lin′), *adj. Heraldry.* (of a cross) having arms of equal length, split and curved back at the ends, used esp. as the cadency mark of an eighth son: *a cross moline.* See illus. under **cross.** [1555–65; < AF **moliné,* equiv. to *molin* MILL[1] + *-é* < L *-ātus* -ATE[1]]

Mo•line (mō lēn′), *n.* a city in NW Illinois, on the Mississippi. 45,709.

Mo•li•nism (mō′lə niz′əm, mol′ə-), *n.* the theological doctrine, formulated by Luis Molina, that the consent of the human will is necessary for divine grace to be effective. [1660–70; MOLIN(A) + -ISM] **—Mo′li•nist,** *n.*

Mo•li•nos (mə lē′nōs; *Sp.* mô lē′nôs), *n.* **Mi•guel de** (mē gel′ de), c1640–c95, Spanish priest and mystic: chief exponent of quietism.

Mo•li•o•nes (mə lī′ə nēz′), *n. Class. Myth.* Cteatus and Eurytus, the twin sons of Molione, sometimes said to have been joined at the waist. They were fathered by Poseidon and reared by Actor.

moll (mol), *n. Slang.* **1.** See **gun moll. 2.** *Archaic.* a prostitute. [special use of MOLL]

moll (môl), *adj. German.* (in music) written in a minor key; minor.

Moll (mol), *n.* a female given name.

mol•lah (mol′ə), *n.* mullah.

Mol•len•do (mô yen′dô), *n.* a seaport in S Peru. 15,000.

mol•les•cent (mə les′ənt), *adj.* softening or tending to soften. [1815–25; < L *mollescent-* (s. of *mollēscēns*) (prp. of *mollēscere* to soften), equiv. to *moll(is)* soft + *-ēscent-* -ESCENT] **—mol•les′cence,** *n.*

Mol•let (mō lā′; *Fr.* mô le′), *n.* **Guy** (gī; *Fr.* gē), 1905–75, French political leader.

Moll′ Flan′ders, (*The Fortunes and Misfortunes of the Famous Moll Flanders*) a novel (1722) by Daniel Defoe.

Mol•lie (mol′ē), *n.* a female given name, form of **Mary** or **Milicent.**

Mol′lier di′agram (môl′yā), *Thermodynam.* a graph showing the enthalpy of a substance as a function of its entropy when some physical property of the substance, as temperature or pressure, is kept at a specified constant value. [named after Richard *Mollier* (d. 1935), German engineer]

mol•li•fy (mol′ə fī′), *v.t.,* **-fied, -fy•ing. 1.** to soften in feeling or temper, as a person; pacify; appease. **2.** to mitigate or reduce; soften: *to mollify one's demands.* [1350–1400; ME < MF *mollifier* < LL *mollificāre,* equiv. to L *molli(s)* soft + *-ficāre* -FY] **—mol′li•fi•ca′tion,** *n.* **—mol′li•fi′er,** *n.* **—mol′li•fy′ing•ly,** *adv.* **—mol′li•fi′•a•ble,** *adj.*

mol•li•sol (mol′ə sôl′, -sol′), *n.* a productive agricultural soil common to the world's grasslands, characterized by a dark surface layer rich in organic matter. Cf. **brown soils.** [1970–75; < L *molli(s)* soft + -SOL]

Mol•lus•ca (mə lus′kə), *n.* the phylum comprising the mollusks. [1790–1800; < NL, neut. pl. of L *molluscus* soft; akin to *mollis* soft]

mol•lus•coid (mə lus′koid), *adj.* belonging or pertaining to the phylum Molluscoidea, in certain classifications comprising the bryozoans and brachiopods. [1850–55; < NL *Molluscoidea.* See MOLLUSCA, -OID]

mol•lus•cum (mə lus′kəm), *n., pl.* **-ca** (-kə). *Pathol.* any of various skin conditions characterized by soft, rounded tumors. [1805–15; < NL, L: fungus, n. use of neut. of *molluscus* soft; akin to *mollis* soft] **—mol•lus′•cous,** *adj.*

mol•lusk (mol′əsk), *n.* any invertebrate of the phylum Mollusca, typically having a calcareous shell of one, two, or more pieces that wholly or partly enclose the soft, unsegmented body, including the chitons, snails, bivalves, squids, and octopuses. Also, **mol′lusc.** [1775–85; < F *mollusque* < NL *Mollusca;* see MOLLUSCA] **—mol•lus•kan, mol•lus•can** (mə lus′kən), *adj., n.* **—mol′lusk•like′,** *adj.*

Moll′wei•de projec′tion (môl′vī də). See **homolographic projection.** [1935–40; named after K. B. *Mollweide* (1774–1825), German astronomer and mathematician]

mol•ly (mol′ē), *n., pl.* **-lies.** any of certain livebearing freshwater fishes of the genus *Mollienisia,* popular in home aquariums. [shortened from NL *Mollienisia,* irreg. named after Count F.N. *Mollien* (1758–1850); see -IA]

Mol•ly (mol′ē), *pl.* **-lies.** *Trademark.* a brand of expansion bolt having a split, sleevelike sheath threaded at one end so that when inserted snugly into masonry the turning of the bolt draws the ends of the sheath together, thus spreading the sides.

Mol•ly (mol′ē), *n.* a female given name, form of **Mary** or **Milicent.**

mol•ly•cod•dle (mol′ē kod′l), *n., v.,* **-dled, -dling.** **—n. 1.** a man or boy who is used to being coddled; a milksop. **—*v.t.* 2.** to coddle; pamper. [1825–35; MOLLY + CODDLE] **—mol′ly•cod′dler,** *n.*
—Syn. 2. spoil, indulge, cosset.

Mol′ly Ma•guire′ (mə gwīər′), **1.** *Irish Hist.* a member of a secret terrorist society organized in Ireland in 1843 to prevent evictions by the government: so called because the members disguised themselves as women. **2.** *U.S. Hist.* a member of a former secret association, organized about 1865, that terrorized the mine operators' agents in an effort to get relief from oppressive conditions in the anthracite coal-mining regions of Pennsylvania: ceased to function about 1877. [1865–70, *Amer.*]

mol•ly•mawk (mol′ē môk′), *n.* any of various oceanic birds, as the fulmar or albatross. Also, **mallemuck, mol•ly•moke** (mol′ē mōk′). [1685–95; < D *mallemok,* equiv. to *malle,* var. of *mal* foolish + *mok* < Norw *mak* MEW[2]]

Mol′ly Mil′ler, a blenny, *Scartella cristata,* of Atlantic seas. [orig. uncert.]

Mol•nár (mōl′när; *Hung.* môl′när), *n.* **Fe•renc** (fe′rents), 1878–1952, Hungarian playwright, novelist, and short-story writer.

Mol•ni•ya (mōl′nē ə; *Russ.* môl′nyi yə), *n.* one of a series of Soviet communications satellites. [< Russ *Mól-niya* lit., lightning]

Mo•loch (mō′lok, mol′ək), *n.* **1.** a deity whose worship was marked by the propitiatory sacrifice of children by their own parents. II Kings 23:10; Jer. 32:35. **2.** anything conceived of as requiring appalling sacrifice: *the Moloch of war.* **3.** (*l.c.*) a spiny agamid lizard, *Moloch horridus,* of Australian deserts, that resembles the horned lizard. Also, **Molech** (for defs. 1, 2). [< LL (Vulgate) *Moloch* < Gk (Septuagint) *Móloch* < Heb *Mōlekh,* var. of *melekh* king]

Mo•lo•ka•i (mō′lə kī′, -kä′ē, mol′ə-), *n.* an island in central Hawaii: leper colony. 5261; 259 sq. mi. (670 sq. km).

Mol•o•kan (mol′ə kän′), *n.* a member of an ascetic religious sect, founded in Russia in the 18th century by former Doukhobors, opposing sacraments and ritual and stressing the authority of the Bible. [< Russ *molokán* (now usually *molokánin,* pl. *-áne*), equiv. to *molok(ó)* MILK + *-an* n. suffix; orig. so named because they ate dairy products on fast days, contrary to Orthodox observance]

Mo•lo•po (mə lō′pō), *n.* a river in S Africa, flowing SW along the S Botswana-N South Africa border to the Orange River. ab. 600 mi. (965 km) long.

Mo•lo•tov (mol′ə tôf′, -tof′, mō′lə-, mô′-; *Russ.* mô′lə təf), *n.* **1. Vya•che•slav Mi•khai•lo•vich** (vē ä′chə släf mi kī′lə vich; *Russ.* vyi chyi släf′ myi khī′lə-vyich), (*Vyacheslav Mikhailovich Skryabin*), 1890–1986, Russian statesman: commissar of foreign affairs 1939–49, 1953–56. **2.** former name of **Perm.**

Mo′lotov cock′tail, a crude incendiary grenade consisting of a bottle filled with a flammable liquid and a wick that is ignited before throwing: used originally for setting fire to enemy tanks during the Spanish Civil War. [1935–40; named after V. M. MOLOTOV]

Mo•lo•tovsk (mô′lə təfsk), *n.* former name of **Severodvinsk.**

molt (mōlt), *v.i.* **1.** (of birds, insects, reptiles, etc.) to cast or shed the feathers, skin, or the like, that will be replaced by a new growth. **—*v.t.* 2.** to cast or shed (feathers, skin, etc.) in the process of renewal. **—*n.* 3.** an act, process, or an instance of molting. **4.** something that is dropped in molting. Also, *esp. Brit.,* **moult.** [1300–50; earlier *mout* (with intrusive *-l-;* cf. FAULT, ASSAULT), ME *mouten,* OE *-mūtian* to change (in *bimūtian* to exchange for) < L *mūtāre* to change; see MUTATE] **—molt′er,** *n.*

mol•ten (mōl′tn), *v.* **1.** a pp. of **melt.** **—*adj.* 2.** liquefied by heat; in a state of fusion; melted: *molten lead.* **3.** produced by melting and casting: *a molten image.* [1250–1300; ME; old ptp. of MELT[1]] **—mol′ten•ly,** *adv.*

Molt•ke (môlt′kə), *n.* **1. Hel•muth Karl** (hel′mōōt kärl), 1800–91, Prussian field marshal: chief of staff 1858–88. **2.** his nephew, **Helmuth Jo•han•nes** (yō hä′nəs), **Count von,** 1848–1916, German general: chief of staff 1906–14.

mol•to (mōl′tō; *It.* môl′tô), *adv. Music.* very: *molto adagio; molto allegro.* [1795–1805; < It < L *multum,* adv. use of acc. sing. neut. of *multus* much]

Mo•luc•cas (mə luk′əz), *n.* (*used with a plural v.*) a group of islands in Indonesia, between Sulawesi (Celebes) and New Guinea. 995,000; ab. 30,000 sq. mi. (78,000 sq. km). Also called **Moluc′ca Is′lands, Spice Islands.** **—Mo•luc′can,** *adj., n.*

mol•vi (mōl′vē), *n.* maulvi.

CONCISE PRONUNCIATION KEY: act, cāpe, dâre, pärt; set, ēqual; if, īce; ox, ōver, ôrder, oil, bŏŏk, bōōt, out; up, ûrge; child; sing; shoe; thin, *th*at; zh as in *treasure.* ə = *a* as in *alone, e* as in *system, i* as in *easily, o* as in *gallop, u* as in *circus;* ə as in *fire* (fīər), *hour* (ouər). l and n can serve as syllabic consonants, as in *cradle* (krād′l), and *button* (but′n). See the full key inside the front cover.

mol. wt., molecular weight.

mo·ly[1] (mō′lē), *n., pl.* **-lies.** *Class. Myth.* an herb given to Odysseus by Hermes to counteract the spells of Circe. [< L *mōly* < Gk *mōly*]

mol·y[2] (mol′ē), *n. Informal.* molybdenum. [by shortening]

mo·lyb·date (mə lib′dāt), *n. Chem.* a salt of any molybdic acid. [1785–95; MOLYBD(IC) + -ATE[2]]

molyb′date or′ange, *Chem.* a pigment consisting of a solid solution of sulfate, molybdate, and chromate compounds of lead. Also called **molyb′date chrome′ or′ange, molyb′denum or′ange.** [1940–45]

mo·lyb·de·nite (mə lib′də nīt′), *n.* a soft, graphitelike mineral, molybdenum sulfide, MoS_2, occurring in foliated masses or scales: the principal ore of molybdenum. [1790–1800; obs. *molybden(a)* MOLYBDENUM + -ITE[1]]

mo·lyb·de·no·sis (mə lib′də nō′sis), *n. Vet. Pathol.* a disease of ruminants, esp. cattle, caused by dietary intake of excessive molybdenum with resultant copper deficiency, characterized by persistent diarrhea and, esp. around the eyes, a fading of coat pigment. [MOLYBDEN(UM) + -OSIS]

mo·lyb·de·nous (mə lib′də nəs), *adj. Chem.* containing bivalent molybdenum. [MOLYBDEN(UM) + -OUS]

mo·lyb·de·num (mə lib′də nəm), *n. Chem.* a silver-white metallic element, used as an alloy with iron in making hard, high-speed cutting tools. *Symbol:* Mo; *at. wt.:* 95.94; *at. no.:* 42; *sp. gr.:* 10.2. [1810–20; < NL, alter. of earlier *molybdēna* < L *molybdaena* < Gk *molýbdaina* galena, equiv. to *mólybd(os)* lead + *-aina* suffix of appurtenance]

molyb′denum disul′fide, *Chem.* a black crystalline powder, MoS_2, insoluble in water, used as a lubricant and as a hydrogenation catalyst. Also called **molyb′denum sul′fide.** [1930–35]

molyb′denum triox′ide, *Chem.* a white, crystalline, sparingly water-soluble powder, MoO_3, used chiefly in the manufacture of molybdenum compounds. Also called **molyb′dic anhy′dride, molyb′dic ox′ide.**

mo·lyb·dic (mə lib′dik), *adj. Chem.* of or containing molybdenum, esp. in the trivalent or hexavalent states, as molybdic acid, H_2MoO_4. [1790–1800; MOLYBD(ENUM) + -IC]

mo·lyb·dous (mə lib′dəs), *adj. Chem.* of or containing molybdenum, esp. in its lower valences. [1790–1800; MOLYBD(ENUM) + -OUS]

mom (mom), *n. Informal.* mother. [short for MOMMA]

m.o.m., middle of month.

mom-and-pop (mom′ən pop′), *adj., n., pl.* **-pops.** **—***adj.* **1.** of or pertaining to a small retail business, usually owned and operated by members of a family: *a mom-and-pop grocery.* **2.** of or indicating something, as an enterprise, investment, or project, that is independent, small in scope, and modestly financed. **—***n.* **3.** a small-scale, owner-operated business. [1950–55, *Amer.*]

Mom·ba·sa (mom bä′sä, -bas′ə), *n.* **1.** an island in S Kenya. **2.** a seaport on this island. 320,000.

mome (mōm), *n. Archaic.* a fool; blockhead. [1545–55; orig. uncert.]

mo·ment (mō′mənt), *n.* **1.** an indefinitely short period of time; instant: *I'll be with you in a moment.* **2.** the present time or any other particular time (usually prec. by *the*): *He is busy at the moment.* **3.** a definite period or stage, as in a course of events; juncture: *at this moment in history.* **4.** importance or consequence: *a decision of great moment.* **5.** a particular time or period of success, excellence, fame, etc.: *His big moment came in the final game.* **6.** *Statistics.* the mean or expected value of the product formed by multiplying together a set of one or more variates or variables each to a specified power. **7.** *Philos.* **a.** an aspect of a thing. **b.** *Obs.* an essential or constituent factor. **8.** *Mech.* **a.** a tendency to produce motion, esp. about an axis. **b.** the product of a physical quantity and its directed distance from an axis: *moment of area; moment of mass.* [1300–50; ME < L *mōmentum* motion, cause of motion, hence, influence, importance, essential factor, moment of time, equiv. to *mō-* (var. s. of *movēre* to MOVE) + *-mentum* -MENT]
—Syn. 1. second, jiffy, trice, flash, twinkling. See **minute**[1]. **4.** significance, weight, gravity. See **importance.**

mo·men·tar·i·ly (mō′mən târ′ə lē, mō′mən ter′-), *adv.* **1.** for a moment; briefly: *to pause momentarily.* **2.** at any moment; imminently: *expected to occur momentarily.* **3.** instantly. [1645–55; MOMENTARY + -LY]

mo·men·tar·y (mō′mən ter′ē), *adj.* **1.** lasting but a moment; very brief; fleeting: *a momentary glimpse.* **2.** that might occur at any moment; ever impending: *to live in fear of momentary annihilation.* **3.** effective or recurring at every moment; constant. [1425–75; late ME *momentare* < L *mōmentārius.* See MOMENT, -ARY] **—mo′men·tar′i·ness,** *n.*

mo·ment·ly (mō′mənt lē), *adv.* **1.** with every moment; from moment to moment. **2.** for a moment; momentarily. **3.** at any moment; momentarily. [1670–80; MOMENT + -LY]

mo·men·to (mə men′tō, mō-), *n., pl.* **-tos, -toes.** memento.
—Usage. See **memento.**

mo′ment of iner′tia, *Physics.* the sum of the products of the mass and the square of the perpendicular distance to the axis of rotation of each particle in a body rotating about an axis. [1820–30]

mo′ment of momen′tum, *Physics.* See **angular momentum.**

mo′ment of sail′, *Naval Archit.* the product of a given area of sail, taken as the maximum safe area, and the vertical distance from the center of effort and the center of lateral resistance.

mo′ment of truth′, **1.** the moment in a bullfight at which the matador is about to make the kill. **2.** the moment at which one's character, courage, skill, etc., is put to an extreme test; critical moment. [1930–35]

mo·men·tous (mō men′təs), *adj.* of great or far-reaching importance or consequence: *a momentous day.* [1645–55; MOMENT + -OUS] **—mo·men′tous·ly,** *adv.* **—mo·men′tous·ness,** *n.*
—Syn. vital, critical, crucial, serious. See **heavy.**

mo·men·tum (mō men′təm), *n., pl.* **-ta** (-tə), **-tums.** **1.** force or speed of movement; impetus, as of a physical object or course of events: *The car gained momentum going downhill. Her career lost momentum after two unsuccessful films.* **2.** *Mech.* a quantity expressing the motion of a body or system, equal to the product of the mass of a body and its velocity, and for a system equal to the vector sum of the products of mass and velocity of each particle in the system. **3.** *Philos.* moment (def. 7). [1690–1700; < L *mōmentum;* see MOMENT]

mom·ism (mom′iz əm), *n.* (*sometimes cap.*) excessive adulation of the mother and undue dependence on maternal care or protection, resulting in absence or loss of maturity and independence. [MOM + -ISM; coined by U.S. author Philip Wylie (1902–71) in *A Generation of Vipers* (1942)]

mom·ma (mom′ə), *n.* mama.

mom·me (mom′ē), *n., pl.* **mom·me.** a Japanese unit of weight equal to 3.75 grams. [< Japn, equiv. to *mon* letter (< MChin, equiv. to Chin *wén*) + *-me(y)* eye]

Momm·sen (mom′sən; *Ger.* môm′zən), *n.* **The·o·dor** (tā′ô dōʀ′), 1817–1903, German classical historian: Nobel prize for literature 1902.

mom·my (mom′ē), *n., pl.* **-mies.** *Informal.* mother[1] (defs. 1, 2, 4). Also, **mom′mie.** [1900–05, *Amer.*; MOMM(A) + -Y[2]. Cf. MAMMY, MUMMY[2]]

mom′my track′, a path of career advancement for women who are willing to forgo promotions, raises, etc., so as to spend more time with their children. [1989]

Mo·mo·ya·ma (mô′mô yä′mä), *n.* See **Azuchi-Momoyama.**

Mom·pós (môm pôs′), *n.* a city in NW Colombia, on the Magdalena. 43,415.

mom·ser (mom′zər), *n.* mamzer. Also, **mom′zer.**

Mo·mus (mō′məs), *n., pl.* **-mus·es, -mi** (-mī) for 2. **1.** Also, **Mo·mos** (mō′mos). *Class. Myth.* the god of ridicule. **2.** (*sometimes l.c.*) a faultfinder; a carping critic. [< L *Mōmus* < Gk *Mômos,* special use of *mômos* blame]

mon (mon), *n. Scot. and North Eng.* man.

Mon (mōn), *n.* an Austroasiatic language used chiefly in Burma in the vicinity of Moulmein.

mon-, var. of **mono-** before a vowel: *monacid.*

Mon., **1.** Monday. **2.** Monsignor.

mon., **1.** monastery. **2.** monetary.

Mo·na (mō′nə), *n.* a female given name.

Mon·a·can (mon′ə kən, mə nä′kən), *n.* **1.** a native or inhabitant of Monaco. **—***adj.* **2.** of or pertaining to Monaco. Also, **Monegasque.** [MONAC(O) + -AN]

mon·ac·e·tin (mon as′i tin), *n.* acetin. [1855–60; MON- + ACETIN]

mon·a·chal (mon′ə kəl), *adj.* of or pertaining to monks or their life; monastic. [1580–90; < LL *monachālis,* equiv. to LL *monach(us)* MONK + *-ālis* -AL[1]]

mon·a·chism (mon′ə kiz′əm), *n.* monasticism. [1570–80; < LL *monach(us)* MONK + -ISM] **—mon′a·chist,** *adj.*

mon·ac·id (mon as′id), *adj., n. Chem.* monoacid. **—mon′a·cid′ic,** *adj.*

mo·na·cil·lo (mon′ə sē′ō; *Sp.* mô′nä sē′yô), *n., pl.* **-cil·los** (-sē′ōz; *Sp.* -sē′yôs). a low shrub, *Malvaviscus arboreus,* of tropical America, having scarlet flowers and berrylike fruit that is sticky when young. [< AmerSp, Sp: lit., altar-boy, earlier *monazillo, monaziello* < VL **monachellus,* equiv. to LL *monach(us)* MONK + *-ellus* dim. suffix; see -ELLE]

Mon·a·co (mon′ə kō′, mə nä′kō; *Fr.* mô nA kō′; *It.* mô′nä kô′), *n.* **1.** a principality on the Mediterranean coast, bordering SE France. 25,000; ½ sq. mi. (1.3 sq. km). **2.** the capital of this principality. 1685.

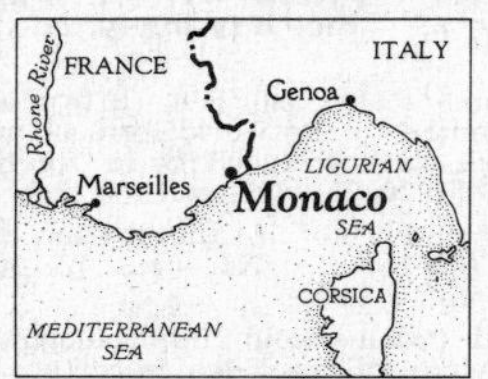

mon·ad (mon′ad, mō′nad), *n.* **1.** *Biol.* **a.** any simple, single-celled organism. **b.** any of various small, flagellate, colorless ameboids with one to three flagella, esp. of the genus *Monas.* **2.** *Chem.* an element, atom, or group having a valence of one. Cf. **dyad** (def. 3), **triad** (def. 2a). **3.** *Philos.* **a.** (in the metaphysics of Leibniz) an unextended, indivisible, and indestructible entity that is the basic or ultimate constituent of the universe and a microcosm of it. **b.** (in the philosophy of Giordano Bruno) a basic and irreducible metaphysical unit that is spatially and psychically individuated. **c.** any basic metaphysical entity, esp. having an autonomous life. **4.** a single unit or entity. [1605–15; < LL *monad-* (s. of *monas*) < Gk (s. of *monás*): unity. See MON-, -AD[1]] **—mo·nad·ic** (mə nad′ik), **mo·nad′i·cal, mo·nad′al,** *adj.* **—mo·nad′i·cal·ly,** *adv.*

mon·a·del·phous (mon′ə del′fəs), *adj. Bot.* **1.** (of stamens) united into one bundle or set by their filaments. **2.** (of a plant or flower) having the stamens so united. [1800–10; MON- + -ADELPHOUS]

monadelphous flower of hollyhock, *Alcea rosea*

mon·a·des (mon′ə dēz′), *n.* pl. of **monas.**

mon·ad·ism (mon′ə diz′əm, mō′nad iz′əm), *n. Philos.* **1.** the doctrine of monads as ultimate units of being. **2.** (*sometimes cap.*) the philosophy of Leibniz. Also, **mon·ad·ol·o·gy** (mon′ə dol′ə jē, mō′na-). [1870–75; MONAD + -ISM] **—mon′ad·is′tic,** *adj.*

mo·nad·nock (mə nad′nok), *n.* **1.** *Physical Geog.* a residual hill or mountain standing well above the surface of a surrounding peneplain. **2.** (*cap.*) **Mount,** a mountain peak in SW New Hampshire. 3186 ft. (971 m). [1735–45, *Amer.*; after (*Grand*) *Monadnock* (earlier name of Mount Monadnock) < a S New England Algonquian name, lit., isolated mountain]

Mon·a·ghan (mon′ə gən, -han′), *n.* a county in the NE Republic of Ireland. 51,174; 498 sq. mi. (1290 sq. km). *Co. seat:* Monaghan.

Mo′na Li′sa (mō′nə lē′sə, lē′zə), (Italian, *La Gioconda*), a portrait (1503?–05?) by Leonardo da Vinci.

mo·nan·drous (mə nan′drəs), *adj.* **1.** of, pertaining to, or characterized by monandry. **2.** *Bot.* **a.** (of a flower) having only one stamen. **b.** (of a plant) having such flowers. [1800–10; < Gk *mónandros.* See MON-, -ANDROUS]

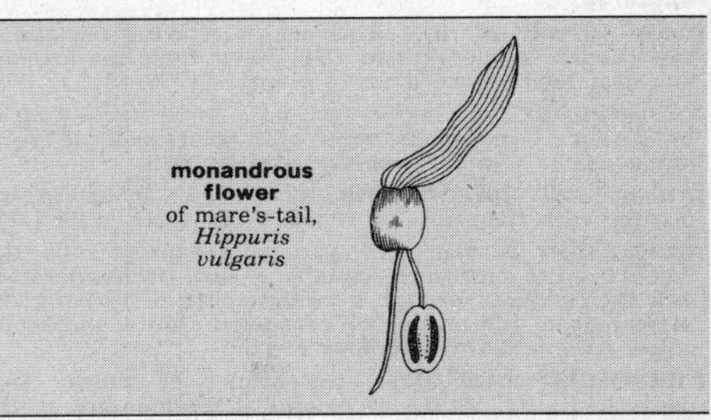
monandrous flower of mare's-tail, *Hippuris vulgaris*

mo·nan·dry (mə nan′drē), *n.* **1.** the practice or condition of having one husband at a time. **2.** (of a female animal) the condition of having one mate at a time. [1850–55; MONANDR(OUS) + -Y[3]]

Mo′na Pas′sage (mō′nə; *Sp.* mô′nä), a strait between Hispaniola and Puerto Rico. 80 mi. (129 km) wide.

mon·arch (mon′ərk, -ärk), *n.* **1.** a hereditary sovereign, as a king, queen, or emperor. **2.** a sole and absolute ruler of a state or nation. **3.** a person or thing that holds a dominant position: *a monarch of international shipping.* **4.** See **monarch butterfly.** [1400–50; late ME < LL *monarcha* < Gk *monárchēs* sole ruler; see MON-, -ARCH]

mo·nar·chal (mə när′kəl), *adj.* **1.** pertaining to, characteristic of, or befitting a monarch: *monarchal pomp.* **2.** having the status of a monarch. Also, **mo·nar·chi·al** (mə när′kē əl). [1580–90; MONARCH + -AL[1]] **—mo·nar′chal·ly,** *adv.*

mon′arch but′terfly, a large, deep-orange butterfly, *Danaus plexippus,* having black and white markings, the larvae of which feed on the leaves of milkweed. Also called **monarch.** [1885–90]

Mo·nar·chi·an·ism (mə när′kē ə niz′əm), *n. Theol.* any of several doctrines of the Christian church in the 2nd and 3rd centuries A.D., emphasizing the unity of God by maintaining that the Father, the Son, and the Holy Ghost are three manifestations or aspects of God. [1835–45; *Monarchian* (< LL *monarchiānus;* see MONARCHY, -AN) + -ISM] **—Mo·nar′chi·an,** *adj., n.* **—Mo·nar′chi·an·ist,** *n.*

mo·nar·chi·cal (mə när′ki kəl), *adj.* **1.** of, like, or pertaining to a monarch or monarchy. **2.** characterized by or favoring monarchy. Also, **mo·nar′chic.** [1570–80; < Gk *monarchik(ós)* (see MONARCH, -IC) + -AL[1]] **—mo·nar′chi·cal·ly,** *adv.*

mon·ar·chism (mon′ər kiz′əm), *n.* **1.** the principles of monarchy. **2.** advocacy of monarchical rule. [1830–40; MONARCH(Y) + -ISM; cf. F *monarchisme,* G *Monarchismus*] **—mon′ar·chist,** *n., adj.* **—mon′ar·chis′tic,** *adj.*

mon·ar·chy (mon′ər kē), *n., pl.* **-chies.** **1.** a state or nation in which the supreme power is actually or nominally lodged in a monarch. Cf. **absolute monarchy, limited monarchy.** **2.** supreme power or sovereignty held by a single person. [1300–50; ME *monarchie* < LL *monarchia* < Gk *monarchía.* See MONARCH, -Y[3]]
—Syn. 1. See **kingdom.**

mo·nar·da (mə när′də), *n.* any aromatic, erect plant belonging to the genus *Monarda,* of the mint family, native to North America, including horsemint and Oswego tea. [1705–15; < NL, named after N. *Monardés* (1493–1588), Spanish botanist; see -A[2]]

mon·as (mon′as, mō′nas), *n., pl.* **mon·a·des** (mon′ə dēz′). monad. [< LL < Gk *monás;* cf. MONAD]

CONCISE ETYMOLOGY KEY: <, descended or borrowed from; >, whence; b., blend of, blended; c., cognate with; cf., compare; deriv., derivative; equiv., equivalent; imit., imitative; obl., oblique; r., replacing; s., stem; sp., spelling, spelled; resp., respelling, respelled; trans., translation; ?, origin unknown; *, unattested; ‡, probably earlier than. See the full key inside the front cover.

mon·as·ter·y (mon′ə ster′ē), *n., pl.* **-ter·ies.** **1.** a house or place of residence occupied by a community of persons, esp. monks, living in seclusion under religious vows. **2.** the community of persons living in such a place. [1350–1400; ME < LL *monastērium* < LGk *monastḗrion* monk house, orig. hermit's cell, equiv. to *monas-*, var. s. of *monázein* to be alone (see MON-) + *-tērion* neut. adj. suffix denoting place] —**mon·as·te·ri·al** (mon′ə stēr′ē əl), *adj.*
—**Syn. 1.** cloister; abbey, priory, friary, lamasery.

mo·nas·tic (mə nas′tik), *adj.* Also, **mo·nas′ti·cal. 1.** of or pertaining to monasteries: *a monastic library.* **2.** of, pertaining to, or characteristic of monks or nuns, their manner of life, or their religious obligations: *monastic vows.* **3.** of, pertaining to, or characteristic of a secluded, dedicated, or austere manner of living. —*n.* **4.** a member of a monastic community or order, esp. a monk. [1400–50; late ME *monastik* < LL *monasticus* < LGk *monastikós*, equiv. to *monas-* (verbid s. of *monázein* to be alone; see MON-) + *-ikos* -IC, with *-t-* by analogy with derivatives of agent nouns in *-tēs* (cf. ATHLETE, ATHLETIC)] —**mo·nas′ti·cal·ly,** *adv.*

mo·nas·ti·cism (mə nas′tə siz′əm), *n.* the monastic system, condition, or mode of life. [1785–95; MONASTIC + -ISM]

Mo·na·stir (mô′nä stēr′), *n.* Turkish name of **Bitolj.**

mon·a·tom·ic (mon′ə tom′ik), *adj. Chem.* **1.** having one atom in the molecule. **2.** containing one replaceable atom or group. **3.** having a valence of one. Also, **monoatomic.** [1840–50; MON- + ATOMIC] —**mon′a·tom′i·cal·ly,** *adv.*

mon·au·ral (mon ôr′əl), *adj.* **1.** monophonic (def. 2). **2.** of, pertaining to, or affecting one ear. [1885–90; MON- + AURAL[2]] —**mon·au′ral·ly,** *adv.*

mon·ax·i·al (mon ak′sē əl), *adj. Bot.* **1.** uniaxial. **2.** having flowers that grow on the primary axis. [1875–80; MON- + AXIAL]

mon·a·zite (mon′ə zīt′), *n.* a reddish- or yellowish-brown mineral, a phosphate of cerium and lanthanum, (Ce,La)PO_4: the principal ore of thorium. [1830–40; < G *Monazit*, equiv. to *monaz-* (< Gk *monázein* to be alone; see MON-) + *-it* -ITE[1]]

Mön·chen·glad·bach (mœn′khən glät′bäkh), *n.* a city in W North Rhine-Westphalia, in W Germany. 249,600. Formerly, **München-Gladbach.**

mon cher (môn sher′), *French.* (referring to men) my dear. Cf. ***ma chère.***

Monck (mungk), *n.* **1. Sir Charles Stanley,** (*4th Viscount Monck, 1st Baron Monck*), 1819–94, British colonial administrator, born in Ireland: governor general of Canada 1861–68. **2.** Also, **Monk. George,** (*1st Duke of Albermarle and Earl of Torrington*), 1608–70, English general.

Mon·clo·va (môNG klô′vä), *n.* a city in NE Mexico. 80,252.

Monc·ton (mungk′tən), *n.* a city in SE New Brunswick, in E Canada. 55,934.

Mon·dale (mon′dāl′), *n.* **Walter Frederick** (*"Fritz"*), born 1928, U.S. politician: senator 1965–77; vice president 1977–81.

Mon·day (mun′dā, -dē), *n.* the second day of the week, following Sunday. [bef. 1000; ME *Mone(n)day*, OE *mōn(an)dæg*, trans. of LL *lūnae diēs* moon's day]

Mon′day morn′ing disease′, *Vet. Pathol.* azoturia (def. 2).

Mon′day morn′ing quar′terback, *Informal.* a person who criticizes the actions or decisions of others after the fact, using hindsight to assess situations and specify alternative solutions. [1940–45] —**Mon′day morn′ing quar′terbacking.**

Mon·days (mun′dāz, -dēz), *adv.* on Mondays.

monde (mônd), *n. French.* the world; people; society.

mon·do (mon dō′), *n., pl.* **-dos.** *Zen.* a question to a student for which an immediate answer is demanded, the spontaneity of which is often illuminating. Cf. **koan.** [1925–30; < Japn *mondō*, earlier *mondau* < MChin, equiv. to Chin *wèn* inquire + *dá* reply]

mon′do grass′ (mon′dō), any of several plants belonging to the genus *Ophiopogon*, of the lily family, native to western Asia, esp. *O. japonicus*, having grasslike leaves and lavender or white flowers. Also called **lilyturf.** [< NL (1763), an earlier genus name, of unexplained orig.]

Mon·dri·an (môn′drē än′, mon′-; *Du.* mon′drē än′), *n.* **Piet** (pēt), (*Pieter Cornelis Mondriaan*) 1872–1944, Dutch painter.

mo·ne·cious (mə nē′shəs, mō-), *adj.* monoecious.

Mon·e·gasque (mon′i gask′), *n., adj.* Monacan. [1880–85; < F *monégasque* < Pr *mounegasc*, deriv. of *Mounegue* Monaco]

Mo·nel′ met′al (mō nel′), *Trademark.* a brand of alloy consisting mainly of nickel and copper.

mo·nen·sin (mō nen′sin), *n. Biochem.* a complex derivative of butyric acid, $C_{36}H_{62}O_{11}$, produced by the bacterium *Streptomyces cinnamonensis* and used as an antibiotic in animals. [1967; < NL (*cinna*)*monens*(*is*) specific epithet of the bacterium (see CINNAMON, -ENSIS; so called from the color of the aerial mycelium) + -IN[2]]

Mo·ne·ra (mə nēr′ə), *n.* (*used with a plural v.*) *Biol.* a taxonomic kingdom of prokaryotic organisms that typically reproduce by asexual budding or fission and have a nutritional mode of absorption, photosynthesis, or chemosynthesis, comprising the bacteria, blue-green algae, and various primitive pathogens. [< NL (1869), pl. of *monēron*, coinage based on Gk *monḗrēs* solitary, single, deriv. of *mónos* alone, only]

mo·ne·ran (mə nēr′ən), *Biol.* —*n.* **1.** any organism of the kingdom Monera. —*adj.* **2.** of or pertaining to the kingdom Monera. [1875–80; MONER(A) + -AN]

mon·er·gism (mon′ər jiz′əm), *n. Theol.* the doctrine that the Holy Ghost acts independently of the human will in the work of regeneration. Cf. **synergism** (def. 3). [1865–70; MON- + Gk *érg*(*on*) work, deed + -ISM] —**mon′er·gist,** *n.* —**mon′er·gis′tic,** *adj.*

mo·ne·sia (mə nē′zhə), *n. Pharm.* a preparation extracted from the bark of a South American tree, *Pradosia lactescens*, and used chiefly as an astringent and as an expectorant. [1835–45; orig. obscure]

Mo·nes·sen (mə nes′ən, mō-), *n.* a city in SW Pennsylvania, on the Monongahela River. 11,928.

mon·es·trous (mon es′trəs), *adj.* of or pertaining to a mammal that has one estrus period per breeding season, as the dog. Also, **monoestrous.** [1895–1900; MON- + ESTROUS]

Mo·net (mō nā′; *Fr.* mô ne′), *n.* **Claude** (klōd; *Fr.* klōd), 1840–1926, French painter.

Mo·ne·ta (mō nā′tə; *It.* mô ne′tä), *n.* **1. Er·ne·sto Te·o·do·ro** (er ne′stô te′ô dô′rô), 1833–1918, Italian journalist: Nobel peace prize 1907. **2.** (in Roman religion) an epithet of Juno.

mon·e·ta·rism (mon′i tə riz′əm, mun′-), *n. Econ.* a doctrine holding that changes in the money supply determine the direction of a nation's economy. [1965–70, *Amer.*; MONETAR(Y) + -ISM] —**mon′e·ta·rist,** *n., adj.*

mon·e·tar·y (mon′i ter′ē, mun′-), *adj.* **1.** of or pertaining to the coinage or currency of a country. **2.** of or pertaining to money; pecuniary: *The necklace has sentimental as opposed to monetary value.* [1795–1805; < LL *monētārius.* See MONEY, -ARY] —**mon·e·tar·i·ly** (mon′i târ′ə lē, mun′-, mon′i ter′ə lē, mun′-), *adv.*
—**Syn. 1.** See **financial.**

mon′etary ag′gregate, a measure of the money in circulation.

mon′etary u′nit, the standard unit of value of the currency of a country, as the dollar in the U.S. and the franc in France. [‡1860–65]

mon·e·tize (mon′i tīz′, mun′-), *v.t.,* **-tized, -tiz·ing. 1.** to legalize as money. **2.** to coin into money: *to monetize gold.* **3.** to give the character of money to. **4.** *Econ.* to convert (a debt, esp. the national debt) into currency, esp. by issuing government securities or notes. Also, *esp. Brit.,* **mon′e·tise′.** [1875–80; < L *monēt*(*a*) MONEY + -IZE] —**mon′e·ti·za′tion,** *n.*

mon·ey (mun′ē), *n., pl.* **mon·eys, mon·ies,** *adj.* —*n.* **1.** any circulating medium of exchange, including coins, paper money, and demand deposits. **2.** See **paper money. 3.** gold, silver, or other metal in pieces of convenient form stamped by public authority and issued as a medium of exchange and measure of value. **4.** any article or substance used as a medium of exchange, measure of wealth, or means of payment, as checks on demand deposit or cowrie. **5.** a particular form or denomination of currency. See table under **currency. 6.** See **money of account. 7.** capital to be borrowed, loaned, or invested: *mortgage money.* **8.** an amount or sum of money: *Did you bring some money?* **9.** wealth considered in terms of money: *She was brought up with money.* **10. moneys** or **monies,** *Chiefly Law.* pecuniary sums. **11.** property considered with reference to its pecuniary value. **12.** pecuniary profit: *not for love or money.* **13. for one's money,** *Informal.* with respect to one's opinion, choice, or wish: *For my money, there's nothing to be gained by waiting.* **14. in the money,** *Informal.* **a.** having a great deal of money; affluent: *You can see he's in the money by all those clothes he buys.* **b.** first, second, or third place in a contest, esp. a horse or dog race. **15. make money,** to make a profit or become rich: *You'll never make money as a poet.* **16. on the money,** *Informal.* **a.** at just the exact spot or time; on target: *The space shuttle landed on the money at 9:55* A.M. **b.** exhibiting or done with great accuracy or expertise: *His weather forecasts are always on the money.* Also, **right on the money. 17. put one's money where one's mouth is,** *Informal.* to prove the truth of one's words by actions or other evidence; demonstrate one's sincerity or integrity: *Instead of bragging about your beautiful house, put your money where your mouth is and invite us over to see it.* —*adj.* **18.** of or pertaining to money. **19.** used for carrying, keeping, or handling money: *Have you seen my little money purse?* **20.** of or pertaining to capital or finance: *the money business.* [1250–1300; ME *moneie* < MF < L *monēta* MINT[2], money] —**mon′ey·less,** *adj.*
—**Syn. 3.** coin, cash, currency, specie, change. **11.** funds, capital, assets, wealth, riches.

mon·ey·bag (mun′ē bag′), *n.* **1.** a bag for money. **2. moneybags,** (*used with a singular v.*) a very wealthy or extravagant person. [1555–65; 1940–45 for def. 2; MONEY + BAG]

mon′ey belt′, a belt with a concealed section for holding money. [1840–50, *Amer.*]

mon′ey box′, 1. a cashbox. **2.** *Chiefly Brit.* a small, lidded receptacle for keeping, collecting, or saving coins, usually with a slot for their insertion. [1575–85]

mon·ey·chang·er (mun′ē chān′jər), *n.* **1.** a person whose business is the exchange of currency, usually of different countries, at a fixed or official rate. **2.** a portable device consisting of conjoined vertical tubes for holding coins of different sizes and a mechanism for dispensing change, usually having a clip for attachment to a belt. Also, **mon′ey chang′er, mon′ey-chang′er.** [1350–1400; ME; see MONEY, CHANGER]

mon′ey chang′ing, the business of exchanging one currency for another, with the deduction of a commission for the service.

mon′ey cow′rie. See under **cowrie.** [1830–40]

mon·eyed (mun′ēd), *adj.* **1.** having much money; wealthy. **2.** of or pertaining to the wealthy: *moneyed interests.* [1425–75; late ME; see MONEY, -ED[3]]
—**Syn. 1.** rich, affluent, prosperous.

mon·ey·er (mun′ē ər), *n.* **1.** *Archaic.* a person employed in the authorized coining of money. **2.** *Obs.* a moneylender or banker. [1250–1300; ME < OF *monier* < LL *monētārius* coiner, minter (n. use of adj.: of money); see MONETARY]

mon′ey fund′, a money-market fund.

mon·ey·grub·ber (mun′ē grub′ər), *n. Informal.* a person who is aggressively engaged in or preoccupied with making or saving money. [1830–40; MONEY + GRUBBER] —**mon′ey·grub′bing,** *adj., n.*

mon·ey·lend·er (mun′ē len′dər), *n.* a person or organization whose business it is to lend money at interest. [1775–85; MONEY + LENDER]

mon′ey machine′. See **automated-teller machine.**

mon·ey·mak·er (mun′ē mā′kər), *n.* **1.** a person engaged in or successful at acquiring much money. **2.** something that produces or yields much pecuniary profit. [1250–1300; ME; see MONEY, MAKER]

mon·ey·mak·ing (mun′ē mā′king), *adj.* **1.** profitable: *a moneymaking scheme.* **2.** capable of making or promising to make money: *the moneymaking part of the deal.* —*n.* **3.** the making of money. [1730–40; MONEY + MAKING]

mon·ey·man (mun′ē man′), *n., pl.* **-men. 1.** an investor; angel; backer. **2.** a person responsible for managing money or financial arrangements of a business, institution, etc. [1565–75; MONEY + MAN[1]]

mon′ey mar′ket, the short-term trade in money, as in the sale and purchase of bonds and certificates. [1925–30]

mon′ey-mar·ket certif′icate (mun′ē mär′kit), **1.** a certificate of deposit held for a specified term earning a fixed interest rate keyed to the interest rate of U.S. Treasury bills. **2.** any type of savings certificate whose interest rate is based on current money-market interest rates.

mon′ey-market fund′, a mutual fund that invests in the money market. [1980–85]

mon′ey of account′, a monetary denomination used in reckoning, esp. one not issued as a coin, as the U.S. mill. [1685–95]

mon′ey of neces′sity, temporary coinage, as siege pieces, issued in areas where regular coinage is unavailable: sometimes of unusual materials, as leather or wood.

mon′ey or′der, an order for the payment of money, as one issued by one bank or post office and payable at another. [1795–1805]

mon′ey play′er, *Slang.* **1.** a person who performs best under pressure, esp. in a competitive situation. **2.** a person skilled in gambling when the stakes are high. [1930–35]

mon′ey shell′. See **butter clam.**

mon′ey supply′, *Econ.* the sum of demand or checking-account deposits and currency in circulation. [1875–80]

mon′ey tree′, 1. a fanciful tree that when shaken sheds coins or paper money. **2.** *Informal.* a good source of money, funds, or revenues; gold mine.

mon·ey·wort (mun′ē wûrt′, -wôrt′), *n.* a creeping plant, *Lysimachia nummularia*, of the primrose family, having roundish leaves and solitary yellow flowers. Also called **creeping Charlie, creeping Jennie, creeping Jenny.** [1570–80; MONEY + WORT[2]]

mong (mung, mong), *n. Australian.* mongrel, esp. a mongrel dog. [shortened form]

Monge (mônzh), *n.* **Gas·pard** (gas par′), **Comte de Pé·luse** (pā lyz′), 1746–1818, French mathematician.

mon·ger (mung′gər, mong′-), *n.* **1.** a person who is involved with something in a petty or contemptible way (usually used in combination): *a gossipmonger.* **2.** *Chiefly Brit.* a dealer in or trader of a commodity (usually used in combination): *fishmonger.* —*v.t.* **3.** to sell; hawk. [bef. 1000; ME (n.); OE *mangere*, equiv. to *mang(ian)* to trade, act as a monger (<< L *mangō* salesman) + *-ere* -ER[1]; c. ON, OHG *mangari*] —**mon′ger·ing,** *n., adj.*

mon·go[1] (mong′gō), *n., pl.* **-gos.** mungo. Also, **mon′·goe.**

mon·go[2] (mong′gō), *n., pl.* **-go, -gos.** an aluminum coin and monetary unit of the Mongolian People's Republic, the 100th part of a tugrik. [< Mod. Mongolian *möngö* lit., silver, money]

Mon·go (mong′gō), *n.* **1.** a member of any of various agricultural peoples of central Zaire. **2.** the Bantu language of the Mongo peoples.

Mon·gol (mong′gəl, -gōl, mon′-), *n.* **1.** a member of a pastoral people now living chiefly in Mongolia. **2.** a person having Mongoloid characteristics. **3.** any Mongolian language. **4.** (*often l.c.*) *Pathol.* (no longer in technical use) a person affected with Down syndrome; Mongoloid. —*adj.* **5.** Mongolian.

Mon′gol Em′pire, an empire founded in the 12th century by Genghis Khan, which reached its greatest territorial extent in the 13th century, encompassing the larger part of Asia and extending westward to the Dnieper River in eastern Europe.

CONCISE PRONUNCIATION KEY: act, cāpe, dâre, pärt; set, ēqual; *if*, īce; ox, ōver, ôrder, oil, bŏŏk, bōōt, out; up, ûrge; child; sing; shoe; thin, *th*at; zh as in *treasure*. ə = *a* as in *alone*, *e* as in *system*, *i* as in *easily*, *o* as in *gallop*, *u* as in *circus*; ′ as in *fire* (fī′r), *hour* (ou′r). l and n can serve as syllabic consonants, as in *cradle* (krād′l), and *button* (but′n). See the full key inside the front cover.

Mon·go·li·a (mong gō′lē ə, mon-), *n.* **1.** a region in Asia including Inner Mongolia of China and the Mongolian People's Republic. **2.** Also, **Nei Monggol.** See **Inner Mongolia. 3. Outer,** former name of **Mongolian People's Republic.**

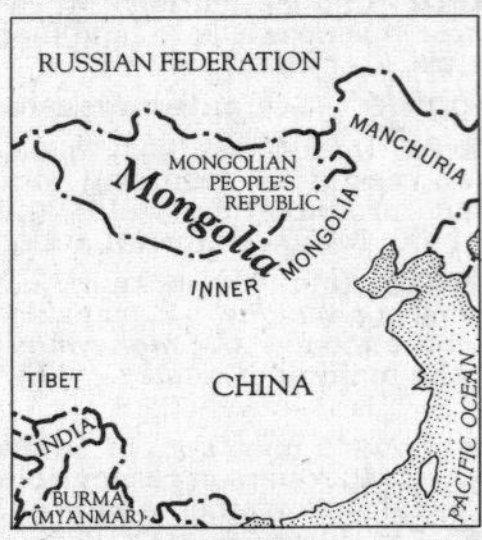

Mon·go·li·an (mong gō′lē ən, mon-), *adj.* **1.** pertaining to Mongolia. **2.** of or pertaining to the Mongol people of inner Asia. **3.** *Anthropol.* Mongoloid. **4.** of or pertaining to Mongolian, a branch of the Altaic languages. —*n.* **5.** a native or inhabitant of the Mongolian People's Republic. **6.** a native or inhabitant of Inner Mongolia. **7.** Also, **Mongolic.** a group of languages including Buriat and Khalkha and constituting a branch of Altaic. **8.** any of the languages of this branch, esp. Khalkha. **9.** a member of the Mongoloid peoples of Asia. [1730–40; MONGOLI(A) + -AN]

Mongo′lian fold′, epicanthus. [1910–15]

Mongo′lian hot′ pot′, *Chinese Cookery.* a stewlike dish of sliced meat, seafood, and vegetables cooked together in hot broth, often in a clay pot, and seasoned with a hot sauce. [1965–70]

Mongo′lian id′iocy, (*often l.c.*) *Pathol.* (no longer in technical use) Down syndrome. [1890–95] —**Mongo′lian id′iot.**

Mongo′lian Peo′ple's Repub′lic, a republic in E central Asia, in N Mongolia. 1,380,000; ab. 600,000 sq. mi. (1,500,000 sq. km). *Cap.:* Ulan Bator. Formerly, **Outer Mongolia.** Also called **Mongolia.**

Mon·gol·ic (mong gol′ik, mon-), *adj.* **1.** Mongolian (def. 4). **2.** Mongoloid (def. 2). —*n.* **3.** Mongolian (def. 7). [1825–35; MONGOL + -IC]

mon·gol·ism (mong′gə liz′əm, mon′-), *n.* (*sometimes cap.*) *Pathol.* (no longer in technical use) Down syndrome. [1895–1900; MONGOL + -ISM]

Mon·gol·oid (mong′gə loid′, mon′-), *adj.* **1.** resembling the Mongols. **2.** *Anthropol.* of, pertaining to, or characteristic of one of the traditional racial divisions of humankind, marked by yellowish complexion, prominent cheekbones, epicanthic folds about the eyes, and straight black hair, and including the Mongols, Manchus, Chinese, Koreans, Japanese, Annamese, Siamese, Burmese, Tibetans, and, to some extent, the Eskimos and the American Indians: no longer in technical use. **3.** (*often l.c.*) *Pathol.* (no longer in technical use) of, affected with, or characteristic of Down syndrome. —*n.* **4.** *Anthropol.* a member of the peoples traditionally classified as the Mongoloid race: no longer in technical use. **5.** (*usually l.c.*) *Pathol.* (no longer in technical use) a person affected with Down syndrome. [1865–70; MONGOL + -OID]

mon·goose (mong′go͞os′, mon′-), *n., pl.* **-goos·es. 1.** a slender, ferretlike carnivore, *Herpestes edwardsi,* of India, that feeds on rodents, birds, and eggs, noted esp. for its ability to kill cobras and other venomous snakes. **2.** any of several other animals of this genus or related genera. [1690–1700; < Marathi *mangūs,* var. of *muṅgūs*]

mongoose, *Herpestes edwardsi,* head and body 1½ ft. (0.5 m); tail 14 in (36 cm)

mon·grel (mung′grəl, mong′-), *n.* **1.** a dog of mixed or indeterminate breed. **2.** any animal or plant resulting from the crossing of different breeds or varieties. **3.** any cross between different things, esp. if inharmonious or indiscriminate. —*adj.* **4.** of mixed breed, nature, or origin; of or like a mongrel. [1425–75; late ME (once): heraldic term for a type of dog; equiv. to *mong(e)* mixture (OE *gemang;* cf. MINGLE) + -REL] —**mon′grel·ism, mon′grel·ness,** *n.* —**mon′grel·ly,** *adv.*
—**Syn. 1.** mutt. **2.** cross, half-breed. See **hybrid.**
—**Ant. 2.** thoroughbred, purebred.

mon·grel·ize (mung′grə līz′, mong′-), *v.t.,* **-ized, -iz·ing. 1.** to subject (a breed, group, etc.) to crossbreeding, esp. with one considered inferior. **2.** to mix the kinds, classes, types, characters, or sources of origin of (people, animals, or things). **3.** to make debased or impure: *The French they speak is mongrelized.* Also, *esp. Brit.,* **mon′grel·ise′.** [1620–30; MONGREL + -IZE] —**mon′grel·i·za′tion,** *n.* —**mon′grel·iz′er,** *n.*

mongst (mungst), *prep.* amongst. Also, **'mongst.** [aph. var. of AMONGST]

Mon·gu (mong go͞o′), *n.* a city in and headquarters of Western Province, W Zambia. 4049.

mo·ni·al (mō′nē əl), *n. Archaic.* a mullion. [1300–50; earlier *muniall,* ME *moniel* < MF *moinel* < ?]

mon·ic (mon′ik), *adj. Math.* (of a polynomial) having the coefficient of the term of highest degree equal to 1. [1935–40; MON- + -IC]

Mon·i·ca (mon′i kə), *n.* a female given name.

mon·ied (mun′ēd), *adj.* moneyed.

mon·ies (mun′ēz), *n.* a pl. of **money.**

mon·i·ker (mon′i kər), *n. Slang.* a person's name, esp. a nickname or alias. Also, **mon′ick·er.** [1850–55; prob. < Shelta *mŭnnik* name (alleged to be a permutation and extension of Ir *ainm* NAME); final *-er* may represent -ER[1] or, as a sp. of *ə,* simply release of the *k*]

mo·nil·i·a (mə nil′ē ə), *n.* a fungus of the genus *Monilia,* of the class Fungi Imperfecti, having spherical or oval conidia in branched chains. [1745–55; < NL, deriv. of L *monīle* necklace; see -IA]

mo·nil·i·al (mə nil′ē əl), *adj.* pertaining to or caused by a fungus of the genus *Monilia.* [1945–50; MONILI(A) + -AL[1]]

mon·i·li·a·sis (mon′ə lī′ə sis, mō′nə-), *n. Pathol.* (formerly) candidiasis. [1915–20; MONIL(IA) + -IASIS; a fungus of this genus was orig. thought to have been the causative agent of the disease]

mo·nil·i·form (mō nil′ə fôrm′), *adj.* **1.** *Bot., Zool.* consisting of or characterized by a series of beadlike swellings alternating with contractions, as certain roots or stems. **2.** resembling a string of beads in shape. [1795–1805; < L *monīli-* (s. of *monīle* necklace) + -FORM] —**mo·nil′i·form′ly,** *adv.*

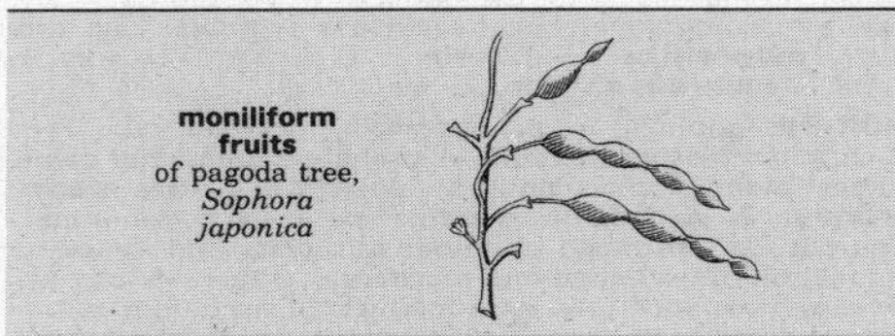
moniliform fruits of pagoda tree, *Sophora japonica*

mon·ish (mon′ish), *v.t. Archaic.* to admonish. [1250–1300; ME *monisshen,* prob. aph. var. of *amonisshen* to ADMONISH]

mon·ism (mon′iz əm, mō′niz əm), *n.* **1.** *Philos.* **a.** (in metaphysics) any of various theories holding that there is only one basic substance or principle as the ground of reality, or that reality consists of a single element. Cf. **dualism** (def. 2), **pluralism** (def. 1a). **b.** (in epistemology) a theory that the object and datum of cognition are identical. Cf. **pluralism** (def. 1b). **2.** the reduction of all processes, structures, concepts, etc., to a single governing principle; the theoretical explanation of everything in terms of one principle. **3.** the conception that there is one causal factor in history; the notion of a single element as primary determinant of behavior, social action, or institutional relations. [1860–65; < G *Monismus.* See MON-, -ISM] —**mon′ist,** *n.* —**mo·nis·tic** (mə nis′tik, mō-), **mo·nis′ti·cal,** *adj.* —**mo·nis′ti·cal·ly,** *adv.*

mo·ni·tion (mə nish′ən, mō-), *n.* **1.** *Literary.* admonition or warning. **2.** an official or legal notice. **3.** *Law.* a court order to a person, esp. one requiring an appearance and answer. Cf. **subpoena. 4.** a formal notice from a bishop requiring the amendment of an ecclesiastical offense. [1350–1400; ME *monicio(u)n* < L *monitiōn-* (s. of *monitiō*) warning, equiv. to *monit(us)* (ptp. of *monēre* to advise, warn) + *-iōn-* -ION]

mon·i·tor (mon′i tər) *n.* **1.** a student appointed to assist in the conduct of a class or school, as to help take attendance or keep order. **2.** a person appointed to supervise students, applicants, etc., taking an examination, chiefly to prevent cheating; proctor. **3.** a person who admonishes, esp. with reference to conduct. **4.** something that serves to remind or give warning. **5.** a device or arrangement for observing, detecting, or recording the operation of a machine or system, esp. an automatic control system. **6.** an instrument for detecting dangerous gases, radiation, etc. **7.** *Radio and Television.* **a.** a receiving apparatus used in a control room, esp. to provide a steady check of the quality of an audio or video transmission. **b.** a similar apparatus placed in various parts of a studio so that an audience can watch a recorded portion of a show, the performer can see the various segments of a program, etc. **c.** any such receiving apparatus used in a closed-circuit system, as in an operating room. **8.** *Computers.* **a.** a component, as a CRT, with a screen for viewing data at a computer terminal. **b.** a control program. Cf. **operating system. c.** a group of systems used to measure the performance of a computer system. **9.** *Naut.* **a.** a former U.S. steam-propelled, armored warship of very low freeboard, having one or more turrets and used for coastal defense. **b.** (*cap., italics*) the first of such warships, used against the Confederate ironclad warship *Merrimac* at Hampton Roads, Va., in 1862. **10.** a raised construction straddling the ridge of a roof and having windows or louvers for lighting or ventilating a building, as a factory or warehouse. **11.** an articulated mounting for a nozzle, usually mechanically operated, which permits a stream of water to be played in any desired direction, as in firefighting or hydraulic mining. **12.** Also called **giant.** (in hydraulic mining) a nozzle for dislodging and breaking up placer deposits with a jet of water. **13.** any of various large lizards of the family Varanidae, of Africa, southern Asia, the East Indies, and Australia, fabled to give warning of the presence of crocodiles: several species are endangered. —*v.t.* **14.** *Radio and Television.* **a.** to listen to (transmitted signals) on a receiving set in order to check the quality of the transmission. **b.** to view or listen to (television or radio transmissions) in order to check the quality of the video or audio. **c.** to listen to (a radio conversation or channel); keep tuned to. **15.** to observe, record, or detect (an operation or condition) with instruments that have no effect upon the operation or condition. **16.** to oversee, supervise, or regulate: *to monitor the administering of a test.* **17.** to watch closely for purposes of control, surveillance, etc.; keep track of; check continually: *to monitor one's eating habits.* —*v.i.* **18.** to serve as a monitor, detector, supervisor, etc. [1540–50; < L: prompter, adviser, equiv. to *moni-,* var. s. of *monēre* to remind, advise, warn + *-tor* -TOR] —**mon′i·tor·ship′,** *n.*

mon·i·to·ri·al (mon′i tôr′ē əl, -tōr′-), *adj.* **1.** of or pertaining to a monitor. **2.** monitory. [1715–25; MONITORY + -AL[1]] —**mon′i·to′ri·al·ly,** *adv.*

mon·i·to·ry (mon′i tôr′ē, -tōr′ē), *adj., n., pl.* **-ries.** —*adj.* **1.** serving to admonish or warn; admonitory. **2.** giving monition. —*n.* **3.** Also called **mon′itory let′ter.** a letter, as one from a bishop, containing a monition. [1400–50; late ME < L *monitōrius* reminding, warning, equiv. to *moni-* (see MONITOR) + *-tōrius* -TORY[1]]

mon·i·tress (mon′i tris), *n.* **1.** a female student who helps keep order or assists a teacher in school. **2.** a girl or woman who admonishes, esp. with reference to conduct. [1740–50; MONIT(O)R + -ESS]
—**Usage.** See **-ess.**

Mo·niz (mô nēsh′), *n.* **An·to·nio Ca·e·ta·no de A·bre·u Fre·i·re E·gas** (än tô′nyo͝o kä′ə tä′no͞o də ə bre′o͞o frā ē′rə ē′gəsh), 1874–1955, Portuguese neurosurgeon: Nobel prize 1949.

monk (mungk), *n.* **1.** (in Christianity) a man who has withdrawn from the world for religious reasons, esp. as a member of an order of cenobites living according to a particular rule and under vows of poverty, chastity, and obedience. **2.** (in any religion) a man who is a member of a monastic order: *a Buddhist monk.* **3.** *Print.* a dark area on a printed page caused by uneven inking of the plate or type. Cf. **friar** (def. 2). [bef. 900; ME; OE *munuc* < LL *monachus* < Gk *monachós* hermit, n. use of adj.: solitary, equiv. to *món(os)* alone + *-achos* adj. suffix]
—**Syn. 1.** brother. MONK, FRIAR refer to members of special male groups whose lives are devoted to the service of the church, esp. in Roman Catholic, Anglican, and Orthodox denominations. A MONK is properly a member of a monastery, under a superior; he is bound by a vow of stability, and is a co-owner of the community property of the monastery. Since the Reformation, MONK and FRIAR have been used as if they were the same. A FRIAR is, however, strictly speaking, a member of a mendicant order, whose members are not attached to a monastery and own no community property.

Monk (mungk), *n.* **1. The·lo·ni·ous** (thə lō′nē əs) **(Sphere),** 1917–1982, U.S. jazz pianist and composer. **2. George.** See **Monck, George.**

monk·er·y (mung′kə rē), *n., pl.* **-er·ies. 1.** the mode of life, behavior, etc., of monks; monastic life. **2.** a monastery. **3. monkeries,** *Disparaging.* the practices, beliefs, etc., of monks. [1530–40; MONK + -ERY]

mon·key (mung′kē), *n., pl.* **-keys,** *v.,* **-keyed, -key·ing.** —*n.* **1.** any mammal of the order Primates, including the guenons, macaques, langurs, and capuchins, but excluding humans, the anthropoid apes, and, usually, the tarsier and prosimians. Cf. **New World monkey, Old World monkey. 2.** the fur of certain species of such long-haired animals. **3.** a person likened to such an animal, as a mischievous, agile child or a mimic. **4.** a dance, deriving from the twist, in which the partners move their hands as if climbing a pole and jerk their heads back and forth. **5.** *Slang.* an addiction to narcotics. **6.** any of various mechanical devices, as the ram of a pile driver. **7.** *Coal Mining.* a small passageway or opening. **8.** *Brit. Slang.* the sum of 500 pounds. **9.** *Australian Informal.* a sheep. **10. a monkey on one's back,** *Slang.* **a.** an addiction to a drug or drugs; narcotic dependency. **b.** an enduring and often vexing habit or urge. **c.** a burdensome problem, situation, or responsibility; personal affliction or hindrance. **11. make a monkey out of,** to cause to appear ridiculous; make a fool of. Also, **make a monkey of.** —*v.i.* **12.** *Informal.* to play or trifle idly; fool (often fol. by *around* or *with*). —*v.t.* **13.** to imitate; ape; mimic. **14.** to mock. [1520–30; appar. < LG; cf. MLG *Moneke* (name of son of Martin the Ape in the story of Reynard), equiv. to *mone-* (akin to obs. F *monne* she-ape, Sp, Pg *mono* ape) + *-ke* dim. suffix] —**mon′key·ish,** *adj.* —**mon′key·ish·ly,** *adv.* —**mon′key·ish·ness,** *n.*

rhesus monkey, *Macaca mulatta,* head and body 20 in. (50 cm); tail 10 in. (25 cm)

mon′key bars′, junglegym. [1950–55]

mon′key block′, *Naut.* a single block that swivels. [1785–95]

mon′key bread′, 1. the gourdlike fruit of the baobab, eaten by monkeys. **2.** the tree itself. [1780–90]

mon′key bridge′, *Naut.* **1.** See **flying bridge. 2.** Also called **flying gangway.** a raised fore-and-aft cat-

CONCISE ETYMOLOGY KEY: <, descended or borrowed from; >, whence; b., blend of, blended; c., cognate with; cf., compare; deriv., derivative; equiv., equivalent; imit., imitative; obl., oblique; r., replacing; s., stem; sp., spelling, spelled; resp., respelling, respelled; trans., translation; ?, origin unknown; *, unattested; ‡, probably earlier than. See the full key inside the front cover.

walk permitting safe passage when the weather deck is washed by heavy seas. [1925–30]

mon′key busi′ness, 1. frivolous or mischievous behavior. **2.** improper or underhanded conduct; trickery.

mon′key dog′, affenpinscher.

mon′key-faced owl′ (mung′kē fāst′). See **barn owl.** [1915–20, *Amer.*]

mon′key fist′. See **monkey's fist.**

mon′key flow′er, any of various plants belonging to the genus *Mimulus,* of the figwort family, as *M. cardinalis* **(scarlet monkey flower),** having spotted flowers that resemble a face. [1780–90]

mon′key flush′, *Poker.* three cards of the same suit, usually not in sequence.

mon′key is′land, *Naut. Slang.* a flying bridge on top of a pilothouse or chart house. [1910–15]

mon′key jack′et, a short, close-fitting jacket or coat, formerly worn by sailors. [so called from its resemblance to a jacket worn by an organ-grinder's monkey]

mon′key link′. See **lap link.**

mon′key nut′, *Slang.* a peanut. [1875–80]

mon′key paw′. See **monkey's fist.**

mon′key pin′scher, affenpinscher.

mon•key•pod (mung′kē pod′), *n.* a tropical American tree, *Samanea saman,* of the legume family, having spreading branches and dense heads of small, pink flowers. Also called **rain tree.** [MONKEY + POD[1]]

mon•key•pot (mung′kē pot′), *n.* the woody, operculate seed vessel of any of certain large South American trees of the genus *Lecythis.* [1840–50; MONKEY + POT[1]]

mon′key puz′zle, a South American, coniferous timber tree, *Araucaria araucana,* having candelabralike branches, stiff sharp leaves, and edible nuts. [1865–70; perh. from the intertwined arrangement of its limbs]

mon′key's fist′, a ball-like knot used as an ornament or as a throwing weight at the end of a line. Also, **monkey fist.** Also called **monkey paw.** [1925–30; so called from fancied resemblance]

mon•key•shine (mung′kē shīn′), *n.* Usually, **monkeyshines.** a frivolous or mischievous prank; monkey business. [1820–30; MONKEY + SHINE]

mon′key suit′, *Slang.* **1.** a tuxedo or full-dress suit. **2.** any uniform. [1885–90; see MONKEY JACKET]

mon′key tail′, *Naut.* any of various light or short ropes or lines. [1825–35]

Mon′key Tri′al. See under **Scopes.**

mon′key wrench′, 1. Also called, *esp. Brit.,* **adjustable spanner.** a wrench having an adjustable jaw permitting it to grasp nuts or the like of different sizes. **2.** something that interferes with functioning; obstacle.

mon•key-wrench, (mung′kē rench′), *v.,* **-wrenched, -wrench•ing.** —*v.t.* **1.** to ruin (plans, a schedule, etc.) unavoidably or, sometimes, deliberately: *The storm monkey-wrenched our plans for a picnic.* —*v.i.* **2.** to prevent, delay, or sabotage industrialization or development of wilderness areas, esp. through vandalism. —**mon′key-wrench′er,** *n.*

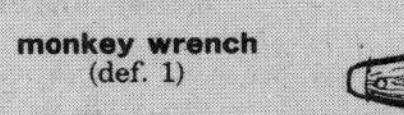

monkey wrench (def. 1)

monk•fish (mungk′fish′), *n., pl.* (*esp. collectively*) **-fish,** (*esp. referring to two or more kinds or species*) **-fish•es.** angler (def. 3). [1600–10; MONK + FISH, appar. alluding to its remote sea-bottom habitat]

Mon-Khmer (mōn′kmâr′, -kə mâr′), *n.* **1.** a group of Austroasiatic languages that includes Mon, of Burma, and Khmer, the language of Cambodia. —*adj.* **2.** of or pertaining to the Mon-Khmer.

monk•hood (mungk′ho͝od), *n.* **1.** the condition or profession of a monk. **2.** monks collectively. [ME *monkehode,* OE *munuchād.* See MONK, -HOOD]

monk•ish (mung′kish), *adj.* of, pertaining to, or resembling a monk: *a monkish manner.* [1540–50; MONK + -ISH[1]] —**monk′ish•ly,** *adv.* —**monk′ish•ness,** *n.*

monk's′ cloth′, a heavy cotton fabric in a basket weave, used for curtains, bedspreads, etc. [1840–50]

monk′ seal′, a small, dark brown, subtropical seal of the genus *Monachus:* the three species, *M. tropicalis* of the Caribbean, *M. schauinslandi* of Hawaiian island regions, and *M. monachus* of the Mediterranean, are endangered. [1835–45; appar. trans. of the NL genus name *Monachus* (see MONK), orig. a specific name (*Phoca monacha*), prob. in allusion to the animal's gray coloration and isolated breeding sites; cf. F *moine,* It *monaco* the monk seal, lit., monk]

monks•hood (mungks′ho͝od′), *n.* a plant belonging to the genus *Aconitum,* of the buttercup family, esp. *A. napellus,* the flowers of which have a large, hood-shaped sepal. [1570–80; MONK + 'S[1] + HOOD[1]]

Monks′ Mound′, the largest of the Cahokia Mounds.

monk's′ pep′per tree′. See **chaste tree.**

Mon•mouth (mon′məth), *n.* **1. James Scott, Duke of,** 1649–85, illegitimate son of Charles II of England and pretender to the throne of James II. **2.** a city in W Illinois. 10,706. **3.** Monmouthshire. **4.** former name of **Freehold.**

Mon•mouth•shire (mon′məth shēr′, -shər), *n.* a historic county in E Wales, now part of Gwent, Mid Glamorgan, and South Glamorgan. Also called **Monmouth.**

Mon•net (mō nā′; *Fr.* mô ne′), *n.* **Jean** (zhäN), 1888–1979, French economist: originator of the European Common Market.

mon•ni•on (mon′ē ən), *n. Armor.* spaulder. [<< OF *moignon* stump (of a limb), hence, that which covers or protects it; akin to Sp *muñón* muscle of the arm]

mon•o[1] (mon′ō), *n. Informal.* infectious mononucleosis. [by shortening]

mon•o[2] (mon′ō), *adj.* monophonic (def. 2). [by shortening]

mono-, a combining form meaning "alone," "single," "one" (*monogamy*); specialized in some scientific terms to denote a monomolecular thickness (*monolayer*) and adapted in chemistry to apply to compounds containing one atom of a particular element (*monohydrate*). Also, *esp. before a vowel,* **mon-.** [< Gk, comb. form of *mónos* alone]

mon•o•ac•e•tin (mon′ō as′i tin), *n. Chem.* acetin. [1855–60; MONO- + ACETIN]

mon•o•ac•id (mon′ō as′id, mon′ō as′id), *Chem.* —*adj.* Also, **monacidic. 1.** having one replaceable hydrogen atom or hydroxyl radical. **2.** capable of reacting with only one equivalent weight of an acid. —*n.* **3.** an acid having one replaceable hydrogen atom. Also, **monacid.** [1860–65; MONO- + ACID]

mon′o•al•pha•bet′ic substitu′tion (mon′ō al′fə bet′ik, mon′ō-), *Cryptography.* a system of substitution that uses only one cipher alphabet in a cryptogram so that each plaintext letter is always represented by the same cipher. Cf. **polyalphabetic substitution.** [1935–40; MONO- + ALPHABETIC]

mon•o•a•mine (mon′ō ə mēn′, -am′in), *n. Biochem.* any of various biogenic amine neurotransmitters having a single amino group, as dopamine, epinephrine, and norepinephrine. [1855–60; MONO- + AMINE]

mon′oamine′ ox′idase, *Biochem.* a copper-containing enzyme that catalyzes the breakdown of monoamines. *Abbr.:* MAO [1950–55]

mon′oamine′ ox′idase inhib′itor, *Pharm.* any of various substances, as isocarboxazid and phenelzine, that block enzymatic breakdown of certain monoamine neurotransmitters: used to treat severe depression. *Abbr.:* MAOI Also called **MAO inhibitor.** [1960–65]

mon′o•am•mo′ni•um phos′phate (mon′ō ə mō′nē əm, mon′-), *Chem.* a white, crystalline, moderately water-soluble compound, $NH_4H_2PO_4$, used as fertilizer, in fire extinguishers, etc. Also called **ammonium phosphate.** [MONO- + AMMONIUM]

mon•o•a•tom•ic (mon′ō ə tom′ik), *adj. Chem.* monatomic.

mon•o•ba•sic (mon′ə bā′sik), *adj.* **1.** *Chem.* (of an acid) containing one replaceable hydrogen atom. **2.** *Biol.* monotypic. [1835–45; MONO- + BASIC] —**mon•o•ba•sic•i•ty** (mon′ə bā sis′i tē), *n.*

monobas′ic potas′sium phos′phate, *Chem.* potassium diphosphate. See under **potassium phosphate.**

monoba′sic so′dium phos′phate, *Chem.* See **sodium phosphate** (def. 1).

mon•o•bath (mon′ə bath′, -bäth′), *n. Photog.* a developer and fixer combined in the same solution. [MONO- + BATH[1]]

mon•o•blas•tic (mon′ə blas′tik), *adj.* having a single layer, as an embryo in the blastula stage or developing from a single layer. [1885–90; MONO- + -BLAST + -IC]

mon•o•bloc (mon′ə blok′), *adj.* denoting or pertaining to the casting of a complex metal object as a single piece rather than in separate parts. [< F; see MONO-, BLOCK]

mon•o•bu•oy (mon′ə bo͞o′ē, -boi′), *n. Naut.* a floating platform anchored offshore in deep water and equipped with pipelines leading to storage tanks onshore, to which large, deep-draft tankers moor to load or unload. Also called **single buoy mooring, single point mooring.** [1970–75; MONO- + BUOY]

mon•o•ca•ble (mon′ə kā′bəl), *n.* an aerial ropeway having a single moving cable. [MONO- + CABLE]

mon•o•car•box•yl•ic (mon′ə kär′bok sil′ik), *adj. Chem.* containing one carboxyl group. [1905–10; MONO- + CARBOXYL + -IC]

mon•o•carp (mon′ə kärp′), *n. Bot.* a plant that dies after having once borne fruit. [MONO- + -CARP]

mon•o•car•pel•lar•y (mon′ə kär′pə ler′ē), *adj. Bot.* consisting of a single carpel. [1860–65; MONO- + CARPELLARY]

mon•o•car•pic (mon′ə kär′pik), *adj. Bot.* producing fruit only once and then dying. [1840–50; MONOCARP + -IC]

mon•o•car•pous (mon′ə kär′pəs), *adj. Bot.* **1.** having a gynoecium that forms only a single ovary. **2.** monocarpic. [1725–35; MONO- + -CARPOUS]

Mo•noc•er•os (mə nos′ər əs), *n., gen.* **-noc•er•o•tis** (-nos′ə rō′tis). *Astron.* the Unicorn, a constellation south of Gemini and east of Orion.

mon•o•cha•si•um (mon′ə kā′zhē əm, -zhəm, -zē əm), *n., pl.* **-si•a** (-zhē ə, -zhə, -zē ə). *Bot.* a form of cymose inflorescence in which the main axis produces only a single branch. [1885–90; < NL; see MONO-, DICHASIUM] —**mon′o•cha′si•al,** *adj.*

mon•o•chlo•ride (mon′ə klôr′id, -klōr′-), *n. Chem.* a chloride containing one atom of chlorine with one atom of another element or a group. [1865–70; MONO- + CHLORIDE]

mon′o•chlo•ro•a•ce•to′tic ac′id (mon′ə klôr′ō ə sē′tik, -ə set′ik, -klōr′-, mon′-), *Chem.* See **chloroacetic acid.** [1850–55; MONO- + CHLOROACETIC ACID]

mon•o•chord (mon′ə kôrd′), *n.* an acoustical instrument dating from antiquity, consisting of an oblong wooden sounding box, usually with a single string, used for the mathematical determination of musical intervals. [1375–1425; late ME *monocorde* < ML *monochordum* < Gk *monóchordon,* n. use of neut. of *monóchordos* with one string. See MONO-, CHORD[1]]

mon•o•chro•ic (mon′ə krō′ik), *adj.* of one color. [1885–90; MONO- + -CHROIC]

mon•o•chro•mat•ic (mon′ə krō mat′ik, -ō krə-), *adj.* **1.** of or having one color. **2.** of, pertaining to, or having tones of one color in addition to the ground hue: *monochromatic pottery.* **3.** *Optics.* pertaining to light of one color or to radiation of a single wavelength or narrow range of wavelengths. **4.** *Ophthalm.* of or pertaining to monochromatism. [1815–25; MONO- + CHROMATIC] —**mon′o•chro•mat′i•cal•ly,** *adv.* —**mon•o•chro•ma•tic•i•ty** (mon′ə krō′mə tis′i tē), *n.*

mon•o•chro•ma•tism (mon′ə krō′mə tiz′əm), *n.* **1.** a monochromatic quality: *the monochromatism of Southern Sung art.* **2.** *Ophthalm.* a defect of vision in which the retina fails to perceive color. Cf. **dichromatism** (def. 2), **trichromatism** (def. 3). Also, **mon•o•chro•ma•sia** (mon′ə krō mā′zhə, -zē ə, -shə, -shē ə). [1860–65; MONO- + CHROMATISM]

mon•o•chro•ma•tor (mon′ə krō′mā tər), *n. Optics.* a spectroscope with a slit that can be moved across the spectrum for viewing individual spectral bands. Also called **mon′ochromat′ic illu′minator.** [1905–10; MONOCHROMAT(IC) + (ILLUMINAT)OR]

mon•o•chrome (mon′ə krōm′), *n.* **1.** a painting or drawing in different shades of a single color. **2.** the art or technique of producing such a painting or drawing. **3.** the state or condition of being painted, decorated, etc., in shades of a single color. —*adj.* **4.** being or made in the shades of a single color: *a blue monochrome seascape.* **5.** having the images reproduced in tones of gray: *monochrome television.* [1655–65; < ML *monochrōma.* See MONO-, -CHROME] —**mon′o•chro′mic, mon′o•chro′mi•cal,** *adj.* —**mon′o•chro′mi•cal•ly,** *adv.* —**mon′o•chrom′ist,** *n.* —**mon′o•chro′my,** *n.*

mon•o•cle (mon′ə kəl), *n.* an eyeglass for one eye. [1855–60; < F, n. use of adj.: one-eyed < LL *monoculus,* equiv. to *mon-* MON- + *oculus* EYE] —**mon′o•cled,** *adj.*

mon•o•cli•nal (mon′ə klīn′l), *Geol.* —*adj.* **1.** noting, pertaining to, or composed of strata dipping in only one direction. —*n.* **2.** monocline. [1835–45; MONO- + Gk *klīn(ein)* to incline + -AL[1]] —**mon′o•cli′nal•ly,** *adv.*

mon•o•cline (mon′ə klīn′), *n. Geol.* a monoclinal structure or fold. [1875–80; back formation from MONOCLINAL]

mon•o•clin•ic (mon′ə klin′ik), *adj. Crystall.* noting or pertaining to a system of crystallization in which the crystals have three unequal axes, with one oblique intersection. Cf. **crystal system.** [1865–70; MONO- + Gk *klīn(ein)* to incline + -IC]

mon•o•cli•nous (mon′ə klī′nəs, mon′ə klī′-), *adj. Bot.* (of a plant, species, etc.) having both the stamens and pistils in the same flower. [1820–30; MONO- + Gk *klín(ē)* bed + -OUS] —**mon′o•cli′nism,** *n.*

mon•o•clo•nal (mon′ə klōn′l), *Biol.* —*adj.* **1.** pertaining to cells or cell products derived from a single clone. —*n.* **2.** a monoclonal antibody or other monoclonal product. [1910–15; MONO- + CLONE + -AL[1]]

mon′oclo′nal an′tibody, *Biotech.* antibody produced by a laboratory-grown cell clone, either of a hybridoma or a virus-transformed lymphocyte, that is more abundant and uniform than natural antibody and is able to bind specifically to a single site on almost any chosen antigen or reveal previously unknown antigen sites: used as an analytic tool in scientific research and medical diagnosis and potentially important in the treatment of certain diseases. *Abbr.:* MAb [1970–75]

mon•o•clo•nal•i•ty (mon′ə klō nal′i tē), *n. Biol., Biotech.* the state or condition of having one specific type of antibody. [MONO- + CLONAL + -ITY]

mon•o•coque (mon′ə kōk′, -kok′), *n.* **1.** a type of boat, aircraft, or rocket construction in which the shell carries most of the stresses. **2.** *Auto.* a type of vehicular construction in which the body is combined with the chassis as a single unit. —*adj.* **3.** of, pertaining to, or being a monocoque. [1910–15; < F, equiv. to *mono-* MONO- + *coque* shell, eggshell (of uncert. orig.)]

mon•o•cot (mon′ə kot′), *n. Bot.* a monocotyledon. Also, **mon•o•cot•yl** (mon′ə kot′l). [shortened form]

mon•o•cot•y•le•don (mon′ə kot′l ēd′n), *n. Bot.* an angiospermous plant of the class Monocotyledones, characterized by producing seeds with one cotyledon and an endogenous manner of growth. Cf. **dicotyledon.** [1720–30; < NL; see MONO-, COTYLEDON]

mon•o•cot•y•le•don•ous (mon′ə kot′l ēd′n əs), *adj.* belonging or pertaining to the monocotyledons. [1760–70; MONOCOTYLEDON + -OUS]

mo•noc•ra•cy (mō nok′rə sē, mə-), *n., pl.* **-cies.** government by only one person; autocracy. [1645–55; MONO- + -CRACY; modeled on ARISTOCRACY, DEMOCRACY] —**mon•o•crat•ic** (mon′ə krat′ik), *adj.*

mon•o•crat (mon′ə krat′), *n.* a person favoring monocracy. [1785–95, *Amer.*; MONO- + -CRAT]

mo•noc•u•lar (mə nok′yə lər), *adj.* **1.** having only one eye. **2.** of, pertaining to, or for the use of only one eye: *a monocular microscope.* —*n.* **3.** a monocular instrument or device. [1630–40; < LL *monocul(us)* one-eyed (see MONOCLE) + -AR[1]] —**mo•noc′u•lar•ly,** *adv.*

mon•o•cul•ture (mon′ə kul′chər), *n. Agric.* the use of land for growing only one type of crop. Also called **mon•o•crop•ping** (mon′ə krop′ing). [1910–15; MONO- + CULTURE] —**mon′o•cul′tur•al,** *adj.*

mon•o•cy•cle (mon′ə sī′kəl), *n.* a one-wheeled vehicle. [1865–70, *Amer.*; MONO- + CYCLE]

mon•o•cy•clic (mon′ə sī′klik, -sik′lik), *adj.* **1.** having one cycle. **2.** *Bot.* arranged in a single whorl, as the parts of certain flowers. **3.** *Chem.* of or pertaining to a

CONCISE PRONUNCIATION KEY: act, cāpe, dâre, pärt; set, ēqual; *if,* īce; ox, ōver, ôrder, oil, bo͝ok, bo͞ot, out; up, ûrge; child; sing; shoe; thin, *th*at; zh as in *treasure.* ə = *a* as in *alone, e* as in *system, i* as in *easily, o* as in *gallop, u* as in *circus;* ᵊ as in *fire* (fīᵊr), *hour* (ouᵊr). l and n can serve as syllabic consonants, as in *cradle* (krād′l), and *button* (but′n). See the full key inside the front cover.

molecular structure containing one ring. [1880–85; MONO- + CYCLIC] —**mon′o·cy′cly,** *n.*

mon·o·cyte (mon′ə sīt′), *n. Cell Biol.* a large, circulating white blood cell, formed in bone marrow and in the spleen, that ingests large foreign particles and cell debris. [1910–15; MONO- + -CYTE] —**mon·o·cyt·ic** (mon′ə sit′ik), *adj.* —**mon′o·cy′toid,** *adj.*

Mo·nod (mô nō′), *n.* **Jacques** (zhäk), 1910–76, French chemist: Nobel prize 1965.

mon·o·dac·ty·lous (mon′ə dak′tl əs), *adj. Zool.* having only one digit or claw. Also, **mon′o·dac′tyl.** [1820–30; < Gk *monodáktylos* one-fingered, one-toed. See MONO-, -DACTYLOUS] —**mon′o·dac′tyl·ism, mon′o·dac′ty·ly,** *n.*

mo·nod·ic (mə nod′ik), *adj. Music.* of or relating to monody. [1810–20; < Gk *monōidikós.* See MONODY, -IC] —**mo·nod′i·cal·ly,** *adv.*

mo·nod·o·mous (mə nod′ə məs), *adj.* living as a community in a single nest, as certain ant colonies. Cf. **polydomous.** [MONO- + Gk *dóm(os)* house + -OUS]

mon·o·dra·ma (mon′ə drä′mə, -dram′ə), *n.* a dramatic piece for only one performer. [1785–95; MONO- + DRAMA] —**mon·o·dra·mat·ic** (mon′ə drə mat′ik), *adj.* —**mon′o·dram′a·tist,** *n.*

mon·o·dy (mon′ə dē), *n., pl.* **-dies. 1.** a Greek ode sung by a single voice, as in a tragedy; lament. **2.** a poem in which the poet or speaker laments another's death; threnody. **3.** *Music.* **a.** a style of composition in which one part or melody predominates; homophony, as distinguished from polyphony. **b.** a piece in this style. **c.** monophony (def. 1). [1580–90; < LL *monōdia* < Gk *monōidía* a solo, monody, equiv. to *monōid(ós)* singing alone (see MON-, ODE) + *-ia* -Y³] —**mon·o·dist** (mon′ə-dist), *n.*

mo·noe·cious (mə nē′shəs), *adj.* **1.** *Biol.* having both male and female organs in the same individual; hermaphroditic. **2.** *Bot.* (of a plant, species, etc.) having the stamens and the pistils in separate flowers on the same plant. Also, **monecious.** [1755–65; < NL (Linnaeus) *Monoeci(a)* name of the group comprising monoecious plants (equiv. to Gk *mon-* MON- + *oîk(os)* house + NL *-ia* -IA) + -OUS] —**mo·noe′cious·ly,** *adv.* —**mo·noe′·cism** (mə nē′siz əm), **mo·noe′cy,** *n.*

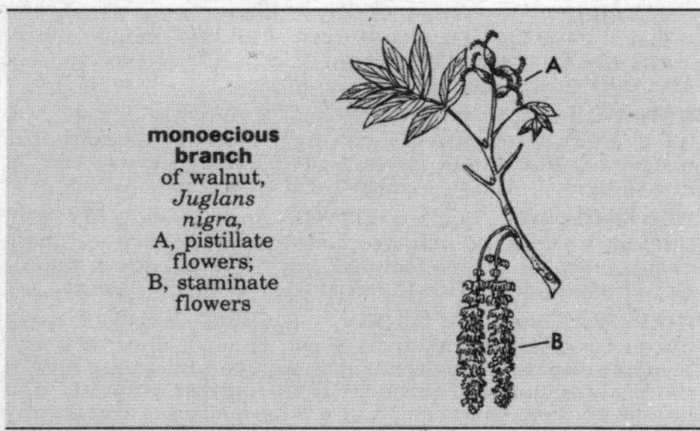

monoecious branch of walnut, *Juglans nigra,* A, pistillate flowers; B, staminate flowers

mon·o·es·ter (mon′ō es′tər), *n. Chem.* a single esterified polybasic acid. [1925–30; MONO- + ESTER]

mon·oes·trous (mon es′trəs, -ē′strəs), *adj.* monestrous.

mon·o·fil·a·ment (mon′ə fil′ə mənt), *n.* **1.** Also, **mon·o·fil** (mon′ə fil′). a single, generally large filament of synthetic fiber. Cf. **multifilament** (def. 2). —*adj.* **2.** made of such a filament: *a monofilament fishing line.* [1945–50; MONO- + FILAMENT]

mon·o·gam·ic (mon′ə gam′ik), *adj.* monogamous. [1830–40; MONOGAM(Y) + -IC]

mo·nog·a·mist (mə nog′ə mist), *n.* a person who practices or advocates monogamy. [1645–50; MONOGAM(Y) + -IST] —**mo·nog′a·mis′tic,** *adj.*

mo·nog·a·mous (mə nog′ə məs), *adj.* **1.** practicing or advocating monogamy. **2.** of or pertaining to monogamy. Also, **monogamic.** [1760–70; < LL *monogamus* < Gk *monógamos* marrying only once. See MONO-, -GAMOUS] —**mo·nog′a·mous·ly,** *adv.* —**mo·nog′a·mous·ness,** *n.*

mo·nog·a·my (mə nog′ə mē), *n.* **1.** marriage with only one person at a time. Cf. **bigamy, polygamy. 2.** *Zool.* the practice of having only one mate. **3.** the practice of marrying only once during life. Cf. **digamy.** [1605–15; < LL *monogamia* < Gk *monogamía.* See MONO-, -GAMY]

mon·o·ge·ne·an (mon′ə jē′nē ən), *n.* any trematode of the order Monogenea, mostly ectoparasites on fish, amphibians, and turtles. [1955–60; < NL *Monogene(a)* order name (equiv. to Gk *mono-* MONO- + *geneá* race, generation; see MONOGENETIC) + -AN]

mon·o·gen·e·sis (mon′ə jen′ə sis), *n.* **1.** the hypothetical descent of the human race from a single pair of individuals. **2.** *Biol.* the hypothetical descent of all living things from a single cell. Also, **mo·nog·e·ny** (mə noj′ə nē). [1860–65; MONO- + -GENESIS]

mon·o·ge·net·ic (mon′ō jə net′ik), *adj.* **1.** of or pertaining to monogenesis; monogenous. **2.** (of certain trematode worms) having only one generation in the life cycle, without an intermediate asexual generation. [1870–75; MONO- + GENETIC]

mon·o·gen·ic (mon′ə jen′ik), *adj.* **1.** *Biol.* bearing either only males or only females. **2.** *Genetics.* pertaining to a character controlled by one pair of genes. [1855–60; MONO- + -GEN or -GEN(Y) or GENE + -IC] —**mon′o·gen′i·cal·ly,** *adv.*

mo·nog·e·nism (mə noj′ə niz′əm), *n.* the theory that the human race has descended from a single pair of individuals or a single ancestral type. [1860–65; MONO- + -GEN + -ISM] —**mo·nog′e·nist,** *n.* —**mo·nog′e·nis′·tic,** *adj.*

mo·nog·e·nous (mə noj′ə nəs), *adj.* monogenetic. [1855–60; MONO- + -GENOUS]

mon·o·glot (mon′ə glot′), *adj.* **1.** knowing only one language; monolingual: *monoglot travelers.* **2.** composed in only one language. —*n.* **3.** a person with a knowledge of only one language. [1820–30; MONO- + -GLOT]

mon·o·glyc·er·ide (mon′ə glis′ə rīd′, -ər id), *n. Chem.* an ester obtained from glycerol by the esterification of one hydroxyl group with a fatty acid. Cf. **glyceride.** [1855–60; MONO- + GLYCERIDE]

mon·o·gram (mon′ə gram′), *n., v.,* **-grammed, -gramming.** —*n.* **1.** a design consisting of two or more alphabetic letters combined or interlaced, commonly one's initials, often printed on stationery, embroidered on clothing, etc. **2.** a single emblematic or decorative letter; applied initial. —*v.t.* **3.** to decorate with a monogram. [1600–10; < LL *monogramma,* irreg. < LGk *monógrammon.* See MONO-, -GRAM¹] —**mon·o·gram·mat·ic** (mon′ə grə mat′ik), **mon′o·gram·mat′i·cal, mon′o·gram′mic,** *adj.*

mon·o·graph (mon′ə graf′, -gräf′), *n.* **1.** a treatise on a particular subject, as a biographical study or study of the works of one artist. **2.** a highly detailed and thoroughly documented study or paper written about a limited area of a subject or field of inquiry: *scholarly monographs on medieval pigments.* **3.** an account of a single thing or class of things, as of a species of organism. —*v.t.* **4.** to write a monograph about. [1815–25; MONO- + -GRAPH] —**mo·nog·ra·pher** (mə nog′rə fər), **mo·nog′ra·phist,** *n.* —**mon·o·graph·ic** (mon′ə graf′ik), **mon′o·graph′i·cal,** *adj.* —**mon′o·graph′i·cal·ly,** *adv.*

monograph′ic se′ries, a series of monographs issued in uniform style or format and related by subject or by issuing agency.

mon·o·gy·noe·cial (mon′ō ji nē′shəl, -gi-), *adj.* (of a fruit) developing from a single pistil. [1875–80; MONO- + GYNOECI(UM) + -AL¹]

mo·nog·y·ny (mə noj′ə nē), *n.* **1.** the practice or condition of having only one wife at a time. **2.** (of a male animal) the condition of having only one mate at a time. **3.** (in social insects) the condition of having one functioning queen in a colony. **4.** *Bot.* the condition of having one pistil. [1875–80; MONO- + Gk *-gynia,* equiv. to *gyn(ē)* woman, wife + *-ia* -Y³] —**mo·nog′y·nous, mon·o·gyn·ic** (mon′ə jin′ik), **mon′o·gyn′i·ous,** *adj.* —**mo·nog′y·nist,** *n.*

mon·o·hull (mon′ə hul′), *adj.* **1.** (of a vessel) having a single hull. —*n.* **2.** a monohull vessel, as distinguished from a multihull vessel. [1965–70; MONO- + HULL²]

mon·o·hy·brid (mon′ə hī′brid), *Genetics.* —*n.* **1.** the offspring of individuals that differ with respect to a particular gene pair. **2.** Also called **monohy′brid cross′.** a genetic cross made to examine the distribution of one specific set of alleles in the resulting offspring. —*adj.* **3.** of or pertaining to such an offspring. [1900–05; MONO- + HYBRID]

mon·o·hy·drate (mon′ə hī′drāt), *n. Chem.* a hydrate that contains one molecule of water, as ammonium carbonate, $(NH_4)_2CO_3 \cdot H_2O$. [1850–55; MONO- + HYDRATE] —**mon′o·hy′drat·ed,** *adj.*

mon·o·hy·dric (mon′ə hī′drik), *adj. Chem.* (esp. of alcohols and phenols) monohydroxy. [1855–60; MONO- + HYDR(OXYL) + -IC]

mon·o·hy·drox·y (mon′ə hī drok′sē), *adj. Chem.* (of a molecule) containing one hydroxyl group. [1940–45; MONO- + HYDROXY]

mon·oid (mon′oid), *n. Math.* groupoid. [1860–65; MON- + -OID]

mon·o·kine (mon′ə kīn′), *n. Immunol.* any substance secreted by a monocyte or macrophage and affecting the function of other cells. [MONO- + (LYMPHO)KINE]

mon·o·ki·ni (mon′ə kē′nē), *n.* a topless bikini. [1960–65; MONO- + (BI)KINI]

mo·nol·a·try (mə nol′ə trē), *n.* the worship of only one god although other gods are recognized as existing. [1880–85; MONO- + -LATRY] —**mo·nol·a·ter** (mə nol′ə-tər), **mo·nol′a·trist,** *n.* —**mo·nol′a·trous,** *adj.*

mon·o·lay·er (mon′ə lā′ər), *n. Physical Chem.* See **molecular film.** [1930–35; MONO- + LAYER]

mon·o·lin·gual (mon′ə ling′gwəl *or, Can.,* -ling′gyōō-əl), *adj.* **1.** knowing or able to use only one language; monoglot. **2.** spoken or written in only one language. —*n.* **3.** a monolingual person. [1950–55; MONO- + LINGUAL] —**mon′o·lin′gual·ism,** *n.*

mon·o·lith (mon′ə lith), *n.* **1.** an obelisk, column, large statue, etc., formed of a single block of stone. **2.** a single block or piece of stone of considerable size, esp. when used in architecture or sculpture. **3.** something having a uniform, massive, redoubtable, or inflexible quality or character. [1820–30; < L *monolithus* < Gk *monólithos* made of one stone. See MONO-, -LITH] —**mon′o·lith′ism,** *n.*

mon·o·lith·ic (mon′ə lith′ik), *adj.* **1.** of or pertaining to a monolith. **2.** made of only one stone: *a monolithic column.* **3.** consisting of one piece; solid or unbroken: *a boat with a monolithic hull.* **4.** constructed of monoliths or huge blocks of stone: *the monolithic monuments of the New Stone Age.* **5.** characterized by massiveness, total uniformity, rigidity, invulnerability, etc.: *a monolithic society.* **6.** *Electronics.* of or pertaining to an integrated circuit formed in a single chip. [1815–25; MONOLITH + -IC] —**mon′o·lith′i·cal·ly,** *adv.*

mon·o·logue (mon′ə lôg′, -log′), *n.* **1.** a form of dramatic entertainment, comedic solo, or the like by a single speaker: *a comedian's monologue.* **2.** a prolonged talk or discourse by a single speaker, esp. one dominating or monopolizing a conversation. **3.** any composition, as a poem, in which a single person speaks alone. **4.** a part of a drama in which a single actor speaks alone; soliloquy. Also, **mon′o·log′.** [1615–25; < F, on the model of *dialogue* DIALOGUE; cf. Gk *monólogos* speaking alone] —**mon·o·log·ic** (mon′ə loj′ik), **mon′o·log′i·cal,** *adj.* —**mon·o·log·ist** (mon′ə lô′gist, -log′ist, mə nol′ə jist), **mon·o·logu·ist** (mon′ə lô′gist, -log′ist), *n.*

mo·nol·o·gy (mə nol′ə jē), *n., pl.* **-gies. 1.** the act or habit of soliloquizing. **2.** *Obs.* a monologue. [1600–10; < Gk *monología.* See MONO-, -LOGY]

mon·o·ma·ni·a (mon′ə mā′nē ə, -mān′yə), *n.* **1.** (no longer in technical use) a psychosis characterized by thoughts confined to one idea or group of ideas. **2.** an inordinate or obsessive zeal for or interest in a single thing, idea, subject, or the like. [1815–25; < NL; see MONO-, -MANIA] —**mon·o·ma·ni·ac** (mon′ə mā′nē ak′), *n.* —**mon·o·ma·ni·a·cal** (mon′ə mə nī′ə kəl), *adj.*

mon·o·mer (mon′ə mər), *n. Chem.* a molecule of low molecular weight capable of reacting with identical or different molecules of low molecular weight to form a polymer. [1910–15; MONO- + -MER] —**mon·o·mer·ic** (mon′ə mer′ik), *adj.*

mo·nom·er·ous (mə nom′ər əs), *adj.* **1.** consisting of one part. **2.** *Bot.* (of flowers) having one member in each whorl. [1820–30; < Gk *monomer(ḗs)* consisting of one part (*mono-* MONO- + *mér(os)* part + *-ēs* adj. suffix) + -OUS]

mon·o·me·tal·lic (mon′ō mə tal′ik), *adj.* **1.** of or using one metal. **2.** pertaining to monometallism. [1875–80; MONO- + METALLIC]

mon·o·met·al·lism (mon′ə met′l iz′əm), *n.* **1.** the use of one metal only, as gold or silver, as a monetary standard. **2.** the doctrine or actions supporting such a standard. [1875–80; MONO- + (BI)METALLISM] —**mon′o·met′al·list,** *n.*

mo·nom·e·ter (mə nom′i tər), *n. Pros.* a line of verse of one measure or foot. [1840–50; < LL: composed in one meter < Gk *monómetros,* equiv. to *mono-* MONO- + *métr(on)* METER² + *-os* adj. suffix] —**mon·o·met·ri·cal** (mon′ə me′tri kəl), **mon′o·met′ric,** *adj.*

mon·o·meth·yl·a·mine (mon′ə meth′əl ə mēn′, -me thil′ə min), *n. Chem.* methylamine. [MONO- + METHYLAMINE]

mo·no·mi·al (mō nō′mē əl, mə-), *adj.* **1.** *Algebra.* **a.** consisting of one term only. **b.** (of a matrix) having exactly one non-zero term in each row and each column. **2.** *Biol.* noting or pertaining to a name that consists of a single word or term. —*n.* **3.** *Algebra.* a monomial expression or quantity. [1700–10; MON- + (BIN)OMIAL]

mon·o·mo·lec·u·lar (mon′ō mə lek′yə lər), *adj.* **1.** noting or pertaining to a thickness of one molecule. **2.** having a thickness of one molecule. [1875–80; MONO- + MOLECULAR] —**mon′o·mo·lec′u·lar·ly,** *adv.*

mon·o·mor·phe·mic (mon′ō môr fē′mik), *adj.* containing only one morpheme, as the words *wait* and *gorilla.* [1935–40; MONO- + MORPHEMIC]

mon·o·mor·phic (mon′ə môr′fik), *adj.* **1.** *Biol.* having only one form. **2.** of the same or of an essentially similar type of structure. Also, **mon′o·mor′phous.** [1875–80; MONO- + -MORPHIC]

mon·o·mor·phism (mon′ə môr′fiz əm), *n. Math.* a one-to-one homomorphism. [1955–60; MONO- + -MORPHISM]

Mo·non·ga·he·la (mə nong′gə hē′lə), *n.* a river flowing from N West Virginia through SW Pennsylvania into the Ohio River. 128 mi. (205 km) long.

mon·o·nu·cle·ar (mon′ə nōō′klē ər, -nyōō′- *or, by metathesis,* -kyə lər), *adj.* **1.** Also, **mon′o·nu′cle·ate.** *Cell Biol.* having only one nucleus. **2.** *Chem.* (of hydrocarbons) monocyclic. [1885–90; MONO- + NUCLEAR] —**Pronunciation.** See **nuclear.**

mon·o·nu·cle·o·sis (mon′ə nōō′klē ō′sis, -nyōō′-), *n. Pathol.* **1.** the presence of an abnormally large number of mononuclear leukocytes, or monocytes, in the blood. **2.** See **infectious mononucleosis.** [1915–20; MONONUCLE(AR) + -OSIS]

mon·o·pet·al·ous (mon′ə pet′l əs), *adj. Bot.* **1.** gamopetalous. **2.** having only one petal, as a corolla. [1685–95; MONO- + PETALOUS]

mon·o·pha·gia (mon′ə fā′jə, -jē ə), *n.* the eating of or craving for only one kind of food. [MONO- + Gk *-phagia* -PHAGY]

mo·noph·a·gous (mə nof′ə gəs), *adj.* feeding on only one kind of food. [1865–70; MONO- + -PHAGOUS] —**mo·noph·a·gy** (mə nof′ə jē), *n.*

mon·o·pha·sic (mon′ə fā′zik), *adj.* having one phase. [1895–1900; MONO- + PHASE + -IC]

mon·o·pho·bi·a (mon′ə fō′bē ə), *n.* an abnormal fear of being alone. [MONO- + -PHOBIA]

mon·o·phon·ic (mon′ə fon′ik), *adj.* **1.** *Music.* of or pertaining to monophony. **2.** Also, **monaural, mono.** of or noting a system of sound recording and reproduction using only a single channel. Cf. **quadraphonic, stereophonic.** [1880–85; MONOPHON(Y) + -IC] —**mon′o·phon′i·cal·ly,** *adv.*

mo·noph·o·ny (mə nof′ə nē), *n., pl.* **-nies. 1.** a musical style employing a single melodic line without accompaniment. **2.** monody (def. 3a). [1885–90; MONO- + -PHONY]

mon·o·phos·phate (mon′ə fos′fāt), *n. Chem.* a salt containing only one phosphate group. [MONO- + PHOSPHATE]

mon·oph·thong (mon′əf thông′, -thong′), *n. Phonet.* a vowel retaining the same quality throughout its duration. Cf. **diphthong.** [1610–20; < Gk *monóphthongos* equiv. to *mono-* MONO- + *phthóngos* sound] —**mon·oph·thon·gal** (mon′əf thông′gəl, -thong′-), *adj.*

CONCISE ETYMOLOGY KEY: <, descended or borrowed from; >, whence; b., blend of, blended; c., cognate with; cf., compare; deriv., derivative; equiv., equivalent; imit., imitative; obl., oblique; r., replacing; s., stem; sp., spelling, spelled; resp., respelling, respelled; trans., translation; ?, origin unknown; *, unattested; ‡, probably earlier than. See the full key inside the front cover.

mon·oph·thong·ize (mon′əf thông īz′, -gīz′, -thong-), *v.*, **-ized, -iz·ing.** *Phonet.* —*v.t.* **1.** to change into or pronounce as a monophthong. —*v.i.* **2.** to become a monophthong. Also, *esp. Brit.*, **mon′oph·thong·ise′.** [1875–80; MONOPHTHONG + -IZE] —**mon′oph·thong′i·za′tion,** *n.*

mon·o·phy·let·ic (mon′ō fī let′ik), *adj. Biol.* consisting of organisms descended from a single taxon. [1870–75; MONO- + PHYLETIC] —**mon·o·phy·le·tism** (mon′ə fī′li tiz′əm, -fil′i-), **mon′o·phy′le·ty,** *n.*

mon·o·phyl·lous (mon′ə fil′əs), *adj. Bot.* **1.** consisting of one leaf, as a calyx. **2.** having only one leaf. [1740–50; < Gk *monóphyllos.* See MONO-, -PHYLLOUS]

Mo·noph·y·site (mə nof′ə sīt′), *n. Theol.* a person who maintains that Christ has one nature, partly divine and partly human. Cf. **Dyophysite.** [1690–1700; < LL *monophysīta* < LGk *monophysítēs,* equiv. to Gk *mono-* MONO- + *phý(is)* nature + *-itēs* -ITE[1]] —**Mo·noph·y·sit·ic** (mə nof′ə sit′ik), *adj.* —**Mo·noph′y·sit′ism, Mo·noph′y·sism,** *n.*

mon·o·plane (mon′ə plān′), *n.* **1.** an airplane with one main sustaining surface or one set of wings. **2.** *Naut.* a planing craft the bottom of which is in an unbroken fore-and-aft line. [1905–10; MONO- + PLANE[1]] —**mon′o·plan′ist,** *n.*

mon·o·ple·gi·a (mon′ə plē′jē ə, -plē′jə), *n. Pathol.* paralysis of one extremity, muscle, or muscle area. [1885–90; MONO- + -PLEGIA] —**mon·o·ple·gic** (mon′ə-plē′jik, -plej′ik), *adj.*

mon·o·ploid (mon′ə ploid′), *Biol.* —*adj.* **1.** having the basic or haploid number of chromosomes. —*n.* **2.** a monoploid cell or organism. [1925–30; MONO- + -PLOID]

mon·o·pod (mon′ə pod′), *n.* a single-legged support used to steady a hand-held camera. [1960–65; MONO- + (TRI)POD]

mon·o·pode (mon′ə pōd′), *adj.* **1.** having one foot. —*n.* **2.** a creature having one foot. **3.** (*sometimes cap.*) one of a fabled race of people having only one foot. **4.** *Bot.* monopodium. [1810–20; < LL *monopodius* one-footed, equiv. to *monopod-* (< Gk; see MONO-, -POD) + *-ius* adj. suffix]

mon·o·po·di·um (mon′ə pō′dē əm), *n., pl.* **-di·a** (-dē ə). *Bot.* a single main axis that continues to extend at the apex in the original line of growth, giving off lateral branches beneath in acropetal succession. Cf. **sympodium.** [1870–75; MONO- + -PODIUM] —**mon′o·po′di·al,** *adj.* —**mon′o·po′di·al·ly,** *adv.*

mo·nop·o·dy (mə nop′ə dē), *n., pl.* **-dies.** *Pros.* a measure consisting of one foot. [1835–45; < Gk *monopodía.* See MONOPODE, -Y[3]] —**mon·o·pod·ic** (mon′ə-pod′ik), *adj.*

mon·o·pole (mon′ə pōl′), *n.* See **magnetic monopole.**

mo·nop·o·lism (mə nop′ə liz′əm), *n.* the existence or prevalence of monopolies. [1880–85; MONOPOL(Y) + -ISM]

mo·nop·o·list (mə nop′ə list), *n.* **1.** a person who has a monopoly. **2.** an advocate of monopoly. [1595–1605; MONOPOL(Y) + -IST] —**mo·nop′o·lis′tic,** *adj.* —**mo·nop′o·lis′ti·cal·ly,** *adv.*

mo·nop·o·lize (mə nop′ə līz′), *v.t.*, **-lized, -liz·ing.** **1.** to acquire, have, or exercise a monopoly of. **2.** to obtain exclusive possession of; keep entirely to oneself: *Children monopolize one's time.* Also, *esp. Brit.*, **mo·nop′o·lise′.** [1605–15; MONOPOL(Y) + -IZE] —**mo·nop′o·li·za′tion,** *n.* —**mo·nop′o·liz′er,** *n.*

mo·nop·o·ly (mə nop′ə lē), *n., pl.* **-lies.** **1.** exclusive control of a commodity or service in a particular market, or a control that makes possible the manipulation of prices. Cf. **duopoly, oligopoly.** **2.** an exclusive privilege to carry on a business, traffic, or service, granted by a government. **3.** the exclusive possession or control of something. **4.** something that is the subject of such control, as a commodity or service. **5.** a company or group that has such control. **6.** the market condition that exists when there is only one seller. **7.** (*cap.*) *Trademark.* a board game in which a player attempts to gain a monopoly of real estate by advancing around the board and purchasing property, acquiring capital by collecting rent from other players whose pieces land on that property. [1525–35; < L *monopōlium* < Gk *monopṓlion* right of exclusive sale, equiv. to *mono-* MONO- + *pōl(eîn)* to sell + *-ion* n. suffix] —**mo·nop′o·loid′,** *adj.*

mon·o·pol·y·logue (mon′ə pol′i lôg′, -log′), *n.* a theatrical entertainment in which the same performer plays several parts or characters. [1815–25; MONO- + POLY- + *-logue,* as in MONOLOGUE, DIALOGUE]

mon·o·prot·ic (mon′ə prot′ik), *adj. Chem.* (of an acid) having one transferable proton. [MONO- + PROT(ON) + -IC]

mo·nop·so·ny (mə nop′sə nē), *n., pl.* **-nies.** the market condition that exists when there is one buyer. Cf. **duopsony, oligopsony.** [1930–35; MON- + Gk *opsōnía* shopping, purchase of provisions] —**mo·nop′so·nist,** *n.* —**mo·nop′so·nis′tic,** *adj.*

mo·nop·ter·al (mo nop′tər əl, mō-), *adj.* **1.** having the form of a monopteron. **2.** of or pertaining to a monopteron. [1815–25; < L *monopter(os)* (see MONOPTERON) + -AL[1]]

mo·nop·te·ron (mo nop′tə ron′, mō-), *n., pl.* **-te·ra** (-tər ə). a classical building having a single outer colonnade surrounding a central structure or a courtyard. Also called **monopteros.** [1700–10; n. use of neut. of L *monopteros* < Gk *monópteros,* equiv. to *mono-* MONO- + *-pteros* -PTEROUS]

mo·nop·te·ros (mo nop′tə ros′, mō-), *n., pl.* **-te·roi** (-tə roi′). monopteron.

mon·o·rail (mon′ə rāl′), *n.* **1.** a single rail functioning as a track for wheeled vehicles, as railroad or other cars, balanced upon or suspended from it. **2.** a railroad or other transportation system using such a rail. **3.** a vehicle traveling on such a rail. [1895–1900; MONO- + RAIL[1]]

mon·o·rhi·nous (mon′ə rī′nəs), *adj. Zool.* having a single, median nostril, as the cyclostomes. Also, **mon′o·rhi′nal, mon′o·rhine′.** [1900–05; MONO- + *-rhinous* < Gk *-rhinos* -nosed, adj. deriv. of *rhīs,* s. *rhin-* nose; see -OUS]

mon·o·rhyme (mon′ə rīm′), *n. Pros.* a poem or stanza in which all the lines rhyme with each other. [1725–35; MONO- + RHYME]

mon·o·sac·cha·ride (mon′ə sak′ə rīd′, -ər id), *n. Chem.* a carbohydrate that does not hydrolyze, as glucose, fructose, or ribose, occurring naturally or obtained by the hydrolysis of glycosides or polysaccharides. Also, **mon·o·sac·cha·rose** (mon′ə sak′ə rōs′). Also called **simple sugar.** [1895–1900; MONO- + SACCHARIDE]

mon·o·scope (mon′ə skōp′), *n.* a cathode-ray tube that provides a signal of a fixed pattern for testing television equipment. [1935–40; MONO- + -SCOPE]

mon·o·sep·al·ous (mon′ə sep′ə ləs), *adj. Bot.* **1.** gamosepalous. **2.** having only one sepal, as a calyx. [1820–30; MONO- + -SEPALOUS]

mon·o·so·di·um (mon′ə sō′dē əm), *adj. Chem.* containing one atom of sodium. [1855–60; MONO- + SODIUM]

monoso′dium glu′tamate, *Chem.* a white, crystalline, water-soluble powder, $C_5H_8NNaO_4 \cdot H_2O$, used to intensify the flavor of foods. Also called **MSG, sodium glutamate.** Cf. **glutamic acid.** [1925–30]

mon·o·some (mon′ə sōm′), *n. Genetics.* **1.** a chromosome having no homologue, esp. an unpaired X chromosome. **2.** a protein-synthetic complex involving the translation of a messenger RNA molecule by a single ribosome. **3.** a monosomic individual. [1920–25; MONO- + -SOME[3]]

mon·o·so·mic (mon′ə sō′mik), *adj. Genetics.* having one less than the usual diploid number of chromosomes. [1925–30; MONOSOME + -IC]

mon·o·sper·mous (mon′ə spûr′məs), *adj. Bot.* having one seed. Also, **mon′o·sper′mal.** [1720–30; < NL *monospermus.* See MONO-, SPERMOUS]

mon·o·sper·my (mon′ə spûr′mē), *n.* the fertilization of an ovum by only one spermatozoon. [1900–05; MONO- + -SPERM + -Y[3]] —**mon′o·sper′mic,** *adj.*

mon·o·sta·ble (mon′ə stā′bəl), *adj.* (of an electric or electronic circuit) having only one stable state. [MONO- + STABLE[2]]

mon·o·ste·a·rate (mon′ə stē′ə rāt′, -stēr′āt), *n. Chem.* a stearate containing one $C_{22}H_{35}CO-$ group, derived from stearic acid. [MONO- + STEARATE]

mon·o·stich (mon′ə stik′), *n.* **1.** a poem or epigram consisting of a single metrical line. **2.** a single line of poetry. [1570–80; < LL *monostichum* < Gk *monóstichon,* n. use of neut. of *monóstichos* consisting of one line of verse. See MONO-, STICH] —**mon′o·stich′ic,** *adj.*

mon·o·stome (mon′ə stōm′), *adj.* having a single mouth, pore, or stoma. Also, **mo·nos·to·mous** (mə nos′tə məs). [1840–50; MONO- + -STOME]

mo·nos·tro·phe (mə nos′trə fē, mon′ə strōf′), *n.* a poem in which all the strophes or stanzas are of the same metrical form. [1885–90; < Gk *monóstrophos* consisting of one strophe. See MONO-, STROPHE]

mon·o·stroph·ic (mon′ə strof′ik, -strō′fik), *adj.* **1.** consisting of stanzas or strophes all having the same metrical structure. —*n.* **2. monostrophics,** monostrophic verses. [1665–75; < Gk *monostrophikós.* See MONOSTROPHE, -IC]

mon·o·sty·lous (mon′ə stī′ləs), *adj. Bot.* having only one style. [MONO- + *-stylous;* see -STYLE[1], -OUS]

mon·o·sub·sti·tut·ed (mon′ə sub′sti tōō′tid, -tyōō′-), *adj. Chem.* containing one substituent. [1885–90; MONO- + SUBSTITUTED]

mon·o·syl·lab·ic (mon′ə si lab′ik), *adj.* **1.** having only one syllable, as the word *no.* **2.** having a vocabulary composed primarily of monosyllables or short, simple words. **3.** very brief; terse or blunt: *a monosyllabic reply.* [1815–25; < ML *monosyllabicus,* equiv. to LL *monosyllab(on)* monosyllable (< Gk *monosýllabon,* n. use of neut. of *monosýllabos* monosyllabic) + *-icus* -IC] —**mon′o·syl·lab′i·cal·ly,** *adv.* —**mon·o·syl·la·bic·i·ty** (mon′ə sil′ə bis′i tē), *n.*

mon·o·syl·la·bism (mon′ə sil′ə biz′əm), *n.* **1.** monosyllabic character. **2.** the use of monosyllables. [1795–1805; < LL *monosyllab(on)* monosyllable + -ISM]

mon·o·syl·la·ble (mon′ə sil′ə bəl), *n.* a word of one syllable, as *yes* or *no.* [1525–35; MONO- + SYLLABLE]

mon·o·sym·met·ric (mon′ə si me′trik), *adj. Biol., Bot.* zygomorphic. Also, **mon′o·sym·met′ri·cal.** [1875–80; MONO- + SYMMETRIC] —**mon′o·sym·met′ri·cal·ly,** *adv.* —**mon·o·sym·met·ry** (mon′ə sim′i trē), *n.*

mon·o·tech·nic (mon′ə tek′nik), *adj.* of or offering instruction in a single scientific or technical subject. [1900–05; MONO- + (POLY)TECHNIC]

mon·o·the·ism (mon′ə thē iz′əm), *n.* the doctrine or belief that there is only one God. [1650–60; MONO- + (POLY)THEISM] —**mon′o·the′ist,** *n., adj.* —**mon′o·the·is′tic, mon′o·the·is′ti·cal,** *adj.* —**mon′o·the·is′ti·cal·ly,** *adv.*

Mo·noth·e·lite (mə noth′ə līt′), *n. Theol.* a person who maintains that Christ has a single theanthropic will. Cf. **Dyothelite.** [1540–50; < ML *monothelita* < LGk *monothelḗtēs,* equiv. to Gk *mono-* MONO- + *thelḗtēs* willer, equiv. to *thelē-* (var. s. of *thélein* to will) + *-tēs* agent suffix] —**Mo·noth·e·lit·ic** (mə noth′ə lit′ik), *adj.* —**Mo·noth·e·lit·ism** (mə noth′ə lī tiz′əm), **Mo·noth′e·lism,** *n.*

mon·o·the·mat·ic (mon′ə thē mat′ik), *adj.* having a single theme. [1885–90; MONO- + THEMATIC]

mon·o·tint (mon′ə tint′), *n.* monochrome. [1885–90; MONO- + TINT]

mon·o·to·nal (mon′ə tōn′l), *adj. Print.* having equal tone throughout, as sans-serif type. [MONOTONE + -AL[1]]

mon·o·tone (mon′ə tōn′), *n.* **1.** a vocal utterance or series of speech sounds in one unvaried tone. **2.** a single tone without harmony or variation in pitch. **3.** recitation or singing of words in such a tone. **4.** a person who is unable to discriminate between or to reproduce differences in musical pitch, esp. in singing. **5.** sameness of tone or color, sometimes to a boring degree. —*adj.* **6.** monotonous. **7.** consisting of or characterized by a uniform tone of one color: *a monotone drape.* Cf. **monochromatic** (defs. 1, 2). **8.** *Math.* monotonic (def. 2). [1635–45; < F *monotone* < LGk *monótonos* MONOTONOUS]

mon·o·ton·ic (mon′ə ton′ik), *adj.* **1.** of, pertaining to, or uttered in a monotone: *a monotonic delivery of a lecture.* **2.** *Math.* **a.** (of a function or of a particular set of values of a function) increasing or decreasing. **b.** (of an ordered system of sets) consisting of sets such that each set contains the preceding set or such that each set is contained in the preceding set. [1790–1800; MONOTONE + -IC] —**mon′o·ton′i·cal·ly,** *adv.*

mo·not·o·nous (mə not′n əs), *adj.* **1.** lacking in variety; tediously unvarying: *the monotonous flat scenery.* **2.** characterizing a sound continuing on one note. **3.** having very little inflection; limited to a narrow pitch range. [1770–80; < LGk *monótonos.* See MONO-, TONE, -OUS] —**mo·not′o·nous·ly,** *adv.* —**mo·not′o·nous·ness,** *n.*
—**Syn. 1.** tedious, humdrum, boring, dull.

mo·not·o·ny (mə not′n ē), *n.* **1.** wearisome uniformity or lack of variety, as in occupation or scenery. **2.** the continuance of an unvarying sound; monotone. **3.** sameness of tone or pitch, as in speaking. [1700–10; < LGk *monotonía,* equiv. to *monóton(os)* MONOTONOUS + *-ia* -Y[3]]

mon·o·trem·a·tous (mon′ə trem′ə təs, -trē′mə-), *adj.* of or pertaining to a monotreme. [1825–35; < NL *monotrematus* lit., single-holed, equiv. to *mono-* MONO- + *-trematus* -holed, adj. use of Gk *trêma,* s. *trēmat-* hole, perforation; see -OUS]

mon·o·treme (mon′ə trēm′), *n.* any animal of the Monotremata, the most primitive order of mammals, characterized by certain birdlike and reptilian features, as hatching young from eggs, and having a single opening for the digestive, urinary, and genital organs, comprising only the duckbill and the echidnas of Australia and New Guinea. [1825–35; < F *monotrème* < NL *monotrema,* assumed sing. of *Monotremata,* neut. pl. of *monotrematus* MONOTREMATOUS]

mo·not·ri·chate (mə no′tri kit), *adj.* (of bacteria) having a single flagellum at one pole. Also, **mo·not′ri·chous, mon·o·trich·ic** (mon′ə trik′ik). [MONO- + *trichate;* see TRICH-, -ATE[1]]

mon·o·tri·glyph (mon′ə trī′glif), *n.* (in the Doric order) any intercolumniation having one whole triglyph. [1700–10; < LL *monotriglyphus.* See MONO-, TRIGLYPH] —**mon′o·tri·glyph′ic,** *adj.*

mo·not·ro·py (mə no′trə pē), *n., pl.* **-pies.** *Crystall.* polymorphism that is irreversible. Cf. **enantiotropy.** [1900–05; MONO- + -TROPY] —**mon·o·trop·ic** (mon′ə-trop′ik, -trō′pik), *adj.* —**mon′o·trop′i·cal·ly,** *adv.*

mon·o·type (mon′ə tīp′), *n.* **1.** the only print made from a metal or glass plate on which a picture is painted in oil color, printing ink, or the like. **2.** the method of producing such a print. **3.** *Biol.* the only type of its group, as a single species constituting a genus. [1880–85; MONO- + -TYPE]

Mon·o·type (mon′ə tīp′), *Print., Trademark.* a brand of machine for setting and casting type, consisting of a separate keyboard for producing a paper tape containing holes in a coded pattern so that when this tape is fed into the casting unit each code evokes a unique letter cast from hot metal by a special matrix.

mon·o·typ·ic (mon′ə tip′ik), *adj.* **1.** having only one type. **2.** of the nature of a monotype. **3.** *Biol.* having only one representative, as a genus with a single species. [1875–80; MONO- + TYPIC]

mon·o·un·sat·u·rate (mon′ō un sach′ər it), *n.* a monounsaturated fat or fatty acid, as olive oil. [MONO- + UNSATURATE]

mon·o·un·sat·u·rat·ed (mon′ō un sach′ə rā′tid), *adj. Nutrition.* of or noting a class of fats that lack a hydrogen bond at one point on the carbon chain and that are associated with a low cholesterol content of the blood. [1935–40; MONO- + UNSATURATED]

mon·o·va·lent (mon′ə vā′lənt), *adj.* **1.** *Chem.* univalent. **2.** *Immunol.* **a.** containing only one kind of antibody. **b.** pertaining to an antibody fragment with one antigen-binding site. [1865–70; MONO- + -VALENT] —**mon′o·va′lence, mon′o·va′len·cy,** *n.*

mon·o·vi·sion (mon′ə vizh′ən), *n.* the condition of seeing with one eye. [MONO- + VISION]

mon′ovision lens′es, *Ophthalm.* contact lenses that adjust one eye for farsightedness and the other for nearsightedness, used as an alternative to bifocal lenses.

mon·ox·ide (mon ok′sīd, mə nok′-), *n. Chem.* an oxide containing one oxygen atom in each molecule. [1865–70; MON- + OXIDE]

mon·o·zy·got·ic (mon′ə zī got′ik), *adj.* developed from a single fertilized ovum, as identical twins. Also, **mon·o·zy·gous** (mon′ə zī′gəs). [1915–20; MONO- + ZYGOTIC] —**mon·o·zy·gote** (mon′ə zī′gōt), *n.*

Mon·roe (mən rō′), *n.* **1. Harriet,** 1861?–1936, U.S. editor and poet. **2. James,** 1758–1831, 5th president of the U.S. 1817–25. **3. Marilyn** (*Norma Jean Baker* or *Mortenson*), 1926–62, U.S. film actress. **4.** a city in N

Louisiana. 57,597. **5.** a city in SE Michigan, on Lake Erie. 23,531. **6.** a town in SW Connecticut. 14,010. **7.** a city in S North Carolina. 12,639. **8.** a town in S Wisconsin. 10,027. **9. Fort.** See **Fort Monroe. 10.** a male given name.

Monroe′ Doc′trine, *U.S. Hist.* the policy, as stated by President Monroe in 1823, that the U.S. opposed further European colonization of and interference with independent nations in the Western Hemisphere.

Mon·roe·ville (mən rō′vil), *n.* a city in SW Pennsylvania, near Pittsburgh. 30,977.

Mon·ro·vi·a (mən rō′vē ə), *n.* **1.** a seaport in and the capital of Liberia, in W Africa. 204,000. **2.** a city in SW California. 30,531.

mons (monz), *n., pl.* **mon·tes** (mon′tēz). *Anat.* **1.** an area of the body that is higher than neighboring areas. **2.** See **mons pubis. 3.** See **mons veneris.** [1615–25; < NL; L *mōns* mountain, hill; see MOUNT²]

Mons (môNs), *n.* a city in Belgium. 61,732.

Mons., Monsieur.

Mon·sar·rat (mon′sə rat′), *n.* **Nicholas,** 1910–79, English novelist in Canada.

Mon·sei·gneur (môN se nyœr′), *n., pl.* **Mes·sei·gneurs** (mā se nyœr′). **1.** a French title of honor given to princes, bishops, and other persons of eminence. **2.** a person bearing this title. Also, **mon·sei·gneur′.** [1590–1600; < F: my lord; see SEIGNEUR]

mon·sieur (mə syûr′; *Fr.* mə syœ′), *n., pl.* **mes·sieurs** (mās yûrz′, mes′ərz; *Fr.* me syœ′). the conventional French title of respect and term of address for a man, corresponding to *Mr.* or *sir.* [1490–1500; < F: lit., my lord (orig. applied only to men of high station); see SIRE]

Mon·si·gnor (mon sē′nyər; *It.* môn′sē nyôr′), *n., pl.* **Mon·si·gnors,** *It.* **Mon·si·gno·ri** (môn′sē nyô′rē). *Rom. Cath. Ch.* **1.** a title conferred upon certain prelates. **2.** a person bearing this title. Also, **mon·si′gnor.** [1635–45; < It < F *Monseigneur* MONSEIGNEUR; see SIGNOR] **—mon·si·gno·ri·al** (mon′sēn yôr′ē əl, -yōr′-), *adj.*

mon·soon (mon sōōn′), *n.* **1.** the seasonal wind of the Indian Ocean and southern Asia, blowing from the southwest in summer and from the northeast in winter. **2.** (in India and nearby lands) the season during which the southwest monsoon blows, commonly marked by heavy rains; rainy season. **3.** any wind that changes directions with the seasons. **4.** any persistent wind established between water and adjoining land. [1575–85; < D *monssoen* (now obs.) < Pg *monção,* earlier *moução* < Ar *mawsim* season] **—mon·soon′al,** *adj.*

mon′soon low′, the seasonal low found over most continents in summer and, to a lesser extent, over adjacent ocean areas in winter.

mons pu·bis (monz′ pyōō′bis), *pl.* **mon·tes pu·bis** (mon′tēz pyōō′bis). *Anat.* a rounded prominence of fatty tissue over the pubic symphysis, covered with hair after puberty. Also called **mons.** Cf. **mons veneris.** [< NL: elevation of the pubes; see MONS, PUBES¹]

mon·ster (mon′stər), *n.* **1.** a legendary animal combining features of animal and human form or having the forms of various animals in combination, as a centaur, griffin, or sphinx. **2.** any creature so ugly or monstrous as to frighten people. **3.** any animal or human grotesquely deviating from the normal shape, behavior, or character. **4.** a person who excites horror by wickedness, cruelty, etc. **5.** any animal or thing huge in size. **6.** *Biol.* **a.** an animal or plant of abnormal form or structure, as from marked malformation or the absence of certain parts or organs. **b.** a grossly anomalous fetus or infant, esp. one that is not viable. **7.** anything unnatural or monstrous. **—***adj.* **8.** huge; enormous; monstrous: *a monster tree.* [1250–1300; ME *monstre* < L *mōnstrum* portent, unnatural event, monster, equiv. to *mon(ēre)* to warn + *-strum* n. suffix] **—mon′ster·like′,** *adj.*
—Syn. 4. fiend, brute, demon, devil, miscreant.

mon·ster·a (mon′stər ə), *n.* any of various tropical American climbing plants belonging to the genus *Monstera,* of the arum family, esp. *M. deliciosa,* having split or perforated leaves and often grown as a houseplant. [< NL (1763), appar. irreg. deriv. of L *mōnstrum* MONSTER; see -A²]

mon·strance (mon′strəns), *n. Rom. Cath. Ch.* a receptacle in which the consecrated Host is exposed for adoration. Also called **ostensorium, ostensory.** [1250–1300; ME < ML *mōnstrantia,* equiv. to *mōnstr(āre)* to show (see MUSTER) + *-antia* -ANCE]

mon·stros·i·ty (mon stros′i tē), *n., pl.* **-ties. 1.** the state or character of being monstrous. **2.** a monster or something monstrous. [1545–55; < LL *mōnstrōsitās,* equiv. to L *mōnstrōs(us)* MONSTROUS + *-itās* -ITY]

mon·strous (mon′strəs), *adj.* **1.** frightful or hideous, esp. in appearance; extremely ugly. **2.** shocking or revolting; outrageous: *monstrous cruelty.* **3.** extraordinarily great; huge; immense: *a monstrous building.* **4.** deviating grotesquely from the natural or normal form or type. **5.** having the nature or appearance of a fabulous monster. **—***adv.* **6.** extremely; exceedingly; very. [1350–1400; ME < L *mōnstrōsus.* See MONSTER, -OUS] **—mon′strous·ly,** *adv.* **—mon′strous·ness,** *n.*
—Syn. 1, 2. horrible, atrocious. **3.** See **gigantic.**

mons ve·ne·ris (monz′ ven′ər is), *pl.* **mon·tes ve·ne·ris** (mon′tēz ven′ər is), *Anat.* the mons pubis of the human female. Also called **mons.** [1615–25; < NL: lit., Venus's mount]

Mont., Montana.

Mon·ta·dale (mon′tə dāl′), *n.* one of a breed of white-faced, hornless sheep developed in the U.S. by crossing Cheviot rams and Columbia ewes, noted for their meat and heavy fleece. [1945–50; MONTA(NA) + *-dale,* as in CORRIEDALE]

mon·tage (mon täzh′; *Fr.* môN tazh′), *n., pl.* **-tag·es** (-tä′zhiz; *Fr.* -tazh′), *v.,* **-taged** (-täzhd), **tag·ing** (-tä′zhing). **—***n.* **1.** the technique of combining in a single composition pictorial elements from various sources, as parts of different photographs or fragments of printing, either to give the illusion that the elements belonged together originally or to allow each element to retain its separate identity as a means of adding interest or meaning to the composition. Cf. **collage** (def. 1). **2.** photomontage. **3.** *Motion Pictures, Television.* **a.** juxtaposition or partial superimposition of several shots to form a single image. **b.** a technique of film editing in which this is used to present an idea or set of interconnected ideas. **4.** any combination of disparate elements that forms or is felt to form a unified whole, single image, etc. **—***v.t.* **5.** to make or incorporate into a montage. [1920–25; < F, equiv. to *mont(er)* to MOUNT¹ + *-age* -AGE]

Mon·ta·gnais (mon′tən yā′, môN′-), *n., pl.* **-ta·gnais** (-tən yā′, -yāz′) for 1. **1.** a member of an American Indian people of Quebec and Labrador. **2.** the Algonquian language of the Montagnais, closely related to Cree.

Mon·ta·gnard (mon′tən yärd′, -yär′), *n., pl.* **-gnards,** (*esp. collectively*) **-gnard.** (*sometimes l.c.*) a member of a dark-skinned people of mixed ethnic origins inhabiting the highland areas of Vietnam. [1835–45; < F: lit., mountaineer. See MOUNTAIN, -ARD]

Mon·ta·gu (mon′tə gyōō′), *n.* **1. Ashley** (*Montague Francis Ashley Montagu*), born 1905, U.S. anthropologist and writer, born in England. **2. Charles, 1st Earl of Halifax,** 1661–1715, British statesman: prime minister 1714–15. **3. Lady Mary Wort·ley** (wûrt′lē), (*Mary Pierrepont*), 1689–1762, English author.

Mon·ta·gue (mon′tə gyōō′), *n.* **1.** (in Shakespeare's *Romeo and Juliet*) the family name of Romeo. Cf. **Capulet. 2. William Pep·per·ell** (pep′ər əl), 1873–1953, U.S. philosopher. **3.** a male given name.

Mon·taigne (mon tān′; *Fr.* môN ten′yᵊ), *n.* **Mi·chel Ey·quem** (mē shel′ e kem′), **Seigneur de,** 1533–92, French essayist.

Mon·ta·le (môn tä′le), *n.* **E·u·ge·nio** (e′ōō je′nyô), 1896–1981, Italian poet: Nobel prize 1975.

Mon·tal·vo (môn täl′vô), *n.* **Gar·ci Or·dó·ñez de** (gäR thē′ ôR thô′nyeth the), 15th-century Spanish writer.

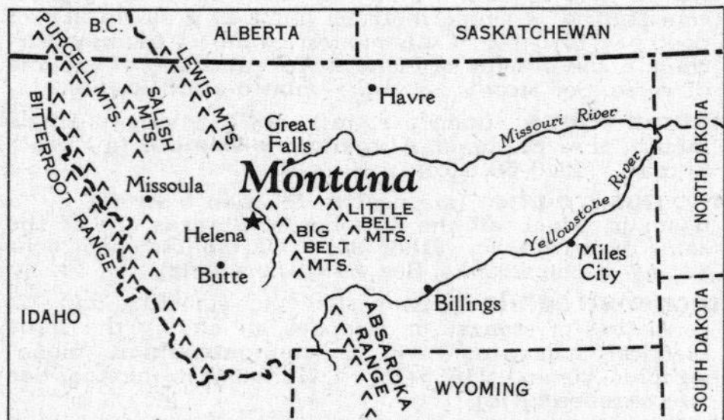

Mon·tan·a (mon tan′ə), *n.* a state in the NW United States. 786,690; 147,138 sq. mi. (381,085 sq. km). *Cap.:* Helena. *Abbr.:* MT (for use with zip code), Mont. **—Mon·tan′an,** *adj., n.*

mon·tane (mon′tān), *Ecol.* **—***adj.* **1.** pertaining to, growing in, or inhabiting mountainous regions. **—***n.* **2.** the lower vegetation belt on mountains. [1860–65; < L *montānus,* equiv. to *mont-* (s. of *mōns*) MOUNT² + *-ānus* -ANE]

mon·ta·ni sem·per li·be·ri (mōn tä′nē sem′peR lē′be Rē; *Eng.* mon tā′nī sem′pər lib′ə rī′), *Latin.* mountaineers (are) always free: motto of West Virginia.

mon′tan wax′ (mon′tan), a dark-brown bituminous wax extracted from lignite and peat: used chiefly in polishes and waxes for furniture, shoes, etc. Also called **lignite wax.** [1905–10; < L *montānus* of a mountain (see MONTANE)]

Mon·tau·ban (môN tō bäN′), *n.* a city in and the capital of Tarn-et-Garonne, in S France, N of Toulouse. 50,420.

Mon′tauk Point′ (mon′tôk), the SE end of Long Island, in SE New York.

Mont Blanc (môN bläN′), a mountain in SE France, near the Italian border: highest peak of the Alps, 15,781 ft. (4810 m). Italian, **Monte Bianco.**

Mont·calm (mont käm′; *Fr.* môN kalm′), *n.* **Louis Jo·seph** (lwē zhō zef′), 1712–59, French general in Canada.

Mont Cer·vin (môN seR vaN′), French name of **Matterhorn.**

Mont·clair (mont clâr′), *n.* **1.** a city in NE New Jersey. 38,321. **2.** a city in SE California. 22,628.

Mont-de-Mar·san (môNdᵊ maR säN′), *n.* a city in and the capital of Landes in SW France. 30,171.

mont-de-pié·té (môNdᵊ pyā tā′), *n., pl.* ***monts-de-pié·té*** (môNdᵊ pyā tā′). *French.* a public pawnbroking establishment that lends money on reasonable terms, esp. to the poor.

mon·te (mon′tē), *n. Cards.* **1.** Also called **mon′te bank′.** a gambling game played with a 40-card pack in which players bet that one of two layouts, each consisting of two cards drawn from either the top or bottom of the deck and turned face up, will be matched in suit by the next card turned up. **2.** See **three-card monte** (def. 1). [1815–25; < Sp: mountain, hence, heap (of cards); see MOUNT²]

Mon·te (mon′tē), *n.* a male given name.

Mon·te Al·bán (môn′te äl bän′), a major ceremonial center of the Zapotec culture, near the city of Oaxaca, Mexico, occupied from 600 B.C. to A.D. 700.

Mon·te·bel·lo (mon′tə bel′ō), *n.* a city in SW California, SE of Los Angeles. 52,929.

Mon·te Bian·co (môn′te byäng′kô), Italian name of **Mont Blanc.**

mon·te·bra·site (mon′tē brä′zīt), *n.* a mineral, lithium aluminum hydroxyl phosphate, $LiAlPO_4(OH)$, isomorphous with amblygonite, used as an ore of lithium. [1870–75; after *Montebras,* locale in central France (Creuse); see -ITE¹]

Mon·te Car·lo (mon′tē kär′lō, -ti; *It.* môn′te kär′lô), **1.** a town in Monaco principality, in SE France: gambling resort. 10,000. **2.** *Statistics.* of, pertaining to, or using a Monte Carlo method, as a Monte Carlo simulation or solution.

Mon′te Car′lo meth′od, *Statistics.* a technique for numerically approximating the solution of a mathematical problem by studying the distribution of some random variable, often generated by a computer. [1945–50; alluding to the randomness of such a method, as characteristic of the games of chance played at MONTE CARLO]

Mon·te Cas·si·no (môn′te käs sē′nô), a monastery at Cassino, Italy: founded A.D. c530 by St. Benedict and destroyed by Allied bombings in 1944.

Mon·te Cor·no (môn′te kôR′nô), a mountain in central Italy: highest peak in the Apennines, 9585 ft. (2922 m).

Mon·te Cris·to (mon′tē kris′tō), a sandwich containing slices of ham, chicken, and Swiss cheese, dipped in beaten egg and fried until brown.

Mon·te·fia·sco·ne (môn′te fyäs kô′ne), *n.* a town in central Italy: wine-growing area. 12,214.

Mon·te′go Bay′ (mon tē′gō), a city in NW Jamaica: seaside resort. 50,000.

mon·teith (mon tēth′), *n.* **1.** a large punch bowl, usually of silver, having a notched rim for suspending punch cups. **2.** Also called **bonnet glass.** a small stemless glass of the 18th century, having a bowl with a compoundly curved profile upon a broad foot. [1675–85; said to have been named after *Monteigh,* a Scotsman who wore a coat or cloak with a notched hem]

Mon·te·ne·gro (mon′tə nē′grō, -neg′rō), *n.* a constituent republic of Yugoslavia, in the SW part: an independent kingdom 1878–1918. 615,000; 5333 sq. mi. (13,812 sq. km). *Cap.:* Podgorica. Serbo-Croatian, **Crna Gora. —Mon·te·ne·grin** (mon′tə nē′grin, -neg′rin), *adj., n.*

Mon·te·rey (mon′tə rā′), *n.* **1.** a city in W California, on Monterey Bay: the capital of California until 1847. 27,558. **2.** See **Monterey Jack.**

Mon′terey Bay′, an inlet of the Pacific in W California. 26 mi. (42 km) long.

Mon′terey cy′press, a tree, *Cupressus macrocarpa,* of southern California, being pyramid-shaped in youth, but spreading in age: occurs naturally in only two groves on the coast of Monterey County, California, but is cultivated extensively. [1870–75]

Mon′terey Jack′, a mild, moist cheddar, made from whole, skimmed, or partially skimmed milk: first made in Monterey County, California. Also called **jack cheese.** [1945–50, *Amer.*]

Mon′terey Park′, a city in SW California, E of Los Angeles. 54,338.

Mon′terey pine′, a pine tree, *Pinus radiata,* native to coastal California, having cones that open to germinate only in the heat of a forest fire, used for reforestation and as a timber tree. [1825–35]

Mon·te·rí·a (môn′tə Rē′ä), *n.* a city in N Colombia. 123,600.

mon·te·ro (mon târ′ō; *Sp.* môn te′Rô), *n., pl.* **-te·ros** (-târ′ōz; *Sp.* -te′Rôs). a Spanish hunter's cap, round in shape and having an earflap. [1615–25; < Sp, special use of *montero* huntsman, lit., mountaineer, equiv. to *monte* MOUNT² + *-ero* < L *-ārius* -ARY]

Mon·ter·rey (mon′tə rā′; *Sp.* môn′teR Rā′), *n.* a city in and the capital of Nuevo León, in NE Mexico: battle 1846. 1,500,000.

Mon·tes Ap·en·ni·nus (mon′təs ap′ə nī′nəs), a mountain range in the first and second quadrants of the visible face of the moon, forming the SE border of Mare Imbrium: about 600 miles (970 km) long.

Mon·tes Cla·ros (môN′tis klä′Rōōs), a city in E Brazil. 121,428.

Mon·tes·pan (mon′tə span′; *Fr.* môN tes päN′), *n.* **Marquise de** (*Françoise Athénaïs de Rochechouart*), 1641–1707, mistress of Louis XIV of France.

CONCISE ETYMOLOGY KEY: <, descended or borrowed from; >, whence; b., blend of, blended; c., cognate with; cf., compare; deriv., derivative; equiv., equivalent; imit., imitative; obl., oblique; r., replacing; s., stem; sp., spelling, spelled; resp., respelling, respelled; trans., translation; ?, origin unknown; *, unattested; ‡, probably earlier than. See the full key inside the front cover.

Mon•tes•quieu (mon′tə skyōō′; *Fr.* môɴ tes kyœ′), *n.* (*Charles Louis de Secondat, Baron de la Brède et de Montesquieu*) 1689–1755, French philosophical writer.

Mon•tes Riph•ae•us (mon′tēz rif′ē əs), a mountain range in the third quadrant of the visible face of the moon.

Mon•tes•so•ri (mon′tə sôr′ē, -sōr′ē; *It.* môn′tes sô′rē), *n.* **Ma•ri•a** (mə rē′ə; *It.* mä rē′ä), 1870–1952, Italian educator.

Montesso′ri meth′od, a system for teaching young children, in which the fundamental aim is self-motivated education by the children themselves, as they are encouraged to move freely through individualized instruction and physical exercises, accompanied by special emphasis on the training of the senses and the early development of reading and writing skills. Also called **Montesso′ri sys′tem.** [1910–15; named after M. MONTESSORI] —**Mon′tes•so′ri•an,** *adj.*

Mon•teux (mon tœ′; *Fr.* môɴ tœ′), *n.* **Pierre** (pyer), 1875–1964, U.S. symphony orchestra conductor born in France.

Mon•te•ver•di (mon′tə vâr′dē; *It.* môn′te ver′dē), *n.* **Clau•dio** (klou′dyô), 1567–1643, Italian composer.

Mon•te•vi•de•o (mon′tə vi dā′ō, -vid′ē ō′; *Sp.* môn′te vē the′ô), *n.* a seaport in and the capital of Uruguay. 1,229,748.

Mon•tez (mon′tez, mon tez′), *n.* **Lola** (*Marie Dolores Eliza Rosanna Gilbert*), 1818?–61, British dancer, born in Ireland: gained notoriety as mistress of Franz Liszt, Alexandre Dumas *père,* and Louis I of Bavaria (1786–1868).

Mon•te•zu•ma II (mon′tə zōō′mə), c1470–1520, last Aztec emperor of Mexico 1502–20. Also, **Moctezuma.** [< Sp < Nahuatl *Motēuczōmah, Motēcuhzōmah,* equiv. to *mo-* reflexive pron. + *tēuc(tli)* lord, nobleman + *zōmah* frowned in anger, i.e., the one who became angry like a nobleman]

Montezu′ma's revenge′, *Slang.* traveler's diarrhea, esp. as experienced by some visitors to Mexico. [1960–65, *Amer.*; in allusion to MONTEZUMA II, who was killed by invading Europeans]

Mont•fort (mont′fərt; *Fr.* môɴ fôr′), *n.* **1. Si•mon de** (sē môɴ′ də), c1160–1218, French leader of the crusade against the Albigenses. **2.** his son **Simon de, Earl of Leicester,** 1208?–65, English soldier and statesman: leader of the Barons' War.

mont•gol•fi•er (mont gol′fē ər; *Fr.* môɴ gôl fyā′), *n., pl.* **-fi•ers** (-fē ərz; *Fr.* -fyā′). a balloon raised by air heated from a fire in the lower part. [1775–85; named after Joseph and Jacques MONTGOLFIER]

Mont•gol•fi•er (mont gol′fē ər; *Fr.* môɴ gôl fyā′), *n.* **Jacques É•tienne** (zhäk ā tyen′), 1745–99, and his brother **Jo•seph Mi•chel** (zhô zef′ mē shel′), 1740–1810, French aeronauts: inventors of the first practical balloon 1783.

Mont•gom•er•y (mont gum′ə rē, -gum′rē), *n.* **1. Bernard Law, 1st Viscount Montgomery of Alamein** ("*Monty*"), 1887–1976, British field marshal: World War II commander of British 8th Army in Africa and Europe. **2. Richard,** 1736–75, American Revolutionary general. **3.** a city in and the capital of Alabama, in the central part, on the Alabama River. 178,157. **4.** a town in SW Ohio. 10,088. **5.** Montgomeryshire. **6.** a male given name.

Mont•gom•er•y•shire (mont gum′ə rē shēr′, -shər, -gum′rē-), *n.* a historic county in Powys, in central Wales. Also called **Montgomery.**

Montgom′ery Vil′lage, a city in central Maryland. 18,725.

month (munth), *n.* **1.** Also called **calendar month.** any of the twelve parts, as January or February, into which the calendar year is divided. **2.** the time from any day of one calendar month to the corresponding day of the next. **3.** a period of four weeks or 30 days. **4.** Also called **solar month.** one-twelfth of a solar or tropical year. **5.** Also called **lunar month.** the period of a complete revolution of the moon around the earth, as the period between successive new moons **(synodic month),** equal to 29.531 days, or the period between successive conjunctions with a star **(sidereal month),** equal to 27.322 days, or the period between successive perigees **(anomalistic month),** equal to 27.555 days, or the period between successive similar nodes **(nodical month** or **draconic month),** equal to 27.212 days. **6.** an unusually long period of time of indefinite length: *I haven't seen him for months.* [bef. 900; ME; OE *mōnath;* c. OHG *mānōd,* ON *mānathr.* See MOON]

Mon•ther•lant (môɴ ter läɴ′), *n.* **Hen•ry de** (äɴ rē′ də), 1896–1972, French author.

month•ly (munth′lē), *adj., n., pl.* **-lies,** *adv.* —*adj.* **1.** pertaining to a month, or to each month. **2.** done, happening, appearing, etc., once a month: *a monthly magazine.* **3.** computed or determined by the month: *a monthly salary.* **4.** continuing or lasting for a month. —*n.* **5.** a periodical published once a month. **6.** Sometimes, **monthlies.** *Informal.* a menstrual period. —*adv.* **7.** once a month; by the month. [1525–35; MONTH + -LY]

month′ly meet′ing, (*often caps.*) a district unit of local congregations of the Society of Friends. [1765–75]

month's′ mind′, *Rom. Cath. Ch.* a Requiem Mass said on the thirtieth day after a person's death or burial. [1425–75; late ME *moneth mynde*]

mon•ti•cel•lite (mon′tə sel′īt, -chel′-), *n.* a mineral, silicate of magnesium and calcium, $CaMgSiO_4$, belonging to the olivine group and often occurring in contact metamorphosed limestones. [1825–35; named after T. *Monticelli* (1758–1846), Italian mineralogist; see -ITE[1]]

Mon•ti•cel•lo (mon′ti chel′ō, -sel′ō), *n.* the estate and residence of Thomas Jefferson, in central Virginia, near Charlottesville.

mon•ti•cule (mon′ti kyōōl′), *n.* **1.** a subordinate volcanic cone. **2.** a small mountain, hill, or mound. [1790–1800; < LL *monticulus,* equiv. to L *monti-* (s. of *mōns*) MOUNT[2] + *-culus* -CULE[1]] —**mon•tic•u•late** (mon tik′yə lit), **mon•tic′u•lous,** *adj.*

mon•til•la (mon til′ə; *Sp.* môn tē′lyä), *n.* a dry, rather bitter wine of Spain. [1785–95; after *Montilla,* Spanish town]

Mont•lu•çon (môɴ ly sôɴ′), *n.* a city in central France. 58,824.

Mont•ma•gny (*Fr.* môɴ ma nyē′), *n.* a city in S Quebec, in E Canada, on the St. Lawrence. 12,405.

Mont•mar•tre (môɴ mar′trᵊ), *n.* a hilly section in the N part of Paris, France: noted for the artists who have frequented and lived in the area.

Mont•mo•ren•cy (mont′mə ren′sē; *Fr.* môɴ mô räɴ sē′), *n.* **Anne** (an; *Fr.* an), **Duc de,** 1493–1567, French marshal: constable of France 1537.

mont•mo•ril•lon•ite (mont′mə ril′ə nīt′), *n.* any of a group of clay minerals characterized by the ability to expand when they absorb large quantities of water. Also called **smectite.** [1850–55; named after *Montmorillon,* France, where it was found; see -ITE[1]] —**mont•mo•ril•lon•it•ic** (mont′mə ril′ə nit′ik), *adj.*

Mont•par•nasse (môɴ par nas′), *n.* a district in S Paris, France, on the left bank of the Seine: noted for its cafés and the artists and writers who have frequented and lived in the area.

Mont•pel•ier (mont pēl′yər), *n.* a city in and the capital of Vermont, in the central part. 8241.

Mont•pel•lier (môɴ pe lyā′), *n.* a city in and the capital of Hérault, in S France, near the Mediterranean. 195,603.

Mon•tra•chet (mōn′trə shā′, mon′-; *Fr.* môɴ ra she′), a full-bodied dry white wine from the Montrachet vineyard in Burgundy.

Mont•re•al (mon′trē ôl′, mun′-), *n.* a seaport in S Quebec, in E Canada, on an island **(Mon′treal Is′land)** in the St. Lawrence. 1,080,546. French, **Mont•ré•al** (môɴ rā al′). —**Mont′re•al′er,** *n.*

Mon′treal′ canoe′, *Canadian.* a large freight canoe having a raised gunwale at the bow and stern. [1785–95]

Mon′treal North′, a city in S Quebec, in E Canada, N of Montreal. 94,914. French, **Mont•ré•al-Nord** (môɴ rā al nôr′).

Mon•treuil (môɴ trœ′yᵊ), *n.* a suburb of Paris, in N France. 96,684.

Mont•rose (mon trōz′), *n.* **James Graham, Marquis of,** 1612–50, Scottish supporter of Charles I.

Mont-Roy•al (*Fr.* môɴ rwa yal′), *n.* a town in S Quebec, in E Canada: suburb of Montreal. 19,247.

Mont-Saint-Mi•chel (môɴ saɴ mē shel′), *n.* a rocky islet near the coast of NW France, in an inlet of the Gulf of St. Malo: famous abbey and fortress. Also, **Mont Saint Michel′.**

Mont•ser•rat (mont′sə rat′; *for 2 also Sp.* môn′ser-rät′), *n.* **1.** an island in the Leeward Islands, in the SE West Indies: a British crown colony. 12,162; 39½ sq. mi. (102 sq. km). *Cap.:* Plymouth. **2.** a mountain in NE Spain, NW of Barcelona: the site of Montserrat Monastery. 4058 ft. (1237 m).

Mont•ville (mont′vil), *n.* a town in SE Connecticut. 16,455.

mon•u•ment (*n.* mon′yə mənt; *v.* mon′yə ment′), *n.* **1.** something erected in memory of a person, event, etc., as a building, pillar, or statue: *the Washington Monument.* **2.** any building, megalith, etc., surviving from a past age, and regarded as of historical or archaeological importance. **3.** any enduring evidence or notable example of something: *a monument to human ingenuity.* **4.** an exemplar, model, or personification of some abstract quality, esp. when considered to be beyond question: *a monument of middle-class respectability.* **5.** an area or a site of interest to the public for its historical significance, great natural beauty, etc., preserved and maintained by a government. **6.** a written tribute to a person, esp. a posthumous one. **7.** *Survey.* an object, as a stone shaft, set in the ground to mark the boundaries of real estate or to mark a survey station. **8.** a person considered as a heroic figure or of heroic proportions: *He became a monument in his lifetime.* **9. a.** *Obs.* a tomb; sepulcher. **b.** a statue. —*v.t.* **10.** to build a monument or monuments to; commemorate: *to monument the nation's war dead.* **11.** to build a monument on: *to monument a famous site.* [1250–1300; ME < L *monumentum,* equiv. to *mon-* (s. of *monēre* to remind, warn) + *-u-* (var. of *-i-* -I- before labials) + *-mentum* -MENT] —**mon′u•ment•less,** *adj.*

mon•u•men•tal (mon′yə men′tl), *adj.* **1.** resembling a monument; massive or imposing. **2.** exceptionally great, as in quantity, quality, extent, or degree: *a monumental work.* **3.** of historical or enduring significance: *a monumental victory.* **4.** *Fine Arts.* having the quality of being larger than life; of heroic scale. **5.** of or pertaining to a monument or monuments. **6.** serving as a monument. [1595–1605; < LL *monumentālis.* See MONUMENT, -AL[1]] —**mon′u•men′tal•ism,** *n.* —**mon′u•men•tal′i•ty,** *n.* —**mon′u•men′tal•ly,** *adv.*
—**Syn. 1.** immense, colossal.

mon•u•men•tal•ize (mon′yə men′tl īz′), *v.t.,* **-ized, -iz•ing.** to establish an enduring memorial or record of. Also, *esp. Brit.,* **mon′u•men′tal•ise′.** [1855–60; MONUMENTAL + -IZE] —**mon′u•men′tal•i•za′tion,** *n.*

mon•y (mon′ē), *adj., n. Scot. and North Eng.* many.

-mony, a suffix found on abstract nouns borrowed from Latin, usually denoting a status, role, or function (*matrimony; testimony*), or a personal quality or kind of behavior (*acrimony; sanctimony*). [< L *-mōnium* (denominal), *-mōnia* (usually deadjectival), presumably orig. derivatives with *-ium* -IUM, *-ia* -IA of *-mōn-,* an adj. or n. suffix, c. Gk *-mōn* (see HEGEMONY); cf. ALIMONY]

Mon•za (mon′zə; *It.* môn′tsä), *n.* a city in N Italy, NNE of Milan. 121,155.

Mon•zam•ba•no (*Ger.* mōn′tsäm bä′nō), *n.* **Se•ve•ri•nus de** (*Ger.* zā′vā rē′nōōs de), pseudonym of Samuel von Pufendorf.

mon•zo•nite (mon′zə nīt′), *n.* any of a group of granular igneous rocks having approximately equal amounts of orthoclase and plagioclase feldspar, intermediate in composition between syenite and diorite. [1880–85; < G *Monzonit,* named after *Monzoni,* mountain in Tyrol; see -ITE[1]] —**mon•zo•nit•ic** (mon′zə nit′ik), *adj.*

moo (mōō), *v.,* **mooed, moo•ing,** *n., pl.* **moos.** —*v.i.* **1.** to utter the characteristic deep sound of a cow; low. —*n.* **2.** a mooing sound. [1540–50; imit.]

mooch (mōōch), *Slang.* —*v.t.* **1.** to borrow (a small item or amount) without intending to return or repay it. **2.** to get or take without paying or at another's expense; sponge: *He always mooches cigarettes.* **3.** to beg. **4.** to steal. —*v.i.* **5.** to skulk or sneak. **6.** to loiter or wander about. —*n.* **7.** Also, **mooch′er.** a person who mooches. Also, **mouch.** [1425–75; late ME, appar. var. of ME *michen* < OF *muchier* to skulk, hide]

mood[1] (mōōd), *n.* **1.** a state or quality of feeling at a particular time: *What's the boss' mood today?* **2.** a distinctive emotional quality or character: *The mood of the music was almost funereal.* **3.** a prevailing emotional tone or general attitude: *the country's mood.* **4.** a frame of mind disposed or receptive, as to some activity or thing: *I'm not in the mood to see a movie.* **5.** a state of sullenness, gloom, or bad temper. [bef. 900; ME; OE *mōd* mind, spirit; courage; c. G *Mut,* Goth *mōths* courage, ON *mōthr* anger]
—**Syn. 1.** temper, humor, disposition, inclination.

mood[2] (mōōd), *n.* **1.** *Gram.* **a.** a set of categories for which the verb is inflected in many languages, and that is typically used to indicate the syntactic relation of the clause in which the verb occurs to other clauses in the sentence, or the attitude of the speaker toward what he or she is saying, as certainty or uncertainty, wish or command, emphasis or hesitancy. **b.** a set of syntactic devices in some languages that is similar to this set in function or meaning, involving the use of auxiliary words, as *can, may, might.* **c.** any of the categories of these sets: *the Latin indicative, imperative, and subjunctive moods.* **2.** *Logic.* a classification of categorical syllogisms by the use of three letters that name, respectively, the major premise, the minor premise, and the conclusion. Also called **mode.** [1525–35; special use of MOOD[1] by influence of MODE[1]]

mood-al•ter•ing (mōōd′ôl′tər ing), *adj.* (esp. of drugs) capable of changing one's emotional state.

mood′ mu′sic, music comprised chiefly of popular songs in lush orchestral arrangements, intended to provide a relaxing, soothing atmosphere. [1935–40]

mood•y (mōō′dē), *adj.,* **mood•i•er, mood•i•est. 1.** given to gloomy, depressed, or sullen moods; ill-humored. **2.** proceeding from or showing such a mood: *a moody silence.* **3.** expressing or exhibiting sharply varying moods; temperamental. [bef. 900; ME *mody,* OE *mōdig.* See MOOD[1], -Y[1]] —**mood′i•ly,** *adv.* —**mood′i•ness,** *n.*
—**Syn. 1.** sulky, morose, brooding; glowering.

Moo•dy (mōō′dē), *n.* **1. Dwight Ly•man** (lī′mən), 1837–99, U.S. evangelist. **2. Helen Wills.** See **Wills, Helen Newington. 3. William Vaughn** (vôn), 1869–1910, U.S. poet and playwright.

moo goo gai pan (mōō′ gōō′ gī′ pan′), *Cantonese Cookery.* a dish of sliced chicken stir-fried with button mushrooms and, often, assorted vegetables. [< dial. Chin; cf. Chin *mógu* Mongolian-type mushroom (prob. < Mongolian; cf. Dagur (Mongolian language of NW Manchuria) *muugee* mushroom), *ji* chicken (Guangdong dial. *gāi*), *piān* slice(s)]

Moog′ syn′thesizer (mōg), *Music, Trademark.* an electronic synthesizer. Also called **Moog.** [1965–70; named after Robert A. Moog (b. 1934), U.S. engineer]

moo′ juice′, *Facetious.* cow's milk.

mool (mōōl), *n. Scot. and North Eng.* **1.** soft, crumbly soil rich in mold or humus. **2.** earth from or for a grave. **3.** a grave. [1570–80; var. of MOLD[3]]

moo•la (mōō′lə), *n. Slang.* money. Also, **moo′lah.** [1905–10, *Amer.*; orig. uncert.]

mool•vee (mōōl′vē), *n.* maulvi. Also, **mool′vi.**

moon (mōōn), *n.* **1.** the earth's natural satellite, orbiting the earth at a mean distance of 238,857 miles (384,393 km) and having a diameter of 2160 miles (3476 km). **2.** this body during a particular lunar month, or during a certain period of time, or at a certain point of time, regarded as a distinct object or entity. Cf. **full moon, half-moon, new moon, waning moon, waxing moon.** See diag. on next page. **3.** a lunar month, or, in general, a month. **4.** any planetary satellite: *the moons of Jupiter.* **5.** something shaped like an orb or a crescent. **6.** moonlight. **7.** a platyfish. **8.** *Slang.* the buttocks, esp. when bared. **9. blue moon,** a very long period of time: *Such a chance comes once in a blue moon.* —*v.i.* **10.** to act or wander abstractedly or listlessly: *You've been mooning about all day.* **11.** to sentimentalize or remember nostalgically: *He spent the day mooning about his lost love.* **12.** to gaze dreamily or sentimentally at something or someone: *They sat there mooning into each other's eyes.* **13.** *Slang.* to expose one's buttocks suddenly and publicly as a prank or gesture of disrespect. —*v.t.* **14.** to spend (time) idly: *to moon the afternoon away.* **15.** to illuminate by or align against the moon. **16.** *Slang.* to expose one's buttocks to as a prank or gesture of disrespect. [bef. 900; ME *mone,* OE *mōna;* c. OHG *māno,* ON *māni,* Goth *mena;* akin to G *Mond* moon, L *mēnsis* month, Gk *mḗnē* moon, Skt *māsa* moon, month] —**moon′er,** *n.* —**moon′less,** *adj.*

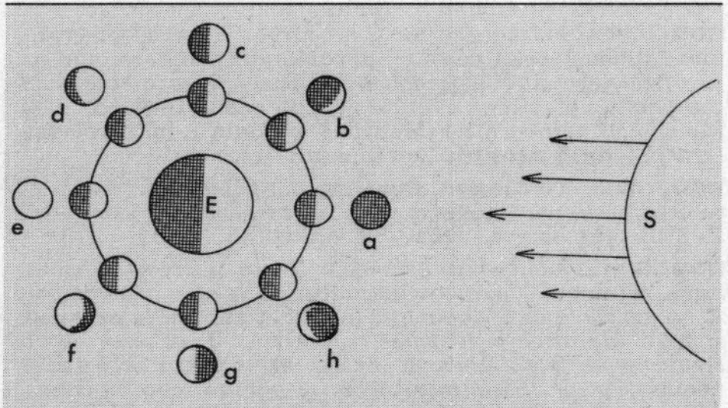

phases of the moon
figures on the inner circle show the moon in its orbit; those on the outer circle represent the moon's corresponding phases as seen from the earth; a, new moon (invisible); b, crescent (waxing moon); c, first quarter (half-moon); d, gibbous; e, full moon; f, gibbous; g, last quarter (half-moon); h, crescent (waning moon); S, sun; E, earth

Moon (mo͞on), *n.* **Sun Myung** (sun myung), born 1920, Korean religious leader: founder of the Unification Church.

Moon′ and Six′pence, The, a novel (1919) by W. Somerset Maugham.

moon•ball (mo͞on′bôl′), *n. Informal.* a high lob in tennis.

moon•beam (mo͞on′bēm′), *n.* a ray of moonlight. [1580–90; MOON + BEAM]

moon-blind (mo͞on′blīnd′), *adj. Vet. Pathol.* (of horses) afflicted with moon blindness; moon-eyed.

moon′ blind′ness, *Vet. Pathol.* a disease of horses in which the eyes suffer from recurring attacks of inflammation, eventually resulting in opacity and blindness. [1710–20]

moon•bow (mo͞on′bō′), *n.* a rainbow caused by the refraction and reflection of light from the moon. Also called **lunar rainbow.** [1890–95; MOON + (RAIN)BOW]

moon•calf (mo͞on′kaf′, -käf′), *n., pl.* **-calves. 1.** a congenitally grossly deformed and mentally defective person. **2.** a foolish person. **3.** a person who spends time idly daydreaming. [1555–65; MOON + CALF[1]]

moon•child (mo͞on′chīld′), *n., pl.* **-chil•dren.** a person born under the zodiacal sign of Cancer. [1965–70; MOON + CHILD; so called because of the astrological pairing of the moon with Cancer]

moon′ dog′, paraselene. [1660–70]

mooned (mo͞ond), *adj.* **1.** ornamented with moons or crescents. **2.** orb- or crescent-shaped. [MOON + -ED[3]]

moon•eye (mo͞on′ī′), *n., pl.* **-eyes. 1.** *Vet. Pathol.* an eye of a horse affected with moon blindness. **2.** any silvery, herringlike fish of the family Hiodontidae, esp. *Hiodon tergisus,* found in fresh waters from Hudson Bay to the lower Mississippi, having large eyes. [1600–10; MOON + EYE]

moon-eyed (mo͞on′īd′), *adj.* **1.** having the eyes open wide, as in fear or wonder; wide-eyed. **2.** *Vet. Pathol.* moon-blind. [1780–90 for def. 1; 1885–90 for def. 2]

moon-faced (mo͞on′fāst′), *adj.* having a very round face, regarded as resembling a full moon. [1610–20]

moon•fish (mo͞on′fish′), *n., pl.* (*esp. collectively*) **-fish,** (*esp. referring to two or more kinds or species*) **-fish•es. 1.** Also called **horsefish, horsehead.** any of several silvery marine fishes of the genus *Selene,* having a very compressed body and inhabiting shallow coastal waters. **2.** the opah. **3.** any of various other rounded, silvery fishes. [1640–50; MOON + FISH]

moon•flow•er (mo͞on′flou′ər), *n.* a plant, *Ipomoea alba,* of the morning glory family, having fragrant white flowers that bloom at night. [1780–90; MOON + FLOWER]

moon′ gate′, (in Chinese architecture) a circular gateway in a wall.

Moon•ie (mo͞o′nē), *n.* a member or follower of the Unification Church. [1970–75; Sun Myung Moon + -IE, with pun on MOONY]

moon•ish (mo͞o′nish), *adj.* **1.** capricious; inconstant. **2.** fully round or plump. [1375–1425; late ME *monish.* See MOON, -ISH[1]] —**moon′ish•ly,** *adv.*

moon′ jel′lyfish, a coelenterate, *Aurelia aurita,* inhabiting all seas, having a luminescent milky-pink or milky-orange, umbrellalike disk 3–9 in. (8–23 cm) in diameter. Also called **moon′ jel′ly.**

moon′ knife′, *Tanning.* a crescent-shaped knife used to scrape hides. [1880–85]

moon•let (mo͞on′lit), *n.* a small natural or artificial satellite, as one of a number of natural satellites thought to be embedded in the ring system of Saturn. [1825–35; MOON + -LET]

moon′ let′ter, *Arabic Gram.* any letter, as *bā* or *mīm,* representing a consonant that does not assimilate the *l* of a prefixed definite article. Cf. **sun letter.** [trans. of Ar *al-ḥurūf al-qamarīyah,* so called from the use of *al-qamar* (the moon) to illustrate nonassimilation of *l* in *al* the]

CONCISE ETYMOLOGY KEY: <, descended or borrowed from; >, whence; b., blend of, blended; c., cognate with; cf., compare; deriv., derivative; equiv., equivalent; imit., imitative; obl., oblique; r., replacing; s., stem; sp., spelling, spelled; resp., respelling, respelled; trans., translation; ?, origin unknown; *, unattested; ‡, probably earlier than. See the full key inside the front cover.

moon•light (mo͞on′līt′), *n., adj., v.,* **-light•ed, -light•ing.** —*n.* **1.** the light of the moon. —*adj.* **2.** pertaining to moonlight. **3.** illuminated by moonlight. **4.** occurring by moonlight, or at night. —*v.i.* **5.** to work at an additional job after one's regular, full-time employment, as at night. [1325–75; 1950–55 for def. 5; ME *monelight*] —**moon′light′er,** *n.*

moon•lit (mo͞on′lit′), *adj.* lighted by the moon. [1820–30; MOON + LIT[1]]

moon′ pil′lar, *Astron.* a halo phenomenon in which a vertical streak of light appears above and below the moon, believed to be caused by the reflection of moonlight by ice crystals with vertical axes. Cf. **sun pillar.**

moon•probe (mo͞on′prōb′), *n.* an information-gathering spacecraft designed to pass close by or land on the lunar surface. [1955–60; MOON + (SPACE) PROBE]

moon•quake (mo͞on′kwāk′), *n.* a seismic vibration of the moon's surface. [1935–40; MOON + (EARTH)QUAKE]

moon•rak•er (mo͞on′rā′kər), *n.* **1.** Also called **moonsail** (mo͞on′səl, -sāl′). *Naut.* a light square sail set above a skysail. **2.** a simpleton. [1780–90; MOON + RAKER]

moon•rise (mo͞on′rīz′), *n.* **1.** the rising of the moon above the horizon. **2.** the time at which the moon rises above the horizon. [1720–30; MOON + (SUN)RISE]

moon•rock (mo͞on′rok′), *n.* a sample of lunar material. [1965–70; MOON + ROCK[1]]

moon•roof (mo͞on′ro͞of′, -ro͝of′), *n., pl.* **-roofs.** a transparent section of an automobile roof that can be propped open, removed entirely, or remain fixed within the roof. Cf. **sunroof.** [1965–70; MOON + ROOF]

moon•scape (mo͞on′skāp′), *n.* **1.** the general appearance of the surface of the moon. **2.** an artistic representation of it. **3.** a land area that resembles the surface of the moon, esp. in barrenness and desolation. [1925–30; MOON + (LAND)SCAPE]

moon•seed (mo͞on′sēd′), *n.* **1.** any climbing plant of the genus *Menispermum,* having greenish-white flowers and crescent-shaped seeds. **2.** See **Carolina moonseed.** [1730–40; MOON + SEED]

moon•set (mo͞on′set′), *n.* **1.** the setting of the moon below the horizon. **2.** the time at which the moon disappears below the horizon. [1835–45; MOON + (SUN)SET]

moon•shee (mo͞on′shē), *n.* munshi.

moon′ shell′, 1. any marine gastropod of the family Naticidae, having a rounded, short-spired, smooth shell. **2.** the shell itself. [1935–40]

moon•shine (mo͞on′shīn′), *n.* **1.** *Informal.* smuggled or illicitly distilled liquor, esp. corn liquor as illicitly distilled chiefly in rural areas of the southern U.S. **2.** empty or foolish talk, ideas, etc.; nonsense. **3.** the light of the moon; moonlight. [1375–1425; late ME: moonlight. See MOON, SHINE]

moon•shin•er (mo͞on′shī′nər), *n. Informal.* **1.** a person who distills or sells liquor, esp. corn liquor, illegally. **2.** a person who pursues any illegal trade or activity at night. [1855–60, *Amer.;* MOONSHINE + -ER[1]]

moon•shot (mo͞on′shot′), *n.* the act or procedure of launching a rocket or spacecraft to the moon. Also, **moon′ shot′.** [1955–60, *Amer.;* MOON + SHOT[1]]

moon•stone (mo͞on′stōn′), *n.* **1.** Also called **precious moonstone.** a semitransparent or translucent, opalescent, pearly-blue variety of adularia, used as a gem. **2.** any of several adularescent feldspars, as certain varieties of albite, labradorite, or oligoclase, used as gems. **3.** (not used technically) any milky or girasol stone used as a gem. [1625–35; MOON + STONE]

moon•struck (mo͞on′struk′), *adj.* **1.** mentally deranged, supposedly by the influence of the moon; crazed. **2.** dreamily romantic or bemused. Also, **moon•strick•en** (mo͞on′strik′ən). [1665–75; MOON + STRUCK]

moon•walk (mo͞on′wôk′), *n.* **1.** an exploratory walk by an astronaut on the surface of the moon. —*v.i.* **2.** (of an astronaut) to walk on the surface of the moon. [1965–70, *Amer.;* MOON + WALK] —**moon′walk′er,** *n.*

moon•ward (mo͞on′wərd), *adv.* **1.** Also, **moon′wards.** toward the moon: *turned their eyes moonward.* —*adj.* **2.** directed toward the moon: *the moonward flight of the rocket.* [1850–55; MOON + -WARD]

moon•wort (mo͞on′wûrt′, -wôrt′), *n.* **1.** any fern of the genus *Botrychium,* esp. *B. lunaria,* a rare fern having fronds with crescent-shaped leaflets. **2.** honesty (def. 4). [1570–80; MOON + WORT[2]]

moon•y (mo͞o′nē), *adj.,* **moon•i•er, moon•i•est. 1.** dreamy, listless, or silly. **2.** pertaining to or characteristic of the moon. **3.** moonlit. [1580–90; MOON + -Y[1]] —**moon′i•ly,** *adv.* —**moon′i•ness,** *n.*

moor[1] (mo͝or), *n.* **1.** a tract of open, peaty, wasteland, often overgrown with heath, common in high latitudes and altitudes where drainage is poor; heath. **2.** a tract of land preserved for game. [bef. 900; ME *more,* OE *mōr;* c. D *moer,* G *Moor* marsh] —**moor′y,** *adj.*

moor[2] (mo͝or), *v.t.* **1.** to secure (a ship, boat, dirigible, etc.) in a particular place, as by cables and anchors or by lines. **2.** to fix firmly; secure. —*v.i.* **3.** to moor a ship, small boat, etc. **4.** to be made secure by cables or the like. —*n.* **5.** the act of mooring. [1485–95; earlier *more,* akin to OE *mǣrels-* in *mǣrelsrāp* rope for mooring a ship; see MARLINE]

Moor (mo͝or), *n.* **1.** a Muslim of the mixed Berber and Arab people inhabiting NW Africa. **2.** a member of this group that invaded Spain in the 8th century A.D. and occupied it until 1492. [1350–1400; ME *More* < MF, var. of *Maure* < L *Maurus* < Gk *Maûros*]

moor•age (mo͝or′ij), *n.* **1.** a place for mooring. **2.** a charge or payment for the use of moorings. **3.** an act or instance of mooring or the state of being moored. [1640–50; MOOR[2] + -AGE]

moor•bird (mo͝or′bûrd′), *n.* moorfowl. [1805–15; MOOR[1] + BIRD]

moor′cock′, *Chiefly Brit.* the male red grouse. [1300–50; ME]

Moore (mo͝or, môr, mōr), *n.* **1. Archibald Lee** (*Archie*), born 1916?, U.S. boxer. **2. Clement Clarke,** 1779–1863, U.S. scholar and writer. **3. Douglas Stuart,** 1893–1969, U.S. composer. **4. E•li•a•kim Hastings** (i lī′ə kim), 1862–1932, U.S. mathematician. **5. George,** 1852–1933, Irish novelist, critic, and dramatist. **6. G(eorge) E(dward),** 1873–1958, English philosopher. **7. Gerald,** 1899–1987, British pianist. **8. Henry,** 1898–1986, English sculptor. **9. Sir John,** 1761–1809, British general. **10. John Bas•sett** (bas′it, -et), 1860–1947, U.S. jurist. **11. Marianne (Craig),** 1887–1972, U.S. poet and critic. **12. Stanford,** 1913–82, U.S. biochemist: Nobel prize for chemistry 1972. **13. Thomas,** 1779–1852, Irish poet. **14.** a city in central Oklahoma. 35,063.

moor•fowl (mo͝or′foul′), *n., pl.* **-fowls,** (*esp. collectively*) **-fowl.** *Chiefly Brit.* the red grouse. Also called **moorbird.** [1500–10; MOOR[1] + FOWL]

Moor•head (mo͝or′hed′, môr′-, mōr′-), *n.* a city in W Minnesota. 29,998.

moor•hen (mo͝or′hen′), *n.* **1.** Also called **water hen.** a common species of gallinule, *Gallinule chloropus,* of nearly worldwide distribution. **2.** any of several related gallinules. **3.** *Chiefly Brit.* the female red grouse. [1250–1300; ME *mor-hen.* See MOOR[1], HEN]

moor•ing (mo͝or′ing), *n.* **1.** the act of a person or thing that moors. **2.** Usually, **moorings.** the means by which a ship, boat, or aircraft is moored. **3. moorings,** a place where a ship, boat, or aircraft may be moored. **4.** Usually, **moorings.** one's stability or security: *After the death of his wife he lost his moorings.* [1375–1425; late ME; cf. MD *moor;* see MOOR[2], -ING[1]]

moor′ing bu′oy, *Naut.* a buoy to which ships or boats can be moored. [1800–10]

moor′ing mast′, the mast or tower to which a dirigible is moored. Also called **moor′ing tow′er.** [1915–20]

moor′ing rack′, *Naut.* a row of piles, connected at the tops, to which ships or boats can be moored.

moor′ing screw′, *Naut.* a broad, augerlike anchor used for securing buoys in soft-bottomed lakes, rivers, etc. Also called **screw anchor, screw mooring.**

Moor•ish (mo͝or′ish), *adj.* **1.** of or pertaining to the Moors. **2.** in the style of the Moors, as architecture or decoration. [1400–50; late ME *morys.* See MOOR, -ISH[1]]

Moor′ish arch′. See **horseshoe arch.**

Moor′ish i′dol, a black, white, and yellow fish, *Zanclus cornutus* (or *canescens*), inhabiting the tropical Indian and Pacific oceans, having a long snout and an elongated dorsal fin.

moor•land (mo͝or′lənd, -land′), *n. Chiefly Brit.* an area of moors, esp. country abounding in heather. [bef. 950; ME *more lond,* OE *mōrlond.* See MOOR[1], -LAND]

moor′ myr′tle. See **sweet gale.**

moose (mo͞os), *n., pl.* **moose. 1.** a large, long-headed mammal, *Alces alces,* of the deer family, having circumpolar distribution in the Northern Hemisphere, the male of which has enormous palmate antlers. **2.** (*cap.*) a member of a fraternal and benevolent organization **(Loyal Order of Moose).** [1595–1605, *Amer.;* < Eastern Abenaki *mos,* reinforced by cognates in other Algonquian languages, all < Proto-Algonquian **mo·swa*]

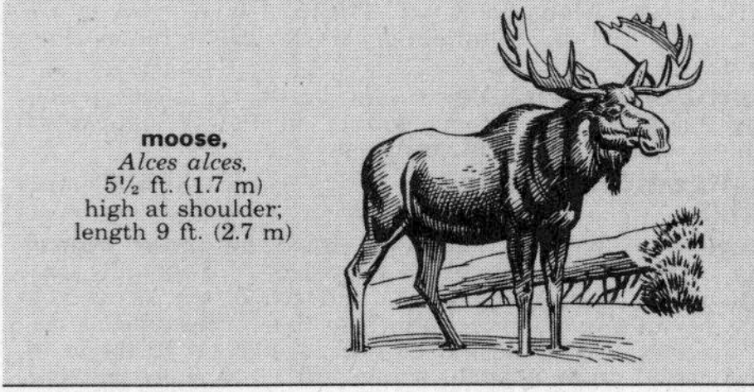

moose,
Alces alces,
5½ ft. (1.7 m)
high at shoulder;
length 9 ft. (2.7 m)

Moose′head Lake′ (mo͞os′hed′), a lake in central Maine. 42 mi. (68 km) long; 300 sq. mi. (780 sq. km).

Moose′ Jaw′, a city in S Saskatchewan, in SW Canada. 32,581.

moose•milk (mo͞os′milk′), *n. Canadian.* **1.** homemade or bootleg whiskey. **2.** a cocktail of whiskey or rum and milk. [1915–20; MOOSE + MILK]

moose•wood (mo͞os′wo͝od′), *n.* **1.** See **striped maple. 2.** leatherwood. [1770–80, *Amer.;* MOOSE + WOOD[1]]

moot[1] (mo͞ot), *adj.* **1.** open to discussion or debate; debatable; doubtful: *a moot point.* **2.** of little or no practical value or meaning; purely academic. **3.** *Chiefly Law.* not actual; theoretical; hypothetical. —*v.t.* **4.** to present or introduce (any point, subject, project, etc.) for discussion. **5.** to reduce or remove the practical significance of; make purely theoretical or academic. **6.** *Archaic.* to argue (a case), esp. in a mock court. —*n.* **7.** an assembly of the people in early England exercising political, administrative, and judicial powers. **8.** an argument or discussion, esp. of a hypothetical legal case. **9.** *Obs.* a debate, argument, or discussion. [bef. 900; ME *mot(e)* meeting, assembly, OE *gemōt;* c. ON *mōt,* D *gemoet* meeting. See MEET[1]] —**moot′er,** *n.* —**moot′ness,** *n.*
—**Syn. 1.** disputable, disputed, unsettled. **4.** debate, dispute, discuss. —**Ant. 1.** indisputable. **4.** agree.

moot[2] (mo͞ot), *n.* **1.** a ring gauge for checking the diameters of treenails. —*v.t.* **2.** to bring (a treenail) to the proper diameter with a moot. [1805–15; special use of dial. *moot* tree-stump, block of wood; c. D *moot* piece]

moot′ court′, a mock court for the conduct of hypothetical legal cases, as for students of law. [1780–90]

moot′ hall′, a building in some English villages where moots were once held; town hall. [1350–1400; ME]

mop[1] (mop), *n., v.,* **mopped, mop•ping.** —*n.* **1.** a bundle of coarse yarn, a sponge, or other absorbent material, fastened at the end of a stick or handle for washing floors, dishes, etc. **2.** a thick mass of hair. **3.** a polishing wheel having several layers of cloth secured by a boss. —*v.t.* **4.** to rub, wipe, clean, or remove with a mop (often fol. by *up*): *to mop up a spill.* **5.** to wipe as if with a mop: *to mop the face with a handkerchief.* —*v.i.* **6.** to clean or wipe with or as if with a mop (often fol. by *up*): *First he swept, then he mopped up.* **7. mop the floor with.** See **floor** (def. 15). **8. mop up, a.** *Mil.* to clear (ground, trenches, towns, etc.) of scattered or remaining enemy combatants after attacking forces have conquered the area. **b.** *Informal.* to dispose of; complete; finish: *He mopped up the rest of his business and went on a vacation.* [1375–1425; earlier *map,* late ME *mappe,* apocopated var. of *mappel* < ML *mappula* a cloth, equiv. to L *mapp(a)* napkin + *-ula* -ULE]

mop[2] (mop), *v.,* **mopped, mop•ping,** *n.* —*v.i.* **1.** to make a disappointed or unhappy face; grimace: *an unruly child that mops and mows.* —*n.* **2.** a wry face; grimace. [1560–70; akin to D *moppen* to pout]

mop•board (mop′bôrd′, -bōrd′), *n.* baseboard (def. 1). [1850–55, *Amer.*; MOP[1] + BOARD, so called because it adjoins the floor surface, which is cleaned by a mop]

mope (mōp), *v.,* **moped, mop•ing,** *n.* —*v.i.* **1.** to be sunk in dejection or listless apathy; sulk; brood. —*v.t.* **2.** to make dejected, listless, or apathetic. —*n.* **3.** a person who mopes or is given to moping. **4. mopes,** depressed spirits; blues. [1560–70; var. of MOP[2]] —**mop′er,** *n.* —**mop′ing•ly,** *adv.*

mo•ped (mō′ped′), *n.* a motorized bicycle that has pedals in addition to a low-powered gasoline engine designed for low-speed operation. [1955–60; < G, ult. < Sw (*trampcykel med*) *mo(tor och) ped(aler)* pedal cycle with engine and pedals]

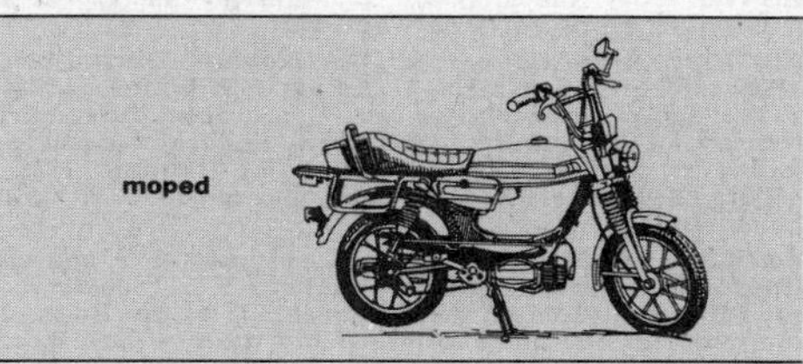
moped

mop•er•y (mō′pə rē), *n.* **1.** mopish behavior. **2.** *Slang.* a violation of a minor or imaginary law or rule. [MOPE + -ERY]

mop•ey (mō′pē), *adj.,* **mop•i•er, mop•i•est.** languishing, listless, droopy, or glum. Also, **mopy.** [1820–30; MOPE + -Y[1]] —**mop′i•ness,** *n.*

mop•ish (mō′pish), *adj.* given to moping; listless, apathetic, or dejected. [1615–25; MOPE + -ISH[1]] —**mop′ish•ly,** *adv.* —**mop′ish•ness,** *n.*

mop•per-up (mop′ər up′), *n., pl.* **mop•pers-up.** a person or thing that mops up. [1930–35; v. phrase *mop up* + -ER[1]]

mop•pet (mop′it), *n.* a young child. [1900–05; obs. *mop* rag doll, baby (see MOP[1]) + -ET]

mop•ping-up (mop′ing up′), *adj.* **1.** serving to complete or put the finishing touches to a phase of a particular action. **2.** serving to complete a military campaign by killing or capturing any remaining enemy troops: *a mopping-up operation.* [1905–10; *mop up* + -ING[1], used attributively]

M.Opt., Master of Optometry.

mop-up (mop′up′), *n.* the act, process, or an instance of mopping up; completion of an operation or action. [1895–1900; n. use of v. phrase *mop up*]

mop•y (mō′pē), *adj.,* **mop•i•er, mop•i•est.** mopey.

mo•quette (mō ket′), *n.* a type of fabric with a thick, velvety pile, used for carpets and in upholstering. [1755–65; < F, equiv. to *moc(ade)* imitation velvet + *-ette* -ETTE]

Mo•qui (mō′kē), *n., pl.* **-quis,** (*esp. collectively*) **-qui.** Moki.

MOR, middle-of-the-road (defs. 2, 3).

mor., morocco.

mo•ra (môr′ə, mōr′ə), *n., pl.* **mo•rae** (môr′ē, mōr′ē), **mo•ras.** *Pros.* the unit of time equivalent to the ordinary or normal short sound or syllable. [1560–70; < L: delay, hence, space of time]

mo•ra•ceous (mô rā′shəs, mō-), *adj.* belonging to the Moraceae, the mulberry family of plants. Cf. **mulberry family.** [< NL, *Morace(ae)* the type genus (L *mōrus* black mulberry tree) + *-aceae* -ACEAE) + -OUS]

Mo•ra•da•bad (môr′ə də bad′, mōr′-, mə rä′də bäd′), *n.* a city in N Uttar Pradesh, in N India. 272,355.

mo•rae•a (mə rē′ə), *n.* any of various plants belonging to the genera *Moraea* and *Dietes,* of the iris family, native to tropical Africa. [< NL (1758), irreg. after Robert *More* (1703–80), English plant collector; see -EA]

Mo•ra•ga (mə rä′gə), *n.* a city in W California. 15,014.

mo•raine (mə rān′), *n.* **1.** a ridge, mound, or irregular mass of unstratified glacial drift, chiefly boulders, gravel, sand, and clay. **2.** a deposit of such material left on the ground by a glacier. [1780–90; < F < Savoyard dial. *morêna* rise in the ground along the lower edge of a sloping field, equiv. to *mour(o)* mound, accumulation of earth (< **murr-* mound, elevation, appar. pre-L) + *-ena* suffix of landforms, prob. of pre-L orig.; cf. Upper It (Piedmont) *morena* heap of organic detritus, Sp *moreña* heap of stones, moraine] —**mo•rain′al, mo•rain′ic,** *adj.*

mor•al (môr′əl, mor′-), *adj.* **1.** of, pertaining to, or concerned with the principles or rules of right conduct or the distinction between right and wrong; ethical: *moral attitudes.* **2.** expressing or conveying truths or counsel as to right conduct, as a speaker or a literary work; moralizing: *a moral novel.* **3.** founded on the fundamental principles of right conduct rather than on legalities actment, or custom: *moral obligations.* **4.** capab conforming to the rules of right conduct: *a moral b* **5.** conforming to the rules of right conduct (oppose *immoral*): *a moral man.* **6.** virtuous in sexual mat chaste. **7.** of, pertaining to, or acting on the mind, ings, will, or character: *moral support.* **8.** resting upon convincing grounds of probability; virtual: *a moral certainty.* —*n.* **9.** the moral teaching or practical lesson contained in a fable, tale, experience, etc. **10.** the embodiment or type of something. **11. morals,** principles or habits with respect to right or wrong conduct. [1300–50; ME < L *mōrālis,* equiv. to *mōr-* (s. of *mōs*) usage, custom + *-ālis* -AL[1]] —**mor′al•less,** *adj.*
—**Syn. 5.** upright, honest, straightforward, open, virtuous, honorable. **11.** integrity, standards, morality. MORALS, ETHICS refer to rules and standards of conduct and practice. MORALS refers to generally accepted customs of conduct and right living in a society, and to the individual's practice in relation to these: *the morals of our civilization.* ETHICS now implies high standards of honest and honorable dealing, and of methods used, esp. in the professions or in business: *ethics of the medical profession.*

mo•rale (mə ral′), *n.* emotional or mental condition with respect to cheerfulness, confidence, zeal, etc., esp. in the face of opposition, hardship, etc.: *the morale of the troops.* [1745–55; < F, n. use of fem. of *moral* MORAL]

mor′al haz′ard, *Insurance.* an insurance company's risk as to the insured's trustworthiness and honesty. [1915–20]

mor•al•ism (môr′ə liz′əm, mor′-), *n.* **1.** the habit of moralizing. **2.** a moral maxim. **3.** emphasis, esp. undue emphasis, on morality. **4.** the practice of morality, as distinct from religion. [1820–30; MORAL + -ISM]

mor•al•ist (môr′ə list, mor′-), *n.* **1.** a person who teaches or inculcates morality. **2.** a philosopher concerned with the principles of morality. **3.** a person who practices morality. **4.** a person concerned with regulating the morals of others, as by imposing censorship. [1615–25; MORAL + -IST] —**mor′al•is′tic,** *adj.* —**mor′•al•is′ti•cal•ly,** *adv.*

mo•ral•i•ty (mə ral′i tē, mô-), *n., pl.* **-ties** for 4–6. **1.** conformity to the rules of right conduct; moral or virtuous conduct. **2.** moral quality or character. **3.** virtue in sexual matters; chastity. **4.** a doctrine or system of morals. **5.** moral instruction; a moral lesson, precept, discourse, or utterance. **6.** See **morality play.** [1350–1400; ME *moralite* < LL *mōrālitās.* See MORAL, -ITY]
—**Syn. 1.** See **goodness.**

moral′ity play′, an allegorical form of the drama current from the 14th to 16th centuries and employing such personified abstractions as Virtue, Vice, Greed, Gluttony, etc. Cf. **miracle play, mystery play.** [1925–30]

mor•al•ize (môr′ə līz′, mor′-), *v.,* **-ized, -iz•ing.** —*v.i.* **1.** to reflect on or express opinions about something in terms of right and wrong, esp. in a self-righteous or tiresome way. —*v.t.* **2.** to explain in a moral sense, or draw a moral from. **3.** to improve the morals of. Also, *esp. Brit.,* **mor′al•ise′.** [1350–1400; ME *moralisen* < ML *mōrālizāre.* See MORAL, -IZE] —**mor′al•i•za′tion,** *n.* —**mor′al•iz′er,** *n.* —**mor′al•iz′ing•ly,** *adv.*

mor•al•ly (môr′ə lē, mor′-), *adv.* **1.** in a moral manner. **2.** from a moral point of view: *morally reprehensible.* **3.** virtuously. **4.** virtually; practically. [1350–1400; ME; see MORAL, -LY]

Mor′al Major′ity, a political action group formed mainly of Protestant fundamentalists to further strict conservative aims, as strong antiabortion laws, the restoration of school prayer, the teaching of creationism in public schools, and the curbing of books and television programs considered antireligious or immoral. —**Mo′•ral Ma•jor•i•tar′i•an** (mə jôr′i târ′ē ən, -jor′-).

mor′al philos′ophy, philosophy dealing with the principles of morality; ethics. [1600–10]

Mor′al Re-Ar′ma•ment (rē är′mə mənt), a worldwide movement initiated by Frank Buchman in 1938 as a successor to the Oxford Group, and maintaining that the practice of high morality in public and private life is the key to world betterment. *Abbr.:* MRA

mor′al sense′, the ability to determine the rightness or wrongness of actions. [1690–1700]

mor′al theol′ogy, the branch of theology dealing with principles of moral conduct. [1900–05]

mor′al tur′pitude, 1. conduct that is regarded as immoral. **2.** an instance of such conduct. [1875–80]

Mo•ran•di (mô rän′dē), *n.* **Gior•gio** (jôr′jô), 1890–1964, Italian painter.

mo•rass (mə ras′), *n.* **1.** a tract of low, soft, wet ground. **2.** a marsh or bog. **3.** marshy ground. **4.** any confusing or troublesome situation, esp. one from which it is difficult to free oneself; entanglement. [1645–55; < D *moeras,* alter. (by assoc. with *moer* marsh; cf. MOOR[1]) of MD *maras* < OF *mareis* < Gmc. See MARSH]

mor•a•to•ri•um (môr′ə tôr′ē əm, -tōr′-, mor′-), *n., pl.* **-to•ri•a** (-tôr′ē ə, -tōr′-), **-to•ri•ums. 1.** a suspension of activity: *a moratorium on the testing of nuclear weapons.* **2.** a legally authorized period to delay payment of money due or the performance of some other legal obligation, as in an emergency. **3.** an authorized period of delay or waiting. [1870–75; < NL, LL *morātōrium,* n. use of neut. of *morātōrius* MORATORY]

mor•a•to•ry (môr′ə tôr′ē, -tōr′ē, mor′-), *adj.* authorizing delay of payment: *a moratory law.* [1890–95; < LL *morātōrius* dilatory, equiv. to *morā(rī)* to delay; see MORA + *-tōrius* -TORY[1]]

Mo•ra•tu•wa (mô rä′to͝o wə), *n.* a city in W Sri Lanka. 86,000.

Mo•ra•va (*Czech., Serbo-Croatian.* mô′rä vä), *n.* **1.** German, **March.** a river in central Europe flowing S from the NE Czech Republic, along part of the border between the Czech Republic and Slovakia, and Slovakia and Austria, into the Danube W of Bratislava. 240 mi. (385 km) long. **2.** a river in E Yugoslavia, flowing N to the Danube. 134 mi. (216 km) long. **3.** Czech name of **Moravia.**

Mo•ra•vi•a (mô rā′vē ə, -rä′-, mō-; *for 1 also It.* mô-rä′vyä), *n.* **1. Al•ber•to** (äl ber′tô), (*Alberto Pincherle*), 1907–90, Italian writer. **2.** Czech, **Morava.** German, **Mähren.** a region in the E Czech Republic: former province of Austria.

Mo•ra•vi•an (mô rā′vē ən, mō-), *adj.* **1.** pertaining to Moravia or its inhabitants. **2.** of or pertaining to the religious denomination of Moravians. —*n.* **3.** a native or inhabitant of Moravia. **4.** Also called **Herrnhuter.** a member of a Christian denomination descended from the Bohemian Brethren and holding that the Scriptures are the only rule of faith and practice. **5.** a dialect of Czech spoken in Moravia. [1545–55; MORAVI(A) + -AN] —**Mo•ra′vi•an•ism,** *n.*

Mora′vian Breth′ren, the Moravian Church.

Mora′vian Gate′, a mountain pass between the Sudeten Mountains and the Tatra range of the Carpathians, leading from S Poland into N Moravia in the NE Czech Republic.

Mo•rav•ská Os•tra•va (mô′räf skä ôs′trä vä), former name of **Ostrava.** German, **Mährisch-Ostrau.**

Mor•ax•el•la (môr′ək sel′ə), *n. Bacteriol.* a genus of rod-shaped, aerobic bacteria, certain species of which, as *M. lacunata,* are parasitic and pathogenic for humans and other warm-blooded animals. [< NL (1939), after Victor *Morax* (1899–1935), Swiss ophthalmologist, who isolated the type species; see -ELLA]

mo•ray (môr′ā, mor′ā; mô rā′, mō-), *n., pl.* **-rays.** any of numerous chiefly tropical eels of the family Muraenidae, having porelike gill openings and no pectoral fins. Also called **mo′ray eel′.** [1615–25, *Amer.*; < Pg *moréia* < L *mūraena* < Gk *mýraina* lamprey]

Mor•ay (mûr′ē), *n.* a historic county in NE Scotland, on Moray Firth. Formerly, **Elgin.**

Mor′ay Firth′, an arm of the North Sea projecting into the NE coast of Scotland. Inland portion ab. 30 mi. (48 km) long.

Mo•ra•zán (mô rä sän′), *n.* **Fran•cis•co** (frän sēs′kô), 1799–1842, Central American statesman and soldier, born in Honduras.

mor•bid (môr′bid), *adj.* **1.** suggesting an unhealthy mental state or attitude; unwholesomely gloomy, sensitive, extreme, etc.: *a morbid interest in death.* **2.** affected by, caused by, causing, or characteristic of disease. **3.** pertaining to diseased parts: *morbid anatomy.* **4.** gruesome; grisly. [1650–60; < L *morbidus* sickly, equiv. to *morb(us)* sickness + *-idus* -ID[4]] —**mor′bid•ly,** *adv.* —**mor′bid•ness,** *n.*
—**Syn. 2.** unwholesome, diseased, unhealthy, sick, sickly; tainted, corrupted, vitiated. —**Ant. 1.** cheerful. **2.** healthy.

mor•bi•dez•za (môr′bi det′sə; *It.* môr bē det′tsä), *n. Fine Arts.* the effect of extreme softness and delicacy in pictorial and sculptural representations. [1615–25; < It, equiv. to *morbid(o)* delicate (see MORBID) + *-ezza* -ICE]

mor•bid•i•ty (môr bid′i tē), *n.* **1.** a morbid state or quality. **2.** the proportion of sickness or of a specific disease in a geographical locality. [1715–25; MORBID + -ITY]

mor•bif•ic (môr bif′ik), *adj.* causing disease. Also, **mor•bif′i•cal.** [1645–55; < NL *morbificus,* equiv. to *morb(us)* sickness + *-i-* -I- + *-ficus* -FIC] —**mor•bif′i•cal•ly,** *adv.*

Mor•bi•han (môr bē än′), *n.* a department in W France. 563,588; 2738 sq. mi. (7090 sq. km). *Cap.:* Vannes.

mor•bil•li (môr bil′ī), *n.* (*used with a singular v.*) *Pathol.* measles (def. 1). [1685–95; < ML, pl. of *morbillus* pustule, equiv. to L *morb(us)* sickness + *-illus* dim. suffix]

mor•ceau (môr sō′), *n., pl.* **-ceaux** (-sō′). *French.* **1.** piece; morsel. **2.** an excerpt or passage of poetry or music.

mor•da•cious (môr dā′shəs), *adj.* **1.** biting or given to biting. **2.** sharp or caustic in style, tone, etc. [1640–50; < L *mordāci-* (s. of *mordāx* given to biting) + -OUS] —**mor•da′cious•ly,** *adv.* —**mor•dac•i•ty** (môr-das′i tē), *n.*

mor•dan•cy (môr′dn sē), *n.* the quality of being mordant; sharpness. [1650–60; MORD(ANT) + -ANCY]

mor•dant (môr′dnt), *adj.* **1.** sharply caustic or sarcastic, as wit or a speaker; biting. **2.** burning; corrosive. **3.** having the property of fixing colors, as in dyeing. —*n.* **4.** a substance used in dyeing to fix the coloring matter, esp. a metallic compound, as an oxide or hydroxide, that combines with the organic dye and forms an insoluble colored compound or lake in the fiber. **5.** an adhesive substance for binding gold or silver leaf to a surface. **6.** an acid or other corrosive substance used in etching to eat out the lines, areas, etc. **7.** *Music.* mordent. —*v.t.* **8.** to impregnate or treat with a mordant. [1425–75; late

ME < MF, prp. of *mordre* to bite << L *mordēre;* see -ANT] —**mor′dant·ly,** *adv.*
—**Syn. 1.** cutting, stinging, acerbic, scathing.

mor′dant rouge′, a solution of aluminum acetate in acetic acid, used in dyeing and calico printing. Also called **red liquor.**

Mor·de·cai (môr′di kī′, môr′di kā′ī), *n.* **1.** the cousin and guardian of Esther who delivered the Jews from the destruction planned by Haman. Esther 2–8. **2.** a male given name.

mor·dent (môr′dnt), *n. Music.* **1.** a melodic embellishment consisting of a rapid alternation of a principal tone with the tone a half or a whole step below it, called *single* or *short* when the auxiliary tone occurs once and *double* or *long* when this occurs twice or more. **2.** See **inverted mordent.** Also, **mordant.** [1800–10; < G < It *mordente* biting < L *mordent-,* s. of *mordēns,* prp. of *mordēre* to bite; see -ENT]

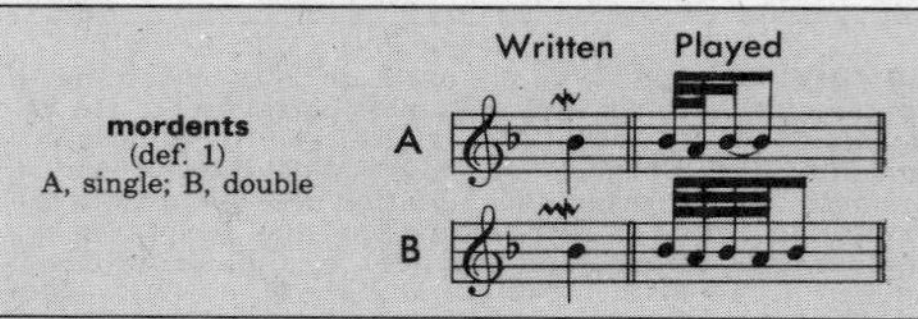

mordents (def. 1)
A, single; B, double

mor·di·da (môr thē′thä), *n., pl.* **-das** (-thäs). *Mexican Spanish.* a bribe or kickback. [lit., bite]

Mor·do′vi·an Auton′omous Repub′lic (môr dō′vē ən), an autonomous republic in the Russian Federation in Europe. 964,000; 9843 sq. mi. (25,493 sq. km). *Cap.:* Saransk. Also, **Mordvinian Autonomous Republic.**

Mor·dred (môr′dred), *n.* Modred.

Mord·vin (môrd′vin), *n.* **1.** a member of a Uralic people living in scattered communities in the middle Volga basin, esp. between Nizhni Novgorod and Saratov. **2.** the Finnic language of the Mordvin, with two major dialects, sometimes considered distinct languages. Also, **Mord·vin·i·an** (môrd vin′ē ən). [< Russ *mordvín,* deriv. of the collective n. *mordvá,* of uncert. orig.]

Mordvin′ian Auton′omous Repub′lic. See **Mordovian Autonomous Republic.**

more (môr, mōr), *adj., compar. of* **much** *or* **many** *with* **most** *as superl.* **1.** in greater quantity, amount, measure, degree, or number: *I need more money.* **2.** additional or further: *Do you need more time? More discussion seems pointless.* —*n.* **3.** an additional quantity, amount, or number: *I would give you more if I had it. He likes her all the more. When I could take no more of such nonsense, I left.* **4.** a greater quantity, amount, or degree: *More is expected of him. The price is more than I thought.* **5.** something of greater importance: *His report is more than a survey.* **6.** (*used with a plural v.*) a greater number of a class specified, or the greater number of persons: *More will attend this year than ever before.* —*adv. compar. of* **much** *with* **most** *as superl.* **7.** in or to a greater extent or degree (in this sense often used before adjectives and adverbs, and regularly before those of more than two syllables, to form comparative phrases having the same force and effect as the comparative degree formed by the termination *-er*): *more interesting; more slowly.* **8.** in addition; further; longer; again: *Let's talk more another time. We couldn't stand it any more.* **9.** moreover. **10. more and more,** to an increasing extent or degree; gradually more: *They became involved more and more in stock speculation.* **11. more or less, a.** to some extent; somewhat: *She seemed more or less familiar with the subject.* **b.** about; in substance; approximately: *We came to more or less the same conclusion.* [bef. 900; ME; OE *māra;* c. OHG *mēro,* ON *meiri,* Goth *maiza.* See MOST] —**more′ness,** *n.*

More (môr, mōr), *n.* **1. Hannah,** 1745–1833, English writer on religious subjects. **2. Paul Elmer,** 1864–1937, U.S. essayist, critic, and editor. **3. Sir Thomas,** 1478–1535, English humanist, statesman, and author: canonized in 1935.

Mo·ré (mə rā′), *n.* Mossi (def. 2).

Mo·re·a (mô rē′ə, mō-), *n.* Peloponnesus.

Mo·reau (mô rō′; *Fr.* mô rō′), *n.* **1. Gustave** (gys tav′), 1826–98, French painter. **2. Jeanne** (zhän), born 1928, French film actress. **3. Jean Vic·tor** (zhän vēk tôr′), 1763–1813, French general.

more dict., (in prescriptions) in the manner directed. Also, **mor. dict.** [< L *mōre dictū*]

mo·reen (mə rēn′), *n.* a heavy fabric of wool, or wool and cotton, with a ribbed face and a moiré finish, used for curtains, petticoats, etc. [1685–95; *mor-* (perh. var. of MOIRE) + (VELVET)EEN]

mo·rel[1] (mə rel′), *n.* any edible mushroom of the genus *Morchella,* esp. *M. esculenta.* [1665–75; < F, MF *morille,* perh. < VL **mauricula,* deriv. of ML *maurus* brown, dark-colored; see MOREL[2], -CULE[1]]

mo·rel[2] (mə rel′), *n.* any of several nightshades, esp. the black nightshade. Also, **mo·relle′.** [1350–1400; ME *morel(l)e* < AF < ML *morella,* equiv. to *maur(us)* brown, dark-colored (adj. use of L *Maurus* MOOR) + *-ella* -ELLE]

Mo·rel (mô rel′; *Fr.* mô rel′), *n.* **Jean** (zhän), 1903–75, French orchestra conductor.

Mo·re·lia (mô re′lyä), *n.* a city in and the capital of Michoacán, in central Mexico. 209,014.

mo·rel·lo (mə rel′ō), *n., pl.* **-los. 1.** a variety of sour cherry having dark-colored skin and juice. **2.** the tree bearing this fruit. [1640–50; perh. < It *amarello* AMARELLE, confused (in E) with It *morello* blackish. See MOREL[2]]

Mo·re·los (mô re′lôs), *n.* a state in S central Mexico. 866,000; 1916 sq. mi. (4960 sq. km). *Cap.:* Cuernavaca.

Mo·re·los y Pa·vón (mô re′lôs ē pä vôn′), **Jo·sé Ma·rí·a** (hô se′ mä rē′ä), 1765–1815, Mexican priest and revolutionary leader.

more·o·ver (môr ō′vər, mōr-, môr′ō′vər, mōr′-), *adv.* in addition to what has been said; further; besides. [1325–75; ME *more over.* See MORE, OVER]
—**Syn.** See **besides.**

Mo·re′ra's the′orem (mô râr′əz), *Math.* the theorem that a function is analytic in a simply connected domain if its integral is zero around every simple closed curve of finite length in the domain. [after Italian mathematician and physicist Giacinto *Morera* (1856–1909), who formulated it]

mo·res (môr′āz, -ēz, mōr′-), *n.pl. Sociol.* folkways of central importance accepted without question and embodying the fundamental moral views of a group. [1905–10; < L *mōres,* pl. of *mōs* usage, custom]
—**Syn.** customs, conventions, practices.

more sol., (in prescriptions) in the usual manner. Also, **mor. sol.** [< L *mōre solitō*]

Mo·resque (mə resk′), *adj.* Moorish. [1605–15; < MF < It *moresco,* equiv. to *Mor(o)* MOOR + *-esco* -ESQUE]

Mor·ga·gni (môr gä′nyē), *n.* **Gio·van·ni Bat·tis·ta** (jô vän′nē bät tēs′tä), 1682–1771, Italian anatomist.

Mor·gain le Fay (môr′gān lə fā′, môr′gən). See **Morgan le Fay.**

Mor·gan (môr′gən), *n.* one of a breed of light carriage and saddle horses descended from the stallion *Justin Morgan.* [1865–70; named after the original sire owned by Justin *Morgan* (1747–98), a New England teacher]

Mor·gan (môr′gən), *n.* **1. Charles Lang·bridge** (lang′brij′), 1894–1958, English novelist and critic. **2. Daniel,** 1736–1802, American Revolutionary general. **3. Sir Henry,** 1635?–88, Welsh buccaneer in the Americas. **4. John Hunt,** 1826–64, Confederate general in the American Civil War. **5. J(ohn) P(ier·pont)** (pēr′pont), 1837–1913, U.S. financier and philanthropist. **6.** his son **John Pierpont,** 1867–1943, U.S. financier. **7. Lewis Henry,** 1818–81, U.S. ethnologist and anthropologist. **8. Thomas Hunt,** 1866–1945, U.S. zoologist: Nobel prize for medicine 1933. **9.** a male or female given name.

mor·ga·nat·ic (môr′gə nat′ik), *adj.* of or pertaining to a form of marriage in which a person of high rank, as a member of the nobility, marries someone of lower station with the stipulation that neither the low-ranking spouse nor their children, if any, will have any claim to the titles or entailed property of the high-ranking partner. [1720–30; < NL *morganāticus* (adj.), for ML phrase (*mātrimōnium*) *ad morganāticam* (marriage) to the extent of morning-gift (*morganātica* repr. Gmc **morgangeba* (fem.); cf. OE *morgengiefu* gift from husband to wife on day after wedding)] —**mor′ga·nat′i·cal·ly,** *adv.*

Mor′gan Cit′y, a city in S Louisiana: headquarters for offshore oil drilling and base for shrimp fleet. 16,114.

Mor′gan Hill′, a town in W California. 17,060.

mor·gan·ite (môr′gə nīt′), *n.* rose-colored beryl. [1910–15; named after J. P. MORGAN; see -ITE[1]]

Mor·gan le Fay (môr′gən lə fā′), *Celtic and Arthurian Legend.* the fairy sister of King Arthur. Also, **Morgain le Fay.**

Mor·gan·ton (môr′gən tən), *n.* a town in central North Carolina. 13,763.

Mor·gan·town (môr′gən toun′), *n.* a city in N West Virginia. 27,605.

mor·gen (môr′gən), *n.* **1.** a unit of land measure equal to about two acres (0.8 hectare), formerly in use in Holland and the Dutch colonies and still used in South Africa. **2.** a unit equal to about two-thirds of an acre (0.3 hectare), formerly used in Prussia, Norway, and Denmark. [1620–30, *Amer.;* < D *morgen* and G *Morgen* morgen, morning (as much land as one plows in a morning)]

Mor·gen·thau (môr′gən thô′ *or, for 1,* -tou′), *n.* **1. Henry,** 1856–1946, U.S. financier and diplomat, born in Germany. **2.** his son **Henry, Jr.,** 1891–1967, U.S. statesman: Secretary of the Treasury 1934–45.

morgue (môrg), *n.* **1.** a place in which bodies are kept, esp. the bodies of victims of violence or accidents, pending identification or burial. **2.** a reference file of old clippings, mats, books, etc., in a newspaper office. **3.** the room containing such a reference file. **4.** any place, as a room or file, where records, information, or objects are kept for unexpected but possible future use. **5.** such records, information, or objects. [1815–25; < F; name of building in Paris housing unidentified dead bodies]

Mo·ri·ah (mô rī′ə, mō-), *n.* **1.** a mountainous region in S Palestine, where Abraham prepared to sacrifice Isaac. Gen. 22:3. **2.** Also, *Douay Bible,* **Mo·ri′a.** a site usually identified with Zion, where Solomon built the Temple. II Chron. 3:1.

mor·i·bund (môr′ə bund′, mor′-), *adj.* **1.** in a dying state; near death. **2.** on the verge of extinction or termination. **3.** not progressing or advancing; stagnant: *a moribund political party.* [1715–25; < L *moribundus* dying, equiv. to *mori-* (s. of *morī* to die) + *-bundus* adj. suffix] —**mor′i·bun′di·ty,** *n.* —**mor′i·bund′ly,** *adv.*

Mö·ri·ke (mœ′ri kə), *n.* **E·du·ard** (ā′do͞o ärt′), 1804–75, German poet.

Mo·ri·ni (mô rē′nē), *n.* **Erika,** born 1906, U.S. violinist, born in Austria.

mo·ri·on[1] (môr′ē on′, mōr′-), *n.* an open helmet of the 16th and early 17th centuries, worn by common soldiers and usually having a flat or turned-down brim and a crest from front to back. [1555–65; < MF < Sp *morrión,* equiv. to *morr(o)* top of head + *-ión* n. suffix]

morion[1]
(16th century)

mo·ri·on[2] (môr′ē on′, mōr′-), *n.* a variety of smoky quartz of a dark-brown or nearly black color. [1740–50; < L *mōrion,* misreading of *mormorion* a kind of crystal]

Mo·ris·co (mə ris′kō), *adj., n., pl.* **-cos, -coes.** —*adj.* **1.** Moorish. —*n.* **2.** a Moor, esp. one of the Moors of Spain. [1540–50; < Sp, equiv. to *Mor(o)* MOOR + *-isco* adj. suffix]

Mor·i·son (môr′ə sən, mor′-), *n.* **Samuel Eliot,** 1887–1976, U.S. historian.

Mo·ri·sot (mô rē zō′), *n.* **Berthe** (bert), 1841–95, French Impressionist painter.

mo·ri·tu·ri te sa·lu·ta·mus (mō′ri to͞o′re te sä′lo͞o tä′mo͝os; *Eng.* môr′i to͝or′ī tē sal′yo͞o tā′məs, -tyo͝or′ī, -to͝or′ē, -tyo͝or′ē), *Latin.* we who are about to die salute you: said by Roman gladiators to the emperor.

Mo·ritz (*Ger.* mō′rits), *n.* **1.** Maurice (def. 1). **2.** a male given name, form of **Maurice.**

Mor·ley (môr′lē), *n.* **1. Christopher Darlington,** 1890–1957, U.S. writer. **2. Edward Williams,** 1838–1923, U.S. chemist and physicist. **3. John, Viscount Morley of Blackburn,** 1838–1923, English statesman, journalist, biographer, and critic. **4. Thomas,** 1557–1603?, English composer, esp. of madrigals. **5.** a male given name.

Mor·mon (môr′mən), *n.* **1.** a member of a church (**Mor′mon Church′**), founded in the U.S. in 1830 by Joseph Smith and based on the teachings of the Book of Mormon. **2.** See under **Book of Mormon.** —*adj.* **3.** of or pertaining to the Mormons or their religious system: *the Mormon view of Creation.* —**Mor′mon·dom,** *n.* —**Mor′mon·ism,** *n.*

Mor′mon crick′et, a flightless, long-horned grasshopper, *Anabrus simplex,* of the western U.S., that is destructive to range grasses and cultivated crops. [so named because found where the Mormons settled]

mor·my·rid (môr mī′rid), *n.* **1.** any of numerous African freshwater fishes of the family Mormyridae, many species of which have an elongated snout and are capable of producing an electric discharge. —*adj.* **2.** belonging or pertaining to the family Mormyridae. [1895–1900; < NL *Mormyridae,* equiv. to *Mormyr(us)* genus name (< Gk *mormýros* a species of fish) + *-idae* -ID[2]]

morn (môrn), *n. Literary.* morning. [bef. 900; ME *morn(e),* OE *morne* (dat. of *morgen* morning); c. D, G *Morgen*]

Mor·nay (môr nā′ *for 1;* môr nā′ *for 2*), *n.* **1.** Also called **Duplessis-Mornay. Phi·lippe de** (fē lēp′ də), **Sei·gneur du Ples·sis-Mar·ly** (se nyœr′ dy ple sē mar lē′), (*"Pope of the Huguenots"*), 1549–1623, French statesman and Protestant leader. **2.** (*often l.c.*) Also called **Mornay′ sauce′.** a béchamel, or white sauce, containing cheese, esp. Parmesan and Gruyère.

morn·ing (môr′ning), *n.* **1.** the first part or period of the day, extending from dawn, or from midnight, to noon. **2.** the beginning of day; dawn: *Morning is almost here.* **3.** the first or early period of anything; beginning: *the morning of life.* —*adj.* **4.** of or pertaining to morning: *the morning hours.* **5.** occurring, appearing, used, etc., in the morning: *a morning coffee break.* [1200–50; ME; see MORN, -ING[1]; modeled on EVENING]
—**Syn. 2.** morn, daybreak, sunrise.

morn′ing af′ter, *pl.* **mornings after. 1.** a period, as in the morning, when the aftereffects of excessive self-indulgence during the previous evening are felt, esp. the aftereffects of excessive drinking of alcoholic beverages. **2.** a moment or period of realization in which the consequences of an earlier ill-advised action are recognized or brought home to one. [1880–85]

morn′ing-af′ter pill′ (môr′ning af′tər, -äf′-), *Pharm.* a contraceptive pill containing only an estrogen and used by women within a few hours after sexual intercourse. [1955–60]

morn′ing coat′, a man's cutaway for wear as part of morning dress. [1930–35]

morn′ing dress′, 1. formal daytime apparel for men, including striped pants, a cutaway, and a silk hat. **2.** a simple dress for wear in the home; housedress. Cf. **evening dress.** [1690–1700]

morn′ing glo′ry, 1. any of various plants, esp. of the genera *Ipomoea* and *Convolvulus,* as *I. purpurea,* a twining plant having cordate leaves and funnel-shaped flowers of various colors, often opening only in the morning. **2.** a racehorse that runs faster in morning workouts than in afternoon races. Also, **morn′ing-glo′ry.** [1805–15, *Amer.*]

morn′ing glo′ry fam′ily, the plant family Convulvulaceae, characterized by twining herbaceous vines, shrubs, and trees having alternate, simple, or compound leaves, funnel-shaped, often showy flowers, and fruit in the form of a berry or capsule, and including bindweed, dodder, moonflower, morning glory, and sweet potato.

morn′ing gun′, *Mil.* **1.** a gun fired at the first note of reveille. **2.** the firing of this gun. [1735–45]

morn′ing line′, a list of entries for a horse race with the probable betting odds as estimated by a bookmaker

CONCISE ETYMOLOGY KEY: <, descended or borrowed from; >, whence; b., blend of, blended; c., cognate with; cf., compare; deriv., derivative; equiv., equivalent; imit., imitative; obl., oblique; r., replacing; s., stem; sp., spelling, spelled; resp., respelling, respelled; trans., translation; ?, origin unknown; *, unattested; ‡, probably earlier than. See the full key inside the front cover.

or track handicapper, usually issued the morning of the race, before wagering begins. [1930–35]

morn′ing loan′. See **day loan.**

Morn′ing Prayer′, matin (def. 1c).

morn·ings (môr′ningz), *adv.* in or during the morning regularly. [1610–20]

morn′ing sick′ness, nausea occurring in the early part of the day, esp. as a characteristic symptom in the first months of pregnancy. [1875–80]

morn′ing star′, **1.** a bright planet, esp. Venus, seen in the east immediately before sunrise. **2.** Also called **holy water sprinkler, holy water sprinkle.** a medieval shafted weapon having a head in the form of a spiked ball. [1525–35]

morn′ing watch′, *Naut.* the watch from 4 A.M. until 8 A.M. [1525–35]

Mo·ro (môr′ō, mōr′ō), *n., pl.* **-ros,** (*esp. collectively*) **-ro.** a member of any of the various tribes of Muslim Malays in the southern Philippines. [< Sp < L *Maurus* MOOR]

Mo·ro (môr′ō, mor′ō; *It.* mô′Rô), *n.* **Al·do** (al′dō; *It.* äl′dô), 1916–78, Italian lawyer, author, and statesman: prime minister 1963–68, 1974–76.

Mo·roc·co (mə rok′ō), *n.* **1.** French, **Maroc.** Spanish, **Marruecos.** a kingdom in NW Africa: formed from a sultanate that was divided into two protectorates (**French Morocco** and **Spanish Morocco**) and an international zone. 17,000,000; 172,104 sq. mi. (445,749 sq. km). *Cap.:* Rabat. Cf. **Tangier Zone. 2.** former name of **Marrakesh. 3.** (*l.c.*) a fine, pebble-grained leather, originally made in Morocco from goatskin tanned with sumac. **4.** (*l.c.*) any leather made in imitation of this. Also called **moroc′co leath′er** (for defs. 3, 4). —**Mo·roc·can** (mə rok′ən), *adj., n.*

Mo·ro·go·ro (môr′ə gôr′ō, mōr′ə gōr′ō), *n.* a city in E Tanzania. 25,262.

mo·ron (môr′on, mōr′-), *n.* **1.** a person who is notably stupid or lacking in good judgment. **2.** *Psychol.* a person of borderline intelligence in a former classification of mental retardation, having an intelligence quotient of 50 to 69. Cf. **feeble-minded.** [*Amer.;* < Gk *mōrón,* neut. of *mōrós* foolish, dull] —**mo·ron·ic** (mə ron′ik), *adj.* —**mo·ron′i·cal·ly,** *adv.* —**mo′ron·ism,** *n.*

Mo·ro·ni (mô rō′nē), *n.* a town in and the capital of the Comoros. 12,000.

mo·ror (*Seph.* mä RÔR′; *Ashk.* mô′RŌR), *n. Hebrew.* maror.

Mo·ros (môr′os, mōr′-), *n. Class. Myth.* a child of Nyx, and the personification of fate.

mo·rose (mə rōs′), *adj.* **1.** gloomily or sullenly ill-humored, as a person or mood. **2.** characterized by or expressing gloom. [1555–65; < L *mōrōsus* fretful, peevish, willful, equiv. to *mōr-* (s. of *mōs*) will, inclination + *-ōsus* -OSE[1]] —**mo·rose′ly,** *adv.* —**mo·rose′ness,** *n.*
—**Syn. 1.** moody, sour, sulky, surly. See **glum.**

morph (môrf), *n.* **1.** *Ling.* a sequence of phonemes constituting a minimal unit of grammar or syntax, and, as such, a representation, member, or contextual variant of a morpheme in a specific environment. Cf. **allomorph** (def. 2). **2.** *Biol.* an individual of one particular form, as a worker ant, in a species that occurs in two or more forms. [1945–50; back formation from MORPHEME, or independent use of -MORPH] —**mor′phic,** *adj.*

morph-, var. of **morpho-** before a vowel: *morpheme.*

-morph, a combining form meaning "form, structure," of the kind specified by the initial element: *isomorph.* [< Gk *-morphos;* see -MORPHOUS]

mor·phac·tin (môr fak′tin), *n. Biochem.* any of various synthetic compounds, derived from fluorine and carboxylic acid, that regulate the growth and development of plants. [1965–70; prob. MORPH- + ACT(IVE) or ACT(IVATE) + -IN[2]]

mor·phal·lax·is (môr′fə lak′sis), *n., pl.* **-lax·es** (-lak′sēz). *Biol.* the regeneration of a destroyed body part by the reorganization of its remaining cells. [1900–05; MORPH- + Gk *állaxis* exchange, barter (cf. *allássein* to change, exchange, ult. deriv. of *állos* other, ALLO-); coined by T. H. Morgan]

mor·pheme (môr′fēm), *n. Ling.* any of the minimal grammatical units of a language, each constituting a word or meaningful part of a word, that cannot be divided into smaller independent grammatical parts, as *the, write,* or the *-ed* of *waited.* Cf. **allomorph** (def. 2), **morph** (def. 1). [1895–1900; < F *morphème;* see MORPH-, -EME] —**mor·phe′mic,** *adj.* —**mor·phe′mi·cal·ly,** *adv.*

mor′pheme struc′ture condi′tion, *Ling.* (in generative phonology) a constraint on the occurrence of sounds or sequences of sounds in the phonological representation of morphemes.

mor·phe·mics (môr fē′miks), *n.* (*used with a singular v.*) *Ling.* **1.** the study of the classification, description, and functions of morphemes; morphology. **2.** the manner by which morphemes combine to form words. [1945–50; see MORPHEME, -ICS]

Mor·phe·us (môr′fē əs, -fyōōs), *n.* **1.** *Class. Myth.* a son of Hypnos and the god of dreams. **2. in the arms of Morpheus,** asleep. [1325–75; ME < L < Gk *morph(ḗ)* form + L *-eus* n. suffix; coined by Ovid, with allusion to the forms seen in dreams] —**Mor′phe·an,** *adj.*

-morphic, var. of **-morphous:** *anthropomorphic.* [-MORPH + -IC]

mor·phine (môr′fēn), *n. Pharm.* a white, bitter, crystalline alkaloid, $C_{17}H_{19}NO_3{\cdot}H_2O$, the most important narcotic and addictive principle of opium, obtained by extraction and crystallization and used chiefly in medicine as a pain reliever and sedative. Also, **mor·phi·a** (môr′fē ə). [1820–30; < G *Morphin.* See MORPHEUS, -INE[2]] —**mor·phin·ic** (môr fin′ik), *adj.*

morph·ing (môr′fing), *n.* the smooth transformation of one image into another by computer, as in a motion picture. [1985–90]

-morphism, a combining form occurring in nouns that correspond to adjectives ending in **-morphic** or **-morphous:** *monomorphism.* [see -MORPHOUS, -ISM]

morpho-, a combining form meaning "form, structure," used in the formation of compound words: *morphology.* Also, *esp. before a vowel,* **morph-.** Cf. **-morph, -morphic, -morphism, -morphous.** [< Gk, comb. form of *morphḗ*]

mor·pho·gen·e·sis (môr′fə jen′ə sis), *n. Embryol.* the development of structural features of an organism or part. [1880–85; MORPHO- + GENESIS] —**mor·pho·ge·net·ic** (môr′fō jə net′ik), **mor′pho·gen′ic,** *adj.*

morphol., morphology.

mor·pho·line (môr′fə lēn′, -lin), *n. Chem.* a colorless, hygroscopic liquid, C_4H_9NO, used chiefly as a solvent for dyes, resins, and waxes. [1885–90; MORPH- + -OL[2] + -INE[2]]

morpholog′ic construc′tion, *Gram.* a construction that forms a compound or complex word. Cf. **syntactic construction** (def. 1).

mor·phol·o·gy (môr fol′ə jē), *n.* **1.** the branch of biology dealing with the form and structure of organisms. **2.** the form and structure of an organism considered as a whole. **3.** *Ling.* **a.** the patterns of word formation in a particular language, including inflection, derivation, and composition. **b.** the study and description of such patterns. **c.** the study of the behavior and combination of morphemes. **4.** *Physical Geog.* geomorphology. **5.** the form or structure of anything: *to gain an insight into the morphology of our political system.* **6.** the study of the form or structure of anything. [1820–30; MORPHO- + -LOGY; first formed in G] —**mor·pho·log·ic** (môr′fə loj′ik), **mor′pho·log′i·cal,** *adj.* —**mor′pho·log′i·cal·ly,** *adv.* —**mor·phol′o·gist,** *n.*

mor·pho·nol·o·gy (môr′fə nol′ə jē), *n.* morphophonemics (def. 1). [1925–30; by haplology from MORPHOPHONOLOGY, prob. after F *morphonologie*]

mor·pho·pho·neme (môr′fə fō′nēm, môr′fō-), *n. Ling.* **1.** an abstract phonological unit representing corresponding phonemes in different allomorphs of one morpheme. In English the symbol *F* may be used to represent a morphophoneme occurring in two related allomorphs, as *f* in *leaf,* but *v* in the plural *leaves.* **2.** a phonological entity comprising a bundle of distinctive features used in the representation of a morpheme. **3.** a symbol for a phonological alternation. [1930–35; MORPHO- (as comb. form for MORPHEME) + PHONEME]

mor·pho·pho·ne·mic (môr′fō fə nē′mik, -fō nē′-), *adj. Ling.* noting or pertaining to morphophonemics or morphophonemes. [1940–45; MORPH(EME) + -O- + PHONEMIC]

mor·pho·pho·ne·mics (môr′fō fə nē′miks, -fō nē′-), *n.* (*used with a singular v.*) *Ling.* **1.** Also called **morphonology, morphophonology.** the study of the relations between morphemes and their phonological realizations, components, or mappings. **2.** the body of data concerning these relations in a given language. [1935–40; see MORPHOPHONEMIC, -ICS]

mor·pho·pho·nol·o·gy (môr′fō fə nol′ə jē, -fō-nol′-), *n.* morphophonemics (def. 1). [1930–35; MORPHO- (as comb. form for MORPHOLOGY OR MORPHEME) + PHONOLOGY]

mor·pho·sis (môr fō′sis), *n., pl.* **-ses** (-sēz). *Biol.* the sequence or manner of development or change in an organism or any of its parts. [1665–75; < NL < Gk *mórphōsis,* equiv. to *morph(oûn)* to shape + *-ōsis* -OSIS] —**mor·phot·ic** (môr fot′ik), *adj.*

mor·pho·syn·tac·tic (môr′fō sin tak′tik), *adj. Ling.* involving both morphology and syntax. [1955–60; MORPHO- (as comb. form for MORPHOLOGY) + SYNTACTIC]

mor·pho·to·ne·mics (môr′fō tə nē′miks, -tō-), *n.* (*used with a singular v.*) *Ling.* the morphophonemics of tonal phenomena. [b. MORPHOPHONEMICS and TONE] —**mor′pho·to·ne′mic,** *adj.*

-morphous, a combining form with the meaning "having the shape, form, or structure" of the kind or number specified by the initial element, used in the formation of compound words: *polymorphous.* Also, **-morphic.** Cf. **morpho-.** [repr. Gk *-morphos,* adj. deriv. of *morphḗ* form; see -OUS]

Mor·phy (môr′fē), *n.* **Paul Charles,** 1837–84, U.S. chess player.

Mor′rill Act′ (môr′il, mor′-), *U.S. Hist.* **1.** an act of Congress (1862) granting each state 30,000 acres (12,000 hectares) of land for each member it had in Congress, 90 percent of the gross proceeds of which were to be used for the endowment and maintenance of colleges and universities teaching agricultural and mechanical arts and other subjects. **2.** either of two supplementary acts (1890 and 1907) in which Congress made direct financial grants to assist the land-grant colleges and universities. [named after Justin Smith *Morrill* (1810–98), congressman and senator from Vermont]

Mor·ris (môr′is, mor′-), *n.* **1. Gouv·er·neur** (guv′ər-nēr′), 1752–1816, U.S. statesman. **2. Robert,** 1734–1806, U.S. financier and statesman, born in England. **3. William,** 1834–96, English painter, furniture designer, poet, and socialist writer. **4. Wright,** born 1910, U.S. novelist. **5.** a male given name, form of **Maurice.**

Mor′ris chair′, a large armchair having an adjustable back and loose, removable cushions. [1895–1900; named after William MORRIS]

Morris chair

mor′ris dance′ (môr′is, mor′-), a rural folk dance of north English origin, performed in costume traditionally by men who originally represented characters of the Robin Hood legend, esp. in May Day festivities. Also called **mor′ris.** [1425–75; late ME *moreys daunce* Moorish dance; see MOORISH]

Mor·ri·son (môr′ə sən, mor′-), *n.* **1. Herbert Stanley,** 1888–1965, English labor leader and statesman. **2. Toni,** born 1931, U.S. novelist: Nobel prize 1993. **3.** a male given name.

Mor′ris Plan′ bank′, a private banking organization, formerly common in the U.S., designed primarily to grant small loans to industrial workers.

Mor·ris·town (môr′is toun′, mor′-), *n.* **1.** a city in E Tennessee. 19,683. **2.** a city in N New Jersey: Washington's winter headquarters 1776–77, 1779–80. 16,614.

Mor′ro Cas′tle (môr′ō, mor′ō; *Sp.* môR′Rô), a historic fort at the entrance to the harbor of Havana, Cuba.

mor·row (môr′ō, mor′ō), *n.* **1.** *Literary.* **a.** tomorrow. **b.** the next day. **2.** *Archaic.* the morning. [1225–75; ME *morwe,* var. of *morwen,* OE *morgen* morning. See MORN]

Mor·row (môr′ō, mor′ō), *n.* **Hon·o·ré Will·sie** (on′ə-rā′ wil′sē, on′ə rā′), 1880–1940, U.S. novelist.

morse (môrs), *n. Eccles.* an ornamented metal clasp or brooch for fastening a cope in front. [1375–1425; late ME *mors* < OF < L *morsus* fastening, lit., act of biting, equiv. to *mord(ēre)* to bite + *-tus,* suffix of v. action]

Morse (môrs), *n.* **1. Jed·i·di·ah** (jed′i dī′ə), 1761–1826, U.S. geographer and Congregational clergyman (father of Samuel F. B. Morse). **2. Samuel F(in·ley) B(reese)** (fin′lē brēz), 1791–1872, U.S. artist and inventor: developer of the first successful telegraph in the U.S.; inventor of the most commonly used telegraphic code system. **3.** See **Morse code. 4.** a male given name, form of **Maurice.** —*adj.* **5.** noting or pertaining to the Morse code or the system of communications using it. **6.** pertaining to any code resembling the Morse code.

Morse′ code′, either of two systems of clicks and pauses, short and long sounds, or flashes of light, used to represent the letters of the alphabet, numerals, etc.: now used primarily in radiotelegraphy by ham operators. Also called **Morse′ al′phabet.** [1830–40; after S. F. B. MORSE]

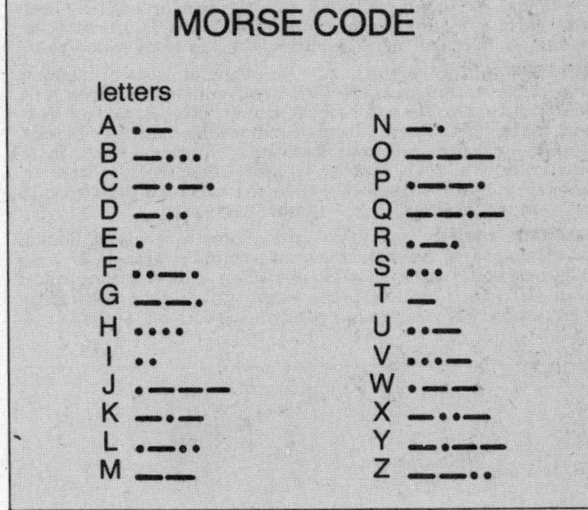

mor·sel (môr′səl), *n.* **1.** a bite, mouthful, or small portion of food, candy, etc. **2.** a small piece, quantity, or amount of anything; scrap; bit. **3.** something very appetizing; treat or tidbit. **4.** a person or thing that is attractive or delightful. —*v.t.* **5.** to distribute in or divide into tiny portions (often fol. by *out*): *to morsel out the last pieces of meat.* [1250–1300; ME < OF, equiv. to *mors* a bite (< L *morsum* something bitten off, n. use of neut. of *morsus,* ptp. of *mordēre* to bite) + *-el* < L *-ellus* dim. suffix; see -ELLE]

Morse′ lamp′, a blinker lamp for signaling in Morse code.

mort[1] (môrt), *n.* **1.** *Hunting.* the note played on a hunting horn signifying that the animal hunted has been killed. **2.** *Obs.* death. [1300–50; ME < MF < L *mort-* (s. of *mors*) death]

mort[2] (môrt), *n.* a three-year-old salmon. [1520–30; orig. uncert.]

mort[3] (môrt), *n. Brit. Dial.* lard. [1600–10; orig. uncert.]

Mort (môrt), *n.* a male given name, form of **Mortimer** or **Morton.**

mor·ta·del·la (môr′tə del′ə), *n.* a large Italian sausage of pork, beef, and pork fat chopped fine, seasoned with garlic and pepper, cooked, and smoked. [1605–15; < It < L *murtātum* sausage seasoned with myrtle (*murt(um)* myrtle-berry + *-ātum,* neut. of *-ātus* -ATE[1]) + *-ella* dim. suffix]

mor·tal (môr′tl), *adj.* **1.** subject to death; having a transitory life: *all mortal creatures.* **2.** of or pertaining to human beings as subject to death; human: *this mortal life.* **3.** belonging to this world. **4.** deadly or implacable; relentless: *a mortal enemy.* **5.** severe, dire, grievous, or bitter: *in mortal fear.* **6.** causing or liable to cause death; fatal: *a mortal wound.* **7.** to the death: *mortal combat.* **8.** of or pertaining to death: *the mortal hour.* **9.** involving spiritual death (opposed to *venial*): *mortal sin.* **10.** long and wearisome. **11.** extreme; very great: *in a mortal hurry.* **12.** conceivable; possible: *of no mortal value to the owners.* —*n.* **13.** a human being. **14.** the condition of being subject to death. [1325–75; ME < L *mortālis,* equiv. to *mort-* (s. of *mors*) death + *-ālis* -AL[1]] —**mor′tal·ly,** *adv.*
—**Syn. 6.** See **fatal.**

mor·tal·i·ty (môr tal′i tē), *n., pl.* **-ties. 1.** the state or condition of being subject to death; mortal character, nature, or existence. **2.** the relative frequency of deaths in a specific population; death rate. **3.** mortal beings collectively; humanity. **4.** death or destruction on a large scale, as from war, plague, or famine. **5.** *Obs.* death. [1300–50; ME *mortalite* < MF < L *mortālitās.* See MORTAL, -ITY]

mortal′ity ta′ble, *Insurance.* an actuarial table showing the percentage of persons who die at any given age, compiled from statistics on selected population groups or on former policyholders. Also called **life table.** [1875–80]

mor′tal mind′, *Christian Science.* the illusion that mind and life arise from matter and are subject to death. Cf. **mind** (def. 19). [1870–75]

mor′tal sin′, *Rom. Cath. Ch.* a willfully committed, serious transgression against the law of God, depriving the soul of divine grace. Cf. **venial sin.**

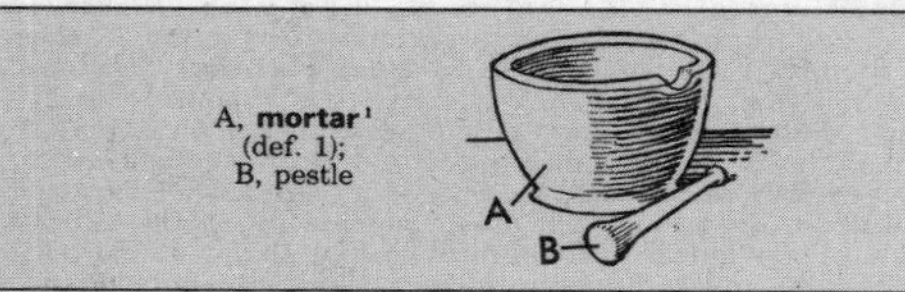

A, mortar[1] (def. 1); B, pestle

mor·tar[1] (môr′tər), *n.* **1.** a receptacle of hard material, having a bowl-shaped cavity in which substances are reduced to powder with a pestle. **2.** any of various mechanical appliances in which substances are pounded or ground. **3.** a cannon very short in proportion to its bore, for throwing shells at high angles. **4.** some similar contrivance, as for throwing pyrotechnic bombs or a lifeline. —*v.t., v.i.* **5.** to attack with mortar fire or shells. [bef. 1000; ME, OE *mortere* and OF *mortier* < L *mortārium;* in defs. 3, 4 trans. of F *mortier* < L, as above; see -AR[2]]

mor·tar[2] (môr′tər), *n.* **1.** a mixture of lime or cement or a combination of both with sand and water, used as a bonding agent between bricks, stones, etc. **2.** any of various materials or compounds for bonding together bricks, stones, etc.: *Bitumen was used as a mortar.* —*v.t.* **3.** to plaster or fix with mortar. [1250–1300; ME *morter* < AF; OF *mortier* MORTAR[1], hence the mixture produced in it] —**mor′tar·less,** *adj.* —**mor′tar·y,** *adj.*

mor·tar·board (môr′tər bôrd′, -bōrd′), *n.* **1.** a board, usually square, used by masons to hold mortar. **2.** Also called **cap.** a cap with a close-fitting crown surmounted by a stiff, flat, square piece from which a tassel hangs, worn as part of academic costume. [1850–55; MORTAR[2] + BOARD]

mortarboard (def. 2)

mor′tar ketch′, *Naut.* See **bomb ketch.**

mort·gage (môr′gij), *n., v.,* **-gaged, -gag·ing.** —*n.* **1.** a conveyance of an interest in property as security for the repayment of money borrowed. **2.** the deed by which such a transaction is effected. **3.** the rights conferred by it, or the state of the property conveyed. —*v.t.* **4.** *Law.* to convey or place (real property) under a mortgage. **5.** to place under advance obligation; pledge: *to mortgage one's life to the defense of democracy.* [1350–1400; earlier *morgage,* ME < OF *mortgage,* equiv. to *mort* dead (< L *mortuus*) + *gage* pledge, GAGE[1]]

CONCISE ETYMOLOGY KEY: <, descended or borrowed from; >, whence; b., blend of, blended; c., cognate with; cf., compare; deriv., derivative; equiv., equivalent; imit., imitative; obl., oblique; r., replacing; s., stem; sp., spelling, spelled; resp., respelling, respelled; trans., translation; ?, origin unknown; *, unattested; ‡, probably earlier than. See the full key inside the front cover.

mort′gage bond′, a bond secured by a mortgage on real estate or other property. [1885–90]

mort·ga·gee (môr′gə jē′), *n.* a person to whom property is mortgaged. [1575–85; MORTGAGE + -EE]

mortgagee′ clause′, *Insurance.* a clause attached to a fire-insurance policy for protecting a mortgagee against loss or damage.

mort·ga·gor (môr′gə jər), *n.* a person who mortgages property. Also, **mort′gag·er.** [1575–85; MORTGAGE + -OR[2]]

mor·tice (môr′tis), *n., v.t.,* **-ticed, -tic·ing.** mortise.

mor·ti·cian (môr tish′ən), *n.* See **funeral director.** [1890–95, *Amer.;* MORT(UARY) + -ICIAN]

mor·tif·er·ous (môr tif′ər əs), *adj.* deadly; fatal. [1525–35; < L *mortiferus* death-bearing, equiv. to *morti-* (s. of *mors*) death + *-ferus* -FEROUS] —**mor·tif′er·ous·ness,** *n.*

mor·ti·fi·ca·tion (môr′tə fi kā′shən), *n.* **1.** a feeling of humiliation or shame, as through some injury to one's pride or self-respect. **2.** a cause or source of such humiliation or shame. **3.** the practice of asceticism by penitential discipline to overcome desire for sin and to strengthen the will. **4.** *Pathol.* the death of one part of the body while the rest is alive; gangrene; necrosis. [1350–1400; ME *mortificacion* < LL *mortificātiōn-* (s. of *mortificātiō*), equiv. to *morti-* (see MORTIFY) + *-ficātiōn-* -FICATION]
—**Syn. 1.** See **shame.**

mor·ti·fy (môr′tə fī′), *v.,* **-fied, -fy·ing.** —*v.t.* **1.** to humiliate or shame, as by injury to one's pride or self-respect. **2.** to subjugate (the body, passions, etc.) by abstinence, ascetic discipline, or self-inflicted suffering. **3.** *Pathol.* to affect with gangrene or necrosis. —*v.i.* **4.** to practice mortification or disciplinary austerities. **5.** *Pathol.* to undergo mortification; become gangrened or necrosed. [1350–1400; ME *mortifien* < MF *mortifier* < LL *mortificāre* to put to death, equiv. to L *morti-* (s. of *mors*) death + *-ficāre* -FY] —**mor′ti·fied′ly,** *adv.* —**mor′ti·fi′er,** *n.* —**mor′ti·fy′ing·ly,** *adv.*
—**Syn. 1.** humble, abase. **2.** subdue, restrain.

Mor·ti·mer (môr′tə mər), *n.* **1. Roger de** (də), **8th Baron of Wig·more** (wig′môr′, -mōr′) and **1st Earl of March,** 1287–1330, English rebel leader: paramour of Isabella, queen of Edward II of England. **2.** a male given name.

mor·tise (môr′tis), *n., v.,* **-tised, -tis·ing.** —*n.* **1.** a notch, hole, groove, or slot made in a piece of wood or the like to receive a tenon of the same dimensions. **2.** a deep recess cut into wood for any of several other purposes, as for receiving a mortise lock. **3.** *Print.* a space cut out of a plate, esp. for the insertion of type or another plate. —*v.t.* **4.** to secure with a mortise and tenon. **5.** to cut or form a mortise in (a piece of wood or the like). **6.** to join securely. **7.** *Print.* **a.** to cut metal from (a plate). **b.** to cut out metal from a plate and insert (new material) in its place. Also, **mortice.** [1350–1400; ME *morteys, mortaise* < AF *mortais(e),* OF *mortoise,* of obscure orig.] —**mor′tis·er,** *n.*

mor′tise block′, *Mach.* a block having a shell cut from a single piece of wood.

mor′tise chis′el. See **framing chisel.** [1670–80]

mor′tise joint′, any of various joints between two pieces of timber or the like in which a tenon is housed in or secured to a mortise. Also called **mor′tise and ten′on joint′.** [1880–85]

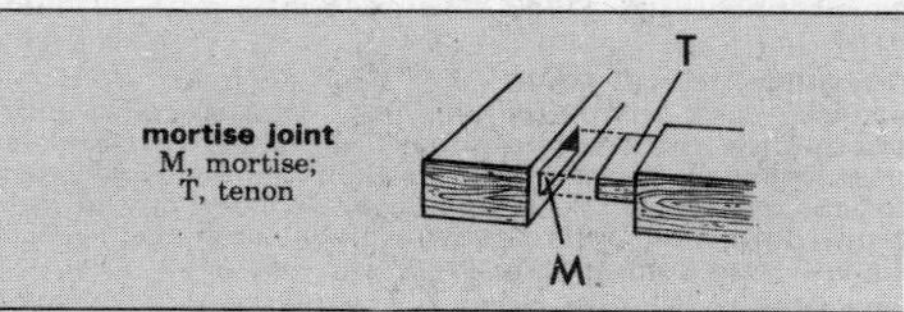

mortise joint
M, mortise;
T, tenon

mor′tise lock′, a lock housed within a mortise in a door or the like, so that the lock mechanism is covered on both sides. [1770–80]

mort·ling (môrt′ling), *n. Brit.* wool obtained from dead sheep. [1400–50; earlier *morling,* late ME; prob. by suffix substitution from *mor(t)kin* dead animal < AF *mortekine,* for OF *mortecine* (<< L *morticīnus* (of an animal) having died naturally) with final conformed to ME *-kin* -KIN; see -LING[1]]

mort·main (môrt′mān′), *n. Law.* **1.** the condition of lands or tenements held without right of alienation, as by an ecclesiastical corporation; inalienable ownership. **2.** the perpetual holding of land, esp. by a corporation or charitable trust. [1250–1300; ME *mort(e)mayn(e)* < AF *mortemain,* trans. of ML *mortua manus* dead hand]

Mor·ton (môr′tn), *n.* **1. Jelly Roll** (*Ferdinand Morton*), 1885–1941, U.S. jazz pianist, composer, and band leader. **2. Le·vi Par·sons** (lē′vī pär′sənz), 1824–1920, vice president of the U.S. 1889–93; governor of New York 1895–96. **3. William Thomas Green,** 1819–68, U.S. dentist: first to employ ether as an anesthetic. **4.** a town in central Illinois. 14,178. **5.** a male given name: a family name taken from a Norman placename meaning "town on the moor."

Mor′ton Grove′, a city in NE Illinois, near Chicago. 23,747.

mor·tu·ar·y (môr′chōō er′ē), *n., pl.* **-ar·ies,** *adj.* —*n.* **1.** See **funeral home. 2.** a customary gift formerly claimed by and due to the incumbent of a parish in England from the estate of a deceased parishioner. —*adj.* **3.** of or pertaining to the burial of the dead. **4.** pertaining to or connected with death. [1350–1400; ME *mortuarie* < ML *mortuārium,* n. use of neut. of L *mortuārius* of the dead, equiv. to *mortu(us)* dead + *-ārius* -ARY]

mor·u·la (môr′ŏŏ lə, -yŏŏ-), *n., pl.* **-las, -lae** (-lē′). *Embryol.* the mass of cells resulting from the cleavage of the ovum before the formation of a blastula. [1855–60; < NL, equiv. to L *mōr(um)* mulberry + *-ula* -ULE] —**mor′u·lar,** *adj.*

MOS, *Electronics.* metal oxide semiconductor.

mos., months.

mo·sa·ic (mō zā′ik), *n., adj., v.,* **-icked, -ick·ing.** —*n.* **1.** a picture or decoration made of small, usually colored pieces of inlaid stone, glass, etc. **2.** the process of producing such a picture or decoration. **3.** something resembling such a picture or decoration in composition, esp. in being made up of diverse elements: *a mosaic of borrowed ideas.* **4.** Also called **aerial mosaic, photomosaic.** an assembly of aerial photographs matched in such a way as to show a continuous photographic representation of an area **(mosaic map). 5.** *Archit.* (in an architectural plan) a system of patterns for differentiating the areas of a building or the like, sometimes consisting of purely arbitrary patterns used to separate areas according to function but often consisting of plans of flooring, reflected ceiling plans, overhead views of furnishings and equipment, or other items really included in the building or building plan. **6.** Also called **mosa′ic disease′.** *Plant Pathol.* any of several diseases of plants, characterized by mottled green or green and yellow areas on the leaves, caused by certain viruses. **7.** *Biol.* an organism exhibiting mosaicism. **8.** *Television.* a light-sensitive surface in a television camera tube, consisting of a thin mica sheet coated on one side with a large number of small globules of silver and cesium insulated from each other. The image to be televised is focused on this surface and the resulting charges on the globules are scanned by an electron beam. —*adj.* **9.** pertaining to, resembling, or used for making a mosaic or mosaic work: *a mosaic tile.* **10.** composed of a combination of diverse elements. —*v.t.* **11.** to make a mosaic of or from. **12.** to decorate with mosaic. [1350–1400; ME < MF *mosaïque* < It *mosaico* < ML *musaicum,* reformation of LL *musīvum (opus),* L *musēum, musaeum* mosaic work (quantity of *u* uncert.), of obscure orig.; variants may show an assumed relationship with Gk *mouseîon* shrine of the Muses, MUSEUM, by analogy with *archi(v)um* (see ARCHIVE), though classical Gk word is not attested in sense "mosaic"] —**mo·sa′i·cal·ly,** *adv.*

Mo·sa·ic (mō zā′ik), *adj.* of or pertaining to Moses or the writings, laws, and principles attributed to him: *Mosaic ethics.* Also, **Mo·sa′i·cal.** [1655–65; < NL *Mosaicus,* equiv. to LL *Mōs(ēs)* MOSES + *-aicus,* on the model of *Hebraicus* Hebraic]

mosa′ic glass′, glass having a polychrome pattern made by fusing colors or variously colored canes, rods, strips, or squares together.

mosa′ic gold′, 1. *Chem.* See **stannic sulfide. 2.** ormolu (def. 1). [1720–30; so called because used in mosaic work]

mo·sa·i·cism (mō zā′ə siz′əm), *n. Biol.* a condition in which an organism or part is composed of two or more genetically distinct tissues owing to experimental manipulation or to faulty distribution of genetic material during mitosis. [1925–30; MOSAIC + -ISM]

mo·sa·i·cist (mō zā′ə sist), *n.* a person who works in mosaic. [1840–50; MOSAIC + -IST]

Mosa′ic Law′, 1. the ancient law of the Hebrews, ascribed to Moses. **2.** the part of the Scripture containing this law; the Pentateuch. [1695–1705]

mosa′ic map′. See under **mosaic** (def. 4). [1915–20]

mosa′ic vi′sion, a type of vision hypothesized for the insect compound eye, in which the image is formed by hundreds of separate ommatidia. [1875–80]

mo·sa·saur (mō′sə sôr′), *n.* any of several extinct carnivorous marine lizards from the Cretaceous Period, having the limbs modified into broad, webbed paddles. [< NL *Mosasaurus* (1823) genus name, equiv. to L *Mosa* the MEUSE river (where a species was first discovered) + NL *-saurus* -SAUR]

Mos·bach·er (môs′bak ər, mos′-), *n.* **Emil, Jr.** (*"Bus"*), born 1922, U.S. yacht racer.

Mos·by (mōz′bē), *n.* **John Sin·gle·ton** (sing′gəl tən), 1833–1916, Confederate cavalry colonel.

mos·chate (mos′kāt, -kit), *adj.* having a musky smell. [1820–30; < NL *moschātus,* equiv. to ML *mosch(us)* musk + L *-ātus* -ATE[1]]

mos·cha·tel (mos′kə tel′, mos′kə tel′), *n.* a small plant, *Adoxa moschatellina,* having greenish or yellowish flowers with a musky odor. [1725–35; < F *moscatelle* < It *moscatella,* equiv. to *moscat(o)* musk + *-ella* -ELLE; *-h-* from botanical name]

Mos·co·ni (mo skō′nē), *n.* **William Joseph** (*Willie*), 1913–93, U.S. billiards and pool player.

Mos·cow (mos′kō *or, for 1, 2,* -kou), *n.* **1.** Russian, **Moskva.** the capital of the Russian Federation: capital of the former Soviet Union, located in the central part. 8,967,000. **2.** Also called **Grand Duchy of Moscow.** Muscovy (def. 1). **3.** a city in W Idaho. 16,513.

Mos′cow Art′ The′ater, a Russian theatrical company founded in 1898 principally by Konstantin Stanislavski and famous for its naturalistic acting. [trans. of Russ *Moskóvskiĭ Khudózhestvennyĭ teátr*]

Mos′cow mule′, a cocktail of vodka, lime juice, and ginger beer, traditionally served in a copper mug.

Mose·ley (mōz′lē), *n.* **Henry Gwyn Jeffreys** (gwin), 1887–1915, English physicist: pioneer in x-ray spectroscopy.

Mose′ley's law′, *Physics.* the observed law that the square root of the frequencies of lines in atomic x-ray spectra depends linearly on the atomic number of the emitting atom. [named after H. G. J. MOSELEY]

Mo·selle (mō zel′), *n.* **1.** German, **Mo·sel** (mō′zəl). a river in W central Europe, flowing from the Vosges Mountains in NE France into the Rhine at Coblenz in W Germany. 320 mi. (515 km) long. **2.** a department in NE France. 1,006,373. 2406 sq. mi. (6230 sq. km). *Cap.:* Metz. **3.** a light, white wine made along the Moselle in Germany.

Mo•ser (mō′zər), *n.* **Jo•hann Ja•kob** (yō′hän yä′kôp), 1701–85, German jurist and publicist.

Mo•ses (mō′ziz, -zis), *n.* **1.** the Hebrew prophet who led the Israelites out of Egypt and delivered the Law during their years of wandering in the wilderness. **2.** a male given name.

Mo•ses (mō′ziz, -zis), *n.* **1. Anna Mary Robertson** (*"Grandma Moses"*), 1860–1961, U.S. painter. **2. Robert,** 1888–1981, U.S. public official: New York City Commissioner of Parks 1934–60.

Mo•ses-in-the-cra•dle (mō′ziz in thə krā′dəl, mō′-zis), *n.* a plant, *Rhoeo spathacea,* native to the West Indies and Central America, having leaves with purple undersides and white flowers enclosed in a boat-shaped envelope formed by two bracts. Also called **Mo•ses-on-a-raft** (mō′ziz on ə raft′, -räft′, -ôn-, mō′zis-), **boat lily, oyster plant.**

Mo′ses Lake′, a city in central Washington, on the eastern shore of Moses Lake. 10,629.

mo•sey (mō′zē), *v.i.,* **-seyed, -sey•ing.** *Informal.* **1.** to wander or shuffle about leisurely; stroll; saunter (often fol. by *along, about,* etc.). **2.** to leave quickly; decamp. [1820–30, *Amer.*; orig. uncert.]

MOSFET (mos′fet′), *n. Electronics.* metal oxide semiconducter field-effect transistor.

mo•shav (mō shäv′), *n., pl.* **mo•sha•vim** (mō′shä-vēm′). a cooperative community in Israel made up of small farm units. Cf. **kibbutz.** [1930–35; < Mod Heb *moshav,* Heb *mōshābh* dwelling]

Mo•shi (mō′shē), *n.* a city in N Tanzania. 26,864.

Mo•shoe•shoe II (mō shwā′shwā), (*Constantine Bereng Seeiso*) born 1938, king of Lesotho 1966–90.

Mo•skva (mu skvä′), *n.* Russian name of **Moscow.**

Mos•lem (moz′ləm, mos′-), *adj., n., pl.* **-lems, -lem.** Muslim (defs. 1, 2).

Mos•lem•ism (moz′lə miz′əm, mos′-), *n.* the Muslim religion; Islam. [MOSLEM + -ISM]

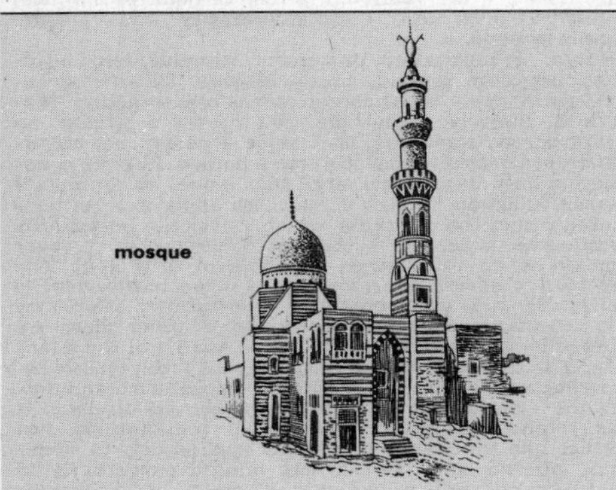
mosque

mosque (mosk, môsk), *n.* a Muslim temple or place of public worship. [1600–10; earlier *mosquee* < MF < It *moschea* << Ar *masjid,* deriv. of *sajada* to worship, lit., prostrate oneself; the *-ee* seems to have been taken as dim. suffix and dropped]

mos•qui•to (mə skē′tō), *n., pl.* **-toes, -tos. 1.** any of numerous dipterous insects of the family Culicidae, the females of which suck the blood of animals and humans, some species transmitting certain diseases, as malaria and yellow fever. **2.** (*cap.*) *Mil.* a twin-engined, two-seat British fighter and bomber of World War II, made largely of plywood and having a top speed of 380 mph (610 km/h). [1575–85; < Sp, equiv. to *mosc(a)* fly (< L *musca*) + *-ito* dim. suffix] **—mos•qui′to•ey,** *adj.*

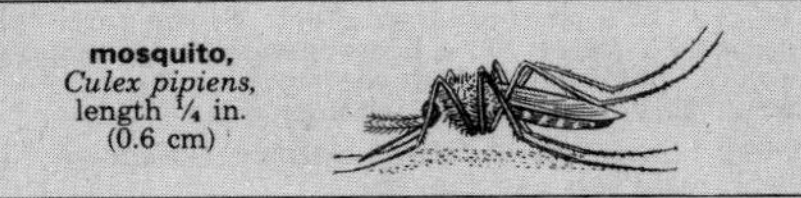
mosquito, *Culex pipiens,* length ¼ in. (0.6 cm)

Mos•qui•to (mə skē′tō), *n., pl.* **-tos,** (*esp. collectively*) **-to.** Miskito.

mosqui′to boat′. See **PT boat.** [1910–15]

Mosqui′to Coast′, a coastal region in Central America bordering on the Caribbean Sea, E of Honduras and Nicaragua.

mos•qui•to•fish (mə skē′tō fish′), *n., pl.* (*esp. collectively*) **-fish,** (*esp. referring to two or more kinds or species*) **-fish•es.** any of several fishes that feed on mosquito larvae, as *Gambusia affinis,* found in the southeastern U.S., now introduced into other parts of the world for mosquito control. [1925–30; MOSQUITO + FISH]

mosqui′to fleet′, a group or fleet of PT boats or other small, armed boats. [1795–1805]

mosqui′to hawk′, 1. nighthawk (def. 1). **2.** *Chiefly Southern U.S.* Also called **skeeter hawk.** dragonfly (def. 1). [1700–10, *Amer.*; so called because it feeds on nocturnal insects such as mosquitoes]
—Regional Variation. 2. See **dragonfly.**

mosqui′to net′, a screen, curtain, or canopy of net, gauze, or the like, for keeping out mosquitoes. [1735–45]

mosqui′to net′ting, netting used in the making of mosquito nets. [1735–45]

moss (môs, mos), *n.* **1.** any tiny, leafy-stemmed, flowerless plant of the class Musci, reproducing by spores and growing in tufts, sods, or mats on moist ground, tree trunks, rocks, etc. **2.** a growth of such plants. **3.** any of various similar plants, as Iceland moss or club moss. **4.** *Chiefly Scot. and North Eng.* a swamp or bog. **—*v.t.* 5.** to cover with a growth of moss: *to moss a crumbling wall.* [bef. 1000; ME *mos(se),* OE *mos* moss, bog; akin to G *Moos,* ON *mýrr* MIRE] **—moss′like′,** *adj.*

Mos•sad (mō säd′) *n.* the Israeli intelligence service, established in 1951.

Mos•sa•degh (mō′sä dek′), *n.* **Mohammed,** 1880–1967, Iranian statesman: premier 1951–53.

moss′ ag′ate, a kind of agate or chalcedony containing brown or black mosslike dendritic markings from various impurities. [1790–1800]

moss′ an′imal, bryozoan. [1880–85]

moss•back (môs′bak′, mos′-), *n.* **1.** *Informal.* **a.** a person holding very antiquated notions; reactionary. **b.** a person living in the backwoods; rustic. **2.** an old turtle. **3.** *Angling.* a large and old fish, as a bass. **4.** a wild bull or cow. [1870–75, *Amer.*; MOSS + BACK[1]]

Möss•bau•er (môs′bou ər, mos′-; *Ger.* mœs′bou ər), *n.* **Ru•dolf L.** (ro͞o′dôlf), born 1929, German physicist: Nobel prize 1961.

Möss′bauer effect′, *Physics.* the phenomenon in which an atom in a crystal undergoes no recoil when emitting a gamma ray, giving all the emitted energy to the gamma ray, resulting in a sharply defined wavelength. [1955–60; named after R. MÖSSBAUER]

moss•bunk•er (môs′bung′kər, mos′-), *n.* the menhaden. [1785–95, *Amer.*; < D *marsbanker*]

moss′ cam′pion, 1. See **cushion pink. 2.** a related garden plant, *Silene schafta,* of the Caucasus, having rose-colored or purple flowers. [1785–95]

moss′ green′, a moderate to dark yellow-green color. [1880–85] **—moss′-green′,** *adj.*

moss-grown (môs′grōn′, mos′-), *adj.* **1.** overgrown with moss. **2.** old-fashioned; antiquated: *moss-grown traditions.* [1350–1400; ME]

moss′ hag′, *Scot.* an area, pit, or hole from which peat has been dug. [1810–20]

Mos•si (mos′ē), *n., pl.* **-sis,** (*esp. collectively*) **-si** for 1. **1.** an agricultural people of Africa living mainly in Burkina Faso. **2.** Also called **Moré.** the language of the Mossi people, a Gur language of the Niger-Congo family.

mos•so (mō′sō; *It.* môs′sô), *adj. Music.* rapid; fast. [1875–80; < It, ptp. of *muovere* to MOVE]

Mos•so•ró (mo͝o so͞o RÔ′), *n.* a city in NE Brazil. 53,114.

moss′ pink′, a phlox, *Phlox subulata,* of the eastern U.S., having showy pink to purple flowers. [1855–60]

Moss′ Point′, a town in SE Mississippi. 18,998.

moss′ rose′, 1. a variety of rose, *Rosa centrifolia muscosa,* having a mosslike growth on the calyx and stem. **2.** See **rose moss.** [1725–35]

moss•troop•er (môs′tro͞o′pər, mos′-), *n.* **1.** a marauder who operated in the mosses, or bogs, of the border between England and Scotland in the 17th century. **2.** any marauder. [1645–55; MOSS + TROOPER] **—moss′troop′er•y,** *n.* **—moss′troop′ing,** *n., adj.*

moss•y (môs′ē, mos′ē), *adj.,* **moss•i•er, moss•i•est. 1.** overgrown with or abounding in moss: *a mossy stone.* **2.** covered with a mosslike growth. **3.** appearing as if covered with moss. **4.** resembling moss: *a mossy softness.* **5.** old or outdated; antiquated: *mossy ideas.* [1540–50; MOSS + -Y[1]] **—moss′i•ness,** *n.*

moss′y horn′, *Western U.S.* **1.** an old steer, esp. a longhorn with scaly horns. **2.** an aged cowboy. Also, **moss′ horn′.** [1880–85]

most (mōst), *adj., superl. of* **much** *or* **many** *with* **more** *as compar.* **1.** in the greatest quantity, amount, measure, degree, or number: *to win the most votes.* **2.** in the majority of instances: *Most operations are successful.* **3.** greatest, as in size or extent: *the most talent.* **4. for the most part.** See **part** (def. 18). **—*n.* 5.** the greatest quantity, amount, or degree; the utmost: *The most I can hope for is a passing grade.* **6.** the greatest number or the majority of a class specified: *Most of his writing is rubbish.* **7.** the greatest number: *The most this room will seat is 150.* **8.** the majority of persons: *to be more sensitive than most.* **9. at the most,** at the maximum. Also, **at most. 10. make the most of,** to use to greatest advantage; utilize fully: *to make the most of an opportunity.* **11. the most,** *Slang.* the ultimate in something: *He's the most. That movie was the most.* **—*adv., superl. of* much** *with* **more** *as compar.* **12.** in or to the greatest extent or degree (in this sense often used before adjectives and adverbs, and regularly before those of more than two syllables, to form superlative phrases having the same force and effect as the superlative degree formed by the termination *-est*): *most rapid; most wisely.* **13.** very: *a most puzzling case.* **14.** *Informal.* almost or nearly. [bef. 900; ME *most(e),* OE *māst;* r. ME *mest(e),* OE *mǣst;* c. G *meist,* Goth *maists.* See MORE]
—Syn. 14. See **almost.**
—Usage. 14. The adverb MOST, a shortened form of *almost,* is far from being either a recent development or an Americanism. It goes back to the 16th century in England, where it is now principally a dialect form. In American English it occurs before such pronouns as *all, anyone, anybody, everyone,* and *everybody;* the adjectives *all, any,* and *every;* and adverbs like *anywhere* and *everywhere: Most everyone around here is related to everyone else. You can find that plant most anywhere.* This use of MOST is often objected to, but it is common in the informal speech of educated persons. It is less common in edited writing except in representations of speech.

-most, a combining form of **most** occurring in a series of superlatives: *foremost; utmost.* [ME *-most;* r. ME, OE *-mest,* double superl. suffix, equiv. to *-ma* superl. suffix (as in OE *forma* first; cf. L *primus*) + -EST[1]; later identified with MOST]

most•est (mō′stist), *adj., n. Slang.* most. [1880–85; MOST + -EST[1]]

most-fa•vored-na•tion (mōst′fā′vərd nā′shən), *adj.* of or pertaining to the status, treatment, terms, etc., that are embodied in or conferred by a most-favored-nation clause. [1750–60]

most′-fa′vored-na′tion clause′, a clause in a commercial treaty or contract by which each signatory agrees to give the other the same treatment that is or will be accorded any other nation.

most•ly (mōst′lē), *adv.* **1.** for the most part; in the main: *The work is mostly done.* **2.** chiefly; principally. **3.** generally; customarily. [1585–95; MOST + -LY]

Most′ Rev′erend, the official form of address for cardinals, heads of religious orders, and certain prelates, as archbishops and bishops.

most′ signif′icant dig′it, the digit farthest to the left in a number. *Abbr.:* MSD Cf. **least significant digit.**

most′ want′ed list′, an actual or supposed listing of the names of persons who are urgently being sought for a specific reason, as apprehension for an alleged crime.

Mo•sul (mō so͞ol′), *n.* a city in N Iraq, on the Tigris, opposite the ruins of Nineveh. 243,311.

Mosz•kow•ski (mōsh kôf′skē, -kof′-), *n.* **Mo•ritz** (môr′its, mōr′its), 1854–1925, Polish composer and pianist.

mot (mō), *n.* **1.** a pithy or witty remark; bon mot. **2.** *Archaic.* a note on a horn, bugle, etc. [1625–35; < F < LL *muttum* utterance. See MOTTO]

Mo•ta•gua (mô tä′gwä), *n.* a river in S central Guatemala, flowing NE to the Caribbean Sea. ab. 250 mi. (315 km) long.

mote[1] (mōt), *n.* **1.** a small particle or speck, esp. of dust. **2.** moit. [bef. 1000; ME, OE *mot* speck; c. D *mot* grit, sawdust, Norw *mutt* speck] **—mote′y,** *adj.*

mote[2] (mōt), *v., pt.* **moste** (mōst). *Archaic.* may or might. [ME *mot(e),* OE *mōt;* c. G *muss.* See MUST[1]]

mo•tel (mō tel′), *n.* a hotel providing travelers with lodging and free parking facilities, typically a roadside hotel having rooms adjacent to an outside parking area or an urban hotel offering parking within the building. [1920–25; b. MOTOR and HOTEL]

mote′ spoon′, a small spoon with a pierced bowl for removing tea leaves from a cup of tea.

mo•tet (mō tet′), *n. Music.* a vocal composition in polyphonic style, on a Biblical or similar prose text, intended for use in a church service. [1350–1400; ME < MF; see MOT, -ET]

moth (môth, moth), *n., pl.* **moths** (môthz, mothz, môths, moths). **1.** any of numerous insects of the order Lepidoptera, generally distinguished from the butterflies by having feathery antennae and by having crepuscular or nocturnal habits. **2.** See **clothes moth.** [bef. 950; ME *motthe,* OE *moththe;* akin to G *Motte,* ON *motti*]

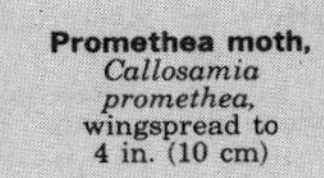
Promethea moth, *Callosamia promethea,* wingspread to 4 in. (10 cm)

moth•ball (môth′bôl′, moth′-), *n.* **1.** a small ball of naphthalene or sometimes of camphor for placing in closets or other storage areas to repel moths from clothing, blankets, etc. **2. in mothballs, a.** in disuse or in storage, esp. with reference to standby equipment. **b.** (of ideas) dismissed as unworthy of further deliberation. **—*v.t.* 3.** to put into storage or reserve; inactivate. **—*adj.* 4.** inactive; unused; stored away: *a mothball fleet.* [1905–10; MOTH + BALL[1]]

moth′ bean′, a low, trailing Indian plant, *Vigna aconitifolia,* of the legume family, having yellow flowers grown for forage and edible seeds. [1880–85]

moth-eat•en (môth′ēt′n, moth′-), *adj.* **1.** eaten or damaged by or as if by the larvae of moths. **2.** decayed or worn out. **3.** out of fashion; antiquated. [1350–1400; ME]

moth•er[1] (muth′ər), *n.* **1.** a female parent. **2.** (*often cap.*) one's female parent. **3.** a mother-in-law, stepmother, or adoptive mother. **4.** a term of address for a female parent or a woman having or regarded as having the status, function, or authority of a female parent. **5.** a term of familiar address for an old or elderly woman. **6.** See **mother superior. 7.** a woman exercising control, influence, or authority like that of a mother: *to be a mother to someone.* **8.** the qualities characteristic of a mother, as maternal affection: *It is the mother in her showing itself.* **9.** something or someone that gives rise to or exercises protecting care over something else; origin or source. **10.** (in disc recording) a mold from which stampers are made. **11. mother of all,** the greatest or most notable example of: *the mother of all mystery novels.* **—*adj.* 12.** being a mother: *a mother bird.* **13.** of, pertaining to, or characteristic of a mother: *mother love.* **14.** derived from or as if from one's mother; native: *his mother culture.* **15.** bearing a relation like that of a mother, as in being the origin, source, or protector: *the mother company and its affiliates; the mother computer and its network of terminals.* **—*v.t.* 16.** to be the mother of; give origin or rise to. **17.** to acknowledge oneself the author of; assume as one's own. **18.** to care for or protect like a mother; act maternally toward. **—*v.i.* 19.** to perform the tasks or duties of a female parent; act maternally: *a woman with a need to mother.* [bef. 900; ME *mother, moder,* OE *mōdor;* c. D *moeder,* G

Mutter, ON *mōthir,* L *māter,* Gk *mḗtēr,* Skt *mātar-.* As in *father, th* was substituted for *d,* possibly on the model of *brother*] **—moth′er•less,** *adj.* **—moth′er•less•ness,** *n.*

—Syn. 18. tend, nurse, mind, raise.

moth•er[2] (muth′ər), *n.* a stringy, mucilaginous substance consisting of various bacteria, esp. *Mycoderma aceti,* that forms on the surface of a fermenting liquid and causes fermentation when added to other liquids, as in changing wine or cider to vinegar. Also called **mother of vinegar.** [1530–40; prob. special use of MOTHER[1], but perh. another word, akin to D *modder* dregs, MLG *moder* swampy land; see MUD]

moth•er[3] (muth′ər), *n. Slang* (*vulgar*). **1.** motherfucker. **2.** a person or thing that is very large, powerful, or impressive. [1945–50; euphemistic shortening]

moth•er•board (muth′ər bôrd′, -bōrd′), *n. Computers.* a rigid, slotted board upon which other boards that contain the basic circuitry of a computer or of a computer component can be mounted. Cf. **board** (def. 14). [MOTHER[1] + BOARD]

Moth′er Car′ey's chick′en (kâr′ēz), any of various small petrels, esp. the stormy petrel, *Oceanites oceanicus.* [1760–70; orig. uncert.]

moth′er church′, 1. a church from which other churches have had their origin or derived their authority. **2.** a cathedral or a metropolitan church. **3.** the church attended in one's youth or for the greater part of one's life. [1275–1325; ME]

moth′er coun′try, 1. the country of one's birth or ancestry. **2.** the country of origin of settlers or colonists in a place. [1580–90]

moth′er earth′, 1. the earth regarded as the source of all animate and inanimate things. **2.** the land or soil. [1580–90]

moth•er•fuck•er (muth′ər fuk′ər), *n. Slang* (*vulgar*). **1.** a mean, despicable, or vicious person. **2.** anything considered to be despicable, frustrating, etc. (used as a general expression of contempt or anger). [1955–60; MOTHER[1] + FUCKER] **—moth′er•fuck′ing,** *adj.*

Moth′er God′dess, *Hinduism.* **1.** Kālī. **2.** Pārvatī.

Moth′er Goose′, the fictitious author of a collection of nursery rhymes first published in London (about 1760) under the title of *Mother Goose's Melody.*

moth′er hen′, a person who attends to the welfare of others, esp. one who is fussily protective. [1950–55]

moth•er•hood (muth′ər ho͝od′), *n.* **1.** the state of being a mother; maternity. **2.** the qualities or spirit of a mother. **3.** mothers collectively. *—adj.* **4.** having or relating to an inherent worthiness, justness, or goodness that is obvious or unarguable: *legislation pushed through on a motherhood basis.* [1375–1425; late ME *moderhed.* See MOTHER[1], -HOOD]

moth′er house′, *Rom. Cath. Ch.* **1.** a convent housing a mother superior of a community of nuns. **2.** a self-governing convent having authority over other houses. [1665–75]

Moth′er Hub′bard (hub′ərd), **1.** a full, loose gown, usually fitted at the shoulders, worn by women. **2.** a character in a nursery rhyme.

moth•er•ing (muth′ər ing), *n.* **1.** the nurturing of an infant or small child by its mother. **2.** (in rural England) the custom of visiting one's parents on Laetare Sunday with a present. [1640–50; MOTHER[1] + -ING[1]]

Moth′ering Sun′day, *Brit.* See **Laetare Sunday.**

moth•er-in-law (muth′ər in lô′), *n., pl.* **moth•ers-in-law.** the mother of one's husband or wife. [1350–1400; ME *modyr in lawe*]

moth′er-in-law plant′. See **dumb cane.**

moth•er•land (muth′ər land′), *n.* **1.** one's native land. **2.** the land of one's ancestors. **3.** a country considered as the origin or source of something. [1705–15; MOTHER[1] + LAND]

moth′er lan′guage, a language from which another language is descended; parent language. Also called **mother tongue.**

moth′er liq′uor, the portion of a solution remaining after crystallization of its important component. [1790–1800]

moth′er lode′, 1. *Mining.* a rich or important lode. **2.** a major or profitable source or supply: *New York City is a mother lode of actors.* [1855–60]

moth•er•ly (muth′ər lē), *adj.* **1.** pertaining to, characteristic of, or befitting a mother; maternal: *motherly solicitude.* **2.** like a mother: *to take a motherly interest in an orphan.* *—adv.* **3.** in the manner of a mother. [bef. 1000; ME *moderly,* OE *mōdorlic.* See MOTHER[1], -LY] **—moth′er•li•ness,** *n.*

moth•er-na•ked (muth′ər nā′kid), *adj.* stark naked; as naked as when born. [1350–1400; ME]

moth′er of coal′. See **mineral charcoal.** [1865–70]

Moth′er of God′, a title of the Virgin Mary. [1375–1425; late ME]

moth•er-of-pearl (muth′ər əv pûrl′), *n.* **1.** a hard, iridescent substance that forms the inner layer of certain mollusk shells, used for making buttons, beads, etc.; nacre. *—adj.* **2.** of or having the qualities of mother-of-pearl, as being iridescent or pearly: *mother-of-pearl buttons.* [1500–10; cf. It *madreperla,* obs. F *mère perle*]

moth′er-of-pearl′ cloud′. See **nacreous cloud.** [1930–35]

moth′er-of-pearl′ glass′. See **satin glass.**

moth•er-of-thou•sands (muth′ər əv thou′zəndz), *n., pl.* **-sands.** (*used with a singular or plural v.*) See **strawberry geranium.** [1850–55]

moth•er-of-thyme (muth′ər əv tīm′), *n., pl.* **-thymes.** a branched, woody, prostrate plant, *Thymus serpyllum,* of the mint family, native to Eurasia and northern Africa, having wiry stems that root at the joints and small, purplish flowers. [1590–1600]

moth′er of vin′egar, mother[2]. [1595–1605]

moth′er's boy′. See **mama's boy.** [1875–80]

Moth′er's Day′, a day, usually the second Sunday in May, set aside in honor of mothers.

moth′er's help′er, a person who is hired to assist in household chores, esp. caring for children.

moth′er ship′, a vessel or craft that services others operating far from a home port or center. [1885–90]

moth′er spleen′wort, a fern, *Asplenium bulbiferum,* of tropical Africa and Australasia, the fronds often bearing bulbils that sprout into new plants while still attached, grown as an ornamental. [‡ 1960–65]

moth′er supe′rior, *pl.* **mother superiors, mothers superior.** the head of a Christian religious community for women. [1905–10]

moth•er tongue′ (muth′ər tung′ *for 1;* muth′ər tung′ *for 2*), **1.** the language first learned by a person; native language. **2.** See **mother language.** [1350–1400; ME *moder tonge*]

Moth•er•well (muth′ər wel′, -wəl), *n.* **1. Robert,** 1915–91, U.S. painter. **2.** an administrative district in the Strathclyde region, in S Scotland. 161,104.

Moth′erwell and Wish′aw (wish′ô), a burgh in the Motherwell district, in S Scotland. 74,038.

moth′er wit′, natural or practical intelligence, wit, or sense. [1400–50; late ME *moderis wytte*]

moth•er•wort (muth′ər wûrt′, -wôrt′), *n.* a European plant, *Leonorus cardiaca,* of the mint family, an introduced weed in the U.S., having cut leaves with a whorl of lavender flowers in the axils. [1350–1400; ME *moderwort* (see MOTHER[1], WORT[2]), so called because believed helpful for diseases of the womb]

moth′er yaw′, *Pathol.* the initial lesion of yaws, occurring at the site of inoculation. [1815–25]

moth′ mul′lein, a weedy, European mullein, *Verbascum blattaria,* of the figwort family, having lance-shaped leaves and loose spikes of white or yellow flowers. [1570–80; from its mothlike appearance]

moth′ or′chid, any orchid of the genus *Phalaenopsis,* having thick, leathery leaves and loose clusters of flowers, usually white or tinged with rose or purple. [1875–80]

moth•proof (môth′pro͞of′, moth′-), *adj.* **1.** resistant to attack by moths. *—v.t.* **2.** to render (fabric, clothing, etc.) mothproof. [1890–95; MOTH + -PROOF] **—moth′•proof′er,** *n.*

moth•y (mô′thē, moth′ē), *adj.,* **moth•i•er, moth•i•est.** **1.** containing moths. **2.** moth-eaten. [1590–1600; MOTH + -Y[1]]

Mo Ti (mô′ dē′), Mo-tze.

mo•tif (mō tēf′), *n.* **1.** a recurring subject, theme, idea, etc., esp. in a literary, artistic, or musical work. **2.** a distinctive and recurring form, shape, figure, etc., in a design, as in a painting or on wallpaper. **3.** a dominant idea or feature: *the profit motif of free enterprise.* [1840–50; < F; see MOTIVE]

mo•tile (mōt′l, mō′til), *adj. Biol.* moving or capable of moving spontaneously: *motile cells; motile spores.* [1860–65; < L *mōt*(*us*) (ptp. of *movēre* to move, set in motion) + -ILE] **—mo•til•i•ty** (mō til′i tē), *n.*

mo•tion (mō′shən), *n.* **1.** the action or process of moving or of changing place or position; movement. **2.** power of movement, as of a living body. **3.** the manner of moving the body in walking; gait. **4.** a bodily movement or change of posture; gesture. **5.** a proposal formally made to a deliberative assembly: *to make a motion to adjourn.* **6.** *Law.* an application made to a court or judge for an order, ruling, or the like. **7.** a suggestion or proposal. **8.** an inward prompting or impulse; inclination: *He will go only of his own motion.* **9.** *Music.* melodic progression, as the change of a voice part from one pitch to another. **10.** *Mach.* **a.** a piece of mechanism with a particular action or function. **b.** the action of such a mechanism. **11. go through the motions,** to do something halfheartedly, routinely, or as a formality or façade. **12. in motion,** in active operation; moving: *The train was already in motion when he tried to board it.* *—v.t.* **13.** to direct by a significant motion or gesture, as with the hand: *to motion a person to a seat.* *—v.i.* **14.** to make a meaningful motion, as with the hand; gesture; signal: *to motion to someone to come.* [1350–1400; ME *mocio*(*u*)*n* < L *mōtiōn-* (s. of *mōtiō*), equiv. to *mōt*(*us*) (ptp. of *movēre* to MOVE) + *-iōn-* -ION] **—mo′tion•al,** *adj.* **—mo′tion•er,** *n.*

—Syn. 1. MOTION, MOVE, MOVEMENT refer to change of position in space. MOTION denotes change of position, either considered apart from, or as a characteristic of, something that moves; usually the former, in which case it is often a somewhat technical or scientific term: *perpetual motion.* The chief uses of MOVE are founded upon the idea of moving a piece, in chess or a similar game, for winning the game, and hence the word denotes any change of position, condition, or circumstances for the accomplishment of some end: *a shrewd move to win votes.* MOVEMENT is always connected with the person or thing moving, and is usually a definite or particular motion: *the movements of a dance.* **3.** bearing, carriage.

mo•tion•less (mō′shən lis), *adj.* without motion: *a motionless statue.* [1590–1600; MOTION + -LESS] **—mo′•tion•less•ly,** *adv.* **—mo′tion•less•ness,** *n.*

—Syn. still, stationary, unmoving, inert, stable, fixed, quiescent, quiet. **—Ant.** active.

mo′tion pic′ture, 1. a sequence of consecutive pictures of objects photographed in motion by a specially designed camera **(mo′tion-pic′ture cam′era)** and thrown on a screen by a projector **(mo′tion-pic′ture projec′tor)** in such rapid succession as to give the illusion of natural movement. **2.** a play, event, or the like, presented in this form. **3. motion pictures,** the art, technique, or business of producing motion pictures. Also called **movie, moving picture.** [1890–95] **—mo′•tion-pic′ture,** *adj.*

mo′tion sick′ness, *Pathol.* a feeling of nausea and dizziness, sometimes accompanied by vomiting, resulting from stimulation by motion of the semicircular canals of the ear during travel by car, plane, etc. [1940–45]

mo′tion stud′y. See **time and motion study.** [1910–15]

mo′tion work′, clockwork by which the hour hand is driven from the shaft of the minute hand. [1785–95]

mo•ti•vate (mō′tə vāt′), *v.t.,* **-vat•ed, -vat•ing.** to provide with a motive or motives; incite; impel. [1860–65; MOTIVE + -ATE[1]] **—mo′ti•va′tor, n.**

—Syn. induce, move, provoke, prompt, cause.

mo•ti•va•tion (mō′tə vā′shən), *n.* **1.** the act or an instance of motivating. **2.** the state or condition of being motivated. **3.** something that motivates; inducement; incentive. [1870–75; MOTIVE + -ATION] **—mo′ti•va′•tion•al,** *adj.* **—mo′ti•va′tive,** *adj.*

motiva′tion research′, the application of the knowledge and techniques of the social sciences, esp. psychology and sociology, to understanding consumer attitudes and behavior: used as a guide in advertising and marketing. Also, **motiva′tional research′.** [1950–55]

mo•tive (mō′tiv), *n., adj., v.,* **-tived, -tiv•ing.** *—n.* **1.** something that causes a person to act in a certain way, do a certain thing, etc.; incentive. **2.** the goal or object of a person's actions: *Her motive was revenge.* **3.** (in art, literature, and music) a motif. *—adj.* **4.** causing, or tending to cause, motion. **5.** pertaining to motion. **6.** prompting to action. **7.** constituting a motive or motives. *—v.t.* **8.** to motivate. [1325–75; (adj.) ME (< MF *motif*) < ML *mōtīvus* serving to move, equiv. to L *mōt*(*us*) (ptp. of *movēre* to MOVE) + *-īvus* -IVE; (n.) ME (< MF *motif*) < ML *mōtīvum,* n. use of neut. of *mōtīvus*] **—mo′tive•less,** *adj.* **—mo′tive•less•ly,** *adv.* **—mo′•tive•less•ness,** *n.*

—Syn. 1. motivation, incitement, stimulus, spur; influence, occasion, ground, cause. MOTIVE, INCENTIVE, INDUCEMENT apply to whatever moves one to action. MOTIVE is, literally, something that moves a person; an INDUCEMENT, something that leads a person on; an INCENTIVE, something that inspires a person. MOTIVE is applied mainly to an inner urge that moves or prompts a person to action, though it may also apply to a contemplated result, the desire for which moves the person: *His motive was a wish to be helpful.* INDUCEMENT is never applied to an inner urge, and seldom to a goal: *The pleasure of wielding authority may be an inducement to get ahead.* It is used mainly of opportunities offered by the acceptance of certain conditions, whether these are offered by a second person or by the factors of the situation: *The salary offered me was a great inducement.* INCENTIVE was once used of anything inspiring or stimulating the emotions or imagination: *incentives to piety;* it has retained of this its emotional connotations, but (rather like INDUCEMENT) is today applied only to something offered as a reward, and offered particularly to stimulate competitive activity: *to create incentives for higher achievement.* **2.** See **reason.**

-motive, a combining form of **motive:** *automotive.*

mo′tive pow′er, 1. any power used to impart motion; any source of mechanical energy. **2.** *Railroads.* locomotives or other vehicles that supply tractive power. [1615–25]

mo•tiv•i•ty (mō tiv′i tē), *n.* the power of initiating or producing motion. [1680–90; MOTIVE + -ITY]

mot juste (mō zhʏst′), *pl.* ***mots justes*** (mō zhʏst′). *French.* the exact, appropriate word.

mot•ley (mot′lē), *adj., n., pl.* **-leys.** *—adj.* **1.** exhibiting great diversity of elements; heterogeneous: *a motley crowd.* **2.** being of different colors combined; parti-colored: *a motley flower border.* **3.** wearing a parti-colored garment: *a motley fool.* *—n.* **4.** a combination of different colors. **5.** a parti-colored effect. **6.** the parti-colored garment of a jester. **7.** a heterogeneous assemblage. **8.** a medley. [1350–1400; ME; see MOTE[1], -LY]

—Syn. 1. varied, mixed, incongruous.

Mot•ley (mot′lē), *n.* **John Lo•throp** (lō′thrəp), 1814–77, U.S. historian and diplomat.

mot•mot (mot′mot), *n.* any of several tropical and subtropical American birds of the family Momotidae, related to the kingfishers, having a serrate bill and chiefly greenish and bluish plumage. [1625–35; < AmerSp; repetitive compound, imitating the bird's note]

mo•to (mō′tō), *n., pl.* **-tos.** one of the heats in a motocross. [1970–75; see MOTOCROSS]

mo•to•cross (mō′tō krôs′, -kros′), *n.* a timed motorcycle race over a closed course consisting of a winding dirt trail with hills, jumps, sharp turns, and often muddy terrain. [< F: equiv. to *moto*(*cycle*) MOTORCYCLE + *cross*(*-country*) CROSS-COUNTRY]

mo•ton (mōt′n), *n. Armor.* besague. [1480–90; orig. uncert.]

mo•to•neu•ron (mō′tə no͝or′on, -nyo͝or′-), *n. Cell Biol., Physiol.* motor neuron. [1905–10; *moto-* (comb. form repr. MOTOR) + NEURON]

mo•tor (mō′tər), *n.* **1.** a comparatively small and powerful engine, esp. an internal-combustion engine in an automobile, motorboat, or the like. **2.** any self-powered vehicle. **3.** a person or thing that imparts motion, esp. a contrivance, as a steam engine, that receives and modifies energy from some natural source in order to utilize it in driving machinery. **4.** Also called **electric motor.** *Elect.* a machine that converts electrical energy into mechanical energy, as an induction motor. **5. motors,** stocks or bonds in automobile companies. *—adj.* **6.** pertaining to or operated by a motor. **7.** of, for, by, or pertaining to motor vehicles: *motor freight.* **8.** designed

CONCISE ETYMOLOGY KEY: <, descended or borrowed from; >, whence; b., blend of, blended; c., cognate with; cf., compare; deriv., derivative; equiv., equivalent; imit., imitative; obl., oblique; r., replacing; s., stem; sp., spelling, spelled; resp., respelling, respelled; trans., translation; ?, origin unknown; *, unattested; ‡, probably earlier than. See the full key inside the front cover.

or for automobiles, their drivers, or their passengers: *The hotel has a motor lobby in its parking garage for picking up and discharging passengers.* **9.** causing or producing motion. **10.** *Physiol.* conveying an impulse that results or tends to result in motion, as a nerve. **11.** *Psychol., Physiol.* Also, **motoric.** of, pertaining to, or involving muscular movement: *a motor response; motor images.* —*v.i.* **12.** to ride or travel in an automobile; drive: *They motored up the coast.* —*v.t.* **13.** *Chiefly Brit.* to drive or transport by car: *He motored his son to school.* [1580–90; < L *mōtor* mover, equiv. to *mō-* (var. s. of *movēre* to MOVE) + *-tor* -TOR]

mo′tor apha′sia, *Pathol.* See **Broca's aphasia.**

mo•tor•bike (mō′tər bīk′), *n., v.,* **-biked, -bik•ing.** —*n.* **1.** a small, lightweight motorcycle. **2.** a bicycle that is propelled by an attached motor. —*v.i.* **3.** to go by motorbike; drive or ride a motorbike. Also called **mo•tor•bi•cy•cle** (mō′tər bī′si kəl, -sik əl, -sī kəl). [1900–05; MOTOR + BIKE[1]] —**mo′tor•bik′er,** *n.*

mo•tor•boat (mō′tər bōt′), *n.* **1.** a boat propelled by an inboard or outboard motor. —*v.i.* **2.** to travel in or operate a motorboat: *to motorboat from Hyannis to Martha's Vineyard.* [1900–05; MOTOR + BOAT] —**mo′tor•boat′er,** *n.*

mo•tor•boat•ing (mō′tər bō′ting), *n.* **1.** the recreational activity of operating or traveling in a motorboat. **2.** a malfunction in audio equipment resulting in sounds like those produced by an outboard motor. [1925–30; MOTORBOAT + -ING[1]]

mo•tor•bus (mō′tər bus′), *n., pl.* **-bus•es, -bus•ses.** a passenger bus powered by a motor. Also called **mo′tor coach′.** [1900–05; MOTOR + BUS[1]]

mo•tor•cade (mō′tər kād′), *n., v.,* **-cad•ed, -cad•ing.** —*n.* **1.** a procession or parade of automobiles or other motor vehicles. —*v.i.* **2.** to travel by or in a motorcade. [1910–15; MOTOR + -CADE]

mo•tor•car (mō′tər kär′), *n.* **1.** *Chiefly Brit.* an automobile. **2.** *Railroads.* a self-propelled car for freight or passengers. [1885–90, *Amer.*; MOTOR + CAR[1]]

mo′tor cor′tex, the region of the cerebral cortex concerned with transmitting impulses to the voluntary muscles. [1885–90]

mo′tor court′, motel. [1935–40, *Amer.*]

mo•tor•cy•cle (mō′tər sī′kəl), *n., v.,* **-cled, -cling.** —*n.* **1.** a motor vehicle similar to a bicycle but usually larger and heavier, chiefly for one rider but sometimes having two saddles or an attached sidecar for passengers. —*v.i.* **2.** to ride on or operate a motorcycle. [1890–95, *Amer.*; MOTOR + CYCLE] —**mo•tor•cy•clist** (mō′tər sī′klist), *n.*

motorcycle (def. 1)

mo′tor drive′, a mechanical system, including an electric motor, used to operate a machine or machines. [1905–10] —**mo•tor-driv•en** (mō′tər driv′ən), *adj.*

mo•tor•drome (mō′tər drōm′), *n.* a rounded course or track for automobile and motorcycle races. [1905–10; MOTOR + -DROME]

mo•tored (mō′tərd), *adj.* having a motor or motors, esp. of a specified number or type (usually used in combination): *a bimotored airplane.* [1925–30; MOTOR + -ED[3]]

mo′tor gen′erator, *Elect.* one or more motors mechanically coupled to one or more generators for converting or transforming electric current into mechanical energy. Also called **mo′tor gen′erator set′.** [1885–90]

mo′tor home′, a small bus or trucklike vehicle with a roomlike area behind the driver's seat outfitted as living quarters. Also, **mo′tor•home′.** [1965–70]

mo•tor•ic (mō tôr′ik, -tor′-), *adj.* **1.** motor (def. 11). **2.** (of music or musical performance) full of movement or energy. [1925–30; MOTOR + -IC] —**mo•tor′i•cal•ly,** *adv.*

mo•tor•ing (mō′tər ing), *n.* traveling in a car, esp. when considered as a recreation. [MOTOR + -ING[1]]

mo•tor•ist (mō′tər ist), *n.* a person who drives or travels in a privately owned automobile. [1895–1900; MOTOR + -IST]

mo•tor•ize (mō′tə rīz′), *v.t.,* **-ized, -iz•ing.** **1.** to furnish with a motor, as a vehicle. **2.** to supply with motor-driven vehicles, usually in the place of horses and horse-drawn vehicles. Also, *esp. Brit.,* **mo′tor•ise′.** [1910–15; MOTOR + -IZE] —**mo′tor•i•za′tion,** *n.*

mo′tor lodge′, motel. [1960–65]

mo′tor lor′ry, *Brit.* a motor truck, esp. one with open sides. [1900–05]

mo•tor•man (mō′tər mən), *n., pl.* **-men.** **1.** a person who operates or drives an electrically operated vehicle, as a streetcar or subway train. **2.** a person who operates a motor. [1885–90, *Amer.*; MOTOR + -MAN]
—**Usage.** See **-man.**

mo•tor-mind•ed (mō′tər mīn′did), *adj.* disposed to perceive one's environment in terms of mechanical or muscular activity. Cf. **ear-minded, eye-minded.** [1895–1900] —**mo′tor-mind′ed•ness,** *n.*

mo•tor-mouth (mō′tər mouth′), *n., pl.* **-mouths** (-mouths′, mouthz′). *Slang.* a person who is a constant or irrepressible talker.

mo′tor neu′ron, *Cell Biol., Physiol.* a nerve cell that conducts impulses to a muscle, gland, or other effector. Also, **motoneuron.** [1895–1900]

mo′tor pool′, a standby fleet of motor vehicles available for temporary use by appropriate personnel, as at a military or governmental installation. [1940–45, *Amer.*]

mo′tor root′. See under **nerve root.** [1830–40]

mo′tor sail′er, *Naut.* a yacht having sails and an engine as an alternative or auxiliary means of propulsion.

mo′tor scoot′er, scooter[1] (def. 2). [1915–20]

mo•tor•ship (mō′tər ship′), *n.* a ship driven by a diesel or other internal-combustion engine. Also called **mo′•tor ves′sel.** [1900–05]

mo•tor•sports (mō′tər spôrts′, -spōrts′), *n.pl.* competitions, esp. races, involving motor vehicles, as automobiles, motorboats, or motorcycles. [MOTOR + SPORTS]

mo′tor torpe′do boat′. See **PT boat.** [1935–40]

mo′tor truck′, truck[1] (def. 1). Also, **mo′tor•truck′.**

mo′tor u′nit, *Cell Biol., Physiol.* a motor neuron and the muscle fibers innervated by its axon. [1965–70]

mo′tor van′, *Brit.* a motor truck, esp. one enclosed to protect the cargo. [1895–1900]

mo′tor ve′hicle, an automobile, truck, bus, or similar motor-driven conveyance. [1885–90]

mo′tor vo′ter law′, a law that enables prospective voters to register when they obtain or renew a driver's license. [1990–93]

mo•tor•way (mō′tər wā′), *n. Brit.* an expressway. [1900–05; MOTOR + WAY[1]]

Mo•town (mō′toun′), *n.* **1.** Detroit, Michigan: a nickname. **2.** Also called **Mo′town sound′.** an upbeat, often pop-influenced style of rhythm and blues associated with the city of Detroit and with numerous black vocalists and vocal groups since the 1950's and characterized by compact, danceable arrangements.

Mo•tril (mô trēl′), *n.* a town in S Spain: resort center. 31,716.

Mo•trin (mō′trin), *Pharm., Trademark.* a brand of ibuprofen.

Mo-tse (*Chin.* mô′dzu′), *n.* Mo-tze. Also, **Mo′ Tse′.**

mot•ser (mot′sər), *n. Australian Slang.* a large amount of money, esp. a sum won in gambling. Also, **motzer, motza.** [1940–45; perh. alter. of Polari *medzers, medzies, metzes* money, pl. of *medzer, madzer* halfpenny, ult. < It *mezzo* half, MEZZO]

Mott (mot), *n.* **1. John Raleigh,** 1865–1955, U.S. religious leader: Nobel peace prize 1946. **2. Lucretia Coffin,** 1793–1880, U.S. social reformer: advocate of women's rights. **3. Sir Nev•ill Francis** (nev′əl), 1905–96, British physicist: developer of solid-state circuitry; Nobel prize 1977.

motte (mot), *n. Chiefly Southwestern U.S.* a grove or clump of trees in prairie land or open country. Also, **mott.** [1830–40, *Amer.*; < MexSp *mata;* Sp: grove, plantation, perh. < LL *matta* MAT[1]]

Mot•tel•son (mot′l sən, -sôn′), *n.* **Ben R(oy),** born 1926, Danish physicist, born in the U.S.: Nobel prize 1975.

mot•tle (mot′l), *v.,* **-tled, -tling,** *n.* —*v.t.* **1.** to mark or diversify with spots or blotches of a different color or shade. —*n.* **2.** a diversifying spot or blotch of color. **3.** mottled coloring or pattern. [1670–80; prob. back formation from MOTLEY] —**mot′tle•ment,** *n.* —**mot′tler,** *n.*

mot•tled (mot′ld), *adj.* spotted or blotched in coloring. [1670–80; MOTTLE + -ED[2]]

mot′tled enam′el, *Dentistry.* fluorosis (def. 2).

mot•to (mot′ō), *n., pl.* **-toes, -tos.** **1.** a maxim adopted as an expression of the guiding principle of a person, organization, city, etc. **2.** a sentence, phrase, or word expressing the spirit or purpose of a person, organization, city, etc., and often inscribed on a badge, banner, etc. [1580–90; < It < LL *muttum* sound, utterance. See MOT]

mot•tram•ite (mo′trə mīt′), *n. Mineral.* a copper and lead vanadate. [1875–80; named after *Mottram* St. Andrew's, Cheshire, England, where it was found; see -ITE[1]]

mo•tu pro•pri•o (mō′to͞o prō′prē ō′), *Latin.* of one's own accord: used of certain documents issued by the pope without counsel from others.

Mo-tze (mô′dzu′), *n.* (*Mo Ti*) fl. 5th century B.C., Chinese philosopher. Also, **Mo′ Tzu′, Mo-tse, Mo Tse.**

mot•zer (mot′sər), *n.* motser. Also, **mot•za** (mot′sə).

mouch (mo͞och), *v.i., v.t., n. Slang.* mooch.

mou•chette (mo͞o shet′), *n. Archit.* a daggerlike form, esp. in tracery, created by a segmental and an ogee curve so that it is pointed at one end and circular at the other. [1925–30; < F: orig., the fillet below an ovolo, projecting part of a cornice; hence, with the common sense "what protrudes," prob. deriv. of *moucher* to cut or knock off (something protruding) (see -ETTE), appar. extended sense of *moucher* to wipe (a person's) nose < VL **muccāre,* deriv. of L *muccus, mūcus* MUCUS]

mou•choir (mo͞o shwär′), *n., pl.* ***-choirs*** (-shwär′). *French.* a handkerchief.

moue (mo͞o), *n., pl.* **moues** (mo͞o). a pouting grimace. [< F; OF *moe;* see MOW[3]]

mouf•lon (mo͞of′lon), *n.* a wild sheep, *Ovis musimon,* inhabiting the mountainous regions of Sardinia and Corsica, the male of which has large curving horns. Also, **mouf′flon.** [1765–75; < F < It *muflone,* orig. dial.; cf. Corsican *muffolo,* Sardinian *murone,* LL *mufrō,* s. *mufrōn-,* presumably < a pre-L substratal language]

mought (môt), *South Midland and Southern U.S.* a pt. of **may.**

mouil•lé (mo͞o yā′), *adj. Phonet.* **1.** palatal or palatalized, esp. referring to sounds spelled *ll* and *ñ* in Spanish, *gl* and *gn* in Italian, etc. **2.** (of French sounds) spelled *l* or *ll* and pronounced as a *y* sound. [1825–35; < F, ptp. of *mouiller* to wet < VL **molliāre* to soften by wetting, deriv. of L *mollis* soft; see MOLLIFY]

mou•jik (mo͞o zhik′, mo͞o′zhik), *n.* muzhik.

mou•lage (mo͞o läzh′), *n.* **1.** the making of a mold, esp. with plaster of Paris, of objects, footprints, tire tracks, etc., as for the purpose of identification. **2.** the mold itself. [1900–05; < F, equiv. to *moul(er)* to mold (deriv. of *moule* MOLD[1]) + *-age* -AGE]

mould (mōld), *n., v.t., v.i. Chiefly Brit.* mold.

mould•y (mōl′dē), *n., pl.* **mould•ies.** *Brit. Mil. Slang.* a torpedo. [1915–20; prob. identical with Scot and north dial. *moudie* a mole]

mou•lin (mo͞o laN′), *n.* a nearly vertical shaft or cavity worn in a glacier by surface water falling through a crack in the ice. [1855–60; < F < LL *molinum* MILL[1]]

Mou•lin Rouge (*Fr.* mo͞o laN ro͞ozh′), a dance hall in the Montmartre section of Paris, France, opened in 1889 and famous for its cancan dancers and the drawings of its performers and customers made there by Toulouse-Lautrec. [< F: lit., red mill]

Moul•mein (mo͞ol mān′, mōl-), *n.* a seaport in S Burma at the mouth of the Salween River. 171,767. Also, **Maulmain.**

moult (mōlt), *v.i., v.t., n. Brit.* molt.

Moul•trie (mōl′trē, mo͞ol′-), *n.* **1. William,** 1730–1805, U.S. general. **2.** a city in S Georgia. 15,708. **3. Fort.** See **Fort Moultrie.**

moul•vi (moul′vē), *n.* maulvi.

mound[1] (mound), *n.* **1.** a natural elevation of earth; a hillock or knoll. **2.** an artificial elevation of earth, as for a defense work or a dam or barrier; an embankment. **3.** a heap or raised mass: *a mound of papers; a mound of hay.* **4.** *Baseball.* the slightly raised ground from which the pitcher delivers the ball. Cf. **rubber** (def. 13). **5.** an elevation formed of earth, sand, stones, etc., esp. over a grave or ruins. **6.** a tumulus or other raised work of earth dating from a prehistoric or long-past period. —*v.t.* **7.** to form into a mound; heap up. **8.** to furnish with a mound of earth, as for a defense. [1505–15; earlier: hedge or fence used as a boundary or protection, (v.) to enclose with a fence; cf. OE *mund* hand, hence protection, protector; c. ON *mund,* MD *mond* protection]

mound[2] (mound), *n.* a globe topped with a cross that symbolizes power and constitutes part of the regalia of an English sovereign. [1250–1300; ME: world < OF *monde* < L *mundus* world]

mound•bird (mound′bûrd′), *n.* megapode. [1850–55; MOUND[1] + BIRD; so called because it covers its eggs with mounds of dirt and compost]

mound′ build′er, megapode. [1835–45]

Mound′ Build′ers, the various American Indian tribes who, in prehistoric and early historic times, erected the burial mounds and other earthworks of the Mississippi drainage basin and southeastern U.S. [1830–40, *Amer.*]

mounds•man (moundz′mən), *n., pl.* **-men.** *Baseball Slang.* pitcher[2] (def. 2). [1910–15; MOUND[1] + 's[1] + MAN[1]]

Mounds′ View′, a town in E Minnesota. 12,593.

Mounds•ville (moundz′vil), *n.* a city in NW West Virginia, on the Ohio River. 12,419.

mount[1] (mount), *v.t.* **1.** to go up; climb; ascend: *to mount stairs.* **2.** to get up on (a platform, a horse, etc.). **3.** to set or place at an elevation: *to mount a house on stilts.* **4.** to furnish with a horse or other animal for riding. **5.** to set or place (a person) on horseback. **6.** to organize, as an army. **7.** to prepare and launch, as an attack or a campaign. **8.** to raise or put into position for use, as a gun. **9.** (of a fortress or warship) to have or carry (guns) in position for use. **10.** to go or put on guard, as a sentry or watch. **11.** to attach to or fix on or in a support, backing, setting, etc.: *to mount a photograph; to mount a diamond in a ring.* **12.** to arrange for display: *to mount a museum exhibit.* **13.** to provide (a play, musical comedy, opera, etc.) with scenery, costumes, and other equipment for production. **14.** to prepare (an animal body or skeleton) as a specimen. **15.** (of a male animal) to climb upon (a female) for copulation. **16.** *Micros.* **a.** to prepare (a slide) for microscopic investigation. **b.** to prepare (a sample) for examination by a microscope, as by placing it on a slide. —*v.i.* **17.** to increase in amount or intensity (often fol. by *up*): *The cost of all those small purchases mounts up.* **18.** to get up on the back of a horse or other animal for riding. **19.** to rise or go to a higher position, level, degree, etc.; ascend. **20.** to get up on something, as a platform. —*n.* **21.** the act or a manner of mounting. **22.** a horse, other animal, or sometimes a vehicle, as a bicycle, used, provided, or available for riding. **23.** an act or occasion of riding a horse, esp. in a race. **24.** a support, backing, setting, or the like, on or in which something is, or is to be, mounted or fixed. **25.** an ornamental metal piece applied to a piece of wooden furniture. **26.** *Micros.* a prepared slide. **27.** a distinctive metal feature on a sheath or scabbard, as a locket or chape. **28.** *Philately.* hinge (def. 4). **29.** *Print.* a wooden or metal block to which a plate is secured for printing. [1300–50; ME *mounten* < OF *munter, monter* < VL **montāre,* deriv. of L *mont-* (s. of *mōns*) MOUNT[2]] —**mount′a•ble,** *adj.* —**mount′less,** *adj.*
—**Syn. 1.** scale. See **climb. 19.** soar. **22.** steed, charger, palfrey. —**Ant. 1, 19.** descend.

mount[2] (mount), *n. Chiefly Literary.* a mountain: often used as part of a placename. [bef. 900; ME, OE *munt* < L *mont-* (s. of *mōns*) mountain, hill]

moun•tain (moun′tn), *n.* **1.** a natural elevation of the earth's surface rising more or less abruptly to a summit, and attaining an altitude greater than that of a hill, usually greater than 2000 ft. (610 m). See table on next page. **2.** a large mass of something resembling this, as in shape

CONCISE PRONUNCIATION KEY: act, cāpe, dâre, pärt; set, ēqual; if, ice; ox, ōver, ôrder, oil, bo͝ok, bo͞ot, out; up, ûrge; child; sing; shoe; thin, *th*at; zh as in *treasure.* ə = *a* as in *alone, e* as in *system, i* as in *easily, o* as in *gallop, u* as in *circus;* ᵊ as in *fire* (fīᵊr), *hour* (ouᵊr). l and n can serve as syllabic consonants, as in *cradle* (krād′l), and *button* (but′n). See the full key inside the front cover.

NOTABLE MOUNTAIN PEAKS OF THE WORLD

Name	Country or Region	Range or Location	Altitude ft.	Altitude m
Mt. Everest	Nepal-Tibet	Himalaya Mountains	29,028	8848
K2	Kashmir	Karakoram Range	28,250	8611
Kanchenjunga	Nepal-Sikkim	Himalaya Mountains	28,146	8579
Makalu	Nepal-Tibet	Himalaya Mountains	27,790	8470
Dhaulagiri	Nepal	Himalaya Mountains	26,826	8180
Nanga Parbat	Kashmir	Himalaya Mountains	26,660	8125
Annapurna	Nepal	Himalaya Mountains	26,503	8078
Gasherbrum	Kashmir	Karakoram Range	26,470	8068
Gosainthan	Tibet	Himalaya Mountains	26,291	8013
Nanda Devi	India	Himalaya Mountains	25,661	7820
Tirich Mir	Pakistan	Hindu Kush	25,230	7690
Muztagh Ata	China	Muztagh Ata Mountains	24,757	7546
Communism Peak	Tadzhikistan	Pamirs	24,590	7495
Pobeda Peak	Kirghizia-China	Tien Shan	24,406	7439
Lenin Peak	Kirghizia-Tadzhikistan	Trans Alai	23,382	7127
Aconcagua	Argentina	Andes	22,834	6960
Huascarán	Peru	Andes	22,205	6768
Illimani	Bolivia	Andes	21,188	6458
Chimborazo	Ecuador	Andes	20,702	6310
Mt. McKinley	United States (Alaska)	Alaska Range	20,320	6194
Mt. Logan	Canada (Yukon)	St. Elias Mountains	19,850	6050
Cotopaxi	Ecuador	Andes	19,498	5943
Kilimanjaro	Tanzania	N Tanzania	19,321	5889
El Misti	Peru	Andes	19,200	5880
Demavend	Iran	Elburz Mountains	18,606	5671
Orizaba (Citlaltepetl)	Mexico	Sierra Madre Oriental	18,546	5653
Mt. Elbrus	Russian Federation	Caucasus Mountains	18,465	5628
Popocatépetl	Mexico	Altiplano de Mexico	17,887	5450
Ixtaccihuatl	Mexico	Altiplano de Mexico	17,342	5286
Mt. Kenya	Kenya	Central Kenya	17,040	5194
Ararat	Turkey	E Turkey	16,945	5165
Mt. Ngaliema (Mt. Stanley)	Zaire-Uganda	Ruwenzori	16,790	5119
Mont Blanc	France	Alps	15,781	4810
Mt. Wilhelm	Papua New Guinea	Bismarck Range	15,400	4694
Monte Rosa	Italy-Switzerland	Pennine Alps	15,217	4638
Mt. Kirkpatrick	Antarctica	Queen Alexandra Range	14,855	4528
Weisshorn	Switzerland	Pennine Alps	14,804	4512
Matterhorn	Switzerland	Pennine Alps	14,780	4505
Mt. Whitney	United States (California)	Sierra Nevada	14,495	4418
Mt. Elbert	United States (Colorado)	Rocky Mountains	14,431	4399
Mt. Rainier	United States (Washington)	Cascade Range	14,408	4392
Longs Peak	United States (Colorado)	Rocky Mountains	14,255	4345
Mt. Shasta	United States (California)	Cascade Range	14,161	4315
Pikes Peak	United States (Colorado)	Rocky Mountains	14,108	4300
Mauna Kea	United States (Hawaii)	Island of Hawaii	13,784	4201
Grand Teton	United States (Wyoming)	Teton Range	13,766	4196
Mauna Loa	United States (Hawaii)	Island of Hawaii	13,680	4170
Jungfrau	Switzerland	Bernese Alps	13,668	4166
Mt. Victoria	Papua New Guinea	Owen Stanley Range	13,240	4036
Mt. Erebus	Antarctica	Ross Island	13,202	4024
Eiger	Switzerland	Bernese Alps	13,025	3970
Mt. Robson	Canada (B.C.)	Rocky Mountains	12,972	3954
Mt. Fuji	Japan	Central Honshu Island	12,395	3778
Mt. Cook	New Zealand	South Island	12,349	3764
Mt. Hood	United States (Oregon)	Cascade Range	11,253	3430
Mt. Etna	Italy	Eastern Sicily	10,758	3280
Lassen Peak	United States (California)	Cascade Range	10,465	3190
Haleakala	United States (Hawaii)	Island of Maui	10,032	3058
Mt. Olympus	Greece	Thessaly/Macedonia	9730	2966
Mt. Kosciusko	Australia	Australian Alps	7316	2230

or size. **3.** a huge amount: *a mountain of incoming mail.* **4.** (*cap.*) a steam locomotive having a four-wheeled front truck, eight driving wheels, and a two-wheeled rear truck. See table under **Whyte classification.** **5.** Also called **moun′tain wine′.** *Brit. Archaic.* a sweet Malaga wine. **6. make a mountain out of a molehill.** See **molehill** (def. 2). —*adj.* **7.** of or pertaining to mountains: *mountain air.* **8.** living, growing, or located in the mountains: *mountain people.* **9.** resembling or suggesting a mountain, as in size. [1175–1225; ME *mountaine* < OF *montaigne* < VL **montānea,* n. use of fem. of **montāneus,* equiv. to L *montān(us)* mountainous (*mont-,* s. of *mōns* mountain + *-ānus* -AN) + *-eus* adj. suffix] —**moun′tain·less,** *adj.*

moun′tain ash′, **1.** any of several small trees of the genus *Sorbus,* of the rose family, having flat-topped clusters of small, white flowers and bright-red to orange berries. **2.** any of certain other trees, as several Australian species of eucalyptus. [1590–1600]

moun′tain av′ens, any evergreen plant of the genus *Dryas,* of the rose family, growing in northern or alpine regions of the Northern Hemisphere and having showy, solitary, white or yellow flowers. [1790–1800]

moun′tain bea′ver, a small, burrowing rodent, *Aplodontia rufa,* of the Pacific coastal region of North America, considered the most primitive living rodent. Also called **sewellel.** [1880–85, *Amer.*]

moun′tain blue′bird, a bluebird, *Sialia currucoides,* of western North America. [1855–60, *Amer.*]

moun′tain blu′et, a European composite plant, *Centaurea montana,* having raylike blue flowerheads.

Moun′tain Brook′, a city in central Alabama, near Birmingham. 17,400.

moun′tain cat′, **1.** a cougar. **2.** a bobcat. [1655–65]

moun′tain chain′. See **mountain system.** [1815–25]

moun′tain climb′ing, mountaineering. [1870–75] —**moun′tain climb′er.**

moun′tain cran′berry, a low-growing shrub, *Vaccinium vitis-idaea,* of the heath family, growing in northern regions and having tart, red, edible berries. Also called **cowberry, lingonberry, lowbush cranberry.** [1840–50, *Amer.*]

CONCISE ETYMOLOGY KEY: <, descended or borrowed from; >, whence; b., blend of, blended; c., cognate with; cf., compare; deriv., derivative; equiv., equivalent; imit., imitative; obl., oblique; r., replacing; s., stem; sp., spelling, spelled; resp., respelling, respelled; trans., translation; ?, origin unknown; *, unattested; ‡, probably earlier than. See the full key inside the front cover.

moun′tain cur′rant, an ornamental shrub, *Ribes alpinum,* of Europe, having greenish-yellow flowers and scarlet fruit. Also called **Alpine currant.**

moun′tain da′isy. See **mountain sandwort.** [1855–60]

moun′tain dew′, illegally distilled corn liquor; moonshine. [1810–20]

moun′tain dog′wood. See **Pacific dogwood.**

moun′tain eb′ony. See **orchid tree.** [1715–25]

moun·tain·eer (moun′tn ēr′), *n.* **1.** an inhabitant of a mountainous district. **2.** a climber of mountains, esp. for sport. —*v.i.* **3.** to climb mountains, esp. for sport. [1600–10; MOUNTAIN + -EER]

moun·tain·eer·ing (moun′tn ēr′ing), *n.* the sport of climbing mountains. [1795–1805; MOUNTAINEER + -ING[1]]

moun′tain fet′terbush, an erect shrub, *Pieris floribunda,* of the heath family, found from Virginia to Georgia, having white flowers in nodding clusters. [1795–1805]

moun′tain goat′. See **Rocky Mountain goat.** [1825–35, *Amer.*]

moun′tain goril′la. See under **gorilla.**

moun′tain hol′ly fern′, a hardy, evergreen fern, *Polystichum lonchitis,* of North America, Europe, and Asia, having stiff and leathery fronds.

moun′tain lau′rel, a North American laurel, *Kalmia latifolia,* having terminal clusters of rose to white flowers: the state flower of Connecticut and Pennsylvania. Also called **calico bush.** [1750–60, *Amer.*]

moun′tain li′on, cougar. [1855–60, *Amer.*]

moun′tain magno′lia, a tree, *Magnolia fraseri,* of the southeastern U.S., having fragrant, creamy-white flowers from 9 to 11 in. (23 to 28 cm) across. [1880–85]

moun′tain mahog′any, any of several western North American shrubs or small trees of the genus *Cercocarpus,* of the rose family, having simple, leathery leaves and small, whitish flowers. [1800–10, *Amer.*]

moun′tain man′, **1.** mountaineer (def. 1). **2.** a man who lives and works in the mountains or wilderness, esp. a frontiersman or pioneer, as in the early American West. [1685–95]

moun′tain ma′ple, a shrub, *Acer spicatum,* of eastern North America, having small, greenish-yellow flowers and winged fruit, the foliage turning to orange and scarlet in autumn. [1775–85, *Amer.*]

moun′tain mint′, any of various pungently aromatic North American mints of the genus *Pycnanthemum,* having large, flat clusters of small, whitish flowers. [1665–75]

moun·tain·ous (moun′tn əs), *adj.* **1.** abounding in mountains: *a mountainous wilderness.* **2.** of the nature of a mountain. **3.** resembling a mountain or mountains, as being very large and high: *mountainous waves.* [1400–50; late ME *mounteynous.* See MOUNTAIN, -OUS] —**moun′tain·ous·ly,** *adv.* —**moun′tain·ous·ness,** *n.*

moun′tain oys′ter, the testis of a calf, sheep, pig, etc., used as food. Also called **Rocky Mountain oyster.** Cf. **prairie oyster.** [1885–90, *Amer.*]

moun′tain range′, **1.** a series of more or less connected mountains ranged in a line. **2.** a series of mountains, or of more or less parallel lines of mountains, closely related, as in origin. **3.** an area in which the greater part of the land surface is in considerable degree of slope, upland summits are small or narrow, and there are great differences in elevations within the area (commonly over 2000 ft., or 610 m). [1825–35]

moun′tain rose′bay, a showy, evergreen shrub, *Rhododendron catawbiense,* of the heath family, found in the mountainous regions from Virginia to Georgia, having bell-shaped, rose or purple flowers. [1940–45, *Amer.*]

moun′tain sand′wort, a sandwort, *Arenaria groenlandica,* of the pink family, native to Greenland and North America, having very numerous small leaves and small, white flowers, growing in rocky soil. Also called **mountain daisy.**

moun′tain sheep′, **1.** the bighorn. **2.** any of various wild sheep inhabiting mountains. [1795–1805, *Amer.*]

moun′tain sick′ness, *Pathol.* See **altitude sickness.** [1840–50]

moun·tain·side (moun′tn sīd′), *n.* the side or slope of a mountain. [1300–50; ME. See MOUNTAIN, SIDE[1]]

Moun′tain State′, Montana (used as a nickname).

moun′tain sys′tem, a series of interconnected or geologically related mountain ranges. Also called **mountain chain.** [1880–85]

Moun′tain time′. See under **standard time.** Also called **Moun′tain Stand′ard Time′.** [1880–85; *Amer.*]

moun·tain·top (moun′tn top′), *n.* **1.** the top or summit of a mountain. —*adj.* **2.** situated at the top or summit of a mountain: *a mountaintop house.* [1585–95; MOUNTAIN + TOP[1]]

Moun′tain View′, a city in central California, S of San Francisco. 58,655.

moun′tain visca′cha, viscacha (def. 2).

moun′tain wave′, the wavelike effect, characterized by severe updrafts and downdrafts, that occurs when rapidly flowing air encounters the steep front of a mountain range. Also called **lee wave.**

moun′tain white′fish, a whitefish, *Prosopium williamsoni,* inhabiting mountain streams and lakes of the western U.S. and Canada. Also called **Rocky Mountain whitefish.**

moun′tain wind′ (wind), a wind descending a mountain valley at night. Cf. **valley wind.** [1600–10]

moun·tain·y (moun′tn ē), *adj.* **1.** having mountains; mountainous. **2.** pertaining to or living in the mountains. [1605–15; MOUNTAIN + -Y[1]]

Mount′ Ar′arat, Ararat.

Mount·bat·ten (mount bat′n), *n.* **Louis, 1st Earl Mountbatten of Burma,** 1900–79, British admiral: viceroy of India 1947; governor general of India 1947–48.

Mount′ Car′mel man′, an early human of Neanderthaloid type, known from skeletal remains from the late Pleistocene Epoch, c50,000–40,000 B.C., found in Palestine.

Mount′ Clem′ens (klem′ənz), a city in SE Michigan. 18,806.

Mount′ Des′ert Is′land (dez′ərt, di zûrt′), an island off the coast of E central Maine: summer resort; forms part of Acadia National Park. 14 mi. (23 km) long; 8 mi. (13 km) wide.

moun·te·bank (moun′tə bangk′), *n.* **1.** a person who sells quack medicines, as from a platform in public places, attracting and influencing an audience by tricks, storytelling, etc. **2.** any charlatan or quack. —*v.i.* **3.** to act or operate as a mountebank. [1570–80; (< MF) < It *montimbanco* one who climbs on a bench, equiv. to *mont(are)* to climb (see MOUNT[1]) + *-im-,* var. of *in* on + *banco* bench (see BANK[2])] —**moun·te·bank·er·y** (moun′tə bangk′ə rē), *n.*
—**Syn. 1.** pitchman. **2.** phony, pretender, fraud.

mount·ed (moun′tid), *adj.* **1.** seated or riding on a horse or other animal. **2.** serving on horseback or on some special mount, as soldiers or police. **3.** *Mil.* (formerly) permanently equipped with horses or vehicles for transport. Cf. **mobile** (def. 3). **4.** having or set in a mounting: *mounted gems.* **5.** put into position for use, as guns. [1575–85; MOUNT[1] + -ED[2]]
—**Ant. 1.** afoot.

mount·er (moun′tər), *n.* a person or thing that mounts. [1600–10; MOUNT[1] + -ER[1]]

Mount′ Ev′erest, **1.** Everest (def. 1). **2.** something regarded as the most difficult or challenging of its kind: *the Mount Everest of international sailing.*

Mount′ Gam′bier (gam′bēr), a city in S Australia. 19,880.

Moun·tie (moun′tē), *n. Informal.* a member of the Royal Canadian Mounted Police. Also, **Mounty.** [1885–90; MOUNT(ED) + -IE]

mount·ing (mounʹting), *n.* **1.** the act of a person or thing that mounts. **2.** something that serves as a mount, support, setting, or the like: *a new mounting for an heirloom jewel.* [1400–50; late ME; see MOUNT[1], -ING[1]]

Mountʹlake Terʹrace (mountʹlākʹ), a town in NW Washington. 16,534.

Mountʹ Leb·anon, a town in SW Pennsylvania, SW of Pittsburgh. 34,414.

Mountʹ McKinʹley Naʹtional Parkʹ, former name of **Denali National Park.**

Mountʹ Pearlʹ, a town in Newfoundland, in E Canada, on the SE part of the island, S of St. John's. 11,543.

Mountʹ Pleasʹant, 1. a city in central Michigan. 23,746. **2.** a town in SE South Carolina. 13,838. **3.** a town in NE Texas. 11,003.

Mountʹ Prosʹpect, a city in NE Illinois, near Chicago. 52,634.

Mountʹ Rai·nierʹ (rā nērʹ, rə-, rāʹnēr), See **Rainier, Mount.**

Mountʹ Rainierʹ Naʹtional Parkʹ, a national park in W Washington, including Mount Rainier. 378 sq. mi. (980 sq. km).

Mountʹ Robʹson Parkʹ (robʹsən), a national park in the Rocky Mountains of E British Columbia, Canada.

Mountʹ Rushʹmore Naʹtional Memoʹrial. See under **Rushmore.**

Mountʹ Shasʹta. See **Shasta, Mount.**

Mountʹ Verʹnon, 1. the home and tomb of George Washington in NE Virginia, on the Potomac, 15 mi. (24 km) below Washington, D.C. **2.** a city in SE New York, near New York City. 66,713. **3.** a city in S Illinois. 16,995. **4.** a city in central Ohio. 14,380. **5.** a town in NW Washington. 13,009.

Mountʹ Washʹington. See **Washington, Mount.**

Mountʹ Wilʹson Observʹatory, an astronomical observatory on Mount Wilson, near Los Angeles, California, having a 100-in. (254-cm) reflecting telescope.

Mount·y (mounʹtē), *n., pl.* **Mount·ies.** Mountie.

mourn (môrn, mōrn), *v.i.* **1.** to feel or express sorrow or grief. **2.** to grieve or lament for the dead. **3.** to show the conventional or usual signs of sorrow over a person's death. —*v.t.* **4.** to feel or express sorrow or grief over (misfortune, loss, or anything regretted); deplore. **5.** to grieve or lament over (the dead). **6.** to utter in a sorrowful manner. [bef. 900; ME *mo(u)rnen,* OE *murnan;* c. OHG *mornēn,* ON *morna,* Goth *maurnan*] **—Syn. 1.** bewail, bemoan. See **grieve. —Ant. 1.** laugh, rejoice.

mourn·er (môrʹnər, mōrʹ-), *n.* **1.** a person who mourns. **2.** a person who attends a funeral to mourn for the deceased. **3.** (at religious revival meetings) a person who professes penitence for sin, with desire for salvation. [1350–1400; ME; see MOURN, -ER[1]]

mournʹers' benchʹ, (at religious revival meetings) a bench or seat at the front of the church or room, set apart for mourners or penitent sinners seeking salvation. [1835–45, *Amer.*]

Mournʹer's Kadʹdish, *Judaism.* Kaddish (def. 2).

mourn·ful (môrnʹfəl, mōrnʹ-), *adj.* **1.** feeling or expressing sorrow or grief; sorrowful; sad. **2.** of or pertaining to mourning for the dead. **3.** causing grief or lament: *a mournful occasion.* **4.** gloomy, somber, or dreary, as in appearance or character: *mournful shadows.* [1375–1425; late ME *morneful.* See MOURN, -FUL] **—mournʹful·ly,** *adv.* **—mournʹful·ness,** *n.*

mourn·ing (môrʹning, mōrʹ-), *n.* **1.** the act of a person who mourns; sorrowing or lamentation. **2.** the conventional manifestation of sorrow for a person's death, esp. by the wearing of black clothes or a black armband, the hanging of flags at half-mast, etc. **3.** the outward symbols of such sorrow, as black garments. **4.** the period or interval during which a person grieves or formally expresses grief, as by wearing black garments. —*adj.* **5.** of, pertaining to, or used in mourning. [bef. 900; ME (n., adj.); OE *murnung* (n.). See MOURN, -ING[1], -ING[2]] **—mournʹing·ly,** *adv.* **—Ant. 1.** rejoicing.

mournʹing bandʹ, a piece of black cloth that is worn, esp. as a band encircling the upper arm, to indicate mourning. [1610–20]

Mournʹing Becomesʹ Elecʹtra, a three-part tragedy (1931) by Eugene O'Neill, including *Homecoming, The Hunted,* and *The Haunted.*

mournʹing brideʹ. See **sweet scabious.**

mournʹing cloakʹ, an anglewing butterfly, *Nymphalis antiopa,* widely distributed in Europe and North America, having velvety, dark-brown wings with purple spots and pale-yellow edges. Also called **Camberwell beauty.** [1600–10]

mournʹing doveʹ, a dove, *Zenaidura macroura,* of North America, noted for its plaintive cooing. [1825–35, *Amer.*]

mournʹing iʹris, an iris, *Iris susiana,* of Asia Minor and Iran, having solitary, grayish flowers with a black patch and a brownish beard. [1880–85]

mournʹing warʹbler, a North American wood warbler, *Oporornis philadelphia,* olive-green above, yellow below, and with a gray head and throat. [1800–10, *Amer.*]

house mouse, *Mus musculus,* head and body 3½ in. (8.9 cm); tail to 3½ in. (8.9 cm)

mouse (*n.* mous; *v.* mouz), *n., pl.* **mice** (mīs), *v.,* **moused, mous·ing.** —*n.* **1.** any of numerous small Old World rodents of the family Muridae, esp. of the genus *Mus,* introduced widely in other parts of the world. **2.** any similar small animal of various rodent and marsupial families. **3.** a quiet, timid person. **4.** *Computers.* a palm-sized, button-operated device that can be slid on wheels or ball bearings over a desktop to move the cursor on a CRT to any position, or slid over a drawing in order to recreate the drawing on a CRT. Cf. **joystick** (def. 2). **5.** *Informal.* a swelling under the eye, caused by a blow or blows; black eye. **6.** *Slang.* a girl or woman. —*v.t.* **7.** to hunt out, as a cat hunts out mice. **8.** *Naut.* to secure with a mousing. —*v.i.* **9.** to hunt for or catch mice. **10.** to prowl about, as if in search of something: *The burglar moused about for valuables.* **11.** to seek or search stealthily or watchfully, as if for prey. [bef. 900; ME *mous* (pl. *mis*), OE *mūs* (pl. *mȳs*); c. G *Maus,* ON *mūs,* L *mūs,* Gk *mŷs*] **—mouseʹlikeʹ,** *adj.*

mouse·bird (mousʹbûrdʹ), *n.* coly. [1815–25; MOUSE + BIRD]

mouseʹ deerʹ, chevrotain. [1830–40]

mouse-dun (mousʹdunʹ), *n.* a dark brownish-gray color. [1375–1425; late ME]

mouse-ear (mousʹērʹ), *n.* any of various plants having small, hairy leaves, as the hawkweed, *Hieracium pilosella,* or the forget-me-not, *Myosotis palustris.* [1225–75; ME *mous-ere.* See MOUSE, EAR[1]]

mouseʹ-ear chickʹweed, any of several weedy plants belonging to the genus *Cerastium,* of the pink family, as *C. vulgatum,* having small, hairy leaves and tiny, white flowers. [1725–35]

mouse·fish (mousʹfishʹ), *n., pl.* (*esp. collectively*) **-fish,** (*esp. referring to two or more kinds or species*) **-fish·es.** sargassumfish. [1875–80; MOUSE + FISH]

mouse·hole (mousʹhōlʹ), *n.* **1.** the burrow of a mouse. **2.** the entrance to a mouse's burrow. **3.** a small hole resembling this. [1425–75; late ME; see MOUSE, HOLE]

mouseʹ oposʹsum. See **murine opossum.**

mouse·poxʹ (mousʹpoksʹ), *n. Vet. Pathol.* ectromelia (def. 2). Also, **mouseʹ poxʹ.** [1945–50; MOUSE + POX]

mous·er (mouʹzər), *n.* **1.** an animal that catches mice: *Our cat is a good mouser.* **2.** a person or thing that seeks or prowls, as if for prey. [1350–1400; ME; see MOUSE, -ER[1]]

mouse·trap (mousʹtrapʹ), *n., v.,* **-trapped, -trap·ping.** —*n.* **1.** a trap for mice, esp. one consisting of a rectangular wooden base on which a metal spring is mounted. **2.** a device, machine, or the like whose structure or function suggests a trap for mice. **3.** a device, system, or stratagem for detecting and catching someone in an unauthorized or illegal act. **4.** *Football.* trap[1] (def. 11). **5. build a better mousetrap,** to make or offer a superior product. —*v.t.* **6.** *Informal.* **a.** to trap or snare: *traffic cops mousetrapping drunken drivers.* **b.** to manipulate by devious or clever means; trick or outwit: *to mousetrap the witness into a contradiction.* **7.** *Football.* trap[1] (def. 20). [1400–50; late ME *mous trappe.* See MOUSE, TRAP[1]]

mous·ey (mouʹsē, -zē), *adj.,* **mous·i·er, mous·i·est.** mousy. **—mousʹi·ly,** *adv.* **—mousʹi·ness,** *n.*

mous·ing (mouʹzing), *n. Naut.* a wrapping of several turns of small stuff around the shank end of a hook. [1825–35; MOUSE + -ING[1]]

mous·que·taire (mo͞osʹkə târʹ), *n.* musketeer. [< F]

mous·sa·ka (mo͞o säʹkə, mo͞oʹsä käʹ), *n. Greek Cookery.* a baked dish consisting of layers of sautéed slices of eggplant and ground lamb usually flavored with tomatoes, onions, and cinnamon, and covered with a custard sauce sprinkled with grated cheese. Also, **mussaka.** [1930–35; < ModGk *mousakâs* < Turk *musakka*]

mousse (mo͞os), *n.* **1.** *Cookery.* **a.** a sweetened dessert with whipped cream as a base, often stabilized with gelatin and chilled in a mold: *chocolate mousse.* **b.** an aspic, unsweetened and containing meat, vegetables, or fish: *salmon mousse.* **2.** a foamy preparation used on the hair to help hold it in place, applied usually to damp hair before grooming or styling and worked in until absorbed. [1890–95; < F: moss, froth < Gmc; see MOSS]

mousse·line (mo͞os lēnʹ), *n.* **1.** Also called **Chantilly, Chantilly sauce.** hollandaise sauce mixed with whipped cream. **2.** any prepared dish made light and fluffy or airy, as by the mixing in of whipped cream or beaten egg whites. —*adj.* **3.** prepared or served with whipped cream. [< F: lit., MUSLIN]

mousse·line (mo͞os lēnʹ), *n. French.* muslin.

mousse·line de laine (mo͞os lēn də lenʹ), *French.* a thin worsted fabric, often having a printed pattern. Also called **muslin delaine.** [lit., muslin of wool]

mousse·line de soie (mo͞os lēn də swäʹ), *French.* a thin, stiff silk or rayon fabric. [lit., muslin of silk]

Mous·sorg·sky (mo͝o sôrgʹskē, -zôrgʹ-; *Russ.* mo͞oʹsərk skyə), *n.* **Mo·dest Pe·tro·vich** (mō destʹ pi trôʹvich; *Russ.* mu dyestʹ pyi trôʹvyich), 1839–81, Russian composer. Also, **Mous·sorgʹski, Mussorgski, Mussorgsky.**

mous·tache (musʹtash, mə stashʹ), *n.* mustache. **—mousʹtached,** *adj.*

mousʹtache cupʹ. See **mustache cup.**

Mous·te·ri·an (mo͞o stērʹē ən), *adj. Anthropol.* **1.** of or pertaining to a Middle Paleolithic culture of Neanderthal man dating to the early upper Pleistocene Epoch (c100,000–40,000 B.C.) and consisting of five or more stone-artifact traditions in Europe whose characteristic tools are side scrapers and points. **2.** pertaining to Paleolithic human relics having the workmanship, finish, and character of the flint scrapers found in the sands of Moustier, France. Also, **Mous·tieʹri·an.** [1885–90; < F *moust(i)érien;* see -IAN]

mous·y (mouʹsē, -zē), *adj.,* **mous·i·er, mous·i·est. 1.** resembling or suggesting a mouse, as in color or odor. **2.** drab and colorless. **3.** meek; timid: *A drill sergeant can't be mousy!* **4.** quiet; noiseless: *a mousy tread.* **5.** infested with mice. Also, **mousey.** [1805–15; MOUSE + -Y[1]] **—mousʹi·ly,** *adv.* **—mousʹi·ness,** *n.* **—Syn. 3.** fearful, shy, bashful, timorous.

mouth (*n.* mouth; *v.* mouth), *n., pl.* **mouths** (mouthz), *v.* —*n.* **1.** *Anat., Zool.* **a.** the opening through which an animal or human takes in food. **b.** the cavity containing the structures used in mastication. **c.** the structures enclosing or being within this cavity, considered as a whole. **2.** the masticating and tasting apparatus. **3.** a person or animal dependent on someone for sustenance: *another mouth to feed.* **4.** the oral opening or cavity considered as the source of vocal utterance. **5.** utterance or expression: *to give mouth to one's thoughts.* **6.** talk, esp. loud, empty, or boastful talk: *That man is all mouth.* **7.** disrespectful talk or language; back talk; impudence. **8.** a grimace made with the lips. **9.** an opening leading out of or into any cavity or hollow place or thing: *the mouth of a cave; a bottle's mouth.* **10.** the outfall at the lower end of a river or stream, where flowing water is discharged, as into a lake, sea, or ocean: *the mouth of the Nile.* **11.** the opening between the jaws of a vise or the like. **12.** the lateral hole of an organ pipe. **13.** the lateral blowhole of a flute. **14. down in** or **at the mouth,** *Informal.* dejected; depressed; disheartened: *Ever since he lost his job, he has been looking very down in the mouth.* **15. run off at the mouth,** *Informal.* to talk incessantly or indiscreetly. **16. talk out of both sides of one's mouth,** to make contradictory or untruthful statements. —*v.t.* **17.** to utter in a sonorous or pompous manner, or with excessive mouth movements: *to mouth a speech.* **18.** to form (a word, sound, etc.) with the lips without actually making an utterance: *She silently mouthed her answer so as not to wake her napping child.* **19.** to utter or pronounce softly and indistinctly; mumble: *Stop mouthing your words and speak up.* **20.** to put or take into the mouth, as food. **21.** to press, rub, or chew at with the mouth or lips: *The dog mouthed the toys.* **22.** to accustom (a horse) to the use of the bit and bridle. —*v.i.* **23.** to speak sonorously and oratorically, or with excessive mouth movement. **24.** to grimace with the lips. **25. mouth off,** *Slang.* **a.** to talk back; sass: *He mouthed off to his mother.* **b.** to express one's opinions, objections, or the like in a forceful or uninhibited manner, esp. in public. [bef. 900; ME; OE *mūth;* c. G *Mund,* ON *munnr*] **—mouthʹer,** *n.* **—mouthʹless,** *adj.* **—Syn. 5.** voice, speech.

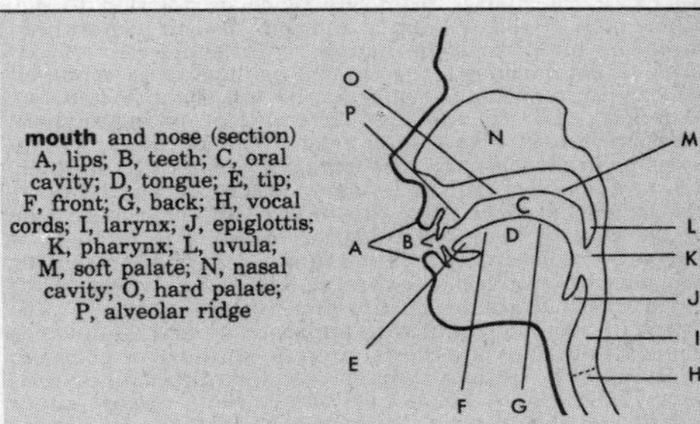

mouth and nose (section) A, lips; B, teeth; C, oral cavity; D, tongue; E, tip; F, front; G, back; H, vocal cords; I, larynx; J, epiglottis; K, pharynx; L, uvula; M, soft palate; N, nasal cavity; O, hard palate; P, alveolar ridge

mouth·breed·er (mouthʹbrēʹdər), *n.* **1.** any of several fishes of the genera *Tilapia* and *Haplochromis,* that hatch and care for their young in the mouth. **2.** any of several fishes in various genera of the Anabantidae, Apogonidae, Cichlidae, and other teleost fish families that hold their eggs or young in their mouths. [1925–30; MOUTH + BREEDER]

mouthed (mouthd, moutht), *adj.* **1.** having a mouth of a specified kind (often used in combination): *a small-mouthed man.* **2.** having a way of speaking of a specified kind (often used in combination): *a mealy-mouthed speaker; a loud-mouthed brat.* [1250–1300; ME. See MOUTH, -ED[3]]

mouth·ful (mouthʹfo͝olʹ), *n., pl.* **-fuls. 1.** the amount a mouth can hold. **2.** the amount taken into the mouth at one time. **3.** a small quantity. **4.** *Informal.* a spoken remark of great truth, relevance, effectiveness, etc.: *You said a mouthful!* **5.** a long word or group of words, esp. one that is hard to pronounce. [1375–1425; late ME. See MOUTH, -FUL] **—Usage.** See **-ful.**

mouthʹ harpʹ, *South Midland and Southern U.S.* harmonica (def. 1). Also called **harp.** [1900–05, *Amer.*]

mouthʹ orʹgan, harmonica (def. 1). [1660–70]

mouth·part (mouthʹpärtʹ), *n.* Usually, **mouthparts.**

the appendages surrounding or associated with the mouth of arthropods. [1790–1800; MOUTH + PART]

mouth•piece (mouth′pēs′), *n.* **1.** a piece placed at or forming the mouth, as of a receptacle or tube. **2.** a piece or part, as of an instrument, to which the mouth is applied or which is held in the mouth: *the mouthpiece of a trumpet.* **3.** the part of a bit or bridle, as for a horse, that passes through the animal's mouth. **4.** a person, newspaper, etc., that conveys the opinions or sentiments of others; spokesperson. **5.** *Slang.* a lawyer, esp. a criminal lawyer. [1675–85; MOUTH + PIECE]

mouth′-to-mouth′ resuscita′tion (mouth′tə-mouth′), a method of artificial respiration in which a person rhythmically blows air into the victim's lungs, either directly, by placing the mouth over the patient's, or through a tube. [1960–65]

mouth•wash (mouth′wôsh′, -wosh′), *n.* a solution, often containing antiseptic, astringent, and breath-sweetening agents, used for cleansing the mouth and teeth, and for gargling. Also called **collutory, collutorium.** [1830–40; MOUTH + WASH]

mouth-wa•ter•ing (mouth′wô′tər ing, -wot′ər-), *adj.* very appetizing in appearance, aroma, or description: *a mouth-watering dessert.* [1815–25]

mouth•y (mou′thē, -thē), *adj.,* **mouth•i•er, mouth•i•est.** garrulous, often in a bombastic manner. [1580–90; MOUTH + -Y[1]] **—mouth′i•ly,** *adv.* **—mouth′i•ness,** *n.*

mou•ton (mo͞o′ton), *n.* sheepskin that has been processed to resemble another fur, esp. seal or beaver. [1940–45; < F: sheep, sheepskin; see MUTTON]

mov•a•ble (mo͞o′və bəl), *adj.* **1.** capable of being moved; not fixed in one place, position, or posture. **2.** *Law.* (of property) **a.** not permanent in reference to place; capable of being moved without injury. **b.** personal, as distinguished from real. **3.** changing from one date to another in different years: *a movable holiday.* **4.** (of type or matrices) able to be rearranged. **—***n.* **5.** an article of furniture that is not fixed in place. **6.** Often, **movables.** *Law.* an article of personal property not attached to land. Also, **moveable.** [1350–1400; ME *mevable, movable* < AF *movable.* See MOVE, -ABLE] **—mov′a•bil′i•ty, mov′a•ble•ness,** *n.* **—mov′a•bly,** *adv.*

mov′a•ble-do′ sys′tem (mo͞o′və bəl dō′), *Music.* a system of solmization in which the syllable *do* can be transposed to the tonic of any key. Cf. **fixed-do system.**

mov′able feast′, a religious feast that does not occur on the same date each year. [1275–1325; ME]

mov′able type′, *Print.* type from which text is printed directly in which each character is on a separate piece of metal. [1760–70]

move (mo͞ov), *v.,* **moved, mov•ing,** *n.* **—***v.i.* **1.** to pass from one place or position to another. **2.** to go from one place of residence to another: *They moved from Tennessee to Texas.* **3.** to advance or progress: *The red racing car moved into the lead.* **4.** to have a regular motion, as an implement or a machine; turn; revolve. **5.** to sell or be sold: *That new model is moving well.* **6.** to start off or leave: *It's time to be moving.* **7.** to transfer a piece in a game, as chess or checkers. **8.** (of the bowels) to discharge or eject the feces; evacuate. **9.** to be active in a particular sphere: *to move in musical society.* **10.** to take action; proceed. **11.** to make a formal request, application, or proposal: *to move for a new trial.* **—***v.t.* **12.** to change from one place or position to another. **13.** to set or keep in motion. **14.** to prompt, actuate, or impel to some action: *What moved you to do this?* **15.** to arouse or excite the feelings or passions of; affect with emotion (usually fol. by *to*): *to move someone to anger.* **16.** to affect with tender or compassionate emotion; touch: *The tale of tragedy moved her.* **17.** to transfer (a piece in a game) from one position to another. **18.** to dispose of (goods) by sale. **19.** to cause (the bowels) to discharge or eject the feces. **20.** to propose formally, as to a court or judge, or for consideration by a deliberative assembly. **21.** to submit a formal request or proposal to (a court, a sovereign, etc.). **22. move in,** to begin to occupy a place in which to live or work. **23. move in on,** *Informal.* **a.** to approach or make advances toward usurping another's success, authority, position, or the like. **b.** to take aggressive steps to control or possess: *The company has not yet moved in on the consumer market.* **24. move on,** to approach or attack as a military target: *The army is moving on the capital itself.* **25. move out,** to leave a place in order to start or continue a planned march, maneuver, journey, etc.: *The troops will move out of the encampment at dawn.* **26. move over,** to change or cause to change to another position, esp. to make room for another: *to make space by moving over.* **27. move up,** to advance to a higher level. **—***n.* **28.** an act or instance of moving; movement. **29.** a change of location or residence. **30.** an action toward an objective or goal; step: *a move toward a higher tax.* **31.** (in chess, checkers, etc.) a player's right or turn to make a play. **32.** a play or maneuver, as in a game or sport. **33. get a move on,** *Informal.* **a.** to begin; act: *We'd better get a move on before it rains.* **b.** to hurry; hasten. **34. make one's move,** *Informal.* to act, esp. to assert oneself at an opportune time. **35. on the move, a.** busy; active: *on the move from morning till night.* **b.** going from place to place: *Infantry units have been on the move all day.* **c.** advancing; progressing: *an industry on the move.* **36. put moves on,** *Slang.* to make sexual advances toward. Also, **make a move on.** [1200–50; ME *meven, moven* < AF *mover* << L *movēre*] **—Syn. 1.** stir, budge. See **advance. 2.** remove. **4.** spin, gyrate, rotate, operate. **12.** shift, transfer; propel. **13.** agitate. **14.** influence, induce, incite, instigate, lead. **28.** See **motion.** **—Ant. 12.** fix.

move•a•ble (mo͞o′və bəl), *adj., n.* movable.

CONCISE ETYMOLOGY KEY: <, descended or borrowed from; >, whence; b., blend of, blended; c., cognate with; cf., compare; deriv., derivative; equiv., equivalent; imit., imitative; obl., oblique; r., replacing; s., stem; sp., spelling, spelled; resp., respelling, respelled; trans., translation; ?, origin unknown; *, unattested; ‡, probably earlier than. See the full key inside the front cover.

move-in (mo͞ov′in′), *n. Informal.* an act or instance of occupying a living or working place: *The offices will be ready for move-in soon.* [n. use of v. phrase *move in*]

move•less (mo͞ov′lis), *adj.* lacking movement: *the still night with its moveless branches.* [1570–80; MOVE + -LESS] **—move′less•ly,** *adv.* **—move′less•ness,** *n.*

move•ment (mo͞ov′mənt), *n.* **1.** the act, process, or result of moving. **2.** a particular manner or style of moving. **3.** Usually, **movements.** actions or activities, as of a person or a body of persons. **4.** *Mil., Naval.* a change of position or location of troops or ships. **5.** abundance of events or incidents. **6.** rapid progress of events. **7.** the progress of events, as in a narrative or drama. **8.** *Fine Arts.* the suggestion of motion in a work of art, either by represented gesture in figurative painting or sculpture or by the relationship of structural elements in a design or composition. **9.** a progressive development of ideas toward a particular conclusion: *the movement of his thought.* **10.** a series of actions or activities intended or tending toward a particular end: *the movement toward universal suffrage.* **11.** the course, tendency, or trend of affairs in a particular field. **12.** a diffusely organized or heterogeneous group of people or organizations tending toward or favoring a generalized common goal: *the antislavery movement; the realistic movement in art.* **13.** the price change in the market of some commodity or security: *an upward movement in the price of butter.* **14.** See **bowel movement. 15.** the working parts or a distinct portion of the working parts of a mechanism, as of a watch. **16.** *Music.* **a.** a principal division or section of a sonata, symphony, or the like. **b.** motion; rhythm; time; tempo. **17.** *Pros.* rhythmical structure or character. [1350–1400; ME < MF; see MOVE, -MENT] **—Syn. 1.** See **motion. 5.** eventfulness. **—Ant. 1.** inertia, stasis.

move-out (mo͞ov′out′), *n.* an act or instance of vacating a living or working place: *With so many business move-outs, the local economy is suffering.* [n. use of v. phrase *move out*]

mov•er (mo͞o′vər), *n.* **1.** a person or thing that moves. **2.** Often, **movers.** a person or company whose business is the moving of household effects or office equipment from one location to another. **3.** a powerful and influential person, as in politics or business. **4.** a person who is energetic and ambitious; go-getter. **5. movers and shakers,** *Informal.* powerful and influential people, as in politics and business. [1350–1400; ME *mevere.* See MOVE, -ER[1]]

mov•ie (mo͞o′vē), *n.* **1.** See **motion picture. 2.** motion-picture theater (often prec. by *the*): *The movie is next-door to the hardware store.* **3. movies, a.** motion pictures, as an industry (usually prec. by *the*): *The movies have had to raise prices.* **b.** motion pictures, as a genre of art or entertainment: *gangster movies.* **c.** the exhibition of a motion picture: *an evening at the movies.* [1905–10; MOV(ING PICTURE) + -IE]

mov•ie•dom (mo͞o′vē dəm), *n.* filmdom. [1915–20, *Amer.;* MOVIE + -DOM]

mov•ie•go•ing (mo͞o′vē gō′ing), *n.* **1.** the practice or act of going to see motion pictures. **—***adj.* **2.** characterized by going to see motion pictures often: *the moviegoing public.* [1935–40; MOVIE + GOING] **—mov′ie•go′er,** *n.*

mov′ie house′, a motion-picture theater. [1910–15]

mov•ie•land (mo͞o′vē land′), *n.* **1.** a place where many motion pictures are made, esp. Hollywood, California. **2.** the motion-picture industry, esp. considered as including the people who work in it, their attitudes, way of life, etc.: *Movieland has yet to produce low-budget films that are consistently good.* [1910–15; MOVIE + LAND]

mov•ie•mak•er (mo͞o′vē mā′kər), *n.* filmmaker. [MOVIE + MAKER] **—mov′ie•mak′ing,** *n.*

mov′ie the′ater, a motion-picture theater. [1910–15]

mov•ing (mo͞o′ving), *adj.* **1.** capable of or having movement: *a moving object.* **2.** causing or producing motion. **3.** involved in changing the location of possessions, a residence, office, etc.: *moving expenses.* **4.** involving a motor vehicle in motion. **5.** actuating, instigating, or impelling: *the moving spirit behind the party.* **6.** stirring or evoking strong feelings or emotions, esp. touchingly or pathetically: *a moving story.* [1300–50; ME *meving.* See MOVE, -ING[2]] **—mov′ing•ly,** *adv.* **—Syn. 6.** touching, affecting, pathetic, poignant.

mov′ing av′erage, *Statistics.* one of a succession of averages of data from a time series, where each average is calculated by successively shifting the interval by the same period of time. [1910–15]

mov′ing pic′ture. See **motion picture.**

mov′ing side′walk, a moving surface, similar to a conveyor belt, for carrying pedestrians. [1905–10]

mov′ing stair′way, escalator (def. 1). Also called **mov′ing stair′case.** [1905–10]

mov′ing tar′get in′dicator, *Electronics.* a Doppler-radar presentation that indicates moving targets only, stationary objects reflecting signals that the system rejects. *Abbr.:* MTI [1965–70]

mov′ing van′, a large truck or trailer used for transporting furnishings from one residence or office to another. [1895–1900, *Amer.*]

mov′ing viola′tion, any of various traffic violations committed while a vehicle is in motion, as speeding, driving through a red light, or going the wrong direction on a one-way street.

Mo•vi•o•la (mo͞o′vē ō′lə), *Motion Pictures, Trademark.* a brand of projection device for a motion-picture film allowing one person to see the film through a viewer and control its motion and speed, used in film editing, preparation of titles, etc.

mow[1] (mō), *v.,* **mowed, mowed** or **mown, mow•ing.** **—***v.t.* **1.** to cut down (grass, grain, etc.) with a scythe or a machine. **2.** to cut grass, grain, etc., from: *to mow the lawn.* **—***v.i.* **3.** to cut down grass, grain, etc. **4. mow down, a.** to destroy or kill indiscriminately or in great numbers, as troops in battle. **b.** to defeat, overwhelm, or overcome: *The team mowed down its first four opponents.* **c.** to knock down. [bef. 900; ME *mowen,* OE *māwan;* c. G *mähen*]

mow[2] (mou), *n.* **1.** the place in a barn where hay, sheaves of grain, etc., are stored. **2.** a heap or pile of hay or of sheaves of grain in a barn. **—***v.t.* **3.** *Chiefly Northern and North Midland U.S.* to store (hay) in a barn. [bef. 900; ME *mow(e),* OE *mūwa, mūha, mūga;* c. ON *mūgi* swath]

mow[3] (mou, mō), *Archaic.* **—***n.* **1.** a wry or derisive grimace. **—***v.i.* **2.** to make mows, mouths, or grimaces. Also, **mowe.** [1275–1325; ME *mowe* < MF *moue* lip, pout, OF *moe* < Frankish; akin to MD *mouwe* protruded lip]

mowe (mou, mō), *n., v.i.,* **mowed, mow•ing.** *Archaic.* mow[3].

mow•er (mō′ər), *n.* **1.** See **lawn mower. 2.** See **mowing machine.** [1400–50; late ME: one who mows; see MOW[1], -ER[1]]

mow′er deck′ (mō′ər). See **cutter deck.**

mow•ing (mō′ing), *n.* **1.** the act of leveling or cutting down grass, grain, etc., with a mowing machine or scythe. **2.** the quantity of grass, grain, etc., cut in a specified period. [1375–1425; late ME; see MOW[1], -ING[1]]

mow′ing machine′ (mō′ing), a machine for mowing or cutting down grass, grain, etc. Also called **mower.** [1815–25, *Amer.*]

mown (mōn), *v.* a pp. of **mow[1].**

mow•rah (mou′rə), *n.* mahua. Also, **mow′ra.** [1865–70]

mow′rah fat′, a yellow, semifluid fat expressed from the seeds of several trees of the genus *Madhuca,* used in making soap and as an adulterant in butter. Also called **mow′rah but′ter, mow′rah oil′.**

mox•a (mok′sə), *n.* **1.** a flammable substance or material obtained from the leaves of certain Chinese and Japanese wormwood plants, esp. *Artemisia moxa.* **2.** this substance or a similar one of cotton, wool, or the like, placed on the skin usually in the form of a cone or cylinder and ignited for use as a counterirritant. [1670–80; by uncert. mediation < Japn *mogusa,* equiv. to *mo(y)e* burn + *-gusa,* comb. form of *kusa* herb]

mox•ie (mok′sē), *n. Slang.* **1.** vigor; verve; pep. **2.** courage and aggressiveness; nerve. **3.** skill; know-how. [1925–30, *Amer.;* after *Moxie,* a trademark (name of a soft drink)]

mo•yen âge (mwA ye näzh′), *French.* See **Middle Ages.**

Mo•yo•bam•ba (mô′yô bäm′bä), *n.* a city in NW Peru. 10,000.

Mozamb., Mozambique.

Mo•zam•bi•can (mō′zəm bē′kən), *n.* **1.** a native or inhabitant of the territory or city of Mozambique. **—***adj.* **2.** of or pertaining to the territory or city of Mozambique or its natives or inhabitants. [1870–75; MOZAMBIQUE + -AN]

Mo•zam•bique (mō′zam bēk′, -zəm-), *n.* **1.** Formerly, **Portuguese East Africa.** a republic in SE Africa: formerly an overseas province of Portugal; gained independence in 1975. 9,900,000; 297,731 sq. mi. (771,123 sq. km). *Cap.:* Maputo. **2.** a seaport on an island just off the NE coast of this republic. 55,000. Portuguese, **Moçambique.**

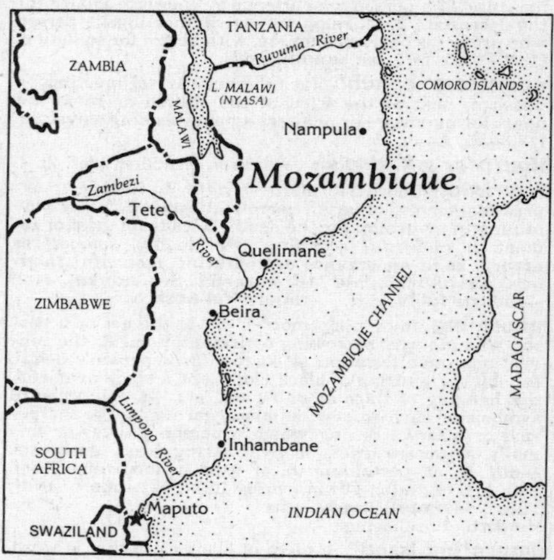

Mo′zambique Chan′nel, a channel in SE Africa, between Mozambique and Madagascar. 950 mi. (1530 km) long; 250–550 mi. (400–885 km) wide.

Mo′zambique Cur′rent. See **Agulhas Current.**

Moz•ar•ab (mō zar′əb), *n.* a Christian in Spain who, during the Muslim domination, was permitted to practice his or her own religion. [1780–90; < Sp *mozárabe* < Ar *musta′rib* one assimilated to the Arabs]

Moz•ar•a•bic (mō zar′ə bik), *adj.* **1.** of, pertaining to, or characteristic of the Mozarabs: *Mozarabic culture.* **2.** of or pertaining to a style of Spanish church architecture produced from the 9th to the 15th centuries and characterized chiefly by the horseshoe arch. **—***n.* **3.** any of the Romance dialects, descended from the Vulgar Latin of the Visigothic kingdom, that were spoken in the portions of Spain under Moorish control, were strongly influenced by Arabic, and subsequently had a significant impact on the development of Spanish. [1700–10; MOZARAB + -IC]

Mo·zart (mōt′särt), *n.* **Wolf·gang A·ma·de·us** (wŏŏlf′-gang am′ə dā′əs; *Ger.* vôlf′gäng ä′mä dā′ŏŏs), 1756–91, Austrian composer. —**Mo·zar′te·an, Mo·zar′ti·an,** *adj.*

Mo·zi (*Chin.* mô′zœ′), *n. Pinyin.* Mo-tze.

mo·zo (mō′zō), *n., pl.* **-zos.** *Southwestern U.S.* a waiter or male household servant. [1830–40; < Sp: lit., youth, servant, of obscure orig.]

moz·za·rel·la (mot′sə rel′lə, mōt′-), *n.* a mild, white, semisoft Italian cheese. [1910–15; < It, equiv. to *mozza* a kind of cheese (lit., a cut; cf. *mozzare* to cut off) + *-rella* -REL]

moz·zet·ta (mō zet′ə; *It.* môt tset′tä), *n., pl.* **-tas,** *It.* ***moz·zet·te*** (môt tset′te). *Rom. Cath. Ch.* a short cape that covers the shoulders and can be buttoned over the breast, and to which a hood is attached, worn by the pope and by cardinals, bishops, abbots, and other dignitaries. Also, **mo·zet′ta.** [1765–75; < It, aph. var. of *almozzetta,* equiv. to *almozz(a)* (cf. ML *almutia* AMICE[2]) + *-etta* -ETTE]

MP, 1. Military Police. **2.** Military Policeman. **3.** Mounted Police.

mp, *Music.* mezzo piano.

M.P., 1. Member of Parliament. **2.** Metropolitan Police. **3.** Military Police. **4.** Military Policeman. **5.** Mounted Police.

m.p., 1. melting point. **2.** (in prescriptions) in the manner prescribed; as directed. [< L *modō praescriptō*]

M.P.A., 1. Master of Professional Accounting. **2.** Master of Public Administration. **3.** Master of Public Affairs.

M.P.E., Master of Physical Education.

MPers, Middle Persian.

mpg, miles per gallon. Also, **m.p.g., M.P.G., MPG**

mph, miles per hour. Also, **m.p.h., MPH**

M.Ph., Master of Philosophy.

M.P.H., Master of Public Health.

Mpha·hle·le (əm pä hlā′lā, -lā′lā), *n.* **Ezekiel,** born 1919, South African writer.

M.Pharm., Master of Pharmacy.

MR, 1. motivation research. **2.** Moral Re-Armament. Also, **M.R.**

mR, milliroentgen; milliroentgens. Also, **mr**

Mr. (mis′tər), *pl.* **Messrs.** (mes′ərz). **1.** mister: a title of respect prefixed to a man's name or position: *Mr. Lawson; Mr. President.* **2.** a title prefixed to a mock surname that is used to represent possession of a particular attribute, identity, etc., esp. in an idealized or excessive way: *Mr. Democrat; Mr. Perfect; Mr. Macho.*

MRA, Moral Re-Armament.

M-ra·di·a·tion (em′rā′dē ā′shən), *n. Physics.* See under **M-line.**

Mr. Big, *Slang.* a man having the highest authority, control, prestige, or influence in a group, field, situation, or the like, esp. in the underworld. [1935–40]

MRBM, medium-range ballistic missile.

Mr. Bones, the end man in a minstrel troupe who plays the bones. Cf. **Mr. Tambo.**

Mr. Charlie, *Slang (disparaging and offensive).* See **Mister Charlie.**

Mr. Clean, *Informal.* **1.** an actual or idealized person with an impeccable record, reputation, or image, esp. a politician (sometimes used with *Miss, Ms.,* or *Mrs.* instead of *Mr.* when referring to a female). **2.** such a person regarded as excessively virtuous; goody-goody (sometimes used with *Miss, Ms.,* or *Mrs.* instead of *Mr.* when referring to a female). [1970–75; popularized as the trademark of a liquid cleaner]

Mr. Cool, *Informal.* a person who is ideally or excessively self-possessed, poised, or reserved (sometimes used with *Miss, Ms.,* or *Mrs.* instead of *Mr.* when referring to a female).

M.R.E., Master of Religious Education.

mrem, millirem; millirems.

Mr. Fix·it (fiks′it), *Informal.* **1.** a person who characteristically repairs or tinkers with things, as household appliances (sometimes used with *Miss, Ms.,* or *Mrs.* instead of *Mr.* when referring to a female). **2.** a person who epitomizes the ability or tendency to manage situations or solve problems (sometimes used with *Miss, Ms.,* or *Mrs.* instead of *Mr.* when referring to a female). [1920–25; from v. phrase *fix it*]

MRI, *Med.* **1.** Also called **NMR.** magnetic resonance imaging: a noninvasive diagnostic procedure employing an MR scanner to obtain detailed sectional images of the internal structure of the body. **2.** magnetic resonance imager. See **MR scanner.**

mri·dan·ga (mrē däng′gə), *n.* an ancient drum of India shaped like a long conical barrel with two tuned heads of different sizes. Also, **mri·dan·gam** (mrē däng′-gəm). [1885–1900]

mRNA, messenger RNA.

Mr. Nice Guy, *Informal.* a typically pleasant, likable person who avoids causing trouble or dissension (sometimes used with *Miss, Ms.,* or *Mrs.* instead of *Mr.* when referring to a female).

M roof, a roof having the form of two parallel gable roofs. Also called **trough roof.** [1875–80]

M.R.P., Master in Regional Planning or Master of Regional Planning.

Mr. Right, a man who is viewed as an ideal romantic partner or potential spouse (sometimes used with *Miss, Ms.,* or *Mrs.* instead of *Mr.* when referring to a female). [1920–25]

Mrs. (mis′iz, miz′iz), *pl.* **Mmes.** (mā däm′, -dam′). **1.** a title of respect prefixed to the name of a married woman: *Mrs. Jones.* **2.** a title prefixed to a mock surname that is used to represent possession of a particular attribute, identity, etc., esp. in an idealized or excessive way: *Mrs. Punctuality.* [abbr. of MISTRESS]

—**Usage.** See **Ms.**

—**Pronunciation.** MRS., first recorded in the early 17th century, was originally, like *Miss,* an abbreviation of *mistress.* MRS. and *mistress* were at first used interchangeably in all contexts, but by the second half of that century, the written form of the abbreviation was largely confined to use as a title preceding a woman's surname. By the early 19th century, reduction of the medial consonant cluster had contracted the usual pronunciation of the title from (mis′tris) to (mis′iz) or (mis′iz). The contracted pronunciation used other than as a title was not considered standard, and today, locutions like *Let me discuss it with the missis* are perceived as old-fashioned. Currently, two main types of pronunciation for the abbreviation occur in the United States; (mis′iz) and sometimes (mis′is) are the common forms in the North and North Midland, while in the South Midland and South, the prevalent types are (miz′iz) and (miz), the latter homophonous with the usual pronunciation of the abbreviation *Ms.*

MR scan, 1. a medical examination performed with an MR scanner. **2.** an image obtained by examination with an MR scanner. Also, **MRI scan.** Also called **NMR scan.**

MR scanner, a diagnostic device employing nuclear magnetic resonance to display computer-generated sectional images of the body, consisting of a large, body-encircling magnet that generates a strong, uniform magnetic field which interacts with radio waves to excite the nuclei of hydrogen atoms, or other specific atoms, and a detection system that picks up the signals from the body and transforms them into a visual image. Also called **MR imager, MRI scanner, NMR scanner.**

Mr. Tam·bo (tam′bō), the end man in a minstrel troupe who plays the tambourine. Cf. **Mr. Bones.**

MRV, *Mil.* See **multiple reentry vehicle.** Also, **M.R.V.**

MS, 1. Mississippi (approved esp. for use with zip code). **2.** motorship. **3.** multiple sclerosis.

ms, millisecond; milliseconds.

Ms. (miz), *pl.* **Mses.** (miz′əz). **1.** a title of respect prefixed to a woman's name or position: unlike *Miss* or *Mrs.,* it does not depend upon or indicate her marital status. **2.** a title prefixed to a mock surname that is used to represent possession of a particular attribute, identity, etc., esp. in an idealized or excessive way: *Ms. Cooperation.*

—**Usage.** Ms. came into use in the 1950's as a title before a woman's surname when her marital status was unknown or irrelevant. In the early 1970's, the use of Ms. was adopted and encouraged by the women's movement, the reasoning being that since a man's marital status is not revealed by the title MR., there is no reason that a woman's status should be revealed by her title. Since then Ms. has gained increasing currency, especially in business and professional use. Some women prefer the traditional MISS (still fully standard for a woman whose marital status is unknown and for an unmarried woman) or, when appropriate, MRS.

Newspaper editors sometimes reject Ms. except in quoted matter. Others use whichever of the three titles a woman prefers if her preference is known. Increasingly, newspapers avoid the use of all three titles by referring to women by their full names in first references (*Sarah Brady; Margaret Bourke-White*) and by surname only, as with men, in subsequent references: *Brady, Bourke-White.* Since all three titles—Ms., MISS, and MRS.—remain in use, the preference of the woman being named or addressed or the practice of the organization or publication in which the name is to appear is often followed.

—**Pronunciation.** Ms. is pronounced (miz), a pronunciation that is identical with one standard South Midland and Southern U.S. pronunciation of MRS.

MS., *pl.* **MSS.** manuscript.

ms., *pl.* **mss.** manuscript.

M/S, 1. *Com.* months after sight. **2.** motorship.

m/s, meter per second; meters per second.

M.S., 1. mail steamer. **2.** Master of Science. **3.** Master in Surgery. **4.** motorship.

m.s., 1. modification of the stem of. **2.** *Com.* months after sight.

M.S.A., Master of Science in Agriculture.

M.S.A.E., Master of Science in Aeronautical Engineering.

M.S.A.M., Master of Science in Applied Mechanics.

M.S.Arch., Master of Science in Architecture.

MSAT, Minnesota Scholastic Aptitude Test.

M.S.B.A., Master of Science in Business Administration.

M.S.B.C., Master of Science in Building Construction.

M.S.Bus., Master of Science in Business.

M.Sc., Master of Science.

M.Sc.D., Doctor of Medical Science.

M.S.C.E., Master of Science in Civil Engineering.

M.S.Ch.E., Master of Science in Chemical Engineering.

M.Sc.Med., Master of Medical Science.

M.S.Cons., Master of Science in Conservation.

M.S.C.P., Master of Science in Community Planning.

MSD, See **most significant digit.**

M.S.D., 1. Doctor of Medical Science. **2.** Master of Science in Dentistry.

M.S.Dent., Master of Science in Dentistry.

MS DOS (em′es′ dôs′, -dos′), *Trademark.* a microcomputer operating system. Also, **MS-DOS**

M.S.E., 1. Master of Science in Education. **2.** Master of Science in Engineering.

msec, millisecond; milliseconds.

m/sec, meter per second; meters per second.

M.S.Ed., Master of Science in Education.

M.S.E.E., Master of Science in Electrical Engineering.

M.S.E.M., 1. Master of Science in Engineering Mechanics. **2.** Master of Science in Engineering of Mines.

M.S.Ent., Master of Science in Entomology.

M-se·ries (em′sēr′ēz), *n. Physics.* See under **M-line.**

M.S.F., Master of Science in Forestry.

M.S.F.M., Master of Science in Forest Management.

M.S.For., Master of Science in Forestry.

MSG, See **monosodium glutamate.**

msg., message.

M.S.Geol.E., Master of Science in Geological Engineering.

M.S.G.M., Master of Science in Government Management.

M.S.G.Mgt., Master of Science in Game Management.

Msgr., 1. Monseigneur. **2.** Monsignor.

M.Sgt., master sergeant.

MSH, 1. Also called **melanocyte-stimulating hormone, melanotropin.** *Biochem.* a hormone, produced in vertebrates by the pituitary gland, that causes dispersal of the black pigment melanin of melanocytes. **2.** *Mineral.* See **Mohs scale.**

M.S.H.A., Master of Science in Hospital Administration.

M.S.H.E., Master of Science in Home Economics. Also, **M.S.H.Ec.**

M-shell (em′shel′), *n. Physics.* the third shell of electrons surrounding the nucleus of an atom and containing, when filled, 18 electrons having principal quantum number three. Cf. **K-shell, L-shell, N-shell.** [1920–25]

M.S.Hort., Master of Science in Horticulture.

M.S.Hyg., Master of Science in Hygiene.

MSI, *Electronics.* medium-scale integration: the technology for concentrating up to a thousand semiconductor devices in an integrated circuit. Cf. **SSI, LSI.**

M.S.I.E., Master of Science in Industrial Engineering.

m'sieur (mə syœ′), *French.* contraction of *monsieur.*

M.S.J., Master of Science in Journalism.

M.S.L., 1. Master of Science in Linguistics. **2.** Also, **m.s.l.** mean sea level.

M.S.M., 1. Master of Sacred Music. **2.** Master of Science in Music.

M.S.M.E., Master of Science in Mechanical Engineering.

M.S.Met.E., Master of Science in Metallurgical Engineering.

M.S.Mgt.E., Master of Science in Management Engineering.

M.S.N., Master of Science in Nursing.

M.S.P.E., Master of Science in Physical Education.

M.S.P.H., Master of Science in Public Health.

M.S.Phar., Master of Science in Pharmacy. Also, **M.S.Pharm.**

M.S.P.H.E., Master of Science in Public Health Engineering.

M.S.P.H.Ed., Master of Science in Public Health Education.

MSS., manuscripts. Also, **MSS, Mss, mss.**

M.S.S., 1. Master of Social Science. **2.** Master of Social Service.

M.S.Sc., Master of Social Science.

M.S.S.E., Master of Science in Sanitary Engineering.

MST, Mountain Standard Time. Also, **m.s.t.**

M.S.T., 1. Master of Science in Teaching. **2.** Mountain Standard Time.

M star, *Astron.* a relatively cool, red star, as Antares or Betelgeuse, having a surface temperature of less than 3600 K and an absorption spectrum dominated by molecular bands, esp. titanium oxide. Cf. **spectral type.**

MSTS, Military Sea Transportation Service (U.S. Navy).

M.S.W., 1. Master of Social Welfare. **2.** Master of Social Work or Master in Social Work. Also, **MSW**

MT, 1. mechanical translation. **2.** megaton; megatons. **3.** Montana (approved esp. for use with zip code). **4.** Mountain time.

Mt., 1. mount: *Mt. Rainier.* **2.** mountain. Also, **mt.**

M.T., 1. metric ton. **2.** Also, **m.t.** Mountain time.

mtg., 1. meeting. **2.** mortgage.

mtge., mortgage.

M.Th., Master of Theology.

MTI, See **moving target indicator.**

mtn, mountain.

MTO, *Mil.* (in World War II) Mediterranean Theater of Operations.

MTP, *Mil.* Mobilization Training Program.

Mt. Rev., Most Reverend.

MTS, multichannel television sound: a system adopted in the U.S. for broadcasting two or more stereo or unrelated audio channels over a single television station.

Mts., mountains. Also, **mts.**

MTV, *Trademark.* Music Television: a cable television subscription service featuring a format of music videos.

Mtwa·ra (əm twär′ə), *n.* a seaport in SE Tanzania. 20,413.

mu (myo͞o, mo͞o), *n.* **1.** the 12th letter of the Greek alphabet (M, μ). **2.** the consonant sound represented by this letter. **3.** micron (def. 1). [1895–1900; < Gk *mŷ*]

Mu (myo͞o, mo͞o), *n.* a legendary lost continent supposed to have sunk into the SW Pacific Ocean at about the same time that Atlantis disappeared into the Atlantic Ocean.

Mu·ba·rak (mo͞o bär′ək), *n.* **(Mohammed) Hos·ni** (hoz′nē, hos′-), born 1928, Egyptian political leader: president since 1981.

muc-, var. of **muco-** before a vowel: *mucin.*

MU car, *Railroads.* See **multiple-unit car.**

mu·ced·i·nous (myo͞o sed′n əs), *adj.* of or resembling mold or mildew. [1855–60; < NL *mūcēdin-* (s. of *mūcēdō* mucus; used in name of family of mold fungi; equiv. to *mūc(ēre)* to be moldy + *-ēdō* fem. n. suffix) + -OUS]

much (much), *adj.,* **more, most,** *n., adv.,* **more, most.** —*adj.* **1.** great in quantity, measure, or degree: *too much cake.* —*n.* **2.** a great quantity, measure, or degree: *Much of his research was unreliable.* **3.** a great, important, or notable thing or matter: *The house is not much to look at.* **4. make much of, a.** to treat, represent, or consider as of great importance: *to make much of trivial matters.* **b.** to treat with great consideration; show fondness for; flatter. —*adv.* **5.** to a great extent or degree; greatly; far: *to talk too much; much heavier.* **6.** nearly, approximately, or about: *This is much like the others.* **7. much as, a.** almost the same as: *We need exercise, much as we need nourishment.* **b.** however much: *Much as she wanted to stay at the party, she had to leave.* [1150–1200; ME *muche, moche,* apocopated var. of *muchel, mochel,* OE *mycel;* r. ME *miche(l),* OE *micel* great, much (cf. MICKLE), c. ON *mikill,* Goth *mikils,* Gk *mégal-,* suppletive s. of *mégas* great]

Much′ Ado′ About′ Noth′ing, a comedy (1598?) by Shakespeare.

much·ness (much′nis), *n. Archaic.* greatness, as in quantity, measure, or degree. [1350–1400; ME *mochenesse.* See MUCH, -NESS]

muci-, var. of **muco-:** *muciferous.*

mu·cic (myo͞o′sik), *adj. Chem.* of or derived from mucic acid. [1800–10; MUC- + -IC]

mu′cic ac′id, *Chem.* a white, crystalline, water-soluble powder, $C_6H_{10}O_8$, obtained by the oxidation of certain gums, milk sugar, or galactose, and used chiefly in organic synthesis. Also called **saccharolactic acid.**

mu·cid (myo͞o′sid), *adj. Archaic.* moldy; musty. [1650–60; < L *mūcidus* musty, moldy, equiv. to *mūc-* (see MUCOR) + *-idus* -ID[4]] —**mu′cid·ness,** *n.*

mu·cif·er·ous (myo͞o sif′ər əs), *adj.* secreting or containing mucus. Also, **mu·cig·en·ous** (myo͞o sij′ə nəs), **muciparous.** [1835–45; MUC- + -I- + -FEROUS]

mu·ci·lage (myo͞o′sə lij), *n.* **1.** any of various, usually liquid, preparations of gum, glue, or the like, used as an adhesive. **2.** any of various gummy secretions or gelatinous substances present in plants. [1350–1400; ME *muscilage* < MF *musillage* < LL *mūcilāgō* a musty juice, akin to *mūcēre* to be musty. See MUCOR]

mu·ci·lag·i·nous (myo͞o′sə laj′ə nəs), *adj.* **1.** of, pertaining to, or secreting mucilage. **2.** of the nature of or resembling mucilage; moist, soft, and viscid. [1640–50; < LL *mūcilāgin-* (s. of *mūcilāgō*) MUCILAGE + -OUS] —**mu′ci·lag′i·nous·ly,** *adv.*

mu·cin (myo͞o′sin), *n. Biochem.* any of a class of glycoproteins found in saliva, gastric juice, etc., that form viscous solutions and act as lubricants or protectants on external and internal surfaces of the body. [1825–35; MUC- + -IN[2]] —**mu′cin·oid′,** *adj.* —**mu·ci·nous** (myo͞o′sə nəs), *adj.*

mu·cip·a·rous (myo͞o sip′ər əs), *adj.* muciferous. [1825–35; MUC- + -I- + -PAROUS]

muck (muk), *n.* **1.** moist farmyard dung, decaying vegetable matter, etc.; manure. **2.** a highly organic, dark or black soil, less than 50 percent combustible, often used as a manure. **3.** mire; mud. **4.** filth, dirt, or slime. **5.** defamatory or sullying remarks. **6.** a state of chaos or confusion: *to make a muck of things.* **7.** *Chiefly Brit. Informal.* something of no value; trash. **8.** (esp. in mining) earth, rock, or other useless matter to be removed in order to get out the mineral or other substances sought. —*v.t.* **9.** to manure. **10.** to make dirty; soil. **11.** to remove muck from (sometimes fol. by *out*). **12.** *Informal.* **a.** to ruin; bungle (often fol. by *up*). **b.** to put into a state of complete confusion (often fol. by *up*). **13. muck about** or **around,** *Informal.* to idle; waste time; loiter. [1200–50; ME *muc, muk* < ON *myki* cow dung]

muck-a-muck (muk′ə muk′), *n.* **1.** *Slang.* high-muck-a-muck. **2.** *Northwestern U.S.* food. [1840–50, *Amer.;* see HIGH MUCK-A-MUCK]

muck′ bar′, *Metall.* a rough bar of wrought iron, rolled from blooms of iron extracted from a puddling furnace. [1865–70, *Amer.*]

CONCISE ETYMOLOGY KEY: <, descended or borrowed from; >, whence; b., blend of, blended; c., cognate with; cf., compare; deriv., derivative; equiv., equivalent; imit., imitative; obl., oblique; r., replacing; s., stem; sp., spelling, spelled; resp., respelling, respelled; trans., translation; ?, origin unknown; *, unattested; ‡, probably earlier than. See the full key inside the front cover.

muck·er (muk′ər), *n.* **1.** *Slang.* a vulgar, illbred person. **2.** *Informal.* a person who often does or says the wrong thing; bungler. **3.** (esp. in mining) a person who removes muck. [1890–95, *Amer.;* MUCK + -ER[1]] —**muck′er·ish,** *adj.* —**muck′er·ism,** *n.*

muck·ing (muk′ing), *adj., adv. Brit. Slang.* damned. [1595–1605; MUCK + -ING[2]]

muck·land (muk′land′), *n. Agric.* fertile farmland characterized by soil **(muck′ soil′)** that contains a high percentage (between 20 percent and 50 percent) of organic matter. [1840–50, *Amer.;* MUCK + -LAND]

muck·le (muk′əl), *adj. Brit. Dial.* mickle. [ME *mukel,* var. of *muchel;* see MUCH]

muck·luck (muk′luk), *n.* mukluk.

muck·rake (muk′rāk′), *v.i.,* **-raked, -rak·ing.** to search for and expose real or alleged corruption, scandal, or the like, esp. in politics. [1675–85; obs. *muck rake* a rake for use on muck or dung. See MUCK, RAKE[1]] —**muck′rak′er,** *n.*

muck-up (muk′up′), *n. Informal.* a bungled or disordered situation; foul-up. [1925–30; n. use of v. phrase *muck up*]

muck·worm (muk′wûrm′), *n.* **1.** (not in technical use) the larva of any of several insects, as the dung beetle, which lives in or beneath manure. **2.** a miser. [1590–1600; MUCK + WORM]

muck·y (muk′ē), *adj.,* **muck·i·er, muck·i·est. 1.** of or like muck. **2.** filthy, dirty, or slimy. **3.** *Brit. Informal.* **a.** obscene: *a mucky story.* **b.** nasty; mean or contemptible: *a mucky trick.* **c.** (of weather) oppressively humid. [1530–40; MUCK + -Y[1]]

muc·luc (muk′luk), *n.* mukluk.

muco-, a combining form representing **mucus** or **mucous** in compound words: *mucopurulent.* Also, **muc-, muci-.**

mu·coid (myo͞o′koid), *n.* **1.** *Biochem.* any of a group of substances resembling the mucins, occurring in connective tissue, cysts, etc. —*adj.* **2.** Also, **mu·coi·dal** (myo͞o koid′l). resembling mucus. [1840–50; MUC(IN) + -OID]

mu·co·lyt·ic (myo͞o′kə lit′ik), *adj. Biochem.* denoting or pertaining to enzymes that break down mucus. [1935–40; MUCO- + -LYTIC]

mu·co·pol·y·sac·cha·ride (myo͞o′kō pol′ē sak′ə rīd′, -rid), *n.* (formerly) glycosaminoglycan. [1935–40; MUCO- + POLYSACCHARIDE]

mu·co·pro·tein (myo͞o′kə prō′tēn, -tē in), *n. Biochem.* a protein that yields carbohydrates as well as amino acids on hydrolysis. [1920–25; MUCO- + PROTEIN]

mu·co·pu·ru·lent (myo͞o′kə pyo͝or′yə lənt, -pyo͝or′ə-), *adj. Med.* containing or composed of mucus and pus. [1835–45; MUCO- + PURULENT]

mu·cor (myo͞o′kər), *n.* any phycomycetous fungus of the genus *Mucor,* that forms a furry coating on foodstuffs and dead and decaying vegetable matter. [1650–60; < NL, L: moldiness, equiv. to *mūc(ēre)* to be moldy or musty + *-or* -OR[1]]

mu·co·sa (myo͞o kō′sə, -zə), *n., pl.* **-sae** (-sē, -zē). *Anat.* See **mucous membrane.** [1875–80; < NL, n. use of fem. of L *mūcōsus* MUCOUS] —**mu·co′sal,** *adj.*

mu·cous (myo͞o′kəs), *adj.* **1.** pertaining to, consisting of, or resembling mucus. **2.** containing or secreting mucus. [1640–50; < L *mūcōsus* slimy, mucous, equiv. to *mūc(us)* snot (see MUCUS) + *-ōsus* -OUS] —**mu·cos·i·ty** (myo͞o kos′i tē), *n.*

mu′cous mem′brane, a lubricating membrane lining an internal surface or an organ, as the alimentary, respiratory, and genitourinary canals. [1805–15]

mu·co·vis·ci·do·sis (myo͞o′kō vis′i dō′sis), *n. Pathol.* See **cystic fibrosis.** [1940–45; < NL; see MUCO-, VISCID, -OSIS]

mu·cro (myo͞o′krō), *n., pl.* **mu·cro·nes** (myo͞o krō′nēz). *Bot., Zool.* a short point projecting abruptly, as at the end of a leaf. [1640–50; < NL, L *mucrō* sharp point]

mu·cro·nate (myo͞o′krə nit, -nāt′), *adj. Bot., Zool.* having an abruptly projecting point, as a feather or leaf. Also, **mu′cro·nat′ed.** [1770–80; < NL, L *mūcrōnātus* pointed, equiv. to *mūcrōn-* (s. of *mūcrō*) point, edge + *-ātus* -ATE[1]] —**mu′cro·na′tion,** *n.*

mu·cus (myo͞o′kəs), *n.* a viscous, slimy mixture of mucins, water, electrolytes, epithelial cells, and leukocytes that is secreted by glands lining the nasal, esophageal, and other body cavities and serves primarily to protect and lubricate surfaces. [1655–65; < L *mūcus* snot; akin to Gk *myktēr* nose, *mýxa* slime]

mud (mud), *n., v.,* **mud·ded, mud·ding.** —*n.* **1.** wet, soft earth or earthy matter, as on the ground after rain, at the bottom of a pond, or along the banks of a river; mire. **2.** *Informal.* scandalous or malicious assertions or information: *The opposition threw a lot of mud at our candidate.* **3.** *Slang.* brewed coffee, esp. when strong or bitter. **4.** a mixture of chemicals and other substances pumped into a drilling rig chiefly as a lubricant for the bit and shaft. —*v.t.* **5.** to cover, smear, or spatter with mud: *to mud the walls of a hut.* **6.** to stir up the mud or sediment in: *waders mudding the clear water.* —*v.i.* **7.** to hide in or burrow into mud. [1300–50; ME *mudde, mode* < MLG *mudde, mode.* Cf. MOTHER[2]]

mud′ berth′, *Naut.* a mooring place in which a vessel rests on the bottom at low tide.

mud′ bug′, *Chiefly Mississippi Delta.* a crayfish.

mud·cap (mud′kap′), *v.t.,* **-capped, -cap·ping.** to blast (a rock) with an explosive attached to it with a capping of clay. [MUD + CAP[1]]

mud·cat (mud′kat′), *n.* See **flathead catfish.** [1810–20, *Amer.;* MUD + CAT[1]]

mud′ crack′, *Geol.* a fracture, part of a desiccation pattern, caused by the drying out and shrinking of silt or clay. [1890–95]

mud′ daub′er, any of several wasps of the family Sphecidae that build a nest of mud cells and provision it with spiders or insects. [1855–60, *Amer.*]

mud·der (mud′ər), *n.* **1.** a racehorse able to perform well on a wet, muddy track. **2.** an athlete who performs well in muddy conditions. [1900–05; MUD + -ER[1]]

mud·dle (mud′l), *v.,* **-dled, -dling,** *n.* —*v.t.* **1.** to mix up in a confused or bungling manner; jumble. **2.** to cause to become mentally confused. **3.** to cause to become confused or stupid with or as if with an intoxicating drink. **4.** to make muddy or turbid, as water. **5.** to mix or stir (a cocktail, chocolate, etc.). **6.** *Ceram.* to smooth (clay) by rubbing it on glass. —*v.i.* **7.** to behave, proceed, or think in a confused or aimless fashion or with an air of improvisation: *Some people just muddle along, waiting for their big break.* **8. muddle through,** to achieve a certain degree of success but without much skill, polish, experience, or direction: *None of us knew much about staging a variety show, so we just had to muddle through.* —*n.* **9.** the state or condition of being muddled, esp. a confused mental state. **10.** a confused, disordered, or embarrassing condition; mess. [1540–50; MUD + -LE; c. MD *moddelen* to muddy] —**mud′dled·ness, mud′dle·ment,** *n.* —**mud′dling·ly,** *adv.*
—**Syn. 1.** confuse, botch, bungle, spoil.

mud·dle·head (mud′l hed′), *n. Informal.* a stupid person; blunderer. [1850–55; MUDDLE + HEAD]

mud·dle·head·ed (mud′l hed′id), *adj.* confused in one's thinking; blundering: *a muddleheaded assertion.* [1750–60; MUDDLE + HEADED]

mud·dler (mud′lər), *n.* **1.** a swizzle stick with an enlarged tip for stirring drinks, crushing fruit or sugar, etc. **2.** a person who muddles or muddles through. **3.** a miller's thumb. [1850–55; MUDDLE + -ER[1]]

mud·dy (mud′ē), *adj.,* **-di·er, -di·est,** *v.,* **-died, -dy·ing.** —*adj.* **1.** abounding in or covered with mud. **2.** not clear or pure: *muddy colors.* **3.** cloudy with sediment: *muddy coffee.* **4.** dull, as the complexion. **5.** not clear mentally. **6.** obscure or vague, as thought, expression, or literary style. **7.** *Horse Racing.* denoting the condition of a track after a heavy, continuous rainfall has ceased and been completely absorbed into the surface, leaving it the consistency of thick mud. —*v.t.* **8.** to make muddy; soil with mud. **9.** to make turbid. **10.** to cause to be confused or obscure. —*v.i.* **11.** to become muddy. [1375–1425; late ME *muddi.* See MUD, -Y[1]] —**mud′di·ly,** *adv.* —**mud′di·ness,** *n.*

mud′ eel′, a salamander, *Siren lacertina,* having external gills, tiny front legs, and no hind legs, inhabiting shallow waters in the southeastern U.S. Also called **greater siren.** [1815–25]

Mu·dé·jar (*Sp.* mo͞o thĕ′här), *n., pl.* **-ja·res** (-hä res′), *adj.* —*n.* **1.** a Muslim permitted to remain in Spain after the Christian reconquest, esp. during the 8th to the 13th centuries. —*adj.* **2.** of or pertaining to a style of Spanish architecture from the 13th to 16th centuries, a fusion of Romanesque and Gothic with Arabic. [1860–65; < Sp < Ar *muddajjan* permitted to stay]

mud·fat (mud′fat′), *adj. Brit., Australian.* (of animals) very fat. [1885–90; from phrase *as fat as mud*]

mud·fish (mud′fish′), *n., pl.* (*esp. collectively*) **-fish,** (*esp. referring to two or more kinds or species*) **-fish·es.** any of various fishes that live in muddy waters, as the bowfin or mummichog. [1495–1505; MUD + FISH]

mud′ flat′, **1.** a mud-covered, gently sloping tract of land, alternately covered and left bare by tidal waters. **2.** the muddy, nearly level bed of a dry lake. [1805–15]

mud·flow (mud′flō′), *n. Geol.* **1.** a flow of mixed earth debris containing a large amount of water. **2.** the dried-out product of such a flow. Also called **mud slide, mudspate.** [1900–05; MUD + FLOW]

mud·guard (mud′gärd′), *n.* **1.** Also called **mud′ flap′.** splash guard. **2.** fender (def. 3). [MUD + GUARD]

mud′ hen′, any of various marsh-inhabiting birds, esp. the American coot. Also, **mud′hen′.** [1800–10]

mud·hole (mud′hōl′), *n.* a depression in which mud collects. [1745–55, *Amer.;* MUD + HOLE]

mud·lark (mud′lärk′), *n.* **1.** *Chiefly Brit.* a person who gains a livelihood by searching for iron, coal, old ropes, etc., in mud or low tide. **2.** *Chiefly Brit. Informal.* a street urchin. **3.** either of two black and white birds, *Grallina cyanoleuca,* of Australia, or *G. bruijni,* of New Guinea, that builds a large, mud nest. —*v.i.* **4.** to grub or play in mud. [1790–1800; MUD + LARK[1]]

mud·lump (mud′lump′), *n.* a small, short-lived island of clay or silt that forms within a river delta. [1865–70, *Amer.*]

mud·min·now (mud′min′ō), *n., pl.* (*esp. collectively*) **-now,** (*esp. referring to two or more kinds or species*) **-nows.** any of several small, carnivorous fishes of the genera *Umbra* and *Novumbra,* found in muddy streams and pools. [1865–70, *Amer.;* MUD + MINNOW]

mud·pack (mud′pak′), *n.* a pastelike preparation, as one consisting of fuller's earth, astringents, etc., used on the face as a cosmetic restorative. [1930–35; MUD + PACK[1]]

mud′ pot′, *Geol.* a hot spring filled with boiling mud. Cf. **paint pot** (def. 2). [1895–1900, *Amer.*]

mud·pup·py (mud′pup′ē), *n., pl.* **-pies. 1.** any of several often large, aquatic salamanders of the genus *Necturus,* of eastern North America, having bushy, red gills and well-developed limbs. **2.** any of several North American salamanders of the genus *Ambystoma.* [1880–85, *Amer.;* MUD + PUPPY]

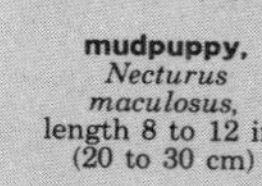

mudpuppy, *Necturus maculosus,* length 8 to 12 in. (20 to 30 cm)

mu•dra (mə drä′), *n.* **1.** *Hinduism, Buddhism.* any of a series of arm and hand positions expressing an attitude or action of the deity. **2.** any of various similar gestures used in India's classical dancing to represent specific feelings. [1805–15; < Skt *mudrā* sign]

mud′ room′, a vestibule or other area in a house, in which wet and muddy clothes or footwear are removed. Also, **mud′room′.** [1945–50]

mud•sill (mud′sil′), *n.* the lowest sill of a structure, usually placed in or on the ground. Also called **foot-plate.** [1675–85; MUD + SILL]

mud•skip•per (mud′skip′ər), *n.* any of several gobies of the genera *Periophthalmus* and *Boleophthalmus,* of tropical seas from Africa to the East Indies and Japan, noted for the habit of remaining out of water on mud flats for certain periods and jumping about when disturbed. Also called **mudspringer.** [1855–60; MUD + SKIPPER[2]]

mudskipper, *Periophthalmus barbarus,* length 5½ in. (14 cm)

mud′ slide′, *Geol.* mudflow. [1920–25]

mud•sling•ing (mud′sling′ing), *n.* an attempt to discredit one's competitor, opponent, etc., by malicious or scandalous attacks. [1880–85; MUD + SLINGING] —**mud′sling′er,** *n.*

mud′ snake′, an iridescent black and red snake, *Farancia abacura,* of southeastern and south-central U.S., having a sharp, stiff tail tip used in manipulating prey into position for swallowing. Cf. **hoop snake.**

mud•spate (mud′spāt′), *n. Geol.* mudflow. [MUD + SPATE]

mud•spring•er (mud′spring′ər), *n.* mudskipper. [MUD + SPRINGER]

mud•stone (mud′stōn′), *n. Geol.* a clayey rock with the texture and composition of shale but little or no lamination. [1730–40; MUD + STONE]

mud′ stream′, *Geol.* mudflow.

mud•suck•er (mud′suk′ər), *n.* a goby, *Gillichthys mirabilis,* of California, used as bait. [1680–90; MUD + SUCKER]

mud′ tur′tle, any of several small, freshwater turtles of the family Kinosternidae, of North and South America, as the dark-brown *Kinosternon subrubrum,* of the U.S. [1775–85, *Amer.*]

mud′ volca′no, a vent in the earth's surface through which escaping gas and vapor issue, causing mud to boil and occasionally to overflow, forming a conical mound around the vent. [1810–20]

mud′ wasp′, *Chiefly North Midland and Western U.S.* any of several wasps, as the mud dauber, that construct a nest of mud. [1815–25, *Amer.*]

mud•wres•tling (mud′res′ling), *n.* wrestling in an enclosure with a floor or base of wet mud, staged as a public display and competitive event.

mu ehr (mo͞o′ âr′, myo͞o′). See **cloud ear.** [< Chin *mùěr,* equiv. to *mù* tree + *ěr* ear(s)]

Muel•ler (myo͞o′lər, mul′ər, mil′-), *n.* **Paul,** 1899–1965, Swiss chemist: Nobel prize for medicine 1948.

muen•ster (mun′stər, mo͝on′-), *n.* (*often cap.*) a white, semisoft, mild cheese made from whole milk. [1900–05; after *Müenster* in France (Haut-Rhin)]

mu•ez•zin (myo͞o ez′in, mo͞o-), *n.* the crier who, from a minaret or other high part of a mosque, at stated hours five times daily, intones aloud the call summoning Muslims to prayer. [1575–85; < Turk *müezzin* < Ar *mu'adhdhin*]

MUF, material unaccounted for.

muff (muf), *n.* **1.** a thick, tubular case for the hands, covered with fur or other material, used by women and girls for warmth and as a handbag. **2.** a bungled or clumsy action or performance. **3.** *Sports.* a failure to hold onto a ball that may reasonably be expected to be caught successfully. **4.** a tuft of feathers on the sides of the head of certain fowls. **5.** *Slang* (*vulgar*). a woman's pubic area. **6.** See under **muff glass.** —*v.t.* **7.** *Informal.* to bungle; handle clumsily: *He muffed a good opportunity.* **8.** *Sports.* to fail to hold onto (a ball that may reasonably be expected to be caught successfully); fumble. —*v.i.* **9.** *Informal.* to bungle; perform clumsily. [1590–1600; < D *mof,* earlier *moffel, muffel* mitten, muff < ONF *moufle* < early ML *muffula,* perh. < Frankish] —**muff′y,** *adj.*

muff′ glass′, sheet glass made from a blown cylinder **(muff)** that is split and flattened.

muf•fin (muf′in), *n.* **1.** an individual cup-shaped quick bread made with wheat flour, cornmeal, or the like, and baked in a pan **(muf′fin pan′)** containing a series of cuplike forms. **2.** See **English muffin.** [1695–1705; orig. uncert.]

muf•fin•eer (muf′ə nēr′), *n.* a caster for sprinkling sugar or other condiments on food. [1800–10; MUFFIN + -EER]

muf′fin stand′, a small stand having several tiers for holding muffins, cakes, etc., and a tea service.

muf•fle[1] (muf′əl), *v.,* **-fled, -fling,** *n.* —*v.t.* **1.** to wrap with something to deaden or prevent sound: *to muffle drums.* **2.** to deaden (sound) by wrappings or other means. **3.** to wrap or envelop in a cloak, shawl, coat, etc., esp. to keep warm or protect the face and neck (often fol. by *up*): *Muffle up the children before they go out.* **4.** to wrap (oneself) in a garment or other covering: *muffled in silk.* **5.** to alter temporarily the profile of (a plaster mold) in order to run a base coat of plaster that will later be covered by a finish coat having the true profile. —*n.* **6.** something that muffles. **7.** muffled sound. **8.** an oven or arched chamber in a furnace or kiln, used for heating substances without direct contact with the fire. [1400–50; late ME *mufeln,* perh. aph. form of AF **amoufler,* for OF *enmoufler* to wrap up, muffle, deriv. of *moufle* mitten (see EN-[1], MUFF); (def. 8) directly < F *moufle* lit., mitten]

muf•fle[2] (muf′əl), *n.* the thick, bare part of the upper lip and nose of ruminants and rodents. [1595–1605; < MF *mufle* muzzle, snout, prob. b. *moufle* chubby face (obscurely akin to G *Muffel* snout) and *museau* snout, MUZZLE]

muf′fle col′or, *Ceram.* a color fired onto an object in a muffle kiln.

muf•fler (muf′lər), *n.* **1.** a scarf worn around one's neck for warmth. **2.** any of various devices for deadening sound, as the sound of escaping gases of an internal-combustion engine. **3.** anything used for muffling. **4.** *Armor.* a mittenlike glove worn with a mail hauberk. [1525–35; MUFFLE + -ER[1]]

muf•ti (muf′tē), *n., pl.* **-tis.** **1.** civilian clothes, in contrast with military or other uniforms, or as worn by a person who usually wears a uniform. **2.** a Muslim jurist expert in the religious law. **3.** (in the Ottoman Empire) a deputy of the chief Muslim legal adviser to the Sultan. **4.** (*cap.*) See **Grand Mufti.** [1580–90; < Ar *muftī* lit., a person who delivers a judgment, orig. a Muslim legal adviser; sense of def. 1 arises from the legal adviser being a civil official]

Mu•fu•li•ra (mo͞o′fə lēr′ə), *n.* a city in N central Zambia, on the Zaire border. 142,000.

mug (mug), *n., v.,* **mugged, mug•ging.** —*n.* **1.** a drinking cup, usually cylindrical in shape, having a handle, and often of a heavy substance, as earthenware. **2.** the quantity it holds. **3.** *Slang.* **a.** the face. **b.** the mouth. **c.** an exaggerated facial expression; grimace, as in acting. **d.** a thug, ruffian, or other criminal. **4.** *Brit. Slang.* a gullible person; dupe; fool. —*v.t.* **5.** to assault or menace, esp. with the intention of robbery. **6.** *Slang.* to photograph (a person), esp. in compliance with an official or legal requirement. —*v.i.* **7.** *Slang.* to grimace; exaggerate a facial expression, as in acting. [1560–70; prob. < Scand; cf. Sw *mugg,* Norw, Dan *mugge* drinking cup; sense "face" appar. transferred from cups adorned with grotesque faces; sense "to assault" from earlier pugilistic slang "to strike in the face, fight"]

Mu•ga•be (mo͞o gä′bē, -bā), *n.* **Robert (Gabriel),** born 1924, Zimbabwean political leader: prime minister 1980–87; president since 1987.

mug•gee (mu gē′), *n.* a person who is attacked by a mugger; the victim of a mugging. [1970–75; MUG + -EE]

mug•ger[1] (mug′ər), *n.* a person who mugs, esp. one who assaults a person in order to rob him or her. [1860–65, *Amer.*; MUG + -ER[1]]

mug•ger[2] (mug′ər), *n.* a broad-snouted crocodile, *Crocodylus palustris,* of southern Asia, that grows to a length of about 16 ft. (4.88 m). Also, **mug′gar, mug′gur.** [1835–45; < Hindi *magar*]

mug•ging (mug′ing), *n.* an assault or threat of violence upon a person, esp. with intent to rob. [1840–50; MUG + -ING[1]]

mug•gins (mug′inz), *n.* **1.** a convention in cribbage in which a player scores points overlooked by an opponent. **2.** a game of dominoes, in which any player who can make the sum of two ends of the line equal five or a multiple of five adds the number so made to his or her score. **3.** *Brit. Slang.* a fool. [1850–55; prob. special use of proper name; def. 3 by assoc. with MUG]

mug•gy (mug′ē), *adj.,* **-gi•er, -gi•est.** (of the atmosphere, weather, etc.) oppressively humid; damp and close. [1725–35; *mug* to drizzle (n. and v.) (< Scand; cf. ON *mugga* mist, drizzle) + -Y[1]] —**mug′gi•ly,** *adv.* —**mug′gi•ness,** *n.*

Mu•ghal (mo͞o′gəl), *n., adj.* Mogul (defs. 1, 2, 6).

mu′gho pine′ (myo͞o′gō, mo͞o′-), a prostrate, shrubby pine, *Pinus mugo mugo,* native to Europe, cultivated as an ornamental. Also called **mu′go pine′.** [1750–60; < F *mugho* < It *mugo,* of dial. orig. (Trentino, Valtellina); further etym. uncert.]

mug's′ game′, a foolish, useless, or ill-advised venture. [1905–10]

mug′ shot′, *Slang.* **1.** an identifying photograph of a suspect or criminal, often one of a set showing a frontal view, a profile view, and a view of the back of the head. **2.** any closeup photograph of one's face. [1945–50]

mug•wort (mug′wûrt′, -wôrt′), *n.* any of certain weedy composite plants of the genus *Artemisia,* esp. *A. vulgaris,* having aromatic leaves and small, greenish flower heads. [bef. 1000; ME; OE *mucgwyrt.* See MIDGE, WORT[2]]

mug•wump (mug′wump′), *n.* **1.** a Republican who refused to support the party nominee, James G. Blaine, in the presidential campaign of 1884. **2.** a person who is unable to make up his or her mind on an issue, esp. in politics; a person who is neutral on a controversial issue. [1830–35, *Amer.*; artificial 19th-cent. revival of Massachusett (E sp.) *mugquomp,* syncopated form of *muggumquomp* war leader (equiv. to Proto-Algonquian **memekw-* perh., swift + **-a·pe·w* man)] —**mug′wump′er•y, mug′wump′ism,** *n.* —**mug′wump′i•an,** *adj.* —**mug′wump′ish,** *adj.*

Mu•ha•ji•run (mo͝o hä′jə ro͞on′, -hä′jə ro͞on′), *n.pl., sing.* **Mu•ha•jir** (mo͝o hä′jir). those who accompanied Muhammad on the Hijra. [< Ar *muhājirūna*]

Mu•ham•mad (mo͝o ham′əd, -hä′məd), *n.* **1.** Also, **Mohammed, Mahomet.** A.D. 570–632, Arab prophet: founder of Islam. **2. Elijah** (*Elijah Poole*), 1897–1975, U.S. clergyman: leader of the Black Muslims 1934–75. **3.** a male given name.

Muham′mad Ah′med (am′əd), (*"the Mahdi"*) 1844–85, Muslim leader in Anglo-Egyptian Sudan.

Mu•ham•mad•an (mo͝o ham′ə dn), *n., adj.* Muslim (defs. 1, 2). Also, **Mu•ham′med•an.** [1960–65; MUHAMMAD + -AN]

Muham′madan cal′endar. See **Muslim Calendar.**

Mu•ham•mad•an•ism (mo͝o ham′ə dn iz′əm), *n.* Islam. [1805–15; MUHAMMADAN + -ISM]

Muham′mad Gho•ri′ (gô rē′, gō-). See **Mohammed of Ghor.**

Muham′mad Ri•za′ Pah•la•vi′ (ri zä′ pä lä vē′, pal′ə vē). See **Pahlavi** (def. 1).

Mu•har•ram (mo͞o har′əm), *n.* Moharram.

Mühl•bach (myl′bäкн), *n.* **Lu•i•se** (lo͞o ē′zə), (*Klara Müller Mundt*), 1814–73, German novelist.

Muh•len•berg (myo͞o′lən bûrg′), *n.* **1. Frederick Augustus Conrad,** 1750–1801, U.S. clergyman and statesman: first Speaker of the House 1789–91, 1793–95. **2.** his father, **Henry Mel•chi•or** (mel′kē ôr′), 1711–87, American Lutheran clergyman, born in Germany.

Muir (myo͝or), *n.* **John,** 1838–1914, U.S. naturalist, explorer, and writer; born in Scotland.

Muir′ Gla′cier, a glacier in SE Alaska, flowing SE from Mt. Fairweather into Glacier Bay. 350 sq. mi. (905 sq. km).

mu•ja•he•din (mo͞o jä′he dēn′), *n.pl.* (*sometimes cap.*) Muslim guerrilla fighters, esp. in Afghanistan and Iran. Also, **mu•ja′hed•din′, mu•ja′hi•deen′.**

mu•jik (mo͞o zhik′, mo͞o′zhik), *n.* muzhik.

muj•ta•hid (mo͞oj tä′hid), *n. Islam.* a person who has been certified as capable of interpreting religious law. [1805–15; < Ar: lit., one who exerts himself; see IJTIHAD]

Mu•kal•la (mo͞o kal′ə), *n.* a seaport in SE Yemen, on the Gulf of Aden. 158,000.

Muk•den (mo͝ok′den′, mo͝ok′-), *n.* a former name of **Shenyang.**

Mu•kha (mo͞o kä′), *n.* Mocha.

muk•luk (muk′luk), *n.* **1.** a soft boot worn by Eskimos, often lined with fur and usually made of sealskin or reindeer skin. **2.** a similar boot with a soft sole, usually worn for lounging. Also, **mucluc, muckluck.** [1865–70, *Amer.*; < Yupik *maklak* bearded seal, incorrectly taken to mean "sealskin," then transferred to boots made of sealskin]

muk•ti (mo͝ok′tē), *n. Hinduism.* moksha. [1775–85; < Skt]

mu•lat•to (mə lat′ō, -lä′tō, myo͞o-), *n., pl.* **-toes,** *adj.* —*n.* **1.** the offspring of one white parent and one black parent: not in technical use. **2.** a person whose ancestry is a mixture of Negro and Caucasian. —*adj.* **3.** of a light-brown color. [1585–95; < Sp *mulato* young mule, equiv. to *mul*(o) MULE[1] + *-ato* of unclear orig.]

mul•ber•ry (mul′ber′ē, -bə rē), *n., pl.* **-ries.** **1.** the edible, berrylike collective fruit of any tree of the genus *Morus.* **2.** a tree of this genus, as *M. rubra* **(red mulberry** or **American mulberry)** bearing dark-purple fruit, *M. nigra* **(black mulberry)** bearing dark-colored fruit, or *M. alba* **(white mulberry)** bearing nearly white fruit and having leaves used as food for silkworms. Cf. **mulberry family.** [1225–75; ME *mulberie,* dissimilated var. of *murberie,* OE *mōrberie,* equiv. to *mōr-* (< L *mōrum* mulberry) + *berie* BERRY]

mul′berry fam′ily, the plant family Moraceae, characterized by deciduous or evergreen trees, shrubs, and herbaceous plants having simple, alternate leaves, often milky sap, dense clusters of small flowers, and fruit in the form of a fleshy berry, usually hollow in the center, and including the fig, mulberry, Osage orange, and rubber plant.

mulch (mulch), *n.* **1.** a covering, as of straw, compost, or plastic sheeting, spread on the ground around plants to prevent excessive evaporation or erosion, enrich the soil, inhibit weed growth, etc. —*v.t.* **2.** to cover with mulch. [1650–60; n. use of obs. *mulch* (adj.), ME *molsh* soft, OE *myl(i)sc* mellow; c. dial. G *molsch* soft, overripe]

mulch•er (mul′chər), *n.* **1.** a person or thing that mulches. **2.** a machine or device that cuts up grass, leaves, etc., for use as mulch. [MULCH + -ER[1]]

mulct (mulkt), *v.t.* **1.** to deprive (someone) of something, as by fraud, extortion, etc.; swindle. **2.** to obtain (money or the like) by fraud, extortion, etc. **3.** to punish (a person) by fine, esp. for a misdemeanor. —*n.* **4.** a fine, esp. for a misdemeanor. [1475–85; < L *mul(c)ta* penalty involving loss of property]

Mul•doon (mul do͞on′), *n.* **Robert David,** born 1921, New Zealand political leader: prime minister 1975–84.

mule[1] (myo͞ol), *n.* **1.** the sterile offspring of a female horse and a male donkey, valued as a work animal, having strong muscles, a body shaped like a horse, and donkeylike long ears, small feet, and sure-footedness. Cf. **hinny[1].** See illus. on next page. **2.** any hybrid between the donkey and the horse. **3.** *Informal.* a very stubborn person. **4.** *Bot.* any sterile hybrid. **5.** *Slang.* a person paid to carry or transport contraband, esp. drugs, for a smuggler. **6.** a small locomotive used for pulling rail cars, as in a coal yard or on an industrial site, or for towing, as of ships through canal locks. **7.** Also called **spinning mule.** a machine for spinning cotton or other fibers into yarn and winding the yarn on spindles. **8.** *Naut.* a large triangular staysail set between two masts and having its clew set well aft. **9.** *Numis.* a hybrid coin having the obverse of one issue and the reverse of the succeed-

CONCISE PRONUNCIATION KEY: act, cāpe, dâre, pärt; set, ēqual; if, īce; ox, ōver, ôrder, oil, bo͝ok, bo͞ot, out; up, ûrge; child; sing; shoe; thin, *th*at; zh as in *treasure.* ə = *a* as in *alone, e* as in *system, i* as in *easily, o* as in *gallop, u* as in *circus;* ᵊ as in *fire* (fīᵊr), *hour* (ouᵊr). l and n can serve as syllabic consonants, as in *cradle* (krād′l), and *button* (but′n). See the full key inside the front cover.

ingissue,orviceversa. **10.** *Biol.* a hybrid, esp. one between the canary and some other finch. [bef. 1000; ME < OF < L *mūla* mule (fem.); r. OE *mūl* < L *mūlus* (masc.)]

mule[1], *Equus asinus × caballus,* 5 ft. (1.5 m) high at shoulder

mule[2] (myo͞ol), *n.* a lounging slipper that covers the toes and instep or only the instep. [1350–1400; ME: sore spot on the heel, chilblain, perh. < MD *mūle*]

mule′ chest′, a low chest with drawers, mounted on a low frame. [1910–15]

mule′ deer′, a deer, *Odocoileus hemionus,* of western North America, having large ears and a gray coat. [1795–1805, *Amer.*]

mule deer, *Odocoileus hemionus,* 3½ ft. (1.1 m) high at shoulder; head and body 5 ft. (1.5 m); tail 7½ in. (19 cm)

mule-ears (myo͞ol′ērz′), *n., pl.* **-ears.** (*used with a singular or plural v.*) any of several composite plants of the genus *Wyethia,* of the western U.S., having large leaves and broad flower heads with yellow rays. Also, **mule's′-ears′.**

mule-fat (myo͞ol′fat′), *n.* a composite shrub, *Baccharis viminea,* of California, having willowlike leaves and clustered flowers, growing in riverbeds. [1930–35; so called from its being a source of food for mule deer]

mule·head·ed (myo͞ol′hed′id), *adj. South Midland and Southern U.S.* stubborn; intractable. [1880–85; MULE[1] + HEAD + -ED[3]]

mule′ skin′ner, *Informal.* a muleteer. [1865–70, *Amer.*]

mule′ spin′ning, a process of spinning that produces extremely fine yarn by drawing and twisting the roving, and winding the resultant yarn onto a bobbin or spindle in the form of a cop. Cf. **ring spinning.** [1815–25]

mu·le·ta (mo͞o lā′tə, -let′ə), *n.* a red cloth similar to but smaller than a capa and manipulated by a stick set into one of the three holes in or near the center, for use by a matador in guiding the course of the bull's attack in the stage of the fight preparatory to the kill. [1830–40; < Sp: prop, support, muleta, dim. of *mula* (fem.) MULE[1]]

mu·le·teer (myo͞o′lə tēr′), *n.* a driver of mules. [1530–40; < MF *muletier,* equiv. to *mulet* (see MULE[1], -ET) + *-ier* -IER[2]; see -EER]

mule′ train′, a line of pack mules or a line of wagons drawn by mules. [1840–50, *Amer.*]

mul·ey (myo͞o′lē, mo͝ol′ē), *adj., n., pl.* **-eys.** —*adj.* **1.** (of cattle or deer) hornless; polled. —*n.* **2.** any cow. Also, **mulley.** [1565–75; var. of dial. *moiley* < Ir *maol* or Welsh *moel* bald, hornless + -EY[1], -EY[2]]

mul′ey saw′, a saw having a long, stiff blade that is not stretched in a gate, but whose motion is directed by clamps at each end mounted on guide rails. [1850–55, *Amer.*]

mul·ga (mul′gə), *n., pl.* **-gas, -ga. 1.** an Australian shrub or small tree, *Acacia aneura,* forming dense growths in some areas and having foliage used as forage for livestock. **2.** an object, as an Aboriginal shield or club, made from the wood of this tree. [1830–40; < Yuwaalaraay (Australian Aboriginal language spoken near Lightning Ridge, N New South Wales) *malga*]

CONCISE ETYMOLOGY KEY: <, descended or borrowed from; >, whence; b., blend of, blended; c., cognate with; cf., compare; deriv., derivative; equiv., equivalent; imit., imitative; obl., oblique; r., replacing; s., stem; sp., spelling, spelled; resp., respelling, respelled; trans., translation; ?, origin unknown; *, unattested; ‡, probably earlier than. See the full key inside the front cover.

Mul·ha·cén (mo͞ol′ä then′), *n.* a mountain in S Spain: the highest peak in Spain. 11,411 ft. (3478 m).

Mül·heim an der Ruhr (myl′hīm än dɛr ro͞or′), a city in North Rhine-Westphalia, W Germany, near Essen. 176,100.

Mul·house (my lo͞oz′), *n.* a city in E France, near the Rhine. 119,326. German, **Mül·hau·sen** (myl hou′zən).

mu·li·eb·ri·ty (myo͞o′lē eb′ri tē), *n.* **1.** womanly nature or qualities. **2.** womanhood. [1585–95; < LL *muliēbritās* womanhood, equiv. to L *muliēbri(s)* womanly (deriv. of *mulier* woman) + *-tās* -TY[2]] —**mu′li·eb′·ral,** *adj.*

mu·li·er[1] (myo͞o′lē ər), *n. Old Eng. Law.* a woman or wife. [1325–75; ME < AF << L: woman]

mu·li·er[2] (myo͞o′lē ər), *n. Old Eng. Law.* a legitimate child. [1350–1400; ME *mulire, moylere* < AF *mulieré* born in wedlock, legitimate < ML *mulierātus.* See MULIER[1], -ATE[1]]

mu′lier puis′ne, *Old Eng. Law.* the legitimate son of parents whose first son was illegitimate. Cf. **bastard eigne.** [1620–30]

mu·li·er·ty (myo͞o′lē ər tē), *n. Old Eng. Law.* the state of being of legitimate birth. [1620–30; < AF *muliertie.* See MULIER[2], -TY[2]]

mul·ish (myo͞o′lish), *adj.* of or like a mule, as being very stubborn, obstinate, or intractable. [1745–55; MULE[1] + -ISH[1]] —**mul′ish·ly,** *adv.* —**mul′ish·ness,** *n.*

mull[1] (mul), *v.i.* **1.** to study or ruminate; ponder. —*v.t.* **2.** to think about carefully; consider (often fol. by *over*): *to mull over an idea.* **3.** to make a mess or failure of. [1815–25; perh. identical with dial. *mull* to crumble, pulverize; see MULL[4]] —**Syn. 1.** consider, weigh.

mull[2] (mul), *v.t.* to heat, sweeten, and flavor with spices for drinking, as ale or wine. [1610–20; orig. uncert.]

mull[3] (mul), *n.* a soft, thin muslin. [1790–1800; earlier *mulmul* < Hindi *malmal*]

mull[4] (mul), *v.t. Metall.* to mix (clay and sand) under a roller for use in preparing a mold. [1400–50; cf. dial.: to crumble, pulverize, ME *mollen, mullen,* orig., to moisten, soften by wetting; see MOIL]

Mull (mul), *n.* an island in the Hebrides, in W Scotland. 3185; ab. 351 sq. mi. (910 sq. km).

mul·lah (mul′ə, mo͝ol′ə, mo͞o′lə), *n.* **1.** (in Islamic countries) a title of respect for a person who is learned in, teaches, or expounds the sacred law. **2.** (in Turkey) a provincial judge. Also, **mul′la, mollah.** [1605–15; < Pers or Urdu *mullā* < Ar *mawlā;* see MAULVI]

mul·lein (mul′ən), *n.* **1.** any of various plants belonging to the genus *Verbascum,* of the figwort family, native to the Old World, esp. *V. thapsus,* a tall plant with woolly leaves and a dense spike of yellow flowers. **2.** any of several similar plants. Also, **mul′len.** [1325–75; ME *moleine* < AF, perh. deriv. of *mol* soft < L *mollis*]

mul′lein pink′. See **rose campion.** [1830–40]

mul·ler[1] (mul′ər), *n.* **1.** an implement of stone or other substance with a flat base for grinding paints, powders, etc., on a slab of stone or the like. **2.** any of various mechanical devices for grinding. [1375–1425; late ME *molour;* see MULL[4], -OR[2], -ER[1]]

mull·er[2] (mul′ər), *n.* **1.** a person or thing that mulls. **2.** a container for mulling an alcoholic beverage over a fire. [1855–60; MULL[2] + -ER[1]]

Mul·ler (myo͞o′lər, mul′ər, mil′-), *n.* **Hermann Joseph,** 1890–1967, U.S. geneticist: Nobel prize for medicine 1946.

Mül·ler (mul′ər; *Ger.* my′lər), *n.* **1. Frie·drich Max** (frē′drik maks; *Ger.* frē′drikh mäks), 1823–1900, English Sanskrit scholar and philologist born in Germany. **2. Jo·hann** (yō′hän), (*"Regiomontanus"*), 1436–76, German mathematician and astronomer. **3. Jo·han·nes Pe·ter** (yō hä′nəs pā′tər), 1801–58, German physiologist and comparative anatomist. **4. Wil·helm** (vil′helm), 1794–1827, German poet.

Mül·le′ri·an mim′icry (myo͞o lēr′ē ən, mu-, mi-), *Ecol.* the resemblance in appearance of two or more unpalatable species, which are avoided by predators to a greater degree than any one of the species would be otherwise. Also, **Mulle′rian mim′icry.** Cf. **Batesian mimicry.** [after German-born Brazilian biologist Fritz *Müller* (1821–97), who described it in 1878; see -IAN]

Mül′ler-Ly′er illu′sion (mul′ər lī′ər, myo͞o′lər-, mil′ər-; *Ger.* myl′ər lē′ər), a geometric illusion in which two lines of equal length appear unequal depending on whether angular lines forming arrowheads at each end point toward or away from each other. [after Franz-Karl *Müller-Lyer* (1857–1916), German sociologist, who described the illusion in 1889]

mul·let[1] (mul′it), *n., pl.* (*esp. collectively*) **-let,** (*esp. referring to two or more kinds or species*) **-lets. 1.** any of several marine or freshwater, usually gray fishes of the family Mugilidae, having a nearly cylindrical body. **2.** a goatfish. **3.** a sucker, esp. of the genus *Moxostoma.* [1400–50; late ME *mulet* < MF < L *mullus* red mullet; see -ET]

mul·let[2] (mul′it), *n. Heraldry.* a starlike charge having five points unless a greater number is specified, used esp. as the cadency mark of a third son. Also, **molet.** Also called **American star, Scottish star.** [1350–1400; ME *molet* < OF *molete* rowel of a spur, equiv. to *mole* millstone (F *meule*) + *-ette* -ETTE]

mul·ley (mo͝ol′ē), *adj., n., pl.* **-leys.** muley.

mul·li·gan (mul′i gən), *n.* **1.** Also called **mul′ligan stew′.** a stew containing meat, vegetables, etc., esp. one made of any available ingredients. **2.** *Golf.* a shot not counted against the score, permitted in unofficial play to a player whose previous shot was poor. [1900–05; special use of proper name]

mul·li·ga·taw·ny (mul′i gə tô′nē), *n.* a curry-flavored soup of East Indian origin, made with chicken or meat stock. [1775–85; < Tamil *miḷakutaṇṇīr* lit., pepper water]

mul·li·grubs (mul′i grubz′), *n.* (*used with a singular or plural v.*) *Southern U.S.* ill temper; colic; grumpiness. [1590–1600; earlier *mulligrums,* appar. alter. of MEGRIMS]

Mul·li·ken (mul′i kən), *n.* **Robert San·der·son** (san′dər sən), 1896–1986, U.S. chemist and physicist: Nobel prize for chemistry 1966.

mul·lion (mul′yən), *Archit.* —*n.* **1.** a vertical member, as of stone or wood, between the lights of a window, the panels in wainscoting, or the like. **2.** one of the radiating bars of a rose window or the like. —*v.t.* **3.** to furnish with, or to form into divisions by the use of, mullions. [1560–70; metathetic var. of MONIAL]

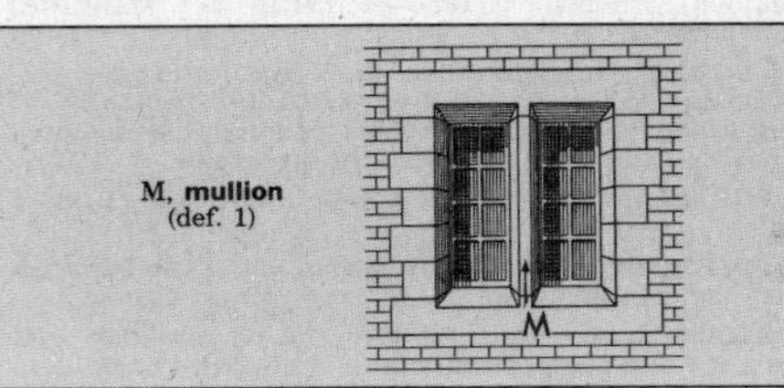

M, mullion (def. 1)

mull·ite (mul′īt), *n.* a rare clay mineral, aluminum silicate, $Al_6Si_2O_{13}$, produced artificially during various melting and firing processes: used as a refractory. Also called **porcelainite.** [1924; after MULL, source of the rocks in which it was first identified; see -ITE[1]]

mul·lock (mul′ək), *n.* **1.** (in Australasia) refuse or rubbish, as rock or earth, from a mine; muck. **2. poke mullock at,** *Australian.* to ridicule. [1350–1400; orig. dial. E; ME *mullok,* equiv. to *mul* dust, mold, rubbish (cf. OE *myl* dust; vowel perh. from ME *mullen;* see MULL[4]) + *-ok* -OCK] —**mul′lock·y,** *adj.*

mul·lo·way (mul′ə wā′), *n.* a large Australian saltwater fish, *Sciaena antarctica.* regarded as a culinary delicacy. [orig. uncert.]

Mul·ro·ney (mul rō′nē), *n.* **(Martin) Brian,** born 1939, Canadian political leader: prime minister 1984–93.

mult-, var. of **multi-** before a vowel: *multangular.*

Mul·tan (mo͝ol tän′), *n.* a city in E central Pakistan. 730,000.

mul·tan·gu·lar (mul tang′gyə lər), *adj.* having many angles; polyangular. Also, **mul·ti·an·gu·lar** (mul′tē ang′gyə lər, mul′tī-). [1670–80; < L *multangul(us)* many-cornered (see MULT-, ANGLE[1]) + -AR[1]]

mul·ti (mul′tē, -tī), *n., pl.* **-tis,** *adj. Informal.* —*n.* **1.** a pattern of several colors or hues, usually in stripes: *This dress comes in pink or green multi.* —*adj.* **2.** multicolored. [by shortening of MULTICOLOR or MULTICOLORED]

multi-, a combining form meaning "many," "much," "multiple," "many times," "more than one," "more than two," "composed of many like parts," "in many respects," used in the formation of compound words: *multiply; multivitamin.* Also, *esp. before a vowel,* **mult-.** [ME < L, comb. form of *multus* much, many]

—**Note.** The lists at the bottom of this and following pages provide the spelling, syllabification, and stress for words whose meanings may be easily inferred by combining the meaning of MULTI- and an attached base word, or base word plus a suffix. Appropriate parts of speech are also shown. Words prefixed by MULTI- that have special meanings or uses are entered in their proper alphabetical places in the main vocabulary or as derived forms run on at the end of a main vocabulary entry.

mul·ti·cel·lu·lar (mul′tē sel′yə lər, mul′tī-), *adj.* composed of several or many cells. [1855–60; MULTI- + CELLULAR]

mul·ti·coil (mul′ti koil′), *adj.* having more than one coil, as an electrical device. [MULTI- + COIL[1]]

mul·ti·col·or (mul′ti kul′ər), *adj.* **1.** of many colors; multicolored. **2.** (of a printing press) capable of printing more than two colors simultaneously or in a single operation. —*n.* **3.** an arrangement or design of many colors. [1840–50; back formation from MULTICOLORED]

mul′ti·a·re′o·late, *adj.*
mul′ti·ar·tic′u·lar, *adj.*
mul′ti·ar·tic′u·late, *adj.*
mul′ti·ar·tic′u·lat′ed, *adj.*
mul′ti·au′thored, *adj.*
mul′ti·ax′i·al, *adj.;* **-ly,** *adv.*
mul′ti·birth′, *n.*
mul′ti·blade′, *n.*
mul′ti·blad′ed, *adj.*
mul′ti·branched′, *adj.*
mul′ti·bran′chi·ate, *adj.*
mul′ti·busi′ness, *adj.*
mul′ti·cap′i·tate′, *adj.*
mul′ti·cap′su·lar, *adj.*
mul′ti·car′i·nate′, *adj.*
mul′ti·car′i·nat′ed, *adj.*
mul′ti·cast′ing, *n.*
mul′ti·cen′tral, *adj.;* **-ly,** *adv.*
mul′ti·cen′tric, *adj.*
mul′ti·chan′nel, *n., adj.*
mul′ti·chan′neled, *adj.*
mul′ti·chan′nelled, *adj.*
mul′ti·charge′, *n.*
mul′ti·chord′, *n.*
mul′ti·chrome′, *n.*
mul′ti·cil′i·ate, *adj.*
mul′ti·cil′i·at′ed, *adj.*
mul′ti·cir′cuit, *n.*
mul′ti·cir′cuit·ed, *adj.*
mul′ti·coat′ed, adj.
mul′ti·con·duc′tor, *adj.*
mul′ti·con′ic, *adj.*
mul′ti·cor′date, *adj., n.*
mul′ti·core′, *n.*
mul′ti·cor′ne·al, *adj.*
mul′ti·cor′po·ra′tion, *n.*
mul′ti·cos′tate, *adj.*
mul′ti·course′, *n.*
mul′ti·crys′tal·line, *adj.*
mul′ti·cul′ture, *n.*
mul′ti·cus′pid, *n.*
mul′ti·cus′pi·date′, *adj.*
mul′ti·cus′pi·dat′ed, *adj.*
mul′ti·den·tic′u·late, *adj.*
mul′ti·den·tic′u·lat′ed, *adj.*
mul′ti·des′ti·na′tion, *adj.*
mul′ti·dig′i·tate′, *adj.*
mul′ti·di·men′sion·al, *adj.*
mul′ti·dis′ci·pline, *n.*
mul′ti·dwell′ing, *n. adj.*
mul′ti·en′gine, *n.*
mul′ti·en′gined, *adj.*
mul′ti·ex·haust′, *n.*
mul′ti·faced′, *adj.*
mul′ti·faith′, *adj.*
mul′ti·fea′tured, *adj.*
mul′ti·fe·ta′tion, *n.*
mul′ti·fi′bered, *adj.*
mul′ti·fi′brous, *adj.*
mul′ti·fis′tu·lar, *adj.*
mul′ti·fis′tu·lous, *adj.*
mul′ti·flag′el·late, *adj.*
mul′ti·flag′el·lat′ed, *adj.*
mul′ti·func′tion, *adj.*
mul′ti·func′tion·al, *adj.*
mul′ti·fur′cate, *adj.*
mul′ti·gan′gli·on′ic, *adj.*

mul·ti·col·ored (mul′ti kul′ərd, mul′tī kul′ərd), *adj.* of several or many colors. [1835–45; MULTI- + COLORED]

mul·ti·cul·tur·al (mul′tē kul′chər əl, mul′tī-), *adj.* of, pertaining to, or representing several different cultures or cultural elements: *a multicultural society.* [1940–45; MULTI- + CULTURAL]

mul·ti·cul·tur·al·ism (mul′tē kul′chər ə liz′əm, mul′tī-), *n.* **1.** the state or condition of being multicultural. **2.** the preservation of different cultures or cultural identities within a unified society, as a state or nation. [1960–65; MULTICULTURAL + -ISM]

mul·ti·cyl·in·der (mul′tē sil′in dər, mul′tī-), *adj.* having more than one cylinder, as an internal-combustion or steam engine. Also, **mul′ti·cyl′in·dered.** [1900–05; MULTI- + CYLINDER]

mul·ti·den·tate (mul′tē den′tāt, mul′tī-), *adj.* having several or many teeth or toothlike processes. [1810–20; MULTI- + DENTATE]

mul·ti·di·rec·tion·al (mul′tē di rek′shə nl, -dī rek′-, mul′tī-), *adj.* extending or operating in several directions at the same time; functioning or going in more than one direction: *a multidirectional stereo speaker system.* [1940–45; MULTI- + DIRECTIONAL]

mul·ti·dis·ci·pli·nar·y (mul′tē dis′ə plə ner′ē, mul′tī-), *adj.* composed of or combining several usually separate branches of learning or fields of expertise: *a multidisciplinary study of the 18th century.* Also, **mul′ti·dis′ci·plined.** [1945–50; MULTI- + DISCIPLINARY]

mul·ti·eth·nic (mul′tē eth′nik, mul′tī-), *adj.* involving or pertaining to two or more distinct ethnic groups. [1965–70; MULTI- + ETHNIC]

mul·ti·fac·et·ed (mul′tē fas′i tid, mul′tī-), *adj.* **1.** having many facets, as a gem. **2.** having many aspects or phases: *a multifaceted problem.* [1865–70; MULTI- + FACETED]

mul·ti·fac·to·ri·al (mul′tē fak tôr′ē əl, -tōr′-, mul′tī-), *adj.* having or stemming from a number of different causes or influences: *Some medical researchers regard cancer as a multifactorial disease.* [1915–20; MULTI- + FACTOR + -IAL] —**mul′ti·fac·to′ri·al·ly,** *adv.*

multifacto′rial inher′itance, *Genetics.* See **polygenic inheritance.** [1955–60]

mul·ti·fam·i·ly (mul′tē fam′ə lē, -fam′lē, mul′tī-), *adj.* designed or suitable for the use of several or many families: *multifamily apartment buildings.* [MULTI- + FAMILY]

mul·ti·far·i·ous (mul′tə fâr′ē əs), *adj.* **1.** having many different parts, elements, forms, etc. **2.** numerous and varied; greatly diverse or manifold: *multifarious activities.* [1585–95; < LL *multifārius* many-sided, manifold, equiv. to L *multifāri(am)* on many sides + *-us* adj. suffix (see -OUS); see MULTI-, BIFARIOUS] —**mul′ti·far′i·ous·ly,** *adv.* —**mul′ti·far′i·ous·ness,** *n.*

mul·ti·fid (mul′tə fid), *adj.* cleft into many parts, divisions, or lobes. [1745–55; < L *multifidus* divided into many parts. See MULTI-, -FID] —**mul′ti·fid·ly,** *adv.*

mul·ti·fil·a·ment (mul′tə fil′ə mənt), *adj.* **1.** having two or more filaments: *multifilament yarn.* —*n.* **2.** Also, **mul·ti·fil** (mul′tə fil). yarn constructed of a number of filaments in excess of the standard quantity. Cf. **monofilament** (def. 1). [1935–40; MULTI- + FILAMENT]

mul·ti·flo·ra (mul′tə flôr′ə, -flōr′ə), *n.* any of several plant varieties or hybrids characterized by many single, relatively small flowers, as certain kinds of petunias or roses. [1820–30; < NL, a typical specific epithet of flowering plants; see MULTIFLORA ROSE]

mul′tiflo′ra rose′, a climbing or trailing rose, *Rosa multiflora,* of Japan and Korea, having hooked prickles and fragrant, dense clusters of flowers. [1820–30; *multiflora* < NL, fem. of ML *multiflōrus* MULTIFLOROUS]

mul·ti·flo·rous (mul′tə flôr′əs, -flōr′-), *adj. Bot.* bearing many flowers, as a peduncle. [1750–60; < ML *multiflōrus.* See MULTI-, -FLOROUS]

mul·ti·fo·cal (mul′tē fō′kəl, mul′tī-), *adj.* **1.** having several focuses. **2.** (of an eyeglass lens) having several focusing areas that correct for both nearsightedness and farsightedness. [1915–20; MULTI- + FOCAL]

mul·ti·foil (mul′tə foil′), *Archit.* —*n.* **1.** a foil, esp. one having more than five lobes. —*adj.* **2.** (of an arch, window opening, etc.) having the form of a foil with more than five lobes. [1825–35; MULTI- + FOIL[2]]

mul·ti·fold (mul′tə fōld′), *adj.* numerous and varied; greatly diverse; manifold. [1800–10; MULTI- + -FOLD]

mul·ti·fo·li·ate (mul′tə fō′lē it, -āt′), *adj. Bot.* having many leaves or leaflets. [1855–60; MULTI- + FOLIATE]

mul·ti·form (mul′tə fôrm′), *adj.* having many different shapes, forms, or kinds. [1595–1605; < L *multiformis.* See MULTI-, -FORM] —**mul·ti·for·mi·ty** (mul′tə fôr′mi tē), *n.*

mul·ti·gen·er·a·tion·al (mul′tē jen′ə rā′shə nl, mul′tī-), *adj.* of or pertaining to several generations, as of a family, or society: *a multigenerational novel covering 300 years.* [MULTI- + GENERATION + -AL[1]]

Mul·ti·graph (mul′ti graf′, -gräf′), **1.** *Trademark.* a brand name for a rotary typesetting and printing machine, commonly used in making many copies of written matter. —*v.t., v.i.* **2.** (*l.c.*) to print with such a machine.

mul·ti·grav·i·da (mul′ti grav′i də), *n., pl.* **-das, -dae** (-dē′). *Obstet.* a pregnant woman who has been pregnant two or more times. [1885–90; MULTI- + GRAVIDA] —**mul·ti·gra·vid·i·ty** (mul′ti grə vid′i tē), *n.*

mul·ti·hull (mul′tē hul′, mul′tī-), *adj.* **1.** (of a vessel) having more than one hull joined by a single deck. —*n.* **2.** a multihull vessel, as distinguished from a monohull vessel. [1955–60; MULTI- + HULL[2]]

mul·ti·lat·er·al (mul′ti lat′ər əl), *adj.* **1.** having several or many sides; many-sided. **2.** participated in by more than two nations, parties, etc.; multipartite: *multilateral agreements on disarmament.* [1690–1700; MULTI- + LATERAL] —**mul′ti·lat′er·al·ism,** *n.* —**mul′ti·lat′er·al·ist,** *adj., n.* —**mul′ti·lat′er·al·ly,** *adv.*

mul·ti·lat·er·al·ize (mul′ti lat′ər ə līz′), *v.t.,* **-ized, -iz·ing.** to open to participation by several nations, organizations, etc.: *to multilateralize trade agreements.* Also, *esp. Brit.,* **mul′ti·lat′er·al·ise′.** [1945–50; MULTILATERAL + -IZE] —**mul′ti·lat′er·al·i·za′tion,** *n.*

mul·ti·lay·er (*adj.* mul′tē lā′ər, mul′tī-; *n.* mul′ti lā′ər), *adj.* **1.** multilayered. —*n.* **2.** *Physical Chem.* a film consisting of two or more monolayers of different substances. [1920–25; MULTI- + LAYER]

mul·ti·lay·ered (mul′tē lā′ərd, mul′tī-, mul′tē lā′ərd, mul′tī-), *adj.* **1.** having two or more layers. **2.** offering several viewpoints, solutions, degrees of complexity, etc.: *the multilayered problem of urban development.* Also, **multilayer.** [1930–35; MULTI- + LAYER + -ED[3]]

mul·ti·lev·el (mul′ti lev′əl), *adj.* having different levels or planes: *a multilevel stage set.* Also, **mul′ti·lev′·eled.** [1950–55; MULTI- + LEVEL]

mul′ti·lin′e·ar form′ (mul′ti lin′ē ər, mul′tī-), *Math.* a function or functional of several variables such that when all variables but one are held fixed, the function is linear in the remaining variable. [MULTI- + LINEAR]

mul′ti·line insur′er (mul′ti līn′), an insurance company that is engaged in more than two fields of insurance. [MULTI- + LINE[1]]

mul·ti·lin·gual (mul′tē ling′gwəl, mul′tī- *or, Can.,* -ling′gyo͞o əl), *adj.* **1.** using or able to speak several or many languages with some facility. **2.** spoken or written in several or many languages: *a multilingual broadcast.* **3.** dealing with or involving several or many languages: *a multilingual dictionary of business terms.* —*n.* **4.** a multilingual person. [1830–40; MULTI- + LINGUAL] —**mul′ti·lin′gual·ly,** *adv.* —**mul′ti·lin′gual·ism,** *n.*

Mul·ti·lith (mul′ti lith), **1.** *Trademark.* a brand name for a small photo-offset printing machine. —*v.t., v.i.* **2.** (*l.c.*) to print with such a machine.

mul·ti·lob·u·lar (mul′ti lob′yə lər), *adj.* having several or many lobules. [1870–75; MULTI- + LOBULAR]

mul·ti·lo·ca·tion (mul′tē lō kā′shən, mul′tī-), *n.* the state or power of being in more than two places at the same time. Cf. **bilocation.** [MULTI- + LOCATION]

mul·ti·loc·u·lar (mul′ti lok′yə lər), *adj.* having or consisting of many cells or vesicles. [1805–15; MULTI- + LOCULAR]

mul·ti·me·di·a (mul′tē mē′dē ə, mul′tī-), *n.* (*used with a singular v.*) **1.** the combined use of several media, as sound and full-motion video in computer applications. —*adj.* **2.** of, pertaining to, or involving multimedia. **3.** having or offering the use of various communications or promotional media: *a multimedia corporation that owns TV stations and newspapers.* [1960–65; MULTI- + MEDIA[1]] —**mul′ti·me′di·al,** *adj.*

mul·tim·e·ter (mul tim′i tər), *n. Elect.* a device consisting of one or more meters, as an ammeter and voltmeter, used to measure two or more electrical quantities in an electric circuit, as voltage, resistance, and current. Also called **circuit analyzer.** [1905–10; MULTI- + -METER]

mul·ti·mil·lion·aire (mul′tē mil′yə nâr′, mul′tī-), *n.* a person who possesses a fortune that amounts to many millions of dollars, francs, etc. [1855–60, *Amer.*; MULTI- + MILLIONAIRE]

mul·ti·mod·al (mul′tē mōd′l, mul′tī-), *adj.* **1.** having more than one mode. **2.** *Statistics.* having more than one modal value: *a multimodal distribution.* **3.** *Transp.* intermodal. [1900–05; MULTI- + MODAL]

mul·ti·na·tion·al (mul′tē nash′ə nl, mul′tī-), *n.* **1.** a large corporation with operations and subsidiaries in several countries. —*adj.* **2.** of, pertaining to, or involving several nations. **3.** noting or pertaining to multinationals. [1925–30; MULTI- + NATIONAL] —**mul′ti·na′·tion·al·ism,** *n.* —**mul′ti·na′tion·al·ly,** *adv.*

mul·ti·no·mi·al (mul′ti nō′mē əl), *n. Algebra. Now Rare.* polynomial (def. 3c). [1600–10; MULTI- + *-nomial,* on the model of POLYNOMIAL, BINOMIAL]

mul·ti·nom·i·nal (mul′ti nom′ə nl), *adj.* having several or many names. [1650–60; MULTI- + NOMINAL]

mul·ti·pack (mul′ti pak′), *n.* a packaged item containing two or more products sold as a unit. [MULTI- + PACK[1]]

mul·tip·a·ra (mul tip′ər ə), *n., pl.* **-a·ras, -a·rae** (-ə rē′). *Obstet.* a woman who has borne two or more children, or who is parturient for the second time. [1870–75; n. use of fem. of NL *multiparus* MULTIPAROUS]

mul·tip·a·rous (mul tip′ər əs), *adj.* **1.** of or pertaining to a multipara. **2.** producing more than one at a birth. **3.** *Bot.* (of a cyme) having many lateral axes. [1640–50; < NL *multiparus* bearing many young at a birth. See MULTI-, -PAROUS] —**mul·ti·par·i·ty** (mul′ti par′i tē), *n.*

mul·ti·par·tite (mul′ti pär′tīt), *adj.* **1.** divided into several or many parts; having several or many divisions. **2.** multilateral (def. 2). [1715–25; < L *multipartītus* divided into many parts. See MULTI-, PARTITE]

mul·ti·par·ty (mul′tē pär′tē, mul′tī-), *adj.* of or pertaining to more than two political parties. [1905–10; MULTI- + PARTY]

mul·ti·ped (mul′ti ped′), *adj.* having many feet. Also, **mul·ti·pede** (mul′ti pēd′). [1595–1605; < L *multiped-* (s. of *multipēs*) many-footed. See MULTI-, -PED]

mul·ti·phase (mul′ti fāz′), *adj.* having many phases, stages, aspects, or the like. Also, **mul′ti·pha′sic.** [1885–90; MULTI- + PHASE]

mul·ti·ple (mul′tə pəl), *adj.* **1.** consisting of, having, or involving several or many individuals, parts, elements, relations, etc.; manifold. **2.** *Elect.* **a.** (of circuits) arranged in parallel. **b.** (of a circuit or circuits) having a number of points at which connection can be made. **3.** *Bot.* (of a fruit) collective. —*n.* **4.** *Math.* a number that contains another number an integral number of times without a remainder: *12 is a multiple of 3.* **5.** *Elect.* a group of terminals arranged to make a circuit or group of circuits accessible at a number of points at any one of which connection can be made. [1570–80; < F < LL *multiplus* manifold. See MULTI-, DUPLE]

mul′tiple alleles′, *Genetics.* a series of three or more alternative or allelic forms of a gene, only two of which can exist in any normal, diploid individual. [1935–40] —**mul′tiple allel′ism.**

mul·ti·ple-choice (mul′tə pəl chois′), *adj.* **1.** consisting of several possible answers from which the correct one must be selected: *a multiple-choice question.* **2.** made up of multiple-choice questions: *a multiple-choice exam.* [1925–30]

mul′tiple crop′ping, *Agric.* the use of the same field for two or more crops, whether of the same or of different kinds, successively during a single year.

mul′tiple drill′, a drilling machine having a number of vertical spindles for drilling several holes in a piece simultaneously. Cf. **gang drill.**

mul′tiple fac′tors, *Genetics.* a series of two or more pairs of genes responsible for the development of complex, quantitative characters, as size or yield. [1910–15]

mul′tiple fis′sion, *Biol.* fission into more than two new organisms. Cf. **binary fission.** [1910–15]

mul′tiple in′depend′ently tar′getable reen′try ve′hicle, *Mil.* a reentry vehicle that breaks up into several nuclear warheads, each capable of reaching a different target. *Abbr.:* MIRV, M.I.R.V.

mul′tiple in′tegral, *Math.* an integral in which the integrand involves a function of more than one variable and which requires for evaluation repetition of the integration process. [1835–45]

mul′tiple list′ing, the listing of a home for sale with a number of real-estate brokers who participate in a shared listing service.

Mul′tiple Mir′ror Tel′escope, *Astron.* a reflecting telescope on Mount Hopkins, in Arizona, that features six computer-linked mirrors set on a single mount. *Abbr.:* MMT

mul′tiple myelo′ma, *Pathol.* a malignant plasma cell tumor of the bone marrow that destroys bone tissue. [1895–1900; MYEL- + -OMA]

mul′tiple neuri′tis, *Pathol.* polyneuritis.

mul′tiple personal′ity, *Psychiatry.* a rare disorder in which an individual displays several functionally dissociated personalities, each of a complexity comparable to that of a normal individual. Also called **split personality.** [1900–05]

mul′tiple reen′try ve′hicle, *Mil.* a reentry vehicle equipped with multiple warheads that cannot be directed to separate targets. *Abbr.:* MRV, M.R.V.

mul′tiple sclero′sis, *Pathol.* a chronic degenerative, often episodic disease of the central nervous system marked by patchy destruction of the myelin that surrounds and insulates nerve fibers, usually appearing in young adulthood and manifested by one or more mild to severe neural and muscular impairments, as spastic

CONCISE PRONUNCIATION KEY: act, cāpe, dâre, pärt; set, ēqual; *if,* īce; ox, ōver, ôrder, oil, bo͝ok, bo͞ot, out; up, ûrge; child; sing; shoe; thin, *th*at; zh as in *treasure.* ə = a as in *alone,* e as in *system,* i as in *easily,* o as in *gallop,* u as in *circus;* ᵊ as in *fire* (fīᵊr), *hour* (ouᵊr). l and n can serve as syllabic consonants, as in *cradle* (krād′l), and *button* (but′n). See the full key inside the front cover.

mul′ti·gauge′, *adj.*
mul′ti·glazed′, *adj.*
mul′ti·grade′, *adj.*
mul′ti·grain′, *n., adj.*
mul′ti·gran′u·lar, *adj.*
mul′ti·gran′u·lat′ed, *adj.*
mul′ti·gy′rate, *adj.*
mul′ti·hand′i·capped′, *adj.*
mul′ti·head′, *n.*
mul′ti·hearth′, *n.*
mul′ti·hos′pi·tal, *adj.*
mul′ti·hued′, *adj.*
mul′ti·jet′, *n.*
mul′ti·ju′gate, *adj.*
mul′ti·la·cin′i·ate′, *adj.*
mul′ti·la·mel′lar, *adj.*
mul′ti·lam′el·late′, *adj.*
mul′ti·lam′i·nar, *adj.*
mul′ti·lam′i·nate′, *adj.*
mul′ti·lam′i·nat′ed, *adj.*
mul′ti·lane′, *n., adj.*
mul′ti·light′ed, *adj.*
mul′ti·lin′e·al, *adj.*
mul′ti·lo′bar, *adj.*
mul′ti·lo′bate, *adj.*
mul′ti·lobe′, *n.*
mul′ti·lobed′, *adj.*
mul′ti·mac′u·lar, *adj.*
mul′ti·mar′ket, *adj.*
mul′ti·meg′a·ton′, *n.*
mul′ti·me·tal′lic, *adj.*
mul′ti·mil′lion, *n.*
mul′ti·mo·dal′i·ty, *n.*
mul′ti·mode′, *adj.*
mul′ti·mo·lec′u·lar, *adj.*
mul′ti·mo′tor, *n.*
mul′ti·mo′tored, *adj.*
mul′ti·nerv′ate, *adj.*
mul′ti·nod′al, *adj.*
mul′ti·no′dous, *adj.*
mul′ti·nod′u·lar, *adj.*
mul′ti·nu′cle·ar, *adj.*
mul′ti·nu′cle·ate, *adj.*
mul′ti·nu·cle′o·lar, *adj.*
mul′ti·nu′cle·o·late′, *adj.*
mul′ti·nu′cle·o·lat′ed, *adj.*
mul′ti·or′gan, *adj.*
mul′ti·ov′u·lar, *adj.*
mul′ti·ov′u·late′, *adj.*
mul′ti·ov′u·lat′ed, *adj.*
mul′ti·part′, *adj.*
mul′ti·par′ti·san, *n.*
mul′ti·path′, *n.*
mul′ti·per′fo·rate, *adj.*
mul′ti·per′fo·rat′ed, *adj.*
mul′ti·per′il, *adj., n.*
mul′ti·per′son, *adj.*
mul′ti·per′son·al, *adj.*
mul′ti·pho·tog′ra·phy, *n.*
mul′ti·piece′, *adj.*
mul′ti·pin′nate, *adj.*
mul′ti·plat′ed, *adj.*
mul′ti·point′, *adj.*
mul′ti·point′ed, *adj.*
mul′ti·port′ed, *adj.*
mul′ti·po·si′tion·a·ble, *adj.*

weakness in one or more limbs, local sensory losses, bladder dysfunction, or visual disturbances. [1880–85]

mul′tiple shop′, *Brit.* See **chain store.** Also called **mul′tiple store′.** [1905–10]

mul′tiple star′, *Astron.* three or more stars lying close together in the celestial sphere and usually united in a single gravitational system. [1840–50]

mul·ti·plet (mul′tə plet′, -plit), *n. Physics.* a group of several related spectral lines, usually of nearly the same wavelengths. Also called **mul′tiplet line′.** [1920–25; MULTI- + (TRI)PLET]

mul′tiple-u′nit car′ (mul′tə pəl yo͞o′nit), a self-propelled railroad car, generally used in commuting service, equipped so that a train of such cars can be operated from any one of them. Also called **MU car.**

mul·ti·ple-val·ued (mul′tə pəl val′yo͞od), *adj. Math.* many-valued. [1880–85]

mul′tiple-val′ued func′tion, *Math.* function (def. 4b).

mul′tiple vot′ing, the casting of ballots in more than one constituency in one election, as in England before the election reform of 1918. [1900–05]

mul·ti·plex (mul′tə pleks′), *adj.* **1.** having many parts or aspects: *the multiplex problem of drug abuse.* **2.** manifold; multiple: *the multiplex opportunities in high technology.* **3.** *Telecommunications.* of, pertaining to, or using equipment permitting the simultaneous transmission of two or more trains of signals or messages over a single channel. —*v.t.* **4.** *Telecommunications.* **a.** to arrange (a circuit) for use by multiplex telegraphy. **b.** to transmit (two or more signals or messages) by a multiplex system, circuit, or the like. —*v.i.* **5.** to send several messages or signals simultaneously, as by multiplex telegraphy. —*n.* **6.** a multiplex electronics system. **7.** (in map making) a stereoscopic device that makes it possible to view pairs of aerial photographs in three dimensions. **8.** Also called **mul′tiplex cin′ema, mul′tiplex the′ater.** a group of two or more motion-picture theaters on the same site or in the same building, esp. a cluster of adjoining theaters. [1550–60; < L; see MULTI-, -PLEX] —**mul′ti·plex′er, mul′ti·plex′or,** *n.*

mul·ti·pli·a·ble (mul′tə plī′ə bəl), *adj.* capable of being multiplied. Also, **mul·ti·plic·a·ble** (mul′tə plik′ə-bəl). [1615–25; MULTIPLY + -ABLE]

mul·ti·pli·cand (mul′tə pli kand′), *n. Arith.* a number to be multiplied by another. [1585–95; < L *multiplicandum,* n. use of neut. of *multiplicandus* to be multiplied, gerundive of *multiplicāre* to MULTIPLY]

mul·ti·pli·cate (mul′tə pli kāt′), *adj.* multiple; manifold. [1375–1425; late ME < L *multiplicātus,* ptp. of *multiplicāre* to MULTIPLY, increase. See MULTI-, PLICATE]

mul·ti·pli·ca·tion (mul′tə pli kā′shən), *n.* **1.** the act or process of multiplying or the state of being multiplied. **2.** *Arith.* a mathematical operation, symbolized by $a \times b$, $a \cdot b$, $a * b$, or ab, and signifying, when a and b are positive integers, that a is to be added to itself as many times as there are units in b; the addition of a number to itself as often as is indicated by another number, as in 2×3 or 5×10. **3.** *Math.* any generalization of this operation applicable to numbers other than integers, as fractions or irrational numbers. [1350–1400; ME *multiplicacio(u)n* < L *multiplicātiōn-* (s. of *multiplicātiō*). See MULTI-, PLICATION] —**mul′ti·pli·ca′tion·al,** *adj.*

multiplica′tion sign′, *Arith.* the symbol (·), (×), or (*) between two mathematical expressions, denoting multiplication of the second expression by the first. In certain algebraic notations the sign is suppressed and multiplication is indicated by immediate juxtaposition or contiguity, as in *ab.* Also called **times sign.** [1905–10]

multiplica′tion ta′ble, *Arith.* a tabular listing of the products of any two numbers of a set, usually of the integers 1 through 10 or 1 through 12. [1665–75]

mul·ti·pli·ca·tive (mul′tə pli kā′tiv, mul′tə plik′ə-), *adj.* **1.** tending to multiply or increase. **2.** having the power of multiplying. [1645–55; < ML *multiplicātīvus.* See MULTIPLICATE, -IVE] —**mul′ti·pli·ca′tive·ly,** *adv.*

mul′tiplicative ax′iom, *Math. Chiefly Brit.* See **axiom of choice.**

mul′tiplicative group′, *Math.* a group in which the operation of the group is multiplication.

mul′tiplicative iden′tity, *Math.* an identity that when used to multiply a given element in a specified set leaves that element unchanged, as the number 1 for the real-number system. [1955–60]

mul′tiplicative in′verse, *Math.* reciprocal (def. 9).

mul·ti·plic·i·ty (mul′tə plis′i tē), *n., pl.* **-ties.** **1.** a large number or variety: *a multiplicity of errors.* **2.** the state of being multiplex or manifold; manifold variety. [1580–90; < LL *multiplicitās,* equiv. to *multiplic-* (s. of *multiplex*) MULTIPLEX + *-itās* -ITY]

CONCISE ETYMOLOGY KEY: <, descended or borrowed from; >, whence; b., blend of, blended; c., cognate with; cf., compare; deriv., derivative; equiv., equivalent; imit., imitative; obl., oblique; r., replacing; s., stem; sp., spelling, spelled; resp., respelling, respelled; trans., translation; ?, origin unknown; *, unattested; ‡, probably earlier than. See the full key inside the front cover.

mul·ti·pli·er (mul′tə plī′ər), *n.* **1.** a person or thing that multiplies. **2.** *Arith.* a number by which another is multiplied. **3.** *Physics.* a device for intensifying some effect. [1425–75; late ME; see MULTIPLY, -ER[1]]

mul·ti·ply (mul′tē plī′, mul′tī-), *adj.* having or composed of several plies: *a multi-ply fabric.* [1935–40]

mul·ti·ply[1] (mul′tə plī′), *v.,* **-plied, -ply·ing.** —*v.t.* **1.** to make many or manifold; increase the number, quantity, etc., of. **2.** *Arith.* to find the product of by multiplication. **3.** to breed (animals). **4.** to propagate (plants). **5.** to increase by procreation. —*v.i.* **6.** to grow in number, quantity, etc.; increase. **7.** *Arith.* to perform the process of multiplication. **8.** to increase in number by procreation or natural generation. [1225–75; ME *multiplien* < OF *multiplier* < L *multiplicāre.* See MULTI-, PLY[2]] —**Syn. 6.** magnify, enlarge, intensify.

mul·ti·ply[2] (mul′tə plē), *adv.* in several or many ways; in a multiple manner; manifoldly. [1880–85; MULTIPLE + -LY]

mul·ti·ply-con·nect·ed (mul′tə plē kə nek′tid), *adj. Math.* connected but not simply-connected. [1880–85]

mul·ti·po·lar (mul′tē pō′lər, mul′tī-), *adj.* **1.** having several or many poles. **2.** (of nerve cells) having more than two dendrites. [1855–60; MULTI- + POLAR] —**mul·ti·po·lar·i·ty** (mul′tē pō lar′i tē, -pə-, mul′tī-), *n.*

mul·tip·o·tent (mul tip′ə tənt), *adj.* having power to produce or influence several effects or results. Also, **mul·ti·po·ten·tial** (mul′ti pə ten′shəl). [MULTI- + POTENT[1]]

mul·ti·proc·ess·ing (mul′tē pros′es ing, -ə sing *or, esp. Brit.,* -prō′ses ing, -sə sing), *n. Computers.* the simultaneous execution of two or more programs or instruction sequences by separate CPUs under integrated control. [1930–35; MULTI- + PROCESS + -ING[1]] —**mul′·ti·proc′es·sor,** *n.*

mul·ti·pro·gram·ming (mul′tē prō′gram ing, -grə-ming, mul′tī-), *n. Computers.* the overlapped or interleaved execution of two or more programs by a single CPU. [1955–60; MULTI- + PROGRAM + -ING[1]]

mul·ti·pronged (mul′ti prôngd′, -prongd′), *adj.* **1.** having or composed of several prongs: *a multipronged electric plug.* **2.** of, pertaining to, or made by several separate forces or elements or from several directions or points of view: *a multipronged assault on the enemy.* [1955–60; MULTI- + PRONG + -ED[3]]

mul·ti·pur·pose (mul′tē pûr′pəs, mul′tī-), *adj.* able to be used for several purposes: *a multipurpose lawn spray.* [1930–35; MULTI- + PURPOSE]

mul·ti·ra·cial (mul′tē rā′shəl, mul′tī-), *adj.* of, pertaining to, or representing more than one race. [1920–25; MULTI- + RACIAL] —**mul′ti·ra′cial·ism,** *n.* —**mul′·ti·ra′cial·ly,** *adv.*

mul′ti-scene control′ board′ (mul′tē sēn′, mul′-tī-). See **preset board.**

mul·ti·spec·tral (mul′tē spek′trəl, mul′tī-), *adj.* (of an airborne camera or scanner) capable of sensing and recording radiation from invisible as well as visible parts of the electromagnetic spectrum. [1965–70; MULTI- + SPECTRAL]

mul·ti·stage (mul′ti stāj′), *adj.* (of a rocket or guided missile) having more than one stage. [1900–05; MULTI- + STAGE]

mul·ti·state (mul′ti stāt′), *adj.* of or operating in several states of a nation: *a multistate corporation.* [1940–45; MULTI- + STATE]

mul′ti·step hy′droplane (mul′ti step′), *Naut.* a motorship having a flat bottom built as a series of planes inclined forward, the ship planing on each from stem to stern as its speed increases. [MULTI- + STEP]

mul·ti·sto·ry (mul′ti stôr′ē, -stōr′ē), *adj.* (of a building) having several or many stories. Also, **mul′ti·sto′·ried.** [1915–20; MULTI- + STORY[2]]

mul·ti·syl·lab·ic (mul′ti si lab′ik), *adj.* polysyllabic. [1650–60; MULTI- + SYLLABIC]

mul·ti·syl·la·ble (mul′ti sil′ə bəl), *n.* polysyllable. [1960–65; MULTI- + SYLLABLE]

mul·ti·task·ing (mul′tē tas′king, -tä′sking, mul′tī-), *n. Computers.* the concurrent or interleaved execution of two or more jobs by a single CPU. Also, **mul′ti-task′·ing.** [MULTI- + TASKING]

mul·ti·track·ing (mul′tē trak′ing, mul′tī-), *n.* the process of recording separate audio tracks for later mixing into a single audio track. [MULTI- + TRACK + -ING[1]]

mul·ti·tu·ber·cu·late (mul′tē to͞o bûr′kyə lit, -lāt′, -tyo͞o-, mul′tī-), *n.* **1.** a rodentlike mammal of the extinct order Multituberculata, which lived from the late Jurassic Period to the Oligocene Epoch, reaching the size of a woodchuck and having molars with two or three rows of simple pointed cusps. —*adj.* **2.** of or pertaining to the multituberculates. **3.** having teeth with many simple, pointed cusps. [< NL *Multituberculata* (1884); see MULTI-, TUBERCULATE, -ATA[1]]

mul·ti·tude (mul′ti to͞od′, -tyo͞od′), *n.* **1.** a great number; host: *a multitude of friends.* **2.** a great number of people gathered together; crowd; throng. **3.** the state or character of being many; numerousness. **4. the multitude,** the common people; the masses. [1275–1325; ME < L *multitūdō.* See MULTI-, -TUDE] —**Syn. 2.** mass. Se **crowd.**

mul·ti·tu·di·nous (mul′ti to͞od′n əs, -tyo͞od′-), *adj.* **1** forming a multitude or great number; existing, occur ring, or present in great numbers; very numerous. **2** comprising many items, parts, or elements. **3.** *Archaic* crowded or thronged. [1595–1605; < L *multitūdin-* (s. o *multitūdō*) MULTITUDE + -OUS] —**mul′ti·tu′di·nous·ly,** *adv.* —**mul′ti·tu′di·nous·ness,** *n.*

mul·ti·us′er sys′tem (mul′tē yo͞o′zər, mul′tī-), a computer system in which multiple terminals connect to a host computer that handles processing tasks.

mul·ti·va·lent (mul′ti vā′lənt, mul tiv′ə lənt), *adj.* **1.** *Chem.* having a valence of three or higher. **2.** *Immunol.* **a.** containing several kinds of antibody. **b.** pertaining to an antibody that contains many antigen-binding sites. **c.** pertaining to an antibody that has many determinants [1870–75; MULTI- + -VALENT] —**mul′ti·va′lence,** *n.*

mul·ti·val·ued (mul′ti val′yo͞od), *adj.* possessing several or many values. [1930–35; MULTI- + VALUED]

mul·ti·valve (mul′ti valv′), *adj.* **1.** (of a shell) composed of more than two valves or pieces. —*n.* **2.** a multivalve mollusk or its shell. [1745–55; MULTI- + VALVE]

mul·ti·var·i·ate (mul′ti vâr′ē it), *adj. Statistics.* (of a combined distribution) having more than one variate or variable. [1925–30; MULTI- + VARIATE]

mul·ti·ver·si·ty (mul′ti vûr′si tē), *n., pl.* **-ties.** a university with several campuses, each of which has many schools, divisions, etc. [1960–65; MULTI- + (UNI)VERSITY]

mul·ti·vi·ta·min (mul′ti vī′tə min), *adj.* **1.** containing or consisting of several vitamins: *multivitamin capsules.* —*n.* **2.** a compound of several vitamins. [1940–45; MULTI- + VITAMIN]

mul·tiv·o·cal (mul tiv′ə kəl), *adj.* having many or different meanings of equal probability or validity: *a multivocal word.* [1800–10; MULTI- + VOCAL]

mul·ti·vol·tine (mul′ti vōl′tēn, -tn), *adj. Entomol.* producing several broods in one year, as certain silkworm moths; polyvoltine. [1870–75; MULTI- + It *volt(a)* turn, time + -INE[1]]

mul·ti·vol·ume (mul′tē vol′yo͞om, mul′tī-), *adj.* consisting of or encompassing several volumes: *a multivolume encyclopedia.* Also, **mul′ti·vol′umed.** [1935–40; MULTI- + VOLUME]

mul·ti·wall (mul′ti wôl′), *adj.* **1.** having a wall or casing composed of layers of material, often pressed closely together: *multiwall bags for shipping grain.* —*n.* **2.** a multiwall bag or sack. [1935–40; MULTI- + WALL]

mul·tum in par·vo (mo͝ol′to͝om in pär′wō; *Eng.* mul′təm in pär′vō), *Latin.* much in little; a great deal in a small space or in brief.

mul·ture (mul′chər), *n. Scots Law.* a toll or fee given to the proprietor of a mill for the grinding of grain, usually consisting of a fixed proportion of the grain brought or of the flour made. [1250–1300; ME *multir* < OF *molture* < ML *molitūra* a grinding, equiv. to L *molit(us)* (ptp. of *molere*) to grind + *-ūra* -URE]

mum[1] (mum), *adj.* **1.** silent; not saying a word: *to keep mum.* —*interj.* **2.** say nothing! be silent! **3. mum's the word,** do not reveal what you know (about something); keep silent: *Mum's the word, or the surprise party won't be a surprise.* [1350–1400; ME *momme;* imit.]

mum[2] (mum), *v.i.,* **mummed, mum·ming.** **1.** to say "mum"; call for silence. **2.** to act as a mummer. Also, **mumm.** [1350–1400; ME *mommen,* v. use of MUM[1]; cf. MD *mommen* to act the mummer's part]

mum[3] (mum), *n.* chrysanthemum. [shortened form]

mum[4] (mum), *n. Chiefly Brit.* mother. [1815–25; nursery word; see MOM]

mum[5] (mum), *n.* a strong beer or ale, first made in Brunswick, Germany. [1630–40; < G *Mumme,* said to have been named after the brewer who made it]

mum[6] (mum), *n. Chiefly Brit.* madam. [var. of MA'AM]

mum·ble (mum′bəl), *v.,* **-bled, -bling,** *n.* —*v.i.* **1.** to speak in a low indistinct manner, almost to an unintelligible extent; mutter. **2.** to chew ineffectively, as from loss of teeth: *to mumble on a crust.* —*v.t.* **3.** to say or utter indistinctly, as with partly closed lips: *He mumbled something about expenses.* **4.** to chew, or try to eat, with difficulty, as from loss of teeth. —*n.* **5.** a low, indistinct utterance or sound. [1275–1325; ME *momelen,* equiv. to *mom(me)* MUM[1] + *-elen* -LE; cf. D *mommelen,* G *mummeln*] —**mum′bler,** *n.* —**mum′bling·ly,** *adv.*
—**Syn. 1, 3.** See **murmur.** —**Ant. 1.** articulate.

mum·ble·ty·peg (mum′bəl tē peg′), *n.* a children's game played with a pocketknife, the object being to cause the blade to stick in the ground or a wooden surface by flipping the knife in a number of prescribed ways or from a number of prescribed positions. Also, **mum·ble·de·peg, mum·ble·dy·peg** (mum′bəl dē peg′), **mum′ble peg′, mum·ble-the-peg** (mum′bəl *th*ə peg′), **mum′ble·ty-peg′, mum·bly·peg** (mum′blē peg′). [1620–30; from phrase *mumble the peg* (see MUMBLE); so named because the losing player was formerly required to pull a peg from the ground with his or her teeth]

mum·bo jum·bo (mum′bō jum′bō), *pl.* **mum·bo jum·**

mul′ti·prod′uct, *adj.*
mul′ti·pro·pel′lant, *n.*
mul′ti·ra′di·al, *adj.*
mul′ti·ra′di·ate, *adj.*
mul′ti·ra′di·at′ed, *adj.*
mul′ti·rad′i·cal, *adj.*
mul′ti·ram′i·fied′, *adj.*
mul′ti·ra′mose, *adj.*
mul′ti·ra′mous, *adj.*
mul′ti·rec′re·a′tion·al, *adj.*
mul′ti·re′flex, *n.*
mul′ti·role′, *adj.*
mul′ti·root′ed, *adj.*
mul′ti·sac′cate, *adj.*
mul′ti·sac′cu·late′, *adj.*
mul′ti·sac′cu·lat′ed, *adj.*
mul′ti·sea′son·al, *adj.*
mul′ti·sec′tion, *adj.*
mul′ti·sec′tion·al, *adj.*
mul′ti·seg′ment, *adj.*
mul′ti·seg·men′tal, *adj.*
mul′ti·seg′ment·ed, *adj.*
mul′ti·sen′so·ry, *adj.*
mul′ti·sep′tate, *adj.*
mul′ti·se′ri·ate, *adj.*
mul′ti·se′ries, *n. pl.* **-ries.**
mul′ti·serv′ice, *adj.*
mul′ti·shot′, *n.*
mul′ti·skilled′, *adj.*
mul′ti·son′ic, *adj.*
mul′ti·so·no′rous, *adj.;* **-ly,** *adv.;* **-ness,** *n.*
mul′ti·so′nous, *adj.*
mul′ti·speed′, *adj.*
mul′ti·sper′mous, *adj.*
mul′ti·spic′u·lar, *adj.*
mul′ti·spic′u·late, *adj.*
mul′ti·spin′dled, *adj.*
mul′ti·spi′nous, *adj.*
mul′ti·spi′ral, *adj.*
mul′ti·spired′, *adj.*
mul′ti·stam′i·nate, *adj.*
mul′ti·stem′, *adj.*
mul′ti·stop′, *adj.*
mul′ti·strat′i·fied′, *adj.*
mul′ti·stri′ate, *adj.*
mul′ti·sul′cate, *adj.*
mul′ti·sul′cat·ed, *adj.*
mul′ti·tal′ent·ed, *adj.*
mul′ti·ten′ta·cled, *adj.*
mul′ti·test′er, *n.*
mul′ti·thread′ed, *adj.*
mul′ti·tiered′, *adj.*
mul′ti·tit′u·lar, *adj.*
mul′ti·toed′, *adj.*
mul′ti·toned′, *adj.*
mul′ti·tool′, *n.*
mul′ti·track′, *v.t.*
mul′ti·trunked′, *adj.*
mul′ti·tube′, *adj.*
mul′ti·tu′bu·lar, *adj.*
mul′ti·u′nit, *adj.*
mul′ti·use′, *adj.*
mul′ti·us′er, *adj., n.*
mul′ti·val′vu·lar, *adj.*
mul′ti·vane′, *adj.*
mul′ti·view′, *adj.*
mul′ti·view′ing, *adj.*
mul′ti·voiced′, *adj.*
mul′ti·year′, *adj.*

bos. **1.** meaningless incantation or ritual. **2.** senseless or pretentious language, usually designed to obscure an issue, confuse a listener, or the like. **3.** an object of superstitious awe or reverence. **4.** (*caps.*) the guardian of western Sudan villages symbolized by a masked man who combats evil and punishes women for breaches of tribal laws. [1730–40; of disputed orig.]

mu′ me′son, *Physics.* (no longer in technical use) muon. [1945–50]

Mu·met·al (mo͞o′met′l, myo͞o′-), *n.* an alloy containing nickel, iron, and copper, characterized by high magnetic permeability and low hysteresis losses. [formerly a trademark; MU (repr. the Greek letter, a conventional symbol for permeability) + METAL]

Mum·ford (mum′fərd), *n.* **Lewis,** 1895–1990, U.S. author and social scientist.

Mu′·min (mo͞o′min), *n. Islam.* one of the devout. [< Ar: believer]

mumm (mum), *v.i.* mum².

mum·mer (mum′ər), *n.* **1.** a person who wears a mask or fantastic costume while merrymaking or taking part in a pantomime, esp. at Christmas and other festive seasons. **2.** an actor, esp. a pantomimist. [1400–50; late ME *mommer.* See MUM², -ER¹]

mum·mer·y (mum′ə rē), *n., pl.* **-mer·ies. 1.** the performance of mummers. **2.** any performance, ceremony, etc., regarded as absurd, false, or ostentatious. [1520–30; MUMMER + -Y³]

mum·mi·chog (mum′i chog′), *n. Coastal New England.* a silver and black killifish, *Fundulus heteroclitus,* found in fresh, brackish, and salt water along the Atlantic coast of the U.S. [1780–90, *Amer.*; < Narragansett (E sp.) *moamitteaūg*]

mum·mi·fy (mum′ə fī′), *v.,* **-fied, -fy·ing.** —*v.t.* **1.** to make (a dead body) into a mummy, as by embalming and drying. **2.** to make (something) resemble a mummy. —*v.i.* **3.** to dry or shrivel up. [1620–30; MUMMY¹ + -FY] —**mum′mi·fi·ca′tion,** *n.*

mum·my¹ (mum′ē), *n., pl.* **-mies,** *v.,* **-mied, -my·ing.** —*n.* **1.** the dead body of a human being or animal preserved by the ancient Egyptian process or some similar method of embalming. **2.** a dead body dried and preserved by nature. **3.** a withered or shrunken living being. **4.** a dry, shriveled fruit, tuber, or other plant organ, resulting from any of several fungous diseases. —*v.t.* **5.** to make into or cause to resemble a mummy; mummify. [1350–1400; ME *mummie* < ML *mummia* < Ar *mūmiyah* mummy, lit., bitumen < Pers *mūm* wax]

mum·my² (mum′ē), *n., pl.* **-mies.** *Chiefly Brit.* mother. [1815–25; MUM⁴ + -Y²]

mum′my bag′, a snug-fitting sleeping bag tapered from the shoulders to the feet, enclosing both the body and head except for a small opening for the face. [so called because its shape resembles a wrapped Egyptian mummy]

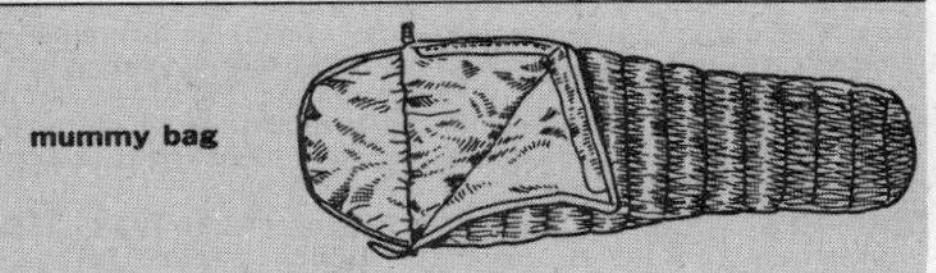

mump¹ (mump, mo͝omp), *Brit. Dial.* —*v.t.* **1.** to mumble; mutter. —*v.i.* **2.** to sulk; mope. **3.** to grimace. [1580–90; imit., appar. akin to MUM¹; cf. D *mompen* to mumble, G *mimpfeln* to mumble while eating, Icel *mumpa* to take into the mouth, eat greedily]

mump² (mump, mo͝omp), *Brit. Dial.* —*v.t.* **1.** to cheat. —*v.i.* **2.** to beg. [1645–55; < D *mompen* (obs.)]

mumps (mumps), *n.* (*used with a singular v.*) *Pathol.* an infectious disease characterized by inflammatory swelling of the parotid and usually other salivary glands, and sometimes by inflammation of the testes or ovaries, caused by a paramyxovirus. [1590–1600; MUMP¹ + -S³]

mump·si·mus (mump′sə məs), *n., pl.* **-mus·es** for 2. **1.** adherence to or persistence in an erroneous use of language, memorization, practice, belief, etc., out of habit or obstinacy (opposed to *sumpsimus*). **2.** a person who persists in a mistaken expression or practice (opposed to *sumpsimus*). [1520–30; from a story, which perh. originated with Erasmus, of an illiterate priest who said *mumpsimus* rather than *sūmpsimus* (1st pl. perfect indic. of L *sūmere* to pick up; see CONSUME) while reciting the liturgy, and refused to change the word when corrected]

mu·mu (mo͞o′mo͞o), *n.* muumuu.

mun., **1.** municipal. **2.** municipality.

munch (munch), *v.t.* **1.** to chew with steady or vigorous working of the jaws, often audibly. —*v.i.* **2.** to chew steadily or vigorously, often audibly. **3. munch out,** *Slang.* to snack esp. extensively or frequently. —*n.* **4.** *Informal.* a snack. [1375–1425; late ME *monchen,* var. of *mocchen;* imit.] —**munch′er,** *n.*

Munch (mo͝ongk), *n.* **Ed·vard** (ed′värd), 1863–1944, Norwegian painter and graphic artist.

Münch (mynsh), *n.* **Charles,** 1891–1968, French conductor in the U.S.

Mun′chausen syn′drome, *Psychiatry.* a factitious disorder in which otherwise healthy individuals seek to hospitalize themselves with feigned or self-induced pathology in order to receive surgical or other medical treatment. [1950–55; named after Baron von MÜNCHAUSEN, whose fictionalized accounts of his own experiences suggest symptoms of the disorder]

Mun′chausen syn′drome by prox′y, *Psychiatry.* a form of Munchausen syndrome in which a person induces or claims to observe a disease in another, usu. a close relative, in order to attract the doctor's attention to herself or himself.

Mün·chen (myn′KHən), *n.* German name of **Munich.**

Mün·chen-Glad·bach (myn′KHən glät′bäKH), *n.* former name of **Mönchengladbach.**

Münch·hau·sen (mynKH′hou′zən), *n.* **Karl Friedrich Hi·e·ro·ny·mus** (kärl frē′drIKH hē′ā RÔ′NY mo͝os′), **Baron von** (fən), 1720–97, German soldier, adventurer, and teller of tales. English, **Mun·chau·sen** (mun′chou′zən, munch′hou′-, mun chô′-). —**Mun′chau′sen·ism,** *n.*

munch·kin (munch′kin), *n.* (*often cap.*) a small person, esp. one who is dwarfish or elfin in appearance. [after the *Munchkins,* a dwarflike race portrayed in L. Frank Baum's *The Wonderful Wizard of Oz* (1900) and other fantasy novels]

munch·y (mun′chē), *adj.,* **munch·i·er, munch·i·est,** *n., pl.* **munch·ies.** —*adj.* Also, **munch′ie. 1.** (of food) **a.** crunchy or chewy. **b.** *Informal.* for snacking: *munchy foods like popcorn and cookies.* —*n.* **2. munchies,** *Informal.* food suitable or meant for snacking: *Munchies were served before dinner.* **3. the munchies,** *Slang.* hunger, esp. a craving for sweets or snacks: *suffering from the munchies.* [1915–20; MUNCH + -Y¹ or -Y²] —**munch′i·ness,** *n.*

Mun·cie (mun′sē), *n.* a city in E Indiana. 77,216.

Mun·da (mo͝on′də), *n.* a small family of languages spoken in east-central India.

mun·dane (mun dān′, mun′dān), *adj.* **1.** of or pertaining to this world or earth as contrasted with heaven; worldly; earthly: *mundane affairs.* **2.** common; ordinary; banal; unimaginative. **3.** of or pertaining to the world, universe, or earth. [1425–75; < L *mundānus,* equiv. to *mund(us)* world + *-ānus* -ANE; r. late ME *mondeyne* < MF *mondain* < L, as above] —**mun·dane′ly,** *adv.* —**mun·dane′ness,** *n.*
—**Syn. 1.** secular, temporal. See **earthly.**

mundane′ astrol′ogy, the astrology of worldly events, in contrast to the astrology of the individual: used esp. in interpretations and forecasts involving politics, the stock market, weather, and disasters.

mun·dan·i·ty (mun dan′i tē), *n., pl.* **-ties. 1.** the condition or quality of being mundane. **2.** an instance of being mundane. [1495–1505; MUNDANE + -ITY]

Mun·de·lein (mun′dl īn′), *n.* a city in NE Illinois. 17,053.

mun·di·fy (mun′də fī′), *v.t.,* **-fied, -fy·ing. 1.** to cleanse; deterge: *to mundify a wound.* **2.** to purge or purify: *to mundify a person of past sins.* [1375–1425; late ME < LL *mundificāre,* equiv. to L *mundi-,* s. of *mundus* clean + *-ficare* -FY]

Mun·du·gu·mor (mun do͞o′gə môr′), *n., pl.* **-mors,** (*esp. collectively*) **-mor.** a member of a Papuan people of Papua New Guinea.

mun·dun·gus (mun dung′gəs), *n. Archaic.* malodorous tobacco. [1630–40; Latinized var. of Sp *mondongo* tripe]

mu·neu·tri·no (myo͞o′no͞o trē′nō, -nyo͞o-, mo͞o′-), *n., pl.* **-nos.** *Physics.* muon-neutrino.

mung′ bean′ (mung), **1.** a plant, *Vigna radiata,* of the legume family, cultivated for its edible seeds, pods, and young sprouts. **2.** the seed or pod of this plant. Also called **gram, green gram.** [1905–10; earlier *moong* < Hindi *mūg,* var. of *mūg;* cf. Pali, Prakrit *mugga,* Skt *mudga*]

mun·go (mung′gō), *n., pl.* **-gos.** a low-grade wool from felted rags or waste. Also, **mongo, mongoe.** Cf. **shoddy** (def. 1). [1800–10; orig. uncert.]

Mun·hall (mun′hôl′), *n.* a city in W Pennsylvania, near Pittsburgh. 14,532.

mu·ni (myo͞o′nē), *Informal.* —*adj.* **1.** municipal; operated by a municipal government: *a muni bus company.* —*n.* **2.** a municipal bond. Also, **muny.** [by shortening]

Mu·ni (myo͞o′nē), *n.* **Paul** (*Muni Weisenfreund*), 1895–1967, U.S. actor, born in Austria.

mu′ni bond′ fund′, *Informal.* See **municipal bond fund.**

munic., **1.** municipal. **2.** municipality.

Mu·nich (myo͞o′nik), *n.* **1.** German, **München.** a city in and the capital of Bavaria, in SW Germany. 1,188,800. **2.** any dishonorable appeasement. Cf. **Munich Pact.**

Mu′nich Pact′, the pact signed by Great Britain, France, Italy, and Germany on September 29, 1938, by which the Sudetenland was ceded to Germany: often cited as an instance of unwise and unprincipled appeasement of an aggressive nation. Also called **Mu′nich Agree′ment.**

mu·nic·i·pal (myo͞o nis′ə pəl), *adj.* **1.** of or pertaining to a town or city or its local government: *municipal elections.* **2.** *Archaic.* pertaining to the internal affairs of a state or nation rather than to international affairs. —*n.* **3.** a municipal bond. [1530–40; < L *mūnicipālis,* equiv. to *mūnicip-* (s. of *mūniceps*) citizen of a free town (*mūni(a)* duties + *-cip-,* comb. form of *capere* to take) + *-ālis* -AL¹] —**mu·nic′i·pal·ly,** *adv.*

munic′ipal bond′, a bond issued by a state or local authority to finance projects.

munic′ipal bond′ fund′, a mutual fund that invests in municipal bonds.

munic′ipal corpora′tion, a city, town, etc., that operates under a corporate charter granted by the state.

munic′ipal court′, a court whose jurisdiction is confined to a city or municipality, with criminal jurisdiction usually corresponding to that of a police court and civil jurisdiction over small causes. [1820–30]

mu·nic·i·pal·ism (myo͞o nis′ə pə liz′əm), *n.* **1.** the principle or system of home rule by a municipality. **2.** advocacy of such a principle or system. [1850–55; MUNICIPAL + -ISM] —**mu·nic′i·pal·ist,** *n.*

mu·nic·i·pal·i·ty (myo͞o nis′ə pal′i tē), *n., pl.* **-ties. 1.** a city, town, or other district possessing corporate existence and usually its own local government. **2.** a community under municipal jurisdiction. **3.** the governing body of such a district or community. [1780–90; < F *municipalité.* See MUNICIPAL, -ITY]

mu·nic·i·pal·ize (myo͞o nis′ə pə līz′), *v.t.,* **-ized, -iz·ing. 1.** to make a municipality of. **2.** to bring under municipal ownership or control. Also, *esp. Brit.,* **mu·nic′i·pal·ise′.** [1875–80; MUNICIPAL + -IZE] —**mu·nic′i·pal·i·za′tion,** *n.*

mu·nif·i·cent (myo͞o nif′ə sənt), *adj.* **1.** extremely liberal in giving; very generous. **2.** characterized by great generosity: *a munificent bequest.* [1575–85; back formation from L *mūnificentia* generosity, munificence, equiv. to *mūnific(us)* generous (*muni-,* comb. form of *mūnus* gift + *-ficus* -FIC) + *-entia* -ENCE] —**mu·nif′i·cence, mu·nif′i·cent·ness,** *n.* —**mu·nif′i·cent·ly,** *adv.*
—**Syn. 1.** bountiful, bounteous, lavish. See **generous.**

mu·ni·ment (myo͞o′nə mənt), *n.* **1. muniments,** *Law.* a document, as a title deed or a charter, by which rights or privileges are defended or maintained. **2.** *Archaic.* a defense or protection. [1375–1425; late ME < ML *mūnimentum* document (e.g., title, deed) for use in defense against a claimant, L: defense, protection, orig., fortification, equiv. to *mūni(re)* to fortify + *-mentum* -MENT]

mu′niment room′, *Brit.* a storage or display room in a castle, church, university, or the like, where pertinent historical documents and records are kept.

Mu·nin (mo͞o′nin), *n. Scand. Myth.* one of the two ravens of Odin that brought him news from the whole world. Cf. **Hugin.** [< ON, equiv. to *mun-* noun from base of *muna* to remember + *-inn* definite article]

mu·nite (myo͞o nīt′), *v.t.,* **-nit·ed, -nit·ing.** *Obs.* to fortify. [1400–50; late ME: fortified < L *mūnītus,* ptp. of *mūnire* to wall (a town), fortify; see -ITE²]

mu·ni·tion (myo͞o nish′ən), *n.* **1.** Usually, **munitions.** materials used in war, esp. weapons and ammunition. **2.** material or equipment for carrying on any undertaking. —*v.t.* **3.** to provide with munitions. [1525–35; < L *mūnītiōn-* (s. of *mūnītiō*) a fortifying, equiv. to *mūnīt(us)* fortified (see MUNITE) + *-iōn* -ION]

muni′tion ar′mor, armor made in quantity for common soldiers.

Mun·ká·csy (mo͝on′kä chi), *n.* **Mi·hály von** (mi′hī fən), (*Michael Lieb*), 1844–1900, Hungarian painter.

mun·nion (mun′yən), *n.* a mullion or muntin. [1585–95; assimilated var. of MULLION]

Mu·ñoz Ma·rín (mo͞o nyôs′ mä RēN′), **Luis** (lwēs), 1898–1980, Puerto Rican political leader: governor 1948–64.

Mun·ro (mən rō′), *n.* **H(ector) H(ugh)** (*"Saki"*), 1870–1916, Scottish novelist and short-story writer, born in Burma.

Mun·roe (mən rō′), *n.* **Charles Edward,** 1849–1938, U.S. chemist.

Munroe′ effect′, *Mil.* the reinforcement of shock waves in the concave, hollow end of a shaped charge, producing a greater resultant wave and concentrating the explosion along the axis of the charge. [named after C. E. MUNROE]

Mun·see (mun′sē), *n., pl.* **-sees,** (*esp. collectively*) **-see** for 1. **1.** a member of a North American Indian people, one of the Delaware group. **2.** the Eastern Algonquian language of the Munsee and closely related peoples, originally spoken in the lower Hudson Valley and upper Delaware Valley.

Mun·sey (mun′sē), *n.* **Frank Andrew,** 1854–1925, U.S. publisher.

mun·shi (mo͞on′shē), *n. Anglo-Indian.* **1.** a native interpreter or language instructor. **2.** a native secretary or assistant. Also, **moonshee.** [1770–80; < Hindi *munshī* < Ar *munshī'* writer]

mun·ster (mun′stər, mo͝on′-), *n.* (*often cap.*) muenster.

Mun·ster (mun′stər), *n.* **1.** a province in SW Republic of Ireland. 997,948. 9316 sq. mi. (24,130 sq. km). **2.** a town in NW Indiana. 20,671.

Mün·ster (myn′stəR), *n.* a city in NW Germany: treaty of Westphalia 1648. 246,300.

Mün·ster·berg (mo͝on′stər bûrg′; *Ger.* myn′stəR-berK′), *n.* **Hu·go** (hyo͞o′gō; *Ger.* ho͞o′gō), 1863–1916, German psychologist and philosopher in the U.S.

mun·tin (mun′tn), *n.* **1.** Also called **sash bar.** a bar for holding the edges of window panes within a sash. See diag. under **double-hung. 2.** (formerly) a vertical bar in a window sash. **3.** a stile within the frame of a door or the like. [1300–50; earlier *mountan, montan,* ME *mountaun, mountain* < MF *montant,* n. use of prp. of *monter* to MOUNT¹; cf. D *munting*]

munt·jac (munt′jak), *n.* **1.** any of various small deer of the genus *Muntiacus,* of southern and eastern Asia and the adjacent islands, esp. *M. muntjac,* of Java, India, etc., having well-developed horns on bony pedicels. **2.** any of the small deer of the related genus *Elaphodus,* of China and Tibet, having minute horns. Also, **munt′jak.** Also called **barking deer.** [1790–1800; (< D) < Sundanese *mənčək* a kind of chevrotain; reason for subsequent application to this deer uncert.]

Muntz′ met′al (munts). See **alpha-beta brass.** [1860–65; named after its inventor, G. F. Muntz, 19th-century English metallurgist and manufacturer]

mu·ny (myo͞o′nē), *adj., n.* muni.

mu·on (myo͞o′on), *n. Physics.* a lepton similar in most respects to the electron except that it is unstable, it may

CONCISE PRONUNCIATION KEY: act, cāpe, dâre, pärt; set, ēqual; *if,* īce; ox, ōver, ôrder, oil, bo͝ok, bo͞ot, out; up, ûrge; child; sing; shoe; thin, *th*at; zh as in *treasure.* ə = *a* as in *alone, e* as in *system, i* as in *easily, o* as in *gallop, u* as in *circus;* ᵊ as in *fire* (fīᵊr), *hour* (ouᵊr). l and n can serve as syllabic consonants, as in *cradle* (krād′l), and *button* (but′n). See the full key inside the front cover.

be positively charged, and its mass is approximately 207 times greater; the positively charged muon is the antiparticle of the negatively charged muon. *Symbol:* μ [1950–55; by shortening of MU MESON; see MU, -ON[1]] —**mu·on′ic,** *adj.*

mu·o·ni·um (myōō ō′nē əm), *n. Physics.* an electron and a positively charged muon bound together by electrical attraction in the same manner as the electron and proton in a hydrogen atom. [1955–60; MU(ON) + *-onium,* prob. extracted from POSITRONIUM]

mu·on·neu·tri·no (myōō′on nōō trē′nō, -nyōō-), *n., pl.* **-nos.** *Physics.* a type of neutrino that obeys a conservation law together with the muon, with the total number of muons and muon-neutrinos minus the total number of their antiparticles remaining constant. Also called **mu-neutrino, muon′ic neutri′no.** Cf. **lepton.**

M.U.P., Master of Urban Planning.

mu·ra (mŏŏr′ə), *n.* (in Japan) a village; hamlet. [< Japn]

mu·rae·nid (myŏŏ rē′nid), *n.* **1.** any fish of the family Muraenidae, comprising the morays. —*adj.* **2.** belonging or pertaining to the morays. [1840–50; < NL *Muraenidae* name of the family, equiv. to *Muraen(a)* a genus (L *mūraena, mūrēna* moray eel < Gk *mýraina*) + *-idae* -ID[2]]

mu·rage (myŏŏr′ij), *n. Eng. Law.* a toll or tax for the repair or construction of the walls or fortifications of a town. [1225–75; ME < OF, equiv. to *mur(er)* to wall about (see MURE) + *-age* -AGE]

mu·ral (myŏŏr′əl), *n.* **1.** a large picture painted or affixed directly on a wall or ceiling. **2.** a greatly enlarged photograph attached directly to a wall. **3.** a wallpaper pattern representing a landscape or the like, often with very widely spaced repeats so as to produce the effect of a mural painting on a wall of average size; a trompe-l'oeil. —*adj.* **4.** of, pertaining to, or resembling a wall. **5.** executed on or affixed to a wall: *mural inscriptions.* **6.** pertaining to any of several astronomical instruments that were affixed to a wall aligned on the plane of a meridian, and were formerly used to measure the altitude of celestial bodies: *a mural quadrant; a mural circle.* [1400–50; late ME < L *mūrālis,* equiv. to *mūr(us)* wall + *-ālis* -AL[1]]

mu′ral crown′, **1.** a golden crown formed with indentations to resemble a battlement, bestowed by the ancient Romans on the soldiers who first mounted the wall of a besieged place and there lodged a standard. **2.** Also called **mu′ral cor′onet.** *Heraldry.* a representation of an embattled coronet, often appearing on municipal arms. [1540–50] —**mu′ral·ly,** *adv.*

mu·ral·ism (myŏŏr′ə liz′əm), *n.* (*sometimes cap.*) an artistic movement identified chiefly with the Mexican painters José Orozco, Diego Rivera, and David Siqueiros and exemplified by their grand-scale, narrative murals on humanitarian, social, and political themes. [MURAL + -ISM; cf. Sp *muralismo*]

mu·ral·ist (myŏŏr′ə list), *n.* **1.** an artist who paints murals, esp. an artist associated with muralism. —*adj.* **2.** of, pertaining to, or characteristic of muralism. [MURAL + -IST]

Mu·ra·no (mŏŏ rä′nō; *It.* mōō Rä′nô), *n.* an island suburb of Venice: cathedral; noted for Venetian glass manufacture.

Mu·ra·sa·ki Shi·ki·bu (mōō′Rä sä′kē shē′kē bōō′), **Lady,** 978?–1031?, Japanese poet and novelist.

Mu·rat (MY RA′), *n.* **Jo·a·chim** (zhô A kēm′), 1767?–1815, French marshal: king of Naples 1808–15.

Mu·rat (mŏŏ rät′), *n.* a river in E Turkey, flowing W to the Euphrates. 425 mi. (685 km) long. Also called **Murad Su** (mŏŏ räd′ sōō′).

Mur·cia (mŏŏr′shə; *Sp.* mōōR′thyä), *n.* **1.** a city in SE Spain. 243,759. **2.** a region in SE Spain: formerly a kingdom.

mur·cott (mûr′kot), *n.* a thin-skinned, juicy variety of tangerine. Also, **mur′cot.** [allegedly named after Charles *Murcott* Smith, Florida grower]

mur·der (mûr′dər), *n.* **1.** *Law.* the killing of another human being under conditions specifically covered in law. In the U.S., special statutory definitions include murder committed with malice aforethought, characterized by deliberation or premeditation or occurring during the commission of another serious crime, as robbery or arson (**first-degree murder**), and murder by intent but without deliberation or premeditation (**second-degree murder**). **2.** *Slang.* something extremely difficult or perilous: *That final exam was murder!* **3. get away with murder,** *Informal.* to engage in a deplorable activity without incurring harm or punishment: *The new baby-sitter lets the kids get away with murder.* **4. murder will out,** a secret will eventually be exposed. **5. yell** or **scream bloody murder, a.** to scream loudly in pain, fear, etc. **b.** to protest loudly and angrily: *If I don't get a good raise I'm going to yell bloody murder.* —*v.t.* **6.** *Law.* to kill by an act constituting murder. **7.** to kill or slaughter inhumanly or barbarously. **8.** to spoil or mar by bad performance, representation, pronunciation, etc.: *The tenor murdered the aria.* —*v.i.* **9.** to commit murder. [1300–50; ME *mo(u)rdre, murder,* var. (influenced by OF *murdre* < Gmc) of *murthre* MURTHER]
—**Syn. 6.** See **kill**[1].

mur·der·ee (mûr′də rē′), *n.* a murderer's victim or intended victim. [1915–20; MURDER + -EE]

mur·der·er (mûr′dər ər), *n.* a person who commits murder. [1300–50; ME *mortherer, mord(e)rer;* see MURDER, -ER[1]]

mur·der·ess (mûr′dər is), *n.* a woman who commits murder. [1350–1400; ME *moerdrice, morderes;* see MURDER, -ESS]
—**Usage.** See **-ess.**

Mur′der in the Cathe′dral, a verse drama (1935) by T. S. Eliot.

mur′der one′, first-degree murder. See under **murder** (def. 1).

mur·der·ous (mûr′dər əs), *adj.* **1.** of the nature of or involving murder: *a murderous deed.* **2.** guilty of, bent on, or capable of murder. **3.** extremely difficult, dangerous, or unpleasant: *murderous heat.* [1525–35; MURDER + -OUS] —**mur′der·ous·ly,** *adv.* —**mur′der·ous·ness,** *n.*

mur′der two′, second-degree murder. See under **murder** (def. 1).

Mur·doch (mûr′dok), *n.* a male given name.

mur·drum (mûr′drəm), *n. Old Eng. Law.* **1.** the killing of a human being in a secret manner. **2.** the fine payable to the king by the hundred where such a killing occurred, unless the killer was produced or the victim proved to be a Saxon. [< ML < OF *murdre* MURDER]

mure (myŏŏr), *n., v.,* **mured, mur·ing.** —*n.* **1.** *Obs.* a wall. —*v.t.* **2.** to immure. [1400–50; late ME *muren* (v.) < MF *murer* < LL *mūrāre* v. deriv. of L *mūrus* wall]

Mu·res (mŏŏr′esh), *n.* a river in SE central Europe, flowing W from the Carpathian Mountains in central Rumania to the Tisza River in S Hungary. 400 mi. (645 km) long. Hungarian, **Maros.** Rumanian, **Mu·reş** (mŏŏ′-resh).

mu·rex (myŏŏr′eks), *n., pl.* **mu·ri·ces** (myŏŏr′ə sēz′), **mu·rex·es. 1.** any marine gastropod of the genus *Murex,* common in tropical seas, certain species of which yield the royal purple dye valued by the ancients. **2.** a shell used as a trumpet, as in representations of Tritons in art. **3.** purplish red. [1580–90; < NL, L *mūrex* the shellfish that yielded Tyrian purple dye]

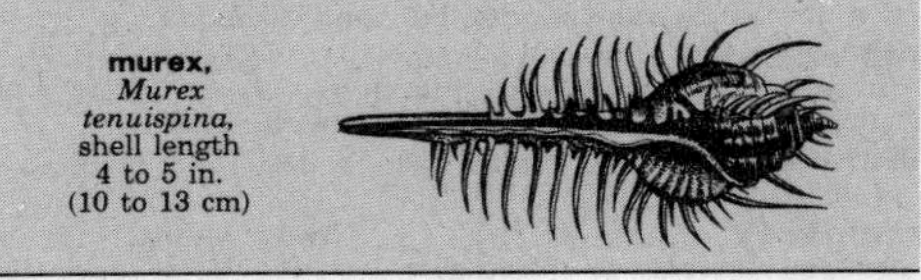
murex, *Murex tenuispina,* shell length 4 to 5 in. (10 to 13 cm)

mu·rex·ide (myŏŏ rek′sīd, -sid), *n. Chem.* a reddish-purple, crystalline, sparingly water-soluble solid, $C_8H_8N_6O_6$, having a green luster, formerly used as a dye. Also called **ammonium purpurate.** [1830–40; MUREX + -IDE]

murex′ide test′, *Biochem.* a test in which treatment of a substance, usually urine, with nitric acid and ammonia indicates the presence of uric acid by formation of murexide.

Mur·frees·bor·o (mûr′frēz bûr′ō, -bur′ō), *n.* a city in central Tennessee: battle of Stone River (or Murfreesboro) 1862. 32,845.

mur·geon (mûr′jən), *n. Scot.* a grimace; a wry face. [1490–1500; orig. uncert.]

mu·ri·ate (myŏŏr′ē āt′, -it), *n.* (not in scientific use) any chloride, esp. potassium chloride, KCl, used as a fertilizer. [1780–90; back formation from MURIATIC]

mu·ri·at·ic (myŏŏr′ē at′ik), *adj.* (not in scientific use) of or derived from muriatic acid. [1665–75; < L *muriāticus* pickled, lying in brine, equiv. to *muri(a)* brine + *-āticus;* see -ATE[1], -IC]

mu′riat′ic ac′id, (not in scientific use) See **hydrochloric acid.** [1780–90]

mu·ri·cate (myŏŏr′i kāt′), *adj. Bot., Zool.* covered with short, sharp points. Also, **mu′ri·cat′ed.** [1655–65; < L *mūricātus* like a murex, equiv. to *mūric-* (s. of *mūrex*) MUREX + *-ātus* -ATE[1]]

Mu·ri·el (myŏŏr′ē əl), *n.* a female given name.

Mu·ril·lo (myŏŏ ril′ō, mŏŏ rē′ō, myŏŏ-; *Sp.* mōō Rē′-lyō), *n.* **Bar·to·lo·mé Es·te·ban** (bäR′tô lô me′ es te′-vän), 1617–82, Spanish painter.

mu·rine (myŏŏr′in, -in), *adj.* **1.** belonging or pertaining to the Muridae, the family of rodents that includes the mice and rats. —*n.* **2.** a murine rodent. [1600–10; < L *mūrinus* of mice, equiv. to *mūr-* (s. of *mūs*) MOUSE + *-inus* -INE[1]]

mu′rine opos′sum, any of several grayish, brownish, or russet opossums of the genus *Marmosa,* inhabiting forests of Central and South America, often having a black, masklike marking on the face. Also called **mouse opossum.** [1790–1800]

Murj·ite (mûr′jīt), *n. Islam.* a member of a sect asserting that a man cannot be judged by his present or past actions and that such judgment must be left to God. [< Ar *murji'ah* body of believers in the doctrines of the sect; see -ITE[1]]

murk (mûrk), *n.* **1.** darkness; gloom: *the murk of a foggy night.* —*adj.* **2.** *Archaic.* dark; murky. Also, **mirk.** [bef. 900; ME *mirke, myrke* < ON *myrkr* dark, darkness, r. OE *myrce* dark]

murk·y (mûr′kē), *adj.,* **murk·i·er, murk·i·est. 1.** dark, gloomy, and cheerless. **2.** obscure or thick with mist, haze, etc., as the air. **3.** vague; unclear; confused: *a murky statement.* Also, **mirky.** [1300–50; ME *mirky.* See MURK, -Y[1]] —**murk′i·ly,** *adv.* —**murk′i·ness,** *n.*
—**Syn. 1.** See **dark. 2.** cloudy, dusky, lowering, misty, hazy. —**Ant. 1, 2.** bright, clear.

Mur·man′ Coast′ (mŏŏr män′), an Arctic coastal region in the NW Russian Federation in Europe, on the Kola Peninsula.

Mur·mansk (mŏŏr mänsk′; *Russ.* mōōR′mənsk), *n.* an ice-free seaport and railroad terminus in the NW Russian Federatrion, on the Murman Coast. 432,000.

mur·mur (mûr′mər), *n.* **1.** a low, continuous sound, as of a brook, the wind, or trees, or of low, indistinct voices. **2.** a mumbled or private expression of discontent. **3.** Also called **heart murmur.** *Med.* **a.** an abnormal sound heard on listening to the heart, usually through a stethoscope, produced by the blood passing through deformed cardiac valves. **b.** in some persons a similar sound heard when blood passes through normal valves. **4.** *Phonet.* a voice quality in which vibration of the vocal cords is accompanied by the escape of a great deal of air, as in the (h) of *ahead;* breathy voice. —*v.i.* **5.** to make a low or indistinct sound, esp. continuously. **6.** to speak in a low tone or indistinctly. **7.** to complain in a low tone or in private. —*v.t.* **8.** to sound by murmurs. **9.** to utter in a low tone: *He murmured a threat as he left the room.* [1275–1325; (v.) ME *murmuren* < L *murmurāre;* (n.) ME < L] —**mur′mur·er,** *n.* —**mur′mur·less,** *adj.* —**mur′mur·less·ly,** *adv.*
—**Syn. 1.** grumble, susurration, mumble, complaint, mutter. **6.** MURMUR, MUMBLE, MUTTER mean to make sounds that are not fully intelligible. To MURMUR is to utter sounds or words in a low, almost inaudible tone, as in expressing affection or dissatisfaction: *to murmur disagreement.* To MUMBLE is to utter imperfect or inarticulate sounds with the mouth partly closed, so that the words can be distinguished only with difficulty: *to mumble the answer to a question.* To MUTTER is to utter words in a low, grumbling way, often voicing complaint or discontent, not meant to be fully audible: *to mutter complaints.* **7.** grouse.

mur·mur·a·tion (mûr′mə rā′shən), *n.* **1.** an act or instance of murmuring. **2.** a flock of starlings. [1350–1400; ME < L *murmurātiōn-* (s. of *murmurātiō*). See MURMUR, -ATION]

mur·mur·ous (mûr′mər əs), *adj.* **1.** abounding in or characterized by murmurs. **2.** murmuring; indistinctly low: *murmurous waters.* [1575–85; MURMUR + -OUS] —**mur′mur·ous·ly,** *adv.*

Mu·rom (mōō′rəm), *n.* a city in the W Russian Federation in Europe, SW of Nizhni Novgorod. 120,000.

mur·phy (mûr′fē), *n., pl.* **-phies,** *v.,* **-phied, -phy·ing.** *Slang.* —*n.* **1.** an Irish or white potato. **2.** any of various confidence games in which a victim is left with a sealed envelope supposedly containing money, but which contains only newspaper or scrap paper cut to the same size as paper money. —*v.t.* **3.** to victimize or dupe in such a manner. [1805–15; special uses of *Murphy,* a typical Irish surname]

Mur·phy (mûr′fē), *n.* **1. Frank,** 1890–1949, U.S. statesman and jurist: associate justice of the U.S. Supreme Court 1940–49. **2. Isaac,** 1861–96, U.S. thoroughbred racehorse jockey. **3. William Par·ry** (par′ē), born 1892, U.S. physician: Nobel prize for medicine 1934.

Mur′phy bed′, a bed constructed so that it can be folded or swung into a closet. [1920–25; named after William L. *Murphy* (1876–1959), American inventor]

Mur′phy's Law′, the facetious proposition that if something can go wrong, it will. Also called **Mur′phy's First′ Law′.** [*Amer.;* after a fictitious *Murphy,* allegedly the name of a bungling mechanic in U.S. Navy educational cartoons of the 1950's]

mur·ra (mûr′ə), *n.* a mineral or stone used in ancient Rome for making fine vases, cups, etc.: believed to have been fluorite. Also, **mur′rha.** [1590–1600; < L *murr(h)a,* appar. back formation from *murrinus* MURRHINE]

mur·rain (mûr′in), *n.* **1.** *Vet. Pathol.* any of various diseases of cattle, as anthrax, foot-and-mouth disease, and Texas fever. **2.** *Obs.* a plague or pestilence. [1300–50; ME *moreine, moryne* < MF *morine* a plague, equiv. to *mor(ir)* to die (<< L *mori*) + *-ine* -INE[2]]

Mur·ray (mûr′ē, mur′ē), *n.* **1. Sir (George) Gilbert (Ai·mé)** (ā mā′), 1866–1957, English classical scholar. **2. Sir James Augustus Henry,** 1837–1915, Scottish lexicographer and philologist. **3. Lind·ley** (lin′lē, lind′-), 1745–1826, English grammarian, born in the U.S. **4. Philip,** 1886–1952, U.S. labor leader: president of the CIO 1940–52. **5.** a river in SE Australia, flowing W along the border between Victoria and New South Wales, through SE South Australia into the Indian Ocean. 1200 mi. (1930 km) long. **6.** a city in N Utah, S of Salt Lake City. 25,750. **7.** a town in SW Kentucky. 14,248. **8.** a male given name.

murre (mûr), *n.* **1.** either of two black and white diving birds of the genus *Uria,* of northern seas, *U. aalge* (**com′mon murre′**) or *U. lomvia* (**thick′-billed murre′**). **2.** See **razor-billed auk.** [1595–1605; orig. uncert.]

murre·let (mûr′lit), *n.* any of several small, chunky diving birds of the family Alcidae, of North Pacific coasts. [1870–75, *Amer.;* MURRE + -LET]

mur·rey (mûr′ē), *n.* a dark purplish-red color. [1375–1425; late ME *murrey, morrey* < MF *moré* (adj. and n.), *morée* (n.) < ML *mōrātum, mōrāta,* neut. and fem. of *mōrātus,* equiv. to L *mōr(um)* mulberry + *-ātus* -ATE[1]]

mur·rhine (mûr′in, -in), *adj.* of, pertaining to, or manufactured of murra. Also, **mur′rine.** [1570–80; < L *murr(h)inus,* for Gk *mourrinē,* equiv. to *mórr(ia)* murra + *-inē* fem. n. suffix; see -INE[1]]

CONCISE ETYMOLOGY KEY: <, descended or borrowed from; >, whence; b., blend of, blended; c., cognate with; cf., compare; deriv., derivative; equiv., equivalent; imit., imitative; obl., oblique; r., replacing; s., stem; sp., spelling, spelled; resp., respelling, respelled; trans., translation; ?, origin unknown; *, unattested; ‡, probably earlier than. See the full key inside the front cover.

mur′rhine glass′, 1. glassware believed to resemble the murrhine cups of ancient Rome. 2. a ware composed of glass in which metals, precious stones, or the like are embedded.

Mur·row (mûr′ō, mur′ō), *n.* **Edward R(oscoe),** 1908–65, U.S. news broadcaster and commentator.

Mur·rum·bidg·ee (mûr′əm bij′ē), *n.* a river in SE Australia, flowing W through New South Wales to the Murray River. 1050 mi. (1690 km) long.

Mur·ry (mûr′ē, mur′ē), *n.* a male given name, form of **Murray.**

Mur·rys·ville (mûr′ēz vil′, mur′-), *n.* a city in SW Pennsylvania. 16,036.

mur·ther (mûr′thər), *n., v.t., v.i. Obs.* murder. [bef. 900; ME *morther,* OE *morthor;* c. Goth *maurthr.* See MORTAL]

mus., 1. museum. 2. music. 3. musical. 4. musician.

mu·sa·ceous (myo͞o zā′shəs), *adj.* belonging to the Musaceae, the banana family of plants. Cf. **banana family.** [1850–55; < NL *Musace(ae)* family name (*Mus(a)* genus name (< Ar *mawzah* banana, perh. < Skt *mocaḥ*) + *-aceae* -ACEAE) + -OUS]

Mu·saf (mo͞o′säf), *n. Hebrew.* the religious service celebrated by Jews in addition to and immediately after the morning service on the Sabbath and festivals. [*mūsāph* lit., addition]

Mus.B., Bachelor of Music. Also, **Mus. Bac.** [< NL *Mūsicae Baccalaureus*]

Mus·ca (mus′kə), *n., gen.* **Mus·cae** (mus′ē). *Astron.* the Fly, a small southern constellation between Crux and Chamaeleon. [< NL, L: a fly]

mus·ca·del (mus′kə del′), *n.* muscatel. Also, **mus′ca·delle′.**

Mus·ca·det (mus′kə dā′; *Fr.* mys ka de′), *n.* 1. a white grape grown esp. in the lower Loire Valley region of France. 2. a dry white wine made from this grape. [< F *muscadet,* MF: wine with musklike taste; see MUSCATEL, -ET]

mus·ca·din (mus′kə din; *Fr.* my skä dan′), *n., pl.* **-dins** (-dins; *Fr.* -dan′). 1. a person with monarchical sympathies during the French Revolution, esp. from 1794 to 1796. 2. a French fop or dandy of this period. [1785–95; < F: dandy, fop, lit., lozenge containing musk (used by such dandies) < It *moscardino,* deriv. (with *-ardino;* see -ARD, -IN[1]) of *moscado, moscato,* equiv. to *mosc-* (< LL; see MUSK) + *-ato* -ATE[1]]

mus·ca·dine (mus′kə din, -dīn′), *n.* a grape, *Vitis rotundifolia,* of the southern U.S., having dull purple, thick-skinned musky fruit and being the origin of many grape varieties. [1535–45; MUSCAD(EL) + -INE[1]]

mus·ca·ri (mus kâr′ī, -kâr′ē), any plant of the genus *Muscari,* which includes the grape hyacinth. [1590–1600; < NL, perh. < early ModGk **moschari* grape hyacinth, deriv. of LGk *móschos* MUSK]

mus·ca·rine (mus′kər in, -kə rēn′), *n. Chem.* a poisonous compound, $C_8H_{19}NO_3$, found in certain mushrooms, esp. fly agaric, and in decaying fish. [1870–75; < L *muscār(ius)* of flies (*musc(a)* fly + *-ārius* -ARY) + -INE[1]]

mus·ca·rin·ic (mus′kə rin′ik), *adj.* 1. of or pertaining to muscarine. 2. related to or imitating the action of muscarine on neurons, esp. in blocking cholinergic effects. [MUSCARINE + -IC]

mus·cat (mus′kət, -kat), *n.* 1. a variety of grape having a pronounced sweet aroma and flavor, used for making wine and raisins. 2. the vine bearing this fruit. [1570–80; short for *muscat wine* or *grape* < MF *muscat* musky < OPr, equiv. to *musc* (< LL *muscus* MUSK) + *-at* -ATE[1]]

Mus·cat (mus kat′), *n.* a seaport in and the capital of Oman. 70,000. Arabic, **Masqat.**

Muscat′ and Oman′, former name of **Oman.**

mus·ca·tel (mus′kə tel′, mus′kə tel′), *n.* 1. a sweet wine made from muscat grapes. 2. a muscat grape. 3. a raisin made from muscat grapes. Also, **muscadel, muscadelle.** [1350–1400; < MF, equiv. to *muscat* MUSCAT + *-el* n. suffix; r. ME *muscadel(le)* < MF, equiv. to *muscad-* (< OPr *muscade,* fem. of *muscat* musky) + *-elle,* fem. of *-el* n. suffix]

Mus·ca·tine (mus′kə tēn′, mus′kə tēn′), *n.* a city in E Iowa, on the Mississippi. 23,467.

mus·ca·va·do (mus′kə vā′dō, -vä′-), *n.* muscovado.

mus·ca vol·i·tans (mus′kə vol′i tanz′), *pl.* **mus·cae vol·i·tan·tes** (mus′kē vol′i tan′tēz, mus′ē). *Ophthalm.* floater (def. 6). [< NL; L: fly flying about]

mus·cid (mus′id), *adj.* 1. belonging or pertaining to the Muscidae, the family of dipterous insects that includes the common housefly. —*n.* 2. any muscid fly. [1890–95; < NL *Muscidae* name of the family. See MUSCA, -ID[2]]

mus·cle (mus′əl), *n., v.,* **-cled, -cling,** *adj.* —*n.* 1. a tissue composed of cells or fibers, the contraction of which produces movement in the body. 2. an organ, composed of muscle tissue, that contracts to produce a particular movement. 3. muscular strength; brawn: *It will take a great deal of muscle to move this box.* 4. power or force, esp. of a coercive nature: *They put muscle into their policy and sent the marines.* 5. lean meat. 6. *Slang.* a. a hired thug or thugs. b. a bodyguard or bodyguards: *a gangster protected by muscle.* 7. a necessary or fundamental thing, quality, etc.: *The editor cut the muscle from the article.* —*v.t.* 8. *Informal.* to force or compel others to make way for: *He muscled his way into the conversation.* 9. to make more muscular: *The dancing lessons muscled her legs.* 10. to strengthen or toughen; put muscle into. 11. *Informal.* to accomplish by muscular force: *to muscle the partition into place.* 12. *Informal.* to force or compel, as by threats, promises, influence, or the like: *to muscle a bill through Congress.* —*v.i.* 13. *Informal.* to make one's way by force or fraud (often fol. by *in* or *into*). —*adj.* 14. *Informal.* (of a machine, engine, or vehicle) being very powerful or capable of high-speed performance: *a muscle power saw.* [1525–35; < L *mūsculus* lit., little mouse (from fancied resemblance to some muscles), equiv. to *mūs* MOUSE + *-culus* -CLE[1]] —**mus′cle·less,** *adj.* —**mus′cly,** *adj.*
—**Syn.** 3. power, vigor, might, force.

mus′cle beach′, a beach where young men display their muscles, engage in calisthenics, etc.

mus·cle·bound (mus′əl bound′), *adj.* 1. having enlarged and inelastic muscles, as from excessive exercise. 2. rigid; inflexible: *musclebound rules.* [1875–80; MUSCLE + -BOUND[1]]

mus′cle fi′ber, one of the structural cells of a muscle. [1875–80]

mus·cle·man (mus′əl man′), *n., pl.* **-men.** 1. *Informal.* a man with a muscular or brawny physique, esp. a bodybuilder. 2. *Slang.* a bodyguard, esp. one hired to intimidate others, often by strong-arm methods. [1925–30, *Amer.;* MUSCLE + MAN[1]]

mus′cle sense′, *Psychol., Physiol.* a sense of movement derived from afferent nerves originating in tendons, muscle tissue, skin, and joints; proprioception. [1890–95]

Mus′cle Shoals′, former rapids of the Tennessee River in SW Alabama, changed into a lake by Wilson Dam: part of the Tennessee Valley Authority.

mus′cle spin′dle, *Cell Biol.* a proprioceptor in skeletal muscle, composed of striated muscle fibers and sensory nerve endings in a connective tissue sheath, that conveys information via the spinal nerves on the state of muscle stretch, important in the reflex mechanism that maintains body posture. [1890–95]

mus·cone (mus′kōn), *n. Chem.* an oily, very slightly water-soluble, large cyclic ketone containing a 15-membered ring, $C_{16}H_{30}O$, obtained from musk: used in the perfume industry. Also, **muskone.** [< LL *musc(us)* MUSK + -ONE]

mus·co·va·do (mus′kə vā′dō, -vä′-), *n.* raw or unrefined sugar, obtained from the juice of the sugar cane by evaporating and draining off the molasses. Also, **muscavado.** [1635–45; (< Sp (*azúcar*) *mascabado*) < Pg (*açúcar*) *mascavado,* ptp. of *mascavar* to separate raw sugar, earlier *meoscabar,* reduced form of *menoscabar* to belittle, detract from, c. Sp *menoscabar* to diminish, reduce < VL **minuscapāre,* equiv. to L *minus* smaller, less (see MINUS) + VL **-capāre,* deriv. of **capum,* for L *caput* head; cf. ACHIEVE, MISCHIEF]

Mus·co·vite (mus′kə vīt′), *n.* 1. a native or inhabitant of Moscow. 2. a native or inhabitant of the Grand Duchy of Muscovy. 3. (*l.c.*) *Mineral.* common light-colored mica, essentially $KAl_3Si_3O_{10}(OH)_2$, used as an electrical insulator. 4. *Archaic.* a Russian. —*adj.* 5. of, pertaining to, or characteristic of Moscow, Muscovy, or the Muscovites. [1545–55; MUSCOV(Y) + -ITE[1]]

Mus·co·vy (mus′kə vē), *n.* 1. Also called **Grand Duchy of Muscovy.** a principality founded c1271 and centered on the ancient city of Moscow. Its rulers gradually gained control over the neighboring Great Russian principalities and established the Russian Empire under the czars. 2. *Archaic.* Moscow. 3. *Archaic.* Russia.

Mus′covy duck′, a large, crested, wild duck, *Cairina moschata,* of tropical America, that has been widely domesticated. Also called **musk duck.** [1650–60]

mus·cu·lar (mus′kyə lər), *adj.* 1. of or pertaining to muscle or the muscles: *muscular strain.* 2. dependent on or affected by the muscles: *muscular strength.* 3. having well-developed muscles; brawny. 4. vigorously and forcefully expressed, executed, performed, etc., as if by the use of a great deal of muscular power: *a muscular response to terrorism.* 5. broad and energetic, esp. with the implication that subtlety and grace are lacking: *a muscular style.* 6. reflected in physical activity and work: *a muscular religion.* 7. *Informal.* having or showing power; powerful: *a muscular vehicle.* [1675–85; < L *mūscul(us)* MUSCLE + -AR[1]] —**mus′cu·lar′i·ty,** *n.* —**mus′cu·lar·ly,** *adv.*
—**Syn.** 3. sinewy; strong, powerful; stalwart, sturdy.

mus′cular dys′trophy, *Pathol.* a hereditary disease characterized by gradual wasting of the muscles with replacement by scar tissue and fat, sometimes also affecting the heart. [1865–70]

mus·cu·la·ture (mus′kyə lə chər, -cho͝or′), *n.* the muscular system of the body or of its parts. [1870–75; *musculat(ion)* muscular system (see MUSCLE, -ATION) + -URE]

musculo-, a combining form representing **muscle** in compound words: *musculoskeletal.* [< L *mūscul(us)* MUSCLE + -O-]

mus·cu·lo·skel·e·tal (mus′kyə lō skel′i tl), *adj.* concerning, involving, or made up of both the muscles and the bones: *the musculoskeletal system.* [1940–45; MUSCULO- + SKELETAL]

Mus.D., Doctor of Music. Also, **Mus.Doc., Mus.Dr.** [< NL *Mūsicae Doctor*]

muse (myo͞oz), *v.,* **mused, mus·ing.** —*v.i.* 1. to think or meditate in silence, as on some subject. 2. *Archaic.* to gaze meditatively or wonderingly. —*v.t.* 3. to meditate on. 4. to comment thoughtfully or ruminate upon. [1300–50; ME *musen* to mutter, gaze meditatively on, be astonished < MF *muser,* perh. ult. deriv. of ML *mūsum* MUZZLE] —**mus′er,** *n.*
—**Syn.** 1. cogitate, ruminate, think; dream. 1, 3. ponder, contemplate, deliberate.

Muse (myo͞oz), *n.* 1. *Class. Myth.* a. any of a number of sister goddesses, originally given as Aoede (song), Melete (meditation), and Mneme (memory), but latterly and more commonly as the nine daughters of Zeus and Mnemosyne who presided over various arts: Calliope (epic poetry), Clio (history), Erato (lyric poetry), Euterpe (music), Melpomene (tragedy), Polyhymnia (religious music), Terpsichore (dance), Thalia (comedy), and Urania (astronomy); identified by the Romans with the Camenae. b. any goddess presiding over a particular art. 2. (*sometimes l.c.*) the goddess or the power regarded as inspiring a poet, artist, thinker, or the like. 3. (*l.c.*) the genius or powers characteristic of a poet. [1350–1400; ME *Muse* < MF < L *Mūsa* < Gk *Moûsa*]

muse·ful (myo͞oz′fəl), *adj. Archaic.* deeply thoughtful; pensive. [1610–20; MUSE + -FUL] —**muse′ful·ly,** *adv.*

mu·se·ol·o·gy (myo͞o′zē ol′ə jē), *n.* the systematic study of the organization, management, and function of a museum. [1880–85; MUSE(UM) + -O- + -LOGY] —**mu·se·o·log·i·cal** (myo͞o′zē ə loj′i kəl), *adj.* —**mu′se·ol′o·gist,** *n.*

mu·sette (myo͞o zet′), *n.* 1. Also called **musette′ bag′.** a small leather or canvas bag with a shoulder strap, used for carrying personal belongings, food, etc., while hiking, marching, or the like. 2. a French bagpipe of the 17th and early 18th centuries, with several chambers and drones, and with the wind supplied by a bellows rather than a blowpipe. 3. a woodwind instrument similar to but smaller than a shawm. 4. a short musical piece with a drone bass, often forming the middle section of a gavotte. [1350–1400; ME < MF, equiv. to *muse* bagpipe (deriv. of *muser* to play the bagpipe < L *mussāre* to hum; see MUSE[1]) + *-ette* -ETTE]

mu·se·um (myo͞o zē′əm), *n.* a building or place where works of art, scientific specimens, or other objects of permanent value are kept and displayed. [1605–15; < L *mūsēum* place sacred to the Muses, building devoted to learning or the arts (referring esp. to the scholarly institute founded in Alexandria about 280 B.C.) < Gk *Mouseîon,* equiv. to *Moûs(a)* MUSE + *-eion* suffix of place]

mu·se·um·go·er (myo͞o zē′əm gō′ər), *n.* a frequent visitor to museums. [1925–30; MUSEUM + GOER]

muse′um piece′, 1. something suitable for keeping and exhibiting in a museum. 2. something very old-fashioned or decrepit: *That car he drives is a museum piece.* [1900–05]

mush[1] (mush *or, esp. for 2–5,* mo͝osh), *n.* 1. meal, esp. cornmeal, boiled in water or milk until it forms a thick, soft mass, or until it is stiff enough to mold into a loaf for slicing and frying. 2. any thick, soft mass. 3. mawkish sentimentality or amorousness. 4. anything unpleasantly or contemptibly lacking in coherence, force, dignity, etc.: *His entire argument was simply mush.* —*v.t.* 5. to squeeze or crush; crunch: *to mush all the candy together in a sticky ball.* [1665–75, *Amer.;* obscurely akin to MASH[1]]

mush[2] (mush), *v.i.* 1. to go or travel, esp. over snow with a dog team and sled. —*v.t.* 2. to drive or spur on (sled dogs or a sled drawn by dogs). —*interj.* 3. go! (used as an order to start or speed up a dog team) —*n.* 4. a trip or journey, esp. across snow and ice with a dog team. [1895–1900; perh. orig. as phrasal v. *mush on!* < CanF, F *marchons!* let's go!; see MARCH[1]]

mush·er (mush′ər), *n. Alaska and Northern Canada.* a person who competes in cross-country races with dog team and sled. [1895–1900; MUSH[2] + -ER[1]]

mush·head (mush′hed′, mo͝osh′-), *n. Slang.* a stupid person. [1885–90, *Amer.;* MUSH[1] + HEAD]

Mu·shin (mo͞o′shin), *n.* a city in SW Nigeria, NW of Lagos. 197,000.

mush·mel·on (mush′mel′ən), *n. Older Use.* muskmelon.

mush·mouth (mush′mouth′, mo͝osh′-), *n., pl.* **-mouths** (-mouths′, -mouthz′). *Slang.* a person who speaks indistinctly. Also, **mush′-mouth′.** [MUSH[1] + MOUTH]

mushroom,
A, pileus; B, annulus; C, stem; D, volva; E, gills

mush·room (mush′ro͞om, -ro͝om), *n.* 1. any of various fleshy fungi including the toadstools, puffballs, coral fungi, morels, etc. 2. any of several edible species, esp. of the family Agaricaceae, as *Agaricus campestris* **(meadow mushroom** or **field mushroom),** cultivated for food in the U.S. 3. anything of similar shape or correspondingly rapid growth. 4. a large, mushroom-shaped cloud of smoke or rubble, formed in the atmosphere as a result of an explosion, esp. a nuclear explosion. —*adj.* 5. of, consisting of, or containing mushrooms: *a mushroom omelet.* 6. resembling a mushroom in shape or form. 7. of rapid growth and often brief duration: *mushroom towns of the gold-rush days.* —*v.i.* 8. to spread, grow, or develop quickly. 9. to gather mushrooms. 10. to have or assume the shape of a mushroom. [1350–1400; alter. (by folk etym.) of ME *muscheron, musseroun* < MF *mousseron* << LL *mussiriōn-,* s. of *mussiriō*] —**mush′room·like′,** *adj.* —**mush′room·y,** *adj.*

mush′room an′chor, *Naut.* a stockless anchor having a bowlike head, used chiefly for semipermanent moorings. See illus. under **anchor.** [1835–45]

mush′room cloud′, mushroom (def. 4). [1940–45]

mush′room slab′ construc′tion, beamless rein-

CONCISE PRONUNCIATION KEY: *act, cāpe, dâre, pärt; set, ēqual; if, īce; ox, ōver, ôrder, oil, bo͝ok, bo͞ot, out; up, ûrge; child; sing; shoe; thin, that;* zh as in *treasure.* ə = *a* as in *alone, e* as in *system, i* as in *easily, o* as in *gallop, u* as in *circus;* ə as in *fire* (fīər), *hour* (ouər). l and n can serve as syllabic consonants, as in *cradle* (krād′l), and *button* (but′n). See the full key inside the front cover.

forced-concrete floor and roof construction employing columns with widely flaring heads having horizontal rings of reinforcement to support the floor or roof slab. [1960–65]

mush′room ven′tilator, a ventilator having at the top of a vertical shaft a broad rounded cap that can be screwed down to close it.

mush·y (mush′ē, mo͝osh′ē), *adj.,* **mush·i·er, mush·i·est.** **1.** resembling mush; pulpy. **2.** *Informal.* overly emotional or sentimental: *mushy love letters.* [1830–40; MUSH[1] + -Y[1]] —**mush′i·ly,** *adv.* —**mush′i·ness,** *n.*

mush·y·head·ed (mush′ē hed′id, mo͝osh′-), *adj. Informal.* **1.** inadequately thought out: *mushyheaded ideas.* **2.** having vague, unsubstantiated, or unrealistic ideas or opinions: *a mushyheaded idealist.* [MUSHY + HEADED]

Mu·si·al (myo͞o′zē əl, -zhē əl, -zhəl), *n.* **Stanley Frank** (*"Stan the Man"*), born 1920, U.S. baseball player.

mu·sic (myo͞o′zik), *n.* **1.** an art of sound in time that expresses ideas and emotions in significant forms through the elements of rhythm, melody, harmony, and color. **2.** the tones or sounds employed, occurring in single line (melody) or multiple lines (harmony), and sounded or to be sounded by one or more voices or instruments, or both. **3.** musical work or compositions for singing or playing. **4.** the written or printed score of a musical composition. **5.** such scores collectively. **6.** any sweet, pleasing, or harmonious sounds or sound: *the music of the waves.* **7.** appreciation of or responsiveness to musical sounds or harmonies: *Music was in his very soul.* **8.** *Fox Hunting.* the cry of the hounds. **9. face the music,** to meet, take, or accept the consequences of one's mistakes, actions, etc.: *He's squandered his money and now he's got to face the music.* [1200–50; ME *musike* < L *mūsica* < Gk *mousikḗ* (*téchnē*) (the art) of the Muse, fem. of *mousikós,* equiv. to *Moûs*(*a*) MUSE + *-ikos* -IC] —**mu′sic·less,** *adj.*

mu·si·ca fic·ta (myo͞o′zi kə fik′tə; *Lat.* mo͞o′si kä′ fik′tä), the use of chromatically altered tones in the contrapuntal music of the 10th to the 16th centuries. Also, **mu′si·ca fal′sa** (myo͞o′zi kə fôl′sə; *Lat.* mo͞o′si-kä′ fäl′sä). [1795–1805; < ML *mūsica ficta,* lit., fashioned music]

mu·si·cal (myo͞o′zi kəl), *adj.* **1.** of, pertaining to, or producing music: *a musical instrument.* **2.** of the nature of or resembling music; melodious; harmonious. **3.** fond of or skilled in music. **4.** set to or accompanied by music: *a musical entertainment.* —*n.* **5.** Also called **musical comedy.** a play or motion picture in which the story line is interspersed with or developed by songs, dances, and the like. [1375–1425; late ME < ML *mūsicālis.* See MUSIC, -AL[1]] —**mu′si·cal·ly,** *adv.* —**mu′si·cal′i·ty, mu′si·cal·ness,** *n.*
—**Syn. 1.** tuneful, dulcet, sweet, lyric.

mu′sical box′, *Chiefly Brit.* See **music box.** [1820–30]

mu′sical chairs′, 1. Also called **going to Jerusalem.** a game in which players march to music around two rows of chairs placed back to back, there being one chair less than the number of players, the object being to find a seat when the music stops abruptly. The player failing to do so is removed from the game, together with one chair, at each interval. **2.** *Informal.* a situation or series of events in which jobs, decisions, prospects, etc., are changed with confusing rapidity. [1875–80]

mu′sical com′edy, musical (def. 5). [1755–65]

mu·si·cale (myo͞o′zi kal′), *n.* a music program forming the main part of a social occasion. [1840–50, *Amer.*; < F, short for *soirée musicale* musical evening]

mu′sical glass′es, a set of drinking glasses filled with varying amounts of water to produce ringing tones of different pitches when the player's finger is rubbed around the wet rims. Cf. **glass harmonica.** [1760–70]

mu·si·cal·ize (myo͞o′zi kə līz′), *v.t.,* **-ized, -iz·ing.** to write or produce a musical version of (a book, play, etc.): *an attempt to musicalize one of Shakespeare's comedies.* Also, *esp. Brit.,* **mu′si·cal·ise′.** [1915–20; MUSICAL + -IZE] —**mu′si·cal·i·za′tion,** *n.*

mu′sical saw′, a handsaw played as a musical instrument with a violin bow or a hammer while the saw is bent with varying tension to change the pitch. [1925–30]

mu′sic box′, a box or case containing an apparatus for producing music mechanically, as by means of a comblike steel plate with tuned teeth sounded by small pegs or pins in the surface of a revolving cylinder or disk. Also, *esp. Brit.,* **musical box.** [1765–75]

mu′sic dra′ma, an opera having more or less continuous musical and dramatic activity without arias, recitatives, or ensembles. Cf. **number opera.** [1875–80]

mu′sic hall′, 1. an auditorium for concerts and musical entertainments. **2.** a vaudeville or variety theater. [1835–45]

mu·si·cian (myo͞o zish′ən), *n.* **1.** a person who makes music a profession, esp. as a performer of music. **2.** any person, whether professional or not, skilled in music. [1350–1400; ME *musicien* < MF. See MUSIC, -IAN] —**mu·si′cian·ly,** *adj.*

mu·si·cian·ship (myo͞o zish′ən ship′), *n.* knowledge, skill, and artistic sensitivity in performing music. [1865–70; MUSICIAN + -SHIP]

mu′sic of the spheres′, a music, imperceptible to human ears, formerly supposed to be produced by the movements of the spheres or heavenly bodies. [1600–10]

mu·si·col·o·gy (myo͞o′zi kol′ə jē), *n.* the scholarly or scientific study of music, as in historical research, musical theory, or the physical nature of sound. [1905–10; MUSIC + -O- + -LOGY] —**mu·si·co·log·i·cal** (myo͞o′zi-kə loj′i kəl), *adj.* —**mu′si·co·log′i·cal·ly,** *adv.* —**mu′si·col′o·gist,** *n.*

mu′sic roll′, a roll of perforated paper for actuating a player piano. [1905–10]

mu′sic stand′, a pedestal or rack designed to hold a score or sheet of music in position for reading. [1755–65]

mu′sic vid′eo, a commercial videotape featuring a performance of a popular song, often through a stylized dramatization by the performers with lip-synching and special effects. Also called **video, video record.**

Mu·si·gny (mo͞o zēn yē′; *Fr.* my zē nyē′), *n.* a dry, red wine of the Burgundy region in France.

Mu·sil (mo͞o′sil, -zil), *n.* **Robert,** 1880–1942, Austrian writer.

mus·ing (myo͞o′zing), *adj.* **1.** absorbed in thought; meditative. —*n.* **2.** contemplation; reflection. [1350–1400; ME; see MUSE, -ING[2], -ING[1]] —**mus′ing·ly,** *adv.*

mu·sique con·crète (my zēk kôN kret′), *French.* tape-recorded musical and natural sounds, often electronically distorted, arranged in planned combinations, sequences, and rhythmic patterns to create an artistic work. Cf. **electronic music.** [lit., concrete music]

mus·jid (mus′jid), *n. Arabic.* masjid.

musk (musk), *n.* **1.** a substance secreted in a glandular sac under the skin of the abdomen of the male musk deer, having a strong odor, and used in perfumery. **2.** an artificial imitation of the substance. **3.** a similar secretion of other animals, as the civet, muskrat, and otter. **4.** the odor of musk or some similar odor. **5.** *Bot.* any of several plants, as the monkey flower, having a musky fragrance. [1350–1400; ME *musk*(*e*) (< MF *musc*) < LL *muscus* (ML *moschus*) < LGk *móskos, móschos* < Pers *mushk*]

mus·kal·longe (mus′kə lonj′), *n., pl.* **-longe.** muskellunge.

musk′ bag′, the musk-secreting gland of a male musk deer. Also called **musk gland.** [1675–85]

musk′ deer′, a small, hornless deer, *Moschus moschiferus,* of central Asia, the male of which secretes musk: now rare. [1675–85]

musk′ duck′, 1. See **Muscovy duck. 2.** an Australian duck, *Biziura lobata,* having a musky odor. [1765–75]

mus·keg (mus′keg), *n.* a bog of northern North America, commonly having sphagnum mosses, sedge, and sometimes stunted black spruce and tamarack trees. [1765–75; < Cree *maske·k* < Proto-Algonquian **maš-kye·kwi* swamp]

Mus·ke·go (mus kē′gō), *n.* a city in SE Wisconsin. 15,277.

Mus·ke·gon (mus kē′gən), *n.* a port in W Michigan, on Lake Michigan. 40,823.

Muske′gon Heights′, a city in W Michigan, on Lake Michigan. 14,611.

mus·kel·lunge (mus′kə lunj′), *n., pl.* **-lung·es,** (*esp. collectively*) **-lunge.** a large game fish, *Esox masquinongy,* of the pike family, found in the lakes and rivers of eastern and middle western North America. Also, **maskalonge, maskinonge, muskallonge.** [1780–90, *Amer.*; earlier *muskinunge, masquenongez* (F sp.), etc., < CanF *maskinongé* < Ojibwa *ma·skino·še·, ma·škino·še·* (equiv. to Proto-Algonquian **mya·ši* similar to, kind of + **kenwešye·wa* northern pike)]

mus·ket (mus′kit), *n.* **1.** a heavy, large-caliber smoothbore gun for infantry soldiers, introduced in the 16th century: the predecessor of the modern rifle. **2.** the male sparrow hawk, *Accipiter nisus.* [1580–90; < MF *mousquet* < It *moschetto* crossbow arrow, later musket, orig. kind of hawk, equiv. to *mosch*(*a*) fly (< L *musca*) + *-etto* -ET]

mus·ket·eer (mus′ki tēr′), *n.* a soldier armed with a musket. [1580–90; MUSKET + -EER; cf. F *mousquetaire,* equiv. to *mousquet* musket + *-aire* -ARY]

mus·ket·ry (mus′ki trē), *n.* **1.** *Mil.* the technique of bringing fire from a group of rifle and automatic weapons to bear on specified targets. **2.** muskets collectively. **3.** musketeers collectively. [1640–50; < F *mousqueterie.* See MUSKET, -RY]

musk′ flow′er. See **musk plant.**

musk′ gland′. See **musk bag.**

musk′ hog′, the collared peccary. See under **peccary.** [1765–75]

mus·kie (mus′kē), *n.* muskellunge. [1890–95; MUSK(ELLUNGE) + -IE]

Mus·kie (mus′kē), *n.* **Edmund (Sixtus),** born 1914, U.S. politician: senator 1959–80; Secretary of State 1980–81.

musk′ mal′low, 1. Also called **musk rose.** a European mallow, *Malva moschata,* introduced into North America, having musk-scented white or lavender flowers. **2.** abelmosk. [1775–85]

musk·mel·on (musk′mel′ən), *n.* **1.** a round or oblong melon, occurring in many varieties, having a juicy, often aromatic, sweet, yellow, white, or green, edible flesh. **2.** the plant, *Cucumis melo reticulatus,* of the gourd family, bearing this fruit. **3.** cantaloupe (def. 1). Also, **mushmelon.** [1565–75; MUSK + MELON]

Mus·ko·ge·an (mus kō′gē ən), *n.* a family of American Indian languages of the southeastern U.S., including Choctaw, Chickasaw, Creek, and several less well-known languages. Also, **Mus·kho′ge·an.**

Mus·ko·gee (mus kō′gē), *n., pl.* **-gees,** (*esp. collectively*) **-gee** for 2. **1.** a city in E Oklahoma. 40,011. **2.** a member of an American Indian people formerly constituting part of the Creek Confederacy in Georgia and Alabama and now living in Oklahoma. **3.** Creek (def. 2).

mus·kone (mus′kōn), *n. Chem.* muscone.

musk·ox (musk′oks′), *n., pl.* **-ox·en** (-ok′sən). a bovine ruminant, *Ovibos moschatus,* of arctic regions of North America and Greenland, that is between an ox and a sheep in size and anatomy. Also, **musk′ ox′.** [1735–45; MUSK + OX, so called from its odor]

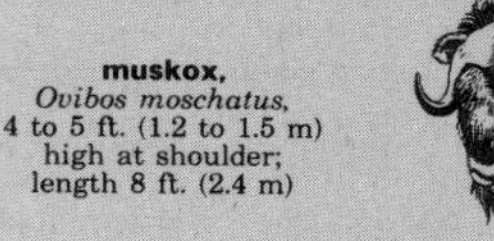

muskox,
Ovibos moschatus,
4 to 5 ft. (1.2 to 1.5 m)
high at shoulder;
length 8 ft. (2.4 m)

musk′ plant′, a sticky-hairy plant, *Mimulus moschata,* of the figwort family, native to northern and western North America, having pale-yellow flowers and a musky odor. Also called **musk flower.** [1775–85]

musk·rat (musk′rat′), *n., pl.* **-rats,** (*esp. collectively*) **-rat. 1.** a large, aquatic, North American rodent, *Ondatra zibethica,* having a musky odor. **2.** its thick, light-brown fur, used for coats, for hats, as a trimming, etc. [1680–90, *Amer.*; alter., by folk etym., of MUSQUASH]

muskrat,
Ondatra zibethica,
head and body
1 ft. (0.3 m);
tail to 11 in.
(28 cm)

musk′ rose′, 1. a rose, *Rosa moschata,* of the Mediterranean region, having white, musk-scented flowers. **2.** See **musk mallow** (def. 1). [1570–80]

musk′ this′tle, a composite plant, *Carduus nutans,* having heads of nodding, rose-purple flowers, introduced into the U.S. from Eurasia. [1725–35]

musk′ tur′tle, any of several aquatic turtles of the genus *Sternotherus,* of North America, which, when disturbed, emit a musky secretion. [1865–70, *Amer.*; so called from its musky smell]

musk·y[1] (mus′kē), *adj.,* **musk·i·er, musk·i·est.** of or like musk, as an odor: *a musky perfume.* [1600–10; MUSK + -Y[1]] —**musk′i·ness,** *n.*

mus·ky[2] (mus′kē), *n., pl.* **-kies.** muskellunge. [MUSK(ELLUNGE) + -Y[2]]

Mus·lem (muz′ləm, mo͝oz′-, mo͝os′-), *adj., n., pl.* **-lems, -lem.** Muslim.

Mus·lim (muz′lim, mo͝oz′-, mo͝os′-), *adj., n., pl.* **-lims, -lim.** —*adj.* **1.** of or pertaining to the religion, law, or civilization of Islam. —*n.* **2.** an adherent of Islam. **3.** See **Black Muslim.** Also, **Moslem, Muslem** (for defs. 1, 2). [< Ar, lit., a person who submits. See ISLAM]

Mus′lim Broth′ers, Soci′ety of the, an organization founded in Egypt in 1928 by Hasan al-Banna (1906–49), calling for a return to rigid orthodoxy, the overthrow of secular governments, and a restoration of the theocratic state. Also called **Mus′lim Broth′erhood.** [trans. of Ar *al-ilchwān al-muslimūn*]

Mus′lim cal′endar, the lunar calendar used by Muslims and reckoned from A.D. 622: the calendar year consists of 354 days and contains 12 months: Moharram, Safar, Rabi I, Rabi II, Jumada I, Jumada II, Rajab, Shaban, Ramadan, Shawwal, Dhu 'l-Qa'da, and Dhu 'l-hijjah. In leap years the month Dhu 'l-hijjah contains one extra day. Also called **Islamic calendar.** See table under **calendar.**

Mus′lim E′ra, the period since the flight of Muhammad from Mecca in A.D. 622; Hijra.

mus·lin (muz′lin), *n.* a cotton fabric made in various degrees of fineness and often printed, woven, or embroidered in patterns, esp. a cotton fabric of plain weave, used for sheets and for a variety of other purposes. [1600–10; < F *mousseline* < It *mussolina,* equiv. to *Mussol*(*o*) Mosul, Iraq (where first made) + *-ina* -INE[1]]

mus′lin delaine′. See **mousseline de laine.** [1835–45]

mus′lin kail′, *Scot.* barley broth or barley and vegetable soup. [1775–85; MUSLIN (perh. in the sense "thin")]

Mus.M., Master of Music. [< L *Mūsicae Magister*]

mus·nud (mus′nəd), *n.* (in India) a seat or throne of cushions used by native princes. [1755–65; < Urdu < Ar *masnad* cushion]

mus·quash (mus′kwosh), *n. Chiefly Brit.* the fur of the muskrat. [1770–80, *Amer.*; < Massachusett cognate of Western Abenaki *mòskwas* (perh. equiv. to Proto-Algonquian **mo·šk-* bobbing above the surface of the water + **-exkwe·* head + derivational elements, i.e., the one whose head bobs above the water)]

mus′quash root′. See **spotted cowbane.** [1605–15, *Amer.*]

muss (mus), *n.* **1.** a state of disorder or untidiness. —*v.t.* **2.** to put into disorder; make messy; rumple (often fol. by *up*). [1820–30; perh. b. MESS and FUSS]
—**Syn. 2.** mess, disturb, tangle, bedraggle.

mus·sa·ka (mo͞o sä′kə, mo͞o′sä kä′), *n. Greek Cookery.* moussaka.

mus·sel (mus′əl), *n.* any bivalve mollusk, esp. an edible marine bivalve of the family Mytilidae and a freshwater clam of the family Unionidae. See illus. on next page. [bef. 1000; ME, OE *muscle* < VL **mūscula,* var. of L *mūsculus* little mouse, sea mussel. See MUSCLE]

CONCISE ETYMOLOGY KEY: <, descended or borrowed from; >, whence; b., blend of, blended; c., cognate with; cf., compare; deriv., derivative; equiv., equivalent; imit., imitative; obl., oblique; r., replacing; s., stem; sp., spelling, spelled; resp., respelling, respelled; trans., translation; ?, origin unknown; *, unattested; ‡, probably earlier than. See the full key inside the front cover.

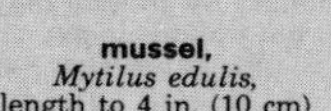

mussel,
Mytilus edulis,
length to 4 in. (10 cm)

mus′sel crab′, a pea crab, *Pinnotheres maculatus,* the female of which lives as a commensal within the mantle cavity of mussels. [1890–95]

mus′sel shrimp′. See **seed shrimp.**

Mus·set (MY sā′), *n.* **(Louis Charles) Al·fred de** (lwē SHARL AL FRED′ də), 1810–57, French poet, dramatist, and novelist.

mus·si·tate (mus′i tāt′), *v.i.,* **-tat·ed, -tat·ing.** *Obs.* to mutter; mumble. [1620–30; < L *mussitātus* (ptp. of *mussitāre* to mutter), equiv. to *muss(āre)* to mutter + *-it-* freq. suffix + *-ātus* -ATE[1]]

mus·si·ta·tion (mus′i tā′shən), *—n.* **1.** silent movement of the lips in simulation of the movements made in audible speech. **2.** muttering; mumbling; murmuring. [1640–50; < LL *mussitātiōn-* (s. of *mussitātiō*). See MUSSITATE, -ION]

Mus·so·li·ni (mo͞os′ə lē′nē, mo͞o′sə-; *It.* mo͞os′sô lē′nē), *n.* **Be·ni·to** (bə nē′tō; *It.* be nē′tô), ("*Il Duce*"), 1883–1945, Italian Fascist leader: premier of Italy 1922–43.

Mus·sorg·sky (mo͞o sôrg′skē, -zôrg′-; *Russ.* mo͞o′-sərg skyē), *n.* **Mo·dest Pe·tro·vich** (mō dest′ pi trô′-vich; *Russ.* mu dyest′ pyi TRÔ′vyich). See **Moussorgsky, Modest Petrovich.** Also, **Mus·sorg′ski.**

Mus·sul·man (mus′əl mən), *n., pl.* **-mans.** a Muslim. [1555–65; < Pers *Musulmān* (pl.) < Ar *Muslimūn,* pl. of *Muslim* MUSLIM]

muss·y (mus′ē), *adj.,* **muss·i·er, muss·i·est.** untidy, messy, or rumpled. [1855–60, *Amer.;* MUSS + -Y[1]] **—muss′i·ly,** *adv.* **—muss′i·ness,** *n.*

must[1] (must), *auxiliary verb.* **1.** to be obliged or bound to by an imperative requirement: *I must keep my word.* **2.** to be under the necessity to; need to: *Animals must eat to live.* **3.** to be required or compelled to, as by the use or threat of force: *You must obey the law.* **4.** to be compelled to in order to fulfill some need or achieve an aim: *We must hurry if we're to arrive on time.* **5.** to be forced to, as by convention or the requirements of honesty: *I must say, that is a lovely hat.* **6.** to be or feel urged to; ought to: *I must buy that book.* **7.** to be reasonably expected to; is bound to: *It must have stopped raining by now. She must be at least 60.* **8.** to be inevitably certain to; be compelled by nature: *Everyone must die.* *—v.i.* **9.** to be obliged; be compelled: *Do I have to go? I must, I suppose.* **10.** *Archaic.* (sometimes used with ellipsis of *go, get,* or some similar verb readily understood from the context): *We must away.* *—adj.* **11.** necessary; vital: *A raincoat is must clothing in this area.* *—n.* **12.** something necessary, vital, or required: *This law is a must.* [bef. 900; ME *most(e),* OE *mōste* (past tense); c. G *musste.* See MOTE[2]]
—Syn. 1. MUST, OUGHT, SHOULD express necessity or duty. MUST expresses necessity or compulsion: *I must attend to those patients first. Soldiers must obey orders.* OUGHT (weaker than MUST) expresses obligation, duty, desirability: *You ought to tell your mother.* SHOULD expresses obligation, expectation, or probability: *You are not behaving as you should. Children should be taught to speak the truth. They should arrive at one o'clock.*

must[2] (must), *n.* new wine; the unfermented juice as pressed from the grape or other fruit. [bef. 900; ME, OE < L *mustum,* short for *vīnum mustum* new wine]

must[3] (must), *n.* mold; moldiness; mustiness: *a castle harboring the must of centuries.* [1595–1605; back formation from MUSTY[1]]

must[4] (must), *n.* musth.

must[5] (must), *Obs.* *—n.* **1.** musk, esp. a powder made from musk. *—v.t.* **2.** to powder (the hair). [1480–90; earlier *moist* < MF *must,* var. of *musc* MUSK]

mus·tache (mus′tash, mə stash′), *n.* **1.** the hair growing on the upper lip **2.** such hair on men, allowed to grow without shaving, and often trimmed in any of various shapes. **3.** hairs or bristles growing near the mouth of an animal. **4.** a stripe of color, or elongated feathers, suggestive of a mustache on the side of the head of a bird. **5.** something resembling a mustache, as food or drink adhering to the upper lip: *a mustache of milk.* Also, **moustache.** [1575–85; < MF *moustache* < It *mostaccio;* see MUSTACHIO] **—mus′tached,** *adj.*

mus′tache cup′, a cup having a straight piece inside, just below the rim, for holding back a man's mustache while he is drinking. [1885–90]

mus·ta·chio (mə stä′shō, -shē ō′, -stash′ō, -stash′ē-ō′), *n., pl.* **-chios.** a mustache. [1545–55; < Sp *mostacho* and its source, It *mostaccio,* var. of *mostacchio* < MGk *moustáki,* Doric Gk *mýstax,* s. *mystak-* upper lip, mustache] **—mus·ta′chioed,** *adj.*

Mus·ta·fa Ke·mal (mo͞os′tä fä kə mäl′). See **Kemal Atatürk.**

Mus·tagh (mo͞os täKH′), *n.* Karakoram (def. 1).

mus·tang (mus′tang), *n.* **1.** a small, hardy horse of the American plains, descended from Spanish stock. **2.** *U.S. Navy Slang.* a naval officer who received his commission while still an enlisted man. *—v.i.* **3.** to round up wild horses, esp. in order to sell them illegally to slaughterhouses. [1800–10, *Amer.;* < Sp *mestengo* stray or ownerless beast, n. use of masc. adj.: pertaining to a mixed lot of beasts, equiv. to *mest(a)* such a mixed lot (< L (*animālia*) *mixta* mixed (beasts), neut. pl. adj., taken as fem. sing. noun; see MIXED) + *-engo* adj. suffix]

mus·tang·er (mus′tang ər), *n.* a person who engages in mustanging. [1845–50; *Amer.;* MUSTANG + -ER[1]]

mus·tard (mus′tərd), *n.* **1.** a pungent powder or paste prepared from the seed of the mustard plant, used as a food seasoning or condiment, and medicinally in plasters, poultices, etc. **2.** any of various acrid or pungent plants, esp. of the genus *Brassica,* as *B. juncea* **(leaf mustard),** the leaves of which are used for food and is the chief source of commercial mustard, and *Sinapis alba* **(white mustard).** Cf. **mustard family. 3.** See **nitrogen mustard. 4. cut the mustard,** *Slang.* to reach or surpass the desired standard of performance: *a pitcher who cuts the mustard with his fastball.* [1300–50; ME < OF *moustarde* a relish orig. made of mustard seed and must, equiv. to *moust* MUST[2] + *-arde* -ARD]

mus′tard fam′ily, the plant family Cruciferae (or Brassicaceae), characterized by herbaceous plants having alternate leaves, acrid or pungent juice, clusters of four-petaled flowers, and fruit in the form of a two-parted capsule, and including broccoli, cabbage, candytuft, cauliflower, cress, mustard, radish, sweet alyssum, turnip, and wallflower.

mus′tard gas′, an oily liquid, $C_4H_8Cl_2S$, used as a chemical-warfare gas, blistering the skin and damaging the lungs, often causing blindness and death: introduced by the Germans in World War I. Also called **dichlorodiethyl sulfide.** [1915–20; so called from its mustard-like odor]

mus′tard oil′, oil expressed from the seed of mustard, used chiefly in making soap. [1840–50]

mus′tard plas′ter, a black mixture of mustard and rubber placed on a cloth and applied to the skin as a counterirritant. [1855–60]

mus·tee (mu stē′, mus′tē), *n.* **1.** the offspring of a white person and a quadroon; octoroon. **2.** a half-breed. [1690–1700; short var. of MESTIZO]

mus·te·lid (mus′tl id), *n.* **1.** any of numerous carnivorous mammals of the family Mustelidae, comprising the weasels, martens, skunks, badgers, and otters. *—adj.* **2.** belonging or pertaining to the family Mustelidae. [1905–10; < NL *Mustelidae* family name, equiv. to *Mustel(a)* a genus (L *mustēla* weasel) + *-idae* -ID[2]]

mus·te·line (mus′tl īn′, -in), *adj.* **1.** belonging or pertaining to the family Mustelidae, including the martens, skunks, minks, weasels, badgers, and otters. **2.** resembling a weasel. **3.** tawny or brown, like a weasel in summer. [1650–60; < L *mustēlinus,* equiv. to *mustēl(a)* weasel + *-inus* -INE[1]]

mus·ter (mus′tər), *v.t.* **1.** to assemble (troops, a ship's crew, etc.), as for battle, display, inspection, orders, or discharge. **2.** to gather, summon, rouse (often fol. by *up*): *He mustered all his courage.* *—v.i.* **3.** to assemble for inspection, service, etc., as troops or forces. **4.** to come together; collect; assemble; gather. **5. muster in,** to enlist into service in the armed forces. **6. muster out,** to discharge from service in the armed forces: *He will be mustered out of the army in only two more months.* *—n.* **7.** an assembling of troops or persons for formal inspection or other purposes. **8.** an assemblage or collection. **9.** the act of mustering. **10.** Also called **mus′ter roll′.** (formerly) a list of the persons enrolled in a military or naval unit. **11. pass muster, a.** to pass a cursory inspection. **b.** to measure up to a certain standard; be adequate: *Your grades don't pass muster.* [1250–1300; ME *mostren* (v.) < OF *mostrer* < L *mōnstrāre* to show, deriv. of *mōnstrum* portent; see MONSTER]
—Syn. 1. convoke. See **gather. 1, 4.** convene; congregate. **7.** gathering, assembly, convention. **—Ant. 1, 4.** scatter, separate.

Mus′ter Day′, *U.S. Hist.* the annual day for enrollment in the militia of all able men aged 18 to 45, according to a law established in 1792 and in effect until after the Civil War.

musth (must), *n.* a state or condition of violent, destructive frenzy occurring with the rutting season in male elephants, accompanied by the exudation of an oily substance from glands between the eyes and mouth. Also, **must.** [1870–75; < Urdu *mast* < Pers: lit., drunk]

must·n't (mus′ənt), contraction of *must not.*
—Usage. See **contraction.**

must-see (must′sē′), *n. Informal.* something, as a remarkable sight or entertainment, that should be seen or attended: *The new play is a must-see.*

mus·ty[1] (mus′tē), *adj.,* **-ti·er, -ti·est. 1.** having an odor or flavor suggestive of mold, as old buildings, long-closed rooms, or stale food. **2.** obsolete; outdated; antiquated: *musty laws.* **3.** dull; apathetic. [1520–30; perh. var. of *moisty* (ME; see MOIST, -Y[1]) with loss of *i* before *s* as in *master*] **—mus′ti·ly,** *adv.* **—mus′ti·ness,** *n.*
—Syn. 1. dank, moldy, stale.

mus·ty[2] (mus′tē), *n., pl.* **-ties.** (formerly) a kind of snuff having a musty flavor. [1700–10; n. use of MUSTY[1]]

mut[1] (mut), *n.* mutt.

mut[2] (mut), *n. Print.* mutton[2]. [by shortening]

mut., 1. mutilated. **2.** mutual.

mu·ta·ble (myo͞o′tə bəl), *adj.* **1.** liable or subject to change or alteration. **2.** given to changing; constantly changing; fickle or inconstant: *the mutable ways of fortune.* [1350–1400; ME < L *mūtābilis,* equiv. to *mūtā(re)* to change + *-bilis* -BLE] **—mu′ta·bil′i·ty, mu′ta·ble·ness,** *n.* **—mu′ta·bly,** *adv.*
—Syn. 1. changeable, variable. **2.** unstable, vacillating, unsettled, wavering, unsteady. **—Ant. 2.** stable.

mu′table sign′, any of the four astrological signs, Gemini, Virgo, Sagittarius, or Pisces, that are grouped together because of their placement at the end of the seasons and characterized by the attribute of adaptability to circumstances. Cf. **quadruplicity.**

mu·ta·gen (myo͞o′tə jən, -jen′), *n.* a substance or preparation capable of inducing mutation. [1945–50; MUTA(TION) + -GEN]

mu·ta·gen·e·sis (myo͞o′tə jen′ə sis), *n.* the origin and development of a mutation. [1950–55; < NL; see MUTATION, -GENESIS] **—mu·ta·ge·net·ic** (myo͞o′tə jə-net′ik), *adj.*

mu·ta·gen·ic (myo͞o′tə jen′ik), *adj. Genetics.* capable of inducing mutation or increasing its rate. [1945–50; MUTA(TION) + -GENIC] **—mu′ta·gen′i·cal·ly,** *adv.* **—mu·ta·ge·nic·i·ty** (myo͞o′tə jə nis′i tē), *n.*

mu·tant (myo͞ot′nt), *adj.* **1.** undergoing or resulting from mutation. *—n.* **2.** a new type of organism produced as the result of mutation. [1900–05; < L *mūtant-* (s. of *mūtāns*), prp. of *mūtāre* to change; see -ANT]

Mu·ta·re (mo͞o tär′ē, -tär′ä), *n.* a city in E Zimbabwe. 62,000. Formerly, **Umtali.**

mu·ta·ro·ta·tion (myo͞o′tə rō tā′shən), *n. Chem.* a gradual change in the optical rotation of freshly prepared solutions of reducing sugars. [1895–1900; < L *mūtā(re)* to change + ROTATION]

mu·tate (myo͞o′tāt), *v.,* **-tat·ed, -tat·ing.** *—v.t.* **1.** to change; alter. **2.** *Phonet.* to change by umlaut. *—v.i.* **3.** to change; undergo mutation. [1810–20; < L *mūtātus,* ptp. of *mūtāre* to change; see -ATE[1]] **—mu·ta·tive** (myo͞o′tə tiv), *adj.*

mu·ta·tion (myo͞o tā′shən), *n.* **1.** *Biol.* **a.** a sudden departure from the parent type in one or more heritable characteristics, caused by a change in a gene or a chromosome. **b.** an individual, species, or the like, resulting from such a departure. **2.** the act or process of changing. **3.** a change or alteration, as in form or nature. **4.** *Phonet.* umlaut. **5.** *Ling.* (in Celtic languages) syntactically determined morphophonemic phenomena that affect initial sounds of words. [1325–75; ME *mutacio(u)n* < L *mūtātiōn-* (s. of *mūtātiō*) a changing. See MUTATE, -ION] **—mu·ta′tion·al,** *adj.* **—mu·ta′tion·al·ly,** *adv.*

mu·ta·tis mu·tan·dis (mo͞o tä′tēs mo͞o tän′dēs; *Eng.* myo͞o tā′tis myo͞o tan′dis), *Latin.* the necessary changes having been made.

mu·ta·to no·mi·ne (mo͞o tä′tō nō′mi ne; *Eng.* myo͞o-tā′tō nom′ə nē), *Latin.* the name having been changed.

Mu·ta·zi·la (mo͞o tä′zə lə), *n.* See under **Mutazilite.**

Mu·ta·zi·lite (mo͞o tä′zə līt′), *n. Islam.* a member of a medieval theological sect **(Mutazila)** that maintained that nothing but eternity could be asserted regarding Allah, that the eternal nature of the Koran was questionable, and that humans have free will. [1720–30; < Ar *mu'tazil(ah)* + -ITE[1]] **—Mu·ta′zi·lism,** *n.*

mutch (much), *n. Brit. Dial.* a close-fitting linen or muslin cap, as worn by elderly women or babies. [1425–75; late ME (dial.) *much* < MD *mutse;* c. G *Mütze* cap. See AMICE[2]]

mutch·kin (much′kin), *n.* **1.** *Scot.* a unit of liquid measure equal to a little less than a U.S. liquid pint. **2.** a container, usually of pewter, holding this quantity. [1375–1425; late ME (Scots) *muchekyn* < MD *mudseken,* equiv. to *mudse* (dim. of *mudde* << L *modius* measure of grain) + *-ken* -KIN]

mut′ dash′, *Print.* a dash equal in length to one side of an em quad; em dash.

mute (myo͞ot), *adj.,* **mut·er, mut·est,** *n., v.,* **mut·ed, mut·ing.** *—adj.* **1.** silent; refraining from speech or utterance. **2.** not emitting or having sound of any kind. **3.** incapable of speech; dumb. **4.** (of letters) silent; not pronounced. **5.** *Law.* (of a person who has been arraigned) making no plea or giving an irrelevant response when arraigned, or refusing to stand trial (used chiefly in the phrase *to stand mute*). **6.** *Fox Hunting.* (of a hound) hunting a line without giving tongue or cry. *—n.* **7.** a person incapable of speech. **8.** an actor whose part is confined to dumb show. **9.** *Law.* a person who stands mute when arraigned. **10.** Also called **sordino.** a mechanical device of various shapes and materials for muffling the tone of a musical instrument. **11.** *Phonet.* a stop. **12.** *Brit. Obs.* a hired mourner at a funeral; a professional mourner. *—v.t.* **13.** to deaden or muffle the sound of. **14.** to reduce the intensity of (a color) by the addition of another color. [1325–75; < L *mūtus* dumb; r. ME *muet* < MF, equiv. to OF *mu* (< L *mūtus*) + unexplained suffix *-et;* cf. -ET] **—mute′ly,** *adv.* **—mute′ness,** *n.*
—Syn. 3. still. See **dumb. —Ant. 1.** talkative.

mut·ed (myo͞o′tid), *adj.* of low intensity and reduced volume; softened: *She spoke in muted tones.* [1860–65; MUTE + -ED[2]] **—mut′ed·ly,** *adv.*

mu·tein (myo͞o′tēn, -tē in), *n. Biochem.* a mutationally altered protein. [appar. MUT(ATION) + (PROT)EIN]

mute′ swan′, a commonly domesticated soundless white swan, *Cygnus olor,* of Europe and Asia. See illus. under **swan.** [1775–85]

mu·ti·cous (myo͞o′ti kəs), *adj.* **1.** *Bot.* having no pointed process or awn; awnless. **2.** Also, **mu·tic** (myo͞o′tik). *Zool.* lacking certain defensive structures, as spines or claws. Also, **mu·ti·cate** (myo͞o′tə kāt′, -kit). [1855–60; < L *muticus* curtailed; cf. MUTILATE]

mu·ti·late (myo͞ot′l āt′), *v.t.,* **-lat·ed, -lat·ing. 1.** to injure, disfigure, or make imperfect by removing or irreparably damaging parts: *Vandals mutilated the painting.* **2.** to deprive (a person or animal) of a limb or other essential part. [1525–35; < L *mutilātus* (ptp. of *mutilāre* to cut off, maim), equiv. to *mutil(us)* maimed, mutilated + *-ātus* -ATE[1]] **—mu′ti·la′tion,** *n.* **—mu′ti·la′tive, mu·ti·la·to·ry** (myo͞ot′l ə tôr′ē, -tōr′ē), *adj.* **—mu′ti·la′tor,** *n.*
—Syn. 1. damage, mar, cripple. **2.** See **maim.**

mu·ti·neer (myo͞ot′n ēr′), *n.* a person who mutinies. [1600–10; < MF *mutinier,* equiv. to *mutin* mutiny, mutinous (*meut(e)* mutiny < VL **movita,* fem. of **movitus,* var. of L *mōtus,* ptp. of *movēre* to MOVE + *-in* -INE[1]) + *-ier* -IER[2]; see -EER]

mu·ti·nous (myo͞ot′n əs), *adj.* **1.** disposed to, engaged in, or involving revolt against authority. **2.** characterized by mutiny; rebellious. **3.** difficult to control: *mutinous feelings.* [1570–80; obs. *mutine* mutiny (< MF *mutin;* see MUTINEER) + -OUS] **—mu′ti·nous·ly,** *adv.* **—mu′ti·nous·ness,** *n.*
—Syn. 1. seditious, insurrectionary, revolutionary, insurgent. **2.** refractory, insubordinate, riotous, disaffected. **—Ant. 1.** patriotic. **2.** obedient.

mu·ti·ny (myo͞ot′n ē), *n., pl.* **-nies,** *v.,* **-nied, -ny·ing.** **—***n.* **1.** revolt or rebellion against constituted authority, esp. by sailors against their officers. **2.** rebellion against any authority. **—***v.i.* **3.** to commit the offense of mutiny; revolt against authority. [1560–70; obs. *mutine* to mutiny (< MF *mutiner,* deriv. of *mutin* mutiny; see MUTINEER) + -Y[3]]
—Syn. 2. uprising, overthrow, coup, takeover.

mut·ism (myo͞o′tiz əm), *n. Psychiatry.* an inability to speak, due to a physical defect, conscious refusal, or psychogenic inhibition. [1815–25; < NL *mūtismus.* See MUTE, -ISM]

Mu·tsu·hi·to (mo͞o′tso͝o hē′tô), *n.* 1852–1912, emperor of Japan 1867–1912.

mutt (mut), *n. Slang.* **1.** a dog, esp. a mongrel. **2.** a stupid or foolish person; simpleton. Also, **mut.** [1900–05, *Amer.;* short for MUTTONHEAD]

Mutt′ and Jeff′, a very short and a very tall person who are paired as companions, teammates, or associates. [1915–20; after the characters in a cartoon strip of the same name created by U.S. cartoonist Harry C. "Bud" Fisher (1885–1954)]

mut·ter (mut′ər), *v.i.* **1.** to utter words indistinctly or in a low tone, often as if talking to oneself; murmur. **2.** to complain murmuringly; grumble. **3.** to make a low, rumbling sound. **—***v.t.* **4.** to utter indistinctly or in a low tone: *to mutter complaints.* **—***n.* **5.** the act or utterance of a person who mutters. [1325–75; ME *moteren,* perh. freq. of MOOT[1] (OE *mōtian* to speak); see -ER[6]] **—mut′ter·er,** *n.* **—mut′ter·ing·ly,** *adv.*
—Syn. 1. See **murmur.**

mut·ton[1] (mut′n), *n.* the flesh of sheep, esp. full-grown or more mature sheep, used as food. [1250–1300; ME *moton* sheep < OF < Celtic; cf. MIr *molt,* Welsh *mollt,* Breton *maout* wether] **—mut′ton·y,** *adj.*

mut·ton[2] (mut′n), *n. Print.* em (def. 2). Also called **mut.** [1935–40; code term, coined to differentiate the pronunciation of *em quad* from *en quad*]

mut′ton bird′, any of several long-winged seabirds, often used as food, esp. *Puffinus tenuirostris* **(short-tailed shearwater)** of Australia and *Puffinus griseus* **(sooty shearwater),** which breeds in the Southern Hemisphere and winters in the Northern Hemisphere. Also, **mut′ton-bird′.** [1840–50]

mut·ton·chops (mut′n chops′), *n.pl.* side whiskers that are narrow at the temples and broad and trimmed short at the jawline, the chin being shaved both in front and beneath. Also called **mut′tonchop whisk′ers.** [1860–65; MUTTON[1] + CHOP[1] + -S[3]; so called from their shape]

mut′ton corn′, *South Atlantic States.* sweet corn, esp. when ripe and ready for eating on the cob.

mut·ton·fish (mut′n fish′), *n., pl.* (*esp. collectively*) **-fish,** (*esp. referring to two or more kinds or species*) **-fish·es.** **1.** See **ocean pout.** **2.** See **mutton snapper.** [1725–35, *Amer.;* MUTTON[1] + FISH, so called for its muttonlike taste]

mut·ton·head (mut′n hed′), *n. Informal.* a slow-witted, foolish, or stupid person; dolt. [1795–1805; MUTTON[1] + HEAD] **—mut′ton·head′ed,** *adj.*

mut′ton snap′per, a snapper, *Lutjanus analis,* inhabiting the warmer parts of the western Atlantic Ocean, valued as food and game. [1865–70]

Mut·tra (mu′trə), *n.* former name of **Mathura.**

mu·tu·al (myo͞o′cho͞o əl), *adj.* **1.** possessed, experienced, performed, etc., by each of two or more with respect to the other; reciprocal: *to have mutual respect.* **2.** having the same relation each toward the other: *to be mutual enemies.* **3.** of or pertaining to each of two or more; held in common; shared: *mutual interests.* **4.** having or pertaining to a form of corporate organization in which there are no stockholders, and profits, losses, expenses, etc., are shared by members in proportion to the business each transacts with the company: *a mutual company.* **—***n.* **5.** *Informal.* a mutual fund. [1470–80; < MF *mutuel* < L *mūtu(us)* mutual, reciprocal (*mūt(āre)* to change (see MUTATE) + *-uus* deverbal adj. suffix) + MF *-el* (< L *-ālis*) -AL[1]] **—mu′tu·al·ly,** *adv.*
—Syn. 1. MUTUAL, RECIPROCAL agree in the idea of an exchange or balance between two or more persons or groups. MUTUAL indicates an exchange of a feeling, obligation, etc., between two or more people, or an interchange of some kind between persons or things: *mutual esteem; in mutual agreement.* RECIPROCAL indicates a relation in which one act, thing, feeling, etc., balances or is given in return for another: *reciprocal promises or favors.*
—Usage. The earliest (15th century) and still a current meaning of MUTUAL is "reciprocal," specifying the relation of two or more persons or things to each other: *Their admiration is mutual. Teachers and students sometimes suffer from a mutual misunderstanding.* MUTUAL soon developed the sense of "having in common, shared": *Their mutual objective is peace.* This latter sense has been in use since the 16th century and is entirely standard. It is occasionally criticized, not on the grounds of ambiguity but on the grounds that the later sense development is somehow wrong. MUTUAL in the sense of "shared" may have been encouraged by the title of Charles Dickens's novel *Our Mutual Friend* (1864–65), but Dickens was not the innovator. The fact that *common* also has the sense "ordinary, unexceptional" and "coarse, vulgar" may have contributed to the use of MUTUAL instead of *common* in designating a shared friend.

mu′tual aid′, *Sociol.* the cooperative as opposed to the competitive factors operating in the development of society. [1530–40]

Mu′tual Assured′ Destruc′tion, a U.S. doctrine of reciprocal deterrence resting on the U.S. and Soviet Union each being able to inflict unacceptable damage on the other in retaliation for a nuclear attack. Also called **MAD.**

mu′tual fund′, an investment company that issues shares continuously and is obligated to repurchase them from shareholders on demand. Also called **open-end investment company.** Cf. **closed-end investment company.** [1790–1800]

mu′tual imped′ance, *Elect.* the ratio of the potential difference between either of two pairs of terminals to the current applied at the other pair of terminals when the circuit is open. [1965–70]

mu′tual induct′ance, *Elect.* the ratio of the electromotive force in one of two circuits to the rate of change of current in the other circuit. Cf. **inductive coupling.** [1885–90]

mu′tual induc′tion, *Elect.* the production of an electromotive force in one circuit by a change in current in another circuit. [1860–65]

mu′tual insur′ance, insurance in which those insured become members of a company who reciprocally engage, by payment of certain amounts into a common fund, to indemnify one another against loss.

mu·tu·al·ism (myo͞o′cho͞o ə liz′əm), *n.* **1.** a relationship between two species of organisms in which both benefit from the association. **2.** the doctrine that the interdependence of social elements is the primary determinant of individual and social relations, esp. the theory that common ownership of property, or collective effort and control governed by sentiments of brotherhood and mutual aid, will be beneficial to both the individual and society. **3.** *Sociol.* the force or principle of mutual aid. [1860–65; MUTUAL + -ISM] **—mu′tu·al·ist,** *n.* **—mu′tu·al·is′tic,** *adj.*

mu·tu·al·i·ty (myo͞o′cho͞o al′i tē), *n.* condition or quality of being mutual; reciprocity; mutual dependence. [1580–90; MUTUAL + -ITY]

mu·tu·al·ize (myo͞o′cho͞o ə līz′), *v.,* **-ized, -iz·ing.** **—***v.t.* **1.** to make mutual. **2.** to incorporate as a mutual company. **—***v.i.* **3.** to become mutual. Also, *esp. Brit.,* **mu′tu·al·ise′.** [1805–15; MUTUAL + -IZE] **—mu′tu·al·i·za′tion,** *n.*

mu′tually exclu′sive, of or pertaining to a situation involving two or more events, possibilities, etc., in which the occurrence of one precludes the occurrence of the other: *mutually exclusive plans of action.* [1870–75]

mu′tual sav′ings bank′, a noncapitalized savings bank that distributes its net earnings to depositors.

mu·tu·el (myo͞o′cho͞o əl), *n.* pari-mutuel (def. 1). [prob. by false construal of *pari* as a prefix or adj.]

mu·tule (myo͞o′cho͞ol), *n. Archit.* a projecting flat block under the corona of the Doric cornice, corresponding to the modillion of other orders. [1555–65; < L *mūtulus* modillion] **—mu·tu·lar** (myo͞o′chə lər), **mu·tu·la·ry** (myo͞o′chə ler′ē), *adj.*

mutule (Grecian Doric)

muu·muu (mo͞o′mo͞o′), *n.* **1.** a long, loose-hanging dress, usually brightly colored or patterned, worn esp. by Hawaiian women. **2.** a similar dress worn as a housedress. [1920–25; < Hawaiian *mu′umu′u* name of the dress, lit., cut-off; so called because it originally lacked a yoke]

Muy·bridge (mī′brij), *n.* **Ead·weard** (ed′wərd), (*Edward James Muggeridge*), 1830–1904, U.S. photographer, born in England: pioneered in photographic studies of animals and humans in motion.

Mu·zak (myo͞o′zak), *Trademark.* recorded background music transmitted by radio, telephone, or satellite to built-in sets in offices, restaurants, waiting rooms, etc.

mu·zhik (mo͞o zhik′, mo͞o′zhik), *n.* a Russian peasant. Also, **moujik, mujik, mu·zjik′.** [1560–70; < Russ *muzhík,* equiv. to *muzh* husband, man (OCS *mǫžĭ,* akin to MAN[1]) + *-ik* dim. suffix]

muzz (muz), *Brit. Slang.* **—***v.i.* **1.** to study intensely; grind. **—***v.t.* **2.** to confuse (someone); make (someone) muzzy. [1765–75; back formation from MUZZY]

muz·zle (muz′əl), *n., v.,* **-zled, -zling.** **—***n.* **1.** the mouth, or end for discharge, of the barrel of a gun, pistol, etc. **2.** the projecting part of the head of an animal, including jaws, mouth, and nose. See diag. under **dog.** **3.** a device, usually an arrangement of straps or wires, placed over an animal's mouth to prevent the animal from biting, eating, etc. **—***v.t.* **4.** to put a muzzle on (an animal or its mouth) so as to prevent biting, eating, etc. **5.** to restrain from speech, the expression of opinion, etc.: *The censors muzzled the press.* **6.** *Naut.* to attach the cable to the stock of (an anchor) by means of a light line to permit the anchor to be pulled loose readily. [1350–1400; ME *musel* < MF < ML *mūsellum,* dim. of *mūsum* snout < ?]
—Syn. 5. silence, quiet, still, supress.

muz·zle·load·er (muz′əl lō′dər), *n.* a firearm that is loaded through the muzzle. Also, **muz′zle-load′er.** [1855–60; MUZZLE + LOADER] **—muz′zle·load′ing,** *adj.*

muz·zler (muz′lər), *n.* **1.** a person or thing that muzzles. **2.** Also called **nose ender.** *Naut.* a strong opposing wind. [1645–55; MUZZLE + -ER[1]]

muz′zle veloc′ity, *Ordn.* the speed of a projectile, usually expressed in feet or meters per second, as it leaves the muzzle of a gun. [1875–80]

muz·zy (muz′ē), *adj.,* **-zi·er, -zi·est.** *Informal.* **1.** confused; muddled. **2.** dull; mentally hazy. [1720–30; perh. b. MUDDLED and FUZZY] **—muz′zi·ly,** *adv.* **—muz′zi·ness,** *n.*

MV, 1. main verb. **2.** megavolt; megavolts. **3.** motor vessel.

Mv, *Symbol, Chem.* mendelevium.

mV, millivolt; millivolts.

m.v., 1. market value. **2.** mean variation. **3.** *Music.* mezza voce.

M.V.Ed., Master of Vocational Education.

MVP, Most Valuable Player. Also, **M.V.P.**

MW, *Elect.* megawatt; megawatts.

mW, *Elect.* milliwatt; milliwatts.

M.W.A., Modern Woodmen of America.

Mwam·bu·tsa IV (mwäm bo͞o′tsä), 1912–77, king of Burundi 1962–66.

Mwan·za (mwän′zä), *n.* a city in N Tanzania, on Lake Victoria. 35,000.

Mwe·ru (mwā′ro͞o), *n.* a lake in S central Africa, between Zaire and Zambia. 68 mi. (109 km) long.

M.W.T., Master of Wood Technology.

MX, missile experimental: a ten-warhead U.S. intercontinental ballistic missile.

Mx, *Elect.* maxwell; maxwells.

my (mī), *pron.* **1.** (a form of the possessive case of **I** used as an attributive adjective): *My soup is cold.* **—***interj.* **2.** Also, **my-my.** (used as an exclamation of mild surprise or dismay): *My, what a big house this is! My-my, how old he looks!* [1125–75; ME *mī,* var. of *mīn,* OE *mīn;* see MINE[1]] **—Usage.** See **me.**

my-, var. of **myo-** before some vowels: *myalgia.*

my·al·gi·a (mī al′jē ə, -jə), *n. Pathol.* pain in the muscles; muscular rheumatism. Also called **myoneuralgia.** [1855–60; MY- + -ALGIA] **—my·al′gic,** *adj.*

my·all (mī′ôl), *n.* any of several Australian acacias, esp. *Acacia pendula* **(weeping myall),** having gray foliage and drooping branches. [1835–45; appar. to be identified with *myall* wild, uncivilized < Dharuk *miyal* stranger, Aborigine from another tribe]

My·an·mar (mī än′mär), *n.* **Union of,** official name of **Burma.**

my·a·sis (mī′ə sis), *n., pl.* **-ses** (-sēz′). *Pathol., Vet. Pathol.* myiasis.

my·as·the·ni·a (mī′əs thē′nē ə), *n. Pathol.* muscle weakness. [1855–60; MY- + ASTHENIA] **—my·as·then·ic** (mī′əs then′ik), *adj.*

my′asthe′nia gra′vis, *Pathol.* a disease of impaired transmission of motor nerve impulses, characterized by episodic muscle weakness and easy fatigability, esp. of the face, tongue, neck, and respiratory muscles: caused by autoimmune destruction of acetylcholine receptors. *Abbr.:* MG [1895–1900; < NL: serious muscle weakness]

my·a·to·ni·a (mī′ə tō′nē ə), *n. Pathol.* deficient muscle tone. [MY- + ATONIA]

my·at·ro·phy (mī a′trə fē), *n. Pathol.* myoatrophy.

myc-, var. of **myco-** before a vowel: *mycelium.*

my·ce·li·um (mī sē′lē əm), *n., pl.* **-li·a** (-lē ə). *Mycol.* the mass of hyphae that form the vegetative part of a fungus. [< NL, equiv. to Gk *myk-* MYC- + (*h*)*ēl*(*os*) wart, nail + NL *-ium* -IUM] **—my·ce′li·al,** *adj.*

My·ce·nae (mī sē′nē), *n.* an ancient city in S Greece, in Argolis: important ruins.

My·ce·nae·an (mī′si nē′ən), *adj.* **1.** of or pertaining to the ancient city of Mycenae. **2.** denoting or pertaining to the ancient civilization at Mycenae, dating from c2000 to c1100 B.C. **—***n.* **3.** Also called **My′cenae′an Greek′.** the earliest recorded Greek dialect, written in the Linear B syllabary and dating from the 15th through the 13th centuries B.C. [1590–1600; MYCENAE + -AN]

Myc·e·ri·nus (mis′ə rī′nəs), *n.* king of ancient Egypt c2600–2570 B.C.: builder of the third great pyramid at El Giza. Also, **Mykerinos.** Also called **Menkure.**

-mycete a combining form meaning "mushroom, fungus," taken as the singular of the plural taxonomic combining form **-mycetes.**

-mycetes, a combining form meaning "mushrooms, fungi," used in the formation of taxonomic names of fungi, esp. classes: *Myxomycetes.* [< NL < Gk *mykētes,* pl. of *mýkēs* mushroom, fungus. See MYCETO-]

my·ce·tism (mī′si tiz′əm), *n.* poisoning due to mushrooms. Also, **my·ce·tis·mus** (mī′si tiz′məs). [< Gk *mykēt-,* s. of *mýkēs* mushroom + -ISM]

my·ce·to·ma (mī′si tō′mə), *n., pl.* **-mas, -ma·ta** (-mə tə). *Pathol.* a chronic tumorous infection caused by any of various soil-dwelling fungi, usually affecting the foot. Also called **maduramycosis.** [1870–75; < Gk *myket-* (see MYCETISM) + -OMA] —**my′ce·to′ma·tous,** *adj.*

-mycin, a combining form used in the names of antibiotics, usually fungal derivatives: *neomycin.* [perh. orig. in ACTINOMYCIN; see MYC-, -IN[2]]

myco-, a combining form meaning "mushroom, fungus," used in the formation of compound words: *mycology.* Also, *esp. before a vowel,* **myc-.** [comb. form repr. Gk *mýkēs* mushroom, fungus]

my·co·bac·te·ri·um (mī′kō bak tēr′ē əm), *n., pl.* **-te·ri·a** (-tēr′ē ə). *Bacteriol.* any of several rod-shaped aerobic bacteria of the genus *Mycobacterium,* certain species of which, as *M. tuberculosis,* are pathogenic for humans and animals. [< NL (1896); see MYCO-, BACTERIUM]

my·co·bi·ont (mī′kō bī′ont), *n.* the fungal component of a lichen. [1957; MYCO- + Gk *biont-,* s. of *biôn,* prp. of *bioûn* to live; cf. SYMBIONT]

my·co·ce·cid·i·um (mī′kō sə sid′ē əm), *n. Mycol.* a gall caused by a parasitic fungus. [< NL, equiv. to *myco-* MYCO- + *cecidium* gall < Gk *kēkídion* ink-gall, equiv. to *kēkíd-,* s. of *kēkís* oak-gall, a dye made therefrom + *-ion* dim. suffix]

my·co·flo·ra (mī′kō flôr′ə, -flōr′ə), *n. Ecol.* the fungi characteristic of a particular environment. [1740–45; MYCO- + FLORA]

my·cog·e·nous (mī koj′ə nəs), *adj. Bot.* arising from or inhabiting fungi. [MYCO- + -GENOUS]

mycol., mycology.

my·col·o·gy (mī kol′ə jē), *n.* **1.** the branch of biology dealing with fungi. **2.** the fungi found in an area. [1830–40; MYCO- + -LOGY] —**my·co·log·i·cal** (mī′kə loj′i kəl), **my′co·log′ic,** *adj.* —**my′co·log′i·cal·ly,** *adv.* —**my·col′o·gist,** *n.*

my·co·par·a·site (mī′kō par′ə sīt′), *n.* a parasitic fungus whose host is another fungus. [MYCO- + PARASITE]

my·coph·a·gist (mī kof′ə jist), *n.* **1.** a fungus-eating organism. **2.** an epicure whose interest is mushrooms. [1860–65; MYCO- + -PHAGE or -PHAG(Y) + -IST]

my·coph·a·gous (mī kof′ə gəs), *adj.* feeding on fungi. [1920–25; MYCO- + -PHAGOUS]

my·co·plas·ma (mī′kō plaz′mə), *n.* any of numerous parasitic microorganisms of the class Mollicutes, comprising the smallest self-reproducing prokaryotes, lacking a true cell wall and able to survive without oxygen: a common cause of pneumonia and urinary tract infections. [1950–55; < NL; see MYCO-, PLASMA]

my·cor·rhi·za (mī′kə rī′zə), *n., pl.* **-zae** (-zē), **-zas.** *Plant Pathol.* a symbiotic association of the mycelium of a fungus, esp. a basidiomycete, with the roots of certain plants, in which the hyphae form a closely woven mass around the rootlets or penetrate the cells of the root. Also, **my′co·rhi′za.** Also called **fungus root.** [1890–95; MYCO- + -RRHIZA] —**my′cor·rhi′zal, my′co·rhi′zal,** *adj.*

my·co·sis (mī kō′sis), *n. Pathol.* **1.** the presence of parasitic fungi in or on any part of the body. **2.** the condition caused by the presence of such fungi. [1875–80; MYC- + -OSIS] —**my·cot·ic** (mī kot′ik), *adj.*

my·co·so·zin (mī′kō sō′zin), *n. Biochem.* any sozin that kills microorganisms. [MYCO- + SOZIN]

my·co·stat (mī′kō stat′), *n.* a substance or preparation that prevents or inhibits the growth of molds. [MYCO- + -STAT] —**my′co·stat′ic,** *adj.*

My·co·stat·in (mī′kō stat′n), *Pharm., Trademark.* a brand of nystatin.

My·co·ta (mī kō′tə), *n.* an alternative taxonomic name for the kingdom Fungi. [< NL; see MYC-, -OTA]

my·cot·ic (mī kot′ik), *adj.* of, pertaining to, or caused by a fungus. [MYC- + -OTIC]

my·co·tox·i·co·sis (mī′kō tok′si kō′sis), *n., pl.* **-ses** (-sēz). *Pathol.* poisoning resulting from exposure to fungal toxins. [1948; MYCO- + TOXICOSIS]

my·co·tox·in (mī′kō tok′sin), *n. Pathol.* a toxin produced by a fungus. [1960–65; MYCO- + TOXIN]

my·cot·ro·phy (mī ko′trə fē), *n.* the symbiotic relationship between a fungus and a living plant. [< G *Mykotrophie* (1923); see MYCO-, -TROPHY]

my·co·vi·rus (mī′kō vī′rəs), *n., pl.* **-rus·es.** any fungus-infecting virus. [MYCO- + VIRUS]

my·dri·a·sis (mi drī′ə sis, mī-), *n. Med.* excessive dilatation of the pupil of the eye, as the result of disease, drugs, or the like. Cf. **miosis.** [1650–60; < L *mydriāsis* < Gk *mydríāsis*]

mydr·i·at·ic (mid′rē at′ik), *adj.* **1.** pertaining to or producing mydriasis. —*n.* **2.** a mydriatic drug. [1850–55; MYDRIA(SIS) + -TIC]

myel-, var. of **myelo-** before a vowel: *myelitis.*

my·el·en·ceph·a·lon (mī′ə len sef′ə lon′), *n., pl.* **-lons, -la** (-lə). *Anat.* the posterior section of the hindbrain comprising the medulla oblongata. [1835–45; MYEL- + ENCEPHALON] —**my·el·en·ce·phal·ic** (mī′ə len′sə fal′ik), *adj.*

my·e·lin (mī′ə lin), *n. Biol.* a soft, white, fatty material in the membrane of Schwann cells and certain neuroglial cells: the substance of the myelin sheath. Also, **my·e·line** (mī′ə lēn′). [1865–70; MYEL- + -IN[2]] —**my′e·lin′ic,** *adj.*

my·e·li·nat·ed (mī′ə lə nā′tid), *adj. Anat.* (of a nerve) having a myelin sheath; medullated. [1895–1900; MYELIN + -ATE[1] + -ED[2]]

my·e·li·na·tion (mī′ə lə nā′shən), *n. Anat.* the formation of a myelin sheath. Also, **my·e·lin·i·za·tion** (mī′ə lin ə zā′shən). [1895–1900; MYELIN + -ATION]

my′elin sheath′, *Anat.* a wrapping of myelin around certain nerve axons, serving as an electrical insulator that speeds nerve impulses to muscles and other effectors. See diag. under **neuron.** [1895–1900]

my·e·li·tis (mī′ə lī′tis), *n. Pathol.* **1.** inflammation of the substance of the spinal cord. **2.** inflammation of the bone marrow. [1825–35; MYEL- + -ITIS]

myelo-, a combining form meaning "marrow," "of the spinal cord," used in the formation of compound words: *myelocyte.* Also, *esp. before a vowel,* **myel-.** [comb. form repr. Gk *myelós* marrow]

my·e·lo·blast (mī′ə lə blast′), *n. Cell Biol.* an immature myelocyte. [1900–05; MYELO- + -BLAST] —**my′e·lo·blas′tic,** *adj.*

my·e·lo·cyte (mī′ə lə sīt′), *n. Anat.* a cell of the bone marrow, esp. one developing into a granulocyte. [1865–70; MYELO- + -CYTE] —**my·e·lo·cyt·ic** (mī′ə lə sit′ik), *adj.*

my·e·lo·fi·bro·sis (mī′ə lō fī brō′sis), *n. Pathol.* the replacement of bone marrow by fibrous tissue, characteristic of leukemia and certain other diseases. [1945–50; MYELO- + FIBROSIS]

my·e·lo·gen·ic (mī′ə lə jen′ik), *adj.* produced in the bone marrow. Also, **my·e·log·e·nous** (mī′ə loj′ə nəs). [1875–80; MYELO- + -GENIC]

my·e·lo·gram (mī′ə lə gram′), *n. Med.* an x-ray photograph of the spinal cord, following administration of a radiopaque substance into the spinal subarachnoid space. [1935–40; MYELO- + -GRAM[1]]

my·e·log·ra·phy (mī′ə log′rə fē), *n. Med.* the production of myelograms. [1935–40; MYELO- + -GRAPHY] —**my·e·lo·graph·ic** (mī′ə lə graf′ik), *adj.* —**my′e·lo·graph′i·cal·ly,** *adv.*

my·e·loid (mī′ə loid′), *adj. Anat.* **1.** pertaining to the spinal cord. **2.** marrowlike. **3.** pertaining to marrow. [1855–60; MYEL- + -OID]

my·e·lo·ma (mī′ə lō′mə), *n., pl.* **-mas, -ma·ta** (-mə tə). *Pathol.* a tumor of plasma cells, arising in bone marrow, and often occurring at multiple sites, as in the vertebrae and flat skull bones. Cf. **multiple myeloma.** [1855–60; MYEL- + -OMA]

my·e·lop·a·thy (mī′ə lop′ə thē), *n., pl.* **-thies.** *Pathol.* any disorder of the spinal cord or of bone marrow. [1890–95; MYELO- + -PATHY] —**my·e·lo·path·ic** (mī′ə lə path′ik), *adj.*

my·ia·sis (mī′ə sis), *n., pl.* **-ses** (-sēz′). *Pathol., Vet. Pathol.* any disease that results from the infestation of tissues or cavities of the body by larvae of flies. Also, **myasis.** [1830–40; < Gk *myî(a)* fly + -ASIS]

Myin·gyan (myin′jän), *n.* a city in central Burma. 40,000.

Myk·e·ri·nos (mik′ə rī′nəs), *n.* Mycerinus.

My·ko·nos (mik′ə nos′, -nōs′, mē′kə-), *n.* a mountainous island in SE Greece, in the S Aegean: resort. 3823; 35 sq. mi. (90 sq. km). Greek, **Mikonos.**

My Lai (mē′ lī′), a hamlet in S Vietnam: U.S. forces' massacre of South Vietnamese civilians 1968.

My·lar (mī′lär), *Trademark.* a brand of strong, thin polyester film used in photography, recording tapes, and insulation.

My·lit·ta (mi lit′ə), *n.* Ishtar.

my·lo·hy·oid (mī′lō hī′oid), *Anat.* —*adj.* **1.** Also, **my·lo·hy·oi·de·an** (mī′lō hī oi′dē ən). of, pertaining to, or situated near the lower molar teeth and the hyoid bone. —*n.* **2.** a flat, triangular muscle that forms the floor of the mouth. [1685–95; *mylo-* (< Gk *mýlo(s)* molar, lit., mill) + HYOID]

my·lo·nite (mī′lə nīt′, mil′ə-), *n. Geol.* a rock that has been crushed and sheared to such an extent that its original texture has been destroyed. [1885–90; *mylon-* (repr. Gk *mýlos* mill) + -ITE[1]]

my-my (mī′mī′), *interj.* my (def. 2).

my·na (mī′nə), *n.* any of several Asian birds of the starling family Sturnidae, esp. those of the genera *Acridotheres* and *Gracula,* certain species of which have the ability to mimic speech and are kept as pets. Also, **my′nah, mina, minah.** [1760–70; < Hindi *mainā*]

My·nes (mī′nēz), *n.* (in the *Iliad*) a king of Lyrnessus killed by Achilles in the Trojan War.

Myn·heer (mīn hâr′, -hēr′), *n.* **1.** *Dutch.* the term of address and title of respect corresponding to *sir* and *Mr.* **2.** (*l.c.*) a Dutchman. [1645–55; sp. var. of D *mijnheer,* equiv. to *mijn* MINE[1] + *heer* lord, sir, Mr.; see HERR]

myo-, a combining form meaning "muscle," used in the formation of compound words: *myology.* Also, *esp. before a vowel,* **my-.** [comb. form repr. Gk *mŷs* mouse, muscle]

my·o·at·ro·phy (mī′ō a′trə fē), *n. Pathol.* atrophy of muscle. Also, **myatrophy.** [MYO- + ATROPHY]

M.Y.O.B., mind your own business.

my·o·blast (mī′ə blast′), *n. Embryol.* any of the cells derived from the mesoderm in the vertebrate embryo that develop into muscle tissue. [1880–85; MYO- + -BLAST]

myocar′dial infarc′tion, *Pathol.* See **heart attack.** Also, **my′ocar′dial in′farct.** *Abbr.:* MI

my·o·car·di·o·gram (mī′ə kär′dē ə gram′), *n.* the graphic record produced by a myocardiograph. [MYO- + CARDIOGRAM]

my·o·car·di·o·graph (mī′ə kär′dē ə graf′, -gräf′), *n.* an instrument for recording the movements of the heart. [1930–35; MYO- + CARDIOGRAPH]

my·o·car·di·tis (mī′ō kär dī′tis), *n. Pathol.* inflammation of the myocardium. [1865–70; MYO- + CARDITIS]

my·o·car·di·um (mī′ə kär′dē əm), *n., pl.* **-di·a** (-dē ə). *Anat.* the muscular substance of the heart. [1875–80; MYO- + -CARDIUM] —**my′o·car′di·al,** *adj.*

my·o·clo·ni·a (mī′ə klō′nē ə), *n. Pathol.* a disease characterized by myoclonus. [MYOCLON(US) + -IA] —**my·o·clon·ic** (mī′ə klon′ik), *adj.*

my·oc·lo·nus (mī ok′lə nəs), *n. Pathol.* an abrupt spasm or twitch of a muscle or group of muscles, occurring in some neurological diseases. [1880–85; MYO- + CLONUS]

my·o·cyte (mī′ə sīt′), *n.* a contractile cell, esp. an elongated cell in sponges that forms a sphincter around body openings. [1885–90; MYO- + -CYTE]

my·o·e·lec·tric (mī′ō i lek′trik), *adj.* **1.** of or pertaining to electrical impulses, generated by muscles of the body, which may be amplified and used esp. to control artificial limbs. **2.** of or pertaining to an artificial limb under myoelectric control. [1915–20; MYO- + ELECTRIC]

my·o·fi·bril (mī′ə fī′brəl, -fib′rəl), *n. Cell Biol.* a contractile fibril of skeletal muscle, composed mainly of actin and myosin. [1895–1900; MYO- + FIBRIL]

my·o·fil·a·ment (mī′ə fil′ə mənt), *n. Cell Biol.* a threadlike filament of actin or myosin that is a component of a myofibril. [1945–50; MYO- + FILAMENT]

my·o·gen·ic (mī′ə jen′ik), *adj.* **1.** originating in muscle, as an impulse or sensation. **2.** producing muscle tissue. [1875–80; MYO- + -GENIC] —**my·o·ge·nic·i·ty** (mī′ə jə nis′i tē), *n.*

my·o·glo·bin (mī′ə glō′bin, mī′ə glō′-), *n. Biochem.* hemoglobin of muscle, weighing less and carrying more oxygen and less carbon monoxide than blood hemoglobin. Also, **my·o·he·mo·glo·bin** (mī′ə hē′mə glō′bin, -hem′ə-). [1920–25; MYO- + GLOBIN]

my·o·gram (mī′ə gram′), *n.* the graphic record produced by a myograph. [1885–90; MYO- + -GRAM[1]]

my·o·graph (mī′ə graf′, -gräf′), *n.* an instrument for recording the contractions and relaxations of muscles. [1865–70; MYO- + -GRAPH] —**my·o·graph·ic** (mī′ə graf′ik), *adj.* —**my′o·graph′i·cal·ly,** *adv.* —**my·og·ra·phy** (mī og′rə fē), *n.*

my·o·kym·i·a (mī′ə kim′ē ə), *n. Pathol.* twitching of individual segments of a muscle. [MYO- + *-kymia,* equiv. to Gk *kŷm(a)* something swollen + -IA]

my·ol·o·gy (mī ol′ə jē), *n.* the science or branch of anatomy dealing with muscles. [1640–50; < NL *myologia.* See MYO-, -LOGY] —**my·o·log·ic** (mī′ə loj′ik), **my′o·log′i·cal,** *adj.* —**my·ol′o·gist,** *n.*

my·o·ma (mī ō′mə), *n., pl.* **-mas, -ma·ta** (-mə tə). *Pathol.* a tumor composed of muscular tissue. [1870–75; MY- + -OMA] —**my·om·a·tous** (mī om′ə təs, -ō′mə-), *adj.*

my·o·mec·to·my (mī′ə mek′tə mē), *n., pl.* **-mies.** the surgical removal of a myoma, esp. the excision of a fibroid tumor from the uterus. [1885–90; MYOM(A) + -ECTOMY]

my·o·neu·ral (mī′ə nŏŏr′əl, -nyŏŏr′-), *adj.* of or pertaining to both muscle and nerve. [1900–05; MYO- + NEURAL]

my·o·neu·ral·gia (mī′ō nŏŏ ral′jə, -nyŏŏ-), *n. Pathol.* myalgia. [MYO- + NEURALGIA]

my·op·a·thy (mī op′ə thē), *n. Pathol.* any abnormality or disease of muscle tissue. [1840–50; MYO- + -PATHY] —**my·o·path·ic** (mī′ə path′ik), *adj.*

my·o·pi·a (mī ō′pē ə), *n.* **1.** *Ophthalm.* a condition of the eye in which parallel rays are focused in front of the retina, objects being seen distinctly only when near to the eye; nearsightedness (opposed to *hyperopia*). **2.** lack of foresight or discernment; obtuseness. **3.** narrow-mindedness; intolerance. [1685–95; < NL < Gk *myōpía,* equiv. to *myōp-* (s. of *mýōps*) near-sighted, lit., blinking (*my(ein)* to shut + *ōps* EYE) + *-ia* -IA]

my·op·ic (mī op′ik, -ō′pik), *adj.* **1.** *Ophthalm.* pertaining to or having myopia; nearsighted. **2.** unable or unwilling to act prudently; shortsighted. **3.** lacking tolerance or understanding; narrow-minded. [1790–1800; MYOP(IA) + -IC] —**my·op′i·cal·ly,** *adv.*

my·op·o·rum (mī op′ər əm), *n.* any of several shrubs or trees of the genus *Myoporum,* chiefly of Australia and New Zealand, cultivated in warm regions as hedges or ornamentals. [< NL (1786) < Gk *mý(ein)* to shut (the eyes) + NL *-porum,* deriv. of LL *porus* PORE[2], alluding to the spots on the leaves, suggesting closed pores]

my·o·psy·chop·a·thy (mī′ō sī kop′ə thē), *n. Pathol.* myopathy associated with mental weakness or change. [MYO- + PSYCHOPATHY]

my·o·scope (mī′ə skōp′), *n.* an instrument for observing muscular contraction. [1875–80; MYO- + -SCOPE]

my·o·sin (mī′ə sin), *n. Biochem.* the principal contractile protein of muscle. [1865–70; MY- + -OSE[2] + -IN[2]]

my·o·sis (mī ō′sis), *n. Med.* miosis.

my·o·so·tis (mī′ə sō′tis), *n.* any plant belonging to the genus *Myosotis,* of the borage family, having basal leaves and pink or white flowers, as the forget-me-not. Also, **my·o·sote** (mī′ə sōt′). [1700–10; < NL, L *myosōtis* < Gk *myosōtís* the plant mouse-ear, equiv. to *myós* (gen. of *mŷs*) MOUSE + *-ōt-* (s. of *oûs*) ear + *-is* n. suffix]

my·ot·ic (mī ot′ik), *adj., n.* miotic.

my·ot·o·my (mī ot′ə mē), *n., pl.* **-mies.** *Surg.* incision of a muscle. [1670–80; < NL *myotomia.* See MYO-, -TOMY]

my·o·to·ni·a (mī′ə tō′nē ə), *n. Pathol.* tonic muscle spasm or muscular rigidity. [1895–1900; MYO- + -TONIA] —**my·o·ton·ic** (mī′ə ton′ik), *adj.*

My·ra (mī′rə), *n.* **1.** an ancient city in SW Asia Minor, in Lycia. **2.** a female given name: from a Latin word meaning "extraordinary."

Myr·dal (mėr′däl, -dôl, mûr′-; *Sw.* MYR′däl), *n.* **1.** **Al·va (Rei·mer)** (al′və rā′mər; *Sw.* äl′vä RĀ′mər), 1902–86, Swedish sociologist and diplomat: Nobel peace prize 1982 (wife of Gunnar Myrdal). **2.** **(Karl) Gun·nar** (kärl gun′ər, gŏŏn′-; *Sw.* kärl gŏŏn′när), 1898–1987,

CONCISE PRONUNCIATION KEY: act, cāpe, dâre, pärt; set, ēqual; *if,* ice; ox, ōver, ôrder, oil, bŏŏk, bōōt, out; up, ûrge; child; sing; shoe; thin, *th*at; zh as in *treasure.* ə = *a* as in *alone, e* as in *system, i* as in *easily, o* as in *gallop, u* as in *circus;* ᵊ as in *fire* (fīᵊr), *hour* (ouᵊr). l and n can serve as syllabic consonants, as in *cradle* (krād′l), and *button* (but′n). See the full key inside the front cover.

Swedish sociologist and economist: Nobel prize for economics 1974.

myria-, a combining form meaning "10,000," used esp. in the names of metric units equal to 10,000 of the unit denoted by the base word: *myriagram; myriameter.* [comb. form repr. Gk *mȳriás* ten thousand; see MYRIAD]

myr·i·ad (mir′ē əd), *n.* **1.** a very great or indefinitely great number of persons or things. **2.** ten thousand. —*adj.* **3.** of an indefinitely great number; innumerable: *the myriad stars of a summer night.* **4.** having innumerable phases, aspects, variations, etc.: *the myriad mind of Shakespeare.* **5.** ten thousand. [1545–55; < Gk *mȳriad-* (s. of *mȳriás*) ten thousand; see -AD[1]] —**myr′i·ad·ly,** *adv.*
—**Syn. 4.** countless, boundless, infinite, untold.

myr·i·ad-leaf (mir′ē əd lēf′), *n., pl.* **-leaves.** an aquatic plant, *Myriophyllum verticillatum,* of the North Temperate Zone, having hairlike, submerged leaves.

myr·i·a·pod (mir′ē ə pod′), *n.* **1.** any arthropod of the group Myriapoda, having an elongated segmented body with numerous paired, jointed legs, formerly classified as a class comprising the centipedes and millipedes. —*adj.* **2.** Also, **myr·i·ap·o·dous** (mir′ē ap′ə dəs). belonging or pertaining to the myriapods. **3.** having very numerous legs. Also, **myr′i·o·pod′.** [1820–30; < NL *Myriapoda.* See MYRIA-, -POD]

my·ri·ca (mi rī′kə), *n.* **1.** the bark of the wax myrtle. **2.** the bark of the bayberry. [1700–10; < L < Gk *myrīkē* a shrub, the tamarisk]

myr·in·got·o·my (mir′in got′ə mē, -ing-), *n., pl.* **-mies.** surgical incision of the tympanic membrane. [1875–80; < NL *myring(a)* tympanic membrane (cf. ML *miringa* membrane enclosing the brain, dissimilated form of LL *mēninga* < Gk *mêninx,* s. *mēning-* membrane) + -O- + -TOMY]

my·ris′tic ac′id (mə ris′tik), *Chem.* an oily, white crystalline compound, $C_{14}H_{28}O_2$, insoluble in water, soluble in alcohol and ether: used in soaps, cosmetics, and in the synthesis of esters for flavors and perfumes. [1840–50; < NL *Myristica* the nutmeg genus (the acid is a constituent of oil derived from nutmeg and related plants) < Gk *myristikḗ,* fem. of *myristikós* fragrant, akin to *mýron* perfume, unguent]

myr·me·col·o·gy (mûr′mi kol′ə jē), *n.* the branch of entomology dealing with ants. [< Gk *myrmēk-,* s. of *mýrmēx* ant + -O- + -LOGY] —**myr·me·co·log·i·cal** (mûr′mi kə loj′i kəl), *adj.* —**myr′me·col′o·gist,** *n.*

Myr·mi·don (mûr′mi don′, -dn), *n., pl.* **Myr·mi·dons, Myr·mid·o·nes** (mûr mid′n ēz′). **1.** *Class. Myth.* one of the warlike people of ancient Thessaly who accompanied Achilles to the Trojan War. **2.** (*l.c.*) a person who executes without question or scruple a master's commands. [ME < L *Myrmidones* (pl.) < Gk *Myrmidónes*]

Myr·na (mûr′nə), *n.* a female given name.

my·rob·a·lan (mī rob′ə lən, mi-), *n.* **1.** the dried plumlike fruit of certain tropical trees of the genus *Phyllanthus,* used in dyeing, tanning, and making ink. **2.** See **cherry plum.** [1350–1400; ME < L *myrobalanum* < Gk *myrobálanos* kind of fruit, equiv. to *mýro(n)* balsam + *bálanos* acorn]

my·ron (mē′rôn; *Eng.* mī′ron), *n. Gk. Ch.* chrism. [< Gk *mýron* unguent, perfume]

My·ron (mī′rən), *n.* **1.** fl. c450 B.C., Greek sculptor. **2.** a male given name: from a Greek word meaning "pleasant."

myrrh (mûr), *n.* an aromatic resinous exudation from certain plants of the genus *Myrrhis,* esp. *M. odorata,* a small spiny tree: used for incense, perfume, etc. [bef. 900; ME, OE *myrre* < L *myrrha* < Gk *mýrra* << Akkadian *murru;* akin to Heb *mōr,* Ar *murr*] —**myrrhed,** *adj.* —**myrrh′ic,** *adj.*

Myr·rha (mēr′ə), *n. Class. Myth.* a daughter of King Cinyras of Cyprus who had incestuous relations with her father and was changed into a myrrh tree by the gods. Their child, Adonis, was born from the split trunk of the tree. Also called **Smyrna.**

myr·ta·ceous (mûr tā′shəs), *adj.* **1.** belonging to the Myrtaceae, the myrtle family of plants. Cf. **myrtle family.** **2.** of, pertaining to, or resembling the myrtle. [1825–35; < NL *Myrtace(ae)* family name (NL, L *myrt(us)* MYRTLE + *-aceae* -ACEAE) + -OUS]

myr·tle (mûr′tl), *n.* **1.** any plant of the genus *Myrtus,* esp. *M. communis,* a shrub of southern Europe having evergreen leaves, fragrant white flowers, and aromatic berries: anciently held sacred to Venus and used as an emblem of love. Cf. **myrtle family.** **2.** any of certain unrelated plants, as the periwinkle, *Vinca minor,* and California laurel, *Umbellularia californica.* **3.** Also called **myr·tle·wood** (mûr′tl wo͝od′). the hard, golden-brown wood of the California laurel. **4.** Also called **myr′tle green′.** dark green with bluish tinge. [1350–1400; ME *mirtile* < ML *myrtillus,* equiv. to L *myrt(us)* (< Gk *mýrtos*) + NL *-illus* dim. suffix]

Myr·tle (mûr′tl), *n.* a female given name.

Myr′tle Beach′, a town in E South Carolina. 18,758.

myr′tle fam′ily, the plant family Myrtaceae, characterized by mostly tropical trees and shrubs having aromatic, simple, usually opposite leaves, clusters of flowers, and fruit in the form of a berry or capsule, and including allspice, clove, eucalyptus, guava, and myrtles of the genus *Myrtus.*

myr′tle war′bler. See under **yellow-rumped warbler.** [1890–95, *Amer.*]

my·self (mī self′), *pron., pl.* **our·selves** (är selvz′, ouər-, ou′ər-). **1.** (used as an intensive of **me** or **I**): *I myself will challenge the winner.* **2.** (used reflexively in place of **me** as the object of a preposition or as the direct or indirect object of a verb): *I gave myself a good rubdown. She asked me for a picture of myself.* **3.** *Informal.* (used in place of **I** or **me,** esp. in compound subjects, objects, and complements): *My wife and myself fully agree. She wanted John and myself to take charge. The originators of the plan were my partner and myself.* **4.** (used in place of **I** or **me** after *as, than,* or *but*): *He knows as much about the matter as myself.* **5.** my normal or customary self: *After a few days of rest, I expect to be myself again.* [bef. 900; MY + SELF; r. ME *meself,* OE *mē selfum* (dat.)]
—**Usage.** There is no disagreement over the use of MYSELF and other -SELF forms when they are used intensively (*I myself cannot agree*) or reflexively (*He introduced himself proudly*). Questions are raised, however, when the -SELF forms are used instead of the personal pronouns (*I, me,* etc.) as subjects, objects, or complements.
MYSELF occurs only rarely as a single subject in place of I: *Myself was the one who called.* The recorded instances of such use are mainly poetic or literary. It is also uncommon as a simple object in place of ME: *Since the letter was addressed to myself, I opened it.* As part of a compound subject, object, or complement, MYSELF and to a lesser extent the other -SELF forms are common in informal speech and personal writing, somewhat less common in more formal speech and writing: *The manager and myself completed the arrangements. Many came to welcome my husband and myself back to Washington.*
MYSELF and other -SELF forms are also used, alone or with other nouns or pronouns, in constructions after *as, than,* or *but* in all varieties of speech and writing: *The captain has far more experience than myself in such matters. Orders have arrived for everyone but the orderlies and yourself.*
There is ample precedent, going as far back as Chaucer and running through the whole range of British and American literature and other serious formal writing, for all these uses. Many usage guides, however, state that to use MYSELF in any construction in which I or ME could be used instead (as *My daughter and myself play the flute* instead of *My daughter and I,* or *a gift for my husband and myself* instead of *for my husband and me*) is characteristic only of informal speech and that such use ought not to occur in writing. See also **me.**

My·si·a (mish′ē ə), *n.* an ancient country in NW Asia Minor. —**My′si·an,** *adj., n.*

my·sid (mī′sid), *n.* **1.** any member of the malacostracan order Mysidacea, the opossum shrimps, esp. of the genus *Mysis.* —*adj.* **2.** of or pertaining to such shrimps. [1940–45; < NL *Mysidae* a family of the order, equiv. to *Mys(is)* the type genus (< Gk *mýsis* shutting (*mý(ein)* to shut (the mouth, eyes, or other openings) + *-sis* -SIS)) + *-idae* -ID[2]]

my·so·phil·i·a (mī′sə fil′ē ə), *n. Psychiatry.* a pathological attraction to dirt or filth. [1955–60; < NL, equiv. to *myso-* (< Gk *mýsos* filth) + *-philia* -PHILIA]

my·so·pho·bi·a (mī′sə fō′bē ə), *n. Psychiatry.* a dread of dirt or filth. [1875–80; < NL, equiv. to *myso-* (< Gk *mýs(os)* filth) + -O- + *-phobia* -PHOBIA] —**my′so·pho′bic,** *adj.*

My·sore (mī sôr′, -sōr′), *n.* **1.** a city in S Karnataka, in S India. 355,636. **2.** former name of **Karnataka.**

mys·ta·gogue (mis′tə gôg′, -gog′), *n.* **1.** someone who instructs others before initiation into religious mysteries or before participation in the sacraments. **2.** a person whose teachings are said to be founded on mystical revelations. [1540–50; < L *mystagōgus* < Gk *mystagōgós,* equiv. to *mýst(ēs)* (see MYSTIC) + *agōgós* -AGOGUE] —**mys·ta·go·gy** (mis′tə gō′jē, -goj′ē), **mys·ta·gogu·er·y** (mis′tə gô′gə rē, -gog′ə-), *n.* —**mys·ta·gog·ic** (mis′tə goj′ik), **mys′ta·gog′i·cal,** *adj.* —**mys′ta·gog′i·cal·ly,** *adv.*

mys·te·ri·ous (mi stēr′ē əs), *adj.* **1.** full of, characterized by, or involving mystery: *a mysterious occurrence.* **2.** implying or suggesting a mystery: *a mysterious smile.* **3.** of obscure nature, meaning, origin, etc.; puzzling; inexplicable: *a mysterious inscription on the ancient tomb.* [1610–20; MYSTERY[1] + -OUS] —**mys·te′ri·ous·ly,** *adv.* —**mys·te′ri·ous·ness,** *n.*
—**Syn. 1.** secret, esoteric, occult, cryptic. MYSTERIOUS, INSCRUTABLE, MYSTICAL, OBSCURE refer to that which is not easily comprehended or explained. That which is MYSTERIOUS, by being unknown or puzzling, excites curiosity, amazement, or awe: *a mysterious disease.* INSCRUTABLE applies to that which is impenetrable, so enigmatic that one cannot interpret its significance: *an inscrutable smile.* That which is MYSTICAL has a secret significance, such as that attaching to certain rites or signs: *mystical symbols.* That which is OBSCURE is discovered or comprehended dimly or with difficulty: *obscure motives.* **3.** unfathomable, unintelligible, incomprehensible, enigmatic, impenetrable.

mys·ter·y[1] (mis′tə rē, -trē), *n., pl.* **-ter·ies.** **1.** anything that is kept secret or remains unexplained or unknown: *the mysteries of nature.* **2.** any affair, thing, or person that presents features or qualities so obscure as to arouse curiosity or speculation: *The masked guest is an absolute mystery to everyone.* **3.** a novel, short story, play, or film whose plot involves a crime or other event that remains puzzlingly unsettled until the very end: *a mystery by Agatha Christie.* **4.** obscure, puzzling, or mysterious quality or character: *the mystery of Mona Lisa's smile.* **5.** any truth that is unknowable except by divine revelation. **6.** (in the Christian religion) **a.** a sacramental rite. **b.** the Eucharist. **7.** an incident or scene in connection with the life of Christ, regarded as of special significance: *the mysteries of the Passion.* **8.** any of the 15 events in the lives of Christ and the Virgin Mary meditated upon during the recitation of the rosary. **9.** **mysteries, a.** ancient religions that admitted candidates by secret rites and rituals the meaning of which was known only to initiated worshipers. **b.** any rites or secrets known only to those initiated: *the mysteries of Freemasonry.* **c.** (in the Christian religion) the Eucharistic elements. **10.** See **mystery play.** [1275–1325; ME *mysterie* < L *mystērium* < Gk *mystḗrion,* equiv. to *mýs(tēs)* (see MYSTIC) + *-tērion* n. suffix]
—**Syn. 4.** puzzle, problem, secret, riddle.

mys·ter·y[2] (mis′tə rē), *n., pl.* **-ter·ies.** *Archaic.* **1.** a craft or trade. **2.** a guild, as of merchants. [1325–75; ME *mistery* < ML *misterium,* var. of L *ministerium* MINISTRY]

mys′tery play′, a medieval dramatic form based on a Biblical story, usually dealing with the life, death, and resurrection of Christ. Cf. **miracle play, morality play.** [1850–55]

mys·tic (mis′tik), *adj.* **1.** involving or characterized by esoteric, otherworldly, or symbolic practices or content, as certain religious ceremonies and art; spiritually significant; ethereal. **2.** of the nature of or pertaining to mysteries known only to the initiated: *mystic rites.* **3.** of occult character, power, or significance: *a mystic formula.* **4.** of obscure or mysterious character or significance. **5.** of or pertaining to mystics or mysticism. —*n.* **6.** a person who claims to attain, or believes in the possibility of attaining, insight into mysteries transcending ordinary human knowledge, as by direct communication with the divine or immediate intuition in a state of spiritual ecstasy. **7.** a person initiated into religious mysteries. [1275–1325; ME *mystik* < L *mysticus* < Gk *mystikós,* equiv. to *mýst(ēs)* an initiate into the mysteries + *-ikos* -IC; akin to *myeîn* to initiate, teach] —**mys·tic·i·ty** (mi stis′i tē), *n.* —**mys′tic·ly,** *adv.*

Mys·tic (mis′tik), *n.* a section of Groton, in SE Connecticut: maritime museum. 2333.

mys·ti·cal (mis′ti kəl), *adj.* **1.** mystic; occult. **2.** of or pertaining to mystics or mysticism: *mystical writings.* **3.** spiritually symbolic. **4.** *Rare.* obscure in meaning; mysterious. [1425–75; late ME. See MYSTIC, -AL[1]] —**mys′ti·cal·ly,** *adv.* —**mys′ti·cal′i·ty, mys′ti·cal·ness,** *n.*
—**Syn. 1.** See **mysterious.**

mys′tical theol′ogy, the branch of theology dealing with mysticism and mystical experiences. [1605–15]

mys·ti·cete (mis′tə sēt′), *n. Zool.* any whale of the suborder Mysticeti, as finback and humpback whales, characterized by a symmetrical skull, paired blowholes, and rows of baleen plates for feeding on plankton. Cf. **odontocete.** [1825–35; < NL *Mysticeti,* pl. of *Mysticetus* < Gk *mystíkētos* or *mŷs tò kêtos* whalebone whale, lit., mouse-whale (term used in extant texts of Aristotle, perh. a corruption of *mystakókētos mustache-whale; see MUSTACHIO, CET-)]

mys·ti·cism (mis′tə siz′əm), *n.* **1.** the beliefs, ideas, or mode of thought of mystics. **2.** a doctrine of an immediate spiritual intuition of truths believed to transcend ordinary understanding, or of a direct, intimate union of the soul with God through contemplation or ecstasy. **3.** obscure thought or speculation. [1730–40; MYSTIC + -ISM]

mys·ti·cize (mis′tə sīz′), *v.,* **-cized, -ciz·ing.** —*v.t.* **1.** to make mystical; give mystical meaning to: *to mysticize natural phenomena.* —*v.i.* **2.** to speak or write on mystical subjects. Also, *esp. Brit.,* **mys′ti·cise′.** [1670–80; MYSTIC + -IZE]

mys·ti·fy (mis′tə fī′), *v.t.,* **-fied, -fy·ing.** **1.** to perplex (a person) by playing upon the person's credulity; bewilder purposely. **2.** to involve in mystery or obscurity. [1805–15; < F *mystifier,* equiv. to *mysti-* (irreg. comb. form of *mystique* MYSTIC or *mystère* MYSTERY[1]) + *-fier* -FY] —**mys′ti·fi·ca′tion,** *n.* —**mys′ti·fied′ly,** *adv.* —**mys′ti·fi′er,** *n.* —**mys′ti·fy′ing·ly,** *adv.*
—**Syn. 1.** fool, mislead, elude, puzzle.

mys·tique (mi stēk′), *n.* **1.** a framework of doctrines, ideas, beliefs, or the like, constructed around a person or object, endowing the person or object with enhanced value or profound meaning: *the mystique of Poe.* **2.** an aura of mystery or mystical power surrounding a particular occupation or pursuit: *the mystique of nuclear science.* [1890–95; < F (adj.); see MYSTIC]

myth (mith), *n.* **1.** a traditional or legendary story, usually concerning some being or hero or event, with or without a determinable basis of fact or a natural explanation, esp. one that is concerned with deities or demigods and explains some practice, rite, or phenomenon of nature. **2.** stories or matter of this kind: *realm of myth.* **3.** any invented story, idea, or concept: *His account of the event is pure myth.* **4.** an imaginary or fictitious thing or person. **5.** an unproved or false collective belief that is used to justify a social institution. [1820–30; < LL *mȳthos* < Gk *mŷthos* story, word]
—**Syn. 1.** See **legend. 3.** fiction, fantasy, talltale.

myth., **1.** mythological. **2.** mythology.

myth·i·cal (mith′i kəl), *adj.* **1.** pertaining to, of the nature of, or involving a myth. **2.** dealt with in myth, as a prehistoric period. **3.** dealing with myths, as writing. **4.** existing only in myth, as a person. **5.** without foundation in fact; imaginary; fictitious: *The explanation was entirely mythical.* Also, **myth′ic.** [1670–80; < LL *mȳthicus* < Gk *mythikós* of myths (see MYTH, -IC) + -AL[1]] —**myth′i·cal·ly,** *adv.* —**myth′i·cal·ness,** *n.*

myth·i·cize (mith′ə sīz′), *v.t.,* **-cized, -ciz·ing.** to turn into, treat, or explain as a myth. Also, *esp. Brit.,* **myth′i·cise′.** [1830–40; MYTHIC + -IZE] —**myth′i·ci·za′tion,** *n.* —**myth′i·ciz′er,** *n.*

myth·i·fy (mith′ə fī′), *v.t.,* **-fied, -fy·ing.** to create a myth about (a person, place, tradition, etc.); cause to become a myth. [1905–10; MYTH + -IFY] —**myth·i·fi·ca·tion** (mith′ə fi kā′shən), *n.*

myth·mak·er (mith′mā′kər), *n.* a creator of myths. [1870–75; MYTH + MAKER] —**myth′mak′ing,** *n.*

mytho-, a combining form representing **myth** in compound words: *mythogenesis.* [< Gk, comb. form of *mŷthos* MYTH]

myth·o·clast (mith′ə klast′), *n.* a destroyer or debunker of myths. [1885–90; MYTHO- + -CLAST] —**myth′o·clas′tic,** *adj.*

CONCISE ETYMOLOGY KEY: <, descended or borrowed from; >, whence; b., blend of, blended; c., cognate with; cf., compare; deriv., derivative; equiv., equivalent; imit., imitative; obl., oblique; r., replacing; s., stem; sp., spelling, spelled; resp., respelling, respelled; trans., translation; ?, origin unknown; *, unattested; ‡, probably earlier than. See the full key inside the front cover.

myth·o·gen·ic (mith′ə jen′ik), *adj.* producing or capable of producing myths. [1960–65; MYTHO- + -GENIC]

my·thog·ra·pher (mi thog′rə fər), *n.* a person who collects or records myths in writing. Also, **my·thog′ra·phist.** [1650–60; < Gk *mȳthográph(os)* mythographer (see MYTHO-, -GRAPH) + -ER[1]]

my·thog·ra·phy (mi thog′rə fē), *n., pl.* **-phies. 1.** a written collection of myths. **2.** expression of myths in artistic, esp. plastic, form. **3.** description of myths. [1850–55; < Gk *mȳthographía.* See MYTHO-, -GRAPHY]

myth·oi (mith′oi, mī′thoi), *n.* pl. of **mythos.**

mythol., 1. mythological. **2.** mythology.

my·thol·o·gem (mi thol′ə jəm), *n.* a basic theme, as of revenge, self-sacrifice, or betrayal, that is shared by cultures throughout the world. [1880–85; < Gk *mȳthológēma* mythical narrative, equiv. to *mȳthologē-* (var. s. of *mȳthologeîn* to tell as a legend; see MYTHO-, LOGOS) + *-ma* n. suffix]

myth·o·log·i·cal (mith′ə loj′i kəl), *adj.* **1.** of or pertaining to mythology. **2.** imaginary; fictitious. Also, **myth′o·log′ic.** [1605–15; < LL *mȳthologic(us)* < Gk *mȳthologikós* (see MYTHOLOGY, -IC) + -AL[1]] —**myth′o·log′i·cal·ly,** *adv.*

my·thol·o·gist (mi thol′ə jist), *n.* **1.** an expert in mythology. **2.** a writer of myths. [1625–35; < Gk *mȳthológ(os)* story-teller (see MYTHO-, LOGO-) + -IST]

my·thol·o·gize (mi thol′ə jīz′), *v.,* **-gized, -giz·ing.** —*v.i.* **1.** to classify, explain, or write about myths. **2.** to construct or narrate myths. —*v.t.* **3.** to make into or explain as a myth; make mythical. Also, *esp. Brit.,* **my·thol′o·gise′.** [1595–1605; MYTHOLOG(Y) + -IZE; cf. F *mythologiser*] —**my·thol′o·gi·za′tion,** *n.* —**my·thol′o·giz′er,** *n.*

my·thol·o·gy (mi thol′ə jē), *n., pl.* **-gies. 1.** a body of myths, as that of a particular people or that relating to a particular person: *Greek mythology.* **2.** myths collectively. **3.** the science or study of myths. **4.** a set of stories, traditions, or beliefs associated with a particular group or the history of an event, arising naturally or deliberately fostered: *the Fascist mythology of the inter-war years.* [1375–1425; late ME *mythologie* < LL *mȳthologia* < Gk *mȳthología.* See MYTHO-, -LOGY]

myth·o·mane (mith′ə mān′), *n.* **1.** a person with a strong or irresistible propensity for fantasizing, lying, or exaggerating. —*adj.* **2.** of, pertaining to, or characteristic of a mythomane. [1950–55; perh. back formation from MYTHOMANIA]

myth·o·ma·ni·a (mith′ə mā′nē ə), *n. Psychiatry.* lying or exaggerating to an abnormal degree. [1905–10; MYTHO- + -MANIA] —**myth·o·ma·ni·ac** (mith′ə mā′nē ak′), *n., adj.*

myth·o·poe·ia (mith′ə pē′ə), *n.* a mythopoeic act, circumstance, characteristic, etc. [1955–60; < LL < Gk *mȳthopoiía* making of fables, invention, equiv. to *mȳtho-* MYTHO- + *-poiia* (*poi(eîn)* to make + *-ia* n. suffix)]

myth·o·poe·ic (mith′ə pē′ik), *adj.* of or pertaining to the making of myths; causing, producing, or giving rise to myths. Also, **myth·o·po·et·ic** (mith′ə pō et′ik). [1840–50; < Gk *mȳthopoi(ós)* making tales (*mȳtho-* MYTHO- + *-poios* making (*poi(eîn)* to make + *-os* adj. suffix) + -IC] —**myth′o·poe′ism,** *n.* —**myth′o·poe′·ist,** *n.*

myth·o·po·et·ize (mith′ə pō′i tīz′), *v.i.,* **-ized, -iz·ing.** to produce myths or mythological poetry. Also, *esp. Brit.,* **myth′o·po′et·ise′.** [1890–95; MYTHO- + POETIZE]

myth·os (mith′os, mī′thos), *n., pl.* **myth·oi** (mith′oi, mī′thoi). **1.** the underlying system of beliefs, esp. those dealing with supernatural forces, characteristic of a particular cultural group. **2.** myth (def. 1). **3.** mythology (def. 1). [1745–55; < Gk *mȳ́thos;* see MYTH]

Myt·i·le·ne (mit′l ē′nē; *Gk.* mē′tē lē′nē), *n.* **1.** Also called **Lesbos.** a Greek island in the NE Aegean. 97,000; 836 sq. mi. (2165 sq. km). **2.** Also called **Kastro.** the capital of this island. 24,157.

My·ti·shchi (mi tē′shē; *Russ.* mi tyē′shchyi), *n.* a city in the W Russian Federation in Europe, NE of Moscow. 150,000.

myx-, var. of **myxo-** before a vowel: *myxasthenia.*

myx·a·me·ba (mik′sə mē′bə), *n., pl.* **-bas, -bae** (-bē). the amebalike, usually nonflagellated, uninucleate haploid individual of a sporocarp that is released upon spore germination and feeds by engulfing bacteria and yeast: a typical stage in the life cycle of cellular slime molds. Also, **myx′a·moe′ba.** [1885–90; MYX- + AMEBA]

myx·as·the·ni·a (mik′səs thē′nē ə, mik sas′thə nī′ə), *n. Pathol.* defective secretion of mucus. [MYX- + ASTHENIA]

myx·e·de·ma (mik′si dē′mə), *n. Pathol.* a condition characterized by thickening of the skin, blunting of the senses and intellect, and labored speech, associated with hypothyroidism. Also, **myx′oe·de′ma.** [1875–80; MYX- + EDEMA] —**myx·e·dem·a·tous** (mik′si dem′ə təs, -dē′mə-), *adj.* —**myx·e·dem·ic** (mik′si dem′ik), *adj.*

myxo-, a combining form meaning "mucus" or "slime," used in the formation of compound words: *myxoneurosis.* Also, *esp. before a vowel,* **myx-.** [comb. form repr. Gk *mýxa*]

myx·o·bac·te·ri·a (mik′sō bak tēr′ē ə), *n.pl., sing.* **-te·ri·um** (-tēr′ē əm). *Bacteriol.* See **gliding bacteria.** [1930–35; MYXO- + BACTERIA, based on the genus name *Myxobacter;* see -BACTER]

myx·oid (mik′soid), *adj.* resembling mucus. [MYX- + -OID]

myx·o·ma (mik sō′mə), *n., pl.* **-mas, -ma·ta** (-mə tə). *Pathol.* a soft tumor composed of connective and mucoid tissue. [1865–70; < NL; see MYX-, -OMA] —**myx·om·a·tous** (mik som′ə təs), *n.*

myx·o·ma·to·sis (mik′sə mə tō′sis), *n.* **1.** *Pathol.* **a.** a condition characterized by the presence of many myxomas. **b.** myxomatous degeneration. **2.** *Vet. Pathol.* a highly infectious viral disease of rabbits, artificially introduced into Great Britain and Australia to reduce the rabbit population. [1925–30; < NL *myxomat-* (s. of *myxoma;* see MYX-, -OMA) + -OSIS]

myx·o·my·cete (mik′sō mī′sēt, -mī sēt′), *n.* an organism of the phylum Myxomycota (or, in some classifications, the class Myxomycetes), comprising the slime molds. [1875–80; < NL *Myxomycetes;* see MYXO-, -MYCETE]

myx·o·my·ce·tous (mik′sō mī sē′təs), *adj.* of or pertaining to a slime mold. [1880–85; MYXOMYCET(ES) + -OUS]

myx·o·spore (mik′sə spôr′, -spōr′), *n. Mycol.* a spore produced within any of various fruiting bodies of myxomycetes. [1850–55; MYXO- + SPORE]

myx·o·vi·rus (mik′sə vī′rəs, mik′sə vī′-), *n., pl.* **-rus·es.** any of a group of medium-sized, RNA-containing viruses having a helical envelope, infectious to humans and other animals and a cause of influenza. Cf. **paramyxovirus.** [1950–55; < NL; see MYXO-, VIRUS]

CONCISE PRONUNCIATION KEY: *act, cāpe, dâre, pärt; set, ēqual; if, īce; ox, ōver, ôrder, oil, bŏŏk, bōōt, out; up, ûrge; child; sing; shoe; thin, that;* zh as in *treasure.* ə = *a* as in *alone, e* as in *system, i* as in *easily, o* as in *gallop, u* as in *circus;* ᵊ as in *fire* (fīᵊr), *hour* (ouᵊr). l and n can serve as syllabic consonants, as in *cradle* (krād′l), and *button* (but′n). See the full key inside the front cover.

DEVELOPMENT OF MAJUSCULE								
NORTH SEMITIC	GREEK		ETR.	LATIN		MODERN		
						GOTHIC	ITALIC	ROMAN

N

DEVELOPMENT OF MINUSCULE					
ROMAN CURSIVE	ROMAN UNCIAL	CAROL. MIN.	MODERN		
			GOTHIC	ITALIC	ROMAN

The fourteenth letter of the English alphabet, developed from North Semitic *nun*, has preserved its original form, with little change, through Greek *nu* (ν). It has usually followed M, and during most of its history, paralleling that letter, it has retained its similarity to it.

N, n (en), *n., pl.* **N's** or **Ns, n's** or **ns. 1.** the 14th letter of the English alphabet, a consonant. **2.** any spoken sound represented by the letter *N* or *n*, as in *now, dinner, son,* etc. **3.** something having the shape of an N. **4.** a written or printed representation of the letter *N* or *n*. **5.** a device, as a printer's type, for reproducing the letter *N* or *n*.

'n (ən), *conj. Pron. Spelling.* and: *Stop 'n save. Look 'n listen.* Also, **'n'.**

N, 1. *Physics.* newton; newtons. **2.** north. **3.** northern.

N, *Symbol.* **1.** the 14th in order or in a series, or, when *I* is omitted, the 13th. **2.** (*sometimes l.c.*) the medieval Roman numeral for 90. Cf. **Roman numerals. 3.** *Chem.* nitrogen. **4.** *Biochem.* asparagine. **5.** *Math.* an indefinite, constant whole number, esp. the degree of a quantic or an equation, or the order of a curve. **6.** *Chess.* knight. **7.** *Print.* en. **8.** *Chem.* See **Avogadro's number. 9.** See **neutron number.**

n, *Symbol.* **1.** *Physics.* neutron. **2.** *Optics.* See **index of refraction.**

n-, *Chem.* an abbreviated form of **normal,** used in the names of hydrocarbon compounds that have a normal or straight chain of carbon atoms: *n-3 fatty acid.*

-n, var. of **-an** after a vowel: *Virginian.*

N., 1. Nationalist. **2.** Navy. **3.** New. **4.** Noon. **5.** *Chem.* normal (strength solution). **6.** Norse. **7.** north. **8.** northern. **9.** *Finance.* note. **10.** November.

n., 1. name. **2.** born. [< L *nātus*] **3.** nephew. **4.** *Com.* net. **5.** neuter. **6.** new. **7.** nominative. **8.** noon. **9.** *Chem.* normal (strength solution). **10.** north. **11.** northern. **12.** *Finance.* note. **13.** noun. **14.** number.

na (nä, nə), *Chiefly Scot.* **—adv. 1.** no. **2.** not; in no way; by no means. **—conj. 3.** nor; neither. [bef. 900; ME (north and Scots); in part repr. OE *nā* (*n*(*e*) not, nor + *ā* ever; cf. AY[1]); in part var. of *ne;* cf. NO[1]]

NA, 1. not applicable. **2.** not available.

Na, *Symbol, Chem.* sodium. [< NL *natrium*]

n/a, no account.

N.A., 1. National Army. **2.** North America. **3.** not applicable. **4.** *Micros.* See **numerical aperture.**

NAA, National Aeronautic Association.

NAACP, National Association for the Advancement of Colored People. Also, **N.A.A.C.P.**

Naaf•i (naf′ē), *n. Brit.* **1.** Navy, Army, and Air Force Institutes: an organization that provides social facilities, stores, etc., to British military personnel. **2.** a canteen run by this organization. Also, **NAAFI**

nab (nab), *v.t.,* **nabbed, nab•bing.** *Informal.* **1.** to arrest or capture. **2.** to catch or seize, esp. suddenly. **3.** to snatch or steal. [1675–85; earlier *nap;* perh. < Scand; cf. Dan *nappe,* Norw, Sw *nappa* to snatch] **—nab′ber,** *n.*

NAB, 1. Also, **N.A.B.** National Association of Broadcasters. **2.** See **New American Bible.**

Na•bal (nā′bəl), *n.* a wealthy Calebite, husband of Abigail, who refused rightful tribute to King David for protecting Nabal's flocks. I Sam. 25. **—Na′bal•ism,** *n.* **—Na′bal•ite′,** *n.* **—Na•bal•it•ic** (nā′bə lit′ik), *adj.*

Nab•a•tae•an (nab′ə tē′ən), *n.* **1.** a subject of an ancient Arab kingdom in Palestine that became a Roman province in A.D. 106. **2.** the Aramaic dialect of the Nabataeans. **—adj. 3.** of or pertaining to the Nabataeans, their kingdom, or their dialect. Also, **Nab′a•te′an.** [1595–1605; < L *Nabatae*(*a*) name of kingdom + -AN]

nabe (nāb), *n.* Usually, **nabes.** *Slang.* a neighborhood movie theater. [shortening and resp. of NEIGHBORHOOD]

CONCISE ETYMOLOGY KEY: <, descended or borrowed from; >, whence; b., blend of, blended; c., cognate with; cf., compare; deriv., derivative; equiv., equivalent; imit., imitative; obl., oblique; r., replacing; s., stem; sp., spelling, spelled; resp., respelling, respelled; trans., translation; ?, origin unknown; *, unattested; ‡, probably earlier than. See the full key inside the front cover.

Na•be•rezh•nye Chel•ny (nä′bə rezh′nē ə chel nē′; *Russ.* nä′byi ʀyi zhni yə chyil nī′), a port in the Tatar Autonomous Republic, in the Russian Federation in Asia, E of Kazan, on the Kama River. 501,000. Also, **Na′be•re′zhny•ye Chel•ny′.**

na•bi (nä′bē), *n. Islam.* a prophet. [1875–80; < Ar *nabī*]

Nab•lus (nab′ləs, nä′bləs), *n.* modern name of **Shechem.**

na•bob (nā′bob), *n.* **1.** any very wealthy, influential, or powerful person. **2.** Also, **nawab.** a person, esp. a European, who has made a large fortune in India or another country of the East. **3.** nawab (def. 1). [1605–15; < Hindi *nawāb.* See NAWAB] **—na•bob•er•y** (nā′bob ə rē, nā bob′ə rē), **na′bob•ism,** *n.* **—na′bob•ish, na•bob′i•cal,** *adj.* **—na′bob•ish•ly, na•bob′i•cal•ly,** *adv.* **—na′bob•ship′,** *n.*

Na•bo•kov (nə bô′kəf, nab′ə kôf′, -kof′; *Russ.* nu bô′-kəf), *n.* **Vla•di•mir Vla•di•mi•ro•vich** (vlad′ə mēr′ vlad′ə mēr′ə vich; *Russ.* vlu dyē′myiʀ vlu dyē′myi ʀə-vyich), 1899–1977, U.S. novelist, short-story writer, and poet, born in Russia.

Nab•o•ko•vi•an (nab′ə kō′vē ən), *adj.* of, pertaining to, characteristic of, or resembling the literary style of Vladimir Nabokov: *a sly, Nabokovian sense of the absurd.* [1955–60; NABOKOV + -IAN]

Nab•o•nas•sar (nab′ō nas′ər), *n.* died 733? B.C., king of Babylon 747?–733?. Assyrian, **Nab′ū-nas′ir.**

Nab•o•ni•dus (nab′ō nī′dəs), *n.* died 539? B.C., last king of Babylonia 556–539 (father of Belshazzar).

Na•both (nā′both, -bôth), *n.* the owner of a vineyard coveted by Ahab, slain by the scheming of Jezebel so that Ahab could secure the vineyard. I Kings 21.

Nab•u•cho•don•o•sor (nab′ə kō don′ə sôr′), *n. Douay Bible.* Nebuchadnezzar (def. 1).

NACA, National Advisory Committee for Aeronautics. Also, **N.A.C.A.**

na•celle (nə sel′), *n.* **1.** the enclosed part of an airplane, dirigible, etc., in which the engine is housed or in which cargo or passengers are carried. **2.** the car of a balloon. [1475–85; < F: a small boat < LL *nāvicella,* for L *nāvicula,* equiv. to *nāvi*(*s*) ship (see NAVE) + *-cula* -CULE[1]]

na•cho (nä′chō), *n., pl.* **-chos.** *Mexican Cookery.* a snack or appetizer consisting of a small piece of tortilla topped with cheese, hot peppers, etc., and broiled. [1965–70; < MexSp; ulterior orig. uncert.]

Nac•og•do•ches (nak′ə dō′chəz), *n.* a city in N Texas. 27,149.

na•cre (nā′kər), *n.* mother-of-pearl. [1590–1600; < ML *nacrum, nacer,* var. of *nacara* < OIt *naccara* kind of drum, nacre < Ar *naqqārah* drum]

na•cred (nā′kərd), *adj.* lined with or resembling nacre. [1590–1600; NACRE + -ED[3]]

na•cre•ous (nā′krē əs), *adj.* **1.** of or pertaining to nacre. **2.** resembling nacre; lustrous; pearly. [1830–40; NACRE + -OUS]

na′creous cloud′, a rarely seen, luminous, iridescent cloud shaped like a cirrus or altocumulus, approximately 15 mi. (24 km) above the earth, and of unknown composition. Also called **mother-of-pearl cloud.**

NAD, *Biochem.* nicotinamide adenin[illegible]ucleotide: a coenzyme, $C_{21}H_{27}N_7O_{14}P_2$, involved in [illegible]ellular oxidation-reduction reactions.

N.A.D., National Academy of Desi[illegible]

Na•dab (nā′dab), *n.* a son of Aar[illegible]f. **Abihu.**

Na-De•ne (nä dā′nē, nä′dā nā′[illegible] group of North American Indian languages, [illegible]e Athabaskan family, Eyak, Tlingit, and [illegible]etically considered to be descendants of [illegible]nguage: the genetic relationship of eith[illegible]aida to Athabaskan and Eyak is now dis[illegible]ypothesized protolanguage itself. **—adj.** [illegible] to, or pertaining to Na-Dene. Also, **Na•de′ne.** [1915; name coined by Edward Sapir from assumed reflexes of a single Na-Dene root: Haida *na* to live, house, Tlingit *na* people, Athabaskan **-ne* in *dene,* repr. a word in Athabaskan languages for "person, people," e.g., Navajo *diné*]

Na•der (nā′dər), *n.* **Ralph,** born 1934, U.S. lawyer, author, political reformer, and consumer advocate.

NADH, *Biochem.* an abbreviation for the reduced form of NAD in electron transport reactions. [NAD + *H,* for hydrogen]

Na•dine (nā dēn′, nə-), *n.* a female given name.

na•dir (nā′dər, nā′dēr), *n.* **1.** *Astron.* the point on the celestial sphere directly beneath a given position or observer and diametrically opposite the zenith. **2.** *Astrol.* the point of a horoscope opposite the midheaven: the cusp of the fourth house. **3.** the lowest point; point of greatest adversity or despair. [1350–1400; ME << Ar *naẓīr* over against, opposite to (the zenith)] **—na′dir•al,** *adj.*
—Syn. 3. bottom, floor, foot, depths.

NADP, *Biochem.* nicotinamide adenine dinucleotide phosphate: a coenzyme, $C_{21}H_{28}N_7O_{17}P_3$, similar in function to NAD in many oxidation-reduction reactions.

nae (nā), *Scot. and North Eng.* **—adv. 1.** no; not. **—adj. 2.** no. [1715–25; var. of NA]

nae•thing (nā′thing), *n., adv. Scot.* nothing.

Na•fl (nä′fl[ə]), *n. Islam.* a prayer, charitable act, etc., that goes beyond the requirements of one's religion. Also, **Na•fi•la, Na•fi•lah** (nä′fə lə). [< Ar]

NAFTA (naf′tə), *n.* North American Free Trade Agreement. Also, **Nafta.**

Na•fud (na fōōd′), *n.* See **Nefud Desert.**

nag[1] (nag), *v.,* **nagged, nag•ging,** *n.* **—v.t. 1.** to annoy by persistent faultfinding, complaints, or demands. **2.** to keep in a state of troubled awareness or anxiety, as a recurrent pain or problem: *She had certain misgivings that nagged her.* **—v.i. 3.** to find fault or complain in an irritating, wearisome, or relentless manner (often fol. by *at*): *If they start nagging at each other, I'm going home.* **4.** to cause pain, discomfort, distress, depression, etc. (often fol. by *at*): *This headache has been nagging at me all day.* **—n. 5.** Also, **nagger.** a person who nags, esp. habitually. **6.** an act or instance of nagging. [1815–25; < ON *nagga* to rub, grumble, quarrel; akin to MLG *naggen* to irritate. See GNAW]
—Syn. 1. pester, harass, hector, irritate, vex.

nag[2] (nag), *n.* **1.** an old, inferior, or worthless horse. **2.** *Slang.* any horse, esp. a racehorse. **3.** a small riding horse or pony. [1350–1400; late ME *nagge;* connected with D *neg(ge)* small horse, itself attested late and of obscure orig.; said to be akin to NEIGH]

Na•ga (nā′gä), *n.* a city on E Cebu, in the S central Philippines. 90,712.

Na•ga (nä′gä), *n., pl.* **-gas,** (*esp. collectively*) **-ga** for 1. **1.** a member of any of the disparate tribal peoples of Nagaland and bordering areas of Burma. **2.** any of the Tibeto-Burman languages spoken by the Naga.

Na•ga•land (nä′gə land′), *n.* a state in NE India. 56,000; 6366 sq. mi. (16,488 sq. km). *Cap.:* Kohima.

na•ga′mi kum′quat (nə gä′mē). See **oval kumquat.** [*nagami* < Japn, equiv. to *naga* long, oblong + *mi* fruit]

na•ga•na (nə gä′nə), *n. Vet. Pathol.* **1.** a disease of horses and other animals, widespread in parts of Africa, caused by the organism *Trypanosoma brucei,* and transmitted by a variety of tsetse fly. **2.** any trypanosomal disease of animals that is transmitted by the tsetse fly. Also, **n'gana.** [1890–95; < Nguni; cf. Zulu *unukane, ulunakane, izinakane*]

Na•ga•no (nä gä′nô), *n.* a city on central Honshu, in central Japan. 324,360.

Na•ga•ri (nä′gə rē), *n.* **1.** a group of related scripts, including Devanagari, derived from Brahmi and used for the writing of many of the languages of India. **2.** Devanagari.

Na·ga·sa·ki (nä′gə sä′kē, nag′ə sak′ē; *Japn.* nä′gä-sä′kē), *n.* a seaport on W Kyushu, in SW Japan: second military use of the atomic bomb August 9, 1945. 446,000.

nag·ger (nag′ər), *n.* nag¹ (def. 5). [1880–85; NAG¹ + -ER¹]

nag·ging (nag′ing), *adj.* **1.** continually faultfinding, complaining, or petulant: *a nagging parent.* **2.** persistently recurring; unrelenting: *a nagging backache.* [1830–40; NAG¹ + -ING²] —**nag′ging·ness,** *n.*

nag·gish (nag′ish), *adj.* tending to nag; somewhat nagging. [1880–85; NAG¹ + -ISH¹]

nag·gy (nag′ē), *adj.,* **-gi·er, -gi·est.** naggish. [1690–1700; NAG¹ + -Y¹]

Na·gor′no-Ka·ra·bakh′ Auton′omous Re′gion (nə gôr′nō kär′ə bäk′; *Russ.* nu gôʀ′nə kə ʀu bäkʜ′), an autonomous region in SW Azerbaijan. 188,000; 1700 sq. mi. (4400 sq. km). *Cap.:* Stepanakert.

Na·go·ya (nə goi′ə; *Japn.* nä′gô yä′), *n.* a city on S Honshu, in central Japan. 2,087,884.

Nag·pur (näg′po͝or), *n.* a city in NE Maharashtra, in central India: former capital of the Central Provinces and Berar. 866,144.

na·gual (nä gwäl′, -wäl′), *n.* a guardian spirit among Mexican and Central American Indians, believed to reside in an animal. [< MexSp *nagual, nahual* < Nahuatl *nāhualli*] —**na·gual′ism,** *n.*

Na·guib (nə gēb′), *n.* **Mohammed,** born 1901, Egyptian general and political leader: premier 1952–54; president 1953–54.

Na·gur·ski (nə gûr′skē), *n.* **Bron·is·law** (bron′ə slof′), (*"Bronko"*), born 1908, U.S. football player.

Nagy (nod′yᵊ, noj), *n.* **Im·re** (im′ʀe), 1896–1958, Hungarian political leader: premier 1953–55, 1956.

Nagy·vá·rad (nod′yᵊ vä′ʀod, noj′-), *n.* Hungarian name of **Oradea.**

Nah., Nahum.

Na·ha (nä′hä), *n.* a port on SW Okinawa, in S Japan. 295,801.

NAHB, National Association of Home Builders.

nah·co·lite (nä′kə līt′), *n.* a carbonate mineral, naturally occurring sodium bicarbonate, $NaHCO_3$. [1925–30; *$NaHCO_3$*, its chemical name + -LITE]

Na·hua (nä′wä), *n., pl.* **-huas,** (*esp. collectively*) **-hua,** *adj.* Nahuatl.

Na·hua·tl (nä′wät l), *n., pl.* **-hua·tls,** (*esp. collectively*) **-hua·tl,** *adj.* —*n.* **1.** a member of any of various peoples of ancient origin ranging from southeastern Mexico to parts of Central America and including the Aztecs. **2.** a Uto-Aztecan language spoken by over half a million people mostly in central Mexico. Cf. **Aztec** (def. 2). —*adj.* **3.** of or pertaining to the Nahuatl language or peoples. [1815–25; < Sp *nāhuatl* < Nahuatl *nāhuatl* something that makes an agreeable sound, a second-language speaker of one's own language]

Na·hua·tlan (nä′wät lən), *n.* **1.** Nahuatl in all its dialects, often taken as a group of languages, spoken in large areas of central Mexico and El Salvador and in various small, widely dispersed areas throughout southern Mexico and Central America. —*adj.* **2.** of or pertaining to Nahuatl or Nahuatlan. [1900–05; NAHUATL + -AN]

Na·hum (nā′həm), *n.* **1.** a Minor Prophet of the 7th century B.C. **2.** a book of the Bible bearing his name. *Abbr.:* Nah.

nai·ad (nā′ad, -əd, nī′-), *n., pl.* **-ads, -a·des** (-ə dēz′). **1.** (*sometimes cap.*) *Class. Myth.* any of a class of nymphs presiding over rivers and springs. **2.** the juvenile form of the dragonfly, damselfly, or mayfly. **3.** a female swimmer, esp. an expert one. **4.** *Bot.* a plant of the genus *Najas,* having narrow leaves and solitary flowers. **5.** *Entomol.* an aquatic nymph. **6.** a freshwater mussel. [< L *Nāïad-* (s. of *Nāïas*) < Gk *Nāïás* a water nymph]

Nai·da (nā′də), *n.* a female given name.

na·ïf (nä ēf′), *n.* **1.** a naive or inexperienced person. —*adj.* **2.** naive. Also, **na·if′.** [< MF; masc. of NAÏVE]

nail (nāl), *n.* **1.** a slender, typically rod-shaped rigid piece of metal, usually in any of numerous standard lengths from a fraction of an inch to several inches and having one end pointed and the other enlarged and flattened, for hammering into or through wood, other building materials, etc., as used in building, in fastening, or in holding separate pieces together. **2.** a thin, horny plate, consisting of modified epidermis, growing on the upper side of the end of a finger or toe. **3.** a former measure of length for cloth, equal to 2¼ in. (6.4 cm). **4. hit the nail on the head,** to say or do exactly the right thing; be accurate or correct: *Your analysis really hit the nail on the head.* **5. on the nail,** *Informal.* **a.** of present interest; under discussion. **b.** without delay; on the spot; at once: *He was offered a job on the nail.* —*v.t.* **6.** to fasten with a nail or nails: *to nail the cover on a box.* **7.** to enclose or confine (something) by nailing (often fol. by *up*): *to nail up oranges in a crate.* **8.** to make fast or keep firmly in one place or position: *Surprise nailed him to the spot.* **9.** *Informal.* **a.** to secure by prompt action; catch or seize: *The police nailed him with the goods.* **b.** to catch (a person) in some difficulty, lie, etc. **c.** to detect and expose (a lie, scandal, etc.). **10.** *Slang.* to hit (a person): *He nailed him on the chin with an uppercut in the first round.* **11.** to focus intently on an object or subject: *She kept her eyes nailed on the suspicious customer.* **12.** *Obs.* to stud with or as if with nails. **13. nail down,** to make final; settle once and for all: *Signing the contract will nail down our agreement.* [bef. 900; (n.) ME *nail(l), nayl(l),* OE *nægl,* c. OFris *neil,* OS, OHG *nagal,* D *nagel,* G *Nagel,* ON *nagl* fingernail, all < Gmc **naglaz;* akin as deriv. to Lith *nāgas, nagà* hoof, OPruss *nage* foot, OCS *noga* leg, foot (Serbo-Croatian *nòga,* Czech *noha,* Russ *nogá;* prob. orig. jocular reference to the foot as a hoof), OCS *nogŭtĭ,* Tocharian A *maku,* B *mekwa* fingernail, claw, all < North European IE **H₃nogʷh-;* further akin to OIr *ingen,* Welsh *ewin,* Breton *ivin* < Celtic **ŋgʷhinā,* L *unguis* < Italo-Celtic **H₃ngʷhi-;* Gk *ónyx,* s. *onych-,* Armenian *elungn* < **H₃nogʷh-;* (v.) ME *nail(l)(e), nayl(l)e(n),* OE *næglian,* c. OS *neglian,* OHG *negilen,* ON *negla* < Gmc **nagl-janaⁿ;* cf. Goth *ganagljan*] —**nail′less,** *adj.* —**nail′like′,** *adj.*
—**Syn. 8.** fix, secure, pin, fasten.

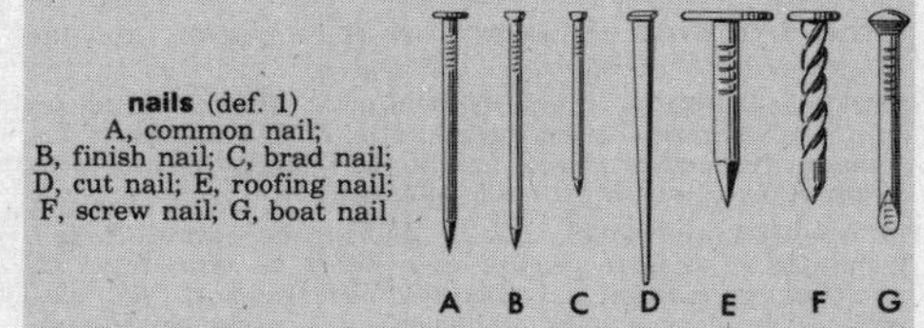

nails (def. 1) A, common nail; B, finish nail; C, brad nail; D, cut nail; E, roofing nail; F, screw nail; G, boat nail

nail-bit·ing (nāl′bī′ting), *n.* **1.** the act or practice of biting one's fingernails, esp. as the result of anxiety or nervousness. **2.** *Informal.* nervousness: *The announcement that the trade agreement had been signed ended a week of nail-biting on Wall Street.* —*adj.* **3.** *Informal.* causing nervousness: *The nail-biting part of the canoe trip was through the stretches of white water.* [1890–95] —**nail′-bit′er,** *n.*

nail′ bomb′, an explosive device packed with nails or similar metal objects that act as shrapnel. [1970–75]

nail·brush (nāl′brush′), *n.* a small brush with stiff bristles, used to clean the fingernails. [1795–1805; NAIL + BRUSH¹]

nail·clip·per (nāl′klip′ər), *n.* Often, **nailclippers.** a small mechanical device for clipping the fingernails or toenails. [1940–45; NAIL + CLIPPER]

nail′ enam′el. See **nail polish.** [1905–10]

nail·er (nā′lər), *n.* a person or thing that drives nails, as a machine that drives nails automatically. [1400–50; late ME; see NAIL, -ER¹]

nail′er joist′, a steel joist having a permanently attached nailing strip, as for securing wooden flooring.

nail′ file′, a small file of metal or cardboard, for trimming, smoothing, or shaping the fingernails and sometimes having a point for removing dirt from under them. [1870–75, *Amer.*]

nail·head (nāl′hed′), *n.* **1.** the enlarged top of a nail, usually flattened but sometimes rounded. **2.** an ornament that suggests or resembles the enlarged top of a nail. [1675–85; NAIL + HEAD] —**nail′-head′ed,** *adj.*

nail′ing strip′, a strip of wood or other partly yielding material attached to a hard surface, as of steel or concrete, so that objects may be nailed to the surface.

nail′ pol′ish, a polish of quick-drying lacquer, either clear or colored, used to paint the fingernails or toenails. [1905–10]

nail′ scis′sors, (*usually used with a plural v.*) small scissors with short curved blades for trimming the fingernails or toenails. [1850–55]

nail′ set′, a short rod of steel used to drive a nail below or flush with a surface. [1895–1900]

nail-sick (nāl′sik′), *adj.* *Naut.* iron-sick. [1860–65] —**nail′sick′ness,** *n.*

nail′ var′nish, *Brit.* See **nail polish.** [1925–30]

nail′ violin′, a musical instrument consisting of a wooden cylinder or half cylinder with a number of nails or U-shaped metal pins inserted into its surface, played with one or two fiddle bows. [1880–85]

Na·i·ma (nä ē′mə), *n.* a female given name: from an Arabic word meaning "benevolent."

nain·sook (nān′so͝ok, nan′-), *n.* a fine, soft-finished cotton fabric, usually white, used for lingerie and infants' wear. [1780–90; < Urdu, Hindi *nainsukh,* equiv. to *nain* the eye + *sukh* pleasure]

nai·ra (nī′rə), *n.* a paper money and monetary unit of Nigeria, equal to 100 kobo: replaced the pound in 1973.

Nairn (nârn), *n.* a historic county in N Scotland. Also called **Nairn·shire** (nârn′shēr′, -shər).

Nai·ro·bi (nī rō′bē), *n.* a city in and the capital of Kenya, in the SW part. 650,000.

Nai·smith (nā′smith), *n.* **James,** 1861–1939, U.S. physical-education teacher and originator of basketball, born in Canada.

nais·sance (nā′səns), *n.* a birth, an origination, or a growth, as that of a person, an organization, an idea, or a movement. [1480–90; < F, MF, equiv. to *nais-* (s. of *naître* to be born < VL **nāscere,* for L *nāscī*) + *-ance* -ANCE]

na·ive (nä ēv′), *adj.* **1.** having or showing unaffected simplicity of nature or absence of artificiality; unsophisticated; ingenuous. **2.** having or showing a lack of experience, judgment, or information; credulous: *She's so naive she believes everything she reads. He has a very naive attitude toward politics.* **3.** having or marked by a simple, unaffectedly direct style reflecting little or no formal training or technique: *valuable naive 19th-century American portrait paintings.* **4.** not having previously been the subject of a scientific experiment, as an animal. Also, **na·ïve′.** [1645–55; < F, fem. of *naïf,* OF *naif* natural, instinctive < L *nātīvus* NATIVE] —**na·ive′ly,** *adv.* —**na·ive′ness,** *n.*
—**Syn. 1.** simple, unaffected, unsuspecting, artless, guileless, candid, open, plain. —**Ant. 1.** sophisticated, artful.

naive′ re′alism, *Philos.* the theory that the world is perceived exactly as it is. Also called **commonsense realism, natural realism.** [1880–85] —**naive′ re′alist.**

na·ive·té (nä ēv tā′, -ē′və tā′, -ēv′tā, -ē′və-), *n.* **1.** the quality or state of being naive; natural or artless simplicity. **2.** a naive action, remark, etc. Also, **na·ive·té′, na·ive·te′.** [1665–75; < F; see NAIVE, -ITY²]

na·ive·ty (nä ēv′tē, -ē′və-), *n., pl.* **-ties.** naiveté. Also, **na·ïve′ty.**

Na·jaf (naj′af), *n.* a city in central Iraq: holy city of the Shi'ites; shrine contains tomb of Ali (A.D. c600–661), founder of the Shi'ite sect. 134,027. Also, **An-Najaf.**

Na·ka·so·ne (nä′kä sô′ne), *n.* **Ya·su·hi·ro** (yä′so͞o-hē′ʀô), born 1918, Japanese political leader: prime minister 1982–87.

na·ked (nā′kid), *adj.* **1.** being without clothing or covering; nude: *naked children swimming in the lake.* **2.** without adequate clothing: *a naked little beggar.* **3.** bare of any covering, overlying matter, vegetation, foliage, or the like: *naked fields.* **4.** bare, stripped, or destitute (usually fol. by *of*): *The trees were suddenly naked of leaves.* **5.** without the customary covering, container, or protection: *a naked sword; a naked flame.* **6.** without carpets, hangings, or furnishings, as rooms or walls. **7.** (of the eye, sight, etc.) unassisted by a microscope, telescope, or other instrument: *visible to the naked eye.* **8.** defenseless; unprotected; exposed: *naked to invaders.* **9.** plain; simple; unadorned: *the naked realities of the matter.* **10.** not accompanied or supplemented by anything else: *a naked outline of the facts.* **11.** exposed to view or plainly revealed: *the naked threat in the letter; a naked vein of coal.* **12.** plain-spoken; blunt: *the naked truth.* **13.** *Law.* unsupported, as by authority or consideration: *a naked promise.* **14.** *Bot.* **a.** (of seeds) not enclosed in an ovary. **b.** (of flowers) without a calyx or perianth. **c.** (of stalks, branches, etc.) without leaves. **d.** (of stalks, leaves, etc.) without hairs or pubescence. **15.** *Zool.* having no covering of hair, feathers, shell, etc. [bef. 900; ME *naked(e),* OE *nacod;* c. D *naakt,* G *nackt,* Goth *naqths;* akin to ON *nakinn,* L *nūdus,* Gk *gymnós,* Skt *nagnás*] —**na′ked·ly,** *adv.* —**na′ked·ness,** *n.*
—**Syn. 1.** uncovered, undressed, unclothed. **4.** denuded. **5.** unsheathed, exposed. **6.** unfurnished. **8.** unarmed, open. **11.** manifest, evident, undisguised. **12.** direct, outspoken. —**Ant. 1.** dressed. **8.** protected.

Na′ked and the Dead′, The, a novel (1948) by Norman Mailer.

na′ked la′dies, *Brit.* See **autumn crocus.**

na′ked la′dy, amaryllis (def. 2).

na′ked mole′ rat′, a nearly hairless rodent, *Heterocephalus glaber,* of eastern African dry steppes and savannas, having two protruding upper and lower front teeth and living entirely underground in colonies, based on a single breeding female and specialized workers of both sexes. Also called **sand rat, sand puppy.**

naked mole rat, *Heterocephalus glaber,* head and body 3½ in. (8.9 cm); tail 1½ in. (3.8 cm)

Na·khi·che·van′ Auton′omous Repub′lic (nä′-kə chə vän′; *Russ.* nə kʜyi chyi vän′), an autonomous republic of Azerbaijan, surrounded by Armenia, Iran and Turkey. 295,000; 2277 sq. mi. (5500 sq. km). *Cap.:* Nakhichevan.

Na·khod·ka (nu kʜôt′kə), *n.* a port in the SE Russian Federation in Asia, SE of Vladivostok, on the Sea of Japan. 148,000.

Na·khon Rat·cha·si·ma (nä′kôn rä′chə sē′mä), a city in central Thailand. 77,397.

Na·khon Sa·wan (nä′kôn sə wän′), a city in W central Thailand, on the Chao Phraya River. 46,135.

nal·bu·phine (nal′byo͞o fēn′), *n.* *Pharm.* a potent synthetic narcotic, $C_{21}H_{27}NO_4$, used as an analgesic for moderate to severe pain. [by rearrangement of parts of its chemical name]

Nal·chik (näl′chik; *Russ.* näl′chyik), *n.* a city in and the capital of the Kabardino-Balkar Autonomous Republic in the S Russian Federation. 235,000.

na·led (nā′led), *n.* *Chem.* a synthetic insecticide and miticide, $C_4H_7Br_2Cl_2O_4$, having relatively low toxicity to mammals. [1960–65; generic name of uncert. orig.]

na′li·dix′ic ac′id (nā′li dik′sik, nā′-), *Pharm.* a substance, $C_{12}H_{12}N_2O_3$, that has antibacterial activity against many susceptible Gram-negative organisms, esp. used in the treatment of urinary tract infections. [1960–65; by shortening and rearrangement of *naphthyridine* and *carboxylic acid,* components of its chemical name]

Nal·line (nal′ēn), *Pharm., Trademark.* a brand of nalorphine.

nal·or·phine (nal′ər fēn′, nal ôr′fēn), *n.* *Pharm.* a white, crystalline, water-soluble powder, $C_{19}H_{21}NO_3$, used to nullify respiratory depression due to narcotics and for the diagnosis of addiction to narcotics. [1950–55; *N-al(lyln)or(mor)phine;* see ALLYL, NOR-, MORPHINE]

nal·ox·one (nə lok′sōn, nal′ək sōn′), *n.* *Pharm.* a narcotic analgesic antagonist, $C_{19}H_{21}NO_4$, used in the reversal of acute narcotic analgesic respiratory depression. [1960–65; by shortening and rearrangement of *dihydroxy-, morphinan-,* and *-one,* components of its chemical name]

nal·trex·one (nal trek′sōn), *n.* *Pharm.* a nonaddictive substance, $C_{20}H_{23}NO_4$, used in the treatment of heroin addiction and opiate overdose. [1970–75; by rearrangement of parts of its chemical name]

Nam (näm), *n.* a former name of **Chao Phraya.**

Nam (näm, nam), *n.* *Informal.* Vietnam. Also, **'Nam.** [1965–70; by shortening]

CONCISE PRONUNCIATION KEY: act, cāpe, dâre, pärt; set, ēqual; if, īce; ox, ōver, ôrder, oil, bo͝ok, bo͞ot, out; up, ûrge; child; sing; shoe; thin, *th*at; zh as in *treasure.* ə = *a* as in *alone, e* as in *system, i* as in *easily, o* as in *gallop, u* as in *circus;* ᵊ as in *fire* (fīᵊr), *hour* (ouᵊr). l and n can serve as syllabic consonants, as in *cradle* (krād′l), and *button* (but′n). See the full key inside the front cover.

NAM, National Association of Manufacturers. Also, **N.A.M.**

Na·ma (nä′mä, -mə), *n., pl.* **-mas,** (*esp. collectively*) **-ma.** for 1. **1.** a member of a Khoikhoi people of Namaqualand, in SW Africa. **2.** the language of the Nama.

nam·a·ble (nā′mə bəl), *adj.* nameable.

Na·man·gan (nä′mən gän′; *Russ.* nə mun gän′), *n.* a city in E Uzbekistan, NW of Andizhan. 291,000.

Na·ma·qua·land (nə mä′kwə land′), *n.* a coastal region in the S part of Namibia, extending into the Cape of Good Hope province of the Republic of South Africa: inhabited by the Nama. Also called **Na·ma·land** (nä′mə-land′).

na·ma·ste (num′ə stā′), *n.* a conventional Hindu expression on meeting or parting, used by the speaker usually while holding the palms together vertically in front of the bosom. [1945–50; < Skt: hail, lit., (a) bow to thee]

nam·ay·cush (nam′ī kush′, nam′ā-), *n., pl.* **-cush·es,** (*esp. collectively*) **-cush.** a lake trout. [1735–45; < Cree *name·kos* < Proto-Algonquian **name·kwehsa*]

nam·by-pam·by (nam′bē pam′bē), *adj., n., pl.* **-bies** for 4. —*adj.* **1.** without firm methods or policy; weak or indecisive: *namby-pamby handling of juvenile offenders.* **2.** lacking in character, directness, or moral or emotional strength: *namby-pamby writing.* **3.** weakly sentimental, pretentious, or affected; insipid. —*n.* **4.** a namby-pamby person: *written by and for namby-pambies.* **5.** namby-pamby sentiment: *the harmless namby-pamby of a birthday card.* **6.** a namby-pamby verse or prose. [1726; rhyming compound based on the first syll. of *Ambrose* Philips; first used as a nickname for Philips in the title of a poem by Henry Carey (1687?–1743) ridiculing his verse] **—nam′by-pam′bi·ness, nam′by-pam′by·ism,** *n.* **—nam′by-pam′by·ish,** *adj.*

name (nām), *n., v.,* **named, nam·ing,** *adj.* —*n.* **1.** a word or a combination of words by which a person, place, or thing, a body or class, or any object of thought is designated, called, or known. **2.** mere designation, as distinguished from fact: *He was a king in name only.* **3.** an appellation, title, or epithet, applied descriptively, in honor, abuse, etc. **4.** a reputation of a particular kind given by common opinion: *to protect one's good name.* **5.** a distinguished, famous, or great reputation; fame: *to make a name for oneself.* **6.** a widely known or famous person; celebrity: *She's a name in show business.* **7.** an unpleasant or derogatory appellation or expression: *Don't call your brother names! Sticks and stones may break my bones but names will never hurt me.* **8.** a personal or family name as exercising influence or bringing distinction: *With that name they can get a loan at any bank in town.* **9.** a body of persons grouped under one name, as a family or clan. **10.** the verbal or other symbolic representation of a thing, event, property, relation, or concept. **11.** (*cap.*) a symbol or vehicle of divinity: *to take the Name in vain; the power of the Name.* **12. by name, a.** personally; individually: *She was always careful to address every employee by name.* **b.** not personally; by repute: *I know him by name only.* **13. call names,** to scold or speak abusively of or to a person: *Better not to call names unless one is larger and considerably stronger than one's adversary.* **14. in the name of, a.** with appeal to: *In the name of mercy, stop that screaming!* **b.** by the authority of: *Open, in the name of the law!* **c.** on behalf of: *to purchase something in the name of another.* **d.** under the name or possession of: *money deposited in the name of a son.* **e.** under the designation or excuse of: *murder in the name of justice.* **15. to one's name,** in one's possession: *I haven't a penny to my name.* —*v.t.* **16.** to give a name to: *to name a baby.* **17.** to accuse: *He was named as the thief.* **18.** to call by an epithet: *They named her speedy.* **19.** to identify, specify, or mention by name: *Three persons were named in the report.* **20.** to designate for some duty or office; nominate or appoint: *I have named you for the position.* **21.** to specify; suggest: *Name a price.* **22.** to give the name of: *Can you name the capital of Ohio?* **23.** to speak of. **24.** *Brit.* (in the House of Commons) to cite (a member) for contempt. **25. name names,** to specify people by name, esp. those who have been accomplices in a misdeed: *The witness in the bribery investigation threatened to name names.* —*adj.* **26.** famous; widely known: *a name author.* **27.** designed for or carrying a name. **28.** giving its name or title to a collection or anthology containing it: *the name piece.* [bef. 900; ME; OE *nama;* c. G *Name,* Goth *namō;* akin to ON *nafn,* L *nōmen,* Gk *ónoma,* OIr *ainm,* Pol *imię,* Czech *jméno*] **—nam′er,** *n.*
—Syn. 1. NAME, TITLE both refer to the label by which a person is known. NAME is the simpler and more general word for appellation: *The name is John.* A TITLE is an official or honorary term bestowed on a person or the specific designation of a book, article, etc.: *He now has the title of Doctor.* Treasure Island *is the title of a book.* **4.** repute, character, credit. **5.** note, distinction, renown, eminence. **6.** personality. **18.** nickname, dub, denominate. **20.** choose. **21.** mention.

name·a·ble (nā′mə bəl), *adj.* **1.** capable of or susceptible to being named or identified; identifiable. **2.** worth mentioning by name; notable; memorable. Also, **nam·a·ble.** [1770–80; NAME + -ABLE] **—name′a·bil′i·ty,** *n.*

name·board (nām′bôrd′, -bōrd′), *n.* **1.** a signboard that identifies a place or object. **2.** a name painted, stenciled, etc., on something, as on the side of a ship. [1840–50; NAME + BOARD]

name-brand (nām′brand′), *adj.* **1.** brand-name (def. 1). —*n.* **2.** See **brand name** (def. 2). [1940–45]

name-call·er (nām′kô′lər), *n.* a person who constantly resorts to name-calling.

name-call·ing (nām′kô′ling), *n.* the use of abusive names to belittle or humiliate another person in a political campaign, an argument, etc. [1890–95]

name′ day′, 1. the feast day of the saint after whom a person is named. **2.** the day on which a person is christened. [1715–25]

name-drop (nām′drop′), *v.i.,* **-dropped, -drop·ping.** to indulge in name-dropping. [1950–55]

name-drop·per (nām′drop′ər), *n.* a person who indulges in name-dropping. [1945–50]

name-drop·ping (nām′drop′ing), *n.* the introduction into one's conversation, letters, etc., of the names of famous or important people as alleged friends or associates in order to impress others. [1945–50]

name·less (nām′lis), *adj.* **1.** having no name. **2.** left unnamed: *a certain person who shall be nameless.* **3.** anonymous: *a nameless source of information.* **4.** incapable of being specified or described: *a nameless charm.* **5.** too shocking or vile to be specified: *a nameless crime.* **6.** having no legitimate paternal name, as a child born out of wedlock. **7.** unknown to fame; obscure: *a nameless poet; nameless defenders of the country.* [1275–1325; ME; see NAME, -LESS] **—name′less·ly,** *adv.* **—name′less·ness,** *n.*

name·ly (nām′lē), *adv.* that is to say; explicitly; specifically; to wit: *an item of legislation, namely, the housing bill.* [1125–75; ME *namely,* earlier *nameliche.* See NAME, -LY]

name′ of the game′, *Informal.* the essential element, consideration, or ultimate purpose; key: *Profit is the name of the game in business.* [1965–70]

name·plate (nām′plāt′), *n.* **1.** a flat, usually rectangular piece of metal, wood, or plastic on which the name of a person, company, etc., is printed or engraved: *She has a large office with her nameplate on the door.* **2.** masthead (def. 2). [1880–85; NAME + PLATE[1]]

name·sake (nām′sāk′), *n.* **1.** a person named after another. **2.** a person having the same name as another. [1640–50; alter. of *name's* (NAME + -'S[1]) SAKE[1]]

name·tag (nām′tag′), *n.* an identification tag or label showing one's name and sometimes one's address or business affiliation, attached to an article of clothing or worn around the neck or wrist. Also, **name′ tag′.** [1945–50; NAME + TAG[1]]

name′ tape′, a fabric tape on which a person's name is written, woven, or printed: for affixing to garments and other personal belongings to identify ownership. [1895–1900]

Nam·hoi (näm′hoi′), *n. Older Spelling.* Nanhai.

Na′mib Des′ert (nä′mib), a desert region in SW Africa, extending along the coast from SW Angola to W South Africa. 1200 mi. (1930 km) long, 30–100 mi. (48–160 km) wide; 50,000 sq. mi. (129,500 sq. km).

Na·mib·i·a (nə mib′ē ə), *n.* a republic in SW Africa: a former German protectorate; a mandate of South Africa 1920–66; gained independence 1990. 1,400,000; 318,261 sq. mi. (824,296 sq. km). *Cap.:* Windhoek. Formerly, **German Southwest Africa** (1884–1919), **South-West Africa** (1920–68). **—Na·mib′i·an,** *adj., n.*

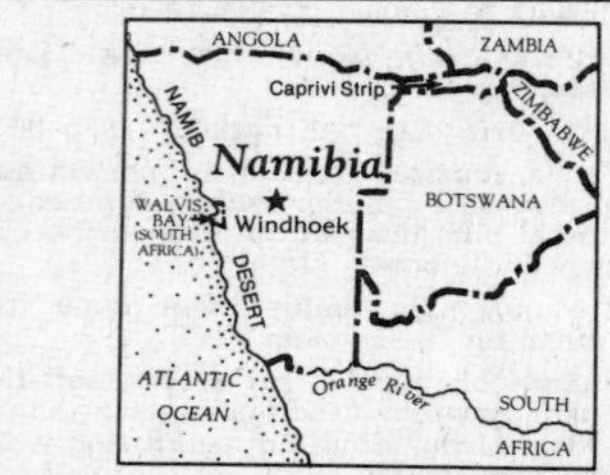

nam′ma hole′ (nam′ə), *Australian.* See **gnamma hole.** [< Nyungar *ŋama*]

Nam·mu (nä′mo͞o), *n.* a Sumerian goddess personifying the primeval sea: the mother of the gods and of heaven and earth.

Nam·pa (nam′pə), *n.* a city in W Idaho. 25,112.

Nam·pu·la (nam po͞o′lə), *n.* a city in E Mozambique. 18,000.

Nam·tar (näm′tär), *n.* the Sumerian and Akkadian demon personifying death.

Na·mur (nä mo͝or′; *Fr.* NA MYR′), *n.* **1.** a province in S Belgium. 390,442; 1413 sq. mi. (3660 sq. km). **2.** a city in and capital of this province, on the Sambre and Meuse rivers. 31,302.

Nan (nan), *n.* **1.** a word formerly used in communications to represent the letter *N.* **2.** a female given name.

nan-, var. of **nano-** before a vowel: *nanoid.*

nan·a (nan′ə), *n.* **1.** *Chiefly Northeastern U.S.* grandmother; grandma. **2.** *Gulf States.* godmother. **3.** *Chiefly Southeastern U.S.* a child's nursemaid; nanny. [1835–45; nursery word; cf. NANNY]

Na·nai (nə nī′), *n., pl.* **-nais,** (*esp. collectively*) **-nai.** Nanay.

Na·nai·mo (nə nī′mō), *n.* a port in SW British Columbia, in SW Canada, on the SE part of Vancouver Island. 47,069.

Na·nak (nä′nək), *n.* (*"Guru"*) 1469–1539, Indian religious leader: founder of Sikhism.

Na·nay (nə nī′), *n., pl.* **-nays,** (*esp. collectively*) **-nay** for 1. **1.** a member of a Tungusic people, traditionally hunters and fishermen, who inhabit the lower Amur Valley in southeastern Siberia and northeastern Manchuria. **2.** the language of the Nanays. Also, **Nanai.** Also called **Goldi, Gold.**

nance (nans), *n. Slang* (*disparaging and offensive*). **1.** an effeminate male. **2.** a homosexual male. [1905–10; shortened from given name *Nancy*]

Nan·chang (nän′chäng′), *n. Pinyin, Wade-Giles.* a city in and the capital of Jiangxi province, in SE China. 675,000.

Nan·ching (*Chin.* nän′jing′), *n. Wade-Giles.* Nanjing.

Nan·chong (nän′chông′), *n. Pinyin.* a city in E central Sichuan province, in central China. 164,700. Also, *Wade-Giles,* **Nan·chung** (nän′cho͝ong′).

Nan·cy (nan′sē; *Fr.* NÄN sē′), *n.* **1.** a city in and the capital of Meurthe-et-Moselle, in NE France: battles 1477, 1914, 1944. 111,493. **2.** Also, **Nan′cee, Nan′cie.** a female given name, form of **Ann** or **Anna. 3.** (*sometimes l.c.*) *Slang* (*disparaging and offensive*). nance.

Nan·da De·vi (nun′dä dā′vē), a mountain in N India, in Uttar Pradesh: a peak of the Himalayas. 25,661 ft. (7820 m).

NAND′ cir′cuit (nand), *Computers.* a circuit that is energized when any one of its inputs is not energized. Also called **NAND′ gate′.** [1955–60]

Nan·di (nän′dē), *n.* a town on W Viti Levu, in the Fiji Islands: airport.

Nan·di (nän′dē) *n. Hinduism.* the bull companion of Shiva.

Nan·di (nän′dē), *n., pl.* **-dis,** (*esp. collectively*) **-di** for 1. **1.** a member of an agricultural people of southwestern Kenya. **2.** the Nilotic language spoken by the Nandi.

nan·di·na (nan dī′nə, -dē′nə), *n.* a Chinese and Japanese evergreen shrub, *Nandina domestica,* of the barberry family, having pinnate leaves and bright red berries, cultivated as an ornamental. Also, **nan·din** (nan′din). Also called **heavenly bamboo, sacred bamboo.** [< NL (1781), the genus name < Japn dial. *nanden,* Japn *nanten* < MChin, equiv. to Chin *nántiān(zhú); nán* south + *tiān* heaven + *zhú* bamboo; see -A[2]]

ñan·du·ti (nyän′də tē′), *n.* a fine, intricate lace made in Paraguay, usually of cotton, and resembling a spiderweb. [< AmerSp *ñandutí* < Guarani: spiderweb, equiv. to *ñandu* spider + *tí* point]

nane (nān), *pron., adv., adj. Scot.* none.

Na·nette (na net′), *n.* a female given name, form of **Ann.**

Nan·ga Par·bat (nung′gə pur′but), a mountain in NW Kashmir, in the Himalayas. 26,660 ft. (8125 m).

Nan Hai (nän′ hī′), *Pinyin.* See **South China Sea.**

Nan·hai (nän′hī′), *n. Pinyin, Wade-Giles.* former name of **Foshan.** Also, **Namhoi.** Also called **Fatshan, Foshan.**

na·nism (nā′niz əm, nan′iz-), *n. Med.* the condition of being unusually or abnormally small in size or stature; dwarfism. [1855–60; < F *nanisme,* equiv. to Gk *nân(os)* dwarf + F *-isme* -ISM]

Nan·jing (nän′jing′), *n. Pinyin.* a port in and the capital of Jiangsu province, in E China, on the Chang Jiang: a former capital of China. 1,750,000. Also, **Nanching, Nanking.**

nan·keen (nan kēn′), *n.* **1.** a firm, durable, yellow or buff fabric, formerly made from a natural-colored Chinese cotton. **2.** a twilled material made from other cotton and dyed in imitation of this fabric. **3. nankeens,** garments made of this material. **4.** a yellow or buff color. **5.** Also called **Nan′keen por′celain, Nan′king chi′na, Nan′king′ ware′.** a type of Chinese porcelain having blue ornament on a white ground. Also, **nan·kin** (nan′-kin). [1745–55; named after *Nankin* NANKING, where first made]

nan′keen lil′y, a lily, *Lilium testaceum,* having drooping, fragrant, pink-tinged, yellowish or apricot-colored flowers with recurved petals.

Nan·king (nan′king′; *Chin.* nän′king′), *n. Older Spelling.* Nanjing.

Nan Ling (nän′ ling′), *Pinyin, Wade-Giles.* a mountain range in S China, separating Guangdong province from Hunan province and Guangxi Zhuang region.

Nan·na (nän′nä), *n. Scand. Myth.* the wife of Balder.

Nan·na (nä′nä), *n.* the Sumerian god of the moon: the counterpart of the Akkadian god Sin.

Nan·ning (nan′ning′; *Chin.* nän′ning′), *n. Pinyin, Wade-Giles.* a city in and the capital of Guangxi Zhuang region, in S China. 375,000. Formerly, **Yongning.**

nan·no·fos·sil (nan′ə fos′əl), *n.* any fossil so small that it is near or below the limit of resolution of a light microscope. [1965–70; NANNO- + FOSSIL]

nan·no·plank·ton (nan′ə plangk′tən), *n.* the smallest of the microplankton; the aquatic organisms that can pass through fine mesh plankton nets. Also, **nanoplankton.** [1910–15; NANNO- + PLANKTON]

nan·ny (nan′ē), *n., pl.* **-nies.** a child's nursemaid. [1785–95; nursery word; cf. Welsh *nain* grandmother, Gk *nánna* aunt, Russ *nyánya* nursemaid]

Nan·ny (nan′ē), *n.* a female given name.

nan·ny·ber·ry (nan′ē ber′ē), *n., pl.* **-ries.** sheepberry. Also called **nan′ny plum′.** [1780–90; NANNY (GOAT) + BERRY]

nan·ny·gai (nan′ē gī′), *n.* a small red saltwater fish, *Trachichthodes affinis,* of Australian waters. [1870–75; perh. < an Australian Aboriginal language of New South Wales]

nan′ny goat′, a female goat. [1780–90; NANNY]

nano-, a combining form with the meaning "very small, minute," used in the formation of compound words (*nanoplankton*); in the names of units of measure it has the specific sense "one billionth" (10^{-9}): *nanomole; nanosecond.* Also, **nanno-;** *esp. before a vowel,* **nan-.** [comb. form repr. Gk *nânos, nánnos* dwarf]

CONCISE ETYMOLOGY KEY: <, descended or borrowed from; >, whence; b., blend of, blended; c., cognate with; cf., compare; deriv., derivative; equiv., equivalent; imit., imitative; obl., oblique; r., replacing; s., stem; sp., spelling, spelled; resp., respelling, respelled; trans., translation; ?, origin unknown; *, unattested; ‡, probably earlier than. See the full key inside the front cover.

nan·o·gram (nan′ə gram′, nā′nə-), *n.* one billionth of a gram. *Abbr.:* ng [1950–55; NANO- + -GRAM[2]]

nan·oid (nan′oid, nā′noid), *adj. Med.* dwarfish. [1855–60; < Gk *nân(os)* dwarf + -OID]

nan·o·me·ter (nan′ə mē′tər, nā′nə-), *n.* one billionth of a meter. *Abbr.:* nm Cf. **millimicron.** [1960–65; NANO- + METER[1]]

nan·o·mole (nan′ə mōl′, nā′nə-), *n. Chem.* one billionth of a mole. [1965–70; NANO- + MOLE[4]]

nan·o·plank·ton (nan′ə plangk′tən, nā′nə-), *n.* nannoplankton.

nan·o·sec·ond (nan′ə sek′ənd, nā′nə-), *n.* one billionth of a second. *Abbr.:* ns, nsec [1955–60; NANO- + SECOND[2]]

nan·o·tech·nol·o·gy (nan′ə tek nol′ə jē, nā′nə-), *n.* any technology on the scale of nanometers. [1987]

Nan·sen (nan′sən; *Norw.* nän′sən), *n.* **Fridt·jof** (frit′-yof), 1861–1930, Norwegian arctic explorer, zoologist, and statesman: Nobel peace prize 1922.

Nan′sen bot′tle, *Oceanog.* a waterproof container for taking samples of ocean water, several usually being lowered open on a line and each being closed at the desired depth by the action of a falling weight. [named after F. NANSEN]

Nan′sen pass′port, a passport issued after World War I by the League of Nations to refugees unable to establish citizenship. [1920–25; after F. NANSEN]

Nan Shan (nän′ shän′), *Pinyin, Wade-Giles.* former name of **Qilian Shan.**

Nan·terre (näɴ tɛʀ′), *n.* a city in and the capital of Hauts-de-Seine, in N France: W suburb of Paris. 96,004.

Nantes (nants; *Fr.* näɴt), *n.* **1.** a seaport in and the capital of Loire-Atlantique, in W France, at the mouth of the Loire River. 263,689. **2. Edict of,** *Fr. Hist.* a law, promulgated by Henry IV in 1598, granting considerable religious and civil liberty to the Huguenots: revoked by Louis XIV in 1685.

Nan·ti·coke (nan′ti kōk′ *or, for 1,* -kō′), *n.* **1.** a city in SE Ontario, in S Canada, on Lake Erie. 19,816. **2.** a city in E Pennsylvania. 13,044.

Nan·ti·coke (nan′ti kōk′), *n., pl.* **-cokes,** (*esp. collectively*) **-coke. 1.** a member of an extinct North American Indian people who inhabited Maryland, Delaware, and Pennsylvania. **2.** the Algonquian language of the Nanticoke. **3.** a member of a group of people of southern Delaware of mixed white, black, and Indian ancestry.

Nan·tong (nän′tông′), *n. Pinyin.* a city in SE Jiangsu province, in E China, on the Chang Jiang. 300,000. Also, *Wade-Giles,* **Nan·tung** (nän′tŏŏng′). Formerly, **Tongzhou.**

Nan·tuck·et (nan tuk′it), *n.* an island off SE Massachusetts: summer resort. 5087; 15 mi. (24 km) long.

Naoi·se (nē′sē, nā′-), *n. Irish Legend.* the husband of Deirdre and a nephew of Conchobar, by whom he was treacherously killed.

Na·o·mi (nā ō′mē, -mī, nā′ō mī′, -mē′), *n.* **1.** the mother-in-law of Ruth and the great-grandmother of David. Ruth 1. **2.** a female given name: from a Hebrew word meaning "pleasant."

na·os (nā′os), *n., pl.* **-oi** (-oi). **1.** a temple. **2.** *Archit.* cella. [1765–75; < Gk *naós* dwelling of a god, inner part of a temple, shrine]

nap[1] (nap), *v.,* **napped, nap·ping,** *n.* —*v.i.* **1.** to sleep for a short time; doze. **2.** to be off one's guard: *The question caught him napping.* —*v.t.* **3.** to sleep or doze through (a period of time, an activity, etc.) (usually fol. by *away*): *I napped the afternoon away. He naps away most of his classes.* —*n.* **4.** a brief period of sleep, esp. one taken during daytime: *Has the baby had her nap?* [bef. 900; ME *nappen* (v.), *nap* (n.), OE *hnappian* to sleep; c. MHG *napfen*]
—**Syn. 1.** nod, rest, catnap.

nap[2] (nap), *n., v.,* **napped, nap·ping.** —*n.* **1.** the short fuzzy ends of fibers on the surface of cloth, drawn up in napping. **2.** any downy coating, as on plants. —*v.t.* **3.** to raise a nap on. [1400–50; late ME *noppe,* OE *-hnoppa* (as in *wullknoppa,* mistake for **wullhnoppa* tuft of wool), c. MD, MLG *noppe;* akin to OE *hnoppian* to pluck] —**nap′less,** *adj.* —**nap′less·ness,** *n.*

nap[3] (nap), *n.* napoleon (defs. 2, 3). [shortened form]

-nap, a combining form extracted from **kidnap,** with the general sense "abduct or steal in order to collect a ransom": *artnap; petnap; starnap.*

na·pa (nä′pə), *n.* See **Chinese cabbage.** [of undetermined orig.]

Nap·a (nap′ə), *n.* a city in W California: center of wine-producing region. 50,879.

Na·pae·ae (nə pē′ē), *n.pl. Rom. Legend.* the nymphs of a dell.

na·palm (nā′päm), *n.* **1.** a highly incendiary jellylike substance used in fire bombs, flamethrowers, etc. —*v.t.* **2.** to drop bombs containing napalm on (troops, a city, or the like). [1940–45, *Amer.;* NA(PHTHENE) + PALM(ITATE)]

nape (nāp, nap), *n.* the back of the neck (usually used in the phrase *nape of the neck*). [1300–50; ME]

Na·per·ville (nā′pər vil′), *n.* a city in NE Illinois. 42,330.

na·per·y (nā′pə rē), *n.* **1.** table linen, as tablecloths or napkins. **2.** any linen for household use. [1350–1400; ME *naprye* < MF, equiv. to *nape,* var. of *nappe* tablecloth (see **NAPKIN**) + *-erie* -ERY]

Naph·ta·li (naf′tə lī′), *n.* **1.** the sixth son of Jacob and Bilhah. Gen. 30:7,8. **2.** one of the 12 tribes of Israel, traditionally descended from Naphtali.

Naph·ta·lite (naf′tə līt′), *n.* a member of the tribe of Naphtali. [NAPHTAL(I) + -ITE[1]]

naphth-, a combining form representing **naphtha** or **naphthalene** in compound words: *naphthol.*

naph·tha (naf′thə, nap′-), *n.* **1.** a colorless, volatile petroleum distillate, usually an intermediate product between gasoline and benzine, used as a solvent, fuel, etc. Cf. **mineral spirits. 2.** any of various similar liquids distilled from other products. **3.** petroleum. [1565–75; < L < Gk *náphthas,* perh. < Iranian **nafta,* deriv. of **nab-* to be damp; cf. Avestan *napta-* damp, Persian *naft* naphtha] —**naph′thous,** *adj.*

naph·tha·cene (naf′thə sēn′, nap′-), *n. Chem.* an explosive solid compound, $C_{18}H_{12}$, derived from anthracene and coal tar: used for detonating high explosives, as TNT. Also, **tetracene, tetrazene.** [NAPHTHA + (TETRA)CENE]

naph·tha·lene (naf′thə lēn′, nap′-), *n. Chem.* a white, crystalline, water-insoluble hydrocarbon, $C_{10}H_8$, usually obtained from coal tar: used in making dyes, as a moth repellant, etc. Also, **naph′tha·line′, naph·tha·lin** (naf′thə lin, nap′-). [1865–70; NAPHTH- + -AL[3] + -ENE] —**naph·thal·ic** (naf thal′ik, nap-), **naph·tha·len·ic** (naf′thə len′ik, nap′-), *adj.*

naph·tha·lize (naf′thə līz′, nap′-), *v.t.,* **-lized, -liz·ing.** to mix or saturate with naphtha. Also, *esp. Brit.,* **naph′·tha·lise′.** [1835–45; NAPHTHAL(ENE) + -IZE]

naph·thene (naf′thēn, nap′-), *n. Chem.* any of a group of hydrocarbon ring compounds of the general formula, C_nH_{2n}, derivatives of cyclopentane and cyclohexane, found in certain petroleums. [1840–50; NAPHTH- + -ENE] —**naph·the·nic** (naf thē′nik, -then′ik, nap-), *adj.*

naph·thol (naf′thôl, -thol, nap′-), *n. Chem.* either of two isomeric hydroxyl derivatives, $C_{10}H_7OH$, of naphthalene **(alpha-naphthol** or **1-naphthol** and **beta-naphthol** or **2-naphthol),** white or yellowish crystals, with a phenolic odor, that darken on exposure to light: used chiefly in dyes, drugs, perfumes, and insecticides. Also called **hydroxynaphthalene.** [1840–50; NAPHTH- + -OL[1]]

naph·thyl (naf′thil, nap′-), *adj. Chem.* containing the naphthyl group. [1865–70; NAPHTH- + -YL]

naph′thyl group′, *Chem.* **1.** Also called **alpha-naphthyl group, alpha-naphthyl radical.** the univalent group $C_{10}H_7$–, having a replaceable hydrogen atom in the first, or alpha, position; 1-naphthyl group. **2.** Also called **beta-naphthyl group, beta-naphthyl radical.** the univalent group $C_{10}H_7$–, having a replaceable hydrogen atom in the second, or beta, position; 2-naphthyl group. Also called **naph′thyl rad′ical.**

na·pi·er (nā′pē ər), *n. Physics.* neper.

Na·pi·er (nā′pē ər *or, for 1–3,* nə pēr′), *n.* **1. Sir Charles James,** 1782–1853, British general. **2.** Also, **Neper. John,** 1550–1617, Scottish mathematician: inventor of logarithms. **3. Robert Cornelis** (kôr nē′lis), (*1st Baron Napier of Magdala*), 1810–90, English field marshal. **4.** former name of **Napier-Hastings.**

na′pier grass′, a tall, leafy grass, *Pennisetum purpureum,* native to Africa, grown as a forage plant. Also called **elephant grass.** [1910–15; named after *Napier,* South Africa]

Na·pi·er-Has·tings (nā′pē ər hā′stingz), *n.* a seaport on E North Island, in New Zealand. 109,010. Formerly, **Napier.**

Na·pier·i·an (nə pēr′ē ən), *adj.* of, pertaining to, or formulated by John Napier. [1810–20; NAPIER + -IAN]

Napier′ian log′arithm, *Math.* See **natural logarithm.** [1810–20]

Na′pier's bones′, *Math.* a form of multiplication table originally marked on sticks of bone or ivory that could be rearranged to carry out the operations of multiplication or division. Also called **Na′pier's rods′.** [1650–60; named after their developer, J. NAPIER]

na·pi·form (nā′pə fôrm′), *adj.* round at the top and tapering sharply below; turnip-shaped, as a root. [1840–50; < L *nāp(us)* a kind of turnip + -I- + -FORM]

nap·kin (nap′kin), *n.* **1.** a small piece of cloth or paper, usually square, for use in wiping the lips and fingers and to protect the clothes while eating. **2.** See **sanitary napkin. 3.** *Chiefly Brit.* a diaper. **4.** *Scot. and North Eng.* a handkerchief. **5.** *Scot.* a kerchief or neckerchief. [1350–1400; ME, equiv. to *nape* tablecloth (< MF *nappe* < L *mappa* napkin) + -KIN; cf. MAP]

nap′kin ring′, a ring or band of metal, wood, plastic, etc., through which a folded napkin is inserted, often as part of a place setting. [1680–90]

Na·ples (nā′pəlz), *n.* **1.** Italian, **Napoli.** a seaport in SW Italy. 1,223,342. **2. Bay of,** Italian, **Gol·fo di Na·po·li** (gôl′fô dē nä′pô lē). a bay in SW Italy: Naples located here. 22 mi. (35 km) long. **3.** a town in S Florida. 17,581.

Na′ples yel′low, a poisonous pigment used in painting and enameling, consisting chiefly of lead antimoniate and characterized by its fugitive yellow color, rapid drying rate, and strong film-forming properties. Also called **antimony yellow.** [1730–40; after NAPLES, Italy]

Na·po (nä′pô), *n.* a South American river flowing from central Ecuador through NE Peru to the Amazon River. ab. 700 mi. (1125 km) long.

na·po·le·on (nə pō′lē ən, -pōl′yən), *n.* **1.** a pastry consisting of thin layers of puff paste interlaid with a cream or custard filling. **2.** a former gold coin of France, equal to 20 francs and bearing a portrait either of Napoleon I or of Napoleon III. **3.** *Cards.* **a.** a game in which the players bid for the privilege of naming the trump, stating the number of tricks they propose to win. **b.** a bid in this game to take all five tricks of a hand. [1805–15; < F *napoléon*]

Na·po·le·on (nə pō′lē ən, -pōl′yən), *n.* **1. Louis** (lo͞o′-ē; *Fr.* lwē). See **Napoleon III. 2.** a male given name.

Napoleon I, (*Napoleon Bonaparte*) (*"the Little Corporal"*) 1769–1821, French general born in Corsica: emperor of France 1804–15.

Napoleon II, (*François Charles Joseph Bonaparte*) (*Duke of Reichstadt*) 1811–32, titular king of Rome (son of Napoleon I).

Napoleon III, (*Louis Napoleon*) (*Charles Louis Napoleon Bonaparte*) (lo͞o′ē; *Fr.* lwē) 1808–73, president of France 1848–52, emperor of France 1852–70 (nephew of Napoleon I).

Na·po·le·on·ic (nə pō′lē on′ik), *adj.* pertaining to, resembling, or suggestive of Napoleon I, or, less often, Napoleon III, or their dynasty: *the Napoleonic era; a Napoleonic attitude toward one's employees.* [1860–65; NAPOLEON + -IC] —**Na·po′le·on′i·cal·ly,** *adv.*

Napo′leon′ic Code′. See **Code Napoléon.**

Napo′leon′ic Wars′, the intermittent wars (1796–1815) waged by France principally against England, Prussia, Austria, and Russia.

Na·po·li (nä′pô lē), *n.* Italian name of **Naples.**

nappe (nap), *n.* **1.** *Geol.* a large mass of rock thrust a considerable distance along a nearly horizontal fault plane or in an overturned anticlinal fold. **2.** *Geom.* one of the two equal sections of a cone. [1905–10, *Amer.;* < F: lit., tablecloth, cloth; OF *nappe, nape* < L *mappa;* cf. NAPKIN]

nap·per[1] (nap′ər), *n.* **1.** a textile worker who naps cloth. **2.** a machine for putting a nap on cloth. [1760–70; NAP[2] + -ER[1]]

nap·per[2] (nap′ər), *n.* a person who naps or dozes. [1350–1400; ME; see NAP[1], -ER[1]]

nap·py[1] (nap′ē), *n. Chiefly Scot.* liquor, esp. ale. [1425–75; late ME *noppi.* See NAP[2], -Y[1]]

nap·py[2] (nap′ē), *n., pl.* **-pies.** a small shallow dish, usually round and often of glass, with a flat bottom and sloping sides, for serving food. Also, **nap′pie.** [1870–75, *Amer.; nap* (ME; OE *hnæp* bowl) + -Y[2]]

nap·py[3] (nap′ē), *adj.,* **-pi·er, -pi·est. 1.** covered with nap; downy. **2.** (of hair) kinky. [1490–1500; NAP[2] + -Y[1]] —**nap′pi·ness,** *n.*

nap·py[4] (nap′ē), *n., pl.* **-pies.** *Chiefly Brit.* a diaper. [1925–30; NAP(KIN) + -Y[2]]

na·prap·a·thy (nə prap′ə thē), *n.* a system or method of treating disease that employs no medications but uses manipulation of muscles, joints, ligaments, etc., to stimulate the natural healing process. [1915–20; < Czech *náprav(va)* correction + -PATHY] —**nap·ra·path** (nap′rə path′), *n.*

na·prox·en (nə prok′sən), *n. Pharm.* a nonsteroidal anti-inflammatory substance, $C_{14}H_{14}O_3$, used chiefly in the management of certain types of arthritis and as a painkiller. [by shortening and rearrangement of *methoxy-, naphthyl-,* and *propionic,* components of one of its chemical names]

Na·ra (nä rä′), *n.* **1.** a city on S Honshu, in central Japan: chief Buddhist center of ancient Japan; first capital of Japan A.D. 710–84. 297,893. **2.** a period of Japanese history, A.D. 710–784, characterized by the adoption of Chinese culture and forms of government.

Nar·a·ka (nur′ə kə), *n. Hinduism.* a place of torment for the spirits of the wicked.

Na·ra·yan·ganj (nə rä′yən gunj′), *n.* a port in SE Bangladesh, SE of Dacca. 186,769.

Nar·ba·da (nər bud′ə), *n.* a river flowing W from central India to the Arabian Sea. 800 mi. (1290 km) long. Also, **Nerbudda.**

Nar·bonne (naʀ bôn′), *n.* a city in S France: an important port in Roman times. 40,543.

narc (närk), *n. Slang.* a government agent or detective charged with the enforcement of laws restricting the use of narcotics. Also, **nark.** [1965–70, *Amer.;* shortening of NARCOTIC]

narc-, var. of **narco-** before a vowel: *narcoma.*

nar·ce·ine (när′sē ēn′, -in), *n. Pharm.* a narcotic alkaloid, $C_{23}H_{27}NO_8$, occurring in opium and acting as a mild relaxant on smooth muscle. [< F *narcéine* (1832), irreg. < Gk *nárkē* numbness (see NARCO-) + F *-ine* -INE[2]]

nar·cis·sism (när′sə siz′əm), *n.* **1.** inordinate fascination with oneself; excessive self-love; vanity. **2.** *Psychoanal.* erotic gratification derived from admiration of one's own physical or mental attributes, being a normal condition at the infantile level of personality development. Also, **nar·cism** (när′siz əm). [1815–25; < G *Narzissismus.* See NARCISSUS, -ISM] —**nar′cis·sist, nar′·cist,** *n.* —**nar′cis·sis′tic, nar·cis′tic,** *adj.*
—**Syn. 1.** self-centeredness, smugness, egocentrism.

narcissis′tic personal′ity, *Psychiatry.* a personality disorder characterized by extreme self-centeredness and self-absorption, fantasies involving unrealistic goals, an excessive need for attention and admiration, and disturbed interpersonal relationships. [1970–75]

nar·cis·sus (när sis′əs), *n., pl.* **-cis·sus, -cis·sus·es, -cis·si** (-sis′ē, -sis′ī) for 1, 2. **1.** any bulbous plant belonging to the genus *Narcissus,* of the amaryllis family, having showy yellow or white flowers with a cup-shaped corona. **2.** the flower of any of these plants. **3.** (*cap.*) *Class. Myth.* a youth who fell in love with his own image reflected in a pool and wasted away from unsatisfied desire, whereupon he was transformed into the flower. [1540–50; < L < Gk *nárkissos* plant name, traditionally connected, by virtue of plant's narcotic effects, with *nárkē* numbness, torpor. See NARCOTIC]

nar·co (när′kō), *n., pl.* **-cos.** *Slang.* narc. [shortening of NARCOTIC; cf. -O]

narco-, a combining form meaning "stupor," "narcosis," used in the formation of compound words: *narcodiagnosis.* Also, *esp. before a vowel,* **narc-.** [< Gk *nárk(ē)* numbness, stiffness + -O-]

nar·co·a·nal·y·sis (när′kō ə nal′ə sis), *n.* a method of psychological investigation in which the conscious or

CONCISE PRONUNCIATION KEY: *act, cāpe, dâre, pärt; set, ēqual; if, īce; ox, ōver, ôrder, oil, bo͝ok, bo͞ot, out; up, ûrge; child; sing; shoe; thin, that;* zh as in *treasure.* ə = *a* as in *alone, e* as in *system, i* as in *easily, o* as in *gallop, u* as in *circus;* ᵊ as in *fire* (fīᵊr), *hour* (ouᵊr). l and n can serve as syllabic consonants, as in *cradle* (krād′l), and *button* (but′n). See the full key inside the front cover.

unconscious unwillingness of a subject to express memories or feelings is diminished by the use of a barbiturate drug. Cf. **truth serum.** [1935–40; NARCO- + ANALYSIS]

nar·co·di·ag·no·sis (när′kō dī′ag nō′sis), *n. Psychiatry.* the use of drugs to produce narcosis as an aid in diagnosis. [NARCO- + DIAGNOSIS]

nar·co·lep·sy (när′kə lep′sē), *n. Pathol.* a condition characterized by frequent and uncontrollable periods of deep sleep. [1875–80; NARCO- + (EPI)LEPSY] —**nar′co·lep′tic,** *adj., n.*

nar·co·ma (när kō′mə), *n., pl.* **-mas, -ma·ta** (-mə tə). *Med.* stupor produced by narcotics. [NARC- + -OMA] —**nar·com·a·tous** (när kom′ə təs), *adj.*

nar·co·ma·ni·a (när′kə mā′nē ə), *n. Psychiatry.* abnormal craving for a drug to deaden pain. [1885–90]

nar·cose (när′kōs), *adj.* characterized by stupor; stuporous. [NARC- + -OSE[1]]

nar·co·sis (när kō′sis), *n.* **1.** a state of stupor or drowsiness. **2.** a state of stupor or greatly reduced activity produced by a drug. Cf. **nitrogen narcosis.** Also called **narcotism.** [1685–95; < NL < Gk *nárkōsis.* See NARC-, -OSIS]

nar·co·syn·the·sis (när′kō sin′thə sis), *n.* a treatment for psychiatric disturbances that uses narcotics. [1940–45; NARCO- + SYNTHESIS]

nar·co·ter·ror·ism (när′kō ter′ə riz′əm), *n.* terrorist tactics employed by dealers in illicit drugs, as against competitors or government agents. [1985–90] —**nar′co·ter′ror·ist,** *n., adj.*

nar·co·ther·a·py (när′kō ther′ə pē), *n. Psychiatry.* an infrequently used method of treating mental disorders by intravenous injection of barbiturates. [1965–70]

nar·cot·ic (när kot′ik), *n.* **1.** any of a class of substances that blunt the senses, as opium, morphine, belladonna, and alcohol, that in large quantities produce euphoria, stupor, or coma, that when used constantly can cause habituation or addiction, and that are used in medicine to relieve pain, cause sedation, and induce sleep. **2.** anything that exercises a soothing or numbing effect or influence: *Television is a narcotic for many people.* —*adj.* **3.** of or having the power to produce narcosis, as a drug. **4.** pertaining to or of the nature of narcosis. **5.** of or pertaining to narcotics or their use. **6.** used by, or in the treatment of, narcotic addicts. [1350–1400; ME *narcotik(e)* (n.) < ML *narcōticum* < Gk *narkōtikón,* n. use of neut. of *narkōtikós* benumbing, equiv. to *narkō-* (var. s. of *narkoûn* to benumb; see NARCO-) + *-tikos* -TIC] —**nar·cot′i·cal·ly,** *adv.*

nar·co·tism (när′kə tiz′əm), *n.* **1.** habitual use of narcotics. **2.** the action or influence of narcotics. **3.** narcosis. [1825–35; earlier *narcoticism.* See NARCOTIC, -ISM] —**nar′co·tist,** *n.*

nar·co·tize (när′kə tīz′), *v.,* **-tized, -tiz·ing.** —*v.t.* **1.** to subject to or treat with a narcotic; stupefy. **2.** to make dull; stupefy; deaden the awareness of: *He had used liquor to narcotize his anxieties.* —*v.i.* **3.** to act as a narcotic: *a remedy that does not heal but merely narcotizes.* Also, *esp. Brit.,* **nar′co·tise′.** [1835–45; NARCOT(IC) + -IZE] —**nar′co·ti·za′tion,** *n.*

nard (närd), *n.* **1.** an aromatic Himalayan plant, believed to be the spikenard, *Nardostachys jatamansi,* the source of an ointment used by the ancients. **2.** the ointment. [1350–1400; ME *narde* < L *nardus* < Gk *nárdos* < Sem; cf. Heb *nērd*] —**nar·dine** (när′din, -dīn), *adj.*

nar·es (nâr′ēz), *n.pl., sing.* **nar·is** (nâr′is). *Anat.* the nostrils or the nasal passages. [1685–95; < L *nārēs,* pl. of *nāris* a nostril; see NOSE]

Na·rew (nä′ʀef), *n.* a river in NE Poland, flowing S and SW into the Bug River: battle 1915. 290 mi. (465 km) long. Russian, **Na·rev** (nä′ʀyif).

nar·ghi·le (när′gə lē, -lā′), *n.* a Middle Eastern tobacco pipe in which the smoke is drawn through water before reaching the lips; hookah. Also, **nar′gi·le, nar′gi·leh.** [1830–40; < Turk *nargile* < Pers *nārgīleh,* deriv. of *nārgīl* coconut, from which the bowl was formerly made]

nar·i·al (nâr′ē əl), *adj. Anat.* of or pertaining to the nares or nostrils. Also, **nar·ine** (nâr′in, -īn). [1865–70; < L *nāri(s)* nostril (see NARES) + -AL[1]]

nark[1] (närk), *n.* **1.** *Brit. Slang.* a stool pigeon or informer. **2.** *Chiefly Australian Slang.* an annoying person. —*v.i.* **3.** *Brit. Slang.* to act as a police informer or stool pigeon. **4.** *Chiefly Australian Slang.* to become annoyed. [1860–65; < Romany *nāk* nose]

nark[2] (närk), *n.* narc.

Nar·mer (när′mər), *n.* a king of Egypt identified by modern scholars as the Menes of tradition and depicted as the unifier of Upper and Lower Egypt on an ancient slate tablet **(Nar′mer Pal′ette** or **Palette of Narmer),** c3200 B.C. with relief carvings on both sides. Cf. **Menes.**

Nar·ra·gan·set (nar′ə gan′sit), *n., pl.* **-sets,** (*esp. collectively*) **-set.** Narragansett.

Nar·ra·gan·sett (nar′ə gan′sit), *n., pl.* **-setts,** (*esp. collectively*) **-sett.** **1.** a member of a North American Indian tribe of the Algonquian family formerly located in Rhode Island but now almost extinct. **2.** an Algonquian language, the language of the Narragansett Indians. **3.** a town in S Rhode Island: includes a resort **(Nar′·ragan′sett Pier′).** 12,088.

Nar′ragan′sett Bay′, an inlet of the Atlantic in E Rhode Island. 28 mi. (45 km) long.

nar·rate (nar′āt, na rāt′), *v.,* **-rat·ed, -rat·ing.** —*v.t.* **1.** to give an account or tell the story of (events, experiences, etc.). **2.** to add a spoken commentary to (a film, television program, etc.): *to narrate a slide show.* —*v.i.* **3.** to relate or recount events, experiences, etc., in speech or writing. [1650–60; < L *narrātus* (ptp. of *narrāre* to relate, tell, say), equiv. to *nār(us)* knowing, acquainted with (var. of *gnārus;* see COGNITION) + *-ātus* -ATE[1]] —**nar′rat·a·ble,** *adj.* —**nar·ra·tor, nar·rat·er** (nar′ā tər, na rā′-, nar′ə-), *n.*
—**Syn. 1.** detail, recite. See **describe.**

nar·ra·tion (na rā′shən), *n.* **1.** something narrated; an account, story, or narrative. **2.** the act or process of narrating. **3.** a recital of events, esp. in chronological order, as the story narrated in a poem or the exposition in a drama. **4.** *Rhet.* (in classical speech) the third part, the exposition of the question. [1400–50; late ME < L *narrātiōn-* (s. of *narrātiō*), equiv. to *narrāt(us)* (see NARRATE) + *-iōn-* -ION] —**nar·ra′tion·al,** *adj.*

nar·ra·tive (nar′ə tiv), *n.* **1.** a story or account of events, experiences, or the like, whether true or fictitious. **2.** a book, literary work, etc., containing such a story. **3.** the art, technique, or process of narrating: *Somerset Maugham was a master of narrative.* —*adj.* **4.** consisting of or being a narrative: *a narrative poem.* **5.** of or pertaining to narration: *narrative skill.* **6.** *Fine Arts.* representing stories or events pictorially or sculpturally: *narrative painting.* Cf. **anecdotal** (def. 2). [1555–65; < L *narrātīvus* suitable for narration. See NARRATE, -IVE] —**nar′ra·tive·ly,** *adv.*
—**Syn. 1.** chronicle, tale. NARRATIVE, ACCOUNT, RECITAL, HISTORY are terms for a story of an event or events. NARRATIVE is the general term (for a story long or short; of past, present, or future; factual or imagined; told for any purpose; and with or without much detail). The other three terms apply primarily to factual stories of time already past. An ACCOUNT is usually told informally, often for entertainment, with emphasis on details of action, whether about an incident or a series of happenings. A RECITAL is an extended narrative usually with an informative purpose, emphasizing accuracy and exhaustive details of facts and figures. A HISTORY, usually written and at some length, is characterized by a tracing of causes and effects, and by an attempt to estimate, evaluate, and interpret facts.

nar·row (nar′ō), *adj.,* **-er, -est,** *v., n.* —*adj.* **1.** of little breadth or width; not broad or wide; not as wide as usual or expected: *a narrow path.* **2.** limited in extent or space; affording little room: *narrow quarters.* **3.** limited in range or scope: *a narrow sampling of public opinion.* **4.** lacking breadth of view or sympathy, as persons, the mind, or ideas: *a narrow man, knowing only his professional specialty; a narrow mind.* **5.** with little margin to spare; barely adequate or successful; close: *a narrow escape.* **6.** careful, thorough, or minute, as a scrutiny, search, or inquiry. **7.** limited in amount; small; meager: *narrow resources.* **8.** straitened; impoverished: *narrow circumstances.* **9.** *New Eng.* stingy or parsimonious. **10.** *Phonet.* **a.** (of a vowel) articulated with the tongue laterally constricted, as the *ee* of *beet,* the *oo* of *boot,* etc.; tense. Cf. **lax** (def. 7). **b.** (of a phonetic transcription) utilizing a unique symbol for each phoneme and whatever supplementary diacritics are needed to indicate its subphonemic varieties. Cf. **broad** (def. 14). **11.** (of livestock feeds) proportionately rich in protein. —*v.i.* **12.** to decrease in width or breadth: *This is where the road narrows.* —*v.t.* **13.** to make narrower. **14.** to limit or restrict (often fol. by *down*): *to narrow an area of search; to narrow down a contest to three competitors.* **15.** to make narrow-minded: *Living in that village has narrowed him.* —*n.* **16.** a narrow part, place, or thing. **17.** a narrow part of a valley, passage, or road. **18.** **narrows,** (*used with a singular or plural v.*) a narrow part of a strait, river, ocean current, etc. **19. The Narrows,** a narrow strait from upper to lower New York Bay, between Staten Island and Long Island. 2 mi. (3.2 km) long; 1 mi. (1.6 km) wide. [bef. 900; ME; OE *nearu;* c. OS *naru* narrow, D *naar* unpleasant; akin to G *Narbe* scar, lit., narrow mark] —**nar′row·ly,** *adv.* —**nar′row·ness,** *n.*
—**Syn. 4.** biased, limited, shallow, small-minded.

nar′row-an·gle glauco′ma (nar′ō ang′gəl). *Ophthalm.* angle-closure glaucoma. See under **glaucoma.**

nar·row·cast (nar′ō kast′, -käst′), *v.i.,* **-cast** or **-cast·ed, -cast·ing.** *Radio and Television.* to aim a program or programming at a specific, limited audience or sales market. [1770–80, for an earlier sense; *narrow (broad)-cast*]

nar·row-fist·ed (nar′ō fis′tid), *adj.* tight-fisted.

nar′row gauge′. See under **gauge** (def. 13). [1835–45] —**nar′row-gauge′;** *esp. in technical use,* **nar′·row-gage′,** *adj.* —**nar′row-gauged′;** *esp. in technical use,* **nar′row-gaged′,** *adj.*

nar′row-leaved bot′tle tree′ (nar′ō lēvd′). See under **bottle tree.**

nar·row-mind·ed (nar′ō mīn′did), *adj.* **1.** having or showing a prejudiced mind, as persons or opinions; biased. **2.** not receptive to new ideas; having a closed mind. **3.** extremely conservative and morally self-righteous. [1615–25] —**nar′row-mind′ed·ly,** *adv.* —**nar′·row-mind′ed·ness,** *n.*
—**Syn. 1.** bigoted, partial, intolerant, illiberal. —**Ant. 1.** tolerant.

Nar·rows (nar′ōz), *n.* **The,** narrow (def. 19).

nar·thex (när′theks), *n. Archit.* an enclosed passage between the main entrance and the nave of a church. [1665–75; < LGk *nárthēx,* Gk: giant fennel] —**nar·the·cal** (när thē′kəl), *adj.*

Nar·va (när′və), *n.* a city in NE Estonia: Swedish defeat of Russians 1700. 82,300.

Nar·vá·ez (när vä′eth, -vä′es), *n.* **Pán·fi·lo de** (päm′fē lô′ *th*e), 1478?–1528, Spanish soldier and adventurer in America.

Nar·vik (när′vik), *n.* a seaport in N Norway. 13,297.

nar·whal (när′wəl), *n.* a small arctic whale, *Monodon monoceros,* the male of which has a long, spirally twisted tusk extending forward from the upper jaw. Also, **nar′·wal, nar·whale** (när′hwāl′, -wāl′). [1650–60; < Scand; cf. Norw, Sw, Dan *nar(h)val,* reshaped from ON *nāhvalr,* equiv. to *nār* corpse + *hvalr* WHALE[1]; allegedly so called because its skin resembles that of a human corpse] —**nar·whal·i·an** (när hwä′lē ən, -wä′-, -wol′ē-), *adj.*

narwhal, *Monodon monoceros,* length 14 ft. (4.3 m); tusk 9 ft. (2.7 m)

nar·y (nâr′ē), *adj. Older Use.* not any; no; never a: *nary a sound..* [1740–50; var. of *ne'er a* never a]

N.A.S., 1. See **National Academy of Sciences. 2.** naval air station. Also, **NAS**

NASA (nas′ə), *n.* See **National Aeronautics and Space Administration.**

na·sal[1] (nā′zəl), *adj.* **1.** of or pertaining to the nose: *the nasal cavity.* **2.** *Phonet.* pronounced with the voice issuing through the nose, either partly, as in French nasal vowels, or entirely (as in *m, n,* or the *ng* of *song*). —*n.* **3.** *Phonet.* a nasal speech sound. [1375–1425; late ME (adj.) < ML **nāsālis,* equiv. to L *nās(us)* NOSE + *-ālis* -AL[1]] —**na·sal·i·ty** (nā zal′i tē), **na′sal·ism,** *n.*

na·sal[2] (nā′zəl), *n. Armor.* a bar or narrow plate used with an open helmet as a defense for the nose. [1470–80; late ME < ML *nāsāle,* n. use of neut. of **nāsālis* NASAL[1]; r. ME *nasel* < MF < ML, as above]

na′sal con′cha, turbinate (def. 5).

na′sal gleet′, *Vet. Pathol.* gleet (def. 2).

na′sal in′dex, 1. *Craniom.* (of the skull) the ratio of the distance from nasion to the lower margin of the nasal aperture to that of the maximum breadth of the nasal aperture. **2.** *Cephalom.* (of the head) the ratio of the maximum breadth of the external nose to its height from the nasal root to where the septum is confluent with the upper lip. [1895–1900]

na·sal·ize (nā′zə līz′), *v.,* **-ized, -iz·ing.** *Phonet.* —*v.t.* **1.** to pronounce as a nasal sound. —*v.i.* **2.** to pronounce normally oral sounds as nasal sounds. Also, *esp. Brit.,* **na′sal·ise′.** [1840–50; NASAL[1] + -IZE] —**na′sal·i·za′·tion,** *n.*

na·sal·ly (nā′zə lē, -zəl lē), *adv.* **1.** in a nasal manner. **2.** by inhaling through the nose: *to take drugs nasally.* [1840–50; NASAL[1] + -LY]

na′sal spray′, a liquid medication that can be atomized and inhaled into or through the nose.

Nas·by (naz′bē), *n.* **Petroleum V.,** pen name of David Ross Locke.

Nas·ca (näs′kä, -kə), *adj.* Nazca.

NASCAR (nas′kär), *n.* National Association for Stock Car Auto Racing. Also, **N.A.S.C.A.R.**

nas·cent (nas′ənt, nā′sənt), *adj.* **1.** beginning to exist or develop: *the nascent republic.* **2.** *Chem.* (of an element) in the nascent state. [1615–25; < L *nāscent-* (s. of *nāscēns*), prp. of *nāscī* to be born, arise, equiv. to *nā(tus)* born (var. of *gnātus*) + *-sc-* inchoative suffix + *-ent-* -ENT] —**nas′cence, nas′cen·cy,** *n.*

nas′cent state′, *Chem.* the condition of an element at the instant it is set free from a combination in which it has previously existed. Also called **nas′cent condi′·tion.** [1790–1800]

NASD, National Association of Securities Dealers. Also, **N.A.S.D.**

NASDAQ (nas′dak, naz′-), *n.* National Association of Securities Dealers Automated Quotations: a system for quoting over-the-counter securities.

nase·ber·ry (nāz′ber′ē, -bə rē), *n., pl.* **-ries. 1.** the fruit of the sapodilla, *Manilkara zapota.* **2.** the sapodilla tree. [1690–1700; alter. (by folk etym.) of Sp or Pg *néspera* < L *mespila* MEDLAR]

Nase·by (nāz′bē), *n.* a village in W Northamptonshire, in central England: Royalist defeat 1645.

Nash (nash), *n.* **1. John,** 1752–1835, English architect and city planner. **2. Ogden,** 1902–71, U.S. writer of humorous verse. **3.** Also, **Nashe. Thomas,** (*"Pasquil"*), 1567–1601, English dramatist, novelist, and satirical pamphleteer.

Nash·u·a (nash′o͞o ə), *n.* a city in S New Hampshire, on the Merrimack River. 67,865.

Nash·ville (nash′vil), *n.* a city in and the capital of Tennessee, in the central part: battle 1864. 455,651.

Nash′ville war′bler, a North American wood warbler, *Vermivora ruficapilla,* having a gray head, an olive-green back, and yellow underparts. [1805–15, *Amer.*]

Na·si (nä′sē), *n. Jewish Hist.* the head or president of the Sanhedrin. [< Heb *nāsī* chief]

Nä·si (nas′ē), *n.* **Lake,** a lake in SW Finland: city of Tampere located on its S shore. 20 mi. (32 km) long; 2–8 mi. (3.2–12.9 km) wide.

Na·sik (nä′sik), *n.* a city in W Maharashtra, in W central India: pilgrimage city of the Hindus. 176,091.

na·si·on (nā′zē on′), *n. Craniom.* the intersection of the internasal suture with the nasofrontal suture in the midsagittal plane. [1885–90; < NL, equiv. to L *nās(us)* NASO- + Gk *-ion,* dim. suffix] —**na′si·al,** *adj.*

Nas·ka·pi (nas′kə pē), *n., pl.* **-pis,** (*esp. collectively*) **-pi** for 1. **1.** a member of a North American Indian people of Labrador and Quebec. **2.** the eastern Algonquian language spoken by the Naskapi.

Nas·khi (nas′kē), *n.* the cursive variety of Arabic script from which was derived the variety used in modern printed works. [1765–75; < Ar *naskhī,* akin to *nasakha* to copy]

naso-, a combining form meaning "nose," used in the formation of compound words: *nasology.* [< L *nās(us)* NOSE + -O-]

na·so·gas·tric (nā′zō gas′trik), *adj.* of, pertaining to, or involving the nose and stomach. [1955–60; NASO- + GASTRIC]

na·so·lac·ri·mal (nā′zō lak′rə məl), *adj. Anat.* of or pertaining to the lacrimal structures and the nose. Also, **na′so·lach′ry·mal.** [1830–40; NASO- + LACRIMAL]

na′solac′rimal duct′, *Anat.* a membranous canal extending from the lacrimal sac to the nasal cavity, through which tears are discharged into the nose. See diag. under **lacrimal gland.**

na·sol·o·gy (nā zol′ə jē), *n.* the scientific study of noses. [1850–55; NASO- + -LOGY] —**na·so·log·i·cal** (nā′zə loj′i kəl), *adj.* —**na·sol′o·gist,** *n.*

na·so·phar·ynx (nā′zō far′ingks), *n., pl.* **-pha·ryn·ges** (-fə rin′jēz), **-phar·ynx·es.** *Anat.* the part of the pharynx behind and above the soft palate, directly continuous with the nasal passages. Cf. **oropharynx** (def. 2). [1875–80; NASO- + PHARYNX] —**na·so·pha·ryn·ge·al** (nā′zō fə rin′jē əl, -jəl, -far′ən jē′əl), *adj.*

Nas·sau (nas′ô; *for 2, 3, also Ger.* nä′sou), *n.* **1.** a seaport on New Providence Island: capital of the Bahamas; seaside resort. 100,000. **2.** a district in central Germany: formerly a duchy, now a part of Hesse. **3.** a member of a European royal family that ruled chiefly in Germany and the Netherlands until the 19th century. **4.** *Golf.* an eighteen-hole match in which one point each is awarded to the players having the lowest score for the first nine holes, for the second nine holes, and for the entire round.

Nas′sau group′er a colorful food and game fish, *Epinephelus striatus,* common off the Florida Keys.

Nas′sau Moun′tains, former name of **Maoke Mountains.**

Nas·ser (nä′sər, nas′ər), *n.* **1. Ga·mal Ab·del** (gə mäl′ ab′dŏŏl, jə-), 1918–70, Egyptian military and political leader: prime minister of Egypt 1954–56; president of Egypt 1956–58; president of the United Arab Republic 1958–70. **2. Lake,** a reservoir in SE Egypt, formed in the Nile River S of the Aswan High Dam; S part, in N Sudan, named **Lake Nubia.** ab. 300 mi. (500 km) long; 6 mi. (10 km) wide.

Nast (nast), *n.* **Thomas,** 1840–1902, U.S. illustrator and cartoonist.

nas·tic (nas′tik), *adj. Bot.* of or showing sufficiently greater cellular force or growth on one side of an axis to change the form or position of the axis. [1900–10; < Gk *nast(ós)* pressed close, stamped down, firm (equiv. to *nad-* s. of *nássein* to press, squeeze + *-tos* ptp. suffix, with *dt* > *st*) + -IC]

-nastic, a combining form occurring in adjectives corresponding to nouns ending in **-nasty:** *hyponastic.* [see NASTIC]

nas·tur·tium (na stûr′shəm, nə-), *n.* any plant of the genus *Tropaeolum,* cultivated for its showy, usually orange, red, or yellow flowers or for its fruit, which is pickled and used like capers. [1560–70; < L *nāsturtium, nāsturcium* a kind of cress, taken to mean, perh. by folk etym., something that wrings the nose (referring to its acrid smell). See NOSE, TORT, -IUM]

nas·ty (nas′tē), *adj.,* **-ti·er, -ti·est,** *n., pl.* **-ties.** —*adj.* **1.** physically filthy; disgustingly unclean: *a nasty pigsty of a room.* **2.** offensive to taste or smell; nauseating. **3.** offensive; objectionable: *a nasty habit.* **4.** vicious, spiteful, or ugly: *a nasty dog; a nasty rumor.* **5.** bad or hard to deal with, encounter, undergo, etc.; dangerous; serious: *a nasty cut; a nasty accident.* **6.** very unpleasant or disagreeable: *nasty weather.* **7.** morally filthy; obscene; indecent: *a nasty word.* **8.** *Slang.* formidable: *The young pitcher has a good fast ball and a nasty curve.* —*n.* **9.** *Informal.* a nasty person or thing. [1350–1400; ME < ?] —**nas′ti·ly,** *adv.* —**nas′ti·ness,** *n.*
—**Syn. 1.** dirty, foul, loathsome. **2.** sickening, repulsive, repellent. **6.** stormy, inclement. **7.** smutty, pornographic. —**Ant. 1.** clean, pure.

-nasty, a combining form with the meaning "nastic pressure," of the kind or in the direction specified by the initial element: *hyponasty.* [< Gk *nast(ós)* pressed close (see NASTIC) + -Y[3]]

na·sute (nā sōōt′), *n. Entomol.* a soldier termite characterized by a beaklike snout through which a sticky secretion repellent to other insects is emitted. [1645–55 for earlier sense "big-nosed"; < L *nāsūtus* big-nosed, equiv. to *nāsū-* (comb. form of *nāsus* NOSE) + *-tus* adj. suffix] —**na·sute′ness,** *n.*

Nat (nat), *n.* a male given name, form of **Nathan** or **Nathaniel.**

nat., **1.** national. **2.** native. **3.** natural. **4.** naturalist.

na·tal (nāt′l), *adj.* **1.** of or pertaining to a person's birth: *celebrating one's natal day.* **2.** presiding over or affecting a person at birth: *natal influences.* **3.** (of places) native: *nostalgia for one's natal town.* [1350–1400; ME < L *nātālis* of, belonging to one's birth, natal, equiv. to *nāt(us)* an offspring (var. of *gnātus,* ptp. of *nāscī* to be born) + *-ālis* -AL[1]]

Na·tal (nə tal′, -täl′; *for 2 also Port.* nə tôl′), *n.* **1.** a province in the E part of the Republic of South Africa. 4,236,700; 35,284 sq. mi. (91,886 sq. km). *Cap.:* Pietermaritzburg. **2.** a seaport in E Brazil. 250,787. —**Na·tal′i·an,** *adj., n.*

na′tal chart′, *Astrol.* the horoscope based on an individual's birth. Also called **na′tal hor′oscope.**

Nat·a·lie (nat′l ē), *n.* a female given name: from a Latin word meaning "birthday." Also, **Na·tal·ia** (nə tal′yə, -täl′-).

na·tal·i·ty (nā tal′i tē, nə-), *n.* birthrate. [1885–90; < F *natalité;* see NATAL, -ITY]

Natal′ or′ange, a spiny shrub, *Strychnos spinosa,* of the logania family, of central and southern Africa, having yellowish-white flowers and edible, berrylike, yellow fruit.

Natal′ plum′, **1.** a southern African bushy shrub, *Carissa grandiflora,* of the dogbane family, having forked spines, white flowers, and egg-shaped, red berries. **2.** the fruit of this shrub. Also called **amatungula.** [1855–60]

na·tant (nāt′nt), *adj.* **1.** swimming; floating. **2.** *Bot.* floating on water, as the leaf of an aquatic plant. [1700–10; < L *natant-* (s. of *natāns*), prp. of *natāre* to swim; see -ANT] —**na′tant·ly,** *adv.*

Na·ta·sha (nə tä′shə), *n.* a female given name, Russian form of **Natalie.** Also, **Na·ta′scha.**

na·ta·tion (nā tā′shən, na-), *n.* an act or the skill of swimming. [1535–45; < L *natātiōn-* (s. of *natātiō*), equiv. to *natāt(us)* (ptp. of *natāre* to swim) + *-iōn-* -ION] —**na·ta′tion·al,** *adj.*

na·ta·tor (nā′tə tər), *n.* a swimmer. [1815–25; < L, equiv. to *natā(re)* to swim + *-tor* -TOR]

na·ta·to·ri·al (nā′tə tôr′ē əl, -tōr′-, nat′ə-), *adj.* pertaining to, adapted for, or characterized by swimming: *natatorial birds.* Also, **na′ta·to′ry.** [1810–20; NATAT(ION) + -ORIAL]

na·ta·to·ri·um (nā′tə tôr′ē əm, -tōr′-, nat′ə-), *n., pl.* **-to·ri·ums, -to·ri·a** (-tôr′ē ə, -tōr′-). a swimming pool, esp. one that is indoors. [1885–90; < LL *natātōrium* swimming place, equiv. to L *natā(re)* to swim + *-tōrium* -TORY[2]]

natch (nach), *adv. Slang.* of course; naturally. [shortening and resp. of NATURALLY]

Natch·ez (nach′iz), *n., pl.* **-ez** for 2. **1.** a port in SW Mississippi, on the Mississippi River. 22,015. **2.** a member of an extinct Muskhogean Indian tribe once living on the lower Mississippi River.

Natch′ez Trace′, *U.S. Hist.* a road begun in 1806 between Natchez, Miss., and Nashville, Tenn.: about 500 mi. (800 km) long.

Natch·i·toches (nak′i tosh′), *n.* a city in NW Louisiana. 16,664.

na·tes (nā′tēz), *n.* (*used with a plural v.*) buttocks; rump. [1675–85; < L *natēs,* pl. of *natis;* generally used in the pl.; akin to Gk *nôton* the back]

Nath·a·lie (nat′l ē; *Fr.* NA TA LĒ′), *n.* a female given name.

Na·than (nā′thən), *n.* **1.** a prophet during the reigns of David and Solomon. II Sam. 12; I Kings 1:34. **2. George Jean,** 1882–1958, U.S. drama critic, author, and editor. **3. Robert,** 1894–1985, U.S. novelist and poet. **4.** a male given name: from a Hebrew word meaning "gift."

Na·than·a·el (nə than′ē əl, -than′yəl), *n.* a disciple of Jesus, possibly Bartholomew. John 1:45–51.

Na·than·iel (nə than′yəl), *n.* **1.** Bartholomew (def. 1). **2.** a male given name: from a Hebrew word meaning "gift of God."

Na·thans (nā′thənz), *n.* **Daniel,** born 1928, U.S. biologist: Nobel prize for medicine 1978.

nathe·less (nāth′lis, nath′-), *Archaic. adv.* nevertheless. Also, **nath·less** (nath′lis). [bef. 900; ME; OE *nā thē lǣs,* equiv. to *nā* not (see NA) + *thē,* var. of *thȳ* instrumental sing. definite article (see THE[2]) + *lǣs* LESS]

Na·tick (nā′tik), *n.* **1.** a town in E Massachusetts, W of Boston. 29,461. **2.** a dialect of the Massachusett language.

na·tion (nā′shən), *n.* **1.** a large body of people, associated with a particular territory, that is sufficiently conscious of its unity to seek or to possess a government peculiarly its own: *The president spoke to the nation about the new tax.* **2.** the territory or country itself: *the nations of Central America.* **3.** a member tribe of an American Indian confederation. **4.** an aggregation of persons of the same ethnic family, often speaking the same language or cognate languages. [1250–1300; ME < L *nātiōn-* (s. of *nātiō*) birth, tribe, equiv. to *nāt(us)* (ptp. of *nāscī* to be born) + *-iōn-* -ION] —**na′tion·hood′,** *n.* —**na′tion·less,** *adj.*
—**Syn. 1.** See **race[2]. 2.** state, commonwealth, kingdom, realm.

Na·tion (nā′shən), *n.* **Carry** or **Carrie (Amelia Moore),** 1846–1911, U.S. temperance leader.

na·tion·al (nash′ə nl, nash′nəl), *adj.* **1.** of, pertaining to, or maintained by a nation as an organized whole or independent political unit: *national affairs.* **2.** owned, preserved, or maintained by the federal government: *a national wildlife refuge.* **3.** peculiar or common to the whole people of a country: *national customs.* **4.** devoted to one's own nation, its interests, etc.; patriotic: *to stir up national pride.* **5.** nationalist. **6.** concerning or encompassing an entire nation: *a national radio network.* **7.** limited to one nation. —*n.* **8.** a citizen or subject of a particular nation who is entitled to its protection: *U.S. nationals living abroad.* **9.** Often, **nationals.** a national competition, tournament, or the like: *We're invited to Minneapolis for the nationals.* **10.** a national company or organization. [1590–1600; NATION + -AL[1]] —**na′tion·al·ly,** *adv.*

Na′tional Acad′emy of Sci′ences, a private organization, created by an act of Congress (1863), that furthers science and advises the U.S. government on scientific and technical issues. *Abbr.:* N.A.S., NAS

Na′tional Aeronau′tics and Space′ Adminis·tra′tion, the federal agency that institutes and administers the civilian programs of the U.S. government that deal with aeronautical research and the development of launch vehicles and spacecraft. *Abbr.:* NASA

Na′tional Associa′tion for the Advance′ment of Col′ored Peo′ple, an interracial U.S. organization working for political and civil equality of black people: organized in 1910. *Abbr.:* NAACP

na′tional bank′, **1.** a bank chartered by the U.S. government and formerly authorized to issue notes that served as money. **2.** a bank owned and administered by the government, as in some European countries. [1780–90, *Amer.*]

Na′tional Book′ Award′, any of several awards given annually, 1949–79, to an author whose book was judged the best in its category: administered by the Association of American Publishers. *Abbr.:* NBA, N.B.A. Cf. **American Book Award.**

Na′tional Bu′reau of Stand′ards, *U.S. Govt.* the federal agency that establishes the standards for units used in measuring the physical properties of substances. *Abbr.:* NBS, N.B.S.

na′tional cem′etery, a cemetery, maintained by the U.S. government, for persons who have served honorably in the armed forces. [1865–70, *Amer.*]

Na′tional Char′ter. See under **Chartism.**

na′tional church′, an independent church within a country, usually representing the prevalent religion. Cf. **established church.** [1645–55]

Na′tional Cit′y, a city in SW California, near San Diego. 48,772.

Na′tional Con′ference of Chris′tians and Jews′, an organization founded in 1928 to promote better understanding among Protestants, Catholics, and Jews: headquarters in New York City.

Na′tional Conven′tion, **1.** *Fr. Hist.* the legislature of France 1792–95. **2.** *U.S. Politics.* a convention held every four years by each of the major political parties to nominate a presidential candidate.

Na′tional Cov′enant, an agreement (1638) among Scottish Presbyterians to uphold their faith in Scotland. Cf. **Solemn League and Covenant.**

na′tional debt′, the financial obligations of a national government resulting from deficit spending. Also called **public debt.** [1775–85, *Amer.*]

Na′tional Endow′ment for the Arts′, *U.S. Govt.* an independent agency that stimulates the growth and development of the arts in the U.S. by awarding grants to individuals and organizations.

Na′tional Endow′ment for the Human′ities, *U.S. Govt.* an independent agency that stimulates the growth and development of the humanities in the U.S. by awarding grants to individuals and organizations.

na′tional for′est, forested land owned, maintained, and preserved by the U.S. government. [1880–85]

Na′tional Founda′tion on the Arts′ and the Human′ities, *U.S. Govt.* an independent agency, created in 1965, that develops a national policy of support for the arts and humanities.

Na′tional Guard′, state military forces, in part equipped, trained, and quartered by the U.S. government, and paid by the U.S. government, that become an active component of the army when called into federal service by the president in civil emergencies. Cf. **militia** (def. 2).

Na′tional Guards′man, guardsman (def. 2).

na′tional hol′iday, **1.** a holiday that is observed throughout a nation. **2.** a holiday that is legally established by a national government rather than by a municipal or state government. [1865–70, *Amer.*]

na′tional in′come, the total net earnings from the production of goods and services in a country over a period of time, usually one year, and consisting essentially of wages, salaries, rent, profits, and interest. Cf. **gross national product, net national product.** [1875–80]

Na′tional Indus′trial Recov′ery Act′, an act of Congress (1933, declared unconstitutional in 1936) that enabled the president and the National Recovery Administration to formulate and execute measures for reducing industrial unemployment. *Abbr.:* NIRA, N.I.R.A.

na·tion·al·ism (nash′ə nl iz′əm, nash′nə liz′-), *n.* **1.** national spirit or aspirations. **2.** devotion and loyalty to one's own nation; patriotism. **3.** excessive patriotism; chauvinism. **4.** the desire for national advancement or independence. **5.** the policy or doctrine of asserting the interests of one's own nation, viewed as separate from the interests of other nations or the common interests of all nations. **6.** an idiom or trait peculiar to a nation. **7.** a movement, as in the arts, based upon the folk idioms, history, aspirations, etc., of a nation. [1830–40; NATIONAL + -ISM]

na·tion·al·ist (nash′ə nl ist, nash′nə list), *n.* **1.** a person devoted to nationalism. **2.** (*cap.*) a member of a political group advocating or fighting for national independence, a strong national government, etc. —*adj.* **3.** Also, **na′tion·al·is′tic.** of, pertaining to, or promoting nationalism: *the beginnings of a nationalist movement.* **4.** (*cap.*) of, pertaining to, or noting a political group advocating or fighting for national independence, a strong national government, etc. [1705–15; NATIONAL + -IST] —**na′tion·al·is′ti·cal·ly,** *adv.*

Na′tionalist Chi′na. See **China, Republic of.**

na·tion·al·i·ty (nash′ə nal′i tē), *n., pl.* **-ties** for 1, 2, 5, 6. **1.** the status of belonging to a particular nation, whether by birth or naturalization: *the nationality of an immigrant.* **2.** the relationship of property, holdings, etc., to a particular nation, or to one or more of its members: *the nationality of a ship.* **3.** nationalism. **4.** existence as a distinct nation; national independence: *a small colony that has just achieved nationality.* **5.** a nation or people: *the nationalities of the Americas.* **6.** a national quality or character: *Nationalities tend to submerge and disappear in a metropolis.* [1685–95; NATIONAL + -ITY]

na·tion·al·ize (nash′ə nl īz′, nash′nə līz′), *v.,* **-ized, -iz·ing.** —*v.t.* **1.** to bring under the ownership or control of a nation, as industries and land: *a movement to nationalize the oil industry.* **2.** to make into a nation. **3.** to naturalize. **4.** to make national in extent or scope: *a magazine article that nationalized a local problem.* —*v.i.* **5.** to become nationalized or naturalized: *Those* *who remain in the country must nationalize.* Also, *esp. Brit.,* **na′tion·al·ise′.** [1790–1800; NATIONAL + -IZE] —**na′tion·al·i·za′tion,** *n.* —**na′tion·al·iz′er,** *n.*

Na′tional La′bor Rela′tions Act′, an act of Congress (1935) that forbade any interference by employers with the formation and operation of labor unions. Also called **Wagner Act.** Cf. **Taft-Hartley Act.**

Na′tional La′bor Rela′tions Board′, *U.S. Govt.* a board consisting of five members, originally set up under the National Labor Relations Act to guarantee workers' rights to organize and to prevent unfair labor practices. *Abbr.:* NLRB

Na′tional League′, the older of the two major professional U.S. baseball leagues, established in 1876. *Abbr.:* N.L.

Na′tional Libera′tion Front′, 1. the name taken by nationalist insurgent groups in various countries. **2.** Also called **Na′tional Libera′tion Front′ of South′ Vietnam′.** a political organization formed by the Vietcong in South Vietnam in 1960 to carry out an insurgent policy.

na′tional li′brary, a library established and funded by a national government with the designation *national,* to serve the needs of this government, often to function as a library of record for the nation's publishing output, and in some cases to act as a central agency for library and bibliographic development in the nation.

Na′tional Mer′it Schol′arship, one of some 6000 college scholarships awarded annually since 1956, by the nonprofit, grant-supported National Merit Scholarship Corporation, to high-school students (**Na′tional Mer′it Schol′ars**) on the basis of scholastic record, personal character, and score on a test administered nationally.

na′tional mon′ument, a monument, as a historic site or geographical area, owned and maintained in the public interest by the federal government. [1905–10, *Amer.*]

Na′tional Ocean′ic and Atmospher′ic Administra′tion, *U.S. Govt.* a division of the Department of Commerce, created in 1970, that conducts research on the world's oceans and atmosphere. *Abbr.:* NOAA

Na′tional Organiza′tion for Wom′en, a women's rights organization founded in 1966. *Abbr.:* NOW

na′tional park′, an area of scenic beauty, historical importance, or the like, owned and maintained by a national government for the use of the people. See table below. [1865–70, *Amer.*]

Na′tional Park′ Serv′ice, *U.S. Govt.* a division of the Department of the Interior, created in 1916, that administers national parks, monuments, historic sites, and recreational areas.

Na′tional Progres′sive par′ty. See **Progressive party** (def. 1).

Na′tional Pub′lic Ra′dio, *n.* a nationwide network of nonprofit radio stations supported in part by U.S. government funds distributed by the Corporation for Public Broadcasting, often affiliated with a public television station or educational institution. *Abbr.:* NPR

CONCISE ETYMOLOGY KEY: <, descended or borrowed from; >, whence; b., blend of, blended; c., cognate with; cf., compare; deriv., derivative; equiv., equivalent; imit., imitative; obl., oblique; r., replacing; s., stem; sp., spelling, spelled; resp., respelling, respelled; trans., translation; ?, origin unknown; *, unattested; ‡, probably earlier than. See the full key inside the front cover.

Na′tional Ra′dio Astron′omy Observ′atory, an observatory founded in 1956 by the National Science Foundation, currently with three sites of operation: one near Green Bank, W. Va., having 300-ft. (91-m) and 140-ft. (43-m) paraboloidal dishes; one on Kitt Peak in Arizona having a 36-ft. (11-m) radio telescope; and the Very Large Array in New Mexico.

Na′tional Recov′ery Administra′tion. See **NRA.**

Na′tional Sci′ence Founda′tion, *U.S. Govt.* an independent agency of the executive branch, created in 1950, that promotes and supports research and education in the sciences. *Abbr.:* NSF

na′tional sea′shore, (*sometimes caps.*) an area of seacoast set aside and maintained by the U.S. government for purposes of recreation or wildlife study. [1960–65]

Na′tional Secur′ity Coun′cil, *U.S. Govt.* the council, composed of the President, Vice President, Secretary of State, Secretary of Defense, director of the Central Intelligence Agency and the Chairman of the Joint Chiefs of Staff, that determines means by which domestic, foreign, and military policy can best be integrated for safeguarding the national security. *Abbr.:* NSC

Na′tional So′cialism, the principles and practices of the Nazi party in Germany. —**Na′tional So′cialist.**

Na′tional Transporta′tion Safe′ty Board′, *U.S. Govt.* an independent agency, created in 1975, that promotes safe transportation in the U.S. through accident investigations, studies, and recommendations. *Abbr.:* NTSB

Na′tional War′ La′bor Board′, *U.S. Govt.* the board (1942–45) that mediated and arbitrated labor disputes. *Abbr.:* NWLB, WLB Also, **War Labor Board.**

Na′tional Weath′er Serv′ice, an agency of the National Oceanic and Atmospheric Administration that is responsible for meteorological observations, weather forecasts, storm and flood warnings, etc. Formerly, **Weather Bureau.**

na·tion·hood (nā′shən ho͝od′), *n.* the state or quality of having status as a separate and independent nation: *an African colony that achieved nationhood.* [1840–50; NATION + -HOOD]

Na′tion of Islam′, an organization composed chiefly of American blacks, advocating the teachings of Islam and originally favoring the separation of races: members are known as Black Muslims.

na·tion-state (nā′shən stāt′), *n.* a sovereign state inhabited by a relatively homogeneous group of people who share a feeling of common nationality. [1915–20]

na·tion·wide (nā′shən wīd′), *adj.* extending throughout the nation: *The incident aroused nationwide interest.* [1910–15; NATION + -WIDE]

na·tive (nā′tiv), *adj.* **1.** being the place or environment in which a person was born or a thing came into being: *one's native land.* **2.** belonging to a person by birth or to a thing by nature; inherent: *native ability; native grace.* **3.** belonging by birth to a people regarded as indigenous to a certain place, esp. a preliterate people: *Native guides accompanied the expedition through the rain forest.* **4.** of indigenous origin, growth, or production: *native pottery.* **5.** of, pertaining to, or characteristic of the indigenous inhabitants of a place or country: *native customs; native dress.* **6.** born in a particular place or country: *a native New Yorker.* **7.** of or pertaining to a language acquired by a person before or to the exclusion of any other language: *Her native language is Greek.* **8.** pertaining to or characteristic of a person using his or her native language: *a native speaker of English; native command of a language.* **9.** under the rule of natives: *a native government.* **10.** occupied by natives: *the native quarter of Algiers.* **11.** remaining or growing in a natural state; unadorned or unchanged: *the native beauty of a desert island.* **12.** forming the source or origin of a person or thing: *He returned to his native Kansas.* **13.** originating naturally in a particular country or region, as animals or plants. **14.** found in nature rather than produced artificially, as a mineral substance: *the difference between native and industrial diamonds.* **15.** *Chem., Mineral.* (of metals) occurring in nature pure or uncombined: *native copper.* **16.** belonging to a person as a birthright: *to deprive a person of his native rights.* **17.** *Archaic.* closely related, as by birth. **18. go native,** *Informal.* to adopt or affect the manners or way of life of a place or environment that is different from one's own, esp. a less developed country: *After living on the island for a year, we went native and began to wear the local costume.* —*n.* **19.** one of the people indigenous to a place or country, esp. as distinguished from strangers, foreigners, colonizers, etc.: *the natives of Chile.* **20.** a person born in a particular place or country: *a native of Ohio.* **21.** an organism indigenous to a particular region. **22.** *Brit.* an oyster reared in British waters, esp. in an artificial bed. **23.** *Astrol.* a person born under a particular planet, [1325–75; < L *nātīvus* inborn, natural, equiv. to *nāt(us)* (ptp. of *nāscī* to be born) + *-īvus* -IVE; r. ME *natif* (adj.) < MF < L, as above] —**na′tive·ly,** *adv.* —**na′tive·ness,** *n.*
—**Syn. 2.** inherited, innate, inbred, congenital. **4.** autochthonous, aboriginal. **11.** real, genuine, original. **19.** aborigine. —**Ant. 2.** acquired. **19.** alien

na′tive Amer′ican, a person born in the United States. [1835–45, *Amer.*] —**na′tive-A·mer′i·can,** *adj.*

Na′tive Amer′ican, Indian (def. 1).
—**Usage.** See **Indian, Eskimo.**

na·tive-born (nā′tiv bôrn′), *adj.* born in the place or country indicated: *a native-born Australian.* [1490–1500]

na′tive Cana′dian, *Canadian.* **1.** a person born in Canada of American Indian or Inuit descent. **2.** any person born in Canada.

na′tive cat′, any of several catlike dasyures of the genus *Dasyurus,* of Australia and Tasmania: most populations are now rare. [1875–80]

na′tive compan′ion, *Ornith.* brolga. [1810–20]

na′tive elm′ bark′ bee′tle. See **elm bark beetle** (def. 2).

na′tive immu′nity. See **natural immunity.**

na′tive son′, a person born in a particular place: *The delegation from Iowa nominated a native son.* [1825–35, *Amer.*]

Na′tive Son′, a novel (1940) by Richard Wright.

Na′tive States′. See **Indian States and Agencies.**

na·tiv·ism (nā′ti viz′əm), *n.* **1.** the policy of protecting the interests of native inhabitants against those of immigrants. **2.** the policy or practice of preserving or reviving an indigenous culture. **3.** *Philos.* the doctrine that innate ideas exist. **4.** See **innateness hypothesis.** [1835–45, *Amer.;* NATIVE + -ISM] —**na′tiv·ist,** *n., adj.* —**na′tiv·is′tic,** *adj.*

na·tiv·i·ty (nə tiv′i tē, nā-), *n., pl.* **-ties. 1.** birth. **2.** birth with reference to place or attendant circumstances: *of Irish nativity.* **3.** (*cap.*) the birth of Christ. **4.** (*cap.*) the church festival commemorating the birth of Christ; Christmas. **5.** (*cap.*) a representation of the birth of Christ, as in art. **6.** *Astrol.* a horoscope of a person's birth. [bef. 1150; ME *nativite* < MF < LL *nātīvitāt-* (s. of *nātīvitās;* see NATIVE, -ITY); r. late OE *nativiteth* < OF *nativited* < LL, as above]

natl., national.

NATO (nā′tō), *n.* an organization formed in Washington, D.C. (1949), comprising the 12 nations of the Atlantic Pact together with Greece, Turkey, and the Federal Republic of Germany, for the purpose of collective defense against aggression. [*N(orth) A(tlantic) T(reaty) O(rganization)*]

na·tri·um (nā′trē əm), *n.* (formerly) sodium. [1835–45; < G; see NATRON, -IUM]

na·tri·u·re·sis (nā′trə yo͞o rē′sis), *n.* excretion of sodium in the urine. [1957; NATRI(UM) + *-uresis* < Gk *oúrēsis* urination, equiv. to *ourē-,* var. s. of *oureîn* to urinate + *-sis* -SIS] —**na·tri·u·ret·ic** (nā′trə yo͞o ret′ik), *adj., n.*

nat·ro·lite (na′trə līt′, nā′-), *n.* a white or colorless zeolite mineral, a hydrous silicate of sodium and aluminum, $Na_2Al_2Si_3O_{10}\cdot 2H_2O$, often occurring in acicular crystals. [1795–1805; NATRO(N) + -LITE]

na·tron (nā′tron, -trən), *n.* a mineral, hydrated sodium carbonate, $Na_2CO_3\cdot 10H_2O$. [1675–85; < F < Sp < Ar *natrūn,* var. of *nitrūn* < Gk *nítron* NITER; cf. also Egyptian *ntry,* Heb *nether*]

Na·tsu·me (nä′tso͞o me′), *n.* **So·se·ki** (sô′se kē′), (*Kinnosuke Natsume*), 1867–1916, Japanese novelist.

Nat·ta (nät′tä), *n.* **Giu·lio** (jo͞o′lyô), 1903–79, Italian chemist and engineer: Nobel prize for chemistry 1963.

nat·ter (nat′ər), *v.i.* **1.** to talk incessantly; chatter. —*n.* **2.** a conversation; chat. [1820–30; var. of earlier *gnatter* < ?]

nat·ter·jack (nat′ər jak′), *n.* a European toad, *Bufo calamita,* that moves by running. [1760–70; orig. uncert.]

nat·ty (nat′ē), *adj.,* **-ti·er, -ti·est.** neatly or trimly smart in dress or appearance; spruce: *a natty white uniform.* [1775–85; perh. var. of NEAT[1] + -Y[1]] —**nat′ti·ly,** *adv.* —**nat′ti·ness,** *n.*

nat·u·ral (nach′ər əl, nach′rəl), *adj.* **1.** existing in or formed by nature (opposed to *artificial*): *a natural bridge.* **2.** based on the state of things in nature; con-

MAJOR NATIONAL PARKS OF THE UNITED STATES

Park	Location	Highlights
Acadia	S Maine	Granite mountains; coastal scenery
Badlands	SW South Dakota	Fossils; prairie grasslands; rugged, eroded slopes
Big Bend	SW Texas	Mountain and desert scenery
Bryce Canyon	SW Utah	Canyon with brilliantly colored pinnacles
Canyonlands	SE Utah	Red rock canyons; sandstone structures
Carlsbad Caverns	SE New Mexico	Huge natural caves
Crater Lake	SW Oregon	Clear blue lake in extinct volcano
Denali*	S central Alaska	Mount McKinley, highest peak in North America
Everglades	S Florida	Mangrove swamps; rare birds and plants
Glacier	NW Montana	Mountain scenery with lakes and glaciers
Glacier Bay	SE Alaska	Tidewater glaciers; wildlife
Grand Canyon	NW Arizona	Huge river gorge with varicolored cliffs
Grand Teton	NW Wyoming	Snow-capped peaks; evergreen forests
Great Smoky Mountains	E Tennessee/W North Carolina	Mountain scenery; primeval hardwood forests
Haleakala	Maui Isl., Hawaii	Large dormant volcano
Hawaii Volcanoes	Isl. of Hawaii	Active volcanoes
Hot Springs	W central Arkansas	Forty-seven mineral hot springs
Isle Royale	N Michigan	Forested islands
Kings Canyon	E central California	Imposing peaks and canyons; giant sequoias
Lassen Volcanic	N California	Recently active volcano; hot springs; geysers
Mammoth Cave	S central Kentucky	Limestone caverns; underground river and lakes
Mesa Verde	SW Colorado	Prehistoric cliff dwellings; pueblo houses
Mount Rainier	W central Washington	Glacier system; dense forests
North Cascades	NW Washington	Alpine region; glaciers; jagged peaks
Olympic	NW Washington	Temperate rainforest; mountain wilderness
Petrified Forest	N Arizona	Petrified wood in brilliant colors
Rocky Mountain	N central Colorado	Heart of Colorado Rockies; wildlife; alpine tundra
Sequoia	E central California	Stands of sequoias; lakes; high mountains
Shenandoah	N Virginia	Skyline drive along crest of Blue Ridges
Virgin Islands	E Caribbean	Tropical area; prehistoric and historic relics
Wind Cave	SW South Dakota	Limestone caverns; buffalo herd
Wrangell-St. Elias	E Alaska	Glaciers; high peaks
Yellowstone	NW Wyoming	Geysers; hot springs; lakes; waterfalls; wildlife
Yosemite	E central California	Lofty cliffs; domes; high waterfalls; giant sequoias
Zion	SW Utah	Colorful canyons; picturesque sandstone cliffs

*Formerly, Mount McKinley

stituted by nature: *Growth is a natural process.* **3.** of or pertaining to nature or the universe: *natural beauty.* **4.** of, pertaining to, or occupied with the study of natural science: *conducting natural experiments.* **5.** in a state of nature; uncultivated, as land. **6.** growing spontaneously, without being planted or tended by human hand, as vegetation. **7.** having undergone little or no processing and containing no chemical additives: *natural food; natural ingredients.* Cf. **organic** (def. 11). **8.** having a real or physical existence, as opposed to one that is spiritual, intellectual, fictitious, etc. **9.** of, pertaining to, or proper to the nature or essential constitution: *natural ability.* **10.** proper to the circumstances of the case: *a natural result of his greed.* **11.** free from affectation or constraint: *a natural manner.* **12.** arising easily or spontaneously: *a natural courtesy to strangers.* **13.** consonant with the nature or character of. **14.** in accordance with the nature of things: *It was natural that he should hit back.* **15.** based upon the innate moral feeling of humankind: *natural justice.* **16.** in conformity with the ordinary course of nature; not unusual or exceptional. **17.** happening in the ordinary or usual course of things, without the intervention of accident, violence, etc. **18.** related only by birth; of no legal relationship; illegitimate: *a natural son.* **19.** related by blood rather than by adoption. **20.** based on what is learned from nature rather than on revelation. **21.** true to or closely imitating nature: *a natural representation.* **22.** unenlightened or unregenerate: *the natural man.* **23.** being such by nature; born such: *a natural fool.* **24.** *Music.* **a.** neither sharp nor flat. **b.** changed in pitch by the sign ♮. **25.** not treated, tanned, refined, etc.; in its original or raw state: *natural wood; natural cowhide.* **26.** (of a horn or trumpet) having neither side holes nor valves. **27.** not tinted or colored; undyed. **28.** having a pale tannish or grayish-yellow color, as many woods and untreated animal skins. **29.** *Cards.* **a.** being a card other than a wild card or joker. **b.** (of a set or sequence of cards) containing no wild cards. **30.** having or showing feelings, as affection, gratitude, or kindness, considered part of basic human nature. **31.** Afro (def. 1). —*n.* **32.** any person or thing that is or is likely or certain to be very suitable to and successful in an endeavor without much training or difficulty. **33.** *Music.* **a.** a white key on a piano, organ, or the like. **b.** the sign ♮, placed before a note, canceling the effect of a previous sharp or flat. **c.** a note affected by a ♮, or a tone thus represented. **34.** an idiot. **35.** *Cards.* blackjack (def. 2b). **36.** Afro (def. 2). **37.** (in craps) a winning combination of seven or eleven made on the first cast. **38.** a natural substance or a product made with such a substance: *an ointment containing mink oil and other naturals.* [1300–50; ME < L *nātūrālis* (see NATURE, -AL[1]); r. ME *naturel* < MF < L, as above] —**nat′u•ral•ness,** *n.*
—**Syn. 11.** spontaneous, unaffected, genuine, unmannered.

nat′ural aids′, *Manège.* aid (def. 6a).

nat•u•ral-born (nach′ər əl bôrn′, nach′rəl-), *adj.* **1.** native-born. **2.** by virtue of one's nature, qualities, or innate talent: *a natural-born musician.* [1575–85]

Nat′ural Bridge′, a natural limestone bridge in western Virginia. 215 ft. (66 m) high; 90 ft. (27 m) span.

Nat′ural Bridg′es, a national monument in SE Utah containing three natural bridges. Largest, 222 ft. (68 m) high; 261 ft. (80 m) span.

nat′ural child′, **1.** *Law.* **a.** an illegitimate child; one born of illicit intercourse. **b.** (esp. in Louisiana) an illegitimate child who has been lawfully acknowledged by its father. **2.** See **biological child.** [1860–65]

nat′ural child′birth, childbirth involving little or no use of drugs or anesthesia and usually involving a program in which the mother is psychologically and physically prepared for the birth process. Cf. **psychoprophylaxis.** [1930–35]

nat′ural death′, death that occurs from natural causes, as disease or old age, rather than from violence or an accident. [1570–80]

nat′ural gas′, a combustible mixture of gaseous hydrocarbons that accumulates in porous sedimentary rocks, esp. those yielding petroleum, consisting usually of over 80 percent methane together with minor amounts of ethane, propane, butane, nitrogen, and, sometimes, helium: used as a fuel and to make carbon black, acetylene, and synthesis gas. [1815–25]

nat′ural gen′der, *Gram.* gender based on the sex or, for neuter, the lack of sex of the referent of a noun, as English *girl* (feminine) is referred to by the feminine pronoun *she, boy* (masculine) by the masculine pronoun *he,* and *table* (neuter) by the neuter pronoun *it.* Cf. **grammatical gender.**

nat′ural harmon′ics, *Music.* harmonics of a note produced on a stringed instrument by lightly touching an open or unstopped sounded string. Cf. **artificial harmonics.**

nat′ural his′tory, **1.** the sciences, as botany, mineralogy, or zoology, dealing with the study of all objects in nature: used esp. in reference to the beginnings of these sciences in former times. **2.** the study of these sciences. [1560–70] —**nat′ural histo′rian.**

nat′ural immu′nity, immunity that is present without prior immunization. Also called **native immunity.**

nat•u•ral•ism (nach′ər ə liz′əm, nach′rə-), *n.* **1.** *Literature.* **a.** a manner or technique of treating subject matter that presents, through volume of detail, a deterministic view of human life and actions. **b.** a deterministic theory of writing in which it is held that a writer should adopt an objective view toward the material written about, be free of preconceived ideas as to form and content, and represent with clinical accuracy and frankness the details of life. Cf. **realism** (def. 4b). **c.** a representation of natural appearances or natural patterns of speech, manner, etc., in a work of fiction. **d.** the depiction of the physical environment, esp. landscape or the rural environment. **2.** (in a work of art) treatment of forms, colors, space, etc., as they appear or might appear in nature. Cf. **idealism** (def. 4), **realism** (def. 3a). **3.** action arising from or based on natural instincts and desires alone. **4.** *Philos.* **a.** the view of the world that takes account only of natural elements and forces, excluding the supernatural or spiritual. **b.** the belief that all phenomena are covered by laws of science and that all teleological explanations are therefore without value. **5.** *Theol.* **a.** the doctrine that all religious truth is derived from a study of natural processes and not from revelation. **b.** the doctrine that natural religion is sufficient for salvation. **6.** adherence or attachment to what is natural. [1635–45; NATURAL + -ISM]

nat•u•ral•ist (nach′ər ə list, nach′rə-), *n.* **1.** a person who studies or is an expert in natural history, esp. a zoologist or botanist. **2.** an adherent of naturalism in literature or art. [1580–90; NATURAL + -IST]

nat•u•ral•is•tic (nach′ər ə lis′tik, nach′rə-), *adj.* **1.** imitating nature or the usual natural surroundings. **2.** pertaining to naturalists or natural history. **3.** pertaining to naturalism, esp. in literature and art. [1830–40; NATURAL + -ISTIC] —**nat′u•ral•is′ti•cal•ly,** *adv.*

nat•u•ral•ize (nach′ər ə līz′, nach′rə-), *v.,* **-ized, -iz•ing.** —*v.t.* **1.** to confer upon (an alien) the rights and privileges of a citizen. **2.** to introduce (organisms) into a region and cause them to flourish as if native. **3.** to introduce or adopt (foreign practices, words, etc.) into a country or into general use: *to naturalize a French phrase.* **4.** to bring into conformity with nature. **5.** to regard or explain as natural rather than supernatural: *to naturalize miracles.* **6.** to adapt or accustom to a place or to new surroundings. —*v.i.* **7.** to become naturalized. **8.** to adapt as if native to a new environment, set of circumstances, etc. **9.** to study or carry on research in natural history. Also, *esp. Brit.,* **nat′u•ral•ise′.** [1585–95; NATURAL + -IZE] —**nat′u•ral•i•za′tion,** *n.* —**nat′u•ral•iz′er,** *n.*

nat′ural kill′er cell′, *Immunol.* a small killer cell that destroys virus-infected cells or tumor cells without activation by an immune system cell or antibody. Cf. **killer T cell.**

nat′ural lan′guage, a language used as a native tongue by a group of speakers. [1875–80]

nat′ural law′, a principle or body of laws considered as derived from nature, right reason, or religion and as ethically binding in human society. Cf. **positive law.** [1350–1400; ME]

na′tural lev′ee, a deposit of sand or mud built up along, and sloping away from, either side of the flood plain of a river or stream. Also called **levee.**

nat′ural log′arithm, *Math.* a logarithm having *e* as a base. *Symbol:* ln Also called **Napierian logarithm.** Cf. **common logarithm.** [1810–20]

nat•u•ral•ly (nach′ər ə lē, -əl lē, nach′rə lē, -rəl lē), *adv.* **1.** in a natural or normal manner. **2.** by nature; innately or inherently. **3.** of course; as would be expected; needless to say. [1400–50; late ME; see NATURAL, -LY]

nat′ural num′ber, a positive integer or zero. [1755–65]

nat′ural par′ent. See **biological parent.**

nat′ural per′son, *Law.* See under **person** (def. 11).

nat′ural philos′ophy, **1.** See **natural science.** **2.** See **physical science.** [1425–75; late ME] —**nat′ural philos′opher.**

nat′ural re′alism. See **naive realism.** —**nat′ural re′alist.**

nat′ural reli′gion, religion based on principles derived solely from reason and the study of nature. Cf. **revealed religion.** [1665–75]

nat′ural resist′ance, *Immunol.* See **natural immunity.**

nat′ural re′sources, the natural wealth of a country, consisting of land, forests, mineral deposits, water, etc. [1865–70]

nat′ural right′, any right that exists by virtue of natural law. [1680–90]

nat′ural rub′ber, rubber[1] (def. 1).

nat′ural sci′ence, a science or knowledge of objects or processes observable in nature, as biology or physics, as distinguished from the abstract or theoretical sciences, as mathematics or philosophy. [1350–1400; ME]

nat′ural selec′tion, the process by which forms of life having traits that better enable them to adapt to specific environmental pressures, as predators, changes in climate, or competition for food or mates, will tend to survive and reproduce in greater numbers than others of their kind, thus ensuring the perpetuation of those favorable traits in succeeding generations. Cf. **survival of the fittest.** [1855–60]

nat′ural theol′ogy, theology based on knowledge of the natural world and on human reason, apart from revelation. Cf. **revealed theology.** [1670–80] —**nat′ural theolo′gian.**

nat′ural var′nish. See under **varnish** (def. 2).

nat′ural vir′tue, (esp. among the scholastics) any moral virtue of which humankind is capable, esp. the cardinal virtues: justice, temperance, prudence, and fortitude. Cf. **theological virtue.**

na•tu•ra non fa•cit sal•tum (nä to͞o′rä nōn fä′kit säl′to͝om; *Eng.* nə to͝or′ə non fā′sit sal′təm, -tyo͝or′-), *Latin.* nature makes no leap.

na•ture (nā′chər), *n.* **1.** the material world, esp. as surrounding humankind and existing independently of human activities. **2.** the natural world as it exists without human beings or civilization. **3.** the elements of the natural world, as mountains, trees, animals, or rivers. **4.** natural scenery. **5.** the universe, with all its phenomena. **6.** the sum total of the forces at work throughout the universe. **7.** reality, as distinguished from any effect of art: *a portrait true to nature.* **8.** the particular combination of qualities belonging to a person, animal, thing, or class by birth, origin, or constitution; native or inherent character: *human nature.* **9.** the instincts or inherent tendencies directing conduct: *a man of good nature.* **10.** character, kind, or sort: *two books of the same nature.* **11.** characteristic disposition; temperament: *a self-willed nature; an evil nature.* **12.** the original, natural, uncivilized condition of humankind. **13.** the biological functions or the urges to satisfy their requirements. **14.** a primitive, wild condition; an uncultivated state. **15.** a simple, uncluttered mode of life without the conveniences or distractions of civilization: *a return to nature.* **16.** (*cap., italics*) a prose work (1836), by Ralph Waldo Emerson, expounding transcendentalism. **17.** *Theol.* the moral state as unaffected by grace. **18. by nature,** as a result of inborn or inherent qualities; innately: *She is by nature a kindhearted person.* **19. in a state of nature, a.** in an uncivilized or uncultured condition. **b.** without clothes; nude; naked. **20. of or in the nature of,** having the character or qualities of: *in the nature of an apology.* [1200–50; ME *natur(e)* < OF < L *nātūra* conditions of birth, quality, character, natural order, world, equiv. to *nāt(us)* (ptp. of *nāscī* to be born) + *-ūra* -URE] —**na′ture•like′,** *adj.*

na′ture's call′. See **call of nature.**

na′ture stud′y, the study of plants and animals, esp. by amateurs. [1895–1900]

na′ture trail′, a path through a forest, wildlife preserve, or the like, esp. one designed to provide opportunities for observing and learning about the flora and fauna. [1925–30]

na′ture walk′, **1.** a walk on a nature trail, esp. with an experienced guide. **2.** See **nature trail.** [1930–35]

na′ture wor′ship, **1.** a system of religion based on the deification and worship of natural forces and phenomena. **2.** love of nature. [1865–70] —**na′ture wor′shiper.**

na•tur•ist (nā′chər ist), *n.* **1.** a person who appreciates the beauty and benefits of nature. **2.** a nudist. [1675–85; NATURE + -IST] —**na′tur•ism,** *n.*

na•tur•op•a•thy (nā′chə rop′ə thē, nach′ə-), *n.* a system or method of treating disease that employs no surgery or synthetic drugs but uses special diets, herbs, vitamins, massage, etc., to assist the natural healing processes. [1900–05; NATURE + -O- + -PATHY] —**na•tur•o•path** (nā′chər ə path′, nach′ər-), *n.* —**na′tur•o•path′ic,** *adj.*

Nau•cra•tis (nô′krə tis), *n.* an ancient Greek city in N Egypt, on the Nile delta. Greek, **Nau′kra•tis.**

Nau•ga•hyde (nô′gə hīd′), *Trademark.* a brand of strong vinyl-coated fabric made to look like leather and used for upholstery, luggage, etc.

Nau•ga•tuck (nô′gə tuk′), *n.* a city in central Connecticut. 26,456.

naught (nôt), *n.* **1.** nothing. **2.** a cipher (0); zero. **3. come to naught,** to come to nothing; be without result or fruition; fail. **4. set at naught,** to regard or treat as of no importance; disdain: *He entered a milieu that set his ideals at naught.* —*adj.* **5.** lost; ruined. **6.** *Archaic.* worthless; useless. **7.** *Obs.* morally bad; wicked. —*adv.* **8.** *Obs.* not. Also, **nought.** [bef. 900; ME; OE *nauht, nāwiht* (nā NO[1] + *wiht* thing). See NOUGHT, WIGHT[1], WHIT]

naugh•ty (nô′tē), *adj.,* **-ti•er, -ti•est.** **1.** disobedient; mischievous (used esp. in speaking to or about children): *Weren't we naughty not to eat our spinach?* **2.** improper, tasteless, indecorous, or indecent: *a naughty word.* **3.** *Obs.* wicked; evil. [1350–1400; ME; see NAUGHT, -Y[1]] —**naugh′ti•ly,** *adv.* —**naugh′ti•ness,** *n.*
—**Syn. 1.** willful, wayward, misbehaving.

nau•ma•chi•a (nô mā′kē ə), *n., pl.* **-chi•ae** (-kē ē′), **-chi•as.** **1.** a mock sea fight, given as a spectacle among the ancient Romans. **2.** a place for presenting such spectacles. [1590–1600; < L: mock naval battle < Gk *naumachía* a sea fight, equiv. to *naû(s)* ship + *mách(ē)* battle, fight + *-ia* -IA]

nau•ma•chy (nô′mə kē), *n., pl.* **-chies.** naumachia.

nau•mann•ite (nô′mə nīt′, nou′-), *n.* a mineral, silver-lead selenide, $(Ag_2Pb)Se$, usually occurring in iron-black cubic crystals. [1840–50; named after Karl F. *Naumann,* (1797–1873), German mineralogist; see -ITE[1]]

nau•pli•us (nô′plē əs), *n., pl.* **-pli•i** (-plē ī′). (in many crustaceans) a larval form with three pairs of appendages and a single median eye, occurring usually as the first stage of development after leaving the egg. [1830–40; < L: a kind of shellfish] —**nau′pli•al, nau′pli•form′, nau′pli•oid′,** *adj.*

Na•u•ru (nä o͞o′ro͞o), *n.* **Republic of,** an island republic in the Pacific, near the equator, W of the Gilbert Islands: administered by Australia before 1968. 8007; 8¼ sq. mi. (21 sq. km). Formerly, **Pleasant Island.** —**Na•u′ru•an,** *n., adj.*

nau•se•a (nô′zē ə, -zhə, -sē ə, -shə), *n.* **1.** sickness at the stomach, esp. when accompanied by a loathing for food and an involuntary impulse to vomit. **2.** extreme disgust; loathing; repugnance. [1560–70; < L *nausea, nausia* < Gk **nausiā* (Ionic *nausíē*) seasickness, deriv. of *naûs* ship; see -IA]

nau•se•ant (nô′zē ənt, -zhē-, -sē-, -shē-), *Med.* —*adj.* **1.** producing nausea. —*n.* **2.** a nauseant agent. [1840–50; < L *nauseant-* (s. of *nauseāns*) prp. of *nauseāre* to be seasick. See NAUSEA, -ANT]

nau•se•ate (nô′zē āt′, -zhē-, -sē-, -shē-), *v.,* **-at•ed, -at•ing.** —*v.t.* **1.** to affect with nausea; sicken. **2.** to cause to feel extreme disgust: *His vicious behavior toward the dogs nauseates me.* —*v.i.* **3.** to become

CONCISE PRONUNCIATION KEY: act, cāpe, dâre, pärt; set, ēqual; if, īce; ox, ōver, ôrder, oil, bo͝ok, bo͞ot, out; up, ûrge; child; sing; shoe; thin, *th*at; zh as in *treasure.* ə = *a* as in *alone, e* as in *system, i* as in *easily, o* as in *gallop, u* as in *circus;* ᵊ as in *fire* (fīᵊr), *hour* (ouᵊr). l and n can serve as syllabic consonants, as in *cradle* (krād′l), and *button* (but′n). See the full key inside the front cover.

affected with nausea. [1630–40; < L *nauseātus* (ptp. of *nauseāre* to be seasick). See NAUSEA, -ATE[1]]
—Syn. 2. revolt. **—Ant. 2.** attract, delight.
—Usage. See **nauseous.**

nau·se·at·ing (nô′zē ā′ting, -zhē-, -sē-, -shē-), *adj.* **1.** causing sickness of the stomach; nauseous. **2.** such as to cause contempt, disgust, loathing, etc.: *I had to listen to the whole nauseating story.* [1635–45; NAUSEATE + -ING[2]] **—nau′se·at′ing·ly,** *adv.*
—Usage. See **nauseous.**

nau·seous (nô′shəs, -zē əs), *adj.* **1.** affected with nausea; nauseated: *to feel nauseous.* **2.** causing nausea; sickening; nauseating. **3.** disgusting; loathsome: *a nauseous display of greed.* [1595–1605; < L *nauseōsus.* See NAUSEA, -OUS] **—nau′seous·ly,** *adv.* **—nau′seous·ness,** *n.*
—Syn. 3. revolting, nasty, repellent, abhorrent, detestable, despicable, offensive. **—Ant. 3.** delightful.
—Usage. The two literal senses of NAUSEOUS, "causing nausea" (*a nauseous smell*) and "affected with nausea" (*to feel nauseous*), appear in English at almost the same time in the early 17th century, and both senses are in standard use at the present time. NAUSEOUS is more common than NAUSEATED in the sense "affected with nausea," despite recent objections by those who imagine the sense to be new. In the sense "causing nausea," either literally or figuratively, NAUSEATING has become more common than NAUSEOUS: *a nauseating smell.*

naut., nautical.

nautch (nôch), *n.* **1.** (in India) an exhibition of dancing by professional dancing girls. **2.** Also called **nautch′ dance′.** a sinuous dance of the Orient, resembling the cooch. [1800–10; < Hindi *nāch* < Prakrit *nachcha* dancing]

Nau·tes (nô′tēz, nō′-), *n.* (in the *Aeneid*) an aged Trojan and advisor to Aeneas.

nau·ti·cal (nô′ti kəl, not′i-), *adj.* of or pertaining to sailors, ships, or navigation: *nautical terms.* [1545–55; < L *nautic(us)* pertaining to ships or sailors (< Gk *nautikós,* equiv. to *naû(s)* ship + *-tikos* -TIC) + -AL[1]] **—nau·ti·cal·i·ty** (nô′ti kal′i tē, not′i-), *n.* **—nau′ti·cal·ly,** *adv.*
—Syn. seagoing, marine, maritime.

nau′tical archaeol′ogy. See **marine archaeology.**

nau′tical day′, a period from noon of one day to noon of the next, used in reckoning time aboard ship. [1865–70]

nau′tical mile′, a unit of distance used chiefly in navigation, equal to 6080.20 feet (1853.25 meters) in the U.S., now replaced by the international nautical mile. Also called **geographical mile, sea mile.** [1625–35]

nau·ti·lus (nôt′l əs, not′-), *n., pl.* **nau·ti·lus·es, nau·ti·li** (nôt′l ī′, not′-) for 1, 2. **1.** Also called **chambered nautilus, pearly nautilus.** any cephalopod of the genus *Nautilus,* having a spiral, chambered shell with pearly septa. **2.** See **paper nautilus. 3.** (*cap.*) the first nuclear-powered submarine launched by the U.S. Navy. [1595–1605; < L < Gk *nautílos* paper nautilus, lit., sailor, deriv. of *naûs* ship; the webbed dorsal arms of the paper nautilus were thought to have been used as sails]

nautilus, *Nautilus macromphalus,* shell length 8 in. (20 cm)

nau·to·phone (nô′tə fōn′, not′ə-), *n. Naut.* an electrically operated horn for giving fog warnings. [< Gk *nauto-,* comb. form of *naûs* ship or *naútēs* sailor + -PHONE]

nav., **1.** naval. **2.** navigable. **3.** navigation.

Nav·a·ho (nav′ə hō′, nä′və-), *n., pl.* **-hos, -hoes,** (*esp. collectively*) **-ho,** *adj.* Navajo.

nav·aid (nav′ād′), *n.* an electronic aid to navigation. [1955–60; NAV(IGATIONAL) + AID]

Nav·a·jo (nav′ə hō′, nä′və-), *n., pl.* **-jos, -joes,** (*esp. collectively*) **-jo** for 1, *adj.* **—*n.* 1.** a member of the principal tribe of the southern division of the Athabaskan stock of North American Indians, located in New Mexico and Arizona, and now constituting the largest tribal group in the U.S. **2.** the Athabaskan language of the Navajo. **—*adj.* 3.** of, pertaining to, or characteristic of the Navajo, their language, or their culture: *a Navajo blanket.* Also, **Navaho.**

na·val (nā′vəl), *adj.* **1.** of or pertaining to warships: *a naval battle; naval strength.* **2.** of or pertaining to ships of all kinds: *naval architecture; naval engineer.* **3.** belonging to, pertaining to, or connected with a navy: *naval affairs.* **4.** possessing a navy: *the great naval powers.* [1585–95; < L *nāvālis,* equiv. to *nāv(is)* ship + *-ālis* -AL[1]] **—na′val·ly,** *adv.*

na′val acad′emy, a collegiate institution for training naval officers. [1805–15, *Amer.*]

na′val ar′chitecture, the science of designing ships and other waterborne craft. [1700–10] **—na′val ar′chitect.**

na′val brass′, an alloy of about 60 percent copper and 40 percent zinc, with traces of lead, tin, arsenic, and iron, used in marine and steam-generating equipment. [1880–85]

na′val mine′, mine[2] (def. 5).

Na′val Observ′atory, an astronomical observatory located in Washington, D.C., operated by the U.S. government, and responsible for the U.S. time service.

na′val stores′, **1.** supplies for warships. **2.** various products of the pine tree, as resin, pitch, or turpentine, used in building and maintaining wooden ships. [1670–80]

Nav. Arch., Naval Architect.

Nav·a·ri·no (nav′ə rē′nō), *n.* a seaport in the SW Peloponnesus, in SW Greece: Turkish and Egyptian fleets defeated near here in a naval battle 1827. Greek, **Pylos, Pilos.**

Na·varre (nə vär′; *Fr.* NA VAR′), *n.* a former kingdom in SW France and N Spain. Spanish, **Na·var·ra** (nä-vär′rä). **—Na·varr′i·an,** *adj.*

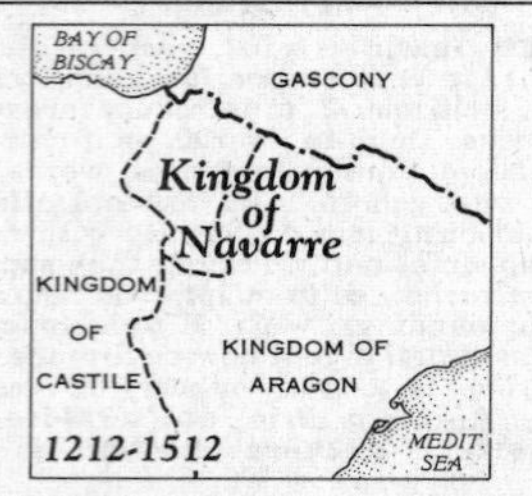

nave (nāv), *n.* the principal longitudinal area of a church, extending from the main entrance or narthex to the chancel, usually flanked by aisles of less height and breadth: generally used only by the congregation. See diag. under **basilica.** [1665–75; < ML *nāvis,* L: ship; so called from the resemblance in shape]

Nav. E., Naval Engineer.

na·vel (nā′vəl), *n.* **1.** umbilicus (def. 1). **2.** the central point or middle of any thing or place. **3.** *Heraldry.* nombril. [bef. 900; ME; OE *nafela;* c. D *navel,* G *Nabel,* ON *nafli;* akin to Skt *nābhila,* L *umbilicus,* Gk *omphalós*]

na′vel ill′, *Vet. Pathol.* See **joint ill.** [1825–35]

na′vel or′ange, a seedless variety of orange having at the apex a navellike formation containing a small secondary fruit. [1885–90]

na·vel·wort (nā′vəl wûrt′, -wôrt′), *n.* **1.** a European plant, *Umbilicus rupestris,* of the stonecrop family, having fleshy, round leaves and yellowish-green flowers. **2.** any of several low, hairy Eurasian plants belonging to the genus *Omphalodes,* of the borage family, having loose clusters of white or blue flowers. [1400–50; late ME; see NAVEL, WORT[2]]

na·vette (na vet′; *Fr.* NA vet′), *n., pl.* **-vettes** (-vets′; *Fr.* -vet′). *Jewelry.* a gem, usually not a diamond, cut as a marquise. [1905–10; < F: weaver's shuttle; lit., little ship. See NAVE, -ETTE]

na·vic·u·lar (nə vik′yə lər), *Anat.* **—*adj.* 1.** boat-shaped, as certain bones. **—*n.*** Also, **na·vic·u·lar·e** (nə vik′yə lâr′ē, -lär′ē). **2.** the bone at the radial end of the proximal row of the bones of the carpus. **3.** the bone in front of the talus on the inner side of the foot. [1535–45; < LL *nāviculāris* of, relating to shipping, equiv. to L *nāvicul(a)* a small ship (*nāvi(s)* ship + *-cula* -CULE[1]) + *-āris* -AR[1]]

navig., navigation.

nav·i·ga·ble (nav′i gə bəl), *adj.* **1.** deep and wide enough to provide passage to ships: *a navigable channel.* **2.** capable of being steered or guided, as a ship, aircraft, or missile. [1520–30; < L *nāvigābilis,* equiv. to *nāvigā(re)* to sail (see NAVIGATE) + *-bilis* -BLE] **—nav′i·ga·bil′i·ty, nav′i·ga·ble·ness,** *n.* **—nav′i·ga·bly,** *adv.*

nav′igable sem′icircle, *Naut.* the less violent half of a cyclone; the half blowing in the direction opposite to that in which the cyclone is moving and in which a vessel can run before the wind.

nav·i·gate (nav′i gāt′), *v.,* **-gat·ed, -gat·ing. —*v.t.* 1.** to move on, over, or through (water, air, or land) in a ship or aircraft: *to navigate a river.* **2.** to direct or manage (a ship, aircraft, or guided missile) on its course. **3.** to ascertain or plot and control the course or position of (a ship, aircraft, etc.). **4.** to pass over (the sea or other body of water), as a ship does. **5.** to walk or find one's way on, in, or across: *It was difficult to navigate the stairs in the dark.* **—*v.i.* 6.** to direct or manage a ship, aircraft, or guided missile on its course. **7.** to pass over the water, as a ship does. **8.** to walk or find one's way. **9.** to travel by ship or boat; sail. [1580–90; < L *nāvigātus,* ptp. of *nāvigāre* to sail, deriv. of *nāvis* ship; for formation, see FUMIGATE]

nav·i·ga·tion (nav′i gā′shən), *n.* **1.** the act or process of navigating. **2.** the art or science of plotting, ascertaining, or directing the course of a ship, aircraft, or guided missile. [1520–30; < L *nāvigātiōn-* (s. of *nāvigātiō*) a voyage. See NAVIGATE, -ION] **—nav′i·ga′tion·al,** *adj.*

Naviga′tion Act′, *Eng. Hist.* any of several acts of Parliament between 1651 and 1847 designed primarily to expand British trade and limit trade by British colonies with countries that were rivals of Great Britain.

naviga′tional sat′ellite, a satellite designed to enable operators of aircraft, vehicles, or vessels to determine their geographical position. Also, **naviga′tion set′ellite.** Also called **NAVSAT.** [1960–65]

naviga′tion weir′, stanch[1] (def. 5).

nav·i·ga·tor (nav′i gā′tər), *n.* **1.** a person who navigates. **2.** a person who practices, or is skilled in, navigation, as of ships or aircraft. **3.** a person who conducts explorations by sea. **4.** *Brit.* a navvy. [1580–90; < L *nāvigātor* a sailor, mariner. See NAVIGATE, -TOR]

Nav′igator Is′lands, former name of **Samoa.**

Náv·pak·tos (näf′päk tôs), *n.* Greek name of **Lepanto.**

Nav·ra·ti·lo·va (nav′rə ti lō′və, näv′-), *n.* **Martina,** born 1956, U.S. tennis player, born in Czechoslovakia.

NAVSAT (nav′sat′), *n.* See **navigational satellite.**

NAV′STAR Glo′bal Posi′tioning Sys′tem (nav′-stär′), a global system of U.S. navigational satellites developed to provide precise positional and velocity data and global time synchronization for air, sea, and land travel. [*nav(igation) s(ystem using) t(ime) a(nd) r(anging)*]

nav·vy (nav′ē), *n., pl.* **-vies.** *Brit. Informal.* an unskilled manual laborer. [1825–35; short for NAVIGATOR]

na·vy (nā′vē), *n., pl.* **-vies. 1.** the whole body of warships and auxiliaries belonging to a country or ruler. **2.** (*often cap.*) the complete body of such warships together with their officers and enlisted personnel, equipment, yards, etc., constituting the sea power of a nation. **3.** (*often cap.*) the department of government charged with its management. **4.** See **navy blue. 5.** *Archaic.* a fleet of ships. [1300–50; ME *navie* < MF < VL **navia,* equiv. to L *nāv(is)* ship + *-ia* -Y[3]]

na′vy bean′, a small, white bean, dried for prolonged storage and prepared for eating by soaking and cooking. [1885–60, *Amer.;* so called from wide use in the U.S. Navy]

na′vy blue′, a dark blue. [1830–40] **—na′vy-blue′,** *adj.*

Na′vy Cross′, a U.S. Navy decoration awarded for outstanding heroism in operations against an enemy.

na′vy plug′, a strong, dark tobacco in plug form. [1865–70, *Amer.*]

na′vy yard′, a government dockyard where naval ships are built, repaired, and fitted out, and naval supplies and munitions are laid up. [1765–75]

na·wab (nə wob′, -wôb′), *n.* **1.** Also, **nabob.** a viceroy or deputy governor under the former Mogul empire in India. **2.** an honorary title conferred upon Muslims of distinction in India and Pakistan. **3.** nabob (def. 3). [1750–60; < Urdu *nawwāb* < Ar *nuwwāb,* pl. of *nā'ib* deputy, viceroy]

Nax·os (nak′sos, -sōs, -səs; *Gk.* nä′ksôs), *n.* a Greek island in the S Aegean: the largest of the Cyclades group. 14,201; 169 sq. mi. (438 sq. km).

nay (nā), *adv.* **1.** and not only so but; not only that but also; indeed: *many good, nay, noble qualities.* **2.** *Archaic.* no (used in dissent, denial, or refusal). **—*n.* 3.** a denial or refusal. **4.** a negative vote or voter. [1125–75; ME *nai, nei* < ON *nei* no, contr. of *ne* not + *ei* ever; see NA, AY[1]]

na·ya pai·sa (nə yä′ pī sä′), *pl.* **na·ye pai·se** (nə yā′ pī sä′). a former monetary unit of India and Bhutan, the 100th part of a rupee. [1955–60; < Hindi: lit., new pice]

Na·ya·rit (nä′yä rēt′), *n.* a state in W Mexico. 699,000; 10,442 sq. mi. (27,045 sq. km). *Cap.:* Tepic.

nay·say (nā′sā′), *v.t.,* **-said, -say·ing.** to say nay to; deny; reject; oppose. [1765–75; NAY + SAY[1], or by back formation from NAYSAYER]

nay·say·er (nā′sā′ər), *n.* a person who habitually expresses negative or pessimistic views: *Despite a general feeling that things were going well, a few naysayers tried to cast gloom.* [1715–25; NAY + SAY[1] + -ER[1]]

Naz·a·rene (naz′ə rēn′, naz′ə rēn′), *n.* **1.** a native or inhabitant of Nazareth. **2.** a member of a sect of early Jewish converts to Christianity who retained the Mosaic ritual. **3. the Nazarene,** Jesus Christ. **—*adj.* 4.** of or pertaining to Nazareth or the Nazarenes. [1225–75; ME < LL *Nazarēnus* < Gk *Nazarēnós,* equiv. to *Nazar(ét)* NAZARETH + *-ēnos* suffix of origin]

Naz·a·reth (naz′ər əth), *n.* a town in N Israel: the childhood home of Jesus. 41,200.

Naz·a·rite (naz′ə rit′), *n.* **1.** (among the ancient Hebrews) a person who had taken certain strict religious vows, usually for a limited period. **2.** *Rare.* a Nazarene. **3.** *Rare.* Christ. **4.** *Obs.* a Christian. Also, **Nazirite.** [1550–60; < LL *Nāzar(aeus)* (< Gk *Nāzeraîos,* equiv. to *nāzēr* (< Heb *nāzīr* consecrated person) + *-aios* suffix) + -ITE[1]] **—Naz·a·rit·ic** (naz′ə rit′ik), *adj.*

Naz·ca (näs′kä, -kə), *adj.* of or pertaining to a pre-Incan culture of SW Peru, dating from c200 B.C., characterized by polychrome pottery and the employment of irrigation techniques in agriculture. Also, **Nasca.**

Naz′ca Plate′, *Geol.* a tectonic division of the earth's crust, coincident with the suboceanic Peru Basin, and bounded on the north by the Cocos Plate, separated from the South American Plate by the Peru-Chile Trench, from the Pacific Plate by the East Pacific Rise, and from the Antarctic Plate by the Chile Rise.

Naze (nāz), *n.* **The,** Lindesnes.

Na·zi (nät′sē, nat′-), *n., pl.* **-zis,** *adj.* **—*n.* 1.** a member of the National Socialist German Workers' party of Germany, which in 1933, under Adolf Hitler, seized political control of the country, suppressing all opposition and establishing a dictatorship over all cultural, economic, and political activities of the people, and promulgated belief in the supremacy of Hitler as Führer, aggressive anti-Semitism, the natural supremacy of the German people, and the establishment of Germany by superior force as a dominant world power. The party was officially abolished in 1945 at the conclusion of World War II. **2.** (*often l.c.*) a person elsewhere who holds similar views. **—*adj.* 3.** of or pertaining to the Nazis. [1925–30; < G *Nazi(onalsozialist)* National Socialist]

na·zi·fy (nät′si fī′, nat′-), *v.t.,* **-fied, -fy·ing.** (*often cap.*) to place under Nazi control or influence. [1930–35; NAZI + -FY] **—na′zi·fi·ca′tion,** *n.*

Na•zi•mo•va (nə zim′ə və; *Russ.* nu zyĕ′mə və), *n.* **Al•la** (ä′lə), 1879–1945, Russian actress in the U.S.

na•zir (nä′zir), *n.* **1.** (in Muslim countries) the title of any of various public officials. **2.** (formerly) a title of certain officials serving native rulers in India. [1670–80; earlier *nasar, naser* < Urdu *nāzir* < Pers *nāẓir* < Ar: inspector] **—na′zir•ship′,** *n.*

Naz•i•rite (naz′ə rīt′), *n.* Nazarite.

Na•zism (nät′siz əm, nat′-), *n.* the principles or methods of the Nazis. Also, **Na•zi•ism** (nät′sē iz′əm, nat′-). [1930–35; NAZ(I) + -ISM]

NB, See **nota bene.**

Nb, *Symbol, Chem.* niobium.

N.B., **1.** New Brunswick. **2.** See **nota bene.**

NBA, **1.** National Basketball Association. **2.** Also, **N.B.A.** See **National Book Award.** **3.** National Boxing Association.

NbE, See **north by east.**

N-bomb (en′bom′), *n.* See **neutron bomb.**

NBS, See **National Bureau of Standards.** Also, **N.B.S.**

NbW, See **north by west.**

n/c, no charge.

NC, **1.** no charge. **2.** North Carolina (approved esp. for use with zip code). **3.** numerical control. **4.** *Mil.* Nurse Corps.

N.C., **1.** no charge. **2.** North Carolina.

NCAA, National Collegiate Athletic Association. Also, **N.C.A.A.**

N.C.C., National Council of Churches. Also, **NCC**

NCCJ, See **National Conference of Christians and Jews.**

N.C.O., Noncommissioned Officer.

NCPAC, National Conservative Political Action Committee.

NC-17 (en′sē′sev′ən tēn′), *Trademark.* no children under 17: a motion-picture rating advising that persons under the age of 17 will not be admitted to the film. Compare **G** (def. 7), **PG, PG-13, R** (def. 5), **X** (def. 8).

NCTE, National Council of Teachers of English.

ND, North Dakota (approved esp. for use with zip code).

Nd, *Symbol, Chem.* neodymium.

nd, *Stock Exchange.* (esp. of bonds) next day (delivery).

n.d., no date.

NDAC, National Defense Advisory Commission.

N.Dak., North Dakota. Also, **N.D.**

Nde•be•le (ən də bē′lē), *n., pl.* **-les,** (*esp. collectively*) **-le** for 1. **1.** Also called **Matabele.** a member of a Nguni people of the Transvaal and Zimbabwe. **2.** the Bantu language of these people.

N′Dja•me•na (ən jä mā′nä), *n.* a city in and the capital of Chad, in the SW part. 192,962. Formerly, **Fort-Lamy.**

Ndo•la (ən dō′lə), *n.* a city in N Zambia. 240,000.

NDSL, National Direct Student Loan.

NE, **1.** Nebraska (approved esp. for use with zip code). **2.** northeast. **3.** northeastern.

Ne, *Symbol, Chem.* neon.

ne-, var. of **neo-** esp. before a vowel: *neencephalon.*

N.E., **1.** naval engineer. **2.** New England. **3.** northeast. **4.** northeastern.

n.e., **1.** northeast. **2.** northeastern.

N.E.A., National Education Association. Also, **NEA**

Neal (nēl), *n.* a male given name.

Ne•an•der•thal (nē an′dər thôl′, -tôl′, -täl′; nā än′dər täl′), *adj.* **1.** of or pertaining to Neanderthal man. **2.** (*often l.c.*) *Informal.* primitive, unenlightened, or reactionary; culturally or intellectually backward. **—*n.*** **3.** See **Neanderthal man.** **4.** (*often l.c.*) *Informal.* **a.** an unenlightened or ignorant person; barbarian. **b.** a reactionary; a person with very old-fashioned ideas. Also, **Ne•an•der•tal** (nē an′dər tôl′, -täl′; nā än′dər täl′) (for defs. 1, 3). [1860–65; named after *Neanderthal,* valley in Germany, near Düsseldorf, where evidence of Neanderthal man was first found] **—Ne•an′der•thal′er,** *n.*

Nean′derthal man′, a member of an extinct subspecies of powerful, physically robust humans, *Homo sapiens neanderthalensis,* that inhabited Europe and western and central Asia c100,000–40,000 B.C. See illus. under **hominid.** [1860–65]

Ne•an•der•thal•oid (nē an′dər thô′loid, -tô′-, -tä′-; nā än′dər tä′loid), *Anthropol.* **—*adj.*** **1.** resembling or characteristic of the physical type of Neanderthal man. **—*n.*** **2.** a fossil human having characteristics like those of Neanderthal man. [1885–90; NEANDERTHAL + -OID]

ne•an•throp•ic (nē′an throp′ik), *adj. Anthropol.* of or pertaining to modern forms of humans as compared with extinct species of the genus *Homo.* Also, **neoanthropic.** Cf. **paleoanthropic.** [1890–95; NE- + ANTHROPIC]

neap[1] (nēp), *adj.* **1.** designating tides midway between spring tides that attain the least height. **—*n.*** **2.** neap tide. See diag. under **tide**[1]. [bef. 900; ME *neep,* OE *nēp-,* in *nēpflōd* neap tide]

neap[2] (nēp), *n. New Eng.* the pole or tongue of a cart, wagon, etc., drawn by two animals side by side. [1545–55 orig. uncert.]

neaped (nēpt), *adj. Naut.* grounded until the next cycle of spring tides. [1695–1705; NEAP[1] + -ED[3]]

Ne•a•pol•i•tan (nē′ə pol′i tn), *adj.* **1.** of, pertaining to, or characteristic of Naples: *a Neapolitan love song.* **—*n.*** **2.** a native or inhabitant of Naples. [1375–1425; late ME *Neopolitan* < L *Neāpolitānus.* See NAPLES (< Gk *Neápolis* lit., new town), -ITE[1], -AN]

Ne′apol′itan ice′ cream′, variously flavored and colored ice cream frozen in layers. [1875–80, *Amer.*]

near (nēr), *adv.,* **-er, -est,** *adj.,* **-er, -est,** *prep., v.* **—*adv.*** **1.** close; to a point or place not far away: *Come near so I won't have to shout.* **2.** at, within, or to a short distance. **3.** close in time: *The New Year draws near.* **4.** close in relation; closely with respect to connection, similarity, intimacy, etc. (often used in combination): *a near-standing position.* **5.** all but; almost; nearly: *a period of near 30 years.* **6.** *Naut.* close to the wind. **7.** *Archaic.* in a thrifty or stingy manner. **—*adj.*** **8.** being close by; not distant: *the near fields.* **9.** being the lesser in distance: *the near side.* **10.** short or direct: *the near road.* **11.** close in time: *the near future.* **12.** closely related or connected: *our nearest relatives.* **13.** close to an original: *a near translation.* **14.** closely affecting one's interests or feelings: *a matter of near consequence to one.* **15.** intimate or familiar: *a near friend.* **16.** narrow or close: *a near escape.* **17.** thrifty or stingy: *near with one's pocketbook.* **18.** (of two draft animals hitched together) being on the driver's left (as opposed to *off*): *The near horse is going lame.* **19. near at hand, a.** in the immediate vicinity: *There is a shopping area near at hand.* **b.** in the near future; soon: *The departure is near at hand.* **—*prep.*** **20.** at, to, or within a short distance, or no great distance, from or of: *regions near the equator.* **21.** close to in time: *near the beginning of the year.* **22.** close to a condition or state: *He is near death.* **—*v.t., v.i.*** **23.** to come or draw near; approach: *The boat neared the dock. Storm clouds neared.* [bef. 900; ME *nere,* OE *nēar,* comp. of *nēah* NIGH] **—near′ness,** *n.*
—Syn. **11.** imminent, impending, approaching. **17.** tight, miserly.

near′ beer′, any of several malt beverages that are similar to beer but are usually considered nonalcoholic because they have an alcoholic content of less than ½ percent. [1905–10, *Amer.*]

near•by (nēr′bī′), *adj.* **1.** close at hand; not far off; adjacent; neighboring: *a nearby village.* **—*adv.*** **2.** in the neighborhood or vicinity; close by: *She works nearby.* [1425–75; late ME; see NEAR, BY]

Ne•arc•tic (nē ärk′tik, -är′-), *adj. Biogeog.* belonging or pertaining to a geographical division comprising temperate Greenland and arctic North America, sometimes including high mountainous regions of the northern Temperate Zone. [1855–60; NE- + ARCTIC]

Near′ East′, an indefinite geographical or regional term, usually referring to the countries of SW Asia, including Turkey, Lebanon, Syria, Iraq, Israel, Jordan, and Saudi Arabia and the other nations of the Arabian Peninsula. Cf. **Middle East** (def. 1). **—Near′ East′ern.**

Near′er Tibet′, the eastern part of Tibet.

near•ly (nēr′lē), *adv.* **1.** all but; almost: *nearly dead with cold.* **2.** with close approximation: *a nearly perfect likeness.* **3.** with close agreement or resemblance: *a plan nearly like our own.* **4.** with close kinship, interest, or connection; intimately: *nearly associated in business; two women nearly related.* [1530–40; NEAR + -LY]
—Syn. **1.** See **almost.** **4.** closely.

near′ miss′, **1.** a strike by a missile that is not a direct hit but is close enough to damage the target. **2.** an instance of two vehicles, aircraft, etc., narrowly avoiding a collision. **3.** something that falls narrowly short of its object or of success: *an interesting movie, but a near miss.* Also, **near′-miss′.**

near′ mon′ey, any asset easily made liquid, as government bonds or savings deposits. [1940–45]

near-point (nēr′point′), *n. Ophthalm.* the point nearest the eye at which an object is clearly focused on the retina when accommodation of the eye is at a maximum. Cf. **far-point.** [1875–80]

near′ rhyme′. See **slant rhyme.**

near•shore (nēr′shôr′, -shōr′), *adj.* extending from or occurring along a shore. [1895–1900; NEAR + SHORE]

near•sight•ed (nēr′sī′tid, -sī′-), *adj.* **1.** seeing distinctly at a short distance only; myopic. **2.** shortsighted. [1680–90; NEAR + SIGHT + -ED[3]] **—near′sight′ed•ly,** *adv.* **—near′sight′ed•ness,** *n.*

near-term (nēr′tûrm′), *adj.* for, covering, or involving the very near future: *the near-term prospects for lower interest rates.* [1955–60]

neat[1] (nēt), *adj.,* **-er, -est,** *adv.* **—*adj.*** **1.** in a pleasingly orderly and clean condition: *a neat room.* **2.** habitually orderly and clean in appearance or habits: *a neat person.* **3.** of a simple, pleasing appearance, style, design, etc.: *a neat cottage.* **4.** cleverly effective in character or execution: *a neat scheme; a neat solution.* **5.** *Slang.* great; wonderful; fine: *What a neat car!* **6.** clever, dexterous, or apt: *She gave a neat characterization of the old woman.* **7.** straight (def. 33). **8.** *Building Trades.* **a.** (of cement) without sand or other aggregate. **b.** (of plaster) without any admixture except hair or fiber. **9.** net: *neat profits.* **—*adv.*** **10.** *Informal.* neatly. [1300–50; ME *net* spruce, trim, clean < MF < L *nitidus* shining, spruce, equiv. to *nit(ēre)* to shine + *-idus* -ID[4]] **—neat′ly,** *adv.* **—neat′ness,** *n.*
—Syn. **1.** spruce, smart. **4.** finished, well-planned. **6.** adroit. **7.** unmixed, pure. **—Ant.** **1.** sloppy.

neat[2] (nēt), *n., pl.* **neat.** an animal of the genus *Bos;* a bovine, as a cow or ox. [bef. 900; ME *neet,* OE *nēat,* c. ON *naut,* MD *noot;* akin to OE *nēotan* to use, possess]

neat•en (nēt′n), *v.t.* to make neat: *a day spent neatening the kitchen shelves.* [1895–1900; NEAT[1] + -EN[1]]

neath (nēth, nēth), *prep. Chiefly Literary.* beneath. Also, **′neath.** [1780–90; aph. var. of BENEATH]

neat•herd (nēt′hûrd′), *n. Obs.* cowherd. [1350–1400; ME; see NEAT[2], HERD[2]]

neat′ line′, a line defining a limit or edge of an excavation, cut stone, etc. Also called **net line.**

neat•o (nē′tō), *adj. Slang.* neat[1] (def. 5). [NEAT[1] + -O]

neat's′-foot oil′ (nēts′fo͝ot′), a pale-yellow fixed oil made by boiling the feet and shinbones of cattle, used chiefly as a dressing for leather. [1570–80]

neb (neb), *n. Scot.* **1.** a bill or beak, as of a bird. **2.** the nose, esp. of an animal. **3.** the tip or pointed end of anything. **4.** the nib of a pen. **5.** *Obs.* a person's mouth. [bef. 900; ME *nebbe,* OE *nebb,* c. MD, MLG *nebbe,* ON *nef.* See NIB]

Neb., Nebraska.

neb•bish (neb′ish), *n. Slang.* a pitifully ineffectual, luckless, and timid person. [1890–95; < Yiddish *nebekh* poor, unfortunate, prob. < Slavic; cf. Czech *nebohý* poor; sp. with *-sh* perh. < Western Yiddish forms of the word] **—neb′bish•y,** *adj.*

NEbE, See **northeast by east.**

Ne•bi•im (*Seph.* nə vē ēm′; *Ashk.* nə vē′im), *n. Hebrew.* Neviim. Cf. **Tanach.**

NEbN, See **northeast by north.**

Ne•bo (nē′bō), *n.* **Mt.** See under **Pisgah.**

Nebr., Nebraska.

Ne•bras•ka (nə bras′kə), *n.* a state in the central United States. 1,570,006; 77,237 sq. mi. (200,044 sq. km). *Cap.:* Lincoln. *Abbr.:* NE (for use with zip code), Nebr., Neb.

Ne•bras•kan (nə bras′kən), *adj.* **1.** of or pertaining to Nebraska. **2.** *Geol.* of or pertaining to the Nebraskan. **—*n.*** **3.** a native or inhabitant of Nebraska. **4.** *Geol.* the first stage of the glaciation of North America during the Pleistocene. [1870–75; NEBRASK(A) + -AN]

neb•ris (neb′ris), *n.* a fawn skin worn in Greek mythology by Dionysus and his followers. [1770–80; < L < Gk *nebrís* fawn-skin; akin to *nebrós* fawn]

Neb•u•chad•nez•zar (neb′ə kəd nez′ər, neb′yo͝o-), *n.* **1.** Also, **Neb•u•chad•rez•zar** (neb′ə kəd rez′ər, neb′yo͝o-) a king of Babylonia, 604?–561? B.C., and conqueror of Jerusalem. II Kings 24, 25. **2.** (*sometimes l.c.*) a bottle for wine holding 20 quarts (18.9 liters).

neb•u•la (neb′yə lə), *n., pl.* **-lae** (-lē′, -lī′), **-las.** **1.** *Astron.* **a.** Also called **diffuse nebula.** a cloud of interstellar gas and dust. Cf. **dark nebula, emission nebula, reflection nebula.** **b.** (formerly) any celestial object that appears nebulous, hazy, or fuzzy, and extended in a telescope view. **2.** *Pathol.* **a.** a faint opacity in the cornea. **b.** cloudiness in the urine. **3.** any liquid medication prepared for use as a spray. [1655–65; < L: a mist, vapor, cloud; akin to Gk *nephélē* cloud, G *Nebel* fog, haze] **—neb′u•lar,** *adj.*

neb′ular hypoth′esis, *Astron.* the theory that the solar system evolved from a mass of nebular matter: prominent in the 19th century following its precise formulation by Laplace. [1830–40]

neb•u•lat•ed (neb′yə lā′tid), *adj.* having dim or indistinct markings, as a bird or other animal. [1480–90; < ML *nebulāt(us)* (L *nebul(a)* cloud + *-ātus* -ATE[1]) + -ED[3]; see NEBULA]

ne•bu•li•um (nə byo͞o′lē əm), *n. Astron.* a hypothetical element once thought to be present in emission nebulae because of certain unidentified spectral lines, now known to be forbidden transitions of oxygen and nitrogen ions. [1895–1900; NEBUL(A) + -IUM]

neb•u•lize (neb′yə līz′), *v.,* **-lized, -liz•ing.** **—*v.t.*** **1.** to reduce to fine spray; atomize. **—*v.i.*** **2.** to become vague, indistinct, or nebulous. Also, *esp. Brit.,* **neb′u•lise′.** [1870–75; NEBUL(A) + -IZE] **—neb′u•li•za′tion,** *n.* **—neb′u•liz′er,** *n.*

neb•u•lose (neb′yə lōs′, -lōs′), *adj.* **1.** cloudlike; nebulous. **2.** hazy or indistinct; nebulous. **3.** having cloudlike markings. [1795–1805; < L *nebulōsus* full of mist, foggy, cloudy. See NEBULA, -OSE]

neb•u•los•i•ty (neb′yə los′i tē), *n., pl.* **-ties.** **1.** nebulous or nebular matter. **2.** a nebulous form, shape, or mass. **3.** the state or condition of being nebulous. [1755–65; < LL *nebulōsitās.* See NEBULOSE, -ITY]

neb•u•lo•sus (neb′yə lō′səs), *adj. Meteorol.* (of a cloud) having indistinct details. [< L *nebulōsus* NEBULOUS]

neb•u•lous (neb′yə ləs), *adj.* **1.** hazy, vague, indistinct, or confused: *a nebulous recollection of the meeting; a nebulous distinction between pride and conceit.* **2.** cloudy or cloudlike. **3.** of or resembling a nebula or nebulae; nebular. [1375–1425; late ME < L *nebulōsus* full of mist, foggy, cloudy. See NEBULA, -OUS] **—neb′u•lous•ly,** *adv.* **—neb′u•lous•ness,** *n.*

n.e.c., not elsewhere classified.

nec•es•sar•i•an (nes′ə sâr′ē ən), *n., adj.* necessitarian. [NECESSARY + -AN] **—nec′es•sar′i•an•ism,** *n.*

nec•es•sar•i•ly (nes′ə sâr′ə lē, -ser′-), *adv.* **1.** by or of necessity; as a matter of compulsion or requirement: *You don't necessarily have to attend.* **2.** as a necessary, logical, or inevitable result: *That conclusion doesn't necessarily follow.* [1400–50; late ME; see NECESSARY, -LY]

nec•es•sar•y (nes′ə ser′ē), *adj., n., pl.* **-sar•ies.** **—*adj.***

CONCISE PRONUNCIATION KEY: act, cāpe, dâre, pärt; set, ēqual; if, īce; ox, ōver, ôrder, oil, bo͝ok, bo͞ot, out; up, ûrge; child; sing; shoe; thin, *th*at; zh as in *treasure.* ə = *a* as in *alone, e* as in *system, i* as in *easily, o* as in *gallop, u* as in *circus;* ᵊ as in *fire* (fīᵊr), *hour* (ouᵊr). l and n can serve as syllabic consonants, as in *cradle* (krād′l), and *button* (but′n). See the full key inside the front cover.

1. being essential, indispensable, or requisite: *a necessary part of the motor.* **2.** happening or existing by necessity: *a necessary change in our plans.* **3.** acting or proceeding from compulsion or necessity; not free; involuntary: *a necessary agent.* **4.** *Logic.* **a.** (of a proposition) such that a denial of it involves a self-contradiction. **b.** (of an inference or argument) such that its conclusion cannot be false if its supporting premises are true. **c.** (of a condition) such that it must exist if a given event is to occur or a given thing is to exist. Cf. **sufficient** (def. 2). —*n.* **5.** something necessary or requisite; necessity. **6.** **necessaries,** *Law.* food, clothing, etc., required by a dependent or incompetent and varying with his or her social or economic position or that of the person upon whom he or she is dependent. **7.** *Chiefly New Eng.* a privy or toilet. [1300–50; ME *necessarie* < L *necessārius* unavoidable, inevitable, needful, equiv. to *necess(e)* (neut. indeclinable adj.) unavoidable, necessary + *-ārius* -ARY] —**nec′es·sar′i·ness,** *n.*
—**Syn. 1.** required, needed. NECESSARY, ESSENTIAL, INDISPENSABLE, REQUISITE indicate something vital for the fulfillment of a need. NECESSARY applies to that without which a condition cannot be fulfilled or to an inevitable consequence of certain events, conditions, etc.: *Food is necessary to life. Multiplicity is a necessary result of division.* INDISPENSABLE applies to something that cannot be done without or removed from the rest of a unitary condition: *Food is indispensable to living things. He made himself indispensable as a companion.* That which is ESSENTIAL forms a vitally necessary condition of something: *Air is essential to red-blooded animals. It is essential to understand the matter clearly.* REQUISITE applies to what is thought necessary to fill out, complete, or perfect something: *She had all the requisite qualifications for a position.* **5.** requirement, requisite, essential. —**Ant. 1.** dispensable.

nec′essary stool′, close-stool. [1755–65]

ne·ces·si·tar·i·an (nə ses′i târ′ē ən), *n.* **1.** a person who advocates or supports necessitarianism (distinguished from *libertarian*). —*adj.* **2.** pertaining to necessitarians or necessitarianism. Also, **necessarian.** [1790–1800; NECESSIT(Y) + -ARIAN]

ne·ces·si·tar·i·an·ism (nə ses′i târ′ē ə niz′əm), *n.* the doctrine that all events, including acts of the will, are determined by antecedent causes; determinism. [1850–55; NECESSITARIAN + -ISM]

ne·ces·si·tate (nə ses′i tāt′), *v.t.,* **-tat·ed, -tat·ing. 1.** to make necessary or unavoidable: *The breakdown of the car necessitated a change in our plans.* **2.** to compel, oblige, or force: *The new wage demand will necessitate a price increase.* [1620–30; < ML *necessitātus,* ptp. of *necessitāre* to compel, constrain. See NECESSITY, -ATE[1]] —**ne·ces′si·ta′tion,** *n.* —**ne·ces′si·ta′tive,** *adj.*

ne·ces·si·tous (nə ses′i təs), *adj.* **1.** destitute or impoverished; needy; indigent: *to aid a necessitous young mother.* **2.** being essential or unavoidable: *a necessitous discharge of responsibilities.* **3.** requiring immediate attention or action; urgent: *the necessitous demands of the oil shortage.* [1605–15; NECESSIT(Y) + -OUS] —**ne·ces′si·tous·ly,** *adv.* —**ne·ces′si·tous·ness,** *n.*

ne·ces·si·tude (nə ses′i to͞od′, -tyo͞od′), *n. Archaic.* necessity. [1605–15; < L *necessitūdō,* equiv. to *necessi-,* comb. form of *necesse* NECESSARY + *-tūdō* -TUDE]

ne·ces·si·ty (nə ses′i tē), *n., pl.* **-ties. 1.** something necessary or indispensable: *food, shelter, and other necessities of life.* **2.** the fact of being necessary or indispensable; indispensability: *the necessity of adequate housing.* **3.** an imperative requirement or need for something: *the necessity for a quick decision.* **4.** the state or fact of being necessary or inevitable: *to face the necessity of testifying in court.* **5.** an unavoidable need or compulsion to do something: *not by choice but by necessity.* **6.** a state of being in financial need; poverty: *a family in dire necessity.* **7.** *Philos.* the quality of following inevitably from logical, physical, or moral laws. **8.** **of necessity,** as an inevitable result; unavoidably; necessarily: *Our trip to China must of necessity be postponed for a while.* [1325–75; ME *necessite* < L *necessitās,* equiv. to *necess(e)* needful + *-itās* -ITY]
—**Syn. 3.** demand. See **need. 6.** neediness, indigence, want.

Ne·cho (nē′kō), *n.* **Prince of Sais** and **Prince of Memphis,** fl. 633? B.C., chief of the Egyptian delta lords (father of Psamtik I). Also called **Necho I.**

neck (nek), *n.* **1.** the part of the body of an animal or human being that connects the head and the trunk. **2.** the part of a garment encircling, partly covering, or closest to the neck; neckline. **3.** the length of the neck of a horse or other animal as a measure in racing. **4.** the slender part near the top of a bottle, vase, or similar object. **5.** any narrow, connecting, or projecting part suggesting the neck of an animal. **6.** a narrow strip of land, as an isthmus or a cape. **7.** a strait. **8.** the longer and more slender part of a violin or similar stringed instrument, extending from the body to the head. **9.** *Building Trades, Mach.* the part on a shank of a bolt next to the head, esp. when it has a special form. **10.** *Anat.* a narrowed part of a bone, organ, or the like. **11.** *Dentistry.* the slightly narrowed region of a tooth between the crown and the root. **12.** *Print.* beard (def. 5). **13.** *Archit.* a cylindrical continuation of the shaft of a column above the lower astragal of the capital, as in the Roman Doric and Tuscan orders. **14.** Also called **volcanic neck.** *Geol.* the solidified lava or igneous rock filling a conduit leading either to a vent of an extinct volcano or to a laccolith. **15.** **be up to one's neck,** *Informal.* to have a surfeit; be overburdened: *Right now she's up to her neck in work.* **16.** **break one's neck,** *Informal.* to make a great effort: *We broke our necks to get there on time.* **17.** **get it in the neck,** *Slang.* **a.** to suffer punishment or loss: *The trend is to consolidation and small businesses are getting it in the neck.* **b.** to be rejected or dismissed: *The employees got it in the neck when the company moved overseas.* **c.** to be sharply reprimanded or scolded. **18.** **neck and neck,** even or very close; indeterminate as to the outcome: *They were coming toward the finish line neck and neck.* **19.** **neck of the woods,** *Informal.* neighborhood, area, or vicinity: *Next time you're in this neck of the woods, drop in.* **20.** **stick one's neck out,** *Informal.* to expose oneself to danger, disaster, failure, disgrace, etc.; take a risk: *He stuck his neck out by supporting an unpopular candidate.* **21.** **win by a neck, a.** to win by a small amount or narrow margin. **b.** *Racing.* to be first by a head and neck; finish closely. —*v.i.* **22.** *Informal.* (of two persons) to embrace, kiss, and caress one another amorously. —*v.t.* **23.** *Informal.* to embrace, kiss, and caress (someone) amorously. **24.** to strangle or behead. [bef. 900; ME *nekke,* OE *hnecca,* c. D *nek* nape of neck; akin to G *Nacken,* ON *hnakki* nape of neck] —**neck′er,** *n.* —**neck′less,** *adj.* —**neck′like′,** *adj.*

Neck·ar (nek′ər; *Ger.* ne′kär), *n.* a river in SW Germany, flowing N and NE from the Black Forest, then W to the Rhine River. 246 mi. (395 km) long.

neck·band (nek′band′), *n.* **1.** a band of cloth at the neck of a garment. **2.** a band, esp. one of ornamental design, worn around the neck, affixed to a bottle, etc. [1400–50; late ME *nekband.* See NECK, BAND[2]]

neck·cloth (nek′klôth′, -kloth′), *n., pl.* **-cloths** (-klôthz′, -klothz′, -klôths′, -kloths′). *Obs.* cravat (def. 2). [1630–40; NECK + CLOTH]

neck′ cord′, lash[1] (def. 7).

necked (nekt), *adj.* having a neck of a kind specified (usually used in combination): *a square-necked blouse.* [1350–1400; ME. See NECK, -ED[3]]

Neck·er (nek′ər; *Fr.* ne ker′), *n.* **Jacques** (zhäk), 1732–1804, French statesman, born in Switzerland.

neck·er·chief (nek′ər chif, -chēf′), *n.* a cloth or scarf worn round the neck. [1350–1400; ME; see NECK, KERCHIEF]

neck·ing (nek′ing), *n.* **1.** *Informal.* the act of embracing, kissing, and caressing amorously; petting. **2.** *Archit.* **a.** a molding or group of moldings between the projecting part of a capital of a column and the shaft. **b.** gorgerin. [1795–1805; NECK + -ING[1]]

neck·lace (nek′lis), *n.* a piece of jewelry consisting of a string of stones, beads, jewels, or the like, or a chain of gold, silver, or other metal, for wearing around the neck. [1580–90; NECK + LACE (def. 2)]

neck·let (nek′lit), *n.* something worn around the neck for ornamentation, as a fur piece. [1860–65; NECK + -LET]

neck·line (nek′līn′), *n.* the opening at the neck of a garment, esp. of a woman's garment, with reference to its shape or its position on the body: *a V-neckline; a high neckline.* [1900–05; NECK + LINE[1]]

neck·piece (nek′pēs′), *n.* a scarf, esp. one of fur. [1595–1605; NECK + PIECE]

neck-rein (nek′rān′), *v.t.* **1.** to guide or direct (a horse) with the pressure of a rein on the opposite side of the neck from the direction in which the rider wishes to travel. —*v.i.* **2.** (of a horse) to respond to such pressure from a rein by going in the desired direction. [1925–30]

neck′ sweet′bread, sweetbread (def. 2).

neck·tie (nek′tī′), *n.* **1.** a band of decorative fabric worn around the neck, under the collar, and tied in front to hang down the front of a shirt or to form a small bow. **2.** any band, scarf, or tie fastened at the front of the neck. **3.** *Slang.* a hangman's rope. [1830–40; NECK + TIE] —**neck′tie′less,** *adj.*

neck′tie par′ty, *Older Slang.* a lynching or other execution by hanging. [1830–40]

neck·wear (nek′wâr′), *n.* articles of dress worn round or at the neck. [1875–80; NECK + WEAR]

necro-, a combining form meaning "the dead," "corpse," "dead tissue," used in the formation of compound words: *necrology.* Also, *esp. before a vowel,* **necr-.** [< Gk *nekro-,* comb. form of *nekrós* dead person, corpse, (adj.) dead]

nec·ro·bac·il·lo·sis (nek′rō bas′ə lō′sis), *n. Vet. Pathol.* any disease of cattle, horses, sheep, and swine marked by necrotic areas in which a bacillus, *Fusobacterium necrophorum,* is found. [1905–10; NECRO- + BACILLOSIS] —**nec·ro·bac·il·lar·y** (nek′rō bas′ə ler′ē), *adj.*

nec·ro·bi·o·sis (nek′rō bī ō′sis), *n. Med.* the death of cells or tissue caused by aging or disease. Cf. **necrosis.** [1875–80; NECRO- + -BIOSIS] —**nec·ro·bi·ot·ic** (nek′rō bī ot′ik), *adj.*

ne·crol·a·try (nə krol′ə trē, ne-), *n.* worship of the dead. [1820–30; NECRO- + -LATRY]

ne·crol·o·gy (nə krol′ə jē, ne-), *n., pl.* **-gies. 1.** a list of persons who have died within a certain time. **2.** a notice of death; obituary. [1720–30; NECRO- + -LOGY] —**nec·ro·log·i·cal** (nek′rə loj′i kəl), **nec′ro·log′ic,** *adj.* —**nec′ro·log′i·cal·ly,** *adv.* —**ne·crol′o·gist,** *n.*

nec·ro·man·cy (nek′rə man′sē), *n.* **1.** a method of divination through alleged communication with the dead; black art. **2.** magic in general, esp. that practiced by a witch or sorcerer; sorcery; witchcraft; conjuration. [1250–1300; NECRO- + -MANCY; r. ME *nigromancie* < ML *nigromantia* for LL *necromantia* < Gk *nekromanteía;* by folk etymology *nigro-* (comb. form of L *niger* black) was substituted in ML for original *necro-*] —**nec′ro·man′cer,** *n.* —**nec′ro·man′tic;** *Obs.,* **nec′ro·man′ti·cal,** *adj.* —**nec′ro·man′ti·cal·ly,** *adv.*
—**Syn. 2.** See **magic.**

nec·ro·mi·me·sis (nek′rō mi mē′sis), *n. Psychiatry.* a pathological state in which a person believes himself or herself to be dead. [NECRO- + MIMESIS]

nec·ro·phil·i·a (nek′rə fil′ē ə), *n. Psychiatry.* an erotic attraction to corpses. [1890–95; < NL; see NECRO-, -PHILIA] —**nec·ro·phile** (nek′rə fīl′), *n.* —**nec·ro·phil·i·ac** (nek′rə fil′ē ak′), **nec′ro·phil′ic,** *adj., n.*

ne·croph·i·lism (nə krof′ə liz′əm, ne-), *n. Psychiatry.* necrophilia. [1860–65; NECRO- + -PHILISM]

nec·ro·pho·bi·a (nek′rə fō′bē ə), *n. Psychiatry.* **1.** an abnormal fear of death; thanatophobia. **2.** an abnormal fear of dead bodies. [1825–35; < NL; see NECRO-, -PHOBIA] —**nec′ro·pho′bic,** *adj.*

ne·crop·o·lis (nə krop′ə lis, ne-), *n., pl.* **-lis·es. 1.** a cemetery, esp. one of large size and usually of an ancient city. **2.** a historic or prehistoric burial ground. [1810–20; < Gk *nekrópolis* burial place (lit., city of the dead). See NECRO-, -POLIS] —**nec·ro·pol·i·tan** (nek′rə pol′i-tn), *adj.*

nec·rop·sy (nek′rop sē), *n., pl.* **-sies.** the examination of a body after death; autopsy. [1855–60; NECR- + -OPSY[1]]

ne·cros·co·py (nə kros′kə pē, ne-), *n., pl.* **-pies.** necropsy. [1835–45; NECRO- + -SCOPY]

ne·crose (nə krōs′, ne-, nek′rōs), *v.t., v.i.,* **-crosed, -cros·ing.** *Pathol.* to affect or be affected with necrosis. [1870–75; back formation from NECROSIS]

ne·cro·sis (nə krō′sis, ne-), *n.* death of a circumscribed portion of animal or plant tissue. [1655–65; < NL < Gk *nékrōsis* mortification, state of death. See NECR-, -OSIS] —**ne·crot·ic** (nə krot′ik, ne-), *adj.*

nec·ro·tize (nek′rə tīz′), *v.,* **-tized, -tiz·ing.** —*v.i.* **1.** to undergo necrosis. —*v.t.* **2.** to cause necrosis in (a tissue, an organ, etc.). Also, *esp. Brit.,* **nec′ro·tise′.** [1870–75; NECROT(IC) + -IZE]

ne·crot·o·my (nə krot′ə mē, ne-), *n., pl.* **-mies. 1.** *Surg.* the excision of necrosed bone. **2.** the dissection of dead bodies. [1895–1900; NECRO- + -TOMY]

nec·tar (nek′tər), *n.* **1.** the saccharine secretion of a plant, which attracts the insects or birds that pollinate the flower. **2.** the juice of a fruit, esp. when not diluted, or a blend of fruit juices: *pear nectar; tropical nectar.* **3.** *Class. Myth.* the life-giving drink of the gods. Cf. **ambrosia** (def. 1). **4.** any delicious drink. [1545–55; < L < Gk *néktar*] —**nec′tar·like′,** *adj.*

nec·tar·e·ous (nek târ′ē əs), *adj.* nectarous. Also, **nec·tar′e·an.** [1700–10; < L *nectareus* of, belonging to nectar < Gk *nektáreos* like nectar, divinely fragrant, equiv. to *néktar* NECTAR + *-eos* adj. suffix; see -EOUS] —**nec·tar′e·ous·ly,** *adv.* —**nec·tar′e·ous·ness,** *n.*

nec·tar·if·er·ous (nek′tə rif′ər əs), *adj. Bot.* producing nectar. [1750–60; NECTAR + -I- + -FEROUS]

nec·tar·ine (nek′tə rēn′, nek′tə rēn′), *n.* a variety or mutation of peach having a smooth, downless skin. [1610–20; NECTAR + -INE[1]]

nec·tar·ize (nek′tə rīz′), *v.t.,* **-ized, -iz·ing.** to mix or saturate with nectar. Also, *esp. Brit.,* **nec′tar·ise′.** [1585–95; NECTAR + -IZE]

nec·tar·ous (nek′tər əs), *adj.* **1.** of the nature of or resembling nectar. **2.** delicious or sweet. Also, **nectareous, nectarean.** [1660–70; NECTAR + -OUS]

nec·ta·ry (nek′tə rē), *n., pl.* **-ries. 1.** *Bot.* an organ or part that secretes nectar. **2.** *Entomol.* a cornicle (formerly thought to secrete honeydew). [1590–1600; < NL *nectarium.* See NECTAR, -Y[3]] —**nec′ta·ried,** *adj.*

nec·to·pod (nek′tə pod′), *n.* (in certain mollusks) an appendage modified for swimming. [1895–1900; < Gk *nektó(s)* swimming (equiv. to *néch(ein)* to swim + *-tos* deverbal adj. suffix, with *cht* > *kt*) + -POD]

Ned (ned), *n.* a male given name, form of **Edward.**

N.E.D., New English Dictionary. Also, **NED**

Ned·da (ned′ə), *n.* a female given name.

ned·dy (ned′ē), *n., pl.* **-dies. 1.** *Brit. Informal.* donkey. **2.** *Australian Slang.* a horse. [1780–90; appar. generic use of personal name *Neddy;* see NED, -Y[2]]

Ne·der·land (nā′dər länt′ *for 1;* nē′dər land′ *for 2*), *n.* **1.** Dutch name of the **Netherlands. 2.** a city in SE Texas. 16,855.

nee (nā), *adj.* born (placed after the name of a married woman to introduce her maiden name): *Madame de Staël, nee Necker.* Also, **née.** [1750–60; < F, fem. of *né* (ptp. of *naître* to be born) << L *nātus* (see NATIVE)]

need (nēd), *n.* **1.** a requirement, necessary duty, or obligation: *There is no need for you to go there.* **2.** a lack of something wanted or deemed necessary: *to fulfill the needs of the assignment.* **3.** urgent want, as of something requisite: *He has no need of your charity.* **4.** necessity arising from the circumstances of a situation or case: *There is no need to worry.* **5.** a situation or time of difficulty; exigency: *to help a friend in need; to be a friend in need.* **6.** a condition marked by the lack of something requisite: *the need for leadership.* **7.** destitution; extreme poverty: *The family's need is acute.* **8.** **if need be,** should the necessity arise: *If need be, I can type the letters myself.* —*v.t.* **9.** to have need of; require: *to need money.* —*v.i.* **10.** to be under an obligation (used as an auxiliary, typically in an interrogative or in a negative statement, and fol. by infinitive, in certain cases without *to;* in the 3d pers. sing. the form is *need,* not *needs*): *He need not go.* **11.** to be in need or want. **12.** to be necessary: *There needs no apology.* [bef. 900; (n.) ME *nede,* OE *nēd* (WSaxon *nied*), c. G *Not,* ON *nauth,* Goth *nauths;* (v.) ME *neden,* OE *nēodian,* deriv. of the n.] —**need′er,** *n.*
—**Syn. 2, 3.** See **lack. 3.** requirement. **4.** NEED, NECESSITY imply a want, a lack, or a demand, which must be filled. NEED, a word of Old English origin, has connotations that make it strong in emotional appeal: *the need to be appreciated.* NECESSITY, a word of Latin origin, is more formal and impersonal or objective; though much stronger than NEED in expressing urgency or imperative demand, it is less effective in appealing to the emotions: *Water is a necessity for living things.* **5.** emergency. **7.** neediness, indigence, penury, privation. See **poverty. 9.** want, lack. —**Ant. 7.** wealth.

need·fire (nēd′fīᵊr′), *n.* **1.** See **spontaneous com-**

bustion. **2.** luminescence, as of rotted or decayed wood. [1525–35; NEED + FIRE]

need·ful (nēd′fəl), *adj.* **1.** necessary or required: *needful supplies.* **2.** needy. —*n.* **3. the needful,** *Slang.* money, esp. immediately available cash: *They haven't the needful for a car right now.* [1125–75; ME; see NEED, -FUL] —**need′ful·ly,** *adv.* —**need′ful·ness,** *n.*

Need·ham (nē′dəm), *n.* a town in E Massachusetts, near Boston. 27,901.

need·i·ness (nē′dē nis), *n.* a condition of want or need; poverty; indigence. [1350–1400; ME *nedynes.* See NEEDY, -NESS]

nee·dle (nēd′l), *n., v.,* **-dled, -dling.** —*n.* **1.** a small, slender, rodlike instrument, usually of polished steel, with a sharp point at one end and an eye or hole for thread at the other, for passing thread through cloth to make stitches in sewing. **2.** any of various similar, usually considerably larger, implements for making stitches, as one for use in knitting or one hooked at the end for use in crocheting. **3.** *Med.* **a.** a slender, pointed, steel instrument used in sewing or piercing tissues, as in suturing. **b.** See **hypodermic needle. 4.** *Informal.* an injection of a drug or medicine; shot. **5.** any of various objects resembling or suggesting a needle. **6.** the tapered stylus at the end of a phonographic tonearm, used to transmit vibrations from a record groove to a transducer for conversion to audible signals. **7.** *Elect.* See **magnetic needle. 8.** a pointed instrument, or stylus, used in engraving, etching, or the like. **9.** *Bot.* a needle-shaped leaf, as of a conifer: *a pine needle.* **10.** *Zool.* a slender sharp spicule. **11.** *Chem., Mineral.* a needlelike crystal. **12.** a sharp-pointed mass or pinnacle of rock. **13.** an obelisk or a tapering, four-sided shaft of stone: *Cleopatra's Needle.* **14.** Also called **nee′dle beam′.** *Building Trades.* a short beam passed through a wall as a temporary support. **15. on the needle,** *Slang.* taking drugs by injection, esp. habitually. **16. the needle,** *Informal.* irritating abuse; teasing; heckling (used esp. in the phrases *give someone the needle* and *get the needle*). —*v.t.* **17.** to sew or pierce with or as if with a needle: *to needle a patch on a sleeve.* **18.** *Informal.* **a.** to prod or goad (someone) to a specified action: *We needled her into going with us.* **b.** to tease: *We needled him about his big ears.* **19.** *Slang.* to add alcohol or ether to (a beverage): *to needle beer.* —*v.i.* **20.** to form needles in crystallization. **21.** to work with a needle. [bef. 900; 1880–85 for def. 18; ME *nedle,* OE *nǣdl,* c. G *Nadel;* akin to L *nēre* to spin] —**nee′dle·like′,** *adj.*

nee′dle bi′opsy, the removal of a small amount of tissue or cellular material with a long hollow surgical needle, performed for diagnostic purposes.

nee·dle·craft (nēd′l kraft′, -kräft′), *n.* needlework. [1350–1400; ME *nedle craft.* See NEEDLE, CRAFT]

nee·dle·fish (nēd′l fish′), *n., pl.* (*esp. collectively*) **-fish,** (*esp. referring to two or more kinds or species*) **-fish·es. 1.** any fish of the family Belonidae, of warm seas and coastal fresh waters, having a sharp beak and needlelike teeth. **2.** a pipefish. [1595–1605; NEEDLE + FISH]

nee·dle·point (nēd′l point′), *n.* **1.** embroidery upon canvas, usually with uniform spacing of stitches in a pattern. —*adj.* **2.** done or executed in needlepoint: *a needlepoint cushion.* **3.** noting a lace **(nee′dlepoint lace′)** in which a needle works out the design upon parchment or paper. —*v.t., v.i.* **4.** to execute or create in needlepoint: *to needlepoint an evening bag; to needlepoint as a hobby.* [1690–1700; NEEDLE + POINT] —**nee′dle·point′·er,** *n.*

Nee·dles (nēd′lz), *n.* a town in SE California: on Colorado River at Arizona line. 4120.

need·less (nēd′lis), *adj.* unnecessary; not needed or wanted: *a needless waste of food.* [1175–1225; ME *nedles.* See NEED, -LESS] —**need′less·ly,** *adv.* —**need′less·ness,** *n.*
—**Syn.** unessential, gratuitous, pointless, uncalled-for.

nee′dle trades′, the occupations and organizations involved in the manufacture of clothing. [1860–65]

nee′dle valve′, *Mach.* a valve with a needlelike part, a fine adjustment, or a small opening, esp. a valve in which the opening is controlled by a needlelike or conical point that fits into a conical seat. [1900–05]

nee·dle·wom·an (nēd′l wo͝om′ən), *n., pl.* **-wom·en.** a woman who does needlework. [1605–15; NEEDLE + WOMAN]
—**Usage.** See **-woman.**

nee·dle·work (nēd′l wûrk′), *n.* **1.** the art, process, or product of working with a needle, esp. in embroidery, needlepoint, tapestry, quilting, and appliqué. **2.** the occupation or employment of a person skilled in embroidery, needlepoint, etc. Also called **needlecraft, stitchery.** [1350–1400; ME *nedle werk.* See NEEDLE, WORK]

need·n't (nēd′nt), contraction of *need not.*
—**Usage.** See **contraction.**

needs (nēdz), *adv.* of necessity; necessarily (usually prec. or fol. by *must*): *It must needs be so. It needs must be.* [bef. 1000; ME *nedis,* OE *nēdes,* orig. gen. of *nēd* NEED; see -S[1]]

need·y (nē′dē), *adj.,* **need·i·er, need·i·est,** *n.* —*adj.* **1.** in a condition of need or want; poverty-stricken; impoverished; extremely poor; destitute. —*n.* **2.** (*used with a plural v.*) needy persons collectively (usually prec. by *the*): *Help the needy.* [1125–75; ME *nedi;* see NEED, -Y[1]] —**need′i·ly,** *adv.*

Né·el (nā el′), *n.* **Louis Eu·gène Fé·lix** (lwē œ zhen′ fā lēks′), born 1904, French physicist: Nobel prize 1970.

neem (nēm), *n.* **1.** a product of the seeds of a tropical tree, *Azadirachta indica,* of the mahogany family, that disrupts reproduction in insects, used as an insecticide. **2.** Also called **neem′ tree′, nim tree, margosa.** the tree itself. [1805–15; < Hindi *nīm* < Skt *nimba*]

Nee·nah (nē′nə), *n.* a city in E Wisconsin. 23,272.

ne·en·ceph·a·lon (nē′en sef′ə lon′, -lən), *n., pl.* **-lons, -la** (-lə). the more recent part of the brain in the evolutionary development of animals, including the cerebral cortex and its related structures. Also, **neoencephalon.** Cf. **paleencephalon.** [1915–20; NE- + ENCEPHALON] —**ne·en·ce·phal·ic** (nē′en sə fal′ik), *adj.*

neep (nēp), *n. Scot.* a turnip. [bef. 900; ME *nepe,* OE *nēp, nǣp* < L *nāpus* TURNIP]

ne'er (nâr), *adv. Literary.* never.

ne'er-do-well (nâr′do͞o wel′), *n.* **1.** an idle, worthless person; a person who is ineffectual, unsuccessful, or completely lacking in merit; good-for-nothing. —*adj.* **2.** worthless; ineffectual; good-for-nothing. [1730–40]
—**Syn. 1.** idler, loafer, wastrel.

nef (nef), *n.* a silver or gold table furnishing in the form of a ship, either for holding various utensils or for ornament. [1680–90; < F: ship < L *nāvis.* See NAVE]

ne·far·i·ous (ni fâr′ē əs), *adj.* extremely wicked or villainous; iniquitous: *a nefarious plot.* [1595–1605; < L *nefārius* wicked, vile, equiv. to *nefās* offense against divine or moral law (*ne-* negative prefix + *fās* law, right) + *-ius* -IOUS, with intervocalic *s* > *r*] —**ne·far′i·ous·ly,** *adv.* —**ne·far′i·ous·ness,** *n.*
—**Syn.** flagitious, heinous, infamous; vile, atrocious, execrable. —**Ant.** good, honest.

Ne·fer·tem (nā′fər tem′), *n. Egyptian Relig.* Ptah, as the personification of the lotus that keeps Ra alive with its fragrance.

Nef·er·ti·ti (nef′ər tē′tē), *n.* fl. early 14th century B.C., Egyptian queen: wife of Amenhotep IV. Also, **Nef·re·te·te** (nef′ri tē′tē), **Nofretete.**

Ne·fud′ Des′ert (nə fo͞od′), a desert in N Saudi Arabia: areas of reddish sand. ab. 50,000 sq. mi. (129,500 sq. km). Also called **An Nafud, Nafud, Ne·fud′, Nufud, Red Desert.**

neg (neg), *n. Informal.* a photographic negative. [by shortening]

neg., 1. negative. **2.** negatively.

ne·gate (ni gāt′, neg′āt), *v.,* **-gat·ed, -gat·ing.** —*v.t.* **1.** to deny the existence, evidence, or truth of: *an investigation tending to negate any supernatural influences.* **2.** to nullify or cause to be ineffective: *Progress on the study has been negated by the lack of funds.* —*v.i.* **3.** to be negative; bring or cause negative results: *a pessimism that always negates.* [1615–25; < L *negātus* (ptp. of *negāre* to deny, refuse), equiv. to *neg-* (var. of *nec* not; see NEGLECT) + *-ā-* theme vowel + *-tus* ptp. suffix] —**ne·ga′tor, ne·gat′er,** *n.*

ne·ga·tion (ni gā′shən), *n.* **1.** the act of denying: *He shook his head in negation of the charge.* **2.** a denial: *a negation of one's former beliefs.* **3.** something that is without existence; nonentity. **4.** the absence or opposite of something that is actual, positive, or affirmative: *Darkness is the negation of light.* **5.** a negative statement, idea, concept, doctrine, etc.; a contradiction, refutation, or rebuttal: *a shameless lie that demands a negation.* [1375–1425; late ME < L *negātiōn-* (s. of *negātiō*) denial. See NEGATE, -ION] —**ne·ga′tion·al,** *adj.* —**ne·ga′tion·ist,** *n.*

neg·a·tive (neg′ə tiv), *adj., n., adv., v.,* **-tived, -tiv·ing,** *interj.* —*adj.* **1.** expressing or containing negation or denial: *a negative response to the question.* **2.** refusing consent, as to a proposal: *a negative reply to my request.* **3.** expressing refusal to do something: *He maintained a negative attitude about cooperating.* **4.** prohibitory, as a command or order. **5.** characterized by the absence of distinguishing or marked qualities or features; lacking positive attributes (opposed to *positive*): *a dull, lifeless, negative character.* **6.** lacking in constructiveness, helpfulness, optimism, cooperativeness, or the like: *a man of negative viewpoint.* **7.** being without rewards, results, or effectiveness: *a search of the premises proved negative.* **8.** *Math., Physics.* **a.** involving or noting subtraction; minus. **b.** measured or proceeding in the direction opposite to that which is considered as positive. **9.** *Photog.* noting an image in which the brightness values of the subject are reproduced so that the lightest areas are shown as the darkest. **10.** *Elect.* **a.** of, pertaining to, or characterized by negative electricity. **b.** indicating a point in a circuit that has a lower potential than that of another point, the current flowing from the point of higher potential to the point of lower potential. **11.** *Med.* failing to show a positive result in a test for a specific disease caused by either bacteria or viruses. **12.** *Chem.* (of an element or group) tending to gain electrons and become negatively charged; acid. **13.** *Physiol.* responding in a direction away from the stimulus. **14.** of, pertaining to, or noting the south pole of a magnet. **15.** *Logic.* (of a proposition) denying the truth of the predicate with regard to the subject. —*n.* **16.** a negative statement, answer, word, gesture, etc.: *The ship signaled back a negative.* **17.** a refusal of assent: *to answer a request with a negative.* **18.** the negative form of statement. **19.** a person or number of persons arguing against a resolution, statement, etc., esp. a team upholding the negative side in a formal debate. **20.** a negative quality or characteristic. **21.** disadvantage; drawback: *The plan is generally brilliant, but it has one or two negatives.* **22.** *Math.* **a.** a minus sign. **b.** a negative quantity or symbol. **23.** *Photog.* a negative image, as on a film, used chiefly for making positives. **24.** *Elect.* the negative plate or element in a voltaic cell. **25.** *Archaic.* a veto, or right of veto: *The delegation may exercise its negative.* **26. in the negative,** in the form of a negative response, as a refusal, denial, or disagreement; no: *The reply, when it finally came, was in the negative.* —*adv.* **27.** (used to indicate a negative response): *"You won't come with us?" "Negative."* —*v.t.* **28.** to deny; contradict. **29.** to refute or disprove (something). **30.** to refuse assent or consent to; veto. **31.** to neutralize or counteract. —*interj.* **32.** (used to indicate disagreement, denial of permission, etc.): *Negative, pilot—complete your mission as directed.* [1350–1400; < L *negātīvus* denying (see NEGATE, -IVE); r. ME *negatif* (n. and adj.) < MF < L as above] —**neg′a·tive·ly,** *adv.* —**neg′a·tive·ness, neg′a·tiv′i·ty,** *n.*
—**Syn. 6.** uncooperative, antagonistic, hostile.

neg′ative amortiza′tion, the increase of the principal of a loan by the amount by which periodic loan payments fall short of the interest due, usually as a result of an increase in the interest rate after the loan has begun.

neg′ative cat′alyst, *Chem.* an inhibitor. [1900–05]

neg′ative electric′ity, the electricity present in a body or substance that has an excess of electrons, as the electricity developed on a resin when rubbed with flannel. Cf. **positive electricity.** [1745–55]

neg′ative eugen′ics. See under **eugenics.** [1905–10]

neg′ative feed′back, *Electronics.* See under **feedback** (def. 1).

neg′ative flag′, the letter *N* in the International Code of Signals, signifying "no" when flown by itself: a square flag having four rows of alternate blue and white squares. [1905–10]

neg′ative glow′, *Physics.* the luminous region between the Crookes dark space and the Faraday dark space in a vacuum tube, occurring when the pressure is low. [1885–90]

neg′ative in′come, invested income that has produced a loss and hence may yield a tax deduction.

neg′ative in′come tax′, a system of income subsidy through which persons having less than a certain annual income receive money from the government rather than pay taxes to it.

neg′ative i′on, *Physics, Chem.* See under **ion** (def. 1).

neg′ative lens′, *Optics.* See **diverging lens.**

neg′ative op′tion, a clause in a sales contract, as for a series of books or records, that provides that merchandise will be sent periodically to the subscriber unless he or she notifies the company in writing that it is not wanted. [1970–75] —**neg′ative-op′tion,** *adj.*

neg′ative trans′fer, *Psychol.* the obstruction of or interference with new learning because of previous learning, as when a U.S. tourist in England learns to drive on the left side of the road. [1920–25]

neg·a·tiv·ism (neg′ə ti viz′əm), *n.* **1.** a negative or pessimistic attitude. **2.** *Psychol.* a tendency to resist external commands, suggestions, or expectations, or internal stimuli, as hunger, by doing nothing or something contrary or unrelated to the stimulus. **3.** any system of negative philosophy, as agnosticism or skepticism. [1815–25; NEGATIVE + -ISM] —**neg′a·tiv·ist,** *n.* —**neg′a·tiv·is′tic,** *adj.*

neg·a·ton (neg′ə ton′), *n.* (not in technical use) electron (def. 1). Also called **neg·a·tron** (neg′ə tron′). [1928; NEGAT(IVE) + -ON[1]]

neg·a·to·ry (neg′ə tôr′ē, -tōr′ē), *adj.* marked by negation; denying; negative. [1570–80; < LL *negātōrius.* See NEGATE, -TORY[1]]

Neg·ev (neg′ev), *n.* a partially reclaimed desert region and district in S Israel, bordering on the Sinai Peninsula. 4700 sq. mi. (12,173 sq. km). *Cap.:* Beersheba. Also, **Neg·eb** (neg′eb).

ne·glect (ni glekt′), *v.t.* **1.** to pay no attention or too little attention to; disregard or slight: *The public neglected his genius for many years.* **2.** to be remiss in the care or treatment of: *to neglect one's family; to neglect one's appearance.* **3.** to omit, through indifference or carelessness: *to neglect to reply to an invitation.* **4.** to fail to carry out or perform (orders, duties, etc.): *to neglect the household chores.* **5.** to fail to take or use: *to neglect no precaution.* —*n.* **6.** an act or instance of neglecting; disregard; negligence: *The neglect of the property was shameful.* **7.** the fact or state of being neglected: *a beauty marred by neglect.* [1520–30; < L *neglēctus,* var. of *neclēctus* (ptp. of *neglegere, neclegere* to disregard, ignore, slight), equiv. to *nec* not + *leg-,* base of *legere* to pick up + *-tus* ptp. suffix] —**ne·glect′ed·ly,** *adv.* —**ne·glect′ed·ness,** *n.* —**ne·glect′er, ne·glec′tor,** *n.*
—**Syn. 1.** ignore. See **slight. 6, 7.** default, inattention, heedlessness. NEGLECT, DERELICTION, NEGLIGENCE, REMISSNESS imply carelessness, failure, or some important omission in the performance of one's duty, a task, etc. NEGLECT and NEGLIGENCE are occasionally interchangeable, but NEGLECT commonly refers to an instance, NEGLIGENCE to the habit or trait, of failing to attend to or perform what is expected or required: *gross neglect of duty; negligence in handling traffic problems.* DERELICTION implies culpable or reprehensible neglect or failure in the performance of duty: *dereliction in a position of responsibility.* REMISSNESS implies the omission or the careless or indifferent performance of a duty: *remissness in filing a report on the accident.* —**Ant. 6.** attention, care.

ne·glect·ful (ni glekt′fəl), *adj.* characterized by neglect; disregardful; careless; negligent (often fol. by *of*): *neglectful of one's health.* [1615–25; NEGLECT + -FUL] —**ne·glect′ful·ly,** *adv.* —**ne·glect′ful·ness,** *n.*
—**Syn.** remiss, inattentive, heedless, thoughtless.
—**Ant.** careful, thoughtful.

neg·li·gee (neg′li zhā′, neg′li zhā′), *n.* **1.** a dressing gown or robe, usually of sheer fabric and having soft, flowing lines, worn by women. **2.** easy, informal attire. Also, **neg′li·gée′, neg′li·gé′.** [1745–55, *Amer.;* < F *négligé* carelessness, undress, lit., neglected, ptp. of *négliger* < L *negligere,* var. of *neglegere* to NEGLECT]

neg·li·gence (neg′li jəns), *n.* **1.** the quality, fact, or result of being negligent; neglect: *negligence in discharging one's responsibilities.* **2.** an instance of being negligent: *a downfall brought about by many negligences.* **3.**

CONCISE PRONUNCIATION KEY: act, cāpe, dâre, pärt; set, ēqual; *if,* ice; ox, ōver, ôrder, oil, bo͝ok, bo͞ot, out; up, ûrge; child; sing; shoe; thin, *th*at; zh as in *treasure.* ə = *a* as in *alone, e* as in *system, i* as in *easily, o* as in *gallop, u* as in *circus;* ə as in *fire* (fīər), *hour* (ouər). l and n can serve as syllabic consonants, as in *cradle* (krād′l), and *button* (but′n). See the full key inside the front cover.

Law. the failure to exercise that degree of care that, in the circumstances, the law requires for the protection of other persons or those interests of other persons that may be injuriously affected by the want of such care. —*adj.* **4.** *Law.* pertaining to or involving a civil action for compensation for damages filed by a person who claims to have suffered an injury or loss in an accident caused by another's negligence: *a negligence suit; a large negligence award.* [1300–50; ME, var. of *necligence* < L *necligentia.* See NEGLIGENT, -ENCE]
—Syn. 1. See **neglect.**

neg·li·gent (neg′li jənt), *adj.* **1.** guilty of or characterized by neglect, as of duty: *negligent officials.* **2.** lazily careless; offhand: *a negligent wave of his manicured hand.* [1350–1400; ME, var. of *necligent* < L *negligent-, necligent-,* s. of *negligēns,* prp. of *negligere,* var. of *neglegere* to NEGLECT; see -ENT] **—neg′li·gent·ly,** *adv.*
—Syn. 1. neglectful.

neg·li·gi·ble (neg′li jə bəl), *adj.* so small, trifling, or unimportant that it may safely be neglected or disregarded: *The extra expenses were negligible.* [1820–30; < L *neglig(ere)* to NEGLECT + -IBLE] **—neg′li·gi·bil′i·ty, neg′li·gi·ble·ness,** *n.* **—neg′li·gi·bly,** *adv.*

ne·go·ti·a·ble (ni gō′shē ə bəl, -shə bəl), *adj.* **1.** capable of being negotiated: *a negotiable salary demand.* **2.** (of bills, securities, etc.) transferable by delivery, with or without endorsement, according to the circumstances, the title passing to the transferee. —*n.* **3. negotiables,** negotiable bonds, stocks, etc. [1750–60; NEGOTI(ATE) + -ABLE] **—ne·go′ti·a·bil′i·ty,** *n.*

ne·go·ti·ant (ni gō′shē ənt, -shənt), *n.* a person who negotiates; negotiator. [1605–15; < L *negōtiant-,* s. of *negōtiāns,* n. use of prp. of *negōtiārī.* See NEGOTIATE, -ANT]

ne·go·ti·ate (ni gō′shē āt′), *v.,* **-at·ed, -at·ing.** —*v.i.* **1.** to deal or bargain with another or others, as in the preparation of a treaty or contract or in preliminaries to a business deal. —*v.t.* **2.** to arrange for or bring about by discussion and settlement of terms: *to negotiate a loan.* **3.** to manage; transact; conduct: *He negotiated an important business deal.* **4.** to move through, around, or over in a satisfactory manner: *to negotiate a difficult dance step without tripping: to negotiate sharp curves.* **5.** to transfer (a draft, promissory note, etc.) to a new owner by endorsement and delivery or by delivery. [1590–1600; < L *negōtiātus* (ptp. of *negōtiārī* to trade), equiv. to *negōti(um)* business (*neg-* not + *ōtium* leisure) + *-ātus* -ATE[1]] **—ne·go′ti·a′tor,** *n.*
—Syn. 5. convey, transmit, sign over.

ne·go·ti·a·tion (ni gō′shē ā′shən, -sē-), *n.* **1.** mutual discussion and arrangement of the terms of a transaction or agreement: *the negotiation of a treaty.* **2.** the act or process of negotiating. **3.** an instance or the result of negotiating. [1570–80; < L *negōtiātiōn-* (s. of *negōtiātiō*) a doing of business, equiv. to *negōtiāt(us)* (see NEGOTIATE) + *-iōn-* -ION]

Ne·gress (nē′gris), *n. Usually Offensive.* a black woman or girl. [1780–90; < F *négresse.* See NEGRO, -ESS]
—Usage. See **-ess.**

Ne′gri bod′y (nā′grē), any of the microscopic bodies found in the nerve cells of animals affected with rabies. [1900–05; after A. *Negri* (1876–1912), Italian physician]

Ne·gril·lo (ni gril′ō), *n., pl.* **-los,** (*esp. collectively*) **-lo.** a member of any of various small-statured, indigenous peoples of Africa, as a Pygmy. [1850–55; < Sp *negrillo,* dim. of *negro* black]

Ne·gri Sem·bi·lan (nā′grē sem bē′län, sem′bē län′, nə grē′), a state in Malaysia, on the SW Malay Peninsula. 481,563; 2580 sq. mi. (6682 sq. km). *Cap.:* Seremban.

Ne·grit·ic (ni grit′ik), *adj.* of or pertaining to blacks or to the Negritos. [1875–80; NEGRIT(O) + -IC]

Ne·gri·to (ni grē′tō), *n., pl.* **-tos, -toes.** a member of any of various small-statured, indigenous peoples of Africa, the Philippines, the Malay Peninsula, the Andaman Islands, and southern India. [1805–15; < Sp *negrito,* equiv. to *negr(o)* black + *-ito* dim. suffix]

Neg·ri·tude (neg′ri to͞od′, -tyo͞od′, nē′gri-), *n.* (*sometimes l.c.*) the historical, cultural, and social heritage considered common to blacks collectively. [1945–50; < F *négritude;* see NEGRO, -I-, -TUDE]

Ne·gro (nē′grō), *n., pl.* **-groes,** *adj.* —*n.* **1.** *Anthropol.* a member of the peoples traditionally classified as the Negro race, esp. those who originate in sub-Saharan Africa: no longer in technical use. —*adj.* **2.** of, pertaining to, or characteristic of one of the traditional racial divisions of humankind, generally marked by brown to black skin pigmentation, dark eyes, and woolly or crisp hair and including esp. the indigenous peoples of Africa south of the Sahara. **3.** being a member of the black peoples of humankind, esp. those who originate in sub-Saharan Africa. [1545–55; < Sp and Pg *negro* black < L *nigrum,* masc. acc. of *niger* black]
—Usage. See **black.**

Ne·gro (nā′grō; *Sp.* ne′grô; *Port.* ne′gro͝o), *n.* **1.** a river in NW South America, flowing SE from E Colombia through N Brazil into the Amazon. 1400 mi. (2255 km) long. **2.** a river in S Argentina, flowing E from the Andes to the Atlantic. 700 mi. (1125 km) long. **3.** a river in SE South America, flowing S from Brazil and W through Uruguay, to the Uruguay River. ab. 500 mi. (800 km) long. Also called **Ne′gro Riv′er.** Portuguese, **Rio Negro.** Spanish, **Río Negro.**

Ne·groid (nē′groid), *adj.* **1.** of, pertaining to, or characteristic of the peoples traditionally classified as the Negro race. —*n.* **2.** a member of such peoples. [1855–60; NEGR(O)- + -OID]

CONCISE ETYMOLOGY KEY: <, descended or borrowed from; >, whence; b., blend of, blended; c., cognate with; cf., compare; deriv., derivative; equiv., equivalent; imit., imitative; obl., oblique; r., replacing; s., stem; sp., spelling, spelled; resp., respelling, respelled; trans., translation; ?, origin unknown; *, unattested; ‡, probably earlier than. See the full key inside the front cover.

Ne·gro·ism (nē′grō iz′əm), *n.* (*sometimes l.c.*) **1.** the doctrine or advocacy of equal rights for blacks. **2.** a quality or manner, as a speech pattern or pronunciation, considered characteristic of blacks. [1840–50, *Amer.*]

Ne·gro·ize (nē′grō īz′), *v.t.,* **-ized, -iz·ing. 1.** to cause to include black people or to have the qualities or characteristics of blacks. **2.** to infuse or imbue with Negroism. Also, *esp. Brit.,* **Ne′gro·ise′.** [1885–90]

ne·gro·ni (ni grō′nē), *n., pl.* **-nis.** a cocktail made from sweet vermouth, gin, and bitters. [1945–50; < It, said to be after a nobleman named *Negroni,* who first made the drink ca. 1935]

Ne·gro·phile (nē′grə fīl′, -fil), *n.* (*sometimes l.c.*) a white or other nonblack person who is esp. sympathetic to or supportive of blacks. Also, **Ne·gro·phil** (nē′grə fil). [1795–1805; NEGRO + -PHILE] **—Ne·groph·i·lism** (ni grof′ə liz′əm), *n.* **—Ne·groph′i·list,** *n.*

Ne·gro·phobe (nē′grə fōb′), *n.* (*sometimes l.c.*) a person who strongly fears or dislikes black people. [1895–1900; NEGRO + -PHOBE]

Ne·gro·pho·bi·a (nē′grə fō′bē ə), *n.* (*sometimes l.c.*) strong fear or dislike of black people. [1810–20; NEGRO + -PHOBIA]

Neg·ro·pont (neg′rō pont′), *n.* Euboea. Italian, **Ne·gro·pon·te** (ne′grô pôn′te).

Ne·gros (nā′grōs; *Sp.* ne′grôs), *n.* an island of the central Philippines. 2,749,700; 5043 sq. mi. (13,061 sq. km).

ne·gus[1] (nē′gəs), *n., pl.* **-gus·es. 1.** a title of Ethiopian royalty. **2.** (*cap.*) the Emperor of Ethiopia. [1585–95; < Amharic *nəgus* king < Geez, participle of *nägšä* to reign]

ne·gus[2] (nē′gəs), *n.* a beverage made of wine and hot water, with sugar, nutmeg, and lemon. [1735–45; named after Colonel Francis *Negus* (d. 1732), Englishman who invented it]

NEH, National Endowment for the Humanities.

Neh., Nehemiah.

Ne·he·mi·ah (nē′ə mī′ə), *n.* **1.** a Hebrew leader of the 5th century B.C. **2.** a book of the Bible bearing his name. *Abbr.:* Neh. **3.** a male given name. Also, *Douay Bible,* **Ne·he·mi·as** (nē′ə mī′əs) (for defs. 1, 2).

Neh·ru (nā′ro͞o, ne′ro͞o), *n.* **1. Ja·wa·har·lal** (jə wä′hər läl), 1889–1964, Hindu political leader in India: first prime minister of the republic of India 1947–64 (father of Indira Gandhi). **2.** his father **Mo·ti·lal** (mō′ti läl), 1861–1931, Indian lawyer and statesman. —*adj.* **3.** indicating a man's close-fitting jacket or coat with long sleeves, a Mandarin-type collar, and front buttons to the neckline, as usually worn by J. Nehru. **4.** indicating a man's suit consisting of such a jacket and very narrow trousers.

neigh (nā), *v.i.* **1.** to utter the cry of a horse; whinny. —*n.* **2.** the cry of a horse; whinny. [bef. 1000; ME *ney(gh)en,* OE *hnǣgan,* c. MD *neyen,* OS *hnēgian,* MHG *nēgen,* OHG *hneigen,* ON *hneggja;* akin to OS *hnechian;* MD *nighen,* MLG *nigen,* MHG *nyhen;* and, with intrusion in the initial, ON *gneggja,* Norw *kneggja.* See NAG[2]]

neigh·bor (nā′bər), *n.* **1.** a person who lives near another. **2.** a person or thing that is near another. **3.** one's fellow human being: *to be generous toward one's less fortunate neighbors.* **4.** a person who shows kindliness or helpfulness toward his or her fellow humans: *to be a neighbor to someone in distress.* **5.** (used as a term of address, esp. as a friendly greeting to a stranger): *Tell me, neighbor, which way to town?* —*adj.* **6.** situated or living near another: *one of our neighbor nations.* —*v.t.* **7.** to live or be situated near to; adjoin; border on. **8.** to place or bring near. —*v.i.* **9.** to live or be situated nearby. **10.** to associate with or as if with one's neighbors; be neighborly or friendly (often fol. by *with*). Also, *esp. Brit.,* **neigh′bour.** [bef. 900; ME; OE *neahgebūr, nēahbūr* (*nēah* NIGH + *(ge)būr* farmer; see BOER, BOOR); akin to D *nabuur,* G *Nachbar,* ON *nābūi*] **—neigh′bor·less,** *adj.*

neigh·bor·hood (nā′bər ho͝od′), *n.* **1.** the area or region around or near some place or thing; vicinity: *the kids of the neighborhood; located in the neighborhood of Jackson and Vine streets.* **2.** a district or locality, often with reference to its character or inhabitants: *a fashionable neighborhood; to move to a nicer neighborhood.* **3.** a number of persons living near one another or in a particular locality: *The whole neighborhood was there.* **4.** neighborly feeling or conduct. **5.** nearness; proximity: *to sense the neighborhood of trouble.* **6.** *Math.* an open set that contains a given point. **7. in the neighborhood of,** approximately; nearly; about: *She looks to be in the neighborhood of 70.* [1400–50; late ME *neighborehode.* See NEIGHBOR, -HOOD]
—Syn. 2. community, area, locale, vicinity.

neigh′borhood watch′, a neighborhood surveillance program or group in which residents keep watch over one another's houses, patrol the streets, etc., in an attempt to prevent crime.

neigh·bor·ing (nā′bər ing), *adj.* situated or living near; adjacent: *to visit the neighboring towns.* [1595–1605; NEIGHBOR + -ING[2]]

neigh·bor·ly (nā′bər lē), *adj.* having or showing qualities befitting a neighbor; friendly. [1515–25; NEIGHBOR + -LY] **—neigh′bor·li·ness,** *n.*

Neil (nēl), *n.* a male given name: from an Irish word meaning "champion."

Ne·i·lah (*Seph.* nə ē lä′; *Ashk.* nē′lə), *n. Hebrew.* the Jewish religious service marking the conclusion of Yom Kippur.

Neil·son (nēl′sən), *n.* **William Allan,** 1869–1946, U.S. educator and lexicographer, born in Scotland.

Nei′ Mon′gol (nā). See **Inner Mongolia.** Also, *Pinyin,* **Nei·meng·gu** (nā′mœng′gY′); **Nei′ Mong′gol′** (mong′gōl′, mon′-).

Neis·se (nī′sə), *n.* a river in N Europe, flowing N from the NW Czech Republic along part of the boundary between Germany and Poland to the Oder River. 145 mi. (233 km) long.

neis·se·ri·a (nī sēr′ē ə), *n., pl.* **-se·ri·ae** (-sēr′ē ē′). *Bacteriol.* any of several spherical bacteria of the genus *Neisseria,* certain species of which, as *N. gonorrhoeae,* are pathogenic for humans. [< NL; named after A.L.S. *Neisser* (1855–1916), German physician; see -IA]

nei·ther (nē′thər, nī′-), *conj.* **1.** not either, as of persons or things specified (usually fol. by *nor*): *Neither John nor Betty is at home.* **2.** nor; nor yet; no more: *Bob can't go, and neither can I. If she doesn't want it, neither do I.* —*adj.* **3.** not either; not the one or the other: *Neither statement is true.* —*pron.* **4.** not either; not one person or the other; not one thing or the other: *Neither of the suggestions will do. Neither is to be trusted.* [1150–1200; ME, equiv. to *ne* not + EITHER; r. ME *nawther,* OE *nāwther, nāhwæther* (*nā* not, NO[1] + *hwæther* which of two; see WHETHER)]

—Usage. As an adjective or pronoun meaning "not either," NEITHER is usually followed by a singular verb and referred to by a singular personal pronoun: *Neither lawyer prepares her own briefs. Neither performs his duties for reward.* When NEITHER is followed by a prepositional phrase with a plural object, there has been, ever since the 17th century, a tendency, especially in speech and less formal writing, to use a plural verb and personal pronoun: *Neither of the guards were at their stations.* In edited writing, however, singular verbs and pronouns are more common in such constructions: *Neither of the guards was at his station.*

As a correlative conjunction, NEITHER is almost always followed by *nor,* not *or: Neither the liberals nor the conservatives had originally supported the winner.* Subjects connected by NEITHER . . . NOR take singular verbs and pronouns when both subjects are singular (*Neither Diane nor Nicole has her own apartment*), plural when both are plural: *Neither the Yankees nor the Dodgers got much help from their bull pens that year.* Usage guides commonly say that when a singular and a plural subject are joined by these correlative conjunctions, the noun or pronoun nearer the verb should determine the number of the verb: *Neither the mayor nor the council members have yielded on the issue. Neither the council members nor the mayor has yielded on the issue.* Practice in this matter varies, however, and often the presence of one plural, no matter what its position, results in a plural verb.

In edited writing the construction following NEITHER is parallel to the one following NOR: *The great days of American political oratory are neither dead nor waning* (not *neither are dead nor waning*). *This sale sacrifices neither quality nor availability* (not *This sale neither sacrifices quality nor availability*).

Although some usage guides say that NEITHER may introduce a series of no more than two, it often is used to introduce a series of three or more: *The head of that department is neither skillful nor well-prepared nor honest.* See also **either.**
—Pronunciation. See **either.**

Nei·va (nā′vä), *n.* a city in W Colombia. 105,476.

Nejd (nejd, näd), *n.* one of the two major regions of Saudi Arabia in the E central part: formerly a sultanate of Arabia. ab. 400,000 sq. mi. (1,000,000 sq. km). Also, **Najd.**

Nekh·bet (nek′bet), *n. Egyptian Relig.* the guardian goddess of Upper Egypt, often represented as a vulture. Also, **Nekh·e·bet** (nek′ə bet′), **Nekh·e·bit** (nek′ə bit), **Ne·khebt** (ne kebt′).

nek·ton (nek′ton, -tən), *n.* the aggregate of actively swimming aquatic organisms in a body of water, able to move independently of water currents. [1890–95; < G, n. use of neut. of *nēktós* swimming (verbal of *nḗchein* to swim; see NECTOPOD)] **—nek·ton′ic,** *adj.*

Nel·da (nel′də), *n.* a female given name.

Nell (nel), *n.* a female given name, form of **Helen.**

Nel·lie (nel′ē), *n.* **1.** a female given name, form of **Helen. 2.** (*l.c.*) *Slang.* a fussily effeminate male. **3.** *Slang* (*disparaging and offensive*). a male homosexual. Also, **Nel′ly.**

Nel′lis Air′ Force′ Base′ (nel′is), the largest air base in the U.S. Air Force's Tactical Air Command, located near Las Vegas, Nev., and developed from what began in 1941 as a U.S. Army Air Corps field.

nel·ly (nel′ē), *n. Australian Slang.* inferior or cheap wine. [1940–45; of uncert. orig.]

nel·son (nel′sən), *n. Wrestling.* a hold in which pressure is applied to the head, back of the neck, and one or both arms of the opponent. Cf. **full nelson, half nelson, quarter nelson, three-quarter nelson.** [1885–90; special use of name *Nelson*]

Nel·son (nel′sən), *n.* **1. Viscount Horatio,** 1758–1805, British admiral. **2. (John) Byron,** born 1911, U.S. golf player. **3.** a river in central Canada, flowing NE from Lake Winnipeg to Hudson Bay. 400 mi. (645 km) long. **4.** a seaport on N South Island, in New Zealand. 42,433. **5.** a male given name.

ne·lum·bo (nə lum′bō), *n., pl.* **-bos.** lotus (def. 3). [< NL < Sinhalese *neluma*] **—ne·lum′bi·an,** *adj.*

Ne·man (nem′ən, nyem′-, nē′mən), *n.* a river rising in central Byelorussia (Belarus), flowing W through Lithuania into the Baltic. 582 mi. (937 km) long. Lithuanian, **Ne·mu·nas** (nye′mo͝o näs′).

nemat-, var. of **nemato-** before a vowel or *h: nematic.*

nem·a·the·ci·um (nem′ə thē′shē əm, -sē əm), *n., pl.* **-ci·a** (-shē ə, -sē ə). a wartlike protuberance on the thallus of certain red algae, containing tetraspores, antheridia, or cystocarps. [1820–30; < NL, irreg. < Gk *nêma* thread + *thēkíon* THECIUM] **—nem·a·the·cial** (nem′ə thē′shəl, -shē əl, -sē-), *adj.*

nem·a·thel·minth (nem′ə thel′minth), *n.* any worm of the phylum Nemathelminthes (now usually broken up into several phyla), including the nematodes and hairworms, having an elongated, unsegmented, cylindrical body. [1885–90; NEMAT- + HELMINTH]

ne•mat•ic (ni mat′ik), *adj. Physical Chem.* (of liquid crystals) noting a mesomorphic state in which the arrangement of the molecules is linear. Cf. **smectic.** [1920–25; NEMAT- + -IC]

nemato-, a combining form with the meaning "thread," "threadlike organism, esp. a nematode," used in the formation of compound words: *nematocyst.* Also, *esp. before a vowel or h,* **nemat-.** [comb. form repr. Gk *nēmat-* (s. of *nêma*) thread, yarn; see -O-]

nem•a•to•cide (nem′ə tə sīd′, ni mat′ə-), *n.* a substance or preparation used for killing nematodes parasitic to plants. Also, **nem′a•ti•cide′.** [1895–1900; NEMATO- + -CIDE] —**nem′a•to•cid′al, nem′a•ti•cid′al,** *adj.*

nem•a•to•cyst (nem′ə tə sist′, ni mat′ə-), *n. Zool.* an organ in coelenterates consisting of a minute capsule containing an ejectable thread that causes a sting. [1870–75; NEMATO- + -CYST] —**nem′a•to•cys′tic,** *adj.*

nem•a•tode (nem′ə tōd′), *n.* **1.** any unsegmented worm of the phylum Nematoda, having an elongated, cylindrical body; a roundworm. —*adj.* **2.** pertaining to the Nematoda. [1860–65; NEMAT- + -ODE[1]]

nem•a•tol•o•gy (nem′ə tol′ə jē), *n.* the branch of zoology dealing with nematodes. [1925–30; NEMATO- + -LOGY] —**nem•a•to•log•i•cal** (nem′ə tl oj′i kəl, ni-mat′ə-), *adj.* —**nem′a•tol′o•gist,** *n.*

nem•a•to•morph (nem′ə tə môrf′, nə mat′ə-), *n. Zool.* any member of the phylum Nematomorpha, having a threadlike body, comprising the horsehair worms. [< NL *Nematomorpha;* see NEMATO-, -MORPH]

Nem•bu•tal (nem′byə tôl′, -tal′), *Pharm., Trademark.* a brand of pentobarbital.

Nem•bu•tsu (nem bo͞o′tso͞o), *n. Japanese.* meditation on the name of Amida.

nem. con., nemine contradicente.

nem. diss., nemine dissentiente.

Ne•me•a (nē′mē ə), *n.* a valley in SE Greece, in ancient Argolis. —**Ne•me•an** (ni mē′ən, nē′mē-), *adj.*

Neme′an Games′, one of the great national festivals of ancient Greece, held at Nemea in the second and fourth year of each Olympiad. [1650–60]

Neme′an li′on, *Class. Myth.* a powerful lion strangled by Hercules as one of his labors.

Nem•e•rov (nem′ə rôf′, -rof′), *n.* **Howard,** 1920–91, U.S. poet, novelist, and essayist: U.S. poet laureate 1988–90.

ne•mer•te•an (ni mûr′tē ən), *n.* any member of the invertebrate phylum Nemertea, comprising the ribbon worms. Also called **ribbon worm.** [1860–65; < NL *Nemerte(a),* deriv. of *Nemertes* a genus (< Gk *Nēmertḗs* name of a Nereid; see -A[2]) + -AN] —**ne•mer•tine** (ni mûr′tēn), *adj.*

nem•e•sis (nem′ə sis), *n., pl.* **-ses** (-sēz′). **1.** something that a person cannot conquer, achieve, etc.: *The performance test proved to be my nemesis.* **2.** an opponent or rival whom a person cannot best or overcome. **3.** (*cap.*) *Class. Myth.* the goddess of divine retribution. **4.** an agent or act of retribution or punishment. [< L < Gk *némesis* lit., a dealing out, verbid of *némein* to dispense (justice); see -SIS] —**Syn. 1.** Waterloo. **4.** downfall, undoing, ruin, Waterloo.

ne•mi•ne con•tra•di•cen•te (ne′mi ne′ kōn′trä di-ken′te; *Eng.* nem′ə nē′ kon′trə di sen′tē), *Latin.* no one contradicting; unanimously.

ne•mi•ne dis•sen•ti•en•te (ne′mi ne′ di sen′tē en′-te; *Eng.* nem′ə nē′ di sen′shē en′tē), *Latin.* no one dissenting; unanimously.

ne•mo (nē′mō), *n., pl.* **-mos.** *Radio and Television.* remote (def. 10). [1935–40, *Amer.;* perh. < L *nēmō* nobody, reinforced by sound assoc. with REMOTE]

ne•mo me im•pu•ne la•ces•sit (ne′mō me im-po͞o′ne lä kes′sit; *Eng.* nē′mō mē im pyo͞o′nē lə ses′-it), *Latin.* no one attacks me with impunity: motto of Scotland.

ne•mor•i•cole (ni môr′i kōl′, nem′ər i-), *adj.* living in a grove. Also, **nem•o•ric•o•line** (nem′ə rik′ə līn′, -lin), **nem•o•ric•o•lous** (nem′ə rik′ə ləs). [< L *nemori-* (s. of *nemus*) grove + *-cola;* see -COLOUS]

Nem•rod (nem′rod), *n. Douay Bible.* Nimrod (def. 1).

Ne•mu•nas (nye′mo͝o näs′), *n.* Lithuanian name of **Neman.**

ne•ne (nā′nā), *n., pl.* **-ne.** a barred, gray-brown wild goose, *Nesochen sandvicensis,* native to Hawaii, where it is the state bird. Also called **Hawaiian goose.** [1900–05; < Hawaiian *nēnē*]

Nen•ets (nen′ets), *n., pl.* **Nen•tsi, Nen•tsy** (nent′sē), (*esp. collectively*) **Nen•ets. 1.** a member of a reindeer-herding Uralic people of far northern European Russia and adjacent areas of Siberia as far as the Yenisei River delta. **2.** the Samoyedic language of the Nenets. Also called **Yurak.** [< Russ *nénets* (with *-ets* falsely construed as the Russ suffix) < Nenets *ńenetś* man, Nenets]

N. Eng., Northern England.

Nen•ni (nen′nē), *n.* **Pie•tro** (pye′trô), 1891–1980, Italian socialist leader and author.

neo-, 1. a combining form meaning "new," "recent," "revived," "modified," used in the formation of compound words: *neo-Darwinism; Neolithic; neoorthodoxy; neophyte.* **2.** *Chem.* a combining form used in the names of isomers having a carbon atom attached to four carbon atoms: *neoarsphenamine.* Also, *esp. before a vowel,* **ne-.** [< Gk, comb. form of *néos;* akin to NEW]

ne•o•an•throp•ic (nē′ō an throp′ik), *adj.* neanthropic. [1890–95; NEO- + ANTHROPIC]

ne•o-Cath•o•lic (nē′ō kath′ə lik, -kath′lik), *adj.* **1.** of or pertaining to those Anglicans who avowedly prefer the doctrines, rituals, etc., of the Roman Catholic Church to those of the Anglican communion. —*n.* **2.** a neo-Catholic person. [1835–45] —**ne•o-Ca•thol•i•cism** (nē′-ō kə thol′ə siz′əm), *n.*

Ne•o•cene (nē′ə sēn′), *adj., n. Geol.* Neogene. [1890–95; NEO- + -CENE]

ne•o-Chris•ti•an•i•ty (nē′ō kris′chē an′i tē), *n.* any interpretation of Christianity based on the prevalent philosophy of a given period. [1855–60]

ne•o•clas•sic (nē′ō klas′ik), *adj.* **1.** (*sometimes cap.*) belonging or pertaining to a revival of classic styles or something that is held to resemble classic styles, as in art, literature, music, or architecture. **2.** (*usually cap.*) *Fine Arts.* of, pertaining to, or designating a style of painting and sculpture developed principally from the mid-18th through the mid-19th centuries, characterized chiefly by an iconography derived from classical antiquity, a hierarchical conception of subject matter, severity of composition and, esp. in painting, by an oblique lighting of forms in the early phase and a strict linear quality in the later phase of the style. **3.** *Archit.* of, pertaining to, or designating neoclassicism. **4.** (*sometimes cap.*) *Literature.* of, pertaining to, or designating a style of poetry or prose, developed chiefly in the 17th and 18th centuries, rigidly adhering to canons of form that were derived mainly from classical antiquity, that were exemplified by decorum of style or diction, the three unities, etc., and that emphasized an impersonal expression of universal truths as shown in human actions, representing them principally in satiric and didactic modes. Also, **ne′o•clas′si•cal, ne′o-clas′sic, ne′o-clas′si•cal.** [1875–80; NEO- + CLASSIC] —**ne′o•clas′si•cist, ne′o-clas′si•cist,** *n.*

ne•o•clas•si•cism (nē′ō klas′ə siz′əm), *n.* **1.** (*often cap.*) *Archit.* the trend or movement prevailing in the architecture of Europe, America, and various European colonies at various periods during the late 18th and early 19th centuries, characterized by the introduction and widespread use of Greek orders and decorative motifs, the subordination of detail to simple, strongly geometric overall compositions, the presence of light colors or shades, frequent shallowness of relief in ornamental treatment of façades, and the absence of textural effects. **2.** (*sometimes cap.*) the principles of the neoclassic style in art, literature, etc. **3.** (*sometimes cap.*) any of various movements based on neoclassic principles in the arts, literature, etc., of the late 17th to mid-19th centuries. [1890–95; NEO- + CLASSICISM]

ne•o•co•lo•ni•al•ism (nē′ō kə lō′nē ə liz′əm), *n.* the policy of a strong nation in seeking political and economic hegemony over an independent nation or extended geographical area without necessarily reducing the subordinate nation or area to the legal status of a colony. [1960–65; NEO- + COLONIALISM] —**ne′o•co•lo′ni•al,** *adj., n.* —**ne′o•co•lo′ni•al•ist,** *n., adj.*

ne•o•con (nē′ō kon′), *n.* a neoconservative. [by shortening]

ne•o-Con•fu•cian (nē′ō kən fyo͞o′shən), *adj.* **1.** of or pertaining to an eclectic philosophical movement of the 12th to the 16th centuries, incorporating Taoist and Buddhist elements with an adaptation of Confucianism. —*n.* **2.** an advocate or follower of neo-Confucianism. Also called **neo-Ju.** [1945–50] —**ne′o-Con•fu′cian•ism,** *n.*

ne•o-Con•fu•cian•ist (nē′ō kən fyo͞o′shə nist), *adj.* **1.** of or pertaining to neo-Confucians or neo-Confucianism. —*n.* **2.** neo-Confucian (def. 2).

ne•o•con•serv•a•tism (nē′ō kən sûr′və tiz′əm), *n.* moderate political conservatism espoused or advocated by former liberals or socialists. [1960–65; NEO- + CONSERVATISM] —**ne′o•con•serv′a•tive,** *n., adj.*

ne•o•cor•tex (nē′ō kôr′teks), *n., pl.* **-ti•ces** (-tə sēz′). the largest and evolutionarily most recent portion of the cerebral cortex, composed of complex, layered tissue, the site of most of the higher brain functions. Also called **neopallium.** [1905–10; NEO- + CORTEX] —**ne•o•cor•ti•cal** (nē′ō kôr′ti kəl), *adj.*

ne•o•cy•a•nine (nē′ō sī′ə nēn′, -nin), *n.* a dye used to make photographic emulsions sensitive to infrared radiation. [1975–80; NEO- + CYANINE]

ne•o•da•da (nē′ō dä′dä), *n.* a minor art movement chiefly of the 1960's reviving some of the objectives of dada but placing emphasis on the importance of the work of art produced rather than on the concept generating the work. Also, **ne′o-Da′da.** Also called **ne′o•da′-da•ism.** [1960–65] —**ne′o•da′da•ist,** *n., adj.*

ne•o-Dar•win•ism (nē′ō där′wi niz′əm), *n. Biol.* **1.** the theory of evolution as expounded by later students of Charles Darwin, esp. Weismann, holding that natural selection accounts for evolution and denying the inheritance of acquired characters. **2.** any modern theory of evolution holding that species evolve by natural selection acting on genetic variation. [1900–05] —**ne′o-Dar•win′i•an,** *adj., n.* —**ne′o-Dar′win•ist,** *n.*

ne•o•dym•i•um (nē′ō dim′ē əm), *n. Chem.* a rare-earth, metallic, trivalent element occurring with cerium and other rare-earth metals, and having rose-colored to violet-colored salts. *Symbol:* Nd; *at. wt.:* 144.24; *at. no.:* 60; *sp. gr.:* 6.9 at 20°C. [1880–85; < NL; see NEO-, DIDYMIUM]

ne•o•en•ceph•a•lon (nē′ō en sef′ə lon′, -lən), *n., pl.* **-lons, -la** (-lə). neencephalon.

ne•o-ex•pres•sion•ism (nē′ō ik spresh′ə niz′əm), *n.* an art movement, chiefly in painting, that developed in Germany, Italy, and the U.S. in the late 1970's, emphasized large heavy forms and thick impasto, and typically dealt with historical narrative in terms of symbolism, allegory, and myth. Also, **Ne′o-Ex•pres′sion•ism.** Also called **new expressionism.** [1960–65] —**ne′o-ex•pres′sion•ist,** *n., adj.*

ne•o•fas•cism (nē′ō fash′iz əm), *n.* **1.** any of various political movements or beliefs inspired by or reminiscent of fascism or Nazism. **2. neo-Fascism,** an Italian political movement that seeks to reestablish Fascism. [1945–50] —**ne′o•fas′cist, ne′o-Fas′cist,** *adj., n.*

ne•o•for•ma•tion (nē′ō fôr mā′shən), *n. Pathol.* a new and abnormal growth of tissue; tumor; neoplasm. [NEO- + FORMATION] —**ne•o•for•ma•tive** (nē′ō fôr′-mə tiv), *adj.*

ne•o-Freu•di•an (nē′ō froi′dē ən), **1.** *adj.* of or pertaining to a group of psychoanalytic thinkers whose modifications of Freudian analytic theory place increased emphasis on ego functions and interpersonal relationships. —*n.* **2.** a psychoanalyst advocating such a view. [1940–45]

Ne•o•gae•a (nē′ə jē′ə), *n.* a biogeographical division comprising the Neotropical region. Also, **Ne′o•ge′a.** [< NL; see NEO-, GAEA] —**Ne′o•gae′an, Ne′o•ge′an, Ne′o•gae′al, Ne′o•ge′al, Ne′o•gae′ic, Ne′o•ge′ic,** *adj.*

Ne•o•gene (nē′ə jēn′), *Geol.* —*adj.* **1.** noting or pertaining to an interval of time corresponding to the Miocene and Pliocene epochs and accorded the status of a period when the Tertiary is considered an era. Cf. **Paleogene.** —*n.* **2.** the Neogene Period or System. Also, **Neocene.** [1855–60; NEO- + *-gene* (see -GEN)]

ne•o•gen•e•sis (nē′ō jen′ə sis), *n. Physiol.* the regeneration of tissue. [1900–05; NEO- + -GENESIS]

ne•o•gla•ci•a•tion (nē′ō glā′shē ā′shən, -sē-), *n. Geol.* a phase of renewed glaciation associated with a readvance of ice sheets between the postglacial phase and the present. [1950–55; NEO- + GLACIATION]

ne•o•goth•ic (nē′ō goth′ik), *adj.* of, pertaining to, or designating chiefly a style of architecture in which gothic motifs and forms are imitated. [1890–95]

ne•o•gram•mar•i•an (nē′ō grə mâr′ē ən), *Ling.* —*n.* **1.** a member of the *Junggrammatiker.* —*adj.* **2.** of or pertaining to the *Junggrammatiker.* [1880–85; trans. of G *Junggrammatiker*]

ne•o-He•gel•i•an•ism (nē′ō hā gā′lē ə niz′əm, -hi-jē′-), *n. Philos.* Hegelianism as modified by various philosophers of the latter half of the 19th century. [1915–20] —**ne′o-He•gel′i•an,** *n., adj.*

ne•o•im•pres•sion•ism (nē′ō im presh′ə niz′əm), *n.* (*sometimes cap.*) *Fine Arts.* the theory and practice of a group of post-impressionists of about the middle 1880's, characterized chiefly by a systematic juxtaposition of dots or points of pure color according to a concept of the optical mixture of hues. Cf. **pointillism.** [1890–95; NEO- + IMPRESSIONISM] —**ne′o•im•pres′sion•ist,** *n., adj.*

ne•o•i•so•la•tion•ism (nē′ō ī′sə lā′shə niz′əm), *n.* (in U.S. politics) a revival of isolationism arising from increased anti-Soviet and anti-European sentiment and a reluctance to involve the nation in further political and military commitments abroad. [1950–55; NEO- + ISOLATIONISM] —**ne′o•i′so•la′tion•ist,** *adj., n.*

ne•o-Ju (nē′ō zho͞o′), *adj., n.* neo-Confucian.

ne•o-Kant•i•an•ism (nē′ō kan′tē ə niz′əm, -kän′-), *n. Philos.* Kantianism as modified by various philosophers. [1885–90] —**ne′o-Kant′i•an,** *n., adj.*

ne•o-La•marck•ism (nē′ō lə mär′kiz əm), *n. Biol.* Lamarckism as expounded by later biologists who hold esp. that some acquired characters of organisms may be inherited by descendants, but that natural selection also is a factor in evolution. —**ne′o-La•marck′i•an,** *adj., n.* —**ne′o-La•marck′ist,** *n.*

Ne•o-Lat•in (nē′ō lat′n), *n.* **1.** Also called **New Latin.** the Latin that became current, notably in scientific literature, after the Renaissance, c1500. **2.** romance[1] (def. 8). —*adj.* **3.** romance[1] (def. 12). *Abbr.:* NL [1840–50]

ne•o•lib•er•al•ism (nē′ō lib′ər ə liz′əm, -lib′rə-), *n.* an outgrowth of the U.S. liberal movement, beginning in the late 1960's, that modified somewhat its traditional endorsement of all trade unions and opposition to big business and military buildup. [NEO- + LIBERAL + -ISM] —**ne′o•lib′er•al,** *adj., n.*

ne•o•lin•guis•tics (nē′ō ling gwis′tiks), *n.* (*used with a singular v.*) a school of linguistics centered in Italy emphasizing the importance of linguistic geography in diachronic studies. [1945–50; NEO- + LINGUISTICS, as trans. of It *neolinguistica*] —**ne′o•lin′guist,** *n.* —**ne′o•lin•guis′tic,** *adj.*

ne•o•lith (nē′ə lith), *n.* a Neolithic stone implement. [1880–85; back formation from NEOLITHIC]

Ne•o•lith•ic (nē′ə lith′ik), *adj.* **1.** (*sometimes l.c.*) *Anthropol.* of, pertaining to, or characteristic of the last phase of the Stone Age, marked by the domestication of animals, the development of agriculture, and the manufacture of pottery and textiles: commonly thought to have begun c9000–8000 B.C. in the Middle East. Cf. **Mesolithic, Paleolithic. 2.** (*usually l.c.*) belonging to or remaining from an earlier era; outdated; passé. [1860–65; NEO- + -LITHIC]

ne•o•lo•cal (nē′ō lō′kəl), *adj. Anthropol.* living or located away from both the husband's and the wife's relatives: *a neolocal family.* Cf. **matrilocal, virilocal.** [1945–50; NEO- + LOCAL]

ne•ol•o•gism (nē ol′ə jiz′əm), *n.* **1.** a new word, meaning, usage, or phrase. **2.** the introduction or use of new words or new senses of existing words. **3.** a new doctrine, esp. a new interpretation of sacred writings. **4.** *Psychiatry.* a new word, often consisting of a combination of other words, that is understood only by the speaker: occurring most often in the speech of schizophrenics. [1790–1800; < F *néologisme.* See NEOLOGY, -ISM] —**ne•ol′o•gist,** *n.* —**ne•ol′o•gis′tic, ne•ol′o•gis′ti•cal,** *adj.*

ne•ol•o•gize (nē ol′ə jīz′), *v.i.,* **-gized, -giz•ing. 1.** to make or use new words or create new meanings for existing words. **2.** to devise or accept new religious doctrines. Also, *esp. Brit.,* **ne•ol′o•gise′.** [1840–50; NEOLOG(Y) + -IZE]

ne•ol•o•gy (nē ol′ə jē), *n., pl.* **-gies.** neologism. [1790–

CONCISE PRONUNCIATION KEY: act, cāpe, dâre, pärt; set, ēqual; if, īce; ox, ōver, ôrder, oil, bo͝ok, bo͞ot, out; up, ûrge; child; sing; shoe; thin, *th*at; zh as in *treasure.* ə = *a* as in *alone, e* as in *system, i* as in *easily, o* as in *gallop, u* as in *circus;* ə as in *fire* (fīər), *hour* (ouər). l and n can serve as syllabic consonants, as in *cradle* (krād′l), and *button* (but′n). See the full key inside the front cover.

1800; < F *néologie.* See NEO-, -LOGY] **—ne•o•log•i•cal** (nē′ə loj′i kəl), **ne′o•log′ic,** *adj.* **—ne′o•log′i•cal•ly,** *adv.*

ne•o-Lu•ther•an•ism (nē′ō lo͞o′thər ə niz′əm, -lo͞oth′rə-), *n.* a movement begun in the 19th century in Germany and Scandinavia to revive the orthodox principles, beliefs, and practices of the Lutheran Church. [1875–80] **—ne′o-Lu′ther•an,** *adj., n.*

ne•o•lyte (nē′ə līt′), *n.* a durable, semiflexible synthetic material used for the heels and soles of shoes. [sp. var. of *Neolite* a trademark]

Ne•o-Mel•a•ne•sian (nē′ō mel′ə nē′zhən, -shən), *n.* a pidgin language based on English and spoken in Melanesia, New Guinea, and NE Australia. Also called **Beach-la-mar, bêche-de-mer.** [1960–65]

ne•o•mer•can•til•ism (nē′ō mûr′kən ti liz′əm, -tē-, -tī-), *n.* an economic doctrine or policy during the early 20th century that set high tariffs and other import restrictions in order to protect domestic industries.

ne•o•my•cin (nē′ō mī′sin), *n. Pharm.* an antibiotic produced by an actinomycete, *Streptomyces fradiae,* administered orally or locally, used chiefly for skin, urinary tract, and eye infections and as a surgical antiseptic. [1945–50; NEO- + -MYCIN]

ne•on (nē′on), *n.* **1.** *Chem.* a chemically inert gaseous element occurring in small amounts in the earth's atmosphere, used chiefly in a type of electrical lamp. *Symbol:* Ne; *at. wt.:* 20.183; *at. no.:* 10; *density:* 0.9002 g/l at 0°C and 760 mm pressure. **2.** See **neon lamp. 3.** a sign or advertising sign formed from neon lamps. **—***adj.* **4.** using or containing the gas neon. **5.** made of or formed by a neon lamp or lamps: *a neon sign.* **6.** of, pertaining to, or characteristic of a tawdry urban district or of gaudy nighttime entertainment. [1895–1900; < NL < Gk *néon* new, recent (neut. of *néos*); see -ON[1]]

ne•o•na•tal (nē′ō nāt′l), *adj.* of or pertaining to newborn children. [1900–05; NEO- + NATAL] **—ne′o•na′tal•ly,** *adv.*

Neona′tal Behav′ioral Assess′ment Scale′, Brazelton.

ne•o•nate (nē′ə nāt′), *n.* a newborn child, or one in its first 28 days. [1930–35; NEO- + *-nate* < L *nātus* born; see NATIVE]

ne•o•na•tol•o•gy (nē′ō nā tol′ə jē), *n.* the study of the development and disorders of newborn children. [1955–60; NEONATE + -O- + -LOGY] **—ne′o•na•tol′o•gist,** *n.*

ne•o-Na•zi (nē′ō nät′sē, -nat′-), *n., pl.* **-zis.** (since 1945) a person who belongs to a political organization whose beliefs are inspired by or reminiscent of Nazism. [1945–50] **—ne•o-Na•zism** (nē′ō nät′siz əm, -nat′-), **ne′o-Na′zi•ism,** *n.*

ne′on lamp′, a gas-discharge bulb containing two electrodes in neon gas and emitting a glow when a voltage is applied across the electrodes. [1910–15]

ne′on tet′ra, a small, brightly colored red and blue characin fish, *Pracheirodon innesi,* native to parts of the Amazon basin: a popular aquarium fish. [1935–40]

ne•o•or•tho•dox (nē′ō ôr′thə doks′), *adj.* **1.** adhering to the principles of neoorthodoxy. **2.** advocating a return to older, proven methods or institutions. Also, **ne′o-or′tho•dox′.** [1955–60; NEO- + ORTHODOX]

ne•o•or•tho•dox•y (nē′ō ôr′thə dok′sē), *n.* a movement in Protestant theology, beginning after World War I, stressing the absolute sovereignty of God and chiefly characterized by a reaction against liberal theology and a reaffirmation of certain doctrines of the Reformation. Also, **ne′o-or′tho•dox′y.** Cf. **crisis theology, dialectical theology.** [1950–55; NEO- + ORTHODOXY]

ne•o•pa•gan•ism (nē′ō pā′gə niz′əm), *n.* a 20th-century revival of interest in the worship of nature, fertility, etc., as represented by various deities. [1875–80]

ne•o•pal•li•um (nē′ō pal′ē əm), *n., pl.* **-pal•li•a** (-pal′ē ə), **-pal•li•ums.** neocortex. [1900–05; < NL; see NEO-, PALLIUM] **—ne′o•pal′li•al,** *adj.*

ne•o-Pen•te•cos•tal (nē′ō pen′ti kôs′tl, -kos′-), *adj.* **1.** charismatic (def. 2). **—***n.* **2.** a member of a charismatic or neo-Pentecostal movement. [1970–75] **—ne′o-Pen′te•cos′tal•ist,** *adj., n.*

ne•o•phyte (nē′ə fīt′), *n.* **1.** a beginner or novice: *He's a neophyte at chess.* **2.** *Rom. Cath. Ch.* a novice. **3.** a person newly converted to a belief, as a heathen, heretic, or nonbeliever; proselyte. **4.** *Primitive Church.* a person newly baptized. [1540–50; < LL *neophytus* newly planted < Gk *neóphytos.* See NEO-, -PHYTE] **—ne•o•phyt•ic** (nē′ə fit′ik), **ne•o•phyt•ish** (nē′ə fī′tish), *adj.* **—ne•o•phyt•ism** (nē′ə fī tiz′əm), *n.*
—Syn. 1. greenhorn, tyro.

ne•o•pi•li•na (nē′ō pi lī′nə, -lē′-), *n.* any primitive mollusk of the genus *Neopilina,* having a serial repetition of internal organs that suggests a close relationship to the annelids. [< NL, equiv. to *neo-* NEO- + *Pilina* genus of mollusks]

ne•o•pla•sia (nē′ō plā′zhə, -zhē ə, -zē ə), *n.* **1.** *Pathol.* tumor growth. **2.** the formation and growth of new tissue. [1885–90; NEO- + -PLASIA]

ne•o•plasm (nē′ə plaz′əm), *n. Pathol.* a new, often uncontrolled growth of abnormal tissue; tumor. [1860–65; NEO- + PLASM] **—ne•o•plas•tic** (nē′ə plas′tik), *adj.*

ne•o•plas•ti•cism (nē′ō plas′tə siz′əm), *n.* (*sometimes cap.*) *Fine Arts.* the theory and practice of the de Stijl group, chiefly characterized by an emphasis on the formal structure of a work of art, and restriction of spatial or linear relations to vertical and horizontal movements as well as restriction of the artist's palette to black, white, and the primary colors. [< F *néo-plasticisme* (1920); see NEO-, PLASTICISM] **—ne′o•plas′tic,** *adj.* **—ne′o•plas′ti•cist,** *n.*

Ne•o•pla•to•nism (nē′ō plāt′n iz′əm), *n.* (*sometimes l.c.*) a philosophical system, originated in the 3rd century A.D. by Plotinus, founded chiefly on Platonic doctrine and Oriental mysticism, with later influences from Christianity. It holds that all existence consists of emanations from the One with whom the soul may be reunited. [1835–45; NEO- + PLATONISM] **—Ne•o•pla•ton•ic** (nē′ō plə ton′ik), *adj.* **—Ne′o•pla′to•nist,** *n.*

ne•o•pop•u•list (nē′ō pop′yə list), *adj.* pertaining to a revival of populism, esp. a sophisticated form appealing to commonplace values and prejudices. [1975–80] **—ne′o•pop′u•lism,** *n.*

ne•o•prene (nē′ə prēn′), *n. Chem.* an oil-resistant synthetic rubber: used chiefly in paints, putties, linings for tanks and chemical apparatus, and in crepe soles for shoes. [1935–40; NEO- + (CHLORO)PRENE]

Ne•op•tol•e•mus (nē′op tol′ə məs), *n. Class. Myth.* the son of Achilles, who slew Priam at the fall of Troy. Also called **Pyrrhus.**

ne•o-Py•thag•o•re•an•ism (nē′ō pi thag′ə rē′ə niz′əm), *n.* a philosophical system, established in Alexandria and Rome in the second century B.C., consisting mainly of revived Pythagorean doctrines with elements of Platonism and Stoicism. [1860–65] **—ne′o-Py•thag′o•re′an,** *n., adj.*

ne•o•re•al•ism (nē′ō rē′ə liz′əm), *n.* **1.** (*sometimes cap.*) any of various movements in literature, art, etc., that are considered as a return to a more realistic style. **2.** a philosophy developed chiefly by 20th-century American philosophers, including Montague and Santayana, characterized by a presentationist epistemology and by the assertion of the real status of universals. **3.** *Motion Pictures.* a style of filming prominent in Italy after World War II, characterized by a concern for social issues and often shot on location with untrained actors. Also called **New Realism** (for defs. 1, 2). [1915–20; NEO- + REALISM] **—ne′o•re′al•ist,** *n., adj.*

Ne•o•ri•can (nē′ō rē′kən) *n.* **1.** a Puerto Rican living in New York or one who has lived in New York and returned to Puerto Rico. **—***adj.* **2.** of or pertaining to Neoricans. Also, **Nuyorican.** [1970–75; NEO- + (PUERTO) RICAN]

ne•o•ro•man•ti•cism (nē′ō rō man′tə siz′əm), *n.* **1.** (*sometimes cap.*) *Fine Arts.* a style of painting developed in the 20th century, chiefly characterized by forms or images that project a sense of nostalgia and fantasy. **2.** any of various movements or styles in literature, motion-picture directing, architecture, etc., considered as a return to a more romantic style. [1880–85; NEO- + ROMANTICISM] **—ne′o•ro•man′tic,** *adj., n.*

ne•o-Scho•las•ti•cism (nē′ō skə las′tə siz′əm), *n. Philos., Theol.* a contemporary application of Scholasticism to modern problems and life. [1910–15] **—ne′o-Scho•las′tic,** *adj., n.*

Ne•o•spo•rin (nē′ō spôr′in, -spōr′-), *Pharm., Trademark.* a brand name for a solution primarily used in the local treatment of skin and eye infections.

ne•o•stig•mine (nē′ō stig′mēn, -min), *n. Pharm.* a synthetic anticholinesterase, $C_{12}H_{19}N_2O_2$, used in the treatment of myasthenia gravis, glaucoma, and postoperative urinary bladder distention. [1940–45; NEO- + *-stigmine* (after PROSTIGMIN; see -INE[2])]

ne•o•style (nē′ə stīl′), *n., v.,* **-styled, -styl•ing.** **—***n.* **1.** a manifolding device similar to the cyclostyle. **—***v.t.* **2.** to reproduce (copies, facsimiles, etc.) by means of a neostyle. [NEO- + STYLE]

Ne•o-Syn•eph•rine (nē′ō si nef′rin, -rēn), *Pharm., Trademark.* a brand of phenylephrine.

ne•ot•e•ny (nē ot′n ē), *n. Biol.* **1.** Also called **pedogenesis.** the production of offspring by an organism in its larval or juvenile form; the elimination of the adult phase of the life cycle. **2.** a slowing of the rate of development with the consequent retention in adulthood of a feature or features that appeared in an earlier phase in the life cycle of ancestral individuals. [1900–05; < NL *neotēnia* < Gk *neo-* NEO- + *teín(ein)* to stretch + *-ia* -Y[3]] **—ne•ot•e•nous** (nē ot′n əs), *adj.*

ne•o•ter•ic (nē′ə ter′ik), *adj.* **1.** modern; new; recent. **—***n.* **2.** a new or modern writer, thinker, etc. [1590–1600; < LL *neōtericus* new, modern < Gk *neōterikós* young, youthful, equiv. to *neṓter(os)* younger (comp. of *néos* NEW) + *-ikos* -IC] **—ne′o•ter′i•cal•ly,** *adv.*

ne•ot•er•ism (nē ot′ə riz′əm), *n.* **1.** an innovation in language, as a new word, term, or expression. **2.** the use of new words, terms, or expressions. [1870–75; < Gk *neōterismós* an attempt to change, equiv. to *neōter(ízein)* to make innovations (see NEOTERIZE) + *-ismos* -ISM]
—Syn. 1, 2. neologism.

ne•ot•er•ize (nē ot′ə rīz′), *v.i.,* **-ized, -iz•ing.** to coin new words, terms, or expressions; neologize. Also, *esp. Brit.,* **ne•ot′er•ise′.** [1870–75; < Gk *neōterízein,* equiv. to *neṓter(os)* (see NEOTERIC) + *-izein* -IZE]

Ne•o•trop•i•cal (nē′ō trop′i kəl), *adj. Biogeog.* belonging or pertaining to a geographical division comprising that part of the New World extending from the tropic of Cancer southward. [1855–60; NEO- + TROPICAL]

ne•o•type (nē′ə tīp′), *n. Biol.* a specimen selected to replace a holotype that has been lost or destroyed. [1850–55; NEO- + -TYPE]

ne•o•vas•cu•lar•i•za•tion (nē′ō vas′kyə lər ə zā′shən), *n.* the development of new blood vessels, esp. in tissues where circulation has been impaired by trauma or disease. [1975–80; NEO- + VASCULARIZATION]

ne•o•yt•ter•bi•um (nē′ō i tûr′bē əm), *n. Chem.* (formerly) ytterbium. [NEO- + YTTERBIUM]

NEP (nep), *n.* See **New Economic Policy.** Also, **Nep, N.E.P.**

Ne•pal (nə pôl′, -päl′, -pal′, nā-), *n.* a constitutional monarchy in the Himalayas between N India and Tibet. 13,000,000; ab. 54,000 sq. mi. (140,000 sq. km). *Cap.:* Katmandu.

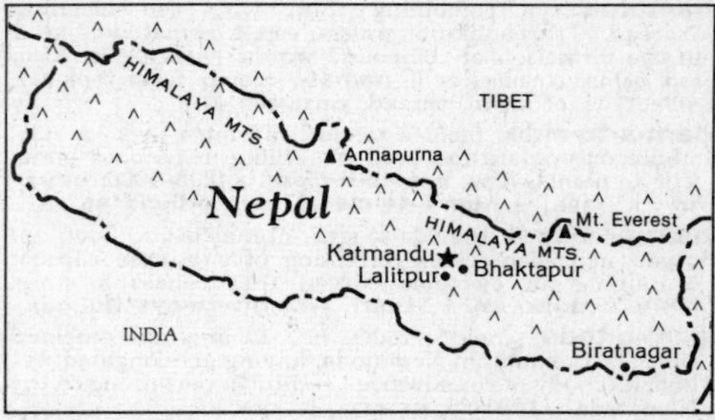

Nep•a•lese (nep′ə lēz′, -lēs′), *adj., n., pl.* **-lese** for 2. **—***adj.* **1.** of or pertaining to Nepal, its inhabitants, or their language. **—***n.* **2.** a native or inhabitant of Nepal. **3.** Nepali (def. 1). [1810–20; NEPAL + -ESE]

Ne•pal•i (nə pô′lē, -pä′-, -pal′ē, nā-), *n., pl.* **-lis, -li** for 2. **1.** Also, **Nepalese.** an Indic language spoken in Nepal. **2.** Nepalese (def. 2). **—***adj.* **3.** Nepalese (def. 1).

ne•pen•the (ni pen′thē), *n.* **1.** a drug or drink, or the plant yielding it, mentioned by ancient writers as having the power to bring forgetfulness of sorrow or trouble. **2.** anything inducing a pleasurable sensation of forgetfulness, esp. of sorrow or trouble. [1590–1600; < L *nēpenthes* < Gk *nēpenthés* herb for soothing, n. use of neut. of *nēpenthḗs* sorrowless, equiv. to *nē-* not + *pénth(os)* sorrow + *-ēs* adj. suffix] **—ne•pen′the•an,** *adj.*

ne•pen•thes (ni pen′thēz), *n., pl.* **-thes. 1.** nepenthe. **2.** any of various tropical Asian and Australian pitcher plants of the genus *Nepenthes,* having leaves usually in the form of cylindrical tubes. [< NL; see NEPENTHE]

ne•per (nē′pər, nā′-), *n. Physics.* the unit used to express the ratio of two amplitudes as a natural logarithm: equal to 8.68 dB. *Abbr.:* Np Also, **napier.** [1920–25; named after J. NEPER; see NAPIER]

Ne•per (nā′pər), *n.* **John.** See **Napier, John.**

neph-, var. of **nepho-** before a vowel: *nephanalysis.*

neph•a•nal•y•sis (nef′ə nal′ə sis), *n., pl.* **-ses** (-sēz′). **1.** a map or chart showing the distribution of types and amounts of clouds and precipitation at a given time. **2.** the preparation of such a map or chart. [1940–45; NEPH- + ANALYSIS]

Neph•e•le (nef′ə lē′), *n. Class. Myth.* a woman formed from a cloud by Zeus as a counterfeit of Hera, in order to deceive the lustful Ixion: mother by Ixion of the centaurs.

neph•e•line (nef′ə lin), *n.* a feldspathoid mineral, essentially sodium aluminum silicate, $NaAlSiO_4$, occurring in alkali-rich volcanic rocks. Also, **neph•e•lite** (nef′ə līt′). [1805–15; < F *néphéline,* equiv. to *néphél-* (< Gk *nephélē* cloud) + *-ine* -INE[2]]

neph•e•lin•ite (nef′ə lə nīt′), *n. Petrog.* a fine-grained, dark rock of volcanic origin, essentially a basalt containing nepheline but no feldspar and little or no olivine. [1860–65; NEPHELINE + -ITE[1]] **—neph•e•li•nit•ic** (nef′ə lə nit′ik), *adj.*

neph•e•lom•e•ter (nef′ə lom′i tər), *n.* **1.** *Bacteriol.* an apparatus containing a series of barium chloride standards used to determine the number of bacteria in a suspension. **2.** *Physical Chem.* an instrument for studying the density of suspended particles in a liquid by measuring the degree to which the suspension scatters light. [1880–85; *nephel-* (comb. form repr. Gk *nephélē* cloud; see NEBULA) + -O- + -METER] **—neph•e•lo•met•ric** (nef′ə lə me′trik), **neph′e•lo•met′ri•cal,** *adj.* **—neph′e•lo•met′ri•cal•ly,** *adv.* **—neph′e•lom′e•try,** *n.*

neph•ew (nef′yo͞o *or, esp. Brit.,* nev′yo͞o), *n.* **1.** a son of one's brother or sister. **2.** a son of one's spouse's brother or sister. **3.** an illegitimate son of a clergyman who has vowed celibacy (used as a euphemism). **4.** *Obs.* a direct descendant, esp. a grandson. **5.** *Obs.* a remote male descendant, as a grandnephew or cousin. [1250–1300; ME *neveu* < OF < L *nepōtem,* acc. of *nepōs* nephew, grandson; akin to OE *nefa,* D *neef,* G *Neffe,* ON *nefi;* the pseudo-etymological sp. with *ph* has influenced pron.]

nepho-, a combining form meaning "cloud," used in the formation of compound words: *nephometer.* Also, *esp. before a vowel,* **neph-.** [< Gk *néphos* a cloud, mass of clouds; see NEBULA]

ne•phom•e•ter (ne fom′i tər), *n.* an instrument for measuring the amount of cloud cover in the sky. [1905–10; NEPHO- + -METER]

neph•o•scope (nef′ə skōp′), *n.* an instrument for determining the speed and direction of cloud motion. [1880–85; NEPHO- + -SCOPE]

nephr-, var. of **nephro-** before a vowel: *nephralgia.*

ne•phral•gi•a (nə fral′jē ə, -jə), *n. Pathol.* kidney pain. [1790–1800; NEPHR- + -ALGIA] **—ne•phral′gic,** *adj.*

ne•phrec•to•mize (nə frek′tə mīz′), *v.t.,* **-mized, -miz•ing.** *Surg.* to perform a nephrectomy upon. Also, *esp. Brit.,* **ne•phrec′to•mise′.** [1895–1900; NEPHRECTOM(Y) + -IZE]

ne•phrec•to•my (nə frek′tə mē), *n., pl.* **-mies.** *Surg.* excision of a kidney. [1875–80; NEPHR- + -ECTOMY]

neph•ric (nef′rik), *adj.* renal. [1885–90; NEPHR- + -IC]

ne•phrid•i•um (nə frid′ē əm), *n., pl.* **-phrid•i•a** (-frid′ē ə). *Zool.* the excretory organ of many invertebrates, consisting of a tubule with one end opening into the body

CONCISE ETYMOLOGY KEY: <, descended or borrowed from; >, whence; b., blend of, blended; c., cognate with; cf., compare; deriv., derivative; equiv., equivalent; imit., imitative; obl., oblique; r., replacing; s., stem; sp., spelling, spelled; resp., respelling, respelled; trans., translation; ?, origin unknown; *, unattested; ‡, probably earlier than. See the full key inside the front cover.

cavity and the other opening into a pore at the body surface. [1875–80; < NL; see NEPHR-, -IDIUM] **—ne•phrid′•i•al,** *adj.*

neph•rite (nef′rīt), *n. Mineral.* a compact or fibrous variety of actinolite, varying from whitish to dark green: a form of jade. [1785–95; < G *Nephrit.* See NEPHR-, -ITE[1]]

ne•phri•tis (nə frī′tis), *n. Pathol.* inflammation of the kidneys, esp. in Bright's disease. [1570–80; < LL *nephrītis* a disease of the kidneys < Gk *nephrîtis.* See NEPHR-, -ITIS] **—ne•phrit•ic** (nə frit′ik), *adj.*

nephro-, a combining form meaning "kidney," used in the formation of compound words: *nephrolith.* Also, *esp. before a vowel,* **nephr-.** [comb. form repr. Gk *nephrós* kidney, kidneys]

neph•ro•lith (nef′rə lith), *n. Pathol.* a renal calculus; kidney stone. [NEPHRO- + -LITH] **—neph′ro•lith′ic,** *adj.*

neph•ro•li•thot•o•my (nef′rō li thot′ə mē), *n., pl.* **-mies.** *Surg.* incision or opening of a kidney pelvis for removal of a calculus. [1840–50; NEPHROLITH + -O- + -TOMY]

ne•phrol•o•gy (nə frol′ə jē), *n.* the branch of medical science that deals with the kidney. [1835–45; NEPHRO- + -LOGY] **—ne•phrol′o•gist,** *n.*

neph•ron (nef′ron), *n. Anat., Zool.* the filtering and excretory unit of the kidney, consisting of the glomerulus and tubules. [1930–35; < G; alter. of Gk *nephrós* kidney]

ne•phrop•a•thy (nə frop′ə thē), *n. Pathol.* any disease of the kidney. [1915–20; NEPHRO- + -PATHY] **—neph•ro•path•ic** (nef′rə path′ik), *adj.*

ne•phro•sis (nə frō′sis), *n. Pathol.* kidney disease, esp. marked by noninflammatory degeneration of the tubular system. [1915–20; < NL; see NEPHR-, -OSIS] **—ne•phrot•ic** (nə frot′ik), *adj.*

neph•ro•stome (nef′rə stōm′), *n.* **1.** *Zool.* the ciliated opening of a nephridium into the coelom. **2.** *Embryol.* a similar opening from the coelom into a tubule of the embryonic kidney. [1885–90; NEPHRO- + -STOME] **—ne•phros•to•mous** (nə fros′tə məs), **neph′ro•sto′mi•al,** *adj.*

ne•phrot•o•my (nə frot′ə mē), *n., pl.* **-mies.** *Surg.* incision into the kidney, as for the removal of a calculus. [1690–1700; < NL *nephrotomia.* See NEPHRO-, -TOMY]

Neph•ta•li (nef′tə lī′), *n. Douay Bible.* Naphtali.

ne plus ul•tra (ne′ plo͞os′ o͞ol′trä; *Eng.* nē′ plus′ ul′trə, nā′), *Latin.* **1.** the highest point; acme. **2.** the most intense degree of a quality or state.

nep•man (nep′mən), *n., pl.* **-men.** (in the Soviet Union) a person who engaged briefly in private enterprise during the New Economic Policy of the 1920's. [< Russ *nèpman,* equiv. to *nèp,* acronym from *Nóvaya èkonomícheskaya polítika* NEW ECONOMIC POLICY + *-man* < G *-mann* or E -MAN] **—Usage.** See **-man.**

Ne•pos (nē′pos, nep′os), *n.* **Cornelius,** 99?–24? B.C., Roman biographer and historian.

nep•o•tism (nep′ə tiz′əm), *n.* patronage bestowed or favoritism shown on the basis of family relationship, as in business and politics: *She was accused of nepotism when she made her nephew an officer of the firm.* [1655–65; < It *nepotismo.* See NEPHEW, -ISM] **—ne•pot•ic** (nə pot′ik), **nep′o•tis′tic, nep′o•tis′ti•cal,** *adj.* **—nep′o•tist,** *n.*

nep•tune (nep′to͞on, -tyo͞on), *n.* any whelk of the genus *Neptunea,* esp. *N. decemcostata,* common along the eastern coast of North America and having a shell with seven to ten raised reddish-brown spiral ridges on a pale beige or yellow background. [< NL *Neptunea;* see NEPTUNE, -EA]

Nep•tune (nep′to͞on, -tyo͞on), *n.* **1.** the ancient Roman god of the sea, identified with the Greek god Poseidon. **2.** the sea or ocean: *Neptune's mighty roar.* **3.** *Astron.* the planet eighth in order from the sun, having an equatorial diameter of 30,200 mi. (48,600 km), a mean distance from the sun of 2794.4 million mi. (4497.1 million km), a period of revolution of 164.81 years, and two moons. See table under **planet** (def. 1). **4.** a township in E New Jersey. 28,366.

Nep•tu•ni•an (nep to͞o′nē ən, -tyo͞o′-), *adj.* **1.** pertaining to Neptune or the sea. **2.** pertaining to the planet Neptune. **3.** (*often l.c.*) *Geol.* formed by the action of water. [1650–60; NEPTUNE + -IAN]

nep•tu•ni•um (nep to͞o′nē əm, -tyo͞o′-), *n. Chem., Physics.* a transuranic element produced in nuclear reactors by the neutron bombardment of U-238: decays rapidly to plutonium and then to U-235. *Symbol:* Np; *at. no.:* 93. [1940–45; NEPTUNE + -IUM]

ne•ral (nēr′al), *n.* citral b. See under **citral.** [1935–40; NER(OL) + -AL[3]]

Ner•bud•da (nər bud′ə), *n.* Narbada.

nerd (nûrd), *n. Slang.* **1.** a stupid, irritating, ineffectual, or unattractive person. **2.** an intelligent but single-minded person obsessed with a nonsocial hobby or pursuit: *a computer nerd.* Also, **nurd.** [1960–65, *Amer.*; obscurely derived expressive formation]

nerd•y (nûr′dē), *adj.,* **nerd•i•er, nerd•i•est.** *Slang.* of or like a nerd. [1975–80; NERD + -Y[1]]

ne•re•id (nēr′ē id), *n.* **1.** any elongate cylindrical worm of the polychaete family Nereididae, including clamworms. —*adj.* **2.** of or pertaining to the family Nereididae. [1830–40; < NL *Nereididae* family name; see NEREID, -IDAE]

Ne•re•id (nēr′ē id), *n.* **1.** (*sometimes l.c.*) *Class. Myth.* any of the 50 daughters of Nereus; a sea nymph. **2.** *Astron.* a moon of the planet Neptune. [< L *Nērēid-* (s. of *Nērēis*) < Gk, s. of *Nērēís.* See NEREUS, -ID[1]]

Ne•re•us (nēr′ē əs, nēr′yo͞os), *n. Class. Myth.* a sea god, the son of Pontus and Gaea and father of the Nereids.

Ner•gal (nâr′gäl), *n.* (in Akkadian mythology) the god ruling, with Ereshkigal, the world of the dead.

Ne•ri (nâr′ē; *It.* ne′RE), *n.* **Saint Philip** (*Filippo Neri*), 1515–95, Italian priest: founder of Congregation of the Oratory.

ne•ri•ne (nə rī′nē), *n.* any of several bulbous plants belonging to the genus *Nerine,* of the amaryllis family, native to southern Africa, having funnel-shaped red, pink, or white flowers. [< NL (1820); L *Nērīnē* a Nereid]

ne•rit•ic (nə rit′ik), *adj.* of or pertaining to the region of water lying directly above the sublittoral zone of the sea bottom. Cf. **oceanic, pelagic.** [< G *neritisch* (1890), appar. after Gk *Nērēís* NEREID or *Nēreús* NEREUS, though derivation is unclear; see -IC]

Nernst (nârnst, nûrnst; *Germ.* nernst), *n.* **Wal•ther Her•man** (väl′tər her′män), 1864–1941, German physicist and chemist: Nobel prize for chemistry 1920.

Ne•ro (nēr′ō), *n.* **1.** (*Lucius Domitius Ahenobarbus*) (*"Nero Claudius Caesar Drusus Germanicus"*) A.D. 37–68, emperor of Rome 54–68, known for his cruelty and depravity. **2.** a male given name.

ne•rol (nēr′ôl, -ol, ner′-), *n. Chem.* a colorless, liquid, unsaturated alcohol, $C_{10}H_{18}O$, an isomeric form of geraniol occurring in neroli oil, used in perfumery. [1900–05; NER(OLI OIL) + -OL[1]]

ner′o•li oil′ (ner′ə lē, nēr′-), a brown essential oil derived from the flowers of the orange tree, *Citrus aurantium,* used in the manufacture of perfumes. Also called **orange flower oil.** [1720–30; < F *néroli* < It *neroli,* after Anne-Marie de la Tremouille de Noirmontier, Princess of *Nerola,* who is said to have discovered it ca. 1670]

Ne•ro•nize (nēr′ō nīz′), *v.t.,* **-nized, -niz•ing. 1.** to characterize (a person) as resembling Nero. **2.** to make depraved in the manner of Nero. **3.** to rule over, tyrannize, or oppress in the manner of Nero. Also, *esp. Brit.,* **Ne′ro•nise′.** [1665–75; < L *Nerōn-* (s. of *Nerō* NERO) + -IZE]

Ner Ta•mid (*Seph.* neR′ tä mēd′; *Ashk.* nâR′ tô mid′; *Eng.* nâr′ tä′mid), *Hebrew.* a lamp that is set above and in front of the Holy Ark in a synagogue and is kept burning constantly. [*nēr tāmīdh* eternal light]

Ner•thus (nûr′thəs), *n. Germanic Myth.* goddess of fertility, described by Tacitus in his *Germania:* later appeared in Scandinavian mythology as the god Njord. Cf. **Njord.**

nerts (nûrts), *interj. Older Slang.* nuts (def. 1). Also, **nertz.** [1930–35; by alter.]

Ne•ru•da (ne Ro͞o′thä; *Eng.* nə ro͞o′də), *n.* **Pa•blo** (pä′vlō; *Eng.* pä′blō), (*Neftalí Ricardo Reyes Basoalto*), 1904–73, Chilean poet and diplomat: Nobel prize for literature 1971.

Ner•va (nûr′və), *n.* **Marcus Coc•ce•ius** (kok sē′yəs), A.D. 32?–98, emperor of Rome 96–98.

nerv•al (nûr′vəl), *adj.* neural. [1630–40; < LL *nervālis* of, belonging to nerves, equiv. to L *nerv(us)* NERVE + *-ālis* -AL[1]]

Ner•val (neR vAl′), *n.* **Gé•rard de** (zhā RAR′ də), (*Gérard Labrunie*), 1808–55, French writer.

ner•va•tion (nûr vā′shən), *n.* venation. Also, **ner•va•ture** (nûr′və cho͝or′, -chər). [1715–25; NERVE + -ATION]

nerve (nûrv), *n., v.,* **nerved, nerv•ing.** —*n.* **1.** one or more bundles of fibers forming part of a system that conveys impulses of sensation, motion, etc., between the brain or spinal cord and other parts of the body. **2.** a sinew or tendon: *to strain every nerve.* **3.** firmness or courage under trying circumstances: *an assignment requiring nerve.* **4.** boldness; audacity; impudence; impertinence: *He had the nerve to say that?* **5. nerves,** nervousness: *an attack of nerves.* **6.** strength, vigor, or energy: *a test of nerve and stamina.* **7.** (not in technical use) pulp tissue of a tooth. **8.** *Bot.* a vein, as in a leaf. **9.** a line, or one of a system of lines, extending across something. **10. get on one's nerves,** to irritate, annoy, or provoke one: *Boisterous children get on my nerves.* —*v.t.* **11.** to give strength, vigor, or courage to: *Encouragement had nerved him for the struggle.* [1350–1400; ME: nerve, tendon < L *nervus* sinew, tendon; akin to Gk *neûron* (see NEURON); r. ME *nerf* < MF < L, as above] **—Syn. 3.** steadfastness, intrepidity, fortitude, resolution. **6.** power, force, might. **11.** strengthen, fortify, invigorate, steel, brace. **—Ant. 6.** weakness. **11.** weaken.

nerve′ block′, *Med.* an arrest of the passage of impulses through a nerve by means of pressure on the nerve or by injection of an anesthetic into or around the nerve. [1920–25]

nerve′ cell′, neuron. [1855–60]

nerve′ cen′ter, 1. a group of nerve cells closely connected with one another and acting together in the performance of some function. **2.** a source of information, authority, action, etc.: *The communications room is the nerve center of a battleship.* [1865–70]

nerve′ cord′, 1. a single hollow tract of nervous tissue that constitutes the central nervous system of chordates and develops into the spinal cord and brain in vertebrates. **2.** a solid double strand of nerve fibers along the length of the body in elongate invertebrates, as earthworms and insects, connecting with a pair of nerve ganglia at each body segment. [1875–80]

nerve′ fi′ber, *Anat., Physiol.* a process, axon, or dendrite of a nerve cell. [1830–40]

nerve′ gas′, any of several poison gases, derived chiefly from phosphoric acid, that weaken or paralyze the nervous system, esp. that part of the system controlling respiration. [1935–40]

nerve′ growth′ fac′tor, *Biochem.* a protein that promotes the growth, organization, and maintenance of sympathetic and some sensory nerve cells. *Abbr.:* NGF [1965–70]

nerve′ im′pulse, *Physiol.* a progressive wave of electric and chemical activity along a nerve fiber that stimulates or inhibits the action of a muscle, gland, or other nerve cell. [1895–1900]

nerve•less (nûrv′lis), *adj.* **1.** without nervousness, as in emergencies; calm; collected. **2.** lacking strength or vigor; feeble; weak. **3.** lacking firmness or courage; spiritless; cowardly. **4.** *Anat., Bot.* having no nerves. [1725–35; NERVE + -LESS] **—nerve′less•ly,** *adv.* **—nerve′less•ness,** *n.*

nerve′ net′, a diffuse branching network of nerve cells connecting the sensory and muscular cells of coelenterates and primitive flatworms. [1900–05]

nerve-rack•ing (nûrv′rak′ing), *adj.* extremely irritating, annoying, or trying: *a nerve-racking day; a nerve-racking noise.* Also, **nerve′-wrack′ing.** [1805–15]

nerve′ root′, *Anat.* a nerve fiber bundle that emerges from either side of the spinal cord and joins with a complementary bundle to form each spinal nerve in the series of spinal nerves: the root at the rear of the spinal cord **(dorsal root** or **sensory root)** conveys sensations to the central nervous system, and the root at the front **(ventral root** or **motor root)** conveys impulses to the muscles. [1875–80]

nerve′ trunk′, *Anat.* the main stem of a nerve. [1850–55]

nerv•ine (nûr′vēn, -vīn), *adj.* **1.** of or pertaining to the nerves. **2.** acting on or relieving disorders of the nerves; soothing the nerves. —*n.* **3.** a nervine medicine. [1655–65; < NL *nervīnus,* equiv. to L *nerv(us)* NERVE + *-īnus* -INE[1]]

ner•vos•i•ty (nûr vos′i tē), *n.* the quality of being nervous; nervousness. [1605–15 in sense "strength"; NERV(OUS) + -OSITY; cf. L *nervōsitās* strength]

nerv•ous (nûr′vəs), *adj.* **1.** highly excitable; unnaturally or acutely uneasy or apprehensive: *to become nervous under stress.* **2.** of or pertaining to the nerves: *nervous tension.* **3.** affecting the nerves: *nervous diseases.* **4.** suffering from, characterized by, or originating in disordered nerves. **5.** characterized by or attended with acute uneasiness or apprehension: *a nervous moment for us all.* **6.** having or containing nerves. **7.** sinewy or strong. **8.** *Archaic.* vigorous or spirited. [1350–1400; ME < L *nervōsus* sinewy, equiv. to *nerv(us)* NERVE + *-ōsus* -OUS] **—nerv′ous•ly,** *adv.* **—nerv′ous•ness,** *n.* **—Syn. 1.** fearful, timid, timorous. **—Ant. 1.** confident, bold.

nerv′ous break′down, (not in technical use) any disabling mental disorder requiring treatment. [1900–05, *Amer.*]

nerv′ous exhaus′tion, extreme mental and physical fatigue caused by excessive emotional stress; neurasthenia. Also called **nerv′ous prostra′tion.** [1925–30]

nerv′ous Nel′lie, *Informal.* a constantly nervous, worried, or timid person. [1925–30]

nerv′ous sys′tem, *Anat., Zool.* **1.** the system of nerves and nerve centers in an animal or human, including the brain, spinal cord, nerves, and ganglia. **2.** a particular part of this system. Cf. **autonomic nervous system, central nervous system, peripheral nervous system.** [1730–40]

ner•vule (nûr′vyo͞ol), *n. Zool.* a small branch of a nerve in the wing of an insect. [1885–90; NERVE + -ULE]

ner•vu•ra•tion (nûr′vyə rā′shən), *n. Entomol.* the arrangement of the veins in the wing of an insect. Also, **ner•vu•la•tion** (nûr′vyə lā′shən). [1895–1900; NERVURE + -ATION]

ner•vure (nûr′vyo͝or), *n. Bot., Zool.* a vein, as of a leaf or the wing of an insect. [1810–20; < F: rib. See NERVE, -URE]

nerv•y (nûr′vē), *adj.,* **nerv•i•er, nerv•i•est. 1.** brashly presumptuous or insolent; pushy: *a nervy thing to say; a nervy trick to pull.* **2.** having or showing courage; brave or bold: *the nervy feats of the mountaineers.* **3.** strong; sinewy; vigorous: *a hard, nervy physique.* **4.** *Chiefly Brit.* straining one's patience or forbearance; trying. **5.** nervous; excitable; on edge. [1600–10; NERVE + -Y[1]] **—nerv′i•ly,** *adv.* **—nerv′i•ness,** *n.*

n.e.s., not elsewhere specified. Also, **N.E.S.**

nesc•ience (nesh′əns, nesh′ē əns, nes′ē-), *n.* **1.** lack of knowledge; ignorance. **2.** agnosticism. [1605–15; < LL *nescientia* ignorance, equiv. to *ne-* not + *scientia* knowledge; see SCIENCE] **—nes′cient,** *adj.*

ne•so•sil•i•cate (nē′sō sil′i kit, -kāt′, nes′ō-), *n. Mineral.* any silicate, as olivine, in which the SiO_4 tetrahedra are not interlinked. Cf. **cyclosilicate, inosilicate, sorosilicate, tektosilicate.** [< Gk *nêso(s)* island + SILICATE]

ness (nes), *n.* a headland; promontory; cape. [bef. 900; ME *-nes(se)* (in place names), in part continuing OE *næs,* in part < ON *nes;* akin to NOSE]

-ness, a native English suffix attached to adjectives and participles, forming abstract nouns denoting quality and state (and often, by extension, something exemplifying a quality or state): *darkness; goodness; kindness; obligingness; preparedness.* [ME, OE *-nes, -nis,* c. G *-nis,* Goth *-(n)assus;* suffix orig. **-assus; -n-* by false division of words with adj. and ptp. stems ending in *-n-;* cf. OE *efnes* (later *efen-nys*) EVENNESS]

Nes•sel•rode (nes′əl rōd′), *n.* a mixture of preserved fruits, nuts, etc., used as a sauce or in pies, puddings, ice

CONCISE PRONUNCIATION KEY: *act, cāpe, dâre, pärt; set, ēqual; if, īce; ox, ōver, ôrder, oil, bo͝ok, bo͞ot, out; up, ûrge; child; sing; shoe; thin, that;* zh as in *treasure.* ə = *a* as in *alone, e* as in *system, i* as in *easily, o* as in *gallop, u* as in *circus;* ᵊ as in *fire* (fīᵊr), *hour* (ouᵊr). l and n can serve as syllabic consonants, as in *cradle* (krād′l), and *button* (but′n). See the full key inside the front cover.

cream, or the like. [1835–45; said to have been invented by chef of NESSELRODE]

Nes·sel·rode (nes′əl rōd′), *n.* **Count Karl Robert** (*Karl Vasilyevich*), 1780–1862, Russian diplomat and statesman.

Nes·sie (nes′ē), *n. Informal.* See **Loch Ness Monster.** [(LOCH) NESS + -IE]

ness·ler·ize (nes′lə rīz′), *v.*, **-ized, -iz·ing.** *v.t.* (*sometimes cap.*) to test (water, liquid solutions, etc.) for ammonia by means of Nessler's reagent. Also, *esp. Brit.*, **ness′ler·ise′.** [1870–75; named after Julius Nessler (1827–1905), German chemist; see -IZE]

Ness′ler's rea′gent (nes′lərz), an aqueous solution of potassium iodide, mercuric chloride, and potassium hydroxide, used as a test for the presence of ammonia. Also called **Ness′ler's solu′tion.** [1870–75; see NESSLERIZE]

Nes·sus (nes′əs), *n. Class. Myth.* a centaur who, on attempting to seduce Deianira, the wife of Hercules, was shot by Hercules with a poisoned arrow. Before Nessus died, he gave to Deianira the poisoned tunic that ultimately caused Hercules' death. Also, **Nes′sos.**

nest (nest), *n.* **1.** a pocketlike, usually more or less circular structure of twigs, grass, mud, etc., formed by a bird, often high in a tree, as a place in which to lay and incubate its eggs and rear its young; any protected place used by a bird for these purposes. **2.** a place used by insects, fishes, turtles, rabbits, etc., for depositing their eggs or young. **3.** a number of birds, insects, animals, etc., inhabiting one such place. **4.** a snug retreat or refuge; resting place; home. **5.** an assemblage of things lying or set close together, as a series of boxes or trays, that fit within each other: *a nest of tables.* **6.** a place where something bad is fostered or flourishes: *a nest of vice; a robber's nest.* **7.** the occupants or frequenters of such a place. —*v.t.* **8.** to settle or place (something) in or as if in a nest: *to nest dishes in straw.* **9.** to fit or place one within another: *to nest boxes for more compact storage.* —*v.i.* **10.** to build or have a nest: *The swallows nested under the eaves.* **11.** to settle in or as if in a nest. **12.** to fit together or within another or one another: *bowls that nest easily for storage.* **13.** to search for or collect nests: *to go nesting.* **14.** *Computers.* to place a routine inside another routine that is at a higher hierarchical level. [bef. 900; ME, OE (c. D, G *nest;* akin to L *nīdus* nest, OIr *net,* Welsh *nyth,* Skt *nīḍa* lair) << IE *nizdo- bird's nest, equiv. to *ni down (see NETHER) + *zd-, var. of *sd-, ablaut var. of *sed-, v. base meaning "sit" (see SIT) + *-o- theme vowel] —**nest′a·ble,** *adj.* —**nest′er,** *n.* —**nest′like′,** *adj.* —**nest′y,** *adj.*

nest·ed (nes′tid), *adj. Math.* (of an ordered collection of sets or intervals) having the property that each set is contained in the preceding set and the length or diameter of the sets approaches zero as the number of sets tends to infinity. [1720–30; NEST + -ED[3]]

nest′ egg′, 1. money saved and held in reserve for emergencies, retirement, etc. **2.** a natural or artificial egg placed in a nest to induce a hen to continue laying eggs there. [1600–10]

nest′ing ta′ble, one of a set of usually three or four small tables that are graduated in size so that they may be stacked on top of one another. Also called **stack table.** [1930–35]

nes·tle (nes′əl), *v.*, **-tled, -tling.** —*v.i.* **1.** to lie close and snug, like a bird in a nest; snuggle or cuddle. **2.** to lie or be located in a sheltered spot; be naturally or pleasantly situated: *a cottage nestling in a pine grove.* **3.** *Archaic.* **a.** to make or have a nest. **b.** to make one's home; settle in a home. —*v.t.* **4.** to settle or ensconce snugly: *He nestled himself into the hay for a short nap.* **5.** to put or press confidingly or affectionately: *She nestled her head on his shoulder.* **6.** to provide with or settle in a nest, as a bird. [bef. 1000; ME *nestlen,* OE *nestlian,* c. D *nestelen.* See NEST, -LE] —**nes′tler,** *n.*

nest·ling (nest′ling, nes′ling), *n.* **1.** a young bird not yet old enough to leave the nest. **2.** a young child or infant. [1350–1400; ME; see NEST, -LING[1]]

nest′ of draw′ers, a miniature chest of drawers made in the 18th century, often set on top of a desk or table. [1695–1705]

Nes·tor (nes′tər, -tôr), *n. Class. Myth.* the oldest and wisest of the Greeks in the Trojan War and a king of Pylos.

Nes·to·ri·an (ne stôr′ē ən, -stōr′-), *n.* one of a sect of followers of Nestorius who denied the hypostatic union and were represented as maintaining the existence of two distinct persons in Christ. [1400–50; late ME < LL *Nestoriānus.* See NESTORIUS, -AN] —**Nes·to′ri·an·ism,** *n.*

Nes·to·ri·us (ne stôr′ē əs, -stōr′-), *n.* died A.D. 451?, Syrian ecclesiastic: patriarch of Constantinople 428–431.

net[1] (net), *n., v.,* **net·ted, net·ting.** —*n.* **1.** a bag or other contrivance of strong thread or cord worked into an open, meshed fabric, for catching fish, birds, or other animals: *a butterfly net.* **2.** a piece of meshed fabric designed to serve a specific purpose, as to divide a court in racket games or protect against insects: *a tennis net; a mosquito net.* **3.** anything serving to catch or ensnare: *a police net to trap the bank robber.* **4.** a lacelike fabric with a uniform mesh of cotton, silk, rayon, nylon, etc., often forming the foundation of any of various laces. **5.** (in tennis, badminton, etc.) a ball that hits the net. **6.** Often, **nets.** the goal in hockey or lacrosse. **7.** any network or reticulated system of filaments, lines, veins, or the like. **8.** *Math.* the abstraction, in topology, of a sequence; a map from a directed set to a given space. **9.** any network containing computers and telecommunications equipment. **10.** (*cap.*) *Astron.* the constellation Reticulum. **11.** *Informal.* a radio or television network. —*v.t.* **12.** to cover, screen, or enclose with a net or netting: *netting the bed to keep out mosquitoes.* **13.** to take with a net: *to net fish.* **14.** to set or use nets in (a river, stream, etc.), as for catching fish. **15.** to catch or ensnare: *to net a dangerous criminal.* **16.** (in tennis, badminton, etc.) to hit (the ball) into the net. [bef. 900; ME *net* (n.), *netten* (v.), OE *net(t)* (n.); c. D, ON *net,* Goth *nati,* G *Netz*] —**net′ta·ble,** *adj.* —**net′like′,** *adj.*
—**Syn. 15.** seize, capture, trap.

net[2] (net), *adj., n., v.,* **net·ted, net·ting.** —*adj.* **1.** remaining after deductions, as for charges or expenses (opposed to *gross*): *net earnings.* **2.** sold at a stated price with all parts and charges included and with all deductions having been made. **3.** final; totally conclusive: *After all that work, what was the net result?* **4.** (of weight) after deduction of tare, tret, or both. —*n.* **5.** net income, profit, or the like. —*v.t.* **6.** to gain or produce as clear profit. [1300–50; ME; var. of NEAT[1]] —**net′ta·ble,** *adj.*

NET, National Educational Television.

net′ as′sets, the total assets of a business minus its total liabilities. Also called **net worth.**

net·ball (net′bôl′), *n.* **1.** *Tennis.* a ball, on a return shot, that hits the top of the net and drops on the other side of the court, thus remaining in play. **2.** *Brit.* a game similar to basketball, played with a soccer ball, usually outdoors. [1895–1900; NET[1] + BALL[1]]

net′ blotch′, *Plant Pathol.* a disease of barley, characterized by a brown, netlike discoloration of the leaves, caused by fungi of the genus *Helminthosporium.*

Neth., Netherlands.

neth·er (neth′ər), *adj.* **1.** lying or believed to lie beneath the earth's surface; infernal: *the nether regions.* **2.** lower or under: *his nether lip.* [bef. 900; ME *nethere,* OE *neothera, nithera,* deriv. of *nither* down (c. G *nieder*), lit., further down, equiv. to *ni-* down + *-ther* comp. suffix] —**neth′er·ward,** *adj.*

Neth·er·land·ic (neth′ər lan′dik), *n.* **1.** Dutch (def. 8). —*adj.* **2.** of or pertaining to the Netherlands.

Neth·er·lands (neth′ər ləndz), *n.* **the,** (*used with a singular or plural v.*) a kingdom in W Europe, bordering on the North Sea, West Germany, and Belgium. 14,208,600; 13,433 sq. mi. (34,790 sq. km). *Capitals:* Amsterdam and The Hague. Also called **Holland.** Dutch, **Nederland.** —**Neth·er·land·er** (neth′ər lan′dər, -lən-), *n.* —**Neth′er·land′i·an,** *adj.*

Neth′erlands Antil′les, a Netherlands overseas territory in the Caribbean Sea, N and NE of Venezuela; includes the islands of Aruba, Bonaire, Curaçao, Saba, and St. Eustatius, and the S part of St. Martin: considered an integral part of the Dutch realm. 247,148; 366 sq. mi. (948 sq. km). *Cap.:* Willemstad. Formerly, **Curaçao, Neth′erlands West′ In′dies, Dutch West Indies.** —**Neth′erlands Antil′lean.**

Neth′erlands East′ In′dies, a former name of the Republic of Indonesia.

Neth′erlands Guian′a, a former name of Suriname.

Neth′erlands New′ Guin′ea, a former name of **Irian Jaya.**

neth·er·most (neth′ər mōst′, -məst), *adj.* lowest; farthest down: *the nethermost depths of the ocean.* [1250–1300; ME *nethermast.* See NETHER, -MOST]

neth′er world′, 1. the infernal regions; hell. **2.** the afterworld, or the hereafter. Also, **neth′er·world′.** [1630–40]

Né·thou (*Fr.* nā to͞o′), *n.* **Pic de** (*Fr.* pēk də), a mountain in NE Spain: highest peak of the Pyrenees. 11,165 ft. (3400 m). Spanish, **Pico de Aneto.**

net′ in′come, the excess of revenues and gains of a business over expenses and losses during a given period of time. [1760–70]

ne·ti ne·ti (nā′ti nā′ti), *Sanskrit.* neither this nor that (used in Hinduism to describe the undifferentiated and ineffable nature of Brahman).

net′ line′. See **neat line.**

net·man (net′man′, -mən), *n., pl.* **-men** (-men′, -mən). **1.** a tennis player. **2.** *Tennis.* the partner in a doubles game who stands near the net in the forward part of the court. [NET[1] + MAN[1]]

net′ na′tional prod′uct, the gross national product less allowance for depreciation of capital goods. *Abbr.:* NNP Cf. **national income.** [1940–45]

net′ prof′it, the actual profit made on a business transaction, sale, etc., or during a specific period of business activity, after deducting all costs from gross receipts. [1660–70]

net′ reg′ister ton′. See **net ton** (def. 1).

net′ reg′ister ton′nage. See **net tonnage.**

net′ silk′, *Chiefly Brit.* See **thrown silk.**

ne·tsu·ke (net′skē, -skā; *Japn.* ne′tso͝o ke′), *n.* (in Japanese art) a small figure of ivory, wood, metal, or ceramic, originally used as a buttonlike fixture on a man's sash, from which small personal belongings were hung. [1880–85; < Japn, equiv. to *ne* root + *tsuke* (earlier *tuke(y)* attach]

net′ted mel′on, a variety of muskmelon, *Cucumis melo reticulatus,* of the gourd family, having reticulate markings on the skin and green to reddish-orange flesh. Also called **nutmeg melon.**

net·ting (net′ing), *n.* any of various kinds of net fabric: *fish netting; mosquito netting.* [1560–70; NET[1] + -ING[1]]

net′ting knot′. See **sheet bend.**

net·tle (net′l), *n., v.,* **-tled, -tling.** —*n.* **1.** any plant of the genus *Urtica,* covered with stinging hairs. Cf. **nettle family. 2.** any of various allied or similar plants. **3. grasp the nettle,** *Australian.* to undertake or tackle an unpleasant task. —*v.t.* **4.** to irritate, annoy, or provoke. **5.** to sting as a nettle does. [bef. 900; ME; OE *netele* (n.); c. D *netel,* G *Nessel,* Norw *netla*] —**net′tle·like′,** *adj.* —**net′tler,** *n.* —**net′tly,** *adj.*

net′tle cell′, *Zool.* a nematocyst. [1865–70]

net′tle fam′ily, the plant family Urticaceae, characterized by herbaceous plants, trees, and shrubs, sometimes covered with stinging hairs, having alternate or opposite simple leaves, clusters of small flowers, and small, dry, seedlike fruit, and including baby's-tears, clearweed, nettles of the genus *Urtica,* and ramie.

net·tle·fish (net′l fish′), *n., pl.* (*esp. collectively*) **-fish,** (*esp. referring to two or more kinds or species*) **-fish·es.** jellyfish. [1885–90; NETTLE + FISH]

net′tle rash′, *Pathol.* urticaria resulting from contact with various plants causing local irritation. [1730–40]

net·tle·some (net′l səm), *adj.* **1.** causing irritation, vexation, or annoyance: *to cope with a nettlesome situation.* **2.** easily provoked or annoyed: *to become nettlesome over trivial matters.* [1760–70; NETTLE + -SOME[1]]

net′ ton′, 1. Also called **net register ton.** *Naut.* one gross ton registered as taxable. **2.** See **short ton.**

net′ ton′nage, the taxable gross tonnage of a merchant ship. Also called **net register tonnage.**

net-veined (net′vānd′), *adj. Bot.* having branched veins that form a network, as the leaves of most dicotyledonous plants. Cf. **parallel-veined.** [1860–65]

net-winged (net′wingd′), *adj. Entomol.* having reticulate wing venation. [1885–90]

net·work (net′wûrk′), *n.* **1.** any netlike combination of filaments, lines, veins, passages, or the like: *a network of arteries; a network of sewers under the city.* **2.** *Radio and Television.* **a.** a group of transmitting stations linked by wire or microwave relay so that the same program can be broadcast or telecast by all. **b.** a company or organization that provides programs to be broadcast over these stations: *She was hired by the network as program coordinator.* **3.** a system of interrelated buildings, offices, stations, etc., esp. over a large area or throughout a country, territory, region, etc.: *a network of supply depots.* **4.** *Elect.* an arrangement of conducting elements, as resistors, capacitors, or inductors, connected by conducting wire. **5.** a netting or net. **6.** *Telecommunications, Computers.* a system containing any combination of computers, computer terminals, printers, audio or visual display devices, or telephones interconnected by telecommunication equipment or cables: used to transmit or receive information. **7.** an association of individuals having a common interest, formed to provide mutual assistance, helpful information, or the like: *a network of recent college graduates.* —*v.i.* **8.** to cultivate people who can be helpful to one professionally, esp. in finding employment or moving to a higher position: *His business lunches were taken up with networking.* —*v.t.* **9.** to place (as a program from a local radio or television station) in or on a network: *The station will try to network the local cooking show.* **10.** to connect to a network. **11.** to distribute widely: *We charge a small fee for networking your résumé.* **12.** to cover with or as if with a network: *to network a bay with buoy markers.* **13.** to organize into a network: *to network the state's independent stations.* **14.** to broadcast (a program) over a radio or television network. [1550–60; 1910–15 for def. 2; NET[1] + WORK] —**net′work′er,** *n.*

net′work anal′ysis, a mathematical method of analyzing complex problems, as in transportation or project scheduling, by representing the problem as a network of lines and nodes. [1925–30]

net·work·ing (net′wûr′king), *n.* **1.** a supportive system of sharing information and services among individuals and groups having a common interest: *Working mothers in the community use networking to help themselves manage successfully.* **2.** the design, establishment, or utilization of a computer network. —*adj.* **3.** of or pertaining to a network or networking: *networking software, a networking system.* [1935–40; NETWORK + -ING[1]]

net′ worth′. See **net assets.** [1925–30]

Neu·châ·tel (no͞o′shə tel′, nyo͞o′-, no͞o′shə tel′, nyo͞o′-; *Fr.* nœ shä tel′), *n.* **1.** a canton in W Switzerland. 166,100; 309 sq. mi. (800 sq. km). **2.** the capital of this canton, on the Lake of Neuchâtel. 36,400. **3. Lake of,** a lake in W Switzerland. 85 sq. mi. (220 sq. km). German, **Neu·en·burg** (noi′ən bo͝ork′).

Neuf·châ·tel (no͞o′shə tel′, nyo͞o′-, no͞o′shə tel′, nyo͞o′-; *Fr.* nœ shä tel′), *n.* a soft, white cheese similar to cream cheese, made from whole or partly skimmed

CONCISE ETYMOLOGY KEY: <, descended or borrowed from; >, whence; b., blend of, blended; c., cognate with; cf., compare; deriv., derivative; equiv., equivalent; imit., imitative; obl., oblique; r., replacing; s., stem; sp., spelling, spelled; resp., respelling, respelled; trans., translation; ?, origin unknown; *, unattested; ‡, probably earlier than. See the full key inside the front cover.

milk in Neufchâtel, a town in N France. Also called **Neuf′châtel cheese′.** [1860–65]

Neuil·ly (nœ yē′), *n.* a suburb of Paris, in N France: treaty of peace (1919) between the Allies and Bulgaria. 66,095. Also called **Neuil·ly-sur-Seine** (nœ yē syr sen′).

neuk (nyo͞ok), *n. Scot.* nook.

Neu·mann (no͞o′mən, nyo͞o′- *for 1;* noi′män, -mən *for 2*), *n.* **1. Saint John Ne·pom·u·cene** (nə pom′ə sēn′), 1811–60, U.S. Roman Catholic clergyman and educator, born in Czechoslovakia: canonized 1977. **2. John von.** See **Von Neumann, John.**

neumes

neume (no͞om, nyo͞om), *n.* any of various symbols representing from one to four notes, used in the musical notation of the Middle Ages but now employed solely in the notation of Gregorian chant in the liturgical books of the Roman Catholic Church. [1400–50; late ME < ML *neuma* < Gk *pneûma* breath] —**neu·mat·ic** (no͞o mat′ik, nyo͞o-), **neu′mic,** *adj.*

Neu·pest (noi′pest), *n.* German name of **Ujpest.**

neur-, var. of **neuro-** before a vowel: *neuritis.*

neu·ral (no͝or′əl, nyo͝or′-), *adj.* of or pertaining to a nerve or the nervous system. [1830–40; NEUR- + -AL[1]] —**neu′ral·ly,** *adv.*

neu′ral crest′, *Embryol.* a group of ectodermal cells that develop into a variety of tissues, including spinal and autonomic ganglia, connective tissue around the brain and spinal cord, and parts of the facial bones.

neu·ral·gia (no͝o ral′jə, nyo͝o-), *n. Pathol.* sharp and paroxysmal pain along the course of a nerve. [1815–25; NEUR- + -ALGIA] —**neu·ral′gic,** *adj.*

neu′ral net′work, *n.* **1.** any group of neurons that conduct impulses in a coordinated manner, as the assemblages of brain cells that record a visual stimulus. **2.** Also called **neu′ral net′.** a computer model designed to simulate the behavior of biological neural networks, as in pattern recognition, language processing, and problem solving, with the goal of self-directed information processing. [1985–90]

neu′ral tube′, *Embryol.* a tube formed by the closure of ectodermal tissue in the early vertebrate embryo that later develops into the brain, spinal cord, nerves, and ganglia. [1885–90]

neu′ral tube′ de′fect, *Pathol.* any of a group of congenital abnormalities involving the brain and spinal cord, including spina bifida and meningocele, caused by failure of the neural tube to close properly during embryonic development. [1885–90]

neur·as·the·ni·a (no͝or′əs thē′nē ə, nyo͝or′-), *n.* nervous debility and exhaustion occurring in the absence of objective causes or lesions; nervous exhaustion. [1855–60; NEUR- + ASTHENIA]

neur·as·then·ic (no͝or′əs then′ik, nyo͝or′-), *adj.* **1.** pertaining to or suffering from neurasthenia. —*n.* **2.** a person suffering from neurasthenia. [1875–80; NEURASTHEN(IA) + -IC] —**neur′as·then′i·cal·ly,** *adv.*

neu·ra·tion (no͝o rā′shən, nyo͝o-), *n.* venation, as of an insect's wings. [1820–30; NEUR- + -ATION]

neu·ra·xon (no͝o rak′son, nyo͝o-), *n. Anat.* axon. Also, **neu·rax·one** (no͝o rak′sōn, nyo͝o-). [NEUR- + AXON]

neu·rec·to·my (no͝o rek′tə mē, nyo͝o-), *n., pl.* **-mies.** *Surg.* the removal of part or all of a nerve. [1855–60; NEUR- + -ECTOMY]

neu·ri·lem·ma (no͝or′ə lem′ə, nyo͝or′-), *n. Anat.* the delicate outermost membrane of the myelin sheath of a myelinated nerve cell. [1815–25; alter. of F *névrilème* (< Gk *neur-* NEUR- + *eílēma* covering), by assoc. with LEMMA[2]] —**neu′ri·lem′mal, neu·ri·lem·mat·ic** (no͝or′ə lə mat′ik, nyo͝or′-), **neu′ri·lem′ma·tous,** *adj.*

neu·ris·tor (no͝o ris′tər, nyo͝o-), *n.* a microelectronic fiberlike device used in information processing. [1955–60; NEUR- + *-istor,* as in *transistor;* so named because it acts like a nerve fiber]

neu·ri·tis (no͝o rī′tis, nyo͝o-), *n. Pathol.* **1.** inflammation of a nerve. **2.** continuous pain in a nerve, associated with paralysis and sensory disturbances. [1830–40; NEUR- + -ITIS] —**neu·rit·ic** (no͝o rit′ik, nyo͝o-), *adj.*

neuro-, a combining form meaning "nerve," "nerves," "nervous system," used in the formation of compound words: *neurology.* Also, *esp. before a vowel,* **neur-.** [< Gk *neuro-,* comb. form of *neûron;* akin to L *nervus*]

neu·ro·a·nat·o·my (no͝or′ō ə nat′ə mē, nyo͝or′-), *n., pl.* **-mies. 1.** the branch of anatomy dealing with the nervous system. **2.** the nerve structure of an organism. [1895–1900; NEURO- + ANATOMY] —**neu′ro·a·nat′o·mist,** *n.* —**neu·ro·an·a·tom·i·cal** (no͝or′ō an′ə tom′i kəl, nyo͝or′-), **neu′ro·an′a·tom′ic,** *adj.*

neu·ro·be·hav·ior·al (no͝or′ō bi hāv′yər əl, nyo͝or′-), *adj.* of or pertaining to an approach to studying behavior that stresses the importance of nerve and brain function. [NEURO- + BEHAVIORAL]

neu·ro·bi·ol·o·gy (no͝or′ō bī ol′ə jē, nyo͝or′-), *n.* the branch of biology that is concerned with the anatomy and physiology of the nervous system. [1905–10] —**neu·ro·bi·o·log·i·cal** (no͝or′ō bī′ə loj′i kəl), *adj.* —**neu′ro·bi′o·log′i·cal·ly,** *adv.* —**neu′ro·bi·ol′o·gist,** *n.*

neu·ro·blast (no͝or′ə blast′, nyo͝or′-), *n.* an immature nerve cell. [1890–95; NEURO- + -BLAST] —**neu′ro·blas′tic,** *adj.*

neu·ro·blas·to·ma (no͝or′ō bla stō′mə, nyo͝or′-), *n., pl.* **-mas, -ma·ta** (-mə tə). *Pathol.* a malignant tumor of immature nerve cells that usually starts in the autonomic nervous system or adrenal gland and spreads quickly, most often affecting young children. [1905–10; NEURO- + BLASTOMA]

neu·ro·chem·i·cal (no͝or′ō kem′i kəl, nyo͝or′-), *adj.* **1.** of or pertaining to neurochemistry. **2.** (of a drug or other substance) affecting the nervous system. —*n.* **3.** a drug or other substance that affects the nervous system. [1945–50; NEURO- + CHEMICAL]

neu·ro·chem·is·try (no͝or′ō kem′ə strē, nyo͝or′-), *n.* the branch of science that is concerned with the chemistry of the nervous system. [1920–25] —**neu′ro·chem′·ist,** *n.*

neu·ro·cir′cu·la·to·ry asthe′nia (no͝or′ō sûr′kyə lə tôr′ē, -tōr′ē, nyo͝or′-), *Pathol.* See **cardiac neurosis.** [1915–20; NEURO- + CIRCULATORY]

neu·ro·coele (no͝or′ə sēl′, nyo͝or′-), *n. Embryol.* the system of cavities of the embryonic brain and spinal cord. Also, **neu′ro·coel′, neu′ro·cele′.** [1885–90; NEURO- + -COELE] —**neu′ro·coel′i·an, neu′ro·cel′i·an,** *adj.*

neu·ro·de·pres·sive (no͝or′ō di pres′iv, nyo͝or′-), *adj.* **1.** (of a drug) depressing nerve-cell function. —*n.* **2.** any such substance. [1965–70; NEURO- + DEPRESSIVE]

neu·ro·em·bry·ol·o·gy (no͝or′ō em′brē ol′ə jē, nyo͝or′-), *n.* the branch of embryology dealing with the origin and development of the nervous system. [1930–35; NEURO- + EMBRYOLOGY] —**neu·ro·em·bry·o·log·i·cal** (no͝or′ō em′brē ə loj′i kəl, nyo͝or′-), **neu′ro·em′bry·o·log′ic,** *adj.* —**neu′ro·em′bry·ol′o·gist,** *n.*

neu·ro·en·do·crine (no͝or′ō en′də krin, -krīn′, -krēn′, nyo͝or′-), *adj.* of or pertaining to the interactions between the nervous and endocrine systems, esp. in relation to hormones. [1920–25; NEURO- + ENDOCRINE]

neu·ro·en·do·cri·nol·o·gy (no͝or′ō en′dō krə nol′ə jē, -krī-, nyo͝or′-), *n.* the study of the anatomical and physiological interactions between the nervous and endocrine systems. [1920–25; NEURO- + ENDOCRINOLOGY] —**neu′ro·en′do·cri·nol′o·gist,** *n.*

neu·ro·ep·i·the·li·um (no͝or′ō ep′i thē′lē əm, nyo͝or′-), *n., pl.* **-li·ums, -li·a** (-lē ə). **1.** *Embryol.* the part of the embryonic ectoderm that gives rise to the nervous system. **2.** *Anat.* tissue composed of epithelial cells that are specialized to serve a sensory function, as the nasal mucosa and retina. [NEURO- + EPITHELIUM]

neu·ro·fi·bril (no͝or′ə fī′brəl, -fib′rəl, nyo͝or′-), *n. Anat.* a fibril of a nerve cell. [1895–1900; NEURO- + FIBRIL] —**neu′ro·fi′bril·lar, neu′ro·fi′bril·lar′y,** *adj.*

neu·ro·fi·bro·ma (no͝or′ō fī brō′mə, nyo͝or′-), *n., pl.* **-mas, -ma·ta** (-mə tə). *Pathol.* a benign neoplasm composed of the fibrous elements of a nerve. [1890–95; NEURO- + FIBROMA]

neu·ro·fi·bro·ma·to·sis (no͝or′ō fī brō′mə tō′sis, nyo͝or′-), *n. Pathol.* a dominantly inherited genetic disorder characterized by flat brown patches on the skin, neurofibromas of the skin and internal organs, and in some cases skeletal deformity. [1895–1900; < NL *neurofibromat-,* s. of *neurofibroma* NEUROFIBROMA + -OSIS]

neu·ro·gen·ic (no͝or′ə jen′ik, nyo͝or′-), *adj. Med.* originating in a nerve or nerve tissue. Also, **neu·rog·e·nous** (no͝o roj′ə nəs, nyo͝o-). [1900–05; NEURO- + -GENIC]

neu·rog·li·a (no͝o rog′lē ə, nyo͝o-), *n. Anat., Cell Biol.* a class of cells in the brain and spinal cord that form a supporting structure for the neurons and provide them with insulation. Also called **glia.** [1870–75; NEURO- + LGk *glía* glue] —**neu·rog′li·al, neu·rog′li·ar,** *adj.*

neu·ro·hor·mo·nal (no͝or′ō hôr mōn′l, nyo͝or′-), *adj.* **1.** pertaining to or controlled by a neurohormone. **2.** pertaining to, affecting, or controlled by neurons or neurotransmitters and hormones. [1930–35; NEURO- + HORMONAL]

neu·ro·hor·mone (no͝or′ō hôr′mōn, nyo͝or′-), *n. Biochem.* any of various substances, as antidiuretic hormone, formed in the nervous system and delivered to an effector organ through blood circulation. [1940–45]

neu·ro·hy·poph·y·sis (no͝or′ō hī pof′ə sis, -hi-, nyo͝or′-), *n., pl.* **-ses** (-sēz′). *Anat.* See under **pituitary gland.** [1910–15; NEURO- + HYPOPHYSIS] —**neu·ro·hy·po·phys·e·al** (no͝or′ō hī′pə fiz′ē əl, -hip′ə-, -hī pof′ə-sē′əl, -hi-, nyo͝or′-), *adj.*

neu·ro·im·mu·nol·o·gy (no͝or′ō im′yə nol′ə jē, nyo͝or′-), *n.* a branch of immunology concerned with the interactions between immunological and nervous system functions, esp. as they apply to various autoimmune diseases. [1980–85]

neurol., neurology; neurological.

neu·ro·lept·an·al·ge·si·a (no͝or′ə lept an′l jē′zē ə, -sē ə, nyo͝or′-), *n. Pharm.* a semiconscious nonreactive state induced by certain drug combinations, as fentanyl with droperidol. [NEUROLEPT(IC) + ANALGESIA]

neu·ro·lep·tic (no͝or′ə lep′tik, nyo͝or′-), *n., adj.* antipsychotic. [1955–60; < F *neuroleptique,* equiv. to *neuro-* NEURO- + *-leptique* < Gk *lēptikós* disposed to take, equiv. to *lēp-* (verbid s. of *lambánein* to seize) + *-tikos* -TIC; see -LEPSY]

neu·ro·lin·guis·tics (no͝or′ō ling gwis′tiks, nyo͝or′-), *n.* (*used with a singular v.*) the study of the neurological processes underlying the development and use of language. [1960–65; NEURO- + LINGUISTICS] —**neu′ro·lin′guist,** *n.* —**neu′ro·lin·guis′tic,** *adj.*

neu·rol·o·gist (no͝o rol′ə jist, nyo͝o-), *n.* a physician specializing in neurology. [1825–35]

neu·rol·o·gy (no͝o rol′ə jē, nyo͝o-), *n.* the science of the nerves and the nervous system, esp. of the diseases affecting them. [1675–85; < NL *neurologia.* See NEURO-, -LOGY] —**neu·ro·log·i·cal** (no͝or′ə loj′i kəl, nyo͝or′-), *adj.* —**neu′ro·log′i·cal·ly,** *adv.*

neu·rol·y·sis (no͝o rol′ə sis, nyo͝o-), *n.* **1.** *Pathol.* **a.** disintegration of nerve tissue. **b.** exhaustion of a nerve by excess stimulation. **2.** *Surg.* separation of adhesions from a nerve fiber. [NEURO- + -LYSIS] —**neu·ro·lyt·ic** (no͝or′ə lit′ik, nyo͝or′-), *adj.*

neu·ro·ma (no͝o rō′mə, nyo͝o-), *n., pl.* **-mas, -ma·ta** (-mə tə). *Pathol.* a tumor formed of nerve tissue. [1830–40; NEUR- + -OMA] —**neu·rom·a·tous** (no͝o rom′ə təs, nyo͝o-), *adj.*

neu·ro·mast (no͝or′ə mast′, nyo͝or′-), *n.* a group of innervated sensory cells occurring along the lateral line of fishes and aquatic amphibians. [1910–15; NEURO- + *-mast* < Gk *mastós* hillock, lit., breast] —**neu′ro·mas′·tic,** *adj.*

neu·ro·mech·an·ism (no͝or′ō mek′ə niz′əm, nyo͝or′-), *n.* the function of the nervous system as it relates to its structure. [NEURO- + MECHANISM]

neu·ro·mod·u·la·tor (no͝or′ō moj′ə lā′tər), *n. Biochem.* any of various substances, as certain hormones and amino acids, that influence the function of neurons but do not act as neurotransmitters.

neu·ro·mo·tor (no͝or′ō mō′tər, nyo͝or′-), *adj.* **1.** neuromuscular. **2.** of or pertaining to the effects of nerve impulses on muscles. [1910–15; NEURO- + MOTOR]

neu·ro·mus·cu·lar (no͝or′ō mus′kyə lər, nyo͝or′-), *adj.* pertaining to or affecting both nerves and muscles. [1875–80; NEURO- + MUSCULAR]

neu·ron (no͝or′on, nyo͝or′-), *n. Cell Biol.* a specialized, impulse-conducting cell that is the functional unit of the nervous system, consisting of the cell body and its processes, the axon and dendrites. Also called **nerve cell.** Also, *esp. Brit.,* **neu·rone** (no͝or′ōn, nyo͝or′-). Cf. **synapse.** [1880–85; < Gk *neûron* sinew, cord, nerve] —**neu·ron·al** (no͝or′ə nl, nyo͝or′-, no͝o rōn′l, nyo͝o-), *adj.*

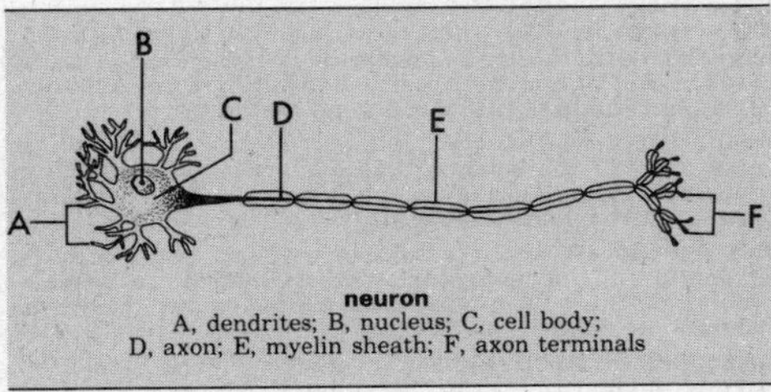

neuron
A, dendrites; B, nucleus; C, cell body;
D, axon; E, myelin sheath; F, axon terminals

neu·ro·oph·thal·mol·o·gy (no͝or′ō of′thəl mol′ə jē, -thə-, -thal-, -op′-, nyo͝or′ō-), *n.* the branch of ophthalmology that deals with the optic nerve and other nervous system structures involved in vision.

neu·ro·pa·thol·o·gy (no͝or′ō pə thol′ə jē, nyo͝or′-), *n.* the pathology of the nervous system. [1850–55; NEURO- + PATHOLOGY] —**neu·ro·path·o·log·i·cal** (no͝or′ō-path′ə loj′i kəl), *adj.* —**neu′ro·pa·thol′o·gist,** *n.*

neu·rop·a·thy (no͝o rop′ə thē, nyo͝o-), *n.* any diseased condition of the nervous system. [1855–60; NEURO- + -PATHY] —**neu·ro·path·ic** (no͝or′ə path′ik, nyo͝or′-), *adj.* —**neu′ro·path′i·cal·ly,** *adv.*

neu·ro·pep·tide (no͝or′ō pep′tīd, nyo͝or′-), *n.* any of various short-chain peptides, as endorphins, that function as neuromodulators in the nervous system and as hormones in the endocrine system. [1970–75]

neu·ro·phar·ma·col·o·gy (no͝or′ō fär′mə kol′ə jē, nyo͝or′-), *n. Pharm.* the branch of pharmacology concerned with the effects of drugs on the nervous system. [1945–50; NEURO- + PHARMACOLOGY] —**neu·ro·phar·ma·co·log·ic** (no͝or′ō fär′mə kə loj′ik, nyo͝or′-), **neu′ro·phar′ma·co·log′i·cal,** *adj.* —**neu′ro·phar′ma·co·log′·i·cal·ly,** *adv.* —**neu′ro·phar′ma·col′o·gist,** *n.*

neu·ro·phys·i·ol·o·gy (no͝or′ō fiz′ē ol′ə jē, nyo͝or′-), *n.* the branch of physiology dealing with the functions of the nervous system. [1865–70; NEURO- + PHYSIOLOGY] —**neu·ro·phys·i·o·log·i·cal** (no͝or′ō fiz′ē ə loj′i kəl, nyo͝or′-), **neu′ro·phys′i·o·log′ic,** *adj.* —**neu′ro·phys′i·o·log′i·cal·ly,** *adv.* —**neu′ro·phys′i·ol′o·gist,** *n.*

neu·ro·plasm (no͝or′ə plaz′əm, nyo͝or′-), *n. Anat.* the cytoplasm of a nerve cell. [1890–95; NEURO- + -PLASM] —**neu·ro·plas·mat·ic** (no͝or′ō plaz mat′ik, nyo͝or′-), **neu′ro·plas′mic,** *adj.*

neu·ro·psy·chi·a·try (no͝or′ō si kī′ə trē, -sī-, nyo͝or′-), *n.* the branch of medicine dealing with diseases involving the mind and nervous system. [1915–20] —**neu·ro·psy·chi·at·ric** (no͝or′ō sī′kē a′trik, nyo͝or′-), *adj.* —**neu′ro·psy·chi′a·trist,** *n.*

neu·rop·ter·an (no͝o rop′tər ən, nyo͝o-), *adj.* **1.** neuropterous. —*n.* **2.** Also, **neu·rop′ter·on.** a neuropterous insect. [1835–45; < NL *Neuropter(a),* neut. pl. of *neuropterus* (see NEUROPTEROUS) + -AN]

neu·rop·ter·ous (no͝o rop′tər əs, nyo͝o-), *adj.* belonging or pertaining to the Neuroptera, an order of insects characterized by four membranous wings having netlike venation, comprising the ant lions, lacewings, dobsonflies, alderflies, fishflies, snakeflies, mantispids, and spongillaflies. [1795–1805; < NL *Neuropter(a),* neut. pl. of *neuropterus* nerve-winged + -OUS. See NEURO-, -PTEROUS]

neu·ro·sci·ence (no͝or′ō sī′əns, nyo͝or′-), *n.* the field of study encompassing the various scientific disciplines dealing with the structure, development, function, chemistry, pharmacology, and pathology of the nervous system. [1960–65; NEURO- + SCIENCE] —**neu′ro·sci′en·tif′ic,** *adj.* —**neu′ro·sci′en·tist,** *n.*

neu·ro·se·cre·tion (no͝or′ō si krē′shən, nyo͝or′-), *n.* a chemical secreted by a nerve cell. [1940–45; NEURO- + SECRETION] —**neu′ro·se·cre′to·ry,** *adj.*

neu·ro·sen·so·ry (no͝or′ō sen′sə rē, nyo͝or′-), *adj.* of or pertaining to the sensory role of the nervous system. [1925–30; NEURO- + SENSORY]

neu·ro·sis (no͝o rō′sis, nyo͝o-), *n., pl.* **-ses** (-sēz). *Psy-*

chiatry. **1.** Also called **psychoneurosis.** a functional disorder in which feelings of anxiety, obsessional thoughts, compulsive acts, and physical complaints without objective evidence of disease, in various degrees and patterns, dominate the personality. **2.** a relatively mild personality disorder typified by excessive anxiety or indecision and a degree of social or interpersonal maladjustment. [1770–80; < NL; see NEUR-, -OSIS]

neu•ro•sur•ger•y (nŏŏr′ō sûr′jə rē, nyŏŏr′-), *n.* surgery of the brain or other nerve tissue. [1900–05; NEURO- + SURGERY] —**neu•ro•sur•geon** (nŏŏr′ō sûr′jən, nyŏŏr′-), *n.* —**neu′ro•sur′gi•cal,** *adj.*

neu•rot•ic[1] (nŏŏ rot′ik, nyŏŏ-), *Psychiatry.* —*adj.* **1.** of, pertaining to, or characteristic of neurosis. —*n.* **2.** a neurotic person. [1870–75; NEUR(OSIS) + -OTIC] —**neu•rot′ic•al•ly,** *adv.*

neu•rot•ic[2] (nŏŏ rot′ik, nyŏŏ-), *adj. Pathol.* pertaining to the nerves or to nerve disease; neural: no longer in technical use. [1765–75; NEURO- + -TIC]

neu•rot•i•cism (nŏŏ rot′ə siz′əm, nyŏŏ-), *n.* the state of having traits or symptoms characteristic of neurosis. [1895–1900; NEUROTIC + -ISM]

neu•rot•o•my (nŏŏ rot′ə mē, nyŏŏ-), *n., pl.* **-mies.** *Surg.* the cutting of a nerve, as to relieve neuralgia. [1695–1705; NEURO- + -TOMY] —**neu•ro•tom•i•cal** (nŏŏr′ə tom′i kəl, nyŏŏr′-), *adj.* —**neu•rot′o•mist,** *n.*

neu•ro•tox•ic (nŏŏr′ō tok′sik, nyŏŏr′-), *adj.* poisonous to nerve tissue, as to the brain or spinal cord. [1900–05; NEURO- + TOXIC]

neu•ro•tox•ic•i•ty (nŏŏr′ō tok sis′i tē, nyŏŏr′-), *n.* **1.** the degree to which a substance is poisonous to nerve tissue. **2.** *Pathol.* the condition resulting from exposure to a neurotoxin. [1945–50; NEURO- + TOXICITY]

neu•ro•tox•i•col•o•gy (nŏŏr′ə tok′si kol′ə jē, nyŏŏr′-), *n.* the science that deals with the effects of poisons on the nervous system. [NEURO- + TOXICOLOGY] —**neu′ro•tox′i•col′o•gist,** *n.*

neu•ro•tox•in (nŏŏr′ō tok′sin, nyŏŏr′-, nŏŏr′ō tok′-, nyŏŏr′-), *n.* a neurotoxic substance, as rattlesnake venom or the poison of a black widow spider. [1900–05; NEURO- + TOXIN]

neu•ro•trans•mis•sion (nŏŏr′ō trans mish′ən, -tranz-, nyŏŏr′-), *n.* the transmission of a nerve impulse across a synapse. [1960–65; NEURO- + TRANSMISSION]

neu•ro•trans•mit•ter (nŏŏr′ō trans′mit ər, -tranz′-, nyŏŏr′-), *n.* any of several chemical substances, as epinephrine or acetylcholine, that transmit nerve impulses across a synapse to a postsynaptic element, as another nerve, muscle, or gland. [1960–65; NEURO- + TRANSMITTER]

neu•ro•troph•ic (nŏŏr′ə trof′ik, -trō′fik, nyŏŏr′-), *adj.* **1.** of or pertaining to the effect of nerves on the nutritive processes. **2.** neurotropic. [1895–1900; NEURO- + -TROPHIC]

neu•rot•ro•phy (nŏŏ ro′trə fē, nyŏŏ-), *n.* the influence of the nerves on the nutrition and maintenance of body tissue. [NEURO- + -TROPHY]

neu•ro•trop•ic (nŏŏr′ə trop′ik, -trō′pik, nyŏŏr′-), *adj. Med.* having an affinity for nerve cells or tissue: *a neurotropic virus; a neurotropic drug.* [1900–05; NEURO- + -TROPIC]

neu•rot•ro•pism (nŏŏ ro′trə piz′əm, nyŏŏ-), *n.* the quality of being neurotropic. Also, **neu•rot′ro•py.** [1900–05; NEURO- + -TROPISM]

neu•ro•vas•cu•lar (nŏŏr′ō vas′kyə lər, nyŏŏr′-), *adj. Anat.* of, pertaining to, or involving the nerves and blood vessels. [1885–90; NEURO- + VASCULAR]

neu•ru•la (nŏŏr′ə lə, nyŏŏr′-), *n., pl.* **-las, -lae** (-lē′, -lī′). *Embryol.* an embryo in the stage of development in which part of the ectoderm is differentiated into neural tissue and in which the neural tube, which develops into the brain and spinal cord, is formed. [1905–10; < NL; see NEUR-, -ULE] —**neu′ru•lar,** *adj.*

neu•ru•la•tion (nŏŏr′ə lā′shən, nyŏŏr′-), *n.* the formation of a neurula. [1885–90; NEURUL(A) + -ATION]

Neu•satz (noi′zäts), *n.* German name of **Novi Sad.**

Neuss (nois), *n.* a city in W Germany, near Düsseldorf. 142,200.

neus•ton (nŏŏ′ston, nyŏŏ′-), *n.* the aggregate of minute aquatic organisms that float or swim in the surface film of a body of water. [1925–30; < G; n. use of neut. of Gk *neustós* swimming, verbal of *neîn* to swim] —**neus′•tic, neus•ton•ic** (nŏŏ ston′ik, nyŏŏ-), *adj.*

Neus•tri•a (nŏŏ′strē ə, nyŏŏ′-), *n.* the W part of the Frankish kingdom, corresponding roughly to N and NW France. —**Neus′tri•an,** *adj.*

neut., neuter.

neu•ter (nŏŏ′tər, nyŏŏ′-), *adj.* **1.** *Gram.* **a.** noting or pertaining to a gender that refers to things classed as neither masculine nor feminine. **b.** (of a verb) intransitive. **2.** *Biol.* having no organs of reproduction; without sex; asexual. **3.** *Zool.* having imperfectly developed sexual organs, as the worker bees and ants. **4.** *Bot.* having neither stamens nor pistils; asexual. **5.** neutral; siding with no one. —*n.* **6.** *Gram.* **a.** the neuter gender. **b.** a noun of that gender. **c.** another element marking that gender. **d.** an intransitive verb. **7.** an animal made sterile by castration or spaying. **8.** *Zool.* a neuter insect. **9.** a person or thing that is neutral. —*v.t.* **10.** *Vet. Sci.* to spay or castrate (a dog, cat, etc.). [1350–1400; < L *neuter* neither (of two), equiv. to *ne* not + *uter* either (of two); r. ME *neutre* < MF < L, as above]

neu•ter•cane (nŏŏ′tər kān′, nyŏŏ′-), *n.* a storm resembling a small hurricane but obtaining part of its energy by the same mechanism as a frontal cyclone. [1970–75; NEUTER + (HURRI)CANE, with *hurr-* punningly taken as *her*]

CONCISE ETYMOLOGY KEY: <, descended or borrowed from; >, whence; b., blend of, blended; c., cognate with; cf., compare; deriv., derivative; equiv., equivalent; imit., imitative; obl., oblique; r., replacing; s., stem; sp., spelling, spelled; resp., respelling, respelled; trans., translation; ?, origin unknown; *, unattested; ‡, probably earlier than. See the full key inside the front cover.

Neu•tra (noi′trə), *n.* **Richard Joseph,** 1892–1970, U.S. architect, born in Austria.

neu•tral (nŏŏ′trəl, nyŏŏ′-), *adj.* **1.** not taking part or giving assistance in a dispute or war between others: *a neutral nation during World War II.* **2.** not aligned with or supporting any side or position in a controversy: *The arbitrator was absolutely neutral.* **3.** of or belonging to a neutral state or party: *neutral territory.* **4.** of no particular kind, characteristics, etc.; indefinite: *a neutral personality that made no impression whatever; a sex-neutral job title.* **5.** (of a color or shade) **a.** gray; without hue; of zero chroma; achromatic. **b.** matching well with many or most other colors or shades, as white or beige. **6.** *Bot., Zool.* neuter. **7.** not causing or reflecting a change in something: *It is believed that the new tax law will be revenue neutral.* **8.** *Chem.* exhibiting neither acid nor alkaline qualities: *neutral salts.* **9.** *Physics.* **a.** (of a particle) having no charge. **b.** (of an atom, molecule, collection of particles, fluid, or solid) having no net charge; electroneutral; not electrified. **c.** not magnetized. **10.** *Phonet.* (of a vowel) pronounced with the tongue relaxed in a central position, as the *a* in *alive;* reduced. —*n.* **11.** a person or a nation that remains neutral, as in a controversy or war. **12.** a citizen of a neutral nation during a war. **13.** *Mach., Auto.* the position or state of disengaged gears or other interconnecting parts: *in neutral.* **14.** a neutral color. [1400–50; late ME < L *neutrālis* grammatically neuter. See NEUTER, -AL[1]] —**neu′•tral•ly,** *adv.*
—**Syn. 2.** impartial, disinterested, dispassionate, uninvolved, unbiased.

neu′tral acrifla′vine, *Chem.* acriflavine.

neu′tral ax′is, an imaginary line in the cross section of a beam, shaft, or the like, along which no stresses occur. [1835–45]

neu′tral cor′ner, *Boxing.* either of the two corners of the ring not used by the boxers between rounds. [1950–55]

neu′tral ground′, *Gulf States.* **1.** a median strip on a highway or boulevard, esp. one planted with grass. **2.** the strip of grass between a street and sidewalk. [1815–25, *Amer.*, for an earlier sense]

neu•tral•ism (nŏŏ′trə liz′əm, nyŏŏ′-), *n.* **1.** the policy or advocacy of maintaining strict neutrality in foreign affairs. **2.** *Biol.* the theory that some changes in evolution are governed by random mutations that become fixed in populations by chance rather than by natural selection. [1570–80; NEUTRAL + -ISM]

neu•tral•ist (nŏŏ′trə list, nyŏŏ′-), *n.* **1.** a person who advocates or adheres to a policy of strict neutrality in foreign affairs. **2.** a person who advocates or adheres to a policy or theory of neutralism. —*adj.* **3.** of, pertaining to, or advocating neutralism. [1615–25; NEUTRAL + -IST]

neu•tral•i•ty (nŏŏ tral′i tē, nyŏŏ-), *n.* **1.** the state of being neutral. **2.** the policy or status of a nation that does not participate in a war between other nations: *the continuous neutrality of Switzerland.* **3.** neutral status, as of a seaport during a war. [1425–75; late ME; see NEUTRAL, -ITY]

neu•tral•i•za•tion (nŏŏ′trə lə zā′shən, nyŏŏ′-), *n.* **1.** the act, process, or an instance of neutralizing. **2.** the quality or condition of being neutralized. **3.** *Ling.* the loss of a distinctive feature of one of a pair of phonemes that are otherwise differentiated on the basis of that feature, as the loss of voice as a distinctive feature between the *-t-* and *-d-* of *latter* and *ladder.* [1800–10; NEUTRALIZE + -ATION]

neu•tral•ize (nŏŏ′trə līz′, nyŏŏ′-), *v.,* **-ized, -iz•ing.** —*v.t.* **1.** to make neutral; cause to undergo neutralization. **2.** to make (something) ineffective; counteract; nullify: *carelessness that neutralized our efforts.* **3.** *Mil.* to put out of action or make incapable of action: *to neutralize an enemy position.* **4.** to declare neutral; invest with neutrality in order to exempt from involvement during a war: *to neutralize a city to prevent bombing.* **5.** to add an acid to a basic solution or a base to an acidic solution until the resulting solution is chemically neutral (pH = 7). **6.** *Elect.* to render electrically or magnetically neutral. —*v.i.* **7.** to become neutral or neutralized; undergo neutralization: *With this additive the solution begins to neutralize.* Also, *esp. Brit.,* **neu′tral•ise′.** [1655–65; NEUTRAL + -IZE] —**neu′tral•iz′er,** *n.*

neu′tral mon′ism, *Philos.* the theory that mind and matter consist of different relations between entities that are themselves neither mental nor physical. [1910–15] —**neu′tral mon′ist.**

neu′tral spir′its, nonflavored alcohol of 95 percent, or 190 proof, obtained chiefly from grain or molasses or redistilled from brandy, rum, etc., used for blending with straight whiskies and in the making of gin, cordials, liqueurs, and the like. [1915–20]

neu′tral zone′, *Ice Hockey.* the area of a rink between the two blue lines. Cf. **end zone** (def. 2). [1900–05, in sense "zone between the two scrimmage lines in football"]

neu•tri•no (nŏŏ trē′nō, nyŏŏ-), *n., pl.* **-nos.** *Physics.* any of the massless or nearly massless electrically neutral leptons. There is a distinct kind of neutrino associated with each of the massive leptons. Cf. **antineutrino, lepton, conservation of lepton number.** [< It (1933), equiv. to *neutr(o)* NEUTER, neutral + *-ino* -INE[2]; coined by E. Fermi]

neutri′no astron′omy, the branch of astronomy dealing with the detection and measurement of neutrinos emitted by the sun and other celestial objects. [1975–80]

neutro-, a combining form representing **neutral** in compound words: *neutrosphere.* [see NEUTER, -O-]

neu•tron (nŏŏ′tron, nyŏŏ′-), *n. Physics.* an elementary particle having no charge, mass slightly greater than that of a proton, and spin of ½: a constituent of the nuclei of all atoms except those of hydrogen. *Symbol:* n [1920–25; NEUTR(O)- + -ON[1]]

neu′tron activa′tion anal′ysis. See **activation analysis.**

neu′tron bomb′, a nuclear bomb designed to release radiation consisting mainly of neutrons, thus causing extensive loss of life but relatively little damage to buildings and property and only brief radioactive contamination. Also called **neu′tron radia′tion weap′on, N-bomb.** [1955–60]

neu′tron num′ber, *Physics.* the number of neutrons in the nucleus of an atom, equal to the mass number minus the atomic number of the atom. *Symbol:* N [1950–55]

neu′tron star′, *Astron.* an extremely dense, compact star composed primarily of neutrons, esp. the collapsed core of a supernova: the neutrons are believed to form when electrons and protons fuse during gravitational collapse. Cf. **pulsar.** [1930–35]

neu•tro•phil (nŏŏ′trə fil, nyŏŏ′-), *adj. Histol.* **1.** (of a cell or cell part) having an affinity for neutral dyes. —*n.* **2.** *Immunol.* a phagocytic white blood cell having a lobulate nucleus and neutrophil granules in the cytoplasm. Also, **neu•tro•phile** (nŏŏ′trə fīl′, nyŏŏ′-). [1885–90; NEUTRO- + -PHIL]

neu•tro•sphere (nŏŏ′trə sfēr′, nyŏŏ′-), *n.* the part of the atmosphere whose constituents are, for the most part, electrically neutral, extending from the earth's surface to the base of the ionosphere. [NEUTRO- + SPHERE]

Nev., Nevada.

Ne•va (nē′və; *Russ.* nyi vä′), *n.* a river in the NW Russian Federation in Europe, flowing from Lake Ladoga through St. Petersburg into the Gulf of Finland: canalized for ships. 40 mi. (65 km) long.

Ne•vad•a (nə vad′ə, -vä′də), *n.* a state in the W United States. 799,184; 110,540 sq. mi. (286,300 sq. km). *Cap.:* Carson City. *Abbr.:* NV (for use with zip code), Nev. —**Ne•vad′an, Ne•vad′i•an,** *adj., n.*

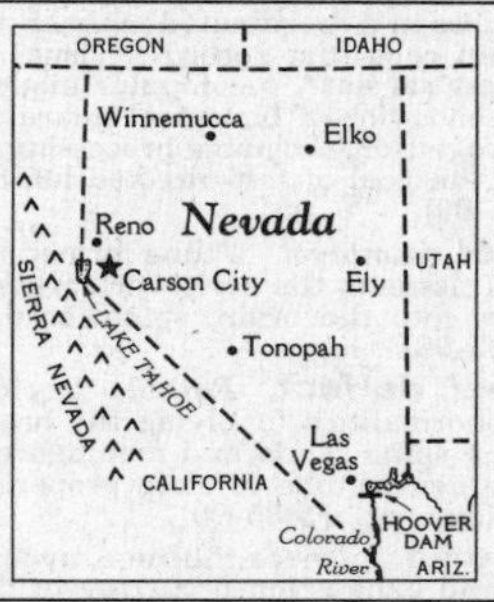

Ne•va•do del Ruiz (ne vä′thô thel rwēs′), a volcano in W central Colombia, in the Andes: eruption 1985. 17,720 ft. (5401 m).

né•vé (nā vā′), *n.* **1.** granular snow accumulated on high mountains and subsequently compacted into glacial ice. **2.** a field of such snow. Also called **firn.** [1850–55; < Franco-Provençal < VL **nivātum,* n. use of neut. of L *nivātus* snow-cooled, equiv. to *niv-* (s. of *nix* SNOW) + *-ātus* -ATE[1]]

Nev•el•son (nev′əl sən), *n.* **Louise,** born 1899, U.S. sculptor, born in Russia.

nev•er (nev′ər), *adv.* **1.** not ever; at no time: *Such an idea never occurred to me.* **2.** not at all; absolutely not: *never mind; This will never do.* **3.** to no extent or degree: *He was never the wiser for his experience.* [bef. 900; ME; OE *nǣfre,* equiv. to *ne* not + *ǣfre* EVER]

nev•er•land (nev′ər land′), *n.* See **never-never land.** [1900–05; NEVER + LAND]

nev•er•mind (nev′ər mīnd′, nev′ər mīnd′), *n. Older Use.* **1.** attention; heed; notice (usually used in negative constructions): *Pay him no nevermind.* **2.** business; affair; responsibility (usually used in negative constructions): *It's no nevermind of yours.* [1930–35; n. use of v. phrase *never mind*]

nev•er•more (nev′ər môr′, -mōr′), *adv.* never again; never thereafter: *And nevermore were the elves seen in that town.* [1175–1225; ME; see NEVER, MORE]

nev•er-nev•er (nev′ər nev′ər), *n.* **1.** See **never-never land. 2.** *Brit. Slang.* See **hire-purchase system.** —*adj.* **3.** not real or true; imaginary or ideal; illusory: *the never-never world of the cinema.* [1880–85]

nev′er-nev′er land′, 1. an unreal, imaginary, or ideal state, condition, place, etc. **2.** any remote, isolated, barren, or sparsely settled region. Also called **neverland, never-never.** [1875–85 for def. 2; redupl. of NEVER]

Ne•vers (nə ver′), *n.* a city in and the capital of Nièvre, in central France, on the Loire River: Romanesque church. 47,730.

nev•er•the•less (nev′ər *th*ə les′), *adv.* nonetheless; notwithstanding; however; in spite of that: *a small but nevertheless important change.* [1250–1300; ME; r. *natheles, notheles* NATHELESS; see NEVER, THE[2], LESS]
—**Syn.** See **but**[1].

Ne•vi•im (*Seph.* nə vē ēm′; *Ashk.* nə vē′im), *n. Hebrew.* the Prophets, being the second of the three Jewish divisions of the Old Testament. Also, **Nebiim.** Cf. **Tanach.**

Nev•il (nev′əl), *n.* a male given name, form of **Neville.**

Nev•ille (nev′əl), *n.* **1. Richard.** See **Warwick, Earl of. 2.** a male given name: an Old North French family name, taken from a place-name.

Nev·in (nev′in), *n.* **Ethelbert Woodbridge,** 1862–1901, U.S. composer.

Ne·vin·no·myssk (nə vin′ə misk′; *Russ.* nyi vyi nu-misk′), *n.* a city in the SW RSFSR, in the SW Soviet Union in Europe, S of Stavropol. 104,000.

Nev·ins (nev′inz), *n.* **Allan,** 1890–1971, U.S. historian.

Ne·vis (nē′vis, nev′is), *n.* **1.** one of the Leeward Islands, in the E West Indies: part of St. Kitts-Nevis; formerly a British colony. 11,900; 50 sq. mi. (130 sq. km). Cf. **St. Kitts-Nevis-Anguilla. 2. Ben.** See **Ben Nevis.**

Nev·ski (nev′skē, nef′-; *Russ.* nyef′skyē), *n.* **Alexander.** See **Alexander Nevsky.**

ne·vus (nē′vəs), *n., pl.* **-vi** (-vī). *Med.* any congenital anomaly of the skin, including moles and various types of birthmarks. [1685–95; sp. var. of L *naevus* mole] **—ne·void** (nē′void), *adj.*

new (no͞o, nyo͞o), *adj.,* **-er, -est,** *adv., n.*—*adj.* **1.** of recent origin, production, purchase, etc.; having but lately come or been brought into being: *a new book.* **2.** of a kind now existing or appearing for the first time; novel: *a new concept of the universe.* **3.** having but lately or but now come into knowledge: *a new chemical element.* **4.** unfamiliar or strange (often fol. by *to*): *ideas new to us; to visit new lands.* **5.** having but lately come to a place, position, status, etc.: *a reception for our new minister.* **6.** unaccustomed (usually fol. by *to*): *people new to such work.* **7.** coming or occurring afresh; further; additional: *new gains.* **8.** fresh or unused: *to start a new sheet of paper.* **9.** (of physical or moral qualities) different and better: *The vacation made a new man of him.* **10.** other than the former or the old: *a new era; in the New World.* **11.** being the later or latest of two or more things of the same kind: *the New Testament; a new edition of Shakespeare.* **12.** (*cap.*) (of a language) in its latest known period, esp. as a living language at the present time: *New High German.* **—***adv.* **13.** recently or lately (usually used in combination): *The valley was green with new-planted crops.* **14.** freshly; anew or afresh (often used in combination): *roses new washed with dew; new-mown hay.* **—***n.* **15.** something that is new; a new object, quality, condition, etc.: *Ring out the old, ring in the new.* [bef. 900; ME *newe* (adj., adv., and n.), OE *nēowe, nīewe, nīwe* (adj. and adv.); c. D *nieuw,* G *neu,* ON *nýr,* Goth *niujis,* OIr *núe,* Welsh *newydd,* Gk *neîos;* akin to L *novus,* Gk *néos*] **—new′ness,** *n.*
—Syn. 1. modern; late. NEW, FRESH, NOVEL describe something that is not old. NEW applies to something that has not been long in existence: *a new broom, dress* (one recently made or bought). FRESH suggests a condition of newness, not yet affected by use or the passage of time: *a fresh towel, dress* (newly clean). NOVEL suggests newness that has an unexpected quality, or is strange or striking, but generally pleasing: *a novel experience.*
—Pronunciation. Following the alveolar consonants (t), (d), and (n), two main types of pronunciation occur for the "long" vowel represented by the spellings *u, ue,* discontinuous *u...e,* and *ew,* as in STUDENT, DUE, NUDE, and NEW. In the North and North Midland U.S. (o͞o) immediately follows the alveolar consonant: (sto͞od′nt), (do͞o), (no͞od), and (no͞o). In the South Midland and Southern U.S., pronunciations of the type (styo͞od′nt), (dyo͞o), (nyo͞od), and (nyo͞o) predominate. Both these types are traceable to England, as well as some less common ones, for example, those in which the high front vowel (i) substitutes for the (y). A belief that the (yo͞o) pronunciations are more prestigious sometimes leads to hypercorrection, the insertion of the *y* sound where historically it does not belong, leading to such pronunciations as (nyo͞on) for *noon.* Currently in the United States, a (y) following (s), (z), (th), and (l), as in *sue* (syo͞o), *resume* (ri zyo͞om′), *enthusiasm* (en thyo͞o′sē az′əm), and *illusion* (i lyo͞o′-zhən), is used by some speakers, but is considered affected by others.

New′ Age′, 1. of or pertaining to a movement espousing a broad range of philosophies and practices traditionally viewed as occult, metaphysical, or paranormal. **2.** of or pertaining to an unintrusive style of music using both acoustic and electronic instruments and drawing on classical music, jazz, and rock. **3.** the New Age movement. [1970–75] **—New′ Ag′er.**

New′ Al′bany, a city in S Indiana, on the Ohio River. 37,103.

New′ Amer′ican Bi′ble, an English translation (1970) of the Bible based on the original languages, prepared by Catholic Biblical scholars. *Abbr.:* NAB

New′ Am′ster·dam (am′stər dam′), **1.** a former Dutch town on Manhattan Island: the capital of New Netherland; renamed New York by the British in 1664. **2.** a city in NE Guyana, on the Berbice River. 18,199.

Ne·war (ni wär′), *n., pl.* **-wars,** (*esp. collectively*) **-war.** a member of a Mongoloid people of Nepal.

new′ archaeol′ogy, a reorientation of archaeology, first current in the 1960's, that emphasizes an explicitly scientific, problem-oriented, deductive approach to research and uses among other devices the methods of statistics and technology. **—new′ archaeol′ogist.**

Ne·wa·ri (ni wär′ē), *n.* a Sino-Tibetan language, the language of the Newar. [1875–80]

New·ark (no͞o′ərk, nyo͞o′- *for 1–3, 5;* no͞o′ärk′, nyo͞o′- *for 4; for 1 also locally* no͝ork, nyo͝ork), *n.* **1.** a city in NE New Jersey, on Newark Bay. 329,248. **2.** a city in central Ohio. 41,200. **3.** a town in W California. 32,126. **4.** a city in N Delaware. 25,247. **5.** a town in W New York. 10,017.

New′ Atlan′tis, a political allegory by Francis Bacon, published in 1627.

New′ark Bay′, a bay in NE New Jersey. 6 mi. (10 km) long; 1 mi. (1.6 km) wide.

new′ ball′ game′, *Informal.* a new or changed situation: *The microcomputer created a new ball game in the field of data analysis.*

New′ Bed′ford, a seaport in SE Massachusetts: formerly a chief whaling port. 98,478.

New·berg (no͞o′bûrg, nyo͞o′-), *n.* a town in NW Oregon. 10,394.

New′ Ber′lin, a city in SE Wisconsin, near Milwaukee. 30,529.

New′ Bern′, a city in E North Carolina. 14,557.

New·ber·y (no͞o′ber ē, -bə rē, nyo͞o′-), *n.* **John,** 1713–67, English publisher.

New′bery Award′, an annual award for the most distinguished book for juveniles.

new′ biol′ogy. See **molecular biology.**

New·bold (no͞o′bōld, nyo͞o′-), *n.* a male given name.

New·bolt (no͞o′bōlt, nyo͞o′-), *n.* **Sir Henry John,** 1862–1938, English poet, novelist, historian, and critic.

new·born (no͞o′bôrn′, nyo͞o′-), *adj., n., pl.* **-born, -borns.** **—***adj.* **1.** recently or only just born. **2.** born anew; reborn: *a newborn faith in human goodness.* **—***n.* **3.** a newborn infant; neonate. [1250–1300; ME]

New′ Braun′fels (broun′fəlz), a city in S Texas, near San Antonio. 22,402.

New′ Brigh′ton, a town in E Minnesota. 23,269.

New′ Brit′ain, 1. the largest island in the Bismarck Archipelago, Papua New Guinea, in the W central Pacific Ocean. 175,369. ab. 14,600 sq. mi. (37,814 sq. km). *Cap.:* Rabaul. **2.** a city in central Connecticut. 73,840.

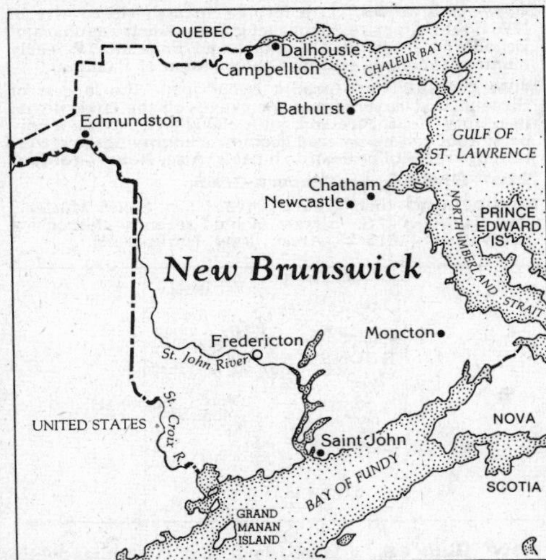

New′ Bruns′wick, 1. a province in SE Canada, E of Maine. 664,525; 27,985 sq. mi. (72,480 sq. km). *Cap.:* Fredericton. **2.** a city in central New Jersey. 41,442.

New·burg (no͞o′bûrg, nyo͞o′-), *adj.* (of seafood) cooked with a sauce of cream, egg yolk, butter, and usually sherry: *lobster Newburg.* [1900–05, *Amer.*; named after *Newburgh,* a fishing village in Scotland]

New·burgh (no͞o′bûrg, nyo͞o′-), *n.* a city in SE New York, on the Hudson. 23,438.

New·bur·y·port (no͞o′bə rē pôrt′, -pōrt′, -ber′ē-, nyo͞o′-), *n.* a city in NE Massachusetts. 15,900.

New′ Caledo′nia, (kal′i dō′nē ə, -dōn′yə), **1.** an island in the S Pacific, ab. 800 mi. (1290 km) E of Australia. 113,680; 6224 sq. mi. (16,120 sq. km). **2.** an overseas territory of France comprising this island and other smaller islands: formerly a penal colony. 131,665; 7200 sq. mi. (18,650 sq. km). *Cap.:* Nouméa.

New′ Ca′naan, a town in SW Connecticut. 17,931.

New′ Car′rollton, a city in S central Maryland, near Washington, D.C. 12,632.

New′ Castile′, a region in central Spain: formerly a province. 27,933 sq. mi. (72,346 sq. km). Spanish, **Castilla la Nueva.**

New′ Cas′tle, 1. a city in W Pennsylvania. 33,621. **2.** a city in E Indiana. 20,056.

New·cas·tle (no͞o′kas′əl, -kä′səl, nyo͞o′-), *n.* **1. 1st Duke of.** See **Pelham-Holles, Thomas. 2.** Also called **New·cas·tle-up·on-Tyne** (no͞o′kas′əl ə pon′tīn′, -ə pôn′-, -kä′səl-, nyo͞o′-). a seaport in Tyne and Wear, in NE England, on the Tyne River: shipbuilding; major coal center. 295,700. **3.** a seaport in E New South Wales, in SE Australia. 146,900. **4.** a town in SE Ontario, in S Canada, NE of Toronto, on Lake Ontario. 32,229. **5. carry coals to Newcastle, a.** to take something to a place where its kind exists in great quantity. **b.** to do something wholly unnecessary.

New′castle disease′, *Vet. Pathol.* a rapidly spreading virus-induced disease of birds and domestic fowl, as chickens, marked by respiratory difficulty, reduced egg production and, in chicks, paralysis. Also called **avian pneumoencephalitis.** [after *Newcastle*-upon-Tyne, near which the disease was first reported in 1927]

New′ Church′. See **New Jerusalem Church.**

New·chwang (no͞o′chwäng′, nyo͞o′-), *n.* Niuzhuang.

New′ Cit′y, a city in SE New York. 35,859.

new-col·lar (no͞o′kol′ər, nyo͞o′), *adj.* pertaining to or designating middle-class wage earners holding jobs in a service industry. Cf. **blue-collar.** [1985–90]

New·comb (no͞o′kəm, nyo͞o′-), *n.* **Simon,** 1835–1909, U.S. astronomer.

New′ Com′edy, Greek comedy arising toward the end of the 4th century B.C. that employed stock characters and plots drawn from contemporary bourgeois life, the formulas of which were adopted by later Roman writers for the comic stage. Cf. **Middle Comedy, Old Comedy.** [1840–50]

New·com·en (no͞o kum′ən, nyo͞o-), *n.* **Thomas,** 1663–1729, English inventor.

new·com·er (no͞o′kum′ər, nyo͞o′-), *n.* a person or thing that has recently arrived; new arrival: *She is a newcomer to our city. The firm is a newcomer in the field of advertising.* [1585–95; NEW + COMER]

new′ cov′enant, (*sometimes caps.*) (in Christian exegesis) the promises of salvation made by God to humans individually, based on divine grace rather than Mosaic Law.

new′ crit′icism, (*often caps.*) an approach to the critical study of literature that concentrates on textual explication and rejects historical and biographical study as irrelevant to an understanding of the total formal organization of a work. Cf. ***explication de texte.*** [1940–45] **—new′ crit′ic, New′ Crit′ic.**

new′ cuisine′. See ***nouvelle cuisine.***

New′ Deal′, 1. the principles of the progressive wing of the Democratic party, esp. those advocated under the leadership of President Franklin D. Roosevelt for economic recovery and social reforms. **2.** the domestic program of the Franklin D. Roosevelt administration, esp. during the period from 1933 to 1941. Cf. **Fair Deal, Great Society, New Frontier.** [1830–35, as political catchphrase during the Jackson presidency] **—New′ Deal′er.**

New′ Del′hi (del′ē), the capital city of India, in the N part, adjacent to Delhi. 301,800. Cf. **Delhi** (def. 2).

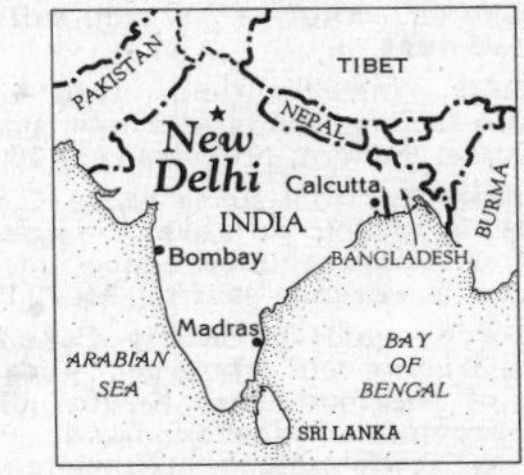

New′ Econom′ic Pol′icy, (in the Soviet Union) a program in effect from 1921 to 1928, reviving the wage system and private ownership of some factories and businesses, and abandoning grain requisitions.

new′ econom′ics, Keynesianism. [1925–30, *Amer.*]

N, newel (def. 2)

new·el (no͞o′əl, nyo͞o′-), *n.* **1.** See **newel post. 2.** a central pillar or upright from which the steps of a winding stair radiate. **3.** (on an escalator) the horizontal section of railing at the upper or lower end. [1325–75; earlier *nuel,* ME *nowel* < MF *no(u)el* kernel, newel < LL **nucāle,* n. use of neut. of *nucālis* of a nut, nutlike, equiv. to L *nuc-* (s. of *nux*) nut + *-ālis* -AL[1]]

new′el post′, a post supporting one end of a handrail at the top or bottom of a flight of stairs. [1790–1800]

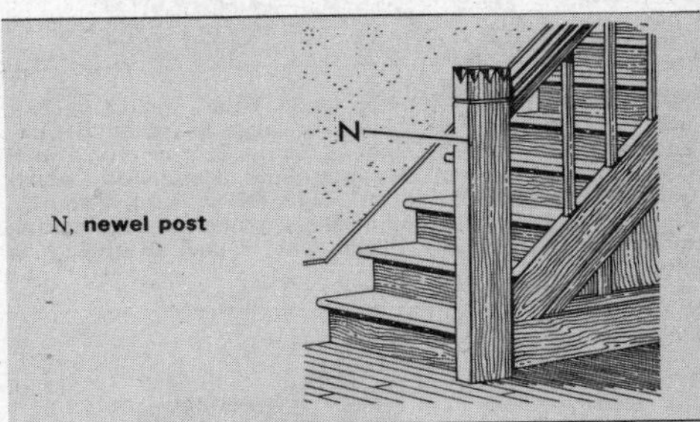

N, newel post

New′ Em′pire. See **New Kingdom.**

New′ Eng′land, an area in the NE United States, including the states of Connecticut, Maine, Massachusetts, New Hampshire, Rhode Island, and Vermont. **—New′ Eng′land·er. —New′ Eng′land·ish.**

CONCISE PRONUNCIATION KEY: *act, cāpe, dâre, pärt; set, ēqual; if, īce; ox, ōver, ôrder, oil, bo͝ok, bo͞ot, out; up, ûrge; child; sing; shoe; thin, that;* zh as in *treasure.* ə = *a* as in *alone, e* as in *system, i* as in *easily, o* as in *gallop, u* as in *circus;* ᵊ as in *fire* (fīᵊr), *hour* (ouᵊr). l and n can serve as syllabic consonants, as in *cradle* (krād′l), and *button* (but′n). See the full key inside the front cover.

New′ Eng′land as′ter, a tall composite plant, *Aster novae-angliae,* of the northeastern U.S., the flowers of which have lavender to deep-purple rays. [1805–15, *Amer.*]

New′ Eng′land boiled′ din′ner. See **boiled dinner.** [1935–40]

New′ Eng′land clam′ chow′der, a thick chowder made from clams, potatoes, onions, sometimes salt pork, and milk or cream. Cf. **Manhattan clam chowder.** [1880–85]

New′ Eng′land theol′ogy, Calvinism as modified and interpreted by the descendants of the Puritans in New England, esp. Jonathan Edwards, becoming the dominant theology there from about 1730 to 1880. [1895–1900]

New′ Eng′lish. See **Modern English.** [1625–35, *Amer.*]

New′ Eng′lish Bi′ble, an English translation (1970) of the Bible into contemporary idiom, directed by Anglican and other Protestant churches of Great Britain.

new′ expres′sionism, neo-expressionism. Also, **New′ Expres′sionism.**

Newf (nōōf, nyōōf), *n. Chiefly Canadian Slang (sometimes disparaging and offensive).* a native or inhabitant of Newfoundland. [by shortening]

Newf., Newfoundland.

New′ Fair′field, a town in SW Connecticut. 11,260.

new·fan·gled (nōō′fang′gəld, -fang′-, nyōō′-), *adj.* **1.** of a new kind or fashion: *newfangled ideas.* **2.** fond of or given to novelty. [1425–75; late ME, equiv. to *newefangel* fond of or taken by what is new (*newe* NEW + *-fangel,* OE **fangol* inclined to take, equiv. to *fang-,* s. of *fōn* to take (cf. FANG[2]) + *-ol* adj. suffix) + -ED[3]] —**new′fan′gled·ness,** *n.*

new-fash·ioned (nōō′fash′ənd, nyōō′-), *adj.* **1.** lately come into fashion; made in a new style, fashion, etc. **2.** up-to-date; modern; progressive. [1605–15]

new′ fed′eralism, (*sometimes caps.*) *U.S. Govt.* a plan, announced in 1969, to turn over the control of some federal programs to state and local governments and institute block grants, revenue sharing, etc. [1965–70]

New·fie (nōō′fē, nyōō′-), *Chiefly Canadian Slang (sometimes disparaging and offensive).* —*n.* **1.** a native or inhabitant of Newfoundland; Newfoundlander. **2.** the Canadian province of Newfoundland. —*adj.* **3.** of or pertaining to Newfoundland. [NEWF(OUNDLAND) + -IE]

New′ For′est, a forest region in S England, in Hampshire: national park. 145 sq. mi. (376 sq. km).

new·found (nōō′found′, nyōō′-), *adj.* newly found or discovered: *newfound friends.* [1490–1500; NEW + FOUND[1]]

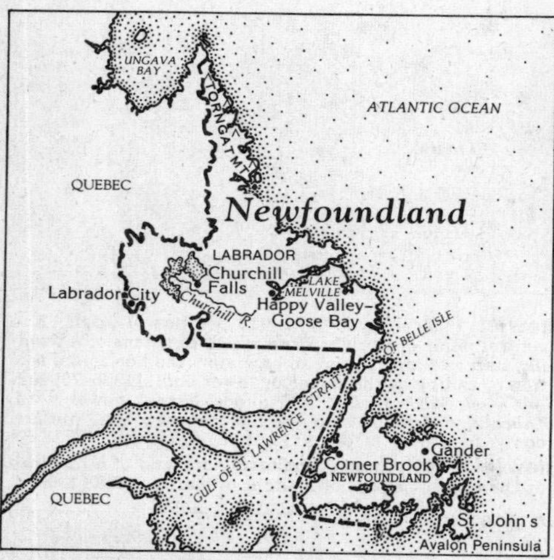

New·found·land (nōō′fən lənd, -land′, -fənd-, nyōō′-; nōō found′lənd, nyōō-), *n.* **1.** a large island in E Canada. 42,734 sq. mi. (110,680 sq. km). **2.** a province in E Canada, composed of Newfoundland island and Labrador. 557,725; 155,364 sq. mi. (402,390 sq. km). *Cap.:* St. John's. **3.** one of a breed of large, powerful dogs having a dense, oily, usually black coat, raised originally in Newfoundland.

Newfoundland (def. 3), 28 in. (71 cm) high at shoulder

CONCISE ETYMOLOGY KEY: <, descended or borrowed from; >, whence; b., blend of, blended; c., cognate with; cf., compare; deriv., derivative; equiv., equivalent; imit., imitative; obl., oblique; r., replacing; s., stem; sp., spelling, spelled; resp., respelling, respelled; trans., translation; ?, origin unknown; *, unattested; ‡, probably earlier than. See the full key inside the front cover.

New·found·land·er (nōō′fən lən′dər, -lan′-, -fənd-, nyōō′-), *n.* a native or inhabitant of Newfoundland. [1605–15; NEWFOUNDLAND + -ER[1]]

New′foundland time′, a form of civil time observed on the island of Newfoundland, one and one-half hours later than Eastern time and a half hour later than Atlantic time.

New′ France′, the French colonies and possessions in North America up to 1763.

New′ Frontier′, the principles and policies of the liberal wing of the Democratic party under the leadership of President John F. Kennedy. Cf. **Fair Deal, Great Society, New Deal.** [as a political catchphrase, appar. first used by Henry Wallace in a book of the same title (1934)]

New′ Frontiers′man, an advocate or follower of the New Frontier, esp. one in public service. [1960–65]

New·gate (nōō′gāt′, -git, nyōō′-), *n.* a prison in London, England: torn down 1902.

New′ Gen′eral Cat′alogue, *Astron.* See **NGC.**

New′ Geor′gia, 1. a group of islands in the Solomon Islands. **2.** the chief island of this group. 50 mi. (80 km) long; 20 mi. (32 km) wide.

New′ Glas′gow, a city in N central Nova Scotia, in E Canada. 10,672.

New′ Grana′da, 1. a former Spanish viceroyalty in NW South America, comprising the present republics of Ecuador, Venezuela, Colombia, and Panama. **2.** early name of Colombia (before the secession of Panama).

New·grange (nōō′grānj′, nyōō′-), *n.* the largest of three mound-covered passage graves on the river Boyne in county Meath, Ireland, built c3000 B.C., having a corbeled roof and hammered geometric engravings and containing traces of cremation burials. Also, **New′ Grange′.**

New′ Greek′. See **Modern Greek.**

new·ground (nōō′ground′, nyōō′-), *n. South Midland and Southern U.S.* a tract of land recently cleared for cultivation. [1615–25, *Amer.*; NEW + GROUND[1]]

New′ Guin′ea, a large island N of Australia, politically divided into the Indonesian province of Irian Jaya (West Irian) and the independent country of Papua New Guinea. 2,800,000; ab. 316,000 sq. mi. (818,000 sq. km). —**New′ Guin′ean.**

New·ham (nōō′əm, nyōō′-), *n.* a borough of Greater London, England. 232,600.

New′ Hamp′shire, (hamp′shər, -shēr), **1.** a state in the NE United States. 920,610; 9304 sq. mi. (24,100 sq. km). *Cap.:* Concord. *Abbr.:* NH (for use with zip code), N.H. **2.** one of an American breed of chestnut-red chickens raised for meat and eggs. —**New′ Hamp′shirite** (hamp′shə rīt′), **New′ Hamp′shire·man.**

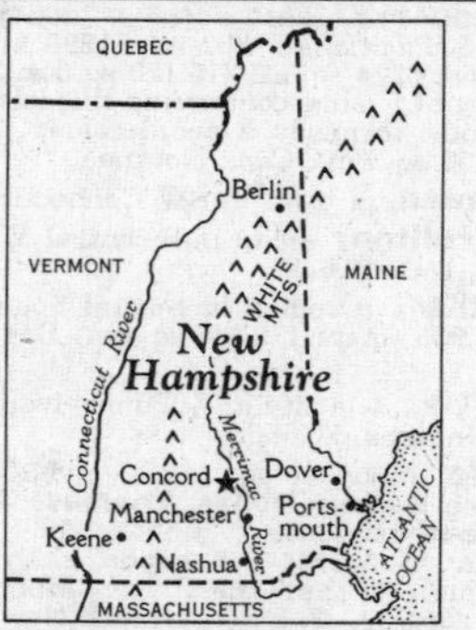

New′ Har′mony, a town in SW Indiana: socialistic community established by Robert Owen 1825. 945.

New′ Ha′ven, a seaport in S Connecticut, on Long Island Sound. 126,109.

New′ Ha′ven Col′ony, *Amer. Hist.* a settlement founded in 1638 by John Davenport and Theophilus Eaton at Quinnipiac (now New Haven, Conn.).

New′ Ha′ven stem′, *Naut.* a straight stem for flat-bottomed boats in which the ends of the side planking are mitered and covered with a sheet of metal, the stem piece being wholly inside.

New′ Ha′ven theol′ogy, Taylorism.

New′ He′brew. See **Modern Hebrew.**

New′ Heb′rides, former name of **Vanuatu.**

New′ High′ Ger′man, the High German language since c1500.

New′ Hope′, a town in SE Minnesota, near Minneapolis. 23,087.

New·house (nōō′hous′, nyōō′-), *n.* **Samuel I(rving),** 1895–1979, U.S. publisher.

New′ Ibe′ria, a city in S Louisiana. 32,766.

Ne Win (ne′ win′), **U** (ōō), (*Maung Shu Maung*), born 1911, Burmese soldier and political leader: prime minister 1958–60, 1962–74; president 1974–81.

New·ing·ton (nōō′ing tən, nyōō′-), *n.* a town in S Connecticut. 28,841.

New′ Ire′land, an island in the Bismarck Archipelago, in the W central Pacific Ocean NE of New Guinea: part of Papua New Guinea. 59,543; ab. 3800 sq. mi. (9800 sq. km).

new·ish (nōō′ish, nyōō′-), *adj.* rather new. [1560–70]

New′ Jer′sey, a state in the E United States, on the Atlantic coast. 7,364,158; 7836 sq. mi. (20,295 sq. km). *Cap.:* Trenton. *Abbr.:* NJ (for use with zip code), N.J. —**New′ Jer′sey·ite** (jûr′zē īt′), **New′ Jer′sey·an.**

New′ Jer′sey plan′, *Amer. Hist.* a plan, unsuccessfully proposed at the Constitutional Convention, providing for a single legislative house with equal representation for each state. Cf. **Connecticut Compromise, Virginia plan.**

New′ Jer′sey tea′, a North American shrub, *Ceanothus americanus,* of the buckthorn family, the leaves of which were used as a substitute for tea during the American Revolution. [1750–60]

New′ Jeru′salem, the abode of God and His saints; heaven. Rev. 21:2. Also called **Heavenly City, Celestial City.**

New′ Jeru′salem Church′, the church composed of the followers of Swedenborg; the Swedenborgian church. Also called **Church of the New Jerusalem, New Church.**

New′ Jour′nalism, journalism containing the writer's personal opinions and reactions and often fictional asides as added color. [1965–70] —**New′ Jour′nalist.**

New′ Ken′sington, a city in W Pennsylvania. 17,660.

New′ King′dom, the period in the history of ancient Egypt, 1580–1085 B.C., comprising the 18th to 20th dynasties, characterized by the predominance of Thebes. Also called **New Empire.** Cf. **Middle Kingdom, Old Kingdom.**

New′ Lat′in, Neo-Latin.

new′ learn′ing, the humanist revival of classical Greek and Latin studies and the development of Biblical scholarship in the 15th and 16th centuries in Europe.

New′ Left′, (*sometimes l.c.*) a radical leftist political movement active esp. during the 1960's and 1970's, composed largely of college students and young intellectuals, whose goals included racial equality, de-escalation of the arms race, nonintervention in foreign affairs, and other major changes in the political, economic, social, and educational systems. [1960; phrase appar. introduced by U.S. sociologist C. Wright Mills (1916–62)] —**New′ Left′ist.**

New′ Lon′don, a seaport in SE Connecticut, on the Thames River: naval base. 28,842.

new′ look′, 1. a new or changed appearance, approach, etc., esp. one characterized by marked departure from the previous or traditional one. **2.** (*usually caps.*) a style of women's clothing introduced by the designer Christian Dior in 1947, characterized by a silhouette with broad shoulders, a narrow waist, a long, full skirt, and often emphasized hips. —**new′-look′,** *adj.*

new·ly (nōō′lē, nyōō′-), *adv.* **1.** recently; lately: *a newly married couple.* **2.** anew or afresh: *a newly repeated slander.* **3.** in a new manner or form: *a room newly decorated.* [bef. 900; ME; OE *nīwlice.* See NEW, -LY]

new·ly·wed (nōō′lē wed′, nyōō′-), *n.* a person who has recently married. [1915–20; NEWLY + WED]

New·man (nōō′mən, nyōō′-), *n.* **John Henry, Cardinal,** 1801–90, English theologian and author.

New·man·ism (nōō′mə niz′əm, nyōō′-), *n. Theol., Eccles.* the views and theories of John Henry Newman before his conversion to the Roman Catholic Church, in which he held that the Thirty-nine Articles of the Church of England are compatible with Roman Catholicism. [1830–40; NEWMAN + -ISM]

New·man·ite (nōō′mə nīt′, nyōō′-), *n.* **1.** an adherent of John Henry Newman. **2.** a supporter of Newmanism. [1830–40; NEWMAN + -ITE[1]]

New·man·ize (nōō′mə nīz′, nyōō′-), *v.i.,* **-ized, -iz·ing.** to adopt or follow Newmanism. [1830–40]

New·mar·ket (nōō′mär′kit, nyōō′-), *n.* **1.** a town in SE Ontario, in S Canada, NW of Toronto. 29,753. **2.** a town in W Suffolk, in E England, E of Cambridge: horse races. 12,934. **3.** (*often l.c.*) Also called **New′market coat′.** a long, close-fitting coat worn in the 19th century as an overcoat by women and as a riding coat by men. **4.** *Brit.* the card game Michigan.

new′ math′, a unified, sequential system of teaching arithmetic and mathematics in accord with set theory so as to reveal basic concepts: used in some U.S. schools, esp. in the 1960's and 1970's. Also called **new′ mathemat′ics.** [1965–70]

New′ Mex′ico, a state in the SW United States. 1,299,968; 121,666 sq. mi. (315,115 sq. km). *Cap.:* Santa Fe. *Abbr.:* NM (for use with zip code), N. Mex., N.M. —**New′ Mex′i·can.**

New′ Mil′ford, 1. a town in W Connecticut. 19,420. **2.** a city in NE New Jersey. 16,876.

new-mint (nōō′mint′, nyōō′-), *v.t.* **1.** to mint or coin afresh. **2.** to give a new meaning or sense to (a word, term, or expression). [1585–95]

new′ moon′, 1. the moon either when in conjunction with the sun or soon after, being either invisible or visible only as a slender crescent. **2.** the phase of the moon at this time. See diag. under **moon.** [bef. 1000; ME; OE]

new-mown (nōō′mōn′, nyōō′-), *adj.* recently mown or cut: *the refreshing smell of new-mown hay.* [1425–75; late ME]

New·nan (nōō′nən, nyōō′-), *n.* a city in W Georgia. 11,449.

New′ Neth′erland, a Dutch colony in North America (1613–64), comprising the area along the Hudson River and the lower Delaware River. By 1669 all of the land comprising this colony was taken over by England. *Cap.:* New Amsterdam.

New′ Norse′, Nynorsk.

new′ or′der, 1. a new or revised system of operation, form of government, plan of attack, or the like. **2.** (*caps.*) the system of political and economic control and of social organization that prevailed in Germany and its subject countries during the Nazi era; National Socialism. [1835–45]

New′ Or′le·ans (ôr′lē ənz, ôr lēnz′, ôr′lənz), a seaport in SE Louisiana, on the Mississippi: British defeated (1815) by Americans under Andrew Jackson. 557,482. —**New′ Or·lea′ni·an** (ôr lē′nē ən, -lēn′yən).

New′ Or′leans lug′ger, a half-decked fishing boat, formerly used on the Gulf of Mexico near New Orleans, having a rather broad hull with centerboard and a single mast with a large dipping lugsail.

New′ Or′leans style′, a style of jazz developed in New Orleans early in the 20th century, influenced by blues, ragtime, marching band music, and minstrelsy and marked by polyphonic group improvisation. [1930–35]

new′ pen′ny, penny (def. 2). [1965–70]

New′ Philadel′phia, a city in E Ohio. 16,883.

New′ Plym′outh, a seaport on W North Island, in New Zealand. 43,914.

New′ Pol′itics, (*sometimes l.c.*) politics concerned more with grass-roots participation in the political process than with party loyalty or affiliation: identified esp. with the candidacies of Senators Eugene McCarthy and George McGovern. [1965–70]

New·port (nōō′pôrt′, -pōrt′, nyōō′-), *n.* **1.** a seaport in Gwent, in SE Wales, near the Severn estuary. 133,500. **2.** a seaport and summer resort in SE Rhode Island: naval base. 29,259. **3.** a city on the Isle of Wight, in S England. 22,286. **4.** a city in central Kentucky, on the Ohio River, opposite Cincinnati, Ohio. 21,587.

New′port Beach′, a city in SW California, SE of Los Angeles. 63,475.

New′port East′, a town in SE Rhode Island. 11,030.

New′port News′, (nōō′pôrt′, -pōrt′, -pərt, nyōō′-), a seaport in SE Virginia: shipbuilding and ship-repair center. 144,903.

New′ Port′ Rich′ey (rich′ē), a town in central Florida. 11,196.

New′ Prov′idence, 1. an island in the N Bahamas. 101,503; 58 sq. mi. (150 sq. km). **2.** a borough in NE New Jersey. 12,426.

New′ Re′alism, *Philos.* neorealism. [1905–10] —**New′ Re′alist.**

new-rich (nōō′rich′, nyōō′-), *adj.* **1.** newly or suddenly wealthy. **2.** characteristic of a newly or suddenly wealthy person: *a new-rich display of expensive jewelry.* —*n.* **3.** See **nouveau riche.** [1885–90]

New′ Right′, (*sometimes l.c.*) a group of conservatives whose views diverge from those of traditional conservatives, as in being more staunchly opposed to abortion or defense cuts. [1965–70] —**New′ Right′ist.**

New′ Ro·chelle′ (rə shel′, rō-), a city in SE New York, near New York City. 70,794.

New′ Rom′ney, a seaport town in E Kent, in SE England: one of the Cinque Ports. 3414. Formerly, **Romney.**

news (nōōz, nyōōz), *n.* (*usually used with a singular v.*) **1.** a report of a recent event; intelligence; information: *His family has had no news of his whereabouts for months.* **2.** the presentation of a report on recent or new events in a newspaper or other periodical or on radio or television. **3.** such reports taken collectively; information reported: *There's good news tonight.* **4.** a person, thing, or event considered as a choice subject for journalistic treatment; newsworthy material. Cf. **copy** (def. 5). **5.** newspaper. **6.** newscast. [1425–75; late ME *newis,* pl. of *newe* new thing, novelty (see NEW); on the model of MF *noveles* (pl. of *novele*), or ML *nova* (pl. of *novum*); see NOVEL[2]] —**news′less,** *adj.* —**news′less·ness,** *n.*

news′ a′gency, 1. a business organization that gathers news for transmittal to its subscribers. Cf. **press association. 2.** a business that sells newspapers at retail. [1870–75, *Amer.*]

news·a·gent (nōōz′ā′jənt, nyōōz′-), *n. Chiefly Brit.* newsdealer. [1850–55; NEWS + AGENT]

news′ an′alyst, commentator (def. 1).

news·beat (nōōz′bēt′, nyōōz′-), *n.* beat (def. 52b). [NEWS + BEAT]

news·board (nōōz′bôrd′, -bōrd′, nyōōz′-), *n. Brit.* See **bulletin board.** [1920–25; NEWS + BOARD]

news·boy (nōōz′boi′, nyōōz′-), *n.* a person, typically a boy, who sells or delivers newspapers. [1755–65; NEWS + BOY]

news·break (nōōz′brāk′, nyōōz′-), *n.* **1.** a newsworthy event or incident. **2.** *Radio and Television.* a station break that consists typically of two or three short news items. [1950–55; NEWS + BREAK]

news′ case′, *Print.* one of a pair of wooden, metal, or plastic trays divided into compartments for the sorting of type. Cf. **case[2]** (def. 8).

news·cast (nōōz′kast′, -käst′, nyōōz′-), *n.* a broadcast of news on radio or television. [1925–30; NEWS + (BROAD)CAST] —**news′cast′er,** *n.* —**news′cast′ing,** *n.*

news′ con′ference, a press conference, esp. one held by a government official. [1965–70]

New′ Scot′land Yard′. See under **Scotland Yard** (def. 1).

news·deal·er (nōōz′dē′lər, nyōōz′-), *n.* a person who sells newspapers and periodicals. [1860–65; NEWS + DEALER]

news·desk (nōōz′desk′, nyōōz′-), *n.* the department of a newspaper, television, etc., that writes, edits, or releases news, esp. late-breaking news or important bulletins. [1945–50; NEWS + DESK]

news′ flash′, *Journalism.* flash (def. 6). [1900–05]

news·girl (nōōz′gûrl′, nyōōz′-), *n.* a girl who sells or delivers newspapers. [1865–70; NEWS + GIRL]

news·hawk (nōōz′hôk′, nyōōz′-), *n. Informal.* a newspaper reporter, esp. one who is energetic and aggressive. Also called **news·hound** (nōōz′hound′, nyōōz′-). [1930–35, *Amer.*; NEWS + HAWK]

New′ Shrews′bury, former name of **Tinton Falls.**

New′ Sibe′rian Is′lands, a group of islands in the Arctic Ocean, N of the Russian Federation in Asia: part of the Yakut Autonomous Republic. 14,826 sq. mi. (38,400 sq. km).

news·let·ter (nōōz′let′ər, nyōōz′-), *n.* **1.** a written report, usually issued periodically, prepared by or for a group or institution, as a business firm, charitable organization, or government agency, to present information to employees, contributors, stockholders, or the like, and often to the press and public. **2.** a written report and analysis of the news, often providing forecasts, typically directed at a special audience, as business people, and mailed to subscribers: *a stock-market newsletter.* [1665–75; NEWS + LETTER]

news·mag·a·zine (nōōz′mag′ə zēn′, nyōōz′-), *n.* **1.** a periodical specializing in reports and commentaries on current events, usually issued weekly. **2.** *Radio and Television.* magazine (def. 5a). [1920–25; NEWS + MAGAZINE]

news·mak·er (nōōz′mā′kər, nyōōz′-), *n.* a person, thing, or event that is newsworthy: *a weekly magazine devoted to stories on newsmakers.* [1965–70; NEWS + MAKER]

news·man (nōōz′man′, -mən, nyōōz′-), *n., pl.* **-men** (-men′, -mən). **1.** a person employed to gather news, as for a newspaper, magazine, or radio or television news bureau; reporter. **2.** a person who reports the news on radio or television. **3.** a person who sells or distributes newspapers, periodicals, etc.; newsdealer. [1590–1600; NEWS + MAN[1]]
—**Usage.** See **-man.**

news′ me′dia, media[1] (def. 2). [1960–65]

news·mon·ger (nōōz′mung′gər, -mong′-, nyōōz′-), *n.* a person who spreads gossip or idle talk; a gossip or gossipmonger. [1590–1600; NEWS + MONGER]

New′ Smyr′na Beach′, a town in NE Florida. 13,557.

New′ South′ Wales′, a state in SE Australia. 5,126,217; 309,433 sq. mi. (801,430 sq. km). *Cap.:* Sydney.

New′ Spain′, the former Spanish possessions in the Western Hemisphere, at one time including South America (except Brazil), Central America, Mexico, the West Indies, Florida, and most of the land in the U.S. west of the Mississippi River.

news·pa·per (nōōz′pā′pər, nyōōz′-, nōōs′-, nyōōs′-), *n.* **1.** a publication issued at regular and usually close intervals, esp. daily or weekly, and commonly containing news, comment, features, and advertising. **2.** a business organization publishing such a publication. **3.** a single issue or copy of such a publication. **4.** newsprint. [1660–70; NEWS + PAPER] —**news′pa′per·dom,** *n.* —**news′pa′per·ish,** *adj.*

news·pa·per·man (nōōz′pā′pər man′, nyōōz′-, nōōs′-, nyōōs′-), *n., pl.* **-men. 1.** a person employed by a newspaper or wire service as a reporter, writer, editor, etc. **2.** the owner or operator of a newspaper or news service. [1800–10; NEWSPAPER + -MAN]
—**Usage.** See **-man.**

news·pa·per·wom·an (nōōz′pā′pər wŏŏm′ən, nyōōz′-, nōōs′-, nyōōs′-), *n., pl.* **-wom·en. 1.** a woman employed by a newspaper or wire service as a reporter, writer, editor, etc. **2.** a woman who is the owner or operator of a newspaper or news service. [1880–85; NEWSPAPER + WOMAN]
—**Usage.** See **-woman.**

new·speak (nōō′spēk′, nyōō′-), *n.* (*sometimes cap.*) an official or semiofficial style of writing or saying one thing in the guise of its opposite, esp. in order to serve a political or ideological cause while pretending to be objective, as in referring to "increased taxation" as "revenue enhancement." [NEW + SPEAK, coined by George Orwell in his novel, *1984* (1949)]

news′ peg′, 1. a news story that forms the basis of or justification for a feature story, editorial, political cartoon, or the like. **2.** the reference in a feature story, editorial, or the like, to the newsworthy event that underlies or justifies it. Also called **peg.** [1955–60]

news·per·son (nōōz′pûr′sən, nyōōz′-), *n.* a newsman or newswoman; reporter. [1970–75; NEWS + -PERSON]
—**Usage.** See **-person.**

news·print (nōōz′print′, nyōōz′-), *n.* a low-grade, machine-finished paper made from wood pulp and a small percentage of sulfite pulp, used chiefly for newspapers. Also called **newspaper.** [1895–1900; NEWS + PRINT]

new-sprung (nōō′sprung′, nyōō′-), *adj.* newly or suddenly come into existence. [1585–95; NEW + SPRUNG]

news·read·er (nōōz′rē′dər, nyōōz′-), *n. Chiefly Brit.* a person who presents the news on a radio or television news broadcast; newscaster. [1920–25; NEWS + READER]

news·reel (nōōz′rēl′, nyōōz′-), *n.* a short motion picture presenting current or recent events. [1915–20; NEWS + REEL[1]]

news′ release′. See **press release.**

news·room (nōōz′rōōm′, -rŏŏm′, nyōōz′-), *n.* a room in the offices of a newspaper, news service, or broadcasting organization in which the news is processed. Also, **news′ room′.** [1810–20]

news′ serv′ice, an agency that gathers news stories for its members or subscribers. Cf. **news agency** (def. 1), **press association, wire service.** [1890–95, *Amer.*]

news·stand (nōōz′stand′, nyōōz′-), *n.* a stall or other place at which newspapers and often periodicals are sold, as on a street corner or in a building lobby. [1870–75, *Amer.*; NEWS + STAND]

news′ sto′ry, a news report of any length, usually presented in a straightforward style and without editorial comment. Also called **story.** Cf. **editorial, feature story** (def. 1).

New′ Stone′ Age′, the Neolithic period.

New′ Style′, time reckoned according to the Gregorian calendar. Cf. **old style** (def. 2). [1605–15]

news·ven·dor (nōōz′ven′dər, nyōōz′-), *n. Chiefly Brit.* a person who sells newspapers or periodicals. [1825–35; NEWS + VENDOR]

New′ Swe′den, a colony established by Swedish settlers in 1638 along the Delaware River and captured by the Dutch in 1655: the only Swedish colony in America.

news·week·ly (nōōz′wēk′lē, nyōōz′-), *n., pl.* **-lies.** a newsmagazine or newspaper published weekly. [1945–50; NEWS + WEEKLY]

news·wire (nōōz′wīᵊr′, nyōōz′-), *n.* **1.** a service transmitted esp. by teletypewriter and providing late-breaking news stories, stock-market results, or other up-to-the-minute information: *We took the story off the newswires.* **2.** a teletypewriter or other machine by which such information is transmitted or received. [NEWS + WIRE]

news·wom·an (nōōz′wŏŏm′ən, nyōōz′-), *n., pl.* **-wom·en. 1.** a woman employed to gather news, as for a newspaper, magazine, or radio or television news bureau. **2.** a woman who reports the news on radio or television. **3.** a woman who sells or distributes newspapers, periodicals, etc. [1925–30; NEWS + -WOMAN]
—**Usage.** See **-woman.**

news·wor·thy (nōōz′wûr′thē, nyōōz′-), *adj.* of sufficient interest to the public or a special audience to warrant press attention or coverage. [1930–35; NEWS + -WORTHY] —**news′wor′thi·ness,** *n.*

news·writ·ing (nōōz′rī′ting, nyōōz′-), *n.* writing for publication in a newspaper, often reporting current events; journalism. [1915–20; NEWS + WRITING]

news·y[1] (nōō′zē, nyōō′-), *adj.,* **news·i·er, news·i·est.** *Informal.* **1.** full of news: *a nice long newsy letter.* **2.** gossipy. [1825–35; NEWS + -Y[1]] —**news′i·ness,** *n.*

news·y[2] (nōō′zē, nyōō′-), *n., pl.* **news·ies.** *Informal.* a person who sells or distributes newspapers. [1870–75; NEWS + -Y[2]]

newt (nōōt, nyōōt), *n.* **1.** any of several brilliantly colored salamanders of the family Salamandridae, esp. those of the genera *Triturus* and *Notophthalmus,* of

CONCISE PRONUNCIATION KEY: *act, cāpe, dâre, pärt; set, ēqual; if, īce; ox, ōver, ôrder, oil, bŏŏk, bōōt, out; up, ûrge; child; sing; shoe; thin, that;* zh as in *treasure.* ə = *a* as in *alone, e* as in *system, i* as in *easily, o* as in *gallop, u* as in *circus;* ᵊ as in *fire* (fīᵊr), *hour* (ouᵊr). l and n can serve as syllabic consonants, as in *cradle* (krād′l), and *button* (but′n). See the full key inside the front cover.

North America, Europe, and northern Asia. **2.** any of various other small salamanders. [1375–1425; late ME *newte,* for *ewte* (the phrase *an ewte* being taken as *a newte;* cf. NICKNAME), var. of *evet,* OE *efete* EFT[1]]

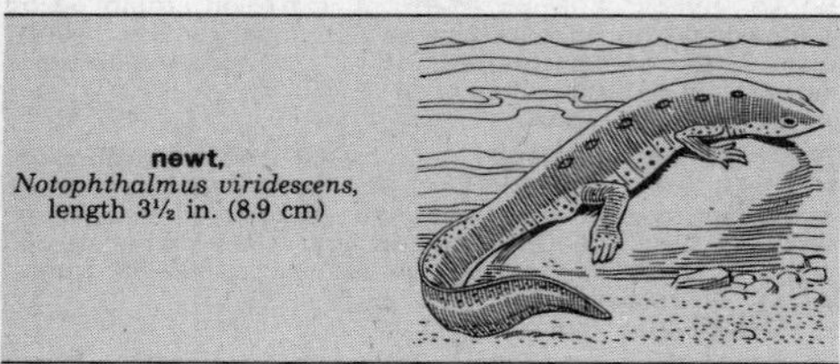

newt, *Notophthalmus viridescens,* length 3½ in. (8.9 cm)

New′ Ter′ritories. See under **Hong Kong** (def. 1).

New Test., New Testament.

New′ Tes′tament, 1. the collection of the books of the Bible that were produced by the early Christian church, comprising the Gospels, Acts of the Apostles, the Epistles, and the Revelation of St. John the Divine. See table under **Bible. 2.** the covenant between God and humans in which the dispensation of grace is revealed through Jesus Christ.

new′ theol′ogy, a movement away from orthodox or fundamentalist theological thought, originating in the late 19th century and aimed at reconciling modern concepts and discoveries with theology.

new′ thing′. See **free jazz.**

New′ Thought′, a system of doctrine and practice originating in the 19th century and stressing the power of thought to control physical and mental events. [1885–90] **—New′ Thought′er, New′ Thought′ist.**

new·ton (no͞ot′n, nyo͞ot′n), *n. Physics.* the SI unit of force, equal to the force that produces an acceleration of one meter per second per second on a mass of one kilogram. *Abbr.:* N [1900–05; after I. NEWTON]

New·ton (no͞ot′n, nyo͞ot′n), *n.* **1. Sir Isaac,** 1642–1727, English philosopher and mathematician: formulator of the law of gravitation. **2.** a city in E Massachusetts, near Boston. 83,622. **3.** a city in central Kansas. 16,332. **4.** a city in central Iowa, E of Des Moines. 15,292. **5.** a male given name: a family name taken from a place-name meaning "new town."

New·to·ni·an (no͞o tō′nē ən, nyo͞o-), *adj.* of or pertaining to Sir Isaac Newton or to his theories or discoveries: *Newtonian physics.* [1705–15; NEWTON + -IAN]

Newto′nian flu′id, *Hydrodynam.* any fluid exhibiting a linear relation between the applied shear stress and the rate of deformation. [NEWTON + -IAN]

Newto′nian mechan′ics. *Physics.* See **classical mechanics.**

Newto′nian tel′escope, a reflecting telescope in which a mirror or reflecting prism is mounted on the axis near the eyepiece so that the image may be viewed from outside the telescope tube at right angles to the axis. [1755–65]

new·ton-me·ter (no͞ot′n mē′tər, nyo͞ot′-), *n. Physics.* joule.

New′ton's law′ of mo′tion, *Physics.* See **law of motion.**

New′ton's meth′od, *Math.* a process for approximating the roots of an equation by replacing the curve representing the equation by its tangent and finding the intersection of the tangent with the x-axis and iterating this process. [named after I. NEWTON]

New′ton's rings′, *Optics.* the pattern of light interference produced by the contact of the convex surface of a lens with a plane glass plate, appearing as a series of concentric, alternately bright and dark rings, which are colored if the light source is white. [1825–35; after I. NEWTON, who discovered them]

new′ town′, (*sometimes caps.*) a comprehensively planned, self-sufficient urban community that provides housing, educational, recreational, and commercial facilities and often serves to absorb residents from a nearby overcrowded metropolis. [1915–20]

New·town (no͞o′toun′, nyo͞o′-), *n.* a town in SW Connecticut. 19,107.

New′ Ulm′ (ulm), a city in S Minnesota. 13,755.

new′ wave′, 1. a movement, trend, or vogue, as in art, literature, or politics, that breaks with traditional concepts, values, techniques, or the like. **2.** (*often caps.*) a group of leaders or representatives of such a movement, esp. of French film directors of the late 1950's and early 1960's. Cf. ***nouvelle vague.*** **3.** (*often caps.*) a largely minimalist but emotionally intense style of rock music, being an outgrowth of punk rock in the late 1970's, typified by spare or repetitive arrangements, and emphasizing energetic, unpolished performance. [1955–60] **—new′-wave′,** *adj.* **—new′wav′er.**

New′ West′minster, a city in SW British Columbia, in SW Canada, on the Fraser River: suburb of Vancouver. 38,550.

New′ World′. See **Western Hemisphere** (def. 1).

New′ World′ mon′key, any of various arboreal anthropoid primates of the group or superfamily Platyrrhini, inhabiting forests from Mexico to Argentina and typically having a hairy face, widely separated nostrils, long arms, and a long, prehensile tail, and including the capuchin, douroucouli, howler monkey, marmoset, saki, spider monkey, squirrel monkey, and woolly monkey.

CONCISE ETYMOLOGY KEY: <, descended or borrowed from; >, whence; b., blend of, blended; c., cognate with; cf., compare; deriv., derivative; equiv., equivalent; imit., imitative; obl., oblique; r., replacing; s., stem; sp., spelling, spelled; resp., respelling, respelled; trans., translation; ?, origin unknown; *, unattested; ‡, probably earlier than. See the full key inside the front cover.

new′ world′ or′der, (*sometimes caps.*) the post-Cold War organization of power in which nations tend to cooperate rather than foster conflict. [1990]

new′ year′, 1. the year approaching or newly begun. **2.** See **New Year's Day. 3.** (*caps.*) the first day or few days of a year in any of various calendars. [1150–1200]

New′ Year's′, 1. See **New Year's Day. 2.** See **New Year's Eve.**

New′ Year's′ Day′, January 1, celebrated as a holiday in many countries. [1150–1200; ME]

New′ Year's′ Eve′, the night of December 31, often celebrated with merrymaking to usher in the new year at midnight. [1350–1400; ME]

New′ York′, 1. Also called **New York State.** a state in the NE United States. 17,557,288; 49,576 sq. mi. (128,400 sq. km). *Cap.:* Albany. *Abbr.:* NY (for use with zip code), N.Y. **2.** Also called **New′ York′ Cit′y.** a seaport in SE New York at the mouth of the Hudson: comprising the boroughs of Manhattan, Queens, Brooklyn, the Bronx, and Staten Island. 7,071,639. **3. Greater,** New York City, the counties of Nassau, Suffolk, Rockland, and Westchester in New York, and the counties of Bergen, Essex, Hudson, Middlesex, Morris, Passaic, Somerset, and Union in New Jersey: the metropolitan area as defined by the U.S. census. 17,412,652. **—New′ York′er.**

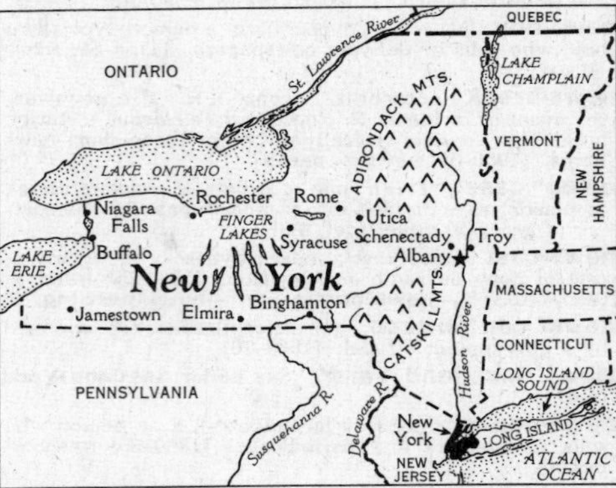

New′ York′ Bay′, a bay of the Atlantic at the mouth of the Hudson, W of Long Island and E of Staten Island and New Jersey.

New′ York′ Curb′ Exchange′, former name of the **American Stock Exchange.**

New′ York′ cut′. See **shell steak.**

New′ York·ese′ (yôr kēz′, -kēs′), the speech thought to be characteristic of a person from New York City, as in pronunciation or vocabulary. [1890–95, *Amer.;* NEW YORK + -ESE]

New′ York′ school′, a loosely associated group of American and European artists and sculptors, esp. abstract expressionist painters, active in and near New York City chiefly in the 1940's and 1950's.

New′ York′ State′. See **New York** (def. 1).

New′ York′ State′ Barge′ Canal′, 1. a New York State waterway system. 575 mi. (925 km) long. **2.** the main canal of this system, between the Hudson River and Lake Erie: consists of the rebuilt Erie Canal. 352 mi. (565 km) long.

New′ York′ steak′. See **shell steak.**

New′ York′ Stock′ Exchange′, the largest stock exchange in the U.S., located in New York City. *Abbr.:* NYSE, N.Y.S.E. Cf. **American Stock Exchange.**

New′ York′ strip′. See **shell steak.**

New′ Zea′land (zē′lənd), a country in the S Pacific, SE of Australia, consisting of North Island, South Island, and adjacent small islands: a member of the Commonwealth of Nations. 3,129,383; 103,416 sq. mi. (267,845 sq. km). *Cap.:* Wellington. **—New′ Zea′land·er.**

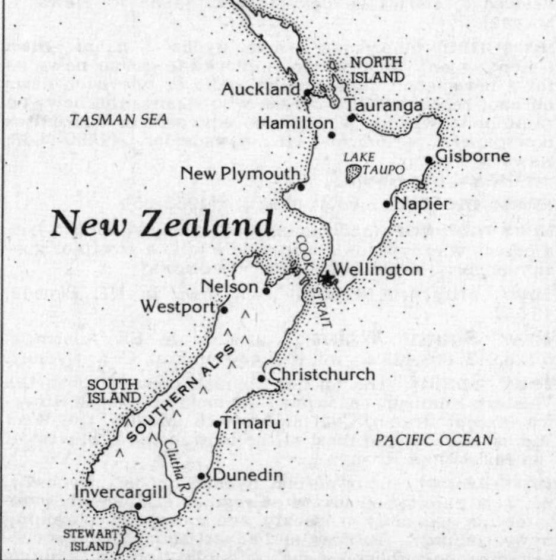

New′ Zea′land flax′, a large New Zealand plant, *Phormium tenax,* of the agave family, having showy, red-margined, leathery leaves and dull-red flowers, grown as an ornamental and for the fiber-yielding leaves. Also called **flax lily.** [1805–15]

New′ Zea′land spin′ach, a plant, *Tetragonia tetragonioides,* of warm regions, cultivated for its edible leaves, eaten as a vegetable. [1815–25]

Nex·ö (nek′sœ), *n.* **Mar·tin An·der·sen** (mär′ten ä′-nəʀ sən), 1869–1954, Danish novelist.

next (nekst), *adj.* **1.** immediately following in time, order, importance, etc.: *the next day; the next person in line.* **2.** nearest or adjacent in place or position: *the next room.* **3.** nearest in relationship or kinship. **4. next door to, a.** in an adjacent house, apartment, office, etc.; neighboring. **b.** in a position of proximity; near to: *They are next door to poverty.* **5. next to, a.** adjacent to: *He sat next to his sister.* **b.** almost; nearly: *next to impossible.* **c.** aside from: *Next to cake, ice cream is my favorite dessert.* —*adv.* **6.** in the place, time, importance, etc., nearest or immediately following: *We're going to London next. This is my next oldest daughter.* **7.** on the first occasion to follow: *when next we meet.* **8. get next to (someone),** *Informal.* to get into the favor or good graces of; become a good friend of. —*prep.* **9.** adjacent to; nearest: *It's in the closet next the blackboard.* [bef. 900; ME *next(e),* OE *nēxt, nēhst, niehst,* superl. of *nēah* NIGH (see -EST[1]); c. Icel *næstr,* G *nächst;* cf. NEAR]

next-door (*adv.* neks′dôr′, -dōr′, nekst′-; *adj.* neks′-dôr′, -dōr′, nekst′-), *adv.* **1.** Also, **next′ door′.** to, at, or in the next house on the street, esp. if it is very close by, or the adjacent apartment, office, room, or the like: *Go next-door and get your sister. Your sister is next-door. Her brother lives next-door.* —*adj.* **2.** being situated or living next-door: *next-door neighbors.* [1475–85]

next′ friend′, *Law.* a person other than a duly appointed guardian who acts on behalf of an infant or other person not fully qualified by law to act on his or her own behalf. Also called **prochein ami.** Cf. **guardian ad litem.** [bef. 900; ME; OE]

next′ of kin′, 1. a person's nearest relative or relatives: *The newspaper did not publish the names of casualties until the next of kin had been notified.* **2.** *Law.* the nearest relative or relatives who share in the estate of a person who dies intestate. [1760–70]

nex·us (nek′səs), *n., pl.* **nex·us. 1.** a means of connection; tie; link. **2.** a connected series or group. **3.** the core or center, as of a matter or situation. **4.** *Cell Biol.* a specialized area of the cell membrane involved in intercellular communication and adhesion. [1655–65; < L *nexus* a binding, joining, fastening, equiv. to *nect(ere)* to bind, fasten, tie + *-tus* suffix of v. action, with *tt* > *s*]

Ney (nā), *n.* **Mi·chel** (mē shel′), **Duke of El·ching·en** (el′ᴋʜing ən), 1769–1815, French revolutionary and Napoleonic military leader: marshal of France 1805–15.

Nez Per·cé (nez′ pûrs′; *Fr.* nā peʀ sā′), *pl.* **Nez Per·cés** (nez′ pûr′siz; *Fr.* nā peʀ sā′), (*esp. collectively*) **Nez Per·cé** for 1. **1.** a member of a North American Indian people of the Sahaptin family. **2.** the Sahaptin language of the Nez Percé. [1805–15; < F: lit., pierced nose]

Nez′ Percé′ War′, a war (1877) fought in the northwestern U.S. between the U.S. and a band of Nez Percé Indians.

NF, 1. no funds. **2.** Norman French.

n/f, no funds. Also, **N/F**

N.F., 1. Newfoundland. **2.** no funds. **3.** Norman French.

NFC, National Football Conference.

NFD., Newfoundland. Also, **Nfd., Nfld.**

NFL, National Football League.

NFS, not for sale. Also, **N.F.S.**

NG, 1. *Chem.* nitroglycerin. **2.** *Anat.* nasogastric.

ng, nanogram; nanograms.

N.G., 1. National Guard. **2.** New Guinea. **3.** no good.

n.g., no good.

Nga·dju (əng gä′jo͞o), *n., pl.* **-djus,** (*esp. collectively*) **-dju** for 1. **1.** a member of any of several Dayak tribes of southern Borneo. **2.** the Austronesian language of the Ngadju. Also, **Nga′ju.** Also called **Nga′dju Day′ak.**

Nga·li·e·ma (əng gä′lē ā′mə), *n.* **Mount,** a mountain with two summits, in central Africa, between Uganda and Zaire: highest peak in the Ruwenzori group. 16,790 ft. (5119 m). Formerly, **Mount Stanley.**

n′ga·na (nə gä′nə), *n. Vet. Pathol.* nagana.

NGC, *Astron.* New General Catalogue: a catalog of clusters, nebulae, and galaxies compiled by Danish astronomer Johan Ludwig Dreyer (1852–1926) and published in 1888.

NGF, nerve growth factor.

NGk, New Greek. Also, **N.Gk.**

NGNP, nominal gross national product.

Ngo Dinh Diem (ngō′ dēn′ dyem′, dzyem′, nō′ dēn′), 1901–1963, South Vietnamese statesman: president of the Republic of South Vietnam 1956–63.

Ngo·ni (əng gō′nē), *n., pl.* **-nis,** (*esp. collectively*) **-ni** for 1, 3. **1.** a member of an Nguni people of Tanzania, Malawi, and Zambia. **2.** the Bantu language of the Ngoni. **3.** Nguni.

NGU, See **nongonococcal urethritis.**

ngul·trum (əng gul′trəm), *n.* a paper money, cupronickel coin, and monetary unit of Bhutan, equal to 100 chetrums.

Ngu·ni (əng go͞o′nē), *n., pl.* **-nis,** (*esp. collectively*) **-ni** for 1. **1.** a member of a group of culturally and linguistically related peoples of southern and eastern Africa, including the Xhosa, Zulu, Ndebele, and Swazi. **2.** the group of Bantu languages spoken by these peoples, sometimes considered dialects of a single language. Also, **Ngoni.**

Ngu·yen Van Thieu (ngo͞o′yen′ vän′ tyo͞o′, no͞o′-yen′), born 1923, South Vietnamese political leader: president 1967–75, when South Vietnam capitulated to North Vietnam.

ngwee (əng gwē′), *n., pl.* **ngwee.** a bronze coin and monetary unit of Zambia, the 100th part of a kwacha.

NH, New Hampshire (approved esp. for use with zip code).

N.H., New Hampshire.

NHA, National Housing Agency. Also, **N.H.A.**

Nha Trang (nyä′ träng′), a port in SW Vietnam. 216,227.

N. Heb., New Hebrides.

NHG, New High German. Also, **NHG., N.H.G.**

NHI, *Brit.* National Health Insurance.

NHL, National Hockey League.

NHS, *Brit.* National Health Service.

NHTSA, National Highway Traffic Safety Administration.

Ni, *Symbol, Chem.* nickel.

N.I., Northern Ireland.

NIA, **1.** National Intelligence Authority. **2.** Newspaper Institute of America.

ni·a·cin (nī′ə sin), *n. Biochem.* See **nicotinic acid.** [1935–40; NI(COTINIC) AC(ID) + -IN²]

ni·a·cin·a·mide (nī′ə sin′ə mīd′), *n. Biochem.* nicotinamide. [1950–55; NIACIN + AMIDE]

Ni·ag·a·ra (nī ag′rə, -ag′ər ə), *n.* **1.** a river on the boundary between W New York and Ontario, Canada, flowing from Lake Erie into Lake Ontario. 34 mi. (55 km) long. **2.** See **Niagara Falls. 3. Fort,** a fort in W New York, at the mouth of the Niagara River. **4.** (*l.c.*) anything taken as resembling Niagara Falls in force and relentlessness; avalanche: *a niagara of criticism.* **5.** *Hort.* **a.** a variety of white grape, grown for table use. **b.** the vine bearing this fruit.

Niag′ara Falls′, 1. the falls of the Niagara River: in Canada, the Horseshoe Falls, 158 ft. (48 m) high; 2600 ft. (792 m) wide; in the U.S., American Falls, 167 ft. (51 m) high; 1000 ft. (305 m) wide. **2.** a city in W New York, on the U.S. side of the falls. 71,384. **3.** a city in SE Ontario, on the Canadian side of the falls. 69,423.

Niag′ara green′, a light bluish green. Also, **niag′ara green′.** [1930–35]

Ni·ag·a·ra-on-the-Lake (nī ag′rə on *th*ə lāk′, -ôn-, -ag′ər ə), *n.* a town in SE Ontario, in S Canada, on Lake Ontario, at the mouth of the Niagara River, on the border between Canada and New York. 12,186.

Ni′ah Cave′ (nē′ə), a limestone cave in Sarawak, Borneo, the site of the discovery of one of the earliest anatomically modern *Homo sapiens* skulls, dated c38,000 B.C.

Nia·mey (nyä mā′), *n.* a port in and the capital of Niger, in the SW part, on the Niger River. 102,000.

Ni·ar·chos (nē är′kōs; *Gk.* nē′är khôs), *n.* **Stav·ros Spy·ros** (stäv′rôs spē′rôs), born 1909, Greek businessman.

nib (nib), *n.* **1.** the point of a pen, or either of its divisions. **2.** a penpoint for insertion into a penholder. **3.** a point of anything: *a cutting tool with a diamond nib.* **4.** a bill or beak, as of a bird; neb. **5.** any pointed extremity. **6.** *Metall.* **a.** a piece of sintered tungsten carbide used as a die for drawing wire or the like. **b.** (in powder metallurgy) a compact at any stage of its manufacture. [1575–85; perh. var. of NEB; cf. D *nib,* MLG *nibbe* (var. of *nebbe*) beak, ON *nibba* sharp point. See NIBBLE] **—nib′like′,** *adj.*

nib·ba·na (nib bä′nə), *n. Pali.* nirvana (def. 1).

nib·ble (nib′əl), *v.,* **-bled, -bling,** *n.* **—***v.i.* **1.** to bite off small bits. **2.** to eat or chew in small bites: *Give him a graham cracker to nibble on.* **3.** to bite, eat, or chew gently and in small amounts (usually fol. by *at*): *She was so upset she could only nibble at her food.* **—***v.t.* **4.** to bite off small bits of (something). **5.** to eat (food) by biting off small pieces. **6.** to bite in small bits: *He nibbled each morsel with great deliberation.* **7. nibble away at,** to cause to decrease or diminish bit by bit: *Inflation was nibbling away at her savings. The rains nibbled at the loam.* Also, **nibble at. —***n.* **8.** a small morsel or bit: *Each nibble was eaten with the air of an epicure.* **9.** an act or instance of nibbling. **10.** a response by a fish to bait on a fishing line. **11.** any preliminary positive response or reaction. [1425–75; late ME *nebillen* to peck away at, nibble, try, perh. < MLG *nibbelen* to pick with the beak; cf. NIB, -LE]
—Syn. 8. tidbit, bite, taste, crumb.

nib·bler (nib′lər), *n.* **1.** a person or thing that nibbles. **2.** any of several fishes of the family Girellidae, inhabiting shallow coastal waters on both sides of the Pacific Ocean, having thin, incisorlike teeth. [1590–1600; NIBBLE + -ER¹]

Ni·be·lung (nē′bə lo͝ong′), *n., pl.* **-lungs, -lung·en.** *Teutonic Legend.* **1.** any of a race of dwarfs who possessed a treasure captured by Siegfried. **2.** the followers of Siegfried.

Ni·be·lung·en·lied (nē′bə lo͝ong′ən lēt′), *n.* a Middle High German epic of c1200, related to the Scandinavian *Volsunga Saga* and telling of the life of Siegfried, his marriage to Kriemhild, his wooing of Brunhild on behalf of Gunther, his murder by Hagen, and the revenge of Kriemhild. [< G; see NIBELUNG, LIED²]

nib·lick (nib′lik), *n. Golf.* a club with an iron head, the face of which has the greatest slope of all the irons, for hitting the ball with maximum loft. Also called **number nine iron.** [1855–60; perh. NIBBLE + *-ick,* var. of -OCK]

nibs (nibz), *n.* **his** or **her nibs,** *Informal* (*often facetious*). a person in authority, esp. one who is demanding and tyrannical: *His nibs wants fresh strawberries in December.* [1815–25; orig. uncert.]

ni·cad (nī′kad′), *n.* See **nickel-cadmium battery.** [by shortening]

Ni·cae·a (nī sē′ə), *n.* an ancient city in NW Asia Minor: Nicene Creed formulated here A.D. 325.

Ni·cae·an (nī sē′ən), *adj.* Nicene.

HONDURAS
Coco River
Nicaragua
Rio Grande
Matagalpa
Chinandega
León
LAKE MANAGUA
Managua
Masaya
Granada
LAKE NICARAGUA
Bluefields
CARIBBEAN SEA
PACIFIC OCEAN
San Juan River
COSTA RICA

Nic·a·ra·gua (nik′ə rä′gwə), *n.* **1.** a republic in Central America. 2,253,095; 57,143 sq. mi. (148,000 sq. km). *Cap.:* Managua. **2. Lake.** Spanish, **Lago de Nicaragua.** a lake in SW Nicaragua. 92 mi. (148 km) long; 34 mi. (55 km) wide; 3060 sq. mi. (7925 sq. km). **—Nic′a·ra′guan,** *n., adj.*

nic·co·lite (nik′ə līt′), *n. Mineral.* nickeline. [1865–70; < NL *niccol(um)* nickel + -ITE¹]

NiCd battery. See **nickel-cadmium battery.**

nice (nīs), *adj.,* **nic·er, nic·est. 1.** pleasing; agreeable; delightful: *a nice visit.* **2.** amiably pleasant; kind: *They are always nice to strangers.* **3.** characterized by, showing, or requiring great accuracy, precision, skill, tact, care, or delicacy: *nice workmanship; a nice shot; a nice handling of a crisis.* **4.** showing or indicating very small differences; minutely accurate, as instruments: *a job that requires nice measurements.* **5.** minute, fine, or subtle: *a nice distinction.* **6.** having or showing delicate, accurate perception: *a nice sense of color.* **7.** refined in manners, language, etc.: *Nice people wouldn't do such things.* **8.** virtuous; respectable; decorous: *a nice girl.* **9.** suitable or proper: *That was not a nice remark.* **10.** carefully neat in dress, habits, etc. **11.** (esp. of food) dainty or delicate. **12.** having fastidious, finicky, or fussy tastes: *They're much too nice in their dining habits to enjoy an outdoor barbecue.* **13.** *Obs.* coy, shy, or reluctant. **14.** *Obs.* unimportant; trivial. **15.** *Obs.* wanton. **16. nice and,** sufficiently: *It's nice and warm in here.* [1250–1300; ME: foolish, stupid < OF: silly, simple < L *nescius* ignorant, incapable, equiv. to *ne-* negative prefix + *sci-* (s. of *scire* to know; see SCIENCE) + *-us* adj. suffix] **—nice′ly,** *adv.* **—nice′ness,** *n.*
—Syn. 2. friendly. **3.** delicate, exact, exacting, critical, scrupulous, discriminating, discerning, particular. **7.** polite. **10, 12.** finical. **—Ant. 1.** unpleasant. **2.** unkind. **3.** careless. **9.** improper.
—Usage. The semantic history of NICE is quite varied, as the etymology and the obsolete senses attest, and any attempt to insist on only one of its present senses as correct will not be in keeping with the facts of actual usage. If any criticism is valid, it might be that the word is used too often and has become a cliché lacking the qualities of precision and intensity that are embodied in many of its synonyms.

Nice (nēs), *n.* a port in and the capital of Alpes-Maritimes, in SE France, on the Mediterranean: resort. 346,620.

Ni·cene (nī sēn′, nī′sēn), *adj.* of or pertaining to Nicaea. Also, **Nicaean.** [1350–1400; ME < LL *Nicēnus,* var. of *Nicaenus* < Gk *Nikaîos* (*Níkai(a)* Nicaea + *-os* adj. suffix), with *-n-* from L adj. suffix *-ānus* -AN]

Ni′cene Coun′cil, either of two church councils that met at Nicaea, the first in A.D. 325 to deal with the Arian heresy, the second in A.D. 787 to consider the question of the veneration of images. [1350–1400; ME]

Ni′cene Creed′, 1. a formal statement of the chief tenets of Christian belief, adopted by the first Nicene Council. **2.** a later creed of closely similar form (**Niceno-Constantinopolitan Creed** or **Constantinopolitan Creed**) referred, perhaps erroneously, to the Council of Constantinople (A.D. 381), received universally in the Eastern Church and, with an addition introduced in the 6th century A.D., accepted generally throughout western Christendom. [1560–70]

nice′ nel′ly (nel′ē), **1.** a person who professes or exhibits excessive modesty, prudishness, or the like: *too much of a nice nelly to have any fun.* **2.** nice-nellyism (def. 2). Also, **nice′ Nel′ly.**

nice-nel·ly (nīs′nel′ē), *adj.* **1.** characterized by prudishness or excessive modesty: *The entrance of his nice-nelly friend stopped the flow of risqué stories.* **2.** being a euphemism; euphemistic: *nice-nelly expressions.* Also, **nice′-Nel′ly.** [1920–25, *Amer.*]

nice-nel·ly·ism (nīs′nel′ē iz′əm), *n.* **1.** excessive modesty; prudishness. **2.** a euphemism: *an evasive style of writing, full of circumlocutions and nice-nellyisms.* Also, **nice′-Nel′ly·ism.** [1935–40; NICE NELLY + -ISM]

Ni·ce′no-Con·stan·ti·no·pol′i·tan Creed′ (nī-sē′nō kon stan′tn ō pol′i tn). See under **Nicene Creed** (def. 2).

Ni·ce·tas (nī sē′təs), *n.* See **Ignatius, Saint** (def. 2).

ni·ce·ty (nī′si tē), *n., pl.* **-ties. 1.** a delicate or fine point; punctilio: *niceties of protocol.* **2.** a fine distinction; subtlety; detail: *the niceties of the filigree work.* **3.** Usually, **niceties.** a refined, elegant, or choice feature, as of manner or living: *working hard to acquire the niceties of life.* **4.** exactness or precision. **5.** the quality of being nice; niceness. **6.** delicacy of character, as of something requiring care or tact: *a matter of considerable nicety.* [1275–1325; ME: silliness, extravagance, cleverness < OF *niceté.* See NICE, -TY]

niche (nich), *n., v.,* **niched, nich·ing. —***n.* **1.** an ornamental recess in a wall or the like, usually semicircular in plan and arched, as for a statue or other decorative object. **2.** a place or position suitable or appropriate for a person or thing: *to find one's niche in the business world.* **3.** *Ecol.* the position or function of an organism in a community of plants and animals. **—***v.t.* **4.** to place (something) in a niche. [1605–15; < F, MF, back formation from *nicher* to make a nest < VL **nīdiculāre,* deriv. of L *nīdus* NEST]
—Syn. 2. calling, vocation, slot, berth.

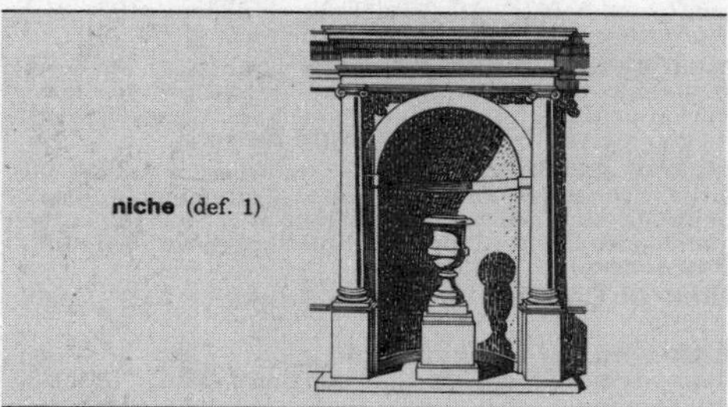
niche (def. 1)

Ni′chi·ren Bud′dhism (nich′ər ən), a doctrine of salvation based on the Lotus Sutra. [after *Nichiren* (1222–82), a Japanese Buddhist monk who advocated the doctrine]

Nich·o·las (nik′ə ləs, nik′ləs), *n.* **1. of Cu·sa** (kyo͞o′-zə), 1401–1464, German cardinal, mathematician, and philosopher. German, **Nikolaus von Cusa. 2. Grand Duke,** 1856–1929, Russian general in World War I. **3. Saint,** fl. 4th century A.D., bishop in Asia Minor: patron saint of Russia; protector of children and prototype of the legendary Santa Claus. **4.** a male given name: from Greek words meaning "victory" and "people."

Nicholas I, 1. Saint (*"Nicholas the Great"*), died A.D. 867, Italian ecclesiastic: pope 858–867. **2.** 1796–1855, czar of Russia 1825–55.

Nicholas II, 1. (*Gerard*) died 1061, pope 1058–61. **2.** 1868–1918, czar of Russia 1894–1917: executed 1918.

Nicholas III, (*Giovanni Gaetani Orsini*) died 1280, Italian ecclesiastic: pope 1277–80.

Nicholas IV, (*Girolamo Masci*) died 1292, Italian ecclesiastic: pope 1288–92.

Nicholas V, (*Thomas Parentucelli*) 1397?–1455, Italian ecclesiastic: pope 1447–55.

Nich·o·las·ville (nik′ə ləs vil′, nik′ləs-), *n.* a town in central Kentucky. 10,400.

Ni·chole (ni kōl′), *n.* a female given name.

Nich·ol·son (nik′əl sən), *n.* **1. Ben,** 1894–1982, British abstract painter. **2. Sir Francis,** 1655–1728, English colonial administrator in America.

Ni·chrome (nī′krōm′), *Trademark.* a brand name for a nickel-base alloy, containing chromium and iron, having high electrical resistance and stability at high temperatures.

nicht wahr (nɪKHt vär′), *German.* isn't that so?

Ni·ci·as (nish′ē əs), *n.* died 413 B.C., Athenian statesman and general.

nick (nik), *n.* **1.** a small notch, groove, chip, or the like, cut into or existing in something. **2.** a hollow place produced in an edge or surface, as of a dish, by breaking, chipping, or the like: *I didn't notice those tiny nicks in the vase when I bought it.* **3.** a small dent or wound. **4.** a small groove on one side of the shank of a printing type, serving as a guide in setting or to distinguish different types. See diag. under **type. 5.** *Biochem.* a break in one strand of a double-stranded DNA or RNA molecule. **6.** *Brit. Slang.* prison. **7. in the nick of time,** at the right or vital moment, usually at the last possible moment: *The fire engines arrived in the nick of time.* **—***v.t.* **8.** to cut into or through: *I nicked my chin while shaving.* **9.** to hit or injure slightly. **10.** to make a nick or nicks in (something); notch, groove, or chip. **11.** to record by means of a notch or notches. **12.** to incise certain tendons at the root of (a horse's tail) to give it a higher carrying position; make an incision under the tail of (a horse). **13.** to hit, guess, catch, etc., exactly. **14.** *Slang.* to trick, cheat, or defraud: *How much did they nick you for that suit?* **15.** *Brit. Slang.* **a.** to arrest (a criminal or suspect). **b.** to capture; nab. **c.** to steal: *Someone nicked her pocketbook on the bus.* [1475–85; obscurely akin to OE *gehnycned* wrinkled, ON *hnykla* to wrinkle]

Nick (nik), *n.* **1.** See **Old Nick. 2.** a male given name, form of **Nicholas.**

nick·el (nik′əl), *n., v.,* **-eled, -el·ing** or (*esp. Brit.*) **-elled, -el·ling,** *adj.* **—***n.* **1.** *Chem.* a hard, silvery-white, ductile and malleable metallic element, allied to iron and cobalt, not readily oxidized: used chiefly in alloys, in electroplating, and as a catalyst in organic synthesis. *Symbol:* Ni; *at. wt.:* 58.71; *at. no.:* 28; *sp. gr.:* 8.9 at 20°C. **2.** a cupronickel coin of the U.S., the 20th part of

CONCISE PRONUNCIATION KEY: act, cāpe, dâre, pärt; set, ēqual; *if,* īce; ox, ōver, ôrder, oil, bo͝ok, bo͞ot, out; up, ûrge; child; sing; shoe; thin, *th*at; zh as in *treasure.* ə = *a* as in *alone, e* as in *system, i* as in *easily, o* as in *gallop, u* as in *circus;* ᵊ as in *fire* (fīᵊr), *hour* (ouᵊr). l and n can serve as syllabic consonants, as in *cradle* (krād′l), and *button* (but′n). See the full key inside the front cover.

a dollar, equal to five cents. **3.** a nickel coin of Canada, the 20th part of a dollar, equal to five cents. —*v.t.* **4.** to cover or coat with nickel; nickel-plate. —*adj.* **5.** *Slang.* costing or worth five dollars: *a nickel bag of heroin.* [1745–55; < Sw, abstracted from *kopparnickel* < G *Kupfernickel* niccolite, lit., copper demon (so called because though looking like copper it yielded none); *Nickel* demon, special use of short form of *Nikolaus* proper name. Cf. OLD NICK, PUMPERNICKEL]

nick′el ac′etate, *Chem.* a green, crystalline, water-soluble solid, $C_4H_6NiO_4$, used chiefly in nickel-plating.

nick•el-and-dime (nik′əl ən dīm′), *adj., v.,* **nick•el-and-dimed** or **nick•eled-and-dimed, nick•el-and-dim•ing** or **nick•el•ing-and-dim•ing.** *Informal.* —*adj.* **1.** of little or no importance; trivial; petty: *a nickel-and-dime business that soon folded.* —*v.t.* **2.** to expose to financial hardship or bankruptcy by the accumulation of small expenses, bills, etc.: *We're being nickel-and-dimed to death by these small weekly expenses.* **3.** to hinder, annoy, or harass with trivialities or nonessentials: *to be nickeled-and-dimed by petty criticisms.* [1965–70]

nick′el-cad′mi•um bat′tery (nik′əl kad′mē əm), a storage battery, with an alkaline electrolyte, having nickel oxide as the positive element and cadmium as the negative. Also called **nicad, NiCd battery.**

nick′el car′bonyl, *Chem.* a colorless or yellow, volatile, water-insoluble, poisonous, flammable liquid, $Ni(CO)_4$, obtained by the reaction of nickel and carbon monoxide, and used for nickel-plating. Also called **nickel tetracarbonyl.** [1930–35]

Nick′el Cen′tre, a town in S Ontario, in S Canada. 12,318.

nick•el•ic (ni kel′ik, nik′ə lik), *adj. Chem.* of or containing nickel, esp. in the trivalent state. [1820–30; NICKEL + -IC]

nickel′ic ox′ide, *Chem.* a gray-black, water-insoluble powder, Ni_2O_3, which, at 600°C, decomposes to nickel oxide: used chiefly in storage batteries as an oxidizing agent. Also called **black nickel oxide, nickel sesquioxide.**

nick•el•if•er•ous (nik′ə lif′ər əs), *adj.* containing or yielding nickel. [1815–25; NICKEL + -I- + -FEROUS]

nick•el•ine (nik′ə lēn′), *n.* a usually massive, pale copper-red mineral, nickel arsenide, NiAs, with a metallic luster. Also called **niccolite.** [1780–90; NICKEL + -INE[2]]

nick•el•ize (nik′ə līz′), *v.t.,* **-ized, -iz•ing.** to nickel-plate. Also, *esp. Brit.,* **nick′el•ise′.** [1870–75; NICKEL + -IZE]

nick•el•o•de•on (nik′ə lō′dē ən), *n.* **1.** an early motion-picture theater where a film or a variety show could be seen, usually for the admission price of a nickel. **2.** an early jukebox that was operated by inserting nickels. [1885–90, *Amer.;* NICKEL (def. 2) + (MEL)ODEON]

nick•el•ous (nik′ə ləs), *adj. Chem.* containing bivalent nickel. [1875–80; NICKEL + -OUS]

nick′el ox′ide, *Chem.* a green, water-insoluble powder, NiO, used chiefly in the manufacture of nickel salts and in green pigments for ceramic paints. Also called **nick′el monox′ide, nick′elous ox′ide, nick′el protox′ide.**

nick′el plate′, a thin coating of nickel deposited on the surface of a piece of metal, as by electroplating. [1870–75]

nick•el-plate (nik′əl plāt′), *v.t.,* **-plat•ed, -plat•ing.** to coat with nickel by electroplating or other process. [1880–85]

nick′el sesquiox′ide, *Chem.* See **nickelic oxide.**

nick′el sil′ver. See **German silver.** [1855–60]

nick′el steel′, steel to which up to 9 percent nickel has been added. [1890–95]

nick′el tet•ra•car′bon•yl (te′trə kär′bə nil), *Chem.* See **nickel carbonyl.** [TETRA- + CARBONYL]

nick•el•type (nik′əl tīp′), *n. Print.* an electrotype with a deposit of nickel. [NICKEL + -TYPE]

nick•er[1] (nik′ər), *n.* a person or thing that nicks. [1660–70; NICK + -ER[1]]

nick•er[2] (nik′ər), *v.i., n. Chiefly Midland and Southern U.S.* **1.** neigh. **2.** laugh; snicker. [1785–95; appar. var. of *nicher, neigher,* freq. of NEIGH; see -ER[6]]

nick•er[3] (nik′ər), *n., pl.* **-er, -ers** for 1. **1.** *Brit. Slang.* one pound sterling. **2.** *Australian.* money. [1905–10; perh. special use of NICKER[1]]

Nick•laus (nik′ləs), *n.* **Jack (William),** born 1940, U.S. golfer.

nick•nack (nik′nak′), *n.* knickknack.

nick•name (nik′nām′), *n., v.,* **-named, -nam•ing.** —*n.* **1.** a name added to or substituted for the proper name of a person, place, etc., as in affection, ridicule, or familiarity: *He has always loathed his nickname of "Whizzer."* **2.** a familiar form of a proper name, as *Jim* for *James* and *Peg* for *Margaret.* —*v.t.* **3.** to give a nickname to (a person, town, etc.); call by a nickname. **4.** *Archaic.* to call by an incorrect or improper name; misname. [1400–50; late ME *nekename,* for *ekename* (the phrase *an ekename* being taken as *a nekename*). See EKE[2], NAME; cf. NEWT] —**nick′nam′er,** *n.*

Nick•y (nik′ē), *n.* **1.** a female given name, form of **Nicole. 2.** a male given name, form of **Nicholas.**

Nic•o•bar•ese (nik′ə bär′ēz, -ēs, -bä rēz′, -rēs′), *n., pl.* **-ese. 1.** a member of a people or group of peoples inhabiting the Nicobar Islands. **2.** the group of Austroasiatic languages spoken by the Nicobarese. [1870–75; NICOBAR (ISLANDS) + -ESE]

CONCISE ETYMOLOGY KEY: <, descended or borrowed from; >, whence; b., blend of, blended; c., cognate with; cf., compare; deriv., derivative; equiv., equivalent; imit., imitative; obl., oblique; r., replacing; s., stem; sp., spelling, spelled; resp., respelling, respelled; trans., translation; ?, origin unknown; *, unattested; ‡, probably earlier than. See the full key inside the front cover.

Nic′o•bar Is′lands (nik′ə bär′), a group of islands of India in the E part of the Bay of Bengal, forming the S part of the Andaman and Nicobar Islands. 30,433; 635 sq. mi. (1645 sq. km).

Nic•o•de•mus (nik′ə dē′məs), *n.* a Pharisee and member of the Sanhedrin who became a secret follower of Jesus. John 3:1–21; 7:50–52; 19:39.

ni•çoise (nē swäz′; *Fr.* nē SWAZ′), *adj.* **1.** in the style of Nice, France. **2.** garnished or prepared with tomatoes, and often anchovies, black olives, capers, etc.: *salade niçoise.* [ellipsis of F *à la niçoise* (*niçoise,* fem. of *niçois,* equiv. to *Nice* NICE + *-ois,* OF *-eis* < L *-ēnsis* -ENSIS)]

Nic•o•la•i (nik′ə lī′; *Ger.* nē′kō lä′ē), *n.* **(Carl) Ot•to (Eh•ren•fried)** (kärl ôt′ō ā′rən frēt′), 1810–49, German composer.

Nic•o•lay (nik′ə lā′), *n.* **John George,** 1832–1901, U.S. biographer.

Ni•cole (ni kōl′; *Fr.* nē kôl′), *n.* a female given name: from Greek words meaning "victory" and "people."

Ni•co•let (nik′ə lā′; *Fr.* nē kô le′), *n.* **Jean** (zhäN), 1598–1642, French explorer in America.

Ni•co•lette (nik′ə let′; *Fr.* nē kô let′), *n.* a female given name, form of **Nicole.**

Ni•colle (nē kôl′), *n.* **Charles** (sharl), 1866–1936, French physician: Nobel prize 1928.

Nic′ol prism′ (nik′əl), *Optics.* one of a pair of prisms used to produce and analyze plane-polarized light in a polarizing microscope. Also called **Nic′ol.** Cf. **polarizer** (def. 1). [1870–75; named after William *Nicol* (1768–1851), British physicist, its inventor]

Nic•ol•son (nik′əl sən), *n.* **1. Sir Harold George,** 1886–1968, English diplomat, biographer, and journalist (husband of Victoria Mary Sackville-West). **2. Marjorie Hope,** born 1894, U.S. scholar, educator, and author.

Nic•o•si•a (nik′ə sē′ə), *n.* a city on and the capital of Cyprus, in the central part. 115,700.

Ni•cos•tra•tus (nī kos′trə təs), *n. Class. Myth.* a son of Menelaus and Helen who, with his illegitimate brother Megapenthes, expelled Helen from Sparta when Menelaus died. Also, **Ni•kos′tra•tos.**

ni•co•ti•a•na (ni kō′shē ā′nə, -an′ə, -ä′nə), *n.* any plant belonging to the genus *Nicotiana,* of the nightshade family, esp. one grown for its ornamental value, as flowering tobacco. [1590–1600; < NL (*herba*) *nicotiana* Nicot's (herb) (named after Jacques *Nicot* (1530–1600), said to have introduced tobacco into France); see -IAN, -A[2]]

nic•o•tin•a•mide (nik′ə tin′ə mīd′, -mid, -tē′nə-), *n. Biochem.* a colorless, crystalline, water-soluble solid, $C_6H_6N_2O$, the amide of nicotinic acid, and a component of the vitamin-B complex, found in meat, liver, fish, whole wheat, and eggs: used in medicine chiefly as an agent for preventing or treating human pellagra or animal black tongue. Also called **niacinamide, nicotin′ic ac′id am′ide.** [1890–95; NICOTINE + AMIDE]

nicotin′amide ad′enine dinu′cleotide, *Biochem.* See NAD [1960–65; DI-[1] + NUCLEOTIDE]

nicotin′amide ad′enine dinu′cleotide phos′•phate, *Biochem.* See NADP [1960–65]

nic•o•tine (nik′ə tēn′, -tin, nik′ə tēn′), *n. Chem.* a colorless, oily, water-soluble, highly toxic, liquid alkaloid, $C_{10}H_{14}N_2$, found in tobacco and valued as an insecticide. [1810–20; < F; see NICOTIANA, -INE[2]] —**nic′o•tined′,** *adj.* —**nic′o•tine′less,** *adj.*

nic•o•tin•ic (nik′ə tin′ik, -tē′nik), *adj.* **1.** of, pertaining to, or containing nicotine. **2.** related to or imitating the action of nicotine on neurons, esp. in blocking the cholinergic receptors of the autonomic ganglia. [1870–75; NICOTINE + -IC]

nic′otin′ic ac′id, *Biochem.* a crystalline acid, $C_6H_5NO_2$, that is a component of the vitamin-B complex, found in fresh meat, yeast, etc., produced by the oxidation of nicotine, and used in the prevention and treatment of pellagra. Also called **niacin, vitamin B_3.** [1885–90]

nic•o•tin•ism (nik′ə tē niz′əm, -ti-, nik′ə tē′niz-), *n.* a pathological condition caused by excessive use of tobacco, and characterized by depression of the central and autonomic nervous systems; nicotine poisoning. [1890–95; NICOTINE + -ISM]

nic•o•tin•ize (nik′ə tē nīz′, nik′ə tē′nīz), *v.t.,* **-ized, -iz•ing.** to drug or impregnate with nicotine. Also, *esp. Brit.,* **nic′o•tin•ise′.** [1860–65; NICOTINE + -IZE]

Ni•co′ya Penin′sula (ni koi′ə; *Sp.* nē kô′yä), a peninsula in NW Costa Rica, on the Pacific Ocean.

Nic•the•roy (nik′tə roi′, nē′-), *n.* Niterói.

nic•ti•tate (nik′ti tāt′), *v.i.,* **-tat•ed, -tat•ing.** to wink. Also, **nic′tate.** [1815–25; < ML *nictitātus,* ptp. of *nictitāre,* freq. of L *nictāre* to wink, freq. of *nicere* to beckon; see -ATE[1]] —**nic′ti•tant,** *adj.*

nic′titating mem′brane, a thin membrane, or inner or third eyelid, present in many animals, capable of being drawn across the eyeball, as for protection. [1705–15; NICTATE + -ING[2]]

Nid•a (nid′ə), *n.* a female given name, form of **Nydia.**

ni•da•na (ni dä′nə), *n. Buddhism.* any of 12 aspects of Samsara, or the cycle of birth and death, often compared to 12 spokes of a wheel. [< Skt *nidāna* cause, source]

Ni•da•ros (nē′də rōs′), *n.* former name of **Trondheim.**

ni•da•tion (nī dā′shən), *n. Embryol.* implantation of an embryo in the lining of the uterus. [1870–75 for an earlier sense; NID(US) + -ATION]

nide (nīd), *n.* a nest or brood, esp. of pheasants. [1670–80; < L *nidus* NEST]

nidge (nij), *v.t.,* **nidged, nidg•ing.** *Masonry.* to dress (a stone) with a pick or kevel. [1835–45; orig. uncert.]

Nid•hogg (nēd′hôg′), *n. Scand. Myth.* a serpent in Niflheim who gnaws upon the lowermost root of Yggdrasil. Also, **Nid•hug** (nēd′hœg). [< ON *Níthhǫgg,* equiv. to *níth* evil + *hǫgg* hewer]

ni•dic•o•lous (nī dik′ə ləs), *adj.* remaining in the nest for a period after hatching. Cf. **nidifugous.** [1900–05; < L *nīd-* (s. of *nīdus*) NEST + -I- + -COLOUS]

nid•i•fi•cate (nid′ə fi kāt′), *v.i.,* **-cat•ed, -cat•ing.** to build a nest. [1810–20; < L *nīdificātus* (ptp. of *nīdificāre* to build a nest); see NIDIFY, -ATE[1]] —**nid′i•fi•ca′tion,** *n.* —**nid′i•fi•ca′tion•al,** *adj.*

ni•dif•u•gous (nī dif′yə gəs), *adj.* leaving the nest shortly after hatching. Cf. **nidicolous.** [1900–05; < L *nīd-* (s. of *nīdus*) NEST + *-i-* -I- + *fug(ere)* to flee, take flight + -OUS]

nid•i•fy (nid′ə fī′), *v.i.,* **-fied, -fy•ing.** nidificate. [1650–60; < L *nīdificāre* to build a nest, equiv. to *nīd-* (s. of *nīdus*) NEST + *-ificāre* -IFY]

ni•dus (nī′dəs), *n., pl.* **-di** (-dī). **1.** a nest, esp. one in which insects, spiders, etc., deposit their eggs. **2.** a place or point in an organism where a germ or other organism can develop or breed. [1735–45; < L *nīdus* NEST] —**ni′•dal,** *adj.*

Nid•wal•den (nēt′väl′dən), *n.* a demicanton of Unterwalden, in central Switzerland. 26,200; 106 sq. mi. (275 sq. km). *Cap.:* Stans.

Nie•buhr (nē′bo͝or; *for 1 also Ger.* nē′bo͝or), *n.* **1. Barthold Ge•org** (bär′tôlt gā ôrk′), 1776–1831, German historian. **2. Rein•hold** (rīn′hōld), 1892–1971, U.S. theologian and philosopher.

niece (nēs), *n.* **1.** a daughter of a person's brother or sister. **2.** a daughter of a person's spouse's brother or sister. [1250–1300; ME *nece* < OF < VL **neptia,* for L *neptis* granddaughter; r. ME *nifte,* OE *nift* niece (c. OFris, OHG *nift,* D *nicht,* ON *nipt*) < Gmc; akin to Lith *neptė̃,* Skt *naptī;* cf. NEPHEW]

Nie•der•sach•sen (nē′dər zäk′sən), *n.* German name of **Lower Saxony.**

ni•el•lo (nē el′ō), *n., pl.* **-el•li** (-el′ē), *v.,* **-el•loed, -el•lo•ing.** —*n.* **1.** a black metallic substance, consisting of silver, copper, lead, and sulfur, with which an incised design or ground is filled to produce an ornamental effect on metal. **2.** ornamental work so produced. **3.** a specimen of such work. **4.** a print on paper made from an incised metal plate before the application of niello and associated esp. with 15th-century Italy. —*v.t.* **5.** to decorate by means of niello; treat with niello or by the niello process. [1810–20; < It < L *nigellus* blackish, dim. of *niger* black] —**ni•el′list,** *n.*

Niel•sen (nēl′sən), *n.* **1. Carl Au•gust** (kärl ou′go͞ost), 1865–1931, Danish composer. **2.** *Informal.* See **Nielsen rating.**

Niel′sen rat′ing, an estimate of the total number of viewers for a particular television program, expressed as a percentage of the total number of viewers whose television sets are on at the time and based on a monitoring of the sets of a preselected sample of viewers. [1960–65; named after the A.C. *Nielsen* Co., its originator]

Nie•man (nē′mən; *Pol.* nye′men), *n.* Polish name of **Neman.**

Nie′mann-Pick′ disease′ (nē′mən pik′), *Pathol.* a rare, hereditary lipid-storage disease, occurring primarily among Ashkenazic Jews, in which abnormal lipid metabolism results in enlargement of the liver, spleen, and lymph nodes, and in progressive mental and physical deterioration. [described independently by German physicians Albert *Niemann* (1880–1921) in 1914 and Ludwig *Pick* (1868–1935?) in 1926]

Nie•mey•er (nē′mī ər), *n.* **Oscar,** born 1907, Brazilian architect.

Nie•moel•ler (nē′mœ lər), *n.* **Mar•tin** (mär′tēn), 1892–1984, German Lutheran clergyman: resisted Nazism. Also, **Nie′möl•ler.**

Niepce (nyeps), *n.* **Jo•seph Ni•cé•phore** (zhô zef nē sā fôr′), 1765–1833, French inventor.

Nier (nēr), *n.* **Alfred Otto Carl,** born 1911, U.S. physicist.

Nier•stein (nēr′stīn; *Ger.* nēr′shtīn′), *n.* a village in central West Germany, SSE of Mainz: noted for its wines.

Nie•tzsche (nē′chə, -chē), *n.* **Frie•drich Wil•helm** (frē′drikh vil′helm), 1844–1900, German philosopher.

Nie•tzsche•ism (nē′chē iz′əm), *n.* the philosophy of Nietzsche, emphasizing the will to power as the chief motivating force of both the individual and society. Also, **Nie′tzsche•an•ism.** [1905–10; NIETZSCHE + -ISM] —**Nie′tzsche•an,** *n., adj.*

Niè•vre (nye′vrᵊ), *n.* a department in central France. 245,212; 2659 sq. mi. (6885 sq. km). *Cap.:* Nevers.

Ni•fl•heim (niv′əl hām′), *n. Scand. Myth.* a place of eternal cold, darkness, and fog, ruled over by Hel: abode of those who die of illness or old age. [< ON *Niflheimr,* equiv. to *nifl-* (c. OE *nifol* darkness, OHG *nebal* mist, cloud, L *nebula* (see NEBULA)) + *heimr* world, HOME]

nif•ty (nif′tē), *adj.,* **-ti•er, -ti•est,** *n., pl.* **-ties.** *Informal.* —*adj.* **1.** attractively stylish or smart: *a nifty new dress for Easter.* **2.** very good; fine; excellent: *a nifty idea.* **3.** substantial; sizable: *We sold the car for a nifty profit.* —*n.* **4.** something nifty, as a clever remark or joke. [1860–65, *Amer.;* of obscure orig.] —**nif′ti•ly,** *adv.*

nig (nig), *v.t.,* **nigged, nig•ging.** *Masonry.* nidge.

Ni•gel (nī′jəl), *n.* a male given name, form of **Neil.**

Ni•ger (nī′jər; *Fr.* nē zher′), *n.* **1.** a republic in NW Africa: formerly part of French West Africa. 4,239,000; 458,976 sq. mi. (1,188,748 sq. km). *Cap.:* Niamey. See map on next page. **2.** a river in W Africa, rising in S Guinea, flowing NE through Mali, and then SE through Nigeria into the Gulf of Guinea. 2600 mi. (4185 km) long. See map on next page. —**Ni•ge•ri•en** (nī jēr′ē en′), *adj., n.*

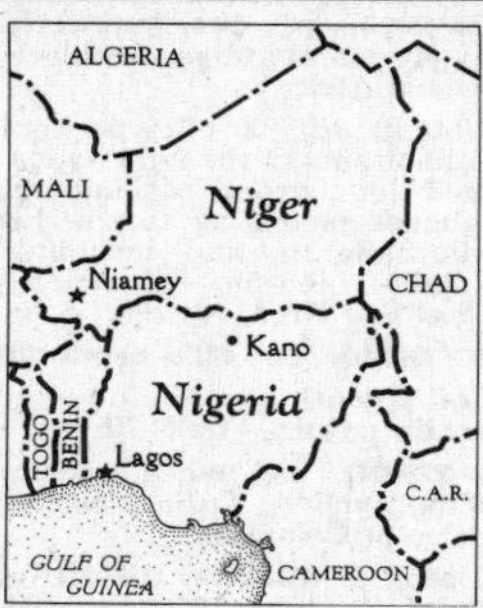

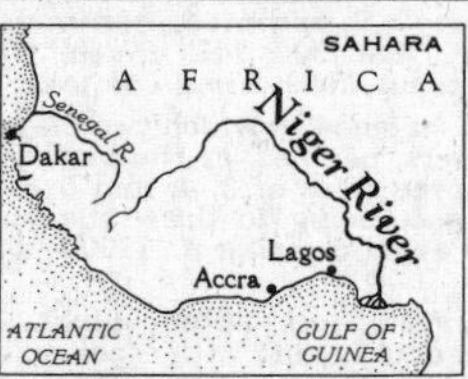

Ni·ger-Con·go (nī′jər kong′gō), *n.* **1.** a subfamily of Niger-Kordofanian, that comprises a large number of languages of Africa, as Ewe, Ibo, Yoruba, and the Bantu languages, spoken in nearly all of the equatorial forest region and in much of southern Africa. —*adj.* **2.** of, belonging to, or constituting Niger-Congo.

Ni·ge·ri·a (nī jēr′ē ə), *n.* a republic in W Africa: member of the Commonwealth of Nations; formerly a British colony and protectorate. 88,500,000; 356,669 sq. mi. (923,773 sq. km). *Cap.:* Abuja. Official name, **Fed′eral Repub′lic of Nige′ria.** See map above. —**Ni·ge′ri·an,** *adj., n.*

Ni·ger-Kor·do·fan·i·an (nī′jər kôr′də fan′ē ən), *n.* a language family comprising Niger-Congo and Kordofanian.

Ni′ger seed′, the black seed of a tropical African composite plant, *Guizotia abyssinica,* yielding an oil used as food, in the manufacture of soap, etc. [1885–90]

nig·gard (nig′ərd), *n.* **1.** an excessively parsimonious, miserly, or stingy person. —*adj.* **2.** niggardly; miserly; stingy. [1325–75; ME *nyggard,* equiv. to *nig* niggard (< Scand; cf. dial. Sw *nygg;* akin to OE *hnēaw* stingy) + -ARD]

nig·gard·ly (nig′ərd lē), *adj.* **1.** reluctant to give or spend; stingy; miserly. **2.** meanly or ungenerously small or scanty: *a niggardly tip to a waiter.* —*adv.* **3.** in the manner of a niggard. [1520–30; NIGGARD + -LY] —**nig′·gard·li·ness,** *n.*
—**Syn. 1.** penurious, miserly, mean, tight, avaricious, mercenary, illiberal, close. **2.** poor.

nig·ger (nig′ər), *n.* **1.** *Slang: Extremely Disparaging and Offensive.* **a.** (a contemptuous term used to refer to a black person.) **b.** (a contemptuous term used to refer to a member of any dark-skinned people.) **2.** *Slang: Extremely Disparaging and Offensive.* **a.** (a contemptuous term used to refer to a person of any race or origin regarded as comtemptible, inferior, ignorant, etc.) **3.** a victim of prejudice similar to that suffered by blacks; a person who is economically, politically, or socially disenfranchised. [1640–50; < F *nègre* < Sp *negro* black]

nig·gle (nig′əl), *v.i.,* **-gled, -gling. 1.** to criticize, esp. constantly or repeatedly, in a peevish or petty way; carp: *to niggle about the fine points of interpretation; preferring to niggle rather than take steps to correct a situation.* **2.** to spend too much time and effort on inconsequential details: *It's difficult to be meticulous and not niggle.* **3.** to work ineffectively; trifle: *to niggle with an uninteresting task.* [1610–20; < Scand; cf. Norw *nigla* to be penurious (ult. < ON *hnøggr* stingy, c. OE *hnēaw*); cf. NIGGARD] —**nig′gler,** *n.*

nig·gling (nig′ling), *adj.* **1.** petty; trivial; inconsequential: *to quibble about a niggling difference in terminology.* **2.** demanding too much care, attention, time, etc.: *niggling chores about the house.* [1590–1600; NIGGLE + -ING[2]] —**nig′gling·ly,** *adv.*

nigh (nī), *adv., adj.,* **nigh·er, nigh·est,** *prep., v.* —*adv.* **1.** near in space, time, or relation: *The time draws nigh.* **2.** nearly; almost; (often fol. by *on* or *onto*): *nigh onto twenty years.* —*adj.* **3.** near; approaching: *Evening is nigh.* **4.** short or direct: *to take the nighest route.* **5.** (of an animal or vehicle) being on the left side: *to be astride the nigh horse.* **6.** *Archaic.* parsimonious; stingy. —*prep.* **7.** near. —*v.i., v.t.* **8.** *Archaic.* to approach. [bef. 900; ME *nigh(e), neye,* OE *nēah, nēh,* c. D *na,* G *nahe,* ON *nā-,* Goth *nehw, nehwa;* cf. NEAR, NEXT]

night (nīt), *n.* **1.** the period of darkness between sunset and sunrise. **2.** the beginning of this period; nightfall. **3.** the darkness of night; the dark. **4.** a condition or time of obscurity, ignorance, sinfulness, misfortune, etc.: *the long night of European history known as the Dark Ages.* **5.** (*sometimes cap.*) an evening used or set aside for a particular event, celebration, or other special purpose: *a night on the town; poker night; New Year's Night.* **6. night and day,** unceasingly; continually: *She worked night and day until the job was done.* —*adj.* **7.** of or pertaining to night: *the night hours.* **8.** occurring, appearing, or seen at night: *a night raid; a night bloomer.* **9.** used or designed to be used at night: *to take a night coach; the night entrance.* **10.** working at night: *night nurse; the night shift.* **11.** active at night: *the night feeders of the jungle.* [bef. 900; ME; OE *niht, neaht,* c. G *Nacht,* Goth *nahts,* L *nox* (s. *noct-*), Gk *nýx* (s. *nykt-*)] —**night′less,** *adj.* —**night′less·ly,** *adv.* —**night′like′,** *adj.*

night′ blind′ness, *Ophthalm.* a condition of the eyes in which vision is normal in daylight but abnormally poor at night or in a dim light; nyctalopia. [1745–55] —**night′blind′,** *adj.*

night′-bloom·ing ce′reus (nīt′blo͞o′ming), any of various cacti of the genera *Hylocereus, Peniocereus, Nyctocereus,* or *Selenicereus,* having large, usually white flowers that open at night. [1800–10]

night′ bolt′. See **night latch.** [1775–85]

night·cap (nīt′kap′), *n.* **1.** *Informal.* an alcoholic drink taken at bedtime or at the end of a festive evening. **2.** a cap for the head, intended primarily to be worn in bed. **3.** *Sports Informal.* the last event of the program for the day, esp. the second game of a doubleheader in baseball or the last race of the day in horse racing. [1350–1400; ME; see NIGHT, CAP[1]] —**night′capped′,** *adj.*

night·clothes (nīt′klōz′, -klōthz′), *n.pl.* garments for wearing in bed, as pajamas or nightgowns. [1595–1605; NIGHT + CLOTHES]

night·club (nīt′klub′), *n., v.,* **-clubbed, -club·bing.** —*n.* **1.** Also, **night′ club′.** an establishment for evening entertainment, generally open until the early morning, that serves liquor and usually food and offers patrons music, comedy acts, a floor show, or dancing; nightspot. —*v.i.* **2.** to visit nightclubs. [1880–85, *Amer.*; NIGHT + CLUB] —**night′club′ber,** *n.*

night′ coach′, the class of airline coach at a lower fare than regularly offered, often restricted to late-night journeys. Also, **night′coach′.** Cf. **day coach** (def. 2). [1835–45; NIGHT + COACH]

night′ court′, a criminal court that convenes at night for the quick disposition of charges and the granting of bail. [1930–35]

night′ crawl′er, *Chiefly Northern, North Midland, and Western U.S.* an earthworm. [1920–25, *Amer.*]
—**Regional Variation.** See **earthworm.**

night·dress (nīt′dres′), *n.* **1.** nightclothes. **2.** a nightgown. [1705–15; NIGHT + DRESS]

night′ ed′itor, an editor responsible for getting a morning newspaper to press, for the night operations of a wire service, or the like. [1865–70]

night·fall (nīt′fôl′), *n.* the coming of night; the end of daylight; dusk. [1605–15; NIGHT + FALL]
—**Syn.** twilight, sundown.

night·glow (nīt′glō′), *n.* See under **airglow.** [1950–55; NIGHT + GLOW]

night·gown (nīt′goun′), *n.* **1.** a loose gown, worn in bed by women or children. **2.** *Archaic.* a dressing gown. [1350–1400; ME; see NIGHT, GOWN]

night·hawk (nīt′hôk′), *n.* **1.** any of several long-winged, American goatsuckers of the genus *Chordeiles,* related to the whippoorwill, esp. *C. minor,* having variegated black, white, and buff plumage. **2.** the European goatsucker or nightjar, *Caprimulgus europaeus.* **3.** *Informal.* a person who is habitually up or moving about late at night; night owl. [1605–15; NIGHT + HAWK[1]]

night′ her′on, any of several thick-billed, crepuscular or nocturnal herons of the genus *Nycticorax* and related genera, as *N. nycticorax* **(black-crowned night heron),** of the Old and New Worlds, and *Nyctanassa violacea* **(yellow-crowned night heron),** of America. [1775–85]

night·ie (nī′tē), *n. Informal.* a nightgown. Also, **nighty.** [1890–95; NIGHT(GOWN) + -IE]

night·in·gale (nīt′n gāl′, nī′ting-), *n.* any of several small, Old World, migratory birds of the thrush family, esp. *Luscinia megarhynchos,* of Europe, noted for the melodious song of the male, given chiefly at night during the breeding season. [1200–50; ME *nightyngale,* nasalized var. of *nightegale,* OE *nihtegale,* c. G *Nachtigall,* lit., night singer (cf. OE *galan* sing; akin to YELL)]

nightingale, *Luscinia megarhynchos,* length 6½ in. (17 cm)

Night·in·gale (nīt′n gāl′, nī′ting-), *n.* **Florence** (*"the Lady with the Lamp"*), 1820–1910, English nurse: reformer of hospital conditions and procedures; reorganizer of nurse's training programs.

night·jar (nīt′jär′), *n.* **1.** a nocturnal European bird, *Caprimulgus europaeus,* of the family Caprimulgidae, having a short bill and a wide mouth and feeding on insects captured in the air. **2.** Also called **goatsucker.** any other nocturnal or crepuscular bird of the family Caprimulgidae. [1620–30; NIGHT + JAR[2] (from its harsh cry)]

night′ jas′mine, 1. Also called **hursinghar, sad tree, tree of sadness.** a jasminelike, Indian shrub or small tree, *Nyctanthes arbor-tristis,* of the verbena family, having fragrant, white and orange flowers that bloom at night. **2.** Also called **night′ jes′samine.** a West Indian shrub, *Cestrum nocturnum,* of the nightshade family, having fragrant, creamy-white flowers that bloom at night. [1865–70]

Night′ Jour′ney, *Islam.* the journey in which Muhammad was carried from Mecca to Jerusalem and ascended into heaven. Cf. **Isra′, Mi′raj.**

night′ key′, a key for a night latch. [1830–40, *Amer.*]

night′ latch′, a door lock operated from the inside by a knob and from the outside by a key. Also called **night bolt.** [1850–55]

night′ let′ter, former name of **overnight telegram.** *Abbr.:* NL [1910–15]

night·life (nīt′līf′), *n.* **1.** the activity of people seeking nighttime diversion, as at a nightclub, theater, or the like. **2.** the entertainment available to them. Also, **night′ life′.** [1850–55; NIGHT + LIFE]

night-light (nīt′līt′), *n.* a usually dim light kept burning at night, as in a child's bedroom. [1640–50]

night′ liz′ard, any of several nocturnal lizards of the family Xantusiidae, of southwestern North America and Cuba, which bear live young.

night·long (*adj.* nīt′lông′, -long′; *adv.* nīt′lông′, -long′), *adj.* **1.** lasting all night: *a nightlong snowfall.* —*adv.* **2.** through the entire night: *They typed nightlong to finish the reports.* [bef. 1000; ME; OE *nihtlang* (adv.) for the space of a night. See NIGHT, LONG[1]]

night·ly (nīt′lē), *adj.* **1.** coming or occurring each night: *his nightly walk to the newsstand.* **2.** coming, occurring, appearing, or active at night: *nightly revels.* **3.** of, pertaining to, or characteristic of night: *the nightly gloom before a storm.* —*adv.* **4.** on every night: *performances given nightly.* **5.** at or by night: *an animal that is seen nightly.* [bef. 900; ME; OE *nihtlīc.* See NIGHT, -LY]

night·mare (nīt′mâr′), *n.* **1.** a terrifying dream in which the dreamer experiences feelings of helplessness, extreme anxiety, sorrow, etc. **2.** a condition, thought, or experience suggestive of a nightmare: *the nightmare of his years in prison.* **3.** (formerly) a monster or evil spirit believed to oppress persons during sleep. [1250–1300; ME; see NIGHT, MARE[2]]
—**Syn. 1.** phantasmagoria. See **dream.**

night·mar·ish (nīt′mâr′ish), *adj.* resembling a nightmare, esp. in being terrifying, exasperating, or the like: *his nightmarish experience in a concentration camp.* [1825–35; NIGHTMARE + -ISH[1]] —**night′mar′ish·ly,** *adv.* —**night′mar′ish·ness,** *n.*

night′ mon′key, douroucouli. [1870–75]

night-night (*interj.* nīt′nīt′, -nīt′; *adv.* nīt′nīt′), *interj.* **1.** *Informal.* good night. —*adv.* **2. go night-night,** *Baby Talk.* to go to bed or to sleep. [1895–1900]

night′ of′fice, *Eccles.* the office for matins. [1760–70]

night′ owl′, *Informal.* a person who often stays up late at night; nighthawk. [1585–95]

night′ per′son, a person who prefers to stay up late or who functions best during the nighttime hours.

night′ ra′ven, a bird that cries in the night. [bef. 900; ME; OE *nihthræfn, næhthræfn.*]

night·rid·er (nīt′rī′dər), *n.* one of a band of mounted men, esp. in the southern U.S. during Reconstruction, who committed nocturnal acts of violence and intimidation against blacks and black sympathizers. [1875–80; NIGHT + RIDER] —**night′rid′ing,** *n.*

night′ robe′, nightgown. [1545–55] —**night′-robed′,** *adj.*

nights (nīts), *adv.* at or during the night regularly or frequently: *He worked during the day and wrote nights.* [bef. 900; ME *nightes,* OE *nihtes.* See NIGHT, -S[1]]

night′ school′, a school held in the evening, esp. for working adults and others who are unable to attend school during the day. Also called **evening school.** [1520–30]

night·shade (nīt′shād′), *n.* **1.** any of various plants of the genus *Solanum,* esp. the black nightshade or the bittersweet. **2.** any of various other related plants, as the deadly nightshade. [bef. 1000; ME; OE *nihtscada.* See NIGHT, SHADE]

night′shade fam′ily, the plant family Solanaceae, characterized by herbaceous plants, trees, shrubs, and vines having alternate, simple or pinnate leaves, conspicuous flowers, and fruit in the form of a berry or capsule, and including belladonna, eggplant, nightshade, peppers of the genus *Capsicum,* petunia, potato, tobacco, and tomato.

night′ shift′, 1. the work force, as of a factory, scheduled to work during the nighttime. **2.** the scheduled period of labor for this work force. [1700–10]

night·shirt (nīt′shûrt′), *n.* a loose shirtlike garment reaching to the knees or lower, for wearing in bed. [1840–50; NIGHT + SHIRT]

night·side (nīt′sīd′), *n.* **1.** *Journalism.* the night shift of a newspaper. **2.** *Astron.* the dark side of a planet or moon. Cf. **dayside.** [1840–50 for an earlier sense; NIGHT + SIDE[1]]

night′-sky light′ (nīt′skī′), the faint glow of the night sky, caused by such phenomena as airglow and zodiacal light. [1975–80]

night′ snake′, a nocturnal, mildly venomous New World snake, *Hypsiglena torquata,* having a gray or yellowish body marked with dark brown spots.

night′ soil′, human excrement collected and used as fertilizer. [1765–75]

night·spot (nīt′spot′), *n.* a nightclub. [1935–40; NIGHT + SPOT]

night·stand (nīt′stand′), *n.* See **night table.** [1960–65; NIGHT + STAND]

CONCISE PRONUNCIATION KEY: act, cāpe, dâre, pärt; set, ēqual; if, īce; ox, ōver, ôrder, oil, bo͝ok, bo͞ot, out; up, ûrge; child; sing; shoe; thin, *th*at; zh as in *treasure.* ə = *a* as in *alone, e* as in *system, i* as in *easily, o* as in *gallop, u* as in *circus;* ə as in *fire* (fīər), *hour* (ouər). l and n can serve as syllabic consonants, as in *cradle* (krād′l), and *button* (but′n). See the full key inside the front cover.

night′ stick′, a special club carried by a policeman; billy. [1885–90, *Amer.*]

night′ sweats′, *Pathol.* heavy sweating during sleep, esp. as a symptom of certain diseases, as tuberculosis.

night′ ta′ble, a small table, chest, etc., for use next to a bed. Also called **bedstand, bed table, nightstand.** [1780–90]

night′ ter′ror, *Psychiatry.* a sudden feeling of extreme fear that awakens a sleeping person, usually during slow-wave sleep, and is not associated with a dream or nightmare. Also called **sleep-terror disorder.** [1895–1900]

night•tide (nīt′tīd′), *n. Literary.* nighttime. [1845–50; NIGHT + TIDE[1]]

night•time (nīt′tīm′), *n.* **1.** the time between evening and morning. —*adj.* **2.** occurring, done, presented, etc., during the night, esp. the hours before midnight. Cf. **daytime.** [1350–1400; ME; see NIGHT, TIME]

night•walk•er (nīt′wô′kər), *n.* **1.** a person who walks or roves about at night, esp. a thief, prostitute, etc. **2.** *New Eng.* an earthworm. [1475–85; NIGHT + WALKER] —**night′walk′ing,** *adj., n.*
—**Regional Variation. 2.** See **earthworm.**

night′ watch′, **1.** a watch or guard kept during the night. **2.** a person or the persons keeping such a watch. **3.** Usually, **night watches.** the periods or divisions into which the night was divided in ancient times. [bef. 1000; ME; OE] —**night′ watch′ing.**

Night′ Watch′, The, a painting (1642) by Rembrandt.

night′ watch′man, **1.** watchman. **2.** *Cricket.* a batsman who is sent in to bat just before the end of a day's play and continues his innings on the next day of play. Also, **night′-watch′man.** [1860–65]

night•wear (nīt′wâr′), *n.* night clothes.

night•y (nī′tē), *n., pl.* **night•ies.** nightie.

night•y-night (nī′tē nīt′), *interj. Informal.* See **good night.** [1875–80; redupl. of (*good*) *night;* see -Y[2]]

ni•gi•ri•zu•shi (ni gēr′ē zo͞o′shē), *n.* See under **sushi.** [< Japn]

ni•gres•cent (ni gres′ənt), *adj.* tending toward black; blackish. [1745–55; < L *nigrēscent-* (s. of *nigrēscēns,* prp. of *nigrēscere* to turn black, grow dark), equiv. to *nigr-* (s. of *niger*) black + *-ēscent-* (see -ESCE, -ENT)] —**ni•gres′cence,** *n.*

nig•ri•fy (nig′rə fī′), *v.t.,* **-fied, -fy•ing.** to blacken. [1650–60; < L *nigrificāre* to make black, blacken, equiv. to *nigr-* (s. of *niger*) black + *-i-* -I- + *-ficāre* -FY] —**nig′ri•fi•ca′tion,** *n.*

nig•ri•tude (nig′ri to͞od′, -tyo͞od′, nī′gri-), *n.* complete darkness or blackness. [1645–55; < L *nigritūdō* blackness, black color, equiv. to *nigr-* (s. of *niger*) black + *-i-* -I- + *-tūdō* -TUDE]

ni•gro•sine (nī′grə sēn′, -sin), *n. Chem.* any of the class of deep blue or black dyes obtained by the oxidation of aniline, used as coloring agents in inks and shoe polishes and for dyeing leather, wood, textiles, and furs. Also, **ni•gro•sin** (nī′grə sin). [1890–95; < L *nigr-* (s. of *niger*) black, dark + -OSE + -INE[1]]

NIH, National Institutes of Health.

ni•hil•ism (nī′ə liz′əm, nē′-), *n.* **1.** total rejection of established laws and institutions. **2.** anarchy, terrorism, or other revolutionary activity. **3.** total and absolute destructiveness, esp. toward the world at large and including oneself: *the power-mad nihilism that marked Hitler's last years.* **4.** *Philos.* **a.** an extreme form of skepticism: the denial of all real existence or the possibility of an objective basis for truth. **b.** nothingness or nonexistence. **5.** (*sometimes cap.*) the principles of a Russian revolutionary group, active in the latter half of the 19th century, holding that existing social and political institutions must be destroyed in order to clear the way for a new state of society and employing extreme measures, including terrorism and assassination. **6.** annihilation of the self, or the individual consciousness, esp. as an aspect of mystical experience. [1810–20; < L *nihil* nothing (var. of *nihilum;* see NIL) + -ISM] —**ni′hil•ist,** *n., adj.* —**ni′hil•is′tic,** *adj.*

ni•hil ob•stat (nī′hil ob′stat, nē′-), *Rom. Cath. Ch.* permission to publish a book, granted by an official censor who, upon examining it, has certified that it contains nothing contrary to faith or morals. [1885–90; < L: lit., nothing stands in the way]

Ni•hon (nē′hôn′), *n.* a Japanese name of **Japan.**

Ni•i•ga•ta (nē′ē gä′tä), *n.* a seaport on NW Honshu, in central Japan. 457,783.

Ni•i•ha•u (nē′ē hä′o͞o, nē′hou), *n.* an island in NW Hawaii, W of Kauai. 237; 72 sq. mi. (186 sq. km).

Ni•jin•sky (ni zhin′skē, -jin′-; *Russ.* nyi zhin′skyē), *n.* **Vas•lav** or **Was•law** (vä′sləf), 1890–1950, Russian ballet dancer and choreographer.

Nij•me•gen (nī′mā gən; *Du.* nī′mā KHən, -KHə), *n.* a city in the E Netherlands, on the Waal River: peace treaty 1678. 221,684. German, **Nimwegen.** Formerly, **Nymwegen.**

-nik, a suffix of nouns that refer, usually derogatorily, to persons who support or are concerned or associated with a particular political cause or group, cultural attitude, or the like: *beatnik, filmnik; no-goodnik; peacenik.* [< Yiddish (cf. NUDNIK) < Slavic: a personal suffix in Slavic languages in contact with Yiddish]

Ni•ke (nī′kē), *n.* **1.** the ancient Greek goddess of victory. **2.** one of a series of antiaircraft or antimissile missiles having two or three rocket stages. [< Gk *nī́kē* victory, conquest]

Ni′ke Her′cules, a 40 ft. (12 m) U.S. surface-to-air missile effective at medium to high altitudes and having a range of more than 87 mi. (140 km).

Ni′ke of Sam′othrace. See **Winged Victory.**

Nik•kei (nē′kā), *n.* **1.** an index showing the average closing prices of 225 stocks on the Tokyo Stock Exchange. **2.** an American of Japanese descent. [1980–85; < Japn]

Nik•ko (nēk′kō; *Eng.* nik′ō, nē′kō), *n.* a city on central Honshu, in central Japan: famous for shrines and temples. 28,502.

Nik′ko fir′, a tall evergreen tree, *Abies homolepis,* native to mountainous areas of Japan, having dark-green needles and purple cones, cultivated as an ornamental.

nik•kud (nē ko͞od′), *n., pl.* **nik•ku•dim** (nē′ko͞o dēm′). any of the combinations of dots and lines sometimes placed above or below Hebrew consonant symbols to indicate the pronunciation of vowels accompanying and usually following the consonants; vowel point. [< Heb *niqqūdh* pointing, vowelling]

Nik•ky (nik′ē), *n.* **1.** a female given name, form of **Nicole. 2.** a male given name, form of **Nicholas.**

Ni•ko•laus von Cu•sa (*Ger.* nē′kō lous fən ko͞o′zä *or, often,* nē′kō lä′o͞os). Nicholas (def. 1).

Ni•ko•la•yev (nik′ə lä′yəf; *Russ.* nyi ku lä′yif), *n.* a city in S Ukraine, on the Bug River. 503,000. Also, **Ni′ko•la′ev.** Formerly, **Vernoleninsk.**

Ni•kon (nē′kôn; *Russ.* nyē′kən), *n.* 1605–81, patriarch of Russian Orthodox Church 1652–66.

Ni•ko•pol (ni kô′pəl; *Russ.* nyē′kə pəl), *n.* a city in SE Ukraine, on the Dnieper River. 154,000.

nil (nil), *n.* **1.** nothing; naught; zero. —*adj.* **2.** having no value or existence: *His credit rating is nil.* [1805–15; < L *nīl,* var. (by apocope) *of nilum,* contr. of *nihilum* nothing, equiv. to *ni* (var. of *ne* not) + *hīlum* trifle]

nil ad•mi•ra•ri (nēl′ äd′mē RÄ′Rē; *Eng.* nil′ ad′mi-râr′ī, -râr′ē), *Latin.* to wonder at nothing.

nil de•spe•ran•dum (nēl′ des′pe RÄN′do͝om; *Eng.* nil′ des′pə ran′dəm), *Latin.* never despair.

Nile (nīl), *n.* a river in E Africa, the longest in the world, flowing N from Lake Victoria to the Mediterranean. 3473 mi. (5592 km) long; from the headwaters of the Kagera River, 4000 mi. (6440 km) long. Cf. **Blue Nile, White Nile.**

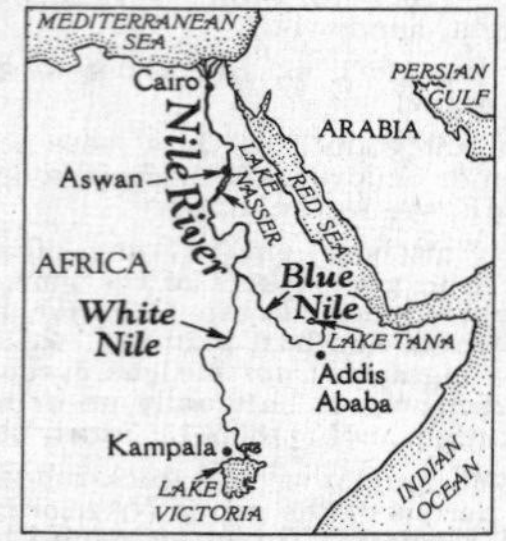

Nile′ blue′, pale greenish blue. [1880–85]

Nile′ croc′odile, the common African crocodile, *Crocodylus niloticus,* sometimes growing to a length of 20 ft. (6.1 m): in some areas it is greatly reduced in number and now rare. Also, **Nilotic crocodile.** See illus. under **crocodile.** [1895–1900]

Nile′ green′, pale bluish green. [1885–90]

Niles (nīlz), *n.* **1.** a city in NE Illinois, near Chicago. 30,363. **2.** a city in NE Ohio. 23,088. **3.** a city in SW Michigan. 13,115. **4.** a male given name, form of **Neil.**

nil•gai (nil′gī), *n., pl.* **-gais,** (*esp. collectively*) **-gai.** a large, Indian antelope, *Boselaphus tragocamelus,* the male of which is bluish gray with small horns, the female tawny and hornless. Also, **nylghai, nylghau.** Also called **blue bull.** [1880–85; < Hindi *nīlgāy* lit., blue cow]

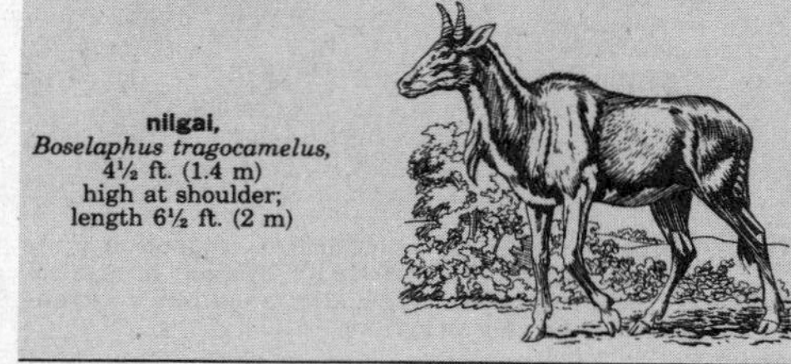
nilgai, *Boselaphus tragocamelus,* 4½ ft. (1.4 m) high at shoulder; length 6½ ft. (2 m)

Nil′gi•ri Hills′ (nil′gə rē), a group of mountains in S India, in Madras state. Highest peak, Mt. Dodabetta, 8760 ft. (2670 m).

nill (nil), *v.,* **nilled, nill•ing.** *Archaic.* —*v.i.* **1.** to be unwilling: *will he, nill he.* —*v.t.* **2.** to refuse or reject. [bef. 900; ME *nillen,* OE *nyllan,* contr. of *nwillan,* contr. of phrase *ne willan;* see NA, WILL[1], WILLY-NILLY]

Ni•ló•po•lis (ni lô′po͝o lis), *n.* a city in SE Brazil, NW of Rio de Janeiro. 128,524.

Ni•lo-Sa•har•an (nī′lō sə har′ən, -hâr′-, -här′-), *n.* a family of African languages, including the Central and Eastern Sudanic groups as well as Kanuri, Songhai, and other languages, spoken from the Sahara southward to Zaire and Tanzania.

Ni•lo•te (nī lō′tē), *n., pl.* **-tes,** (*esp. collectively*) **-te.** a member of any of several indigenous black peoples of the Sudan and eastern Africa.

Ni•lot•ic (nī lot′ik), *adj.* **1.** of or pertaining to the Nile River or the inhabitants of the Nile region. **2.** of or pertaining to the Nilotic group of languages. —*n.* **3.** a group of languages belonging to the Eastern Sudanic branch of Nilo-Saharan, and including Dinka, Luo, Masai, and Nandi. [1645–55; < L *Nīlōticus* of the Nile < Gk *Neilōtikós.* See NILE, -OTIC]

Nilot′ic croc′odile. See **Nile crocodile.** [1850–55]

nil•po•tent (nil pōt′nt), *adj. Math.* equal to zero when raised to a certain power. [1865–70; NIL + POTENT]

nil si•ne nu•mi•ne (nēl sin′e no͞o′mi ne; *Eng.* nil sin′ē no͞o′mi nē, nyo͞o′-), *Latin.* nothing without the divine will: motto of Colorado.

Nils•son (nil′sən), *n.* **(Mär•ta) Bir•git** (mär′tä biʀ′git; *Eng.* mär′tə bûr′git), born 1918, Swedish soprano.

nim[1] (nim), *v.t., v.i.,* **nimmed, nim•ming.** *Archaic.* to steal or pilfer. [bef. 900; ME *nimen,* OE *niman,* c. G *nehmen,* ON *nema,* Goth *niman* to take; cf. NUMB]

nim[2] (nim), *n.* a game in which two players alternate in drawing counters, pennies, or the like, from a set of 12 arranged in three rows of 3, 4, and 5 counters, respectively, the object being to draw the last counter, or, sometimes, to avoid drawing it. [1900–05; special use of NIM[1]]

nim•ble (nim′bəl), *adj.,* **-bler, -blest. 1.** quick and light in movement; moving with ease; agile; active; rapid: *nimble feet.* **2.** quick to understand, think, devise, etc.: *a nimble mind.* **3.** cleverly contrived: *a story with a nimble plot.* [bef. 1000; late ME *nymel,* earlier *nemel,* OE *næmel* capable, equiv. to *næm-* (var. s. of *niman* to take; see NIM[1]) + *-el* -LE] —**nim′ble•ness,** *n.* —**nim′•bly,** *adv.*
—**Syn. 1.** lively, brisk, swift. **2.** alert.

nimbo-, a combining form representing **nimbus** in compound words: *nimbostratus.*

nim•bo•stra•tus (nim′bō strā′təs, -strat′əs), *n., pl.* **-tus.** a cloud of a class characterized by a formless layer that is almost uniformly dark gray; a rain cloud of the layer type, of low altitude, usually below 8000 ft. (2440 m). [1885–90; NIMBO- + STRATUS]

nim•bus (nim′bəs), *n., pl.* **-bi** (-bī), **-bus•es. 1.** *Class. Myth.* a shining cloud sometimes surrounding a deity when on earth. **2.** a cloud, aura, atmosphere, etc., surrounding a person or thing: *The candidate was encompassed with a nimbus of fame.* **3.** halo (def. 1). **4.** the type of dense clouds or cloud mass with ragged edges, that yields rain or snow; a rain cloud. **5.** (*cap.*) *U.S. Aerospace.* one of a series of polar-orbiting meteorological and environmental research satellites, the last of which Nimbus 7, launched 1978, was the first satellite designed to monitor atmospheric pollutants. [1610–20; < L: a rainstorm, rain cloud, thundercloud, cloud; akin to L *nebula* and Gk *nephélē, néphos* cloud] —**nim′bused,** *adj.*

NIMBY (*usually* nim′bē), not in my backyard: used to express opposition by local citizens to the locating in their neighborhood of a civic project, as a jail, garbage dump, or drug rehabilitation center, that, though needed by the larger community, is considered unsightly, dangerous, or likely to lead to decreased property values. Also, **Nim′by.** [1980–85] —**Nim′by•ism,** *n.*

Ni•mei•ry (nə mâr′ē), *n.* **Gaa•far Muhammad al-** (gä′fär; al), born 1930, Sudanese political leader: president 1969–85. Also, **Ni•mei′ri.**

Nîmes (nēm), *n.* a city in and the capital of Gard, in S France: Roman ruins. 133,942.

NIMH, National Institute of Mental Health.

ni•mi•e•ty (ni mī′i tē), *n., pl.* **-ties. 1.** excess; overabundance: *nimiety of mere niceties in conversation.* **2.** an instance of this. [1555–65; < LL *nimietās,* equiv. to *nimi(us)* too much + *-etās,* var. (after *i*) of *-itās* -ITY]

nim•i•ny-pim•i•ny (nim′ə nē pim′ə nē), *adj.* affectedly delicate or refined; mincing; effeminate: *A niminy-piminy shyness makes frankness impossible.* [1795–1805; rhyming compound; cf. NAMBY-PAMBY] —**nim′i•ny-pim′i•ni•ness,** *n.* —**nim′i•ny-pim′i•ny•ism,** *n.*

Nim•itz (nim′its), *n.* **Chester William,** 1885–1966, U.S. admiral.

Nim•rod (nim′rod), *n.* **1.** the great-grandson of Noah: noted as a great hunter. Gen. 10:8–10. **2.** (*sometimes l.c.*) a person expert in or devoted to hunting. —**Nim•rod′i•an, Nim•rod′ic, Nim•rod′i•cal,** *adj.*

Nim•rud (nim ro͞od′), *n.* modern name of the site of the ancient city of Kalakh.

nim′ tree′, neem (def. 2). [1875–80]

Nim•we•gen (nim′vā gən), *n.* German name of **Nijmegen.**

ni•ña (nē′nyä), *n., pl.* **-ñas** (-nyäs). *Spanish.* girl; child.

Ni•na (nē′nə, nī′-), *n.* a female given name, Russian form of **Anna.**

Ni•ña (nēn′yə, nē′nə; *Sp.* nē′nyä), *n.* one of the three ships under the command of Columbus when he made his first voyage of discovery to America in 1492.

nin•com•poop (nin′kəm po͞op′, ning′-), *n.* a fool or simpleton. [1670–80; orig. uncert.] —**nin′com•poop′•er•y,** *n.* —**nin′com•poop′ish,** *adj.*

nine (nīn), *n.* **1.** a cardinal number, eight plus one. **2.** a symbol for this number, as 9 or IX. **3.** a set of this many persons or things. **4.** a baseball team. **5.** a playing card with nine pips. **6. dressed to the nines,** looking one's best; dressed smartly, splendidly, etc.: *All the girls were dressed to the nines for the party.* **7. the Nine,** the Muses. —*adj.* **8.** amounting to nine in number. [bef. 900; ME; OE *nigan, nigon,* c. D *negen,* akin to G *neun,* ON *nīu,* Goth *niun,* L *novem,* Gk *ennéa,* Skt *náva*]

nine′ ball′, a variation of pool played with nine numbered object balls that must be pocketed in order by number. Also, **nine′ball′.** [1965–70]

CONCISE ETYMOLOGY KEY: <, descended or borrowed from; >, whence; b., blend of, blended; c., cognate with; cf., compare; deriv., derivative; equiv., equivalent; imit., imitative; obl., oblique; r., replacing; s., stem; sp., spelling, spelled; resp., respelling, respelled; trans., translation; ?, origin unknown; *, unattested; ‡, probably earlier than. See the full key inside the front cover.

nine′-band′ed armadil′lo (nīn′band′did), an armadillo, *Dasypus novemcinctus*, of the southern U.S. to Argentina, having nine hinged bands of bony plates, the female of which usually gives birth to quadruplets that are always of the same sex. Also called **peba, Texas armadillo.** See illus. under **armadillo.** [1905–10]

nine•bark (nīn′bärk′), *n.* any of several shrubs belonging to the genus *Physocarpus*, of the rose family, having bark that separates into thin layers. [1775–85, *Amer.*; NINE + BARK[2]]

nine′ days′ won′der, an event or thing that arouses considerable but short-lived interest or excitement. [1585–95]

nine•fold (*adj.* nīn′fōld′; *adv.* nīn′fōld′), *adj.* **1.** nine times as great or as much. **2.** having nine elements or parts. —*adv.* **3.** in a ninefold manner or measure; to or by nine times as much: *to increase one's income ninefold.* [bef. 1000; NINE + -FOLD; cf. OE *nigonfeald* in same sense (not attested in ME)]

900 number, a telephone number preceded by the three-digit code "900," used to provide information or entertainment for a fee charged directly to the caller's telephone bill. [1985–90]

nine•pence (nīn′pens′, -pəns), *n.* **1.** (*used with a plural v.*) *Brit.* nine pennies. **2.** a former shilling of Great Britain, issued under Elizabeth I for use in Ireland, debased so that it was used in England as a ninepenny piece. [1540–50; NINE + PENCE]

nine•pen•ny (nīn′pen′ē; *for 2 also* nīn′pə nē), *adj.* **1.** noting a nail 2¾ in. (7 cm) long. *Symbol:* 9d **2.** of the value of ninepence. [1820–30; NINE + PENNY]

nine•pins (nīn′pinz′), *n.* **1.** (*used with a singular v.*) tenpins played without the head pin. **2. ninepin,** a pin used in this game. [1570–80; NINE + PINS]

nine′ plus′ two′ array′, *Cell Biol.* the arrangement of microtubules in a flagellum or cilium, consisting of a ring of nine evenly spaced couplets surrounding two central singlets. *Symbol:* 9 + 2.

nine′ plus′ ze′ro array′, *Cell Biol.* the arrangement of microtubules characteristic of basal bodies and centrioles, consisting of nine evenly spaced triplets between the outer and inner walls of the structure and having no central microtubules. *Symbol:* 9 + 0.

nin•er (nī′nər), *n. Slang.* nine. [NINE + -ER[1]]

nine-spot (nīn′spot′), *n. Slang.* a playing card the face of which bears nine pips.

nine•teen (nīn′tēn′), *n.* **1.** a cardinal number, ten plus nine. **2.** a symbol for this number, as 19 or XIX. **3.** a set of this many persons or things. **4. talk nineteen to the dozen,** to talk very rapidly or vehemently. —*adj.* **5.** amounting to nineteen in number. [bef. 1000; ME *nintene*, OE *nigontȳne.* See NINE, -TEEN]

1984, an antiutopian novel (1949) by George Orwell.

nine•teenth (nīn′tēnth′), *adj.* **1.** next after the eighteenth; being the ordinal number for 19. **2.** being one of 19 equal parts. —*n.* **3.** a nineteenth part, esp. of one (1/19). **4.** the nineteenth member of a series. [bef. 900; ME *nyntenthe* (see NINETEEN, -TH[2]); r. *nientethe*, OE *nigonteotha;* see NINE, TITHE]

Nine′teenth Amend′ment, an amendment to the U.S. Constitution, ratified in 1920, guaranteeing women the right to vote.

nine′teenth hole′, *Informal.* a place where golfers gather after play to relax. [1900–05]

nine•ti•eth (nīn′tē ith), *adj.* **1.** next after the eighty-ninth; being the ordinal number for 90. **2.** being one of 90 equal parts. —*n.* **3.** a ninetieth part, esp. of one (1/90). **4.** the ninetieth member of a series. [bef. 1100; ME *nyntithe*, OE *nigenteotha.* See NINETY, -ETH[2]]

nine-to-five (nīn′tə fīv′), *adj. Informal.* **1.** of, pertaining to, or during the workday, esp. the hours from 9 A.M. to 5 P.M. when offices are characteristically open for business: *the nine-to-five grind.* **2.** exhibiting a lack of willingness to work beyond the required amount of time or with more than minimal effort: *a nine-to-five mentality.* [1955–60] —**nine′-to-fiv′er,** *n.*

Ni•nette (ni net′), *n.* a female given name.

nine•ty (nīn′tē), *n., pl.* **-ties,** *adj.* —*n.* **1.** a cardinal number, ten times nine. **2.** a symbol for this number, as 90 or XC. **3.** a set of this many persons or things. **4. nineties,** the numbers, years, degrees, or the like, from 90 through 99, as in referring to numbered streets, indicating the years of a lifetime or of a century, or degrees of temperature: *His grandmother is in her nineties.* —*adj.* **5.** amounting to 90 in number. [bef. 1000; ME *nineti*, OE *nigontig.* See NINE, -TY[1]]

nine′ty-day won′der (nīn′tē dā′), *Informal.* an officer commissioned in a branch of the armed forces after an unusually short training period. [1915–20, *Amer.*]

nine•ty-eight (nīn′tē āt′), *n.* **1.** a cardinal number, 90 plus 8. **2.** a symbol for this number, as 98 or XCVIII. **3.** a set of this many persons or things. —*adj.* **4.** amounting to 98 in number.

nine•ty-eighth (nīn′tē ātth′, -āth′), *adj.* **1.** next after the ninety-seventh; being the ordinal number for 98. **2.** being one of 98 equal parts. —*n.* **3.** a ninety-eighth part, esp. of one (1/98). **4.** the ninety-eighth member of a series.

nine•ty-fifth (nīn′tē fifth′), *adj.* **1.** next after the ninety-fourth; being the ordinal number for 95. **2.** being one of 95 equal parts. —*n.* **3.** a ninety-fifth part, esp. of one (1/95). **4.** the ninety-fifth member of a series.

nine•ty-first (nīn′tē fûrst′), *adj.* **1.** next after the ninetieth; being the ordinal number for 91. **2.** being one of 91 equal parts. —*n.* **3.** a ninety-first part, esp. of one (1/91). **4.** the ninety-first member of a series.

nine•ty-five (nīn′tē fīv′), *n.* **1.** a cardinal number, 90 plus 5. **2.** a symbol for this number, as 95 or XCV. **3.** a set of this many persons or things. —*adj.* **4.** amounting to 95 in number.

Nine′ty-Five The′ses, the theses of Luther against the sale of indulgences in the Roman Catholic Church, posted by him on the door of a church in Wittenberg, October 31, 1517.

nine•ty-four (nīn′tē fôr′, -fōr′), *n.* **1.** a cardinal number, 90 plus 4. **2.** a symbol for this number, as 94 or XCIV. **3.** a set of this many persons or things. —*adj.* **4.** amounting to 94 in number.

nine•ty-fourth (nīn′tē fôrth′, -fōrth′), *adj.* **1.** next after the ninety-third; being the ordinal number for 94. **2.** being one of 94 equal parts. —*n.* **3.** a ninety-fourth part, esp. of one (1/94). **4.** the ninety-fourth member of a series.

nine•ty-nine (nīn′tē nīn′), *n.* **1.** a cardinal number, 90 plus 9. **2.** a symbol for this number, as 99 or XCIX. **3.** a set of this many persons or things. —*adj.* **4.** amounting to 99 in number.

nine•ty-ninth (nīn′tē nīnth′), *adj.* **1.** next after the ninety-eighth; being the ordinal number for 99. **2.** being one of 99 equal parts. —*n.* **3.** a ninety-ninth part, esp. of one (1/99). **4.** the ninety-ninth member of a series.

nine•ty-one (nīn′tē wun′), *n.* **1.** a cardinal number, 90 plus 1. **2.** a symbol for this number, as 91 or XCI. **3.** a set of this many persons or things. —*adj.* **4.** amounting to 91 in number.

nine•ty-sec•ond (nīn′tē sek′ənd), *adj.* **1.** next after the ninety-first; being the ordinal number for 92. **2.** being one of 92 equal parts. —*n.* **3.** a ninety-second part, esp. of one (1/92). **4.** the ninety-second member of a series.

nine•ty-sev•en (nīn′tē sev′ən), *n.* **1.** a cardinal number, 90 plus 7. **2.** a symbol for this number, as 97 or XCVII. **3.** a set of this many persons or things. —*adj.* **4.** amounting to 97 in number.

nine•ty-sev•enth (nīn′tē sev′ənth), *adj.* **1.** next after the ninety-sixth; being the ordinal number for 97. **2.** being one of 97 equal parts. —*n.* **3.** a ninety-seventh part, esp. of one (1/97). **4.** the ninety-seventh member of a series.

nine•ty-six (nīn′tē siks′), *n.* **1.** a cardinal number, 90 plus 6. **2.** a symbol for this number, as 96 or XCVI. **3.** a set of this many persons or things. —*adj.* **4.** amounting to 96 in number.

nine•ty-sixth (nīn′tē siksth′), *adj.* **1.** next after the ninety-fifth; being the ordinal number for 96. **2.** being one of 96 equal parts. —*n.* **3.** a ninety-sixth part, esp. of one (1/96). **4.** the ninety-sixth member of a series.

nine•ty-third (nīn′tē thûrd′), *adj.* **1.** next after the ninety-second; being the ordinal number for 93. **2.** being one of 93 equal parts. —*n.* **3.** a ninety-third part, esp. of one (1/93). **4.** the ninety-third member of a series.

nine•ty-three (nīn′tē thrē′), *n.* **1.** a cardinal number, 90 plus 3. **2.** a symbol for this number, as 93 or XCIII. **3.** a set of this many persons or things. —*adj.* **4.** amounting to 93 in number.

nine•ty-two (nīn′tē to͞o′), *n.* **1.** a cardinal number, 90 plus 2. **2.** a symbol for this number, as 92 or XCII. **3.** a set of this many persons or things. —*adj.* **4.** amounting to 92 in number.

Nin•e•veh (nin′ə və), *n.* the ancient capital of Assyria: its ruins are opposite Mosul, on the Tigris River, in N Iraq. —**Nin•e•vite** (nin′ə vīt′), *n.* —**Nin•e•vit•i•cal** (nin′ə vit′i kəl), *adj.* —**Nin•e•vit•ish** (nin′ə vī′tish), *adj.*

Nine′ Wor′thies, three pagan, three Jewish, and three Christian heroes mentioned together in medieval romances, usually including Hector, Alexander the Great, Julius Caesar, Joshua, David, Judas Maccabaeus, Arthur, Charlemagne, and Godefroy de Bouillon.

Ning•bo (ning′bô′), *n. Pinyin.* a seaport in E Zhejiang province, in E China. 350,000. Also, *Wade-Giles,* **Ning•po** (ning′bô′). Formerly, **Yinxian.**

Ning•hsien (ning′shyun′), *n. Older Spelling.* Yinxian.

Ning•xia (ning′shyä′), *n. Pinyin.* a former province in NW China, now part of Inner Mongolia. Also, *Wade-Giles,* **Ning′hsia′**; *Older Spelling,* **Ning′sia′.**

Ning′xia′ Hui′ (hwē), *Pinyin.* an administrative division in N China. 2,000,000; 25,640 sq. mi. (66,400 sq. km). *Cap.:* Yinchuan. Also, *Wade-Giles,* **Ning′hsia′ Hui′**; *Older Spelling,* **Ning′sia′ Hui′.** Official name, **Ning′xia′ Hui′ Auton′omous Re′gion.**

nin•hy•drin (nin hī′drin), *n. Chem.* a white or yellow, toxic, crystalline or powdery compound, $C_9H_4O_3{\cdot}H_2O$, that reddens when heated above 100°C, a monohydrate, soluble in water or alcohol: used primarily as a reagent to detect the presence of various amino acids. [< G]

Ni•nib (nē′nib), *n. Obs.* Ninurta.

Ni•ni•gi (nē nē′gē), *n. Japanese Legend.* the grandson of Amaterasu and first ruler of Japan.

nin•ja (nin′jə), *n., pl.* **-ja, -jas.** (*often cap.*) a member of a feudal Japanese society of mercenary agents, highly trained in martial arts and stealth **(ninjutsu),** who were hired for covert purposes ranging from espionage to sabotage and assassination. [< Japn, equiv. to *nin-* endure + *-ja,* comb. form of *-sha* person (< MChin, equiv. to Chin *rěn* + *zhě*)]

nin•jut•su (nin jut′so͞o, -jo͝ot′-), *n.* See under **ninja.** Also, **nin•jit•su** (nin jit′so͞o). [< Japn, equiv. to *nin-* endure + *-jutsu* technique; see NINJA]

nin•ny (nin′ē), *n., pl.* **-nies.** a fool or simpleton. [1585–95; perh. generic use of pet form of *Innocent* proper name; see -Y[2]] —**nin′ny•ish,** *adj.*

nin•ny•ham•mer (nin′ē ham′ər), *n.* a fool or simpleton; ninny. [1585–95; NINNY + HAMMER]

ni•ño (nē′nyô; *Eng.* nēn′yō), *n., pl.* **ni•ños** (nē′nyôs; *Eng.* nēn′yōz). *Spanish.* boy; child.

ni•non (nē′non; *Fr.* nē nôN′), *n.* a sturdy chiffon or voile generally used in the manufacture of women's garments, curtains, and drapery. [1910–15; < F: generic use of nickname for ANNE proper name]

Nin•ten•do (nin ten′dō), *Trademark.* **1.** a system for playing video games. **2.** any game designed for this system.

ninth (nīnth), *adj.* **1.** next after the eighth; being the ordinal number for nine. **2.** being one of nine equal parts. —*n.* **3.** a ninth part, esp. of one (1/9). **4.** the ninth member of a series. **5.** *Music.* **a.** a tone distant from another tone by an interval of an octave and a second. **b.** the interval between such tones. **c.** harmonic combination of such tones. —*adv.* **6.** in the ninth place. [bef. 900; ME *ninthe* (see NINE, -TH[2]), r. ME *niend* (OE *nigend*), *neogethe, nigethe* (OE *nigotha*); akin to OS *niguntho*, ON *níundi*, Goth *niunda*] —**ninth′ly,** *adv.*

Ninth′ Amend′ment, an amendment to the U.S. Constitution, ratified in 1791 as part of the Bill of Rights, guaranteeing that the rights enumerated in the Constitution would not be construed as denying or jeopardizing other rights of the people.

ninth′ chord′, *Music.* a chord formed by the superposition of four thirds. [1945–50]

Ninth′ Command′ment, "Thou shalt not bear false witness against thy neighbor": ninth of the Ten Commandments. Cf. **Ten Commandments.**

Ninth′ of Av′, *Judaism.* See **Tishah b'Av.** Also, **Ninth′ of Ab′.**

Ni•nur•ta (ni no͝or′tä), *n.* a Sumerian and Babylonian hero god.

Ni•nus (nī′nəs), *n.* the legendary husband of Semiramis and founder of Nineveh.

ni•o•bate (nī′ə bāt′), *n. Chem.* any salt of niobic acid; columbate. [1835–45; NIOB(IUM) + -ATE[2]]

Ni•o•be (nī′ō bē′), *n. Class. Myth.* the daughter of Tantalus and wife of Amphion of Thebes. She provoked Apollo and Artemis to vengeance by taunting their mother, Leto, with the number and beauty of her own children; Niobe's children were slain and Zeus turned her into stone, in which state she continued to weep over her loss. —**Ni′o•be′an,** *adj.*

ni•o•bic (nī ō′bik, -ob′ik), *adj. Chem.* **1.** of or pertaining to niobium; columbic. **2.** of or derived from niobic acid. [1835–45; NIOB(IUM) + -IC]

nio′bic ac′id, *Chem.* a white, water-insoluble solid, $Nb_2O_5{\cdot}nH_2O$. [1835–45]

Ni•o•bid (nī′ō bid), *n. Class. Myth.* any of the children of Niobe.

ni•o•bi•um (nī ō′bē əm), *n. Chem.* a steel-gray metallic element resembling tantalum in its chemical properties; becomes a superconductor below 9 K; used chiefly in alloy steels. *Symbol:* Nb; *at. no.:* 41; *at. wt.:* 92.906; *sp. gr.:* 8.4 at 20°C. [1835–45; < NL; see NIOBE, -IUM]

ni•o•bous (nī ō′bəs), *adj.* **1.** *Chem.* containing trivalent niobium, as niobous chloride, $NbCl_3$. **2.** of or pertaining to niobium. [1860–65; NIOB(IUM) + -OUS]

Ni•o•brar•a (nī′ə brâr′ə), *n.* a river flowing E from E Wyoming through Nebraska to the Missouri. 431 mi. (692 km) long.

Niort (nyôr), *n.* a city in and the capital of Deux-Sèvres, in W France. 63,965.

Ni•os (nē′ōs), *n.* **Lake,** a volcanic lake in Cameroon, at the NW border: eruption 1986. Also, **Nyos.**

NIOSH (nī′osh), *n.* National Institute for Occupational Safety and Health.

nip[1] (nip), *v.,* **nipped, nip•ping,** *n.* —*v.t.* **1.** to squeeze or compress tightly between two surfaces or points; pinch; bite. **2.** to take off by pinching, biting, or snipping (usually fol. by *off*): *He nipped off a piece of steak and gave it to the dog.* **3.** to check in growth or development. **4.** to affect sharply and painfully or injuriously, as a very cold temperature: *a cold wind that nips the fingers.* **5.** *Informal.* to snatch away suddenly. **6.** *Informal.* to defeat (an opponent) by a very close margin; edge. **7.** *Informal.* to steal or pilfer. **8.** *Naut.* **a.** (of ice) to press (a ship) from opposite sides. **b.** to seize (a taut rope) to another rope. —*v.i.* **9.** *Chiefly Brit. Slang.* to leave stealthily; sneak away; flee (often fol. by *away*). **10. nip in the bud.** See **bud**[1] (def. 6). —*n.* **11.** an act of nipping; a pinch or small bite: *The dog took several nips at our heels.* **12.** a biting quality, as in cold or frosty air: *There's a nip in the air this morning.* **13.** sharp cold; a sharp touch of frost: *The trees had felt the first nip of winter.* **14.** a sharp or biting remark. **15.** a biting taste or tang, esp. in some cheese. **16.** a small bit or quantity of anything: *a nip of bread to stave off hunger.* **17.** *Naut.* **a.** an abrupt turn or twist in a rope. **b.** a part of a rope or chain bound by a seizing or nipper. **18.** Usually, **nips.** nipper (def. 2). **19. nip and tuck,** with each competitor equaling or closely contesting the speed, scoring, or efforts of the other: *It was nip and tuck as to which sailboat would reach port first.* [1350–1400; ME *nyppe* to pinch < ON *hnippa* to poke, thrust]
—**Syn. 4.** freeze, bite, pierce, cut, chill.

nip[2] (nip), *n., v.,* **nipped, nip•ping.** —*n.* **1.** a small drink of alcoholic liquor; sip: *a person who relishes an occasional nip.* **2.** *Chiefly Brit.* split (def. 29). —*v.t., v.i.* **3.** to drink (alcoholic liquor) in small sips, esp. repeatedly. [1690–1700; < D *nippen* to sip; in def. 2, short for earlier *nipperkin* vessel holding half-pint or less]

Nip (nip), *n., adj. Slang* (*disparaging and offensive*). Japanese. [short for NIPPONESE]

ni•pa (nē′pə), *n.* a palm, *Nypa fruticans,* of India, the Philippines, etc., whose foliage is used for thatching, basketry, etc. [1580–90; < NL < Malay *nipah*]

Nip•i•gon (nip′i gon′), *n.* **Lake,** a lake in SW Ontario, in S central Canada. ab. 1870 sq. mi. (4845 sq. km).

Nip•is•sing (nip′ə sing), *n.* a lake in SE Canada, in Ontario, N of Georgian Bay. 330 sq. mi. (855 sq. km).

Nip•muck (nip′muk), *n., pl.* **-mucks,** (*esp. collectively*)

CONCISE PRONUNCIATION KEY: act, cāpe, dâre, pärt; set, ēqual; *if,* īce; ox, ōver, ôrder, oil, bo͝ok, bo͞ot, out; up, ûrge; child; sing; shoe; thin, *th*at; zh as in *treasure.* ə = *a* as in *alone, e* as in *system, i* as in *easily, o* as in *gallop, u* as in *circus;* ᵊ as in *fire* (fīᵊr), *hour* (ouᵊr). l and n can serve as syllabic consonants, as in *cradle* (krād′l), and *button* (but′n). See the full key inside the front cover.

-muck. a member of an Algonquian Indian people living in the vicinity of Worcester, Mass.

nip·per (nip′ər), *n.* **1.** a person or thing that nips. **2.** Usually, **nippers.** a device for nipping, as pincers or forceps. **3.** one of the two large claws of a crustacean. **4.** *Metalworking.* dog (def. 13). **5. nippers,** *Older Slang.* handcuffs. **6.** *Informal.* **a.** a small boy. **b.** *Chiefly Brit.* a costermonger's helper or assistant. **7.** *Naut.* a short rope for seizing an anchor cable to a messenger from a capstan. [1525–35; NIP[1] + -ER[1]]

nip·ping (nip′ing), *adj.* **1.** sharp or biting, as cold. **2.** sarcastic; caustic. [1540–50; NIP[1] + -ING[2]] **—nip′ping·ly,** *adv.*

nip·ple (nip′əl), *n.* **1.** a protuberance of the mamma or breast where, in the female, the milk ducts discharge; teat. **2.** something resembling it, as the mouthpiece of a nursing bottle or pacifier. **3.** a short piece of pipe with threads on each end, used for joining valves. [1520–30; earlier *neble, nib(b)le, nepil;* perh. akin to NIB; cf. Dan *nip* point; see -LE] **—nip′ple·less,** *adj.*

Nip·pon (nē pôn′; *Eng.* ni pon′, nip′on), *n.* a Japanese name of **Japan.** [< Japn, earlier *nit-pon* < MChin, equiv. to Chin *rì* sun + *běn* origin]

Nip·pon·ese (nip′ə nēz′, -nēs′), *n., pl.* **-ese,** *adj.* Japanese. [1855–60; NIPPON + -ESE] **—Nip·pon·ism** (nip′ə niz′əm), *n.*

Nip·pur (ni po͝or′), *n.* an ancient Sumerian and Babylonian city in SE Iraq: partially excavated.

nip·py (nip′ē), *adj.,* **-pi·er, -pi·est.** **1.** chilly or cold: *morning air that feels a bit nippy.* **2.** sharp or biting; tangy: *This cheese has a good, nippy taste.* **3.** *Chiefly Brit. Informal.* nimble; agile. [1565–75; NIP[1] + -Y[1]]

nip-up (nip′up′), *n.* a calisthenic routine or gymnastic move of springing to one's feet from a supine position. [1935–40; n. use of v. phrase *nip up*]

NIRA, National Industrial Recovery Act. Also, **N.I.R.A.**

Nir·en·berg (nir′ən bûrg′), *n.* **Marshall Warren,** born 1927, U.S. biochemist: pioneered studies on the genetic code; Nobel prize for medicine 1968.

ni·rid·a·zole (nī rid′ə zōl′), *n. Pharm.* an anthelmintic substance, $C_6H_6N_4O_3S$, used in the treatment of schistosomiasis. [by rearrangement of parts of its chemical name]

Nir·ma·lin (nir mä′lin), *n.* one of a group of Sikh ascetics devoted to the study of sacred writings.

nir·va·na (nir vä′nə, -van′ə, nər-), *n.* **1.** (*often cap.*) Pali, ***nibbana.*** *Buddhism.* freedom from the endless cycle of personal reincarnations, with their consequent suffering, as a result of the extinction of individual passion, hatred, and delusion: attained by the Arhat as his goal but postponed by the Bodhisattva. **2.** (*often cap.*) *Hinduism.* salvation through the union of Atman with Brahma; moksha. **3.** a place or state characterized by freedom from or oblivion to pain, worry, and the external world. [1830–40; < Skt *nirvāṇa*] **—nir·va′nic,** *adj.*

Niš (nēsh), *n.* a city in SE Serbia, in SE Yugoslavia: a former capital of Serbia. 230,711. Also, **Nish.**

Ni·san (nē′sän, nis′ən, nē sän′), *n.* the seventh month of the Jewish calendar. Also, **Nissan.** Cf. **Jewish calendar.**

Ni·sei (nē′sā, nē sā′), *n., pl.* **-sei.** a person of Japanese descent, born and educated in the U.S. or Canada. Also, **ni′sei′.** Cf. **Issei, Kibei, Sansei.** [1940–45, *Amer.;* < Japn: lit., second generation; earlier *ni-seï* < MChin, equiv. to Chin *èr* two, second + *shēng* birth]

Ni·sha·pur (nē′shä po͝or′), *n.* a town in NE Iran: the birthplace of Omar Khayyám. 33,482.

Ni·shi·no·mi·ya (nē′shē nô′mē yä′), *n.* a city on S Honshu, in S Japan. 410,329.

ni·si (nī′sī, nē′sē), *adj.* not yet final or absolute (used, esp. in law, to indicate that a judgment or decree will become final on a particular date unless set aside or invalidated by certain specified contingencies): *a decree nisi.* [< L: if not, unless (conj.)]

ni·si pri·us (nī′sī prī′əs, nē′sē prē′əs), *Law.* **1.** Also called **ni′si pri′us court′.** a trial court for the hearing of civil cases before a judge and jury. **2.** *Brit. Law.* **a.** a writ commanding a sheriff of a county to summon a jury and bring it to the court in Westminster on a certain day, unless the judges of assizes previously came to that county. **b.** the clause with the words "nisi prius" introducing this writ. **c.** the system of judicial circuits to which judges are assigned for local trials of civil and criminal cases. [1300–50; ME < L: lit., unless previously, unless before] **—ni′si-pri′us,** *adj.*

Nis·san (nē′sän, nis′ən, nē sän′), *n.* Nisan.

Nis′sen hut′ (nis′ən), a prefabricated, tunnel-shaped shelter made of corrugated metal and having a concrete floor; Quonset hut: first used by the British army in World War I. [1915–20; named after Lieutenant Colonel Peter N. *Nissen* (1871–1930), Canadian military engineer who invented it]

Nis·tru (nē′stro͞o), *n.* Rumanian name of **Dniester.**

ni·sus (nī′səs), *n., pl.* **-sus.** an effort or striving toward a particular goal or attainment; impulse. [1690–1700; < L *nīsus* act of planting the feet, effort, equiv. to *nīt(ī)* to support or exert oneself + *-tus* suffix of v. action, with *tt* > s]

nit[1] (nit), *n.* **1.** the egg of a parasitic insect, esp. of a louse, often attached to a hair or a fiber of clothing. **2.** the young of such an insect. [bef. 900; ME *nite,* OE *hnitu,* c. D *neet,* G *Niss,* Norw *nit*]

CONCISE ETYMOLOGY KEY: <, descended or borrowed from; >, whence; b., blend of, blended; c., cognate with; cf., compare; deriv., derivative; equiv., equivalent; imit., imitative; obl., oblique; r., replacing; s., stem; sp., spelling, spelled; resp., respelling, respelled; trans., translation; ?, origin unknown; *, unattested; ‡, probably earlier than. See the full key inside the front cover.

nit[2] (nit), *n. Physics.* a unit of luminous intensity equal to one candela per square meter. *Abbr.:* nt [1950–55; extracted from L *nitor* brightness; see NITID, -OR[1]]

nit[3] (nit), *n. Chiefly Brit.* a nitwit. [by shortening]

nit·chie (nē′chē), *n. Chiefly Canadian Slang* (*disparaging and offensive*). an Indian. [1785–95; < Ojibwa *ni·či·* my friend, extracted from the phrase *po·žo· ni·či·* "greetings, friend!", a common salutation among men]

nite (nīt), *n.* an informal, simplified spelling of **night.**

ni·ter (nī′tər), *n.* **1.** See **potassium nitrate. 2.** See **sodium nitrate.** Also, *esp. Brit.,* **nitre.** [1375–1425; late ME *nitre* < L *nitrum* < Gk *nítron* NATRON]

Ni·te·rói (nē′tə roi′), *n.* a seaport in and the capital of Rio de Janeiro state, in SE Brazil. 291,970. Also, **Nictheroy.**

nit·er·y (nī′tə rē), *n., pl.* **-er·ies.** *Informal.* a nightclub. [1930–35, *Amer.; nite* (resp. of NIGHT) + -ERY]

nit·fly (nit′flī′), *n., pl.* **-flies.** *Midland U.S. and Gulf States.* botfly. [NIT[1] + FLY[2]]

nit·id (nit′id), *adj.* bright; lustrous. [< L *nitidus* shining, bright, equiv. to *nit(ēre)* to glisten + *-idus* -ID[4]] **—ni·tid·i·ty** (ni tid′i tē), *n.*

ni·ti·nol (nit′n ôl′, -ol′), *n.* a paramagnetic alloy of nickel and titanium that, after heating and deformation, resumes its original shape when reheated. [1965–70; NI(CKEL) + TI(TANIUM) + *N(aval) O(rdnance) L(aboratory),* Silver Spring, Maryland, where the alloy was developed]

nit-lamp (nit′lamp′), *n. Canadian.* See **jack light.**

ni·ton (nī′ton), *n.* (formerly) radon. *Symbol:* Nt [1910–15; < L *nit(ēre)* to shine + -ON[1]]

nit·pick (nit′pik′), *v.i.* **1.** to be excessively concerned with or critical of inconsequential details. **—***v.t.* **2.** to criticize by focusing on inconsequential details. **—***n.* **3.** a carping, petty criticism. **—***adj.* **4.** of, pertaining to, or characteristic of a nitpicker or nitpicking. Also, **nit′-pick′.** [1965–70; NIT[1] + PICK[1]]

nit·pick·er (nit′pik′ər), *n.* a person who nitpicks, esp. habitually. [1950–55; NIT[1] + PICK[1] + -ER[1]] Also, **nit′-pick′er.**

nitr-, var. of **nitro-** before a vowel: *nitramine.*

Ni·tral·loy (nī′trə loi′), *Trademark.* a brand of nitriding steel.

ni·tra·mine (nī′trə mēn′, nī tram′in), *n. Chem.* **1.** any of a class of compounds containing the nitramino group. **2.** tetryl. [NITR- + AMINE]

ni·tra·mi·no (nī′trə mē′nō, nī tram′ə nō′), *adj. Chem.* containing the nitramino group. [NITR- + AMINO]

nitrami′no group′, *Chem.* the univalent group $-NHNO_2$. Also called **nitrami′no rad′ical.**

ni·trate (*n.* nī′trāt, -trit; *v.* nī′trāt), *n., v.,* **-trat·ed, -trat·ing.** **—***n.* **1.** *Chem.* a salt or ester of nitric acid, or any compound containing the univalent group $-ONO_2$ or NO_3. **2.** fertilizer consisting of potassium nitrate or sodium nitrate. **3.** cellulose nitrate, a substance used as a film base in the early days of filmmaking. **4.** *Informal.* See **nitrate film. —***v.t.* **5.** to treat with nitric acid or a nitrate. **6.** to convert into a nitrate. [1785–95; NITR- + -ATE[2]] **—ni·tra′tion,** *n.*

ni′trate film′, **1.** film stock using a base of cellulose nitrate: extremely flammable and tending to erode at a relatively early age. **2.** a motion picture made with or printed on this film. [1920–25]

ni·tra·tine (nī′trə tēn′, -tin), *n. Mineral.* See **soda niter.** [1840–50; NITRATE + -INE[2]]

ni·tre (nī′tər), *n. Chiefly Brit.* niter.

ni·tric (nī′trik), *adj. Chem.* **1.** containing nitrogen, usually in the pentavalent state. **2.** of or pertaining to niter. [1785–95; NITR- + -IC, modeled on F *nitrique*]

ni′tric ac′id, *Chem.* a colorless or yellowish, fuming, suffocating, caustic, corrosive, water-soluble liquid, HNO_3, having powerful oxidizing properties, usually obtained from ammonia or from Chile saltpeter: used chiefly in the manufacture of explosives and fertilizers and in organic synthesis. Also called **aqua fortis.** [1785–95]

ni′tric ox′ide, *Chem.* a colorless, slightly water-soluble gas, NO, formed by the action of dilute nitric acid on copper, and by the direct combination of atmospheric oxygen and nitrogen at the high temperatures of an electric arc: an intermediate in the manufacture of nitric acid. [1800–10]

ni·tride (nī′trīd, -trid), *n. Chem.* a compound, containing two elements only, of which the more electronegative one is nitrogen. [1840–50; NITR- + -IDE]

ni·trid·ing (nī′trī ding), *n. Metall.* a process of casehardening in which nitrogen is introduced into the metal by keeping it at a suitable temperature in the presence of a nitrogen source. [NITRIDE + -ING[1]]

ni′triding steel′, any steel suitable for casehardening by nitriding. [1930–35]

ni·tri·fi·ca·tion (nī′trə fi kā′shən), *n.* the act of nitrifying. [1820–30; NITR- + -I- + -FICATION]

ni·tri·fi·er (nī′trə fī′ər), *n.* a person or thing that nitrifies. [1900–05; NITRIFY + -ER[1]]

ni·tri·fy (nī′trə fī′), *v.t.,* **-fied, -fy·ing.** **1.** to oxidize (ammonia, ammonium compounds, or atmospheric nitrogen) to nitrites, nitrates, or their respective acids, esp. by bacterial action. **2.** to impregnate with nitrogen or nitrogen compounds. **3.** to treat or combine with nitrogen or its compounds. **4.** (formerly) to convert into niter. [1820–30; < F *nitrifier.* See NITR-, NITER, -I-, -FY] **—ni′·tri·fi′a·ble,** *adj.*

ni·trile (nī′tril, -trēl, -trīl), *n. Chem.* any of a class of organic compounds with the general formula RC≡N. [1840–50; NITR- + *-ile,* perh. var. of -YL]

ni′trile rub′ber, *Chem.* a synthetic rubber obtained by the copolymerization of acrylonitrile and butadiene, noted for its oil resistance. [1945–50]

ni·trite (nī′trīt), *n.* **1.** *Chem.* a salt or ester of nitrous acid. **2.** *Nutrition.* See **sodium nitrite.** [1790–1800; NITR- + -ITE[1]]

ni·tro (nī′trō), *adj.* **1.** *Chem.* containing the nitro group. **—***n.* **2.** nitroglycerin. [1855–60; see NITRO-]

nitro-, a combining form used in the names of chemical compounds in which the nitro group is present: *nitroglycerin.* Also, *esp. before a vowel,* **nitr-.** [comb. form of Gk *nítron.* See NITER]

ni·tro·bac·te·ri·a (nī′trō bak tēr′ē ə), *n.pl., sing.* **-te·ri·um** (-tēr′ē əm). certain bacteria in the soil involved in nitrifying processes. [1890–95; NITRO- + BACTERIA]

ni·tro·ben·zene (nī′trō ben′zēn, -ben zēn′), *n. Chem.* a pale yellow, toxic, water-soluble liquid, $C_6H_5NO_2$, produced by nitrating benzene with nitric acid: used chiefly in the manufacture of aniline. Also called **ni·tro·ben·zol** (nī′trō ben′zôl, -zol). [1865–70; NITRO- + BENZENE]

ni·tro·cel·lu·lose (nī′trə sel′yə lōs′), *n. Chem.* See **cellulose nitrate.** [1880–85; NITRO- + CELLULOSE] **—ni′tro·cel′lu·lo′sic, ni′tro·cel′lu·lous,** *adj.*

ni·tro·chlo·ro·form (nī′trə klôr′ə fôrm′, -klōr′-), *n. Chem.* chloropicrin. [NITRO- + CHLOROFORM]

ni·tro·cot·ton (nī′trō kot′n), *n. Chem.* See **cellulose nitrate.** [1895–1900; NITRO- + COTTON]

ni·tro·fur·an·to·in (nī′trō fyo͞o ran′tō in), *n. Pharm.* an antimicrobial substance, $C_8H_6N_4O_5$, used for the treatment of urinary tract infections. [1950–55; NITRO- + *fur(furyl)* + (HYD)ANTOIN, components of its chemical name]

ni·tro·gel·a·tin (nī′trō jel′ə tn), *n.* See **gelatin dynamite.** [1880–85; NITRO- + GELATIN]

ni·tro·gen (nī′trə jən), *n. Chem.* a colorless, odorless, gaseous element that constitutes about four-fifths of the volume of the atmosphere and is present in combined form in animal and vegetable tissues, esp. in proteins: used chiefly in the manufacture of ammonia, nitric acid, cyanide, explosives, fertilizer, dyes, as a cooling agent, etc. *Symbol:* N; *at. wt.:* 14.0067; *at. no.:* 7; *density:* 1.2506 g/l at 0°C and 760 mm pressure. [1785–95; < F *nitrogène.* See NITRO-, -GEN]

ni·trog·en·ase (nī troj′ə nās′, -nāz′, nī′trə jə-), *n. Biochem.* an enzyme complex that catalyzes the reduction of molecular nitrogen in the nitrogen-fixation process of bacteria. [1930–35; NITROGEN + -ASE]

ni′trogen bal′ance, *Biochem., Physiol.* the difference between the amount of nitrogen taken in and the amount excreted or lost: used to evaluate nutritional balance. [1940–45]

ni′trogen cy′cle, the continuous sequence of events by which atmospheric nitrogen and nitrogenous compounds in the soil are converted, as by nitrification and nitrogen fixation, into substances that can be utilized by green plants, the substances returning to the air and soil as a result of the decay of the plants and denitrification. [1905–10]

ni′trogen diox′ide, *Chem.* a reddish-brown, highly poisonous gas, NO_2, used as an intermediate in the manufacture of nitric and sulfuric acids, and as a nitrating and oxidizing agent; a major air pollutant from the exhaust of internal combustion engines that are not fitted with pollution control devices.

ni′trogen fixa′tion, **1.** any process of combining atmospheric nitrogen with other elements, either by chemical means or by bacterial action: used chiefly in the preparation of fertilizers, industrial products, etc. **2.** this process as performed by certain bacteria found in the nodules of leguminous plants, which make the resulting nitrogenous compounds available to their host plants. [1890–95]

ni′trogen fix′er, any of various microorganisms in the soil involved in the process of nitrogen fixation.

ni·tro·gen-fix·ing (nī′trə jən fik′sing), *adj.* involved in or aiding the process of nitrogen fixation. [1895–1900]

ni·trog·en·ize (nī troj′ə nīz′, nī′trə jə-), *v.t.,* **-ized, -iz·ing.** to combine with nitrogen or add nitrogenous material to. Also, *esp. Brit.,* **ni·trog′en·ise′.** [1895–1900; NITROGEN + -IZE] **—ni·trog′en·i·za′tion, ni′tro·ge·na′·tion,** *n.*

ni′trogen mus′tard, *Chem.* any of the class of poisonous, blistering compounds, as $C_5H_{11}Cl_2N$, analogous in composition to mustard gas but containing nitrogen instead of sulfur: used in the treatment of cancer and similar diseases; mechlorethamine. [1945–50]

ni′trogen narco′sis, *Pathol.* a semistupor, lightheadedness, or euphoria experienced by deep-sea divers when nitrogen from air enters the blood at higher than atmospheric pressure. Also called **rapture of the deep.** [1935–40]

ni·trog·e·nous (nī troj′ə nəs), *adj.* containing nitrogen. [1830–40; NITROGEN + -OUS]

ni′trogen tetrox′ide, *Chem.* a poisonous compound, N_2O_4, occurring as a colorless, water-soluble solid or liquid, dissociating into NO_2: used chiefly as an oxidizer, esp. in rocket fuels, as a nitrating agent, and as an intermediate in the manufacture of nitric acid.

ni·tro·glyc·er·in (nī′trə glis′ər in), *n. Chem., Pharm.* a colorless, thick, oily, flammable, highly explosive, slightly water-soluble liquid, $C_3H_5N_3O_9$, prepared from glycerol with nitric and sulfuric acids: used chiefly as a constituent of dynamite and other explosives, in rocket propellants, and in medicine as a vasodilator in the treatment of angina pectoris. Also, **ni·tro·glyc·er·ine** (nī′trə glis′ər in, -ə rēn′). Also called **glonoin, glyceryl trinitrate, trinitroglycerin.** [1855–60; NITRO- + GLYCERIN]

ni′tro group′, *Chem.* the univalent group $-NO_2$. Also called **nitro radical.** [1885–90]

ni′tro·hy·dro·chlo′ric ac′id (nī′trə hī′drə klôr′ik, -klōr′-, nī′-), *Chem.* See **aqua regia.** [1830–40; NITRO- + HYDROCHLORIC ACID]

ni·trol·ic (nī trol′ik), *adj. Chem.* of or noting a series of acids of the type $RC(=NOH)NO_2$, whose salts form deep-red solutions. [1890–95; NITR- + -OL[1] + -IC]

ni·tro·man·ni·tol (nī′trə man′i tôl′, -tol′), *n. Chem.* See **mannitol hexanitrate.** Also, **ni·tro·man·nite** (nī′trə man′īt). [NITRO- + MANNITOL]

ni·tro·mer·sol (nī′trə mûr′sôl, -sol), *n. Chem.* a brownish-yellow or yellow, granular, water-insoluble powder, $C_7H_5HgNO_3$: used in alkaline solution chiefly as an antiseptic. [NITRO- + MER(CURIC) + (CREO)SOL]

ni·trom·e·ter (nī trom′i tər), *n.* an apparatus for determining the amount of nitrogen or nitrogen compounds in a substance or mixture. [1820–30; NITRO- + -METER] —**ni·tro·met·ric** (nī′trō me′trik), *adj.*

ni·tro·meth·ane (nī′trə meth′ān), *n. Chem.* a colorless, oily, slightly water-soluble, poisonous liquid, CH_3NO_2, used chiefly as a solvent, rocket fuel, and gasoline additive and in organic synthesis. [1870–75; NITRO- + METHANE]

ni·tro·par·af·fin (nī′trə par′ə fin), *n. Chem.* any of a class of compounds derived from the methane series in which a hydrogen atom is replaced by a nitro group. [1890–95; NITRO- + PARAFFIN]

ni·tro·phe·nol (nī′trə fē′nôl, -nol), *n. Chem.* **1.** any compound derived from phenol by the replacement of one or more of its ring hydrogen atoms by the nitro group. **2.** any of three water-soluble, crystalline isomers of such a derivative, having the formula $C_6H_5NO_3$, occurring in yellow **(ortho-nitrophenol),** pale-yellow **(meta-nitrophenol),** and yellowish **(para-nitrophenol)** solids, used chiefly as intermediates in organic synthesis and as indicators. [1850–55; NITRO- + PHENOL]

ni′tro rad′ical. See **nitro group.**

ni·tros·a·mine (nī trō′sə mēn′, nī′trōs am′in), *n. Chem.* any of a series of compounds with the type formula R_2NNO, some of which are carcinogenic, formed in cured meats by the conversion of nitrite. [1875–80; NITROS- + AMINE]

ni·tro·so (nī trō′sō), *adj. Chem.* (esp. of organic compounds) containing the nitroso group; nitrosyl. [1880–85; independent use of NITROSO-]

nitroso-, a combining form of the nitroso group: *nitrosobenzene.* Also, *esp. before a vowel,* **nitros-.** [comb. form of L *nitrōsus* full of natron, equiv. to *nitr(um)* native soda, NATRON (< Gk *nítron* soda) + *-ōsus* -OSE[1]; see -O-]

ni·tro·so·ben·zene (nī trō′sō ben′zēn, -ben zēn′), *n. Chem.* a blue, crystalline, water-insoluble solid, C_6H_5NO, that is green as a molten solid or in solution. [NITROSO- + BENZENE]

nitro′so group′, *Chem.* the univalent group O=N–. Also called **nitro′so rad′ical.** [1905–10]

ni·tro·so·u·re·a (nī trō′sō yŏŏ rē′ə), *n. Pharm.* any of various lipid-soluble, synthetic or naturally occurring alkylating agents that can cross the blood-brain barrier: used in the treatment of certain brain cancers. [NITROSO- + UREA]

ni·tro·starch (nī′trə stärch′), *n. Chem.* an orange powder, $C_{12}H_{12}N_6O_{26}$, soluble in ethanol, used in explosives. [NITRO- + STARCH]

ni·tro·syl (nī′trə sil), *adj. Chem.* nitroso. [NITROS- + -YL]

ni·tro·syl·sul·fu·ric (nī′trə sil sul fyŏŏr′ik), *adj. Chem.* of or derived from nitrosylsulfuric acid. Also, **ni′·tro·syl·sul·phu′ric.** [1830–40; NITROSYL + SULFURIC]

ni′trosylsulfu′ric ac′id, *Chem.* a clear, straw-colored, oily, corrosive liquid, HNO_5S, used chiefly in the manufacture of dyes. [1830–40; NITROSYL + SULFURIC ACID]

ni·trous (nī′trəs), *adj. Chem.* **1.** pertaining to compounds obtained from niter, usually containing less oxygen than the corresponding nitric compounds. **2.** containing nitrogen, usually in the trivalent state. [1595–1605; < L *nitrōsus* full of natron. See NITROSO-]

ni′trous ac′id, *Chem.* an acid, HNO_2, known only in solution. [1670–80]

ni′trous bacte′ria, nitrobacteria that convert ammonia derivatives into nitrites by oxidation.

ni′trous e′ther, *Chem.* See **ethyl nitrite.** [1805–15]

ni′trous ox′ide, *Chem., Pharm.* a colorless, sweet-smelling, sweet-tasting, nonflammable, slightly water-soluble gas, N_2O, that sometimes produces a feeling of exhilaration when inhaled: used chiefly as an anesthetic in dentistry and surgery, in the manufacture of chemicals, and as an aerosol. Also called **laughing gas.** [1790–1800]

ni′tro·xan′thic ac′id (nī′trə zan′thik, nī′-), *Chem.* See **picric acid.** [NITRO- + XANTHIC ACID]

Nit·ti (nēt′tē), *n.* **Fran·ces·co Sa·ve·rio** (frän ches′kô sä ve′ryô), 1868–1953, Italian lawyer, statesman, and economist.

nit·ty (nit′ē), *adj.,* **-ti·er, -ti·est.** full of nits. [1560–70; NIT[1] + -Y[1]]

nit·ty-grit·ty (nit′ē grit′ē), *Slang.* —*n.* **1.** the essential substance or details of a matter; basics; crux: *Let's skip the chitchat and get down to the nitty-gritty.* —*adj.* **2.** fundamental, detailed, or probing: *nitty-gritty questions.* **3.** direct and practical: *nitty-gritty advice; a nitty-gritty system.* [1960–65, *Amer.*; rhyming compound of uncert. orig.]

nit·wit (nit′wit′), *n.* a slow-witted, stupid, or foolish person. [1920–25; *nit* (< G; dial. var. of *nicht* not) + WIT]
—**Syn.** fool, blockhead, dolt, dunce, booby.

Ni·u·e (nē ōō′ā), *n.* an island in the S Pacific between Tonga and Cook Islands: possession of New Zealand. 5128; ab. 100 sq. mi. (260 sq. km). Also called **Savage Island.** —**Ni·u·an** (nē ōō′ən), *adj., n.*

Niu·zhuang (*Chin.* nyY′jwäng′), *n. Pinyin.* former name of **Yingkou.** Also, **Newchwang.**

ni·val (nī′vəl), *adj.* of or growing in snow: *nival flora.* [1650–60; < L *nivālis* of, belonging to snow, snowy, equiv. to *niv-* (s. of *nix*) snow + *-ālis* -AL[1]]

ni·va·tion (nī vā′shən), *n. Geol.* erosion resulting from the action of frost beneath a snowbank. [1895–1900; < L *niv-* (s. of *nix*) snow + -ATION]

niv·e·ous (niv′ē əs), *adj.* resembling snow, esp. in whiteness; snowy. [1615–25; < L *niveus* snowy, snow-white, of, from snow, equiv. to *niv-* (s. of *nix*) snow + *-eus* -EOUS]

Ni·ver·nais (nē veʀ ne′), *n.* a former province in central France. *Cap.:* Nevers.

Nivkh (nēfk, nēfKH), *n., pl.* **Nivkhs, Niv·khi** (nēf′kē, -KHē), (*esp. collectively*) **Nivkh** for 1. **1.** an indigenous people of the Soviet Far East, now living mainly in scattered communities on the lower Amur River and Sakhalin Island. **2.** the Paleosiberian language of the Nivkh. Also called **Gilyak.** [< Russ < Nivkh (Amur dial.) *ńivx* a self-designation]

Ni·vôse (nē vōz′), *n.* (in the French Revolutionary calendar) the fourth month of the year, extending from December 21 to January 19. [1795–1805; < F < L *nivōsus* snowy, equiv. to *niv-* (s. of *nix*) snow + *-ōsus* -OSE[1]]

nix[1] (niks), *Slang.* —*n.* **1.** nothing. —*adv.* **2.** no. —*interj.* **3.** (used as an exclamation, esp. of warning): *Nix, the cops!* —*v.t.* **4.** to veto; refuse to agree to; prohibit: *to nix the project.* [1780–90; < G: var. of *nichts* nothing]

nix[2] (niks), *n., pl.* **nix·es.** (in Germanic folklore) a water spirit that draws its victims into its underwater home. [1825–35; < G *Nix,* OHG *nihhus;* c. OE *nicor* water monster, ON *nykr,* Norw *nøkk,* Sw *näck;* cf. Skt *nenekti* (he) washes]

nix·ie[1] (nik′sē), *n.* a letter or parcel that is undeliverable by the post office because of a faulty or illegible address. [1880–85; NIX[1] + -IE]

nix·ie[2] (nik′sē), *n. Germanic Folklore.* a female water spirit. [1810–20; < G *Nixe* (MHG *nickese,* OHG *nicchessa;* see NIX[2]), perh. construed at time of borrowing as NIX[2] + -IE]

Nix·on (nik′sən), *n.* **Richard M(il·hous)** (mil′hous), 1913–94, 37th president of the U.S., 1969–74 (resigned).

Nix′on Doc′trine, the policy declared by President Nixon in 1969 that the U.S. would supply arms but not military forces to its allies in Asia and elsewhere.

ni·ya·ma (nē′yə mə), *n. Yoga.* one of five observances, composing one of the eight practices, or angas, which are cleanliness of mind and body, equanimity, temperance or tapas, self-appraisal, and attentiveness to God, who is conceived of as a completely free spirit. [< Skt]

Ni·zam (ni zäm′, -zam′, nī-), *n.* **1.** the title of the ruler of Hyderabad from the beginning of the 18th century to 1950. **2.** (*l.c.*) the Turkish regular army or any member of it. [1595–1605; (def. 1) < Urdu *Nizām-al-mulk* governor of the realm; (def. 2) < Turk *nizamiye* regular army; both < Ar *niẓām* order, arrangement]

ni·zam·ate (ni zä′māt, -zam′āt, nī-), *n.* the position held or territory governed by a Nizam. [1885–90]

Ni·zhne·kamsk (nizh′nə kamsk′; *Russ.* nyi zhnyi-kämsk′), *n.* a city in the E Russian Federation in Europe, SE of Kazan. 134,000.

Nizh·ni Nov·go·rod (nizh′nē nov′gə rod′; *Russ.* nyē′zhnyē nôv′gə rət), a city in the Russian Federation in Europe, E of Moscow, on the Volga River. 1,438,000. Formerly (1932–91), **Gorki.**

Nizh·ni Ta·gil (nizh′nē tə gēl′; *Russ.* nyē′zhnyē tə gyēl′), a city in the Russian Federation in Asia, on the E slope of the Ural Mountains. 427,000.

NJ, New Jersey (approved esp. for use with zip code).

N.J., New Jersey.

Njord (nyôrd), *n. Scand. Myth.* the god of winds, navigation, and prosperity, and the father of Frey and Freya; king of the Vanir. Cf. **Nerthus.** [< ON *Njǫrthr;* cf. L *Nerthus,* a Gmc female deity described by Tacitus]

NKGB, in the U.S.S.R., the government's secret-police organization (1941–46). Cf. **Cheka.** [< Russ *N(aródnyĭ) k(omissariát) g(osudárstvennoĭ) b(ezopásnosti)* People's Commissariat for State Security]

Nko·mo (ən kō′mō, əng kō′-), *n.* **Joshua Mqua·bu·ko Nyon·go·lo** (əm kwä bōō′kō nyong gō′lō), born 1917, African nationalist and political leader in Zimbabwe.

Nkru·mah (ən krōō′mə, əng krōō′-), *n.* **Kwa·me** (kwä′mē), 1909–72, president of Ghana 1960–66.

NKVD, in the U.S.S.R., the government's secret-police organization (1934–46). Cf. **Cheka.** [< Russ *N(aródnyĭ) K(omissariát) V(nútrennikh) D(el)* People's Commissariat of Internal Affairs]

NL, 1. Also, **NL.** New Latin; Neo-Latin. **2.** See **night letter.**

N.L., 1. *Baseball.* National League. **2.** New Latin; Neo-Latin.

n.l., 1. *Print.* new line. **2.** non licet. **3.** non liquet.

N. Lat., north latitude. Also, **N. lat.**

N.L.F., See **National Liberation Front.**

NLRB, National Labor Relations Board. Also, **N.L.R.B.**

NM, 1. New Mexico (approved esp. for use with zip code). **2.** *Gram.* noun modifier.

nm, 1. nanometer; nanometers. **2.** nautical mile. **3.** nonmetallic.

N.M., New Mexico. Also, **N. Mex.**

NMI, no middle initial.

NMN, no middle name.

NMR, 1. *Physics.* nuclear magnetic resonance. **2.** See **MRI** (def. 1).

NMR scan. See **MR scan.**

NMR scanner. See **MR scanner.**

NMSQT, National Merit Scholarship Qualifying Test.

NMSS, National Multiple Sclerosis Society.

N.M.U., National Maritime Union. Also, **NMU**

NNE, north-northeast. Also, **N.N.E.**

NNP, See **net national product.**

NNW, north-northwest. Also, **N.N.W.**

no[1] (nō), *adv., adj., n., pl.* **noes, nos,** *v.* —*adv.* **1.** (a negative used to express dissent, denial, or refusal, as in response to a question or request) **2.** (used to emphasize or introduce a negative statement): *Not a single person came to the party, no, not a one.* **3.** not in any degree or manner; not at all (used with a comparative): *He is no better.* **4.** not a (used before an adjective to convey the opposite of the adjective's meaning): *His recovery was no small miracle.* —*adj.* **5.** not a (used before a noun to convey the opposite of the noun's meaning): *She's no beginner on the ski slopes.* —*n.* **6.** an utterance of the word "no." **7.** a denial or refusal: *He responded with a definite no.* **8.** a negative vote or voter: *The noes have it.* **9. no can do,** *Informal.* it can't be done. —*v.t.* **10.** to reject, refuse approval, or express disapproval of. —*v.i.* **11.** to express disapproval. [bef. 900; ME; OE *nā,* equiv. to *ne* not + *ā* ever (see AY[1])]

no[2] (nō), *adj.* **1.** not any: *no money.* **2.** not at all; far from being: *He is no genius.* **3.** very little; negligible: *We got her to the hospital in no time.* [1150–1200; ME; var. of NONE[1]]

No, *Symbol, Chem.* nobelium.

Nō (nō), *n.* classic drama of Japan, developed chiefly in the 14th century, employing verse, prose, choral song, and dance in highly conventionalized formal and thematic patterns derived from religious sources and folk myths. Also, **No, Noh.** Also called ***Nogaku.*** Cf. **kabuki.** [1870–75; < Japn, earlier *noũ* < MChin, equiv. to Chin *néng* ability]

N/O, *Banking.* registered.

no., 1. north. **2.** northern. **3.** number. Also, **No.**

NOAA, See **National Oceanic and Atmospheric Administration.**

no-ac·count (nō′ə kount′), *Informal.* —*adj.* **1.** worthless; good-for-nothing; trifling. —*n.* **2.** a worthless person; good-for-nothing. Also, **no-count.** [1835–45, *Amer.*]

No·a·chi·an (nō ā′kē ən), *adj.* of or pertaining to the patriarch Noah or his time. Also, **No·ach·ic** (nō ak′ik, -ā′kik), **No·ach′i·cal, No·ah·ic** (nō ā′ik). [1670–80; *Noach* (var. of NOAH) + -IAN]

No·ah (nō′ə), *n.* **1.** the patriarch who built a ship **(Noah's Ark)** in which he, his family, and animals of every species survived the Flood. Gen. 5–9. **2.** a male given name: from a Hebrew word meaning "rest."

No′ah's Ark′, 1. See under **Noah** (def. 1). **2.** an ark shell, *Arca noae.* [1605–15]

No′ah's Dove′, *Astron.* the constellation Columba. [1585–95]

nob[1] (nob), *n.* **1.** *Slang.* the head. **2.** *Cribbage.* Sometimes, **his nobs.** the jack of the same suit as the card turned up, counting one to the holder. [1690–1700; perh. var. of KNOB]

nob[2] (nob), *n. Chiefly Brit. Slang.* a person of wealth or social importance. [1745–55; earlier *knabb* (Scots), *nab;* of uncert. orig.]

no′ ball′, *Cricket.* an unfairly bowled ball. [1740–50]

nob·ble (nob′əl), *v.t.,* **-bled, -bling.** *Brit. Slang.* **1.** to drug or disable (a race horse) to prevent its winning a race. **2.** to convince (a person) by fraudulent methods; misrepresent or lie to. **3.** to swindle; defraud. **4.** to seize (a person); hold for arrest. [1840–50; back formation from *nobbler,* var. of HOBBLER (dial. phrase *an 'obbler* being taken as *a nobbler*)] —**nob′bler,** *n.*

nob·by (nob′ē), *adj.,* **-bi·er, -bi·est.** *Brit. Slang.* **1.** fashionable or elegant; stylish; chic. **2.** excellent; first-rate. [1780–90; NOB[2] + -Y[1]] —**nob′bi·ly,** *adv.*

No·bel (nō bel′), *n.* **Al·fred Bern·hard** (äl′fʀed beʀ′-närd), 1833–96, Swedish engineer, manufacturer, and philanthropist.

No·bel·ist (nō bel′ist), *n.* a person who is awarded a Nobel prize. [1940–45; NOBEL (PRIZE) + -IST]

no·bel·i·um (nō bel′ē əm, -bē′lē-), *n. Chem., Physics.* a transuranic element in the actinium series. *Symbol:* No; *at. no.:* 102. [1955–60; < NL; named after NOBEL Institute, where first discovered; see -IUM]

No′bel prize′, any of various awards made annually, beginning in 1901, from funds originally established by Alfred B. Nobel for outstanding achievement in physics, chemistry, medicine or physiology, literature, and the promotion of peace; an annual award in economics was established in 1969 from private funds.

No·bi·le (nô′bē le), *n.* **Um·ber·to** (ŏŏm beʀ′tô), 1885–1978, Italian aeronautical engineer and arctic explorer.

no·bil·i·ar·y (nō bil′ē er′ē, -bil′yə rē), *adj.* of or pertaining to the nobility. [1720–30; < F *nobiliaire.* See NOBLE, -ARY]

no·bil·i·ty (nō bil′i tē), *n., pl.* **-ties. 1.** the noble class or the body of nobles in a country. **2.** (in Britain) the peerage. **3.** the state or quality of being noble. **4.** nobleness of mind, character, or spirit; exalted moral excellence. **5.** grandeur or magnificence. **6.** noble birth or rank. [1350–1400; ME *nobilite* < L *nōbilitās.* See NOBLE, -ITY]

no′ bill′, *Law.* a failure to indict. Cf. **true bill.**

no-bill (nō′bil′), *v.t. Law* to fail to indict (a person).

no·ble (nō′bəl), *adj.*, **-bler, -blest,** *n.* —*adj.* **1.** distinguished by rank or title. **2.** pertaining to persons so distinguished. **3.** of, belonging to, or constituting a hereditary class that has special social or political status in a country or state; of or pertaining to the aristocracy. **4.** of an exalted moral or mental character or excellence; lofty: *a noble thought.* **5.** admirable in dignity of conception, manner of expression, execution, or composition: *a noble poem.* **6.** very impressive or imposing in appearance; stately; magnificent: *a noble monument.* **7.** of an admirably high quality; notably superior; excellent. **8.** famous; illustrious; renowned. **9.** *Chem.* inert; chemically inactive. **10.** *Falconry.* (of a hawk) having excellent qualities or abilities. —*n.* **11.** a person of noble birth or rank; nobleman or noblewoman. **12.** a former gold coin of England, first issued in 1346 by Edward III, equal to half a mark or 6s. 8d., replaced in 1464 under Edward IV by the rose noble. **13.** (in Britain) a peer. [1175–1225; ME < OF < L (*g*)*nōbilis* notable, of high rank, equiv. to (*g*)*nō-*, base of (*g*)*nōscere* to get to know, find out (see KNOW[1]) + *-bilis* -BLE] —**no′ble·ness,** *n.*
—**Syn. 3.** highborn, aristocratic. **4.** honorable. NOBLE, HIGH-MINDED, MAGNANIMOUS agree in referring to lofty principles and loftiness of mind or spirit. NOBLE implies a loftiness of character or spirit that scorns the petty, mean, base, or dishonorable: *a noble deed.* HIGH-MINDED implies having elevated principles and consistently adhering to them: *a high-minded pursuit of legal reforms.* MAGNANIMOUS suggests greatness of mind or soul, esp. as manifested in generosity or in overlooking injuries: *magnanimous toward his former enemies.* **6.** grand, lordly, splendid. **11.** peer, aristocrat.

no′ble fir′, **1.** a fir, *Abies procera,* of the northwestern U.S., which may grow to a height of 250 ft. (76 m). **2.** the soft, light wood of this tree, used for pulpwood and plywood. [1895–1900, *Amer.*]

no′ble gas′, *Chem.* any of the chemically inert gaseous elements of group 8A or 0 of the periodic table: helium, neon, argon, krypton, xenon, and radon. Also called **inert gas.** [1900–05]

no·ble·man (nō′bəl mən), *n., pl.* **-men.** a man of noble birth or rank; noble; peer. [1520–30; NOBLE + -MAN] —**no′ble·man·ly,** *adv.*

no′ble met′al, any of a number of metals, as gold, silver, mercury, or platinum, that resist oxidation when heated in air, and solution by inorganic acids. [1350–1400; ME: precious metal]

no·ble-mind·ed (nō′bəl mīn′did), *adj.* characterized by morally admirable thought or motives; righteous; worthy. [1850–55] —**no′ble-mind′ed·ly,** *adv.* **no′·ble-mind′ed·ness,** *n.*

no′ble o′pal. See **precious opal.** [1850–55]

no′ble rot′, *Winemaking.* the fungus *Botrytis cinerea,* which is cultivated in some winemaking processes, esp. in the making of French Sauternes, where the ripened grapes become shriveled as a result of its introduction, thereby concentrating the juice and increasing the sugar content. Also called **no′ble mold′.** [1920–25]

no·blesse o·blige (nō bles′ ō blēzh′; *Fr.* nô bles′ ô blēzh′), the moral obligation of those of high birth, powerful social position, etc., to act with honor, kindliness, generosity, etc. [1830–40; < F: lit., nobility obliges]

No·bles·ville (nō′bəlz vil′), *n.* a town in central Indiana. 12,056.

no·ble·wom·an (nō′bəl wo͝om′ən), *n., pl.* **-wom·en.** a woman of noble birth or rank. [1565–75; NOBLE + -WOMAN]

no·bly (nō′blē), *adv.* **1.** in a noble manner. **2.** courageously; bravely; gallantly. **3.** splendidly; superbly; magnificently. **4.** of noble ancestry: *nobly born.* [1250–1300; ME *nobliche.* See NOBLE, -LY]

no·bod·y (nō′bod′ē, -bud′ē, -bə dē), *pron., n., pl.* **-bod·ies.** —*pron.* **1.** no person; not anyone; no one: *Nobody answered, so I hung up.* —*n.* **2.** a person of no importance, influence, or power. [1300–50; ME; see NO[2], BODY]

no-brain·er (nō′brā′nər), *n. Informal.* anything requiring little thought or effort; something easy or simple to understand or do. [1975–80]

N.O.C., *Insurance.* not otherwise classified.

no-cal (nō′kal′), *adj.* containing no calories: *a no-cal sweetener.* [1970–75; NO[2] + CAL(ORIE)]

no·car·di·a (nō kär′dē ə), *n. Bacteriol.* any of several filamentous or rod-shaped, aerobic bacteria of the genus *Nocardia,* certain species of which are pathogenic for humans and other animals. [1905–10; < NL; named after Edmond I.E. *Nocard* (1850–1903), French biologist; see -IA] —**no·car′di·al,** *adj.*

no·cent (nō′sənt), *adj.* **1.** harmful; injurious. **2.** *Archaic.* guilty. [1400–50; late ME < L *nocent-,* s. of *nocēns,* prp. of *nocēre* to do harm; see -ENT]

nock (nok), *n.* **1.** a metal or plastic piece at the end of an arrow, having a notch for the bowstring. **2.** a notch or groove at the end of an arrow into which the bowstring fits. **3.** a notch or groove at each end of a bow, to hold the bowstring in place. **4.** *Naut.* throat (def. 6a). —*v.t.* **5.** to furnish with a nock. **6.** to adjust (the arrow) to the bowstring, in readiness to shoot. [1325–75; ME *nok(ke)* (n.); akin to D *nok,* LG *nok(ke)* tip]

no-code (nō′kōd′), *n.* **1.** *Med.* a directive not to alert a hospital team to perform emergency resuscitation on a particular patient. Cf. **code** (def. 9). **2.** *Med. Slang.* a patient to whom a no-code applies.

no′ con′test, *Law.* See **nolo contendere.**

no-count (nō′kount′), *adj., n.* no-account.

noct-, var. of **nocti-** before a vowel.

CONCISE ETYMOLOGY KEY: <, descended or borrowed from; >, whence; b., blend of, blended; c., cognate with; cf., compare; deriv., derivative; equiv., equivalent; imit., imitative; obl., oblique; r., replacing; s., stem; sp., spelling, spelled; resp., respelling, respelled; trans., translation; ?, origin unknown; *, unattested; ‡, probably earlier than. See the full key inside the front cover.

noc·tam·bu·lism (nok tam′byə liz′əm), *n.* somnambulism. Also, **noc·tam′bu·la′tion.** [1855–60; NOCTAMBUL(OUS) + -ISM] —**noc·tam′bu·list, noc·tam·bule** (nok tam′byo͞ol), *n.*

noc·tam·bu·lous (nok tam′byə ləs), *adj.* of, pertaining to, or given to sleepwalking. Also, **noc·tam′bu·lant, noc·tam′bu·lis′tic.** [1725–35; NOCT- + L *ambul(āre)* to walk + -OUS]

nocti-, a combining form meaning "night," used in the formation of compound words: *noctilucent.* Also, *esp. before a vowel,* **noct-.** [< L *nocti-,* comb. form of *nox* NIGHT]

noc·ti·lu·ca (nok′tə lo͞o′kə), *n., pl.* **-cae** (-sē). a dinoflagellate of the genus *Noctiluca,* capable of producing light and, in groups, of causing a luminous appearance of the sea. [1670–80; < NL; L *noctilūca* shiner by night, equiv. to *nocti-* NOCTI- + *-lūca* shiner, deriv. of *lūcēre* to shine] —**noc′ti·lu′can,** *adj.*

noc·ti·lu·cent (nok′tə lo͞o′sənt), *adj. Meteorol.* (of high-altitude clouds) visible during the short night of the summer. [1885–90; NOCTI- + LUCENT] —**noc′ti·lu′·cence,** *n.*

noc·tis (nok′tis), *adj.* (in prescriptions) of the night. [< L, gen. sing. of *nox* night]

noc·to·graph (nok′tə graf′, -gräf′), *n.* a frame used to aid the blind in writing. [1860–65; NOCT- + -O- + -GRAPH]

noc·tu·id (nok′cho͞o id), *n.* **1.** Also called **owlet moth.** any of numerous dull-colored moths of the family Noctuidae, the larvae of which include the armyworms and cutworms. —*adj.* **2.** belonging or pertaining to the family Noctuidae. [1875–80; < NL *Noctuidae,* equiv. to *Noctu(a)* a genus of European moths (L *noctua* the little owl, prob. n. use of fem. of **noctuus,* equiv. to *noct-,* s. of *nox* NIGHT + *-uus* adj. suffix) + *-idae* -ID[2]]

noc·tule (nok′cho͞ol), *n.* a large reddish insectivorous bat, *Nyctalus noctula,* common to Europe and Asia. [1765–75; < F < It *nottola* a bat, owl << L *noctua* night owl. See NOCTUID, -ULE]

noc·turn (nok′tûrn), *n. Rom. Cath. Ch.* the office of matins, consisting of nine psalms and either three or nine lessons. [bef. 1150; ME *nocturne* < ML *nocturna,* n. use of fem. of L *nocturnus* by night; r. OE *noctern* < ML, as above]

noc·tur·nal (nok tûr′nl), *adj.* **1.** of or pertaining to the night (opposed to *diurnal*). **2.** done, occurring, or coming at night: *nocturnal visit.* **3.** active at night (opposed to *diurnal*): *nocturnal animals.* **4.** opening by night and closing by day, as certain flowers (opposed to *diurnal*). —*n.* **5.** *Archaic.* an astrolabe for telling time at night or for determining latitude by the position of certain stars in reference to Polaris. [1475–85; < LL *nocturnālis.* See NOCTURN, -AL[1]] —**noc′tur·nal′i·ty,** *n.* —**noc·tur′nal·ly,** *adv.* —**Syn. 2.** nighttime.

noctur′nal arc′, *Astron.* the portion of the diurnal circle that is below the horizon of a given point. Cf. **diurnal arc.** [1695–1705]

noctur′nal emis′sion, the release of semen during sleep, often during a sexual dream. Also called **wet dream.** [1925–30]

noc·turne (nok′tûrn), *n. Music.* **1.** a piece appropriate to the night or evening. **2.** an instrumental composition of a dreamy or pensive character. [1860–65; < F *nocturne.* See NOCTURN]

noc·u·ous (nok′yo͞o əs), *adj.* likely to cause damage or injury; harmful; noxious. [1625–35; < L *nocuus* harmful, injurious, equiv. to *noc(ēre)* to harm + *-uus* deverbal adj. suffix; see -OUS] —**noc′u·ous·ly,** *adv.* —**noc′u·ous·ness,** *n.*

no′-cut con′tract (nō′kut′), *Informal.* a professional athlete's contract guaranteeing that he or she will remain on the team's roster for a specified time. [1975–80]

nod (nod), *v.,* **nod·ded, nod·ding,** *n.* —*v.i.* **1.** to make a slight, quick downward bending forward of the head, as in assent, greeting, or command. **2.** to let the head fall slightly forward with a sudden, involuntary movement when sleepy. **3.** to doze, esp. in a sitting position: *The speaker was so boring that half the audience was nodding.* **4.** to become careless, inattentive, or listless; make an error or mistake through lack of attention. **5.** (of trees, flowers, plumes, etc.) to droop, bend, or incline with a swaying motion. —*v.t.* **6.** to bend (the head) in a short, quick downward movement, as of assent or greeting. **7.** to express or signify by such a movement of the head: *to nod approval; to nod agreement.* **8.** to summon, bring, or send by a nod of the head. **9.** to cause (something) to lean or sway; incline. **10. nod off,** to fall asleep or doze, esp. in a sitting position: *He was reprimanded for nodding off in class.* **11. nod out,** *Slang.* to fall asleep owing to the effects of a dose of a narcotic analgesic drug. —*n.* **12.** a short, quick downward bending forward of the head, as in assent, greeting, or command or because of drowsiness. **13.** a brief period of sleep; nap. **14.** a bending or swaying movement. **15. give the nod to,** *Informal.* to express approval of; agree to: *The board gave the nod to the new proposal.* **16. on the nod, a.** *Brit. Slang.* on credit. **b.** *Slang.* drowsy following a dose of a narcotic drug. [1350–1400; ME *nodde,* of uncert. orig.] —**nod′der,** *n.* —**nod′ding·ly,** *adv.* —**Syn. 3.** drowse.

Nod (nod), *n.* **1.** the land east of Eden where Cain went to dwell. Gen. 4:16. **2.** See **land of Nod.**

nod·al (nōd′l), *adj.* pertaining to or of the nature of a node. [1825–35; NODE + -AL[1]] —**no·dal′i·ty,** *n.*

nod′al point′, *Optics.* either of two points on the axis of a lens or other optical system, determined by extending an incident oblique ray and the corresponding refracted ray to the axis for the pair of rays that are parallel outside the optical system. Also called **node.** [1835–45]

nod′ding acquain′tance, **1.** a slight, incomplete, or superficial knowledge (of something or someone): *He had only a nodding acquaintance with Italian and didn't trust it to get him through the tour. Although we were neighbors for several years, we had only a nodding acquaintance.* **2.** a person with whom one is only slightly acquainted: *I don't really know what he's like—he's only a nodding acquaintance.* [1860–65]

nod′ding li′lac, a showy Chinese lilac, *Syringa reflexa,* of the olive family, having nodding clusters of pinkish flowers.

nod′ding pogo′nia, a rare orchid, *Triphora trianthophora,* of the eastern U.S., bearing three pink flowers. Also called **three-birds.** [1905–10, *Amer.*]

nod′ding tril′lium, a hardy plant, *Trillium cernuum,* of the lily family, of the eastern coast of North America, having wavy-petalled, white or pinkish flowers on short, recurved stalks hanging beneath the three whorled leaves. [1805–15, *Amer.*]

nod·dle (nod′l), *n. Older Slang.* the head or brain. [1375–1425; late ME *nodel*]

nod·dy (nod′ē), *n., pl.* **-dies.** **1.** any of several dark-bodied terns of the genera *Anous* and *Micranous* found about the coasts and islands in warm seas of both the New and Old Worlds, often so tame as to seem stupid. **2.** a fool or simpleton; noodle. [1520–30; perh. n. use of obs. *noddy* (adj.) silly. See NOD, -Y[1]]

node (nōd), *n.* **1.** a knot, protuberance, or knob. **2.** a centering point of component parts. **3.** *Anat.* a knotlike mass of tissue: *lymph node.* **4.** *Pathol.* circumscribed swelling. **5.** *Bot.* **a.** a joint in a stem. **b.** a part of a stem that normally bears a leaf. **6.** *Math.* knot (def. 12). **7.** *Geom.* a point on a curve or surface at which there can be more than one tangent line or tangent plane. **8.** *Physics.* a point, line, or region in a standing wave at which there is relatively little or no vibration. **9.** *Astron.* either of the two points at which the orbit of a heavenly body intersects a given plane, esp. the plane of the ecliptic or of the celestial equator. Cf. **ascending node, descending node.** **10.** *Ling.* an element of a tree diagram that represents a constituent of a linguistic construction. **11.** *Optics.* See **nodal point.** **12.** *Engin.* See **panel point.** **13.** nodus. [1565–75; < L *nōdus* knot]

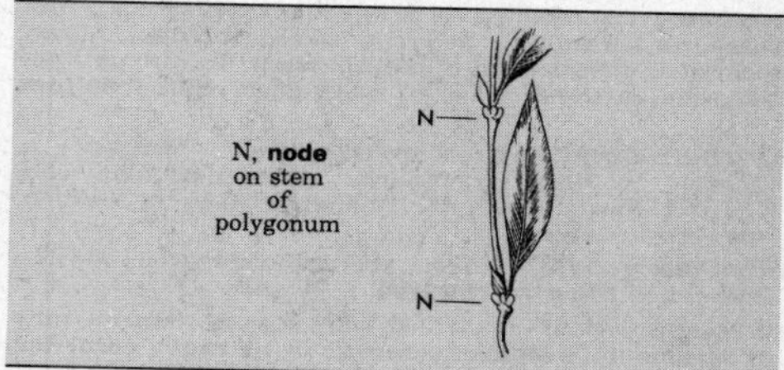

N, **node** on stem of polygonum

node′ of Ran·vier′ (rän vyā′, rän′vyā), *Cell Biol.* a gap occurring at regular intervals between segments of myelin sheath along a nerve axon. [1880–85; named after Louis-Antoine *Ranvier* (1835–1922), French histologist, who described it in 1878]

nod·i·cal (nod′i kəl, nō′di-), *adj. Astron.* of or pertaining to a node or the nodes. [1830–40; NODE + -ICAL]

nod′ical month′. See under **month** (def. 5). [1830–40]

no·dose (nō′dōs, nō dōs′), *adj.* **1.** having nodes. **2.** full of knots; knotty. Also, **no·dous** (nō′dəs). [1715–25; < L *nōdōsus* full of knots, knotty, equiv. to *nōd(us)* NODE + *-ōsus* -OSE[1]] —**no·dos·i·ty** (nō dos′i tē), *n.*

nod·u·lar (noj′ə lər), *adj.* **1.** of, pertaining to, or characterized by nodules. **2.** shaped like or occurring in nodules: *a nodular concretion.* [1785–95; NODULE + -AR[1]]

nod′ular cast′ i′ron, any of various cast irons strengthened by having the graphite content in the form of nodules rather than flakes, and containing cerium or magnesium as well as other additives. Also called **ductile iron.** [1945–50]

nod·ule (noj′o͞ol), *n.* **1.** a small node, knot, or knob. **2.** a small, rounded mass or lump. **3.** *Bot.* a tubercle. [1590–1600; < L *nōdulus* a little knot, equiv. to *nōd(us)* NODE + *-ulus* -ULE]

nod·u·lous (noj′ə ləs), *adj.* having nodules. Also, **nod·u·lose** (noj′ə lōs′, nod′yə-, noj′ə lōs′, nod′yə-). [1835–45; NODULE + -OUS]

nod·u·lus (noj′ə ləs), *n., pl.* **-li** (-lī′). *Anat.* a small node, esp. on the vermis of the cerebellum. [1645–55; < L *nōdulus* little knot; see NODULE]

no·dus (nō′dəs), *n., pl.* **-di** (-dī). a difficult or intricate point, situation, plot, etc. [1350–1400; ME: knot in the flesh < L *nōdus* knot]

No·e (nō′ə), *n. Douay Bible.* Noah (def. 1).

no·e·gen·e·sis (nō′ē jen′ə sis), *n.* the production of new knowledge from sensory or intellectual experience. [1920–25; < Gk *noē-* (comb. form repr. *nóēsis* intelligence, or *nóēma* perception, thought) + -GENESIS] —**no·e·ge·net·ic** (nō′ē jə net′ik), *adj.*

No·el (nō el′ *for 1, 2;* nō′əl, nōl *for 3*), *n.* **1.** the Christmas season; yuletide. **2.** (*l.c.*) a Christmas song or carol. **3.** a male given name. [1805–15; < F << L *nātālis* (*diēs*) birthday; see NATAL]

No·el-Ba·ker (nō′əl bā′kər, nōl′-), *n.* **Philip John,** 1889–1982, British statesman and author: Nobel peace prize 1959.

No·e·mi (nō′ə mī′), *n. Douay Bible.* Naomi (def. 1).

no·e·sis (nō ē′sis), *n.* **1.** (in Greek philosophy) the exercise of reason. **2.** *Psychol.* cognition; the functioning of the intellect. [1880–85; < Gk *nóēsis* thought, intelligence, equiv. to *noē-* (var. s. of *noeîn* to think) + *-sis* -SIS]

no·et·ic (nō et′ik), *adj.* **1.** of or pertaining to the mind. **2.** originating in or apprehended by the reason. [1645–55; < Gk *noētikós* intelligent, equiv. to *nóē(sis)* NOESIS + *-tikos* -TIC]

no•et•ics (nō et′iks), *n.* (*used with a singular v.*) *Logic.* the science of the intellect or of pure thought; reasoning. [1870–75; see NOETIC, -ICS]

No′ Ex′it, (French, *Huis Clos*), a play (1945) by Jean-Paul Sartre.

no-fault (nō′fôlt′), *n.* **1.** Also called **no′-fault insur′•ance.** a form of automobile insurance designed to enable the policyholder in case of an accident to collect a certain basic compensation promptly for economic loss from his or her own insurance company without determination of liability. —*adj.* **2.** of, pertaining to, or requiring no-fault insurance: *a no-fault law; no-fault coverage.* **3.** of, pertaining to, or designating a divorce in which there is no attempt or need to hold either party responsible for the breakup. [1965–70, *Amer.*]

no′-fly′ zone′ (nō′flī′), an area over which no military flights are allowed. [1991]

Nof•re•te•te (nof′ri tē′tē), *n.* Nefertiti.

no-frills (nō′frilz′), *adj.* **1.** providing or including basic services and necessities without any additional features or amenities: *Food and beverages are not covered by the low no-frills air fare.* **2.** no-name. **3.** unadorned; simple; plain; spare: *a straightforward, no-frills package of health-care benefits.* [1955–60]

nog[1] (nog), *n.* **1.** any beverage made with beaten eggs, usually with alcoholic liquor; eggnog. **2.** a strong ale formerly brewed in Norfolk, England. [1685–95; orig. uncert.]

nog[2] (nog), *n., v.,* **nogged, nog•ging.** —*n.* **1.** a block of wood, as one inserted into brickwork to provide a hold for nails. **2.** any wooden peg, pin, or block. **3.** Also, **nogging.** one of a number of wooden pieces fitted between the principal timbers of a half-timbered wall. —*v.t.* **4.** to fill (a framed wall or partition) with small masonry, as bricks or stones. [1605–15; perh. var. of *knag,* ME *knagge* spur, peg]

No•gai (nō′gī), *n., pl.* **-gais,** (*esp. collectively*) **-gai** for 1. **1.** a member of a people living in the Caucasus region of the Soviet Union. **2.** the Turkic language of the Nogai people. Also, **Nogay.**

No•ga•ku (nô′gä ko͞o′), *n.* (*often l.c.*) *Japanese.* Nō.

No•gal•es (nə gal′is), *n.* a town in S Arizona. 15,683.

No•gay (nō′gī), *n., pl.* **-gays,** (*esp. collectively*) **-gay.** Nogai.

nogg (nog), *n. Carpentry.* a shave for shaping dowels and handles. [special use of NOG[2]]

nog•gin (nog′ən), *n.* **1.** a small cup or mug. **2.** a small amount of alcoholic liquor, usually a gill. **3.** *Informal.* a person's head. [1620–30; orig. uncert.]

nog•ging (nog′ing), *n.* **1.** masonry, as bricks, used to fill the spaces between studs or other framing members. **2.** nog (def. 3). [1815–25; NOG[2] + -ING[1]]

No•ginsk (no ginsk′; *Russ.* nu gyēnsk′), *n.* a city in the NW Russian Federation in Europe, E of Moscow. 119,000. Formerly, **Bogorodsk.**

no-go (nō′gō′), *adj. Slang.* **1.** inoperative; canceled. **2.** not ready. **3.** not functioning properly. [1865–70]

no-good (*adj.* nō′go͝od′; *n.* nō′go͝od′), *Informal.* —*adj.* **1.** lacking worth or merit; useless; bad. —*n.* **2.** a person or thing that is worthless or undependable. [1905–10, *Amer.*]

no-good•nik (nō′go͝od′nik), *n. Slang.* a no-good person. Also, **no′good′nik.** [1940–45, *Amer.*; NO-GOOD + -NIK]

no-growth (*adj.* nō′grōth′; *n.* nō′grōth′), *adj.* **1.** failing to or unlikely to grow; showing a lack of progress or development: *a no-growth industry.* **2.** restricting or prohibiting growth or expansion: *a no-growth policy; no-growth rulings.* —*n.* **3.** a policy or practice of curtailing growth, expansion, or development. [1970–75]

No•gu•chi (nə go͞o′chē; *Japn.* nô go͞o′chē), *n.* **1. Hi•de•yo** (hē′de yô′), 1876–1928, Japanese physician and bacteriologist in the U.S. **2. I•sa•mu** (ē′sä mo͞o′), 1904–88, U.S. sculptor and designer.

Noh (nō), *n.* Nō.

no-hit (nō′hit′), *adj. Baseball.* of or noting a game in which a pitcher allows no base hits to the opposing team: *a no-hit pitcher; a no-hit game.* [1910–15, *Amer.*]

no-hit•ter (nō′hit′ər), *n. Baseball.* a no-hit game. Cf. **perfect game.** [1935–40]

no-hop•er (nō′hō′pər), *n. Australian Slang.* a useless person from whom nothing can be expected. [1940–45; *no hope* + -ER[1]]

no-host (nō′hōst′), *adj. Chiefly Western U.S.* requiring patrons and guests to pay a fee for attendance or to pay for any food and drink they consume: *a no-host cocktail party; a no-host dinner-dance.*

no•how (nō′hou′), *adv. Nonstandard.* under no circumstances; in no way (usually prec. by another negative): *I can't learn this nohow.* [1765–75; NO[2] + HOW[1]]

-noia, a combining form appearing in loanwords from Greek, where it meant "thought": *paranoia.* [< Gk *-noia,* equiv. to *nó(os)* mind + *-ia* -Y[3]]

n.o.i.b.n., not otherwise indexed by name.

noil (noil), *n.* a short fiber of cotton, wool, worsted, etc., separated from the long fibers in combing. [1615–25; orig. uncert.] —**noil′y,** *adj.*

noir (nwar), *adj. French.* black; noting the black numbers in roulette. Cf. ***rouge.***

no-i•ron (nō′ī′ərn), *adj.* requiring no ironing or pressing: *a no-iron blouse; no-iron sheets.*

noise (noiz), *n., v.,* **noised, nois•ing.** —*n.* **1.** sound, esp. of a loud, harsh, or confused kind: *deafening noises.* **2.** a sound of any kind: *to hear a noise at the door.* **3.** loud shouting, outcry, or clamor. **4.** a nonharmonious or discordant group of sounds. **5.** an electric disturbance in a communications system that interferes with or prevents reception of a signal or of information, as the buzz on a telephone or snow on a television screen. **6.** *Informal.* extraneous, irrelevant, or meaningless facts, information, statistics, etc.: *The noise in the report obscured its useful information.* **7.** *Obs.* rumor or gossip, esp. slander. **8. make noises,** *Informal.* to speak vaguely; hint: *He is making noises to the press about running for public office.* —*v.t.* **9.** to spread, as a report or rumor; disseminate (usually fol. by *about* or *abroad*): *A new scandal is being noised about.* —*v.i.* **10.** to talk much or publicly. **11.** to make a noise, outcry, or clamor. [1175–1225; ME < OF < L *nausea* seasickness. See NAUSEA]
—**Syn. 1.** clatter, blare, uproar, tumult. NOISE, CLAMOR, DIN, HUBBUB, RACKET refer to unmusical or confused sounds. NOISE is the general word and is applied equally to soft or loud, confused or inharmonious sounds: *street noises.* CLAMOR and HUBBUB are alike in referring to loud noises resulting from shouting, cries, animated or excited tones, and the like; but in CLAMOR the emphasis is on the meaning of the shouting, and in HUBBUB the emphasis is on the confused mingling of sounds: *the clamor of an angry crowd; His voice could be heard above the hubbub.* DIN suggests a loud, resonant noise, painful if long continued: *the din of a boiler works.* RACKET suggests a loud, confused noise of the kind produced by clatter or percussion: *He always makes a racket when he cleans up the dishes.* **2.** See **sound**[1].

noise′ fac′tor, *Radio, Electronics.* the ratio of the noise output of an ideal device to the noise output of the unit being tested. Also called **noise′ fig′ure.** [1935–40]

noise•less (noiz′lis), *adj.* accompanied by or making little or no noise; silent; quiet: *a noiseless step; a noiseless typewriter.* [1595–1605; NOISE + -LESS] —**noise′less•ly,** *adv.* —**noise′less•ness,** *n.*
—**Syn.** inaudible, soundless. See **still**[1].

noise′ lim′iter, *Electronics.* an electronic circuit that cuts off all noise peaks that are stronger than some specific maximum for the desired input signal, thus limiting atmospheric and other interference. Also called **noise suppressor.** [1935–40]

noise•mak•er (noiz′mā′kər), *n.* a person or thing that makes noise, as a reveler on New Year's Eve, Halloween, etc., or a rattle, horn, or similar device used on such an occasion. [1565–75] —**noise′mak′ing,** *n., adj.*

noise′ pollu′tion, unwanted or harmful noise, as from automobiles, airplanes, or industrial workplaces.

noise•proof (noiz′pro͞of′), *adj.* soundproof.

noise′ suppres′sor, *Electronics.* **1.** squelch (def. 8). **2.** See **noise limiter.**

noi•sette (nwä zet′; *Fr.* nwa zet′), *n., pl.* **-settes** (-zets′; *Fr.* -zet′). a loin, fillet, or other lean section of meat: *an entrée of lamb noisettes.* [1890–95; < F: a round, rather thick slice of fillet or loin of lamb or mutton, dim. of *noix* choice part of a cut of meat, lit., nut, kernel < L *nucem,* acc. of *nux;* see -ETTE]

noi•sette′ rose′ (nwä zet′), a hybrid climbing rose, *Rosa noisettiana,* bearing clusters of fragrant yellow, white, or pink flowers. [1830–40; named after P. *Noisette,* who first raised it in the U.S. in the early 19th century]

noi•some (noi′səm), *adj.* **1.** offensive or disgusting, as an odor. **2.** harmful or injurious to health; noxious. [1350–1400; ME *noy* (aph. var. of ANNOY) + -SOME[1]] —**noi′some•ly,** *adv.* —**noi′some•ness,** *n.*
—**Syn. 1.** fetid, putrid, rotten, stinking, mephitic.

nois•y (noi′zē), *adj.,* **nois•i•er, nois•i•est.** **1.** making much noise: *noisy children.* **2.** abounding in or full of noise: *a noisy assembly hall.* **3.** characterized by much noise: *a noisy celebration; a noisy protest.* [1685–95; NOISE + -Y[1]] —**nois′i•ly,** *adv.* —**nois′i•ness,** *n.*
—**Syn. 1.** clamorous, tumultuous, uproarious; vociferous. See **loud.** —**Ant. 1.** quiet.

no-knock (nō′nok′), *adj.* **1.** antiknock. **2.** *Law.* that authorizes law-enforcement officers to enter premises unannounced and without identifying themselves: *a no-knock narcotics policy.* [1965–70, *Amer.*]

no•kyo (nō′kyō, -kē ō′; *Japn.* nô′kyô), *n., pl.* **-kyo.** a Japanese agricultural cooperative. [< Japn *nō-kyō* < MChin, equiv. to Chin *nóng* farming + *gòng* together]

no•lens vo•lens (nō′lens wō′lens; *Eng.* nō′lenz vō′-lenz), *Latin.* whether willing or not; willy-nilly.

no•li me tan•ge•re (nō′lī mē tan′jə rē, nō′lē; *Lat.* nō′lē me täng′ge re′), **1.** a person or thing that must not be touched or interfered with. **2.** a picture representing Jesus appearing to Mary Magdalene after his resurrection. **3.** Also, **no′li-me-tan′ge•re.** the touch-me-not. [< L: do not touch me (Jesus' words to Mary Magdalene)]

nol•le pros•e•qui (nol′ē pros′i kwī′, -kwē′), *Law.* an entry made upon the records of a court when the plaintiff or prosecutor will proceed no further in a suit or action. *Abbr.:* nol. pros. [1675–85; < L: be unwilling to pursue, do not prosecute]

no•lo (nō′lō), *n., pl.* **-los.** *Informal.* See **nolo contendere.**

no•lo con•ten•de•re (nō′lō kən ten′də rē), *Law.* (in a criminal case) a defendant's pleading that does not admit guilt but subjects him or her to punishment as though a guilty plea had been entered, the determination of guilt remaining open in other proceedings. Also, **nolo.** [1870–75; < L: I am unwilling to contend]

nol-pros (nol′pros′), *v.t.,* **-prossed, -pros•sing.** *Law.* to end by a nolle prosequi. [1875–80, *Amer.*]

nol. pros., *Law.* See **nolle prosequi.**

Nol•u•dar (nol′yə där′), *Pharm., Trademark.* a brand of methyprylon.

nom., nominative.

no•ma (nō′mə), *n., pl.* **-mas.** *Pathol.* a gangrenous ulceration of the mouth or genitalia, occurring mainly in debilitated children. [1825–35; < NL, L *nomē* a sore, ulcer < Gk *nomē* a feeding, grazing (akin to *némein* to feed, graze, consume)]

no•mad (nō′mad), *n.* **1.** a member of a people or tribe that has no permanent abode but moves about from place to place, usually seasonally and often following a traditional route or circuit according to the state of the pasturage or food supply. **2.** any wanderer; itinerant. —*adj.* **3.** nomadic. [1580–90; < L *nomad-* < Gk, s. of *nomás* pasturing flocks, akin to *némein* to pasture, graze] —**no′mad•ism,** *n.*

no•mad•ic (nō mad′ik), *adj.* of, pertaining to, or characteristic of nomads. [1810–20; < Gk *nomadikós.* See NOMAD, -IC] —**no•mad′i•cal•ly,** *adv.*

no•mad•ize (nō′ma dīz′), *v.,* **-ized, -iz•ing.** —*v.i.* **1.** to live in the manner of a nomad. —*v.t.* **2.** to cause (a person, tribe, etc.) to become nomadic. Also, *esp. Brit.,* **no′•mad•ise′.** [1790–1800; NOMAD + -IZE]

no′ man's′ land′, **1.** an area between opposing armies, over which no control has been established. **2.** an unowned or unclaimed tract of usually barren land. **3.** an indefinite or ambiguous area where guidelines and authority are not clear: *a no man's land between acceptance and rejection.* **4.** (in tennis, handball, etc.) the area of a court in which a player is at a tactical disadvantage, as the area of a tennis court about midway between the net and the base line. [1300–50; ME]

nom•arch (nom′ärk), *n.* the governor of a nome or a nomarchy. [1650–60; < Gk *nomárchēs* the chief of a province, equiv. to *nom(ós)* a province, district + *-archēs* -ARCH]

nom•ar•chy (nom′är kē), *n., pl.* **-chies.** one of the provinces into which modern Greece is divided. [1650–60; < Gk *nomarchía* rule of a province. See NOMARCH, -Y[3]]

nom•bles (num′bəlz), *n.pl.* numbles.

nom•bril (nom′bril), *n. Heraldry.* the point in an escutcheon between the middle of the base and the fess point. Also called **navel.** [1555–65; < F: lit., navel]

Nom. Cap., nominal capital.

nom de guerre (nom′ də gâr′; *Fr.* nôɴ də geʀ′), *pl.* **noms de guerre** (nomz′ də gâr′; *Fr.* nôɴ də geʀ′). an assumed name, as one under which a person fights, paints, writes, etc.; pseudonym. [< F: lit., war name]

nom de plume (nom′ də plo͞om′; *Fr.* nôɴ də plʏm′), *pl.* **noms de plume** (nomz′ də plo͞om′; *Fr.* nôɴ də plʏm′). See **pen name.** [1815–25; coined in E < F words: lit., pen name]

nome (nōm), *n.* **1.** one of the provinces of ancient Egypt. **2.** nomarchy. [1720–30; < Gk *nomós* a pasture, district, akin to *némein* to pasture]

Nome (nōm), *n.* **1.** a seaport in W Alaska. 2301. **2. Cape,** a cape in W Alaska, on Seward Peninsula, W of Nome.

no•men (nō′men), *n., pl.* **nom•i•na** (nom′ə nə, nō′mə-). (in ancient Rome) the second name of a citizen, indicating his gens, as "Gaius *Julius* Caesar." [1885–90; < L *nōmen* NAME]

no•men•cla•tor (nō′mən klā′tər), *n.* **1.** a person who assigns names, as in scientific classification; classifier. **2.** *Archaic.* a person who calls or announces things or persons by their names. [1555–65; < L *nōmenclātor,* var. of *nōmenculātor* one who announces names, equiv. to *nōmen* NAME + *-culātor,* var. of *calātor* a crier (*calā(re)* to call + *-tor* -TOR)]

no•men•cla•ture (nō′mən klā′chər, nō men′klə chər, -cho͝or′), *n.* **1.** a set or system of names or terms, as those used in a particular science or art, by an individual or community, etc. **2.** the names or terms comprising a set or system. [1600–10; < L *nōmenclātūra* a calling by name, list of names. See NOMENCLATOR, -URE] —**no′•men•cla′tur•al, no•men•cla•to•ri•al** (nō′mən klə tôr′ē-əl, -tōr′-), **no•men•cla•tive** (nō′mən klā′tiv), *adj.*

no•men•kla•tu•ra (nō′mən klä to͝or′ə), *n., pl.* **-ras.** a select list or class of people from which appointees for top-level government positions are drawn, esp. from a Communist Party. [1980–85; < Russ *nomenklatúra* lit., nomenclature]

No•mex (nō′meks), *Trademark.* a brand of lightweight, heat-resistant aramid fiber used in clothing, esp. for firefighters.

nom•i•nal (nom′ə nl), *adj.* **1.** being such in name only; so-called; putative: *a nominal treaty; the nominal head of the country.* **2.** (of a price, consideration, etc.) named as a mere matter of form, being trifling in comparison with the actual value; minimal. **3.** of, pertaining to, or constituting a name or names. **4.** *Gram.* **a.** of, pertaining to, or producing a noun or nouns: *a nominal suffix.* **b.** functioning as or like a noun. **5.** assigned to a person by name: *nominal shares of stock.* **6.** containing, bearing, or giving a name or names. **7.** (of money, income, or the like) measured in an amount rather than in real value: *Nominal wages have risen 50 percent, but real wages are down because of inflation.* **8.** *Aerospace.* performing or achieved within expected, acceptable limits; normal and satisfactory: *The mission was nominal throughout.* **9.** *Slang.* done smoothly as expected: *The space shot was nominal, proceeding without a hitch.* —*n.* **10.** *Gram.* a word or group of words functioning as a noun. [1425–75; late ME *nominalle* of a noun < L *nōminālis* of, belonging to a name, nominal, equiv. to *nōmin-* (s. of *nōmen;* see NOMEN) + *-ālis* -AL[1]]
—**Syn. 1.** titular, formal.

nom′inal dam′ages, *Law.* damages of a small amount awarded to a plaintiff where substantial compensable loss has not been established but whose legal rights were violated. [1790–1800]

nom•i•nal•ism (nom′ə nl iz′əm), *n.* (in medieval phi-

CONCISE PRONUNCIATION KEY: *act, cāpe, dâre, pärt; set, ēqual; if, īce; ox, ōver, ôrder, oil, bo͝ok, bo͞ot, out; up, ûrge; child; sing; shoe; thin, that;* zh as in *treasure.* ə = *a* as in *alone, e* as in *system, i* as in *easily, o* as in *gallop, u* as in *circus;* ᵊ as in *fire* (fīᵊr), *hour* (ouᵊr). l and n can serve as syllabic consonants, as in *cradle* (krād′l), and *button* (but′n). See the full key inside the front cover.

losophy) the doctrine that general or abstract words do not stand for objectively existing entities and that universals are no more than names assigned to them. Cf. **conceptualism, realism** (def. 5a). [1830–40; < F *nominalisme.* See NOMINAL, -ISM] —**nom′i·nal·ist,** *n.* —**nom′i·nal·is′tic,** *adj.* —**nom′i·nal·is′ti·cal·ly,** *adv.*

nom·i·nal·ize (nom′ə nl īz′), *v.t.,* **-ized, -iz·ing. 1.** to convert (another part of speech) into a noun, as in changing the adjective *lowly* into *the lowly* or the verb *legalize* into *legalization.* **2.** to convert (an underlying clause) into a noun phrase, as in changing *he drinks* to *his drinking* in *I am worried about his drinking.* Also, *esp. Brit.,* **nom′i·nal·ise′.** [1650–60; NOMINAL + -IZE] —**nom′i·nal·i·za′tion,** *adj.*

nom·i·nal·ly (nom′ə nl ē), *adv.* by or as regards name; in name; ostensibly: *He was nominally the leader, but others actually ran the organization.* [1655–65; NOMINAL + -LY]

nom′inal par′, *Finance.* See under **par** (def. 4b).

nom′inal sen′tence, *Gram.* a sentence consisting of a subject and complement without a linking verb, as *Very interesting, those books.* [1920–25]

nom′inal val′ue, book or par value, as of securities; face value. [1900–05]

nom′inal wag′es, *Econ.* wages measured in terms of money and not by their ability to command goods and services. Cf. **real wages.** [1895–1900]

nom·i·nate (*v.* nom′ə nāt′; *adj.* nom′ə nit), *v.,* **-nat·ed, -nat·ing,** *adj.* —*v.t.* **1.** to propose (someone) for appointment or election to an office. **2.** to appoint to a duty or office. **3.** to propose for an honor, award, or the like. **4.** *Horse Racing.* to register (a horse) as an entry in a race. **5.** to name; designate. **6.** *Obs.* to specify. —*adj.* **7.** having a particular name. [1475–85; < L *nōminātus* (ptp. of *nōmināre* to name, call by name), equiv. to *nōmin-* (s. of *nōmen;* see NOMEN) + *-ātus* -ATE[1]] —**nom′i·na′tor,** *n.*
—**Syn. 1.** pick, choose.

CONCISE ETYMOLOGY KEY: <, descended or borrowed from; >, whence; b., blend of, blended; c., cognate with; cf., compare; deriv., derivative; equiv., equivalent; imit., imitative; obl., oblique; r., replacing; s., stem; sp., spelling, spelled; resp., respelling, respelled; trans., translation; ?, origin unknown; *, unattested; ‡, probably earlier than. See the full key inside the front cover.

nom·i·na·tion (nom′ə nā′shən), *n.* **1.** an act or instance of nominating, esp. to office: *The floor is open for nomination of candidates for the presidency.* **2.** the state of being nominated. [1375–1425; late ME < L *nōminātiōn-* (s. of *nōminātiō*) a naming, nomination. See NOMINATE, -ION]

nom·i·na·tive (nom′ə nə tiv, nom′nə- *or, for 2, 3,* nom′ə nā′tiv), *adj.* **1.** *Gram.* **a.** (in certain inflected languages, as Sanskrit, Latin, and Russian) noting a case having as its function the indication of the subject of a finite verb, as in Latin *Nauta bonus est* "The sailor is good," with *nauta* "sailor" in the nominative case. **b.** similar to such a case in function or meaning. **2.** nominated; appointed by nomination. **3.** made out in a person's name, as a certificate or security. —*n. Gram.* **4.** the nominative case. **5.** a word in the nominative case. **6.** a form or construction of similar function or meaning. [1350–1400; < L *nōminātīvus* (see NOMINATE, -IVE), r. ME *nominatif* < MF < L as above] —**nom′i·na·tive·ly,** *adv.*

nom′inative ab′solute, *Gram.* a construction consisting in English of a noun, noun phrase, or pronoun in the nominative case followed by a predicate lacking a finite verb, used as a loose modifier of the whole sentence, as *the play done* in *The play done, the audience left the theater.* [1835–45; by analogy with ABLATIVE ABSOLUTE]

nom′inative of address′, *Gram.* a noun naming the person to whom one is speaking.

nom·i·nee (nom′ə nē′), *n.* **1.** a person nominated, as to run for elective office or fill a particular post. **2.** a person in whose name title to real estate or ownership of stock is held but who is not the actual proprietor or holder. [1655–65; NOMIN(ATE) + -EE]

no·mism (nō′miz əm), *n.* religious conduct based on law. [1900–05; NOM(O)- + -ISM] —**no·mis′tic,** *adj.*

nomo-, a combining form meaning "custom," "law," used in the formation of compound words: *nomology.* [< Gk *nomo-,* comb. form of *nómos* law, custom; akin to *némein* to manage, control]

no·mo·can·on (nō′mə kan′ən), *n.* a compendium of Greek Orthodox ecclesiastical laws and Byzantine imperial laws that related to ecclesiastical matters. [1720–30; < MGk *nomokanón.* See NOMO-, CANON]

nom·o·gram (nom′ə gram′, nō′mə-), *n.* **1.** a graph, usually containing three parallel scales graduated for different variables so that when a straight line connects values of any two, the related value may be read directly from the third at the point intersected by the line. **2.** any similar graph used to show the relation between quantities, values, numbers, and so on. Also called **nom·o·graph** (nom′ə graf′, -gräf′, nō′mə-), **alignment chart.** [1905–10; NOMO- + -GRAM[1]]

no·mog·ra·phy (nō mog′rə fē), *n., pl.* **-phies** for 1. **1.** the art of or a treatise on drawing up laws. **2.** the art of making and using a nomogram for solving a succession of nearly identical problems. [1725–35; < Gk *nomographía* the writing of laws. See NOMO-, -GRAPHY] —**no·mog′ra·pher,** *n.* —**nom·o·graph·ic** (nom′ə graf′ik, nō′mə-), **nom′o·graph′i·cal,** *adj.* —**nom′o·graph′i·cal·ly,** *adv.*

no·mol·o·gy (nō mol′ə jē), *n.* **1.** the science of law or laws. **2.** the science of the laws of the mind. [1835–45; NOMO- + -LOGY] —**nom·o·log·i·cal** (nom′ə loj′i kəl, nō′mə-), *adj.* —**no·mol′o·gist,** *n.*

nom·o·thet·ic (nom′ə thet′ik), *adj.* **1.** giving or establishing laws; legislative. **2.** founded upon or derived from law. **3.** *Psychol.* pertaining to or involving the study or formulation of general or universal laws (opposed to *idiographic*). [1650–60; < Gk *nomothetikós.* See NOMO-, THETIC]

No·mu·ra (nô′mo͞o rä′), *n.* **Ki·chi·sa·bu·ro** (kē′chē-sä′bo͞o rô′), 1877–1964, Japanese diplomat.

-nomy, a combining form of Greek origin meaning "distribution," "arrangement," "management,": *astronomy; economy; taxonomy.* [< Gk *-nomia* law. See NOMO-, -Y[3]]

non-, a prefix meaning "not," freely used as an English formative, usually with a simple negative force as implying mere negation or absence of something (rather than the opposite or reverse of it, as often expressed by **un-**[1]): *nonadherence; noninterference; nonpayment; nonprofessional.* [prefix repr. L adv. *nōn* not]
—**Note.** The lists at the bottom of this and following

non′a·ban′don·ment, *n.*
non′ab·di·ca′tion, *n.*
non·ab′di·ca′tive, *adj.*
non′a·bid′ing, *adj.;* **-ly,** *adv.;* **-ness,** *n.*
non′ab·ju·ra′tion, *n.*
non′ab·jur′a·to′ry, *adj.*
non′ab·o·li′tion, *n.*
non′a·bort′ive, *adj.;* **-ly,** *adv.;* **-ness,** *n.*
non′a·bridg′a·ble, *adj.*
non′a·bridg′ment, *n.*
non·ab′ro·ga·ble, *adj.*
non′ab·sen·ta′tion, *n.*
non·ab′so·lute′, *adj., n.;* **-ly,** *adv.;* **-ness,** *n.*
non′ab·so·lu′tion, *n.*
non·ab′so·lut′ist, *n.*
non′ab·so·lu·tis′tic, *adj.*
non′ab·so·lu·tis′ti·cal·ly, *adv.*
non′ab·sorb′a·bil′i·ty, *n.*
non′ab·sorb′a·ble, *adj.*
non′ab·sorb′en·cy, *n.*
non′ab·sorb′ent, *adj., n.*
non′ab·sorb′ing, *adj.*
non′ab·sorp′tion, *n.*
non′ab·sorp′tive, *adj.*
non′ab·stain′er, *n.*
non′ab·stain′ing, *adj.*
non′ab·ste′mi·ous, *adj.;* **-ly,** *adv.;* **-ness,** *n.*
non′ab·sten′tion, *n.*
non·ab′stract, *adj., n.;* **-ly,** *adv.;* **-ness,** *n.*
non′ab·stract′ed, *adj.;* **-ly,** *adv.;* **-ness,** *n.*
non′a·bu′sive, *adj.;* **-ly,** *adv.;* **-ness,** *n.*
non′ac·a·dem′ic, *adj., n.*
non′ac·a·dem′i·cal, *adj.;* **-ly,** *adv.;* **-ness,** *n.*
non′a·cad′e·mi′cian, *n.*
non′ac·ced′ence, *n.*
non′ac·ced′ing, *adj.*
non′ac·cel′er·a′tion, *n.*
non′ac·cel′er·a′tive, *adj.*
non′ac·cel′er·a·to′ry, *adj.*
non·ac′cent, *n.*
non·ac′cent·ed, *adj.*
non·ac′cent·ing, *adj.*
non′ac·cen′tu·al, *adj.;* **-ly,** *adv.*
non′ac·cept′ance, *n.*
non′ac·cept′ant, *adj.*
non′ac·cep·ta′tion, *n.*
non′ac·ces′si·ble, *adj.*
non′ac·ces′sion, *n.*
non′ac·ces′so·ry, *adj., n., pl.* **-ries.**
non′ac·ci·den′tal, *adj., n.;* **-ly,** *adv.;* **-ness,** *n.*
non′ac·com′mo·da·ble, *adj.;* **-bly,** *adv.*
non′ac·com′mo·dat′ing, *adj.;* **-ly,** *adv.;* **-ness,** *n.*
non′ac·com′mo·da′tion, *n.*
non′ac·com′pa·ni·ment, *n.*
non′ac·com′pa·ny·ing, *adj.*
non′ac·cord′, *n.*
non′ac·cord′ant, *adj.;* **-ly,** *adv.*
non′ac·count′a·bil′i·ty, *n.*
non′ac·count′a·ble, *adj.*
non′ac·cred′it·ed, *adj.*
non′ac·cre′tion, *n.*
non′ac·cre′tive, *adj*
non′ac·cru′al, *adj.*
non′ac·crued′, *adj.*
non′ac·cru′ing, *adj.*
non′ac·cul′tu·rat′ed, *adj.*
non′ac·cu′mu·lat′ing, *adj.*
non′ac·cu′mu·la′tion, *n.*
non′ac·cu′mu·la·tive, *adj.;* **-ly,** *adv.;* **-ness,** *n.*
non′ac·cus′ing, *adj.*
non·ac′id, *n., adj.*
non′a·cid′ic, *adj.*
non′a·cid′i·ty, *n.*
non′a·cous′tic, *adj., n.*
non′a·cous′ti·cal, *adj.;* **-ly,** *adv.*
non′ac·quaint′ance, *n.*
non′ac·quaint′ance·ship′, *n.*
non′ac·qui·es′cence, *n.*
non′ac·qui·es′cent, *adj.;* **-ly,** *adv.*
non′ac·qui·esc′ing, *adj.*
non′ac·quis′i·tive, *adj.;* **-ly,** *adv.;* **-ness,** *n.*
non′ac·quit′tal, *n.*
non′ac·tin′ic, *adj.*
non′ac·tin′i·cal·ly, *adv.*
non·ac′tion, *n.*
non·ac′tion·a·ble, *adj.;* **-bly,** *adv.*
non′ac·ti·va′tion, *n.*
non·ac′ti·va′tor, *n.*
non·ac′tive, *adj., n.*
non·ac′tiv·ist, *adj., n.*
non′ac·tiv′i·ty, *n., pl.* **-ties.**
non·ac′tor, *n.*
non·ac′tu·al, *adj.;* **-ness,** *n.*
non′ac·tu·al′i·ty, *n., pl.* **-ties.**
non′a·cu′i·ty, *n.*
non′a·cu′le·ate, *adj.*
non′a·cu′le·at′ed, *adj.*
non′a·cute′, *adj.;* **-ly,** *adv.;* **-ness,** *n.*
non′a·dapt′a·bil′i·ty, *n.*
non′a·dapt′a·ble, *adj.;* **-ness,** *n.*
non′a·dapt′er, *n.*
non′a·dapt′ing, *adj.*
non′ad·ap·ta′tion, *n.*
non′ad·ap·ta′tion·al, *adj.*
non′a·dap′tive, *adj.*
non′a·dap′tor, *n.*
non·ad′dict, *n.*
non′ad·dict′ed, *adj.*
non′ad·dict′ing, *adj.*
non′ad·dic′tive, *adj.*
non′a·dept′, *adj.;* **-ly,** *adv.;* **-ness,** *n.*
non′ad·her′ence, *n.*
non′ad·her′ent, *adj., n.*
non′ad·her′ing, *adj.*
non′ad·he′sion, *n.*
non′ad·he′sive, *adj.;* **-ly,** *adv.;* **-ness,** *n.*
non′ad·ja′cen·cy, *n., pl.* **-cies.**
non′ad·ja′cent, *adj.;* **-ly,** *adv.*
non′ad·jec·ti′val, *adj.;* **-ly,** *adv.*
non·ad′jec·tive·ly, *adv.*
non′ad·join′ing, *adj.*
non′ad·journ′ment, *n.*
non′ad·ju′di·cat′ed, *adj.*
non′ad·ju′di·ca′tion, *n.*
non′ad·ju′di·ca′tive, *adj.;* **-ly,** *adv.*
non′ad·junc′tive, *adj.;* **-ly,** *adv.*
non′ad·just′a·bil′i·ty, *n.*
non′ad·just′a·ble, *adj.;* **-bly,** *adv.*
non′ad·just′er, *n.*
non′ad·just′ment, *n.*
non′ad·jus′tor, *n.*
non′ad·min′is·tra·ble, *adj.*
non′ad·min′is·trant, *adj.*
non′ad·min′is·tra′tive, *adj.;* **-ly,** *adv.*
non′ad·mis′si·bil′i·ty, *n.*
non′ad·mis′si·ble, *adj.;* **-ble·ness,** *n.;* **-bly,** *adv.*
non′ad·mis′sion, *n.*
non′ad·mis′sive, *adj.*
non′ad·mit′ted, *adj., n.;* **-ly,** *adv.*
non′a·dopt′a·ble, *adj.*
non′a·dopt′er, *n.*
non′a·dop′tion, *n.*
non′a·dorn′er, *n.*
non′a·dorn′ing, *adj.*
non′a·dorn′ment, *n.*
non′a·dult′, *adj., n.*
non′ad·vance′ment, *n.*
non′ad·van·ta′geous, *adj.;* **-ly,** *adv.;* **-ness,** *n.*
non′ad·ven·ti′tious, *adj.;* **-ly,** *adv.;* **-ness,** *n.*
non′ad·ven′tur·ous, *adj.;* **-ly,** *adv.;* **-ness,** *n.*
non′ad·ver′bi·al, *adj.;* **-ly,** *adv.*
non′ad·ver·sar′i·al, *adj.*
non′ad·vert′ence, *n.*
non′ad·vert′en·cy, *n.*
non·ad′vo·ca·cy, *n.*
non·ad′vo·cate, *n.*
non·aer′at·ed, *adj.*
non·aer′at·ing, *adj.*
non′aer·o′bic, *adj.*
non′aes·thet′ic, *adj.*
non′aes·thet′i·cal, *adj.;* **-ly,** *adv.*
non′af·fec·ta′tion, *n.*
non′af·fect′ing, *adj.;* **-ly,** *adv.*
non′af·fec′tive, *adj.*
non′af·fil′i·ate, *n.*
non′af·fil′i·at′ed, *adj.*
non′af·fil′i·at′ing, *adj.*
non′af·fil′i·a′tion, *n.*
non′af·fin′i·tive, *adj.*
non′af·fin′i·ty, *n., pl.* **-ties,** *adj.*
non′af·firm′ance, *n.*
non′af·fir·ma′tion, *n.*
non·af′flu·ent, *adj.*
non-Af′ri·can, *adj., n.*
non′ag·glom′er·a′tive, *adj.*
non′ag·glu′ti·nant, *adj., n.*
non′ag·glu′ti·nat′ing, *adj.*
non′ag·glu′ti·na′tive, *adj.*
non′a·grar′i·an, *adj., n.*
non′a·gree′ment, *n.*
non′-Al·ex·an′dri·an, *adj.*
non′al·ge·bra′ic, *adj.*
non′al·ge·bra′i·cal, *adj.;* **-ly,** *adv.*
non·al′ien, *n., adj.*
non·al′ien·at′ing, *adj.*
non·al′ien·a′tion, *n.*
non′a·lign′a·ble, *adj.*
non′a·lined′, *adj.*
non′a·line′ment, *n.*
non·al′ka·loid′, *n., adj.*
non′al·ka·loi′dal, *adj.*
non′al·le·ga′tion, *n.*
non′al·le′giance, *n.*
non′al·le·gor′ic, *adj.*
non′al·le·gor′i·cal, *adj.;* **-ly,** *adv.*
non′al·lel′ic, *adj.*
non′al·li′ance, *n.*
non′al·lied′, *adj.*
non′al·lit′er·at′ed, *adj.*
non′al·lit′er·a′tive, *adj.;* **-ly,** *adv.;* **-ness,** *n.*
non′al·lot′ment, *n.*
non′al·lu′vi·al, *adj., n.*
non′al·pha·bet′ic, *adj.*
non′al·pha·bet′i·cal, *adj.;* **-ly,** *adv.*
non·al′ter·nat′ing, *adj.*
non′al·tru·is′tic, *adj.*
non′al·tru·is′ti·cal·ly, *adv.*
non′am·bi·gu′i·ty, *n., pl.* **-ties.**
non′am·bi′tious, *adj.;* **-ly,** *adv.;* **-ness,** *n.*
non·am′bu·la·to′ry, *adj., n., pl.* **-ties.**
non′a·me′na·bil′i·ty, *n.*
non′a·me′na·ble, *adj.;* **-ble·ness,** *n.;* **-bly,** *adv.*
non′a·mend′a·ble, *adj.*
non′a·mend′ment, *n.*
non′-A·mer′i·can, *adj., n.*
non·am′o·rous, *adj.;* **-ly,** *adv.;* **-ness,** *n.*
non·am′or·tiz′a·ble, *adj.*
non′am·phib′i·an, *adj.*
non′am·phib′i·ous, *adj.;* **-ly,** *adv.;* **-ness,** *n.*
non′am·pu·ta′tion, *n.*
non′a·nach′ro·nis′tic, *adj.*
non′a·nach′ro·nis′ti·cal·ly, *adv.*
non′a·nach′ro·nous, *adj.;* **-ly,** *adv.*
non′a·nae′mic, *adj.*
non′an·a·log′ic, *adj.*
non′an·a·log′i·cal, *adj.;* **-ly,** *adv.;* **-ness,** *n.*
non′a·nal′o·gous, *adj.;* **-ly,** *adv.;* **-ness,** *n.*
non′an·a·lyt′ic, *adj.*
non′an·a·lyt′i·cal, *adj.;* **-ly,** *adv.*
non·an′a·lyz′a·ble, *adj.*
non·an′a·lyzed′, *adj.*
non′an·ar′chic, *adj.*
non′an·ar′chi·cal, *adj.;* **-ly,** *adv.*
non′an·ar·chis′tic, *adj.*
non′an·a·tom′ic, *adj.*
non′an·a·tom′i·cal, *adj.;* **-ly,** *adv.*
non′an·ces′tral, *adj.;* **-ly,** *adv.*
non′a·ne′mic, *adj.*
non′an·es·thet′ic, *adj., n.*
non′an·es′the·tized′, *adj.*
non′an·gel′ic, *adj.*
non-An′gli·can, *adj., n.*
non·an′gling, *adj.*
non·an′guished, *adj.*
non·an′i·mal, *n., adj.*
non′an·i·mal′i·ty, *n.*
non·an′i·mate, *adj.*
non·an′i·mat′ed, *adj.*
non·an′i·mat′ing, *adj.;* **-ly,** *adv.*
non′an·i·ma′tion, *n.*
non′an·nex′a·ble, *adj.*
non′an·nex·a′tion, *n.*
non′an·ni′hi·la·bil′i·ty, *n.*
non′an·ni′hi·la·ble, *adj.*
non′an·nul′ment, *n.*
non′an·o·nym′i·ty, *n.*
non′a·non′y·mous·ness, *n.*
non′an·tag′o·nis′tic, *adj.*
non′an·tag′o·nis′ti·cal·ly, *adv.*
non′an·te′ri·or, *adj.*
non′an·tic′i·pa′tion, *n.*
non′an·tic′i·pa′tive, *adj.;* **-ly,** *adv.*
non′an·tic′i·pa·to′ri·ly, *adv.*
non′an·tic′i·pa·to′ry, *adj.*
non′a·pha′si·ac′, *n.*
non′a·pha′sic, *adj., n.*
non′a·phet′ic, *adj.*
non′aph·o·ris′tic, *adj.*
non′aph·o·ris′ti·cal·ly, *adv.*
non′a·pol′o·get′ic, *adj.*
non′a·pol′o·get′i·cal, *adj.;* **-ly,** *adv.*
non′ap·os·tol′ic, *adj.*
non′ap·os·tol′i·cal, *adj.;* **-ly,** *adv.*
non′ap·par′ent, *adj.;* **-ly,** *adv.;* **-ness,** *n.*
non′ap·pa·ri′tion·al, *adj.*
non′ap·peal′a·bil′i·ty, *n.*
non′ap·peal′a·ble, *adj.*
non′ap·peal′ing, *adj.;* **-ly,** *adv.;* **-ness,** *n.*
non′ap·peas′a·bil′i·ty, *n.*
non′ap·peas′a·ble, *adj.*
non′ap·peas′ing, *adj.*
non′ap·pel′late, *adj.*
non′ap·pend′ance, *n.*
non′ap·pend′ant, *adj.*
non′ap·pend′ence, *n.*
non′ap·pend′ent, *adj.*
non′ap·pen′dic′u·lar, *adj.*
non′ap·pli·ca·bil′i·ty, *n.*
non·ap′pli·ca·ble, *adj.;* **-ness,** *n.*
non′ap·pli·ca′tion, *n.*
non·ap′pli·ca′tive, *adj.*
non·ap′pli·ca·to′ry, *adj.*
non′ap·poin′tive, *adj.*
non′ap·por′tion·a·ble, *adj.*
non′ap·por′tion·ment, *n.*
non′ap·pos′a·ble, *adj.*
non′ap·pre′ci·a′tion, *n.*
non′ap·pre′cia·tive, *adj.;* **-ly,** *adv.;* **-ness,** *n.*
non′ap·pre·hen′si·bil′i·ty, *n.*
non′ap·pre·hen′si·ble, *adj.*
non′ap·pre·hen′sion, *n.*
non′ap·pre·hen′sive, *adj.*

pages provide the spelling, syllabification, and stress for words whose meanings may be easily inferred by combining the meaning of NON- and an attached base word, or base word plus a suffix. Appropriate parts of speech are also shown. Words prefixed by NON- that have special meanings or uses are entered in their proper alphabetical places in the main vocabulary or as derived forms run on at the end of a main vocabulary entry.

no·na (nō′nə), *n. Pathol.* See **sleeping sickness** (def. 2). [< L *nōna* (*hōra*) ninth (hour); i.e., late stage in life of patient]

non·a·bra·sive (non′ə brā′siv, -ziv), *adj.* **1.** not causing abrasion. **2.** preventing abrasion. [NON- + ABRASIVE] **—non′a·bra′sive·ly,** *adv.* **—non′a·bra′sive·ness,** *n.*

non·a·chiev·er (non′ə chē′vər), *n.* **1.** a student who fares poorly in the classroom or has failing grades. **2.** any person who does not succeed or progress, esp. because of lack of interest or motivation. [1970–75; NON- + ACHIEVER]

non·age (non′ij, nō′nij), *n.* **1.** the period of legal minority, or of an age below 21. **2.** any period of immaturity. [1350–1400; late ME < MF (see NON-, AGE); r. ME *nounage* < AF *nounage*; MF as above]

non·a·ge·nar·i·an (non′ə jə nâr′ē ən, nō′nə-), *adj.* **1.** of the age of 90 years, or between 90 and 100 years old. *—n.* **2.** a nonagenarian person. [1795–1805; < L *nōnāgēnāri(us)* containing ninety, consisting of ninety (*nōnāgēn(ī)* ninety each + *-ārius* -ARY) + -AN]

non·ag·gres·sion (non′ə gresh′ən) *n.* **1.** abstention from aggression, esp. by a nation. *—adj.* **2.** of or pertaining to abstention from aggression: *a nonaggression pact.* [1900–05; NON- + AGGRESSION] **—non′ag·gres′sive,** *adj.* **—non′ag·gres′sive·ly,** *adv.* **—non′ag·gres′sive·ness,** *n.*

non·a·gon (non′ə gon′), *n.* a polygon having nine angles and nine sides. Also called **enneagon.** [1680–90; < L *nōn(us)* ninth + *-a-* (extracted from PENTAGON, HEXAGON, etc.) + -GON] **—non·ag·o·nal** (non ag′ə nl), *adj.*

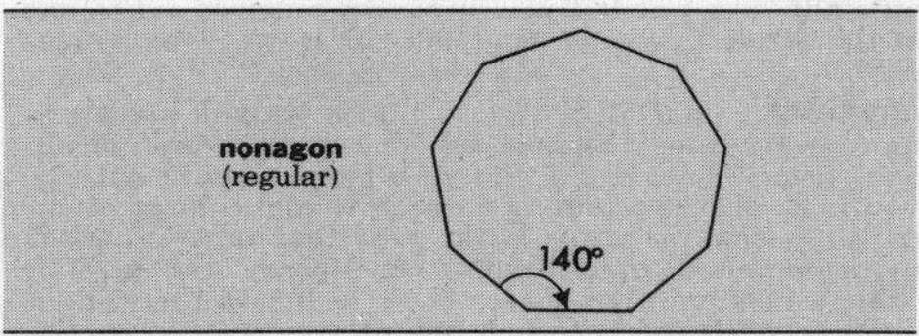

non·ag·ri·cul·tur·al (non′ag ri kul′chər əl), *adj.* not applied to or generally practicing agriculture: *a nonagricultural nation.* [1840–50; NON- + AGRICULTURAL]

non·al·co·hol·ic (non′al kə hô′lik, -hol′ik), *adj.* **1.** not being or containing alcohol: *nonalcoholic beverages.* *—n.* **2.** a person who is not an alcoholic. [1905–10; NON- + ALCOHOLIC]

non·a·ligned (non′ə līnd′), *adj.* **1.** not aligned: *nonaligned machine parts.* **2.** not allied with or favoring any other nation or bloc: *nonaligned African nations.* *—n.* **3.** a nonaligned person or nation. [1955–60; NON- + ALIGNED]

non·a·lign·ment (non′ə līn′mənt), *n.* **1.** the state or condition of being nonaligned. **2.** a national policy repudiating political or military alliance with a world power, as the U.S. or the People's Republic of China. [1930–35; NON- + ALIGNMENT]

non·al·ler·gen·ic (non′al ər jen′ik), *adj.* not causing an allergic reaction: *nonallergenic cosmetics.* [NON- + ALLERGENIC]

non·al·ler·gic (non′ə lûr′jik), *adj. Pathol.* not having an allergy; not sensitive to a particular antigen. [1935–40; NON- + ALLERGIC]

no-name (nō′nām′), *adj.* packaged and sold without a brand name and usually at a lower price than similar items with brand names; generic: *a can of no-name dog food.* [1985–90]

non′a·no′ic ac′id (non′ə nō′ik, non′-), *Chem.* See **pelargonic acid.** [1945–50; *nonane* (< L *nōn(us)* ninth + -ANE) + -o- + -IC]

non-A, non-B hepatitis (non′ā′ non′bē′), *Pathol.* See **hepatitis non-A, non-B.**

non·ap·pear·ance (non′ə pēr′əns), *n.* failure to appear, as in a court. [1425–75; late ME; see NON-, APPEARANCE]

non-art (non ärt′), *n.* antiart. [1935–40]

CONCISE PRONUNCIATION KEY: *act, cāpe, dâre, pärt; set, ēqual; if, īce; ox, ōver, ôrder, oil, bo͝ok, bo͞ot, out; up, ûrge; child; sing; shoe; thin,* t͟hat; zh as in *treasure.* ə = *a* as in *alone, e* as in *system, i* as in *easily, o* as in *gallop, u* as in *circus;* ᵊ as in *fire* (fīᵊr), *hour* (ouᵊr). l and n can serve as syllabic consonants, as in *cradle* (krād′l), and *button* (but′n). See the full key inside the front cover.

non′ap·proach′a·ble, *adj.*; **-ness,** *n.*
non′ap·proach′a·bil′i·ty, *n.*
non′ap·pro′pri·a·ble, *adj.*
non′ap·pro′pri·a·tive, *adj.*
non′ap·prov′al, *n.*
non′ap·proved′, *adj.*
non′a·quat′ic, *adj.*
non·a′que·ous, *adj.*
non-Ar′ab, *n., adj.*
non-Ar′a·bic, *adj.*
non·ar′bi·tra·ble, *adj.*
non·ar′bi·trar′i·ly, *adv.*
non·ar′bi·trar′i·ness, *n.*
non·ar′bi·trar′y, *adj.*
non′ar·chi·tec·ton′ic, *adj.*
non′ar·chi·tec′tur·al, *adj.*; **-ly,** *adv.*
non′ar·gen·tif′er·ous, *adj.*
non·ar′gu·a·ble, *adj.*
non·ar′gu·men′ta·tive, *adj.*; **-ly,** *adv.*; **-ness,** *n.*
non′a·ris′to·crat′ic, *adj.*
non′a·ris′to·crat′i·cal, *adj.*; **-ly,** *adv.*
non′ar·ith·met′ic, *adj.*
non′ar·ith·met′i·cal, *adj.*; **-ly,** *adv.*
non·ar′ma·ment, *n.*
non′ar·mig′er·ous, *adj.*
non′ar·o·mat′ic, *adj.*
non′ar·o·mat′i·cal·ly, *adv.*
non′a·rous′al, *n.*
non′ar·raign′ment, *n.*
non′ar·rest′ing, *adj.*
non′ar·riv′al, *n.*
non·ar′ro·gance, *n.*
non·ar′ro·gan·cy, *n.*
non′ar·sen′ic, *adj.*
non′ar·sen′i·cal, *adj.*
non′ar·te′ri·al, *adj.*
non′ar·tic′u·late, *adj.*; **-ly,** *adv.*; **-ness,** *n.*
non′ar·tic′u·la′tive, *adj.*
non′ar·tis′tic, *adj.*
non′ar·tis′ti·cal, *adj.*; **-ly,** *adv.*
non-Ar′y·an, *n., adj.*
non′as·bes′tine, *adj.*
non′as·cend′ance, *n.*
non′as·cend′an·cy, *n.*
non′as·cend′ant, *adj.*; **-ly,** *adv.*
non′as·cend′ence, *n.*
non′as·cend′en·cy, *n.*
non′as·cend′ent, *adj.*; **-ly,** *adv.*
non′as·cer·tain′a·ble, *adj.*; **-ble·ness,** *n.*; **-bly,** *adv.*
non′as·cer·tain′ment, *n.*
non′as·cet′ic, *n., adj.*
non′as·cet′i·cal, *adj.*; **-ly,** *adv.*
non′as·cet′i·cism, *n.*
non′a·sep′tic, *adj.*
non′a·sep′ti·cal·ly, *adv.*
non-A′sian, *adj., n.*
non′-A·si·at′ic, *adj., n.*
non′as·per′sion, *n.*
non·as′pi·rate, *n., adj.*
non·as′pi·rat′ed, *adj.*
non·as′pi·rat′ing, *adj.*
non′as·pi′ra·to′ry, *adj.*
non′as·pir′ing, *adj.*
non′as·sault′, *n.*
non′as·sent′ing, *adj.*
non′as·ser′tion, *n.*
non′as·ser′tive, *adj.*; **-ly,** *adv.*; **-ness,** *n.*
non′as·sign′a·bil′i·ty, *n.*
non′as·sign′a·ble, *adj.*; **-bly,** *adv.*
non′as·signed′, *adj.*
non′as·sign′ment, *n.*
non′as·sim′i·la·bil′i·ty, *n.*
non′as·sim′i·la·ble, *adj.*
non′as·sim′i·lat′ing, *adj.*
non′as·sim′i·la′tion, *n.*
non′as·sim′i·la′tive, *adj.*
non′as·sim′i·la·to′ry, *adj.*
non′as·sis′tant, *n.*
non′as·sist′er, *n.*
non′as·so′ci·a·bil′i·ty, *n.*
non′as·so′ci·a·ble, *adj.*
non′as·so′ci·at′ed, *adj.*
non′as·so′ci·a′tion, *n.*
non′as·so′ci·a′tion·al, *adj.*
non′as·so′ci·a′tive, *adj.*; **-ly,** *adv.*
non·as′so·nance, *n.*
non·as′so·nant, *adj., n.*
non′as·sumed′, *adj.*
non′as·sump′tion, *n.*
non′as·sump′tive, *adj.*
non′asth·mat′ic, *adj., n.*
non′asth·mat′i·cal·ly, *adv.*
non·as′tral, *adj.*
non′as·trin′gen·cy, *n.*
non′as·trin′gent, *adj.*; **-ly,** *adv.*
non′as·tro·nom′ic, *adj.*
non′as·tro·nom′i·cal, *adj.*; **-ly,** *adv.*
non′a·the·is′tic, *adj.*
non′a·the·is′ti·cal, *adj.*; **-ly,** *adv.*
non·ath′lete, *n.*
non′ath·let′ic, *adj.*
non′ath·let′i·cal·ly, *adv.*
non′at·mos·pher′ic, *adj.*
non′at·mos·pher′i·cal, *adj.*; **-ly,** *adv.*
non′a·tom′ic, *adj.*
non′a·tom′i·cal, *adj.*; **-ly,** *adv.*
non′a·troph′ic, *adj.*
non·at′ro·phied, *adj.*
non′at·tached′, *adj.*
non′at·tach′ment, *n.*
non′at·tack′ing, *adj.*
non′at·tain′a·bil′i·ty, *n.*
non′at·tain′a·ble, *adj.*
non′at·tain′ment, *n., adj.*
non′at·tes·ta′tion, *n.*
non-At′tic, *adj., n.*
non′at·trib′ut·a·ble, *adj.*
non′at·trib′u·tive, *adj.*; **-ly,** *adv.*; **-ness,** *n.*
non′au·di·bil′i·ty, *n.*
non·au′di·ble, *adj.*; **-ble·ness,** *n.*; **-bly,** *adv.*
non′aug·ment′a·tive, *adj., n.*
non′au·ric′u·lar, *adj.*
non′au·rif′er·ous, *adj.*
non′au·then′tic, *adj.*
non′au·then′ti·cal, *adj.*
non′au·then′ti·cat′ed, *adj.*
non′au·then′ti·ca′tion, *n.*
non′au·then·tic′i·ty, *n.*
non′au·thor′i·tar′i·an, *adj.*
non′au·thor′i·ta′tive, *adj.*; **-ly,** *adv.*; **-ness,** *n.*
non′au·to·bi′o·graph′i·cal, *adj.*; **-ly,** *adv.*
non·au′to·mat′ed, *adj.*
non′au·to·mat′ic, *adj.*
non′au·to·mat′i·cal·ly, *adv.*
non′au·to·mo′tive, *adj.*
non′au·ton′o·mous, *adj.*; **-ly,** *adv.*; **-ness,** *n.*
non′a·vail′a·bil′i·ty, *n.*
non′a·void′a·ble, *adj.*; **-ble·ness,** *n.*; **-bly,** *adv.*
non′a·void′ance, *n.*
non′ax·i·o·mat′ic, *adj.*
non′ax·i·o·mat′i·cal, *adj.*; **-ly,** *adv.*
non·bach′e·lor, *n.*
non′bac·te′ri·al, *adj.*; **-ly,** *adv.*
non·bail′a·ble, *adj.*
non·bal′lot·ing, *n.*
non·ban′ish·ment, *n.*
non·bank′a·ble, *adj.*
non-Ban′tu, *n., adj.*
non-Bap′tist, *n., adj.*
non′bar·bar′i·an, *adj., n.*
non′bar·bar′ic, *adj.*
non·bar′ba·rous, *adj.*; **-ly,** *adv.*; **-ness,** *n.*
non′bar·bit′u·rate, *n.*
non′ba·ro′ni·al, *adj.*
non·base′, *n., adj.*
non·ba′sic, *adj.*
non·bath′ing, *adj.*
non·beard′ed, *adj.*
non′be·a·tif′ic, *adj.*
non′be·a·tif′i·cal·ly, *adv.*
non·beau′ty, *n., pl.* **-ties.**
non·be′ing, *n., adj.*
non·bend′ing, *adj.*
non·ben′e·ficed, *adj.*
non′be·nef′i·cence, *n.*
non′be·nef′i·cent, *adj.*; **-ly,** *adv.*
non·ben′e·fi′cial, *adj.*; **-ly,** *adv.*; **-ness,** *n.*
non′be·nev′o·lence, *n.*
non′be·nev′o·lent, *adj.*; **-ly,** *adv.*
non·bi′ased, *adj.*
non-Bib′li·cal, *adj.*; **-ly,** *adv.*
non·bib′u·lous, *adj.*; **-ly,** *adv.*; **-ness,** *n.*
non·big′ot·ed, *adj.*; **-ly,** *adv.*
non′bi·la′bi·ate, *adj.*
non·bil′ious, *adj.*; **-ly,** *adv.*; **-ness,** *n.*
non·bill′a·ble, *adj.*
non·bind′ing, *adj.*; **-ly,** *adv.*; **-ness,** *n.*
non′bi·o·de·grad′a·ble, *adj.*
non′bi·o·graph′i·cal, *adj.*; **-ly,** *adv.*
non′bi·o·log′i·cal, *adj.*; **-ly,** *adv.*
non·bit′ing, *adj.*
non·bit′ter, *adj.*
non′bi·tu′mi·nous, *adj.*
non·black′, *adj., n.*
non·blam′a·ble, *adj.*; **-ble·ness,** *n.*; **-bly,** *adv.*
non·blame′ful, *adj.*; **-ly,** *adv.*; **-ness,** *n.*
non·blas′phe·mous, *adj.*; **-ly,** *adv.*; **-ness,** *n.*
non·blas′phe·my, *n., pl.* **-mies.**
non·bleach′, *n.*
non·bleed′ing, *adj., n.*
non·blend′ed, *adj.*
non·blend′ing, *adj., n.*
non·blind′ing, *adj.*; **-ly,** *adv.*
non′block·ad′ed, *adj.*
non·block′ing, *adj., n.*
non·bloom′ing, *adj., n.*
non·blun′der·ing, *adj., n.*; **-ly,** *adv.*
non·boast′er, *n.*
non·boast′ing, *adj., n.*; **-ly,** *adv.*
non·bod′i·ly, *adj.*
non·bod′ing, *adj.*; **-ly,** *adv.*
non·boil′ing, *adj.*
non-Bol′she·vik, *n.*
non-Bol′she·vism, *n.*
non-Bol′she·vist, *n.*
non′-Bol·she·vis′tic, *adj.*
non·book′ish, *adj.*; **-ly,** *adv.*; **-ness,** *n.*
non·bor′rowed, *adj.*
non·bor′row·er, *n.*
non·bor′row·ing, *adj.*
non′bo·tan′ic, *adj.*
non′bo·tan′i·cal, *adj.*; **-ly,** *adv.*
non′bour·geois′, *n., pl.* **-geois,** *adj.*
non′-Brah·man′ic, *adj.*
non′-Brah·man′i·cal, *adj.*
non′-Brah·min′ic, *adj.*
non′-Brah·min′i·cal, *adj.*
non·brand′, *adj.*
non·brand′ed, *adj.*
non·breach′, *n.*
non·breach′ing, *adj.*
non·break′a·ble, *adj.*
non·breed′er, *n.*
non·breed′ing, *adj., n.*
non·bris′tled, *adj.*
non-Brit′ish, *adj.*
non′bro·mid′ic, *adj.*
non·brood′ing, *adj., n.*
non·brows′er, *n.*
non·brows′ing, *adj., n.*
non·bru′tal, *adj.*; **-ly,** *adv.*
non-Bud′dhist, *n., adj.*
non′-Bud·dhis′tic, *adj.*
non·bud′ding, *adj., n.*
non·budg′et·ar′y, *adj.*
non′bul·ba′ceous, *adj.*
non·bul′bar, *adj.*
non′bul·bif′er·ous, *adj.*
non·bul′bous, *adj.*
non·buoy′an·cy, *n.*
non·buoy′ant, *adj.*; **-ly,** *adv.*
non·bur′den·some, *adj.*; **-ly,** *adv.*; **-ness,** *n.*
non′bu·reau·crat′ic, *adj.*
non′bu·reau·crat′i·cal·ly, *adv.*
non·burg′age, *n.*
non·burn′a·ble, *adj.*
non·burn′ing, *adj., n.*
non·burst′ing, *adj., n.*
non·bus′i·ly, *adv.*
non·busi′ness, *adj.*
non·bus′y, *adj.*
non·bus′y·ness, *n.*
non·but′tressed, *adj.*
non·buy′ing, *adj., n.*
non·ca′denced, *adj.*
non·ca′dent, *adj.*
non·caf·feine′, *n.*
non′caf·fein′ic, *adj.*
non·cak′ing, *adj., n.*
non′cal·car′e·ous, *adj.*
non·cal′ci·fied′, *adj.*
non·cal′cu·la·ble, *adj.*; **-bly,** *adv.*
non·cal′cu·lat′ing, *adj.*
non·cal′cu·la′tive, *adj.*
non′ca·lor′ic, *adj.*
non′ca·lum′ni·at′ing, *adj.*
non′ca·lum′ni·ous, *adj.*
non-Cal′vin·ist, *n., adj.*
non′-Cal·vin·is′tic, *adj.*
non′-Cal·vin·is′ti·cal, *adj.*
non·cam′pus, *adj.*
non·can′cer·ous, *adj.*
non′can·des′cence, *n.*
non′can·des′cent, *adj.*; **-ly,** *adv.*
non′can·ni·bal·is′tic, *adj.*
non′can·ni·bal·is′ti·cal·ly, *adv.*
non′cap·il·lar′i·ty, *n.*
non·cap′il·lar′y, *adj., n., pl.* **-lar·ies.**
non·cap′i·tal, *adj., n.*
non·cap′i·tal·ist, *n.*
non′cap·i·tal·is′tic. *adj.*
non′cap·i·tal·is′ti·cal·ly, *adv.*
non·cap′i·tal·ized′, *adj.*
non′ca·pit′u·la′tion, *n.*
non′ca·pri′cious, *adj.*; **-ly,** *adv.*; **-ness,** *n.*
non·cap′siz′a·ble, *adj.*
non·cap′tious, *adj.*; **-ly,** *adv.*; **-ness,** *n.*
non·cap′tive, *adj.*
non′car·bo·hy′drate, *n.*
non′car·bol′ic, *adj.*
non·car′bon, *n.*
non·car′bo·nate′, *n.*
non·car′bo·nat′ed, *adj.*
non′car·di·o·log′ic, *adj.*
non·car′ing, *adj.*
non′car·niv′o·rous, *adj.*; **-ly,** *adv.*; **-ness,** *n.*
non·car′ri·er, *n.*
non·car′tel·ized′, *adj.*
non·cas′ti·gat′ing, *adj.*
non′cas·ti·ga′tion, *n.*
non′cas·u·is′tic, *adj.*
non′cas·u·is′ti·cal, *adj.*; **-ly,** *adv.*
non′cat·a·clys′mal, *adj.*
non′cat·a·clys′mic, *adj.*
non·cat′a·log′, *adj.*
non′cat·a·lyt′ic, *adj.*
non′cat·a·lyt′i·cal·ly, *adv.*
non′ca·tar′rhal, *adj.*
non′cat·a·stroph′ic, *adj.*
non′cat·e·chis′tic, *adj.*
non′cat·e·chis′ti·cal, *adj.*
non′cat·e·gor′i·cal, *adj.*; **-ly,** *adv.*; **-ness,** *n.*
non′ca·thar′tic, *adj., n.*
non′ca·thar′ti·cal, *adj.*
non-Cath′o·lic, *adj., n.*
non′cath·o·lic′i·ty, *n.*
non′-Cau·ca′sian, *adj., n.*
non-Cau′ca·soid′, *adj., n.*
non·caus′a·ble, *adj.*
non·caus′al, *adj.*; **-ly,** *adv.*
non′cau·sal′i·ty, *n.*
non′cau·sa′tion, *n.*
non·caus′a·tive, *adj.*; **-ly,** *adv.*; **-ness,** *n.*
non·caus′tic, *adj.*
non·caus′ti·cal·ly, *adv.*
non′cel·e·bra′tion, *n.*
non′ce·leb′ri·ty, *n., pl.* **-ties.**
non′ce·les′tial, *adj.*; **-ly,** *adv.*
non·cel′i·bate, *adj.*
non·cel′lu·lous, *adj.*
non-Celt′ic, *adj.*
non·cen′sored, *adj.*
non′cen·so′ri·ous, *adj.*; **-ly,** *adv.*; **-ness,** *n.*
non·cen′sur·a·ble, *adj.*; **-ble·ness,** *n.*; **-bly,** *adv.*
non·cen′tral, *adj.*; **-ly,** *adv.*
non·ce′re·al, *adj., n.*
non·cer′e·bral, *adj.*
non′cer·e·mo′ni·al, *adj.*; **-ly,** *adv.*
non′cer·e·mo′ni·ous, *adj.*; **-ly,** *adv.*; **-ness,** *n.*
non·cer′tain·ty, *n., pl.* **-ties.**
non·cer′tif′i·cat′ed, *adj.*
non′cer·ti·fi·ca′tion, *n.*
non·cer′ti·fied′, *adj.*
non·cer′ti·tude′, *n.*
non·chaf′ing, *adj.*
non·chalk′y, *adj.*
non·chal′leng·er, *n.*
non·chal′leng·ing, *adj.*
non·cham′pi·on, *n.*
non·change′a·ble, *adj.*; **-ble·ness,** *n.*; **-bly,** *adv.*
non·chan′neled, *adj.*
non·chan′nel·ized′, *adj.*

no·na·ry (nō′nə rē), *adj., n., pl.* **-ries.** —*adj.* **1.** consisting of nine. **2.** of, pertaining to, or noting a numerical system based on the number 9. —*n.* **3.** a number in a nonary system. [1660–70; < L *nōnārius* of, belonging to the ninth (hour), equiv. to *nōn(us)* ninth + *-ārius* -ARY]

non·as·sess·a·ble (non′ə ses′ə bəl), *adj.* (of stock) exempting the investor from any expense or liability beyond the amount of his or her investment. [NON- + ASSESSABLE] —**non′as·ses′sa·bil′i·ty,** *n.*

non·at·tend·ance (non′ə ten′dəns), *n.* failure to attend: *Members of the society can be dropped for chronic nonattendance.* [1680–90; NON- + ATTENDANCE]

non·bank (*n.* non′bangk′; *adj.* non′bangk′), *n.* **1.** an institution that is not a bank but engages in certain banking practices, as lending money or holding deposits. —*adj.* **2.** of, pertaining to, or handled by a nonbank: *nonbank loans.* [1945–50; NON- + BANK[2]]

non·bear·ing (non′bâr′ing), *adj.* (of a wall or partition) supporting no load other than its own weight. Also, **non′-bear′ing.** [NON- + BEAR[1] + -ING[2]]

non·be·liev·er (non′bi lē′vər), *n.* a person who lacks belief or faith, as in God, a religion, an idea, or an undertaking. [NON- + BELIEVER] —**non′be·liev′ing,** *adj.*
—**Syn.** doubter, skeptic, questioner, cynic.

CONCISE ETYMOLOGY KEY: <, descended or borrowed from; >, whence; b., blend of, blended; c., cognate with; cf., compare; deriv., derivative; equiv., equivalent; imit., imitative; obl., oblique; r., replacing; s., stem; sp., spelling, spelled; resp., respelling, respelled; trans., translation; ?, origin unknown; *, unattested; ‡, probably earlier than. See the full key inside the front cover.

non·bel·lig·er·en·cy (non′bə lij′ər ən sē), *n.* **1.** the state or status of not participating in a war. **2.** the status or policy of a nation that does not participate openly in a war but supports the cause of one of the belligerents. [1935–40; NON- + BELLIGERENCY]

non·bel·lig·er·ent (non′bə lij′ər ənt), *adj.* **1.** of or pertaining to a country whose status or policy is one of nonbelligerency. —*n.* **2.** a nation that does not engage officially in a war but openly favors or gives aid to one of the active participants. [1905–10; NON- + BELLIGERENT]

non·book (non′bo͝ok′), *n.* **1.** a book without artistic or literary merit or substance, esp. one that has been developed primarily to exploit a fad or make a profit quickly. —*adj.* **2.** of or pertaining to such a book. **3.** of or indicating what is not a book: *pens and other nonbook items for sale in the bookstore.* **4.** *Library Science.* of or being a holding other than a book, as a cassette, film, or art print. [1955–60; NON- + BOOK]

non·call·a·ble (non kô′lə bəl), *adj.* **1.** not capable of being called. **2.** not subject to redemption prior to maturity, as securities. **3.** not subject to payment on demand, as money loaned. [NON- + CALLABLE]

non·can·cel·a·ble (non kan′sə lə bəl), *adj.* not subject to cancellation: *a noncancellable insurance policy.* Also, **non·can′cel·la·ble.** [NON- + CANCELABLE] —**non·can′cel·a·bil′i·ty,** *n.*

non·can·di·date (non kan′di dāt′, -dit), *n.* a person who has not yet announced his or her availability for election to a political office or who has declared himself or herself not a candidate. [1940–45; NON- + CANDIDATE] —**non·can′di·da·cy,** *n.*

non·ca·non·i·cal (non′kə non′i kəl), *adj.* **1.** not included within a canon or group of rules. **2.** not belonging to the canon of Scripture. [NON- + CANONICAL]

non·cash (non kash′), *adj.* of or constituting financial sources other than cash: *a noncash expense.* [NON- + CASH[1]]

non cau·sa pro cau·sa (non kô′zə prō kô′zə; *Lat.* nōn kou′sä prō kou′sä), *Logic.* the fallacy of giving as a reason for a conclusion a proposition not actually relevant to that conclusion. [< L *nōn causa prō causā* lit., no cause for cause]

nonce (nons), *n.* the present, or immediate, occasion or purpose (usually used in the phrase *for the nonce*). [1150–1200; ME *nones,* in phrase *for the nones,* by faulty division of *for then ones* for the once (ME *then* dat. sing. of THE[1]; *ones* ONCE)]

non·cel·lu·lar (non sel′yə lər), *adj.* not composed of or containing cells: *Cytoplasm is noncellular.* [NON- + CELLULAR]

non·cel·lu·lo·sic (non′sel yə lō′sik), *adj.* not derived from or containing cellulose: *Nylon is a noncellulosic fiber.* [1930–35; NON- + CELLULOSE + -IC]

nonce′ word′, a word coined and used only for a particular occasion. Cf. **neologism** (def. 1). [1880–85]

non·cha·lance (non′shə läns′, non′shə läns′, -ləns), *n.* the state or quality of being nonchalant; cool indifference or lack of concern; casualness. [1670–80; < F; see NONCHALANT, -ANCE]

non·cha·lant (non′shə länt′, non′shə länt′, -lənt), *adj.* coolly unconcerned, indifferent, or unexcited; casual: *His nonchalant manner infuriated me.* [1725–35; < F *nonchalant,* prp. of obs. *nonchaloir* to lack warmth (of

non′cha·ot′ic, *adj.*
non′cha·ot′i·cal·ly, *adv.*
non′char·ac·ter·is′tic, *adj.*
non′char·ac·ter·is′ti·cal·ly, *adv.*
non·char′ac·ter·ized′, *adj.*
non·charge′a·ble, *adj.*
non·char·is·mat′ic, *adj.*
non·char′i·ta·ble, *adj.;* **-ble·ness,** *n.;* **-bly,** *adv.*
non·chas′tise·ment, *n.*
non·chas′ti·ty, *n.*
non′-Chau·ce′ri·an, *adj., n.*
non·chem′i·cal, *adj., n.*
non·chem′ist, *n.*
non′chi·mer′ic, *adj.*
non′chi·mer′i·cal, *adj.;* **-ly,** *adv.*
non′-Chi·nese′, *n., pl.* **-nese,** *adj.*
non·chiv′al·ric, *adj.*
non·chiv′al·rous, *adj.;* **-ly,** *adv.;* **-ness,** *n.*
non·chol′er·ic, *adj.*
non-Chris′tian, *adj., n.*
non′chro·mat′ic, *adj.*
non′chro·mat′i·cal·ly, *adv.*
non′chro·mo·so′mal, *adj.*
non·chron′ic, *adj.*
non·chron′i·cal, *adj.;* **-ly,** *adv.*
non·church′, *adj.*
non·churched′, *adj.*
non·church′go′er, *n.*
non·church′go′ing, *adj.*
non·cil′i·ate, *adj.*
non·cil′i·at′ed, *adj.*
non·cir′cuit·ed, *adj.*
non′cir·cu′i·tous, *adj.;* **-ly,** *adv.;* **-ness,** *n.*
non·cir′cu·lar, *adj.;* **-ly,** *adv.*
non·cir′cu·lat′ing, *adj.*
non′cir·cu·la′tion, *n.*
non·cir′cu·la·to′ry, *adj.*
non·cir′cum·scribed′, *adj.*
non′cir·cum·scrip′tive, *adj.*
non·cir′cum·spect′, *adj.;* **-ly,** *adv.;* **-ness,** *n.*
non′cir·cum·stan′tial, *adj.;* **-ly,** *adv.*
non′cir·cum·val′lat·ed, *adj.*
non·cit′a·ble, *adj.*
non′ci·ta′tion, *n.*
non·cite′a·ble, *adj.*
non·cit′i·zen, *n.*
non′ci·vil′ian, *n.*
non·civ′i·liz′a·ble, *adj.*
non·civ′i·lized′, *adj.*
non·claim′a·ble, *adj.*
non·clam′or·ous, *adj.;* **-ly,** *adv.*
non·clar′i·fi′a·ble, *adj.*
non·clar′i·fi·ca′tion, *n.*
non·clar′i·fied′, *adj.*
non·clas′sic, *adj.*
non·clas′si·cal′i·ty, *n.*
non·clas′si·fi′a·ble, *adj.*
non·clas′si·fi·ca′tion, *n.*
non·clas′si·fied′, *adj.*
non·clas′tic, *adj.*
non·clear′ance, *n.*
non′cleis·to·gam′ic, *adj.*
non′cleis·tog′a·mous, *adj.*
non·cler′i·cal, *adj., n.;* **-ly,** *adv.*
non·cli′ent, *adj.*
non′cli·mac′tic, *adj.*
non′cli·mac′ti·cal, *adj.*
non·climb′a·ble, *adj.*
non·climb′ing, *adj.*
non·clin′i·cal, *adj.;* **-ly,** *adv.*
non·clois′tered, *adj.*
non·close′, *adj.*
non·close′ly, *adv.*
non·clo′sure, *n.*
non·clot′ting, *adj.*
non′co·ag′u·la·bil′i·ty, *n.*
non′co·ag′u·la·ble, *adj.*
non′co·ag′u·lat′ing, *adj.*
non′co·ag′u·la′tion, *n.*
non′co·ag′u·la′tive, *adj.*
non′co·a·les′cence, *n.*
non′co·a·les′cent, *adj.*
non′co·a·les′cing, *adj.*
non·cod′i·fied′, *adj.*
non′co·er′ci·ble, *adj.*
non′co·er′cion, *n.*
non′co·er′cive, *adj.;* **-ly,** *adv.;* **-ness,** *n.*
non·co′gen·cy, *n.*
non·co′gent, *adj.;* **-ly,** *adv.*
non·cog′nate, *adj., n.*
non′cog·ni′tion, *n.*
non·cog′ni·tive, *adj.*
non·cog′ni·za·ble, *adj.;* **-bly,** *adv.*
non·cog′ni·zance, *n.*
non·cog′ni·zant, *adj.;* **-ly,** *adv.*
non′co·hab′i·ta′tion, *n.*
non′co·her′ence, *n.*
non′co·her′en·cy, *n.*
non′co·her′ent, *adj.;* **-ly,** *adv.*
non′co·he′sion, *n.*
non′co·he′sive, *adj.;* **-ly,** *adv.;* **-ness,** *n.*
non·coin′age, *n.*
non′co·in′ci·dence, *n.*
non′co·in′ci·dent, *adj.*
non′co·in′ci·den′tal, *adj.;* **-ly,** *adv.*
non·co′la, *n.*
non′col·lab′o·ra′tion, *n.*
non′col·lab′o·ra′tion·ist, *n.*
non′col·laps′a·bil′i·ty, *n.*
non′col·laps′a·ble, *adj.*
non′col·laps′i·ble, *adj.*
non′col·laps′i·bil′i·ty, *n.*
non′col·lect′a·ble, *adj.*
non′col·lect′i·ble, *adj.*
non′col·lec′tion, *n.*
non′col·lec′tive, *adj.;* **-ly,** *adv.*
non′col·lec′tiv·is′tic, *adj.*
non′col·lin′e·ar, *adj.*
non·col′loid, *n.*
non′col·loi′dal, *adj.*
non′col·lu′sion, *n.*
non′col·lu′sive, *adj.;* **-ly,** *adv.;* **-ness,** *n.*
non′co·lo′ni·al, *adj., n.;* **-ly,** *adv.*
non·col′or·a·bil′i·ty, *n.*
non·col′or·a·ble, *adj.;* **-ble·ness,** *n.;* **-bly,** *adv.*
non·col′or·ing, *adj., n.*
non·com·bi·na′tion, *n.*
non′com·bi′na·tive, *adj.*
non′com·bin′ing, *adj.*
non′com·bus′tion, *n.*
non′com·bus′tive, *adj.*
non·com′ic, *adj., n.*
non·com′i·cal, *adj.;* **-ly,** *adv.;* **-ness,** *n.*
non·com′i·cal′i·ty, *n.*
non′com·mem′o·ra′tion, *n.*
non′com·mem′o·ra′tion·al, *adj.*
non′com·mem′o·ra′tive, *adj.;* **-ly,** *adv.*
non′com·mem′o·ra·to′ry, *adj.*
non′com·mence′ment, *n.*
non′com·mend′a·ble, *adj.;* **-ble·ness,** *n.;* **-bly,** *adv.*
non′com·men′da·to′ry, *adj.*
non′com·mer′cial, *adj., n.;* **-ly,** *adv.*
non′com·mer′ci·al′i·ty, *n.*
non′com·mis′er·a′tion, *n.*
non′com·mis′er·a′tive, *adj.;* **-ly,** *adv.*
non′com·mit′ment, *n.*
non′com·mit′ted, *adj.*
non′com·mo′di·ous, *adj.;* **-ly,** *adv.;* **-ness,** *n.*
non′com·mod′i·ty, *adj., n., pl.* **-ties.**
non′com·mu′nal, *adj.;* **-ly,** *adv.*
non′com·mu′ni·cat′ing, *adj.*
non′com·mu′ni·ca′tion, *n.*
non′com·mu′ni·ca′tive, *adj.;* **-ly,** *adv.;* **-ness,** *n.*
non′Com·mu·nis′tic, *adj.*
non′Com·mu·nis′ti·cal, *adj.;* **-ly,** *adv.*
non·com′mu·ta′tive, *adj.*
non′com·pat′i·ble, *adj.;* **-bly,** *adv.;* **-ble·ness,** *n.*
non′com·pen′sa·ble, *adj.*
non·com′pen·sat′ed, *adj.*
non·com′pen·sat′ing, *adj.*
non′com·pen·sa′tion, *n.*
non·com′pen·sa′tive, *adj.*
non′com·pen′sa·to′ry, *adj.*
non·com′pe·ten·cy, *n.*
non·com′pe·tent, *adj.;* **-ly,** *adv.*
non′com·pet′ing, *adj.*
non′com·pe·ti′tion, *adj.*
non′com·pet′i·tive, *adj.;* **-ly,** *adv.;* **-ness,** *n.*
non′com·pla′cence, *n.*
non′com·pla′cen·cy, *n., pl.* **-cies.**
non′com·pla′cent, *adj.;* **-ly,** *adv.*
non′com·plai′sance, *n.*
non′com·plai′sant, *adj.;* **-ly,** *adv.*
non′com·ple′tion, *n.*
non′com·plic′i·ty, *n., pl.* **-ties.**
non′com·pli′er, *n.*
non′com·pos′ite, *adj., n.;* **-ly,** *adv.;* **-ness,** *n.*
non′com·po′sure, *n.*
non′com·pound′a·ble, *adj.*
non′com·pre·hend′i·ble, *adj.*
non′com·pre·hend′ing, *adj.;* **-ly,** *adv.*
non′com·pre·hen′si·ble, *adj.;* **-ly,** *adv.*
non′com·pre·hen′sion, *n.*
non′com·pre·hen′sive, *adj.;* **-ly,** *adv.;* **-ness,** *n.*
non′com·pres′si·bil′i·ty, *n.*
non′com·pres′si·ble, *adj.*
non′com·pres′sion, *n.*
non′com·pres′sive, *adj.;* **-ly,** *adv.*
non′com·pro′mised, *adj.*
non′com·pro·mis′ing, *adj.*
non′com·pul′sion, *n.*
non′com·pul′sive, *adj.;* **-ly,** *adv.*
non′com·pul′so·ri·ly, *adv.;* **-ness,** *n.*
non′com·pul′so·ry, *adj.*
non′com·pu·ta′tion, *n.*
non′com·put′er, *adj.*
non′con·ceal′ment, *n.*
non′con·ceiv′ing, *n., adj.*
non·con′cen·trat′ed, *adj.*
non′con·cen·tra′tion, *n.*
non′con′cen·tra′tive, *adj.;* **-ness,** *n.*
non′con·cen′tric, *adj.*
non′con·cen′tri·cal, *adj.;* **-ly,** *adv.*
non′con·cen·tric′i·ty, *n.*
non′con·cep′tu·al, *adj.;* **-ly,** *adv.*
non′con·ces′sion, *n.*
non′con·ces′sive, *adj.*
non′con·cil′i·at′ing, *adj.*
non′con·cil′i·a·to′ry, *adj.*
non′con·ci′sion, *n.*
non′con·clud′ing, *adj.*
non′con·clu′sion, *n.*
non′con·clu′sive, *adj.;* **-ly,** *adv.;* **-ness,** *n.*
non′con·cord′ant, *adv.;* **-ly,** *adv.*
non′con·dem·na′tion, *n.*
non′con·den′sa·ble, *adj.*
non·con·den·sa′tion, *n.*
non′con·densed′, *adj.*
non′con·den′si·bil′i·ty, *n.*
non′con·den′si·ble, *adj.*
non′con·de·scend′ing, *adj.;* **-ly,** *adv.;* **-ness,** *n.*
non′con·de·scen′sion, *n.*
non·con′di·ment, *n.*
non′con·di·men′tal, *adj.*
non′con·di′tion·al, *adj.*
non′con·di′tioned, *adj.*
non′con·do·na′tion, *n.*
non′con·du′cive, *adj.;* **-ness,** *n.*
non′con·duc′ti·bil′i·ty, *n.*
non′con·duc′ti·ble, *adj.*
non′con·duc′tive, *adj.*
non′con·fed′er·ate, *adj., n.*
non′con·fed′er·a′tion, *n.*
non′con·fer′ra·ble, *adj.*
non·con′fi·dence, *n.*
non·con′fi·dent, *adj.;* **-ly,** *adv.*
non′con·fi·den′tial, *adj.;* **-ly,** *adv.;* **-ness,** *n.*
non′con·fi·den′ti·al′i·ty, *n.*
non′con·fid′ing, *adj.*
non′con·fined′, *adj.*
non′con·fine′ment, *n.*
non′con·fin′ing, *adj.*
non′con·fir·ma′tion, *n.*
non′con·firm′a·tive, *adj.*
non′con·firm′a·to′ry, *adj.*
non′con·firm′ing, *adj.*
non′con·fis′ca·ble, *adj.*
non′con·fis·ca′tion, *n.*
non′con·flict′ing, *adj.*
non′con·flic′tive, *adj.*
non′con·form′ing, *adj.*
non′con·fron·ta′tion, *n.*
non′con·fron·ta′tion·al, *adj.*
non′con·geal′ing, *adj., n.*
non·con′gen′i·tal, *adj.*
non′con·ges′tion, *n.*
non′con·ges′tive, *adj.*
non′con·grat′u·la·to′ry, *adj.*
non′-Con·gre·ga′tion·al, *adj.*
non·con′gre·ga′tive, *adj.*
non′-Con·gres′sion·al, *adj.*
non·con′gru·ence, *n.*
non·con′gru·en·cy, *n.*
non·con′gru·ent, *adj.;* **-ly,** *adv.*
non′con·gru′i·ty, *n., pl.* **-ties.**
non·con′gru·ous, *adj.;* **-ly,** *adv.;* **-ness,** *n.*
non′con·jec′tur·a·ble, *adj.;* **-bly,** *adv.*
non·con′ju·gal, *adj.;* **-ly,** *adv.*
non′con·ju·gal′i·ty, *n.*
non·con′ju·gate, *adj., n.*
non′con·ju·ga′tion, *n.*
non′con·junc′tion, *n.*
non′con·junc′tive, *adj.;* **-ly,** *adv.*
non′con·nec′tive, *adj., n.;* **-ly,** *adv.*
non′con·nec·tiv′i·ty, *n.*
non′con·niv′ance, *n.*
non′con·niv′ence, *n.*
non·con′no·ta′tive, *adj.;* **-ly,** *adv.*
non′con·nu′bi·al, *adj.;* **-ly,** *adv.*
non′con·nu′bi·al′i·ty, *n.*
non·con′sci·en′tious, *adj.;* **-ly,** *adv.;* **-ness,** *n.*
non·con′scious, *adj.;* **-ly,** *adv.;* **-ness,** *n.*
non′con·script′a·ble, *adj.*
non′con·scrip′tion, *n.*
non′con·se·cra′tion, *n.*
non′con·sec′u·tive, *adj.;* **-ly,** *adv.;* **-ness,** *n.*
non′con·sen′su·al, *adj.;* **-ly,** *adv.*
non′con·sent′, *n.*
non′con·sent′ing, *adj., n.*
non·con′se·quence, *n.*
non·con′se·quent, *adj.*
non′con·se·quen′tial, *adj.;* **-ly,** *adv.;* **-ness,** *n.*
non′con·se·quen′ti·al′i·ty, *n.*
non′con·ser·va′tion, *n.*
non′con·ser·va′tion·al, *adj.*
non′con·ser′va·tive, *adj., n.*
non′con·serv′ing, *adj., n.*
non′con·sid′er·a′tion, *n.*
non′con·sign′ment, *n.*
non′con·sis·to′ri·al, *adj.*
non′con·sol′a·ble, *adj.*
non′con·sol′i·da′tion, *n.*
non′con·sol′ing, *adj.;* **-ly,** *adv.*
non·con′so·nance, *n.*
non′con·sort′ing, *adj.*
non′con·spir′a·tor, *n.*
non′con·spir′a·to′ri·al, *adj.*
non′con·spir′ing, *adj.*
non·con′stant, *n., adj.*
non′con·stit′u·ent, *adj., n.*
non·con′sti·tut′ed, *adj.*
non′con·sti·tu′tion·al, *adj.*
non′con·strain′ing, *adj.*
non′con·straint′, *n.*
non′con·strict′ed, *adj.*
non′con·strict′ing, *adj.*
non′con·stric′tive, *adj.*
non′con·stru′a·bil′i·ty, *n.*
non′con·stru′a·ble, *adj.*
non′con·struc′tive, *adj.;* **-ly,** *adv.;* **-ness,** *n.*
non′con·su′lar, *adj.*
non′con·sul′ta·tive, *adj.*
non′con·sul′ta·to′ry, *adj.*
non′con·sum′a·ble, *adj.*
non′con·sum′er, *adj., n.*
non′con·sum′ing, *adj.*
non·con′sum·ma′tion, *n.*
non′con·sump′tion, *n.*
non′con·sump′tive, *adj.;* **-ly,** *adv.;* **-ness,** *n.*
non·con′tact, *n., adj.*
non′con·ta′gion, *n.*
non′con·ta′gious, *adj.;* **-ly,** *adv.;* **-ness,** *n.*
non′con·tain′er·ized′, *adj.*
non′con·tam′i·na·ble, *adj.*
non′con·tam′i·na′tion, *n.*
non′con·tam′i·na′tive, *adj.*
non′con·tem′pla·tive, *adj.;* **-ly,** *adv.;* **-ness,** *n.*
non′con·tem′po·ra′ne·ous, *adj.;* **-ly,** *adv.;* **-ness,** *n.*
non′con·tem′po·rar′y, *adj., n., pl.* **-rar·ies.**
non′con·tempt′i·bil′i·ty, *n.*
non′con·tempt′i·ble, *adj.;* **-ble·ness,** *n.;* **-bly,** *adv.*
non′con·temp′tu·ous, *adj.;* **-ly,** *adv.;* **-ness,** *n.*
non′con·tend′ing, *adj.*
non′con·ten′tion, *n.*

heart), be indifferent, equiv. to *non-* NON- + *chaloir* < L *calēre* to be warm. See -ANT] —**non′cha·lant′ly,** *adv.*
—**Syn.** cool, calm, collected, composed. —**Ant.** excitable.

non·clas·si·cal (non klas′i kəl), *adj.* **1.** not classical or contrary to classical precepts. **2.** *Physics.* pertaining to a law, theory, or observation that cannot be expressed or understood in terms of Newtonian physics. [1925–30; NON- + CLASSICAL] —**non·clas′si·cal·ly,** *adv.*

non·cling (non kling′), *adj.* (of fabric or the like) having little or no tendency to stick to an object, surface, etc., as by static electricity. Also, **non·cling′ing.** [NON- + CLING[1]]

non·col·le·giate (non′kə lē′jit, -jē it), *adj.* **1.** below the level usually associated with college or university study. **2.** (of a university) not composed of colleges. [1675–85; NON- + COLLEGIATE]

non·com (non′kom′), *n. Informal.* a noncommissioned officer. [1740–50; short for NONCOMMISSIONED]

noncom., noncommissioned.

non·com·bat (non kom′bat), *adj.* not including, entailing, or requiring combat: *noncombat duty.* [1940–45; NON- + COMBAT]

non·com·bat·ant (non′kəm bat′nt, non kom′bə tnt), *n.* **1.** a person connected with a military force in some capacity other than that of a fighter, as a surgeon or chaplain. **2.** a person who is not directly involved in combat; a civilian in wartime. —*adj.* **3.** not constituting, designed for, or engaged in combat. [1805–15; NON- + COMBATANT]

non·com·bus·ti·ble (non′kəm bus′tə bəl), *adj.* **1.** not flammable. —*n.* **2.** a noncombustible substance. [1965–70; NON- + COMBUSTIBLE] —**non′com·bus′ti·bil′i·ty,** *n.*

non·com·mis·sioned (non′kə mish′ənd), *adj.* not commissioned, applied esp. to military officers, as sergeants and corporals, ranking below warrant officer. [1695–1705; NON- + COMMISSIONED]

non′commis′sioned of′ficer, *Mil.* an enlisted person, as a sergeant or corporal, holding any of various ranks below commissioned or warrant officers. [1695–1705]

non·com·mit·tal (non′kə mit′l), *adj.* not committing oneself, or not involving committal, to a particular view, course, or the like: *The senator gave us a noncommittal answer.* [1820–30, *Amer.*; NON- + COMMITTAL] —**non′·com·mit′tal·ly,** *adv.*
—**Syn.** indefinite, vague, equivocal, evasive, guarded.

non·com·mu·ni·ca·ble (non′kə myōō′ni kə bəl), *adj.* not communicable, esp. with reference to a disease that is not transmitted through contact with an infected or afflicted person. [NON- + COMMUNICABLE]

non·com·mu·ni·cant (non′kə myōō′ni kənt), *n.* **1.** a person who is not a communicant. **2.** a person who does not communicate. [1595–1605; NON- + COMMUNICANT]

non-Com·mu·nist (non kom′yə nist), *adj.* **1.** not following, belonging to, or associated with the Communist party or Communism. —*n.* **2.** a person who does not belong to or follow the Communist party or Communism. [1915–20]

non·com·pli·ance (non′kəm plī′əns), *n.* failure or refusal to comply, as with a law, regulation, or term of a contract. [1680–90; NON- + COMPLIANCE] —**non′com·pli′ant, non′com·ply′ing,** *adj., n.*

non com·pos (non′ kom′pəs), *Informal.* See ***non compos mentis.*** [1620–30]

non com·pos men·tis (nōn′ kōm′pōs men′tis; *Eng.* non′ kom′pəs men′tis), *Latin.* not of sound mind; mentally incapable of managing one's affairs.

non·con·cur·rence (non′kən kûr′əns, -kur′-), *n.* refusal or failure to concur. [1685–95; NON- + CONCURRENCE] —**non′con·cur′rent,** *adj., n.* —**non′con·cur′·rent·ly,** *adv.*

non′condens′ing en′gine, a steam engine releasing exhaust steam to the atmosphere rather than condensing it to hot feedwater. [1835–45; NON- + CONDENSING]

non·con·duc·tor (non′kən duk′tər), *n.* a substance that does not readily conduct heat, sound, or electricity. [1745–55; NON- + CONDUCTOR] —**non′con·duct′ing,** *adj.*

non·con·form·ance (non′kən fôr′məns), *n.* lack of conformity. [1835–45; NON- + CONFORMANCE]

non·con·form·ist (non′kən fôr′mist), *n.* **1.** a person who refuses to conform, as to established customs, attitudes, or ideas. **2.** (*often cap.*) a Protestant in England who is not a member of the Church of England; dissenter. [1610–20; NON- + CONFORMIST]
—**Syn. 1.** dissenter, dissident, individualist, loner.

CONCISE PRONUNCIATION KEY: *act, cāpe, dâre, pärt; set, ēqual; if, īce; ox, ōver, ôrder, oil, bŏŏk, bōōt, out; up, ûrge; child; sing; shoe; thin, that;* zh as in *treasure.* ə = *a* as in *alone, e* as in *system, i* as in *easily, o* as in *gallop, u* as in *circus;* ə as in *fire* (fīər), *hour* (ouər). l and n can serve as syllabic consonants, as in *cradle* (krād′l), and *button* (but′n). See the full key inside the front cover.

non′con·ten′tious, *adj.*; **-ly,** *adv.*
non′con·ter′mi·nal, *adj.*
non′con·ter′mi·nous, *adj.*; **-ly,** *adv.*
non′con·tes·ta′tion, *n.*
non′con·tex′tu·al, *adj.*; **-ly,** *adv.*
non′con·tex′tu·al·ized′, *adj.*
non′con·ti·gu′i·ty, *n., pl.* **-ties.**
non′con·tig′u·ous, *adj.*; **-ly,** *adv.*; **-ness,** *n.*
non·con′ti·nence, *n.*
non·con′ti·nen·cy, *n.*
non′con·ti·nen′tal, *adj., n.*
non′con·tin′gent, *adj.*; **-ly,** *adv.*
non′con·tin′u·a·ble, *adj.*; **-bly,** *adv.*
non′con·tin′u·ance, *n.*
non′con·tin′u·a′tion, *n.*
non′con·tin·u′i·ty, *n.*
non′con·tin′u·ous, *adj.*; **-ly,** *adv.*; **-ness,** *n.*
non·con′tra·band′, *n., adj.*
non·con′tract, *adj.*
non′con·trac′tion, *n.*
non′con·trac′tu·al, *adj.*
non′con·tra·dic′to·ry, *adj., n., pl.* **-ries.**
non′con·tra·ri′e·ty, *n., pl.* **-ties.**
non′con·trib′ut·a·ble, *adj.*
non′con·trib′ut·ing, *adj.*
non′con·tri·bu′tion, *n.*
non′con·trib′u·tive, *adj.*; **-ly,** *adv.*; **-ness,** *n.*
non′con·trib′u·tor, *n.*
non′con·trib′u·to′ry, *adj., n., pl.* **-ries.**
non′con·triv′ance, *n.*
non′con·trol′la·ble, *adj.*; **-ly,** *adv.*
non′con·trolled′, *adj.*
non′con·trol′ling, *adj.*
non′con·tro·ver′sial, *adj.*; **-ly,** *adv.*
non′con·tu·ma′cious, *adj.*; **-ly,** *adv.*; **-ness,** *n.*
non′con·vec′tive, *adj.*; **-ly,** *adv.*
non′con·ven′tion·al, *adj.*; **-ly,** *adv.*
non′con·ver′gence, *n.*
non′con·ver′gen·cy, *n.*
non′con·ver′gent, *adj.*
non′con·verg′ing, *adj.*
non′con·ver′sa·ble, *adj.*; **-ble·ness,** *n.*; **-bly,** *adv.*
non′con·ver′sance, *n.*
non′con·ver′san·cy, *n.*
non′con·ver′sant, *adj.*; **-ly,** *adv.*
non′con·ver·sa′tion·al, *adj.*; **-ly,** *adv.*
non′con·ver′sion, *n.*
non′con·vert′i·bil′i·ty, *n.*
non′con·vert′i·ble, *adj.*; **-ble·ness,** *n.*; **-bly,** *adv.*
non′con·vey′ance, *n.*
non′con·vic′tion, *n.*
non′con·viv′i·al, *adj.*; **-ly,** *adv.*
non′con·viv′i·al′i·ty, *n.*
non′co·or′di·nat′ing, *adj.*
non′co·or′di·na′tion, *n.*
non′co·pla′nar, *adj.*
non′co·ro′nal, *adj.*
non·cor′po·rate, *adj.*; **-ly,** *adv.*
non′cor·po·ra′tion, *n.*
non·cor′po·ra′tive, *adj.*
non′cor·po′re·al, *adj.*
non′cor·po′re·al′i·ty, *n.*
non′cor·pus′cu·lar, *adj.*
non′cor·rec′tion, *n.*
non′cor·rec′tion·al, *n.*
non′cor·rec′tive, *adj., n.*; **-ly,** *adv.*
non·cor′re·lat′ing, *adj.*
non′cor·re·la′tion, *n.*
non′cor·rel′a·tive, *adj.*; **-ly,** *adv.*; **-ness,** *n.*
non′cor·res·pond′ence, *n.*
non′cor·res·pond′ent, *adj., n.*
non′cor·res·pond′ing, *adj., n.*; **-ly,** *adv.*
non′cor·rob′o·rat′ing, *adj.*
non′cor·rob′o·ra′tion, *n.*
non′cor·rob′o·ra′tive, *adj.*; **-ly,** *adv.*
non′cor·rob′o·ra·to′ry, *adj.*
non′cor·rod′i·ble, *adj.*
non′cor·rod′ing, *adj., n.*
non′cor·ro′sive, *adj.*; **-ly,** *adv.*; **-ness,** *n.*
non′cor·rupt′, *adj.*; **-ly,** *adv.*; **-ness,** *n.*
non′cor·rupt′er, *n.*
non′cor·rupt′i·bil′i·ty, *n.*
non′cor·rupt′i·ble, *adj.*; **-ble·ness,** *n.*; **-bly,** *adv.*
non′cor·rup′tive, *adj.*
non·cor′ti·cal, *adj.*; **-ly,** *adv.*
non·cos′mic, *adj.*
non·cos′mi·cal·ly, *adv.*
non′cos·mo·pol′i·tan, *adj., n.*
non′cos·mo·pol′i·tan·ism, *n.*
non′cos·mop′o·lite′, *n.*
non′cos·mop′o·lit·ism, *n.*
non·cot′tag·er, *n.*
non′cot·y·le′don·al, *adj.*
non′cot·y·le′don·ar′y, *adj.*
non′cot·y·le′don·ous, *adj.*
non′coun·ter·ac′tive, *adj.*
non·coun′ter·feit, *adj.*
non·cov′et·ous, *adj.*; **-ly,** *adv.*; **-ness,** *n.*
non·crank′ing, *adj.*
non′cre·a′tive, *adj.*; **-ly,** *adv.*; **-ness,** *n.*
non′cre·a·tiv′i·ty, *n.*
non·cre′dence, *n.*
non·cre′dent, *adj.*
non′cred·i·bil′i·ty, *n.*
non·cred′i·ble, *adj.*; **-ble·ness,** *n.*; **-bly,** *adv.*
non·cred′it·a·ble, *adj.*; **-ble·ness,** *n.*; **-bly,** *adv.*
non·cred′i·tor, *n.*
non·cred′u·lous, *adj.*; **-ly,** *adv.*; **-ness,** *n.*
non·creep′ing, *adj.*
non·cre′nate, *adj.*
non·cre′nat·ed, *adj.*
non′cre·ta′ceous, *adj.*
non·crim′i·nal, *adj., n.*; **-ly,** *adv.*
non′crim·i·nal′i·ty, *n.*
non·cri′noid, *adj.*
non·crit′i·cal, *adj.*; **-ly,** *adv.*; **-ness,** *n.*
non·crit′i·ciz′ing, *adj., n.*
non·crop′, *adj.*
non·cru′cial, *adj.*; **-ly,** *adv.*
non·cru′ci·form′, *adj.*; **-ly,** *adv.*
non′cru·sad′ing, *adj.*
non′crus·ta′ceous, *adj.*
non·cryp′tic, *adj.*
non·cryp′ti·cal, *adj.*; **-ly,** *adv.*
non·crys′tal·line, *adj.*
non·crys′tal·liz′a·ble, *adj.*
non·crys′tal·lized′, *adj.*
non·crys′tal·liz′ing, *adj.*
non·cul′mi·nat′ing, *adj.*
non′cul·mi·na′tion, *n.*
non′cul·pa·bil′i·ty, *n.*
non·cul′pa·ble, *adj.*; **-ble·ness,** *n.*; **-bly,** *adv.*
non′cul·ti·va·bil′i·ty, *n.*
non·cul′ti·va·ble, *adj.*
non·cul′ti·vat′a·ble, *adj.*
non·cul′ti·vat′ed, *adj.*
non′cul·ti·va′tion, *n.*
non·cul′tur·al, *adj.*; **-ly,** *adv.*
non·cul′ture, *n.*
non·cul′tured, *adj.*
non·cum′brous, *adj.*; **-ly,** *adv.*; **-ness,** *n.*
non·cur′a·tive, *adj.*; **-ly,** *adv.*; **-ness,** *n.*
non·cur′dling, *adj., n.*
non′cu·ri·os′i·ty, *n.*
non·cu′ri·ous, *adj.*; **-ly,** *adv.*; **-ness,** *n.*
non·cur′rent, *adj.*; **-ly,** *adv.*
non·cur′sive, *adj.*; **-ly,** *adv.*
non′cur·tail′ing, *adj.*
non′cur·tail′ment, *n.*
non·cus′pi·date′, *adj.*
non·cus′pi·dat′ed, *adj.*
non′cus·to′di·al, *adj.*
non·cus′tom·ar′i·ly, *adv.*
non·cus′tom·ar′y, *adj.*
non·cus′tom·ized′, *adj.*
non·cut′ting, *adj., n.*
non·cy′clic, *adj.*
non·cy′cli·cal, *adj.*; **-ly,** *adv.*
non-Cym′ric, *adj.*
non-Czech′, *adj., n.*
non′-Czech·o·slo·va′ki·an, *adj., n.*
non·dam′age·a·ble, *adj.*
non·dam′ag·ing, *adj.*; **-ly,** *adv.*
non′dam·na′tion, *n.*
non·danc′er, *n.*
non·dan′ger·ous, *adj.*; **-ly,** *adv.*; **-ness,** *n.*
non-Dan′ish, *adj.*
non·dark′, *adj.*
non′-Dar·win′i·an, *adj., n.*
non′da·ti′val, *adj.*
non·dead′ly, *adj.*
non·deaf′, *adj.*; **-ly,** *adv.*; **-ness,** *n.*
non·deaf′ened, *adj.*
non·deaf′en·ing, *adj.*; **-ly,** *adv.*
non′de·bat′a·ble, *adj.*
non′de·bat′er, *n.*
non′de·bat′ing, *adj.*
non′de·bil′i·tat′ing, *adj.*
non′de·bil′i·ta′tion, *n.*
non′de·bil′i·ta′tive, *adj.*
non·debt′or, *n.*
non·dec′a·dence, *n.*
non·dec′a·den·cy, *n.*
non·dec′a·dent, *adj., n.*
non′de·cal′ci·fi·ca′tion, *n.*
non′de·cal′ci·fied′, *adj.*
non′dec·a·syl·lab′ic, *adj.*
non·dec′a·syl′la·ble, *n.*
non′de·cayed′, *adj.*
non′de·cay′ing, *adj.*
non′de·ceit′, *n.*
non′de·ceiv′a·ble, *adj.*
non′de·ceiv′ing, *adj.*
non′de·cel′er·a′tion, *n.*
non′de·cep′tion, *n.*
non′de·cep′tive, *adj.*; **-ly,** *adv.*; **-ness,** *n.*
non′de·cid′u·ous, *adj.*; **-ly,** *adv.*; **-ness,** *n.*
non′de·ci′sion, *n.*
non′de·ci′sive, *adj.*; **-ly,** *adv.*; **-ness,** *n.*
non′de·clam′a·to′ry, *adj.*
non′dec·la·ra′tion, *n.*
non′de·clar′a·tive, *adj.*; **-ly,** *adv.*
non′de·clar′a·to′ry, *adj.*
non′de·clar′er, *n.*
non′de·cliv′i·tous, *adj.*
non·dec′o·rat′ed, *adj.*
non′dec·o·ra′tion, *n.*
non·dec′o·ra·tive, *adj.*
non·dec′o·rous, *adj.*; **-ly,** *adv.*; **-ness,** *n.*
non·ded′i·cat′ed, *adj.*
non′ded·i·ca′tion, *n.*
non·ded′i·ca′tive, *adj.*
non·ded′i·ca·to′ry, *adj.*
non′de·duc′i·ble, *adj.*
non′de·duct′i·bil′i·ty, *n.*
non′de·duct′i·ble, *adj., n.*
non′de·duc′tion, *n.*
non′de·duc′tive, *adj.*; **-ly,** *adv.*
non·deep′, *adj.*
non′de·fal·ca′tion, *n.*
non′de·fam′a·to′ry, *adj.*
non′de·fault′ing, *adj., n.*
non′de·fea′sance, *n.*
non′de·fea′si·bil′i·ty, *n.*
non′de·fea′si·ble, *adj.*; **-ness,** *n.*
non′de·feat′, *n.*
non′de·fect′ing, *adj.*
non′de·fec′tion, *n.*
non′de·fec′tive, *adj.*; **-ly,** *adv.*; **-ness,** *n.*
non′de·fec′tor, *n.*
non′de·fend′ant, *n.*
non′de·fense′, *n., adj.*
non′de·fen′si·bil′i·ty, *n.*
non′de·fen′si·ble, *adj.*; **-ble·ness,** *n.*; **-bly,** *adv.*
non′de·fen′sive, *adj.*; **-ly,** *adv.*; **-ness,** *n.*
non′de·fer′a·ble, *adj.*
non·def′er·ence, *n.*
non·def′er·ent, *adj.*
non′def·er·en′tial, *adj.*; **-ly,** *adv.*
non′de·fer′ra·ble, *adj.*
non′de·fi′ance, *n.*
non′de·fi′ant, *adj.*; **-ly,** *adv.*; **-ness,** *n.*
non′de·fi′cien·cy, *n., pl.* **-cies.**
non′de·fi′cient, *adj.*; **-ly,** *adv.*
non′de·file′ment, *n.*
non′de·fil′ing, *adj.*
non′de·fin′a·bil′i·ty, *n.*
non′de·fin′a·ble, *adj.*; **-bly,** *adv.*
non′de·fined′, *adj.*
non′de·fin′er, *n.*
non′de·fin′ing, *adj.*
non·def′i·nite, *adj.*; **-ly,** *adv.*; **-ness,** *n.*
non′de·fin′i·tive, *adj.*; **-ly,** *adv.*; **-ness,** *n.*
non′de·fla′tion, *n.*
non′de·fla′tion·ar′y, *adj.*
non′de·flect′ed, *adj.*
non′de·flec′tion, *n.*
non′de·flec′tive, *adj.*
non′de·for·ma′tion, *n.*
non′de·formed′, *adj.*
non′de·for′mi·ty, *n., pl.* **-ties.**
non′de·funct′, *adj.*
non′de·gen′er·a·cy, *n., pl.* **-cies.**
non′de·gen′er·ate, *adj., n.*; **-ly,** *adv.*; **-ness,** *n.*
non′de·gen′er·a′tion, *n.*
non′de·gen′er·a·tive, *adj.*
non′deg·ra·da′tion, *n.*
non′de·grad′ing, *adj.*
non′de·his′cent, *adj.*
non·de′ist, *n.*
non′de·is′tic, *adj.*
non′de·is′ti·cal, *adj.*; **-ly,** *adv.*
non·del′e·ga·ble, *adj.*
non·del′e·gate, *n.*
non′del·e·ga′tion, *n.*
non′del·e·te′ri·ous, *adj.*; **-ly,** *adv.*; **-ness,** *n.*
non′de·lib′er·ate, *adj.*; **-ly,** *adv.*; **-ness,** *n.*
non′de·lib′er·a′tion, *n.*
non·del′i·cate, *adj.*; **-ly,** *adv.*; **-ness,** *n.*
non′de·lin′e·a′tion, *n.*
non′de·lin′e·a′tive, *adj.*
non′de·lin′quent, *adj.*
non′del·i·ques′cence, *n.*
non′del·i·ques′cent, *adj.*
non′de·lir′i·ous, *adj.*; **-ly,** *adv.*; **-ness,** *n.*
non′de·liv′er·ance, *n.*
non′de·liv′er·y, *n., pl.* **-er·ies.**
non′de·lud′ed, *adj.*
non′de·lud′ing, *adj.*
non′de·lu′sive, *adj.*
non′de·mand′ing, *adj.*
non′de·mise′, *n.*
non′de·mo′bi·li·za′tion, *n.*
non′de·moc′ra·cy, *n., pl.* **-cies.**
non′dem·o·crat′ic, *adj.*
non′dem·o·crat′i·cal, *adj.*; **-ly,** *adv.*
non′dem·o·li′tion, *n.*
non′de·mon′stra·bil′i·ty, *n.*
non′de·mon′stra·ble, *adj.*; **-ble·ness,** *n.*; **-bly,** *adv.*
non′de·mon′stra·tive, *adj.*; **-ly,** *adv.*; **-ness,** *n.*
non·den′droid, *adj.*
non′den·droi′dal, *adj.*
non′de·ni′al, *n.*
non′de·nom′i·na′tion·al, *adj.*; **-ly,** *adv.*
non·de′no·ta′tive, *adj.*; **-ly,** *adv.*
non·dense′ness, *n.*
non·den′si·ty, *n.*
non′de·nun′ci·at′ing, *adj.*
non′de·nun′ci·a′tion, *n.*
non′de·nun′ci·a′tive, *adj.*
non′de·nun′ci·a·to′ry, *adj.*
non′de·o′dor·ant, *n., adj.*
non′de·o′dor·iz′ing, *adj.*
non′de·part·men′tal, *adj.*; **-ly,** *adv.*
non′de·par′ture, *n.*
non′de·pend′a·bil′i·ty, *n.*
non′de·pend′a·ble, *adj.*; **-ble·ness,** *n.*; **-bly,** *adv.*
non′de·pend′ance, *n.*
non′de·pend′an·cy, *n., pl.* **-cies.**
non′de·pend′ence, *n.*
non′de·pend′en·cy, *n., pl.* **-cies.**
non′de·plet′a·ble, *adj.*
non′de·ple′tion, *n.*
non′de·ple′tive, *adj.*
non′de·ple′to·ry, *adj.*
non′de·port′a·ble, *adj.*
non′de·por·ta′tion, *n.*
non′de·port′ed, *adj., n.*
non′de·pos′i·tor, *n.*
non′de·pos′i·to′ry, *adj.*
non′dep·ra·va′tion, *n.*
non′de·praved′, *adj.*
non′de·prav′i·ty, *n., pl.* **-ties.**
non·dep′re·cat′ing, *adj.*; **-ly,** *adv.*

non·con·form·i·ty (non′kən fôr′mi tē), *n.* **1.** failure or refusal to conform, as with established customs, attitudes, or ideas. **2.** lack of conformity or agreement. **3.** (*often cap.*) refusal to conform to the Church of England. **4.** *Geol.* an unconformity that separates crystalline rocks, either igneous or metamorphic, from sedimentary rocks. [1610–20; NON- + CONFORMITY]

non·con·tra·dic·tion (non′kon trə dik′shən), *n.* absence or lack of contradiction. [1830–40; NON- + CONTRADICTION]

non·con·tras·tive (non′kən tras′tiv), *adj.* **1.** not contrastive. **2.** *Ling.* in complementary distribution; in free variation. [1960–65; NON- + CONTRASTIVE]

non·co·op·er·a·tion (non′kō op′ə rā′shən), *n.* **1.** failure or refusal to cooperate. **2.** a method or practice, as that established in India by Gandhi, of showing opposition to acts or policies of the government by refusing to participate in civic and political life or to obey governmental regulations. Cf. **civil disobedience** (def. 1), **passive resistance.** Also, **non′co·op′er·a′tion.** [1785–95; NON- + COOPERATION] —**non·co·op·er·a·tive** (non′kō op′ər ə tiv, -ə rā′tiv), *adj.* —**non′co·op′er·a′tor,** *n.* —**non′co·op′er·a′tion·ist,** *n.*

non·cor·rect·ing (non′kə rek′ting), *adj. Ophthalm.* (of eyeglass lenses) ground and polished without a corrective prescription. [NON- + CORRECTING]

CONCISE ETYMOLOGY KEY: <, descended or borrowed from; >, whence; b., blend of, blended; c., cognate with; cf., compare; deriv., derivative; equiv., equivalent; imit., imitative; obl., oblique; r., replacing; s., stem; sp., spelling, spelled; resp., respelling, respelled; trans., translation; ?, origin unknown; *, unattested; ‡, probably earlier than. See the full key inside the front cover.

non·cred·it (non kred′it), *adj.* (of academic courses) carrying or conferring no official academic credit in a particular program or toward a particular degree or diploma. [1960–65; NON- + CREDIT]

non·cum·u·la·tive (non kyōō′myə lə tiv, -lā′tiv), *adj.* of or pertaining to preferred stock the dividends of which are skipped and not accrued. [1905–10; NON- + CUMULATIVE]

non·dair·y (non dâr′ē), *adj.* being a substitute for milk or milk products; containing no dairy ingredients: *nondairy whipped topping for the pie.* [1965–70; NON- + DAIRY]

non·de·creas·ing (non′di krē′sing), *adj.* **1.** not decreasing. **2.** *Math.* increasing (def. 2). [NON- + DECREASING]

non·de·grad·a·ble (non′di grā′də bəl), *adj.* **1.** not subject to or capable of degradation or decomposition: *nondegradable waste.* —*n.* **2.** something that is not degradable, as a chemical compound. [NON- + DEGRADE + -ABLE] —**non′de·grad′a·bil′i·ty,** *n.*

non·dense (non dens′), *adj. Math.* nowhere-dense. [NON- + DENSE]

non·de·script (non′di skript′), *adj.* **1.** of no recognized, definite, or particular type or kind: *a nondescript novel; a nondescript color.* **2.** undistinguished or uninteresting; dull or insipid: *The private detective deliberately wore nondescript clothes.* —*n.* **3.** a person or a thing of no particular or notable type or kind. [1675–85; NON- + L *dēscriptus* (ptp. of *dēscrībere* to describe, define, represent; see DESCRIBE)]
—**Syn. 1.** undistinctive, usual, ordinary, unexceptional.

non·di·rec·tion·al (non′di rek′shə nl, -dī-), *adj.* **1.** functioning equally well in all directions; omnidirectional. **2.** without direction; not directional. [1900–05; NON- + DIRECTIONAL]

non′di·rec′tive ther′apy (non′di rek′tiv, -dī-). See **client-centered therapy.** [NON- + DIRECTIVE]

non·dis·junc·tion (non′dis jungk′shən), *n. Biol.* the failure of chromosomes to separate and segregate into daughter cells at division. [1910–15; NON- + DISJUNCTION]

non·dis·tinc·tive (non′di stingk′tiv), *adj. Ling.* not serving to distinguish meanings: *a nondistinctive difference in sound.* [1915–20; NON- + DISTINCTIVE] —**non′dis·tinc′tive·ly,** *adv.*

non·drink·er (non dring′kər), *n.* a person who abstains from alcoholic beverages. [1925–30; NON- + DRINKER] —**non·drink′ing,** *adj., n.*

non·du·ra·ble (non dŏŏr′ə bəl, -dyŏŏr′-), *adj.* **1.** not resistant to wear, decay, etc.; not sturdy: *nondurable fabrics.* **2.** not lasting or enduring; consumable or perishable. —*n.* **3. nondurables.** goods that are used up quickly or purchased frequently, as food and apparel. Cf. **durable goods.** [NON- + DURABLE] —**non′dur·a·bil′i·ty, non·du′ra·ble·ness,** *n.* —**non·du′ra·bly,** *adv.*

none[1] (nun), *pron.* **1.** no one; not one: *None of the members is going.* **2.** not any, as of something indicated: *None of the pie is left. That is none of your business.* **3.** no part; nothing: *I'll have none of your backtalk!* **4.** (*used with a plural v.*) no or not any persons or things: *I left three pies on the table and now there are none. None were left when I came.* —*adv.* **5.** to no extent; in no way; not at all: *The supply is none too great.* —*adj.*

non·dep′re·ca′tive, *adj.*; **-ly,** *adv.*
non·dep′re·ca·to′ri·ly, *adv.*; **-ness,** *n.*
non·dep′re·ca·to′ry, *adj.*
non′de·pre′ci·a·ble, *adj.*
non′de·pre′ci·at′ing, *adj.*
non′de·pre′ci·a′tion, *n.*
non′de·pre′ci·a′tive, *adj.*; **-ly,** *adv.*
non′de·pre′ci·a·to′ry, *adj.*
non′de·pressed′, *adj.*
non′de·press′ing, *adj.*; **-ly,** *adv.*
non′de·pres′sion, *n.*
non′de·pres′sive, *adj.*; **-ly,** *adv.*
non′de·priv′a·ble, *adj.*
non′dep·ri·va′tion, *n.*
non′dep·ri·va′tion·al, *adj.*
non·der′e·lict, *adj., n.*
non′de·ris′i·ble, *adj.*
non′de·ri′sive, *adj.*
non′de·riv′a·bil′i·ty, *n.*
non′de·riv′a·ble, *adj.*
non′de·riv′a·tive, *adj., n.*; **-ly,** *adv.*
non′der·o·ga′tion, *n.*
non′de·rog′a·tive, *adj.*; **-ly,** *adv.*
non′de·rog′a·to′ri·ly, *adv.*; **-ness,** *n.*
non′de·rog′a·to′ry, *adj.*
non′de·scrib′a·ble, *adj.*
non′de·scrip′tive, *adj.*; **-ly,** *adv.*; **-ness,** *n.*
non′des·e·cra′tion, *n.*
non·des′ig·nate, *adj.*
non·des′ig·na′tive, *adj.*
non′de·signed′, *adj.*
non′de·sir′ous, *adj.*
non′de·sist′ance, *n.*
non′de·sist′ence, *n.*
non′de·sist′ing, *adj., n.*
non′des·pot′ic, *adj.*
non′des·pot′i·cal·ly, *adv.*
non′de·struc′tion, *n.*
non′de·struc′tive, *adj.*; **-ly,** *adv.*; **-ness,** *n.*
non′de·sul′fu·ri·za′tion, *n.*
non′de·sul′fu·rized′, *adj.*
non′de·tach′a·bil′i·ty, *n.*
non′de·tach′a·ble, *adj.*
non′de·tach′ment, *n.*
non′de·tailed′, *adj.*
non′de·ten′tion, *n.*
non′de·ter′gent, *adj.*
non′de·te′ri·o·ra′tion, *n.*
non′de·ter′mi·na·ble, *adj.*
non′de·ter′mi·nant, *n.*
non′de·ter′mi·na′tion, *n.*
non′de·ter′mi·na′tive, *adj., n.*; **-ly,** *adv.*; **-ness,** *n.*
non′de·ter′min·ist, *n., adj.*
non′de·ter′min·is′tic, *adj.*
non′de·ter′rent, *adj.*
non·det′o·nat′ing, *adj.*
non′de·trac′tive, *adj.*; **-ly,** *adv.*
non′de·trac′to·ry, *adj.*
non′det·ri·men′tal, *adj.*; **-ly,** *adv.*
non′de·vel′op·a·ble, *adj.*
non′de·vel′op·ing, *adj.*
non′de·vel′op·ment, *n.*
non′de·vel′op·men′tal, *adj.*; **-ly,** *adv.*
non·de′vi·ant, *adj., n.*
non·de′vi·at′ing, *adj.*
non′de·vi·a′tion, *n.*
non·de′vi·ous, *adj.*; **-ly,** *adv.*; **-ness,** *n.*
non′de·vo′tion·al, *adj.*; **-ly,** *adv.*
non′de·vout′, *adj.*; **-ly,** *adv.*; **-ness,** *n.*
non′dex·ter′i·ty, *n.*
non·dex′ter·ous, *adj.*; **-ly,** *adv.*; **-ness,** *n.*
non·dex′trous, *adj.*
non′di·a·bet′ic, *adj.*
non′di·a·bol′ic, *adj.*
non′di·a·bol′i·cal, *adj.*; **-ly,** *adv.*; **-ness,** *n.*
non′di·ag′o·nal, *adj., n.*; **-ly,** *adv.*
non′di·a·gram·mat′ic, *adj.*
non′di·a·gram·mat′i·cal, *adj.*; **-ly,** *adv.*
non′di·a·lec′tal, *adj.*; **-ly,** *adv.*
non′di·a·lec′tic, *adj., n.*
non′di·a·lec′ti·cal, *adj.*; **-ly,** *adv.*
non·di′a·lyz′ing, *adj.*
non′di·am′e·tral, *adj.*; **-ly,** *adv.*
non′di·aph′a·nous, *adj.*; **-ly,** *adv.*; **-ness,** *n.*
non′di·a·sta′sic, *adj.*
non′di·a·stat′ic, *adj.*
non′di·a·ther′ma·nous, *adj.*
non′di·cho·gam′ic, *adj.*
non′di·chog′a·mous, *adj.*
non′di·chog′a·my, *n.*
non′di·chot′o·mous, *adj.*; **-ly,** *adv.*
non′dic·ta′tion, *n.*
non′dic·ta·to′ri·al, *adj.*; **-ly,** *adv.*; **-ness,** *n.*
non′di·dac′tic, *adj.*
non′di·dac′ti·cal·ly, *adv.*
non·di′et, *adj.*
non·di′et·er, *n.*
non′di·e·tet′ic, *adj.*
non′di·e·tet′i·cal·ly, *adv.*
non·di′et·ing, *adj., n.*
non′dif·fer·en′ti·a·ble, *adj.*
non′dif·fer·en′ti·a′tion, *n.*
non·dif′fi·cult′, *adj.*
non·dif′fi·dence, *n.*
non·dif′fi·dent, *adj.*; **-ly,** *adv.*
non′dif·frac′tive, *adj.*; **-ly,** *adv.*; **-ness,** *n.*
non′dif·fuse′, *adj.*
non′dif·fused′, *adj.*
non′dif·fus′i·ble, *adj.*; **-ble·ness,** *n.*; **-bly,** *adv.*
non′dif·fus′ing, *adj.*
non′dif·fu′sion, *n.*
non′di·gest′i·bil′i·ty, *n.*
non′di·gest′i·ble, *adj.*; **-ble·ness,** *n.*; **-bly,** *adv.*
non′di·gest′ing, *adj.*
non′di·ges′tion, *n.*
non′di·ges′tive, *adj.*
non′di·lap′i·dat′ed, *adj.*
non′di·lat′a·bil′i·ty, *n.*
non′di·lat′a·ble, *adj.*
non′di·la′tion, *n.*
non·dil′i·gence, *n.*
non·dil′i·gent, *adj.*; **-ly,** *adv.*
non′di·lu′tion, *n.*
non′di·men′sioned, *adj.*
non′di·min′ish·ing, *adj.*
non′di·oc′e·san, *adj.*
non′diph·the′ri·al, *adj.*
non′diph·ther′ic, *adj.*
non′diph·the·rit′ic, *adj.*
non′diph·thon′gal, *adj.*
non′di·plo′ma·cy, *n.*
non′dip·lo·mat′ic, *adj.*
non′dip·lo·mat′i·cal·ly, *adv.*
non·dip′ter·ous, *adj.*
non′dir·i·gi·bil′i·ty, *n.*
non·dir′i·gi·ble, *adj., n.*
non′dis·a′bled, *n., adj.*
non′dis·ad·van′taged, *adj., n.*
non′dis·a·gree′ment, *n.*
non′dis·ap·pear′ing, *adj.*
non′dis·ar′ma·ment, *n.*
non′dis·as′trous, *adj.*; **-ly,** *adv.*; **-ness,** *n.*
non′dis·burs′a·ble, *adj.*
non′dis·bursed′, *adj.*
non′dis·burse′ment, *n.*
non′dis·cern′ing, *adj.*
non′dis·cern′ment, *n.*
non′dis·charg′ing, *adj., n.*
non·dis′ci·plin′a·ble, *adj.*
non·dis′ci·pli·nar′y, *adj.*
non·dis′ci·plined, *adj.*
non·dis′ci·plin′ing, *adj.*
non′dis·clo′sure, *n.*
non′dis·con·tin′u·ance, *n.*
non′dis·cord′ant, *adj.*
non·dis′count, *adj.*
non′dis·count′a·ble, *adj.*
non′dis·count·ed, *adj.*
non′dis·cov′er·a·ble, *adj.*
non′dis·cov′er·y, *n., pl.* **-er·ies.**
non′dis·cre′tion·ar′y, *adj.*
non′dis·crim′i·nat′ing, *adj.*; **-ly,** *adv.*
non′dis·crim′i·na′tion, *n.*
non′dis·crim′i·na′tive, *adj.*; **-ly,** *adv.*
non′dis·crim′i·na·to′ry, *adj.*
non′dis·cur′sive, *adj.*; **-ly,** *adv.*; **-ness,** *n.*
non′dis·cus′si·ble, *adj.*
non′dis·eased′, *adj.*
non′dis·fig′ure·ment, *n.*
non′dis·fran′chised, *adj.*
non′dis·guised′, *adj.*
non′dis·in·gen′u·ous, *adj.*; **-ly,** *adv.*; **-ness,** *n.*
non′dis·in′te·grat′ing, *adj.*
non′dis·in′te·gra′tion, *n.*
non′dis·in′ter·est·ed, *adj.*
non′dis·junc′tive, *adj.*; **-ly,** *adv.*
non′dis·mem′ber·ment, *n.*
non′dis·mis′sal, *n.*
non′dis·par′ag·ing, *adj.*
non·dis′pa·rate, *adj.*; **-ly,** *adv.*; **-ness,** *n.*
non′dis·par′i·ty, *n., pl.* **-ties.**
non′dis·pens′a·ble, *adj.*
non′dis·pen·sa′tion, *n.*
non′dis·pen·sa′tion·al, *adj.*
non′dis·pens′i·ble, *adj.*
non′dis·per′sal, *n.*
non′dis·per′sion, *n.*
non′dis·per′sive, *adj.*
non′dis·pos′a·ble, *adj.*
non′dis·pos′al, *n.*
non′dis·posed′, *adj.*
non′dis·pu·ta′tious, *adj.*; **-ly,** *adv.*; **-ness,** *n.*
non′dis·qual′i·fy′ing, *adj.*
non′dis·rupt′ing, *adj.*; **-ly,** *adv.*
non′dis·rup′tive, *adj.*
non′dis·sem′i·na′tion, *n.*
non′dis·sent′ing, *adj., n.*
non·dis′si·dence, *n.*
non·dis′si·dent, *adj., n.*
non·dis′si·pat′ed, *adj.*; **-ly,** *adv.*; **-ness,** *n.*
non·dis′si·pa′tive, *adj.*
non′dis·so·lu′tion, *n.*
non′dis·solv′ing, *adj.*
non′dis·till′a·ble, *adj.*
non′dis·til·la′tion, *n.*
non′dis·tin′guish·a·ble, *adj.*; **-ble·ness,** *n.*; **-bly,** *adv.*
non′dis·tin′guished, *adj.*
non′dis·tin′guish·ing, *adj.*
non′dis·tort′ed, *adj.*; **-ly,** *adv.*; **-ness,** *n.*
non′dis·tort′ing, *adj.*; **-ly,** *adv.*
non′dis·tor′tion, *n.*
non′dis·tor′tive, *adj.*
non′dis·tract′ed, *adj.*; **-ly,** *adv.*
non′dis·tract′ing, *adj.*; **-ly,** *adv.*
non′dis·trac′tive, *adj.*
non′dis·tri·bu′tion, *n.*
non′dis·tri·bu′tion·al, *adj.*
non′dis·trib′u·tive, *adj.*; **-ly,** *adv.*; **-ness,** *n.*
non′dis·turb′ance, *n.*
non′dis·turb′ing, *adj.*
non′di·ver′gence, *n.*
non′di·ver′gen·cy, *n., pl.* **-cies.**
non′di·ver′gent, *adj.*; **-ly,** *adv.*
non′di·verg′ing, *adj.*
non′di·ver′si·fi·ca′tion, *n.*
non′di·ver′si·fied′, *adj.*
non′di·vin′i·ty, *n., pl.* **-ties.**
non′di·vis′i·bil′i·ty, *n.*
non′di·vis′i·ble, *adj.*
non′di·vi′sion, *n.*
non′di·vi′sion·al, *adj.*
non′di·vi′sive, *adj.*; **-ly,** *adv.*; **-ness,** *n.*
non′di·vorce′, *n.*
non′di·vorced′, *adj.*
non′di·vul′gence, *n.*
non′di·vulg′ing, *adj.*
non′doc·tri·naire′, *adj.*
non·doc′tri·nal, *adj.*; **-ly,** *adv.*
non′doc·u·men′tal, *adj.*
non′doc·u·men′ta·ry, *adj., n., pl.* **-ries.**
non·doc′u·ment′ed, *adj., n.*
non′dog·mat′ic, *adj.*
non′dog·mat′i·cal, *adj.*; **-ly,** *adv.*
non′do·mes′tic, *adj., n.*
non′do·mes′ti·cal·ly, *adv.*
non′do·mes′ti·cat′ed, *adj.*
non′do·mes′ti·cat′ing, *adj.*
non·dom′i·nance, *n.*
non·dom′i·nant, *adj., n.*
non·dom′i·nat′ing, *adj.*
non′dom·i·na′tion, *n.*
non′dom·i·neer′ing, *adj.*
non·dor′mant, *adj.*
non·doubt′a·ble, *adj.*
non·doubt′er, *n.*
non·doubt′ing, *adj.*; **-ly,** *adv.*
non′dra·mat′ic, *adj.*
non′dra·mat′i·cal·ly, *adv.*
non·drink′a·ble, *adj.*
non·drip′, *adj.*
non·driv′a·ble, *adj.*
non·drive′a·ble, *adj.*
non·driv′er, *n.*
non·drop′si·cal, *adj.*
non·drop′si·cal·ly, *adv.*
non-Dru′id, *n.*
non′dru·id′ic, *adj.*
non′dru·id′i·cal, *adj.*
non·dry′ing, *adj., n.*
non·du′al·ism, *n.*
non′du·al·is′tic, *adj.*
non′du·al·is′ti·cal·ly, *adv.*
non′du·al′i·ty, *n.*
non·duc′tile, *adj.*
non′duc·til′i·ty, *n.*
non·du′pli·cat′ing, *adj.*
non′du·pli·ca′tion, *n.*
non·du′pli·ca′tive, *adj.*
non′du·plic′i·ty, *n.*
non·du′ti·a·ble, *adj.*
non′dy·nam′ic, *adj.*
non′dy·nam′i·cal, *adj.*; **-ly,** *adv.*
non′dy·nas′tic, *adj.*
non′dy·nas′ti·cal, *adj.*; **-ly,** *adv.*
non′dys·pep′tic, *adj.*
non′dys·pep′ti·cal, *adj.*; **-ly,** *adv.*
non·ea′ger, *adj.*; **-ly,** *adv.*; **-ness,** *n.*
non·earn′ing, *adj., n.*
non·east′ern, *adj.*
non·eat′a·ble, *adj.*
non′e·bul′lience, *n.*
non′e·bul′lien·cy, *n.*
non′e·bul′lient, *adj.*; **-ly,** *adv.*
non′ec·cen′tric, *adj.*
non′ec·cen′tri·cal·ly, *adv.*
non′ec·cle′si·as′tic, *adj., n.*
non′ec·cle′si·as′ti·cal, *adj.*; **-ly,** *adv.*
non′e·cho′ic, *adj.*
non′ec·lec′tic, *adj., n.*
non′ec·lec′ti·cal·ly, *adv.*
non′e·clipsed′, *adj.*
non′e·clips′ing, *adj.*
non′e·clip′tic, *adj.*
non′e·clip′ti·cal, *adj.*; **-ly,** *adv.*
non′e·co·nom′ic, *adj.*
non′e·co·nom′i·cal, *adj.*; **-ly,** *adv.*
non′e·con′o·my, *n., pl.* **-mies.**
non′ec·stat′ic, *adj.*
non′ec·stat′i·cal·ly, *adv.*
non′ec·u·men′ic, *adj.*
non′ec·u·men′i·cal, *adj.*
non·ed′i·bil′i·ty, *n.*
non·ed′i·ble, *adj., n.*; **-ness,** *n.*
non·ed′i·fied′, *adj.*
non′ed·i·to′ri·al, *adj.*; **-ly,** *adv.*
non·ed′u·ca·ble, *adj.*
non·ed′u·cat′ed, *adj.*
non′ed·u·ca′tion, *n.*
non′ed·u·ca′tion·al, *adj.*; **-ly,** *adv.*
non·ed′u·ca′tive, *adj.*
non·ed′u·ca·to′ry, *adj.*
non′ef·fer·ves′cent, *adj.*; **-ly,** *adv.*
non′ef·fete′, *adj.*; **-ly,** *adv.*; **-ness,** *n.*
non′ef·fi·ca′cious, *adj.*; **-ly,** *adv.*
non·ef′fi·ca·cy, *n.*
non′ef·fi′cien·cy, *n.*
non′ef·fi′cient, *adj.*; **-ly,** *adv.*
non′ef·fu′sion, *n.*
non′ef·fu′sive, *adj.*; **-ly,** *adv.*; **-ness,** *n.*
non′e·go·cen′tric, *adj.*
non′e·go·is′tic, *adj.*
non′e·go·is′ti·cal, *adj.*; **-ly,** *adv.*
non′e·go·tis′tic, *adj.*
non′e·go·tis′ti·cal, *adj.*; **-ly,** *adv.*
non′e·gre′gious, *adj.*; **-ly,** *adv.*; **-ness,** *n.*
non′-E·gyp′tian, *adj., n.*
non′ei·det′ic, *adj.*
non′e·jac′u·la·to′ry, *adj.*
non′e·ject′ing, *adj.*
non′e·jec′tion, *n.*
non′e·jec′tive, *adj.*
non′e·lab′o·rate, *adj.*; **-ly,** *adv.*; **-ness,** *n.*
non′e·lab′o·rat′ing, *adj.*
non′e·lab′o·ra′tive, *adj.*
non′e·las′tic, *adj.*

6. *Archaic.* not any; no (usually only before a vowel or *h*): *Thou shalt have none other gods but me.* [bef. 900; ME *non,* OE *nān,* equiv. to *ne* not + *ān* ONE]
—Usage. Since NONE has the meanings "not one" and "not any," some insist that it always be treated as a singular and be followed by a singular verb: *The rescue party searched for survivors, but none was found.* However, NONE has been used with both singular and plural verbs since the 9th century. When the sense is "not any persons or things" (as in the example above), the plural is more common: . . . *none were found.* Only when NONE is clearly intended to mean "not one" or "not any" is it followed by a singular verb: *Of all my articles, none has received more acclaim than my latest one.*

none[2] (nōn), *n.* nones[1]. [1175–1225; ME; OE *nōn* < L *nōna* (*hōra*) ninth (hour). See NOON]

non•ef•fec•tive (non′i fek′tiv), *adj.* **1.** not effective. **2.** not fit for duty or active service, as a soldier or sailor. —*n.* **3.** a noneffective person. [1750–60; NON- + EFFECTIVE]

non•emp•ty (non emp′tē), *adj. Math.* (of a set, group, collection, etc.) containing at least one element. [1935–40; NON- + EMPTY]

non•en•ti•ty (non en′ti tē), *n., pl.* **-ties. 1.** a person or thing of no importance. **2.** something that does not exist or exists only in imagination. **3.** nonexistence. [1590–1600; NON- + ENTITY]
—Syn. 1. nobody, cipher, mediocrity, zero, nullity.

nones[1] (nōnz), *n. Eccles.* the fifth of the seven canonical hours, or the service for it, originally fixed for the ninth hour of the day (or 3 P.M.). [1375–1425; late ME; pl. of NONE[2]]

nones[2] (nōnz), *n.* (*used with a singular or plural v.*) (in the ancient Roman calendar) the ninth day before the ides, both days included: the seventh of March, May, July, and October, and the fifth of the other months. [1375–1425; late ME; Anglicization of L *nōnae,* orig. fem. pl. of *nōnus* ninth]

none-so-pret•ty (nun′sō prit′ē, -prit′ē), *n., pl.* **-ties.** See **sweet william catchfly.** [1690–1700]

non•es•sen•tial (non′ə sen′shəl), *adj.* **1.** not essential; not necessary: *Nonessential use of gasoline was forbidden during the war.* —*n.* **2.** a nonessential thing or person. [1745–55; NON- + ESSENTIAL]
—Syn. 1. unnecessary, incidental, extrinsic.

non est (non′ est′), *Law.* the returning of a sheriff's writ when the person to be arrested or served with it cannot be found in the sheriff's jurisdiction. [1865–70; < L: short for *non est inventus* (he) was not found]

none•such (nun′such′), *n.* a person or thing without equal; paragon. Also, **nonsuch.** [1550–60; NONE[1] + SUCH]
—Syn. 1. ideal, model, pattern, nonpareil.

no•net (nō net′), *n. Music.* **1.** a group of nine performers or instruments. **2.** a composition for a nonet. [1860–65; < It *nonetto,* deriv. of *nono* ninth < L *nōnus.* See -ET]

none•the•less (nun′thə les′), *adv.* however; nevertheless. [1840–50; from the phrase *none the less*]

non•eth•nic (non eth′nik), *adj.* not of or associated with any particular ethnic background or group: *some of the best nonethnic cooking in town.* Also, **non•eth′ni•cal.** [NON- + ETHNIC] **—non•eth′ni•cal•ly,** *adv.*

non-Eu•clid•e•an (non′yōō klid′ē ən), *adj.* differing from the postulates of Euclid or based upon postulates other than those of Euclid. [1870–75]

non′-Euclid′ean geom′etry, geometry based upon one or more postulates that differ from those of Euclid, esp. from the postulate that only one line may be drawn through a given point parallel to a given line. [1870–75; NON- + EUCLIDEAN]

non•e•vent (non′i vent′), *n.* **1.** an event or situation that is anticipated but does not occur or occurs with much less than the expected impact, esp. one that has been widely publicized; anticlimax. **2.** an occurrence of only superficial interest or content; a dull or insignificant occasion. [1960–65; NON- + EVENT]

non•ex•ist•ence (non′ig zis′təns), *n.* **1.** absence of existence. **2.** a thing that has no existence. [1640–50; NON- + EXISTENCE] **—non′ex•ist′ent,** *adj.*

non•ex•por•ta•tion (non′ek spôr tā′shən, -spōr-), *n.* failure or refusal to export. [1765–75, *Amer.*; NON- + EXPORTATION]

non•fat (non′fat′), *adj.* without fat or fat solids; having the fat solids removed, as skim milk: *nonfat milk.* [1965–70; NON- + FAT]

non•fea•sance (non fē′zəns), *n. Law.* the omission of some act that ought to have been performed. Cf. **malfea-**

CONCISE PRONUNCIATION KEY: *act, cāpe, dâre, pärt; set, ēqual; if, īce; ox, ōver, ôrder, oil, bŏŏk, bōōt, out; up, ûrge; child; sing; shoe; thin, that;* zh as in *treasure.* ə = *a* as in *alone, e* as in *system, i* as in *easily, o* as in *gallop, u* as in *circus;* ᵊ as in *fire* (fīᵊr), *hour* (ouᵊr). l and n can serve as syllabic consonants, as in *cradle* (krād′l), and *button* (but′n). See the full key inside the front cover.

non′e•las′ti•cal•ly, *adv.*
non′e•las•tic′i•ty, *n.*
non•eld′er•ly, *n.*
non′e•lect′, *n.*
non′e•lec′tion, *n.*
non′e•lec′tive, *adj., n.;* **-ly,** *adv.;* **-ness,** *n.*
non′e•lec′tor, *n.*
non′e•lec′tric, *adj., n.*
non′e•lec′tri•cal, *adj.;* **-ly,** *adv.*
non′e•lec′tri•fi•ca′tion, *n.*
non′e•lec′tri•fied′, *adj.*
non′e•lec′trized, *adj.*
non′e•lec′tro•lyte′, *n.*
non′e•lec′tro•lyt′ic, *adj.*
non′e•lec•tron′ic, *adj., n.*
non′el•ee•mos′y•nar′y, *adj.*
non′el•e•men′tal, *adj.;* **-ly,** *adv.*
non′el•e•men′ta•ry, *adj.*
non•el′e•vat′ing, *adj.*
non′el•e•va′tion, *n.*
non′e•lic′it•ed, *adj.*
non′el•i•gi•bil′i•ty, *n.*
non•el′i•gi•ble, *adj.;* **-bly,** *adv.*
non′e•lim′i•na′tion, *n.*
non′e•lim′i•na′tive, *adj.*
non′e•lim′i•na•to′ry, *adj.*
non′e•lite′, *n.*
non′e•lit′ist, *adj., n.*
non′el•lip′tic, *adj.*
non′el•lip′ti•cal, *adj.;* **-ly,** *adv.*
non′e•lon•ga′tion, *n.*
non′e•lope′ment, *n.*
non•el′o•quence, *n.*
non•el′o•quent, *adj.;* **-ly,** *adv.*
non′e•lu′ci•dat′ing, *adj.*
non′e•lu′ci•da′tion, *n.*
non′e•lu′ci•da′tive, *adj.*
non′e•lu′sive, *adj.;* **-ly,** *adv.;* **-ness,** *n.*
non•em′a•nant, *adj.*
non•em′a•nat′ing, *adj.*
non′e•man′ci•pa′tion, *n.*
non′e•man′ci•pa′tive, *adj.*
non′em•bar•ka′tion, *n.*
non′em•bel′lished, *adj.*
non′em•bel′lish•ing, *adj.*
non′em•bel′lish•ment, *n.*
non′em•bez′zle•ment, *n.*
non′em•bry•o′nal, *adj.*
non′em•bry•on′ic, *adj.*
non′em•bry•on′i•cal•ly, *adv.*
non′e•mend′a•ble, *adj.*
non′e•men•da′tion, *n.*
non′e•mer′gence, *n.*
non′e•mer′gen•cy, *adj., n., pl.* **-cies.**
non′e•mer′gent, *adj.*
non•em′i•grant, *n., adj.*
non′em•i•gra′tion, *n.*
non•em′i•nent, *adj.*
non′e•mis′sion, *n.*
non′e•mo′tion•al, *adj.;* **-ly,** *adv.*
non′e•mo′tion•al•ism, *n.*
non′e•mo′tive, *adj.;* **-ly,** *adv.;* **-ness,** *n.*
non′em•path′ic, *adj.*
non′em•path′i•cal•ly, *adv.*
non′em•pir′ic, *n., adj.*
non′em•pir′i•cal, *adj.;* **-ly,** *adv.*
non′em•pir′i•cism, *n.*
non′em•ploy′ing, *adj.*
non′em•ploy′ment, *n.*
non•em•u•la′tion, *n.*
non•em′u•la′tive, *adj.*
non•em′u•lous, *adj.;* **-ly,** *adv.;* **-ness,** *n.*
non′en•act′ment, *n.*
non′en•clo′sure, *n.*
non′en•croach′ment, *n.*
non′en•cy′clo•pae′dic, *adj.*
non′en•cy′clo•pe′dic, *adj.*
non′en•cy′clo•pe′di•cal, *adj.*
non′en•dem′ic, *adj.*
non′en•dorse′ment, *n.*
non′en•dow′ment, *n.*
non′en•dur′a•ble, *adj.*
non′en•dur′ing, *adj.*
non•en′e•my, *n., pl.* **-mies.**
non′en•er•get′ic, *adj.*
non′en•er•get′i•cal•ly, *adv.*
non•en′er•vat′ing, *adj.*
non′en•force′a•ble, *adj.*
non′en•forced′, *adj.*
non′en•for′ced•ly, *adv.*
non′en•force′ment, *n.*
non′en•forc′ing, *adj.*
non′en•gage′ment, *n.*
non•en′gi•neer′ing, *n., adj.*
non-Eng′lish, *adj., n.*
non′en•gross′ing, *adj.;* **-ly,** *adv.*
non′en•ig•mat′ic, *adj.*
non′en•ig•mat′i•cal, *adj.;* **-ly,** *adv.*
non′en•light′ened, *adj.*
non′en•light′en•ing, *adj.*
non′en•rolled′, *adj.*
non′en•tailed′, *adj.*
non′en•ter′ic, *adj.*
non•en′ter•pris′ing, *adj.*
non•en′ter•tain′ing, *adj.*
non•en′ter•tain′ment, *n., adj.*
non′en•thu′si•as′tic, *adj.*
non′en•thu′si•as′ti•cal•ly, *adv.*
non′en•tic′ing, *adj.;* **-ly,** *adv.*
non′en•to•mo•log′ic, *adj.*
non′en•to•mo•log′i•cal, *adj.*
non•en′trant, *n.*
non′en•treat′ing, *adj.;* **-ly,** *adv.*
non′en•tre•pre•neur′i•al, *adj.*
non•en′try, *n., pl.* **-tries.**
non′e•nu′mer•at′ed, *adj.*
non′e•nu′mer•a′tive, *adj.*
non′e•nun′ci•a′tion, *n.*
non′e•nun′ci•a′tive, *adj.*
non′e•nun′ci•a•to′ry, *adj.*
non•en′vi•a•ble, *adj.;* **-ble•ness,** *n.;* **-bly,** *adv.*
non•en′vi•ous, *adj.;* **-ly,** *adv.;* **-ness,** *n.*
non′en•vi′ron•men′tal, *adj.;* **-ly,** *adv.*
non′e•phem′er•al, *adj.;* **-ly,** *adv.*
non•ep′ic, *adj., n.*
non•ep′i•cal, *adj.;* **-ly,** *adv.*
non′ep•i•cu•re′an, *adj., n.*
non′ep•i•gram•mat′ic, *adj.*
non′ep•i•gram•mat′i•cal•ly, *adv.*
non′ep•i•lep′tic, *adj., n.*
non′e•pis′co•pal, *adj.;* **-ly,** *adv.*
non′e•pis′co•pa′lian, *adj.*
non′-E•pis′co•pa′lian, *n.*
non′ep•i•sod′ic, *adj.*
non′ep•i•sod′i•cal, *adj.;* **-ly,** *adv.*
non′ep•i•the′li•al, *adj.*
non•ep′och•al, *adj.*
non′eq•ua•bil′i•ty, *n.*
non•eq′ua•ble, *adj.;* **-ble•ness,** *n.;* **-bly,** *adv.*
non•e′qual, *adj., n.*
non′e•qual•i•za′tion, *n.*
non•e′qual•ized′, *adj.*
non•e′qual•iz′ing, *adj.*
non′e•qua′tion, *n.*
non′e•qua•to′ri•al, *adj.;* **-ly,** *adv.*
non′e•ques′tri•an, *adj., n.*
non′e•qui•lat′er•al, *adj.;* **-ly,** *adv.*
non′e•qui•lib′ri•um, *n.*
non•eq′ui•ta•ble, *adj.;* **-bly,** *adv.*
non′e•quiv′a•lence, *n.*
non′e•quiv′a•len•cy, *n.*
non′e•quiv′a•lent, *adj., n.;* **-ly,** *adv.*
non′e•quiv′o•cal, *adj.;* **-ly,** *adv.*
non′e•quiv′o•cat′ing, *adj.*
non′e•rad′i•ca•ble, *adj.*
non′e•rad′i•ca′tive, *adj.*
non′e•ras′a•ble, *adj.*
non′e•ra′sure, *n.*
non′e•rect′ing, *adj.*
non′e•rec′tion, *n.*
non′e•rod′ed, *adj.*
non′e•rod′ent, *adj.*
non′e•rod′ing, *adj.*
non′e•ro′sive, *adj.*
non′e•rot′ic, *adj.*
non′e•rot′i•cal•ly, *adv.*
non•er′rant, *adj.;* **-ly,** *adv.*
non′er•rat′ic, *adj., n.*
non′er•rat′i•cal•ly, *adv.*
non′er•ro′ne•ous, *adj.;* **-ly,** *adv.,* **-ness,** *n.*
non•er′u•dite′, *adj.;* **-ly,** *adv.;* **-ness,** *n.*
non′er•u•di′tion, *n.*
non′e•rup′tion, *n.*
non′e•rup′tive, *adj.*
non•es′ca•lat′ing, *adj.*
non•es′ca•la•to′ry, *adj.*
non′es•o•ter′ic, *adj.*
non′es•o•ter′i•cal•ly, *adv.*
non•es′pi•o•nage′, *n.*
non′es•pous′al, *n.*
non′es•tab′lish•ment, *n., adj.*
non′es•thet′ic, *adj.*
non′es•thet′i•cal, *adj.;* **-ly,** *adv.*
non•es′ti•ma•ble, *adj.;* **-ble•ness,** *n.;* **-bly,** *adv.*
non′e•su′ri•ent, *adj.;* **-ly,** *adv.*
non′e•ter′nal, *adj.;* **-ly,** *adv.;* **-ness,** *n.*
non′e•ter′ni•ty, *n.*
non′e•the′re•al, *adj.;* **-ly,** *adv.;* **-ness,** *n.*
non′e•the′re•al′i•ty, *n.*
non•eth′ic, *adj.*
non•eth′i•cal, *adj.;* **-ly,** *adv.;* **-ness,** *n.*
non′eth•no•log′ic, *adj.*
non′eth•no•log′i•cal, *adj.;* **-ly,** *adv.*
non•eth′yl, *n.*
non′eu•gen′ic, *adj.*
non′eu•gen′i•cal, *adj.;* **-ly,** *adv.*
non′eu•pho′ni•ous, *adj.;* **-ly,** *adv.;* **-ness,** *n.*
non′-Eu•ro•pe′an, *adj., n.*
non′e•vac′u•a′tion, *n.*
non′e•vad′a•ble, *adj.*
non′e•vad′i•ble, *adj.*
non′e•vad′ing, *adj.;* **-ly,** *adv.*
non′e•val′u•a′tion, *n.*
non′e•val′u•a′tive, *adj.*
non′ev•a•nes′cent, *adj.;* **-ly,** *adv.*
non′e•van•gel′ic, *adj.*
non′e•van•gel′i•cal, *adj.;* **-ly,** *adv.*
non′e•vap′o•ra•ble, *adj.*
non′e•vap′o•rat′ing, *adj.*
non′e•vap′o•ra′tion, *n.*
non′e•vap′o•ra′tive, *adj.*
non′e•va′sion, *n.*
non′e•va′sive, *adj.;* **-ly,** *adv.;* **-ness,** *n.*
non′e•vic′tion, *n.*
non•ev′i•dent, *adj.*
non′ev•i•den′tial, *adj.*
non′ev•i•den′tia•ry, *adj.*
non•e′vil, *adj.;* **-ly,** *adv.;* **-ness,** *n.*
non′e•vin′ci•ble, *adj.*
non′e•vin′cive, *adj.*
non′e•voc′a•tive, *adj.*
non′ev•o•lu′tion•al, *adj.;* **-ly,** *adv.*
non′ev•o•lu′tion•ar′y, *adj.*
non′ev•o•lu′tion•ist, *n.*
non′e•volv′ing, *adj.*
non′ex•act′a•ble, *adj.*
non′ex•act′ing, *adj.;* **-ly,** *adv.;* **-ness,** *n.*
non′ex•ac′tion, *n.*
non′ex•ag′ger•at′ed, *adj.;* **-ly,** *adv.*
non′ex•ag′ger•at′ing, *adj.*
non′ex•ag′ger•a′tion, *n.*
non′ex•ag′ger•a′tive, *adj.*
non′ex•ag′ger•a•to′ry, *adj.*
non′ex•ca•va′tion, *n.*
non′ex•cept′ed, *adj.*
non′ex•cept′ing, *adj.*
non′ex•cep′tion•al, *adj.;* **-ly,** *adv.*
non′ex•ces′sive, *adj.;* **-ly,** *adv.;* **-ness,** *n.*
non′ex•change′a•bil′i•ty, *n.*
non′ex•change′a•ble, *adj.*
non′ex•cit′a•ble, *adj.;* **-ble•ness,** *n.;* **-bly,** *adv.*
non′ex•cit′a•tive, *adj.*
non′ex•cit′a•to′ry, *adj.*
non′ex•cit′ing, *adj.*
non′ex•clam′a•to′ry, *adj.*
non′ex•clu′sion, *n.*
non′ex•clu′sive, *adj.*
non′ex•cul′pa•ble, *adv.*
non′ex•cul•pa′tion, *n.*
non′ex•cul′pa•to′ry, *adj.*
non′ex•cus′a•ble, *adj.;* **-ble•ness,** *n.;* **-bly,** *adv.*
non•ex′e•cut′a•ble, *adj.*
non′ex•e•cu′tion, *n.*
non′ex•ec′u•tive, *adj., n.*
non′ex•em′pla•ry, *adj.*
non′ex•em′pli•fi•ca′tion, *n.*
non′ex•empt′, *adj., n.*
non′ex•emp′tion, *n.*
non•ex′er•cis′a•ble, *adj.*
non•ex′er•cise′, *n.*
non•ex′er•cis′er, *n.*
non′ex•er′tion, *n.*
non′ex•er′tive, *adj.*
non′ex•haust′ed, *adj.*
non′ex•haust′i•ble, *adj.*
non′ex•haus′tive, *adj.;* **-ly,** *adv.;* **-ness,** *n.*
non′ex•hi•bi′tion, *n.*
non′ex•hi•bi′tion•ism, *n.*
non′ex•hi•bi′tion•is′tic, *adj.*
non′ex•hib′i•tive, *adj.*
non′ex•hor•ta′tion, *n.*
non′ex•hor′ta•tive, *adj.*
non′ex•hor′ta•to′ry, *adj.*
non•ex′i•gent, *adj.;* **-ly,** *adv.*
non′ex•is•ten′tial, *adj.;* **-ly,** *adv.*
non′ex•is•ten′tial•ism, *n.*
non′ex•ist′ing, *adj.*
non′ex•ot′ic, *adj.*
non′ex•ot′i•cal•ly, *adv.*
non′ex•pand′ed, *adj.*
non′ex•pand′ing, *adj.*
non′ex•pan′si•bil′i•ty, *n.*
non′ex•pan′si•ble, *adj.*
non′ex•pan′sile, *adj.*
non′ex•pan′sion, *n.*
non′ex•pan′sive, *adj.;* **-ly,** *adv.;* **-ness,** *n.*
non′ex•pect′ant, *adj.;* **-ly,** *adv.*
non′ex•pe′di•ence, *n.*
non′ex•pe′di•en•cy, *n.*
non′ex•pe′di•ent, *adj.;* **-ly,** *adv.*
non′ex•pe′di•en′tial, *adj.*
non′ex•pe•di′tious, *adj.;* **-ly,** *adv.;* **-ness,** *n.*
non′ex•pend′a•ble, *adj.*
non′ex•pe′ri•enced, *adj.*
non′ex•pe′ri•en′tial, *adj.;* **-ly,** *adv.*
non′ex•per′i•men′tal, *adj.;* **-ly,** *adv.*
non•ex′pert, *n., adj.*
non′ex′pi•a•ble, *adj.*
non′ex•pi•a′tion, *n.*
non•ex′pi•a•to′ry, *adj.*
non′ex•pi•ra′tion, *n.*
non′ex•pir′ing, *adj.*
non′ex•pi′ry, *n., pl.* **-ries.**
non′ex•plain′a•ble, *adj.*
non′ex•plan′a•tive, *adj.*
non′ex•plan′a•to′ry, *adj.*
non•ex′pli•ca•ble, *adj.*
non•ex′pli•ca′tive, *adj.*
non′ex•ploit′a•ble, *adj.*
non′ex•ploi•ta′tion, *n.*
non′ex•ploit′a•tive, *adj.*
non′ex•ploi′tive, *adj.*
non′ex•plor′a•tive, *adj.*
non′ex•plor′a•to′ry, *adj.*
non′ex•plo′si•bil′i•ty, *n.*
non′ex•plo′sive, *adj., n.;* **-ly,** *adv.;* **-ness,** *n.*
non′ex•po•nen′tial, *adj.;* **-ly,** *adv.*
non′ex•po′ni•ble, *adj.*
non′ex•port′a•ble, *adj.*
non′ex•po′sure, *n.*
non′ex•pres′sion•is′tic, *adj.*
non′ex•pres′sive, *adj.;* **-ly,** *adv.;* **-ness,** *n.*
non′ex•pul′sion, *n.*
non′ex•pul′sive, *adj.*
non•ex′tant, *adj.*
non′ex•tem′po•re, *adv., adj.*
non′ex•tend′ed, *adj.*
non′ex•tend′i•ble, *adj.;* **-ble•ness,** *n.*
non′ex•ten′si•bil′i•ty, *n.*
non′ex•ten′si•ble, *adj.;* **-ness,** *n.*
non′ex•ten′sile, *adj.*
non′ex•ten′sion, *n.*
non′ex•ten′sion•al, *adj.*
non′ex•ten′sive, *adj.;* **-ly,** *adv.;* **-ness,** *n.*
non′ex•ten′u•at′ing, *adj.;* **-ly,** *adv.*
non′ex•ten′u•a′tive, *adj.*
non′ex•ter′mi•na′tion, *n.*
non′ex•ter′mi•na′tive, *adj.*
non′ex•ter′mi•na•to′ry, *adj.*
non′ex•ter′nal, *adj., n.;* **-ly,** *adv.*
non′ex•ter•nal′i•ty, *n.*
non′ex•ter′nal•ized′, *adj.*
non′ex•tinct′, *adj.*
non′ex•tinc′tion, *n.*
non′ex•tin′guish•a•ble, *adj.*
non′ex•tin′guished, *adj.*
non′ex•tor′tion, *n.*
non′ex•tor′tive, *adj.*
non′ex•tract′a•ble, *adj.*
non′ex•tract′ed, *adj.*
non′ex•tract′i•ble, *adj.*
non′ex•trac′tion, *n.*
non′ex•trac′tive, *adj.*

sance, misfeasance (def. 2). [1590–1600; NON- + obs. *feasance;* see MALFEASANCE]

non·fer·rous (non fer′əs), *adj.* **1.** (of a metal) containing little or no iron. **2.** noting or pertaining to metals other than iron or steel. [1885–90; NON- + FERROUS]

non·fic·tion (non fik′shən), *n.* **1.** the branch of literature comprising works of narrative prose dealing with or offering opinions or conjectures upon facts and reality, including biography, history, and the essay (opposed to *fiction* and distinguished from *poetry* and *drama*). **2.** works of this class: *She had read all of his novels but none of his nonfiction.* **3.** (esp. in cataloging books, as in a library or bookstore) all writing or books not fiction, poetry, or drama, including nonfictive narrative prose and reference works; the broadest category of written works. [1905–10; NON- + FICTION] **—non·fic′tion·al,** *adj.* **—non·fic′tion·al·ly,** *adv.*

non·fi′nite clause′ (non fī′nīt), a clause with a nonfinite verb or with no verb, as *the hour being late* in *The hour being late, we left.* [1970–75]

nonfi′nite verb′, a verb form that does not indicate person or number; in English, the infinitive and participles. [1970–75]

non·flam·ma·ble (non flam′ə bəl), *adj.* not flammable; not combustible or easily set on fire. [1960–65; NON- + FLAMMABLE]

CONCISE ETYMOLOGY KEY: <, descended or borrowed from; >, whence; b., blend of, blended; c., cognate with; cf., compare; deriv., derivative; equiv., equivalent; imit., imitative; obl., oblique; r., replacing; s., stem; sp., spelling, spelled; resp., respelling, respelled; trans., translation; ?, origin unknown; *, unattested; ‡, probably earlier than. See the full key inside the front cover.

non·for′fei·ture val′ue (non fôr′fi chər), *Insurance.* any benefit, as cash or other form of insurance, available to a life-insurance policyholder who discontinues premium payments on the policy. Also called **nonfor′·feiture ben′efit.** [NON- + FORFEITURE]

non·freez·ing (non frē′zing), *adj.* not given or subject to freezing. [NON- + FREEZING]

non·ful·fill·ment (non′fo͝ol fil′mənt), *n.* **1.** neglect or failure to fulfill or carry out as required. **2.** lack of fulfillment. [1795–1805; NON- + FULFILLMENT]

nong (nong), *n. Australian and New Zealand Informal.* a foolish, incompetent person. [1940–45; prob. by shortening of Australian and earlier Brit. slang *ning-nong, ning-nang* fool, perh. expressive vars. of earlier *nigmenog* fool, of obscure orig.]

non·gon·o·coc′cal urethri′tis (non gon′ə kok′əl), *Pathol.* a widespread sexually transmitted infection of the urethra, caused by the parasite *Chlamydia trachomatis,* or the mycoplasm *Ureaplasma urealyticum,* characterized in males by painful urination and discharge from the penis and in females by frequent, painful urination and cervical erosion. *Abbr.:* NGU Also called **nonspecific urethritis.** Cf. **chlamydia.** [NON- + GONOCOCCAL]

non·grad·ed (non grā′did), *adj.* **1.** without grade levels: *a nongraded school.* **2.** without rating grades. [1965–70; NON- + GRADED]

non·gram·mat·i·cal (non′grə mat′i kəl), *adj.* (of a sentence or expression) not conforming to the grammatical rules of a given language. [1950–55; NON- + GRAMMATICAL]

non gra·ta (non grä′tə, grā′-; *Lat.* nōn grä′tä), not welcome: *Reporters were non grata at the diplomatic reception.* Cf. **persona non grata.** [1925–30; abstracted from PERSONA NON GRATA]

non′har·mon′ic tone′ (non′här mon′ik, non′-), *Music.* a tone sounding with a chord of which it is not a chord tone. [NON- + HARMONIC]

non·he·ro (non hēr′ō), *n., pl.* **-roes.** antihero. [1935–40; NON- + HERO]

non·hu·man (non hyo͞o′mən *or, often,* -yo͞o′-), *adj.* **1.** not human. **2.** not displaying the emotions, sympathies, intelligence, etc., of most human beings. **3.** not intended for consumption by humans: *nonhuman products such as soaps and detergents.* [NON- + HUMAN] **—non·hu′·man·ness,** *n.*

non·i·de·al (non′ī dē′əl, -dēl′), *adj. Physics.* (of a gas or solution) differing in behavior from that of an ideal gas or solution. [NON- + IDEAL]

no·nil·lion (nō nil′yən), *n., pl.* **-lions,** (*as after a numeral*) **-lion,** *adj.* **—***n.* **1.** a cardinal number represented in the U.S. by 1 followed by 30 zeros, and in Great Britain by 1 followed by 54 zeros. **—***adj.* **2.** amounting to one nonillion in number. [1680–90; < F, equiv. to *non-* (< L *nōnus* ninth) + *-illion,* as in *million* MILLION] **—no·nil′lionth,** *n., adj.*

non·im·por·ta·tion (non′im pôr tā′shən, -pōr-), *n.* failure or refusal to import. [1760–70, *Amer.;* NON- + IMPORTATION]

non·in·creas·ing (non′in krē′sing), *adj.* **1.** not in-

non·ex′tra·dit′a·ble, *adj.*
non′ex·tra·di′tion, *n.*
non′ex·tra′ne·ous, *adj.;* **-ly,** *adv.;* **-ness,** *n.*
non·ex′tri·ca·ble, *adj.;* **-bly,** *adv.*
non′ex·tri·ca′tion, *n.*
non′ex·trin′sic, *adj.*
non′ex·trin′si·cal, *adj.;* **-ly,** *adv.*
non′ex·tru′sive, *adj.*
non′ex·u′ber·ance, *n.*
non′ex·u′ber·an·cy, *n.*
non′ex·ud′ing, *adj.*
non′ex·ult′ant, *adj.;* **-ly,** *adv.*
non′ex·ul·ta′tion, *n.*
non′fa·ce′tious, *adj.;* **-ly,** *adv.;* **-ness,** *n.*
non′fa·cil′i·ty, *n., pl.* **-ties.**
non·fac′tious, *adj.;* **-ly,** *adv.;* **-ness,** *n.*
non′fac·ti′tious, *adj.;* **-ly,** *adv.;* **-ness,** *n.*
non·fac′tu·al, *adj.;* **-ly,** *adv.*
non·fac′ul·ta′tive, *adj.*
non·fad′dist, *n.*
non·fail′ure, *n.*
non′fal·la′cious, *adj.;* **-ly,** *adv.;* **-ness,** *n.*
non·fal′si·fi′a·ble, *adj.*
non·fal′ter·ing, *adj.;* **-ly,** *adv.*
non′fa·mil′ial, *adj.*
non′fa·mil′iar, *adj.;* **-ly,** *adv.*
non′fa·nat′ic, *n.*
non′fa·nat′i·cal, *adj.;* **-ly,** *adv.*
non·fan′ta·sy, *n., pl.* **-sies.**
non·far′ci·cal, *adj.;* **-ly,** *adv.;* **-ness,** *n.*
non′far·ci·cal′i·ty, *n.*
non·farm′, *adj.*
non′fas′cist, *n.*
non·fash′ion·a·ble, *adj.;* **-ble·ness,** *n.;* **-bly,** *adv.*
non′fas·tid′i·ous, *adj.;* **-ly,** *adv.;* **-ness,** *n.*
non·fa′tal, *adj.;* **-ly,** *adv.;* **-ness,** *n.*
non′fa·tal·is′tic, *adj.*
non′fa·tal′i·ty, *n., pl.* **-ties.**
non·fat′i·ga·ble, *adj.*
non·fault′y, *adj.*
non·fa′vor·a·ble, *adj.;* **-ble·ness,** *n.;* **-bly,** *adv.*
non·fa′vored, *adj.*
non·fa′vor·ite, *n.*
non′fe′al·ty, *n., pl.* **-ties.**
non′fea·si·bil′i·ty, *n.*
non·fea′si·ble, *adj.;* **-ble·ness,** *n.;* **-bly,** *adv.*
non·fea′tured, *adj.*
non·fe′brile, *adj.*
non·fe′cund, *adj.*
non′fe·cun′di·ty, *n.*
non·fed′, *adj.*
non·fed′er·al, *adj.*
non·fed′er·at′ed, *adj.*
non·fee′ble, *adj.;* **-ble·ness,** *n.;* **-bly,** *adv.*
non·feed′ing, *adj.*
non·feel′ing, *adj.;* **-ly,** *adv.*
non′feld·spath′ic, *adj.*
non′fe·lic′i·tous, *adj.;* **-ly,** *adv.;* **-ness,** *n.*
non′fe·lic′i·ty, *n.*
non′fe·lo′ni·ous, *adj.;* **-ly,** *adv.;* **-ness,** *n.*
non·fem′i·nist, *adj., n.*
non·fe′nes′trat·ed, *adj.*
non′fer·ment′a·bil′i·ty, *n.*
non′fer·ment′a·ble, *adj.*
non′fer·men·ta′tion, *n.*
non′fer·men′ta·tive, *adj.*
non′fer·ment′ed, *adj.*
non′fer·ment′ing, *adj.*
non′fe·ro′cious, *adj.;* **-ly,** *adv.;* **-ness,** *n.*
non′fe·roc′i·ty, *n.*
non·fer′tile, *adj.*
non′fer·til′i·ty, *n.*
non·fer′vent, *adj.;* **-ly,** *adv.;* **-ness,** *n.*
non·fer′vid, *adj.;* **-ly,** *adv.;* **-ness,** *n.*
non·fes′tive, *adj.;* **-ly,** *adv.;* **-ness,** *n.*
non·feu′dal, *adj.;* **-ly,** *adv.*
non·fe′ver·ish, *adj.;* **-ly,** *adv.;* **-ness,** *n.*
non·fe′ver·ous, *adj.;* **-ly,** *adv.*
non·fi′brous, *adj.*
non′fic·ti′tious, *adj.;* **-ly,** *adv.;* **-ness,** *n.*
non·fic′tive, *adj.;* **-ly,** *adv.*
non′fi·del′i·ty, *n.*
non′fi·du′ci·ar′y, *adj., n., pl.* **-ar·ies.**
non·fight′er, *n.*
non·fig′ur·a·tive, *adj.;* **-ly,** *adv.;* **-ness,** *n.*
non′fil·a·men′tous, *adj.*
non·fil′er, *n.*
non·fil′i·al, *adj.*
non·fil′ter, *n.*
non·fil′ter·a·ble, *adj.*
non·fim′bri·ate, *adj.*
non·fim′bri·at′ed, *adj.*
non′fi·nan′cial, *adj.;* **-ly,** *adv.*
non·find′ing, *n.*
non·fin′ish·ing, *adj., n.*
non·fi′nite, *adj., n.;* **-ly,** *adv.;* **-ness,** *n.*
non·fire′proof′, *adj.*
non·fis′cal, *adj.;* **-ly,** *adv.*
non·fish′er·man, *n., pl.* **-men.**
non·fis′sile, *adj.*
non′fis·sil′i·ty, *n.*
non·fis′sion·a·ble, *adj.*
non′fix·a′tion, *n.*
non·flag′el·late, *adj.*
non·flag′el·lat′ed, *adj.*
non′fla·gi′tious, *adj.;* **-ly,** *adv.;* **-ness,** *n.*
non·fla′grance, *n.*
non·fla′gran·cy, *n.*
non·fla′grant, *adj.;* **-ly,** *adv.*
non·flak′i·ly, *adv.;* **-ness,** *n.*
non·flak′y, *adj.*
non·flat′u·lence, *n.*
non·flat′u·len·cy, *n.*
non·flat′u·lent, *adj.;* **-ly,** *adv.*
non·flawed′, *adj.*
non-Flem′ish, *adj., n.*
non′flex·i·bil′i·ty, *n.*
non·flex′i·ble, *adj.;* **-ble·ness,** *n.;* **-bly,** *adv.*
non′flir·ta′tious, *adj.;* **-ly,** *adv.;* **-ness,** *n.*
non·float′ing, *adj.;* **-ly,** *adv.*
non′flo·rif′er·ous, *adj.*
non·flow′er·ing, *adj.*
non·fluc′tu·at′ing, *adj.*
non′fluc·tu·a′tion, *n.*
non·flu′en·cy, *n.*
non·flu′ent, *adj.;* **-ly,** *adv.;* **-ness,** *n.*
non·flu′id, *n.;* **-ly,** *adv.*
non′flu·id′ic, *adj.*
non′flu·id′i·ty, *n.*
non′fluo·res′cence, *n.*
non′fluo·res′cent, *adj.*
non·flux′, *n.*
non·fly′a·ble, *adj.*
non·fly′ing, *adj.*
non·fol′low·ing, *adj.*
non·food′, *n., adj.*
non′for·bear′ance, *n.*
non′for·bear′ing, *adj.;* **-ly,** *adv.*
non′fore·clos′ing, *adj.*
non′fore·clo′sure, *n.*
non·for′eign, *adj.;* **-ness,** *n.*
non′fo·ren′sic, *adj.*
non′fo·ren′si·cal·ly, *adv.*
non·for′est, *n.*
non·for′est·ed, *adj.*
non′for·feit′a·ble, *adj.*
non′for·feit′ing, *adj.*
non′for·giv′ing, *adj.*
non·form′, *n.*
non·for′mal, *adj.;* **-ly,** *adv.;* **-ness,** *n.*
non·for′mal·ism, *n.*
non′for·mal·is′tic, *adj.*
non′for·ma′tion, *n.*
non·form′a·tive, *adj.;* **-ly,** *adv.*
non′for·mi·da·bil′i·ty, *n.*
non·for′mi·da·ble, *adj.;* **-ble·ness,** *n.;* **-bly,** *adv.*
non·form′ing, *adj.*
non′for·mu·la′tion, *n.*
non·for′ti·fi′a·ble, *adj.*
non′for·ti·fi·ca′tion, *n.*
non·for′ti·fy′ing, *adj.*
non′for·tu′i·tous, *adj.;* **-ly,** *adv.;* **-ness,** *n.*
non′fos·sil·if′er·ous, *adj.*
non·foul′ing, *adj.*
non·frag′ile, *adj.;* **-ly,** *adv.;* **-ness,** *n.*
non′fra·gil′i·ty, *n.*
non·frag′ment·ed, *adj.*
non·fra′grant, *adj.*
non′fran·gi·bil′i·ty, *n.*
non·fran′gi·ble, *adj.*
non′fra·ter′nal, *adj.;* **-ly,** *adv.*
non′fra·ter′ni·ty, *n., pl.* **-ties.**
non·fraud′u·lence, *n.*
non·fraud′u·len·cy, *n.*
non·fraud′u·lent, *adj.;* **-ly,** *adv.*
non·free′dom, *n.*
non·free′man, *n., pl.* **-men.**
non·freez′a·ble, *adj.*
non-French′, *adj., n.*
non′fre·net′ic, *adj.*
non′fre·net′i·cal·ly, *adv.*
non·fre′quence, *n.*
non·fre′quen·cy, *n.*
non·fre′quent, *adj.;* **-ly,** *adv.*
non·fric′a·tive, *adj., n.*
non·fric′tion, *n.*
non·friend′, *n.*
non·fright′en·ing, *adj.;* **-ly,** *adv.*
non·frig′id, *adj.;* **-ly,** *adv.;* **-ness,** *n.*
non′fri·gid′i·ty, *n.*
non·frost′ed, *adj.*
non·frost′ing, *adj.*
non·fru′gal, *adj.;* **-ly,** *adv.;* **-ness,** *n.*
non′fru·gal′i·ty, *n.*
non′fru·i′tion, *n.*
non′frus·tra′tion, *n.*
non·fu′el, *adj.*
non·fu′gi·tive, *adj., n.;* **-ly,** *adv.;* **-ness,** *n.*
non·ful′mi·nat′ing, *adj.*
non·func′tion·al, *adj.;* **-ly,** *adv.*
non·func′tion·ing, *adj.*
non′fun·da·men′tal, *adj., n.;* **-ly,** *adv.*
non′fun·da·men′tal·ist, *n.*
non·fund′ed, *adj.*
non·fun′gi·ble, *adj.*
non·fused′, *adj.*
non′fu·si·bil′i·ty, *n.*
non·fu′si·ble, *adj.*
non·fu′sion, *n.*
non·fu′tile, *adj.*
non′fu·tur·is′tic, *adj.*
non-Gael′ic, *adj.*
non′ga·lac′tic, *adj.*
non·gal′va·nized′, *adj.*
non·gam′bler, *n.*
non′gan·gli·on′ic, *adj.*
non·gan′gre·nous, *adj.*
non′gar·ru′li·ty, *n.*
non·gar′ru·lous, *adj.;* **-ly,** *adv.;* **-ness,** *n.*
non·gas′, *n., pl.* **-gas·es.**
non·gas′e·ous, *adj.;* **-ness,** *n.*
non·gas′sy, *adj.*
non·gay′, *adj.*
non′ge·lat′i·niz′ing, *adj.*
non′ge·lat′i·nous, *adj.;* **-ly,** *adv.;* **-ness,** *n.*
non·gel′ling, *adj.*
non·gem′i·nate, *adj., n.*
non′ge·ne·a·log′ic, *adj.*
non′ge·ne·a·log′i·cal, *adj.;* **-ly,** *adv.*
non·gen′er·al·ized′, *adj.*
non·gen′er·at′ing, *adj.*
non·gen′er·a′tive, *adj.*
non′ge·ner′ic, *adj.*
non′ge·ner′i·cal, *adj.;* **-ly,** *adv.*
non′ge·net′ic, *adj.*
non′ge·net′i·cal, *adj.;* **-ly,** *adv.*
non·gen′tile, *adj., n.*
non·gen′u·ine, *adj.;* **-ly,** *adv.;* **-ness,** *n.*
non′ge·o·graph′ic, *adj.*
non′ge·o·graph′i·cal, *adj.;* **-ly,** *adv.*
non′ge·o·log′ic, *adj.*
non′ge·o·log′i·cal, *adj.;* **-ly,** *adv.*
non′ge·o·met′ric, *adj.*
non′ge·o·met′ri·cal, *adj.;* **-ly,** *adv.*
non-Ger′man, *adj., n.*
non′ger·mane′, *adj.*
non′-Ger·man′ic, *adj.*
non·ger′mi·nal, *adj.*
non·ger′mi·nat′ing, *adj.*
non′ger·mi·na′tion, *n.*
non·ger′mi·na′tive, *adj.*
non′ge·run′di·al, *adj.*
non′ge·run′dive, *adj.;* **-ly,** *adv.*
non·ges′tic, *adj.*
non·ges′ti·cal, *adj.*
non·gild′ed, *adj.*
non·gilled′, *adj.*
non·giv′ing, *adj.*
non·gla′cial, *adj.;* **-ly,** *adv.*
non·glan′dered, *adj.*
non·glan′du·lar, *adj.*
non·glan′du·lous, *adj.*
non·glare′, *n., adj.*
non·glar′ing, *adj.*
non·glass′, *adj.*
non·glazed′, *adj.*
non·glob′u·lar, *adj.;* **-ly,** *adv.*
non·glom′er·ate, *adj.;* **-ly,** *adv.*
non·gloss′y, *adj.*
non·glu′cose, *n.*
non·glu′te·nous, *adj.*
non·god′, *n.*
non·gold′, *n., adj.*
non·golf′er, *n.*
non·gos′pel, *adj.*
non-Goth′ic, *adj.*
non-Goth′i·cal·ly, *adv.*
non·gov′ern·ance, *n.*
non·gov′ern·ment, *n.*
non′gov·ern·men′tal, *adj.*
non·grace′ful, *adj.;* **-ly,** *adv.;* **-ness,** *n.*
non′gra·ci·os′i·ty, *n.*
non·gra′cious, *adj.;* **-ly,** *adv.;* **-ness,** *n.*
non·grad′u·ate, *n.*
non·grad′u·at′ed, *adj.*
non′grad·u·a′tion, *n.*
non·grain′, *n.*
non·grained′, *adj.*
non·gran′u·lar, *adj.*
non·gran′u·lat′ed, *adj.*
non·graph′ic, *adj.*
non·graph′i·cal, *adj.;* **-ly,** *adv.;* **-ness,** *n.*
non′gra·phit′ic, *adj.*
non′grat·i·fi·ca′tion, *n.*
non·grat′i·fy′ing, *adj.;* **-ly,** *adv.*
non′gra·tu′i·tous, *adj.;* **-ly,** *adv.;* **-ness,** *n.*
non·grav′en, *adj.*
non′grav·i·ta′tion, *n.*
non′grav·i·ta′tion·al, *adj.;* **-ly,** *adv.*
non·grav′i·ta′tive, *adj.*
non·grav′i·ty, *n., pl.* **-ties.**
non·greas′y, *adj.*
non-Greek′, *adj., n.*
non·green′, *adj.*
non′gre·gar′i·ous, *adj.;* **-ly,** *adv.;* **-ness,** *n.*
non·grieved′, *adj.*
non·griev′ing, *adj.*
non·griev′ous, *adj.;* **-ly,** *adv.;* **-ness,** *n.*
non·groom′ing, *adj.*
non·ground′ed, *adj.*
non·ground′ing, *adj.*
non′guar·an·tee′, *n.*
non·guar′an·ty′, *n., pl.* **ties.**
non·guid′a·ble, *adj.*
non·guid′ance, *n.*
non·guilt′, *n.*
non·gut′tur·al, *adj.;* **-ly,** *adv.;* **-ness,** *n.*
non·gym′nast, *n.*
non-Gyp′sy, *n., pl.* **-sies.**
non·hab′it·a·bil′i·ty, *n.*
non·hab′it·a·ble, *adj.;* **-ble·ness,** *n.;* **-bly,** *adv.*
non′hab·i·ta′tion, *n.*
non′ha·bit′u·al, *adj.;* **-ly,** *adv.;* **-ness,** *n.*
non·hack′neyed, *adj.*
non′hal·lu′ci·na′tion, *n.*
non′hal·lu′ci·nat′ed, *adj.*
non′hal·lu′ci·na·to′ry, *adj.*
non′-Ha·mit′ic, *adj.*
non·hand′i·cap′, *n.*
non·hand′i·capped′, *adj.*
non′har·mon′ic, *adj.*
non′har·mo′ni·ous, *adj.;* **-ly,** *adv.;* **-ness,** *n.*
non·har′mo·ny, *n., pl.* **-nies.**
non·haz′ard·ous, *adj.;* **-ly,** *adv.;* **-ness,** *n.*
non·head′ing, *n.*
non·hea′then, *n., pl.* **-thens, -then,** *adj.*
non′-He·bra′ic, *adj.*
non′-He·bra′i·cal·ly, *adv.*
non-He′brew, *n., adj.*
non·hec′tic, *adj.*
non·hec′ti·cal·ly, *adv.*
non′he·don′ic, *adj.*
non′he·don′i·cal·ly, *adv.*
non′he·do·nis′tic, *adj.*

creasing. **2.** *Math.* decreasing (def. 2). [1960–65; NON- + INCREASING]

non·in·duc·tive (non′in duk′tiv), *adj. Elect.* not inductive: *a noninductive resistance.* [1895–1900; NON- + INDUCTIVE] —**non′in·duc′tive·ly,** *adv.* —**non′in·duc·tiv′i·ty,** *n.*

non-in′su·lin-de·pend·ent diabe′tes (non in′sə lin di pen′dənt, -ins′yə-), diabetes (def. 4).

non·in·ter·course (non in′tər kôrs′, -kōrs′), *n.* suspension of interchange in relations, esp. commercial or political relations. [1785–95, *Amer.*; NON- + INTERCOURSE]

Nonin′tercourse Act′, *U.S. Hist.* the act of Congress (1809) prohibiting all shipping and trade between the United States and British- or French-controlled ports.

non·in·ter·fer·ence (non′in tər fēr′əns), *n.* the policy or practice of refraining from interference, esp. in political affairs. [1820–30; NON- + INTERFERENCE]

non·in·ter·ven·tion (non′in tər ven′shən), *n.* **1.** abstention by a nation from interference in the affairs of other nations or in those of its own political subdivisions. **2.** failure or refusal to intervene. [1820–30; NON- + INTERVENTION] —**non′in·ter·ven′tion·al,** *adj.* —**non′in·ter·ven′tion·al·ist,** *n.* —**non′in·ter·ven′tion·ism,** *n.* —**non′in·ter·ven′tion·ist,** *n., adj.*

non·in·va·sive (non′in vā′siv), *adj. Med.* **1.** not invading adjacent healthy cells, blood vessels, or tissues; localized: *a noninvasive tumor.* **2.** not entering or penetrating the body or disturbing body tissue, esp. in a diagnostic procedure. [1970–75; NON- + INVASIVE] —**non′·in·va′sive·ly,** *adv.*

non·i·on′ic deter′gent (non′ī on′ik), a detergent that is polar but does not ionize in aqueous solution. [1945–50; NON- + IONIC]

non·i·ron (non ī′ərn), *adj. Brit.* drip-dry. [1955–60; NON- + IRON]

non·is·sue (non ish′o͞o *or, esp. Brit.,* -is′yo͞o), *n.* a matter or issue of little or no interest or importance: *Whether the candidate is a woman or a man should be a nonissue.* [1960–65; NON- + ISSUE]

non·join·der (non join′dər), *n. Law.* omission to join, as of a person who should have been a party to an action. [1825–35; NON- + JOINDER]

non·judg·men·tal (non′juj men′tl), *adj.* not judged or judging on the basis of one's personal standards or opinions: *They tried to adopt a nonjudgmental attitude that didn't reflect their own biases. My guidance counselor in high school was sympathetic and nonjudgmental.* [1960–65; NON- + JUDGMENTAL] —**non′judg·men′tal·ly,** *adv.*

non·ju·ror (non jo͝or′ər), *n.* **1.** a person who refuses to take a required oath, as of allegiance. **2.** (*often cap.*) *Eng. Hist.* any of the clergymen of the Church of England who in 1689 refused to swear allegiance to William and Mary. [1685–95; NON- + JUROR]

non·lead·ed (non led′id), *adj.* lead-free. [1950–55; NON- + LEAD[2] + -ED[3]]

non·le·gal (non lē′gəl), *adj.* not related to, qualified for, or phrased in the manner of the practice of law (distinguished from *illegal*): *a nonlegal explanation.* [NON- + LEGAL]

non li·cet, (non′ lī′sit), *Law.* it is not permitted or lawful. [1615–25; < L]

non·life (non līf′), *n.* lack or absence of life. [1725–35; NON- + LIFE]

non·lin·e·ar·i·ty (non′lin ē ar′i tē), *n.* **1.** *Math.* the quality of a function that expresses a relationship that is not one of direct proportion. **2.** *Elect.* deviation of an input-output relationship from one of direct proportionality. [1925–30; NON- + LINEARITY]

non li·quet (non′ lī′kwit), *Law.* (of evidence, a cause, etc.) it is not clear or evident. [1650–60; < L *nōn liquet*]

non·lit·er·ate (non lit′ər it), *adj. Anthropol.* preliterate. [1945–50; NON- + LITERATE] —**non·lit′er·a·cy,** *n.*

non·match·ing (non mach′ing), *adj.* **1.** not matching: *a nonmatching set of furniture.* **2.** (of a financial grant, donation, or the like) available or given without requiring the recipient to obtain a complementary amount from another source. [1960–65; NON- + MATCHING]

non·ma·te·ri·al (non′mə tēr′ē əl), *adj.* **1.** not material or composed of matter. **2.** not involving, seeking, or primarily concerned with riches or material things; involving or concerned with the spiritual, intellectual, or cultural aspects of life. **3.** of or pertaining to the spirit or soul; spiritual: *to minister to a person's nonmaterial needs.* [1935–40; NON- + MATERIAL]

non′mate′rial cul′ture, *Sociol.* the aggregate of values, mores, norms, etc., of a society; the ideational

CONCISE PRONUNCIATION KEY: act, cāpe, dâre, pärt; set, ēqual; *if,* ice; ox, ōver, ôrder, oil, bo͝ok, bo͞ot, out; up, ûrge; child; sing; shoe; thin, *th*at; zh as in *treasure.* ə = *a* as in *alone, e* as in *system, i* as in *easily, o* as in *gallop, u* as in *circus;* ᵊ as in *fire* (fīᵊr), *hour* (ouᵊr). l and n can serve as syllabic consonants, as in *cradle* (krād′l), and *button* (but′n). See the full key inside the front cover.

non′he·do·nis′ti·cal·ly, *adv.*
non·hei′nous, *adj.;* **-ly,** *adv.;* **-ness,** *n.*
non′-Hel·len′ic, *adj.*
non′he·mat′ic, *adj., n.*
non′he·mo·phil′ic, *adj.*
non′he·pat′ic, *adj., n.*
non′he·red′i·ta·bil′i·ty, *n.*
non′he·red′i·ta·ble, *adj.;* **-bly,** *adv.*
non′he·red′i·tar′i·ly, *adv.*
non′he·red′i·tar′i·ness, *n.*
non′he·red′i·tar′y, *adj.*
non′he·ret′i·cal, *adj.;* **-ly,** *adv.*
non·her′it·a·bil′i·ty, *n.*
non·her′it·a·ble, *adj.;* **-bly,** *adv.*
non·her′i·tor, *n.*
non′he·ro′ic, *adj.*
non′he·ro′i·cal, *adj.;* **-ly,** *adv.;* **-ness,** *n.*
non′he·ro′ic·ness, *n.*
non·hes′i·tant, *adj.;* **-ly,** *adv.*
non′heu·ris′tic, *adj.*
non′-Hi·ber′ni·an, *adj., n.*
non′hi·er·ar′chic, *adj.*
non′hi·er·ar′chi·cal, *adj.;* **-ly,** *adv.*
non′hi·er·at′ic, *adj.*
non′hi·er·at′i·cal, *adj.;* **-ly,** *adv.*
non-Hin′du, *n., adj.*
non′-His·pan′ic, *adj.*
non′his·tor′ic, *adj.*
non′his·tor′i·cal, *adj.;* **-ly,** *adv.;* **-ness,** *n.*
non′his·tri·on′ic, *adj.*
non′his·tri·on′i·cal, *adj.;* **-ly,** *adv.;* **-ness,** *n.*
non·hit′, *n.*
non′-Ho·mer′ic, *adj.*
non′hom·i·let′ic, *adj.*
non′ho·mo·ge·ne′i·ty, *n.*
non′ho·mo·ge′ne·ous, *adj.;* **-ly,** *adv.;* **-ness,** *n.*
non′ho·mog′e·nous, *adj.*
non′ho·mol′o·gous, *adj.*
non·hos′tile, *adj.;* **-ly,** *adv.*
non′hos·til′i·ty, *n.*
non·house′hold′er, *n.*
non′hu·bris′tic, *adj.*
non·hu′ma·nist, *n.*
non′hu·man·is′tic, *adj.*
non·hu′man·ized′, *adj.*
non·hu′mor·ous, *adj.;* **-ly,** *adv.;* **-ness,** *n.*
non·hu′mus, *n.*
non·hunt′ing, *adj.*
non·hy′drat·ed, *adj.*
non′hy·drau′lic, *adj.*
non′hy·drog′e·nous, *adj.*
non′hy·dro·pho′bic, *adj.*
non′hy·gro·met′ric, *adj.*
non′hy·gro·scop′ic, *adj.*
non′hy·gro·scop′i·cal·ly, *adv.*
non′hy·gi·en′ic, *adj.*
non′hy·per·bol′ic, *adj.*
non′hy·per·bol′i·cal, *adj.;* **-ly,** *adv.*
non′hyp·not′ic, *adj., n.*
non′hyp·not′i·cal·ly, *adv.*
non′hy·po·stat′ic, *adj.*
non′hy·po·stat′i·cal, *adj.;* **-ly,** *adv.*
non′i·con′o·clas′tic, *adj.*
non′i·con′o·clas′ti·cal·ly, *adv.*
non′i·de′al·is′tic, *adj.*
non′i·de′al·is′ti·cal·ly, *adv.*
non′i·de·a′tion·al, *adj.;* **-ly,** *adv.*
non′i·den′ti·cal, *adj.*
non′i·den′ti·fi·ca′tion, *n.*
non′i·den′ti·ty, *n.*
non′i·de·o·log′ic, *adj.*
non′i·de·o·log′i·cal, *adj.;* **-ly,** *adv.*
non′id·i·o·mat′ic, *adj.*
non′id·i·o·mat′i·cal, *adj.;* **-ly,** *adv.;* **-ness,** *n.*
non′i·dol′a·trous, *adj.;* **-ly,** *adv.;* **-ness,** *n.*
non′i·dyl′lic, *adj.*
non′i·dyl′li·cal·ly, *adv.*
non·ig′ne·ous, *adj.*
non′ig·nit′a·bil′i·ty, *n.*
non′ig·nit′a·ble, *adj.*
non′ig·nit′i·bil′i·ty, *n.*
non′ig·nit′i·ble, *adj.*
non′ig·no·min′i·ous, *adj.;* **-ly,** *adv.;* **-ness,** *n.*
non·ig′no·rant, *adj.;* **-ly,** *adv.*
non·il′la·tive, *adj.;* **-ly,** *adv.*
non′il·lu′mi·nant, *n.*
non′il·lu′mi·nat′ing, *adj.;* **-ly,** *adv.*
non′il·lu′mi·na′tion, *n.*
non′il·lu′mi·na′tive, *adj.*
non′il·lu′sion·al, *adj.*
non′il·lu′sive, *adj.;* **-ly,** *adv.;* **-ness,** *n.*
non′il·lus·tra′tion, *n.*
non′il·lus′tra·tive, *adj.;* **-ly,** *adv.*
non′im·ag′i·nar′i·ly, *adv.;* **-ness,** *n.*
non′im·ag′i·nar′i·ness, *n.*
non′im·ag′i·nar′y, *adj.*
non′im·ag′i·na′tion·al, *adj.*
non·im′bri·cate, *adj.;* **-ly,** *adv.*
non·im′bri·cat′ed, *adj.*
non·im′bri·cat′ing, *adj.*
non·im′bri·ca′tive, *adj.*
non·im′i·ta·bil′i·ty, *n.*
non·im′i·ta·ble, *adj.*
non·im′i·tat′ing, *adj.*
non′im·i·ta′tion·al, *adj.*
non·im′i·ta′tive, *adj.;* **-ly,** *adv.;* **-ness,** *n.*
non·im′ma·nence, *n.*
non·im′ma·nen·cy, *n.*
non·im′ma·nent, *adj.;* **-ly,** *adv.*
non′im·mer′sion, *n.*
non·im′mi·grant, *n., adj.*
non′im·mi·gra′tion, *n.*
non′im·mune′, *adj.*
non′im·mu′ni·ty, *n., pl.* **-ties.**
non′im·mu·ni·za′tion, *n.*
non·im′mu·nized′, *adj.*
non·im′pact, *n., adj.*
non′im·pact′ed, *adj.*
non′im·pair′ment, *n.*
non′im·par·ta′tion, *n.*
non′im·part′ment, *n.*
non′im·peach′a·bil′i·ty, *n.*
non′im·peach′a·ble, *adj.*
non′im·peach′ment, *n.*
non′im·ped′i·men′tal, *adj.*
non′im·ped′i·men′ta·ry, *adj.*
non′im·per′a·tive, *adj.;* **-ly,** *adv.;* **-ness,** *n.*
non′im·pe′ri·al, *adj.;* **-ly,** *adv.;* **-ness,** *n.*
non′im·pe′ri·al·is′tic, *adj.*
non′im·pe′ri·al·is′ti·cal·ly, *adv.*
non′im·pe′ri·ous, *adj.;* **-ly,** *adv.;* **-ness,** *n.*
non·im′ple·ment, *n.*
non′im·ple·men′tal, *adj.*
non′im·pli·ca′tion, *n.*
non·im′pli·ca′tive, *adj.;* **-ly,** *adv.*
non·im′port, *n.*
non′im·po·si′tion, *n.*
non′im·preg′nat·ed, *adj.*
non′im·pres′sion·a·bil′i·ty, *n.*
non′im·pres′sion·a·ble, *adj.;* **-ness,** *n.*
non′im·pres′sion·is′tic, *adj.*
non′im·prove′ment, *n.*
non′im·pul′sive, *adj.;* **-ly,** *adv.;* **-ness,** *n.*
non′im·put′a·bil′i·ty, *n.*
non′im·put′a·ble, *adj.;* **-ble·ness,** *n.;* **-bly,** *adv.*
non′im·put′a·tive, *adj.;* **-ly,** *adv.;* **-ness,** *n.*
non′in·can·des′cence, *n.*
non′in·can·des′cent, *adj.;* **-ly,** *adv.*
non′in·car′nate, *adj.*
non′in·car′nat·ed, *adj.*
non′in·cen′tive, *adj.*
non′in·ces′tu·ous, *adj.;* **-ly,** *adv.;* **-ness,** *n.*
non·in′ci·dent, *n., adj.*
non′in·ci·den′tal, *adj.;* **-ly,** *adv.*
non′in·cite′ment, *n.*
non′in·clin′a·ble, *adj.*
non′in·cli·na′tion, *n.*
non′in·cli·na′tion·al, *adj.*
non′in·cli′na·to′ry, *adj.*
non′in·clu′sion, *n.*
non′in·clu′sive, *adj.;* **-ly,** *adv.;* **-ness,** *n.*
non′in·cor′po·rat′ed, *adj.*
non′in·cor′po·ra′tive, *adj.*
non′in·creas′a·ble, *adj.*
non·in′crease, *n.*
non′in·crim′i·nat′ing, *adj.*
non′in·crim′i·na′tion, *n.*
non′in·crim′i·na·to′ry, *adj.*
non′in·crust′ing, *adj., n.*
non′in·cum′bent, *n., adj.*
non′in·de·pend′ent, *adj.;* **-ly,** *adv.*
non·in′dexed, *adj.*
non-In′di·an, *adj., n.*
non′in·dict′a·ble, *adj.*
non′in·dict′ment, *n.*
non′in·dig′e·nous, *adj.*
non′in·di·vid′u·al, *adj.*
non′in·di·vid′u·al·is′tic, *adj.*
non′in·di·vid′u·al′i·ty, *n., pl.* **-ties.**
non-In′do-Eu′ro·pe′an, *adj., n.*
non′in·duced′, *adj.*
non′in·duc′i·ble, *adj.*
non′in·dul′gence, *n.*
non′in·dul′gent, *adj.;* **-ly,** *adv.*
non·in′du·rat′ed, *adj.*
non·in′du·ra′tive, *adj.*
non′in·dus′tri·al, *adj.;* **-ly,** *adv.*
non′in·dus′tri·al·i·za′tion, *n.*
non′in·dus′tri·al·ized′, *adj.*
non′in·dus′tri·ous, *adj.;* **-ly,** *adv.;* **-ness,** *n.*
non·in′dus·try, *n.*
non′in·ert′, *adj.;* **-ly,** *adv.;* **-ness,** *n.*
non′in·er′tial, *adj.*
non′in·fal′li·bil′i·ty, *n.*
non′in·fal′li·ble, *adj.;* **-ble·ness,** *n.;* **-bly,** *adv.*
non·in′fan·try, *n.*
non′in·fect′ed, *adj.*
non′in·fect′ing, *adj.*
non′in·fec′tion, *n.*
non′in·fec′tious, *adj.;* **-ly,** *adv.;* **-ness,** *n.*
non′in·fer′a·ble, *adj.;* **-bly,** *adv.*
non·in′fer·en′tial, *adj.;* **-ly,** *adv.*
non·in′fi·nite, *adj., n.;* **-ly,** *adv.;* **-ness,** *n.*
non′in·flam′ma·bil′i·ty, *n.*
non′in·flam′ma·ble, *adj.;* **-ble·ness,** *n.;* **-bly,** *adv.*
non′in·flam′ma·to′ry, *adj.*
non′in·fla′tion, *n.*
non′in·fla′tion·ar′y, *adj.*
non′in·flect′ed, *adj.*
non′in·flec′tion·al, *adj.;* **-ly,** *adv.*
non·in′flu·ence, *n.*
non′in·flu·en′tial, *adj.;* **-ly,** *adv.*
non′in·for·ma′tion·al, *adj.*
non′in·for′ma·tive, *adj.;* **-ly,** *adv.;* **-ness,** *n.*
non′in·frac′tion, *n.*
non′in·fu′si·bil′i·ty, *n.*
non′in·fu′si·ble, *adj.;* **-ness,** *n.*
non′in·hab′it·a·bil′i·ty, *n.*
non′in·hab′it·a·ble, *adj.*
non′in·hab′it·ance, *n.*
non′in·hab′it·an·cy, *n., pl.* **-cies.**
non′in·her′ence, *n.*
non′in·her′ent, *adj.;* **-ly,** *adv.*
non′in·her′it·a·bil′i·ty, *n.*
non′in·her′it·a·ble, *adj.;* **-ness,** *n.*
non′in·her′it·ed, *adj.*
non′in·hib′i·tive, *adj.*
non′in·hib′i·to′ry, *adj.*
non′in·i′ti·ate, *n.*
non′in·ju′ri·ous, *adj.;* **-ly,** *adv.;* **-ness,** *n.*
non·in′ju·ry, *n., pl.* **-ries.**
non′in·oc′u·la′tion, *n.*
non′in·oc′u·la′tive, *adj.*
non′in·quir′ing, *adj.;* **-ly,** *adv.*
non·in′sect, *n.*
non′in·sec′ti·cid′al, *adj.*
non′in·ser′tion, *n.*
non′in·sist′ence, *n.*
non′in·sist′en·cy, *n., pl.* **-cies.**
non′in·sist′ent, *adj.*
non′in·spis′sat·ing, *adj.*
non′in·stall′ment, *adj.*
non′in·stinc′tive, *adj.;* **-ly,** *adv.*
non′in·stinc′tu·al, *adj.;* **-ly,** *adv.*
non′in·sti·tu′tion, *n.*
non′in·sti·tu′tion·al, *adj.;* **-ly,** *adv.*
non′in·struc′tion·al, *adj.;* **-ly,** *adv.*
non′in·struc′tive, *adj.;* **-ly,** *adv.;* **-ness,** *n.*
non′in·stru·men′tal, *adj.;* **-ly,** *adv.*
non′in·stru·men′tal·is′tic, *adj.*
non·in′su·la′tor, *n.*
non·in′su·lat′ing, *adj.*
non′in·sur′ance, *n.*
non·in′te·ger, *n.*
non·in′te·gra·ble, *adj.*
non·in′te·grat′ed, *adj.*
non′in·te·gra′tion, *n.*
non′in·tel·lec′tu·al, *adj., n.;* **-ly,** *adv.;* **-ness,** *n.*
non′in·tel·lec′tu·al·ism, *n.*
non′in·tel′li·gence, *n.*
non′in·tel′li·gent, *adj.;* **-ly,** *adv.*
non′in·ter·ac′tive, *adj.*
non′in·ter·cept′ing, *adj.*
non′in·ter·cep′tive, *adj.*
non′in·ter·change′a·bil′i·ty, *n.*
non′in·ter·change′a·ble, *adj.;* **-ble·ness,** *n.;* **-bly,** *adv.*
non′in·ter·de·pend′ence, *n.*
non′in·ter·de·pend′en·cy, *n.*
non′in·ter·de·pend′ent, *adj.;* **-ly,** *adv.*
non′in·ter·fer′ing, *adj.;* **-ly,** *adv.*
non′in·ter·mit′tence, *n.*
non′in·ter·mit′tent, *adj.;* **-ly,** *adv.;* **-ness,** *n.*
non′in·ter·na′tion·al, *adj.;* **-ly,** *adv.*
non′in·ter′po·lat′ing, *adj.*
non′in·ter′po·la′tion, *n.*
non′in·ter′po·la′tive, *adj.*
non′in·ter·po·si′tion, *n.*
non′in·ter′pret·a·bil′i·ty, *n.*
non′in·ter′pret·a·ble, *adj.*
non′in·ter′pre·ta′tion·al, *adj.*
non′in·ter′pre·ta′tive, *adj.;* **-ly,** *adv.*
non′in·ter′pre·tive, *adj.;* **-ly,** *adv.;* **-ness,** *n.*
non′in·ter·rupt′ed, *adj.;* **-ly,** *adv.;* **-ness,** *n.*
non′in·ter·rupt′i·ble, *adj.*
non′in·ter·rup′tive, *adj.*
non′in·ter·sect′ing, *adj.*
non′in·ter·sec′tion·al, *adj.*
non·in′ter·state′, *adj.*
non′in·ter·ven′er, *n.*
non′in·ter·ve′nor, *n.*
non′in·tox′i·cant, *adj.*
non′in·tox′i·cat′ing, *adj.;* **-ly,** *adv.*
non′in·tox′i·ca′tive, *adj.*
non′in·tro·spec′tive, *adj.;* **-ly,** *adv.;* **-ness,** *n.*
non′in·tro·ver′sive, *adj.;* **-ly,** *adv.;* **-ness,** *n.*
non·in′tro·vert′ed, *adj.;* **-ly,** *adv.;* **-ness,** *n.*
non′in·tru′sive, *adj.;* **-ly,** *adv.*
non′in·tu′i·tive, *adj.;* **-ly,** *adv.;* **-ness,** *n.*
non′in·vert′ed, *adj.*
non′in·ves′tor, *n.*
non′in·vid′i·ous, *adj.;* **-ly,** *adv.;* **-ness,** *n.*
non′in·vin′ci·bil′i·ty, *n.*
non′in·vin′ci·ble, *adj.;* **-ble·ness,** *n.;* **-bly,** *adv.*
non′in·volved′, *adj.*
non′in·volve′ment, *n.*
non·i′o·dized′, *adj.*
non′-I·on′ic, *adj., n.*
non·i′on·ized′, *adj.*
non·i′on·iz′ing, *adj.*
non·i′rate′, *adj.;* **-ly,** *adv.*
non′i·ren′ic, *adj.*
non′i·ren′i·cal, *adj.*
non′ir·i·des′cence, *n.*
non′ir·i·des′cent, *adj.;* **-ly,** *adv.*
non-I′rish, *adj., n., pl.* **-I·rish.**
non′i·ron′ic, *adj.*
non′i·ron′i·cal, *adj.;* **-ly,** *adv.;* **-ness,** *n.*
non·ir′ra′di·at′ed, *adj.*
non′ir·ra′tion·al, *adj., n.;* **-ly,** *adv.;* **-ness,** *n.*
non′ir·rev′o·ca·bil′i·ty, *n.*
non′ir·rev′o·ca·ble, *adj.;* **-ble·ness,** *n.;* **-bly,** *adv.*
non·ir′ri·ga·ble, *adj.*
non·ir′ri·gat′ed, *adj.*
non·ir′ri·gat′ing, *adj.*
non′ir·ri·ga′tion, *n.*
non′ir·ri·ta·bil′i·ty, *n.*
non·ir′ri·ta·ble, *adj.;* **-ble·ness,** *n.;* **-bly,** *adv.*
non·ir′ri·tan·cy, *n.*
non·ir′ri·tant, *adj.*
non·ir′ri·tat′ing, *adj.*
non′-Is·lam′ic, *adj.*
non′-Is·lam·it′ic, *adj.*
non′i·so·e·las′tic, *adj.*
non·i′so·la·ble, *adj.*
non′i·so·lat′a·bil′i·ty, *n.*

structure of a culture that provides the values and meanings by which it functions. Cf. **material culture.** [1935–40]

non·mem·ber (non mem′bər), *n.* a person who is not a member: *The election meeting of the club is not open to nonmembers.* [1640–50; NON- + MEMBER] —**non·mem′ber·ship′,** *n.*

non·met·al (non met′l), *n. Chem.* **1.** an element not having the character of a metal, as carbon or nitrogen. **2.** an element incapable of forming simple positive ions in solution. [1865–70; NON- + METAL]

non·me·tal·lic (non′mə tal′ik), *adj. Chem.* **1.** of or relating to a nonmetal. **2.** not of a metallic quality: *a nonmetallic appearance.* [1805–15; NON- + METALLIC]

non·mis·ci·ble (non mis′ə bəl), *adj.* not capable of being mixed. [NON- + MISCIBLE] —**non·mis·ci·bil·i·ty** (non′mis ə bil′i tē), *n.*

non·mor·al (non môr′əl, -mor′-), *adj.* having no relation to morality; neither moral nor immoral: *It was a completely nonmoral problem and involved only judgments as to efficacy.* [1865–70; NON- + MORAL] —**non′mo·ral′i·ty,** *n.* —**non·mor′al·ly,** *adv.*
—**Syn.** See **immoral.**

non·na·sal (non nā′zəl), *adj.* **1.** not nasal. **2.** *Phonet.* oral (def. 5). [1875–80; NON- + NASAL] —**non′na·sal′i·ty,** *n.* —**non·na′sal·ly,** *adv.*

non·neg·a·tive (non neg′ə tiv), *adj. Math.* (of a real number) greater than or equal to zero. [1880–85; NON- + NEGATIVE]

non·ni·trog·e·nous (non′nī troj′ə nəs), *adj.* containing no nitrogen. [1870–75; NON- + NITROGENOUS]

non·nu·clear (non no͞o′klē ər, -nyo͞o′- or, *by metathesis,* -kyə lər), *adj.* not utilizing nuclear power, nuclear weapons, etc.: *to fight a nonnuclear war.* [1950–55; NON- + NUCLEAR]
—**Pronunciation.** See **nuclear.**

non·ny-non·ny (non′ē non′ē), *interj. Archaic.* (used as a nonsense expression, esp. in Elizabethan songs and verses): *with a hey nonny-nonny.*

no-no (nō′nō′), *n., pl.* **-nos, -no's.** *Informal.* anything that is forbidden or not advisable, as because of being improper or unsafe: *If you want to lose weight, rich desserts are a no-no.* [1940–45, *Amer.*; redupl. of NO[1]]

non·o·be·di·ence (non′ō bē′dē əns), *n.* absence or lack of obedience. [1575–85; NON- + OBEDIENCE] —**non′o·be′di·ent,** *adj.* —**non′o·be′di·ent·ly,** *adv.*

non·ob·jec·tive (non′əb jek′tiv), *adj.* **1.** not objective. **2.** *Fine Arts.* not representing objects known in physical nature; nonrepresentational: *some nonobjective works by Kandinsky and Mondrian.* [1900–05; NON- + OBJECTIVE]

non·ob·serv·ance (non′əb zûr′vəns), *n.* absence or lack of observance. [1735–45; NON- + OBSERVANCE] —**non′ob·serv′ant,** *adj.* —**non′ob·serv′ant·ly,** *adv.*

non obst., non obstante.

non ob·stan·te (nōn ōb stän′te; *Eng.* non ob stan′tē), *Latin.* notwithstanding. [short for AL, L *nōn obstante aliquō statūtō in contrārium* any statute to the contrary notwithstanding]

non·oc·cur·rence (non′ə kûr′əns, -kur′-), *n.* absence or lack of occurrence. [1800–10; NON- + OCCURRENCE]

no-non·sense (nō′non′sens, -səns), *adj.* **1.** not tolerating anything frivolous or trifling; firm and businesslike: *a no-nonsense approach to money matters; a no-nonsense teacher with well-behaved classes.* **2.** economical or utilitarian; practical: *a no-nonsense car that gets excellent gas mileage.* **3.** plain and simple; not fancy, complicated, or elegant: *no-nonsense recipes for easy preparation.* [1925–30]
—**Syn. 1.** earnest, diligent, resolute, purposeful.

non·ox·y·nol-9 (no nok′sə nôl′nīn′, -nol′-), *n. Pharm.* the active ingredient of spermicides. [by rearrangement of parts of its chemical name]

non·par·a·met·ric (non′par ə me′trik), *adj. Statistics.* (of a test or method) not requiring assertions about parameters or about the form of the underlying distribution. [1940–45; NON- + PARAMETRIC]

non·pa·reil (non′pə rel′), *adj.* **1.** having no equal; peerless. —*n.* **2.** a person or thing having no equal. **3.** a small pellet of colored sugar for decorating candy, cake, and cookies. **4.** a flat, round, bite-sized piece of chocolate covered with this sugar. **5.** See **painted bunting.** **6.** *Print.* **a.** a 6-point type. **b.** a slug occupying 6 points of space between lines. [1400–50; late ME *nonparaille* < MF *nonpareil,* equiv. to *non-* NON- + *pareil* equal < VL **pariculum* (L *pari-* (s. of *pār*) equal + *-culum* -CULE[1])]

CONCISE ETYMOLOGY KEY: <, descended or borrowed from; >, whence; b., blend of, blended; c., cognate with; cf., compare; deriv., derivative; equiv., equivalent; imit., imitative; obl., oblique; r., replacing; s., stem; sp., spelling, spelled; resp., respelling, respelled; trans., translation; ?, origin unknown; *, unattested; ‡, probably earlier than. See the full key inside the front cover.

non′i·so·trop′ic, *adj.*
non′i·sot′ro·pous, *adj.*
non-Is′ra·el·ite′, *n.*
non′-Is·ra·el·it′ic, *adj.*
non-Is′ra·el·it′ish, *adj.*
non·is′su·a·ble, *adj.*; **-bly,** *adv.*
non′-I·tal′ian, *adj., n.*
non′-I·tal′ic, *adj., n.*
non·i′tem·ized′, *adj.*
non·i′tem·iz′er, *n.*
non·jail′a·ble, *adj.*
non′-Jap·an·ese′, *adj., n., pl.* **-ese.**
non-Jew′, *n.*
non-Jew′ish, *adj.*
non′jour·nal·is′tic, *adj.*
non′jour·nal·is′ti·cal·ly, *adv.*
non·ju′di·ca·ble, *adj.*
non·ju′di·ca′tive, *adj.*
non·ju′di·ca·to′ry, *adj., n., pl.* **-ries.**
non′ju·di′ci·a·ble, *adj.*
non′ju·di′cial, *adj.*; **-ly,** *adv.*
non′ju·rid′ic, *adj.*
non′ju·rid′i·cal, *adj.*; **-ly,** *adv.*
non·ju′ried, *adj.*
non′ju·ris′tic, *adj.*
non′ju·ris′ti·cal, *adj.*; **-ly,** *adv.*
non·ju′ry, *adj., n., pl.* **-ries.**
non′jus·ti′ci·a·bil′i·ty, *n.*
non′jus·ti′ci·a·ble, *adj.*
non-Kaf′fir, *n.*
non′ki·net′ic, *adj.*
non·knowl′edge·a·ble, *adj.*
non·ko′sher, *adj., n.*
non·la′bel·ing, *adj., n.*
non·la′bel·ling, *adj., n.*
non·la′bor, *adj.*
non·lac′te·al, *adj.*; **-ly,** *adv.*
non·lac′te·ous, *adj.*
non′lac·tes′cent, *adj.*
non·lac′tic, *adj.*
non·lam′i·na·ble, *adj.*
non·lam′i·nat′ed, *adj.*
non·lam′i·na′ting, *adj., n.*
non·lam′i·na′tive, *adj.*
non·lar′ce·nous, *adj.*
non-Lat′in, *adj., n.*
non·law′yer, *n.*
non·lay′ered, *adj.*
non·lay′ing, *adj.*
non·leak′ing, *adj.*
non′le·ga′to, *adj.*
non·leg′is·la′tive, *adj.*; **-ly,** *adv.*
non′le·git′i·ma·cy, *n.*
non′le·git′i·mate, *adj.*
non·leg′ume, *n.*
non′le·gu′mi·nous, *adj.*
non′lep·i·dop′ter·al, *adj.*
non′lep·i·dop′ter·an, *adj., n.*
non′lep·i·dop′ter·ous, *adj.*
non·lep′rous, *adj.*; **-ly,** *adv.*
non·le′thal, *adj.*; **-ly,** *adv.*
non′le·thar′gic, *adj.*
non′le·thar′gi·cal, *adj.*; **-ly,** *adv.*
non·lev′el, *adj.*
non·lev′er·aged, *adj.*
non·lev′u·lose′, *adj.*
non′li·a·bil′i·ty, *n., pl.* **-ties.**
non·li′a·ble, *adj.*
non·li′bel·ous, *adj.*; **-ly,** *adv.*
non·lib′er·al, *adj.*
non·lib′er·al·ism, *n.*
non′lib·er·a′tion, *n.*
non′li·bid′i·nous, *adj.*; **-ly,** *adv.*; **-ness,** *n.*
non·li′cens·a·ble, *adj.*
non·li′censed, *adj.*
non′li·cen′ti·ate, *n.*
non′li·cen′tious, *adj.*; **-ly,** *adv.*; **-ness,** *n.*
non·lick′ing, *adj.*
non′lim·i·ta′tion, *n.*
non·lim′i·ta′tive, *adj.*
non·lim′it·ing, *adj.*
non·lin′e·al, *adj.*
non·lin′e·ar, *adj.*
non′lin·guis′tic, *adj.*
non·link′age, *adj.*
non·liq′ue·fi′a·ble, *adj.*
non·liq′ue·fy′ing, *adj.*
non·liq′uid, *adj., n.*; **-ly,** *adv.*
non·liq′ui·dat′ing, *adj.*
non′liq·ui·da′tion, *n.*
non·list′ing, *adj.*
non·lit′er·al, *adj.*; **-ly,** *adv.*; **-ness,** *n.*
non·lit′er·ar′i·ly, *adv.*; **-ness,** *n.*
non·lit′er·ar′i·ness, *n.*
non·lit′er·ar′y, *adj.*
non′lit·i·ga′tion, *n.*
non′li·ti′gious, *adj.*; **-ly,** *adv.*; **-ness,** *n.*
non′li·tur′gic, *adj.*
non′li·tur′gi·cal, *adj.*; **-ly,** *adv.*
non·live′, *adj.*
non·liv′ing, *adj., n.*
non′lix·iv′i·at′ed, *adj.*
non′lix·iv′i·a′tion, *n.*
non·load′-bear′ing, *adj.*
non·lo′cal, *adj., n.*; **-ly,** *adv.*
non·lo′cal·iz′a·ble, *adj.*
non·lo′cal·ized′, *adj.*
non′lo·ca′tion, *n.*
non·log′ic, *n.*
non·log′i·cal, *adj.*; **-ly,** *adv.*; **-ness,** *n.*
non′log·i·cal′i·ty, *n.*
non′lo·gis′tic, *adj.*
non′lo·gis′ti·cal, *adj.*
non·los′a·ble, *adj.*
non·los′er, *n.*
non·lov′er, *n.*
non·lov′ing, *adj.*
non′lox·o·drom′ic, *adj.*
non′lox·o·drom′i·cal, *adj.*
non·loy′al, *adj.*; **-ly,** *adv.*
non·loy′al·ty, *n., pl.* **-ties.**
non·lu′bri·cant, *n.*
non·lu′bri·cat′ing, *adj.*
non′lu·bri′cious, *adj.*; **-ly,** *adv.*; **-ness,** *n.*
non·lu′cid, *adj.*; **-ly,** *adv.*; **-ness,** *n.*
non′lu·cid′i·ty, *n.*
non·lu′cra·tive, *adj.*; **-ly,** *adv.*; **-ness,** *n.*
non′lu·gu′bri·ous, *adj.*; **-ly,** *adv.*; **-ness,** *n.*
non′lu·mi·nes′cence, *n.*
non′lu·mi·nes′cent, *adj.*
non′lu·mi·nos′i·ty, *n.*
non·lu′mi·nous, *adj.*; **-ly,** *adv.*; **-ness,** *n.*
non·lus′ter, *n.*
non·lus′trous, *adj.*; **-ly,** *adv.*; **-ness,** *n.*
non-Lu′ther·an, *adj., n.*
non′lym·phat′ic, *adj.*
non·lyr′ic, *adj.*
non·lyr′i·cal, *adj.*; **-ly,** *adv.*; **-ness,** *n.*
non·lyr′i·cism, *n.*
non′mag·net′ic, *adj.*
non′mag·net′i·cal, *adj.*; **-ly,** *adv.*
non·mag′net·ized′, *adj.*
non-Mag′yar, *n., adj.*
non·main′te·nance, *n.*
non′ma·jor′i·ty, *n., pl.* **-ties.**
non·make′up′, *adj.*
non′ma·lar′i·al, *adj.*
non′ma·lar′i·an, *adj.*
non′ma·lar′i·ous, *adj.*
non′-Ma′lay, *adj., n.*
non′-Ma·lay′an, *adj., n.*
non′ma·li′cious, *adj.*; **-ly,** *adv.*; **-ness,** *n.*
non′ma·lig′nance, *n.*
non′ma·lig′nan·cy, *n., pl.* **-cies.**
non′ma·lig′nant, *adj.*; **-ly,** *adv.*
non′ma·lig′ni·ty, *n.*
non·mal′le·a·bil′i·ty, *n.*
non·mal′le·a·ble, *adj.*; **-ness,** *n.*
non′-Mal·thu′si·an, *adj., n.*
non′mam·ma′li·an, *n., adj.*
non·man′age·ment, *n., adj.*
non′man·a·ge′ri·al, *adj.*
non·man′da·to′ry, *adj., n., pl.* **-ries.**
non·man′i·fest′, *adj.*; **-ly,** *adv.*; **-ness,** *n.*
non′man·i·fes·ta′tion, *n.*
non′ma·nip′u·la′tive, *adj.*
non′ma·nip′u·la·to′ry, *adj.*
non·man′nered, *adj.*
non′man·ner·is′tic, *adj.*
non·man′u·al, *adj.*; **-ly,** *adv.*
non′man·u·fac′ture, *n.*
non′man·u·fac′tured, *adj.*
non′man·u·fac′tur·ing, *n.*
non′ma·rine′, *adj., n.*
non·mar′i·tal, *adj.*; **-ly,** *adv.*
non·mar′i·time′, *adj.*
non·mar′ket, *n., adj.*
non′mar′ket·a·bil′i·ty, *n.*
non·mar′ket·a·ble, *adj., n.*
non·mar′riage, *n.*
non′mar′riage·a·bil′i·ty, *n.*
non·mar′riage·a·ble, *adj.*; **-ness,** *n.*
non·mar′ry·ing, *adj.*
non·mar′tial, *adj.*; **-ly,** *adv.*; **-ness,** *n.*
non-Marx′ist, *adj., n.*
non·mas′cu·line, *adj.*; **-ly,** *adv.*; **-ness,** *n.*
non′mas·cu·lin′i·ty, *n.*
non·ma′son, *n.*
non·mas′ter·y, *n., pl.* **-ter·ies.**
non′ma·te′ri·al·is′tic, *adj.*
non′ma·te′ri·al·is′ti·cal·ly, *adv.*
non′ma·ter′nal, *adj.*; **-ly,** *adv.*
non′math·e·mat′ic, *adj.*
non′math·e·mat′i·cal, *adj.*; **-ly,** *adv.*
non′math·e·ma·ti′cian, *n.*
non′ma·tric′u·lant, *n.*
non′mat·ri·mo′ni·al, *adj.*; **-ly,** *adv.*
non·mat′ter, *n.*
non′mat·u·ra′tion, *n.*
non′mat′u·ra′tive, *adj.*
non′ma·ture′, *adj.*; **-ly,** *adv.*; **-ness,** *n.*
non′ma·tu′ri·ty, *n.*
non′meas·ur·a·bil′i·ty, *n.*
non·meas′ur·a·ble, *adj.*; **-ble·ness,** *n.*; **-bly,** *adv.*
non′me·chan′i·cal, *adj.*; **-ly,** *adv.*; **-ness,** *n.*
non′mech·a·nis′tic, *adj.*
non′me·dal′lic, *adj.*
non′me·di·a′tion, *n.*
non·me′di·a′tive, *adj.*
non·med′i·ca·ble, *adj.*
non·med′i·cal, *adj.*; **-ly,** *adv.*
non·med′i·ca′tive, *adj.*
non′me·dic′i·nal, *adj.*; **-ly,** *adv.*
non·med′i·ta′tive, *adj.*; **-ly,** *adv.*; **-ness,** *n.*
non′-Med·i·ter·ra′ne·an, *n., adj.*
non·med′ul·lat′ed, *adj.*
non′me·lod′ic, *adj.*
non′me·lod′i·cal·ly, *adv.*
non′me·lo′di·ous, *adj.*; **-ly,** *adv.*; **-ness,** *n.*
non′mel·o·dra·mat′ic, *adj.*
non′mel·o·dra·mat′i·cal·ly, *adv.*
non·melt′a·ble, *adj.*
non·melt′ing, *adj.*
non·men′ac·ing, *adj.*
non′-Men·de′li·an, *adj.*
non·men′di·can·cy, *n.*
non·men′di·cant, *adj.*
non·me′ni·al, *adj.*; **-ly,** *adv.*
non·men′tal, *adj.*; **-ly,** *adv.*
non·mer′can·tile′, *adj.*
non·mer′cen·ar′y, *adj., n., pl.* **-ar·ies.**
non′met·al·lif′er·ous, *adj.*
non′met·al·lur′gic, *adj.*
non′met·al·lur′gi·cal, *adj.*; **-ly,** *adv.*
non′met·a·mor′phic, *adj.*
non′met·a·mor′pho·sis, *n., pl.* **-ses.**
non′met·a·mor′phous, *adj.*
non′met·a·phor′ic, *adj.*
non′met·a·phor′i·cal, *adj.*; **-ly,** *adv.*
non′met·a·phys′i·cal, *adj.*; **-ly,** *adv.*
non′me·te·or′ic, *adj.*
non′me·te·or′i·cal·ly, *adv.*
non′me·te·or·o·log′ic, *adj.*
non′me·te·or·o·log′i·cal, *adj.*; **-ly,** *adv.*
non′me·thod′ic, *adj.*
non′me·thod′i·cal, *adj.*; **-ly,** *adv.*; **-ness,** *n.*
non-Meth′od·ist, *n., adj.*
non′-Meth·od·is′tic, *adj.*
non·met′ric, *adj.*
non·met′ri·cal, *adj.*; **-ly,** *adv.*
non′met·ro·pol′i·tan, *adj., n.*
non′mi·cro′bic, *adj.*
non′mi·cro·scop′ic, *adj.*
non′mi·cro·scop′i·cal, *adj.*; **-ly,** *adv.*
non·mi′grant, *adj., n.*
non·mi′grat·ing, *adj., n.*
non′mi·gra′tion, *n.*
non·mi′gra·to′ry, *adj.*
non·mil′i·tan·cy, *n.*
non·mil′i·tant, *adj., n.*; **-ly,** *adv.*
non·mil′i·tar′y, *adj.*
non′mil·lion·aire′, *n.*
non′mi·met′ic, *adj.*
non′mi·met′i·cal·ly, *adv.*
non·min′er·al, *n., adj.*
non′min·er·al·og′i·cal, *adj.*; **-ly,** *adv.*
non·min′i·mal, *adj.*
non′min·is·te′ri·al, *adj.*; **-ly,** *adv.*
non′min·is·tra′tion, *n.*
non′mi·nor′i·ty, *adj.*
non′mi·rac′u·lous, *adj.*; **-ly,** *adv.*; **-ness,** *n.*
non·mis′chie·vous, *adj.*; **-ly,** *adv.*; **-ness,** *n.*
non·mis′sion·ar′y, *adj., n., pl.* **-ar·ies.**
non′mit·i·ga′tion, *n.*
non·mit′i·ga′tive, *adj.*
non·mit′i·ga·to′ry, *adj.*
non·mo′bile, *adj.*
non′mo·bil′i·ty, *n.*
non·mod′al, *adj.*; **-ly,** *adv.*
non·mod′er·ate, *adj., n.*; **-ly,** *adv.*; **-ness,** *n.*
non·mod′ern, *adj., n.*; **-ly,** *adv.*; **-ness,** *n.*
non′mod·ern·is′tic, *adj.*
non·mod′i·fi·ca′tive, *adj.*
non·mod′i·fi·ca′to·ry, *adj.*
non·mod′i·fy′ing, *adj.*
non′-Mo·ham′med·an, *adj., n.*
non·mo′lar, *adj., n.*
non′mo·lec′u·lar, *adj.*
non·mo′men·tar′i·ness, *n.*
non·mo′men·tar′y, *adj.*
non′mo·nar′chal, *adj.*; **-ly,** *adv.*
non′mo·nar′chi·al, *adj.*
non′mo·nar′chic, *adj.*
non′mo·nar′chi·cal·ly, *adv.*
non·mon′ar·chist, *n.*
non′mon·ar·chis′tic, *adj.*
non′mo·nas′tic, *adj.*
non′mo·nas′ti·cal·ly, *adv.*
non·mon′e·tar′y, *adj.*
non·mon′ey, *adj.*
non-Mon′gol, *n., adj.*
non′-Mon·go′li·an, *adj., n.*
non·mon′ist, *n.*
non′mo·nis′tic, *adj.*
non′mo·nis′ti·cal·ly, *adv.*
non′mo·nog′a·mous, *adj.*; **-ly,** *adv.*
non′mo·nop′o·lis′tic, *adj.*
non-Mor′mon, *n., adj.*
non·mor′tal, *adj., n.*; **-ly,** *adv.*
non-Mos′lem, *adj., n., pl.* **-lems, -lem.**
non·mo′tile, *adj.*
non′mo·til′i·ty, *n.*
non·mo′tion, *n.*
non·mo′ti·vat′ed, *adj.*
non′mo·ti·va′tion, *n.*
non′mo·ti·va′tion·al, *adj.*
non·mo′tor·ing, *adj.*
non·mo′tor·ist, *n.*
non·mo′tor·ized′, *adj.*
non·moun′tain·ous, *adj.*; **-ly,** *adv.*
non′mov·a·bil′i·ty, *n.*
non·mov′a·ble, *adj.*; **-ble·ness,** *n.*; **-bly,** *adv.*
non′mu·ci·lag′i·nous, *adj.*
non·mu′cous, *adj.*
non′-Mu·ham′mad·an, *adj., n.*
non′-Mu·ham′med·an, *adj., n.*
non·mulched′, *adj.*
non·mul′ti·ple, *adj., n.*
non′mul·ti·pli·ca′tion, *n.*
non′mul·ti·pli·ca′tion·al, *adj.*
non·mul′ti·pli·ca′tive, *adj.*; **-ly,** *adv.*
non′mu·nic′i·pal, *adj.*; **-ly,** *adv.*
non·mur′der·ous, *adj.*
non·mus′cu·lar, *adj.*; **-ly,** *adv.*
non·mu′si·cal, *adj.*; **-ly,** *adv.*; **-ness,** *n.*
non-Mus′lem, *adj., n., pl.* **-lems, -lem.**
non-Mus′lim, *adj., n., pl.* **-lims, -lim.**
non′mu·ta·bil′i·ty, *n.*
non·mut′a·ble, *adj.*; **-ble·ness,** *n.*; **-bly,** *adv.*
non′mu·ta′tion·al, *adj.*; **-ly,** *adv.*
non·mu′ta·tive, *adj.*
non·mu′ti·nous, *adj.*; **-ly,** *adv.*; **-ness,** *n.*
non·mu′tu·al, *adj.*; **-ly,** *adv.*
non′mu·tu·al′i·ty, *n.*
non′my·op′ic, *adj.*
non′my·op′i·cal·ly, *adv.*

—**Syn. 1.** unparalleled. **2.** nonesuch. —**Ant. 1.** ordinary.

non•par•ous (non par′əs), *adj. Physiol.* having borne no children. [NON- + -PAROUS]

non•par•tic•i•pant (non′pär tis′ə pənt), *n.* a person who does not participate. [1880–85; NON- + PARTICIPANT]

non•par•tic•i•pat•ing (non′pär tis′ə pā′ting), *adj.* **1.** not participating. **2.** *Insurance.* having or imparting no right to dividends or to a distribution of surplus. [NON- + PARTICIPATING]

non•par•tic•i•pa•tion (non′pär tis′ə pā′shən), *n.* absence of participation: *Nonparticipation of citizens in political matters hampers efforts toward better government.* [NON- + PARTICIPATION]

non•par•ti•san (non pär′tə zən), *adj.* **1.** not partisan; objective. **2.** not supporting or controlled by a political party, special interest group, or the like. —*n.* **3.** a person who is nonpartisan. Also, **non•par′ti•zan.** [1880–85; NON- + PARTISAN] —**non•par′ti•san•ship′,** *n.*
—**Syn. 2.** uninvolved, disinterested, unimplicated.

Nonpar′tisan League′, a political organization of farmers, founded in North Dakota in 1915, and extending to many states west of the Mississippi, with the aim of influencing agricultural legislation in state legislatures.

non•pay•ment (non pā′mənt), *n.* failure or neglect to pay: *His property was confiscated for nonpayment of taxes.* [1400–50; late ME; see NON-, PAYMENT]

non•peak (non pēk′), *adj.* off-peak. [1910–15; NON- + PEAK[1]]

non•per•form•ance (non′pər fôr′məns), *n.* failure or neglect to perform. [1500–10; NON- + PERFORMANCE]

non•per•form•er (non′pər fôr′mər), *n.* **1.** a person or thing that is not performing well or properly. **2.** a person who does not perform, esp. on stage or before a camera, as a crew member of a stage production. [NON- + PERFORMER]

non•per•form•ing (non′pər fôr′ming), *adj.* **1.** not performing well or properly. **2.** *Banking.* noting or pertaining to a debt on which interest payments have been missed or slow, or for which the interest rate has been voluntarily lowered: *the rise in nonperforming loans.* [NON- + PERFORMING]

non•per•ish•a•ble (non per′i shə bəl), *adj.* **1.** not subject to rapid deterioration or decay: *A supply of nonperishable food was kept for emergencies.* —*n.* **2.** Usually, **nonperishables.** articles or items, esp. of food, not subject to rapid spoilage. [1920–25; NON- + PERISHABLE]

non•per•son (non pûr′sən), *n.* **1.** someone whose existence or presence is not recognized. **2.** someone whose existence is denied or ignored by a government, political party, or the like, often as a punishment for disloyalty or dissent and sometimes resulting in the loss of personal liberty; unperson. [1905–10; NON- + PERSON]

non pla•cet (nōn plä′ket; *Eng.* non plā′sit), *Latin.* it is not pleasing.

non•plus (non plus′, non′plus), *v.,* **-plussed** or **-plused, -plus•sing** or **-plus•ing,** *n.* —*v.t.* **1.** to render utterly perplexed; puzzle completely. —*n.* **2.** a state of utter perplexity. [1575–85; (n.) < L *nōn plūs* lit., not more, no further, i.e., a state in which nothing more can be done]
—**Syn. 1.** perplex, confuse, confound, disconcert.

non•point (non′point′), *adj.* of or pertaining to a source of pollution that is not readily and specifically identifiable, as water runoff. [NON- + POINT]

non•po•lar (non pō′lər), *adj. Physical Chem.* containing no permanently dipolar molecules; lacking a dipole. [1890–95; NON- + POLAR]

non•pos•i•tive (non poz′i tiv), *adj. Math.* (of a real number) less than or equal to zero. [NON- + POSITIVE]

non pos•su•mus (nōn pō′so͞o mo͞os′; *Eng.* non pos′ə məs), *Latin.* we cannot.

non•prac•tic•ing (non prak′tə sing), *adj.* not currently practicing one's profession, religion, etc.: *a nonpracticing physician.* [NON- + PRACTICING]

non•pre•scrip•tion (non′pri skrip′shən), *adj.* (of drugs, medication, etc.) legally available for purchase without a doctor's prescription; over-the-counter. [1955–60; NON- + PRESCRIPTION]

non•print (non print′), *adj.* of, pertaining to, or consisting of other than printed matter: *Slide shows, slide-tape presentations, and video are nonprint media.* [1970–75; NON- + PRINT]

non•pro (non prō′), *n., pl.* **-pros,** *adj. Informal.* nonprofessional. [see NON-, PRO[2]]

non•pro•duc•tive (non′prə duk′tiv), *adj.* **1.** not pro-

CONCISE PRONUNCIATION KEY: *act, cāpe, dâre, pärt; set, ēqual; if, īce; ox, ōver, ôrder, oil, bo͝ok, bo͞ot, out; up, ûrge; child; sing; shoe; thin, that;* zh as in *treasure.* ə = *a* as in *alone, e* as in *system, i* as in *easily, o* as in *gallop, u* as in *circus;* ᵊ as in *fire* (fīᵊr), *hour* (ouᵊr). l and n can serve as syllabic consonants, as in *cradle* (krād′l), and *button* (but′n). See the full key inside the front cover.

non•mys′tic, *adj., n.*
non•mys′ti•cal, *adj.;* **-ly,** *adv.;* **-ness,** *n.*
non•mys′ti•cism, *n.*
non•myth′i•cal, *adj.;* **-ly,** *adv.*
non′myth•o•log′ic, *adj.*
non′myth•o•log′i•cal, *adj.;* **-ly,** *adv.*
non•nar′cism, *n.*
non•nar′cis•sism, *n.*
non′nar•cis•sis′tic, *adj.*
non′nar•cot′ic, *adj., n.*
non′nar•ra′tion, *n.*
non•nar′ra•tive, *adj., n.*
non•na′tion•al, *adj., n.;* **-ly,** *adv.*
non•na′tion•al•ism, *n.*
non′na•tion•al•is′tic, *adj.*
non′na•tion•al•is′ti•cal•ly, *adv.*
non•na′tion•al•i•za′tion, *n.*
non•na′tive, *adj., n.;* **-ly,** *adv.;* **-ness,** *n.*
non•nat′ti•ly, *adv.;* **-ness,** *n.*
non•nat′ty, *adj.*
non•nat′u•ral, *adj.;* **-ly,** *adv.;* **-ness,** *n.*
non•nat′u•ral•ism, *n.*
non•nat′u•ral•ist, *n.*
non•nat•u•ral•is′tic, *adj.*
non•nau′ti•cal, *adj.;* **-ly,** *adv.*
non•na′val, *adj.*
non•nav′i•ga•bil′i•ty, *n.*
non•nav′i•ga•ble, *adj.;* **-ble•ness,** *n.;* **-bly,** *adv.*
non•nav′i•ga′tion, *n.*
non•neb′u•lar, *adj.*
non•neb′u•lous, *adj.;* **-ly,** *adv.;* **-ness,** *n.*
non′ne•ces′si•tous, *adj.;* **-ly,** *adv.;* **-ness,** *n.*
non′ne•ces′si•ty, *n., pl.* **-ties.**
non′ne•ga′tion, *n.*
non•neg′a•tiv•ism, *n.*
non′neg•a•tiv•is′tic, *adj.*
non′neg•a•tiv′i•ty, *n.*
non•neg′li•gence, *n.*
non•neg′li•gent, *adj.;* **-ly,** *adv.*
non•neg′li•gi•bil′i•ty, *n.*
non•neg′li•gi•ble, *adj.;* **-ble•ness,** *n.;* **-bly,** *adv.*
non′ne•go′ti•a•bil′i•ty, *n.*
non′ne•go′ti•a•ble, *adj.*
non′ne•go′ti•a′tion, *n.*
non′-Ne•grit′ic, *adj.*
non-Ne′gro, *n., pl.* **-groes,** *adj.*
non′ne•phrit′ic, *adj.*
non•ner′vous, *adj.;* **-ly,** *adv.;* **-ness,** *n.*
non•nes′cience, *n.*
non•nes′cient, *adj.*
non•net′work′, *adj.*
non•neu′ral, *adj.*
non′neu•rot′ic, *adj., n.*
non•neu′tral, *adj., n.;* **-ly,** *adv.*
non′neu•tral′i•ty, *n.*
non′-New•to′ni•an, *adj., n.*
non′-Ni•cene′, *adj.*
non′nic•o•tin′ic, *adj.*
non•ni′hil•ism, *n.*
non•ni′hil•ist, *n.*
non′ni•hil•is′tic, *adj.*
non•ni′tric, *adj.*
non•ni′tro•gen•ized′, *adj.*
non•ni′trous, *adj.*
non′no•bil′i•ty, *n.*
non•no′ble, *adj.*
non′noc•tur′nal, *adj.;* **-ly,** *adv.*
non•no′mad, *n.*
non′no•mad′ic, *adj.*
non′no•mad′i•cal•ly, *adv.*
non′nom•i•nal•is′tic, *adj.*
non′nom•i•na′tion, *n.*
non-Nor′dic, *adj., n.*
non•nor′mal, *adj.;* **-ly,** *adv.;* **-ness,** *n.*
non′nor•mal′i•ty, *n., pl.* **-ties.**
non-Nor′man, *n., adj.*
non-Norse′, *adj., n., pl.* **-Norse.**
non•not′a•ble, *adj.;* **-ble•ness,** *n.;* **-bly,** *adv.*
non′no•ta′tion•al, *adj.*
non′no•ti•fi•ca′tion, *n.*
non•no′tion•al, *adj.*
non•nou′me•nal, *adj.;* **-ly,** *adv.*
non•nour′ish•ing, *adj.*
non•nour′ish•ment, *n.*
non•nov′el, *n.*
non′nul•li•fi•ca′tion, *n.*
non•nu′mer•al, *n., adj.*
non•nurs′ing, *adj.*
non•nur′tur•ant, *adj.*
non•nu′tri•ent, *adj., n.*
non•nu′tri•ment, *n.*
non′nu•tri′tious, *adj.;* **-ly,** *adv.;* **-ness,** *n.*
non•nu′tri•tive, *adj.;* **-ly,** *adv.;* **-ness,** *n.*
non′ob•jec′ti•fi•ca′tion, *n.*
non′ob•jec′tion, *n.*
non′ob•jec′ti•vis′tic, *adj.*
non•ob′li•gat′ed, *adj.*
non′ob•lig′a•to′ri•ly, *adv.*
non′ob•lig′a•to′ry, *adj.*
non′ob•scu′ri•ty, *n., pl.* **-ties.**
non′ob•serv′a•ble, *adj.;* **-bly,** *adv.*
non′ob•ser•va′tion, *n.*
non′ob•ser•va′tion•al, *adj.*
non′ob•serv′ing, *adj.;* **-ly,** *adv.*
non′ob•ses′sion, *n.*
non′ob•ses′sion•al, *adj.*
non′ob•ses′sive, *adj.;* **-ly,** *adv.;* **-ness,** *n.*
non′ob•so•lete′, *adj.*
non′ob•stet′ric, *adj.*
non′ob•stet′ri•cal, *adj.;* **-ly,** *adv.*
non′ob•struc′tive, *adj.;* **-ly,** *adv.;* **-ness,** *n.*
non•ob′vi•ous, *adj.;* **-ly,** *adv.;* **-ness,** *n.*
non′oc•ci•den′tal, *adj.;* **-ly,** *adv.*
non′oc•clu′sion, *n.*
non′oc•clu′sive, *adj.*
non′oc•cult′, *adj.*
non′oc•cult′ing, *adj.*
non•oc′cu•pant, *n.*
non′oc•cu•pa′tion, *n.*
non′oc•cu•pa′tion•al, *adj.*
non•o′dor•if′er•ous, *adj.;* **-ly,** *adv.;* **-ness,** *n.*
non•o′dor•ous, *adj.;* **-ly,** *adv.;* **-ness,** *n.*
non′oec•u•men′ic, *adj.*
non′oec•u•men′i•cal, *adj.*
non′of•fend′er, *n.*
non′of•fen′sive, *adj.;* **-ly,** *adv.;* **-ness,** *n.*
non•of′fer, *n.*
non•of′fice•hold′er, *n.*
non′of•fi′cial, *adj.;* **-ly,** *adv.*
non′of•fic′i•nal, *adj.*
non•oil′y, *adj.*
non•ol′fac′to•ry, *adj., n., pl.* **-ries.**
non•ol′i•gar′chic, *adj.*
non′ol•i•gar′chi•cal, *adj.*
non′o•mis′si•ble, *adj.*
non′o•mis′sion, *n.*
non•on′er•ous, *adj.;* **-ly,** *adv.;* **-ness,** *n.*
non′o•pac′i•ty, *n., pl.* **-ties.**
non•op′er•a•ble, *adj.*
non′op•er•at′ic, *adj.*
non′op•er•at′i•cal•ly, *adv.*
non•op′er•at′ing, *adj.*
non′op•er•a′tion•al, *adj.*
non•op′er•a•tive, *adj.*
non′o•pin′ion•at′ed, *adj.;* **-ness,** *n.*
non′o•pin′ion•a′tive, *adj.;* **-ly,** *adv.;* **-ness,** *n.*
non′op•pos′a•ble, *adj.*
non′op•pos′ing, *adj.*
non′op•po•si′tion, *n.*
non′op•pres′sion, *n.*
non′op•pres′sive, *adj.;* **-ly,** *adv.;* **-ness,** *n.*
non′op•pro′bri•ous, *adj.;* **-ly,** *adv.;* **-ness,** *n.*
non•op′tic, *adj.*
non•op′ti•cal, *adj.;* **-ly,** *adv.*
non′op•ti•mis′tic, *adj.*
non′op•ti•mis′ti•cal, *adj.;* **-ly,** *adv.*
non•op′tion•al, *adj.;* **-ly,** *adv.*
non•o′ral, *adj.;* **-ly,** *adv.*
non•or′bit•ing, *adj.*
non′or•ches′tral, *adj.;* **-ly,** *adv.*
non•or′dered, *adj.*
non′or•di•na′tion, *n.*
non′or•gan′ic, *adj.*
non′or•gan′i•cal•ly, *adv.*
non′or•gan•i•za′tion, *n.*
non′or•gas′mic, *adj.*
non•o′ri•en′ta•ble, *adj.*
non′o•ri•en′tal, *adj., n.*
non′o•ri•en•ta′tion, *n.*
non′o•rig′i•nal, *adj., n.;* **-ly,** *adv.*
non′or•na•men′tal, *adj.;* **-ly,** *adv.*
non′or•na•men•tal′i•ty, *n.*
non•or′tho•dox′, *adj.;* **-ly,** *adv.*
non′or•tho•graph′ic, *adj.*
non′or•tho•graph′i•cal, *adj.;* **-ly,** *adv.*
non′or•tho•pe′dic, *adj.*
non-Os′can, *adj., n.*
non•os′cine, *adj.*
non′os•mot′ic, *adj.*
non′os•mot′i•cal•ly, *adv.*
non′os•ten′si•ble, *adj.;* **-bly,** *adv.*
non′os•ten′sive, *adj.;* **-ly,** *adv.*
non′os•ten•ta′tion, *n.*
non•out′law′ry, *n., pl.* **-ries.**
non•o′ver•head′, *n., adj.*
non′o•ver•lap′ping, *adj., n.*
non•own′er, *n.*
non•own′ing, *adj.*
non•ox′i•dat′ing, *adj.*
non′ox•i•da′tion, *n.*
non•ox′i•da′tive, *adj.*
non•ox′i•diz′a•ble, *adj.*
non′ox•i•di•za′tion, *n.*
non•ox′i•diz′ing, *adj.*
non•ox′y•gen•at′ed, *adj.*
non•pac′i•fi′a•ble, *adj.*
non′pa•cif′ic, *adj.*
non′pa•cif′i•cal, *adj.;* **-ly,** *adv.*
non′pac•i•fi•ca′tion, *n.*
non′pa•cif′i•ca•to′ry, *adj.*
non•pac′i•fist, *n.*
non′pac•i•fis′tic, *adj.*
non•pa′gan, *n., adj.*
non•pa′gan•ish, *adj.*
non•paid′, *adj.*
non•paint′er, *n.*
non•pal′at•a•bil′i•ty, *n.*
non•pal′at•a•ble, *adj.;* **-ble•ness,** *n.;* **-bly,** *adv.*
non•pal′a•tal, *adj., n.*
non′pal•a•tal•i•za′tion, *n.*
non•pal′li•a′tion, *n.*
non•pal′li•a′tive, *adj.;* **-ly,** *adv.*
non′pal•pa•bil′i•ty, *n.*
non•pal′pa•ble, *adj.;* **-bly,** *adv.*
non′pan•the•is′tic, *adj.*
non′pan•the•is′ti•cal, *adj.;* **-ly,** *adv.*
non•pa•pal, *adj.*
non•pa′pist, *n.*
non′pa•pis′tic, *adj.*
non′pa•pis′ti•cal, *adj.*
non•par′, *n., adj.*
non′par•a•bol′ic, *adj.*
non′par•a•bol′i•cal, *adj.;* **-ly,** *adv.*
non′par•a•dox′i•cal, *adj.;* **-ly,** *adv.;* **-ness,** *n.*
non•par′al•lel′, *adj., n.*
non•par′al•lel′ism, *n.*
non′pa•ral′y•sis, *n., pl.* **-ses.**
non′par•a•lyt′ic, *adj., n.*
non′par•a•sit′ic, *adj.*
non′par•a•sit′i•cal, *adj.;* **-ly,** *adv.*
non•par′a•sit′ism, *n.*
non•par′don•ing, *adj.*
non•par′ent, *n.*
non′pa•ren′tal, *adj.;* **-ly,** *adv.*
non•par′ent•hood′, *n.*
non′pa•rish′ion•er, *n.*
non′-Pa•ri′sian, *adj., n.*
non•par′i•ty, *n.*
non′par•lia•men′ta•ry, *adj.*
non′pa•ro′chi•al, *adj.;* **-ly,** *adv.*
non′pa•rod′ic, *adj.*
non′pa•rod′i•cal, *adj.*
non•par′tial, *adj.;* **-ly,** *adv.*
non′par•ti•al′i•ty, *n., pl.* **-ties.**
non•par′ti•ble, *adj.*
non′par•tic′u•late, *adj.*
non•part′ner, *n.*
non•par′ty, *adj., n., pl.* **-ties.**
non•pas′sen•ger, *n.*
non•pas′ser•ine, *adj., n.*
non•pas′si•ble, *adj.*
non•pas′sion•ate, *adj.;* **-ly,** *adv.;* **-ness,** *n.*
non•pas′to•ral, *adj., n.;* **-ly,** *adv.*
non′pat•ent•a•bil′i•ty, *n.*
non•pat′ent•a•ble, *adj.*
non•pat′ent•ed, *adj.*
non•pat′ent•ly, *adv.*
non′pa•ter′nal, *adj.;* **-ly,** *adv.*
non′path•o•gen′ic, *adj.*
non′path•o•log′ic, *adj.*
non′path•o•log′i•cal, *adj.;* **-ly,** *adv.*
non•pa•tri•ot′ic, *adj.*
non′pa•tri•ot′i•cal•ly, *adv.*
non•pa′tron•iz′ing, *adj.*
non•pat′terned, *adj.*
non•pause′, *n.*
non•pay′ing, *adj.*
non•peace′, *n.*
non•peaked′, *adj.*
non′pe•cu′ni•ar′y, *adj.*
non′ped•a•gog′ic, *adj.*
non′ped•a•gog′i•cal, *adj.;* **-ly,** *adv.*
non′pe•des′tri•an, *n., adj.*
non•ped′i•greed′, *adj.*
non′pe•jo′ra•tive, *adj.;* **-ly,** *adv.*
non′pe•lag′ic, *adj.*
non•pel′tast, *n.*
non•pe′nal, *adj.*
non•pe′nal•ized′, *adj.*
non•pend′ant, *adj.*
non•pend′en•cy, *n.*
non•pend′ent, *adj.;* **-ly,** *adv.*
non•pend′ing, *adj.*
non′pen•e•tra•bil′i•ty, *n.*
non•pen′e•tra•ble, *adj.;* **-bly,** *adv.*
non•pen′e•trat′ing, *adj.*
non′pen•e•tra′tion, *n.*
non•pen′i•tent, *adj., n.*
non•pen′sion•a•ble, *adj.*
non•pen′sion•er, *n.*
non′per•ceiv′a•ble, *adj.;* **-bly,** *adv.*
non′per•ceiv′ing, *adj.*
non′per•cep′ti•bil′i•ty, *n.*
non′per•cep′ti•ble, *adj.;* **-ble•ness,** *n.;* **-bly,** *adv.*
non′per•cep′tion, *n.*
non′per•cep′tion•al, *adj.*
non′per•cep′tive, *adj.;* **-ly,** *adv.;* **-ness,** *n.*
non′per•cep•tiv′i•ty, *n.*
non′per•cep′tu•al, *adj.*
non′per•cip′i•ence, *n.*
non′per•cip′i•en•cy, *n.*
non′per•cip′i•ent, *adj.*
non′per•cus′sive, *adj.*
non′per•fect′ed, *adj.*
non′per•fect′i•bil′i•ty, *n.*
non′per•fect′i•ble, *adj.*
non′per•fec′tion, *n.*
non•per′fo•rat′ed, *adj.*
non•per′fo•rat′ing, *adj.*
non•per′il•ous, *adj.;* **-ly,** *adv.*
non′pe•ri•od′ic, *adj.*
non′pe•ri•od′i•cal, *adj., n.;* **-ly,** *adv.*
non•per′ish•ing, *adj.*
non•per′jured, *adj.*
non•per′ju•ry, *n., pl.* **-ries.**
non•per′ma•nence, *n.*
non•per′ma•nen•cy, *n.*
non•per′ma•nent, *adj.;* **-ly,** *adv.*
non′per•me•a•bil′i•ty, *n.*
non•per′me•a•ble, *adj.*
non′per•me•a′tion, *n.*
non•per′me•a′tive, *adj.*
non′per•mis′si•bil′i•ty, *n.*
non′per•mis′si•ble, *adj.;* **-bly,** *adv.*
non′per•mis′sion, *n.*
non′per•mis′sive, *adj.;* **-ly,** *adv.;* **-ness,** *n.*
non′per•mit′ted, *adj.*
non′per•pen•dic′u•lar, *adj., n.;* **-ly,** *adv.*
non′per•pen•dic′u•lar′i•ty, *n.*
non′per•pe•tra′tion, *n.*
non′per•pet′u•al, *adj.;* **-ly,** *adv.*
non′per•pet′u•ance, *n.*
non′per•pe•tu′i•ty, *n., pl.* **-ties.**
non•per′se•cut′ing, *adj.*
non′per•se•cu′tion, *n.*
non•per′se•cu′tive, *adj.*
non•per′se•cu•to′ry, *adj.*
non′per•se•ver′ing, *adj.*
non′per•sist′ence, *n.*
non′per•sist′en•cy, *n.*
non′per•sist′ent, *adj.;* **-ly,** *adv.*
non′per•sist′ing, *adj.*
non•per′son•age, *n.*
non•per′son•al, *adj.;* **-ly,** *adv.*
non′per•son′i•fi•ca′tion, *n.*
non′per•spec′tive, *n., adj.*
non′per•suad′a•ble, *adj.*
non′per•sua′si•ble, *adj.*
non′per•sua′sive, *adj.;* **-ly,** *adv.;* **-ness,** *n.*
non•per′ti•nence, *n.*
non•per′ti•nen•cy, *n.*

ductive; unproductive. **2.** not worthwhile or beneficial; not leading to practical or beneficial results. **3.** not producing goods directly, as employees in charge of personnel or inspectors. [1920–25; NON- + PRODUCTIVE] —**non′pro·duc′tive·ly,** *adv.* —**non′pro·duc′·tive·ness, non·pro·duc·tiv·i·ty** (non′prō duk tiv′i tē, -prod ək-), *n.*

non·pro·fes·sion·al (non′prə fesh′ə nl), *adj.* **1.** not a member of or trained in a specific profession. **2.** *Sports.* not offering or engaged in for payment or a monetary prize; amateur: *a nonprofessional league; a nonprofessional player.* —*n.* **3.** a person who is not a professional. **4.** an amateur athlete. [1795–1805; NON- + PROFESSIONAL] —**non′pro·fes′sion·al·ism,** *n.*

non·pro·fi·cien·cy (non′prə fish′ən sē), *n.* absence or lack of proficiency. [1585–95; NON- + PROFICIENCY] —**non′pro·fi′cient,** *adj.*

non·prof·it (non prof′it), *adj.* **1.** not established for the purpose of making a profit; not entered into for money: *a nonprofit institution.* —*n.* **2.** a nonprofit organization, institution, corporation, or other entity. [1900–05; NON- + PROFIT]

non·pro·lif·er·a·tion (non′prō lif′ə rā′shən), *n.* **1.** the action or practice of curbing or controlling an excessive, rapid spread: *nonproliferation of nuclear weapons.* **2.** failure or refusal to proliferate, as in budding or cell division. —*adj.* **3.** pertaining to diplomatic agreements limiting the spread of nuclear weapons. [1960–65; NON- + PROLIFERATION]

CONCISE ETYMOLOGY KEY: <, descended or borrowed from; >, whence; b., blend of, blended; c., cognate with; cf., compare; deriv., derivative; equiv., equivalent; imit., imitative; obl., oblique; r., replacing; s., stem; sp., spelling, spelled; resp., respelling, respelled; trans., translation; ?, origin unknown; *, unattested; ‡, probably earlier than. See the full key inside the front cover.

non-pros (non′pros′), *v.t.,* **-prossed, -pros·sing.** *Law.* to adjudge (a plaintiff) in default. [1665–75; shortened form of NON PROSEQUITUR]

non pros., non prosequitur.

non pro·se·qui·tur (non′ prō sek′wi tər), *Law.* a judgment entered against the plaintiff in a suit when the plaintiff does not appear in court to prosecute it. [1760–70; < L *nōn prōsequitur* lit., he does not pursue (prosecute)]

non·qual·i·fied (non kwol′ə fīd′), *adj.* **1.** unqualified (def. 1). **2.** not meeting the requirements in the pertinent provisions of the applicable regulations, as for tax or pension plan considerations. [NON- + QUALIFIED]

non·read·a·ble (non rē′də bəl), *adj.* **1.** unreadable. **2.** pertaining to letter mail with addresses and zip codes incapable of being read by optical scanning devices. [NON- + READABLE] —**non′read·a·bil′i·ty,** *n.* —**non·read′a·ble·ness,** *n.* —**non·read′a·bly,** *adv.*

non·rec·og·ni·tion (non′rek əg nish′ən), *n.* absence or lack of recognition. [1840–50; NON- + RECOGNITION]

non·re′course loan′ (non rē′kôrs, -kōrs, non′ri-kôrs′, -kōrs′), *Finance.* a loan for which the borrower cannot be held responsible for any amount in excess of the security for the loan, even if the value of such security falls below the level it had or that had been anticipated for it at the time of the loan. [NON- + RECOURSE]

non·re·cur·rent (non′ri kûr′ənt, -kur′), *adj.* not recurrent. [1920–25; NON- + RECURRENT]

non·re·cur·ring (non′ri kûr′ing, -kur′), *adj.* **1.** not occurring or happening again, esp. often or periodically. **2.** noting or pertaining to an income or charge considered of a nature not likely to occur or happen again. [1965–70; NON- + RECURRING]

non·re·gent (non rē′jənt), *n.* (at English universities) a Master of Arts whose regency has terminated. [1495–1505; NON- + REGENT]

non′rel·a·tiv·is′tic quan′tum mechan′ics (non′-rel ə ti vis′tik, non′-), *Physics.* a form of quantum mechanics that excludes relativistic effects and is approximately applicable to low-energy problems, as the structure of atoms and molecules. Cf. **matrix mechanics, Schrödinger equation.** [NON- + RELATIVISTIC]

non rep., non repetatur.

non′re·peat′ing dec′imal (non′ri pē′ting, non′-), *Math.* a decimal representation of any irrational number, having the property that no sequence of digits is repeated ad infinitum. [NON- + REPEATING]

non re·pe·ta·tur (non rep′i tā′tər), (in prescriptions) do not repeat. [< L *nōn repetātur* it is not repeated]

non·rep·re·sen·ta·tion·al (non′rep ri zen tā′shə nl), *adj.* not resembling or portraying any object in physical nature: *a nonrepresentational painting.* [1920–25; NON- + REPRESENTATIONAL] —**non′rep·re·sen·ta′tion·al·ism,** *n.* —**non′rep·re·sen·ta′tion·al·ist,** *n.*

non·res·i·dent (non rez′i dənt), *adj.* **1.** not resident in a particular place. **2.** not residing where official duties require a person to reside. —*n.* **3.** a person who is

non·per′ti·nence, *n.*
non·per′ti·nen·cy, *n.*
non·per′ti·nent, *adj.;* **-ly,** *adv.*
non′per·turb′a·ble, *adj.*
non′per·turb′ing, *adj.*
non′-Pe·ru′vi·an, *adj., n.*
non′per·verse′, *adj.;* **-ly,** *adv.;* **-ness,** *n.*
non′per·ver′sion, *n.*
non′per·ver′si·ty, *n., pl.* **-ties.**
non′per·ver′sive, *adj.*
non′per·vert′ed, *adj.;* **-ly,** *adv.*
non′per·vert′i·ble, *adj.*
non′pes·si·mis′tic, *adj.*
non′pes·si·mis′ti·cal·ly, *adv.*
non·pes′ti·lent, *adj.;* **-ly,** *adv.*
non′pes·ti·len′tial, *adj.*
non′pet·ro·lif′er·ous, *adj.*
non′phag·o·cyt′ic, *adj.*
non′phar·ma·ceu′tic, *adj.*
non′phar·ma·ceu′ti·cal, *adj.;* **-ly,** *adv.*
non′phe·no′lic, *adj.*
non′phe·nom′e·nal, *adj.;* **-ly,** *adv.*
non′phil·an·throp′ic, *adj.*
non′phil·an·throp′i·cal, *adj.*
non′phil·o·log′ic, *adj.*
non′phil·o·log′i·cal, *adj.*
non′phil·o·soph′ic, *adj.*
non′phil·o·soph′i·cal, *adj.;* **-ly,** *adv.*
non′phi·los′o·phy, *n., pl.* **-phies.**
non·pho′bic, *adj.*
non′pho·ne′mic, *adj.*
non′pho·ne′mi·cal·ly, *adv.*
non′pho·net′ic, *adj.*
non′pho·net′i·cal, *adj.;* **-ly,** *adv.*
non′phos·phat′ic, *adj.*
non′phos′pho·rous, *adj.*
non′pho·to·graph′ic, *adj.*
non′pho·to·graph′i·cal, *adj.;* **-ly,** *adv.*
non·pho′to·syn·thet′ic, *adj.*
non′phre·net′ic, *adj.*
non′phre·net′i·cal·ly, *adv.*
non·phys′i·cal, *adj.;* **-ly,** *adv.*
non′phys·i·o·log′ic, *adj.*
non′phys·i·o·log′i·cal, *adj.;* **-ly,** *adv.*
non′phy·to·tox′ic, *adj.*
non′pic·to′ri·al, *adj.;* **-ly,** *adv.*
non·pig′ment·ed, *adj.*
non′pi·na′ceous, *adj.*
non′pla·cen′tal, *adj.*
non·plan′e·tar′y, *adj.*
non·plas′tic, *adj., n.*
non′plas·tic′i·ty, *n.*
non·plat′ed, *adj.*
non′plat·i·tu′di·nous, *adj.;* **-ly,** *adv.*
non′plau·si·bil′i·ty, *n.*
non·plau′si·ble, *adj.;* **-ble·ness,** *n.;* **-bly,** *adv.*
non·play′er, *n.*
non·play′ing, *adj.*
non·plead′a·ble, *adj.*
non·plead′ing, *adj.;* **-ly,** *adv.*
non′pli·a·bil′i·ty, *n.*
non·pli′a·ble, *adj.;* **-ble·ness,** *n.;* **-bly,** *adv.*
non·pli′an·cy, *n.*
non·pli′ant, *adj.;* **-ly,** *adv.;* **-ness,** *n.*
non′plu·ral·is′tic, *adj.*
non′plu·ral′i·ty, *n., pl.* **-ties.**
non′plu·to·crat′ic, *adj.*
non′plu·to·crat′i·cal, *adj.*
non′pneu·mat′ic, *adj.*
non′pneu·mat′i·cal·ly, *adv.*
non·po′et, *n.*
non′po·et′ic, *adj.*
non·poi′son·ous, *adj.;* **-ly,** *adv.;* **-ness,** *n.*
non′po·lar′i·ty, *n.*
non·po′lar·iz′a·ble, *adj.*
non·po′lar·ized′, *adj.*
non·po′lar·iz′ing, *adj.*
non′po·lem′ic, *n., adj.*
non′po·lem′i·cal, *adj.;* **-ly,** *adv.*
non-Pol′ish, *adj., n.*
non′po·lit′i·cal, *adj.;* **-ly,** *adv.*
non·pol′i·ti′cian, *n.*
non′po·lit′i·ci·za′tion, *n.*
non·pol′i·tick′ing, *n.*
non′pol·lu′tant, *adj., n.*
non′pol·lut′ing, *adj.*
non′pon·der·a·bil′i·ty, *n.*
non·pon′der·a·ble, *adj.*
non′pon·der·os′i·ty, *n.*
non·pon′der·ous, *adj.;* **-ly,** *adv.;* **-ness,** *n.*
non·poor′, *n.*
non·pop′u·lar, *adj.;* **-ly,** *adv.*
non′pop·u·lar′i·ty, *n.*
non·pop′u·lous, *adj.;* **-ly,** *adv.;* **-ness,** *n.*
non′por·no·graph′ic, *adj.*
non·po′rous, *adj.;* **-ness,** *n.*
non′por·phy·rit′ic, *adj.*
non′port·a·bil′i·ty, *n.*
non·port′a·ble, *adj.*
non′por·ten′tous, *adj.;* **-ly,** *adv.;* **-ness,** *n.*
non′por·tray′a·ble, *adj.*
non′por·tray′al, *n.*
non′-Por·tu·guese′, *adj., n., pl.* **-guese.**
non′pos·i·tiv·is′tic, *adj.*
non′pos·sessed′, *adj.*
non′pos·ses′sion, *n.*
non′pos·ses′sive, *adj.;* **-ly,** *adv.;* **-ness,** *n.*
non·pos′si·ble, *adj.;* **-ly,** *adv.*
non·post′hu·mous, *adj.*
non′post·pon′a·ble, *adj.*
non′post·pone′ment, *n.*
non·po′ta·ble, *adj., n.*
non′po·ten′tial, *adj., n.*
non·pow′ered, *adj.*
non′prac·ti·ca·bil′i·ty, *n.*
non·prac′ti·ca·ble, *adj.;* **-ble·ness,** *n.;* **-bly,** *adv.*
non·prac′ti·cal, *adj.;* **-ly,** *adv.;* **-ness,** *n.*
non′prac·ti·cal′i·ty, *n.*
non·prac′tice, *n.*
non·prac′ticed, *adj.*
non′prag·mat′ic, *adj., n.*
non′prag·mat′i·cal, *adj.;* **-ly,** *adv.*
non·preach′ing, *adj., n.*
non·prec′e·dent, *n.*
non′pre·ced′ent, *adj.*
non′prec·e·den′tial, *adj.*
non·pre′cious, *adj.;* **-ly,** *adv.;* **-ness,** *n.*
non′pre·cip′i·ta′tion, *n.*
non′pre·cip′i·ta′tive, *adj.*
non·pred′a·to′ri·ly, *adv.;* **-ness,** *n.*
non·pred′a·to′ry, *adj.*
non·pred′i·ca′tive, *adj.;* **-ly,** *adv.*
non′pre·dict′a·ble, *adj.*
non′pre·dic′tive, *adj.*
non′pref·er·a·bil′i·ty, *n.*
non·pref′er·a·ble, *adj.;* **-ble·ness,** *n.;* **-bly,** *adv.*
non·pref′er·ence, *n.*
non′pref·er·en′tial, *adj.;* **-ly,** *adv.*
non′pref·er·en′tial·ism, *n.*
non′pre·formed′, *adj.*
non·preg′nant, *adj.*
non′pre·hen′sile, *adj.*
non·prej′u·diced, *adj.*
non′prej·u·di′cial, *adj.;* **-ly,** *adv.*
non′pre·lat′ic, *adj.*
non·pre′mi·um, *n.*
non′prep·a·ra′tion, *n.*
non′pre·par′a·tive, *adj.*
non′pre·par′a·to′ry, *adj.*
non′prep·o·si′tion·al, *adj.;* **-ly,** *adv.*
non·pres′by·ter, *n.*
non′-Pres·by·te′ri·an, *adj., n.*
non·pre′sci·ent, *adj.;* **-ly,** *adv.*
non′pre·scribed′, *adj.*
non′pre·scrib′er, *n.*
non′pre·scrip′tive, *adj.*
non·pres′ence, *n.*
non·pres′ent, *adj.*
non′pre·sent′a·bil′i·ty, *n.*
non′pre·sent′a·ble, *adj.;* **-ble·ness,** *n.;* **-bly,** *adv.*
non′pres·en·ta′tion, *n.*
non′pres·en·ta′tion·al, *adj.*
non′pre·serv′a·ble, *adj.*
non′pres·er·va′tion, *n.*
non′pre·serv′a·tive, *adj.*
non′pres·i·den′tial, *adj.*
non·press′ing, *adj.*
non·pres′sure, *n., adv.*
non′pre·sump′tive, *adj.;* **-ly,** *adv.*
non·prev′a·lence, *n.*
non·prev′a·lent, *adj.;* **-ly,** *adv.*
non′pre·vent′a·ble, *adj.*
non′pre·vent′i·ble, *adj.*
non′pre·ven′tion, *n.*
non′pre·ven′tive, *adj.;* **-ly,** *adv.;* **-ness,** *n.*
non·priest′ly, *adj.*
non·pri′mal, *adj.*
non·prime′, *adj.*
non·prim′i·tive, *adj., n.;* **-ly,** *adv.;* **-ness,** *n.*
non·prin′ci·pled, *adj.*
non·print′a·ble, *adj.*
non·print′ing, *adj.*
non′pri·or′i·ty, *adj.*
non·priv′i·leged, *adj.*
non′priv′i·ty, *n., pl.* **-ties.**
non′prob·a·bil′i·ty, *n., pl.* **-ties.**
non·prob′a·ble, *adj.;* **-bly,** *adv.*
non′pro·ba′tion, *n.*
non·pro′ba·tive, *adj.*
non·pro′ba·to′ry, *adj.*
non′prob·lem·at′ic, *adj.*
non′prob·lem·at′i·cal, *adj.;* **-ly,** *adv.*
non′pro·ce′dur·al, *adj.*
non′pro·ces′sion·al, *adj.*
non′pro·cre·a′tion, *n.*
non·pro′cre·a′tive, *adj.*
non′pro·cur′a·ble, *adj.*
non′proc·u·ra′tion, *n.*
non′pro·cure′ment, *n.*
non′pro·duc′er, *n.*
non′pro·duc′i·ble, *adj.*
non′pro·duc′ing, *adj.*
non′pro·duc′tion, *n., adj.*
non′pro·fane′, *adj.;* **-ly,** *adv.;* **-ness,** *n.*
non′pro·fan′i·ty, *n., pl.* **-ties.**
non′pro·fessed′, *adj.*
non′pro·fes′sion, *n.*
non′pro·fes·so′ri·al, *adj.;* **-ly,** *adv.*
non′prof·it·a·bil′i·ty, *n.*
non·prof′it·a·ble, *adj.;* **-ly,** *adv.;* **-ness,** *n.*
non′prof·it·eer′ing, *n.*
non′prog·nos′ti·ca′tive, *adj.*
non′pro·gram′ma·ble, *adj.*
non′pro·gram·mat′ic, *adj.*
non′pro·gres′sive, *adj., n.;* **-ly,** *adv.;* **-ness,** *n.*
non′pro·hi·bi′tion, *n.*
non′pro·hib′i·tive, *adj.;* **-ly,** *adv.*
non′pro·hib′i·to′ri·ly, *adv.*
non′pro·hib′i·to′ry, *adj.*
non′pro·ject′ing, *adj.*
non′pro·jec′tion, *n.*
non′pro·jec′tive, *adj.*
non′pro·le·tar′i·an, *adj., n.*
non′pro·le·tar′i·at, *n.*
non′pro·lif′er·ous, *adj.*
non′pro·lif′ic, *adj.;* **-ness,** *n.*
non′pro·lif′i·ca·cy, *n.*
non′pro·lif′i·cal·ly, *adv.*
non′pro·lix′, *adj.;* **-ly,** *adv.;* **-ness,** *n.*
non′pro·lix′i·ty, *n.*
non′pro·lon·ga′tion, *n.*
non·prom′i·nence, *n.*
non·prom′i·nent, *adj.;* **-ly,** *adv.*
non′pro·mis′cu·ous, *adj.;* **-ly,** *adv.;* **-ness,** *n.*
non·prom′is·so′ry, *adj.*
non′pro·mo′tion, *n.*
non′pro·mo′tive, *adj.*
non′prom·ul·ga′tion, *n.*
non′pro·nun′ci·a′tion, *n.*
non·prop′a·ga·ble, *adj.*
non′prop·a·gan′dist, *n., adj.*
non′prop·a·ga′tion, *n.*
non·prop′a·ga′tive, *adj.*
non′pro·pel′lent, *adj., n.*
non′pro·phet′ic, *adj.*
non′pro·phet′i·cal, *adj.;* **-ly,** *adv.*
non′pro·pi′ti·a·ble, *adj.*
non′pro·pi′ti·a′tion, *n.*
non′pro·pi′ti·a′tive, *adj.*
non′pro·por′tion·a·ble, *adj.*
non′pro·por′tion·al, *adj.;* **-ly,** *adv.*
non′pro·por′tion·ate, *adj.;* **-ly,** *adv.;* **-ness,** *n.*
non′pro·por′tioned, *adj.*
non′pro·pri′e·tar′y, *adj., n., pl.* **-tar·ies.**
non′pro·pri′e·tor, *n.*
non′pro·pri′e·ty, *n., pl.* **-ties.**
non′pro·ro·ga′tion, *n.*
non′pro·sa′ic, *adj.;* **-ness,** *n.*
non′pro·sa′i·cal·ly, *adv.*
non′pro·scrip′tion, *n.*
non′pro·scrip′tive, *adj.;* **-ly,** *adv.*
non′pros·e·cut′a·ble, *adj.*
non′pros·e·cu′tion, *n.*
non·pros′pect, *n.*
non′pros·per′i·ty, *n.*
non·pros′per·ous, *adj.;* **-ly,** *adv.;* **-ness,** *n.*
non′pro·tect′ing, *adj.*
non′pro·tec′tion, *n.*
non′pro·tec′tive, *adj.;* **-ly,** *adv.*
non·pro′tein, *n.*
non-Prot′es·tant, *n., adj.*
non′prot·es·ta′tion, *n.*
non′pro·test′ing, *adj.*
non′pro·trac′tile, *adj.*
non′pro·trac′tion, *n.*
non′pro·trud′ing, *adj.*
non′pro·tru′sion, *n.*
non′pro·tru′sive, *adj.;* **-ly,** *adv.;* **-ness,** *n.*
non′pro·tu′ber·ance, *n.*
non′pro·tu′ber·an·cy, *n., pl.* **-cies.**
non′pro·tu′ber·ant, *adj.;* **-ly,** *adv.*
non·prov′a·ble, *adj.*
non′pro·vid′ed, *adj.*
non·prov′i·dent, *adj.;* **-ly,** *adv.*
non′prov·i·den′tial, *adj.;* **-ly,** *adv.*
non′pro·vid′er, *n.*
non′pro·vin′cial, *adj.;* **-ly,** *adv.*
non′pro·vi′sion·al, *adj.;* **-ly,** *adv.*
non′pro·vi′sion·ar′y, *adj.*
non′prov·o·ca′tion, *n.*
non′pro·voc′a·tive, *adj.;* **-ly,** *adv.;* **-ness,** *n.*
non′prox·im′i·ty, *n.*
non·pru′dence, *n.*
non·pru′dent, *adj.;* **-ly,** *adv.*
non′pru·den′tial, *adj.;* **-ly,** *adv.*
non-Prus′sian, *n., adj.*
non′psy·chi·at′ric, *adj.*
non·psy′chic, *adj., n.*
non·psy′chi·cal, *adj.;* **-ly,** *adv.*
non′psy·cho·an′a·lyt′ic, *adj.*
non′psy·cho·an′a·lyt′i·cal, *adj.;* **-ly,** *adv.*
non′psy·cho·log′ic, *adj.*
non′psy·cho·log′i·cal, *adj.;* **-ly,** *adv.*
non′psy·cho·path′ic, *adj.*
non′psy·cho·path′i·cal·ly, *adv.*
non′psy·chot′ic, *adj.*
non·pub′lic, *adj.*
non′pub·li·ca′tion, *n.*
non′pub·lic′i·ty, *n.*
non·pub′lish·a·ble, *adj.*
non·pu′er·ile, *adj.;* **-ly,** *adv.*
non′pu·er·il′i·ty, *n., pl.* **-ties.**
non·pul′mo·nar′y, *adj.*
non·pulp′a·ble, *adj.*
non·pul′sat·ing, *adj.*
non′pul·sa′tion, *n.*
non·pul′sa·tive, *adj.*
non·punc′tu·al, *adj.;* **-ly,** *adv.;* **-ness,** *n.*
non·punc′tu·at′ing, *adj.*
non′punc·tu·a′tion, *n.*
non·punc′tur·a·ble, *adj.*
non·pun′gen·cy, *n.*
non·pun′gent, *adj.;* **-ly,** *adv.*
non·pun′ish·a·ble, *adj.*
non·pun′ish·ing, *adj.*
non·pun′ish·ment, *n.*
non·pu′ni·tive, *adj.*
non·pu′ni·to′ry, *adj.*
non′pur·chas·a·bil′i·ty, *n.*
non·pur′chas·a·ble, *adj.*
non·pur′chase, *n.*
non·pur′chas·er, *n.*
non′pur·ga′tion, *n.*
non·pur′ga·tive, *adj.;* **-ly,** *adv.*
non·pur′ga·to′ri·al, *adj.*
non′pu·ri·fi·ca′tion, *n.*
non·pu′ri·fy′ing, *adj.*
non′pu·ris′tic, *adj.*
non·pur′pos·ive, *adj.;* **-ly,** *adv.;* **-ness,** *n.*
non·pur′su·ance, *n.*
non·pur·su′ant, *adj.;* **-ly,** *adv.*
non·pu′ru·lence, *n.*
non·pu′ru·lent, *adj.;* **-ly,** *adv.*
non′pur·vey′ance, *n.*
non′pu·tres′cence, *n.*
non′pu·tres′cent, *adj.*
non′pu·tres′ci·ble, *adj.*

nonresident. [1520–30; NON- + RESIDENT] —**non·res′i·dence, non·res′i·den·cy,** *n.*

non·re·sis·tance (non′ri zis′təns), *n.* the policy or practice of not resisting violence or established authority, even when tyrannical, by force. [1635–45; NON- + RESISTANCE]

non·re·sis·tant (non′ri zis′tənt), *adj.* **1.** not able, conditioned, or constructed to withstand the effect of something, as a disease, a specific change in temperature, or harsh treatment; susceptible to damage or ill effects. **2.** not resistant; passively obedient. —*n.* **3.** a person who does not resist force. **4.** a person who maintains that violence or established authority, even when tyrannical, should not be resisted by force. [1695–1705; NON- + RESISTANT]

non·re·straint (non′ri strānt′), *n.* absence or lack of restraint. [1840–50; NON- + RESTRAINT]

non·re·stric·tive (non′ri strik′tiv), *adj.* **1.** not restrictive or limiting. **2.** *Gram.* descriptive of a modified element rather than limiting of the element's meaning: *a nonrestrictive modifier.* Cf. **restrictive** (def. 4). [1920–25; NON- + RESTRICTIVE]

non′restric′tive clause′, *Gram.* a relative clause that describes or supplements but is not essential in establishing the identity of the antecedent and is usually set off by commas in English. In *This year, which has been dry, is bad for crops* the clause *which has been dry* is a nonrestrictive clause. Also called **descriptive clause.** Cf. **restrictive clause.** [1925–30]

non·re·turn·a·ble (non′ri tûr′nə bəl), *adj.* **1.** not returnable. **2.** (of an empty bottle or container) not returnable to a vendor for refund of a deposit. —*n.* **3.** something that is not eligible or acceptable for return. [1900–05; NON- + RETURNABLE]

non·rig·id (non rij′id), *adj.* **1.** not rigid. **2.** designating a type of airship having a flexible gas container without a supporting structure and held in shape only by the pressure of the gas within. [1905–10; NON- + RIGID]

non·sched·uled (non skej′o͞old, -o͞old, -o͞o əld; *Brit.* non shed′yo͞old, -shej′o͞old), *adj.* **1.** not scheduled; not entered on or having a schedule; unscheduled: *nonscheduled activities.* **2.** (of an airline) authorized to carry passengers or freight between specified points as demand warrants, rather than on a regular schedule. [1945–50, *Amer.*; NON- + SCHEDULED]

non·sec·tar·i·an (non′sek târ′ē ən), *adj.* not affiliated with or limited to a specific religious denomination. [1825–35; NON- + SECTARIAN]

non·self (non self′), *n. Immunol.* any antigen-bearing foreign material that enters the body and normally stimulates an attack by the body's immune system (distinguished from *self*). [1870–75; NON- + SELF]

non·self-an·ti·gen (non self′an′ti jən, -jen′), *n. Immunol.* any of the antigens present in an individual that originate outside the body (contrasted with *self-antigen*). Also, **nonself′ an′tigen.**

non·sense (non′sens, -səns), *n.* **1.** words or language having little or no sense or meaning. **2.** conduct, action, etc., that is senseless, foolish, or absurd: *to have tolerated enough nonsense.* **3.** impudent, insubordinate, or otherwise objectionable behavior: *He doesn't have to take that nonsense from you.* **4.** something absurd or fatuous: *the utter nonsense of such a suggestion.* **5.** anything of trifling importance or of little or no use. **6.** *Genetics.* a DNA sequence that does not code for an amino acid and is not transcribed (distinguished from *sense*). [1605–15; NON- + SENSE] —**non·sen·si·cal** (non sen′si kəl), *adj.* —**non·sen′si·cal·ly,** *adv.* —**non·sen′si·cal·ness,** *n.* —**Syn. 1.** twaddle, balderdash, moonshine, absurdity.

non′sense syl′lable, *Psychol.* any of numerous letter combinations without meaning, used in learning experiments. [1885–90]

non′sense verse′, a form of light verse, usually for children, depicting imaginative characters in amusing situations of fantasy, whimsical in tone and with a rhythmic appeal, often employing fanciful phrases and meaningless made-up words. [1790–1800]

non seq. See **non sequitur.**

non se·qui·tur (non sek′wi tər, -to͝or′; *Lat.* nōn se′kwi to͝or′), **1.** *Logic.* an inference or a conclusion that does not follow from the premises. **2.** a statement containing an illogical conclusion. [< L: it does not follow]

non·sex·ist (non sek′sist), *adj.* **1.** not showing prejudice on the basis of sex: *nonsexist language.* **2.** not suggesting, advocating, or involving traditional stereotypes regarding what is appropriate for or exclusive to males or females: *nonsexist toys.*

non·sight·ed (non sī′tid), *adj.* having no eyesight; unsighted; blind. [NON- + SIGHT + -ED[3]]

CONCISE PRONUNCIATION KEY: *act, cāpe, dâre, pärt; set, ēqual; if, īce; ox, ōver, ôrder, oil, bo͝ok, bo͞ot, out; up, ûrge; child; sing; shoe; thin, that;* zh as in *treasure.* ə = *a* as in *alone, e* as in *system, i* as in *easily, o* as in *gallop, u* as in *circus;* ᵊ as in *fire* (fīᵊr), *hour* (ouᵊr). l and n can serve as syllabic consonants, as in *cradle* (krād′l), and *button* (but′n). See the full key inside the front cover.

non′py·o·gen′ic, *adj.*
non-Quak′er, *n., adj.*
non-Quak′er·ish, *adj.*
non′qual·i·fi·ca′tion, *n.*
non·qual′i·fy′ing, *adj.*
non·qual′i·ta′tive, *adj.;* **-ly,** *adv.*
non·qual′i·ty, *n., pl.* **-ties.**
non·quan′ti·fi′a·ble, *adj.*
non·quan′ti·ta′tive, *adj.;* **-ly,** *adv.;* **-ness,** *n.*
non·rab·bin′i·cal, *adj.*
non·ra′cial, *adj.;* **-ly,** *adv.*
non·ra′cial·ism, *n.*
non·ra′di·ance, *n.*
non·ra′di·an·cy, *n.*
non·ra′di·ant, *adj.;* **-ly,** *adv.*
non·ra′di·at′ing, *adj.*
non′ra·di·a′tion, *n.*
non·ra′di·a′tive, *adj.*
non·rad′i·cal, *adj., n.;* **-ness,** *n.*
non·rad′i·cal·ly, *adv.*
non′ra·di·o·ac′tive, *adj.*
non·rail′road′, *adj.*
non·rais′a·ble, *adj.*
non·raise′a·ble, *adj.*
non·raised′, *adj.*
non·ran′dom, *adj.;* **-ly,** *adv.;* **-ness,** *n.*
non·rang′ing, *adj.*
non′rap·port′, *n.*
non′rat·a·bil′i·ty, *n.*
non·rat′a·ble, *adj.;* **-ble·ness,** *n.;* **-bly,** *adv.*
non′rate·a·bil′i·ty, *n.*
non·rate′a·ble, *adj.;* **-ble·ness,** *n.;* **-bly,** *adv.*
non·rat′ed, *adj.*
non′rat·i·fi·ca′tion, *n.*
non·rat′i·fy′ing, *adj.*
non·ra′tion·al, *adj.;* **-ly,** *adv.*
non·ra′tion·al·ism, *n.*
non·ra′tion·al·ist, *n.*
non′ra·tion·al·is′tic, *adj.*
non′ra·tion·al·is′ti·cal, *adj.;* **-ly,** *adv.*
non′ra·tion·al′i·ty, *n.*
non′ra·tion·al·i·za′tion, *n.*
non·ra′tion·al·ized′, *adj.*
non′re·act′ing, *adj.*
non′re·ac′tion, *n.*
non′re·ac′tion·ar′y, *adj., n., pl.* **-ar·ies.**
non′re·ac′tive, *adj.*
non′re·ac′tor, *n.*
non·read′er, *n.*
non·read′ing, *n.*
non·re′al·ism, *n.*
non·re′al·ist, *n.*
non′re·al·is′tic, *adj.*
non′re·al·is′ti·cal·ly, *adv.*
non′re·al′i·ty, *n., pl.* **-ties.**
non·re′al·iz′a·ble, *adj.*
non′re·al·i·za′tion, *n.*
non·re′al·iz′ing, *adj.*
non·rea′son, *n.*
non′rea·son·a·bil′i·ty, *n.*
non·rea′son·a·ble, *adj.;* **-ble·ness,** *n.;* **-bly,** *adv.*
non·rea′son·er, *n.*
non·rea′son·ing, *adj.*
non·reb′el, *n., adj.*
non′re·bel′lion, *n.*
non′re·bel′lious, *adj.;* **-ly,** *adv.;* **-ness,** *n.*
non′re·cal′ci·trance, *n.*
non′re·cal′ci·tran·cy, *n.*
non′re·cal′ci·trant, *adj.*
non′re·ceipt′, *n.*
non′re·ceiv′a·ble, *adj., n.*
non′re·ceiv′ing, *adj.*
non′re·cep′tion, *n.*
non′re·cep′tive, *adj.;* **-ly,** *adv.;* **-ness,** *n.*
non′re·cep·tiv′i·ty, *n.*
non′re·cess′, *n.*
non′re·ces′sion, *n.*
non′re·ces′sive, *adj.*
non′re·charge′a·ble, *adj.*
non′re·cip′i·ence, *n.*
non′re·cip′i·en·cy, *n.*
non′re·cip′i·ent, *adj., n.*
non′re·cip′ro·cal, *adj., n.;* **-ly,** *adv.*
non′re·cip′ro·cat′ing, *adj.*
non′rec·i·proc′i·ty, *n.*
non′re·ci′sion, *n.*
non′re·cit′al, *n., adj.*
non′rec·i·ta′tion, *n.*
non′re·cit′a·tive, *adj.*
non′re·claim′a·ble, *adj.*
non′rec·la·ma′tion, *n.*
non′re·clu′sive, *adj.*
non·rec′og·nized′, *adj.*
non′re·coil′, *n.*
non′re·coil′ing, *adj.*
non′rec·ol·lec′tion, *n.*
non′rec·ol·lec′tive, *adj.*
non′rec·on·cil′a·bil′i·ty, *n.*
non′rec′on·cil′a·ble, *adj.;* **-ble·ness,** *n.;* **-bly,** *adv.*
non′rec·on·cil′i·a′tion, *n.*
non′re·coup′a·ble, *adj.*
non′re·cov′er·a·ble, *adj.*
non′rec·tan′gu·lar, *adj.;* **-ly,** *adv.*
non′rec·tan′gu·lar′i·ty, *n.*
non′rec′ti·fi′a·ble, *adj.*
non′rec′ti·fied′, *adj.*
non′re·cu′per·a′tion, *n.*
non′re·cu′per·a′tive, *adj.;* **-ness,** *n.*
non′re·cu′per·a·to′ry, *adj.*
non′re·cy′cla·ble, *adj.*
non′re·deem′a·ble, *adj.*
non′re·demp′ti·ble, *adj.*
non′re·demp′tion, *n.*
non′re·demp′tive, *adj.*
non′re·dress′ing, *adj., n.*
non′re·duced′, *adj.*
non′re·duc′i·bil′i·ty, *n.*
non′re·duc′i·ble, *adj.;* **-bly,** *adv.*
non′re·duc′ing, *adj.*
non′re·duc′tion, *n.*
non′re·duc′tion·al, *adj.*
non′re·duc′tive, *adj.*
non·ref′er·ence, *n.*
non′re·fill′a·ble, *adj.*
non′re·fined′, *adj.*
non′re·fine′ment, *n.*
non′re·flect′ed, *adj.*
non′re·flect′ing, *adj.*
non′re·flec′tion, *n.*
non′re·flec′tive, *adj.;* **-ly,** *adv.;* **-ness,** *n.*
non′re·flec′tor, *n.*
non′ref·or·ma′tion, *n.*
non′ref·or·ma′tion·al, *adj.*
non′re·fract′ing, *adj.*
non′re·frac′tion, *n.*
non′re·frac′tion·al, *adj.*
non′re·frac′tive, *adj.;* **-ly,** *adv.;* **-ness,** *n.*
non′re·frig′er·ant, *adj., n.*
non′re·frig′er·at′ed, *adj.*
non′re·fu′el·ing, *adj.*
non′re·fu′el·ling, *adj.*
non′re·fund′a·bil′i·ty, *n.*
non′re·fund′a·ble, *adj.*
non′re·fut′al, *n.*
non′ref·u·ta′tion, *n.*
non′re·gen′er·ate, *adj.*
non′re·gen′er·at′ing, *adj.*
non′re·gen′er·a′tion, *n.*
non′re·gen′er·a·tive, *adj.;* **-ly,** *adv.*
non′reg·i·men′tal, *adj.*
non·reg′i·ment′ed, *adj.*
non·reg′is·tered, *adj.*
non·reg′is·tra·ble, *adj.*
non·reg′is·trant, *n.*
non′reg·is·tra′tion, *n.*
non′re·gres′sion, *n.*
non′re·gres′sive, *adj.;* **-ly,** *adv.*
non·reg′u·lat′ed, *adj.*
non′reg·u·la′tion, *n.*
non·reg′u·la′tive, *adj.*
non·reg′u·la·to′ry, *adj.*
non′re·ha·bil′i·ta′tion, *n.*
non′re·ha·bil′i·ta′tive, *adj.*
non·reign′ing, *adj.*
non′re·im·bursed′, *adj.*
non′re·im·burse′ment, *n.*
non′re·in·force′ment, *n.*
non′re·in·state′ment, *n.*
non′re·in·vest′ment, *n.*
non′re·jec′tion, *n.*
non′re·join′der, *n.*
non′re·lat′ed, *adj.*
non′re·la′tion, *n.*
non′re·la′tion·al, *adj.*
non·rel′a·tive, *n., adj.;* **-ly,** *adv.;* **-ness,** *n.*
non′rel·a·tiv′i·ty, *n.*
non′re·lax·a′tion, *n.*
non′re·lease′, *n.*
non′re·lent′ing, *adj.*
non·rel′e·vant, *adj.*
non′re·li′a·bil′i·ty, *n.*
non′re·li′a·ble, *adj.;* **-ble·ness,** *n.;* **-bly,** *adv.*
non′re·li′ance, *n.*
non′re·liev′ing, *adj.*
non′re·li′gion, *n.*
non′re·li′gious, *adj.;* **-ly,** *adv.;* **-ness,** *n.*
non′re·lin′quish·ment, *n.*
non′re·me′di·a·bil′i·ty, *n.*
non′re·me′di·a·ble, *adj.;* **-bly,** *adv.*
non′re·me′di·al, *adj.;* **-ly,** *adv.*
non·rem′e·dy, *n., pl.* **-dies.**
non′re·mem′brance, *n.*
non′re·mis′si·ble, *adj.*
non′re·mis′sion, *n.*
non′re·mit′ta·ble, *adj.;* **-bly,** *adv.*
non′re·mon′strance, *n.*
non′re·mon′strant, *adj.*
non′re·mov′a·ble, *adj.*
non′re·mu′ner·a′tion, *n.*
non′re·mu′ner·a′tive, *adj.;* **-ly,** *adv.*
non′ren·di′tion, *n.*
non′re·new′a·ble, *adj.*
non′re·new′al, *n.*
non′re·nounc′ing, *adj.*
non′re·nun′ci·a′tion, *n.*
non′re·pair′, *n.*
non′re·pair′a·ble, *adj.*
non·rep′a·ra·ble, *adj.*
non′rep·a·ra′tion, *n.*
non′re·pa′tri·a·ble, *adj.*
non′re·pa′tri·a′tion, *n.*
non′re·pay′a·ble, *adj.*
non′re·pay′ing, *adj.*
non′re·peal′a·ble, *adj.*
non′re·peat′, *n.*
non′re·peat′ed, *adj.*
non′re·peat′er, *n.*
non′re·pel′lence, *n.*
non′re·pel′len·cy, *n.*
non′re·pel′lent, *adj.*
non′re·pel′ler, *n.*
non′re·pent′ance, *n.*
non′re·pent′ant, *adj.;* **-ly,** *adv.*
non′rep·e·ti′tion, *n.*
non′rep·e·ti′tious, *adj.;* **-ly,** *adv.;* **-ness,** *n.*
non′re·pet′i·tive, *adj.;* **-ly,** *adv.*
non′re·place′a·ble, *adj.*
non′re·place′ment, *n.*
non′re·plen′ish·a·ble, *adj.*
non·rep′li·cate, *adj.*
non·rep′li·cat′ed, *adj.*
non′rep·li·ca′tion, *n.*
non′re·port′a·ble, *adj.*
non′re·port′ed, *adj.*
non′rep·re·hen′si·bil′i·ty, *n.*
non′rep·re·hen′si·ble, *adj.;* **-ble·ness,** *n.;* **-bly,** *adv.*
non′rep·re·sent′a·ble, *adj.*
non′rep·re·sen·ta′tion, *n.*
non′rep·re·sent′a·tive, *n., adj.;* **-ly,** *adv.;* **-ness,** *n.*
non′re·pressed′, *adj.*
non′re·press′i·ble, *adj.;* **-ble·ness,** *n.;* **-bly,** *adv.*
non′re·pres′sion, *n.*
non′re·pres′sive, *adj.*
non′re·pris′al, *n.*
non′re·pro·duc′i·ble, *adj.*
non′re·pro·duc′tion, *n.*
non′re·pro·duc′tive, *adj.;* **-ly,** *adv.;* **-ness,** *n.*
non′re·pub′li·can, *adj., n.*
non′re·pu′di·a·ble, *adj.*
non′re·pu′di·a′tion, *n.*
non′re·pu′di·a′tive, *adj.*
non·rep′ut·a·ble, *adj.;* **-bly,** *adv.*
non′re·quir′a·ble, *adj.*
non′re·quire′ment, *n.*
non·req′ui·site, *adj., n.;* **-ly,** *adv.;* **-ness,** *n.*
non′req·ui·si′tion, *n.*
non′re·quit′al, *n.*
non′re·scis′si·ble, *adj.*
non′re·scis′sion, *n.*
non′re·scis′so·ry, *adj.*
non·res′cue, *n.*
non′re·sem′blance, *n.*
non′re·serv′a·ble, *adj.*
non′res·er·va′tion, *n.*
non′re·serve′, *n., adj.*
non′res·i·den′tial, *adj.*
non′re·sid′u·al, *adj., n.*
non′res·ig·na′tion, *n.*
non′re·sil′i·ence, *n.*
non′re·sil′i·en·cy, *n.*
non′re·sil′i·ent, *adj.;* **-ly,** *adv.*
non′re·sist′i·bil′i·ty, *n.*
non′re·sist′i·ble, *adj.*
non′re·sist′ing, *adj.*
non′re·sis′tive, *adj.*
non′res·o·lu′tion, *n.*
non′re·solv′a·bil′i·ty, *n.*
non′re·solv′a·ble, *adj.;* **-ness,** *n.;* **-bly,** *adv.*
non·res′o·nant, *adj.;* **-ly,** *adv.*
non′re·spect′a·bil′i·ty, *n., pl.* **-ties.**
non′re·spect′a·ble, *adj.;* **-ble·ness,** *n.;* **-bly,** *adv.*
non′re·spir′a·ble, *adj.*
non′re·spon′si·bil′i·ty, *n., pl.* **-ties.**
non′re·spon′si·ble, *adj.;* **-ble·ness,** *n.;* **-bly,** *adv.*
non′re·spon′sive, *adj.;* **-ly,** *adv.*
non′res·ti·tu′tion, *n.*
non′res·to·ra′tion, *n.*
non′re·stor′a·tive, *adj., n.*
non′re·strained′, *adj.*
non′re·strict′ed, *adj.;* **-ly,** *adv.*
non′re·strict′ing, *adj.*
non′re·stric′tion, *n.*
non′re·sump′tion, *n.*
non′res·ur·rec′tion, *n.*
non′res·ur·rec′tion·al, *adj.*
non′re·sus′ci·ta·ble, *adj.*
non′re·sus′ci·ta′tion, *n.*
non′re·sus′ci·ta′tive, *adj.*
non·re′tail, *adj.*
non·re′tail·er, *n.*
non′re·tain′a·ble, *adj.*
non′re·tain′ment, *n.*
non′re·tal′i·a′tion, *n.*
non′re·tar·da′tion, *n.*
non′re·tard′a·tive, *adj.*
non′re·tard′a·to′ry, *adj.*
non′re·tard′ed, *adj.*
non′re·tard′ment, *n.*
non′re·ten′tion, *n.*
non′re·ten′tive, *adj.;* **-ly,** *adv.;* **-ness,** *n.*
non·ret′i·cence, *n.*
non·ret′i·cent, *adj.;* **-ly,** *adv.*
non·ret′i·nal, *adj.*
non′re·tired′, *adj.*
non′re·tire′ment, *n.*
non′re·tir′ing, *adj.*
non′re·trace′a·ble, *adj.*
non′re·trac′tile, *adj.*
non′re·trac·til′i·ty, *n.*
non′re·trac′tion, *n.*
non′re·trench′ment, *n.*
non′re·triev′a·ble, *adj.*
non′ret·ro·ac′tive, *adj.;* **-ly,** *adv.*
non′ret·ro·ac·tiv′i·ty, *n.*
non′re·turn′, *adj.*
non′re·us′a·ble, *adj., n.*
non′re·val′u·a′tion, *n.*
non′re·veal′ing, *adj.*
non′rev·e·la′tion, *n.*
non′re·venge′, *n.*
non′re·veng′er, *n.*
non·rev′e·nue′, *adj., n.*
non′rev′er·ence, *n.*
non·rev′er·ent, *adj.;* **-ly,** *adv.*
non′rev·er·en′tial, *adj.;* **-ly,** *adv.*
non′re·verse′, *adj., n.*
non′re·versed′, *adj.*
non′re·vers′i·bil′i·ty, *n.*
non′re·vers′i·ble, *adj.;* **-ble·ness,** *n.;* **-bly,** *adv.*
non′re·vers′ing, *adj.*
non′re·ver′sion, *n.*
non′re·vert′i·ble, *adj.*
non′re·ver′tive, *adj.*
non′re·view′a·bil′i·ty, *n.*
non′re·view′a·ble, *adj.*
non′re·vi′sion, *n.*
non′re·viv′al, *n.*
non′re·viv′al·ist, *n.*
non′rev·o·ca·bil′i·ty, *n.*
non·rev′o·ca·ble, *adj.;* **-bly,** *adv.*
non′rev·o·ca′tion, *n.*
non′re·vok′a·ble, *adj.*
non′re·volt′ing, *adj.;* **-ly,** *adv.*
non′rev·o·lu′tion, *n.*
non′rev·o·lu′tion·ar′y, *adj., n., pl.* **-ar·ies.**
non′re·volv′ing, *adj.*
non′rhe·tor′i·cal, *adj.;* **-ly,** *adv.*
non′rheu·mat′ic, *adj., n.*
non·rhyme′, *n.*
non·rhymed′, *adj.*
non·rhym′ing, *adj.*
non·rhythm′, *n.*
non·rhyth′mic, *adj.*
non·rhyth′mi·cal, *adj.;* **-ly,** *adv.*
non·rid′ing, *adj., n.*
non·ri′ot·er, *n.*

non·sin·gu·lar (non sing′gyə lər), *adj. Math.* not singular. Cf. **singular** (def. 7). [1875–80; NON- + SINGULAR]

non·sked (non′sked′), *n. Informal.* a nonscheduled airline or plane: *He got his training with the nonskeds.* [1945–50, *Amer.*; NON- + *sked* (shortening and resp. of SCHEDULE)]

non·skid (non′skid′), *adj.* designed or constructed to prevent or reduce skidding: *nonskid tires; nonskid driveways and sidewalks.* [1905–10; NON- + SKID]

non·smok·er (non smō′kər), *n.* **1.** a person who does not smoke. **2.** a railroad car, room, or area reserved for those who do not smoke. [1840–50; NON- + SMOKER]

non·smok·ing (non smō′king), *adj.* **1.** having restrictions against the smoking of tobacco: *a nonsmoking section of an airplane.* **2.** not using cigarettes, cigars, or other smoking materials: *nonsmoking persons.* Also, **non·smok′ing, no-smoking.** [1890–95; NON- + SMOKING]

non·sol·vent (non sol′vənt), *n. Chem.* a substance incapable of dissolving a given component of a solution or mixture. [1615–25; NON- + SOLVENT] —**non·sol′ven·cy,** *n.*

non·spe·cif′ic u·re·thri′tis, (non′spi sif′ik), *Pathol.* See **nongonococcal urethritis.** [NON- + SPECIFIC]

non·sport′ing dog′ (non spôr′ting, -spōr′-), one of any of several breeds of variously sized dogs that may have been developed to hunt or work but now are usually bred for show or as a pet, including the Bichon Frise, bulldog, dalmatian, chow chow, keeshond, and poodle. Also, **non·sport′ing dog′.** [1955–60]

non·stand·ard (non′stan′dərd), *adj.* **1.** not standard. **2.** not conforming in pronunciation, grammar, vocabulary, etc., to the usage characteristic of and considered acceptable by most educated native speakers; lacking in social prestige or regionally or socially limited in use: *a nonstandard dialect; nonstandard English.* Cf. **standard** (def. 27). **3.** *Math.* of or pertaining to a generalized system of numbers that includes the real numbers but also includes infinite and infinitesimal numbers: *nonstandard analysis.* [1920–25; NON- + STANDARD]

non·sta·tive (non stā′tiv), *adj. Gram.* (of a verb) expressing an action or process, as *run* or *grow,* and able to be used in either simple or progressive tenses: *I run every day. I am running home now.* Also, **dynamic.** Cf. **stative.** [NON- + STATIVE]

non·ste·roi·dal (non′ste roid′l, -sti-), *Pharm.* —*adj.* **1.** of or pertaining to a substance that is not a steroid but has certain similar physiological effects. —*n.* **2.** any such substance, esp. a nonsteroidal anti-inflammatory drug, as ibuprofen. [1960–65; NON- + STEROIDAL]

non·stick (non′stik′), *adj.* having or providing a finish designed to prevent food from sticking during cooking or baking: *a nonstick saucepan; a nonstick cooking spray.* [1955–60; NON- + STICK[2]]

non·stop (*adj., adv.* non′stop′; *n.* non′stop′), *adj.* **1.** being without a single stop en route: *a nonstop bus; a nonstop flight from New York to Paris.* **2.** happening, done, or held without a stop or pause or without offering relief or respite: *The ambassador faced a nonstop schedule of meetings and interviews during her visit.* —*adv.* **3.** without a single stop en route. **4.** *Informal.* without a pause or interruption or without respite; continually: *My back ached nonstop for three days.* —*n.* **5.** a long-distance airline flight that makes no stops between the starting point and the destination. [1900–05; NON- + STOP]

non·stri·at·ed (non strī′ā tid), *adj.* not striated; unstriped, as certain muscular tissue. [1865–70; NON- + STRIATED]

non·such (non′such′, nun′-), *n.* nonesuch.

non·suit (non sōōt′), *Law.* —*n.* **1.** a judgment given against a plaintiff who neglects to prosecute, or who fails to show a legal cause of action or to bring sufficient evidence. —*v.t.* **2.** to subject to a nonsuit. [1350–1400; NON- + SUIT; r. ME *nounsuyt* < AF *nounsute*]

non·sul·fide (non sul′fīd), *adj.* (of minerals) not containing a sulfide. Also, **non·sul′phide.** [NON- + SULFIDE]

non·sup·port (non′sə pôrt′, -pōrt′), *n. Law.* failure to support a spouse, child, or other dependent as required by law. [1905–10; NON- + SUPPORT]

non·syl·lab·ic (non′si lab′ik), *adj.* (of a speech sound) not forming a syllable or the nucleus of a syllable. [1905–10; NON- + SYLLABIC]

non·tar·get (non tär′git), *adj.* not being the subject or goal of a particular action, program, maneuver, or the like; not designated for use, observation, attack, etc. [1940–45; NON- + TARGET] —**non·tar′get·a·ble,** *adj.*

non·ten·ured (non ten′yərd), *adj. Educ.* not having tenure. [NON- + TENURED]

CONCISE ETYMOLOGY KEY: <, descended or borrowed from; >, whence; b., blend of, blended; c., cognate with; cf., compare; deriv., derivative; equiv., equivalent; imit., imitative; obl., oblique; r., replacing; s., stem; sp., spelling, spelled; resp., respelling, respelled; trans., translation; ?, origin unknown; *, unattested; ‡, probably earlier than. See the full key inside the front cover.

non·ri′ot·ing, *adj.*
non′ri·par′i·an, *adj., n.*
non′rit·u·al·is′tic, *adj.*
non′rit·u·al·is′ti·cal·ly, *adv.*
non·ri′val, *n., adj.*
non-Ro′man, *adj., n.*
non′ro·man′tic, *adj., n.*
non′ro·man′ti·cal·ly, *adv.*
non′ro·man′ti·cism, *n.*
non·ro′tat·a·ble, *adj.*
non·ro′tat·ing, *adj.*
non′ro·ta′tion, *n.*
non′ro·ta′tion·al, *adj.*
non·ro′ta·tive, *adj.*
non·round′, *adj.*
non·rous′ing, *adj.*
non′rou·tine′, *adj., n.*
non·roy′al, *adj.; -ly, adv.*
non·roy′al·ist, *n.*
non·roy′al·ty, *n., pl.* **-ties.**
non·rub′ber, *n.*
non′ru·di·men′tal, *adj.*
non′ru·di·men′ta·ri·ly, *adv.;* **-ness,** *n.*
non′ru·di·men′ta·ry, *adj.*
non·ru′in·a·ble, *adj.*
non·ru′in·ous, *adj.;* **-ly,** *adv.;* **-ness,** *n.*
non·rul′ing, *n., adj.*
non·ru′mi·nant, *n., adj.*
non·ru′mi·nat′ing, *adj.;* **-ly,** *adv.*
non′ru·mi·na′tion, *n.*
non·ru′mi·na′tive, *adj.*
non·run′, *adj.*
non·rup′tur·a·ble, *adj.*
non·rup′ture, *n.*
non·ru′ral, *adj.;* **-ly,** *adv.*
non-Rus′sian, *adj., n.*
non·rust′a·ble, *adj.*
non·rus′tic, *adj.*
non·rus′ti·cal·ly, *adv.*
non′-Sab·bat′ic, *adj., n.*
non′-Sab·bat′i·cal, *adj., n.;* **-ly,** *adv.*
non·sac′cha·rin, *adj., n.*
non·sac′cha·rine, *adj., n.*
non′sac·cha·rin′i·ty, *n.*
non′sac·er·do′tal, *adj.;* **-ly,** *adv.*
non′sac·ra·men′tal, *adj.*
non·sa′cred, *adj.;* **-ly,** *adv.;* **-ness,** *n.*
non·sac′ri·fice′, *n.*
non′sac·ri·fi′cial, *adj.*
non·sac′ri·fic′ing, *adj.*
non′sac·ri·le′gious, *adj.;* **-ly,** *adv.;* **-ness,** *n.*
non·sail′or, *n.*
non′sal·a·bil′i·ty, *n.*
non·sal′a·ble, *adj.;* **-bly,** *adv.*
non·sal′a·ried, *adj.*
non·sale′, *n.*
non′sale·a·bil′i·ty, *n.*
non·sale′a·ble, *adj.;* **-bly,** *adv.*
non·sa′line, *adj.*
non′sa·lin′i·ty, *n.*
non′sa·lu′bri·ous, *adj.;* **-ly,** *adv.;* **-ness,** *n.*
non·sal′u·tar′i·ly, *adv.;* **-ness,** *n.*
non·sal′u·tar′i·ness, *n.*
non·sal′u·tar′y, *adj.*
non′sal·u·ta′tion, *n.*
non·sal′vage·a·ble, *adj.*
non′sal·va′tion, *n.*
non·san′a·tive, *adj.*
non′sanc·ti·fi·ca′tion, *n.*
non′sanc·ti·mo′ni·ous, *adj.;* **-ly,** *adv.;* **-ness,** *n.*
non·sanc′ti·mo′ny, *n.*
non·sanc′tion, *n.*
non·sanc′tioned, *adj.*
non·sanc′ti·ty, *n., pl.* **-ties.**
non·sane′, *adj.;* **-ly,** *adv.;* **-ness,** *n.*
non·san′guine, *adj.;* **-ly,** *adv.;* **-ness,** *n.*
non·san′i·ty, *n.*
non′-San·skrit′ic, *adj.*
non′sa·pon′i·fi′a·ble, *adj.*
non′sa·pon′i·fi·ca′tion, *n.*
non′sap·o·rif′ic, *adj.*
non′sa·ti·a·bil′i·ty, *n.*
non·sa′ti·a·ble, *adj.*
non′sa·ti·a′tion, *n.*
non·sat′ire, *n.*
non′sa·tir′ic, *adj.*
non′sa·tir′i·cal, *adj.;* **-ly,** *adv.;* **-ness,** *n.*
non·sat′i·riz′ing, *adj.*
non′sat·is·fac′tion, *n.*
non·sat′is·fy′ing, *adj.*
non·sat′u·rat′ed, *adj.*
non′sat·u·ra′tion, *n.*
non·sav′ing, *adj.*
non·saw′ing, *adj.*
non-Sax′on, *n., adj.*
non·scald′ing, *adj.*
non·scal′ing, *adj.*
non·scan′dal·ous, *adj.;* **-ly,** *adv.*
non′-Scan·di·na′vi·an, *adj., n.*
non·scar′ci·ty, *n., pl.* **-ties.**
non·scent′ed, *adj.*
non′sche·mat′ic, *adj.*
non′sche·mat′i·cal·ly, *adv.*
non·sche′ma·tized′, *adj.*
non′schis·mat′ic, *adj.*
non′schis·mat′i·cal, *adj.*
non′schiz·o·phren′ic, *adj.*
non·schol′ar, *n.;* **-ly,** *adj.*
non′scho·las′tic, *adj.*
non′scho·las′ti·cal, *adj.;* **-ly,** *adv.*
non·school′ing, *n.*
non′sci·at′ic, *adj.*
non·sci′ence, *n.*
non′sci·en·tif′ic, *adj.*
non′sci·en·tif′i·cal·ly, *adv.*
non·sci′en·tist, *n.*
non·scor′ing, *adj.*
non·scrap′ing, *adj.*
non·scrip′tur·al, *adj.*
non·scrub′ba·ble, *adj.*
non·scru′ti·ny, *n., pl.* **-nies.**
non·sculp′tur·al, *adj.;* **-ly,** *adv.*
non·sculp′tured, *adj.*
non·sea′son·a·ble, *adj.;* **-ble·ness,** *n.;* **-bly,** *adv.*
non·sea′son·al, *adj.;* **-ly,** *adv.*
non·sea′soned, *adj.*
non′se·ces′sion, *n.*
non′se·ces′sion·al, *adj.*
non′se·clud′ed, *adj.;* **-ly,** *adv.;* **-ness,** *n.*
non′se·clu′sion, *n.*
non′se·clu′sive, *adj.;* **-ly,** *adv.;* **-ness,** *n.*
non·se′cre·cy, *n., pl.* **-cies.**
non·se′cret, *adj., n.;* **-ly,** *adv.*
non′sec·re·tar′i·al, *adj.*
non′se·cre′tion, *n.*
non′se·cre′tion·ar′y, *adj.*
non′se·cre′tive, *adj.;* **-ly,** *adv.*
non′se·cre′to·ry, *adj., n., pl.* **-ries.**
non·sec′tion·al, *adj.;* **-ly,** *adv.*
non·sec·to′ri·al, *adj.*
non·sec′u·lar, *adj.*
non′se·cu′ri·ty, *n., pl.* **-ties.**
non′sed·en·tar′i·ly, *adv.*
non·sed′en·tar′i·ness, *n.*
non·sed′en·tar′y, *adj.*
non′se·di′tious, *adj.;* **-ly,** *adv.;* **-ness,** *n.*
non′seg·men′tal, *adj.;* **-ly,** *adv.*
non·seg′men·tar′y, *adj.*
non′seg·men·ta′tion, *n.*
non·seg′ment·ed, *adj.*
non·seg′re·ga·ble, *adj.*
non·seg′re·gat′ed, *adj.*
non′seg·re·ga′tion, *n.*
non·seg′re·ga′tive, *adj.*
non·seis′mic, *adj.*
non·sei′zure, *n.*
non′se·lect′ed, *adj.*
non′se·lec′tion, *n.*
non′se·lec′tive, *adj.*
non·self-gov′ern·ing, *adj.*
non·sell′ing, *adj.*
non′se·man′tic, *adj.*
non′se·man′ti·cal·ly, *adv.*
non-Sem′ite, *n.*
non′-Se·mit′ic, *adj.*
non·sen·a·to′ri·al, *adj.*
non·sen′sate, *adj.*
non′sen·sa′tion, *n.*
non′sen·sa′tion·al·is′tic, *adj.*
non·sen′si·bil′i·ty, *n., pl.* **-ties.**
non·sen′si·ble, *adj.;* **-ble·ness,** *n.;* **-bly,** *adv.*
non·sen′si·tive, *adj.;* **-ly,** *adv.;* **-ness,** *n.*
non′sen·si·tiv′i·ty, *n., pl.* **-ties.**
non·sen′si·ti·za′tion, *n.*
non·sen′si·tized′, *adj.*
non·sen′si·tiz′ing, *adj.*
non′sen·so′ri·al, *adj.*
non·sen′so·ry, *adj.*
non·sen′su·al, *adj.;* **-ly,** *adv.*
non′sen·su·al·is′tic, *adj.*
non′sen·su·al′i·ty, *n.*
non·sen′su·ous, *adj.;* **-ly,** *adv.;* **-ness,** *n.*
non′sen·ten′tious, *adj.;* **-ly,** *adv.;* **-ness,** *n.*
non·sen′tience, *n.*
non·sen′tien·cy, *n.*
non·sen′tient, *adj.;* **-ly,** *adv.*
non′sep·a·ra·bil′i·ty, *n.*
non·sep′a·ra·ble, *adj.;* **-ble·ness,** *n.;* **-bly,** *adv.*
non·sep′a·rat′ing, *adj.*
non′sep·a·ra′tion, *n.*
non·sep′a·ra′tive, *adj.*
non·sep′tate, *adj.*
non·sep′tic, *adj.*
non′se·qua′cious, *adj.;* **-ly,** *adv.;* **-ness,** *n.*
non′se·quac′i·ty, *n.*
non·se′quent, *adj.*
non′se·quen′tial, *adj.;* **-ly,** *adv.*
non′se·quen′ti·al′i·ty, *n.*
non′se·ques′tered, *adj.*
non′se·ques·tra′tion, *n.*
non′se·raph′ic, *adj.*
non′se·raph′i·cal, *adj.;* **-ly,** *adv.*
non·se′ri·al, *n., adj.;* **-ly,** *adv.*
non·se′ri·ate, *adj.;* **-ly,** *adv.*
non·se′ri·ous, *adj.;* **-ly,** *adv.;* **-ness,** *n.*
non·se′rous, *adj.*
non·serv′ice, *adj.*
non′serv·ice·a·bil′i·ty, *n.*
non·serv′ice·a·ble, *adj.;* **-ble·ness,** *n.;* **-bly,** *adv.*
non·ser′vile, *adj.;* **-ly,** *adv.;* **-ness,** *n.*
non·set′ting, *adj.*
non·set′tle·ment, *n.*
non·sev′er·a·ble, *adj.*
non·sev′er·ance, *n.*
non′se·ver′i·ty, *n., pl.* **-ties.**
non·sex′-linked′, *adj.*
non·sex′u·al, *adj., n.;* **-ly,** *adv.*
non′-Shake·spear′e·an, *adj.*
non′-Shake·spear′i·an, *adj.*
non·share′hold′er, *n.*
non·shar′ing, *adj., n.*
non·shat′ter, *n.*
non·shat′ter·ing, *adj.*
non·shed′ding, *adj.*
non·ship′per, *n.*
non·ship′ping, *adj.*
non·shop′per, *n.*
non·shred′ding, *adj.*
non·shrink′a·ble, *adj.*
non·shrink′ing, *adj.;* **-ly,** *adv.*
non·sib′i·lance, *n.*
non·sib′i·lan·cy, *n.*
non·sib′i·lant, *adj., n.;* **-ly,** *adv.*
non·sic′ca·tive, *adj., n.*
non′si·de′re·al, *adj.*
non·sign′a·ble, *adj.*
non·sig′na·to′ry, *adj., n., pl.* **-ries.**
non′sig·nif′i·cance, *n.*
non′sig·nif′i·can·cy, *n.*
non′sig·nif′i·cant, *adj.;* **-ly,** *adv.*
non′sig·ni·fi·ca′tion, *n.*
non′sig·nif′i·ca′tive, *adj.*
non·sil′i·cate, *n.*
non′si·li′ceous, *adj.*
non′si·li′cious, *adj.*
non·sil′ver, *n., adj.*
non·sim′i·lar, *adj.;* **-ly,** *adv.*
non′sim·i·lar′i·ty, *n., pl.* **-ties.**
non′si·mil′i·tude′, *n.*
non′sim·plic′i·ty, *n., pl.* **-ties.**
non′sim·pli·fi·ca′tion, *n.*
non·sim′u·lar, *n., adj.*
non·sim′u·late, *adj.*
non′sim·u·la′tion, *n.*
non·sim′u·la′tive, *adj.*
non′si·mul·ta′ne·ous, *adj.;* **-ly,** *adv.*
non·sing′er, *n.*
non′sin·gu·lar′i·ty, *n., pl.* **-ties.**
non·sink′a·ble, *adj.*
non·sis′ter, *n.*
non·skel′e·tal, *adj.;* **-ly,** *adv.*
non·skep′tic, *adj., n.*
non·skep′ti·cal, *adj.*
non·skilled′, *adj.*
non·skip′ping, *adj., n.*
non·slan′der·ous, *adj.*
non·slave′hold′ing, *adj., n.*
non-Slav′ic, *adj.*
non·slip′, *adj.*
non·slip′per·y, *adj.*
non·slip′ping, *adj., n.*
non·so′ber, *adj.;* **-ly,** *adv.;* **-ness,** *n.*
non·so′ber·ing, *adj.*
non′so·bri′e·ty, *n.*
non′so·cia·bil′i·ty, *n.*
non·so′cia·ble, *adj.;* **-ble·ness,** *n.;* **-bly,** *adv.*
non·so′cial, *adj.;* **-ly,** *adv.;* **-ness,** *n.*
non·so′cial·ist, *n., adj.*
non′so·cial·is′tic, *adj.*
non′so·ci·al′i·ty, *n.*
non′so·ci′e·tal, *adj.*
non′so·ci′e·ty, *n., pl.* **-ties.**
non′so·ci·o·log′i·cal, *adj.*
non·so′lar, *adj.*
non·sol′dier, *n.*
non′so·lic′i·ta′tion, *n.*
non′so·lic′i·tous, *adj.;* **-ly,** *adv.;* **-ness,** *n.*
non·sol′id, *adj., n.;* **-ly,** *adv.*
non′sol·i·dar′i·ty, *n.*
non′so·lid′i·fi·ca′tion, *n.*
non′so·lid′i·fied′, *adj.*
non′so·lid′i·fy′ing, *adj.*
non·sol′u·ble, *adj.;* **-ble·ness,** *n.;* **-bly,** *adv.*
non′so·lu′tion, *n.*
non·solv′a·bil′i·ty, *n.*
non·solv′a·ble, *adj.;* **-ble·ness,** *n.*
non·so′nant, *adj., n.*
non′so·no′rant, *adj., n.*
non′so·phis′tic, *adj.*
non′so·phis′ti·cal, *adj.;* **-ly,** *adv.;* **-ness,** *n.*
non′sop·or·if′ic, *adj., n.*
non·sov′er·eign, *n., adj.;* **-ly,** *adv.*
non·spa′cious, *adj.;* **-ly,** *adv.;* **-ness,** *n.*
non·spall′ing, *adj.*
non-Span′ish, *adj., n.*
non·spar′ing, *adj.*
non·spark′ing, *adj.*
non·spar′kling, *adj.*
non-Spar′tan, *adj., n.*
non·spa′tial, *adj.;* **-ly,** *adv.*
non′spa·ti·al′i·ty, *n.*
non·speak′er, *n.*
non·speak′ing, *adj.*
non·spe′cial, *adj., n.;* **-ly,** *adv.*
non·spe′cial·ist, *n., adj.*
non·spe′cial·ized′, *adj.*
non·spe′cial·iz′ing, *adj.*
non·spec′i·fi′a·ble, *adj.*
non′spe·cif′i·cal·ly, *adv.*
non′spec·i·fi·ca′tion, *n.*
non′spec·i·fic′i·ty, *n.*
non·spec′i·fied′, *adj.*
non·spe′cious, *adj.;* **-ly,** *adv.;* **-ness,** *n.*
non′spec·tac′u·lar, *adj.;* **-ly,** *adv.*
non·spec′tral, *adj.;* **-ly,** *adv.*
non′spec·tral′i·ty, *n.*
non′spec·u·la′tion, *n.*
non·spec′u·la′tive, *adj.;* **-ly,** *adv.;* **-ness,** *n.*
non·spec′u·la·to′ry, *adj.*
non·spher′al, *adj.*
non·spher′ic, *adj.*
non·spher′i·cal, *adj.;* **-ly,** *adv.*
non′spher·i·cal′i·ty, *n.*
non·spill′, *adj.*
non·spill′a·ble, *adj.*
non·spi′nal, *adj.*
non·spin′ning, *n., adj.*
non·spi′nose, *adj.;* **-ly,** *adv.*
non′spi·nos′i·ty, *n.*
non·spin′y, *adj.*
non·spi′ral, *adj., n.*
non·spir′it, *n.*
non·spir′it·ed, *adj.;* **-ly,** *adv.;* **-ness,** *n.*
non·spir′it·ous, *adj.*
non·spir′it·u·al, *adj., n.;* **-ly,** *adv.;* **-ness,** *n.*
non′spir·it·u·al′i·ty, *n.*
non·spir′it·u·ous, *adj.;* **-ness,** *n.*
non′spon·ta′ne·ous, *adj.;* **-ly,** *adv.;* **-ness,** *n.*
non·spore′-form′ing, *adj.*
non·sport′ing, *adj.;* **-ly,** *adv.*
non·spot′ta·ble, *adj.*
non·sprout′ing, *adj.*
non·spu′ri·ous, *adj.;* **-ly,** *adv.;* **-ness,** *n.*
non·sta′bile, *adj.*
non′sta·bil′i·ty, *n.*
non·sta′ble, *adj.;* **-ble·ness,** *n.;* **-bly,** *adv.*
non·staff′, *adj.*
non·stain′a·ble, *adj.*
non·stain′er, *n.*

non·ter′mi·nat·ing dec′imal (non tûr′mə nā′ting), *Math.* a decimal numeral that does not end in an infinite sequence of zeros (contrasted with *terminating decimal*). Also called **infinite decimal.** [1905–10; NON- + TERMINATING]

non·triv·i·al (non triv′ē əl), *adj.* **1.** not trivial. **2.** *Math.* noting a solution of a linear equation in which the value of at least one variable of the equation is not equal to zero. [1910–15; NON- + TRIVIAL]

non trop·po (non trop′ō, trō′pō, nōn trō′pō; *It.* nôn trôp′pô), *Music.* not too much: *allegro non troppo.* [1850–55; < It]

non-U (non yōō′), *adj.* not characteristic of or appropriate to the upper class, esp. of Great Britain: *certain words and phrases that are considered absolutely non-U.* [NON- + U (adj.)]

non·un·ion (non yōōn′yən), *adj.* **1.** not belonging to a labor union: *nonunion workers.* **2.** not recognizing or accepting a labor union or union policy: *a nonunion factory.* **3.** not manufactured by labor union workers. **4.** antiunion. —*n.* **5.** *Med.* failure of a broken bone to heal. [1860–65; NON- + UNION]

non·un·ion·ism (non yōōn′yə niz′əm), *n.* disregard of or opposition to trade unions. [1890–95; NON- + UNIONISM] —**non·un′ion·ist,** *n.*

non′union shop′, a shop or business in which the employer fixes terms and conditions of employment unilaterally without recognizing or dealing with a union. Cf. **union shop.**

non·u·ple (non′yə pəl), *adj. Music.* having nine beats to the measure: *a nonuple rhythm.* [< NL *nōnuplus,* equiv. to L *nōn(us)* ninth + *-uplus* as in *duplus* DUPLE]

non·us·er (non yōō′zər), *n.* a person who does not use or partake of something, as drugs or alcoholic beverages. [1640–50; NON- + USER]

non·vi·a·ble (non vī′ə bəl), *adj.* **1.** not capable of living, growing, and developing, as an embryo, seed, or plant. **2.** not practicable or workable: *a nonviable plan.* [1875–80; NON- + VIABLE] —**non′vi·a·bil′i·ty,** *n.*

non·vi·o·lence (non vī′ə ləns), *n.* **1.** absence or lack of violence; state or condition of avoiding violence. **2.** the policy, practice, or technique of refraining from the use of violence, esp. when reacting to or protesting against oppression, injustice, discrimination, or the like. Cf. **passive resistance.** [1915–20; NON- + VIOLENCE]

non·vi·o·lent (non vī′ə lənt), *adj.* **1.** not violent; free of violence. **2.** peacefully resistant, as in response to or protest against injustice, esp. on moral or philosophical grounds. [1915–20; NON- + VIOLENT] —**non·vi′o·lent·ly,** *adv.*

non·vis·cous (non vis′kəs), *adj.* inviscid. [NON- + VISCOUS] —**non·vis′cous·ly,** *adv.* —**non·vis′cous·ness,** *n.*

non·vol·a·tile (non vol′ə tl, -til *or, esp. Brit.,* -tīl′), *adj.* **1.** not volatile. **2.** (of computer memory) having the property of retaining data when electrical power fails or is turned off. [NON- + VOLATILE]

non·vot·er (non vō′tər), *n.* **1.** a person who does not vote. **2.** a person who is not eligible to vote. [NON- + VOTER] —**non·vot′ing,** *adj.*

non·white (non hwīt′, -wīt′), *n.* **1.** a person who is not Caucasoid. —*adj.* **2.** not Caucasoid: *the nonwhite peoples of Africa and Asia.* **3.** of or pertaining to nonwhite persons or peoples. [1920–25; NON- + WHITE]

non·wood·y (non wŏŏd′ē), *adj. Hort.* herbaceous. [NON- + WOODY]

non·word (non wûrd′), *n.* **1.** a word that is not recognized or accepted as legitimate, as one produced by a spelling or typographical error. **2.** a word whose meaning or use is not approved in a given circumstance: *"Failure" is a nonword in her vocabulary.* [1960–65; NON- + WORD]

non·work·ing (non wûr′king) *adj.* **1.** not employed for a salary, fees, or wages; not producing or generating income: *Our employee medical plan also covers nonworking spouses.* **2.** not involved in or deriving from labor; not engaged in or directed toward work, esp. as an employee: *What are some of your nonworking activities?* **3.** not functioning or operating: *a nonworking coffee grinder.* [1850–55; NON- + WORKING]

non·wo·ven (non wō′vən), *adj.* (of a fabric) made of fibers autogenously bonded through the action of a chemical agent or heating device, or adhering by means of resinous substances. [1940–45; NON- + WOVEN]

non′yl al′cohol (non′il, -ēl, nō′nil, -nēl), *Chem.* any of several colorless or light-yellow, liquid, water-soluble isomers of the formula $C_9H_{20}O$, esp. having a roselike odor: used chiefly in perfumery and flavoring. [1865–70; *non(ane)* (see NONANOIC) + -YL]

CONCISE PRONUNCIATION KEY: *act, cāpe, dâre, pärt; set, ēqual; if, īce; ox, ōver, ôrder, oil, bŏŏk, bōōt, out; up, ûrge; child; sing; shoe; thin, that;* zh as in *treasure.* ə = *a* as in *alone, e* as in *system, i* as in *easily, o* as in *gallop, u* as in *circus;* ° as in *fire* (fī°r), *hour* (ou°r). l and n can serve as syllabic consonants, as in *cradle* (krād′l), and *button* (but′n). See the full key inside the front cover.

non·stain′ing, *adj.*
non·stamp′a·ble, *adj.*
non·stand′ard·i·za′tion, *n.*
non·stand′ard·ized′, *adj.*
non′stan·za′ic, *adj.*
non·sta′ple, *n.*
non·start′er, *n.*
non·start′ing, *adj.*
non·state′ment, *n.*
non·stat′ic, *adj.*
non·sta′tion·ar′y, *adj., n., pl.* **-ar·ies.**
non′sta·tis′tic, *adj.*
non′sta·tis′ti·cal, *adj.;* **-ly,** *adv.*
non·sta′tus, *adj.*
non·stat′u·ta·ble, *adj.*
non·stat′u·to′ry, *adj.*
non·steal′a·ble, *adj.*
non·stel′lar, *adj.*
non·ster′e·o·typed′, *adj.*
non·ster′e·o·typ′ic, *adj.*
non·ster′e·o·typ′i·cal, *adj.*
non·ster′ile, *adj.;* **-ly,** *adv.*
non′ste·ril′i·ty, *n.*
non·ster′i·li·za′tion, *n.*
non·stick′y, *adj.*
non·stim′u·la·ble, *adj.*
non·stim′u·lant, *n., adj.*
non·stim′u·lat′ing, *adj.*
non′stim·u·la′tion, *n.*
non·stim′u·la′tive, *adj.*
non′stip·u·la′tion, *n.*
non·stock′, *n., adj.*
non-Sto′ic, *adj., n.*
non·sto′i·cal, *adj.;* **-ly,** *adv.;* **-ness,** *n.*
non·stoop′ing, *adj.*
non·stor′a·ble, *adj.*
non·stor′age, *n.*
non′stra·te′gic, *adj.*
non′stra·te′gi·cal, *adj.;* **-ly,** *adv.*
non·strat′i·fied′, *adj.*
non·stress′, *n.*
non·stretch′a·ble, *adj.*
non·stric′tured, *adj.*
non·stri′dent, *adj.*
non·strike′, *adj.*
non·strik′er, *n.*
non·strik′ing, *adj.*
non·strin′gent, *adj.*
non·striped′, *adj.*
non·stroph′ic, *adj.*
non·struc′tur·al, *adj.;* **-ly,** *adv.*
non·struc′ture, *n.*
non·struc′tured, *adj.*
non·stu′dent, *n.*
non·stud′ied, *adj.*
non·stu′di·ous, *adj.;* **-ly,** *adv.;* **-ness,** *n.*
non·stud′y, *n., pl.* **-stud·ies.**
non′stul·ti·fi·ca′tion, *n.*
non′sty·li·za′tion, *n.*
non·styl′ized, *adj.*
non·styp′tic, *adj.*
non·styp′ti·cal, *adj.*
non′stip·tic′i·ty, *n.*
non′sub·con′scious, *adj.;* **-ly,** *adv.;* **-ness,** *n.*
non·sub′ject, *n., adj.*
non′sub·ject′ed, *adj.*
non′sub·jec′ti·fi·ca′tion, *n.*
non′sub·jec′tion, *n.*
non′sub·jec′tive, *adj.;* **-ly,** *adv.;* **-ness,** *n.*
non′sub·jec·tiv′i·ty, *n.*
non·sub′ju·ga·ble, *adj.*
non′sub·ju·ga′tion, *n.*
non′sub·li·ma′tion, *n.*
non′sub·lim′i·nal, *adj.;* **-ly,** *adv.*
non′sub·merged′, *adj.*
non′sub·mer′gence, *n.*
non′sub·mer′gi·bil′i·ty, *n.*
non′sub·mer′gi·ble, *adj.*
non′sub·mers′i·ble, *adj.*
non′sub·mis′si·ble, *adj.*
non′sub·mis′sion, *n.*
non′sub·mis′sive, *adj.;* **-ly,** *adv.;* **-ness,** *n.*
non′sub·or′di·nate, *adj.*
non′sub·or′di·nat′ing, *adj.*
non′sub·or′di·na′tion, *n.*
non′sub·scrib′er, *n.*
non′sub·scrib′ing, *adj.*
non′sub·scrip′tion, *n.*
non′sub·sid′i·ar′y, *adj., n., pl.* **-ar·ies.**
non′sub·sid′ing, *adj.*
non·sub′si·dized′, *adj.*
non·sub′si·dy, *n., pl.* **-dies.**
non′sub·sist′ence, *n.*
non′sub·sist′ent, *adj.*
non′sub·stan′tial, *adj.;* **-ly,** *adv.;* **-ness,** *n.*
non′sub·stan′ti·al′i·ty, *n.*
non′sub·stan′ti·a′tion, *n.*
non′sub·stan·ti′val, *adj.;* **-ly,** *adv.*
non·sub′stan·tive, *adj.;* **-ly,** *adv.;* **-ness,** *n.*
non·sub′sti·tut′ed, *adj.*
non′sub·sti·tu′tion, *n.*
non′sub·sti·tu′tion·al, *adj.;* **-ly,** *adv.*
non′sub·sti·tu′tion·ar′y, *adj.*
non·sub′sti·tu′tive, *adj.*
non·sub′tile, *adj.;* **-ly,** *adv.;* **-ness,** *n.*
non′sub·til′i·ty, *n.*
non·sub′tle, *adj.;* **-tle·ness,** *n.;* **-tly,** *adv.*
non·sub′tle·ty, *n., pl.* **-ties.**
non′sub·trac′tion, *n.*
non′sub·trac′tive, *adj.;* **-ly,** *adv.*
non·sub·ur′ban, *adj., n.*
non′sub·ver′sion, *n.*
non′sub·ver′sive, *adj.;* **-ly,** *adv.;* **-ness,** *n.*
non′suc·cess′, *n.*
non′suc·cess′ful, *adj.;* **-ly,** *adv.*
non′suc·ces′sion, *n.*
non′suc·ces′sion·al, *adj.;* **-ly,** *adv.*
non′suc·ces′sive, *adj.;* **-ly,** *adv.;* **-ness,** *n.*
non·suc′cor, *n.*
non·suc′tion, *n.*
non′suc·to′ri·al, *adj.*
non·suds′ing, *adj.*
non·suf′fer·a·ble, *adj.;* **-ble·ness,** *n.;* **-bly,** *adv.*
non·suf′fer·ance, *n.*
non·suf′frage, *n.*
non·sug′ar, *n.*
non′sug·gest′i·ble, *adj.*
non′sug·ges′tion, *n.*
non′sug·ges′tive, *adj.;* **-ly,** *adv.;* **-ness,** *n.*
non·sul′fur·ous, *adj.*
non·sul′phur·ous, *adj.*
non·sum′mons, *n.*
non·su′per·vis′ing, *adj.*
non′su·per·vi′sion, *n.*
non′su·per·vi′so·ry, *adj.*
non′sup·ple·men′tal, *adj.;* **-ly,** *adv.*
non′sup·ple·men′ta·ry, *adj.*
non·sup′pli·cat′ing, *adj.*
non′sup·pli·ca′tion, *n.*
non′sup·port′a·bil′i·ty, *n.*
non′sup·port′a·ble, *adj.;* **-ble·ness,** *n.;* **-bly,** *adv.*
non′sup·port′er, *n.*
non′sup·port′ing, *adj.*
non′sup·port′ive, *adj.*
non′sup·posed′, *adj.*
non′sup·pos′ing, *adj.*
non′sup·po·si′tion·al, *adj.;* **-ly,** *adv.*
non′sup·pos′i·tive, *adj., n.;* **-ly,** *adv.*
non′sup·pressed′, *adj.*
non′sup·pres′sion, *n.*
non′sup·pres′sive, *adj.;* **-ly,** *adv.;* **-ness,** *n.*
non·sup′pu·ra′tive, *adj.*
non·sur′face, *n., adj.*
non·sur′gi·cal, *adj.;* **-ly,** *adv.*
non′sur·re′al·is′tic, *adj.*
non′sur·re′al·is′ti·cal·ly, *adv.*
non′sur·ren′der, *n.*
non′sur·viv′a·ble, *adj.*
non′sur·viv′al, *n.*
non′sur·vi′vor, *n.*
non′sus·cep′ti·bil′i·ty, *n.*
non′sus·cep′ti·ble, *adj.;* **-ble·ness,** *n.;* **-bly,** *adv.*
non′sus·cep′tive, *adj.;* **-ness,** *n.*
non′sus·cep·tiv′i·ty, *n.*
non′sus′pect, *n., adj.*
non′sus·pend′ed, *adj.*
non′sus·pen′sion, *n.*
non′sus·pen′sive, *adj.;* **-ly,** *adv.;* **-ness,** *n.*
non′sus·tain′a·ble, *adj.*
non′sus·tained′, *adj.*
non′sus·tain′ing, *adj.*
non·sus′te·nance, *n.*
non·sweat′ing, *adj.*
non-Swed′ish, *adj., n.*
non·sweet′, *adj.*
non·sweet′ened, *adj.*
non·swim′mer, *n.*
non·swim′ming, *adj.*
non-Swiss′, *adj., n., pl.* **-Swiss.**
non′syl·lo·gis′tic, *n., adj.*
non′syl·lo·gis′ti·cal, *adj.;* **-ly,** *adv.*
non·syl′lo·giz′ing, *adj.*
non′sym·bi·ot′ic, *adj.*
non′sym·bi·ot′i·cal, *adj.;* **-ly,** *adv.*
non′sym·bol′ic, *adj.*
non′sym·bol′i·cal, *adj.;* **-ly,** *adv.;* **-ness,** *n.*
non′sym·met′ri·cal, *adj.*
non·sym′me·try, *n., pl.* **-tries.**
non′sym·pa·thet′ic, *adj.*
non′sym·pa·thet′i·cal·ly, *adv.*
non·sym′pa·thiz′er, *n.*
non·sym′pa·thiz′ing, *adj.;* **-ly,** *adv.*
non·sym′pa·thy, *n., pl.* **-thies.**
non′sym·phon′ic, *adj.*
non′sym·phon′i·cal·ly, *adv.*
non′sym·pho′ni·ous, *adj.;* **-ly,** *adv.;* **-ness,** *n.*
non′symp·to·mat′ic, *adj.*
non·syn′chro·nal, *adj.*
non′syn·chron′ic, *adj.*
non′syn·chron′i·cal, *adj.;* **-ly,** *adv.*
non·syn′chro·nous, *adj.;* **-ly,** *adv.;* **-ness,** *n.*
non′syn·co·pa′tion, *n.*
non·syn′di·cat′ed, *adj.*
non′syn·di·ca′tion, *n.*
non′syn·es·thet′ic, *adj.*
non′syn·od′ic, *adj.*
non′syn·od′i·cal, *adj.;* **-ly,** *adv.*
non′syn·on′y·mous, *adj.;* **-ly,** *adv.*
non′syn·op′tic, *adj., n.*
non′syn·op′ti·cal, *adj.;* **-ly,** *adv.*
non′syn·tac′tic, *adj.*
non′syn·tac′ti·cal, *adj.;* **-ly,** *adv.*
non·syn′the·sis, *n., pl.* **-ses.**
non·syn′the·sized′, *adj.*
non′syn·thet′ic, *adj.*
non′syn·thet′i·cal, *adj.;* **-ly,** *adv.*
non′syn·ton′ic, *adj.*
non′syn·ton′i·cal, *adj.;* **-ly,** *adv.*
non-Syr′i·an, *adj., n.*
non′sys·tem·at′ic, *adj.*
non′sys·tem·at′i·cal, *adj.;* **-ly,** *adv.*
non·sys′tem·a·tized′, *adj.*
non′sys·tem′ic, *adj.*
non·tab′u·lar, *adj.;* **-ly,** *adv.*
non·tab′u·lat′ed, *adj.*
non·tack′y, *adj.*
non·tac′tic, *n., adj.*
non·tac′ti·cal, *adj.;* **-ly,** *adv.*
non·tac′tile, *adj.*
non′tac·til′i·ty, *n.*
non·tal′ent·ed, *adj.*
non·talk′a·tive, *adj.;* **-ly,** *adv.;* **-ness,** *n.*
non·talk′er, *n.*
non·tan′, *adj.*
non′tan·gen′tal, *adj.*
non′tan·gen′tial, *adj.;* **-ly,** *adv.*
non·tan′gi·ble, *adj.;* **-ble·ness,** *n.;* **-bly,** *adv.*
non·tan′nic, *adj.*
non·tan′nin, *n.*
non·tan′ning, *adj.*
non·tar′nish·a·ble, *adj.*
non·tar′nished, *adj.*
non·tar′nish·ing, *adj.*
non·tarred′, *adj.*
non-Tar′tar, *n., adj.*
non′tau·to·log′i·cal, *adj.;* **-ly,** *adv.*
non′tau·to·mer′ic, *adj.*
non′tau·tom′er·iz′a·ble, *adj.*
non·tax′, *n., adj.*
non·tax·a·bil′i·ty, *n.*
non·tax′a·ble, *adj., n.;* **-ble·ness,** *n.;* **-bly,** *adv.*
non′tax·a′tion, *n.*
non·tax′er, *n.*
non′tax·o·nom′ic, *adj.*
non′tax·o·nom′i·cal, *adj.;* **-ly,** *adv.*
non·teach·a·bil′i·ty, *n.*
non·teach′a·ble, *adj.;* **-ble·ness,** *n.;* **-bly,** *adv.*
non·teach′er, *n.*
non·teach′ing, *adj.*
non·tech′ni·cal, *adj.;* **-ly,** *adv.;* **-ness,** *n.*
non′tech·no·log′ic, *adj.*
non′tech·no·log′i·cal, *adj.;* **-ly,** *adv.*
non′tee·to′tal·er, *n.*
non′tee·to′tal·ist, *n.*
non′tel·e·graph′ic, *adj.*
non′tel·e·graph′i·cal, *adj.;* **-ly,** *adv.*
non′tel·e·o·log′i·cal, *adj.;* **-ly,** *adv.*
non′tel·e·path′ic, *adj.*
non′tel·e·path′i·cal·ly, *adv.*
non′tel·e·phon′ic, *adj.*
non′tel·e·phon′i·cal·ly, *adv.*
non′tel·e·scop′ic, *adj.*
non·tel′e·scop′ing, *adj.*
non·tel′ic, *adj.*
non·tem′per·a·ble, *adj.*
non′tem·per·a·men′tal, *adj.;* **-ly,** *adv.*
non·tem′per·ate, *adj.;* **-ly,** *adv.;* **-ness,** *n.*
non·tem′pered, *adj.*
non·tem′po·ral, *adj., n.;* **-ly,** *adv.*
non′tem·po·rar′i·ly, *adv.*
non·tem′po·rar′i·ness, *n.*
non·tem′po·rar′y, *adj.*
non·tem′po·riz′ing, *adj.;* **-ly,** *adv.*
non′temp·ta′tion, *n.*
non′ten·a·bil′i·ty, *n.*
non·ten′a·ble, *adj.;* **-ble·ness,** *n.;* **-bly,** *adv.*
non·ten′ant, *n.*
non·ten′ant·a·ble, *adj.*
non·ten′sile, *adj.*
non′ten·sil′i·ty, *n.*
non·ten′ta·tive, *adj.;* **-ly,** *adv.;* **-ness,** *n.*
non·ten′ured, *adj.*
non′ten·u′ri·al, *adj.;* **-ly,** *adv.*
non·ter′mi·na·bil′i·ty, *n.*
non·ter′mi·na·ble, *adj.;* **-ble·ness,** *n.;* **-bly,** *adv.*
non·ter′mi·nal, *adj.;* **-ly,** *adv.*
non·ter′mi·na′tion, *n.*
non·ter′mi·na′tive, *adj.;* **-ly,** *adv.*
non′ter·res′tri·al, *adj., n.*
non′ter·ri·to′ri·al, *adj.;* **-ly,** *adv.*
non′ter·ri·to′ri·al′i·ty, *n.*
non·test′a·ble, *adj.*
non′tes·ta·men′ta·ry, *adj.*
non·test′ing, *adj.*
non-Teu′ton, *n., adj.*
non′-Teu·ton′ic, *adj.*
non·tex′tu·al, *adj.;* **-ly,** *adv.*
non·tex′tur·al, *adj.;* **-ly,** *adv.*
non·the′a·ter, *adj.*
non′the·at′ric, *adj.*
non′the·at′ri·cal, *adj.;* **-ly,** *adv.*
non′the·is′tic, *adj.*
non′the·is′ti·cal, *adj.;* **-ly,** *adv.*
non′the·mat′ic, *adj.*
non′the·mat′i·cal·ly, *adv.*
non′the·o·crat′ic, *adj.*
non′the·o·crat′i·cal, *adj.;* **-ly,** *adv.*
non′the·o·log′ic, *adj.*
non′the·o·log′i·cal, *adj.;* **-ly,** *adv.*
non′the·o·ret′ic, *adj.*
non′the·o·ret′i·cal, *adj.;* **-ly,** *adv.*
non′the·o·soph′ic, *adj.*
non′the·o·soph′i·cal, *adj.;* **-ly,** *adv.*
non′ther·a·peu′tic, *adj.*
non′ther·a·peu′ti·cal, *adj.;* **-ly,** *adv.*
non·ther′mal, *adj.;* **-ly,** *adv.*
non′ther·mo·plas′tic, *adj., n.*
non·think′er, *n.*
non·think′ing, *adj., n.*
non·thirst′y, *adj.*
non′tho·rac′ic, *adj.*
non·thread′ed, *adj.*
non·threat′en·ing, *adj.;* **-ly,** *adv.*
non·thrift′, *adj.*
non·tid′al, *adj.*
non·till′a·ble, *adj.*
non·tim′bered, *adj.*
non·tint′ed, *adj.*
non′ti·tan·if′er·ous, *adj.*
non·ti′tle, *adj.*
non·ti′tled, *adj.*
non·tit′u·lar, *adj.;* **-ly,** *adv.*
non·tol′er·a·ble, *adj.;* **-ble·ness,** *n.;* **-bly,** *adv.*
non·tol′er·ance, *n.*

non•ze•ro (non zēr′ō), *adj.* not equal to zero. [1900–05; NON- + ZERO]

noodge (no͝oj), *v.t., v.i.,* **noodged, noodg•ing,** *n.* nudge².

noo•dle¹ (no͞od′l), *n.* a narrow strip of unleavened egg dough that has been rolled thin and dried, boiled, and served alone or in soups, casseroles, etc.; a ribbon-shaped pasta. [1770–80; < G *Nudel*]

noo•dle² (no͞od′l), *n.* **1.** *Slang.* the head. **2.** a fool or simpleton. [1745–55; perh. var. of NODDLE (with oo from FOOL)]

noo•dle³ (no͞od′l), *v.,* **-dled, -dling.** —*v.i.* **1.** to improvise a musical passage in a casual manner, esp. as a warm-up exercise. **2.** *Informal.* **a.** to play; toy: *to noodle with numbers as a hobby.* **b.** to improvise, experiment, or think creatively: *The writers noodled for a week and came up with a better idea for the ad campaign.* —*v.t.* **3.** *Informal.* **a.** to manipulate or tamper with: *She denied that she had noodled the statistics to get a favorable result.* **b.** to make or devise freely as an exercise or experiment (sometimes fol. by *up*): *The architects noodled up a model of a solar house.* **4. noodle around,** *Informal.* to play, experiment, or improvise. [1935–40, *Amer.*; orig. uncert.]

noo•dle•head (no͞od′l hed′), *n.* a fool or simpleton; dolt; blockhead. [NOODLE² + HEAD] —**noo′dle•head′•ed,** *adj.*

CONCISE ETYMOLOGY KEY: <, descended or borrowed from; >, whence; b., blend of, blended; c., cognate with; cf., compare; deriv., derivative; equiv., equivalent; imit., imitative; obl., oblique; r., replacing; s., stem; sp., spelling, spelled; resp., respelling, respelled; trans., translation; ?, origin unknown; *, unattested; ‡, probably earlier than. See the full key inside the front cover.

noog•ie (no͝og′ē), *n. Slang.* a light blow or jab, usually to a person's head, back, or upper arm and accompanied by a twisting motion, with the extended knuckle of the curled-up second or third finger: done as a gesture of affection or painfully as a prank. Also, **nuggie, nugie.** [1975–80; appar. expressive alter. of KNUCKLE; see -Y²]

nook (no͝ok), *n.* **1.** a corner, as in a room. **2.** any secluded or obscure corner. **3.** any small recess: *a breakfast nook.* **4.** any remote or sheltered spot: *a shady nook that was ideal for a picnic.* [1250–1300; ME *nok*] —**nook′like′,** *adj.*

nook•er•y (no͝ok′ə rē), *n., pl.* **-er•ies.** a snug, secure, or cozy nook. [1815–25; NOOK + -ERY]

nook•y¹ (no͝ok′ē), *n., pl.* **nook•ies** for 2. *Slang (vulgar)* **1.** coitus; sexual intercourse. **2.** a female regarded as a sexual partner. Also, **nook′ie.** [1925–30; of uncert. orig.; D *neuken* "to have intercourse" has been proposed as a source (cf. dial. D *neuk* a push, punch), but it is unclear in what context it could have been borrowed]

nook•y² (no͝ok′ē), *adj.* **nook•i•er, nook•i•est.** full of nooks. [1805–15; NOOK + -Y¹]

noon (no͞on), *n.* **1.** midday. **2.** twelve o'clock in the daytime. **3.** the highest, brightest, or finest point or part: *the noon of one's career.* **4.** *Archaic.* midnight: *the noon of night.* [bef. 900; ME *none,* OE *nōn* < L *nōna* ninth hour. See NONE²]

noon•day (no͞on′dā′), *adj.* **1.** of or at noon or midday: *the usual noonday meal.* —*n.* **2.** midday; noon. [1525–35; NOON + DAY]

no′ one′, no person; not anyone; nobody: *No one is home.* Also, **no′-one′.** [1595–1605] —**Usage.** See **each.**

No. 1 (num′bər wun′), number one. [1595–1605]

noon•er (no͞o′nər), *n. Informal.* **1.** an activity undertaken during the lunch hour. **2.** a brief midday sexual encounter. [NOON + -ER¹]

noon•hour (no͞on′ouᵊr′, -ou′ər), *n.* **1.** the hour between 12 noon and 1 P.M. **2.** lunchtime. [1885–90, *Amer.*; NOON + HOUR]

noon•ing (no͞o′ning), *n. Chiefly Inland North.* **1.** noontime. **2.** an interval at noon for rest or food. **3.** a rest or meal at noon. [1425–75; late ME; see NOON, -ING¹]

noon•tide (no͞on′tīd′), *n.* **1.** the time of noon; midday. **2.** the highest or best point or part: *the noontide of one's theatrical career.* **3.** *Literary.* midnight. [bef. 1000; ME *nonetyde,* OE *nōntīd.* See NOON, TIDE]

noon•time (no͞on′tīm′), *n.* noon; noontide; noonday: *Will he be home at noontime?* [1350–1400; ME *none tyme.* See NOON, TIME]

noose (no͞os), *n., v.,* **noosed, noos•ing.** —*n.* **1.** a loop with a running knot, as in a snare, lasso, or hangman's halter, that tightens as the rope is pulled. **2.** a tie or bond; snare. —*v.t.* **3.** to secure by or as by a noose. **4.** to make a noose with or in (a rope or the like). [1400–50; late ME *nose* < ?] —**noos′er,** *n.*

no•o•sphere (nō′ə sfēr′), *n. Ecol.* the biosphere including and modified by such human activities as agriculture, forestry, animal husbandry, urbanization, and industrialization. Also called **anthroposphere.** [1940–45; < F *noösphere* < Gk *nóo(s)* mind + F *sphère* SPHERE]

non•tol′er•ant, *adj.*; **-ly,** *adv.*
non•tol′er•at′ed, *adj.*
non′tol•er•a′tion, *n.*
non•tol′er•a′tive, *adj.*
non′to•nal′i•ty, *n.*
non•toned′, *adj.*
non•ton′ic, *adj.*
non•top′o•graph′i•cal, *adj.*
non•tor′tu•ous, *adj.*; **-ly,** *adv.*
non′to•tal′i•tar′i•an, *adj.*
non•tour′ist, *n.*
non•tox′ic, *adj.*
non•tox′i•cal•ly, *adv.*
non′tox•ic′i•ty, *n.*
non′trace•a•bil′i•ty, *n.*
non•trace′a•ble, *adj.*; **-ble•ness,** *n.*; **-bly,** *adv.*
non′trac•ta•bil′i•ty, *n.*
non•trac′ta•ble, *adj.*; **-ble•ness,** *n.*; **-bly,** *adv.*
non•trac′tion, *n.*
non•trade′, *n.*
non•trad′er, *n.*
non•trad′ing, *adj.*
non′tra•di′tion, *n.*
non′tra•di′tion•al, *adj.*; **-ly,** *adv.*
non′tra•di′tion•al•ist, *n., adj.*
non′tra•di′tion•al•is′tic, *adj.*
non′tra•di′tion•ar′y, *adj.*
non•trag′e•dy, *n., pl.* **-dies.**
non•trag′ic, *adj.*
non•trag′i•cal, *adj.*; **-ly,** *adv.*; **-ness,** *n.*
non•trail′ing, *adj.*
non•trained′, *adj.*
non•train′ing, *adj., n.*
non•trai′tor•ous, *adj.*; **-ly,** *adv.*; **-ness,** *n.*
non′tran•scrib′ing, *adj.*
non′tran•scrip′tion, *n.*
non′tran•scrip′tive, *adj.*
non′trans•fer′a•bil′i•ty, *n.*
non′trans•fer′a•ble, *adj.*
non′trans•fer′ence, *n.*
non′trans•fer•en′tial, *adj.*
non′trans•for•ma′tion, *n.*
non′trans•form′ing, *adj.*
non′trans•gres′sion, *n.*
non′trans•gres′sive, *adj.*; **-ly,** *adv.*
non•tran′sience, *n.*
non•tran′sien•cy, *n.*
non•tran′sient, *adj.*; **-ly,** *adv.*; **-ness,** *n.*
non′tran•si′tion•al, *adj.*; **-ly,** *adv.*
non•tran′si•tive, *adj., n.*; **-ly,** *adv.*; **-ness,** *n.*
non′trans•lo•ca′tion, *n.*
non′trans•mis′sion, *n.*
non′trans•mit′tal, *n., adj.*
non′trans•mit′tance, *n.*
non′trans•mit′ti•ble, *adj.*
non′trans•par′ence, *n.*
non′trans•par′en•cy, *n.*
non′trans•par′ent, *adj.*; **-ly,** *adv.*; **-ness,** *n.*
non′trans•port′a•bil′i•ty, *n.*
non′trans•port′a•ble, *adj.*
non′trans•por•ta′tion, *n.*
non′trans•pos′a•ble, *adj.*
non′trans•pos′ing, *adj.*
non′trans•po•si′tion, *n.*
non•trav′el•er, *n.*
non•trav′el•ing, *adj.*
non•trav′el•ler, *n.*
non•trav′el•ling, *adj.*
non′tra•vers′a•ble, *adj.*
non′trea′son•a•ble, *adj.*; **-ble•ness,** *n.*; **-bly,** *adv.*
non•treat′a•ble, *adj.*
non•treat′ed, *adj.*
non•treat′ment, *n.*
non•trea′ty, *n., pl.* **-ties.**
non•tres′pass, *n.*
non•tri′al, *n.*
non•trib′al, *adj.*; **-ly,** *adv.*
non•tribes′man, *n., pl.* **-men.**
non•trib′u•tar′y, *adj.*
non•tri′er, *n.*
non′trig•o•no•met′ric, *adj.*
non′trig•o•no•met′ri•cal, *adj.*; **-ly,** *adv.*
non′-Trin•i•tar′i•an, *adj., n.*
non′triv•i•al′i•ty, *n., pl.* **-ties.**
non•trop′ic, *adj.*
non•trop′i•cal, *adj.*; **-ly,** *adv.*
non•trou′bling, *adj.*
non•tru′an•cy, *n.*
non•tru′ant, *n., adj.*
non•trunked′, *adj.*
non•trust′, *n.*
non•trust′ing, *adj.*
non•truth′, *n.*
non′tu•ber′cu•lar, *adj.*; **-ly,** *adv.*
non′tu•ber′cu•lous, *adj.*
non•tu′bu•lar, *adj.*
non•tu′mor•ous, *adj.*
non′tu•mul′tu•ous, *adj.*; **-ly,** *adv.*; **-ness,** *n.*
non•tuned′, *adj.*
non•tur′bi•nate, *adj.*
non•tur′bi•nat′ed, *adj.*
non-Turk′, *n.*
non-Tur′kic, *adj.*
non-Turk′ish, *adj., n.*
non-Tus′can, *adj., n.*
non′tu•to′ri•al, *adj.*; **-ly,** *adv.*
non′ty•phoi′dal, *adj.*
non•typ′i•cal, *adj.*; **-ly,** *adv.*; **-ness,** *n.*
non′ty•po•graph′ic, *adj.*
non′ty•po•graph′i•cal, *adj.*; **-ly,** *adv.*
non′ty•ran′nic, *adj.*
non′ty•ran′ni•cal, *adj.*; **-ly,** *adv.*; **-ness,** *n.*
non•tyr′an•nous, *adj.*; **-ly,** *adv.*; **-ness,** *n.*
non′u•biq′ui•tar′y, *adj.*
non′u•biq′ui•tous, *adj.*; **-ly,** *adv.*; **-ness,** *n.*
non′-U•krain′i•an, *adj., n.*
non•ul′cer•ous, *adj.*; **-ly,** *adv.*; **-ness,** *n.*
non′um•bil′i•cal, *adj.*
non-Um′bri•an, *adj., n.*
non′u•nan′i•mous, *adj.*; **-ly,** *adv.*; **-ness,** *n.*
non′un•der•grad′u•ate, *n., adj.*
non′un•der•stand′a•ble, *adj.*
non′un•der•stand′ing, *adj., n.*; **-ly,** *adv.*
non′un•der•stood′, *adj.*
non•un′du•lant, *adj.*
non•un′du•late, *adj.*
non•un′du•lat′ing, *adj.*
non•un′du•la•to′ry, *adj.*
non′u•ni•fi•ca′tion, *n.*
non•u′ni•fied′, *adj.*
non•u′ni•form′, *adj.*
non′u•ni•form′i•ty, *n., pl.* **-ties.**
non′u•nique′, *adj.*; **-ly,** *adv.*; **-ness,** *n.*
non•u′ni•son, *n.*
non•u•nit′a•ble, *adj.*
non′u•ni•tar′i•an, *n.*
non′-U•ni•tar′i•an, *adj., n.*
non′u•nite′a•ble, *adj.*
non′u•nit′ed, *adj.*
non′u•nit′ing, *adj.*
non•u′ni•ty, *n., pl.* **-ties.**
non′u•ni•ver′sal, *adj., n.*; **-ly,** *adv.*
non′u•ni•ver′sal•ist, *n., adj.*
non′u•ni•ver•sal′i•ty, *n.*
non′u•ni•ver′si•ty, *n., pl.* **-ties,** *adj.*
non•up′right′, *adj., n.*; **-ly,** *adv.*; **-ness,** *n.*
non′-U•ra′li•an, *n.*
non•ur′ban, *adj.*
non•ur′ban•ite′, *n.*
non•ur′ban•ized′, *adj.*
non•ur′gent, *adj.*; **-ly,** *adv.*
non•us′a•ble, *adj.*
non•us′age, *n.*
non•use′, *n.*
non•use′a•ble, *adj.*
non•us′ing, *adj.*
non′u•su′ri•ous, *adj.*; **-ly,** *adv.*; **-ness,** *n.*
non′u•surp′ing, *adj.*; **-ly,** *adv.*
non•u′ter•ine, *adj.*
non′u•til′i•tar′i•an, *adj., n.*
non′u•til′i•ty, *n., pl.* **-ties.**
non•u′til•i•za′tion, *n.*
non•u′til•ized′, *adj.*
non•ut′ter•ance, *n.*
non•va′can•cy, *n., pl.* **-cies.**
non•va′cant, *adj.*; **-ly,** *adv.*
non′vac•ci•na′tion, *n.*
non•vac′il•lat′ing, *adj.*
non′vac•il•la′tion, *n.*
non•vac′u•ous, *adj.*; **-ly,** *adv.*; **-ness,** *n.*
non•vac′u•um, *adj., n., pl.* **-vac•u•ums, -vac•u•a.**
non•vag′i•nal, *adj.*
non•va′gran•cy, *n., pl.* **-cies.**
non•va′grant, *adj.*; **-ly,** *adv.*; **-ness,** *n.*
non•val′id, *adj.*; **-ly,** *adv.*; **-ness,** *n.*
non•val′i•da′tion, *n.*
non′va•lid′i•ty, *n., pl.* **-ties.**
non•val′or•ous, *adj.*; **-ly,** *adv.*; **-ness,** *n.*
non•val′u•a•ble, *adj.*
non•val′ue, *n.*
non•val′ued, *adj.*
non•van′ish•ing, *adj.*
non•va′por•os′i•ty, *n.*
non•va′por•ous, *adj.*; **-ly,** *adv.*; **-ness,** *n.*
non•var′i•a•bil′i•ty, *n.*
non•var′i•a•ble, *adj.*; **-ble•ness,** *n.*; **-bly,** *adv.*
non•var′i•ance, *n.*
non•var′i•ant, *adj., n.*
non•var′i•a′tion, *n.*
non•var′ied, *adj.*
non′va•ri′e•ty, *n., pl.* **-ties.**
non•var′i•ous, *adj.*; **-ly,** *adv.*; **-ness,** *n.*
non•vas′cu•lar, *adj.*; **-ly,** *adv.*
non•vas′cu•lose′, *adj.*
non•vas′cu•lous, *adj.*
non•vas′sal, *n.*
non-Ve′dic, *adj.*
non•veg′e•ta•ble, *n., adj.*
non′veg•e•tar′i•an, *adj., n.*
non′veg•e•ta′tion, *n.*
non•veg′e•ta′tive, *adj.*; **-ly,** *adv.*; **-ness,** *n.*
non•veg′e•tive, *adj.*
non•ve′he•ment, *adj.*; **-ly,** *adv.*
non′ve•hic′u•lar, *adj.*
non•ve′nal, *adj.*; **-ly,** *adv.*
non′vend•i•bil′i•ty, *n.*
non•vend′i•ble, *adj.*; **-ble•ness,** *n.*; **-bly,** *adv.*
non′ve•ne′re•al, *adj.*
non′-Ve•ne′tian, *adj., n.*
non•ven′om•ous, *adj.*; **-ly,** *adv.*; **-ness,** *n.*
non•ve′nous, *adj.*; **-ly,** *adv.*; **-ness,** *n.*
non′ven•ti•la′tion, *n.*
non•ven′ti•la′tive, *adj.*
non′ve•ra′cious, *adj.*; **-ly,** *adv.*; **-ness,** *n.*
non′ve•rac′i•ty, *n., pl.* **-ties.**
non•ver′bal, *adj.*; **-ly,** *adv.*
non•ver′bal•ized′, *adj.*
non•ver•bos′i•ty, *n.*
non•ver′i•fi′a•ble, *adj.*
non•ver′i•fi•ca′tion, *n.*
non•ver′i•ta•ble, *adj.*; **-ble•ness,** *n.*; **-bly,** *adv.*
non•ver′min•ous, *adj.*; **-ly,** *adv.*; **-ness,** *n.*
non′ver•nac′u•lar, *adj.*
non′ver•sa•til′i•ty, *n.*
non•ver′te•bral, *adj.*
non•ver′te•brate′, *adj., n.*
non•ver′ti•cal, *adj.*; **-ly,** *adv.*; **-ness,** *n.*
non′ver•ti•cal′i•ty, *n.*
non′ve•sic′u•lar, *adj.*; **-ly,** *adv.*
non•vest′ed, *adj.*
non•vest′ing, *adj., n.*
non•ves′ture, *n.*
non•vet′er•an, *n.*
non•vet′er•i•nar′y, *adj., n., pl.* **-nar•ies.**
non′vex•a′tious, *adj.*; **-ly,** *adv.*; **-ness,** *n.*
non•vi′bra•tile, *adj.*
non•vi′brat•ing, *adj.*
non′vi•bra′tion, *n.*
non•vi′bra•tor, *n.*
non•vi′bra•to′ry, *adj.*
non′vi•car′i•ous, *adj.*; **-ly,** *adv.*; **-ness,** *n.*
non•vic′tim, *n.*
non•vic′to•ry, *n., pl.* **-ries.**
non•view′er, *n.*
non•vig′i•lance, *n.*
non•vig′i•lant, *adj.*; **-ly,** *adv.*; **-ness,** *n.*
non•vil′lag•er, *n.*
non•vil′lain•ous, *adj.*; **-ly,** *adv.*; **-ness,** *n.*
non•vin′di•ca•ble, *adj.*
non′vin•di•ca′tion, *n.*
non′vi•nos′i•ty, *n.*
non•vi′nous, *adj.*
non•vin′tage, *adj., n.*
non′vi•o•la•bil′i•ty, *n.*
non•vi′o•la•ble, *adj.*; **-ble•ness,** *n.*; **-bly,** *adv.*
non′vi•o•la′tion, *n.*
non•vi′o•la′tive, *adj.*
non•vir′gin•al, *adj.*; **-ly,** *adv.*
non′-Vir•gin′ian, *adj., n.*
non•vir′ile, *adj.*
non′vi•ril′i•ty, *n.*
non•vir′tue, *n.*
non•vir′tu•ous, *adj.*; **-ly,** *adv.*; **-ness,** *n.*
non•vir′u•lent, *adj.*; **-ly,** *adv.*
non•vis′cer•al, *adj.*
non•vis′cid, *adj.*; **-ly,** *adv.*; **-ness,** *n.*
non′vis•cid′i•ty, *n.*
non′vis•i•bil′i•ty, *n., pl.* **-ties.**
non•vis′i•ble, *adj.*; **-bly,** *adv.*
non•vi′sion•al, *adj.*
non•vi′sion•ar′y, *adj., n.*
non•vis′it•ing, *adj.*
non•vis′u•al, *adj.*
non•vis′u•al•ized′, *adj.*
non•vi′tal, *adj.*; **-ly,** *adv.*; **-ness,** *n.*
non′vi•tal′i•ty, *n.*
non•vi′tal•ized′, *adj.*
non′vi•ti•a′tion, *n.*
non•vit′ri•fied′, *adj.*
non′vit•ri•ol′ic, *adj.*
non′vi•tu′per•a′tive, *adj.*; **-ly,** *adv.*
non′viv•i•par′i•ty, *n.*
non′vi•vip′a•rous, *adj.*; **-ly,** *adv.*; **-ness,** *n.*
non•vo′ca•ble, *adj.*
non•vo′cal, *adj., n.*; **-ly,** *adv.*; **-ness,** *n.*
non′vo•cal′ic, *adj.*
non′vo•cal′i•ty, *n.*
non′vo•cal•i•za′tion, *n.*
non′vo•ca′tion•al, *adj.*; **-ly,** *adv.*
non•void′, *adj., n.*
non•void′a•ble, *adj.*
non•vo′lant, *adj.*
non•vol′a•til′i•ty, *n.*
non•vol′a•til•iz′a•ble, *adj.*
non•vol′a•til•ized′, *adj.*
non′vol•can′ic, *adj.*
non′vo•li′tion, *n.*
non′vo•li′tion•al, *adj.*
non′vol•u•bil′i•ty, *n.*
non•vol′u•ble, *adj.*; **-ble•ness,** *n.*; **-bly,** *adv.*
non•vol′un•tar′y, *adj.*
non•vul′can•ized′, *adj.*
non′vul•gar′i•ty, *n., pl.* **-ties.**
non•vul′val, *adj.*
non•vul′var, *adj.*
non•waiv′a•ble, *adj.*
non•walk′ing, *adj., n.*
non•war′, *n.*
non•war′rant•a•ble, *adj.*; **-bly,** *adv.*
non•war′rant•ed, *adj.*
non•wash′a•ble, *adj.*
non•wast′ing, *adj., n.*
non•wa′ter•tight′, *adj.*
non•wa′ver•ing, *adj.*
non•wax′ing, *adj.*
non•weak′ness, *n.*
non-Welsh′, *adj., n.*
non•west′ern, *adj., n.*
non•wet′ted, *adj.*
non•whal′ing, *adj.*
non•winged′, *adj.*
non•win′ner, *n.*
non′with•draw′a•ble, *adj.*
non•with′er•ing, *adj.*
non•wool′, *adj.*
non•work′, *n.*
non•work′er, *n.*
non•yield′ing, *adj.*
non•zeal′ous, *adj.*; **-ly,** *adv.*; **-ness,** *n.*
non-Zi′on•ist, *n., adj.*
non′zo•di′a•cal, *adj.*
non•zon′al, *adj.*; **-ly,** *adv.*
non•zon′ate, *adj.*
non•zon′at•ed, *adj.*
non′zo•o•log′ic, *adj.*
non′zo•o•log′i•cal, *adj.*; **-ly,** *adv.*

Noot·ka (no͞ot′kə, no͝ot′-), *n., pl.* **-kas,** (*esp. collectively*) **-ka** for 2. **1.** a Wakashan language spoken in SW Canada on the western coast of Vancouver Island. **2.** a member of an Indian people of Washington and Vancouver Island speaking this language.

Noot′ka fir′, (in the Pacific Northwest) See **Douglas fir.** [1795–1805, *Amer.*]

NOP, not our publication. Also, **N.O.P.**

no·pal (nō′pəl, nō päl′, -pal′), *n.* **1.** any of several cacti of the genus *Nopalea,* resembling the prickly pear. **2.** the fruit of such a cactus, or of a similar cactus, as the prickly pear. [1720–30; < MexSp < Nahuatl *nohpalli*]

no-par (nō′pär′), *adj.* without par or face value: *no-par stock.* [1920–25; special use of phrase *no par* (*value*)]

nope (nōp), *adv. Informal.* no. [1885–90, *Amer.*; var. of NO[1]; cf. YUP]

no·place (nō′plās′), *adv.* nowhere. [1925–30; NO[2] + PLACE]

—Usage. See **anyplace.**

nor (nôr; *unstressed* nər), *conj.* **1.** (used in negative phrases, esp. after *neither,* to introduce the second member in a series, or any subsequent member): *Neither he nor I will be there. They won't wait for you, nor for me, nor for anybody.* **2.** (used to continue the force of a negative, as *not, no, never,* etc., occurring in a preceding clause): *He left and I never saw him again, nor did I regret it.* **3.** (used after an affirmative clause, or as a continuative, in the sense of *and not*): *They are happy, nor need we worry.* **4.** *Older Use.* than. **5.** *Archaic.* (used without a preceding *neither,* the negative force of which is understood): *He nor I was there.* **6.** *Archaic.* (used instead of *neither* as correlative to a following *nor*): *Nor he nor I was there.* [1300–50; ME, contr. of *nother,* OE *nōther,* equiv. to *ne* not + *ōther* (contr. of *ōhwæther*) either; cf. OR[1]]

—Usage. See **neither.**

nor-, a combining form used in the names of chemical compounds which are the normal or parent forms of the compound denoted by the base words: *l-norepinephrine.* [short for NORMAL]

Nor., 1. Norman. **2.** North. **3.** Northern. **4.** Norway. **5.** Norwegian.

nor., 1. north. **2.** northern.

No·ra (nôr′ə, nōr′ə), *n.* a female given name, form of **Honora.**

NORAD (nôr′ad), *n.* a joint U.S.-Canadian air force command responsible for detecting aircraft and space vehicles deemed a threat to the continental airspace. [*Nor*(*th American*) *A*(*ir*) *D*(*efence Command*).]

nor·a·dren·a·line (nôr′ə dren′l in, -ēn′), *n.* norepinephrine. Also, **nor·a·dren·a·lin** (nôr′ə dren′l in). [1930–35; NOR- + ADRENALINE]

Nor·bert (nôr′bərt), *n.* a male given name.

NOR′ cir′cuit (nôr), *Computers.* a circuit that is energized only when none of its inputs are energized. Also called **NOR gate.** [1955–60]

Nor·co (nôr′kō), *n.* a town in S California. 21,126.

Nord (nôʀ), *n.* a department in N France. 2,510,738; 2229 sq. mi. (5770 sq. km). *Cap.:* Lille.

Nor·dau (nôr′dou), *n.* **Max Si·mon** (mäks zē′mōn), 1849–1923, Hungarian author, physician, and leader in the Zionist movement.

Nor·den·skjöld (nôr′dn shōld′, -shəld; *Sw.* no͞oʀ′dən-shœld′), *n.* **1. Baron Nils A·dolf E·rik** (nils ä′dôlf ā′ʀik), 1832–1901, Swedish arctic explorer, geographer, and geologist; born in Finland. **2.** his nephew **Nils Ot·to Gus·taf** (nils ôt′o͞o go͞os′täv), 1869–1928, Swedish arctic and antarctic explorer.

Nor′den·skjöld Sea′. See **Laptev Sea.**

Nord·hau·sen (nôʀt′hou′zən), *n.* a city in SW East Germany: site of a former Nazi concentration camp. 46,404.

Nor·dic (nôr′dik), *adj.* **1.** of, pertaining to, or characteristic of a Germanic people of northern European origin, exemplified by the Scandinavians. **2.** having or suggesting the physical characteristics associated with these people, typically tall stature, blond hair, blue eyes, and elongated head. **3.** (*sometimes l.c.*) of or pertaining to skiing events involving ski jumping and cross-country skiing. Cf. **Alpine.** —*n.* **4.** a member of the Nordic people, esp. a Scandinavian. [1895–1900; < F *nordique,* equiv. to *nord* NORTH + *-ique* -IC] **—Nor·dic·i·ty** (nôr-dis′i tē), *n.*

Nor·di·ca (nôr′di kə), *n.* **Lillian** (*Lillian Norton*), 1859–1914, U.S. soprano.

Nor′dic combined′, a competition for Nordic skiers comprising ski jumping and cross-country skiing events, the winner having the highest combined score.

Nord′kyn Cape′ (nôʀ′kyn, no͞oʀ′-), a cape in N Norway: the northernmost point of the European mainland.

Nord·land (nôʀ′län, no͞oʀ′-), *n.* a county in N Norway. 243,200; 14,797 sq. mi. (38,325 sq. km). *Co. seat:* Bodö.

Nor·doff (nôr′dof, -dôf), *n.* **Charles Bernard,** 1887–1947, U.S. novelist.

Nord-Ost·see Ka·nal (nôʀt′ ôst′zā kä näl′), German name of **Kiel Canal.**

Nord·rhein-West·fa·len (nôʀt′ʀīn vest′fä′lən), *n.* German name of **North Rhine-Westphalia.**

nor′east·er (nôr′ē′stər), *n.* northeaster. [1830–40]

No·reen (nô rēn′, nôr′ēn), *n.* a female given name, Irish diminutive of **Nora.** Also, **No·rene′.**

nor·ep·i·neph·rine (nôr′ep ə nef′rin, -rēn), *n.* **1.** Also called **noradrenaline.** *Physiol.* a neurotransmitter, released by adrenergic nerve terminals in the autonomic and possibly the central nervous system, that has such effects as constricting blood vessels, raising blood pressure, and dilating bronchi. **2.** *Pharm.* a commercial form of this substance used for emergency treatment of lowered blood pressure. [1940–45; NOR- + EPINEPHRINE]

nor·eth·in·drone (nôr eth′in drōn′), *n. Pharm.* an orally active progestin, $C_{20}H_{26}O_2$, used as a progesterone, esp. as an oral contraceptive in combination with an estrogen. [by shortening and alter. of parts of its chemical name]

nor·e·thy·no·drel (nôr′ə thī′nə drəl, nô reth′ə nə-drel′), *n. Pharm.* a progestin, $C_{20}H_{26}O_2$, used in combination with an estrogen in some oral contraceptives. [1955–60; NOR- + *ethyn*(*yl*), components of 2 versions of its chemical name + *-odrel,* of uncert. derivation]

no-re·turn (nō′ri tûrn′), *adj.* nonreturnable (def. 2).

Nor·folk (nôr′fək; *for 2, 3 also* nôr′fôk), *n.* **1.** a county in E England. 659,300; 2068 sq. mi. (5355 sq. km). **2.** a seaport in SE Virginia: naval base. 266,979. **3.** a city in NE Nebraska. 19,449.

Nor′folk Is′land, an island in the S Pacific between New Caledonia and New Zealand: a territory of Australia. 1683; 13 sq. mi. (34 sq. km).

Nor′folk Is′land pine′, a coniferous evergreen tree, *Araucaria heterophylla* (or *A. excelsa*), having whorled branches and needlelike foliage, widely cultivated as a houseplant. Also called **Australian pine, Nor′folk pine′.** [1795–1805]

Nor′folk jack′et, a loosely belted single-breasted jacket, with box pleats in front and back. Also called **Nor′folk coat′.** [1865–70; named after NORFOLK county in England]

Nor′folk ter′rier, one of an English breed of small short-legged hunting terriers having a straight, wiry, red, black and tan, or grizzle coat, and dropped ears that distinguish it from the Norwich terrier. [1960–65]

NOR′ gate′, *Computers.* See **NOR circuit.** [1965–70]

Nor·ge (nôr′gə), *n.* Norwegian name of **Norway.**

nor·ges·trel (nôr jes′trəl), *n. Pharm.* a synthetic progestin, $C_{21}H_{28}O_2$, used in some oral contraceptives either alone or in combination with an estrogen. [1965–70; NOR- + (PRO)GEST(OGEN) + *-rel,* of uncert. derivation]

no·ri·a (nôr′ē ə, nōr′-), *n.* a device consisting of a series of buckets on a wheel, used in Spain and the Orient for raising water. [1785–95; < Sp < Ar *nā'ūra*]

Nor·i·cum (nôr′i kəm, nor′-), *n.* an ancient Roman province in central Europe, roughly corresponding to the part of Austria south of the Danube.

No·rilsk (nə rēlsk′; *Russ.* nu ʀyēlsk), *n.* a city in the N Russian Federation in Asia, near the mouth of the Yenisei River. 181,000.

nor·ite (nôr′īt), *n.* a granular igneous rock consisting of a mix of light and dark minerals, the former being calcic plagioclase feldspars, and the latter orthorhombic pyroxenes. [1875–80; < Norw *norit.* See NORWAY, -ITE[1]] **—nor·it·ic** (nô rit′ik), *adj.*

nor·land (nôr′lənd), *n. Chiefly Brit. Dial.* northland. [1570–80; reduced form]

norm (nôrm), *n.* **1.** a standard, model, or pattern. **2.** general level or average: *Two cars per family is the norm in most suburban communities.* **3.** *Educ.* **a.** a designated standard of average performance of people of a given age, background, etc. **b.** a standard based on the past average performance of a given individual. **4.** *Math.* **a.** a real-valued, nonnegative function whose domain is a vector space, with properties such that the function of a vector is zero only when the vector is zero, the function of a scalar times a vector is equal to the absolute value of the scalar times the function of the vector, and the function of the sum of two vectors is less than or equal to the sum of the functional values of each vector. The norm of a real number is its absolute value. **b.** the greatest difference between two successive points of a given partition. [1815–25; < L *norma* carpenter's square, rule, pattern] **—norm′less,** *adj.*

Norm., Norman.

Nor·ma (nôr′mə), *n., gen.* **-mae** (-mē). *Astron.* the Rule, a small southern constellation between Lupus and Ara. [< L; see NORM]

Nor·ma (nôr′mə), *n.* **1.** (*italics*) an opera (1831) with music by Vincenzo Bellini. **2.** a female given name.

nor·mal (nôr′məl), *adj.* **1.** conforming to the standard or the common type; usual; not abnormal; regular; natural. **2.** serving to establish a standard. **3.** *Psychol.* **a.** approximately average in any psychological trait, as intelligence, personality, or emotional adjustment. **b.** free from any mental disorder; sane. **4.** *Biol., Med.* **a.** free from any infection or other form of disease or malformation, or from experimental therapy or manipulation. **b.** of natural occurrence. **5.** *Math.* **a.** being at right angles, as a line; perpendicular. **b.** of the nature of or pertaining to a mathematical normal. **c.** (of an orthogonal system of real functions) defined so that the integral of the square of the absolute value of any function is 1. **d.** (of a topological space) having the property that corresponding to every pair of disjoint closed sets are two disjoint open sets, each containing one of the closed sets. **e.** (of a subgroup) having the property that the same set of elements results when all the elements of the subgroup are operated on consistently on the left and consistently on the right by any element of the group; invariant. **6.** *Chem.* **a.** (of a solution) containing one equivalent weight of the constituent in question in one liter of solution. **b.** pertaining to an aliphatic hydrocarbon having a straight unbranched carbon chain, each carbon atom of which is joined to no more than two other carbon atoms. **c.** of or pertaining to a neutral salt in which any replaceable hydroxyl groups or hydrogen atoms have been replaced by other groups or atoms, as sodium sulfate, Na_2SO_4. —*n.* **7.** the average or mean: *Production may fall below normal.* **8.** the standard or type. **9.** *Math.* **a.** a perpendicular line or plane, esp. one perpendicular to a tangent line of a curve, or a tangent plane of a surface, at the point of contact. **b.** the portion of this perpendicular line included between its point of contact with the curve and the *x*-axis. [1520–30; < L *normālis* made according to a carpenter's square, equiv. to *norm*(*a*) (see NORM) + *-ālis* -AL[1]] **—nor·mal′i·ty, nor′mal·ness,** *n.*

Nor·mal (nôr′məl), *n.* a city in central Illinois. 35,672.

nor′mal curve′, *Statistics.* a bell-shaped curve showing a particular distribution of probability over the values of a random variable. Also called **Gaussian curve, probability curve.** Cf. illus. under **bell-shaped curve.** [1890–95]

nor·mal·cy (nôr′məl sē), *n.* the quality or condition of being normal, as the general economic, political, and social conditions of a nation; normality: *After months of living in a state of tension, all yearned for a return to normalcy.* [1855–60; NORMAL + -CY]

nor′mal distribu′tion, *Statistics.* a theoretical frequency distribution represented by a normal curve. Also called **Gaussian distribution.** [1895–1900]

nor′mal divi′sor, *Math.* a normal subgroup.

nor′mal equiv′alent de′viate, *Statistics.* a value *x* such that the integral of a normal curve over all those values of the independent variable less than *x* is equal to the given probability.

nor′mal fault′, *Geol.* See **gravity fault.** [1875–80]

nor·mal·ize (nôr′mə līz′), *v.,* **-ized, -iz·ing.** —*v.t.* **1.** to make normal. **2.** to establish or resume (relations) in a normal manner, as between countries. **3.** *Metall.* to heat (a steel alloy) to a suitable temperature above the transformation range and then to cool in still air at ambient temperature. —*v.i.* **4.** to become normal; resume a normal state: *Prices soon normalized after the war.* Also, *esp. Brit.,* **nor′mal·ise′.** [1860–65; NORMAL + -IZE] **—nor′mal·i·za′tion,** *n.*

nor·mal·iz·er (nôr′mə lī′zər), *n.* **1.** a person or thing that normalizes. **2.** *Math.* **a.** the subgroup consisting of elements that commute with a given element. **b.** the set of elements of a group that commute with every element of a given subgroup. [1925–30; NORMALIZE + -ER[1]]

nor·mal·ly (nôr′mə lē), *adv.* **1.** in a normal or regular way: *The wound is healing normally.* **2.** according to rule, general custom, etc.; as a rule; ordinarily; usually. [1590–1600; NORMAL + -LY]

nor′mal magnifica′tion, *Optics.* the magnification produced by a telescope or microscope such that the diameter of the exit pupil of the instrument is equal to the diameter of the pupil of the eye.

nor′mal orthog′onal, *Math.* orthonormal.

nor′mal pen′tane, *Chem.* pentane (def. 2).

nor′mal pitch′, *Mach.* See under **pitch**[1] (def. 49a). [1895–1900]

nor′mal sa′line solu′tion, *Pharm.* See **isotonic sodium chloride solution.**

nor′mal school′, (formerly) a school offering a two-year course and certification to high-school graduates preparing to be teachers, esp. elementary-school teachers. Cf. **teachers college.** [1825–35]

nor′mal se′ries, *Math.* a collection of subgroups of a given group so arranged that the first subgroup is the identity, the last subgroup is the group itself, and each subgroup is a normal subgroup of the succeeding subgroup.

nor′mal Zee′man effect′, *Physics, Optics.* See under **Zeeman effect.**

Nor·man (nôr′mən), *n.* **1.** a member of that branch of the Northmen or Scandinavians who in the 10th century conquered Normandy. **2.** Also called **Norman French.** one of the mixed Scandinavian and French people who inhabited Normandy and conquered England in 1066. **3.** a native or inhabitant of Normandy. **4.** See **Norman French** (def. 1). **5.** a city in central Oklahoma. 68,020. **6.** a male given name. —*adj.* **7.** of or pertaining to the Normans. **8.** noting or pertaining to a variety of Romanesque architecture built by the Normans, esp. in England after 1066. [1175–1225; ME < OF *Normant* < ON *Northmathr* Northman]

Nor′man Con′quest, the conquest of England by the Normans, under William the Conqueror, in 1066.

Nor·man·dy (nôr′mən dē), *n.* a region in N France along the English Channel: invaded and settled by Scandinavians in the 10th century, becoming a duchy in A.D. 911; later a province, the capital of which was Rouen; Allied invasion in World War II began here June 6, 1944.

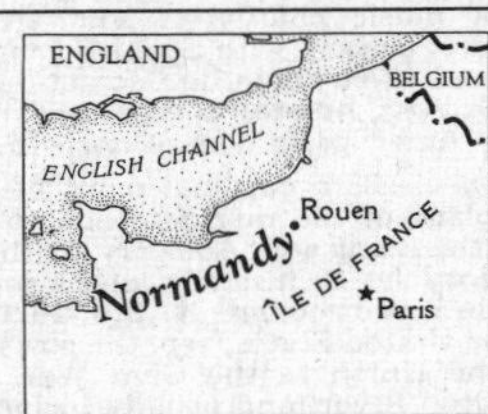

Nor′man dy′nasty, a succession of English kings founded by Duke William of the duchy of Normandy in northern France, who conquered England in 1066 and whose successors ruled the country to 1154.

Nor·man·esque (nôr′mə nesk′), *adj.* in the style of Norman architecture, a variety of Romanesque architecture. [1835–45; NORMAN + -ESQUE]

Nor′man French′, 1. Also called **Norman.** the French dialect of the Normans or of Normandy. **2.** Norman (def. 2). [1595–1605] **—Nor′man-French′,** *adj.*

Nor·man·ize (nôr′mə nīz′), *v.t., v.i.,* **-ized, -iz·ing.** to make or become Norman in customs, language, etc. [1615–25] **—Nor′man·i·za′tion,** *n.*

CONCISE PRONUNCIATION KEY: act, cāpe, dâre, pärt; set, ēqual; *if,* ice; ox, ōver, ôrder, oil, bo͝ok, bo͞ot, out; up, ûrge; child; sing; shoe; thin, *th*at; zh as in *treasure.* ə = *a* as in *alone,* e as in *system,* i as in *easily,* o as in *gallop,* u as in *circus;* ° as in *fire* (fī°r), *hour* (ou°r). l and n can serve as syllabic consonants, as in *cradle* (krād′l), and *button* (but′n). See the full key inside the front cover.

Nor′man Wells′, a settlement in the W Northwest Territories, in NW Canada, on the Mackenzie River: oil wells. 200.

nor·ma·tive (nôr′mə tiv), *adj.* **1.** of or pertaining to a norm, esp. an assumed norm regarded as the standard of correctness in behavior, speech, writing, etc. **2.** tending or attempting to establish such a norm, esp. by the prescription of rules: *normative grammar.* **3.** reflecting the assumption of such a norm or favoring its establishment: *a normative attitude.* [1875–80; NORM + -ATIVE] —**nor′ma·tive·ly,** *adv.* —**nor′ma·tive·ness,** *n.*

normed′ space′, *Math.* any vector space on which a norm is defined. [1970–75]

normo-, a combining form with the meaning "normal, close to the norm," used in the formation of compound words: *normocyte.* [NORM or NORM(AL) + -O-]

nor·mo·cyte (nôr′mə sīt′), *n. Anat.* an erythrocyte of normal size. [1895–1900; NORMO- + -CYTE] —**nor·mo·cyt·ic** (nôr′mə sit′ik), *adj.*

nor·mo·ten·sive (nôr′mō ten′siv), *Pathol.* —*adj.* **1.** characterized by normal arterial tension or blood pressure. —*n.* **2.** a normotensive person. [1940–45; NORMO- + TENSIVE, on the model of HYPERTENSIVE, HYPOTENSIVE]

Norn (nôrn), *n. Scand. Myth.* any of three goddesses of fate, goddess of the past **(Urd),** goddess of the present **(Verdandi),** and goddess of the future **(Skuld).**

Norn (nôrn), *n.* an extinct Norse dialect, spoken until early modern times in the Shetland and Orkney Islands and in parts of northern Scotland. [< ON *norrœnn,* earlier *northrœnn* Norwegian, lit., NORTHERN]

nor·nic·o·tine (nôr nik′ə tēn′), *n.* an alkaloid, $C_9H_{12}N_2$, extracted from tobacco and related to nicotine but having a lower toxicity: used as an agricultural and horticultural insecticide. [NOR- + NICOTINE]

No·ro·dom Si·ha·nouk (nôr′ə dom′ sē′ə no͝ok′, -dəm), **Prince,** born 1922, Cambodian statesman: premier 1952–60; chief of state 1960–70 and 1975–76.

Nor·plant (nôr′plant′), *Trademark.* a long-term contraceptive for women, usu. effective for 5 years, consisting of several small slow-release capsules of progestin implanted under the skin. [1985–90]

Nor·ridge (nôr′ij, nor′-), *n.* a city in NE Illinois, near Chicago. 16,483.

Nor·ris (nôr′is, nor′-), *n.* **1. Charles Gilman,** 1881–1945, U.S. novelist and editor. **2. Frank,** 1870–1902, U.S. novelist (brother of Charles Gilman). **3. George William,** 1861–1944, U.S. senator 1913–43. **4. Kathleen (Thompson),** 1880–1966, U.S. novelist and short-story writer (wife of Charles Gilman). **5.** a male given name.

Nor·rish (nôr′ish, nor′-), *n.* **Ronald George Wreyford** (rā′fərd), 1897–1978, British chemist: Nobel prize 1967.

Nor·ris·town (nôr′is toun′, nor′-), *n.* a borough in SE Pennsylvania, near Philadelphia. 34,684.

Norr·kö·ping (nôʀ′chœ′ping), *n.* a seaport in SE Sweden. 119,238.

Norse (nôrs), *adj.* **1.** of or pertaining to ancient Scandinavia, its inhabitants, or their language. **2.** Norwegian (def. 1). —*n.* **3.** (*used with a plural v.*) the Norwegians, esp. the ancient Norwegians. **4.** (*used with a plural v.*) the Northmen or ancient Scandinavians generally. **5.** the Norwegian language, esp. in its older forms. Cf. **Old Norse.** [1590–1600; perh. < D *noorsch,* obs. var. of *noordsch* (now *noords*), equiv. to *noord* NORTH + *-sch* -ISH[1]. Cf. Norw, Sw, Dan *Norsk* Norwegian, Norse]

Norse·man (nôrs′mən), *n., pl.* **-men.** Northman. [1810–20; NORSE + MAN[1]]

Nor·stad (nôr′stad, -städ), *n.* **Lau·ris** (lôr′is, lōr′-), born 1907, U.S. Air Force general: Supreme Allied Commander of NATO 1956–63.

nor·te·a·me·ri·ca·no (nôʀ′te ä me′ʀē kä′nô), *n., pl.* **-nos** (-nôs), *adj. Spanish.* —*n.* **1.** a citizen or inhabitant of the U.S., esp. as distinguished from the peoples of Spanish-speaking America. —*adj.* **2.** of, pertaining to, or characteristic of the *norteamericano.*

nor·te·ña (nôr tān′yə; *Sp.* nôʀ te′nyä), *n.* a lively, polkalike folk music chiefly of southern Texas and northern Mexico, usually with Spanish lyrics and played on accordion and 12-string guitar, sometimes with fiddle and saxophone. Also, **nor·te·no** (nôr tān′yō). Also called **Tex-Mex.** [< AmerSp; Sp: fem of *norteño* northern(er)]

north (nôrth), *n.* **1.** a cardinal point of the compass, lying in the plane of the meridian and to the left of a person facing the rising sun. *Abbr.:* N **2.** the direction in which this point lies. **3.** (*usually cap.*) a region or territory situated in this direction. **4. the North,** the northern area of the United States, esp. the states that fought to preserve the Union in the Civil War, lying to the north of the Ohio River, and usually including Missouri and Maryland. **5.** (*cap.*) See **North Country. 6.** the north wind. —*adj.* **7.** in, toward, or facing, the north: *the north gate.* **8.** directed or proceeding toward the north: *a north course.* **9.** coming from the north: *a north wind.* **10.** (*usually cap.*) designating the northern part of a region, nation, country, etc.: *North Atlantic.* —*adv.* **11.** to, toward, or in the north: *sailing north.* [bef. 900; ME, OE, c. D *noord,* G *Nord,* ON *northr*]

North (nôrth), *n.* **1. Christopher,** pen name of John Wilson. **2. Frederick, 2nd Earl of Guil·ford** (gil′fərd) (*"Lord North"*), 1732–92, British statesman: prime minister 1770–82. **3. Sir Thomas,** 1535?–1601?, English translator.

North′ Ad′ams, a city in NW Massachusetts. 18,063.

North′ Af′rica, the northern part of Africa, esp. the region north of the tropical rain forest and comprised of Morocco, Algeria, Tunisia, Libya, and that part of Egypt west of the Gulf of Suez. —**North′ Af′rican.**

North′ Amer′ica, the northern continent of the Western Hemisphere, extending from Central America to the Arctic Ocean. Highest point, Mt. McKinley, 20,300 ft. (6187 m); lowest, Death Valley, 276 ft. (84 m) below sea level. 400,000,000 including Central America; ab. 9,360,000 sq. mi. (24,242,400 sq. km). —**North′ Amer′ican.**

North′ Amer′ican Plate′, *Geol.* a major tectonic division of the earth's crust, comprising Greenland and the continent of North America and the suboceanic Labrador and North American Basins, and bounded on the east by the Mid-Atlantic Ridge, on the south by the Caribbean and South American Plates, and on the west by the San Andreas fault and Aleutian Trench.

North·amp·ton (nôr thamp′tən, nôrth hamp′-), *n.* **1.** a city in Northamptonshire, in central England. 139,900. **2.** a city in central Massachusetts. 29,286. **3.** Northamptonshire.

North·amp·ton·shire (nôr thamp′tən shēr′, -shər, nôrth hamp′-), *n.* a county in central England. 500,100; 914 sq. mi. (2365 sq. km). Also called **Northampton.**

North′ An′dover, a city in NE Massachusetts. 20,129.

North′an·ger Ab′bey (nôrth′ān jər, -ang gər), a novel (1818) by Jane Austen.

North′ Ar′lington, a city in NE New Jersey. 16,587.

North′ Atlan′tic Cur′rent, an ocean current flowing NE toward the British Isles, formed by the convergence of the Gulf Stream and the Labrador Current SE of Newfoundland. Also called **North′ Atlan′tic Drift′.**

North′ Atlan′tic Trea′ty, the treaty (1949) signed by 12 countries, providing for the establishment of NATO. Also called **North′ Atlan′tic Pact′.**

North′ Atlan′tic Trea′ty Organiza′tion. See **NATO.**

North′ At′tle·bor·ough (at′l bûr′ō, -bur′ō), a city in SE Massachusetts. 21,095.

North′ Augus′ta, a city in W South Carolina. 13,593.

North′ Austral′ia, a former division of Australia; now part of the Northern Territory. —**North′ Austral′ian.**

North′ Bab′ylon, a city on S Long Island, in SE New York. 19,019.

North′ Bat′tle·ford (bat′l fôrd′, -fōrd′, -fərd), a city in W central Saskatchewan, in central Canada. 13,158.

North′ Bay′, a city in SE Ontario, in S Canada. 51,639.

North′ Bay′ Shore′, a city on S Long Island, in SE New York. 35,020.

North′ Bed′fordshire, a city in Bedfordshire, in central England. 130,500. Formerly, **Bedford.**

North′ Bell′more, (bel′môr, -mōr), a town on W Long Island, in SE New York. 20,630.

North′ Bel′mont, a town in S North Carolina. 10,759.

North′ Ber′gen, a township in NE New Jersey. 47,019.

North′ Bor′neo, a former name of **Sabah.**

North·bor·ough (nôrth′bûr′ō, -bur′ō), *n.* a town in central Massachusetts. 10,568.

north·bound (nôrth′bound′), *adj.* going toward the north: *northbound traffic.* [1880–85, *Amer.*; NORTH + -BOUND[2]]

North′ Brabant′, a province in S Netherlands. 2,071,885; 1965 sq. mi. (5090 sq. km). *Cap.:* 's Hertogenbosch.

North′ Bran′ford, a town in S Connecticut. 11,554.

North·bridge (nôrth′brij′), *n.* a town in S Massachusetts. 12,246.

North·brook (nôrth′bro͝ok′), *n.* a city in NE Illinois. 30,735.

north′ by east′, *Navig., Survey.* a point on the compass 11°15′ east of north. *Abbr.:* NbE

north′ by west′, *Navig., Survey.* a point on the compass 11°15′ west of north. *Abbr.:* NbW

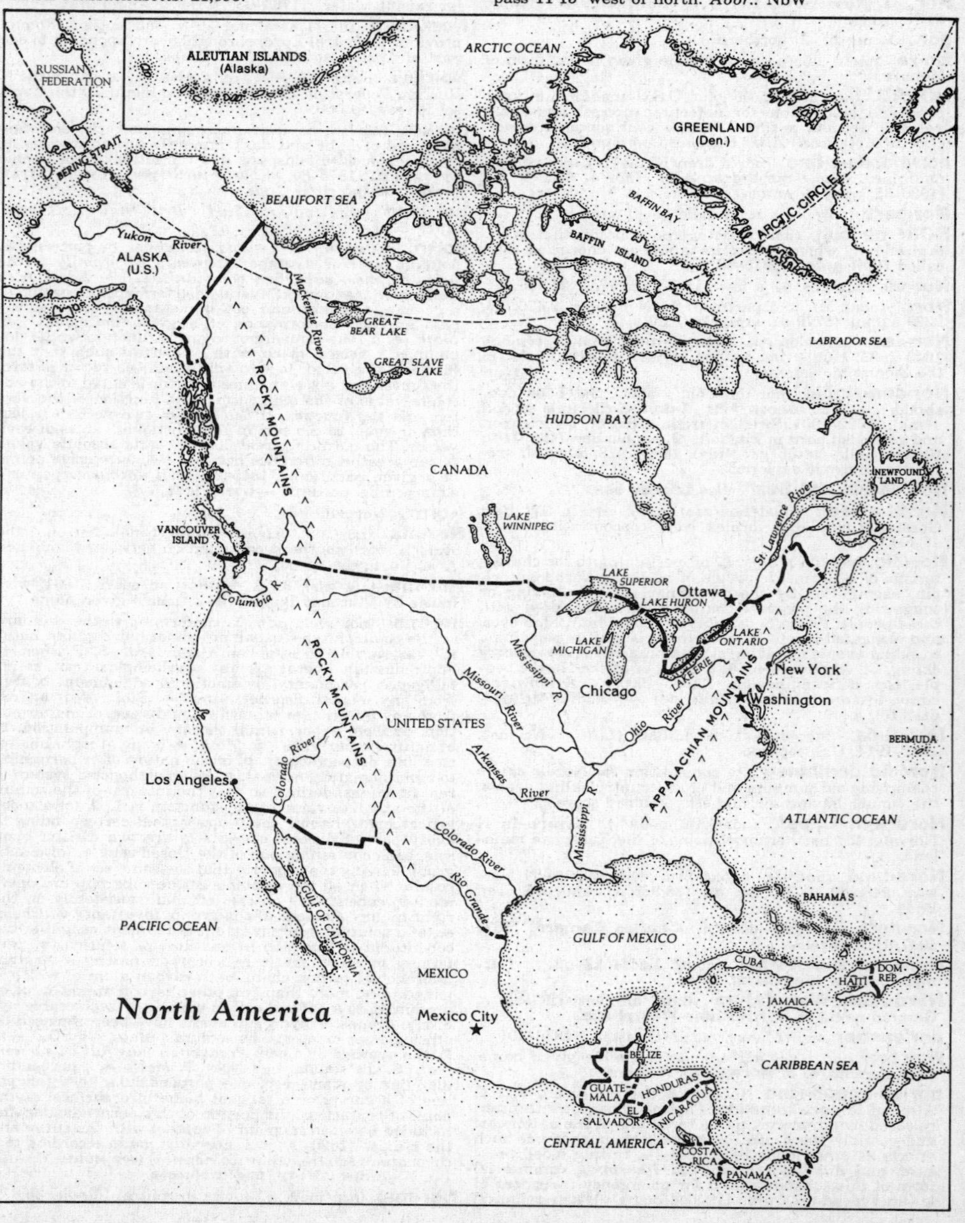

CONCISE ETYMOLOGY KEY: <, descended or borrowed from; >, whence; b., blend of, blended; c., cognate with; cf., compare; deriv., derivative; equiv., equivalent; imit., imitative; obl., oblique; r., replacing; s., stem; sp., spelling, spelled; resp., respelling, respelled; trans., translation; ?, origin unknown; *, unattested; ‡, probably earlier than. See the full key inside the front cover.

North′ Can′ton (kan′tn), a town in central Ohio. 14,228.

North′ Cape′, 1. a point of land on an island at the N tip of Norway: the northernmost point of Europe. 2. the northern end of North Island, New Zealand.

North′ Caroli′na, a state in the SE United States, on the Atlantic coast. 5,874,429; 52,586 sq. mi. (136,198 sq. km). *Cap.:* Raleigh. *Abbr.:* NC (for use with zip code), N.C. —**North′ Carolin′ian.**

North′ Cascades′, a national park in NW Washington: site of glaciers and mountain lakes. 789 sq. mi. (2043 sq. km).

North′ Cauca′sian, 1. a language family including all the Caucasian languages north of the Caucasian divide, as Kabardian and the Circassian language proper, and a few between the divide and the Black Sea, as Abkhazian. 2. of or pertaining to this language family.

North′ Cau′casus, a region in the S Soviet Union in Europe, E of the Black Sea.

North′ Chan′nel, a strait between SW Scotland and NE Ireland. 14 mi. (23 km) wide at the narrowest point.

North′ Charles′ton, a city in SE South Carolina. 65,630.

North′ Chica′go, a city in NE Illinois, on Lake Michigan. 38,774.

North•cliffe (nôrth′klif), *n.* **Viscount.** See **Harmsworth, Alfred Charles William.**

North′ Col′lege Hill′, a city in SW Ohio. 10,990.

North′ Coun′try, 1. the part of England north of the Humber estuary. 2. Alaska and the Yukon territory of Canada (as a geographical and economic unit).

North′ Dako′ta, a state in the N central United States. 652,695; 70,665 sq. mi. (183,020 sq. km). *Cap.:* Bismarck. *Abbr.:* ND (for use with zip code), N. Dak. —**North′ Dako′tan.**

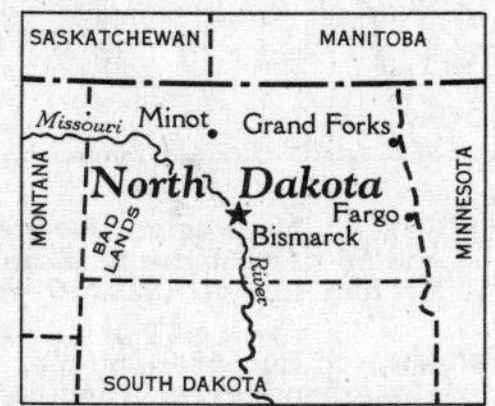

north•east (nôrth′ēst′; *Naut.* nôr′ēst′), *n.* 1. a point on the compass midway between north and east. *Abbr.:* NE 2. a region in this direction. 3. **the Northeast,** the northeastern part of the United States. —*adv.* 4. toward or in the northeast: *sailing northeast.* —*adj.* 5. coming from the northeast: *a northeast wind.* 6. directed toward the northeast: *a northeast course.* [bef. 950; ME, OE; see NORTH, EAST] —**north′east′ern,** *adj.*

northeast′ by east′, *Navig., Survey.* a point on the compass 11°15′ east of northeast. *Abbr.:* NEbE

northeast′ by north′, *Navig., Survey.* a point on the compass 11°15′ north of northeast. *Abbr.:* NEbN

North′east Cor′ridor, the long, narrow strip of land between Boston, New York City, and Washington, D.C., containing many adjacent urban areas.

north•east•er (nôrth′ē′stər; *Naut.* nôr′ē′stər), *n.* 1. *New Eng. and South Atlantic States.* a wind or gale from the northeast. 2. *Meteorol.* See **northeast storm.** Also, **nor′easter.** [1765–75; NORTHEAST + -ER[1]]

north•east•er•ly (nôrth′ē′stər lē; *Naut.* nôr′ē′stər lē), *adj.* 1. of or located in the northeast. 2. toward or from the northeast. —*adv.* 3. toward or from the northeast. [1730–40; NORTH + EASTERLY]

north•east•ern•er (nôrth′ē′stər nər), *n.* 1. a native or inhabitant of the northeast. 2. (*cap.*) a native or inhabitant of the northeastern part of the U.S. [1960–65; NORTHEASTERN + -ER[1]]

North′ East′ New′ Guin′ea, the NE part of the former Australian Territory of New Guinea; now part of Papua New Guinea.

North′east Pas′sage, a ship route along the N coast of Europe and Asia, between the North Sea and the Pacific.

north′east storm′, a cyclonic storm that moves northeastward within several hundred miles of the eastern coast of the U.S. and Canada, particularly in fall and winter, its often strong northeast winds causing high seas and coastal damage and bearing rain or snow. Also called **northeaster, nor′easter.**

north•east•ward (nôrth′ēst′wərd; *Naut.* nôr′ēst′wərd), *adv., adj.* 1. Also, **north′east′ward•ly.** toward the northeast. —*n.* 2. the northeast. [1545–55; NORTHEAST + -WARD]

north•east•wards (nôrth′ēst′wərdz; *Naut.* nôr′ēst′wərdz), *adv.* northeastward. [NORTHEASTWARD + -S[1]]

North′ Equato′rial Cur′rent, a westward-flowing ocean current occurring N of the equator in the Atlantic and Pacific oceans.

north•er (nôr′thər), *n.* 1. *Chiefly Texas and Oklahoma.* a cold gale from the north, formed during the winter by a vigorous outbreak of continental polar air behind a cold front. 2. a wind or storm from the north. Also, **northerner.** [1770–80, *Amer.;* NORTH + -ER[1]]

north•er•ly (nôr′thər lē), *adj., adv., n., pl.* **-lies.** —*adj.* 1. moving, directed, or situated toward the north. 2. (esp. of a wind) coming from the north: *a northerly gale.* —*adv.* 3. toward the north. 4. from the north. —*n.* 5. a wind that blows from the north. [1545–55; NORTH + *-erly,* modeled on EASTERLY] —**north′er•li•ness,** *n.*

north•ern (nôr′thərn), *adj.* 1. lying toward or situated in the north. 2. directed or proceeding northward. 3. coming from the north, as a wind. 4. (*often cap.*) of or pertaining to the North, esp. the northern U.S. 5. *Astron.* north of the celestial equator or of the zodiac: *a northern constellation.* —*n.* 6. a person living in a northern region or country. 7. (*cap.*) a steam locomotive having a four-wheeled front truck, eight driving wheels, and a four-wheeled rear truck. See table under **Whyte classification.** [bef. 900; ME, OE; see NORTH, -ERN] —**north′ern•ness,** *n.*

North′ern blot′, *Biol., Med.* a procedure for studying the activity of a specific gene, as in testing for a hereditary defect: RNA fragments in an extract of a cell population or a tissue are separated by gel electrophoresis, transferred to a filter, and then hybridized with labeled DNA or RNA derived from a laboratory-engineered copy of the gene in order to identify the size and abundance of the RNA expressed by that gene. [1977; orig. as a facetious counterpart to SOUTHERN BLOT]

north′ern bobwhite′. See under **bobwhite.**

North′ern Cameroons′. See under **Cameroons** (def. 2).

north′ern canoe′, *Canadian.* a large, heavy canoe used to transport supplies. Cf. **York boat.** [1810–20]

north′ern corn′-leaf blight′ (kôrn′lēf′). See **northern leaf blight.**

north′ern corn′ root′worm. See **corn rootworm.** [1960–65]

North′ern Cross′, *Astron.* six stars in the constellation Cygnus, arranged in the form of a cross. [1905–10]

North′ern Crown′, *Astron.* the constellation Corona Borealis. [1585–95]

North•ern•er (nôr′thər nər), *n.* 1. (*sometimes l.c.*) a native or inhabitant of the North, esp. the northern U.S. 2. (*l.c.*) norther. [1825–35; NORTHERN + -ER[1]]

north′ern har′rier, a hawk of North America and Europe, *Circus cyaneus,* that frequents marshes and meadows. Also called **marsh hawk;** *Brit.,* **hen harrier.**

north′ern har′vestfish. See under **harvestfish** (def. 1).

North′ern Hem′isphere, the half of the earth between the North Pole and the equator. [1885–90]

north′ern hog′ suck′er. See **black sucker.**

North′ern Ire′land, a political division of the United Kingdom, in the NE part of the island of Ireland. 1,537,200; 5238 sq. mi. (13,565 sq. km). *Cap.:* Belfast.

North•ern•ize (nôr′thər nīz′), *v.t.,* **-ized, -iz•ing.** (*sometimes l.c.*) to make northern; impart qualities considered typical of the North, esp. of the northern part of U.S. Also, *esp. Brit.,* **North′ern•ise′.** [1855–60; NORTHERN + -IZE]

north′ern king′fish, *Ichthyol.* a croaker, *Menticirrhus saxatilis,* inhabiting Atlantic coastal waters of the U.S. Also called **king-whiting, northern whiting.**

north′ern leaf′ blight′, *Plant Pathol.* a disease of corn caused by the fungus *Exsherohilum turcicum,* characterized by elongate tan-gray elliptical spots with subsequent blighting and necrosis of leaves. Also called **northern corn-leaf blight.**

north′ern lights′. See **aurora borealis.** [1715–25]

North′ern Mich′igan. See **Upper Peninsula.**

North′ern Min′, Foochow (def. 2).

north•ern•most (nôr′thərn mōst′ *or, esp. Brit.,* -məst), *adj.* farthest north. [1710–20; NORTHERN + -MOST]

north′ern o′riole, an oriole, *Icterus galbula,* of North America, with highly distinctive eastern and western subspecies that interbreed in the Great Plains region. Cf. **Baltimore oriole, Bullock's oriole.**

North′ern Paiute′, 1. a member of an American Indian people of Nevada, Oregon, and California, allied to the Paiute. 2. See under **Paiute** (def. 2).

north′ern par′ula. See under **parula.**

north′ern pike′, a pike, *Esox lucius,* of North American and Eurasian waters, valued as a game fish. See illus. under **pike.** [1855–60, *Amer.*]

north′ern red′belly dace′. See under **redbelly dace.**

North′ern Rhode′sia, former name of **Zambia.** —**North′ern Rhode′sian.**

north′ern sen′net. See under **sennet**[1].

North′ern Spor′ades. See under **Sporades.**

North′ern Spy′, an American variety of red-striped apple that ripens in autumn or early winter. [1840–50, *Amer.*]

north′ern stud′fish. See under **studfish.**

North′ern Ter′ritories, a former British protectorate in W Africa; now a part of N Ghana.

North′ern Ter′ritory, a territory in N Australia. 123,324; 523,620 sq. mi. (1,356,175 sq. km). *Cap.:* Darwin.

north′ern white′ ce′dar. See under **white cedar** (def. 1). [1925–30]

north′ern whit′ing. See **northern kingfish.** [1930–35]

North•field (nôrth′fēld′), *n.* a town in SE Minnesota. 12,562.

North′ Frig′id Zone′, the part of the earth's surface between the Arctic Circle and the North Pole. See diag. under **zone.**

North′ Fri′sian Is′lands. See under **Frisian Islands.**

North′ German′ic, the subbranch of Germanic that includes the languages of Scandinavia and Iceland. Also called **Scandinavian.** [1925–30]

North•glenn (nôrth′glen′), *n.* a city in NE central Colorado. 29,847.

North′ Ha′ven, a town in S Connecticut. 22,080.

North′ High′lands, a town in central California, near Sacramento. 37,825. —**North′ High′lander.**

North′ Hol′land, a province in W Netherlands. 2,315,676; 1163 sq. mi. (3010 sq. km). *Cap.:* Haarlem.

north•ing (nôr′thing, -thing), *n. Navig.* 1. northward movement or deviation. 2. distance due north made on any course tending northward. [1660–70; NORTH + -ING[1]]

North′ Is′land, the northernmost principal island of New Zealand. 2,268,393; 44,281 sq. mi. (114,690 sq. km).

North′ Kings′town (kingz′tən, -toun′, king′stən), a town in S central Rhode Island. 21,938.

North′ Kore′a, a country in E Asia: formed 1948 after the division of the former country of Korea at 38° N. 16,000,000; 50,000 sq. mi. (129,500 sq. km). *Cap.:* Pyongyang. Cf. **Korea.** Official name, **Democratic People's Republic of Korea.** —**North′ Kore′an.**

North•lake (nôrth′lāk′), *n.* a city in NE Illinois: suburb of Chicago. 12,166.

north•land (nôrth′lənd, -land′), *n.* 1. the land or region in the north. 2. the northern part of a country. 3. (*cap.*) the peninsula containing Norway and Sweden. [bef. 900; ME, OE; see NORTH, -LAND] —**north′land•er,** *n.*

North′ Las′ Ve′gas, a city in S Nevada. 42,739.

North′ Lau′derdale, a city in SE Florida. 18,479.

North′ Lit′tle Rock′, a city in central Arkansas, on the Arkansas River. 64,419.

North•man (nôrth′mən), *n., pl.* **-men.** one of the ancient Scandinavians, esp. a member of the group that from about the 8th to the 11th century made many raids and established settlements in Great Britain, Ireland, many parts of continental Europe, and probably in parts of North America. Also, **Norseman.** [bef. 900; OE *northman(n)* (not recorded in ME); see NORTH, -MAN]

North′ Maria′na Is′lands, a group of islands in the W Pacific Ocean, N of Guam: formerly a part of the Trust Territory of the Pacicfic Islands; since 1986 a commonwealth associated with the U.S. 18,400; 184 sq. mi. (477 sq. km). *Cap.:* Saipan.

North′ Massape′qua, a city on S Long Island, in SE New York. 21,385.

North′ Mer′rick, a town on S Long Island, in SE New York. 12,848.

North′ Miam′i, a city in SE Florida. 42,566.

North′ Miam′i Beach′, a city in SE Florida. 36,481.

north•most (nôrth′mōst′ *or, esp. Brit.,* -məst), *adj.* northernmost. [bef. 900; OE *northmest* (not recorded in ME); see NORTH, -MOST]

North′ New′ Hyde′ Park′, a town on W Long Island, in SE New York. 15,114.

north′ node′, (*often caps.*) *Astrol.* the ascending node of the moon.

north-north•east (nôrth′nôrth′ēst′; *Naut.* nôr′nôr′ēst′), *n.* 1. the point on the compass midway between north and northeast. *Abbr.:* NNE —*adj.* 2. coming from this point: *facing a north-northeast wind.* 3. directed toward this point: *a north-northeast course.* —*adv.* 4.toward this point: *sailing north-northeast.* [1400–50; late ME *north north est;* see NORTH, NORTHEAST]

north-north•east•ward (nôrth′nôrth′ēst′wərd; *Naut.* nôr′nôr′ēst′wərd), *adv., adj.* toward the north-northeast. Also, **north′-north′east′ward•ly.**

north-north•west (nôrth′nôrth′west′; *Naut.* nôr′nôr′west′), *n.* 1. the point on the compass midway between north and northwest. *Abbr.:* NNW —*adj.* 2. coming from this point: *a north-northwest wind.* 3. directed toward this point: *a north-northwest course.* —*adv.* 4. toward this point: *sailing north-northwest.* [1350–1400; ME; see NORTH, NORTHWEST]

north-north•west•ward (nôrth′nôrth′west′wərd, *Naut.* nôr′nôr′west′wərd), *adv., adj.* toward the north-northwest. Also, **north′-north′west′ward•ly.** [1775–85]

North′ Olm′sted (um′sted, -stid), a city in NE Ohio, near Cleveland. 36,486.

North′ Osse′tian Auton′omous Repub′lic, an autonomous republic in the Russian Federation in SE Europe. 634,000; 3088 sq. mi. (8000 sq. km). *Cap.:* Ordzhonikidze.

North′ Pacif′ic Cur′rent, a warm current flowing eastward across the Pacific Ocean.

North′ Palm′ Beach′, a town in E Florida. 11,344.

North′ Plain′field, a city in NE New Jersey. 19,108.

North′ Platte′, 1. a river flowing from N Colorado through SE Wyoming and W Nebraska into the Platte. 618 mi. (995 sq. km) long. 2. a city in central Nebraska. 24,479.

North′ Pole′, **1.** *Geog.* the end of the earth's axis of rotation, marking the northernmost point on the earth. **2.** *Astron.* the point at which the extended axis of the earth cuts the northern half of the celestial sphere, about 1° from the North Star; the north celestial pole. **3.** (*l.c.*) the pole of a magnet that seeks the earth's north magnetic pole. **4.** (*l.c.*) See under **magnetic pole** (def. 1). [1350–1400; ME]

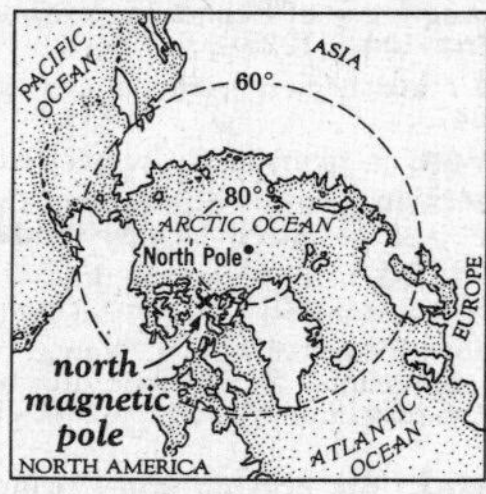

North·port (nôrth′pôrt′, -pōrt′), *n.* a town in central Alabama. 14,291.

North′ Prov′idence, a town in NE Rhode Island. 29,188.

North′ Read′ing (red′ing), a city in NE Massachusetts. 11,455.

North′ Rhine′-West·pha′li·a (rīn′west fā′lē ə, -fāl′yə), a state in W Germany; formerly a part of Rhine province. 16,874,000; 13,154 sq. mi. (34,070 sq. km). *Cap.:* Düsseldorf. German, **Nordrhein-Westfalen.**

North′ Rich′land Hills′, a town in N Texas. 30,592.

North′ Ridge′ville (rij′vil), a town in N Ohio. 21,522.

North′ Ri′ding (rī′ding), a former administrative division of Yorkshire, in N England, now part of North Yorkshire, Cleveland, and Durham.

North′ Riv′er, a part of the Hudson River between NE New Jersey and SE New York.

Nor·throp (nôr′thrəp), *n.* **John Howard,** born 1891, U.S. biochemist: Nobel prize for chemistry 1946.

North′ Roy′al·ton (roi′əl tən), a town in N Ohio. 17,671.

Nor·thrup (nôr′thrəp), *n.* a male given name.

North′ Sea′, an arm of the Atlantic between Great Britain and the European mainland. ab. 201,000 sq. mi. (520,600 sq. km); greatest depth, 1998 ft. (610 m). Formerly, **German Ocean.**

North′ Slope′, the northern coastal area of Alaska, rich in oil and natural gas: so called because it is N of the Brooks Range sloping down to the Arctic Ocean.

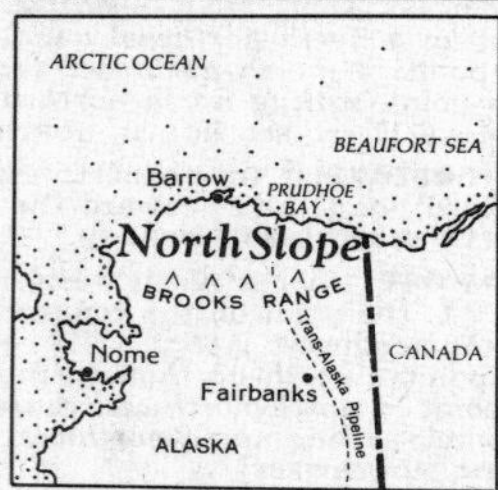

North′ Star′, *Astron.* Polaris. [1350–1400; ME]

North St. Paul, a town in E Minnesota. 11,921.

North′ Tem′perate Zone′, the part of the earth's surface between the tropic of Cancer and the Arctic Circle. See diag. under **zone.**

North′ Tonawan′da, a city in W New York. 35,760.

North·um·ber·land (nôr thum′bər lənd), *n.* a county in NE England. 286,700; 1943 sq. mi. (5030 sq. km).

Northum′berland Strait′, the part of the Gulf of St. Lawrence that separates Prince Edward Island from New Brunswick and Nova Scotia, in SE Canada. ab. 200 mi. (320 km) long; 9–30 mi. (15–48 km) wide.

North·um·bri·a (nôr thum′brē ə), *n.* an early English kingdom extending N from the Humber to the Firth of Forth. See map under **Mercia.**

CONCISE ETYMOLOGY KEY: <, descended or borrowed from; >, whence; b., blend of, blended; c., cognate with; cf., compare; deriv., derivative; equiv., equivalent; imit., imitative; obl., oblique; r., replacing; s., stem; sp., spelling, spelled; resp., respelling, respelled; trans., translation; ?, origin unknown; *, unattested; ‡, probably earlier than. See the full key inside the front cover.

North·um·bri·an (nôr thum′brē ən), *adj.* **1.** of or pertaining to Northumbria, Northumberland, or the inhabitants or dialect of either. —*n.* **2.** a native or inhabitant of Northumbria or Northumberland. **3.** the English dialect of Northumbria or Northumberland. [1615–25; NORTHUMBRI(A) + -AN]

North′ Val′ley Stream′, a town on W Long Island, in SE New York. 14,530.

North′ Vancou′ver, a city in SW British Columbia, in SW Canada. 33,952.

North′ Vietnam′, that part of Vietnam N of about 17° N; formerly a part of French Indochina; separate republic 1954–75. Cf. **Vietnam, South Vietnam.**

north·ward (nôrth′wərd; *Naut.* nôr′thərd), *adv.* **1.** Also, **north′wards.** toward the north. —*adj.* **2.** moving, bearing, facing, or situated toward the north. —*n.* **3.** the northward part, direction, or point. Also, **north′·ward·ly** (for defs. 1, 2). [bef. 1100; ME; OE *northweard.* See NORTH, -WARD]

north·west (nôrth′west′; *Naut.* nôr′west′), *n.* **1.** a point on the compass midway between north and west. *Abbr.:* NW **2.** a region in this direction. **3. the Northwest, a.** the northwestern part of the United States, esp. Washington, Oregon, and Idaho. **b.** the northwestern part of the United States when its western boundary was the Mississippi River. **c.** the northwestern part of Canada. —*adj.* **4.** Also, **north′west′ern.** coming from the northwest: *a northwest wind.* **5.** directed toward the northwest: *sailing a northwest course.* —*adv.* **6.** from the northwest. **7.** toward the northwest: *sailing northwest.* [bef. 900; ME, OE; see NORTH, WEST]

northwest′ by north′, *Navig., Survey.* a point on the compass, 11°15′ north of northwest. *Abbr.:* NWbN [1675–85]

northwest′ by west′, *Navig., Survey.* a point on the compass, 11°15′ west of northwest. *Abbr.:* NWbW [1715–25]

north·west·er (nôrth′wes′tər; *Naut.* nôr′wes′tər), *n.* *New Eng. and South Atlantic States.* a wind or gale from the northwest. Also, **nor′wester.** [1725–35; NORTHWEST + -ER[1]]

north·west·er·ly (nôrth′wes′tər lē; *Naut.* nôr′wes′-tər lē), *adj., adv.* toward or from the northwest. [1605–15; NORTHWESTER + -LY]

north·west·ern·er (nôrth′wes′tər nər), *n.* **1.** a native or inhabitant of the northwest. **2.** (*cap.*) a native or inhabitant of the northwestern part of the U.S. [1920–25; NORTHWESTERN + -ER[1]]

North′-West Frontier′ Prov′ince (nôrth′west′, -west′), a province in Pakistan, bordering Punjab and Kashmir on the west: a former province of British India. 10,885,000; 28,773 sq. mi. (77,516 sq. km). *Cap.:* Peshawar.

North′west In′dian Confedera′tion. See under **Fallen Timbers.**

North′west Or′dinance, the act of Congress in 1787 providing for the government of the Northwest Territory and setting forth the steps by which its subdivisions might become states.

North′west Pas′sage, a ship route along the Arctic coast of Canada and Alaska, joining the Atlantic and Pacific oceans. [1545–55]

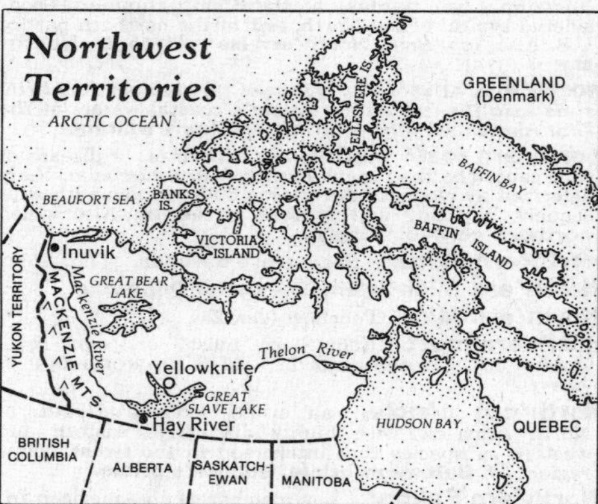

North′west Ter′ritories, a territory of Canada lying N of the provinces and extending E from Yukon territory to Davis Strait. 42,237; 1,304,903 sq. mi. (3,379,700 sq. km). *Cap.:* Yellowknife. Also called **Old Northwest.**

North′west Ter′ritory, the region north of the Ohio River, organized by Congress in 1787, comprising present-day Ohio, Indiana, Illinois, Michigan, Wisconsin, and the eastern part of Minnesota.

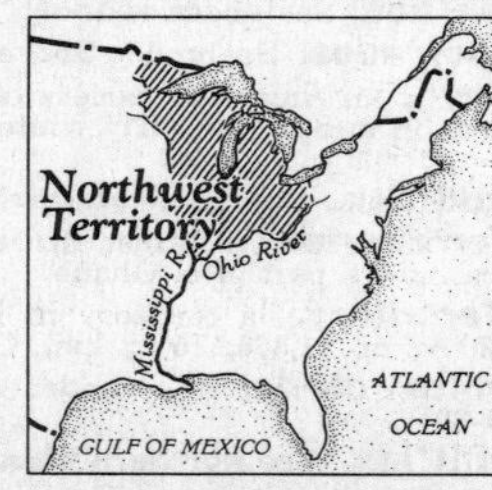

north·west·ward (nôrth′west′wərd; *Naut.* nôr′-west′wərd), *adv., adj.* **1.** Also, **north′west′ward·ly.** toward the northwest. —*n.* **2.** the northwest. [1350–1400; ME; see NORTHWEST, -WARD]

north·west·wards (nôrth′west′wərdz; *Naut.* nôr′-west′wərdz), *adv.* northwestward.

North′ York′shire, a county in NE England. 646,100; 3208 sq. mi. (8309 sq. km).

Nor·ton (nôr′tn), *n.* **1. Charles Eliot,** 1827–1908, U.S. scholar. **2. Thomas,** 1532–84, English author. **3.** a town in SE Massachusetts. 12,690. **4.** a city in NE Ohio. 12,242. **5.** a male given name: an Old English family name taken from a place-name meaning "north town."

Nor′ton Shores′, a city in W Michigan, on Lake Michigan. 22,025.

nor·trip·ty·line (nôr trip′tə lēn′), *n. Pharm.* a tricyclic antidepressant drug, $C_{19}H_{21}N$, used to treat depression. [1960–65; perh. NOR- + TRI(CYCLIC) + (*cyclohe*)*p*-*t*(*ene*) a chemical component + -YL + -INE[2]]

Norw., **1.** Norway. **2.** Norwegian.

Nor·walk (nôr′wôk), *n.* **1.** a city in SW California. 85,232. **2.** a city in SW Connecticut. 77,767. **3.** a city in N Ohio. 14,358.

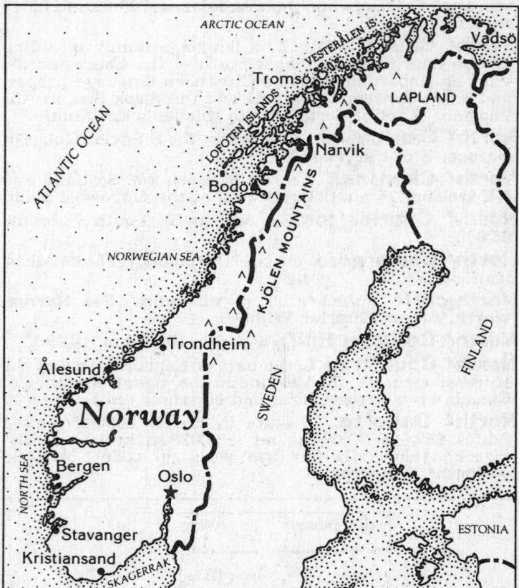

Nor·way (nôr′wā), *n.* Norwegian, **Norge.** a kingdom in N Europe, in the W part of the Scandinavian Peninsula. 4,017,101; 124,555 sq. mi. (322,597 sq. km). *Cap.:* Oslo.

Nor′way ma′ple, a European maple, *Acer platanoides,* having bright-green leaves, grown as a shade tree in the U.S. [1790–1800]

Nor′way pine′. See **red pine.** [1710–20]

Nor′way rat′, an Old World rat, *Rattus norvegicus,* having a grayish-brown body with whitish underparts and a long, scaly tail, now common in the U.S. in or near homes, barns, wharves, etc. See illus. under **rat.** Also called **brown rat.** [1745–55]

Nor′way spruce′, a European spruce, *Picea abies,* having shiny, dark-green needles, grown as an ornamental. [1725–35]

Nor·we·gian (nôr wē′jən), *adj.* **1.** of or pertaining to Norway, its inhabitants, or their language. —*n.* **2.** a native or inhabitant of Norway. **3.** the language of Norway, a Germanic language spoken in two different dialects known as Bokmål and Nynorsk. *Abbr.:* Norw [1595–1605; earlier *Norvegian* < ML *Norvegi*(*a*) NORWAY + -AN]

Norwe′gian Cur′rent, an ocean current formed from the terminus of the North Atlantic Current, flowing N along the Norwegian coast into the Barents Sea.

Norwe′gian elk′hound, one of a breed of dogs having a short, compact body, short, pointed ears, and a thick, gray coat, raised originally in Norway for hunting elk and other game. [1925–30]

Norwe′gian salt′peter, *Chem.* See **calcium nitrate.**

Norwe′gian Sea′, part of the Arctic Ocean, N and E of Iceland and between Greenland and Norway.

nor′west·er (nôr′wes′tər), *n.* **1.** sou'wester (defs. 1, 2). **2.** northwester. [1695–1705; NOR(TH)WESTER]

Nor·wich (nôr′ich, -ij, nor′- *for 1;* nôr′wich *for* 2), *n.* **1.** a city in E Norfolk, in E England: cathedral. 121,800. **2.** a city in SE Connecticut, on the Thames River. 38,074.

Nor′wich ter′rier, one of an English breed of small, short-legged terriers having a straight, wiry, red, gray, or black-and-tan coat, and erect ears that distinguish it from the Norfolk terrier. [1930–35]

Nor·wood (nôr′wŏŏd′), *n.* **1.** a town in E Massachusetts. 29,711. **2.** a city in SW Ohio, near Cincinnati. 26,342.

nos-, var. of **noso-** before a vowel.

nos., numbers. Also, **Nos.**

n.o.s., not otherwise specified.

nos·ce te ip·sum (nōs′ke tā ip′so͝om; *Eng.* no′sē tē ip′səm), *Latin.* know thyself.

nose (nōz), *n., v.,* **nosed, nos·ing.** —*n.* **1.** the part of

the face or facial region in humans and certain animals that contains the nostrils and the organs of smell and functions as the usual passageway for air in respiration: in humans it is a prominence in the center of the face formed of bone and cartilage, serving also to modify or modulate the voice. **2.** this part as the organ of smell. **3.** the sense of smell: *fragrances appealing to the nose.* **4.** anything regarded as resembling the nose of a person or animal, as a spout or nozzle. **5.** the prow of a ship. **6.** the forward end of an aircraft. **7.** the forward edge of the head of a golf club. **8.** a projecting part of anything: *the nose of a pair of pliers.* **9.** a faculty of perceiving or detecting: *to have a nose for news.* **10.** the human nose regarded as a symbol of meddling or prying: *Why can't he keep his nose out of my business?* **11.** the length of a nose: *The horse won the race by a nose.* **12.** the bouquet of an alcoholic drink, esp. the distinctive aroma of a wine. **13. count noses,** to count the number of people in attendance: *Each time the troop left an exhibit the leader counted noses.* **14. cut off one's nose to spite one's face,** to create a disadvantage to oneself through one's own spiteful action. **15. follow one's nose, a.** to go forward in a straight course. **b.** to guide oneself by instinct: *I found the house by following my nose.* **16. keep one's nose clean,** to behave oneself; avoid trouble or scandal: *Did he keep his nose clean after he got out of prison?* **17. keep one's nose to the grindstone.** See **grindstone** (def. 3). **18. lead** or **lead around by the nose,** to exercise complete control over; dominate totally: *He lets his brother lead him by the nose.* **19. look down one's nose at,** to regard with disdain or condescension: *He had always looked down his nose at those who were poorer than he.* **20. on the nose,** *Informal.* **a.** precisely, correctly, or perfectly. **b.** exactly on time: *We made it at ten o'clock on the nose.* **c.** (of a bet) for win only. **d.** *Australian Informal.* decayed or putrid; stinking. **e.** *Australian Informal.* distasteful or unpleasant; of doubtful validity or propriety. **21. pay through the nose,** to pay an excessive price: *They patronize small and exclusive shops where they cheerfully pay through the nose.* **22. put someone's nose out of joint, a.** to annoy or irritate greatly. **b.** to supersede a person in another's regard, devotion, etc. **c.** to thwart someone; spoil someone's plans. **23. rub someone's nose in,** to persecute or tease someone persistently about; nag someone about: *I know I was wrong but you don't have to rub my nose in it.* **24. turn up one's nose at,** to regard with contempt; scorn: *My friend turns up his nose at anyone who hasn't had a college education.* **25. under someone's nose,** plainly visible to; in full view of; in bold defiance of: *The theft took place right under the detective's nose.* Also, **under someone's very nose.**
—*v.t.* **26.** to perceive by or as by the nose or the sense of smell: *a cheese that could be nosed at some distance.* **27.** to approach the nose to, as in smelling or examining; sniff. **28.** to move or push forward with or as with the nose: *The dog nosed its pup back into the yard. The boat nosed its way toward shore.* **29.** to touch or rub with the nose; nuzzle.
—*v.i.* **30.** to smell or sniff. **31.** to seek as if by smelling or scent: *The dogs nosed after their quarry.* **32.** to move or push forward: *to nose into the wind.* **33.** to meddle or pry (often fol. by *about, into,* etc.): *They are always nosing about in other people's business.* **34. nose out, a.** to defeat, esp. by a narrow margin: *The other candidates had been nosed out in the final returns.* **b.** to learn or discover, esp. by snooping or prying: *to nose out a secret.* [bef. 900; ME (n.); OE *nosu;* akin to D *neus,* G *Nase,* L *nāsus,* Skt *nāsā*] **—nose′less,** *adj.* **—nose′like′,** *adj.*

nose′ bag′. See **feed bag** (def. 1). [1790–1800]

nose•band (nōz′band′), *n.* that part of a bridle or halter that passes over the animal's nose. See illus. under **harness.** [1605–15] **—nose′band′ed,** *adj.*

nose•bleed (nōz′blēd′), *n.* **1.** bleeding from the nose. **2.** See **red trillium.** [1400–50 as plant name; 1850–55 for def. 1; late ME; see NOSE, BLEED]

nose′ can′dy, *Slang.* cocaine. [1930–35, *Amer.*]

nose′ cone′, *Rocketry.* the cone-shaped forward section of a rocket or guided missile, including a heat shield and containing the payload. [1945–50]

nose•count (nōz′kount′), *n. Informal.* the counting of individual persons, as for a census. [1935–40]

nose•dive (nōz′dīv′), *n., v.,* **-dived** or **-dove, -dived, -div•ing.** —*n.* Also, **nose′ dive′. 1.** a plunge of an aircraft with the forward part pointing downward. **2.** a sudden sharp drop or rapid decline: *a time when market values were in a nosedive.* —*v.i.* Also, **nose′-dive′. 3.** to go into a nosedive: *a warning that prices might nosedive.* [1910–15; NOSE + DIVE]

nose′ drops′, medication applied through the nostrils with a dropper. [1940–45]

nose′ end′er, *Naut.* muzzler (def. 2). [1850–55]

no-see-um (nō sē′əm), *n. Northern and Western U.S.* punkie. [1840–50, *Amer.*; pseudo-AmerInd E version of *you can't see them*]

nose•gay (nōz′gā′), *n.* a small bunch of flowers; bouquet; posy. [1375–1425; late ME: lit., a *gay* (obs., something pretty; see GAY) for the NOSE (i.e., to smell)]

nose′ glass′es, eyeglasses held in place by a spring that clamps them to the bridge of the nose; pince-nez.

nose′ guard′, *Football.* See **middle guard.** [1975–80]

nose′ job′, *Informal.* cosmetic surgery of the nose; rhinoplasty. [1965–70]

nose′ leaf′, a leaflike outgrowth of skin on the nose of various bats, thought to be sensitive to vibrations of the air. [1830–40]

nose•piece (nōz′pēs′), *n.* **1.** the part of a frame for eyeglasses that passes over the bridge of the nose. **2.** the part of a microscope to which the objectives are attached. See diag. under **microscope. 3.** a piece of armor serving as a protective cover for the nose. **4.** a noseband. [1605–15; NOSE + PIECE]

nose′ ring′, 1. a ring inserted in the nose of an animal, to facilitate leading it. **2.** a ring worn as an ornament in the nose. [1780–90]

nose•wheel (nōz′hwēl′, -wēl′), *n.* the landing wheel under the nose of an aircraft. [1930–35; NOSE + WHEEL]

nose•wing (nōz′wing′), *n.* the flared portion of each side of the nose; a nasal ala. [NOSE + WING]

nos•ey (nō′zē), *adj.,* **nos•i•er, nos•i•est.** nosy.

Nos•ey Par•ker (nō′zē pär′kər), *Informal.* See **Nosy Parker.** Also, **nos′ey Par′ker.**

nosh (nosh), *Informal.* —*v.i.* **1.** to snack or eat between meals. —*v.t.* **2.** to snack on: *They noshed peanuts and cookies while watching television.* —*n.* **3.** a snack. [1955–60; < Yiddish *nashn;* MHG *naschen,* OHG *nascōn* to nibble, gnaw; c. Dan *naske,* Sw *snaska*]

nosh•er (nosh′ər), *n. Informal.* a person who snacks, esp. one who does so often or continuously. [1955–60; < Yiddish; see NOSH, -ER[1]]

nosh•er•ei (nosh′ə rī′), *n. Slang.* food for snacking or noshing. [< Yiddish *nasheray* tidbit, equiv. to *nash(n)* NOSH + *-eray* < MHG *-er* -ER[1] + *-īe* < OF *-ie* (see -Y[3])]

no-show (nō′shō′), *n.* **1.** a person who makes a reservation and neither uses nor cancels it. **2.** a person who purchases an admission ticket and doesn't use it. **3.** any absentee. —*adj.* **4.** not appearing as scheduled or expected. [1940–45, *Amer.*; NO[2] + SHOW]

nos•ing (nō′zing), *n. Archit.* a projecting edge, as the part of the tread of a step extending beyond the riser or a projecting part of a buttress. [1765–75; NOSE + -ING[1]]

no-smok•ing (nō′smō′king), *adj.* nonsmoking.

noso-, a combining form meaning "disease," used in the formation of compound words: *nosology.* Also, *esp. before a vowel,* **nos-.** [comb. form repr. Gk *nósos* disease]

nos•o•co•mi•al (nos′ə kō′mē əl), *adj.* (of infections) contracted as a result of being hospitalized; hospital-acquired. [1850–55; < NL *nosocomi(um)* hospital (< LGk *nosokomeîon,* equiv. to Gk *noso-* NOSO- + *kom-* (base with sense "care, attendance," as in *gērokómos* caring for the old) + *-eion* suffix of location) + -AL[1]]

nos•o•gen•e•sis (nos′ə jen′ə sis), *n.* pathogenesis. Also, **no•sog•e•ny** (nō soj′ə nē). [NOSO- + GENESIS] **—nos•o•ge•net•ic** (nos′ə jə net′ik), *adj.*

nos•o•ge•og•ra•phy (nos′ō jē og′rə fē), *n.* the study of the geographical causes and distribution of diseases. Also called **nos•och•tho•nog•ra•phy** (nos′ok thə nog′rə fē). [NOSO- + GEOGRAPHY] **—nos•o•ge•o•graph•ic** (nos′ō jē′ə graf′ik), **nos′o•ge′o•graph′i•cal,** *adj.*

no•sog•ra•phy (nō sog′rə fē), *n.* the systematic description of diseases. [1645–55; NOSO- + -GRAPHY] **—no•sog′ra•pher,** *n.* **—no•so•graph•ic** (nō′sə graf′ik, nos′ə-), **no′so•graph′i•cal,** *adj.* **—no′so•graph′i•cal•ly,** *adv.*

no•sol•o•gy (nō sol′ə jē), *n.* **1.** the systematic classification of diseases. **2.** the knowledge of a disease. [1715–25; < NL *nosologia.* See NOSO-, -LOGY] **—nos•o•log•i•cal** (nos′ə loj′i kəl), *adj.* **—nos′o•log′i•cal•ly,** *adv.* **—no•sol′o•gist,** *n.*

nos•o•pho•bi•a (nos′ə fō′bē ə), *n. Psychiatry.* an abnormal fear of disease. [1885–90; NOSO- + -PHOBIA]

nos•tal•gia (no stal′jə, -jē ə, nə-), *n.* **1.** a wistful desire to return in thought or in fact to a former time in one's life, to one's home or homeland, or to one's family and friends; a sentimental yearning for the happiness of a former place or time: *a nostalgia for his college days.* **2.** something that elicits or displays nostalgia. [1770–80; < NL < Gk *nóst(os)* a return home + *-algia* -ALGIA] **—nos•tal′gic,** *adj.* **—nos•tal′gi•cal•ly,** *adv.*

nos•tal•gist (no stal′jist, nə-), *n.* a person who collects or buys and sells items preserved from an earlier era. [1950–55; NOSTALG(IA) + -IST]

nos•tal•gy (no stal′jē, nə-), *n., pl.* **-gies.** *Archaic.* nostalgia. [1840–50; Anglicized form of NOSTALGIA; see -Y[3]]

no-stick (nō′stik′), *adj.* nonstick: *a no-stick skillet.*

nos•toc (nos′tok), *n.* any freshwater, blue-green alga of the genus *Nostoc,* often occurring in jellylike colonies in moist places. [1640–50; < NL, coined by Paracelsus]

nos•tol•o•gy (no stol′ə jē), *n.* geriatrics. [< Gk *nósto(s)* a return home + -LOGY] **—nos•to•log•ic** (nos′tə loj′ik), *adj.*

nos•to•ma•ni•a (nos′tə mā′nē ə, -mān′yə), *n.* intense homesickness; an irresistible compulsion to return home. [1850–55; < Gk *nósto(s)* a return home + -MANIA]

Nos•tra•da•mus (nos′trə dā′məs, -dä′-, nō′strə-), *n.* (*Michel de Nostredame*), 1503–66, French astrologer. **—Nos•tra•dam•ic** (nos′trə dam′ik, nō′strə-), *adj.*

no-strike (nō′strīk′), *adj.* of, pertaining to, or containing a provision that workers are not permitted to strike under certain terms and conditions: *a no-strike clause.*

nos•tril (nos′trəl), *n.* either of the two external openings of the nose. [bef. 1000; ME *nostrill,* OE *nosterl,* var. of *nosthyrl,* equiv. to *nos(u)*) NOSE + *thyrel* hole; see THIRL]

no-strings (nō′stringz′), *adj.* done without conditions or limitations: *a no-strings proposal.* [‡1965–70]

Nos•tro•mo (no strō′mō), *n.* a novel (1904) by Joseph Conrad.

nos•trum (nos′trəm), *n.* **1.** a medicine sold with false or exaggerated claims and with no demonstrable value; quack medicine. **2.** a scheme, theory, device, etc., esp. one to remedy social or political ills; panacea. **3.** a medicine made by the person who recommends it. **4.** a patent medicine. [1595–1605; < L *nostrum* our, ours (neut. sing. of *noster*); referring to the seller's calling the drug "our" drug]

no-sweat (nō′swet′), *adj. Informal.* requiring little effort; easy: *a no-sweat job.*

nos•y (nō′zē), *adj.,* **nos•i•er, nos•i•est.** unduly curious about the affairs of others; prying; meddlesome. Also, **nosey.** [1880–85; NOSE + -Y[1]] **—nos′i•ly,** *adv.* **—nos′i•ness,** *n.*

Nos•y Par•ker (nō′zē pär′kər), *Informal.* a persistently nosy, prying person; busybody. Also, **Nosey Parker.** [1905–10]

not (not), *adv.* **1.** (used to express negation, denial, refusal, or prohibition): *You must not do that. It's not far from here.* **2.** *U.S. Slang.* (used jocularly as a postpositive interjection to indicate that a previous statement is untrue): *That's a lovely dress. Not!* [1275–1325; ME; weak var. of NOUGHT]

not-, var. of **noto-** before a vowel.

NOTA, none of the above.

no•ta be•ne (nō′tä be′ne; *Eng.* nō′tə bā′nē, ben′ē, bē′nē), *Latin.* note well; take notice.

no•ta•bil•i•a (nō′tə bil′ē ə), *n.pl.* matters, events, or items worthy of note. [< L, neut. pl. of *notābilis* remarkable, noteworthy]

no•ta•bil•i•ty (nō′tə bil′i tē), *n., pl.* **-ties** for 2. **1.** the state or quality of being notable; distinction; prominence. **2.** a notable or prominent person. [1350–1400; ME *notabilite.* See NOTABLE, -ITY]

no•ta•ble (nō′tə bəl), *adj.* **1.** worthy of note or notice; noteworthy: *a notable success; a notable theory.* **2.** prominent, important, or distinguished: *many notable artists.* **3.** *Archaic.* capable, thrifty, and industrious. —*n.* **4.** a prominent, distinguished, or important person. **5.** (*usually cap.*) *Fr. Hist.* **a.** one of a number of prominent men, usually of the aristocracy, called by the king on extraordinary occasions. **b. Notables,** Also called **Assembly of the Notables.** an assembly of high-ranking nobles, ecclesiastics, and state functionaries having deliberative but not legislative or administrative powers, convoked by the king principally in 1554, 1786, and 1788, in the lattermost year to establish the manner for selecting the States-General. **6.** *Obs.* a notable fact or thing. [1300–50; ME *notab(i)le* < L *notābilis.* See NOTE, -ABLE] **—no′ta•ble•ness,** *n.* **—no′ta•bly,** *adv.*
—Syn. 1, 2. conspicuous, memorable, great, remarkable, noticeable, noted, outstanding, unusual, uncommon, eminent. **2.** celebrated, famous. **—Ant. 1.** ordinary.

no•taph•i•ly (nō taf′ə lē), *n.* the collecting of bank notes as a hobby. [irreg. < L *nota* NOTE + -PHILY] **—no•taph′i•list,** *n.*

no•tar•i•al (nō târ′ē əl), *adj.* **1.** of, pertaining to, or characteristic of a notary public. **2.** drawn up or executed by a notary public. [1475–85; NOTARY + -AL[1]] **—no•tar′i•al•ly,** *adv.*

no•ta•rize (nō′tə rīz′), *v.t.,* **-rized, -riz•ing.** to certify (a document, contract, etc.) or cause to become certified through a notary public. Also, *esp. Brit.,* **no′ta•rise′.** [1925–30; NOTAR(Y) + -IZE] **—no′ta•ri•za′tion,** *n.*

no•ta•ry (nō′tə rē), *n., pl.* **-ries.** See **notary public.** [1275–1325; ME < L *notārius* clerk, equiv. to *not(āre)* to NOTE, mark + *-ārius* -ARY] **—no′ta•ry•ship′,** *n.*

no′tary pub′lic, *pl.* **notaries public.** a public officer or other person authorized to authenticate contracts, acknowledge deeds, take affidavits, protest bills of exchange, take depositions, etc. [1490–1500]

no•ta•tion (nō tā′shən), *n.* **1.** a system of graphic symbols for a specialized use, other than ordinary writing: *musical notation.* **2.** the process or method of noting or setting down by means of a special system of signs or symbols. **3.** the act of noting, marking, or setting down in writing. **4.** a note, jotting, or record; annotation: *notations in the margin.* [1560–70; < L *notātiōn-* (s. of *notātiō*) a marking, equiv. to *notāt(us)* (ptp. of *notāre* to NOTE) + *-iōn-* -ION] **—no•ta′tion•al,** *adj.*

notch (noch), *n.* **1.** an angular or V-shaped cut, indentation, or slit in an object, surface, or edge. **2.** a cut or nick made in a stick or other object for record, as in keeping a tally. **3.** *New Eng. and Upstate New York.* a deep, narrow opening or pass between mountains; gap; defile. **4.** *Informal.* a step, degree, or grade: *This camera is a notch better than the other.* **5.** *Metall.* a taphole in a blast furnace: *iron notch; cinder notch.* —*v.t.* **6.** to cut or make a notch in. **7.** to record by notches: *He notched each kill on the stick.* **8.** to score, as in a game: *He notched another win.* **9. notch up** or **down,** to move up or down or increase or decrease by notches or degrees. [1570–80; *a notch* (by false division) for *an* **otch* < OF *oche* notch] **—notch′y,** *adj.*

notch′ba′by, a person who was born in the U.S. between 1917 and 1921 and as a retiree received lower cost-of-living increases in Social Security than others after Congress readjusted Social Security benefits in 1977. [1985–90; *Amer.*]

notch•back (noch′bak′), *n.* **1.** a style of back for an automobile in which there is a sharp vertical drop-off from the roof line to the trunk. **2.** an automobile having such a back. Cf. **fastback.** [1960–65; NOTCH + BACK[1], on the model of HATCHBACK, FASTBACK, etc.]

notched′ col′lar, a collar forming a notch with the lapels of a garment at the seam where collar and lapels join. Also called **notched′ lapel′.**

notched collar

CONCISE PRONUNCIATION KEY: *act, cāpe, dâre, pärt; set, ēqual; if, īce; ox, ōver, ôrder, oil, bŏŏk, bōōt, out; up, ûrge; child; sing; shoe; thin, that;* zh as in *treasure.* ə = *a* as in *alone, e* as in *system, i* as in *easily, o* as in *gallop, u* as in *circus;* ə as in *fire* (fīər), *hour* (ouər). l and n can serve as syllabic consonants, as in *cradle* (krād′l), and *button* (but′n). See the full key inside the front cover.

NOT′ cir′cuit (not), *Computers.* a circuit that is energized when its input is not. Also called **NOT gate.** [1945–50]

note (nōt), *n., v.,* **not·ed, not·ing.** —*n.* **1.** a brief record of something written down to assist the memory or for future reference. **2. notes,** a record or outline of a speech, statement, testimony, etc., or of one's impressions of something. **3.** an explanatory or critical comment, or a reference to some authority quoted, appended to a passage in a book or the like: *a note on the origin of the phrase.* **4.** a brief written or printed statement giving particulars or information. **5.** *Library Science.* additional information about a work, such as its special series or some other significant identification, included on the library catalog entry. **6.** a short, informal letter: *a thank-you note.* **7.** a formal diplomatic or official communication in writing: *a note delivered by the ambassador.* **8.** a paper acknowledging a debt and promising payment; promissory note. **9.** a certificate, as of a government or a bank, accepted as money. **10.** eminence, distinction, or reputation: *a man of note.* **11.** importance or consequence: *few events of particular note.* **12.** notice, observation, or heed: *to take note of warning signs; to be worthy of note.* **13.** a characteristic or distinguishing feature: *a note of whimsy in the design of the house.* **14.** a mark, quality, or indication of something, esp. as a submerged but ubiquitous element: *There was just a note of bitterness in his films.* **15.** a characteristic way of speaking or thinking: *His critics had begun to change their note.* **16.** a signal, announcement, or intimation: *a note of warning in her voice.* **17.** *Music.* **a.** a sign or character used to represent a tone, its position and form indicating the pitch and duration of the tone. **b.** a key, as of a piano. **18.** a tone sounded on a musical instrument. **19.** a musical sound or tone. **20.** a melody, tune, or song. **21.** a sound of musical quality, as one uttered by a bird: *attentive to the thrush's note.* **22.** any call, cry, or sound of a bird, fowl, etc. **23.** a new or unexpected element in a situation. **24.** a mark or sign, as of punctuation, used in writing or printing. **25. compare notes,** to exchange views, ideas, or impressions: *The returning tourists were sitting on the sun deck comparing notes.* —*v.t.* **26.** to write or mark down briefly; make a memorandum of: *to note the places of interest.* **27.** to make particular mention of in a writing: *She noted their extra efforts in her report.* **28.** to annotate. **29.** to observe carefully; give attention or heed to: *Note the fine brushwork in this painting.* **30.** to take notice of; perceive: *We noted his concern at the announcement.* **31.** to set down in or furnish with musical notes. **32.** to indicate or designate; signify; denote. [1175–1225; (n.) ME (< OF) < ML *nota* sign for musical tone, L: mark, sign, lettering; (v.) ME *noten* < OF *noter* to mark < L *notāre,* deriv. of the n.] —**not′er,** *n.*
—**Syn. 1.** memorandum, minute. **3.** commentary, annotation. See **remark. 9.** bill. **10.** repute, celebrity, fame, renown, name. **26.** register, record. **30.** see, spot, remark. **32.** mention.

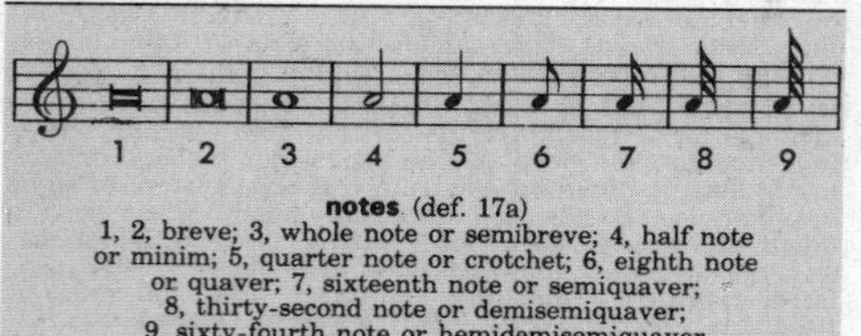

notes (def. 17a)
1, 2, breve; 3, whole note or semibreve; 4, half note or minim; 5, quarter note or crotchet; 6, eighth note or quaver; 7, sixteenth note or semiquaver; 8, thirty-second note or demisemiquaver; 9, sixty-fourth note or hemidemisemiquaver

note·book (nōt′bo͝ok′), *n.* **1.** a book of or for notes. **2.** a book or binder of blank, often ruled, pages for recording notes, esp. one used by students in class. **3.** a book in which promissory notes are entered, registered, recorded, etc. [1570–80; NOTE + BOOK]

note′ bro′ker, *Finance.* a broker who buys and sells commercial paper. [1865–70, *Amer.*]

note·case (nōt′kās′), *n. Chiefly Brit.* billfold. [1830–40; NOTE + CASE²]

not·ed (nō′tid), *adj.* **1.** well-known; celebrated; famous: *a noted scholar.* **2.** provided with musical notation, a musical score, etc.: *The text is illustrated with noted examples from the symphonies.* [1350–1400; ME; see NOTE, -ED²] —**not′ed·ly,** *adv.* —**not′ed·ness,** *n.*
—**Syn. 1.** distinguished, renowned, eminent. —**Ant. 1.** obscure, unknown.

note·hold·er (nōt′hōl′dər), *n.* a person who holds or owns a note, as a promissory or Treasury note. [1925–30; NOTE + HOLDER]

note·less (nōt′lis), *adj.* **1.** not noted; undistinguished; unnoticed. **2.** unmusical or voiceless. [1610–20; NOTE + -LESS] —**note′less·ly,** *adv.* —**note′less·ness,** *n.*

note′ of hand′. See **promissory note.** [1760–70]

note·pad (nōt′pad′), *n.* a pad of blank pages for writing notes. [1920–25; NOTE + PAD¹]

note·pa·per (nōt′pā′pər), *n.* writing paper, esp. that used in writing notes or personal correspondence and usually less than 8½ × 11 in. (21.6 × 27.9 cm) in size. [1840–50; NOTE + PAPER]

note′ row′ (rō), *Music.* See **tone row.** [1950–55]

note ver·bale (nôt ver bal′), *pl.* ***notes ver·bales*** (nôt ver bal′). *French.* a diplomatic communication prepared in the third person and unsigned: less formal than a note but more formal than an aide-mémoire.

CONCISE ETYMOLOGY KEY: <, descended or borrowed from; >, whence; b., blend of, blended; c., cognate with; cf., compare; deriv., derivative; equiv., equivalent; imit., imitative; obl., oblique; r., replacing; s., stem; sp., spelling, spelled; resp., respelling, respelled; trans., translation; ?, origin unknown; *, unattested; ‡, probably earlier than. See the full key inside the front cover.

note·wor·thy (nōt′wûr′thē), *adj.* worthy of notice or attention; notable; remarkable: *a noteworthy addition to our collection of rare books.* [1545–55; NOTE + WORTHY] —**note′wor′thi·ly,** *adv.* —**note′wor′thi·ness,** *n.*
—**Syn.** distinguished, outstanding, significant.

not-for-prof·it (not′fər prof′it), *adj.* nonprofit. [1965–70]

NOT′ gate′, *Computers.* See **NOT circuit.** [1955–60]

noth·ing (nuth′ing), *n.* **1.** no thing; not anything; naught: *to say nothing.* **2.** no part, share, or trace (usually fol. by *of*): *The house showed nothing of its former magnificence.* **3.** something that is nonexistent. **4.** nonexistence; nothingness: *The sound faded to nothing.* **5.** something or someone of no importance or significance: *Money is nothing when you're without health.* **6.** a trivial action, matter, circumstance, thing, or remark: *to exchange a few nothings when being introduced.* **7.** a person of little or no importance; a nobody. **8.** something that is without quantity or magnitude. **9.** a cipher or naught: *Nothing from nine leaves nine.* **10.** (used in conventional responses to expressions of thanks): *Think nothing of it. It's nothing. Nothing to it.* **11. for nothing, a.** free of charge. **b.** for no apparent reason or motive. **c.** futilely; to no avail: *They had gone to a great deal of expense for nothing.* **12. in nothing flat,** in very little time: *Dinner was finished in nothing flat.* **13. make nothing of, a.** to treat lightly; regard as easy. **b.** to be unsuccessful in comprehending: *He could make nothing of the complicated directions.* **14. nothing but,** nothing other than; only: *We could see nothing but fog.* **15. nothing doing, a.** *Informal.* emphatically no; certainly not. **b.** no activity, inducement, advantage, etc., present to the eye: *We drove through the town but there seemed to be nothing doing.* **16. nothing less than** or **short of,** absolutely; completely: *She was used to nothing less than the best.* **17. think nothing of, a.** to treat casually. **b.** to regard as insignificant: *He thinks nothing of lying to conceal his incompetence.* —*adv.* **18.** in no respect or degree; not at all: *It was nothing like that. Nothing dismayed, he repeated his question.* —*adj.* **19.** amounting to nothing, as in offering no prospects for satisfaction, advancement, or the like: *She was stuck in a nothing job.* [bef. 900; ME; OE *nānthing, nathing;* see NO², THING¹]

noth·ing·ness (nuth′ing nis), *n.* **1.** the state of being nothing. **2.** something that is nonexistent: *a view of humanity as suspended between infinity and nothingness.* **3.** lack of being; nonexistence: *The sound faded into nothingness.* **4.** unconsciousness or death: *She remembered a dizzy feeling, then nothingness.* **5.** utter insignificance, emptiness, or worthlessness; triviality: *The days followed one another in an endless procession of nothingness.* **6.** something insignificant or without value. [1625–35; NOTHING + -NESS]

no·tice (nō′tis), *n., v.,* **-ticed, -tic·ing.** —*n.* **1.** an announcement or intimation of something impending; warning: *a day's notice.* **2.** a note, placard, or the like conveying information or a warning: *to post a notice about the fire laws.* **3.** information or warning of something, esp. for wide attention: *to give notice of one's departure.* **4.** a notification of the termination, at a specified time, of an agreement, as for renting or employment, given by one of the parties to the agreement: *The sales manager suddenly gave notice and headed for Acapulco.* **5.** observation, perception, attention, or heed: *a book worthy of notice.* **6.** interested or favorable attention: *to take notice of an unusual feature in the design of a building.* **7.** critical attention, appraisal, or evaluation: *Only a few of the entries were singled out for notice.* **8.** a brief written review or critique, as of a newly published book; review: *The notices of the play were mostly favorable.* —*v.t.* **9.** to pay attention to or take notice of: *Did you notice her hat?* **10.** to perceive; become aware of: *Did you notice the anger in his voice?* **11.** to acknowledge acquaintance with: *She noticed him merely with a nod.* **12.** to mention or refer to; point out: *a circumstance that was noticed in an earlier chapter.* **13.** to give notice to; serve with a notice: *to notice a person that his taxes are overdue.* [1400–50; late ME < MF < L *nōtitia* a knowing, a being known, deriv. of *nōtus* known (see NOTIFY)] —**no′tic·er,** *n.*
—**Syn. 2.** sign, poster. **3.** advice, news, notification, announcement. **5.** note, cognizance. **7.** comment, mention. **9.** see, regard, heed, observe. **10.** note, mark, remark; descry, distinguish, discriminate, recognize, understand. NOTICE, DISCERN, PERCEIVE imply becoming aware of, and paying attention to, something. To NOTICE is to become aware of something that has caught one's attention: *to notice a newspaper headline; to notice a road sign.* DISCERN suggests distinguishing (sometimes with difficulty) and recognizing a thing for what it is, discriminating it from its surroundings: *In spite of the fog, we finally discerned the outline of the harbor.* PERCEIVE, often used as a formal substitute for see or notice, may convey also the idea of understanding meanings and implications: *After examining the evidence he perceived its significance.*

no·tice·a·ble (nō′ti sə bəl), *adj.* **1.** attracting notice or attention; capable of being noticed: *a noticeable lack of interest.* **2.** worthy or deserving of notice or attention; noteworthy: *a book that is noticeable for its vivid historical background.* [1790–1800; NOTICE + -ABLE] —**no′tice·a·bil′i·ty,** *n.* —**no′tice·a·bly,** *adv.*
—**Syn. 1.** conspicuous, prominent **2.** notable. —**Ant. 1.** inconspicuous.

no·ti·fi·ca·tion (nō′tə fi kā′shən), *n.* **1.** a formal notifying or informing. **2.** an act or instance of notifying, making known, or giving notice; notice. **3.** a written or printed notice, announcement, or warning: *Notifications were mailed to the winners.* [1325–75; ME *notificacioun* < ML *nōtificātiōn-* (s. of *nōtificātiō*). See NOTIFY, -ATION]

no·ti·fy (nō′tə fī′), *v.t.,* **-fied, -fy·ing. 1.** to inform (someone) or give notice to: *to notify the police of a crime.* **2.** *Chiefly Brit.* to make known; give information of: *The sale was notified in the newspapers.* [1325–75; ME *notifien* < MF *notifier* < L *nōtificāre,* equiv. to (*g*)*nōt*(*us*) (ptp. of (*g*)*nōscere* to come to know; see KNOW¹) + *-ificāre* -IFY] —**no′ti·fi′a·ble,** *adj.* —**no′ti·fi′er,** *n.*
—**Syn. 1.** apprise, advise, tell.

no-till·age (nō′til′ij), *n.* the planting of crops by direct seeding without plowing, using herbicides as necessary to control weeds. Also, **no′-till′.** Also called **minimum tillage, zero tillage.** [1965–70]

no·tion (nō′shən), *n.* **1.** a general understanding; vague or imperfect conception or idea of something: *a notion of how something should be done.* **2.** an opinion, view, or belief: *That's his notion, not mine.* **3.** conception or idea: *his notion of democracy.* **4.** a fanciful or foolish idea; whim: *She had a notion to swim in the winter.* **5.** an ingenious article, device, or contrivance; knickknack. **6. notions,** small articles, as buttons, thread, ribbon, and other personal items, esp. such items displayed together for sale, as in a department store. [1560–70; < L *nōtiōn-* (s. of *nōtiō*) examination, idea, equiv. to *nōt*(*us*) ptp. of *nōscere* (see NOTIFY) + *-iōn-* -ION] —**no′tion·less,** *adj.*
—**Syn. 1, 3.** See **idea.**

no·tion·al (nō′shə nl), *adj.* **1.** pertaining to or expressing a notion or idea. **2.** of the nature of a notion or idea: *a notional response to the question.* **3.** abstract, theoretical, or speculative, as reflective thought. **4.** not real or actual; ideal or imaginary: *to create a notional world for oneself.* **5.** given to or full of foolish or fanciful ideas or moods. **6.** *Gram.* **a.** relating to the meaning expressed by a linguistic form. **b.** having full lexical meaning, in contrast to relational. **7.** *Semantics.* belonging to a class of words that express clear concepts rather than relations between concepts; presentive. Cf. **relational** (def. 3), **symbolic** (def. 4). [1590–1600; NOTION + -AL¹] —**no′tion·al′i·ty,** *n.* —**no′tion·al·ly,** *adv.*

no·tion·ate (nō′shə nit), *adj. Chiefly Midland and Southern U.S.* **1.** strong-willed or stubborn. **2.** having foolish and fanciful notions. [1840–50; NOTION + -ATE¹]

noto-, a combining form meaning "the back," used in the formation of compound words: *notochord.* Also, *esp. before a vowel,* **not-.** [comb. form repr. Gk *nôton* the back]

no·to·chord (nō′tə kôrd′), *n. Embryol.* a rodlike cord of cells that forms the chief axial supporting structure of the body of the lower chordates, as amphioxus and the cyclostomes, and of the embryos of the vertebrates. [1840–50; NOTO- + CHORD] —**no′to·chord′al,** *adj.*

No·to·gae·a (nō′tə jē′ə), *n.* a biogeographical division comprising the Australian region. Also, **No′to·ge′a.** [< NL < Gk *nóto*(*s*) the south + *gaîa* earth, land] —**No′to·gae′an,** *n., adj.* —**No′to·gae′al, No′to·gae′ic,** *adj.*

no·to·ri·e·ty (nō′tə rī′i tē), *n., pl.* **-ties. 1.** the state, quality, or character of being notorious or widely known: *a craze for notoriety.* **2.** *Chiefly Brit.* a notorious or celebrated person. [1585–95; < ML *nōtōrietās,* equiv. to *nōtōri*(*us*) NOTORIOUS + *-etās,* var. (after *-i-*) of -ITY]
—**Syn. 1.** disrepute, ill-repute, shame, infamy.

no·to·ri·ous (nō tôr′ē əs, -tōr′-, nə-), *adj.* **1.** widely and unfavorably known: *a notorious gambler.* **2.** publicly or generally known, as for a particular trait: *a newspaper that is notorious for its sensationalism.* [1540–50; < ML *nōtōrius* evident, equiv. to *nō*(*scere*) to get to know (see NOTIFY) + *-tōrius* -TORY¹] —**no·to′ri·ous·ly,** *adv.* —**no·to′ri·ous·ness,** *n.*

no·tor·nis (nō tôr′nis), *n.* a rare, flightless gallinule-like bird, *Notornis mantelli,* of New Zealand. Also called **takahe.** [1840–50; < NL: name of the genus < Gk *nó-t*(*os*) the south + *órnis* bird]

no·to·un·gu·late (nō′tō ung′gyə lit, -lāt′), *n.* **1.** one of the herbivorous, hoofed mammals of the extinct order Notoungulata, best known from the Paleocene to the Pleistocene Epochs of South America. —*adj.* **2.** belonging or pertaining to the Notoungulata. Also, **notungulate.** [< NL *Notoungulata.* See NOTUNGULATE]

No·tre Dame (nō′trə dām′, dăm′, nō′tər), **1.** Also called **Notre Dame de Paris** (*Fr.* nô trᵉ dam də pa-rē′), a famous early gothic cathedral in Paris (started 1163). **2.** the Virgin Mary, mother of Jesus. [< F: our lady]

no-trump (nō′trump′), *Bridge.* —*adj.* **1.** (of a hand, bid, or contract) without a trump suit; noting a bid or contract to be played without naming a trump suit. —*n.* **2.** the declaration to play a no-trump contract. [1895–1900]

Not·ting·ham (not′ing əm *or, U.S. often* -ham′), *n.* **1.** a city in SW Nottinghamshire, in central England. 287,800. **2.** Nottinghamshire.

Not·ting·ham·shire (not′ing əm shēr′, -shər *or, U.S. often* -ham-), *n.* a county in central England. 982,700; 854 sq. mi. (2210 sq. km). Also **Nottingham, Notts** (nots).

not·tur·no (nə to͝or′nō, nō-; *It.* nôt to͞or′nô), *n., pl.* **-ni** (-nē). *Music.* **1.** an 18th-century composition for chamber orchestra, similar to a serenade or a divertimento. **2.** nocturne. [< It: of the night < L *nocturnus.* See NOCTURN]

no·tum (nō′təm), *n., pl.* **-ta** (-tə). a dorsal plate or sclerite of the thorax of an insect. [1875–80; < NL < Gk *nôton* the back] —**no′tal,** *adj.*

no·tun·gu·late (nō tung′gyə lit, -lāt′), *n., adj.* notoungulate. [< NL *Notungulata* (var. of *Notoungulata*) name of order, equiv. to *not*(*o*)- (< Gk *nótos* the south) + *ungulata* UNGULATE]

No·tus (nō′təs), *n.* the ancient Greek personification of the south wind. [< L < Gk *Nótos,* special use of *nótos* the south]

not·with·stand·ing (not′with stan′ding, -with-), *prep.* **1.** in spite of; without being opposed or prevented by: *Notwithstanding a brilliant defense, he was found guilty. She went to the game anyway, doctor's orders notwithstanding.* —*conj.* **2.** in spite of the fact that; although: *It was the same material, notwithstanding the texture seemed different.* —*adv.* **3.** nevertheless; anyway; yet: *We were invited notwithstanding.* [1350–1400; ME (prep., adv., and conj.); see NOT, WITHSTAND, -ING²]

—Syn. 1. NOTWITHSTANDING, DESPITE, IN SPITE OF imply that something is true even though there are obstacles or opposing conditions. The three expressions may be used practically interchangeably. NOTWITHSTANDING suggests, however, a hindrance of some kind: *Notwithstanding the long delay, I shall still go.* DESPITE indicates that there is an active opposition: *Despite procrastination and disorganization, they finished the project.* IN SPITE OF implies meeting strong opposing forces or circumstances that must be taken into account: *She succeeded in spite of many discouragements.* **—Ant. 1.** because of, on account of.

Noua•dhi•bou (nwä′di bo͞o′), *n.* a seaport in SW Mauritania. 25,000. Formerly, **Port-Étienne.**

Nouak•chott (nwäk shot′), *n.* a city in and the capital of Mauritania, on the W coast. 130,000.

nou•gat (no͞o′gət, no͞o′gä), *n.* a chewy or brittle candy containing almonds or other nuts and sometimes fruit. [1820–30; < F < Pr << VL **nucātum,* n. use of neut. of **nucātus,* equiv. to L *nuc-* (s. of *nux*) nut + *-ātus* -ATE¹]

nou•ga•tine (no͞o′gə tēn′), *n.* a chocolate-coated nougat. [1890–95; NOUGAT + -INE¹]

nought (nôt), *n., adj., adv.* naught. [bef. 900; ME; OE *nōht,* contr. of *nōwiht,* equiv. to *ne* not + *ōwiht* AUGHT¹]

noughts-and-cross•es (nôts′ən krô′siz, -kros′iz), *n.* (*used with a singular v.*) *Brit.* tick-tack-toe (def. 1). [1890–95]

Nou•mé•a (no͞o mā′ə), *n.* a city in and the capital of New Caledonia, on the SW coast. 59,869.

nou•me•nal (no͞o′mə nl), *adj.* ontic. [1795–1805; NOUMEN(ON) + -AL¹] **—nou′me•nal•ism,** *n.* **—nou′me•nal•ist,** *n.* **—nou′me•nal′i•ty,** *n.* **—nou′me•nal•ly,** *adv.*

nou•me•non (no͞o′mə non′), *n., pl.* **-na** (-nə). **1.** the object, itself inaccessible to experience, to which a phenomenon is referred for the basis or cause of its sense content. **2.** a thing in itself, as distinguished from a phenomenon or thing as it appears. **3.** *Kantianism.* something that can be the object only of a purely intellectual, nonsensuous intuition. [1790–1800; < Gk *nooúmenon* a thing being perceived, n. use of neut. of prp. passive of *noeîn* to perceive; akin to NOUS]

noun (noun), *Gram.* **—n. 1.** any member of a class of words that are formally distinguished in many languages, as in English, typically by the plural and possessive endings and that can function as the main or only elements of subjects or objects, as *cat, belief, writing, Ohio, darkness.* Nouns are often thought of as referring to persons, places, things, states, or qualities. **—adj. 2.** Also, **noun′al.** of or resembling a noun. [1350–1400; ME *nowne* < AF *noun* < L *nōmen* NAME] **—noun′al•ly,** *adv.*

noun′ ad′junct, *Gram.* a noun that occurs before and modifies another noun, as *toy* in *toy store* or *tour* in *tour group.* [1960–65]

noun′ clause′, *Gram.* a subordinate clause that functions as a noun within a main clause.

noun′ phrase′, *Gram.* a construction that functions syntactically as a noun, consisting of a noun and any modifiers, as *all the men in the room who are reading books,* or of a noun substitute, as a pronoun. [1950–55]

nou•rice (no͞o′ris), *n. Obs.* a nurse. [1175–1225; ME; see NURSE]

nour•ish (nûr′ish, nur′-), *v.t.* **1.** to sustain with food or nutriment; supply with what is necessary for life, health, and growth. **2.** to cherish, foster, keep alive, etc.: *He had long nourished the dream of living abroad.* **3.** to strengthen, build up, or promote: *to nourish discontent among the workers; to nourish the arts in one's community.* [1250–1300; ME *norisshe* < OF *noriss-,* long s. of *norir* < L *nūtrīre* to feed; see NURSE, -ISH²] **—nour′ish•a•ble,** *adj.* **—nour′ish•er,** *n.*
—Syn. 1. See **nurse. 3.** encourage, help, aid, back, advance. **—Ant. 3.** discourage.

nour•ish•ing (nûr′i shing, nur′-), *adj.* promoting or sustaining life, growth, or strength: *a nourishing diet.* [1350–1400; ME (ger.); see NOURISH, -ING²] **—nour′ish•ing•ly,** *adv.*

nour•ish•ment (nûr′ish mənt, nur′-), *n.* **1.** something that nourishes; food, nutriment, or sustenance. **2.** the act of nourishing. **3.** the state of being nourished. **4.** a process, system, method, of, providing or administering nourishment: *a treatise on the nourishment of international trade.* [1375–1425; late ME *norysshement* < MF *norissement.* See NOURISH, -MENT]

nous (no͞os, nous), *n.* **1.** *Gk. Philos.* mind or intellect. **2.** *Neoplatonism.* the first and purest emanation of the One, regarded as the self-contemplating order of the universe. [1670–80; < Gk *noûs,* contracted var. of *nóos* mind]

nou•veau (no͞o′vō, no͞o vō′), *adj.* newly or recently created, developed, or come to prominence: *The sudden success of the firm created several nouveau millionaires.* [1805–15; < F: new; OF *novel* < L *novellus;* see NOVEL²]

nou•veau pau•vre (no͞o vō pō′vʀᵊ), *pl.* ***nou•veaux pau•vres*** (no͞o vō pō′vʀᵊ). *French.* a newly poor person.

nou•veau riche (no͞o′vō rēsh′; *Fr.* no͞o vō ʀēsh′), *pl.* **nou•veaux riches** (no͞o′vō rēsh′; *Fr.* no͞o vō ʀēsh′). a person who is newly rich: *the ostentation of the nouveaux riches of the 1920's.* [1805–15; < F: new rich (person)]

nou•veau•té (no͞o vō tā′), *n., pl.* ***-tés*** (-tā′). *French.* newness; novelty.

nou•velle (no͞o vel′), *adj.* pertaining to or characteristic of *nouvelle cuisine.* [extracted from NOUVELLE CUISINE]

nou•velle cui•sine (no͞o vel kwē zēn′), (*sometimes caps.*) *French.* a modern style of French cooking that emphasizes the use of the finest and freshest ingredients simply and imaginatively prepared, often with fresh herbs, the artful arrangement and presentation of food, and the use of reduced stocks in place of flour-thickened sauces. [lit., new cooking]

nou•velles (no͞o vel′), *n.pl. French.* news.

nou•velle vague (no͞o vel vAg′), *pl.* ***nou•velles vagues*** (no͞o vel vAg′). *French.* **1.** a new wave, trend, movement, phase, etc., esp. in an art form. **2.** the films of a group of young French and Italian filmmakers, beginning in the late 1950's, who emphasized conscious manipulation of film techniques and psychological probing instead of plot. [lit., new wave]

Nov., November.

nov., novelist.

no•va (nō′və), *n., pl.* **-vas, -vae** (-vē). *Astron.* a star that suddenly becomes thousands of times brighter and then gradually fades to its original intensity. Cf. **supernova.** [1680–90; < NL: n. use of fem. of L *novus* NEW] **—no′va•like′,** *adj.*

No•va (nō′və), *n.* **1.** Also called **No′va Salm′on.** a Pacific salmon cured in the style of Nova Scotia salmon. **2.** (*l.c.*) (loosely) any smoked salmon. Cf. **Nova Scotia salmon.**

No•va•chord (nō′və kôrd′), *Trademark.* a brand name for a keyboard instrument resembling in shape an upright piano, operating by electronic tone generation and providing a great variety of tone colors.

no•vac•u•lite (nō vak′yə līt′), *n. Petrol.* a very hard sedimentary rock, similar to chert, composed essentially of microcrystalline quartz. [1790–1800; < L *novācul(a)* a sharp knife, razor + -ITE¹]

No•va I•gua•çu (nō′vä ē′gwä so͞o′), a city in SE Brazil, NW of Rio de Janeiro. 931,954.

No•va•lis (nō vä′lis), *n.* (pen name of *Friedrich von Hardenberg*), 1772–1801, German poet.

No•va Lis•bo•a (*Port.* nô′və lēzh bô′ə), *n.* former name of **Huambo.**

No•va•ra (nō vär′ə; *It.* nô vä′ʀä), *n.* a city in NE Piedmont, in NW Italy. 102,135.

No•va Sco•tia (nō′və skō′shə), **1.** a peninsula and province in SE Canada: once a part of the French province of Acadia. 812,127; 21,068 sq. mi. (54,565 sq. km). *Cap.:* Halifax. **2.** *Informal.* See **Nova Scotia salmon.** **—No′va Sco′tian.**

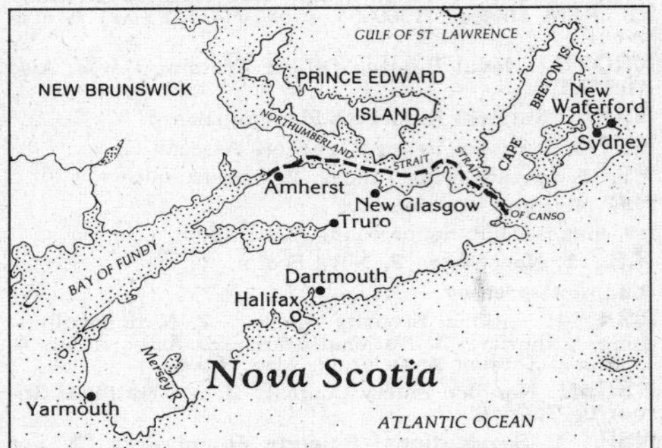

No′va Sco′tia lox′. See under **lox¹.**

No′va Sco′tia salm′on, an Atlantic salmon, esp. from the waters off Nova Scotia, cured in the local manner. Cf. **lox¹.**

no•va•tion (nō vā′shən), *n.* **1.** *Law.* the substitution of a new obligation for an old one, usually by the substitution of a new debtor or of a new creditor. **2.** the introduction of something new; innovation. [1525–35; < L *novātiōn-* (s. of *novātiō*) a renewing, equiv. to *novāt(us)* (ptp. of *novāre* to renew, deriv. of *novus* NEW) + *-iōn-* -ION]

No•va•to (nə vä′tō), *n.* a city in W California, N of San Francisco. 43,916.

No•va•ya Zem•lya (nō′və yə zem′lē ä′; *Russ.* nô′və yə zyim lyä′), two large islands in the Arctic Ocean, N of and belonging to the Russian Federation. 35,000 sq. mi. (90,650 sq. km).

nov•el¹ (nov′əl), *n.* **1.** a fictitious prose narrative of considerable length and complexity, portraying characters and usually presenting a sequential organization of action and scenes. **2.** (formerly) novella (def. 1). [1560–70; < It *novella* (*storia*) new kind of story. See NOVEL²] **—nov′el•like′,** *adj.*

nov•el² (nov′əl), *adj.* of a new kind; different from anything seen or known before: *a novel idea.* [1375–1425; late ME (< MF, OF) < L *novellus* fresh, young, novel, dim. of *novus* NEW]
—Syn. See **new.**

nov•el³ (nov′əl), *n.* **1.** *Roman Law.* **a.** an imperial enactment subsequent and supplementary to an imperial compilation and codification of authoritative legal materials. **b.** Usually, **Novels,** imperial enactments subsequent to the promulgation of Justinian's Code and supplementary to it: one of the four divisions of the Corpus Juris Civilis. **2.** *Civil Law.* an amendment to a statute. [1605–15; < LL *novella* (*constitūtiō*) a new (regulation, order). See NOVEL²]

nov•el•ette (nov′ə let′), *n.* a brief novel or long short story. [1805–15; NOVEL¹ + -ETTE]

nov•el•ist (nov′ə list), *n.* a person who writes novels. [1575–85; NOVEL¹ + -IST]

nov•el•is•tic (nov′ə lis′tik), *adj.* of, pertaining to, or characteristic of novels. [1825–35; NOVEL¹ + -ISTIC] **—nov′el•is′ti•cal•ly,** *adv.*

nov•el•ize (nov′ə līz′), *v.t.,* **-ized, -iz•ing. 1.** to put into the form of a novel: *He tried to novelize one of Shakespeare's plays.* **2.** to make fictional; fictionalize. Also, *esp. Brit.,* **nov′el•ise′.** [1625–35; NOVEL¹ + -IZE] **—nov′el•i•za′tion,** *n.* **—nov′el•iz′er,** *n.*

no•vel•la (nō vel′ə), *n., pl.* **-vel•las, -vel•le** (-vel′ē, -vel′ā). **1.** a tale or short story of the type contained in the *Decameron* of Boccaccio. **2.** a fictional prose narrative that is longer and more complex than a short story; a short novel. [1900–05; < It; see NOVEL¹]

nov•el•ty (nov′əl tē), *n., pl.* **-ties,** *adj.* **—n. 1.** state or quality of being novel, new, or unique; newness: *the novelty of a new job.* **2.** a novel occurrence, experience, or proceeding: *His sarcastic witticisms had ceased being an entertaining novelty.* **3.** an article of trade whose value is chiefly decorative, comic, or the like and whose appeal is often transitory: *a store catering to tourists who loaded up with souvenir pennants and other novelties.* **—adj. 4.** *Textiles.* **a.** (of a weave) consisting of a combination of basic weaves. **b.** (of a fabric or garment) having a pattern or design produced by a novelty weave. **c.** (of yarn) having irregularities within the fibrous structure. **5.** of or pertaining to novelties as articles of trade: *novelty goods; novelty items.* **6.** having or displaying novelties: *novelty shop.* [1350–1400; ME *novelte* < MF *novelete* < LL *novellitās* newness. See NOVEL², -ITY]

nov′elty sid′ing. See **drop siding.**

No•vem•ber (nō vem′bər), *n.* **1.** the eleventh month of the year, containing 30 days. **2.** a word used in communications to represent the letter *N. Abbr.:* Nov. [bef. 1000; ME, OE < L: the ninth month of the early Roman calendar, compound with *novem* NINE; for final element see DECEMBER]

no•vem•de•cil•lion (nō′vəm di sil′yən), *n., pl.* **-lions,** (*as after a numeral*) **-lion,** *adj.* **—n. 1.** a cardinal number represented in the U.S. by 1 followed by 60 zeros, and in Great Britain by 1 followed by 114 zeros. **—adj. 2.** amounting to one novemdecillion in number. [1935–40; < L *novemdec(im)* nineteen (*novem* NINE + *decem* TEN) + *-illion,* as in *million*] **—no′vem•de•cil′lionth,** *adj., n.*

no•ve•na (nō vē′nə, nə-), *n., pl.* **-nae** (-nē), **-nas.** *Rom. Cath. Ch.* a devotion consisting of nine separate days of prayers or services. [1850–55; < ML *novēna,* n. use of fem. sing. of L *novēnus* nine each]

no•ver•cal (nō vûr′kəl), *adj.* of, like, or befitting a stepmother. [1615–25; < L *novercālis,* equiv. to *noverc(a)* stepmother + *-ālis* -AL¹]

Nov•go•rod (nov′gə rod′; *Russ.* nôv′gə ʀət), *n.* a city in the W Russian Federation in Europe, SE of St. Petersburg: a former capital of Russia. 228,000.

No•vi (nō′vī), *n.* a town in SE Michigan. 22,525.

no•via (nô′vyä; *Eng.* nō′vē ə), *n., pl.* ***-vias*** (-vyäs; *Eng.* -vē əz). *Spanish.* **1.** a fiancée or bride. **2.** a girlfriend or sweetheart.

nov•ice (nov′is), *n.* **1.** a person who is new to the circumstances, work, etc., in which he or she is placed; beginner; tyro: *a novice in politics.* **2.** a person who has been received into a religious order or congregation for a period of probation before taking vows. **3.** a person newly become a church member. **4.** a recent convert to Christianity. [1300–50; ME *novyce* < MF *novice* < ML *novītius* convent novice, var. of L *novīcius* newly come into a particular status, deriv. of *novus* NEW. See -ITIOUS] **—nov′ice•hood′,** *n.* **—nov′ice•like′,** *adj.*
—Syn. 1. newcomer. **1, 2.** neophyte.

no•vi•lle•ro (nō′vil yâr′ō, -vəl yâr′ō; *Sp.* nô′vē ye′ʀô, -lye′-), *n., pl.* **-vi•lle•ros** (-vē âr′ōz, -vəl yâr′ōz; *Sp.* -vē-ye′ʀôs, -lye′-). a young bullfighter who has not yet been named a matador. [1920–25; < Sp, equiv. to *novill(o)* a fighting bull less than three years old (< L *novellus;* see NOVEL²) + *-ero* (< L *-ārius* -ARY); such bulls are typically fought by novice bullfighters]

no•vio (nô′vyô; *Eng.* nō′vē ō′), *n., pl.* ***-vios*** (-vyôs; *Eng.* -vē ōz′). *Spanish.* **1.** a fiancé or bridegroom. **2.** a boyfriend or sweetheart.

No•vi Sad (nô′vē säd′), a city in and the capital of Vojvodina, in N Yugoslavia, on the Danube. 257,685. German, **Neusatz.**

no•vi•ti•ate (nō vish′ē it, -āt′), *n.* **1.** the state or period of being a novice of a religious order or congregation. **2.** the quarters occupied by religious novices during probation. **3.** the state or period of being a beginner in anything. **4.** a novice. Also, **no•vi′ci•ate.** [1590–1600; < ML, equiv. to *novīti(us)* NOVICE + *-ātus* -ATE³]

No•vo•cain (nō′və kān′), *Pharm., Trademark.* a brand of procaine.

No•vo•cher•kassk (nō′və chər käsk′; *Russ.* nə və-chyiʀ käsk′), *n.* a city in the SW Russian Federation in Europe, NE of Rostov. 188,000.

No•vo•kui•by•shevsk (nō′və kwē′bə shefsk′; *Russ.* nə və ko͞oi′bi shifsk), *n.* a city in the SW Russian Federation in Europe, SW of Kuibyshev. 109,000.

No•vo•kuz•netsk (nō′və ko͝oz netsk′; *Russ.* nə və-ko͞o znyetsk′), *n.* a city in the S Russian Federation in central Asia: an industrial center is located here because of coal deposits of the Kuznetsk Basin. 600,000. Formerly, **Stalinsk.**

No•vo•mos•kovsk (nō′və mos kôfsk′, -kofsk′; *Russ.* nə və mu skôfsk′), *n.* a city in the W Russian Federation in Europe, S of Moscow. 147,000.

No•vo•ros•siysk (nō′və rə sēsk′; *Russ.* nə və ʀu-syēsk′), *n.* a seaport in the SW Russian Federation in Europe, on the Black Sea. 179,000. Also, **No′vo•ros•siisk′.**

No•vo•shakh•tinsk (nō′və shäk′tinsk; *Russ.* nə və-shäkʜ′tyinsk), *n.* a city in the S Russian Federation in Europe, NE of the Sea of Azov. 104,000.

No•vo•si•birsk (nō′və sə bērsk′; *Russ.* nə və syi-byēʀsk′), *n.* a city in the SW Russian Federation in

CONCISE PRONUNCIATION KEY: act, cāpe, dâre, pärt; set, ēqual; *if,* īce; ox, ōver, ôrder, oil, bo͝ok, bo͞ot, out; up, ûrge; child; sing; shoe; thin, *th*at; zh as in *treasure.* ə = *a* as in *alone, e* as in *system, i* as in *easily, o* as in *gallop, u* as in *circus;* ᵊ as in *fire* (fīᵊr), *hour* (ouᵊr). l and n can serve as syllabic consonants, as in *cradle* (krād′l), and *button* (but′n). See the full key inside the front cover.

Asia, on the Ob. 1,436,000. Formerly, **No·vo·ni·ko·la·yevsk** (nō′və nik′ə lä′yefsk; *Russ.* nə və nyi ku lä′yifsk).

No·vot·ný (nə vot′nē; *Czech.* nô′vôt nē′), *n.* **An·to·nín** (an′tə nin; *Czech.* än′tô nyēn′), 1904–75, Czech political leader: president 1957–68.

No·vum Or·ga·num (nō′vəm ôr′gə nəm, ôr gä′nəm, -gan′əm; *Lat.* nō′wo͝om ôʀ′gä no͝om′), a philosophical work in Latin (1620) by Francis Bacon, presenting an inductive method for scientific and philosophical inquiry.

no·vus or·do se·clo·rum (nō′wo͞os ōʀ′dō se klō′ro͞om; *Eng.* nō′vəs ôr′dō se klôr′əm, -klōr′-), *Latin.* a new order of the ages (is born): motto on the reverse of the great seal of the United States (adapted from Vergil's *Eclogues* IV:5).

now (nou), *adv.* **1.** at the present time or moment: *You are now using a dictionary.* **2.** without further delay; immediately; at once: *Either do it now or not at all.* **3.** at this time or juncture in some period under consideration or in some course of proceedings described: *The case was now ready for the jury.* **4.** at the time or moment immediately past: *I saw him just now on the street.* **5.** in these present times; nowadays: *Now you rarely see horse-drawn carriages.* **6.** under the present or existing circumstances; as matters stand: *I see now what you meant.* **7.** (used to introduce a statement or question): *Now, you don't really mean that.* **8.** (used to strengthen a command, entreaty, or the like): *Now stop that!* **9. now and again,** occasionally. Also, **now and then. 10. now that,** inasmuch as; since: *Now that she is rich and famous, she is constantly being besieged by appeals for aid.* —*conj.* **11.** inasmuch as; since: *Now you're here, why not stay for dinner?* —*n.* **12.** the present time or moment: *Up to now no one has volunteered.* —*adj.* **13.** up-to-the-minute; encompassing the latest ideas, fads, or fashions: *the now look; the now generation.* [bef. 900; 1965–70 for def. 13; ME; OE *nū,* c. ON, Goth *nū;* akin to G *nun,* L *num,* Skt *nu,* Gk *ný, nŷn*] —**now′ness,** *n.*

NOW, 1. See **National Organization for Women. 2.** *Banking.* negotiable order of withdrawal.

now·a·days (nou′ə dāz′), *adv.* **1.** at the present day; in these times: *Few people do their laundry by hand nowadays.* —*n.* **2.** the present: *The kitchens of nowadays are much more efficient than when I was a boy.* [1325–75; ME *nou adaies;* see NOW, A-[1], DAY, -S[1]]

no′ way′, *Informal.* absolutely not; no. [1965–70]

no·way (nō′wā′), *adv.* in no way, respect, or degree; not at all; nowise: *He was noway responsible for the accident.* Also, **no′ways′.** [1275–1325; ME; see NO[2], WAY]

now·el (nō el′), *n. Archaic.* Noel (def. 2). [1300–50; ME < MF *no(u)el* NOEL]

no·where (nō′hwâr′, -wâr′), *adv.* **1.** in or at no place; not anywhere: *The missing pen was nowhere to be found.* **2.** to no place: *We went nowhere last weekend.* **3. nowhere near,** not nearly: *There's nowhere near enough food to go around.* —*n.* **4.** the state of nonexistence or seeming nonexistence: *A gang of thieves appeared from nowhere.* **5.** anonymity or obscurity: *She came from nowhere to win the championship.* **6.** an unknown, remote, or nonexistent place or region. **7. miles from nowhere,** in a remote, isolated, or inaccessible area. —*adj. Informal.* **8.** being or leading nowhere; pointless; futile: *to be stuck in a nowhere job.* **9.** worthless or useless: *That's a nowhere idea if I ever heard one.* [bef. 1000; ME (adv.); OE *nāhwǣr, nōhwǣr.* See NO[1], WHERE]
—**Usage.** See **anyplace.**

no·where-dense (nō′hwâr dens′, -wâr-), *adj. Math.* (of a set in a topological space) having a closure that contains no open set with any points in it; nondense.

no·wheres (nō′hwârz, -wârz), *adv. Nonstandard.* nowhere. [see NOWHERE, -S[1]]

no·wheres·ville (nō′hwârz vil′, -wârz-), *n. Slang.* **1.** a remote or isolated town or village. **2.** a job, position, rank, etc., completely lacking in status, recognition, or a chance for advancement. **3.** anything unrealistic, impractical, or useless. Also, **No′wheres·ville′.** [NOWHERE + 's[1] or -s[1] + *-ville,* extracted from place names with this element]

no·whith·er (nō′hwith′ər, -with′-), *adv.* to no place; nowhere: *paths leading nowhither.* [bef. 900; ME *nohwider,* OE *nāhwider.* See NO[1], WHITHER]

no-win (nō′win′), *adj. Informal.* denoting a condition in which one cannot benefit, succeed, or win: *a no-win situation; a no-win war.* [1960–65]

no·wise (nō′wīz′), *adv.* noway. [1350–1400; ME. See NO[2], -WISE]

nown (nōn), *adj. Obs.* own.

Now·ruz (nou ro͞oz′), *n.* **1.** the Persian New Year's Day. **2.** *Zoroastrianism.* the seventh feast of obligation, devoted to fire, the seventh creation.

nowt[1] (nout), *n., pl.* **nowt.** *Scot. and North Eng.* **1.** an ox. **2.** a herd of cattle. [1150–1200; ME < Scand; cf. ON *naut,* NEAT[2]]

nowt[2] (nōt), *n. Brit. Dial.* naught; nothing.

now·y (nou′ē, nō′ē), *adj. Heraldry.* noting a partition line or charge in which one or more curves interrupt a normally straight line or lines, usually halfway along their length: *per fess nowy; a cross nowy.* [1555–65; < MF *noue* knotted < L *nōdātus.* See NODE, -ATE[1]]

nox·ious (nok′shəs), *adj.* **1.** harmful or injurious to health or physical well-being: *noxious fumes.* **2.** morally harmful; corrupting; pernicious: *a noxious plan to spread dissension.* [1605–15; < L *noxius* harmful, hurtful, injurious, equiv. to *nox(a)* harm, hurt, injury (akin to *nocēre* to do harm, inflict injury; see INNOCENT) + *-ius* -IOUS] —**nox′ious·ly,** *adv.* —**nox′ious·ness,** *n.*
—**Syn. 1.** hurtful, unwholesome, unhealthy, nocuous, detrimental, deleterious. **2.** corruptive. —**Ant. 1, 2.** harmless.

no·yade (nwä yäd′; *Fr.* nwa yad′), *n.* destruction or execution by drowning, esp. as practiced at Nantes, France, in 1793–94, during the Reign of Terror. [1810–20; < F: drowning, equiv. to *noy(er)* to drown (< L *necāre* to kill) + *-ade* -ADE[1]]

Noyes (noiz), *n.* **1. Alfred,** 1880–1958, English poet. **2. John Humphrey,** 1811–86, U.S. social reformer: founder of the Oneida Community.

noz·zle (noz′əl), *n.* **1.** a projecting spout, terminal discharging pipe, or the like, as of a hose or bellows. **2.** *Slang.* the nose. **3.** the spout of a teapot. **4.** the socket of a candlestick. [1600–10; earlier *nosle;* see NOSE, -LE]

NP, 1. noun phrase. **2.** nurse-practitioner.

Np, *Physics.* neper; nepers.

Np, *Symbol, Chem.* neptunium.

N.P., 1. new paragraph. **2.** nisi prius. **3.** no protest. **4.** notary public.

n.p., 1. net proceeds. **2.** new paragraph. **3.** nisi prius. **4.** no pagination. **5.** no place of publication. **6.** no protest. **7.** notary public.

NPK, *Hort.* nitrogen, phosphorus, and potasium.

n.p. or d., no place or date.

NPR, See **National Public Radio.** Also, **N.P.R.**

NPT, nonproliferation treaty.

n.p.t., normal pressure and temperature. Also, **npt**

nr., near.

NRA, 1. *U.S. Govt.* National Recovery Administration: the former federal agency (1933–36) charged with administering the provisions of the National Industrial Recovery Act. **2.** National Recreation Area. **3.** National Rifle Association. Also, **N.R.A.**

NRAB, National Railroad Adjustment Board.

NRC, 1. National Research Council. **2.** See **Nuclear Regulatory Commission.**

NREM sleep (en′rem′), *adj.* See **slow-wave sleep.** Cf. **REM sleep.** [1960–65; *n(on-)r(apid) e(ye) m(ovement)*]

NROTC, Naval Reserve Officer Training Corps. Also **N.R.O.T.C.**

NRPB, National Resources Planning Board.

NRTA, National Retired Teachers Association.

NS, 1. not sufficient (funds). **2.** nuclear ship.

Ns, *Meteorol.* nimbostratus.

ns, nanosecond; nanoseconds. Also, **nsec**

N.S., 1. New Style. **2.** Nova Scotia.

n.s., not specified.

NSA, 1. National Security Agency. **2.** National Shipping Authority. **3.** National Standards Association. **4.** National Student Association. Also, **N.S.A.**

NSC, 1. National Safety Council. **2.** See **National Security Council.**

NSF, 1. See **National Science Foundation. 2.** not sufficient funds. Also, **N.S.F.**

N/S/F, not sufficient funds.

N-shell (en′shel′), *n. Physics.* the fourth shell of electrons surrounding the nucleus of an atom and containing, when filled, 32 electrons having principal quantum number 4. Cf. **K-shell, L-shell, M-shell.** [1920–25]

N.S.P.C.A., National Society for the Prevention of Cruelty to Animals.

N.S.P.C.C., National Society for the Prevention of Cruelty to Children.

n.s.p.f., not specifically provided for.

NSU, nonspecific urethritis. See **nongonococcal urethritis.**

N.S.W., New South Wales.

-n't, a contraction of **not:** *didn't; hadn't; couldn't; shouldn't; won't; mustn't.*

NT, New Testament.

Nt, *Symbol, Chem.* niton.

nt, *Physics.* nit; nits.

N.T., 1. New Testament. **2.** Northern Territory.

N terminus, *Biochem.* the amino end of a protein molecule. Also, **N terminal.** Cf. **C terminus.** [abbrev. for *nitrogen* or $-NH_2$] —**N-ter·mi·nal** (en′tûr′mə nl), *adj.*

nth (enth), *adj.* **1.** being the last in a series of infinitely decreasing or increasing values, amounts, etc. **2.** (of an item in a series of occurrences, planned events, things used, etc., that is thought of as being infinitely large) being the latest, or most recent: *This is the nth time I've told you to eat slowly.* **3. the nth degree** or **power, a.** a high degree or power. **b.** the utmost degree or extent: *The new hotel was luxurious to the nth degree.* [1850–55; N (symbol, def. 5) + -TH[2]]

n-3 fatty acid (en′thrē′), *Biochem.* See **omega-3 fatty acid.**

NTIA, National Telecommunications and Information Administration.

NTSB, See **National Transportation Safety Board.**

n-tu·ple (en to͞o′pəl, -tyo͞o′-, -tup′əl; en′to͞o pəl, -tyo͞o-), *n. Math.* a set of *n* objects or quantities, where *n* is an integer, esp. such a set arranged in a specified order **(ordered n-tuple).** [N (symbol, def. 5) + *-tuple* (extracted from words such as *quintuple, octuple*)]

nt. wt., net weight.

nu[1] (no͞o, nyo͞o), *n.* **1.** the 13th letter of the Greek alphabet (N, ν). **2.** the consonant sound represented by this letter. [1885–90; < Gk *nŷ* < Sem; cf. NUN[2]]

nu[2] (no͞o), *interj.* well? so? so what? [1890–95; < Yiddish; c. OHG, MHG *nū* (adv. and conj.), G *nu* (dial. and colloquial) well! well now! See NOW]

Nu (no͞o), *n.* **U** (o͞o), (*Thakin Nu*), born 1907, Burmese political leader: prime minister 1948–56, 1957–58, 1960–62.

nu·ance (no͞o′äns, nyo͞o′-, no͞o äns′, nyo͞o-; *Fr.* ny-äns′), *n., pl.* **-anc·es** (-än siz, -än′siz; *Fr.* -äns′). **1.** a subtle difference or distinction in expression, meaning, response, etc. **2.** a very slight difference or variation in color or tone. [1775–85; < F: shade, hue, equiv. to *nu(er)* to shade (lit., to cloud < VL **nūbāre,* deriv. of **nūba,* for L *nūbēs* cloud) + *-ance* -ANCE] —**nu′anced,** *adj.*
—**Syn. 1.** subtlety, nicety, hint, refinement.

nub (nub), *n.* **1.** the point, gist, or heart of something. **2.** a knob or protuberance. **3.** a lump or small piece: *a nub of coal; a nub of pencil.* **4.** a small mass of fibers produced on a card, dyed brilliant colors, and introduced into yarn during the spinning process. Also, **knub.** [1585–95; < LG, MLG *knubbe;* cf. KNOB]

nub·bin (nub′in), *n.* **1.** a small lump or stunted piece; stub. **2.** a small or imperfect ear of corn. **3.** an undeveloped fruit. [1685–95, *Amer.;* perh. NUB + *-in,* var. of -ING[1]]

nub·ble (nub′əl), *n.* **1.** a small lump or piece. **2.** a small knob or protuberance. [1810–20; NUB + -LE (dim. suffix)]

nub·bly (nub′lē), *adj.,* **-bli·er, -bli·est. 1.** full of small protuberances. **2.** in the form of small lumps. Also, **knubbly.** [1820–30; NUBBLE + -Y[1]]

nub·by (nub′ē), *adj.,* **-bi·er, -bi·est.** having nubs; knobby or lumpy. Also, **knubby, nubbed, knubbed.** [1875–80; NUB + -Y[1]]

nu·bi·a (no͞o′bē ə, nyo͞o′-), *n.* a light, knitted woolen head scarf for women. [1855–60; < L *nūb(ēs)* a cloud + -IA]

Nu·bi·a (no͞o′bē ə, nyo͞o′-), *n.* **1.** a region in S Egypt and the Sudan, N of Khartoum, extending from the Nile to the Red Sea. **2. Kingdom of,** an ancient state in Nubia, 2000 B.C.–A.D. 1400. **3. Lake.** See **Nasser, Lake.**

Nu·bi·an (no͞o′bē ən, nyo͞o′-), *n.* **1.** a member of any of the various peoples inhabiting Nubia. **2.** the Nilo-Saharan language of the Nubians. **3.** a Nubian or black slave. **4.** a Nubian horse. —*adj.* **5.** of, pertaining to, or characteristic of Nubia, its people, or their language. [1350–1400; ME; see NUBI(A), -AN]

Nu′bian Des′ert, an arid region in the NE Sudan.

Nu′bian goat′, one of a breed of large, long-eared North African goats having a Roman nose and predominantly brown or black hair: noted for their rich milk. [1875–80]

nu·bile (no͞o′bil, -bīl, nyo͞o′-), *adj.* **1.** (of a young woman) suitable for marriage, esp. in regard to age or physical development; marriageable. **2.** (of a young woman) sexually developed and attractive: *the nubile girls in their bikinis.* [1635–45; < L *nūbilis,* equiv. to *nūb(ere)* to marry (see NUPTIAL) + *-ilis* -ILE] —**nu·bil·i·ty** (no͞o bil′i tē, nyo͞o-), *n.*

nu·bi·lous (no͞o′bə ləs, nyo͞o′-), *adj.* **1.** cloudy or foggy. **2.** obscure or vague; indefinite. [1525–35; < L *nūbilus,* equiv. to *nūb(ēs)* cloud + *-ilus* adj. suffix. See -OUS]

nu·cel·lus (no͞o sel′əs, nyo͞o-), *n., pl.* **-cel·li** (-sel′ī). *Bot.* the central cellular mass of the body of the ovule, containing the embryo sac. [1880–85; < NL, equiv. to L *nuc-* (s. of *nux*) nut + *-ella* -ELLE] —**nu·cel′lar,** *adj.*

NUCFLASH (no͞ok′flash′, nyo͞ok′-), *n.* a report of highest precedence notifying the president, secretary of defense, or their deputies of an accidental or unauthorized nuclear-weapon launch or of a nuclear attack. [*nuc(lear) flash*]

nu·cha (no͞o′kə, nyo͞o′-), *n., pl.* **-chae** (-kē). nape. [1350–1400; < ML: nape of neck < Ar *nukhā′* spinal marrow]

nuci-, a combining form meaning "nut," used in the formation of compound words: *nuciform.* [comb. form repr. L *nuci-* (s. of *nux*) nut]

nu·ci·form (no͞o′sə fôrm′, nyo͞o′-), *adj.* nut-shaped. [1855–60; NUCI- + -FORM]

nu·cle·ar (no͞o′klē ər, nyo͞o′- *or, by metathesis,* -kyə-lər), *adj.* **1.** pertaining to or involving atomic weapons: *nuclear war.* **2.** operated or powered by atomic energy: *a nuclear submarine.* **3.** (of a nation or group of nations) having atomic weapons. **4.** of, pertaining to, or forming a nucleus. **5.** of, pertaining to, or like the nuclear family: *nuclear bonds.* —*n. Informal.* **6.** nuclear energy: *switching to nuclear as a power source.* [1840–50; NUCLE(US) + -AR[1]; cf. F *nucléaire*]
—**Pronunciation.** In pronouncing NUCLEAR, the second and third syllables are most commonly said as (-klē ər), a sequence of sounds that directly reflects the spelled sequence -CLE·AR. In recent years, a somewhat controversial pronunciation has come to public attention, with these two final syllables said as (-kyə lər). Since (-klē ər), the common pronunciation of -CLE·AR, might also be represented, broadly, as (-klə yər), the (-kyə lər) pronunciation can be seen as coming from a process of metathesis, in which the (l) and the (y) change places. The resulting pronunciation is reinforced by analogy with such words as *molecular, particular,* and *muscular,* and although it occurs with some frequency among highly educated speakers, including scientists, professors, and government officials, it is disapproved of by many.

nu′clear cross′ sec′tion, *Physics.* See **cross section** (def. 7).

nu′clear emul′sion, *Physics.* a photographic emulsion in the form of a thick block, used to record the tracks of elementary particles. [1945–50]

nu′clear en′ergy, energy released by reactions within atomic nuclei, as in nuclear fission or fusion. Also called **atomic energy.** [1925–30]

CONCISE ETYMOLOGY KEY: <, descended or borrowed from; >, whence; b., blend of, blended; c., cognate with; cf., compare; deriv., derivative; equiv., equivalent; imit., imitative; obl., oblique; r., replacing; s., stem; sp., spelling, spelled; resp., respelling, respelled; trans., translation; ?, origin unknown; *, unattested; ‡, probably earlier than. See the full key inside the front cover.

nu′clear fam′ily, a social unit composed of father, mother, and children. Cf. **extended family.** [1945–50]

nu′clear fis′sion, fission (def. 2). [1885–90]

nu′clear fu′el, **1.** *Physics.* fissile or fertile material that undergoes fission in a nuclear reactor. **2.** any light element, as hydrogen or helium, that undergoes fusion and gives off energy within the interior of stars. [1945–50]

nu′clear fu′sion, fusion (def. 4). [1895–1900]

nu·cle·ar·ism (nōō′klē ə riz′əm, nyōō′- *or, by metathesis,* -kyə lə-), *n.* a political philosophy maintaining that nuclear weapons are the best means of assuring peace and of attaining political goals. [1965–70; NUCLEAR + -ISM] —**nu′cle·ar·ist,** *n.* —**nu′cle·ar·is′tic,** *adj.*
—**Pronunciation.** See **nuclear.**

nu′clear i′somer, *Physics.* isomer (def. 2). [1965–70]

nu′clear isom′erism, *Physics.* isomerism (def. 2).

nu·cle·ar·ize (nōō′klē ə rīz′, nyōō′- *or, by metathesis,* -kyə lə-), *v.t.*, **-ized, -iz·ing.** to equip with nuclear weapons; give nuclear capability to: *a fear that armed forces on both sides would become nuclearized.* Also, *esp. Brit.,* **nu′cle·ar·ise′.** [1955–60; NUCLEAR + -IZE] —**nu′cle·ar·i·za′tion,** *n.*
—**Pronunciation.** See **nuclear.**

nu′clear magnet′ic res′onance, *Physics.* the selective absorption of electromagnetic radiation by an atomic nucleus in the presence of a strong, static, magnetic field: used in research and in medicine to monitor tissue metabolism and to distinguish between normal and abnormal cells. Cf. **MRI.** *Abbr.:* NMR [1940–45]

nu′clear mag′neton, *Physics.* a unit of magnetic moment, used to measure proton spin and approximately equal to 1/1836 Bohr magneton. [1930–35]

nu′clear med′icine, diagnostic and therapeutic medical techniques using radionuclides or radioisotopes. [1950–55]

nu′clear mem′brane, *Biol.* the double membrane surrounding the nucleus within a cell. Also called **nu′·clear en′velope.** [1885–90]

nu′clear phys′ics, the branch of physics that deals with the behavior, structure, and component parts of atomic nuclei. [1930–35] —**nu′clear phys′icist.**

nu′clear pow′er, power derived from nuclear energy. Also called **atomic power.** [1925–30]

nu′clear radia′tion, *Physics.* radiation in the form of elementary particles emitted by an atomic nucleus, as alpha rays or gamma rays, produced by decay of radioactive substances or by nuclear fission.

nu′clear reac′tion, reaction (def. 8).

nu′clear reac′tor, *Physics.* reactor (def. 4). Also called **nu′clear pile′.** [1940–45]

Nu′clear Reg′ulatory Commis′sion, *U.S. Govt.* an independent agency, created in 1975, that licenses and regulates the nonmilitary use of nuclear energy. *Abbr.:* NRC

Nu′clear Test′-Ban Trea′ty, an agreement signed by Britain, the Soviet Union, and the U.S. in 1963, committing nations to halt atmospheric tests of nuclear weapons: by the end of 1963, 96 additional nations had signed the treaty.

nu′clear war′head. a warhead containing a fission or fusion bomb. [1950–55]

nu′clear waste′. See **radioactive waste.**

nu′clear weap′on, an explosive device whose destructive potential derives from the release of energy that accompanies the splitting or combining of atomic nuclei. [1945–50]

nu′clear win′ter, the general devastation of life, along with worldwide darkness and extreme cold, that some scientists believe would result from a global dust cloud screening out sunlight following large-scale nuclear detonations. [1980–85]

nu·cle·ase (nōō′klē ās′, -āz′, nyōō′-), *n. Biochem.* any enzyme that catalyzes the hydrolysis of nucleic acids. [1900–05; NUCLE(IC) + -ASE]

nu·cle·ate (*adj.* nōō′klē it, -āt′, nyōō′-; *v.* nōō′klē āt′, nyōō′-), *adj., v.,* **-at·ed, -at·ing.** —*adj.* **1.** having a nucleus. —*v.t.* **2.** to form (something) into a nucleus. —*v.i.* **3.** to form a nucleus. [1860–65; < L *nucleātus* having a kernel or stone. See NUCLEUS, -ATE[1]] —**nu·cle·a·tion** (nōō′klē ā′shən, nyōō′-), *n.* —**nu′cle·a′tor,** *n.*

nu·cle·i (nōō′klē ī′, nyōō′-), *n.* pl. of **nucleus.** [< L *nucleī*, nom. pl. of *nucleus;* see NUCLEUS]

nu·cle′ic ac′id (nōō klē′ik, -klā′-, nyōō-), *Biochem.* any of a group of long, linear macromolecules, either DNA or various types of RNA, that carry genetic information directing all cellular functions: composed of linked nucleotides. [1890–95; NUCLE(US) + -IC; cf. G *Nucleinsäure* (1889)]

nucleo-, a combining form representing **nucleus, nuclear,** or **nucleic acid** in compound words: *nucleoprotein.*

nu·cle·o·cap·sid (nōō′klē ə kap′sid, nyōō′-), *n. Microbiol.* the nucleic acid core and surrounding capsid of a virus; the basic viral structure. [1960–65; NUCLEO- + CAPSID]

nu·cle·oid (nōō′klē oid′, nyōō′-), *Microbiol.* —*n.* **1.** the central region in a prokaryotic cell, as a bacterium, that contains the chromosomes and that has no surrounding membrane. —*adj.* **2.** resembling a nucleus. [1850–55; NUCLE(US) + -OID]

nu·cle·o·lar (nōō klē′ə lər, nyōō-, nōō′klē ō′-, nyōō′-), *adj. Cell Biol.* of, pertaining to, or forming a nucleolus. [1860–65; NUCLEOL(US) + -AR[1]]

nu·cle·o·lat·ed (nōō′klē ə lā′tid, nyōō′-, nōō klē′ə-, nyōō-), *adj.* containing a nucleolus or nucleoli. Also, **nu′cle·o·late′.** [1840–50; NUCLEOL(US) + -ATE[1] + -ED[3]]

nu·cle·o·lus (nōō klē′ə ləs, nyōō-), *n., pl.* **-li** (-lī′). *Cell Biol.* a conspicuous, rounded body within the nucleus of a cell. See diag. under **cell.** [1835–45; < LL: small kernel, equiv. to *nucle(us)* kernel (see NUCLEUS) + *-olus* -OLE[1]]

nu·cle·on (nōō′klē on′, nyōō′-), *n. Physics.* a proton or neutron, esp. when considered as a component of a nucleus. [1935–40; NUCLE(US) + -ON[1]] —**nu′cle·on′ic,** *adj.*

nu·cle·on·ics (nōō′klē on′iks, nyōō′-), *n.* (*used with a singular v.*) the branch of science that deals with nuclear phenomena, as radioactivity, fission, or fusion, esp. practical applications, as in industrial engineering. [1940–45; NUCLEON + -ICS]

nu·cle·o·phil·ic (nōō′klē ə fil′ik, nyōō′-), *adj. Chem.* of or pertaining to electron contribution in covalent bonding (opposed to *electrophilic*). [1930–35; NUCLEO- + -PHILIC] —**nu·cle·o·phile** (nōō′klē ə fil′, nyōō′-), *n.*

nu·cle·o·plasm (nōō′klē ə plaz′əm, nyōō′-), *n. Cell Biol.* the protoplasm of the nucleus of a cell. Also called **karyoplasm.** [1885–90; NUCLEO- + -PLASM] —**nu′cle·o·plas′mic, nu·cle·o·plas·mat·ic** (nōō′klē ō plaz mat′ik, nyōō′-), *adj.*

nu·cle·o·pro·tein (nōō′klē ə prō′tēn, -tē in, nyōō′-), *n. Biochem.* any of the class of conjugated proteins occurring in cells and consisting of a protein combined with a nucleic acid, essential for cell division and reproduction. [1905–10; NUCLEO- + PROTEIN]

nu·cle·o·sid·ase (nōō′klē ə sī′dās, -dāz, nyōō′-), *n. Biochem.* any of the class of enzymes that catalyze the hydrolysis of nucleosides. [1910–15; NUCLEOSIDE + -ASE]

nu·cle·o·side (nōō′klē ə sīd′, nyōō′-), *n. Biochem.* any of the class of compounds derived by the hydrolysis of nucleic acids or nucleotides, consisting typically of deoxyribose or ribose combined with adenine, guanine, cytosine, uracil, or thymine. [1910–15; NUCLE(IC) + -OSE[2] + -IDE]

nu·cle·o·some (nōō′klē ə sōm′, nyōō′-), *n. Cell Biol.* any of the repeating subunits of chromatin occurring at intervals along a strand of DNA, consisting of DNA coiled around histone. [1960–65; NUCLEO- + -SOME[3]]

nu·cle·o·syn·the·sis (nōō′klē ō sin′thə sis, nyōō′-), *n. Physics, Astron.* the formation of new atomic nuclei by nuclear reactions, thought to occur in the interiors of stars and in the early stages of development of the universe. [1955–60; NUCLEO- + SYNTHESIS] —**nu·cle·o·syn·thet·ic** (nōō′klē ō sin thet′ik, nyōō′-), *adj.*

nu·cle·o·tide (nōō′klē ə tīd′, nyōō′-), *n. Biochem.* any of a group of molecules that, when linked together, form the building blocks of DNA or RNA: composed of a phosphate group, the bases adenine, cytosine, guanine, and thymine, and a pentose sugar, in RNA the thymine base being replaced by uracil. [1905–10; alter. of NUCLEOSIDE]

nu·cle·us (nōō′klē əs, nyōō′-), *n., pl.* **-cle·i** (-klē ī′), **-cle·us·es. 1.** a central part about which other parts are grouped or gathered; core: *A few faithful friends formed the nucleus of the club.* **2.** *Biol.* a specialized, usually spherical mass of protoplasm encased in a double membrane, and found in most living eukaryotic cells, directing their growth, metabolism, and reproduction, and functioning in the transmission of genic characters. See illus. under **ameba. 3.** *Physics.* the positively charged mass within an atom, composed of neutrons and protons, and possessing most of the mass but occupying only a small fraction of the volume of the atom. **4.** *Anat.* a mass of nerve cells in the brain or spinal cord in which nerve fibers form connections. **5.** Also called **condensation nucleus.** *Meteorol.* a particle upon which condensation of water vapor occurs to form water drops or ice crystals. **6.** *Chem.* a fundamental arrangement of atoms, as the benzene ring, that may occur in many compounds by substitution of atoms without a change in structure. **7.** *Astron.* the condensed portion of the head of a comet. **8.** *Phonet.* **a.** the central, most prominent segment in a syllable, consisting of a vowel, diphthong, or vowellike consonant, as the *a*-sound in *cat* or the *l*-sound in *bottled;* peak. **b.** the most prominent syllable in an utterance or stress group; tonic syllable. [1695–1705; < L: kernel, syncopated var. of *nuculeus,* equiv. to *nucu(la)* little nut (*nuc-*, s. of *nux* nut + *-ula* -ULE) + *-leus* n. suffix]
—**Syn. 1.** center, kernel, heart.

nu′cleus count′er. See **dust counter.**

nu·clide (nōō′klīd, nyōō′-), *n. Physics.* **1.** an atomic species in which the atoms all have the same atomic number and mass number. **2.** an individual atom in such a species. [1945–50; NUCL(EO)- + *-ide* < Gk *eîdos* shape]

Nudd (*Welsh.* nyth), *n.* Lludd.

nude (nōōd, nyōōd), *adj.*, **nud·er, nud·est,** *n.* —*adj.* **1.** naked or unclothed, as a person or the body. **2.** without the usual coverings, furnishings, etc.; bare: *a nude stretch of land laid waste by brush fires.* **3.** (of a photograph, painting, statue, etc.) being or prominently displaying a representation of the nude human figure. **4.** *Law.* made without a consideration or other legal essential: *a nude contract.* **5.** having the color nude. —*n.* **6.** a sculpture, painting, etc., of a nude human figure. **7.** an unclothed human figure. **8.** the condition of being unclothed: *to sleep in the nude.* **9.** a light grayish-yellow brown to brownish-pink color. [1525–35; < L *nūdus;* see NAKED] —**nude′ly,** *adv.* —**nude′ness,** *n.*
—**Syn. 1.** uncovered, undressed, undraped, exposed.
—**Ant. 1.** covered.
—**Pronunciation.** See **new.**

nude′ mouse′, a virtually hairless mutant laboratory-bred mouse having a major immune system deficiency caused by a lack of T cells, and able to accept grafts of foreign tissue. [1965–70]

nudge[1] (nuj), *v.*, **nudged, nudg·ing,** *n.* —*v.t.* **1.** to push slightly or gently, esp. with the elbow, to get someone's attention, prod someone into action, etc. —*v.i.* **2.** to give a nudge. —*n.* **3.** a slight or gentle push or jog, esp. with the elbow. [1665–75; var. of dial. *(k)nidge,* akin to OE *cnucian, cnocian* to KNOCK] —**nudg′er,** *n.*
—**Syn. 1.** elbow, poke, jog.

nudge[2] (nŏŏj), *v.*, **nudged, nudg·ing,** *n.* —*v.t.* **1.** to annoy with persistent complaints, criticisms, or pleas; nag: *He was always nudging his son to move to a better neighborhood.* —*v.i.* **2.** to nag, whine, or carp. —*n.* **3.** a person who nudges; pest. Also, **noodge, nudzh.** [1875–80; < Yiddish, s. of *nudyen* to bore < Pol *nudzić;* cf. NUDNIK]

nudg·y (nŏŏj′ē), *adj.*, **nudg·i·er, nudg·i·est. 1.** of, pertaining to, or like a nudge or nag. **2.** nervous; edgy. [NUDGE[2] + -Y[1]]

nudi-, a combining form meaning "naked," "bare," used in the formation of compound words: *nudicaul.* [comb. form repr. L *nūdus* naked; see -I-]

nu·di·branch (nōō′də brangk′, nyōō′-), *n.* a shell-less, marine snail of the suborder Nudibranchia, having external, often branched respiratory appendages on the back and sides. [1835–45; < F *nudibranche,* equiv. to *nudi-* NUDI- + *branche* gill (< L *branchia* BRANCHIA)]

nu·di·bran·chi·ate (nōō′də brang′kē it, -āt′, nyōō′-), *n.* **1.** nudibranch. —*adj.* **2.** belonging or pertaining to the nudibranchiates. Also, **nu·di·bran·chi·an** (nōō′də-brang′kē ən, nyōō′-). [1830–40; < NL *Nudibranchiata* name of suborder of mollusks. See NUDI-, BRANCHIATE]

nu·di·caul (nōō′di kôl′, nyōō′-), *adj. Bot.* having leafless stems. Also, **nu′di·cau′lous.** [NUDI- + CAUL]

nud·ie (nōō′dē, nyōō′-), *Informal.* —*n.* **1.** a film, performance, or magazine featuring nude performers or photographs. **2.** a nude person. —*adj.* **3.** featuring nude performers or photographs: *nudie photo layouts.* [1930–35; NUDE + -IE]

nud·ism (nōō′diz əm, nyōō′-), *n.* the practice of going nude, esp. in places that allow sexually mixed groups, in the belief that such practice benefits health. [1925–30; NUDE + -ISM] —**nud′ist,** *n., adj.*

nu·di·ty (nōō′di tē, nyōō′-), *n., pl.* **-ties** for 2. **1.** the state or fact of being nude; nakedness. **2.** something nude or naked. [1605–15; < L *nūditās.* See NUDE, -ITY]

nud·nik (nŏŏd′nik), *n. Slang.* a persistently dull, boring pest. [1945–50, *Amer.;* < Yiddish, equiv. to *nud-* base of *nudyen* (see NUDGE[2]) + *-nik* -NIK]

nu·dum pac·tum (nōō′dəm pak′təm, nyōō′-), *Law.* a simple contract or promise involving no legal consideration. [< L *nūdum pāctum* lit., bare pact]

nudzh (nŏŏj), *v.t., v.i., n.* nudge[2].

Nu·e·ces (nōō ā′səs, nyōō-), *n.* a river in S Texas, flowing SE to Corpus Christi Bay, on the Gulf of Mexico. 338 mi. (545 km) long.

nu·ée ar·dente (*Fr.* ny ā ar dänt′), *pl.* **nu·ées ar·dentes** (*Fr.* ny ā zar dänt′). *Geol.* (in a volcanic eruption) a swiftly flowing, dense cloud of hot gases, ashes, and lava fragments. [1900–05; < F: lit., burning cloud]

Nu·er (nōō′ər), *n., pl.* **-ers,** (*esp. collectively*) **-er** for 1. **1.** a member of a tribal people who live along the Nile in southern Sudan and subsist chiefly by raising cattle. **2.** the Nilotic language of the Nuer people.

Nue·va Ge·ro·na (nwe′vä he rô′nä), a town on the Isle of Pines, S of Cuba. 9000.

Nue·va O·co·te·pe·que (nwe′vä ô kô′te pe′ke), a town in W Honduras. 4608.

Nue·va San Sal·va·dor (nwā′və san sal′və dôr′, nōō ā′-; *Sp.* nwe′vä sän säl′vä thôr′). See **Santa Tecla.**

Nue·vo La·re·do (nwā′vō lə rā′dō, nōō ā′-; *Sp.* nwe′vô lä re′thô), a city in NE Mexico, on the Rio Grande opposite Laredo, Texas. 193,145.

Nue·vo Le·ón (nwā′vō lā ōn′, nōō ā′-; *Sp.* nwe′vô le ôn′), a state in NE Mexico. 2,344,000; 25,136 sq. mi. (65,102 sq. km). *Cap.:* Monterrey.

′nuff (nuf), *n. Informal.* enough. [by aphesis and resp.]

Nuf′field Ra′dio Astron′omy Lab′oratories (nuf′ēld). See under **Jodrell Bank.**

Nu·fud (nə fōōd′), *n.* See **Nefud Desert.** [1815–25]

nu·ga·cious (nōō gā′shəs, nyōō-), *adj.* trivial; unimportant or insignificant; nugatory. [1645–55; < L *nūgāc-*, s. of *nūgāx* bungling (*nūg(ārī)* to trifle, quibble + *-āx* adj. suffix) + -IOUS] —**nu·ga′cious·ness,** *n.*

nu·gac·i·ty (nōō gas′i tē, nyōō-), *n., pl.* **-ties** for 2. **1.** triviality; insignificance. **2.** something insignificant or inconsequential; a trifle. [1585–95; < LL *nūgācitās,* equiv. to *nūgāc-* (see NUGACIOUS) + *-itās* -ITY]

nu·gae (nōō′gī; *Eng.* nōō′jē, nyōō′-), *n.pl. Latin.* trifles.

nu·ga·to·ry (nōō′gə tôr′ē, -tōr′ē, nyōō′-), *adj.* **1.** of no real value; trifling; worthless. **2.** of no force or effect; ineffective; futile; vain. **3.** not valid. [1595–1605; < L *nūgātōrius* worthless, useless, trifling, equiv. to *nūgā(rī)* to trifle + *-tōrius* -TORY[1]]
—**Syn. 1.** trivial, insignificant, frivolous. **2.** useless, inoperative.

nug·get (nug′it), *n.* **1.** a lump of something, as of precious metal. **2.** a lump of native gold. **3.** anything of great value, significance, or the like: *nuggets of wisdom.* **4.** a bite-size piece of chicken, fish, etc., usually batter-fried. **5.** *Welding.* (in a spot-weld) the metal fused. **6.** *Australian.* **a.** a powerful, heavy animal. **b.** a strong, thickset man. [1850–55; perh. dim. of obs. *nug* small piece, var. of NOG[2]; see -ET] —**nug′get·y,** *adj.*

CONCISE PRONUNCIATION KEY: act, cāpe, dâre, pärt; set, ēqual; if, ice; ox, ōver, ôrder, oil, bŏŏk, bōōt, out; up, ûrge; child; sing; shoe; thin, that; zh as in *treasure.* ə = *a* as in *alone, e* as in *system, i* as in *easily, o* as in *gallop, u* as in *circus;* ᵊ as in *fire* (fīᵊr), *hour* (ouᵊr). l and n can serve as syllabic consonants, as in *cradle* (krād′l), and *button* (but′n). See the full key inside the front cover.

nug·gie (no͝og′ē), *n.* noogie. Also, **nug′ie.**

nui·sance (no͞o′səns, nyo͞o′-), *n.* **1.** an obnoxious or annoying person, thing, condition, practice, etc.: *a monthly meeting that was more nuisance than pleasure.* **2.** *Law.* something offensive or annoying to individuals or to the community, esp. in violation of their legal rights. [1375–1425; late ME *nu(i)sa(u)nce* < AF, equiv. to *nuis(er)* to harm (<< L *nocēre*) + *-ance* -ANCE]

nui′sance ground′, *Canadian Dial.* a garbage dump. [1885–90]

nui′sance tax′, a tax paid in small but frequent amounts, usually by consumers. [1920–25]

nuke (no͞ok, nyo͞ok), *n., adj., v.,* **nuked, nuk·ing.** *Informal.* —*n.* **1.** a nuclear or thermonuclear weapon. **2.** a nuclear power plant or nuclear reactor. **3.** nuclear energy: *to convert from coal to nuke.* —*adj.* **4.** of or pertaining to a nuclear or thermonuclear weapon or to a nuclear plant. —*v.t.* **5.** to attack, defeat, or destroy with or as if with nuclear weapons. **6.** *Slang.* to cook or bake in a microwave oven. [1945–50; by shortening and resp.]

Nü-kua (ny′kwä′), *n.* a Chinese goddess who repaired and restored order to heaven and earth when they were damaged, and who created the human race.

Nu·ku·a·lo·fa (no͞o′ko͞o ə lô′fə), *n.* a seaport in and the capital of Tonga, in the S Pacific Ocean. 15,545.

NUL, National Urban League. Also **N.U.L.**

null (nul), *adj.* **1.** without value, effect, consequence, or significance. **2.** being or amounting to nothing; nil; lacking; nonexistent. **3.** *Math.* (of a set) **a.** empty. **b.** of measure zero. **4.** being or amounting to zero. **5. null and void,** without legal force or effect; not valid: *This contract is null and void.* —*n.* **6.** *Electronics.* a point of minimum signal reception, as on a radio direction finder or other electronic meter. —*v.t.* **7.** to cancel; make null. [1555–65; < L *nūllus,* equiv. to *n(e)* not + *ūllus* any]

nul·lah (nul′ə), *n.* (in the East Indies) **1.** an intermittent watercourse. **2.** a gully or ravine. [1770–80; < Hindi *nālā* brook, ravine]

nul·la-nul·la (nul′ə nul′ə), *n. Australian.* an Aboriginal club or cudgel for use in hunting and war. [1830–40; < Dharuk *ŋa-la-ŋa-la*]

null′ hypoth′esis, (in the statistical testing of a hypothesis) the hypothesis to be tested. Cf. **alternative hypothesis.** [1930–35]

nulli-, a combining form meaning "none," "null": *nullipara.* [< LL *nūlli-* not any, none, no (comb. form of *nūllus* NULL)]

nul·li·fi·ca·tion (nul′ə fi kā′shən), *n.* **1.** an act or instance of nullifying. **2.** the state of being nullified. **3.** (*often cap.*) the failure or refusal of a U.S. state to aid in enforcement of federal laws within its limits, esp. on Constitutional grounds. [1620–30; < LL *nūllificātiōn-* (s. of *nūllificātiō*) contempt, equiv. to *nūllificāt(us)* (ptp. of *nūllificāre* to despise) + *-iōn-* -ION. See NULLIFY] —**nul′li·fi·ca′tion·ist, nul′li·fi·ca′tor,** *n.*

nul·li·fid·i·an (nul′ə fid′ē ən), *n.* a person who has no faith or religion; skeptic. [1555–65; NULLI- + L *fid-* (s. of *fidēs*) faith + -IAN]

nul·li·fy (nul′ə fī′), *v.t.,* **-fied, -fy·ing. 1.** to render or declare legally void or inoperative: *to nullify a contract.* **2.** to deprive (something) of value or effectiveness; make futile or of no consequence. [1585–95; < LL *nūllificāre* to despise. See NULLI-, -FY] —**nul′li·fi′er,** *n.*
—**Syn. 1, 2.** invalidate, annul, void, cancel.

nul·ling (nul′ing), *n.* knulling.

nul·lip·a·ra (nu lip′ər ə), *n., pl.* **-a·rae** (-ə rē′). *Obstet.* a woman who has never borne a child. [1870–75; < NL, equiv. to *nūlli-* NULLI- + *-para,* fem. of *-parus* -PAROUS] —**nul·li·par·i·ty** (nul′ə par′i tē), *n.* —**nul·lip′a·rous,** *adj.*

nul·li·pore (nul′ə pôr′, -pōr′), *n. Bot.* any of the coralline algae with a crustlike plant body. [1830–40; NULLI- + PORE[2]] —**nul·lip·o·rous** (nu lip′ər əs, nul′ə pôr′əs, -pōr′-), *adj.*

nul·li·ty (nul′i tē), *n., pl.* **-ties** for 2–4. **1.** the state or quality of being null; nothingness; invalidity. **2.** something null. **3.** something of no legal force or validity. **4.** a person of negligible importance. [1560–70; < ML *nūllitās.* See NULL, -ITY]

nul·li·us fi·li·us (no͞ol′lē o͞os′ fē′lē o͞os′; *Eng.* nul′ē əs fē′lē əs), *Latin.* (esp. in law) son of nobody; bastard.

nul·li·us ju·ris (no͞ol′lē o͞os′ yo͞o′ris; *Eng.* nul′ē əs jo͝or′is), *Latin.* (esp. in old English law) of no legal force.

null′ meth′od, a method of measurement using an electrical device, as a Wheatstone bridge, in which the quantity to be measured is balanced by an opposing known quantity that is varied until the resultant of the two is zero. [1870–75]

nul·lo (nul′ō), *n., pl.* **-los.** (in certain card games) a bid to take no tricks. [1590–1600; < It: none < L *nūllus* NULL]

null′ se′quence, *Math.* a sequence that has zero as its limit.

null-space (nul′spās′), *n. Math.* the set of elements of a vector space that a given linear transformation maps to zero. Also called **null-man·i·fold** (nul′man′ə fōld′). [1880–85]

Num., Numbers.

num., **1.** number. **2.** numeral; numerals.

Nu·man·ti·a (no͞o man′shē ə, -shə, nyo͞o-), *n.* an ancient city in N Spain: besieged and taken 134–133 B.C. by Scipio the Younger.

CONCISE ETYMOLOGY KEY: <, descended or borrowed from; >, whence; b., blend of, blended; c., cognate with; cf., compare; deriv., derivative; equiv., equivalent; imit., imitative; obl., oblique; r., replacing; s., stem; sp., spelling, spelled; resp., respelling, respelled; trans., translation; ?, origin unknown; *, unattested; ‡, probably earlier than. See the full key inside the front cover.

Nu·ma Pom·pil·i·us (no͞o′mə pom pil′ē əs, nyo͞o′-), died 673? B.C., 2nd legendary Sabine king of Rome 715–673?

numb (num), *adj.,* **-er, -est,** *v.* —*adj.* **1.** deprived of physical sensation or the ability to move: *fingers numb with cold.* **2.** manifesting or resembling numbness: *a numb sensation.* **3.** incapable of action or of feeling emotion; enervated; prostrate: *numb with grief.* **4.** lacking or deficient in emotion or feeling; indifferent: *She was numb to their pleas for mercy.* —*v.t.* **5.** to make numb. [1400–50; late ME *nome* lit., taken, seized, var. of *nomen, numen,* OE *numen,* ptp. of *niman* to take, NIM[1]] —**numb′ly,** *adv.* —**numb′ness,** *n.*

num·bat (num′bat), *n.* See **banded anteater.** [1920–25; < Nyungar *numbat*]

num·ber (num′bər), *n.* **1.** a numeral or group of numerals. **2.** the sum, total, count, or aggregate of a collection of units, or the like: *A number of people were hurt in the accident. The number of homeless children in the city has risen alarmingly.* **3.** a word or symbol, or a combination of words or symbols, used in counting or in noting a total. **4.** the particular numeral assigned to an object so as to designate its place in a series: *house number; license number.* **5.** one of a series of things distinguished by or marked with numerals. **6.** a certain collection, company, or quantity not precisely reckoned, but usually considerable or large: *I've gone there a number of times.* **7.** the full count of a collection or company. **8.** a collection or company. **9.** a quantity of individuals: *Their number was more than 20,000.* **10. numbers, a.** a considerable amount or quantity; many: *Numbers flocked to the city to see the parade.* **b.** metrical feet; verse. **c.** musical periods, measures, or groups of notes. **d.** See **numbers pool** (def. 1). **e.** *Informal.* the figures representing the actual cost, expense, profit, etc.: *We won't make a decision until we see the numbers.* **f.** *Obs.* arithmetic. **11.** quantity as composed of units: *to increase the number of eligible voters.* **12.** numerical strength or superiority; complement: *The garrison is not up to its full number.* **13.** a tune or arrangement for singing or dancing. **14.** a single or distinct performance within a show, as a song or dance: *The comic routine followed the dance number.* **15.** a single part of a program made up of a group of similar parts: *For her third number she played a nocturne.* **16.** any of a collection of poems or songs. **17.** a distinct part of an extended musical work or one in a sequence of compositions. **18.** conformity in music or verse to regular beat or measure; rhythm. **19.** a single part of a book published in a series of parts. **20.** a single issue of a periodical: *several numbers of a popular magazine.* **21.** a code of numerals, letters, or a combination of these assigned to a particular telephone: *Did you call the right number?* **22.** *Gram.* a category of noun, verb, or adjective inflection found in many languages, as English, Latin, and Arabic, used to indicate whether a word has one or more than one referent. There may be a two-way distinction in number, as between singular and plural, three-way, as between singular, dual, and plural, or more. **23.** *Informal.* person; individual: *the attractive number standing at the bar.* **24.** *Informal.* an article of merchandise, esp. of wearing apparel, offered for sale: *Put those leather numbers in the display window.* **25.** mathematics regarded as a science, a basic concept, and a mode of thought: *Number is the basis of science.* **26. by the numbers, a.** according to standard procedure, rules, customs, etc.; orthodoxly; by the book: *We're going to run things here by the numbers.* **b.** together or in unison to a called-out count: *calisthenics by the numbers.* **27. do a number on,** *Slang.* **a.** to undermine, defeat, humiliate, or criticize thoroughly: *The committee really did a number on the mayor's proposal.* **b.** to discuss or discourse about, esp. in an entertaining way: *She could do a number on anything from dentistry to the Bomb.* **28. do one's number, a.** to give a performance; perform: *It's time for you to get on stage and do your number.* **b.** *Slang.* to behave in a predictable or customary manner: *Whenever I call, he does his number about being too busy to talk.* **29. get** or **have someone's number,** *Informal.* to become informed about someone's real motives, character, intentions, etc.: *He was only interested in her fortune, but she got his number fast.* **30. have one's number on it,** *Slang.* to be thought of as the instrument of fate in the death of a person: *That bullet had his number on it.* **31. one's number is (was, will be) up,** *Slang.* **a.** one is (was, will be) in serious trouble. **b.** one is (was, will be) on the point of death: *Convinced that her number was up anyway, she refused to see doctors.* **32. without number,** of unknown or countless number; vast: *stars without number.*
—*v.t.* **33.** to mark with or distinguish by numbers: *Number each of the definitions.* **34.** to amount to or comprise in number; total: *The manuscript already numbers 425 pages.* **35.** to consider or include in a number: *I number myself among his friends.* **36.** to count over one by one; tell: *to number one's blessings.* **37.** to mention individually or one by one; enumerate: *They numbered the highlights of their trip at length.* **38.** to set or fix the number of; limit in number; make few in number: *The sick old man's days are numbered.* **39.** to live or have lived (a number of years). **40.** to ascertain the number of; count. **41.** to apportion or divide: *The players were numbered into two teams.*
—*v.i.* **42.** to make a total; reach an amount: *Casualties numbered in the thousands.* **43.** to be numbered or included (usually fol. by *among* or *with*): *Several eminent scientists number among his friends.* **44.** to count. [1250–1300; 1940–45 for def. 23; (n.) ME, var. of *nombre* < OF < L *numerus;* (v.) ME *nombren* < OF *nombrer* < L *numerāre* (deriv. of *numerus*)] —**num′ber·a·ble,** *adj.* —**num′ber·er,** *n.*
—**Syn. 1.** digit, figure. **2.** NUMBER, SUM both imply the total of two or more units. NUMBER applies to the result of a count or estimate in which the units are considered as individuals; it is used of groups of persons or things: *to have a number of items on the agenda.* SUM applies to the result of addition, in which only the total is considered: *a large sum of money.* **20.** copy, edition.
—**Usage. 2.** As a collective noun, NUMBER, when preceded by *a,* is most often treated as a plural: *A number of legislators have voiced their dissent.* When preceded by *the,* it is usually used as a singular: *The number of legislators present was small.* See also **amount, collective noun.**

num·ber-crunch·er (num′bər krun′chər), *n. Informal.* a person or thing that performs a great many numerical calculations, as a financial analyst, statistician, computer, or computer program. Also, **num′ber cruncher.** [1965–70] —**num′ber-crunch′ing,** *adj.*

num′bered account′, *Finance.* a bank account whose owner is identified by a number for the purpose of preserving anonymity. [1960–65]

num′ber eight′ i′ron, *Golf.* See **pitching niblick.**

num′ber five′ i′ron, *Golf.* mashie.

num′ber four′ i′ron, *Golf.* See **mashie iron.**

num′ber four′ wood′, *Golf.* baffy.

num·ber·less (num′bər lis), *adj.* **1.** innumerable; countless; myriad. **2.** without a number. [1565–75; NUMBER + -LESS]
—**Syn. 1.** uncounted, untold; numerous.

num′ber line′, *Math.* a straight line on which there is indicated a one-to-one correspondence between points on the line and the set of real numbers. Also called **real line.** [1955–60]

num′ber nine′ i′ron, *Golf.* niblick.

num′ber one′, **1.** oneself, esp. one's own well-being or interests: *to look out for number one.* **2.** a person, company, etc., that is first in rank, order, or prestige: *Our team is number one.* **3.** of the highest in quality, status, importance, etc.; first-rate: *a number one performance.* **4.** first in rank, order, or prestige: *the number one book on the bestseller list.* **5.** urination: used esp. by or with reference to children. **6. make, do,** or **go number one,** *Informal.* to urinate: used esp. by or with reference to children. [1830–40]

num′ber one′ i′ron, *Golf.* See **driving iron.**

num′ber one′ wood′, *Golf.* driver (def. 4).

num′ber op′era, an opera in which the arias, ensembles, recitatives, and other sections are clearly separated from one another. Cf. **music drama.**

Num·bers (num′bərz), *n.* (*used with a singular v.*) the fourth book of the Old Testament, containing the census of the Israelites after the Exodus from Egypt. *Abbr.:* Num.

num′ber sev′en i′ron, *Golf.* pitcher[2] (def. 3).

num′ber sign′, a symbol (#) for "number" or "numbered": *item #8 on the list.* Cf. **hash mark, pound sign** (def. 2), **space mark.**

num′ber six′ i′ron, *Golf.* See **mashie niblick.**

num′bers pool′, **1.** Also called **numbers, num′bers game′, num′bers rack′et.** an illegal daily lottery in which money is wagered on the appearance of certain numbers in some statistical listing or tabulation published in a daily newspaper, racing form, etc. **2.** policy[2] (def. 2).

num′ber the′ory, *Math.* the study of integers and their relation to one another. Also called **theory of numbers.** [1910–15]

num′ber three′ i′ron, *Golf.* mid-mashie.

num′ber three′ wood′, *Golf.* spoon (def. 5).

num′ber two′, **1.** someone or something that is second in rank, order, or importance. **2.** defecation: used esp. by or with reference to children. **3. make, do,** or **go number two,** *Informal.* to defecate: used esp. by or with reference to children. [1905–10]

num′ber two′ i′ron, *Golf.* midiron.

num′ber two′ wood′, *Golf.* brassie.

numb·fish (num′fish′), *n., pl.* (*esp. collectively*) **-fish,** (*esp. referring to two or more kinds or species*) **-fish·es.** an electric ray, so called from its power of numbing its prey by means of electric shocks. [1705–15; NUMB + FISH]

numb·ing (num′ing), *adj.* causing numbness or insensibility; stupefying: *the numbing effects of grief; a story repeated with numbing regularity.* [1625–35; NUMB + -ING[2]] —**numb′ing·ly,** *adv.*

num·bles (num′bəlz), *n.pl.* certain of the inward parts of an animal, esp. of a deer, used as food. Also, **nombles.** [1275–1325; ME < MF *nombles* fillet of venison, pl. of *nomble,* dissimilated var. of **lomble* < L *lumbulus,* dim. of *lumbus* loin. See LUMB-, -ULE]

numb·skull (num′skul′), *n.* numskull.

nu·men (no͞o′min, nyo͞o′-), *n., pl.* **-mi·na** (-mə nə). divine power or spirit; a deity, esp. one presiding locally or believed to inhabit a particular object. [1620–30; < L *nūmen* a nod, command, divine will or power, divinity; akin to *nūtāre* to nod the head in commanding or assent]

nu·mer·a·ble (no͞o′mər ə bəl, nyo͞o′-), *adj.* capable of being counted, totaled, or numbered. [1560–70; < L *numerābilis* that can be counted, equiv. to *numer(āre)* to NUMBER + *-ābilis* -ABLE] —**nu′mer·a·ble·ness,** *n.* —**nu′mer·a·bly,** *adv.*

nu·me·raire (no͞o′mə râr′, nyo͞o′-), *n.* a basic standard by which values are measured, as gold in the monetary system. [1960–65; < F *numéraire;* see NUMERARY]

nu·mer·al (no͞o′mər əl, nyo͞o′-; no͞om′rəl, nyo͞om′-), *n.* **1.** a word, letter, symbol, or figure, etc., expressing a number; number: *the Roman numerals.* —*adj.* **2.** of, pertaining to, or consisting of numbers or numerals. **3.** expressing or noting a number or numbers. [1520–30; < LL *numerālis* of, belonging to number, equiv. to L *numer(us)* NUMBER + *-ālis* -AL[1]]

nu·mer·ar·y (no͞o′mə rer′ē, nyo͞o′-), *adj.* of or pertaining to a number or numbers. [1720–30; < ML *numerārius* (LL: arithmetician, accountant), equiv. to L *numer(us)* number + *-ārius* -ARY]

nu•mer•ate (*v.* no͞o′mə rāt′, nyo͞o′-; *adj.* no͞o′mər it, nyo͞o′-), *v.*, **-at•ed, -at•ing,** *adj.* —*v.t.* **1.** to represent numbers by symbols. **2.** enumerate (def. 2). —*adj.* **3.** able to use or understand numerical techniques of mathematics. [1400–50; late ME: counted, numbered < L *numerātus* (ptp. of *numerāre* to NUMBER), equiv. to *numer-* NUMBER + *-ātus* -ATE[1]] —**nu′mer•a•cy,** *n.*

nu•mer•a•tion (no͞o′mə rā′shən, nyo͞o′-), *n.* **1.** an act or instance of or the process or result of numbering or counting. **2.** the process or a method of reckoning or calculating. **3.** the act, art, or method of expressing or reading off numbers set down in numerals, esp. those written decimally. [1400–50; late ME < L *numerātiōn-* (s. of *numerātiō*) a counting out, paying, equiv. to *numerāt(us)* NUMERATE + *-iōn-* -ION] —**nu′mer•a′tive,** *adj.*

nu•mer•a•tor (no͞o′mə rā′tər, nyo͞o′-), *n.* **1.** *Arith.* the term of a fraction, usually above the line, that indicates the number of equal parts that are to be added together; the dividend placed over a divisor: *The numerator of the fraction ⅔ is 2.* Cf. **denominator** (def. 1). **2.** a person or thing that numbers. [1535–45; < LL *numerātor* a counter, numberer, equiv. to L *numerā(re)* to NUMBER + *-tor* -TOR]

nu•mer•i•cal (no͞o mer′i kəl, nyo͞o-), *adj.* **1.** of or pertaining to numbers; of the nature of a number. **2.** indicating a number: *numerical symbols.* **3.** bearing or designated by a number. **4.** expressed by numbers instead of letters: *numerical cryptography; numerical equations.* **5.** of or pertaining to one's skill at working with numbers, solving mathematical problems, etc.: *tests for rating numerical aptitude.* **6.** *Math.* absolute (def. 12). Also, **nu•mer′ic.** [1615–25; < L *numer(us)* NUMBER + -ICAL] —**nu•mer′i•cal•ly,** *adv.* —**nu•mer′i•cal•ness,** *n.*

numer′ical anal′ysis, the branch of mathematics dealing with methods for obtaining approximate numerical solutions of mathematical problems. [1925–30]

numer′ical ap′erture, *Micros.* a measure of the resolving power of a microscope, equal to the index of refraction of the medium in which the object is placed multiplied by the sine of the angle made with the axis by the most oblique ray entering the instrument, the resolving power increasing as the product increases. *Abbr.:* N.A. [1875–80]

numer′ical control′, *Computers.* control of a machine tool, or other device used in a manufacturing process, by a computer, other control circuitry, or recorded digital commands. [1950–55] —**numer′ically controlled′.**

numer′ical taxon′omy, classification of organisms by a comparison of large numbers of observable characteristics that are given equal value instead of being weighted according to possible evolutionary significance. Also called **numer′ical phenet′ics.** [1960–65]

numer′ical weath′er predic′tion, a method of predicting weather through the use of high-speed computers, specifically by the time integration of the fundamental equations of hydrodynamics in a mathematically modeled atmosphere. Also called **numer′ical fore′casting.**

numer′ic key′pad, *Computers.* keypad (def. 1). Also, **numer′ic pad′.**

nu•mer•ol•o•gy (no͞o′mə rol′ə jē, nyo͞o′-), *n.* the study of numbers, as the figures designating the year of one's birth, to determine their supposed influence on one's life, future, etc. [1910–15; < L *numer(us)* NUMBER + -O- + -LOGY] —**nu•mer•o•log•i•cal** (no͞o′mər ə loj′i kəl, nyo͞o′-), *adj.* —**nu′mer•ol′o•gist,** *n.*

nu•me•ro u•no (no͞o′mə rō′ o͞o′nō, nyo͞o′-), number one (defs. 1–4). [1970–75; < It]

nu•mer•ous (no͞o′mər əs, nyo͞o′-), *adj.* **1.** very many; being or existing in great quantity: *numerous visits; numerous fish.* **2.** consisting of or comprising a great number of units or individuals: *Recent audiences have been more numerous.* [1580–90; < L *numerōsus* consisting of a great number, numerous, equiv. to *numer(us)* NUMBER + *-ōsus* -OUS] —**nu′mer•ous•ly,** *adv.* —**nu′mer•ous•ness, nu•me•ros•i•ty** (no͞o′mə ros′i tē, nyo͞o′-), *n.*
—**Syn. 1.** See **many.**

Num•ic (num′ik), *n.* **1.** a branch of the Uto-Aztecan family of languages including Northern Paiute, Shoshone, Comanche, Southern Paiute, Ute, and others. —*adj.* **2.** of or pertaining to the Numic languages. [coined from *nïmi* person (in several Numic languages) + -IC]

Nu•mid•i•a (no͞o mid′ē ə, nyo͞o-), *n.* an ancient country in N Africa, corresponding roughly to modern Algeria. —**Nu•mid′i•an,** *adj., n.*

nu•mi•na (no͞o′mə nə, nyo͞o′-), *n.* pl. of **numen.**

nu•mi•nous (no͞o′mə nəs, nyo͞o′-), *adj.* **1.** of, pertaining to, or like a numen; spiritual or supernatural. **2.** surpassing comprehension or understanding; mysterious: *that element in artistic expression that remains numinous.* **3.** arousing one's elevated feelings of duty, honor, loyalty, etc.: *a benevolent and numinous paternity.* [1640–50; < L *nūmin-* (s. of *nūmen*) NUMEN + -OUS]

numis., **1.** numismatic. **2.** numismatics. Also, **numism.**

nu•mis•mat•ic (no͞o′miz mat′ik, -mis-, nyo͞o′-), *adj.* **1.** of, pertaining to, or consisting of coins, medals, paper money, etc. **2.** pertaining to numismatics. Also, **nu′mis•mat′i•cal.** [1785–95; < NL *numismaticus* < Gk *nomismat-* (s. of *nómisma*) currency + L *-icus* -IC; akin to Gk *nómos* usage, law] —**nu′mis•mat′i•cal•ly,** *adv.*

nu•mis•mat•ics (no͞o′miz mat′iks, -mis-, nyo͞o′-), *n.* (*used with a singular v.*) the study or collecting of coins, medals, paper money, etc. [1820–30; see NUMISMATIC, -ICS]

nu•mis•ma•tist (no͞o miz′mə tist, -mis′-, nyo͞o-), *n.* **1.** a specialist in numismatics. **2.** a person who collects numismatic items, esp. coins. [1790–1800; < L *numismat-* (s. of *numisma*) coin + -IST]

num•ma•ry (num′ə rē), *adj.* **1.** of or pertaining to coins or money. **2.** dealing in coins or money. [1650–60; < L *nummārius* of, belonging to money, equiv. to *numm(us)* coin + *-ārius* -ARY]

num•mu•lar (num′yə lər), *adj.* **1.** pertaining to coins or money; nummary. **2.** having the shape of a coin; flat and circular or oval in form. **3.** *Pathol.* composed of round, flat disks: *nummular skin lesions.* [1725–35; < L *nummul(i)* petty cash, small change (*numm(us)* coin + *-ulī*, pl. of *-ulus* -ULE) + -AR[1]]

num•mu•lite (num′yə līt′), *n.* a fossil foraminifer of the genus *Camerina* (*Nummulites*), having a calcareous, usually disklike shell. [1805–15; NUMMUL(AR) + -ITE[1]] —**num•mu•lit•ic** (num′yə lit′ik), *adj.*

num′mulit′ic lime′stone, limestone composed predominantly of fossil nummulites. [1825–35]

num•skull (num′skul′), *n.* a dull-witted or stupid person; dolt. Also, **numbskull.** [1710–20; NUM(B) + SKULL]

nun[1] (nun), *n.* **1.** a woman member of a religious order, esp. one bound by vows of poverty, chastity, and obedience. **2.** any of various birds, esp. a domestic variety of pigeon. [bef. 900; ME, OE *nunne* < ML *nonna*, fem. of *nonnus* monk] —**nun′like′,** *adj.*

nun[2] (no͞on, no͝on), *n.* **1.** the 14th letter of the Hebrew alphabet. **2.** the consonant sound represented by this letter. [1875–80; < Heb *nūn* lit., fish]

nūn (no͝on), *n.* the 25th letter of the Arabic alphabet. [< Ar; see NUN[2], NU[1]]

Nun (no͞on), *n.* the major channel of the Niger River, in W Africa.

Nun (no͞on), *n. Egyptian Relig.* Nunu.

nun•a•tak (nun′ə tak′), *n.* a hill or mountain that has been completely encircled by a glacier. [1875–80; < Inuit (West Greenlandic) *nunataq*]

nun•a•tion (nu nā′shən), *n. Arabic Gram.* the doubling, in writing, of the final vowel symbol to indicate the addition, in speech, of the indefinite suffix *n* to certain nouns. Also, **nunnation.** [< NL *nunnātiōn-* (s. of *nunnātiō*), equiv. to *nūn* (< Ar; see NŪN) + *-ātiōn-* -ATION] —**nun′a•ted,** *adj.*

nun′ bu′oy (nun), a conical, unlighted buoy used as a channel marker, esp. on the starboard side of a channel entering from seaward. Cf. **can buoy.** See illus. under **buoy.** [1695–1705; obs. *nun* spinning top + BUOY]

nunc (no͝ongk; *Eng.* nungk), *adv. Latin.* now.

Nunc Di•mit•tis (nungk′ di mit′is, no͝ongk′), **1.** (*italics*) the canticle beginning with the words of Simeon, in Luke 2:29–32, "Lord, now lettest thou thy servant depart in peace." **2.** (*l.c.*) permission to leave; dismissal or departure. [< L]

nun•cha•ku (nun chä′ko͞o), *n.* Sometimes, **nunchakus.** an Oriental hand weapon for defense against frontal assault, consisting of two foot-long hardwood sticks joined by a chain or thick cord that stretches to body width. Also, **nun-chucks** (nun′chuks′). Also called **karate sticks.** [1965–70; < Okinawan Japn version of a dial. Chin (Taiwan) word for a farm implement, prob. *neng-cak*, equiv. to Chin *lyǎng* pair(ed) + *záo* dig (a hole), i.e., two diggers; with 2nd element interpreted as *zat*, equiv. to Chin *jié* section]

nun•ci•a•ture (nun′shē ə chər, -cho͝or′, -sē-, no͝on′-), *n.* the office or the term of service of a nuncio. [1645–55; < It *nunziatura.* See NUNCIO, -ATE[3], -URE]

nun•ci•o (nun′shē ō′, -sē ō′, no͝on′-), *n., pl.* **-ci•os.** a diplomatic representative of the pope at a foreign court or capital: equal in status to an ambassador. Cf. **apostolic delegate.** [1520–30; < It *nuncio, nunzio* < L *nūncius, nūntius* messenger]

nun•cle (nung′kəl), *n. Chiefly Brit. Dial.* uncle. [1580–90; from the phrase *mine uncle*, taken as *my nuncle*; cf. NEWT]

nun•cu•pa•tive (nung′kyə pā′tiv, nung kyo͞o′pə tiv), *adj.* (esp. of a will) oral; not written. [1540–50; < ML (*testāmentum*) *nuncupātīvum* oral (will), neut. of LL *nuncupātīvus* so-called, nominal, equiv. to L *nuncupāt(us)* ptp. of *nuncupāre* to state formally, utter the name of (prob. < **nōmicupāre*, deriv. of **nōmiceps* one taking a name, equiv. to **nōmi-* comb. form of *nōmen* NAME + *-ceps* taking, possessing; see PRINCE) + *-īvus* -IVE]

nun′cupative will′, *Law.* a will made by the oral and unwritten declaration of the testator, valid only in special circumstances. Cf. **holographic will.** [1540–50]

nun•hood (nun′ho͝od), *n.* the status, vocation, or responsibilities of a nun. Also called **nun′ship.** [1805–15; NUN[1] + -HOOD]

nun•na•tion (nu nā′shən), *n.* nunation. —**nun′nated,** *adj.*

nun•ner•y (nun′ə rē), *n., pl.* **-ner•ies.** a building or group of buildings for nuns; convent. [1225–75; ME *nonnerie.* See NUN[1], -ERY]

nun's′ fid′dle. See **trumpet marine.** [1900–05]

nun's′ veil′ing, a thin, plain-woven, worsted fabric, originally for nuns' veils but now also for dresses, coats, etc. [1880–85]

Nu•nu (no͞o′no͞o), *n. Egyptian Relig.* a god personifying the ocean, the primeval chaos from which the world was formed. Also, **Nun.**

Nu•per•caine (no͞o′pər kān′, nyo͞o′-), *Pharm., Trademark.* a brand of dibucaine.

nup•tial (nup′shəl, -chəl), *adj.* **1.** of or pertaining to marriage or the marriage ceremony: *the nuptial day; nuptial vows.* **2.** of, pertaining to, or characteristic of mating or the mating season of animals: *nuptial behavior.* —*n.* **3.** Usually, **nuptials.** a wedding or marriage. [1480–90; (MF) < L *nuptiālis*, equiv. to *nupti(ae)* marriage, wedding, deriv. of *nubere* to marry (of a woman); cf. NUBILE] —**nup′tial•ly,** *adv.*
—**Syn. 3.** See **marriage.**
—**Pronunciation.** The pronunciations (nup′cho͞o əl) and (nup′sho͞o əl), by analogy with such words as *mutual* and *actual*, are not considered standard.

nup′tial mass′, *Rom. Cath. Ch.* a special mass said at a wedding.

nup′tial plum′age, *Ornith.* the plumage assumed by a male bird during the courtship period, esp. in those species that are more colorful at this period. Also called **breeding plumage.** [1830–40]

nuque (no͞ok, nyo͞ok), *n.* the back of the neck. [1570–80; < F; see NUCHA]

nu•ra•ghe (no͞o rä′gā), *n., pl.* **-ghi** (-gē), **-ghes.** any of the large, tower-shaped, prehistoric stone structures found in Sardinia and dating from the second millennium B.C. to the Roman conquest. [1820–30; < Sardinian; of obscure orig. (presumably pre-L)] —**nu•ra′ghic,** *adj.*

nurd (nûrd), *n.* nerd.

Nu•rem•berg (no͝or′əm bûrg′, nyo͝or′-), *n.* a city in central Bavaria, in SE Germany: site of international trials (1945–46) of Nazis accused of war crimes. 471,800. German, **Nürnberg.**

Nu′remberg egg′, *Horol.* an egg-shaped watch of the 16th century: one of the earliest watches. [1955–60]

Nu′remberg vi′olet. See **manganese violet.**

Nu•re•yev (no͝o rā′ef, -ev; *Russ.* no͞o ryä′yif), *n.* **Rudolf (Ha•me•to•vich)** (KHU mye′tə vyich), 1938–93, Russian ballet dancer and choreographer; Austrian citizen 1982.

Nu•ri•stan (no͝or′ə stan′, -stän′), *n.* a mountainous region in NE Afghanistan. 5000 sq. mi. (12,950 sq. km). Formerly, **Kafiristan.**

Nu•ris•ta•ni (no͝or′ə stä′nē, -stan′ē), *n., pl.* **-nis,** (*esp. collectively*) **-ni** for 1. **1.** Kafir (def. 1). **2.** Kafiri.

nurl (nûrl), *n., v.t.* knurl.

Nur•mi (nûr′mē; *Fin.* no͝or′mi), *n.* **Paa•vo Jo•han•nes** (pä′vô yô′hän nes), 1897–1973, Finnish athlete.

Nürn•berg (NYRN′berk′), *n.* German name of **Nuremberg.**

nurse (nûrs), *n., v.,* **nursed, nurs•ing.** **1.** a person formally educated and trained in the care of the sick or infirm. Cf. **nurse-midwife, nurse-practitioner, physician's assistant, practical nurse, registered nurse.** **2.** a woman who has the general care of a child or children; dry nurse. **3.** a woman employed to suckle an infant; wet nurse. **4.** any fostering agency or influence. **5.** *Entomol.* a worker that attends the young in a colony of social insects. **6.** *Billiards.* the act of maintaining the position of billiard balls in preparation for a carom. —*v.t.* **7.** to tend or minister to in sickness, infirmity, etc. **8.** to try to cure (an ailment) by taking care of oneself: *to nurse a cold.* **9.** to look after carefully so as to promote growth, development, etc.; foster; cherish: *to nurse one's meager talents.* **10.** to treat or handle with adroit care in order to further one's own interests: *to nurse one's nest egg.* **11.** to use, consume, or dispense very slowly or carefully: *He nursed the one drink all evening.* **12.** to keep steadily in mind or memory: *He nursed a grudge against me all the rest of his life.* **13.** to suckle (an infant). **14.** to feed and tend in infancy. **15.** to bring up, train, or nurture. **16.** to clasp or handle carefully or fondly: *to nurse a plate of food on one's lap.* **17.** *Billiards.* to maintain the position of (billiard balls) for a series of caroms. —*v.i.* **18.** to suckle a child, esp. one's own. **19.** (of a child) to suckle: *The child did not nurse after he was three months old.* **20.** to act as nurse; tend the sick or infirm. [1350–1400; (n.) ME, var. of *n(o)urice, norice* < OF < LL *nūtrīcia*, n. use of fem. of L *nūtrīcius* NUTRITIOUS; (v.) earlier *nursh* (reduced form of NOURISH), assimilated to the n.]
—**Syn. 9.** encourage, abet, help, aid, back. **14.** rear, raise. NURSE, NOURISH, NURTURE may be used almost interchangeably to refer to bringing up the young. NURSE, however, suggests attendance and service; NOURISH emphasizes providing whatever is needful for development; and NURTURE suggests tenderness and solicitude in training mind and manners. —**Ant. 7, 9.** neglect.

nurse-cli•ni•cian (nûrs′kli nish′ən), *n.* nurse-practitioner. Also, **nurse′ clini′cian.**

nurse′ crop′, a crop planted in the same field with another crop, esp. to minimize the growth of weeds. [1935–40]

nurse•ling (nûrs′ling), *n.* nursling.

nurse•maid (nûrs′mād′), *n.* **1.** Also called **nurs′er•y•maid′.** a woman or girl employed to care for a child or several children, esp. in a household. —*v.t.* **2.** to act as a nursemaid to; to take care of or look after protectively. [1650–60; NURSE + MAID]

nurse-mid•wife (nûrs′mid′wīf′), *n., pl.* **-wives.** a nurse skilled in assisting women in the prenatal period and in childbirth, esp. at home or in another nonhospital setting.

nurse-prac·ti·tion·er (nûrs′prak tish′ə nər), *n.* a registered nurse who has received special training for diagnosing and treating routine or minor ailments. *Abbr.:* NP Also, **nurse′ practi′tioner.** Also called **nurse-clinician.** Cf. **physician's assistant.** [1975–80]

nurs·er (nûr′sər), *n.* **1.** a person, animal, or thing that nurses. **2.** See **nursing bottle.** [1350–1400; ME; see NURSE, -ER[1]]

nurs·er·y (nûr′sə rē), *n., pl.* **-er·ies.** **1.** a room or place set apart for young children. **2.** a nursery school or day nursery. **3.** a place where young trees or other plants are raised for transplanting, for sale, or for experimental study. **4.** any place in which something is bred, nourished, or fostered: *The art institute has been the nursery of much great painting.* **5.** any situation, condition, circumstance, practice, etc., serving to breed or foster something: *Slums are nurseries for young criminals.* [1350–1400; ME *norcery.* See NURSE, -ERY]

nurs·er·y·man (nûr′sə rē mən), *n., pl.* **-men.** a person who owns or conducts a plant nursery. [1665–75; NURSERY + MAN[1]]
—Usage. See **-man.**

nurs′ery rhyme′, a short, simple poem or song for very young children, as *Hickory Dickory Dock.* [1835–45]

nurs′ery school′, a prekindergarten school for children from about three to five years of age. [1825–35]

nurs·er·y·wom·an (nûr′sə rē wo͝om′ən), *n., pl.* **-wom·en.** a woman who owns or operates a plant nursery. [NURSERY(MAN) + -WOMAN]
—Usage. See **-woman.**

nurse′'s aide′, a person who assists professional nurses, as in a hospital, by performing such routine tasks as making beds and serving meals.

nurse′ shark′, any of several sharks of the family Orectolobidae, esp. *Ginglymostoma cirratum,* occurring in shallow waters from Rhode Island to Brazil and the Gulf of California to Ecuador. [1850–55; allegedly so called because the male habitually hangs on to the female's fin with his teeth]

nurs′ing bot′tle, a bottle with a rubber nipple, from which an infant sucks milk, water, etc. [1860–65]

nurs′ing home′, **1.** a private residential institution equipped to care for persons unable to look after themselves, as the aged or chronically ill. **2.** *Chiefly Brit.* a small private hospital; a small hospital owned by one person or a group of individuals and supported solely by the fees of patients. [1895–1900]

nurs·ling (nûrs′ling), *n.* **1.** an infant, child, or young animal being nursed or being cared for by a nurse. **2.** any person or thing under fostering care, influences, or conditions. Also, **nurseling.** [1550–60; NURSE + -LING[1]]

nur·tur·ance (nûr′chər əns), *n.* warm and affectionate physical and emotional support and care. [1935–40; NURTURE + -ANCE] **—nur′tur·ant,** *adj.*

nur·ture (nûr′chər), *v.,* **-tured, -tur·ing,** *n.* **—***v.t.* **1.** to feed and protect: *to nurture one's offspring.* **2.** to support and encourage, as during the period of training or development; foster: *to nurture promising musicians.* **3.** to bring up; train; educate. **—***n.* **4.** rearing, upbringing, training, education, or the like. **5.** development: *the nurture of young artists.* **6.** something that nourishes; nourishment; food. [1300–50; (n.) ME *norture* < MF, var. of *nourriture* < LL *nūtrītūra* a nourishing, equiv. to L *nūtrīt(us)* (ptp. of *nūtrīre* to feed, NOURISH) + *-ūra* -URE; (v.) deriv. of the n.] **—nur′tur·a·ble,** *adj.* **—nur′·ture·less,** *adj.* **—nur′tur·er,** *n.*
—Syn. 1, 3. See **nurse.**

Nus·ku (no͞os′ko͞o), *n.* a Sumerian and Babylonian deity, originally the vizier of Enlil.

nut (nut), *n., v.,* **nut·ted, nut·ting.** **—***n.* **1.** a dry fruit consisting of an edible kernel or meat enclosed in a woody or leathery shell. **2.** the kernel itself. **3.** *Bot.* a hard, indehiscent, one-seeded fruit, as the chestnut or the acorn. **4.** any of various devices or ornaments resembling a nut. **5.** a block, usually of metal and generally square or hexagonal, perforated with a threaded hole so that it can be screwed down on a bolt to hold together objects through which the bolt passes. **6.** *Slang.* the head. **7.** *Slang.* **a.** a person who is very enthusiastic about something; buff; enthusiast; devotee: *He's a real circus nut.* **b.** an extremely concerned or zealous person: *My boss is a nut on double-checking everything.* **8.** *Slang.* **a.** a foolish, silly, or eccentric person. **b.** *Offensive.* an insane person; psychotic. **9.** *Slang (vulgar).* a testis. **10.** *Informal.* **a.** the operating expenses, usually figured weekly, of a theatrical production or other commercial enterprise; a break-even point. **b.** the total cost of producing a theatrical production or of forming and opening any new business venture. **11.** *Music.* (in instruments of the violin family) **a.** the ledge, as of ebony, at the upper end of the fingerboard, over which the strings pass. **b.** the movable piece at the lower end of the bow, by means of which the hairs may be slackened or tightened. **12.** *Print.* en (def. 2). **13. from soup to nuts.** See **soup** (def. 6). **14. hard nut to crack, a.** a problem difficult to solve; a formidable undertaking. **b.** a person difficult to know, understand, or convince. Also, **tough nut to crack. 15. off one's nut,** *Slang.* **a.** *Sometimes Offensive.* foolish, silly, or insane. **b.** confused; unreasonable. **c.** mistaken or wrong: *You're off your nut if you think such a plan can succeed.* **—***v.i.* **16.** to seek for or gather nuts: *to go nutting in late autumn.* [bef. 900; 1900–05 for def. 8b; ME *nute,* OE *hnutu;* c. D *noot,* G *Nuss,* ON *hnot;* akin to L *nux*] **—nut′like′,** *adj.*

CONCISE ETYMOLOGY KEY: <, descended or borrowed from; >, whence; b., blend of, blended; c., cognate with; cf., compare; deriv., derivative; equiv., equivalent; imit., imitative; obl., oblique; r., replacing; s., stem; sp., spelling, spelled; resp., respelling, respelled; trans., translation; ?, origin unknown; *, unattested; ‡, probably earlier than. See the full key inside the front cover.

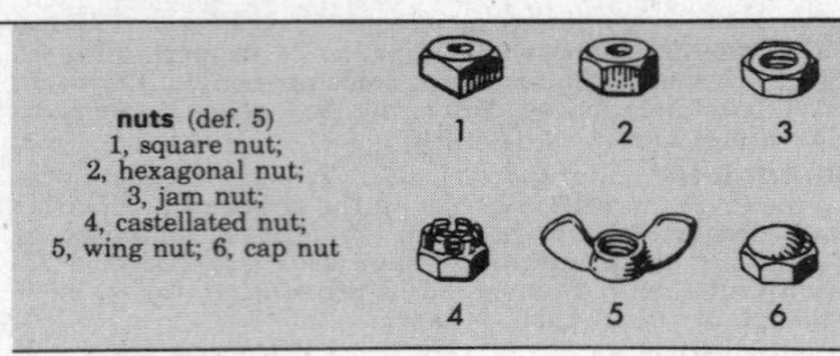

nuts (def. 5)
1, square nut;
2, hexagonal nut;
3, jam nut;
4, castellated nut;
5, wing nut; 6, cap nut

Nut (no͞ot), *n. Egyptian Relig.* the goddess of the sky, sometimes shown as a cow bearing Ra on her back and the stars on her underside.

N.U.T., *Brit.* National Union of Teachers.

nu·tant (no͞ot′nt, nyo͞ot′-), *adj. Bot.* drooping; nodding. [1745–55; < L *nūtant-* (s. of *nūtāns*), prp. of *nūtāre* to nod repeatedly. See NUTATION, -ANT]

nu·tate (no͞o′tāt, nyo͞o′-), *v.i.,* **-tat·ed, -tat·ing.** to undergo or show nutation. [1875–80; back formation from NUTATION]

nu·ta·tion (no͞o tā′shən, nyo͞o-), *n.* **1.** an act or instance of nodding one's head, esp. involuntarily or spasmodically. **2.** *Bot.* spontaneous movements of plant parts during growth. **3.** *Astron.* the periodic oscillation observed in the precession of the earth's axis and the precession of the equinoxes. **4.** *Mech.* the variation of the inclination of the axis of a gyroscope to the vertical. [1605–15; < L *nūtātiōn-* (s. of *nūtātiō*), equiv. to *nūtāt(us)* (ptp. of *nūtāre* to nod repeatedly; *nū-* nod + *-tā-* freq. suffix + *-tus* ptp. ending) + *-iōn-* -ION; cf. NUMEN] **—nu·ta′tion·al,** *adj.*

nut·brown (nut′broun′), *adj.* dark brown, as many nuts when ripe. [1250–1300; ME. See NUT, BROWN]

nut′ case′, *Slang (offensive).* a deranged person; lunatic. [1955–60]

nut′ coal′. See **chestnut coal.**

nut·crack·er (nut′krak′ər), *n.* **1.** an instrument or device for cracking the shells of nuts. **2.** any of several corvine birds of the genus *Nucifraga* that feed on nuts, as the common nutcracker, *N. caryocatactes,* of Europe and Clark's nutcracker, *N. columbiana,* of the western U.S. [1540–50; NUT + CRACKER]

Nut′cracker Suite′, a ballet and concert suite (1892) arranged by Peter Ilyich Tchaikovsky from his orchestral work for a ballet, *The Nutcracker.*

nut′ dash′, *Print.* a dash equal in length to the width of an en quad; en dash.

nut·gall (nut′gôl′), *n.* a nutlike gall or excrescence, esp. one formed on an oak. [1585–95; NUT + GALL[3]]

nut′ grass′, either of two sedges, *Cyperus rotundus* or *C. esculentus,* that have small, nutlike tubers and are often troublesome weeds. Also called **nut sedge.**

nut·hatch (nut′hach′), *n.* any of numerous small, short-tailed, sharp-beaked birds of the family Sittidae that creep on trees and feed on small nuts and insects. [1300–50; ME *notehache, nuthagge, nuthak,* lit., nut hacker. See NUT, HACK[1]]

nuthatch,
Sitta carolinensis,
length 6 in. (15 cm)

nut′ house′, *Slang.* a mental hospital; insane asylum. Also, **nut′house′.** [1900–05]

nut·let (nut′lit), *n.* **1.** a small nut; a small nutlike fruit or seed. **2.** the stone of a drupe. [1855–60; NUT + -LET]

Nut·ley (nut′lē), *n.* a city in NE New Jersey. 28,998.

nut·meat (nut′mēt′), *n.* the kernel of a nut, usually edible. [1910–15; NUT + MEAT]

nut·meg (nut′meg), *n.* **1.** the hard, aromatic seed of the fruit of an East Indian tree, *Myristica fragrans,* used in grated form as a spice. **2.** the similar product of certain other trees of the same genus or other genera. **3.** a tree bearing such seeds. [1300–50; ME *notemug(g)e,* perh. back formation from **notemugede* (*-ede* being taken as -ED[3]), equiv. to *note* NUT + *mugede* < OF < LL *muscāta* musky; see MUSK, -ATE[1]] **—nut′megged,** *adj.*

Nut·meg·ger (nut′meg ər), *n.* a native or inhabitant of Connecticut. [NUTMEG + -ER[1]; see NUTMEG STATE]

nut′meg gera′nium, a southern African plant, *Pelargonium fragrans,* of the geranium family, having hairy leaves with scalloped margins and nutmeg-scented clusters of white flowers, of which the two upper petals are veined deep pink.

nut′meg mel′on. See **netted melon.** [1815–25]

Nut′meg State′, Connecticut (used as a nickname).

nut·pick (nut′pik′), *n.* a thin, sharp-pointed table implement or device for removing the edible kernels from nuts. [1885–90; NUT + PICK[2]]

nut′ pine′, piñon (def. 1). [1835–45, *Amer.*]

nut′ quad′, *Print.* a quad one en wide; en quad.

Nu·tra·Sweet (no͞o′trə swēt′, nyo͞o′-), *Trademark.* a brand of aspartame used in a low-calorie sweetener and in other processed foods, as soft drinks.

nu·tri·a (no͞o′trē ə, nyo͞o′-), *n.* **1.** the coypu. **2.** the fur of the coypu, resembling beaver, used for making coats, hats, suit trimmings, etc. [1810–20, *Amer.;* < Sp: otter, var. of *lutria* < ML, for L *lutra*]

nu·tri·ent (no͞o′trē ənt, nyo͞o′-), *adj.* **1.** nourishing; providing nourishment or nutriment. **2.** containing or conveying nutriment, as solutions or vessels of the body. **—***n.* **3.** a nutrient substance. [1640–50; < L *nūtrient-* (s. of *nūtriēns*), prp. of *nūtrīre* to feed, NOURISH; see -ENT]

nu·tri·ent-dense (no͞o′trē ənt dens′), *adj.* (of food) relatively rich in nutrients for the number of calories contained: *A potato is a nutrient-dense carbohydrate.* **—nu′trient den′sity.**

Nu·tri·lite (no͞o′trə līt′, nyo͞o′-), *Trademark.* any of several preparations of vitamins and minerals used as food supplements.

nu·tri·ment (no͞o′trə mənt, nyo͞o′-), *n.* **1.** any substance or matter that, taken into a living organism, serves to sustain it in its existence, promoting growth, replacing loss, and providing energy. **2.** anything that nourishes; nourishment; food. [1375–1425; late ME < L *nūtrīmentum* nourishment, equiv. to *nūtrī(re)* to NOURISH, feed + *-mentum* -MENT] **—nu·tri·men·tal** (no͞o′trə men′tl, nyo͞o′-), *adj.*

nu·tri·tion (no͞o trish′ən, nyo͞o-), *n.* **1.** the act or process of nourishing or of being nourished. **2.** the science or study of, or a course of study in, nutrition, esp. of humans. **3.** the process by which organisms take in and utilize food material. **4.** food; nutriment. **5.** the pursuit of this science as an occupation or profession. [1375–1425; late ME < LL *nūtrītiōn-* (s. of *nūtrītiō*) a feeding, equiv. to L *nūtrīt(us)* (ptp. of *nūtrīre* to feed, NOURISH) + *-iōn-* -ION] **—nu·tri′tion·al, nu·tri′tion·ar′y,** *adj.* **—nu·tri′tion·al·ly,** *adv.*

nu·tri·tion·ist (no͞o trish′ə nist, nyo͞o-), *n.* a person who is trained or expert in the science of nutrition. [1925–30; NUTRITION + -IST]

nu·tri·tious (no͞o trish′əs, nyo͞o-), *adj.* providing nourishment, esp. to a high degree; nourishing; healthful: *a good, nutritious meal.* [1655–65; < L *nūtrītius* that suckles, nourishes, var. of *nūtrīcius,* equiv. to *nūtrīci-* (s. of *nūtrīx*) nurse (see NURSE) + *-us* adj. suffix (see -OUS)] **—nu·tri′tious·ly,** *adv.* **—nu·tri′tious·ness,** *n.*

nu·tri·tive (no͞o′tri tiv, nyo͞o′-), *adj.* **1.** serving to nourish; providing nutriment; nutritious. **2.** of, pertaining to, or concerned with nutrition: *foods with high nutritive value.* **—***n.* **3.** an item of nourishing food: *a breakfast of cereals, fruits, and other nutritives.* [1350–1400; < ML *nūtrītīvus,* equiv. to *nūtrīt-* (see NUTRITION) + *-īvus* -IVE; r. ME *nutritif* < MF < ML as above] **—nu′tri·tive·ly,** *adv.* **—nu′tri·tive·ness,** *n.*

nuts (nuts), *Slang.* **—***interj.* **1.** Also, **nerts, nertz.** (used to express disgust, defiance, disapproval, despair). **—***adj.* **2.** insane; crazy. **3. be nuts about, a.** to be extremely or excessively enthusiastic about; be fervent in one's admiration of: *Both of them are nuts about chamber music.* **b.** to be deeply in love with: *He's nuts about his new girlfriend.* [1900–05; pl. of NUT]

nuts′ and bolts′, the essential or basic aspects: *to learn the nuts and bolts of a new job.* [1955–60] **—nuts′-and-bolts′,** *adj.*

nut′ sedge′. See **nut grass.** [1905–10]

nut·shell (nut′shel′), *n.* **1.** the shell of a nut. **2. in a nutshell,** in very brief form; in a few words: *Just tell me the story in a nutshell.* [1175–1225; ME *nutescell;* see NUT, SHELL]

nut·sy (nut′sē), *adj.,* **-si·er, -si·est.** nutty (defs. 3, 4). [NUTS + -Y[1]; cf. -SY]

nut·ter (nut′ər), *n.* **1.** a person who gathers nuts. **2.** *Brit. Slang.* an insane person. [1475–85; NUT + -ER[1]]

nut·ting (nut′ing), *n.* the act of seeking or gathering nuts. [1715–25; NUT + -ING[1]]

Nut·ting (nut′ing), *n.* **Wallace,** 1861–1941, U.S. antiquary, author, and illustrator.

nut·ty (nut′ē), *adj.,* **-ti·er, -ti·est.** **1.** abounding in or producing nuts. **2.** nutlike, esp. in flavor. **3.** *Slang.* **a.** silly or ridiculous: *a nutty suggestion.* **b.** eccentric; queer. **c.** insane. **d.** very or excessively interested, excited, or the like: *He's nutty about Mexican food.* **4.** full of flavor or zest; lively; stimulating; meaty: *He offered several rich, nutty ideas on the subject.* [1655–65; NUT + -Y[1]] **—nut′ti·ly,** *adv.* **—nut′ti·ness,** *n.*

nut′ wee′vil, any of several snout beetles of the genus *Balaninus,* the larvae of which live in and feed on nuts and acorns. [1795–1805]

nut·wood (nut′wo͝od′), *n.* **1.** any of various nutbearing trees, as the hickory or walnut. **2.** the wood of such a tree. [1650–60, *Amer.;* NUT + WOOD[1]]

nu·val·ue (no͞o′val′yo͞o, nyo͞o′-), *n. Optics.* See **Abbe number.**

N.U.W.W., *Brit.* National Union of Women Workers.

nux vom·i·ca (nuks′ vom′i kə), **1.** the seed of the orangelike fruit of an East Indian tree, *Strychnos nux-vomica,* of the logania family, containing strychnine, used in medicine. **2.** the tree itself; strychnine. [1570–80; < NL: lit., vomiting nut]

Nu·yo·ri·can (no͞o′yô rē′kən, nyo͞o′-), *n., adj.,* Neorican. [1970–75; by alteration (influence of Sp *Nu(eva) York*)]

Nuyts′ Land′ (nyo͞ots), early name of a region on the southern coast in S Australia, discovered by the Dutch in 1626–27.

nuz·zle (nuz′əl), *v.,* **-zled, -zling,** *n.* **—***v.i.* **1.** to burrow or root with the nose, snout, etc., as an animal does: *a rabbit nuzzling into the snow.* **2.** to thrust the nose, muzzle, etc.: *The dog nuzzled up to his master.* **3.** to lie very close to someone or something; cuddle or snuggle up. **—***v.t.* **4.** to root up with the nose, snout, etc.: *training pigs to nuzzle truffles from the ground.* **5.** to touch or rub with the nose, snout, muzzle, etc. **6.** to thrust the nose, muzzle, snout, etc., against or into: *The horse was nuzzling my pocket for sugar.* **7.** to thrust (the nose or head), as into something. **8.** to lie very close to; cuddle or snuggle up to. **—***n.* **9.** an affectionate embrace or cuddle. [1375–1425; late ME *noselen* to grovel; orig. uncert.]

NV, Nevada (approved esp. for use with zip code).

N/V, *Banking.* no value.

NW, 1. net worth. 2. northwest. 3. northwestern. Also, **N.W., n.w.**

NWbN, See **northwest by north.**

NWbW, See **northwest by west.**

NWC, *Mil.* National War College.

NWLB, National War Labor Board.

NWS, National Weather Service.

n. wt., net weight.

N.W.T., Northwest Territories (Canada).

NY, New York (approved esp. for use with zip code).

N.Y., New York.

NYA, National Youth Administration. Also, **N.Y.A.**

nya·la (nyä′lə), *n.* an antelope, *Tragelaphus angasii,* of southeastern Africa, the male of which has a grayish body marked with white stripes. [1895–1900; < Venda (Bantu language of the Transvaal and Zimbabwe) *(dzi)-nyálà* nyala buck; or < a cognate Bantu word]

Nyan·da (nyän′də), *n.* a former name of **Masvingo.**

Nyan·ja (nyan′jə), *n.* a Bantu language spoken in Malawi and Zambia. [1890–95]

ny·an·za (nē an′zə, nī-), *n.* (in central and East Africa) a large body of water, esp. a lake. [< a Bantu language of the region; cf. Shona *nyanza* lake, sea]

Nya·sa (nyä′sä, nī as′ə), *n.* former name of **Malawi** (def. 2). Also, **Nyas′sa.**

Nya·sa·land (nyä′sä land′, nī as′ə-), *n.* former name of **Malawi** (def. 1).

Nya·ya (nyä′yə), *n.* (in ancient India) a philosophical school emphasizing logical analysis of knowledge, which is considered as deriving from perception, inference, analogy, and reliable testimony. [< Skt *nyāya*]

N.Y.C., New York City. Also, **NYC**

nyck·el·har·pa (nik′əl här′pə), *n.* an old-time Swedish stringed musical instrument, similar to the hurdy-gurdy but sounded with a bow instead of a wheel. [< Sw, equiv. to *nyckel* fret + *harpa* HARP]

NYCSCE, New York Coffee, Sugar and Cocoa Exchange.

nyct-, a combining form meaning "night," used in the formation of compound words: *nyctalgia.* Also, **nycti-, nycto-.** [< Gk *nykt-,* s. of *nýx* night]

nyc·ta·gi·na·ceous (nik′tə jə nā′shəs), *adj.* belonging to the Nyctaginaceae, the four-o'clock family of plants. Cf. **four-o'clock family.** [< NL *Nyctagin-* (s. of *Nyctago* old name of genus, equiv. to *nyct-* NYCT- + L *-āgō* n. suffix) + -ACEOUS]

nyc·tal·gia (nik tal′jə, -jē ə), *n. Pathol.* night pain that occurs in the sleep. [NYCT- + -ALGIA]

nyc·ta·lo·pi·a (nik′tl ō′pē ə), *n. Ophthalm.* **1.** See **night blindness. 2.** hemeralopia. [1675–85; < LL *nyctalōpia* < Gk *nykt-* NYCT- + *al(aós)* blind + *-ōpia* -OPIA] —**nyc·ta·lop·ic** (nik′tl op′ik), *adj.*

nycti-, var. of **nyct-.**

nyc·ti·trop·ic (nik′ti trop′ik, -trō′pik), *adj. Bot.* tending to assume at or just before nightfall positions unlike those maintained during the day, as the leaves or flowers of certain plants. [1875–80; NYCTI- + -TROPIC] —**nyc·tit·ro·pism** (nik ti′trə piz′əm), *n.*

nycto-, var. of **nyct-.**

nyc·to·pho·bi·a (nik′tə fō′bē ə), *n. Psychiatry.* an abnormal fear of night or darkness. [NYCTO- + -PHOBIA]

Nyd·i·a (nid′ē ə), *n.* a female given name.

Nye (nī), *n.* **1. Edgar Wilson** ("*Bill Nye*"), 1850–96, U.S. humorist. **2.** a male given name, form of **Aneurin.**

Nye·man (nye′mən), *n.* Russian name of **Neman.**

Nye·re·re (*Swahili.* nye RE′RE; *Eng.* ni râr′ē), *n.* **Julius Kam·ba·ra·ge** (*Swahili.* käm bä′RÄ gə), born 1921, African statesman: president of Tanzania 1964–85.

nyet (nyet), *adv., n. Russian.* no.

Nyí·regy·há·za (nyē′Redy[ə] hä′zo), *n.* a city in NE Hungary. 91,000.

Ny·kvist (nik′vist; *Sw.* NY′kvist), *n.* **Sven** (sven), born 1922, Swedish cinematographer.

nyl·ghai (nil′gī), *n., pl.* **-ghais,** *(esp. collectively)* **-ghai.** nilgai.

nyl·ghau (nil′gô), *n., pl.* **-ghaus,** *(esp. collectively)* **-ghau.** nilgai.

ny·lon (nī′lon), *n.* **1.** any of a class of thermoplastic polyamides capable of extrusion when molten into fibers, sheets, etc., of extreme toughness, strength, and elasticity, synthesized by the interaction of a dicarboxylic acid with a diamine: used esp. for yarn, fabrics, and bristles, as for brushes. **2. nylons,** stockings made of nylon, esp. sheer, full-length ones for women. [1938; coined as a generic by the du Pont Chemical Co. as distinct from known words and having no prior meaning or use, but with the suffix *-on* suggesting other textile fibers such as RAYON]

ny′lon let′down, *Mil. Slang.* evacuation from an aircraft by means of a parachute.

NYME, New York Mercantile Exchange.

nymph (nimf), *n.* **1.** one of a numerous class of lesser deities of mythology, conceived of as beautiful maidens inhabiting the sea, rivers, woods, trees, mountains, meadows, etc., and frequently mentioned as attending a superior deity. **2.** a beautiful or graceful young woman. **3.** a maiden. **4.** the young of an insect that undergoes incomplete metamorphosis. [1350–1400; ME *nimphe* < L *nympha* < Gk *nýmphē* bride, nymph] —**nymph′al,** **nym·phe·an** (nim′fē ən), *adj.*
—**Syn. 1.** naiad, nereid, oread, dryad, hamadryad. See **sylph.**

nym·pha (nim′fə), *n., pl.* **-phae** (-fē). **1.** *Anat.* one of the inner labia of the vulva. **2.** nymph (def. 4). [1595–1605; < L *nympha* (see NYMPH)]

nym·phae·a·ceous (nim′fē ā′shəs), *adj.* belonging to the Nymphaeaceae, the water lily family of plants. Cf. **water lily family.** [< NL *Nymphaeace(ae)* (*Nymphae(a)* the type genus (L: the water lily (< Gk *nymphaía,* n. use of fem. of *nymphaîos,* sacred to the nymphs; see NYMPHAEUM)) + *-aceae* -ACEAE) + -OUS]

nym·phae·um (nim fē′əm), *n., pl.* **-phae·a** (-fē′ə). **1.** a room or area having a fountain, statues, flowers, etc. **2.** an architecturally treated outlet of a reservoir or aqueduct. [1760–70; < L < Gk *nymphaîon* place sacred to nymphs, n. use of neut. of *nymphaîos,* equiv. to *nýmph(ē)* NYMPH + *-aios* adj. suffix]

nym·pha·lid (nim′fə lid), *n.* **1.** a butterfly of the family Nymphalidae, comprising the brush-footed butterflies. —*adj.* **2.** belonging or pertaining to the family Nymphalidae. [1890–95; < NL *Nymphalidae* name of family, equiv. to *Nymphāl(is)* name of genus (L *nymph(a)* NYMPH + *-ālis* -AL[1]) + *-idae* -ID[2]]

nymph·et (nim fet′, nim′fit), *n.* **1.** a young nymph. **2.** a sexually attractive young girl. **3.** a sexually precocious girl or young woman. [1605–15; < MF *nymphette.* See NYMPH, -ET]

nym·pho (nim′fō), *n., pl.* **-phos,** *adj. Slang.* nymphomaniac. [by shortening; see -O]

nym·pho·lep·sy (nim′fə lep′sē), *n., pl.* **-sies. 1.** an ecstasy supposed by the ancients to be inspired by nymphs. **2.** a frenzy of emotion, as for something unattainable. [1765–75; formed on NYMPHOLEPT, on the model of EPILEPSY] —**nym·pho·lep·tic** (nim′fə lep′tik), *adj.*

nym·pho·lept (nim′fə lept′), *n.* a person seized with nympholepsy. [1805–15; < Gk *nymphóleptos* caught by nymphs, equiv. to *nýmph(ē)* NYMPH + *-o-* -O- + *lēptos,* verbid of *lambánein* to seize]

nym·pho·ma·ni·a (nim′fə mā′nē ə, -mān′yə), *n. Pathol.* abnormally excessive and uncontrollable sexual desire in women. Cf. **Don Juanism, satyriasis.** [1790–1800; < Gk *nympho-* (see NYMPH, -O-) + -MANIA] —**nym·pho·ma·ni·ac** (nim′fə mā′nē ak′), *n., adj.* —**nym·pho·ma·ni·a·cal** (nim′fō mə nī′ə kəl), *adj.*

Nym·we·gen (*Ger.* nim′vā gən), *n.* Nijmegen.

Ny·norsk (nē′nôrsk, -nörsk; *Norw.* NY′nôshk′), *n.* a literary language based on western Norwegian dialects and Old Norse and in 1885 adopted as one of the two official languages of Norway. Also called **Landsmål, New Norse.** Cf. **Bokmål.** [< Norw: lit., new Norwegian]

Ny·os (nē′ōs), *n.* **Lake.** See **Nios, Lake.**

NYP, not yet published. Also, **N.Y.P.**

Ny·sa (nī′sə), *n. Class. Myth.* **1.** the mountain where Zeus sent the infant Dionysus to protect him from the vindictive wrath of Hera. **2.** one of the Nysaean Nymphs.

Ny·sae′an Nymphs′ (nī sē′ən), *Class. Myth.* the nymphs who cared for the infant Dionysus on Nysa. Also called **Ny·se·i·des** (nī sē′i dēz′).

NYSE, New York Stock Exchange. Also, **N.Y.S.E.**

nys·tag·mus (ni stag′məs), *n.* a congenital or acquired persistent, rapid, involuntary, and oscillatory movement of the eyeball, usually from side to side. [1815–25; < NL < Gk *nystagmós* nodding, deriv. of *nystázein* to nod] —**nys·tag′mic,** *adj.*

nys·ta·tin (nis′tə tin), *n. Pharm.* a light-yellow antibiotic powder, $C_{46}H_{77}NO_{19}$, produced by the microorganism *Streptomyces noursei* and used as an antifungal for infections due to various susceptible fungi, esp. those of the genus *Candida* that primarily infect the skin, mucous membranes, gastrointestinal tract, and vagina. [1950–55; *N(ew) Y(ork) Stat(e),* where originated + -IN[2]]

ny·tril (nī′tril), *n.* a synthetic, long-chain polymer fiber that produces a soft, elastic fabric. [*(vi)ny(lidine) (dini)tril(e)*]

Nyun·gar (nyŏŏng′gär) *n.* an Australian Aboriginal language spoken over a large area of southwest Western Australia, including Perth and Albany.

Nyx (niks), *n.* an ancient Greek goddess personifying night.

N.Z., New Zealand. Also, **N. Zeal.**

CONCISE PRONUNCIATION KEY: act, cāpe, dâre, pärt; set, ēqual; if, īce; ox, ōver, ôrder, oil, bŏŏk, bōōt, out; up, ûrge; child; sing; shoe; thin, *th*at; zh as in *treasure.* ə = *a* as in *alone, e* as in *system, i* as in *easily, o* as in *gallop, u* as in *circus;* [ə] as in *fire* (fī[ə]r), *hour* (ou[ə]r). l and n can serve as syllabic consonants, as in *cradle* (krād′l), and *button* (but′n). See the full key inside the front cover.

DEVELOPMENT OF MAJUSCULE								
NORTH SEMITIC	GREEK		ETR.	LATIN		MODERN		
						GOTHIC	ITALIC	ROMAN
O	O	O	O	O	O	O	O	O

DEVELOPMENT OF MINUSCULE					
ROMAN CURSIVE	ROMAN UNCIAL	CAROL. MIN.	MODERN		
			GOTHIC	ITALIC	ROMAN
o	o	o	o	o	o

The fifteenth letter of the English alphabet descended from Greek *omicron* (o). In form, the letter was adopted in Greek from the North Semitic consonant *ayin*, North Semitic having no vowel symbols. Since its appearance in Greek, this sign has changed little throughout its history.

O, o (ō), *n., pl.* **O's** or **Os; o's** or **os** or **oes. 1.** the fifteenth letter of the English alphabet, a vowel. **2.** any spoken sound represented by the letter *O* or *o*, as in *box, note, short,* or *love.* **3.** something having the shape of an O. **4.** a written or printed representation of the letter *O* or *o.* **5.** a device, as a printer's type, for reproducing the letter *O* or *o.*

O (ō), *interj., n., pl.* **O's.** —*interj.* **1.** (used before a name in direct address, esp. in solemn or poetic language, to lend earnestness to an appeal): *Hear, O Israel!* **2.** (used as an expression of surprise, pain, annoyance, longing, gladness, etc.) —*n.* **3.** the exclamation "O." [1125–75; ME < OF < L *ō*]

O, 1. Old. **2.** *Gram.* object.

O, *Symbol.* **1.** the fifteenth in order or in a series. **2.** the Arabic cipher; zero. **3.** (*sometimes l.c.*) the medieval Roman numeral for 11. Cf. **Roman numerals. 4.** *Physiol.* a major blood group, usually enabling a person whose blood is of this type to donate blood to persons of group O, A, B, or AB and to receive blood from persons of group O. Cf. **ABO system. 5.** *Chem.* oxygen. **6.** *Logic.* See **particular negative.**

o' (ə, ō), *prep.* **1.** an abbreviated form of *of*, as in *o'clock* or *will-o'-the-wisp.* **2.** an abbreviated form of *on.* [ME; by shortening.]

O', a prefix meaning "descendant," in Irish family names: *O'Brien; O'Connor.* [repr. Ir *ó* descendant, OIr *au*]

o-[1], *Chem.* an abridgment of **ortho-.**

o-[2], var. of **ob-** before *m: omission.*

o-[3], var. of **oo-:** *oidium.*

-o-, the typical ending of the first element of compounds of Greek origin (as **-i-** is, in compounds of Latin origin), used regularly in forming new compounds with elements of Greek origin and often used in English as a connective irrespective of etymology: *Franco-Italian; geography; seriocomic; speedometer.* Cf. **-i-.** [ME (< OF) < L < Gk]

-o, 1. a suffix occurring as the final element in informal shortenings of nouns (*ammo; combo; condo; limo; promo*); **-o** also forms nouns, usually derogatory, for persons or things exemplifying or associated with that specified by the base noun or adjective (*cheapo; pinko; sicko; weirdo; wino*). **2.** a suffix occurring in colloquial noun or adjective derivatives, usually grammatically isolated, as in address: *cheerio; kiddo; neato; righto.* [perh. orig. the interjection O, appended to words as in def. 2; as a derivational suffix reinforced by clipped forms of words with -o- as a linking element (e.g., PHOTO, STEREO), by Rom nouns ending in *o*, and by personal nouns such as BIMBO and BOZO, of obscure orig.]

O., 1. Ocean. **2.** (in prescriptions) a pint. [< L *octārius*] **3.** octavo. **4.** October. **5.** Ohio. **6.** Old. **7.** Ontario. **8.** Oregon.

o., 1. pint. [< L *octārius*] **2.** octavo. **3.** off. **4.** old. **5.** only. **6.** order. **7.** *Baseball.* out; outs.

OA, office automation.

o/a, on or about.

oaf (ōf), *n.* **1.** a clumsy, stupid person; lout. **2.** a simpleton; dunce; blockhead. **3.** *Archaic.* **a.** a deformed or mentally deficient child. **b.** a changeling. [1615–25; var. of *auf,* ME *alfe,* OE *ælf* ELF; c. G *Alp* nightmare] —**oaf′ish,** *adj.* —**oaf′ish·ly,** *adv.* —**oaf′ish·ness,** *n.* —**Syn. 1.** churl, boor. **2.** dolt, ninny.

O·a·hu (ō ä′ho͞o), *n.* an island in central Hawaii: third largest and most important island of the state; location of Honolulu. 630,528; 589 sq. mi. (1525 sq. km).

CONCISE ETYMOLOGY KEY: <, descended or borrowed from; >, whence; b., blend of, blended; c., cognate with; cf., compare; deriv., derivative; equiv., equivalent; imit., imitative; obl., oblique; r., replacing; s., stem; sp., spelling, spelled; resp., respelling, respelled; trans., translation; ?, origin unknown; *, unattested; ‡, probably earlier than. See the full key inside the front cover.

oak (ōk), *n.* **1.** any tree or shrub belonging to the genus *Quercus,* of the beech family, bearing the acorn as fruit. **2.** the hard, durable wood of such a tree, used in making furniture and in construction. **3.** the leaves of this tree, esp. as worn in a chaplet. **4.** anything made of the wood of this tree, as an item of furniture, a door, etc. **5. sport one's oak,** *Brit.* (of a university student) to indicate that one is not at home to visitors by closing the outer door of one's lodgings. [bef. 900; ME *ook,* OE *āc;* c. D *eik,* G *Eiche*] —**oak′like′,** *adj.*

oak′ ap′ple, See **oak gall.** [1400–50; late ME]

Oak′ Creek′, a town in SE Wisconsin. 16,932.

Oak·dale (ōk′dāl′), *n.* a town in E Minnesota. 12,123.

oak·en (ō′kən), *adj.* **1.** made of oak: *the old oaken bucket.* **2.** of or pertaining to the oak tree. [1300–50; ME; see OAK, -EN[2]]

oak′ fern′, a small woodland fern, *Gymnocarpium dryopteris,* of northern regions, having triangular, pinnate fronds that slant horizontally. [1540–50; trans. of L *dryopteris* < Gk *dryopterís,* equiv. to *dryo-* (comb. form of *drŷs* oak) + *ptéris* fern]

Oak′ For′est, a town in NE Illinois. 26,096.

oak′ gall′, any of various rounded galls produced on oaks, esp. the horned oak gall. Also called **oak apple.** [1760–70]

Oak′ Har′bor, a town in NW Washington. 12,271.

Oak·land (ōk′lənd), *n.* **1.** a seaport in W California, on San Francisco Bay. 339,288. **2.** a town in NE New Jersey. 13,443.

Oak′land Park′, a town in S Florida. 21,939.

Oak′ Lawn′, a city in NE Illinois, near Chicago. 60,590.

oak′ leaf′ clus′ter, a U.S. military decoration in the form of a small bronze twig bearing four oak leaves and three acorns, worn on the ribbon of another decoration for valor, wounds, or distinguished service to signify a second award of the same medal. [1915–20, *Amer.*]

oak′-leaf hydran′gea (ōk′lēf′), a shrub, *Hydrangea quercifolia,* of the southeastern U.S., having lobed leaves and pyramidal clusters of white flowers. [1880–85]

oak′ leath′er, *Mycol.* a thick sheet of mycelium occurring in decayed oak wood. [1745–55]

oak′-leaved gera′nium (ōk′lēvd′), a geranium, *Pelargonium quercifolium,* of southern Africa, having oaklike leaves with purple veins and sparse clusters of purple flowers with darker markings.

Oak·ley (ōk′lē), *n.* **1. Annie** (*Phoebe Anne Oakley Mozee*), 1860–1926, U.S. sharpshooter. **2.** *Slang.* See **Annie Oakley.**

oak·moss (ōk′môs′, -mos′), *n.* a lichen, *Evernia prunastri,* growing on oak and other trees, yielding a resin used in the manufacture of perfumes. [1920–25; OAK + MOSS]

Oak′ Park′, 1. a city in NE Illinois, near Chicago. 54,887. **2.** a city in SE Michigan. 31,537.

Oak′ Ridge′, a city in E Tennessee, near Knoxville: atomic research center. 27,662.

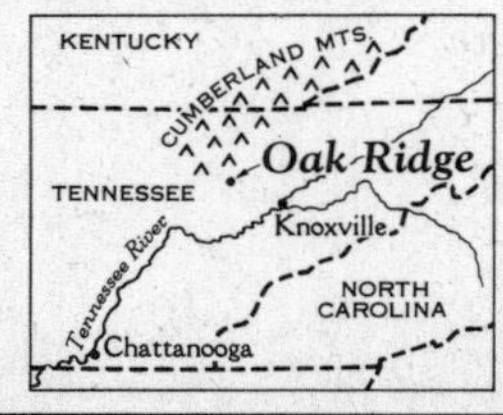

oak′-root rot′ (ōk′ro͞ot′, -ro͝ot′), *Plant Pathol.* a disease of oaks and other trees and woody plants, caused by the fungus *Amillariella mellea* **(oak′-root fun′gus),** the fruiting body of which is the honey mushroom, and characterized by rotting roots, girdling of crown, and eventual death of the tree. Also called **shoestring root rot.**

oak·tag (ōk′tag′), *n.* tagboard. [OAK + TAG[1]]

oa·kum (ō′kəm), *n.* loose fiber obtained by untwisting and picking apart old ropes, used for caulking the seams of ships. [bef. 1000; ME *okome,* OE *ācuma,* var. of *ācumba,* lit., offcombings, equiv. to *ā-* separative prefix (see A-[3]) + *-cumba* (see COMB[1])]

Oak·ville (ōk′vil), *n.* a town in SE Ontario, in S Canada, SW of Toronto, on Lake Ontario. 75,773.

oak′ wax′ scale′. See under **pit scale.** Also called **oak′ scale′.**

oak′ wilt′, *Plant Pathol.* a disease of oaks, characterized by wilting and discoloration of the leaves and defoliation, usually starting at and spreading from the top of the tree and the ends of the branches, caused by a fungus, *Chalara quercina.* [1940–45, *Amer.*]

O and O (ō′ ənd ō′), owned and operated. Also, **O&O**

OAO, *U. S. Aerospace.* Orbiting Astronomical Observatory: one of a series of scientific satellites that studied astronomical phenomena at ultraviolet and x-ray wavelengths.

OAP, *Brit.* old-age pensioner.

OAPC, Office of Alien Property Custodian.

oar (ôr, ōr), *n.* **1.** a long shaft with a broad blade at one end, used as a lever for rowing or otherwise propelling or steering a boat. **2.** something resembling this or having a similar purpose. **3.** a person who rows; oarsman. **4. put in one's oar,** to meddle; interfere: *He put in his oar and was told to mind his own business.* **5. rest on one's oars,** to cease to make an effort; relax after exertion; stop working after success or completing a task: *Once he became president, he was content to rest on his oars.* —*v.t.* **6.** to propel with or as if with oars; row. **7.** to traverse or make (one's way) by, or as if by, rowing. —*v.i.* **8.** to row. **9.** to move or advance as if by rowing. [bef. 900; ME *ore,* OE *ār;* c. ON *ār*] —**oar′less,** *adj.* —**oar′like′,** *adj.*

oared (ôrd, ōrd), *adj.* furnished with oars. [1740–50; OAR + -ED[3]]

oar·fish (ôr′fish′, ōr′-), *n., pl.* (*esp. collectively*) **-fish,** (*esp. referring to two or more kinds or species*) **-fish·es.** any long, ribbon-shaped, silvery fish of the genus *Regalecus,* of deep tropical waters, having a red dorsal fin along the spine that rises to a crest, and reaching a length of 30 ft. (9 m). Also called **ribbonfish.** [1855–60; OAR + FISH]

O, **oarlock**

oar·lock (ôr′lok′, ōr′-), *n.* any of various devices providing a pivot for an oar in rowing, esp. a swiveling, crutchlike or ringlike metal device projecting above a gunwale. Also called **rowlock.** [bef. 1100; ME *orlok,* OE *ārloc.* See OAR, LOCK[1]]

oars (ôrz, ōrz), *interj. Naut.* (used as a command to the crew of a scull or other similar boat to cease rowing and hold the oars horizontal with blades feathered.)

oars·man (ôrz′mən, ōrz′-), *n., pl.* **-men.** a person who rows a boat, esp. a racing boat; rower. [1695–1705; OAR + 'S[1] + -MAN] —**oars′man·ship′,** *n.*

oar·y (ôr′ē, ōr′ē), *adj. Archaic.* oarlike. [1660–70; OAR + -Y¹]

OAS, See **Organization of American States.**

O.A.S.I., Old Age and Survivors Insurance.

o·a·sis (ō ā′sis), *n., pl.* **-ses** (-sēz). **1.** a small fertile or green area in a desert region, usually having a spring or well. **2.** something serving as a refuge, relief, or pleasant change from what is usual, annoying, difficult, etc.: *The library was an oasis of calm in the hectic city.* [1605–15; < LL < Gk *óasis* (Herodotus) < Egyptian *wḥ't* oasis, oasis region] **—o·a·sit·ic** (ō′ə sit′ik), **o·a′sal, o·a·se·an** (ō ā′sē ən), *adj.*
—Syn. 2. haven, harbor, retreat, shelter.

oast (ōst), *n. Chiefly Brit.* a kiln for drying hops or malt. [bef. 1050; ME *ost,* OE *āst;* c. D *eest*]

oast-house (ōst′hous′), *n., pl.* **-hous·es** (-hou′ziz). *Chiefly Brit.* **1.** oast. **2.** a building housing several oasts. [1755–65]

oat (ōt), *n.* **1.** a cereal grass, *Avena sativa,* cultivated for its edible seed. **2.** Usually, **oats.** (*used with a singular or plural v.*) the seed of this plant, used as a food for humans and animals. **3.** any of several plants of the same genus, as the wild oat. **4.** *Archaic.* a musical pipe made of an oat straw. **5. feel one's oats,** *Informal.* **a.** to feel frisky or lively. **b.** to be aware of and use one's importance or power. **6. sow one's wild oats.** See **wild oat** (def. 3). [bef. 900; ME *ote,* OE *āte*] **—oat′like′,** *adj.*

oat·cake (ōt′kāk′), *n.* a cake, usually thin and brittle, made of oatmeal. [1590–1600; OAT + CAKE]

-oate, a combining form used in the names of chemical compounds containing the ester or >C=O group of the compound specified by the initial element: *benzoate.* [*-o(ic)* (as in *benzoic*) + -ATE²]

oat·en (ōt′n), *adj.* **1.** of, pertaining to, or made of oats. **2.** of or made of oatmeal. **3.** made of an oat straw. [1350–1400; ME; see OAT, -EN²]

oat·er (ō′tər), *n. Slang.* a movie, television show, etc., about the frontier days of the U.S. West; western; horse opera. [1945–50; OAT + -ER¹]

Oates (ōts), *n.* **1. Joyce Carol,** born 1938, U.S. novelist and short-story writer. **2. Titus,** 1649–1705, English conspirator and Anglican priest: instigator of the Popish Plot scare.

oat′ grass′, any of several grasses of the genus *Arrhenatherum* or *Danthonia,* esp. *A. elatius,* native to Europe, having a purplish-green flowering panicle. [1570–80]

oath (ōth), *n., pl.* **oaths** (ōthz, ōths). **1.** a solemn appeal to a deity, or to some revered person or thing, to witness one's determination to speak the truth, to keep a promise, etc.: *to testify upon oath.* **2.** a statement or promise strengthened by such an appeal. **3.** a formally affirmed statement or promise accepted as an equivalent of an appeal to a deity or to a revered person or thing; affirmation. **4.** the form of words in which such a statement or promise is made. **5.** an irreverent or blasphemous use of the name of God or anything sacred. **6.** any profane expression; curse; swearword: *He slammed the door with a muttered oath.* **7. take an oath,** to swear solemnly; vow. [bef. 900; ME *ooth,* OE *āth;* c. G *Eid*]
—Syn. 2. vow, pledge. **5.** profanity.

oat·meal (ōt′mēl′, -mēl′), *n.* **1.** meal made from ground or rolled oats. **2.** a cooked breakfast food made from this. **3.** a grayish-fawn color. **—*adj.* 4.** made with or containing oatmeal: *oatmeal cookies.* [1350–1400; ME; see OAT, MEAL²]

OAU, See **Organization of African Unity.** Also, **O.A.U.**

Oa·xa·ca (wə hä′kə; *Sp.* wä hä′kä), *n.* **1.** a state in S Mexico. 2,337,000; 36,375 sq. mi. (94,210 sq. km). **2.** a city in and the capital of this state, in the central part. 118,810.

Ob (ôb, ob; *Russ.* ôp), *n.* **1.** a river in the W Russian Federation in Asia, flowing NW to the Gulf of Ob. 2500 mi. (4025 km) long. **2. Gulf of,** an inlet of the Arctic Ocean. ab. 500 mi. (800 km) long.

OB, **1.** Also, **ob** *Med.* **a.** obstetrical. **b.** obstetrician. **c.** obstetrics. **2.** off Broadway. **3.** opening of books. **4.** ordered back.

ob-, a prefix meaning "toward," "to," "on," "over," "against," orig. occurring in loanwords from Latin, but now used also, with the sense of "reversely," "inversely," to form Neo-Latin and English scientific terms: *object; obligate; oblanceolate.* Also, **o-, oc-, of-, op-.** [ME (< OF) < L, repr. *ob* (prep.); in some scientific terms, < NL, L *ob-*]

ob., **1.** he died; she died. [< L *obiit*] **2.** incidentally. [< L *obiter*] **3.** oboe. **4.** *Meteorol.* observation.

O.B., **1.** opening of books. **2.** ordered back. Also, **O/B**

o·ba (ô′bə), *n.* a hereditary tribal ruler among various peoples in the Benin region of western Africa. [1900–05; < Edo *ɔ̀bá*]

Obad., Obadiah.

O·ba·di·ah (ō′bə dī′ə), *n.* **1.** a Minor Prophet. **2.** a book of the Bible bearing his name. *Abbr.:* Obad.

obb., obbligato.

ob·bli·ga·to (ob′li gä′tō; *It.* ôb′blē gä′tô), *adj., n., pl.* **-tos, -ti** (-tē). *Music.* **—*adj.* 1.** (used as a musical direction) obligatory or indispensable; so important that it cannot be omitted. **—*n.* 2.** an obbligato part or accompaniment. **3.** a continuing or persistent subordinate or background motif. **4.** a subordinate part of a solo. Also, **obligato.** [1715–25; < It: bound, obliged < L *obligātus;* see OBLIGATE]

ob·cla·vate (ob klā′vāt), *adj.* inversely clavate. [1855–60; < NL; see OB-, CLAVATE]

ob·con·i·cal (ob kon′i kəl), *adj. Bot.* conical, with the attachment at the pointed end. Also, **ob·con′ic.** [1800–10; OB- + CONICAL]

ob·cor·date (ob kôr′dāt), *adj. Bot.* heart-shaped, with the attachment at the pointed end, as a leaf. [1765–75; OB- + CORDATE]

ob·cu·ne·ate (ob kyōō′nē āt′, -it), *adj.* inversely cuneate. [1865–70; OB- + CUNEATE]

obdt., obedient.

ob·du·ce (ob dōō′sē, -dyōō′-), *v.imp.* (in prescriptions) cover; conceal; coat. [1650–60; < L]

ob·du·ra·cy (ob′dŏŏ rə sē, -dyŏŏ-), *n.* the state or quality of being obdurate. [1590–1600; OBDUR(ATE) + -ACY]

ob·du·rate (ob′dŏŏ rit, -dyŏŏ-), *adj.* **1.** unmoved by persuasion, pity, or tender feelings; stubborn; unyielding. **2.** stubbornly resistant to moral influence; persistently impenitent: *an obdurate sinner.* [1400–50; late ME *obdurat* < L *obdūrātus* (ptp. of *obdūrāre* to harden), equiv. to *ob-* OB- + *dūr(us)* hard + *-ātus* -ATE¹] **—ob′du·rate·ly,** *adv.* **—ob′du·rate·ness,** *n.*
—Syn. 1. hard, obstinate, callous, unbending, inflexible. **2.** unregenerate, reprobate, shameless. **—Ant. 1.** soft, tractable. **2.** humble, repentant.

O.B.E., **1.** Officer (of the Order) of the British Empire. **2.** Order of the British Empire.

o·be·ah (ō′bē ə), *n.* **1.** a form of belief involving sorcery, practiced in parts of the West Indies, South America, the southern U.S., and Africa. **2.** a fetish or charm used in practicing obeah. Also, **obi.** [1750–60; cf. Gullah, Jamaican E, Guyanan E, Sranan *óbia* magic, charm; < a West African language, though precise source unclear; cf. Twi *ɔ-bayifó* sorcerer (compound with *-fo* person), Igbo *dìbìà* folk healer (compound with *dí-* expert in)]

o·be·che (ō bē′chē), *n.* **1.** a tropical African tree, *Triplochiton scleroxylon.* **2.** the hard, white to pale-yellow wood of this tree, used for making furniture. [1905–10; < Edo *oβεxε*]

o·be·di·ence (ō bē′dē əns), *n.* **1.** the state or quality of being obedient. **2.** the act or practice of obeying; dutiful or submissive compliance: *Military service demands obedience from its members.* **3.** a sphere of authority or jurisdiction, esp. ecclesiastical. **4.** *Chiefly Eccles.* **a.** conformity to a monastic rule or the authority of a religious superior, esp. on the part of one who has vowed such conformance. **b.** the rule or authority that exacts such conformance. [1150–1200; ME < OF < L *oboedientia.* See OBEDIENT, -ENCE]
—Syn. 2. submission, subservience, deference.

obe′dience train′ing, the training of an animal, esp. a dog, to obey certain commands. [1960–65]

obe′dience tri′al, a competitive event at which a dog can progress toward a degree in obedience by demonstrating its ability to follow a prescribed series of commands. [1940–45]

o·be·di·ent (ō bē′dē ənt), *adj.* obeying or willing to obey; complying with or submissive to authority: *an obedient son.* [1175–1225; ME < OF < L *oboedient-* (s. of *oboediēns*), prp. of *oboedīre* to OBEY; see -ENT] **—o·be′·di·ent·ly,** *adv.*
—Syn. compliant, docile, tractable, yielding, deferential, respectful. **—Ant.** recalcitrant.

obe′dient plant′. See **false dragonhead.** [1905–10, *Amer.;* from the fact that the individual blossoms on the flower spike will remain in whatever position they are placed]

O·beid (ō bād′), *n.* See **El Obeid.**

o·bei·sance (ō bā′səns, ō bē′-), *n.* **1.** a movement of the body expressing deep respect or deferential courtesy, as before a superior; a bow, curtsy, or other similar gesture. **2.** deference or homage: *The nobles gave obeisance to the new king.* [1325–75; ME *obeisaunce* < MF *obeissance,* deriv. of OF *obeissant,* prp. of *obeir* to OBEY; see -ANCE] **—o·bei′sant,** *adj.* **—o·bei′sant·ly,** *adv.*

o·be·lia (ō bēl′yə, ō bē′lē ə), *n.* a colonial hydroid of the genus *Obelia,* common in temperate seas and appearing as a delicate, mosslike growth on rocks, pilings, etc. [1865–70; < NL < Gk *obelías* a loaf toasted on a spit, equiv. to *obel(ós)* a spit (see OBELISK) + *-ias* n. suffix]

ob·e·lisk (ob′ə lisk), *n.* **1.** a tapering, four-sided shaft of stone, usually monolithic and having a pyramidal apex. **2.** something resembling such a shaft. **3.** an obelus. **4.** *Print.* dagger (def. 2). [1540–50; < L *obeliscus* < Gk *obelískos* small spit, equiv. to *obel(ós)* spit, pointed pillar + *-iskos* dim. suffix] **—ob′e·lis′cal,** *adj.* **—ob′e·lis′koid,** *adj.*

obelisk (def. 1)

ob·e·lize (ob′ə līz′), *v.t.,* **-lized, -liz·ing.** to mark (a word or passage) with an obelus. Also, *esp. Brit.,* **ob′e·lise′.** [1605–15; < Gk *obelízein,* equiv. to *obel(ós)* OBELUS + *-izein* -IZE] **—ob′e·lism,** *n.*

ob·e·lus (ob′ə ləs), *n., pl.* **-li** (-lī′). a mark (— or ÷) used in ancient manuscripts to point out spurious, corrupt, doubtful, or superfluous words or passages. [1350–1400; ME < LL < Gk *obelós* spit, pointed pillar]

o·ben·to (ō ben′tō; *Japn.* ô ben′tô), *n., pl.* **-tos;** *Japn.* **-to.** bento. Also, **o-ben′to.**

O·ber·am·mer·gau (ō′bər ä′mər gou′), *n.* a village in S Germany, SW of Munich: famous for the passion play performed there every ten years. 4700.

O·ber·hau·sen (ō′bər hou′zən), *n.* a city in W Germany, in the lower Ruhr valley. 235,900.

O·ber·land (ō′bər land′; *Ger.* ō′bər länt′), *n.* a mountain region in central Switzerland, mostly in S Bern canton.

O·ber·lin (*Fr.* ô ber laN′), *n.* **Jean Fré·dé·ric** (*Fr.* zhäN frā dā rēk′), 1740–1826, Alsatian clergyman.

O·ber·on (ō′bə ron′), *n.* **1.** (in medieval folklore) the king of the fairies. **2.** *Astron.* one of the five moons of Uranus.

O·berth (ō′bərt; *Ger.* ō′bert), *n.* **Her·mann Ju·li·us** (hûr′mən jōōl′yəs; *Ger.* her′män yōō′lē ōōs′), born 1894, German physicist: pioneer in rocketry.

o·bese (ō bēs′), *adj.* very fat or overweight; corpulent. [1645–55; < L *obēsus* (ptp. of *obedere* to eat away), equiv. to *ob-* OB- + *ed(ere)* to EAT + *-tus* ptp. suffix, with *dt* > *s*] **—o·bese′ly,** *adv.* **—o·be′si·ty, o·bese′ness,** *n.*

o·bey (ō bā′), *v.t.* **1.** to comply with or follow the commands, restrictions, wishes, or instructions of: *to obey one's parents.* **2.** to comply with or follow (a command, restriction, wish, instruction, etc.). **3.** (of things) to respond conformably in action to: *The car obeyed the slightest touch of the steering wheel.* **4.** to submit or conform in action to (some guiding principle, impulse, one's conscience, etc.). **—*v.i.* 5.** to be obedient: *to agree to obey.* [1250–1300; ME *obeien* < OF *obeir* < L *oboedīre,* equiv. to *ob-* OB- + *audīre* to hear; *-oe-* for expected *-ū-* is unclear] **—o·bey′a·ble,** *adj.* **—o·bey′er,** *n.* **—o·bey′ing·ly,** *adv.*

ob·fus·cate (ob′fə skāt′, ob fus′kāt), *v.t.,* **-cat·ed, -cat·ing. 1.** to confuse, bewilder, or stupefy. **2.** to make obscure or unclear: *to obfuscate a problem with extraneous information.* **3.** to darken. [1525–35; < LL *obfuscātus* (ptp. of *obfuscāre* to darken), equiv. to L *ob-* OB- + *fusc(us)* dark + *-ātus* -ATE¹] **—ob′fus·ca′tion,** *n.* **—ob·fus·ca·to·ry** (ob fus′kə tôr′ē, -tōr′ē), *adj.*
—Syn. 1. muddle, perplex. **2.** cloud. **—Ant. 1.** clarify.

ob-gyn (ō′bē′jē′wī′en′), **1.** obstetrical-gynecological. **2.** obstetrician-gynecologist. **3.** obstetrics and gynecology. Also, **ob/gyn, OB/GYN**

o·bi¹ (ō′bē; *Japn.* ô′bē), *n., pl.* **o·bis, o·bi.** a long, broad sash tied about the waist over a Japanese kimono. [1875–80; < Japn: girdle, gird (v.)]

o·bi² (ō′bē), *n., pl.* **o·bis.** obeah.

O·bie (ō′bē), *n.* one of a group of awards given annually, beginning in 1956, by New York City's *The Village Voice* newspaper for achievement in the off-Broadway theater. [pron. of OB, abbr. of *off Broadway*]

o·bi·it (ō′bi it; *Eng.* ō′bē it, ob′ē-), *Latin.* he died; she died.

o·bit (ō bit′ *for 1;* ō′bit, ob′it *for 2, 3; esp. Brit.* ob′it *for 1–3*), *n.* **1.** *Informal.* an obituary. **2.** the date of a person's death. **3.** *Obs.* a Requiem Mass. [1325–75; ME *obite* < L *obitus* death, equiv. to *obi-* (s. of *obīre* to meet, meet one's death, die; *ob-* OB- + *īre* to go) + *-tus* suffix of v. action]

ob·i·ter dic·tum (ob′i tər dik′təm), *pl.* **ob·i·ter dic·ta** (ob′i tər dik′tə). **1.** an incidental or passing remark, opinion, etc. **2.** *Law.* an incidental or supplementary opinion by a judge in deciding a case, upon a matter not essential to the decision, and therefore not binding as precedent. [1805–15; < L: (a) saying by the way]

o·bit·u·ar·y (ō bich′ōō er′ē), *n., pl.* **-ar·ies,** *adj.* **—*n.* 1.** a notice of the death of a person, often with a biographical sketch, as in a newspaper. **—*adj.* 2.** of, pertaining to, or recording a death or deaths: *the obituary page of a newspaper.* [1700–10; < ML *obituārius,* equiv. to L *obitu(s)* death (see OBIT) + *-ārius* -ARY] **—o·bit′u·ar·ist,** *n.*

obj., **1.** object. **2.** objection. **3.** objective.

ob·ject (*n.* ob′jikt, -jekt; *v.* əb jekt′), *n.* **1.** anything that is visible or tangible and is relatively stable in form. **2.** a thing, person, or matter to which thought or action is directed: *an object of medical investigation.* **3.** the end toward which effort or action is directed; goal; purpose: *Profit is the object of business.* **4.** a person or thing with reference to the impression made on the mind or the feeling or emotion elicited in an observer: *an object of curiosity and pity.* **5.** anything that may be apprehended intellectually: *objects of thought.* **6.** *Optics.* the thing of which a lens or mirror forms an image. **7.** *Gram.* (in many languages, as English) a noun, noun phrase, or noun substitute representing by its syntactical position either the goal of the action of a verb or the goal of a preposition in a prepositional phrase, as *ball* in *John hit the ball, Venice* in *He came to Venice, coin* and *her* in *He gave her a coin.* Cf. **direct object, indirect object. 8.** *Metaphys.* something toward which a cognitive act is directed. **—*v.i.* 9.** to offer a reason or argument in opposition. **10.** to express or feel disapproval, dislike, or distaste; be averse. **11.** to refuse or attempt to refuse to permit some action, speech, etc. **—*v.t.* 12.** to state, claim, or cite in opposition; put forward in objection: *Some persons objected that the proposed import duty would harm world trade.* **13.** *Archaic.* to bring forward or adduce in opposition. [1325–75; (n.) ME: something perceived, purpose, objection < ML *objectum* something thrown down or presented (to the mind), n. use of neut. of L *objectus* (ptp. of *objicere*), equiv. to *ob-* OB- + *jec-* (comb. form of *jacere* to throw; see JET¹) + *-tus* ptp. suffix; (v.) ME *objecten* to argue against (< MF *obje(c)ter*) < L *objectāre* to throw or put before, oppose] **—ob·jec′tor,** *n.*
—Syn. 3. objective, target, destination, intent, intention, motive. See **aim.**

CONCISE PRONUNCIATION KEY: act, cāpe, dâre, pärt; set, ēqual; *if,* ice; ox, ōver, ôrder, oil, bŏŏk, bōōt, out; up, ûrge; child; sing; shoe; thin, *th*at; zh as in *treasure.* ə = *a* as in *alone, e* as in *system, i* as in *easily, o* as in *gallop, u* as in *circus;* ᵊ as in *fire* (fīᵊr), *hour* (ouᵊr). l and n can serve as syllabic consonants, as in *cradle* (krād′l), and *button* (but′n). See the full key inside the front cover.

object., 1. objection. 2. objective.

ob′ject ball′, *Billiards, Pool.* 1. the first ball struck by the cue ball in making a carom. Cf. **carom ball.** 2. a ball to be struck by the cue ball; any ball except the cue ball. [1855–60]

ob′ject code′, *Computers.* the machine-language output of a compiler or assembler that is ready for execution.

ob′ject com′plement, *Gram.* a word or a group of words used in the predicate following a factitive verb and referring to its direct object, as *treasurer* in *We appointed him treasurer, white* in *They painted the house white,* or *an interesting speaker* in *They thought him an interesting speaker.* Also called **objective complement.** [1905–10]

ob′ject dis′tance, *Photog.* the distance between the lens of a camera and an object being photographed.

ob′ject glass′, *Optics.* objective (def. 3). [1655–65]

ob•jec•ti•fy (əb jek′tə fī′), *v.t.,* **-fied, -fy•ing.** to present as an object, esp. of sight, touch, or other physical sense; make objective; externalize. [1830–40; OBJECT + -IFY] **—ob•jec′ti•fi•ca′tion,** *n.*

ob•jec•tion (əb jek′shən), *n.* 1. a reason or argument offered in disagreement, opposition, refusal, or disapproval. 2. the act of objecting. 3. a ground or cause for objecting. 4. a feeling of disapproval, dislike, or disagreement. [1350–1400; ME *objeccioun* (< AF) < LL *objectiōn-* (s. of *objectiō*), equiv. to L *object(us)* (see OBJECT) + *-iōn-* -ION]
—Syn. 4. complaint, protest, criticism.

ob•jec•tion•a•ble (əb jek′shə nə bəl), *adj.* 1. causing or tending to cause an objection, disapproval, or protest. 2. offending good taste, manners, etiquette, propriety, etc.; offensive: *objectionable behavior.* [1775–85; OBJECTION + -ABLE] **—ob•jec′tion•a•bil′i•ty, ob•jec′tion•a•ble•ness,** *n.* **—ob•jec′tion•a•bly,** *adv.*
—Syn. 2. unacceptable, offensive, vile, odious.

ob•jec•tive (əb jek′tiv), *n.* 1. something that one's efforts or actions are intended to attain or accomplish; purpose; goal; target: *the objective of a military attack; the objective of a fund-raising drive.* 2. *Gram.* a. Also called **objective case.** (in English and some other languages) a case specialized for the use of a form as the object of a transitive verb or of a preposition, as *him* in *The boy hit him,* or *me* in *He comes to me with his troubles.* b. a word in that case. 3. Also called **object glass, object lens, objective lens.** *Optics.* (in a telescope, microscope, camera, or other optical system) the lens or combination of lenses that first receives the rays from the object and forms the image in the focal plane of the eyepiece, as in a microscope, or on a plate or screen, as in a camera. See diag. under **microscope.** *—adj.* 4. being the object or goal of one's efforts or actions. 5. not influenced by personal feelings, interpretations, or prejudice; based on facts; unbiased: *an objective opinion.* 6. intent upon or dealing with things external to the mind rather than with thoughts or feelings, as a person or a book. 7. being the object of perception or thought; belonging to the object of thought rather than to the thinking subject (opposed to *subjective*). 8. of or pertaining to something that can be known, or to something that is an object or a part of an object; existing independent of thought or an observer as part of reality. 9. *Gram.* a. pertaining to the use of a form as the object of a transitive verb or of a preposition. b. (in English and some other languages) noting the objective case. c. similar to such a case in meaning. d. (in case grammar) pertaining to the semantic role of a noun phrase that denotes something undergoing a change of state or bearing a neutral relation to the verb, as *the rock* in *The rock moved* or in *The child threw the rock.* 10. being part of or pertaining to an object to be drawn: *an objective plane.* 11. *Med.* (of a symptom) discernible to others as well as the patient. [1610–20; < ML *objectivus,* equiv. to L *object(us)* (see OBJECT) + *-ivus* -IVE] **—ob•jec′tive•ly,** *adv.* **—ob•jec′tive•ness,** *n.*
—Syn. 1. object, destination, aim. 5. impartial, fair, impersonal, disinterested. **—Ant.** 5. personal.

objec′tive case′, objective (def. 2a).

objec′tive com′plement. See **object complement.** [1865–70]

objec′tive correl′ative, *Literature.* a completely depicted situation or chain of events that objectifies a particular emotion in such a way as to produce or evoke that emotion in the reader. [1840–50]

objec′tive ide′alism, *Philos.* a form of idealism asserting that the act of experiencing has a reality combining and transcending the natures of the object experienced and of the mind of the observer. Cf. **subjective idealism. —objec′tive ide′alist.**

objec′tive lens′, *Optics.* objective (def. 3).

objec′tive prism′, *Astron.* a large prism placed in front of the objective lens or mirror of a telescope, allowing the simultaneous acquisition of the spectra of many stars.

objec′tive rel′ativism, *Epistemology.* the doctrine that knowledge of real objects is relative to the individual. **—objec′tive rel′ativist.**

objec′tive spir′it, *Hegelianism.* the human spirit, insofar as it has become capable of a rational identification of its individual self with the community of other spirits but is not yet capable of the identification with the absolute idea that characterizes the absolute spirit.

objec′tive test′, *Educ.* a test consisting of factual questions requiring extremely short answers that can be quickly and unambiguously scored by anyone with an answer key, thus minimizing subjective judgments by both the person taking the test and the person scoring it.

CONCISE ETYMOLOGY KEY: <, descended or borrowed from; >, whence; b., blend of, blended; c., cognate with; cf., compare; deriv., derivative; equiv., equivalent; imit., imitative; obl., oblique; r., replacing; s., stem; sp., spelling, spelled; resp., respelling, respelled; trans., translation; ?, origin unknown; *, unattested; ‡, probably earlier than. See the full key inside the front cover.

ob•jec•tiv•ism (əb jek′tə viz′əm), *n.* 1. a tendency to lay stress on the objective or external elements of cognition. 2. the tendency, as of a writer, to deal with things external to the mind rather than with thoughts or feelings. 3. a doctrine characterized by this tendency. [1850–55; OBJECTIVE + -ISM] **—ob•jec′tiv•ist,** *n., adj.* **—ob•jec′ti•vis′tic,** *adj.*

ob•jec•tiv•i•ty (ob′jik tiv′i tē, -jek-), *n.* 1. the state or quality of being objective: *He tries to maintain objectivity in his judgment.* 2. intentness on objects external to the mind. 3. external reality. [1795–1805; OBJECTIVE + -ITY]

ob•jec•tiv•ize (əb jek′tə vīz′), *v.t.,* **-ized, -iz•ing.** to cause to become concrete or objective; objectify. Also, *esp. Brit.,* **ob•jec′tiv•ise′.** [1855–60; OBJECTIVE + -IZE] **—ob•jec′ti•vi•za′tion,** *n.*

ob′ject lan′guage, the language to which a metalanguage refers. [1930–35]

ob′ject lens′, *Optics.* objective (def. 3). [1825–35]

ob•ject•less (ob′jikt lis, -jekt-), *adj.* 1. not directed toward any goal; purposeless; aimless. 2. having no object: *an objectless preposition.* [1795–1805; OBJECT + -LESS] **—ob′ject•less•ly,** *adv.* **—ob′ject•less•ness,** *n.*

ob′ject les′son, a practical or concrete illustration of a principle. [1825–35]

ob•jet d'art (ôb zhe dᴀʀ′), *pl.* ***ob•jets d'art*** (ôb zhe dᴀʀ′). *French.* an object of artistic worth or curiosity, esp. a small object. Also called ***ob•jet′.***

ob•jet trou•vé (ôb zhe trōō vā′), *pl.* ***ob•jets trou•vés*** (ôb zhe trōō vā′). *French.* See **found object.**

ob•jur•gate (ob′jər gāt′, əb jûr′gāt), *v.t.,* **-gat•ed, -gat•ing.** to reproach or denounce vehemently; upbraid harshly; berate sharply. [1610–20; < L *objūrgātus,* ptp. of *objūrgāre* to rebuke, equiv. to *ob-* OB- + *jūrgāre, jurigāre* to rebuke, equiv. to *jūr-* (s. of *jūs*) law + *-ig-,* comb. form of *agere* to drive, do + *-ātus* -ATE[1]] **—ob′jur•ga′tion,** *n.* **—ob′jur•ga′tor,** *n.* **—ob•jur•ga•to•ri•ly** (əb jûr′gə tôr′ə lē, -tōr′-), **ob•jur′ga•tive•ly,** *adv.* **—ob•jur′ga•to′ry, ob•jur′ga•tive,** *adj.*

obl., 1. oblique. 2. oblong.

ob•lan•ce•o•late (ob lan′sē ə lit, -lāt′), *adj. Bot.* inversely lanceolate, as a leaf. [1840–50; OB- + LANCEOLATE]

o•blast (ob′last, -läst; *Russ.* ô′bləst), *n., pl.* **o•blasts,** *Russ.* ***o•bla•sti*** (ô′blə styē). 1. (in Russia and the Soviet Union) an administrative division corresponding to an autonomous province. 2. region; province. [1885–90; < Russ *óblast′,* ORuss *oblastĭ,* equiv. to *ob-* against, on + *vlastĭ* authority, power; see VOLOST]

ob•late[1] (ob′lāt, o blāt′), *adj.* flattened at the poles, as a spheroid generated by the revolution of an ellipse about its shorter axis (opposed to *prolate*). See diag. under **prolate.** [1695–1705; < NL *oblātus* lengthened, equiv. to L *ob-* OB- + *(prō)lātus* PROLATE] **—ob′late•ly,** *adv.*

ob•late[2] (ob′lāt, o blāt′), *n.* 1. a person offered to the service of and living in a monastery, but not under monastic vows or full monastic rule. 2. a lay member of any of various Roman Catholic societies devoted to special religious work. [1860–65; < ML *oblātus,* suppletive ptp. of *offerre* to OFFER]

ob•la•tion (o blā′shən), *n.* 1. the offering to God of the elements of bread and wine in the Eucharist. 2. the whole office of the Eucharist. 3. the act of making an offering, esp. to a deity. 4. any offering for religious or charitable uses. [1375–1425; late ME *oblacion* < LL *oblātion-* (s. of *oblātiō*), equiv. to *oblāt(us)* (see OBLATE[2]) + *-iōn-* -ION] **—ob•la•to•ry** (ob′lə tôr′ē, -tōr′ē), **ob•la′tion•al,** *adj.*

ob•li•gate (*v.* ob′li gāt′; *adj.* ob′li git, -gāt′), *v.* **-gat•ed, -gat•ing,** *adj.* *—v.t.* 1. to bind or oblige morally or legally: *to obligate oneself to purchase a building.* 2. to pledge, commit, or bind (funds, property, etc.) to meet an obligation. *—adj.* 3. morally or legally bound; obliged; constrained. 4. necessary; essential. 5. *Biol.* restricted to a particular condition of life, as certain organisms that can survive only in the absence of oxygen: *obligate anaerobe* (opposed to *facultative*). [1400–50; late ME *obligat* (adj.) < L *obligātus* (ptp. of *obligāre* to bind), equiv. to *ob-* OB- + *ligātus;* see LIGATE] **—ob•li•ga•ble** (ob′li gə bəl), *adj.* **—ob′li•ga′tor,** *n.*

ob•li•ga•tion (ob′li gā′shən), *n.* 1. something by which a person is bound or obliged to do certain things, and which arises out of a sense of duty or results from custom, law, etc. 2. something that is done or is to be done for such reasons: *to fulfill one's obligations.* 3. a binding promise, contract, sense of duty, etc. 4. the act of binding or obliging oneself by a promise, contract, etc. 5. *Law.* a. an agreement enforceable by law, originally applied to promises under seal. b. a document containing such an agreement. c. a bond containing a penalty, with a condition annexed for payment of money, performance of covenants, etc. 6. any bond, note, bill, certificate, or the like, as of a government or a corporation, serving as evidence of indebtedness. 7. an indebtedness or amount of indebtedness. 8. a favor, service, or benefit for which gratitude is due. 9. a debt of gratitude: *He felt an obligation to his teacher.* 10. the state of being under a debt, as of gratitude, for a favor, service, or benefit. [1250–1300; ME *obligacioun* < OF *obligation* < L *obligātiōn-* (s. of *obligātiō*) a binding, equiv. to *obligāt(us)* bound (see OBLIGATE) + *-iōn-* -ION]
—Syn. 1. responsibility. See **duty.** 5. contract, covenant.

ob•li•ga•tion•al (ob′li gā′shə nl), *adj.* obligatory. [OBLIGATION + -AL[1]]

obliga′tional author′ity, the necessary authority that precedes budget spending by a government agency or department, granted by Congress through appropriations.

ob•li•ga•tive (ob′li gā′tiv), *adj.* implying or involving obligation: *an obligative commitment.* [1590–1600; < L *obligāt(us)* (see OBLIGATE) + -IVE]

ob•li•ga•to (ob′li gä′tō), *adj., n., pl.* **-tos, -ti** (tē). obbligato.

o•blig•a•to•ry (ə blig′ə tôr′ē, -tōr′ē, ob′li gə-), *adj.* 1. required as a matter of obligation; mandatory: *A reply is desirable but not obligatory.* 2. incumbent or compulsory (usually fol. by *on* or *upon*): *duties obligatory on all.* 3. imposing moral or legal obligation; binding: *an obligatory promise.* 4. creating or recording an obligation, as a document. [1425–75; late ME < LL *obligātōrius* binding, equiv. to L *obligā(re)* to bind (see OBLIGATE) + *-tōrius* -TORY[1]] **—ob•lig•a•to•ri•ly** (ə blig′ə tôr′ə lē, -tōr′-, ob′li gə-, ə blig′ə tôr′ə lē, -tōr′-, ob′li gə-), *adv.* **—o•blig′a•to′ri•ness,** *n.*
—Syn. 2. necessary, imperative. **—Ant.** 2. voluntary.

o•blige (ə blīj′), *v.,* **o•bliged, o•blig•ing.** *—v.t.* 1. to require or constrain, as by law, command, conscience, or force of necessity. 2. to bind morally or legally, as by a promise or contract. 3. to place under a debt of gratitude for some benefit, favor, or service: *I'm much obliged for the ride.* 4. to put (one) in a debt of gratitude, as by a favor or accommodation: *Mr. Weems will oblige us with a song.* 5. to make (an action, policy, etc.) necessary or obligatory: *Your carelessness obliges firmness on my part.* *—v.i.* 6. to be kindly accommodating: *I'll do anything within reason to oblige.* [1250–1300; ME *obligen* < OF *obligier* < L *obligāre* to bind. See OBLIGATE] **—o•blig•ed•ly** (ə blī′jid lē), *adv.* **—o•blig′ed•ness,** *n.* **—o•blig′er,** *n.*
—Syn. 1. compel, force. 2. obligate. 4. OBLIGE, ACCOMMODATE imply making a gracious and welcome gesture of some kind. OBLIGE emphasizes the idea of conferring a favor or benefit (and often of taking some trouble to do it): *to oblige someone with a loan.* ACCOMMODATE emphasizes doing a service or furnishing a convenience: *to accommodate someone with lodgings and meals.*

ob•li•gee (ob′li jē′), *n.* 1. *Law.* a. a person to whom another is obligated or bound. b. a person to whom a bond is given. 2. a person who is under obligation for a favor, service, or benefit. [1565–75; OBLIGE + -EE]

o•blig•ing (ə blī′jing), *adj.* 1. willing or eager to do favors, offer one's services, etc.; accommodating: *The clerk was most obliging.* 2. obligating. [1630–40; OBLIGE + -ING[2]] **—o•blig′ing•ly,** *adv.* **—o•blig′ing•ness,** *n.*
—Syn. 1. helpful, kind, friendly.

ob•li•gor (ob′li gôr′, ob′li gôr′), *n. Law.* 1. a person who is bound to another. 2. a person who gives a bond. [1535–45; OBLIGE + -OR[2]]

o•blique (ə blēk′, ō blēk′; *Mil.* ə blīk′, ō blīk′), *adj., adv., v.,* **o•bliqued, o•bliqu•ing,** *n.* *—adj.* 1. neither perpendicular nor parallel to a given line or surface; slanting; sloping. 2. (of a solid) not having the axis perpendicular to the plane of the base. 3. diverging from a given straight line or course. 4. not straight or direct, as a course. 5. indirectly stated or expressed; not straightforward: *oblique remarks about the candidate's honesty.* 6. indirectly aimed at or reached, as ends or results; deviously achieved. 7. morally, ethically, or mentally wrong; underhand; perverse. 8. *Typography.* (of a letter) slanting toward the right, as a form of sans-serif, gothic, or square-serif type. 9. *Rhet.* indirect (applied to discourse in which the original words of a speaker or writer are assimilated to the language of the reporter). 10. *Anat.* pertaining to muscles running obliquely in the body as opposed to those running transversely or longitudinally. 11. *Bot.* having unequal sides, as a leaf. 12. *Gram.* noting or pertaining to any case of noun inflection except nominative and vocative: *Latin genitive, dative, accusative, and ablative cases are said to be oblique.* 13. *Drafting.* designating a method of projection **(oblique projection)** in which a three-dimensional object is represented by a drawing **(oblique′ draw′ing)** in which the face, usually parallel to the picture plane, is represented in accurate or exact proportion, and all other faces are shown at any convenient angle other than 90°. Cf. **axonometric, cabinet** (def. 19), **isometric** (def. 5). See illus. under **isometric.** *—adv.* 14. *Mil.* at an angle of 45°. *—v.i.* 15. *Mil.* to change direction obliquely. *—n.* 16. something that is oblique. 17. *Gram.* an oblique case. 18. *Anat.* any of several oblique muscles, esp. in the walls of the abdomen. [1400–50; late ME *oblike* < L *obliquus* slanting; see OB- (second element obscure)] **—o•blique′ness,** *n.*
—Syn. 5, 6. indirect, veiled, masked, covert.

oblique′ an′gle, an angle that is not a right angle; an acute or obtuse angle. [1685–95] **—o•blique′-an′gled,** *adj.*

oblique′ cir′cular cone′, *Geom.* a cone whose surface is generated by lines joining a fixed point to the points of a circle, the fixed point lying on a line that is not perpendicular to the circle at its center. Cf. **right circular cone.** [‡1950–55]

oblique′ cir′cular cyl′inder, *Geom.* a cylinder generated by the revolution of a parallelogram other than a rectangle about one of its sides. Cf. **right circular cylinder.**

oblique′ coor′dinates, *Math.* a coordinate system in which the axes do not meet at right angles.

o•blique•ly (ə blēk′lē, ō blēk′-; *Mil.* ə blīk′lē, ō blīk′-), *adv.* in an oblique manner or direction. [1565–75; OBLIQUE + -LY]

oblique′ mo′tion, *Music.* the relative motion of two melodic parts in which one remains in place or moves relatively little while the other moves more actively. [1805–15]

oblique′ projec′tion, *Drafting.* See under **oblique** (def. 13).

oblique′ sail′ing, the navigation of a vessel on a point of the compass other than one of the cardinal points. [1700–10]

oblique′ sec′tion, a representation of an object as it would appear if cut by a plane that is other than parallel or perpendicular to its longest axis.

oblique′ tri′angle, any triangle that does not have a right angle (contrasted with *right triangle*).

o•bliq•ui•ty (ə blik′wi tē, ō blik′-), *n., pl.* **-ties. 1.** the state of being oblique. **2.** divergence from moral conduct, rectitude, etc.; immorality, dishonesty, or the like. **3.** an instance of such divergence. **4.** mental perversity. **5.** an instance of mental perversity. **6.** an inclination or a degree of inclination. **7.** a confusing or obscure statement or passage of writing, esp. one deliberately made obscure. **8.** Also called **obliq′uity of the eclip′tic.** *Astron.* the angle between the plane of the earth's orbit and that of the earth's equator, equal to 23°27′; the inclination of the earth's equator. [1375–1425; late ME *obliquitee* < MF *obliquite* < L *obliquitās,* equiv. to *obliqu(us)* OBLIQUE + *-itās* -ITY] **—o•bliq′ui•tous,** *adj.*

ob•lit•er•ate (ə blit′ə rāt′), *v.t.,* **-at•ed, -at•ing. 1.** to remove or destroy all traces of; do away with; destroy completely. **2.** to blot out or render undecipherable (writing, marks, etc.); efface. [1590–1600; < L *oblitterātus* (ptp. of *oblitterāre,* efface, cause to be forgotten), equiv. to *ob-* OB- + *litter(a)* LETTER + *-ātus* -ATE[1]] **—ob•lit•er•a•ble** (ə blit′ər ə bəl), *adj.* **—o•blit′•er•a′tor,** *n.*
—Syn. 2. expunge. See **cancel.**

ob•lit•er•a•tion (ə blit′ə rā′shən), *n.* **1.** the act of obliterating or the state of being obliterated. **2.** *Pathol., Surg.* the removal of a part as a result of disease or surgery. [1650–60; < L *oblitterātiōn-* (s. of *oblitterātiō*), equiv. to *oblitterāt(us)* (see OBLITERATE) + *-iōn-* -ION] **—ob•lit•er•a•tive** (ə blit′ə rā′tiv, -ər ə tiv), *adj.*

ob•li•ves•cence (ob′lə ves′əns), *n.* the process of forgetting. [< L *oblīv(isci)* to forget + -ESCENCE]

ob•liv•i•on (ə bliv′ē ən), *n.* **1.** the state of being completely forgotten or unknown: *a former movie star now in oblivion.* **2.** the state of forgetting or of being oblivious: *the oblivion of sleep.* **3.** official disregard or overlooking of offenses; pardon; amnesty. [1350–1400; ME < MF < L *oblīviōn-* (s. of *oblīviō*), equiv. to *obliv(isci)* to forget + *-iōn-* -ION; see OB-]

ob•liv•i•ous (ə bliv′ē əs), *adj.* **1.** unmindful; unconscious; unaware (usually fol. by *of* or *to*): *She was oblivious of his admiration.* **2.** forgetful; without remembrance or memory: *oblivious of my former failure.* **3.** *Archaic.* inducing forgetfulness. [1400–50; late ME < L *obliviōsus* forgetful, equiv. to *oblivi(sci)* to forget + *-ōsus* -OUS] **—ob•liv′i•ous•ly,** *adv.* **—ob•liv′i•ous•ness,** *n.*
—Syn. 2. See **absent-minded.**

ob•long (ob′lông′, -long′), *adj.* **1.** elongated, usually from the square or circular form. **2.** in the form of a rectangle one of whose dimensions is greater than the other. —*n.* **3.** an oblong figure. [1375–1425; late ME *oblonge* < L *oblongus* rather long, equiv. to *ob-* OB- + *longus* LONG[1]] **—ob′long•ish,** *adj.* **—ob′long•ly,** *adv.* **—ob′long•ness,** *n.*

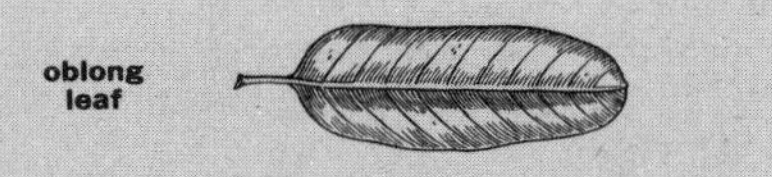
oblong leaf

ob•long•a•ta (ob′lông gä′tə, -long-), *n., pl.* **-tas, -tae** (-tē). See **medulla oblongata.** [< NL: lit., OBLONG; see -ATE[1]]

ob•lo•quy (ob′lə kwē), *n., pl.* **-quies. 1.** censure, blame, or abusive language aimed at a person or thing, esp. by numerous persons or by the general public. **2.** discredit, disgrace, or bad repute resulting from public blame, abuse, or denunciation. [1425–75; late ME < LL *obloquium* contradiction, equiv. to L *obloqu(ī)* to contradict (*ob-* OB- + *loquī* to speak) + *-ium* -IUM] **—ob•lo•qui•al** (o blō′kwē əl), *adj.*
—Syn. 1. reproach, calumny; aspersion, revilement. **—Ant. 1.** praise. **2.** credit.

ob•nounce (ob nouns′), *v.i.,* **-nounced, -nounc•ing.** (in ancient Rome) to announce an unfavorable omen. [1735–45; < L *obnūntiāre,* equiv. to *ob-* OB- + *nūntiāre* to tell (*nūnti(us)* messenger + *-āre* inf. suffix)]

ob•nox•ious (əb nok′shəs), *adj.* **1.** highly objectionable or offensive; odious: *obnoxious behavior.* **2.** annoying or objectionable due to being a showoff or attracting undue attention to oneself: *an obnoxious little brat.* **3.** *Archaic.* exposed or liable to harm, evil, or anything objectionable. **4.** *Obs.* liable to punishment or censure; reprehensible. [1575–85; < L *obnoxiōsus* harmful, equiv. to *ob-* OB- + *noxiōsus* NOXIOUS] **—ob•nox′ious•ly,** *adv.* **—ob•nox′ious•ness,** *n.*
—Syn. 1. See **hateful. —Ant. 1.** delightful.

ob•nu•bi•late (ob nōō′bə lāt′, -nyōō′-), *v.t.,* **-lat•ed, -lat•ing.** to cloud over; becloud; obscure. [1575–85; < L *obnūbilātus,* ptp. of *obnūbilāre* to darken, obscure, equiv. to *ob-* OB- + *nūbilāre* to become cloudy, v. deriv. of *nūbilus* cloudy; see NUBILOUS] **—ob•nu′bi•la′tion,** *n.*

o•boe[1] (ō′bō), *n.* **1.** a woodwind instrument having a slender conical, tubular body and a double-reed mouthpiece. **2.** (in an organ) a reed stop with a sound like that of an oboe. **3.** (a word formerly used in communications to represent the letter *O.*) [1690–1700; < It < F *hautbois,* equiv. to *haut* high + *bois* wood; see HAUTBOY]

oboe (def. 1)

o•boe[2] (ō′bō), *n.* (*sometimes cap*). a navigation system utilizing two radar ground stations that measure the distance to an aircraft and then radio the information to the aircraft. [1940–45; special use of OBOE[1]]

o′boe d'a•mour′ (də mōōr′), an oboe with a bulb-shaped bell that is pitched a minor third below the range of the conventional oboe and was much used in music of the Baroque period. [1875–80; < It *oboe d'amore* lit., oboe of love]

o•bo•ist (ō′bō ist), *n.* a player of the oboe. [1860–65; OBOE[1] + -IST]

ob•ol (ob′əl), *n.* **1.** a silver coin of ancient Greece, the sixth part of a drachma. **2.** obole. [1660–70; see OBOLUS]

ob•ole (ob′ōl), *n.* a silver-alloy coin of France issued during the Middle Ages, the 24th part of a sol, or one-half denier. Also, **obol, obolus.** [1595–1605; < F < L *obolus* OBOLUS]

ob•o•lus (ob′ə ləs), *n., pl.* **-li** (-lī′). **1.** a modern Greek unit of weight equal to 0.1 gram. **2.** obole. [1350–1400; ME < L < Gk *obolós* small coin, weight]

O•bo•te (ō bō′tā), *n.* **(Apollo) Milton,** born 1924, Ugandan political leader: president 1966–71 and 1980–85.

ob•o•vate (ob ō′vāt), *adj.* inversely ovate; ovate with the narrow end at the base. [1775–85; OB- + OVATE]

obovate leaf

ob•o•void (ob ō′void), *adj.* inversely ovoid; ovoid with the narrow end at the base, as certain fruits. [1810–20; OB- + OVOID]

O'Boyle (ō boil′), *n.* **Patrick Aloysius,** born 1896, U.S. Roman Catholic clergyman: archbishop of Washington, D.C., 1947–73.

ob•pyr•i•form (ob pir′ə fôrm′), *adj.* inversely pear-shaped; pear-shaped with the narrow end at the base. [1865–75; OB- + PYRIFORM]

O•brecht (ō′bʀeкнт), *n.* **Ja•cob** (yä′kôp), 1430–1505, Dutch composer and conductor. Also, **Hobrecht.**

O•bre•gón (ô′vʀe gôn′), *n.* **Al•va•ro** (äl′vä ʀô), 1880–1928, Mexican general and statesman: president 1920–24.

O•bre•no•vić (*Serbo-Croatian.* ô′bʀe nô vich), *n.* **A•le•ksan•dar** (*Serbo-Croatian.* ä′le kän′däʀ). See **Alexander I** (def. 3).

O•bren•o•vich (ō bren′ə vich′), *n.* **Alexander.** See **Alexander I** (def. 3).

ob•rep•tion (o brep′shən), *n.* **1.** *Canon Law.* fraud in obtaining or attempting to obtain something from an official. Cf. **subreption** (def. 1). **2.** *Scots Law.* the act of obtaining something, as an escheat, by falsehood. Cf. **subreption** (def. 2). [1605–15; < L *obreptiōn-* (s. of *obreptiō*) a surprise, equiv. to *ob-* OB- + *rept(us)* (see REPTILE) + *-iōn-* -ION] **—ob•rep•ti•tious** (ob′rep tish′əs), *adj.* **—ob′rep•ti′tious•ly,** *adv.*

O'Bri′en pota′toes (ō brī′ən), *Cookery.* home fries prepared with diced green pepper. [perh. from the conventional association between the Irish and potatoes, *O'Brien* being taken as a typical Irish surname]

OBrit, Old British.

ob•ro•ga•tion (ob′rə gā′shən), *n.* *Civil Law.* the annulment or alteration of a law by the enactment of a new one. [1650–60; < L *obrogātiōn-* (s. of *obrogātiō*), equiv. to *ob-* OB- + *rogātiōn-* ROGATION]

obs., 1. observation. **2.** observatory. **3.** obsolete. Also, **Obs.**

ob•scene (əb sēn′), *adj.* **1.** offensive to morality or decency; indecent; depraved: *obscene language.* **2.** causing uncontrolled sexual desire. **3.** abominable; disgusting; repulsive. [1585–95; < L *obscēnus, obscaenus*] **—ob•scene′ly,** *adv.* **—ob•scene′ness,** *n.*

ob•scen•i•ty (əb sen′i tē, -sē′ni-), *n., pl.* **-ties** for 2, 3. **1.** the character or quality of being obscene; indecency; lewdness. **2.** something obscene, as a picture or story. **3.** an obscene word or expression, esp. when used as an invective. [1600–10; < F *obscenité* < L *obscēnitās,* equiv. to *obscēn(us)* OBSCENE + *-itās* -ITY]

ob•scu•rant (əb skyōōr′ənt), *n.* **1.** a person who strives to prevent the increase and spread of knowledge. **2.** a person who obscures. —*adj.* **3.** pertaining to or characteristic of obscurants. **4.** tending to make obscure. [1790–1800; < L *obscūrant-* (s. of *obscūrāns,* prp. of *obscūrāre*), equiv. to *obscūr(us)* dark + *-ant-* -ANT]

ob•scu•rant•ism (əb skyōōr′ən tiz′əm, ob′skyōō ran′tiz əm), *n.* **1.** opposition to the increase and spread of knowledge. **2.** deliberate obscurity or evasion of clarity. [1825–35; < F *obscurantisme;* see OBSCURANT, -ISM] **—ob•scu′rant•ist,** *n., adj.*

ob•scu•ra•tion (ob′skyōō rā′shən), *n.* **1.** the act of obscuring. **2.** the state of being obscured. [1425–75; late ME < L *obscūrātiōn-* (s. of *obscūrātiō*) a darkening, equiv. to *obscūrāt(us),* ptp. of *obscūrāre* (*obscūr(us)* dark + *-ātus* -ATE[1]) + *-iōn-* -ION; see -ATION]

ob•scure (əb skyōōr′), *adj.,* **-scur•er, -scur•est,** *v.,* **-scured, -scur•ing,** *n.* —*adj.* **1.** (of meaning) not clear or plain; ambiguous, vague, or uncertain: *an obscure sentence in the contract.* **2.** not clear to the understanding; hard to perceive: *obscure motivations.* **3.** (of language, style, a speaker, etc.) not expressing the meaning clearly or plainly. **4.** indistinct to the sight or any other sense; not readily seen, heard, etc.; faint. **5.** inconspicuous or unnoticeable: *the obscure beginnings of a great movement.* **6.** of little or no prominence, note, fame, or distinction: *an obscure French artist.* **7.** far from public notice, worldly affairs, or important activities; remote; retired: *an obscure little town.* **8.** lacking in light or illumination; dark; dim; murky: *an obscure back room.* **9.** enveloped in, concealed by, or frequenting darkness. **10.** not bright or lustrous; dull or darkish, as color or appearance. **11.** (of a vowel) having the reduced or neutral sound usually represented by the schwa (ə). —*v.t.* **12.** to conceal or conceal by confusing (the meaning of a statement, poem, etc.). **13.** to make dark, dim, indistinct, etc. **14.** to reduce or neutralize (a vowel) to the sound usually represented by a schwa (ə). —*n.* **15.** obscurity. [1350–1400; ME < OF *oscur, obscur* < L *obscūrus* dark] **—ob•scur•ed•ly** (əb skyōōr′id lē), **ob•scure′ly,** *adv.* **—ob•scure′ness,** *n.*
—Syn. 1. doubtful, dubious. See **mysterious. 4.** blurred, veiled. **6.** undistinguished, unnoted, unknown. **7.** secluded, inconspicuous, unnoticeable, unnoticed. **8.** cloudy, dusky, somber. See **dark. —Ant. 1.** certain. **4.** clear. **6.** noted. **7.** conspicuous. **8.** bright.

ob•scu•ri•ty (əb skyōōr′i tē), *n., pl.* **-ties. 1.** the state or quality of being obscure. **2.** the condition of being unknown: *He lived in obscurity for years before winning acclaim.* **3.** uncertainty of meaning or expression; ambiguity. **4.** an unknown or unimportant person or thing. **5.** darkness; dimness; indistinctness. [1470–80; late ME < MF *obscurite* < L *obscūritās,* equiv. to *obscūr(us)* OBSCURE + *-itās* -ITY]

ob•se•crate (ob′si krāt′), *v.t.,* **-crat•ed, -crat•ing.** to entreat solemnly; beseech; supplicate. [1590–1600; < L *obsecrātus* (ptp. of *obsecrāre* to supplicate), equiv. to *ob-* OB- + *secr-* (comb. form of *sacr-,* s. of *sacer* SACRED) + *-ātus* -ATE[1]] **—ob′se•cra′tion,** *n.*

ob•se•quence (ob′si kwəns), *n.* willingness or eagerness to comply, please, serve, etc.; obsequiousness. Also, **ob•se•que•ence** (ob sē′kwē əns). [1595–1605; < L *obsequentia,* equiv. to *obsequent-,* s. of *obsequēns* prp. of *obsequī* to comply with (see OBSEQUIOUS) + *-ia* -IA]

ob′se•quent stream′ (ob′si kwənt), *Geol.* a stream flowing in a direction opposite to that of the dip of the local strata. Cf. **consequent stream.** [1890–95]

ob•se•qui•ous (əb sē′kwē əs), *adj.* **1.** characterized by or showing servile complaisance or deference; fawning: *an obsequious bow.* **2.** servilely compliant or deferential: *obsequious servants.* **3.** obedient; dutiful. [1375–1425; late ME < L *obsequiōsus,* equiv. to *obsequi(um)* compliance (*obsequ(ī)* to comply with (*ob-* OB- + *sequī* to follow) + *-ium* -IUM) + *-ōsus* -OUS] **—ob•se′qui•ous•ly,** *adv.* **—ob•se′qui•ous•ness,** *n.*
—Syn. 1. sycophantic, flattering. **2.** cringing, submissive. See **servile.**

ob•se•quy (ob′si kwē), *n., pl.* **-quies.** Usually, **obsequies.** a funeral rite or ceremony. [1350–1400; ME *obseque* < MF < LL *obsequiae,* alter. (by confusion with *exsequiae* funeral rites) of *obsequia,* pl. of L *obsequium;* see OBSEQUIOUS]

ob•serv•a•ble (əb zûr′və bəl), *adj.* **1.** capable of being or liable to be observed; noticeable; visible; discernible: *an observable change in attitude.* **2.** worthy or important enough to be celebrated, followed, or observed: *an observable holiday.* **3.** deserving of attention; noteworthy. [1600–10; < L *observābilis* remarkable, equiv. to *observā(re)* to OBSERVE + *-bilis* -BLE] **—ob•serv′a•bil′i•ty, ob•serv′a•ble•ness,** *n.* **—ob•serv′a•bly,** *adv.*

ob•serv•ance (əb zûr′vəns), *n.* **1.** an act or instance of following, obeying, or conforming to: *the observance of traffic laws.* **2.** a keeping or celebration by appropriate procedure, ceremonies, etc.: *the observance of the Sabbath.* **3.** a procedure, ceremony, or rite, as for a particular occasion: *patriotic observances.* **4.** a rule or custom to be followed or obeyed; a customary practice. **5.** *Rom. Cath. Ch.* **a.** a rule or discipline for a religious house or order. **b.** a house or order observing a rule or discipline. **6.** an act or instance of watching, noting, or perceiving; observation. **7.** respectful attention or service. **8.** *Archaic.* courteous attention as to a person; dutiful service. [1175–1225; ME *observaunce* < OF < LL *observantia,* L: esteem, attention, deriv. of *observant-* (s. of *observāns*), prp. of *observāre.* See OBSERVE, -ANCE]
—Syn. 1. compliance, adherence, heedfulness.

ob•serv•ant (əb zûr′vənt), *adj.* **1.** quick to notice or perceive; alert. **2.** looking at, watching, or regarding attentively; watchful. **3.** careful in the observing of a law, custom, religious ritual, or the like. —*n.* **4.** an observer of law or rule. **5.** (*cap.*) Also, **Ob•ser•van•tine** (ob zûr′vən tin, -tēn′). a member of a Franciscan order that observes the strict rule of St. Francis. [1425–75; late ME < F, prp. of *observer.* See OBSERVE, -ANT] **—ob•serv′ant•ly,** *adv.*
—Syn. 1. perceptive. **2.** attentive, heedful, mindful, aware. **3.** obedient. **—Ant. 1.** dull, slow. **2.** heedless.

ob•ser•va•tion (ob′zûr vā′shən), *n.* **1.** an act or instance of noticing or perceiving. **2.** an act or instance of regarding attentively or watching. **3.** the faculty or habit of observing or noticing. **4.** notice: *to escape a person's observation.* **5.** an act or instance of viewing or noting a fact or occurrence for some scientific or other special purpose: *the observation of blood pressure under stress.* **6.** the information or record secured by such an act. **7.** something that is learned in the course of observing things: *My observation is that such clouds mean a storm.* **8.** a remark, comment, or statement based on what one has noticed or observed. **9.** the condition of being observed. **10.** *Navig.* **a.** the measurement of the altitude or azimuth of a heavenly body for navigational purposes. **b.** the information obtained by such a measurement. **11.** *Obs.* observance, as of the law. [1350–1400; ME < L *observātiōn-* (s. of *observātiō*), equiv. to *observāt(us)* (ptp. of *observāre* to OBSERVE) + *-iōn-* -ION]
—Syn. 3. attention. **8.** pronouncement, opinion. See **remark.**

ob•ser•va•tion•al (ob′zûr vā′shə nl), *adj.* of, pertaining to, or founded on observation, esp. founded on observation rather than experiment. [1825–35; OBSERVATION + -AL[1]] **—ob′ser•va′tion•al•ly,** *adv.*

CONCISE PRONUNCIATION KEY: *act, cāpe, dâre, pärt; set, ēqual; if, īce; ox, ōver, ôrder, oil, bŏŏk, bōōt, out; up, ûrge; child; sing; shoe; thin, that;* zh as in *treasure.* ə = *a* as in *alone, e* as in *system, i* as in *easily, o* as in *gallop, u* as in *circus;* ᵊ as in *fire* (fīᵊr), *hour* (ouᵊr). l and n can serve as syllabic consonants, as in *cradle* (krād′l), and *button* (but′n). See the full key inside the front cover.

observa′tion car′, a railroad passenger car having a lounge or platform from which the scenery can be viewed. [1870–75, *Amer.*]

observa′tion post′, *Mil.* a forward position, often on high ground, from which enemy activity can be observed and, particularly, from which artillery or mortar fire can be directed.

ob·serv·a·to·ry (əb zûr′və tôr′ē, -tōr′ē), *n., pl.* **-ries.** **1.** a place or building equipped and used for making observations of astronomical, meteorological, or other natural phenomena, esp. a place equipped with a powerful telescope for observing the planets and stars. **2.** an institution that controls or carries on the work of such a place. **3.** a place or structure that provides an extensive view; lookout. [1670–80; < L *observā(re)* to OBSERVE + -TORY[2]]

ob·serve (əb zûrv′), *v.,* **-served, -serv·ing.** —*v.t.* **1.** to see, watch, perceive, or notice: *He observed the passersby in the street.* **2.** to regard with attention, esp. so as to see or learn something: *I want you to observe her reaction to the judge's question.* **3.** to watch, view, or note for a scientific, official, or other special purpose: *to observe an eclipse.* **4.** to state by way of comment; remark: *He observed frequently that clerks were not as courteous as they used to be.* **5.** to keep or maintain in one's action, conduct, etc.: *You must observe quiet.* **6.** to obey, comply with, or conform to: *to observe laws.* **7.** to show regard for by some appropriate procedure, ceremony, etc.: *to observe Palm Sunday.* **8.** to perform duly or solemnize (ceremonies, rites, etc.). **9.** to note or inspect closely for an omen or sign of future events. —*v.i.* **10.** to notice. **11.** to act as an observer. **12.** to remark or comment (usually fol. by *on* or *upon*). [1350–1400; ME *observen* < MF *observer* < L *observāre* to watch, regard, attend to, equiv. to *ob-* OB- + *servāre* to keep, save, pay heed to] —**ob·serv·ed·ly** (əb zûr′vid lē), *adv.* —**ob·serv′ing·ly,** *adv.*
—**Syn. 2.** note. OBSERVE, WITNESS imply paying strict attention to what one sees or perceives. Both are "continuative" in action. To OBSERVE is to mark or be attentive to something seen, heard, etc.; to consider carefully; to watch steadily: *to observe the behavior of birds, a person's pronunciation.* To WITNESS, formerly to be present when something was happening, has added the idea of having observed with sufficient care to be able to give an account as evidence: *to witness an accident.* **4.** mention, say. **6.** follow, fulfill. **7.** celebrate, keep. —**Ant. 1–3, 6–8.** ignore.

ob·serv·er (əb zûr′vər), *n.* **1.** someone or something that observes. **2.** a delegate to an assembly or gathering, who is sent to observe and report but not to take part officially in its activities. **3.** *U.S. Air Force.* **a.** a member of an aircrew, other than the pilot, holding an aeronautical rating. **b.** a person who maintains observation in an aircraft during flight. **4.** Also called **air observer, aircraft observer.** *U.S. Army.* a person who serves in an aircraft as a reconnoiterer and directs artillery fire. [1545–55; OBSERVE + -ER[1]] —**ob·serv′er·ship′,** *n.*

ob·sess (əb ses′), *v.t.* **1.** to dominate or preoccupy the thoughts, feelings, or desires of (a person); beset, trouble, or haunt persistently or abnormally: *Suspicion obsessed him.* —*v.i.* **2.** to think about something unceasingly or persistently; dwell obsessively upon something. [1495–1505; < L *obsessus,* ptp. of *obsidēre* to occupy, frequent, besiege, equiv. to *ob-* OB- + *-sid(ēre)* comb. form of *sedēre* to SIT] —**ob·sess′ing·ly,** *adv.* —**ob·ses′sor,** *n.*
—**Syn. 1.** possess, control, haunt.

ob·sessed (əb sest′), *adj.* **1.** having an obsession (usually fol. by *with* or *by*): *He is obsessed with eliminating guilt.* **2.** having or displaying signs of an obsession: *The audiophile entered the record store wearing an obsessed smile.* [1835–45; OBSESS + -ED[2]]

ob·ses·sion (əb sesh′ən), *n.* **1.** the domination of one's thoughts or feelings by a persistent idea, image, desire, etc. **2.** the idea, image, desire, feeling, etc., itself. **3.** the state of being obsessed. **4.** the act of obsessing. [1505–15; < L *obsessiōn-* (s. of *obsessiō*) blockade, siege, equiv. to *obsess(us)* (see OBSESS) + *-iōn-* -ION] —**ob·ses′sion·al,** *adj.*

ob·ses·sive (əb ses′iv), *adj.* **1.** being, pertaining to, or resembling an obsession: *an obsessive fear of illness.* **2.** causing an obsession. **3.** excessive, esp. extremely so. —*n.* **4.** someone who has an obsession or obsessions; a person who thinks or behaves in an obsessive manner. [1910–15; OBSESS(ION) + -IVE] —**ob·ses′sive·ly,** *adv.* —**ob·ses′sive·ness,** *n.*

ob·ses·sive-com·pul·sive (əb ses′iv kəm pul′siv), *adj.* **1.** of or pertaining to a personality style characterized by perfectionism, indecision, conscientiousness, concern with detail, rigidity, and inhibition. **2.** *Psychiatry.* of or pertaining to a neurosis characterized by persistent intrusion of unwanted thoughts (obsessions) or the performance of actions, as repeated hand-washing, that one is unable to stop (compulsions). —*n.* **3.** a person having such a personality style. [1925–30]

ob·sid·i·an (əb sid′ē ən), *n.* a volcanic glass similar in composition to granite, usually dark but transparent in thin pieces, and having a good conchoidal fracture. [1350–1400; < L *Obsidiānus,* printer's error for *Obsiānus* pertaining to *Obsius,* the discoverer (according to Pliny) of a similar mineral in Ethiopia; r. ME *obsianus* < L; see -AN]

obsid′ian dat′ing, *Archaeol.* a method of dating obsidian artifacts or debitage by calculating how long it has taken to produce a given thickness of a hydration layer within such matter. [1965–70]

ob·sid′i·o·nal coin′ (əb sid′ē ə nl). See **siege piece.** [1800–10; < L *obsidiōnālis* of a siege, equiv. to *obsid(ēre)* to besiege + *-iōn-* -ION + *-ālis* -AL[1]]

CONCISE ETYMOLOGY KEY: <, descended or borrowed from; >, whence; b., blend of, blended; c., cognate with; cf., compare; deriv., derivative; equiv., equivalent; imit., imitative; obl., oblique; r., replacing; s., stem; sp., spelling, spelled; resp., respelling, respelled; trans., translation; ?, origin unknown; *, unattested; ‡, probably earlier than. See the full key inside the front cover.

obsolesc., obsolescent.

ob·so·lesce (ob′sə les′), *v.i.* **-lesced, -lesc·ing.** to be or become obsolescent. [1870–75; < L *obsolescere;* see OBSOLETE]

ob·so·les·cence (ob′sə les′əns), *n.* the state, process, or condition of being or becoming obsolete. [1820–30; OBSOLESC(ENT) + -ENCE]

ob·so·les·cent (ob′sə les′ənt), *adj.* **1.** becoming obsolete; passing out of use, as a word: *an obsolescent term.* **2.** becoming outdated or outmoded, as machinery or weapons. **3.** *Biol.* gradually disappearing or imperfectly developed, as vestigial organs. [1745–55; < L *obsolēscent-* (s. of *obsolēscēns,* prp. of *obsolēscere* to fall into disuse). See OBSOLETE, -ESCENT] —**ob′so·les′cent·ly,** *adv.*

ob·so·lete (ob′sə lēt′, ob′sə lēt′), *adj., v.,* **-let·ed, -let·ing.** —*adj.* **1.** no longer in general use; fallen into disuse: *an obsolete expression.* **2.** of a discarded or outmoded type; out of date: *an obsolete battleship.* **3.** (of a linguistic form) no longer in use, esp., out of use for at least the past century. Cf. **archaic. 4.** effaced by wearing down or away. **5.** *Biol.* imperfectly developed or rudimentary in comparison with the corresponding character in other individuals, as of the opposite sex or of a related species. —*v.t.* **6.** to make obsolete by replacing with something newer or better; antiquate: *Automation has obsoleted many factory workers.* [1570–80; < L *obsolētus,* ptp. of *obsolēscere* to fall into disuse, perh. equiv. to *ob-* OB- + *sol(ēre)* to be accustomed to + *-ēscere* -ESCE] —**ob′so·lete′ly,** *adv.* —**ob′so·lete′ness,** *n.*
—**Syn. 2.** antiquated, ancient, old. —**Ant. 1, 2.** new, modern.

ob·sta·cle (ob′stə kəl), *n.* something that obstructs or hinders progress. [1300–50; ME < OF < L *obstāculum,* equiv. to *obstā(re)* to face, block, hinder (*ob-* OB- + *stāre* to STAND) + *-culum* -CLE[2]]
—**Syn.** OBSTACLE, OBSTRUCTION, HINDRANCE, IMPEDIMENT refer to something that interferes with or prevents action or progress. An OBSTACLE is something, material or nonmaterial, that stands in the way of literal or figurative progress: *Lack of imagination is an obstacle to one's advancement.* An OBSTRUCTION is something that more or less completely blocks a passage: *A blood clot is an obstruction to the circulation.* A HINDRANCE keeps back by interfering and delaying: *Interruptions are a hindrance to one's work.* An IMPEDIMENT interferes with proper functioning: *an impediment in one's speech.* —**Ant.** help.

ob′stacle course′, **1.** a military training area having obstacles, as hurdles, ditches, and walls, that must be surmounted or crossed in succession. **2.** *Informal.* an event, situation, course of action, or the like that presents many challenges or difficulties.

ob′stacle race′, a foot race in which the contestants are prevented in a specific way from covering the full course at top speed, as by having hurdles to jump, sacks enclosing the legs, or potatoes to pick up. [1865–70] —**ob′stacle rac′er.**

obstet., **1.** obstetric. **2.** obstetrics.

ob·stet·ri·cal (əb ste′tri kəl), *adj.* **1.** of or pertaining to the care and treatment of women in childbirth and during the period before and after delivery. **2.** of or pertaining to childbirth or obstetrics. *Abbr.:* OB, ob Also, **ob·stet′ric.** [1735–45; < NL *obstetrīcus* pertaining to a midwife, alter. of L *obstetrīcius,* deriv. of *obstetrīx,* equiv. to *ob-* OB- + *ste-* (comb. form of *stāre* to STAND) + *-trix* -TRIX] —**ob·stet′ri·cal·ly,** *adv.*

ob·ste·tri·cian (ob′sti trish′ən), *n.* a physician who specializes in obstetrics. *Abbr.:* OB, ob [1820–30; < L *obstetrīci(a)* midwifery (n. use of fem. of *obstetrīcius;* see OBSTETRICAL) + -AN]

ob·stet·rics (əb ste′triks), *n.* (*used with a singular v.*) the branch of medical science concerned with childbirth and caring for and treating women in or in connection with childbirth. *Abbr.:* OB, ob [1810–20; see OBSTETRICAL, -ICS]

ob·sti·na·cy (ob′stə nə sē), *n., pl.* **-cies** for 5. **1.** the quality or state of being obstinate; stubbornness. **2.** unyielding or stubborn adherence to one's purpose, opinion, etc. **3.** stubborn persistence: *The garrison fought on with incredible obstinacy.* **4.** resistance to cure, relief, or treatment, as a disease. **5.** an instance of being obstinate; an obstinate act, viewpoint, etc. [1350–1400; ME < ML *obstinātia,* deriv. of L *obstinātus* (see OBSTINATE); see -CY]

ob·sti·nate (ob′stə nit), *adj.* **1.** firmly or stubbornly adhering to one's purpose, opinion, etc.; not yielding to argument, persuasion, or entreaty. **2.** characterized by inflexible persistence or an unyielding attitude; inflexibly persisted in or carried out: *obstinate advocacy of high tariffs.* **3.** not easily controlled or overcome: *the obstinate growth of weeds.* **4.** not yielding readily to treatment, as a disease. [1350–1400; ME < L *obstinātus* (ptp. of *obstināre* to set one's mind on, be determined), equiv. to *ob-* OB- + *-stin-,* comb. form of *stan-* (deriv. of *stāre* to STAND) + *-ātus* -ATE[1]] —**ob′sti·nate·ly,** *adv.* —**ob′sti·nate·ness,** *n.*
—**Syn. 1.** mulish, obdurate, unyielding, unbending, intractable, perverse, inflexible, refractory, pertinacious. See **stubborn.** —**Ant. 1.** submissive, tractable.

ob·sti·pa·tion (ob′stə pā′shən), *n. Med.* obstinate constipation. [1590–1600; < LL *obstīpātiōn-* (s. of *obstīpātiō*) close pressure, equiv. to *ob-* OB- + *stīpāt(us)* (ptp. of *stīpāre* to press) + *-iōn-* -ION]

ob·strep·er·ous (əb strep′ər əs), *adj.* **1.** resisting control or restraint in a difficult manner; unruly. **2.** noisy, clamorous, or boisterous: *obstreperous children.* [1590–1600; < L *obstreperus* clamorous, akin to *obstrepere* to make a noise at (*ob-* OB- + *strepere* to rattle); see -OUS] —**ob·strep′er·ous·ly,** *adv.* —**ob·strep′er·ous·ness, ob·strep·e·ros·i·ty** (əb strep′ə ros′i tē), *n.*
—**Syn. 1.** uncontrolled, refractory. —**Ant. 1.** obedient. **2.** calm.

ob·struct (əb strukt′), *v.t.* **1.** to block or close up with an obstacle; make difficult to pass: *Debris obstructed the road.* **2.** to interrupt, hinder, or oppose the passage, progress, course, etc., of. **3.** to block from sight; to be in the way of (a view, passage, etc.). [1605–15; < L *obstructus* (ptp. of *obstruere* to build or pile up in the way, bar). See OB-, CONSTRUCT] —**ob·struct′ed·ly,** *adv.* —**ob·struct′er, ob·struc′tor,** *n.* —**ob·struct′ing·ly,** *adv.* —**ob·struc′tive,** *adj.* —**ob·struc′tive·ly,** *adv.* —**ob·struc′tive·ness, ob·struc·tiv·i·ty** (ob′struk tiv′i tē), *n.*
—**Syn. 1.** stop, choke, clog, hinder, impede, prevent; check, slow, retard, arrest. —**Ant. 1.** encourage, further.

ob·struc·tion (əb struk′shən), *n.* **1.** something that obstructs, blocks, or closes up with an obstacle or obstacles; obstacle or hindrance: *obstructions to navigation.* **2.** an act or instance of obstructing. **3.** the state of being obstructed. **4.** the delaying or preventing of business before a deliberative body, esp. a legislative group, by parliamentary contrivances. [1525–35; < L *obstructiōn-* (s. of *obstructiō*) barrier. See OBSTRUCT, -ION]
—**Syn. 1.** barrier, bar, impediment. See **obstacle. 3.** stoppage. —**Ant. 1, 3.** encouragement.

ob·struc·tion·ist (əb struk′shə nist), *n.* **1.** a person who deliberately delays or prevents progress. **2.** a person who delays or obstructs the business before a legislative body by parliamentary contrivances or legalistic maneuvers. [1840–50; OBSTRUCTION + -IST] —**ob·struc′tion·ism,** *n.* —**ob·struc′tion·is′tic,** *adj.*

ob·stru·ent (ob′stro͞o ənt), *adj.* **1.** *Med.* (of a substance) producing an obstruction. **2.** *Phonet.* (of a speech sound) characterized by stoppage or obstruction of the flow of air from the lungs. Cf. **sonorant.** —*n.* **3.** *Med.* a medicine that closes the natural passages of the body. **4.** *Phonet.* an obstruent speech sound; a stop, fricative, or affricate. Cf. **sonorant** (def. 2). [1660–70; < L *obstruent-* (s. of *obstruēns,* prp. of *obstruere*); see OBSTRUCT, -ENT]

ob·tain (əb tān′), *v.t.* **1.** to come into possession of; get, acquire, or procure, as through an effort or by a request: *to obtain permission; to obtain a better income.* **2.** *Obs.* to attain or reach. —*v.i.* **3.** to be prevalent, customary, or in vogue; prevail: *the morals that obtained in Rome.* **4.** *Archaic.* to succeed. [1375–1425; late ME *obteinen* < MF *obtenir* < L *obtinēre* to take hold of, equiv. to *ob-* OB- + *-tinēre* (comb. form of *tenēre* to hold)] —**ob·tain′a·ble,** *adj.* —**ob·tain′a·bil′i·ty,** *n.* —**ob·tain′er,** *n.* —**ob·tain′ment,** *n.*
—**Syn. 1.** gain, achieve, earn, win, attain. See **get.** —**Ant. 1.** lose, forgo.

ob·tect (ob tekt′), *adj.* (of a pupa) having the antennae, legs, and wings glued to the surface of the body. Also, **ob·tect′ed.** Cf. **exarate.** [1810–20; < L *obtēctus* (ptp. of *obtegere,* var. of *obtigere* to cover over), equiv. to *ob-* OB- + *teg(ere)* to cover (see THATCH, TOGA) + *-tus* ptp. suffix]

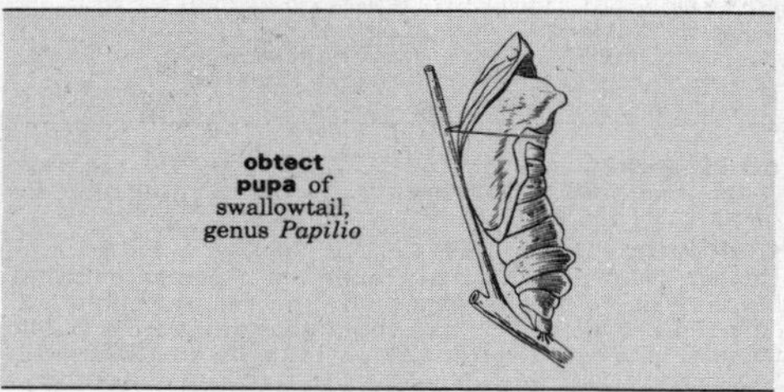
obtect pupa of swallowtail, genus *Papilio*

ob·test (ob test′), *v.t.* **1.** to invoke as witness. **2.** to supplicate earnestly; beseech. —*v.i.* **3.** to protest. **4.** to make supplication; beseech. [1540–50; < L *obtestārī,* equiv. to *ob-* OB- + *test(is)* a witness + *-ārī* inf. suffix] —**ob′tes·ta′tion,** *n.*

ob·trude (əb tro͞od′), *v.,* **-trud·ed, -trud·ing.** —*v.t.* **1.** to thrust (something) forward or upon a person, esp. without warrant or invitation: *to obtrude one's opinions upon others.* **2.** to thrust forth; push out. —*v.i.* **3.** to thrust forward, esp. unduly; intrude. [1545–55; < L *obtrūdere* to thrust against, equiv. to *ob-* OB- + *trūdere* to thrust] —**ob·trud′er,** *n.*
—**Syn. 1.** impose, force. **3.** shove, push.

ob·tru·sion (əb tro͞o′zhən), *n.* **1.** the act of obtruding. **2.** something obtruded. [1570–80; < LL *obtrūsiōn-* (s. of *obtrūsiō*), equiv. to L *obtrūs(us)* (*obtrūd(ere)* to OBTRUDE + *tus* ptp. suffix, with $dt > s$) + *-iōn-* -ION] —**ob·tru′sion·ist,** *n.*

ob·tru·sive (əb tro͞o′siv), *adj.* **1.** having or showing a disposition to obtrude, as by imposing oneself or one's opinions on others. **2.** (of a thing) obtruding itself: *an obtrusive error.* **3.** protruding; projecting. [1660–70; < L *obtrūs(us)* (see OBTRUSION) + -IVE] —**ob·tru′sive·ly,** *adv.* —**ob·tru′sive·ness,** *n.*
—**Syn. 1.** interfering, meddlesome, officious, presumptuous. **2.** blatant.

ob·tund (ob tund′), *v.t.* to blunt; dull; deaden. [1350–1400; ME < L *obtundere* to beat at, equiv. to *ob-* OB- + *tundere* to strike] —**ob·tund′ent,** *adj.* —**ob·tun′di·ty,** *n.*

ob·tu·rate (ob′tə rāt′, -tyə-), *v.t.,* **-rat·ed, -rat·ing.** **1.** to stop up; close. **2.** *Ordn.* to close (a hole or cavity) so as to prevent a flow of gas through it, esp. the escape of explosive gas from a gun tube during firing. [1550–60; < L *obtūrātus,* ptp. of *obtūrāre* to block, stop up] —**ob′tu·ra′tion,** *n.* —**ob′tu·ra′tor,** *n.*

ob·tuse (əb to͞os′, -tyo͞os′), *adj.* **1.** not quick or alert in perception, feeling, or intellect; not sensitive or observant; dull. **2.** not sharp, acute, or pointed; blunt in form. **3.** (of a leaf, petal, etc.) rounded at the extremity. **4.** indistinctly felt or perceived, as pain or sound. [1500–10; < L *obtūsus* dulled (ptp. of *obtundere*), equiv. to *ob-* OB- + *tūd-,* var. s. of *tundere* to beat + *-tus* ptp. suffix, with $dt > s$] —**ob·tuse′ly,** *adv.* —**ob·tuse′ness,** *n.*

—Syn. 1. unfeeling, tactless, insensitive; blind, imperceptive, unobservant; gauche, boorish; slow, dim.

obtuse′ an′gle, an angle greater than 90° but less than 180°. See diag. under **angle.** [1560–70] **—ob·tuse′-an′gled, ob·tuse-an·gu·lar** (əb to͞os′ang′gyə lər, -tyo͞os′), *adj.*

obtuse′ bisec′trix, *Crystall.* See under **bisectrix** (def. 1). [1895–1900]

obtuse′ tri′angle, *Geom.* a triangle with one obtuse angle. See diag. under **triangle.**

O·bu·da (ō′bo͝o do), *n.* See under **Budapest.**

OBulg., Old Bulgarian. Also, **OBulg**

ob·um·brant (ob um′brənt), *adj. Zool.* overhanging; projecting over another part. [1820–30; < L *obumbrant-* (s. of *obumbrāns*) (prp. of *obumbrāre* to overshadow), equiv. to *ob-* OB- + *umbr(āre)* to shade (deriv. of *umbra* shadow) + *-ant-* -ANT]

ob·um·brate (ob um′brāt), *v.,* **-brat·ed, -brat·ing,** *adj.* **—***v.t.* **1.** to darken, overshadow, or cloud. **—***adj.* **2.** *Obs.* overshadowed, darkened. [1505–15; < *obumbrātus,* ptp. of *obumbrāre,*; see OBUMBRANT, -ATE[1]] **—ob′um·bra′·tion,** *n.*

ob·verse (*n.* ob′vûrs; *adj.* ob vûrs′, ob′vûrs), *n.* **1.** the side of a coin, medal, flag, etc., that bears the principal design (opposed to *reverse*). **2.** the front or principal surface of anything. **3.** a counterpart. **4.** *Logic.* a proposition obtained from another by obversion. **—***adj.* **5.** facing the observer. **6.** corresponding to something else as a counterpart. **7.** having the base narrower than the top, as a leaf. [1650–60; < L *obversus* turned toward or against (ptp. of *obvertere*), equiv. to *ob-* OB- + *vert(ere)* to turn + *-tus* ptp. suffix, with *tt* > *s*]

ob·ver·sion (ob vûr′zhən, -shən), *n.* **1.** an act or instance of obverting. **2.** something that is obverted. **3.** *Logic.* a form of inference in which a negative proposition is obtained from an affirmative, or vice versa, as "None of us is immortal" is obtained by obversion from "All of us are mortal." [1840–50; < LL *obversiōn-* (s. of *obversiō*) a turning toward, equiv. to *obvers(us)* (see OBVERSE) + *-iōn-* -ION]

ob·vert (ob vûrt′), *v.t.* **1.** to turn (something) so as to show a different surface. **2.** *Logic.* to change (a proposition) by obversion. [1615–25; < L *obvertere* to turn toward, equiv. to *ob-* OB- + *vertere* to turn]

ob·vi·ate (ob′vē āt′), *v.t.,* **-at·ed, -at·ing.** to anticipate and prevent or eliminate (difficulties, disadvantages, etc.) by effective measures; render unnecessary: *to obviate the risk of serious injury.* [1590–1600; < L *obviātus,* ptp. of *obviāre* to act contrary to, deriv. of *obvius;* see OBVIOUS, -ATE[1]] **—ob·vi·a·ble** (ob′vē ə bəl), *adj.* **—ob′·vi·a′tion,** *n.* **—ob′vi·a′tor,** *n.*
—Syn. preclude, avert, anticipate.

ob·vi·ous (ob′vē əs), *adj.* **1.** easily seen, recognized, or understood; open to view or knowledge; evident: *an obvious advantage.* **2.** lacking in subtlety. **3.** *Obs.* being or standing in the way. [1580–90; < L *obvius* in the way, lying in the path, equiv. to *ob-* OB- + *vi(a)* WAY + *-us* adj. suffix (see -OUS)] **—ob′vi·ous·ly,** *adv.* **—ob′vi·ous·ness,** *n.*
—Syn. 1. plain, manifest, clear, palpable, unmistakable. See **apparent. —Ant. 1.** hidden.

ob·vo·lute (ob′və lo͞ot′), *adj.* **1.** rolled or turned in. **2.** *Bot.* noting or pertaining to a vernation in which two leaves are folded together in the bud so that one half of each is exterior and the other interior. [1750–60; < L *obvolūtus* (ptp. of *obvolvere* to cover by wrapping up), equiv. to *ob-* OB- + *volū-,* base of *volvere* to turn, roll + *-tus* ptp. suffix; see VOLUTE] **—ob′vo·lu′tion,** *n.* **—ob′·vo·lu′tive,** *adj.*

Ob·wal·den (*Ger.* ôp′väl′dən), *n.* one of the two divisions of the canton of Unterwalden, in central Switzerland. 25,100; 189 sq. mi. (490 sq. km). *Cap.:* Sarnen.

oc-, var. of **ob-** (by assimilation) before *c: occident.*

Oc., ocean. Also, **oc.**

o/c, overcharge.

O.C., *Philately.* original cover.

o.c., 1. *Archit.* on center. See **center** (def. 20). **2.** in the work cited. [< L *opere citātō*]

o·ca (ō′kə), *n.* **1.** a wood sorrel, *Oxalis tuberosa,* of the Andes, cultivated in South America for its edible tubers. **2.** a tuber of this plant. Also, **oka.** [1595–1605; < Sp < Quechua *oqa*]

O·cal·a (ō kal′ə), *n.* a city in central Florida. 37,170.

ocarina

oc·a·ri·na (ok′ə rē′nə), *n.* a simple musical wind instrument shaped somewhat like an elongated egg with a mouthpiece and finger holes. Also called **sweet potato.** [< It, orig. dial. (Emilia), dim. of *oca* goose (< LL *auca,* contr. of **avica,* deriv. of L *avis* bird), so called from the instrument's shape; appar. the name given to it by Giuseppe Donati of Budrio, near Bologna, who popularized a ceramic version c1860] **—oc′a·ri′nist,** *n.*

O'Ca·sey (ō kā′sē), *n.* **Sean** (shôn, shän), 1880–1964, Irish playwright.

occ., 1. occasional. **2.** occasionally. **3.** occident. **4.** occidental. **5.** occupation.

Oc·cam (ok′əm), *n.* **William of,** died 1349?, English scholastic philosopher. Also, **Ockham. —Oc′cam·ism,** *n.* **—Oc′cam·ist, Oc′cam·ite′,** *n.* **—Oc′cam·is′tic,** *adj.*

Oc′cam's ra′zor, the maxim that assumptions introduced to explain a thing must not be multiplied beyond necessity. [1900–05; after William of OCCAM]

occas., 1. occasional. **2.** occasionally.

oc·ca·sion (ə kā′zhən), *n.* **1.** a particular time, esp. as marked by certain circumstances or occurrences: *They met on three occasions.* **2.** a special or important time, event, ceremony, celebration, etc.: *His birthday will be quite an occasion.* **3.** a convenient or favorable time, opportunity, or juncture: *This slack period would be a good occasion to take inventory.* **4.** the immediate or incidental cause or reason for some action or result: *What is the occasion for this uproar?* **5.** (in the philosophy of Alfred North Whitehead) the coincidence of the eternal objects forming a specific point-event. **6. occasions,** *Obs.* **a.** needs or necessities. **b.** necessary business matters: *to go about one's lawful occasions.* **7. on occasion,** now and then; from time to time; occasionally: *She visits New York on occasion.* **—***v.t.* **8.** to give occasion or cause for; bring about. [1350–1400; ME *occasioun* < OF *occasion* < L *occāsiōn-* (s. of *occāsiō*), equiv. to *oc-* OC- + *cās(us)* (ptp. of *cadere* to fall, befall) + *-iōn-* -ION]
—Syn. 3. chance, opening. **4.** motive, inducement, influence. See **cause. 8.** motivate, originate, produce, create.

oc·ca·sion·al (ə kā′zhə nl), *adj.* **1.** occurring or appearing at irregular or infrequent intervals; occurring now and then: *an occasional headache.* **2.** intended for supplementary use when needed: *an occasional chair.* **3.** pertaining to, arising out of, or intended for the occasion: *occasional verses.* **4.** acting or serving for the occasion or only on particular occasions. **5.** serving as the occasion or incidental cause. [1560–70; OCCASION + -AL[1]] **—oc·ca′sion·al·ness, oc·ca′sion·al′i·ty,** *n.*

oc·ca·sion·al·ism (ə kā′zhə nl iz′əm), *n. Philos.* a theory that there is no natural interaction between mind and matter, but that God makes mental events correspond to physical perceptions and actions. [1835–45; OCCASIONAL + -ISM] **—oc·ca′sion·al·ist,** *n.* **—oc·ca′·sion·al·is′tic,** *adj.*

oc·ca·sion·al·ly (ə kā′zhə nl ē), *adv.* at times; from time to time; now and then. [1615–25; OCCASIONAL + -LY]

Oc·ci·dent (ok′si dənt), *n.* **1. the Occident, a.** the West; the countries of Europe and America. **b.** See **Western Hemisphere. 2.** (*l.c.*) the west; the western regions. [ME < MF < L *occident-* (s. of *occidēns*) prp. of *occidere* to fall, (of the sun) to set, equiv. to *oc-* OC- + *cid-* (comb. form of *cadere* to fall) + *-ent-* -ENT]

oc·ci·den·tal (ok′si den′tl), *adj.* **1.** (*usually cap.*) of, pertaining to, or characteristic of the Occident or its natives and inhabitants. **2.** western. **—***n.* **3.** (*usually cap.*) a native or inhabitant of the Occident. [1350–1400; ME < L *occidentālis* western, equiv. to *occident-* OCCIDENT + *-ālis* -AL[1]] **—oc′ci·den·tal′i·ty,** *n.* **—oc′ci·den′tal·ly,** *adv.*

Oc·ci·den·tal·ism (ok′si den′tl iz′əm), *n.* Occidental character or characteristics. [1830–40; OCCIDENTAL + -ISM] **—Oc′ci·den′tal·ist,** *n., adj.*

Oc·ci·den·tal·ize (ok′si den′tl īz′), *v.t.,* **-ized, -iz·ing.** to make Occidental. Also, *esp. Brit.,* **Oc′ci·den′tal·ise′.** [1865–70; OCCIDENTAL + -IZE] **—Oc′ci·den′tal·i·za′·tion,** *n.*

oc·cip·i·tal (ok sip′i tl), *Anat.* **—***adj.* **1.** of, pertaining to, or situated near the occiput or the occipital bone. **—***n.* **2.** any of several parts of the occiput, esp. the occipital bone. [1535–45; < ML *occipitālis,* equiv. to L *occipit-* (s. of *occiput*) OCCIPUT + *-ālis* -AL[1]] **—oc·cip′i·tal·ly,** *adv.*

occip′ital bone′, *Anat.* a curved, compound bone forming the back and part of the base of the skull. See diag. under **skull.** [1670–80]

occip′ital con′dyle, *Anat.* a protrusion on the occipital bone of the skull that forms a joint with the first cervical vertebra, enabling the head to move relative to the neck. [1855–60]

occip′ital lobe′, *Anat.* the most posterior lobe of each cerebral hemisphere, behind the parietal and temporal lobes. [1885–90]

oc·ci·put (ok′sə put′, -pət), *n., pl.* **oc·ci·puts, oc·cip·i·ta** (ok sip′i tə). *Anat.* the back part of the head or skull. [1350–1400; ME < L, equiv. to *oc-* OC- + *-ciput,* comb. form of *caput* head]

Oc·ci·tan (ok′si tan′), *n.* Provençal (def. 3).

Oc·cleve (ok′lēv), *n.* Hoccleve.

oc·clude (ə klo͞od′), *v.,* **-clud·ed, -clud·ing. —***v.t.* **1.** to close, shut, or stop up (a passage, opening, etc.). **2.** to shut in, out, or off. **3.** *Physical Chem.* (of certain metals and other solids) to incorporate (gases and other foreign substances), as by absorption or adsorption. **—***v.i.* **4.** *Dentistry.* to shut or close, with the cusps of the opposing teeth of the upper and lower jaws fitting together. **5.** *Meteorol.* to form an occluded front. [1590–1600; < L *occlūdere* to shut up, close up, equiv. to *oc-* OC- + *-clūdere,* comb. form of *claudere* to CLOSE] **—oc·clud′ent,** *adj.*
—Syn. 1. obstruct, clog, block, plug.

occlud′ed front′, *Meteorol.* a composite front formed when a cold front overtakes a warm front and forces it aloft. Also called **occlusion.** [1965–70]

oc·clu·sion (ə klo͞o′zhən), *n.* **1.** the act or state of occluding or the state of being occluded. **2.** *Dentistry.* the fitting together of the teeth of the lower jaw with the corresponding teeth of the upper jaw when the jaws are closed. **3.** *Pathol.* closure or blockage of a blood vessel: *coronary occlusion.* **4.** *Phonet.* momentary complete closure at some area in the vocal tract, causing stoppage of the flow of air and accumulation of pressure. **5.** *Meteorol.* **a.** the formation of an occluded front. **b.** See **occluded front.** [1635–45; < L *occlūs(us)* (ptp. of *occlūdere* to OCCLUDE) + -ION] **—oc·clu·sal** (ə klo͞o′səl, -zəl), *adj.*

oc·clu·sive (ə klo͞o′siv), *adj.* **1.** occluding or tending to occlude. **2.** *Phonet.* characterized by or having occlusion. **—***n. Phonet.* **3.** a stop that is unreleased, as the *p*-sound in *stop,* or deviously released, as the *k*-sound in *acme, acne,* or *action,* the *t*-sound of *catnip,* the *g*-sound of *pygmy* or *ugly.* **4.** (not in technical use) any stop sound. [1885–90; < L *occlūs(us)* (see OCCLUSION) + -IVE] **—oc·clu′sive·ness,** *n.*

oc·cult (ə kult′, ok′ult), *adj.* **1.** of or pertaining to magic, astrology, or any system claiming use or knowledge of secret or supernatural powers or agencies. **2.** beyond the range of ordinary knowledge or understanding; mysterious. **3.** secret; disclosed or communicated only to the initiated. **4.** hidden from view. **5.** (in early science) **a.** not apparent on mere inspection but discoverable by experimentation. **b.** of a nature not understood, as physical qualities. **c.** dealing with such qualities; experimental: *occult science.* **6.** *Med.* present in amounts too small to be visible: *a chemical test to detect occult blood in the stool.* **—***n.* **7.** the supernatural or supernatural agencies and affairs considered as a whole (usually prec. by *the*). **8.** occult studies or sciences (usually prec. by *the*). **—***v.t.* **9.** to block or shut off (an object) from view; hide. **10.** *Astron.* to hide (a celestial body) by occultation. **—***v.i.* **11.** to become hidden or shut off from view. [1520–30; < L *occultus* (ptp. of *occulere* to hide from view, cover up), equiv. to *oc-* OC- + *-cul-,* akin to *cēlāre* to CONCEAL + *-tus* ptp. suffix] **—oc·cult′er,** *n.* **—oc·cult′ly,** *adv.* **—oc·cult′ness,** *n.*
—Syn. 2. metaphysical, supernatural. **3.** concealed, unrevealed; veiled, shrouded; mystical, cabalistic.

oc·cul·ta·tion (ok′ul tā′shən), *n.* **1.** *Astron.* the passage of one celestial body in front of another, thus hiding the other from view: applied esp. to the moon's coming between an observer and a star or planet. **2.** disappearance from view or notice. **3.** the act of blocking or hiding from view. **4.** the resulting hidden or concealed state. [1375–1425; late ME < L *occultātiōn-* (s. of *occultātiō*) a hiding, equiv. to *occultāt(us)* (ptp. of *occultāre* to conceal, keep something hidden, freq. of *occulere;* see OCCULT) + *-iōn-* -ION]

occult′ bal′ance, asymmetrical balance of visual elements in an artistic composition.

occult′ing light′, *Navig.* a beacon having a light covered briefly at regular intervals. [1890–95]

oc·cult·ism (ə kul′tiz əm), *n.* **1.** belief in the existence of secret, mysterious, or supernatural agencies. **2.** the study or practice of occult arts. [1880–85; OCCULT + -ISM] **—oc·cult′ist,** *n., adj.*

oc·cu·pan·cy (ok′yə pən sē), *n., pl.* **-cies. 1.** the act, state, or condition of being or becoming a tenant or of living in or taking up quarters or space in or on something: *Continued occupancy of the office depends on a rent reduction.* **2.** the possession or tenancy of a property: *You can have occupancy on June 1st.* **3.** the act of taking possession, as of a property. **4.** the term during which one is an occupant. **5.** the condition of being occupied: *Occupancy of the auditorium is limited to 1200 people.* **6.** the use to which property is put. **7.** exercise of dominion over property that has no owner so as to become the legal owner. [1590–1600; OCCUP(ANT) + -ANCY]
—Syn. 1. tenancy, occupation, possession.

oc·cu·pant (ok′yə pənt), *n.* **1.** a person, family, group, or organization that lives in, occupies, or has quarters or space in or on something: *the occupant of a taxicab; the occupants of the building.* **2.** a tenant of a house, estate, office, etc.; resident. **3.** *Law.* **a.** an owner through occupancy. **b.** one who is in actual possession. [1590–1600; < MF *occupant,* prp. of *occuper.* See OCCUPY, -ANT]

oc·cu·pa·tion (ok′yə pā′shən), *n.* **1.** a person's usual or principal work or business, esp. as a means of earning a living; vocation: *Her occupation was dentistry.* **2.** any activity in which a person is engaged. **3.** possession, settlement, or use of land or property. **4.** the act of occupying. **5.** the state of being occupied. **6.** the seizure and control of an area by military forces, esp. foreign territory. **7.** the term of control of a territory by foreign military forces: *Danish resistance during the German occupation.* **8.** tenure or the holding of an office or official function: *during his occupation of the vice presidency.* [1250–1300; ME *occupacioun* < MF *occupation* < L *occupātiōn-* (s. of *occupātiō*), equiv. to *occupāt(us)* (ptp. of *occupāre;* see OCCUPY) + *-iōn-* -ION] **—oc′cu·pa′tion·less,** *adj.* **—oc′cu·pa′tive,** *adj.*
—Syn. 1. employment, pursuit, craft, métier. OCCUPATION, BUSINESS, PROFESSION, TRADE refer to the activity to which one regularly devotes oneself, esp. one's regular work, or means of getting a living. OCCUPATION is the general word: *a pleasant or congenial occupation.* BUSINESS esp. suggests a commercial or mercantile occupation: *the printing business.* PROFESSION implies an occupation requiring special knowledge and training in some field of science or learning: *the profession of teaching.* TRADE suggests an occupation involving manual training and skill: *one of the building trades.* **3.** occupancy.

oc·cu·pa·tion·al (ok′yə pā′shə nl), *adj.* **1.** of or pertaining to an occupation, trade, or calling: *occupational guidance.* **2.** of or pertaining to occupation: *occupational troops.* [1840–50; OCCUPATION + -AL[1]] **—oc′cu·pa′tion·al·ly,** *adv.*

occupa′tional disease′, 1. Also called **industrial disease.** a disease caused by the conditions or hazards of a particular occupation. **2.** a trait or tendency that develops among members of a particular profession:

CONCISE PRONUNCIATION KEY: act, cāpe, dâre, pärt; set, ēqual; if, īce; ox, ōver, ôrder, oil, bo͝ok, bo͞ot, out; up, ûrge; child; sing; shoe; thin, *th*at; zh as in *treasure.* ə = *a* as in *alone, e* as in *system, i* as in *easily, o* as in *gallop, u* as in *circus;* ᵊ as in *fire* (fīᵊr), *hour* (ouᵊr). l and n can serve as syllabic consonants, as in *cradle* (krād′l), and *button* (but′n). See the full key inside the front cover.

Cynicism was thought to be an occupational disease of reporters. [1900–05]

oc′cupa′tional haz′ard, a danger or hazard to workers that is inherent in a particular occupation: *Silicosis is an occupational hazard of miners.* [1950–55]

Occupa′tional Safe′ty and Health′ Administra′tion. See **OSHA.**

occupa′tional ther′apy, a form of therapy in which patients are encouraged to engage in vocational tasks or expressive activities, as art or dance, usually in a social setting. [1910–15]

occupa′tion lay′er, (on an archaeological site) a layer of remains left by a single culture, from which the culture can be dated or identified. Also called **occupa′tion lev′el.** [1950–55]

oc•cu•py (ok′yə pī′), *v.*, **-pied, -py•ing.** —*v.t.* **1.** to take or fill up (space, time, etc.): *I occupied my evenings reading novels.* **2.** to engage or employ the mind, energy, or attention of: *Occupy the children with a game while I prepare dinner.* **3.** to be a resident or tenant of; dwell in: *We occupied the same house for 20 years.* **4.** to take possession and control of (a place), as by military invasion. **5.** to hold (a position, office, etc.). —*v.i.* **6.** to take or hold possession. [1300–50; ME *occupien* < MF *occuper* < L *occupāre* to seize, take hold, take up, make one's own, equiv. to *oc-* OC- + *-cup-*, comb. form of *capere* to take, seize + *-āre* inf. suffix] —**oc′cu•pi′a•ble,** *adj.* —**oc′cu•pi′er,** *n.*
—**Syn. 1, 2, 4, 5.** See **have. 2.** use, busy. **4.** capture, seize.

oc•cur (ə kûr′), *v.i.*, **-curred, -cur•ring. 1.** to happen; take place; come to pass: *When did the accident occur?* **2.** to be met with or found; present itself; appear. **3.** to suggest itself in thought; come to mind (usually fol. by *to*): *An idea occurred to me.* [1520–30; < L *occurrere* to run to meet, arrive, meet, equiv. to *oc-* OC- + *currere* to run]
—**Syn. 1.** befall. See **happen. 2.** arise, offer.

oc•cur•rence (ə kûr′əns, ə kur′-), *n.* **1.** the action, fact, or instance of occurring. **2.** something that happens; event; incident: *We were delayed by several unexpected occurrences.* [1530–40; OCCURR(ENT) + -ENCE; cf. ML *occurrentia*] —**oc•cur′rent,** *adj.*
—**Syn. 2.** circumstance. See **event.**

OCD, Office of Civil Defense.

OCDM, See **Office of Civil and Defense Mobilization.**

o•cean (ō′shən), *n.* **1.** the vast body of salt water that covers almost three fourths of the earth's surface. **2.** any of the geographical divisions of this body, commonly given as the Atlantic, Pacific, Indian, Arctic, and Antarctic oceans. See table below. **3.** a vast expanse or quantity: *an ocean of grass.* [1250–1300; ME *ocean(e)* (< OF) < L *ōceanus*, special use of *Ōceanus* OCEANUS < Gk *ōkeanós, Ōkeanós*] —**o′cean•like′,** *adj.*

o•cea•nar•i•um (ō′shə nâr′ē əm), *n., pl.* **-nar•i•ums, -nar•i•a** (-nâr′ē ə). a large saltwater aquarium for the display and observation of fish and other marine life. [1935–40; OCEAN + -ARIUM, modelled on AQUARIUM]

o•cea•naut (ō′shə nôt′, -not′), *n.* aquanaut. [1960–65, *Amer.*; b. OCEAN and AQUANAUT]

O′cean Cit′y, a town in SE New Jersey. 13,949.

o′cean engineer′ing, the branch of engineering that deals with the development of equipment and techniques for the exploration of the ocean floor and exploitation of its resources. Also called **o•cea•neer•ing** (ō′shə nēr′ing). [1960–65]

o′cean farm′ing, mariculture.

o•cean•front (ō′shən frunt′), *n.* **1.** the land along the shore of an ocean. —*adj.* **2.** pertaining to or located on such land: *an oceanfront condominium.* [1930–35; OCEAN + FRONT]

CONCISE ETYMOLOGY KEY: <, descended or borrowed from; >, whence; b., blend of, blended; c., cognate with; cf., compare; deriv., derivative; equiv., equivalent; imit., imitative; obl., oblique; r., replacing; s., stem; sp., spelling, spelled; resp., respelling, respelled; trans., translation; ?, origin unknown; *, unattested; ‡, probably earlier than. See the full key inside the front cover.

o•cean•go•ing (ō′shən gō′ing), *adj.* **1.** (of a ship) designed and equipped to travel on the open sea. **2.** noting or pertaining to sea transportation: *oceangoing traffic.* Also, **o′cean-go′ing.** [1880–85; OCEAN + GOING]

O•ce•an•i•a (ō′shē an′ē ə, -ä′nē ə), *n.* the islands of the central and S Pacific, including Micronesia, Melanesia, Polynesia, and traditionally Australasia. 23,400,000; ab. 3,450,000 sq. mi. (8,935,500 sq. km). Also, **O•ce•an•i•ca** (ō′shē an′i kə). —**O′ce•an′i•an,** *adj., n.*

o•ce•an•ic (ō′shē an′ik), *adj.* **1.** of, living in, or produced by the ocean: *oceanic currents.* **2.** of or pertaining to the region of water lying above the bathyal, abyssal, and hadal zones of the sea bottom. Cf. **neritic, pelagic. 3.** immensely large; vast: *an oceanic expanse of stars.* **4.** (*cap.*) of or pertaining to Oceania, its peoples, or their languages. [1650–60; < ML *ōceanicus*, equiv. to L *ōcean(us)* OCEAN + *-icus* -IC]

o•cea•nic•i•ty (ō′shə nis′i tē, ō′shē ə-), *n.* the degree to which the climate of a place is influenced by the sea. Also called **o•ce•an•i•ty** (ō′shē an′i tē). Cf. **continentality.** [1945–50; OCEANIC + -ITY]

ocean′ic white′tip shark′. See **whitetip shark** (def. 2).

O•ce•a•nid (ō sē′ə nid), *n., pl.* **O•ce•a•nids, O•ce•an•i•des** (ō′sē an′i dēz′). *Class. Myth.* any of the daughters of Oceanus and Tethys; a sea nymph. [< Gk *Ōkeanídes* daughters of Oceanus (nom. pl. of *Ōkeanís*), equiv. to *Ōkean(ós)* OCEANUS + *-ides* -ID[1]]

o′cean lin′er, an oceangoing passenger ship, operating either as one unit of a regular scheduled service or as a cruise ship. [1830–40, *Amer.*]

o′cean marine′ insur′ance, insurance covering risks involving the transporting of persons or goods on the high seas. Cf. **inland marine insurance.**

oceanog., oceanography.

o•cea•nog•ra•phy (ō′shə nog′rə fē, ō′shē ə-), *n.* the branch of physical geography dealing with the ocean. [1855–60; OCEAN + -O- + -GRAPHY] —**o′cea•nog′ra•pher,** *n.* —**o•cea•no•graph•ic** (ō′shə nə graf′ik), **o′cea•no•graph′i•cal,** *adj.* —**o′cea•no•graph′i•cal•ly,** *adv.*

o•cea•no•log•ic (ō′shə nl oj′ik), *adj.* of or pertaining to the ocean and its study. Also, **o′cea•no•log′i•cal.** [OCEANOLOG(Y) + -IC]

o•cea•nol•o•gy (ō′shə nol′ə jē, ō′shē ə-), *n.* the practical application of oceanography. [1860–65, *Amer.*; OCEAN + -O- + -LOGY] —**o′cea•nol′o•gist,** *n.*

o′cean perch′, redfish (def. 1).

o′cean pout′, an eelpout, *Macrozoarces americanus*, common along the northeastern coast of North America.

O•cean•side (ō′shən sīd′), *n.* **1.** a city in SW California. 56,003. **2.** a town on SW Long Island, in SE New York. 33,639.

O′cean Springs′, a town in SE Mississippi. 14,504.

o′cean sun′fish, a brown and gray mola, *Mola mola*, inhabiting tropical and temperate seas, having the posterior half of the body sharply truncated behind the elongated dorsal and anal fins. Also called **headfish.** [1620–30]

O•ce•a•nus (ō sē′ə nəs), *n. Class. Myth.* **1.** a Titan who was the son of Uranus and Gaea, the consort of Tethys, and the father of the river gods and Oceanids. **2.** a great stream of water encircling the earth and believed to be the source of all rivers, lakes, etc.

O•ce•a•nus Pro•cel•la•rum (ō′sē ä′nəs prō′sə lär′əm, -an′əs, ō′shē-), (*Ocean of Storms*) the largest dark plain on the face of the moon, in the second and third quadrants: about 2 million square miles (5.2 million sq. km).

o•cel•lar (ō sel′ər), *adj.* pertaining to an ocellus. [1885–90; OCELL(US) + -AR[1]]

oc•el•lat•ed (os′ə lā′tid, ō sel′ā tid), *adj.* **1.** (of a spot or marking) eyelike. **2.** having ocelli, or eyelike spots. Also, **oc•el•late** (os′ə lāt′, ō sel′it, -āt). [1705–15; < NL *ocellāt(us)* (*ocell(us)* OCELLUS + *-ātus* -ATE[1]) + -ED[2]]

GREAT OCEANS AND SEAS OF THE WORLD

Ocean or Sea	Area sq. mi.	Area sq. km	Location
Pacific Ocean	70,000,000	181,300,000	Bounded by N and S America, Asia, and Australia
Atlantic Ocean	31,530,000	81,663,000	Bounded by N and S America, Europe, and Africa
Indian Ocean	28,357,000	73,444,630	S of Asia, E of Africa, and W of Australia
Arctic Ocean	5,540,000	14,350,000	N of North America, Asia, and the Arctic Circle
Mediterranean Sea	1,145,000	2,965,550	Between Europe, Africa, and Asia
South China Sea	895,000	2,318,050	Part of N Pacific, off coast of SE Asia
Bering Sea	878,000	2,274,000	Part of N Pacific, between N North America and N Asia
Caribbean Sea	750,000	1,943,000	Between Central America, West Indies, and South America
Gulf of Mexico	700,000	1,813,000	Arm of N Atlantic, off SE coast of North America
Sea of Okhotsk	582,000	1,507,380	Arm of N Pacific, off E coast of Asia
East China Sea	480,000	1,243,200	Part of N Pacific, off E coast of Asia
Yellow Sea	480,000	1,243,200	Part of N Pacific, off E coast of Asia
Sea of Japan	405,000	1,048,950	Arm of N Pacific, between Asia mainland and Japanese Isles
Hudson Bay	400,000	1,036,000	N North America
Andaman Sea	300,000	777,000	Part of Bay of Bengal (Indian Ocean), off S coast of Asia
North Sea	201,000	520,600	Arm of N Atlantic, off coast of NW Europe
Red Sea	170,000	440,300	Arm of Indian Ocean, between N Africa and Arabian Peninsula
Black Sea	164,000	424,760	SE Europe-SW Asia
Baltic Sea	160,000	414,000	N Europe
Persian Gulf	92,200	238,800	Between Iran and Arabian Peninsula
Gulf of St. Lawrence	92,000	238,280	Arm of N Atlantic, between mainland of SE Canada and Newfoundland
Gulf of California	62,600	162,100	Arm of N Pacific, between W coast of Mexico and peninsula of Lower California

ocellated marking on peacock feather

oc′ellated tur′key, a wild turkey, *Agriocharis ocellata*, of Yucatán, Belize, and Guatemala, typically having green, blue, reddish-brown, and yellowish-brown plumage of a metallic luster and eyelike spots on the tail. [1860–65]

oc•el•la•tion (os′ə lā′shən), *n.* **1.** an eyelike spot or marking. **2.** the state of having eyelike markings. [1840–50; OCELLATE + -ION]

o•cel•lus (ō sel′əs), *n., pl.* **o•cel•li** (ō sel′ī). **1.** a type of simple eye common to invertebrates, consisting of retinal cells, pigments, and nerve fibers. **2.** an eyelike spot, as on a peacock feather. [1810–20; < L: little eye, dim. of *oculus* EYE; see -ELLE]

oc•e•lot (os′ə lot′, ō′sə-), *n.* a spotted leopardlike cat, *Felis pardalis*, ranging from Texas through South America: now greatly reduced in number and endangered in the U.S. [1765–75; < F, appar. arbitrary shortening of Nahuatl *tlālōcēlōtl* ocelot, equiv. to *tlāl(li)* earth, land + *ōcēlōtl* jaguar] —**oc′e•loid′,** *adj.*

ocelot, *Felis pardalis,* head and body 3 ft. (0.9 m); tail 14 in. (36 cm)

och (OKH), *interj. Scot., Irish Eng.* (used as an expression of surprise, disapproval, regret, etc.) [1520–30; < ScotGael, Ir]

o•cher (ō′kər), *n., adj., v.,* **o•chered, o•cher•ing.** —*n.* **1.** any of a class of natural earths, mixtures of hydrated oxide of iron with various earthy materials, ranging in color from pale yellow to orange and red, and used as pigments. **2.** the color of this, ranging from pale yellow to an orangish or reddish yellow. **3.** *Obs.* money, esp. gold coin. —*adj.* **4.** of the color of ocher. —*v.t.* **5.** to color or mark with ocher. Also, **ochre.** [1350–1400; ME *oker* < OF *ocre* < L *ōchra* < Gk *ōchrā* yellow ocher] —**o′cher•ous, o′cher•y,** *adj.*

och•le•sis (ok lē′sis), *n. Pathol.* any disease caused by overcrowding. [1855–60; < Gk *óchlēsis* disturbance, distress, equiv. to *ochlé*, var. s. of *ochleîn* to disturb + *-sis* -SIS] —**och•le•sit•ic** (ok′lə sit′ik), **och•let•ic** (ok let′ik), *adj.*

och•loc•ra•cy (ok lok′rə sē), *n.* government by the mob; mob rule; mobocracy. [1475–85; < Gk *ochlokratía*, equiv. to *óchl(os)* mob + *-o-* -O- + *-kratia* -CRACY] —**och•lo•crat** (ok′lə krat′), *n.* —**och′lo•crat′ic, och′lo•crat′i•cal,** *adj.* —**och′lo•crat′i•cal•ly,** *adv.*

och•lo•pho•bi•a (ok′lə fō′bē ə), *n. Psychiatry.* an abnormal fear of crowds. [1890–95; < Gk *óchl(os)* mob + *-o-* -O- + -PHOBIA] —**och′lo•pho′bist,** *n.*

O•cho•a (ō chō′ə; *Sp.* ō chô′ä), *n.* **Se•ve•ro** (sə vâr′ō; *Sp.* se ve′rô), born 1905, U.S. biochemist, born in Spain: Nobel prize for medicine 1959.

o•chone (ə KHōn′), *interj. Scot. and Irish Eng.* ohone.

O•cho Ri•os (ō′chō rē′əs), a seaport in N Jamaica: resort. 6900.

Och•o•zath (ok′ə zath′), *n. Douay Bible.* Ahuzzath.

Och•o•zi•as (ok′ə zī′əs), *n. Douay Bible.* Ahaziah.

och•ra•tox•in (ō′krə tok′sin), *n.* a toxin produced by *Aspergillus ochraceus* and several other molds that commonly contaminate cereal grains: causes intestinal inflammation and kidney and liver degeneration when ingested by animals. [1970–75; < NL *ochra(ceus)* specific epithet of the mold, lit., like ocher (see OCHER, -ACEOUS) + TOXIN]

o•chre (ō′kər), *n., adj., v.t.,* **o•chred, o•chring.** ocher. —**o•chre•ous** (ō′kər əs, ō′krē əs), **o•chrous** (ō′krəs), **o•chry** (ō′krē), *adj.*

och•re•a (ok′rē ə), *n., pl.* **-re•ae** (-rē ē′). ocrea.

o•chroid (ō′kroid), *adj.* yellow as ocher. [1895–1900; < Gk *ōchroeidḗs* pallid, equiv. to *ōchr-* OCHER + *-oeidēs* -OID]

Ochs (oks), *n.* **Adolph Simon,** 1858–1935, U.S. newspaper publisher.

-ock, a native English suffix of nouns, used to form descriptive names (*ruddock*, lit., the red one) and diminutives (*hillock*). [ME *-ok*, OE *-oc*, *-uc*]

Ock•e•ghem (ok′ə gem′), *n.* **Jo•han•nes** (yō hä′nəs). See **Okeghem, Jean d′** or **Jan van.** Also, **Ock•en•heim** (ok′ən hīm′, ō′kən-).

ock•er (ok′ər), *Australian Informal.* —*n.* **1.** an uncultured Australian male. **2.** an uncouth, offensive male chauvinist. —*adj.* **3.** of or pertaining to such a person. **4.** typically Australian. [1970–75; after *Ocker*, a character in an Australian television series]

Ock•ham (ok′əm), *n.* **William of.** See **Occam.**

Ock′ham's ra′zor. See **Occam's razor.**

o'clock (ə klok′), *adv.* **1.** of, by, or according to the clock (used in specifying the hour of the day): *It is now 4 o'clock.* **2.** according to a method for indicating relative position whereby a plane in space is considered to be numbered as a clock's face, with 12 o'clock considered as directly ahead in horizontal position or straight up in vertical position. [1710–20; see o', CLOCK[1]]

o·co·nee-bells (ə kō′nē belz′), *n., pl.* **-bells.** (*used with a singular or plural v.*) a plant, *Shortia galacifolia,* of the southeastern U.S., having glossy, rounded leaves and white or pink bell-shaped flowers with fringed petals. [from its abundance along the *Oconee* River in NE Georgia]

O'Con·nell (ō kon′l), *n.* **Daniel,** 1775–1847, Irish nationalist leader and orator.

O'Con·nor (ō kon′ər), *n.* **1. Frank** (*Michael Donovan*), 1903–66, Irish writer. **2. (Mary) Flannery,** 1925–64, U.S. novelist and short-story writer. **3. John Joseph, Cardinal,** born 1920, U.S. Roman Catholic clergyman: archbishop of New York since 1984. **4. Sandra Day,** born 1930, U.S. jurist: associate justice of the U.S. Supreme Court since 1981 and first woman appointed to that position. **5. Thomas Power,** 1848–1929, Irish journalist, author, and political leader.

o·co·til·lo (ō′kə tēl′yō; *Sp.* ô′kô tē′yô), *n., pl.* **-til·los** (-tēl′yōz; *Sp.* -tē′yôs). a spiny, woody shrub, *Fouqueria splendens,* of arid regions of the southwestern U.S. and Mexico, having a tight cluster of red flowers at the tip of each branch. [1855–60, *Amer.*; < MexSp, dim. of *ocote* kind of pine < Nahuatl *ocotl*]

OCR, *Computers.* **1.** optical character reader. **2.** optical character recognition.

oc·re·a (ok′rē ə, ō′krē ə), *n., pl.* **oc·re·ae** (ok′rē ē′, ō′krē ē′). *Bot., Zool.* a sheathing part, as a pair of stipules united about a stem. Also, **ochrea.** [1820–30; < L: greave, legging]

O, **ocrea**

oc·re·ate (ok′rē it, -āt′, ō′krē-), *adj.* having an ocrea or ocreae; sheathed. [1820–30; < L *ocreātus* greaved, equiv. to *ocre(a)* greave (see OCREA) + *-ātus* -ATE[1]]

OCS, 1. *Mil.* officer candidate school. **2.** Old Church Slavonic. **3.** outer continental shelf.

oct-, var. of **octa-** or **octo-** before a vowel: *octal.*

Oct., October.

oct., octavo.

octa-, a combining form occurring in loanwords from Greek and Latin, where it meant "eight" (*octagon; octastyle*), on this model, used in the formation of compound words, and in chemical terms specialized to mean "having eight atoms" (*octavalent*). Also, **oct-, octo-.** [< Gk *okta-,* comb. form of *oktṓ* EIGHT]

oc·ta·chord (ok′tə kôrd′), *n.* **1.** any musical instrument with eight strings. **2.** a diatonic series of eight tones. [1750–60; < Gk *oktáchordos* having eight strings. See OCTA-, CHORD[1]] —**oc′ta·chor′dal,** *adj.*

oc·tad (ok′tad), *n.* **1.** a group or series of eight. **2.** *Chem.* an element, atom, or group having a valence of eight. [1835–45; < Gk *oktad-* (s. of *oktás*) group of eight, equiv. to *okt-* OCT- + *-ad* -AD[1]] —**oc·tad′ic,** *adj.*

oc′ta·dec·a·no′ic ac′id (ok′tə dek′ə nō′ik, ok′-), *Chem.* See **stearic acid.** [OCTA- + DECANE + -O- + -IC]

oc·ta·gon (ok′tə gon′, -gən), *n.* a polygon having eight angles and eight sides. Also called **octangle.** [1650–60; < L *octagōnon* < Gk *oktágōnon,* n. use of neut. of *oktágōnos* octangular; see OCTA-, -GON]

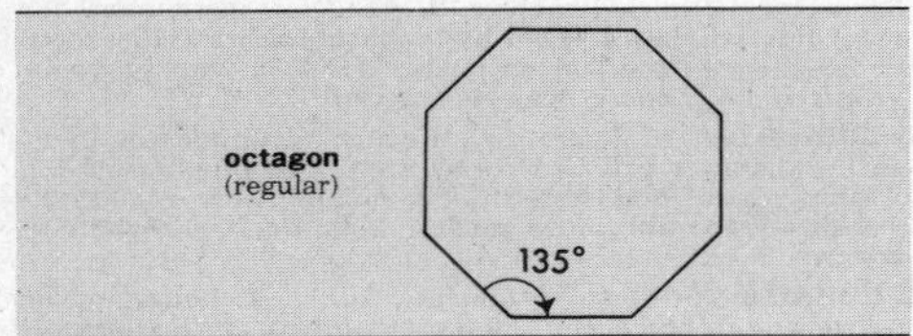

octagon (regular)

oc·tag·o·nal (ok tag′ə nl), *adj.* having eight angles and eight sides. [1565–75; OCTAGON + -AL, r. earlier *octogonal* < NL *octōgōnālis,* equiv. to *octō-* OCTO- + Gk *gōn(ía)* angle + *-ālis* -AL[1]] —**oc·tag′o·nal·ly,** *adv.*

oc′tagon house′, a type of American house, c. 1850, having an octagonal perimeter to reduce exterior wall area.

oc′tagon scale′, *Carpentry.* a scale used in laying out octagonal figures of various sizes.

oc·ta·he·dral (ok′tə hē′drəl), *adj.* having the form of an octahedron. [1750–60; OCTAHEDR(ON) + -AL[1]]

oc·ta·he·drite (ok′tə hē′drit), *n. Mineral.* anatase. [1795–1805; < LL *octahedr(os)* eight-sided < Gk *oktáedron* (see OCTAHEDRON) + -ITE[1]]

oc·ta·he·dron (ok′tə hē′drən), *n., pl.* **-drons, -dra** (-drə). a solid figure having eight faces. [1560–70; < Gk *oktáedron* eight-sided (neut. of *oktáedros*), equiv. to *okta-* OCTA- + *-edron* -HEDRON]

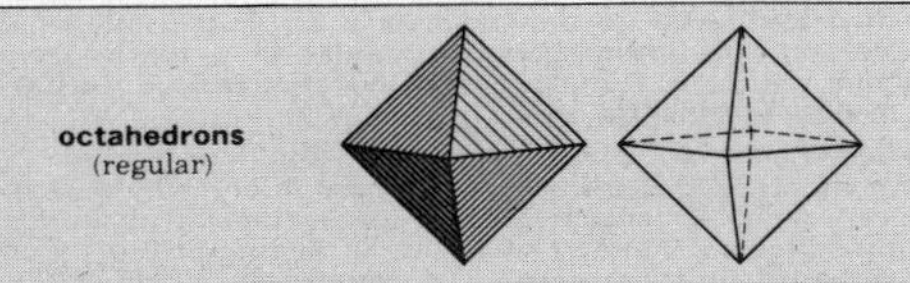
octahedrons (regular)

oc·tal (ok′tl), *adj.* **1.** Also, **octonary.** of or pertaining to the number system with base 8, employing the numerals 0 through 7. **2.** relating to or encoded in an octal system, especially for use by a digital computer. **3.** (of an electronic device) having eight pins in its base for electrical connections. —*n.* **4.** octonary (def. 6). [1935–40; OCT- + -AL[1]]

oc·ta·mer (ok′tə mər), *n. Biochem.* an eight-molecule complex. [OCTA- + -MER]

oc·tam·er·ous (ok tam′ər əs), *adj.* **1.** consisting of or divided into eight parts. **2.** *Bot.* (of flowers) having eight members in each whorl. Also, **octomerous.** [1860–65; < Gk *oktamerḗs* having eight parts (equiv. to *okta-* OCTA- + *mér(os)* -MEROUS + *-ēs* adj. suffix) + -OUS] —**oc·tam·er·ism** (ok tam′ə riz′əm), *n.*

oc·tam·e·ter (ok tam′i tər), *Pros.* —*adj.* **1.** consisting of eight measures or feet. —*n.* **2.** Also, **octometer.** an octameter verse. [1840–50; < LL < Gk *oktámetros* (adj.), equiv. to *okta-* OCTA- + *métr(on)* -METER + *-os* adj. suffix]

oc·tan (ok′tən), *adj.* **1.** (of a fever) occurring every eighth day. —*n.* **2.** an octan fever. [1895–1900; < F *octane,* MF *octaine,* deriv. of L *octō* EIGHT, on the model of *quartaine* QUARTAN]

oc·tane (ok′tān), *n. Chem.* **1.** any of 18 isomeric saturated hydrocarbons having the formula C_8H_{18}, some of which are obtained in the distillation and cracking of petroleum. **2.** See **octane number.** [1870–75; OCT- + -ANE]

oc′tane num′ber, (of gasoline) a designation of antiknock quality, numerically equal to the percentage of isooctane by volume in a mixture of isooctane and normal heptane that matches the given gasoline in antiknock characteristics. Also called **oc′tane rat′ing.** [1930–35]

oc·tan·gle (ok′tang gəl), *adj.* **1.** octangular. —*n.* **2.** octagon. [1605–15; < LL *octangulus* eight-angled, equiv. to L *oct-* OCT- + *angulus* ANGLE]

oc·tan·gu·lar (ok tang′gyə lər), *adj.* having eight angles. [1635–45; < LL *octangul(us)* (see OCTANGLE) + -AR[1]] —**oc·tan′gu·lar·ness,** *n.*

oc′ta·no′ic ac′id (ok′tə nō′ik, ok′-), *Chem.* See **caprylic acid.** [1905–10; OCTANE + *-oic* denoting an organic acid containing a carboxyl group, appar. after CAPROIC ACID]

Oc·tans (ok′tanz), *n., gen.* **Oc·tan·tis** (ok tan′tis). *Astron.* the Octant, a southern constellation that contains the south celestial pole. [< LL: eighth part of a circle, equiv. to *oct-* OCT- + *-āns,* as in *quadrāns* QUADRANT]

oc·tant (ok′tənt), *n.* **1.** the eighth part of a circle. **2.** *Math.* any of the eight parts into which three mutually perpendicular planes divide space. **3.** an instrument having an arc of 24°, used by navigators for measuring angles up to 90°. **4.** the position of one heavenly body when 45° distant from another. **5.** (*cap.*) *Astron.* the constellation Octans. [1680–90; < L *octant-* (s. of *octāns*); see OCTANS] —**oc·tan·tal** (ok tan′tl), *adj.*

oc·tar·chy (ok′tär kē), *n., pl.* **-chies. 1.** a government by eight persons. **2.** a group of eight states or kingdoms. [1795–1805; OCT- + -ARCHY]

oc·ta·teuch (ok′tə to͝ok′, -tyo͝ok′), *n.* the first eight books of the Old Testament, consisting of Genesis, Exodus, Leviticus, Numbers, Deuteronomy, Joshua, Judges, and Ruth, or a volume containing them. [1670–80; < LL *octateuchus* < Gk *oktáteuchos,* equiv. to *okta-* OCTA- + *teûchos* container for scrolls]

oc·ta·va·lent (ok′tə vā′lənt), *adj. Chem.* having a valence of eight. [1875–80; OCTA- + -VALENT]

oc·tave (ok′tiv, -tāv), *n.* **1.** *Music.* **a.** a tone on the eighth degree from a given tone. **b.** the interval encompassed by such tones. **c.** the harmonic combination of such tones. **d.** a series of tones, or of keys of an instrument, extending through this interval. **2.** a pipe-organ stop whose pipes give tones an octave above the normal pitch of the keys used. **3.** a series or group of eight. **4.** Also called **octet.** *Pros.* **a.** a group of eight lines of verse, esp. the first eight lines of a sonnet in the Italian form. Cf. **sestet** (def. 1). **b.** a stanza of eight lines. **5.** the eighth of a series. **6.** *Eccles.* **a.** the eighth day from a feast day, counting the feast day as the first. **b.** the period of eight days beginning with a feast day. **7.** one eighth of a pipe of wine. **8.** *Fencing.* the eighth of eight defensive positions. —*adj.* **9.** pitched an octave higher. [1300–50; ME < L *octāva* eighth part, n. use of fem. of *octāvus,* equiv. to *oct-* OCT- + *-āvus* adj. suffix] —**oc·ta·val** (ok tā′vəl, ok′tə-), *adj.*

Oc·ta·vi·a (ok tā′vē ə), *n.* **1.** died 11 B.C., sister of Roman emperor Augustus and wife of Marc Antony. **2.** A.D. c42–62 Roman empress, wife of Nero. **3.** a female given name.

Oc·ta·vi·an (ok tā′vē ən), *n.* Augustus.

Oc·ta·vi·us (ok tā′vē əs), *n.* a male given name.

oc·ta·vo (ok tā′vō, -tä′-), *n., pl.* **-vos** for 2, *adj.* —*n.* **1.** a book size of about 6 × 9 in. (16 × 23 cm), determined by printing on sheets folded to form 8 leaves or 16 pages. *Symbol:* 8vo, 8° **2.** a book of this size. —*adj.* **3.** in octavo. [1575–85; short for NL *in octāvō* in an eighth (of a sheet)]

oc·ta·vus (ōk tä′wo͞os; *Eng.* ok tā′vəs), *adj. Latin.* eighth.

oc·ten·ni·al (ok ten′ē əl), *adj.* **1.** occurring every eight years. **2.** of or for eight years. [1650–60; < LL *octenni(um)* eight-year period (*oct-* OCT- + *-enn-,* comb. form of *annus* year + *-ium* -IUM) + -AL[1]] —**oc·ten′ni·al·ly,** *adj.*

oc·tet (ok tet′), *n.* **1.** a company of eight singers or musicians. **2.** a musical composition for eight voices or instruments. **3.** *Pros.* octave (def. 4). **4.** any group of eight. Also, **oc·tette′.** [1860–65; OCT- + *-et,* as in *duet*]

oc·til·lion (ok til′yən), *n., pl.* **-lions,** (*as after a numeral*) **-lion,** *adj.* —*n.* **1.** a cardinal number represented in the U.S. by 1 followed by 27 zeros, and in Great Britain by 1 followed by 48 zeros. —*adj.* **2.** amounting to one octillion in number. [1680–90; < F, equiv. to *oct-* OCT- + *-illion,* as in *million*] —**oc·til′lionth,** *n., adj.*

octo-, var. of **octa-:** *octosyllabic.*

Oc·to·ber (ok tō′bər), *n.* **1.** the tenth month of the year, containing 31 days. *Abbr.:* Oct. **2.** *Brit.* ale or beer traditionally brewed in this month. [bef. 1050; ME, OE < L *Octōber* the eighth month of the early Roman year, equiv. to *octō-* OCTO- + *-ber,* on the model of *September, November, December;* see DECEMBER]

Oc·to·ber·fest (ok tō′bər fest′), *n.* Oktoberfest.

Octo′ber Revolu′tion. See **Russian Revolution** (def. 2).

Oc·to·brist (ok tō′brist), *n.* **1.** a member of a Russian political party that advocated constitutional monarchism: so called because it was organized after the Czar's manifesto in October, 1905. **2.** a member of a communist organization in the Soviet Union for children ranging in age from eight to ten. Cf. **Komsomol, Pioneer.** [trans. of Russ *oktyabríst*]

oc·to·cen·ten·ar·y (ok′tō sen ten′ə rē, -sen′tn er′ē *or, esp. Brit.,* -sen tē′nə rē), *adj., n., pl.* **-ar·ies.** —*adj.* **1.** pertaining to 800 or a period of 800 years; marking the completion of 800 years. —*n.* **2.** an 800th anniversary or its celebration. [1885–90; OCTO- + CENTENARY]

oc·to·de·cil·lion (ok′tō di sil′yən), *n., pl.* **-lions,** (*as after a numeral*) **-lion,** *adj.* —*n.* **1.** a cardinal number represented in the U.S. by 1 followed by 57 zeros, and in Great Britain by 1 followed by 108 zeros. —*adj.* **2.** amounting to one octodecillion in number. [1935–40; < L *octōdec(im)* eighteen + E *-illion,* as in *million*] —**oc′to·de·cil′lionth,** *adj., n.*

oc·to·dec·i·mo (ok′tə des′ə mō′), *n., pl.* **-mos** for 2, *adj.* —*n.* **1.** a book size of about 4 × 6 ¼ in. (10 × 16 cm), determined by printing on sheets folded to form 18 leaves or 36 pages. *Symbol:* 18mo, 18° **2.** a book of this size. —*adj.* **3.** in octodecimo. Also called **eighteenmo.** [1855–60; short for NL *in octōdecimō* in an eighteenth (of a sheet)]

oc·to·foil (ok′tə foil′), *n. Heraldry.* See **double quatrefoil.** [1885–90; OCTO- + FOIL[2]]

oc·to·ge·nar·i·an (ok′tə jə nâr′ē ən), *adj.* Also, **oc·tog·e·nar·y** (ok toj′ə ner′ē). **1.** of the age of 80 years. **2.** between 80 and 90 years old. —*n.* **3.** a person who is between 80 and 90 years old. [1805–15; < L *octōgēnāri(us)* comprising eighty, eighty years old (equiv. to *octōgēn(ī)* eighty each + *-ārius* -ARY) + -AN] —**oc′to·ge·nar′i·an·ism,** *n.*

oc·tom·er·ous (ok tom′ər əs), *adj.* octamerous.

oc·tom·e·ter (ok tom′i tər), *n.* octameter.

oc·to·nar·y (ok′tə ner′ē), *adj., n., pl.* **-nar·ies.** —*adj.* **1.** pertaining to the number 8. **2.** consisting of eight. **3.** proceeding by eight. **4.** octal (def. 1). —*n.* **5.** a group of eight; an ogdoad. **6.** Also, **octal.** *Pros.* a stanza of eight lines. **7.** a number in an octonary system. [1525–35; < L *octōnārius* consisting of eight, equiv. to *octōn(ī)* eight each + *-ārius* -ARY]

oc·to·pod (ok′tə pod′), *n.* any eight-armed cephalopod mollusk of the order or suborder Octopoda, including the octopuses and paper nautiluses. [1820–30; < NL *Octopoda* name of the order < Gk *oktṓpoda* neut. pl. of *oktṓpous* eight-footed. See OCTO-, -POD]

oc·to·pus (ok′tə pəs), *n., pl.* **-pus·es, -pi** (-pī′). **1.** any octopod of the genus *Octopus,* having a soft, oval body and eight sucker-bearing arms, living mostly at the bottom of the sea. **2.** something likened to an octopus, as an organization with many forms of far-reaching influence or control. [1750–60; < NL < Gk *oktṓpous* (pl. *oktṓpodes*) eight-footed; see OCTO-, -POD]

octopus, *Octopus vulgaris,* radial span about 10 ft. (3 m)

oc·to·roon (ok′tə ro͞on′), *n.* a person having one-eighth black ancestry; the offspring of a quadroon and a white. [1855–60, *Amer.*; OCTO- + (QUAD)ROON]

oc·to·syl·lab·ic (ok′tō si lab′ik), *adj.* **1.** consisting of or pertaining to eight syllables. —*n.* **2.** an octosyllable. [1765–75; < LL *octōsyllab(us)* (< Gk, equiv. to *oktō-* OCTO- + *-syllabos* SYLLABIC) + -IC]

oc·to·syl·la·ble (ok′tə sil′ə bəl), *n.* a word or line of verse of eight syllables. [1765–75; part trans. of LL *octōsyllabus;* see OCTOSYLLABIC, SYLLABLE]

oc·troi (ok′troi; *Fr.* ôk TRWA′), *n., pl.* **-trois** (-troiz; *Fr.* -TRWA′). **1.** (formerly esp. in France and Italy) a local tax levied on certain articles, such as foodstuffs, on their entry into a city. **2.** the place at which such a tax is collected. **3.** the officials collecting it. **4.** the act of a sovereign in granting to subjects a constitution or other charter. [1605–15; < F, n. deriv. of *octroyer* to grant, partial Latinization of OF *otreier* < ML *auctorizāre;* see AUTHORIZE]

oc·tu·ple (ok′to͞o pəl, -tyo͞o-; ok to͞o′pəl, -tyo͞o′-), *adj., v.,* **-pled, -pling,** *n.* —*adj.* **1.** eightfold; eight times as great. **2.** having eight effective units or elements. —*v.t.* **3.** to make eight times as great. —*n.* **4.** *Rowing.* a shell rowed by a crew of eight, each rower using a pair of oars. [1595–1605; < L *octuplus,* equiv. to *octu-,* var. (before labials) of *octō-* OCTO- + *-plus* -FOLD]

oc•tup•let (ok tup′lit, -to͞o′plit, -tyo͞o′-; ok′to͞o plit, -tyo͞o-), *n.* **1.** a group, series, or combination of eight related items. **2.** *Music.* a group of eight notes that are to be played or sung in the same time as six notes of equal value. [1850–55; OCTUPLE + -ET]

oc•tu•pli•cate (*n., adj.* ok to͞o′pli kit, -kāt′, -tyo͞o′-, -tup′li-; *v.* ok to͞o′pli kāt′, -kit, -tyo͞o′-, -tup′li-), *n., adj., v.,* **-cat•ed, -cat•ing.** —*n.* **1.** a group, series, or set of eight identical copies (usually prec. by *in*). —*adj.* **2.** having or consisting of eight identical parts; eightfold. **3.** noting the eighth copy or item. —*v.t.* **4.** to make eight copies of. **5.** to make eight times as great, as by multiplying. [< L *octuplicātus,* equiv. to *octupl(us)* OCTUPLE + *plicātus* folded (see PLICATE), on the model of *quadruplus, quadruplicātus*]

oc′tyl al′cohol (ok′tl), *Chem.* any of a group of isomers having the formula $C_8H_{18}O$, esp. used in making perfumes and as a solvent. [1870–75; OCT(ANE) + -YL]

oc′tyl phe′nol, *Chem.* a white to pink, water-insoluble, flaky substance having the formula $C_{14}H_{22}O$, used chiefly in the manufacture of commercial surface-active agents.

ocul-, var. of **oculo-** before a vowel: *oculist.*

oc•u•lar (ok′yə lər), *adj.* **1.** of, pertaining to, or for the eyes: *ocular movements.* **2.** of the nature of an eye: *an ocular organ.* **3.** performed or perceived by the eye or eyesight. —*n.* **4.** *Optics.* eyepiece. [1565–75; < L *oculāris,* equiv. to *ocul(us)* EYE + *-āris* -AR[1]] —**oc′u•lar•ly,** *adv.*

oc•u•list (ok′yə list), *n.* (formerly) **1.** ophthalmologist. **2.** optometrist. [1605–15; < F *oculiste.* See OCUL-, -IST] —**oc′u•lis′tic,** *adj.*
—**Syn.** See **eye doctor.**

oculo-, a combining form meaning "eye," "ocular," used in the formation of compound words: *oculomotor.* Also, *esp. before a vowel,* **ocul-.** [comb. form of L *oculus* EYE; see -O-]

oc•u•lo•mo•tor (ok′yə lō mō′tər), *adj.* moving or tending to move the eyeball: *an oculomotor muscle.* [1880–85; OCULO- + MOTOR]

oculomo′tor nerve′, *Anat.* either one of the third pair of cranial nerves, consisting chiefly of motor fibers that innervate most of the muscles of the eyeball. See diag. under **brain.** [1880–85]

oc•u•lus (ok′yə ləs), *n., pl.* **-li** (-lī′). **1.** an eye. **2.** *Archit.* a circular opening, esp. one at the apex of a dome. **3.** *Archaeol.* a design representing an eye, as on funerary pottery found in megalithic tombs of Europe. [< NL, L: EYE]

od (od, ōd), *n.* a hypothetical force formerly held to pervade all nature and to manifest itself in magnetism, mesmerism, chemical action, etc. Also, **odyl, odyle.** [1840–50; arbitrary name coined by Karl von Reichenbach (1788–1869), German scientist]

Od (od), *interj. Archaic.* a shortened form of "God" (used interjectionally and in minced oaths). Also, **'Od, Odd.** [1590–1600]

OD (ō′dē′), *n., pl.* **ODs** or **OD's,** *v.,* **OD'd** or **ODed** or **OD'ed, OD'ing** or **OD•ing.** —*n.* **1.** an overdose of a drug, esp. a fatal one. **2.** a person who has taken an overdose of a drug, esp. one who has become seriously ill or has died from such an overdose. —*v.i.* **3.** to take an overdose of a drug. **4.** to die from an an overdose of a drug. **5.** to have or experience an excessive amount or degree of something. [1955–60]

OD, 1. See **officer of the day. 2.** Old Dutch. **3.** Ordnance Department. **4.** outside diameter.

od, 1. on demand. **2.** outside diameter. **3.** outside dimensions. **4.** overdraft. **5.** overdrawn.

OD., Old Dutch.

O.D., 1. Doctor of Optometry. **2.** (in prescriptions) the right eye. [< L *oculus dexter*] **3.** See **officer of the day. 4.** Old Dutch. **5.** (of a military uniform) olive drab. **6.** ordinary seaman. **7.** outside diameter. **8.** overdraft. **9.** overdrawn.

o.d., 1. (in prescriptions) the right eye. [< L *oculus dexter*] **2.** olive drab. **3.** on demand. **4.** outside diameter.

o•da (ō′də, ō dä′), *n., pl.* **o•das, o•da, o•da•lar** (ō′də-lär′). a room within a harem. [1615–25; < Turk: room]

o•dah (ō′də, ō dä′), *n., pl.* **o•dahs, o•dah.** oda.

o•da•lisque (ōd′l isk), *n.* **1.** a female slave or concubine in a harem, esp. in that of the sultan of Turkey. **2.** (*cap.*) any of a number of representations of such a woman or of a similar subject, as by Ingres or Matisse. Also, **o′da•lisk.** [1675–85; < F, alter. of earlier *odalique* (with *-s-* perh. from *-esque* -ESQUE) < Turk *odalık* concubine, equiv. to *oda* room + *-lık* n. suffix of appurtenance]

odd (od), *adj.,* **-er,-est,** *n.* —*adj.* **1.** differing in nature from what is ordinary, usual, or expected: *an odd choice.* **2.** singular or peculiar in a strange or eccentric way: *an odd person; odd manners.* **3.** fantastic; bizarre: *Her taste in clothing was rather odd.* **4.** leaving a remainder of 1 when divided by 2, as a number (opposed to *even*): *Numbers like 3, 15, and 181 are odd numbers.* **5.** more or less, esp. a little more (used in combination with a round number): *I owe three hundred-odd dollars.* **6.** being a small amount in addition to what is counted or specified: *I have five gross and a few odd dozens.* **7.** being part of a pair, set, or series of which the rest is lacking: *an odd glove.* **8.** remaining after all others are paired, grouped, or divided into equal numbers or parts: *Everybody gets two hamburgers and I get the odd one.* **9.** left over after all others are used, consumed, etc. **10.** (of a pair) not matching: *Do you know you're wearing an odd pair of socks?* **11.** not forming part of any particular group, set, or class: *to pick up odd bits of information.* **12.** not regular, usual, or full-time; occasional; casual: *odd jobs.* **13.** out-of-the-way; secluded: *a tour to the odd parts of the Far East.* **14.** *Math.* (of a function) having a sign that changes when the sign of each independent variable is changed at the same time. —*n.* **15.** something that is odd. **16.** *Golf.* **a.** a stroke more than the opponent has played. **b.** *Brit.* a stroke taken from a player's total score for a hole in order to give him or her odds. [1300–50; ME *odde* < ON *oddi* odd (number)] —**odd′ly,** *adv.* —**odd′ness,** *n.*
—**Syn. 1.** extraordinary, unusual, rare, uncommon. See **strange.** —**Ant. 1.** ordinary, usual, common.

CONCISE ETYMOLOGY KEY: <, descended or borrowed from; >, whence; b., blend of, blended; c., cognate with; cf., compare; deriv., derivative; equiv., equivalent; imit., imitative; obl., oblique; r., replacing; s., stem; sp., spelling, spelled; resp., respelling, respelled; trans., translation; ?, origin unknown; *, unattested; ‡, probably earlier than. See the full key inside the front cover.

odd′ and e′ven. See **odd or even.** [1830–40]

odd•ball (od′bôl′), *Informal.* —*n.* **1.** a person or thing that is atypical, bizarre, eccentric, or nonconforming, esp. one having beliefs that are unusual but harmless. —*adj.* **2.** whimsically free-spirited; eccentric; atypical: *an oddball scheme.* [1940–45, *Amer.*; ODD + BALL[1]]

odd′-e′ven check′ (od′ē′vən). See **parity check.**

Odd′ Fel′low, a member of a social and benevolent society that originated in England in the 18th century. Also, **Odd′fel′low.** [1785–95] —**Odd′fel′low•ship′,** *n.*

odd•ish (od′ish), *adj.* rather odd; queer. [1695–1705; ODD + -ISH[1]]

odd•i•ty (od′i tē), *n., pl.* **-ties** for 1, 3. **1.** an odd or remarkably unusual person, thing, or event. **2.** the quality of being odd; singularity, strangeness, or eccentricity. **3.** an odd characteristic or trait; peculiarity. [1705–15; ODD + -ITY]
—**Syn. 1.** rarity, curiosity, wonder.

odd-job (od′job′), *v.i.,* **-jobbed, -job•bing.** to work at a series of unrelated or unspecialized jobs, often of a low-paying or menial nature. [1855–60] —**odd′ job′ber.** —**odd′-job′ber,** *n.*

odd′ lot′, 1. a quantity or amount less than the conventional unit of trading. **2.** *Stock Exchange.* (in a transaction) a quantity of stock less than the established 100-share unit for active issues or the 10-share unit for designated inactive issues. Also called **broken lot.** Cf. **round lot.** [1895–1900] —**odd′-lot′,** *adj.*

odd-lot•ter (od′lot′ər), *n.* a person who buys or sells odd lots. Also, **odd′ lot′ter.** [1965–70; ODD LOT + -ER[1]]

odd′ man′ out′, 1. a method of selecting or eliminating a person from a group, as by matching coins, esp. in preparation for playing a game. **2.** the person so selected or eliminated. **3.** a game consisting of this method. **4.** outsider (def. 2). Also, **odd′-man′-out′.** [1885–90]

odd•ment (od′mənt), *n.* **1.** an odd article, bit, remnant, or the like. **2.** an article belonging to a broken or incomplete set. **3.** *Print.* any individual portion of a book excluding the text, as the frontispiece or index. [1790–1800; ODD + -MENT]

odd′ or e′ven, any of various games of chance in which one bets on an odd or even number, as one in which two players alternately draw from a pile of an odd number of counters any desired number up to a prearranged limit, the object being to have drawn an odd number of counters at the end of the game. Also, **odd and even, odds or evens.**

odd′ permuta′tion, *Math.* a permutation of a set of *n* elements, $x_1, x_2, \ldots, x_n$, which permutes the product of all differences of the form $(x_i - x_j)$, where *i* is less than *j*, into the negative of the product. Cf. **even permutation.** [1925–30]

odd-pin•nate (od′pin′āt, -it), *adj. Bot.* pinnate with an odd terminal leaflet. [1885–90]

odds (odz), *n.* (*usually used with a plural v.*) **1.** the probability that something is so, will occur, or is more likely to occur than something else: *The odds are that it will rain today.* **2.** the ratio of probability that something is so, will occur, or is more likely to occur than something else. **3.** this ratio used as the basis of a bet; the ratio by which the bet of one party to a wager exceeds that of the other, granted by one of two betting opponents to equalize the chances favoring one of them: *The odds are two-to-one that it won't rain today.* **4.** an equalizing allowance, as that given the weaker person or team in a contest; handicap. **5.** an advantage or degree of superiority on the side of two contending parties; a difference favoring one of two contestants. **6.** an amount or degree by which one thing is better or worse than another. **7. at odds,** at variance; in disagreement: *They were usually at odds over political issues.* **8. by all odds,** in every respect; by far; undoubtedly: *She is by all odds the brightest child in the family.* Also, **by long odds, by odds.** [1490–1500; special use of ODD]

odds′ and ends′, 1. miscellaneous items, matters, etc. **2.** fragments; remnants; scraps; bits. [1740–50]

Odds•bod•i•kins (odz bod′i kinz), *interj. Archaic.* Gadsbodikins.

odd•side (od′sīd′), *n. Metall.* a temporary support for a pattern below the joint of a mold, used while the mold is being made. [1830–40; ODD + SIDE[1]]

odds•mak•er (odz′mā′kər), *n.* a person who calculates or predicts the outcome of a contest, as in sports or politics, and sets betting odds. Also, **odds′-mak′er.** [ODDS + MAKER]

odds-on (odz′on′, -ôn′), *adj.* being the one more or most likely to win, succeed, attain, or achieve something: *the odds-on favorite.* [1885–90]

odds′ or e′vens. See **odd or even.**

odd′ trick′, 1. *Bridge.* each trick exceeding six that is taken by the declarer. **2.** *Whist.* the seventh trick taken by a partnership. [1700–10]

ode (ōd), *n.* **1.** a lyric poem typically of elaborate or irregular metrical form and expressive of exalted or enthusiastic emotion. **2.** (originally) a poem intended to be sung. Cf. **Horatian ode, Pindaric ode.** [1580–90; < MF < LL *ōda* < Gk *ōidḗ,* contr. of *aoidḗ* song, deriv. of *aeídein* to sing]

-ode[1], a suffix of nouns, appearing in loanwords from Greek, where it meant "like"; used in the formation of compound words: *phyllode.* Cf. **-oid.** [< Gk *-ōdēs,* prob. generalized from adjectives describing smells, as *kēṓdēs* smelling like incense; base *ōd-* of *ózein* to smell, give off odor]

-ode[2], a combining form meaning "way," "road," used in the formation of compound words: *anode; electrode.* [< Gk *-odos,* comb. form of *hodós*]

O•dels•ting (ōd′ls ting′), *n.* See under **Storting.** Also, **O′dels•thing′.** [< Norw, modern formation from *odel* (ON *ōthal*) allodial rights + *-s* 's[1] + *ting* (ON *thing*) THING[2]]

O•den•se (ō′thən sə), *n.* a seaport on Fyn island, in S Denmark. 168,178.

Ode′ on a Gre′cian Urn′, a poem (1819) by Keats.

O•der (ō′dər), *n.* a river in central Europe, flowing from the NE Czech Republic, N through SW Poland and along the border between Germany and Poland into the Baltic. 562 mi. (905 km) long.

O′der-Neis′se Line′ (ō′dər nī′sə), the boundary between Poland and East Germany after World War II.

O•des•sa (ō des′ə; *for 1 also Russ.* u dye′sə), *n.* **1.** a seaport in S Ukraine, on the Black Sea: 1,046,000. **2.** a city in W Texas. 90,027.

Ode′ to a Night′ingale, a poem (1819) by Keats.

Ode′ to the West′ Wind′, a poem (1820) by Shelley.

O•dets (ō dets′), *n.* **Clifford,** 1906–63, U.S. dramatist.

O•det•ta (ō det′ə), *n.* **1.** (*Odetta Holmes*), born 1930, U.S. folk singer. **2.** a female given name.

O•dette (ō det′), *n.* a female given name.

o•de•um (ō dē′əm), *n., pl.* **o•de•a** (ō dē′ə). **1.** a hall, theater, or other structure for musical or dramatic performances. **2.** (in ancient Greece and Rome) a roofed building for musical performances. [1595–1605; < *ōdēum* music hall < Gk *ōideîon,* equiv. to *ōid(ḗ)* song, ODE + *-eion* suffix denoting place]

od•ic (ō′dik), *adj.* of an ode. [1860–65; ODE + -IC] —**od′i•cal•ly,** *adv.*

O•din (ō′din), *n. Scand. Myth.* the ruler of the Aesir and god of war, poetry, knowledge, and wisdom; Wotan: the chief god. Also, **Othin.** [< ON *Ōthinn;* c. OE *Wōden,* OS *Woden,* OHG *Wuotan;* see WODEN] —**O•din′i•an, O•din′ic, O′din•it′ic,** *adj.* —**O′din•ism,** *n.* —**O′din•ist,** *n.*

o•di•ous (ō′dē əs), *adj.* **1.** deserving or causing hatred; hateful; detestable. **2.** highly offensive; repugnant; disgusting. [1350–1400; ME < L *odiōsus,* equiv. to *od(ium)* hatred, ODIUM + *-ōsus* -OUS] —**o′di•ous•ly,** *adv.* —**o′di•ous•ness,** *n.*
—**Syn. 1.** abominable, objectionable, despicable, execrable. See **hateful. 2.** loathsome, repellent, repulsive. —**Ant. 1.** attractive, lovable.

o•di•um (ō′dē əm), *n.* **1.** intense hatred or dislike, esp. toward a person or thing regarded as contemptible, despicable, or repugnant. **2.** the reproach, discredit, or opprobrium attaching to something hated or repugnant: *He had to bear the odium of neglecting his family.* **3.** the state or quality of being hated. [1595–1605; < L: hatred, equiv. to *od(isse)* to hate + *-ium* -IUM]
—**Syn. 1.** detestation, abhorrence, antipathy. **2.** obloquy. —**Ant. 1.** love.

O•do•a•cer (ō′dō ā′sər), *n.* A.D. 434?–493, first barbarian ruler of Italy 476–493. Also, **Odovacar.**

o•do•graph (ō′də graf′, -gräf′), *n.* **1.** a recording odometer. **2.** a pedometer. **3.** *Naut.* an instrument for recording courses steered by a vessel with the distances or lengths of time run on each. [1880–85; var. of *hodograph* < Gk *hodó(s)* way + -GRAPH]

o•dom•e•ter (ō dom′i tər), *n.* an instrument for measuring distance traveled, as by an automobile. [1785–95, *Amer.*; var. of *hodometer* < Gk *hodó(s)* way + -METER] —**o•do•met•ri•cal** (ō′də me′tri kəl), *adj.* —**o•dom′e•try,** *n.*

o•do•nate (ōd′n āt′, ō don′āt), *adj.* **1.** belonging or pertaining to the order Odonata, comprising the damselflies and dragonflies. —*n.* **2.** any of numerous large predatory aquatic insects of the order Odonata, occurring worldwide and characterized by two pairs of membranous wings. [< NL *Odonata* (1792), irreg. < Gk *odṓn* TOOTH + NL *-ata* -ATA[1]]

odont-, var. of **odonto-** before a vowel: *odontiasis.*

-odont, a combining form meaning "having teeth" of the kind or number specified by the initial element: *diphyodont; selenodont.* Cf. **-odus.** [< Gk *-odont-,* s. of *-odous* or *-odōn* -toothed, having teeth, adj. deriv. of *odoús, odṓn* TOOTH]

o•don•tal•gia (ō′don tal′jə, -jē ə), *n. Dentistry.* pain in a tooth; toothache. [1645–55; ODONT- + -ALGIA] —**o′don•tal′gic,** *adj.*

o•don•ti•a•sis (ō′don tī′ə sis), *n. Dentistry.* dentition (def. 2). [1700–10; < Gk *odontiā(n)* to cut teeth + -SIS]

odonto-, a combining form meaning "tooth," used in the formation of compound words: *odontology.* Also, *esp. before a vowel,* **odont-.** Cf. **-odont, -odus.** [< Gk *odont-,* s. of *odoús* or *odṓn* TOOTH + -O-]

o•don•to•blast (ō don′tə blast′), *n. Anat.* one of a layer of cells lining the pulp cavity of a tooth, from which dentin is formed. [1875–80; ODONTO- + -BLAST] —**o•don′to•blas′tic,** *adj.*

o•don•to•cete (ō don′tə sēt′), *n. Zool.* any whale of the suborder Odontoceti, as dolphins, killer whales, and sperm whales, characterized by an asymmetrical skull, a single blowhole, and rows of teeth, feeding primarily on fish, squid, and crustaceans. Cf. **mysticete.** [1880–85; <

NL *Odontoceti,* equiv. to *odonto-* ODONTO- + *ceti,* pl. of *cetus* whale, L *cētus* < Gk *kētos*]

o·don·tog·e·ny (ō′don toj′ə nē), *n. Dentistry.* the development of teeth. Also, **o·don·to·gen·e·sis** (ō don′tə jen′ə sis). [1850–55; ODONTO- + -GENY] **—o·don·to·gen·ic** (ō don′tə jen′ik), *adj.*

o·don·to·glos·sum (ō don′tə glos′əm), *n.* any epiphytic orchid of the genus *Odontoglossum,* of the mountainous regions from Bolivia to Mexico. [< NL (1816) < Gk *odonto-* ODONTO- + *glôss(a)* tongue + NL *-um* neut. n. suffix]

o·don·to·graph (ō don′tə graf′, -gräf′), *n.* an instrument for laying out the forms of gear teeth or ratchets. [1855–60; ODONTO- + -GRAPH] **—o·don·to·graph·ic** (ō don′tə graf′ik), *adj.* **—o·don·tog·ra·phy** (ō′don-tog′rə fē), *n.*

o·don·toid (ō don′toid), *adj.* of or resembling a tooth; toothlike. [1700–10; < Gk *odontoeidḗs* toothlike. See ODONT-, -OID]

o·don·to·lite (ō don′tl īt′), *n.* See **bone turquoise.** [1810–20; < F; see ODONTO-, -LITE]

o·don·tol·o·gy (ō′don tol′ə jē, od′on-), *n.* the science dealing with the study of the teeth and their surrounding tissues and with the prevention and cure of their diseases. [1810–20; ODONTO- + -LOGY] **—o·don·to·log·i·cal** (ō don′tl oj′i kəl), *adj.* **—o′don·tol′o·gist,** *n.*

o·don·to·phore (ō don′tə fôr′, -fōr′), *n. Zool.* a structure in the mouth of most mollusks over which the radula is drawn backward and forward in the process of breaking up food. [1865–70; < Gk *odontophóros* bearing teeth. See ODONTO-, -PHORE] **—o·don·toph·o·ral** (ō′don-tof′ər əl), **o·don·toph·o·rine** (ō′don tof′ə rīn′, -ər in), **o′don·toph′or·ous,** *adj.*

o·dor (ō′dər), *n.* **1.** the property of a substance that activates the sense of smell: *to have an unpleasant odor.* **2.** a sensation perceived by the sense of smell; scent. **3.** an agreeable scent; fragrance. **4.** a disagreeable smell. **5.** a quality or property characteristic or suggestive of something: *An odor of suspicion surrounded his testimony.* **6.** repute: *in bad odor with the whole community.* **7.** *Archaic.* something that has a pleasant scent. Also, *esp. Brit.,* **odour.** [1250–1300; ME < OF < L] **—o′dor·ful,** *adj.* **—o′dor·less,** *adj.*
—Syn. 3. aroma, redolence, perfume. ODOR, SMELL, SCENT, STENCH all refer to sensations perceived through the nose by the olfactory nerves. ODOR and SMELL in literal contexts are often interchangeable. Figuratively, ODOR also usually occurs in positive contexts: *the odor of sanctity.* SMELL is the most general and neutral of these two terms, deriving connotation generally from the context in which it is used: *the tempting smell of fresh-baked bread; the rank smell of rotting vegetation.* In figurative contexts SMELL may be either positive or negative: *the sweet smell of success; a strong smell of duplicity pervading the affair.* SCENT refers either to delicate and pleasing aromas or to faint, barely perceptible smells: *the scent of lilacs on the soft spring breeze; deer alarmed by the scent of man.* STENCH is strongly negative, referring both literally and figuratively to what is foul, sickening, or repulsive: *the stench of rotting flesh; steeped in the stench of iniquity and treason.*

o·dor·ant (ō′dər ənt), *n.* an odorous substance or product. [1425–75; late ME: fragrant; see ODOR , -ANT]

o·dor·if·er·ous (ō′də rif′ər əs), *adj.* yielding or diffusing an odor. [1425–75; late ME < ML *odōriferus* smelling of (something), equiv. to *odōr-* ODOR + *-i-* -I- + *-ferus* -FEROUS] **—o′dor·if′er·ous·ly,** *adv.* **—o′dor·if′er·ous·ness, o·dor·if·er·os·i·ty** (ō′də rif′ə ros′i tē), *n.*
—Syn. odorous, fragrant, aromatic, perfumed, redolent.

o·dor·ize (ō′də rīz′), *v.t.,* **-ized, -iz·ing.** to make odorous; add scent to: *to odorize natural gas to make leaks detectable.* Also, *esp. Brit.,* **o′dor·ise′.** [1880–85; ODOR + -IZE] **—o′dor·iz′er,** *n.*

o·dor·ous (ō′dər əs), *adj.* odoriferous. [1540–50; < L *odōrus* fragrant. See ODOR, -OUS] **—o′dor·ous·ly,** *adv.* **—o′dor·ous·ness, o·dor·os·i·ty** (ō′də ros′i tē), *n.*

o·dour (ō′dər), *n. Chiefly Brit.* odor.

O·do·va·car (ō′dō vā′kər), *n.* Odoacer.

Ods·bod·i·kins (odz bod′i kinz), *interj. Archaic.* Gadsbodikins. Also, **Ods·bod·kins** (odz bod′kinz), **Odds-bodikins.** [1700–10]

ODT, Office of Defense Transportation.

-odus, var. of **-odont,** esp. in the names of genera in zoology: *ceratodus.* [< NL < Gk *-odous;* see -ODONT]

od·yl (od′il, ō′dil), *n.* od. Also, **od′yle.** [1840–50; OD + *-yl* < Gk *hýlē* matter; see -YL] **—o·dyl·ic** (ō dil′ik), *adj.* **—od′yl·ism,** *n.* **—od′yl·ist,** *n.*

-odynia, a combining form meaning "pain," of the kind or in the place specified by the initial element: *pododynia.* Cf. **-algia.** [< NL < Gk, equiv. to *odýn(ē)* pain + *-ia* -Y[3]]

O·dys·se·us (ō dis′ē əs, ō dis′yōōs), *n. Class. Myth.* king of Ithaca; son of Laertes; one of the heroes of the *Iliad* and protagonist of the *Odyssey:* shrewdest of the Greek leaders in the Trojan War. Latin, **Ulysses.**

Od·ys·sey (od′ə sē), *n., pl.* **-seys** for 2. **1.** (*italics*) an epic poem attributed to Homer, describing Odysseus's adventures in his ten-year attempt to return home to Ithaca after the Trojan War. **2.** (*often l.c.*) a long series of wanderings or adventures, esp. when filled with notable experiences, hardships, etc. **—Od′ys·se′an,** *adj.*

Od·zooks (od zōōks′, -zōōks′), *interj.* Gadzooks. Also, **Od·zook·ers** (od zōōk′ərz, -zōō′kərz). [1685–95]

oe (oi), *n. Scot.* oy.

OE, Old English (def. 1). Also, **OE.**

Oe, *Elect.* oersted; oersteds.

O.E., **1.** Old English (def. 1). **2.** *Com.* omissions excepted.

o.e., *Com.* omissions excepted. Also, **oe**

OECD, Organization for Economic Cooperation and Development.

oec·u·men·i·cal (ek′yōō men′i kəl *or, esp. Brit.,* ē′kyōō-), *adj.* ecumenical. Also, **oec′u·men′ic.**

oe·cus (ē′kəs), *n., pl.* **oe·ci** (ē′sī). (in an ancient Roman house) an apartment, esp. a dining room, decorated with columns. [< L < Gk *oîkos* house]

OED, Oxford English Dictionary. Also, **O.E.D.**

oe·de·ma (i dē′mə), *n., pl.* **-ma·ta** (-mə tə). *Pathol.* edema.

oed·i·pal (ed′ə pəl, ē′də-), *adj.* (*often cap.*) of, characterized by, or resulting from the Oedipus complex. [1935–40; OEDIP(US COMPLEX) + -AL[1]]

Oed·i·pe·an (ed′ə pē′ən), *adj.* of, pertaining to, or characteristic of Oedipus or the Oedipus complex. [1615–25; OEDIP(US) + *-ean,* var. of -IAN]

Oed·i·pus (ed′ə pəs, ē′də-), *n. Gk. Legend.* a king of Thebes, the son of Laius and Jocasta, and the father by Jocasta of Eteocles, Polynices, Antigone, and Ismeme: as was prophesied at his birth, he unwittingly killed his father and married his mother and, in penance, blinded himself and went into exile.

Oed′ipus at Co·lo′nus (kə lō′nəs), a tragedy by Sophocles, written toward the end of his life and produced posthumously in 401? B.C.

Oed′ipus com′plex, *Psychoanal.* the unresolved desire of a child for sexual gratification through the parent of the opposite sex, esp. the desire of a son for his mother. This involves, first, identification with and, later, hatred for the parent of the same sex, who is considered by the child as a rival. Cf. **Electra complex.** [1890–95]

Oed′ipus Rex′, a tragedy (c430 B.C.) by Sophocles. Also called ***Oed′ipus Ty·ran′nus*** (ti ran′əs).

OEEC, Organization for European Economic Cooperation.

oeil-de-boeuf (*Fr.* œ′yᵊ də bœf′), *n., pl.* **oeils-de-boeuf** (*Fr.* œ′yᵊ də bœf′). a comparatively small round or oval window, as in a frieze. Also called **oxeye.** [< F: lit., bull's eye]

oeil·lade (œ yad′), *n., pl.* ***oeil·lades*** (œ yad′). *French.* an amorous glance; ogle.

OEM, See **original equipment manufacturer.**

Oe·ne·us (ē′nē əs, -nyōōs), *n. Class. Myth.* a king of Calydon believed to have been the first man to cultivate grapes.

oe·noch·o·e (ē nok′ō ē′), *n., pl.* **oe·noch·o·es, oe·noch·o·ai** (ē nok′ō ī′). oinochoe.

oe·nol·o·gy (ē nol′ə jē), *n.* the science of viniculture. Also, **enology.** [1805–15; < Gk *oîn(os)* WINE + *-o-* + -LOGY] **—oe·no·log·i·cal** (ēn′l oj′i kəl), *adj.* **—oe·nol′o·gist,** *n.*

oe·no·mel (ē′nə mel′, en′ə-), *n.* **1.** a drink made of wine mixed with honey. **2.** something combining strength with sweetness. [1565–75; < LL *oenomeli* < Gk *oinómeli,* equiv. to *oîno(s)* WINE + *méli* honey]

Oe·no·ne (ē nō′nē), *n. Class. Myth.* a nymph of Mount Ida who was the wife of Paris, but was deserted by him for Helen.

oe·no·phile (ē′nə fīl′), *n.* a person who enjoys wines, usually as a connoisseur. Also, **oe·noph·i·list** (ē nof′ə-list). [1925–30; < F < Gk *oîn(os)* WINE + *-o-* -O- + F *-phile* -PHILE] **—oe·no·phil·i·a** (ē′nə fil′ē ə), *n.* **—oe′no·phil′ic,** *adj.*

OEO, See **Office of Economic Opportunity.**

o'er (ôr, ōr), *prep., adv. Literary.* over.

oer·sted (ûr′sted), *n. Elect.* **1.** the centimeter-gram-second unit of magnetic intensity, equal to the magnetic pole of unit strength when undergoing a force of one dyne in a vacuum. *Abbr.:* Oe **2.** (formerly) the unit of magnetic reluctance equal to the reluctance of a centimeter cube of vacuum between parallel surfaces. *Abbr.:* Oe [1875–80; named after H. C. OERSTED]

Oer·sted (ûr′sted; *Dan.* œʀ′stith), *n.* **Hans Chris·tian** (häns kʀis′tyän), 1777–1851, Danish physicist.

OES, **1.** Office of Economic Stabilization. **2.** Order of the Eastern Star.

Oe·sel (œ′zəl), *n.* German name of **Saaremaa.**

oesophag-, var. of **esophag-.**

oe·soph·a·ge·al (i sof′ə jē′əl, ē′sə faj′ē əl), *adj.* esophageal.

oes·trous (es′trəs, ē′strəs), *adj.* estrous. [OESTR(US) + -OUS]

oes·trus (es′trəs, ē′strəs), *n.* estrus. [1690–1700; < L < Gk *oîstros* gadfly, sting, madness]

oeu·vre (œ′vʀᵊ), *n., pl.* ***oeu·vres*** (œ′vʀᵊ). *French.* **1.** the works of a writer, painter, or the like, taken as a whole. **2.** any one of the works of a writer, painter, or the like.

of[1] (uv, ov; *unstressed* əv *or, esp. before consonants,* ə), *prep.* **1.** (used to indicate distance or direction from, separation, deprivation, etc.): *within a mile of the church; south of Omaha; to be robbed of one's money.* **2.** (used to indicate derivation, origin, or source): *a man of good family; the plays of Shakespeare; a piece of cake.* **3.** (used to indicate cause, motive, occasion, or reason): *to die of hunger.* **4.** (used to indicate material, component parts, substance, or contents): *a dress of silk; an apartment of three rooms; a book of poems; a package of cheese.* **5.** (used to indicate apposition or identity): *Is that idiot of a salesman calling again?* **6.** (used to indicate specific identity or a particular item within a category): *the city of Chicago; thoughts of love.* **7.** (used to indicate possession, connection, or association): *the king of France; the property of the church.* **8.** (used to indicate inclusion in a number, class, or whole): *one of us.* **9.** (used to indicate the objective relation, the object of the action noted by the preceding noun or the application of a verb or adjective): *the ringing of bells; He writes her of home; I'm tired of working.* **10.** (used to indicate reference or respect): *There is talk of peace.* **11.** (used to indicate qualities or attributes): *an ambassador of remarkable tact.* **12.** (used to indicate a specified time): *They arrived of an evening.* **13.** *Chiefly Northern U.S.* before the hour of; until: *twenty minutes of five.* **14.** on the part of: *It was very mean of you to laugh at me.* **15.** in respect to: *fleet of foot.* **16.** set aside for or devoted to: *a minute of prayer.* **17.** *Archaic.* by: *consumed of worms.* [bef. 900; ME, OE: of, off; c. G *ab,* L *ab,* Gk *apó.* See OFF, A-[2], O']
—Usage. OF is sometimes added to phrases beginning with the adverb *how* or *too* followed by a descriptive adjective: *How long of a drive will it be? It's too hot of a day for tennis.* This construction is probably modeled on that in which *how* or *too* is followed by *much,* an unquestionably standard use in all varieties of speech and writing: *How much of a problem will that cause the government? There was too much of an uproar for the speaker to be heard.* The use of OF with descriptive adjectives after *how* or *too* is largely restricted to informal speech. It occurs occasionally in informal writing and written representations of speech. See also **couple, off.**

of[2] (əv), *auxiliary v. Pron. Spelling.* have: *He should of asked me first.* Cf. **a**[4].
—Pronunciation. Because the preposition OF, when unstressed (*a piece of cake*), and the unstressed or contracted auxiliary verb HAVE (*could have gone, could've gone*) are both pronounced (əv) or (ə) in connected speech, inexperienced writers commonly confuse the two words, spelling HAVE as OF (*I would of handed in my book report, but the dog ate it*). Professional writers have been able to exploit this spelling deliberately, especially in fiction, to help represent the speech of the uneducated: *If he could of went home, he would of.*

of-, var. of **ob-** (by assimilation) before *f: offend.*

OF, Old French. Also, **OF., O.F.**

O'Fal·lon (ō fal′ən), *n.* a town in SW Illinois. 10,217.

O'Fao·láin (ō fā′lən, ō fal′ən), *n.* **Seán** (shôn), 1900–91, Irish writer and teacher.

o·fay (ō′fā), *n. Slang* (*disparaging and offensive*). a white person. Also, **fay.** [1920–25, *Amer.;* of obscure orig.; the popular notion that the word is a Pig Latin deformation of *foe* is very dubious]

off (ôf, of), *adv.* **1.** so as to be no longer supported or attached: *This button is about to come off.* **2.** so as to be no longer covering or enclosing: *to take a hat off; to take the wrapping off.* **3.** away from a place: *to run off; to look off toward the west.* **4.** away from a path, course, etc.; aside: *This road branches off to Grove City.* **5.** so as to be away or on one's way: *to start off early; to cast off.* **6.** away from what is considered normal, regular, standard, or the like: *to go off on a tangent.* **7.** from a charge or price: *He took 10 percent off for all cash purchases.* **8.** at a distance in space or future time: *to back off a few feet; Summer is only a week off.* **9.** out of operation or effective existence: *Turn the lights off.* **10.** into operation or action: *The alarm goes off at noon.* **11.** so as to interrupt continuity or cause discontinuance: *Negotiations have been broken off.* **12.** in absence from work, service, a job, etc.: *two days off at Christmas.* **13.** completely; utterly: *to kill off all the inhabitants.* **14.** with prompt or ready performance: *to dash a letter off.* **15.** to fulfillment, or into execution or effect: *The contest came off on the appointed day.* **16.** into nonexistence or nothingness: *My headache passed off soon.* **17.** so as to be delineated, divided, or apportioned: *Mark it off into equal parts.* **18.** away from a state of consciousness: *I must have dozed off.* **19.** *Naut.* away from the land, a ship, the wind, etc. **20. get it off.** See **get** (def. 45). **21. get off on.** See **get** (def. 49). **22. off and on, a.** Also, **on and off.** with intervals between; intermittently: *to work off and on.* **b.** *Naut.* on alternate tacks. **23. off with, a.** take away; remove: *Off with those muddy boots before you step into this kitchen!* **b.** cut off: *Off with his head!*
—prep. **24.** so as no longer to be supported by, attached to, on, resting on, or unified with: *Take your feet off the table! Break a piece of bread off the loaf.* **25.** deviating from: *off balance; off course.* **26.** below or less than the usual or expected level or standard: *20 percent off the marked price; I was off my golf game.* **27.** away, disengaged, or resting from: *to be off duty on Tuesdays.* **28.** *Informal.* refraining or abstaining from; denying oneself the pleasure, company, practice, etc., of: *He's off gambling.* **29.** away from; apart or distant from: *a village off the main road.* **30.** leading into or away from: *an alley off 12th Street.* **31.** not fixed on or directed toward, as the gaze, eyes, etc.: *Their eyes weren't off the king for a moment.* **32.** *Informal.* from (a specified source): *I bought it off a street vendor.* **33.** from or of, indicating material or component parts: *to lunch off cheese and fruit.* **34.** from or by such means or use of: *living off an inheritance; living off his parents.* **35.** *Naut.* at some distance to seaward of: *off Cape Hatteras.* **36. off of,** *Informal.* off: *Take your feet off of the table!*
—adj. **37.** in error; wrong: *You are off on that point.* **38.** slightly abnormal or not quite sane: *He is a little off, but he's really harmless.* **39.** not up to standard; not so good or satisfactory as usual; inferior or subnormal: *a good play full of off moments.* **40.** no longer in effect, in operation, or in process: *The agreement is off.* **41.** stopped from flowing, as by the closing of a valve: *The electricity is off.* **42.** in a specified state, circumstance, etc.: *to be badly off for money.* **43.** (of time) free from work or duty; nonworking: *a pastime for one's off hours.* **44.** not working at one's usual occupation: *We're off Wednesdays during the summer.* **45.** of less than the ordinary activity, liveliness, or lively interest; slack: *an off season in the tourist trade.* **46.** unlikely; remote; doubtful: *on the off chance that we'd find her at home.* **47.** more distant; farther: *the off side of a wall.* **48.** (of a

vehicle, single animal, or pair of animals hitched side by side) of, being, or pertaining to the right as seen from the rider's or driver's viewpoint (opposed to *near*): *the off horse; the off side.* **49.** starting on one's way; leaving: *I'm off to Europe on Monday. They're off and running in the third race at Aqueduct.* **50.** lower in price or value; down: *Stock prices were off this morning.* **51.** *Naut.* noting one of two like things that is the farther from the shore; seaward: *the off side of the ship.* **52.** *Cricket.* noting or pertaining to that side of the wicket or of the field opposite that on which the batsman stands. —*n.* **53.** the state or fact of being off. **54.** *Cricket.* the off side. —*v.i.* **55.** to go off or away; leave (used imperatively): *Off, and don't come back!* —*v.t.* **56.** *Slang.* to kill; slay. [orig. stressed var. of OF[1]]

—**Usage.** The phrasal preposition OFF OF is old in English, going back to the 16th century. Although usage guides reject it as redundant, recommending OFF without OF, the phrase is widespread in speech, including that of the educated: *Let's watch as the presidential candidates come off of the rostrum and down into the audience.* OFF OF is rare in edited writing except to give the flavor of speech.

-off, a suffixal use of the adverb **off,** forming nouns that denote competitions, esp. between the finalists of earlier competitions or as a means of deciding a tie: *cookoff; playoff; runoff.*

off., 1. offered. 2. office. 3. officer. 4. official.

of·fal (ô′fəl, of′əl), *n.* **1.** the parts of a butchered animal that are considered inedible by human beings; carrion. **2.** the parts of a butchered animal removed in dressing; viscera. **3.** refuse; rubbish; garbage. [1350–1400; ME, equiv. to *of* OFF + *fal* FALL; cf. D *afval*]

Of·fa·ly (ô′fə lē, of′ə-), *n.* a county in Leinster, in the central Republic of Ireland. 51,829; 760 sq. mi. (1970 sq. km). *Co. seat:* Tullamore.

off-base (ôf′bās′, of′-), *adj.* located outside the perimeters of a military base: *off-base housing for officers.* [1935–40]

off·beat (*adj.* ôf′bēt′, of′-; *n.* ôf′bēt′, of′-), *adj.* **1.** differing from the usual or expected; unconventional: *an offbeat comedian.* —*n.* **2.** *Music.* an unaccented beat of a measure. [1925–30; OFF + BEAT]

off-board (ôf′bôrd′, -bōrd′, of′-), *adj., adv. Stock Exchange.* outside of a major exchange, as over the counter or between private parties: *an off-board transaction.* Also, **off-the-board.** [1945–50]

off-brand (ôf′brand′, of′-), *adj.* **1.** not having a recognized or popular brand or name: *an off-brand TV set.* **2.** being a cheap or inferior brand or grade: *off-brand batteries that never work when you need them.* —*n.* **3.** a brand or name that is unrecognized or relatively unfamiliar. **4.** a cheap or inferior brand.

off′ Broad′way, professional drama produced in New York City in small theaters often away from the Broadway area and characterized by experimental productions. Also, **Off′ Broad′way.** [1950–55, *Amer.*] —**off′-Broad′way,** *adj., adv.*

off-bud·get (ôf′buj′it, of′-), *adj. U.S. Govt.* not included in the regular federal budget; funded through separate agencies.

off-cam·er·a (ôf′kam′ər ə, -kam′rə, of′-), *adj.* **1.** occurring as part of a film or program but outside the range of the motion-picture or television camera: *the off-camera shouts of a mob.* —*adv.* **2.** out of the range of a motion-picture or television camera: *The star walked off-camera at the end of his monologue.* **3.** (of an actor) in one's private rather than professional life: *Off-camera the movie star liked to cook.*

off-cam·pus (ôf′kam′pəs, of′-), *adj.* **1.** located or available outside a campus. —*adv.* **2.** outside or away from a campus. [1950–55, *Amer.*]

off·cast (ôf′kast′, -käst′, of′-), *adj.* **1.** discarded or rejected; castoff: *his offcast suits.* —*n.* **2.** a castoff person or thing. [1565–75; adj., n. use of v. phrase *cast off*]

off-cen·ter (ôf′sen′tər, of′-), *adj.* Also, **off′-cen′·tered. 1.** not centered; diverging from the exact center. **2.** unconventional; eccentric: *off-center characters who disrupt other people's lives.* [1925–30]

off-col·or (ôf′kul′ər, of′-), *adj.* **1.** not having the usual or standard color: *an off-color gem.* **2.** of doubtful propriety or taste; risqué: *an off-color joke.* **3.** not in one's usual health: *to feel off-color.* Also, *esp. Brit.,* **off′-col′our.** Also, **off′-col′ored** (for defs. 1, 2). [1855–60]

—**Syn. 2.** racy, spicy, salty, earthy, blue.

off-du·ty (ôf′do͞o′tē, -dyo͞o′-, of′-), *adj.* **1.** not engaged in the performance of one's usual work: *an off-duty police officer.* **2.** of, pertaining to, or during a period when a person is not at work. [1850–55]

Of·fen·bach (ô′fən bäk′, of′ən-; *for 1 also Fr.* ô fenbak′; *for 2 also Ger.* ôf′ən bäKH′), *n.* **1. Jacques** (zhäk), 1819–80, French composer. **2.** a city in S Hesse, in central Germany, on the Main River, near Frankfurt. 114,200.

of·fence (ə fens′, ô′fens, of′ens), *n.* offense.

of·fend (ə fend′), *v.t.* **1.** to irritate, annoy, or anger; cause resentful displeasure in: *Even the hint of prejudice offends me.* **2.** to affect (the sense, taste, etc.) disagreeably. **3.** to violate or transgress (a criminal, religious, or moral law). **4.** to hurt or cause pain to. **5.** (in Biblical use) to cause to fall into sinful ways. —*v.i.* **6.** to cause resentful displeasure; irritate, annoy, or anger: *a remark so thoughtless it can only offend.* **7.** to err in conduct; commit a sin, crime, or fault. [1275–1325; ME *offenden* < MF *offendre* < L *offendere* to strike against, displease, equiv. to *of-* OF- + *-fendere* to strike] —**of·fend′a·ble,** *adj.* —**of·fend′ed·ly,** *adv.* —**of·fend′ed·ness,** *n.* —**of·fend′er,** *n.*

—**Syn. 1.** provoke, chafe, nettle, affront, insult. **7.** transgress. —**Ant. 1.** please.

of·fense (ə fens′ *or, for 7–9,* ô′fens, of′ens), *n.* **1.** a violation or breaking of a social or moral rule; transgression; sin. **2.** a transgression of the law; misdemeanor. **3.** a cause of transgression or wrong. **4.** something that offends or displeases. **5.** the act of offending or displeasing. **6.** the feeling of resentful displeasure caused: *to give offense.* **7.** the act of attacking; attack or assault: *weapons of offense.* **8.** a person, army, etc., that is attacking. **9.** *Sports.* **a.** the players or team unit responsible for attacking or scoring in a game. **b.** the players possessing or controlling the ball, puck, etc., or the aspects or period of a game when this obtains. **c.** a pattern or style of scoring attack: *single-wing offense; fast-break offense.* **d.** offensive effectiveness; ability to score: *a total breakdown in offense.* **10.** *Archaic.* injury, harm, or hurt. Also, **offence.** [1325–75; ME *offence, offense;* in part < MF *offens* < L *offēnsus* collision, knock, equiv. to *offend(ere)* (see OFFEND) + *-tus* suffix of v. action; in part < MF *offense* << L *offēnsa,* fem. ptp. of *offendere*]

—**Syn. 1, 2.** trespass, felony, fault. See **crime. 6.** umbrage, resentment, wrath, indignation. **7.** aggression. **8.** besiegers, attackers, enemy, foe. —**Ant. 6.** pleasure. **7.** defense.

of·fense·less (ə fens′lis), *adj.* **1.** without offense. **2.** incapable of offense or attack. **3.** not offensive. Also, **of·fence′less.** [1595–1605; OFFENSE + -LESS] —**of·fense′less·ly,** *adv.*

of·fen·sive (ə fen′siv *or, for 4, 5,* ô′fen-, of′en-), *adj.* **1.** causing resentful displeasure; highly irritating, angering, or annoying: *offensive television commercials.* **2.** unpleasant or disagreeable to the sense: *an offensive odor.* **3.** repugnant to the moral sense, good taste, or the like; insulting: *an offensive remark; an offensive joke.* **4.** pertaining to offense or attack: *the offensive movements of their troops.* **5.** characterized by attack; aggressive: *offensive warfare.* —*n.* **6.** the position or attitude of aggression or attack: *to take the offensive.* **7.** an aggressive movement or attack: *a carefully planned naval offensive.* [1540–50; < ML *offēnsīvus,* equiv. to L *offēns(us)* ptp. of *offendere* (see OFFEND) + *-īvus* -IVE] —**of·fen′sive·ly,** *adv.* —**of·fen′sive·ness,** *n.*

—**Syn. 1.** displeasing, vexatious, vexing, unpleasant. See **hateful. 2, 3.** distasteful, disgusting, revolting, repellent. **3.** repulsive, shocking. **4.** invading, attacking. —**Ant. 1, 2.** pleasing. **4.** defensive.

of·fer (ô′fər, of′ər), *v.t.* **1.** to present for acceptance or rejection; proffer: *He offered me a cigarette.* **2.** to propose or put forward for consideration: *to offer a suggestion.* **3.** to propose or volunteer (to do something): *She offered to accompany me.* **4.** to make a show of intention (to do something): *We did not offer to go first.* **5.** to give, make, or promise: *She offered no response.* **6.** to present solemnly as an act of worship or devotion, as to God, a deity or a saint; sacrifice. **7.** to present for sale: *He offered the painting to me at a reduced price.* **8.** to tender or bid as a price: *to offer ten dollars for a radio.* **9.** to attempt or threaten to do, engage in, or inflict: *to offer battle.* **10.** to put forth; exert: *to offer resistance.* **11.** to present to sight or notice. **12.** to introduce or present for exhibition or performance. **13.** to render (homage, thanks, etc.). **14.** to present or volunteer (oneself) to someone as a spouse. —*v.i.* **15.** to present itself; occur: *Whenever an opportunity offered, he slipped off to town.* **16.** to present something as an act of worship or devotion; sacrifice. **17.** to make a proposal or suggestion. **18.** to suggest oneself to someone for marriage; propose. **19.** *Archaic.* to make an attempt (fol. by *at*). —*n.* **20.** an act or instance of offering: *an offer of help.* **21.** the condition of being offered: *an offer for sale.* **22.** something offered. **23.** a proposal or bid to give or pay something as the price of something else; bid: *an offer of $90,000 for the house.* **24.** *Law.* a proposal that requires only acceptance in order to create a contract. **25.** an attempt or endeavor. **26.** a show of intention. **27.** a proposal of marriage. [bef. 900; ME *offren,* OE *offrian* to present in worship < L *offerre,* equiv. to *of-* OF- + *ferre* to bring, BEAR[1]] —**of′fer·a·ble,** *adj.* —**of′fer·er, of′·fer·or,** *n.*

—**Syn. 1.** OFFER, PROFFER, TENDER mean to present for acceptance or refusal. OFFER is a common word in general use for presenting something to be accepted or rejected: *to offer assistance.* PROFFER, with the same meaning, is now chiefly a literary word: *to proffer one's services.* TENDER (no longer used in reference to concrete objects) is a ceremonious term for a more or less formal or conventional act: *to tender one's resignation.* **2.** give, move, propose. —**Ant. 1.** withdraw, withhold. **20.** refusal, denial.

of·fer·ing (ô′fər ing, of′ər-), *n.* **1.** something offered in worship or devotion, as to a deity; an oblation or sacrifice. **2.** a contribution given to or through the church for a particular purpose, as at a religious service. **3.** anything offered as a gift. **4.** something presented for inspection or sale. **5.** a sale: *our spring offering of furniture.* **6.** the act of one who offers. [bef. 1000; ME; OE *offrung.* See OFFER, -ING[1]]

of′fering price′, the price quoted when something is offered for sale, esp. the price per share, as of an investment security or mutual fund being sold to the public.

of·fer·to·ry (ô′fər tôr′ē, -tōr′ē, of′ər-), *n., pl.* **-ries. 1.** (*sometimes cap.*) the offering of the unconsecrated elements that is made to God by the celebrant in a Eucharistic service. **2.** *Eccles.* **a.** the verses, anthem, or music said, sung, or played while the offerings of the people are received at a religious service. **b.** that part of a service at which offerings are made. **c.** the offerings themselves. [1350–1400; ME *offertorie* < ML *offertōrium* place to which offerings are brought, offering, oblation, equiv. to L *offer(re)* (see OFFER) + *-tōrium* -TORY[2]; cf. OBLATION] —**of′fer·to′ri·al,** *adj.*

off-glide (ôf′glīd′, of′-), *n. Phonet.* **1.** a transitional sound produced as the vocal organs move from a previous speech sound to an inactive position or to the position of a following sound. Cf. **on-glide. 2.** the final, weaker part of a complex vowel, such as a diphthong, as the (i) sound of the (oi) in *boy.* [1875–80]

off·hand (ôf′hand′, of′-), *adv.* **1.** cavalierly, curtly, or brusquely: *to reply offhand.* **2.** without previous thought or preparation; extempore: *to decide offhand to take a trip.* —*adj.* **3.** informal, casual, curt, or brusque: *an offhand manner.* **4.** Also, **off′hand′ed.** done or made offhand. **5.** *Glassmaking.* working manually and without the use of molds: *offhand blowing.* [1685–95; OFF + HAND] —**off′hand′ed·ly,** *adv.* —**off′hand′ed·ness,** *n.*

—**Syn. 1.** short, shortly, abruptly. **3, 4.** impromptu, extempore. —**Ant. 4.** considered.

off-hour (*n.* ôf′ouər′, -ou′ər, -ouər′, -ou′ər, of′-; *adj.* ôf′ouər′, -ou′ər, of′-), *n.* **1.** an hour or other period when a person is not at a job: *I spend my off-hours reading.* **2.** a period outside of rush hours or greatest activity: *I travel by subway during the off-hours.* —*adj.* **3.** of, pertaining to, or during an off-hour: *The off-hour traffic will be lighter.* [1930–35]

of·fice (ô′fis, of′is), *n.* **1.** a room, set of rooms, or building where the business of a commercial or industrial organization or of a professional person is conducted: *the main office of an insurance company; a doctor's office.* **2.** a room assigned to a specific person or a group of persons in a commercial or industrial organization: *Her office is next to mine.* **3.** a business or professional organization: *He went to work in an architect's office.* **4.** the staff or designated part of a staff at a commercial or industrial organization: *The whole office was at his wedding.* **5.** a position of duty, trust, or authority, esp. in the government, a corporation, a society, or the like: *She was elected twice to the office of president.* **6.** employment or position as an official: *to seek office.* **7.** the duty, function, or part of a particular person or agency: *to act in the office of adviser.* **8.** (*cap.*) an operating agency or division of certain departments of the U.S. Government: *Office of Community Services.* **9.** (*cap.*) *Brit.* a major administrative unit or department of the national government: *the Foreign Office.* **10.** *Slang.* hint, signal, or warning; high sign. **11.** Often, **offices.** something, whether good or bad, done or said for or to another: *He obtained a position through the offices of a friend.* **12.** *Eccles.* **a.** the prescribed order or form for a service of the church or for devotional use. **b.** the services so prescribed. **c.** Also called **divine office.** the prayers, readings from Scripture, and psalms that must be recited every day by all who are in major orders. **d.** a ceremony or rite, esp. for the dead. **13.** a service or task to be performed; assignment; chore: *little domestic offices.* **14. offices,** *Chiefly Brit.* **a.** the parts of a house, as the kitchen, pantry, or laundry, devoted mainly to household work. **b.** the stables, barns, cowhouses, etc., of a farm. **15.** *Older Slang.* privy. [1200–50; ME < OF < L *officium* service, duty, ceremony, presumably contr. of *opificium,* equiv. to *opi-,* comb. form akin to *opus* OPUS + *-fic-,* comb. form of *facere* to make, DO[1] + *-ium* -IUM] —**of′fice·less,** *adj.*

—**Syn. 5.** post, station, berth, situation. See **appointment. 7.** responsibility, charge, trust. **13.** work, duty.

of′fice automa′tion, a method or system of using automated or electronic equipment, as word processors and computers, in the operations of an office. —**of′·fice-au′to·ma′tion,** *adj.*

of′fice block′, *Brit.* a large office building. [1940–45]

of′fice-block bal′lot (ô′fis blok′, of′is-), a ballot on which the candidates are listed alphabetically, with or without their party designations, in columns under the office for which they were nominated. Cf. **Indiana ballot, Massachusetts ballot.**

of′fice boy′, a person, traditionally a boy, employed in an office to run errands, do odd jobs, etc. [1840–50]

of·fice·hold·er (ô′fis hōl′dər, of′is-), *n.* a person filling a governmental position; public official. [1850–55; OFFICE + HOLDER]

of′fice hours′, 1. the hours during which a professional person or an office conducts regular business. **2.** the hours a person spends working in an office. [1795–1805]

Of′fice of Civ′il and Defense′ Mobiliza′tion, the former division (1958–61) of the Executive Office of the President that administered all federal programs dealing with the defense by civilians of their homes, families, communities, etc., in the event of enemy attack. *Abbr.:* OCDM

Of′fice of Defense′ Transporta′tion, the World War II federal agency (1941–45) that regulated the transport over public routes of goods considered vital to the war effort. *Abbr.:* ODT

Of′fice of Econom′ic Opportun′ity, a former name of the **Community Services Administration.** *Abbr.:* OEO

Of′fice of Man′agement and Budg′et. See **OMB.**

Of′fice of Price′ Administra′tion. See **OPA.**

Of′fice of Technol′ogy Assess′ment, *U.S. Govt.* a bipartisan agency, created in 1972, that informs and advises Congress about scientific and technical developments bearing on national policy. *Abbr.:* OTA

Of′fice of War′ Informa′tion. See **OWI.**

of′fice park′, a commercial complex consisting of an office building set in parklike surroundings, often with such facilities as parking lots, restaurants, and recreational areas. Also called **business park, executive park, of′fice pla′za.**

of·fi·cer (ô′fə sər, of′ə-), *n.* **1.** a person who holds a position of rank or authority in the army, navy, air force, or any similar organization, esp. one who holds a commission. **2.** a member of a police department or a constable. **3.** a person licensed to take full or partial responsibility for the operation of a merchant ship or other large civilian ship; a master or mate. **4.** a person ap-

CONCISE ETYMOLOGY KEY: <, descended or borrowed from; >, whence; b., blend of, blended; c., cognate with; cf., compare; deriv., derivative; equiv., equivalent; imit., imitative; obl., oblique; r., replacing; s., stem; sp., spelling, spelled; resp., respelling, respelled; trans., translation; ?, origin unknown; *, unattested; ‡, probably earlier than. See the full key inside the front cover.

pointed or elected to some position of responsibility or authority in the government, a corporation, a society, etc. **5.** (in some honorary orders) a member of any rank except the lowest. **6.** *Obs.* an agent. —*v.t.* **7.** to furnish with officers. **8.** to command or direct as an officer does. **9.** to direct, conduct, or manage. [1275–1325; ME < AF; MF *officier* < ML *officiārius,* equiv. to L *offici(um)* OFFICE + *-ārius* -ARY; see -ER[2], -IER[2]] —**of′fi·cer·i·al** (ô′fə sēr′ē əl, of′ə-), *adj.* —**of′fi·cer·less,** *adj.* —**of′fi·cer·ship′, of′fi·cer·hood′,** *n.*

of′ficer of arms′, an officer with the duties of a herald, esp. one charged with the devising, granting, or confirming of armorial bearings. [1490–1500]

of′ficer of the day′, *Mil.* an officer who has charge of the guard and prisoners on an assigned day at a military installation. *Abbr.:* OD, O.D., O.O.D. [1835–45]

of′ficer of the deck′, a naval duty officer responsible for the operation of the ship in the absence of the captain or the executive officer. *Abbr.* O.O.D.

of′ficer of the guard′, *Mil.* an officer, acting under the officer of the day, who is responsible for the instruction, discipline, and performance of duty of the guard in a post, camp, or station. *Abbr.:* OG, O.G.

of′ficer of the watch′, *Naut.* the officer primarily responsible for the navigation of a ship, in the absence of the captain, during a certain watch.

of′fice seek′er, a person who seeks appointment or election to some government position. [1805–15, *Amer.*]

of·fi·cial (ə fish′əl), *n.* **1.** a person appointed or elected to an office or charged with certain duties. —*adj.* **2.** of or pertaining to an office or position of duty, trust, or authority: *official powers.* **3.** authorized or issued authoritatively: *an official report.* **4.** holding office. **5.** appointed or authorized to act in a designated capacity: *an official representative.* **6.** (of an activity or event) intended for the notice of the public and performed or held on behalf of officials or of an organization; formal: *the official opening of a store.* **7.** *Pharm.* noting drugs or drug preparations that are recognized by and that conform to the standards of the *United States Pharmacopeia* or the *National Formulary.* [1300–50; ME < LL *officiālis* of duty, equiv. to L *offici(um)* OFFICE + *-ālis* -AL[1]] —**of·fi′cial·ly,** *adv.*

of·fi·cial·dom (ə fish′əl dəm), *n.* **1.** the class or entire body of officials; officials as a whole. **2.** the position or domain of officials. [1860–65; OFFICIAL + -DOM]

of·fi·cial·ese (ə fish′ə lēz′, -lēs′), *n.* a style of language used in some official statements, often criticized for its use of polysyllabic jargon and obscure, pretentiously wordy phrasing. [1880–85; OFFICIAL + -ESE]

offi′cial fam′ily, the executives or officials chiefly responsible for the operation of an organization or government. [1900–05, *Amer.*]

of·fi·cial·ism (ə fish′ə liz′əm), *n.* **1.** excessive attention to official regulations and routines. **2.** official methods or systems. **3.** officials collectively. [1855–60; OFFICIAL + -ISM]

of·fi·cial·ize (ə fish′ə līz′), *v.t.,* **-ized, -iz·ing.** to make official; place under official authority or control. Also, *esp. Brit.,* **of·fi′cial·ise′.** [1840–50; OFFICIAL + -IZE] —**of·fi′cial·i·za′tion,** *n.*

of·fi·ci·ant (ə fish′ē ənt), *n.* a person who officiates at a religious service or ceremony. [1835–45; < ML *officiant-* (s. of *officiāns*), prp. of *officiāre* to serve, equiv. to L *offici(um)* OFFICE + *-ant-* -ANT]

of·fi·ci·ar·y (ə fish′ē er′ē), *adj.* **1.** pertaining to or derived from an office, as a title. **2.** having a title or rank derived from an office, as a dignitary. [1605–15; < L *offici(um)* OFFICE + -ARY]

of·fi·ci·ate (ə fish′ē āt′), *v.,* **-at·ed, -at·ing.** —*v.i.* **1.** to perform the office of a member of the clergy, as at a divine service. **2.** to perform the duties or function of some office or position. **3.** to serve as referee, umpire, or other official in a sports contest or game. —*v.t.* **4.** to serve as the priest or minister of (a divine service, religious ceremony, etc.). **5.** to perform, carry out, or fulfill (an official duty or function). **6.** to act as a referee, umpire, timekeeper, or other official for (a sports contest or game). [1625–35; < ML *officiātus* (ptp. of *officiāre* to serve), equiv. to L *offici(um)* OFFICE + *-ātus* -ATE[1]] —**of·fi′ci·a′tion,** *n.* —**of·fi′ci·a′tor,** *n.*

of·fic·i·nal (ə fis′ə nl), *adj.* **1.** kept in stock by apothecaries, as a drug. Cf. **magistral** (def. 1). **2.** recognized by a pharmacopoeia. —*n.* **3.** an officinal medicine. [1710–20; < ML *officīnālis* of a store or workshop, equiv. to L *officīn(a)* workshop, presumably contr. of *opificīna* (*opific-,* s. of *opifex* artisan, equiv. to *opi-,* comb. form akin to *opus* work + *-fic-,* comb. form of *facere* to make, DO[1] + *-īna* -INE[1]; cf. OFFICE) + *-ālis* -AL[1]] —**of·fic′i·nal·ly,** *adv.*

of·fi·cious (ə fish′əs), *adj.* **1.** objectionably aggressive in offering one's unrequested and unwanted services, help, or advice; meddlesome: *an officious person.* **2.** marked by or proceeding from such forwardness: *officious interference.* **3.** *Obs.* ready to serve; obliging. [1555–65; < L *officiōsus* obliging, dutiful, equiv. to *offici(um)* OFFICE + *-ōsus* -OUS] —**of·fi′cious·ly,** *adv.* —**of·fi′cious·ness,** *n.*
—**Syn. 1.** interfering, meddling. —**Ant. 1.** retiring.

offi′cious will′, *Law.* a will by which the testator gives his or her property to the natural objects of such bounty, as the family. Also called **offi′cious tes′tament.** Cf. **inofficious will.**

off·ing (ô′fing, of′ing), *n.* **1.** the more distant part of the sea seen from the shore, beyond the anchoring ground. **2.** a position at a distance from shore. **3. in the offing, a.** at a distance but within sight. **b.** in the projected future; likely to happen: *A wedding is in the offing.* [1620–30; OFF + -ING[1]]

off·ish (ô′fish, of′ish), *adj. Informal.* aloof; unapproachable; standoffish. [1825–35, *Amer.*; OFF + -ISH[1]] —**off′ish·ly,** *adv.* —**off′ish·ness,** *n.*

off-is·land (ôf′ī′lənd, of′-), *adj.* **1.** located or tending away from the shore of an island: *an off-island current.* —*adv.* **2.** away from the shore of an island: *The ship sank about two miles off-island.* [1915–20]

off-is·land·er (ôf′ī′lən dər, of′-), *n.* **1.** a temporary or seasonal resident of an island; island visitor or tourist. **2.** a person living on an offshore island. [1880–85]

off-key (ôf′kē′, of′-), *adj.* **1.** deviating from the correct tone or pitch; out of tune. **2.** *Informal.* somewhat irregular, abnormal, or incongruous. [1925–30]

off·lap (ôf′lap′, of′-), *n. Geol.* **1.** the retreat of a sea from its shore. **2.** a sequence of layers of sedimentary rock formed during a retreat of the sea. [1905–10; OFF + LAP[3]]

off-li·cense (ôf′lī′səns, of′-), *Brit.* —*n.* **1.** a license permitting the sale of sealed bottles of alcoholic beverages to be taken away from the premises by the purchaser. **2.** a store having such a license. —*adj.* **3.** having such a license. Also, **off′-li′cence.** [1890–95]

off-lim·its (ôf′lim′its, of′-), *adj.* forbidden to be patronized, frequented, used, etc., by certain persons: *The tavern is off-limits to soldiers.* [1950–55, *Amer.*]

off-line (ôf′līn′, of′-), *adj.* **1.** *Computers.* operating independently of, or disconnected from, an associated computer (opposed to *on-line*). **2.** *Radio.* (of a network) not supplying affiliated stations with programming but allowing each station to program its own shows, usually within a specific format. **3.** *Television.* of or pertaining to the preliminary planning and editing of a videotaped program. **4.** located in or serving a place not on a regular route of a railroad, bus, or air carrier: *an off-line ticket office.* Cf. **on-line.** Also, **off′line′, off′ line′.** [1925–30]

off-load (ôf′lōd′, of′-), *v.t., v.i.* to unload. Also, **off′load′.** [1840–50] —**off′-load′er,** *n.*

off-mike (ôf′mīk′, of′-), *adj.* located at a distance from or not projected directly into a microphone: *off-mike sound effects.* [1935–40]

off′ off′ Broad′way, experimental or avant-garde drama produced in New York City, in small theaters, halls, churches, etc. Also, **Off′ Off′ Broad′way.** —**off′-off′-Broad′way,** *adj., adv.*

off-peak (ôf′pēk′, of′-), *adj.* **1.** of, pertaining to, or during a period of less than maximum frequency, demand, intensity, or use: *the off-peak travel season; off-peak train fares.* **2.** lower than the maximum: *off-peak production.* [1915–20]

off-price (ôf′prīs′, of′-), *adj.* **1.** offering or dealing in goods, esp. brand-name apparel, at prices lower than those at regular retail stores or discount stores. **2.** designating, of, or pertaining to such merchandise: *off-price designer jeans.* [1980–85]

off-pric·er (ôf′prī′sər, of′-), *n.* a seller of off-price merchandise. [OFF-PRICE + -ER[1]]

off·print (ôf′print′, of′-), *n.* **1.** Also called **separate.** a reprint of an article that originally appeared as part of a larger publication. —*v.t.* **2.** to reprint separately, as an article from a larger publication. [1880–85; trans. of G *Abdruck*]

off-put·ting (ôf′po͝ot′ing, of′-), *adj.* provoking uneasiness, dislike, annoyance, or repugnance; disturbing or disagreeable. [1820–30; OFF + PUTTING, after v. phrase *put off*] —**off′-put′ting·ly,** *adv.*

off-ramp (ôf′ramp′, of′-), *n.* an exit lane for traffic from a turnpike or freeway to a street. Also, **off′ramp′.** Cf. **on-ramp.** [1950–55, *Amer.*]

off-road (ôf′rōd′, of′-), *adj.* **1.** designed, built, or used for traveling off public roads, esp. on unpaved roads, trails, beaches, or rough terrain: *an off-road vehicle.* **2.** taking place on such roads or terrain: *off-road racing.* **3.** used for or suitable to an off-road vehicle: *off-road tires.* —*adv.* **4.** on a road or terrain other than a public road: *to travel off-road.* [1960–65]

off·scour·ing (ôf′skouᵊr′ing, -skou′ər-, of′-), *n.* **1.** Often, **offscourings.** something scoured off; filth; refuse. **2.** a social outcast. [1520–30; OFF + SCOURING, after v. phrase *scour off*]

off·screen (ôf′skrēn′, of′-), *adj.* **1.** occurring, existing, or done away from the motion-picture or television screen: *an offscreen voice.* **2.** in real life rather than on the motion-picture or television screen: *the newscaster's offscreen personality.* —*adv.* **3.** apart or away from motion-picture or television performances; in actual life: *Offscreen he's a racing-car enthusiast.* [1930–35; OFF + SCREEN]

off-sea·son (ôf′sē′zən, of′-), *n.* **1.** a time of year other than the regular or busiest one for a specific activity: *Fares are lower in the off-season.* **2.** a time of year when business, manufacturing activity, etc., is less than normal or at an unusually low point. —*adj.* **3.** of, pertaining to, or during the off-season: *off-season hotel rates.* —*adv.* **4.** in or during the off-season: *Traveling off-season is the easiest way to save vacation money.* [1840–50]

off·set (*n., adj.* ôf′set′, of′-; *v.* ôf′set′, of′-), *n., adj., v.,* **-set, -set·ting.** —*n.* **1.** something that counterbalances, counteracts, or compensates for something else; compensating equivalent. **2.** the start, beginning, or outset. **3.** a short lateral shoot by which certain plants are propagated. **4.** an offshoot or branch of a family or race. **5.** any offshoot; branch. **6.** Also called **offset printing, offset lithography.** *Lithog.* **a.** a process in which a lithographic stone or metal or paper plate is used to make an inked impression on a rubber blanket that transfers it to the paper being printed, instead of being made directly on the paper. **b.** the impression itself. **7.** Also called **setoff.** *Print.* an unintentional transfer of excess or undried ink from one printed sheet to another. **8.** *Geol.* **a.** (in faults) the magnitude of displacement between two previously aligned bodies. **b.** a spur of a mountain range. **9.** *Mach.* a jog or short displacement in an otherwise straight and continuous line, as in a pipe, lever, or rod, made to avoid objects or to connect with other parts. **10.** *Archit.* setoff (def. 3). **11.** *Survey.* **a.** a short distance measured perpendicularly from a main survey line. **b.** Also called **off′set line′.** a line a short distance from and parallel to a main survey line. **12.** *Naval Archit.* any of the coordinates by which any point on a hull being planned is located. —*adj.* **13.** of, noting, or pertaining to an offset. **14.** *Lithog.* pertaining to, printed by, or suitable for printing by offset. **15.** placed away from a center line; off-center. **16.** placed at an angle to something, as to the axis of a form, shape, or object; not parallel. —*v.t.* **17.** to counterbalance as an equivalent does; compensate for: *The gains offset the losses.* **18.** to juxtapose with something else, as for purposes of comparison: *to offset advantages against disadvantages.* **19.** *Print.* **a.** to make an offset of. **b.** to print by the process of offset lithography. **20.** *Archit.* to build with a setoff, as a wall. **21.** *Survey.* to establish (a line) parallel to a main survey line at an offset. —*v.i.* **22.** to project as an offset or branch. **23.** to counterbalance or compensate. **24.** *Print.* to make an offset. [1545–55; after v. phrase *set off*]
—**Syn. 2.** onset. **17.** match, parallel; counterweight, counterpoise; counteract.

off′set lithog′raphy, *Lithog.* offset (def. 6). [1955–60]

off′set print′ing, *Lithog.* offset (def. 6).

off·shoot (ôf′sho͞ot′, of′-), *n.* **1.** a branch or lateral shoot from a main stem, as of a plant. **2.** anything conceived of as springing or proceeding from a main stock: *an offshoot of a discussion.* **3.** a branch, descendant, or scion of a family or race. [1665–75; OFF + SHOOT]

off·shore (ôf′shôr′, -shōr′, of′-), *adv.* **1.** off or away from the shore: *They pushed the boat offshore.* **2.** at a distance from the shore, on a body of water: *looking for oil offshore.* **3.** in a foreign country. —*adj.* **4.** moving or tending away from the shore toward or into a body of water: *an offshore wind.* **5.** located or operating on a body of water, at some distance from the shore: *offshore fisheries.* **6.** registered, located, conducted, or operated in a foreign country: *an off-shore investment company; off-shore manufacture of car parts.* [1710–20; OFF + SHORE[1]]

off′shore dock′, *Naut.* a floating dock moored to pilings, dolphins, etc., used for cleaning and repairing medium-sized vessels.

off·shore·man (ôf′shôr′mən, -shōr′-, of′-), *n., pl.* **-men.** a person who works offshore, esp. on an offshore oil rig. [OFFSHORE + -MAN]
—**Usage.** See **-man.**

off·side (ôf′sīd′, of′-), *adj., adv.* **1.** *Sports.* illegally beyond a prescribed line or area or in advance of the ball or puck at the beginning of or during play or a play: *The touchdown was nullified because the offensive left tackle was offside.* **2.** with or in doubtful propriety or taste; risqué: *an offside joke.* [1840–50; OFF + SIDE[1]]

off·sid·er (ôf′sī′dər, of′-), *n. Australian.* **1.** an assistant or helper. **2.** a follower or supporter of a person or cause. [1875–80; OFFSIDE + -ER[1]]

off·spring (ôf′spring′, of′-), *n., pl.* **-spring, -springs.** **1.** children or young of a particular parent or progenitor. **2.** a child or animal in relation to its parent or parents. **3.** a descendant. **4.** descendants collectively. **5.** the product, result, or effect of something: *the offspring of an inventive mind.* [bef. 950; ME; OE *ofspring;* see OFF, OF[1], SPRING (v.)]

off·stage (ôf′stāj′, of′-), *adv.* **1.** off the stage or in the wings; away from the view of the audience (opposed to *onstage*). **2.** in one's private life rather than on the stage: *Offstage the actress seemed rather plain.* —*adj.* **3.** not in view of the audience; backstage, in the wings, etc.: *an offstage crash.* **4.** withheld from public view or attention; private: *offstage political meetings.* [1920–25; OFF + STAGE]

off′ stump′, *Cricket.* the outside stump opposite the one at which the batsman stands. Cf. **leg stump, middle stump.**

off·take (ôf′tāk′, of′-), *n.* a pipe or passage for conducting smoke, a current of air, or the like, to an uptake or downtake. [1870–75; after v. phrase *take off*]

off-the-board (ôf′thə bôrd′, -bōrd′, of′-), *adj., adv.* off-board.

off-the-books (ôf′thə bo͝oks′, of′-), *adj.* not recorded in account books or not reported as taxable income.

off-the-cuff (ôf′thə kuf′, of′-), *adj.* with little or no preparation; extemporaneous; impromptu: *a speaker with a good off-the-cuff delivery.* [1940–45]

off-the-face (ôf′thə fās′, of′-), *adj.* **1.** (of a woman's hat) made without a brim. **2.** (of a woman's hairdo) not covering, framing, or shading the face. [1905–10]

off-the-job (ôf′thə job′, of′-), *adj.* **1.** done, received, or happening away from or while not at one's job: *off-the-job research.* **2.** temporarily not employed: *off-the-job union members.* [1965–70]

off-the-peg (ôf′thə peg′, of′-), *adj. Brit.* ready-to-wear. [1875–80]

off-the-rack (ôf′thə rak′, of′-), *adj.* **1.** (of clothing) not made to specific or individual requirements; ready-made: *off-the-rack men's suits.* **2.** *Slang.* off-the-wall. [1965–70]

off-the-rec·ord (ôf′thə rek′ərd, of′-), *adj.* **1.** not for publication; not to be quoted: *a candidate's off-the-record remarks to reporters.* **2.** confidential: *off-the-record information.* [1930–35]

off-the-shelf (ôf′thə shelf′, of′-), *adj.* **1.** readily available from merchandise in stock. **2.** made according to a standardized format; not developed for specialized or individual needs; ready-made: *off-the-shelf computer programs.* [1945–50]

off-the-wall (ôf′*th*ə wôl′, of′-), *adj. Informal.* markedly unconventional; bizarre; oddball: *an unpredictable, off-the-wall personality.* [1970–75]

off·track (ôf′trak′, of′-), *adj.* occurring or carried on away from a racetrack: *offtrack betting.* [1940–45; OFF + TRACK]

off-white (ôf′hwīt′, -wīt′, of′-), *adj.* **1.** white mixed with a small amount of gray, yellow, or other light color. —*n.* **2.** an off-white color. [1925–30]

off′ year′, **1.** a year without a major, esp. presidential, election. **2.** a year marked by reduced or inferior production or activity in a particular field, as farming, business, or sports: *With its wet, cold summer, this was an off year for grapes.* —**off′-year′**, *adj.* [1870–75]

Of Hu′man Bond′age, a novel (1915) by W. Somerset Maugham.

of·lag (ôf′läg′, of′-), *n.* a World War II German internment camp for war prisoners of officer rank. [< G, for *Of(fizier)lag(er)* officer camp]

O′Fla·her·ty (ō fla′hər tē), *n.* **Li·am** (lē′əm), 1896–1984, Irish novelist.

OFlem, Old Flemish. Also, **OFlem.**

O.F.M., Order of Friars Minor (Franciscan). [< L *Ōrdō Frātrum Minōrum*]

Of Mice′ and Men′, a novel (1937) and play (1938) by John Steinbeck.

OFr., Old French. Also, **OFr**

OFris., Old Frisian. Also, **OFris**

oft (ôft, oft), *adv. Literary.* often. [bef. 900; ME *oft(e)*, OE *oft;* c. OFris *ofta*, OS *oft(o)*, G *oft*, ON *opt*]

of·ten (ô′fən, of′ən; ôf′tən, of′-), *adv.* **1.** many times; frequently: *He visits his parents as often as he can.* **2.** in many cases. —*adj.* **3.** *Archaic.* frequent. [1300–50; ME *oftin*, var. before vowels of *ofte* OFT] —**of′ten·ness,** *n.*
—**Syn. 1, 2.** repeatedly, customarily. OFTEN, FREQUENTLY, GENERALLY, USUALLY refer to experiences that are customary. OFTEN and FREQUENTLY may be used interchangeably in most cases, but OFTEN implies numerous repetitions and, sometimes, regularity of recurrence: *We often go there;* FREQUENTLY suggests esp. repetition at comparatively short intervals: *It happens frequently.* GENERALLY refers to place and means universally: *It is generally understood. He is generally liked;* but it is often used as a colloquial substitute for USUALLY. In this sense, GENERALLY, like USUALLY, refers to time, and means in numerous instances. GENERALLY, however, extends in range from the merely numerous to a majority of possible instances; whereas USUALLY means practically always: *The train is generally on time. We usually have hot summers.* —**Ant. 1, 2.** seldom.
—**Pronunciation.** OFTEN was pronounced with a *t*-sound until the 17th century, when a pronunciation without the (t) came to predominate in the speech of the educated, in both North America and Great Britain, and the earlier pronunciation fell into disfavor. Common use of a spelling pronunciation has since restored the (t) for many speakers, and today (ô′fən) and (ôf′tən) [or (of′ən) and (of′tən)] exist side by side. Although it is still sometimes criticized, OFTEN with a (t) is now so widely heard from educated speakers that it has become fully standard once again.

of·ten·times (ô′fən tīmz′, of′ən-; ôf′tən, of′-), *adv.* often. Also, **oft·times** (ôft′tīmz′, oft′-, ôf′-, of′-). [1350–1400; ME; see OFTEN, TIME, -S[1]]

Of Time′ and the Riv′er, a novel (1935) by Thomas Wolfe.

o·fu·ro (ō fo͝or′ō; *Japn.* ô fo͞o′rô), *n., pl.* **o·fu·ros,** *Japn.* **o·fu·ro** (ô fo͞o′rô). furo. Also, **o-fu′ro.** [< Japn *o-* honorific prefix + *furo* FURO]

OG, See **officer of the guard.**

O.G., **1.** See **officer of the guard.** **2.** *Archit.* ogee. **3.** *Philately.* See **o.g.** (def. 1).

o.g., **1.** Also, **O.G.** *Philately.* original gum: the gum on the back of a stamp when it is issued to the public. **2.** *Archit.* ogee.

O·ga·den (ō gä′den), *n.* an arid region in SE Ethiopia.

o·gam (og′əm, ô′gəm), *n.* ogham.

O·ga·sa·wa·ra Ji·ma (ô′gä sä wä′rä jē′mä), Japanese name of **Bonin Islands.**

O gauge, (ō) **1.** a model-railroad gauge of 1¼ in. (32 mm). **2.** Also called **Q gauge.** a model-railroad gauge of $1\frac{3}{16}$ in. (30 mm). [1900–05]

Og·bo·mo·sho (og′bə mō′shō), *n.* a city in SW Nigeria. 392,000.

Og·burn (og′bûrn), *n.* **William Fielding,** 1886–1959, U.S. sociologist and educator.

Og·den (ôg′dən, og′-), *n.* **1. Charles Kay,** 1889–1957, British psychologist and linguist, inventor of Basic English. **2.** a city in N Utah. 64,407. **3.** a male given name.

Og·dens·burg (ôg′dənz bûrg′, og′-), *n.* a city in NE New York, on the St. Lawrence River. 12,375.

og·do·ad (og′dō ad′), *n.* **1.** the number eight. **2.** a group of eight. [1615–25; < LL *ogdoad-* (s. of *ogdoas*) < Gk *ogdoás*, deriv. of *ógdoos* eighth; see -AD[1]]

o·gee (ō jē′, ō′jē), *n.* **1.** a double curve, resembling the letter *S*, formed by the union of a concave and a convex line. **2.** Also called **gula.** *Archit.* a molding with such a curve for a profile; cyma. *Abbr.:* O.G., o.g. [1275–1325; ME *ogeus, oggez* (pl.), var. (by assimilation of *f*) of *oggifs*, presumed sing. *oggif* diagonal rib of a vault < AF, OF *ogive* OGIVE]

CONCISE ETYMOLOGY KEY: <, descended or borrowed from; >, whence; b., blend of, blended; c., cognate with; cf., compare; deriv., derivative; equiv., equivalent; imit., imitative; obl., oblique; r., replacing; s., stem; sp., spelling, spelled; resp., respelling, respelled; trans., translation; ?, origin unknown; *, unattested; ‡, probably earlier than. See the full key inside the front cover.

o′gee arch′, *Archit.* an arch, each haunch of which is an ogee with the concave side uppermost. See illus. under **arch.** [1810–20]

og·ham (og′əm, ô′gəm), *n.* **1.** an alphabetical script used originally for inscriptions in an archaic form of Irish, from about the 5th to the 10th centuries. **2.** any of the 20 characters of this script, each consisting of one or more strokes for consonants and of notches for vowels cut across or upon a central line on a stone or piece of wood. **3.** an inscription employing this script. Also, **ogam.** [1620–30; < Ir; MIr *ogum, ogom*]

O·gil·vie (ō′gəl vē), *n.* **John,** 1797–1867, Scottish lexicographer.

o·give (ō′jīv, ō jīv′), *n.* **1.** *Archit.* **a.** a diagonal vaulting rib. **b.** a pointed arch. **2.** *Statistics.* the distribution curve of a frequency distribution. **3.** *Rocketry.* the curved nose of a missile or rocket. [1605–15; < F, MF *ogive, augive* < Sp *aljibe* < SpAr *al-jibb* the well]

Og·la·la (og lä′lə), *n., pl.* **-las,** (*esp. collectively*) **-la** for **1.** **1.** a member of a North American Indian people belonging to the Teton branch of the Dakota Indians. **2.** the language of the Oglala, a dialect of Dakota.

o·gle (ō′gəl), *v.,* **o·gled, o·gling,** *n.* —*v.t.* **1.** to look at amorously, flirtatiously, or impertinently. **2.** to eye; look or stare at. —*v.i.* **3.** to look amorously, flirtatiously, or impertinently. **4.** to look or stare. —*n.* **5.** an amorous, flirtatious, or impertinent glance or stare. [1670–80; appar. < D, freq. (see -LE) of *oogen* to make eyes at, deriv. of *oog* EYE (cf. LG *oegeln*, G *äugeln*)] —**o′gler,** *n.*

O·gle·thorpe (ō′gəl thôrp′), *n.* **James Edward,** 1696–1785, British general: founder of the colony of Georgia.

Og·ma (og′mə), *n. Irish Myth.* a god of poetry and eloquence and the inventor of the ogham letters: one of the Tuatha De Danann.

Og·mi·os (og′mē ōs′), *n.* the ancient Gallic god of eloquence, identified by the Romans with Mercury.

OGO, *U.S. Aerospace.* Orbiting Geophysical Observatory: one of a series of scientific satellites that studied sun-earth relationships and the earth's atmosphere, ionosphere, and magnetosphere.

OGPU (og′po͞o), *n.* (in the U.S.S.R.) the government's secret-police organization (1923–1934). Also, **Og′pu.** Cf. **Cheka, KGB.** [< Russ *Ógpu*, for *Ob″edinënnoe gosudárstvennoe politícheskoe upravlénie* Unified State Political Directorate]

o·gre (ō′gər), *n.* **1.** a monster in fairy tales and popular legend, usually represented as a hideous giant who feeds on human flesh. **2.** a monstrously ugly, cruel, or barbarous person. [1705–15; < F; perh. << L *Orcus* ORCUS] —**o·gre·ish** (ō′gər ish), **o·grish** (ō′grish), *adj.* —**o′gre·ish·ly, o′grish·ly,** *adv.* —**o′gre·ism, o′grism,** *n.*
—**Syn. 2.** fiend, tyrant, despot.

o·gress[1] (ō′gris), *n.* **1.** a female monster in fairy tales and popular legend, usually represented as a hideous giant who feeds on human flesh. **2.** a monstrously ugly, cruel, or barbarous woman. [1705–15; < F *ogresse.* See OGRE, -ESS]
—**Usage.** See **-ess.**

o·gress[2] (ō′gris), *n. Heraldry.* a roundel sable. Also called **pellet.** [1565–75; orig. uncert.]

oh (ō), *interj., n., pl.* **oh's, ohs,** *v.* —*interj.* **1.** (used as an expression of surprise, pain, disapprobation, etc.) **2.** (used in direct address to attract the attention of the person spoken to): *Oh, John, will you take these books?* —*n.* **3.** the exclamation "oh." —*v.i.* **4.** to utter or exclaim "oh." [later sp. of O, from mid-16th century]

Oh (ō), *n.* **Sa·da·ha·ru** (sä′də här′o͞o), born 1940, Chinese baseball player in Japan.

OH, Ohio (approved esp. for use with zip code).

O′Har·a (ō hâr′ə, ō har′ə), *n.* **John (Henry),** 1905–70, U.S. journalist, novelist, short-story writer, and scenarist.

O′Hare (ō hâr′), *n.* an airport in Chicago.

OHC, *Auto.* See **overhead camshaft.**

O. Hen·ry (ō hen′rē), pen name of William S. Porter.

OHG, Old High German. Also, **OHG., O.H.G.**

o·hi′a lehu′a (ō hē′ə), lehua (def. 1). [1885–90; < Hawaiian *′ōhi′a-lehua*]

O′Hig·gins (ō hig′inz; *Sp.* ô ē′gēns), *n.* **1. Am·bro·sio** (äm brô′syô), (*Marqués de Osorno*), 1720?–1801, Irish soldier and administrator in South America. **2.** his son, **Ber·nar·do** (beʀ när′*th*ô), (*Liberator of Chile*), 1778–1842, Chilean general and statesman.

O·hi·o (ō hī′ō), *n.* **1.** a state in the NE central United States: a part of the Midwest. 10,797,419; 41,222 sq. mi. (106,765 sq. km). *Cap.:* Columbus. *Abbr.:* OH (for use with zip code), O. **2.** a river formed by the confluence of the Allegheny and Monongahela rivers, flowing SW from Pittsburgh, Pa., to the Mississippi in S Illinois. 981 mi. (1580 km) long. —**O·hi′o·an,** *adj., n.*

Ohi′o buck′eye. See under **buckeye** (def. 1).

Oh·lin (ō′lin; *Sw.* o͞o lēn′), *n.* **Ber·til** (bûr′til; *Sw.* bâr′-til), 1899–1979, Swedish economist: Nobel prize 1977.

ohm (ōm), *n.* the SI unit of electrical resistance, defined to be the electrical resistance between two points of a conductor when a constant potential difference applied between these points produces in this conductor a current of one ampere. The resistance in ohms is numerically equal to the magnitude of the potential difference. *Symbol:* Ω [1861; named after G. S. OHM] —**ohm·ic** (ō′mik), *adj.*

Ohm (ōm), *n.* **Ge·org Si·mon,** (gā ôʀk′ zē′môn) 1787–1854, German physicist.

ohm·age (ō′mij), *n. Elect.* electric resistance expressed in ohms. [1895–1900; OHM + -AGE]

ohm′ic resist′ance, *Elect.* resistance (def. 3a).

ohm·me·ter (ōm′mē′tər), *n. Elect.* an instrument for measuring electric resistance in ohms. [1895–1900]

O.H.M.S., On His Majesty's Service; On Her Majesty's Service.

Ohm's′ law′, *Elect.* the law that for any circuit the electric current is directly proportional to the voltage and is inversely proportional to the resistance. [1840–50; named after G. S. OHM]

o·ho (ō hō′), *interj.* (used as an exclamation to express surprise, taunting, exultation, etc.) [1300–50; ME]

-oholic, var. of **-aholic:** *cokeoholic.*

o·hone (ō KHōn′), *interj. Scot. and Irish Eng.* alas! Also, **ochone.** [1470–80; < ScotGael *ochan*, Ir *ochón;* cf. OCH]

O horizon, the layer of loose leaves and organic debris at the surface of soil.

O·hře (ôr′zhə; *Czech.* ô′ʜʀzhe), *n.* a river in central Europe, flowing NE from Germany through the W Czech Republic to the Elbe. 193 mi. (310 km) long. German, **Eger.**

O·hrid (ō′krid, ō′krēd; *Serbo-Croatian.* ô′KHRid), *n.* **Lake,** a lake between E Albania and SW Macedonia, emptying into the Drin River. ab. 20 mi. (32 km) long.

Ohr·mazd (ôr′məzd), *n. Zoroastrianism.* See **Ahura Mazda.**

oi (oi), *interj.* oy[1].

OI, opportunistic infection.

OIC, officer in charge.

OIcel, Old Icelandic.

-oid, a suffix meaning "resembling," "like," used in the formation of adjectives and nouns (and often implying an incomplete or imperfect resemblance to what is indicated by the preceding element): *alkaloid; anthropoid; cardioid; cuboid; lithoid; ovoid; planetoid.* Cf. **-ode**[1]. [< Gk *-oeidēs*, equiv. to *-o-* -O- + *-eidēs* having the form of, deriv. of *eîdos* form]

-oidea, a suffix used in the names of zoological classes or entomological superfamilies. [< NL, pl. of Gk *-oeidēs* -OID; see -A[1]]

o·id·i·um (ō id′ē əm), *n., pl.* **o·id·i·a** (ō id′ē ə). *Mycol.* **1.** one of the conidia that are borne in chains by certain fungi. **2.** (in certain fungi) a thin-walled spore derived from the fragmentation of a hypha into its component cells. [1855–60; < NL < Gk *ōi(ón)* EGG (cf. L *ovum;* see OO-) + *-idium* -IDIUM] —**o·id′i·oid′,** *adj.*

oik (oik), *n., pl.* **oicks, oiks.** *Brit. Slang.* oaf; lout. [1920–25; of obscure orig.]

oil (oil), *n.* **1.** any of a large class of substances typically unctuous, viscous, combustible, liquid at ordinary temperatures, and soluble in ether or alcohol but not in water: used for anointing, perfuming, lubricating, illuminating, heating, etc. **2.** a substance of this or similar consistency. **3.** refined or crude petroleum. **4.** *Painting.* **a.** See **oil color. b.** See **oil painting. 5.** *Informal.* unctuous hypocrisy; flattery. **6.** an oilskin garment. **7.** *Australian and New Zealand Slang.* facts or news; information: *good oil.* **8. pour oil on troubled waters,** to attempt to calm a difficult or tense situation, as an argument. **9. strike oil, a.** to discover oil, esp. to bring in a well. **b.** to have good luck, esp. financially; make an important and valuable discovery: *They struck oil only after years of market research.* —*v.t.* **10.** to smear, lubricate, or supply with oil. **11.** to bribe. **12.** to make unctuous or smooth: *to oil his words.* **13.** to convert into oil by melting, as butter. —*adj.* **14.** pertaining to or resembling oil. **15.** using oil, esp. as a fuel: *an oil furnace.* **16.** concerned with the production or use of oil: *an offshore oil rig.* **17.** made with oil. **18.** obtained from oil. [1125–75; ME *olie, oile* < OF < L *oleum, olivum* (olive) oil < **oleivum* (cf. DEUS) < dial. Gk **elaíwon* (Attic *élaion*), deriv. of **elaíwā* OLIVE] —**oil′less,** *adj.* —**oil′less·ness,** *n.* —**oil′like′,** *adj.*

oil′ bee′tle, any of several blister beetles of the genus *Meloe* that exude an oily fluid from the joints of their legs when disturbed. [1650–60]

oil·bird (oil′bûrd′), *n.* guacharo. [1890–95; OIL + BIRD]

oil′ burn′er, a furnace, boiler, or other device that burns fuel oil. [1895–1900]

oil′ cake′, a cake or mass of linseed, cottonseed, soybean, or the like, from which the oil has been extracted or expressed, used as food for livestock. [1735–45]

oil·can (oil′kan′), *n.* a can having a long spout through which oil is poured or squirted to lubricate machinery or the like. [1830–40; OIL + CAN[2]]

Oil′ Cit′y, a city in NW Pennsylvania, on the Allegheny River. 13,881.

oil·cloth (oil′klôth′, -kloth′), *n., pl.* **-cloths** (-klô*th*z′, -klo*th*z′, -klôths′, -kloths′) for 2. —*n.* **1.** a cotton fabric made waterproof by being treated with oil and pigment, for use as tablecloths, shelf coverings, and the like. **2.** a piece of this fabric. [1690–1700; OIL + CLOTH]

oil′ col′or, a paint made by grinding a pigment in oil, usually linseed oil. [1530–40]

oil•cup (oil′kup′), *n.* a closed cup or can supplying lubricant to a bearing or bearings. Also called **grease cup.** [1840–50; OIL + CUP]

Oil•dale (oil′dāl′), *n.* a town in SW California. 23,382.

oil′ der′rick, derrick (def. 2). [1860–65]

oiled (oild), *adj.* **1.** lubricated or smeared with or as if with oil. **2.** *Slang.* drunk; intoxicated. [1525–35; OIL + -ED[2], -ED[3]]

oil•er (oi′lər), *n.* **1.** a person or thing that oils. **2.** a worker employed to oil machinery. **3.** any of several devices, other than pressure devices, for feeding lubricating oil to a bearing. **4.** an oilcan. **5.** Often, **oilers.** an oilskin garment, esp. a coat. **6.** a ship using oil as fuel. **7.** See **oil tanker. 8.** an oil well. [1545–55; OIL + -ER[1]]

oil′ field′, an area in which there are large deposits of oil. [1890–95]

oil•fish (oil′fish′), *n., pl.* **-fish•es,** (*esp. collectively*) **-fish.** a snake mackerel, *Ruvettus pretiosus,* commonly inhabiting deep, marine waters. [OIL + FISH]

oil′ gild′ing, gilding of glass or ceramic ware by using a size of japan or lacquer. Also, **oil′-gild′ing.** [1840–50]

oil′ gland′, 1. See **uropygial gland. 2.** See **sebaceous gland.** [1825–35]

oil-hard•en (oil′här′dn), *v.t. Metall.* to quench (steel) in a bath of oil. Cf. **water-harden.** [1900–05]

oil′-im•mer•sion objec′tive (oil′i mûr′zhən, -shən), *Optics.* See **immersion objective.** [1880–85]

oil•let (oi′lit), *n.* eyelet (def. 5). [1350–1400; ME *oilet*]

oil•lion•aire (oil′yə nâr′), *n. Canadian Informal.* a millionaire whose wealth is derived from the petroleum industry. [b. OIL and MILLIONAIRE]

oil•man (oil′man′, -mən), *n., pl.* **-men** (-men′, -mən). **1.** a person who owns or operates oil wells or an executive in the petroleum industry. **2.** a person who retails or delivers oil, esp. fuel oil for furnaces. [1400–50; late ME; see OIL, MAN[1]]
—Usage. See **-man.**

oil′ meal′, oil cake ground into small particles for livestock feed. [1885–90]

oil′ of an′ise. See under **aniseed.** Also called **anise oil, aniseed oil.** [1860–65]

oil′ of cade′. See under **cade**[1]. [1875–80]

oil′ of catechu′mens, holy oil used in baptism, the ordination of a cleric, the coronation of a sovereign, or in the consecration of a church.

oil′ of lav′ender, an essential oil distilled from lavender flowers, esp. *Lavandula angustifolia* and *L. stoechas,* and used in perfumery.

oil′ of the sick′, holy oil used in the sacrament of extreme unction.

oil′ of tur′pentine, a colorless, flammable, volatile essential oil having a penetrating odor and a pungent, bitter taste, obtained from turpentine oleoresin by distillation: used in paints and varnishes, and in medicine as a carminative, vermifuge, expectorant, rubefacient, and, formerly, as a diuretic. Also called **spirits of turpentine, turpentine.** [1590–1600]

oil′ of vit′riol, *Chem.* See **sulfuric acid.** [1570–80]

oil′ of win′tergreen. See **methyl salicylate.** [1835–45]

oil′ paint′, 1. See **oil color. 2.** a commercial paint in which a drying oil is the vehicle. [1780–90]

oil′ paint′ing, 1. the art or technique of painting with oil colors. **2.** a painting executed in oil colors. [1775–85] **—oil′ paint′er.**

oil′ palm′, an African feather palm, *Elaeis guineensis,* the fruits of which yield palm oil. [1715–25]

oil′ pan′, the bottom part of the crankcase of an internal-combustion engine in which the oil used to lubricate the engine accumulates. [1905–10]

oil•pa•per (oil′pā′pər), *n.* a paper made waterproof and translucent by treatment with oil. [1830–40; OIL + PAPER]

oil′ patch′, *Slang.* **1.** an area in which oil is produced. **2.** the petroleum industry. [1960–65]

oil-plant (oil′plant′), *n.* any of several plants, as the castor-oil plant or sesame, the seeds of which yield an oil. [1840–50]

Oil′ Riv′ers, a region in W Africa, comprising the vast Niger River delta: formerly a British protectorate; now a part of Nigeria.

oil′ sand′, *Geol.* a sand or sandstone containing oil or tarry residue in the pore spaces. [1880–85, *Amer.*]

oil•seed (oil′sēd′), *n.* any of several seeds, as the castor bean, sesame, or cottonseed, from which an oil is expressed. [1555–65; OIL + SEED]

oil′ shale′, *Geol.* a black or dark-brown shale or siltstone rich in bitumens, from which shale oil is obtained by destructive distillation. [1870–75]

oil•skin (oil′skin′), *n.* **1.** a cotton fabric made waterproof by treatment with oil and used for rain gear and fishermen's clothing. **2.** a piece of this. **3.** Often, **oilskins,** a garment made of this, esp. a long, full-cut raincoat or a loose-fitting suit of pants and jacket as worn by sailors for protection against rain. [1805–15; OIL + SKIN]

oil′ slick′, a smooth area on the surface of water caused by the presence of oil. [1885–90]

oil′ spill′, an accidental release of oil into a body of water, as from a tanker, offshore drilling rig, or underwater pipeline, often presenting a hazard to marine life and the environment. [1965–70]

oil′spot glaze′ (oil′spot′), a brown or black ceramic glaze dotted with silvery spots caused by impurities. [1920–25; OIL + SPOT]

oil•stone (oil′stōn′), *n.* a block of fine-grained stone, usually oiled, for putting the final edge on certain cutting tools by abrasion. [1575–85; OIL + STONE]

oil′ tank′er, a large ship specifically designed for transporting crude oil in bulk across the oceans. [1915–20]

oil tanker

oil•tight (oil′tīt′), *adj.* constructed to be impervious to oil: *an oiltight bulkhead.* [1855–60; OIL + TIGHT]

oil′ var′nish. See under **varnish** (def. 1).

oil′ well′, a well that yields or has yielded oil. [1840–50, *Amer.*]

oil•y (oi′lē), *adj.,* **oil•i•er, oil•i•est,** *adv.* —*adj.* **1.** smeared or covered with oil; greasy: *an oily road surface.* **2.** of the nature of, consisting of, or resembling oil. **3.** of or pertaining to oil. **4.** full of or containing oil. **5.** smooth or unctuous, as in manner or speech: *an oily hypocrite.* —*adv.* **6.** in an oily manner. [1520–30; OIL + -Y[1]] **—oil′i•ness,** *n.*
—Syn. 5. fawning, smarmy, bootlicking.

oink (oingk), *v.i.* **1.** to make the characteristic sound of a pig; grunt. —*n.* **2.** the squealing or grunting sound made by a pig. [1940–45; imit.]

oinochoe

oi•noch•o•e (oi nok′ō ē′), *n., pl.* **-noch•o•es, -noch•o•ai** (-nok′ō ī′). *Gk. and Rom. Antiq.* a wine pitcher or jug, characterized by a curved handle extending from the lip to the shoulder, and a round or trefoil mouth. Also, **oenochoe.** [1870–75; < Gk *oinochóē* wine jug, equiv. to *oîno(s)* WINE + *choē* a pouring, liquid offering (deriv. of *cheîn* to pour)]

oint•ment (oint′mənt), *n. Pharm.* a soft, unctuous preparation, often medicated, for application to the skin; unguent. [1250–1300; obs. *oint* (aph. var. of ANOINT) + -MENT; r. ME *oignement* < OF < VL **unguimentum* for L *unguentum;* see UNGUENT]
—Syn. salve, balm; nard.

OIr, Old Irish. Also, **OIr.**

Oir•each•tas (ēr′əkh təs), *n.* **1.** the parliament of the Republic of Ireland, consisting of the president, the Dail Eireann, and the Seanad Eireann. **2.** an annual assembly, usually in Dublin, held by Gaelic-speaking people to celebrate, exhibit, and encourage the use of the Gaelic language, traditions, and arts. [< Ir: assembly, festival]

Oise (wáz), *n.* **1.** a river in W Europe, flowing SW from S Belgium through N France to the Seine, near Paris. 186 mi. (300 km) long. **2.** a department in N France. 606,320; 2273 sq. mi. (5885 sq. km). *Cap.:* Beauvais.

Oi•sin (u shēn′), *n.* Ossian.

Oi•strakh (oi′sträk, -sträkh), *n.* **Da•vid** (dä′vid), 1908–74, Russian violinist.

OIt, Old Italian.

O•i•ta (ô′ē tä′), *n.* a seaport on NE Kyushu, in S Japan. 360,484.

oi•ti•ci•ca (oi′tə sē′kə), *n.* a Brazilian tree, *Licania rigida,* of the rose family, the seeds of which yield oiticica oil. [1915–20; < Pg < Tupi]

oitici′ca oil′, a light yellow drying oil expressed from the seeds of the oiticica tree, used as a vehicle for paints, varnishes, etc. [1915–20]

OJ, *Informal.* orange juice. Also, **O.J., o.j.**

O•jib•wa (ō jib′wā, -wə), *n., pl.* **-was,** (*esp. collectively*) **-wa. 1.** a member of a large tribe of North American Indians found in Canada and the U.S., principally in the region around Lakes Huron and Superior but extending as far west as Saskatchewan and North Dakota. **2.** an Algonquian language used by the Ojibwa, Algonquin, and Ottawa Indians. Also, **Ojibway.** Also called **Chippewa.** [1690–1700, *Amer.;* < Ojibwa *očipwe·,* orig. the name of a single local group]

O•jib•way (ō jib′wā), *n., pl.* **-ways,** (*esp. collectively*) **-way.** Ojibwa.

o•jo ca•lien•te (ō′hō käl yen′tā), *Southwestern U.S.* a hot spring. [1835–45, *Amer.;* < Sp]

OJT, on-the-job training. Also, **O.J.T.**

OK, Oklahoma (approved esp. for use with zip code).

OK (ō′kā′, ō′kā′, ō′kā′), *adj., adv., interj., n., pl.* **OK's,** *v.,* **OK'd, OK'ing.** —*adj.* **1.** all right; proceeding normally; satisfactory or under control: *Things are OK at the moment.* **2.** correct, permissible, or acceptable; meeting standards: *Is this suit OK to wear to a formal party?* **3.** doing well or in good health; managing adequately: *She's been OK since the operation.* **4.** adequate but unexceptional or unremarkable; tolerable: *The job they did was OK, nothing more.* **5.** estimable, dependable, or trustworthy; likable: *an OK person.* —*adv.* **6.** all right; well enough; successfully; fine: *She'll manage OK on her own. He sings OK, but he can't tap dance.* **7.** (used as an affirmative response) yes; surely. **8.** (used as an interrogative or interrogative tag) all right?; do you agree? —*interj.* **9.** (used to express agreement, understanding, acceptance, or the like): *OK, I'll get it for you.* **10.** (used as an introductory or transitional expletive): *OK, now where were we?* —*n.* **11.** an approval, agreement, or endorsement: *They gave their OK to her leave of absence.* —*v.t.* **12.** to put one's endorsement on or indicate one's approval of (a request, piece of copy, bank check, etc.); authorize; initial: *Would you OK my application?* Also, **O.K., okay.** [initials of a facetious folk phonetic spelling, e.g., *oll* or *orl korrect* representing *all correct,* first attested in Boston, Massachusetts, in 1839, then used in 1840 by Democrat partisans of Martin Van Buren during his election campaign, who allegedly named their organization, the *O.K. Club,* in allusion to the initials of *Old Kinderhook,* Van Buren's nickname, derived from his birthplace *Kinderhook,* New York]
—Usage. Few Americanisms have been more successful than OK, which survived the political campaign of 1840 that fostered it, quickly lost its political significance, and went on to develop use as a verb, adverb, noun, and interjection. The expression was well known in England by the 1880's. Today OK has achieved worldwide recognition and use. It occurs in all but the most formal speech and writing.

o•ka[1] (ō′kə), *n.* **1.** a unit of weight in Turkey and neighboring countries, equal to about 2¾ pounds (1.25 kilograms). **2.** a unit of liquid measure, equal to about 1⅓ U.S. liquid quarts (1.26 liters). Also, **oke.** [1615–25; < It *occa* < Turk *okka* < Ar (cf. *ūquiyya*) < Gk *ounkía;* c. L *uncia;* see OUNCE[1]]

o•ka[2] (ō′kə), *n.* oca.

O•ka (ō kä′; *Russ.* u kä′), *n.* a river in the central Russian Federation in Europe, flowing NE to the Volga at Nizhni Novgorod. 950 mi. (1530 km) long.

o•ka•pi (ō kä′pē), *n., pl.* **-pis,** (*esp. collectively*) **-pi.** an African mammal, *Okapia johnstoni,* closely related to and resembling the giraffe, but smaller and with a much shorter neck. [1900; < Bambuba (Mvu'ba), a Central Sudanic language of NE Zaire (or < a related Pygmy dial.), according to English Africanist Harry Johnston (1858–1927), author of the first zoological descriptions of the animal]

okapi, *Okapia johnstoni,* 5 ft. (1.5 m) high at shoulder; head and body 6 ft. (1.8 m); tail 16 in. (41 cm)

O•ka•van•go (ō′kə vang′gō, -väng′-), *n.* a river in central Africa, flowing SE from Angola to Botswana. ab. 1000 mi. (1610 km) long. Portugese, **Cubango.** Formerly, **Okovango, Okovanggo.**

o•kay (ō′kā′, ō′kā′, ō′kā′), *adj., adv., interj., n., v.t.* OK.

O•ka•ya•ma (ô′kä yä′mä), *n.* a city on SW Honshu, in SW Japan. 545,737.

O•ka•za•ki (ô′kä zä′kē), *n.* a city on S central Honshu, in central Japan. 262,370.

oke[1] (ōk), *n.* oka.

oke[2] (ōk), *adj. Informal.* OK; all right. [1925–30, *Amer.;* appar. shortening of OK]

O•kee•cho•bee (ō′ki chō′bē), *n.* **Lake.** a lake in S Florida, in the N part of the Everglades. 35 mi. (56 km) long; 30 mi. (48 km) wide. Also called **O′kee•cho′bee.**

O'Keeffe (ō kēf′), *n.* **Georgia,** 1887–1986, U.S. painter.

O•ke•fe•no′kee Swamp′ (ō′kə fə nō′kē), a large wooded swamp area in SE Georgia.

O•ke•ghem (ō′kə gem′), *n.* **Jean** (zhäɴ) **d′** or **Jan van** (yän vän), c1430–c95, Flemish composer. Also, **Ockeghem, Ockenheim.**

O'Kel•ley (ō kel′ē), *n.* **Seán Thomas** (shôn, shän), 1882–1966, Irish statesman: president 1945–59.

O•ken (ō′kən), *n.* **Lorenz** (*Lorenz Ockenfuss*), 1779–1851, German naturalist and philosopher.

o•key-doke (ō′kē dōk′), *adj., adv., interj.* OK. Also, **o•key-do•key** (ō′kē dō′kē), **okle-dokle.** [1930–35, *Amer.;* rhyming redupl. of OKE[2]]

O•khotsk (ō kotsk′; *Russ.* u khôtsk′), *n.* **Sea of,** an arm of the N Pacific enclosed by the Kamchatka Peninsula, the Kurile Islands, Sakhalin, and the Russian Federation in Asia. 582,000 sq. mi. (1,507,380 sq. km); greatest depth, 10,554 ft. (3217 m).

Okhotsk′ Cur′rent. See **Oyashio Current.**

O•kie (ō′kē), *n. Usually Disparaging and Offensive.* **1.** a migrant worker from Oklahoma, esp. during the Great Depression. **2.** a native or inhabitant of Oklahoma. **3.** a migrant farm worker. [1930–35; OK(LAHOMA) + -IE]

O•kie (ō′kē), *Disparaging and Offensive.* —*n.* **1.** a native of Okinawa. —*adj.* **2.** belonging to the Okinawan people. [1935–40; OK(INAWA) + -IE]

CONCISE PRONUNCIATION KEY: act, cāpe, dâre, pärt; set, ēqual; if, īce; ox, ōver, ôrder, oil, bŏŏk, bōōt, out; up, ûrge; child; sing; shoe; thin, *th*at; zh as in *treasure.* ə = *a* as in *alone, e* as in *system, i* as in *easily, o* as in *gallop, u* as in *circus;* ᵊ as in *fire* (fīᵊr), *hour* (ouᵊr). l and n can serve as syllabic consonants, as in *cradle* (krād′l), and *button* (but′n). See the full key inside the front cover.

O·ki·na·wa (ō′kə nou′wə, -nä′wə; *Japn.* ô′kē nä′wä), *n.* the largest of the Ryukyu Islands, in the N Pacific, SW of Japan: taken by U.S. forces April–June 1945 in the last major amphibious campaign of World War II. 748,632; 544 sq. mi. (1409 sq. km). **—O′ki·na′wan,** *adj., n.*

Okla., Oklahoma.

O·kla·ho·ma (ō′klə hō′mə), *n.* a state in the S central U.S. 3,025,266. 69,919 sq. mi. (181,090 sq. km). *Cap.:* Oklahoma City. *Abbr.:* OK (for use with zip code), Okla. **—O′kla·ho′man,** *adj., n.*

O′klaho′ma Cit′y, a city in and the capital of Oklahoma, in the central part. 403,213.

o·kle-do·kle (ō′kəl dō′kəl), *adj., adv., interj.* okeydoke. [by alter.]

Ok·mul·gee (ōk mul′gē), *n.* a city in E Oklahoma. 16,263.

o·kou·me (ō′kə mā′), *n.* gaboon. [1920–25; < F *okoumé,* prob. < Mpongwe (Bantu language of Gabon)]

O·ko·van·go (ō′kə vang′gō, -väng′-), *n.* a former name of **Okavango.** Also, **O′ko·vang′go.**

o·kra (ō′krə), *n.* **1.** a shrub, *Abelmoschus esculentus,* of the mallow family, bearing beaked pods. **2.** the pods, used in soups, stews, etc. **3.** a dish made with the pods. Also called **gumbo.** [1670–80; said to be of West African origin, though precise source unknown; cf. Igbo *ókùrù* okra]

Ok·to·ber·fest (ok tō′bər fest′), *n.* **1.** a traditional festival held each October in Munich, Germany. **2.** any similar festival held usually in the autumn. Also, **Oc·toberfest.** [< G; see OCTOBER, -FEST]

O·ku·ni·nu·shi (ô ko͞o′nē no͞o′shē), *n. Japanese Legend.* a son of Susanowo and, in some legends, creator of the world.

-ol[1], a suffix used in the names of chemical derivatives, representing "alcohol" (*glycerol; naphthol; phenol*), or sometimes "phenol" or less definitely assignable phenol derivatives (*resorcinol*). [short for ALCOHOL or PHENOL]

-ol[2], var. of **-ole**[2].

OL, Old Latin. Also, **OL.**

Ol., (in prescriptions) oil. [< L *oleum*]

O.L., **1.** Also, **o.l.** (in prescriptions) the left eye. [< L *oculus laevus*] **2.** Old Latin.

-ola, **1.** a formative of no precise significance found in a variety of commercial coinages (*Crayola; granola; Victrola*) and jocular variations of words (*crapola*). **2.** a suffix extracted from **payola,** used in coinages that have the general sense "bribery, esp. covert payments to an entertainment figure in return for promoting a product, making an appearance, etc." (*playola; plugola*). [appar. < It or L *-ola* dim. suffix; see -OLE[1], -ULE]

O·laf I (o͞o′läf; *Eng.* ō′ləf), (*Olaf Tryggvessön*), A.D. 969–1000, king of Norway 995–1000. Also, **Olav I.**

Olaf II, **Saint** (*Olaf Haraldssön*), A.D. 995–1030, king of Norway from 1016 to 1029; patron saint of Norway. Also, **Olav II.**

ol·al·lie·ber·ry (ol′ə lē ber′ē), *n., pl.* **-ries.** a blackberry that is a cross between the loganberry and the youngberry, cultivated in California and Oregon. [*olallie* < Chinook Jargon: berries < Lower Chinook *úlali* (*ú-lalx* camass + *-ix* deictic suffix, indicating a patch or region of something) + BERRY]

Ö·land (œ′länd′), *n.* an island in SE Sweden, separated from the mainland by Kalmar Sound. 26,750; 519 sq. mi. (1345 sq. km).

O·la·the (ō lā′thə), *n.* a city in E Kansas. 37,258.

O·lav V (o͞o′läf; *Eng.* ō′ləf, ō′ləv), 1903–91, king of Norway, 1957–91. Also, **Olaf V.**

Ol·bers (ōl′bərz; *Ger.* ôl′bərs), *n.* **Hein·rich Wil·helm Mat·thä·us** (hīn′rɪkh vil′helm mä te′o͞os), 1758–1840, German astronomer and physician.

Ol′bers' par′adox (ōl′bərz), *Astron.* the paradox that if the universe consisted of an infinite number of stars equally distributed through space, then every line of sight would come from a star and the night sky would glow uniformly, which is observationally not true. [1950–55; after H.W.M. OLBERS]

Ol·cott (ol′kət), *n.* **Chauncey** (*Chancellor John Olcott*), 1860–1932, U.S. tenor, actor, and songwriter.

old (ōld), *adj.,* **old·er, old·est** or **eld·er, eld·est,** *n.* **—***adj.* **1.** far advanced in the years of one's or its life: *an old man; an old horse; an old tree.* **2.** of or pertaining to the latter part of the life or term of existence of a person or thing: *old age.* **3.** as if or appearing to be far advanced in years: *Worry had made him old.* **4.** having lived or existed for a specified time: *a man 30 years old; a century-old organization.* **5.** having lived or existed as specified with relation to younger or newer persons or things: *Jim is our oldest boy.* **6.** having been aged for a specified time: *This whiskey is eight years old.* **7.** having been aged for a comparatively long time: *old brandy.* **8.** long known or in use: *the same old excuse.* **9.** belonging to the past: *the good old days.* **10.** having been in existence since the distant past: *a fine old family.* **11.** no longer in general use: *This typewriter is an old model.* **12.** acquired, made, or in use by one prior to the acquisition, making, or use of something more recent: *When the new house was built, we sold the old one.* **13.** of, pertaining to, or originating at an earlier period or date: *old maps.* **14.** prehistoric; ancient: *There may have been an old land bridge between Asia and Alaska.* **15.** (*cap.*) (of a language) in its oldest known period, as attested by the earliest written records: *Old Czech.* **16.** experienced: *He's an old hand at welding.* **17.** of long standing; having been such for a comparatively long time: *an old and trusted employee.* **18.** (of colors) dull, faded, or subdued: *old rose.* **19.** deteriorated through age or long use; worn, decayed, or dilapidated: *old clothes.* **20.** *Physical Geog.* (of landforms) far advanced in reduction by erosion or the like. **21.** sedate, sensible, mature, or wise: *That child seems old beyond his years.* **22.** (used to indicate affection, familiarity, disparagement, or a personalization): *good old Bob; that dirty old jalopy.* **23.** *Informal.* (used as an intensive) great; uncommon: *a high old time.* **24.** former; having been so formerly: *a dinner for his old students.* **—***n.* **25.** (*used with a plural v.*) old persons collectively (usually prec. by *the*): *appropriations to care for the old.* **26.** a person or animal of a specified age or age group (used in combination): *a class for six-year-olds; a horse race for three-year-olds.* **27.** old or former time, often time long past: *days of old.* [bef. 900; ME; OE *eald, ald;* c. D *old,* G *alt,* Goth *altheis;* akin to ON *ala* to nourish] **—old′ness,** *n.*

—Syn. 1. OLD, AGED, ELDERLY all mean well along in years. An OLD person has lived long, nearly to the end of the usual period of life. An AGED person is very far advanced in years, and is usually afflicted with the infirmities of age. An ELDERLY person is somewhat old, but usually has the mellowness, satisfactions, and joys of age ahead. **9.** olden, early. **—Ant. 1.** young.

old′ Ad′am, (in Christian theology) human nature lacking in grace; humans in their unredeemed state. Also called **old man.** [1540–50]

old′ age′, the last period of human life, now often considered to be the years after 65. [1300–50; ME] **—old′-age′,** *adj.*

Old′ Bai′ley (bā′lē), the main criminal court of London, England.

Old′ Believ′er, Raskolnik. [1805–15]

old boy (ōld′ boi′ *for 1, 2;* ōld′ boi′ *for 3;* ōld′ boi′ *for 4*), **1.** *Informal (sometimes disparaging).* an adult male, esp. a Southerner. Cf. **good old boy.** **2.** a lively elderly man. **3.** *Chiefly Brit.* an alumnus, esp. of a boys' preparatory or public school. **4.** *Chiefly Brit.* See **old chap.** [1595–1605]

old-boy·ism (ōld′boi′iz əm), *n.* support of or participation in an old-boy network. [OLD BOY + -ISM]

old′-boy′ net′work (ōld′boi′), an exclusive network that links members of a profession, social class, or organization or the alumni of a particular school through which the individuals assist one another in business, politics, etc. [1955–60]

Old′ Brit′ish, Brythonic as used before A.D. 800.

Old′ Bulgar′ian, the Bulgarian language of the Middle Ages. Cf. **Old Church Slavonic.**

Old′ Cai′ro, al-Fustat.

Old′ Cas·tile′ (ka stēl′), a region in N Spain: formerly a province. Spanish, **Castilla la Vieja.**

Old·cas·tle (ōld′kas′əl, -kä′səl), *n.* **Sir John** (**Lord Cobham**), 1377–1417, English martyr: leader of a Lollard conspiracy; executed for treason and heresy; model for Shakespeare's Falstaff.

Old′ Cath′olic, **1.** a member of any of several European churches professing to be truly Catholic but rejecting certain modern Roman Catholic doctrines, dogmas, and practices, esp. the dogma of papal infallibility. **2.** a member of any of several minor churches, esp. in the U.S., differing from the Roman Catholic Church chiefly in their rejection of the ecclesiastical authority of the Roman Catholic hierarchy. [1840–50]

old′ chap′, *Chiefly Brit.* (used in informal direct address). Also, **old boy, old fellow.** [1815–25]

Old′ Church′ Slavon′ic, the oldest attested Slavic language, an ecclesiastical language written first by Cyril and Methodius in a Bible translation of the 9th century and continued in use for about two centuries. It represents the South Slavic, Bulgarian dialect of 9th-century Salonika with considerable addition of other South and West Slavic elements. *Abbr.:* OCS Also called **Old Church′ Slav′ic, Old Slavic, Old Slavonic.** Cf. **Church Slavic.** [1875–80]

Old′ Com′edy, Greek comedy of the 5th century B.C., which derived from fertility rites in honor of Dionysus and combined robust humor with biting personal and political satire. Cf. **Middle Comedy, New Comedy.** [1840–50]

old′ coun′try, the original home country of an immigrant or a person's ancestors, esp. a European country. [1775–85] **—old′-coun′try,** *adj.*

old′ cov′enant, (in Christian exegesis) **1.** the covenant between God and the ancient Israelites, based on the Mosaic Law. **2.** (*cap.*) the Old Testament.

Old′ Curios′ity Shop′, The, a novel (1840–41) by Dickens.

Old′ Del′hi, Delhi (def. 2).

Old′ Domin′ion, the state of Virginia (used as a nickname). [1770–80, *Amer.*]

Old′ Dutch′, the Dutch language before c1100. *Abbr.:* OD, OD., O.D.

old·en (ōl′dən), *adj. Literary.* **1.** of or pertaining to the distant past or bygone times; ancient. **2.** old. [1350–1400; ME; see OLD, -EN[2]]

Ol·den·burg (ōl′dən bûrg′; *for 2, 3 also Ger.* ōl′dən-bo͝ork′), *n.* **1.** **Claes (Thu·re)** (klous to͞or′ə), born 1929, U.S. sculptor, born in Sweden. **2.** a former state in NW Germany, now part of Lower Saxony. **3.** a city in Lower Saxony, in NW Germany: former capital of Oldenburg. 140,200.

Old′ Eng′lish, **1.** Also called **Anglo-Saxon.** the English language of A.D. c450–c1150. *Abbr.:* OE **2.** *Print.* a style of black letter.

Old′ Eng′lish cut′, *Jewelry.* See **single cut.**

Old′ Eng′lish pat′tern, a spoon pattern having a stem curving backward at the end. [1905–10]

Old′ Eng′lish sheep′dog, one of an English breed of large working dogs having a long, shaggy, gray or blue-merle and white coat that hangs over the eyes, and a bobbed tail, originally developed to drive sheep and cattle. [1885–90]

Old English sheepdog, 22 in. (56 cm) high at shoulder

old·er (ōl′dər), *adj.* a comparative of **old.**
—Syn. OLDER, ELDER imply having greater age than something or someone else. OLDER is the usual form of the comparative of old: *This building is older than that one.* ELDER, now greatly restricted in application, is used chiefly to indicate seniority in age as between any two people but especially priority of birth as between children born of the same parents: *The elder brother became king.* **—Ant.** newer, younger.

old·est (ōl′dist), *adj.* a superlative of **old.**

Old′ Faith′ful, one of the best known geysers of Yellowstone National Park. [so named because of the longevity and regularity of its activity]

old·fan·gled (ōld′fang′gəld), *adj.* old-fashioned; of an older or former kind. [1835–45; formed after NEWFANGLED] **—old′fan′gled·ness,** *n.*

old′ fart′, fart (def. 2).

old′ fash′ioned, (*sometimes caps.*) a cocktail made with whiskey, bitters, water, and sugar, and garnished with citrus-fruit slices and a cherry. [1900–05]

old-fash·ioned (ōld′fash′ənd), *adj.* **1.** of a style or kind that is no longer in vogue: *an old-fashioned bathing suit.* **2.** favored or prevalent in former times: *old-fashioned ideas.* **3.** having the conservative behavior, ways, ideas, or tastes of earlier times: *a delightfully old-fashioned gentleman.* [1645–55] **—old′-fash′ioned·ly,** *adv.* **—old′-fash′ioned·ness,** *n.*
—Syn. 1. outmoded, obsolete. See **ancient**[1].

old′ fel′low, *Chiefly Brit.* See **old chap.** [1810–20]

old′ field′, land no longer under cultivation because the fertility of the soil has been exhausted. [1625–35, *Amer.*]

Old·field (ōld′fēld′), *n.* **Ber·na Eli** (bûr′nə), ("*Barney*"), 1878–1946, U.S. racing-car driver.

Old′ Flem′ish, the Flemish language before c1300.

old′ fo′gy, a person who is excessively old-fashioned in attitude, ideas, manners, etc. Also, **old′ fo′gey.** [1825–35] **—old′-fo′gy·ish, old′-fo′gey·ish,** *adj.*

Old′ Franco′nian, the Franconian language before 1100; Frankish.

Old′ French′, the French language of the 9th through the 13th centuries. *Abbr.:* OF [1885–90]

Old′ Fri′sian, the Frisian language before c1500. *Abbr.:* OFris

old′ fus′tic, fustic (defs. 1–3).

old′-girl′ net′work (ōld′gûrl′), an association among women that is comparable to or modeled on an old-boy network. [1950–55]

Old′ Glo′ry. See **Stars and Stripes.**

old′ goat′, *Informal.* **1.** an elderly man who is disliked, esp. for being mean to or disapproving of younger people. **2.** a lecherous man, esp. one considerably older than those to whom he is attracted. [1960–65]

old′ gold′, a color ranging in hue from medium yellow to light olive brown. [1875–80]

old′ growth′, **1.** forest growth consisting of mature or overmature trees. **2.** virgin timber. [1880–85] **—old′-growth′,** *adj.*

Old′ Guard′, **1.** the imperial guard created in 1804 by Napoleon: it made the last French charge at Waterloo. **2.** (in the U.S.) the conservative element of any political party, esp. the Republican party. **3.** (*usually l.c.*) the in-

CONCISE ETYMOLOGY KEY: <, descended or borrowed from; >, whence; b., blend of, blended; c., cognate with; cf., compare; deriv., derivative; equiv., equivalent; imit., imitative; obl., oblique; r., replacing; s., stem; sp., spelling, spelled; resp., respelling, respelled; trans., translation; ?, origin unknown; *, unattested; ‡, probably earlier than. See the full key inside the front cover.

fluential, established, more conservative members of any body, group, movement, etc.: *the old guard of New York society.* [trans. of F *Vieille Garde*]

Old′ Guard′ism (gär′dĭz əm), political conservatism. [1940–45, *Amer.*; OLD GUARD + -ISM] —**Old′ Guard′ist.**

Old·ham (ōl′dəm; *locally* ou′dəm), *n.* a city in Greater Manchester, in NW England. 228,400.

old′ hand′, a person who is experienced in or familiar with a subject, area, procedure, etc.: *The guide you just hired is an old hand at leading safaris.* [1775–85]

Old′ Har′ry, *Older Use.* the devil; Satan. [1730–40]

old′ hat′, **1.** old-fashioned; dated. **2.** trite from having long been used or known. [1745–55]

Old′ High′ Ger′man, High German before 1100. *Abbr.:* OHG [1885–90]

Old′ Icelan′dic, Old Norse as used in Iceland. *Abbr.:* OIcel

old·ie (ōl′dē), *n. Informal.* a popular song, joke, movie, etc., that was in vogue at a time in the past. Also, **oldy.** [1870–75; OLD + -IE]

Old′ Ion′ic, epic (def. 9). [1885–90]

Old′ I′rish, the Irish language before c900. *Abbr.:* OIr [1885–90]

Old′ I′ronsides, the U.S. frigate *Constitution* (used as a nickname).

old·ish (ōl′dĭsh), *adj.* somewhat old: *an oldish man.* [1660–70; OLD + -ISH[1]]

Old′ Ital′ian, the Italian language of the 10th to the 14th centuries. *Abbr.:* OIt

Old′ King′dom, the period in the history of ancient Egypt, 2780–2280 B.C., comprising the 3rd to 6th dynasties, characterized by the predominance of Memphis. Cf. **Middle Kingdom, New Kingdom.** [1900–05]

old′ la′dy, *Informal.* **1.** a mother, usually one's own. **2.** a wife. **3.** a girlfriend or female lover, esp. a female lover with whom one cohabits. [1775–85]

Old′ La′dy of Thread′nee·dle Street′ (thred′-nēd′l), the Bank of England (used as a nickname).

Old′ Lat′in, the Latin language in use from the earliest inscriptions to c100 B.C. *Abbr.:* OL, OL., O.L. [1885–90]

old-line (ōld′līn′), *adj.* **1.** following or supporting conservative or traditional ideas, beliefs, customs, etc. **2.** long established; traditional: *old-line society.* [1855–60]

Old′ Line′ State′, Maryland (used as a nickname).

Old′ Low′ Fran·co′ni·an (frang kō′nē ən), a Low German dialect of the Franks of the lower Rhine valley before c1100. Also called **Old′ Low′ Frank′ish.**

Old′ Low′ Ger′man, the language of the German lowlands before c1100. *Abbr.:* OLG

old′ maid′, **1.** *Usually Disparaging and Offensive.* an elderly or confirmed spinster. **2.** a fussy, timid, prudish person. **3.** *Cards.* **a.** a simple game, played with a deck having one card removed, in which the players draw from one another to match pairs and the one holding an odd queen at the end loses. **b.** the loser of such a game. [1520–30]

old-maid·ish (ōld′mā′dĭsh), *adj.* characteristic of or resembling an old maid. [1750–60]

old′ man′, *Informal.* **1.** a father, usually one's own: *His old man's letting him have the car for the prom.* **2.** a husband: *The office is giving my old man a retirement party.* **3.** a boyfriend or male lover, esp. a male lover with whom one cohabits. **4.** (*sometimes caps.*) a person in a position of authority, esp. an employer or a commanding officer: *The Old Man has ordered an inspection for Saturday morning.* **5.** (used affectionately in addressing a man). **6.** See **old Adam. 7.** southernwood.

Old′ Man′ and the Sea′, The, a novel (1952) by Ernest Hemingway.

old-man-and-wom·an (ōld′man′ən wo͝om′ən), *n.* houseleek (def. 1).

old′-man cac′tus (ōld′man′), a Mexican cactus, *Cephalocereus senilis,* having a columnar body from 30 to 40 ft. (9 to 12 m) high with thatchlike, long, white hairs on the top, and red flowers with white centers. [1895–1900, *Amer.*]

Old′ Man′ of the Sea′, **1.** (in *The Arabian Nights' Entertainments*) an old man who clung to the shoulders of Sindbad the Sailor for many days and nights. **2.** a burden, annoyance, care, or the like, from which it is extremely difficult to free oneself.

old′ man′ of the woods′, an edible, mild-tasting mushroom, *Strobilomyces floccopus,* occurring in coniferous woodlands of eastern North America.

old-man's-beard (ōld′manz′bērd′), *n.* **1.** See **fringe tree. 2.** beard moss. **3.** traveler's-joy. [1735–45]

old′ mas′ter, **1.** an eminent artist of an earlier period, esp. from the 15th to the 18th centuries. **2.** a work by such an artist. [1945–50]

old′ mine′ cut′, *Jewelry.* a brilliant cut, common in the 19th century, retaining a relatively high proportion of the original stone and having a large culet and small table compared to modern brilliants.

old′ mon′ey, **1.** inherited wealth, esp. wealth that confers status and social acceptance. **2.** a family or forebears possessing such wealth. —**old′-mon′ey,** *adj.*

old′ moon′. See **waning moon.** [1580–90]

Old′ Nick′, *Informal* the devil; Satan. [1660–70]

Old′ Norse′, the Germanic language of medieval Scandinavia. *Abbr.:* ON [1835–45]

Old′ North′ French′, the dialect of Old French spoken in northern France. *Abbr.:* ONF [1925–30]

Old′ Northwest′. See **Northwest Territories.**

Old′ Or′chard Beach′, a resort town in S Maine. 6291.

Ol·do·wan (ōl′də wən, ôl′-), *adj. Archaeol.* of or designating a Lower and Middle Pleistocene industrial complex of eastern Africa, characterized by assemblages of stone tools about two million years old that are the oldest well-documented artifacts yet known. [1930–35; *Oldow(ay)* (G sp. of *Olduvai*) + -AN]

Old′ Per′mic. See under **Permic.**

Old′ Per′sian, an ancient West Iranian language attested by cuneiform inscriptions. *Abbr.:* OPers

Old′ Pretend′er. See **Stuart, James Francis Edward.**

Old′ Provençal′, the Provençal language as found in documents from the 11th to the 16th centuries. *Abbr.:* OPr

Old′ Prus′sian, a Baltic language extinct since the 17th century. *Abbr.:* OPruss [1870–75]

Old′ Rit′ualist, Raskolnik. [1880–85]

old′ riv′er, a river bed left dry because the river has changed its course. [1685–95, *Amer.*]

old′ rose′, rose color with a purplish or grayish cast. [1880–85] —**old′-rose′,** *adj.*

Old′ Rus′sian, Russian as used in documents before 1600. *Abbr.:* ORuss

Olds (ōldz), *n.* **Ransom Eli,** 1864–1950, U.S. automobile pioneer and manufacturer.

Old′ Sax′on, the Saxon dialect of Low German in use before c1100. *Abbr.:* OS

old′ school′, advocates or supporters of established custom or of conservatism: *a military man of the old school.* [1790–1800] —**old′-school′,** *adj.*

old′ school′ tie′, **1.** a necktie striped in the colors of a specific English public school, esp. as worn by a graduate to indicate his educational background. **2.** an alumnus of an English public school. **3.** the clannishness and conservative manners, dress, and attitudes associated with students and graduates of the English public schools. **4.** snobbishness, clannishness, or extreme conservatism. [1930–35]

Old′ Scratch′, *Chiefly South Midland and Southern U.S.* the devil; Satan. [1755–65]

old′ shoe′, *Informal.* a person or thing that is comfortably familiar and unpretentious: *Uncle Will is a lovable old shoe.* —**old′-shoe′,** *adj.*

Old′ Slav′ic. See **Old Church Slavonic.** Also called **Old′ Slavon′ic.**

old′ sledge′. See **all fours** (def. 2). [1820–30, *Amer.*]

Old′ South′, the U.S. South before the Civil War.

Old′ Span′ish, the Spanish language of the 12th to the 16th centuries. *Abbr.:* OSp

Old′ Span′ish Trail′, *Amer. Hist.* an overland route from Santa Fe, N. Mex., to Los Angeles, Calif., first marked out in 1776 by Spanish explorers and missionaries.

old′ squaw′, a sea duck, *Clangula hyemalis,* of arctic and subarctic regions. Also, **old′squaw′.** [1830–40, *Amer.*]

old′ stag′er, stager (def. 1). [1705–15]

old·ster (ōld′stər), *n.* **1.** an old or elderly person. **2.** (in the British navy) a midshipman of four years' standing. [1810–20; OLD + -STER, modeled on *youngster*]

Old′ Sto′a (stō′ə), the earliest phase of Stoicism, lasting from the latter part of the 4th century to the early part of the 3rd century B.C.

Old′ Stone′ Age′, the Paleolithic period.

old′ style′, **1.** Also, **old′style′.** *Print.* a type style differentiated from modern by the more or less uniform thickness of all strokes and by slanted serifs. **2.** (*caps.*) time reckoned according to the Julian calendar. Cf. **New Style. 3.** Also, **old′-style′.** *Typography.* noting or descriptive of a font of numerals of which some part extends below the baseline. [1865–70]

Old Test., Old Testament.

Old′ Tes′tament, **1.** the first of the two main divisions of the Christian Bible, comprising the Law, the Prophets, and the Hagiographa. In the Vulgate translation all but two books of the Apocrypha are included in the Old Testament. See table under **Bible. 2.** this testament considered as the complete Bible of the Jews. **3.** the covenant between God and Israel on Mount Sinai, constituting the basis of the Hebrew religion. Ex. 19–24; Jer. 31:31–34; II Cor. 3:6, 14. [1300–50; ME; trans. of LL *Vetus Testamentum,* trans. of Gk *Palaià Diathḗkē*]

old-time (ōld′tīm′), *adj.* **1.** belonging to or characteristic of old or former times, methods, ideas, etc.: *old-time sailing ships; an old-time piano player.* **2.** being long established: *old-time residents.* [1815–25]

old-tim·er (ōld′tī′mər), *n. Informal.* **1.** a person whose residence, membership, or experience began long ago and has been continuing for a considerable length of time; veteran. **2.** an old person. **3.** an old-fashioned person or thing. **4.** *Sometimes Offensive.* (used as a form of familiar direct address to an elderly man.) [1855–60; OLD-TIME + -ER[1]]

Old′ Turk′ic, the Turkic languages or dialects spoken in Central Asia from the 8th to the 10th centuries.

Ol′du·vai Gorge′ (ôl′do͝o vī′), a gorge in Tanzania in which is located a site containing Australopithecine and human skeletal and cultural remains.

Old′ Welsh′, the Welsh language of the period before c1150 A.D.

Old′ West′, the western region of the U.S., esp. in the frontier period of the 19th century.

old·wife (old′wīf′), *n., pl.* **-wives. 1.** any of various fishes, as the alewife, the menhaden, or a West Indian fish of the family Balistidae. **2.** See **old squaw.** [1580–90; OLD + WIFE]

Old′ Wives′ sum′mer, a period of fine, summerlike weather occurring in Europe in autumn. Cf. **Indian summer.**

old′ wives′ tale′, a traditional belief, story, or idea that is often of a superstitious nature. [1670–80]

old-wom·an·ish (ōld′wo͝om′ə nĭsh), *adj. Sometimes Offensive.* having characteristics considered typical of an old woman, as excessive fussiness or timidity. [1765–75] —**old′-wom′an·ish·ness,** *n.*

Old′ World′, **1.** Europe, Asia, and Africa. **2.** See **Eastern Hemisphere.**

old-world (ōld′wûrld′), *adj.* **1.** of or pertaining to the ancient world or to a former period of history. **2.** of or pertaining to the Old World: *old-world customs.* **3.** characteristic of the Old World; quaint; traditional. [1705–15] —**old′-world′ly,** *adj.* —**old′-world′li·ness,** *n.*

Old′ World′ mon′key, any of various anthropoid primates of the family Cercopithecidae, of Africa, the Arabian peninsula, and Asia, typically having a hairless face, forward- or downward-directed nostrils, relatively short arms, flat nails, and either having a rudimentary tail or using the tail for balance rather than grasping, and including the baboon, colobus monkey, guenon, langur, macaque, mandrill, mangabey, patas, proboscis, and talapoin. [1860–65]

Old′ World′ scops′ owl′. See under **scops owl.**

old·y (ōl′dē), *n., pl.* **old·ies.** oldie.

o·lé (ō lā′), *interj.* **1.** (used as a shout of approval, triumph, or encouragement). —*n.* **2.** a cry of "olé." [< Sp (*h*)*ole,* prob. of expressive orig.]

-ole[1], a suffix found in French loanwords of Latin origin, usually diminutives, and later in adaptations of words borrowed directly from Latin or in Neo-Latin coinages: *areole; centriole; vacuole.* [< F < L *-olus, -ola, -olum,* var. of *-ulus* -ULE with stems ending in a vowel]

-ole[2], a suffix used in names of chemical compounds, esp. five-membered, unsaturated rings (*carbazole; indole; thiazole*) and, less systematically, aromatic ethers (*anisole; safrole*). Also, **-ol**[2]. [< F < L *oleum* OIL]

o·le·a·ceous (ō′lē ā′shəs), *adj.* belonging to the Oleaceae, the olive family of plants. Cf. **olive family.** [1855–60; < NL *Oleace(ae)* (*Ole(a)* the olive genus (L *olea, oliva* olive, olive tree; see OLIVE, OIL) + *-aceae* -ACEAE) + -OUS]

o·le·ag·i·nous (ō′lē aj′ə nəs), *adj.* **1.** having the nature or qualities of oil. **2.** containing oil. **3.** producing oil. **4.** unctuous; fawning; smarmy. [1625–35; < L *oleāginus* of the olive, deriv. of *olea* OLIVE] —**o′le·ag′i·nous·ness,** *n.*

O·le·an (ō′lē an′), *n.* a city in SW New York. 18,207.

o·le·an·der (ō′lē an′dər, ō′lē an′-), *n.* a poisonous shrub, *Nerium oleander,* of the dogbane family, native to southern Eurasia, having evergreen leaves and showy clusters of pink, red, or white flowers, and widely cultivated as an ornamental. [1540–50; < ML *oleander, oliandrum,* obscurely akin to LL *laurandrum,* perh. a conflation of L *laurus* LAUREL and *rhododendron* RHODODENDRON]

o·le·as·ter (ō′lē as′tər), *n.* an ornamental shrub or small tree, *Elaeagnus angustifolia,* of Eurasia, having fragrant yellow flowers and an olivelike fruit. Also called **Russian olive.** [bef. 1000; ME < L: wild olive tree, deriv. of *olea* OLIVE]

o·le·ate (ō′lē āt′), *n.* **1.** *Chem.* an ester or a salt of oleic acid. **2.** *Pharm.* a preparation, as an ointment, composed of medicated oleic acid. [1825–35; OLE(IC ACID) + -ATE[2]]

o·lec·ra·non (ō lek′rə non′, ō′li krā′non), *n. Anat.* the part of the ulna beyond the elbow joint. [1720–30; < NL < Gk *ōlékrānon* point of the elbow, short for *ōlenókrānon,* equiv. to *ōlén(ē)* elbow + *-o-* -o- + *krān(íon)* head (see CRANIUM) + *-on* neut. n. suffix] —**o·lec·ra·nal** (ō lek′rə nl, ō′li krān′l), **o′le·cra′ni·al, o′le·cra′ni·an, o′le·cra′ni·oid′,** *adj.*

o·le·fi′ant gas′ (ō′lə fī′ənt, ō lē′fē-, ō lef′ē-), ethylene (def. 2). [1800–10; part trans. of F *gaz oléfiant,* equiv. to *olé-* (< L *oleum* OIL) + *-fiant,* prp. of *-fier* -FY; see -ANT]

o·le·fin (ō′lə fĭn), *n. Chem.* any member of the alkene series. Also, **o·le·fine** (ō′lə fĭn, -fēn′). [1855–60; < F *oléf(iant)* (see OLEFIANT GAS) + -IN[2]] —**o′le·fin′ic,** *adj.*

o′lefin fi′ber, any of a group of synthetic textile fibers, as Herculon, formed from long-chain polymers no less than 85 percent ethylene, propylene, or other olefin units.

o′lefin se′ries, *Chem.* See **alkene series.** [1875–80]

o·le·ic (ō lē′ĭk, ō′lē ĭk), *adj. Chem.* pertaining to or derived from oleic acid. [1810–20; < L *ole(um)* OIL + -IC]

ole′ic ac′id, *Chem.* a colorless, odorless, liquid, water-insoluble, unsaturated acid, $C_{18}H_{34}O_2$, obtained from animal tallow and natural vegetable oils, in which it occurs as the glycerol ester: used chiefly in the manufacture of soap, commercial oleates, and cosmetics. [1810–20]

o·le·if·er·ous (ō′lē ĭf′ər əs), *adj.* giving rise to oil, as certain seeds or hypha. [1795–1805; < L *ole(um)* OIL + -I- + -FEROUS]

o·le·in (ō′lē ĭn), *n. Chem.* **1.** Also called **glyceryl trioleate, triolein.** a colorless to yellowish, oily, water-insoluble liquid, $C_{57}H_{104}O_6$, the triglyceride of oleic acid, present in many vegetable oils. **2.** the oily or lower-melting fractions of a fat as distinguished from the solid or higher-melting constituents. [1830–40; < F *oléine,* equiv. to *olé-* (< L *oleum* OIL) + *-ine* -IN[2]]

CONCISE PRONUNCIATION KEY: *act, cāpe, dâre, pärt; set, ēqual; if, īce; ox, ōver, ôrder, oil, bo͝ok, bo͞ot, out; up, ûrge; child; sing; shoe; thin, that;* zh as in *treasure.* ə = *a* as in *alone, e* as in *system, i* as in *easily, o* as in *gallop, u* as in *circus;* ᵊ as in *fire* (fīᵊr), *hour* (ouᵊr). l and n can serve as syllabic consonants, as in *cradle* (krād′l), and *button* (but′n). See the full key inside the front cover.

o•le•o (ō′lē ō′), *n.* margarine. [1880–85; by shortening of OLEOMARGARINE]

oleo-, a combining form meaning "oil," used in the formation of compound words: *oleograph.* [< L, comb. form repr. *oleum* OIL]

o•le•o•graph (ō′lē ə graf′, -gräf′), *n.* a chromolithograph printed in oil colors on canvas or cloth. [1870–75; OLEO- + -GRAPH] **—o•le•o•graph•ic** (ō′lē ə graf′ik), *adj.* **—o•le•og•ra•phy** (ō′lē og′rə fē), *n.*

o•le•o•mar•ga•rine (ō′lē ō mär′jə rin, -rēn′, -märj′rin, -rēn), *n.* margarine. Also, **o′le•o•mar′ga•rin.** [1870–75; < F *oléomargarine.* See OLEO-, MARGARINE] **—o•le•o•mar•gar•ic** (ō′lē ō mär gär′ik), *adj.*

o′leo oil′, a product obtained from beef fat and consisting chiefly of a mixture of olein and palmitin, used for making butterlike foods. [1880–85, *Amer.*]

o•le•o•phil•ic (ō′lē ō fil′ik), *adj. Chem.* of or pertaining to a substance that has an affinity for oils and not for water. Cf. **hydrophobic** (def. 2). [1955–60; OLEO- + -PHILIC]

o•le•o•res•in (ō′lē ō rez′ən), *n.* **1.** a mixture of an essential oil and a resin, found in nature. **2.** *Pharm.* an oil holding resin in solution, extracted from a substance, as ginger, by means of alcohol, ether, or acetone. [1850–55; OLEO- + RESIN]

o•le•o•res•in•ous (ō′lē ō rez′ə nəs), *adj.* **1.** pertaining to, characteristic of, or containing oleoresin. **2.** (of a varnish or paint vehicle) consisting of drying oils and resins that usually have been cooked. [1860–65; OLEORESIN + -OUS]

o′leo strut′, a hydraulic device used as a shock absorber in the landing gear of aircraft, consisting of an oil-filled cylinder fitted with a hollow, perforated piston into which oil is slowly forced when a compressive force is applied to the landing gear, as in a landing.

ol•er•i•cul•ture (ol′ər i kul′chər), *n.* the cultivation of vegetables for the home or market. [1885–90; < L *(h)oler-,* s. of *(h)olus* vegetable, kitchen herb + -I- + CULTURE] **—ol′er•i•cul′tur•al,** *adj.* **—ol′er•i•cul′tur•al•ly,** *adv.* **—ol′er•i•cul′tur•ist,** *n.*

o•le•threu•tid (ō′lə thrōō′tid), *n.* **1.** any of numerous brown or gray moths of the family Olethreutidae having mottled or banded wings and forewings, each with a truncated tip, including many crop pests, as the codling moth or oriental fruit moth. **—*adj.* 2.** belonging or pertaining to the family Olethreutidae. [< NL *Olethreutidae* name of the family, equiv. to *Olethreut(es)* genus (< Gk *olethreú(ein)* to destroy, deriv. of *ólethros* destruction + *-tēs* agent suffix) + *-idae* -ID[2]]

o•le•um (ō′lē əm), *n., pl.* **o•le•a** (ō′lē ə) for 1, **o•le•ums** for 2. **1.** *Pharm.* oil. **2.** *Chem.* See **pyrosulfuric acid.** [1900–05; < L: OIL]

O lev•el (ō′ lev′əl), *Brit.* **1.** a public examination for secondary-school students, usually 15 to 16 years old, testing basic knowledge in various subjects, required before advancing to more specialized courses of study. **2.** a pass in this examination. Cf. **A level.** [*O(rdinary) level*]

o•le′yl al′cohol (ō lē′il), *Chem.* an unsaturated, fatty alcohol, derived from oleic acid, $C_{18}H_{36}O$, used chiefly in organic synthesis. [1900–05; OLE(UM) + -YL]

ol•fac•tion (ol fak′shən, ōl-), *n.* **1.** the act of smelling. **2.** the sense of smell. [1840–50; < L *olfact(us)* ptp. of *olfacere* to smell (see OLFACTORY) + -ION]

ol•fac•tom•e•ter (ol′fak tom′i tər, ōl′-), *n.* a device for estimating the keenness of the sense of smell. [1885–90; < L *olfact(us)* (see OLFACTION) + -O- + -METER]

ol•fac•to•ry (ol fak′tə rē, -trē, ōl-), *adj., n., pl.* **-ries.** **—*adj.* 1.** of or pertaining to the sense of smell: *olfactory organs.* **—*n.* 2.** Usually, **olfactories.** an olfactory organ. **3.** See **olfactory nerve.** [1650–60; < L *olfactōrius,* equiv. to *olfac(ere)* to smell at, sniff *(ol(ēre)* to smell (akin to ODOR) + *facere* to make, do) + *-tōrius* -TORY[1]] **—ol•fac′to•ri•ly,** *adv.*

olfac′tory bulb′, *Anat.* the enlarged terminal part of each olfactory lobe from which the olfactory nerve originates. [1865–70]

olfac′tory lobe′, *Anat.* the anterior part of each cerebral hemisphere, involved with olfactory functions. [1855–60]

olfac′tory nerve′, *Anat.* either one of the first pair of cranial nerves, consisting of sensory fibers that conduct to the brain the impulses from the mucous membranes of the nose. [1660–70]

OLG, Old Low German. Also, **O.L.G.**

O.L.G., Old Low German.

Ol•ga (ol′gə, ōl′-; *Russ.* ôl′gə), *n.* **1. Saint,** died A.D. 968?, regent of Kiev until 955; saint of the Russian Orthodox Church. **2.** a female given name: from a Scandinavian word meaning "holy."

o•lib•a•num (ō lib′ə nəm), *n.* frankincense. [1350–1400; ME < ML, for LL *libanus* < Gk *líbanos,* of Sem orig.; cf. Heb *ləbhōnāh*]

olig-, var. of **oligo-** before a vowel: *oligarchy.*

ol•i•garch (ol′i gärk′), *n.* one of the rulers in an oligarchy. [1600–10; < Gk *oligárchēs,* equiv. to *olig(os)* OLIG- + *-archēs* -ARCH]

ol•i•gar•chic (ol′i gär′kik), *adj.* of, pertaining to, or having the form of an oligarchy. Also, **ol′i•gar′chi•cal.** [1640–50; < Gk *oligarchikós,* equiv. to *oligarch(ía)* OLIGARCHY + *-ikos* -IC] **—ol′i•gar′chi•cal•ly,** *adv.*

ol•i•gar•chy (ol′i gär′kē), *n., pl.* **-chies. 1.** a form of government in which all power is vested in a few persons or in a dominant class or clique; government by the few. **2.** a state or organization so ruled. **3.** the persons or class so ruling. [1570–80; < ML *oligarchia* < Gk *oligarchía.* See OLIG-, -ARCHY]

oligo-, a combining form meaning "few," "little," used in the formation of compound words: *oligopoly.* Also, *esp. before a vowel,* **olig-.** [< Gk, comb. form of *olígos* little, few (in pl.)]

Ol•i•go•cene (ol′i gō sēn′), *Geol.* **—*adj.* 1.** noting or pertaining to an epoch of the Tertiary Period, occurring from 40 to 25 million years ago. See table under **geologic time.** **—*n.* 2.** the Oligocene Epoch or Series. [1855–60; OLIGO- + -CENE]

ol•i•go•chaete (ol′i gō kēt′), *n.* any of various annelids of the family Oligochaeta, including earthworms and certain small, freshwater species, having locomotory setae sunk directly in the body wall. [1875–80; < NL *Oligochaeta;* see OLIGO-, CHAETA] **—ol′i•go•chae′tous,** *adj.*

ol•i•go•clase (ol′i gō klās′), *n. Mineral.* a kind of plagioclase feldspar occurring commonly in white crystals, sometimes shaded with gray, green, or red. [1825–35; OLIGO- + -CLASE]

ol•i•go•don•tia (ol′i gō don′shə, -shē ə), *n. Dentistry.* an abnormal condition in which fewer than the normal number of teeth develop. [< NL; see OLIG-, -ODONT, -IA]

ol•i•go•gene (ol′i gō jēn′, ə lig′ə-), *n. Genetics.* a gene that produces or significantly affects the expression of a qualitative heritable characteristic, acting either alone or with a few other genes. [OLIGO- + GENE]

ol•i•go•men•or•rhe•a (ol′i gō men′ə rē′ə), *n. Pathol.* **1.** abnormally infrequent menstruation. **2.** abnormally scanty blood flow in menstruation. Also, **ol′i•go•men′or•rhoe′a.** [1880–85; OLIGO- + MENORRHEA]

o•lig•o•mer (ə lig′ə mər), *n. Chem.* a polymer molecule consisting of a small number of monomers. Cf. **dimer, tetramer, trimer.** [1965–70; OLIGO- + -MER] **—o•lig•o•mer•ic** (ə lig′ə mer′ik), *adj.*

ol•i•go•nu•cle•o•tide (ol′i gō nōō′klē ə tīd′, -nyōō′-), *n. Biochem.* a chain of a few nucleotides. [1940–45; OLIGO- + NUCLEOTIDE]

ol•i•go•phre•ni•a (ol′i gō frē′nē ə, ə lig′ə-), *n. Pathol.* less than normal mental development. [1895–1900; < NL; see OLIGO-, PHREN-, -IA] **—ol•i•go•phren•ic** (ol′i gō-fren′ik, ə lig′ə-), *adj.*

ol•i•gop•o•ly (ol′i gop′ə lē), *n.* the market condition that exists when there are few sellers, as a result of which they can greatly influence price and other market factors. Cf. **duopoly, monopoly** (def. 1). [1890–95; OLIGO- + (MONO)POLY] **—ol•i•gop•o•lis•tic** (ol′i gop′ə-lis′tik), *adj.*

ol•i•gop•so•ny (ol′i gop′sə nē), *n.* the market condition that exists when there are few buyers, as a result of which they can greatly influence price and other market factors. Cf. **duopsony, monopsony.** [1940–45; OLIG- + Gk *opsōnía* purchase of provisions, shopping] **—ol′i•gop′so•nis′tic,** *adj.*

ol•i•go•sac•cha•ride (ol′i gō sak′ə rīd′, -rid), *n. Chem.* any carbohydrate yielding few monosaccharides on hydrolysis, as two, three, or four. [1925–30; OLIGO- + SACCHARIDE]

ol•i•go•troph•ic (ol′i gō trof′ik, -trō′fik), *adj. Ecol.* (of a lake) characterized by a low accumulation of dissolved nutrient salts, supporting but a sparse growth of algae and other organisms, and having a high oxygen content owing to the low organic content. [1925–30; OLIGO- + TROPHIC]

ol•i•got•ro•phy (ol′i go′trə fē), *n. Ecol.* the state of being oligotrophic. [1700–10; OLIGO- + -TROPHY]

ol•i•gu•ri•a (ol′i gyŏŏr′ē ə), *n. Pathol.* scantiness of urine due to diminished secretion. Also, **ol•i•gu•re•sis** (ol′i gyŏŏ rē′sis). [1895–1900; OLIG- + -URIA] **—ol•i•gu•ret•ic** (ol′i gyŏŏ ret′ik), *adj.*

O•lin (ō′lin), *n.* a male given name.

O•lin•da (ō lin′də; *Port.* ŏŏ lēN′dä), *n.* a city in NE Brazil, N suburb of Recife, on the Atlantic coast: beach resort. 250,704.

o•lin•go (ō ling′gō), *n., pl.* **-gos.** *n.* any raccoonlike, nocturnal, fruit-eating mammal of the genus *Bassaricyon,* inhabiting tropical jungles from Nicaragua to Peru and Bolivia and having large eyes and a long, ringed tail. [1915–20; of unexplained orig.]

o•li•o (ō′lē ō′), *n., pl.* **o•li•os. 1.** a dish of many ingredients. **2.** *Informal.* See **olla podrida** (def. 2). **3.** a mixture of heterogeneous elements; hodgepodge. **4.** a medley or potpourri, as of musical or literary selections; miscellany. **5.** *Theat.* **a.** a specialty act performed downstage while the upstage set is changed. **b.** a performance, as a musical number, presented between scenes or acts. **c.** See **drop scene** (def. 1). **d.** a program of variety acts, esp. the second half of a minstrel show. [1635–45; < Sp *olla* pot, stew < L *olla, ōla* pot, jar]

Ol•i•phant (ol′ə fənt), *n.* **Margaret Wilson,** 1828–97, Scottish novelist.

ol•i•va•ceous (ol′ə vā′shəs), *adj.* of a deep shade of green; olive. [1770–80; < NL *olivāceus,* equiv. to L *olīv(a)* OLIVE + *-āceus* -ACEOUS]

ol•i•va•ry (ol′ə ver′ē), *adj.* **1.** shaped like an olive. **2.** of or pertaining to an olivary body [1535–45; < L *olivārius* belonging to olives. See OLIVE, -ARY]

ol′ivary bod′y, *Anat.* one of two oval bodies or prominences composed of nerve tissue, one on each side of the anterior surface of the medulla oblongata. [1830–40]

ol•ive (ol′iv), *n.* **1.** an evergreen tree, *Olea europaea,* of Mediterranean and other warm regions, cultivated chiefly for its fruit. Cf. **olive family. 2.** the fruit of this tree, a small oval drupe, eaten as a relish and used as a source of oil. **3.** Also called **olive wood.** the wood of this tree, valued for ornamental work. **4.** the foliage of this tree. **5.** a wreath of it. **6.** any of various related or similar trees. **7.** See **olive branch. 8.** the ocher green or dull yellow green of the unripe olive fruit. **—*adj.* 9.** of, pertaining to, or made of olives, their foliage, or their fruit. **10.** of the color olive. **11.** tinged with this color: *an olive complexion.* [1150–1200; ME < OF < L *oliva,* by-form of *olea* < dial. Gk **elaíwa* olive, olive tree; cf. OIL, OLEACEOUS]

Ol•ive (ol′iv), *n.* a female given name.

ol′ive-backed thrush′ (ol′iv bakt′). See **Swainson's thrush.** [1835–45, *Amer.*]

ol′ive branch′, 1. a branch of the olive tree as an emblem of peace. **2.** any token of peace. [1275–1325; ME]

ol′ive drab′, *pl.* **olive drabs** for 3. **1.** a deep olive color. **2.** woolen cloth of this color, used esp. for U.S. Army uniforms. **3.** a military uniform made from this cloth. [1895–1900]

ol′ive fam′ily, the plant family Oleaceae, characterized by trees and shrubs having opposite, simple or pinnately compound leaves, usually small and sometimes showy flowers, and fruit in the form of a berry, capsule, or winged seed, and including the ash, forsythia, lilac, olive, and privet.

ol•ive-green (ol′iv grēn′), *n., adj.* green with a yellowish or brownish tinge. [1750–60]

o•liv•en•ite (ō liv′ə nīt′, ol′ə və-), *n.* a mineral, basic copper arsenate, $Cu_4As_2O_8(OH)_2$, occurring in crystals and in masses, usually olive-green in color. [1810–20; < G *Oliven(erz)* olive (ore) + -ITE[1]]

ol′ive oil′, an oil expressed from the olive fruit, used in cooking, in salad dressings, in medicine, etc. [1765–75]

Ol•i•ver (ol′ə vər), *n.* **1.** one of the 12 paladins of Charlemagne. Cf. **Roland. 2. Joseph** (*"King"*), 1885?–1938, U.S. cornet player, bandleader, and composer: pioneer in jazz. **3.** a male given name.

Ol′iver Twist′, a novel (1838) by Dickens.

Ol•ives (ol′ivz), *n.* **Mount of,** a small ridge E of Jerusalem, in what is now Jordan. Highest point, 2737 ft. (834m). Also, **Ol•i•vet** (ol′ə vet′, -vit).

ol′ive shell′, 1. any marine gastropod of the family Olividae, having a polished, highly colored, elongated shell and a large mantle that, when extended, surrounds the shell. **2.** the shell itself. [1880–85]

ol•i•vette (ol′ə vet′), *n. Theat.* a large floodlight having a single bulb. Also, **ol•i•vet** (ol′ə vet′, ol′ə vet′). [< F; see OLIVE, -ETTE]

ol′ive wood′, olive (def. 3).

O•liv•i•a (ō liv′ē ə), *n.* a female given name, form of **Olive.**

O•liv•i•er (ō liv′ē ā′), *n.* **Laurence (Kerr)** (kûr; *Brit.* kär, kâr), (*Baron Olivier of Brighton*), 1907–89, English actor and director.

ol•i•vine (ol′ə vēn′, ol′ə vēn′), *n. Mineral.* any of a group of magnesium iron silicates, $(Mg,Fe)_2SiO_4$, occurring in olive-green to gray-green masses as an important constituent of basic igneous rocks. Also called **chrysolite.** [1785–95; < G *Olivin,* equiv. to *Olive* OLIVE + *-in* -INE[2]] **—ol•i•vin•ic** (ol′ə vin′ik), **ol•i•vin•it•ic** (ol′ə vi-nit′ik), *adj.*

o•lla (ô′lyä, ô′yä; *Eng.* ol′ə), *n. Spanish.* **1.** a pot, esp. an earthen pot for holding water, cooking, etc. **2.** a stew.

OLLA, Office of Lend Lease Administration.

ol•la po•dri•da (ol′ə pə drē′də; *Sp.* ô′lyä pô thrē′thä, ô′yä), **1.** a spicy Spanish stew of sausage and other meat, chickpeas, and often tomatoes and other vegetables. **2.** an incongruous mixture or miscellany; olio. [1590–1600; < Sp: lit., rotten pot]

Ol•lie (ol′ē), *n.* **1.** a male given name, form of **Oliver. 2.** a female given name, form of **Olive.**

Ol•mec (ol′mek, ōl′-), *adj., n., pl.* **-mecs,** (*esp. collectively*) **-mec.** *Archaeol.* **—*adj.* 1.** of or designating a Mesoamerican civilization, c1000–400 B.C., along the southern Gulf coast of Mexico, characterized by extensive agriculture, a dating system, long-distance trade networks, pyramids and ceremonial centers, and very fine jade work. **—*n.* 2.** a member of the ancient people who belonged to the Olmec civilization.

Olm•sted (ōm′stid, -sted), *n.* **Frederick Law,** 1822–1903, U.S. landscape architect.

ol•o•gy (ol′ə jē), *n., pl.* **-gies.** *Informal or facetious.* any science or branch of knowledge. [1795–1805; extracted from words like BIOLOGY, GEOLOGY where the element -LOGY is preceded by *-o-;* see -O-]

o•lo•li•u•qui (ō′lō lē ōō′kē), *n.* a woody vine, *Turbina corymbosa,* of the morning glory family, native to Central America, having seeds that are hallucinogenic and are used in some Indian rituals. [< MexSp *ololiuque* < Nahuatl *ololiuhqui* lit., something rolled into a ball, collected]

O•lo•mouc (ô′lô mōts), *n.* a city in central Moravia, in the E Czech Republic. 107,000. German, **Ol•mütz** (ôl′-myts).

O•lon•ga•po (ō lông′gə pō′), *n.* a port in the Philippines, on SW Luzon. 156,430.

O•lo•nos (*Gk.* ô′lô nôs′), *n.* Erymanthus.

o•lo•ro•so (ō′lə rō′sō), *n.* a medium-dry sherry of Spain. [1875–80; < Sp: lit., sweet-smelling, equiv. to *olor* smell (< L (var. of *odor* ODOR), equiv. to *ol(ēre)* to give off a smell + *-or* -OR[1]) + *-oso* -OUS]

ol•pe (ol′pē), *n., pl.* **-pes, -pae** (-pē). a form of the oinochoe. [1880–85; < Gk *ólpē* oil-flask]

CONCISE ETYMOLOGY KEY: <, descended or borrowed from; >, whence; b., blend of, blended; c., cognate with; cf., compare; deriv., derivative; equiv., equivalent; imit., imitative; obl., oblique; r., replacing; s., stem; sp., spelling, spelled; resp., respelling, respelled; trans., translation; ?, origin unknown; *, unattested; ‡, probably earlier than. See the full key inside the front cover.

Ol•sztyn (ôl′shtin), *n.* a city in NE Poland. 107,500. German, **Allenstein.**

Ol•wen (ol′wen), *n. Welsh Legend.* a princess, the daughter of Ysbaddaden Chief-giant.

ol•y•koek (ol′i ko͝ok′), *n. Hudson Valley* (*older use*). doughnut. [1800–10, *Amer.*; < New York D; cf. D *oliekoek* oilseed cake, equiv. to *olie* OIL + *koek* cake (see COOKIE)]

O•lym•pi•a (ə lim′pē ə, ō lim′-), *n.* **1.** a plain in ancient Elis, Greece, where the ancient Olympic Games were held. **2.** a city in and the capital of Washington, in the W part, on Puget Sound. 27,447. **3.** (*sometimes l.c.*) a common oyster, *Ostrea lurida,* of the Pacific coast of North America. **4.** a female given name: from a Greek word meaning "of Olympus."

O•lym•pi•ad (ə lim′pē ad′, ō lim′-), *n.* (*often l.c.*) **1.** a period of four years reckoned from one celebration of the Olympic Games to the next, by which the Greeks computed time from 776 B.C. **2.** a celebration of the modern Olympic Games. [1350–1400; ME < L *Olympiad-,* s. of *Olympias* < Gk *Olympiás* n. use of the adj.: of Olympus. See OLYMPIA, -AD[1]] —**O•lym′pi•ad′ic,** *adj.*

O•lym•pi•an (ə lim′pē ən, ō lim′-), *adj.* **1.** pertaining to Mount Olympus or dwelling thereon, as the gods of classical Greece. **2.** pertaining to Olympia in Elis. **3.** of, resembling, characteristic of, or suitable to the gods of Olympus; majestic or aloof: *an Olympian landscape; an Olympian disdain.* —*n.* **4.** an Olympian deity. **5.** a contender in the Olympic Games. **6.** a native or inhabitant of Olympia. [1585–95; < LL *Olympiānus,* equiv. to L *Olympi(us)* (< Gk *Olýmpios,* deriv. of *Ólympos* OLYMPUS) + *-ānus* -AN] —**O•lym′pi•an•ly,** *adv.*

O•lym•pic (ə lim′pik, ō lim′-), *adj.* **1.** of or pertaining to the Olympic Games: *an Olympic contender.* **2.** of or pertaining to Olympia, in Greece. **3.** pertaining to Mount Olympus, in Greece. **4.** Olympian (def. 3). —*n.* **5.** an Olympian deity. **6. Olympics.** See **Olympic Games.** (def. 2). [1590–1600; < L *Olympicus* of Olympus, of Olympia < Gk *Olympikós.* See OLYMPUS, -IC]

Olym′pic Games′, **1.** Also called **Olym′pian Games′.** the greatest of the games or festivals of ancient Greece, held every four years in the plain of Olympia in Elis, in honor of Zeus. **2.** a modern international sports competition, held once every four years. [1600–10]

Olym′pic Moun′tains, a mountain system in NW Washington, part of the Coast Range. Highest peak, Mt. Olympus, 7954 ft. (2424 m).

Olym′pic Na′tional Park′, a national park in NW Washington. 1323 sq. mi. (3425 sq. km).

O•lym•pic-size (ə lim′pik sīz′, ō lim′-), *adj.* **1.** of the dimensions or length prescribed for the Olympic Games and other major athletic competitions: *an Olympic-size speed-skating oval.* **2.** (of a swimming pool) having a length of 55 yds. (50 m) and a width of at least 23 yds. (21 m). Also, **O•lym′pic-sized′.** [1965–70]

O•lym•pi•o (ə lim′pē ō′), *n.* **Syl•va•nus** (sil vā′nəs), 1902–63, African statesman: first president of the Republic of Togo 1961–63.

O•lym•pus (ə lim′pəs, ō lim′-), *n.* **Mount, 1.** a mountain in NE Greece, on the boundary between Thessaly and Macedonia: mythical abode of the greater Grecian gods. 9730 ft. (2966 m). **2.** a mountain in NW Washington: highest peak of the Olympic Mountains. 7954 ft. (2424 m).

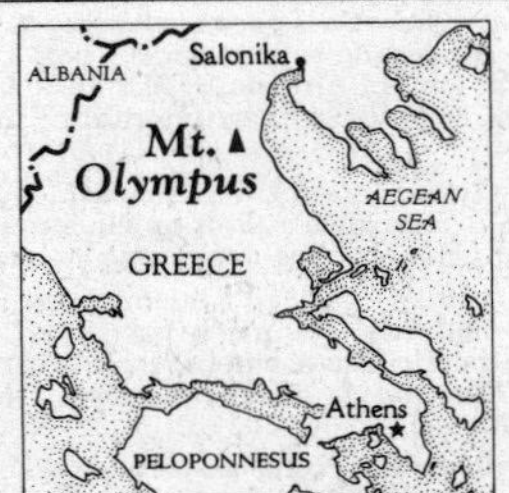

O•lyn•thus (ō lin′thəs), *n.* an ancient city in NE Greece, on the Chalcidice Peninsula. —**O•lyn•thi•ac** (ō lin′thē ak′), **O•lyn′thi•an,** *adj., n.*

Om (ôm), *n. Hinduism.* a mantric word thought to be a complete expression of Brahman and interpreted as having three sounds representing Brahma or creation, Vishnu or preservation, and Siva or destruction, or as consisting of the same three sounds, representing waking, dreams, and deep sleep, along with the following silence, which is fulfillment. Also, **Aum.** [1780–90; < Skt]

Om., Ostmark.

O.M., *Brit.* Order of Merit.

OMA, orderly marketing agreement.

-oma, *pl.* **-omas, -omata.** a noun suffix used to form names of tumors, of the kind specified by the base: *fibroma; melanoma.* [prob. extracted from CARCINOMA or SARCOMA]

O•ma•ha (ō′mə hô′, -hä′), *n., pl.* **-has,** (*esp. collectively*) **-ha** for 2. **1.** a city in E Nebraska, on the Missouri River. 311,681. **2.** a member of a North American Indian people of northeastern Nebraska. **3.** the Siouan language of the Omaha, mutually intelligible with Ponca. **4.** *Mil.* the World War II Allied code name for one of the five D-Day invasion beaches on France's Normandy coast, attacked by American troops.

O•man (ō män′), *n.* **1. Sultanate of.** Formerly, **Muscat and Oman.** an independent sultanate in SE Arabia. 800,000; ab. 82,800 sq. mi. (212,380 sq. km). *Cap.:* Muscat. **2. Gulf of,** a NW arm of the Arabian Sea, at the entrance to the Persian Gulf.

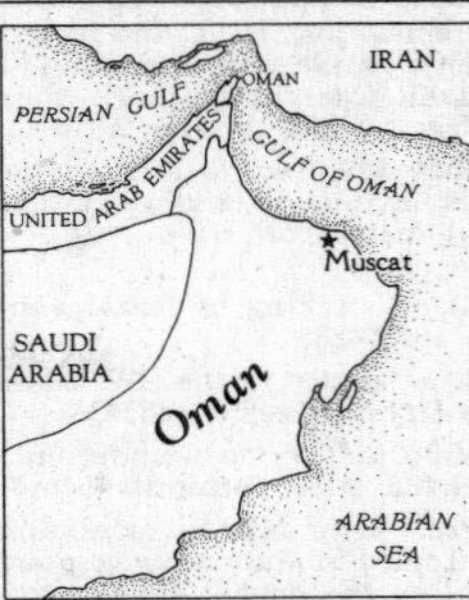

O•ma•ni (ō mä′nē), *adj.* **1.** of or pertaining to Oman or its people. —*n.* **2.** a native or inhabitant of Oman.

O•mar (ō′mär), *n.* a male given name.

O•mar Khay•yám (ō′mär kī yäm′, -yam′, ō′mər), died 1123?, Persian poet and mathematician.

o•ma•sum (ō mā′səm), *n., pl.* **-sa** (-sə), the third stomach of a ruminant, between the reticulum and the abomasum; the manyplies. See diag. under **ruminant.** [1700–10; < NL, L *omāsum* bullock's tripe]

O•may•yad (ō mī′ad), *n., pl.* **-yads, -ya•des** (-ə dēz′). **1.** a member of the dynasty that ruled at Damascus A.D. 661–750, claiming descent from Omayya, cousin of the grandfather of Muhammad the Prophet. **2.** a member of the dynasty of caliphs that ruled in southern Spain, A.D. 756–1031: related to the Damascus dynasty. Also, **Ommiad, Umayyad.**

OMB, *U.S. Govt.* Office of Management and Budget: the division of the Executive Office of the President that prepares and administers the federal budget and improves management in the executive branch. Also, **O.M.B.** Formerly, **Bureau of the Budget.**

OMBE, Office of Minority Business Enterprise.

om•ber (om′bər), *n.* **1.** a card game popular in the 17th and 18th centuries and played, usually by three persons, with 40 cards. **2.** the player undertaking to win the pool in this game. Also, **hombre;** *esp. Brit.,* **om′bre.** [1650–60; < F *(h)ombre* < Sp *hombre* lit., man < L *hominem,* acc. of *homō* man. See HOMO]

om•brel•li•no (om′brə lē′nō), *n., pl.* **-nos.** *Western Ch.* the white silk canopy held over the Eucharist while transferring it from one place to another, esp. from the main altar to a side altar. [1840–50; < It: lit., parasol, sunshade]

om•bu (om bo͞o′), *n.* a South American tree, *Phytolacca dioica,* having a thick trunk and large, evergreen leaves. [< AmerSp *ombú* < Guarani *umbú*]

om•buds•man (om′bədz mən, -man′, -bo͝odz-, ôm′-, om bo͝odz′mən, -man′, ôm-), *n., pl.* **-men** (-mən, -men′). **1.** a government official who hears and investigates complaints by private citizens against other officials or government agencies. **2.** a person who investigates and attempts to resolve complaints and problems, as between employees and an employer or between students and a university. [1910–15; < Sw: legal representative, equiv. to *ombud* agent, attorney + *-s* 's[1] + *-man* -MAN]
—**Usage.** See **-man.**

om•buds•per•son (om′bədz pûr′sən, -bo͝odz-, ôm′-), *n.* ombudsman (def. 2). [OMBUDS(MAN) + -PERSON]
—**Usage.** See **-person.**

om•buds•wom•an (om′bədz wo͝om′ən, -bo͝odz-, ôm′-), *n., pl.* **-wom•en.** a woman employed to investigate complaints against government or institutional officials, employers, etc. [1960–65; OMBUDS(MAN) + -WOMAN]
—**Usage.** See **-woman.**

Om•dur•man (om′do͝or män′), *n.* a city in central Sudan, on the White Nile opposite Khartoum: British victory 1898. 305,308.

o•me•ga (ō mē′gə, ō mā′-, ō meg′ə), *n.* **1.** the 24th and last letter of the Greek alphabet (Ω, ω). **2.** the vowel sound represented by this letter. **3.** the last of any series; the end. [< Gk *ō méga* lit., great *o.* Cf. OMICRON]

o•me′ga-mi′nus par′ticle (ō mē′gə mī′nəs, -mā′-, ō meg′ə-), *Physics.* a baryon with strangeness −3, isotopic spin 0, and negative charge; predicted from the mathematics of the Eightfold Way and subsequently discovered. *Symbol:* Ω^- [1960–65]

o•me′ga-3 fat′ty ac′id (ō mē′gə thrē′, ō mā′-, ō meg′ə-), a polyunsaturated fatty acid, essential for normal retinal function, that influences various metabolic pathways, resulting in lowered cholesterol and triglyceride levels, inhibited platelet clotting, and reduced inflammatory and immune reactions. Also called **n-3 fatty acid.** [so named because its 1st double bond occurs after the 3d carbon atom counting from the methyl or *omega* end of the molecule]

om•e•let (om′lit, om′ə-), *n.* eggs beaten until frothy, often combined with other ingredients, as herbs, chopped ham, cheese, or jelly, and cooked until set. Also, **om′e•lette.** [1605–15; < F *omelette,* earlier *amelette,* metathetic form of *alemette,* var. of *alemelle* lit., thin plate, var. of OF *lemelle* < L *lāmella.* See LAMELLA, -ET]

o•men (ō′mən), *n.* **1.** anything perceived or happening that is believed to portend a good or evil event or circumstance in the future; portent. **2.** a prognostic. **3.** prophetic significance; presage: *a bird of ill omen.* —*v.t.* **4.** to be an omen of; portend. **5.** to divine, as if from omens. [1575–85; < L *ōmen*]
—**Syn. 1.** augury, foreboding. See **sign.**

o•men•tum (ō men′təm), *n., pl.* **-ta** (-tə). *Anat.* a fold of the peritoneum connecting the stomach and the abdominal viscera forming a protective and supportive covering. Cf. **greater omentum, lesser omentum.** [1535–45; < L *ōmentum* caul surrounding the intestines] —**o•men′tal,** *adj.*

o•mer (ō′mər; *Seph. Heb.* ô meʀ′; *Ashk. Heb.* ō′meʀ), *n.* **1.** a Hebrew unit of dry measure, the tenth part of an ephah. **2.** (*usually cap.*) *Judaism.* the period of 49 days extending from the second day of Passover to the first day of Shavuoth. [< Heb *'ōmer*]

o•mer•tà (ô′meʀ tä′; *Eng.* ō mer′tə), *n. Italian.* secrecy sworn to by oath; code of silence.

O•mi (ō′mē; *Japn.* ô′mē), *n.* Biwa.

om•i•cron (om′i kron′, ō′mi-), *n.* **1.** the 15th letter of the Greek alphabet (O, o). **2.** the vowel sound represented by this letter. [< Gk *ō mikrón,* lit., small *o.* Cf. OMEGA]

om•i•nous (om′ə nəs), *adj.* **1.** portending evil or harm; foreboding; threatening; inauspicious: *an ominous bank of dark clouds.* **2.** having the significance of an omen. [1580–90; < L *ōminōsus* portentous, equiv. to *ōmin-* (s. of *ōmen*) OMEN + *-ōsus* -OUS] —**om′i•nous•ly,** *adv.* —**om′i•nous•ness,** *n.*
—**Syn.** OMINOUS, PORTENTOUS, THREATENING, MENACING, FATEFUL are adjectives describing that which forebodes a serious, significant, and often harmful outcome. OMINOUS, derived from *omen* "a predictor of outcomes," usually suggests evil or damaging eventualities: *ominous storm clouds; an ominous silence.* PORTENTOUS, although it may suggest evil results, often stresses a momentous or very important outcome: *a portentous moment in history; a portentous escalation of hostilities.* THREATENING may suggest calamity or great harm but sometimes mere unpleasantness: *a threatening rumble from the volcano; A threatening look from his brother caused him to quickly change the subject.* MENACING always suggests serious damage as an outcome: *a disease menacing the entire population; He advanced with a menacing swagger.* FATEFUL most often stresses the great or decisive importance of what it describes: *a fateful encounter between two future leaders; a fateful day that changed our world.*

o•mis•si•ble (ō mis′ə bəl), *adj.* capable of being or allowed to be omitted. [1810–20; < L *omiss(us)* (see OMISSION) + -IBLE]

o•mis•sion (ō mish′ən), *n.* **1.** the act of omitting. **2.** the state of being omitted. **3.** something left out, not done, or neglected: *an important omission in a report.* [1350–1400; ME < LL *omissiōn-* (s. of *omissiō*), equiv. to *omiss(us)* (ptp. of *omittere* to let go; see OMIT) + *-iōn-* -ION; see MISSION]

o•mis•sive (ō mis′iv), *adj.* neglecting; leaving out. [1620–30; < L *omiss(us)* (see OMISSION) + -IVE] —**o•mis′sive•ly,** *adv.*

o•mit (ō mit′), *v.t.,* **o•mit•ted, o•mit•ting.** **1.** to leave out; fail to include or mention: *to omit a name from a list.* **2.** to forbear or fail to do, make, use, send, etc.: *to omit a greeting.* [1400–50; late ME *omitten* < L *omittere* to let go, equiv. to *o-* o-[2] + *mittere* to send] —**o•mit′•ter,** *n.*

O•mi•ya (ō′mē yä′), *n.* a city on E Honshu, in Japan, NW of Tokyo. 354,082.

om•ma•te•um (om′ə tē′əm), *n., pl.* **-te•a** (-tē′ə). *Zool.* See **compound eye.** [1880–85; < NL < Gk *ommat-* (s. of *ómma*) eye + NL *-eum* n. suffix] —**om′ma•te′al,** *adj.*

om•ma•tid•i•um (om′ə tid′ē əm), *n., pl.* **-tid•i•a** (-tid′ē ə). *Zool.* one of the radial elements composing a compound eye. [1880–85; < NL < Gk *ommat-* (s. of *ómma* eye) + NL *-idium* -IDIUM] —**om′ma•tid′i•al,** *adj.*

om•mat•o•phore (ə mat′ə fôr′, -fōr′), *n. Zool.* a tentacle or movable stalk bearing an eye, as in certain snails. [1875–80; < Gk *ommat-* eye (see OMMATEUM) + -o- + -PHORE] —**om•ma•toph•or•ous** (om′ə tof′ər əs), *adj.*

Om•mi•ad (ō mī′ad), *n., pl.* **-ads, -a•des** (-ə dēz′). Omayyad.

omn. bih., (in prescriptions) every two hours. [< L *omnī bihōriō*]

omn. hor., (in prescriptions) every hour. [< L *omnī hōrā*]

omni-, a combining form meaning "all," used in the formation of compound words: *omnifarious; omnipotence; omniscient.* [< L, comb. form of *omnis*]

om•ni•a mu•tan•tur, nos et mu•ta•mur in il•lis (ôm′nē ä′ mo͞o tän′to͝or nōs et mo͞o tä′mo͝or in il′lēs; *Eng.* om′nē ə myo͞o tan′tər nōs et myo͞o tā′mər in il′is), *Latin.* all things change, and we change with them.

om•ni•a vin•cit a•mor (ōm′nē ä′ wĕng′kit ä′mōʀ; *Eng.* om′nē ə vin′sit ā′môr), *Latin.* love conquers all.

om•ni•bear•ing (om′nə bâr′ing), *n. Navig.* the magnetic bearing of an omnirange station. [OMNI- + BEARING]

om•ni•bus (om′nə bus′, -bəs), *n., pl.* **-bus•es,** or, for 1, **-bus•ses,** *adj.* —*n.* **1.** bus (def. 1). **2.** a volume of reprinted works of a single author or of works related in interest or theme. —*adj.* **3.** pertaining to, including, or dealing with numerous objects or items at once: *an omnibus bill submitted to a legislature.* [1820–30; < F < L: for all (dat. pl. of *omnis*)]

om′nibus clause′, *Insurance.* a clause, esp. in an automobile liability policy, extending coverage to persons other than the insured named in the policy.

om•ni•di•rec•tion•al (om′nē di rek′shə nl), *adj. Electronics.* sending or receiving signals in all directions: *an omnidirectional microphone.* [1925–30; OMNI- + DIRECTIONAL]

om•ni•dis•tance (om′ni dis′təns), *n. Navig.* the distance between an omnirange station and a receiver. [OMNI- + DISTANCE]

om•ni•far•i•ous (om′nə fâr′ē əs), *adj.* of all forms, varieties, or kinds. [1645–55; < LL *omnifārius* (deriv. of L *omnifāriam* on all sides), equiv. to L *omni-* OMNI- + *-fārius;* see BIFARIOUS] **—om′ni•far′i•ous•ly,** *adv.* **—om′ni•far′i•ous•ness,** *n.*

om•nif•i•cent (om nif′ə sənt), *adj.* creating all things; having unlimited powers of creation. Also, **om•nif•ic** (om nif′ik). [1670–80; OMNI- + *-ficent,* as in *beneficent*] **—om•nif′i•cence,** *n.*

om•ni•graph (om′ni graf′, -gräf′), *n.* a device for converting Morse Code signals that are punched on a tape into audio signals, used in the training of telegraph operators. [1860–65; OMNI- + -GRAPH]

om•nip•o•tence (om nip′ə təns), *n.* **1.** the quality or state of being omnipotent. **2.** (*cap.*) God. [1560–70; < LL *omnipotentia,* equiv. to L *omnipotent-* OMNIPOTENT + *-ia;* see -ENCE]

om•nip•o•tent (om nip′ə tənt), *adj.* **1.** almighty or infinite in power, as God. **2.** having very great or unlimited authority or power. —*n.* **3.** an omnipotent being. **4. the Omnipotent,** God. [1275–1325; ME < L *omnipotent-* (s. of *omnipotēns*), equiv. to *omni-* OMNI- + *potent-* (see POTENT[1])] **—om•nip′o•tent•ly,** *adv.*
—Syn. 2. powerful, mighty, supreme. **—Ant. 2.** impotent, powerless, helpless.

om•ni•pres•ent (om′nə prez′ənt), *adj.* present everywhere at the same time: *the omnipresent God.* [1600–10; < ML *omnipraesent-* (s. of *omnipraesēns*), equiv. to L *omni-* OMNI- + *praesent-* PRESENT[1]] **—om′ni•pres′•ence,** *n.*
—Syn. OMNIPRESENT, UBIQUITOUS refer to the quality of being everywhere. OMNIPRESENT emphasizes in a lofty or dignified way the power, usually divine, of being present everywhere at the same time, as though all-enveloping: *Divine law is omnipresent.* UBIQUITOUS is applied to that which seems to appear in many and all sorts of places, or in an undignified or humorous way is "all over the place," often when unwanted: *A bore seems to be ubiquitous.*

om•ni•range (om′nə rānj′), *n.* a radio navigational aid in which stations emit distinctive signals on each of 360 degrees, giving the bearing of each degree with reference to magnetic north. Also called **VOR** [1945–50; OMNI- + RANGE]

om•nis•cience (om nish′əns), *n.* **1.** the quality or state of being omniscient. **2.** infinite knowledge. **3.** (*cap.*) God. [1605–15; < ML *omniscientia,* equiv. to L *omni-* OMNI- + *scientia* knowledge; see SCIENCE]

om•nis•cient (om nish′ənt), *adj.* **1.** having complete or unlimited knowledge, awareness, or understanding; perceiving all things. —*n.* **2.** an omniscient being. **3. the Omniscient,** God. [1595–1605; < NL *omniscient-,* s. of *omnisciēns,* equiv. to L *omni-* OMNI- + *scient-* knowing; see SCIENCE] **—om•nis′cient•ly,** *adv.*

om•ni•um-gath•er•um (om′nē əm gath′ər əm), *n., pl.* **-ums.** a miscellaneous collection. [1520–30; < L *omnium* of all (gen. pl. of *omnis*) + pseudo-L *gatherum* a gathering]

om•ni•vore (om′nə vôr′, -vōr′), *n.* **1.** someone or something that is omnivorous. **2.** an omnivorous animal. [1885–90; < F, on the model of CARNIVORE, etc.]

om•niv•o•rous (om niv′ər əs), *adj.* **1.** eating both animal and plant foods. **2.** eating all kinds of foods indiscriminately. **3.** taking in everything, as with the mind: *an omnivorous reader.* [1650–60; < L *omnivorus,* equiv. to *omni-* OMNI- + *-vorus* -VOROUS] **—om•niv′o•rism,** *n.* **—om•niv′o•rous•ly,** *adv.* **—om•niv′o•rous•ness,** *n.* **—om•niv′o•rism,** *n.*

omn. man., (in prescriptions) every morning. Also, **omn man** [< L *omnī māne*]

omn. noct., (in prescriptions) every night. Also, **omn noct** [< L *omnī nocte*]

omn. quadr. hor., (in prescriptions) every quarter of an hour. Also, **omn quadr hor** [< L *omnī quadrante hōrae*]

O•mo•la•ra (ō mō′lä rä′), *n.* a male given name: from a West African word meaning "child born at the right time."

O•moo (ō mo͞o′), *n.* a novel (1847) by Herman Melville.

o•mo•pha•gia (ō′mə fā′jə, -jē ə), *n.* the eating of raw food, esp. raw meat. [1700–10; < NL < Gk *ōmophagía,* equiv. to *ōmó(s)* raw + *-phagia* -PHAGY] **—o•mo•phag•ic** (ō′mə faj′ik), **o•moph•a•gous** (ō mof′ə gəs), *adj.* **—o•moph•a•gist** (ō mof′ə jist), *n.*

o•mo•pho•ri•on (ō′mə fôr′ē ən, -fōr′-, om′ə-), *n., pl.* **-pho•ri•a** (-fôr′ē ə, -fōr′-). *Eastern Ch.* a liturgical stole, resembling a pallium, worn by bishops. [1865–70; < LGk *ōmophórion,* equiv. to Gk *ōmo-* (deriv. of *ōmos* shoulder) + LGk *-phorion,* deriv. of Gk *phérein* to bear]

O•mot•ic (ō mot′ik), *n.* a proposed branch of the Afroasiatic family comprising a group of languages spoken in Ethiopia and often included within the Cushitic branch.

om•pha•cite (om′fə sīt′), *n. Mineral.* a pale-green variety of pyroxene similar to olivine, found in eclogite. [1820–30; < G *Omphazit* < Gk *omphakítēs* green stone, equiv. to *omphak-* (s. of *ómphax*) unripe grape + *-ītēs* -ITE[1]]

CONCISE ETYMOLOGY KEY: <, descended or borrowed from; >, whence; b., blend of, blended; c., cognate with; cf., compare; deriv., derivative; equiv., equivalent; imit., imitative; obl., oblique; r., replacing; s., stem; sp., spelling, spelled; resp., respelling, respelled; trans., translation; ?, origin unknown; *, unattested; ‡, probably earlier than. See the full key inside the front cover.

om•pha•los (om′fə ləs), *n.* **1.** the navel; umbilicus. **2.** the central point. **3.** *Gk. Antiq.* a stone in the temple of Apollo at Delphi, thought to mark the center of the earth. [1840–50; < Gk *omphalós;* akin to NAVEL]

om•pha•lo•skep•sis (om′fə lō skep′sis), *n.* contemplation of one's navel as part of a mystical exercise. [< Gk *omphal(ós)* OMPHALOS + *-o-* -O- + *sképsis* act of looking]

Om•ri (om′rī), *n.* a king of Israel and the father of Ahab. I Kings 16:16–28.

Omsk (ômsk), *n.* a city in the SW Russian Federation in Asia on the Irtysh River. 1,148,000.

O•mu•ta (ô′mo͞o tä′), *n.* a seaport on W Kyushu, in SW Japan. 169,485. Also, **O•mu•da** (ô′mo͞o dä′).

on (on, ôn), *prep.* **1.** so as to be or remain supported by or suspended from: *Put your package down on the table; Hang your coat on the hook.* **2.** so as to be attached to or unified with: *Hang the picture on the wall. Paste the label on the package.* **3.** so as to be a covering or wrapping for: *Put the blanket on the baby. Put aluminum foil on the lamb chops before freezing them.* **4.** in connection, association, or cooperation with; as a part or element of: *to serve on a jury.* **5.** so as to be a supporting part, base, backing, etc., of: *a painting on canvas; mounted on cardboard; legs on a chair.* **6.** (used to indicate place, location, situation, etc.): *a scar on the face; the book on the table; a house on 19th Street.* **7.** (used to indicate immediate proximity): *a house on the lake; to border on absurdity.* **8.** in the direction of: *on the left; to sail on a southerly course.* **9.** (used to indicate a means of conveyance or a means of supporting or supplying movement): *on the wing; This car runs on electricity. Can you walk on your hands? I'll be there on the noon plane.* **10.** by the agency or means of: *drunk on wine; talking on the phone; I saw it on television.* **11.** in addition to: *millions on millions of stars.* **12.** with respect or regard to (used to indicate the object of an action directed against or toward): *Let's play a joke on him. Write a critical essay on Shakespeare.* **13.** in a state or condition of; in the process of: *on strike; The house is on fire!* **14.** subject to: *a doctor on call.* **15.** engaged in or involved with: *He's on the second chapter now.* **16.** (used to indicate a source or a person or thing that serves as a source or agent): *a duty on imported goods; She depends on her friends for encouragement.* **17.** (used to indicate a basis or ground): *on my word of honor; The movie is based on the book.* **18.** (used to indicate risk or liability): *on pain of death.* **19.** (used to indicate progress toward or completion of an objective): *We completed the project on budget.* **20.** assigned to or occupied with; operating: *Who's on the switchboard this afternoon?* **21.** *Informal.* so as to disturb or affect adversely: *My hair dryer broke on me.* **22.** *Informal.* paid for by, esp. as a treat or gift: *Dinner is on me.* **23.** taking or using as a prescribed measure, cure, or the like: *The doctor had her on a low-salt diet.* **24.** regularly taking or addicted to: *He was on drugs for two years.* **25.** *Informal.* with; carried by: *I have no money on me.* **26.** (used to indicate time or occasion): *on Sunday; We demand cash on delivery.* **27.** (used to indicate the object or end of motion): *to march on the capital.* **28.** (used to indicate the object or end of action, thought, desire, etc.): *to gaze on a scene.* **29.** (used to indicate subject, reference, or respect): *views on public matters.* **30.** (used to indicate an encounter): *The pickpocket crept up on a victim.* **31. on the bow,** *Naut.* bow[3] (def. 7).
—*adv.* **32.** in, into, or onto a position of being supported or attached: *Sew the buttons on.* **33.** in, into, or onto a position of covering or wrapping: *Put your raincoat on.* **34.** fast to a thing, as for support: *Hold on!* **35.** toward a place, point, activity, or object: *to look on while others work.* **36.** forward, onward, or along, as in any course or process: *further on.* **37.** with continuous activity: *to work on.* **38.** into or in active operation or performance: *Turn the gas on.* **39. on and off,** off (def. 22a). **40. on and on,** at great length, so as to become tiresome: *They rambled on and on about their grandchildren.*
—*adj.* **41.** operating or in use: *The television set was on. Is your brake on?* **42.** taking place; occurring: *Don't you know there's a war on?* **43.** performing or broadcasting: *The radio announcer told us we were on.* **44.** *Informal.* **a.** behaving in a theatrical, lively, or ingratiating way: *Around close friends, one doesn't have to be on every minute.* **b.** functioning or performing at one's best: *When she's on, no other tennis player is half as good.* **45.** scheduled or planned: *Anything on after supper?* **46.** *Baseball.* positioned on a base or bases: *They had two men on when he hit the home run.* **47.** *Cricket.* noting that side of the wicket, or of the field, on which the batsman stands. **48. on to,** aware of the true nature, motive, or meaning of: *I'm on to your little game.*
—*n.* **49.** *Cricket.* the on side. [bef. 900; ME *on, an,* OE: on, in, to; c. D *aan,* G *an,* ON *ā,* Goth *ana;* akin to Gk *aná* up, upon (see ANA-)]

On (on), *n.* Biblical name of **Heliopolis.**

ON, Old Norse. Also, **ON., O.N.**

-on[1], a suffix used in the names of subatomic particles (*gluon; meson; neutron*), quanta (*graviton*), and other minimal entities or components (*cistron; codon; magneton; photon*). [prob. extracted from ION; cf. PROTON]

-on[2], a suffix used in the naming of inert gaseous elements: *neon.* [<< Gk *-on,* neut. of *-os* adj. ending]

O•na (ō′nə), *n., pl.* **O•nas,** (*esp. collectively*) **O•na** for def. 1. **1.** a member of a people of Tierra del Fuego. **2.** a female given name.

on-a•gain, off-a•gain (on′ə gen′ ôf′ə gen′, of′-, ôn′-), being in force or inoperative by turns, esp. spasmodically and unpredictably: *an on-again, off-again romance.* Also, **on′-a•gain′-off′-a•gain′.** [1945–50]

on•a•ger (on′ə jər), *n., pl.* **-gri** (-grī′), **-gers. 1.** a wild ass, *Equus hemionus,* of southwestern Asia. **2.** an ancient and medieval military catapult for throwing stones. [1300–50; ME < LL: machine for throwing projectiles, L *onager, onagrus* wild ass < Gk *ónagros* (in both senses), alter. of *ónos ágrios* ass of the fields, wild ass (see ACRE)]

onager, *Equus hemionus,* 4½ ft. (1.4 m) high at shoulder

on•a•gra•ceous (on′ə grā′shəs), *adj.* belonging to the Onagraceae, the evening primrose family of plants. Cf. **evening primrose family.** [1835–45; < NL *Onagrace(ae)* (*Onagr(a)* the type genus (< Gk *onágra* oleander) + *-aceae* -ACEAE) + -OUS]

on-air (on′âr′, ôn′-), *adj.* broadcasting: *an announcer with five years of on-air experience.* [1970–75]

o•nan•ism (ō′nə niz′əm), *n.* **1.** withdrawal of the penis in sexual intercourse so that ejaculation takes place outside the vagina; coitus interruptus. **2.** masturbation. [1720–30; after *Onan,* son of Judah (Gen. 38:9); see -ISM] **—o′nan•ist,** *n.* **—o′nan•is′tic,** *adj.*

O•nas•sis (ō nas′is, ō nä′sis), *n.* **1. Aristotle Socrates,** 1906–75, Greek businessman, born in Turkey. **2. Jacqueline (Lee Bou•vi•er Kennedy)** (bo͞o′vē ā′), ("*Jackie*"), 1929–94, wife of John F. Kennedy (1953–63) and Aristotle Onassis (1968–75).

O•ña•te (ô nyä′te), *n.* **Juan de** (hwän de), 1550?–1624, Spanish explorer who colonized New Mexico.

on-board (on′bôrd′, -bōrd′, ôn′-), *adj.* **1.** provided, occurring, etc., on a vehicle: *among the ship's many onboard services.* **2.** installed and functional within a vehicle: *on-board computers for aircraft.* Also, **on′board′.** [1965–70; adj. use of adv. phrase *on board*]

on-cam•er•a (on′kam′ər ə, -kam′rə, ôn′-), *adj., adv.* within the range of a motion-picture or television camera; while being filmed or televised: *on-camera blunders; The assassination happened on-camera.* [1960–65]

once (wuns), *adv.* **1.** at one time in the past; formerly: *I was a farmer once; a once powerful nation.* **2.** a single time: *We ate there just once. We go to a movie once a week.* **3.** even a single time; at any time; ever: *If the facts once become known, it will be just too bad.* **4.** by a single step, degree, or grade: *a cousin once removed.* **5. once and again,** repeatedly: *He has been told once and again not to slam the door.* **6. once and for all,** decisively; finally: *Let's settle this problem once and for all.* Also, **once for all. 7. once in a while,** at intervals; occasionally: *She stops in to see us once in a while.* **8. once or twice,** a very few times; infrequently: *I've seen her in the elevator once or twice.* **9. once upon a time,** at some unspecified past time, esp. a long time ago: *Once upon a time, in a faraway land, there lived a prince and princess.* —*adj.* **10.** former; having at one time been: *the once and future king.* —*conj.* **11.** if or when at any time; if ever. **12.** whenever; as soon as: *Once you're finished, you can leave.* —*n.* **13.** a single occasion; one time only: *Once is enough.* **14. all at once, a.** simultaneously: *The children were running, screaming, and throwing things all at once.* **b.** suddenly: *All at once the rain came down.* **15. at once, a.** at the same time; simultaneously: *Don't all speak at once.* **b.** immediately; promptly: *Tell him to come at once!* [bef. 1150; ME *ones,* OE *ānes,* orig. gen. of *ān* ONE; r. ME *enes,* OE *ǣnes* once, equiv. to *ǣne* once (orig. instrumental of *ān*) + *-es* adv. suffix; see -S[1]]

once-o•ver (wuns′ō′vər), *n. Informal.* **1.** a quick look, examination, or appraisal. **2.** a quick, superficial job: *He gave the car just a once-over with a rag.* [1910–15, *Amer.*]

once-o•ver-light•ly (wuns′ō′vər līt′lē), *n. Informal.* a hasty or superficial treatment, look, examination, etc.; once-over: *The maid gave the room the once-over lightly.* [1940–45]

on•cho•cer•ci•a•sis (ong′kō sər kī′ə sis), *n. Pathol.* an infestation with filarial worms of the genus *Onchocerca,* common in tropical America and Africa, transmitted by black flies, and characterized by nodules under the skin, an itchy rash, eye lesions, and in severe cases, elephantiasis. Also, **on•cho•cer•co•sis** (ong′kō-sər kō′sis). Also called **river blindness.** [1910–15; < NL *Onchocerc(a)* a genus of filarioid worms (*oncho-* (correctly *onco-* < Gk *ónk(os)* barb + *-o-* -O-) + *-cerca* fem. of *-cercus* -tailed < Gk, adj. deriv. of *kérkos* tail) + -IASIS]

on•cid•i•um (on sid′ē əm), *n.* any of numerous tropical American orchids of the genus *Oncidium,* having clusters of flowers showing great variety in size, form, and color. Also called **dancing lady orchid.** [< NL (1800), equiv. to Gk *onk(o)-* (comb. form of *ónkos* barb of an arrow) + NL *-idium* -IDIUM; so called from the crests on the labellum]

onco- a combining form meaning "tumor," "mass," used in the formation of compound words: *oncogenic.* [comb. form of Gk *ónkos* mass, bulk]

on•co•gene (ong′kə jēn′), *n. Genetics.* any gene that is a causative factor in the initiation of cancerous growth. [1965–70; ONCO- + GENE]

on•co•gen•e•sis (ong′kə jen′ə sis), *n.* the generation of tumors. [1930–35; ONCO- + -GENESIS] **—on′co•gen′•ic, on•co•ge•net•ic** (ong′kə jə net′ik), *adj.*

on•co•ge•nic•i•ty (ong′kə jə nis′i tē), *n.* the capability of inducing tumor formation. [1940–45; ONCOGENIC + -ITY]

on•col•o•gy (ong kol′ə jē), *n.* **1.** the branch of medical science dealing with tumors, including the origin, development, diagnosis, and treatment of malignant neoplasms. **2.** the study of cancer. [1855–60; ONCO- +

-LOGY] **—on·co·log·ic** (ong′kə loj′ik), **on′co·log′i·cal,** *adj.* **—on·col′o·gist,** *n.*

on·com·ing (on′kum′ing, ôn′-), *adj.* **1.** approaching; nearing: *the oncoming train; the oncoming holiday season.* **2.** emerging: *the oncoming generation of leaders.* —*n.* **3.** approach; onset: *the oncoming of winter.* [1835–45; ON + COMING, after v. phrase *come on*]

on·cor·na·vi·rus (ong kôr′nə vī′rəs, -kôr′nə vī′-), *n., pl.* **-rus·es.** *Pathol.* any of various RNA viruses that cause tumors in humans and other animals. Also, **on′co·vi′rus** (ong′kə-). [1965–70; ONCO- + RNA + VIRUS]

on·dine (on dēn′, ôn-; *for 2 also Fr.* ôn dēn′), *n.* **1.** undine. **2.** (*cap., italics*) a play (1939) by Jean Giraudoux. **3.** (*cap., italics*) a ballet (1958) choreographed by Frederick Ashton, with musical score by Hans W. Henze.

on·ding (on′ding), *n. Scot.* the act of continued outpouring or falling; a continuing torrent, as of rain. [1770–80; ON + DING[2]]

on·do·graph (on′də graf′, -gräf′), *n.* an instrument for graphically recording oscillatory variations, as in alternating currents. [< F *ondographe,* equiv. to *onde* wave (< L *unda*) + *-o-* -O- + *-graphe* -GRAPH]

one (wun), *adj.* **1.** being or amounting to a single unit or individual or entire thing, item, or object rather than two or more; a single: *one woman; one nation; one piece of cake.* **2.** being a person, thing, or individual instance or member of a number, kind, group, or category indicated: *one member of the party.* **3.** existing, acting, or considered as a single unit, entity, or individual. **4.** of the same or having a single kind, nature, or condition: *We belong to one team; We are of one resolve.* **5.** noting some indefinite day or time in the future: *You will see him one day.* **6.** a certain (often used in naming a person otherwise unknown or undescribed): *One John Smith was chosen.* **7.** being a particular, unique, or only individual, item, or unit: *I'm looking for the one adviser I can trust.* **8.** noting some indefinite day or time in the past: *We all had dinner together one evening last week.* **9.** of no consequence as to the character, outcome, etc.; the same: *It's all one to me whether they go or not.* —*n.* **10.** the first and lowest whole number, being a cardinal number; unity. **11.** a symbol of this number, as 1 or I. **12.** a single person or thing: *If only problems would come one at a time!* **13.** a die face or a domino face having one pip. **14.** a one-dollar bill: *to change a five-dollar bill for five ones.* **15.** (*cap.*) *Neoplatonism.* the ultimate reality, seen as a central source of being by whose emanations all entities, spiritual and corporeal, have their existence, the corporeal ones containing the fewest of the emanations. **16. at one, a.** in a state of agreement; of one opinion. **b.** united in thought or feeling; attuned: *He felt at one with his Creator.* **17. one and all,** everyone: *They came, one and all, to welcome him home.* **18. one by one,** singly and successively: *One by one the children married and moved away.* **19. one for the road.** See **road** (def. 8). —*pron.* **20.** a person or thing of a number or kind indicated or understood: *one of the Elizabethan poets.* **21.** (in certain pronominal combinations) a person unless definitely specified otherwise: *every one.* **22.** (with a defining clause or other qualifying words) a person or a personified being or agency: *the evil one; the one I love.* **23.** any person indefinitely; anyone: *as good as one would desire.* **24.** *Chiefly Brit.* (used as a substitute for the pronoun I): *Mother had been ailing for many months, and one should have realized it.* **25.** a person of the speaker's kind; such as the speaker himself or herself: *to press one's own claims.* **26.** something or someone of the kind just mentioned: *The portraits are fine ones. Your teachers this semester seem to be good ones.* **27.** something available or referred to, esp. in the immediate area: *Here, take one—they're delicious. The bar is open, so have one on me!* [bef. 900; ME *oon,* OE *ān;* c. D *een,* G *ein,* Goth *ains,* L *ūnus* (OL *oinos*); akin to Gk *oínē* ace on a die]

—Usage. ONE as an indefinite pronoun meaning "any person indefinitely, anyone" is more formal than YOU, which is also used as an indefinite pronoun with the same sense: *One (or you) should avoid misconceptions. One (or you) can correct this fault in three ways.* When the construction requires that the pronoun be repeated, either ONE or *he* or *he or she* is used; *he* or *he or she* is the more common in the United States: *Wherever one looks, he (or he or she) finds evidence of pollution.* In speech or informal writing, a form of *they* sometimes occurs: *Can one read this without having their emotions stirred?*

In constructions of the type *one of those who* (or *that* or *which*), the antecedent of *who* is considered to be the plural noun or pronoun, correctly followed by a plural verb: *He is one of those people who work for the government.* Yet the feeling that ONE is the antecedent is so strong that a singular verb is commonly found in all types of writing: *one of those people who works for the government.* When ONE is preceded by *only* in such a construction, the singular verb is always used: *the only one of her sons who visits her in the hospital.*

The substitution of ONE for *I,* a typically British use, is usually regarded as an affectation in the United States. See also **he[1], they.**

-one, a suffix used in the names of ketones and analogous chemical compounds: *lactone; quinone.* [perh. < Gk *-ōnē* fem. patronymic]

one-a-cat (wun′ə kat′), *n.* See **one old cat.**

one-act·er (wun′ak′tər), *n. Informal.* a short play consisting of one act. Also, **one-act** (wun′akt′). [1890–95]

one′ anoth′er, each other. [1520–30]

—Usage. See **each other.**

one′-armed ban′dit (wun′ärmd′), *Informal.* See **slot machine** (def. 1). Also, **one′arm ban′dit.** [1935–40, *Amer.*]

one-bag·ger (wun′bag′ər), *n. Baseball Informal.* single (def. 23). [1950–55]

one′-base hit′ (wun′bās′), *Baseball.* single (def. 23).

one-di·men·sion·al (wun′di men′shə nl), *adj.* **1.** having one dimension only. **2.** having no depth or scope: *a novel with one-dimensional characters.* [1880–85]

one-eight·y (wun′ā′tē), *n., pl.* **-eight·ies.** *Informal.* a turn or reversal of 180 degrees.

one-eyed (wun′īd′), *adj.* **1.** having but one eye. **2.** *Cards.* being, of, pertaining to, or using a face card or cards on which the figure is shown in profile, such cards being the jack of spades, the jack of hearts, and the king of diamonds in standard packs of cards: *One-eyed jacks are wild.* [bef. 1000; ME, OE]

one·fold (wun′fōld′), *adj.* whole; complete. [1425–75; late ME. See ONE, -FOLD]

O·ne·ga (ō neg′ə; *Russ.* u nye′gə), *n.* **1. Lake,** a lake in the NW Russian Federation in Europe: second largest lake in Europe. 3764 sq. mi. (9750 sq. km). **2.** a river in the NW Russian Federation in Europe, flowing N to Onega Bay. 250 mi. (405 km) long.

One′ga Bay′, a bay in the NW Russian Federation in Europe, at the SW end of the White Sea. 100 mi. (160 km) long.

O·neg Shab·bat (ō′neg shä bät′), *Hebrew.* a Jewish celebration in honor of the Sabbath that takes place on Friday evening or Saturday afternoon and usually includes a program of songs, a lecture, and refreshments. [lit., Sabbath delight]

one-hand·ed (wun′han′did), *adj.* **1.** having or using only one hand: *The left fielder made a one-handed catch of the fly ball.* —*adv.* **2.** with one hand: *to drive one-handed.* [1400–50; late ME]

one-horse (wun′hôrs′, -hōrs′), *adj.* **1.** using or having only a single horse: *a one-horse carriage.* **2.** small and unimportant; limited: *a one-horse town.* [1740–50]

101 (wun′ō wun′), *adj.* comprising the introductory material in or as if in a course of study (used postpositively): *Economics 101; Life 101; It's Jungle 101 on a trip up the Amazon.* [1985–90]

O·nei·da (ō nī′də), *n., pl.* **-das,** (*esp. collectively*) **-da** for 1. **1.** a member of an Iroquois people formerly inhabiting the region east of Oneida Lake. **2.** the Iroquoian language spoken by the Oneida Indians. **3.** a city in central New York. 10,810. [< Oneida *onę·yóteʔ* erected stone, the name of the main Oneida settlement, at successive locations, near which, traditionally, a large syenite boulder always appeared]

Onei′da Commu′nity, a society of religious perfectionists established by John Humphrey Noyes, in 1848 at Oneida, N.Y., on the theory that sin can be eliminated through social reform: dissolved and reorganized in 1881 as a joint-stock company.

Onei′da Lake′, a lake in central New York. 20 mi. (32 km) long; 5 mi. (8 km) wide.

O'Neill (ō nēl′), *n.* **1. Eugene (Gladstone),** 1888–1953, U.S. playwright: Nobel prize 1936. **2. Thomas P(hilip)** ("*Tip*"), born 1912, U.S. politician: congressman 1953–87; speaker of the House 1977–87.

o·nei·ric (ō nī′rik), *adj.* of or pertaining to dreams. [1855–60; < Gk *óneir(os)* dream + -IC]

o·nei·ro·crit·ic (ō nī′rə krit′ik), *n.* an interpreter of dreams. [1605–15; < Gk *oneirokritikós* pertaining to the interpretation of dreams, equiv. to *óneir(os)* dream + *-o-* -O- + *kritikós* skilled in judgment; see CRITIC] **—o·nei′·ro·crit′i·cal,** *adj.* **—o·nei′ro·crit′i·cal·ly,** *adv.*

o·nei·ro·crit·i·cism (ō nī′rə krit′ə siz′əm), *n.* the art of interpreting dreams. [1605–15; ONEIROCRITIC + -ISM]

o·nei·ro·man·cy (ō nī′rə man′sē), *n.* divination through dreams. [1645–55; < Gk *óneiro(s)* dream + -MANCY] **—o·nei′ro·man′cer,** *n.*

one-legged (wun′legd′, -leg′id), *adj.* **1.** having only one leg. **2.** one-sided, as an argument or point of view. **3.** ineffectual because certain basic elements, measures, etc., are lacking: *one-legged legislation.* [1835–45]

one-lin·er (wun′lī′nər), *n.* a brief joke or amusing remark. [1965–70, *Amer.*; *one line* + -ER[1]]

one-lung (wun′lung′), *adj.* **1.** having or equipped with only one lung. **2.** *Slang.* (of an engine, automobile, etc.) having only one cylinder. Also, **one′-lunged′.**

one-lung·er (wun′lung′ər), *n. Slang.* a one-cylinder internal-combustion engine. [1905–10; *one lung* + -ER[1]]

one-man (wun′man′), *adj.* **1.** of or pertaining to, or operated, performed, or used by one person: *a one-man office; a one-man band.* **2.** preferring or seeking romantic involvement with one man only: *a one-man woman.* [1835–45]

one-man·y (wun′men′ē; *usually read as* wun′tə-men′ē), *adj. Logic, Math.* (of a relation) having the property that an element may be assigned to several elements but that given an element, only one may be assigned to it. [1905–10]

1-naph·thol (wun′naf′thôl, -thol, -nap′-), *n. Chem.* alpha-naphthol. See under **naphthol.**

one·ness (wun′nis), *n.* **1.** the quality of being one; singleness. **2.** uniqueness. **3.** sameness; identity. **4.** unity of thought, feeling, belief, aim, etc.; agreement; concord. **5.** a strong feeling of closeness or affinity; union: *He feels a oneness with God.* [bef. 900; ME *onnesse;* OE *ānnes;* see ONE, -NESS]

one-night·er (wun′nī′tər), *n.* See **one-night stand.** [1920–25]

one′-night stand′ (wun′nīt′), **1.** a single performance in one locale, as by a touring theatrical company, before moving on to the next engagement. **2.** a place where such a performance is given. **3.** *Informal.* **a.** a single, unrepeated sexual encounter, as one lasting for just one night. **b.** a participant in such an encounter.

one old cat (wun′ə kat′), *Games.* a form of baseball in which there is a home plate and one other base, and in which a player remains at bat and scores runs by hitting the ball and running to the base and back without being put out. Also, **one′ o′ cat′, one-a-cat.** [1840–50, *Amer.*]

one-one (wun′wun′; *usually read as* wun′tə wun′), *adj.* one-to-one (def. 1).

one-on-one (wun′on wun′, -ôn-), *adj.* **1.** consisting of or involving direct individual competition, confrontation, or communication; person-to-person: *a one-on-one discussion.* —*adv.* **2.** in direct encounter: *I'd rather settle this with her one-on-one.* **3. go one-on-one with,** *Sports.* to play directly against (an opposing player). —*n.* **4.** a meeting or confrontation between two persons. [1965–70, *Amer.*]

O·ne·on·ta (ō′nē on′tə), *n.* a city in E central New York. 14,933.

one-piece (wun′pēs′), *adj.* **1.** complete in one piece, as a garment: *a one-piece snowsuit.* —*n.* **2.** Also called **one′-piec′er.** a one-piece garment. [1875–80]

one′-point perspec′tive (wun′point′). See under **linear perspective.**

one-reel·er (wun′rē′lər), *n.* a motion picture, esp. a cartoon or comedy, of 10 to 12 minutes' duration and contained on one reel of film: popular esp. in the era of silent films. [1915–20; *one reel* + -ER[1]]

on·er·ous (on′ər əs, ō′nər-), *adj.* **1.** burdensome, oppressive, or troublesome; causing hardship: *onerous duties.* **2.** having or involving obligations or responsibilities, esp. legal ones, that outweigh the advantages: *an onerous agreement.* [1350–1400; ME < L *onerōsus,* equiv. to *oner-* (s. of *onus*) burden + *-ōsus* -OUS] **—on′·er·ous·ly,** *adv.* **—on′er·ous·ness, o·ne·ros·i·ty** (ō′nə-ros′i tē), *n.*

—Syn. 1. heavy, crushing, grievous; irksome, galling.

one·self (wun self′, wunz-), *pron.* **1.** a person's self (used for emphasis or reflexively): *One often hurts oneself accidentally.* **2. be oneself, a.** to be in one's normal state of mind or physical condition. **b.** to be unaffected and sincere: *One makes more friends by being oneself than by putting on airs.* **3. by oneself, a.** without a companion; alone. **b.** through one's own efforts; unaided: *to become a millionaire by oneself.* **4. come to oneself, a.** Also, **come to.** to regain consciousness. **b.** to regain one's self-possession; come to one's senses. Also, **one's′ self′.** [1540–50; shortened form of *one's self*]

one-shot (wun′shot′), *n.* Also, **one′ shot′. 1.** a magazine, brochure, or the like that is published only one time, with no subsequent issues intended, usually containing articles and photographs devoted to one topical subject. **2.** a single appearance by a performer, as in a play, motion picture, or television program. **3.** a close-up camera shot of one person. **4.** something occurring, done, used, etc., only once. —*adj.* **5.** occurring, done, etc., only once. **6.** achieved or accomplished with a single try: *a one-shot solution.* [1905–10]

one-sid·ed (wun′sī′did), *adj.* **1.** considering but one side of a matter or question; partial or unfair: *a one-sided judgment.* **2.** with one party, contestant, side, etc., vastly superior; unbalanced; unequal: *a one-sided fight.* **3.** existing or occurring on one side only. **4.** having but one side, or but one developed or finished side. **5.** having one side larger or more developed than the other. **6.** *Law.* involving the action of one person only. **7.** having the parts all on one side, as an inflorescence. **—one′-sid′ed·ly,** *adv.* **—one′-sid′ed·ness,** *n.* [1805–15]

one-spot (wun′spot′), *n.* the upward face of a die bearing one pip or a domino one half of which bears one pip.

one-star (wun′stär′), *adj.* of or being a brigadier general, as indicated by one star on an insignia.

one-step (wun′step′), *n.* **1.** a round dance performed by couples to ragtime. **2.** a piece of music for this dance. —*v.i.* **3.** to dance the one-step. [1910–15]

one-stop (wun′stop′), *adj.* that can be accomplished in one stop: *a store offering one-stop shopping.* [1930–35, *Amer.*]

one-suit·er (wun′sōō′tər), *n.* a piece of luggage designed to hold one suit and other smaller items, as underwear or socks. Also called **single-suiter.** [1960–65, *Amer.*; *one suit* + -ER[1]]

one-time (wun′tīm′), *adj.* **1.** having been as specified at one time; former: *my one-time partners.* **2.** occurring, done, or accomplished only once: *his one-time try at elective office.* Also, **one′time′.** [1880–85]

—Syn. 1. previous, earlier, past.

one-to-one (wun′tə wun′), *adj.* **1.** Also, **one-one.** (of the relationship between two or more groups of things) corresponding element by element. **2.** one-on-one. [1870–75]

one-track (wun′trak′), *adj.* **1.** having only one track. **2.** unable or unwilling to cope with more than one idea, action, etc., at a time; narrow: *a one-track mind.* [1925–30]

O·net·ti (ō net′ē; *Sp.* ô ne′tē), *n.* **Juan Car·los** (wän kär′lōs, -ləs; *Sp.* hwän kär′lôs), 1909–94, Uruguayan novelist and short-story writer.

one-two (wun′tōō′), *n.* **1.** Also called **one′-two′ punch′.** *Boxing.* a left-hand jab immediately followed by a right cross. **2.** *Informal.* any strong or effective combination of two people or things: *The old one-two of a good passer and a good receiver is the best way to win football games.* **3.** *Fencing.* a type of attack made up of two movements. —*adj.* **4.** employing or suggesting a one-two; with one major or powerful thing or person combined with or following another. [1800–10]

one′ up′, 1. having gained an advantage in some way that betokens success, esp. over rivals. **2.** leading an opponent by one point or one scoring unit: *The home team was one up on the visitors.* **3.** one each; tied at a score of one: *The score was one up in the ninth inning.* **4.** *Print.* with only one reproduction of a form per sheet or on a given sheet: *We must print this job one up.* **5.** *Journalism.* using one more column of space than of type.

CONCISE PRONUNCIATION KEY: act, cāpe, dâre, pärt; set, ēqual; *if,* ice; ox, ōver, ôrder, oil, bŏŏk, bōōt, out; up, ûrge; child; sing; shoe; thin, that; zh as in *treasure.* ə = *a* as in *alone,* e as in *system,* i as in *easily,* o as in *gallop,* u as in *circus;* ′ as in *fire* (fī′r), *hour* (ou′r). l and n can serve as syllabic consonants, as in *cradle* (krād′l), and *button* (but′n). See the full key inside the front cover.

one-up (wun′up′), *v.t.*, **-upped, -up·ping.** to get the better of; succeed in being a point, move, step, etc., ahead of (someone): *They one-upped the competition.* [1960–65]

one-up·man·ship (wun′up′mən ship′), *n.* the art or practice of achieving, demonstrating, or assuming superiority in one's rivalry with a friend or opponent by obtaining privilege, status, status symbols, etc.: *the one-upmanship of getting into the president's car pool.* Also, **one-ups·man·ship** (wun′ups′mən ship′). Also called **upmanship, upsmanship.** [1950–55; ONE UP + -MANSHIP]

one-way (wun′wā′), *adj.* **1.** moving, or allowing movement in one direction only: *a one-way street.* **2.** valid for travel in one direction only: *a one-way ticket.* Cf. **round trip. 3.** without a reciprocal feeling, responsibility, relationship, etc.: *It's a one-way friendship.* **4.** not intended for return to a seller, dealer, etc., for reuse; disposable: *one-way bottles.* [1815–25]

one-wom·an (wun′wo͝om′ən), *adj.* **1.** used, operated, performed, etc., by one woman: *a one-woman show.* **2.** preferring or seeking romantic involvement with one woman only: *a one-woman man.* [1890–95]

one-world·er (wun′wûrl′dər), *n.* **1.** a person who supports or believes in any of various movements to establish a world government or a federation of nations stronger than any individual nation, for the purpose of promoting the common good. **2.** a person who believes in the possibility of peaceful cooperation among nations. [1945–50; *one world* + -ER[1]]

ONF, Old North French.

ONFr., Old North French.

on-glide (on′glīd′, ôn′-), *n. Phonet.* a transitional sound produced by the vocal organs in moving from an inactive position or a previous sound to the articulatory position necessary for producing a following sound. Cf. **off-glide** (def. 1). [1885–90]

on·go·ing (on′gō′ing, ôn′-), *adj.* continuing without termination or interruption: *ongoing research projects.* [1855–60; ON + GOING, after the v. phrase *go on*]
—**Syn.** proceeding, uninterrupted, unbroken.

ONI, Office of Naval Intelligence.

-onic, a suffix used in forming names of acids, esp. carboxylic acids obtained by oxidation of aldoses: *gluconic acid.* [perh. generalized from *lactonic acid* as trans. of G *Lactonsäure;* see LACTOSE, -ONE, -IC]

o·ni·o·ma·ni·a (ō′nē ə mā′nē ə, -mān′yə), *n.* an uncontrollable desire to buy things. [< NL < Gk *ōni(os)* for sale (deriv. of *ônos* price) + -o- -o- + LL *mania* -MANIA] —**o·ni·o·ma·ni·ac** (ō′nē ə mā′nē ak′), *n.*

on·ion (un′yən), *n.* **1.** a plant, *Allium cepa,* of the amaryllis family, having an edible, succulent, pungent bulb. **2.** any of certain similar plants. **3.** the bulb of the onion plant. **4.** the flavor or odor of this bulb. **5.** *Slang.* a person: *He's a tough onion.* **6. know one's onions,** *Slang.* to know one's subject or business thoroughly; be capable or proficient. —*adj.* **7.** containing or cooked with onions: *onion soup.* **8.** of, pertaining to, or resembling an onion. [1325–75; ME *onyon* < OF *oignon* < L *ūniōn-* (s. of *ūniō*) a unity, large pearl, onion; see UNION] —**on′ion·like′,** *adj.* —**on′ion·y,** *adj.*

on′ion dome′, *Archit.* a bulbous, domelike roof ending in a sharp point, characteristically used in Russian Orthodox church architecture to cover cupolas or towers. [1955–60]

on′ion rings′, *Cookery.* rings of sliced onion, dipped in batter and deep-fried. [1950–55]

On·ions (un′yənz), *n.* **Charles Tal·but** (tôl′bət, tal′-), 1873–1965, English lexicographer and philologist.

on·ion·skin (un′yən skin′), *n.* a thin, lightweight, translucent, glazed paper, used esp. for making carbon copies. [1875–80, *Amer.;* ONION + SKIN]

O·nit·sha (ō nich′ə), *n.* a city in SW Nigeria, on the Niger River. 220,000.

-onium, *Chem.* a suffix used in the names of complex cations: *oxonium.* [extracted from AMMONIUM]

On·ke·los (ong′kə los′), *n.* fl. 2nd century A.D., author of a Targum of the Pentateuch known as the Targum of Onkelos.

on·kus (ong′kəs), *adj. Australian Slang.* unpleasant, unattractive, or unacceptable; bad. [1910–15; orig. uncert.]

on·lap (on′lap′, ôn′-), *n. Geol.* **1.** the advance of a sea beyond its former shore. **2.** the layer or layers of sedimentary rock formed on a sea floor as a result of this advance. Cf. **offlap.** [1945–50; ON + LAP[3]]

on·lay (*n.* on′lā′, ôn′-; *v.* on lā′, ôn-), *n., v.,* **-laid, -lay·ing.** —*n.* **1.** an overlay, esp. one in relief. **2.** *Dentistry.* an inlay that restores the occlusal surface of a tooth. —*v.t.* **3.** to place or mount (an onlay) on a surface, esp. for decorative purposes. [1875–80; ON + LAY[1], after v. phrase *lay on*]

On′ Lib′erty, a treatise (1859) by John Stuart Mill on the rights of the individual within the state.

on·li·est (ōn′lē ist), *adj. Nonstandard.* only: used as an intensive. [1575–85; ONLY + -EST[1]]

on-lim·its (on′lim′its, ôn′-), *adj.* open or not prohibited to certain persons, as military personnel: *an on-limits area.*

on-line (on′līn′, ôn′-), *adj.* **1.** *Computers.* operating under the direct control of, or connected to, a main computer (opposed to *off-line*). **2.** *Radio.* (of a network) supplying affiliated stations with all or a substantial part of their programming. **3.** *Television.* of or pertaining to the final editing of a videotaped program. **4.** done or accomplished while in operation or active service: *on-line maintenance.* **5.** located on major routes or rail lines: *on-line industries.* Cf. **off-line.** Also, **on′ line′, on′line′.** [1945–50]

on′-line cat′alog, a bibliographic record of a library's holdings, available in machine-readable form.

on·look·er (on′lo͝ok′ər, ôn′-), *n.* spectator; observer; witness. [1600–10; ON + LOOKER, after v. phrase *look on*]

on·look·ing (on′lo͝ok′ing, ôn′-), *adj.* **1.** looking on; observing; perceiving. **2.** looking onward or foreboding. [1655–65; ON + LOOKING, after v. phrase *look on*]

on·ly (ōn′lē), *adv.* **1.** without others or anything further; alone; solely; exclusively: *This information is for your eyes only.* **2.** no more than; merely; just: *If it were only true! I cook only on weekends.* **3.** as recently as: *I read that article only yesterday.* **4.** in the final outcome or decision: *You will only regret your harsh words to me.* **5. only too, a.** as a matter of fact; extremely: *I am only too glad to go.* **b.** unfortunately; very: *It is only too likely to happen.* —*adj.* **6.** being the single one or the relatively few of the kind: *This is the only pencil I can find.* **7.** having no sibling or no sibling of the same sex: *an only child; an only son.* **8.** single in superiority or distinction; unique; the best: *the one and only Muhammad Ali.* —*conj.* **9.** but (introducing a single restriction, restraining circumstance, or the like): *I would have gone, only you objected.* **10.** *Older Use.* except; but: *Only for him you would not be here.* [bef. 900; ME; OE *ānlich, ǣnlich.* See ONE, -LY]
—**Syn. 6.** solitary, lone. **8.** peerless; exclusive.
—**Ant. 6.** plentiful, common.
—**Usage.** The placement of ONLY as a modifier is more a matter of style and clarity than of grammatical rule. In a sentence like *The doctor examined the children,* varying the placement of ONLY results in quite different meanings: *The doctor only examined the children* means that the doctor did nothing else. And *The doctor examined only the children* means that no one else was examined. Especially in formal writing, the placement of ONLY immediately before what it modifies is often observed: *She sold the stock only because she needed the money.* However, there has long been a tendency in all varieties of speech and writing to place ONLY before the verb (*She only sold the stock because she needed the money*), and such placement is rarely confusing.

on-mike (on′mīk′, ôn′-), *adj.* projected by the microphone.

on·na·ga·ta (on′ə gä′tə; *Japn.* ôn′nä gä′tä), *n.* a male actor in kabuki who performs female roles. [1900–05; < Japn]

on·o·ma·si·ol·o·gy (on′ə mā′sē ol′ə jē, -mā′zē-), *n.* the study of the means of expressing a given concept. [1930–35; < G *Onomasiologie,* equiv. to Gk *ònomasí(a)* name, expression (deriv. of *ónoma, ónyma* name) + -o- -o- + *-logie* -LOGY] —**on·o·ma·si·o·log·ic** (on′ə mā′sē-ə loj′ik, -mā′zē-), **on′o·ma′si·o·log′i·cal,** *adj.*

on·o·mas·tic (on′ə mas′tik), *adj.* **1.** of or pertaining to proper names. **2.** of or pertaining to onomastics. **3.** *Law.* (of a signature) written in the handwriting other than that of the document, instrument, etc., to which it is appended. [1600–10; < Gk *onomastikós,* deriv. of *onomázein* to NAME; see -TIC]

on·o·mas·ti·con (on′ə mas′ti kon′, -kən), *n.* **1.** a list or collection of proper names. **2.** a list or collection of specialized terms, as those used in a particular field or subject area. [1700–10; < Gk *onomastikòn* (*bíblion*) vocabulary arranged by subjects; see ONOMASTIC]

on·o·mas·tics (on′ə mas′tiks), *n.* (*used with a singular v.*) the study of the origin, history, and use of proper names. [1930–35; see ONOMASTIC, -ICS] —**on·o·mas·ti·cian** (on′ə mə stish′ən), *n.*

on·o·ma·tol·o·gy (on′ə mə tol′ə jē), *n.* onomastics. [1840–50; < MGk *onomatología,* equiv. to Gk *onomatológ(os)* collector of words (*onomato-,* comb. form of *ónoma* NAME + *-logos;* see LOGOS) + *-ia* -IA; see -LOGY] —**on·o·mat·o·log·ic** (on′ə mat′l oj′ik), **on′o·mat′o·log′i·cal,** *adj.* —**on′o·mat′o·log′i·cal·ly,** *adv.* —**on′o·ma·tol′o·gist,** *n.*

on·o·mat·o·poe·ia (on′ə mat′ə pē′ə, -mä′tə-), *n.* **1.** the formation of a word, as *cuckoo* or *boom,* by imitation of a sound made by or associated with its referent. **2.** a word so formed. **3.** *Rhet.* the use of imitative and naturally suggestive words for rhetorical effect. [1570–80; < LL < Gk *onomatopoiía* making of words, equiv. to *onomato-* (comb. form of *ónoma* NAME) + *poi-* (s. of *poieîn* to make; see POET) + *-ia* -IA] —**on′o·mat′o·poe′ic, on·o·mat·o·po·et·ic** (on′ə mat′ə pō et′ik, -mä′-tə-), **on·o·mat·o·poi·et·ic** (on′ə mat′ə poi et′ik, -mä′-tə-), **on′o·mat′o·poe′ial,** *adj.* —**on′o·mat′o·poe′i·cal·ly, on′o·mat′o·po·et′i·cal·ly,** *adv.*

On·on·da·ga (on′ən dô′gə, -dä′-, -dā′-), *n., pl.* **-gas,** (*esp. collectively*) **-ga** for 1. **1.** a member of a tribe of Iroquoian Indians formerly inhabiting the region of Onondaga Lake. **2.** the dialect of the Seneca language spoken by these Indians. **3. Lake,** a salt lake in central New York. 5 mi. (8 km) long; 1 mi. (1.6 km) wide. [< Onondaga *onǫ́·tà?ke* on the hill, the name of the main Onondaga town, at successive locations] —**On′on·da′gan,** *adj.*

on-peak (on′pēk′, ôn′-), *adj.* peak (def. 17). [by analogy with OFF-PEAK]

ONR, Office of Naval Research.

on-ramp (on′ramp′, ôn′-), *n.* an entrance lane for traffic from a street to a turnpike or freeway. Also, **on′ramp′.** Cf. **off-ramp.** [by analogy with OFF-RAMP]

on-rec·ord (on′rek′ərd, ôn′-), *adj.* **1.** intended for publication, esp. as news: *an on-record comment.* **2.** official or public: *on-record policy.* Also, **on-the-record.**

on·rush (on′rush′, ôn′-), *n.* a strong forward rush, flow, etc. [1835–45; ON + RUSH[1], after the v. phrase *rush on*] —**on′rush′ing,** *adj.*
—**Syn.** onset, torrent, flood, charge.

On·sa·ger (on′sä gər, ôn′-), *n.* **Lars,** 1903–76, U.S. chemist, born in Norway: Nobel prize 1968.

on-screen (on′skrēn′, ôn′-), *adj.* **1.** occurring within a motion picture or television show or in an actor's professional life: *a raucous on-screen personality that was at odds with his quiet private life.* **2.** displayed on a television screen; supplied by means of television: *an on-screen course in economics.* —*adv.* **3.** in a motion picture or television program or in one's professional life: *On-screen he's a villain.* [1950–55]

on-seam (on′sēm′, ôn′-), *adj.* inseam (def. 3.).

on-sea·son (on′sē′zən, ôn′-), *adj.* **1.** being a time of year that is the busiest or most popular for a specific activity; in season: *on-season airfares.* —*adv.* **2.** in or during the busiest season: *to travel on-season.* —*n.* **3.** a time of year that is the busiest or most popular for a specific activity: *We stayed at the resort in the on-season.* [by analogy with OFF-SEASON]

on·set (on′set′, ôn′-), *n.* **1.** a beginning or start: *the onset of winter.* **2.** an assault or attack: *an onset of the enemy.* **3.** *Phonet.* the segment of a syllable preceding the nucleus, as the *gr* in *great.* Cf. **coda** (def. 5), **core** (def. 14). [1525–35; ON + SET, after the v. phrase *set on*]

on·shore (on′shôr′, -shōr′, ôn′-), *adv.* **1.** onto or in the direction of the shore from a body of water: *a breeze blowing onshore.* **2.** in or on a body of water, close to or parallel with the shore: *to sail a boat onshore.* **3.** on land, esp. within the area adjoining a port; ashore: *to land and shop onshore.* —*adj.* **4.** moving or proceeding toward shore or onto land from a body of water: *an onshore breeze.* **5.** located on or close to the shore: *an onshore lighthouse; an onshore buoy.* **6.** done or taking place on land: *onshore liberty for the crew.* [1870–75; ON + SHORE[1]]

on·side (on′sīd′, ôn′-), *adj., adv. Sports.* not offside; being within the prescribed line or area at the beginning of or during play or a play. [1840–50; ON + SIDE[1]]

on′side kick′, *Football.* a kickoff deliberately kicked a short distance in an attempt by the kicking team to regain possession of the ball by recovering it after it has traveled forward the legally required distance of 10 yards, beyond the 50-yard line. Also, **on′sides kick′.** [1925–30]

on-site (on′sīt′, ôn′-), *adj.* accomplished or located at the site of a particular activity or concern: *on-site medical treatment for accident victims.* [1955–60]

on·slaught (on′slôt′, ôn′-), *n.* an onset, assault, or attack, esp. a vigorous one. [1615–25; < D *aanslag* a striking, (earlier) attack (equiv. to *aan* ON + *slag* blow, stroke; akin to SLAY), with assim. to obs. *slaught* SLAUGHTER]

on·stage (on′stāj′, ôn′-), *adv.* **1.** on or onto the stage (opposed to *offstage*): *The director shouted, "Onstage, everybody!"* —*adj.* **2.** of, pertaining to, or used in the acting area, or that part of the stage that is in view of the audience. [1925–30; ON + STAGE]

on-stream (*adv.* on′strēm′, ôn′-; *adj.* on′strēm′, ôn′-), *adv.* **1.** in or into regular operation, esp. as part of a system, assembly line, or the like: *When the new printing press goes on-stream, we'll be able to print twice as many newspapers a day.* —*adj.* **2.** operating on a regular basis or at full capacity: *on-stream production.* [1925–30]

Ont., Ontario.

on-tar·get (on′tär′git, ôn′-), *adj.* correct, accurate, or adhering closely to an anticipated outcome: *an on-target forecast for the weekend weather.*

On·tar·i·o (on târ′ē ō′), *n.* **1.** a province in S Canada, bordering on the Great Lakes. 8,131,618; 412,582 sq. mi. (1,068,585 sq. km). *Cap.:* Toronto. **2. Lake,** a lake between the NE United States and S Canada, between New York and Ontario province: the smallest of the Great Lakes. 193 mi. (310 km) long; 7540 sq. mi. (19,530 sq. km). **3.** a city in SW California, E of Los Angeles. 88,820. —**On·tar′i·an, On·tar′ic** (on tar′ik), *adj., n.*

on-the-job (on′thə job′, ôn′-), *adj.* done, received, or happening while in actual performance of one's work: *on-the-job training.* [1935–40]

on-the-rec·ord (on′thə rek′ərd, ôn′-), *adj.* on-record.

on-the-scene (on′thə sēn′, ôn′-), *adj.* being at the very place of occurrence: *an on-the-scene newscast.*

on-the-spot (on′thə spot′, ôn′-), *adj.* done or occurring at the time or place in question: *an on-the-spot recording.* [1885–90]

on·tic (on′tik), *adj. Philos.* possessing the character of

CONCISE ETYMOLOGY KEY: <, descended or borrowed from; >, whence; b., blend of, blended; c., cognate with; cf., compare; deriv., derivative; equiv., equivalent; imit., imitative; obl., oblique; r., replacing; s., stem; sp., spelling, spelled; resp., respelling, respelled; trans., translation; ?, origin unknown; *, unattested; ‡, probably earlier than. See the full key inside the front cover.

real rather than phenomenal existence; noumenal. [1940–45; < Gk *ont-* (see ONTO-) + -IC]

on•to (on′to͞o, ôn′-; *unstressed* on′tə, ôn′-), *prep.* **1.** to a place or position on; upon; on: *to get onto a horse.* **2.** *Informal.* in or into a state of awareness about: *I'm onto your scheme.* —*adj.* **3.** Also, **surjective.** *Math.* pertaining to a function or map from one set to another set, the range of which is the entire second set. [1575–85; ON + TO]

onto-, a combining form meaning "being," used in the formation of compound words: *ontogeny.* [< NL < Gk *ont-* (s. of *ṓn,* neut. prp. of *eînai* to be) + *-o-* -O-]

on′to func′tion, *Math.* a function from one set to a second set, the range of which is the entire second set. Also called **surjection.**

on•tog•e•ny (on toj′ə nē), *n. Biol.* the development or developmental history of an individual organism. Also, **on•to•gen•e•sis** (on′tə jen′ə sis). Cf. **phylogeny.** [1870–75; ONTO- + -GENY] —**on•to•ge•net•ic** (on′tə jə net′ik), **on′to•ge•net′i•cal, on′to•gen′ic,** *adj.* —**on′to•ge•net′i•cal•ly, on′to•gen′i•cal•ly,** *adv.* —**on•tog′e•nist,** *n.*

on′tolog′ical ar′gument, *Philos.* an a priori argument for the existence of God, asserting that as existence is a perfection, and as God is conceived of as the most perfect being, it follows that God must exist; originated by Anselm, later used by Duns Scotus, Descartes, and Leibniz. Also called **on′tolog′ical proof′.** [1875–80]

on•tol•o•gism (on tol′ə jiz′əm), *n. Theol.* the doctrine that the human intellect has an immediate cognition of God as its proper object and the principle of all its cognitions. [1860–65; ONTOLOG(Y) + -ISM]

on•tol•o•gize (on tol′ə jīz′), *v.t.,* **-gized, -giz•ing.** to express in ontological terms; regard from an ontological viewpoint. Also, *esp. Brit.,* **on•tol′o•gise′.** [1840–50; ONTOLOG(Y) + -IZE]

on•tol•o•gy (on tol′ə jē), *n.* **1.** the branch of metaphysics that studies the nature of existence or being as such. **2.** (loosely) metaphysics. [1715–25; < NL *ontologia.* See ONTO-, -LOGY] —**on•to•log•i•cal** (on′tl oj′i-kəl), **on′to•log′ic, on•tol•o•gis•tic** (on tol′ə jis′tik), *adj.* —**on•tol′o•gist,** *n.*

o•nus (ō′nəs), *n., pl.* **o•nus•es.** **1.** a difficult or disagreeable obligation, task, burden, etc. **2.** burden of proof. Cf. ***onus probandi.*** **3.** blame or responsibility. [1630–40; < L: load, burden]
—**Syn.** **1.** responsibility, weight, duty, load.

o•nus pro•ban•di (ō′no͝os prō bän′dē; *Eng.* ō′nəs prō ban′dī, -dē), *Latin.* the burden of proof.

on•ward (on′wərd, ôn′-), *adv.* Also, **on′wards.** **1.** toward a point ahead or in front; forward, as in space or time. **2.** at a position or point in advance. —*adj.* **3.** directed or moving onward or forward; forward. [1350–1400; ME; see ON, -WARD]
—**Syn.** **1.** See **forward.** —**Ant.** **1, 3.** backward.

o•nych•i•a (ō nik′ē ə), *n. Pathol.* inflammation of the matrix of the nail. [1855–60; < NL, equiv. to Gk *onych-,* s. of *onyx* nail (see ONYX) + NL *-ia* -IA]

on•y•cho•pha•gia (on′i kō fā′jə, -jē ə), *n. Psychiatry.* the practice of biting one's nails, esp. when done habitually and as a symptom of emotional disturbance. [1895–1900; < Gk *onycho-* (comb. form of *ónyx* nail, claw; see ONYX) + -PHAGIA] —**on•y•choph•a•gist** (on′ə kof′ə-jist), *n.*

on•y•choph•o•ran (on′i kof′ər ən), *n.* any small, predatory, caterpillarlike animal of the phylum Onychophora, common in tropical forests, having stubby legs ending in pincers. [1885–90; < NL *Onychophor(a)* phylum name (< Gk *onycho-,* comb. form of *ónyx;* see ONYX) + NL *-phora,* neut. pl. of *-phorus* -PHORE + -AN]

-onym, a combining form of Greek origin, meaning "word," "name": *pseudonym.* [ult. < Gk *-ōnymos* having the kind of name specified, comb. form repr. *ónyma,* dial. var. of *ónoma* NAME]

on•yx (on′iks, ō′niks), *n.* **1.** *Mineral.* a variety of chalcedony having straight parallel bands of alternating colors. Cf. **Mexican onyx.** **2.** (not used technically) an unbanded chalcedony dyed for ornamental purposes. **3.** black, esp. a pure or jet black. **4.** *Med.* a nail of a finger or toe. —*adj.* **5.** black, esp. jet black. [1250–1300; ME *onix* < L *onyx* < Gk *ónyx* nail, claw, veined gem]

o•nyx•is (ō nik′sis), *n. Pathol.* an ingrowing of a fingernail or toenail. [< Gk *onych-* (s. of *ónyx*) nail (see ONYX) + -SIS]

on′yx mar′ble, **1.** See **Mexican onyx.** **2.** any compact, banded calcareous tufa that can be given a high polish. [1890–95]

o-o (ō′ō), *n., pl.* **o-os.** any of several species of Hawaiian honey eaters of the genus *Moho,* esp. the extinct *M. nobilis,* of the island of Hawaii, that had black plumage and two tufts of yellow plumes used to make ceremonial robes for the Hawaiian kings. Also, **o′o, o′’o.** [1885–90; < Hawaiian *‘ō‘ō*]

oo-, a combining form meaning "egg," used in the formation of compound words: *oogamous.* [< Gk *ōio-,* comb. form of *ōión* EGG[1]]

o•o•blast (ō′ə blast′), *n.* a primordial cell from which the ovum is developed. [OO- + -BLAST]

o•o•cyst (ō′ə sist′), *n. Biol.* the encysted zygotic stage in the life cycle of some sporozoans. [1870–75; OO- + -CYST]

o•o•cyte (ō′ə sīt′), *n. Cell Biol.* an immature egg cell of the animal ovary; in humans, one oocyte matures during the menstrual cycle, becoming an ootid and then an ovum, while several others partially mature and then disintegrate. [1890–95; OO- + -CYTE]

O.O.D., **1.** See **officer of the deck.** **2.** See **officer of the day.**

oo•dles (o͞od′lz), *n.* (*sometimes used with a singular v.*) *Informal.* a large quantity: *oodles of love; oodles of money.* [1865–70; orig. uncert.]

o•o•gam•ete (ō ə gam′ēt, -gə mēt′), *n. Cell Biol.* one of a pair of structurally dissimilar gametes, the female gamete being large and nonmotile and the male gamete being small and motile. [1890–95; OO- + GAMETE] —**o•og•a•mous** (ō og′ə məs), *adj.* —**o•og′a•my,** *n.*

OO gauge, (ō′ō′),a model railroad gauge of ¾ in. (19 mm). [1920–25]

o•o•gen•e•sis (ō′ə jen′ə sis), *n. Cell Biol.* the origin and development of the ovum. [1890–95; OO- + -GENESIS] —**o•o•ge•net•ic** (ō′ə jə net′ik), *adj.*

o•o•go•ni•um (ō′ə gō′nē əm), *n., pl.* **-ni•a** (-nē ə), **-ni•ums.** *Biol.* **1.** one of the undifferentiated germ cells giving rise to oocytes. **2.** the one-celled female reproductive organ in certain thallophytes, usually a more or less spherical sac containing one or more eggs. [1865–70; < NL; see OO-, -GONIUM] —**o′o•go′ni•al** *adj.*

ooh (o͞o), *interj.* **1.** (used to express amazement, satisfaction, excitement, etc.) —*n.* **2.** the exclamation "ooh." —*v.i.* **3.** to utter or exclaim "ooh." **4.** **ooh and aah,** to exclaim in wonder or admiration: *The crowds oohed and aahed at the spectacular fireworks.* [1915–20]

o•o•ki•ne•sis (ō′ə ki nē′sis, -kī-), *n. Cell Biol.* the series of nuclear changes occurring in the ovum during maturation and fertilization. [OO- + -KINESIS] —**o•o•ki•net•ic** (ō′ə ki net′ik, -kī-), *adj.*

oo•la•chan (o͞o′lə kän′), *n., pl.* **-chans,** (*esp. collectively*) **-chan.** *Chiefly Canadian.* eulachon.

o•o•lite (ō′ə līt′), *n. Geol.* a limestone composed of minute rounded concretions resembling fish roe, in some places altered to ironstone by replacement with iron oxide. Also called **egg stone.** [1775–85; (< F *oölithe*) < NL *oölithēs.* See OO-, -LITE] —**o•o•lit•ic** (ō′ə lit′ik), *adj.*

o•o•lith (ō′ə lith), *n. Geol.* any of the component concretions of a piece of oolite. [1780–90; OO- + -LITH]

o•ol•o•gy (ō ol′ə jē), *n.* the branch of ornithology that studies birds' eggs. [1825–35; OO- + -LOGY] —**o•o•log•i•cal** (ō′ə loj′i kəl), *adj.* —**o•ol′o•gist,** *n.*

oo•long (o͞o′lông′, -long′), *n.* a brown or amber tea grown in China and Taiwan and partially fermented before being dried. [1850–55; < Chin *wūlóng* lit., black dragon, or < a cognate dial. form]

oom•pah (o͞om′pä, o͝om′-), *n.* **1.** a repetitious bass accompaniment in music typically provided by brasses. —*adj.* **2.** marked by an oompah: *oompah band.* Also, **oom•pah-pah** (o͞om′pä pä′, o͝om′-). [1875–80; imit.]

Oom Pa•ul (o͞om pō′o͝ol). See **Kruger, Stephanus Johannes Paulus.**

oomph (o͝omf), *n. Informal.* **1.** energy; vitality; enthusiasm. **2.** sex appeal. [1935–40, *Amer.*; imit. of the sound made during exertion, as in lifting a heavy object]

o•o•my•cete (ō′ə mī′sēt, -mī sēt′), *n.* any of various algaelike fungi constituting the phylum Oomycota of the kingdom Fungi (or the class Oomycetes of the kingdom Plantae), characterized by the formation of oospores. [< NL *Oomycetes;* see OO-, -MYCETE]

o•o•my•co•ta (ō′ə mī kō′tə), *n.pl.* the oomycetes considered as belonging to the phylum Oomycota of the kingdom Fungi. [< NL; see OO-, MYC-, -OTA]

-oon, a suffix occurring in words borrowed from French and other Romance languages (*bassoon; balloon; dragoon; pontoon*), and on this model occasionally used in the formation of new nouns in English (*spittoon*). [as an English formative (e.g., in *spittoon*), extracted from words of various origins (*buffoon, lagoon,* etc.) but repr. chiefly F *-on* in words stressed on the final syllable; cf. Sp. *-on,* It. *-one,* L *-ōn-*]

Oo•na (o͞o′nə), *n.* a female given name. Also, **Oo′nagh.**

o•o•pho•rec•to•my (ō′ə fə rek′tə mē), *n., pl.* **-mies.** *Surg.* the operation of removing one or both ovaries; ovariectomy. [1870–75; < NL *oophor(on)* ovary (neut. of Gk *ōiophóros* egg-bearing; see OO-, -PHORE) + -ECTOMY]

o•o•pho•ri•tis (ō′ə fə rī′tis), *n. Pathol.* inflammation of an ovary, usually combined with an inflammation of the Fallopian tubes; ovaritis. [1870–75; < NL *oophor(on)* ovary (see OOPHORECTOMY) + -ITIS]

o•o•phyte (ō′ə fīt′), *n. Bot.* the gametophyte of a moss, fern, or liverwort, resulting from the development of a fertilized egg. [1885–90; OO- + -PHYTE] —**o•o•phyt•ic** (ō′ə fit′ik), *adj.*

oops (o͝ops, o͞ops), *interj.* (used to express mild dismay, chagrin, surprise, etc., as at one's own mistake, a clumsy act, or social blunder.) [1925–30; orig. uncert.]

Oort′ cloud′ (ôrt, ōrt), *Astron.* a region of the solar system far beyond the orbit of Pluto in which billions of comets move in nearly circular orbits unless one is pulled into a highly eccentric elliptical orbit by a passing star. [1975–80; after Dutch astronomer Jan Hendrik *Oort* (1900–1992), who proposed its existence]

oo•ry (o͝or′ē), *adj. Scot.* ourie.

o•o•sphere (ō′ə sfēr′), *n. Biol.* an unfertilized egg within an oogonium. [1870–75; OO- + -SPHERE]

o•o•spore (ō′ə spôr′, -spōr′), *n. Biol.* a fertilized egg within an oogonium. [1860–65; OO- + -SPORE] —**o•o•spor•ic** (ō′ə spôr′ik, -spor′-), **o•os•por•ous** (ō os′pər əs, ō′ə spôr′əs, -spōr′-), *adj.*

Oost (ōst), *n.* **Ja•cob van** (yä′kôp vän), 1600?–71, and his son, **Jacob van,** 1639?–1713, Flemish painters.

OOT, out of town. Also, **O.O.T.**

o•o•the•ca (ō′ə thē′kə), *n., pl.* **-cae** (-sē). a case or capsule containing eggs, as that of certain gastropods and insects. Also, called **egg case.** [1850–55; < NL; see OO-, THECA] —**o′o•the′cal,** *adj.*

o•o•tid (ō′ə tid), *n. Cell Biol.* the cell that results from the meiotic divisions of an oocyte and matures into an ovum. [1905–10; OO- + (SPERMA)TID]

ooze[1] (o͞oz), *v.,* **oozed, ooz•ing,** *n.* —*v.i.* **1.** (of moisture, liquid, etc.) to flow, percolate, or exude slowly, as through holes or small openings. **2.** to move or pass slowly or gradually, as if through a small opening or passage: *The crowd oozed toward the entrance.* **3.** (of a substance) to exude moisture. **4.** (of something abstract, as information or courage) to appear or disappear slowly or imperceptibly (often fol. by *out* or *away*): *His cockiness oozed away during my rebuttal speech.* **5.** to display some characteristic or quality: *to ooze with piety.* —*v.t.* **6.** to make by oozing. **7.** to exude (moisture, air, etc.) slowly. **8.** to display or dispense freely and conspicuously: *He can ooze charm when it serves his interest.* —*n.* **9.** the act of oozing. **10.** something that oozes. **11.** an infusion of oak bark, sumac, etc., used in tanning. [bef. 1000; ME *wos(e)* (n.), *wosen* (v.), OE *wōs* juice, moisture]
—**Syn.** **10.** slime, mud, muck, sludge.

ooze[2] (o͞oz), *n.* **1.** *Geol.* a calcareous or siliceous mud composed chiefly of the shells of one-celled organisms, covering parts of the ocean bottom. **2.** soft mud, or slime. **3.** a marsh or bog. [bef. 900; ME *wose,* OE *wāse* mud]

ooze′ leath′er, leather prepared from calfskin or other skin and having a soft, velvety finish on the flesh side. [1885–90]

ooz•y[1] (o͞o′zē), *adj.,* **ooz•i•er, ooz•i•est.** **1.** exuding moisture. **2.** damp with moisture. [1705–15; OOZE[1] + -Y[1]] —**ooz′i•ness,** *n.*

ooz•y[2] (o͞o′zē), *adj.,* **ooz•i•er, ooz•i•est.** of or like ooze, soft mud, or slime. [1350–1400; ME *wosi.* See OOZE[2], -Y[1]] —**ooz′i•ly,** *adv.* —**ooz′i•ness,** *n.*

op (op), *n.* See **op art.**

OP, observation post. Also, **O.P.**

op-, var. of **ob-** (by assimilation) before *p: oppose.*

Op., opus.

op., **1.** opera. **2.** operation. **3.** opposite. **4.** opus.

O.P., **1.** observation post. **2.** *Brit. Theat.* See **opposite prompt.** **3.** Order of Preachers (Dominican). [< L *Ōrdo Praedicātōrum*] **4.** out of print. **5.** overproof.

o.p., out of print.

OPA, *U.S. Govt.* Office of Price Administration: the federal agency (1941–46) charged with regulating rents and the distribution and prices of goods during World War II.

o•pac•i•fy (ō pas′ə fī′), *v.,* **-fied, -fy•ing.** —*v.t.* **1.** to cause to become opaque. —*v.i.* **2.** to become opaque. [1910–15; < L *opāc(us)* shaded + -IFY] —**o•pac′i•fi•ca′•tion,** *n.* —**o•pac′i•fi′er,** *n.*

o•pac•i•ty (ō pas′i tē), *n., pl.* **-ties.** **1.** the state or quality of being opaque. **2.** something opaque. **3.** the degree to which a substance is opaque; capacity for being opaque. **4.** *Photog.* the proportion of the light that is absorbed by the emulsion on any given area of a film or plate. **5.** obscurity of meaning. **6.** mental dullness. **7.** *Med.* an opaque spot or area in normally clear or transparent tissue, as a cataract of the eye. [1550–60; < L *opācitās* shade. See OPAQUE, -ITY]

o•pa•cus (ō pā′kəs), *adj. Meteorol.* (of a cloud) dense enough to obscure the sun or moon. [1615–25; < NL, L *opācus;* see OPAQUE]

o•pah (ō′pə), *n.* a large, deep-bodied, brilliantly colored, oceanic food fish, *Lampris regius.* [1740–50; < an unidentified West African source]

o•pal (ō′pəl), *n.* **1.** a mineral, an amorphous form of silica, SiO_2 with some water of hydration, found in many varieties and colors, including a form that is milky white. **2.** an iridescent variety of this that is used as a gem. **3.** a gem of this. [1350–1400; ME < L *opalus* < Gk *opállios* opal, gem; prob. from a source akin to Skt *upala* precious stone]

O•pal (ō′pəl), *n.* a female given name.

o•pal•esce (ō′pə les′), *v.i.,* **-esced, -esc•ing.** to exhibit a play of colors like that of the opal. [1810–20; back formation from OPALESCENT]

o•pal•es•cent (ō′pə les′ənt), *adj.* **1.** exhibiting a play of colors like that of the opal. **2.** having a milky iridescence. [1805–15; OPAL + -ESCENT] —**o′pal•es′cence,** *n.* —**o′pal•es′cent•ly,** *adv.*

o•pal•eye (ō′pəl ī′), *n., pl.* **-eyes,** (*esp. collectively*) **-eye.** a green game fish, *Girella nigricans,* common off rocky shores from California southward, having opalescent blue eyes. Also called **greenfish.** [OPAL + EYE]

o′pal glass′, a translucent or opaque glass, usually of a milky white hue. [1865–70]

o•pal•ine (ō′pə lin, -lēn′, -līn′), *adj.* of or like opal; opalescent. [1775–85; OPAL + -INE[1]]

O•pa-Lock•a (ō′pə lok′ə), *n.* a town in S Florida. 14,460.

o•paque (ō pāk′), *adj., n., v.,* **o•paqued, o•paqu•ing.** —*adj.* **1.** not transparent or translucent; impenetrable to light; not allowing light to pass through. **2.** not transmitting radiation, sound, heat, etc. **3.** not shining or bright; dark; dull. **4.** hard to understand; not clear or lucid; obscure: *The problem remains opaque despite explanations.* **5.** dull, stupid, or unintelligent. —*n.* **6.** something that is opaque. **7.** *Photog.* a coloring matter, usually black or red, used to render part of a negative opaque. —*v.t.* **8.** *Photog.* to cover up blemishes on (a negative), esp. for making a printing plate. **9.** to cause to become opaque. [1375–1425; late ME *opake* < L *opācus* shaded] —**o•paque′ly,** *adv.* —**o•paque′ness,** *n.*
—**Syn.** **1.** murky, cloudy, muddy.

opaque′ projec′tor, a machine for projecting opaque objects, as books, on a screen, by means of reflected light. [1950–55] —**opaque′ project′ing.**

op′ art′, a style of abstract art in which lines, forms, and space are organized in such a way as to provide optical illusions of an ambiguous nature, as alternately advancing and receding squares on a flat surface. Also,

Op′ Art′. Also called **op, optical art.** [1960–65; OP(TICAL)] **—op′-art′,** *adj.* **—op′ art′ist.**

op. cit. (op′ sit′), in the work cited. [< L *opere citātō*]

ope (ōp), *adj., v.t., v.i.,* **oped, op·ing.** *Literary.* open.

OPEC (ō′pek), *n.* an organization founded in 1960 of nations that export large amounts of petroleum: formed to establish oil-exporting policies and set prices. [*O(rganization of) P(etroleum) E(xporting) C(ountries)*]

O·pech·an·ca·nough (ō pech′ən kä′nō), *n.* c1545–1644, Algonquian leader, brother of Powhatan: led Jamestown massacre 1622.

Op-Ed (op′ed′), *n.* a newspaper page devoted to signed articles by commentators, essayists, humorists, etc., of varying viewpoints: *the Op-Ed of today's* New York Times. Also called **Op′-Ed page′.** [1965–70, *Amer.*; *op(posite) ed(itorial page)*]

O·pe·li·ka (ō′pə lī′kə), *n.* a city in E Alabama. 21,896.

Op·e·lou·sas (op′ə lo͞o′səs), *n.* a city in S Louisiana. 18,903.

o·pen (ō′pən), *adj.* **1.** not closed or barred at the time, as a doorway by a door, a window by a sash, or a gateway by a gate: *to leave the windows open at night.* **2.** (of a door, gate, window sash, or the like) set so as to permit passage through the opening it can be used to close. **3.** having no means of closing or barring: *an open portico.* **4.** having the interior immediately accessible, as a box with the lid raised or a drawer that is pulled out. **5.** relatively free of obstructions to sight, movement, or internal arrangement: *an open floor plan.* **6.** constructed so as to be without cover or enclosure on the top or on some or all sides: *an open boat.* **7.** having relatively large or numerous spaces, voids, or intervals: *an open architectural screen; open ranks of soldiers.* **8.** perforated or porous: *an open texture.* **9.** relatively unoccupied by buildings, fences, trees, etc.: *open country.* **10.** not covered or closed; with certain parts apart: *open eyes; open mouth.* **11.** without a covering, esp. a protective covering; unprotected; unenclosed; exposed: *an open wound; open electrical wires.* **12.** extended or unfolded: *an open newspaper.* **13.** without restrictions as to who may participate: *an open competition; an open session.* **14.** accessible or available to follow: *the only course still open to us.* **15.** not taken or filled; not preempted; available; vacant: *Which job is open?* **16.** ready for or carrying on normal trade or business: *The new store is now open. The office is open on Saturdays.* **17.** not engaged or committed: *Have you any open time on Monday?* **18.** accessible, as to appeals, ideas, or offers: *to be open to suggestion.* **19.** exposed to general view or knowledge; existing, carried on, etc., without concealment: *open disregard of the rules.* **20.** acting publicly or without concealment, as a person. **21.** unreserved, candid, or frank, as persons or their speech, aspect, etc.: *an open manner.* **22.** generous, liberal, or bounteous: *to give with an open hand.* **23.** liable or subject: *open to question; open to retaliation.* **24.** undecided; unsettled: *several open questions.* **25.** without effective or enforced legal, commercial, or moral regulations: *an open town.* **26.** unguarded by an opponent: *an open wide receiver.* **27.** noting the part of the sea beyond headlands or enclosing areas of land: *to sail on the open seas.* **28.** free of ice, as a body of water or a seaport. **29.** free of navigational hazards: *an open coast.* **30.** (of a seaport) available for foreign trade; not closed by government regulations or by considerations of health. **31.** (of a microphone) in operation; live. **32.** (of a delimiting punctuation mark) occurring at the beginning of a group of words or characters that is set off, as from surrounding text: *open parenthesis; open quotes.* Cf. **close** (def. 56). **33.** not yet balanced or adjusted, as an account. **34.** not constipated, as the bowels. **35.** *Phonet.* **a.** (of a vowel) articulated with a relatively large opening above the tongue or with a relatively large oral aperture, as the vowel sound of *cot* compared with that in *caught.* **b.** (of a syllable) ending with a vowel. **c.** (of a consonant) continuant (opposed to *stopped*). **36.** *Ling.* (of a class of items) readily admitting new members, as the class of nouns, verbs, or adjectives (opposed to *closed*). **37.** *Print.* **a.** (of type) in outline form. **b.** widely spaced or leaded, as printed matter. **38.** *Music.* **a.** (of an organ pipe) not closed at the far end. **b.** (of a string) not stopped by a finger. **c.** (of a note) produced by such a pipe or string or, on a wind instrument, without the aid of a slide, key, etc. **39.** *Math.* **a.** (of an interval) containing neither endpoint. **b.** (of a set) consisting of points having neighborhoods wholly contained in the set, as the set of points within a circle. **c.** (of a map from one topological space to another) having the property that the image of an open set is an open set. **40.** free from frost; mild or moderate: *an open winter.* **41.** *Animal Husb.* (of a female animal) not pregnant. **42.** *Textiles.* (of a fabric or weave) so loosely woven that spaces are visible between warp and filling yarns.
—*v.t.* **43.** to move (a door, window sash, etc.) from a shut or closed position so as to admit of passage. **44.** to render (a doorway, gateway, window, etc.) unobstructed by moving a door, window sash, etc., away from it. **45.** to render the interior of (a box, drawer, etc.) readily accessible. **46.** to clear (a passage, channel, etc.) of obstructions. **47.** to clear (areas or passages in the body). **48.** to give access to; make accessible or available, as for use: *to open a port for trade.* **49.** to establish for business purposes or for public use: *to open an office.* **50.** to set in action, begin, start, or commence (sometimes fol. by *up*): *to open a campaign.* **51.** to uncover, lay bare, or expose to view. **52.** to expand, unfold, or spread out: *to open a map.* **53.** to make less compact, less closely spaced, or the like: *to open ranks.* **54.** to disclose, reveal, or divulge. **55.** to render accessible to knowledge, enlightenment, sympathy, etc.: *to open one's mind.* **56.** to cut, blast, or break into: *to open a safe with nitro.* **57.** to make or produce (an opening) by cutting or breaking, or by pushing aside or removing obstructions: *to open a way through a crowd.* **58.** to make an incision or opening in: *to open a boil.* **59.** *Law.* **a.** to recall or revoke (a judgment, decree, etc.) for the purpose of allowing further contest or delay. **b.** to make the first statement of (a case) to the court or jury. **60.** *Cards.* to begin a hand by making (the first bid), placing (the first bet), or playing (a given card or suit) as the lead. **61.** *Naut.* to sail (a course) so that the apparent location of a distant fixed object changes with relation to a nearer fixed object (sometimes fol. by *out*).
—*v.i.* **62.** to become open, as a door, building, box, or enclosure. **63.** to afford access: *a door that opens into a garden.* **64.** to have an opening, passage, or outlet: *The room opens into a corridor.* **65.** (of a building, theater, etc.) to open its doors to the public: *The museum opens at one o'clock.* **66.** to begin a session or term, as a school. **67.** to begin a season, series of performances, or tour, as a theatrical company: *The play will open in Boston.* **68.** to begin, start, or commence an activity: *The game opened with the national anthem.* **69.** to part, or seem to part, so as to allow or reveal a passage: *At last the cliffs opened to show us that we were heading for the sea.* **70.** to become disclosed or revealed. **71.** to come into view; become more visible or plain. **72.** to become receptive to knowledge, sympathy, etc., as the mind. **73.** to disclose or reveal one's knowledge, thoughts, feelings, etc. **74.** to unfold or expand, as a blossom, so as to reveal the interior. **75.** to spread out or expand, as the hand or a fan. **76.** to spread apart or separate, as pages of a book, newspaper, etc.: *Open to page 32.* **77.** to spread or come apart; burst: *The wound opened.* **78.** to become less compact, less closely spaced, or the like: *The ranks began to open.* **79.** *Cards.* to make the first bet, bid, or lead in beginning a hand. **80.** *Hunting.* (of hounds) to begin to bark, as on the scent of game. **81.** **open up, a.** to become or make open. **b.** to expand, esp. before the eye: *A breathtaking panorama opened up as we reached the top of the hill.* **c.** to achieve the initial development of: *to open up a business office; to open up trade with China.* **d.** *Slang.* to increase speed or the speed of (a vehicle).
—*n.* **82.** an open or clear space. **83.** the open air. **84.** the open water, as of the sea. **85.** an opening or aperture. **86.** an opening or opportunity. **87.** a contest or tournament in which both amateurs and professionals may compete, esp. in golf. **88.** **the open, a.** the unenclosed or unobstructed country. **b.** the outdoors: *Vacations in the open are fine for the entire family.* **c.** the condition of being unconcealed, recognized, or publicly known: *The scandal is now out in the open.* [bef. 900; (adj.) ME, OE; c. OS *opan* (D *open*), OHG *offan* (G *offen*), ON *opinn,* akin to UP; (v.) ME *openen,* OE *openian;* c. OS *opanon* (D *openen*), OHG *offanōn* (G *öffnen*)] **—o′pen·ly,** *adv.* **—o′pen·ness,** *n.*
—Syn. 21. See **frank**[1].

o·pen·a·ble (ō′pə nə bəl), *adj.* capable of being opened. [1815–25; OPEN + -ABLE] **—o′pen·a·bil′i·ty,** *n.*

o′pen account′. See **current account** (def. 1). [1895–1900]

o′pen admis′sions, *Educ.* a policy of admitting applicants to an institution, esp. a university, regardless of previous academic record or grades. Also called **o′pen ac′cess, open enrollment.** [1965–70]

o′pen air′, the outdoors. [1520–30]

o·pen-air (ō′pən âr′), *adj.* existing in, taking place in, or characteristic of the open air; outdoor: *The orchestra gave three open-air concerts last summer.* [1820–30] **—o′pen-air′ish,** *adj.* **—o′pen-air′ish·ness,** *n.* **—o′pen-air′ness,** *n.*

o·pen-and-shut (ō′pən ən shut′), *adj.* immediately obvious upon consideration; easily decided: *an open-and-shut case of murder.* [1835–45, *Amer.*]

o′pen-an·gle glauco′ma (ō′pən ang′gəl), *Ophthalm.* See under **glaucoma.**

o′pen bar′, a bar at a reception that serves drinks whose cost has been borne by the host, an admission charge, a sponsor, etc.: *Before the banquet there will be an open bar from 5 to 7* P.M. Cf. **cash bar.** [1970–75]

o′pen book′, someone or something easily understood or interpreted; something very clear: *The child's face is an open book.* [1850–55]

o′pen call′, an audition, esp. for actors or dancers, open to anyone wishing to try out.

o·pen-cast (ō′pən kast′, -käst′), *adj. Brit. Mining.* open-cut. [1705–15]

o′pen chain′, *Chem.* a series of atoms linked in a chain not joined together at its ends, and so represented in its structural formula. Cf. **closed chain.** [1880–85] **—o′pen-chain′,** *adj.*

o′pen cir′cuit, *Elect.* a discontinuous circuit through which no current can flow. Cf. **closed circuit.** [1820–30] **—o′pen-cir′cuit,** *adj.*

o′pen cit′y, 1. a city that, during a war, is offically declared demilitarized and open to occupation, and that will consequently not be defended, in order to spare it, under international law, from bombardment or other military attack. **2.** a city or autonomous city-state that gives equal access and status to inhabitants and visitors of all faiths, races, and nationalities. [1910–15]

o′pen class′room, *Educ.* **1.** a spacious instructional area shared by several groups or classes in elementary school, permitting more individualized, less supervised project learning and movement of pupils from one activity to another. **2.** a method or system utilizing such spacious classrooms and informal, flexible formats for learning and discussion. [1970–75]

o′pen clus′ter, *Astron.* a comparatively young, irregularly shaped group of stars, often numbering up to several hundred, and held together by mutual gravitation; usually found along the central plane of the Milky Way and other galaxies. Also, **galactic cluster.** Cf. **globular cluster, stellar association.**

o′pen commun′ion, *Eccles.* a communion service in which members of all denominations can participate. Cf. **close communion, intercommunion.**

o′pen conven′tion, *U.S. Politics.* a party convention at which delegates are free to vote for the candidate of their choice. Cf. **brokered convention.** [1955–60]

o′pen cou′plet, a couplet that concludes with a run-on line. Cf. **closed couplet.**

o′pen cov′er, *Math.* a cover of a set consisting entirely of open sets.

o·pen-cut (ō′pən kut′), *adj. Mining.* noting or pertaining to a type of surface mining in which coal and other flat-lying mineral deposits are removed by the excavation of long, narrow trenches. [1880–85]

o′pen dat′ing, the practice of putting a freshness date on food packages. [1970–75]

o′pen diapa′son. See under **diapason** (def. 4). [1870–75]

o′pen die′, *Metalworking.* a die of flat, concave, or hollow V shape that only minimally restricts lateral flow.

o′pen door′, 1. the policy of admitting people of all nationalities or ethnic groups to a country upon equal terms, as for immigration. **2.** the policy or practice of trading with all nations on an equal basis. **3.** admission or access; unrestricted opportunity: *His experience had given him an open door to success in his field.* [1520–30] **—o′pen-door′,** *adj.*

o·pen-end (ō′pən end′), *adj.* **1.** of, pertaining to, or like an open-end investment company. **2.** open-ended (def. 2). [1905–10]

o·pen-end·ed (ō′pən en′did), *adj.* **1.** not having fixed limits; unrestricted; broad: *an open-ended discussion.* **2.** allowing for future changes, revisions, or additions: *open-ended agreements.* **3.** having no fixed answer: *an open-ended question.* [1815–25; OPEN + END[1] + -ED[3]] **—o′pen-end′ed·ness,** *n.*

o′pen-end invest′ment com′pany. See **mutual fund.**

o′pen-end′ mort′gage, a mortgage agreement against which new sums of money may be borrowed under certain conditions.

o′pen enroll′ment, 1. See **open admissions. 2.** enrollment at a public school of choice rather than compulsory assignment to a particular school because of where one lives. [1960–65]

o·pen·er (ō′pə nər), *n.* **1.** a person or thing that opens. **2.** a device for opening sealed containers: *can opener.* **3.** the first of several theatrical numbers, variety acts, sports events, etc.: *a humorous monologue as an opener.* **4.** **openers,** *Poker.* cards in a hand, as a pair of jacks or better, that according to a given standard are worth enough to enable the holder to make the first bet of a deal. **5.** **for openers,** as an initially stated reason or argument; at the outset; to begin with: *Well, for openers, I don't have the money.* [1540–50; OPEN + -ER[1]]

o·pen-eyed (ō′pən īd′), *adj.* **1.** having the eyes open. **2.** having the eyes wide open, as in wonder. **3.** watchful; observant; alert. **4.** deliberate; conscious; knowing: *an open-eyed commission of a crime.* [1595–1605] **—o·pen-ey·ed·ly** (ō′pən ī′id lē, -īd′-), *adv.*

o·pen-faced (ō′pən fāst′), *adj.* **1.** having a frank or ingenuous face. **2.** Also, **o′pen-face′.** designating an open sandwich. **3.** (of a watch) having the dial covered only by the crystal. Cf. **hunting case.** [1600–10]

o′pen field′, *Football.* any area of the playing field away from the heavily trafficked line of scrimmage, in which the defense is widely scattered. Also called **broken field.**

o′pen flash′, *Photog.* a photographic technique employing a flash fired while the camera shutter is held open.

o′pen frac′ture. See **compound fracture.**

o′pen frame′, *Bowling.* a frame in which a bowler fails to make a strike or a spare.

o·pen·hand·ed (ō′pən han′did), *adj.* generous; liberal: *openhanded hospitality.* [1595–1605; *open hand* + -ED[3]] **—o′pen·hand′ed·ly,** *adv.* **—o′pen·hand′ed·ness,** *n.*
—Syn. magnanimous, bountiful, lavish, unstinting.

o′pen hand′ knot′. See **loop knot.**

o·pen-heart·ed (ō′pən här′tid), *adj.* **1.** unreserved, candid, or frank: *open-hearted advice.* **2.** kindly; benevolent: *an open-hearted gift to charity.* [1605–15] **—o′pen-heart′ed·ly,** *adv.* **—o′pen-heart′ed·ness,** *n.*

o·pen-hearth (ō′pən härth′), *adj.* noting, pertaining to, or produced by the open-hearth process. [1880–85]

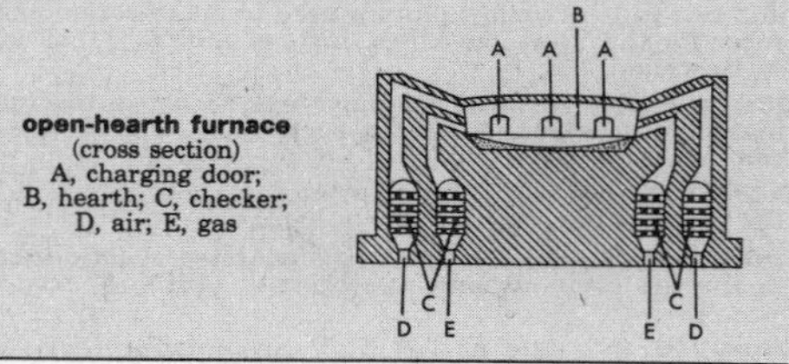

open-hearth furnace
(cross section)
A, charging door;
B, hearth; C, checker;
D, air; E, gas

o′pen-hearth′ proc′ess, a process of steelmaking in which the charge is laid in a furnace **(o′pen-hearth′ fur′nace)** on a shallow hearth and heated directly by burning gas as well as radiatively by the furnace walls. [1885–90]

o′pen-heart′ sur′gery (ō′pən härt′), surgery performed on the exposed heart while a heart-lung machine pumps and oxygenates the blood and diverts it from the heart. [1975–80]

CONCISE ETYMOLOGY KEY: <, descended or borrowed from; >, whence; b., blend of, blended; c., cognate with; cf., compare; deriv., derivative; equiv., equivalent; imit., imitative; obl., oblique; r., replacing; s., stem; sp., spelling, spelled; resp., respelling, respelled; trans., translation; ?, origin unknown; *, unattested; ‡, probably earlier than. See the full key inside the front cover.

o′pen house′, 1. a party or reception during which anyone who wishes may visit to share in a celebration, meet a special guest, etc. 2. a time during which a school, institution, etc., is open to the public for exhibition or for some specific occasion. 3. a house hospitably open to all friends who may wish to visit it. 4. **keep open house,** to be prepared to entertain visitors at any time: *They keep open house for artists and writers.* [1520–30]

o′pen hous′ing, the sale and rental of private housing free of discriminatory practices or policies. Also called **fair housing.** [1965–70, *Amer.*] —**o′pen-hous′ing,** *adj.*

o•pen•ing (ō′pə ning), *n.* 1. an act or instance of making or becoming open. 2. the act of a person or thing that opens. 3. an unobstructed or unoccupied space or place. 4. a void in solid matter; a gap, hole, or aperture. 5. a tract of land thinly wooded as compared with adjoining forest tracts. 6. the act of beginning; start; commencement: *the opening of a new session of Congress.* 7. the first part or initial stage of anything. 8. an employment vacancy; an unfilled position or job: *There are no openings for clerks today.* 9. an opportunity; chance. 10. a formal or official beginning, as of a sport season or a season's sale of goods: *the opening of the deer-hunting season; Swimsuits sold well at the summer opening.* 11. the first performance of a theatrical production. 12. the first public showing or use of something: *the opening of an art exhibition.* 13. a celebration of the first public showing or performance or of the first use or start of something: *The new supermarket is going to give away prizes at its opening.* 14. *Law.* the statement of the case made by counsel to the court or jury preliminary to adducing evidence. 15. a mode of beginning a game: *a manual of chess openings.* [1125–75; ME; see OPEN, -ING[1]]
—**Syn.** 4. orifice; slit, breach, rift, chasm, cleft, fissure, rent. —**Ant.** 1. closing.

o′pening night′, the first performance of a theatrical attraction, taking place in the evening: *The audience was full of celebrities on opening night.* Also called **first night.** [1805–15]

o′pen junc′ture, *Phonet.* a transition between successive sounds marked by a break in articulatory continuity, as by a pause or the modification of a preceding or following sound, and often indicating a division between words; presence of juncture (opposed to *close juncture*). Also called **plus juncture.** Cf. **close juncture, juncture** (def. 7a), **terminal juncture.** [1940–45]

o′pen let′ter, a letter, often of protest or criticism, addressed to a specific person, but intended to be brought to public attention. [1875–80] —**o′pen-let′ter,** *adj.*

o•pen-line (ō′pən līn′), *adj.* (of a radio or TV show) maintaining open telephone lines to permit listeners or viewers to phone a program with comments, questions, requests, etc.; call-in. [1965–70]

o′pen mar′ket, an unrestricted competitive market in which any buyer and seller is free to participate. [1760–70] —**o′pen-mar′ket,** *adj.*

o′pen mar′riage, a marriage in which the partners agree that each is free to have sexual relationships with other partners. [1970–75]

o•pen-mind•ed (ō′pən mīn′did), *adj.* 1. having or showing a mind receptive to new ideas or arguments. 2. unprejudiced; unbigoted; impartial. [1820–30] —**o′pen-mind′ed•ly,** *adv.* —**o′pen-mind′ed•ness,** *n.*

o•pen-mouthed (ō′pən mouŧħd′, -moutht′), *adj.* 1. having the mouth open. 2. gaping, as with surprise or astonishment. 3. greedy, ravenous, or rapacious. 4. clamoring at the sight of game or prey, as hounds. 5. vociferous or clamorous. 6. having a wide mouth, as a pitcher or jar. [1525–35] —**o•pen-mouth•ed•ly** (ō′pən-mou′ŧħid lē, -moutht′lē), *adv.* —**o′pen-mouth′ed•ness,** *n.*
—**Syn.** 2. dumbfounded, flabbergasted, confounded, thunderstruck.

o′pen or′der, *Mil.* a troop formation for drill or basic combat training, the intervals between the individuals being greater than those in close order. Also called **extended order.** [1615–25]

o•pen-pit (ō′pən pit′), *adj. Mining.* noting or pertaining to a type of surface mining in which massive, usually metallic mineral deposits are removed by cutting benches in the walls of a broad, deep funnel-shaped excavation. [1910–15]

o′pen plan′, a floor plan without fully enclosed spaces for distinct rooms. Cf. **closed plan.** [1935–40] —**o′pen-plan′,** *adj.*

o′pen pol′icy, *Insurance.* a continuous policy covering goods of a class subject to changes in volume, usually requiring periodic reports of values. [1875–80]

o•pen-pol•li•nat•ed (ō′pən pol′ə nā′tid), *adj. Bot.* (of a flower) pollinated without human agency. [1920–25] —**o′pen pollina′tion.**

o′pen posi′tion, 1. *Music.* the arrangement of a chord with wide intervals between the parts. 2. (in ballet, modern dance, and jazz dance) any position in which the feet are separated.

o′pen pri′mary, a direct primary election in which voters need not meet a test of party membership. [1930–35, *Amer.*]

o′pen quote′, 1. the quotation mark used to begin a quotation (" or '). 2. (used by a speaker to signify that a quotation will follow). Also, **o′pen quotes′.**

o′pen-reel tape′ (ō′pən rēl′), audiotape, usually ¼ in. (64 mm) wide, wound on a single reel and requiring a separate take-up reel for playing or recording. Also called **reel-to-reel tape.** [1965–70]

o′pen reg′istry, 1. ship registration under a national flag available to all ships regardless of nationality. 2. a national ship registry open to ships of all nations. —**o′pen-reg′istry,** *adj.*

o′pen sand′wich, a sandwich served on only one slice of bread, without a covering slice. [1945–50]

o′pen sea′, the main body of a sea or ocean, esp. the part that is outside territorial waters and not enclosed, or partially enclosed, by land.

o′pen sea′son, 1. a specific season or time of year when it is legal to catch or hunt for fish or game protected at all other times by the law. 2. a period of time in which a person or thing is exposed to criticism, attack, or recrimination: *Election year is open season on all incumbents.* [1895–1900, *Amer.*]

o′pen se′cret, something supposedly secret but actually known quite generally. [1875–80]

o′pen sen′tence, 1. *Math.* an equation or inequality containing one or more variables in which its truth or falsehood depends upon the values assumed by the variables in a particular instance, as the equation $x + 3 = 8$. 2. *Logic.* a propositional function that contains a free variable, as "*x* is a man." [1935–40]

o′pen ses′ame, any marvelously effective means for bringing about a desired result: *Wealth is the open sesame to happiness.* [1785–95; from the use of these words by Ali Baba to open the door of the robbers' den]

o•pen-shelf (ō′pən shelf′), *adj.* open-stack. [1815–25]

o′pen shop′, a factory, office, or other business establishment in which a union, chosen by a majority of the employees, acts as representative of all the employees in making agreements with the employer, but in which union membership is not a condition of employment. [1895–1900] —**o′pen-shop′,** *adj.*

o•pen-sid•ed (ō′pən sī′did), *adj.* having a side or sides open.

o′pen sight′, (on a firearm) a rear sight consisting of a notch across which the gunner aligns the front sight on the target. Cf. **peep sight.** [1585–95]

o′pen space′, *Ecol.* undeveloped land that is protected from development by legislation. [1820–30]

o•pen-stack (ō′pən stak′), *adj. Library Science.* having or being a system of library management in which patrons have direct access to stacks for browsing and selecting books; open-shelf. Cf. **closed-stack.**

o′pen stance′, *Baseball.* a batting stance in which the front foot is farther from the inside of the batter's box than the back foot.

o′pen stock′, merchandise, esp. china, silverware, and glassware, sold in sets with additional individual pieces available from stock for future purchases, as for replacement. [1895–1900]

o′pen string′, a staircase string whose top follows the profile of the steps in such a way that the treads project beyond its outer face.

o′pen sys′tem, *Thermodynam.* a region separated from its surroundings by a boundary that admits a transfer of matter or energy across it. Cf. **closed system.** [1935–40]

o•pen-tim•bered (ō′pən tim′bərd), *adj.* (of a roof, ceiling, etc.) constructed so that the timbers are exposed.

o′pen trail′er, any dog that barks or bays on the trail of its quarry. Cf. **still trailer.**

o′pen un′ion, a labor union that does not impose rigid restrictions on the admission of new members. Cf. **closed union.**

o′pen u′niverse, *Astron.* a model of the universe in which the universe expands forever because there is not enough mass to counteract the expansion by means of gravitational attraction. Cf. **closed universe.** [1975–80]

O′pen Univer′sity, *Trademark.* a largely self-instructional university founded in England in 1969, offering education through such means as television, computers, and mailed course materials.

o•pen-web (ō′pən web′), *adj.* (of a metal joist or girder) having a web of zigzag or crisscross lacing. [1870–75]

o•pen•work (ō′pən wûrk′), *n.* any kind of work, esp. ornamental, as of embroidery, lace, metal, stone, or wood, having a latticelike nature or showing openings through its substance. [1590–1600; OPEN + WORK]

OPer., Old Persian.

op•er•a[1] (op′ər ə, op′rə), *n.* 1. an extended dramatic composition, in which all parts are sung to instrumental accompaniment, that usually includes arias, choruses, and recitatives, and that sometimes includes ballet. Cf. **comic opera, grand opera.** 2. the form or branch of musical and dramatic art represented by such compositions. 3. the score or the words of such a composition. 4. a performance of one: *to go to the opera.* 5. (*sometimes cap.*) an opera house or resident company: *the Paris Opera.* [1635–45; < It: work, opera < L, pl. of *opus* service, work, a work, OPUS]

o•pe•ra[2] (ō′pər ə, op′ər ə), *n. Chiefly Music.* a pl. of **opus.**

op•er•a•ble (op′ər ə bəl, op′rə-), *adj.* 1. that can be treated by a surgical operation. Cf. **inoperable** (def. 2). 2. capable of being put into use, operation, or practice. [1640–50; < LL *operābilis,* equiv. to *operā(ri)* to work + *-bilis* -BLE] —**op′er•a•bil′i•ty,** *n.* —**op′er•a•bly,** *adv.*

o•pé•ra bouffe (op′ər ə bo͞of′, op′rə; *Fr.* ô pā ʀᴀ bo͞of′), *pl.* **o•pé•ra bouffes, o•pé•ras bouffe,** *Fr.* **o•pé•ras bouffes** (ô pā ʀᴀ bo͞of′). a comic opera, esp. of farcical character. [1865–70; < F]

o•pe•ra buf•fa (op′ər ə bo͞o′fə, op′rə; *It.* ô′pe rä bo͞of′fä), *pl.* **o•pe•ra buf•fas, o•pe•ras buf•fa,** *It.* **o•pe•re buf•fe** (ô′pe re bo͞of′fe). 1. an Italian farcical comic opera originating in the 18th century and containing recitativo secco, patter songs, and ensemble finales. 2. the operatic genre comprising such works. [1795–1805; < It]

o•pé•ra co•mique (op′ər ə ko mēk′, op′rə; *Fr.* ô pā ʀᴀ kô mēk′), *pl.* **o•pé•ra co•miques, o•pé•ras co•mique,** *Fr.* **o•pe•ras co•miques** (ô pā ʀᴀ kô mēk′). See **comic opera.** [1735–45; < F]

op′era glass′es, a small, low-power pair of binoculars for use at plays, concerts, and the like. Also, **op′era glass′.** [1730–40]

op•er•a•go•er (op′ər ə gō′ər, op′rə-), *n.* a person who attends opera performances. [1840–50; OPERA[1] + GOER]

op′era hat′, a man's tall, collapsible top hat, held open or in shape by springs and usually covered with a black, silky fabric. Also called **gibus.** Cf. **beaver**[1] (def. 4), **silk hat, top hat.** [1800–10]

op′era house′, 1. a theater devoted chiefly to operas. 2. *Older Use.* a theater, esp. a large, ornate one. [1710–20]

op•er•and (op′ə rand′), *n. Math.* a quantity upon which a mathematical operation is performed. [1885–90; < LL *operandum,* ger. of *operārī;* see OPERATE]

op•er•ant (op′ər ənt), *adj.* 1. operating; producing effects. —*n.* 2. a person or thing that operates. [1595–1605; < LL *operant-* (s. of *operāns,* prp. of *operārī;* see OPERATE); see -ANT]

op′erant condi′tioning, conditioning (def. 1). [1940–45]

o•pe•ra se•ri•a (op′ər ə sēr′ē ə, op′rə; *It.* ô′pe rä se′ryä), *pl.* **o•pe•ra se•rias, o•pe•ras se•ria,** *It.* **o•pe•re se•rie** (ô′pe re se′rye). Italian dramatic opera of the 18th century based typically on a classical subject and characterized by extensive use of the aria da capo and recitative. [1875–80; < It: lit., serious opera]

op•er•ate (op′ə rāt′), *v.,* **-at•ed, -at•ing.** —*v.i.* 1. to work, perform, or function, as a machine does: *This engine does not operate properly.* 2. to work or use a machine, apparatus, or the like. 3. to act effectively; produce an effect; exert force or influence (often fol. by *on* or *upon*): *Their propaganda is beginning to operate on the minds of the people.* 4. to perform some process of work or treatment. 5. *Surg.* to perform a surgical procedure. 6. (of a drug) to produce the effect intended. 7. *Mil.* **a.** to carry on operations in war. **b.** to give orders and accomplish military acts, as distinguished from doing staff work. 8. to carry on transactions in securities, or some commodity, esp. speculatively or on a large scale. 9. *Informal.* to use devious means for one's own gain; insinuate oneself; finagle: *a man who knows how to operate with the ladies.* —*v.t.* 10. to manage or use (a machine, device, etc.): *to operate a switchboard.* 11. to put or keep (a factory, industrial system, ranch, etc.) working or in operation: *to operate a coal mine.* 12. to bring about, effect, or produce, as by action or the exertion of force or influence. [1600–10; < LL *operātus,* ptp. of *operārī, -āre* to work, be efficacious, effect, produce, L: to busy oneself, v. deriv. of *opera* effort, work, akin to *opus* work; see -ATE[1]] —**op′er•at′a•ble,** *adj.*

op•er•at•ic (op′ə rat′ik), *adj.* 1. of or pertaining to opera: *operatic music.* 2. resembling or suitable for opera: *a voice of operatic caliber.* —*n.* 3. Usually, **operatics.** (*used with a singular or plural v.*) **a.** the technique or method of producing or staging operas. **b.** exaggerated or melodramatic behavior, often thought to be characteristic of operatic acting. [1740–50; OPERA[1] + -TIC, after *drama, dramatic*] —**op′er•at′i•cal•ly,** *adv.*

op•er•at•ing (op′ə rā′ting), *adj.* 1. used or engaged in performing operations: *an operating surgeon.* 2. of, for, or pertaining to operations: *an operating budget.* 3. of or pertaining to the proper operation of a machine, appliance, etc.: *a manual of operating instructions.* 4. *Railroads.* of, pertaining, or belonging to railroad workers, as engineers or firemen, who are directly engaged in the mechanical operation of trains: *an operating union.* [1800–10; OPERATE + -ING[1]]

op′erating in′come, revenue from business operations after operating expenses are deducted from gross income. Also called **operations income.**

op′erating room′, a specially equipped room, usually in a hospital, where surgical procedures are performed. *Abbr.:* OR [1885–90]

op′erating sys′tem, *Computers.* the collection of software that directs a computer's operations, controlling and scheduling the execution of other programs, and managing storage, input/output, and communication resources. *Abbr.:* OS [1960–65]

op•er•a•tion (op′ə rā′shən), *n.* 1. an act or instance, process, or manner of functioning or operating. 2. the state of being operative (usually prec. by *in* or *into*): *a rule no longer in operation.* 3. the power to act; efficacy, influence, or force. 4. the exertion of force, power, or influence; agency: *the operation of alcohol on the mind.* 5. a process of a practical or mechanical nature in some form of work or production: *a delicate operation in watchmaking.* 6. a course or procedure of productive or industrial activity: *building operations.* 7. a particular process or course: *mental operations.* 8. a business transaction, esp. one of a speculative nature; deal: *a shady operation.* 9. a business, esp. one run on a large scale: *a multinational operation.* 10. *Surg.* a procedure aimed at restoring or improving the health of a patient, as by correcting a malformation, removing diseased parts, implanting new parts, etc. 11. *Math.* **a.** a mathematical process, as addition, multiplication, or differentiation. **b.** the action of applying a mathematical process to a quantity or quantities. 12. *Mil.* **a.** a campaign, mission, maneuver, or action. **b.** Usually, **operations.** the conduct of a campaign, mission, etc. **c. operations,** a headquarters, office, or place from which a military campaign, air traffic to and from an airfield, or any of various other activities, is planned, conducted, and controlled. **d. operations,** the people who work at such a headquarters. [1350–1400; ME *operacioun* < L *operā-*

tiōn- (s. of *operātiō*), equiv. to *operāt(us)* (see OPERATE) + *-iōn-* -ION]

op•er•a•tion•al (op′ə rā′shə nl), *adj.* **1.** able to function or be used; functional: *How soon will the new factory be operational?* **2.** *Mil.* **a.** of, pertaining to, or involved in military operations. **b.** on active service or combat duty: *All units of the command are operational.* **3.** of or pertaining to operations or an operation. [1920–25; OPERATION + -AL[1]] **—op′er•a′tion•al•ly,** *adv.*

opera′tional am′plifier, *Electronics.* a high-gain, high-input impedance amplifier, usually an integrated circuit, that can perform mathematical operations when suitably wired. [1945–50]

opera′tional cal′culus, *Math.* a method for solving a differential equation by treating differential operators as ordinary algebraic quantities, thus obtaining a simpler problem.

op•er•a•tion•al•ism (op′ə rā′shə nl iz′əm), *n. Philos.* the doctrine that the meaning of a scientific term, concept, or proposition consists of the operation or operations performed in defining or demonstrating it. Also, **op′er•a′tion•ism.** [1930–35; OPERATIONAL + -ISM] **—op′er•a′tion•al•ist,** *n.* **—op′er•a′tion•al•is′tic,** *adj.*

opera′tions in′come. See **operating income.**

opera′tions research′, the analysis, usually involving mathematical treatment, of a process, problem, or operation to determine its purpose and effectiveness and to gain maximum efficiency. [1940–45, *Amer.*]

op•er•a•tive (op′ər ə tiv, op′rə tiv, op′ə rā′tiv), *n.* **1.** a person engaged, employed, or skilled in some branch of work, esp. productive or industrial work; worker. **2.** a detective. **3.** a secret agent; spy. **—***adj.* **4.** operating, or exerting force, power, or influence. **5.** having force; being in effect or operation: *laws operative in this city.* **6.** effective or efficacious. **7.** engaged in, concerned with, or pertaining to work or productive activity. **8.** significant; key: *The operative word in that sentence is "sometimes."* **9.** *Med.* concerned with, involving, or pertaining to surgical operations. [1590–1600; < MF *operatif* < L *operāt(us)* (see OPERATE) + MF *-if* -IVE] **—op′er•a•tive•ly,** *adv.* **—op′er•a•tive•ness, op•er•a•tiv•i•ty** (op′ər ə tiv′i tē), *n.*
—Syn. 1. workman, factory hand. **2.** investigator, agent. **6.** effectual, serviceable.

op•er•a•tor (op′ə rā′tər), *n.* **1.** a person who operates a machine, apparatus, or the like: *a telegraph operator.* **2.** a person who operates a telephone switchboard, esp. for a telephone company. **3.** a person who manages a working or industrial establishment, enterprise, or system: *the operators of a mine.* **4.** a person who trades in securities, esp. speculatively or on a large scale. **5.** a person who performs a surgical operation; a surgeon. **6.** *Math.* **a.** a symbol for expressing a mathematical operation. **b.** a function, esp. one transforming a function, set, etc., into another: *a differential operator.* **7.** *Informal.* **a.** a person who accomplishes his or her purposes by devious means; faker; fraud. **b.** a person who is adroit at overcoming, avoiding, or evading difficulties, regulations, or restrictions. **c.** a person who is extremely successful with or smoothly persuasive to members of the opposite sex. **8.** *Genetics.* a segment of DNA that interacts with a regulatory molecule, preventing transcription of the adjacent region. [1590–1600; < LL, equiv. to *operā(rī)* to work, effect (see OPERATE) + L *-tor* -TOR]

op•er•a•to•ry (op′ər ə tôr′ē, -tōr′ē), *n., pl.* **-ries,** *adj.* **—***n.* **1.** a room or other area with special equipment and facilities, as for dental surgery, scientific experiments, or the like. **—***adj.* **2.** operative. [1645–55; OPERATE + -ORY[1], -ORY[2]; cf. LL *operātōrius* working, acting]

op′era win′dow, a narrow, fixed window on each side of the rear passenger compartment of an automobile. [1970–75]

o•per•cle (ō′pər kəl), *n.* an operculum, esp. the posterior bone of the operculum of a fish. [1590–1600; < L *operculum* cover. See OPERCULUM, -CLE[2]]

o•per•cu•late (ō pûr′kyə lit, -lāt′), *adj.* having an operculum. Also, **o•per′cu•lat′ed.** [1765–75; < L *operc ul(um)* cover (see OPERCULUM) + -ATE[1]]

o•per•cu•lum (ō pûr′kyə ləm), *n., pl.* **-la** (-lə), **-lums.** **1.** *Bot., Zool.* a part or organ serving as a lid or cover, as a covering flap on a seed vessel. **2.** *Zool.* **a.** the gill cover of fishes and amphibians. See diag. under **fish. b.** (in many gastropods) a horny plate that closes the opening of the shell when the animal is retracted. [1705–15; < NL, L: lid, cover, equiv. to *oper(ire)* to cover + *-culum* -CULE[2]] **—o•per′cu•lar,** *adj.*

o•pe•re ci•ta•to (ō′pe RE′ ki tä′tō; *Eng.* op′ə rē′ sī tā′tō, si tä′tō), *Latin.* See **op. cit.**

op•er•et•ta (op′ə ret′ə), *n.* a short opera, usually of a light and amusing character. [1760–70; < It, dim. of *opera* OPERA[1]] **—op′er•et′tist,** *n.*

op•er•on (op′ə ron′), *n. Genetics.* a set of two or more adjacent cistrons whose transcription is under the coordinated control of a promoter, an operator, and a regulator gene. [1960–65; < F *opéron,* equiv. to *opér(er)* to work, OPERATE + *-on* -ON[1]]

op•er•ose (op′ə rōs′), *adj.* **1.** industrious, as a person. **2.** done with or involving much labor. [1660–70; < L *operōsus* busy, active, equiv. to *oper-* (s. of *opus*) work + *-ōsus* -OSE[1]] **—op′er•ose′ly,** *adv.* **—op′er•ose′•ness,** *n.*

OPers, Old Persian.

O•phel•ia (ō fēl′yə), *n.* a female given name.

O•phel•tes (ə fel′tēz), *n. Class. Myth.* the son of King Lycurgus of Nemea who was killed in infancy by a serpent and in whose memory the Nemean games were held. Also called **Archemorus.**

oph•i•cleide (of′i klīd′), *n.* a musical wind instrument, a development of the old wooden serpent, consisting of a conical metal tube bent double. [1825–35; < F *ophicléide* < Gk *óphi(s)* serpent + *kleid-* (s. of *kleís*) key (akin to L *clavis;* see CLAVICLE)] **—oph′i•clei′de•an,** *adj.*

o•phid•i•an (ō fid′ē ən), *adj.* **1.** belonging or pertaining to the suborder Ophidia (Serpentes), comprising the snakes. **—***n.* **2.** a snake. [1820–30; < NL *Ophidi(a)* (pl.) name of the suborder (< Gk *ophídion* (sing.), equiv. to *óph(is)* serpent + *-idion* dim. suffix) + -AN]

o•phid•i•id (ō fid′ē id, of′i dī′id, ō′fi-), *n.* **1.** any fish of the family Ophidiidae, comprising the cusk-eels. **—***adj.* **2.** belonging or pertaining to the family Ophidiidae. [< NL *Ophidiidae* name of the family, equiv. to *Ophidi(on)* genus name (< L *ophidion* snakelike fish < Gk; see OPHIDIAN) + *-idae* -ID[2]]

oph•i•ol•a•try (of′ē ol′ə trē, ō′fē-), *n.* the worship of snakes. [1860–65; < Gk *óphi(s)* snake + (ID)OLATRY] **—oph′i•ol′a•ter,** *n.* **—oph′i•ol′a•trous,** *adj.*

oph•i•o•lite (of′ē ə līt′, ō′fē-), *n. Geol.* an assemblage of mafic igneous rocks representing remnants of former oceanic crust. [1840–50; < Gk *óphi(s)* snake + *-o-* + -LITE; cf. OPHITE]

oph•i•ol•o•gy (of′ē ol′ə jē, ō′fē-), *n.* the branch of herpetology dealing with snakes. [1810–20; < Gk *óphi(s)* snake + *-o-* + -LOGY] **—oph•i•o•log•i•cal** (of′ē ə loj′i kəl, ō′fē-), **oph′i•o•log′ic,** *adj.* **—oph′i•ol′o•gist,** *n.*

O•phir (ō′fər), *n.* a country of uncertain location, possibly southern Arabia or the eastern coast of Africa, from which gold and precious stones and trees were brought for Solomon. I Kings 10:11.

oph•ite (of′īt, ō′fīt), *n. Petrol.* a diabase in which elongate crystals of plagioclase are embedded in pyroxene. [1350–1400; ME *ophites* < L *ophītēs* serpentine stone < Gk *ophī́tēs* (*líthos*) serpentine (stone), equiv. to *óph(is)* serpent + *-ītēs* -ITE[1]] **—o•phit•ic** (ō fit′ik), *adj.*

Oph•i•u•chus (of′ē yo͞o′kəs, ō′fē-), *n., gen.* **-chi** (-kī). *Astron.* the Serpent Bearer, a constellation on the celestial equator between Libra and Aquila.

oph•i•ur•oid (of′ē yo͝or′oid, ō′fē-), *n.* **1.** any echinoderm of the subclass Ophiuroidea, including brittle stars, basket stars, and others, characterized by elongate arms radiating from the disk. **—***adj.* **2.** of or pertaining to the subclass Ophiuroidea. [1885–90; < NL *Ophiuroidea* the class, equiv. to *Ophiur(a)* the type genus (< Gk *ophíoura,* fem. of *ophíouros* serpent-tailed (*ophí(s)* snake + *-ouros* adj. deriv. of *ourá* tail)) + *-oidea* -OIDEA]

ophthal., 1. ophthalmologist. **2.** ophthalmology.

ophthalm-, var. of **ophthalmo-** before a vowel: *ophthalmitis.*

ophthalm., ophthalmology. Also, **ophthalmol.**

oph•thal•mi•a (of thal′mē ə, op-), *n.* inflammation of the eye, esp. of its membranes or external structures. [1350–1400; < LL < Gk *ophthalmía,* equiv. to *ophthalm(ós)* eye + *-ia* -IA; r. ME *obtalmia* < ML, LL as above] **—oph•thal•mi•ac** (of thal′mē ak′, op-), *n.*

ophthal′mia ne•o•na•to′rum (nē′ə nə tôr′əm, -tōr′-), *Pathol.* inflammation of the eyes of a newborn child due to an infectious disease, as gonorrhea, contracted during birth from the infected mother. [< NL: ophthalmia of the newborn (pl.)]

oph•thal•mic (of thal′mik, op-), *adj.* of or pertaining to the eye; ocular. [1595–1605; < L *ophthalmicus* < Gk *ophthalmikós,* equiv. to *ophthalm(ós)* eye + *-ikos* -IC]

oph•thal•mi•tis (of′thal mī′tis, -thəl-, op′-), *n. Ophthalm.* ophthalmia. [1815–25; < NL; see OPHTHALM-, -ITIS] **—oph•thal•mit•ic** (of′thal mit′ik, -thəl-, op′-), *adj.*

ophthalmo-, a combining form meaning "eye," used in the formation of compound words: *ophthalmology.* Also, *esp. before a vowel,* **ophthalm-.** [< Gk, comb. form of *ophthalmós*]

oph•thal•mo•dy•na•mom•e•ter (of thal′mō dī′nə mom′i tər, -din′ə-, op-), *n.* **1.** a device for measuring the blood pressure of the retinal blood vessels. **2.** a device for determining the nearest point of ocular convergence. [OPHTHALMO- + DYNAMOMETER]

oph•thal•mol•o•gist (of′thəl mol′ə jist, -thə-, -thal-, op′-), *n.* a doctor of medicine specializing in ophthalmology. [1825–35; OPHTHALMO- + -LOG(Y) + -IST]
—Syn. See **eye doctor.**

oph•thal•mol•o•gy (of′thəl mol′ə jē, -thə-, -thal-, op′-), *n.* the branch of medical science dealing with the anatomy, functions, and diseases of the eye. [1835–45; OPHTHALMO- + -LOGY] **—oph•thal•mo•log•i•cal** (of-thal′mə loj′i kəl, op-), **oph•thal′mo•log′ic,** *adj.*

oph•thal•mom•e•ter (of′thəl mom′i tər, -thə-, -thal-, op′-), *n.* an instrument for measuring the reflection of an image on the surface of the cornea and other capacities of the eye, used chiefly for determining the presence and degree of astigmatism. [1835–45; OPHTHALMO- + -METER] **—oph•thal•mo•met•ric** (of thal′mə me′trik, op-), **oph•thal′mo•met′ri•cal,** *adj.* **—oph′thal•mom′e•try,** *n.*

oph•thal•mo•scope (of thal′mə skōp′, op-), *n.* an instrument for viewing the interior of the eye or examining the retina. [1855–60; OPHTHALMO- + -SCOPE] **—oph•thal•mo•scop•ic** (of thal′mə skop′ik, op-), **oph•thal′mo•scop′i•cal,** *adj.*

oph•thal•mos•co•py (of′thal mos′kə pē, -thəl-, op′-), *n., pl.* **-pies.** the use of or technique of using an ophthalmoscope. [1720–30; OPHTHALMO- + -SCOPY] **—oph′•thal•mos′co•pist,** *n.*

O•phüls (ō′fəls; *Ger.* ô′fyls), *n.* **Max** (maks; *Ger.* mäks), (*Max Oppenheimer*), 1902–57, German film director, in Germany, France, and the U.S.

-opia, a combining form occurring in compound words denoting a condition of sight or of the visual organs: *diplopia; hemeralopia; myopia.* Also, **-opsia.** [< Gk *-ōpia,* akin to *ṓpē* view, look, *ṓps* eye, face]

o•pi•ate (*n., adj.* ō′pē it, -āt′; *v.* ō′pē āt′), *n., adj., v.,* **-at•ed, -at•ing.** **—***n.* **1.** a drug containing opium or its derivatives, used in medicine for inducing sleep and relieving pain. **2.** any sedative, soporific, or narcotic. **3.** anything that causes dullness or inaction or that soothes the feelings. **—***adj.* **4.** mixed or prepared with opium. **5.** inducing sleep; soporific; narcotic. **6.** causing dullness or inaction. **—***v.t.* **7.** to subject to an opiate; stupefy. **8.** to dull or deaden. [1535–45; < ML *opiātus* bringing sleep, equiv. to L *opi(um)* OPIUM + *-ātus* -ATE[1]]
—Syn. 2. drug. **3.** anodyne. **5.** sedative. **—Ant. 2.** stimulant.

o•pi•at•ic (ō′pē at′ik), *adj.* of, pertaining to, or resembling opiates. [1670–80; OPIATE + -IC]

o•pine (ō pīn′), *v.t., v.i.,* **o•pined, o•pin•ing.** to hold or express an opinion. [1575–85; < L *opīnārī* to think, deem]
—Syn. say, suggest, allow, guess, imagine.

o•pin•i•cus (ō pin′i kəs), *n., pl.* **-cus•es.** a heraldic monster having the head, neck, and wings of an eagle, the body of a lion, and the tail of a bear. [1770–80; orig. uncert.]

o•pin•ion (ə pin′yən), *n.* **1.** a belief or judgment that rests on grounds insufficient to produce complete certainty. **2.** a personal view, attitude, or appraisal. **3.** the formal expression of a professional judgment: *to ask for a second medical opinion.* **4.** *Law.* the formal statement by a judge or court of the reasoning and the principles of law used in reaching a decision of a case. **5.** a judgment or estimate of a person or thing with respect to character, merit, etc.: *to forfeit someone's good opinion.* **6.** a favorable estimate; esteem: *I haven't much of an opinion of him.* [1250–1300; ME < OF < L *opīniōn-* (s. of *opīniō*), deriv. of *opīnārī* to OPINE]
—Syn. 1. persuasion, notion, idea, impression. OPINION, SENTIMENT, VIEW are terms for one's conclusion about something. An OPINION is a belief or judgment that falls short of absolute conviction, certainty, or positive knowledge; it is a conclusion that certain facts, ideas, etc., are probably true or likely to prove so: *political opinions; an opinion about art; In my opinion this is true.* SENTIMENT (usually *pl.*) refers to a rather fixed conviction, usually based on feeling or emotion rather than reasoning: *These are my sentiments.* VIEW is an estimate of something, an intellectual judgment, a critical survey based on a mental examination, particularly of a public matter: *views on governmental planning.*

o•pin•ion•at•ed (ə pin′yə nā′tid), *adj.* obstinate or conceited with regard to the merit of one's own opinions; conceitedly dogmatic. [1595–1605; obs. *opinionate* to possess or form an opinion (see OPINION, -ATE[1]) + -ED[2]] **—o•pin′ion•at′ed•ly,** *adv.* **—o•pin′ion•at′ed•ness,** *n.*
—Syn. prejudiced, biased; bigoted; stubborn.

o•pin•ion•a•tive (ə pin′yə nā′tiv), *adj.* **1.** of, pertaining to, or of the nature of opinion. **2.** opinionated. [1540–50; OPINION + -ATIVE] **—o•pin′ion•a′tive•ly,** *adv.* **—o•pin′ion•a′tive•ness,** *n.*

o•pin•ioned (ə pin′yənd), *adj.* **1.** having an opinion, esp. of a specified kind. **2.** obstinate or dogmatic in one's opinions; opinionated. [1575–85; OPINION + -ED[3]]

o•pi•oid (ō′pē oid′), *n. Biochem, Pharm.* **1.** any opiumlike substance. **2.** any of a group of natural substances, as the endorphins, produced by the body in increased amounts in response to stress and pain. **3.** any of several synthetic compounds, as methadone, having effects similar to natural opium alkaloids and their derivatives. **—***adj.* **4.** pertaining to such a substance. [1955–60; OPI(UM) + -OID]

opistho-, a combining form meaning "back," "behind," "rear," used in the formation of compound words: *opisthograph.* [< Gk, comb. form of *ópisthen* behind, at the back]

o•pis•tho•branch (ə pis′thə brangk′), *n.* **1.** any gastropod mollusk of the order Opisthobranchia, as the sea slugs, sea butterflies, and sea hares, characterized by a vestigial or absent mantle and shell and two pairs of tentacles. **—***adj.* **2.** of or pertaining to the opisthobranches. Also, **o•pis•tho•bran•chi•ate** (ə pis′thə brang′kē it, -āt′). [1850–55; < NL *Opisthobranchia* the subclass; see OPISTHO-, BRANCHIA]

op•is•thod•o•mos (op′is thod′ə məs, -mos′), *n., pl.* **-mos•es.** **1.** Also called **posticum.** a small room in the cella of a classical temple, as for a treasury. **2.** epinaos. [1690–1700; < Gk *opisthódomos,* equiv. to *opistho-* OPISTHO- + *dómos* house]

op•is•thog•na•thous (op′is thog′nə thəs), *adj. Zool.* having receding jaws. [1860–65; OPISTHO- + -GNATHOUS] **—op′is•thog′na•thism,** *n.*

o•pis•tho•graph (ə pis′thə graf′, -gräf′), *n.* a manuscript, parchment, or book having writing on both sides of the leaves. Cf. **anopisthograph.** [1615–25; < L *opisthographus* < Gk *opisthógraphos;* see OPISTHO-, -GRAPH]

o•pi•um (ō′pē əm), *n.* **1.** the dried, condensed juice of a poppy, *Papaver somniferum,* that has a narcotic, soporific, analgesic, and astringent effect and contains morphine, codeine, papaverine, and other alkaloids used in medicine in their isolated or derived forms: a narcotic substance, poisonous in large doses. **2.** anything that causes dullness or inaction or that soothes the mind or emotions. [1350–1400; ME < L < Gk *ópion* poppy juice, equiv. to *op(ós)* sap, juice + *-ion* dim. suffix]

o•pi•um•ism (ō′pē ə miz′əm), *n.* **1.** the addictive use of opium as a stimulant or intoxicant. **2.** the pathological condition caused by the addictive use of opium. [OPIUM + -ISM]

o′pium pop′py, a Eurasian poppy, *Papaver somniferum,* having white, pink, red, or purple flowers, cultivated as the source of opium, for its oily seeds, and as an ornamental. [1860–65]

O′pium War′, a war between Great Britain and China that began in 1839 as a conflict over the opium trade and ended in 1842 with the Chinese cession of Hong Kong to

CONCISE ETYMOLOGY KEY: <, descended or borrowed from; >, whence; b., blend of, blended; c., cognate with; cf., compare; deriv., derivative; equiv., equivalent; imit., imitative; obl., oblique; r., replacing; s., stem; sp., spelling, spelled; resp., respelling, respelled; trans., translation; ?, origin unknown; *, unattested; ‡, probably earlier than. See the full key inside the front cover.

the British, the opening of five Chinese ports to foreign merchants, and the grant of other commercial and diplomatic privileges in the Treaty of Nanking.

OPM, 1. Office of Personnel Management. **2.** operations per minute. **3.** *Slang.* other people's money.

O·por·to (ō pôr′tō, ō pōr′-), *n.* a port in NW Portugal, near the mouth of the Douro River. 300,925. Portuguese, **Pôrto.**

o·pos·sum (ə pos′əm, pos′əm), *n., pl.* **-sums,** (*esp. collectively*) **-sum. 1.** a prehensile-tailed marsupial, *Didelphis virginiana,* of the eastern U.S., the female having an abdominal pouch in which its young are carried: noted for the habit of feigning death when in danger. **2.** any of various animals of related genera. Cf. **possum.** [1600–10, *Amer.*; < Virginia Algonquian (E sp.) *opassom, opussum, aposoum* (equiv. to Proto-Algonquian **wa·p-* white + *-*aʔθemw-* dog)]

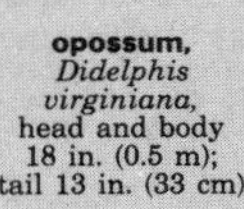

opossum, *Didelphis virginiana,* head and body 18 in. (0.5 m); tail 13 in. (33 cm)

opos′sum shrimp′, any small, shrimplike crustacean of the order Mysidacea, the females of which carry their eggs in a pouch between the legs. [1835–45]

op·o·ther·a·py (op′ə ther′ə pē), *n.* organotherapy. [1895–1900; < Gk *opó(s)* juice + THERAPY]

Opp., opuses; opera.

opp., 1. opposed. **2.** opposite.

Op·pen·heim (op′ən hīm′), *n.* **E(dward) Phillips,** 1866–1946, English novelist.

Op·pen·heim·er (op′ən hī′mər), *n.* **J(ulius) Robert,** 1904–67, U.S. nuclear physicist.

op·pi·dan (op′i dən), *adj.* **1.** of a town; urban. **—*n.* 2.** a townsman. [1530–40; < L *oppidānus,* equiv. to *oppid(um)* town + *-ānus* -AN]

op·pi·late (op′ə lāt′), *v.t.,* **-lat·ed, -lat·ing.** to stop up; fill with obstructing matter; obstruct. [1540–50; < L *oppilātus* (ptp. of *oppilāre* to stop up), equiv. to *op-* OP- + *pil-* (cf. COMPILE) + *-ātus* -ATE¹] **—op′pi·la′tion,** *n.*

op·po·nen·cy (ə pō′nən sē), *n.* **1.** an act or instance of opposing. **2.** the state of being an opponent. [1720–30; OPPON(ENT) + -ENCY]

op·po·nent (ə pō′nənt), *n.* **1.** a person who is on an opposing side in a game, contest, controversy, or the like; adversary. **—*adj.* 2.** being opposite, as in position. **3.** opposing; adverse; antagonistic. **4.** *Anat.* bringing parts together or into opposition, as a muscle. [1580–90; < L *oppōnent-* (s. of *oppōnēns,* prp. of *oppōnere* to place over, against, or in front of, make an obstacle), equiv. to *op-* OP- + *pōn(ere)* to place, set, put + *-ent-* -ENT]
—Syn. 1. antagonist. OPPONENT, COMPETITOR, RIVAL refer to persons engaged in a contest. OPPONENT is the most impersonal, meaning merely one who opposes; perhaps one who continually blocks and frustrates or one who happens to be on the opposite side in a temporary contest: *an opponent in a debate.* COMPETITOR emphasizes the action in striving against another, or others, for a definite, common goal: *competitors in business.* RIVAL has both personal and emotional connotations; it emphasizes the idea that (usually) two persons are struggling to attain the same object: *rivals for an office.* **—Ant. 1.** ally, friend.

op·por·tune (op′ər tōōn′, -tyōōn′), *adj.* **1.** appropriate, favorable, or suitable: *an opportune phrase for the occasion.* **2.** occurring or coming at an appropriate time; well-timed: *an opportune warning.* [1375–1425; late ME < L *opportūnus* convenient, equiv. to *op-* OP- + *portu-,* s. of *portus* access, PORT¹ + *-nus* adj. suffix (*u* lengthened as in *tribūnus* TRIBUNE)] **—op′por·tune′ly,** *adv.* **—op′por·tune′ness,** *n.*
—Syn. 1. apt; fortunate, propitious. **2.** convenient. OPPORTUNE, SEASONABLE, TIMELY refer to something that is particularly fitting or suitable for a certain time. OPPORTUNE refers to something that is well-timed and meets exactly the demands of the time or occasion: *an opportune remark.* Something that is SEASONABLE is right or proper for the time or season or occasion: *seasonable weather.* Something that is TIMELY occurs or is done at an appropriate time, esp. in time to meet some need: *timely intervention.*

op·por·tun·ism (op′ər tōō′niz əm, -tyōō′-), *n.* **1.** the policy or practice, as in politics, business, or one's personal affairs, of adapting actions, decisions, etc., to expediency or effectiveness regardless of the sacrifice of ethical principles. **2.** action or judgment in accordance with this policy. [1865–70; < It *opportunismo,* equiv. to *opportun(o)* (< L *opportūnus;* see OPPORTUNE) + *-ismo* -ISM] **—op′por·tun′ist,** *n.*

op·por·tun·is·tic (op′ər tōō nis′tik, -tyōō-), *adj.* **1.** adhering to a policy of opportunism; practicing opportunism. **2.** *Pathol.* **a.** (of a microorganism) causing disease only under certain conditions, as when a person's immune system is impaired. **b.** (of a disease or infection) caused by such an organism: *Pneumocystis pneumonia is an opportunistic disease that often strikes victims of AIDS.* [1890–95; OPPORTUNIST + -IC] **—op′por·tun·is′ti·cal·ly,** *adv.*

op·por·tu·ni·ty (op′ər tōō′ni tē, -tyōō′-), *n., pl.* **-ties. 1.** an appropriate or favorable time or occasion: *Their meeting afforded an opportunity to exchange views.* **2.** a situation or condition favorable for attainment of a goal. **3.** a good position, chance, or prospect, as for advancement or success. [1350–1400; ME *opportunite* < MF < L *opportūnitās* convenience, fitness, equiv. to *opportūn(us)* (see OPPORTUNE) + *-itās-* -ITY]

op·pos·a·ble (ə pō′zə bəl), *adj.* **1.** capable of being placed opposite to something else: *the opposable thumb of primates.* **2.** capable of being resisted, fought, or opposed. [1660–70; OPPOSE + -ABLE] **—op·pos′a·bil′i·ty,** *n.*

op·pose (ə pōz′), *v.,* **-posed, -pos·ing. —*v.t.* 1.** to act against or provide resistance to; combat. **2.** to stand in the way of; hinder; obstruct. **3.** to set as an opponent or adversary. **4.** to be hostile or adverse to, as in opinion: *to oppose a resolution in a debate.* **5.** to set as an obstacle or hindrance. **6.** to set against in some relation, esp. as to demonstrate a comparison or contrast: *to oppose advantages to disadvantages.* **7.** to use or take as being opposite or contrary. **8.** to set (something) over against something else in place, or to set (two things) so as to face or be opposite to one another. **—*v.i.* 9.** to be or act in opposition. [1350–1400; ME < OF *opposer,* b. L *oppōnere* to set against and OF *poser* to POSE¹, associated with the L ptp. *oppositus*] **—op·pos′er,** *n.* **—op·pos′ing·ly,** *adv.*
—Syn. 1. confront, contravene. OPPOSE, RESIST, WITHSTAND imply setting up a force against something. The difference between OPPOSE and RESIST is somewhat that between offensive and defensive action. To OPPOSE is mainly to fight against, in order to thwart, certain tendencies or procedures of which one does not approve: *The lobbyists opposed the passage of the bill.* RESIST suggests that the subject is already threatened by the forces, or by the imminent possibility, against which he or she struggles: *to resist temptation.* Again, whereas OPPOSE always suggests an attitude of great disapproval, RESIST may imply an inner struggle in which the will is divided: *She tried unsuccessfully to resist the temptation to eat dessert.* WITHSTAND generally implies successful resistance; it may refer to endurance that allows one to emerge unharmed (*to withstand a shock*), as well as to active resistance: *to withstand an attack.* **2.** prevent. **4.** contradict. **—Ant. 1.** support, help.

op·posed′-pis′ton en′gine (ə pōzd′pis′tən), a reciprocating engine, as a diesel engine, in which each cylinder has two pistons that move simultaneously away from or toward the center. Also called **opposed′ en′gine.** [1965–70]

op·pose·less (ə pōz′lis), *adj. Archaic.* tolerating no opposition or resistance; irresistible. [1595–1605; OPPOSE + -LESS]

op·po·site (op′ə zit, -sit), *adj.* **1.** situated, placed, or lying face to face with something else or each other, or in corresponding positions with relation to an intervening line, space, or thing: *opposite ends of a room.* **2.** contrary or radically different in some respect common to both, as in nature, qualities, direction, result, or significance; opposed: *opposite sides in a controversy; opposite directions.* **3.** *Bot.* **a.** situated on diametrically opposed sides of an axis, as leaves when there are two on one node. **b.** having one organ vertically above another; superimposed. **4.** adverse or inimical. **—*n.* 5.** a person or thing that is opposite or contrary. **6.** an antonym. **7.** *Archaic.* an opponent; antagonist. **—*prep.* 8.** across from; facing: *The guest of honor sat opposite me at the banquet.* **9.** in a role parallel or complementary to: *He has played opposite many leading ladies.* **—*adv.* 10.** on opposite sides. **11.** on the opposite side: *I was at one end and she sat opposite.* **12.** to the opposite side; in the opposite direction: *I went to the left balcony, and he went opposite.* [1350–1400; ME < MF < L *oppositus,* ptp. of *oppōnere* to set against. See OPPOSE, -ITE²] **—op′po·site·ly,** *adv.* **—op′po·site·ness,** *n.*
—Syn. 1. facing. **2.** incompatible, irreconcilable, unlike, differing. OPPOSITE, CONTRARY, REVERSE imply that two things differ from each other in such a way as to indicate a definite kind of relationship. OPPOSITE suggests symmetrical antithesis in position, action, or character: *opposite ends of a pole, sides of a road, views.* CONTRARY sometimes adds to OPPOSITE the idea of conflict or antagonism: *contrary statements, beliefs.* REVERSE suggests something that faces or moves in the opposite direction: *the reverse side of a coin; a reverse gear.* **—Ant. 2.** same, like.

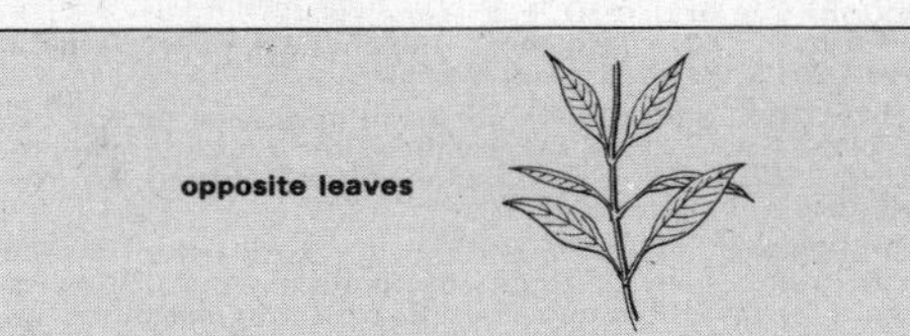

opposite leaves

op′posite num′ber, counterpart; equivalent: *New members with an interest in folk art will find their opposite numbers in the association's directory.* [1905–10]

op′posite prompt′, *Chiefly Brit. Theat.* the offstage area to the right as one faces the audience. *Abbr.:* O.P. Also, **op′posite prompt′ side′.**

op·po·si·tion (op′ə zish′ən), *n.* **1.** the action of opposing, resisting, or combating. **2.** antagonism or hostility. **3.** a person or group of people opposing, criticizing, or protesting something, someone, or another group. **4.** (*sometimes cap.*) the major political party opposed to the party in power and seeking to replace it. **5.** the act of placing opposite, or the state or position of being placed opposite. **6.** the act of opposing, or the state of being opposed by way of comparison or contrast. **7.** *Logic.* **a.** the relation between two propositions that have the same subject and predicate, but which differ in quantity or quality, or in both. **b.** the relation between two propositions in virtue of which the truth or falsity of one of them determines the truth or falsity of the other. **8.** *Astron.* the situation of two heavenly bodies when their longitudes or right ascensions differ by 180°: *The moon is in opposition to the sun when the earth is directly between them.* **9.** *Astrol.* the situation of two heavenly bodies or groups of heavenly bodies whose celestial longitudes differ by 180°, conducive to confrontation or revelation: an astrological aspect. **10.** *Elect.* the condition that exists when two waves of the same frequency are out of phase by one-half of a period. **11.** *Ling.* **a.** the relationship between any two alternative units within a linguistic system, esp. between minimally distinct phonemes. **b.** the feature that constitutes the difference between two such units. [1350–1400; < L *oppositiōn-* (s. of *oppositiō*), equiv. to *opposit(us)* (see OPPOSITE) + *-iōn-* -ION; r. ME *opposicioun* < OF *opposicion* < L as above] **—op′po·si′tion·al, op′po·si′tion·ar′y,** *adj.* **—op′po·si′tion·less,** *adj.*

op·po·si·tion·ist (op′ə zish′ə nist), *n.* a person who offers opposition; a member of an opposition. [1765–75; OPPOSITION + -IST]

op·press (ə pres′), *v.t.* **1.** to burden with cruel or unjust impositions or restraints; subject to a burdensome or harsh exercise of authority or power: *a people oppressed by totalitarianism.* **2.** to lie heavily upon (the mind, a person, etc.): *Care and sorrow oppressed them.* **3.** to weigh down, as sleep or weariness does. **4.** *Archaic.* to put down; subdue or suppress. **5.** *Archaic.* to press upon or against; crush. [1300–50; ME *oppressen* < MF *oppresser* < ML *oppressāre,* deriv. of L *oppressus* ptp. of *opprimere* to squeeze, suffocate, equiv. to *op-* OP- + *-primere* (comb. form of *premere*) to PRESS¹] **—op·press′i·ble,** *adj.* **—op·pres′sor,** *n.*
—Syn. 1, 2. OPPRESS, DEPRESS, both having the literal meaning to press down upon, to cause to sink, are today mainly limited to figurative applications. To OPPRESS is usually to subject (a people) to burdens, to undue exercise of authority, and the like; its chief application, therefore, is to a social or political situation: *a tyrant oppressing his subjects.* DEPRESS suggests mainly the psychological effect, upon the individual, of unpleasant conditions, situations, etc., that sadden and discourage: *depressed by the news.* When OPPRESS is sometimes used in this sense, it suggests a psychological attitude of more complete hopelessness: *oppressed by a sense of failure.* **1.** maltreat, persecute. **—Ant. 2.** uphold, encourage.

op·pres·sion (ə presh′ən), *n.* **1.** the exercise of authority or power in a burdensome, cruel, or unjust manner. **2.** an act or instance of oppressing. **3.** the state of being oppressed. **4.** the feeling of being heavily burdened, mentally or physically, by troubles, adverse conditions, anxiety, etc. [1300–50; ME *oppressioun* < MF < L *oppressiōn-* (s. of *oppressiō*) a pressing down, equiv. to *oppress(us)* (see OPPRESS) + *-iōn-* -ION]
—Syn. 1. tyranny, despotism, persecution. **3, 4.** hardship, suffering. **—Ant. 1.** kindness, justice.

op·pres·sive (ə pres′iv), *adj.* **1.** burdensome, unjustly harsh, or tyrannical: *an oppressive king; oppressive laws.* **2.** causing discomfort by being excessive, intense, elaborate, etc.: *oppressive heat.* **3.** distressing or grievous: *oppressive sorrows.* [1620–30; < ML *oppressīvus,* equiv. to *oppress(us)* (see OPPRESS) + *-īvus* -IVE] **—op·pres′sive·ly,** *adv.* **—op·pres′sive·ness,** *n.*

op·pro·bri·ous (ə prō′brē əs), *adj.* **1.** conveying or expressing opprobrium, as language or a speaker: *opprobrious invectives.* **2.** outrageously disgraceful or shameful: *opprobrious conduct.* [1350–1400; ME < LL *opprobriōsus,* equiv. to L *opprobri(um)* OPPROBRIUM + *-ōsus* -OUS] **—op·pro′bri·ous·ly,** *adv.* **—op·pro′bri·ous·ness,** *n.*
—Syn. 1. reproachful, abusive, vituperative, contemptuous. **2.** dishonorable, ignominious. **—Ant. 1.** laudatory. **2.** reputable.

op·pro·bri·um (ə prō′brē əm), *n.* **1.** the disgrace or the reproach incurred by conduct considered outrageously shameful; infamy. **2.** a cause or object of such disgrace or reproach. [1650–60; < L: reproach, equiv. to *op-* OP- + *probr(um)* infamy, disgrace + *-ium* -IUM]

op·pugn (ə pyōōn′), *v.t.* **1.** to assail by criticism, argument, or action. **2.** to call in question; dispute. [1400–50; late ME < L *oppugnāre* to oppose, attack, equiv. to *op-* OP- + *pugnāre* to fight, deriv. of *pugnus* fist; see PUGILISM] **—op·pugn′er,** *n.*

op·pug·nant (ə pug′nənt), *adj.* opposing; antagonistic; contrary. [1505–15; < L *oppugnant-* (s. of *oppugnāns*), prp. of *oppugnāre* to oppose. See OPPUGN, -ANT] **—op·pug′nan·cy,** *n.*

OPr, Old Provençal.

OPruss, Old Prussian.

op·ry (op′rē), *n., pl.* **-ries,** *adj. Dial.* opera¹. [1910–15; *Amer.*]

Ops (ops), *n.* the ancient Roman goddess of plenty, and the wife of Saturn and mother of Jupiter: identified with the Greek goddess Rhea.

OPS, Office of Price Stabilization. Also, **O.P.S.**

-opsia, var. of **-opia:** *hemianopsia.* Also, **-opsy².**

op·sin (op′sin), *n. Biochem.* any of several compounds that form the protein component of the light-sensitive retina pigment, rhodopsin. [1950–55; prob. back formation from RHODOPSIN]

-opsis, a combining form meaning "likeness," used esp. in the names of living organisms and organic structures that resemble the thing named by the initial element: *coreopsis.* [< Gk *ópsis* appearance, sight]

op·son·ic (op son′ik), *adj. Immunol.* of, pertaining to, or influenced by opsonin; capable of promoting phagocytosis. [1900–05; OPSON(IN) + -IC]

op·son·i·fy (op son′ə fī′), *v.t.,* **-fied, -fy·ing.** *Immunol.* to facilitate phagocytosis of (a microorganism, as a bacterium) by treatment with opsonin. [OPSON(IN) + -IFY]

op·so·nin (op′sə nin), *n. Immunol.* a constituent of normal or immune blood serum that makes invading bacteria more susceptible to the destructive action of the phagocytes. [1900–05; < L *opsōn(ium)* victuals (< Gk *opsōnía,* deriv. of *opsōneîn* to buy provisions) + -IN²] **—op′so·noid′,** *adj.*

op•so•nize (op′sə nīz′), *v.t.*, **-nized, -niz•ing.** *Immunol.* to increase the susceptibility of (bacteria) to ingestion by phagocytes. Also, *esp. Brit.,* **op′so•nise′.** [OPSON(IN) + -IZE] —**op′so•ni•za′tion,** *n.*

-opsy[1], a combining form occurring in compound words denoting a medical examination or inspection: *biopsy; necropsy.* [generalized from AUTOPSY]

-opsy[2], var. of **-opsia:** *achromatopsy.*

opt (opt), *v.i.* **1.** to make a choice; choose (usually fol. by *for*). **2. opt out,** to decide to leave or withdraw: *to opt out of the urban rat race and move to the countryside.* [1875–80; < F *opter* to choose, divide < L *optāre* to wish for, desire, pray for, choose, select]
—**Syn. 1.** select, pick, elect, prefer.

opt., 1. optative. **2.** optical. **3.** optician. **4.** optics. **5.** optional.

op•ta•tive (op′tə tiv), *Gram.* —*adj.* **1.** designating or pertaining to a verb mood, as in Greek, that has among its functions the expression of a wish, as Greek *ioimen* "may we go, we wish we might go." —*n.* **2.** the optative mood. **3.** a verb in the optative mood. [1520–30; < LL *optātīvus,* equiv. to L *optāt(us)* (ptp. of *optāre;* see OPT, -ATE[1]) + *-īvus* -IVE] —**op′ta•tive•ly,** *adv.*

op•tic (op′tik), *adj.* **1.** of or pertaining to the eye or sight. **2.** optical. —*n.* **3.** the eye. **4.** a lens of an optical instrument. [1535–45; < ML *opticus* < Gk *optikós,* equiv. to *opt(ós)* seen (verbid of *ópsesthai* to see) + *-ikos* -IC]

op•ti•cal (op′ti kəl), *adj.* **1.** of, pertaining to, or applying optics or the principles of optics. **2.** constructed to assist sight or to correct defects in vision. **3.** of or pertaining to sight or vision; visual. **4.** of or pertaining to the eye. **5.** of or pertaining to an optician or opticians or to their products, esp. eyeglasses: *an optical service.* **6.** dealing with or skilled in optics. —*n.* **7. opticals.** See **optical effects.** [1560–70; OPTIC + -AL[1]] —**op′ti•cal•ly,** *adv.*

op′tical activ′ity, *Physical Chem.* the ability of a substance to rotate the plane of polarization of plane-polarized light. [1875–80]

op′tical art′. See **op art.** Also, **Op′tical Art′.** [1960–65]

op′tical astron′omy, the branch of observational astronomy using telescopes to observe or photograph celestial objects in visible light. [1965–70] —**op′tical astron′omer.**

op′tical bench′, an apparatus, as a special table or rigid beam, for the precise positioning of light sources, screens, and optical instruments used for optical and photometric studies, having a ruled bar to which these devices can be attached and along which they can be readily adjusted. [1880–85]

op′tical cen′ter, *Print.* a point about ten percent above the exact center of a printed page or layout. Also called **optic center.**

op′tical char′acter recogni′tion, *Computers.* the process or technology of reading data in printed form by a device (**op′tical char′acter read′er**) that scans and identifies characters. *Abbr.:* OCR [1960–65]

op′tical comput′er, an experimental computer that uses photons rather than electrical impulses to process data a thousand times faster than with conventional integrated circuits.

op′tical disk′, *Computers, Television.* **1.** Also, **op′tical disc′.** Also called **laser disk.** a grooveless disk on which digital data, as text, music, or pictures, is stored as tiny pits in the surface and is read or replayed by a laser beam scanning the surface. **2.** videodisk. Cf. **compact disk.**

op′tical dou′ble star′. See under **double star.**

op′tical effects′, *Motion Pictures, Television.* special visual effects, as the wipe or dissolve, created in the camera or esp. in a film laboratory by technicians using complex optical and electronic equipment. Also called **opticals.**

op′tical fi′ber, a very thin, flexible glass or plastic strand along which large quantities of information can be transmitted in the form of light pulses: used in telecommunications, medicine, and other fields. Also called **light guide.** Cf. **fiber optics, waveguide.** [1960–65]

op′tical glass′, *Optics.* any of several types of high-quality, homogeneous, color-free glass, as flint or crown glass, having specified refractive properties, used in lenses and other components of optical systems. [1740–50]

op′tical illu′sion. See under **illusion** (def. 4). [1785–95]

op′tical i′somer, *Chem.* any of two or more isomers exhibiting optical isomerism. [1890–95]

op′tical isom′erism, *Chem.* stereoisomerism in which the isomers are identical in molecular weight and most chemical and physical properties but differ in their effect on the rotation of polarized light. Cf. **dextrorotatory, levorotatory, racemism.** [1890–95]

op′tical ma′ser, *Physics.* laser.

op′tical path′, the path of light through a medium, having a magnitude equal to the geometric distance through the system times the index of refraction of the medium. [1890–95]

op′tical print′er, a film printer used in making optical effects, consisting basically of a camera that photographs the image with special lenses to enlarge, reduce, distort, etc., and a projector that transfers the image to the print stock, as distinguished from a contact printer. [1940–45]

CONCISE ETYMOLOGY KEY: <, descended or borrowed from; >, whence; b., blend of, blended; c., cognate with; cf., compare; deriv., derivative; equiv., equivalent; imit., imitative; obl., oblique; r., replacing; s., stem; sp., spelling, spelled; resp., respelling, respelled; trans., translation; ?, origin unknown; *, unattested; ‡, probably earlier than. See the full key inside the front cover.

op′tical pump′ing, *Physics, Optics.* a method for increasing the number of atoms or molecules occupying higher energy levels by irradiating them with light of the proper frequencies to raise them to those levels. [1950–55]

op′tical rota′tion, *Physical Chem.* the angle at which the plane of polarized light is rotated when passed through an optically active substance. [1890–95]

op′tical scan′ning, the process of interpreting data in printed, handwritten, bar-code, or other visual form by a device (**op′tical scan′ner** or **read′er**) that scans and identifies the data. Cf. **optical character recognition.** [1955–60]

op′tical sound′, *Motion Pictures.* sound recorded on and subsequently played back from an optical or photographic soundtrack, as opposed to a magnetic soundtrack. [1930–35]

op′tical sound′track, the final soundtrack on a motion picture, which appears as a band of black and white serrations along a strip of film to the left of the composite print. Light is shined through the serrations and is converted to audible sound. Also called **op′tical track′.**

op′tical tool′ing, the technique of establishing precise reference lines and planes by means of telescopic sights, esp. for the purpose of aligning machinery, machine-shop work, etc.

op′tical wedge′, a wedge-shaped filter whose transmittance decreases from one end to the other: used as an exposure control device in sensitometry. Also called **wedge.**

op′tic ax′is, *Crystall.* (in a crystal exhibiting double refraction) the direction or directions, uniaxial or biaxial, respectively, along which this phenomenon does not occur. [1655–65]

op′tic cen′ter. *Print.* See **optical center.**

op′tic chias′ma, a site at the base of the forebrain where the inner half of the fibers of the left and right optic nerves cross to the opposite side of the brain. Also, **op′tic chi′asm.** [1870–75]

op•ti•cian (op tish′ən), *n.* **1.** a person who makes or sells eyeglasses and, usually, contact lenses, for remedying defects of vision in accordance with the prescriptions of ophthalmologists and optometrists. **2.** a maker or seller of optical glass and instruments. [1680–90; < F *opticien* < ML *optic(a)* (see OPTICS) + F *-ien* -IAN]
—**Syn. 1.** See **eye doctor.**

op•ti•cist (op′tə sist), *n. Now Rare.* a person engaged in the fields of theoretical or applied optics. [1880–85, *Amer.;* OPTIC(S) + -IST]

op′tic nerve′, *Anat.* either one of the second pair of cranial nerves, consisting of sensory fibers that conduct impulses from the retina to the brain. See illus. under **eye.** [1605–15]

op•tics (op′tiks), *n.* (*used with a singular v.*) the branch of physical science that deals with the properties and phenomena of both visible and invisible light and with vision. [1605–15; < ML *optica* < Gk *optiká,* n. use of neut. pl. of *optikós;* see OPTIC, -ICS]

op•ti•mal (op′tə məl), *adj.* optimum (def. 3). [1885–90; OPTIM(UM) + -AL[1]] —**op′ti•mal•ly,** *adv.*

op•ti•me (op′tə mē′), *n.* (formerly at Cambridge University, England) a student taking second or third honors in the mathematical tripos. Cf. **wrangler** (def. 2). [1700–10; extracted from L phrase *optimē* (*disputasti*) (you have argued) very well]

op•ti•mism (op′tə miz′əm), *n.* **1.** a disposition or tendency to look on the more favorable side of events or conditions and to expect the most favorable outcome. **2.** the belief that good ultimately predominates over evil in the world. **3.** the belief that goodness pervades reality. **4.** the doctrine that the existing world is the best of all possible worlds. [1730–40; < F *optimisme* < L *optim(um)* (see OPTIMUM) + F *-isme* -ISM]
—**Syn. 1.** confidence, hopefulness, cheerfulness.
—**Ant. 1, 2.** pessimism, cynicism.

op•ti•mist (op′tə mist), *n.* **1.** an optimistic person. **2.** a person who holds the belief or the doctrine of optimism. [1760–70; < F *optimiste* < L *optim(um)* (see OPTIMUM) + F *-iste* -IST]

op•ti•mis•tic (op′tə mis′tik), *adj.* **1.** disposed to take a favorable view of events or conditions and to expect the most favorable outcome. **2.** reflecting optimism: *an optimistic plan.* **3.** of or pertaining to optimism. Also, **op′ti•mis′ti•cal.** [1840–50; OPTIMIST + -IC] —**op′ti•mis′ti•cal•ly,** *adv.*

op•ti•mi•za•tion (op′tə mə zā′shən), **1.** the fact of optimizing; making the best of anything. **2.** the condition of being optimized. **3.** *Math.* a mathematical technique for finding a maximum or minimum value of a function of several variables subject to a set of constraints, as linear programming or systems analysis. [1855–60; OPTIMIZE + -ATION]

op•ti•mize (op′tə mīz′), *v.,* **-mized, -miz•ing.** —*v.t.* **1.** to make as effective, perfect, or useful as possible. **2.** to make the best of. **3.** *Computers.* to write or rewrite (the instructions in a program) so as to maximize efficiency and speed in retrieval, storage, or execution. **4.** *Math.* to determine the maximum or minimum values of (a specified function that is subject to certain constraints). —*v.i.* **5.** to be optimistic. Also, *esp. Brit.,* **op′ti•mise′.** [1835–45; OPTIM(UM) + -IZE]

op•ti•mum (op′tə məm), *n., pl.* **-ma** (-mə), **-mums,** *adj.* —*n.* **1.** the best or most favorable point, degree, amount, etc., as of temperature, light, and moisture for the growth or reproduction of an organism. **2.** the greatest degree or best result obtained or obtainable under specific conditions. —*adj.* **3.** most favorable or desirable; best: *optimum conditions.* [1875–80; < L: n. use of neut. of *optimus* best, suppletive superl. of *bonus* good]
—**Syn. 3.** ideal, perfect, optimal.

op′timum pro′gramming, *Computers.* See **minimum access programming.**

op•tion (op′shən), *n.* **1.** the power or right of choosing. **2.** something that may be or is chosen; choice. **3.** the act of choosing. **4.** an item of equipment or a feature that may be chosen as an addition to or replacement for standard equipment and features: *a car with a long list of extra-cost options; a telephoto lens option for a camera.* **5.** See **stock option. 6.** a privilege acquired, as by the payment of a premium or consideration, of demanding, within a specified time, the carrying out of a transaction upon stipulated terms; the right, as granted in a contract or by an initial payment, of acquiring something in the future: *We bought one lot and took a 90-day option on an adjoining one.* **7.** *Football.* a play in which a back has a choice of either passing or running with the ball. —*v.t.* **8.** to acquire or grant an option on: *The studio has optioned his latest novel for film adaptation.* **9.** to provide with optional equipment: *The car can be fully optioned at additional cost.* [1595–1605; < L *optiōn-* (s. of *optiō*) choice, equiv. to *opt(āre)* to select (see OPT) + *-iōn-* -TION] —**op′tion•a•ble,** *adj.*
—**Syn. 2.** See **choice. 2, 3.** selection, election.

op•tion•al (op′shə nl), *adj.* **1.** left to one's choice; not required or mandatory: *Formal dress is optional.* **2.** leaving something to choice. [1755–65; OPTION + -AL[1]] —**op′tion•al′i•ty,** *n.* —**op′tion•al•ly,** *adv.*
—**Syn. 1.** discretional, elective, voluntary.

op•tion•ee (op′shə nē′), *n.* a person who acquires or holds a legal option. [OPTION + -EE]

opto-, a combining form meaning "optic" or "vision," used in the formation of compound words: *optometry.* [< Gk *optós* visible; akin to *ṓps* face; cf. EYE]

op•to•e•lec•tron•ics (op′tō i lek tron′iks, -ē′lek-), *n.* (*used with a singular v.*) the branch of electronics dealing with devices that generate, transform, transmit, or sense optical, infrared, or ultraviolet radiation, as cathode-ray tubes, electroluminescent and liquid crystal displays, lasers, and solar cells. [1955–60; OPTO- + ELECTRONICS] —**op′to•e•lec•tron′ic,** *adj.*

op•tom•e•ter (op tom′i tər), *n.* any of various instruments for measuring the refractive error of an eye. [1730–40; OPTO- + -METER]

op•tom•e•trist (op tom′i trist), *n.* a licensed professional who practices optometry. [1900–05; OPTOMETR(Y) + -IST]
—**Syn.** See **eye doctor.**

op•tom•e•try (op tom′i trē), *n.* the practice or profession of examining the eyes, by means of suitable instruments or appliances, for defects in vision and eye disorders in order to prescribe corrective lenses or other appropriate treatment. [1890–95; OPTO- + -METRY] —**op•to•met•ri•cal** (op′tə me′tri kəl), *adj.*

op•to•phone (op′tə fōn′), *n.* an electronic device that scans ordinary printed characters and produces combinations of sounds, enabling a blind reader to recognize the characters. [OPTO- + -PHONE]

op•to•type (op′tə tīp′), *n. Ophthalm.* type used on an eye chart. [1885–90; OPTO- + -TYPE]

op•u•lence (op′yə ləns), *n.* **1.** wealth, riches, or affluence. **2.** abundance, as of resources or goods; plenty. **3.** the state of being opulent. Also, **op′u•len•cy.** [1500–10; < L *opulentia* wealth. See OPULENT, -ENCE]

op•u•lent (op′yə lənt), *adj.* **1.** characterized by or exhibiting opulence: *an opulent suite.* **2.** wealthy, rich, or affluent. **3.** richly supplied; abundant or plentiful: *opulent sunshine.* [1595–1605; < L *opulentus* wealthy, equiv. to *op-* (s. of *ops* power, wealth) + *-ulentus* -ULENT] —**op′u•lent•ly,** *adv.*
—**Syn. 1.** sumptuous, luxurious. —**Ant. 1.** poor; squalid.

o•pus (ō′pəs), *n., pl.* **o•pus•es** or, esp. for 1, 2, **o•pe•ra** (ō′pər ə, op′ər ə). **1.** a musical composition. **2.** one of the compositions of a composer, usually numbered according to the order of publication. **3.** a literary work or composition, as a book: *Have you read her latest opus? Abbr.:* op. [1695–1705; < L: work, labor, a work]

o•pus•cule (ō pus′kyōōl), *n.* **1.** a small or minor work. **2.** a literary or musical work of small size. [1650–60; < F < L *opusculum,* equiv. to *opus* work + *-culum* -CULE[1]] —**o•pus′cu•lar,** *adj.*

o•pus•cu•lum (ō pus′kyə ləm), *n., pl.* **-la** (-lə). opuscule.

-opy, var. of **-opia.**

o•quas•sa (ō kwas′ə, ō kwä′sə), *n., pl.* **-sas,** (*esp. collectively*) **-sa.** a small, dark-blue brook trout, *Salvelinus oquassa,* of Maine. [1880–85; < Eastern Abenaki *àkʷəsse*]

or[1] (ôr; *unstressed* ər), *conj.* **1.** (used to connect words, phrases, or clauses representing alternatives): *books or magazines; to be or not to be.* **2.** (used to connect alternative terms for the same thing): *the Hawaiian, or Sandwich, Islands.* **3.** (used in correlation): *either . . . or; or . . . or; whether . . . or.* **4.** (used to correct or rephrase what was previously said): *His autobiography, or rather memoirs, will soon be ready for publication.* **5.** otherwise; or else: *Be here on time, or we'll leave without you.* **6.** *Logic.* the connective used in disjunction. [1150–1200; ME, orig. the second, unstressed member of correlative *other . . . or,* earlier *other . . . other,* OE *āther . . . oththe, ā-hwæther . . . oththe,* for *oththe . . . oththe* either . . . or; cf. AY[1], WHETHER]
—**Usage.** See **and/or, either.**

or[2] (ôr), *prep., conj. Chiefly Irish, Scot., and Eng.* before; ere. [bef. 950; ME, OE *ār* soon, early; c. ON *ár,* Goth *air* early; cf. OE *ǣr* soon, before, ERE]

or[3] (ôr), *Heraldry.* —*n.* **1.** the tincture, or metal, gold: represented either by gold or by yellow. —*adj.* **2.** of the tincture, or metal, gold: *a lion or.* [1400–50; late ME < MF < L *aurum* gold]

OR, 1. *Law.* on (one's own) recognizance. **2.** operating room. **3.** operations research. **4.** Oregon (approved esp. for use with zip code). **5.** owner's risk.

-or[1], a suffix occurring in loanwords from Latin, directly or through Anglo-French, usually denoting a condition or property of things or persons, sometimes corresponding to qualitative adjectives ending in **-id**[4] (*ardor; honor; horror; liquor; pallor; squalor; torpor; tremor*); a few other words that originally ended in different suffixes have been assimilated to this group (*behavior; demeanor; glamour*). [< L; in some cases continuing ME *-our* < AF, OF < L *-ōr-*, s. of *-or*, earlier *-os*]

—Usage. While the *-or* spelling of the suffix **-or**[1] is characteristic of American English, there are occasional exceptions, as in advertising copy, where spellings such as *colour* and *favour* seek to suggest the allure and exclusiveness of a product. The spelling *glamour* is somewhat more common than *glamor*—not actually an instance of **-or**[1], but conformed to it orthographically in the course of the word's history. In British English *-our* is still the spelling in most widespread use, *-or* being commonly retained when certain suffixes are added, as in *col*oration, *hon*orary, *hon*orific, *lab*orious, *od*oriferous. The English of the Southern Hemisphere (Australia, New Zealand, South Africa) tends to mirror British practice, whereas Canadian English shares with the U.S. a preference for *-or* but with *-our* spellings as freely used variants.

The suffix **-or**[2] is now spelled *-or* in all forms of English, with the exception of the word *savior*, often spelled *saviour* in the U.S. as well as in Britain, esp. with reference to Jesus.

-or[2], a suffix forming animate or inanimate agent nouns, occurring originally in loanwords from Anglo-French (*debtor; lessor; tailor; traitor*); it now functions in English as an orthographic variant of **-er**[1], usually joined to bases of Latin origin, in imitation of borrowed Latin words containing the suffix **-tor** (and its alternant *-sor*). The association with Latinate vocabulary may impart a learned look to the resultant formations, which often denote machines or other less tangible entities which behave in an agentlike way: *descriptor; plexor; projector; repressor; sensor; tractor.* [ME < AF, OF *-o(u)r* < L *-ōr-*, s. of *-or*, extracted from *-tōr* -TOR by construing the *t* as the ending of the ptp. (hence L *factor* maker, equiv. to *fac(ere)* to make + *-tor*, was analyzed as *fact(us)*, ptp. of *facere* + *-or*); merged with AF, OF *-ēo(u)r* < L *-ātōr-* -ATOR; cf. -EUR]

O.R., owner's risk.

o·ra[1] (ôr′ə, ōr′ə), *n.* pl. of **os**[2].

o·ra[2] (ôr′ə, ōr′ə), *n., pl.* **o·ras, o·rae** (ôr′ē, ōr′ē). a money of account of Anglo-Saxon England, introduced by the Danes and equal to about two shillings. [bef. 950; < OE *ōra* < ON pl. *aurar* monetary unit < L *aureus* AUREUS]

or·ach (ôr′əch, or′-), *n.* any plant of the genus *Atriplex*, esp. *A. hortensis*, of the goosefoot family, cultivated for use like spinach. Also, **or′ache.** [1350–1400; ME *orage, arage* < OF *arache* < VL **atripica*, var. of L *atriplic-* (s. of *atriplex*) << Gk *atráphaxys*]

or·a·cle (ôr′ə kəl, or′-), *n.* **1.** (esp. in ancient Greece) an utterance, often ambiguous or obscure, given by a priest or priestess at a shrine as the response of a god to an inquiry. **2.** the agency or medium giving such responses. **3.** a shrine or place at which such responses were given: *the oracle of Apollo at Delphi.* **4.** a person who delivers authoritative, wise, or highly regarded and influential pronouncements. **5.** a divine communication or revelation. **6.** any person or thing serving as an agency of divine communication. **7.** any utterance made or received as authoritative, extremely wise, or infallible. **8. oracles,** the Scriptures. **9.** the holy of holies of the Temple built by Solomon in Jerusalem. I Kings 6:16, 19–23. [1350–1400; ME < OF < L *ōrāculum*, equiv. to *ōrā(re)* to plead (see ORATION) + *-culum* -CLE[2]]

or′acle bones′, a group of inscribed animal bones and shells discovered in China and used originally in divination by the ancient Chinese, esp. during the Shang dynasty. [1910–15]

o·rac·u·lar (ô rak′yə lər, ō rak′-), *adj.* **1.** of the nature of, resembling, or suggesting an oracle: *an oracular response.* **2.** giving forth utterances or decisions as if by special inspiration or authority. **3.** uttered or delivered as if divinely inspired or infallible; sententious. **4.** ambiguous; obscure. **5.** portentous; ominous. [1625–35; < L *ōrācul(um)* ORACLE + -AR[1]] **—o·rac′u·lar·ly,** *adv.* **—o·rac·u·lar·i·ty** (ô rak′yə lar′i tē, ō rak′-), **o·rac′u·lar·ness,** *n.*

—Syn. 1. prophetic. **2.** authoritative, dogmatic. **4.** equivocal.

o·ra·cy (ôr′ə sē, ōr′-), *n.* the ability to express oneself in and understand spoken language. [1960–65; OR(AL) + (LITER)ACY]

o·rad (ôr′ad, ōr′-), *adv. Anat., Zool.* toward the mouth or the oral region. [1890–95; < L *ōr-* (s. of *ōs*) mouth + -AD[3]]

O·ra·dea (ô rä′dyä), *n.* a city in NW Rumania. 178,407. Also called **Ora′dea Ma′re** (mä′re). German, **Grosswardein.** Hungarian, **Nagyvárad.**

o·ral (ôr′əl, ōr′-), *adj.* **1.** uttered by the mouth; spoken: *oral testimony.* **2.** of, using, or transmitted by speech: *oral methods of language teaching; oral traditions.* **3.** of, pertaining to, or involving the mouth: *the oral cavity.* **4.** done, taken, or administered through the mouth: *an oral dose of medicine.* **5.** *Phonet.* articulated with none of the voice issuing through the nose, as the normal English vowels and the consonants *b* and *v.* **6.** *Psychoanal.* **a.** of or pertaining to the earliest phase of infantile psychosexual development, lasting from birth to one year of age or longer, during which pleasure is obtained from eating, sucking, and biting. **b.** of or pertaining to the sublimation of feelings experienced during the oral stage of childhood: *oral anxiety.* **c.** of or pertaining to gratification by stimulation of the lips or membranes of the mouth, as in sucking, eating, or talking. **7.** *Zool.* pertaining to that surface of polyps and marine animals that contains the mouth and tentacles. **—n. 8.** an oral examination in a school, college, or university, given esp. to a candidate for an advanced degree. [1615–25; < L *ōr-* (s. of *ōs*) mouth (c. Skt *āsya*) + -AL[1]] **—o·ral′i·ty,** *n.* **—o′ral·ly,** *adv.*

—Usage. 1. See **verbal.**

o′ral contracep′tive, *Pharm.* See **birth-control pill.** [1955–60]

o·ra·le (ô rä′lē, ō rä′-), *n. Eccles.* fanon (def. 2). [1835–45; < ML *ōrāle*, equiv. to L *ōr-* (s. of *ōs*) mouth + *-āle*, neut. of *-ālis* -AL[1]]

o′ral her′pes, *Pathol.* a disease caused by herpes simplex virus type 1, characterized primarily by a cluster of small, transient blisters chiefly at the edge of the lip or nostril; herpes labialis. Cf. **cold sore.**

o′ral his′tory, 1. information of historical or sociological importance obtained usually by tape-recorded interviews with persons whose experiences and memories are representative or whose lives have been of special significance. **2.** a book, article, recording, or transcription of such information. [1970–75] **—o′ral histo′rian.**

o′ral hy′giene, the state or practice of keeping the mouth cavity in a healthy condition, as by a regular program of brushing and flossing the teeth combined with periodic examinations by a dentist. Also called **dental hygiene.**

o′ral interpreta′tion, the study and practice of vocally expressing the meaning of written compositions, esp. of literature.

o·ral·ism (ôr′ə liz′əm, ōr′-), *n.* the theory, practice, or advocacy of education for the deaf chiefly or exclusively through lipreading, training in speech production, and training of residual hearing. Cf. **manualism.** [1880–85; ORAL + -ISM]

o·ral·ist (ôr′ə list, ōr′-), *n.* **1.** an advocate of oralism. **2.** a deaf person who communicates through lipreading and speech. **—adj. 3.** of or pertaining to oralism. Cf. **manualist.** [1865–70; ORAL + -IST]

o·ral·i·ty (ô ral′i tē, ō ral′-), *n. Psychoanal.* the condition or quality of being oral; collectively, the personality traits characteristic of the oral phase of psychosexual development. [1660–70; ORAL + -ITY]

o′ral sur′gery, 1. the branch of dentistry or of surgery dealing with the surgical treatment or repair of various conditions of the mouth or jaws. **2.** surgical treatment of any problematic or pathological condition of the mouth or jaws. **—o′ral sur′geon.**

-orama a combining form extracted from **panorama, diorama,** or **cyclorama,** occurring as the final element in compounds, often nonce words used in advertising or journalism. Though the semantic content of the compound is often lent solely by the initial element, the entire formation generally denotes a display or spectacle, or the space, such as a store or hall, containing these: *audiorama; scoutorama; smellorama.* Also, **-ama, -arama, -rama.**

O·ran (ô ran′, ō ran′; Fr. ô RäN′), *n.* a seaport in NW Algeria. 1,075,000.

o·rang (ô rang′, ō rang′), *n.* orangutan.

or·ange (ôr′inj, or′-), *n.* **1.** a globose, reddish-yellow, bitter or sweet, edible citrus fruit. **2.** any white-flowered, evergreen citrus trees of the genus *Citrus*, bearing this fruit, as *C. aurantium* **(bitter orange, Seville orange,** or **sour orange)** and *C. sinensis* **(sweet orange),** cultivated in warm countries. **3.** any of several other citrus trees, as the trifoliate orange. **4.** any of several trees or fruits resembling an orange. **5.** a color between yellow and red in the spectrum, an effect of light with a wavelength between 590 and 610 nm; reddish yellow. **6.** *Art.* a secondary color that has been formed by the mixture of red and yellow pigments. **—adj. 7.** of or pertaining to the orange. **8.** made or prepared with oranges or orangelike flavoring: *orange sherbet.* **9.** of the color orange; reddish-yellow. [1300–50; ME: the fruit or tree < OF *orenge*, c. Sp *naranja* < Ar *nāranj* < Pers *nārang* < Skt *nāraṅga*]

Or·ange (ôr′inj, or′-; *Fr.* ô RäNzh′ *for 3, 6*), *n.* **1.** a member of a European princely family ruling in the United Kingdom from 1688 to 1694 and in the Netherlands since 1815. **2.** a river in the Republic of South Africa, flowing W from Lesotho to the Atlantic. 1300 mi. (2095 km) long. **3.** a former small principality of W Europe: now in the SE part of France. **4.** a city in SW California, near Los Angeles. 91,788. **5.** a city in NE New Jersey, near Newark. 31,136. **6.** a town in SE France, near Avignon: Roman ruins. 26,468. **7.** a city in SE Texas. 23,628. **8.** a town in S Connecticut. 13,237. **9. Fort.** See **Fort Orange.**

orange III, *Chem.* See **methyl orange.**

or·ange·ade (ôr′inj ād′, -in jād′, or′-), *n.* a beverage consisting of orange juice, sweetener, and water, sometimes carbonated. [1700–10; < F; see ORANGE, -ADE[2]]

or′ange blos′som, 1. the white flower of an orange tree, esp. of the genus *Citrus*, much used in wreaths, bridal bouquets, etc.: the state flower of Florida. **2.** a cocktail made of gin, orange juice, and sugar, shaken together with ice. [1780–90]

Or·ange·burg (ôr′inj bûrg′, or′-), *n.* a city in central South Carolina. 14,933.

or′ange flow′er oil′. See **neroli oil.** [1830–40]

Or′ange Free′ State′, a province in central Republic of South Africa: a Boer republic 1854–1900; a British colony **(Or′ange Riv′er Col′ony)** 1900–10. 1,716,350. 49,647 sq. mi. (128,586 sq. km). *Cap.:* Bloemfontein.

or′ange hawk′weed, a European composite plant, *Hieracium aurantiacum*, having orange, dandelionlike flowers, growing as a weed, esp. in eastern North America. Also called **devil's paintbrush.** [1895–1900]

Or·ange·ism (ôr′in jiz′əm, or′-), *n.* the principles and practices of the Orangemen. [1815–25; ORANGE + -ISM] **—Or′ange·ist,** *n.*

or′ange lil′y, a bulbous lily, *Lilium bulbiferum*, of the mountainous regions of southern Europe, having erect, crimson-spotted, orange flowers. [1855–60]

Or·ange·man (ôr′inj mən, or′-), *n., pl.* **-men. 1.** a member of a secret society formed in the north of Ireland in 1795, having as its object the maintenance and political ascendancy of Protestantism. **2.** a Protestant of Northern Ireland. [1790–1800; ORANGE + -MAN]

Or′angemen's Day′, July 12, an annual celebration in Northern Ireland and certain cities having a large Irish section, esp. Liverpool, to mark both the victory of William III over James II at the Battle of the Boyne, July 1, 1690, and the Battle of Augbrim, July 12, 1690.

or′ange milk′weed. See **butterfly weed** (def. 1).

Or′ange Moun′tains, former name of **Jayawijaya.**

or′ange pe′koe, 1. a black tea composed of the smallest top leaves and grown in India and Ceylon. **2.** any India or Ceylon tea of good quality. [1875–80]

or′ange rust′, *Plant Pathol.* a disease of blackberries and raspberries, characterized by an orange, powdery mass of spores on the undersides of the leaves and stunted, misshapen foliage, caused by a rust fungus, *Gymnoconia interstitialis.*

or·ange·ry (ôr′inj rē, or′-), *n., pl.* **-ries.** a warm place, as a greenhouse, in which orange trees are cultivated in cool climates. [1655–65; < F *orangerie*, equiv. to *orang(er)* orange tree (deriv. of *orange* ORANGE) + *-erie* -ERY]

or′ange stick′, a slender, rounded stick, originally of orangewood, having tapered ends and used in manicuring, esp. to push back the cuticles or clean the fingernails. [1910–15, *Amer.*]

or′ange sul′fur. See **alfalfa butterfly.**

Or·ange·vale (ôr′inj vāl′, or′-), *n.* a town in central California, near Sacramento. 20,585.

Or·ange·ville (ôr′inj vil′, or′-), *n.* a town in SE Ontario, in S Canada. 13,740.

or·ange·wood (ôr′inj wŏŏd′, or′-), *n.* the hard, fine-grained, yellowish wood of the orange tree, used in inlaid work and fine turnery. [1880–85; ORANGE + WOOD[1]]

o·rang·u·tan (ô rang′ŏŏ tan′, ō rang′-, ə rang′-), *n.* a large, long-armed anthropoid ape, *Pongo pygmaeus*, of arboreal habits, inhabiting Borneo and Sumatra: an endangered species. Also, **o·rang′-u·tan′, o·rang·u·tang, o·rang·ou·tang** (ô rang′ŏŏ tang′, ō rang′-, ə rang′-). Also called **orang.** [1690–1700; < NL, D *orang outang*, appar. < pidgin or bazaar Malay: lit., forest man (Malay *orang* man, person + *(h)utan* forest]

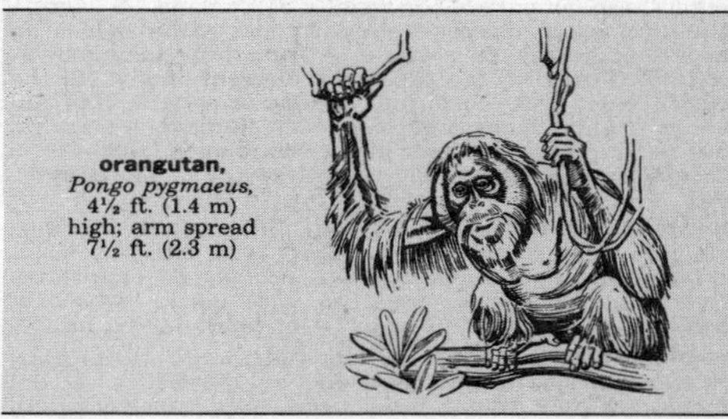

orangutan, *Pongo pygmaeus,* 4½ ft. (1.4 m) high; arm spread 7½ ft. (2.3 m)

or·ang·y (ôr′in jē, or′-), *adj.* resembling or suggesting an orange, as in taste, appearance, or color: *decorated with orangy-pink flowers.* Also, **or′ang·ey, or′ang·ish.** [1770–80; ORANGE + -Y[1]]

O·ran·i·an (ô rā′nē ən, ō rā′-), *adj.* Ibero-Maurusian. [presumably < F *oranien*, equiv. to *Oran*, seaport in NW Algeria + *-ien* -IAN]

o·rans (ôr′anz, ōr′-), *n., pl.* **o·ran·tes** (ô ran′tēz, ō ran′-), orant.

o·rant (ôr′ənt, ōr′-), *n. Fine Arts.* a representation of a female figure, with outstretched arms and palms up in a gesture of prayer, in outward and early Christian art. Also, **o·ran·te** (ô ran′tē, ō ran′-), **orans.** [1895–1900; < ML *ōrant-* (s. of *ōrāns*), prp. of *ōrāre* to plead. See ORATION, -ANT]

o·ra pro no·bis (ôr′ä prō nō′bis, ōr′ä), *Latin.* pray for us.

o·rar·i·on (ə râr′ē ən), *n., pl.* **o·rar·i·a** (ə râr′ē ə). *Eastern Ch.* a stole worn by deacons. Also, **orarium.** [1700–10; < MGk *ōrárion* < LL *ōrārium*, L: napkin, equiv. to *ōr-* (s. of *ōs*) mouth + *-ārium* -ARY]

o·rar·i·um (ə râr′ē əm), *n., pl.* **o·rar·i·a** (ə râr′ē ə). orarion.

o·rate (ô rāt′, ō rāt′, ôr′āt, ōr′āt), *v.i., v.t.,* **-rat·ed, -rat·ing.** to deliver an oration; speak pompously; declaim. [1590–1600; back formation from ORATION]

o·ra·te fra·tres (ō rä′te frä′tres), *Rom. Cath. Ch.* the call to prayer, addressed by the celebrant of the Mass to the people just before the Secret. [< L *ōrāte frātrēs* pray, brothers]

o·ra·tion (ô rā′shən, ō rā′-), *n.* **1.** a formal public speech, esp. one delivered on a special occasion, as on an anniversary, at a funeral, or at academic exercises. **2.** a public speech characterized by a studied or elevated style, diction, or delivery. [1325–75; ME *oracion* < L *ōrātiōn-* (s. of *ōrātiō*) speech, prayer, equiv. to *ōrāt(us)* (ptp. of *ōrāre* to plead, deriv. of *ōr-*, s. of *ōs* mouth) + *-iōn-* -ION]

—Syn. 1. See **speech. 2.** discourse, declamation.

or·a·tor (ôr′ə tər, or′-), *n.* **1.** a person who delivers an oration; a public speaker, esp. one of great eloquence: *Demosthenes was one of the great orators of ancient Greece.* **2.** *Law.* a plaintiff in a case in a court of equity.

CONCISE PRONUNCIATION KEY: act, cāpe, dâre, pärt; set, ēqual; if, īce; ox, ōver, ôrder, oil, bŏŏk, bōōt, out; up, ûrge; child; sing; shoe; thin, *th*at; zh as in *treasure.* ə = *a* as in *alone*, *e* as in *system*, *i* as in *easily*, *o* as in *gallop*, *u* as in *circus*; ᵊ as in *fire* (fīᵊr), *hour* (ouᵊr). l and n can serve as syllabic consonants, as in *cradle* (krād′l), and *button* (but′n). See the full key inside the front cover.

[1325–75; < L *ōrātor* speaker, suppliant, equiv. to *ōrā(re)* (see ORATION) + *-tor* -TOR; r. ME *oratour* < AF < L, as above] **—or′a·tor·like′,** *adj.* **—or′a·tor·ship′,** *n.*

Or·a·to·ri·an (ôr′ə tôr′ē ən, -tōr′-, or′-), *Rom. Cath. Ch.* —*n.* **1.** a member of an Oratory. —*adj.* **2.** of or pertaining to the Oratorians. [1635–45; ORATORY[2] + -AN]

or·a·tor·i·cal (ôr′ə tôr′i kəl, or′ə tor′-), *adj.* **1.** of, pertaining to, or characteristic of an orator or oratory: *His oratorical prowess has led to political success.* **2.** given to oratory: *an oratorical speaker.* [1610–20; ORATOR, ORATOR(Y)[1] + -ICAL] **—or′a·tor′i·cal·ly,** *adv.*

or·a·to·ri·o (ôr′ə tôr′ē ō′, -tōr′-, or′-), *n., pl.* **-ri·os.** an extended musical composition with a text more or less dramatic in character and usually based upon a religious theme, for solo voices, chorus, and orchestra, and performed without action, costume, or scenery. [1625–35; < It: small chapel < LL *ōrātōrium* ORATORY[2]; so named from the musical services in the church of the Oratory of St. Philip Neri in Rome]

or·a·to·ry[1] (ôr′ə tôr′ē, -tōr′ē, or′-), *n.* **1.** skill or eloquence in public speaking: *The evangelist moved thousands to repentance with his oratory.* **2.** the art of public speaking, esp. in a formal and eloquent manner. [1580–90; < L *ōrātōria,* n. use of fem. of *ōrātōrius* of an orator. See ORATOR, -TORY[1]]
—Syn. 1. rhetoric, delivery, declamation.

or·a·to·ry[2] (ôr′ə tôr′ē, -tōr′ē, or′-), *n., pl.* **-ries. 1.** a place of prayer, as a small chapel or a room for private devotions. **2.** (*cap.*) *Rom. Cath. Ch.* any of the religious societies of secular priests who live in religious communities but do not take vows. [1300–50; ME < LL *ōrātōrium* place of prayer. See ORATOR, -TORY[2]]

or·a·trix (ôr′ə triks, or′-), *n., pl.* **or·a·tri·ces** (ôr′ə trī′sēz, or′-). a woman who delivers an oration; a public speaker, esp. one of great eloquence. Also, **or·a·tress** (ôr′ə tris, or′-). [1425–75; late ME < L *ōrātrīx,* fem. of *ōrātor* ORATOR; see -TRIX]
—Usage. See **-trix.**

orb (ôrb), *n.* **1.** a sphere or globe: *a Christmas tree hung with brightly colored orbs.* **2.** the eyeball or eye: *He looks with blind orbs on an indifferent world.* **3.** any of the heavenly bodies, as the sun or moon: *He lay on the grass, warmed by that orb of day, the sun.* **4.** a globe bearing a cross; the mound or emblem of sovereignty, esp. as part of the regalia of England. **5.** *Astrol.* the number of degrees from exactness within which an aspect operates. **6.** a circle or something circular. **7.** *Astron.* (formerly) the orbit of a heavenly body. **8.** the earth. —*v.t.* **9.** to form into a circle or sphere. **10.** *Archaic.* to encircle; enclose. —*v.i.* **11.** to move in an orbit. **12.** to form into an orb or globe; round out. [1520–30; < L *orbis* circle, disk, orb] **—orb′less,** *adj.* **—orb′like′,** *adj.*

or·bic·u·lar (ôr bik′yə lər), *adj.* like an orb; circular; ringlike; spherical; rounded. [1375–1425; late ME < LL *orbiculāris* circular, equiv. to L *orbicul(us)* small disk (*orbi(s)* ORB + *-culus* -CULE[1]) + *-āris* -AR[1]] **—or·bic′u·lar′i·ty, or·bic′u·lar·ness,** *n.* **—or·bic′u·lar·ly,** *adv.*

or·bic·u·late (ôr bik′yə lit, -lāt′), *adj.* orbicular; rounded. Also, **or·bic′u·lat′ed.** [1750–60; < L *orbiculātus* gone round in a circle (ptp. of *orbiculārī*), equiv. to *orbicul(us)* small disk (see ORBICULAR) + *-ātus* -ATE[1]] **—or·bic′u·late·ly,** *adv.* **—or·bic′u·la′tion,** *n.*

or·bit (ôr′bit), *n.* **1.** the curved path, usually elliptical, described by a planet, satellite, spaceship, etc., around a celestial body, as the sun. **2.** the usual course of one's life or range of one's activities. **3.** the sphere of power or influence, as of a nation or person: *a small nation in the Russian orbit.* **4.** *Physics.* (in Bohr theory) the path traced by an electron revolving around the nucleus of an atom. **5.** an orb or sphere. **6.** *Anat.* **a.** the bony cavity of the skull that contains the eye; eye socket. **b.** the eye. **7.** *Zool.* the part surrounding the eye of a bird or insect. —*v.t.* **8.** to move or travel around in an orbital or elliptical path: *The earth orbits the sun once every 365.25 days.* **9.** to send into orbit, as a satellite. —*v.i.* **10.** to go or travel in an orbit. [1350–1400; ME < L *orbita* wheel track, course, circuit] **—or′bit·ar′y,** *adj.*

or·bit·al (ôr′bi tl), *adj.* **1.** of or pertaining to an orbit. —*n.* **2.** *Physics, Chem.* **a.** a wave function describing the state of a single electron in an atom **(atomic orbital)** or in a molecule **(molecular orbital). b.** the electron in that state. [1535–45; < NL, ML *orbitālis;* see ORBIT, -AL[1]]

or′bital an′gular momen′tum, *Physics.* the component of angular momentum of an electron in an atom or a nucleon in a nucleus, arising from its orbital motion rather than from its spin.

or·bi·ta·le (ôr′bi tā′lē), *n.* *Craniom., Cephalom.* the lowermost point on the lower margin of the left orbit, located instrumentally on the skull or by palpation on the head. [1915–20; < NL, ML *orbitāle,* neut. of *orbitālis* ORBITAL]

or′bital in′dex, *Craniom.* the ratio of the maximum breadth to the maximum height of the orbital cavity multiplied by 100. [1875–80]

or′bital quan′tum num′ber, *Physics.* See **azimuthal quantum number.**

or′bital sand′er, a sander that uses a section of sandpaper clamped to a metal pad that moves at high speed in a very narrow orbit, driven by an electric motor. Cf. **belt sander, disk sander.**

or′bital veloc′ity, the minimum velocity at which a body must move to maintain a given orbit. Cf. **circular velocity.**

or·bit·er (ôr′bi tər), *n.* *U.S. Aerospace.* **1.** Also called **space shuttle orbiter.** the crew- and payload-carrying component of the space shuttle. **2.** a space probe designed to orbit a planetary body or moon. Cf. **lander.** [1950–55, *Amer.;* ORBIT + -ER[1]]

Or′biting Astronom′ical Observ′atory. See **OAO.**

Or′biting Geophys′ical Observ′atory. See **OGO.**

Or′biting So′lar Observ′atory. See **OSO.**

orb′ weav′er, any of numerous spiders of the family Argiopidae, characterized by loosely woven, spiraling webs that have support lines radiating outward from the center. [1885–90]

orb·y (ôr′bē), *adj.,* **orb·i·er, orb·i·est.** *Archaic.* like or pertaining to an orb. [1605–15; ORB + -Y[1]]

orc (ôrk), *n.* **1.** any of several cetaceans, as a grampus. **2.** a mythical monster, as an ogre. [1510–20; < L *orca*]

O.R.C., Officers' Reserve Corps.

or·ca (ôr′kə), *n.* the killer whale, *Orcinus orca.* [1865–70; < NL, L; see ORC]

or·ce·in (ôr′sē in), *n.* *Chem.* a red dye, the principal coloring matter of cudbear and orchil, obtained by oxidizing an ammoniacal solution of orcinol. [1830–40; arbitrary alter. of *orcin;* see ORCINOL]

orch., orchestra.

or·chard (ôr′chərd), *n.* **1.** an area of land devoted to the cultivation of fruit or nut trees. **2.** a group or collection of such trees. [bef. 900; ME *orch(i)ard,* OE *orceard;* r. *ortyard,* ME *ortyerd,* OE *ortigeard* (cf. Goth *aurtigards* garden), equiv. to *ort-* (comb. form akin to WORT[2]; later identified with L *hortus* garden) + *geard* YARD[2]]

or′chard grass′, a weedy grass, *Dactylis glomerata,* often grown for pastures. Also called **cock's foot.** [1755–65]

or·chard·ist (ôr′chər dist), *n.* a person who owns, manages, or cultivates an orchard. [1785–95; ORCHARD + -IST]

or′chard o′riole, a North American oriole, *Icterus spurius,* the male of which is chestnut and black. [1800–10, *Amer.*]

or′chard valve′, an alfalfa valve of lesser diameter than the pipe it closes.

or·chec·to·my (ôr kek′tə mē), *n., pl.* **-mies.** *Surg.* orchiectomy.

or·ches·tra (ôr′kə strə), *n.* **1.** a group of performers on various musical instruments, including esp. stringed instruments of the viol class, clarinets and flutes, cornets and trombones, drums, and cymbals, for playing music, as symphonies, operas, popular music, or other compositions. **2.** (in a modern theater) **a.** the space reserved for the musicians, usually the front part of the main floor **(or′chestra pit′). b.** the entire main-floor space for spectators. **c.** the parquet. **3.** (in the ancient Greek theater) the circular space in front of the stage, allotted to the chorus. **4.** (in the Roman theater) a similar space reserved for persons of distinction. [1590–1600; < L *orchēstra* < Gk *orchḗstra* the space on which the chorus danced, deriv. of *orcheîsthai* to dance]

or·ches·tral (ôr kes′trəl), *adj.* **1.** of, pertaining to, or resembling an orchestra. **2.** composed for or performed by an orchestra: *orchestral works.* [1805–15; ORCHESTR(A) + -AL[1]] **—or·ches′tral·ly,** *adv.*

or·ches·trate (ôr′kə strāt′), *v.t., v.i.,* **-trat·ed, -trat·ing. 1.** to compose or arrange (music) for performance by an orchestra. **2.** to arrange or manipulate, esp. by means of clever or thorough planning or maneuvering: *to orchestrate a profitable trade agreement.* [1875–80; < F *orchestr(er)* (deriv. of *orchestre* ORCHESTRA) + -ATE[1]] **—or′ches·tra′tion,** *n.* **—or′ches·tra′tor, or′ches·trat′er,** *n.*

or·ches·tri·on (ôr kes′trē ən), *n.* a mechanical musical instrument, resembling a barrel organ but more elaborate, for producing the effect of an orchestra. [1830–40; ORCHESTR(A) + *-ion,* as in *accordion*]

orchi-, var. of **orchido-.**

or·chid (ôr′kid), *n.* **1.** any terrestrial or epiphytic plant of the family Orchidaceae, of temperate and tropical regions, having usually showy flowers. Cf. **orchid family. 2.** the flower of any of these plants. **3.** a bluish to reddish purple. [1835–45; < NL *Orchideae* (later *Orchidaceae*) family name, equiv. to L *orch(is)* a plant (see ORCHIS) + *-ideae,* irreg. suffix (cf. -IDAE); see -ID[2]]

orchid, genus *Cattleya*

orchid-, var. of **orchido-** before a vowel: *orchidology.*

or·chi·da·ceous (ôr′ki dā′shəs), *adj.* belonging to the plant family Orchidaceae. Cf. **orchid family.** [1830–40; < NL *Orchidace(ae)* (see ORCHID, -ACEAE) + -OUS]

or′chid cac′tus, epiphyllum.

or·chi·dec·to·my (ôr′ki dek′tə mē), *n., pl.* **-mies.** *Surg.* orchiectomy.

or′chid fam′ily, the plant family Orchidaceae, characterized by terrestrial or epiphytic herbaceous plants having simple, parallel-veined, usually alternate leaves, complex and often large and showy flowers pollinated primarily by insects, and fruit in the form of a capsule containing numerous minute seeds, and including calypso, fringed orchis, lady's-slipper, pogonia, rattlesnake plantain, vanilla, as well as numerous tropical orchids such as those of the genera *Cattleya, Cymbidium, Dendrobium, Phalaenopsis,* and *Vanda.*

orchido-, a combining form used, with the meaning "orchid," "testicle," in the formation of compound words: *orchidology; orchidotomy.* Also, **orchi-, orchid-.** [*orchid-* (erroneously taken as s. of Gk *órchis* ORCHIS; cf. ORCHID) + -O-]

or·chid·ol·o·gy (ôr′ki dol′ə jē), *n.* the branch of botany or horticulture dealing with orchids. [1880–85; ORCHIDO- + -LOGY] **—or′chid·ol′o·gist,** *n.*

or·chi·dot·o·my (ôr′ki dot′ə mē), *n., pl.* **-mies.** *Surg.* incision of a testis. Also, **orchotomy.** [1890–95; ORCHIDO- + -TOMY]

or′chid tree′, a tree, *Bauhinia variegata,* of the legume family, native to southeastern Asia, having lavender or purple flowers clustered in the leaf axils, cultivated in warm regions. Also called **mountain ebony.**

or·chi·ec·to·my (ôr′kē ek′tə mē), *n., pl.* **-mies.** *Surg.* excision of one or both testes; castration. Also, **orchectomy, orchidectomy.** [ORCHI- + -ECTOMY]

or·chil (ôr′kil, -chil), *n.* **1.** a violet coloring matter obtained from certain lichens, chiefly species of *Roccella.* **2.** any lichen yielding this dye. Also called **archil, orseille.** [1475–85; < OF]

or·chis (ôr′kis), *n.* **1.** any orchid. **2.** any of various terrestrial orchids, esp. of the genus *Orchis,* of temperate regions, having spikelike flowers. **3.** See **fringed orchis.** [1555–65; < L < Gk *órchis* testicle, plant with roots like testicles]

or·chi·tis (ôr kī′tis), *n.* *Pathol.* inflammation of the testis. Also, **or·chi·di·tis** (ôr′ki dī′tis). [1790–1800; < NL; see ORCHI-, -ITIS] **—or·chit·ic** (ôr kit′ik), *adj.*

or·chot·o·my (ôr kot′ə mē), *n., pl.* **-mies.** *Surg.* orchidotomy. [< Gk *órch(is)* testicle + -O- + -TOMY]

or·ci·nol (ôr′sə nôl′, -nol′), *n.* *Chem.* a white, crystalline, water-soluble solid, $C_7H_8O_2$, sweet but unpleasant in taste, that reddens on exposure to air: obtained from many lichens or produced synthetically and used chiefly as a reagent for certain carbohydrates. Also, **or·cin** (ôr′sin). [1875–80; < NL *orcin(a)* (< It *orcello* ORCHIL, by alter.) + -OL[2]]

OR′ cir′cuit (ôr), *Computers.* a circuit that is energized when any of its inputs are energized. Also called **OR gate.** [so called from the disjunctive operation of such circuits; see OR[1] (def. 6)]

Or·cus (ôr′kəs), *n.* **1.** the ancient Roman god of the underworld, identified with the Greek Pluto, or Hades. **2.** the ancient Roman underworld; Hades; Dis.

Or·czy (ôrt′sē), *n.* **Em·mus·ka** (em′mo͝osh ko), **Baroness,** 1865–1947, English novelist, born in Hungary.

ord., **1.** order. **2.** ordinal. **3.** ordinance. **4.** ordinary. **5.** ordnance.

or·dain (ôr dān′), *v.t.* **1.** to invest with ministerial or sacerdotal functions; confer holy orders upon. **2.** to enact or establish by law, edict, etc.: *to ordain a new type of government.* **3.** to decree; give orders for: *He ordained that the restrictions were to be lifted.* **4.** (of God, fate, etc.) to destine or predestine: *Fate had ordained the meeting.* —*v.i.* **5.** to order or command: *Thus do the gods ordain.* **6.** to select for or appoint to an office. **7.** to invest someone with sacerdotal functions. [1250–1300; ME *ordeinen* < OF *ordener* < L *ordināre* to order, arrange, appoint. See ORDINATION] **—or·dain′a·ble,** *adj.* **—or·dain′er,** *n.* **—or·dain′ment,** *n.*
—Syn. 3. order, prescribe, determine. **4.** predetermine.

or·dain·ee (ôr dā′nē, ôr′dā nē′), *n.* a person who has been recently ordained as a new member of the clergy. [ORDAIN + -EE]

or·deal (ôr dēl′, -dē′əl, ôr′dēl), *n.* **1.** any extremely severe or trying test, experience, or trial. **2.** a primitive form of trial to determine guilt or innocence by subjecting the accused person to fire, poison, or other serious danger, the result being regarded as a divine or preternatural judgment. [bef. 950; ME *ordal,* OE *ordāl;* c. D *oordeel,* G *Urteil.* See A-[3], DOLE[1]]

ordeal′ bean′. See **Calabar bean.** [1880–85; so called because it was allegedly administered as a test to persons suspected of witchcraft]

ordeal′ tree′, any of several trees having poisonous seeds, leaves, etc., used in primitive trials by ordeal.

or·der (ôr′dər), *n.* **1.** an authoritative direction or instruction; command; mandate. **2.** a command of a court or judge. **3.** a command or notice issued by a military organization or a military commander to troops, sailors, etc. **4.** the disposition of things following one after another, as in space or time; succession or sequence: *The names were listed in alphabetical order.* **5.** a condition in which each thing is properly disposed with reference to other things and to its purpose; methodical or harmonious arrangement: *You must try to give order to your life.* **6.** formal disposition or array: *the order of the troops.* **7.** proper, satisfactory, or working condition. **8.** state or condition generally: *His financial affairs were in good order.* **9.** conformity or obedience to law or established authority; absence of disturbance, riot, revolt, unruliness, etc.: *A police officer was there to maintain order.* **10.** customary mode of procedure; established practice or usage. **11.** the customary or prescribed mode of proceeding in debates or the like, or in the conduct of deliberative or legislative bodies, public meetings, etc.: *parliamentary rules of order.* **12.** prevailing course or arrangement of things; established system or regime: *The old order is changing.* **13.** conformity to this. **14.** a direction or commission to make, provide, or furnish something: *The salesclerk will take your order.* **15.** a quantity of goods or items purchased or sold: *The druggist is sending the order right over.* **16.** *Gram.* **a.** the arrangement of the elements of a construction in a particular sequence, as the placing of *John* before the verb and of *George* after it in *John saw George.* **b.** the hierarchy of grammatical rules applying to a construction. **c.** the rank of immediate constituents. **17.** any of the nine grades of angels in medieval angelology. Cf. **angel** (def. 1). **18.** *Math.* **a.** degree, as in algebra. **b.** the number of rows or columns of a square matrix or de-

terminant. **c.** the number of times a function has been differentiated to produce a given derivative: *a second order derivative.* **d.** the order of the highest derivative appearing in a given differential equation: $d^2y/dx^2 + 3y(dy/dx) - 6 = 0$ is a differential equation of order two. **e.** the number of elements of a given group. **f.** the smallest positive integer such that a given element in a group raised to that integer equals the identity. **g.** the least positive integer *n* such that permuting a given set *n* times under a given permutation results in the set in its original form. **19.** any class, kind, or sort, as of persons or things, distinguished from others by nature or character: *talents of a high order.* **20.** *Biol.* the usual major subdivision of a class or subclass in the classification of organisms, consisting of several families. **21.** a rank, grade, or class of persons in a community. **22.** a group or body of persons of the same profession, occupation, or pursuits: *the clerical order.* **23.** a body or society of persons living by common consent under the same religious, moral, or social regulations. **24.** *Eccles.* any of the degrees or grades of clerical office. Cf. **major order, minor order. 25.** a monastic society or fraternity: *the Franciscan order.* **26.** a written direction to pay money or deliver goods, given by a person legally entitled to dispose of it: *delivery order; exchange order.* **27.** *Archit.* **a.** any arrangement of columns with an entablature. **b.** any of five such arrangements typical of classical architecture, including the Doric, Ionic, and Corinthian orders invented by the Greeks and adapted by the Romans, the Tuscan order, invented by the Romans, and the Composite order, first named during the Renaissance. **c.** any of several concentric rings composing an arch, esp. when each projects beyond the one below. See illus. under **tympanum. 28. orders,** the rank or status of an ordained Christian minister. **29.** Usually, **orders.** the rite or sacrament of ordination. **30.** a prescribed form of divine service or of administration of a rite or ceremony. **31.** the service itself. **32.** the visible structures essential or desirable to the nature of the church, involving esp. ministry, polity, and sacraments. **33.** a society or fraternity of knights, of combined military and monastic character, as, in the Middle Ages, the Knights Templars. **34.** a modern organization or society more or less resembling the knightly orders: *fraternal orders.* **35.** *(cap.) Brit.* **a.** a special honor or rank conferred by a sovereign upon a person for distinguished achievement. **b.** the insignia worn by such persons. **36.** *Chiefly Brit.* a pass for admission to a theater, museum, or the like. **37. a tall order,** a very difficult or formidable task, requirement, or demand: *Getting the crop harvested with so few hands to help was a tall order.* Also, **a large order. 38. call to order,** to begin (a meeting): *The meeting was called to order at 3 o'clock.* **39. in order, a.** fitting; appropriate: *It appears that an apology is in order.* **b.** in a state of proper arrangement, preparation, or readiness: *Everything is in order for the departure.* **c.** correct according to the rules of parliamentary procedure: *Questions from the floor are now in order.* **40. in order that,** so that; to the end that: *We ought to leave early in order that we may not miss the train.* **41. in order to,** as a means to; with the purpose of: *She worked summers in order to save money for college.* **42. in short order,** with promptness or speed; rapidly: *The merchandise arrived in short order.* **43. on order,** ordered but not yet received: *We're out of stock in that item, but it's on order.* **44. on the order of, a.** resembling to some extent; like: *I would like a dress on the order of the one in the window.* **b.** approximately; about: *On the order of 100,000 people attended the rally.* **45. out of order, a.** inappropriate; unsuitable: *His remark was certainly out of order.* **b.** not operating properly; in disrepair: *The air conditioner is out of order again.* **c.** incorrect according to the rules of parliamentary procedure: *The chairwoman told him that he was out of order.* **46. to order,** according to one's individual requirements or instructions: *a suit made to order; carpeting cut to order.*
—*v.t.* **47.** to give an order, direction, or command to: *The infantry divisions were ordered to advance.* **48.** to direct or command to go or come as specified: *to order a person out of one's house.* **49.** to prescribe: *The doctor ordered rest for the patient.* **50.** to direct to be made, supplied, or furnished: *to order a copy of a book.* **51.** to regulate, conduct, or manage: *to order one's life for greater leisure.* **52.** to arrange methodically or suitably: *to order chessmen for a game.* **53.** *Math.* to arrange (the elements of a set) so that if one element precedes another, it cannot be preceded by the other or by elements that the other precedes. **54.** to ordain, as God or fate does. **55.** to invest with clerical rank or authority. —*v.i.* **56.** to give an order or issue orders: *I wish to order, but the waiter is busy.* [1175–1225; ME *ordre* (n.), *ordren* (v., deriv. of the n.) < OF *ordre* (n.) < L *ordin-* (s. of *ordō*) row, rank, regular arrangement] **—or′der•a•ble,** *adj.* **—or′der•er,** *n.* **—or′der•less,** *adj.*
—Syn. 1. ukase, ordinance, prescription, decree, injunction. **5.** regularity. **21.** degree. **23.** fraternity, community. **47.** instruct, bid, require, ordain. See **direct. 51.** run, operate, adjust, arrange, systematize.

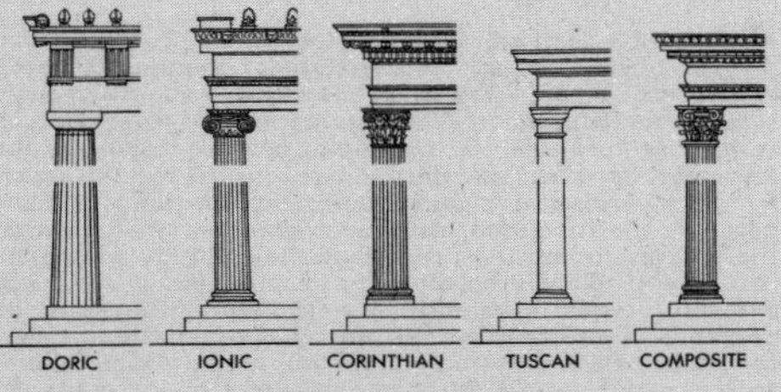

orders (def. 27b)

or′der arms′, 1. (in the manual of arms in close-order drill) a position in which the rifle is held at the right side, with its butt on the ground. **2.** (as an interjection) the command to move the rifle to this position. [1835–45]

or′der bill′ of lad′ing, a bill of lading that is issued to the order of a shipper or consignee for delivery of the goods and that can be transferred by endorsement to third parties. Cf. **straight bill of lading.**

or•dered (ôr′dərd), *adj.* **1.** neatly or conveniently arranged; well-organized: *an ordered office.* **2.** done according to specific principles or procedures: *an ordered method of assembling the parts.* **3.** conducted according to certain precepts or rules: *an ordered way of life.* [ORDER + -ED[2]] **—or′dered•ness,** *n.*

or′dered field′, *Math.* a field containing a subset of elements closed under addition and multiplication and having the property that every element in the field is either zero, in the subset, or has its additive inverse in the subset. [1940–45]

or′dered n-tu′ple, *Math.* See under **n-tuple.** [1960–65]

or′dered pair′, *Math.* two quantities written in such a way as to indicate that one quantity precedes or is to be considered before the other, as (3, 4) indicates the Cartesian coordinates of a point in the plane. [1950–55]

or•der•ly (ôr′dər lē), *adj., adv., n., pl.* **-lies.** *—adj.* **1.** arranged or disposed in a neat, tidy manner or in a regular sequence: *an orderly desk.* **2.** observant of or governed by system or method, as persons or the mind. **3.** characterized by or observant of law, rule, or discipline; well-behaved; law-abiding: *an orderly assemblage of citizens.* **4.** pertaining to or charged with the communication or execution of orders. *—adv.* **5.** methodically; regularly. **6.** according to established order or rule. *—n.* **7.** *Mil.* an enlisted soldier assigned to perform various chores for a commanding officer or group of officers. **8.** a hospital attendant having general, nonmedical duties. [1470–80 as adv.; 1570–80 as adj.; 1795–1805 as n.; ORDER + -LY] **—or′der•li•ness,** *n.*
—Syn. 1, 2. ORDERLY, METHODICAL, SYSTEMATIC characterize that which is neat, in order, and planned. These three words are sometimes used interchangeably. However, ORDERLY emphasizes neatness of arrangement: *an orderly array of books.* METHODICAL suggests a logical plan, a definite order of actions or method from beginning to end: *a methodical examination.* SYSTEMATIC suggests thoroughness, an extensive and detailed plan, together with regularity of action: *a systematic review.* **—Ant. 1.** chaotic, disorderly, haphazard.

or′derly mar′keting agree′ment, any of various formal arrangements by which the volume of certain imported commodities, as steel or textiles, is voluntarily reduced. *Abbr.:* OMA

or′derly of′ficer, *Mil.* officer of the day, as in the British army or, formerly, in the U.S. Army. [1765–75]

or′derly room′, the administrative office of a small military unit. [‡1975–80]

or′der of busi′ness, a task assigned or to be dealt with: *Our first order of business is to reduce expenses.* [1905–10]

or′der of the day′, 1. the agenda for an assembly, meeting, group, or organization. **2.** the activity or feature of primary importance: *Good cheer and celebrations will be the order of the day.* [1690–1700]

Or′der of the Gar′ter, the highest order of British knighthood, instituted by Edward III about 1348.

or′der port′, a port at which a merchant vessel calls for orders regarding the loading or discharge of cargo.

or•di•nal[1] (ôr′dn əl), *adj.* **1.** of or pertaining to an order, as of animals or plants. **2.** of or pertaining to order, rank, or position in a series. *—n.* **3.** an ordinal number or numeral. [1590–1600; < LL *ordinālis* in order, equiv. to L *ordin-* (s. of *ordō*) ORDER + *-ālis* -AL[1]] **—or′di•nal•ly,** *adv.*

or•di•nal[2] (ôr′dn əl), *n.* **1.** a directory of ecclesiastical services. **2.** a book containing the forms for the ordination of priests, consecration of bishops, etc. [1350–1400; ME < ML *ordināle,* n. use of neut. of *ordinālis* in order. See ORDINAL[1]]

or′dinal num′ber, 1. Also called **or′dinal nu′meral.** any of the numbers that express degree, quality, or position in a series, as *first, second,* and *third* (distinguished from *cardinal number*). **2.** *Math.* a symbol denoting both the cardinal number and the ordering of a given set, being identical for two ordered sets having elements that can be placed into one-to-one correspondence, the correspondence preserving the order of the elements. [1600–10]

or•di•nance (ôr′dn əns), *n.* **1.** an authoritative rule or law; a decree or command. **2.** a public injunction or regulation: *a city ordinance against excessive horn blowing.* **3.** something believed to have been ordained, as by a deity or destiny. **4.** *Eccles.* **a.** an established rite or ceremony. **b.** a sacrament. **c.** the communion. [1275–1325; ME *ordinaunce* (< OF *ordenance*) < ML *ordinantia,* deriv. of L *ordinant-* (s. of *ordināns*), prp. of *ordināre* to arrange. See ORDINATION, -ANCE]
—Syn. 1, 2. order.

or•di•nand (ôr′dn and′), *n. Eccles.* a candidate for ordination. [1835–45; < LL *ordinandus,* gerundive of *ordināre* to ORDAIN]

or•di•nar•i•ate (ôr′dn âr′ē it, -āt′), *n. Rom. Cath. Ch.* (formerly) a province in which the faithful of an Eastern rite were under the rule of a prelate of their rite who had no territorial jurisdiction. [ORDINARY (n.) + -ATE[1]]

or•di•nar•i•ly (ôr′dn âr′ə lē, ôr′dn er′ə lē), *adv.* **1.** most of the time; generally; usually: *Ordinarily he wakes at seven.* **2.** in an unexceptional manner or fashion; modestly: *a wealthy child who was dressed ordinarily.* **3.** to the usual extent; reasonably: *to expect someone to be ordinarily honest.* [1525–35; ORDINARY + -LY]

or•di•nar•y (ôr′dn er′ē), *adj., n., pl.* **-nar•ies.** *—adj.* **1.** of no special quality or interest; commonplace; unexceptional: *One novel is brilliant, the other is decidedly ordinary; an ordinary person.* **2.** plain or undistinguished: *ordinary clothes.* **3.** somewhat inferior or below average; mediocre. **4.** customary; usual; normal: *We plan to do the ordinary things this weekend.* **5.** *Chiefly South Midland and Southern U.S.* common, vulgar, or disreputable. **6.** (of jurisdiction) immediate, as contrasted with something that is delegated. **7.** (of officials) belonging to the regular staff or the fully recognized class. *—n.* **8.** the commonplace or average condition, degree, etc.: *ability far above the ordinary.* **9.** something regular, customary, or usual. **10.** *Eccles.* **a.** an order or form for divine service, esp. that for saying Mass. **b.** the service of the Mass exclusive of the canon. **11.** *Hist.* a member of the clergy appointed to prepare condemned prisoners for death. **12.** *Eng. Eccles. Law.* a bishop, archbishop, or other ecclesiastic or his deputy, in his capacity as an ex officio ecclesiastical authority. **13.** (in some U.S. states) a judge of a court of probate. **14.** *Brit.* (in a restaurant or inn) a complete meal in which all courses are included at one fixed price, as opposed to à la carte service. **15.** a restaurant, public house, or dining room serving all guests and customers the same standard meal or fare. **16.** a high bicycle of an early type, with one large wheel in front and one small wheel behind. **17.** *Heraldry.* **a.** any of the simplest and commonest charges, usually having straight or broadly curved edges. **b.** See **honorable ordinary. 18. in ordinary,** in regular service: *a physician in ordinary to the king.* **19. out of the ordinary, a.** exceptional; unusual: *Having triplets is certainly out of the ordinary.* **b.** exceptionally good; unusually good: *The food at this restaurant is truly out of the ordinary.* [1250–1300; ME *ordinarie* (n. and adj.) < L *ordinārius* regular, of the usual order, equiv. to *ordin-* (see ORDER) + *-ārius* -ARY] **—or′di•nar′i•ness,** *n.*
—Syn. 3. See **common. 4.** regular, accustomed. **—Ant. 1.** extraordinary, unusual.

or′dinary differen′tial equa′tion, *Math.* an equation containing derivatives but not partial derivatives. Cf. **partial differential equation.**

or′dinary in′come, taxable income, as salary and wages, other than capital gains.

or′dinary ju′bilee. See under **jubilee** (def. 5a).

or′di•nar•y-lan′guage philos′ophy (ôr′dn er′ē-lang′gwij). See **linguistic analysis.** [1955–60]

or′dinary life′ insur′ance, life insurance with premiums paid throughout the lifetime of the insured. Also called **straight life insurance, whole life insurance.**

or′dinary point′, *Math.* a point in a domain in which a given function of a complex variable is analytic. Cf. **singular point.**

or′dinary ray′, *Optics, Crystall.* the part of a doubly refracted ray whose velocity within a crystal is the same in any direction.

or′dinary sea′man, a seaman insufficiently skilled to be classified as an able-bodied seaman. *Abbr.:* O.D., O.S., o.s. [1695–1705]

or′dinary share′, *Brit.* a share of common stock. [1865–70]

or′dinary stock′, *Brit.* See **common stock.** [1865–70]

or′dinary wave′, *Radio.* (of the two waves into which a radio wave is divided in the ionosphere under the influence of the earth's magnetic field) the wave with characteristics more nearly resembling those that the undivided wave would have exhibited in the absence of the magnetic field. Cf. **extraordinary wave.**

or•di•nate (ôr′dn it′, -āt′), *n. Math.* (in plane Cartesian coordinates) the y-coordinate of a point: its distance from the x-axis measured parallel to the y-axis. Cf. **abscissa.** [1670–80; extracted from NL *(linea) ordināte (applicāta)* (line applied) in order; *ordināte* (adv.), deriv. of L *ordinātus* arranged. See ORDINATION]

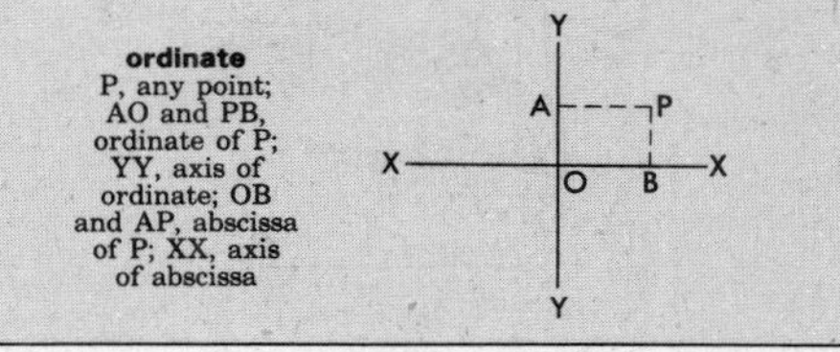

ordinate P, any point; AO and PB, ordinate of P; YY, axis of ordinate; OB and AP, abscissa of P; XX, axis of abscissa

or•di•na•tion (ôr′dn ā′shən), *n.* **1.** *Eccles.* the act or ceremony of ordaining. **2.** the fact or state of being ordained. **3.** a decreeing. **4.** the act of arranging. **5.** the resulting state; disposition; arrangement: *the ordination of animal species.* [1350–1400; ME *ordinacioun* < LL *ordinātiōn-* (s. of *ordinātiō*) ordainment, L: a putting in order, appointment, equiv. to *ordināt(us)* (ptp. of *ordināre* to order, arrange, deriv. of *ordō,* s. *ordin-,* order) + *-iōn-* -ION]

ordn., ordnance.

ord•nance (ôrd′nəns), *n.* **1.** cannon or artillery. **2.** military weapons of all kinds with their equipment, ammunition, etc. **3.** the branch of an army that procures, stores, and issues weapons, munitions, and combat vehicles and maintains arsenals for their development and testing. [1620–30; syncopated var. of ORDINANCE]

CONCISE PRONUNCIATION KEY: *act, cāpe, dâre, pärt; set, ēqual; if, īce; ox, ōver, ôrder, oil, bo͝ok, bo͞ot, out; up, ûrge; child; sing; shoe; thin, that;* zh as in *treasure.* ə = *a* as in *alone, e* as in *system, i* as in *easily, o* as in *gallop, u* as in *circus;* ′ as in *fire* (fīər), *hour* (ouər). l and n can serve as syllabic consonants, as in *cradle* (krād′l), and *button* (but′n). See the full key inside the front cover.

or·do (ôr′dō), *n., pl.* **or·di·nes** (ôr′dn ēz′). *Rom. Cath. Ch.* a booklet containing short and abbreviated directions for the contents of the office and Mass of each day in the year. [1840–50; < ML, L *ordō* series, row, order]

Or·dó·ñez (ôʀ tʜô′nyeth, -nyes), *n.* **An·to·nio** (än tô′nyô), born 1932, Spanish bullfighter.

or·don·nance (ôr′dn əns; *Fr.* ôʀ dô näɴs′), *n., pl.* **-don·nanc·es** (-dn ən siz; *Fr.* -dô näɴs′). **1.** arrangement or disposition of parts, as of a building, a picture, or a literary work. **2.** an ordinance, decree, or law. [1635–45; < F, alter. of OF *ordenance* ORDINANCE, by influence of *donner* to give] —**or′don·nant,** *adj.*

Or·do·vi·cian (ôr′də vish′ən), *Geol.* —*adj.* **1.** noting or pertaining to a period of the Paleozoic Era, from 500 to 425 million years ago, notable for the advent of fish. See table under **geologic time.** —*n.* **2.** the Ordovician Period or System. [1875–80; named after the *Ordovices* (pl.) (< L) an ancient British tribe in northern Wales; see -IAN]

or·dure (ôr′jər, -dyŏŏr), *n.* dung; manure; excrement. [1300–50; ME < OF, equiv. to *ord* filthy (< L *horridus* HORRID) + *-ure* -URE] —**or′dur·ous,** *adj.*

Or·dzho·ni·ki·dze (ôr′jon i kid′zə; *Russ.* uʀ jə nyi-kyē′dzyi), *n.* **1.** Also, **Orjonikidze.** former name of **Vladikavkaz. 2.** former name of **Yenakiyevo.**

ore (ôr, ōr), *n.* **1.** a metal-bearing mineral or rock, or a native metal, that can be mined at a profit. **2.** a mineral or natural product serving as a source of some nonmetallic substance, as sulfur. [bef. 900; conflation of two words: ME *ore* (with close *o*, giving obs. E *ure, our(e), oor(e)*), continuing OE *ōra* ore, unreduced metal; and ME *or(e)* (with open *o*, giving the present pron.) ore, metal, continuing OE *ār* brass (c. OS, OHG *ēr*, ON *eir*, Goth *aiz*; cf. L *aes* bronze, coin, money)]

ö·re (œ′ʀə), *n., pl.* **ö·re. 1.** a bronze coin of Norway, the 100th part of a krone. **2.** a zinc or bronze coin of Denmark, the 100th part of a krone. **3.** a bronze coin of Sweden, the 100th part of a krona. **4.** a fractional currency of the Faeroe Islands, the 100th part of a krona. Also, **ø·re** (œ′ʀə) (for defs. 1, 2). [1600–10; << L *aureus* a gold coin]

Ore., Oregon.

o·re·ad (ôr′ē ad′, ōr′-), *n. Class. Myth.* any of a group of mountain nymphs who were the companions of Artemis. [< L *Oreăd-* (s. of *Oreas*) < Gk *Oreiad-* (s. of *Oreiás*), n. use of *oreiás* of the mountains, equiv. to *órei-(os)* of the mountains (deriv. of *óros* mountain) + *-as* fem. patronymic suffix]

ore·bod·y (ôr′bod′ē, ōr′-), *n., pl.* **-bod·ies.** a well-defined mass of ore-bearing rock. [1870–75; ORE + BODY]

ore′ bridge′, a gantry crane used for transferring ore to and from stockpiles.

Ö·re·bro (œ′ʀə bʀŏŏ′), *n.* a city in S Sweden. 117,473.

o·rec·tic (ô rek′tik, ō rek′-), *adj. Philos.* of or pertaining to desire; appetitive. [1665–75; < Gk *orektikós* appetitive, equiv. to *orekt(ós)* stretched out, longed for (deriv. of *orégein* to grasp for, desire) + *-ikos* -IC]

ore′ dress′ing, *Metall.* the mechanical processes by which valuable minerals are separated from ore. [1860–65]

Oreg., Oregon.

o·reg·a·no (ə reg′ə nō′, ô reg′-), *n.* an aromatic herb, *Origanum vulgare,* of the mint family, having leaves used as seasoning in cooking. Also called **pot marjoram.** Cf. **marjoram.** [1765–75; < AmerSp *orégano*, Sp: wild marjoram < L *origanum.* See ORIGAN]

Or·e·gon (ôr′i gən, -gon′, or′-), *n.* **1.** a state in the NW United States, on the Pacific coast. 2,632,663. 96,981 sq. mi. (251,180 sq. km). *Cap.:* Salem. *Abbr.:* Oreg., Ore., OR (for use with zip code). **2.** a city in NW Ohio. 18,675. [1870–75] —**Or·e·go·ni·an** (ôr′i gō′nē ən, or′-), *adj., n.*

Or′egon ce′dar. See **Port Orford cedar.** [1870–75]

Or′egon Cit′y, a town in NW Oregon, on the Willamette River. 14,673.

Or′egon crab′ ap′ple, a shrub or small tree, *Malus fusca,* of the rose family, of the northwestern coast of North America, having hairy leaves, white flowers, and yellow or green oblong fruit.

Or′egon fir′. See **Douglas fir.** [1900–05]

Or′egon grape′, 1. an evergreen shrub, *Mahonia aquifolium,* of the barberry family, of the western coast of the U.S., having yellow flowers and small, blue, edible berries: the state flower of Oregon. **2.** the berry itself. [1850–55]

Or′egon ma′ple. See **bigleaf maple.**

CONCISE ETYMOLOGY KEY: <, descended or borrowed from; >, whence; b., blend of, blended; c., cognate with; cf., compare; deriv., derivative; equiv., equivalent; imit., imitative; obl., oblique; r., replacing; s., stem; sp., spelling, spelled; resp., respelling, respelled; trans., translation; ?, origin unknown; *, unattested; ‡, probably earlier than. See the full key inside the front cover.

Or′egon myr′tle. See **California laurel** (def. 2).

Or′egon pine′. See **Douglas fir.** [1835–45]

Or′egon Trail′, a route used during the westward migrations, esp. in the period from 1840 to 1860, starting in Missouri and ending in Oregon. ab. 2000 mi. (3200 km) long.

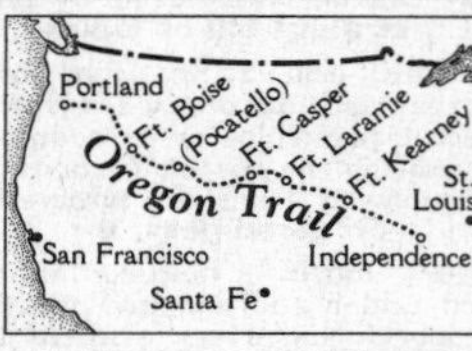

ore′ hearth′, a small blast furnace for smelting lead. Also called **Scotch furnace, Scotch hearth.** [1815–25]

o·re·ide (ôr′ē id′, ōr′-), *n. Metall.* oroide. [< F *oréide,* equiv. to *or* gold (< L *aurum*) + *-éide* (< Gk *-eidēs* having the form of, deriv. of *eîdos* form)]

O·re·kho·vo-Zu·ye·vo (ôr′ə kō′və zōō′ yev′ō; *Russ.* u ʀye′ᴋʜə və zōō′yi və), *n.* a city in the W Russian Federation in Europe, E of Moscow. 132,000.

O·rel (ô rel′, ō rel′; *Russ.* u ʀyôl′), *n.* a city in the W Russian Federation in Europe, on the left bank of the Oka River, S of Moscow. 335,000.

O·rem (ôr′əm, ōr′-), *n.* a city in N Utah. 52,399.

O·ren·burg (ôr′ən bûrg′, ōr′-; *Russ.* u ʀyin bŏŏʀᴋ′), *n.* a city in the SW Russian Federation in Asia, on the Ural River. 547,000. Formerly, **Chkalov.**

o·ren·da (ô ren′də, ō ren′-), *n.* a supernatural force believed by the Iroquois Indians to be present, in varying degrees, in all objects or persons, and to be the spiritual force by which human accomplishment is attained or accounted for. [1902; coined by U.S. ethnologist J.N.B. Hewitt from the supposed Huron cognate of Mohawk *orę̨·na*ʔ inherent power (akin to *karę̨·na*ʔ song; cf. Seneca *oęnǫ*ʔ power, song with power, *kaęnǫ*ʔ song)]

O·ren·se (ô ʀen′se), *n.* a city in N Spain, NW of Madrid. 73,379.

O·re·o (ôr′ē ō′, ōr′-), *n., pl.* **O·re·os.** *Slang (disparaging and offensive).* a black person who is regarded as having adopted the attitudes, values, and behavior thought to be characteristic of middle-class white society, often at the expense of his or her own heritage. Also, **o′re·o.** [1965–70, *Amer.*; from trademark name of a chocolate cookie with a white, cream filling]

Or·e·o·pith·e·cus (ôr′ē ō pith′i kəs, -pə thē′kəs, ōr′-), *n.* a genus of fossil primate from the Miocene coal deposits of Italy, formerly considered to be a possible hominid. [< NL < Gk *ore-* (s. of *óros*) hill, mountain + *-o-* *-o-* + *píthēkos* ape]

o·re ro·tun·do (ō′ʀe ʀō tŏŏn′dō; *Eng.* ôr′ē rō tun′dō, ōr′ē), *Latin.* with full, round voice.

ore·shoot (ôr′shōōt′, ōr′-), *n.* a rich concentration in an orebody. [1875–80; ORE + SHOOT]

O·res·te·ia (ôr′e stē′ə, ōr′-), *n.* a trilogy of tragic dramas (458 B.C.) by Aeschylus, consisting of the *Agamemnon,* the *Choëphori,* and the *Eumenides.*

O·res·tes (ô res′tēz, ō res′-), *n.* **1.** *Class. Myth.* the son of Agamemnon and Clytemnestra, and the brother of Electra and Iphigenia: he avenged the murder of Agamemnon by killing Clytemnestra and her lover, Aegisthus, then was pursued by the Furies until saved by Athena. **2.** (*italics*) a tragedy (408 B.C.) by Euripides.

Ores′tes com′plex, *Psychoanal.* an unconscious desire of a son to kill his mother.

Ö·re·sund (œ′ʀə sŏŏnd′), *n.* Swedish and Danish name of The Sound.

ore′ tank′er, a ship built to carry ore.

-orexia, a combining form meaning "desire," "appetite," as specified by the initial element: *anorexia.* [< Gk *-orexia.* See OREXIS, -IA]

o·rex·is (ô rek′sis, ō rek′-), *n. Psychol.* the affective and conative character of mental activity as contrasted with its cognitive aspect; the appetitive aspect of an act. [1610–20; < L: longing, appetite < Gk *órexis* desire, equiv. to *orég(ein)* to desire + *-sis* -SIS] —**o·rec·tic** (ô rek′tik, ō rek′-), *adj.*

Or·fe·o ed E·u·ri·di·ce (*It.* ôʀ fe′ô ed e ōō ʀē dē′che), an opera (1762), with music by Christoph Willibald von Gluck.

Orff (ôrf), *n.* **Carl,** 1895–1982, German composer, conductor, and music educator.

org., 1. organic. **2.** organization. **3.** organized.

or·gan (ôr′gən), *n.* **1.** Also called **pipe organ.** a musical instrument consisting of one or more sets of pipes sounded by means of compressed air, played by means of one or more keyboards, and capable of producing a wide range of musical effects. **2.** any of various similar instruments, as a reed organ or an electronic organ. **3.** a barrel organ or hand organ. **4.** *Biol.* a grouping of tissues into a distinct structure, as a heart or kidney in animals or a leaf or stamen in plants, that performs a specialized task. **5.** penis. **6.** a newspaper, magazine, or other means of communicating thoughts, opinions, etc., esp. in behalf of some organization, political group, or the like. **7.** an instrument or means, as of action or performance: *This committee will be the chief organ of administration.* **8.** *Archaic.* any of various musical instruments, esp. wind instruments. [bef. 1000; ME: musical instrument, pipe organ, organ of the body, tool (< ML, L *organum* mechanical device, instrument) < Gk *órganon* implement, tool, bodily organ, musical instrument, akin to *érgon* WORK]
—**Syn. 6.** publication, journal, instrument, channel.

or·ga·na[1] (ôr′gə nə), *n.* a pl. of **organon.**

or·ga·na[2] (ôr′gə nə), *n.* a pl. of **organum.**

or·gan·dy (ôr′gən dē), *n.* a fine, thin, cotton fabric usually having a durable crisp finish, white, dyed, or printed: used for blouses, dresses, curtains, trimmings, etc. Also, **or′gan·die.** [1825–35; < F *organdi,* of obscure orig.]

or·gan·elle (ôr′gə nel′, ôr′gə nel′), *n. Cell Biol.* a specialized part of a cell having some specific function; a cell organ. [1905–10; < NL *organella,* dim. of L *organum* ORGAN; see -ELLE]

or′gan grind′er, an itinerant street musician who earns a living by playing a hand organ or hurdy-gurdy. [1800–10]

or·gan·ic (ôr gan′ik), *adj.* **1.** noting or pertaining to a class of chemical compounds that formerly comprised only those existing in or derived from plants or animals, but that now includes all other compounds of carbon. Cf. **inorganic** (def. 3). **2.** characteristic of, pertaining to, or derived from living organisms: *organic remains found in rocks.* **3.** of or pertaining to an organ or the organs of an animal, plant, or fungus. **4.** of, pertaining to, or affecting living tissue: *organic pathology.* **5.** *Psychol.* caused by neurochemical, neuroendocrinologic, structural, or other physical impairment or change: *organic disorder.* Cf. **functional** (def. 5). **6.** *Philos.* having an organization similar in its complexity to that of living things. **7.** characterized by the systematic arrangement of parts; organized; systematic: *elements fitting together into a unified, organic whole.* **8.** of or pertaining to the constitution or structure of a thing; constitutional; structural: *The flaws in your writing are too organic to be easily remedied.* **9.** developing in a manner analogous to the natural growth and evolution characteristic of living organisms; arising as a natural outgrowth. **10.** viewing or explaining something as having a growth and development analogous to that of living organisms: *an organic theory of history.* **11.** pertaining to, involving, or grown with fertilizers or pesticides of animal or vegetable origin, as distinguished from manufactured chemicals: *organic farming; organic fruits.* **12.** *Law.* of or pertaining to the constitutional or essential law or laws organizing the government of a state. **13.** *Archit.* noting or pertaining to any work of architecture regarded as analogous to plant or animal forms in having a structure and a plan that fulfill perfectly the functional requirements for the building and that form in themselves an intellectually lucid, integrated whole. **14.** *Fine Arts.* of or pertaining to the shapes or forms in a work of art that are of irregular contour and seem to resemble or suggest forms found in nature. —*n.* **15.** a substance, as a fertilizer or pesticide, of animal or vegetable origin. [1350–1400; ME: pertaining to an organ of the body < L *organicus* by or employing a mechanical device, instrumental < Gk *organikós,* equiv. to *órgan(on)* ORGAN + *-ikos* -IC] —**or·gan′i·cal·ness, or·ga·nic·i·ty** (ôr′gə-nis′i tē), *n.*
—**Syn. 8.** inherent, fundamental, basic. —**Ant. 1.** inorganic.

or·gan·i·cal·ly (ôr gan′ik lē), *adv.* **1.** in an organic manner. **2.** by or with organs. **3.** with reference to organic structure. [1675–85; ORGANIC + -AL[1] + -LY]

organ′ic chem′istry, the branch of chemistry, originally limited to substances found only in living organisms, dealing with the compounds of carbon.

organ′ic disease′, *Pathol.* a disease in which there is a structural alteration (opposed to *functional disease*). [1835–45]

or·gan·i·cism (ôr gan′ə siz′əm), *n.* **1.** *Philos.* the view that some systems resemble organisms in having parts that function in relation to the whole to which they belong. Cf. **holism. 2.** *Pathol.* the doctrine that all symptoms arise from organic disease. **3.** a view of society as an autonomous entity analogous to and following the same developmental pattern as a biological organism. [1850–55; ORGANIC + -ISM] —**or·gan′i·cis′mal, or·gan′i·cis′tic,** *adj.* —**or·gan′i·cist,** *n.*

organ′ic solidar′ity, *Sociol.* social cohesiveness that is based on division of labor and interdependence and is characteristic of complex, industrial societies. Cf. **mechanical solidarity.**

or·gan·ism (ôr′gə niz′əm), *n.* **1.** a form of life composed of mutually interdependent parts that maintain various vital processes. **2.** any life form considered as an entity; an animal, plant, fungus, protistan, or moneran. **3.** any organized body or system conceived of as analogous to a living being: *the governmental organism.* **4.** any complex thing or system having properties and functions determined not only by the properties and relations of its individual parts, but by the character of the whole that they compose and by the relations of the parts to the whole. [1655–65; ORGAN + -ISM] —**or′gan·is′mic, or′gan·is′mal,** *adj.* —**or′gan·is′mi·cal·ly,** *adv.*
—**Syn. 4.** organization, network, entity, structure.

or·gan·ist (ôr′gə nist), *n.* a person who plays the organ. [1585–95; < ML *organista,* equiv. to *organ(um)* ORGAN + *-ista* -IST]

or·gan·i·za·tion (ôr′gə nə zā′shən), *n.* **1.** the act or process of organizing. **2.** the state or manner of being organized. **3.** something that is organized. **4.** organic structure; composition: *The organization of this painting is quite remarkable.* **5.** a group of persons organized for some end or work; association: *a nonprofit organization.* **6.** the administrative personnel or apparatus of a business. **7.** the functionaries of a political party along with the offices, committees, etc., that they fill. **8.** an organism. —*adj.* **9.** of or pertaining to an organization. **10.** *Informal.* conforming entirely to the standards, rules, or demands of an organization, esp. that of one's employer: *an organization mentality.* [1375–1425; late ME *organizacion* < ML *organizātiōn-* (s. of *organizātiō*), equiv. to *organizāt(us)* (ptp. of *organizāre;* see ORGANIZE, -ATE[2]) + *-iōn-* -ION] —**or′gan·i·za′tion·al,** *adj.* —**or′gan·i·za′tion·al·ly,** *adv.*

organiza′tion chart′, a diagrammatic representation showing how departments or divisions in an organization, as a large corporation, are related to one another along lines of authority. [1940–45]

Organiza′tion for Econom′ic Coopera′tion and Devel′opment, an organization formed in 1966, succeeding the Organization for European Economic Cooperation, to promote economic growth and global trade. *Abbr.:* OECD

Organiza′tion for Europe′an Econom′ic Coopera′tion, the predecessor organization (1948–66) of the Organization for Economic Cooperation and Development. *Abbr.:* OEEC

Organiza′tion of Af′rican U′nity, an organization of African nations formed in Addis Ababa, Ethiopia (1963), for the purpose of coordinating policy and promoting unity among African peoples. *Abbr.:* OAU, O.A.U.

Organiza′tion of Amer′ican States′, an organization formed in 1948 for the purpose of coordinated action in economic, political, and military matters: members are Antigua and Barbuda, Argentina, Bahamas, Barbados, Belize, Bolivia, Brazil, Canada, Chile, Colombia, Costa Rica, Cuba, Dominica, Dominican Republic, Ecuador, El Salvador, Grenada, Guatemala, Guyana, Haiti, Honduras, Jamaica, Mexico, Nicaragua, Panama, Paraguay, Peru, St. Kitts-Nevis, St. Lucia, St. Vincent and the Grenadines, Suriname, Trinidad and Tobago, United States, Uruguay, and Venezuela. *Abbr.:* OAS

Organiza′tion of Petro′leum Ex′porting Coun′tries. See **OPEC.**

or·gan·ize (ôr′gə nīz′), *v.,* **-ized, -iz·ing.** —*v.t.* **1.** to form as or into a whole consisting of interdependent or coordinated parts, esp. for harmonious or united action: *to organize a committee.* **2.** to systematize: *to organize the files of an office.* **3.** to give organic structure or character to: *to organize the elements of a composition.* **4.** to enlist or attempt to enlist into a labor union: *to organize workers.* **5.** to enlist the employees of (a company) into a labor union; unionize: *to organize a factory.* **6.** *Informal.* to put (oneself) in a state of mental competence to perform a task: *We can't have any slip-ups, so you'd better get organized.* —*v.i.* **7.** to combine in an organized company, party, or the like. **8.** to form a labor union: *Management resisted all efforts to organize.* **9.** to assume organic structure. Also, *esp. Brit.,* **or′gan·ise′.** [1375–1425; late ME *organysen* < ML *organizāre* to contrive, arrange, equiv. to L *organ(um)* ORGAN + *-izāre* -IZE] —**or′gan·iz′a·ble,** *adj.* —**or′gan·iz′a·bil′i·ty,** *n.*
—**Syn. 1.** dispose, frame. **2.** order. —**Ant. 1.** destroy.

or·gan·ized (ôr′gə nīzd′), *adj.* **1.** affiliated in an organization, esp. a union: *organized dockworkers.* **2.** having a formal organization or structure, esp. to coordinate or carry out widespread activities: *organized medicine; organized crime.* [1810–20; ORGANIZE + -ED[2]]

or′ganized fer′ment, ferment (def. 1).

or′ganized la′bor, 1. all workers who are organized in labor unions. **2.** these unions considered as a political force. [1880–85, *Amer.*]

or′ganized mili′tia, a former military organization functioning under both state and federal authority.

or·gan·iz·er (ôr′gə nī′zər), *n.* **1.** a person who organizes, esp. one who forms and organizes a group. **2.** a person whose job is to enlist employees into membership in a union. **3.** a person who organizes or schedules work: *You would get this job done sooner if you were a better organizer.* **4.** a multiple folder or, sometimes, a notebook in which correspondence, papers, etc., are sorted by subject, date, or otherwise, for systematic handling. **5.** *Embryol.* any part of an embryo that stimulates the development and differentiation of another part. [1840–50; ORGANIZE + -ER[1]]

organo-, a combining form of Greek origin used, with the meaning "organ (of the body)," "musical instrument," or as a combining form of **organic** in the formation of compound words: *organology; organosilicon.* [< Gk, comb. form of *órganon* ORGAN]

or′gan of Cor′ti (kôr′tē), *Anat., Zool.* a structure in the cochlea of a mammal, consisting of hair cells that serve as receptors for auditory stimuli. [1880–85; named after A. CORTI]

or·ga·no·gen·e·sis (ôr′gə nō jen′ə sis, ôr gan′ō-), *n. Biol.* the origin and development of an organ. Also, **or·ga·nog·e·ny** (ôr′gə noj′ə nē). [1855–60; ORGANO- + -GENESIS] —**or·ga·no·ge·net·ic** (ôr′gə nō jə net′ik, ôr gan′ō-), *adj.* —**or′ga·no·ge·net′i·cal·ly,** *adv.*

or·ga·nog·ra·phy (ôr′gə nog′rə fē), *n., pl.* **-phies.** *Biol., Med.* the description or visual depiction of organs. [1550–60; ORGANO- + -GRAPHY] —**or·ga·no·graph·ic** (ôr′gə nə graf′ik, ôr gan′ə-), **or′ga·no·graph′i·cal,** *adj.* —**or′ga·nog′ra·phist,** *n.*

or·ga·no·lep·tic (ôr′gə nl ep′tik, ôr gan′l ep′-), *adj.* **1.** perceived by a sense organ. **2.** capable of detecting a sensory stimulus. [1850–55; ORGANO- + *-leptic* < Gk *lēptikós* disposed to accept; see -LEPSY, -TIC]

or·ga·nol·o·gy (ôr′gə nol′ə jē), *n.* the branch of biology that deals with the structure and functions of the organs of living things. [1805–15; ORGANO- + -LOGY] —**or·ga·no·log·ic** (ôr′gə nl oj′ik, ôr gan′l oj′-), **or′ga·no·log′i·cal,** *adj.* —**or′ga·nol′o·gist,** *n.*

or·ga·no·mag·ne·si·um (ôr′gə nō mag nē′zē əm, -zhəm, -shē əm, ôr gan′ō-), *adj. Chem.* pertaining to or noting an organic compound, esp. an organic halide, containing magnesium linked to carbon. [1900–05; ORGANO- + MAGNESIUM]

or·ga·no·me·tal·lic (ôr′gə nō mə tal′ik, ôr gan′ō-), *adj. Chem.* pertaining to or noting an organic compound containing a metal or a metalloid linked to carbon. Also, **metallo-organic.** [1850–55; ORGANO- + METALLIC]

or·ga·non (ôr′gə non′), *n., pl.* **-na** (-nə), **-nons. 1.** an instrument of thought or knowledge. **2.** *Philos.* a system of rules or principles of demonstration or investigation. [1580–90; < Gk *órganon;* see ORGAN]

or·ga·no·phos·phate (ôr′gə nō fos′fāt, ôr gan′ə-), *n. Biochem.* any of a variety of organic compounds that contain phosphorus and often have intense neurotoxic activity: originally developed as nerve gases, now widely used as insecticides and fire retardants. Also called **or·ga·no·phos′pho·rus com′pounds** (ôr′gə nō fos′fər əs, ôr gan′ə-). [1945–50; ORGANO- + PHOSPHATE]

or·ga·no·sil·i·con (ôr′gə nō sil′i kən, -kon′, ôr gan′ō-), *adj. Chem.* pertaining to or noting an organic compound containing silicon, esp. where attached directly to a carbon atom. [1940–45; ORGANO- + SILICON]

or·ga·no·si·lox·ane (ôr′gə nō si lok′sān, ôr gan′ō-), *adj. Chem.* a siloxane containing an organic group. [1945–50; ORGANO- + SILOXANE]

or·ga·no·ther·a·py (ôr′gə nō ther′ə pē, ôr gan′ō-), *n.* the branch of therapeutics that deals with the use of remedies prepared from the organs of animals, as from the thyroid gland, the pancreas, or the suprarenal bodies. [1895–1900; ORGANO- + THERAPY]

or·ga·not·ro·pism (ôr′gə no′trə piz′əm), *n. Physiol.* the attraction of microorganisms or chemical substances to particular organs or tissues of the body. [ORGANO- + -TROPISM] —**or·ga·no·trop·ic** (ôr′gə nə trop′ik, -trō′-pik, ôr gan′ə-), *adj.*

or′gan pipe′, 1. one of the pipes of a pipe organ. **2.** something resembling such a pipe. [1425–75; late ME]

or′gan-pipe cac′tus (ôr′gən pīp′), a treelike or columnar cactus, *Lemaireocereus marginatus,* of Mexico, having a central, erect spine surrounded by spreading spines in clusters of five to eight, and funnel-shaped, brownish-purple flowers. [1905–10]

or′gan-pipe cor′al, an alcyonarian coral of the genus *Tubipora,* occurring in tropical waters, and forming a complex colony of brick-red, vertical tubules joined at intervals by transverse plates. [1825–35]

or′gan point′. See **pedal point.**

or′gan screen′, 1. an ornamental screen closing off an organ chamber in a church. **2.** a rood screen or the like supporting an organ.

or·ga·num (ôr′gə nəm), *n., pl.* **-na** (-nə), **-nums. 1.** an organon. **2.** *Music.* **a.** the doubling, or simultaneous singing, of a melody at an interval of either a fourth, a fifth, or an octave. **b.** the second part in such singing. [1605–15; < L; see ORGAN]

or′gan whis′tle, a steam or air whistle in which the jet is forced up against the thin edge of a pipe closed at the top.

or·gan·za (ôr gan′zə), *n.* a sheer rayon, nylon, or silk fabric constructed in plain weave and with a crisp finish, used in the manufacture of evening dresses, trimmings, etc. [1810–20; orig. uncert.]

or·gan·zine (ôr′gən zēn′), *n.* silk that has been additionally twisted in opposite directions, used warpwise in weaving silk fabrics. Cf. **tram.** [1690–1700; < F *organsin* < It *organzino*]

or·gasm (ôr′gaz əm), *n.* **1.** the physical and emotional sensation experienced at the peak of sexual excitation, usually resulting from stimulation of the sexual organ and usually accompanied in the male by ejaculation. **2.** an instance of experiencing this. **3.** intense or unrestrained excitement. **4.** an instance or occurrence of such excitement. —*v.i.* **5.** to have an orgasm. [1640–50; < NL *orgasmus* < Gk *orgasmós,* deriv. of *orgân* to swell, be excited] —**or·gas′mic, or·gas′tic,** *adj.*

OR′ gate′ (ôr), *Computers.* See **OR circuit.**

or·geat (ôr′zhat; *Fr.* ôr zhA′), *n.* a syrup or drink made originally from barley but later from almonds, prepared with sugar and an extract of orange flowers. [1745–55; < F < Pr *orjat,* deriv. of *orge* barley < L *hordeum*]

Or·get·o·rix (ôr jet′ə riks), *n.* fl. c60 B.C., Helvetian chieftain.

or·gi·as·tic (ôr′jē as′tik), *adj.* **1.** of, pertaining to, or having the nature of an orgy. **2.** tending to arouse or excite unrestrained emotion: *orgiastic rhythms.* **3.** *Sociol.* (of an expressive crowd) reaching a peak of emotional intensity, often of an ecstatic nature and frequently expressed by uninhibited behavior. [1690–1700; < Gk *orgiastikós,* deriv. (with *-tikos* -TIC) of *orgiázein* to celebrate orgies (deriv. of *órgia* secret rites; see ORGY)]
—**Syn. 1.** wanton, licentious, debauched, riotous.

or′gone box′ (ôr′gōn), a cabinetlike device constructed of layers of wood and other materials, as tin, claimed by its inventor, Wilhelm Reich, to restore orgone energy to persons sitting in it, thereby aiding in the cure of impotence, cancer, the common cold, etc. Also called **or′gone-en·er·gy accu′mulator** (ôr′gōn en′ər jē). [1940–45; prob. ORG(ANISM) + -ONE]

or′gone en′ergy, (in Wilhelm Reich's theory) a vital, primal, nonmaterial element believed to permeate the universe. Also called **orgone.** [1945–50]

or·gu·lous (ôr′gyə ləs, -gə-), *adj. Archaic.* haughty; proud. [1200–50; ME *orguillous, orguilleus* < OF *orgueillos,* equiv. to *orgueil* pride (earlier *orgoil* < Gmc **urgōli;* cf. OHG *urguol* outstanding, OE *orgol* pride) + *-os* -OUS] —**or′gu·lous·ly,** *adv.*

or·gy (ôr′jē), *n., pl.* **-gies. 1.** wild, drunken, or licentious festivity or revelry. **2.** any actions or proceedings marked by unbridled indulgence of passions: *an orgy of killing.* **3. orgies,** (in ancient Greece) esoteric religious rituals, used esp. in the worship of Demeter and Dionysus, characterized in later times by wild dancing, singing, and drinking. **4.** *Informal.* a boisterous, rowdy party. [1580–90; < MF *orgie* < L *orgia* (neut. pl.) secret rites < Gk *órgia,* akin to *érgon* WORK]

-orial, a suffix used to form adjectives corresponding to nouns ending in **-tor** or **-tory**[2]: *gladiatorial; purgatorial.* [ME *-oriale.* See -OR[2], -ORY[2], -AL[1]]

or·i·bi (ôr′ə bē, or′-), *n., pl.* **-bis.** a small tan-colored antelope, *Ourebia ourebi,* of south and east Africa, with spikelike horns. [1785–95; < Afrik < Khoikhoi, perh. to be identified with Nama *!gore-b*]

or·i·chal·cum (ôr′i kal′kəm), *n.* a brass rich in zinc, prepared by the ancients. [1640–50; < L < Gk *oreíchalkos* lit., mountain-copper, equiv. to *orei-,* comb. form of *óros* mountain + *chalkós* copper]

o·ri·el (ôr′ē əl, ōr′-), *n.* **1.** a bay window, esp. one cantilevered or corbeled out from a wall. **2.** (in medieval architecture) a large bay window of a hall or chamber. [1350–1400; ME < OF *oriol* porch, passage, gallery, perh. << L *aureolus* gilded]

oriel (def. 1)

o·ri·ent (*n., adj.* ôr′ē ənt, ôr′ē ent′, ōr′-; *v.* ôr′ē ent′, ōr′-), *n.* **1. the Orient, a.** the countries of Asia, esp. East Asia. **b.** (formerly) the countries to the E of the Mediterranean. **2.** *Jewelry.* **a.** an orient pearl. **b.** the iridescence of a pearl. **3.** the east; the eastern region of the heavens or the world. —*v.t.* **4.** to adjust with relation to, or bring into due relation to, surroundings, circumstances, facts, etc. **5.** to familiarize (a person) with new surroundings, circumstances, or the like: *lectures designed to orient the new students.* **6.** to place in any definite position with reference to the points of the compass or other locations: *to orient a building north and south.* **7.** to direct or position toward a particular object: *Orient it toward that house.* **8.** to determine the position of in relation to the points of the compass; get the bearings of. **9.** to place so as to face the east, esp. to build (a church) with the chief altar to the east and the chief entrance to the west. **10.** *Survey.* to set (the horizontal circle of a surveying instrument) so that readings give correct azimuths. **11.** *Math.* to assign to (a surface) a constant, outward direction at each point. —*v.i.* **12.** to turn toward the east or in any specified direction. —*adj.* **13.** (of a gem or pearl) exceptionally fine and lustrous; oriental. **14.** *Archaic.* eastern or oriental. **15.** *Archaic.* rising or appearing, esp. as from below the horizon: *the orient sun.* [1350–1400; ME (n.) < MF < L *orient-* (s. of *oriēns*) the east, sunrise, n. use of prp. of *orīrī* to rise; see -ENT] —**o′ri·ent′er,** *n.*
—**Syn. 5.** accustom, relate, orientate.

o·ri·en·tal (ôr′ē en′tl, ōr′-), *adj.* **1.** (*usually cap.*) of, pertaining to, or characteristic of the Orient, or East; Eastern. **2.** of the orient or east; eastern. **3.** (*cap.*) *Zoogeog.* belonging to a geographical division comprising southern Asia and the Malay Archipelago as far as and including the Philippines, Borneo, and Java. **4.** *Jewelry.* **a.** (*usually cap.*) designating various gems that are varieties of corundum: *Oriental aquamarine; Oriental ruby.* **b.** fine or precious; orient: *oriental agate; oriental garnet.* **c.** designating certain natural saltwater pearls found esp. in the Orient. —*n.* **5.** (*usually cap.*) a native or inhabitant of the Orient. [1350–1400; ME < MF < L *orientālis,* equiv. to *orient-* the east (see ORIENT) + *-ālis* -AL[1]] —**o′ri·en′tal·ly,** *adv.*

O′rien′tal al′abaster, alabaster (def. 2). [1750–60]

O′rien′tal bee′tle, a scarab beetle, *Anomala orientalis,* introduced into the U.S. from the Orient, the larvae of which feed on the roots of sugarcane and other grasses. Also called **Asiatic beetle.**

O′rien′tal car′pet. See **Oriental rug.** [1865–70]

O′rien′tal cat's′-eye, *Jewelry.* a chatoyant variety of chrysoberyl, used as a gem.

O′rien′tal cock′roach, a dark-brown cockroach, *Blatta orientalis,* thought to have originated in the Orient but now nearly cosmopolitan in distribution. Also called **o′rien′tal roach′, blackbeetle.**

O′rien′tal fruit′ moth′, a moth, *Grapholitha molesta,* introduced into the U.S. from the Orient, the larvae of which infest and feed on the twigs and fruits of peach, plum, and related trees. Also called **peach moth.** [1920–25]

O·ri·en·ta·li·a (ôr′ē ən tā′lē ə, -tāl′yə, ōr′-), *n.pl.* books, manuscripts, and other objects pertaining to the Orient and Oriental art, culture, history, folklore, or the like. [1915–20; < NL, n. use of neut. pl. of L *orientālis* ORIENTAL]

O·ri·en·tal·ism (ôr′ē en′tl iz′əm, ōr′-), *n.* (*often l.c.*) **1.** a peculiarity or idiosyncrasy of the Oriental peoples. **2.** the character or characteristics of the Oriental peoples. **3.** the knowledge and study of Oriental languages, literature, etc. [1760–70; ORIENTAL + -ISM] —**O′ri·en′tal·ist,** *n.*

O·ri·en·tal·ize (ôr′ē en′tl īz′, ōr′-), *v.t., v.i.,* **-ized, -iz·ing.** (*often l.c.*) to make or become Oriental. Also, *esp. Brit.,* **O′ri·en′tal·ise′.** [1815–25; ORIENTAL + -IZE] —**O′ri·en′tal·i·za′tion,** *n.*

O′rien′tal pop′py, a poppy, *Papaver orientale,* of Asia, having bristly stems and leaves and showy scarlet,

CONCISE PRONUNCIATION KEY: *act, cāpe, dâre, pärt; set, ēqual; if, īce; ox, ōver, ôrder, oil, bo͝ok, bo͞ot, out; up, ûrge; child; sing; shoe; thin, that;* zh as in *treasure.* ə = a as in *alone,* e as in *system,* i as in *easily,* o as in *gallop,* u as in *circus;* ə as in *fire* (fīər), *hour* (ouər). l and n can serve as syllabic consonants, as in *cradle* (krād′l), and *button* (but′n). See the full key inside the front cover.

pink, or white flowers, cultivated as an ornamental. [1725–35]

O′rien′tal rug′, a rug or carpet woven usually in Asia and characterized by hand-knotted pile. Also called **Oriental carpet.** Cf. **Persian carpet, Turkish rug, Turkoman rug.** [1880–85]

O′rien′tal scops′ owl′. See under **scops owl.**

o•ri•en•tate (ôr′ē ən tāt′, -en-, ōr′-), *v.t., v.i.,* **-tat•ed, -tat•ing.** to orient. [1840–50; < F *orient(er)* to ORIENT + -ATE[1]]

o•ri•en•ta•tion (ôr′ē ən tā′shən, -en-, ōr′-), *n.* **1.** the act or process of orienting. **2.** the state of being oriented. **3.** an introduction, as to guide one in adjusting to new surroundings, employment, activity, or the like: *New employees receive two days of orientation.* **4.** *Psychol., Psychiatry.* the ability to locate oneself in one's environment with reference to time, place, and people. **5.** one's position in relation to true north, to points on the compass, or to a specific place or object. **6.** the ascertainment of one's true position, as in a novel situation, with respect to attitudes, judgments, etc. **7.** *Chem.* **a.** the relative positions of certain atoms or groups, especially in aromatic compounds. **b.** the determination of the position of substituted atoms or groups in a compound. [1830–40; ORIENTATE + -ION] **—o′ri•en•ta′tive,** *adj.*

O•ri•en•te (ô′ʀē en′te), *n.* **1.** a region in Ecuador, E of the Andes: the border long disputed by Peru. **2.** a province in E Cuba. 2,998,972; 14,132 sq. mi. (36,600 sq. km). *Cap.:* Santiago de Cuba.

o•ri•en•teer•ing (ôr′ē en tēr′ing, ōr′-), *n.* a competitive sport, originating in Sweden, that tests the skills of map reading and cross-country running, in which competitors race through an unknown area to find various checkpoints by using only a compass and topographical map, the winner being the finisher with the lowest elapsed time. [alter. of Sw *orientering* (conformed to -EER), equiv. to *orienter(a)* ORIENT (v.) + *-ing* -ING[1]]

O′rient Express′, an express passenger train in service between Paris and Istanbul from 1883 until 1977, using various routes. Some or parts of the routes continue to be served by regular service and by rail tours.

or•i•fice (ôr′ə fis, or′-), *n.* an opening or aperture, as of a tube or pipe; a mouthlike opening or hole; mouth; vent. [1535–45; < MF < LL *ōrificium,* equiv. to L *ōr-* (s. of *ōs*) mouth + *-i-* -I- + *-fic-,* comb. form of *facere* to make, DO[1] (see -FIC) + *-ium* n. suffix] **—or•i•fi•cial** (ôr′ə fish′əl, or′-), *adj.*

or•i•flamme (ôr′ə flam′, or′-), *n.* **1.** the red banner of St. Denis, near Paris, carried before the early kings of France as a military ensign. **2.** any ensign, banner, or standard, esp. one that serves as a rallying point or symbol. [1425–75; late ME *oriflam* < MF *oriflamme,* OF, equiv. to *orie* golden (< L *aurea,* fem. of *aureus,* deriv. of *aurum* gold) + *flamme* FLAME]

orig., **1.** origin. **2.** original. **3.** originally.

o•ri•ga•mi (ôr′i gä′mē), *n., pl.* **-mis** for 2. **1.** the traditional Japanese art or technique of folding paper into a variety of decorative or representational forms, as of animals or flowers. **2.** an object made by origami. [1920–25; < Japn, equiv. to *ori* fold + *-gami,* comb. form of *kami* paper]

or•i•gan (ôr′i gən, or′-), *n.* an aromatic herb, esp. oregano. [1375–1425; late ME < L *orīganum* < Gk *orī́ganon;* derivation and further etym. uncert.]

Or•i•gen (ôr′i jen′, -jən, or′-), *n.* (*Origenes Admantius*) A.D. 185?–254?, Alexandrian writer, Christian theologian, and teacher. **—Or′i•gen′i•an,** *adj., n.* **—Or′i•gen•ism,** *n.* **—Or′i•gen•ist,** *n.* **—Or′i•gen•is′tic,** *adj.*

or•i•gin (ôr′i jin, or′-), *n.* **1.** something from which anything arises or is derived; source; fountainhead: *to follow a stream to its origin.* **2.** rise or derivation from a particular source: *the origin of a word.* **3.** the first stage of existence; beginning: *the origin of Quakerism in America.* **4.** ancestry; parentage; extraction: *to be of Scottish origin.* **5.** *Anat.* **a.** the point of derivation. **b.** the more fixed portion of a muscle. **6.** *Math.* **a.** the point in a Cartesian coordinate system where the axes intersect. **b.** Also called **pole.** the point from which rays designating specific angles originate in a polar coordinate system with no axes. [1350–1400; ME < L *orīgin-* (s. of *orīgō*) beginning, source, lineage, deriv. of *orīrī* to rise; cf. ORIENT]
—Syn. 1. root, foundation. **4.** birth, lineage, descent.
—Ant. 1. destination, end.

o•rig•i•nal (ə rij′ə nl), *adj.* **1.** belonging or pertaining to the origin or beginning of something, or to a thing at its beginning: *The book still has its original binding.* **2.** new; fresh; inventive; novel: *an original way of advertising.* **3.** arising or proceeding independently of anything else: *an original view of history.* **4.** capable of or given to thinking or acting in an independent, creative, or individual manner: *an original thinker.* **5.** created, undertaken, or presented for the first time: *to give the original performance of a string quartet.* **6.** being something from which a copy, a translation, or the like is made: *The original document is in Washington.* **—*n.*** **7.** a primary form or type from which varieties are derived. **8.** an original work, writing, or the like, as opposed to any copy or imitation: *The original of this is in the British Museum.* **9.** the person or thing represented by a picture, description, etc.: *The original is said to have been the painter's own house.* **10.** a person whose ways of thinking or acting are original: *In a field of brilliant technicians he is a true original.* **11.** *Archaic.* an eccentric person. **12.** *Archaic.* a source of being; an author or originator. [1300–50; ME < L *orīginālis* (adj.) and ML *orīgināle* original document (n. use of neut. adj.), equiv. to *origin-* (see ORIGIN) + *-ālis* -AL[1]]
—Syn. 1. primary, primordial, primeval, primitive, aboriginal. **7.** archetype, pattern, prototype, model.
—Ant. 7. copy.

CONCISE ETYMOLOGY KEY: <, descended or borrowed from; >, whence; b., blend of, blended; c., cognate with; cf., compare; deriv., derivative; equiv., equivalent; imit., imitative; obl., oblique; r., replacing; s., stem; sp., spelling, spelled; resp., respelling, respelled; trans., translation; ?, origin unknown; *, unattested; ‡, probably earlier than. See the full key inside the front cover.

orig′inal equip′ment manufac′turer **1.** a firm that purchases complex equipment, as computers, from manufacturers and modifies or combines different components for resale. **2.** a firm that manufactures components or parts included in the finished product made by another. *Abbr.:* OEM

orig′inal gum′, *Philately.* See **o.g.** (def. 1).

o•rig•i•nal•i•ty (ə rij′ə nal′i tē), *n.* **1.** the quality or state of being original. **2.** ability to think or express oneself in an independent and individual manner; creative ability. **3.** freshness or novelty, as of an idea, method, or performance. [1735–45; < F *originalité.* See ORIGINAL, -ITY]
—Syn. 1, 3. inventiveness, ingenuity, cleverness, creativeness.

o•rig•i•nal•ly (ə rij′ə nl ē), *adv.* **1.** with respect to origin; by origin: *Originally he came from California.* **2.** at the origin; at first: *Originally this was to be in three volumes.* **3.** in the first place; primarily: *Originally nomads, they first learned agriculture from the missionaries.* **4.** in an original, novel, or distinctively individual manner: *Originally planned houses are much in demand.* **5.** *Archaic.* from the beginning; from the first; inherently. [1480–90; ORIGINAL + -LY]

orig′inal sin′, **1.** *Theol.* **a.** a depravity, or tendency to evil, held to be innate in humankind and transmitted from Adam to the race in consequence of his sin. **b.** inclination to evil, inherent in human nature. **2.** *Rom. Cath. Theol.* the privation of sanctifying grace in consequence of the sin of Adam. [1300–50; ME; trans. of ML *peccātum orīgināle*]

o•rig•i•nate (ə rij′ə nāt′), *v.,* **-nat•ed, -nat•ing.** **—*v.i.*** **1.** to take its origin or rise; begin; start; arise: *The practice originated during the Middle Ages.* **2.** (of a train, bus, or other public conveyance) to begin a scheduled run at a specified place: *This train originates at Philadelphia.* **—*v.t.*** **3.** to give origin or rise to; initiate; invent: *to originate a better method.* [1645–55; prob. back formation from *origination* (< F) < L *orīginātiō* etymology; see ORIGIN, -ATE[1], ION] **—o•rig•i•na•ble** (ə rij′ə nə bəl), *adj.* **—o•rig′i•na′tion,** *n.* **—o•rig′i•na′tor,** *n.*
—Syn. 3. See **discover.**

o•rig•i•na•tive (ə rij′ə nā′tiv), *adj.* having or characterized by the power of originating; creative. [1820–30; ORIGINATE + -IVE] **—o•rig′i•na′tive•ly,** *adv.*

Or′igin of Spe′cies, The, (*On the Origin of Species by Means of Natural Selection, or the Preservation of Favoured Races in the Struggle for Life*) a treatise (1859) by Charles Darwin setting forth his theory of evolution.

o•ri•hon (ôr′ē hon′, ōr′-), *n.* **1.** a manuscript scroll having columns running across the width, folded in accordion fashion along the separating margins. **2.** a book consisting of leaves, printed on one side only, uncut at the fore edge. [1905–10; < Japn, equiv. to *ori* fold + *hon* book (< *fon* < MChin, equiv. to Chin *běn*)]

O•ril•lia (ô ril′yə, ō ril′-), *n.* a city in SE Ontario, in S Canada. 23,955.

o•ri•na•sal (ôr′ə nā′zəl, ōr′-), *Phonet.* **—*adj.*** **1.** pronounced with the voice issuing through the mouth and the nose simultaneously, as in the nasalized vowels of French. **—*n.*** **2.** an orinasal sound. Also, **oronasal.** [1865–70; < L *ōr-* (s. of *ōs*) mouth + -I- + NASAL[1]] **—o′ri•na′sal•ly,** *adv.*

O•rin•da (ə rin′də, ô rin′-, ō rin′-), *n.* a town in W California. 16,825.

O-ring (ō′ring′), *n.* a ring of pliable material, as rubber or neoprene, used as a gasket: the failure of an O-ring caused the explosion that destroyed the space shuttle *Challenger* in 1986. [1945–50]

O•ri•no•co (ôr′ə nō′kō, ōr′-; *Sp.* ô′ʀē nô′kô), *n.* a river in N South America, flowing N from the border of Brazil, along the E border of Colombia, and NE through Venezuela to the Atlantic. 1600 mi. (2575 km) long.

o•ri•ole (ôr′ē ōl′, ōr′-), *n.* **1.** any of several usually brightly colored, passerine birds of the family Oriolidae, of the Old World. Cf. **golden oriole.** **2.** any of several brightly colored passerine birds of the family Icteridae, of the New World. Cf. **northern oriole, orchard oriole.** [1770–80; < F *oriol,* OF < ML *oriolus,* var. of L *aureolus* golden, equiv. to *aure(us)* golden (deriv. of *aurum* gold) + *-olus* -OLE[1]]

O•ri•on (ə rī′ən), *n., gen.* **Or•i•o•nis** (ôr′ē ō′nis, or′-, ə rī′ə nis) for 2. **1.** *Class. Myth.* a giant hunter who pursued the Pleiades, was eventually slain by Artemis, and was then placed in the sky as a constellation. **2.** *Astron.* the Hunter, a constellation lying on the celestial equator between Canis Major and Taurus, containing the bright stars Betelgeuse and Rigel. **3.** *Mil.* a land-based U.S. Navy patrol plane with four turboprop engines, used to detect, track, and destroy enemy submarines and armed with missiles, torpedoes, mines, and depth bombs.

O•ri•o•nids (ə rī′ə nidz, ôr′ē ō′-, ōr′-), *n.* (*used with a plural v.*) *Astron.* a collection of meteors comprising a meteor shower (**Ori′onid me′teor show′er**) visible during October, and having its apparent origin in the constellation Orion.

Ori′on Neb′ula, *Astron.* a luminous nebula in the constellation Orion, in the center of Orion's sword. Also called **Great Nebula of Orion.**

O•ris•ka•ny (ô ris′kə nē, ō ris′-), *n.* a village in central New York, near Utica: battle 1777. 1707. **—Or•is•ka•ni•an** (ôr′is kā′nē ən, or′-), *adj., n.*

or•is•mol•o•gy (ôr′iz mol′ə jē, or′-), *n.* the science of defining the technical or special terms of a particular subject or field of study. [1810–20; < Gk *horism(ós)* definition, lit, marking of boundaries (deriv. of *horízein* to delimit, make a boundary; see HORIZON) + -O- + -LOGY, with erroneous omission of initial *h-*]

or•i•son (ôr′ə zən, or′-), *n.* a prayer. [1125–75; ME < OF < LL *ōrātiōn-* (s. of *ōrātiō*) plea, prayer, ORATION]

O•ris•sa (ô ris′ə, ō ris′ə), *n.* a state in E India. 24,870,000; 60,136 sq. mi. (155,752 sq. km). *Cap.:* Bhubaneswar.

O•ri•ya (ô rē′yə), *n.* an Indic language spoken in Orissa. [1795–1805]

O•ri•za•ba (ôr′ə zä′bə, ōr′-; *Sp.* ô′ʀē sä′vä), *n.* **1.** Also called **Citlaltepetl.** an inactive volcano in SE Mexico, in Veracruz state. 18,546 ft. (5653 m). **2.** a city near this peak. 108,283.

Or•jo•ni•ki•dze (ôr′jon i kid′zə; *Russ.* ᴜʀ jə nyi kyē′dzyi), *n.* Ordzhonikidze (def. 1).

Or•khon (ôr′kon), *n.* a river in E central Asia, flowing E, N, and then NE from the N central Mongolian People's Republic to the Selenga River. ab. 400 mi. (645 km) long.

Ork′ney Is′lands (ôrk′nē), an island group off the NE tip of Scotland. 17,675; 340 sq. mi. (880 sq. km).

Or•lan•do (ôr lan′dō; *also, for 1, It.* ôʀ län′dô), *n.* **1.** **Vit•to•rio E•ma•nu•e•le** (vēt tô′ryô e′mä noo e′le), 1860–1952, Italian statesman. **2.** a city in central Florida: resort. 128,394. **3.** a male given name, form of **Roland.**

Or′land Park′ (ôr′lənd), a town in NE Illinois. 23,045.

orle (ôrl), *n.* **1.** *Heraldry.* **a.** a charge in the form of a narrow band following the form of the escutcheon within the edge, so that the extreme outer edge of the escutcheon is of the field tincture. **b.** an arrangement in orle of small charges: *azure, an orle of bezants.* **2.** *Armor.* a thick roll of cloth or leather on a helmet forming a base for an ornamental crest. **3.** Also called **or•let** (ôr lā′), **orlo.** *Archit.* **a.** a border, as one formed by a fillet. **b.** a fillet at the upper end of the shaft of a column. Cf. **cincture** (def. 3). **c.** a fillet between two flutes of a column. [1565–75; < MF: border, edge < VL **ōrulus,* dim. of L *ōra* border]

Or•lé•a•nais (ôʀ lā a ne′), *n.* a former province in N France. *Cap.:* Orléans.

Or•le•an•ist (ôr′lē ə nist), *n.* a supporter of the Orléans branch of the former French royal family and of its claim to the throne of France through descent from the younger brother of Louis XIV. [1825–35, < F *Orléaniste;* see ORLÉANS, -IST] **—Or′le•an•ism,** *n.*

Or•lé•ans (ôr′lē ənz; *Fr.* ôʀ lā äɴ′), *n.* a city in and the capital of Loiret, in central France, SSW of Paris: English siege of the city raised by Joan of Arc 1428. 109,956.

Or•lé•ans, d′ (dôʀ lā äɴ′), *n.* **Louis Phi•lippe Jo•seph** (lwē fē lēp′ zhô zef′), **Duc** (*Philippe Égalité*), 1747–93, French political leader.

orl•fly (ôrl′flī′), *n., pl.* **-flies.** *Brit.* an alderfly, *Sialis lutaria.* Also, **orl′ fly′.** [1740–50; *orl,* dial. var. of ALDER + FLY[2]]

Or•lich (ôr′lich; *Sp.* ôʀ′lēch), *n.* **Fran•cis•co J.** (fʀän sēs′kô), 1906–69, Costa Rican engineer and statesman: president 1962–66.

or•lo (ôr′lō), *n., pl.* **-los.** *Archit.* **1.** a plinth supporting the base of a column. **2.** orle (def. 3). [1605–15; < It: border, deriv. of *orlare* to hem < VL; see ORLE]

Or•lon (ôr′lon), *Trademark.* a brand of synthetic, acrylic textile fiber of light weight, wrinkle resistance, and resistance to weathering and many chemicals.

or•lop (ôr′lop), *n. Naut.* the lowermost of four or more decks above the space at the bottom of a hull. Also called **or′lop deck′.** [1375–1425; late ME *overloppe* < MD *over-loop* covering, lit., an over-leap, equiv. to *over-* OVER- + *-loopen* to run, extend; see LEAP]

Or•ly (ôr′lē; *Fr.* ôʀ lē′), *n.* a suburb SE of Paris, France: international airport. 26,244.

Or•man•dy (ôr′mən dē), *n.* **Eugene,** 1899–1985, U.S. conductor and violinist, born in Hungary.

Or•mazd (ôr′məzd), *n.* See **Ahura Mazda.** Also, **Or′muzd.**

or•mer (ôr′mər), *n.* **1.** an abalone, *Haliotis tuberculata,* living in waters of the Channel Islands. **2.** any abalone. [1665–75; < F *ormier* < L *auris maris* ear of the sea]

or•mo•lu (ôr′mə lo͞o′), *n.* **1.** Also called **mosaic gold.** an alloy of copper and zinc used to imitate gold. **2.** Also called **bronze doré, gilt bronze.** gilded metal, esp. cast brass or bronze gilded over fire with an amalgam of gold and mercury, used for furniture mounts and ornamental objects. **3.** gold or gold powder prepared for use in gilding. [1755–65; < F *or moulu* ground gold, equiv. to *or* (< L *aurum*) + *moulu,* ptp. of *moudre* to grind < L *molere*]

Or′mond Beach′ (ôr′mənd), a town in NE Florida. 21,378.

Or•muz (ôr mo͞oz′, ôr′muz), *n.* **Strait of.** See **Hormuz, Strait of.**

or•na•ment (*n.* ôr′nə mənt; *v.* ôr′nə ment′, -mənt), *n.*

1. an accessory, article, or detail used to beautify the appearance of something to which it is added or of which it is a part: *architectural ornaments.* **2.** a system, category, or style of such objects or features; ornamentation: *a book on Gothic ornament.* **3.** any adornment or means of adornment. **4.** a person or thing that adds to the credit or glory of a society, era, etc. **5.** the act of adorning. **6.** the state of being adorned. **7.** mere outward display: *a speech more of ornament than of ideas.* **8.** *Chiefly Eccles.* any accessory, adjunct, or equipment. **9.** *Music.* a tone or group of tones applied as decoration to a principal melodic tone. —*v.t.* **10.** to furnish with ornaments; embellish: *to ornament a musical composition.* **11.** to be an ornament to: *Several famous scientists were acquired to ornament the university.* [1175–1225; < L *ornāmentum* equipment, ornament, equiv. to *ornā(re)* to equip + *-mentum* -MENT; r. ME *ornement* < OF < L, as above] —**or′na•ment′er,** *n.*
—**Syn. 1.** embellishment. **3, 5.** decoration. **10, 11.** decorate, adorn, grace.

or•na•men•tal (ôr′nə men′tl), *adj.* **1.** used or grown for ornament: *ornamental plants.* **2.** providing ornament; decorative. **3.** of or pertaining to ornament. —*n.* **4.** something ornamental; decoration; adornment. **5.** a plant cultivated for decorative purposes. [1640–50; ORNAMENT + -AL[1]] —**or′na•men•tal′i•ty,** *n.* —**or′na•men′tal•ly,** *adv.*

or•na•men•tal•ism (ôr′nə men′tl iz′əm), *n.* the desire or tendency to feature ornament in the design of buildings, interiors, furnishings, etc. [1860–65; ORNAMENTAL + -ISM]

or•na•men•ta•tion (ôr′nə men tā′shən, -mən-), *n.* **1.** the act of ornamenting. **2.** the state of being ornamented. **3.** something with which a thing is ornamented; embellishment. **4.** ornaments collectively. [1850–55; ORNAMENT + -ATION]

or•na•ment•ed (ôr′nə men′tid, -mən-), *adj. Typography.* (of a character) highly embellished or ornate; altered by embellishment. [1730–40; ORNAMENT + -ED[2]]

or•nate (ôr nāt′), *adj.* **1.** elaborately or sumptuously adorned, often excessively or showily so: *They bought an ornate Louis XIV sofa.* **2.** embellished with rhetoric; florid or high-flown: *an ornate style of writing.* [1375–1425; late ME < L *ornātus* well-equipped, adorned, orig. ptp. of *ornāre* to equip; see -ATE[1]] —**or•nate′ly,** *adv.* —**or•nate′ness,** *n.*
—**Syn. 1.** showy, ostentatious; rich, lavish.

Orne (ôʀn), *n.* a department in NW France. 293,523; 2372 sq. mi. (6145 sq. km). *Cap.:* Alençon.

or•ner•y (ôr′nə rē), *adj.*, **-ner•i•er, -ner•i•est.** *Dial.* **1.** ugly and unpleasant in disposition or temper: *No one can get along with my ornery cousin.* **2.** stubborn: *I can't do a thing with that ornery mule.* **3.** low or vile. **4.** inferior or common; ordinary. [1790–1800; contr. of ORDINARY] —**or′ner•i•ness,** *n.*
—**Syn. 1.** mean, ill-tempered, ill-natured, surly, testy.

or•nis (ôr′nis), *n., pl.* **or•ni•thes** (ôr ni′thēz). an avifauna. [1860–65; < G < Gk *órnīs* bird; akin to OE *earn* eagle (see ERNE), G *Aar*]

ornith-, var. of **ornitho-** before a vowel: *ornithoid.*

ornith., **1.** ornithological. **2.** ornithology.

or•nith•ic (ôr nith′ik), *adj.* of or pertaining to birds. [1850–55; < Gk *ornīthikós* birdlike, equiv. to *ornīth-* ORNITH- + *-ikos* -IC]

or•ni•thine (ôr′nə thēn′), *n. Biochem.* an amino acid, $H_2N(CH_2)_3CH(NH_2)COOH$, obtained by the hydrolysis of arginine and occurring as an intermediate compound in the urea cycle of mammals. [1880–85; *ornith(uric acid),* secreted by birds + -INE[2]]

or•nith•is•chi•an (ôr′nə this′kē ən), *n.* **1.** any herbivorous dinosaur of the order Ornithischia, having a pelvis resembling that of a bird. Cf. **saurischian.** —*adj.* **2.** belonging or pertaining to the Ornithischia. [1900–05; < NL *Ornithischi(a)* (*ornith-* ORNITH- + *-ischia* < Gk *ischíon* ISCHIUM) + -AN]

ornitho-, a combining form meaning "bird," used in the formation of compound words: *ornithology.* Also, *esp. before a vowel,* **ornith-.** [comb. form repr. Gk *ornīth-* (s. of *órnis*) bird]

or•ni•thoid (ôr′nə thoid′), *adj.* resembling a bird. [1855–60, *Amer.*; ORNITH- + -OID]

ornithol., **1.** ornithological. **2.** ornithology.

or•ni•thol•o•gy (ôr′nə thol′ə jē), *n.* the branch of zoology that deals with birds. [1645–55; < NL *ornithologia.* See ORNITHO-, -LOGY] —**or•ni•tho•log•i•cal** (ôr′nə thə loj′i kəl), **or′ni•tho•log′ic,** *adj.* —**or′ni•tho•log′i•cal•ly,** *adv.* —**or′ni•thol′o•gist,** *n.*

or•ni•tho•pod (ôr′nə thə pod′, ôr ni′thə-), *n.* any herbivorous dinosaur of the suborder Ornithopoda whose members usually walked erect on their hind legs. [1885–90; < NL *Ornithopoda* (pl.). See ORNITHO-, -POD]

or•ni•thop•ter (ôr′nə thop′tər), *n.* a heavier-than-air craft designed to be propelled through the air by flapping wings. [< F *ornithoptère* (1908), equiv. to *ornitho-* ORNITHO- + *-ptère* < Gk *-pteros* -PTEROUS]

or•ni•tho•rhyn•chus (ôr′nə thə ring′kəs), *n.* the platypus. [1790–1800; < NL: genus name, equiv. to *ornitho-* ORNITHO- + *-rhynchus* < Gk *rhýnchos* bill]

or•ni•tho•sis (ôr′nə thō′sis), *n. Vet. Pathol.* psittacosis, esp. of birds other than those of the parrot family. [1830–40; < NL; see ORNITH-, -OSIS]

o•ro (ô′ʀô), *n. Spanish.* gold.

oro-[1], a combining form meaning "mountain," used in the formation of compound words: *orography.* [< Gk, comb. form of *óros*]

oro-[2], a combining form meaning "mouth," used in the formation of compound words: *oropharynx.* [comb. repr. L *ōs,* s. *ōr-*]

or•o•ban•cha•ceous (ôr′ō bang kā′shəs, or′-), *adj.* belonging to the Orobanchaceae, the broomrape family of plants. Cf. **broomrape family.** [< NL *Orobanchac(eae)* family name (L *orobanch(ē)* broomrape (< Gk *orobánchē*) + *-aceae* -ACEAE) + -OUS]

or•o•gen (ôr′ə jen′, -jən, ŏr′-), *n. Geol.* an extensive belt of rocks deformed by orogeny, associated in places with plutonic and metamorphic rocks. [< G (1921); see ORO-[1], -GEN]

o•rog•e•ny (ô roj′ə nē, ō roj′-), *n. Geol.* the process of mountain making or upheaval. Also called **or•o•gen•e•sis** (ôr′ə jen′ə sis, or′ə-). [1885–90; ORO-[1] + -GENY] —**or•o•gen•ic** (ôr′ə jen′ik, or′ə-), **or′o•ge•net′ic,** *adj.*

or′ograph′ic cloud′, any cloud whose existence and form are largely controlled by the disturbed flow of air over and around mountains, as the banner cloud and crest cloud. [1975–80]

orograph′ic precipita′tion, precipitation caused by the lifting of moist air over a mountain barrier. [1965–70]

o•rog•ra•phy (ô rog′rə fē, ō rog′-), *n.* the branch of physical geography dealing with mountains. Also called **o•rol•o•gy** (ô rol′ə jē, ō rol′-). [1840–50; ORO-[1] + -GRAPHY] —**or•o•graph•ic** (ôr′ə graf′ik, or′ə-), **or′o•graph′i•cal,** *adj.* —**or′o•graph′i•cal•ly,** *adv.*

or•o•ide (ôr′ō id′, ŏr′-), *n.* an alloy containing copper, tin, etc., used to imitate gold. Also, **oreide.** [1865–70, *Amer.*; < F *or* gold (< L *aurum*) + *-oide* -OID]

o•rom•e•ter (ô rom′i tər, ō rom′-), *n.* an aneroid barometer with a scale giving elevations above sea level, used to determine land-surface altitudes. [1875–80; ORO-[1] + -METER] —**or′o•met′ric,** *adj.*

O•ro•mo (ô rō′mō), *n., pl.* **-mos,** (*esp. collectively*) **-mo** for 1. **1.** a member of a nomadic, pastoral people of Ethiopia and Kenya. **2.** the Cushitic language of the Oromo. Also called **Galla.**

o•ro•na•sal (ôr′ō nā′zəl, ŏr′ō-), *adj.* **1.** of or pertaining to the mouth and the nose. **2.** *Phonet.* orinasal (def. 1). —*n.* **3.** *Phonet.* orinasal (def. 2). [1885–90; ORO-[2] + NASAL[1]] —**o′ro•na′sal•ly,** *adv.*

O•ro•no (ôr′ə nō′, ŏr′-), *n.* a town in S Maine. 10,578.

O•ron•tes (ô ron′tēz, ō ron′-), *n.* a river in W Asia, flowing N from Lebanon through NW Syria and then SW past Antioch, Turkey, to the Mediterranean. 250 mi. (405 km) long.

o•ro•pen•do•la (ôr′ə pen′dl ə, ŏr′ə-), *n.* any of several birds of the genus *Gymnostinops,* related to crows and feeding primarily on fruit and nectar, noted esp. for their hanging nests. [1895–1900; < Sp *oropéndola* the golden oriole, equiv. to *oro* gold (< L *aurum*) + *péndola,* by-form of *péñola* feather, quill < L *pinnula,* dim. of *pinna* feather, wing; see PINNA, -ULE]

o•ro•phar•ynx (ôr′ō far′ingks, ŏr′-), *n., pl.* **-pha•ryn•ges** (-fə rin′jēz), **-phar•ynx•es.** *Anat.* **1.** the part of the pharynx between the soft palate and the upper edge of the epiglottis. **2.** the pharynx as distinguished from the nasopharynx and laryngeal pharynx. [1885–90; ORO-[2] + PHARYNX] —**o•ro•pha•ryn•ge•al** (ôr′ō fə rin′jē əl, -far′-in jē′əl, ŏr′-), *adj.*

O•ro•si•us (ô rō′zhē əs), *n.* **Pau•lus** (pô′ləs), fl. 5th century A.D., Spanish theologian and historian.

o•ro•tund (ôr′ə tund′, ŏr′-), *adj.* **1.** (of the voice or speech) characterized by strength, fullness, richness, and clearness. **2.** (of a style of speaking) pompous or bombastic. [1785–95; contr. of L phrase *ōre rotundō,* with round mouth] —**o•ro•tun•di•ty** (ôr′ə tun′di tē, ŏr′-), *n.*

o•ro y pla•ta (ô′ʀô ē plä′tä; *Eng.* ôr′ō ē plä′tə), *Spanish.* gold and silver: motto of Montana.

O•roz•co (ô ʀôs′kô), *n.* **Jo•sé Cle•men•te** (hô se′ klemen′te), 1883–1949, Mexican painter.

Or•pen (ôr′pən), *n.* **Sir William New•en•ham Monta•gue** (no͞o′ə nəm, nyo͞o′-), 1878–1931, Irish painter.

or•phan (ôr′fən), *n.* **1.** a child who has lost both parents through death, or, less commonly, one parent. **2.** a young animal that has been deserted by or has lost its mother. **3.** a person or thing that is without protective affiliation, sponsorship, etc.: *The committee is an orphan of the previous administration.* **4.** *Print.* **a.** (esp. in word processing) the first line of a paragraph when it appears alone at the bottom of a page. **b.** widow (def. 3b). —*adj.* **5.** bereft of parents. **6.** of or for orphans: *an orphan home.* **7.** not authorized, supported, or funded; not part of a system; isolated; abandoned: *an orphan research project.* **8.** lacking a commercial sponsor, an employer, etc.: *orphan workers.* —*v.t.* **9.** to deprive of parents or a parent through death: *He was orphaned at the age of four.* **10.** *Informal.* to deprive of commercial sponsorship, an employer, etc.: *The recession has orphaned many experienced workers.* [1425–75; late ME (n.) < LL *orphanus* destitute, without parents < Gk *orphanós* bereaved; akin to L *orbus* bereaved] —**or′phan•hood′,** *n.*

or•phan•age (ôr′fə nij), *n.* **1.** an institution for the housing and care of orphans. **2.** the state of being an orphan; orphanhood. **3.** *Archaic.* orphans collectively. [1530–40; ORPHAN + -AGE]

or′phan drug′, *Pharm.* a drug that remains undeveloped or untested or is otherwise neglected because of limited potential for commercial gain. [1975–80]

or′phans′ court′, a probate court in certain U.S. states. [1705–15]

Or•phe•us (ôr′fē əs, -fyo͞os), *n.* **1.** *Gk. Legend.* a poet and musician, a son of Calliope, who followed his dead wife, Eurydice, to the underworld. By charming Hades, he obtained permission to lead her away, provided he did not look back at her until they returned to earth. But at the last moment he looked, and she was lost to him forever. **2.** (*italics*) a ballet (1947) with music by Stravinsky and choreography by Balanchine. —**Or•phe•an** (ôr fē′ən, ôr′fē ən), *adj.*

Or•phic (ôr′fik), *adj.* **1.** of or pertaining to Orpheus. **2.** resembling the music attributed to Orpheus; entrancing. **3.** pertaining to a religious or philosophical school maintaining a form of the cult of Dionysus, or Bacchus, ascribed to Orpheus as founder: *Orphic mysteries.* **4.** (*often l.c.*) mystic; oracular. [1670–80; < Gk *Orphikós* (c. L *Orphicus*), equiv. to *Orph(eús)* ORPHEUS + *-ikos* -IC] —**Or′phi•cal•ly,** *adv.*

Or•phism (ôr′fiz əm), *n.* **1.** the religious or philosophical system of the Orphic school. **2.** (*often l.c.*) Also called **or′phic cub′ism.** *Fine Arts.* a short-lived but influential artistic movement of the early 20th century arising from analytic cubism and the work of Robert Delaunay and having as conspicuous characteristics the use of bold color, the dynamic, prismatic juxtaposition and overlapping of nonobjective geometric forms and planes, and a lightness and lyricism dissociated from its cubist origins. Cf. **synchromism.** [(def. 2) < F *orphisme,* equiv. to *Orph(ée)* ORPHEUS + *-isme* -ISM; term introduced by G. Apollinaire c1913] —**Or′phist,** *n., adj.*

or•phrey (ôr′frē), *n., pl.* **-phreys. 1.** an ornamental band or border, esp. on an ecclesiastical vestment. **2.** gold embroidery. **3.** rich embroidery of any sort. **4.** a piece of richly embroidered material. [1300–50; ME *orfreis* (later construed as pl.) < OF < ML *aurifrisium,* var. of *aurifrigium,* for L phrase *aurum Phrygium* gold embroidery, lit., Phrygian gold] —**or′phreyed,** *adj.*

or•pi•ment (ôr′pə mənt), *n.* a mineral, arsenic trisulfide, As_2S_3, found usually in soft, yellow, foliated masses, used as a pigment. [1350–1400; ME < OF < L *auripigmentum* pigment of gold; see AURI-[1], PIGMENT]

or•pine (ôr′pin), *n.* a plant, *Sedum telephium,* of the stonecrop family, having purplish flowers. Also, **or′pin.** [1350–1400; ME < MF, back formation from *orpiment* ORPIMENT]

Or•ping•ton (ôr′ping tən), *n.* one of a breed of large, white-skinned chickens. [1890–95; after *Orpington,* town in Kent, England]

Orr (ôr), *n.* **1. Sir John Boyd.** See **Boyd Orr, Sir John. 2. Robert Gordon** (*Bobby*), born 1948, Canadian ice-hockey player.

or•ra (ôr′ə, or′ə), *adj. Scot.* not regular or scheduled; odd: *orra work.* Also, **orrow.** [1720–30; orig. uncert.]

or•rer•y (ôr′ə rē, or′-), *n., pl.* **-rer•ies. 1.** an apparatus for representing the positions, motions, and phases of the planets, satellites, etc., in the solar system. **2.** any of certain similar machines, as a planetarium. [1705–15; named after Charles Boyle, Earl of *Orrery* (1676–1731), for whom it was first made]

Or•rin (ôr′in, or′-), *n.* a male given name.

or•ris[1] (ôr′is, or′-), *n.* an iris, *Iris germanica florentina,* having a fragrant rootstock. Also, **or′rice.** [1535–45; unexplained alter. of IRIS]

or•ris[2] (ôr′is, or′-), *n.* **1.** a lace or braid made of gold or silver, much used in the 18th century. **2.** a galloon used in upholstering. [1695–1705; perh. alter. (by influence of *arras* tapestry) of earlier *orfrays* ORPHREY]

or•ris•root (ôr′is ro͞ot′, -ro͝ot′, or′-), *n.* the rootstock of the orris, used in perfumery, medicine, etc. [1590–1600; ORRIS[1] + ROOT[1]]

or•row (ôr′ə, or′ə), *adj. Scot.* orra.

or•seille (ôr sāl′, -sā′, -sel′), *n.* orchil. [< F]

Or•sha (ôʀ′shə), *n.* a city in NE Byelorussia (Belarus), on the Dnieper River, NE of Minsk. 112,000.

Orsk (ôʀsk), *n.* a city in the S Russian Federation in Europe, on the Ural River. 273,000.

Or•son (ôr′sən), *n.* a male given name: from an Old French word meaning "bearlike."

ort (ôrt), *n.* Usually, **orts.** a scrap or morsel of food left at a meal. [1400–50; late ME; c. LG *ort,* early D *oorete;* cf. OE *or-* out-, *ǣt* food (see EAT)]

Or•te•gal (ôr′te gäl′), *n.* **Cape,** a cape in NW Spain, on the Bay of Biscay.

Or•te•ga Sa•a•ve•dra (ôʀ te′gä sä′ä ve′thʀä), (**José**) **Da•niel** (hô se′ dä nyel′), born 1945, Nicaraguan political leader: president 1985–90.

Or•te•ga y Gas•set (ôr tā′gə ē gä set′; *Sp.* ôʀ te′gä ē gäs set′), **Jo•sé** (hô se′), 1883–1955, Spanish philosopher, journalist, and critic.

orth-, var. of **ortho-** before a vowel: *orthicon.*

Orth., Orthodox.

orth., **1.** orthopedic **2.** orthopedics.

or•thi•con (ôr′thi kon′), *n. Television.* a camera tube, more sensitive than the iconoscope, in which a beam of low-velocity electrons scans a photoemissive mosaic. Also, **or•thi•con•o•scope** (ôr′thi kon′ə skōp′). [1935–40; ORTH- + ICON(OSCOPE)]

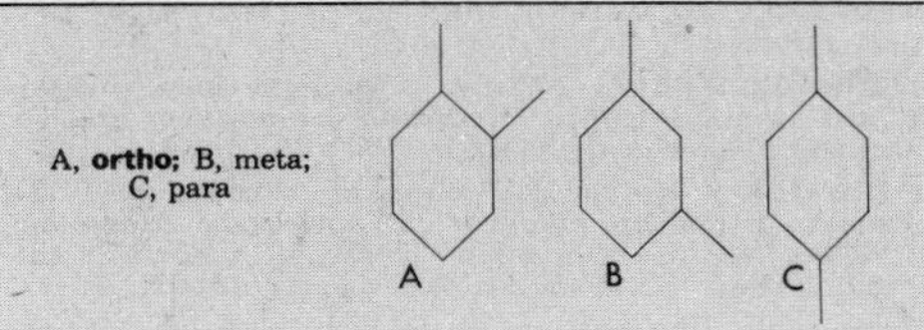

A, **ortho**; B, meta; C, para

or•tho (ôr′thō), *adj. Chem.* pertaining to or occupying two adjacent positions in the benzene ring. Cf. **meta**[2], **para**[3]. [1875–80; independent use of ORTHO-]

ortho-, **1.** a combining form occurring in loanwords from Greek, where it meant "straight," "upright," "right," "correct" (*orthodox*) and on this model used in the formation of compound words (*orthopedic*). **2.**

CONCISE PRONUNCIATION KEY: act, cāpe, dâre, pärt; set, ēqual; if, īce; ox, ōver, ôrder, oil, bo͝ok, bo͞ot, out; up, ûrge; child; sing; shoe; thin, *th*at; zh as in *treasure.* ə = *a* as in *alone, e* as in *system, i* as in *easily, o* as in *gallop, u* as in *circus;* ᵊ as in *fire* (fīᵊr), *hour* (ouᵊr). l and n can serve as syllabic consonants, as in *cradle* (krād′l), and *button* (but′n). See the full key inside the front cover.

Chem. **a.** a combining form used in the name of that acid in a given series of acids that contains the most water (*orthoboric acid*). Cf. **meta-, pyro-. b.** a combining form used in the names of the salts of these acids: if the acid ends in *-ic*, the corresponding salt ends in *-ate* (*orthoboric acid* (H_3BO_3) and *potassium orthoborate* (K_3BO_3)); if the acid ends in *-ous*, the corresponding salt ends in *-ite* (*orthoantimonous acid* (H_3SbO_3) and *potassium orthoantimonite* (K_3SbO_3)). Also, *esp. before a vowel,* **orth-.** [< Gk, comb. form of *orthós* straight, upright, correct]

or′tho·bo′ric ac′id (ôr′thə bôr′ik, -bōr′-, ôr′thə-), *Chem.* See **boric acid** (def. 1). Cf. **ortho-** (def. 2). [ORTHO- + BORIC ACID]

or·tho·cen·ter (ôr′thə sen′tər), *n. Geom.* the point of intersection of the three altitudes of a triangle. [1865–70; ORTHO- + CENTER]

or·tho·ce·phal·ic (ôr′thō sə fal′ik), *adj. Cephalom.* having a medium or intermediate relation between the height of the skull and the breadth or length. Also, **or·tho·ceph·a·lous** (ôr′thə sef′ə ləs). [1860–65; < NL *orthocephal(us)* (see ORTHO-, CEPHAL-) + -IC] **—or′tho·ceph′a·ly,** *n.*

or·tho·chro·mat·ic (ôr′thə krō mat′ik, -thō krə-), *adj. Photog.* **1.** representing correctly the relations of colors as found in a subject; isochromatic. **2.** (of an emulsion) sensitive to all visible colors except red; isochromatic. [1885–90; ORTHO- + CHROMATIC]

or·tho·clase (ôr′thə klās′, -klāz′), *n.* a common white or pink mineral of the feldspar group, $KAlSi_3O_8$, having two good cleavages at right angles, and found in silica-rich igneous rocks: used in the manufacture of porcelain. [1840–50; ORTHO- + *-clase* < Gk *klásis* cleavage, breaking]

or·tho·clas·tic (ôr′thə klas′tik), *adj. Crystall.* (of a crystal) having cleavages at right angles to each other. [1875–80; < G *orthoklastisch*, equiv. to *ortho-* ORTHO- + *-klastisch* CLASTIC]

or·tho-cous·in (ôr′thə kuz′ən, ôr′thə kuz′-), *n.* See **parallel cousin.** [1915–20]

or·tho-di·chlo·ro·ben·zene (ôr′thə dī klôr′ə ben′zēn, -ben zēn′, -klōr′-), *n. Chem.* a colorless liquid with a pleasant odor, $C_6H_4Cl_2$, used as a solvent for a wide range of organic materials. Cf. **dichlorobenzene.**

or·tho·don·tia (ôr′thə don′shə, -shē ə), *n. Dentistry.* **1.** orthodontics. **2.** treatment for the correction of irregularly aligned teeth, usually involving braces and sometimes oral surgery. [1840–50; ORTH- + -ODONT + -IA]

or·tho·don·tics (ôr′thə don′tiks), *n.* (*used with a singular v.*) the branch of dentistry dealing with the prevention and correction of irregular teeth, as by means of braces. [1905–10; ORTH- + -ODONT + -ICS] **—or′tho·don′tic, or′tho·don′tal,** *adj.* **—or′tho·don′tist,** *n.*

or·tho·don·ture (ôr′thə don′chər), *n.* orthodontia (def. 2). [1965–70; appar. b. ORTHODONTIA and DENTURE, prob. orig. (or exclusively) in r-less accents, in which both words end in (ə)]

or·tho·dox (ôr′thə doks′), *adj.* **1.** of, pertaining to, or conforming to the approved form of any doctrine, philosophy, ideology, etc. **2.** of, pertaining to, or conforming to beliefs, attitudes, or modes of conduct that are generally approved. **3.** customary or conventional, as a means or method; established. **4.** sound or correct in opinion or doctrine, esp. theological or religious doctrine. **5.** conforming to the Christian faith as represented in the creeds of the early church. **6.** (*cap.*) of, pertaining to, or designating the Eastern Church, esp. the Greek Orthodox Church. **7.** (*cap.*) of, pertaining to, or characteristic of Orthodox Jews or Orthodox Judaism. [1575–85; < LL *orthodoxus* right in religion < LGk *orthódoxos*, equiv. to *ortho-* ORTHO- + *dóx(a)* belief, opinion + *-os* adj. suffix] **—or′tho·dox′ly,** *adv.* **—or′tho·dox′ness,** *n.*
—Syn. 3. traditional, commonplace, routine, fixed.

Or′thodox Church′, 1. the Christian church comprising the local and national Eastern churches that are in communion with the ecumenical patriarch of Constantinople; Byzantine Church. **2.** (originally) the Christian church of those countries formerly comprising the Eastern Roman Empire and of countries evangelized from it; Greek Orthodox Church.

Or′thodox Jew′, a Jew who adheres faithfully to the principles and practices of traditional Judaism as evidenced chiefly by a devotion to and study of the Torah, daily synagogue attendance if possible, and strict observance of the Sabbath, religious festivals, holy days, and the dietary laws. Cf. **Conservative Jew, Reform Jew.**

Or′thodox Ju′daism, Judaism as observed by Orthodox Jews.

or′thodox sleep′, *Physiol.* dreamless sleep, characterized by a slow alpha rhythm of brain waves and no marked physiological changes. [1965–70]

or·tho·dox·y (ôr′thə dok′sē), *n., pl.* **-dox·ies** for 1. **1.** orthodox belief or practice. **2.** orthodox character. [1620–30; < LL *orthodoxia* < Gk *orthodoxía* right opinion, equiv. to *orthódox(os)* (see ORTHODOX) + *-ia* -Y[3]]

Or′thodoxy Sun′day. See under **Feast of Orthodoxy.** [1840–50]

or·tho·e·py (ôr thō′ə pē, ôr′thō ep′ē), *n.* the study of correct pronunciation. Also, **or·tho′ë·py.** [1660–70; < Gk *orthoépeia* correctness of diction, equiv. to *ortho-* ORTHO- + *epe-* (s. of *épos*) word + *-ia* -Y[3]] **—or·tho·ep·ic** (ôr′thō ep′ik), **or′tho·ep′i·cal,** *adj.* **—or·tho′e·pist,** *n.* **—or′tho·e·pis′tic,** *adj.*

CONCISE ETYMOLOGY KEY: <, descended or borrowed from; >, whence; b., blend of, blended; c., cognate with; cf., compare; deriv., derivative; equiv., equivalent; imit., imitative; obl., oblique; r., replacing; s., stem; sp., spelling, spelled; resp., respelling, respelled; trans., translation; ?, origin unknown; *, unattested; ‡, probably earlier than. See the full key inside the front cover.

or·tho·for·mate (ôr′thə fôr′māt), *n. Chem.* an ester of orthoformic acid. [ORTHO- + FORMATE]

or′tho·for′mic ac′id (ôr′thə fôr′mik, ôr′thə-), *Chem.* a hypothetical acid, $HC(OH)_3$, known only in the form of its esters. [ORTHO- + FORMIC ACID]

or·tho·gen·e·sis (ôr′thə jen′ə sis), *n.* **1.** *Biol.* **a.** Also called **orthoselection.** evolution of a species proceeding by continuous structural changes in a single lineage without presenting a branching pattern of descent. **b.** a theory that the evolution of a species in a continuous, nonbranching manner is due to a predetermined series of alterations intrinsic to the species and not subject to natural selection. **2.** *Sociol.* a hypothetical parallelism between the stages through which every culture necessarily passes, in spite of secondary conditioning factors. [1890–95; < NL; see ORTHO-, GENESIS]

or·tho·ge·net·ic (ôr′thō jə net′ik), *adj.* pertaining to or exhibiting orthogenesis. [1895–1900; < NL *orthogenet-* (s. of *orthogenesis*) ORTHOGENESIS + -IC]

or·tho·gen·ic (ôr′thə jen′ik), *adj.* **1.** *Psychol.* of, concerned with, or providing corrective treatment for mentally retarded or seriously disturbed children: *orthogenic class.* **2.** orthogenetic. [ORTHO- + -GENIC]

or′thognath′ic sur′gery, the surgical correction of deformities or malpositions of the jaw. [ORTHOGNATH(OUS) + -IC]

or·thog·na·thous (ôr thog′nə thəs), *adj. Craniom.* straight-jawed; having the profile of the face vertical or nearly so; having a gnathic index below 98. Also, **or·thog·nath·ic** (ôr′thəg nath′ik, -thog-). [1850–55; ORTHO- + -GNATHOUS] **—or·thog·na·thism** (ôr thog′nə thiz′əm), **or·thog′na·thy,** *n.*

or·thog·o·nal (ôr thog′ə nl), *adj.* **1.** *Math.* **a.** Also, **orthographic.** pertaining to or involving right angles or perpendiculars: *an orthogonal projection.* **b.** (of a system of real functions) defined so that the integral of the product of any two different functions is zero. **c.** (of a system of complex functions) defined so that the integral of the product of a function times the complex conjugate of any other function equals zero. **d.** (of two vectors) having an inner product equal to zero. **e.** (of a linear transformation) defined so that the length of a vector under the transformation equals the length of the original vector. **f.** (of a square matrix) defined so that its product with its transpose results in the identity matrix. **2.** *Crystall.* referable to a rectangular set of axes. [1565–75; obs. *orthogon(ium)* right triangle (< LL *orthogōnium* < Gk *orthogṓnion* (neut.) right-angled, equiv. to *ortho-* ORTHO- + *-gōnion* -GON) + -AL[1]] **—or·thog′o·nal′i·ty,** *n.* **—or·thog′o·nal·ly,** *adv.*

or·thog·o·nal·ize (ôr thog′ə nl īz′), *v.t.*, **-ized, -iz·ing.** *Math.* to make (vectors, functions, etc.) orthogonal. Also, *esp. Brit.,* **or·thog′o·nal·ise′.** [1925–30; ORTHOGONAL + -IZE] **—or·thog′o·nal·i·za′tion,** *n.*

orthog′onal trajec′tory, *Math.* the locus of a point whose path cuts each curve of a family of curves at right angles. [1810–20]

or·thog·ra·pher (ôr thog′rə fər), *n.* **1.** a person versed in orthography or spelling. **2.** a person who spells correctly. Also, **or·thog′ra·phist.** [1590–1600; < LL *orthograph(us)* (adj. and n.) (L *ortho-* ORTHO- + *-graphus* -GRAPH) + -ER[1]]

or·tho·graph·ic (ôr′thə graf′ik), *adj.* **1.** of or pertaining to orthography. **2.** orthogonal (def. 1a). Also, **or′tho·graph′i·cal.** [1660–70; ORTHOGRAPH(Y) + -IC] **—or′tho·graph′i·cal·ly,** *adv.*

orthograph′ic projec′tion, a two-dimensional graphic representation of an object in which the projecting lines are at right angles to the plane of the projection. Also called **orthog′onal projec′tion.** Cf. **isometric** (def. 5). [1660–70]

or·thog·ra·phize (ôr thog′rə fīz′), *v.*, **-phized, -phiz·ing.** *—v.t.* **1.** to spell correctly or according to the rules of orthography. *—v.i.* **2.** to apply the rules of correct spelling. Also, *esp. Brit.,* **or·thog′ra·phise′.** [1605–15; ORTHOGRAPH(Y) + -IZE]

or·thog·ra·phy (ôr thog′rə fē), *n., pl.* **-phies** for 3–5. **1.** the art of writing words with the proper letters, according to accepted usage; correct spelling. **2.** the part of language study concerned with letters and spelling. **3.** a method of spelling, as by the use of an alphabet or other system of symbols; spelling. **4.** a system of such symbols: *Missionaries provided the first orthography for the language.* **5.** an orthographic projection, or an elevation drawn by means of it. [1425–75; late ME *ortografye* < L *orthographia* correct writing, orthogonal projection < Gk *orthographía.* See ORTHO-, -GRAPHY]

or·tho·hy·dro·gen (ôr′thə hī′drə jən), *n. Physics, Chem.* the form of molecular hydrogen in which the nuclei of the two hydrogen atoms contained in the molecule have spins in the same direction. Cf. **parahydrogen.** [1925–30; ORTHO- + HYDROGEN]

or·tho·ker·a·tol·o·gy (ôr′thō ker′ə tol′ə jē), *n. Ophthalm.* a technique for correcting refractive errors in vision by changing the shape of the cornea with the temporary use of progressively flatter hard contact lenses. [1970–75; ORTHO- + KERATO- + -LOGY]

or·tho·mo·lec·u·lar (ôr′thō mə lek′yə lər), *adj.* being or pertaining to the treatment of disease by increasing, decreasing, or otherwise controlling the intake of natural substances, esp. vitamins. Cf. **megavitamin** (def. 1). [1965–70; ORTHO- + MOLECULAR, referring to "the provision of the optimum molecular environment for the mind," according to term's originator, Linus Pauling]

or′tho·mor′phic projec′tion (ôr′thə môr′fik, ôr′-), *Cartog.* See **conformal projection.** [1880–85; ORTHO- + -MORPHIC]

or·tho-ni·tro·phe·nol (ôr′thō nī′trə fē′nôl, -nol), *n.* See under **nitrophenol** (def. 2).

or·tho·nor·mal (ôr′thə nôr′məl), *adj. Math.* **1.** (of a system of functions) normal; normalized. **2.** (of a set of vectors) having the properties that any two vectors are perpendicular and that each vector has a length of one unit. [1930–35; ORTHO- + NORMAL]

Or·tho-No·vum (ôr′thō nō′vəm), *Pharm., Trademark.* a brand name for a tablet containing the progestogen norethindrone and an estrogen, used as an oral contraceptive.

or·tho·pe·dic (ôr′thə pē′dik), *adj.* of or pertaining to orthopedics. Also, **or′tho·pae′dic.** [1830–40; ORTHO- + Gk *paid-* (s. of *paîs*) child + -IC] **—or′tho·pe′di·cal·ly,** *adv.*

or·tho·pe·dics (ôr′thə pē′diks), *n.* (*used with a singular v.*) the medical specialty concerned with correction of deformities or functional impairments of the skeletal system, esp. the extremities and the spine, and associated structures, as muscles and ligaments. Also, **or′tho·pae′dics.** [1850–55; see ORTHOPEDIC, -ICS] **—or′tho·pe′dist,** *n.*

or·tho·phos·phate (ôr′thə fos′fāt), *n. Chem.* a salt or ester of orthophosphoric acid, or any compound containing the trivalent group $-PO_4$. [1855–60; ORTHO- + PHOSPHATE]

or′tho·phos·phor′ic ac′id (ôr′thō fos fôr′ik, -for′-, ôr′-), *Chem.* a colorless, crystalline solid, H_3PO_4, the tribasic acid of pentavalent phosphorus: used chiefly in fertilizers, as a source of phosphorus salts, and in soft drinks as an acidulant and flavoring agent. [1870–75; ORTHO- + PHOSPHORIC ACID]

or′tho·phos′pho·rous ac′id (ôr′thə fos′fər əs, ôr′thō fos fôr′əs, -fōr′-), *Chem.* a white to yellowish, crystalline, hygroscopic, water-soluble solid, H_3PO_3, used chiefly in the synthesis of phosphites. [ORTHO- + PHOSPHOROUS ACID]

or·tho·phthal′ic ac′id (ôr′thə thal′ik, -thəf thal′-). *Chem.* See under **phthalic acid** (def. 1). [ORTHO- + PHTHALIC ACID]

or·tho·phy·ric (ôr′thə fī′rik), *adj. Petrog.* of or pertaining to a texture in which the groundmass is characterized by closely packed, short, quadrilateral crystals of feldspar larger than those in a trachytic groundmass. [ORTHO- + -PHYRE + -IC]

or·thop·ne·a (ôr thop′nē ə, ôr′thop nē′ə, -thəp-), *n. Path.* difficult or painful breathing except in an erect sitting or standing position. Also, **or·thop′noe·a.** [1650–60; < Gk *orthópnoia*, equiv. to *orthópno(os)* breathing upright (*ortho-* ORTHO- + *pno(ē)* breath + *-os* adj. suffix) + *-ia* -IA] **—or′thop·ne′ic, or′thop·noe′ic,** *adj.*

or·tho·pod (ôr′thə pod′), *n. Slang.* an orthopedist. [1955–60; by shortening and alter.; see -POD]

or·tho·prax·i·a (ôr′thə prak′sē ə), *n. Med.* the correction of deformities; orthopedics. Also, **orthopraxy.** [1850–55; ORTHO- + Gk *prâx(is)* PRAXIS + -IA]

or·tho·prax·y (ôr′thə prak′sē), *n.* **1.** correctness or orthodoxy of action or practice. **2.** *Med.* orthopraxia. [1850–55; ORTHO- + PRAX(IS) + -Y[3]]

or·tho·psy·chi·a·try (ôr′thō si kī′ə trē, -sī-), *n.* an approach to psychiatry concerned with the study and treatment of behavioral disorders, esp. of young people. [1920–25; ORTHO- + PSYCHIATRY] **—or·tho·psy·chi·at·ric** (ôr′thō sī′kē a′trik), **or′tho·psy′chi·at′ri·cal,** *adj.* **—or′tho·psy·chi′a·trist,** *n.*

or·thop·ter·an (ôr thop′tər ən), *adj.* **1.** orthopterous. **—*n.* 2.** an orthopterous insect. [1895–1900; < NL *Orthopter(a)* (see ORTHOPTERON) + -AN]

or·thop·ter·on (ôr thop′tə ron′, -tər ən), *n., pl.* **-ter·a** (-tər ə). an orthopterous insect. [1875–80; < NL, sing. of *Orthoptera* name of the order. See ORTHOPTEROUS]

or·thop·ter·ous (ôr thop′tər əs), *adj.* belonging or pertaining to the Orthoptera, an order of insects, including the cockroaches, mantids, walking sticks, crickets, grasshoppers, and katydids, characterized by leathery forewings, membranous hind wings, and chewing mouthparts. [1820–30; < NL *orthopterus* straight-winged. See ORTHO-, -PTEROUS]

or·thop·tic (ôr thop′tik), *adj. Ophthalm.* pertaining to or producing normal binocular vision. [1880–85; ORTH- + OPTIC]

or·thop·tics (ôr thop′tiks), *n.* (*used with a singular v.*) a method of exercising the eye and its muscles in order to cure strabismus or improve vision. [see ORTHOPTIC, -ICS]

or·tho·rhom·bic (ôr′thə rom′bik), *adj. Crystall.* noting or pertaining to a system of crystallization characterized by three unequal axes intersecting at right angles; rhombic; trimetric. Cf. **crystal system.** [1865–70; ORTHO- + RHOMBIC]

or·tho·scope (ôr′thə skōp′), *n. Ophthalm.* (formerly) an instrument for examining the internal structures of the eye through a layer of water that neutralizes the refraction of the cornea. [1890–95; ORTHO- + -SCOPE]

or·tho·scop·ic (ôr′thə skop′ik), *adj. Ophthalm.* pertaining to, characterized by, or produced by normal vision. [1850–55; ORTHO- + -SCOPE + -IC]

or·tho·se·lec·tion (ôr′thō si lek′shən), *n. Biol.* orthogenesis (def. 1a). [ORTHO- + SELECTION]

or·tho·sis (ôr thō′sis), *n., pl.* **-ses** (-sēz). **1.** *Med.* the correction of orthopedic maladjustments. **2.** an orthotic. [1955–60; < Gk *órthōsis* a making straight, guidance, equiv. to *orthō-* (var. s. of *orthoûn* to straighten, v. deriv. of *orthós* straight) + *-sis* -SIS]

or·tho·stat (ôr′thə stat′), *n.* (in a classical temple) any of a number of large stone slabs revetting the lower part of the cella. [1905–10; < Gk *orthostátēs*, equiv. to *ortho-* ORTHO- + *státēs* that stands; see -STAT]

or·thos·ta·tes (ôr thos′tə tēz′), *n., pl.* **-tai** (-tī′). orthostat.

or·tho·stat·ic (ôr′thə stat′ik), *adj.* relating to or caused by erect posture. [1900–05; ORTHO- + STATIC]

orthostat′ic hypoten′sion, *Med.* a fall in blood

pressure associated with an upright position, usually occurring as a result of standing still for a long time or rising from a prolonged stay in bed and often causing faintness, dizziness, and vision disturbances. Also called **postural hypotension.** [1900–05]

or•thos•ti•chy (ôr thos′ti kē), *n., pl.* **-chies.** *Bot.* **1.** a vertical rank or row. **2.** an arrangement of members, as leaves, at different heights on an axis so that their median planes coincide. [1870–75; ORTHO- + Gk *-stichia* alignment, equiv. to *stích(os)* row (see STICH[1]) + *-ia* -Y[3]] —**or•thos′ti•chous,** *adj.*

or•tho•style (ôr′thə stīl′), *adj. Archit.* **1.** (of columns) erected in a straight row. **2.** having columns in a straight row or in straight rows. [1825–35; ORTHO- + -STYLE[2]]

or•thot•ic (ôr thot′ik), *n.* **1.** Also, **orthosis.** a device or support, esp. for the foot, used to relieve or correct an orthopedic problem. —*adj.* **2.** of or pertaining to orthotics. [1960–65; adj. deriv. of ORTHOSIS (on the model of PSYCHOSIS: PSYCHOTIC, etc.); see -TIC]

or•thot•ics (ôr thot′iks), *n.* (*used with a singular v.*) a branch of medicine dealing with the making and fitting of orthotic devices. [1960–65; see ORTHOTIC, -ICS] —**or•thot•ist** (ôr thot′ist, ôr′thə tist), *n.*

or•tho•to•lu•i•dine (ôr′thō tə lo͞o′i dēn′, -din), *n. Chem.* a light-yellow, very slightly water-soluble liquid, C_7H_9N, the ortho isomer of toluidine: used in the manufacture of dyes, saccharin, and other organic compounds, and in textile printing processes.

or•tho•trop•ic (ôr′thə trop′ik, -trō′pik), *adj. Bot.* noting, pertaining to, or exhibiting a mode of vertical growth. [1885–90; ORTHO- + -TROPIC]

or•thot•ro•pism (ôr tho′trə piz′əm), *n. Bot.* orthotropic tendency or growth. [1880–85; ORTHO- + -TROPISM]

or•thot•ro•pous (ôr tho′trə pəs), *adj. Bot.* (of an ovule) straight and symmetrical, with the chalaza at the evident base and the micropyle at the opposite extremity. [1820–30; < NL *orthotropus.* See ORTHO-, -TROPOUS]

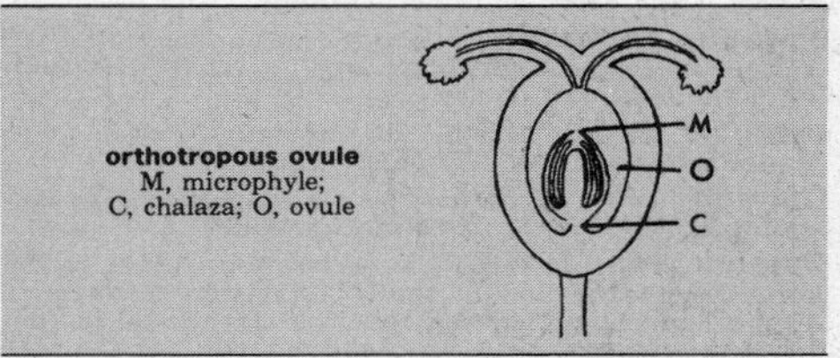

orthotropous ovule
M, microphyle;
C, chalaza; O, ovule

or•tho-xy•lene (ôr′thō zī′lēn), *n. Chem.* a clear, colorless, poisonous, flammable liquid, C_8H_{10}, the ortho isomer of xylene: used chiefly in the synthesis of phthalic anhydride.

or•thros (ôʀ′thʀôs; *Eng.* ôr′thros), *n. Gk. Orth. Ch.* the morning office, corresponding to matins. [< LGk, Gk *órthros* dawn]

Ort•ler (ôrt′lər), *n.* **1.** a range of the Alps in N Italy. **2.** the highest peak of this range. 12,802 ft. (3902 m).

or•to•lan (ôr′tl ən), *n.* **1.** an Old World bunting, *Emberiza hortulana,* esteemed as a table delicacy. **2.** the bobolink. [1520–30; < F < Pr: lit., gardener (i.e., frequenting gardens) < L *hortulānus,* equiv. to *hortul(us)* little garden (*hort(us)* garden + *-ulus* -ULE) + *-ānus* -AN]

O•ru•ro (ô ʀo͞o′ʀô), *n.* a city in W Bolivia: a former capital. 145,410; over 12,000 ft. (3660 m) high.

ORuss, Old Russian.

Or•vi•e•to (ôr′vē ā′tō, -et′ō; *It.* ôʀ vye′tô), *n.* a white wine, from dry to sweet, from Umbria, Italy. [1665–75]

Or•ville (ôr′vil), *n.* a male given name.

Or•well (ôr′wel, -wəl), *n.* **George** (*Eric Arthur Blair*), 1903–50, English novelist and essayist.

Or•well•i•an (ôr wel′ē ən), *adj.* of, pertaining to, characteristic of, or resembling the literary work of George Orwell or the totalitarian future described in his anti-utopian novel *1984* (1949). [1945–50; G. ORWELL + -IAN]

-ory[1], an adjective-forming suffix, joined to bases of Latin origin in imitation of borrowed Latin words containing the suffix **-tory**[1] (and its alternant *-sory*): *excretory; sensory; statutory.* [ME *-orie* < AF; OF *-oire* < L *-ōrius,* extracted from *-tōrius* -TORY[1]; see -OR[2]]

-ory[2], a suffix forming nouns denoting places or receptacles, joined to bases of Latin origin in imitation of borrowed Latin words containing the suffix **-tory**[2] (or its alternant *-sory*): *crematory.* [ME *-orie* < AF; OF *-oire* < L *-ōrium,* extracted from *-tōrium* -TORY[2]; see -ORY[1], -OR[2]]

o•ryx (ôr′iks, ōr′-), *n., pl.* **o•ryx•es,** (*esp. collectively*) **o•ryx. 1.** a large African antelope, *Oryx gazella,* grayish with black markings and having long, nearly straight horns: an endangered species. **2.** gemsbok. [1350–1400; ME < L < Gk *óryx* pickax, oryx]

or•zo (ôr′zō), *n.* pasta in the form of small ricelike grains. [< It: lit., barley < L *hordeum;* cf. GORSE, ORGEAT]

os[1] (os), *n., pl.* **os•sa** (os′ə). *Anat., Zool.* a bone. [1540–50; < L]

os[2] (os), *n., pl.* **o•ra** (ôr′ə, ōr′ə). *Anat., Zool.* a mouth, opening, or entrance. [1730–40; < L *ōs* mouth]

os[3] (ōs), *n., pl.* **o•sar** (ō′sär). *Geol.* an esker, esp. when of great length. [< Sw *ås* (pl. *åsar*) ridge]

OS, 1. Old Saxon. **2.** *Computers.* operating system.

Os, *Symbol, Chem.* osmium.

O/S, (of the calendar) Old Style.

o/s, 1. (of the calendar) Old Style. **2.** out of stock. **3.** (in banking) outstanding.

O.S., 1. (in prescriptions) the left eye. [< L *oculus sinister*] **2.** Old Saxon. **3.** Old School. **4.** Old Series. **5.** (of the calendar) Old Style. **6.** See **ordinary seaman.**

o.s., 1. (in prescriptions) the left eye. [< L *oculus sinister*] **2.** See **ordinary seaman.**

O.S.A., Order of St. Augustine (Augustinian).

O•sage (ō′sāj, ō sāj′), *n., pl.* **O•sag•es,** (*esp. collectively*) **O•sage** for 1. **1.** a member of a North American Indian people formerly of western Missouri, now living in northern Oklahoma. **2.** the Siouan language of the Osage. **3.** a river flowing E from E Kansas to the Missouri River in central Missouri. 500 mi. (800 km) long.

O′sage or′ange, 1. Also called **bois d'arc, bowwood.** a tree, *Maclura pomifera,* of the mulberry family, native to the south-central U.S., having hard, yellowish wood and often cultivated for hedges. **2.** the round, rough-skinned, inedible fruit of this tree. [1810–20]

O•sa•ka (ō sä′kə; *Japn.* ô′sä kä′), *n.* a city on S Honshu, in S Japan. 2,648,158.

o•sar (ō′sär), *n.* pl. of **os**[3].

O•sas•co (o͝o säs′ko͞o), *n.* a city in SE Brazil, NW of São Paulo. 376,689.

O.S.B., Order of St. Benedict (Benedictine).

Os•bert (oz′bərt), *n.* a male given name: from Old English words meaning "god" and "bright."

Os•born (oz′bərn), *n.* **1. Henry Fair•field** (fâr′fēld′), 1857–1935, U.S. paleontologist and author. **2.** a male given name.

Os•borne (oz′bərn), *n.* **1. John (James),** 1929–94, English playwright. **2. Thomas Mott,** 1859–1926, U.S. prison reformer.

Os•can (os′kən), *n.* **1.** one of an ancient people of south-central Italy. **2.** the Indo-European, probably Italic, language of the Oscans, written in an alphabet derived from the Etruscan. —*adj.* **3.** of or pertaining to the Oscans or their language. [1590–1600; L *Osc(i)* the Oscans + -AN]

Os•car (os′kər), *Trademark.* one of a group of statuettes awarded annually by the Academy of Motion Picture Arts and Sciences for achievements in motion-picture production and performance. Cf. **Academy Award.** [allegedly named in 1931 by an employee of the Academy of Motion Picture Arts and Sciences, after her uncle]

Os•car (os′kər), *n.* **1.** a word used in communications to represent the letter *O.* **2.** a male given name: from Old English words meaning "god" and "spear." **3.** *Mil.* the NATO designation for a class of nuclear-powered Soviet attack submarine armed with 24 antiship cruise missiles.

Os•car (os′kər), *n.* one of a series of small communications satellites, launched into polar orbit as piggyback passengers on U.S. launch vehicles, for unrestricted use by radio amateurs. [1980–85; *o(rbiting) s(atellite) c(arrying) a(mateur) r(adio)*]

Oscar II, 1829–1907, king of Sweden 1872–1907; king of Norway 1872–1905.

Os•ce•o•la (os′ē ō′lə, ō′sē-), *n.* 1804–38, U.S. Indian leader: chief of the Seminole tribe.

os•cil•late (os′ə lāt′), *v.,* **-lat•ed, -lat•ing.** —*v.i.* **1.** to swing or move to and fro, as a pendulum does. **2.** to vary or vacillate between differing beliefs, opinions, conditions, etc.: *He oscillates regularly between elation and despair.* **3.** *Physics.* to have, produce, or generate oscillations. **4.** *Math.* (of a function, sequence, etc.) to tend to no limit, including infinity: *The sequence 0, 1, 0, 1, . . . oscillates.* —*v.t.* **5.** to cause to move to and fro; vibrate. [1720–30; < L *oscillātus* (ptp. of *oscillāre* to swing, ride on a swing), equiv. to *oscill(um)* a swing + *-ātus* -ATE[1]] —**Syn. 1.** See **swing**[1]. **2.** fluctuate, waver.

os′cillating en′gine, a steam engine having piston rods connected directly to the crankshaft and cylinders oscillating on trunnions. [1815–25]

os′cillating u′niverse, *Astron.* a variant model of the closed universe in which the universe undergoes cycles of expansion and contraction. Cf. **closed universe, open universe.**

os•cil•la•tion (os′ə lā′shən), *n.* **1.** an act or instance of oscillating. **2.** a single swing or movement in one direction of an oscillating body. **3.** fluctuation between beliefs, opinions, conditions, etc. **4.** *Physics.* **a.** an effect expressible as a quantity that repeatedly and regularly fluctuates above and below some mean value, as the pressure of a sound wave or the voltage of an alternating current. **b.** a single fluctuation between maximum and minimum values in such an effect. **5.** *Math.* **a.** the difference between the least upper bound and the greatest lower bound of the functional values of a function in a given interval. **b.** Also called **saltus.** the limit of the oscillation in an interval containing a given point, as the length of the interval approaches zero. [1650–60; < L *oscillātiōn-* (s. of *oscillātiō*) a swinging, equiv. to *oscillāt(us)* (see OSCILLATE) + *-iōn-* -ION]

os•cil•la•tor (os′ə lā′tər), *n.* **1.** *Electronics.* a circuit that produces an alternating output current of a certain frequency determined by the characteristics of the circuit components. **2.** a device or machine producing oscillations. **3.** a person or thing that oscillates. [1825–35; < NL, equiv. to L *oscillā(re)* to swing (see OSCILLATE) + *-tor* -TOR]

os•cil•la•to•ry (os′ə lə tôr′ē, -tōr′ē), *adj.* characterized by or involving oscillation. [1730–40; < NL *oscillātōrius,* equiv. to L *oscillā(re)* to swing (see OSCILLATE) + *-tōrius* -TORY[1]]

os•cil•lo•gram (ə sil′ə gram′), *n. Elect.* the record produced by the action of an oscillograph or oscilloscope. [1900–05; < L *oscill(āre)* to swing (see OSCILLATE) + -O- + -GRAM[1]]

os•cil•lo•graph (ə sil′ə graf′, -gräf′), *n. Elect.* a device for recording the wave-forms of changing currents, voltages, or any other quantity that can be translated into electric energy, as sound waves. [1870–75; OSCILL(ATE) + -O- + -GRAPH] —**os•cil•lo•graph•ic,** (ə sil′ə-graf′ik), *adj.* —**os•cil•log•ra•phy** (os′ə log′rə fē), *n.*

os•cil•lom•e•ter (os′ə lom′i tər), *n. Med.* an instrument for measuring oscillations, esp. those of the arterial pulse. [1895–1900; OSCILL(ATE) + -O- + -METER] —**os•cil•lo•met•ric** (os′ə lō me′trik, ə sil′ə-), *adj.* —**os′cil•lom′e•try,** *n.*

os•cil•lo•scope (ə sil′ə skōp′), *n. Elect.* a device that uses a cathode-ray tube or similar instrument to depict on a screen periodic changes in an electric quantity, as voltage or current. [1905–10; OSCILL(ATE) + -O- + -SCOPE] —**os•cil•lo•scop•ic** (ə sil′ə skop′ik), *adj.* —**os•cil′lo•scop′i•cal•ly,** *adv.*

os•cine (os′in, -īn), *adj.* **1.** of, belonging to, or pertaining to the suborder Oscines, of the order Passeriformes, comprising the songbirds that have highly developed vocal organs. —*n.* **2.** an oscine bird. [1880–85, *Amer.*; < NL *Oscines* name of the suborder, equiv. to L *oscin-* (s. of *oscen*) songbird, orig. bird that gives omens by its cry (*o(b)s-,* var. of *ob-* OB- + *-cin-,* s. of *-cen,* n. deriv. of *canere* to sing) + *-es* nom. pl. n. suffix]

os•ci•tant (os′i tənt), *adj.* **1.** yawning, as with drowsiness; gaping. **2.** drowsy or inattentive. **3.** dull, lazy, or negligent. [1615–25; < L *ōscitant-* (s. of *ōscitāns*) (prp. of *ōscitāre* to gape, yawn), equiv. to *ōs* mouth + *cit(āre)* to put in motion) + *-ant-* -ANT] —**os′ci•tan•cy, os′ci•tance,** *n.*

Os•co-Um•bri•an (os′kō um′brē ən), *n.* a group of languages, usually classified as Italic, that contains Oscan and Umbrian. [1890–95]

os•cu•lant (os′kyə lənt), *adj.* **1.** united by certain common characteristics. **2.** adhering closely; embracing. [1810–20; < L *ōsculant-* (s. of *ōsculāns*), prp. of *ōsculārī* to kiss; see OSCULATE, -ANT]

os•cu•lar (os′kyə lər), *adj.* **1.** pertaining to an osculum. **2.** pertaining to the mouth or kissing: *oscular stimulation.* [1820–30; < L *ōscul(um)* kiss, mouth (see OSCULUM) + -AR[1]] —**os•cu•lar•i•ty** (os′kyə lar′i tē), *n.*

os•cu•late (os′kyə lāt′), *v.,* **-lat•ed, -lat•ing.** —*v.i.* **1.** to come into close contact or union. **2.** *Geom.* (of a curve) to touch another curve or another part of the same curve so as to have the same tangent and curvature at the point of contact. —*v.t.* **3.** to bring into close contact or union. **4.** *Geom.* (of a curve) to touch (another curve or another part of the same curve) in osculation. **5.** to kiss. [1650–60; < L *ōsculātus* (ptp. of *ōsculārī* to kiss), equiv. to *ōscul(um)* kiss, lit., little mouth (see OSCULUM) + *-ātus* -ATE[1]] —**os•cu•la•to•ry** (os′kyə lə tôr′ē, -tōr′ē), *adj.*

os′culating cir′cle, *Math.* See **circle of curvature.** [1810–20]

os′culating plane′, *Math.* the plane containing the circle of curvature of a point on a given curve. [1860–65]

os•cu•la•tion (os′kyə lā′shən), *n.* **1.** the act of kissing. **2.** a kiss. **3.** close contact. **4.** *Geom.* the contact between two osculating curves or the like. [1650–60; < L *ōsculātiōn-* (s. of *ōsculātiō*) a kissing, equiv. to *ōsculāt(us)* (see OSCULATE) + *-iōn-* -ION]

os•cu•lum (os′kyə ləm), *n., pl.* **-la** (-lə). a small mouthlike aperture, as of a sponge. [1605–15; < NL, L *ōsculum,* equiv. to *ōs* mouth + *-culum* -CULE[1]]

OSD, Office of the Secretary of Defense.

O.S.D., Order of St. Dominic (Dominican).

-ose[1], a suffix occurring in adjectives borrowed from Latin, meaning "full of," "abounding in," "given to," "like": *frondose; globose; jocose; otiose; verbose.* [< L *-ōsus.* Cf. -OUS]

-ose[2], a suffix used in chemical terminology to form the names of sugars and other carbohydrates (*amylose; fructose; hexose; lactose*), and of protein derivatives (*proteose*). [extracted from GLUCOSE]

O•see (ō′zē, ō′sē), *n. Douay Bible.* Hosea.

Ö•sel (œ′zəl), *n.* German name of **Saaremaa.**

O•se•tian (o sē′shən), *adj., n.* Ossetian.

O•set•ic (o set′ik), *adj., n.* Ossetic.

O.S.F., Order of St. Francis (Franciscan).

OSFCW, Office of Solid Fuels Coordinator for War.

Os•good (oz′go͝od), *n.* a male given name.

Osh (ôsh), *n.* a city in W Kirghizia, in the SW Soviet Union in Asia, SE of Andizhan. 169,000.

OSHA (ō′shə, osh′ə), *n. U.S. Govt.* the division of the Department of Labor that sets and enforces occupational health and safety rules. [*O(ccupational) S(afety and) H(ealth) A(dministration)*]

Osh•a•wa (osh′ə wə), *n.* a city in SE Ontario, in S Canada, NE of Toronto, on Lake Ontario. 117,519.

Osh•kosh (osh′kosh), *n.* a city in E Wisconsin, on Lake Winnebago. 49,678.

O•shog•bo (ō shog′bō), *n.* a city in SW Nigeria. 208,966.

o•sier (ō′zhər), *n.* **1.** any of various willows, as the red osier, having tough, flexible twigs or branches that are used for wickerwork. **2.** a twig from such a willow. **3.** any of various North American dogwoods. [1300–50; ME < MF; akin to ML *ausāria* willow bed] —**o′siered,** *adj.* —**o′sier•like′,** *adj.*

O•si•pen•ko (os′ə peng′kō; *Russ.* u syi pyen′kə), *n.* former name of **Berdyansk.**

O•si•ris (ō sī′ris), *n. Egyptian Relig.* the king and judge of the dead, the husband and brother of Isis, and

CONCISE PRONUNCIATION KEY: *act, cāpe, dâre, pärt; set, ēqual; if, ice; ox, ōver, ôrder, oil, bo͝ok, bo͞ot, out; up, ûrge; child; sing; shoe; thin, that;* zh as in *treasure.* ə = *a* as in *alone, e* as in *system, i* as in *easily, o* as in *gallop, u* as in *circus;* ᵊ as in *fire* (fīᵊr), *hour* (ouᵊr). l and n can serve as syllabic consonants, as in *cradle* (krād′l), and *button* (but′n). See the full key inside the front cover.

father (or brother) of Horus, killed by Set but later resurrected (after Horus killed Set): usually depicted as a man, partly wrapped as a mummy, having a beard and wearing the atef-crown. —**O·si·ri·an** (ō sī′rē ən), *adj.*

Osiris

-osis, a suffix occurring in nouns that denote actions, conditions, or states (*hypnosis; leukocytosis; osmosis*), esp. disorders or abnormal states (*chlorosis; neurofibromatosis; tuberculosis*). Cf. **-otic.** [on the model of Gk borrowings ending in Gk *-ōsis,* as *sklērōsis* SCLEROSIS, derived orig. from verbs ending in the formative *-o-* (*-ō-* in n. derivatives), with the suffix *-sis* -SIS]

Os·ka·loo·sa (os′kə lo͞o′sə), *n.* a city in SE central Iowa. 10,629.

OSlav, Old Slavic.

Os·ler (ōs′lər, oz′-), *n.* **Sir William,** 1849–1919, Canadian physician and professor of medicine.

Os·lo (oz′lō, os′-; *Norw.* o͝os′lo͝o), *n.* a seaport in and the capital of Norway, in the SE part, at the head of Oslo Fiord. 463,022. Formerly, **Christiania.**

Os′lo Fiord′, an inlet of the Skagerrak, in SE Norway. 75 mi. (120 km) long.

Os·man (oz′mən, os′-; *Turk.* os män′), *n.* 1259–1326, Turkish emir 1299–1326: founder of the Ottoman dynasty. Also, **Othman.**

Os·man·li (oz man′lē, os-), *n., pl.* **-lis,** *adj.* —*n.* **1.** an Ottoman. **2.** the language of the Ottoman Turks. —*adj.* **3.** Ottoman.

os·mat·ic (oz mat′ik), *adj.* **1.** of or pertaining to the sense of smell. **2.** of or pertaining to animals having a keenly developed sense of smell. [1885–90; < F *osmatique,* equiv. to Gk *osm*(*ḗ*) smell + F *-atique* (see -ATE[1], -IC)]

os·mic (oz′mik), *adj. Chem.* of or containing osmium in its higher valences, esp. the tetravalent state. [1835–45; OSM(IUM) + -IC]

os·mics (oz′miks), *n.* (*used with a singular v.*) the science dealing with the sense of smell. [1920–25; < Gk *osm*(*ḗ*) smell + -ICS]

os·mi·dro·sis (oz′mi drō′sis), *n. Med.* bromhidrosis. [< Gk *osm*(*ḗ*) smell + (H)IDROSIS]

os·mi·ous (oz′mē əs), *adj. Chem.* of or containing osmium in its lower valences. [1840–50; OSMI(UM) + -OUS]

os·mi·rid·i·um (oz′mə rid′ē əm), *n. Chem.* iridosmine. [1875–80; < G; see OSMIUM, IRIDIUM]

os·mi·um (oz′mē əm), *n. Chem.* a hard, heavy, metallic element having the greatest density of the known elements and forming octavalent compounds, as OsO_4 and OsF_8: used chiefly as a catalyst, in alloys, and in the manufacture of electric-light filaments. *Symbol:* Os; *at. wt.:* 190.2; *at. no.:* 76; *sp. gr.:* 22.57. [1795–1805; < NL < Gk *osm*(*ḗ*) smell + *-ium* -IUM; named from the penetrating odor of one of its oxides]

os′mium tetrox′ide, *Chem.* a crystalline or amorphous, colorless, poisonous compound, OsO_4, soluble in water, alcohol, and ether: used for microscopic staining, in photography, and as a catalyst in organic synthesis. Also called **os′mic ac′id.** [1875–80]

osmo- a combining form representing **osmosis** in compound words: *osmoregulation.*

os·mom·e·ter (oz mom′i tər, os-), *n.* an instrument used in osmometry. [1850–55; OSMO- + -METER]

os·mom·e·try (oz mom′i trē, os-), *n. Physical Chem.* measurement of osmotic pressure. [1910–15; OSMO- + -METRY] —**os·mo·met·ric** (oz′mə me′trik, os′-), *adj.* —**os′mo·met′ri·cal·ly,** *adv.*

os·mo·reg·u·la·tion (oz′mō reg′yə lā′shən, os′-), *n.* the process by which cells and simple organisms maintain fluid and electrolyte balance with their surroundings. [1930–35; OSMO- + REGULATION]

os·mose (oz′mōs, os′-), *v.,* **-mosed, -mos·ing,** *n.* —*v.i.* **1.** to undergo osmosis. —*v.t.* **2.** to subject to osmosis. —*n.* **3.** osmosis. [1850–55; back formation from OSMOSIS]

os·mo·sis (oz mō′sis, os-), *n.* **1.** *Physical Chem., Cell Biol.* **a.** the tendency of a fluid, usually water, to pass through a semipermeable membrane into a solution where the solvent concentration is higher, thus equalizing the concentrations of materials on either side of the membrane. **b.** the diffusion of fluids through membranes or porous partitions. Cf. **endosmosis, exosmosis. 2.** a subtle or gradual absorption or mingling: *He never studies but seems to learn by osmosis.* [1865–70; Latinized form of now obs. *osmose* osmosis, extracted from *endosmose* endosmosis, *exosmose* exosmosis < F, equiv. to *end-* END-, *ex-* EX-[2] + Gk *ōsm*(*ós*) push, thrust + F *-ose* -OSIS] —**os·mot·ic** (oz mot′ik, os-), *adj.* —**os·mot′i·cal·ly,** *adv.*

osmot′ic pres′sure, *Physical Chem.* the force that a dissolved substance exerts on a semipermeable membrane, through which it cannot penetrate, when separated by it from pure solvent. [1885–90]

os·mund[1] (oz′mənd, os′-), *n.* any fern of the genus *Osmunda,* esp. the royal fern. [1325–75; ME *osmunde* < AF *osmunde,* OF *osmonde* < ?]

os·mund[2] (oz′mənd, os′-), *n.* a superior quality of iron, formerly used for fishhooks, arrowheads, etc. [1250–1300; ME *osmund, osmond* < MLG *osemunt* < OSw *osmunder* < ?]

Os·na·brück (oz′nə bro͝ok′; *Ger.* ôs′nä brYk′), *n.* a city in Lower Saxony, in NW Germany. 150,900.

os·na·burg (oz′nə bûrg′), *n.* a heavy, coarse cotton in a plain weave, for grain sacks and sportswear and also finished into cretonne. [1535–45; irreg. after OSNABRÜCK, known for its linen]

OSO, *U.S. Aerospace.* Orbiting Solar Observatory: one of a series of scientific satellites, launched between 1962 and 1975, that studied the sun at ultraviolet, x-ray, and gamma-ray wavelengths.

O·sor·no (ô sôr′nô), *n.* a city in S Chile. 78,187.

OSP, he died without issue. [< L *obiit sine prōle*]

OSp, Old Spanish.

os·prey (os′prē), *n., pl.* **-preys. 1.** Also called **fish hawk.** a large hawk, *Pandion haliaetus,* that feeds on fish. **2.** a plume for trimming hats. [1425–75; late ME *ospray*(*e*) << L *ossifraga* OSSIFRAGE; cf. MF *orfraie, offraie,* OF *ospres*]

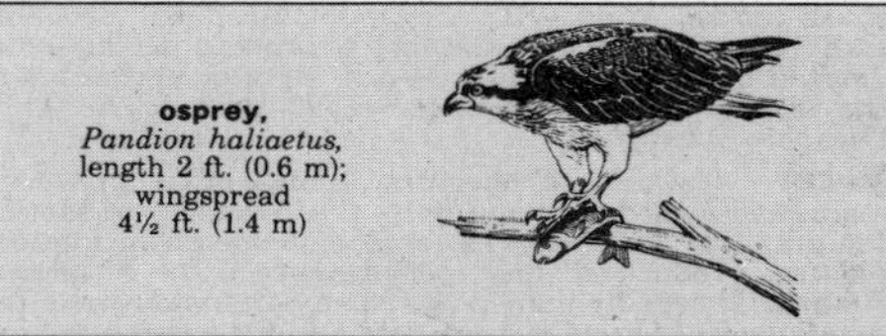
osprey,
Pandion haliaetus,
length 2 ft. (0.6 m);
wingspread
4½ ft. (1.4 m)

OSRD, Office of Scientific Research and Development.

OSS, Office of Strategic Services: a U.S. government intelligence agency during World War II. Also, **O.S.S.**

os·sa (os′ə), *n.* pl. of **os**[1].

Os·sa (os′ə), *n.* a mountain in E Greece, in Thessaly. 6490 ft. (1978 m).

os·se·in (os′ē in), *n. Biochem.* the collagen of bone, remaining after the mineral matter has been removed by treatment with dilute acid. [1855–60; < L *osse*(*us*) OSSEOUS + -IN[2]]

os·se·let (os′ə lit), *n. Vet. Pathol.* a hard nodule on the leg of a horse, esp. one on the inner side of the knee or the outer side of the fetlock. [1680–90; < F: lit., little bone, OF; see OS[1], -LET]

os·se·ous (os′ē əs), *adj.* composed of, containing, or resembling bone; bony. [1675–85; < L *osseus* bony, equiv. to *oss-* (s. of *os*) bone + *-eus* -EOUS] —**os′se·ous·ly,** *adv.*

Os·set (os′it), *n.* a member of an Aryan people of Ossetia whose religion combines features of Islam and Christianity. Also, **Os·sete** (os′ēt), **Ossetian.**

Os·se·tia (o sē′shə; *Russ.* u sye′tyi yə), *n.* a region in Caucasia: divided between the North Ossetian Autonomous Republic of the Russian Federation and the South Ossetian Autonomous Region of the Georgian Republic.

Os·se·tian (o sē′shən), *adj.* **1.** Also, **Ossetic.** of, pertaining to, or characteristic of Ossetia or the Ossets. —*n.* **2.** an Osset. [1805–15; OSSET(IA) or OSSET + -IAN]

Os·set·ic (o set′ik), *adj.* **1.** Ossetian. —*n.* **2.** the Indo-European, Iranian language of the Ossets. [1920–25; OSSET + -IC]

os·si·a (ō sē′ə), *conj.* (indicating an alternative, usually easier, version of a passage in a musical score) or; or else. [1875–80; < It *o sia* or let it be]

Os·sian (osh′ən, os′ē ən), *n. Gaelic Legend.* a legendary hero and poet and son of Finn, who is supposed to have lived during the 3rd century A.D., represented in Gaelic poems and in imitations of them written by James Macpherson in the 18th century. Also, **Oisin.**

Os·si·an·ic (os′ē an′ik, osh′ē-), *adj.* **1.** of, pertaining to, or characteristic of Ossian, the poetry attributed to him, or the rhythmic prose published by James Macpherson in 1762–63, purporting to be a translation from the Scots Gaelic. **2.** grandiloquent; bombastic. [1800–10; OSSIAN + -IC]

os·si·cle (os′i kəl), *n.* a small bone. [1570–80; < L *ossiculum,* equiv. to *ossi-* (comb. form of *os*) bone + *-culum* -CLE[1]] —**os·sic·u·lar** (o sik′yə lər), **os·sic·u·late** (o sik′yə lit), *adj.*

Os·si·etz·ky (ô′sē ets′kē), *n.* **Carl von** (kärl fən), 1889–1938, German pacifist: Nobel peace prize 1935.

os·sif·er·ous (o sif′ər əs), *adj.* containing bones, esp. fossil bones: *ossiferous caves and rock beds.* [1815–25; < L *ossi-* (comb. form of *os*) bone + -FEROUS]

os·si·fi·ca·tion (os′ə fi kā′shən), *n.* **1.** the act or process of ossifying. **2.** the state of being ossified. **3.** something that has ossified; a bony formation. [1690–1700; < L *ossi-,* comb. form of *os* bone + -FICATION]

os·si·fied (os′ə fīd′), *adj.* **1.** hardened like or into bone. **2.** *Slang.* drunk. [1790–1800; OSSIFY + -ED[2]]

os·si·frage (os′ə frij), *n.* **1.** the lammergeier. **2.** *Archaic.* the osprey. [1595–1605; < L *ossifraga* sea eagle, lit., bone-breaker (n. use of fem. of *ossifragus* bone-breaking), equiv. to *ossi-* (comb. form of *os*) bone + *frag-,* var. s. of *frangere* to BREAK + *-a* nom. sing. fem. n. and adj. ending]

os·si·fy (os′ə fī′), *v.,* **-fied, -fy·ing.** —*v.t.* **1.** to convert into or cause to harden like bone. —*v.i.* **2.** to become bone or harden like bone. **3.** to become rigid or inflexible in habits, attitudes, opinions, etc.: *a young man who began to ossify right after college.* [1705–15; < L *ossi-* (s. of *os*) bone + -FY] —**os′si·fi′er,** *n.*

Os·si·ning (os′ə ning), *n.* a town in SE New York, on the Hudson: the site of a state prison formerly known as Sing Sing. 20,196. Formerly, **Sing Sing.**

os·so·bu·co (os′ō bo͞o′kō, ō′sō-; *It.* ôs′sô bo͞o′kô), *n., pl.* **os·si·bu·chi** (os′ē bo͞o′kē, ō′sē-; *It.* ôs′sē bo͞o′kē). *Italian Cookery.* a dish of sliced veal shanks, typically prepared with olive oil, wine, seasonings, tomatoes, etc., and served with rice or other vegetables. [1930–35; < It (Tuscan rendering of Milanese dial. *òss bus*), equiv. to *osso* bone (< L *ossum,* by-form of *os,* s. *oss-*) + *buco* hole, cavity, var. of *buca* (prob. < VL **būca,* by-form of L *bucca* mouth)]

os·su·ar·i·um (osh′o͞o âr′ē əm, os′-), *n., pl.* **-ar·i·a** (-âr′ē ə). ossuary.

os·su·ar·y (osh′o͞o er′ē, os′-), *n., pl.* **-ar·ies.** a place or receptacle for the bones of the dead. Also, **ossuarium.** [1650–60; < LL *ossuārium,* var. of *ossārium,* equiv. to *oss-* (s. of *os*) bone + *-ārium* -ARY]

O star (ō′ stär′), a very hot, massive, blue star of spectral type O, having a surface temperature between 30,000 and 50,000 K and an absorption spectrum with few lines, though the Balmer series of hydrogen lines is present and lines of ionized helium are detectable. Cf. **spectral type.**

oste-, var. of **osteo-** before a vowel: *osteitis.*

os·te·al (os′tē əl), *adj.* osseous. [1875–80; OSTE- + -AL[1]]

os·tec·to·my (o stek′tə mē), *n., pl.* **-mies.** *Surg.* excision of part or all of a bone. Also, **os·te·ec·to·my** (os′tē ek′tə mē). [1890–95; OST(E)- + -ECTOMY]

Os·te·ich·thy·es (os′tē ik′thē ēz′), *n.* the class comprising the bony fishes. [< NL < Gk *osté*(*on*) bone (see OSTE-) + *ichthýes* fish (pl. of *ichthýs*)]

os·te·i·tis (os′tē ī′tis), *n. Pathol.* inflammation of the substance of bone. [1830–40; OSTE- + -ITIS] —**os·te·it·ic** (os′tē it′ik), *adj.*

ostei′tis de·for′mans (di fôr′manz), *Pathol.* See **Paget's disease.** [< NL; deforming osteitis]

Ost·end (os tend′, os′tend), *n.* a seaport in NW Belgium. 69,039. French, **Os·tende** (ôs tänd′).

Ostend′ Manifes′to, a declaration (1854) issued from Ostend, Belgium, by the U.S. ministers to England, France, and Spain, stating that the U.S. would be justified in seizing Cuba if Spain did not sell it to the U.S.

os·ten·si·ble (o sten′sə bəl), *adj.* **1.** outwardly appearing as such; professed; pretended: *an ostensible cheerfulness concealing sadness.* **2.** apparent, evident, or conspicuous: *the ostensible truth of their theories.* [1720–30; < F < L *ostēns*(*us*), var. of *ostentus* (see OSTENSIVE) + F *-ible* -IBLE] —**os·ten′si·bly,** *adv.*

os·ten·sive (o sten′siv), *adj.* **1.** clearly or manifestly demonstrative. **2.** ostensible. [1595–1605; < ML *ostēnsīvus,* equiv. to L *ostēns*(*us*), var. of *ostentus* ptp. of *ostendere* to present, display (*o*(*b*)*s-,* var. of *ob-* OB- + *tend*(*ere*) to stretch + *-tus* ptp. suffix) + *-īvus* -IVE] —**os·ten′sive·ly,** *adv.*

osten′sive defini′tion, *Philos.* the definition of a term by pointing to one or more examples to which the term can be applied. [1920–25]

os·ten·so·ri·um (os′tən sôr′ē əm, -sōr′-), *n., pl.* **-so·ri·a** (-sôr′ē ə, -sōr′ē ə). *Rom. Cath. Ch.* ostensory. [1750–60]

os·ten·so·ry (o sten′sə rē), *n., pl.* **-ries.** *Rom. Cath. Ch.* monstrance. Also, **ostensorium.** [1715–25; < ML *ostēnsōrium;* see OSTENSIVE, -TORY[2]]

os·ten·ta·tion (os′ten tā′shən, -tən-), *n.* **1.** pretentious or conspicuous show, as of wealth or importance; display intended to impress others. **2.** *Archaic.* the act of showing or exhibiting; display. [1425–75; late ME *ostentacioun* < MF *ostentation* < L *ostentātiōn-* (s. of *ostentātiō*), equiv. to *ostentāt*(*us*) ptp. of *ostentāre* to display, exhibit, freq. of *ostendere* to present, display (equiv. to *os-,* var of *ob-* OB- + *ten*(*dere*) to stretch + *-t-* freq. suffix + *-ātus* -ATE[1]) + *-iōn-* -ION]
—**Syn. 1.** pretension, pretense. See **show.**

os·ten·ta·tious (os′ten tā′shəs, -tən-), *adj.* **1.** characterized by or given to pretentious or conspicuous show in an attempt to impress others: *an ostentatious dresser.* **2.** (of actions, manner, qualities exhibited, etc.) intended to attract notice: *Lady Bountiful's ostentatious charity.* [1650–60; OSTENTAT(ION) + -IOUS] —**os′ten·ta′tious·ly,** *adv.* —**os′ten·ta′tious·ness,** *n.*
—**Syn. 1.** See **grandiose.**

osteo-, a combining form meaning "bone," used in the formation of compound words: *osteometry.* Also, *esp. before a vowel,* **oste-.** [< Gk, comb. form of *ostéon*]

os·te·o·ar·thri·tis (os′tē ō är thrī′tis), *n. Pathol.* the most common form of arthritis, usually occurring after middle age, marked by chronic breakdown of cartilage in the joints leading to pain, stiffness, and swelling. Also called **degenerative joint disease.** [1875–80; OSTEO- + ARTHRITIS]

os·te·o·ar·thro·sis (os′tē ō är thrō′sis), *n.* chronic, noninflammatory arthritis. [1930–35; OSTEO- + ARTHR- + -OSIS]

os·te·o·blast (os′tē ə blast′), *n. Anat.* a bone-forming cell. [1870–75; OSTEO- + -BLAST] —**os′te·o·blas′tic,** *adj.*

os·te·o·chon·dri·tis (os′tē ō kon drī′tis), *n. Pathol.* inflammation of bone and cartilage. [OSTEO- + CHONDR- + -ITIS]

os·te·o·chon·dro·sis (os′tē ō kon drō′sis), *n. Pathol.* a disease of bone and cartilage growth centers in children that begins as a necrosis and is followed by regeneration or renewed calcification. [OSTEO- + CHONDR- + -OSIS]

os·te·oc·la·sis (os′tē ok′lə sis), *n.* **1.** *Physiol.* the breaking down or absorption of osseous tissue. **2.** *Surg.* the fracturing of a bone to correct deformity. [< NL; see OSTEO-, -CLASIS]

os·te·o·clast (os′tē ə klast′), *n.* **1.** *Cell Biol.* one of the large multinuclear cells in growing bone concerned with the absorption of osseous tissue, as in the formation of canals. **2.** *Surg.* an instrument for effecting osteoclasis. [1870–75; OSTEO- + *-clast* < Gk *klastós* broken] **—os′te·o·clas′tic,** *adj.*

os·te·o·cope (os′tē ə kōp′), *n. Pathol.* severe pain in the bones, esp. that occurring in syphilitic persons. [1700–10; < Gk *osteokópos,* equiv. to *osteo-* OSTEO- + *kópos* beating, toil, fatigue]

os·te·o·cyte (os′tē ə sīt′), *n. Cell Biol.* a cell of osseous tissue within the bone matrix; a bone cell. [1940–45; OSTEO- + -CYTE]

os·te·o·gen·e·sis (os′tē ə jen′ə sis), *n.* the formation of bone. [1820–30; OSTEO- + GENESIS] **—os·te·o·ge·net·ic** (os′tē ō jə net′ik), **os·te·og·e·nous** (os′tē oj′ə nəs), *adj.*

osteogen′esis im·per·fec′ta (im′pər fek′tə), *Pathol.* a rare hereditary disease in which abnormal connective tissue development leads to fragile bones subject to fracture. [1900–05; < NL: imperfect osteogenesis]

os·te·o·gen·ic (os′tē ə jen′ik), *adj.* **1.** derived from or made up of bone-forming tissue. **2.** of or pertaining to osteogenesis. [1855–60; OSTEO- + -GENIC]

os·te·oid (os′tē oid′), *adj.* **1.** resembling bone; bonelike. **2.** having a skeleton of bones. [1830–40; OSTE- + -OID]

os·te·ol·o·gy (os′tē ol′ə jē), *n.* the branch of anatomy dealing with the skeleton. [1660–70; < NL *osteologia.* See OSTEO-, -LOGY] **—os·te·o·log·i·cal** (os′tē ə loj′i kəl), **os′te·o·log′ic,** *adj.* **—os′te·o·log′i·cal·ly,** *adv.* **—os′te·ol′o·gist,** *n.*

os·te·o·ma (os′tē ō′mə), *n., pl.* **-mas, -ma·ta** (-mə tə). *Pathol.* a benign tumor composed of osseous tissue. [1840–50; OSTE- + -OMA]

os·te·o·ma·la·cia (os′tē ō mə lā′shə, -shē ə, -sē ə), *n. Pathol.* a condition characterized by softening of the bones with resultant pain, weakness, and bone fragility, caused by inadequate deposition of calcium or vitamin D. [1815–25; < NL; see OSTEO-, MALACIA] **—os′te·o·ma·la′cial, os·te·o·ma·lac·ic** (os′tē ō mə las′ik), *adj.*

os·te·om·e·try (os′tē om′i trē), *n.* the anthropometric measurement of bones. [1875–80; OSTEO- + -METRY] **—os·te·o·met·ric** (os′tē ə me′trik), **os′te·o·met′ri·cal,** *adj.*

os·te·o·my·e·li·tis (os′tē ō mī′ə lī′tis), *n. Pathol.* an inflammation of the bone and bone marrow, usually caused by bacterial infection. [1850–55; OSTEO- + MYELITIS]

os·te·o·path (os′tē ə path′), *n.* a physician who practices osteopathy. Also, **os·te·op·a·thist** (os′tē op′ə thist). [1895–1900, *Amer.*; back formation from OSTEOPATHY]

os·te·op·a·thy (os′tē op′ə thē), *n.* a therapeutic system originally based upon the premise that manipulation of the muscles and bones to promote structural integrity could restore or preserve health: current osteopathic physicians use the diagnostic and therapeutic techniques of conventional medicine as well as manipulative measures. [1855–60; OSTEO- + -PATHY] **—os·te·o·path·ic** (os′tē ə path′ik), *adj.* **—os′te·o·path′i·cal·ly,** *adv.*

os·te·o·pe·tro·sis (os′tē ō pi trō′sis), *n. Pathol.* any of several hereditary diseases characterized by increased bone density. [1925–30; OSTEO- + Gk *petrō-,* var. s. of *petroûn* to turn to stone (deriv. of *pétra* stone) + *-sis* -SIS; see -OSIS]

os·te·o·phyte (os′tē ə fīt′), *n. Pathol.* a small osseous excrescence or outgrowth on bone. [1840–50; OSTEO- + -PHYTE] **—os·te·o·phyt·ic** (os′tē ə fit′ik), *adj.*

os·te·o·plas·tic (os′tē ə plas′tik), *adj.* **1.** *Surg.* pertaining to osteoplasty. **2.** *Physiol.* pertaining to bone formation. [1860–65; OSTEO- + -PLASTIC]

os·te·o·plas·ty (os′tē ə plas′tē), *n. Surg.* plastic surgery on a bone to repair a defect or loss. [1860–65; OSTEO- + -PLASTY]

os·te·o·po·ro·sis (os′tē ō pə rō′sis), *n. Pathol.* a disorder in which the bones become increasingly porous, brittle, and subject to fracture, owing to loss of calcium and other mineral components, sometimes resulting in pain, decreased height, and skeletal deformities: common in older persons, primarily postmenopausal women, but also associated with long-term steroid therapy and certain endocrine disorders. [1840–50; OSTEO- + Gk *pór(os)* passage, PORE[2] + -OSIS]

os·te·o·po·rot·ic (os′tē ō pə rot′ik), *adj. Pathol.* **1.** of, pertaining to, or caused by osteoporosis. **2.** suffering from osteoporosis. [1905–10; OSTEOPORO(SIS) + -TIC]

os·te·o·ra·di·o·ne·cro·sis (os′tē ō rā′dē ō nə krō′sis, -ne-), *n. Pathol.* bone tissue death induced by radiation. [OSTEO- + RADIO- + NECROSIS]

os·te·o·sar·co·ma (os′tē ō sär kō′mə), *n., pl.* **-mas, -ma·ta** (-mə tə). *Pathol.* a malignant tumor of the bone. [1800–10; OSTEO- + SARCOMA]

os·te·o·scle·ro·sis (os′tē ō skli rō′sis), *n. Pathol.* abnormal hardening and increase in density of bone. [1855–60; OSTEO- + SCLEROSIS] **—os·te·o·scle·rot·ic** (os′tē ō skli rot′ik), *adj.*

os·te·o·sis (os′tē ō′sis), *n.* the formation of bony tissue, usually infiltrating connective tissue. [OSTEO- + -OSIS]

os·te·o·tome (os′tē ə tōm′), *n. Surg.* a double-beveled chisellike instrument for cutting or dividing bone. [1835–45; < NL *osteotomus.* See OSTEO, -TOME]

os·te·ot·o·my (os′tē ot′ə mē), *n., pl.* **-mies.** *Surg.* the dividing of a bone, or the excision of part of it. [1835–45; OSTEO- + -TOMY] **—os′te·ot′o·mist,** *n.*

Ös·ter·reich (œ′stəʀ ʀīḵʜ′), *n.* German name of **Austria.**

Os·ti·a (os′tē ə; *It.* ô′styä), *n.* a town in central Italy, SW of Rome: ruins from 4th century B.C.; site of ancient port of Rome.

Os·ti·ak (os′tē ak′), *n.* Ostyak.

os·ti·ar·y (os′tē er′ē), *n., pl.* **-ar·ies. 1.** Also called **doorkeeper, porter.** *Rom. Cath. Ch.* **a.** a member of the lowest-ranking of the four minor orders. **b.** the order itself. Cf. **acolyte** (def. 2), **exorcist** (def. 2), **lector** (def. 2). **2.** a doorkeeper, as of a church. [1400–50; late ME *hostiary* < L *ōstiārius* doorkeeper, equiv. to *ōsti(um)* door, entrance (see OSTIUM) + *-ārius* -ARY]

os·ti·na·to (os′ti nä′tō; *It.* ôs′tē nä′tô), *n., pl.* **-tos.** *Music.* a constantly recurring melodic fragment. [1875–80; < It: lit., obstinate < L *obstinātus* OBSTINATE]

os·ti·ole (os′tē ōl′), *n. Biol.* a small opening or pore, esp. in the fruiting body of a fungus. [1825–35; < L *ōstiolum* little door, equiv. to *ōsti(um)* door (see OSTIUM) + *-olum* -OLE[1]] **—os·ti·o·lar** (os′tē ə lər, o stī′-), *adj.*

os·ti·um (os′tē əm), *n., pl.* **-ti·a** (-tē ə). **1.** *Anat., Zool.* a small opening or orifice, as at the end of the oviduct. **2.** *Zool.* one of the tiny holes in the body of a sponge. [1655–65; < L *ōstium* entrance, river mouth]

ost·ler (os′lər), *n.* hostler.

ost·mark (ôst′märk′, ost′-), *n.* (formerly) a cupronickel coin and monetary unit of East Germany: replaced by the Deutsche mark in 1990. [1945–50; < G: east mark]

os·to·my (os′tə mē), *n., pl.* **-mies.** any of various surgical procedures, as a colostomy, in which an artificial opening is made so as to permit the drainage of waste products either into an appropriate organ or to the outside of the body. [1955–60; generalized from words in which *-ostomy* is the final element; see -O-, -STOMY]

os·to·sis (o stō′sis), *n. Physiol.* the formation of bone; ossification. [< NL; see OSTE-, -OSIS]

Ost·po·li·tik (*Ger.* ôst′pô li tēk′), *n.* the German policy toward the Soviet Union and Eastern Europe, esp. the expansionist views of Hitler in the 1930's and the normalization program of the West German government in the 1960's and 1970's. Cf. **Westpolitik.** [1960–65; < G: lit. Eastern policy]

Ost·preus·sen (ôst′proi′sən), *n.* German name of **East Prussia.**

os·tra·cism (os′trə siz′əm), *n.* **1.** exclusion, by general consent, from social acceptance, privileges, friendship, etc. **2.** (in ancient Greece) temporary banishment of a citizen, decided upon by popular vote. [1570–80; < NL *ostracismus* < Gk *ostrakismós* banishment, equiv. to *ostrak(ízein)* to OSTRACIZE + *-ismos* -ISM]

os·tra·cize (os′trə sīz′), *v.t.,* **-cized, -ciz·ing. 1.** to exclude, by general consent, from society, friendship, conversation, privileges, etc.: *His friends ostracized him after his father's arrest.* **2.** to banish (a person) from his or her native country; expatriate. **3.** (in ancient Greece) to banish (a citizen) temporarily by popular vote. Also, *esp. Brit.,* **os′tra·cise′.** [1640–50; < Gk *ostrakízein,* equiv. to *óstrak(on)* potsherd, tile, ballot (akin to *óstreion* OYSTER, shell) + *-izein* -IZE] **—os′tra·ciz′a·ble,** *adj.* **—os′tra·ci·za′tion,** *n.* **—os′tra·ciz′er,** *n.*
—Syn. 1. shun, snub, blacklist. **—Ant. 1.** accept.

os·tra·cod (os′trə kod′), *n.* See **seed shrimp.** [1860–65; < NL *Ostracoda* name of the subclass < Gk *ostrakṓdēs,* equiv. to *óstrak(on)* shell, tile (see OSTRACIZE) + *-ōdēs* -ODE[1]] **—os·tra·co·dan** (os′trə kōd′n), **os′tra·co′dous,** *adj.*

os·tra·co·derm (os′trə kō dûrm′), *n.* any of several extinct jawless fishes of the Ordovician, Silurian, and Devonian periods, having the body enclosed in an armor of bony plates. [1890–95; < NL *Ostracodermi,* pl. of *Ostracodermus* < Gk *ostrakódermos* with a shell, equiv. to *óstrako(n)* shell, tile + *-dermos* -DERM]

os·tra·con (os′trə kon′), *n., pl.* **-ca** (-kə). (in ancient Greece) a potsherd, esp. one used as a ballot on which the name of a person voted to be ostracized was inscribed. Also, **ostrakon.** [1880–85; < Gk *óstrakon;* see OSTRACIZE]

os·tra·kon (os′trə kon′), *n., pl.* **-ka** (-kə). ostracon.

O·stra·va (*Czech.* ô′strä vä), *n.* a city in N Moravia, in the NE Czech Republic. 328,000. Formerly, **Moravská Ostrava.**

os·trich (ô′strich, os′trich), *n.* **1.** a large, two-toed, swift-footed flightless bird, *Struthio camelus,* indigenous to Africa and Arabia, domesticated for its plumage: the largest of living birds. **2.** (not used scientifically) a rhea. **3.** a person who attempts to ignore unpleasant facts or situations. [1175–1225; ME *ostrice, ostriche* < OF *ostrusce* (cf. F *autruche*) < VL **avistrūthius,* for L *avis* bird + LL *strūthiō* < LGk *strouthíōn;* see STRUTHIOUS] **—os′trich·like′,** *adj.*

ostrich,
Struthio camelus,
height 8 ft. (2.4 m);
length 6 ft. (1.8 m)

os·trin·ger (ô′strin jər), *n.* astringer.

Os·tro·goth (os′trə goth′), *n.* a member of the easterly division of the Goths, maintaining a monarchy in Italy, A.D. 493–555. Cf. **Visigoth.** [1640–50; < LL *Ostrogothī, Austrogotī* (pl.) < Gmc, equiv. to **austro-* eastwards (ON *austr,* OS, OHG *ōstar,* MD *ooster,* OE *ēast(er)ra;* cf. EAST) + GOTH] **—Os′tro·goth′ic, Os′tro·goth′i·an,** *adj.*

Ost·wald (ôst′vält), *n.* **Wil·helm** (vil′helm), 1853–1932, German chemist: Nobel prize 1909.

Os·ty·ak (os′tē ak′), *n., pl.* **-aks,** (esp. collectively) **-ak.** Khanty. Also, **Ostiak.** [1715–25; < Russ *ostyák* orig. a Khanty, later used for the Samoyedic Selkup, the Ket, and certain Mansi groups < Khanty *ās-jax,* pl. of *as-xo* one living on the Ob, equiv. to *Ās* the river Ob + *xo* man]

Os·wald (oz′wôld), *n.* **1. Lee Harvey,** 1939–63, designated by a presidential commission to be the lone assassin of John F. Kennedy. **2.** a male given name.

Os·we·go (os wē′gō), *n.* **1.** a town in NW Oregon. 22,868. **2.** a port in W New York, on Lake Ontario. 19,793.

Oswe′go tea′, a North American plant, *Monarda didyma,* of the mint family, having a cluster of showy, bright-red tubular flowers. [1745–55, *Amer.*]

Oś·wię·cim (ôsh vyen′chēm), *n.* Polish name of **Auschwitz.**

ot-, var. of **oto-** before a vowel: *otalgia.*

OT, 1. occupational therapy. **2.** Old Testament. **3.** overnight telegram. **4.** overtime.

O.T., Old Testament.

o.t., overtime.

OTA, See **Office of Technology Assessment.**

-ota, a plural suffix occurring in taxonomic names, esp. of phyla: *Eumycota.* Cf. **-ote.** [< NL < Gk, neut. pl. of *-ōtos,* equiv. to *-ō-* (see -OSIS) + *-tos* adj. suffix; cf. ZYGOTE]

O·ta·hei·te (ō′tə hē′tē, -hā′-), *n.* former name of **Tahiti.**

Otahei′te ap′ple, 1. a Society Islands tree, *Spondias cytherea,* of the cashew family, having whitish flowers and yellow, edible, plumlike fruit. **2.** the fruit itself. Also called **ambarella.** [1855–60]

Otahei′te or′ange, a small citrus bush, *Citrus limonia otaitensis,* having fragrant flowers and small orange fruit, often cultivated as a houseplant.

o·tal·gi·a (ō tal′jē ə, -jə), *n. Pathol.* earache. [1650–60; < NL < Gk *ōtalgía,* equiv. to *ōt-* OT- + *-algia* -ALGIA] **—o·tal′gic,** *adj.*

O·ta·ru (ô′tä ro͞o′), *n.* a city in W Hokkaido, in N Japan. 180,728.

OTB, offtrack betting.

OTC, 1. Also, **O.T.C.** Officers' Training Corps. **2.** over-the-counter.

-ote, a suffix forming singular nouns that correspond to the plural taxonomic suffix **-ota:** *eukaryote.* [< Gk *-ōtos;* see -OTA]

O·tel·lo (*It.* ô tel′lô), *n.* an opera (1887) with music by Giuseppe Verdi and a libretto by Arrigo Boito based on Shakespeare's *Othello.*

O tem·po·ra! O mo·res! (ō tem′pō rä′ ō mō′rās; *Eng.* ō tem′pər ə ō môr′ēz, mōr′-), *Latin.* O times! O customs!

O·thel·lo (ō thel′ō, ə thel′ō), *n.* a tragedy (1604) by Shakespeare.

oth·er (uth′ər), *adj.* **1.** additional or further: *he and one other person.* **2.** different or distinct from the one mentioned or implied: *in some other city; Some other design may be better.* **3.** different in nature or kind: *I would not have him other than he is.* **4.** being the remaining one of two or more: *the other hand.* **5.** (used with plural nouns) being the remaining ones of a number: *the other men; some other countries.* **6.** former; earlier: *sailing ships of other days.* **7.** not long past: *the other night.* **8. every other,** every alternate: *a meeting every other week.* **—n. 9.** the other one: *Each praises the other.* **—pron. 10.** Usually, **others.** other persons or things: *others in the medical profession.* **11.** some person or thing else: *Surely some friend or other will help me.* **—adv. 12.** otherwise; differently (usually fol. by *than*): *We can't collect the rent other than by suing the tenant.* [bef. 900; ME; OE *ōther* (pronoun, adj., and n.); c. G *ander,* Goth *anthar;* akin to Skt *antara-*]

oth·er-di·rect·ed (uth′ər di rek′tid, -dī-), *adj.* guided by a set of values that is derived from current trends or outward influences rather than from within oneself. Cf. **inner-directed.** [1945–50] **—oth′er-di·rect′ed·ness,** *n.* **—oth′er-di·rec′tion,** *n.*

oth·er·guess (uth′ər ges′), *adj. Archaic.* of another kind; different. [1625–35; var. of *othergets,* var. of ME *othergates.* See OTHER, GATE[2], -S[1]]

oth′er half′, 1. the people of an economic class clearly different from one's own or from that to which reference is being made: *a glimpse of how the other half lives.* **2.** *Informal.* one's spouse.

oth′er man′, a man who is romantically or sexually involved with another man's wife or lover, esp. a man who is having an affair with a married woman. [1885–90]

oth·er·ness (uth′ər nis), *n.* the state or fact of being different or distinct. [1580–90; OTHER + -NESS]

oth·er·where (uth′ər hwâr′, -wâr′), *adv. Archaic.*

CONCISE PRONUNCIATION KEY: *act, cāpe, dâre, pärt; set, ēqual; if, īce; ox, ōver, ôrder, oil, bo͝ok, bo͞ot, out; up, ûrge; child; sing; shoe; thin, that;* zh as in *treasure.* ə = *a* as in *alone, e* as in *system, i* as in *easily, o* as in *gallop, u* as in *circus;* ᵊ as in *fire* (fīᵊr), *hour* (ouᵊr). l and n can serve as syllabic consonants, as in *cradle* (krād′l), and *button* (but′n). See the full key inside the front cover.

elsewhere. [1350–1400; ME (north and Scots) *otherquar;* see OTHER, WHERE]

oth•er•while (uth′ər hwīl′, -wīl′), *adv. Archaic.* **1.** at another time or other times. **2.** sometimes. Also, **oth′er•whiles′.** [1125–75; ME *otherwhil, otherwhiles.* See OTHER, WHILE]

oth•er•wise (uth′ər wīz′), *adv.* **1.** under other circumstances: *Otherwise they may get broken.* **2.** in another manner; differently: *Under the circumstances, I can't believe otherwise.* **3.** in other respects: *an otherwise happy life.* —*conj.* **4.** or else; if not: *Button up your overcoat, otherwise you'll catch cold.* —*adj.* **5.** other or different; of another nature or kind: *We hoped his behavior would be otherwise.* **6.** in other or different circumstances: *An otherwise pleasure had become a grinding chore.* [bef. 900; ME; OE (*on*) *ōthre wīsan* (in) another manner. See OTHER, -WISE]

oth′er wom′an, a woman who is romantically or sexually involved with another woman's husband or lover, esp. a woman who is having an affair with a married man. [1850–55]

oth′er world′, the world after death; the future world. [1150–1200; ME]

oth•er•world•ly (uth′ər wûrld′lē), *adj.* of, pertaining to, or devoted to another world, as the world of imagination or the world to come. [1870–75; *other world* + -LY] —**oth′er•world′li•ness,** *n.*

O•thin (ō′thin), *n.* Odin.

Oth•man (oth′mən; *for 1 also Arab.* ŏŏth män′), *n., pl.* **-mans.** **1.** Osman. **2.** Ottoman (defs. 3, 4).

Oth•ni•el (oth′nē əl), *n.* a judge of Israel. Judges 3:9.

O•tho•ni•el (ə thō′nē əl), *n. Douay Bible.* Othniel.

o•tic (ō′tik, ot′ik), *adj. Anat.* of or pertaining to the ear; auricular. [1650–60; < Gk *ōtikós.* See OT-, -IC]

-otic, an adjective suffix of Greek origin, often corresponding to nouns ending in **-osis,** denoting a relationship to an action, process, state, or condition indicated by the preceding element: *hypnotic; neurotic.* See **-tic.** [< Gk *-ōtikos*]

o′tic ves′icle. See **auditory vesicle.**

o•ti•ose (ō′shē ōs′, ō′tē-), *adj.* **1.** being at leisure; idle; indolent. **2.** ineffective or futile. **3.** superfluous or useless. [1785–95; < L *ōtiōsus* at leisure, equiv. to *ōti(um)* leisure + *-ōsus* -OSE[1]] —**o′ti•ose′ly,** *adv.* —**o•ti•os•i•ty** (ō′shē os′i tē, ō′tē-), **o′ti•ose′ness,** *n.*
—**Syn. 1.** lazy, slothful. **2.** idle, vain, profitless. **3.** redundant, worthless, pointless.

O•tis (ō′tis), *n.* **1. Elisha Graves,** 1811–61, U.S. inventor. **2. Harrison Gray,** 1837–1917, U.S. army officer and newspaper publisher. **3. James,** 1725–83, American lawyer and public official who is supposed to have first used the phrase "Taxation without representation" (brother of Mercy Otis Warren). **4.** a male given name.

o•ti•tis (ō tī′tis), *n. Pathol.* inflammation of the ear. [1790–1800; OT- + -ITIS]

oti′tis ex•ter′na (ik stûr′nə), *Pathol.* inflammation of the external ear. [1860–65; < NL: external otitis]

oti′tis in•ter′na (in tûr′nə), *Pathol.* labyrinthitis. [1860–65; < NL: internal otitis]

oti′tis me′di•a (mē′dē ə), *Pathol.* inflammation of the middle ear, characterized by pain, dizziness, and impaired hearing. [1870–75; < NL: middle otitis]

o•ti•um cum dig•ni•ta•te (ō′ti ŏŏm′ kŏŏm dig′ni tä′te; *Eng.* ō′shē əm kum dig′ni tā′tē), *Latin.* leisure with dignity.

O•to (ō′tō), *n., pl.* **O•tos,** (*esp. collectively*) **O•to.** a member of a Siouan-speaking tribe of North American Indians who formerly inhabited the lower Missouri River basin and now live in Oklahoma. Also, **Otoe.**

oto-, a combining form meaning "ear," used in the formation of compound words: *otology.* Also, *esp. before a vowel,* **ot-.** [< Gk *ōto-,* comb. form of *oûs* EAR[1]]

o•to•cyst (ō′tə sist), *n.* **1.** a statocyst. **2.** See **auditory vesicle.** [1875–80; OTO- + -CYST] —**o•to•cys•tic** (ō′tə sis′tik), *adj.*

O•toe (ō′tō), *n., pl.* **O•toes,** (*esp. collectively*) **O•toe.** Oto.

o•to•lar•yn•gol•o•gy (ō′tō lar′ing gol′ə jē), *n.* the branch of medicine that deals with the anatomy, function, and diseases of the ear, nose, and throat. Also called **otorhinolaryngology.** [1895–1900; OTO- + LARYNGOLOGY] —**o′to•lar′yn•gol′o•gist,** *n.* —**o•to•la•ryn•go•log•i•cal** (ō′tō lə ring′gə loj′i kəl), *adj.*

o•to•lith (ōt′l ith), *n.* **1.** *Anat., Zool.* a calcareous concretion in the internal ear of vertebrates. **2.** statolith (def. 1). [1825–35; OTO- + -LITH]

o•tol•o•gy (ō tol′ə jē), *n.* the science of the ear and its diseases. [1835–45; OTO- + -LOGY] —**o•to•log•i•cal** (ōt′l oj′i kəl), *adj.* —**o•tol′o•gist,** *n.*

O•to-Man•gue•an (ō′tō mäng′gē ən, -mang′-), *n.* a family of American Indian languages spoken in central and southern Mexico, including Mixtec, Zapotec, and Otomi. Also, **O′to•man′gue•an.** [*Oto(mian)* a subgroup that includes Otomi + *Manguean* another subgroup; cf. Sp *otomangue*]

O•to•mi (ō′tə mē′), *n., pl.* **-mis,** (*esp. collectively*) **-mi** for 1. **1.** a member of an American Indian people of south-central Mexico. **2.** the Oto-Manguean language of the Otomi. [1780–90; < MexSp *otomí* < Nahuatl *otomih,* pl. of *otomitl;* literal meaning unknown]

o•to•plas•ty (ō′tə plas′tē), *n.* plastic surgery of the external ear. [OTO- + -PLASTY] —**o′to•plas′tic,** *adj.*

o•to•rhi•no•lar•yn•gol•o•gy (ō′tō rī′nō lar′ing gol′ə jē), *n.* otolaryngology. [1895–1900; OTO- + RHINO- + LARYNGOLOGY] —**o•to•rhi•no•la•ryn•go•log•i•cal** (ō′tō rī′nō lə ring′gə loj′i kəl), **o′to•rhi′no•la•ryn′go•log′ic,** *adj.* —**o′to•rhi′no•lar′yn•gol′o•gist,** *n.*

o•tor•rhe•a (ō′tə rē′ə), *n. Pathol.* a mucopurulent discharge from the ear. [1810–20; < NL; see OTO-, -RRHEA]

o•to•scle•ro•sis (ō′tə skli rō′sis), *n. Pathol.* formation of new bone about the stapes or cochlea, resulting in hearing loss. [1895–1900; < NL; see OTO-, SCLEROSIS]

o•to•scope (ō′tə skōp′), *n. Med.* an instrument for examining the external canal and tympanic membrane of the ear. [1840–50; OTO- + -SCOPE] —**o•to•scop•ic** (ō′tə skop′ik), *adj.* —**o•tos•co•py** (ō tos′kə pē), *n.*

o•to•tox•ic (ō′tə tok′sik), *adj.* having a harmful effect on the organs or nerves concerned with hearing and balance. [1950–55; OTO- + TOXIC] —**o•to•tox•ic•i•ty** (ō′tə tok sis′i tē), *n.*

O•tran•to (ō trän′tō; *It.* ô′trän tô), *n.* **Strait of,** a strait between SE Italy and Albania, connecting the Adriatic and the Mediterranean. 44 mi. (71 km) wide.

OTS, Officers' Training School. Also, **O.T.S.**

ot•tar (ot′ər), *n.* attar (def. 1).

ot•ta•va (ō tä′və; *It.* ôt tä′vä), *adv. Music.* (of notes in a score) at an octave higher than written (when placed above the staff) or lower than written (when placed below the staff). *Abbr.:* 8va [1810–20; < It: OCTAVE]

ot•ta•va ri•ma (ō tä′və rē′mə), *pl.* **ot•ta•va ri•mas.** an Italian stanza of eight lines, each of eleven syllables (or, in the English adaptation, of ten or eleven syllables), the first six lines rhyming alternately and the last two forming a couplet with a different rhyme: used in Keats' *Isabella* and Byron's *Don Juan.* [1810–20; < It: octave rhyme]

Ot•ta•wa (ot′ə wə), *n., pl.* **-was,** (*esp. collectively*) **-wa** for 5. **1.** a city in and the capital of Canada, in SE Ontario. 304,462. **2.** a river in SE Canada, flowing SE along the boundary between Ontario and Quebec into the St. Lawrence at Montreal. 685 mi. (1105 km) long. **3.** a city in NE Illinois, SW of Chicago. 18,166. **4.** a town in E Kansas. 11,016. **5.** a member of a tribe of Algonquian Indians of Canada, forced into the Lake Superior and Lake Michigan regions by the Iroquois confederacy. **6.** the Ojibwa language as used by the Ottawa Indians.

ot•ter (ot′ər), *n., pl.* **-ters,** (*esp. collectively*) **-ter. 1.** any of several aquatic, furbearing, weasellike mammals of the genus *Lutra* and related genera, having webbed feet and a long, slightly flattened tail. **2.** the fur of an otter. [bef. 900; ME *otter, oter,* OE *otor, ottor;* c. D, G *otter;* cf. Gk *hýdra* water serpent (see HYDRA), Skt *udra-* otter; akin to WATER]

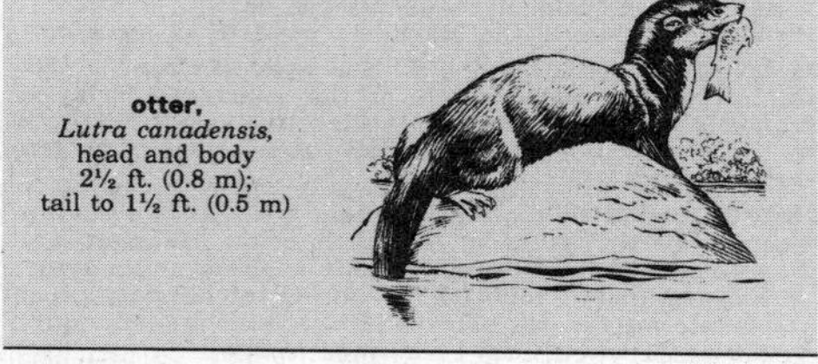
otter, *Lutra canadensis,* head and body 2½ ft. (0.8 m); tail to 1½ ft. (0.5 m)

Ot•ter (ot′ər), *n.* (in the *Volsunga Saga*) a son of Hreidmar, who assumed the form of an otter when fishing, and who was killed by Loki while in that form.

Ot•ter•bein (ot′ər bīn′), *n.* **Philip William,** 1726–1813, American clergyman, founder of the United Brethren, born in Germany.

ot′ter board′, *Naut.* one of a pair of large, heavy, square or rectangular plates or boards of metal or weighted wood attached to the trawl lines on each side of the mouth of a trawl net to maintain lateral spread during trawling. [1765–75]

Ot•ter•burn (ot′ər bûrn′), *n.* a village in central Northumberland, in NE England: battle of Chevy Chase 1388.

ot•ter•hound (ot′ər hound′), *n.* one of an English breed of water dogs having a thick, shaggy, oily coat, trained to hunt otter. [1600–10; OTTER + HOUND[1]]

ot′ter shrew′, a chiefly aquatic insectivore, *Potamogale velox,* of western Africa, that resembles an otter, having sleek, brown fur and a flattened tail. Also called **potamogale.**

ot′ter trawl′, a trawl net equipped with otter boards. Cf. **beam trawl.** [1895–1900]

ot•to (ot′ō), *n.* attar (def. 1).

Ot•to (ot′ō; *Ger.* ôt′ō), *n.* a male given name: from a Germanic word meaning "rich."

Otto I, ("*the Great*") A.D. 912–973, king of the Germans 936–973; emperor of the Holy Roman Empire 962–973.

Otto II, A.D. 955–983, emperor of the Holy Roman Empire 973–983 (son of Otto I).

Otto III, A.D. 980–1002, king of Germany 983–1002; emperor of the Holy Roman Empire 996–1002 (son of Otto II).

Otto IV, c1175–1218, king of Germany 1208–15; emperor of the Holy Roman Empire 1209–15.

Ot′to cy′cle, *Thermodynam.* an idealization of the thermodynamic cycle of the internal combustion engine with air as the working substance: intake of air at atmospheric pressure, then adiabatic compression, then ignition with an increase of pressure and temperature at constant volume, then adiabatic expansion and performance of work, then a drop to atmospheric pressure at constant volume and a rejection of heat to the environment, then the exhaust of air at constant pressure. [1885–90; named after Nikolaus August *Otto,* 1832–91, German engineer and inventor]

Ot•to•man (ot′ə mən), *adj., n., pl.* **-mans.** —*adj.* **1.** of or pertaining to the Ottoman Empire. **2.** of or pertaining to the lands, peoples, and possessions of the Ottoman Empire. —*n.* **3.** a Turk. **4.** a Turk of the family or tribe of Osman. **5.** (*l.c.*) a cushioned footstool. **6.** (*l.c.*) a low cushioned seat without back or arms. **7.** (*l.c.*) a kind of divan or sofa, with or without a back. **8.** (*l.c.*) a corded silk or rayon fabric with large cotton cord for filling. Also, **Othman** (for defs. 3, 4). [1575–85; < F < It *ottomano,* after the founder of the empire (Ar *'uthmān*); in defs. 5–8 < F *ottomane* (fem.)] —**Ot′to•man•like′,** *adj.*

Ot′toman Em′pire, a former Turkish empire that was founded about 1300 by Osman and reached its greatest territorial extent under Suleiman in the 16th century; collapsed after World War I. *Cap.:* Constantinople. Also called **Turkish Empire.**

Ot•to•ni•an (o tō′nē ən), *adj.* **1.** of or pertaining to the German dynasty (Otto I, II, III) that ruled as emperors of the Holy Roman Empire from 962 to 1002. **2.** pertaining to or designating the arts or culture of the Ottonian period, characterized chiefly by the development of forms derived from both Carolingian and Byzantine concepts: *an Ottonian revival.* [1895–1900; < G *Otton(en),* pl. of *Otto* + -IAN]

ot′to of ros′es. See **rose oil.** [1775–85]

ot•tre•lite (o′trə līt′), *n. Mineral.* a brittle mica containing manganese and similar to margarite in physical and chemical properties. [1835–45; < F *ottrélite,* named after *Ottrez,* Belgium, where it is found; see -LITE]

Ot•tum•wa (ə tum′wə), *n.* a city in SE Iowa, on the Des Moines River. 27,381.

Ot•way (ot′wā), *n.* **Thomas,** 1652–85, English dramatist.

o•u (ō′ŏŏ′), *n.* a rare Hawaiian honeycreeper, *Psittirostra psittacea,* having an olive-green body, a parrotlike bill, and in the male a bright yellow head. [1885–90; < Hawaiian *'ō'ū*]

oua•ba•in (wä bä′in), *n. Pharm.* a glycoside occurring as a white, crystalline powder, $C_{29}H_{44}O_{12}$, obtained from the seeds of a shrub, *Strophanthus gratus,* or from the wood of trees of the genus *Acokanthera,* and used in medicine chiefly as a cardiac stimulant. Also called **G-strophanthin.** [1890–95 < F *ouaba(ïo)* (< Somali *waabayyo* arrow poison) + -IN[2]]

Ouach•i•ta (wosh′i tô′, wô′shi-), *n., pl.* **-tas,** (*esp. collectively*) **-ta** for 2. **1.** a river flowing SE from W Arkansas through NE Louisiana to the Red River. 605 mi. (975 km) long. **2.** a member of a former North American Indian tribe, apparently of the Caddoan stock, of NE Louisiana. Also, **Washita.**

Ouach′ita Moun′tains, a range extending from SE Oklahoma to W Arkansas.

Oua•ga•dou•gou (wä′gə dŏŏ′gŏŏ), *n.* a city in and the capital of Burkina Faso, in the central part. 124,779.

Ou•ban•gi (ŏŏ bäɴ gē′), *n.* French name of **Ubangi.**

Ou•ban•gi-Cha•ri (ŏŏ bäɴ gē shä rē′), *n.* French name of **Ubangi-Shari.**

ou•bli•ette (ŏŏ′blē et′), *n.* a secret dungeon with an opening only in the ceiling, as in certain old castles. [1810–20; < F, MF, equiv. to *oubli(er)* to forget, OF *oblider* < VL **oblitāre,* deriv. of L *oblītus* (ptp. of *oblīvīscī* to forget; see OBLIVION) + MF *-ette* -ETTE]

ouch[1] (ouch), *interj.* (used as an exclamation expressing sudden pain or dismay.) [1830–40, *Amer.;* < G *autsch*]

ouch[2] (ouch), *Archaic.* —*n.* **1.** a clasp, buckle, or brooch, esp. one worn for ornament. **2.** the setting of a precious stone. —*v.t.* **3.** to adorn with or as if with ouches. [1325–75; ME *ouche* (n.), for *nouche* (the phrase *a nouche* taken as *an ouche;* cf. APRON) < OF *nosche* << Gmc]

oud (ŏŏd), *n.* a musical instrument of the Middle East and northern Africa belonging to the lute family. [1730–40; < Ar *'ūd* lit., wood; see LUTE]

Oudh (oud), *n.* a former part of the United Provinces of Agra and Oudh in N India: now part of Uttar Pradesh.

Oudts•hoorn (ōts′hôrn′), *n.* a city in the S Cape of Good Hope province, in the S Republic of South Africa. 28,800.

Oué•mé (wā′mā), *n.* a river in Benin, flowing S to the Bight of Benin near Porto Novo. ab. 310 mi. (500 km) long.

Oues•sant (we säɴ′), *n.* French name of **Ushant.**

ought[1] (ôt), *auxiliary verb.* **1.** (used to express duty or moral obligation): *Every citizen ought to help.* **2.** (used to express justice, moral rightness, or the like): *He ought to be punished. You ought to be ashamed.* **3.** (used to express propriety, appropriateness, etc.): *You ought to be home early. We ought to bring her some flowers.* **4.** (used to express probability or natural consequence): *That ought to be our train now.* —*n.* **5.** duty or obligation. [bef. 900; ME *ought, aught,* OE *āhte,* past tense of *āgan* to OWE]
—**Syn. 1.** See **must**[1].
—**Usage.** OUGHT[1] forms its negative in a number of ways. OUGHT NOT occurs in all types of speech and writing and is fully standard: *The conferees ought not to waste time on protocol.* OUGHTN'T, largely a spoken form,

CONCISE ETYMOLOGY KEY: <, descended or borrowed from; >, whence; b., blend of, blended; c., cognate with; cf., compare; deriv., derivative; equiv., equivalent; imit., imitative; obl., oblique; r., replacing; s., stem; sp., spelling, spelled; resp., respelling, respelled; trans., translation; ?, origin unknown; *, unattested; ‡, probably earlier than. See the full key inside the front cover.

is found mainly in the Midland and Southern dialects of the United States, where it is almost the universal form. HADN'T OUGHT is a common spoken form in the Northern dialect area. It is sometimes condemned in usage guides and is uncommon in educated speech except of the most informal variety. DIDN'T OUGHT and SHOULDN'T OUGHT are considered nonstandard.

Both positive and negative forms of OUGHT are almost always followed by the infinitive form: *We ought to go now. You ought not to worry about it.* Occasionally, *to* is omitted after the negative construction: *Congress ought not adjourn without considering this bill.*

ought[2] (ôt), *n., adv.* aught[1].

ought[3] (ôt), *n.* aught[2].

ought•lins (ōKHT′linz), *adv. Scot.* in the least; to the least degree. Also, **aughtlins.** [OUGHT[3] + *-lins* (var. of -LING[2] + -S[1])]

ought•n't (ôt′nt), contraction of *ought not.*
—Usage. See **contraction, ought**[1].

ou•gui•ya (o͞o gē′yə), *n., pl.* **-ya, -yas.** a cupronickel-aluminum coin, paper money, and monetary unit of Mauritania, equal to five khoums. [1970–75; < F< dial. Ar *ūgiya,* akin to Ar *ūqīyah* lit., ounce; see OKA[1]]

oui (wē), *adv., n. French.* yes.

Oui•da (wē′də), *n.* **1.** pen name of Louise de la Ramée. **2.** a female given name.

Oui•ja (wē′jə *or, often,* -jē), *Trademark.* a device consisting of a small board, or planchette, on legs that rest on a larger board marked with words, letters of the alphabet, etc., and that by moving over the larger board and touching the words, letters, etc., while the fingers of spiritualists, mediums, or others rest lightly upon it, is employed to answer questions, give messages, etc. Also called **Oui′ja board′.**

Ouj•da (o͞oj dä′), *n.* a city in NE Morocco. 649,400.

Ou•lu (ō′lo͞o, ou′-; *Fin.* ō′lo͞o), *n.* **1.** a city in W Finland, on the Gulf of Bothnia. 94,680. **2.** a river in central Finland, flowing NE to the Gulf of Bothnia. ab. 65 mi. (105 km) long.

ounce[1] (ouns), *n.* **1.** a unit of weight equal to 437.5 grains or 1/16 pound (28.349 grams) avoirdupois. **2.** a unit of 480 grains, 1/12 pound (31.103 grams) troy or apothecaries' weight. **3.** a fluid ounce. **4.** a small quantity or portion. [1350–1400; ME *unce* < MF < L *uncia* twelfth part, inch, ounce, deriv. of *unus* ONE]

ounce[2] (ouns), *n.* See **snow leopard.** [1300–50; ME *unce* lynx < AF; OF *once,* var. of *lonce* (erroneously taken as *l'once* the ounce) < VL **luncea,* deriv. of L *lync-* (s. of *lynx*) LYNX]

ounc•er (oun′sər), *n.* something weighing a specified number of ounces (used in combination): *The deluxe hamburger is an eight-ouncer.* [1885–90; OUNCE[1] + -ER[1]]

ouphe (ouf, o͞of), *n.* an elf or goblin. [1615–25; scribal var. of OAF]

our (ouᵊr, ou′ər; *unstressed* är), *pron.* (a form of the possessive case of *we* used as an attributive adjective): *Our team is going to win. Do you mind our going on ahead?* Cf. **ours.** [bef. 900; ME *oure,* OE *ūre,* suppletive gen. pl. of *wē* WE from same base as *ūs* US]
—Usage. See **me.**

-our, *Brit.* var. of **-or**[1].
—Usage. See **-or**[1].

Ou•ra•nos (o͞o rä′nəs), *n. Class. Myth.* Uranus (def. 2).

ou•ra•ri (o͞o rär′ē), *n.* curare.

Our′ Fa′ther. See **Lord's Prayer.**

ou•rie (o͝or′ē), *adj. Scot.* **1.** shabby; dingy. **2.** melancholy; languid. Also, **oory.** [1275–1325; ME (north) *ouri,* perh. < ON *ōra* rage, *oerr* mad]

Ou•ri•nhos (ō Rē′nyo͞os), *n.* a city in E Brazil. 40,773.

Our′ La′dy, a title of the Virgin Mary. [1350–1400; ME]

ourn (ouᵊrn, ou′ərn *or, often,* ärn), *pron. Nonstandard.* ours. Also, **our'n.** [1350–1400; ME (South and Midlands) *ouren, ourn,* equiv. to *oure* OUR + *-n* (by analogy with *my, mine; thy, thine*)]

ours (ouᵊrz, ou′ərz *or, often,* ärz), *pron.* **1.** (a form of the possessive case of *we* used as a predicate adjective): *Which house is ours?* **2.** that or those belonging to us: *Ours was given second prize. Ours are in the car.* [1250–1300; ME (orig. north) *ures, oures.* See OUR, 's]

our•self (är self′, ouᵊr-, ou′ər-), *pron.* **1.** one's own person, individuality, etc., considered as private and apart from others: *It is for ourself that we should strive for greater knowledge.* **2.** (a form corresponding to *ourselves,* used of a single person, esp. in the regal or formal style, as **we** for *I*): *We have taken unto ourself such powers as may be necessary.* [1300–50; ME *oure self;* see OUR, SELF]
—Usage. See **myself.**

our•selves (är selvz′, ouᵊr-, ou′ər-), *pron.pl.* **1.** a reflexive form of **we** (used as the direct or indirect object of a verb or the direct object of a preposition): *We are deceiving ourselves. Give us a moment to ourselves.* **2.** (used as an intensive with *we*): *We ourselves would never say such a thing.* **3.** *Informal.* (used in place of **we** or **us,** esp. in compound subjects, objects, and complements): *The children and ourselves thank you kindly. When it satisfies ourselves, it will be ready to market. The ones who really want the new system are the manager and ourselves.* **4.** (used in place of **we** or **us** after *as, than,* or *but*): *How many parents are as fortunate as ourselves? No one loves skiing more than ourselves. Nobody heard it but ourselves.* **5.** our customary, normal, or healthy selves: *After a good rest, we're almost ourselves again.* [1300–50; ME *oure selven;* see OUR, SELF, -EN[4], -S[3]]
—Usage. See **myself.**

Our′ Town′, a play (1938) by Thornton Wilder.

-ous, a suffix forming adjectives that have the general sense "possessing, full of" a given quality (*covetous; glorious; nervous; wondrous*); **-ous** and its variant **-ious** have often been used to Anglicize Latin adjectives with terminations that cannot be directly adapted into English (*atrocious; contiguous; garrulous; obvious; stupendous*). As an adjective-forming suffix of neutral value, it regularly Anglicizes Greek and Latin adjectives derived without suffix from nouns and verbs; many such formations are productive combining forms in English, sometimes with a corresponding nominal combining form that has no suffix; cf. **-fer, -ferous; -phore, -phorous; -pter, -pterous; -vore, -vorous. 2.** a suffix forming adjectival correspondents to the names of chemical elements; specialized, in opposition to like adjectives ending in **-ic,** to mean the lower of two possible valences (*stannous chloride,* $SnCl_2$, and *stannic chloride* $SnCl_4$). [ME < AF, OF < L *-ōsus;* a doublet of -OSE[1]]

Ouse (o͞oz), *n.* **1.** Also called **Great Ouse.** a river in E England, flowing NE to the Wash. 160 mi. (260 km) long. **2.** a river in NE England, in Yorkshire, flowing SE to the Humber. 57 mi. (92 km) long. **3.** a river in SE England, flowing S to the English Channel. 30 mi. (48 km) long.

ou•sel (o͞o′zəl), *n.* ouzel.

Ou•spen•sky (o͞o spen′skē; *Russ.* o͞o spyen′skyē), *n.* **Pe•ter De•mia•no•vich** (pē′tər di myä′nə vich; *Russ.* pyôtʀ′ dyi myä′nə vyich), 1878–1947, Russian philosopher and author.

oust (oust), *v.t.* **1.** to expel or remove from a place or position occupied: *The bouncer ousted the drunk; to oust the Prime Minister in the next election.* **2.** *Law.* to eject or evict; dispossess. [1375–1425; late ME < AF *ouster* to remove, OF *oster* < L *obstāre* to stand in the way, oppose (*ob-* OB- + *stāre* to STAND)]
—Syn. 1. eject, banish, evict, dislodge.

oust•er (ou′stər), *n.* **1.** expulsion or removal from a place or position occupied: *The opposition called for the ouster of the cabinet minister.* **2.** *Law.* **a.** an ejection or eviction; dispossession. **b.** a wrongful exclusion from real property. [1525–35; < AF, n. use of inf. See OUST]

out (out), *adv.* **1.** away from, or not in, the normal or usual place, position, state, etc.: *out of alphabetical order; to go out to dinner.* **2.** away from one's home, country, work, etc., as specified: *to go out of town.* **3.** in or into the outdoors: *to go out for a walk.* **4.** to a state of exhaustion, extinction, or depletion: *to pump a well out.* **5.** to the end or conclusion; to a final decision or resolution: *to say it all out.* **6.** to a point or state of extinction, nonexistence, etc.: *to blow out the candle; a practice on the way out.* **7.** in or into a state of neglect, disuse, etc.; not in current vogue or fashion: *That style has gone out.* **8.** so as not to be in the normal or proper position or state; out of joint: *His back went out after his fall.* **9.** in or into public notice or knowledge: *The truth is out at last.* **10.** seeking openly and energetically to do or have: *to be out for a good time.* **11.** not in present possession or use, as on loan: *The librarian said that the book was still out.* **12.** on strike: *The miners go out at midnight.* **13.** so as to project or extend: *to stretch out; stick your tongue out.* **14.** in or into activity, existence, or outward manifestation: *A rash came out on her arm.* **15.** from a specified source or material: *made out of scraps.* **16.** from a state of composure, satisfaction, or harmony: *to be put out over trifles.* **17.** in or into a state of confusion, vexation, dispute, variance, or unfriendliness: *to fall out about trifles.* **18.** so as to deprive or be deprived: *to be cheated out of one's money.* **19.** so as to use the last part of: *to run out of gas.* **20.** from a number, stock, or store: *to point out the errors.* **21.** aloud or loudly: *to cry out.* **22.** with completeness or effectiveness: *to fill out.* **23.** thoroughly; completely; entirely: *The children tired me out.* **24.** so as to obliterate or make undecipherable: *to cross out a misspelling; to ink out.* **25. all out,** with maximum effort; thoroughly or wholeheartedly: *They went all out to finish by Friday.* **26. out and away,** to a surpassing extent; far and away; by far: *It was out and away the best apple pie she had ever eaten.* **27. out for,** aggressively determined to acquire, achieve, etc.: *He's out for all the money he can get.* **28. out from under,** out of a difficult situation, esp. of debts or other obligations: *The work piled up while I was away and I don't know how I'll ever get out from under.* **29. out of, a.** not within: *out of the house.* **b.** beyond the reach of: *The boat's passengers had sailed out of hearing.* **c.** not in a condition of: *out of danger.* **d.** so as to deprive or be deprived of. **e.** from within or among: *Take the jokers out of the pack.* **f.** because of; owing to: *out of loyalty.* **g.** foaled by (a dam): *Grey Dancer out of Lady Grey.* **30. out of it,** *Informal.* **a.** not part of or acceptable within an activity, social group, or fashion: *She felt out of it because none of her friends were at the party.* **b.** not conscious; drunk or heavily drugged. **c.** not alert or clearheaded; confused; muddled. **d.** eliminated from contention: *If our team loses two more games, we'll be out of it.* **31. out of sight.** See **sight** (def. 19). **32. out of trim,** *Naut.* (of a ship) drawing excessively at the bow or stern.
—adj. **33.** not at one's home or place of employment; absent: *I stopped by to visit you last night, but you were out.* **34.** not open to consideration; out of the question: *I wanted to go by plane, but all the flights are booked, so that's out.* **35.** wanting; lacking; without: *We had some but now we're out.* **36.** removed from or not in effective operation, play, a turn at bat, or the like, as in a game: *He's out for the season because of an injury.* **37.** no longer having or holding a job, public office, etc.; unemployed; disengaged (usually fol. by *of*): *to be out of work.* **38.** inoperative; extinguished: *The elevator is out. Are the lights out?* **39.** finished; ended: *before the week is out.* **40.** not currently stylish, fashionable, or in vogue: *Fitted waistlines are out this season.* **41.** unconscious; senseless: *Two drinks and he's usually out.* **42.** not in power, authority, or the like: *a member of the out party.* **43.** *Baseball.* **a.** (of a batter) not succeeding in getting on base: *He was out at first on an attempted bunt.* **b.** (of a base runner) not successful in an attempt to advance a base or bases: *He was out in attempting to steal second base.* **44.** beyond fixed or regular limits; out of bounds: *The ball was out.* **45.** having a pecuniary loss or expense to an indicated extent: *The company will be out millions of dollars if the new factory doesn't open on schedule.* **46.** incorrect or inaccurate: *His calculations are out.* **47.** not in practice; unskillful from lack of practice: *Your bow hand is out.* **48.** beyond the usual range, size, weight, etc. (often used in combination): *an outsize bed.* **49.** exposed; made bare, as by holes in one's clothing: *out at the knees.* **50.** at variance; at odds; unfriendly: *They are out with each other.* **51.** moving or directed outward; outgoing: *the out train.* **52.** not available, plentiful, etc.: *Mums are out till next fall.* **53.** external; exterior; outer. **54.** located at a distance; outlying: *We sailed to six of the out islands.* **55.** *Cricket.* not having its innings: *the out side.* **56.** of or pertaining to the playing of the first nine holes of an 18-hole golf course (opposed to *in*): *His out score on the second round was 33.*
—prep. **57.** (used to indicate movement or direction from the inside to the outside of something): *He looked out the window. She ran out the door.* **58.** (used to indicate location): *The car is parked out back.* **59.** (used to indicate movement away from a central point): *Let's drive out the old parkway.*
—interj. **60.** begone! away! **61.** (used in radio communications to signify that the sender has finished the message and is not expecting or prepared to receive a reply.) Cf. **over** (def. 61). **62.** *Archaic.* (an exclamation of abhorrence, indignation, reproach, or grief (usually fol. by *upon*): *Out upon you!*
—n. **63.** a means of escape or excuse, as from a place, punishment, retribution, responsibility, etc.: *He always left himself an out.* **64.** a person who lacks status, power, or authority, esp. in relation to a particular group or situation. **65.** Usually, **outs.** persons not in office or political power (distinguished from *ins*). **66.** *Baseball.* a put-out. **67.** (in tennis, squash, handball, etc.) a return or service that does not land within the in-bounds limits of a court or section of a court (opposed to *in*). **68.** something that is out, as a projecting corner. **69.** *Print.* **a.** the omission of a word or words. **b.** the word or words omitted. **70.** *Northern Brit. Dial.* an outing. **71. be on the** or **at outs with,** *Informal.* to be estranged from (another person); be unfriendly or on bad terms with: *He is on the outs with his brother.*
—v.i. **72.** to go or come out. **73.** to become public, evident, known, etc.: *The truth will out.* **74.** to make known; tell; utter (fol. by *with*): *Out with the truth!*
—v.t. **75.** to eject or expel; discharge; oust. [bef. 900; (adv.) ME; OE *ūt;* c. D *uit,* G *aus,* ON, Goth *ūt;* akin to Skt *ud-;* (adj., interjection, and prep.) ME, from the adv.; (v.) ME *outen,* OE *ūtian* to put out, c. OFris *ūtia*]

out-, a prefixal use of **out,** adv., occurring in various senses in compounds (*outcast, outcome, outside*), and serving also to form many transitive verbs denoting a going beyond, surpassing, or outdoing in the particular action indicated (*outbid, outdo, outgeneral, outlast, outstay, outrate*). [ME; OE *ūt-;* see OUT]

CONCISE PRONUNCIATION KEY: *act, cāpe, dâre, pärt; set, ēqual; if, ice; ox, ōver, ôrder, oil, bo͝ok, bo͞ot, out; up, ûrge; child; sing; shoe; thin, that;* zh as in *treasure.* ə = *a* as in *alone, e* as in *system, i* as in *easily, o* as in *gallop, u* as in *circus;* ᵊ as in *fire* (fīᵊr), *hour* (ouᵊr). l and n can serve as syllabic consonants, as in *cradle* (krād′l), and *button* (but′n). See the full key inside the front cover.

out′a•chieve′, *v.t.,* **-chieved, -chiev•ing**
out′awe′, *v.t.,* **-awed, -aw•ing.**
out′bab′ble, *v.t.,* **-bled, -bling.**
out′bake′, *v.t.,* **-baked, -bak•ing.**
out′ban′, *v.t.,* **-banned, -ban•ning.**
out′ban′ter, *v.t.*
out′bar′, *v.t.,* **-barred, -bar•ring.**
out′bar′gain, *v.t.*
out′bark′, *v.t.*
out′bar′ter, *v.t.*
out′bat′, *v.t.,* **-bat•ted, -bat•ting.**
out′bat′ter, *v.t.*
out′bawl′, *v.t.*
out′beam′, *v.t.*
out′beg′, *v.t.,* **-begged, -beg•ging.**
out′belch′, *v.t.*
out′bel′low, *v.t.*
out′bend′, *v.t.,* **-bent, -bend•ing.**
out′bet′ter, *v.t.*
out′blaze′, *v.t.,* **-blazed, -blaz•ing.**
out′bleat′, *v.t.*
out′bleed′, *v.t.,* **-bled, -bleed•ing.**
out′bless′, *v.t.,* **-blessed** or **blest, -bles•sing.**
out′bloom′, *v.t.*
out′blos′som, *v.t.*
out′blot′, *v.t.,* **-blot•ted, -blot•ting.**
out′blow′, *v.t.,* **-blew, -blown, -blow•ing.**
out′blun′der, *v.t.*
out′blush′, *v.t.*
out′blus′ter, *v.t.*
out′boast′, *v.t.*
out′bow′, *v.t.*
out′bowl′, *v.t.*
out′brag′, *v.t.,* **-bragged, -brag•ging.**
out′branch′, *v.t.*
out′brawl′, *v.t.*
out′bray′, *v.t.*
out′bra′zen, *v.t.*
out′breathe′, *v.t.,* **-breathed, -breath•ing.**
out′bribe′, *v.t.,* **-bribed, -brib•ing.**
out′bridge′, *v.t.,* **-bridged, -bridg•ing.**
out′bring′, *v.t.,* **-brought, -bring•ing.**
out′bud′, *v.t.,* **-bud•ded, -bud•ding.**
out′build′, *v.t.,* **-built, -build•ing.**
out′bulge′, *v.,* **-bulged, -bulg•ing.**
out′bulk′, *v.t.*
out′bul′ly, *v.t.,* **-lied, -ly•ing.**
out′burn′, *v.t.,* **-burned** or **-burnt, -burn•ing.**
out′bus′tle, *v.t.,* **-tled, -tling.**
out′buzz′, *v.t.*
out′cant′, *v.t.*
out′ca′per, *v.t.*
out′car′ol, *v.t.,* **-oled, -ol•ing** or (*esp. Brit.*) **-olled, -ol•ling.**
out′catch′, *v.t.,* **-caught, -catch•ing.**
out′cav′il, *v.t.,* **-iled, -il•ing** or (*esp. Brit.*) **-illed, -il•ling.**
out′charge′, *v.t.,* **-charged, -charg•ing.**
out′charm′, *v.t.*
out′chase′, *v.t.,* **-chased, -chas•ing.**
out′chat′ter, *v.t.*
out′cheat′, *v.t.*
out′chide′, *v.t.,* **-chid•ed** or **-chid, -chid•ed** or **chid** or **-chid•den, -chid•ing.**

—Note. The lists beginning at the bottom of the preceding page provide the spelling, syllabification, and stress for words whose meanings may easily be inferred by combining the meanings of OUT- and an attached base word, or base word plus a suffix. Appropriate parts of speech are also shown. Words prefixed by OUT- that have special meanings or uses are entered in their proper alphabetical places in the main vocabulary or as derived forms run on at the end of a main vocabulary entry.

out·act (out/akt/), *v.t.* to outdo in acting. [1635–45; OUT- + ACT]

out·age (ou/tij), *n.* **1.** an interruption or failure in the supply of power, esp. electricity. **2.** the period during which power is lost: *a two-hour outage on the East Coast.* **3.** a stoppage in the functioning of a machine or mechanism due to a failure in the supply of power or electricity. **4.** the quantity of goods lost or lacking from a shipment. Cf. **innage** (def. 1). **5.** *Aeron.* the amount of fuel used during a flight. Cf. **innage** (def. 2). [1900–05, *Amer.*; OUT + -AGE]

out-and-out (out/n out/, -nd out/), *adj.* complete; total; thoroughgoing: *an out-and-out lie.* [1275–1325; ME]

out-and-out·er (out/n ou/tər, -nd ou/-), *n.* **1.** a person who does things with excessive thoroughness; extremist. **2.** a thoroughgoing or perfect example of a kind. [1805–15; OUT-AND-OUT + -ER[1]]

out·ar·gue (out/är/gyo͞o), *v.t.,* **-gued, -gu·ing.** to outdo or defeat in arguing: *That man could outargue the devil himself.* [1740–50; OUT- + ARGUE]

out-a-sight (out/ə sīt/), *adj. Pron. Spelling.* out-of-sight.

out·back (*n.* out/bak/; *adj., adv.* out/bak/), *Chiefly Australian.* —*n.* **1.** (*sometimes cap.*) the back country or remote settlements; the bush (usually prec. by *the*). —*adj.* **2.** of, pertaining to, or located in the back country: *outback settlements.* —*adv.* **3.** in or to the back country: *They moved outback many years ago.* [1875–80; OUT + BACK[2]]

out·bal·ance (out/bal/əns), *v.t.,* **-anced, -anc·ing.** to outweigh. [1635–45; OUT- + BALANCE]

out·bas·ket (out/bas/kit, -bä/skit), *n.* out-box. [1935–40]

out·bid (out/bid/), *v.t.,* **-bid, -bid·den** or **-bid, -bid·ding.** to outdo in bidding; make a higher bid than (another bidder). [1580–90; OUT- + BID] **—out/bid/der,** *n.*

out·bluff (out/bluf/), *v.t.* to surpass in bluffing: *to outbluff one's opponents at poker.* [OUT- + BLUFF[2]]

out·board (out/bôrd/, -bōrd/), *adj.* **1.** located on the exterior of a hull or aircraft. **2.** located farther from the center, as of an aircraft: *the outboard end of a wing.* **3.** (of a motorboat) having an outboard motor. —*adv.* **4.** outside or away from the center of a hull, aircraft, machine, etc.: *The sail swung outboard.* Cf. **inboard.** —*n.* **5.** an outboard motor. **6.** a boat equipped with an outboard motor. [1815–25; OUT- + BOARD]

out/board mo/tor, a portable gasoline engine with propeller and tiller, clamped on the stern of a boat. [1905–10]

out/board pro/file, *Naval Archit.* an exterior side elevation of a vessel, showing all deck structures, rigging, fittings, etc.

out·bond (out/bond/), *adj. Masonry.* composed mainly or entirely of stretchers (opposed to *inbond*). [1835–45; OUT- + BOND[1]]

out·bound (out/bound/), *adj.* outward bound: *an outbound freighter.* [1590–1600; OUT- + -BOUND[2]]

out-box (out/boks/), *n.* a boxlike tray, basket, or the like, as on a desk, for holding outgoing mail, messages, or work. Also called **out-basket.**

out·box (out/boks/), *v.t.* to surpass in boxing: *I've seen the champ outbox better fighters than this one.* [1860–65; OUT- + BOX[2]]

out·brave (out/brāv/), *v.t.,* **-braved, -brav·ing. 1.** to stand up to; face defiantly: *to outbrave charges of misconduct.* **2.** to surpass in bravery, courage, or daring: *None can outbrave the great heroes of the past.* **3.** *Archaic.* to surpass in beauty, splendor, etc. [1580–90; OUT- + BRAVE]

out·break (out/brāk/), *n.* **1.** a sudden breaking out or occurrence; eruption: *the outbreak of war.* **2.** a sudden and active manifestation: *an outbreak of hives.* **3.** an outburst: *an outbreak of temper.* **4.** an insurrection, revolt, or mutiny. **5.** a public disturbance; riot. [1595–1605; OUT- + BREAK]

out·breed (out/brēd/), *v.t.,* **-bred, -breed·ing.** to breed selected individuals outside the limits of the breed or variety. [OUT- + BREED]

CONCISE ETYMOLOGY KEY: <, descended or borrowed from; >, whence; b., blend of, blended; c., cognate with; cf., compare; deriv., derivative; equiv., equivalent; imit., imitative; obl., oblique; r., replacing; s., stem; sp., spelling, spelled; resp., respelling, respelled; trans., translation; ?, origin unknown; *, unattested; ‡, probably earlier than. See the full key inside the front cover.

out·build·ing (out/bil/ding), *n.* a detached building subordinate to a main building. [1620–30; OUT- + BUILDING]

out·burst (out/bûrst/), *n.* **1.** a sudden and violent release or outpouring: *an outburst of tears.* **2.** a sudden spell of activity, energy, etc. **3.** a public disturbance; riot; outbreak. **4.** a bursting forth; eruption. [1650–60; OUT- + BURST]

out·cast[1] (out/kast/, -käst/), *n.* **1.** a person who is rejected or cast out, as from home or society: *In the beginning the area was settled by outcasts, adventurers, and felons.* **2.** a homeless wanderer; vagabond. **3.** rejected matter; refuse. —*adj.* **4.** cast out, as from one's home or society: *an outcast son.* **5.** pertaining to or characteristic of an outcast: *outcast misery.* **6.** rejected or discarded: *outcast opinions.* [1250–1300; ME; see OUT-, CAST]
—Syn. 1. exile, refugee, expatriate; leper, pariah.

out·cast[2] (out/kast/, -käst/), *n. Scot.* a falling out; quarrel. [1590–1600; n. use of v. phrase (Scot) *cast out*]

out·caste (out/kast/, -käst/), *n.* **1.** (in India) a person who has left or been expelled from his or her caste. **2.** a person of no caste. [1875–80; OUT- + CASTE]

out·class (out/klas/, -kläs/), *v.t.* to surpass in excellence or quality, esp. by a wide margin; be superior: *He far outclasses the other runners in the race.* [1865–70; OUT- + CLASS]

out·climb (out/klīm/), *v.t.,* **-climbed** or (*Archaic*) **-clomb; -climbed** or (*Archaic*) **-clomb; -climb·ing.** to surpass or outdo in climbing; climb higher or better than: *As a child, I could outclimb any kid on the block.* [1600–10; OUT- + CLIMB]

out·come (out/kum/), *n.* **1.** a final product or end result; consequence; issue. **2.** a conclusion reached through a process of logical thinking. [1175–1225; ME *utcume.* See OUT-, COME]
—Syn. 1, 2. See **end**[1].

out·coun·try (out/kun/trē), *n.* a remote area or region; hinterland. [1630–40]

out·crop (*n.* out/krop/; *v.* out/krop/), *n., v.,* **-cropped, -crop·ping.** —*n.* **1.** *Geol.* **a.** a cropping out, as of a stratum or vein at the surface of the earth. **b.** the exposed portion of such a stratum or vein. **2.** something that emerges suddenly or violently in the manner of an outcrop; outbreak: *an outcrop of student demonstrations.* —*v.i.* **3.** to crop out, as strata. [1760–70; n. use of v. phrase *crop out*]

out·cross (*v.* out/krôs/, -kros/; *n.* out/krôs/, -kros/), *v.t.* **1.** to cross (animals or plants) by breeding individuals of different strains but, usually, of the same breed. **2.** to produce (a hybrid) by this method. —*n.* **3.** a hybrid animal or plant so produced. **4.** an act of outcrossing. [1885–90; OUT- + CROSS]

out·cry (*n.* out/krī/; *v.,* out/krī/), *n., pl.* **-cries,** *v.,* **-cried, -cry·ing.** —*n.* **1.** a strong and usually public expression of protest, indignation, or the like. **2.** a crying out. **3.** loud clamor. **4.** an auction. —*v.t.* **5.** to outdo in crying; cry louder than. [1350–1400; ME; see OUT-, CRY]
—Syn. 3. uproar, commotion.

out·dare (out/dâr/), *v.t.,* **-dared, -dar·ing. 1.** to surpass in daring. **2.** to defy; brave. [1585–95; OUT- + DARE]

out·date (out/dāt/), *v.t.,* **-dat·ed, -dat·ing.** to put out of date; make antiquated or obsolete: *The advent of the steamship outdated sailing ships as commercial carriers.* [1640–50; prob. back formation from OUTDATED]

out·dat·ed (out/dā/tid), *adj.* no longer in use or fashionable; out-of-date; outmoded; antiquated. [1610–20; OUT- + DATE[1] + -ED[2]]

out·dis·tance (out/dis/təns), *v.t.,* **-tanced, -tanc·ing.** to leave behind, as in running; outstrip: *The winning horse outdistanced the second-place winner by five lengths.* [1855–60; OUT- + DISTANCE]

out·do (out/do͞o/), *v.t.,* **-did, -done, -do·ing.** to surpass in execution or performance: *The cook outdid himself last night.* [1300–50; ME; see OUT-, DO[1]]
—Syn. See **excel.**

out·door (out/dôr/, -dōr/), *adj.* **1.** Also, **outdoors.** characteristic of, located, occurring, or belonging outdoors: *an outdoor barbecue; outdoor sports.* **2.** outdoorsy. [1740–50; OUT- + DOOR]

out·doors (out/dôrz/, -dōrz/), *adv.* **1.** out of doors; in the open air: *He's happiest when he's outdoors.* —*n.* **2.** (*used with a singular v.*) the world outside of or away from houses; open air: *Our whole family likes the outdoors.* —*adj.* **3.** outdoor. [1810–20; earlier *out* (*of*) *doors*]

out·doors·man (out/dôrz/mən, -dōr/-), *n., pl.* **-men. 1.** a person devoted to outdoor sports and recreational activities, as hiking, hunting, fishing, or camping. **2.** a person who spends much time in the outdoors. [1955–60; OUTDOORS + -MAN] **—out/doors/man·ship,** *n.*
—Usage. See **-man.**

out·doors·wom·an (out/dôrz/wo͝om/ən, -dōrz/-), *n., pl.* **-wom·en. 1.** a woman devoted to outdoor sports and recreational activities. **2.** a woman who spends much time in the outdoors. [OUTDOORS(MAN) + -WOMAN]
—Usage. See **-woman.**

out·doors·y (out/dôr/zē, -dōr/-), *adj.* **1.** characteristic of or suitable to the outdoors: *a rugged, outdoorsy life; heavy, outdoorsy clothes.* **2.** unusually fond of outdoor life: *an outdoorsy type who always swam before breakfast.* [1950–55; OUTDOORS + -Y[1]]

out·draw (out/drô/), *v.t.,* **-drew, -drawn, -draw·ing. 1.** to draw a gun, revolver, etc., from a holster, faster than (an opponent or competitor): *She could outdraw any member of the club.* **2.** to prove a greater attraction than; exceed in attracting an audience, patrons, attention, etc.: *She outdraws all male stars at the box office.* [1905–10; OUT- + DRAW]

out·drive (out/drīv/), *adj., n. Naut.* inboard-outboard. [OUT- + DRIVE]

out·dwel·ler (out/dwel/ər), *n.* a person who dwells away from or is remote from a particular place. [1675–85; OUT- + DWELLER]

out·en (out/n), *v.t. Eastern North Midland and South Atlantic U.S.* to turn off (a light) or extinguish (a fire). [1915–20, *Amer.*; OUT + -EN[1]]

out·er (ou/tər), *adj.* **1.** situated on or toward the outside; external; exterior: *outer garments; an outer wall.* **2.** situated farther out or farther from the center: *the outer reaches of space.* **3.** of or pertaining to the external world. [1350–1400; ME; see OUT, -ER[4]] **—out/er·ness,** *n.*

out/er automor/phism, *Math.* an automorphism that is not an inner automorphism.

out/er bar/, *Eng. Law.* a body of the junior counsel who sit and plead outside the dividing bar in the court, ranking below the King's Counsel or Queen's Counsel. Also, **utter bar.** Cf. **inner bar.**

out/er bar/rister, *Eng. Law.* a barrister belonging to the outer bar. Also, **utter barrister.** Cf. **inner barrister.** [1895–1900]

out·er·coat (ou/tər kōt/), *n.* coat (def. 1). [1945–50; OUTER + COAT]

out/er ear/. See **external ear.** [1930–35]

Out/er Heb/rides. See under **Hebrides.**

Out/er Mongo/lia, former name of **Mongolian People's Republic.**

out·er·most (ou/tər mōst/ *or, esp. Brit.,* -məst), *adj.* farthest out; remotest from the interior or center: *the outermost limits.* [1350–1400; ME; see OUTER, -MOST]

out/er plan/et, *Astron.* any of the five planets with orbits outside the orbit of Mars: Jupiter, Saturn, Uranus, Neptune, and Pluto. Cf. **inner planet.** [1940–45]

out/er prod/uct, *Math.* See **cross product.** [1925–30]

out·er·sole (ou/tər sōl/), *n.* outsole. [OUTER + SOLE[2]]

out/er space/, 1. space beyond the atmosphere of the earth. **2.** See **deep space.** [1875–80]

out·er·wear (ou/tər wâr/), *n.* **1.** garments, as raincoats or overcoats, worn over other clothing for warmth or protection outdoors; overclothes. **2.** clothing, as dresses, sweaters, or suits, worn over undergarments. [1925–30; OUTER + WEAR]

out·face (out/fās/), *v.t.,* **-faced, -fac·ing. 1.** to cause to submit by or as if by staring down; face or stare down. **2.** to face or confront boldly; defy. [1520–30; OUT- + FACE]

out·fall (out/fôl/), *n.* the outlet or place of discharge of a river, drain, sewer, etc. [1620–30; OUT- + FALL]

out·field (out/fēld/), *n.* **1.** *Baseball.* **a.** the part of the field beyond the diamond. **b.** the positions played by the right, center, and left fielders. **c.** the outfielders considered as a group (contrasted with *infield*). **2.** *Cricket.* the part of the field farthest from the batsman. **3.** *Agric.* **a.** the outlying land of a farm. **b.** land not regularly tilled but normally used for pasture. Cf. **infield** (def. 3). **4.** an outlying region. [1630–40; OUT- + FIELD]

out·field·er (out/fēl/dər), *n. Sports.* one of the players, esp. in baseball, stationed in the outfield. [1855–60, *Amer.*; OUTFIELD + -ER[1]]

out·fit (out/fit/), *n., v.,* **-fit·ted, -fit·ting.** —*n.* **1.** an assemblage of articles that equip a person for a particular task, role, trade, etc.: *an explorer's outfit.* **2.** a set of usually matching or harmonious garments and accessories worn together; coordinated costume; ensemble: *a new spring outfit.* **3.** a set of articles for any purpose: *a cooking outfit.* **4.** a group associated in an undertaking requiring close cooperation, as a military unit. **5.** a business firm engaged in a particular form of commercial enterprise: *a construction outfit.* **6.** any company, party, or set. **7.** the act of fitting out or equipping for any purpose, as for a voyage, journey, or expedition. **8.** mental, physical, or moral equipment. —*v.t.* **9.** to fur-

out/cit/y, *n., pl.* **-cit·ies.**
out/clam/or, *v.t.*
out/clerk/, *n.*
out/coach/, *v.t.*
out/com/pass, *v.t.*
out/com·pete/, *v.t.,* **-pet·ed, -pet·ing.**
out/com/pli·ment/, *v.t.*
out/court/, *v.t.*
out/crawl/, *v.t.*
out/creep/, *v.t.,* **-crept, -creep·ing.**
out/crick/et, *v.t.*
out/crow/, *v.t.*
out/crowd/, *v.t.*
out/cull/, *v.t.*
out/cure/, *v.t.* **-cured, -cur·ing.**
out/curse/, *v.t.,* **-cursed, -curs·ing.**
out/cut/, *v.t.,* **-cut, -cut·ting.**
out/dance/, *v.t.,* **-danced, -danc·ing.**
out/daz/zle, *v.t.,* **-zled, -zling.**
out/de·bate/, *v.t.,* **-bat·ed, -bat·ing.**
out/de·liv/er, *v.t.*
out/de·sign/, *v.t.*
out/des·patch/, *v.t.*
out/dev/il, *v.t.,* **-iled, -il·ing** or (*esp. Brit.*) **-illed, -il·ling.**
out/dis·patch/, *v.t.*
out/dis/trict, *n.*
out/dodge/, *v.t.,* **-dodged, -dodg·ing.**
out/drag/, *v.t.,* **-dragged, -drag·ging.**
out/dress/, *v.t.*
out/drink/, *v.t.,* **-drank** or (*Nonstandard*) **-drunk; -drunk** or, often, **-drank; -drink·ing.**
out/du/el, *v.t.,* **-eled, -el·ing** or (*esp. Brit.*) **-elled, -el·ling.**
out/dwell/, *v.t.,* **-dwelt** or **-dwelled, -dwell·ing.**
out/earn/, *v.t.*
out/eat/, *v.t.,* **-ate, -eat·en, -eat·ing.**
out/ech/o, *v.t.,* **-ech·oed, -ech·o·ing.**
out/edge/, *v.t.,* **-edged, -edg·ing.**
out/e·quiv/o·cate/, *v.t.,* **-cat·ed, -cat·ing.**
out/ex/e·cute/, *v.t.,* **-cut·ed, -cut·ing.**
out/fa/ble, *v.t.,* **-bled, -bling.**
out/fame/, *v.t.,* **-famed, -fam·ing.**
out/fast/, *v.t.*
out/fawn/, *v.t.*
out/feast/, *v.t.*
out/feed/, *v.t.,* **-fed, -feed·ing.**
out/fence/, *v.t.,* **-fenced, -fenc·ing.**
out/fer/ret, *v.t.*
out/fight/, *v.t.,* **-fought, -fight·ing.**
out/fig/ure, *v.t.,* **-ured, -ur·ing.**
out/fish/, *v.t.*
out/flame/, *v.t.,* **-flamed, -flam·ing.**
out/flare/, *v.t.,* **-flared, -flar·ing.**
out/flash/, *v.t.*
out/flat/ter, *v.t.*
out/flee/, *v.t.,* **-fled, -flee·ing.**
out/fling/, *v.t.,* **-flung, -fling·ing.**
out/float/, *v.t.*
out/flour/ish, *v.t.*
out/fool/, *v.t.*
out/froth/, *v.t.*
out/fum/ble, *v.t.,* **-bled, -bling.**
out/gab/ble, *v.t.,* **-bled, -bling.**

nish with an outfit, equipment, etc.; fit out; equip: *to outfit an expedition to the South Pole.* **10.** *Naut.* to finish equipping (a vessel) at a dock. —*v.i.* **11.** to furnish oneself with an outfit. [1755–65; OUT- + FIT[1]] —**out′fit′ter,** *n.*
—**Syn. 1, 3.** kit. **9.** appoint, supply, rig.

out′fit car′, a railroad car used as a dormitory for construction and maintenance workers. Also called **camp car.**

out•flank (out′flangk′), *v.t.* **1.** to go or extend beyond the flank of (an opposing military unit); turn the flank of. **2.** to outmaneuver or bypass. [1755–65; OUT- + FLANK] —**out′flank′er,** *n.*

out•flow (out′flō′), *n.* **1.** the act of flowing out: *We need flood control to stem the river's outflow.* **2.** something that flows out: *to measure the outflow in gallons per minute.* **3.** any outward movement: *the annual outflow of tourists.* [1790–1800; OUT- + FLOW]

out•flux (out′fluks′), *n.* **1.** the act of flowing out; outflow (opposed to *influx*). **2.** a place of flowing out; outlet. [1730–40; OUT- + FLUX]

out•fly (out′flī′), *v.*, **-flew, -flown, -fly•ing.** —*v.t.* **1.** to surpass in flying, esp. in speed or distance: *to outfly the speed of sound.* —*v.i.* **2.** *Literary.* to fly out or forth. [1585–95; OUT- + FLY[1]]

out•foot (out′fo͝ot′), *v.t.* **1.** to surpass (another person) in running, walking, etc.; outstrip. **2.** to outsail; excel (another boat) in speed. [1730–40; OUT- + FOOT]

out•fox (out′foks′), *v.t.* to outwit; outsmart; outmaneuver: *Politics is often the art of knowing how to outfox the opposition.* [1960–65; OUT- + FOX]

out-front (out′frunt′), *adj. Informal.* candid; frank; honest: *The politician was less than out-front with the interviewer.* [1915–20, *Amer.*]

out•frown (out′froun′), *v.t.* to outdo in frowning; silence, abash, or subdue by frowning. [1595–1605; OUT- + FROWN]

out•gas (out′gas′, out′gas′), *v.*, **-gassed, -gas•sing.** *Chem.* —*v.t.* **1.** to remove (adsorbed or occluded gases), usually by heat or reduced pressure. —*v.i.* **2.** to lose gas. [1920–25; OUT- + GAS]

out•gen•er•al (out′jen′ər əl), *v.t.*, **-aled, -al•ing** or (*esp. Brit.*) **-alled, -al•ling.** to outdo or surpass in generalship. [1760–70; OUT- + GENERAL]

out•giv•ing (out′giv′ing), *adj.* **1.** friendly or responsive; outgoing. —*n.* **2.** *Archaic.* something given out, as a statement or proclamation. [1655–1665; OUT- + GIVE + -ING[1], -ING[2]]

out•go (out′gō′), *n.*, *pl.* **-goes,** *v.*, **-went, -gone, -go•ing.** —*n.* **1.** the act or process of going out: *Her illness occasioned a tremendous outgo of affectionate concern.* **2.** money paid out; expenditure: *a record of income and outgo.* **3.** something that goes out; outflow: *The outgo of electrical energy had to be increased.* —*v.t.* **4.** to go beyond; outdistance: *to outgo the minimum rquirements.* **5.** to surpass, excel, or outdo: *Each child was encouraged to outgo the others.* **6.** *Archaic.* to go faster than; excel in speed. [1520–30; OUT- + GO[1]]

out•go•ing (out′gō′ing *or, for 5,* -gō′-), *adj.* **1.** going out; departing: *outgoing trains.* **2.** leaving or retiring from a position or office: *A farewell party was given for the outgoing members of the board of directors.* **3.** addressed and ready for posting: *outgoing mail.* **4.** of or pertaining to food prepared for delivery or consumption off the premises: *outgoing orders at the pizza parlor.* **5.** interested in and responsive to others; friendly; sociable: *an outgoing personality.* —*n.* **6.** Usually, **outgoings.** *Chiefly Brit.* expenses; money expended. **7.** the act of going out: *The ship's outgoing proved more difficult than its incoming.* **8.** something that goes out; effluence: *an outgoing measured in kilowatt hours.* [1300–50; ME (ger.); see OUT-, GOING]

out-group (out′gro͞op′), *n. Sociol.* people outside one's own group, esp. as considered to be inferior or alien; a group perceived as other than one's own. Cf. **in-group.** [1905–10; OUT- + GROUP]

out•grow (out′grō′), *v.*, **-grew, -grown, -grow•ing.** —*v.t.* **1.** to grow too large for: *to outgrow one's clothes.* **2.** to leave behind or lose in the changes incident to development or the passage of time: *She outgrew her fear of the dark.* **3.** to surpass in growing: *watching one child outgrow another.* —*v.i.* **4.** *Archaic.* to grow out; burst forth; protrude. [1585–95; OUT- + GROW]

out•growth (out′grōth′), *n.* **1.** a natural development, product, or result: *to consider truancy an outgrowth of parental neglect.* **2.** an additional, supplementary result. **3.** a growing out or forth. **4.** something that grows out; offshoot; excrescence. [1830–40; OUT- + GROWTH]

out•guess (out′ges′), *v.t.* to anticipate correctly the actions or intentions of; outwit. [1910–15; OUT- + GUESS]

out•gun (out′gun′), *v.t.*, **-gunned, -gun•ning.** **1.** to exceed in firepower. **2.** to outdo or overwhelm, as by superior forces: *Local manufacturers have been outgunned by the overseas competition.* [1685–95; OUT- + GUN[1]]

out•han•dle (out′han′dəl), *v.t.*, **-dled, -dling.** to handle or operate in a superior way to: *That car outhandles all others in its class.* [OUT- + HANDLE]

out•haul (out′hôl′), *n. Naut.* a rope used for hauling out a sail on a boom, yard, etc. [1830–40; OUT- + HAUL]

out-Her•od (out′her′əd), *v.t.* to outdo in extravagance, violence, or excess: *His cruelty out-Herods Herod.* [1595–1605; OUT- + HEROD (ANTIPAS)]

out•house (out′hous′), *n.*, *pl.* **-hous•es** (-hou′ziz). **1.** an outbuilding with one or more seats and a pit serving as a toilet; privy. **2.** any outbuilding. [1525–35; OUT- + HOUSE]

out•ie (ou′tē), *n. Informal.* **1.** a protruding navel. **2.** a person having such a navel. [OUT + -IE]

out•ing (ou′ting), *n.* **1.** a pleasure trip, excursion, picnic, or the like: *the annual outing for the senior class.* **2.** a public appearance, as by a participant in an athletic contest or event: *The player scored well in his outing with the team.* **3.** the intentional exposure of a secret homosexual, esp. a prominent figure. [1325–75; ME; see OUT, -ING[1]]
—**Syn. 1.** jaunt.

out′ing flan′nel, a light cotton flannel with a short, dense nap. [1885–90, *Amer.*]

out•jock•ey (out′jok′ē), *v.t.*, **-eyed, -ey•ing.** to outmaneuver: *We outjockeyed the competition and got our bid in first.* [1705–15; OUT- + JOCKEY]

out•laid (out′lād′), *v.* pt. and pp. of **outlay.**

out•land (*n.* out′land′; *adj.* out′land′, -lənd), *n.* **1.** Usually, **outlands.** the outlying districts or remote regions of a country; provinces: *a name unknown in the outlands.* **2.** (formerly) the outlying land of a feudal estate, usually granted to tenants. **3.** a foreign land. —*adj.* **4.** outlying, as districts. **5.** foreign. [bef. 950; ME; OE *ūtland.* See OUT-, LAND]

out•land•er (out′lan′dər), *n.* **1.** a foreigner; alien. **2.** an outsider; stranger. [1590–1600; OUTLAND + -ER[1]]

out•land•ish (out lan′dish), *adj.* **1.** freakishly or grotesquely strange or odd, as appearance, dress, objects, ideas, or practices; bizarre: *outlandish clothes; outlandish questions.* **2.** having a foreign appearance. **3.** remote from civilized areas; out-of-the-way: *an outlandish settlement.* **4.** *Archaic.* foreign; alien. [bef. 1000; ME; OE *ūtlendisc.* See OUTLAND, -ISH[1]] —**out•land′ish•ly,** *adv.* —**out•land′ish•ness,** *n.*
—**Syn. 1.** peculiar, queer, eccentric, curious. **3.** backwoods, isolated.

out•last (out′last′, -läst′), *v.t.* **1.** to endure or last longer than: *The pyramids outlasted the civilization that built them.* **2.** to live longer than; outlive. [1565–75; OUT- + LAST[2]]

out•law (out′lô′), *n.* **1.** a lawless person or habitual criminal, esp. one who is a fugitive from the law. **2.** a person, group, or thing excluded from the benefits and protection of the law. **3.** a person under sentence of outlawry. **4.** a person who refuses to be governed by the established rules or practices of any group; rebel; nonconformist: *one of the outlaws of country music.* **5.** *Chiefly Western U.S.* **a.** a horse that cannot be broken; a mean, intractable horse. **b.** any rogue animal. —*v.t.* **6.** to make unlawful or illegal: *The Eighteenth Amendment outlawed the manufacture, sale, or transportation of intoxicating beverages in the U.S.* **7.** to deprive of the benefits and protection of the law: *Members of guerrilla bands who refused to surrender were outlawed.* **8.** to prohibit: *to outlaw smoking in a theater.* **9.** to remove from legal jurisdiction; deprive of legal force. —*adj.* **10.** of, pertaining to, or characteristic of an outlaw. [bef. 1150; ME *outlawe,* OE *ūtlaga* < ON *ūtlagi* one outside the protection of the law; see OUT, LAW[1]]
—**Syn. 1.** desperado, bandit, brigand. **8.** proscribe, ban, forbid.

out•law•ry (out′lô′rē), *n.*, *pl.* **-ries.** **1.** the act or process of outlawing. **2.** the state of being outlawed. **3.** disregard or defiance of the law: *a man whose outlawry had made him a folk hero.* [1350–1400; ME *outlauerie* < AF *utlagerie,* ML *utlagāria* < ME *outlage* OUTLAW + AF *-erie* -RY, ML *-āria* -ARY]

out′law strike′. See **wildcat strike.** [1915–20]

out•lay (*n.* out′lā′; *v.* out′lā′), *n.*, *v.*, **-laid, -lay•ing.** —*n.* **1.** an expending or spending, as of money. **2.** an amount expended; expenditure. —*v.t.* **3.** to expend, as money. [1545–55; OUT- + LAY[1]]

out•leap (out′lēp′), *v.*, **-leaped** or **-leapt, -leap•ing.** —*v.t.* **1.** to leap ahead of or over. **2.** to surpass in leaping. —*v.i.* **3.** to leap forth. [1590–1600; OUT- + LEAP]

out•let (out′let, -lit), *n.* **1.** an opening or passage by which anything is let out; vent; exit. **2.** *Elect.* **a.** a point on a wiring system at which current is taken to supply electric devices. **b.** Also called **out′let box′.** the metal box or receptacle designed to facilitate connections to a wiring system. **3.** a means of expression or satisfaction: *an outlet for one's artistic impulses.* **4.** a market for goods. **5.** a store, merchant, or agency selling the goods of a particular wholesaler or manufacturer. **6.** a local radio or television station that broadcasts the programs of a large network. **7.** a river or stream flowing from a body of water, as a lake or pond. **8.** the channel such a river or stream follows. **9.** the lower end or mouth of a river where it meets a large body of water, as a lake or the sea. [1200–50; ME *utlete.* See OUT, LET[1]]

out•li•er (out′lī′ər), *n.* **1.** a person or thing that lies outside. **2.** a person residing outside the place of his or her business, duty, etc. **3.** *Geol.* a part of a formation left detached through the removal of surrounding parts by erosion. [1600–10; OUT- + LIER]

out•line (out′līn′), *n.*, *v.*, **-lined, -lin•ing.** —*n.* **1.** the line by which a figure or object is defined or bounded; contour. **2.** a drawing or sketch restricted to line without shading or modeling of form. **3.** a general sketch, account, or report, indicating only the main features, as of a book, subject, or project: *an outline of medieval history; an outline of a speech.* **4.** **outlines,** the essential features or main aspects of something under discussion: *At the first meeting, we gave her only the outlines of the project.* **5.** *Print.* an ornamented type in which the outside contours of each character appear in black, with the inside left white. —*v.t.* **6.** to draw the outline of, or draw in outline, as a figure or object. **7.** to give an outline of; sketch the main features of: *On the first day, the professor just outlined the course for us.* [1655–65; OUT- + LINE[1]]
—**Syn. 1.** See **form. 3.** plan, draft, rough, synopsis, summary. **6, 7.** delineate, draft.

out•live (out′liv′), *v.t.*, **-lived, -liv•ing.** **1.** to live longer than; survive (a person, period, etc.): *She outlived her husband by many years.* **2.** to outlast; live or last through: *The ship outlived the storm. He hopes to outlive the stigma of his imprisonment.* [1425–75; late ME *outliven.* See OUT-, LIVE[1]] —**out′liv′er,** *n.*
—**Syn. 1.** See **survive.**

out•look (out′lo͝ok′), *n.* **1.** the view or prospect from a particular place. **2.** mental attitude or view; point of view: *one's outlook on life.* **3.** prospect of the future: *the political outlook.* **4.** the place from which an observer looks out; lookout. **5.** the act or state of looking out. **6.** a watch kept; vigilance; lookout: *a careful outlook to prevent forest fires.* [1660–70; OUT- + LOOK]
—**Syn. 1, 3.** scene. **2.** attitude, viewpoint, position, approach.

out•ly•ing (out′lī′ing), *adj.* **1.** lying at a distance from the center or the main body; remote; out-of-the-way: *outlying military posts.* **2.** lying outside the boundary or limit. [1655–65; OUT- + LYING[2]]

out•man (out′man′), *v.t.*, **-manned, -man•ning.** to surpass in manpower. [1685–95; OUT- + MAN[1]]

out•ma•neu•ver (out′mə no͞o′vər), *v.t.* **1.** to outwit, defeat, or frustrate by maneuvering. **2.** to outdo or surpass in maneuvering or maneuverability. [1790–1800; OUT- + MANEUVER]

out•ma•noeu•vre (out′mə no͞o′vər), *v.t.*, **-vred, -vring.** *Brit.* outmaneuver.

out•march (out′märch′), *v.t.* to march faster or farther than. [1640–50; OUT- + MARCH[1]]

out•match (out′mach′), *v.t.* to be superior to; surpass; outdo: *The home team seems to have been completely outmatched by the visitors.* [1595–1605; OUT- + MATCH[2]]

out•mi•grant (out′mī′grənt), *n.* a person who outmigrates. [1940–45]

out•mi•grate (out′mī′grāt), *v.i.*, **-grat•ed, -grat•ing.** to leave a region, community, etc., to move or settle into a different part of one's country or home territory: *People are no longer out-migrating from the South in such large numbers.* [1950–55] —**out′-mi•gra′tion,** *n.*

out•mode (out′mōd′), *v.*, **-mod•ed, -mod•ing.** —*v.t.* **1.** to cause (something) to go out of style or become obsolete. —*v.i.* **2.** to go out of style or become obsolete. [1900–05; perh. from the phrase *out of mode;* cf. F *démoder*]

out•mod•ed (out′mō′did), *adj.* **1.** gone out of style; no longer fashionable: *outmoded styles.* **2.** not acceptable by present standards; no longer usable; obsolete: *outmoded dwellings; outmoded teaching methods.* [see OUTMODE, -ED[2]]
—**Syn. 1.** unfashionable, dated, old-fashioned.

out•most (out′mōst′ *or, esp. Brit.,* -məst), *adj.* farthest out; outermost. [1300–50; ME; see OUT-, -MOST]

out•mus•cle (out′mus′əl), *v.t.*, **-cled, -cling.** to get the better of or dominate by virtue of superior strength or force. [OUT- + MUSCLE]

out•num•ber (out′num′bər), *v.t.* to exceed in number. [1660–70; OUT- + NUMBER]

out-of-bod•y (out′əv bod′ē), *adj.* of, pertaining to, or

CONCISE PRONUNCIATION KEY: *act, cāpe, dâre, pärt; set, ēqual; if, ice; ox, ōver, ôrder, oil, bo͝ok, bo͞ot, out; up, ûrge; child; sing; shoe; thin, that;* zh as in *treasure.* ə = *a* as in *alone, e* as in *system, i* as in *easily, o* as in *gallop, u* as in *circus;* ᵊ as in *fire* (fīᵊr), *hour* (ouᵊr). l and n can serve as syllabic consonants, as in *cradle* (krād′l), and *button* (but′n). See the full key inside the front cover.

out′gain′, *v.t.*
out′gal′lop, *v.t.*
out′gam′ble, *v.t.*, **-bled, -bling.**
out′game′, *v.t.*, **-gamed, -gam•ing.**
out′gaze′, *v.t.*, **-gazed, -gaz•ing.**
out′glare′, *v.t.*, **-glared, -glar•ing.**
out′gleam′, *v.t.*
out′glit′ter, *v.t.*
out′gloom′, *v.t.*
out′glow′, *v.t.*
out′gnaw′, *v.t.*, **-gnawed, -gnawed** or **-gnawn, -gnaw•ing.**
out′green′, *v.t.*
out′grin′, *v.t.*, **-grinned, -grin•ning.**
out′gross′, *v.t.*
out′gush′, *v.t.*
out′ham′mer, *v.t.*
out′has′ten, *v.t.*
out′hear′, *v.t.*, **-heard, -hear•ing.**
out′hire′, *v.t.*, **-hired, -hir•ing.**
out′hiss′, *v.t.*
out′hit′, *v.t.*, **-hit, -hit•ting.**
out′howl′, *v.t.*
out′hu′mor, *v.t.*
out′hunt′, *v.t.*
out′hurl′, *v.t.*
out′hus′tle, *v.t.*, **-tled, -tling.**
out′hy•per′bo•lize′, *v.t.*, **-lized, -liz•ing.**
out′in′flu•ence, *v.t.*, **-enced, -enc•ing.**
out′in•trigue′, *v.t.*, **-trigued, -tri•guing.**
out′in•vent′, *v.t.*
out′is′sue, *v.t.*, **-sued, -su•ing.**
out′jest′, *v.t.*
out′jet′, *v.t.*, **-jet•ted, -jet•ting.**
out′jinx′, *v.t.*
out′jour′ney, *v.t.*, **-neyed, -ney•ing.**
out′jug′gle, *v.t.*, **-gled, -gling.**
out′jump′, *v.t.*
out′jut′, *v.t.*, **-jut•ted, -jut•ting.**
out′kick′, *v.t.*
out′kill′, *v.t.*
out′king′, *v.t.*
out′kiss′, *v.t.*
out′kitch′en, *n.*
out′la′bor, *v.t.*
out′lance′, *v.t.*, **-lanced, -lanc•ing.**
out′lash′, *v.t.*
out′laugh′, *v.t.*
out′launch′, *v.t.*
out′lead′, *v.t.*, **-led, -lead•ing.**
out′learn′, *v.t.*, **-learned** or **-learnt, -learn•ing.**
out′length′en, *v.t.*
out′light′en, *v.t.*
out′limn′, *v.t.*
out′lin′ger, *v.t.*
out′lip′, *v.t.*, **-lipped, -lip•ping.**
out′love′, *v.t.*, **-loved, -lov•ing.**
out′lus′ter, *v.t.*
out′mal′a•prop′, *v.t.*, **-propped, -prop•ping.**
out′ma•nip′u•late′, *v.t.*, **-lat•ed, -lat•ing.**
out′mar′ry, *v.t.*, **-ried, -ry•ing.**
out′mas′ter, *v.t.*
out′mate′, *v.t.*, **-mat•ed, -mat•ing.**
out′meas′ure, *v.t.*, **-ured, -ur•ing.**
out′mer′chant, *n.*
out′mount′, *v.t.*
out′mouth′, *v.t.*
out′move′, *v.t.*, **-moved, -mov•ing.**
out′of′fice, *n.*

characterized by the dissociative sensation of perceiving oneself from an external vantage point, as though the mind or soul has left the body and is acting on its own: *an alleged out-of-body experience.* [1970–75]

out-of-bounds (out′əv boundz′), *adj.* **1.** *Sports.* being beyond or passing the limits or boundaries of a field, course, etc., marking the area within which the ball, puck, or the like is legally in play. **2.** beyond any established boundaries or prescribed limits; prohibited; forbidden. **3.** further than or beyond established limits, as of behavior or thought. [1855–60]

out-of-court (out′əv kôrt′, -kōrt′), *adj.* conducted or agreed upon between contending parties without court decision: *an out-of-court settlement of a lawsuit.*

out-of-date (out′əv dāt′), *adj.* gone out of style or fashion; outmoded; obsolete: *out-of-date fashions; out-of-date ideas.* [1620–30] **—out′-of-date′ness,** *n.*

out-of-doors (out′əv dôrz′, -dōrz′), *adj.* **1.** Also, **out′-of-door′.** outdoor. **—***n.* **2.** (*used with a singular v.*) outdoors. [1800–10]

out′ of pock′et, 1. lacking money. **2.** having suffered a financial loss.

out-of-pock•et (out′əv pok′it), *adj.* **1.** paid out or owed in cash; necessitating an expenditure of cash: *The out-of-pocket expenses include cab fares.* **2.** without funds or assets: *an out-of-pocket student who stayed with us.* [1880–85]

out-of-print (out′əv print′), *adj.* **1.** being no longer published; no longer printed or reprinted: *a bookstore specializing in out-of-print books.* **—***n.* **2.** a book, pamphlet, etc., that is no longer published. [1665–75]

out-of-round (out′əv round′), *adj.* not perfectly round.

out-of-sight (out′əv sīt′), *adj.* **1.** *Slang.* fantastic; great; marvelous: *an out-of-sight guitarist.* **2.** beyond reason; exceedingly high: *out-of-sight hospital bills.* Also, **out-a-sight.** [1895–1900, *Amer.*]

out-of-state (out′əv stāt′), *adj.* of, pertaining to, or from another state of the U.S.: *a car with an out-of-state license plate; out-of-state vacationers.* [1930–35, *Amer.*]

out-of-stat•er (out′əv stā′tər), *n.* a visitor from another state of the U.S.: *Many out-of-staters come to our summer music festival.* [1935–40, *Amer.*; OUT-OF-STATE + -ER[1]]

out-of-sync (out′əv singk′), *adj., adv.* **1.** *Motion Pictures.* (in the editing or projection of film) referring to any situation in which the sound does not correspond to the lip movements of an actor or to any other sound source on the screen. **2.** not synchronized. [1945–50]

out-of-the-way (out′əv *th*ə wā′), *adj.* **1.** remote from much-traveled, frequented, or populous regions; secluded: *an out-of-the-way inn up in the hills.* **2.** seldom encountered; unusual: *out-of-the-way information.* **3.** giving offense; improper: *an out-of-the-way remark.* [1250–1300; ME]

out-of-town (out′əv toun′), *adj.* **1.** of, pertaining to, or from another city or town: *We're expecting out-of-town visitors tomorrow.* **2.** taking place in another city or town: *the out-of-town tryout of a new play.* [1815–25]

out-of-town•er (out′əv tou′nər), *n.* a visitor from another town or city: *The World's Fair brought many out-of-towners to New Orleans.* [1910–15; OUT-OF-TOWN + -ER[1]]

out•pace (out′pās′), *v.t.,* **-paced, -pac•ing.** to surpass or exceed, as in speed, development, or performance: *a company that has consistently outpaced the competition in sales.* [1565–75; OUT- + PACE[1]]

out•par•ish (out′par′ish), *n.* a parish located outside the boundaries of or at a distance from a town or city; an outlying parish. [1570–80; OUT- + PARISH]

out•pa•tient (out′pā′shənt), *n.* a patient who receives treatment at a hospital, as in an emergency room or clinic, but is not hospitalized. Also, **out′-pa′tient.** [1705–15; OUT- + PATIENT]

out•per•form (out′pər fôrm′), *v.t.* to surpass in excellence of performance; do better than: *a new engine that outperforms the competition; a stock that outperformed all others.* [1955–60; OUT- + PERFORM]

out•place (out′plās′), *v.t.,* **-placed, -plac•ing. 1.** to provide outplacement for. **2.** to displace; supplant: *Suburban shopping malls outplaced urban department stores in many cities.* [1925–30; OUT- + PLACE]

out•place•ment (out′plās′mənt), *n.* **1.** counseling and assistance in finding a new job, provided by a company for an employee who has been or is about to be dismissed. **2.** an act or instance of outplacing. **3.** the state or condition of being outplaced. [1965–70; OUT- + PLACEMENT]

out•play (out′plā′), *v.t.* to play better than. [1640–50; OUT- + PLAY]

out•point (out′point′), *v.t.* **1.** to excel in number of points, as in a competition or contest. **2.** *Naut.* to sail closer to the wind than (another ship). [1585–95; OUT- + POINT]

out•port (out′pôrt′, -pōrt′), *n.* **1.** a secondary seaport close to a larger one but beyond its corporate limits or jurisdiction. **2.** *Canadian.* an isolated fishing village, esp. on the Newfoundland coast. [1635–45; OUT- + PORT[1]]

out•post (out′pōst′), *n.* **1.** a station established at a distance from the main body of an army to protect it from surprise attack: *We keep only a small garrison of men at our desert outposts.* **2.** the body of troops stationed there; detachment or perimeter guard. **3.** an outlying settlement, installation, position, etc. [1750–60; OUT- + POST[2]]

out•pour (*n.* out′pôr′, -pōr′; *v.* out′pôr′, -pōr′), *n.* **1.** outpouring. **—***v.t.* **2.** to pour out. [1665–75; OUT- + POUR] **—out′pour′er,** *n.*

out•pour•ing (out′pôr′ing, -pōr′-), *n.* something that pours out or is poured out; an outflow, overflow, or effusion: *an outpouring of sympathy from her friends.* [1750–60; OUT- + POURING]

out•pull (out′po͝ol′), *v.t.* to exceed in ability to attract an audience, attention, etc.; outdraw: *a film that is outpulling every other movie in town.* [1925–30; OUT- + PULL]

out•put (out′po͝ot′), *n., v.,* **-put•ted** or **-put, -put•ting.** **—***n.* **1.** the act of turning out; production: *the factory's output of cars; artistic output.* **2.** the quantity or amount produced, as in a given time: *to increase one's daily output.* **3.** the material produced or yield; product. **4.** the current, voltage, power, or signal produced by an electrical or electronic circuit or device. Cf. **input** (def. 4). **5.** *Computers.* **a.** information in a form suitable for transmission from internal to external units of a computer, or to an outside medium. **b.** the process of transferring data from internal storage to an external medium, as paper or microfilm. **6.** the power or force produced by a machine. **—***v.t., v.i.* **7.** *Computers.* to transfer (information) from internal storage to an external medium. **8.** to produce; turn out. [1855–60; OUT- + PUT]

out•race (out′rās′), *v.t.,* **-raced, -rac•ing.** to race or run faster than: *The deer outraced its pursuers.* [1650–60; OUT- + RACE[1]]

out•rage (out′rāj), *n., v.,* **-raged, -rag•ing.** **—***n.* **1.** an act of wanton cruelty or violence; any gross violation of law or decency. **2.** anything that strongly offends, insults, or affronts the feelings. **3.** a powerful feeling of resentment or anger aroused by something perceived as an injury, insult, or injustice: *Outrage seized the entire nation at the news of the attempted assassination.* **—***v.t.* **4.** to subject to grievous violence or indignity. **5.** to anger or offend; make resentful; shock: *I am outraged by his whole attitude.* **6.** to offend against (right, decency, feelings, etc.) grossly or shamelessly: *Such conduct outrages our normal sense of decency.* **7.** to rape. [1250–1300; ME < OF *outrage, ultrage,* equiv. to *outr(er)* to push beyond bounds (deriv. of *outre* beyond < L *ultrā*) + *-age* -AGE]
—Syn. 2. offense, abuse, indignity. **7.** violate.

out•ra•geous (out rā′jəs), *adj.* **1.** of the nature of or involving gross injury or wrong: *an outrageous slander.* **2.** grossly offensive to the sense of right or decency: *outrageous behavior; an outrageous remark.* **3.** passing reasonable bounds; intolerable or shocking: *an outrageous price.* **4.** violent in action or temper. **5.** highly unusual or unconventional; extravagant; remarkable: *a child of the most outrageous precocity; a fancy dive performed with outrageous ease.* [1275–1325; ME < MF *outrageus.* See OUTRAGE, -OUS] **—out•ra′geous•ly,** *adv.* **—out•ra′geous•ness,** *n.*
—Syn. 1, 2, 3. See **flagrant. 2.** repugnant, insulting, shocking, revolting. **3.** unthinkable, appalling.

out•ran (out′ran′), *v.* pt. of **outrun.**

ou•trance (o͞o träɴs′), *n. French.* the utmost extremity.

out•rang (out′rang′), *v.* pt. of **outring.**

out•range (out′rānj′), *v.t.,* **-ranged, -rang•ing. 1.** to have a longer or greater range than. **2.** to sail out of the range of (a gun or guns). [1855–60; OUT- + RANGE]

out•rank (out′rangk′), *v.t.* to have a higher rank than: *A major outranks a captain in the army.* [1835–45, *Amer.*; OUT- + RANK[1]]

ou•tré (o͞o trā′), *adj.* passing the bounds of what is usual or considered proper; unconventional; bizarre. [1715–25; < F, ptp. of *outrer* to push beyond bounds (see OUTRAGE)]

out•reach (*v.* out′rēch′; *n., adj.* out′rēch′), *v.t.* **1.** to reach beyond; exceed: *The demand has outreached our supply.* **2.** *Archaic.* to reach out; extend. **—***v.i.* **3.** to reach out. **—***n.* **4.** an act or instance of reaching out. **5.** length or extent of reach. **6.** the act of extending services, benefits, etc., to a wider section of the population, as in community work. **—***adj.* **7.** concerned with extending community services, benefits, etc.: *an educational outreach program.* [1560–70; OUT- + REACH]

out•re•lief (out′ri lēf′), *n. Brit.* public relief administered to people residing in a poorhouse or similar institution. [1890–95]

Ou•tre•mont (o͞o′trə mont′; *Fr.* o͞o trə môɴ′), *n.* a city in S Quebec, in E Canada: suburb of Montreal. 24,338.

out•ride (*v.* out′rīd′; *n.* out′rīd′), *v.,* **-rode, -rid•den, -rid•ing,** *n.* **—***v.t.* **1.** to outdo or outstrip in riding. **2.** (of a ship) to come safely through (a storm) by lying to. **—***v.i.* **3.** to act as an outrider. **—***n.* **4.** *Pros.* an unaccented syllable or syllables added to a metrical foot, esp. in sprung rhythm. [1520–30; OUT- + RIDE]

out•rid•er (out′rī′dər), *n.* **1.** a mounted attendant riding before or beside a carriage. **2.** (at a racetrack) a mounted rider who accompanies or leads a racehorse to the post. **3.** a person who goes in advance of an automobile or person to clear a passage. **4.** a person who leads the way or is a member of a vanguard; forerunner. **5.** a person who rides out or forth, esp. a scout, cowhand, ranch hand, or the like. [1300–50; ME: official in a monastery; see OUT-, RIDER]

out•rig•ger (out′rig′ər), *n.* **1.** a framework extended outboard from the side of a boat, esp., as in South Pacific canoes, supporting a float that gives stability. **2.** a bracket extending outward from the side of a racing shell, to support an oarlock. **3.** the shell itself. **4.** a spar rigged out from a ship's rail or the like, as for extending a sail. **5.** a long, flexible rod, attached to a fishing boat near the stern, along which a fishing line may be threaded to keep it clear of the boat's wake when trolling. **6.** a structure extending outward from a vehicle, vessel, or aircraft to increase stability or provide support for something. **7.** a projecting beam, as for supporting a hoisting tackle. **8.** a horizontal steel beam extending the base of a crane. [1740–50; OUT- + RIG + -ER[1]]

outrigger (def. 1)

out•right (*adj.* out′rīt′; *adv.* out′rīt′, -rīt′), *adj.* **1.** complete or total: *an outright loss.* **2.** downright or unqualified: *an outright refusal.* **3.** without further payments due, restrictions, or qualifications: *an outright sale of the car.* **4.** *Archaic.* directed straight out or on. **—***adv.* **5.** completely; entirely. **6.** without restraint, reserve, or concealment; openly: *Tell me outright what's bothering you.* **7.** at once; instantly: *to be killed outright.* **8.** without further payments due, restrictions, or qualifications: *to own the house outright.* **9.** *Archaic.* straight out or ahead; directly onward. [1250–1300; ME; see OUT, RIGHT] **—out′right′ness,** *n.*
—Syn. 5. downright, utterly, altogether, thoroughly.

out•ring (out′ring′), *v.,* **-rang, -rung, -ring•ing.** **—***v.t.* **1.** to outdo in ringing; ring louder than. **—***v.i.* **2.** to ring out: *church bells outringing over the countryside.* [1325–75; ME (intrans.); see OUT-, RING[2]]

out•row (out′rō′), *v.t.* to surpass in rowing; row faster than. [1520–30; OUT- + ROW[2]]

out•run (out′run′), *v.t.,* **-ran, -run, -run•ning. 1.** to run faster or farther than. **2.** to escape by or as if by running: *They managed to outrun the police.* **3.** to exceed; excel; surpass. [1520–30; OUT + RUN]

out•run•ner (out′run′ər), *n.* **1.** a person or thing that runs ahead or outside. **2.** an attendant who runs before or beside a carriage. **3.** the leader of a team of dogs. **4.** a forerunner. [1590–1600; OUT- + RUNNER]

out•rush (out′rush′), *n.* a rapid or intense outflow: *an outrush of water from a bursting pipe.* [1870–75; OUT- + RUSH[1]]

out•sail (out′sāl′), *v.t.* to outdo in sailing; sail farther, more skillfully, or faster than. [1610–20; OUT- + SAIL]

out•sang (out′sang′), *v.* pt. of **outsing.**

out•sat (out′sat′), *v.* pt. and pp. of **outsit.**

out•sell (out′sel′), *v.t.,* **-sold, -sell•ing. 1.** to exceed in volume of sales; sell more than: *He outsells all our other salespeople.* **2.** to exceed in value or number of sales: *a*

CONCISE ETYMOLOGY KEY: <, descended or borrowed from; >, whence; b., blend of, blended; c., cognate with; cf., compare; deriv., derivative; equiv., equivalent; imit., imitative; obl., oblique; r., replacing; s., stem; sp., spelling, spelled; resp., respelling, respelled; trans., translation; ?, origin unknown; *, unattested; ‡, probably earlier than. See the full key inside the front cover.

out′or′gan•ize′, *v.t.,* **-ized, -iz•ing.**
out′paint′, *v.t.*
out′pass′, *v.t.*
out′path′, *n.*
out′peep′, *v.t.*
out′peo′ple, *v.t.,* **-pled, -pling.**
out′pick′, *v.t.*
out′pipe′, *v.t.,* **-piped, -pip•ing.**
out′pitch′, *v.t.*
out′pit′y, *v.t.,* **-pit•ied, -pit•y•ing.**
out′plan′, *v.t.,* **-planned, -plan•ning.**
out′please′, *v.t.,* **-pleased, -pleas•ing.**
out′plod′, *v.t.,* **-plod•ded, -plod•ding.**
out′plot′, *v.t.,* **-plot•ted, -plot•ting.**
out′poi′son, *v.t.*
out′pol′i•tick, *v.t.*
out′poll′, *v.t.*
out′pop′, *v.t.,* **-popped, -pop•ping.**
out′pop′u•late′, *v.t.,* **-lat•ed, -lat•ing.**
out′prac′tice, *v.t.,* **-ticed, -tic•ing.**
out′praise′, *v.t.,* **-praised, -prais•ing.**
out′pray′, *v.t.*
out′preach′, *v.t.*
out′preen′, *v.t.*
out′pro•duce′, *v.t.,* **-duced, -duc•ing.**
out′prom′ise, *v.t.,* **-ised, -is•ing.**
out′pry′, *v.t.,* **-pried, -pry•ing.**
out′punch′, *v.t.*
out′pu′pil, *n.*
out′purl′, *v.t.*
out′pur•sue′, *v.t.,* **-sued, -su•ing.**
out′push′, *v.t.*
out′quaff′, *v.t.*
out′quar′ters, *n.*
out′que′ry, *v.t.,* **-ried, -ry•ing.**
out′ques′tion, *v.t.*
out′quib′ble, *v.t.,* **-bled, -bling.**
out′quote′, *v.t.,* **-quot•ed, -quot•ing.**
out′rail′, *v.t.*
out′rant′, *v.t.*
out′rap′, *v.t.,* **-rapped, -rap•ping.**
out′rate′, *v.t.,* **-rat•ed, -rat•ing.**
out′rave′, *v.t.,* **-raved, -rav•ing.**
out′read′, *v.t.,* **-read, -read•ing.**
out′rea′son, *v.t.*
out′reck′on, *v.t.*
out′red′den, *v.t.*
out′reign′, *v.t.*
out′rhyme′, *v.t.,* **-rhymed, -rhym•ing.**
out′rib′, *v.t.,* **-ribbed, -rib•bing.**
out′rick′, *v.t.*
out′rig′, *v.t.,* **-rigged, -rig•ging.**
out′ri′val, *v.t.,* **-valed, -val•ing** or (*esp. Brit.*) **-valled, -val•ling.**
out′roar′, *v.t.*
out′rogue′, *v.t.,* **-rogued, -ro•guing.**
out′ro•mance′, *v.t.,* **-manced, -manc•ing.**
out′root′, *v.t.*
out′rove′, *v.t.,* **-roved, -rov•ing.**
out′saint′, *v.t.*
out′sal′ly, *v.t.,* **-lied, -ly•ing.**
out′sat′is•fy′, *v.t.,* **-fied, -fy•ing.**
out′sa′vor, *v.t.*
out′say′, *v.t.,* **-said, -say•ing.**
out′scent′, *v.t.*
out′scheme′, *v.t.,* **-schemed, -schem•ing.**
out′scold′, *v.t.*
out′scoop′, *v.t.*
out′score′, *v.t.,* **-scored, -scor•ing.**
out′scorn′, *v.t.*
out′scream′, *v.t.*

soap that outsells all other brands. 3. *Archaic.* to obtain a higher price than. [1605–15; OUT- + SELL[1]]

out•sert (out′sûrt′), *n. Bookbinding.* an additional folded signature or sheet into which another is bound. Also called **outset, wraparound.** [OUT- + (IN)SERT]

out•set (out′set′), *n.* **1.** the beginning or start: *I wanted to explain the situation at the outset.* **2.** outsert. [1530–40; OUT- + SET]

out•set•tle•ment (out′set′l mənt), *n.* a distant or remote settlement. [1730–40, *Amer.*; OUT- + SETTLEMENT]

out•set•tler (out′set′lər), *n.* a person who inhabits a remote settlement or area. [1750–60, *Amer.*; OUT- + SETTLER]

out•shine (out′shīn′), *v.,* **-shone** or **shined, -shin•ing.** —*v.t.* **1.** to surpass in shining; shine more brightly than. **2.** to surpass in splendor, ability, achievement, excellence, etc.: *a product that outshone all competitors; to outshine one's classmates.* —*v.i.* **3.** to shine out or forth: *a small light outshining in the darkness.* [1590–1600; OUT- + SHINE]

out•shoot (*v.* out′sho͞ot′; *n.* out′sho͞ot′), *v.,* **-shot, -shoot•ing,** *n.* —*v.t.* **1.** to surpass in shooting, as in accuracy or in number of shots made. **2.** to shoot beyond. **3.** to shoot (something) out; send forth: *a tree outshooting its roots.* —*v.i.* **4.** to shoot forth; project: *sparks outshooting from the fire.* —*n.* **5.** an act or instance of shooting out: *an outshoot of his fist that staggered his opponent.* **6.** something that shoots out: *a row of outshoots from the soil.* [1520–30; OUT- + SHOOT]

out•shout (out′shout′), *v.t.* **1.** to surpass (someone) in shouting; shout louder than. **2.** to outdo in advocacy, as of one's position or point of view: *He outshouted all critics of his scheme.* [1655–65; OUT- + SHOUT]

out•side (*n.* out′sīd′, -sīd′; *adj.* out′sīd′, out′-; *adv.* out′sīd′; *prep.* out′sīd′, out′sīd′), *n.* **1.** the outer side, surface, or part; exterior: *The outside of the house needs painting.* **2.** the external aspect or appearance. **3.** the space without or beyond an enclosure, institution, boundary, etc.: *a prisoner about to resume life on the outside.* **4.** a position away or farther away from the inside or center: *The horse on the outside finished second.* **5.** an outside passenger or place on a coach or other vehicle. **6.** *Northern Canada and Alaska.* (*sometimes cap.*) the settled or more populous part of Canada or the U.S. **7. at the outside,** at the utmost limit; at the maximum: *There weren't more than ten at the outside.* —*adj.* **8.** being, acting, done, or originating beyond an enclosure, boundary, etc.: *outside noises; news from the outside world.* **9.** situated on or pertaining to the outside; exterior; external: *an outside television antenna.* **10.** situated away from the inside or center; farther or farthest away from the inside or center: *the outside lane.* **11.** not belonging to or connected with a specified institution, society, etc.: *outside influences; outside help.* **12.** extremely unlikely or remote: *an outside chance for recovery.* **13.** extreme or maximum: *an outside estimate.* **14.** being in addition to one's regular work or duties: *an outside job.* **15.** working on or assigned to the outside, as of a place or organization: *an outside man to care for the grounds.* **16.** *Baseball.* (of a pitched ball) passing, but not going over, home plate on the side opposite the batter: *The fastball was high and outside.* —*adv.* **17.** on or to the outside, exterior, or space without: *Take the dog outside.* **18.** in or to an area that is removed from or beyond a given place or region: *The country's inhabitants seldom travel outside.* —*prep.* **19.** on or toward the outside of: *There was a noise outside the door.* **20.** beyond the confines or borders of: *visitors from outside the country.* **21.** with the exception of; aside from: *She has no interests outside her work.* **22. outside of,** other than; exclusive of; excepting: *Outside of us, no one else came to the party.* [1495–1505; OUT- + SIDE[1]]
—**Syn. 12.** faint, distant, slight.

out′side cal′iper, a caliper whose legs turn inward so that it can measure outside dimensions, as the diameter of a rod. See illus. under **caliper.** [1870–75]

out′side for′ward, *Soccer.* one of two attacking players who usually play on the far side of the field; wing. [1895–1900]

out′side loop′, *Aeron.* a loop during which the back of the airplane is on the outer side of the curve described by the course of flight. Cf. **inside loop.**

out•sid•er (out′sī′dər), *n.* **1.** a person not belonging to a particular group, set, party, etc.: *Society often regards the artist as an outsider.* **2.** a person unconnected or unacquainted with the matter in question: *Not being a parent, I was regarded as an outsider.* **3.** a racehorse, sports team, or other competitor not considered likely to win or succeed. **4.** a person or thing not within an enclosure, boundary, etc. [1790–1800; OUTSIDE + -ER[1]]

out•sight (out′sīt′), *n.* the ability to see and understand external things clearly. Cf. **insight.** [1590–1600; OUT- + SIGHT, on the model of INSIGHT]

out•sing (out′sing′), *v.t.,* **-sang, -sung, -sing•ing. 1.** to sing better than. **2.** to sing louder than. [1595–1605; OUT- + SING]

out•sit (out′sit′), *v.t.,* **-sat, -sit•ting. 1.** to sit longer than; outwait: *He was determined to outsit his rival.* **2.** to sit beyond the time of: *We realized we were outsitting our welcome.* [1650–60; OUT- + SIT]

out•size (out′sīz′), *n.* **1.** an uncommon or irregular size, esp. one larger than average. **2.** a garment of such a size. —*adj.* **3.** Also, **out′sized′.** being unusually or abnormally large, heavy, extensive, etc.: *a rack of outsize dresses; an outsize puppy; pampering an outsize ego.* [1835–45; OUT- + SIZE[1]]

out•skirt (out′skûrt′), *n.* **1.** Often, **outskirts.** the outlying district or region, as of a city, metropolitan area, or the like: *to live on the outskirts of town; a sparsely populated outskirt.* **2.** Usually, **outskirts.** the border or fringes of a specified quality, condition, or the like: *the outskirts of respectability.* [1590–1600; OUT- + SKIRT]

out•sleep (out′slēp′), *v.t.,* **-slept, -sleep•ing. 1.** to sleep through or later than (a specified time). **2.** to sleep until the end of: *to outsleep a thunderstorm.* [1580–90; OUT- + SLEEP]

out•smart (out′smärt′), *v.t.* **1.** to get the better of (someone); outwit. **2. outsmart oneself,** to defeat oneself unintentionally by overly elaborate intrigue, scheming, or the like: *This time he may have outsmarted himself.* [1925–30; OUT- + SMART (adj.)]

out•soar (out′sôr′, -sōr′), *v.t.* to soar beyond. [1665–75; OUT- + SOAR]

out•sold (out′sōld′), *v.* pt. and pp. of **outsell.**

out•sole (out′sōl′), *n.* the outer sole of a shoe. [1880–85; OUT- + SOLE[2]]

out•sourc•ing (out′sôr′sing, -sōr′-), *n. Econ.* the buying of parts of a product to be assembled elsewhere, as in purchasing cheap foreign parts rather than manufacturing them at home. [OUT- + SOURCE + -ING[1]]

out•span (*v.* out′span′; *n.* out′span′), *v.,* **-spanned, -span•ning,** *n. South African Eng.* —*v.t.* **1.** to unyoke or unhitch, as oxen from a wagon. —*v.i.* **2.** to remove the yoke, harness, etc., from animals. —*n.* **3.** the act or a place of outspanning. [1815–25; trans of Afrik *uitspan*; see OUT-, SPAN[2]]

out•speak (out′spēk′), *v.,* **-spoke, -spo•ken, -speak•ing.** —*v.t.* **1.** to outdo or excel in speaking. **2.** to utter frankly or boldly: *to outspeak one's grievances.* —*v.i.* **3.** to speak out: *to outspeak in defense of one's beliefs.* [1595–1605; OUT- + SPEAK]

out•spend (out′spend′), *v.t.,* **-spent, spend•ing. 1.** to outdo in spending; spend more than: *They seemed determined to outspend their neighbors.* **2.** to exceed (one's resources) in spending: *He quickly outspent his fortune.* [1580–90; OUT- + SPEND]

out•spent (out′spent′), *adj.* worn-out; exhausted. [1645–55; OUT- + SPENT]

out•spo•ken (out′spō′kən), *adj.* **1.** uttered or expressed with frankness or without reserve: *outspoken criticism.* **2.** free or unreserved in speech. —*v.* **3.** pp. of **outspeak.** [1800–10; OUT- + SPOKEN] —**out′spo′ken•ly,** *adv.* —**out′spo′ken•ness,** *n.*
—**Syn. 1.** See **frank.** —**Ant. 2.** taciturn.

out•spread (*v.* out′spred′; *adj.* out′spred′; *n.* out′spred′), *v.,* **-spread, -spread•ing,** *adj., n.* —*v.t., v.i.* **1.** to spread out; extend: *an eagle outspreading its wings.* —*adj.* **2.** spread out; stretched out: *outspread arms.* **3.** diffused abroad; widely disseminated: *The outspread news had traveled quickly.* —*n.* **4.** the act of spreading out; expansion: *the rapid outspread of the early American colonists.* **5.** something that is spread out; an expanse: *a vast outspread of rich farmland.* [1300–50; ME *outspredden* (v.). See OUT-, SPREAD]

out•stand (out′stand′), *v.,* **-stood, -stand•ing.** —*v.i.* **1.** to be prominent. —*v.t.* **2.** to stay or remain beyond: *to outstand the hour.* [1565–75; OUT- + STAND]

out•stand•ing (out′stan′ding), *adj.* **1.** prominent; conspicuous; striking: *an outstanding example of courage.* **2.** marked by superiority or distinction; excellent; distinguished: *an outstanding student.* **3.** continuing in existence; remaining unsettled, unpaid, etc.: *outstanding debts.* **4.** (of securities and the like) publicly issued and sold or in circulation. **5.** standing out; projecting: *a stiff, outstanding fabric.* **6.** *Archaic.* that resists or opposes. [1605–15; OUTSTAND + -ING[2]] —**out′stand′ing•ly,** *adv.* —**out′stand′ing•ness,** *n.*
—**Syn. 1.** eminent. **3.** owing, due.

out•stare (out′stâr′), *v.t.,* **-stared, -star•ing. 1.** to outdo in staring; stare down. **2.** to cause (someone) discomfort or embarrassment. [1590–1600; OUT- + STARE]

out•sta•tion (out′stā′shən), *n.* a post, station, or settlement in a remote or outlying area. [1835–45; OUT- + STATION]

out•stay (out′stā′), *v.t.* **1.** to stay longer than. **2.** to stay beyond the time or duration of; overstay: *to outstay one's welcome.* [1590–1600; OUT- + STAY[1]]

out•stretch (out′strech′), *v.t.* **1.** to stretch forth; extend: *to outstretch one's hand in welcome.* **2.** to stretch out; expand: *The rising population has outstretched the city.* **3.** to stretch beyond: *His behavior outstretches my patience.* [1350–1400; ME; see OUT-, STRETCH] —**out′•stretch′er,** *n.*

out•strip (out′strip′), *v.t.,* **-stripped, -strip•ping. 1.** to outdo; surpass; excel. **2.** to outdo or pass in running or swift travel: *A car can outstrip the local train.* **3.** to get ahead of or leave behind in a race or in any course of competition. **4.** to exceed: *a demand that outstrips the supply.* [1570–80; OUT- + STRIP[1]]

out•stroke (out′strōk′), *n.* **1.** a stroke in an outward direction. **2.** (in an engine) the stroke during which the piston rod moves outward from the cylinder. [1850–55; OUT- + STROKE[1]]

out•sung (out′sung′), *v.* pp. of **outsing.**

out•swear (out′swâr′), *v.t.,* **-swore** or (*Archaic*) **-sware; -sworn; -swear•ing.** to outdo in swearing. [1580–90; OUT- + SWEAR]

out•swing•er (out′swing′ər), *n. Cricket.* a ball that when bowled veers from leg side to off side. Cf. **inswinger.** [1915–20; OUT- + SWINGER]

out•take (out′tāk′), *n.* **1.** a segment of film or videotape edited out of the final version, as because of a technical error. **2.** a recording of a song not included in the final release of a record album, as because of a technical error. [1955–60; OUT- + TAKE]

out•talk (out′tôk′), *v.t.* to outdo or overcome in talking. [1590–1600; OUT- + TALK]

out•tell (out′tel′), *v.t.,* **-told, -tell•ing. 1.** to outdo in telling; surpass in effect: *so ridiculous as to outtell any comment.* **2.** to tell to the end; say completely: *He outtold the tale to his amazed listeners.* **3.** to speak out; tell openly; declare: *The guilty heart outtells its inmost thoughts.* [1605–15; OUT- + TELL[1]]

out•think (out′thingk′), *v.t.,* **-thought, -think•ing. 1.** to excel in thinking; think faster, more accurately, or more perceptively than: *outthinking most of her contemporaries in the field of human relations.* **2.** to get the advantage of (someone) by quick or clever thinking; outwit: *only a split second to outthink his opponent.* [1695–1705; OUT- + THINK[1]]

out•throw (out′thrō′), *v.t.,* **-threw, -thrown, -throw•ing. 1.** to throw out or extend: *His arms were outthrown in greeting.* **2.** to surpass in throwing; throw farther or more accurately than: *He can outthrow any other pitcher in the league.* [1250–1300; ME. See OUT-, THROW]

out•thrust (*v., adj.* out′thrust′; *n.* out′thrust′), *v.,* **-thrust, -thrust•ing,** *adj., n.* —*v.t., v.i.* **1.** to thrust out or extend. —*adj.* **2.** thrust or extended outward: *a friendly, outthrust hand.* —*n.* **3.** something that thrusts or extends outward: *an outthrust of the building.* [1350–1400; ME; see OUT-, THRUST]

out•tough (out′tuf′), *v.t.* to get the better of (a competitor) by showing more determination. [OUT- + TOUGH]

out•trade (out′trād′), *v.t.,* **-trad•ed, -trad•ing.** to outdo in trading; get the better of in a trade. [1670–80; OUT- + TRADE]

out•turn (out′tûrn′), *n.* **1.** a quantity produced; output. **2.** the quality or condition of something produced or manufactured. [1790–1800; n. use of v. phrase *turn out*]

out•vote (out′vōt′), *v.t.,* **-vot•ed, -vot•ing.** to outdo or defeat in voting: *The rural districts outvoted the urban districts. The measure was outvoted by the farmers.* [1640–50; OUT- + VOTE]

out•wait (out′wāt′), *v.t.* **1.** to surpass in waiting or expecting; wait longer than. **2.** *Archaic.* to lie in ambush longer than. [1600–10; OUT- + WAIT]

out•walk (out′wôk′), *v.t.* **1.** to outdo in walking; walk faster or farther than. **2.** to walk beyond: *to outwalk the lights of the city.* [1620–30; OUT- + WALK]

out•ward (out′wərd), *adj.* **1.** proceeding or directed toward the outside or exterior, or away from a central point: *the outward flow of gold; the outward part of a voyage.* **2.** pertaining to or being what is seen or apparent, as distinguished from the underlying nature, facts, etc.; pertaining to surface qualities only; superficial: *outward appearances.* **3.** belonging or pertaining to external actions or appearances, as opposed to inner feelings, mental states, etc.: *an outward show of grief.* **4.** that lies toward the outside; that is on the outer side; exterior: *an outward court.* **5.** of or pertaining to the outside, outer surface, or exterior: *to make repairs on the outward walls of a house.* **6.** pertaining to the outside of the body; external. **7.** pertaining to the body, as opposed to the mind or spirit. **8.** belonging or pertaining to what is

CONCISE PRONUNCIATION KEY: act, cāpe, dâre, pärt; set, ēqual; *if,* īce; ox, ōver, ôrder, oil, bo͝ok, bo͞ot, out; up, ûrge; child; sing; shoe; thin, that; zh as in *treasure.* ə = *a* as in *alone,* *e* as in *system,* *i* as in *easily,* *o* as in *gallop,* *u* as in *circus;* ᵊ as in *fire* (fīᵊr), *hour* (ouᵊr). l and n can serve as syllabic consonants, as in *cradle* (krād′l), and *button* (but′n). See the full key inside the front cover.

out′search′, *v.t.*
out′see′, *v.t.,* **-saw, -seen, -see•ing.**
out′seek′, *v.t.,* **-sought, -seek•ing.**
out′shame′, *v.t.,* **-shamed, -sham•ing.**
out′shape′, *v.t.,* **-shaped, -shap•ing.**
out′shoul′der, *v.t.*
out′shove′, *v.t.,* **-shoved, -shov•ing.**
out′show′, *v.t.,* **-showed, -shown** or **-showed, -show•ing.**
out′show′er, *v.t.*
out′shriek′, *v.t.*
out′shrill′, *v.t.*
out′sift′, *v.t.*
out′sigh′, *v.t.*
out′sin′, *v.t.,* **-sinned, -sin•ning.**
out′skate′, *v.t.,* **-skat•ed, -skat•ing.**
out′skill′, *v.t.*
out′skip′, *v.t.,* **-skipped, -skip•ping.**
out′skir′mish, *v.t.*
out′slan′der, *v.t.*
out′slang′, *v.t.*
out′slide′, *v.t.,* **-slid, -slid** or **-slid•den, -slid•ing.**
out′slink′, *v.t.,* **-slunk, -slink•ing.**
out′smell′, *v.t.,* **-smelled** or **-smelt, -smel•ling.**
out′smile′, *v.t.,* **-smiled, -smil•ing.**
out′snatch′, *v.t.*
out′snore′, *v.t.,* **-snored, -snor•ing.**
out′son′net, *v.t.*
out′so•phis′ti•cate′, *v.t.,* **-cat•ed, -cat•ing.**
out′sound′, *v.t.*
out′spar′kle, *v.t.,* **-kled, -kling.**
out′speed′, *v.t.,* **-sped** or **-speed•ed, -speed•ing.**
out′spell′, *v.t.,* **-spelled** or **-spelt, spel•ling.**
out′spill′, *v.t.,* **-spilled** or **-spilt, -spil•ling.**
out′spin′, *v.t.,* **-spun, -spin•ning.**
out′spir′it, *v.t.*
out′spit′, *v.t.,* **-spit,** or **spat, -spit•ting.**
out′splen′dor, *v.t.*
out′sport′, *v.t.*
out′spring′, *v.t.,* **-sprang** or, often, **-sprung; -sprung; -spring•ing.**
out′sprint′, *v.t.*
out′sprue′, *v.t.,* **-sprued, -spru•ing.**
out′spurn′, *v.t.*
out′spurt′, *v.t.*
out′spy′, *v.t.,* **-spied, -spy•ing.**
out′stag′ger, *v.t.*
out′star′tle, *v.t.,* **-tled, -tling.**
out′state′, *v.t.,* **-stat•ed, -stat•ing.**
out′steal′, *v.t.,* **-stole, -sto•len, -steal•ing.**
out′steam′, *v.t.*
out′step′, *v.t.,* **-stepped, -step•ping.**
out′sting′, *v.t.,* **-stung, -sting•ing.**
out′stink′, *v.t.,* **-stank** or, often, **-stunk; -stunk; -stink•ing.**
out′storm′, *v.t.*
out′strain′, *v.t.*
out′stream′, *v.t.*
out′stride′, *v.t.,* **-strode, -strid•den, -strid•ing.**
out′strike′, *v.t.,* **-struck, -struck** or **-strick•en, -strik•ing.**
out′strive′, *v.t.,* **-strove, -striv•en, -striv•ing.**
out′strut′, *v.t.,* **-strut•ted, -strut•ting.**

external to oneself: *outward influences.* —*n.* **9.** that which is external; the external or material world. **10.** outward appearance. —*adv.* Also, **out′wards. 11.** toward the outside; out. **12.** visibly expressing one's inner feelings, mental state, etc. **13.** away from port: *a ship bound outward.* **14.** *Obs.* on the outside; externally. [bef. 900; ME; OE *ūtweard.* See OUT, -WARD] —**out′·ward·ness,** *n.*

Out′ward Bound′, a play (1923) by Sutton Vane.

out·ward-bound (out′wərd bound′), *adj.* headed in an outward direction, as toward foreign ports: *We passed an outward-bound ship as we came into the harbor.* [1595–1605]

out·ward·ly (out′wərd lē), *adv.* **1.** as regards appearance or outward manifestation: *outwardly charming; outwardly considerate.* **2.** on the outside or outer surface; externally: *Outwardly, the fruit was rough to the touch.* **3.** toward the outside: *The pier stretched outwardly from the shore.* [1350–1400; ME; see OUTWARD, -LY]

out·wash (out′wosh′, -wôsh′), *n. Geol.* the material, chiefly sand or gravel, deposited by meltwater streams in front of a glacier. [1890–95; OUT- + WASH]

out′wash plain′, *Geol.* a broad, sloping landform built of coalesced deposits of outwash. [1930–35]

out·watch (out′woch′), *v.t.* **1.** to outdo or surpass in watching. **2.** to watch, or maintain a vigil, until the end of: *The mourners had outwatched the night.* [1620–30; OUT- + WATCH]

out·wear (out′wâr′), *v.t.*, **-wore, -worn, -wear·ing. 1.** to wear or last longer than; outlast: *a well-made product that outwears its competition.* **2.** to exhaust in strength or endurance: *The daily toil had soon outworn him.* **3.** to outlive or outgrow: *Perhaps he will outwear those eccentricities.* **4.** to wear out; destroy by wearing: *A child outwears clothes quickly.* **5.** to pass (time): *trying to outwear the hours by reading.* [1535–45; OUT- + WEAR]

out·weigh (out′wā′), *v.t.* **1.** to exceed in value, importance, influence, etc.: *The advantages of the plan outweighed its defects.* **2.** to exceed in weight: *The champion will probably outweigh his opponent.* **3.** to be too heavy or burdensome for: *Collapse may follow if the load outweighs its supports.* [1590–1600; OUT- + WEIGH]
—**Syn. 1.** surpass, overshadow, eclipse, override.

out·went (out′went′), *v.* pt. of **outgo.**

out·wit (out′wit′), *v.t.*, **-wit·ted, -wit·ting. 1.** to get the better of by superior ingenuity or cleverness; outsmart: *to outwit a dangerous opponent.* **2.** *Archaic.* to surpass in wisdom or knowledge. [1645–55; OUT- + WIT[1]]
—**Syn. 1.** outguess, outfox, outmaneuver, outthink, finesse.

out·work (*v.* out′wûrk′; *n.* out′wûrk′), *v.t.*, **-worked** or **-wrought, -work·ing,** *n.* —*v.t.* **1.** to work harder, better, or faster than. **2.** to work out or carry on to a conclusion; finish: *a problem to be outworked in after generations.* **3.** *Archaic.* to outdo in workmanship. —*n.* **4.** a minor defense built or established outside the principal fortification limits. [1200–50; ME: to complete; see OUT-, WORK] —**out′work′er,** *n.*

out·worn (out′wôrn′, -wōrn′), *adj.* **1.** out-of-date, outmoded, or obsolete: *outworn ideas; outworn methods.* **2.** worn-out, as clothes. **3.** exhausted in strength or endurance, as persons. —*v.* **4.** pp. of **outwear.** [1555–65; OUT- + WORN]

out·write (out′rīt′), *v.t.*, **-wrote** or (*Archaic*) **-writ; -writ·ten** or (*Archaic*) **-writ; -writ·ing.** to write more or better than. [1635–45; OUT- + WRITE]

ou·zel (o͞o′zəl), *n.* dipper (def. 4). Also, **ousel.** [bef. 900; ME *osel* merle, blackbird, OE *ōsle,* c. G *Amsel;* akin to L *merula;* see MERLE[1]]

ou·zo (o͞o′zō; *Gk.* o͞o′zô), *n.* an anise-flavored, colorless liqueur of Greece. [1895–1900; < ModGk *oûzo(n);* etym. uncert.]

o·va (ō′və), *n.* pl. of **ovum.**

o·val (ō′vəl), *adj.* **1.** having the general form, shape, or outline of an egg; egg-shaped. **2.** ellipsoidal or elliptical. —*n.* **3.** an object of oval shape. **4.** a body or plane figure that is oval in shape or outline. **5.** an elliptical field or a field on which an elliptical track is laid out, as for athletic contests. **6.** *Informal.* a football. [1560–70; < NL *ōvālis,* equiv. to L *ōv(um)* EGG[1] + *-ālis* -AL[1]] —**o′val·ly,** *adv.* —**o′val·ness,** *n.*

ov·al·bu·min (ov′al byo͞o′min, ō′val-), *n. Biochem.* the principal protein of egg white. [1825–35; contr. and respelling of LL *ovī albūmen* (L *ovī album*) egg white; see OVUM, ALBUMEN]

CONCISE ETYMOLOGY KEY: <, descended or borrowed from; >, whence; b., blend of, blended; c., cognate with; cf., compare; deriv., derivative; equiv., equivalent; imit., imitative; obl., oblique; r., replacing; s., stem; sp., spelling, spelled; resp., respelling, respelled; trans., translation; ?, origin unknown; *, unattested; ‡, probably earlier than. See the full key inside the front cover.

o·val·i·ty (ō val′i tē), *n., pl.* **-ties. 1.** the quality or state of being oval. **2.** *Metalworking.* distortion in section of drawn wire or the like. [1935–40; OVAL + -ITY]

o′val kum′quat, a spineless shrub or small citrus tree, *Fortunella margarita,* of China, having oval-shaped, orange-yellow fruit with sweet and acid flesh. Also called **nagami kumquat.**

O·va·lle (ô vä′yə), *n.* a city in central Chile. 29,377.

o′val of Cassi′ni, *Geom.* the locus of a point such that the product of the distances from the point to two fixed points is constant. [after Italian geometer and astronomer Giovanni Domenico *Cassini* (1625–1712)]

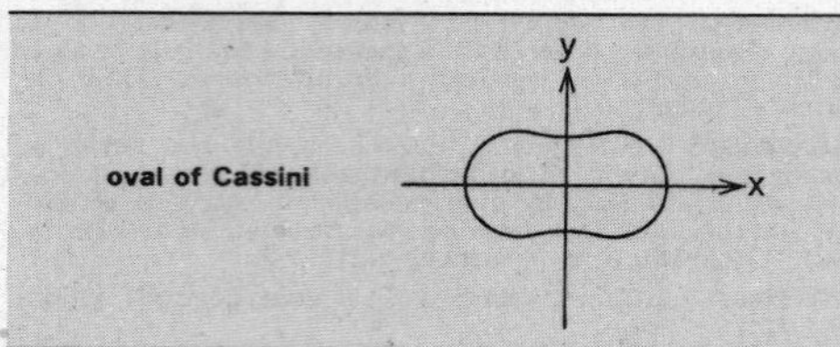

oval of Cassini

O′val Of′fice, 1. the office of the president of the United States, located in the White House. **2.** this office regarded as the seat of executive power in the U.S. federal government. [1960–65; *Amer.*; so called from the shape of the room]

o′val win′dow, *Anat.* an oval opening at the head of the cochlea, connecting the middle and inner ear, through which sound vibrations of the stapes are transmitted. [1675–85]

o·var·i·an (ō vâr′ē ən), *adj.* of or pertaining to an ovary. Also, **o·var′i·al.** [1830–40; OVARY + -AN]

o·var·i·ec·to·my (ō vâr′ē ek′tə mē), *n., pl.* **-mies.** *Surg.* the operation of removing one or both ovaries; oophorectomy. [1885–90; OVARI(UM) + -ECTOMY]

o·var·i·ole (ō vâr′ē ōl′), *n. Entomol.* any of several tubules that compose an insect ovary. [1875–80; < NL *ōvāri(um)* OVARY + L *-ol-* -OLE[1]]

o·var·i·ot·o·my (ō vâr′ē ot′ə mē), *n., pl.* **-mies.** *Surg.* incision into or removal of an ovary. [1835–45; < NL *ōvāriotomia,* equiv. to *ōvāri(um)* OVARY + *-o-* -O- + *-tomia* -TOMY] —**o·var′i·ot′o·mist,** *n.*

o·va·ri·tis (ō′və rī′tis), *n. Pathol.* oophoritis. [1855–60; < NL, equiv. to *ōvār(ium)* OVARY + *-ītis* -ITIS]

o·var·i·um (ō vâr′ē əm), *n., pl.* **o·var·i·a** (ō vâr′ē ə). *Archaic.* ovary. [1685–95; < NL; see OVARY]

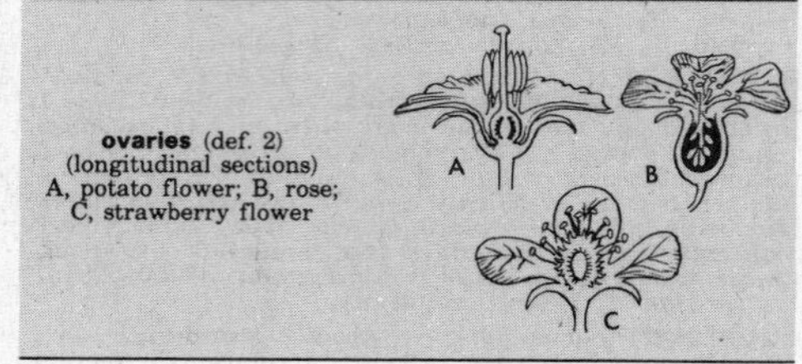

ovaries (def. 2) (longitudinal sections) A, potato flower; B, rose; C, strawberry flower

o·va·ry (ō′və rē), *n., pl.* **-ries. 1.** *Anat., Zool.* the female gonad or reproductive gland, in which the ova and the hormones that regulate female secondary sex characteristics develop. **2.** *Bot.* the enlarged lower part of the pistil in angiospermous plants, enclosing the ovules or young seeds. [1650–60; < NL *ōvārium.* See OVUM, -ARY]

o·vate (ō′vāt), *adj.* **1.** egg-shaped. **2.** *Bot.* **a.** having a shape like the longitudinal section of an egg. **b.** having such a shape with the broader end at the base, as a leaf. [1750–60; < L *ōvātus,* equiv. to *ōv(um)* EGG[1] + *-ātus* -ATE[1]] —**o′vate·ly,** *adv.*

ovate leaf

o·va·tion (ō vā′shən), *n.* **1.** an enthusiastic public reception of a person, marked esp. by loud and prolonged applause. **2.** *Rom. Hist.* the ceremonial entrance into Rome of a commander whose victories were of a lesser degree of importance than that for which a triumph was accorded. Cf. **triumph** (def. 4). [1525–35; < L *ovātiōn-* (s. of *ovātiō*) a rejoicing, shouting, equiv. to *ovāt(us)* (ptp. of *ovāre* to rejoice) + *-iōn-* -ION] —**o·va′tion·al,** *adj.*

ov·en (uv′ən), *n.* a chamber or compartment, as in a stove, for baking, roasting, heating, drying, etc. [bef. 900; ME; OE *ofen;* c. G *Ofen,* ON *ofn*] —**ov′en·like′,** *adj.*

ov·en·bird (uv′ən bûrd′), *n.* **1.** an American warbler, *Seiurus aurocapillus,* that builds an oven-shaped nest of leaves, twigs, etc., on the forest floor. **2.** any of several South American passerine birds of the genus *Furnarius* of the family Furnariidae, certain species of which build an oven-shaped nest. [1815–25; OVEN + BIRD]

ov·en·proof (uv′ən pro͞of′), *adj.* capable of withstanding the heat of an oven; safe for use in cooking in an oven: *an ovenproof dish.* [1935–40; OVEN + -PROOF]

ov·en·ware (uv′ən wâr′), *n.* heat-resistant dishes of glass, pottery, etc., for baking and serving food; bakeware. [1925–30; OVEN + WARE[1]]

ov·en·wood (uv′ən wo͝od′), *n.* brushwood; deadwood fit only for burning. [1785–95; OVEN + WOOD[1]]

o·ver (ō′vər), *prep.* **1.** above in place or position: *the roof over one's head.* **2.** above and to the other side of: *to leap over a wall.* **3.** above in authority, rank, power, etc., so as to govern, control, or have jurisdiction regarding: *There is no one over her in the department now.* **4.** so as to rest on or cover; on or upon: *Throw a sheet over the bed.* **5.** on or upon, so as to cause an apparent change in one's mood, attitude, etc.: *I can't imagine what has come over her.* **6.** on or on top of: *to hit someone over the head.* **7.** here and there on or in; about: *at various places over the country.* **8.** through all parts of; all through: *to roam over the estate; to show someone over the house.* **9.** to and fro on or in; across; throughout: *to travel all over Europe.* **10.** from one side to the other of; to the other side of; across: *to go over a bridge.* **11.** on the other side of; across: *lands over the sea.* **12.** reaching higher than, so as to submerge: *The water is over his shoulders.* **13.** in excess of; more than: *over a mile; not over five dollars.* **14.** above in degree, quantity, etc.: *a big improvement over last year's turnout.* **15.** in preference to: *chosen over another applicant.* **16.** throughout the length of: *The message was sent over a great distance.* **17.** until after the end of: *to adjourn over the holidays.* **18.** throughout the duration of: *over a long period of years.* **19.** in reference to, concerning, or about: *to quarrel over a matter.* **20.** while engaged in or occupied with: *to fall asleep over one's work.* **21.** via; by means of: *He told me over the phone. I heard it over the radio.* **22. over and above,** in addition to; besides: *a profit over and above what they had anticipated.* **23. over the hill.** See **hill** (def. 8).
—*adv.* **24.** beyond the top or upper surface or edge of something: *a roof that hangs over.* **25.** so as to cover the surface, or affect the whole surface: *The furniture was covered over with dust.* **26.** through a region, area, etc.: *He was known the world over.* **27.** at some distance, as in a direction indicated: *They live over by the hill.* **28.** from side to side; across; to the other side: *to sail over.* **29.** across an intervening space: *Toss the ball over, will you?* **30.** across or beyond the edge or rim: *The soup boiled over. The bathtub ran over.* **31.** from beginning to end; throughout: *to read a paper over; Think it over.* **32.** from one person, party, etc., to another: *Hand the money over. He made the property over to his brother.* **33.** on the other side, as of a sea, a river, or any space: *over in Japan.* **34.** so as to displace from an upright position: *to knock over a glass of milk.* **35.** so as to put in the reversed position: *She turned the bottle over. The dog rolled over.* **36.** once more; again: *Do the work over.* **37.** in repetition or succession: *twenty times over.* **38.** in excess or addition: *to pay the full sum and something over.* **39.** in excess of or beyond a certain amount: *Five goes into seven once, with two over.* **40.** throughout or beyond a period of time: *to stay over till Monday.* **41.** to one's residence, office, or the like: *Why don't you come over for lunch?* **42.** so as to reach a place across an intervening space, body of water, etc.: *Her ancestors came over on the* Mayflower **43. all over, a.** over the entire surface of; everywhere: *material printed all over with a floral design.* **b.** thoroughly; entirely. **c.** finished: *The war was all over and the soldiers came home.* **44. all over with,** ended; finished: *It seemed miraculous that the feud was all over with.* **45. over again,** in repetition; once more: *The director had the choir sing one passage over again.* **46. over against.** See **against** (def. 12). **47. over and over,** several times; repeatedly: *They played the same record over and over.* **48. over there,** *Informal.* (in the U.S. during and after World War I) in or to Europe: *Many of the boys who went over there never came back.*
49. over with, finished or done: *Let's get this thing over with, so that we don't have to worry about it any more.*
—*adj.* **50.** upper; higher up. **51.** higher in authority,

out′stud′y, *v.t.*, **-stud·ied, -stud·y·ing.**
out′stunt′, *v.t.*
out′suck′, *v.t.*
out′suf′fer, *v.t.*
out′sulk′, *v.t.*
out′sum′, *v.t.*, **-summed, -sum·ming.**
out′swag′ger, *v.t.*
out′swarm′, *v.t.*
out′sweep′, *v.t.*, **-swept, -sweep·ing.**
out′sweet′en, *v.t.*
out′swim′, *v.*, **-swam, -swum, -swim·ming.**
out′swin′dle, *v.t.*, **-dled, -dling.**
out′swing′, *v.t.*, **-swung, -swing·ing.**
out′swirl′, *v.t.*
out′tear′, *v.t.*, **-tore, -torn, -tear·ing.**
out′tease′, *v.t.*, **-teased, -teas·ing.**
out′thieve′, *v.t.*, **-thieved, -thiev·ing.**
out′threat′en, *v.t.*
out′throb′, *v.t.*, **-throbbed, -throb·bing.**
out′thun′der, *v.t.*
out′thwack′, *v.t.*
out′tin′kle, *v.t.*, **-kled, -kling.**
out′tire′, *v.t.*, **-tired, -tir·ing.**
out′toil′, *v.t.*
out′tongue′, *v.t.*, **-tongued, -tongu·ing.**
out′tow′er, *v.t.*
out′trav′el, *v.t.*, **-eled, -el·ing** or (*esp. Brit.*) **-elled, -el·ling.**
out′trick′, *v.t.*
out′trot′, *v.t.*, **-trot·ted, -trot·ting.**
out′trump′, *v.t.*
out′tyr′an·nize′, *v.t.*, **-nized, -niz·ing.**
out′val′ue, *v.t.*, **-ued, -u·ing.**
out′van′ish, *v.t.*
out′vaunt′, *v.t.*
out′ven′om, *v.t.*
out′vie′, *v.t.*, **-vied, -vy·ing.**
out′vo·cif′er·ate′, *v.t.*, **-at·ed, -at·ing.**
out′voice′, *v.t.*, **-voiced, -voic·ing.**
out′voy′age, *v.t.*, **-aged, -ag·ing.**
out′wal′lop, *v.t.*
out′wan′der, *v.t.*
out′war′, *v.t.*, **-warred, -war·ring.**
out′war′ble, *v.t.*, **-bled, -bling.**
out′waste′, *v.t.*, **-wast·ed, -wast·ing.**
out′wa′ter, *v.t.*
out′wave′, *v.t.*, **-waved, -wav·ing.**
out′weap′oned, *adj.*
out′wea′ry, *v.t.*, **-ried, -ry·ing.**
out′weave′, *v.t.*, **-wove, -wo·ven,** or **-wove, -weav·ing.**
out′weed′, *v.t.*
out′weep′, *v.t.*, **-wept, -weep·ing.**
out′well′, *v.t.*
out′whirl′, *v.t.*
out′wig′gle, *v.t.*, **-gled, -gling.**
out′wile′, *v.t.*, **-wiled, -wil·ing.**
out′will′, *v.t.*
out′wing′, *v.t.*
out′wish′, *v.t.*
out′word′, *v.t.*
out′wran′gle, *v.t.*, **-gled, -gling.**
out′wrench′, *v.t.*
out′wres′tle, *v.t.*, **-tled, -tling.**
out′wrig′gle, *v.t.*, **-gled, -gling.**
out′wring′, *v.t.*, **-wrung, -wring·ing.**
out′yell′, *v.t.*
out′yelp′, *v.t.*
out′yield′, *v.t.*

station, etc. **52.** serving, or intended to serve, as an outer covering; outer. **53.** remaining or additional, surplus; extra. **54.** too great; excessive (usually used in combination): *Insufficient tact and overaggressiveness are two of his problems.* **55.** ended; done; past: *when the war was over.*
—*n.* **56.** an amount in excess or addition; extra. **57.** *Mil.* a shot that strikes or bursts beyond the target. **58.** *Cricket.* **a.** the number of balls, usually six, delivered between successive changes of bowlers. **b.** the part of the game played between such changes.
—*v.t.* **59.** to go or get over; leap over. **60.** *Southern U.S.* to recover from.
—*interj.* **61.** (used in radio communications to signify that the sender has temporarily finished transmitting and is awaiting a reply or acknowledgment.) Cf. **out** (def. 61). [bef. 900; (adv., prep.) ME; OE *ofer;* c. D *over,* G *ober;* (adj.) ME *over(e),* orig. var. of *uver(e)* (E dial. *uver;* cf. LOVE), OE *ufera* (akin to *ofer*), assimilated to the adv. form; akin to L *super,* Gk *hypér,* Skt *upari.* See UP, HYPER-]

over-, a prefixal use of **over,** *prep., adv.,* or *adj.,* occurring in various senses in compounds (*overboard; overcoat; overhang; overlap; overlord; overrun; overthrow*), and especially employed, with the sense of "over the limit," "to excess," "too much," "too," to form verbs, adjectives, adverbs, and nouns (*overact; overcapitalize; overcrowd; overfull; overmuch; oversupply; overweight*), and many others, mostly self-explanatory: a hyphen, which is commonly absent from old or well-established formations, is sometimes used in new coinages or in any words whose component parts it may be desirable to set off distinctly. [ME; OE *ofer-.* See OVER]
—**Note.** The lists at the bottom of this and following pages provide the spelling, syllabification, and stress for words whose meanings may easily be inferred by combining the meanings of OVER- and an attached base word, or base word plus a suffix. Appropriate parts of speech are also shown. Words prefixed by OVER- that have special meanings or uses are entered in their proper alphabetical places in the main vocabulary or as derived forms run on at the end of a main vocabulary entry.

o•ver•a•bun•dance (ō′vər ə bun′dəns), *n.* an excessive amount or abundance; surfeit: *an overabundance of sugar in the diet.* [1350–1400; ME; see OVER-, ABUNDANCE] —**o′ver•a•bun′dant,** *adj.* —**o′ver•a•bun′•dant•ly,** *adv.*
—**Syn.** excess, surplus, plethora, glut, profusion.

o•ver•a•chieve (ō′vər ə chēv′), *v.i.,* **-chieved, -chiev•ing. 1.** to perform, esp. academically, above the potential indicated by tests of one's mental ability or aptitude. **2.** to perform better or achieve more than expected, esp. by others. [1950–55; OVER- + ACHIEVE, or by back formation from *overachiever*] —**o′ver•a•chieve′ment,** *n.* —**o′ver•a•chiev′er,** *n.*

o•ver•act (ō′vər akt′), *v.t., v.i.* to act in an exaggerated manner. [1605–15; OVER- + ACT] —**o′ver•ac′•tion,** *n.*

o•ver•ac•tive (ō′vər ak′tiv), *adj.* exceptionally or excessively active; too active. [1640–50; OVER- + ACTIVE] —**o′ver•ac•tiv′i•ty, o′ver•ac′tive•ness,** *n.*

o•ver•age[1] (ō′vər āj′), *adj.* **1.** beyond the acceptable or desired age: *overage for the draft.* **2.** older than usual or expected for the activity, position, etc.: *an overage baseball player who still outperforms many rookies.* **3.** too old to be serviceable; antiquated: *She drives an overage car.* [1885–90; OVER- + AGE]

o•ver•age[2] (ō′vər ij), *n. Com.* **1.** an excess supply of merchandise. **2.** the value of goods in excess of the amount called for by stock records; money in excess of the amount called for by sales records. [1940–45; OVER- + -AGE]

o•ver•all (*adv.* ō′vər ôl′; *adj., n.* ō′vər ôl′), *adv., adj.* **1.** from one extreme limit of a thing to the other: *the overall length of the bridge.* **2.** covering or including everything: *an overall impression; to view something overall.* —*n.* **3. overalls,** (*used with a plural v.*) **a.** loose, sturdy trousers, usually with a bib or biblike piece to which shoulder straps are attached, originally worn over other trousers to protect them, as by factory workers or farmers. **b.** long waterproof leggings. **4.** *Brit.* a smock or loose-fitting housedress. [bef. 1000; ME *overal* (adv.), OE *ofer eall;* see OVER, ALL]

o•ver•anx•ious (ō′vər angk′shəs, -ang′-), *adj.* excessively anxious. [1735–45; OVER- + ANXIOUS] —**o•ver•anx•i•e•ty** (ō′vər ang zī′i tē), **o′ver•anx′ious•ness,** *n.* —**o′ver•anx′ious•ly,** *adv.*

o•ver•arch (ō′vər ärch′), *v.t.* **1.** to span with or like an arch: *A new bridge overarches the river.* —*v.i.* **2.** to form an arch over something: *a cerulean sky overarching in the early twilight.* [1660–70; OVER- + ARCH[1]]

o•ver•arch•ing (ō′vər är′ching), *adj.* **1.** forming an arch above: *great trees with overarching branches.* **2.** encompassing or overshadowing everything: *The community's overarching needs are more jobs and better housing.* [1710–20; OVERARCH + -ING[2]]

o•ver•arm (ō′vər ärm′), *adj.* thrown or performed by raising the arm above the shoulder: *an overarm pitch; an overarm swimming stroke.* [1860–65, *Amer.;* OVER- + ARM[1]]

o•ver•ate (ō′vər āt′), *v.* pt. of **overeat.**

o•ver•awe (ō′vər ô′), *v.t.,* **-awed, -aw•ing.** to restrain or subdue by inspiring awe; intimidate: *He often uses that imperious scowl to overawe his subordinates.* [1570–80; OVER- + AWE]

o•ver•bal•ance (*v.* ō′vər bal′əns; *n.* ō′vər bal′əns), *v.,* **-anced, -anc•ing,** *n.* —*v.t.* **1.** to outweigh: *The opportunity overbalances the disadvantages of leaving town.* **2.** to cause to lose balance or to fall or turn over: *He accidentally overbalanced a vase.* —*n.* **3.** an excessive weight or amount. **4.** something that more than balances or more than equals: *An overbalance of imports depleted the country's treasury.* [1600–10; OVER- + BALANCE]

o•ver•bank (ō′vər bangk′), *v.i. Horol.* to have the balance staff oscillate so greatly that the fork of the lever fails to engage, rendering the escapement inoperative. [1880–85; OVER- + BANK[1]]

o•ver•bear (ō′vər bâr′), *v.,* **-bore, -borne, -bear•ing.** —*v.t.* **1.** to bear over or down by weight or force: *With his superior strength he easily overbore his opponent in the fight.* **2.** to overcome or overwhelm: *A spirited defense had overborne the enemy attack.* **3.** to prevail over or overrule (wishes, objections, etc.): *She overbore all objections to the new plan.* **4.** to treat in a domineering way; dominate: *to overbear one's children with threats of violence.* **5.** *Naut.* (of a sailing ship) to have the advantage of (another sailing ship) because of an ability to carry more canvas safely. —*v.i.* **6.** to produce fruit or progeny so abundantly as to impair the health. [1525–35; OVER- + BEAR[1]] —**o′ver•bear′er,** *n.*

o•ver•bear•ing (ō′vər bâr′ing), *adj.* **1.** domineering; dictatorial; haughtily or rudely arrogant. **2.** of overwhelming or critical importance. [1590–1600; OVERBEAR + -ING[2]] —**o′ver•bear′ing•ly,** *adv.* —**o′ver•bear′ing•ness,** *n.*

o•ver•bid (*v.* ō′vər bid′; *n.* ō′vər bid′), *v.,* **-bid, -bid•ding,** *n.* —*v.t.* **1.** to bid more than the value of (a thing): *to overbid one's cards.* **2.** to outbid: *She overbid him for the painting.* —*v.i.* **3.** to bid more than the actual value or worth: *a tendency to overbid at auctions; to overbid at bridge.* —*n.* **4.** a higher bid. [1610–20; OVER- + BID[1]]

o•ver•bite (ō′vər bīt′), *n. Dentistry.* occlusion in which the upper incisor teeth overlap the lower ones. [1885–90; OVER- + BITE]

o•ver•blouse (ō′vər blous′, -blouz′), *n.* a blouse designed to be worn outside the waistband of a skirt or a pair of slacks. [1920–25; OVER- + BLOUSE]

o•ver•blow (ō′vər blō′), *v.,* **-blew, -blown, -blow•ing.** —*v.t.* **1.** to give excessive importance or value to: *to overblow one's own writing.* **2.** to overinflate. **3.** to blow over the surface of, as the wind, sand, or the like: *dead leaves overblowing the yard.* **4.** to blow (a wind instrument or an organ pipe) in such a way as to produce overtones. —*v.i.* **5.** to overblow a wind instrument. [1350–1400; ME; see OVER-, BLOW[2]]

o•ver•blown[1] (ō′vər blōn′), *adj.* **1.** overdone or excessive: *overblown praise.* **2.** of unusually large size or proportions: *a majestic, overblown figure.* **3.** overinflated; turgid; bombastic; pretentious: *overblown prose.* —*v.* **4.** pp. of **overblow.** [1590–1600; OVER- + BLOWN[1]]

o•ver•blown[2] (ō′vər blōn′), *adj.* (of a flower) past the stage of full bloom; more than full-blown: *an overblown rose.* [1610–20; OVER- + BLOWN[2]]

o•ver•board (ō′vər bôrd′, -bōrd′), *adv.* **1.** over the side of a ship or boat, esp. into or in the water: *to fall overboard.* **2. go overboard,** to go to extremes, esp. in regard to approval or disapproval of a person or thing: *I think the critics went overboard in panning that new show.* [bef. 1000; ME *over bord,* OE *ofer bord.* See OVER, BOARD]

o•ver•book (ō′vər bŏŏk′), *v.t.* **1.** to accept reservations for in excess of the number that can be accommodated: *The airline routinely overbooks its flights so as to fill its planes even if there are last-minute cancellations.* —*v.i.* **2.** to accept reservations in excess of the number that can be accommodated: *If the hotel has overbooked, some of the conventioners won't have a place to stay.* [1900–05; OVER- + BOOK (v.)]

o•ver•boot (ō′vər bōōt′), *n.* overshoe. [1935–40; OVER- + BOOT[1]]

o•ver•bore (ō′vər bôr′, -bōr′), *v.* pt. of **overbear.**

o•ver•borne (ō′vər bôrn′, -bōrn′), *adj.* **1.** overcome; crushed; oppressed. —*v.* **2.** pp. of **overbear.**

o•ver•bought (ō′vər bôt′), *adj.* **1.** marked by prices considered unjustifiably high because of extensive buying: *The stock market is overbought now.* Cf. **oversold.** —*v.* **2.** pt. and pp. of **overbuy.** [1955–60; OVER- + BOUGHT]

o•ver•brake (ō′vər brāk′), *v.,* **-braked, -brak•ing.** —*v.t.* **1.** to brake (a wheel, vehicle, etc.) excessively. —*v.i.* **2.** to apply an excessive amount of braking power. [OVER- + BRAKE[1]]

o•ver•break (ō′vər brāk′), *n. Civ. Engin.* earth or rock excavated outside of neat lines. Also, **o′ver•break′•age.** [OVER- + BREAK]

o•ver•budg•et (ō′vər buj′it), *adj.* costing or being more than the amount alloted or budgeted: *The building is half-finished and it's already overbudget.* [from prep. phrase *over budget,* erroneously taken as a compound]

o•ver•build (ō′vər bild′), *v.,* **-built, -build•ing.** —*v.t.* **1.** to erect too many buildings in (an area). **2.** to cover or surmount with a building or structure. **3.** to build (a structure) on too great or elaborate a scale. —*v.i.* **4.** to erect too many buildings in an area. [1595–1605; OVER- + BUILD]

o•ver•bur•den (*v.* ō′vər bûr′dn; *n.* ō′vər bûr′dn), *v.t.* **1.** to load with too great a burden; overload: *He was overburdened with cares.* —*n.* **2.** an excessive burden. **3.** Also called **burden, capping.** *Mining.* waste earth and rock covering a mineral deposit. [1570–80; OVER- + BURDEN[1]]

o•ver•bur•den•some (ō′vər bûr′dn səm), *adj.* excessively burdensome. [1605–15; OVER- + BURDENSOME]

o•ver•buy (ō′vər bī′), *v.,* **-bought, -buy•ing.** —*v.t.* **1.** to purchase in excessive quantities. **2.** *Finance.* to buy on margin in excess of one's ability to provide added security in an emergency, as in a falling market. —*v.i.* **3.**

CONCISE PRONUNCIATION KEY: *act, cāpe, dâre, pärt; set, ēqual; if, īce; ox, ōver, ôrder, oil, bŏŏk, bōōt, out; up, ûrge; child; sing; shoe; thin,* t͟h*at;* zh *as in treasure.* ə = *a* as in *alone, e* as in *system, i* as in *easily, o* as in *gallop, u* as in *circus;* ᵊ as in *fire* (fīᵊr), *hour* (ouᵊr). l and n can serve as syllabic consonants, as in *cradle* (krād′l), and *button* (but′n). See the full key inside the front cover.

o′ver•a′ble, *adj.;* **-bly,** *adv.*
o′ver•a•bound′, *v.i.*
o′ver•ab•sorb′, *v.t.*
o′ver•ab•sorp′tion, *n.*
o′ver•ab•stain′, *v.i.*
o′ver•ab•ste′mi•ous, *adj.;* **-ly,** *adv.;* **-ness,** *n.*
o′ver•ab•stract′, *v.t., adj.*
o′ver•a•buse′, *n., v.t.,* **-bused, -bus•ing.**
o′ver•a•bu′sive, *adj.;* **-ly,** *adv.;* **-ness,** *n.*
o′ver•ac•cel′er•ate′, *v.,* **-at•ed, -at•ing.**
o′ver•ac•cel′er•a′tion, *n.*
o′ver•ac•cen′tu•ate′, *v.t.,* **-at•ed, -at•ing.**
o′ver•ac•cen′tu•a′tion, *n.*
o′ver•ac•cu′mu•late′, *v.,* **-lat•ed, -lat•ing.**
o′ver•ac•cu′mu•la′tion, *n.*
o′ver•a•cid′i•ty, *n.*
o′ver•ac′ti•vate′, *v.t.,* **-vat•ed, -vat•ing.**
o′ver•a•cute′, *adj.;* **-ly,** *adv.;* **-ness,** *n.*
o′ver•ad•dic′tion, *n.*
o′ver•a•dorn′, *v.t.*
o′ver•a•dorned′, *adj.*
o′ver•ad•just′, *v.*
o′ver•ad•just′ment, *n.*
o′ver•ad•vance′, *v.,* **-vanced, -vanc•ing,** *n.*
o′ver•ad′ver•tise′, *v.,* **-tised, -tis•ing.**
o′ver•af•fect′, *v.t.*
o′ver•af•fect′, *n.*
o′ver•af•fect′ed, *adj.*
o′ver•af•firm′, *v.*
o′ver•af′fir•ma′tion, *n.*
o′ver•af•firm′a•tive, *adj.;* **-ly,** *adv.*
o′ver•af•flict′, *v.t.*
o′ver•af•flic′tion, *n.*
o′ver•ag′gra•vate′, *v.t.,* **-vat•ed, -vat•ing.**
o′ver•ag′gra•va′tion, *n.*
o′ver•ag•gres′sive, *adj.;* **-ly,** *adv.;* **-ness,** *n.*
o′ver•ag′i•tate′, *v.t.,* **-tat•ed, -tat•ing.**
o′ver•ag′i•ta′tion, *n.*
o′ver•al′co•hol•ize′, *v.t.,* **-ized, -iz•ing.**
o′ver•al•le′giance, *n.*
o′ver•al′le•go•rize′, *v.t.,* **-rized, -riz•ing.**
o′ver•am•bi′tious, *adj.;* **-ly,** *adv.;* **-ness,** *n.*
o′ver•am′pli•fy′, *v.,* **-fied, -fy•ing.**
o′ver•a•nal′y•sis, *n., pl.* **-ses.**
o′ver•an′a•lyt′ic, *adj.*
o′ver•an′a•lyt′i•cal, *adj.;* **-ly,** *adv.*
o′ver•an′a•lyze′, *v.,* **-lyzed, -lyz•ing.**
o′ver•an′gry, *adj.*
o′ver•an′i•mat′ed, *adj.;* **-ly,** *adv.*
o′ver•an′i•ma′tion, *n.*
o′ver•an′no•tate′, *v.,* **-tat•ed, -tat•ing.**
o′ver•ap•par′eled, *adj.*
o′ver•ap•plaud′, *v.*
o′ver•ap′pli•ca′tion, *n.*
o′ver•ap•prais′al, *n.*
o′ver•ap•praise′, *v.t.,* **-praised, -prais•ing.**
o′ver•ap•pre′ci•a′tion, *n.*
o′ver•ap•pre′cia•tive, *adj.;* **-ly,** *adv.;* **-ness,** *n.*
o′ver•ap′pre•hen′sion, *n.*
o′ver•ap′pre•hen′sive, *adj.;* **-ly,** *adv.;* **-ness,** *n.*
o′ver•apt′, *adj.;* **-ly,** *adv.;* **-ness,** *n.*
o′ver•ar′gue, *v.,* **-gued, -gu•ing.**
o′ver•ar′gu•men′ta•tive, *adj.;* **-ly,** *adv.;* **-ness,** *n.*
o′ver•a•rous′al, *n.*
o′ver•ar•range′, *v.,* **-ranged, -rang•ing.**
o′ver•ar•tic′u•late, *adj.*
o′ver•ar•tic′u•late′, *v.,* **-lat•ed, -lat•ing.**
o′ver•ar′ti•fi′cial, *adj.;* **-ly,** *adv.*
o′ver•ar′ti•fi′ci•al′i•ty, *n., pl.* **-ties.**
o′ver•as•sert′, *v.t.*
o′ver•as•ser′tion, *n.*
o′ver•as•ser′tive, *adj.;* **-ly,** *adv.;* **-ness,** *n.*
o′ver•as•sess′, *v.t.*
o′ver•as•sess′ment, *n.*
o′ver•as•sist′, *v.*
o′ver•as•sume′, *v.t.,* **-sumed, -sum•ing.**
o′ver•as•sump′tion, *n.*
o′ver•as•sump′tive, *adj.;* **-ly,** *adv.*
o′ver•as•sured′, *adj.;* **-sur•ed•ly,** *adv.;* **-sur•ed•ness,** *n.*
o′ver•at•tached′, *adj.*
o′ver•at•tach′ment, *n.*
o′ver•at•ten′tion, *n.*
o′ver•at•ten′tive, *adj.;* **-ly,** *adv.;* **-ness,** *n.*
o′ver•at•ten′u•ate′, *v.t.,* **-at•ed, -at•ing.**
o′ver•a•ware′ness, *n.*
o′ver•bait′, *v.t.*
o′ver•bake′, *v.,* **-baked, -bak•ing.**
o′ver•bal′last, *v.t.*
o′ver•bash′ful, *adj.;* **-ly,** *adv.;* **-ness,** *n.*
o′ver•beat′, *v.,* **-beat, -beat•en** or **-beat, -beat•ing.**
o′ver•bet′, *v.,* **-bet** or **-bet•ted, -bet•ting.**
o′ver•bet′, *n.*
o′ver•big′, *adj.;* **-ness,** *n.*
o′ver•bill′, *v.t.*
o′ver•bit′ter, *adj.;* **-ly,** *adv.;* **-ness,** *n.*
o′ver•blame′, *v.t.,* **-blamed, -blam•ing.**
o′ver•blanch′, *v.t.*
o′ver•bleach′, *v.*
o′ver•blind′ly, *adv.*
o′ver•blithe′, *adj.*
o′ver•boast′, *n., v.i.*
o′ver•boast′ful, *adj.;* **-ly,** *adv.;* **-ness,** *n.*
o′ver•boil′, *v.*
o′ver•bold′, *adj.;* **-ly,** *adv.;* **-ness,** *n.*
o′ver•book′ish, *adj.;* **-ly,** *adv.;* **-ness,** *n.*
o′ver•boom′ing, *adj.*
o′ver•bor′row, *v.*
o′ver•boun′te•ous, *adj.;* **-ly,** *adv.;* **-ness,** *n.*
o′ver•brace′, *v.t.,* **-braced, -brac•ing.**
o′ver•brag′, *v.,* **-bragged, -brag•ging.**
o′ver•bra•va′do, *n.*
o′ver•brave′, *adj.;* **-ly,** *adv.;* **-ness,** *n.*
o′ver•brav′er•y, *n.*
o′ver•breed′, *v.t.,* **-bred, -breed•ing.**
o′ver•bright′, *adj.;* **-ly,** *adv.;* **-ness,** *n.*
o′ver•bril′liance, *n.*
o′ver•bril′lian•cy, *n.*
o′ver•bril′liant, *adj.;* **-ly,** *adv.*
o′ver•broad′, *adj.*
o′ver•broad′en, *v.*
o′ver•broil′, *v.*
o′ver•brown′, *v.*
o′ver•browse′, *v.t.,* **-browsed, -brows•ing.**
o′ver•brush′, *v.t.*
o′ver•bru′tal, *adj.;* **-ly,** *adv.*
o′ver•bru•tal′i•ty, *n., pl.* **-ties.**
o′ver•bru′tal•i•za′tion, *n.*
o′ver•bru′tal•ize′, *v.t.,* **-ized, -iz•ing.**
o′ver•bulk′i•ly, *adv.*
o′ver•bulk′i•ness, *n.*
o′ver•bulk′y, *adj.*
o′ver•bump′tious, *adj.;* **-ly,** *adv.;* **-ness,** *n.*
o′ver•burn′, *v.,* **-burned** or **-burnt, -burn•ing.**
o′ver•bus′i•ly, *adv.*
o′ver•bus′i•ness, *n.*

to buy regardless of one's needs or financial means. [1400–50; late ME *overbiggen.* See OVER-, BUY]

o•ver•call (*v.* ō′vər kôl′, ō′vər kôl′; *n.* ō′vər kôl′), *v.t., v.i.* **1.** *Cards.* to make an overcall. —*n.* **2.** *Cards.* a bid higher than the previous bid. **3.** *Bridge.* a bid on a higher level than, or in a higher ranking suit than, the previous bid of an opponent that was not followed by a bid or double by one's partner. **4.** *Theater.* a clause in an investor's agreement whereby the backer agrees to supply an additional amount of money, often 10 to 20 percent of the original amount, should it be required by the producers. [1905–10; OVER- + CALL]

o•ver•came (ō′vər kām′), *v.* pt. of **overcome.**

o•ver•ca•pac•i•ty (ō′vər kə pas′i tē), *n., pl.* **-ties.** capacity beyond what is normal, allowed, or desirable. [1925–30; OVER- + CAPACITY]

o•ver•cap•i•tal•ize (ō′vər kap′i tl īz′), *v.t.,* **-ized, -iz•ing. 1.** to fix the total amount of securities of a corporation in excess of the limits set by law or by sound financial policy. **2.** to overestimate the capital value (of a business property or enterprise). **3.** to provide an excessive amount of capital for (a business enterprise). Also, *esp. Brit.,* **o′ver•cap′i•tal•ise′.** [1885–90; OVER- + CAPITALIZE] —**o′ver•cap′i•tal•i•za′tion,** *n.*

o•ver•care•ful (ō′vər kâr′fəl), *adj.* excessively or unduly careful. [1585–95; OVER- + CAREFUL] —**o′ver•care′ful•ly,** *adv.* —**o′ver•care′ful•ness,** *n.*

o•ver•cast (*adj.* ō′vər kast′, -käst′, ō′vər kast′, -käst′; *v.* ō′vər kast′, -käst′, ō′vər kast′, -käst′; *n.* ō′vər kast′, -käst′), *adj., v.,* **-cast, -cast•ing,** *n.* —*adj.* **1.** overspread or covered with clouds; cloudy: *an overcast day.* **2.** *Meteorol.* (of the sky) more than 95 percent covered by clouds. **3.** dark; gloomy. **4.** *Sewing.* sewn by overcasting. —*v.t.* **5.** to overcloud, darken, or make gloomy: *Ominous clouds began to overcast the sky.* **6.** to sew with stitches passing successively over an edge, esp. long stitches set at intervals to prevent raveling. —*v.i.* **7.** to become cloudy or dark: *By noon it had begun to overcast.* —*n.* **8.** *Meteorol.* the condition of the sky when more than 95 percent covered by clouds. **9.** *Mining.* a crossing of two passages, as airways, dug at the same level, in which one rises to pass over the other without opening into it. Cf. **undercast** (def. 1). [1175–1225; ME (v.); see OVER-, CAST]

o•ver•cast•ing (ō′vər kas′ting, -kä′sting), *n. Sewing.* **1.** the act of sewing along the edges of material with long, spaced stitches to prevent raveling. **2.** the stitch used to overcast. [1880–85; OVERCAST + -ING[1]]

o•ver•cau•tious (ō′vər kô′shəs), *adj.* excessively or unnecessarily cautious: *Sometimes it doesn't pay to be overcautious in business.* [1700–10; OVER- + CAUTIOUS] —**o′ver•cau′tious•ly,** *adv.* —**o′ver•cau′tious•ness,** *n.*

o•ver•cer•ti•fy (ō′vər sûr′tə fī′), *v.t.,* **-fied, -fy•ing.** *Banking.* to certify (a bank check) for an amount greater than the balance in the drawer's account. [OVER- + CERTIFY] —**o′ver•cer′ti•fi•ca′tion,** *n.*

o•ver•charge (*v.* ō′vər chärj′; *n.* ō′vər chärj′), *v.,* **-charged, -charg•ing,** *n.* —*v.t.* **1.** to charge (a purchaser) too high a price: *When the manager realized we'd been overcharged, she gave us a credit for the difference.* **2.** to fill too full; overload. **3.** to exaggerate: *to overcharge the importance of ancestry.* —*v.i.* **4.** to make an excessive charge; charge too much for something. —*n.* **5.** a charge in excess of a stated or just price. **6.** an act of overcharging. **7.** an excessive load. [1275–1325; ME; see OVER-, CHARGE] —**o′ver•charg′er,** *n.*

o•ver•check (ō′vər chek′), *n.* **1.** a textile pattern having one checked design superimposed on another so that both are visible. **2.** a fabric having this pattern. **3.** a checkrein passing from the bit, over a horse's head, to the saddle of a harness. [1870–75; OVER- + CHECK[1]]

CONCISE ETYMOLOGY KEY: <, descended or borrowed from; >, whence; b., blend of, blended; c., cognate with; cf., compare; deriv., derivative; equiv., equivalent; imit., imitative; obl., oblique; r., replacing; s., stem; sp., spelling, spelled; resp., respelling, respelled; trans., translation; ?, origin unknown; *, unattested; ‡, probably earlier than. See the full key inside the front cover.

o•ver•clothes (ō′vər klōz′, -klōthz′), *n.* (*used with a plural v.*) clothing worn outside other garments. [1855–60; OVER- + CLOTHES]

o•ver•cloud (ō′vər kloud′), *v.t.* **1.** to overspread with or as if with clouds: *a summer storm that briefly overclouds the sun; to overcloud one's pleasure with solemn thoughts.* **2.** to darken; obscure; make gloomy: *a childhood that was overclouded by the loss of his parents.* —*v.i.* **3.** to become clouded over or overcast: *Toward evening the sky began to overcloud.* [1585–95; OVER- + CLOUD]

o•ver•coat (*n.* ō′vər kōt′; *v.* ō′vər kōt′, ō′vər kōt′), *n.* **1.** a coat worn over the ordinary indoor clothing, as in cold weather. **2.** Also called **overcoating.** an added coating, as of paint, applied for protection. —*v.t.* **3.** to apply an additional coat of paint to (a surface). [1795–1805; OVER- + COAT]

Overcoat, The, a short story (1842) by Gogol.

o•ver•coat•ing (ō′vər kō′ting), *n.* **1.** material for overcoats. **2.** overcoat (def. 2). [1885–90; OVERCOAT + -ING[1]]

o•ver•coil (ō′vər koil′), *n. Horol.* **1.** a fixed end of a spiral hairspring, consisting of an upwardly and inwardly bent continuation of the outermost coil of the spring: used to offset the asymmetry of the common spiral spring when tight, which impairs isochronism. **2.** a hairspring having such a fixed end. [1880–85; OVER- + COIL[1]]

o•ver•come (ō′vər kum′), *v.,* **-came, -come, -com•ing.** —*v.t.* **1.** to get the better of in a struggle or conflict; conquer; defeat: *to overcome the enemy.* **2.** to prevail over (opposition, a debility, temptations, etc.); surmount: *to overcome one's weaknesses.* **3.** to overpower or overwhelm in body or mind, as does liquor, a drug, exertion, or emotion: *I was overcome with grief.* **4.** *Archaic.* to overspread or overrun. —*v.i.* **5.** to gain the victory; win; conquer: *a plan to overcome by any means possible.* [bef. 900; ME; OE *ofercuman.* See OVER-, COME] —**o′ver•com′er,** *n.*
—**Syn. 1.** vanquish. See **defeat.**

o•ver•com•mit (ō′vər kə mit′), *v.t.,* **-mit•ted, -mit•ting.** to commit more than is feasible, desirable, or necessary. [1950–55; OVER- + COMMIT] —**o′ver•com•mit′•ment,** *n.*

o•ver•com•pen•sate (ō′vər kom′pən sāt′), *v.,* **-sat•ed, -sat•ing.** —*v.t.* **1.** to compensate or reward excessively; overpay: *Some stockholders feel the executives are being overcompensated and that bonuses should be reduced.* —*v.i.* **2.** to exhibit psychological overcompensation; strive to overcome a sense of inferiority through overt, opposite behavior: *The aggressive patient may be overcompensating, and be a profoundly shy person beneath the façade.* [1760–70; OVER- + COMPENSATE; as term in psychology, perh. back formation from OVERCOMPENSATION]

o•ver•com•pen•sa•tion (ō′vər kom′pən sā′shən), *n. Psychoanal.* **1.** a pronounced striving to neutralize and conceal a strong but unacceptable character trait by substituting for it an opposite trait. **2.** compensation to an unnecessary or unreasonable degree: *The pay was overcompensation for the work done.* [1915–20; OVER- + COMPENSATION; as psychoanalytic term, trans. of *Überkompensation,* coined by Alfred Adler] —**o•ver•com•pen•sa•to•ry** (ō′vər kəm pen′sə tôr′ē, -tōr′ē), *adj.*

o•ver•con•fi•dent (ō′vər kon′fi dənt), *adj.* too confident. [1610–20; OVER- + CONFIDENT] —**o′ver•con′fi•dence,** *n.* —**o′ver•con′fi•dent•ly,** *adv.*
—**Syn.** cocksure, brash, arrogant, reckless, heedless.

o•ver•cor•rec•tion (ō′vər kə rek′shən), *n.* correction beyond what is needed or customary, esp. when leading to error; overadjustment: *The pilot made an overcorrection for headwinds.* [1880–85; OVER- + CORRECTION]

o•ver•crit•i•cal (ō′vər krit′i kəl), *adj.* excessively critical; hypercritical. [1850–55; OVER- + CRITICAL] —**o′ver•crit′i•cal•ly,** *adv.* —**o′ver•crit′i•cal•ness,** *n.*

o•ver•crop (*v.* ō′vər krop′; *n.* ō′vər krop′), *v.,* **-cropped, -crop•ping,** *n.* —*v.t.* **1.** *Agric.* to crop (land) to excess; exhaust the fertility of by continuous cropping. —*v.i.* **2.** to produce a crop in excess of what is permitted, agreed on, or normally required, esp. in an attempt to gain added profits by circumventing government regulations. —*n.* **3.** a mark of identification on cattle, which is made by cutting a piece from the upper margin of the ear. [1560–70; OVER- + CROP]

o•ver•crowd (ō′vər kroud′), *v.t., v.i.* to crowd to an uncomfortable or undesirable excess. [1760–70; OVER- + CROWD[1]]

o•ver•cur•rent (ō′vər kûr′ənt, -kur′-), *n. Elect.* a current of a magnitude that is greater than a limiting value, as the value at which a fuse melts. [1930–35; OVER- + CURRENT]

o•ver•date (ō′vər dāt′), *n. Numis.* a coin stamped from a die altered to show a year subsequent to that for which it was cut. [OVER- + DATE[1]]

o•ver•del•i•cate (ō′vər del′i kit), *adj.* extremely or excessively delicate: *an overdelicate digestive system.* [1620–30; OVER- + DELICATE] —**o•ver•del•i•ca•cy** (ō′vər del′i kə sē), **o′ver•del′i•cate•ness,** *n.* —**o′ver•del′i•cate•ly,** *adv.*

o•ver•de•ter•mi•na•tion (ō′vər di tûr′mə nā′shən), *n. Psychoanal.* the concept that a single emotional symptom or event, as a dream or a slip of the tongue, may be caused by more than one factor. [1915–20; OVER- + DETERMINATION, trans. of G *Überdeterminierung* (Freud)]

o•ver•de•ter•mined (ō′vər di tûr′mind), *adj.* excessively or unduly determined. [1915–20; OVER- + DETERMINED]

o•ver•de•vel•op (ō′vər di vel′əp), *v.t., v.i.* to develop to excess: *to overdevelop a photograph; to overdevelop a waterfront area.* [1835–45; OVER- + DEVELOP] —**o′ver•de•vel′op•ment,** *n.*

o•ver•do (ō′vər do͞o′), *v.,* **-did, -done, -do•ing.** —*v.t.* **1.** to do to excess; overindulge in: *to overdo dieting.* **2.** to carry to excess or beyond the proper limit: *He puts on so much charm that he overdoes it.* **3.** to overact (a part); exaggerate. **4.** to overtax the strength of; fatigue; exhaust. **5.** to cook too much or too long; overcook: *Don't overdo the hamburgers.* —*v.i.* **6.** to do too much; go to an extreme: *Exercise is good but you mustn't overdo.* [bef. 1000; ME *overdon,* OE *oferdōn.* See OVER-, DO[1]] —**o′ver•do′er,** *n.*

o•ver•done (ō′vər dun′), *v.* **1.** pp. of **overdo.** —*adj.* **2.** cooked too long or too much: *The roast was overdone. I dislike overdone steak.* **3.** excessive or strained; exaggerated: *Don't you think his politeness is overdone?* **4.** overtaxed; exhausted: *You're looking a bit overdone from that hike.* [OVER- + DONE]

o•ver•door (ō′vər dôr′, -dōr′), *adj.* **1.** situated above a doorway: *an overdoor panel.* —*n.* **2.** an ornamented carving, painting, or section of decorated woodwork over a doorway. [1870–75; OVER- + DOOR]

o•ver•dose (*n.* ō′vər dōs′; *v.* ō′vər dōs′, ō′vər dōs′), *n., v.,* **-dosed, -dos•ing.** See **OD.** [1680–90; OVER- + DOSE]

o•ver•draft (ō′vər draft′, -dräft′), *n.* **1.** an act or instance of overdrawing a checking account. **2.** a check overdrawn on a checking account. **3.** the amount overdrawn. **4.** an excessive drawing on or drawing off of something. **5.** a draft made to pass over a fire, as in a furnace. **6.** a draft passing downward through a kiln. **7.** *Metalworking.* a tendency of a rolled piece to curve upward after passing through a stand, occurring when the lower roll is faster than the upper. Cf. **underdraft.** [1875–80; OVER- + DRAFT]

o′verdraft check′ing account′, a bank account with a credit line permitting checks to be written for an

o′ver•bus′y, *adj.*
o′ver•can′ny, *adj.*
o′ver•ca′pa•bil′i•ty, *n., pl.* **-ties.**
o′ver•ca′pa•ble, *adj.*
o′ver•cap′tious, *adj.;* **-ly,** *adv.;* **-ness,** *n.*
o′ver•care′, *n.*
o′ver•care′less, *adj.;* **-ly,** *adv.;* **-ness,** *n.*
o′ver•cas′u•al, *adj.;* **-ly,** *adv.;* **-ness,** *n.*
o′ver•cas′u•is′tic, *adj.*
o′ver•cas′u•is′ti•cal, *adj.;* **-ly,** *adv.*
o′ver•caus′tic, *adj.*
o′ver•caus′ti•cal•ly, *adv.*
o′ver•caus•tic′i•ty, *n.*
o′ver•cau′tion, *n., v.t.*
o′ver•cen′sor, *v.t.*
o′ver•cen•so′ri•ous, *adj.;* **-ly,** *adv.;* **-ness,** *n.*
o′ver•cen′tral•i•za′tion, *n.*
o′ver•cen′tral•ize′, *v.,* **-ized, -iz•ing.**
o′ver•ce•re′bral, *adj.*
o′ver•chafe′, *v.,* **-chafed, -chaf•ing.**
o′ver•char′i•ta•ble, *adj.;* **-ble•ness,** *n.;* **-bly,** *adv.*
o′ver•char′i•ty, *n.*
o′ver•chase′, *v.,* **-chased, -chas•ing.**
o′ver•cheap′, *adj.;* **-ly,** *adv.;* **-ness,** *n.*
o′ver•cher′ish, *v.t.*
o′ver•cher′ished, *adj.*
o′ver•child′ish, *adj.;* **-ly,** *adv.;* **-ness,** *n.*
o′ver•chill′, *adj.*
o′ver•chill′, *v.*
o′ver•cir′cum•spect′, *adj.*
o′ver•cir′cum•spec′tion, *n.*
o′ver•civ′il, *adj.;* **-ly,** *adv.*
o′ver•ci•vil′i•ty, *n.*
o′ver•civ′i•li•za′tion, *n.*
o′ver•civ′i•lize′, *v.,* **-lized, -liz•ing.**
o′ver•claim′, *v.t.*
o′ver•clas′si•fi•ca′tion, *n.*
o′ver•clas′si•fy′, *v.t.,* **-fied, -fy•ing.**
o′ver•clean′, *adj.;* **-ly,** *adv.;* **-ness,** *n.*
o′ver•clem′en•cy, *n.*
o′ver•clem′ent, *adj.*
o′ver•clev′er, *adj.;* **-ly,** *adv.;* **-ness,** *n.*
o′ver•clin′i•cal, *adj.;* **-ly,** *adv.*
o′ver•clog′, *v.t.,* **-clogged, -clog•ging.**
o′ver•close′, *adj.;* **-ly,** *adv.;* **-ness,** *n.*
o′ver•cloy′, *v.t.*
o′ver•clut′ter, *v.t.*
o′ver•coach′, *v.*
o′ver•cold′, *adj.;* **-ly,** *adv.*
o′ver•col′or, *v.*
o′ver•col′or•a′tion, *n.*
o′ver•com•mend′, *v.t.*
o′ver•com•mer′cial•i•za′tion, *n.*
o′ver•com•mer′cial•ize′, *v.t.,* **-ized, -iz•ing.**
o′ver•com′mon, *adj.;* **-ly,** *adv.;* **-ness,** *n.*
o′ver•com•mu′ni•cate′, *v.,* **-cat•ed, -cat•ing.**
o′ver•com•mu′ni•ca′tion, *n.*
o′ver•com•mu′ni•ca′tive, *adj.*
o′ver•com•pet′i•tive, *adj.;* **-ly,** *adv.;* **-ness,** *n.*
o′ver•com•pla′cence, *n.*
o′ver•com•pla′cen•cy, *n.*
o′ver•com•pla′cent, *adj.;* **-ly,** *adv.*
o′ver•com•plex′, *adj.*
o′ver•com•plex′i•ty, *n.*
o′ver•com•pli′ance, *n.*
o′ver•com•pli′ant, *adj.*
o′ver•com′pli•cate′, *v.t.,* **-cat•ed, -cat•ing.**
o′ver•com•press′, *v.t.*
o′ver•com•pres′sion, *n.*
o′ver•con′cen•trate′, *v.,* **-trat•ed, -trat•ing.**
o′ver•con′cen•tra′tion, *n.*
o′ver•con•cern′, *n., v.t.*
o′ver•con′den•sa′tion, *n.*
o′ver•con•dense′, *v.,* **-densed, -dens•ing.**
o′ver•con′sci•en′tious, *adj.;* **-ly,** *adv.;* **-ness,** *n.*
o′ver•con′scious, *adj.;* **-ly,** *adv.;* **-ness,** *n.*
o′ver•con•serv′a•tism, *n.*
o′ver•con•serv′a•tive, *adj.;* **-ly,** *adv.;* **-ness,** *n.*
o′ver•con•sid′er•ate, *adj.;* **-ly,** *adv.;* **-ness,** *n.*
o′ver•con•sid′er•a′tion, *n.*
o′ver•con′stant, *adj.;* **-ly,** *adv.;* **-ness,** *n.*
o′ver•con•struct′, *v.t.*
o′ver•con•sume′, *v.,* **-sumed, -sum•ing.**
o′ver•con•sump′tion, *n.*
o′ver•con•tent′, *adj.*
o′ver•con•tent′ed, *adj.;* **-ly,** *adv.;* **-ness,** *n.*
o′ver•con•ten′tious, *adj.;* **-ly,** *adv.;* **-ness,** *n.*
o′ver•con•tent′ment, *n.*
o′ver•con•tract′, *v.t.*
o′ver•con•trac′tion, *n.*
o′ver•con•trib′ute, *v.,* **-ut•ed, -ut•ing.**
o′ver•con′tri•bu′tion, *n.*
o′ver•con•trite′, *adj.;* **-ly,** *adv.;* **-ness,** *n.*
o′ver•con•trol′, *v.t.,* **-trolled, -trol•ling,** *n.*
o′ver•cook′, *v.t.*
o′ver•cool′, *adj.;* **-ly,** *adv.;* **-ness,** *n.*
o′ver•co′pi•ous, *adj.;* **-ly,** *adv.;* **-ness,** *n.*
o′ver•cor•rect′, *adj., v.*
o′ver•cor•rupt′, *v., adj.;* **-ly,** *adv.*
o′ver•cor•rup′tion, *n.*
o′ver•cost′li•ness, *n.*
o′ver•cost′ly, *adj.*
o′ver•count′, *v.*
o′ver•count′, *n.*
o′ver•cour′te•ous, *adj.;* **-ly,** *adv.;* **-ness,** *n.*
o′ver•cour′te•sy, *n.*
o′ver•cov′et•ous, *adj.;* **-ly,** *adv.;* **-ness,** *n.*
o′ver•coy′, *adj.;* **-ly,** *adv.;* **-ness,** *n.*
o′ver•cred′it, *v.*
o′ver•cre•du′li•ty, *n.*
o′ver•cred′u•lous, *adj.;* **-ly,** *adv.;* **-ness,** *n.*
o′ver•crit′i•cism, *n.*
o′ver•crit′i•cize′, *v.,* **-cized, -ciz•ing.**
o′ver•crowd′ed, *adj.;* **-ly,** *adv.;* **-ness,** *n.*
o′ver•cull′, *v.t.*
o′ver•cul′ti•vate′, *v.t.,* **-vat•ed, -vat•ing.**
o′ver•cul′ti•va′tion, *n.*
o′ver•cul′tured, *adj.*
o′ver•cum′ber, *v.t.*
o′ver•cun′ning, *adj.;* **-ly,** *adv.;* **-ness,** *n.*
o′ver•cured′, *adj.*
o′ver•cu′ri•os′i•ty, *n.*
o′ver•cu′ri•ous, *adj.;* **-ly,** *adv.;* **-ness,** *n.*
o′ver•dain′ti•ly, *adv.*
o′ver•dain′ti•ness, *n.*
o′ver•dain′ty, *adj.*
o′ver•daz′zle, *v.,* **-zled, -zling.**
o′ver•deal′, *v.,* **-dealt, -deal•ing.**
o′ver•dear′, *adj.;* **-ly,** *adv.;* **-ness,** *n.*
o′ver•de•bate′, *v.,* **-bat•ed, -bat•ing.**
o′ver•de•bil′i•tate′, *v.t.,* **-tat•ed, -tat•ing.**
o′ver•dec′a•dence, *n.*
o′ver•dec′a•dent, *adj.;* **-ly,** *adv.*
o′ver•dec′o•rate′, *v.,* **-rat•ed, -rat•ing.**
o′ver•dec′o•ra′tion, *n.*
o′ver•dec′o•ra•tive, *adj.;* **-ly,** *adv.;* **-ness,** *n.*

amount above the account balance, subject to a finance charge on the overdraft.

o•ver•draft•ing (ō′vər draf′ting, -dräf′-), *n.* the removal of more water from ground and surface basins than is replaced by rain and melting snow. [OVER- + DRAFT + -ING[1]]

o•ver•draw (ō′vər drô′), *v.*, **-drew, -drawn, -draw•ing.** —*v.t.* **1.** to draw upon (an account, allowance, etc.) in excess of the balance standing to one's credit or at one's disposal: *It was the first time he had ever overdrawn his account.* **2.** to strain, as a bow, by drawing too far. **3.** to exaggerate in drawing, depicting, portraying, or describing: *The author has overdrawn the villain to the point of absurdity.* —*v.i.* **4.** to overdraw an account or the like: *It ruins one's credit to overdraw frequently at a bank.* **5.** (of a stove, fireplace, etc.) to draw excessively; have too strong an updraft: *When the flue overdraws, all the heat goes right up the chimney.* [1325–75; ME; see OVER-, DRAW]

o•ver•draw•er (o′vər drô′ər), *n.* a person who overdraws something, esp. a bank account. [1905–10; OVERDRAW + -ER[1]]

o•ver•dress (*v.* ō′vər dres′; *n.* ō′vər dres′), *v.*, **-dressed, -dress•ing,** *n.* —*v.t., v.i.* **1.** to dress with too much display, finery, or formality: *He certainly overdressed for the occasion.* **2.** to put excessive clothing on: *She tends to overdress her children.* —*n.* **3.** a dress worn over another, which it covers either partially or completely. [1700–10; OVER- + DRESS]

o•ver•drive (*v.* ō′vər drīv′; *n.* ō′vər drīv′), *v.*, **-drove, -driv•en, -driv•ing,** *n.* —*v.t.* **1.** to push or carry to excess; overwork. **2.** to drive too hard. —*n.* **3.** *Mach., Auto.* a device containing a gear set at such ratio and arrangement as to provide a drive shaft speed greater than the engine crankshaft speed. **4.** *Informal.* an intense state of activity or productivity: *The political campaign has shifted into overdrive.* [bef. 950; ME *overdriven* to cover over, overpower; OE *oferdrīfan* to drive away, overthrow. See OVER-, DRIVE]

o•ver•dub (*v.* ō′vər dub′; *n.* ō′vər dub′), *v.*, **-dubbed, -dub•bing,** *n.* —*v.i.* **1.** to add other recorded sound or music, as a supplementary instrumental or vocal track, to a taped musical track to complete or enhance a recording. —*v.t.* **2.** to add (a track or tracks) to a musical recording. —*n.* **3.** a recorded segment or layer of instrumental parts, vocalization, or sound effects integrated into a musical recording. [1965–70; OVER- + DUB[4]]

o•ver•due (ō′vər do͞o′, -dyo͞o′), *adj.* **1.** past due, as a delayed train or a bill not paid by the assigned date; late: *two overdue library books.* **2.** too long awaited; needed or expected for some time: *Improvements in our highway system are long overdue.* **3.** more than sufficiently advanced, mature, or ready: *That country is overdue for industrial development.* [1835–45; OVER- + DUE] —**o′ver•due′ness,** *n.*
—**Syn. 1.** tardy, behindhand.

o•ver•dye (ō′vər dī′, ō′vər dī′), *v.t.*, **-dyed, -dy•ing. 1.** to dye too long or too much. **2.** to dye over another color. [1945–50; OVER- + DYE] —**o′ver•dy′er,** *n.*

o′ver eas′y, *Cookery.* (of fried eggs) turned over when nearly done and fried briefly on the reverse side so that the yolk remains somewhat liquid but hard on top. Cf. **sunny-side up.**

o•ver•eat (ō′vər ēt′), *v.*, **-ate, -eat•en, -eat•ing.** —*v.i.* **1.** to eat too much: *If you overeat, you're bound to get fat.* —*v.t.* **2.** to eat more than is good for (oneself): *The food was so tasty we overate ourselves.* [1515–25; OVER- + EAT] —**o′ver•eat′er,** *n.*

o•ver•e•lab•o•rate (*adj.* ō′vər i lab′ər it; *v.* ō′vər i lab′ə rāt′), *adj., v.*, **-rat•ed, -rat•ing.** —*adj.* **1.** excessively or fussily elaborate, ornate, detailed, etc. —*v.t.* **2.** to render or present with excessive or fussy detail: *He so overelaborates his jokes that they lose their humor.* —*v.i.* **3.** to add excessive details, as in writing or speaking: *He overelaborates to an extent that his novels must be cut radically before being published.* [OVER- + ELABORATE] —**o′ver•e•lab′o•rate•ly,** *adv.* —**o′ver•e•lab′o•ra′tion, o′ver•e•lab′o•rate•ness,** *n.*

o•ver•em•pha•sis (ō′vər em′fə sis), *n.* excessive or undue emphasis. [1895–1900; OVER- + EMPHASIS] —**o•ver•em•phat•ic** (ō′vər em fat′ik), *adj.*

o•ver•em•pha•size (ō′vər em′fə sīz′), *v.*, **-sized, -siz•ing.** —*v.t.* **1.** to emphasize excessively. —*v.i.* **2.** to use excessive emphasis. Also, *esp. Brit.,* **o′ver•em′pha•sise′.** [1900–05; OVER- + EMPHASIZE]

o•ver•es•ti•mate (*v.* ō′vər es′tə māt′; *n.* ō′vər es′tə-mit), *v.*, **-mat•ed, -mat•ing,** *n.* —*v.t.* **1.** to estimate at too high a value, amount, rate, or the like: *Don't overestimate the car's trade-in value.* **2.** to hold in too great esteem or to expect too much from: *Don't overestimate him—he's no smarter than you are.* —*n.* **3.** an estimate that is too high. [1815–25; OVER- + ESTIMATE] —**o′ver•es′ti•ma′tion,** *n.*

o•ver•ex•cite (ō′vər ik sīt′), *v.t.*, **-cit•ed, -cit•ing.** to excite too much. [1815–25; OVER- + EXCITE] —**o′ver•ex•cit′a•ble,** *adj.* —**o′ver•ex•cit′a•bil′i•ty,** *n.* —**o′ver•ex•cit′a•bly,** *adv.* —**o′ver•ex•cite′ment,** *n.*

o•ver•ex•ert (ō′vər ig zûrt′), *v.t.* to exert excessively. [1840–50; OVER- + EXERT] —**o′ver•ex•ert′ed•ly,** *adv.* —**o′ver•ex•er′tion,** *n.*

o•ver•ex•pose (ō′vər ik spōz′), *v.t.*, **-posed, -pos•ing. 1.** to expose too much, as to the sun, cold, or light rays (often used reflexively): *Be careful of overexposing yourself to the sun.* **2.** *Photog.* to expose (a film or the like) to too much light. [1865–70; OVER- + EXPOSE]

o•ver•ex•po•sure (ō′vər ik spō′zhər), *n.* **1.** excessive exposure, esp. of photographic film or a sensitized plate to light rays. **2.** the condition of having been seen, heard, or advertised so frequently or for so long that freshness or appeal is diminished. [1870–75; OVER- + EXPOSURE]

o•ver•ex•tend (ō′vər ik stend′), *v.t.* **1.** to extend, reach, or expand beyond a proper, safe, or reasonable point: *a company that overextended its credit to diversify.* **2.** to extend for too long a time: *to overextend a stay.* **3.** to obligate (oneself) to more activities, work, etc., than one has time for or can accomplish well. [1935–40; OVER- + EXTEND] —**o•ver•ex•ten•sion** (ō′vər ik sten′shən), *n.*

o•ver•falls (ō′vər fôlz′), *n.* **1.** *Oceanog.* water made rough by a strong current moving over a shoal, by an opposing current, or by winds blowing against the current. **2.** *Obs.* a cataract or waterfall. [1535–45; OVER- + FALL + -S[3]]

o•ver•fa•tigue (ō′vər fə tēg′) *n.* excessive tiredness from which recuperation is difficult. [1720–30; OVER- + FATIGUE]

o•ver•feed (ō′vər fēd′), *v.t., v.i.*, **-fed, -feed•ing.** to feed or eat to excess. [1600–10; OVER- + FEED]

o•ver•fill (ō′vər fil′), *v.t.* **1.** to fill too full, so as to cause overflowing. —*v.i.* **2.** to become too full. [1200–50; ME *overfillen,* OE *oferfyllan.* See OVER-, FILL]

o•ver•fish (ō′vər fish′), *v.t.* **1.** to fish (an area) excessively; to exhaust the supply of usable fish in (certain waters): *Scientists are concerned that fishing boats may overfish our coastal waters.* —*v.i.* **2.** to fish so as to deplete the supply of fish in certain waters: *If the trawlers are going to overfish here, we'll need legislation to restrict their hauls.* [1865–70; OVER- + FISH]

o•ver•flap (ō′vər flap′), *n.* a protective paper cover for artwork, usually of kraft paper. [1685–95 for an earlier sense; OVER- + FLAP]

o•ver•flight (ō′vər flīt′), *n.* an air flight that passes over a specific area, country, or territory: *Overflights of foreign aircraft are closely monitored.* [1590–1600 as pertaining to the flight of birds; 1955–60 for current sense; OVER- + FLIGHT[1]]

o•ver•flow (*v.* ō′vər flō′; *n.* ō′vər flō′), *v.*, **-flowed, -flown, -flow•ing,** *n.* —*v.i.* **1.** to flow or run over, as rivers or water: *After the thaw, the river overflows and causes great damage.* **2.** to have the contents flowing over or spilling, as an overfull container: *Stop pouring or your glass is going to overflow.* **3.** to pass from one place or part to another as if flowing from an overfull space: *The population overflowed into the adjoining territory.* **4.** to be filled or supplied with in great measure: *a heart overflowing with gratitude; a region overflowing with orchards and vineyards.* —*v.t.* **5.** to flow over; flood; inundate: *The river overflowed several farms.* **6.** to flow over or beyond (the brim, banks, borders, etc.). **7.** to cause to overflow. **8.** to flow over the edge or brim of (a receptacle, container, etc.). **9.** to fill to the point of running over. —*n.* **10.** an overflowing: *the annual overflow of the Nile.* **11.** something that flows or runs over: *to carry off the overflow from a fountain.* **12.** a portion crowded out of an overfilled place: *to house the overflow of the museum's collection in another building.* **13.** an excess or superabundance: *an overflow of applicants for the job.* **14.** an outlet or receptacle for excess liquid: *The tank is equipped with an overflow.* [bef. 900; ME *overflowen,* OE *oferflōwan.* See OVER-, FLOW] —**o′ver•flow′a•ble,** *adj.* —**o′ver•flow′ing•ly,** *adv.*
—**Syn. 13.** overabundance, surplus, plethora, flood, glut.

o•ver•fly (ō′vər flī′), *v.*, **-flew, -flown, -fly•ing.** —*v.t.* **1.** to fly over (a specified area, territory, country, etc.): *The plane lost its way and overflew foreign territory.* **2.** to fly farther than or beyond; overshoot. **3.** to fly over or past instead of making a scheduled stop: *to overfly Philadelphia because of bad weather.* —*v.i.* **4.** to fly over a particular territory, country, etc.: *The plane approached the border but never overflew.* [1550–60; OVER- + FLY[1]]

o•ver•full (ō′vər fo͝ol′), *adj.* excessively full: *The auditorium was overfull.* [bef. 1000; ME; OE *oferfull.* See OVER-, FULL[1]] —**o′ver•full′ness,** *n.*

o•ver•gar•ment (ō′vər gär′mənt), *n.* an outer garment. [1425–75; late ME; see OVER-, GARMENT]

o•ver•gen•er•al•i•za•tion (ō′vər jen′ər ə lə zā′shən), *n.* **1.** the act or process of overgeneralizing. **2.** the result of overgeneralizing. **3.** *Ling.* (in language acquisition) the process of extending the application of a rule to items that are excluded from it in the language norm, as when a child uses the regular past tense verb ending *-ed* of forms like *I walked* to produce forms like **I goed* or **I rided.* [1945–50; OVER- + GENERALIZATION]

o•ver•gen•er•al•ize (ō′vər jen′ər ə līz′), *v.i., v.t.*, **-ized, -iz•ing.** to generalize beyond appropriate or justified limits. Also, *esp. Brit.,* **o′ver•gen′er•al•ise′.** [OVER- + GENERALIZE]

o•ver•gild (ō′vər gild′), *v.t.*, **-gild•ed** or **-gilt, -gild•ing. 1.** to cover with gilding. **2.** to tint with a golden color: *morning sunlight that overgilds the rooftops.* [bef. 1050; ME *overgilden,* OE *ofergyldan.* See OVER-, GILD[1]]

o•ver•glaze (*n., adj.* ō′vər glāz′; *v.* ō′vər glāz′, ō′vər-glāz′), *n., v.*, **-glazed, -glaz•ing,** *adj. Ceram.* —*n.* **1.** a color or glaze applied to an existing glaze. —*v.t.* **2.** to cover or decorate (a ceramic object) with an overglaze. —*adj.* **3.** used as an overglaze. **4.** (of painted or printed decorations) applied over a glaze. [1585–95; OVER- + GLAZE]

o•ver•graze (ō′vər grāz′, ō′vər grāz′), *v.t.*, **-grazed, -graz•ing.** to graze (land) to excess. [OVER- + GRAZE[1]]

o•ver•grow (ō′vər grō′, ō′vər grō′), *v.*, **-grew, -grown, -grow•ing.** —*v.t.* **1.** to grow over; cover with a growth of something. **2.** to grow beyond, grow too large for, or outgrow. **3.** to outdo in growing; choke or supplant by a more exuberant growth. —*v.i.* **4.** to grow to excess; grow too large: *When the vegetable overgrows, it*

CONCISE PRONUNCIATION KEY: act, cāpe, dâre, pärt; set, ēqual; if, ice; ox, ōver, ôrder, oil, bo͝ok, bo͞ot, out; up, ûrge; child; sing; shoe; thin, that; zh as in *treasure.* ə = *a* as in *alone, e* as in *system, i* as in *easily, o* as in *gallop, u* as in *circus;* ᵊ as in *fire* (fīᵊr), *hour* (ouᵊr). l and n can serve as syllabic consonants, as in *cradle* (krād′l), and *button* (but′n). See the full key inside the front cover.

o′ver•ded′i•cate′, *v.t.*, **-cat•ed, -cat•ing.**
o′ver•ded′i•ca′tion, *n.*
o′ver•deep′, *adj.*
o′ver•deep′en, *v.t.*
o′ver•de•fen′sive, *adj.*; **-ly,** *adv.*; **-ness,** *n.*
o′ver•def′er•en′tial, *adj.*; **-ly,** *adv.*
o′ver•de•fi′ant, *adj.*; **-ly,** *adv.*; **-ness,** *n.*
o′ver•de•lib′er•ate′, *v.*, **-at•ed, -at•ing.**
o′ver•de•lib′er•ate, *adj.*; **-ly,** *adv.*; **-ness,** *n.*
o′ver•de•lib′er•a′tion, *n.*
o′ver•de•li′cious, *adj.*; **-ly,** *adv.*; **-ness,** *n.*
o′ver•de•mand′, *v., n.*
o′ver•de•mand′ing, *adj.*; **-ly,** *adv.*
o′ver•de•nun′ci•a′tion, *n.*
o′ver•de•pend′ence, *n.*
o′ver•de•pend′ent, *adj.*
o′ver•de•press′, *v.t.*
o′ver•de•pres′sive, *adj.*; **-ly,** *adv.*; **-ness,** *n.*
o′ver•de•ride′, *v.t.*, **-rid•ed, -rid•ing.**
o′ver•de•ri′sive, *adj.*; **-ly,** *adv.*; **-ness,** *n.*
o′ver•de•scribe′, *v.t.*, **-scribed, -scrib•ing.**
o′ver•de•scrip′tive, *adj.*; **-ly,** *adv.*; **-ness,** *n.*
o′ver•de•sign′, *v.*
o′ver•de•sire′, *n.*
o′ver•de•sir′ous, *adj.*; **-ly,** *adv.*; **-ness,** *n.*
o′ver•de•struc′tive, *adj.*; **-ly,** *adv.*; **-ness,** *n.*
o′ver•de•tailed′, *adj.*
o′ver•de•vot′ed, *adj.*; **-ly,** *adv.*; **-ness,** *n.*
o′ver•dif′fer•en′ti•a′tion, *n.*
o′ver•dif•fuse′, *v.*, **-fused, -fus•ing,** *adj.*; **-ly,** *adv.*; **-ness,** *n.*
o′ver•dif•fu′sion, *n.*
o′ver•di•gest′, *v.*
o′ver•dig′ni•fy′, *v.t.*, **-fied, -fy•ing.**
o′ver•di•late′, *v.*, **-lat•ed, -lat•ing.**
o′ver•di•la′tion, *n.*
o′ver•dil′i•gence, *n.*
o′ver•dil′i•gent, *adj.*; **-ly,** *adv.*; **-ness,** *n.*
o′ver•di•lute′, *v.*, **-lut•ed, -lut•ing.**
o′ver•di•lu′tion, *n.*
o′ver•di•rect′ed, *adj.*
o′ver•dis′ci•pline, *v.*, **-plined, -plin•ing.**
o′ver•dis′count, *v.t.*
o′ver•dis•cour′age, *v.t.*, **-aged, -ag•ing.**
o′ver•dis•cour′age•ment, *n.*
o′ver•dis•creet′, *adj.*; **-ly,** *adv.*; **-ness,** *n.*
o′ver•dis•crim′i•nat′ing, *adj.*; **-ly,** *adv.*
o′ver•dis•cuss′, *v.t.*
o′ver•dis′tant, *adj.*; **-ly,** *adv.*
o′ver•dis•tend′, *v.*
o′ver•dis•ten′tion, *n.*
o′ver•dis•tort′, *v.t.*
o′ver•dis•tor′tion, *n.*
o′ver•dis•trait′, *adj.*
o′ver•dis•traught′, *adj.*
o′ver•di•verse′, *adj.*; **-ly,** *adv.*; **-ness,** *n.*
o′ver•di•ver′si•fi•ca′tion, *n.*
o′ver•di•ver′si•fy′, *v.*, **-fied, -fy•ing.**
o′ver•di•ver′si•ty, *n.*
o′ver•doc′tri•naire′, *adj.*
o′ver•dog•mat′ic, *adj.*
o′ver•dog•mat′i•cal, *adj.*; **-ly,** *adv.*; **-ness,** *n.*
o′ver•dog′ma•tism, *n.*
o′ver•do•mes′ti•cate′, *v.t.*, **-cat•ed, -cat•ing.**
o′ver•dom′i•nate′, *v.t.*, **-nat•ed, -nat•ing.**
o′ver•doubt′, *v.t.*
o′ver•doze′, *v.i.*, **-dozed, -doz•ing.**
o′ver•drain′, *v.t.*
o′ver•drain′age, *n.*
o′ver•dra•mat′ic, *adj.*
o′ver•dra•mat′i•cal•ly, *adv.*
o′ver•dram′a•tize′, *v.*, **-tized, -tiz•ing.**
o′ver•dredge′, *v.t.*, **-dredged, -dredg•ing.**
o′ver•dri′ly, *adv.*
o′ver•drink′, *v.t.*, **-drank** or (*Nonstandard*) **-drunk; -drunk** or, often, **-drank; -drink•ing.**
o′ver•dry′, *adj.*; **-ly,** *adv.*; **-ness,** *n.*
o′ver•ea′ger, *adj.*; **-ly,** *adv.*; **-ness,** *n.*
o′ver•ear′nest, *adj.*; **-ly,** *adv.*; **-ness,** *n.*
o′ver•eas′i•ly, *adv.*
o′ver•eas′y, *adj.*
o′ver•ed′it, *v.*
o′ver•ed′i•to′ri•al•ize′, *v.i.*, **-ized, -iz•ing.**
o′ver•ed′u•cate′, *v.t.*, **-cat•ed, -cat•ing.**
o′ver•ed′u•ca′tion, *n.*
o′ver•ed′u•ca′tive, *adj.*; **-ly,** *adv.*
o′ver•ef′fort, *n.*
o′ver•ef•fu′sive, *adj.*; **-ly,** *adv.*; **-ness,** *n.*
o′ver•e•late′, *v.t.*, **-lat•ed, -lat•ing.**
o′ver•el′e•gance, *n.*
o′ver•el′e•gant, *adj.*; **-ly,** *adv.*
o′ver•el•lip′ti•cal, *adj.*; **-ly,** *adv.*
o′ver•em•bel′lish, *v.t.*
o′ver•em•bel′lish•ment, *n.*
o′ver•em•broi′der, *v.t.*
o′ver•e•mote′, *v.i.*, **-mot•ed, -mot•ing.**
o′ver•e•mo′tion•al, *adj.*; **-ly,** *adv.*
o′ver•e•mo′tion•al′i•ty, *n.*
o′ver•e•mo′tion•al•ize′, *v.t.*, **-ized, -iz•ing.**
o′ver•em•phat′i•cal, *adj.*; **-ly,** *adv.*; **-ness,** *n.*
o′ver•em•pir′i•cal, *adj.*; **-ly,** *adv.*
o′ver•em•ploy′, *v.t.*
o′ver•em•ploy′ment, *n.*
o′ver•emp′ty, *adj.*
o′ver•em′u•late′, *v.t.*, **-lat•ed, -lat•ing.**
o′ver•em′u•la′tion, *n.*
o′ver•en•am′ored, *adj.*
o′ver•en•cour′age, *v.t.*, **-aged, -ag•ing.**
o′ver•en•rolled′, *adj.*
o′ver•en′ter•tained′, *adj.*
o′ver•en•thu′si•asm, *n.*
o′ver•en•thu′si•as′tic, *adj.*
o′ver•en•thu′si•as′ti•cal•ly, *adv.*
o′ver•en′vi•ous, *adj.*; **-ly,** *adv.*; **-ness,** *n.*
o′ver•e•quipped′, *adj.*
o′ver•e•val′u•a′tion, *n.*
o′ver•ex•act′ing, *adj.*
o′ver•ex•ag′ger•ate′, *v.*, **-at•ed, -at•ing.**
o′ver•ex•ag′ger•a′tion, *n.*
o′ver•ex′er•cise′, *v.*, **-cised, -cis•ing.**
o′ver•ex•pand′, *v.*
o′ver•ex•pan′sion, *n.*
o′ver•ex•pan′sive, *adj.*; **-ly,** *adv.*; **-ness,** *n.*
o′ver•ex•pect′, *v.*
o′ver•ex•pect′ant, *adj.*; **-ly,** *adv.*
o′ver•ex′pec•ta′tion, *n.*
o′ver•ex•pend′, *v.*
o′ver•ex•pend′i•ture, *n.*
o′ver•ex•plain′, *v.*

tends to be woody. **5.** to become grown over, as with weeds: *An untended garden will quickly overgrow.* [1300–50; ME *overgrowen.* See OVER-, GROW]

o•ver•growth (ō′vər grōth′), *n.* **1.** a growth overspreading or covering something. **2.** excessive growth: *to prune a young tree so as to prevent overgrowth.* [1595–1605; OVER- + GROWTH]

o•ver•hand (ō′vər hand′), *adj.* **1.** thrown or performed with the hand raised over the shoulder; overarm: *overhand stroke.* **2.** with the hand and part or all of the arm raised above the shoulder: *to pitch overhand.* **3.** (in sewing and embroidery) with close, shallow stitches over two edges. —*adv.* Also, **o′ver•hand′ed. 4.** with the hand over the object: *to grasp one's fork overhand.* —*n.* **5.** an overhand stroke, throw, or delivery. —*v.t.* **6.** to sew overhand. [1860–65; OVER- + HAND]

o′verhand knot′, a simple knot of various uses that slips easily. Also called **single knot.** See illus. under **knot.** [1830–40]

o•ver•hang (*v.* ō′vər hang′; *n.* ō′vər hang′), *v.,* **-hung, -hang•ing,** *n.* —*v.t.* **1.** to hang or be suspended over: *A great chandelier overhung the ballroom.* **2.** to extend, project, or jut over: *A wide balcony overhangs the garden.* **3.** to impend over or threaten, as danger or evil; loom over: *The threat of war overhung Europe.* **4.** to spread throughout; permeate; pervade: *the melancholy that overhung the proceedings.* **5.** *Informal.* to hover over, as a threat or menace: *Unemployment continues to overhang the economic recovery.* —*v.i.* **6.** to hang over; project or jut out over something below: *How far does the balcony overhang?* —*n.* **7.** something that extends or juts out over; projection. **8.** the extent of projection, as of the bow of a ship. **9.** *Informal.* an excess or surplus: *an overhang of office space in midtown.* **10.** a threat or menace: *to face the overhang of foreign reprisals.* **11.** *Archit.* a projecting upper part of a building, as a roof or balcony. [1590–1600; OVER- + HANG]

o•ver•hast•y (ō′vər hā′stē), *adj.* excessively hasty; rash: *overhasty judgment.* [1375–1425; late ME; see OVER-, HASTY] —**o′ver•hast′i•ly,** *adv.* —**o′ver•hast′i•ness,** *n.*

o•ver•haul (*v.* ō′vər hôl′, ō′vər hôl′; *n.* ō′vər hôl′), *v.t.* **1.** to make necessary repairs on; restore to serviceable condition: *My car was overhauled by an expert mechanic.* **2.** to investigate or examine thoroughly for repair or revision: *Next year we're going to overhaul the curriculum.* **3.** to gain upon, catch up with, or overtake, as in a race. **4.** to haul or turn over for examination. **5.** *Naut.* **a.** to slacken (a rope) by hauling in the opposite direction to that in which the rope was drawn taut. **b.** to release the blocks of (a tackle). —*n.* **6.** Also, **o′ver•haul′ing.** a general examination and repair: *The state roads were badly in need of a major overhaul.* [1620–30; OVER- + HAUL] —**o′ver•haul′er,** *n.*

o•ver•head (*adv.* ō′vər hed′; *adj., n.* ō′vər hed′), *adv.* **1.** over one's head; aloft; up in the air or sky, esp. near the zenith: *There was a cloud overhead.* **2.** so as to be completely submerged or deeply involved: *to plunge overhead in water; to sink overhead in debt.* —*adj.* **3.** situated, operating, or passing above, aloft, or over the head: *an overhead sprinkler system.* **4.** of or pertaining to the general cost of running a business: *overhead expenses; an overhead charge.* —*n.* **5.** the general, fixed cost of running a business, as rent, lighting, and heating expenses, which cannot be charged or attributed to a specific product or part of the work operation. **6.** *Accounting.* that part of manufacturing costs for which cost per unit produced is not readily assignable. **7.** (in a hoistway) the distance between the last floor level served and the beam supporting the hoisting sheaves or machinery. **8.** (in racket sports) a stroke in which the ball or shuttlecock is hit with a downward motion from above the head; smash. **9.** an overhead compartment, shelf, etc.: *Pillows are in the overhead above each passenger's seat.* **10.** Also called **o′verhead shot′.** *Motion Pictures, Television.* a shot in which the camera is positioned above the actors, esp. directly overhead. **11.** a ceiling light in a room: *Turn off the overheads when you leave.* **12.** Also called **o′verhead projec′tor.** a projector capable of projecting images above and behind the person operating it, thus allowing a lecturer or speaker to remain facing the audience while using it. **13.** Also called **o′verhead projec′tion.** a picture or image projected in this manner: *a lecture enhanced with overheads.* [1425–75; late ME; see OVER-, HEAD]

CONCISE ETYMOLOGY KEY: <, descended or borrowed from; >, whence; b., blend of, blended; c., cognate with; cf., compare; deriv., derivative; equiv., equivalent; imit., imitative; obl., oblique; r., replacing; s., stem; sp., spelling, spelled; resp., respelling, respelled; trans., translation; ?, origin unknown; *, unattested; ‡, probably earlier than. See the full key inside the front cover.

o′verhead cam′shaft, a camshaft in an automotive engine that is located in the cylinder head over the engine block rather than in the block. *Abbr.:* OHC [1910–15]

o′verhead rail′way, *Brit.* See **elevated railroad.**

o′ver•head-valve′ en′gine (ō′vər hed′valv′). See **I-head engine.** [1965–70]

o•ver•hear (ō′vər hēr′), *v.t.,* **-heard, -hear•ing.** to hear (speech or a speaker) without the speaker's intention or knowledge: *I accidentally overheard what they were saying.* [1540–50; OVER- + HEAR] —**o′ver•hear′•er,** *n.*

o•ver•heat (ō′vər hēt′), *v.t.* **1.** to heat to excess. **2.** to excite or agitate; make vehement: *a crowd overheated by rabble-rousers.* —*v.i.* **3.** to become overheated: *a stove that overheats alarmingly; a temper that overheats with little provocation.* —*n.* **4.** the state or condition of being overheated; excessive heat, agitation, or vehemence. [1350–1400; ME *overheten.* See OVER-, HEAT]

o•ver•hit (ō′vər hit′), *v.i.,* **-hit, -hit•ting.** *Sports.* to hit too hard or too far, as in tennis. [1810–20; OVER- + HIT]

o•ver•hung (*v.* ō′vər hung′; *adj.* ō′vər hung′), *v.* **1.** pt. and pp. of **overhang.** —*adj.* **2.** hung or suspended from above: *an overhung door.* [1700–10; OVER- + HUNG]

O•ver•ijs•sel (ō′vər ī′səl), *n.* a province in the E Netherlands. 985,569. *Cap.:* Zwolle.

o•ver•in•dulge (ō′vər in dulj′), *v.t., v.i.,* **-dulged, -dulg•ing.** to indulge to excess: *to overindulge one's fondness for candy.* [1735–45; OVER- + INDULGE] —**o′ver•in•dul′gence,** *n.* —**o′ver•in•dul′gent,** *adj.* —**o′ver•in•dul′gent•ly,** *adv.*

o•ver•is•sue (ō′vər ish′o͞o *or, esp. Brit.,* -is′yo͞o), *n.* an excessive issue of stocks or bonds, as in excess of the needs of the business or in excess of charter authorization. [1795–1805; OVER- + ISSUE]

o•ver•joy (ō′vər joi′), *v.t.* to cause to feel great joy or delight; elate: *It overjoys me to hear of your good fortune. I was overjoyed at her safe arrival.* [1350–1400; ME; see OVER-, JOY]—**o′ver•joyed′,** *adj.*

o•ver•kill (ō′vər kil′), *n.* **1.** the capacity of a nation to destroy, by nuclear weapons, more of an enemy than would be necessary for a military victory. **2.** an instance of such destruction. **3.** an excess of what is required or suitable, as because of zeal or misjudgment. [1945–50, *Amer.*; OVER- + KILL[1]]

o•ver•lade (ō′vər lād′), *v.t.,* **-lad•ed, -lad•en** or **-lad•ed, -lad•ing.** to overload (usually used in pp. *overladen*): *a table overladen with rich food.* [1175–1225; ME; see OVER-, LADE]

o•ver•laid (ō′vər lād′), *v.* pt. and pp. of **overlay**[1].

o•ver•lain (ō′vər lān′), *v.* pp. of **overlie.**

o•ver•land (ō′vər land′, -lənd), *adv.* **1.** by land; on terrain: *to travel overland rather than by sea.* **2.** over or across the land: *a road that winds overland.* —*adj.* **3.** proceeding, performed, or carried on overland: *the overland route to the West.* [1325–75; ME *overlond.* See OVER-, LAND]

O•ver•land (ō′vər lənd), *n.* a city in E Missouri, near St. Louis. 19,620.

o′verland mail′, *U.S. Hist.* **1.** a government mail service, started in 1848, for sending mail from the Mississippi to the Far West. **2.** (*caps.*) a stagecoach line, established in 1858, linking Memphis, St. Louis, and San Francisco, which was then paid by the government to carry U.S. mail to the Far West. With various changes in ownership, name, and routes it continued until the completion of the transcontinental railroad in 1869.

O′ver•land Park′ (ō′vər lənd), a town in E Kansas, near Kansas City. 81,784.

o′verland stage′, a stagecoach used in the western U.S. during the middle of the 19th century. [1855–60]

O′ver•land Trail′ (ō′vər land′, -lənd), *U.S. Hist.* any of various routes traveled by settlers from the Missouri River to Oregon and California beginning in the 1840's. Cf. **Oregon Trail.**

o•ver•lap (*v.* ō′vər lap′; *n.* ō′vər lap′), *v.,* **-lapped, -lap•ping,** *n.* —*v.t.* **1.** to lap over (something else or each other); extend over and cover a part of; imbricate. **2.** to cover and extend beyond (something else): *The ends of cloth overlap the table.* **3.** to coincide in part with; have in common with: *two lives that overlapped each other.* —*v.i.* **4.** to lap over: *two sales territories that overlap; fields of knowledge that overlap.* —*n.* **5.** an act or instance of overlapping. **6.** the extent or amount of overlapping: *The second story of the building has an overlap of ten feet.* **7.** an overlapping part. **8.** the place of overlapping. **9.** (in yacht racing) the position of two yachts side by side such that the overtaking boat, to pass the other on the opposite side, must fall back, or such that neither can turn toward the other without danger of collision. [1685–95; OVER- + LAP[2]]

o•ver•lay[1] (*v.* ō′vər lā′; *n.* ō′vər lā′), *v.,* **-laid, -lay•ing,** *n.* —*v.t.* **1.** to lay or place (one thing) over or upon another. **2.** to cover, overspread, or surmount with something. **3.** to finish with a layer or applied decoration of something: *wood richly overlaid with gold.* **4.** *Print.* to put an overlay upon. —*n.* **5.** something laid over something else; covering. **6.** a layer or decoration of something applied: *an overlay of gold.* **7.** *Print.* **a.** a shaped piece of paper, or a sheet of paper reinforced at the proper places by shaped pieces, put on the tympan of a press to increase or equalize the impression. **b.** a method of preparing copy for multicolor printing, in which matter for each color is prepared on a transparent sheet that is placed over a key plate, usually the one to be printed in black. **c.** the sheet or sheets so prepared. **8.** a sheet of transparent paper placed over a photograph, a dummy, or other artwork for noting corrections, instructions, mechanical separations, etc. **9.** *Computers.* software or data in external storage and brought into main storage for execution by replacing or augmenting software or data already there. **10.** a transparent sheet giving special military information not ordinarily shown on maps, used by being placed over the map on which it is based. **11.** a decorative piece of leather or other material stitched on a shoe. **12.** *Scot.* a cravat. [1250–1300; ME; see OVER-, LAY[1]]

o•ver•lay[2] (ō′vər lā′), *v.* pt. of **overlie.**

o′verlay glass′. See **case glass.** [1955–60]

O•ver•lea (ō′vər lē), *n.* a town in N Maryland, near Baltimore. 12,965.

o•ver•leaf (ō′vər lēf′), *adv.* on the other side of the page or sheet. [1605–15; OVER- + LEAF]

o•ver•leap (ō′vər lēp′), *v.t.,* **-leaped** or **-leapt, -leap•ing. 1.** to leap over or across: *to overleap a fence.* **2.** to overreach (oneself) by leaping too far: *to overleap oneself with ambition.* **3.** to pass over or omit: *to overleap important steps and reach erroneous conclusions.* **4.** *Archaic.* to leap farther than; outleap. [bef. 900; ME *overlepen,* OE *oferhlēapan.* See OVER-, LEAP]

o•ver•learn (ō′vər lûrn′), *v.t.,* **-learned** (-lûrnd′) or **-learnt, -learn•ing.** *Educ.* to learn or memorize beyond

o′ver•ex′pla•na′tion, *n.*
o′ver•ex•plic′it, *adj.*
o′ver•ex•ploit′, *v.t.*
o′ver•ex′ploi•ta′tion, *n.*
o′ver•ex•press′, *v.t.*
o′ver•ex•pres′sive, *adj.;* **-ly,** *adv.;* **-ness,** *n.*
o′ver•ex•quis′ite, *adj.*
o′ver•ex•tract′, *v.t.*
o′ver•ex•trac′tion, *n.*
o′ver•ex•trap′o•la′tion, *n.*
o′ver•ex•trav′a•gant, *adj.;* **-ly,** *adv.*
o′ver•ex•treme′, *adj.*
o′ver•ex•u′ber•ance, *n.*
o′ver•ex•u′ber•ant, *adj.;* **-ly,** *adv.*
o′ver•fac′ile, *adj.;* **-ly,** *adv.*
o′ver•fa•cil′i•ty, *n.*
o′ver•fac′tious, *adj.;* **-ly,** *adv.;* **-ness,** *n.*
o′ver•fac•ti′tious, *adj.*
o′ver•fag′, *v.,* **-fagged, -fag•ging.**
o′ver•faint′, *adj.;* **-ly,** *adv.;* **-ness,** *n.*
o′ver•faith′ful, *adj.;* **-ly,** *adv.;* **-ness,** *n.*
o′ver•famed′, *adj.*
o′ver•fa•mil′iar, *adj.;* **-ly,** *adv.*
o′ver•fa•mil′i•ar′i•ty, *n.*
o′ver•fa′mous, *adj.*
o′ver•fan′ci•ful, *adj.;* **-ly,** *adv.;* **-ness,** *n.*
o′ver•far′, *adv., adj.*
o′ver•fast′, *adj.*
o′ver•fas•tid′i•ous, *adj.;* **-ly,** *adv.;* **-ness,** *n.*
o′ver•fat′, *adj.*
o′ver•fat′ten, *v.t.*
o′ver•fa′vor, *v.t.*
o′ver•fa′vor•a•ble, *adj.;* **-ble•ness,** *n.;* **-bly,** *adv.*
o′ver•fear′ful, *adj.;* **-ly,** *adv.;* **-ness,** *n.*
o′ver•feast′, *v.*
o′ver•fee′, *n.*
o′ver•feel′, *v.,* **-felt, -feel•ing.**
o′ver•fem′i•nine, *adj.;* **-ly,** *adv.*
o′ver•fem′i•nin′i•ty, *n.*
o′ver•fem′i•nize′, *v.,* **-nized, -niz•ing.**
o′ver•fer′tile, *adj.*
o′ver•fer•til′i•ty, *n.*
o′ver•fer′ti•li•za′tion, *n.*
o′ver•fer′ti•lize′, *v.t.,* **-lized, -liz•ing.**
o′ver•fer′vent, *adj.;* **-ly,** *adv.;* **-ness,** *n.*
o′ver•few′, *adj.*
o′ver•fierce′, *adj.;* **-ly,** *adv.;* **-ness,** *n.*
o′ver•fil′ter, *v.t.*
o′ver•fit′, *adj.*
o′ver•fix′, *v.*
o′ver•flat′, *adj.;* **-ly,** *adv.;* **-ness,** *n.*
o′ver•flat′ten, *v.t.*
o′ver•fla′vor, *v.*
o′ver•fleshed′, *adj.*
o′ver•flex′ion, *n.*
o′ver•flog′, *v.t.,* **-flogged, -flog•ging.**
o′ver•flood′, *v.*
o′ver•flor′id, *adj.;* **-ly,** *adv.;* **-ness,** *n.*
o′ver•flour′, *v.*
o′ver•flu′en•cy, *n.*
o′ver•flu′ent, *adj.;* **-ly,** *adv.;* **-ness,** *n.*
o′ver•fo′cus, *v.t.,* **-cused, -cus•ing** or (*esp. Brit.*) **-cussed, -cus•sing.**
o′ver•fond′, *adj.;* **-ly,** *adv.;* **-ness,** *n.*
o′ver•fon′dle, *v.,* **-dled, -dling.**
o′ver•fool′ish, *adj.;* **-ly,** *adv.;* **-ness,** *n.*
o′ver•force′, *n.*
o′ver•force′, *v.,* **-forced, -forc•ing.**
o′ver•forged′, *adj.*
o′ver•for′mal•ize′, *v.,* **-ized, -iz•ing.**
o′ver•formed′, *adj.*
o′ver•for′ward, *adj.;* **-ly,** *adv.;* **-ness,** *n.*
o′ver•foul′, *adj.;* **-ly,** *adv.;* **-ness,** *n.*
o′ver•frag′ile, *adj.*
o′ver•frag′ment•ed, *adj.*
o′ver•frail′, *adj.;* **-ly,** *adv.;* **-ness,** *n.*
o′ver•frail′ty, *n.*
o′ver•fran′chised, *adj.*
o′ver•frank′, *adj.;* **-ly,** *adv.;* **-ness,** *n.*
o′ver•fraught′, *adj.*
o′ver•free′, *adj.;* **-ly,** *adv.*
o′ver•free′dom, *n.*
o′ver•freight′, *v.t.*
o′ver•fre′quen•cy, *n.*
o′ver•fre′quent, *adj.;* **-ly,** *adv.*
o′ver•fright′en, *v.t.*
o′ver•fru′gal, *adj.;* **-ly,** *adv.*
o′ver•fru•gal′i•ty, *n.*
o′ver•fruit′ful, *adj.;* **-ly,** *adv.;* **-ness,** *n.*
o′ver•frus•tra′tion, *n.*
o′ver•ful•fill′, *v.t.*
o′ver•func′tion•ing, *adj.*
o′ver•fund′, *n.*
o′ver•fund′, *v.t.*
o′ver•fur′nish, *v.t.*
o′ver•fuss′y, *adj.*
o′ver•gam′ble, *v.t.,* **-bled, -bling.**
o′ver•gar′nish, *v.t.*
o′ver•gar′ri•son, *v.t.*
o′ver•gen′er•os′i•ty, *n.*
o′ver•gen′er•ous, *adj.;* **-ly,** *adv.*
o′ver•gen′ial, *adj.;* **-ly,** *adv.;* **-ness,** *n.*
o′ver•ge′ni•al′i•ty, *n.*
o′ver•gen′tle, *adj.*
o′ver•gen′tly, *adv.*
o′ver•ges•tic′u•late′, *v.,* **-lat•ed, -lat•ing.**
o′ver•ges•tic′u•la′tion, *n.*
o′ver•ges•tic′u•la′tive, *adj.;* **-ly,** *adv.*
o′ver•gift′ed, *adj.*
o′ver•gird′, *v.t.,* **-gird•ed** or **-girt, -gird•ing.**
o′ver•glad′, *adj.;* **-ly,** *adv.*
o′ver•glam′or•ize′, *v.t.,* **-ized, -iz•ing.**
o′ver•glam′our•ize′, *v.t.,* **-ized, -iz•ing.**
o′ver•gloom′i•ly, *adv.*
o′ver•gloom′i•ness, *n.*
o′ver•gloom′y, *adj.*
o′ver•glut′, *v.t.,* **-glut•ted, -glut•ting.**
o′ver•gov′ern, *v.t.*
o′ver•gra′cious, *adj.;* **-ly,** *adv.;* **-ness,** *n.*
o′ver•grade′, *v.t.,* **-grad•ed, -grad•ing.**
o′ver•grad′u•at′ed, *adj.*
o′ver•grasp′ing, *adj.*
o′ver•grate′ful, *adj.;* **-ly,** *adv.;* **-ness,** *n.*
o′ver•grat′i•fi•ca′tion, *n.*
o′ver•grat′i•fy′, *v.t.,* **-fied, -fy•ing.**
o′ver•grat′i•tude′, *n.*
o′ver•greas′i•ness, *n.*
o′ver•greas′y, *adj.*
o′ver•great′, *adj.;* **-ly,** *adv.;* **-ness,** *n.*
o′ver•greed′i•ly, *adv.*
o′ver•greed′i•ness, *n.*
o′ver•greed′y, *adj.*
o′ver•grieve′, *v.,* **-grieved, -griev•ing.**
o′ver•griev′ous, *adj.;* **-ly,** *adv.;* **-ness,** *n.*
o′ver•gross′, *adj.;* **-ly,** *adv.;* **-ness,** *n.*
o′ver•guilt′y, *adj.*
o′ver•hand′i•cap′, *v.t.,* **-capped, -cap•ping.**
o′ver•han′dle, *v.t.,* **-dled, -dling.**
o′ver•hap′pi•ly, *adv.*
o′ver•hap′pi•ness, *n.*
o′ver•hap′py, *adj.*
o′ver•har′ass, *v.t.*

the point of proficiency or immediate recall. [1870–75; OVER- + LEARN]

o•ver•lie (ō′vər lī′), *v.t.,* **-lay, -lain, -ly•ing. 1.** to lie over or upon, as a covering or stratum. **2.** to smother (an infant) by lying upon it, as in sleep. [1125–75; ME *overlien, overliggen.* See OVER-, LIE[2]]

o•ver•line (ō′vər līn′), *n. Print., Journ.* **1.** a cutline, usually of one line, appearing over a picture, cartoon, etc. **2.** kicker (def. 10). [1850–55; OVER- + LINE[1]]

o•ver•load (*v.* ō′vər lōd′; *n.* ō′vər lōd′), *v.t.* **1.** to load to excess; overburden: *Don't overload the raft or it will sink.* —*n.* **2.** an excessive load. [1545–55; OVER- + LOAD]

o•ver•look (*v.* ō′vər lo͝ok′; *n.* ō′vər lo͝ok′), *v.t.* **1.** to fail to notice, perceive, or consider: *to overlook a misspelled word.* **2.** to disregard or ignore indulgently, as faults or misconduct: *Only a parent could overlook that kind of behavior.* **3.** to look over, as from a higher position: *a balcony that overlooks the ballroom.* **4.** to afford a view over; look down or out upon: *a hill overlooking the sea.* **5.** to rise above: *The Washington Monument overlooks the tidal basin.* **6.** to excuse; pardon: *a minor infraction we can overlook this time.* **7.** to look over in inspection, examination, or perusal: *They allowed us to overlook the proposed contract.* **8.** to look after, oversee, or supervise: *She has to overlook a large number of employees.* **9.** *Archaic.* to look upon with the evil eye; bewitch. —*n.* **10.** terrain, as on a cliff, that affords an attractive vista or a good view: *Miles of landscape could be seen from the overlook.* [1325–75; ME; see OVER-, LOOK]
—**Syn. 1.** miss. See **slight.**

o•ver•lord (ō′vər lôrd′), *n.* **1.** a person who is lord over another or over other lords: *to obey the will of one's sovereign and overlord.* **2.** a person of great influence, authority, power, or the like: *the overlords of industry.* —*v.t.* **3.** to rule or govern arbitrarily or tyrannically; domineer. [1150–1200; ME; see OVER-, LORD] —**o′ver•lord′ship,** *n.*

o•ver•ly (ō′vər lē), *adv.* excessively; too: *a voyage not overly dangerous.* [bef. 1050; ME; OE *oferlīce.* See OVER, -LY]
—**Syn.** needlessy, immoderately, inordinately.

o•ver•ly•ing (ō′vər lī′ing), *v.* ppr. of **overlie.**

o•ver•man (*n.* ō′vər mən *for 1,* ō′vər man′ *for 2; v.* ō′vər man′), *n., pl.* **-men** (-mən *for 1;* -men′ *for 2*), *v.,* **-manned, -man•ning.** —*n.* **1.** a foreman, supervisor, or overseer. **2.** a superman. —*v.t.* **3.** to oversupply with men, esp. for service: *Indiscriminate hiring had overmanned the factory.* [1200–1250; ME (n.); see OVER-, MAN[1]]

o•ver•man•tel (ō′vər man′tl), *adj.* **1.** situated above a mantelpiece. —*n.* **2.** an ornament or panel situated above a mantelpiece. [1880–85; OVER- + MANTEL]

o•ver•mas•ter (ō′vər mas′tər, -mä′stər), *v.t.* to gain mastery over; conquer; overpower: *The sudden impulse had quite overmastered me.* [1300–50; ME; see OVER-, MASTER] —**o′ver•mas′ter•ing•ly,** *adv.*

o•ver•match (ō′vər mach′), *v.t.* **1.** to be more than a match for; surpass; defeat: *an assignment that clearly overmatched his abilities; an able task force that overmatched the enemy fleet.* **2.** to match (a competitor) against another of superior strength, ability, or the like. [1300–50; ME *overmacchen.* See OVER-, MATCH[2]]

o•ver•mat•ter (ō′vər mat′ər), *n. Print.* overset (def. 6). [1885–90; OVER- + MATTER]

o•ver•meas•ure (ō′vər mezh′ər), *n.* an excessive or surplus measure or amount: *an overmeasure of exuberance.* [1575–85; OVER- + MEASURE]

o•ver•mod•u•la•tion (ō′vər moj′ə lā′shən), *n. Radio.* excessive amplitude modulation, resulting in distortion of a signal. [1925–30; OVER- + MODULATION]

o•ver•much (ō′vər much′), *adj., n., adv.* too much: *He didn't show overmuch concern. We tried not to regret it overmuch.* [1250–1300; ME; see OVER-, MUCH]

o•ver•night (*adv.* ō′vər nīt′; *adj., n.* ō′vər nīt′; *v.* ō′vər nīt′), *adv.* **1.** for or during the night: *to stay overnight.* **2.** on or during the previous evening: *Preparations were made overnight.* **3.** very quickly; suddenly: *New suburbs sprang up overnight.* —*adj.* **4.** done, made, occurring, or continuing during the night: *an overnight stop; an overnight decision.* **5.** staying for one night: *a group of overnight guests.* **6.** designed to be used on a trip or for a journey lasting one night or only a few nights. **7.** intended for delivery on the next day: *overnight letters; an overnight package.* **8.** valid for one night: *The corporal got an overnight pass.* **9.** occurring suddenly or within a very short time: *a comedian who became an overnight sensation.* —*n.* **10.** *Informal.* an overnight stay or trip: *Our daughter had an overnight at a friend's house.* **11.** *Informal.* a permit for overnight absence, as from a college dormitory: *She had an overnight the night of the prom.* **12.** the previous evening. —*v.i.* **13.** to have an overnight stay or trip: *We'll overnight in Denver, then fly on to San Diego.* [1325–75; ME; see OVER-, NIGHT]

overnight′ bag′, a travel bag large enough to hold personal articles and clothing for an overnight trip. Also called **overnight′ case′.** [1920–25]

o•ver•night•er (ō′vər nī′tər), *n.* **1.** an overnight stay or trip. **2.** a traveler or visitor making an overnight stay. **3.** something serving overnight travel, as a special train or an overnight bag. [1955–60; OVERNIGHT + -ER[1]]

overnight′ tel′egram, 1. a type of domestic telegram sent at a reduced rate with a minimum charge for 10 words or less and accepted until midnight for delivery the following day. **2.** the service offering such a telegram. *Abbr.:* OT Cf. **fast telegram, personal-opinion telegram.** Formerly, **night letter.** [1950–55]

o•ver•nu•tri•tion (ō′vər no͞o trish′ən, -nyo͞o-), *n.* the excessive intake of food, esp. in unbalanced proportions. [1895–1900; OVER- + NUTRITION]

o•ver•or•gan•ize (ō′vər ôr′gə nīz′), *v.t.,* **-ized, -iz•ing.** —*v.t.* **1.** to stress formal structure, status, rules, and details excessively. —*v.i.* **2.** to become overorganized. Also, *esp. Brit.,* **o′ver•or′gan•ise′.** [1895–1900; OVER- + ORGANIZE] —**o′ver•or′gan•i•za′tion,** *n.* —**o′ver•or′•gan•iz′er,** *n.*

o•ver•pass (*n.* ō′vər pas′, -päs′; *v.* ō′vər pas′, -päs′), *n., v.,* **-passed** or **-past, -pass•ing.** —*n.* **1.** a road, pedestrian walkway, railroad, bridge, etc., crossing over some barrier, as another road or walkway. —*v.t.* **2.** to pass over or traverse (a region, space, etc.): *We had overpassed the frontier during the night.* **3.** to pass beyond (specified limits, bounds, etc.); exceed; overstep; transgress: *to overpass the bounds of good judgment.* **4.** to get over (obstacles, difficulties, etc.); surmount: *to overpass the early days of privation and uncertainty.* **5.** to go beyond, exceed, or surpass: *Greed had somehow overpassed humanitarianism.* **6.** to pass through (time, experiences, etc.): *to overpass one's apprenticeship.* **7.** to overlook; ignore; disregard; omit: *We could hardly overpass such grievous faults. The board overpassed him when promotions were awarded.* —*v.i.* **8.** to pass over; pass by: *Under the bridge there was the din of cars overpassing.* [1250–1300; ME; see OVER-, PASS]

o•ver•pay (ō′vər pā′), *v.t.,* **-paid, -pay•ing. 1.** to pay more than (an amount due): *I received a credit after overpaying the bill.* **2.** to pay (a person) in excess. [1595–1605; OVER- + PAY[1]] —**o•ver•pay•ment** (ō′vər-pā′mənt, ō′vər pā′mənt), *n.*

o•ver•peo•ple (ō′vər pē′pəl), *v.t.,* **-pled, -pling.** to overpopulate: *The town has been overpeopled by those leaving the farms.* [1675–85; OVER- + PEOPLE]

o•ver•per•suade (ō′vər pər swād′), *v.t.,* **-suad•ed, -suad•ing. 1.** to persuade (a person) against his or her inclination or intention: *By threats and taunts they had overpersuaded him to steal the car.* **2.** to win or bring over by persuasion. [1615–25; OVER- + PERSUADE] —**o′ver•per•sua′sion,** *n.*

o•ver•play (ō′vər plā′), *v.t.* **1.** to exaggerate or overemphasize (one's role in a play, an emotion, an effect, etc.): *The young actor overplayed Hamlet shamelessly. The director of the movie had overplayed the pathos.* **2.** to put too much stress on the value or importance of: *A charitable biographer had overplayed the man's piety and benevolence.* **3.** *Cards.* to overestimate the strength of (the cards in one's hand) with consequent loss. **4.** *Golf.* to hit (the ball) past the putting green. **5.** *Archaic.* outplay. —*v.i.* **6.** to exaggerate one's part, an effect, etc.; overact: *Without a firm director she invariably overplays.* [1640–50; OVER- + PLAY]

o•ver•plus (ō′vər plus′), *n.* an excess over a particular amount; surplus: *After the harvest the overplus was distributed among the tenantry.* [1350–1400; ME; partial trans. of OF *surplus* SURPLUS]

o•ver•pop•u•late (ō′vər pop′yə lāt′), *v.t.,* **-lat•ed, -lat•ing.** to fill with an excessive number of people, straining available resources and facilities: *Expanding industry has overpopulated the western suburbs.* [1865–70; OVER- + POPULATE] —**o′ver•pop′u•la′tion,** *n.*

o•ver•po•ten•tial (ō′vər pə ten′shəl), *n. Elect.* overvoltage. [1915–20; OVER- + POTENTIAL]

o•ver•pow•er (ō′vər pou′ər), *v.t.* **1.** to overcome, master, or subdue by superior force: *to overpower a maniac.* **2.** to overcome or overwhelm in feeling; affect or impress excessively: *overpowered with confusion and desire.* **3.** to gain mastery over the bodily powers or mental faculties of: *a strong drink that quickly overpowered him.* **4.** to furnish or equip with excessive power: *a giant motor that overpowered the pump.* [1585–95; OVER- + POWER]
—**Syn. 1.** vanquish, subjugate, conquer, defeat, beat.

o•ver•pow•er•ing (ō′vər pou′ər ing), *adj.* that overpowers; overwhelming: *an overpowering conviction of the truth.* [1690–1700; OVERPOWER + -ING[2]] —**o′ver•pow′er•ing•ly,** *adv.* —**o′ver•pow′er•ing•ness,** *n.*

o•ver•praise (ō′vər prāz′), *v.,* **-praised, -prais•ing,** *n.* —*v.t.* **1.** to praise excessively or unduly. —*n.* **2.** excessive or undeserved praise. [1350–1400; ME *overpreisen* (v.); see OVER-, PRAISE]

o•ver•pres•sure (ō′vər presh′ər), *n., v.,* **-sured, -sur•ing.** —*n.* **1.** pressure in excess of normal atmospheric pressure, as that caused by an explosion's shock wave or created in an accelerating airplane. —*v.t.* **2.** to cause or expose to overpressure. **3.** to make undue demands on by a regimen, work load, etc.: *students overpressured with heavy academic schedules.* [1635–45; OVER- + PRESSURE] —**o′ver•pres′sur•i•za′tion,** *n.*

o•ver•price (ō′vər prīs′), *v.t.,* **-priced, -pric•ing.** to price excessively high; set too high a price on. [1595–1605; OVER- + PRICE]

o•ver•print (*v.* ō′vər print′; *n.* ō′vər print′), *v.t.* **1.** *Print.* to print additional material or another color on a form or sheet previously printed. —*n.* **2.** *Print.* a quantity of printing in excess of that desired; overrun. **3.** *Philately.* **a.** any word, inscription, or device written or printed on the face of a stamp that alters, limits, or describes its use, place of issue, or character. **b.** a stamp so marked. [1850–55; OVER- + PRINT]

o•ver•prize (ō′vər prīz′), *v.t.,* **-prized, -priz•ing.** to prize too highly; overvalue. [1580–90; OVER- + PRIZE[2]]

o•ver•pro•duce (ō′vər prə do͞os′, -dyo͞os′), *v.t., v.i.,* **-duced, -duc•ing.** to produce in excess of need or stipulated amount. [1890–95; OVER- + PRODUCE] —**o′ver•pro•duc′er,** *n.*

CONCISE PRONUNCIATION KEY: act, cāpe, dâre, pärt; set, ēqual; *if,* īce; ox, ōver, ôrder, oil, bo͝ok, bo͞ot, out; up, ûrge; child; sing; shoe; thin, *th*at; zh as in *treasure.* ə = *a* as in *alone, e* as in *system, i* as in *easily, o* as in *gallop, u* as in *circus;* ᵊ as in *fire* (fīᵊr), *hour* (ouᵊr). l and n can serve as syllabic consonants, as in *cradle* (krād′l), and *button* (but′n). See the full key inside the front cover.

o′ver•har′ass•ment, *n.*
o′ver•hard′, *adj.;* **-ness,** *n.*
o′ver•hard′en, *v.*
o′ver•har′dy, *adj.*
o′ver•harsh′, *adj.;* **-ly,** *adv.;* **-ness,** *n.*
o′ver•has′ten, *v.*
o′ver•haugh′ti•ly, *adv.*
o′ver•haugh′ti•ness, *n.*
o′ver•haugh′ty, *adj.*
o′ver•head′i•ness, *n.*
o′ver•head′y, *adj.*
o′ver•heap′, *v.t.*
o′ver•heart′i•ly, *adv.*
o′ver•heart′i•ness, *n.*
o′ver•heart′y, *adj.*
o′ver•heav′i•ly, *adv.*
o′ver•heav′i•ness, *n.*
o′ver•heav′y, *adj.*
o′ver•help′ful, *adj.;* **-ly,** *adv.;* **-ness,** *n.*
o′ver•high′, *adj.;* **-ly,** *adv.*
o′ver•home′li•ness, *n.*
o′ver•home′ly, *adj.*
o′ver•ho•mog′e•nize′, *v.t.,* **-nized, -niz•ing.**
o′ver•hon′est, *adj.;* **-ly,** *adv.;* **-ness,** *n.*
o′ver•hon′es•ty, *n.*
o′ver•hon′or, *v.t.*
o′ver•hos′tile, *adj.;* **-ly,** *adv.*
o′ver•hos•til′i•ty, *n.*
o′ver•hot′, *adj.;* **-ly,** *adv.*
o′ver•huge′, *adj.;* **-ly,** *adv.;* **-ness,** *n.*
o′ver•hu′man, *adj.*
o′ver•hu•mane′, *adj.*
o′ver•hu•man′i•ty, *n.*
o′ver•hu′man•ize′, *v.,* **-ized, -iz•ing.**
o′ver•hum′ble, *adj.;* **-ble•ness,** *n.;* **-bly,** *adv.*
o′ver•hunt′, *v.t.*
o′ver•hur′ried, *adj.;* **-ly,** *adv.*
o′ver•hur′ry, *v.,* **-ried, -ry•ing.**
o′ver•hype′, *v.t.,* **-hyped, -hyp•ing.**
o′ver•hys•ter′i•cal, *adj.*
o′ver•i•de′al•ism, *n.*
o′ver•i•de′al•is′tic, *adj.*
o′ver•i•de′al•ize′, *v.,* **-ized, -iz•ing.**
o′ver•i•den′ti•fi•ca′tion, *n.*
o′ver•i•den′ti•fy′, *v.,* **-fied, -fy•ing.**
o′ver•i′dle, *adj.;* **-ness,** *n.*
o′ver•i′dly, *adv.*
o′ver•i•dol′a•trous, *adj.;* **-ly,** *adv.;* **-ness,** *n.*
o′ver•il′lus•trate′, *v.t.,* **-trat•ed, -trat•ing.**
o′ver•il′lus•tra′tion, *n.*
o′ver•il•lus′tra•tive, *adj.;* **-ly,** *adv.*
o′ver•im•ag′i•na•tive, *adj.;* **-ly,** *adv.;* **-ness,** *n.*
o′ver•im′i•tate′, *v.t.,* **-tat•ed, -tat•ing.**
o′ver•im′i•ta′tion, *n.*
o′ver•im′i•ta′tive, *adj.;* **-ly,** *adv.;* **-ness,** *n.*
o′ver•im′mu•nize′, *v.t.,* **-nized, -niz•ing.**
o′ver•im•port′, *v.t.*
o′ver•im′por•ta′tion, *n.*
o′ver•im•pose′, *v.t.,* **-posed, -pos•ing.**
o′ver•im•press′, *v.t.*
o′ver•im•press′i•ble, *adj.;* **-bly,** *adv.*
o′ver•im•press′i•bil′i•ty, *n.*
o′ver•im•pres′sion•a•bil′i•ty, *n.*
o′ver•im•pres′sion•a•ble, *adj.;* **-ble•ness,** *n.;* **-bly,** *adv.*
o′ver•in•clin′a•ble, *adj.*
o′ver•in′cli•na′tion, *n.*
o′ver•in•cline′, *v.,* **-clined, -clin•ing.**
o′ver•in•debt′ed•ness, *n.*
o′ver•in′dex, *v.t.*
o′ver•in′dex•ing, *n.*
o′ver•in′di•vid′u•al•ism, *n.*
o′ver•in′di•vid′u•al•is′tic, *adj.*
o′ver•in′di•vid′u•al•is′ti•cal•ly, *adv.*
o′ver•in′di•vid′u•al•i•za′tion, *n.*
o′ver•in•dus′tri•al•ism, *n.*
o′ver•in•dus′tri•al•i•za′tion, *n.*
o′ver•in•dus′tri•al•ize′, *v.,* **-ized, -iz•ing.**
o′ver•in•flate′, *v.t.,* **-flat•ed, -flat•ing.**
o′ver•in•fla′tion, *n.*
o′ver•in•fla′tion•ar′y, *adj.*
o′ver•in′flu•ence, *v.t.,* **-enced, -enc•ing.**
o′ver•in′flu•en′tial, *adj.*
o′ver•in•form′, *v.t.*
o′ver•in•gen′ious, *adj.;* **-ly,** *adv.;* **-ness,** *n.*
o′ver•in•hib′it, *v.t.*
o′ver•in•hib′it•ed, *adj.*
o′ver•in•sist′, *v.i.*
o′ver•in•sist′ence, *n.*
o′ver•in•sist′en•cy, *n., pl.* **-cies.**
o′ver•in•sist′ent, *adj.;* **-ly,** *adv.*
o′ver•in′so•lence, *n.*
o′ver•in′so•lent, *adj.;* **-ly,** *adv.*
o′ver•in•struct′, *v.t.*
o′ver•in•struc′tion, *n.*
o′ver•in•struc′tive, *adj.;* **-ly,** *adv.;* **-ness,** *n.*
o′ver•in•sure′, *v.t.,* **-sured, -sur•ing.**
o′ver•in′tel•lec′tu•al, *adj.;* **-ly,** *adv.;* **-ness,** *n.*
o′ver•in′tel•lec′tu•al•ism, *n.*
o′ver•in′tel•lec′tu•al•i•za′tion, *n.*
o′ver•in′tel•lec′tu•al•ize′, *v.,* **-ized, -iz•ing.**
o′ver•in•tense′, *adj.;* **-ly,** *adv.;* **-ness,** *n.*
o′ver•in•ten′si•fi•ca′tion, *n.*
o′ver•in•ten′si•fy′, *v.,* **-fied, -fy•ing.**
o′ver•in•ten′si•ty, *n.*
o′ver•in′ter•est, *n.*
o′ver•in′ter•est•ed, *adj.;* **-ly,** *adv.;* **-ness,** *n.*
o′ver•in′ter•fer′ence, *n.*
o′ver•in•ter′pre•ta′tion, *n.*
o′ver•in′ven•to′ried, *adj.*
o′ver•in•vest′, *v.*
o′ver•in•vest′ment, *n.*
o′ver•in•volve′, *v.t.,* **-volved, -volv•ing.**
o′ver•i′o•dize′, *v.t.,* **-dized, -diz•ing.**
o′ver•ir′ri•gate′, *v.t.,* **-gat•ed, -gat•ing.**
o′ver•ir′ri•ga′tion, *n.*
o′ver•jade′, *v.t.,* **-jad•ed, -jad•ing**
o′ver•jeal′ous, *adj.;* **-ly,** *adv.;* **-ness,** *n.*
o′ver•joc′u•lar, *adj.;* **-ly,** *adv.*
o′ver•joc′u•lar′i•ty, *n.*
o′ver•joy′ful, *adj.;* **-ly,** *adv.;* **-ness,** *n.*
o′ver•joy′ous, *adj.;* **-ly,** *adv.;* **-ness,** *n.*
o′ver•ju•di′cious, *adj.;* **-ly,** *adv.;* **-ness,** *n.*
o′ver•keen′, *adj.;* **-ly,** *adv.;* **-ness,** *n.*
o′ver•kick′, *v.t.*
o′ver•kind′, *adj.;* **-ly,** *adv.;* **-ness,** *n.*
o′ver•la′bor, *v.t.*
o′ver•lac′tate, *v.i.,* **-tat•ed, -tat•ing.**
o′ver•lac•ta′tion, *n.*
o′ver•lard′, *v.t.*
o′ver•large′, *adj.*
o′ver•las•civ′i•ous, *adj.;* **-ly,** *adv.;* **-ness,** *n.*
o′ver•late′, *adj.;* **-ness,** *n.*
o′ver•lath′er, *v.t.*
o′ver•laud′, *v.t.*
o′ver•lau•da′tion, *n.*
o′ver•laud′a•to′ry, *adj.*
o′ver•lav′ish, *adj.;* **-ly,** *adv.;* **-ness,** *n.*
o′ver•lax′, *adj.;* **-ly,** *adv.;* **-ness,** *n.*

o·ver·pro·duc·tion (ō′vər prə duk′shən), *n.* excessive production; production in excess of need or stipulated amount. [1815–25; OVER- + PRODUCTION]

o·ver·pro·nounce (ō′vər prə nouns′), *v.*, **-nounced, -nounc·ing.** —*v.t.* **1.** to pronounce (a word, syllable, etc.) in an exaggerated, affected, or excessively careful manner. —*v.i.* **2.** to pronounce or speak overcarefully, affectedly, exaggeratedly, etc.: *When he overpronounces that way, he seems to be patronizing his audience.* [OVER- + PRONOUNCE] —**o·ver·pro·nun·ci·a·tion** (ō′vər prə nun′sē ā′shən), *n.*

o·ver·proof (ō′vər pro͞of′), *adj.* containing a greater proportion of alcohol than proof spirit does. [1800–10; OVER- + PROOF]

o·ver·pro·por·tion (*v.* ō′vər prə pôr′shən, -pōr′-; *n.* ō′vər prə pôr′shən, -pōr′-), *v.t.* **1.** to make or measure in excess of the correct, normal, or desired proportion. —*n.* **2.** the excessiveness of something in relation to another or to what is considered correct, desirable, or normal; inequity or imbalance: *the overproportion of insurance to income.* [1635–45; OVER- + PROPORTION] —**o′ver·pro·por′tion·ate,** *adj.* —**o′ver·pro·por′tion·ate·ly,** *adv.* —**o′ver·pro·por′tioned,** *adj.*

o·ver·pro·tec·tive (ō′vər prə tek′tiv), *adj.* unduly protective. [1925–30; OVER- + PROTECTIVE] —**o′ver·pro·tec′tive·ness,** *n.*

o·ver·proud (ō′vər proud′), *adj.* excessively proud. [bef. 1050; ME *over prowde,* OE *ofer-prūt.* See OVER-, PROUD] —**o′ver·proud′ly,** *adv.*

o·ver·qual·i·fied (ō′vər kwol′ə fīd′), *adj.* having more education, training, or experience than is required for a job or position. [1950–55; OVER- + QUALIFIED]

o·ver·quick (ō′vər kwik′), *adj.* too quick: *Let's not be overquick to criticize.* [1530–40; OVER- + QUICK] —**o′ver·quick′ly,** *adv.*

o·ver·rake (ō′vər rāk′), *v.t.*, **-raked, -rak·ing.** *Naut.* (of water) to break over the bow of (a ship) in a solid mass. [1590–1600; OVER- + RAKE[1]]

o·ver·ran (ō′vər ran′), *v.* pt. of **overrun.**

o·ver·rate (ō′vər rāt′), *v.t.*, **-rat·ed, -rat·ing.** to rate or appraise too highly; overestimate: *I think you overrate their political influence.* [1580–90; OVER- + RATE[1]] —**Syn.** overpraise, overesteem, magnify.

o·ver·reach (ō′vər rēch′), *v.t.* **1.** to reach or extend over or beyond: *The shelf overreached the nook and had to be planed down.* **2.** to go beyond, as a thing aimed at or sought: *an arrow that had overreached the target.* **3.** to stretch to excess, as by a straining effort: *to overreach one's arm and strain a muscle.* **4.** to defeat (oneself) by overdoing matters, often by excessive eagerness or cunning: *In trying to promote disunity he had overreached himself.* **5.** to strain or exert (oneself or itself) to the point of exceeding the purpose. **6.** to get the better of, esp. by deceit or trickery; outwit: *Every time you deal with them you wonder if they're overreaching you.* **7.** to overtake. **8.** *Obs.* to overpower. —*v.i.* **9.** to reach or extend over something. **10.** to reach too far: *In grabbing for the rope he overreached and fell.* **11.** to cheat others. **12.** (of a running or walking horse) to strike, or strike and injure, the forefoot with the hind foot. **13.** *Naut.* to sail on a tack longer than is desirable or was intended; overstand. [1250–1300; ME; see OVER-, REACH] —**o′ver·reach′er,** *n.*

o·ver·re·act (ō′vər rē akt′), *v.i.* to react or respond more strongly than is necessary or appropriate. [1960–65; OVER- + REACT] —**o′ver·re·ac′tion,** *n.*

o·ver·re·fine (ō′vər ri fīn′), *v.t.*, **-fined, -fin·ing.** to refine excessively, as with oversubtle distinctions. [1705–15; OVER- + REFINE]

o·ver·re·fine·ment (ō′vər ri fīn′mənt), *n.* excessive or unnecessary refinement. [1705–15; OVER- + REFINEMENT]

o·ver·ride (*v.* ō′vər rīd′; *n.* ō′vər rīd′), *v.*, **-rode, -rid·den, -rid·ing,** *n.* —*v.t.* **1.** to prevail or have dominance over; have final authority or say over; overrule: *to override one's advisers.* **2.** to disregard, set aside, or nullify; countermand: *to override the board's veto.* **3.** to take precedence over; preempt or supersede: *to override any other considerations.* **4.** to extend beyond or spread over; overlap. **5.** to modify or suspend the ordinary functioning of; alter the normal operation of. **6.** to ride over or across. **7.** to ride past or beyond. **8.** to trample or crush; ride down. **9.** to ride (a horse) too much. **10.** *Fox Hunting.* to ride too closely behind (the hounds). —*n.* **11.** a commission on sales or profits, esp. one paid at the executive or managerial level. **12.** budgetary or expense increase; exceeding of an estimate: *work stoppage because of cost overrides.* **13.** an ability or allowance to correct, change, supplement, or suspend the operation of an otherwise automatic mechanism, system, etc. **14.** an auxiliary device for such modification, as a special manual control. **15.** an act of nullifying, canceling, or setting aside: *a Congressional override of the President's veto.* **16.** *Radio and Television Slang.* something that is a dominant or major facet of a program or series, esp. something that serves as a unifying theme: *an entertainment series with a historical override.* [bef. 900; ME *overriden* to ride over or across, OE *oferrīdan.* See OVER-, RIDE]

o·ver·rid·ing (ō′vər rī′ding), *adj.* taking precedence over all other considerations. [1820–30; OVERRIDE + -ING[2]]

o·ver·ripe (ō′vər rīp′), *adj.* too ripe; more than ripe: *overripe tomatoes.* [1665–75; OVER- + RIPE] —**o′ver·ripe′ly,** *adv.* —**o′ver·ripe′ness,** *n.*

o·ver·ruff (*v.* ō′vər ruf′; *n.* ō′vər ruf′), *Cards.* —*v.t., v.i.* **1.** to overtrump. —*n.* **2.** the act of overtrumping. [1805–15; OVER- + RUFF[2]]

o·ver·rule (ō′vər ro͞ol′), *v.t.*, **-ruled, -rul·ing.** **1.** to rule against or disallow the arguments of (a person): *The senator was overruled by the committee chairman.* **2.** to rule or decide against (a plea, argument, etc.); reject: *to overrule an objection.* **3.** to prevail over so as to change the purpose or action: *a delay that overruled our plans.* **4.** to exercise control or influence over: *belief in a beneficent deity that overrules the universe.* [1570–80; OVER- + RULE] —**o′ver·rul′er,** *n.* —**o′ver·rul′ing·ly,** *adv.*

o·ver·run (*v.* ō′vər run′; *n.* ō′vər run′), *v.*, **-ran, -run, -run·ning,** *n.* —*v.t.* **1.** to rove over (a country, region, etc.); invade; ravage: *a time when looting hordes had overrun the province.* **2.** to swarm over in great numbers, as animals, esp. vermin; infest: *The house had been overrun by rats.* **3.** to spread or grow rapidly over, as plants, esp. vines, weeds, etc.: *a garden overrun with weeds.* **4.** to attack and defeat decisively, occupying and controlling the enemy's position; overwhelm. **5.** to spread rapidly throughout, as a new idea or spirit: *a rekindling of scholarship that had overrun Europe.* **6.** to run or go beyond, as a certain limit: *The new jet overran the landing field.* **7.** to exceed, as a budget or estimate: *to overrun one's allotted time.* **8.** to run over; overflow: *During the flood season, the river overruns its banks for several miles.* **9.** *Print.* **a.** to print additional copies of (a book, pamphlet, etc.) in excess of the original or the usual order. **b.** to carry over (type or words) to another page. **10.** *Naut.* **a.** to sail past (an intended stopping or turning point) by accident. **b.** (of a ship) to complete (a schedule of calls) more rapidly than anticipated. **11.** to outrun; overtake in running. —*v.i.* **12.** to run over; overflow: *a stream that always overruns at springtime.* **13.** to exceed the proper, desired, or normal quantity, limit, order, etc.: *Do you want to overrun on this next issue?* —*n.* **14.** an act or instance of overrunning. **15.** an amount in excess; surplus: *an overrun of 10,000 copies of a new book.* **16.** the exceeding of estimated costs in design, development, and production, esp. as estimated in a contract: *a staggering overrun on the new fighter plane.* **17.** the amount exceeded: *an overrun of $500,000 for each fighter plane.* **18.** a run on an item of manufacture beyond the quantity ordered by a customer and often offered at a discount. **19.** the amount by which the volume of a food, as butter or ice cream, is increased above the original volume by the inclusion of air, water, or another substance: *With only a 20 percent overrun, this is an excellent ice cream.* [bef. 900; ME *overrennen,* OE *oferyrnan.* See OVER-, RUN]

o·ver·scale (ō′vər skāl′), *adj.* larger or more extensive than normal or usual; outsize; oversize. [OVER- + SCALE[3]]

o·ver·score (ō′vər skôr′, -skōr′), *v.t.*, **-scored, -scor·ing.** to score over, as with strokes or lines. [1840–50; OVER- + SCORE]

o·ver·scru·pu·lous (ō′vər skro͞o′pyə ləs), *adj.* excessively scrupulous. [1590–1600; OVER- + SCRUPULOUS] —**o′ver·scru′pu·lous·ly,** *adv.* —**o′ver·scru′pu·lous·ness,** *n.*

o·ver·seas (*adv., n.* ō′vər sēz′; *adj.* ō′vər sēz′), *adv.* **1.** over, across, or beyond the sea; abroad: *to be sent overseas.* —*adj.* **2.** of or pertaining to passage over the sea: *overseas travel.* **3.** situated beyond the sea: *overseas territories.* **4.** pertaining to countries, associations, activities, etc., beyond the sea: *overseas military service; overseas commitments.* —*n.* **5.** (*used with a singular v.*) countries or territories across the sea or ocean. Also, *esp. Brit.,* **o·ver·sea** (*adv.* ō′vər sē′; *adj.* ō′vər sē′) (for defs. 1–4). [bef. 1150; *oversea* (ME *overse,* OE *ofer sǣ;* see OVER-, SEA) + -s[3] or -s[1]]

overseas′ cap′, *Mil.* a wedge-shaped cap of cotton or woolen fabric, worn as part of the service uniform. Also called **flight cap, garrison cap.**

o·ver·see (ō′vər sē′), *v.t.*, **-saw, -seen, -see·ing.** **1.** to direct (work or workers); supervise; manage: *He was hired to oversee the construction crews.* **2.** to see or observe secretly or unintentionally: *We happened to oversee the burglar leaving the premises. He was overseen stealing the letters.* **3.** to survey or watch, as from a higher position. **4.** to look over; examine; inspect. [bef. 900; ME *overseen,* OE *oferseōn.* See OVER-, SEE[1]]

o·ver·se·er (ō′vər sē′ər, -sēr′), *n.* a person who oversees; supervisor; manager: *the overseer of a plantation.* [1350–1400; ME; see OVERSEE, -ER[1]] —**Syn.** chief, head, boss, director.

o·ver·sell (ō′vər sel′), *v.*, **-sold, -sell·ing.** —*v.t.* **1.** to sell more of (a stock, product, etc.) than can be delivered. **2.** to sell aggressively, as by using high-pressure merchandising techniques. **3.** to emphasize the good points of excessively and to a self-defeating extent: *She so oversold the picnic that I became convinced I'd have a better time at the movies.* —*v.i.* **4.** to sell something aggressively. **5.** to make extreme claims for something or someone. [1570–80; OVER- + SELL[1]]

o·ver·sen·si·tive (ō′vər sen′si tiv), *adj.* excessively or unduly sensitive. [1840–50; OVER- + SENSITIVE] —**o′ver·sen′si·tiv′i·ty, o′ver·sen′si·tive·ness,** *n.*

o·ver·set (*v.* ō′vər set′; *n.* ō′vər set′), *v.*, **-set, -set·ting,** *n.* —*v.t.* **1.** to upset or overturn; overthrow. **2.** to throw into confusion; disorder physically or mentally. —*v.i.* **3.** to become upset, overturned, or overthrown. **4.** *Print.* **a.** (of type or copy) to set in or to excess. **b.** (of space) to set too much type for. —*n.* **5.** the act or fact of oversetting; upset; overturn. **6.** Also called **overmatter.** *Print.* matter set up in excess of space. [1150–1200; ME *oversetten;* see OVER-, SET] —**o′ver·set′ter,** *n.*

o·ver·sew (ō′vər sō′, ō′vər sō′), *v.t.*, **-sewed, -sewn** or **-sewed, -sew·ing.** to sew with stitches passing successively over an edge, esp. closely, so as to cover the edge or make a firm seam. [1860–65; OVER- + SEW[1]]

CONCISE ETYMOLOGY KEY: <, descended or borrowed from; >, whence; b., blend of, blended; c., cognate with; cf., compare; deriv., derivative; equiv., equivalent; imit., imitative; obl., oblique; r., replacing; s., stem; sp., spelling, spelled; resp., respelling, respelled; trans., translation; ?, origin unknown; *, unattested; ‡, probably earlier than. See the full key inside the front cover.

o′ver·learn′ed, *adj.;* **-ly,** *adv.;* **-ness,** *n.*
o′ver·leg′is·late′, *v.,* **-lat·ed, -lat·ing.**
o′ver·lend′, *v.,* **-lent, -lend′ing.**
o′ver·lib′er·al, *adj;* **-ly,** *adv.*
o′ver·lib′er·al′i·ty, *n.*
o′ver·lib′er·al·i·za′tion, *n.*
o′ver·lib′er·al·ize′, *v.,* **-ized, -iz·ing.**
o′ver·li·cen′tious, *adj.;* **-ly,** *adv.;* **-ness,** *n.*
o′ver·light′, *adj.;* **-ly,** *adv.;* **-ness,** *n.*
o′ver·light′, *n.*
o′ver·lik′ing, *n.*
o′ver·lim′it, *v.t.*
o′ver·lin′ger, *v.i.*
o′ver·lit′er·al, *adj.*
o′ver·lit′er·ar′i·ly, *adv.*
o′ver·lit′er·ar′i·ness, *n.*
o′ver·lit′er·ar′y, *adj.*
o′ver·live′, *v.,* **-lived, -liv·ing.**
o′ver·live′li·ness, *n.*
o′ver·live′ly, *adj.*
o′ver·liv′er, *n.*
o′ver·loan′, *v.t., n.*
o′ver·loath′, *adj.*
o′ver·loft′i·ly, *adv.*
o′ver·loft′i·ness, *n.*
o′ver·loft′y, *adj.*
o′ver·log′i·cal, *adj.;* **-ly,** *adv.;* **-ness,** *n.*
o′ver·log′i·cal′i·ty, *n.*
o′ver·long′, *adj., adv.*
o′ver·loose′, *adj.;* **-ly,** *adv.;* **-ness,** *n.*
o′ver·loud′, *adj.;* **-ly,** *adv.;* **-ness,** *n.*
o′ver·love′, *v.,* **-loved, -lov·ing.**
o′ver·low′ness, *n.*
o′ver·loy′al, *adj.;* **-ly,** *adv.*
o′ver·loy′al·ty, *n., pl.* **-ties.**
o′ver·lu′bri·cate′, *v.t.,* **-cat·ed, -cat·ing.**
o′ver·lu′bri·ca′tion, *n.*
o′ver·lus′cious, *adj.;* **-ly,** *adv.;* **-ness,** *n.*
o′ver·lush′, *adj.;* **-ly,** *adv.;* **-ness,** *n.*
o′ver·lust′i·ness, *n.*
o′ver·lust′y, *adj.*
o′ver·lux·u′ri·ance, *n.*
o′ver·lux·u′ri·ant, *adj.;* **-ly,** *adv.*
o′ver·lux·u′ri·ous, *adj.;* **-ly,** *adv.;* **ness,** *n.*
o′ver·mag·net′ic, *adj.*
o′ver·mag·net′i·cal·ly, *adv.*
o′ver·mag′ni·fi·ca′tion, *n.*
o′ver·mag′ni·fy, *v.t.,* **-fied, -fy·ing.**
o′ver·mag′ni·tude′, *n.*
o′ver·man′age, *v.t.,* **-aged, -ag·ing.**
o′ver·man′nered, *adj.*
o′ver·man′y, *adj.*
o′ver·march′, *v.*
o′ver·mast′, *v.t.*
o′ver·mas′ter·ful, *adj.;* **-ly,** *adv.;* **-ness,** *n.*
o′ver·ma·ture′, *adj.;* **-ly,** *adv.;* **-ness,** *n.*
o′ver·ma·tu′ri·ty, *n.*
o′ver·mean′, *adj.;* **-ly,** *adv.;* **-ness,** *n.*
o′ver·med′dle, *v.i.,* **-dled, -dling.**
o′ver·med′i·cate′, *v.t.,* **-cat·ed, -cat·ing.**
o′ver·med′i·ca′tion, *n.*
o′ver·meek′, *adj.;* **-ly,** *adv.;* **-ness,** *n.*
o′ver·mel′low, *adj.;* **-ly,** *adv.;* **-ness,** *n.*
o′ver·me·lo′di·ous, *adj.;* **-ly,** *adv.;* **-ness,** *n.*
o′ver·melt′, *v.,* **-melt·ed, -melt·ed** or **-mol·ten, -melt·ing.**
o′ver·mer′ci·ful, *adj.;* **-ly,** *adv.;* **-ness,** *n.*
o′ver·mer′it, *v.*
o′ver·mer′ri·ly, *adv.*
o′ver·mer′ri·ment, *n.*
o′ver·mer′ri·ness, *n.*
o′ver·mer′ry, *adj.*
o′ver·met′tled, *adj.*
o′ver·might′y, *adj.*
o′ver·mild′, *adj.*
o′ver·mil′i·ta·ris′tic, *adj.*
o′ver·mil′i·ta·ris′ti·cal·ly, *adv.*
o′ver·milk′, *v.*
o′ver·mill′, *v.t.*
o′ver·mine′, *v.,* **-mined, -min·ing.**
o′ver·mi·nute′, *adj.;* **-ly,** *adv.;* **-ness,** *n.*
o′ver·mit′i·gate′, *v.,* **-gat·ed, -gat·ing.**
o′ver·mix′, *v.*
o′ver·mo′bi·lize′, *v.,* **-lized, -liz·ing.**
o′ver·mod′ern·i·za′tion, *n.*
o′ver·mod′ern·ize′, *v.,* **-ized, -iz·ing.**
o′ver·mod′est, *adj.;* **-ly,** *adv.*
o′ver·mod′est·y, *n.*
o′ver·mod′i·fi·ca′tion, *n.*
o′ver·mod′i·fy′, *v.,* **-fied, -fy·ing.**
o′ver·moist′, *adj.*
o′ver·mois′ten, *v.*
o′ver·mo·nop′o·lize′, *v.t.,* **-lized, -liz·ing.**
o′ver·mor′al, *adj.;* **-ly,** *adv.*
o′ver·mor′al·is′tic, *adj.*
o′ver·mor′al·ize′, *v.,* **-ized, -iz·ing.**
o′ver·mor′al·iz′ing·ly, *adv.*
o′ver·mort′gage, *v.,* **-gaged, -gag·ing.**
o′ver·mourn′, *v.*
o′ver·mourn′ful, *adj.;* **-ly,** *adv.;* **-ness,** *n.*
o′ver·mul′ti·pli·ca′tion, *n.*
o′ver·mul′ti·ply′, *v.,* **-plied, -ply·ing.**
o′ver·mus′cled, *adj.*
o′ver·mys′ti·fi·ca′tion, *n.*
o′ver·mys′ti·fy′, *v.t.,* **-fied, -fy·ing.**
o′ver·nar′row, *adj.;* **-ly,** *adv.;* **-ness,** *n.*
o′ver·na′tion·al·i·za′tion, *n.*
o′ver·na′tion·al·ize′, *v.t.,* **-ized, -iz·ing.**
o′ver·near′, *adj., adv.;* **-ness,** *n.*
o′ver·neat′, *adj.;* **-ly,** *adv.;* **-ness,** *n.*
o′ver·ne·glect′, *v.t.*
o′ver·ne·glect′ful, *adj.;* **-ly,** *adv.;* **-ness,** *n.*
o′ver·neg′li·gence, *n.*
o′ver·neg′li·gent, *adj.;* **-ly,** *adv.*
o′ver·nerv′ous, *adj.;* **-ly,** *adv.;* **-ness,** *n.*
o′ver·neu′tral·i·za′tion, *n.*
o′ver·neu′tral·ize′, *v.t.,* **-ized, -iz·ing.**
o′ver·neu′tral·iz′er, *n.*
o′ver·nice′, *adj.;* **-ly,** *adv.;* **-ness,** *n.*
o′ver·ni′ce·ty, *n., pl.* **-ties.**
o′ver·no′ble, *adj.;* **-ble·ness,** *n.;* **-bly,** *adv.*
o′ver·nor′mal, *adj.;* **-ly,** *adv.*
o′ver·nor·mal′i·ty, *n.*
o′ver·nor′mal·i·za′tion, *n.*
o′ver·nor′mal·ize′, *v.t.,* **-ized, -iz·ing.**
o′ver·nour′ish, *v.t.*
o′ver·nour′ish·ing·ly, *adv.*
o′ver·nour′ish·ment, *n.*
o′ver·nu′mer·ous, *adj.;* **-ly,** *adv.;* **-ness,** *n.*
o′ver·nurse′, *v.t.,* **-nursed, -nurs·ing.**
o′ver·o·be′di·ence, *n.*
o′ver·o·be′di·ent, *adj.;* **-ly,** *adv.*
o′ver·o·bese′, *adj.;* **-ly,** *adv.;* **-ness,** *n.*
o′ver·o·be′si·ty, *n.*
o′ver·ob·ject′, *v.*
o′ver·ob·jec′ti·fi·ca′tion, *n.*
o′ver·ob·jec′ti·fy′, *v.t.,* **-fied, -fy·ing.**
o′ver·ob·se′qui·ous, *adj.;* **-ly,** *adv.;* **-ness,** *n.*

o•ver•sexed (ō′vər sekst′), *adj.* having an unusually strong sexual drive. [1895–1900; OVER- + SEXED]

o•ver•shade (ō′vər shād′), *v.t.,* **-shad•ed, -shad•ing.** **1.** to cast shade over. **2.** to make dark or gloomy. [1580–90; OVER- + SHADE]

o•ver•shad•ow (ō′vər shad′ō), *v.t.* **1.** to be more important or significant by comparison: *For years he overshadowed his brother.* **2.** to cast a shadow over; cover with shadows, clouds, darkness, etc.; darken or obscure: *clouds overshadowing the moon.* **3.** to make sad or hang heavily over; cast a pall on: *a disappointment that overshadowed their last years.* **4.** *Archaic.* to shelter or protect. [bef. 900; ME *overshadewen,* OE *ofersceadwian.* See OVER-, SHADOW] **—o′ver•shad′ow•er,** *n.* **—o′ver•shad′ow•ing•ly,** *adv.*
—Syn. 1. eclipse, outshine, dwarf.

o•ver•shine (ō′vər shīn′), *v.t.,* **-shone** or **-shined, -shin•ing. 1.** to outshine: *One star seemed to overshine all others.* **2.** to surpass in splendor, excellence, etc.: *Her singing overshone that of the opera company's more widely known contraltos.* **3.** to shine over or upon. [bef. 1000; ME *overshinen;* OE *oferscinan.* See OVER-, SHINE]

o•ver•shirt (ō′vər shûrt′), *n.* a pullover sport shirt, worn outside the waistband of a skirt or pair of slacks. [1795–1805; OVER- + SHIRT]

o•ver•shoe (ō′vər shōō′), *n.* a shoe or boot usually worn over another for protection in wet or cold weather, esp. a waterproof outer shoe. Cf. **galosh.** [1570–80; OVER- + SHOE]

o•ver•shoot (*v.* ō′vər shōōt′; *n.* ō′vər shōōt′), *v.,* **-shot, -shoot•ing,** *n.* —*v.t.* **1.** to shoot or go over, beyond, or above; miss: *The missile overshot its target.* **2.** to pass or go by or beyond (a point, limit, etc.): *to overshoot a stop sign.* **3.** to shoot or pour down over: *turbulent water overshooting the top of the dam.* **4.** to overreach (oneself or itself); go further than is intended or proper; go too far: *It looked as though his self-confidence had overshot itself.* **5.** (of an aircraft or pilot) to fly too far along (a landing strip) in attempting to land. —*v.i.* **6.** to fly or go beyond. **7.** to shoot over or above a mark. —*n.* **8.** a shooting beyond a specified point or target: *two overshoots in the missile test series.* **9.** the amount of excessive distance in a trajectory or route: *a two-mile overshoot on the artillery range.* [1325–75; ME; see OVER-, SHOOT]

o•ver•shot (*adj., n.* ō′vər shot′; *v.* ō′vər shot′), *adj.* **1.** driven over the top of, as by water passing over from above. **2.** having the upper jaw projecting beyond the lower, as a dog. —*v.* **3.** pt. and pp. of **overshoot.** —*n.* **4.** (in weaving) a pattern formed when filling threads are passed over several warp threads at a time. [1525–35; OVER- + SHOT[1]]

o′vershot wheel′, a water wheel in which the water enters the buckets tangentially near the top of the wheel. [1665–75]

o•ver•side (ō′vər sīd′), *adv.* **1.** over the side, as of a ship. **2.** on the opposite side (of a phonograph record): *Overside we are given an example of early Ellington.* —*adj.* **3.** effected over the side of a ship: *overside delivery of cargo.* **4.** placed or located on the opposite side (of a phonograph record): *The overside selections are more agreeably sung.* —*n.* **5.** the opposite side (of a phonograph record): *On the overside we have a potpourri of Strauss waltzes.* [1880–85; short for *over the side*]

o•ver•sight (ō′vər sīt′), *n.* **1.** an omission or error due to carelessness: *My bank statement is full of oversights.* **2.** unintentional failure to notice or consider; lack of proper attention: *Owing to my oversight, the letter was sent unsigned.* **3.** supervision; watchful care: *a person responsible for the oversight of the organization.* [1300–50; ME; see OVER-, SIGHT]
—Syn. 1, 2. mistake, blunder, slip. **2.** lapse, neglect, inattention. **3.** management, direction, control; surveillance.

o•ver•sim•pli•fy (ō′vər sim′plə fī′), *v.t., v.i.,* **-fied, -fy•ing.** to simplify to the point of error, distortion, or misrepresentation. [1920–25; OVER- + SIMPLIFY] **—o′ver•sim′pli•fi•ca′tion,** *n.*

o•ver•size (*adj.* ō′vər sīz′; *n.* ō′vər sīz′), *adj.* Also, **o′ver•sized′. 1.** of excessive size; unusually large: *an oversize cigar.* **2.** of a size larger than is necessary or required. —*n.* **3.** something that is oversize; an oversize article or object. **4.** a size larger than the proper or usual size. [1605–15; OVER- + SIZE[1]]

o•ver•skirt (ō′vər skûrt′), *n.* **1.** an outer skirt. **2.** a skirt worn over the skirt of a dress and caught up or draped to reveal it. [1865–70, *Amer.;* OVER- + SKIRT]

o•ver•slaugh (ō′vər slô′), *v.t.* to pass over or disregard (a person) by giving a promotion, position, etc., to another instead. [1765–75; < D *overslaan,* equiv. to *over-* OVER- + *slaan* to strike; cf. G *überschlagen;* see SLAY]

o•ver•sleep (ō′vər slēp′), *v.,* **-slept, -sleep•ing.** —*v.i.* **1.** to sleep beyond the proper or intended time of waking: *He overslept and missed his train.* —*v.t.* **2.** to sleep beyond (a certain hour): *She had overslept her usual time of arising.* **3.** to let (oneself) sleep past the hour of arising: *Of all mornings to oversleep myself!* [1350–1400; ME; see OVER-, SLEEP]

o•ver•slip (ō′vər slip′), *v.t.,* **-slipped** or **-slipt, -slip•ping.** *Obs.* **1.** to leave out; miss. **2.** to elude; evade. [1375–1425; late ME; see OVER-, SLIP[1]]

o•ver•sold (ō′vər sōld′), *v.* **1.** pt. and pp. of **oversell.** —*adj.* **2.** marked by prices considered unjustifiably low because of heavy and extensive selling: *The stock market is oversold.* Cf. **overbought.** [1875–80; OVER- + SOLD]

o•ver•so•lic•i•tous (ō′vər sə lis′i təs), *adj.* too solicitous: *oversolicitous concerning one's health.* [1655–65; OVER- + SOLICITOUS]

o•ver•soul (ō′vər sōl′), *n. Philos.* (esp. in transcendentalism) a supreme reality or mind; the spiritual unity of all being. [1841–44, *Amer.;* OVER- + SOUL]

o•ver•spe•cial•i•za•tion (ō′vər spesh′ə lə zā′shən), *n.* excessive specialization, as in a field of study. [1930–35; OVER- + SPECIALIZATION]

o•ver•spend (ō′vər spend′), *v.,* **-spent, -spend•ing.** —*v.i.* **1.** to spend more than one can afford: *Receiving a small inheritance, she began to overspend alarmingly.* —*v.t.* **2.** to spend in excess of: *He was overspending his yearly salary by several thousand dollars.* **3.** to spend beyond one's means (used reflexively): *When the bills arrived, he realized he had foolishly overspent himself.* **4.** to wear out; exhaust. [1580–90; OVER- + SPEND]

o•ver•spill (*v.* ō′vər spil′; *n.* ō′vər spil′), *v.,* **-spilled** or **-spilt, -spill•ing,** *n.* —*v.i.* **1.** to spill over. —*n.* **2.** the act of spilling over. **3.** something that spills over. **4.** *Brit.* overflow. [1850–55; OVER- + SPILL[1]]

o•ver•spin (ō′vər spin′), *n.* See **top spin.** [1635–45; OVER- + SPIN]

o•ver•spread (ō′vər spred′), *v.t.,* **-spread, -spread•ing.** to spread or diffuse over: *A blush of embarrassment overspread his face.* [bef. 1000; ME *overspreden,* OE *ofersprǣdan.* See OVER-, SPREAD]

o•ver•stand (ō′vər stand′), *v.i.,* **-stood, -stand•ing.** *Naut.* overreach (def. 13). [1300–50; ME *overstonden* to stand over or by; see OVER-, STAND]

o•ver•state (ō′vər stāt′), *v.t.,* **-stat•ed, -stat•ing.** to state too strongly; exaggerate: *to overstate one's position in a controversy.* [1630–40; OVER- + STATE] **—o′ver•state′ment,** *n.*
—Syn. overstress, embroider, magnify.

o•ver•stay (ō′vər stā′), *v.t.* **1.** to stay beyond the time, limit, or duration of; outstay: *to overstay one's welcome.* **2.** *Finance.* to remain in (the market) beyond the point where a sale would have yielded the greatest profit. [1640–50; OVER- + STAY[1]]

o•ver•steer (*n.* ō′vər stēr′; *v.* ō′vər stēr′), *n.* **1.** handling of an automotive vehicle that causes turns that are sharper than the driver intends because the rear wheels slide to the outside of the turn before the front wheels lose traction. —*v.i.* **2.** (of an automotive vehicle) to undergo or handle with an oversteer, esp. excessively. Cf. **understeer.** [1935–40; OVER- + STEER[1]]

o•ver•step (ō′vər step′), *v.t.,* **-stepped, -step•ping.** to go beyond; exceed: *to overstep one's authority.* [bef. 1000; ME *oversteppen,* OE *ofersteppan.* See OVER-, STEP]

o•ver•stitch (*n.* ō′vər stich′; *v.* ō′vər stich′), *Sewing.* —*n.* **1.** a stitch made with a sewing machine, for binding or finishing a raw edge or hem. —*v.t., v.i.* **2.** to sew with overstitches. [OVER- + STITCH]

o•ver•stock (*v.* ō′vər stok′; *n.* ō′vər stok′), *v.t.* **1.** to stock to excess: *We are overstocked on this item.* —*n.* **2.** a stock that is larger than the actual need or demand. [1555–65; OVER- + STOCK]

o•ver•stood (ō′vər stŏŏd′), *v.* pt. and pp. of **overstand.**

o•ver•sto•ry (ō′vər stôr′ē, -stōr′ē), *n., pl.* **-ries.** the uppermost layer of foliage in a forest, forming the canopy. [1480–90, for an earlier sense; 1955–60 for current sense; OVER- + STORY[2]]

o•ver•stress (ō′vər stres′), *v.t.* **1.** overemphasize. **2.** to subject to excessive stress or strain. **3.** *Mech.* to stress (a metal or other body) to the point of deformation. [1915–20; OVER- + STRESS]

o•ver•stretch (*v.* ō′vər strech′; *n.* ō′vər strech′, ō′vər strech′), *v.t.* **1.** to stretch excessively. **2.** to stretch or extend over. —*n.* **3.** an act or instance of overstretching. [1300–50; ME *overstrecchen;* see OVER-, STRETCH]

o•ver•strew (ō′vər strōō′), *v.t.,* **-strewed, -strewn** or **-strewed, -strew•ing.** to strew or scatter over. [1560–70; OVER- + STREW]

o•ver•stride (ō′vər strīd′), *v.t.,* **-strode, -strid•den, -strid•ing. 1.** to surpass: *to overstride one's competitors.* **2.** to stand or sit astride of; bestride: *a great statue overstriding the entrance; to overstride a horse.* **3.** to tower over; dominate: *He overstrides the committee with loud aggressiveness.* **4.** to stride or step over or across: *At its narrowest point, one can easily overstride the stream.* **5.** to stride more rapidly than or beyond: *a downward path where she easily overstrode her companion.* [1150–1200; ME; see OVER-, STRIDE]

o•ver•strike (*v.* ō′vər strīk′; *n.* ō′vər strīk′), *v.,* **-struck, -strik•ing,** *n. Numis.* —*v.t.* **1.** to stamp a new device, value, or inscription on (a coin). —*n.* **2.** a coin that has been overstruck without complete obliteration of the original design. [1900–05; OVER- + STRIKE]

o•ver•string (ō′vər string′), *v.t.,* **-strung; -strung** or (*Rare*) **-stringed; -string•ing. 1.** *Music.* to arrange the strings of (a piano) so that the bass strings cross over the treble. **2.** *Archery.* to string (a bow) too tightly. [1875–80; OVER- + STRING]

o•ver•struc•tured (ō′vər struk′chərd), *adj.* exces-

CONCISE PRONUNCIATION KEY: act, cāpe, dâre, pärt; set, ēqual; *if,* īce; ox, ōver, ôrder, oil, bŏŏk, bōōt, out; up, ûrge; child; sing; shoe; thin, *th*at; zh as in *treasure.* ə = *a* as in *alone, e* as in *system, i* as in *easily, o* as in *gallop, u* as in *circus;* ᵊ as in *fire* (fīᵊr), *hour* (ouᵊr). l and n can serve as syllabic consonants, as in *cradle* (krād′l), and *button* (but′n). See the full key inside the front cover.

o′ver•ob′vi•ous, *adj.*
o′ver•oc′cu•pied′, *adj.*
o′ver•of•fend′, *v.t.*
o′ver•of•fen′sive, *adj.;* **-ly,** *adv.;* **-ness,** *n.*
o′ver•of•fi′cious, *adj.;* **-ly,** *adv.;* **-ness,** *n.*
o′ver•o•pin′ion•at′ed, *adj.;* **-ly,** *adv.;* **-ness,** *n.*
o′ver•op′ti•mism, *n.*
o′ver•op′ti•mist, *n.*
o′ver•op′ti•mis′tic, *adj.*
o′ver•op′ti•mis′ti•cal•ly, *adv.*
o′ver•or′ches•trate′, *v.,* **-trat•ed, -trat•ing.**
o′ver•or′na•ment′, *v.t.*
o′ver•or′na•men′tal, *adj.;* **-ly,** *adv.*
o′ver•or′na•men•tal′i•ty, *n.*
o′ver•ox′i•di•za′tion, *n.*
o′ver•ox′i•dize′, *v.* **-dized, -diz•ing.**
o′ver•pack′, *v.*
o′ver•pained′, *adj.*
o′ver•pain′ful, *adj.;* **-ly,** *adv.;* **-ness,** *n.*
o′ver•pam′per, *v.t.*
o′ver•park′, *v.*
o′ver•par′tial, *adj.;* **-ly,** *adv.;* **-ness,** *n.*
o′ver•par′ti•al′i•ty, *n.*
o′ver•par•tic′u•lar, *adj.;* **-ly,** *adv.*
o′ver•pas′sion•ate, *adj.;* **-ly,** *adv.;* **-ness,** *n.*
o′ver•pa′tient, *adj.*
o′ver•pa′tri•ot′ic, *adj.*
o′ver•pa′tri•ot′i•cal•ly, *adv.*
o′ver•pa′tri•ot•ism, *n.*
o′ver•pe′nal•i•za′tion, *n.*
o′ver•pe′nal•ize′, *v.t.,* **-ized, -iz•ing.**
o′ver•pen′sive, *adj.;* **-ly,** *adv.;* **-ness,** *n.*
o′ver•per•emp′to•ri•ly, *adv.;* **-ness,** *n.*
o′ver•per•emp′to•ry, *adj.*
o′ver•per•form′, *v.*
o′ver•per′se•cute′, *v.t.,* **-cut•ed, -cut•ing.**
o′ver•pes′si•mism, *n.*
o′ver•pes′si•mis′tic, *adj.*
o′ver•pes′si•mis′ti•cal•ly, *adv.*
o′ver•pet′, *v.t.,* **-pet•ted, -pet•ting.**
o′ver•phi•los′o•phize′, *v.i.,* **-phized, -phiz•ing.**
o′ver•pic•to′ri•al•ize′, *v.,* **-ized, -iz•ing.**
o′ver•pit′e•ous, *adj.;* **-ly,** *adv.;* **-ness,** *n.*
o′ver•plain′, *adj.;* **-ly,** *adv.;* **-ness,** *n.*
o′ver•plan′, *v.,* **-planned, -plan•ning.**
o′ver•plant′, *v.t.*
o′ver•plau′si•ble, *adj.;* **-ble•ness,** *n.;* **-bly,** *adv.*
o′ver•please′, *v.,* **-pleased, -pleas•ing.**
o′ver•plen′i•tude′, *n.*
o′ver•plen′te•ous, *adj.;* **ly,** *adv.;* **-ness,** *n.*
o′ver•plen′ti•ful, *adj.;* **-ly,** *adv.;* **-ness,** *n.*
o′ver•plen′ty, *n.*
o′ver•plot′, *v.,* **-plot•ted, -plot•ting.**
o′ver•plow′, *v.*
o′ver•plump′, *adj.;* **-ness,** *n.*
o′ver•ply′, *v.,* **-plied, -ply•ing.**
o′ver•po•et′i•cize′, *v.,* **-cized, -ciz•ing.**
o′ver•po•lem′i•cal, *adj.;* **-ly,** *adv.*
o′ver•po•lice′, *v.t.,* **-liced, -lic•ing.**
o′ver•pol′ish, *v.t.*
o′ver•pol′i•tic, *adj.*
o′ver•po•lit′i•cal, *adj.;* **-ly,** *adv.*
o′ver•pol′li•nate′, *v.t.* **-nat•ed, -nat•ing.**
o′ver•pon′der•ous, *adj.;* **-ly,** *adv.;* **-ness,** *n.*
o′ver•pop′u•lar, *adj.;* **-ly,** *adv.*
o′ver•pop′u•lar′i•ty, *n.*
o′ver•pop′u•lous, *adj.;* **-ly,** *adv.;* **-ness,** *n.*
o′ver•pos′i•tive, *adj.;* **-ly,** *adv.;* **-ness,** *n.*
o′ver•po′ten•cy, *n.*
o′ver•po′tent, *adj.;* **-ly,** *adv.;* **-ness,** *n.*
o′ver•pow′er•ful, *adj.;* **-ly,** *adv.;* **-ness,** *n.*
o′ver•prac′tice, *v.t.,* **-ticed, -tic•ing.**
o′ver•pre•cise′, *adj.;* **-ly,** *adv.;* **-ness,** *n.*
o′ver•pre•ci′sion, *n.*
o′ver•pre•oc′cu•pa′tion, *n.*
o′ver•pre•oc′cu•py′, *v.t.,* **-pied, -py•ing.**
o′ver•pre•scribe′, *v.,* **-scribed, -scrib•ing.**
o′ver•press′, *v.t.*
o′ver•pre•sump′tion, *n.*
o′ver•pre•sump′tive, *adj.;* **-ly,** *adv.*
o′ver•pre•sump′tu•ous, *adj.;* **-ly,** *adv.;* **-ness,** *n.*
o′ver•proc′ess, *v.t.*
o′ver•pro•cras′ti•na′tion, *n.*
o′ver•pro•fi′cien•cy, *n.*
o′ver•pro•fi′cient, *adj.;* **-ly,** *adv.*
o′ver•pro•lif′ic, *adj.;* **-ness,** *n.*
o′ver•pro•lif′i•cal•ly, *adv.*
o′ver•pro•lix′, *adj.;* **-ly,** *adv.;* **-ness,** *n.*
o′ver•pro•lix′i•ty, *n.*
o′ver•prom′i•nence, *n.*
o′ver•prom′i•nent, *adj.;* **-ly,** *adv.*
o′ver•prom′ise, *v.t.,* **-ised, -is•ing.**
o′ver•prompt′, *adj.;* **-ly,** *adv.;* **-ness,** *n.*
o′ver•prone′, *adj.;* **-ness,** *n.*
o′ver•pros′per•ous, *adj.;* **-ly,** *adv.;* **-ness,** *n.*
o′ver•pro•tect′, *v.t.*
o′ver•pro•tec′tion, *n.*
o′ver•pro•tract′, *v.t.*
o′ver•pro•trac′tion, *n.*
o′ver•prove′, *v.t.,* **-proved, -proved** or **-prov•en, -prov•ing.**
o′ver•pro•vide′, *v.t.,* **-vid•ed, -vid•ing.**
o′ver•prov′i•dent, *adj.;* **-ly,** *adv.;* **-ness,** *n.*
o′ver•pro•vi′sion, *n.*
o′ver•prov′o•ca′tion, *n.*
o′ver•pro•voke′, *v.,* **-voked, -vok•ing.**
o′ver•prune′, *v.t.,* **-pruned, -prun•ing.**
o′ver•psy•chol′o•gize′, *v.,* **-gized, -giz•ing.**
o′ver•pub•lic′i•ty, *n.*
o′ver•pub′li•cize′, *v.t.,* **-cized, -ciz•ing.**
o′ver•pu′is•sant, *adj.;* **-ly,** *adv.*
o′ver•pump′, *v.*
o′ver•pun′ish, *v.*
o′ver•pun′ish•ment, *n.*
o′ver•pur′chase, *v.t.,* **-chased, -chas•ing.**
o′ver•qual′i•fi•ca′tion, *n.*
o′ver•qual′i•fy′, *v.,* **-fied, -fy•ing.**
o′ver•qui′et, *adj.;* **-ly,** *adv.;* **-ness,** *n.*
o′ver•rank′, *v.t., adj.;* **-ness,** *n.*
o′ver•rash′, *adj.;* **-ly,** *adv.;* **-ness,** *n.*
o′ver•ra′tion•al, *adj.;* **-ly,** *adv.*
o′ver•ra′tion•al•i•za′tion, *n.*
o′ver•ra′tion•al•ize′, *v.,* **-ized, -iz•ing.**
o′ver•re•ac′tive, *adj.*
o′ver•read′i•ly, *adv.*
o′ver•read′i•ness, *n.*
o′ver•read′y, *adj.*
o′ver•re′al•ism, *n.*
o′ver•re′al•is′tic, *adj.*
o′ver•re′al•is′ti•cal•ly, *adv.*
o′ver•re•duce′, *v.,* **-duced, -duc•ing.**
o′ver•re•duc′tion, *n.*

sively structured or organized. [1965–70; OVER- + STRUCTURED]

o•ver•strung (ō′vər strung′), *adj.* **1.** overly tense or sensitive; strained; on edge: *Their nerves were badly overstrung.* **2.** *Archery.* (of a bow) strung too tightly. [1800–10; OVER- + STRUNG]

o•ver•stud•y (*v.* ō′vər stud′ē; *n.* ō′vər stud′ē), *v.*, **-stud•ied, -stud•y•ing,** *n.* —*v.t., v.i.* **1.** to study too much or too hard (sometimes used reflexively): *to overstudy a letter for hidden meanings; to overstudy to the point of exhaustion; to overstudy oneself and forget half of what has been read.* —*n.* **2.** excessive study. [1635–45; OVER- + STUDY]

o•ver•stuff (ō′vər stuf′), *v.t.* **1.** to force too much into: *If you overstuff your suitcase, the fastenings may not hold.* **2.** *Furniture.* to cover completely with deep upholstery. [1935–40; OVER- + STUFF]

o•ver•stuffed (ō′vər stuft′), *adj.* **1.** stuffed or filled to excess. **2.** *Furniture.* having the entire frame covered by stuffing and upholstery, so that only decorative woodwork or the like is exposed: *an overstuffed sofa.* **3.** filled with tedious or extraneous material; overlong: *an overstuffed biography.* **4.** obese; corpulent: *an overstuffed man who was a compulsive eater.* [1920–25; OVERSTUFF + -ED[2]]

o•ver•sub•scribe (ō′vər səb skrīb′), *v.t.*, **-scribed, -scrib•ing.** to subscribe for more of than is available, expected, or required: *The charity drive was oversubscribed by several thousand dollars.* [1890–95; OVER- + SUBSCRIBE] —**o′ver•sub•scrib′er,** *n.* —**o•ver•sub•scrip•tion** (ō′vər səb skrip′shən), *n.*

o•ver•sup•ply (*n.* ō′vər sə plī′; *v.* ō′vər sə plī′), *n., pl.* **-plies,** *v.*, **-plied, -ply•ing.** —*n.* **1.** an excessive supply. —*v.t.* **2.** to supply in excess. [1825–35; OVER- + SUPPLY[1]]

o•ver•swing (ō′vər swing′), *v.i.*, **-swung, -swing•ing.** *Baseball, Golf.* to swing too hard, hoping to apply more power. [1920–25; OVER- + SWING[1]]

o•vert (ō vûrt′, ō′vûrt), *adj.* **1.** open to view or knowledge; not concealed or secret: *overt hostility.* **2.** *Heraldry.* (of a device, as a purse) represented as open: *a purse overt.* [1275–1325; ME < OF, ptp. of *ouvrir* to open < VL **ōperīre,* for L *aperīre*]
—**Syn. 1.** plain, manifest, apparent, public. —**Ant. 1.** private, concealed.

o•ver•take (ō′vər tāk′), *v.*, **-took, -tak•en, -tak•ing.** —*v.t.* **1.** to catch up with in traveling or pursuit; draw even with: *By taking a cab to the next town, we managed to overtake and board the train.* **2.** to catch up with and pass, as in a race; move by: *He overtook the leader three laps from the finish.* **3.** to move ahead of in achievement, production, score, etc.; surpass: *to overtake all other countries in steel production.* **4.** to happen to or befall someone suddenly or unexpectedly, as night, a storm, or death: *The pounding rainstorm overtook them just outside the city.* —*v.i.* **5.** to pass another vehicle: *Never overtake on a curve.* [1175–1225; ME *overtaken;* see OVER-, TAKE]

o•ver•tax (ō′vər taks′), *v.t.* **1.** to tax too heavily. **2.** to make too great demands on. [1640–50; OVER- + TAX] —**o′ver•tax•a′tion,** *n.*

o•ver-the-air (ō′vər thē âr′), *adj. Radio and Television.* of or pertaining to any means of broadcast transmission. [1970–75]

o′ver the count′er, 1. not transacted through an organized securities exchange; directly to the buyer or from the seller: *He sold his stocks over the counter.* **2.** *Pharm.* without a doctor's prescription but within the law. [1870–75]

CONCISE ETYMOLOGY KEY: <, descended or borrowed from; >, whence; b., blend of, blended; c., cognate with; cf., compare; deriv., derivative; equiv., equivalent; imit., imitative; obl., oblique; r., replacing; s., stem; sp., spelling, spelled; resp., respelling, respelled; trans., translation; ?, origin unknown; *, unattested; ‡, probably earlier than. See the full key inside the front cover.

o•ver-the-count•er (ō′vər thə koun′tər), *adj.* **1.** unlisted on or not part of an organized securities exchange: *over-the-counter stocks; the over-the-counter market. Abbr.:* OTC **2.** *Pharm.* sold legally without a doctor's prescription: *over-the-counter drugs. Abbr.:* OTC [1920–25]

o•ver-the-road (ō′vər thə rōd′), *adj.* of, for, or pertaining to transportation on public highways: *over-the-road trucks.* [1940–45]

o•ver•throw (*v.* ō′vər thrō′; *n.* ō′vər thrō′), *v.*, **-threw, -thrown, -throw•ing,** *n.* —*v.t.* **1.** to depose, as from a position of power; overcome, defeat, or vanquish: *to overthrow a tyrant.* **2.** to put an end to by force, as a government or institution. **3.** to throw or knock down; overturn; topple: *The heavy winds overthrew numerous telephone poles and trees.* **4.** to knock down and demolish. **5.** to throw (something) too far. **6.** *Baseball.* (of a pitcher) to throw too hard, often affecting control or straining the arm. **7.** *Archaic.* to destroy the sound condition of (the mind). —*v.i.* **8.** to throw too far: *If I hadn't overthrown, it would have been a sure putout.* —*n.* **9.** the act of overthrowing; state or condition of being overthrown. **10.** deposition from power. **11.** defeat; destruction; ruin. [1300–50; ME; see OVER-, THROW] —**o′ver•throw′er,** *n.*
—**Syn. 1.** conquer, overpower. **4.** destroy, raze, level. **11.** fall.

o•ver•thrust (ō′vər thrust′), *n. Geol.* **1.** a thrust fault with a low dip and a large slip. **2.** a thrust fault in which the hanging wall was the one that moved (opposed to *underthrust*). [1880–85; OVER- + THRUST]

o′verthrust belt′, (*sometimes caps.*) *Geol.* an elongate area in which thick rock layers have been pushed over one another by compressional forces within the earth's crust.

o•ver•time (*n., adv., adj.* ō′vər tīm′; *v.* ō′vər tīm′), *n., adv., adj., v.*, **-timed, -tim•ing.** —*n.* **1.** working time before or after one's regularly scheduled working hours; extra working time. **2.** pay for such time (distinguished from *straight time*). **3.** time in excess of a prescribed period. **4.** *Sports.* an additional period of play for deciding the winner of a game in which the contestants are tied at the end of the regular playing period. —*adv.* **5.** during overtime: *to work overtime.* —*adj.* **6.** of or for overtime: *overtime pay.* —*v.t.* **7.** to give too much time to (a photographic exposure). [1530–40; OVER- + TIME]

o•ver•tire (ō′vər tīᵊr′), *v.i., v.t.*, **-tired, -tir•ing.** to tire to the point of exhaustion; tire out. [1550–60; OVER- + TIRE[1]]

o•vert•ly (ō vûrt′lē, ō′vûrt lē), *adv.* openly; publicly. [1275–1325; ME; see OVERT, -LY]

o•ver•tone (ō′vər tōn′), *n.* **1.** *Music.* an acoustical frequency that is higher in frequency than the fundamental. **2.** an additional, usually subsidiary and implicit meaning or quality: *an aesthetic theory with definite political overtones.* [1865–70; trans. of G *Oberton.* See OVER-, TONE]
—**Syn. 2.** insinuation, suggestion, intimation, hint.

o•ver•took (ō′vər to͝ok′), *v.* pt. of **overtake.**

o•ver•top (*v.* ō′vər top′; *n.* ō′vər top′), *v.*, **-topped, -top•ping,** *n.* —*v.t.* **1.** to rise over or above the top of: *a skyscraper that overtops all the other buildings.* **2.** to rise above in authority; take precedence over; override: *No individual shall overtop the law.* **3.** to surpass or excel: *a rise in sales that overtopped everyone in the industry.* —*n.* **4.** a top, sometimes sleeveless, designed to be worn over another garment, as a shirt or dress. [1555–65; OVER- + TOP[1]]

o•ver•trade (ō′vər trād′), *v.i.*, **-trad•ed, -trad•ing.** to trade in excess of one's capital or the requirements of the market. [1615–25; OVER- + TRADE]

o•ver•trick (ō′vər trik′), *n. Bridge.* a trick won by declarer in excess of the number of tricks necessary to make the contract. Cf. **undertrick.** [1920–25; OVER- + TRICK]

o•ver•trump (ō′vər trump′, ō′vər trump′), *v.t., v.i. Cards.* to play a higher trump than has already been played. [1740–50; OVER- + TRUMP[1]]

o•ver•ture (ō′vər chər, -cho͝or′), *n., v.*, **-tured, -tur•ing.** —*n.* **1.** an opening or initiating move toward negotiations, a new relationship, an agreement, etc.; a formal or informal proposal or offer: *overtures of peace; a shy man who rarely made overtures of friendship.* **2.** *Music.* **a.** an orchestral composition forming the prelude or introduction to an opera, oratorio, etc. **b.** an independent piece of similar character. **3.** an introductory part, as of a poem; prelude; prologue. **4.** (in Presbyterian churches) **a.** the action of an ecclesiastical court in submitting a question or proposal to presbyteries. **b.** the proposal or question so submitted. —*v.t.* **5.** to submit as an overture or proposal: *to overture conditions for a ceasefire.* **6.** to make an overture or proposal to: *to overture one's adversary through a neutral party.* [1300–50; ME < OF; see OVERT, -URE; doublet of APERTURE]
—**Syn. 1.** See **proposal.**

o•ver•turn (*v.* ō′vər tûrn′; *n.* ō′vər tûrn′), *v.t.* **1.** to destroy the power of; overthrow; defeat; vanquish. **2.** to turn over on its side, face, or back; upset: *to overturn a vase.* —*v.i.* **3.** to turn on its side, face, or back; capsize: *The boat overturned during the storm.* —*n.* **4.** the act of overturning. **5.** the state of being overturned. [1175–1225; ME; see OVER-, TURN] —**o′ver•turn′a•ble,** *adj.*
—**Syn. 1.** conquer. **2.** See **upset.**

o•ver-un•der (ō′vər un′dər), *adj.* **1.** (of double-barreled firearms) with one barrel mounted over the other. —*n.* **2.** such a firearm.

o•ver•use (*v.* ō′vər yo͞oz′; *n.* ō′vər yo͞os′), *v.*, **-used, -us•ing,** *n.* —*v.t.* **1.** to use too much or too often: *to overuse an expression.* —*n.* **2.** excessive use: *to strain one's voice through overuse.* [1670–80; OVER- + USE]

o•ver•val•ue (ō′vər val′yo͞o), *v.t.*, **-ued, -u•ing.** to value too highly; put too high a value on: *They should be careful not to overvalue the property.* [1590–1600; OVER- + VALUE] —**o′ver•val′u•a′tion,** *n.*

o•ver•view (ō′vər vyo͞o′), *n.* a general outline of a subject or situation; survey or summary. [1540–50; OVER- + VIEW]

o•ver•volt•age (ō′vər vōl′tij), *n.* **1.** *Elect.* excess voltage. **2.** *Physics.* the amount by which the voltage applied to an ionization chamber exceeds the Geiger-Müller threshold. [1905–10; OVER- + VOLTAGE]

o•ver•watch (ō′vər woch′), *v.t.* **1.** to watch over. **2.** *Archaic.* to weary by keeping awake. [1555–65; OVER- + WATCH] —**o′ver•watch′er,** *n.*

o•ver•wear (ō′vər wâr′), *v.t.*, **-wore, -worn, -wear•ing.** to use or wear excessively; wear out; exhaust; tax: *needlessly overwearing her best workers; phrases overworn by repetition.* [1570–80; OVER- + WEAR]

o•ver•wea•ry (*adj.* ō′vər wēr′ē; *v.* ō′vər wēr′ē), *adj., v.*, **-ried, -ry•ing.** —*adj.* **1.** excessively weary; tired out. —*v.t.* **2.** to weary to excess; overcome with weariness. [1570–80; OVER- + WEARY]

o•ver•ween (ō′vər wēn′), *v.i. Archaic.* to be conceited or arrogant. [1275–1325; ME *overwenen;* see OVER-, WEEN] —**o′ver•ween′er,** *n.*

o•ver•ween•ing (ō′vər wē′ning), *adj.* **1.** presumptuously conceited, overconfident, or proud: *a brash, insolent, overweening fellow.* **2.** exaggerated, excessive, or arrogant: *overweening prejudice; overweening pride.* [1300–50; ME *overwening(e)* (ger.); see OVERWEEN, -ING[2]] —**o′ver•ween′ing•ly,** *adv.* —**o′ver•ween′ing•ness,** *n.*

o•ver•weigh (ō′vər wā′), *v.t.* **1.** to exceed in weight; overbalance or outweigh: *a respected opinion that overweighs the others.* **2.** to weigh down; oppress; burden: *gloom that overweighs one's spirits.* [1175–1225; ME *overweien;* see OVER-, WEIGH]

o•ver•weight (*adj.* ō′vər wāt′; *n.* ō′vər wāt′; *v.* ō′vər-wāt′), *adj.* **1.** weighing too much or more than is considered normal, proper, etc.: *overweight luggage; an overweight patient; two letters that may be overweight.*

o′ver•re•flec′tion, *n.*
o′ver•re•flec′tive, *adj.;* **-ly,** *adv.;* **-ness,** *n.*
o′ver•reg′i•ment′, *v.t.*
o′ver•reg′i•men•ta′tion, *n.*
o′ver•reg′u•late′, *v.*, **-lat•ed, -lat•ing.**
o′ver•reg′u•la′tion, *n.*
o′ver•re•lax′, *v.*
o′ver•re•li′ance, *n.*
o′ver•re•li′ant, *adj.*
o′ver•re•li′gi•os′i•ty, *n.*
o′ver•re•li′gious, *adj.;* **-ly,** *adv.*
o′ver•re•miss′, *adj.;* **-ly,** *adv.;* **-ness,** *n.*
o′ver•re•port′, *v.*
o′ver•rep′re•sent′, *v.t.*
o′ver•rep′re•sen•ta′tion, *n.*
o′ver•rep′re•sent′a•tive, *adj.;* **-ly,** *adv.;* **-ness,** *n.*
o′ver•re•press′, *v.t.*
o′ver•rep′ri•mand′, *v.t.*
o′ver•re•served′, *adj.;* **-serv•ed•ly,** *adv.;* **-serv•ed•ness,** *n.*
o′ver•re•sist′, *v.*
o′ver•res′o•lute′, *adj.;* **-ly,** *adv.;* **-ness,** *n.*
o′ver•re•spond′, *v.*
o′ver•re•strain′, *v.t.*
o′ver•re•straint′, *n.*
o′ver•re•strict′, *v.t.*
o′ver•re•stric′tion, *n.*
o′ver•re•ten′tion, *n.*
o′ver•re•ward′, *v.*
o′ver•rich′, *adj.;* **-ly,** *adv.;* **-ness,** *n.*
o′ver•rife′, *adj.*
o′ver•rigged′, *adj.*
o′ver•right′eous, *adj.;* **-ly,** *adv.;* **-ness,** *n.*
o′ver•rig′id, *adj.;* **-ly,** *adv.;* **-ness,** *n.*
o′ver•ri•gid′i•ty, *n.*
o′ver•rig′or•ous, *adj.;* **-ly,** *adv.;* **-ness,** *n.*
o′ver•rip′en, *v.*
o′ver•roast′, *v.*
o′ver•ro•man′ti•cize′, *v.*, **-cized, -ciz•ing.**
o′ver•rouge′, *v.*, **-rouged, -roug•ing.**
o′ver•rough′, *adj.;* **-ly,** *adv.;* **-ness,** *n.*
o′ver•rude′, *adj.;* **-ly,** *adv.;* **-ness,** *n.*
o′ver•sac′ri•fi′cial, *adj.;* **-ly,** *adv.*
o′ver•sad′, *adj.;* **-ly,** *adv.;* **-ness,** *n.*
o′ver•salt′, *v.t.*
o′ver•salt′y, *adj.*
o′ver•san′guine, *adj.;* **-ly,** *adv.;* **-ness,** *n.*
o′ver•sate′, *v.t.*, **-sat•ed, -sat•ing.**
o′ver•sa•ti′e•ty, *n.*
o′ver•sat′u•rate′, *v.t.*, **-rat•ed, -rat•ing.**
o′ver•sat′u•ra′tion, *n.*
o′ver•sauce′, *v.t.*, **-sauced, -sauc•ing.**
o′ver•sau′cy, *adj.*
o′ver•scent′ed, *adj.*
o′ver•scep′ti•cal, *adj.;* **-ly,** *adv.;* **-ness,** *n.*
o′ver•scep′ti•cism, *n.*
o′ver•scrub′, *v.*, **-scrubbed, -scrub•bing.**
o′ver•scru′ple, *v.*, **-pled, -pling.**
o′ver•sea′son, *v.t.*
o′ver•se•crete′, *v.t.*, **-cret•ed, -cret•ing.**
o′ver•se•cre′tion, *n.*
o′ver•sec′u•lar•i•za′tion, *n.*
o′ver•sec′u•lar•ize′, *v.t.*, **-ized, -iz•ing.**
o′ver•se•cure′, *adj., v.t.*, **-cured, -cur•ing; -ly,** *adv.*
o′ver•se•cu′ri•ty, *n.*
o′ver•se•da′tion, *n.*
o′ver•seed′, *v.*
o′ver•sen′si•ble, *adj.;* **-ble•ness,** *n.;* **-bly,** *adv.*
o′ver•sen′si•tize′, *v.*, **-tized, -tiz•ing.**
o′ver•sen′ti•men′tal, *adj.;* **-ly,** *adv.*
o′ver•sen′ti•men′tal•ism, *n.*
o′ver•sen′ti•men•tal′i•ty, *n.*
o′ver•sen′ti•men′tal•ize′, *v.*, **-ized, -iz•ing.**
o′ver•se•rene′, *adj.;* **-ly,** *adv.*
o′ver•se•ren′i•ty, *n.*
o′ver•se′ri•ous, *adj.;* **-ly,** *adv.;* **-ness,** *n.*
o′ver•serve′, *v.t.*
o′ver•serv′ice, *v.t.*, **-iced, -ic•ing.**
o′ver•ser′vile, *adj.;* **-ly,** *adv.;* **-ness,** *n.*
o′ver•ser•vil′i•ty, *n.*
o′ver•set′tle, *v.*, **-tled, -tling.**
o′ver•set′tle•ment, *n.*
o′ver•se•vere′, *adj.;* **-ly,** *adv.;* **-ness,** *n.*
o′ver•se•ver′i•ty, *n.*
o′ver•sharp′, *adj.*
o′ver•ship′ment, *n.*
o′ver•short′, *adj.;* **-ness,** *n.*
o′ver•short′en, *v.*
o′ver•shrink′, *v.*, **-shrank** or, often, **-shrunk; -shrunk** or **-shrunk•en; -shrink•ing.**
o′ver•si′lence, *n.*
o′ver•si′lent, *adj.;* **-ly,** *adv.;* **-ness,** *n.*
o′ver•sim′ple, *adj.;* **-ple•ness,** *n.;* **-ply,** *adv.*
o′ver•sim•plic′i•ty, *n.*
o′ver•skep′ti•cal, *adj.;* **-ly,** *adv.;* **-ness,** *n.*
o′ver•skept′ti•cism, *n.*
o′ver•skilled′, *adj.*
o′ver•slack′, *adj.*
o′ver•slav′ish, *adj.;* **-ly,** *adv.;* **-ness,** *n.*
o′ver•slight′, *adj.*
o′ver•slow′, *adj.;* **-ly,** *adv.;* **-ness,** *n.*
o′ver•smooth′, *adj.;* **-ly,** *adv.;* **-ness,** *n.*
o′ver•soak′, *v.*
o′ver•soap′, *v.t.*
o′ver•so′cial, *adj.;* **-ly,** *adv.*
o′ver•so′cial•ize′, *v.t.*, **-ized, -iz•ing.**
o′ver•soft′, *adj.;* **-ly,** *adv.;* **-ness,** *n.*
o′ver•soft′en, *v.*
o′ver•sol′emn, *adj.;* **-ly,** *adv.;* **-ness,** *n.*
o′ver•so•lem′ni•ty, *n.*
o′ver•so•lid′i•fi•ca′tion, *n.*
o′ver•so•lid′i•fy′, *v.t.*, **-fied, -fy•ing.**
o′ver•sooth′ing, *adj.;* **-ly,** *adv.*
o′ver•so•phis′ti•cat′ed, *adj.*
o′ver•so•phis′ti•ca′tion, *n.*
o′ver•sor′row•ful, *adj.;* **-ly,** *adv.;* **-ness,** *n.*
o′ver•sour′, *adj.;* **-ly,** *adv.;* **-ness,** *n.*
o′ver•spa′cious, *adj.;* **-ly,** *adv.;* **-ness,** *n.*
o′ver•spar′ing, *adj.;* **-ly,** *adv.;* **-ness,** *n.*
o′ver•spe′cial•ize′, *v.*, **-ized, -iz•ing.**
o′ver•spec′u•late′, *v.i.*, **-lat•ed, -lat•ing.**
o′ver•spec′u•la′tion, *n.*
o′ver•spec′u•la′tive, *adj.;* **-ly,** *adv.;* **-ness,** *n.*
o′ver•speed′, *v.*, **-sped** or **-speed•ed, -speed•ing.**
o′ver•speed′i•ly, *adv.*
o′ver•speed′i•ness, *n.*
o′ver•speed′y, *adj.*
o′ver•spice′, *v.*, **-spiced, -spic•ing.**
o′ver•spray′, *v.t.*
o′ver•squeam′ish, *adj.;* **-ly,** *adv.;* **-ness,** *n.*
o′ver•sta•bil′i•ty, *n.*
o′ver•staff′, *v.t.*
o′ver•stale′, *adj.;* **-ness,** *n.*
o′ver•starch′, *v.t.*

—*n.* **2.** extra or excess weight above what law or regulation allows, as of baggage or freight: *The overweight will cost us $12.* **3.** weight in excess of that considered normal, proper, healthful, etc.: *Overweight in a child should not be neglected.* **4.** greater effect or importance; preponderance. —*v.t.* **5.** to weight excessively; exceed the weight limit of. **6.** to give too much consideration or emphasis to; stress unduly. [1545–55; OVER- + WEIGHT]

o•ver•whelm (ō′vər hwelm′, -welm′), *v.t.* **1.** to overcome completely in mind or feeling: *overwhelmed by remorse.* **2.** to overpower or overcome, esp. with superior forces; destroy; crush: *Roman troops were overwhelmed by barbarians.* **3.** to cover or bury beneath a mass of something, as floodwaters, debris, or an avalanche; submerge: *Lava from erupting Vesuvius overwhelmed the city of Pompeii.* **4.** to load, heap, treat, or address with an overpowering or excessive amount of anything: *a child overwhelmed with presents; to overwhelm someone with questions.* **5.** to overthrow. [1300–50; ME; see OVER-, WHELM]

o•ver•whelm•ing (ō′vər hwel′ming, -wel′-), *adj.* **1.** that overwhelms; overpowering: *The temptation to despair may become overwhelming.* **2.** so great as to render resistance or opposition useless: *an overwhelming majority.* [1565–75; OVERWHELM + -ING²] **—o′ver•whelm′ing•ly,** *adv.* **—o′ver•whelm′ing•ness,** *n.*

o•ver•wind (ō′vər wīnd′), *v.t.*, **-wound, -wind•ing.** to wind beyond the proper limit; wind too far: *He must have overwound his watch.* [1675–85; OVER- + WIND²]

o•ver•win•ter (ō′vər win′tər), *v.i.* to pass, spend, or survive the winter: *to overwinter on the Riviera.* [1890–95; OVER- + WINTER; prob. trans. of Norw *overvintre*]

o•ver•wire (ō′vər wīᵊr′), *n.* a spiral-bound book in which the spiral is covered by the spine. [OVER- + WIRE]

o•ver•wise (ō′vər wīz′), *adj.* excessively or unusually wise: *overwise for a child of her age.* [1525–35; OVER- + WISE¹]

o•ver•with•hold (ō′vər with hōld′, -with-), *v.*, **-held, -hold•ing.** —*v.t.* **1.** to withhold too much. **2.** to deduct (an amount in withholding tax) in excess of the tax to be paid. —*v.i.* **3.** to withhold oneself excessively. **4.** to deduct too much withholding tax. [1970–75; OVER- + WITHHOLD]

o•ver•word (ō′vər wûrd′), *n.* a word that is repeated, as a refrain in a song. [1490–1500; OVER- + WORD]

o•ver•wore (ō′vər wôr′, -wōr′), *v.* pt. of **overwear.**

o•ver•work (*v.* ō′vər wûrk′; *n.* ō′vər wûrk′), *v.t.* **1.** to cause to work too hard, too much, or too long; weary or exhaust with work (often used reflexively): *Don't overwork yourself on that new job.* **2.** to work up, stir up, or excite excessively: *to overwork a mob to the verge of frenzy.* **3.** to employ or elaborate to excess: *an appeal for sympathy that has been overworked by many speakers.* **4.** to work or decorate all over; decorate the surface of: *white limestone overworked with inscriptions.* —*v.i.* **5.** to work too hard, too much, or too long; work to excess: *You look as though you've been overworking.* —*n.* **6.** work beyond one's strength or capacity. **7.** extra or excessive work. [bef. 1000; OE *oferwyrcan.* See OVER-, WORK]

o•ver•worn (ō′vər wôrn′, -wōrn′), *v.* pp. of **overwear.**

o•ver•write (ō′vər rīt′), *v.*, **-wrote, -writ•ten, -writ•ing.** —*v.t.* **1.** to write in too elaborate, burdensome, diffuse, or prolix a style: *He overwrites his essays to the point of absurdity.* **2.** to write in excess of the requirements, esp. so as to defeat the original intention: *That young playwright tends to overwrite her big scenes.* **3.** to write on or over; cover with writing: *a flyleaf overwritten with a dedication.* —*v.i.* **4.** to write too elaborately: *The problem with so many young authors is that they tend to overwrite.* [1690–1700; OVER- + WRITE]

o•ver•wrought (ō′vər rôt′, ō′vər-), *adj.* **1.** extremely or excessively excited or agitated: *to become overwrought on hearing bad news; an overwrought personality.* **2.** elaborated to excess; excessively complex or ornate: *written in a florid, overwrought style.* **3.** *Archaic.* wearied or exhausted by overwork. [1660–70; OVER- + WROUGHT]
—Syn. 1. overexcited, worked up, wrought up, distracted, frantic.

o•ver•zeal•ous (ō′vər zel′əs), *adj.* too zealous: *overzealous for reform.* [1625–35; OVER- + ZEALOUS] **—o′ver•zeal′ous•ly,** *adv.* **—o′ver•zeal′ous•ness,** *n.*

O•ve•ta (ō vē′tə), *n.* a female given name.

ovi-, a combining form meaning "egg," used in the formation of compound words: *oviferous.* [< L *ōvi-*, comb. form of *ōvum* EGG¹]

o•vi•cide (ō′və sīd′), *n.* a substance or preparation, esp. an insecticide, capable of killing egg cells. [1925–30; OVI- + -CIDE] **—o′vi•cid′al,** *adj.*

Ov•id (ov′id), *n.* (*Publius Ovidius Naso*) 43 B.C.–A.D. 17?, Roman poet. **—O•vid•i•an** (ō vid′ē ən), *adj.*

o•vi•duct (ō′vi dukt′), *n. Anat., Zool.* either of a pair of tubes that transport the ova from the ovary to the exterior, the distal ends of which form the uterus and vagina in higher mammals. Cf. **fallopian tube.** [1830–40; < NL *ōviductus.* See OVI-, DUCT] **—o•vi•du•cal** (ō′vi dōō′kəl, -dyōō′-), **o′vi•duc′tal,** *adj.*

O•vie•do (ô vye′thô), *n.* a city in NW Spain. 154,117.

o•vif•er•ous (ō vif′ər əs), *adj. Anat., Zool.* bearing eggs. [1820–30; OVI- + -FEROUS]

o•vi•form (ō′və fôrm′), *adj.* having a shape resembling that of an egg; egg-shaped; ovoid. [1675–85; OVI- + -FORM]

O•vim•bun•du (ō′vim bōōn′dōō), *n., pl.* **-dus** (*esp. collectively*) **-du.** Mbundu (def. 1).

o•vine (ō′vīn, ō′vin), *adj.* pertaining to, of the nature of, or like sheep. [1820–30; < LL *ovīnus*, equiv. to L *ov(is)* sheep + *-īnus* -INE¹]

o•vip•a•ra (ō vip′ər ə), *n.pl. Zool.* egg-laying animals. [< NL, L, n. use of neut. pl. of *ōviparus* OVIPAROUS]

o•vip•a•rous (ō vip′ər əs), *adj. Zool.* producing eggs that mature and hatch after being expelled from the body, as birds, most reptiles and fishes, and the monotremes. [1640–50; < L *ōviparus.* See OVI-, -PAROUS] **—o•vi•par•i•ty** (ō′və par′i tē), **o•vip′a•rous•ness,** *n.* **—o•vip′a•rous•ly,** *adv.*

o•vi•pos•it (ō′və poz′it, ō′və poz′-), *v.i.* to deposit or lay eggs, esp. by means of an ovipositor. [1810–20; OVI- + *-posit* < L *positus* (see POSIT)] **—o•vi•po•si•tion** (ō′və pə zish′ən), *n.*

o•vi•pos•i•tor (ō′və poz′i tər), *n.* **1.** (in certain female insects) an organ at the end of the abdomen, by which eggs are deposited. **2.** a similar organ in other animals, as certain fishes. [1810–20; OVIPOSIT + -OR²]

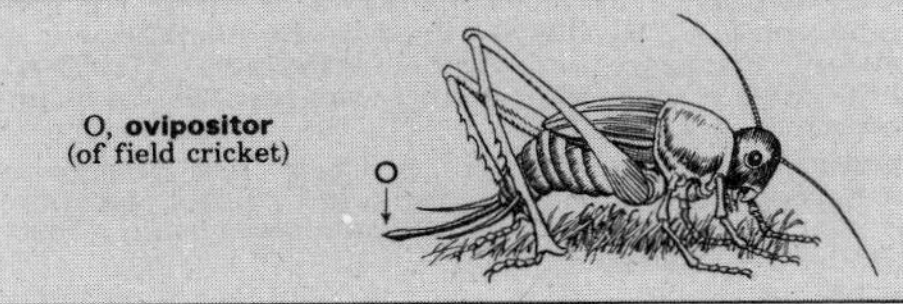

O, **ovipositor** (of field cricket)

o•vi•sac (ō′və sak′), *n. Zool.* a sac or capsule containing an ovum or ova. [1825–35; OVI- + SAC] **—o′vi•sac′like′,** *adj.*

OV language (ō′vē′), *Ling.* a type of language that has direct objects preceding the verb and that tends to have typological traits such as postpositions, suffixes, noun modifiers preceding nouns, adverbs preceding verbs, and auxiliary verbs following main verbs. Cf. **VO language.** [*O*(*bject*) *V*(*erb*)]

o•void (ō′void), *adj.* **1.** egg-shaped; having the solid form of an egg. **2.** ovate (def. 2). —*n.* **3.** an ovoid body. [1820–30; < NL *ōvoidēs.* See OVI-, -OID]

o•vo•lac•tar•i•an (ō′vō lak târ′ē ən), *n.* lacto-ovo-vegetarian. [1970–75; *ovo-*, irreg. for OVI- + LACTARIAN]

o•vo•lac•to•veg•e•tar•i•an (ō′vō lak′tō vej′i târ′ē ən), *n.* lacto-ovo-vegetarian. [1865–70]

o•vo•lo (ō′və lō′), *n., pl.* **-li** (-lī′). *Archit.* a convex molding forming or approximating in section a quarter of a circle or ellipse. See illus. under **molding.** [1655–65; < It, var. (now obs.) of *uovolo*, dim. of *uovo* EGG¹ < L *ōvum*]

o•vo•tes•tis (ō′və tes′tis), *n., pl.* **-tes** (-tēz). *Zool.* the hermaphroditic reproductive organ of some gastropods, containing both an ovary and a testis. [1875–80; *ovo-* (irreg. for OVI-) + TESTIS]

o•vo•vi•tel•lin (ō′vō vi tel′in, -vī-), *n. Biochem.* vitellin. [1905–10; OV(I)- + -O- + VITELLIN]

o•vo•vi•vip•a•rous (ō′vō vī vip′ər əs), *adj. Zool.* producing eggs that are hatched within the body, so that the young are born alive but without placental attachment, as certain reptiles or fishes. [1795–1805; OV(I)- + -O- + VIVIPAROUS] **—o•vo•vi•vip′a•rism, o•vo•vi•vi•par•i•ty** (ō′vō vī′və par′i tē), **o′vo•vi•vip′a•rous•ness,** *n.* **—o′vo•vi•vip′a•rous•ly,** *adv.*

ov•u•lar (ov′yə lər, ō′vyə lər-), *adj.* pertaining to or of the nature of an ovule. [1850–55; < NL *ōvulāris.* See OVULE, -AR¹]

ov•u•late (ov′yə lāt′, ō′vyə lāt′-), *v.i.*, **-lat•ed, -lat•ing.** *Biol.* to produce and discharge eggs from an ovary or ovarian follicle. [1860–65; OVULE + -ATE¹] **—ov′u•la′tion,** *n.* **—ov•u•la•to•ry** (ov′yə lə tôr′ē, -tōr′ē, ō′vyə-), *adj.*.

ov•ule (ov′yōōl, ō′vyōōl), *n.* **1.** *Bot.* **a.** a rudimentary seed. **b.** the plant part that contains the embryo sac and hence the female germ cell, which after fertilization develops into a seed. **2.** *Biol.* a small egg. [1820–30; < L *ōvulum* little egg. See OVUM, -ULE]

o•vum (ō′vəm), *n., pl.* **o•va** (ō′və). **1.** *Cell Biol.* **a.** the female reproductive cell or gamete of animals, which is capable of developing, usually only after fertilization, into a new individual. **b.** the female reproductive cell or gamete of plants. **2.** *Archit.* an oval ornament, as in an egg-and-dart molding. [1700–10; < L *ōvum* EGG¹; c. Gk *ōión*]

ow (ou), *interj.* (used esp. as an expression of intense or sudden pain.)

O•wa•ton•na (ō′wə ton′ə), *n.* a city in S Minnesota. 18,632.

owe (ō), *v.*, **owed, ow•ing.** —*v.t.* **1.** to be under obligation to pay or repay: *to owe money to the bank; to owe the bank interest on a mortgage.* **2.** to be in debt to: *He says he doesn't owe anybody.* **3.** to be indebted (to) as the cause or source of: *to owe one's fame to good fortune.* **4.** to have or bear (a feeling or attitude) toward someone or something: *to owe gratitude to one's rescuers.* **5.** *Obs.* to possess; own. —*v.i.* **6.** to be in debt: *Neither lend nor owe. Who owes for the antipasto?* [bef. 900; ME *owen* to possess, be under obligation, have to pay; OE *āgan* to possess; c. OHG *eigan*, ON *eiga.* See OWN, OUGHT¹]

Ow•en (ō′ən), *n.* **1. Sir Richard,** 1804–92, English zoologist and anatomist. **2. Robert,** 1771–1858, Welsh social reformer in Great Britain and the U.S. **3. Wilfred,** 1893–1918, English poet. **4.** a male given name.

Ow•en•ism (ō′ə niz′əm), *n.* the socialistic philosophy of Robert Owen. [1820–30, *Amer.*; OWEN + -ISM] **—Ow′en•ist, Ow′en•ite′,** *n.*

CONCISE PRONUNCIATION KEY: *act, cāpe, dâre, pärt; set, ēqual; if, īce; ox, ōver, ôrder, oil, bŏŏk, bōōt, out; up, ûrge; child; sing; shoe; thin, that;* zh as in *treasure.* ə = *a* as in *alone, e* as in *system, i* as in *easily, o* as in *gallop, u* as in *circus;* ᵊ as in *fire* (fīᵊr), *hour* (ouᵊr). l and n can serve as syllabic consonants, as in *cradle* (krād′l), and *button* (but′n). See the full key inside the front cover.

o′ver•starched′, *adj.*
o′ver•stead′fast′, *adj.;* **-ly,** *adv.;* **-ness,** *n.*
o′ver•stead′i•ly, *adv.*
o′ver•stead′i•ness, *n.*
o′ver•stead′y, *adj.*
o′ver•stiff′, *adj.;* **-ly,** *adv.;* **-ness,** *n.*
o′ver•stiff′en, *v.*
o′ver•stim′u•late′, *v.*, **-lat•ed, -lat•ing.**
o′ver•stim′u•la′tion, *n.*
o′ver•stim′u•la′tive, *adj.;* **-ly,** *adv.;* **-ness,** *n.*
o′ver•stir′, *v.*, **-stirred, -stir•ring.**
o′ver•stock′ing, *n.*
o′ver•store′, *v.*, **-stored, -stor•ing.**
o′ver•stout′, *adj.;* **-ly,** *adv.;* **-ness,** *n.*
o′ver•straight′, *adj.;* **-ly,** *adv.;* **-ness,** *n.*
o′ver•straight′en, *v.*
o′ver•strain′, *v.*
o′ver•strength′en, *v.*
o′ver•stressed′, *adj.*
o′ver•strict′, *adj.*
o′ver•stri′dence, *n.*
o′ver•stri′den•cy, *n.*
o′ver•stri′dent, *adj.;* **-ly,** *adv.*
o′ver•strive′, *v.i.*, **-strove, -striv•en, -striv•ing.**
o′ver•strong′, *adj.;* **-ly,** *adv.;* **-ness,** *n.*
o′ver•stu′di•ous, *adj.;* **-ly,** *adv.;* **-ness,** *n.*
o′ver•sub′tle, *adj.*
o′ver•sub′tle•ty, *n., pl* **-ties.**
o′ver•sub′tly, *adv.*
o′ver•suf•fi′cien•cy, *n.*
o′ver•suf•fi′cient, *adj.;* **-ly,** *adv.*
o′ver•sup′, *v.*, **-supped, -sup•ping.**
o′ver•su′per•sti′tious, *adj.;* **-ly,** *adv.;* **-ness,** *n.*
o′ver•sure′, *adj.;* **-ly,** *adv.;* **-ness,** *n.*
o′ver•sure′ty, *n.*
o′ver•sus•cep′ti•bil′i•ty, *n.*
o′ver•sus•cep′ti•ble, *adj.;* **-ble•ness,** *n.;* **-bly,** *adv.*
o′ver•sus•pi′cious, *adj.;* **-ly,** *adv.;* **-ness,** *n.*
o′ver•sweet′, *adj.;* **-ly,** *adv.;* **-ness,** *n.*
o′ver•sweet′en, *v.t.*
o′ver•sys′tem•at′ic, *adj.;* **-ness,** *n.*
o′ver•sys′tem•at′i•cal•ly, *adv.*
o′ver•sys′tem•a•tize′, *v.t.*, **-tized, -tiz•ing.**
o′ver•talk′, *v.*
o′ver•talk′a•tive, *adj.;* **-ly,** *adv.;* **-ness,** *n.*
o′ver•tame′, *adj.;* **-ly,** *adv.;* **-ness,** *n.*
o′ver•tart′, *adj.;* **-ly,** *adv.;* **-ness,** *n.*
o′ver•teach′, *v.*, **-taught, -teach•ing.**
o′ver•tech′ni•cal, *adj.;* **-ly,** *adv.*
o′ver•tech′ni•cal′i•ty, *n., pl.* **-ties.**
o′ver•tech•nol′o•gize′, *v.*, **-gized, -giz•ing.**
o′ver•te′di•ous, *adj.;* **-ly,** *adv.;* **-ness,** *n.*
o′ver•te•na′cious, *adj.;* **-ly,** *adv.;* **-ness,** *n.*
o′ver•te•nac′i•ty, *n.*
o′ver•ten′der, *adj.;* **-ly,** *adv.;* **-ness,** *n.*
o′ver•tense′, *adj.;* **-ly,** *adv.;* **-ness,** *n.*
o′ver•ten′sion, *n.*
o′ver•the•at′ri•cal, *adj.;* **-ly,** *adv.;* **-ness;** *n.*
o′ver•the′o•ri•za′tion, *n.*
o′ver•the′o•rize′, *v.i.*, **-rized, -riz•ing.**
o′ver•thick′, *adj.;* **-ly,** *adv.;* **-ness,** *n.*
o′ver•thin′, *adj.;* **-ly,** adv.; **-ness,** *n.*
o′ver•thought′ful, *adj.;* **-ly,** *adv.;* **-ness,** *n.*
o′ver•thrift′i•ly, *adv.*
o′ver•thrift′i•ness, *n.*
o′ver•thrift′y, *adj.*
o′ver•throng′, *v.*
o′ver•tight′, *adj.;* **-ly,** *adv.;* **-ness,** *n.*
o′ver•tight′en, *v.*
o′ver•tim′bered, *adj.*
o′ver•tim′id, *adj.;* **-ly,** *adv.;* **-ness,** *n.*
o′ver•ti•mid′i•ty, *n.*
o′ver•tim′or•ous, *adj.;* **-ly,** *adv.;* **-ness,** *n.*
o′ver•tin′sel, *v.t.*, **-seled, -sel•ing** or (*esp. Brit.*) **-selled, -sel•ling.**
o′ver•tint′, *v.*
o′ver•tint′, *n.*
o′ver•tip′, *v.*, **-tipped, -tip•ping.**
o′ver•tip′ple, *v.i.*, **-pled, -pling.**
o′ver•toil′, *v.*
o′ver•tol′er•ance, *n.*
o′ver•tol′er•ant, *adj.;* **-ly,** *adv.*
o′ver•tor′ture, *v.t.*, **-tured, -tur•ing.**
o′ver•train′, *v.*
o′ver•tread′, *n.*
o′ver•treat′, *v.*
o′ver•treat′ment, *n.*
o′ver•trim′, *v.*, **-trimmed, -trim•ming.**
o′ver•trou′ble, *v.*, **-bled, -bling.**
o′ver•trust′, *v.*
o′ver•trust′ful, *adj.;* **-ly,** *adv.;* **-ness,** *n.*
o′ver•truth′ful, *adj.;* **-ly,** *adv.;* **-ness,** *n.*
o′ver•twist′, *v.*
o′ver•un′ion•ize′, *v.*, **-ized, -iz•ing.**
o′ver•ur′ban•i•za′tion, *n.*
o′ver•ur′ban•ize′, *v.*, **-ized, -iz•ing.**
o′ver•urge′, *v.*, **-urged, -urg•ing.**
o′ver•u′ti•li•za′tion, *n.*
o′ver•u′ti•lize′, *v.t.*, **-lized, -liz•ing.**
o′ver•val′iant, *adj.;* **-ly,** *adv.;* **-ness,** *n.*
o′ver•val′u•a•ble, *adj.;* **-ble•ness,** *n.;* **-bly,** *adv.*
o′ver•var′i•a′tion, *n.*
o′ver•va•ri′e•ty, *n.*
o′ver•var′y, *v.*, **-var•ied, -var•y•ing.**
o′ver•ve′he•mence, *n.*
o′ver•ve′he•ment, *adj.;* **-ly,** *adv.*
o′ver•ven′ti•late′, *v.t.*, **-lat•ed, -lat•ing.**
o′ver•ven′ti•la′tion, *n.*
o′ver•ven′ture•some, *adj.*
o′ver•ven′tur•ous, *adj.;* **-ly,** *adv.;* **-ness,** *n.*
o′ver•vig′or•ous, *adj.;* **-ly,** *adv.;* **-ness,** *n.*
o′ver•vi′o•lent, *adj.;* **-ly,** *adv.;* **-ness,** *n.*
o′ver•viv′id, *adj.;* **-ly,** *adv.;* **-ness,** *n.*
o′ver•war′i•ly, *adv.*
o′ver•war′i•ness, *n.*
o′ver•warmed′, *adj.*
o′ver•war′y, *adj.*
o′ver•wa′ter, *v.*
o′ver•weak′, *adj.;* **-ly,** *adv.;* **-ness,** *n.*
o′ver•wealth′, *n.*
o′ver•wealth′y, *adj.*
o′ver•wet′, *adj., v.t.*, **-wet** or **-wet•ted, -wet•ting;** **-ly,** *adv.;* **-ness,** *n.*
o′ver•whip′, *v.t.*, **-whipped, -whip•ping.**
o′ver•wide′, *adj.;* **-ly,** *adv.;* **-ness,** *n.*
o′ver•wild′, *adj.;* **-ly,** *adv.;* **-ness,** *n.*
o′ver•will′ing, *adj.;* **-ly,** *adv.;* **-ness,** *n.*
o′ver•wil′y, *adj.*
o′ver•with′ered, *adj.*

Ow·ens (ō′ənz), *n.* **Jesse** (*John Cleveland*), 1913–80, U.S. athlete.

Ow·ens·bor·o (ō′ənz bûr′ō, -bur′ō), *n.* a city in NW Kentucky, on the Ohio River. 54,450.

Ow′en Sound′, a city in SE Ontario, in S Canada, on Georgian Bay of Lake Huron: summer resort. 19,883.

Ow′en Stan′ley, a mountain range on New Guinea in SE Papua New Guinea. Highest peak, Mt. Victoria, 13,240 ft. (4036 m).

OWI, 1. Office of War Information: the former U.S federal agency (1942–45) charged with disseminating information about World War II, as changes in Allied military policy or casualty statistics. **2.** operating (a motor vehicle) while intoxicated.

ow·ing (ō′ing), *adj.* **1.** owed, unpaid, or due for payment: *to pay what is owing.* **2. owing to,** because of; as a result of: *Owing to a mistake in the payroll department, some of us were issued incorrect checks.* [1325–75; ME; see OWE, -ING[2]]

owl (oul), *n.* **1.** any of numerous, chiefly nocturnal birds of prey, of the order Strigiformes, having a broad head with large, forward-directed eyes that are usually surrounded by disks of modified feathers: many populations are diminishing owing to loss of habitat. **2.** one of a breed of domestic pigeons having an owllike appearance. **3.** See **night owl. 4.** a person of owllike solemnity or appearance. —*adj.* **5.** operating late at night or all night: *an owl train.* [bef. 900; ME *oule,* OE *ūle;* c. LG *ūle,* D *uil;* akin to G *Eule,* ON *ugla*] —**owl′like′,** *adj.*

great horned owl, *Bubo virginianus,* length 2 ft. (0.6 m)

owl′ but′terfly, any of several South American nymphalid butterflies of the genus *Caligo,* esp. *C. eurylochus,* having a spot like an owl's eye on each hind wing. [1880–85]

owl·et (ou′lit), *n.* **1.** a young owl. **2.** See **little owl.** [1535–45; OWL + -ET]

owl′et moth′, noctuid (def. 1). [1860–65]

owl′et night′jar, any of several birds of the family Aegothelidae, of Australia and Papua New Guinea, related to the nightjars but resembling small owls.

owl·ish (ou′lish), *adj.* resembling or characteristic of an owl: *His thick glasses gave him an owlish appearance.* [1605–15; OWL + -ISH[1]] —**owl′ish·ly,** *adv.* —**owl′ish·ness,** *n.*

owl′ mon′key, douroucouli. [1860–65]

owl's′ clo′ver, any of several western American plants belonging to the genus *Orthocarpus,* of the figwort family, having dense spikes of flowers in a variety of colors with conspicuous bracts. [1895–1900, *Amer.*]

own (ōn), *adj.* **1.** of, pertaining to, or belonging to oneself or itself (usually used after a possessive to emphasize the idea of ownership, interest, or relation conveyed by the possessive): *He spent only his own money.* **2.** (used as an intensifier to indicate oneself as the sole agent of some activity or action, prec. by a possessive): *He insists on being his own doctor.* **3. come into one's own, a.** to take possession of that which is due or owed one. **b.** to receive the recognition that one's abilities merit: *She finally came into her own as a sculptor of the first magnitude.* **4. get one's own back,** to get revenge and thereby a sense of personal satisfaction, as for a slight or a previous setback; get even with somebody or something: *He saw the award as a way of getting his own back for all the snubs by his colleagues.* **5. hold one's own, a.** to maintain one's position or condition: *The stock market seems to be holding its own these days.* **b.** to be equal to the opposition: *He can hold his own in any fight.* **6. of one's own,** belonging to oneself: *She had never had a room of her own.* **7. on one's own, a.** by dint of one's own efforts, resources, or sense of responsibility; independently: *Because she spoke the language, she got around the country very well on her own.* **b.** living or functioning without dependence on others; independent: *My son's been on his own for several years.* —*v.t.* **8.** to have or hold as one's own; possess: *They own several homes.* **9.** to acknowledge or admit: *to own a fault.* **10.** to acknowledge as one's own; recognize as having full claim, authority, power, dominion, etc.: *He owned his child before the entire assembly. They owned the king as their lord.* —*v.i.* **11.** to confess (often fol. by *to, up,* or *up to*): *The one who did it had better own up. I own to being uncertain about that.* [bef. 900; (adj.) ME *owen,* OE *āgen* (c. G *eigen,* ON *eigenn*), orig. ptp. of *āgan* to possess (see OWE); (v.) ME *ownen,* OE *āgnian, āhnian,* deriv. of *āgen*]
—**Syn. 8.** See **have.** —**Ant. 8.** lack, need.

own·er (ō′nər), *n.* a person who owns; possessor; proprietor. [1300–50; ME; see OWN, -ER[1]]

own·er-oc·cu·pied (ō′nər ok′yə pīd′), *adj.* (of a home, apartment, etc.) used as a residence by the owner. [1950–55] —**own′er-oc′cu·pi′er,** *n.*

own·er-op·er·a·tor (ō′nər op′ə rā′tər), *n.* **1.** a driver, esp. of a truck or taxicab, who owns and operates a vehicle used to earn a living. **2.** a person who both owns and operates a business. [1955–60]

own·er·ship (ō′nər ship′), *n.* **1.** the state or fact of being an owner. **2.** legal right of possession; proprietorship. [1575–85; OWNER + -SHIP]

O·wos·so (ō wos′ō), *n.* a city in central Michigan. 16,455.

owse (ous), *n., pl.* **ows·en** (ou′sən, -zən). *Scot. and North Eng.* ox.

ox (oks), *n., pl.* **ox·en** for 1, 2, **ox·es** for 3. **1.** the adult castrated male of the genus *Bos,* used chiefly as a draft animal. **2.** any member of the bovine family. **3.** *Informal.* a clumsy, stupid fellow. [bef. 900; ME *oxe,* OE *oxa;* c. OFris *oxa,* OS, OHG *ohso,* ON *uxi, oxi;* akin to Welsh *ych*] —**ox′like′,** *adj.*

ox-, *Chem.* a combining form meaning "containing oxygen": *oxazine.* [short for OXYGEN]

Ox., Oxford. [< ML *Oxonia*]

ox·a·cil·lin (ok′sə sil′in), *n. Pharm.* a semisynthetic penicillin, $C_{19}H_{19}N_3O_5S$, used in the treatment of serious staphylococcal infections. [1960–65; (*is*)*oxa*(*zole*), a component of its chemical name + (PENI)CILLIN]

ox·a·late (ok′sə lāt′), *n. Chem.* any salt or ester of oxalic acid, occurring in plants, esp. spinach, rhubarb, and certain other vegetables and nuts, and capable of forming an insoluble salt with calcium and interfering with its absorption by the body. [1785–85; OXAL(IC) + -ATE[2]]

ox·al·ic (ok sal′ik), *adj. Chem.* of or derived from oxalic acid. [1785–95; < F *oxalique.* See OXALIS, -IC]

oxal′ic ac′id, *Chem.* a white, crystalline, water-soluble, poisonous acid, $H_2C_2O_4 \cdot 2H_2O$, first discovered in the juice of the wood sorrel species of oxalis and obtained by reacting carbon monoxide with sodium hydroxide or certain carbohydrates with acids or alkalis: used chiefly for bleaching, as a cleanser, and as a laboratory reagent. [1785–95]

ox·a·lis (ok′sə lis, ok sal′is), *n.* any plant of the genus *Oxalis,* comprising the wood sorrels. [1595–1605; < L: garden sorrel, sour wine < Gk *oxalis,* deriv. of *oxýs* sharp]

ox′a·lo·a·ce′tic ac′id (ok′sə lō ə sē′tik, ok′-, ok-sal′ō-, -sal′-), *Biochem.* a crystalline organic acid, $C_4H_4O_5$, that is an important intermediate in the Krebs cycle, where it is formed by the oxidation of malic acid and is acetylated to form citric acid: also a product of transamination reactions of aspartic acid. [1895–1900; OXAL(IC) + -O- + ACETIC ACID]

ox′a·lo·suc·cin′ic ac′id (ok′sə lō sək sin′ik, ok′-, ok sal′ō-, -sal′-), *Biochem.* an organic acid, $C_6H_6O_7$, that is an intermediate formed by the dehydrogenation of isocitric acid in fat and carbohydrate metabolism. [1920–25; OXAL(IC) + -O- + SUCCINIC ACID]

ox·az·e·pam (ok saz′ə pam′), *n. Pharm.* a benzodiazepine, $C_{15}H_{11}ClN_2O_2$, used in the management of anxiety, insomnia, and alcohol withdrawal. [1960–65; (*hydr*)*ox*(*y*) + (*benzodi*)*azep*(*in*), components of its chemical name + AM(IDE)]

ox·a·zine (ok′sə zēn′, -zin), *n. Chem.* any of a group of 13 compounds having the formula C_4H_5NO, the atoms of which are arranged in a six-membered ring. [1895–1900; OX- + AZINE]

ox·blood (oks′blud′), *n.* a deep dull-red color. Also, **ox′blood red′.** [1695–1705; OX + BLOOD]

ox·bow (oks′bō′), *n.* **1.** a U-shaped piece of wood placed under and around the neck of an ox with its upper ends in the bar of the yoke. **2.** *Physical Geog., Geol.* **a.** a bow-shaped bend in a river, or the land embraced by it. **b.** Also called **ox′bow lake′.** a bow-shaped lake formed in a former channel of a river. [1325–75; ME; see OX, BOW[2]]

ox′bow chest′, a chest of drawers having a front convex at the sides and concave in the center without vertical divisions.

ox′bow front′, *Furniture.* a front, as of a chest of drawers, having a curve with a concave section between two convex ones. Also called **yoke front.** Cf. **serpentine front.**

oxbow front

Ox·bridge (oks′brij′), *Chiefly Brit.* —*n.* **1.** Oxford or Cambridge University, or both, esp. in contrast with the redbrick universities of England. **2.** upper-class intellectual life in England, as felt to be under the influence of Oxford and Cambridge universities: *a bitter attack on Oxbridge by the younger writers.* —*adj.* **3.** of, pertaining to, or characteristic of Oxford and Cambridge, or of upper-class, intellectual traditions or manners associated with these universities: *a career formerly open only to Oxbridge graduates; to voice the proper Oxbridge sentiments.*

ox·cart (oks′kärt′), *n.* an ox-drawn cart. [1740–50; OX + CART]

ox·en (ok′sən), *n.* a pl. of **ox.**

Ox·en·stier·na (ŏŏk′sən sheʀ′nä), *n.* **Count Ax·el** (äk′səl), 1583–1654, Swedish statesman. Also, **Ox′en·stjer′na.**

ox·eye (oks′ī′), *n., pl.* **-eyes. 1.** any of several composite plants, esp. of the genera *Heliopsis* and *Buphthalum,* having ray flowers surrounding a conspicuous disk. **2.** *Informal.* any of several shorebirds, as the least sandpiper. **3.** *Archit.* oeil-de-boeuf. [1375–1425; late ME; see OX, EYE]

ox-eyed (oks′īd′), *adj.* having large, round eyes similar to those of an ox. [1615–25; OX + EYED]

ox′eye dai′sy, a composite plant, *Chrysanthemum leucanthemum,* having flowers with white rays and a yellow disk. [1745–55]

ox·ford (oks′fərd), *n.* **1.** Also called **Oxford shoe, Oxford tie.** a low shoe laced over the instep. **2.** Also called **ox′ford cloth′.** a cotton or synthetic fabric, in plain, twill, or basket weave, constructed on a pattern of two fine yarns woven as one warpwise and one loosely twisted yarn weftwise, for shirts, skirts, and summer sportswear. [1580–90; named after OXFORD (def. 2)]

Ox·ford (oks′fərd), *n.* **1. 1st Earl of.** See **Harley, Robert. 2.** a city in S Oxfordshire, in S England, NW of London: university, founded in 12th century. 116,600. **3.** Oxfordshire. **4.** a town in SW Ohio. 17,655. **5.** a town in S Massachusetts. 11,680. **6.** a town in N Mississippi, hometown of William Faulkner. 9882. **7.** Also called **Ox′ford Down′.** one of an English breed of large, hornless sheep, noted for its market lambs and heavy fleece of medium length.

Ox′ford cor′ners, *Print.* ruled border lines about the text of a page that cross and project slightly at the corners. —**Ox′ford cor′nered.**

Ox′ford frame′, a frame for a picture, mirror, etc., consisting of four straight pieces whose ends project beyond the corners. [1870–75]

Ox′ford gray′, medium to dark gray. [1830–40]

Ox′ford Group′, an organization founded at Oxford University in 1921 by Frank Buchman, advocating absolute morality in public and private life. Cf. **Moral Re-Armament.**

Ox′ford move′ment, the movement toward High Church principles within the Church of England, originating at Oxford University in 1833 in opposition to liberalizing, rationalizing, and evangelical tendencies and emphasizing the principles of primitive and patristic Christianity as well as the historic and catholic character of the church. Cf. **Tractarianism.** [1835–45]

Ox′ford rule′, *Typography.* a type that prints a thick line together with and parallel to a thin one.

Ox·ford·shire (oks′fərd shēr′, -shər), *n.* a county in S England. 539,100; 1008 sq. mi. (2610 sq. km). Also called **Oxford, Oxon.**

Ox′ford shoe′, oxford (def. 1). Also called **Ox′ford tie′.** [1840–50]

Ox′ford the′ory, the theory attributing the authorship of Shakespeare's plays to Edward de Vere, Earl of Oxford, 1550–1604. Cf. **Baconian theory.**

ox·heart (oks′härt′), *n.* any large, heart-shaped variety of sweet cherry. [1840–50; OX + HEART]

ox·i·dant (ok′si dənt), *n.* a chemical agent that oxidizes. Also called **oxidizer, oxidizing agent.** [1880–85; OXIDE + -ANT]

ox′i·dant smog′ (ok′si dənt), *Meteorol.* See **photochemical smog.**

ox·i·dase (ok′si dās′, -dāz′), *n. Biochem.* any of a class of oxidoreductases that catalyze the oxidation of a substrate by molecular oxygen with the formation, in most cases, of hydrogen peroxide. [1895–1900; OXIDE + -ASE] —**ox·i·da·sic** (ok′si dā′sik, -zik), *adj.*

ox·i·date (ok′si dāt′), *v.,* **-dat·ed, -dat·ing,** *n. Chem.* —*v.t., v.i.* **1.** to oxidize. —*n.* **2.** *Geochem.* any of the class of sediments consisting chiefly of oxides of iron or manganese. [1780–90; OXIDE + -ATE[1]]

ox·i·da·tion (ok si dā′shən), *n. Chem.* **1.** the process or result of oxidizing. **2.** the deposit that forms on the surface of a metal as it oxidizes. Also, **ox·i·di·za·tion** (ok′si də zā′shən). [1785–95; OXIDE + -ATION] —**ox′i·da′tion·al, ox′i·da′tive,** *adj.*

oxida′tion poten′tial, *Physical Chem.* (in a galvanic cell) the potential of the electrode at which oxidation occurs. Cf. **reduction potential.** [1895–1900]

ox·i·da·tion-re·duc·tion (ok′si dā′shən ri duk′shən), *Chem.* —*n.* **1.** a chemical reaction between two substances in which one substance is oxidized and the other reduced. —*adj.* **2.** of or pertaining to such a reaction. Also called **redox.** [1905–10]

oxida′tion state′, *Chem.* the state of an element or ion in a compound with regard to the electrons gained or lost by the element or ion in the reaction that formed the compound, expressed as a positive or negative number indicating the ionic charge of the element or ion. Also called **oxida′tion num′ber.** [1945–50]

ox′idative phosphoryla′tion, *Biochem.* the aerobic synthesis, coupled to electron transport, of ATP from phosphate and ADP. [1950–55]

ox·ide (ok′sīd, -sid), *n. Chem.* a compound in which oxygen is bonded to one or more electropositive atoms. Also, **ox·id** (ok′sid). [1780–90; < F (now *oxyde*), b. *oxygène* and *acide.* See OXYGEN, ACID] —**ox·id·ic** (ok sid′ik), *adj.*

ox·i·dim·e·try (ok′si dim′i trē), *n.* a technique of analytical chemistry that utilizes oxidizing agents for titrations. [1895–1900; OXIDE + -I- + -METRY] —**ox·i·di·met·ric** (ok′si di me′trik), *adj.*

ox·i·dize (ok′si dīz′), *v.,* **-dized, -diz·ing.** *Chem.* —*v.t.* **1.** to convert (an element) into an oxide; combine with oxygen. **2.** to cover with a coating of oxide or rust. **3.** to take away hydrogen, as by the action of oxygen; add oxygen or any nonmetal. **4.** to remove electrons from (an atom or molecule), thereby increasing the valence. Cf. **reduce** (def. 12). —*v.i.* **5.** to become oxidized. **6.** (esp. of white wine) to lose freshness after prolonged exposure to air and often to darken in color. Also, *esp. Brit.,* **ox′i·dise′.** [1795–1805; OXIDE + -IZE] —**ox′i·diz′a·ble, ox·i·da·ble** (ok′si də bəl), *adj.* —**ox′i·diz′a·bil′i·ty,** *n.*

ox·i·diz·er (ok′si dī′zər), *n. Chem.* oxidant. [1870–75; OXIDIZE + -ER[1]]

ox′idizing a′gent, *Chem.* oxidant.

ox·i·do·re·duc·tase (ok′si dō ri duk′tās, -tāz′), *n. Biochem.* any of a class of enzymes that act as a catalyst, some of them conjointly, causing the oxidation and reduction of compounds. Also, **ox′i·do·re·duc′tase.** [1920–25; OXIDE + -O- + REDUCTASE]

ox·ime (ok′sēm, -sim), *n. Chem.* any of a group of compounds containing the group >C=NOH, produced by the condensation of ketones or aldehydes with hydroxylamine. [1890–95; OX(YGEN) + IM(ID)E]

ox·im·e·ter (ok sim′i tər), *n. Med.* an instrument for measuring the oxygen saturation of the hemoglobin in a sample of blood. [1940–45; OX- + -I- + -METER] **—ox·i·met·ric** (ok′si me′trik), *adj.*

ox·im·e·try (ok sim′i trē), *n. Med.* the measuring of oxygen saturation of the blood by means of an oximeter. [1940–45; OX- + -I- + -METRY]

ox·i·sol (ok′si sôl′, -sol′), *n.* a thick, weathered soil of the humid tropics, largely depleted in the minerals that promote fertility, and characteristic of the Amazon and Congo basins. [1955–60; OX- + -I- + -SOL]

Ox·nard (oks′närd), *n.* a city in SW California, NW of Los Angeles. 108,195.

Ox·on (ok′son, -sən), *n.* Oxfordshire.

Oxon., 1. Oxford. [< ML *Oxonia*] **2.** of Oxford. [< ML *Oxoniēnsis*]

Ox′on Hill′, a city in central Maryland, near Washington, D.C. 36,267.

Ox·o·ni·an (ok sō′nē ən), *adj.* **1.** of or pertaining to Oxford, England, or to Oxford University (in England). —*n.* **2.** a member or graduate of Oxford University. **3.** a native or inhabitant of Oxford. [1530–40; < ML *Oxoni(a)* Oxford + -AN]

ox·o′ni·um com′pound (ok sō′nē əm), *Chem.* a salt formed by the reaction of an acid with an organic compound containing a basic oxygen atom. [OX- + NL *-onium* (abstracted from *ammonium*)]

oxo′nium i′on, *Chem.* See **hydronium ion.**

ox′o proc′ess (ok′sō), *Chem.* a process for producing carbonyl compounds, esp. alcohols and aldehydes, by adding, under high pressure, carbon monoxide and hydrogen to an olefin in the presence of a cobalt catalyst. Also called **ox′o reac′tion.** [OX- + -O-]

ox·peck·er (oks′pek′ər), *n.* either of two African starlings of the genus *Buphagus*, characterized by their habit of riding on large, wild animals and domestic cattle to feed on ticks. [1840–50; OX + PECKER]

ox·tail (oks′tāl′), *n.* the skinned tail of an ox or steer, used as an ingredient in soup, stew, etc. [1675–85; OX + TAIL[1]]

ox·ter (ok′stər), *n. Scot. and North Eng.* the armpit. [1490–1500; akin to OE *ōcusta* armpit, ON *(h)ōstr* throat]

ox′-tongue par′tisan (oks′tung′), a shafted weapon having a long, wide, tapering blade. Also called **langue de boeuf.**

Ox·us (ok′səs), *n.* See **Amu Darya.**

oxy-[1], a combining form meaning "sharp," "acute," "keen," "pointed," "acid," used in the formation of compound words: *oxycephalic; oxygen; oxymoron.* [< Gk, comb. form of *oxýs* sharp, keen, acid]

oxy-[2], a combining form representing **oxygen** in compound words, sometimes as an equivalent of *hydroxy-: oxychloride.*

ox·y·a·cet·y·lene (ok′sē ə set′l ēn′, -in), *adj.* **1.** noting or pertaining to a mixture of oxygen and acetylene: *an oxyacetylene torch.* —*n.* **2.** a mixture of oxygen and acetylene, used in a blowtorch for cutting steel plates or the like. [1905–10; OXY-[2] + ACETYLENE]

ox·y·ac·id (ok′sē as′id), *n. Chem.* an inorganic acid containing oxygen. Also called **oxygen acid.** [1830–40; OXY-[2] + ACID]

ox·y·al·de·hyde (ok′sē al′də hīd′), *n. Chem.* an aldehyde containing the hydroxyl group. [OXY-[2] + ALDEHYDE]

ox·y·ben·zene (ok′si ben′zēn, -ben zēn′), *n. Chem.* phenol (def. 1). [OXY-[2] + BENZENE]

ox·y·cal·ci·um (ok′si kal′sē əm), *adj.* pertaining to or produced by oxygen and calcium. [1860–65; OXY-[2] + CALCIUM]

oxycal′cium light′. See **calcium light.** [1860–65]

ox·y·cel·lu·lose (ok′si sel′yə lōs′), *n. Chem.* any substance formed naturally or synthetically by the oxidation of cellulose. [1880–85; OXY-[2] + CELLULOSE]

ox·y·ceph·a·ly (ok′si sef′ə lē), *n. Pathol.* a malformation in which the head is somewhat pointed, caused by premature closure of the skull sutures. Also called **acrocephaly.** [1890–95; < G *Oxycephalie* < Gk *oxyképhal(os)* sharp-headed (*oxy-* OXY-[1] + *kephal(ḗ)* head + *-os* adj. suffix) + *-ie* -Y[3]] **—ox·y·ce·phal·ic** (ok′sē sə fal′ik), **ox′y·ceph′a·lous,** *adj.*

ox·y·chlo·ride (ok′si klôr′īd, -id, -klōr′-), *n. Chem.* a compound having oxygen and chlorine atoms bonded to another element, as bismuth oxychloride, BiOCl. [1855–60; OXY-[2] + CHLORIDE] **—ox′y·chlo′ric,** *adj.*

ox·y·gen (ok′si jən), *n. Chem.* a colorless, odorless, gaseous element constituting about one-fifth of the volume of the atmosphere and present in a combined state in nature. It is the supporter of combustion in air and was the standard of atomic, combining, and molecular weights until 1961, when carbon 12 became the new standard. *Symbol:* O; *at. wt.:* 15.9994; *at. no.:* 8; *density:* 1.4290 g/l at 0°C and 760 mm pressure. [1780–90; < F *oxygène*, equiv. to *oxy-* OXY-[1] + *-gène* -GEN] **—ox·y·gen·ic** (ok′si jen′ik), **ox·yg·e·nous** (ok sij′ə nəs), *adj.* **—ox·y·gen·ic·i·ty** (ok′si jə nis′i tē), *n.*

ox′ygen ac′id, oxyacid. [1835–45]

ox·y·gen·ase (ok′si jə nās′, -nāz′), *n. Biochem.* an oxidoreductase enzyme that catalyzes the introduction of molecular oxygen into an organic substance. [1900–05; OXYGEN + -ASE]

ox·y·gen·ate (ok′si jə nāt′), *v.t.*, **-at·ed, -at·ing.** to treat, combine, or enrich with oxygen: *to oxygenate the blood.* [1780–90; OXYGEN + -ATE[1]] **—ox′y·gen·a′tion,** *n.* **—ox′y·gen·a′tor,** *n.*

ox′ygen cy′cle, *Ecol.* the process by which oxygen released into the atmosphere by photosynthetic organisms is taken up by aerobic organisms while the carbon dioxide released as a by-product of repiration is taken up for photosynthesis. [1930–35]

ox′ygen debt′, *Physiol.* the body's oxygen deficiency resulting from strenuous physical activity. [1920–25]

ox·y·gen·ize (ok′si jə nīz′), *v.t.*, **-ized, -iz·ing.** oxygenate. Also, *esp. Brit.*, **ox′y·gen·ise′.** [1795–1805; OXYGEN + -IZE] **—ox′y·gen·iz′a·ble,** *adj.* **—ox′y·gen·iz′·er,** *n.*

ox′ygen lance′, a tube for conveying oxygen, used in various thermal cutting or steelmaking operations.

ox′ygen mask′, a masklike device placed or worn over the nose and mouth when inhaling supplementary oxygen from an attached tank. [1915–20]

ox′ygen tent′, a small tentlike canopy placed over a sick person for delivering and maintaining a flow of oxygen at critical periods. [1920–25]

ox·y·he·mo·glo·bin (ok′si hē′mə glō′bin, -hem′ə-), *n. Biochem.* See under **hemoglobin.** [1870–75; OXY-[2] + HEMOGLOBIN]

ox·y·hy·dro·gen (ok′si hī′drə jən), *adj.* **1.** pertaining to or involving a mixture of oxygen and hydrogen. —*n.* **2.** a mixture of oxygen and hydrogen, used in a blowtorch for welding steel plates or the like. [1820–30; OXY-[2] + HYDROGEN]

ox·y·me·taz·o·line (ok′sē mə taz′ə lēn′, -met′ə zō-), *n. Pharm.* a sympathomimetic drug, $C_{16}H_{24}N_2O$, used as a topical, long-lasting nasal decongestant. [by rearrangement of parts of one of its chemical names]

ox·y·mo·ron (ok′si môr′on, -mōr′-), *n., pl.* **-mo·ra** (-môr′ə, -mōr′ə). *Rhet.* a figure of speech by which a locution produces an incongruous, seemingly self-contradictory effect, as in "cruel kindness" or "to make haste slowly." [1650–60; < LL *oxymorum* < presumed Gk **oxýmōron*, neut. of **oxýmōros* sharp-dull, equiv. to *oxý(s)* sharp (see OXY-[1]) + *mōrós* dull (see MORON)] **—ox·y·mo·ron·ic** (ok′sē mə ron′ik), *adj.*

ox·y·mor·phone (ok′si môr′fōn), *n. Pharm.* a potent semisynthetic morphine-derived narcotic analgesic, $C_{17}H_{19}NO_4$, used as a substitute for morphine. [OXY-[2] + MORPH(INE) + -ONE, components of its full chemical name]

ox·y·neu·rine (ok′si no͝or′ēn, -in, -nyo͝or′-), *n. Chem.* betaine. [OXY-[2] + NEUR- + -INE[2]]

ox·y·phil·ic (ok′sə fil′ik), *adj.* acidophilic. [1900–05; OXY-[2] + -PHILIC]

ox·y·salt (ok′si sôlt′), *n. Chem.* **1.** any salt of an oxyacid. **2.** a salt containing oxygen as well as a given anion, as FeOCl or $BiONO_3$. [1830–40; OXY-[2] + SALT[1]]

ox·y·sul·fide (ok′si sul′fīd, -fid), *n. Chem.* a sulfide in which part of the sulfur is replaced by oxygen. [1850–55; OXY-[2] + SULFIDE]

ox·y·te·tra·cy·cline (ok′si te′trə si′klin, -klēn), *n. Pharm.* a dull-yellow, crystalline antibiotic powder, $C_{22}H_{24}N_2O_9$, produced by *Streptomyces rimosus*, used chiefly in treating infections caused by streptococci, staphylococci, Gram-negative bacilli, rickettsiae, and certain protozoans and viruses. [1950–55; OXY-[2] + TETRACYCLINE]

ox·y·to·ci·a (ok′si tō′shē ə, -shə), *n. Med.* rapid childbirth. [< NL, equiv. to *oxy-* OXY-[1] + *toc-* (< Gk *tókos* childbirth) + *-ia* -IA]

ox·y·to·cic (ok′si tō′sik, -tos′ik), *Med.* —*adj.* **1.** of or causing the stimulation of the involuntary muscle of the uterus. **2.** promoting or accelerating childbirth. —*n.* **3.** an oxytocic substance or drug. [1850–55; OXYTOC(IA) + -IC]

ox·y·to·cin (ok′si tō′sən), *n.* **1.** *Biochem.* a polypeptide hormone, produced by the posterior lobe of the pituitary gland, that stimulates contraction of the smooth muscle of the uterus. **2.** *Pharm.* a commercial form of this substance, obtained from beef and hog pituitary glands or esp. by synthesis, and used chiefly in obstetrics to induce labor and to control postnatal hemorrhage. [1925–30; OXYTOC(IC) + -IN[2]]

ox·y·tone (ok′si tōn′), *Class. Gk. Gram.* —*adj.* **1.** having an acute accent on the last syllable. —*n.* **2.** an oxytone word. [1755–65; < Gk *oxýtonos* sharp-toned. See OXY-[1], TONE]

ox·y·u·ri·a·sis (ok′sē yo͝o rī′ə sis), *n. Pathol.* human infection with pinworms. [1905–10; < NL *Oxyur(is)* genus name of pinworms (equiv. to *oxy-* OXY-[1] + Gk *our(á)* tail + NL *-is* n. ending) + -IASIS]

oy[1] (oi), *interj.* (used to express dismay, pain, annoyance, grief, etc.) Also, **oi.** [1890–95; < Yiddish]

oy[2] (oi), *n. Scot.* **1.** a grandchild. **2.** *Obs.* a nephew or niece. Also, **oe.** [1425–75; late ME (north and Scots) *o(o), oy(e)* < ScotGael *ogha;* see O′]

O·ya·ma (ô′yä mä′), *n.* **I·wa·o** (ē′wä ô′), 1842–1916, Japanese field marshal.

O′ya·shi′o Cur′rent (oi′ə shē′ō; *Japn.* ô′yä shē′ô), *n.* a cold ocean current flowing SW from the Bering Sea, E of the Kurile Islands, along the E coast of Japan where it meets the Japan Current. Also called **Okhotsk Current.**

oye·let (oi′lit), *n.* eyelet (def. 5). Also, **oy′let.**

o·yer (ō′yər, oi′ər), *n. Law.* **1.** See **oyer and terminer. 2.** a hearing in open court involving the production of some document pleaded by one party and demanded by the other, the party pleading the document being said to *make profert.* [1375–1425; late ME < AF; OF *oïr* to hear < L *audīre*]

o′yer and ter′mi·ner (tûr′mə nər), *Law.* **1.** (in some U.S. states) any of various higher criminal courts. **2.** *Brit.* **a.** a commission or writ directing the holding of a court to try offenses. **b.** the court itself. [1375–1425; late ME < AF: lit., to hear and determine]

o·yez (ō′yes, ō′yez), *interj.* **1.** hear! attend! (a cry uttered usually twice by a court officer to command silence and attention, as before court is in session, and formerly by public criers). —*n.* **2.** a cry of "oyez." Also, **o′yes.** [1375–1425; late ME < AF, pl. impv. of *oyer;* see OYER]

O·yo (ō′yō), *n.* a city in W Nigeria. 152,000.

oys·ter (oi′stər), *n.* **1.** any of several edible, marine, bivalve mollusks of the family Ostreidae, having an irregularly shaped shell, occurring on the bottom or adhering to rocks or other objects in shallow water. **2.** the oyster-shaped bit of dark meat in the front hollow of the side bone of a fowl. **3.** *Slang.* a closemouthed or uncommunicative person, esp. one who keeps secrets well. **4.** something from which a person may extract or derive advantage: *The world is my oyster.* **5.** See **oyster white.** —*v.i.* **6.** to dredge for or otherwise take oysters. [1325–75; ME *oistre* < MF < L *ostrea* < Gk *óstreon;* see OSTRACIZE]

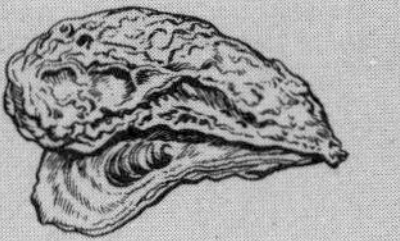

oyster, *Ostrea virginica,* length 2 to 6 in. (5 to 15 cm)

Oys′ter Bay′, a town on the N shore of Long Island, in SE New York. Theodore Roosevelt homestead nearby. 6497.

oys′ter bed′, a place where oysters breed or are cultivated. [1585–95]

oys′ter cap′, an edible, brownish-gray to white mushroom, *Pleurotus ostreatus*, that grows in clusters on fallen trees and their stumps. Also called **oyster mushroom.**

oys·ter·catch·er (oi′stər kach′ər), *n.* any of several long-billed wading birds of the genus *Haematopus* that have chiefly black-and-white plumage and that feed on oysters, clams, mussels, etc. Also, **oys′ter catch′er.** [1725–35, *Amer.*; OYSTER + CATCHER]

oys′ter crab′, a pea crab, *Pinnotheres ostreum*, the female of which lives as a commensal within the mantle cavity of oysters. [1750–60]

oys′ter crack′er, a small, round, usually salted cracker, served with oysters, soup, etc. [1870–75]

oys·tered (oi′stərd), *adj. Furniture.* veneered with matched flitches having a figure of concentric rings. [1910–15; OYSTER + -ED[3]]

oys′ter farm′, a place where oyster beds are kept. [1935–40]

oys·ter·fish (oi′stər fish′), *n., pl.* (*esp. collectively*) **-fish,** (*esp. referring to two or more kinds or species*) **-fish·es.** the oyster toadfish. See under **toadfish** (def. 1). [1605–15; OYSTER + FISH]

oys′ter fork′, a small, three-pronged fork, used esp. in eating seafood.

oys·ter·ing (oi′stər ing), *n.* **1.** veneering of furniture with matched flitches having a figure of concentric rings. **2.** flitches used on an oystered piece. [1910–15; OYSTER + -ING[1]]

oys·ter·man (oi′stər mən), *n., pl.* **-men. 1.** a person who gathers, cultivates, or sells oysters. **2.** a boat specially equipped for gathering oysters. Also called **oys′·ter·er.** [1545–55; OYSTER + -MAN]

oys′ter mush′room. See **oyster cap.** [1870–75]

oys′ter plant′, 1. salsify. **2.** See **sea lungwort. 3.** Moses-in-the-cradle. [1815–25, *Amer.*]

oys′ter-shell scale′ (oi′stər shel′), a scale insect, *Lepidosaphes ulmi*, having a scale shaped like the shell of an oyster, which infests various deciduous trees and shrubs. Also called **oys′ter scale′.** [1875–80, *Amer.*; OYSTER + SHELL]

oys′ters Rock′efeller, *Cookery.* oysters spread with a mixture of spinach, butter, seasonings, and bread crumbs and baked on the half shell. [of unclear orig.; the dish appar. has no direct connection with John D. ROCKEFELLER or his heirs]

oys′ter toad′fish. See under **toadfish** (def. 1). [1960–65]

oys′ter white′, a slightly grayish white; off-white. [1900–05]

oys·ter·wom·an (oi′stər wo͝om′ən), *n., pl.* **-wom·en.** a woman who gathers, cultivates, or sells oysters. [1590–1600; OYSTER + -WOMAN]

Oz (oz), *n. Australian Slang.* Australia. [jocular back formation from AUSSIE (with voiced sibilant)]

Oz (oz), *n.* See **Land of Oz.**

oz., ounce; ounces. [abbr. of It *onza*]

Oz·a·lid (oz′ə lid), **1.** *Trademark.* a process for reproducing line drawings, manuscripts, and the like on a sensitized paper developed by ammonia vapor. —*n.* **2.** (*sometimes l.c.*) a reproduction made by this process. —*adj.* **3.** (*sometimes l.c.*) of or pertaining to the Ozalid process.

CONCISE PRONUNCIATION KEY: act, cāpe, dâre, pärt; set, ēqual; *if*, īce; ox, ōver, ôrder, oil, bo͝ok, bo͞ot, out; up, ûrge; child; sing; shoe; thin, *th*at; zh as in *treasure.* ə = *a* as in *alone*, *e* as in *system*, *i* as in *easily*, *o* as in *gallop*, *u* as in *circus*; ᵊ as in *fire* (fīᵊr), *hour* (ouᵊr). l and n can serve as syllabic consonants, as in *cradle* (krād′l), and *button* (but′n). See the full key inside the front cover.

O·zark (ō′zärk), *n.* a town in SE Alabama. 13,188.

O′zark Moun′tains, a group of low mountains in S Missouri, N Arkansas, and NE Oklahoma. Also called **O′zarks.**

oz. av., ounce avoirdupois.

O·za·wa (ō zä′wə), *n.* **Sei·ji** (sā′jē), born 1935, Japanese conductor in the U.S.

O·zen·fant (ō zäN fäN′), *n.* **A·mé·dée** (A mā dā′), 1886–1966, French painter and writer, in the U.S. after 1938.

ozo-, a combining form meaning "smell," used in the formation of compound words: *ozocerite; ozostomia.* [< Gk, comb. form of Gk *ózein* to smell, have an odor; akin to L *odor* ODOR]

o·zo·ce·rite (ō zō′kə rīt′, -sə rīt′, ō′zō sēr′īt), *n.* a waxlike mineral resin; mineral wax. Also, **o·zo·ke·rite** (ō zō′kə rīt′, ō′zō kēr′īt). [1830–40; < G *Ozokerit* < Gk *ozo-* OZO- + *kēr(ós)* wax + G *-it* -ITE[1]]

ozon-, var. of **ozono-** before a vowel: *ozonide.*

o·zone (ō′zōn, ō zōn′), *n.* a form of oxygen, O_3, with a peculiar odor suggesting that of weak chlorine, produced when an electric spark or ultraviolet light is passed through air or oxygen. It is found in the atmosphere in minute quantities, esp. after a thunderstorm, is a powerful oxidizing agent, and is thus biologically corrosive. In the upper atmosphere, it absorbs ultraviolet rays, thereby preventing them from reaching the surface of the earth. It is used for bleaching, sterilizing water, etc. [< G *Ozon* < Gk *ózōn,* prp. of *ózein* to smell; see OZO-] —**o·zon·ic** (ō zon′ik, ō zō′nik), *adj.*

o′zone hole′, any part of the ozone layer that has become depleted by atmospheric pollution, resulting in excess ultraviolet radiation passing through the atmosphere. [1985–90]

o′zone lay′er, *Meteorol.* the layer of the upper atmosphere where most atmospheric ozone is concentrated, from about 8 to 30 mi. (12 to 48 km) above the earth, with the maximum ozone concentration occurring at an altitude of about 12 mi. (19 km). Also called **o·zo·no·sphere** (ō zō′nə sfēr′).

o′zone sick′ness, *Pathol.* a condition characterized by chest pain, itchy eyes, and drowsiness, caused by exposure to ozone, as experienced in the atmospheres of smog and high-altitude airplanes. [1975–80]

ozon′ic e′ther, *Chem.* a solution of hydrogen peroxide in ethyl ether. [1870–75; OZON- + -IC]

o·zo·nide (ō′zə nīd′, ō′zō-), *n. Chem.* any compound, usually explosive, formed by the addition of ozone to the double or triple bond of an organic compound. [1865–70]

o·zo·nif·er·ous (ō′zə nif′ər əs, ō′zō-), *adj.* containing ozone. [1855–60; OZON- + -I- + -FEROUS]

o·zon·ize (ō′zə nīz′, ō′zō-), *v.,* **-ized, -iz·ing.** —*v.t.* **1.** to impregnate or treat with ozone. **2.** to convert (oxygen) into ozone. —*v.i.* **3.** (of oxygen) to become converted into ozone. Also, *esp. Brit.,* **o′zon·ise′.** [1840–50; OZON- + -IZE] —**o′zon·iza′tion,** *n.*

o·zon·iz·er (ō′zə nī′zər, ō′zō-), *n. Chem.* an apparatus for converting oxygen into ozone. [1870–75; OZONIZE + -ER[1]]

ozono-, a combining form representing **ozone** in compound words: *ozonosphere.* Also, *esp. before a vowel,* **ozon-.**

o·zo·nol·y·sis (ō′zə nol′ə sis, ō′zō-), *n. Chem.* the reaction of ozone with hydrocarbons. [1930–35; OZONO- + -LYSIS]

o·zo·nous (ō′zə nəs, ō′zō-), *adj.* of or containing ozone. [1885–90; OZON- + -OUS]

o·zos·to·mi·a (ō′zə stō′mē ə), *n. Pathol.* bad breath; halitosis. [< NL < Gk *ozóstom(os)* having bad breath (*ozo-* OZO- + *-stomos* -STOMOUS) + *-ia* -IA]

ozs., ounces.

oz. t., ounce troy.

O·zu (ō′zōō), *n.* **Ya·su·ji·ro** (yä′sōō jē′rô), 1903–63, Japanese film director.

Oz·zie (oz′ē), *n.* a male given name, form of **Oswald.**

CONCISE ETYMOLOGY KEY: <, descended or borrowed from; >, whence; b., blend of, blended; c., cognate with; cf., compare; deriv., derivative; equiv., equivalent; imit., imitative; obl., oblique; r., replacing; s., stem; sp., spelling, spelled; resp., respelling, respelled; trans., translation; ?, origin unknown; *, unattested; ‡, probably earlier than. See the full key inside the front cover.

DEVELOPMENT OF MAJUSCULE								
NORTH SEMITIC	GREEK		ETR	LATIN		MODERN		
						GOTHIC	ITALIC	ROMAN
𐤐	ᒣ	Π	ᒣ	Γ	P	𝔓	*P*	P

P

DEVELOPMENT OF MINUSCULE					
ROMAN CURSIVE	ROMAN UNCIAL	CAROL. MIN.	MODERN		
			GOTHIC	ITALIC	ROMAN
p	p	p	𝔭	*p*	p

The sixteenth letter of the English alphabet developed from the North Semitic letter *pe*, which means "mouth," but even in its earliest extant form, the shape of the letter has no obvious connection with this meaning. Its further history can be traced through Etruscan, Greek *pi* (π), and Latin, but except in the case of the last, its present form bears little if any resemblance to its earlier forms. The minuscule (p) is derived from the capital by lengthening the descender.

P, p (pē), *n., pl.* **P's** or **Ps, p's** or **ps. 1.** the sixteenth letter of the English alphabet, a consonant. **2.** any spoken sound represented by the letter *P* or *p*, as in *pet, supper, top,* etc. **3.** something having the shape of a P. **4.** a written or printed representation of the letter *P* or *p*. **5.** a device, as a printer's type, for reproducing the letter *P* or *p*.

P, 1. *Educ.* (as a rating of student performance) passing. **2.** *Chess.* pawn. **3.** *Electronics.* plate. **4.** poor. **5.** *Gram.* predicate. **6.** Protestant.

P, *Symbol.* **1.** the 16th in order or in a series, or, when *I* is omitted, the 15th. **2.** (*sometimes l.c.*) the medieval Roman numeral for 400. Cf. **Roman numerals. 3.** *Genetics.* parental. **4.** *Chem.* phosphorus. **5.** *Physics.* **a.** power. **b.** pressure. **c.** proton. **d.** See **space inversion. e.** poise². **6.** *Biochem.* proline.

p, 1. penny; pence. **2.** *Music.* softly. [< It *piano*]

P-, *Mil.* (in designations of fighter aircraft) pursuit: *P-38.*

p-, *Chem.* para-¹ (def. 2).

P., 1. pastor. **2.** father. [< L *Pater*] **3.** peseta. **4.** peso. **5.** post. **6.** president. **7.** pressure. **8.** priest. **9.** prince. **10.** progressive.

p., 1. page. **2.** part. **3.** participle. **4.** past. **5.** father. [< L *pater*] **6.** *Chess.* pawn. **7.** penny; pence. **8.** per. **9.** *Gram.* person. **10.** peseta. **11.** peso. **12.** *Music.* softly. [< It *piano*] **13.** pint. **14.** pipe. **15.** *Baseball.* pitcher. **16.** pole. **17.** population. **18.** after. [< L *post*] **19.** president. **20.** pressure. **21.** purl.

pa (pä, pô), *n. Informal.* father. [short for PAPA]

PA, 1. paying agent. **2.** Pennsylvania (approved esp. for use with zip code). **3.** physician's assistant. **4.** press agent. **5.** public-address system.

Pa, *Physics.* pascal; pascals.

Pa, *Symbol, Chem.* protactinium.

Pa., Pennsylvania.

P.A., 1. *Insurance.* particular average. **2.** passenger agent. **3.** post adjutant. **4.** power of attorney. **5.** press agent. **6.** public-address system. **7.** publicity agent. **8.** purchasing agent.

p.a., 1. participial adjective. **2.** per annum. **3.** press agent.

p.-a., public-address system.

pa'an·ga (päng′gə, pä äng′-), *n.* a paper money, cupronickel coin, and monetary unit of Tonga equal to 100 seniti. [1965–70; < Tongan *pa'anga* orig., a kind of vine producing large, reddish, disk-shaped seeds, a seed of the vine]

Paa·si·ki·vi (pä′si ki vi), *n.* **Ju·ho Kus·ti** (yo͞o′hô ko͝os′ti), 1870–1956, Finnish statesman: president 1946–56.

PABA, (pä′bə), *n.* para-aminobenzoic acid.

Pa·blo (pä′blō; *Sp.* pä′vlō), *n.* a male given name, Spanish form of **Paul.**

Pab·lum (pab′ləm), **1.** *Trademark.* a brand of soft, bland cereal for infants. **—***n.* **2.** (*l.c.*) trite, naive, or simplistic ideas or writings; intellectual pap.

pab·u·lum (pab′yə ləm), *n.* **1.** something that nourishes an animal or vegetable organism; food; nutriment. **2.** material for intellectual nourishment. **3.** pablum. [1670–80; < L *pābulum* food, nourishment, equiv. to *pā*(*scere*) to feed (akin to FOOD) + *-bulum* n. suffix of instrument]

PABX, an automatically operated PBX. [*p*(*rivate*) *a*(*utomatic*) *b*(*ranch*) *ex*(*change*)]

pac¹ (pak), *n.* pack¹ (def. 1).

pac² (pak), *n.* **1.** Also, **pack.** a soft, flexible, heelless shoe worn as a liner inside a boot or overshoe. **2.** shoepac. [1870–75, *Amer.*; extracted from SHOEPAC by false analysis as SHOE + *pac*]

PAC (pak), *n., pl.* **PAC's, PACs.** political action committee.

Pac., Pacific.

P.A.C., political action committee.

paca, *Agouti paca,* length 2½ ft. (0.8 m)

pa·ca (pä′kə, pak′ə), *n.* a large, white-spotted, almost tailless rodent, *Agouti paca,* of Central and South America, having features resembling a guinea pig and rabbit: valued as food. Also called **spotted cavy.** [1650–60; < Sp or Pg < Tupi]

Pac′a·rai′ma Moun′tains (pak′ə rī′mə, pak′ə-). See **Pakaraima Mountains.**

Pac·ce·ka (pät chā′kə), *n. Pali.* Pratyeka.

pac·cha (pät′chä), *n.* an Incan wooden container for holding liquids. [< Quechua *phaqcha*]

pace¹ (pās), *n., v.,* **paced, pac·ing. —***n.* **1.** a rate of movement, esp. in stepping, walking, etc.: *to walk at a brisk pace of five miles an hour.* **2.** a rate of activity, progress, growth, performance, etc.; tempo. **3.** any of various standard linear measures, representing the space naturally measured by the movement of the feet in walking: roughly 30 to 40 in. (75 cm to 1 m). Cf. **geometrical pace, military pace, Roman pace. 4.** a single step: *She took three paces in the direction of the door.* **5.** the distance covered in a step: *Stand six paces inside the gates.* **6.** a manner of stepping; gait. **7.** a gait of a horse or other animal in which the feet on the same side are lifted and put down together. **8.** any of the gaits of a horse. **9.** a raised step or platform. **10. put through one's paces,** to cause someone to demonstrate his or her ability or to show her or his skill: *The French teacher put her pupils through their paces for the visitors.* **11. set the pace,** to act as an example for others to equal or rival; be the most progressive or successful: *an agency that sets the pace in advertising.* **—***v.t.* **12.** to set the pace for, as in racing. **13.** to traverse or go over with steps: *He paced the floor nervously.* **14.** to measure by paces. **15.** to train to a certain pace; exercise in pacing: *to pace a horse.* **16.** (of a horse) to run (a distance) at a pace: *Hanover II paced a mile.* **—***v.i.* **17.** to take slow, regular steps. **18.** to walk up and down nervously, as to expend nervous energy. **19.** (of a horse) to go at a pace. [1250–1300; ME *pas* < OF < L *passus* step, pace, equiv. to *pad-,* var. s. of *pandere* to spread (the legs, in walking) + *-tus* suffix of v. action, with *dt* > *ss*]
—Syn. 8. step, amble, rack, trot, jog, canter, gallop, walk, run, singlefoot. **17.** PACE, PLOD, TRUDGE refer to a steady and monotonous kind of walking. PACE suggests steady, measured steps as of one completely lost in thought or impelled by some distraction: *to pace up and down.* PLOD implies a slow, heavy, laborious, weary walk: *The mailman plods his weary way.* TRUDGE implies a spiritless but usually steady and doggedly persistent walk: *The farmer trudged to his village to buy his supplies.* **—Ant. 17.** scurry, scamper, skip.

pa·ce² (pā′sē, pä′chā; *Lat.* pä′ke), *prep.* with all due respect to; with the permission of: *I do not, pace my rival, hold with the ideas of the reactionists.* [1860–65; < L *pāce* in peace, by favor (abl. sing. of *pāx* PEACE, favor, pardon, grace)]

pace′ car′ (pās), (in auto racing) an automobile that leads the competing cars through a pace lap or laps and leaves the course before the actual start of the race. [1960–65]

paced (pāst), *adj.* **1.** having a specified or indicated pace (usually used in combination): *fast-paced.* **2.** counted out or measured by paces. **3.** run at a pace set by a pacesetter. [1575–85; PACE¹ + -ED³]

pace′ lap′ (pās), a lap before the beginning of an auto race for warming up the engines and giving the field a moving start. [1970–75]

pace·mak·er (pās′mā′kər), *n.* **1.** pacesetter. **2.** *Med.* an electronic device implanted beneath the skin for providing a normal heartbeat by electrical stimulation of the heart muscle, used in certain heart conditions. **3.** *Anat., Physiol.* any specialized tissue that governs a rhythmic or cyclic biological activity, as the sinoatrial node of the heart that controls heartbeat. [1880–85; PACE¹ + MAKER] **—pace′mak′ing,** *n.*

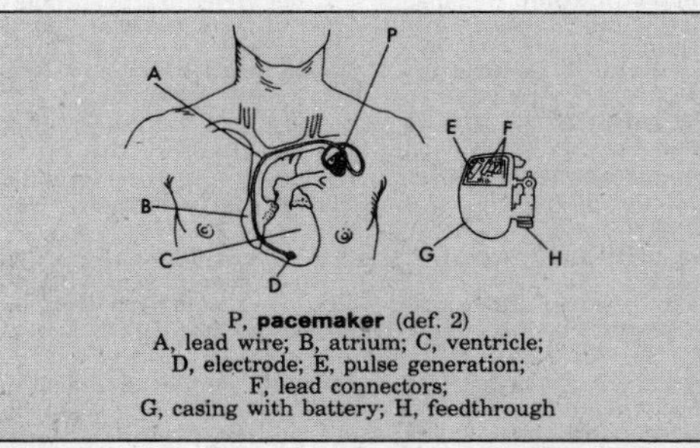

P, **pacemaker** (def. 2)
A, lead wire; B, atrium; C, ventricle; D, electrode; E, pulse generation; F, lead connectors; G, casing with battery; H, feedthrough

pac·er (pā′sər), *n.* **1.** a person or thing that paces. **2.** a standard-bred horse that is used for pacing in harness racing. **3.** a pacemaker. [1650–60; PACE¹ + -ER¹]

pace·set·ter (pās′set′ər), *n.* **1.** a person, group, or organization that is the most progressive or successful and serves as a model to be imitated. **2.** a person or thing that sets the pace, as in racing. Also called **pacemaker.** [1890–95; PACE¹ + SETTER] **—pace′set′ting,** *adj.*

pa·cha (pä′shə, pash′ə, pə shä′), *n.* pasha.

pa·cha·lic (pə shä′lik), *n.* pashalik.

Pach·el·bel (päk′əl bel′; *Ger.* päкн′əl bel′), *n.* **Jo·hann** (yō′hän), 1653–1706, German organist and composer.

Pa Chin (*Chin.* bä′ jin′), *Wade-Giles.* (*Li Fei-kan*). See **Ba Jin.**

pa·chin·ko (pə ching′kō), *n.* a Japanese pinball game played on a vertical machine in which slots struck by the player's ball release other balls that in turn are exchanged for noncash prizes. [1950–55; < Japn, equiv. to *pachin* click! (imit.) + *-ko* dim. suffix]

pa·chi·si (pə chē′zē, pä-), *n.* **1.** a board game, originated in ancient India, in which four players advance four pieces each along a route on a cross-shaped board toward a center square by throws of cowrie shells or dice. **2.** a modern version of this game. Also, **parchesi, parchisi.** [1790–1800; < Hindi *pacīsī,* adj. deriv. of *pacīs* twenty-five]

Pach·mann (päk′mən; *Russ.* päкн′mən), *n.* **Vlad·i·mir de** (vlad′ə mēr′ də; *Russ.* vlu dyē′myiʀ de), 1848–1933, Russian pianist.

Pa·cho·mi·us (pə kō′mē əs), *n.* **Saint,** A.D. 292?–348?, Egyptian ascetic: founder of the cenobitical form of monasticism. **—Pa·cho′mi·an,** *adj., n.*

CONCISE PRONUNCIATION KEY: act, cāpe, dâre, pärt; set, ēqual; *if,* īce; ox, ōver, ôrder, oil, bo͝ok, bo͞ot, out; up, ûrge; child; sing; shoe; thin, *th*at; zh as in *treasure.* ə = *a* as in *alone, e* as in *system, i* as in *easily, o* as in *gallop, u* as in *circus;* ᵊ as in *fire* (fīᵊr), *hour* (ouᵊr). l and n can serve as syllabic consonants, as in *cradle* (krād′l), and *button* (but′n). See the full key inside the front cover.

pach·ou·li (pach′o͝o lē, pə cho͞o′lē), *n.* patchouli.

pa·chu·ca (pə cho͞o′kə; *Sp.* pä cho͞o′kä), *n., pl.* **-cas** (-kəz; *Sp.* -käs). a teenage girl who associates closely with pachucos. [< AmerSp, fem. of *pachuco* PACHUCO]

Pa·chu·ca (pä cho͞o′kä), *n.* a city in and the capital of Hidalgo, in central Mexico: silver mines. 84,543.

pa·chu·co (pə cho͞o′kō; *Sp.* pä cho͞o′kô), *n., pl.* **-cos** (-kōz; *Sp.* -kôs). (esp. among Mexican-Americans) a teenage youth who belongs to a street gang known for its flamboyant style. [1940–45; < AmerSp (U.S. Southwest), MexSp: prob. orig. a resident of EL PASO, equiv. to (*El*) *Pas*(*o*) + -*uco* pejorative n. suffix, with expressive replacement of *s* by *ch;* cf. MexSp *pachuco* worthless card hand, deriv. of *paso* pass]

pach·y·derm (pak′i dûrm′), *n.* **1.** any of the thick-skinned, nonruminant ungulates, as the elephant, hippopotamus, and rhinoceros. **2.** an elephant. **3.** a person who is not sensitive to criticism, ridicule, etc.; a thick-skinned person. [1830–40; < NL *Pachyderma,* assumed sing. of *Pachydermata* (pl.) obs. order name < Gk *pachý*(*s*) thick + -*dérmata,* neut. pl. of -*dermatos* -skinned, adj. deriv. of *dermat-,* s. of *dérma* skin, DERMA[1]] **—pach′y·der′mal, pach′y·der′mous, pach′y·der′·mic, pach′y·der′moid,** *adj.*

pach·y·der·ma·tous (pak′i dûr′mə təs), *adj.* **1.** of, pertaining to, or characteristic of pachyderms. **2.** thick-skinned; insensitive: *a pachydermatous indifference to insults.* [1815–25; < NL *Pachydermat*(*a*) (see PACHYDERM) + -OUS] **—pach′y·der′ma·tous·ly,** *adv.*

pach·y·san·dra (pak′ə san′drə), *n.* any plant of the genus *Pachysandra,* as the Allegheny spurge or Japanese spurge, the leaves of which grow in a rounded clump, widely used as a ground cover in the U.S. [1805–15; < NL: the genus name, irreg. from Gk *pachýs* thick + Gk *andr-* (s. of *anḗr* man; see ANDRO-) + -*a* -A[2]; so called in reference to the thick stamens of the male flowers]

pach·y·tene (pak′i tēn), *n. Cell Biol.* the third stage of prophase in meiosis, during which each chromosome pair separates into sister chromatids with some breakage and crossing over of genes. Also, **pach·y·ne·ma** (pak′ə nē′mə). [< F *pachytène* (1900), equiv. to Gk *pachý*(*s*) thick + -*tène* -TENE]

pa·cif·ic (pə sif′ik), *adj.* **1.** tending to make or preserve peace; conciliatory: *pacific overtures.* **2.** not warlike; peaceable; mild: *a pacific disposition.* **3.** at peace; peaceful: *a pacific era in history.* **4.** calm; tranquil: *The Wabash is a pacific river.* **5.** (*cap.*) of or pertaining to the Pacific Ocean. **6.** (*cap.*) of or pertaining to the region bordering on the Pacific Ocean: *the Pacific states.* —*n.* (*cap.*) **7.** See **Pacific Ocean. 8.** a steam locomotive having a four-wheeled front truck, six driving wheels, and a two-wheeled rear truck. See table under **Whyte classification.** [1540–50; < L *pācificus* lit., peacemaking, equiv. to *pāci-* (comb. form of *pāx*) PEACE + -*ficus* -FIC]
—Syn. 1. appeasing. **2.** quiet, gentle, still. **—Ant. 1.** hostile. **2.** aggressive, bellicose. **4.** agitated.

Pa·cif·i·ca (pə sif′i kə), *n.* a city in W California, S of San Francisco. 36,866.

pa·cif·i·cal·ly (pə sif′ik lē), *adv.* peaceably, mildly, calmly, or quietly. [1785–95; obs. *pacifical* pacific (see PACIFIC, -AL) + -LY]

pa·cif·i·cate (pə sif′i kāt′), *v.t.,* **-cat·ed, -cat·ing.** to pacify. [1640–50; < L *pācificātus* (ptp. of *pācificāre* to make peace). See PACIFY, -ATE[1]] **—pac′i·fi·ca′tion,** *n.* **—pa·cif′i·ca′tor,** *n.* **—pa·cif·i·ca·to·ry** (pə sif′i kə tôr′ē, -tōr′ē), *adj.*

Pacif′ic barracu′da, a small, slender barracuda, *Sphyraena argentea,* of coastal seas from Alaska to Lower California, valued as a food fish. Also called **California barracuda, scooter.**

Pacif′ic cod′, a cod, *Gadus macrocephalus.* Also called **Alaska cod.**

Pacif′ic dog′wood, a dogwood tree, *Cornus nuttallii,* of western North America, having pointed, petallike white or pinkish bracts and clustered scarlet fruits. Also called **mountain dogwood.**

Pacif′ic Grove′, a city in W California, at S end of Monterey Bay. 15,755.

Pacif′ic high′, a semipermanent, atmospheric, high-pressure system of the Pacific Ocean, centered, in the mean, about 1000 mi. (1600 km) northeast of Hawaii: one of the subtropical highs. Also called **Hawaiian high.**

Pacif′ic Is′lands, Trust Territory of the, a U.S. trust territory in the Pacific Ocean, comprising the Mariana, Marshall and Caroline Islands: approved by the United Nations 1947; since 1976 constituents of the trusteeship have established or moved toward self-government. 133,732; 717 sq. mi. (1857 sq. km). Cf. **Belau, Marshall Islands, Micronesia** (def. 2), **Northern Mariana Islands.**

Pacif′ic madro′ne. See under **madrone** (def. 1).

pa·ci·fi·co (pä thē′fē kô′, -sē′-), *n., pl.* **-cos** (-kôs′). *Spanish.* **1.** a peaceful person. **2.** a native of Cuba or the Philippine Islands who did not resist the Spanish occupation.

Pacif′ic O′cean, an ocean bordered by the American continents, Asia, and Australia: largest ocean in the world; divided by the equator into the North Pacific and the South Pacific. 70,000,000 sq. mi. (181,300,000 sq. km); greatest known depth, 35,433 ft. (10,800 m).

Pacif′ic Plate′, *Geol.* one of the major tectonic divisions of the earth's crust, comprising four sea-floor basins; separated from the Nazca, Cocos, and North and South American plates by the East Pacific Rise and San Andreas fault and bounded in the western Pacific Ocean by a series of major ocean deeps, including the Kuril, Japan, Mariana, Kermadec, and Tonga trenches.

Pacif′ic salm′on, any salmon of the genus *Oncorhynchus,* esp. the chinook salmon, *O. tshawytscha.*

Pacif′ic stur′geon. See **white sturgeon.**

Pacif′ic time′. See under **standard time.** Also called **Pacif′ic Stand′ard Time′.** [1880–85, *Amer.*]

Pacif′ic tree′ frog′, a common terrestrial frog, *Hyla regilla,* of western North America, having a dark stripe along each side of the head.

pac·i·fi·er (pas′ə fī′ər), *n.* **1.** a person or thing that pacifies. **2.** a rubber or plastic device, often shaped into a nipple, for a baby to suck or bite on. [1525–35; PACIFY + -ER[1]]

pac·i·fism (pas′ə fiz′əm), *n.* **1.** opposition to war or violence of any kind. **2.** refusal to engage in military activity because of one's principles or beliefs. **3.** the principle or policy that all differences among nations should be adjusted without recourse to war. Also, **pa·cif·i·cism** (pə sif′ə siz′əm). [1905–10; < F *pacifisme.* See PACIFIC, -ISM]

pac·i·fist (pas′ə fist), *n.* **1.** a person who believes in pacifism or is opposed to war or to violence of any kind. **2.** a person whose personal belief in pacifism causes him or her to refuse being drafted into military service. Cf. **conscientious objector.** —*adj.* **3.** pacifistic. [1905–10; < F *pacifiste.* See PACIFIC, -IST]

pac·i·fis·tic (pas′ə fis′tik), *adj.* of or pertaining to pacifism or pacifists. [1925–30; PACIF(IC) + -ISTIC] **—pac′i·fis′ti·cal·ly,** *adv.*

pac·i·fy (pas′ə fī′), *v.t.,* **-fied, -fy·ing. 1.** to bring or restore to a state of peace or tranquillity; quiet; calm: *to pacify an angry man.* **2.** to appease: *to pacify one's appetite.* **3.** to reduce to a state of submission, esp. by military force; subdue. [1425–75; late ME < L *pācificāre* to make peace. See PACIFIC, -FY] **—pac′i·fi′a·ble,** *adj.* **—pac′i·fy′ing·ly,** *adv.*
—Syn. 2. soothe, mollify, assuage. **—Ant. 2.** anger, enrage.

Pa·cin′i·an cor′puscle (pə sin′ē ən), (*sometimes l.c.*) a microscopic, onionlike body consisting of layers of connective tissue wrapped around a nerve ending, located in the deep layers of skin, tendons, etc., and functioning as a sensory receptor of pressure and vibration. [after Filippo *Pacini* (1812–83), Italian anatomist; see -IAN]

pack[1] (pak), *n.* **1.** a group of things wrapped or tied together for easy handling or carrying; a bundle, esp. one to be carried on the back of an animal or a person: *a mule pack; a hiker's pack.* **2.** a definite quantity or standard measure of something wrapped up or otherwise assembled for merchandising (sometimes used in combination): *a pack of cigarettes; a six-pack of beer.* **3.** the quantity of something that is packaged, canned, or the like, at one time, in one season, etc.: *last year's salmon pack.* **4.** a group of people or things: *a pack of fools; a pack of lies.* **5.** a group of certain animals of the same kind, esp. predatory ones: *a pack of wolves.* **6.** *Hunting.* a number of hounds, esp. foxhounds and beagles, regularly used together in a hunt. **7.** a complete set of playing cards, usually 52 in number; deck. **8.** backpack. **9.** a considerable area of pieces of floating ice driven or packed together. **10.** *Metalworking.* a pile of metal sheets for hot-rolling together. **11.** *Med.* **a.** a wrapping of the body in wet or dry clothes for therapeutic purposes. **b.** the cloths so used. **c.** *Obs.* the state of being so wrapped. **12.** *Mining.* **a.** Also called **pack wall.** a rubble wall for supporting a roof. **b.** any of various other roof supports of timber, timber and rubble, or rubble and wire mesh. **13.** a cosmetic material, usually of a paste-like consistency, applied either to the face or to the hair and scalp: *a mud pack; a beauty pack; a henna pack.* **14.** pac[2] (def. 1). **15.** *Obs.* a plot; conspiracy. **16.** *Obs.* a low or worthless person.
—*v.t.* **17.** to make into a pack or bundle. **18.** to form into a group or compact mass. **19.** to fill with anything compactly arranged: *to pack a trunk.* **20.** to put into or arrange compactly in a trunk, valise, etc., as for traveling or storage: *I packed a two-week supply of clothes for the trip.* **21.** to press or crowd together within; cram: *The crowd packed the gallery.* **22.** to prepare for marketing by putting into containers or packages: *to pack fruit for shipping.* **23.** to make airtight, vaportight, or watertight by stuffing: *to pack the piston of a steam engine.* **24.** to cover or envelop with something pressed closely around. **25.** to load, as with packs: *We packed the mules and then set off for the lake.* **26.** to carry or wear, esp. as part of one's usual equipment: *to pack a gun.* **27.** *Informal.* to deliver (a powerful blow, strong message, etc.): *He packs a better punch than any heavyweight in years. His speech packed a powerful plea for peace.* **28.** to treat with a therapeutic pack.
—*v.i.* **29.** to pack goods in compact form, as for transportation or storage (often fol. by *up*). **30.** to place clothes and personal items in a suitcase, trunk, etc., preparatory to traveling. **31.** to be capable of or suitable for compact storage or packing for transportation: *articles that pack well.* **32.** to crowd together, as persons: *The audience packed into the auditorium.* **33.** to become compacted: *Wet snow packs readily.* **34.** to collect into a group: *The grouse began to pack.* **35. pack in** or **up,** to relinquish or give up; quit: *One failure was no reason to pack the whole experiment in. After thirty years of touring, the violinist packed his career up and retired.* **36. pack it in, a.** to give up; abandon one's efforts: *In 1972 we packed it in and moved back to Florida.* **b.** to cease being a nuisance. **37. pack off** or **away, a.** to dispatch: *We packed the kids off to camp for the summer.* **b.** to leave hastily. —*adj.* **38.** transporting, or used in transporting, a pack or load: *pack animals.* **39.** compressed into a pack; packed. **40.** used in or adapted for packing: *pack equipment.* **41.** *Chiefly Scot.* (of animals) tame. [1175–1225; (n.) ME *pak, packe* < MD *pac* or perh. MLG *pak;* (v.) ME *pakken* < MD or MLG]
—Syn. 1. See **package. 4.** band, company, crew. **5.** See **flock**[1].

pack[2] (pak), *v.t.* to choose, collect, arrange, or manipulate (cards, persons, facts, etc.) so as to serve one's own purposes: *to pack the deck; to pack a jury.* [1520–30; perh. var. of PACT]

pack[3] (pak), *adj. Scot.* very friendly or intimate. [1780–90; perh. special use of PACK[1]]

pack·a·ble (pak′ə bəl), *adj.* suitable for packing, esp. for travel: *readily packable clothes.* [1875–80; PACK[1] + -ABLE] **—pack′a·bil′i·ty,** *n.*

pack·age (pak′ij), *n., v.,* **-aged, -ag·ing.** —*n.* **1.** a bundle of something, usually of small or medium size, that is packed and wrapped or boxed; parcel. **2.** a container, as a box or case, in which something is or may be packed. **3.** something conceived of as a compact unit having particular characteristics: *That child is a package of mischief.* **4.** the packing of goods, freight, etc. **5.** a finished product contained in a unit that is suitable for immediate installation and operation, as a power or heating unit. **6.** a group, combination, or series of related parts or elements to be accepted or rejected as a single unit. **7.** a complete program produced for the theater, television, etc., or a series of these, sold as a unit. —*v.t.* **8.** to make or put into a package. **9.** to design and manufacture a package for (a product or series of related products): *They package their soaps in eye-catching wrappers.* **10.** to group or combine (a series of related parts) into a single unit. **11.** to combine the various elements of (a tour, entertainment, etc.) for sale as a unit. [1605–15; < D *pakkage* baggage. See PACK[1], -AGE] **—pack′age·a·ble,** *adj.*
—Syn. 1. PACKAGE, PACK, PACKET, PARCEL refer to a bundle or to something fastened together. A PACKAGE is a bundle of things packed and wrapped: *a package from the drugstore.* A PACK is a large bundle or bale of things put or fastened together, usually wrapped up or in a bag, case, etc., to be carried by a person or a beast of burden: *a peddler's pack.* A PACKET, originally a package of letters or dispatches, is a small package or bundle: *a packet of gems.* A PARCEL is an object or objects wrapped up to form a single, small bundle: *a parcel containing two dresses.* **2.** carton.

pack′age deal′, 1. Also called **pack′age plan′.** an agreement in which the buyer pays a stipulated price for a group of related products or services: *a package deal from a book club.* **2.** the products or services included in such an agreement: *We got a package deal of room, meals, automobile, and guide at the resort hotel.* **3.** an agreement or plan in which the approval of one element is contingent upon the approval of all the others: *The union wanted management to approve a package deal increasing wages, retirement benefits, and the number of paid holidays.* [1945–50]

pack·ag·er (pak′ə jər), *n.* **1.** a person or business firm that packages a product or merchandise for commercial sale: *a soap packager.* **2.** a person or firm that creates and assembles a tour, television show, book, or other product and offers it for sale, use, exhibition, etc., in a completed form: *a packager of European vacations; a packager of rock shows.* [1955–60; PACKAGE + -ER[1]]

pack′age store′, a store selling sealed bottles or other containers of alcoholic beverages that may only be consumed off the premises. [1970–75]

pack′age tour′, a planned tour in which one fee is charged for all expenses: *offering package tours of the chateau country.* Also, **pack′aged tour′.** [1955–60]

pack·ag·ing (pak′ə jing), *n.* **1.** an act or instance of packing or forming packages: *At the end of the production line is a machine for packaging.* **2.** the package in which merchandise is sold or displayed: *Attractive packaging can help sell a product.* [1870–75; PACKAGE + -ING[1]]

pack′ an′imal, a mule, donkey, burro, or horse bred for vigor and hardiness and used for carrying heavy loads. [1840–50]

pack·board (pak′bôrd′, -bōrd′), *n.* a rigid wooden or metal frame, covered with fabric and having shoulder straps, to which equipment can be strapped for carrying. [1935–40; PACK[1] + BOARD]

pack′ date′, the date on which a foodstuff was processed or packed, often shown on the package or label. [1970–75]

packed (pakt), *adj.* **1.** filled to capacity; full: *They've had a packed theater for every performance.* **2.** pressed together; dense; compressed: *packed snow.* **3.** abundantly supplied with a specified element (used in combination): *an action-packed movie.* [1770–80; PACK[1] + -ED[2]]

pack·er (pak′ər), *n.* **1.** a person or thing that packs. **2.** a person who engages in packing as an occupation or business, esp. a person who packs food for market: *a fruit packer.* [1325–75; ME; see PACK[1], -ER[1]]

pack·et (pak′it), *n.* **1.** a small group or package of anything: *a packet of letters.* **2.** Also called **pack′et boat′, pack′et ship′.** a small vessel that carries mail, passengers, and goods regularly on a fixed route, esp. on rivers or along coasts. **3.** *Cards.* a part of a pack of cards after being cut. **4.** *Informal.* a large amount of money. **5.** *Brit. Slang.* **a.** a painful blow or beating. **b.** misfortune or failure. —*v.t.* **6.** to bind up in a package or parcel. [1520–30; < MF *pacquet,* equiv. to *pacqu*(*er*) to PACK[1] + -*et* -ET]
—Syn. 1. See **package.**

pack′et switch′ing, a method of efficient data transmission whereby the initial message is broken into relatively small units that are routed independently and subsequently reassembled. Also, **pack′et-switch′ing.** [1970–75]

pack·frame (pak′frām′), *n.* a framework, usually of lightweight metal tubing, that supports a backpack on the wearer, often by curved extensions that fit over the shoulders. [1950–55; PACK[1] + FRAME]

pack·horse (pak′hôrs′), *n.* **1.** a horse used for carrying goods, freight, supplies, etc. **2.** a person who works hard or bears a heavy load of responsibility. [PACK[1] + HORSE]

pack′ ice′, a large area of floating ice formed over a period of many years and consisting of pieces of ice driven together by wind, current, etc. Also called **ice pack.** [1840–50]

pack•ing (pak′ing), *n.* **1.** the act or work of a person or thing that packs. **2.** the preparation and packaging of foodstuffs, esp. to be sold at wholesale. **3.** the way in which something is packed. **4.** an act or instance of transporting supplies, goods, etc., on the backs of horses, mules, or persons. **5.** material used to cushion or protect goods packed in a container. **6.** material, often in the form of a grease-impregnated fibrous ring, compressed inside a stuffing box or the like to prevent leakage around the moving shaft of an engine, pump, or valve. **7.** *Print.* rubber, paper, or other material fastened to the tympan or cylinder of a press to provide pressure to produce a printed impression. [1350–1400; ME *pakking* (ger.). See PACK¹, -ING¹]

pack′ing case′, a box in which goods are packed for transport or storage. Also called **pack′ing box′.**

pack′ing frac′tion, *Physics.* a measure of the stability of an atomic nucleus, equal to 10^4 multiplied by the mass defect and divided by the mass number. [1925–30]

pack′ing nut′. See **stuffing nut.**

pack′ing plant′, an establishment for processing and packing foods, esp. meat, to be sold at wholesale. Also called **pack′ing house′.** [1825–35]

pack′ing ring′. See **piston ring.**

pack•man (pak′mən), *n., pl.* **-men.** a peddler. [1615–25; PACK¹ + -MAN]

pack′ rat′, **1.** Also called **trade rat.** a large, bushy-tailed rodent, *Neotoma cinerea,* of North America, noted for carrying off small articles to store in its nest. **2.** *Informal.* **a.** a person who collects, saves, or hoards useless small items. **b.** an old prospector or guide. [1840–50]

pack′ roll′ing, *Metalworking.* the hot rolling of metal sheets in two or more thicknesses to produce composite sheets. Also called **ply rolling.**

pack•sack (pak′sak′), *n.* a leather or canvas carrying bag, usually one that can be strapped over the shoulder and used to carry food and personal items when a person is traveling. [1850–55, *Amer.*; PACK¹ + SACK¹]

pack•sad•dle (pak′sad′l), *n.* a saddle specifically designed for holding or supporting the load on a pack animal. [1350–1400; ME *pakke saddil.* See PACK¹, SADDLE]

pack•thread (pak′thred′), *n.* a strong thread or twine for sewing or tying up packages. [1300–50; ME *pakthrede.* See PACK¹, THREAD] —**pack′thread′ed,** *adj.*

pack•train (pak′trān′), *n.* a line or succession of pack animals, as mules or burros, used to transport food and supplies over terrain unsuitable for wagons or other vehicles. [1840–50; PACK¹ + TRAIN]

pack′ wall′, *Mining.* pack (def. 12a). [1865–70]

Pack•wood (pak′wo͝od′), *n.* **Bob,** born 1932, U.S. politician: senator since 1969.

Pac′-Man defense′ (pak′man′), a defensive tactic against a hostile takeover in which the targeted company makes its own bid to take over the hostile firm. [1980–85; after *Pac-Man,* a character in a video game that devours its attackers]

pact (pakt), *n.* **1.** an agreement, covenant, or compact: *We made a pact not to argue any more.* **2.** an agreement or treaty between two or more nations: *a pact between Germany and Italy.* [1400–50; late ME *pact(e)* < MF < L *pactum,* n. use of neut. of ptp. of *pacīscī* to make a bargain, contract]
—**Syn. 1.** contract, bond, bargain, deal.

Pact′ of Steel′, a military alliance concluded between Nazi Germany and Fascist Italy on May 22, 1939, committing each to assist the other in the event of war with another power and pledging that neither would seek a separate peace or armistice.

Pac•to•lus (pak tō′ləs), *n.* a small river in Asia Minor, in ancient Lydia: famous for the gold washed from its sands.

pad¹ (pad), *n., v.,* **pad•ded, pad•ding.** —*n.* **1.** a cushionlike mass of soft material used for comfort, protection, or stuffing. **2.** a soft, stuffed cushion used as a saddle; a padded leather saddle without a tree. **3.** a number of sheets of paper glued or otherwise held together at one edge to form a tablet. **4.** a soft, ink-soaked block of absorbent material for inking a rubber stamp. **5.** *Anat., Zool.* any fleshy mass of tissue that cushions a weight-bearing part of the body, as on the underside of a paw. See diag. under **dog. 6.** the foot, as of a fox, hare, or wolf. **7.** a piece or fold of gauze or other absorbent material for use as a surgical dressing or a protective covering. **8.** *Zool.* a pulvillus, as on the tarsus or foot of an insect. **9.** a lily pad. **10.** *Rocketry.* See **launch pad. 11.** *Slang.* **a.** one's living quarters, as an apartment or room. **b.** one's bed. **c.** a room where people gather to take narcotics; an addicts' den. **12.** *Slang.* **a.** money paid as a bribe to and shared among police officers, as for ignoring law violations. **b.** a list of police officers receiving such money. **13.** *Elect.* a nonadjustable attenuator consisting of a network of fixed resistors. **14.** *Shipbuilding.* **a.** a metal plate riveted or welded to a surface as a base or attachment for bolts, hooks, eyes, etc. **b.** a piece of wood laid on the back of a deck beam to give the deck surface a desired amount of camber. **15.** *Carpentry.* **a.** a handle for holding various small, interchangeable saw blades. **b.** Also, **pod.** a socket in a brace for a bit. **16.** *Metall.* a raised surface on a casting. **17.** a small deposit of weld metal, as for building up a worn surface. **18. on the pad,** *Slang.* (of a police officer) receiving a bribe, esp. on a regular basis. —*v.t.* **19.** to furnish, protect, fill out, or stuff with a pad or padding. **20.** to expand or add to unnecessarily or dishonestly: *to pad a speech; to pad an expense account.* **21.** *Metall.* to add metal to (a casting) above its required dimensions, to insure the flow of enough metal to all parts. —*v.i.* **22.** to insure the proper forging of a piece. [1545–55; orig. special uses of obs. *pad* bundle to lie on, perh. b. PACK¹ and BED]

pad² (pad), *n., v.,* **pad•ded, pad•ding.** —*n.* **1.** a dull, muffled sound, as of footsteps on the ground. **2.** a road horse, as distinguished from a hunting or working horse. **3.** a highwayman. **4.** *Brit. Dial.* a path, lane, or road. —*v.t.* **5.** to travel along on foot. **6.** to beat down by treading. —*v.i.* **7.** to travel on foot; walk. **8.** to walk so that one's footsteps make a dull, muffled sound. [1545–55; (n.) < MD or LG *pad* PATH (orig. argot; hence, appar., "highwayman" and "horse"); (v.) < MD *padden* to make or follow a path, c. OE *pæththan* to traverse, deriv. of *pæth* PATH; defs. 1, 8 perh. represent an independent expressive word that has been influenced by other senses]

PaD, Pennsylvania Dutch.

Pa•dang (pä däng′), *n.* a seaport in W central Sumatra, in W Indonesia. 196,339.

pa•dauk (pə douk′), *n.* padouk. [1830–40]

pad′ded cell′, a room, as in a mental hospital, with padded walls for the confinement of violent inmates.

pad•ding (pad′ing), *n.* **1.** material, as cotton or straw, used to pad something. **2.** something added unnecessarily or dishonestly, as verbiage to a speech or a false charge on an expense account. **3.** the act of a person or thing that pads. [1820–30; PAD¹ + -ING¹]

Pad•ding•ton (pad′ing tən), *n.* a former residential borough of Greater London, England, now part of Westminster.

pad•dle¹ (pad′l), *n., v.,* **-dled, -dling.** —*n.* **1.** a short, flat bladed oar for propelling and steering a canoe or small boat, usually held by both hands and moved more or less through a vertical arc. **2.** any of various similar implements used for mixing, stirring, or beating. **3.** any of various similar but smaller implements with a short handle for holding in one hand and a wide or rounded blade, used for a racket in table tennis, paddle tennis, etc. **4.** such an implement or a similarly shaped makeshift one, used to spank or beat someone. **5.** an implement used for beating garments while washing them in running water, as in a stream. **6.** Also called **float, floatboard.** a blade of a paddle wheel. **7.** See **paddle wheel. 8.** any of the blades by which a water wheel is turned. **9.** a flipper or limb of a penguin, turtle, whale, etc. **10.** an act of paddling. **11.** Also, **pattle.** *Brit. Dial.* a small spade with a long handle, used to dig up thistles. **12.** (in a gate of a lock or sluice) a panel that slides to permit the passage of water. —*v.i.* **13.** to propel or travel in a canoe or the like by using a paddle. **14.** to row lightly or gently with oars. **15.** to move by means of paddle wheels, as a steamer. —*v.t.* **16.** to propel with a paddle: *to paddle a canoe.* **17.** to spank or beat with or as with a paddle. **18.** to stir, mix, or beat with or as with a paddle. **19.** to convey by paddling, as a canoe. **20.** to hit (a table-tennis ball or the like) with a paddle. **21. paddle one's own canoe.** See **canoe** (def. 3). [1375–1425; late ME *padell* (n.)] —**pad′dler,** *n.*

pad•dle² (pad′l), *v.i.,* **-dled, -dling. 1.** to move the feet or hands playfully in shallow water; dabble. **2.** to toy with the fingers. **3.** to toddle. [1520–30; orig. uncert.] —**pad′dler,** *n.*

pad•dle•ball (pad′l bôl′), *n.* a game played on a handball court following the same basic rules as handball, but in which players use short-handled, perforated paddles to hit a ball resembling a tennis ball. [1930–35, *Amer.*; PADDLE¹ + BALL¹]

pad•dle•board (pad′l bôrd′, -bōrd′), *n.* a type of surfboard with one end rounded and the other tapered to a point, used chiefly in surfing and often in lifesaving. [1780–90; PADDLE¹ + BOARD]

pad•dle•boat (pad′l bōt′), *n.* **1.** a boat propelled by a paddle wheel. **2.** See **pedal boat.** [1870–75; PADDLE¹ + BOAT] —**pad′dle•boat′ing,** *n.*

pad′dle box′, a structure enclosing a paddle wheel.

pad•dle•fish (pad′l fish′), *n., pl.* **-fish•es,** (*esp. collectively*) **-fish.** a large ganoid fish, *Polyodon spathula,* of the Mississippi River and its larger tributaries, having a long, flat, paddlelike snout. [1680–90, *Amer.*; PADDLE¹ + FISH]

pad′dle steam′er, a vessel propelled by paddle wheels and driven by steam. [1885–90]

pad′dle ten′nis, a game combining elements of tennis and handball, played with paddles and a rubber ball on a screened court about half the size of and having a lower net than a tennis court. See illus. under **racket².** [1920–25, *Amer.*]

pad′dle wheel′, a wheel for propelling a ship, having a number of paddles entering the water more or less perpendicularly. [1675–85] —**pad′dle-wheel′,** *adj.*

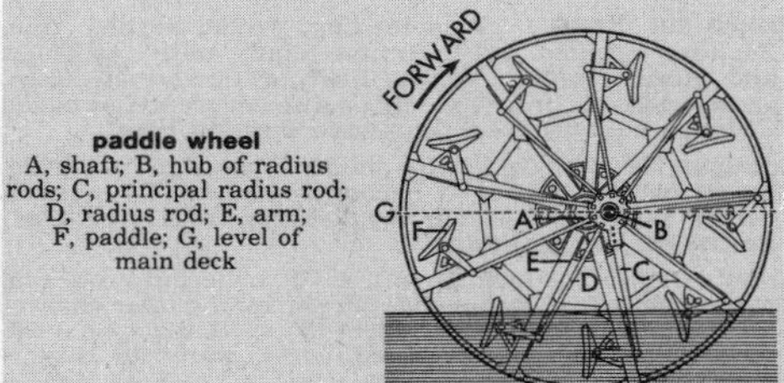

paddle wheel
A, shaft; B, hub of radius rods; C, principal radius rod; D, radius rod; E, arm; F, paddle; G, level of main deck

pad•dock¹ (pad′ək), *n.* **1.** a small, usually enclosed field near a stable or barn for pasturing or exercising animals. **2.** the enclosure in which horses are saddled and mounted before a race. **3.** *Australian.* any enclosed field or pasture. —*v.t.* **4.** to confine or enclose in or as in a paddock. [1540–50; var. of ME *parrok,* with *r* heard as flapped *d;* OE *pearroc* enclosure, orig. fence. See PARK]

pad•dock² (pad′ək), *n. Archaic.* a frog or toad. [1350–1400; ME *paddok(e),* deriv. of early ME *pad* toad (cf. E dial. *pad* frog); akin to D, LG *pad,* ON *padda;* see -OCK]

pad•dy (pad′ē), *n., pl.* **-dies. 1.** a rice field. **2.** rice, esp. in the husk, either uncut or gathered. [1590–1600; < Malay *padi* unhusked rice; currency of this word in E of India perh. due to early assoc. with Kannada *batta, bhatta* unhusked rice (< Indo-Aryan; cf. Hindi, Marathi *bhāt* cooked rice, Skt *bhakhta* food, meal)]

Pad•dy (pad′ē), *n., pl.* **-dies. 1.** *Slang (often disparaging).* an Irishman or a person of Irish descent. **2.** a male given name. [familiar var. of Ir *Padraig* Patrick; see -Y²]

pad•dy•mel•on (pad′ē mel′ən), *n.* pademelon.

pad′dy wag′on, *Informal.* See **patrol wagon.** [1925–30; prob. *paddy* policeman, special use of PADDY]

pad•dy•whack (pad′ē hwak′, -wak′), *n.* **1.** *Informal.* a spanking. —*v.t.* **2.** *Informal.* to spank or beat. Also, **pad•dy•wack** (pad′ē wak′). [1775–85; PADDY + WHACK]

pad•e•mel•on (pad′ē mel′ən), *n.* any of several small Australian wallabies, esp. of the genus *Thylogale.* Also, **paddymelon.** [1820–30; perh. < Dharuk, altered by folk etym.]

Pa•de•rew•ski (*Pol.* pä′de ref′ski; *Eng.* pad′ə ref′skē, -rev′-), *n.* **I•gnace** (*Fr.* ē nyas′) or **Ig•na•cy Jan** (*Pol.* ig nä′tsi yän), 1860–1941, Polish pianist, composer, patriot, and statesman.

pad•eye (pad′ī′), *n., pl.* **-eyes.** a ring fixed to the structure of a ship as a hold for small lines, tackles, etc. Also called **lug pad.** [1905–10; PAD¹ + EYE]

pad′ foot′, *Furniture.* any of various kinds of feet to a cabriole leg, as club, slipper, trifid, or web, having the form of a flattened extension of its lines. [1730–40]

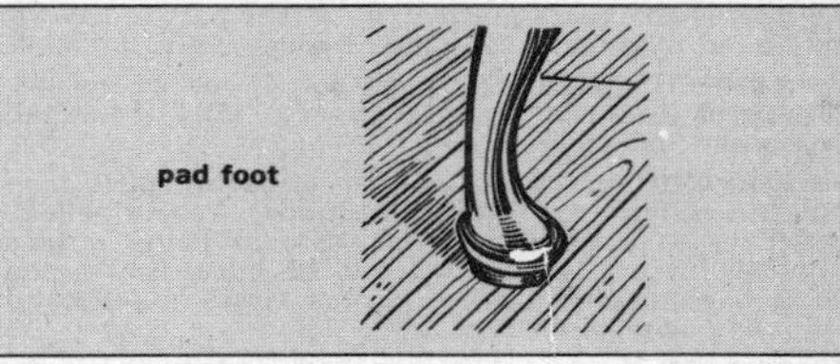
pad foot

pa•di•shah (pä′di shä′, -shô′), *n.* (*often cap.*) great king; emperor (a title applied esp. formerly to the shah of Iran, the sultan of Turkey, and to the British sovereign as emperor in India). [1605–15; < Pers (poetical form), equiv. to *pādi-* (earlier *pati*) lord + *shāh* SHAH]

pad•lock (pad′lok′), *n.* **1.** a portable or detachable lock with a pivoted or sliding shackle that can be passed through a link, ring, staple, or the like. —*v.t.* **2.** to fasten with or as with a padlock. [1425–75; late ME *padlok.* See POD³, LOCK¹]

pa•douk (pə douk′), *n.* **1.** any of several trees belonging to the genus *Pterocarpus,* of the legume family, native to tropical Asia and Africa, having reddish striped or mottled wood used for paneling, furniture, etc. **2.** the wood itself. Also, **padauk.** [1830–40; < Burmese *padauk*]

Pa•do•va (pä′dô vä), *n.* Italian name of **Padua.**

pad′pa•rad′schah sap′phire (päd′pə rä′zhə, päd′-), a rare, yellowish-orange sapphire found in Sri Lanka. [perh. directly < G; obscurely akin to Sinhalese *padmarāgaya* ruby, lit., lotus-colored]

pa•dre (pä′drā, -drē; *Sp.* pä′thre; *It.* pä′dre), *n., pl.* **-dres** (-drāz, -drēz; *Sp.* -thres), **-dri** (*It.* -drē). **1.** father (used esp. in addressing or referring to a priest or member of the clergy). **2.** a chaplain in military or naval service. [1575–85; < Sp, Pg, It: father < L *pater*]

pa•dri•no (pä thrē′nô; *Eng.* pə drē′nō), *n., pl.* ***-nos*** (-nôs; *Eng.* -nōz). *Spanish.* **1.** a godfather. **2.** a person's protector, patron, or mentor.

pa•dro•ne (pə drō′nē, -nā; *It.* pä drô′ne), *n., pl.* **-nes** (-nēz, -nāz), *It.* ***-ni*** (-nē). **1.** a master; boss. **2.** an employer, esp. of immigrant laborers, who provides communal housing and eating arrangements, controls the allocation of pay, etc., in a manner that exploits the workers. **3.** an innkeeper. [1660–70; < It; see PATRON] —**pa•dro•nism** (pə drō′niz əm), *n.*

pad′ saw′, a small compass saw with a pad. [1870–75]

pad′ stone′, *Building Trades.* a stone template.

Pad•u•a (paj′o͞o ə), *n.* a city in NE Italy. 242,130. Italian, **Padova.** —**Pad′u•an,** *adj.*

pad•u•a•soy (paj′o͞o ə soi′), *n., pl.* **-soys. 1.** a slightly corded, strong, rich, silk fabric. **2.** a garment made of this. [1625–35; alter. of F *pou de soie* (var. of *poult de soie* lit., pelt of silk) by assoc. with PADUA]

Pa•du•cah (pə do͞o′kə, -dyo͞o′-), *n.* a city in W Kentucky, at the junction of the Tennessee and Ohio rivers. 29,315.

Pa•dus (pā′dəs), *n.* ancient name of **Po.**

p. ae., (in prescriptions) equal parts. [< L *partēs aequālēs*]

pae•an (pē′ən), *n.* **1.** any song of praise, joy, or triumph. **2.** a hymn of invocation or thanksgiving to Apollo or some other ancient Greek deity. Also, **pean.** [1535–45; < L: religious or festive hymn, special use of *Paean* appellation of Apollo < Gk *Paiā́n* physician of the gods] —**pae′an•ism,** *n.*

paedo-, var. of **pedo-¹.** Also, *esp. before a vowel,* **paed-.**

pa•el•la (pä ā′lə, -āl′yə, pä yel′ə; *Sp.* pä e′lyä, -e′yä), *n.* a Spanish dish prepared by simmering together chicken, seafood, rice, vegetables, and saffron and other

CONCISE PRONUNCIATION KEY: *act, cāpe, dâre, pärt; set, ēqual; if, īce; ox, ōver, ôrder, oil, bo͝ok, bo͞ot, out; up, ûrge; child; sing; shoe; thin, that;* zh as in *treasure.* ə = *a* as in *alone, e* as in *system, i* as in *easily, o* as in *gallop, u* as in *circus;* ᵊ as in *fire* (fīᵊr), *hour* (ouᵊr). l and n can serve as syllabic consonants, as in *cradle* (krād′l), and *button* (but′n). See the full key inside the front cover.

seasonings. [1890–95; < Sp < Catalan: lit., frying pan, pot < MF *paelle* < L *patella* pan. See PATELLA]

pae·nu·la (pēn′yə lə), *n., pl.* **-lae** (-lē′), **-las.** a long, circular cloak, sleeveless and often hooded, worn by the poorer classes in ancient Rome. [1745–55; < L]

pae·on (pē′ən, -on), *n. Class. Pros.* a foot of one long and three short syllables in any order. [1595–1605; < L *paeōn* < Gk *paiṓn,* Attic var. of *paiā́n;* see PAEAN]

Pa·e·siel·lo (*It.* pä′e zyel′lō), *n.* **Gio·van·ni** (*It.* jô-vän′nē). See **Paisiello, Giovanni.**

Paes·tum (pes′təm), *n.* an ancient coastal city of Lucania, in S Italy: the extant ruins include three Greek temples and a Roman amphitheater.

Pá·ez (pä′es), *n.* **Jo·sé An·to·nio** (hô se′ än tô′nyô), 1790–1873, Venezuelan revolutionary and political leader: president 1831–35, 1839–43; dictator 1861–63.

PaG, Pennsylvania German.

pa·gan (pā′gən), *n.* **1.** one of a people or community observing a polytheistic religion, as the ancient Romans and Greeks. **2.** a person who is not a Christian, Jew, or Muslim. **3.** an irreligious or hedonistic person. —*adj.* **4.** pertaining to the worship or worshipers of any religion that is neither Christian, Jewish, nor Muslim. **5.** of, pertaining to, or characteristic of pagans. **6.** irreligious and hedonistic. [1325–75; ME < ML, LL *pāgānus* worshiper of false gods, orig. civilian (i.e., not a soldier of Christ), L: peasant, n. use of *pāgānus* rural, civilian, deriv. of *pāgus* village, rural district (akin to *pangere* to fix, make fast); see -AN] —**pa′gan·ish,** *adj.* —**pa′gan·ish·ly,** *adv.*
—**Syn. 2.** heathen, gentile. **5.** See **heathen.**

pa·gan·dom (pā′gən dəm), *n.* **1.** the part of the world inhabited by pagans. **2.** pagans collectively. [1850–55]

Pa·ga·ni·ni (pag′ə nē′nē, pä′gə-; *It.* pä′gä nē′nē), *n.* **Nic·co·lò** (nik′ə lō′; *It.* nēk′kô lô′), 1784–1840, Italian composer and violinist.

pa·gan·ism (pā′gə niz′əm), *n.* **1.** pagan spirit or attitude in religious or moral questions. **2.** the beliefs or practices of pagans. **3.** the state of being a pagan. [1400–50; late ME *pāgānysme* < LL *pāgānismus,* equiv. to L *pāgān(us)* PAGAN + *-ismus* -ISM] —**pa′gan·ist,** *adj., n.* —**pa′gan·is′tic,** *adj.*

pa·gan·ize (pā′gə nīz′), *v.,* **-ized, -iz·ing.** —*v.t.* **1.** to make pagan. —*v.i.* **2.** to become pagan. Also, *esp. Brit.,* **pa′gan·ise′.** [1605–15] —**pa′gan·i·za′tion,** *n.*

page[1] (pāj), *n., v.,* **paged, pag·ing.** —*n.* **1.** one side of a leaf of something printed or written, as of a book, manuscript, or letter. **2.** the entire leaf of such a printed or written thing: *He tore out one of the pages.* **3.** a single sheet of paper for writing. **4.** any noteworthy or distinctive event or period: *a reign that formed a gloomy page in English history.* **5.** *Print.* the type set and arranged for a page. **6.** *Computers.* **a.** a relatively small block of main or secondary storage, up to about 1024 words. **b.** a block of program instructions or data stored in main or secondary storage. **c.** (in word processing) a portion of a document. —*v.t.* **7.** to paginate. **8.** to turn pages (usually fol. by *through*): *to page through a book looking for a specific passage.* [1580–90; < MF < L *pāgina* column of writing, akin to *pangere* to fix, make fast]

page[2] (pāj), *n., v.,* **paged, pag·ing.** —*n.* **1.** a boy servant or attendant. **2.** a youth in attendance on a person of rank or, in medieval times, a youth being trained for knighthood. **3.** an attendant or employee, usually in uniform, who carries messages, ushers guests, runs errands, etc. **4.** a person employed by a legislature to carry messages and run errands for the members, as in the U.S. Congress. —*v.t.* **5.** to summon formally by calling out the name of repeatedly: *He had his father paged in the hotel lobby.* **6.** to summon or alert by electronic pager. **7.** to control (an electrical appliance, machine, etc.) remotely by means of an electronic signal. **8.** to attend as a page. [1250–1300; ME (n.) < OF < ?]

Page (pāj), *n.* **1. Thomas Nelson,** 1853–1922, U.S. novelist and diplomat. **2. Walter Hines,** 1855–1918, U.S. journalist, editor, and diplomat.

pag·eant (paj′ənt), *n.* **1.** an elaborate public spectacle illustrative of the history of a place, institution, or the like, often given in dramatic form or as a procession of colorful floats. **2.** a costumed procession, masque, allegorical tableau, or the like forming part of public or social festivities. **3.** a show or exhibition, esp. one consisting of a succession of participants or events: *a beauty pageant.* **4.** something comparable to a procession in colorful variety, splendor, or grandeur: *the pageant of Renaissance history.* **5.** a pretentious display or show that conceals a lack of real importance or meaning. **6.** (in medieval times) a platform or stage, usually moving on wheels, on which scenes from mystery plays were presented. **7.** display or pageantry. **8.** *Obs.* a stage bearing any kind of spectacle. [1350–1400; ME *pagyn, pagaunt, pagand* < AL *pāgina* a stage for plays, scene, platform, perh. special use of L *pāgina* PAGE[1]] —**pag′·eant·eer′,** *n.* —**pa·gean·tic** (pə jan′tik), *adj.*

pag·eant·ry (paj′ən trē), *n., pl.* **-ries. 1.** spectacular display; pomp: *the pageantry of a coronation.* **2.** mere show; empty display. **3.** pageants collectively; pageants and the performance of pageants. [1600–10; PAGEANT + -RY]
—**Syn. 1.** spectacle, ceremony, show.

page·boy (pāj′boi′), *n.* **1.** a hair style in which the hair is rolled under, usually at shoulder-length. **2.** a youth or man who works as a page, as at a hotel. Also, **page′ boy′.** [1900–05; PAGE[2] + BOY]

page′ chair′. See **porter chair.**

page′ descrip′tion lan′guage, a high-level programming language for determining the output of a page printer designed to work with it, independent of the printer's internal codes. *Abbr.:* PDL

page′ print′er, *Computers.* a high-speed, high-resolution printer that uses a light source, as a laser beam or electrically charged ions, to print a full page of text or graphics at a time. [1895–1900, for an earlier sense]

page′ proof′, a trial proof printed from type that has been made up in page form, usually after galley corrections have been made, but before plates are made. Cf. **proof** (def. 12). [1880–85]

pag·er[1] (pā′jər), *n.* something, as a book or brochure, having a specified number of pages (usually used in combination): *a 12-pager.* [1965–70; PAGE[1] + -ER[1]]

pag·er[2] (pā′jər), *n.* beeper (def. 3). [1965–70; PAGE[2] + -ER[1]]

Pag·et (paj′it), *n.* **Sir James,** 1814–99, English surgeon and pathologist.

Pag′et's disease′, *Pathol.* a chronic disease characterized by episodic accelerated bone resorption and growth of abnormal replacement bone, causing bone pain, deformation, fractures, and osteosarcoma; osteitis deformans. [1875–80; named after Sir James PAGET, who described it]

page-turn·er (pāj′tûr′nər), *n.* a book so exciting or gripping that one is compelled to read it very rapidly. [1970–75]

pag·i·nal (paj′ə nl), *adj.* **1.** of or pertaining to pages. **2.** consisting of pages. **3.** page for page: *a paginal reprint.* [1640–50; < LL *pāginālis* of, belonging to a page. See PAGE[1], -AL[1]]

pag·i·nate (paj′ə nāt′), *v.,* **-nat·ed, -nat·ing.** —*v.t.* **1.** to indicate the sequence of pages in (a book, manuscript, etc.) by placing numbers or other characters on each leaf; to number the pages of. —*v.i.* **2.** *Computers.* to create pages, as with a word-processing program. [1880–85; < L *pāgin(a)* PAGE[1] + -ATE[1]]

pag·i·na·tion (paj′ə nā′shən), *n.* **1.** *Bibliog.* the number of pages or leaves of a book, manuscript, etc., identified in bibliographical description or cataloging. **2.** the figures by which pages are marked to indicate their sequence. **3.** the act of paginating. **4.** *Print.* **a.** Also called **computer-assisted makeup.** a method of computerized page makeup in which copy and graphic elements are manipulated with the aid of a video display terminal. **b.** composition (def. 17). [1835–45; < L *pāgin(a)* PAGE[1] + -ATION]

pag·ing (pā′jing), *n. Computers.* a technique of storage management that transfers pages from secondary storage to main storage when they are required, and returns them to secondary storage when they are not. Cf. **page**[1] (def. 6a). [1965–70; PAGE[1] + -ING[1]]

Pa·gliac·ci, I (*It.* ē pä lyät′chē), an opera (1892) by Ruggiero Leoncavallo.

pagne (*Fr.* pan′yᵊ), *n., pl.* **pagnes** (*Fr.* pan′yᵊ). a garment worn by some African peoples, consisting of a rectangular strip of cloth fashioned into a loincloth or wrapped on the body so as to form a short skirt. [1690–1700; < F < Sp *paño* cloth << L *pannum*]

Pa·gnol (pa nyôl′), *n.* **Mar·cel** (mar sel′), 1895–1974, French playwright.

pa·go·da (pə gō′də), *n.* **1.** (in India, Burma, China, etc.) a temple or sacred building, usually a pyramidlike tower and typically having upward-curving roofs over the individual stories. **2.** any of several former gold or silver coins of southern India, usually bearing a figure of such a temple, first issued in the late 16th century and later also by British, French, and Dutch traders. [1625–35; < Pg *pagode* temple << Pers *butkada* (*but* idol + *kada* temple, dwelling)] —**pa·go′da·like′,** *adj.*

pagoda (def. 1) (Chinese, 11th century)

pago′da tree′, a spreading, round-headed tree, *Sophora japonica,* of the legume family, native to China and Korea, having yellowish-white flowers in loose, showy clusters, grown widely as a street tree. Also called **Chinese scholar tree, Japanese pagoda tree.**

Pa·go Pa·go (päng′ō päng′ō, päng′gō päng′gō, pä′gō pä′gō), the chief harbor and town of American Samoa, on Tutuila island: naval station. 2491. Also, **Pa′·go·pa′go, Pango Pango.**

pa·gu·ri·an (pə gyŏŏr′ē ən), *n.* **1.** a hermit crab, esp. of the genus *Pagurus.* —*adj.* **2.** pertaining to or characteristic of a hermit crab. [1830–40; < NL *Pagur(us)* the type genus (L: crab < Gk *págouros,* equiv. to *pág(os)* rock, something hard + *our(á)* tail + *-os* n. suffix) + -IAN]

pa·gu·rid (pə gyŏŏr′id, pag′yə rid), *n.* a pagurian. [1890–95; < NL *Pagūridae* name of the family < *Pagūr(us)* (see PAGURIAN) + *-idae* -ID[2]]

-pagus, a combining form used in the names of severely malformed, usually nonviable, conjoined twins, with the site of attachment specified by the initial element: *thoracopagus.* [< NL < Gk *págos* fixation, something fixed or solid]

pah (pä, pa), *interj.* (used as an exclamation of disgust or disbelief.) [1585–95]

Pa·hang (pä häng′, pə hang′), *n.* a state in Malaysia, on the SE Malay Peninsula. 504,945; 13,820 sq. mi. (35,794 sq. km). *Cap.:* Kuantan.

Pa·ha·ri (pä här′ē, pə-), *n., pl.* **-ri, -ris. 1.** one of several hill peoples inhabiting the area in India SW of the Ganges River. **2.** a member of these peoples. **3.** a group of Indic languages or dialects spoken by the Pahari.

Pah·la·vi (pä′lə vē′), *n., pl.* **-vis** for 3. **1. Muhammad Ri·za** (or **Re·za**) (ri zä′), 1919–80, shah of Iran 1941–79; in exile after 1979 (son of Riza Shah Pahlavi). **2. Riza** (or **Reza**) **Shah,** 1877–1944, shah of Iran 1925–41. **3.** (*l.c.*) a former gold coin of Iran, equal to 20 rials. Also, **Pah′le·vi′.**

Pah·la·vi (pä′lə vē′), *n.* **1.** the Indo-European, Iranian language of the Zoroastrian literature of the 3rd to the 10th centuries. **2.** the script used in writing this language, derived from the Aramaic alphabet. [1765–75; < Pers *Pahlavī* Parthian]

pa·ho (pä′hō, -hōō, pä hō′, -hōō′), *n., pl.* **-hos.** a prayer stick of the Hopi Indians. [1880–85, *Amer.;* < Hopi *pá·ho*]

pa·ho·e·ho·e (pə hō′ē hō′ē), *n.* basaltic lava having a smooth or billowy surface. Cf. **aa.** [1855–60; < Hawaiian *pāhoehoe*]

Pa·houin (pä wan′, -wan′), *n., pl.* **-houins,** (*esp. collectively*) **-houin.** *n.* Fang (def. 1).

paid (pād), *v.* a pt. and pp. of **pay**[1].

paid-in (pād′in′), *adj.* having paid the dues, initiation fees, etc., required by an organization or association. [adj. use of v. phrase *pay in*]

paid′-in sur′plus, *Accounting.* surplus paid in by purchasers of stock certificates sold at a premium.

paido-, var. of **pedo-**[1].

paid-up (pād′up′), *adj.* paid in full, as of the present or of a specified date: *a paid-up membership.* [1870–75]

Paige (pāj), *n.* **Leroy Robert** ("*Satchel*"), 1906–82, U.S. baseball player.

pai-hua (bī′hwä′), *n.* a colloquial form of written Chinese based on the spoken language, in use esp. since 1917. Cf. **wen-yen.** [< Chin *báihuà,* equiv. to *bái* plain, pure, white + *huà* word, talk]

pail (pāl), *n.* **1.** bucket. **2.** the amount filling a pail. [bef. 1000; ME *payle* wooden container, continuing OE *pægel* wine container, liquid measure (of unknown orig.; cf. MD, LG *pegel* half pint), by assoc. with OF *paielle* pan < L *patella;* see PATELLA]
—**Regional Variation. 1.** See **bucket.**

pail·ful (pāl′fŏŏl′), *n., pl.* **-fuls.** a quantity sufficient to fill a pail: *a pailful of water.* [1585–95; PAIL + -FUL]
—**Usage.** See **-ful.**

pail·lasse (pal yas′, pal′yas, pal′ē as′, pal′ē as′), *n. Chiefly Brit.* a mattress of straw; pallet. Also, **palliasse.** [1500–10; < F < It *pagliaccio* straw pallet, equiv. to *pagli(a)* straw (< L *palea* chaff) + *-accio* pejorative n. suffix]

pail·lette (pī yet′, pä-, pə let′; *Fr.* pa yet′), *n., pl.* **pail·lettes** (pal yets′, pə lets′; *Fr.* pa yet′). **1.** a spangle for ornamenting a costume. **2.** (in enameling) a decorative piece of gold, silver, or colored foil. [1875–80; < F; see PALLET[1]] —**pail·let′ted,** *adj.*

pail·lon (*Fr.* pä yôN′), *n., pl.* **pail·lons** (*Fr.* pä yôN′). a sheet of thin metallic foil used decoratively in enameling and gilding. [1885–90; < F, special use of *paille* straw (see PALLET[1]) + *-on* n. suffix]

pai-loo (pī′lō′), *n., pl.* **-loo, -loos.** (in Chinese architecture) a decorative or monumental gateway having a trabeated form with three compartments, the central one higher than the others. [1830–40; < Chin *páilou* (*paí* tablet + *lóu* tower)]

Pai′mi·o chair′ (pī′mē ō′), a chair developed by Alvar Aalto between 1930 and 1933, having two continuous, ribbonlike elements made of bent laminated birch veneers forming the arms and legs and supporting a sheet of bent plywood that forms the back and seat. [after *Paimio,* Finland, site of a sanitorium which Aalto was designing when the chair was developed]

pain (pān), *n.* **1.** physical suffering or distress, as due to injury, illness, etc. **2.** a distressing sensation in a particular part of the body: *a back pain.* **3.** mental or emotional suffering or torment: *I am sorry my news causes you such pain.* **4. pains, a.** laborious or careful efforts; assiduous care: *Great pains have been taken to repair the engine perfectly.* **b.** the suffering of childbirth. **5.** *Informal.* an annoying or troublesome person or thing. **6. feel no pain,** *Informal.* to be intoxicated: *After all that free beer, we were feeling no pain.* **7. on, upon,** or **under pain of,** liable to the penalty of: *on pain of death.* **8. pain in the ass,** *Slang* (*vulgar*). pain (def. 5). **9. pain in the neck,** *Informal.* pain (def. 5). —*v.t.* **10.** to cause physical pain to; hurt. **11.** to cause (someone) mental or emotional pain; distress: *Your sarcasm pained me.* —*v.i.* **12.** to have or give pain. [1250–1300; ME *peine* punishment, torture, pain < OF < L *poena* penalty, pain < Gk *poinḗ* penalty]
—**Syn. 1–3.** torture, misery, torment. PAIN, ACHE, AGONY, ANGUISH are terms for sensations causing suffering or torment. PAIN and ACHE usually refer to physical sensations (except *heartache*); AGONY and ANGUISH may be physical or mental. PAIN suggests a sudden sharp twinge: *a pain in one's ankle.* ACHE applies to a continuous pain, whether acute or dull: *headache; muscular aches.* AGONY implies a continuous, excruciating, scarcely endurable pain: *in agony from a wound.* ANGUISH suggests not only extreme and long-continued pain, but also a feeling of despair. **2.** pang, twinge, stitch. **4. a.** See **care. 11.** afflict, torment; trouble, grieve. —**Ant. 3.** joy, delight. **11.** please.

Paine (pān), *n.* **1. Albert Big·e·low** (big′ə lō′), 1861–1937, U.S. author and editor. **2. Robert Treat** (trēt), 1731–1814, U.S. jurist and statesman. **3. Thomas,** 1737–1809, U.S. patriot and writer on government and religion, born in England.

pained (pānd), *adj.* **1.** hurt; injured. **2.** showing or expressing distress, anguish, or resentment: *a pained look in reply to a sarcastic remark.* [1300–50; ME; see PAIN, -ED[2]]

Paines·ville (pānz′vil), *n.* a city in NE Ohio, on Lake Erie. 16,391.

pain·ful (pān′fəl), *adj.* **1.** affected with, causing, or characterized by pain: *a painful wound; a painful night; a painful memory.* **2.** laborious; exacting; difficult: *a painful life.* **3.** *Archaic.* painstaking; careful. [1300–50; ME; see PAIN, -FUL] **—pain′ful·ly,** *adv.* **—pain′ful·ness,** *n.*
—Syn. 1. distressing, torturing, agonizing, tormenting, excruciating. **2.** arduous. **—Ant. 2.** easy.

pain·kill·er (pān′kil′ər), *n.* a drug, treatment, or anything else that relieves pain, esp. an analgesic. [1850–55, *Amer.*; PAIN + KILLER] **—pain′kill′ing,** *adj.*

pain·less (pān′lis), *adj.* **1.** without pain; causing little or no pain: *painless dentistry; a painless cure.* **2.** *Informal.* not difficult; requiring little or no hard work or exertion. [1560–70; PAIN + -LESS] **—pain′less·ly,** *adv.* **—pain′less·ness,** *n.*

pains·tak·ing (pānz′tā′king, pān′stā′-), *adj.* **1.** taking or characterized by taking pains or trouble; expending or showing diligent care and effort; careful: *a painstaking craftsman; painstaking research.* —*n.* **2.** careful and diligent effort. [1550–60; PAIN + -S[3] + TAKING] **—pains′tak′ing·ly,** *adv.* **—pains′tak′ing·ness,** *n.*
—Syn. 1. thorough, scrupulous. PAINSTAKING, CAREFUL, METICULOUS, CONSCIENTIOUS all describe persons or behavior demonstrating attention to detail and effective task performance. PAINSTAKING stresses diligent and assiduous attention to detail in achieving a desired objective: *a painstaking technician; the painstaking editing of a manuscript.* CAREFUL, the most general in sense of these words, implies serious intent to perform well and accurately whatever task one has in hand: *a careful housepainter; a careful study of the social structure of gangs.* METICULOUS suggests extreme attention to details, especially the most minute, coupled with an almost obsessive desire to avoid error: *a meticulous silversmith, every detail finished to perfection; fussily meticulous about matching shoes and clothing.* CONSCIENTIOUS stresses scrupulous effort to obey one's sense of moral obligation to perform tasks well: *a conscientious public defender; a conscientious description of the robbery.*

paint (pānt), *n.* **1.** a substance composed of solid coloring matter suspended in a liquid medium and applied as a protective or decorative coating to various surfaces, or to canvas or other materials in producing a work of art. **2.** an application of this. **3.** the dried surface pigment: *Don't scuff the paint.* **4.** the solid coloring matter alone; pigment. **5.** facial cosmetics, esp. lipstick, rouge, etc., designed to heighten natural color. **6.** *Chiefly Western U.S.* a pied, calico, or spotted horse or pony; pinto. —*v.t.* **7.** to coat, cover, or decorate (something) with paint: *to paint a fence.* **8.** to produce (a picture, design, etc.) in paint: *to paint a portrait.* **9.** to represent in paint, as in oils, tempera, or watercolor: *to paint an actress as the Muse of tragedy.* **10.** to depict as if by painting; describe vividly in words: *The ads painted the resort as a winter wonderland.* **11.** to color by or as if by painting: *Sunset painted the clouds pink.* **12.** to apply a substance to, as a liquid medicine or a cosmetic: *to paint a cut with iodine.* —*v.i.* **13.** to coat or cover anything with paint. **14.** to engage in painting as an art: *She has begun to paint in her spare time.* **15.** to put on or use facial cosmetics. **16. paint the town red,** *Informal.* to celebrate boisterously, esp. by making a round of stops at bars and nightclubs. Also, **paint the town.** [1200–50; ME *peinten* (v.) < OF *peint,* ptp. of *peindre* < L *pingere* to paint; see PICTURE] **—paint′a·ble,** *adj.* **—paint′less,** *adj.*

paint′ bridge′. See under **bridge**[1] (def. 16a).

paint·brush (pānt′brush′), *n.* **1.** a brush for applying paint, as one used in painting houses or one used in painting pictures. **2.** any plant of the genus *Castilleja.* [1820–30; PAINT + BRUSH[1]]

paint·ed (pān′tid), *adj.* **1.** reproduced or represented in paint: *a painted image.* **2.** covered with a coating of paint: *a painted chair.* **3.** unreal; artificial; feigned: *a painted life.* **4.** exaggerated or misrepresented: *a luridly painted version of what really happened.* **5.** covered with makeup, esp. to excess. **6.** brightly colored or multicolored (used in combinations). [1250–1300; ME; see PAINT, -ED[2]]

paint′ed beau′ty, a butterfly, *Vanessa virginiensis,* having brownish-black and orange wings, the hind wings each having two eyespots. [1895–1900]

paint′ed bunt′ing, a brilliantly colored bunting, *Passerina ciris,* of the southern U.S. [1805–15, *Amer.*]

paint′ed cup′, any of several semiparasitic plants of the genus *Castilleja,* of the figwort family, having highly colored dilated bracts about the flowers. Also called **paintbrush.** [1780–90]

Paint′ed Des′ert, a region in N central Arizona, E of the Colorado River: many-colored rock surfaces.

paint′ed green′ling, a greenling, *Oxylebius pictus,* inhabiting the Pacific coastal waters of North America, having a whitish body marked with black bands. Also called **convictfish.**

paint′ed horse′, paint (def. 6). Also called **paint′ed po′ny.**

paint′ed la′dy, a butterfly, *Vanessa cardui,* having brownish-black and orange wings and hind wings each with four eyespots, the larvae of which feed on thistles. [1745–55]

paint′ed snipe′, either of two snipelike birds of the family Rostratulidae, of South America and the Old World tropics, the female of which is larger and more brightly colored than the male. [1805–15]

paint′ed tongue′, a Chilean plant, *Salpiglossis sinuata,* of the nightshade family, having large, funnel-shaped flowers in a variety of colors.

paint′ed tril′lium, a North American trillium, *Trillium undulatum,* having white flowers streaked with pink or purple. [1850–55, *Amer.*]

paint′ed tur′tle, a freshwater turtle, *Chrysemys picta,* common in the U.S., having bright yellow markings on the head and neck and red markings on the margin of the carapace. [1875–80]

paint′ed wom′an, a prostitute; slut.

paint·er[1] (pān′tər), *n.* **1.** an artist who paints pictures. **2.** a person who coats walls or other surfaces with paint, esp. one who does so as an occupation. **3.** (*cap.*) *Astron.* the constellation Pictor. [1300–50; PAINT + -ER[1]; r. ME *peyntour* < AF *peintour*]

paint·er[2] (pān′tər), *n.* a rope, usually at the bow, for fastening a boat to a ship, stake, etc. [1300–50; ME *peyntour,* prob. < MF *pentoir,* var. of *pendoir* rope, cord for hanging things on. See PEND, -ER[2]]

paint·er[3] (pān′tər), *n.* cougar. [1755–65, *Amer.*; var. of PANTHER]

paint·er·ly (pān′tər lē), *adj.* **1.** of, pertaining to, or characteristic of a painter. **2.** *Fine Arts.* characterized by qualities of color, stroke, or texture perceived as distinctive to the art of painting, esp. the rendering of forms and images in terms of color or tonal relations rather than of contour or line. [1580–90; PAINTER[1] + -LY]

paint′er's col′ic, *Pathol.* lead poisoning causing intense intestinal pain. [1815–25]

paint′ horse′, paint (def. 6). Also called **paint′ po′ny.** [1865–70]

paint·ing (pān′ting), *n.* **1.** a picture or design executed in paints. **2.** the act, art, or work of a person who paints. **3.** the works of art painted in a particular manner, place, or period: *a book on Flemish painting.* **4.** an instance of covering a surface with paint. [1175–1225; ME; see PAINT, -ING[1]]

paint′ pot′, **1.** Also, **paint′pot′.** a container, as a jar, pail, or bucket, for holding paint while it is being applied. **2.** *Geol.* a spring or pit filled with boiling colored mud. Cf. **mud pot.** [1830–40]

paint′ roll′er, a roller of absorbent material, mounted on a handle, that is rolled in a trough of paint and then rolled over a flat surface to be painted. [1950–55]

paint·y (pān′tē), *adj.,* **paint·i·er, paint·i·est. 1.** of, coated with, or soiled with paint: *a painty finish; painty overalls.* **2.** having a crudely or clumsily painted surface: *The stage set consisted chiefly of painty scenery.* [1865–70; PAINT + -Y[1]] **—paint′i·ness,** *n.*

pair (pâr), *n., pl.* **pairs, pair,** *v.* —*n.* **1.** two identical, similar, or corresponding things that are matched for use together: *a pair of gloves; a pair of earrings.* **2.** something consisting of or regarded as having two parts or pieces joined together: *a pair of scissors; a pair of slacks.* **3.** two individuals who are similar or in some way associated: *a pair of liars; a pair of seal pups.* **4.** a married, engaged, or dating couple. **5.** two mated animals. **6.** a span or team: *a pair of horses.* **7.** *Govt.* **a.** two members on opposite sides in a deliberative body who for convenience, as to permit absence, arrange together to forgo voting on a given occasion. **b.** the arrangement thus made. **8.** *Cards.* **a.** two cards of the same denomination without regard to suit or color. **b. pairs,** two players who are matched together against different contestants. **9. pairs.** See **pair skating. 10.** Also called **kinematic pair.** *Mech.* two parts or pieces so connected that they mutually constrain relative motion. **11.** *Philately.* two postage stamps joined together either vertically or horizontally. **12.** a set or combination of more than two objects forming a collective whole: *a pair of beads.* —*v.t.* **13.** to arrange or designate in pairs or groups of two: *She paired dancers for the waltz contest.* **14.** to form into a pair, as by matching, joining, etc.; match; couple: *to pair freshly washed socks.* **15.** (of animals) to cause to mate. —*v.i.* **16.** to separate into pairs or groups of two (usually fol. by *off*): *to pair off for a procession.* **17.** to form a pair or pairs. **18.** to be a member of a pair. **19.** to match with or resemble another. **20.** to unite in close association with another, as in a business partnership, friendship, marriage, etc. **21.** (of animals) to mate. **22.** *Govt.* (in a deliberative body) to form or arrange a pair. [1250–1300; ME *paire* < OF < L *pāria,* pl. (taken as fem. sing.) of *pār* a pair. See PAR[1]] **—pair′wise′,** *adv.*
—Syn. 1. PAIR, BRACE, COUPLE, SPAN, YOKE are terms for groups of two. PAIR is used of two things naturally or habitually associated in use, or necessary to each other to make a complete set: *a pair of dice.* It is used also of one thing composed of two similar and complementary parts: *a pair of trousers.* BRACE is a hunter's term, used of a pair of dogs, ducks, etc., or a pair of pistols or slugs: *a brace of partridges.* In COUPLE the idea of combination or interdependence has become greatly weakened; it may be used loosely for two of anything (*a couple of apples*), and even for more than two: *I have to see a couple of people.* SPAN is used of a matched pair of horses harnessed together side by side. YOKE applies to the two animals hitched together under a yoke for drawing and pulling: *a yoke of oxen.*
—Usage. When used without a modifier, PAIRS is the only possible plural: *Pairs of skaters glided over the ice.* When modified by a number, PAIRS is the more common form, especially referring to persons: *Six pairs of masked dancers led the procession.* The unmarked plural PAIR is used mainly in reference to inanimate objects or nonhumans: *He has three pair* (or *pairs*) *of loafers. Two pair* (or *pairs*) *of barn owls have nested on our property.*
PAIR signifying two individuals can take either a singular or plural verb, but it is usually followed by a plural verb and referred to by a plural pronoun: *The guilty pair have not been seen since their escape.*
In the sense "a set or combination of more than two objects forming a collective whole," PAIR occurs chiefly in fixed phrases: *a pair of beads; a pair of stairs.* This use is now somewhat old-fashioned. See also **collective noun, couple.**

pair (peʀ), *adj. French.* noting any even number, esp. in roulette. Cf. **impair.**

pair′ annihila′tion, *Physics.* annihilation (def. 3a).

pair′ bond′, *Animal Behav.* **1.** a partnership between a mating couple that lasts at least one season, serving primarily in the cooperative rearing of young. **2.** the couple that forms such a partnership. [1935–40]

pair-bond (pâr′bond′), *Animal Behav.* —*v.i.* **1.** (of a mating couple) to form and maintain a pair bond. —*n.* **2.** See **pair bond.**

pair·ing (pâr′ing), *n.* **1.** a coupling. **2.** *Cell Biol.* the lining up of the two homologous chromosomes or chromatids of each chromosome pair in meiosis or mitosis. Cf. **base pairing.** [1605–15; PAIR + -ING[1]]

pairle (pârl, perl), *n. Heraldry.* a device representing the front of an ecclesiastical pallium, consisting of a broad Y-shaped form covered with crosses. Also called **pall.** [< F, prob. alter. of OF *paile* PALL[1]]

pair-oar (pâr′ôr′, -ōr′), *n.* a racing shell propelled by two persons, each with one oar. [1850–55] **—pair′-oared′,** *adj.*

pair′ of com′passes, compass (def. 7). [1545–55]

pair′ produc′tion, *Physics.* the simultaneous creation of a particle and its antiparticle by a nucleus or particle in an excited state, as when a photon is absorbed. [1930–35]

pair′ roy′al, *Cribbage.* a set of three cards of the same denomination, worth six points. Cf. **double pair royal.** [1585–95]

pair′ skat′ing, a form of competitive skating in which a man and a woman skate together in performing a choreographed series of jumps, lifts, and other acrobatic moves to a selection of music. Also, **pairs′ skat′ing.** Also called **pairs.**

pai·sa (pī sä′ *for 1;* pī′sä *for 2*), *n., pl.* **-se** (-sā). **1.** Also, **pice.** an aluminum coin and monetary unit, the 100th part of the rupee of India, Nepal, and Pakistan. **2.** poisha. [< Hindi *paisā*]

pai·sa·no (pī sä′nō, -zä′-; *Sp.* pī sä′nô), *n., pl.* **-nos** (-nōz; *Sp.* -nôs). **1.** compatriot. **2.** *Slang.* pal; buddy; comrade. **3.** *Southwestern U.S.* **a.** a rustic or peasant. **b.** a roadrunner. [1835–45, *Amer.*; < Sp < F *paysan.* See PEASANT]

Pai·siel·lo (pī zyel′lô), *n.* **Gio·van·ni** (jô vän′nē), 1741–1816, Italian composer. Also, **Paesiello.**

pais·ley (pāz′lē), *n., pl.* **-leys,** *adj.* —*n.* **1.** a soft woolen fabric woven with a pattern of colorful and minutely detailed figures. **2.** a shawl, scarf, tie, or other article made of this fabric. **3.** a silk print simulating this fabric and weave. **4.** Also called **pais′ley print′.** a pattern resembling the design or figure on this fabric or material. —*adj.* **5.** made of paisley: *a paisley shawl.* **6.** having the pattern of a paisley. Also, **Paisley.** [1825–35; named after PAISLEY]

Pais·ley (pāz′lē), *n.* **1.** a city in the Strathclyde region, in SW Scotland, W of Glasgow: thread factories. 95,067. **2.** paisley.

Pai·ute (pī o͞ot′, pī′o͞ot), *n., pl.* **-utes,** (*esp. collectively*) **-ute. 1.** a member of a group of North American Indians of the Uto-Aztecan family dwelling in California, Nevada, Utah, and Arizona. **2.** either of two mutually unintelligible Uto-Aztecan languages (**Northern Paiute** and **Southern Paiute**). Also, **Piute.**

pa·ja·ma (pə jä′mə, -jam′ə), *adj.* of, pertaining to, or resembling pajamas: *a pajama top; a lounging outfit with pajama pants.* [see PAJAMAS]

paja′ma par′ty. See **slumber party.** [1900–10]

pa·ja·mas (pə jä′məz, -jam′əz), *n.* (*used with a plural v.*) **1.** night clothes consisting of loose-fitting trousers and jacket. **2.** loose-fitting trousers, usually of silk or cotton, worn by both sexes in the Orient. Also, *esp. Brit.,* **pyjamas.** [1870–75; pl. of *pajama* < Hindi, var. of *pāyjāma* < Pers *pāy* leg + *jāma* garment] **—pa·ja′·maed,** *adj.*

pak (pak), *n.* pack; package.

Pa·kan·ba·ru (pä′kän bär′o͞o), *n.* a city on central Sumatra, in W Indonesia. 145,030.

pak·a·poo (pak′ə po͞o′), *n.* a Chinese lottery in which the tickets are sheets of paper bearing densely written characters. Also, **pak′a·pu′.** [1910–15; < dial. Chin, equiv. to Chin *báigē piào* lit., white-pigeon ticket; cf. Guangdong dial. *baahk-gáap* pigeon, *piu* ticket]

pakapoo′ tick′et, *Australian Slang.* something that is indecipherable or confusing: *scrawled over like a pakapoo ticket.*

Pak′a·rai′ma Moun′tains (pak′ə rī′mə, pak′ə-), a mountain range along the W central border of Guyana. Also, **Pacaraima Mountains.**

pak-choi (bäk′choi′), *n., pl.* **-choi, -chois.** See **bok choy.** Also, **pak′choi′.**

Pak·i (pak′ē, pä′kē), *n., pl.* **Pak·is.** *Chiefly Brit. Slang* (*disparaging and offensive*). **1.** a Pakistani, esp. one who has emigrated to Britain. **2.** any emigrant to Britain from the Indian subcontinent. [1960–65; by shortening, with *i* construed as -Y[2]]

Pa·ki·stan (pak′ə stan′, pä′kə stän′), *n.* **1. Islamic Republic of,** a republic in S Asia, between India and Afghanistan: formerly part of British India; known as West Pakistan from 1947–71 to distinguish it from East Pakistan (now Bangladesh). See map on next page.

83,782,000; 310,403 sq. mi. (803,881 sq. km). *Cap.:* Islamabad. **2.** (before 1947) the predominantly Muslim areas of the peninsula of India as distinguished from Hindustan, the predominantly Hindu areas.

Pa·ki·sta·ni (pak′ə stan′ē, pä′kə stä′nē), *n., pl.* **-nis, -ni,** *adj.* —*n.* **1.** a native or inhabitant of Pakistan. —*adj.* **2.** of, pertaining to, or characteristic of Pakistan or its inhabitants.

Pa·kok·ku (pə kôk′ko͞o), *n.* a city in central Burma. 150,000.

Pak·se (päk sā′), *n.* a city in S Laos, on the Mekong River. 44,860.

pal (pal), *n., v.,* **palled, pal·ling.** *Informal.* —*n.* **1.** a very close, intimate friend; comrade; chum. **2.** an accomplice. —*v.i.* **3.** to associate as comrades or chums: *to pal around with the kid next door.* [1675–85; < English Romany: brother, mate, dissimilated var. of continental Romany *phral* << Skt *bhrātṛ* BROTHER]

PAL (pal), *n.* a special air service offered by the U.S. Postal Service for sending parcels from 5 to 30 lb. (2.3 to 13.5 kg) to overseas servicemen: only the regular parcel post rate to the U.S. port of shipment plus $1 is charged. Cf. **SAM** (def. 2). [*P*(*arcel*) *A*(*ir*) *L*(*ift*)]

PAL, Police Athletic League. Also, **P.A.L.**

Pal., Palestine.

pal., **1.** paleography. **2.** paleontology.

pa·la·bra (pä lä′vrä), *n., pl.* ***-bras*** (-vräs). *Spanish.* **1.** a word. **2.** speech; talk.

pal·ace (pal′is), *n.* **1.** the official residence of a king, queen, emperor, bishop, or other sovereign or exalted personage. **2.** a large and stately mansion or building. **3.** a large and usually ornate place for entertainment, exhibitions, etc.: *a movie palace.* [1200–50; ME < ML *palācium,* sp. var. of *palātium,* L: generic use of *Palātium,* name of the hill in Rome on which the emperor's palace was situated; r. ME *paleis* < OF << L *Palātium*] —**pal′aced,** *adj.* —**pal′ace·like′,** *adj.* —**pal′ace·ward,** *adv.*

pal′ace guard′, **1.** the security force protecting a palace. **2.** a group of trusted advisers who often control access to a sovereign, president, or other chief executive. [1885–90]

pal′ace revolu′tion, a challenge to or overthrow of a sovereign or other leader by members of the ruling family or group. Also called **pal′ace revolt′, pal′ace coup′** (ko͞o). [1900–05]

Pa·la·cio Val·dés (pä lä′thyô väl des′), **Ar·man·do** (är män′dô), 1853–1938, Spanish novelist and critic.

Pa·la·de (pə lä′dē), *n.* **George Emil,** born 1912, U.S. biologist, born in Rumania: Nobel prize for medicine 1974.

pal·a·din (pal′ə din), *n.* **1.** any one of the 12 legendary peers or knightly champions in attendance on Charlemagne. **2.** any knightly or heroic champion. **3.** any determined advocate or defender of a noble cause. [1585–95; < F < It *paladino* < LL *palātinus* imperial functionary, n. use of adj.; see PALATINE[1]]

palae-, *Chiefly Brit.* var. of **pale-.** Also, *esp. before a consonant,* **palaeo-.**

palaeo-, *Chiefly Brit.* var. of **paleo-.** Also, *before some vowels,* **palae-.**

Pa·lae·ol·o·gus (pā′lē ol′ə gəs *or, esp. Brit.,* pal′ē-), *n.* family name of Byzantine rulers 1259–1453.

pa·laes·tra (pə les′trə), *n., pl.* **-tras, -trae** (-trē), *Gk. Antiq.* palestra.

pa·lais (pᴀ le′), *n., pl.* ***-lais.*** *French.* a palace, esp. a French government or municipal building.

pal·am·pore (pal′əm pôr′, -pōr′), *n.* a cotton print woven in India and used for clothing, canopies, etc. Also, **pal·am·poor** (pal′əm po͝or′). [1690–1700; prob. named after *Palanpur,* city in Rajputana, India]

pal·an·quin (pal′ən kēn′), *n.* (formerly in India and other Eastern countries) a passenger conveyance, usually for one person, consisting of a covered or boxlike litter carried by means of poles resting on the shoulders of several men. Also, **pal′an·keen′.** [1580–90; < MF < D *pallankin* < Pg *palanquim* << Pali *pallaṅka,* Skt *palyaṅka;* cf. Oriya *pālaṅki*] —**pal′an·quin′er, pal′an·keen′er,** *n.* —**pal′an·quin′ing·ly, pal′an·keen′ing·ly,** *adv.*

pa·la·pa (pə lä′pə; *Sp.* pä lä′pä), *n., pl.* **-pas** (-pəz; *Sp.* -päs). (esp. in Mexico) **1.** a simple, thatched-roof dwelling, usually open on the sides. **2.** any building resembling this, esp. in a resort area, as a restaurant, beach-house, or the like. [perh. < MexSp: a kind of palm tree]

CONCISE ETYMOLOGY KEY: <, descended or borrowed from; >, whence; b., blend of, blended; c., cognate with; cf., compare; deriv., derivative; equiv., equivalent; imit., imitative; obl., oblique; r., replacing; s., stem; sp., spelling, spelled; resp., respelling, respelled; trans., translation; ?, origin unknown; *, unattested; ‡, probably earlier than. See the full key inside the front cover.

pal·at·a·ble (pal′ə tə bəl), *adj.* **1.** acceptable or agreeable to the palate or taste; savory: *palatable food.* **2.** acceptable or agreeable to the mind or feelings: *palatable ideas.* [1660–70; PALATE + -ABLE] —**pal′at·a·bil′i·ty, pal′at·a·ble·ness,** *n.* —**pal′at·a·bly,** *adv.*
—**Syn. 1.** delicious, delectable. PALATABLE, APPETIZING, TASTY, SAVORY all refer to tastes or aromas pleasing to the palate and in some cases to the olfactory nerves. PALATABLE has the least positive connotation of these terms, often referring to food that is merely acceptable and not especially good: *a palatable, if undistinguished, main course; a barely palatable mixture of overcooked vegetables.* APPETIZING suggests stimulation of the appetite by the smell, taste of food, and is the only one of these words that can also refer to food pleasing to the eye: *the appetizing aroma of baking bread; the table contained an appetizing display of meats, cheeses, and salads.* TASTY refers to food that has a notable or especially appealing taste: *mixed with bits of a tasty sausage; an especially tasty sauce.* SAVORY refers most often to well or highly seasoned foods and applies to their appeal in both taste and smell: *a savory, succulent roast of beef, spiced with slivers of garlic; the savory aroma of a simmering duck sauce.* **2.** pleasing, satisfactory. —**Ant. 1.** distasteful.

pal·a·tal (pal′ə tl), *adj.* **1.** *Anat.* of or pertaining to the palate. **2.** *Phonet.* articulated with the blade of the tongue held close to or touching the hard palate. —*n.* **3.** *Phonet.* a palatal consonant. [1820–30; < F; see PALATE, -AL[1]] —**pal′a·tal·ism, pal′a·tal′i·ty,** *n.* —**pal′a·tal·ly,** *adv.*

pal·a·tal·ize (pal′ə tl īz′), *v.,* **-ized, -iz·ing.** *Phonet.* —*v.t.* **1.** to articulate (a consonant other than a normal palatal) as a palatal or with relatively more contact between the blade of the tongue and the hard palate, as in certain pronunciations of the *l*-sound in *million.* —*v.i.* **2.** (of a consonant) to undergo palatalization. Also, *esp. Brit.,* **pal′a·tal·ise′.** [1865–70; PALATAL + -IZE] —**pal′a·tal·i·za′tion,** *n.*

pal·a·tal·ized (pal′ə tl īzd′), *adj. Phonet.* pronounced with secondary palatal articulation. [1865–70; PALATALIZE + -ED[2]]

pal·ate (pal′it), *n.* **1.** *Anat.* the roof of the mouth, consisting of an anterior bony portion **(hard palate)** and a posterior muscular portion **(soft palate)** that separate the oral cavity from the nasal cavity. See diag. under **mouth. 2.** the sense of taste: *a dinner to delight the palate.* **3.** intellectual or aesthetic taste; mental appreciation. [1350–1400; ME *palat* < L *palātum* roof of the mouth] —**pal′ate·less,** *adj.* —**pal′ate·like′,** *adj.*

pa·la·tial (pə lā′shəl), *adj.* **1.** of, pertaining to, or resembling a palace: *a palatial home.* **2.** befitting or suitable for a palace; stately; magnificent: *a palatial tapestry.* [1745–55; < L *palāti*(*um*) PALACE + -AL[1]] —**pa·la′tial·ly,** *adv.* —**pa·la′tial·ness,** *n.*
—**Syn. 1, 2.** noble, regal, imposing, grand. —**Ant. 1, 2.** humble, simple.

Pa·lat·i·nate (pə lat′n āt′, -it), *n.* **1. the.** German, **Pfalz.** either of two historic regions of Germany that constituted an electorate of the Holy Roman Empire: one **(Lower Palatinate** or **Rhine Palatinate)** is now part of Rhineland-Palatinate, and the other **(Upper Palatinate)** is now part of Bavaria. **2.** a native or inhabitant of the Palatinate. **3.** (*l.c.*) the territory under the jurisdiction of a palatine. [PALATINE[1] + -ATE[1]] —**pa·lat′i·nal,** *adj.*

pal·a·tine[1] (pal′ə tīn′, -tin), *adj.* **1.** having royal privileges: *a count palatine.* **2.** of or pertaining to a count palatine, earl palatine, or county palatine. **3.** of or pertaining to a palace; palatial: *a palatine chapel.* **4.** (*cap.*) of or pertaining to the Palatinate. —*n.* **5.** a vassal exercising royal privileges in a province; a count or earl palatine. **6.** an important officer of an imperial palace. **7.** a high official of an empire. **8.** (*cap.*) a native or inhabitant of the Palatinate. **9.** (*cap.*) one of the seven hills on which ancient Rome was built. **10.** a shoulder cape, usually of fur or lace, formerly worn by women. [1400–50; late ME < ML, L *palātinus* of the imperial house, imperial; orig., of the hill *Palātium* in Rome. See PALACE, -INE[1]]

pal·a·tine[2] (pal′ə tīn′, -tin), *adj.* of, near, or in the palate; palatal: *the palatine bones.* [1650–60; < F *palatin, -ine.* See PALATE, -INE[1]]

Pal·a·tine (pal′ə tīn′), *n.* a city in NE Illinois. 32,166.

pa·la·ti·um (pə lā′shē əm, -shəm; *Lat.* pä lä′tē o͝om′), *n., pl.* **-ti·a** (-shē ə, -shə; *Lat.* -tē ä′). a palace, esp. the palace of an ancient Roman emperor. [< L *palātium*]

Pa·lat·ka (pə lat′kə), *n.* a city in NE Florida. 10,175.

palato-, a combining form representing **palate** in compound words: *palatogram.*

pal·a·to·al·ve·o·lar (pal′ə tō al vē′ə lər), *Phonet.* —*adj.* **1.** articulated with the blade or tip of the tongue approaching or touching the alveolar ridge and the main body of the tongue near the hard palate; having a primary alveolar articulation and a secondary palatal articulation. —*n.* **2.** a palato-alveolar sound, as (sh) or (ch). [1930–35]

pal·a·to·gram (pal′ə tə gram′), *n. Phonet.* a diagram or photograph obtained through palatography. [1900–05; PALATO- + -GRAM[1]]

pal·a·tog·ra·phy (pal′ə tog′rə fē), *n. Phonet.* a technique for observing the position of the tongue in relation to the palate during articulation, esp. by placing powder or dye on the palate and then noting the area from which it has been removed by the contact of the tongue with the palate during the production of a speech sound. [1900–05; PALATO- + -GRAPHY]

Pa·lau′ Is′lands (pä lou′), a former name of the Republic of **Belau.**

pa·lav·er (pə lav′ər, -lä′vər), *n.* **1.** a conference or discussion. **2.** a long parley, esp. one between primitive natives and European traders, explorers, colonial officials, etc. **3.** profuse and idle talk; chatter. **4.** persuasive talk; flattery; cajolery. —*v.i.* **5.** to talk profusely and idly. **6.** to engage in a palaver; parley or confer. —*v.t.* **7.** to cajole or persuade. [1720–30; < Pg *palavra* word, speech, talk < LL *parabola* PARABLE] —**pa·lav′er·er, pa·lav′er·ist,** *n.* —**pa·lav′er·ment,** *n.* —**pa·lav′er·ous,** *adj.*

Pa·la·wan (pä lä′wän), *n.* an island in the W Philippines. 371,782; 5697 sq. mi. (14,755 sq. km).

pa·laz·zo (pə lät′sō; *It.* pä lät′tsô), *n., pl.* **-laz·zi** (-lät′sē; *It.* -lät′tsē). an impressive public building or private residence; palace. [< It: lit., PALACE]

pale[1] (pāl), *adj.,* **pal·er, pal·est,** *v.,* **paled, pal·ing.** —*adj.* **1.** lacking intensity of color; colorless or whitish: *a pale complexion.* **2.** of a low degree of chroma, saturation, or purity; approaching white or gray: *pale yellow.* **3.** not bright or brilliant; dim: *the pale moon.* **4.** faint or feeble; lacking vigor: *a pale protest.* —*v.i., v.t.* **5.** to make or become pale: *to pale at the sight of blood.* [1250–1300; ME < MF < L *pallidus* PALLID] —**pale′ly,** *adv.* —**pale′ness,** *n.*
—**Syn. 1.** ashy, ashen. PALE, PALLID, WAN imply an absence of color, esp. from the human countenance. PALE implies a faintness or absence of color, which may be natural when applied to things: *the pale blue of a violet,* but when used to refer to the human face usually means an unnatural and often temporary absence of color, as arising from sickness or sudden emotion: *pale cheeks.* PALLID, limited mainly to the human countenance, implies an excessive paleness induced by intense emotion, disease, or death: *the pallid lips of the dying man.* WAN implies a sickly paleness, as after a long illness: *wan and thin;* the suggestion of weakness may be more prominent than that of lack of color: *a wan smile.* **5.** blanch, whiten. —**Ant. 1.** ruddy. **5.** darken.

pale[2] (pāl), *n., v.,* **paled, pal·ing.** —*n.* **1.** a stake or picket, as of a fence. **2.** an enclosing or confining barrier; enclosure. **3.** an enclosed area. **4.** limits; bounds: *outside the pale of his jurisdiction.* **5.** a district or region within designated bounds. **6.** (*cap.*) Also called **English Pale, Irish Pale.** a district in eastern Ireland included in the Angevin Empire of King Henry II and his successors. **7.** *Heraldry.* an ordinary in the form of a broad vertical stripe at the center of an escutcheon. **8.** *Shipbuilding.* a shore used inside to support the deck beams of a hull under construction. **9. beyond the pale,** beyond the limits of propriety, courtesy, protection, safety, etc.: *Their public conduct is certainly beyond the pale.* —*v.t.* **10.** to enclose with pales; fence. **11.** to encircle or encompass. [1300–50; ME (north), OE *pāl* < L *pālus* stake. See PEEL[3], POLE[1]]

pale-, var. of **paleo-** before most vowels: *paleethnology.* Also, *esp. Brit.,* **palae-.**

pa·le·a (pā′lē ə), *n., pl.* **-le·ae** (-lē ē′). *Bot.* **1.** a chaff-like scale or bract. **2.** the scalelike, membranous organ in the flowers of grasses that is situated upon a secondary axis in the axil of the flowering glume and envelops the stamens and pistil. [1745–55; < NL, special use of L *palea* chaff] —**pa·le·a·ceous** (pā′lē ā′shəs), **pa·le·ate** (pā′lē it, -āt′), *adj.*

pa·le·arc·tic (pā′lē ärk′tik, -är′tik *or, esp. Brit.,* pal′ē-), *adj. Zoogeog.* belonging or pertaining to a geographical division comprising Europe, Africa north of the tropic of Cancer, the northern part of the Arabian Peninsula, and Asia north of the Himalayas. Also, **paleoarctic.** [1855–60; PALE- + ARCTIC]

pale′ chrysan′themum a′phid, greenfly.

pale-dry (pāl′drī′), *adj.* light-colored and medium-sweet: *pale-dry ginger ale.* [1930–35]

pa·le·en·ceph·a·lon (pā′lē en sef′ə lon′ *or, esp. Brit.,* pal′ē-), *n., pl.* **-la** (-lə). (no longer in technical use) the more primitive part of the brain in the evolutionary development of animals, including all parts except the cerebral cortex and its related structures. Also, **paleoencephalon.** Cf. **neencephalon.** [1915–20; < NL; see PALE-, ENCEPHALON]

pa·le·eth·nol·o·gy (pā′lē eth nol′ə jē *or, esp. Brit.,* pal′ē-), *n.* (formerly) the branch of ethnology concerned with the earliest or most primitive races of humankind. [1865–70; PALE- + ETHNOLOGY] —**pa·le·eth·no·log·ic** (pā′lē eth′nl oj′ik *or, esp. Brit.,* pal′ē-), **pa′le·eth′no·log′i·cal,** *adj.* —**pa′le·eth·nol′o·gist,** *n.*

pale·face (pāl′fās′), *n. Slang.* a white person, as distinguished from a North American Indian. [1815–25; PALE[1] + FACE, expression attributed to North American Indians]

Pale′ Horse′, a representation of Death, as in literature or the Bible. [after the Biblical *pale horse* on which Death rides, Rev. 6:8]

Pale′ Horse′, Pale′ Rid′er, a trilogy of short novels (1939) by Katherine Anne Porter.

Pa·lem·bang (pä′lem bäng′), *n.* a city in SE Sumatra, in W Indonesia. 582,961.

Pa·len·que (pä leng′ke), *n.* a village in SE Mexico, in Chiapas state: ruins of an ancient Mayan city.

paleo-, a combining form meaning "old" or "ancient," esp. in reference to former geologic time periods, used in the formation of compound words: *paleobotany.* Also, **pale-,** *esp. Brit.,* **palae-, palaeo-.** [< Gk *palaio-,* comb. form of *palaiós*]

pa·le·o·an·throp·ic (pā′lē ō an throp′ik *or, esp. Brit.,* pal′ē-), *adj.* pertaining to prehistoric humans. [1885–90; PALEO- + ANTHROPIC]

pa·le·o·an·thro·pol·o·gy (pā′lē ō an′thrə pol′ə jē *or, esp. Brit.,* pal′ē-), *n.* the study of the origins and predecessors of the present human species, using fossils and other remains. [1915–20; PALEO- + ANTHROPOLOGY] —**pa′le·o·an′thro·pol′o·gist,** *n.* —**pa·le·o·an·thro·po·log·i·cal** (pā′lē ō an′thrə pə loj′i kəl *or, esp. Brit.,* pal′ē-), *adj.*

pa·le·o·arc·tic (pā′lē ō ärk′tik *or, esp. Brit.,* pal′ē-), *adj.* palearctic.

Pa·le·o·A·si·at·ic (pā′lē ō ā′zhē at′ik, -shē-, -zē- *or, esp. Brit.,* pal′ē-), *n.* **1.** a member of any of various

Mongoloid peoples of northeastern Asia. **2.** Paleosiberian (def. 1).

pa·le·o·bi·o·ge·og·ra·phy (pā′lē ō bī′ō jē og′rə fē *or, esp. Brit.,* pal′ē-), *n.* the study of the distribution of ancient plants and animals and their relation to ancient geographic features. [1930–35; PALEO- + BIOGEOGRAPHY] —**pa·le·o·bi·o·ge·o·graph·ic** (pā′lē ō bī′ō jē′ə graf′ik *or, esp. Brit.,* pal′ē-), **pa′le·o·bi′o·ge′o·graph′i·cal,** *adj.* —**pa′le·o·bi′o·ge′o·graph′i·cal·ly,** *adv.* —**pa′le·o·bi′·o·ge·og′ra·pher,** *n.*

pa·le·o·bi·ol·o·gy (pā′lē ō bī ol′ə jē *or, esp. Brit.,* pal′ē-), *n.* the branch of paleontology dealing with fossil life forms, esp. with reference to their origin, structure, evolution, etc. [1890–95; PALEO- + BIOLOGY] —**pa·le·o·bi·o·log·i·cal** (pā′lē ō bī′ə loj′i kəl *or, esp. Brit.,* pal′ē-), **pa′le·o·bi′o·log′ic,** *adj.* —**pa′le·o·bi·ol′o·gist,** *n.*

pa·le·o·bot·a·ny (pā′lē ō bot′n ē *or, esp. Brit.,* pal′ē-), *n.* the branch of paleontology dealing with fossil plants. [1870–75; PALEO- + BOTANY] —**pa·le·o·bo·tan·i·cal** (pā′lē ō bə tan′i kəl *or, esp. Brit.,* pal′ē-), **pa′le·o·bo·tan′ic,** *adj.* —**pa′le·o·bot′a·nist,** *n.*

Pa·le·o·cene (pā′lē ə sēn′ *or, esp. Brit.,* pal′ē-), *Geol.* —*adj.* **1.** noting or pertaining to an epoch of the Tertiary Period, from 65 to 55 million years ago, and characterized by a proliferation of mammals. See table under **geologic time.** —*n.* **2.** the Paleocene Epoch or Series. [1875–80; PALEO- + -CENE]

pa·le·o·cli·mate (pā′lē ō klī′mit *or, esp. Brit.,* pal′ē-), *n.* the climate of some former period of geologic time. [1920–25; PALEO- + CLIMATE]

pa·le·o·cli·ma·tol·o·gy (pā′lē ō klī′mə tol′ə jē *or, esp. Brit.,* pal′ē-), *n.* the branch of paleogeography dealing with the study of paleoclimates. [1915–20; PALEO- + CLIMATOLOGY] —**pa·le·o·cli·ma·to·log·i·cal** (pā′lē ō-klī′mə tl oj′i kəl *or, esp. Brit.,* pal′ē-), **pa′le·o·cli′ma·to·log′ic,** *adj.* —**pa′le·o·cli′ma·tol′o·gist,** *n.*

pa·le·o·cor·tex (pā′lē ō kôr′teks *or, esp. Brit.,* pal′ē-), *n. Anat.* the olfactory region of the brain. [1905–10; PALEO- + CORTEX] —**pa·le·o·cor·ti·cal** (pā′lē ō kôr′ti-kəl *or, esp. Brit.,* pal′ē-), *adj.*

pa·le·o·en·ceph·a·lon (pā′lē ō en sef′ə lon′ *or, esp. Brit.,* pal′ē-), *n., pl.* **-la** (-lə). paleencephalon.

paleog., paleography.

Pa·le·o·gene (pā′lē ə jēn′ *or, esp. Brit.,* pal′ē-), *Geol.* —*adj.* **1.** noting or pertaining to the earlier part of the Cenozoic Era, in the system adopted by some geologists, occurring from 65 to 25 million years ago and including the Oligocene, Eocene, and Paleocene epochs: corresponds to the earlier part of the Tertiary Period in the system generally used in the U.S. Cf. **Neogene.** —*n.* **2.** the Paleogene Period or System. [1880–85; < G *Paläogen,* equiv. to *paläo-* PALEO- + *-gen* (< Gk *genésthai* to be born); cf. -GEN]

pa·le·o·ge·og·ra·phy (pā′lē ō jē og′rə fē *or, esp. Brit.,* pal′ē-), *n.* the science of representing the earth's geographic features belonging to any part of the geologic past. [1880–85; PALEO- + GEOGRAPHY] —**pa′le·o·ge·og′ra·pher,** *n.* —**pa·le·o·ge·o·graph·ic** (pā′lē ō jē′ə-graf′ik *or, esp. Brit.,* pal′ē-), **pa′le·o·ge′o·graph′i·cal,** *adj.* —**pa′le·o·ge′o·graph′i·cal·ly,** *adv.*

pa·le·o·ge·ol·o·gy (pā′lē ō jē ol′ə jē *or, esp. Brit.,* pal′ē-), *n.* the science of representing geologic conditions of some given time in past earth history. [1930–35; PALEO- + GEOLOGY] —**pa·le·o·ge·o·log·ic** (pā′lē ō jē′ə-loj′ik *or, esp. Brit.,* pal′ē-), *adj.*

pa·le·o·ge·o·phys·ics (pā′lē ō jē′ō fiz′iks *or, esp. Brit.,* pal′ē-), *n.* **1.** (*used with a plural v.*) inferred geophysical conditions or processes of designated periods of the geologic past. **2.** (*used with a singular v.*) the study of these conditions. [1955–60; PALEO- + GEOPHYSICS] —**pa′le·o·ge′o·phys′i·cal,** *adj.* —**pa′le·o·ge′o·phys′i·cal·ly,** *adv.* —**pa′le·o·ge′o·phys′i·cist,** *n.*

pa·le·og·ra·phy (pā′lē og′rə fē *or, esp. Brit.,* pal′ē-), *n.* **1.** ancient forms of writing, as in documents and inscriptions. **2.** the study of ancient writing, including determination of date, decipherment, etc. [1810–20; PALEO- + -GRAPHY] —**pa′le·og′ra·pher,** *n.* —**pa·le·o·graph·ic** (pā′lē ə graf′ik *or, esp. Brit.,* pal′ē-), **pa′le·o·graph′i·cal,** *adj.* —**pa′le·o·graph′i·cal·ly,** *adv.*

Pa·le·o-In·di·an (pā′lē ō in′dē ən *or, esp. Brit.,* pal′-ē-), *adj.* **1.** of, pertaining to, or characteristic of a New World cultural stage, c22,000–6000 B.C., distinguished by fluted-point tools and cooperative hunting methods. —*n.* **2.** a member of the North American Indian people belonging to this cultural stage, who are believed to have migrated originally from Asia and are known to have been expert big-game hunters.

pa·le·o·lim·nol·o·gy (pā′lē ō lim nol′ə jē *or, esp. Brit.,* pal′ē-), *n.* the study of ancient lakes from their sediments and fossils. [1940–45; PALEO- + LIMNOLOGY] —**pa·le·o·lim·no·log·i·cal** (pā′lē ō lim′nl oj′i kəl *or, esp. Brit.,* pal′ē-), **pa′le·o·lim′no·log′ic,** *adj.* —**pa′le·o·lim′no·log′i·cal·ly,** *adv.* —**pa′le·o·lim·nol′o·gist,** *n.*

pa·le·o·lith (pā′lē ə lith *or, esp. Brit.,* pal′ē-), *n.* a paleolithic stone implement. [1875–80; PALEO- + -LITH]

Pa·le·o·lith·ic (pā′lē ə lith′ik *or, esp. Brit.,* pal′ē-), *adj.* (*sometimes l.c.*) *Anthropol.* of, pertaining to, or characteristic of the cultures of the late Pliocene and the Pleistocene epochs, or early phase of the Stone Age, which appeared first in Africa and are marked by the steady development of stone tools and later antler and bone artifacts, engravings on bone and stone, sculpted figures, and paintings and engravings on the walls of caves and rock-shelters: usually divided into three periods (**Lower Paleolithic,** c2,000,000–c200,000 B.C., **Middle Paleolithic,** c150,000–c40,000 B.C., **Upper Paleolithic,** c40,000–c10,000 B.C.). [1860–65; PALEO- + -LITHIC]

Pa′leolith′ic man′, any of the prehistoric populations of humans, as the Cro-Magnon, living in the late Pliocene and the Pleistocene epochs. [1870–75]

pa·le·ol·o·gy (pā′lē ol′ə jē *or, esp. Brit.,* pal′e-), *n.* the study of antiquities. [1820–30; PALEO- + -LOGY] —**pa·le·o·log·i·cal** (pā′lē ə loj′i kəl *or, esp. Brit.,* pal′ē-), *adj.* —**pa′le·ol′o·gist,** *n.*

pa·le·o·mag·net·ism (pā′lē ō mag′ni tiz′əm *or, esp. Brit.,* pal′ē-), *n. Geol.* magnetic polarization acquired by the minerals in a rock at the time the rock was deposited or solidified. Cf. **remanent magnetism.** [1850–55; PALEO- + MAGNETISM] —**pa·le·o·mag·net·ic** (pā′lē ō-mag net′ik *or, esp. Brit.,* pal′ē-), *adj.*

paleon., paleontology.

paleontol., paleontology.

pa·le·on·tol·o·gy (pā′lē ən tol′ə jē *or, esp. Brit.,* pal′-ē-), *n., pl.* **-gies** *for 2.* **1.** the science of the forms of life existing in former geologic periods, as represented by their fossils. **2.** a treatise on paleontology. [1830–40; < F *paléontologie.* See PALE- ONTOLOGY] —**pa·le·on·to·log·ic** (pā′lē on′tl oj′ik *or, esp. Brit.,* pal′ē-), **pa′le·on′·to·log′i·cal,** *adj.* —**pa′le·on′to·log′i·cal·ly,** *adv.* —**pa′le·on·tol′o·gist,** *n.*

pa·le·o·pe·dol·o·gy (pā′lē ō pi dol′ə jē *or, esp. Brit.,* pal′ē-), *n.* the branch of pedology dealing with the soils of past geologic ages. [1925–30; PALEO- + PEDOLOGY]

Pa·le·o·si·be·ri·an (pā′lē ō sī bēr′ē ən *or, esp. Brit.,* pal′ē-), *n.* **1.** a group of languages comprising those languages of Siberia that are not affiliated with Indo-European, Altaic, Uralic, or Eskimo-Aleut and including the Chukotian family and the unrelated language isolates Ket, Nivkh, and Yukaghir; Paleo-Asiatic. **2.** Paleo-Asiatic (def. 1). —*adj.* **3.** of or pertaining to Paleosiberian. [1910–15; PALEO- + SIBERIAN]

pa·le·o·trop·i·cal (pā′lē ō trop′i kəl *or, esp. Brit.,* pal′ē-), *adj. Biogeog.* belonging or pertaining to a geographical division comprising the Ethiopian and Oriental regions. [1855–60; PALEO- + TROPICAL]

Pa·le·o·zo·ic (pā′lē ə zō′ik *or, esp. Brit.,* pal′ē-), *Geol.* —*adj.* **1.** noting or pertaining to an era occurring between 570 million and 230 million years ago, characterized by the advent of fish, insects, and reptiles. See table under **geologic time.** —*n.* **2.** the Paleozoic Era or group of systems. [1830–40; PALEO- + *-zoic* < Gk *zōïkós* pertaining to animals; see ZO-, -IC]

pa·le·o·zo·ol·o·gy (pā′lē ō zō ol′ə jē *or, esp. Brit.,* pal′ē-), *n.* the branch of paleontology dealing with fossil animals. [1855–60; PALEO- + ZOOLOGY] —**pa·le·o·zo·o·log·i·cal** (pā′lē ō zō′ə loj′i kəl *or, esp. Brit.,* pal′ē-), **pa′le·o·zo′o·log′ic,** *adj.* —**pa′le·o·zo·ol′o·gist,** *n.*

Pa·ler·mo (pə lûr′mō, -lâr′-; *It.* pä lėr′mô), *n.* a seaport in and the capital of Sicily, in the NW part. 675,501. —**Pa·ler·mi·tan** (pə lûr′mi tn, -lâr′-), *adj., n.*

Pal·es·tine (pal′ə stīn′ *for 1, 2;* pal′ə stēn′ *for 3*), *n.* **1.** Also called **Holy Land.** Biblical name, **Canaan.** an ancient country in SW Asia, on the E coast of the Mediterranean. **2.** a former British mandate (1923–48) comprising part of this country, divided between Israel, Jordan, and Egypt in 1948: the Jordanian and Egyptian parts were occupied by Israel in 1967. **3.** a city in E Texas. 15,948.

Pal′estine Libera′tion Organiza′tion, an umbrella organization for several Arab groups dedicated to the recovery of Palestine from the state of Israel and the return of refugees from the area to their homeland through diplomatic, military, and terrorist means. *Abbr.:* PLO

Pal·es·tin·i·an (pal′ə stin′ē ən), *n.* **1.** a native or inhabitant of Palestine. **2.** Also called **Palestin′ian Ar′·ab.** an Arab formerly living in Palestine who advocates the establishment of an Arab homeland there. —*adj.* **3.** of or pertaining to Palestine or Palestinians. **4.** of or pertaining to Palestinian Arabs. [PALESTIN(E) + -IAN]

pa·les·tra (pə les′trə), *n., pl.* **-tras, -trae** (-trē). *Gk. Antiq.* a public place for training or exercise in wrestling or athletics. Also, **palaestra.** [1375–1425; late ME *palestre* < L *palaestra* a wrestling school, place of exercise < Gk *palaístra,* equiv. to *palais-,* var. s. of *palaíein* to wrestle + *-tra* fem. n. suffix of place]

Pa·le·stri·na (pal′ə strē′nə; *It.* pä′le strē′nä), *n.* **1.** **Gio·van·ni Pier·lu·i·gi da** (jô vän′nē pyer′lōō ē′jē dä), 1526?–94, Italian composer. **2.** Ancient, **Praeneste.** a town in central Italy, ESE of Rome.

pal·e·tot (pal′i tō′, pal′tō), *n.* any of various loose or fitted coats or jackets for men and women, esp. a close-fitting jacket worn over a dress by women in the 19th century. [1830–40; < F, MF, var. of *paletoc* < ME *paltok* a jacket, peasant's coat]

pal·ette (pal′it), *n.* **1.** a thin and usually oval or oblong board or tablet with a thumb hole at one end, used by painters for holding and mixing colors. **2.** any other flat surface used by a painter for this purpose. **3.** the set of colors on such a board or surface. **4.** the range of colors used by a particular artist. **5.** the variety of techniques or range of any art: *a lush but uneven musical palette.* **6.** the complete range of colors made available by a computer graphics card, from which a user or program may choose those to be displayed. **7.** (in ancient Egyptian art) a somewhat flattish slate object of various shapes, carved with commemorative scenes or motifs or, esp. in the smaller pieces, containing a recessed area probably for holding eye makeup and often used as a votive offering. **8.** Also, **pallette.** *Armor.* a small plate defending the front of the armpit when the arm is lifted; gusset. [1615–25; < F, MF < It *paletta,* dim. of *pala* shovel < L *pāla;* see -ETTE] —**pal′ette·like′,** *adj.*

pal′ette knife′, *Painting.* a thin blade of varying flexibility set in a handle and used for mixing colors or applying them to a canvas. [1750–60]

Pal′ette of Nar′mer. See under **Narmer.**

pale′ west′ern cut′worm, the larva of a noctuid moth, *Agrotis orthogonia,* of the western U.S. and Canada, that seriously damages grains, beets, potatoes, alfalfa, etc., by feeding underground on roots and stems.

Pa·ley (pā′lē), *n.* **1.** **William,** 1743–1805, English theologian, philosopher, and clergyman. **2.** **William S.,** 1901–90, U.S. broadcasting executive.

pal·frey (pôl′frē), *n., pl.* **-freys.** **1.** a riding horse, as distinguished from a war horse. **2.** a saddle horse particularly suitable for a woman. [1200–50; ME *palefrei* < OF < LL *paraverēdus* post horse for byways, prob. lit., spare horse, equiv. to Gk *para-* PARA-[1] + L *verēdus* fast breed of horse < Gaulish < Celtic **woreidos* (> Welsh *gorwydd* horse, charger), equiv. to **wo-* under (< **upo-;* cf. HYPO-) + **reid-,* base of OIr *réidid* (he) rides, *réid* level, smooth, éasy, Welsh *rhwydd* easy; see RIDE] —**pal′freyed,** *adj.*

Pal·grave (pôl′grāv, pal′-), *n.* **Francis Turner,** 1824–97, English critic, poet, and anthologist.

pa·li (pä′lē), *n.* (in Hawaii) a steep slope or cliff. [< Hawaiian]

Pa·li (pä′lē), *n.* the Prakrit language of the Buddhist scriptures. [1685–95; short for Skt *pāli-bhāsa* language of the canonical texts, equiv. to *pāli* line, row, canon + *bhāsa* language]

Pa′li Can′on, *Buddhism.* a collection of scriptures, originally recorded from oral traditions in the 1st century B.C., divided into one of three parts **(Pitaka):** sermons **(*Sutta Pitaka*),** the rules of the Buddhist order **(*Vinaya Pitaka*),** and several treatises on philosophy and psychology **(*Abhidhamma Pitaka*).** Also called **Tripitaka.**

pal·i·kar (pal′i kär′), *n.* a Greek militiaman in the Greek war for independence against the Turks 1821–28. Also, **pellekar.** [1805–15; < ModGk *palikári* lad, youth, var. of LGk *pallēkárion* camp boy (Gk *pallēk-,* s. of *pállēx* a youth + *-arion* dim. suffix)]

pa·li·la (pə lē′lə), *n.* a stout Hawaiian honeycreeper, *Loxioides bailleui,* having a thick, stubby bill, yellow head and breast, and gray back: an endangered species. [< Hawaiian]

pa·lil·o·gy (pə lil′ə jē), *n., pl.* **-gies.** *Rhet.* the technique of repeating a word or phrase for emphasis. Also, **pa·lil′lo·gy.** [1650–60; < Gk *palillogía* recapitulation, equiv. to *pálin* again, back + *-logia* -LOGY]

pal·i·mo·ny (pal′ə mō′nē), *n.* a form of alimony awarded to one of the partners in a romantic relationship after the breakup of that relationship following a long period of living together. [1975–80, *Amer.*; b. PAL and ALIMONY]

pal·imp·sest (pal′imp sest′), *n.* a parchment or the like from which writing has been partially or completely erased to make room for another text. [1655–65; < L *palimpsēstus* < Gk *palímpsēstos* rubbed again (*pálin* again + *psēstós* scraped, rubbed, verbid of *psân* to rub smooth)] —**pal′imp·ses′tic,** *adj.*

pal·im·scope (pal′im skōp′), *n.* a hand instrument that produces concentrated ultraviolet light for reading palimpsests and other research materials. [PALIM(PSEST) + -SCOPE]

pal·in·drome (pal′in drōm′), *n.* **1.** a word, line, verse, number, sentence, etc., reading the same backward as forward, as *Madam, I'm Adam* or *Poor Dan is in a droop.* **2.** *Biochem.* a region of DNA in which the sequence of nucleotides is identical with an inverted sequence in the complementary strand: *GAATTC is a palindrome of CTTAAG.* [1620–30; < Gk *palíndromos* recurring, equiv. to *pálin* again, back + *-dromos* running (see -DROME)] —**pa·lin·dro·mist** (pə lin′drō mist), *n.* —**pal·in·drom·ic** (pal′in drom′ik, -drō′mik), **pal′in·drom′i·cal,** *adj.* —**pal′in·drom′i·cal·ly,** *adv.*

pal·ing (pā′ling), *n.* **1.** Also called **pal′ing fence′.** See **picket fence.** **2.** a pale or picket for a fence. **3.** pales collectively. **4.** the act of building a fence with pales. [1350–1400; ME; see PALE[2], -ING[1]]

pal·in·gen·e·sis (pal′in jen′ə sis), *n.* **1.** rebirth; regeneration. **2.** *Biol.* **a.** embryonic development that reproduces the ancestral features of the species (opposed to *cenogenesis*). **b.** *Obs.* the supposed generation of organisms from others preformed in the germ cells. **3.** baptism in the Christian faith. **4.** the doctrine of transmigration of souls. [1615–25; < NL < Gk *pálin* again + *génesis* GENESIS] —**pal·in·ge·ne·si·an** (pal′in jə nē′zhē-ən, -zhən), **pal·in·ge·net·ic** (pal′in jə net′ik), *adj.* —**pal′in·ge·net′i·cal·ly,** *adv.*

pal·in·gen·e·sist (pal′in jen′ə sist), *n.* a person who believes in a doctrine of rebirth or transmigration of souls. Also, **pal·in·gen·ist** (pal′in jen′ist). [1855–60; PALINGENES(IS) + -IST]

pal·i·node (pal′ə nōd′), *n.* **1.** a poem in which the poet retracts something said in an earlier poem. **2.** a recantation. [1590–1600; < LL *palinōdia* < Gk *palinōidía* a singing again, especially a recanting, equiv. to *pálin* again, back + *ōid(ḗ)* ODE + *-ia* -IA] —**pal′i·nod′·ist,** *n.*

pal·i·sade (pal′ə sād′), *n., v.,* **-sad·ed, -sad·ing.** —*n.* **1.** a fence of pales or stakes set firmly in the ground, as for enclosure or defense. **2.** any of a number of pales or stakes pointed at the top and set firmly in the ground in a close row with others to form a defense. **3.** *Bot.* See **palisade parenchyma.** **4.** **palisades,** a line of cliffs. —*v.t.* **5.** to furnish or fortify with a palisade. [1590–1600; < F *palissade* < OPr *palissada,* equiv. to *paliss(a)* paling (deriv. of *pal* stake, PALE[2]) + *-ada* -ADE[1]]

pal′isade′ paren′chyma, *Bot.* the upper layer of ground tissue in a leaf, consisting of elongated cells beneath and perpendicular to the upper epidermis and constituting the primary area of photosynthesis. Also called **palisade, pal′isade mes′ophyll.** [1880–85]

Pal·i·sades (pal′ə sādz′), *n.* the line of cliffs in NE New Jersey and SE New York extending along the W bank of the lower Hudson River. ab. 15 mi. (24 km) long; 300–500 ft. (91–152 m) high.

Pal′isades Park′, a borough in NE New Jersey. 13,732.

CONCISE PRONUNCIATION KEY: act, cāpe, dâre, pärt; set, ēqual; if, īce; ox, ōver, ôrder, oil, bo͝ok, bo͞ot, out; up, ûrge; child; sing; shoe; thin, *that;* zh as in *treasure.* ə = *a* as in *alone, e* as in *system, i* as in *easily, o* as in *gallop, u* as in *circus;* ᵊ as in *fire* (fīᵊr), *hour* (ouᵊr). l and n can serve as syllabic consonants, as in *cradle* (krād′l), and *button* (but′n). See the full key inside the front cover.

pal·i·sa·do (pal′ə sā′dō), *n., pl.* **-does,** *v.t.,* **-doed, -do·ing.** palisade (defs. 1, 2, 4, 5). [< Sp *palizada*]

pal·i·san·der (pal′ə san′dər, pal′ə san′dər), *n.* See **Brazilian rosewood.** [1835–45; < F *palissandre* < ?]

pal·ish (pā′lish), *adj.* somewhat pale. [1350–1400; ME; see PALE¹, -ISH¹]

Pa·lis·sy (pA lē sē′), *n.* **Ber·nard** (beR naR′), c1510–89, French potter, enameler, and author.

pal·ki (päl′kē), *n. Anglo-Indian.* a palanquin; sedan chair. Also, **pal′kee.** [1670–80; < Hindi *pālkī*]

pall¹ (pôl), *n.* **1.** a cloth, often of velvet, for spreading over a coffin, bier, or tomb. **2.** a coffin. **3.** anything that covers, shrouds, or overspreads, esp. with darkness or gloom. **4.** *Eccles.* **a.** pallium (def. 2b). **b.** a linen cloth or a square cloth-covered piece of cardboard used to cover a chalice. **5.** *Heraldry.* pairle. **6.** *Archaic.* a cloth spread upon an altar; corporal. **7.** *Archaic.* a garment, esp. a robe, cloak, or the like. —*v.t.* **8.** to cover with or as with a pall. [bef. 900; ME; OE *pæll* pope's pallium < L *pallium* cloak] —**pall′-like′,** *adj.*
—**Syn. 3.** shadow, melancholy, oppression.

pall² (pôl), *v.i.* **1.** to have a wearying or tiresome effect (usually fol. by *on* or *upon*). **2.** to become distasteful or unpleasant. **3.** to become satiated or cloyed with something. —*v.t.* **4.** to satiate or cloy. **5.** to make dull, distasteful, or unpleasant. [1350–1400; ME *pallen;* aph. var. of APPALL]
—**Syn. 4.** glut, sate, surfeit.

pal·la (pal′ə), *n., pl.* **pal·lae** (pal′ē). a voluminous square of cloth draped around the body as a mantle or wrap, worn by women of ancient Rome. [1700–10; < L]

Pal·la·di·an (pə lā′dē ən, -lä′-), *adj.* **1.** pertaining to, introduced by, or in the architectural style of Andrea Palladio. —*n.* **2.** a disciple of Andrea Palladio, specifically one of the circle of Lord Burlington in 18th-century England. [1725–35; PALLADI(O) + -AN]

Pal·la·di·an (pə lā′dē ən), *adj.* **1.** of or pertaining to the goddess Athena. **2.** pertaining to wisdom, knowledge, or study. [1555–65; < L *Palladi(us)* of Pallas (< Gk *Palládios;* see PALLADIUM) + -AN]

Pal·la′di·an win′dow (pə lā′dē ən, -lä′-), a window in the form of a round-headed archway with a narrower compartment on either side, the side compartments usually being capped with entablatures on which the arch of the central compartment rests. Also called **Diocletian window, Venetian window.**

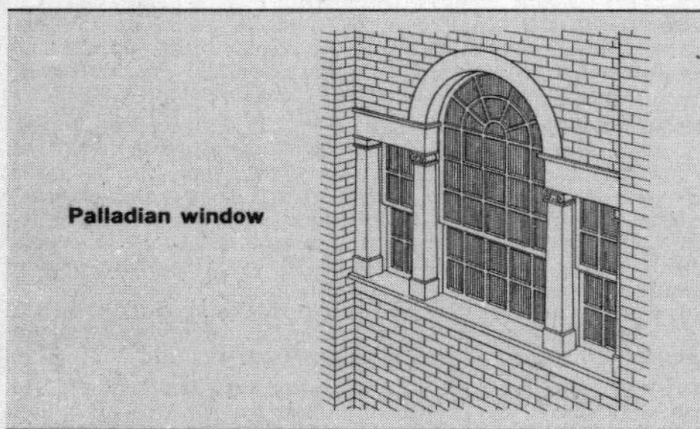
Palladian window

pal·lad·ic (pə lad′ik, -lā′dik), *adj. Chem.* of or containing palladium, esp. in the tetravalent state. Cf. **palladous.** [1855–60; PALLAD(IUM) + -IC]

pal·la·di·nize (pal′ə dn īz′), *v.t.,* **-ized, -iz·ing.** to treat or cover (a surface) with palladium. Also, *esp. Brit.,* **pal′la·di·nise′.** [irreg. < NL *palladium* PALLADIUM; see -IZE]

Pal·la·dio (pə lä′dē ō′; *It.* päl lä′dyô), *n.* **An·dre·a** (än dRe′ä), 1508–80, Italian architect famous for his widely translated *Four Books of Architecture,* 1570.

pal·la·di·um (pə lā′dē əm), *n. Chem.* a rare metallic element of the platinum group, silver-white, ductile and malleable, harder and fusing more readily than platinum: used chiefly as a catalyst and in dental and other alloys. *Symbol:* Pd; *at. wt.:* 106.4; *at. no.:* 46; *sp. gr.:* 12 at 20°C. [special use of PALLADIUM; named (1803) after the asteroid PALLAS, then newly discovered; see -IUM]

Pal·la·di·um (pə lā′dē əm), *n., pl.* **-di·a** (-dē ə). **1.** Also, **Pal·la·di·on** (pə lā′dē on′). a statue of Athena, esp. one on the citadel of Troy on which the safety of the city was supposed to depend. **2.** (*usually l.c.*) anything believed to provide protection or safety; safeguard. [< L *Palladium* < Gk *Pallādion,* n. use of neut. of *Pallādios* of Pallas, equiv. to *Pallad-* (s. of *Pallás*) PALLAS + *-ios* adj. suffix]

pal·la·dous (pə lā′dəs, pal′ə dəs), *adj. Chem.* of or containing bivalent palladium. Cf. **palladic.** [PALLAD(IUM) + -OUS]

Pal·las (pal′əs), *n.* **1.** Also called **Pal′las Athe′na.** *Class. Myth.* Athena (def. 1). **2.** *Astron.* the second largest and one of the four brightest asteroids.

pall·bear·er (pôl′bâr′ər), *n.* one of several persons who carry or attend the coffin at a funeral. [1700–10; PALL¹ + BEARER]

pal·let¹ (pal′it), *n.* **1.** a bed or mattress of straw. **2.** a small or makeshift bed. [1325–75; ME *pailet* < AF *paillete,* equiv. to OF *paille* straw (< L *palea* chaff) + *-ete* -ETTE]

pal·let² (pal′it), *n., v.,* **-let·ed, -let·ing.** —*n.* **1.** a small, low, portable platform on which goods are placed for storage or moving, as in a warehouse or vehicle. **2.** a flat board or metal plate used to support ceramic articles during drying. **3.** *Horol.* **a.** a lever with three projections, two of which intermittently lock and receive impulses from the escape wheel and one which transmits these impulses to the balance. **b.** either of the two projections of this lever that engage and release the escape wheel. See diag. under **lever escapement. 4.** a painter's palette. **5.** (on a pawl) a lip or projection that engages with the teeth of a ratchet wheel. **6.** *Print.* typeholder. **7.** (in gilding) an instrument used to take up the gold leaves from the pillow and to apply and extend them. **8.** a shaping tool used by potters and consisting of a flat blade or plate with a handle at one end. **9.** *Bookbinding.* **a.** a tool for decorating the spine of a book. **b.** the stamping of the name of the binder on the inside covers of a book. —*v.t.* **10.** palletize. [1550–60; < MF *palette* small shovel. See PALETTE]

pal·let·ed (pal′i tid), *adj.* (of the binding of a book) stamped with the name of the binder. [PALLET² + -ED³]

pal·let·ize (pal′i tīz′), *v.,* **-ized, -iz·ing.** —*v.t.* **1.** to place (materials) upon pallets for handling or moving. **2.** to perform (a materials-handling operation) with the aid of pallets. **3.** to equip with pallets or with the ability to handle pallets: *to palletize a truck.* —*v.i.* **4.** to handle cargo or other materials by means of pallets. Also, *esp. Brit.,* **pal′let·ise′.** [1950–55; PALLET² + -IZE] —**pal′let·i·za′tion,** *n.*

pal′let knife′, *Cookery.* a small, flat utensil for picking up and handling pastry paste.

pal·lette (pal′it), *n. Armor.* palette (def. 8).

pal·li·al (pal′ē əl), *adj.* **1.** of or pertaining to the mantle of a mollusk. **2.** of or pertaining to the cerebral cortex. [1830–40; PALLI(UM) + -AL¹]

pal·liasse (pal yas′, pal′yas, pal′ē as′, pal′ē as′), *n. Chiefly Brit.* paillasse.

pal·li·ate (pal′ē āt′), *v.t.,* **-at·ed, -at·ing. 1.** to relieve or lessen without curing; mitigate; alleviate. **2.** to try to mitigate or conceal the gravity of (an offense) by excuses, apologies, etc.; extenuate. [1540–50; < LL *palliātus* cloaked, covered. See PALLIUM, -ATE¹] —**pal′li·a′tion,** *n.* —**pal′li·a′tor,** *n.*

pal·li·a·tive (pal′ē ā′tiv, -ē ə tiv), *adj.* **1.** serving to palliate. —*n.* **2.** something that palliates. [1535–45; < F *palliatif.* See PALLIATE, -IVE] —**pal′li·a′tive·ly,** *adv.*

pal·lid (pal′id), *adj.* **1.** pale; faint or deficient in color; wan: *a pallid countenance.* **2.** lacking in vitality or interest: *a pallid musical performance.* [1580–90; < L *pallidus* sallow, equiv. to *pall(ēre)* to be pale + *-idus* -ID⁴] —**pal′lid·ly,** *adv.* —**pal′lid·ness,** *n.*
—**Syn. 1.** See **pale¹.**

pal·li·um (pal′ē əm), *n., pl.* **pal·li·a** (pal′ē ə), **pal·li·ums. 1.** a large, rectangular mantle worn by men in ancient Greece and Rome. **2.** *Eccles.* **a.** a woolen vestment worn by the pope and conferred by him on archbishops, consisting, in its present form, of a narrow ringlike band that rests on the shoulders, with two dependent bands or lappets, one in front and one behind. **b.** an altar cloth; a pall. **3.** *Anat.* the entire cortex of the cerebrum. **4.** *Zool.* a mantle, as of a mollusk or bird. [bef. 1150; OE < L (not attested in ME); see PALL¹]

Pall Mall (pal′ mal′, pel′ mel′), a street in London, England, famed for its clubs.

pall-mall (pel′mel′, pal′mal′, pôl′môl′), *n.* **1.** a game, popular in the 17th century, in which a ball of boxwood was struck with a mallet in an attempt to drive it through a raised iron ring at the end of a playing alley. **2.** a playing alley on which this game was played. [1560–70; < MF *pallemaille* < It *pallamaglio,* equiv. to *palla* ball (< Langobardic) + *maglio* MALLET (< L *malleus*). See BALL¹, MALL, MELL]

pal·lor (pal′ər), *n.* unusual or extreme paleness, as from fear, ill health, or death; wanness. [1650–60; < L: paleness, equiv. to *pall(ēre)* to be pale + *-or* -OR¹]

pal·ly (pal′ē), *adj.,* **-li·er, -li·est.** *Informal.* friendly; comradely: *old friends being pally at a class reunion.* [1890–95; PAL + -Y¹]

palm¹ (päm), *n.* **1.** the part of the inner surface of the hand that extends from the wrist to the bases of the fingers. **2.** the corresponding part of the forefoot of an animal. **3.** the part of a glove covering this part of the hand. **4.** Also called **sailmaker's palm.** a stiff rawhide or metal shield worn over this part of the hand by sailmakers to serve as a thimble. **5.** a linear measure of from 3 to 4 inches (7½–10 centimeters), based on the breadth of the hand. **6.** a linear measure of from 7 to 10 inches (17½–25 centimeters), based on the length of the hand. **7.** the flat, expanded part of the horn or antler of a deer. **8.** a flat, widened part at the end of an armlike projection. **9.** *Naut.* **a.** the blade of an oar. **b.** the inner face of an anchor fluke. See diag. under **anchor. c.** (loosely) an anchor fluke. **10.** a flat-topped bearing member at the head of a stanchion. **11. grease someone's palm,** to give money to, esp. as a bribe: *Before any work could begin, it was necessary to grease the superintendent's palm.* —*v.t.* **12.** to conceal in the palm, as in cheating at cards or dice or in juggling. **13.** to pick up stealthily. **14.** to hold in the hand. **15.** to impose (something) fraudulently (usually fol. by *on* or *upon*): *to palm stolen jewels on someone.* **16.** to touch or stroke with the palm or hand. **17.** to shake hands with. **18.** *Basketball.* to grip (the ball) momentarily with the hand in the act of dribbling. **19. palm off,** to dispose of by deception, trickery, or fraud; substitute (something) with intent to deceive: *Someone had palmed off a forgery on the museum officials.* [1300–50; < L *palma* (c. OE *folm* hand); r. ME *paume* < MF < L *palma*]

palm² (päm), *n.* **1.** any of numerous plants of the family Palmae, most species being tall, unbranched trees surmounted by a crown of large pinnate or palmately cleft leaves. Cf. **palm family. 2.** any of various other trees or shrubs that resemble this. **3.** a leaf or branch of such a tree, esp. as formerly borne to signify victory or as used on festive occasions. **4.** a representation of such a leaf or branch, as on a military or other decoration of honor, usually indicating a second award of the decoration. **5.** the reward of honor due to a victor: *In oratory she yields the palm to no one.* **6.** victory; triumph; success: *He carried off the palm by sheer perseverance.* [bef. 900; ME, OE < L *palma* palm tree, special use of *palma* PALM¹] —**palm′like′,** *adj.*

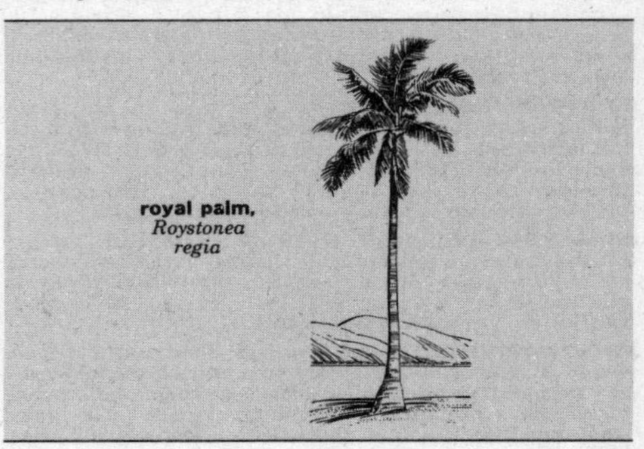
royal palm, *Roystonea regia*

Pal·ma (päl′mä), *n.* **1.** Also called **Palma de Mallorca.** a seaport in and the capital of the Balearic Islands, on W Majorca. 234,098. **2.** one of the Canary Islands, off the NW coast of Africa. 65,000; 281 sq. mi. (728 sq. km). *Cap.:* Santa Cruz de la Palma.

pal·ma·ceous (pal mā′shəs, päl-, pä mā′-), *adj.* belonging to the plant family Palmae. Cf. **palm family.** [1720–30; PALM² + -ACEOUS]

Pal·ma de Ma·llor·ca (*Sp.* päl′mä *th*e mä lyôR′kä), Palma (def. 1).

pal·mar (pal′mər, päl′-, pä′mər), *adj.* of, pertaining to, or located in or on the palm of the hand or to the corresponding part of the forefoot of an animal. [1650–60; < L *palmāris* measuring a hand's breadth. See PALM¹, -AR¹]

pal·ma·ry (pal′mə rē, päl′-, pä′mə-), *adj.* having or deserving to have the palm of victory or success; praiseworthy: *a palmary achievement.* [1650–60; < L *palmārius* of, deserving a palm. See PALM², -ARY]

Pal·mas (päl′mäs), *n.* **Las.** See **Las Palmas.**

pal·mate (pal′māt, -mit, päl′-, pä′māt), *adj.* **1.** shaped like an open palm or like a hand with the fingers extended, as a leaf or an antler. **2.** *Bot.* having four or more lobes or leaflets radiating from a single point. **3.** *Zool.* web-footed. **4.** *Furniture.* **a.** decorated with palmettes. **b.** (in furniture of the 17th century) having bands of semicircles enclosing a radiating leaf form. Also, **pal′mat·ed.** [1750–60; < L *palmātus* shaped like a palm. See PALM¹, -ATE¹] —**pal′mate·ly,** *adv.*

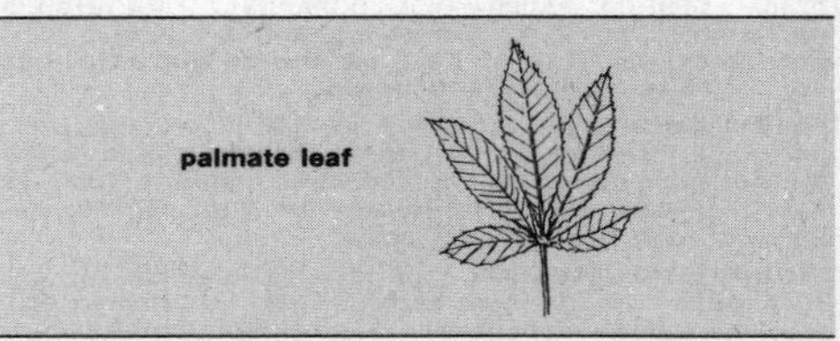
palmate leaf

pal·ma·tion (pal mā′shən, päl-, pä mā′-), *n.* **1.** a palmate state or formation. **2.** a palmate structure. [1680–90; PALMATE + -ION]

Palm′ Bay′, a town in E Florida. 18,560.

Palm′ Beach′, a town in SE Florida: seaside winter resort. 9729.

Palm′ Beach′ Gar′dens, a city in SE Florida, near North Palm Beach. 14,407.

palm′ cab′bage, 1. See **cabbage palm. 2.** the edible bud of a cabbage palm. [1695–1705]

palm′ chat′, a passerine bird, *Dulus dominicus,* of Hispaniola and Gonave, in the West Indies, noted for its huge, communal nest, occupied by several pairs of birds.

palm′ civ′et, any of various small to medium-sized, chiefly arboreal cats of the civet family, of southeastern Asia, the East Indies, etc., with a spotted or striped coat and a long curled tail. Also called **palm′ cat′.** [1840–50]

palm′ crab′. See **coconut crab.** [1880–85]

Palm·dale (päm′dāl′), *n.* a city in SW California. 12,277.

Palm′ Des′ert, a town in S California, near Palm Springs. 11,801.

Pal·me (päl′mə), *n.* **(Sven) O·lof (Jo·a·chim)** (sven o͞o′lôf yo͞o′ä kim), 1927–86, Swedish political leader: prime minister 1969–76, 1982–86; assassinated.

palmed (pämd), *adj.* having a palm or palms of a specified kind (often used in combination): *a wide-palmed hand.* [1350–1400; ME. See PALM¹, -ED³]

palm·er¹ (pä′mər, päl′-), *n.* **1.** a pilgrim, esp. of the Middle Ages, who had returned from the Holy Land bearing a palm branch as a token. **2.** any religious pilgrim. **3.** palmerworm. —*v.i.* **4.** *Scot. and North Eng.* to wander; go idly from place to place. [1250–1300; ME *palmer(e)* < AF *palmer,* OF *palmier* < ML *palmārius,* special use of L *palmārius* PALMARY]

palm·er² (pä′mər), *n.* a person who palms a card, die, or other object, as in cheating at a game or performing a magic trick. [1665–75; PALM¹ + -ER¹]

Palm·er (pä′mər *or, for 5,* päl′-), *n.* **1. Alice Elvira,** 1855–1902, U.S. educator. **2. Arnold,** born 1929, U.S. golfer. **3. Daniel David,** 1845–1913, Canadian originator of chiropractic medicine. **4. George Herbert,** 1842–

CONCISE ETYMOLOGY KEY: <, descended or borrowed from; >, whence; b., blend of, blended; c., cognate with; cf., compare; deriv., derivative; equiv., equivalent; imit., imitative; obl., oblique; r., replacing; s., stem; sp., spelling, spelled; resp., respelling, respelled; trans., translation; ?, origin unknown; *, unattested; ‡, probably earlier than. See the full key inside the front cover.

1933, U.S. educator, philosopher, and author. **5.** a town in S Massachusetts. 11,389.

Palm′er Land′, the southern part of the Antarctic Peninsula.

Palm′er Penin′sula, former name of **Antarctic Peninsula.**

Palm•er•ston (pä′mər stən), *n.* **Henry John Temple, 3rd Viscount,** 1784–1865, British statesman: prime minister 1855–58, 1859–65.

palm•er•worm (pä′mər wûrm′), *n.* the larva of a tineid moth, *Dichomeris ligulella,* of the eastern U.S., that feeds on the leaves of apple and other fruit trees. [1550–60; PALMER[1] + WORM]

pal•mette (pal met′), *n.* a conventionalized shape in the form of palmately spread leaves or sections, used as ornamentation. Cf. **anthemion, lotus** (def. 5). [1835–45; < F; see PALM[2], -ETTE]

pal•met•to (pal met′ō, päl-, pä met′ō), *n., pl.* **-tos, -toes.** any of various palms having fan-shaped leaves, as of the genera *Sabal, Serenoa,* and *Thrinax.* [1555–65; earlier *palmito* < Sp, dim. of *palma* PALM[2]; *-etto* by assoc. with -ETTE]

Palmet′to State′, South Carolina (used as a nickname).

palm′ fam′ily, the plant family Palmae (or Arecaceae; formerly, Palmaceae), characterized by chiefly tropical evergreen trees or shrubs having large compound leaves in featherlike or fanlike fronds, large clusters of small flowers, and fleshy or dry fruit, and including the palmettos, ornamental palms, and palms that are the source of carnauba wax, coconuts, dates, raffia, rattan, sago, and various oils.

Palm•gren (päm′grən; *Fin.* pälm′gʀen), *n.* **Se•lim** (sel′im, sä′lim; *Fin.* se′lim), 1878–1951, Finnish pianist and composer.

Pal•mi•ra (päl mē′ʀä), *n.* a city in W Colombia. 140,481.

palm•is•try (pä′mə strē), *n.* the art or practice of telling fortunes and interpreting character from the lines and configurations of the palm of a person's hand. [1375–1425; late ME *pawmestry,* equiv. to *pawm* PALM[1] + *-estry* (orig. obscure; cf. -Y[3])] **—palm′ist,** *n.*

pal•mi•tate (pal′mi tāt′, päl′-, pä′mi-), *n. Chem.* a salt or ester of palmitic acid. [1870–75; PALMIT(IC ACID) + -ATE[2]]

pal•mit•ic (pal mit′ik, päl-, pä mit′-), *adj. Chem.* of or derived from palmitic acid. [1855–60; < F *palmitique.* See PALM[2], -ITE[1], -IC]

palmit′ic ac′id, *Chem.* a white, crystalline, water-insoluble solid, $C_{16}H_{32}O_2$, obtained by hydrolysis from palm oil and natural fats, in which it occurs as the glyceride, and from spermaceti: used in the manufacture of soap. Also called **cetylic acid, hexadecanoic acid.**

pal•mi•tin (pal′mi tin, päl′-, pä′mi-), *n. Chem.* a white, crystalline, water-insoluble powder, $C_{51}H_{98}O_6$, prepared from glycerol and palmitic acid: used in the manufacture of soap. Also called **glyceryl tripalmitate, tripalmitin.** [1855–60; < F *palmitine.* See PALM[2], -ITE[1], -IN[2]]

pal′mi•to•le′ic ac′id (pal′mī tl ē′ik, pal′-, päl′-, päl′-, pä′mi-, pä′-), *Chem.* a colorless, unsaturated fatty acid, $C_{16}H_{30}O_2$, occurring in oils and fats of plants and animals. [PALMIT(IC) + OLEIC ACID]

palm′ leaf′, the leaf or frond of a palm, esp. that of a fan palm, used in making fans, hats, thatch, mats, etc.

palm′ oil′, **1.** a yellow butterlike oil derived from the fruit of the oil palm and used as an edible fat and for making soap, candles, etc. **2.** oil obtained from various species of palm. [1620–30]

Palm′ Springs′, a city in S California: resort. 32,271.

palm′ sug′ar, sugar from the sap of certain palm trees. [1865–70]

Palm′ Sun′day, the Sunday before Easter, celebrated in commemoration of Christ's triumphal entry into Jerusalem. [bef. 1000; ME; OE]

palm•top (päm′top′), *n.* a battery-powered microcomputer small enough to fit in the palm. [1985–90]

palm′ war′bler, a North American wood warbler, *Dendroica palmarum,* brown above and whitish or yellowish below. [1820–30, *Amer.*]

palm′ wine′, wine made from distilled palm-tree sap. [1605–15]

palm•y (pä′mē), *adj.,* **palm•i•er, palm•i•est. 1.** glorious, prosperous, or flourishing: *the palmy days of yesteryear.* **2.** abounding in or shaded with palms: *palmy islands.* **3.** palmlike. [1595–1605; PALM[2] + -Y[1]]
—Syn. 1. bounteous, booming, halcyon, rosy.

Pal•my•ra (pal mī′rə), *n.* an ancient city in central Syria, NE of Damascus: reputedly built by Solomon. Biblical name, **Tadmor.**

Pal•o Al•to (pal′ō al′tō *for 1;* pä′lō äl′tō *for 2*), **1.** a city in W California, SE of San Francisco. 55,225. **2.** a battlefield in S Texas, near Brownsville: first battle of Mexican War fought here in 1846.

pa•lo•lo (pə lō′lō), *n., pl.* **-los.** See **palolo worm.** [1890–95; < Samoan or Tongan]

palo′lo worm′, a polychaete worm, *Eunice viridis,* that lives in burrows among the coral reefs of several South Pacific islands, producing sperm or eggs in posterior segments that are cast off periodically in enormous numbers. [1890–95]

Pa•lo•ma (pə lō′mə), *n.* a female given name.

Pal•o•mar (pal′ə mär′), *n.* **Mount,** a mountain in S California, NE of San Diego: site of observatory. 6126 ft. (1867 m) high.

Pal′omar Observ′atory, an astronomical observatory situated on Palomar Mountain in S California, having a 200-in. (508-cm) reflecting telescope and a 48-in. (122-cm) Schmidt telescope. Also called **Pal′omar Moun′tain Observ′atory.**

pal•o•met•a (pal′ə met′ə), *n.* **1.** a pompano, *Trachinotus goodei,* of tropical and temperate Atlantic seas, having long, tapering fins. **2.** any of several stromateid butterfishes. [< Sp, dim. of *paloma* dove < L *palumbēs;* see -ET]

pal•o•mi•no (pal′ə mē′nō), *n., pl.* **-nos.** a horse with a golden coat, a white mane and tail, and often white markings on the face and legs, developed chiefly in the southwestern U.S. [1910–15, *Amer.*; < AmerSp, special use of Sp *palomino* of, resembling a dove < L *palumbīnus,* equiv. to *palumb(ēs)* dove + *-īnus* -INE[1]]

pa•loo•ka (pə lo͞o′kə), *n. Slang.* **1.** an athlete, esp. a boxer, lacking in ability, experience, or competitive spirit. **2.** a stupid, clumsy person. [1920–25, *Amer.*; orig. uncert.]

Pa•los (pä′lôs), *n.* a seaport in SW Spain: starting point of Columbus's first voyage westward. 2540.

pal•o san•to (pal′ō san′tō), **1.** a South American tree, *Bulnesia sarmienti,* of the caltrop family, yielding a fragrant essential oil. **2.** a tropical American tree, *Triplaris americana,* of the buckwheat family, having large leaves and showy red female flowers. [< AmerSp: lit., holy wood]

Pa′los Heights′ (pā′ləs), a city in NE Illinois, near Chicago. 11,096.

Pa′los Hills′, a city in NE Illinois, near Chicago. 16,654.

Pal′os Ver′des Estates′ (pal′əs vûr′dis, -dēz), a town in S California. 14,376.

pal•o•ver•de (pal′ō vûr′dē, -vûrd′), *n.* a spiny, desert shrub, *Cercidium floridum,* of the legume family, of the southwestern U.S. and Mexico, having green bark. [1850–55, *Amer.*; < AmerSp: lit., green tree]

palp (palp), *n.* a palpus.

pal•pa•ble (pal′pə bəl), *adj.* **1.** readily or plainly seen, heard, perceived, etc.; obvious; evident: *a palpable lie; palpable absurdity.* **2.** capable of being touched or felt; tangible. **3.** *Med.* perceptible by palpation. [1350–1400; ME < LL *palpābilis* that can be touched, equiv. to *palpā(re)* to stroke, touch, PALPATE[1] + *-bilis* -BLE] **—pal′pa•bil′i•ty, pal′pa•ble•ness,** *n.* **—pal′pa•bly,** *adv.*
—Syn. 1. manifest, plain. **2.** material, corporeal.
—Ant. 1. obscure.

pal•pate[1] (pal′pāt), *v.t.,* **-pat•ed, -pat•ing.** to examine by touch, esp. for the purpose of diagnosing disease or illness. [1840–50; < L *palpātus,* ptp. of *palpāre* to stroke, touch; see PALPUS, -ATE[1]] **—pal•pa′tion,** *n.* **—pal•pa•to•ry** (pal′pə tôr′ē, -tōr′ē), *adj.*

pal•pate[2] (pal′pāt), *adj. Zool.* having a palpus or palpi. [1855–60; PALP(US) + -ATE[1]]

pal•pe•bral (pal′pə brəl, pal pē′brəl, -peb′rəl), *adj.* of or pertaining to the eyelids. [1830–40; < LL *palpebrālis* of, on the eyelids, equiv. to L *palpebr(a)* eyelid (var. of *palpebrum*) + *-ālis* -AL[1]]

pal•pe•brate (pal′pə brāt′, pal pē′brit, -peb′rit), *adj.* having eyelids. [1855–60; < NL *palpebrātus,* equiv. to L *palpebr(a)* eyelid + *-ātus* -ATE[1]]

pal•pi (pal′pī), *n.* pl. of **palpus.**

pal•pi•tant (pal′pi tənt), *adj.* affected or characterized by palpitation. [1835–40; < L *palpitant-* (s. of *palpitāns*), prp. of *palpitāre.* See PALPITATE, -ANT]

pal•pi•tate (pal′pi tāt′), *v.,* **-tat•ed, -tat•ing.** *—v.i.* **1.** to pulsate with unusual rapidity from exertion, emotion, disease, etc.; flutter: *His heart palpitated wildly.* **2.** to pulsate; quiver; throb; tremble. *—v.t.* **3.** to cause to pulsate or tremble. [1615–25; < L *palpitātus,* ptp. of *palpitāre* to pulsate, freq. of *palpāre* to stroke. See PALPUS, -ATE[1]] **—pal′pi•tat′ing•ly,** *adv.*
—Syn. 1. See **pulsate.**

pal•pi•ta•tion (pal′pi tā′shən), *n.* **1.** the act of palpitating. **2.** an unusually or abnormally rapid or violent beating of the heart. [1595–1605; < L *palpitātiōn-* (s. of *palpitātiō*) a throbbing. See PALPITATE, -ION]

pal•pus (pal′pəs), *n., pl.* **-pi** (-pī). an appendage attached to an oral part and serving as an organ of sense in insects, crustaceans, etc. See diag. under **insect.** [1805–15; < NL, special use of L *palpus* a stroking, caress, palm of the hand; akin to FEEL]

pal•sa (päl′sə), *n., pl.* **pal•sen** (päl′sən). *Geol.* a mound of earth pushed up by or formed near the edge of a glacier, found in alpine and arctic areas. [1940–45; (< G) < Sw *pals(e)* < Finnish *palsa* peat knob in a bog, hillock in the tundra < Lappish]

pals•grave (pôlz′grāv, palz′-), *n.* a German count palatine. [1540–50; < early D *paltsgrave* (now *paltsgraaf*); c. G *Pfalzgraf* imperial count. See MARGRAVE, PALATINE[1]]

pals•gra•vine (pôlz′grə vēn′, palz′-), *n.* the wife or widow of a palsgrave. [1825–35; < D *paltsgravin.* See PALSGRAVE, -INE[2]]

pal•sied (pôl′zēd), *adj.* paralyzed; unable to move or control certain muscles. [1960–65; PALSY[1] + -ED[3]]

pal•stave (pôl′stāv′, pal′-), *n. Archaeol.* a bronze celt fitted into a split wooden handle. Also, **pal•staff** (pôl′-staf′, -stäf′, pal′-). [1850–55; < Dan *pålstav,* special use of ON *pālstafr* javelin < OE *palster* spike, taken (by folk etymology) as repr. **pālstæf;* see POLE, STAVE]

pal•sy[1] (pôl′zē), *n., pl.* **-sies,** *v.,* **-sied, -sy•ing.** *—n.* **1.** any of a variety of atonal muscular conditions characterized by tremors of the body parts, as the hands, arms, or legs, or of the entire body. **2.** paralysis (def. 1b). *—v.t.* **3.** to paralyze. [1250–1300; ME, var. of *parlesie* < MF *paralisie* < L *paralysis* PARALYSIS] **—pal′sy•like′,** *adj.*

pal•sy[2] (pal′zē), *adj. Slang.* palsy-walsy. [1925–30; PAL + -SY]

pal•sy-wal•sy (pal′zē wal′zē), *adj. Slang.* friendly or appearing to be friendly in a very intimate or hearty way: *The police kept their eye on him because he was trying to get palsy-walsy with the security guard.* [1930–35; rhyming compound based on PALSY[2]]

pal•ter (pôl′tər), *v.i.* **1.** to talk or act insincerely or deceitfully; lie or use trickery. **2.** to bargain with; haggle. **3.** to act carelessly; trifle. [1530–40 in sense "to speak indistinctly," perh. alter. of FALTER in same sense, with *p-* from PALSY[1]] **—pal′ter•er,** *n.*

pal•try (pôl′trē), *adj.,* **-tri•er, -tri•est. 1.** ridiculously or insultingly small: *a paltry sum.* **2.** utterly worthless. **3.** mean or contemptible: *a paltry coward.* [1560–70; < LG *paltrig* ragged, equiv. to **palter* rag (dial. G *Palter*) + *-ig* -Y[1]] **—pal′tri•ly,** *adv.* **—pal′tri•ness,** *n.*
—Syn. 1. minor, inconsiderable, slight, insignificant. See **petty.** **—Ant. 1.** important, major.

pa•lu•dal (pə lo͞od′l, pal′yə dl), *adj.* **1.** of or pertaining to marshes. **2.** produced by marshes, as miasma or disease. [1810–20; < L *palūd-* (s. of *palūs*) swamp, marsh + -AL[1]]

pa•lu•da•men•tum (pə lo͞o′də men′təm), *n., pl.* **-ta** (-tə). a cloak worn by officials and military officers of ancient Rome, esp. during wartime. Also, **pa•lu•da•ment** (pə lo͞o′də mənt). [1695–1705; < L *palūdāmentum;* akin to PALLA]

pal•u•dism (pal′yə diz′əm), *n. Pathol.* malaria. [1885–90; < L *palūd-* (s. of *palūs*) swamp, marsh + -ISM]

pal•y (pā′lē), *adj. Archaic.* pale. [1550–60; PALE[1] + -Y[1]]

pal•y•nol•o•gy (pal′ə nol′ə jē), *n.* the study of live and fossil spores, pollen grains, and similar plant structures. [1940–45; < Gk *palýn(ein)* to sprinkle, scatter (akin to *pálē* dust, L *pollen;* see POLLEN) + -O- + -LOGY] **—pal•y•no•log•i•cal** (pal′ə nl oj′i kəl), *adj.* **—pal′y•no•log′i•cal•ly,** *adv.* **—pal′y•nol′o•gist,** *n.*

pam (pam), *n. Cards.* **1.** the jack of clubs, esp. in a form of loo in which it is the best trump. **2.** a game in which this card is trump. [1675–85; short for F *pamphile,* special use of *Pamphile* man's name]

Pam (pam), *n.* a female given name, form of **Pamela.**

PAM, 1. *Aerospace.* payload assist module. **2.** *Telecommunications.* pulse-amplitude modulation.

pam., pamphlet.

Pa•ma-Nyun•gan (pä′mə nyo͝ong′gən), *n.* a family of Australian aboriginal languages, the most widespread within the Australian group of languages.

Pam•e•la (pam′ə lə), *n.* a female given name.

Pam•e•la (pam′ə lə), *n.* (or *Virtue Rewarded*) an epistolary novel (1740) by Samuel Richardson.

Pa•mir•i (pä mēr′ī, -mēr′ē), *n., pl.* **-mir•is,** (*esp. collectively*) **-mir•i.** a member of a Caucasian people inhabiting the Pamirs.

Pa•mirs (pä mērz′), *n.* **the,** a mountainous region in central Asia, largely in Tajikistan, where the Hindu Kush, Tien Shan, and Himalaya mountain ranges converge: highest peaks, ab. 25,000 ft. (7600 m). Also called **Pa•mir′.**

Pam′li•co Sound′ (pam′li kō′), a sound between the North Carolina mainland and coastal islands.

Pam•pa (pam′pə), *n.* a city in N Texas. 21,396.

pam•pas (pam′pəz; *attributively* pam′pəs; *Sp.* päm′-päs), *n.pl., sing.* **-pa** (-pə; *Sp.* -pä). the vast grassy plains of southern South America, esp. in Argentina. [1695–1705; < AmerSp, pl. of *pampa* < Quechua: flat, unbounded plain] **—pam•pe•an** (pam pē′ən, pam′pē ən), *adj.*

pam′pas grass′, a tall, ornamental grass, *Cortaderia selloana,* native to South America, having large, thick, feathery, silvery-white panicles. [1840–50]

Pam•pe•lu•na (*Sp.* päm′pe lo͞o′nä), *n.* Pamplona.

pam•per (pam′pər), *v.t.* **1.** to treat or gratify with extreme or excessive indulgence, kindness, or care: *to pamper a child; to pamper one's stomach.* **2.** *Archaic.* to overfeed, esp. with very rich food; glut. [1350–1400; ME *pamperen* < MD; cf. D dial. *pamperen*] **—pam′pered•ly,** *adv.* **—pam′pered•ness,** *n.* **—pam′per•er,** *n.*
—Syn. 1. humor, coddle, baby, spoil.

pam•pe•ro (päm pâr′ō, pam-; *Sp.* päm pe′ʀō), *n., pl.* **-ros** (-rōz; *Sp.* -rôs). a cold and dry southwesterly wind that sweeps down over the pampas of Argentina from the Andes. [1810–20; < AmerSp: lit., of the pampas]

pamph., pamphlet.

pam•phlet (pam′flit), *n.* **1.** a complete publication of generally less than 80 pages stitched or stapled together and usually having a paper cover. **2.** a short treatise or essay, generally a controversial tract, on some subject of contemporary interest: *a political pamphlet.* [1375–1425; late ME *pamflet* < AL *panfletus, pamfletus,* syn-

CONCISE PRONUNCIATION KEY: act, cāpe, dâre, pärt; set, ēqual; *if,* īce; ox, ōver, ôrder, oil, bo͝ok, bo͞ot, out; up, ûrge; child; sing; shoe; thin, *th*at; zh as in *treasure.* ə = *a* as in *alone, e* as in *system, i* as in *easily, o* as in *gallop, u* as in *circus;* ᵊ as in *fire* (fīᵊr), *hour* (ouᵊr). l and n can serve as syllabic consonants, as in *cradle* (krād′l), and *button* (but′n). See the full key inside the front cover.

copated var. of *Pamphiletus,* dim. of ML *Pamphilus,* title of a 12th-century Latin comedy. See -ET] —**pam′·phlet·ar′y,** *adj.*

pam·phlet·eer (pam′fli tēr′), *n.* **1.** a writer or publisher of pamphlets, esp. on controversial issues. —*v.i.* **2.** to write and issue pamphlets. [1690–1700]

pam·phlet·ize (pam′fli tīz′), *v.,* **-ized, -iz·ing.** —*v.i.* **1.** to write a pamphlet. —*v.t.* **2.** to write a pamphlet on (a specific subject). Also, *esp. Brit.,* **pam′phlet·ise′.** [1645–55; PAMPHLET + -IZE]

Pam·phyl·i·a (pam fil′ē ə), *n.* an ancient country in S Asia Minor: later a Roman province.

Pam·plo·na (pam plō′nə; *Sp.* päm plô′nä), *n.* a city in N Spain. 147,168. Also, **Pampeluna.**

pam·pro·dac·ty·lous (pam′prō dak′tə ləs), *adj. Ornith.* having all four toes directed forward, as in swifts and colies. Also, **pam′pro·dac′tyl.** [1895–1900; *pam-* (var. of PAN-) + PRO- + -DACTYLOUS] —**pam′pro·dac′·tyl·ism,** *n.*

Pam·yat (päm′yät), *n.* an ultraconservative Russian nationalist organization founded in 1980 and noted for disseminating anti-Western and anti-Semitic propaganda. [< Russ *Pámyat′* lit., memory]

pan[1] (pan), *n., v.,* **panned, pan·ning.** —*n.* **1.** a broad, shallow container of metal, usually having sides flaring outward toward the top, used in various forms for frying, baking, washing, etc. **2.** any similar receptacle or part, as the scales of a balance. **3.** the amount a pan holds or can hold; panful: *a pan of shelled peas.* **4.** any of various open or closed containers used in industrial or mechanical processes. **5.** a container in which silver ores are ground and amalgamated. **6.** a container in which gold or other heavy, valuable metals are separated from gravel or other substances by agitation with water. **7.** a drifting piece of flat, thin ice, as formed on a shore or bay. **8.** a natural depression in the ground, as one containing water, mud, or mineral salts. **9.** a similar depression made artificially, as for evaporating salt water to make salt. **10.** (in old guns) the depressed part of the lock, holding the priming. **11.** Also, **panning.** an unfavorable review, critique, or appraisal: *The show got one rave and three pans.* **12.** *Slang.* the face. —*v.t.* **13.** *Informal.* to criticize severely, as in a review of a play. **14.** to wash (gravel, sand, etc.) in a pan to separate gold or other heavy valuable metal. **15.** to cook (oysters, clams, etc.) in a pan. —*v.i.* **16.** to wash gravel, sand, etc., in a pan in seeking gold or the like. **17.** to yield gold or the like, as gravel washed in a pan. **18. pan out,** *Informal.* to turn out, esp. successfully: *The couple's reconciliation just didn't pan out.* [bef. 900; ME, OE *panne;* c. D *pan,* G *Pfanne,* ON *panna*] —**pan′ner,** *n.*

pan[2] (pän), *n.* **1.** the leaf of the betel. **2.** a substance, esp. betel nut or a betel-nut mixture, used for chewing. [1610–20; < Hindi *pān;* cf. Pali, Prakrit *paṇṇa,* Skt *parṇa* leaf, betel leaf]

pan[3] (pan), *v.,* **panned, pan·ning,** *n.* —*v.i.* **1.** to photograph or televise while rotating a camera on its vertical or horizontal axis in order to keep a moving person or object in view or allow the film to record a panorama: *to pan from one end of the playing field to the other during the opening of the football game.* **2.** (of a camera) to be moved or manipulated in such a manner: *The cameras panned occasionally during the scene.* —*v.t.* **3.** to move (a camera) in such a manner: *to pan the camera across the scene.* **4.** to photograph or televise (a scene, moving character, etc.) by panning the camera. —*n.* **5.** the act of panning a camera. **6.** Also called **panning shot.** the filmed shot resulting from this. [1920–25; shortening of PANORAMA]

pan[4] (pan), *n.* **1.** a major vertical division of a wall. **2.** a nogged panel of half-timber construction. [1735–45; < F, MF: PANE]

pan[5] (pän), *n. Informal.* panguingue. [by shortening]

pan[6] (pan), *n.* Pan.

Pan (pan), *n.* the ancient Greek god of forests, pastures, flocks, and shepherds, represented with the head, chest, and arms of a man and the legs and sometimes the horns and ears of a goat.

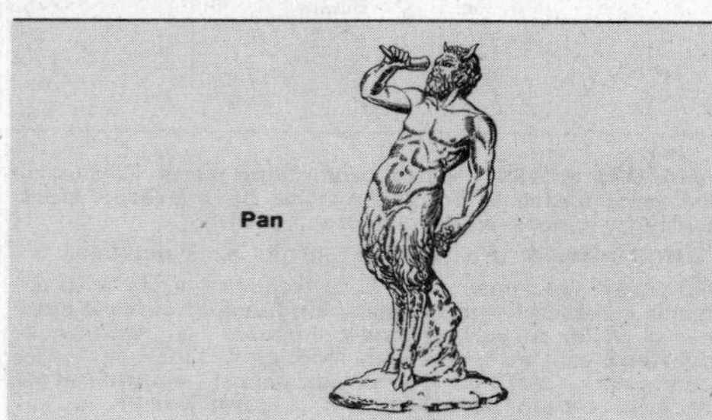

Pan

Pan (pan), *n.* an international distress signal used by shore stations to inform a ship, aircraft, etc., of something vital to its safety or that of one of its passengers. Also, **pan.**

pan-, a combining form meaning "all," occurring originally in loanwords from Greek (*panacea; panoply*), but now used freely as a general formative (*panorama; pantelegraph; pantheism*), and esp. in terms, formed at will, implying the union of all branches of a group (*Pan-Christian; Panhellenic; Pan-Slavism*). The hyphen and the second capital tend with longer use to be lost, unless they are retained in order to set off clearly the component parts. Also, **pant-, panto-.** [< Gk *pan-* comb. form of *pâs* (neut. *pân*) all, every, *pân* everything]

Pan., Panama.

pan·a·ce·a (pan′ə sē′ə), *n.* **1.** a remedy for all disease or ills; cure-all. **2.** an answer or solution for all problems or difficulties: *His economic philosophy is a good one, but he tries to use it as a panacea.* [1540–50; < L < Gk *panákeia,* equiv. to *panake-,* s. of *panakḗs* all-healing (*pan-* PAN- + *akḗs* a cure) + *-ia* -IA] —**pan′a·ce′an,** *adj.*

—**Syn. 1, 2.** elixir, nostrum.

Pan·a·ce·a (pan′ə sē′ə), *n.* an ancient Greek goddess of healing.

pa·nache (pə nash′, -näsh′), *n.* **1.** a grand or flamboyant manner; verve; style; flair: *The actor who would play Cyrano must have panache.* **2.** an ornamental plume of feathers, tassels, or the like, esp. one worn on a helmet or cap. **3.** *Archit.* the surface of a pendentive. [1545–55; var. (after F) of *pennache* < MF < early It *pennachio* < LL *pinnāculum,* dim. of *pinna* wing; identical in form with *pinnāculum* PINNACLE]

pa·na·da (pə nä′də, -nā′-), *n.* a thick sauce or paste made with bread crumbs, milk, and seasonings, often served with roast wild fowl or meat. [1590–1600; < Sp, equiv. to *pan-* bread (< L *pānis*) + *-ada* -ADE[1]]

Pan-Af·ri·can (pan′af′ri kən), *adj.* **1.** of or pertaining to all African nations or peoples. **2.** of or pertaining to Pan-Africanism.

Pan-Af·ri·can·ism (pan′af′ri kə niz′əm), *n.* the idea or advocacy of a political alliance or union of all the African nations. —**Pan′-Af′ri·can·ist,** *n.*

Pa·na·gi·a (pä′nä yē′ä), *n., pl.* **-gi·as** for 1. *Eastern Ch.* **1.** a ceremony in a monastery, commemorating the assumption of the Virgin Mary, in which a loaf of bread on a plate is elevated before being distributed to the monks. **2.** (*l.c.*) an encolpion bearing the image of the Virgin Mary. [1680–90; < LGk *Panágia* the Virgin, fem. of Gk *panágios* all-holy, equiv. to *pan-* PAN- + *hágios* holy]

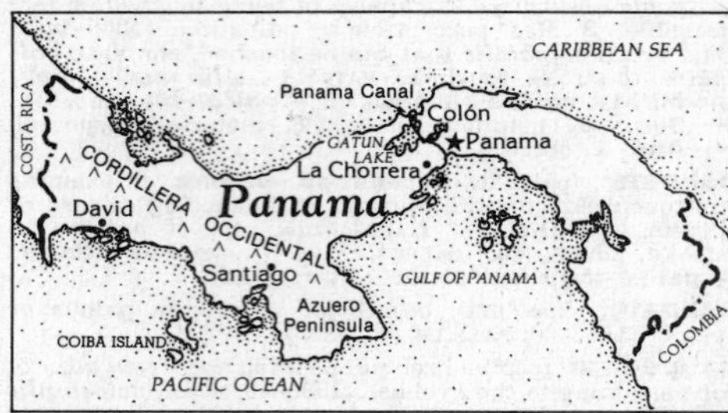

Pan·a·ma (pan′ə mä′, -mô′), *n.* **1.** a republic in S Central America. 1,900,000; 28,575 sq. mi. (74,010 sq. km). **2.** Also called **Panama City.** a city in and the capital of Panama, at the Pacific end of the Panama Canal. 438,000. **3. Isthmus of.** Formerly, **Isthmus of Darien.** an isthmus between North and South America. **4. Gulf of,** the portion of the Pacific in the bend of the Isthmus of Panama. **5.** (*sometimes l.c.*) See **Panama hat.** Also, **Pa·na·má** (*Sp.* pä′nä mä′) (for defs. 1, 2). —**Pan·a·ma·ni·an** (pan′ə mā′nē ən, -mä′-), *adj., n.* —**Pan·am·ic** (pa nam′ik), *adj.*

Pan′ama Canal′, a canal extending SE from the Atlantic to the Pacific across the Isthmus of Panama. 40 mi. (64 km) long.

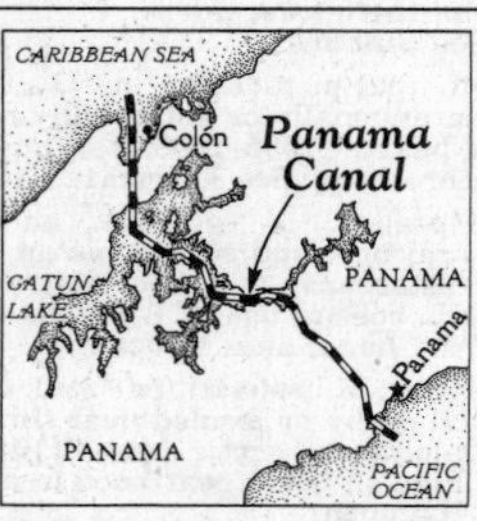

Pan′ama Canal′ Zone′. See **Canal Zone.**

Pan′ama Cit′y, 1. Panama (def. 2). **2.** a city in NW Florida. 33,346.

Pan′ama hat′, a hat made of finely plaited young leaves of the jipijapa, a palmlike plant of Central and South America. Also called **Panama.** [1825–35]

Pan′a·ma-hat′ plant′ (pan′ə mä′hat′, -mô′), jipijapa (def. 1). Also called **Pan′ama-hat′ palm′.** [1970–75; so called because the young leaves are used to make Panama hats]

Pan-A·mer·i·can (pan′ə mer′i kən), *adj.* of, pertaining to, or representing all the countries or people of North, Central, and South America. [1885–90, *Amer.*]

Pan′ Amer′ican Games′, an amateur athletic competition, patterned after the Olympic Games and held every four years in a different host city, involving all the nations of the Western Hemisphere. [1965–70]

Pan-A·mer·i·can·ism (pan′ə mer′i kə niz′əm), *n.* **1.** the idea or advocacy of a political alliance or union of all the countries of North, Central, and South America. **2.** a movement for or the idea or advocacy of close economic, cultural, and military cooperation among the Pan-American countries. [1900–05, *Amer.;* PAN-AMERICAN + -ISM]

Pan′ Amer′ican Un′ion, a former organization of American republics: replaced in 1970 by the secretariat of the Organization of American States.

pan·a·mi·ga (pan′ə mē′gə), *n.* a low South American foliage plant, *Pilea involucrata,* of the nettle family, having toothed, velvety, brownish-green leaves and small, green flowers in clusters. [appar. PAN- or PAN(-AMERICAN) + Sp *amiga* (female) friend (< L *amīca*), the plant having at one time been publicized as "the Pan-American friendship plant"]

Pan′a·mint Moun′tains (pan′ə mint), a mountain range in E California. Highest peak, Telescope Peak, 11,045 ft. (3365 m).

Pan-Ar·ab·ism (pan′ar′ə biz′əm), *n.* the idea or advocacy of a political alliance or union of all the Arab nations. [PAN + ARAB + -ISM] —**Pan′-Ar′ab, Pan′-Ar′·a·bic,** *adj., n.*

Pan-A·sian (pan′ā′zhən, -shən), *adj.* **1.** of or pertaining to all Asian peoples. **2.** of or pertaining to Pan-Asianism. [1965–70]

Pan-A·sian·ism (pan′ā′zhə niz′əm, -shə-), *n.* the idea or advocacy of a political alliance of all the Asian nations. [PAN-ASIAN + -ISM] —**Pan′-A′sian·ist,** *n.*

pan·a·tel·la (pan′ə tel′ə), *n.* panetella. Also, **pan′a·tel′a.**

pan·a·the·ism (pan ā′thē iz′əm), *n.* the belief that because there is no God, nothing can properly be termed sacred or holy. [PAN- + ATHEISM]

Pan·ath·e·nae·a (pan′ath ə nē′ə), *n.* a festival in honor of the goddess Athena, celebrated yearly in ancient Athens, with each fourth year reserved for greater pomp, marked by contests, as in athletics and music, and highlighted by a solemn procession to the Acropolis bearing a peplos embroidered for the goddess. Also, **Pan·ath·e·nai·a** (pan′ath ə nā′ə).

Pan·ath·e·na·ic (pan′ath ə nā′ik), *adj.* (*sometimes l.c.*) of or pertaining to a Panathenaea. Also, **Pan·ath·e·nae·an** (pan′ath ə nē′ən). [1595–1605; PANATHENA(EA) + -IC]

Pa·nay (pä nī′), *n.* an island in the central Philippines. 2,595,314; 4446 sq. mi. (11,515 sq. km). *Cap.:* Iloilo.

pan-broil (pan′broil′), *v.t., v.i.* to cook in an uncovered frying pan over direct heat using little or no fat. Also, **pan′broil′.** [1945–50]

pan·cake (pan′kāk′), *n., v.,* **-caked, -cak·ing.** —*n.* **1.** a thin, flat cake of batter fried on both sides on a griddle or in a frying pan; griddlecake or flapjack. **2.** Also called **pan′cake land′ing.** an airplane landing made by pancaking. —*v.i.* **3.** (of an airplane or the like) to drop flat to the ground after leveling off a few feet above it. —*v.t.* **4.** *Informal.* to flatten, esp. as the result of a collision or other mishap: *The car had been pancaked by the bus.* **5.** to cause (an airplane) to pancake. [1400–50; late ME; see PAN[1], CAKE]

—**Regional Variation. 1.** PANCAKE, HOT CAKE, GRIDDLECAKE, and FLAPJACK, with its derived SLAPJACK, are used interchangeably by many people, regardless of whether a pan or griddle is used for cooking, and each term is widely used throughout the U.S. FLANNEL CAKE, however, is confined chiefly to the North Midland U.S. and BATTERCAKE to South Midland and Southern U.S. The following terms have limited regional use and may refer to flat cakes with different recipes or cooking methods: JOHNNYCAKE, which is used in the Northeastern U.S.; CORNCAKE in the Midland and Southern U.S.; and HOECAKE in the South Midland and Southern U.S.

Pan-Cake (pan′kāk′), *Trademark.* a brand of cosmetic in a semimoist cake of compressed powder, usually applied with a moist sponge.

pan′cake ice′, newly formed ice in flat pieces too small and thin to obstruct navigation. [1810–20]

pan·car·di·tis (pan′kär dī′tis), *n. Pathol.* inflammation of the entire heart: the pericardium, myocardium, and endocardium. [PAN- + CARDITIS]

Pan·chai·a (pän chē′ə), *n.* an area in the northern hemisphere of Mars, appearing as a dark region when viewed telescopically from the earth.

Pan·cha Si·la (pun′chə sē′lə), *Buddhism.* a standard recitation of Hinayanists, including repetitions of formulas and of vows to abstain from anger, lust, cowardice, malevolence, and to abstain from the desire for possessions and unwholesome pleasures. [< Pali *pañca sīlā*]

pan·chax (pan′chaks), *n.* any of a variety of colorful tropical Old World fishes of the genus *Aplocheilus* and related genera: popular in home aquariums. [1960–65; < NL (formerly a genus name); of unexplained orig.]

pan·cha·yat (pən chä′yət), *n.* an elective village council in India. [1880–85; < Hindi *pañcāyat*]

Pan′chen La′ma (pän′chen). See **Tashi Lama.** Also called **Pan′chen Rim·po′che** (rim pō′chā). [1785–95; *panchen* < Chin *bānchán,* transliteration of Skt *paṇḍita;* see PUNDIT]

pan·chet·to (pan chet′ō; *It.* pän ket′tô), *n., pl.* **-tos,** *It.* **-ti** (-tē). *Ital. Furniture.* a Renaissance chair having three splayed legs and a shaped back joined into a solid wooden seat. [< It: stool]

pan·chres·ton (pan kres′tən), *n.* a proposed explanation intended to address a complex problem by trying to account for all possible contingencies but typically proving to be too broadly conceived and therefore oversimplified to be of any practical use. [1625–35; < Gk *pánchrēston,* neut. of *pánchrēstos* good for everything, equiv. to *pan-* PAN- + *chrēs-,* verbid s. of *chrâsthai* to be useful + *-tos* v. adj. suffix]

pan·chro·mat·ic (pan′krō mat′ik, -krə-), *adj.* sensitive to all visible colors, as a photographic film. [1900–05; PAN- + CHROMATIC] —**pan·chro·ma·tism** (pan krō′mə tiz′əm), *n.*

pan·cra·ti·um (pan krā′shē əm), *n., pl.* **-ti·a** (-shē ə). (in ancient Greece) an athletic contest combining wrestling and boxing. [1595–1605; < L < Gk *pankrátion* all-power exercise (n. use of neut. adj.), equiv. to *pan-* PAN- + *krát(os)* strength, mastery + *-ion,* neut. of *-ios* adj. suffix] **—pan·crat·ic** (pan krat′ik), *adj.*

pan·cre·as (pan′krē əs, pang′-), *n. Anat., Zool.* a gland, situated near the stomach, that secretes a digestive fluid into the intestine through one or more ducts and also secretes the hormone insulin. Cf. **islet of Langerhans, pancreatic juice.** [1570–80; < NL < Gk *pán-kreas* sweetbread, equiv. to *pan-* PAN- + *kréas* flesh, meat] **—pan·cre·at·ic** (pan′krē at′ik, pang′-), *adj.*

pancreat-, var. of **pancreato-** before a vowel: *pancreatin.*

pan·cre·a·tec·to·my (pan′krē ə tek′tə mē, pang′-), *n., pl.* **-mies.** *Surg.* excision of part or all of the pancreas. [1895–1900; PANCREAT- + -ECTOMY]

pancreat′ic fibro′sis, *Pathol.* See **cystic fibrosis.**

pan′creat′ic juice′, *Biochem.* a thick, colorless, very alkaline fluid secreted by the pancreas, containing enzymes that break down protein, fat, and starch. [1655–65]

pan·cre·a·tin (pan′krē ə tin, pang′-), *n.* **1.** *Biochem.* a substance containing the pancreatic enzymes, trypsin, amylase, and lipase. **2.** a commercial preparation of this substance, obtained from the pancreas of the hog or ox, and used chiefly as a digestive. [1870–75; PANCREAT- + -IN[2]]

pan·cre·a·ti·tis (pan′krē ə tī′tis, pang′-), *n. Pathol.* inflammation of the pancreas. [1835–45; < NL; see PANCREAT-, -ITIS]

pancreato-, a combining form representing **pancreas** in compound words: *pancreatotomy.* Also, *esp. before a vowel,* **pancreat-.** [< NL < Gk *pankreat-* (s. of *pán-kreas*); see -O-]

pan·cre·a·tot·o·my (pan′krē ə tot′ə mē, pang′-), *n., pl.* **-mies.** *Surg.* incision of the pancreas. [1885–90; PANCREATO- + -TOMY]

pan·da (pan′də), *n.* **1.** Also called **giant panda.** a white-and-black, bearlike mammal, *Ailuropoda melanoleuca,* now rare and restricted to forest areas of central China containing stands of bamboo, on which it mainly subsists: formerly placed with the raccoon family but now classified as a bear subfamily, Ailuropodinae, or as the sole member of a separate family, Ailuropodidae, which diverged from an ancestral bear lineage. **2.** Also called **lesser panda.** a reddish-brown, raccoonlike mammal, *Ailurus fulgens,* of mountain forests in the Himalayas and adjacent eastern Asia, subsisting mainly on bamboo and other vegetation, fruits, and insects, and reduced in numbers by collectors: now considered unrelated to the giant panda and usually classified as the sole member of an Old World raccoon subfamily, Ailurinae, which diverged from an ancestral lineage that also gave rise to the New World raccoons. [1825–35; < F (Cuvier), a name for the lesser panda, perh. < a Tibeto-Burman language of the southeastern Himalayas]

giant panda, *Ailuropoda melanoleuca,* 2 ft. (0.6 m) high at shoulder; length 5 ft. (1.5 m)

lesser panda, *Ailurus fulgens,* head and body 2 ft. (0.6 m); tail 1½ ft. (0.5 m)

pan′da car′, *Brit.* a small patrol car used by the police. [1965–70; from its panda-like coloration]

pan·dal (pan′dl), *n.* (in India) a temporary shed, esp. one used for public meetings. [1710–20; < Tamil *pantal*]

pan·da·nus (pan dā′nəs, -dan′əs), *n., pl.* **-nus·es.** any plant of the genus *Pandanus,* having sword-shaped leaves arranged in a spiral, comprising the screw pines. [1770–80; < NL, based on Malay *pandan* name for such plants]

Pan·da·rus (pan′dər əs), *n. Class. Myth.* a Trojan who attempted to assassinate Menelaus, thereby violating a truce between the Greeks and the Trojans and prolonging the Trojan War: in Chaucerian and other medieval accounts, he is the procurer of Cressida for Troilus. Also, **Pan′da·ros.**

Pan·da·vas (pun′də vəz), *n.* (*used with a plural v.*) (in the *Mahabharata*) the family of Arjuna, at war with their cousins, the Kauravas.

P&E, *Com.* plant and equipment.

Pan·de·an (pan dē′ən, pan′dē ən), *adj.* of or pertaining to the god Pan. [1800–10; PAN + *-d-* (< ?) + *-e-* (< L *-ae(us)*) + -AN]

Pande′an pipes′, panpipe. [1810–20]

pan·dect (pan′dekt), *n.* **1. pandects,** a complete body or code of laws. **2.** a complete and comprehensive digest. **3. Pandects,** *Roman Law.* digest (def. 12b). [1525–35; < LL *Pandectēs* < Gk *pandéktēs* all-receiver (*pan-* PAN- + *déktēs* receiver, container, encyclopedia)]

pan·dem·ic (pan dem′ik), *adj.* **1.** (of a disease) prevalent throughout an entire country, continent, or the whole world; epidemic over a large area. **2.** general; universal: *pandemic fear of atomic war.* —*n.* **3.** a pandemic disease. [1660–70; < LL *pandēm(us)* < Gk *pándēmos* common, public (*pan-* PAN- + *dêm(os)* the people + *-os* adj. suffix) + -IC] **—pan·de·mi·a** (pan dē′mē ə), *n.* **—pan·de·mic·i·ty** (pan′də mis′i tē), *n.*

pan·de·mo·ni·um (pan′də mō′nē əm), *n.* **1.** wild uproar or unrestrained disorder; tumult or chaos. **2.** a place or scene of riotous uproar or utter chaos. **3.** (*often cap.*) the abode of all the demons. **4.** hell. [1660–70; after *Pandaemonium,* Milton's name in *Paradise Lost* for the capital of hell; see PAN-, DEMON, -IUM] **—pan′·de·mo′ni·ac′, pan·de·mo·ni·a·cal** (pan′də mə nī′ə kəl), **pan·de·mon·ic** (pan′də mon′ik), *adj.* **—pan′de·mo′ni·an,** *adj., n.*
—Syn. 1, 2. bedlam, turmoil, babel.

pan·der (pan′dər), *n.* Also, **pan′der·er. 1.** a person who furnishes clients for a prostitute or supplies persons for illicit sexual intercourse; procurer; pimp. **2.** a person who caters to or profits from the weaknesses or vices of others. **3.** a go-between in amorous intrigues. —*v.i.* **4.** to act as a pander; cater basely: *to pander to the vile tastes of vulgar persons.* —*v.t.* **5.** to act as a pander for. [1325–75; earlier *pandar(e),* generalized use of ME name *Pandare* PANDARUS] **—pan′der·age,** *n.* **—pan′der·ing·ly,** *adv.* **—pan′der·ism,** *n.* **—pan′der·ly,** *adj.*

pan·dic·u·la·tion (pan dik′yə lā′shən), *n.* the act of stretching oneself. [1640–50; < L *pandiculāt(us)* ptp. of *pandiculārī* to stretch oneself, deriv. of *pandere* to stretch (see -ATE[1]) + -ION]

pan·dit (pun′dit; *spelling pron.* pan′dit), *n.* a man in India esteemed for his wisdom or learning: often used as a title of respect. Also, **pundit.** [1820–30; < Hindi < Skt *paṇḍita*]

Pan·dit (pun′dit), *n.* **Vi·ja·ya Lak·shmi** (vi jī′ə läk′-shmē), 1900–90, Indian stateswoman (sister of Jawaharlal Nehru).

P. and L., profit and loss. Also, **P. & L., p. and l.**

pan·do·ra (pan dôr′ə, -dōr′ə), *n.* bandore. Also, **pan·dore** (pan dôr′, -dōr′, pan′dôr, -dōr), **pan·dou·ra** (pan-dŏŏr′ə), **pandure.**

Pan·do·ra (pan dôr′ə, -dōr′ə), *n. Class. Myth.* the first woman, created by Hephaestus, endowed by the gods with all the graces and treacherously presented to Epimetheus along with a box (originally a jar) in which Prometheus had confined all the evils that could trouble humanity. As the gods had anticipated, Pandora gave in to her curiosity and opened the box, allowing the evils to escape, thereby frustrating the efforts of Prometheus. In some versions, the box contained blessings, all of which escaped but hope. [< L < Gk *Pandṓra,* equiv. to *pan-* PAN- + *dôr(on)* gift + *-a* fem. n. ending]

Pan·do·rae Fre·tum (pan dôr′ē frē′təm, -dōr′ē), an area in the southern hemisphere of Mars.

Pando′ra's box′, a source of extensive but unforeseen troubles or problems: *The senate investigation turned out to be a Pandora's box for the administration.* [1570–80]

pando′ra shell′, 1. any marine bivalve of the genus *Pandora,* having a scimitar-shaped shell with a pronounced ridge along the hinge. **2.** the shell itself.

pan·dour (pan′dŏŏr), *n.* **1.** *Hist.* a member of a local militia in Croatia, formed as a regiment in the Austrian army in the 18th century and noted for its ruthlessness and cruelty. **2.** a brutal, marauding soldier. [1740–50; < F *pandour(e)* << Serbo-Croatian *pàndūr* community or city policeman, pandour, prob. < Hungarian *pandúr* < Slavic **pǫdarĭ* (> Serbo-Croatian *pùdār* one who guards a vineyard), deriv. of **pǫditi* to drive off, frighten; the Serbo-Croatian var. *bàndūr* (17th century) may result from crossing with ML *banderia* or It *bandiera* troop, lit., BANNER]

pan·dow·dy (pan dou′dē), *n., pl.* **-dies.** *Chiefly New Eng.* See **apple pandowdy.** [1795–1805, *Amer.*; perh. var. of obs. dial. (Somerset) *pandoulde* custard; see PAN[1]]

P&S, purchase and sales (of stocks in a brokerage house).

pan·du·rate (pan′də rāt′, -dər it, -dyə rāt′, -dyər it), *adj.* shaped like a fiddle, as a leaf. Also, **pan·du·ri·form** (pan dŏŏr′ə fôrm′, -dyŏŏr′-). [1765–75; < L *pandūr(a)* musical instrument (see BANDORE) + -ATE[1]]

pandurate leaf

pan·dure (pan′jər, pan dŏŏr′, -dyŏŏr′), *n.* bandore.

pan·dy (pan′dē), *n., pl.* **-dies,** *v.,* **-died, -dy·ing.** *Chiefly Scot.* —*n.* **1.** a stroke on the palm of the hand with a cane or strap given as a punishment in school. —*v.t.* **2.** to hit on the palm of the hand. [1795–1805; < L *pande* stretch out! (impv. of *pandere*), i.e., open your hand to take the blow]

pane (pān), *n.* **1.** one of the divisions of a window or the like, consisting of a single plate of glass in a frame. **2.** a plate of glass for such a division. **3.** a panel, as of a wainscot, ceiling, door, etc. **4.** a flat section, side, or surface, as one of the sides of a bolthead. **5.** *Philately.* a sheet of stamps or any large portion of one, as a half or a quarter, as issued by the post office. [1250–1300; ME *pane, pan* strip of cloth, section < MF *pan* < L *pannus* cloth; akin to OE *fana* flag; see VANE] **—pane′less,** *adj.*

pa·né (pa nā′; *Fr.* pa nā′), *adj.* (of food) prepared with bread crumbs; breaded. [< F]

paned (pānd), *adj.* having panes (usually used in combination): *a diamond-paned window.* [1545–55; PANE + -ED[3]]

pan·e·gyr·ic (pan′i jir′ik, -jī′rik), *n.* **1.** a lofty oration or writing in praise of a person or thing; eulogy. **2.** formal or elaborate praise. [1590–1600; < L, n. use of *panēgyricus* of, belonging to a public assembly < Gk *panēgyrikós,* equiv. to *panḗgyr(is)* solemn assembly (*pan-* PAN- + *-ēgyris,* comb. form of *ágyris* gathering; cf. CATEGORY) + *-ikos* -IC] **—pan′e·gyr′i·cal,** *adj.* **—pan′e·gyr′i·cal·ly,** *adv.*
—Syn. 1. homage, tribute, encomium.

pan·e·gyr·ist (pan′i jir′ist, -jī′rist, pan′i jir′ist, -jī′rist), *n.* a person who panegyrizes; eulogist. [1595–1605; < LL *panēgyrista* < Gk *panēgyristḗs* one who takes part in a public festival or assembly, equiv. to *panēgyr(izein)* to celebrate a public festival (see PANEGYRIZE) + *-istēs* -IST]

pan·e·gy·rize (pan′i jə rīz′), *v.,* **-rized, -riz·ing.** —*v.t.* **1.** to deliver or write a panegyric about; eulogize. —*v.i.* **2.** to indulge in panegyric; bestow praises. Also, *esp. Brit.,* **pan′e·gy·rise′.** [1610–20; < Gk *panēgyrízein* to celebrate a public festival, equiv. to *panḗgyr(is)* (see PANEGYRIC) + *-izein* -IZE]

pan·el (pan′l), *n., v.,* **-eled, -el·ing** or (*esp. Brit.*) **-elled, -el·ling.** —*n.* **1.** a distinct portion, section, or division of a wall, wainscot, ceiling, door, shutter, fence, etc., esp. of any surface sunk below or raised above the general level or enclosed by a frame or border. **2.** a comparatively thin, flat piece of wood or the like, as a large piece of plywood. **3.** a group of persons gathered to conduct a public discussion, judge a contest, serve as advisers, be players on a radio or television game, or the like: *a panel of political scientists meeting to discuss foreign policy.* **4.** a public discussion by such a group. **5.** *Law.* **a.** a list of persons summoned for service as jurors. **b.** the body of persons composing a jury. **c.** (in Scotland) the person or persons arraigned for trial. **6.** a mount for or a surface or section of a machine containing the controls and dials. **7.** *Elect.* a switchboard or control board, or a division of a switchboard or control board containing a set of related cords, jacks, relays, etc. **8.** a broad strip of material set vertically in or on a dress, skirt, etc. **9.** *Painting.* **a.** a flat piece of wood of varying kinds on which a picture is painted. **b.** a picture painted on such a piece of wood. **10.** (in Britain) a list of approved or cooperating doctors available to patients under a health insurance program. **11.** *Aeron.* a lateral subdivision of an airfoil with internal girder construction. **12.** *Engin., Building Trades.* **a.** the space on the chord of a truss between any two adjacent joints made by principal web members with the chord. **b.** the space within the web of a truss between any two such joints and a corresponding pair of joints or a single joint on an opposite chord. **13.** the section between the two bands on the spine of a bound book. **14.** *Mining.* an area of a coal seam separated for mining purposes from adjacent areas by extra thick masses or ribs of coal. **15.** a pad placed under a saddle. **16.** a pad, cloth, or the like, serving as a saddle. **17.** a pane, as in a window. **18.** a slip of parchment. **19.** a photograph much longer in one dimension than the other. —*v.t.* **20.** to arrange in or furnish with a panel or panels. **21.** to ornament with a panel or panels. **22.** to set in a frame as a panel. **23.** to select (a jury). **24.** *Scots Law.* to bring to trial. [1250–1300; ME < OF *panel* a piece (of anything), dim. of *pan* piece of cloth or the like. See PANE, -ELLE]
—Usage. See **collective noun.**

pan·el·board (pan′l bôrd′, -bōrd′), *n.* a compact pressboard for use in constructing sides of cabinets, paneling for walls, and in other nonstructural applications. [1930–35; PANEL + BOARD]

pan′el discus′sion, a formal discussion before an audience for which the topic, speakers, etc., have been selected in advance. [1935–40]

pan′el heat′ing, heating of a room or building by means of wall, ceiling, floor, or baseboard panels containing heating pipes or electrical conductors. [1925–30]

pan′el house′, a brothel having rooms with secret entrances, as sliding panels, for admitting panel thieves. [1840–50, *Amer.*]

pan·el·ing (pan′l ing), *n.* **1.** wood or other material made into panels. **2.** a surface of panels, esp. of decorative wood or woodlike panels. **3.** panels collectively. Also, *esp. Brit.,* **pan′el·ling.** [1815–25; PANEL + -ING[1]]

pan·el·ist (pan′l ist), *n.* a member of a small group of persons gathered for formal public discussion, judging, playing a radio or television game, etc. [1950–55; PANEL + -IST]

pan·el·ized (pan′l īzd′), *adj.* composed of prefabricated sections of walls, floors, or roofs that can be assembled at the building site: *a panelized house.* [PANEL + -IZE + -ED[2]]

pan′el light′ing, lighting of a room or building by means of flat sheets of material that glow brightly when a coating of a phosphor is excited by an electrical charge.

pan′el patch′, a patch made to one of the outer veneers of a sheet of plywood after manufacture.

pan′el point′, *Engin.* a joint between two or more members of a truss. Also called **node.**

pan′el saw′, a small ripsaw or crosscut saw. [1805–15]

pan′el strip′, one of a number of strips of wood or metal laid upon the surface of a wall, ceiling, etc., so as to divide it into a number of broad areas, usually in order to conceal joints between sheets of composition material forming the surface.

pan′el thief′, a thief who secretly robs the customers in a panel house. [1835–45, *Amer.*]

pan′el truck′, a small truck having a fully enclosed body, used mainly to deliver light or small objects. [1935–40, *Amer.*]

pan·e·tel·la (pan′i tel′ə), *n.* a long, slender cigar, usually with straight sides and tapering to a point at the closed end. Also, **pan′e·tel′a, panatella, panatela.** [1900–05; < AmerSp *panetela, panatela* a kind of bread, long, slender biscuit < It *panatella,* dim. of *pane* bread (< L *pānis*); see -ELLE]

pan·e·tière (pan′i tyâr′; *Fr.* pan^ə tyer′), *n., pl.* **-tières**

(-tyârz′; *Fr.* -tyeʀ′). *Fr. Furniture.* a small, decorative livery cupboard, made esp. in Provence in the 18th century. [< F, OF, equiv. to *panet(erie)* bread room (see PANTRY) + *-iere,* fem. of *-ier* -IER[2]]

pan·et·to·ne (pan′i tō′nē; *It.* pä′net tô′ne), *n., pl.* **-nes** (-nēz), *It.* **-ni** (-nē). an Italian yeast-leavened bread, traditionally eaten on holidays, usually made with raisins, candied fruit peels, almonds, and brandy. [1920–25; < It, deriv. of *panetto* little loaf, equiv. to *pan(e)* bread (< L *pānis*) + *-etto* dim. suffix]

Pan-Eu·ro·pe·an (pan′yŏŏr ə pē′ən), *adj.* of or pertaining to all or most of the countries of Europe. [1900–05]

pan·fish (pan′fish′), *n., pl.* **-fish·es,** (*esp. collectively*) **-fish.** any small, freshwater nongame food fish, as a perch or sunfish, usually eaten pan-fried. [1795–1805, *Amer.*; PAN[1] + FISH]

pan′-fried pota′toes (pan′frīd′, -frīd′), *Chiefly Northeastern U.S.* See **home fries.** Also called **pan′ fries′.**

pan-fry (pan′frī′, -frī′), *v.t.,* **-fried, -fry·ing.** to fry in a small amount of fat, as in a skillet or shallow pan; sauté. [1940–45; PAN[1] + FRY[1]]

pan·ful (pan′fŏŏl), *n., pl.* **-fuls.** the amount a pan can hold. [1870–75; PAN[1] + -FUL]
—**Usage.** See **-ful.**

pang (pang), *n.* **1.** a sudden feeling of mental or emotional distress or longing: *a pang of remorse; a pang of desire.* **2.** a sudden, brief, sharp pain or physical sensation; spasm: *hunger pangs.* [1495–1505; orig. uncert.]
—**Syn. 1, 2.** twinge, ache, throb, prick, stab.

pan·ga (päng′gə), *n.* a large, broad-bladed African knife used as a weapon or as an implement for cutting heavy jungle growth, sugar cane, etc.; machete. [1930–35; < Swahili]

Pan·gae·a (pan jē′ə), *n. Geol.* the hypothetical landmass that existed when all continents were joined, from about 300 to 200 million years ago. Also, **Pan·ge′a.** Cf. **supercontinent.** [1920–25; PAN- + Gk *gaîa* earth; allegedly coined by German meteorologist Alfred L. Wegener (1880–1930)]

pan·gen·e·sis (pan jen′ə sis), *n. Biol.* the theory that a reproductive cell contains gemmules or invisible germs that were derived from the individual cells from every part of the organism and that these gemmules are the bearers of hereditary attributes. [1868; PAN- + GENESIS; term introduced by Charles Darwin] —**pan·ge·net·ic** (pan′jə net′ik), *adj.* —**pan′ge·net′i·cal·ly,** *adv.*

Pan-Ger·man·ism (pan′jûr′mə niz′əm), *n.* the idea or advocacy of a union of all the German peoples in a single political organization or state. [1880–85; PAN- + GERMANISM] —**Pan′-Ger′man,** *adj., n.* —**Pan-Ger·man·ic** (pan′jər man′ik), *adj.*

Pang·fou (päng′fō′), *n. Older Spelling.* Bengbu.

Pan·gloss·i·an (pan glos′ē ən, -glô′sē-, pang-), *adj.* characterized by or given to extreme optimism, esp. in the face of unrelieved hardship or adversity. [1825–35; after *Pangloss,* an optimistic character in Voltaire's *Candide;* cf. Gk *panglossía* garrulousness, wordiness (see PAN-, GLOSSO-, -Y[3]); see -IAN]

pan·go′la grass′ (pang gō′lə, pan-), a grass, *Digitaria decumbens,* native to southern Africa, cultivated for hay and forage in the southeastern U.S. [1945–50; var. of *pongola,* after the *Pongola* River, E Transvaal, Republic of South Africa]

pan·go·lin (pang′gə lin, pang gō′-), *n.* any mammal of the order Pholidota, of Africa and tropical Asia, having a covering of broad, overlapping, horny scales and feeding on ants and termites. Also called **scaly anteater.** [1765–75; < Malay *pengguling* (dial. or bazaar Malay name for the animal) one who rolls up, equiv. to *peng-* agentive prefix + *guling* roll up or around; so called from its habit of curling into a ball when threatened]

Malayan pangolin, *Manis javanica,* head and body 2 ft. (0.6 m); tail 2 ft. (0.6 m)

Pang·o Pang·o (päng′ō päng′ō, päng′gō päng′gō). See **Pago Pago.**

pan·gram (pan′grəm, -gram, pang′-), *n.* a sentence, verse, etc., that includes all the letters of the alphabet. [1930–35; PAN- + -GRAM[1]] —**pan·gram·mat·ic** (pan′grə mat′ik, pang′-), *adj.*

pan′ gra′vy, meat juices, as from a roast, seasoned but not thickened. Cf. **dish gravy.**

Pan Gu (pun′ gōō′), *Pinyin.* See **P'an Ku.**

pan·guin·gue (päng gēng′gē), *n.* a card game of the rummy family that is played with from five to eight regular 52-card packs from which the eights, nines, and tens have been removed, the object being to win bonuses by melding certain groups of cards during the play and extra bonuses by melding all the cards in the hand. [< Tagalog *panggînggi*]

Pang·we (päng′wā), *n., pl.* **-wes,** (*esp. collectively*) **-we.** Fang (def. 1).

pan·han·dle[1] (pan′han′dl), *n.* **1.** the handle of a pan. **2.** (*sometimes cap.*) a long, narrow, projecting strip of territory that is not a peninsula, esp. such a part of a specified state: *the panhandle of Alaska; the Texas and Oklahoma panhandles.* [1855–60; PAN[1] + HANDLE]

pan·han·dle[2] (pan′han′dl), *v.,* **-dled, -dling.** *Informal.* —*v.i.* **1.** to accost passers-by on the street and beg from them. —*v.t.* **2.** to accost and beg from. **3.** to obtain by accosting and begging from someone. [1895–1900, *Amer.*; back formation from *panhandler;* so called from the resemblance of the extended arm to a PANHANDLE[1]] —**pan′han′dler,** *n.*

Pan′handle State′, West Virginia (used as a nickname).

pan′ head′, *Photog.* a tripod head permitting vertical or horizontal rotation of a camera to any position.

pan·head (pan′hed′), *n.* a rivet or screw head having the form of a truncated cone. [1865–70; PAN[1] + HEAD] —**pan′head′ed,** *adj.*

Pan·hel·len·ic (pan′hə len′ik, -lē′nik), *adj.* **1.** of or pertaining to all Greeks or to Panhellenism. **2.** of, pertaining to, or noting collegiate fraternities and sororities. Also, **pan′hel·len′ic.** [1840–50; PAN- + HELLENIC]

Pan·hel·len·ism (pan hel′ə niz′əm), *n.* the idea or advocacy of a union of all Greeks in one political body. [1855–60; PAN- + HELLENISM] —**Pan·hel′len·ist,** *n.*

pan·hoss (pän′hos), *n.* pannhas.

pan·hu·man (pan′hyōō′mən *or, often,* -yōō′-), *adj.* of, pertaining to, or affecting all humanity. [1895–1900; PAN- + HUMAN]

pan·ic[1] (pan′ik), *n., adj., v.,* **-icked, -ick·ing.** —*n.* **1.** a sudden overwhelming fear, with or without cause, that produces hysterical or irrational behavior, and that often spreads quickly through a group of persons or animals. **2.** an instance, outbreak, or period of such fear. **3.** *Finance.* a sudden widespread fear concerning financial affairs leading to credit contraction and widespread sale of securities at depressed prices in an effort to acquire cash. **4.** *Slang.* someone or something that is considered hilariously funny: *The comedian was an absolute panic.* —*adj.* **5.** of the nature of, caused by, or indicating panic: *A wave of panic buying shook the stock market.* **6.** (of fear, terror, etc.) suddenly destroying the self-control and impelling to some frantic action. **7.** (*cap.*) of or pertaining to the god Pan. —*v.t.* **8.** to affect with panic; terrify and cause to flee or lose self-control. **9.** *Slang.* to keep (an audience or the like) highly amused. —*v.i.* **10.** to be stricken with panic; become frantic with fear: *The herd panicked and stampeded.* [1595–1605; earlier *panique* < F < Gk *Panikós* of PAN; see -IC] —**pan′ick·y,** *adj.*
—**Syn. 1.** alarm. See **terror.**

pan·ic[2] (pan′ik), *n.* **1.** Also called **pan′ic grass′.** any grass of the genus *Panicum,* many species of which bear edible grain. **2.** the grain. [1375–1425; late ME < L *pānicum* a kind of millet]

pan′ic attack′, *Psychiatry.* an intense attack of anxiety characterized by feelings of impending doom and trembling, sweating, pounding heart, and other physical symptoms.

pan′ic bar′, a bar that spans an emergency exit door on its interior and opens the latch when pressure is applied. Also called **pan′ic bolt′.** [1925–30]

pan′ic but′ton, 1. an alarm button for use in an emergency, as to summon help. **2.** *Informal.* **push** or **hit** or **press the panic button,** to give way to panic in a distressing situation. [allegedly first used in reference to emergency bell systems on World War II bombers such as the B-17 and B-24]

pan′ic disor′der, *Psychiatry.* a disorder in which inappropriate, intense apprehension and physical symptoms of fear occur so frequently as to produce significant impairment.

pan·i·cle (pan′i kəl), *n. Bot.* **1.** a compound raceme. See illus. under **inflorescence. 2.** any loose, diversely branching flower cluster. [1590–1600; < L *pānicula* tuft (on plants), dim. of *pānus* thread wound on a bobbin, a swelling, ear of millet < Doric Gk *pânos* (Attic *pênos*) a web; see -I-, -CLE[1]] —**pan′i·cled,** *adj.*

pan·ic-strick·en (pan′ik strik′ən), *adj.* overcome with, characterized by, or resulting from fear, panic, or the like: *panic-stricken parents looking for their child; a panic-stricken phone call.* Also **pan·ic-struck** (pan′ik-struk′). [1795–1805]

pa·nic·u·late (pə nik′yə lāt′, -lit), *adj. Bot.* arranged in panicles. Also, **pa·nic′u·lat′ed.** [1720–30; < NL *pāniculātus* panicled. See PANICLE, -ATE[1]] —**pa·nic′u·late′ly,** *adv.*

pan·ier (pan′yər, -ē ər), *n.* pannier.

Pa·ni·ni (pä′nē nē *for 1;* pä nē′nē *for 2*), *n.* **1.** fl. c400 B.C., Indian grammarian of Sanskrit. **2.** See **Pannini, Giovanni Paolo.**

pa·ni·o·lo (pä′nē ō′lō), *n., pl.* **-los.** *Hawaiian.* a person who herds cattle; cowboy. [< Hawaiian: cowboy, Spanish, Spaniard, prob. < Sp *español* Spanish]

Pan-Is·lam·ism (pan′is lä′miz əm, -iz-, -is′lə miz′-, -iz′-), *n.* the idea or advocacy of a political union of all Muslim nations. [1880–85; PAN- + ISLAMISM] —**Pan-Is·lam·ic** (pan′is lam′ik, -lä′mik, -iz-), *adj.*

pa·niv·o·rous (pa niv′ər əs), *adj.* subsisting on bread; bread-eating. [1820–30; < L *pān(is)* bread + -I- + -VOROUS]

Pan·ja·bi (pun jä′bē), *n., pl.* **-bis,** *adj.* Punjabi.

pan·jan·drum (pan jan′drəm), *n.* a self-important or pretentious official. [1745–55; pseudo-Latin word (based on PAN-) coined by Samuel Foote (1720–77), English dramatist and actor]

pan′ juice′, Often, **pan juices.** the natural juices exuded by meat, poultry, etc., while baking or roasting: used esp. in basting.

Pank·hurst (pangk′hûrst), *n.* **1. Christabel Harriette,** 1880–1958, English suffragist leader (daughter of Emmeline Pankhurst). **2. Emmeline (Goul·den)** (gōōl′-dn), 1858–1928, English suffragist leader.

P'an Ku (pän′ kōō′), *Chinese Myth.* a being personifying the primeval stuff from which heaven and earth were formed.

pan·leu·ko·pe·ni·a (pan′lōō kə pē′nē ə), *n. Vet. Pathol.* distemper[1] (def. 1c). Also, **pan′leu·co·pe′ni·a.** [1935–40; PAN- + LEUKOPENIA]

pan·lo·gism (pan′lə jiz′əm), *n. Philos.* the doctrine that the universe is a realization or act of the logos. [1870–75; < G *Panlogismus.* See PAN-, LOGOS, -ISM] —**pan·log·i·cal** (pan loj′i kəl), **pan′lo·gis′tic, pan′lo·gis′ti·cal,** *adj.* —**pan′lo·gist,** *adj., n.* —**pan′lo·gis′ti·cal·ly,** *adv.*

pan·mix·i·a (pan mik′sē ə), *n. Animal Behav.* random mating of individuals within a population, the breeding individuals showing no tendency to choose partners with particular traits. Also, **pan·mix·is** (pan-mik′sis). Cf. **assortative mating, disassortative mating.** [1885–90; PAN- + Gk *míx(is)* mingling, mixing (*m(e)ig(nýnai)* to mix + *-sis* -SIS) + -IA] —**pan·mic·tic** (pan mik′tik), *adj.*

Pan·mun·jom (pän′mŏŏn′jom′), *n.* a small community along the boundary between North Korea and South Korea: site of the truce talks at the close of the Korean War.

panne (pan), *n.* a soft, lustrous, lightweight velvet with flattened pile. [1785–95; < F, OF, var. of *pen(n)e,* equiv. to ML *panna, penna* skin, fur, appar. special use of L *penna* feather; cf. MHG *federe* kind of fur]

pann·has (pän′häs), *n. Chiefly Pennsylvania.* scrapple. Also, **panhoss.** [< PaG *pannhâs,* equiv. to *pann* PAN[1] + *hâs* rabbit, HARE; orig. a jocular word, in dials. of the Rhenish Palatinate, for dishes made from scraps or broth mixed with a grain; cf. G *falscher Hase* minced meat, lit., false hare]

pan·nic·u·lus (pə nik′yə ləs), *n., pl.* **-li** (-lī′). *Anat.* a layer of tissue, esp. a subcutaneous layer of fat. [< L: small piece of cloth, rag, equiv. to *pann(us)* cloth, rag (cf. PANE) + -I- -I- + *-culus* -CULE[1]; see PANICLE] —**pan·nic′u·lar,** *adj.*

pan·nier (pan′yər, -ē ər), *n.* **1.** a basket, esp. a large one, for carrying goods, provisions, etc. **2.** a basket for carrying on a person's back, or one of a pair to be slung across the back of a beast of burden. **3.** a similar type of bag, usually one of a pair, fastened over a bicycle's rear wheel. **4.** (on a dress, skirt, etc.) a puffed arrangement of drapery at the hips. **5.** an oval framework formerly used for distending the skirt of a woman's dress at the hips. Also, **panier.** [1250–1300; ME *panier* < MF < L *pānārium* breadbasket, equiv. to *pān(is)* bread + *-ārium* -ARY; see -IER[2]] —**pan′niered,** *adj.*

pan·ni·kin (pan′i kin), *n. Chiefly Brit.* a small pan or metal cup. [1815–25; PAN[1] + -I- + -KIN]

pan′nikin boss′, *Australia and New Zealand Slang* (*disparaging*). an overseer of a small group of workers; person with minor authority. [1895–1900]

pan′ning shot′, pan[3] (def. 6). [1935–40]

Pan·ni·ni (pän nē′nē), *n.* **Gio·van·ni (Pa·o·lo)** (jô vän′-nē pä′ô lô), 1692?–1765, Italian painter. Also, **Panini.**

Pan·no·ni·a (pə nō′nē ə), *n.* an ancient country and Roman province in central Europe, S and W of the Danube, the territory of which is now mostly occupied by Hungary and Yugoslavia. —**Pan·no′ni·an,** *adj., n.* —**Pan·non·ic** (pə non′ik), *adj.*

pan·nose (pan′ōs), *adj. Bot.* having the texture of felt or woolen cloth. [1865–70; < L *pannōsus* full of rags, tattered, equiv. to *pann(us)* cloth, rag (cf. PANE) + *-ōsus* -OSE[1]] —**pan′nose·ly,** *adv.*

pan·nus (pan′əs), *n.* **1.** *Pathol.* **a.** an abnormal vascular thickening of the cornea. **b.** an ingrowth of synovial material into a joint, as in rheumatoid arthritis. **2.** *Meteorol.* a group of ragged cloud fragments hanging below a cloud. [1375–1425; late ME < ML; L: piece of cloth, rag (cf. PANE)]

Pa·no·an (pä′nō ən), *n.* a family of South American Indian languages spoken in Peru, Bolivia, and western Brazil. Also, **Pa·no** (pä′nō).

pa·no·cha (pə nō′chə), *n.* **1.** Also, **penuche.** a coarse grade of sugar made in Mexico. **2.** penuche (def. 1). Also, **pa·no·che** (pə nō′chē). [1840–50; < MexSp; cf. Sp *panocha,* var. of *panoja* ear of grain, panicle < L *pānucula, pānicula;* see PANICLE]

Pa·nof·sky (pa nof′skē), *n.* **Erwin,** 1892–1968, U.S. art historian, born in Germany.

pan·o·ply (pan′ə plē), *n., pl.* **-plies. 1.** a wide-ranging and impressive array or display: *the dazzling panoply of the maharaja's procession; the panoply of European history.* **2.** a complete suit of armor. **3.** a protective covering. **4.** full ceremonial attire or paraphernalia; special dress and equipment. [1570–80; < Gk *panoplía* full complement of arms and armor, equiv. to *pan-* PAN- + *(h)ópl(a)* arms, armor (cf. HOPLITE) + *-ia* -IA] —**pan′o·plied,** *adj.*

pan·op·tic (pan op′tik), *adj.* **1.** permitting the viewing of all parts or elements: *a panoptic stain used in microscopy; a panoptic aerial photograph of an enemy missile base.* **2.** considering all parts or elements; all inclusive: *a panoptic criticism of modern poetry.* Also, **pan·op′ti·cal.** [1820–30; < Gk *panópt(ēs)* all-seeing + -IC. See PAN-, OPTIC] —**pan·op′ti·cal·ly,** *adv.*

pan·op·ti·con (pan op′ti kon′), *n.* a building, as a prison, hospital, library, or the like, so arranged that all parts of the interior are visible from a single point. [1760–70; PAN- + Gk *optikón* sight, seeing (neut. of *optikós;* see OPTIC)]

pan·o·ram·a (pan′ə ram′ə, -rä′mə), *n.* **1.** an unobstructed and wide view of an extensive area in all directions. **2.** an extended pictorial representation or a cyclorama of a landscape or other scene, often exhibited a part at a time and made to pass continuously before the spectators. **3.** a building for exhibiting such a pictorial representation. **4.** a continuously passing or changing scene or an unfolding of events: *the panorama of Chinese history.* **5.** a comprehensive survey, as of a subject.

[1790–1800; PAN- + Gk (h)órāma view, sight, deriv. of *horân* to see, look] —**pan′o·ram′ic,** *adj.* —**pan′o·ram′i·cal·ly,** *adv.*
—**Syn. 1.** scene, vista, prospect.

pan′oram′ic cam′era, a still camera having a movable lens that horizontally scans a view while exposing a long photographic plate or strip of film. [1875–80]

pan′oram′ic sight′, an artillery sight that can be rotated horizontally in a full circle.

pan·pipe (pan′pīp′), *n.* a primitive wind instrument consisting of a series of hollow pipes of graduated length, the tones being produced by blowing across the upper ends. Also, **Pan's′ pipes′, pan′pipes′.** [1810–20; PAN + PIPE[1]]

panpipe

pan·sex·u·al (pan sek′shoo̅ əl), *adj.* **1.** *Psychiatry.* pertaining to the theory that all human behavior is based on sexuality. **2.** expressing or involving sexuality in many different forms or with a variety of sexual outlets. [1925–30; PAN- + SEXUAL] —**pan′sex·u·al′i·ty,** *n.*

Pan·sil (pun′sēl), *n. Buddhism.* See **Pancha Sila.** [< Sinhalese < < Skt]

Pan-Slav·ism (pan′slä′viz əm, -slav′iz-), *n.* the idea or advocacy of a political union of all the Slavic peoples. [1840–50; PAN- + SLAVISM] —**Pan′-Slav′, Pan′-Slav′·ic,** *adj.*

pan·soph·ism (pan′sə fiz′əm), *n.* a claim or pretension to pansophy. [1865–70; < Gk *pánsoph(os)* all-wise + -ISM. See PAN-, SOPHISM] —**pan′so·phist,** *n.*

pan·so·phy (pan′sə fē), *n.* universal wisdom or knowledge. [1635–45; PAN- + -SOPHY] —**pan·soph·ic** (pan sof′ik), **pan·soph′i·cal,** *adj.* —**pan·soph′i·cal·ly,** *adv.*

pan·sper·mi·a (pan spûr′mē ə), *n. Biol.* the theory that life exists and is distributed throughout the universe in the form of germs or spores that develop in the right environment. Also, **pan·sper·ma·tism** (pan spûr′mə tiz′əm), **pan·sper·my** (pan′spûr′mē). [1835–45; < NL < Gk *panspermía* mixture of all seeds. See PAN-, -SPERM, -IA] —**pan·sper′mic,** *adj.*

pan·sy (pan′zē), *n., pl.* **-sies. 1.** a violet, *Viola tricolor hortensis,* cultivated in many varieties, having richly and variously colored flowers. **2.** the flower of this plant. **3.** *Slang (disparaging and offensive).* **a.** a male homosexual. **b.** a weak, effeminate, and often cowardly man. [1490–1500; 1930–35 for def. 3; < MF *pensée* pansy, lit., thought, n. use of fem. of ptp. of *penser* to think < L *pēnsāre* to weigh, consider. See PENSIVE]

Pan·sy (pan′zē), *n.* a female given name.

pan′sy or′chid, miltonia.

pant[1] (pant), *v.i.* **1.** to breathe hard and quickly, as after exertion. **2.** to gasp, as for air. **3.** to long with breathless or intense eagerness; yearn: *to pant for revenge.* **4.** to throb or heave violently or rapidly; palpitate. **5.** to emit steam or the like in loud puffs. **6.** *Naut.* (of the bow or stern of a ship) to work with the shock of contact with a succession of waves. Cf. **work** (def. 30). —*v.t.* **7.** to breathe or utter gaspingly. —*n.* **8.** the act of panting. **9.** a short, quick, labored effort at breathing; gasp. **10.** a puff, as of an engine. **11.** a throb or heave, as of the breast. [1400–50; late ME *panten* < MF *pant(a)is(i)er* < VL **phantasiāre* to have visions < Gk *phantasioûn* to have or form images. See FANTASY] —**pant′ing·ly,** *adv.*
—**Syn. 1.** puff, blow. PANT, GASP suggest breathing with more effort than usual. PANT suggests rapid, convulsive breathing, as from violent exertion or excitement: *to pant after running for the train.* GASP suggests catching one's breath in a single quick intake, as from amazement, terror, and the like, or a series of such quick intakes of breath, as in painful breathing: *to gasp with horror; to gasp for breath.* **3.** thirst, hunger.

pant[2] (pant), *adj.* **1.** of or pertaining to pants: *pant cuffs.* —*n.* **2.** See **pant leg. 3.** pants (defs. 1, 2). [1890–95; sing. of PANTS]

pant-, var. of **panto-** before a vowel.

pan·ta·graph (pan′tə graf′, -gräf′), *n.* pantograph (def. 1).

Pan·tag·ru·el (pan tag′roo̅ el′, -əl, pan′tə groo̅′əl; *Fr.* päɴ ta ɢʀʏ el′), *n.* **1.** (in Rabelais' *Pantagruel*) the huge son of Gargantua, represented as dealing with serious matters in a spirit of broad and somewhat cynical good humor. **2.** (*italics*) a satirical novel (1532) by Rabelais. Cf. **Gargantua.** —**Pan·ta·gru·el·i·an** (pan′tə groo̅el′ē ən), *adj.* —**Pan′ta·gru·el′i·cal·ly,** *adv.* —**Pan·ta·gru·el·ism** (pan′tə groo̅′ə liz′əm, pan tag′roo̅ ə liz′əm), *n.* —**Pan′ta·gru′el·ist,** *n.*

pan·ta·lets (pan′tl ets′), *n.* (*used with a plural v.*) **1.** long drawers extending below the skirt, with a frill or other finish at the bottom of the leg, commonly worn by women and girls in the 19th century. **2.** a pair of separate frilled or trimmed pieces for attaching to the legs of women's drawers. Also, **pan′ta·lettes′.** Also called **trousers.** [1825–35; PANTAL(OON) + -ET + -S[3]] —**pan′ta·let′ted,** *adj.*

pan·ta·loon (pan′tl o̅o̅n′), *n.* **1. pantaloons,** a man's close-fitting garment for the hips and legs, worn esp. in the 19th century, but varying in form from period to period; trousers. **2.** (*usually cap.*) Also, **Pan·ta·lo·ne** (pan′tl ō′nā, pän′-; *It.* pän′tä lô′ne). (in commedia dell'arte) a foolish old Venetian merchant, usually the head of a household, generally lascivious and frequently deceived in the course of lovers' intrigues. **3.** (in the modern pantomime) a foolish, vicious old man, the butt and accomplice of the clown. [1580–90; < MF *Pantalon* < Upper It (Venetian) *Pantalone* nickname for a Venetian, var. of *Pantaleone,* name of a 4th-century saint once a favorite of the Venetians]

pan·tech·ni·con (pan tek′ni kon′, -kən), *n. Brit.* a furniture van; moving van. Also called **pantech′nicon van′.** [1820–30; PAN- + Gk *technikón* artistic, skillful (neut. of *technikós*); see TECHNIC]

Pan·tel·le·ri·a (pän tel′le ʀē′ä), *n.* an Italian island in the Mediterranean between Sicily and Tunisia. 10,000; 32 sq. mi. (83 sq. km). Ancient, **Cosyra.**

Pan-Teu·ton·ism (pan′to̅o̅t′n iz′əm, -tyo̅o̅t′-), *n.* Pan-Germanism. [1890–95]

pan·the·ism (pan′thē iz′əm), *n.* **1.** the doctrine that God is the transcendent reality of which the material universe and human beings are only manifestations: it involves a denial of God's personality and expresses a tendency to identify God and nature. **2.** any religious belief or philosophical doctrine that identifies God with the universe. [1725–35; < F *panthéisme.* See PAN-, THE-ISM] —**pan′the·ist,** *n.* —**pan′the·is′tic, pan′the·is′ti·cal,** *adj.* —**pan′the·is′ti·cal·ly,** *adv.*

Pan·the·on (pan′thē on′, -ən *or, esp. Brit.,* pan thē′-ən), *n.* **1.** a domed circular temple at Rome, erected A.D. 120–124 by Hadrian, used as a church since A.D. 609. **2.** (*l.c.*) a public building containing tombs or memorials of the illustrious dead of a nation. **3.** (*l.c.*) the place of the heroes or idols of any group, individual, movement, party, etc., or the heroes or idols themselves: *to earn a place in the pantheon of American literature.* **4.** (*l.c.*) a temple dedicated to all the gods. **5.** (*l.c.*) the gods of a particular mythology considered collectively. [1375–1425; late ME *panteon* < L *Panthēon* < Gk *Pántheion,* n. use of neut. of *pántheios* of all gods, equiv. to *pan-* PAN- + *the(ós)* god + *-ios* adj. suffix] —**pan′the·on′ic,** *adj.*

Pan·thé·on (päɴ tā ôɴ′), *n.* a national monument in Paris, France, used as a sepulcher for eminent French persons, begun in 1764 by Soufflot as the church of Ste. Geneviève and secularized in 1885. Also called **Panthéon′ Fran·çais′** (fʀäɴ se′).

pan·the·on·ize (pan′thē ə nīz′ *or, esp. Brit.,* pan-thē′-), *v.t.,* **-ized, iz·ing.** to place, esp. to bury, in a pantheon: *The author will be pantheonized following the funeral mass.* Also, *esp. Brit.,* **pan′the·on·ise′.** [PANTHEON + -IZE] —**pan′the·on·i·za′tion,** *n.*

pan·ther (pan′thər), *n., pl.* **-thers,** (*esp. collectively*) **-ther,** *adj.* —*n.* **1.** the cougar or puma, *Felis concolor.* **2.** the leopard, *Panthera pardus.* **3.** any leopard in the black color phase. **4.** *Informal.* a very fierce person. **5.** (*cap.*) *Mil.* a 43-ton (39 m ton) German tank of World War II with a 75mm gun as its main armament. —*adj.* **6.** fierce; strong and violent. [bef. 1000; < L *panthēra* < Gk *pánthēr;* r. ME *pantere* (< OF < L) and OE *pandher* (< L)]

Pan·ther (pan′thər), *n.* See **Black Panther.** [1965–70]

Pan·ther·a (pan′thər ə), *n.* a genus of chiefly large cats that includes the snow leopard, tiger, leopard, jaguar, and lion, most having the ability to roar. Cf. **Felis.** [< NL; see PANTHER]

pan′ther fun′gus, a highly poisonous mushroom, *Amanita pantherina,* with a brownish cap covered with white cottony patches. Also called **pan′ther amani′ta.**

pant·ie (pan′tē), *n.* panties. [var. of PANTY]

pan′tie gir′dle. See **panty girdle.** [1940–45]

pant·ies (pan′tēz), *n.* (*used with a plural v.*) underpants or undershorts for women and children. Also, **pantie, panty.** [1835–45, *Amer.*; pl. of PANTY]

pant·i·hose (pan′tē hōz′), *n.* (*used with a plural v.*) pantyhose. [1960–65; PANTY + HOSE, with *i* from the sp. of the pl. form]

pan·tile (pan′tīl′), *n.* **1.** a roofing tile straight in its length but curved in its width to overlap the next tile. **2.** a tapered, semicylindrical roofing tile laid either convex side up to overlap flanking similar tiles laid concave side up or vice versa. [1630–40; PAN[1] + TILE]

pantiles

pant′ leg′, a leg of a pair of pants. Also called **pant.** [1955–60]

pan·to (pan′tō), *n., pl.* **-tos.** *Brit.* pantomime (def. 2). [by shortening]

panto-, a combining form synonymous with **pan-:** *pantology.* Also, *esp. before a vowel,* **pant-.** [comb. form repr. Gk *pant-* (s. of *pâs*) all]

pan·to·fle (pan′tə fəl, pan tof′əl, -tō′fəl, -to̅o̅′-), *n.* **1.** a slipper. **2.** a cork-soled patten covering the forepart of the foot, worn in the 16th century. Also, **pan′tof·fle.** [1485–95; earlier *pantufle* < MF *pantoufle* < OIt *pantofola* < MGk *pantóphellos* cork shoe, lit., all-cork. See PANTO-, PHELLOGEN]

pan·to·graph (pan′tə graf′, -gräf′), *n.* **1.** Also, **pantagraph.** an instrument for the mechanical copying of plans, diagrams, etc., on any desired scale. **2.** *Elect.* a device usually consisting of two parallel, hinged, double-diamond frames, for transferring current from an overhead wire to a vehicle, as a trolley car or electric locomotive. [1715–25; PANTO- + -GRAPH] —**pan·tog·ra·pher** (pan tog′rə fər), *n.* —**pan·to·graph·ic** (pan′tə graf′ik), **pan′to·graph′i·cal,** *adj.* —**pan′to·graph′i·cal·ly,** *adv.* —**pan·tog′ra·phy,** *n.*

pan·tol·o·gy (pan tol′ə jē), *n.* a systematic view of all human knowledge. [1810–20; PANTO- + -LOGY] —**pan·to·log·ic** (pan′tl oj′ik), **pan′to·log′i·cal,** *adv.* —**pan·tol′o·gist,** *n.*

pan·to·mime (pan′tə mīm′), *n., v.,* **-mimed, -mim·ing.** —*n.* **1.** the art or technique of conveying emotions, actions, feelings, etc., by gestures without speech. **2.** a play or entertainment in which the performers express themselves mutely by gestures, often to the accompaniment of music. **3.** significant gesture without speech. **4.** an actor in dumb show, as in ancient Rome. **5.** Also called **Christmas pantomime.** a form of theatrical spectacle common in England during the Christmas season, generally adapted from a fairy tale and including stock character types who perform songs and dances, tell jokes, etc. —*v.t.* **6.** to represent or express in pantomime. —*v.i.* **7.** to express oneself in pantomime. [1580–90; earlier *pantomimus* < L < Gk *pantómīmos.* See PANTO-, MIME] —**pan·to·mim·ic** (pan′tə mim′ik), **pan′·to·mim′i·cal,** *adj.* —**pan′to·mim′i·cal·ly,** *adv.* —**pan′to·mim′ic·ry,** *n.*

pan·to·mim·ist (pan′tə mī′mist), *n.* **1.** a person who acts in pantomime. **2.** the author of a pantomime. [1830–40; PANTOMIME + -IST]

pan·ton·al (pan tōn′l), *adj. Music.* marked by or using pantonality. [1955–60; PAN- + TONAL]

pan·to·nal·i·ty (pan′tō nal′i tē), *n. Music.* See **twelve-tone technique.** [1955–60; PANTONAL + -ITY]

pan′to·then′ic ac′id (pan′tə then′ik, pan′-), *Biochem.* a hydroxy acid, $C_9H_{17}O_5N$, found in plant and animal tissues, rice, bran, etc., that is part of the B complex of vitamins and is essential for cell growth. [1930–35; < Gk *pántothen* from all quarters (*panto-* PANTO- + *-then* suffix of motion from) + -IC]

pan·to·there (pan′tə thēr′), *n.* any animal of the extinct order Pantotheria that lived during the late Mesozoic Era, believed to be the ancestor of the marsupial and placental mammals. [< NL *Pantotheria* name of order, equiv. to *panto-* PANTO- + *-theria,* pl. of *-therium* -THERE]

pan·toum (pan to̅o̅m′), *n.* a Malay verse form consisting of an indefinite number of quatrains with the second and fourth lines of each quatrain repeated as the first and third lines of the following one. Also, **pantun.** [1880–85; < F, erroneous sp. for *pantoun* < Malay *pantun*]

pan·trop·ic (pan trop′ik, -trō′pik), *adj.* (esp. of viruses) attracted to or affecting many types of body tissues. [1935–40; PAN- + -TROPIC]

pan·trop·i·cal (pan trop′i kəl), *adj.* living or growing throughout the tropics. [PAN- + TROPICAL]

pan·try (pan′trē), *n., pl.* **-tries. 1.** a room or closet in which food, groceries, and other provisions, or silverware, dishes, etc., are kept. **2.** a room between the kitchen and dining room in which food is arranged for serving, glassware and dishes are stored, etc. **3.** a shelter or other place where food is dispensed to the needy, either as groceries or as meals. [1250–1300; ME *panetrie* < AF; OF *paneterie* bread room, equiv. to *panet(er)* to bake bread (deriv. of *pan* bread < L *pānis*) + *-erie* -ERY]

pan·try·man (pan′trē mən), *n., pl.* **-men.** a person who works in or has charge of a pantry, as aboard ship or in a hospital. [1555–65; PANTRY + -MAN]

pants (pants), *n.* (*used with a plural v.*) **1.** trousers (def. 1). **2.** underpants, esp. for women and children; panties. **3.** *Brit.* men's underpants, esp. long drawers. **4. wear the pants,** to have the dominant role; be in charge: *I guess we know who wears the pants in that family.* [1830–40; short for PANTALOONS]

pant·suit (pant′so̅o̅t′), *n.* a woman's suit consisting of slacks and a matching jacket. Also, **pants′ suit′.** Also called **slack suit.** [1960–65; PANT[2] + SUIT]

pan·tun (pan to̅o̅n′), *n.* pantoum.

pant·y (pan′tē), *n., pl.* **pant·ies.** panties. [PANT(S) + -Y[2]]

pant′y gir′dle, a girdle with a crotch. Also, **pantie girdle.** [1940–45]

pant·y·hose (pan′tē hōz′), *n.* (*used with a plural v.*) a one-piece, skintight garment worn by women, combining panties and stockings. Also, **pan′ty hose′, pant·ihose.** [1960–65]

pant′y raid′, a prankish raid by male college students on the living quarters of female students to steal panties as trophies. [1950–55, *Amer.*]

pant·y·waist (pan′tē wāst′), *n.* **1.** *Informal.* a weak, effeminate man; sissy. **2.** formerly, a child's undergarment consisting of short pants and a shirt that buttoned together at the waist. —*adj.* **3.** weak; fainthearted. **4.** *Informal.* childish. [1925–30; PANTY + WAIST]
—**Syn. 1.** weakling, milksop, namby-pamby.

Pá·nu·co (pä′nə kō′; *Sp.* pä′no̅o̅ kô′), *n.* a river in E central Mexico, flowing E to the Gulf of Mexico. ab. 315 mi. (505 km) long.

Pan·urge (pan ûrj′; *Fr.* pa nʏʀzh′), *n.* (in Rabelais' *Pantagruel*) a rascal, the companion of Pantagruel. —**pan·urg′ic,** *adj.*

Pan·za (pan′zə; *Sp.* pän′thä, -sä), *n.* **Sancho.** See **Sancho Panza.**

pan·zer (pan′zər; *Ger.* pän′tsəʀ), *adj.* **1.** (esp. in the German army) armored: *a panzer unit.* **2.** of or pertaining to a panzer division: *a panzer attack.* —*n.* **3.** a vehicle, esp. a tank, forming part of a German panzer division. [1935–40; < G *Panzer* armor; MHG *panzier* < OF *panciere* coat of mail, lit., belly piece. See PAUNCH, -IER²]

pan′zer divi′sion, an armored division of the German army, esp. in World War II, consisting chiefly of tanks and organized for making rapid attacks. [1935–40]

Pao·chi (*Chin.* bou′jē′), *n. Wade-Giles.* Baoji. Also, *Older Spelling,* **Pao·ki** (bou′jē′).

Pão de A·çú·car (pouɴ′ di ä sōō′kär), Portuguese name of **Sugarloaf Mountain.**

Pao·king (*Chin.* bou′king′), *n. Older Spelling.* Baoqing. Also, *Wade-Giles,* **Pao·ch'ing** (bou′ching′).

Pao·shan (bou′shän′), *n. Wade-Giles.* Baoshan.

Pao·ting (bou′ding′), *n. Wade-Giles.* Baoding.

pap¹ (pap), *n.* **1.** soft food for infants or invalids, as bread soaked in water or milk. **2.** an idea, talk, book, or the like, lacking substance or real value. [1400–50; late ME; a nursery word akin to D *pap,* G *Pappe,* L, It *pappa*] —**pap′like′,** *adj.*
—**Syn. 2.** drivel, balderdash, twaddle.

pap² (pap), *n. Chiefly Dial.* **1.** a teat; nipple. **2.** something resembling a teat or nipple. [1150–1200; ME *pappe;* cf. dial. Norw, Sw *pappe,* L *papilla* (see PAPILLA), Lith *pāpas,* all from a base **pap-;* akin to PAP¹]

pa·pa (pä′pə, pə pä′), *n.* **1.** father. **2.** (*cap.*) a code word used in communications, esp. by radio, to represent the letter *P.* [1675–85; < F; MF *pappa* (nursery word); cf. L *pāpa* father (see POPE), ON *pāpi, pabbi* father. See PAP¹]

pa·pa·ble (pā′pə bəl), *adj.* suitable or likely to become pope. [1585–95; < MF < It *papabile,* equiv. to *papa* POPE + *-bile* -BLE] —**pa′pa·bil′i·ty,** *n.*

pa·pa·cy (pā′pə sē), *n., pl.* **-cies.** *Rom. Cath. Ch.* **1.** the office, dignity, or jurisdiction of the pope. **2.** the system of ecclesiastical government in which the pope is recognized as the supreme head. **3.** the period during which a certain pope is in office. **4.** the succession or line of the popes. [1350–1400; ME *papacie* < ML *pāpātia.* See POPE, -ACY]

Pa·pa·ga·yo (pä′pə gī′ō; *Sp.* pä′pä gä′yō), *n.* **1. Gulf of,** an inlet of the Pacific, on the NW coast of Costa Rica. 15 mi. (25 km) long; 25 mi. (40 km) wide. **2.** a violent northerly wind occurring along the W coast of Central America, esp. on the Gulf of Papagayo.

Pap·a·go (pap′ə gō′, pä′pə-), *n., pl.* **-gos,** (*esp. collectively*) **-go** for 1. **1.** a member of a North American Indian people closely related to the Pima and now living mainly in southern Arizona and northwestern Mexico. **2.** the Uto-Aztecan language of the Papago Indians, closely related to Pima. [< Sp *pápago,* earlier *papabo*(s), shortening of *papabi-ootam* < Pima-Papago *bá·bawĭ-ʔóʔodham* Papago(s), equiv. to *bá·bawĭ* tepary beans + *ʔóʔodham* Piman]

pa·pa·in (pə pā′in, -pī′in), *n.* **1.** *Biochem.* a proteolytic enzyme found in the fruit of the papaya tree, *Carica papaya.* **2.** *Pharm.* a commercial preparation of this used as a meat tenderizer and in medicine as a digestant. [1885–90; PAPA(YA) + -IN²]

pa·pal (pā′pəl), *adj.* **1.** of or pertaining to the pope or the papacy: *a papal visit to Canada.* **2.** of or pertaining to the Roman Catholic Church. [1350–1400; ME < ML *pāpālis.* See POPE, -AL¹] —**pa′pal·ly,** *adv.*

pa′pal bull′, bull² (def. 2).

pa′pal cross′, a cross with three horizontal crosspieces. See illus. under **cross.** [1885–90]

pa′pal infallibil′ity, *Rom. Cath. Ch.* the dogma that the pope cannot err in a solemn teaching addressed to the whole church on a matter of faith or morals. [1865–70]

pa·pal·ism (pā′pə liz′əm), *n.* the papal system. [1865–70; PAPAL + -ISM] —**pa′pal·ist,** *adj., n.* —**pa′·pal·is′tic,** *adj.*

pa·pal·ize (pā′pə līz′), *v.i., v.t.,* **-ized, -iz·ing.** to become or render papal. Also, *esp. Brit.,* **pa′pal·ise′.** [1615–25; PAPAL + -IZE] —**pa′pal·i·za′tion,** *n.*

Pa′pal States′, the areas comprising a large district in central Italy ruled as a temporal domain by the popes from A.D. 755 until the greater part of it was annexed in 1860, by Victor Emmanuel II: the remaining part, Rome and its environs, was absorbed into the kingdom of Italy in 1870. Also called **States of the Church.** Cf. **Vatican City.**

Pa·pan·dre·ou (pä′pən drā′ōō), *n.* **1. An·dre·as** (än drā′əs), **(George),** born 1919, Greek political leader: premier 1981–89 (son of George Papandreou). **2. George,** 1888–1968, Greek statesman: premier 1944, 1963–65.

Pa·pa·ni·co·laou′ test′ (pä′pə nē′kə lou′, pap′ə-nik′ə lou′). See **Pap test.**

pa·pa·raz·zo (pä′pə rät′sō; *It.* pä′pä ʀät′tsô), *n., pl.* **-raz·zi** (-rät′sē; *It.* -ʀät′tsē). a freelance photographer, esp. one who takes candid pictures of celebrities for publication. [1965–70; < It, from the surname of such a photographer in Federico Fellini's *La dolce vita* (1959), after the name of a hotelkeeper in George Gissing's *By the Ionian Sea* (1901), read by Fellini in It trans. at the time of the movie's producton]

pa·pav·er·a·ceous (pə pav′ə rā′shəs), *adj.* belonging to the Papaveraceae, the poppy family of plants. Cf. **poppy family.** [1840–50; < NL, L *papāver* POPPY + -ACEOUS]

pa·pav·er·ine (pə pav′ə rēn′, -ər in, pə pā′və rēn′, -vər in), *n. Pharm.* a white, crystalline, nonnarcotic, alkaloidal powder, $C_{20}H_{21}NO_4$, obtained from opium, but not a morphine derivative and not habit-forming or addicting, used in the treatment of spasms of involuntary muscle, esp. of the stomach, bronchi, and arteries. [1855–60; < L *papāver* POPPY + -INE²]

pa·paw (pô′pô, pə pô′), *n.* pawpaw.

pa·pa·ya (pə pä′yə), *n.* **1.** the large, yellow, melonlike fruit of a tropical American shrub or small tree, *Carica papaya,* eaten raw or cooked. **2.** the tree itself. Also called **pawpaw.** [1760–70; < Sp < Carib (Hispaniola)] —**pa·pa′yan,** *adj.*

Pa·pe·e·te (pä′pē ā′tā, pə pē′tē), *n.* a city on NW Tahiti, in the Society Islands: capital of the Society Islands and of French Polynesia. 24,000.

pa·pe·le·ra (pä′pe le′ʀä), *n., pl.* **-ras** (-ʀäs). *Sp. Furniture.* a small Renaissance cabinet for papers and writing materials, mounted on a small stand. [< Sp, equiv. to *papel* PAPER + *-era* (fem.); see -ARY]

Pa·pen (pä′pən), *n.* **Franz von** (fränts fən), 1879–1969, German diplomat, statesman, and soldier.

pa·per (pā′pər), *n.* **1.** a substance made from wood pulp, rags, straw, or other fibrous material, usually in thin sheets, used to bear writing or printing, for wrapping things, etc. **2.** a piece, sheet, or leaf of this. **3.** something resembling this substance, as papyrus. **4.** a written or printed document or the like. **5.** stationery; writing paper. **6.** a newspaper or journal. **7.** an essay, article, or dissertation on a particular topic: *a paper on early Mayan artifacts.* **8.** Often, **papers.** a document establishing or verifying identity, status, or the like: *citizenship papers.* **9.** negotiable notes, bills, etc., as commercial paper or paper money: *Only silver, please, no paper.* **10.** a promissory note. **11. papers, a.** *Naut.* See **ship's papers. b.** See **rolling paper. 12.** wallpaper. **13.** See **toilet paper. 14.** a sheet or card of paper with pins or needles stuck through it in rows. **15.** a set of questions for an examination, an individual set of written answers to them, or any written piece of schoolwork. **16.** *Slang.* a free pass to an entertainment. **17. on paper, a.** in written or printed form. **b.** in theory rather than in practice. **c.** existing only in a preliminary state; in a plan or design: *The university building program is still only on paper.* —*v.t.* **18.** to cover with wallpaper or apply wallpaper to: *They papered the bedroom last summer.* **19.** to line or cover with paper. **20.** to distribute handbills, posters, etc., throughout: *to paper a neighborhood with campaign literature.* **21.** to fold, enclose, or wrap in paper. **22.** to supply with paper. **23.** *Informal.* to deluge with documents, esp. those requiring one to comply with certain technical procedures, as a means of legal harassment: *He papered the plaintiff to force a settlement.* **24.** *Slang.* to fill (a theater or the like) with spectators by giving away free tickets or passes. **25.** *Archaic.* **a.** to write or set down on paper. **b.** to describe in writing. —*v.i.* **26.** to apply wallpaper to walls. **27. paper over,** to patch up or attempt to conceal (a difference, disagreement, etc.) so as to preserve a friendship, present a unified opinion, etc.: *to paper over a dispute.* —*adj.* **28.** made of paper or paperlike material: *a paper bag.* **29.** paperlike; thin, flimsy, or frail. **30.** of, pertaining to, or noting routine clerical duties. **31.** pertaining to or carried on by means of letters, articles, books, etc.: *a paper war.* **32.** written or printed on paper. **33.** existing in theory or principle only and not in reality: *paper profits.* **34.** indicating the first event of a series, as a wedding anniversary. See table under **wedding anniversary. 35.** *Slang.* including many patrons admitted on free passes, as an audience for a theatrical performance: *It's a paper house tonight.* [1325–75; ME *papire* < L *papȳrus* PAPYRUS] —**pa′per·less,** *adj.* —**pa′per·like′,** *adj.*

pa·per·back (pā′pər bak′), *n.* **1.** a book bound in a flexible paper cover, often a lower-priced edition of a hardcover book. —*adj.* **2.** (of a book) bound in a flexible paper cover: *a paperback edition of Orwell's novel.* **3.** of, for, or pertaining to paperbacks: *a paperback bookstore.* Cf. **hardcover.** Also, **softcover; pa·per·bound** (pā′pər bound′), **softbound** (for defs. 1, 2). [1895–1900; PAPER + BACK¹]

pa·per·bark (pā′pər bärk′), *n.* cajeput. [1835–45; PAPER + BARK²]

pa′perbark ma′ple, a shrub or tree, *Acer griseum,* native to China, cultivated for its attractive papery brownish bark. [1925–30]

pa′per birch′, a North American birch, *Betula papyrifera,* having a tough bark and yielding a valuable wood: the state tree of New Hampshire. Also called **canoe birch.** [1800–10, *Amer.*]

pa·per·board (pā′pər bôrd′, -bōrd′), *n.* **1.** a thick, stiff cardboard composed of layers of paper or paper pulp compressed together; pasteboard. —*adj.* **2.** of, pertaining to, or made of paperboard. [1540–50; PAPER + BOARD]

pa·per·boy (pā′pər boi′), *n.* a youth or man who sells newspapers on the street or delivers them to homes; newsboy. [1875–80; PAPER + BOY]

pa′per chase′, **1.** the effort to earn a diploma or college degree, esp. in law, or a professional certificate or license. **2.** the writing of assignments and reports, collecting of supporting documents, filling out of forms, and other paperwork necessary to obtain a college degree or a professional certificate or license, apply for financial aid or a bank loan, etc. **3.** See **hare and hounds.** [1855–60] —**pa′per chas′er.** —**pa′·per-chas′ing,** *adj., n.*

pa′per chromatog′raphy, *Chem.* See under **chromatography.** [1945–50]

pa′per clip′, **1.** a flat wire or plastic clip shaped so that it can hold sheets of paper between two of its loops. **2.** a spring clamp for holding papers. [1870–75]

pa·per-clip (pā′pər klip′), *v.t.,* **-clipped, -clip·ping.** to fasten together with one or more paper clips: *Paperclip these letters and file them.* [1960–65]

pa′per cut′ter, any device for cutting or trimming paper, typically a weighted, powered, or spring-hinged blade mounted on or over a ruled board or table on which many sheets of paper may be aligned for cutting at one time. [1820–30] —**pa′per-cut′ting,** *adj.*

pa′per doll′, **1.** a paper or cardboard, usually two-dimensional, representation of the human figure, used as a child's toy. **2.** Usually, **paper dolls.** a connected series of doll-like figures cut from folded paper. [1840–50]

pa·per·er (pā′pər ər), *n.* **1.** a paperhanger. **2.** a person who lines or covers something with paper. [1835–45; PAPER + -ER¹]

pa·per·girl (pā′pər gûrl′), *n.* a girl who delivers newspapers to homes. [PAPER + GIRL]

pa′per gold′, *Informal.* See **special drawing rights.** [1965–70]

pa·per·hang·er (pā′pər hang′ər), *n.* **1.** a person whose job is covering walls with wallpaper. **2.** *Slang.* a person who passes worthless checks. [1790–1800; PAPER + HANGER]

pa·per·hang·ing (pā′pər hang′ing), *n.* **1.** the activity or business of a paperhanger. **2. paperhangings,** *Archaic.* wallpaper. [1685–95; PAPER + HANGING]

pa′per knife′, **1.** a small, often decorative, knifelike instrument with a blade of metal, ivory, wood, or the like, for slitting open envelopes, the leaves of books, folded papers, etc. **2.** the blade of a paper cutter.

pa·per-mâ·ché (pā′pər mə shā′, -ma-), *n., adj.* papier-mâché.

pa·per·mak·er (pā′pər mā′kər), *n.* a person or thing that makes paper. [1565–75; PAPER + MAKER] —**pa′·per·mak′ing,** *n.*

pa′per match′. See **book match.** [1825–35]

pa′per mon′ey, currency in paper form, such as government and bank notes, as distinguished from metal currency. [1350–1400; ME]

pa′per mul′berry, a mulberry tree, *Broussonetia papyrifera,* of eastern Asia, having alternate leaves that vary in size, round catkins, and orange-red fruit, grown widely as a shade tree. [1770–80; so called because its bark is used to make paper]

pa′per nau′tilus, any dibranchiate cephalopod of the genus *Argonauta,* the female of which has a delicate, white shell. [1825–35]

pa·per·per·son (pā′pər pûr′sən), *n.* a person who delivers newspapers to customers door to door. [PAPER(BOY) + -PERSON]
—**Usage.** See **-person.**

pa′per prof′it, an unrealized profit due to the appreciation of something owned but not yet sold. [1890–95]

pa·per·push·er (pā′pər pŏŏsh′ər), *n. Informal.* **1.** a person who has a routine desk job. **2.** a bureaucrat. Also called **pa·per·shuf·fler** (pā′pər shuf′lər). —**pa′·per-push′ing,** *adj.*

pa·per-shelled (pā′pər sheld′), *adj.* having a thin, easily broken shell: *paper-shelled nuts.* [1880–85]

pa′per tape′, *Computers.* a narrow strip of paper in which holes are punched in designated patterns to represent characters: formerly in common use as an input/-output medium. Also called **punched tape.**

pa·per-thin (pā′pər thin′), *adj.* **1.** extremely thin: *a paper-thin razor blade.* **2.** inadequate or unconvincing; flimsy: *a paper-thin excuse.* [1925–30]

pa′per ti′ger, a person, group, nation, or thing that has the appearance of strength or power but is actually weak or ineffectual. [1945–50]

pa′per trail′, a written or printed record, as of transactions or judicial opinions, esp. when used to incriminate someone. [1975–80]

pa·per-train (pā′pər trān′), *v.t.* to train (a pet) to defecate or urinate on sheets of disposable paper.

pa′per wasp′, any of several social wasps, as the yellow jacket or hornet, that construct a nest of a paperlike substance consisting of chewed plant material. [1850–55, *Amer.*]

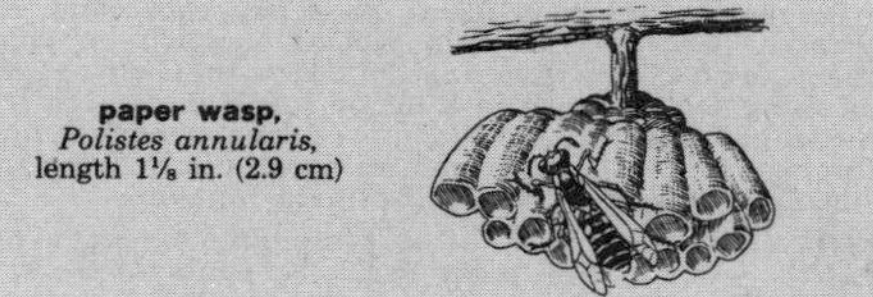
paper wasp, *Polistes annularis,* length 1⅛ in. (2.9 cm)

pa·per·weight (pā′pər wāt′), *n.* a small, heavy object of glass, metal, etc., placed on papers to keep them from scattering. [1855–60; PAPER + WEIGHT]

pa′per-white narcis′sus (pā′pər hwīt′, -wīt′), a white-flowered variety of *Narcissus tazetta,* often forced for indoor bloom. Also called **pa′per-white′.**

pa·per·work (pā′pər wûrk′), *n.* written or clerical work, as records or reports, forming a necessary but often a routine and secondary part of some work or job. [1580–90; PAPER + WORK]

pa·per·y (pā′pə rē), *adj.* like paper; thin or flimsy: *the papery petals of the narcissus.* [1620–30; PAPER + -Y¹] —**pa′per·i·ness,** *n.*

pap·e·terie (pap′i trē; *Fr.* paᴘᵊ tʀē′), *n., pl.* **-teries** (-trēz; *Fr.* -tʀē′). a box for holding stationery, esp. an ornamental one. [1840–50; < F, equiv. to *papet(ier)* papermaker or dealer (deriv. of *papier* PAPER; see -IER²) + *-erie* -ERY]

Pa·phi·an (pā′fē ən), *adj.* **1.** of or pertaining to Paphos, an ancient city of Cyprus sacred to Aphrodite. **2.** of or pertaining to love, esp. illicit sexual love; erotic; wanton. **3.** noting or pertaining to Aphrodite or to her worship or service. —*n.* **4. the Paphian,** Aphrodite: so called from her cult center at Paphos. **5.** (*often l.c.*) a prostitute. [1605–15; < L *Paphi(us)* (< Gk *Páphios* of Paphos, of Aphrodite) + -AN]

Pa′phian God′dess, *Class. Myth.* Aphrodite, worshiped in Cyprus as the goddess of sexual love.

Paph·la·go·ni·a (paf′lə gō′nē ə, -gōn′yə), *n.* an ancient country and Roman province in N Asia Minor, on the S coast of the Black Sea.

Pa·phos (pā′fos), *n.* **1.** an ancient city in SW Cyprus. **2.** Also, **Pa·phus** (pā′fəs). *Class. Myth.* the son of Pygmalion, who inherited the throne of Cyprus.

Pa·pia·men·to (pä′pyä men′tô; *Eng.* pä′pyə men′tō), *n.* a creolized language based on Spanish and spoken on Curaçao.

pa·pier col·lé (*Fr.* pa pyā′ kô lā′), *pl.* **pa·piers col·lés** (*Fr.* pa pyā′ kô lā′). collage. [< F: lit., glued paper]

pa·pier-mâ·ché (pā′pər mə shā′, -ma-; *Fr.* pa pyā-mä shā′), *n.* **1.** a substance made of pulped paper or paper pulp mixed with glue and other materials or of layers of paper glued and pressed together, molded when moist to form various articles, and becoming hard and strong when dry. —*adj.* **2.** made of papier-mâché. **3.** easily destroyed or discredited; false, pretentious, or illusory: *a papier-mâché façade of friendship.* Also, **paper-mâché.** [1745–55; < F: lit., chewed paper]

pa·pil·i·o·na·ceous (pə pil′ē ə nā′shəs), *adj. Bot.* **1.** having an irregular corolla shaped somewhat like a butterfly, as the pea and other leguminous plants. **2.** belonging to the family Papilionaceae (Fabaceae), that is often included as part of the Leguminosae. [1660–70; < L *pāpiliōn-* (s. of *pāpiliō*) butterfly + -ACEOUS]

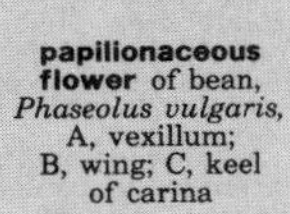

papilionaceous flower of bean, *Phaseolus vulgaris,* A, vexillum; B, wing; C, keel of carina

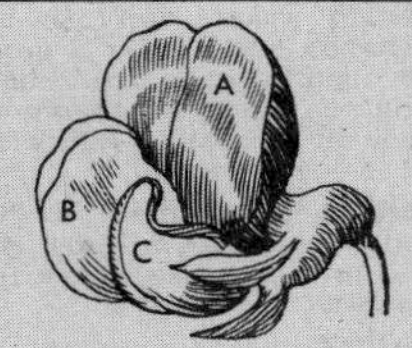

pa·pil·la (pə pil′ə), *n., pl.* **-pil·lae** (-pil′ē). **1.** any small, nipplelike process or projection. **2.** one of certain small protuberances concerned with the senses of touch, taste, and smell: *the papillae of the tongue.* **3.** a small vascular process at the root of a hair. See diag. under **hair. 4.** a papule or pimple. [1400–50; late ME < L: nipple, teat, dim. of *papula* pimple. See PAP²] —**pap·il·lar** (pap′ə lər, pə pil′ər), *adj.*

pap·il·lar·y (pap′ə ler′ē, pə pil′ə rē), *adj.* **1.** of, pertaining to, or of the nature of a papilla or papillae. **2.** having or covered with papillae. [1660–70; < L *papill(a)* nipple + -ARY]

pap′illary mus′cle, *Anat.* one of the small bundles of muscles attached to the ventricle walls and to the chordae tendineae that tighten these tendons during ventricular contraction. [1885–90]

pa·pil·li·form (pə pil′ə fôrm′), *adj.* resembling a papilla. [1820–30; PAPILL(A) + -I- + -FORM]

pap·il·lo·ma (pap′ə lō′mə), *n., pl.* **-ma·ta** (-mə tə), **-mas.** *Pathol.* a benign tumor of the skin or mucous membrane consisting of hypertrophied epithelial tissue, as a wart. [1865–70; < NL; see PAPILLA, -OMA] —**pap′·il·lo′ma·to′sis,** *n.* —**pap·il·lo·ma·tous** (pap′ə lō′mə təs, -lom′ə-), *adj.*

pap·il·lo·ma·vi·rus (pap′ə lō′mə vī′rəs), *n., pl.* **-rus·es.** any of several viruses of the family Papovaviridae, containing circular DNA, causing papillomas in various animals and responsible for human genital warts. [PAPILLOMA + VIRUS]

pap·il·lon (pap′ə lon′; *Fr.* pa pē yôN′), *n., pl.* **-lons** (-lon′; *Fr.* -yôN′). one of a breed of toy spaniels having a long, silky coat and large, erect ears held so that they resemble the wings of a butterfly. [1905–10; < F: butterfly < L *pāpiliōn-* (s. of *pāpiliō*)]

pap·il·lose (pap′ə lōs′), *adj.* full of papillae. [1745–55; PAPILL(A) + -OSE¹] —**pap·il·los·i·ty** (pap′ə los′i tē), *n.*

pap·il·lote (pap′ə lōt′; *Fr.* pa pē yôt′), *n.* **1.** a decorative curled paper placed over the end of the bone of a cutlet or chop. **2.** a wrapping of foil or oiled paper in which food is cooked and served. **3.** See **en papillote.** [1740–50; < F, irreg. deriv. of *papillon* butterfly. See PAPILLON]

Pa·pin·i·an (pə pin′ē ən), *n.* (*Aemilius Papinianus*), died A.D. 212, Roman jurist and writer.

pa·pism (pā′piz əm), *n. Usually Disparaging.* Roman Catholicism. [1540–50; < MF *papisme.* See POPE, -ISM]

pa·pist (pā′pist), *Usually Disparaging.* —*n.* **1.** a Roman Catholic. —*adj.* **2.** papistical. [1515–25; earlier *papista* < NL. See POPE, -IST] —**pa′pist·like′,** *adj.* —**pa′pist·ly,** *adv.*

pa·pis·ti·cal (pā pis′ti kəl, pə-), *adj. Usually Disparaging.* of or pertaining to the Roman Catholic Church. Also, **pa·pis′tic.** [1530–40; prob. < MF *papistique* (see PAPIST, -IC) + -AL¹] —**pa·pis′ti·cal·ly,** *adv.*

pa·pist·ry (pā′pə strē), *n. Usually Disparaging.* the Roman Catholic Church. [1540–50; PAPIST + -RY]

pa·poose (pa po͞os′, pə-), *n.* a North American Indian baby or young child. Also, **pap·poose′.** [1625–35, *Amer.;* < Narragansett (E sp.) *papoòs* baby, or Massachusett (E sp.) *pappouse*]

pa·poose-root (pa po͞os′ro͞ot′, -ro͝ot′, pə-), *n.* the blue cohosh. See under **cohosh.** [1805–15, *Amer.*]

pa·po·va·vi·rus (pə pō′və vī′rəs), *n., pl.* **-rus·es.** *Pathol., Vet. Pathol.* any of a group of DNA-containing human and animal viruses, including polyoma viruses and some papillomaviruses, most of which produce tumors. [1962; PA(PILLOMA) + PO(LYOMA) + *va(cuolating)* (repr. three virus groups in the order in which they became known) + VIRUS]

Papp (pap), *n.* **Joseph** (*Yosl Papirofsky*), 1921–91, U.S. theatrical producer and director.

pap·pen·hei·mer (pap′ən hī′mər, pä′pən-), *n.* a heavy rapier of the 17th century, having a swept guard with two perforated plates. Also called **Walloon sword.** [named after Gottfried Heinrich, Graf zu *Pappenheim* (1594–1632), German leader in the Thirty Years' War; see -ER¹]

pap·pose (pap′ōs), *adj. Bot.* **1.** having or forming a pappus. **2.** downy. Also, **pap·pous** (pap′əs). [1625–35; PAPP(US) + -OSE¹]

pap·pus (pap′əs), *n., pl.* **pap·pi** (pap′ī). *Bot.* a downy, bristly, or other tuftlike appendage of the achene of certain plants, as the dandelion and the thistle. [1695–1705; < NL < Gk *páppos* down, lit., grandfather (taken as greybeard, white hairs, down)]

pap·py¹ (pap′ē), *adj.,* **-pi·er, -pi·est.** like pap; mushy. [1670–80; PAP¹ + -Y¹]

pap·py² (pap′ē), *n., pl.* **-pies.** *Older Use.* father. [1755–65; PAP(A) + -Y²]

pap·ri·ka (pa prē′kə, pə-, pä-, pap′ri kə), *n.* **1.** a red, powdery condiment derived from dried, ripe sweet peppers. —*adj.* **2.** cooked or seasoned with paprika. [1895–1900; < Hungarian < Serbo-Croatian *pàprika* pepper, paprika, deriv. of *pàpar* ground pepper < Slavic **pĭprŭ,* **pipĭrŭ* (cf. OCS *pĭprŭ,* Slovene *péper,* Czech *pepř,* Pol *pieprz*) << L *piper* PEPPER]

Pap′ test′ (pap), **1.** a test for cancer of the cervix, consisting of the staining of cervical cells taken in a cervical or vaginal smear **(Pap′ smear′** or **pap′ smear′)** for examination of exfoliated cells. **2.** a vaginal Pap smear used to evaluate estrogen levels. **3.** an examination of exfoliated cells in any body fluid, as sputum or urine, for cancer cells. Also, **pap′ test′.** Also called **Papanicolaou test.** [1960–65; named after George *Papanicolaou* (1883–1962), U.S. cytologist, born in Greece, who developed the staining method]

Pap·u·a (pap′yo͞o ə, pä′po͞o ä′), *n.* **1.** See **Papua New Guinea. 2. Gulf of,** an inlet of the Coral Sea on the SE coast of New Guinea.

Pap·u·an (pap′yo͞o ən), *adj.* **1.** of or pertaining to New Guinea or to Papua New Guinea. **2.** noting or pertaining to the indigenous black peoples of New Guinea, characterized by a black or dark brown complexion and crisp, frizzled hair. **3.** of or pertaining to any of the unaffiliated languages indigenous to New Guinea and other islands nearby, esp. Timor, the Bismarck Archipelago, the Moluccas, and the Solomons. —*n.* **4.** a native or inhabitant of New Guinea or Papua New Guinea. **5.** any of the Papuan languages. [1805–15; PAPU(A) + -AN]

Pap′ua New′ Guin′ea, an independent republic in the W Pacific Ocean, comprising the E part of New Guinea and numerous near-lying islands, including the Bismarck Archipelago, the Admiralty Islands, the Trobriand Islands, and Bougainville and Buka in the Solomon Islands: a former Australian Trusteeship Territory; independent since 1975; member of the Commonwealth of Nations. 3,000,000; 178,260 sq. mi. (461,693 sq. km). *Cap.:* Port Moresby.

Pap′ua New′ Guin′ean, 1. a native or inhabitant of Papua New Guinea. **2.** of or pertaining to Papua New Guinea or its people. [1970–75; PAPUA NEW GUINE(A) + -AN]

pap·u·la (pap′yə lə), *n., pl.* **-lae** (-lē′). one of the small, ciliated projections of the body wall of an echinoderm, serving for respiration and excretion. [1700–10; < NL, L: pimple, pustule. See PAPULE]

pap·ule (pap′yo͞ol), *n. Pathol.* a small, somewhat pointed elevation of the skin, usually inflammatory but nonsuppurative. [1855–60; < L *papula* pimple, pustule, akin to *papilla* nipple. See PAP², -ULE] —**pap′u·lar,** *adj.* —**pap·u·lose** (pap′yə lōs′), *adj.*

pap·y·ra·ceous (pap′ə rā′shəs), *adj.* papery. [1745–55; < L *papȳr(us)* PAPYRUS + -ACEOUS]

pap·y·rol·o·gy (pap′ə rol′ə jē), *n.* the study of papyrus manuscripts. [1895–1900; PAPYR(US) + -O- + -LOGY] —**pa·py·ro·log·i·cal** (pə pī′rə loj′i kəl, pa pĕr′ə-), *adj.* —**pap′y·rol′o·gist,** *n.*

pa·py·rus (pə pī′rəs), *n., pl.* **-py·ri** (-pī′rī, -rē), **-py·rus·es. 1.** a tall, aquatic plant, *Cyperus papyrus,* of the sedge family, native to the Nile valley: the Egyptian subspecies, *C. papyrus hadidii,* thought to be common in ancient times, now occurs only in several sites. **2.** a material on which to write, prepared from thin strips of the pith of this plant laid together, soaked, pressed, and dried, used by the ancient Egyptians, Greeks, and Romans. **3.** an ancient document, manuscript, or scroll written on this material. [1350–1400; ME *papirus* < L *papȳrus* < Gk *pápȳros*] —**pa·py′ral, pa·pyr·i·an** (pə pir′ē ən), **pa·py·rine** (pə pī′rin), *adj.* —**pap·y·ri·tious** (pap′ə rish′əs), *adj.*

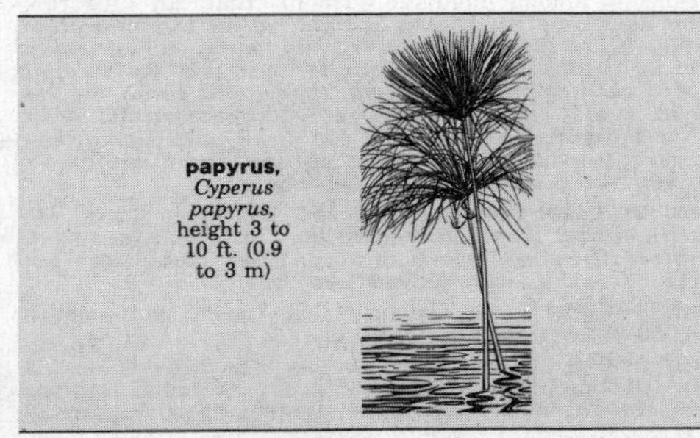

papyrus, *Cyperus papyrus,* height 3 to 10 ft. (0.9 to 3 m)

par¹ (pär), *n., adj., v.,* **parred, par·ring.** —*n.* **1.** an equality in value or standing; a level of equality: *The gains and the losses are on a par.* **2.** an average, usual, or normal amount, degree, quality, condition, standard, or the like: *above par; to feel below par.* **3.** *Golf.* the number of strokes set as a standard for a specific hole or a complete course. **4.** *Finance.* **a.** the legally established value of the monetary unit of one country in terms of that of another using the same metal as a standard of value. **b.** the state of the shares of any business, undertaking, loan, etc., when they may be purchased at the original price **(issue par)** or at their face value **(nominal par). 5. at par,** *Finance.* (of a share) purchasable at issue par or nominal par. **6. par for the course,** exactly what one might expect; typical: *They were late again, but that's par for the course.* —*adj.* **7.** average or normal. **8.** *Finance.* at or pertaining to par: *the par value of a bond.* —*v.t.* **9.** *Golf.* to equal par on (a hole or course). [1615–25; < L *pār* equal]

par² (pär), *adj. Insurance.* of or pertaining to participating insurance. [shortening of PARTICIPATING]

par-, var. of **para-**¹ before a vowel: *parenchyma.*

par., 1. paragraph. **2.** parallel. **3.** parenthesis. **4.** parish.

pa·ra¹ (pä rä′, pär′ä), *n., pl.* **-ras, -ra.** a former copper coin of Turkey, the 40th part of a piaster. [1680–90; < Turk < Pers *pāra* lit., piece]

pa·ra² (pä rä′, pär′ä), *n., pl.* **-ras, -ra.** an aluminum-bronze coin and monetary unit of Yugoslavia, the 100th part of a dinar. [1905–10; < Serbo-Croatian *pȁra* < Turk; see PARA¹]

par·a³ (par′ə), *adj. Chem.* **1.** pertaining to or occupying two positions (1, 4) in the benzene ring that are separated by two carbon atoms. Cf. **ortho, meta². —***n.* **2.** para-dichlorobenzene. [1875–80; independent use of PARA-¹]

par·a⁴ (par′ə), *n. Informal.* **1.** a paraprofessional. **2.** a paratrooper. [1955–60; by shortening of words compounded with PARA-¹, PARA-³]

par·a⁵ (par′ə), *n., pl.* **par·as, par·ae** (par′ē). *Obstetrics.* **1.** Also called **parity.** a woman's status regarding the bearing of viable offspring: usually followed by a Roman numeral designating the number of times the woman has given birth. **2.** the woman herself. Cf. **gravida.** [1880–85; extracted from PRIMAPARA, MULTIPARA, etc.]

Pa·rá (pä rä′), *n.* **1.** an estuary in N Brazil: an arm of the Amazon. 200 mi. (320 km) long; 40 mi. (65 km) wide. **2.** Belém. **3.** See **Pará rubber.**

para-¹, **1.** a prefix appearing in loanwords from Greek, most often attached to verbs and verbal derivatives, with the meanings "at or to one side of, beside, side by side" (*parabola; paragraph; parallel; paralysis*), "beyond, past, by" (*paradox; paragogue*); by extension from these senses, this prefix came to designate objects or activities auxiliary to or derivative of that denoted by the base word (*parody; paronomasia*), and hence abnormal or defective (*paranoia*), a sense now common in modern scientific coinages (*parageusia; paralexia*). As an English prefix, **para-**¹ may have any of these senses; it is also productive in the naming of occupational roles considered ancillary or subsidiary to roles requiring more training, or of a higher status, on such models as **paramedical** and **paraprofessional:** *paralegal; paralibrarian; parapolice.* **2.** *Chem.* a combining form designating the para (1, 4) position in the benzene ring. *Abbr.:* p-. Cf. **meta-** (def. 2c), **ortho-** (def. 2b). See diag. under **ortho-.** Also, *esp. before a vowel,* **par-.** [< Gk *para-,* comb. form repr. *pará* (prep.) beside, alongside of, by, beyond]

para-², a combining form meaning "guard against," occurring in loanwords from French, or, via French, from Italian: *parachute; parasol.* [< F < It *para,* 3d sing. pres. of *parare* to prepare against, ward off < L *parāre* to PREPARE]

para-³, a combining form extracted from **parachute,** forming compounds denoting persons or things utilizing parachutes or landed by parachute: *paradrop; paradoctor; paraglider; paratrooper.*

Para., Paraguay.

par′a-a·mi·no·ben·zo′ic ac′id (par′ə ə mē′nō-ben zō′ik, -am′ə nō-), *Chem., Biochem.* part of the folic acid molecule, a white or yellowish, crystalline, slightly water-soluble solid, $C_7H_7NO_2$, the para isomer of aminobenzoic acid: used chiefly in the manufacture of dyes and pharmaceuticals and in sunscreens to protect against ultraviolet light. *Abbr.:* PABA [1905–10; PARA-¹ + AMINO- + BENZOIC ACID]

pa·rab·a·sis (pə rab′ə sis), *n., pl.* **-ses** (-sēz′). (in ancient Greek drama) a choral ode addressed to the audience, esp. of comedy, and independent of the action of the play: usually following the *agon* and, in the earliest forms of comedy, serving often to end the play. [1810–20; < Gk *parábasis* a going aside, digression; see PARA-¹, BASIS]

par·a·bi·o·sis (par′ə bī ō′sis, -bē-), *n. Biol.* **1.** experimental or natural union of two individuals with exchange of blood. **2.** *Physiol.* the temporary loss of conductivity or excitability of a nerve cell. [1905–10; PARA-¹ + -BIOSIS] —**par·a·bi·ot·ic** (par′ə bī ot′ik, -bē-), *adj.*

par·a·blast (par′ə blast′), *n. Biol.* the nutritive yolk of a meroblastic ovum or egg. [1855–60; PARA-¹ + -BLAST] —**par′a·blas′tic,** *adj.*

par·a·ble (par′ə bəl), *n.* **1.** a short allegorical story designed to illustrate or teach some truth, religious principle, or moral lesson. **2.** a statement or comment that conveys a meaning indirectly by the use of comparison, analogy, or the like. [1275–1325; ME *parabil* < LL *pa-*

CONCISE PRONUNCIATION KEY: act, cāpe, dâre, pärt; set, ēqual; if, ice; ox, ōver, ôrder, oil, bo͝ok, bo͞ot, out; up, ûrge; child; sing; shoe; thin, that; zh as in treasure. ə = a as in alone, e as in system, i as in easily, o as in gallop, u as in circus; ᵊ as in fire (fīᵊr), hour (ouᵊr). l and n can serve as syllabic consonants, as in cradle (krād′l), and button (but′n). See the full key inside the front cover.

rabola comparison, parable, word < Gk *parabolḗ* comparison, equiv. to *para-* PARA-[1] + *bolḗ* a throwing] —**pa·rab′o·list** (pə rab′ə list), *n.*
—**Syn. 1.** allegory, homily, apologue.

pa·rab·o·la (pə rab′ə lə), *n. Geom.* a plane curve formed by the intersection of a right circular cone with a plane parallel to a generator of the cone; the set of points in a plane that are equidistant from a fixed line and a fixed point in the same plane or in a parallel plane. Equation: $y^2 = 2px$ or $x^2 = 2py$. See diag. under **conic section.** [1570–80; < NL < Gk *parabolḗ* an application. See PARABLE]

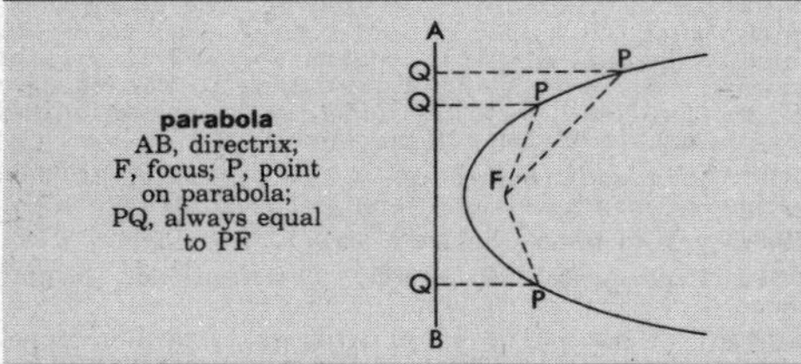

parabola
AB, directrix;
F, focus; P, point on parabola;
PQ, always equal to PF

par·a·bol·ic[1] (par′ə bol′ik), *adj.* **1.** having the form or outline of a parabola. **2.** having a longitudinal section in the form of a paraboloid or parabola: *a parabolic reflector.* **3.** of, pertaining to, or resembling a parabola. [1695–1705; PARABOL(A) + -IC]

par·a·bol·ic[2] (par′ə bol′ik), *adj.* of, pertaining to, or involving a parable. Also, **par′a·bol′i·cal.** [1650–60; < LL *parabolicus* metaphoric < LGk *parabolikós* figurative, equiv. to Gk *parabol(ḗ)* PARABLE + *-ikos* -IC] —**par′a·bol′i·cal·ism,** *n.* —**par′a·bol′i·cal·ly,** *adv.*

pa·rab·o·lize[1] (pə rab′ə līz′), *v.t.,* **-lized, -liz·ing.** to tell or explain in a parable or parables. Also, *esp. Brit.,* **pa·rab′o·lise′.** [1590–1600; < LL *parabol(a)* PARABLE + -IZE] —**pa·rab′o·li·za′tion,** *n.* —**pa·rab′o·liz′er,** *n.*

pa·rab·o·lize[2] (pə rab′ə līz′), *v.t.,* **-lized, -liz·ing.** to form as a parabola or paraboloid. Also, *esp. Brit.,* **pa·rab′o·lise′.** [1865–70; PARABOL(A) + -IZE] —**pa·rab′o·li·za′tion,** *n.* —**pa·rab′o·liz′er,** *n.*

pa·rab·o·loid (pə rab′ə loid′), *n. Geom.* a surface that can be put into a position such that its sections parallel to at least one coordinate plane are parabolas. Cf. **elliptic paraboloid, hyperbolic paraboloid.** [1650–60; PARABOL(A) + -OID] —**pa·rab·o·loi·dal** (pə rab′ə loid′l, par′ə bə-), *adj.*

par·a·brake (par′ə brāk′), *n.* See **parachute brake.** [1950–55; PARA-[3] + BRAKE[1]]

Par·a·cel·sus (par′ə sel′səs), *n.* **1. Phi·lip·pus Au·re·o·lus** (fi lip′əs ō rē′ō ləs), (*Theophrastus Bombastus von Hohenheim*), 1493?–1541, Swiss physician and alchemist. **2.** (*italics*) a dramatic poem (1835) by Robert Browning, based on the life of Paracelsus. —**Par′a·cel′si·an,** *adj., n.* —**Par′a·cel′si·an·ism,** *n.* —**Par′a·cel′sic, Par′a·cel·sis′tic,** *adj.* —**Par′a·cel′sist,** *n.*

par·a·cen·te·sis (par′ə sen tē′sis), *n., pl.* **-ses** (-sēz). *Surg.* puncture of the wall of a cavity to drain off fluid. Also called **tapping.** [1590–1600; < L *paracentēsis* perforation, tapping < Gk *parakéntēsis,* equiv. to *parakentē-,* var. s. of *parakenteîn* to prick beside (*para-* PARA-[1] + *kenteîn* to prick, pierce) + *-sis* -SIS]

par·ac·et·al·de·hyde (par′as i tal′də hīd′), *n. Chem.* paraldehyde. [PAR- + ACETALDEHYDE]

pa·rach·ro·nism (pa rak′rə niz′əm), *n.* a chronological error in which a person, event, etc., is assigned a date later than the actual one. Cf. **anachronism, prochronism.** [1635–45; PARA-[1] + CHRON- + -ISM] —**par·ach′·ro·nis′tic,** *adj.*

par·a·chute (par′ə sho͞ot′), *n., v.,* **-chut·ed, -chut·ing.** —*n.* **1.** a folding, umbrellalike, fabric device with cords supporting a harness or straps for allowing a person, object, package, etc., to float down safely through the air from a great height, esp. from an aircraft, rendered effective by the resistance of the air that expands it during the descent and reduces the velocity of its fall. **2.** See **parachute brake. 3.** *Horol.* a shockproofing device for the balance staff of a watch, consisting of a yielding, springlike support for the bearing at either end. **4.** *Informal.* **a.** the aggregate of benefits, as severance pay or vacation pay, given an employee who is dismissed from a company. **b.** See **golden parachute.** —*v.t.* **5.** to drop or land (troops, equipment, supplies, etc.) by parachute. —*v.i.* **6.** to descend by parachute. [1775–85; < F, equiv. to *para-* PARA-[2] + *chute* fall; see CHUTE[1]] —**par′a·chut′ic,** *adj.* —**par′a·chut′ist, par′a·chut′er,** *n.*

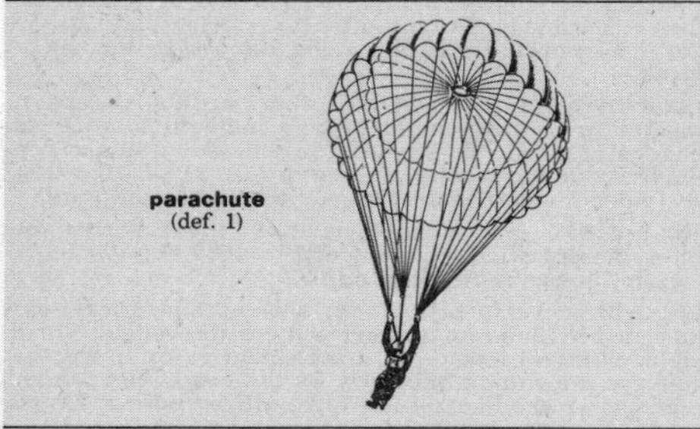
parachute
(def. 1)

CONCISE ETYMOLOGY KEY: <, descended or borrowed from; >, whence; b., blend of, blended; c., cognate with; cf., compare; deriv., derivative; equiv., equivalent; imit., imitative; obl., oblique; r., replacing; s., stem; sp., spelling, spelled; resp., respelling, respelled; trans., translation; ?, origin unknown; *, unattested; ‡, probably earlier than. See the full key inside the front cover.

par′achute brake′, a parachute opened horizontally from the tail of an airplane upon landing, used as an aid in braking. Also called **parabrake.** Cf. **drogue parachute** (def. 2).

par′achute rig′ger, a person who inspects, repairs, and packs or folds parachutes. Also called **rigger.**

par·a·clete (par′ə klēt′), *n.* **1.** an advocate or intercessor. **2.** (*cap.*) the Holy Spirit; the Comforter. [1400–50; < ML, LL *Paraclētus* < LGk *Paráklētos* comforter, lit., (person) called in (to help), verbal of *parakaleîn* (equiv. to *para-* PARA-[1] + *kaleîn* to call); r. late ME *paraclit* < ML *Paraclītus,* repr. MGk *Paráklētos*]

par·a·coc·cid·i·oi·do·my·co·sis (par′ə kok sid′ē oi′dō mī kō′sis), *n. Pathol.* a chronic infection caused by the fungus *Paracoccidioides brasiliensis,* occurring in Mexico and in Central and South America, characterized by mouth and throat ulcers, weight loss, and lesions on the skin, intestines, and genitals. [< NL *Paracoccidioid(es)* a genus of fungi (see PARA-[1], COCCIDIA, -OID) + -O- + MYCOSIS]

par·a·cu·sis (par′ə kyo͞o′sis), *n. Pathol.* defective hearing. Also, **par·a·cu·sia** (par′ə kyo͞o′zhə, -zhē ə, -zē ə). [1650–60; PAR- + Gk *ákousis* hearing; see ACOUSTIC, -SIS] —**par·a·cu·sic,** (par′ə kyo͞o′zik, -sik), *adj.*

par·a·cy·e·sis (par′ə sī ē′sis), *n., pl.* **-ses** (-sēz). *Med.* See **ectopic pregnancy.** [1815–25; PARA-[1] + CYESIS]

par·a·cy·mene (par′ə sī′mēn), *n. Chem.* a colorless liquid, $C_{10}H_{14}$, derived from benzene, found in various essential oils, and obtained as a by-product of papermaking. Cf. **cymene.** [PARA-[1] + CYMENE]

par·a·cys·ti·tis (par′ə si stī′tis), *n. Pathol.* inflammation of the connective tissue around the urinary bladder. [1875–80; PARA-[1] + CYSTITIS]

pa·rade (pə rād′), *n., v.,* **-rad·ed, -rad·ing.** —*n.* **1.** a large public procession, usually including a marching band and often of a festive nature, held in honor of an anniversary, person, event, etc. **2.** a military ceremony involving the formation and marching of troop units, often combined with saluting the lowering of the flag at the end of the day. **3.** the assembly of troops for inspection or display. **4.** a place where troops regularly assemble for inspection or display. **5.** a continual passing by, as of people, objects, or events: *the parade of pedestrians past the office; the parade of the seasons.* **6.** an ostentatious display: *to make a parade of one's religious beliefs.* **7.** *Chiefly Brit.* **a.** a group or procession of promenaders. **b.** a promenade. **8.** *Fort.* the level space forming the interior or enclosed area of a fortification. **9.** *Fencing.* a parry. —*v.t.* **10.** to walk up and down on or in. **11.** to make parade of; display ostentatiously. **12.** to cause to march or proceed for display. —*v.i.* **13.** to march in a procession. **14.** to promenade in a public place, esp. in order to show off. **15.** to assemble in military order for display. **16.** to assume a false or misleading appearance: *international pressure that parades as foreign aid.* [1650–60; < F, MF < Sp *parada* a stop, stopping place, n. use of fem. of *parado,* ptp. of *parar* to stop, end < L *parāre* to set. See COMPARE, PARRY, -ADE[1]] —**pa·rade′ful,** *adj.* —**pa·rade′less,** *adj.* —**pa·rade′·like′,** *adj.* —**pa·rad′er,** *n.* —**pa·rad′ing·ly,** *adv.*
—**Syn. 11.** show, flaunt, flourish. —**Ant. 11.** conceal.

parade′ ar′mor, ornamented armor worn only for ceremonial purposes.

parade′ bed′, *Hist.* a royal bed from which levees were held.

parade′ rest′, *Mil.* **1.** a position assumed by a soldier or sailor in which the feet are 12 in. (30.48 cm) apart, the hands are clasped behind the back, and the head is held motionless and facing forward. **2.** a command to assume this position. [1860–65]

par·a·di·chlo·ro·ben·zene (par′ə dī klôr′ə ben′zēn, -ben zēn′, -klōr′-), *n. Chem.* a white, crystalline, volatile, water-insoluble solid, $C_6H_4Cl_2$, of the benzene series, having a penetrating odor: used chiefly as a moth repellent. Also, **par′a·di·chlo′ro·ben′zene.** Also called **PDB, para.** Cf. **dichlorobenzene.** [1875–80; PARA-[1] + DI-[1] + CHLORO-[2] + BENZENE]

par·a·did·dle (par′ə did′l), *n.* an exercise or sequence performed typically on the snare drum, marked by four basic beats with alternation of the right hand and left hand on successive strong beats, and begun and ended slowly with a dramatic increase in tempo in the middle. [1925–30; staccato syllables partly imit.; cf. DIDDLE[2]; perh. with PARA-[1] facetiously representing the alternation]

par·a·digm (par′ə dīm′, -dim), *n.* **1.** *Gram.* **a.** a set of forms all of which contain a particular element, esp. the set of all inflected forms based on a single stem or theme. **b.** a display in fixed arrangement of such a set, as *boy, boy's, boys, boys'.* **2.** an example serving as a model; pattern. [1475–85; < LL *paradigma* < Gk *parádeigma* pattern (verbid of *paradeiknýnai* to show side by side), equiv. to *para-* PARA-[1] + *deik-,* base of *deiknýnai* to show (see DEICTIC) + *-ma* n. suffix]
—**Syn. 2.** mold, standard; ideal, paragon, touchstone.

par·a·dig·mat·ic (par′ə dig mat′ik), *adj.* **1.** of or pertaining to a paradigm. **2.** *Ling.* pertaining to a relationship among linguistic elements that can substitute for each other in a given context, as the relationship of *sun* in *The sun is shining* to other nouns, as *moon, star,* or *light,* that could substitute for it in that sentence, or of *is shining* to *was shining, shone, will shine,* etc., as well as to *is rising, is setting,* etc. Cf. **syntagmatic.** Also, **par′a·dig·mat′i·cal.** [1655–65; < Gk *paradeigmatikós,* equiv. to *paradeigmat-,* s. of *parádeigma* PARADIGM + *-ikos* -IC] —**par′a·dig·mat′i·cal·ly,** *adv.*

par·a·di·sa·i·cal (par′ə di sā′i kəl, -zā′-, -dī-), *adj.* paradisiacal. Also, **par′a·di·sa′ic.** [1615–25; PARADISE + *-aic* (suffix abstracted from words like *prosaic, algebraic,* etc.) + -AL[1]] —**par′a·di·sa′i·cal·ly,** *adv.*

par·a·dis·al (par′ə dī′səl, -zəl), *adj.* paradisiacal. [1550–60; PARADISE + -AL[1]]

par·a·dise (par′ə dīs′, -dīz′), *n.* **1.** heaven, as the final abode of the righteous. **2.** an intermediate place for the departed souls of the righteous awaiting resurrection. **3.** (*often cap.*) Eden (def. 1). **4.** a place of extreme beauty, delight, or happiness. **5.** a state of supreme happiness; bliss. **6.** *Archit.* **a.** parvis. **b.** an enclosure beside a church, as an atrium or cloister. **7.** (*cap., italics*) Italian, ***Pa·ra·di·so*** (pä′rä dē′zō). the third and concluding part of Dante's *Divine Comedy,* depicting heaven, through which he is guided by Beatrice. Cf. **Inferno** (def. 3), **purgatory** (def. 2). [bef. 1000; ME, OE *paradīs* < LL *paradīsus* < Gk *parádeisos* park, pleasure-grounds < Iranian; cf. Avestan *pairi-daēza* enclosure]

Par·a·dise (par′ə dīs′, -dīz′), *n.* a town in N California. 22,571.

par′adise fish′, any small freshwater fish of the genus *Macropodus,* of southeastern Asia, often kept in aquariums. [1855–60]

par′adise flow′er, a prickly vine, *Solanum wendlandii,* of the nightshade family, native to Costa Rica, having branched clusters of showy lilac-blue flowers. Also called **potato vine.**

Par′adise Lost′, an epic poem (1667) by John Milton.

Par′adise Regained′, an epic poem (1671) by John Milton.

Par′adise Val′ley, a town in SW Arizona. 10,832.

par·a·di·si·a·cal (par′ə di sī′ə kəl, -zī′-), *adj.* of, like, or befitting paradise. Also, **par·a·dis·i·ac** (par′ə dis′ē ak′), **paradisaical.** [1640–50; < LL *paradisiac(us)* < Gk *paradeisiakós* (see PARADISE, -AC) + -AL[1]] —**par′a·di·si′a·cal·ly,** *adv.*

par·a·doc·tor (par′ə dok′tər), *n.* a doctor who parachutes to patients in remote areas. [1940–45; PARA-[3] + DOCTOR]

par·a·dor (par′ə dôr′; *Sp.* pä′rä ᵺôr′), *n., pl.* **-dors,** *Sp.* **-do·res** (-ᵺô′res). a government-sponsored inn in Spain, usually in a scenic or historic area, that offers lodging and meals at reasonable prices. [1835–45; < Sp: wayside inn, hostelry, equiv. to *par(ar)* to stop (see PARADE) + *-ador* -ATOR]

par·a·dos (par′ə dos′), *n. Fort.* a bank of earth built behind a trench or military emplacement to protect soldiers from a surprise attack from the rear. [1825–35; < F; see PARA-[2], REREDOS]

par·a·dox (par′ə doks′), *n.* **1.** a statement or proposition that seems self-contradictory or absurd but in reality expresses a possible truth. **2.** a self-contradictory and false proposition. **3.** any person, thing, or situation exhibiting an apparently contradictory nature. **4.** an opinion or statement contrary to commonly accepted opinion. [1530–40; < L *paradoxum* < Gk *parádoxon,* n. use of neut. of *parádoxos* unbelievable, lit., beyond belief. See PARA-[1], ORTHODOX] —**par′a·dox′i·cal, par′a·dox′·al,** *adj.* —**par′a·dox′i·cal·ly,** *adv.* —**par′a·dox′i·cal·ness, par′a·dox′i·cal′i·ty,** *n.* —**par′a·dox·ol′o·gy,** *n.*
—**Syn. 3.** puzzle, anomaly, riddle.

paradox′ical sleep′, *Physiol.* See **REM sleep.** [1960–65]

par·a·drop (par′ə drop′), *n., v.t.,* **-dropped, -drop·ping.** airdrop. [1945–50; PARA-[3] + DROP]

par·aes·the·sia (par′əs thē′zhə, -zhē ə, -zē ə), *n. Pathol.* paresthesia. —**par·aes·thet·ic** (par′əs thet′ik), *adj.*

par. aff., (in prescriptions) to the part affected. [< L *pars affecta*]

par·af·fin (par′ə fin), *n.* **1.** a white or colorless, tasteless, odorless, water-insoluble, solid substance not easily acted upon by reagents, consisting of a mixture of hydrocarbons chiefly of the alkane series, obtained from crude petroleum: used in candles, for forming preservative coatings and seals, for waterproofing paper, etc. **2.** *Chem.* **a.** any member of the alkane series. **b.** one of the higher members of the alkane series, solid at ordinary temperatures, having a boiling point above 300°C, which largely constitutes the commercial form of this substance. **3.** Also called **par′affin oil′.** *Brit.* kerosene. —*v.t.* **4.** to cover or impregnate with paraffin. [1830–40; < G < L *par(um)* barely + *aff(inis)* connected + -IN[2]; so called from its slight affinity for other substances; see AFFINITY]

par·af·fine (par′ə fin, -fēn′), *n.* paraffin.

par·af·fin·ic (par′ə fin′ik), *adj.* of, noting, or characteristic of paraffin wax or a paraffin hydrocarbon. [1890–95; PARAFFIN + -IC]

par·af·fin·ize (par′ə fi nīz′), *v.t.,* **-ized, -iz·ing.** to paraffin (def. 4). Also, *esp. Brit.,* **par′af·fin·ise′.** [1885–90; PARAFFIN + -IZE]

par·af·fin·oid (par′ə fi noid′), *adj.* resembling a paraffin. [1885–90; PARAFFIN + -OID]

par′affin se′ries, *Chem.* See **alkane series.**

par′affin wax′, paraffin in its solid state. [1870–75]

par·a·foil (par′ə foil′), *n.* a structure, usually made of a strong yet light fabric, having a shape similar to that of an airplane wing, and used as a kite or a parachute. [PARA-[3] + (AIR)FOIL]

par·a·form·al·de·hyde (par′ə fôr mal′də hīd′, -fər-), *n. Chem.* a white, crystalline polymer of formaldehyde, $(HCOH)_n$, from which it is obtained by evaporation of the aqueous solution: used chiefly as an antiseptic. Also called **par·a·form** (par′ə fôrm′). [1930–35; PARA-[1] + FORMALDEHYDE]

par·a·gen·e·sis (par′ə jen′ə sis), *n. Geol.* **1.** the origin of minerals or mineral deposits in contact so as to affect one another's formation. **2.** the order in which the minerals in a rock or vein have crystallized. [1850–55; < NL; see PARA-[1], GENESIS] —**par·a·ge·net·ic** (par′ə jə net′ik), *adj.*

par·a·geu·sia (par′ə gyo͞o′zhə, -zhē ə, -zē ə), *n.* an abnormal or hallucinatory sense of taste. [1895–1900; < NL, equiv. to *para-* PARA-[1] + Gk *geûs(is)* taste + L *-ia* -IA] —**par·a·geu·sic** (par′ə gyo͞o′zik, -sik), *adj.*

par·a·glid·er (par′ə glī′dər), *n.* a steerable glider with inflatable wings proposed for use as an emergency vehicle for travel between a space station and the earth or for the recovery of rocket boosters. Also called **parawing.** [1940–45; PARA-[3] + GLIDER]

par′a·glyph print′ing (par′ə glif), the printing of the positive and negative of a radiograph superimposed in slight misalignment to give the effect of a relief. [< Gk *paraglýphein* to counterfeit. See PARA-[1], GLYPH]

par·a·go·ge (par′ə gō′jē), *n.* the addition of a sound or group of sounds at the end of a word, as in the nonstandard pronunciation of *height* as *height-th* or *once* as *once-t.* [1650–60; < LL *paragōgē* addition to a word, lengthening of a word < Gk *paragōgḗ* a leading by, alteration, change, deriv. of *parágein* to lead by, past. See PARA-[1], -AGOGUE] **—par·a·gog·ic** (par′ə goj′ik), **par′a·gog′i·cal,** *adj.* **—par′a·gog′i·cal·ly,** *adv.*

par·a·gon (par′ə gon′, -gən), *n.* **1.** a model or pattern of excellence or of a particular excellence. **2.** *Print.* a 20-point type. **3.** an unusually large, round pearl. *—v.t.* **4.** to compare; parallel. **5.** to be a match for; rival. **6.** *Obs.* to surpass. **7.** *Obs.* to regard as a paragon. [1540–50; < MF < OIt *paragone* comparison, perh. < Gk *parágōn,* prp. of *parágein* to bring side by side] **—par′a·gon′less,** *adj.*
—Syn. 1. ideal, standard; nonesuch, nonpareil.

pa·rag·o·nite (pə rag′ə nīt′), *n. Mineral.* a mica, similar in composition and appearance to muscovite but containing sodium instead of potassium. [1840–50; < Gk *parágōn* misleading, leading aside (prp. of *parágein;* see PARAGOGE) + -ITE[1]]

Par·a·gould (par′ə gōōld′), *n.* a city in NE Arkansas. 15,214.

par·a·graph (par′ə graf′, -gräf′), *n.* **1.** a distinct portion of written or printed matter dealing with a particular idea, usually beginning with an indentation on a new line. **2.** a paragraph mark. **3.** a note, item, or brief article, as in a newspaper. *—v.t.* **4.** to divide into paragraphs. **5.** to write or publish paragraphs about, as in a newspaper. **6.** to express in a paragraph. [1515–25; earlier *paragraphe* < Gk *paragraphḗ* marked passage; see PARA-[1], GRAPH] **—par′a·graph·ism,** *n.* **—par·a·gra·phis·ti·cal** (par′ə grə fis′ti kəl), *adj.*

par·a·graph·er (par′ə graf′ər, -grä′fər), *n.* a person who writes very short pieces or fillers for a newspaper. Also, *esp. Brit.,* **par′a·graph′ist.** [1815–25; PARAGRAPH[1] + -ER[1]]

par·a·graph·i·a (par′ə graf′ē ə), *n. Psychiatry.* a disorder marked by the writing of words or letters other than those intended, or the loss of the ability to express ideas in writing, usually caused by a brain lesion. [1875–80; < NL; see PARA-[1], -GRAPH, -IA]

par·a·graph·ic (par′ə graf′ik), *adj.* **1.** of, pertaining to, or forming a paragraph. **2.** divided into paragraphs. Also, **par′a·graph′i·cal.** [1780–90; PARAGRAPH + -IC] **—par′a·graph′i·cal·ly,** *adv.*

par′agraph mark′, the character ¶, used in editing and printing to indicate the beginning of a new paragraph; pilcrow. Also called **par′agraph sign′.** [1850–55]

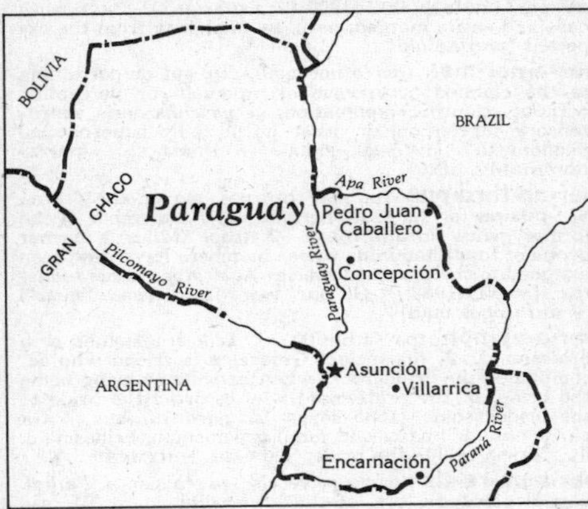

Par·a·guay (par′ə gwī′, -gwā′; *Sp.* pä′rä gwī′), *n.* **1.** a republic in central South America between Bolivia, Brazil, and Argentina. 2,600,000; 157,047 sq. mi. (406,750 sq. km). *Cap.:* Asunción. **2.** a river in central South America, flowing S from W Brazil through Paraguay to the Paraná. 1500 mi. (2400 km) long. **—Par′a·guay′an,** *adj., n.*

Par′aguay tea′, maté. [1720–30]

par·a·hy·dro·gen (par′ə hī′drə jən), *n. Physics, Chem.* the form of molecular hydrogen in which the nuclei of the two hydrogen atoms contained in the molecule have spins in opposite directions. Cf. **orthohydrogen.** [1925–30; PARA-[1] + HYDROGEN]

Pa·ra·í·ba (par′ə ē′bə; *Port.* pä′rä ē′bä), *n.* a state in E Brazil. 2,810,003; 21,760 sq. mi. (56,360 sq. km). *Cap.:* João Pessoa.

par·a·in·flu·en·za (par′ə in′flōō en′zə), *n. Pathol., Vet. Pathol.* an influenzalike respiratory infection of animals and humans, caused by any of several paramyxoviruses. [1955–60; PARA-[1] + INFLUENZA]

par·ai·son (par′ə zon′), *n.* parison.

par·a·jour·nal·ism (par′ə jûr′nl iz′əm), *n.* news reportage that strongly reflects the point of view of the writer or editor or that uses techniques not practiced in conventional journalism. [1960–65, *Amer.;* PARA-[1] + JOURNALISM] **—par′a·jour′nal·ist,** *n.* **—par′a·jour′·nal·is′tic,** *adj.*

par·a·keet (par′ə kēt′), *n.* any of numerous small, slender parrots, usually having a long, pointed, graduated tail, often kept as pets and noted for the ability to mimic speech: several species are endangered. Also, **paraquet, paroquet, parrakeet, parroket, parroquet.** [1575–85; < MF *paroquet* parrot, appar. orig. a dim. of *P(i)errot,* dim. of *Pierre* Peter, as a name for a parrot; the modern form and its earlier vars. have been influenced by It *parrocchetto* and Sp *periquito* (both ult. < MF)]

parakeet (budgerigar), *Melopsittacus undulatus,* length 7 in. (18 cm)

par·a·kit·ing (par′ə kī′ting), *n.* parasailing. [1965–70; PARA(CHUTE) + KITE[1] + -ING[1]]

Par·a·kou (par′ə kōō′, pär′ə-), *n.* a city in E central Benin. 18,000.

par·a·lan·guage (par′ə lang′gwij), *n. Ling.* vocal features that accompany speech and contribute to communication but are not generally considered to be part of the language system, as vocal quality, loudness, and tempo: sometimes also including facial expressions and gestures. Cf. **body language.** [1955–60; PARA-[1] + LANGUAGE]

par·al·de·hyde (pə ral′də hīd′), *n. Chem., Pharm.* a colorless, liquid, cyclic compound, $C_6H_{12}O_3$, having a disagreeable taste but an agreeable odor, produced by the polymerization of acetaldehyde with sulfuric acid: used chiefly in the manufacture of organic chemicals and in medicine as a sedative and hypnotic. Also called **paracetaldehyde.** [1855–60; PAR- + ALDEHYDE]

par·a·le·gal (par′ə lē′gəl), *n.* **1.** an attorney's assistant, not admitted to the practice of law but trained to perform certain legal tasks. *—adj.* **2.** of or pertaining to a paralegal or paralegals: *a paralegal career.* [1970–75; PARA-[1] + LEGAL]

par·a·leip·sis (par′ə līp′sis), *n., pl.* **-ses** (-sēz). paralipsis.

par·a·lep·sis (par′ə lep′sis), *n., pl.* **-ses** (-sēz). paralipsis.

par·a·lex·i·a (par′ə lek′sē ə), *n.* an impairment of reading ability characterized by the transposition of letters or words. [1875–80; < NL, equiv. to *para-* PARA-[1] + Gk *léx(is)* speaking, speech (see LEXIS) + -IA] **—par′a·lex′ic,** *adj.*

par·a·lin·guis·tic (par′ə ling gwis′tik), *adj.* of or pertaining to paralanguage or paralinguistics. [1955–60; PARA-[1] + LINGUISTIC]

par·a·lin·guis·tics (par′ə ling gwis′tiks), *n.* (*used with a singular v.*) the study of paralanguage. [1955–60; PARA-[1] + LINGUISTICS]

par·a·li·pom·e·na (par′ə li pom′ə nə, -lī-), *n.pl.* things omitted or neglected that are added as a supplement. [1665–75; < LL *paralipomena* < Gk (*tà*) *paraleipómena* (things) omitted, not told (prp. passive of *paraleípein*), equiv. to *para-* PARA-[1] + *leíp(ein)* to leave behind + *-omena* neut. pl. prp. mediopassive suffix]

Par·a·li·pom·e·non (par′ə li pom′ə non′, -lī-), *n., pl.* **-na** (-nə). *Douay Bible.* Chronicles. [1300–50; ME < LL *paralipomenon,* sing. of *paralipomena* PARALIPOMENA]

par·a·lip·sis (par′ə lip′sis), *n., pl.* **-ses** (-sēz). *Rhet.* the suggestion, by deliberately concise treatment of a topic, that much of significance is being omitted, as in "not to mention other faults." Also, **paraleipsis, paralepsis.** Also called **preterition.** [1580–90; < LL *paralipsis* < Gk *paráleipsis* an omitting, equiv. to *paraleíp(ein)* to leave on one side (*para-* PARA-[1] + *leípein* to leave) + *-sis* -SIS]

parallac′tic ellipse′, *Astron.* the apparent ellipse, as seen against the background of more distant stars, described annually by a nearby star because of the earth's orbital motion around the sun. Cf. **parallax** (def. 2).

par′allac′tic mo′tion, *Astron.* the apparent motion of stars due to the earth's orbital motion. [1885–90]

par·al·lax (par′ə laks′), *n.* **1.** the apparent displacement of an observed object due to a change in the position of the observer. **2.** *Astron.* the apparent angular displacement of a celestial body due to its being observed from the surface instead of from the center of the earth (**diurnal parallax** or **geocentric parallax**) or due to its being observed from the earth instead of from the sun (**annual parallax** or **heliocentric parallax**). Cf. **parallactic ellipse. 3.** the difference between the view of an object as seen through the picture-taking lens of a camera and the view as seen through a separate viewfinder. **4.** an apparent change in the position of cross hairs as viewed through a telescope, when the focusing is imperfect. [1585–95; < Gk *parállaxis* change, equiv. to *parallak-* (s. of *parallássein* to cause to alternate, equiv. to *para-* PARA-[1] + *allássein* to vary, akin to *állos* other; see ELSE, ALLO-) + *-sis* -SIS] **—par·al·lac·tic** (par′ə lak′tik), *adj.* **—par′al·lac′ti·cal·ly,** *adv.*

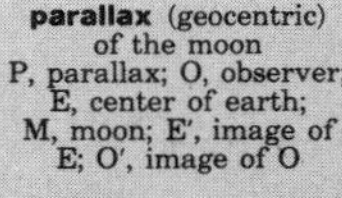

parallax (geocentric) of the moon
P, parallax; O, observer; E, center of earth; M, moon; E′, image of E; O′, image of O

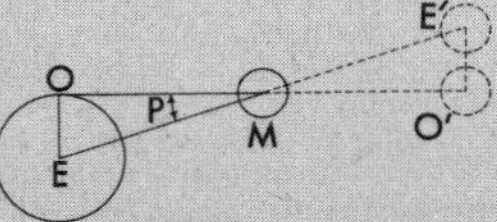

par·al·lel (par′ə lel′, -ləl), *adj., n., v.,* **-leled, -lel·ing** or (*esp. Brit.*) **-lelled, -lel·ling.** *—adj.* **1.** extending in the same direction, equidistant at all points, and never converging or diverging: *parallel rows of trees.* **2.** having the same direction, course, nature, or tendency; corresponding; similar; analogous: *Canada and the U.S. have many parallel economic interests.* **3.** *Geom.* **a.** (of straight lines) lying in the same plane but never meeting no matter how far extended. **b.** (of planes) having common perpendiculars. **c.** (of a single line, plane, etc.) equidistant from another or others (usually fol. by *to* or *with*). **4.** *Elect.* consisting of or having component parts connected in parallel: *a parallel circuit.* **5.** *Music.* **a.** (of two voice parts) progressing so that the interval between them remains the same. **b.** (of a tonality or key) having the same tonic but differing in mode. **6.** *Computers.* **a.** of or pertaining to the apparent or actual performance of more than one operation at a time, by the same or different devices (distinguished from *serial*): *Some computer systems join more than one CPU for parallel processing.* **b.** of or pertaining to the simultaneous transmission or processing of all the parts of a whole, as all the bits of a byte or all the bytes of a computer word (distinguished from *serial*). *—n.* **7.** a parallel line or plane. **8.** anything parallel or comparable in direction, course, nature, or tendency to something else. **9.** Also called **parallel of latitude.** *Geog.* **a.** an imaginary circle on the earth's surface formed by the intersection of a plane parallel to the plane of the equator, bearing east and west and designated in degrees of latitude north or south of the equator along the arc of any meridian. **b.** the line representing this circle on a chart or map. **10.** something identical or similar in essential respects; match; counterpart: *a case history without a known parallel.* **11.** correspondence or analogy: *These two cases have some parallel with each other.* **12.** a comparison of things as if regarded side by side. **13.** *Elect.* an arrangement of the components, as resistances, of a circuit in such a way that all positive terminals are connected to one point and all negative terminals are connected to a second point, the same voltage being applied to each component. Cf. **series** (def. 9). **14.** *Fort.* a trench cut in the ground before a fortress, parallel to its defenses, for the purpose of covering a besieging force. **15.** *Print.* a pair of vertical parallel lines (‖) used as a mark for reference. **16.** *Theat.* a trestle for supporting a platform (**parallel top**). *—v.t.* **17.** to provide or show a parallel for; match. **18.** to go or be in a parallel course, direction, etc., to: *The road parallels the river.* **19.** to form a parallel to; be equivalent to; equal. **20.** to show the identity or similarity of; compare. **21.** to make parallel. [1540–50; < L *parallēlus* < Gk *parállēlos* side by side, equiv. to *par-* PAR- + *állēlos* one another; see ALLO-, ELSE] **—par′al·lel′a·ble,** *adj.* **—par′al·lel′less,** *adj.* **—par′al·lel′ly,** *adv.*
—Syn. 2. like, alike. **10.** equivalent, equal, mate, duplicate, twin, double. **—Ant. 2.** divergent; unlike; unique. **10.** opposite.

par′allel ax′iom, *Geom.* See **parallel postulate.**

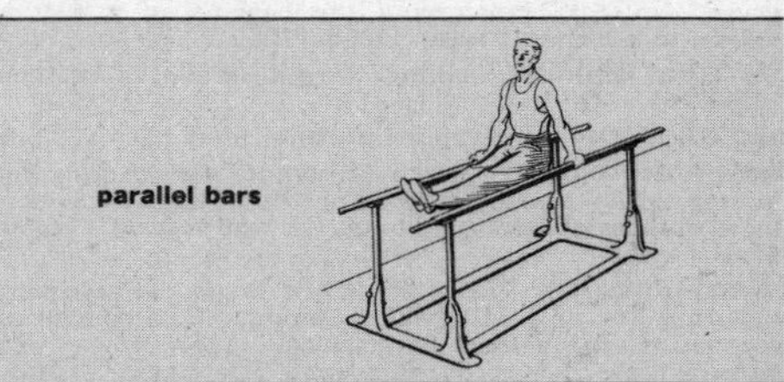

parallel bars

par′allel bars′, a gymnasium apparatus consisting of two wooden bars on uprights, adjustable in height, and used for swinging, vaulting, balancing exercises, etc. [1865–70]

par′allel cous′in, a cousin who is the child either of one's mother's sister or of one's father's brother. Also called **ortho-cousin.** Cf. **cross-cousin.**

par′allel cous′in mar′riage, marriage between the children of two brothers or two sisters. Cf. **cross-cousin marriage.**

par·al·lel·e·pi·ped (par′ə lel′ə pī′pid, -pip′id), *n.* a prism with six faces, all parallelograms. Also, **par·al·lel·e·pip·e·don** (par′ə lel′ə pip′i don′, -dən), **par′al·lel′o·pi′ped.** [1560–70; < Gk *parallēlepípedon* body with parallel surfaces, equiv. to *parállēl(os)* PARALLEL + *epípedon* plane, n. use of neut. of *epípedos* flat, equiv. to *epi-* EPI- + *pédon* ground] **—par·al·lel·e·pip·e·dic** (par′ə lel′ə pip′i dik), **par′al·lel′e·pip′e·don′al, par′al·lel′e·pip′e·dous,** *adj.*

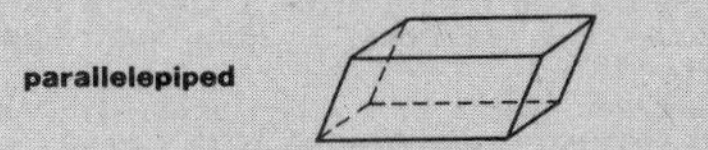

parallelepiped

par′allel evolu′tion, the independent development of closely corresponding adaptive features in two or more groups of organisms that occupy different but equivalent habitats, as marsupial mammals in Australia and placental mammals on other continents. [1960–65]

par′allel forc′es, *Mech.* forces acting along parallel lines of action.

par·al·lel·ism (par′ə le liz′əm, -lə liz′-), *n.* **1.** the position or relation of parallels. **2.** agreement in direction, tendency, or character; the state or condition of being

CONCISE PRONUNCIATION KEY: act, cāpe, dâre, pärt; set, ēqual; if, īce; ox, ōver, ôrder, oil, bŏŏk, bōōt, out; up, ûrge; child; sing; shoe; thin, *th*at; zh as in treasure. ə = *a* as in *alone,* *e* as in *system,* *i* as in *easily,* *o* as in *gallop,* *u* as in *circus;* ə as in *fire* (fīər), *hour* (ouər). l and n can serve as syllabic consonants, as in *cradle* (krād′l), and *button* (but′n). See the full key inside the front cover.

parallel. **3.** a parallel or comparison. **4.** *Metaphys.* the doctrine that mental and bodily processes are concomitant, each varying with variation of the other, but that there is no causal relation of interaction between the two. [1600–10; PARALLEL + -ISM]

par·al·lel·ist (par′ə lel′ist, -lə list), *n.* **1.** a person who seeks or makes a comparison. **2.** an adherent of the metaphysical doctrine of parallelism. [1785–95; PARALLEL + -IST]

par·al·lel·is·tic (par′ə lel is′tik, -lə lis′-), *adj.* **1.** of, pertaining to, or of the nature of a parallelism. **2.** of or pertaining to the metaphysical doctrine of parallelism or to its adherents. **3.** resembling, approaching, or characterized by parallelism. [1865–70; PARALLELIST + -IC]

par·al·lel·ize (par′ə lel īz′, -lə līz′), *v.t.*, **-ized, -iz·ing.** **1.** to make parallel; place so as to be parallel. **2.** to draw a parallelism or analogy between. Also, *esp. Brit.*, **par′·al·lel·ise′.** [1600–10; < Gk *parallēlízein.* See PARALLEL, -IZE] **—par′al·lel′i·za′tion,** *n.*

par′allel mo′tion, a mechanism arranged so as to impart rectilinear motion to a rod connected to a lever that moves through an arc. [1820–30]

par′allel of al′titude, *Astron.* almucantar. [1695–1705]

par′allel of lat′itude, parallel (def. 9). [1660–70]

par·al·lel·o·gram (par′ə lel′ə gram′), *n.* a quadrilateral having both pairs of opposite sides parallel to each other. [1560–70; < LL *parallēlogrammum* < Gk *parallēlógrammon.* See PARALLEL, -O-, -GRAM¹] **—par·al·lel·o·gram·mat·ic,** (par′ə lel′ə grə mat′ik), **par′al·lel′o·gram·mat′i·cal,** *adj.*

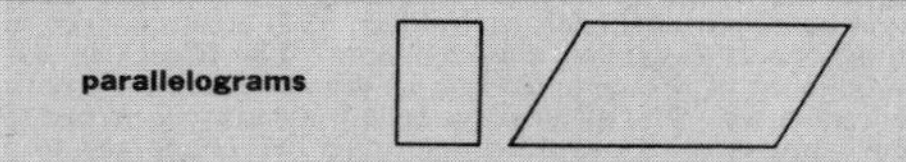
parallelograms

parallel′ogram law′, *Math., Physics.* a rule for adding two vectors, as forces **(parallel′ogram of forc′es),** by placing the point of application of one at the point of origin of the other and obtaining their sum by constructing the line connecting the two remaining end points, the sum being the diagonal of the parallelogram whose adjacent sides are the two vectors.

par′allel pos′tulate, *Geom.* the axiom in Euclidean geometry that only one line can be drawn through a given point so that the line is parallel to a given line that does not contain the point. Also called **parallel axiom.**

par′allel projec′tion, *Geom.* a projection from one plane to a second plane in which the lines joining points on the first plane and corresponding images are parallel.

par′allel rul′ers, a pair of straightedges connected by two pivoted crosspieces of equal length so as to be parallel at all times, used for various navigational purposes, esp. for transferring the bearing of a plotted course to a compass rose. [1695–1705]

par′allel sail′ing, sailing along a parallel of latitude. [1700–10]

par′allel top′. See under **parallel** (def. 16).

par·al·lel-veined (par′ə lel′vānd′, -ləl-), *adj. Bot.* having closely spaced longitudinal veins, as the leaves of most monocotyledonous plants. Cf. **net-veined.** [1860–65; PARALLEL + VEIN + -ED³]

pa·ral·o·gism (pə ral′ə jiz′əm), *n. Logic.* **1.** argument violating principles of valid reasoning. **2.** a conclusion reached through such argument. [1555–65; < LL *paralogismus* < Gk *paralogismós.* See PARA-¹, LOGO-, -ISM] **—pa·ral′o·gist,** *n.* **—pa·ral′o·gis′tic,** *adj.*

pa·ral·o·gize (pə ral′ə jīz′), *v.i.*, **-gized, -giz·ing.** to draw conclusions that do not follow logically from a given set of assumptions. Also, *esp. Brit.*, **pa·ral′o·gise′.** [1590–1600; < ML *paralogizāre* < Gk *paralogízesthai* to reason falsely, equiv. to *parálog(os)* (see PARA-¹, LOGOS) + *-izesthai* -IZE]

pa·ral·y·sis (pə ral′ə sis), *n., pl.* **-ses** (-sēz′). **1.** *Pathol.* **a.** a loss or impairment of voluntary movement in a body part, caused by injury or disease of the nerves, brain, or spinal cord. **b.** a disease characterized by this, esp. palsy. **2.** a state of helpless stoppage, inactivity, or inability to act: *The strike caused a paralysis of all shipping.* [bef. 1150; < L < Gk *parálysis,* equiv. to *paraly-,* var s. of *paralýein* to loosen (i.e., disable) on one side (*para-* PARA-¹ + *lýein* to loosen) + *-sis* -SIS; r. ME *paralisi(e)* < OF < L, as above; r. late OE *paralisin* (acc.) < L, as above; cf. PALSY]

par·a·lyt·ic (par′ə lit′ik), *n.* **1.** a person affected with paralysis. **—*adj.*** **2.** affected with or subject to paralysis. **3.** pertaining to or of the nature of paralysis. [1300–50; ME *paralitik* < L *paralyticus* < Gk *paralytikós,* equiv. to *paraly-* (see PARALYSIS) + *-tikos* -TIC] **—par′a·lyt′i·cal·ly,** *adv.*

par·a·lyze (par′ə līz′), *v.t.*, **-lyzed, -lyz·ing.** **1.** to affect with paralysis. **2.** to bring to a condition of helpless stoppage, inactivity, or inability to act: *The strike paralyzed communications.* Also, *esp. Brit.*, **par′a·lyse′.** [1795–1805; back formation from PARALYSIS, modeled on *analyze*] **—par′a·ly′zant,** *adj., n.* **—par′a·ly·za′tion,** *n.* **—par′a·lyz′er,** *n.* **—par′a·lyz′ing·ly,** *adv.*
—Syn. 2. See **shock¹.**

par·a·mag·net (par′ə mag′nit, par′ə mag′-), *n. Physics.* a body or substance that, placed in a magnetic field, possesses magnetization in direct proportion to the field strength; a substance in which the magnetic moments of the atoms are not aligned. Cf. **antiferromagnetic, diamagnetic, ferromagnetic.** [1905–10; back formation from *paramagnetic;* see PARA-¹, MAGNET] **—par′a·mag′net·ism,** *n.* **—par·a·mag·net·ic** (par′ə mag net′ik), *adj.*

Par·a·mar·i·bo (par′ə mar′ə bō′), *n.* a seaport in and the capital of Suriname, in NE South America. 150,000.

Par·am·at·man (pur′ə mät′mən), *n. Hinduism.* absolute Atman. [< Skt *paramātman* supreme self]

par·a·mat·ta (par′ə mat′ə), *n.* a light, twilled dress fabric, having a silk or cotton warp and a woolen weft. Also, **parramatta.** [1825–35; named after *Parramatta,* town in New South Wales]

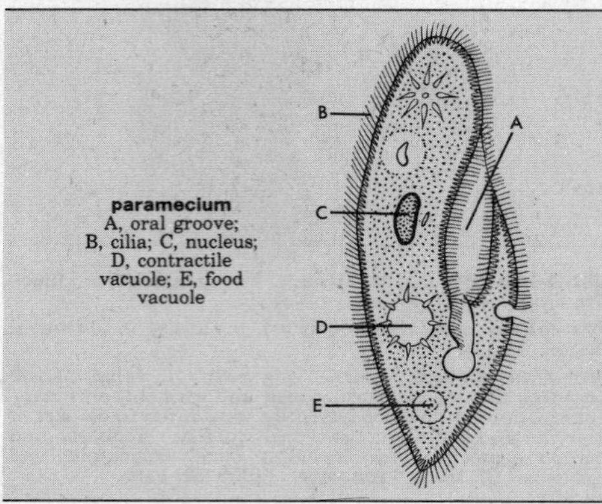

paramecium
A, oral groove;
B, cilia; C, nucleus;
D, contractile
vacuole; E, food
vacuole

par·a·me·ci·um (par′ə mē′shē əm, -shəm, -sē əm), *n., pl.* **-ci·a** (-shē ə, -sē ə). any ciliated freshwater protozoan of the genus *Paramecium,* having an oval body and a long, deep oral groove. [1745–55; < NL < Gk *paramḗk(ēs)* oblong, oval + NL *-ium* n. suffix; see -IUM]

par·a·med·ic¹ (par′ə med′ik), *n.* a person who is trained to assist a physician or to give first aid or other health care in the absence of a physician, often as part of a police, rescue, or firefighting squad. [1950–55, *Amer.*; PARA-¹ + MEDIC¹]

par·a·med·ic² (*n.* par′ə med′ik, par′ə med′-; *adj.* par′ə med′ik), *n.* **1.** *Mil.* a medic in the paratroops. **2.** a doctor who parachutes into remote areas to give medical care. **—*adj.*** **3.** of or pertaining to a paramedic or to paramedics. [1950–55, *Amer.*; PARA-³ + MEDIC¹]

par·a·med·i·cal (par′ə med′i kəl), *adj.* related to the medical profession in a secondary or supplementary capacity. [1920–25; PARA-¹ + MEDICAL]

par·a·ment (par′ə mənt), *n., pl.* **par·a·ments, par·a·men·ta** (par′ə men′tə). **1.** a decoration for a room, as a tapestry. **2.** an ecclesiastical vestment. [1350–1400; ME < LL *parāmentum* an ornament, equiv. to *parā(re)* to adorn (L: to PREPARE) + *-mentum* -MENT]

pa·ram·e·ter (pə ram′i tər), *n.* **1.** *Math.* **a.** a constant or variable term in a function that determines the specific form of the function but not its general nature, as a in $f(x) = ax$, where a determines only the slope of the line described by $f(x)$. **b.** one of the independent variables in a set of parametric equations. **2.** *Statistics.* a variable entering into the mathematical form of any distribution such that the possible values of the variable correspond to different distributions. **3.** *Computers.* a variable that must be given a specific value during the execution of a program or of a procedure within a program. **4.** Usually, **parameters.** limits or boundaries; guidelines: *the basic parameters of our foreign policy.* **5.** characteristic or factor; aspect; element: *a useful parameter for judging long-term success.* [1650–60; < NL *parametrum.* See PARA-¹, -METER] **—par·a·met·ric** (par′ə me′trik), **par′a·met′ri·cal,** *adj.*
—Usage. 4, 5. Some object strongly to the use of PARAMETER in these newer senses. Nevertheless, the criticized uses are now well established both in educated speech and in edited writing.

pa·ram·e·ter·ize (pə ram′i tə rīz′), *v.t.*, **-ized, -iz·ing.** to describe (a phenomenon, problem, curve, surface, etc.) by the use of parameters. Also, **parametrize;** *esp. Brit.*, **pa·ram′e·ter·ise′.** [1935–40; PARAMETER + -IZE] **—pa·ram′e·ter·i·za′tion,** *n.*

par′amet′ric am′plifier, *Electronics.* a device, as an electron tube or transistor, that amplifies a high-frequency input signal by sinusoidally varying the reactance of the circuit. [1955–60]

par′amet′ric equa′tion, *Math.* one of two or more equations expressing the location of a point on a curve or surface by determining each coordinate separately. [1905–10]

pa·ram·e·trize (pə ram′i trīz′), *v.t.*, **-trized, -triz·ing.** parameterize. Also, *esp. Brit.*, **pa·ram′e·trise′.**

par·a·mil·i·tar·y (par′ə mil′i ter′ē), *adj., n., pl.* **-tar·ies.** **—*adj.*** **1.** noting or pertaining to an organization operating as, in place of, or as a supplement to a regular military force: *a paramilitary police unit.* **—*n.*** **2.** Also, **par·a·mil·i·ta·rist** (par′ə mil′i tər ist). a person employed in such a force. [1930–35; PARA-¹ + MILITARY]

pa·ra·mi·ta (pä rum′i tə), *n. Buddhism.* any of the practices prescribed for one aspiring to nirvana. [< Skt and Pali *pāramitā* perfection]

par·am·ne·sia (par′am nē′zhə), *n.* **1.** *Psychiatry.* a distortion of memory in which fact and fantasy are confused. **2.** the inability to recall the correct meaning of a word. [1885–90; < NL; see PAR-, AMNESIA]

pa·ra·mo (par′ə mō′, pär′ə-), *n., pl.* **-mos.** a high, cold plateau of South America. [1750–60; < AmerSp; Sp *páramo* barren plain; presumably of pre-L orig.]

par·a·morph (par′ə môrf′), *n. Mineral.* a pseudomorph formed by a change in crystal structure but not in chemical composition. Also called **allomorph.** [1875–80; PARA-¹ + -MORPH] **—par′a·mor′phic, par′a·mor′phous,** *adj.*

par·a·mor·phine (par′ə môr′fēn), *n. Chem.* thebaine. [PARA-¹ + MORPHINE]

par·a·mor·phism (par′ə môr′fiz əm), *n.* **1.** the process by which a paramorph is formed. **2.** the state of being a paramorph. [1865–70; PARA-¹ + -MORPHISM]

par·a·mount (par′ə mount′), *adj.* **1.** chief in importance or impact; supreme; preeminent: *a point of paramount significance.* **2.** above others in rank or authority; superior in power or jurisdiction. **—*n.*** **3.** a supreme ruler; overlord. [1525–35; < AF *paramont* above, equiv. to *par* PER- + *a mont* < L *ad montem* to the mountain, hence, in OF: upward, above; see AD-, MOUNT²] **—par′a·mount′cy,** *n.* **—par′a·mount′ly,** *adv.*
—Syn. 1. See **dominant.** **—Ant. 1.** unimportant.

Par·a·mount (par′ə mount′), *n.* a city in SW California, near Los Angeles. 36,407.

par·a·mour (par′ə mo͝or′), *n.* **1.** an illicit lover, esp. of a married person. **2.** any lover. [1250–1300; ME, from the phrase *par amour* by or through love < OF]

Pa·ram·us (pə ram′əs), *n.* a city in NE New Jersey. 26,474.

par·a·myx·o·vi·rus (par′ə mik′sə vī′rəs, -mik′sə vī′-), *n., pl.* **-rus·es.** any of various RNA-containing viruses that are similar to but larger than the myxoviruses, including the viruses that cause mumps, measles, parainfluenza, and Newcastle disease. [1960–65; PARA-¹ + MYXOVIRUS]

Pa·ra·ná (par′ə nä′; *Port.* pä′Rä nä′), *n.* **1.** a river in central South America, flowing from S Brazil along the SE boundary of Paraguay and through E Argentina into the Río de la Plata. 2050 mi. (3300 km) long. **2.** a city in E Argentina, on the Paraná River: the capital of Argentina 1852–61. 159,581.

Pa·ra·na·guá (pä′Rä nä gwä′), *n.* a seaport in S Brazil. 65,178.

par·a·na·sal (par′ə nā′zəl), *adj. Anat.* situated near the nasal cavities. [1905–10; PARA-¹ + NASAL¹]

pa·rang (pär′äng), *n.* a large, heavy knife used as a tool or a weapon in Malaysia and Indonesia. [1850–55; < Malay]

par·a·ni·tro·phe·nol (par′ə nī′trə fē′nôl, -nol), *n.* See under **nitrophenol** (def. 2).

par·a·noi·a (par′ə noi′ə), *n.* **1.** *Psychiatry.* a mental disorder characterized by systematized delusions and the projection of personal conflicts, which are ascribed to the supposed hostility of others, sometimes progressing to disturbances of consciousness and aggressive acts believed to be performed in self-defense or as a mission. **2.** baseless or excessive suspicion of the motives of others. Also, **par·a·noe·a** (par′ə nē′ə). [1805–15; < NL < Gk *paránoia* madness. See PARA-, NOUS, -IA]

par·a·noid (par′ə noid′), *adj.* **1.** of, like, or suffering from paranoia. **—*n.*** **2.** a person suffering from paranoia. Also, **par·a·noi·ac** (par′ə noi′ak, -ik), **par·a·noe·ac** (par′ə nē′ak, -ik). [1900–05; PARANOI(A) + -OID, with base and suffix merged, perh. by haplology from the expected **paranoioid*]

par·a·nor·mal (par′ə nôr′məl), *adj.* of or pertaining to the claimed occurrence of an event or perception without scientific explanation, as psychokinesis, extrasensory perception, or other purportedly supernatural phenomena. [1915–20; PARA-¹ + NORMAL] **—par′a·nor′mal·ly,** *adv.*

par·an·thro·pus (pə ran′thrə pəs, par′ən thrō′-), *n., pl.* **-pus·es** for 1. **1.** (*sometimes cap.*) a member of the former genus *Paranthropus.* **2.** (*cap., italics*) a former genus of fossil hominids whose members have now been assigned to the proposed species *Australopithecus robustus.* [< NL (1938) < Gk *par-* PAR- (in the sense "near") + *ánthrōpos* man]

par·a·nymph (par′ə nimf′), *n.* **1.** a groomsman or a bridesmaid. **2.** (in ancient Greece) **a.** a friend who accompanied the bridegroom when he went to bring home the bride. **b.** the bridesmaid who escorted the bride to the bridegroom. [1585–95; < LL *paranymphus* < Gk *paránymphos* (masc. and fem.) groomsman, bridesmaid, lit., person beside the bride. See PARA-¹, NYMPH]

par·a·pa·re·sis (par′ə pə rē′sis, -par′ə sis), *n. Pathol.* partial paralysis, esp. of the lower limbs. [< NL; see PARA-¹, PARESIS]

par·a·pet (par′ə pit, -pet′), *n.* **1.** *Fort.* **a.** a defensive wall or elevation, as of earth or stone, in a fortification. See diag. under **bastion. b.** an elevation raised above the main wall or rampart of a permanent fortification. **2.** any low protective wall or barrier at the edge of a balcony, roof, bridge, or the like. [1575–85; < It *parapetto,* equiv. to *para-* PARA-² + *petto* chest, breast < L *pectus*] **—par′a·pet·ed,** *adj.* **—par′a·pet·less,** *adj.*

par·aph (par′əf, pə raf′), *n.* a flourish made after a signature, as in a document, originally as a precaution against forgery. [1350–1400; ME *paraf* < It *parafo* or MF *paraphe* paragraph mark (by syncope; see PARAGRAPH)]

par′a·phase am′plifier (par′ə fāz′), *Electronics.* an amplifier that produces a push-pull output from a single input. [PARA-¹ + PHASE]

par·a·phe·net·i·dine (par′ə fə net′i dēn′, -din), *n. Chem.* See under **phenetidine.**

par·a·pher·na·lia (par′ə fər nāl′yə, -fə nāl′-), *n.* **1.** (*sometimes used with a singular v.*) equipment, apparatus, or furnishing used in or necessary for a particular activity: *a skier's paraphernalia.* **2.** (*used with a plural v.*) personal belongings. **3.** (*used with a singular v.*) *Law.* the personal articles, apart from dower, reserved by law to a married woman. [1470–80; < ML *paraphernālia* (*bona*) a bride's goods, beyond her dowry, equiv. to LL *parapherna(a)* a bride's property (< Gk *parápherna,* equiv. to *para-* PARA-¹ + *phern(ḗ)* dowry, deriv. of *phérein* to BEAR¹ + *-a* neut. pl. n. suffix) + L *-ālia,* n.

CONCISE ETYMOLOGY KEY: <, descended or borrowed from; >, whence; b., blend of, blended; c., cognate with; cf., compare; deriv., derivative; equiv., equivalent; imit., imitative; obl., oblique; r., replacing; s., stem; sp., spelling, spelled; resp., respelling, respelled; trans., translation; ?, origin unknown; *, unattested; ‡, probably earlier than. See the full key inside the front cover.

use of neut. pl. of *-ālis* -AL[1]] **—par′a·pher·na′lian, par·a·pher·nal** (par′ə fûr′nl), *adj.*
—Syn. 1. appointments, appurtenances, accouterments, trappings. **2.** effects.

par·a·phil·i·a (par′ə fil′ē ə), *n. Psychiatry.* a type of mental disorder characterized by a preference for or obsession with unusual sexual practices, as pedophilia, sadomasochism, or exhibitionism. Also called **sexual deviation.** [1920–25; PARA-[1] + -PHILIA, on the model of PARANOIA]

par·a·phrase (par′ə frāz′), *n., v.,* **-phrased, -phras·ing.** —*n.* **1.** a restatement of a text or passage giving the meaning in another form, as for clearness; rewording. **2.** the act or process of restating or rewording. —*v.t.* **3.** to render the meaning of in a paraphrase: *to paraphrase a technical paper for lay readers.* —*v.i.* **4.** to make a paraphrase or paraphrases. [1540–50; < MF < L *paraphrasis* < Gk *paráphrasis.* See PARA-[1], PHRASE] **—par′a·phras′a·ble,** *adj.* **—par′a·phras′er,** *n.*
—Syn. 1. See **translation. 3.** summarize; explain.

pa·raph·ra·sis (pə raf′rə sis), *n., pl.* **-ses** (-sēz′). paraphrase. [< L]

par·a·phrast (par′ə frast′), *n.* a person who paraphrases. [1540–50; < LL *paraphrastēs* < Gk *paraphrastḗs,* deriv. of *paraphrázein* to retell in other words, equiv. to *para-* PARA-[1] + *phrad-,* base of *phrázein* to tell, declare + *-tēs* agent n. suffix, with *dt* > *st*]

par·a·phras·tic (par′ə fras′tik), *adj.* having the nature of a paraphrase. [1615–25; < ML *paraphrasticus* < Gk *paraphrastikós.* See PARAPHRAST, -IC] **—par′a·phras′ti·cal·ly,** *adv.*

pa·raph·y·sis (pə raf′ə sis), *n., pl.* **-ses** (-sēz′). *Bot., Mycol.* one of the erect, sterile filaments often growing among the reproductive organs in many fungi, mosses, and ferns. [1855–60; < NL < Gk *paráphysis* lit., a growing beside, by-growth, equiv. to *para-* PARA-[1] + *phýsis* growth, nature; see PHYSIC] **—pa·raph′y·sate,** *adj.*

par·a·ple·gi·a (par′ə plē′jē ə, -jə), *n. Pathol.* paralysis of both lower limbs due to spinal disease or injury. [1650–60; < NL < Gk *paraplēgía.* See PARA-[1], -PLEGIA] **—par·a·ple·gic** (par′ə plē′jik, -plej′ik), *adj., n.*

par·a·po·di·um (par′ə pō′dē əm), *n., pl.* **-di·a** (-dē ə). *Zool.* one of the unjointed rudimentary limbs or processes of locomotion of many worms, as annelids. [1875–80; PARA-[1] + -PODIUM] **—par′a·po′di·al,** *adj.*

par·a·prax·is (par′ə prak′sis), *n., pl.* **-prax·es** (-prak′sēz). *Psychol.* a slip of the tongue or pen, forgetfulness, misplacement of objects, or other error thought to reveal unconscious wishes or attitudes. Cf. **Freudian slip.** [1935–40; PARA- + Gk *prâxis* act, action; cf. PRAXIS]

par·a·pro·fes·sion·al (par′ə prə fesh′ə nl), *n.* **1.** a person trained to assist a doctor, lawyer, teacher, or other professional, but not licensed to practice in the profession. —*adj.* **2.** of or pertaining to paraprofessionals. [1965–70; PARA-[1] + PROFESSIONAL]

par·a·psy·chol·o·gy (par′ə sī kol′ə jē), *n.* the branch of psychology that deals with the investigation of purportedly psychic phenomena, as clairvoyance, extrasensory perception, telepathy, and the like. [1925–30; PARA-[1] + PSYCHOLOGY] **—par′a·psy′cho·log′i·cal,** *adj.* **—par′a·psy·chol′o·gist,** *n.*

par·a·quat (par′ə kwät′), *n. Chem.* a toxic herbicide, $C_{12}H_{14}N_2{\cdot}2CH_3SO_4$, applied to food and flower crops and to highway borders as a defoliant and weed-killer. [1960–65; PARA-[1] + QUAT(ERNARY), in reference to the bond between the two pyridyl groups, which is in the para position with respect to their quaternary nitrogen atoms]

par·a·quet (par′ə ket′), *n.* parakeet.

par·a·res·cue (par′ə res′kyōō), *n.* a rescue, as of persons caught in a disaster, accomplished by parachutists. [1945–50; PARA-[3] + RESCUE]

Pará′ rhat′any. See under **rhatany** (def. 1). [see PARÁ RUBBER]

Pará′ rub′ber, India rubber obtained from the tree *Hevea brasiliensis,* of the spurge family, and other species of the same genus of tropical South America. [1895–1900; named after PARÁ]

par·a·sail (par′ə sāl′), *n.* **1.** a special parachute, kept open with wing-tip holders to help provide lift, used in parasailing. —*v.i.* **2.** to engage in parasailing. [PARA-[3] + SAIL]

par·a·sail·ing (par′ə sā′ling), *n.* the sport of soaring while harnessed to a parasail that is towed by a motorboat, car, or other fast-moving vehicle, from which one often releases oneself to float freely. Also, **par′a·sail′·ing.** Also called **parakiting.** [PARA-[3] + SAILING]

par·a·sce·ni·um (par′ə sē′nē əm), *n., pl.* **-ni·a** (-nē ə). either of two wings flanking and extending forward from the skene of an ancient Greek theater. [1700–10; < NL < Gk *paraskḗnion* space at sides of stage. See PARA-[1], SCENE]

par·a·se·le·ne (par′ə si lē′nē), *n., pl.* **-nae** (-nē). *Meteorol.* a bright moonlike spot on a lunar halo; a mock moon. Also called **moondog.** Cf. **parhelion.** [1645–55; < NL, equiv. to *para-* PARA-[1] + Gk *selḗnē* the moon] **—par·a·se·le·nic** (par′ə si lē′nik, -len′ik), *adj.*

parasex′ual reproduc′tion, *Biol.* reproduction by recombination of genes from genetically dissimilar nuclei within binucleate or multinucleate cells, as in filamentous fungi.

Pa·ra·shah (pär′ə shä′, pär′shə; *Seph. Heb.* pä rä-shä′; *Ashk. Heb.* pä′rə shə), *n., pl.* **Pa·ra·shoth, Pa·ra·shot** (*Seph. Heb.* pä rä shōt′), **Pa·ra·shi·oth, Pa·ra·shi·ot** (*Seph. Heb.* pä rä shē ōt′), *Eng.,* *Ashk. Heb.* **Pa·ra·shahs** (pär′ə shäz′, pär′shəz; *Ashk. Heb.* pä′rə shəz). *Judaism.* **1.** a portion of the Torah chanted or read each week in the synagogue on the Sabbath. **2.** a selection from such a portion, chanted or read in the synagogue on Mondays, Thursdays, and holy days. [< Heb *pārāshāh* lit., section, division]

Par·a·shu·ra·ma (par′ə shōō rä′mə), *n. Hindu Myth.* a Rama and avatar of Vishnu who rid the earth of Kshatriyas.

par·a·site (par′ə sīt′), *n.* **1.** an organism that lives on or in an organism of another species, known as the host, from the body of which it obtains nutriment. **2.** a person who receives support, advantage, or the like, from another or others without giving any useful or proper return, as one who lives on the hospitality of others. **3.** (in ancient Greece) a person who received free meals in return for amusing or impudent conversation, flattering remarks, etc. [1530–40; < L *parasītus* < Gk *parásītos* one who eats at another's table, orig. adj.: feeding beside, equiv. to *para-* PARA-[1] + *sît(os)* grain, food + *-os* adj. suffix]
—Syn. 2. sycophant, toady, leech, sponge, hanger-on.

par′asite drag′, *Aeron.* the component of drag caused by skin friction and the shape of the surfaces not contributing to lift. [1925–30]

par·a·sit·ic (par′ə sit′ik), *adj.* **1.** of, pertaining to, or characteristic of parasites. **2.** (of diseases) due to parasites. **3.** *Phonet.* excrescent (def. 2). Also, **par′a·sit′i·cal.** [1620–30; < L *parasīticus* < Gk *parasītikós.* See PARASITE, -IC] **—par′a·sit′i·cal·ly,** *adv.* **—par′a·sit′i·cal·ness,** *n.*

par·a·sit·i·cide (par′ə sit′ə sīd′), *n.* **1.** an agent or preparation that destroys parasites. —*adj.* **2.** destructive to parasites. [1860–65; PARASITE + -I- + -CIDE] **—par′a·sit′i·cid′al,** *adj.*

par·a·sit·ism (par′ə sī tiz′əm, -si-), *n.* **1.** *Biol.* a relation between organisms in which one lives as a parasite on another. **2.** a parasitic mode of life or existence. **3.** *Pathol.* a diseased condition due to parasites. **4.** (in some totalitarian countries) **a.** unemployment or refusal to work. **b.** employment in work considered nonessential by the state. [1605–15; PARASITE + -ISM]

par·a·sit·ize (par′ə si tīz′, -sī-), *v.t.,* **-ized, -iz·ing.** to live on (a host) as a parasite. Also, *esp. Brit.,* **par′a·si·tise′.** [1885–90; PARASITE + -IZE]

par·a·sit·oid (par′ə si toid′, -sī-), *n.* **1.** an organism that practices parasitoidism. —*adj.* **2.** of or pertaining to a parasite, esp. one practicing parasitoidism. [1920–25; < NL *Parasitoidea* (1913); see PARASITE, -OID]

par·a·sit·oid·ism (par′ə si toi diz′əm, -sī-), *n.* the feeding by certain insect larvae on host tissues such that the host remains alive until larval development is complete and then usually dies. [PARASITOID + -ISM]

par·a·si·tol·o·gy (par′ə sī tol′ə jē, -si-), *n.* the branch of biology dealing with parasites and the effects of parasitism. [1880–85; PARASITE + -O- + -LOGY] **—par·a·si·to·log·i·cal** (par′ə sīt′l oj′i kəl), *adj.* **—par′·a·si·tol′o·gist,** *n.*

par·a·si·to·sis (par′ə sī tō′sis, -si-), *n. Pathol.* parasitism (def. 3). [1895–1900; PARASITE + -OSIS]

par·a·sol (par′ə sôl′, -sol′), *n.* a lightweight umbrella used, esp. by women, as a sunshade. [1610–20; < F, MF < It *parasole.* See PARA-[2], SOL] **—par′a·soled′,** *adj.*

par′asol ant′. See **leaf-cutting ant.** [1775–85]

par′asol mush′room, a common edible field mushroom, *Macrolepiota* (*Lepiota*) *procera,* having a light-brown, scaly cap.

par′asol pine′, **1.** See **stone pine** (def. 1). **2.** See **umbrella pine.** [1860–65]

par·a·stat·al (par′ə stāt′l), *adj.* **1.** working with the government in an unofficial capacity. —*n.* **2.** a parastatal company or group. [1965–70; PARA-[1] + STATE + -AL[1]]

pa·ras·ti·chy (pi ras′ti kē), *n., pl.* **-chies.** *Bot.* one of a number of seemingly secondary spirals or oblique ranks winding around the stem or axis to the right and left in a spiral arrangement of leaves, scales, etc., where the internodes are short and the members closely crowded, as in the houseleek and the pine cone. [1870–75; PARA-[1] + STICH[1] + -Y[3]]

par·a·sym·pa·thet·ic (par′ə sim′pə thet′ik), *Anat., Physiol., adj.* pertaining to that part of the autonomic nervous system consisting of nerves and ganglia that arise from the cranial and sacral regions and function in opposition to the sympathetic system, as in inhibiting heartbeat or contracting the pupil of the eye. [1900–05; PARA-[1] + SYMPATHETIC]

par·a·syn·ap·sis (par′ə si nap′sis), *n. Biol.* the conjugation of chromosomes side by side; synapsis. [1905–10; PARA-[1] + SYNAPSIS] **—par′a·syn·ap′tic,** *adj.* **—par′a·syn·ap′tist,** *n.*

par·a·syn·the·sis (par′ə sin′thə sis), *n. Gram.* **1.** the formation of a word by the addition of a derivational suffix to a phrase or compound, as of *greathearted,* which is *great heart* plus *-ed.* **2.** the formation of a word by the addition of both a prefix and a derivational suffix to a word or stem, as *demoralize.* [1860–65; PARA-[1] + SYNTHESIS] **—par·a·syn·thet·ic** (par′ə sin-thet′ik), *adj.*

par·a·tax·ic (par′ə tak′sik), *adj. Psychol.* **1.** of or characterized by emotional maladjustment. **2.** of or related to a lack of harmony between attitudes, ideas, etc., and other aspects of an individual's personality. [1935–40; PARATAX(IS) + -IC]

paratax′ic distor′tion, *Psychiatry.* a distortion in perception, esp. of interpersonal relationships, based on a tendency to perceive others in accordance with a pattern determined by previous experiences. [1960–65]

par·a·tax·is (par′ə tak′sis), *n. Gram.* the placing together of sentences, clauses, or phrases without a conjunctive word or words, as *Hurry up, it is getting late! I came—I saw—I conquered.* Cf. **hypotaxis.** [1835–45; < NL < Gk *parátaxis* an arranging in order for battle. See PARA-[1], -TAXIS] **—par·a·tac·tic** (par′ə tak′tik), **par′a·tac′ti·cal,** *adj.* **—par′a·tac′ti·cal·ly,** *adv.*

par·a·thi·on (par′ə thī′on), *n. Chem.* a deep-brown to yellow, poisonous liquid, $C_{10}H_{14}NO_5PS$, used as an insecticide. [1945–50; PARA-[1] + THI- + -ON(E)]

Par·a·thor·mone (par′ə thôr′mōn), *Pharm., Trademark.* a brand of parathyroid extract.

par·a·thy·roid (par′ə thī′roid), *Anat.* —*adj.* **1.** situated near the thyroid gland. —*n.* **2.** See **parathyroid gland.** [1895–1900; PARA-[1] + THYROID]

par·a·thy·roid·ec·to·my (par′ə thī′roi dek′tə mē), *n., pl.* **-mies.** *Surg.* the excision of a parathyroid gland. [1900–05; PARATHYROID + -ECTOMY]

par′athy′roid ex′tract, *Pharm.* an aqueous preparation obtained from the parathyroid gland of cattle, used in medicine chiefly in cases of parathyroid deficiency and in veterinary medicine in the treatment of tetanic convulsions.

parathy′roid gland′, *Anat.* any of several small oval glands usually lying near or embedded in the thyroid gland. [1900–05]

parathy′roid hor′mone, *Biochem., Physiol.* a polypeptide hormone, produced in the parathyroid glands, that helps regulate the blood levels of calcium and phosphate. *Abbr.:* PTH

par·a·to·lu·i·dine (par′ə tə lōō′i dēn′, -din), *n. Chem.* a white, flaky, lustrous, very slightly water-soluble solid, C_7H_9N, the para isomer of toluidine, used in the manufacture of dyes, in organic synthesis, and as a reagent in tests for nitrite, lignin, and phloroglucinol.

par·a·trans·it (par′ə tran′sit, -zit), *n.* public or group transportation, as by automobile, van, or minibus, organized to relieve the congestion of mass transportation. [1970–75; PARA-[1] + TRANSIT]

par·a·troop (par′ə trōōp′), *adj.* **1.** of or pertaining to a paratrooper or a parachute unit: *paratroop boots.* —*n.* **2.** paratrooper. [1935–40; back formation from PARATROOPER]

par·a·troop·er (par′ə trōō′pər), *n.* a member of a military infantry unit trained to attack or land in combat areas by parachuting from airplanes. [1940–45; PARA-[3] + TROOPER]

par·a·troph·ic (par′ə trof′ik, -trō′fik), *adj.* obtaining nourishment from living organic matter; parasitic. [1855–60; PARA-[1] + -TROPHIC]

par·a·tu·ber·cu·lo·sis (par′ə tōō bûr′kyə lō′sis, -tyōō-), *n. Vet. Pathol.* See **Johne's disease.** [< NL; see PARA-[1], TUBERCULOSIS] **—par·a·tu·ber·cu·lous** (par′ə tōō bûr′kyə ləs, -tyōō-), *adj.*

par·a·ty·phoid (par′ə tī′foid), *Pathol.* —*n.* **1.** Also called **paraty′phoid fe′ver.** an infectious disease, similar in some of its symptoms to typhoid fever but usually milder, caused by any of several bacilli of the genus *Salmonella* other than *S. typhi.* —*adj.* **2.** of or pertaining to paratyphoid. **3.** resembling typhoid. [1900–05; PARA-[1] + TYPHOID]

par·a·u·re′thral gland′ (par′ə yōō rē′thrəl), any of a group of vestigial glands located in the posterior wall of the urethra in women. [PARA-[1] + URETHRAL]

par·a·vail (par′ə vāl′, par′ə vāl′), *adj. Old Eng. Law.* being below or inferior to all others; specifically, being a tenant of one who holds land of another who is also a tenant: *a tenant paravail.* [1525–35; < OF *par aval* down (of direction, position), equiv. to *par* through, by (see PER-) + *aval, a val* down < L *ad vallem* lit., to the valley]

par·a·vane (par′ə vān′), *n.* an underwater defensive device against mines, consisting of a pair of torpedo-shaped vanes towed at the bow of a ship, usually a minesweeper, by cables that can cut the cable of a moored mine, causing the mine to rise to the surface, where it can be destroyed or removed from the water. [1915–20; PARA-[1] + VANE]

par·a·vent (par′ə vent′), *n.* a screen against a draft or the wind. [< F: lit., against wind, equiv. to *para-* PARA-[2] + *vent* WIND[1]]

pa·ra·vid·ya (pär′ə vid′yä), *n. Hinduism.* transcendental knowledge. Cf. **aparavidya.** [< Skt *parā vidyā*]

par a·vion (pa ʀa vyôɴ′), *French.* by plane (used esp. as a designation on matter to be sent by airmail).

par·a·wing (par′ə wing′), *n. Aerospace.* paraglider. [1965–70; PARA-[3] + WING]

par·ax·i·al (par ak′sē əl), *adj. Optics.* making a small angle with and lying close to the axis of an optical system: *paraxial ray.* [1860–65; PAR- + AXIAL]

par·a·zo·an (par′ə zō′ən), *Zool.* —*n.* **1.** any member of a group of invertebrates comprising the phylum Porifera, the sponges. —*adj.* **2.** of or pertaining to a parazoan organism. [< NL *parazo(a)* (see PARA-[1], -ZOA) + -AN]

par·boil (pär′boil′), *v.t.* to boil partially or for a short time; precook. [1400–50; late ME *parboylen* to boil partly, (rarely) to boil fully < MF *parboillir* < LL *perbullīre* to boil through and through (see PER-, BOIL); change of meaning by confusion of *par-* with *part*]

par·buck·le (pär′buk′əl), *n., v.,* **-led, -ling.** —*n.* **1.** a kind of tackle for raising or lowering a cask or similar object along an inclined plane or a vertical surface, consisting of a rope looped over a post or the like, with its two ends passing around the object to be moved. **2.** a kind of double sling made with a rope, as around a cask to be raised or lowered. —*v.t.* **3.** to raise, lower, or move with a parbuckle. [1620–30; earlier *parbunkel,* of uncert. orig.]

Par·ca (pär′kə), *n.* **1.** an ancient Roman goddess of childbirth and destiny. Cf. **Parcae. 2.** any one of the Parcae.

Par·cae (pär′sē, -kī), *n.pl., sing.* **-ca** (-kə). the three Fates of ancient Rome, developed out of the goddess

Parca by identification with the Moerae of Greek mythology.

par•cel (pär′səl), *n., v.,* **-celed, -cel•ing** or (*esp. Brit.*) **-celled, -cel•ling,** *adv.* —*n.* **1.** an object, article, container, or quantity of something wrapped or packed up; small package; bundle. **2.** a quantity or unit of something, as of a commodity for sale; lot. **3.** a group, collection, or assemblage of persons or things. **4.** a distinct, continuous portion or tract of land. **5.** a part, portion, or fragment. —*v.t.* **6.** to divide into or distribute in parcels or portions (usually fol. by *out*). **7.** to make into a parcel or wrap as a parcel. **8.** *Naut.* to cover or wrap (a rope) with strips of canvas. —*adv.* **9.** *Archaic.* in part; partially. [1275–1325; ME < MF *parcelle* < LL *particella, fresh formation for L *particula;* see PARTICLE, PASSEL]
—**Syn. 1.** See **package. 3.** batch, assortment. **6.** mete, apportion, deal, allot.

par′cel gild′ing, the gilding of only some areas or ornaments of a piece of furniture. [1865–70] —**par′cel-gild′er,** *n.* —**par′cel-gilt′,** *adj.*

par•cel•ing (pär′sə ling), *n.* **1.** the act of separating or dividing into parts and distributing; allotting or apportioning. **2.** *Naut.* strips of canvas, usually coated with tar, for wrapping around a rope to protect it. [1400–50; late ME; see PARCEL, -ING[1]]

par′cel post′, **1.** (in the U.S. Postal Service) nonpreferential mail consisting of packages and parcels, weighing one pound or more sent at fourth-class rates. Cf. **fourth class. 2.** the branch of a postal service that processes and delivers parcels. **3.** the service this branch renders. [1855–60]

par′cel tank′er, *Naut.* a tanker designed to carry an assortment of liquids, as chemicals, or different grades of a liquid, as petroleum, at one time. [1970–75]

par•ce•nar•y (pär′sə ner′ē), *n. Law.* joint heirship or coheirship; the undivided holding of land by two or more coheirs. Cf. **coparcenary.** [1475–85; < AF *parcenarie,* OF *parçonerie* coheirship, equiv. to *parçon* (see PARCENER) + *-erie* -ERY]

par•ce•ner (pär′sə nər), *n. Law.* a joint heir; coheir. [1250–1300; ME < AF: coheir, equiv. to *parcen* (OF *parçon* < VL *partion-, for L *partītiōn-* PARTITION) + *-er* -ER[2]]

parch (pärch), *v.t.* **1.** to make extremely, excessively, or completely dry, as heat, sun, and wind do. **2.** to make dry, hot, or thirsty: *Walking in the sun parched his throat.* **3.** to dry (peas, beans, grain, etc.) by exposure to heat without burning; to toast or roast slightly: *A staple of the Indian diet was parched corn.* **4.** to dry or shrivel with cold. —*v.i.* **5.** to suffer from heat, thirst, or need of water. **6.** to become parched; undergo drying by heat. **7.** to dry (usually fol. by *up*). [1350–1400; ME *perchen* < ?] —**parch′a•ble,** *adj.* —**parch•ed•ly** (pär′chid lē, pärcht′-), *adv.* —**parch′ed•ness,** *n.* —**parch′ing•ly,** *adv.*
—**Syn. 1.** dry, shrivel, dessicate. —**Ant.** wet, moisten.

Par•chee•si (pär chē′zē), *Trademark.* a brand of the game pachisi.

parch•ment (pärch′mənt), *n.* **1.** the skin of sheep, goats, etc., prepared for use as a material on which to write. **2.** a manuscript or document on such material. **3.** a stiff, off-white paper resembling this material. **4.** a diploma. [1275–1325; late ME < MF, OF (*parche* < L *Parthica* (*pellis*) Parthian (leather) + -MENT (cf. ML *percamentum,* D *perkament*)); r. ME *parchemin* < OF (*-min* < ML *pergamīnum,* var. of *pergamēnum,* for LL *Pergamēna charta* paper of PERGAMUM)] —**parch′ment•like′, parch′ment•y,** *adj.*

parch•ment•ize (pärch′mən tīz′), *v.t.,* **-ized, -iz•ing.** to treat (paper or the like) so that it resembles parchment. Also, *esp. Brit.,* **parch′ment•ise′.** [1875–80; PARCHMENT + -IZE]

parch′ment pa′per, a waterproof and grease-resistant paper produced by treating ordinary paper with concentrated sulfuric acid. [1855–60]

parch′ment worm′, any of several polychaete worms of the genus *Chaetopterus* that secrete and live in a U-shaped, parchmentlike tube.

par•close (pär′klōz′), *n.* (in a church) a screen dividing one area from another, as a chapel from an aisle. Also, **perclose.** Cf. **rood screen.** [1300–50; ME < MF, n. use of fem. of *parclos,* ptp. of *parclore* to enclose fully. See PER-, CLOSE]

par•cours (PAR kōōr′), *n., pl.* ***-cours*** (-kōōr′). *French.* parcourse.

par•course (pär′côrs′, -cōrs′), *n.* an outdoor exercise track or course, esp. for joggers, equipped with a series of stations along the way where one is to stop and perform a specific exercise. [partial trans. of F *parcours* course, route, circuit, OF: calque on ML, LL *percursus,* n. deriv. of *percurrere* (see PER-, COURSE); E sense reflects F *parcours du combattant* military obstacle course, or a like phrase]

pard[1] (pärd), *n. Literary.* a leopard or panther. [1250–1300; ME *parde* (< OF *pard*) < L *pardus* < Gk *párdos* (masc.), deriv. of *párdalis* (fem.); cf. OE (rare) *pardus*] —**pard•ine** (pär′din, -dīn), *adj.*

pard[2] (pärd), *n. Informal.* partner; companion. [1840–50, *Amer.*; by alter. and shortening of PARTNER]

par•dah (pûr′də), *n.* purdah.

par•da•lote (pär′dl ōt′), *n.* any of several tiny, short-tailed Australian songbirds of the genus *Pardalotus,* having short bills and most having brilliant plumage with gemlike specks on the dark upper parts. Also called **diamond bird.** [< NL *Pardalotus* (1816) < Gk *pardalōtós* spotted like a pard, deriv. of *pardális* pard]

par•di (pär dē′), *adv., interj. Archaic.* verily; indeed. Also, **par•die′, pardy, perdie.** [1200–50; late ME *pardie,* ME *parde* < OF *par De* < L *per Deum* by God]

pard•ner (pärd′nər), *n. U.S. Dial.* **1.** (in direct address) friend. **2.** partner. [1785–95, *Amer.*; alter. of PARTNER reproducing voiced flap, here with nasal release, of American medial *t* between voiced sounds]

par•don (pär′dn), *n.* **1.** kind indulgence, as in forgiveness of an offense or discourtesy or in tolerance of a distraction or inconvenience: *I beg your pardon, but which way is Spruce Street?* **2.** *Law.* **a.** a release from the penalty of an offense; a remission of penalty, as by a governor. **b.** the document by which such remission is declared. **3.** forgiveness of a serious offense or offender. **4.** *Obs.* a papal indulgence. —*v.t.* **5.** to make courteous allowance for or to excuse: *Pardon me, madam.* **6.** to release (a person) from liability for an offense. **7.** to remit the penalty of (an offense): *The governor will not pardon your crime.* —*interj.* **8.** (used, with rising inflection, as an elliptical form of *I beg your pardon,* as when asking a speaker to repeat something not clearly heard or understood.) [1250–1300; ME (n. and v.) < OF *pardon* (n.) remission, indulgence, n. deriv. of *pardoner* (v.) < ML *perdōnāre* to remit, overlook, lit., to forgive, equiv. to L *per-* FOR- (see PER-) + *dōnāre* to give; see DONATE; ML v. perh. a trans. from Gmc] —**par′don•a•ble,** *adj.* —**par′don•a•ble•ness,** *n.* —**par′don•a•bly,** *adv.* —**par′don•less,** *adj.*
—**Syn. 3.** absolution, remission. PARDON, AMNESTY, REPRIEVE are nouns referring to the cancellation, or delay with the possibility of eventual cancellation, of a punishment or penalty assigned for the violation of a military regulation or a civil law; absolution from guilt is not implied, merely a remission of the penalty. A PARDON is granted to an individual, often by the action of a government official such as a governor, president, or monarch, and releases the individual from any punishment due for the infraction of the law, as a death sentence, prison term, or fine: *to be released from prison with a full pardon.* An AMNESTY is a pardon granted to a group of persons for past offenses against a government; it often includes an assurance of no future prosecution: *to grant amnesty to political prisoners; an amnesty period for delinquent taxpayers during which no penalties are assessed.* A REPRIEVE is a delay of impending punishment, especially a death sentence; it does not cancel or remit the punishment, it simply delays it, usually for a specific period of time or until a decision can be arrived at as to the possibility of pardon or reduction of sentence: *a last-minute reprieve, allowing the filing of an appeal to the Supreme Court.* **6.** acquit, clear. See **excuse. 7.** forgive, absolve, condone, overlook. —**Ant. 5.** censure, blame.

par•don•er (pär′dn ər), *n.* **1.** a person who pardons. **2.** (during the Middle Ages) an ecclesiastical official authorized to sell indulgences. [1325–75; ME; see PARDON, -ER[1]]

par•dy (pär dē′), *adv., interj. Archaic.* pardi.

pare (pâr), *v.t.,* **pared, par•ing. 1.** to cut off the outer coating, layer, or part of. **2.** to remove (an outer coating, layer, or part) by cutting (often fol. by *off* or *away*). **3.** to reduce or remove by or as by cutting; diminish or decrease gradually (often fol. by *down*): *to pare down one's expenses.* [1275–1325; ME *paren* < MF *parer* to make ready, trim < L *parāre* to PREPARE] —**pare′a•ble,** *adj.*
—**Syn. 1.** See **peel**[1]. **3.** clip, shave, lessen. —**Ant. 3.** increase.

Pa•ré (PA RĀ′), *n.* **Am•broise** (äN BRWAZ′), 1510–90, French surgeon.

pa•re•cious (pə rē′shəs), *adj. Bot.* paroicous.

pa•reg•me•non (pə reg′mə non′), *n. Rhet.* the juxtaposition of words that have a common derivation, as in "sense and sensibility." [1670–80; < Gk *paregménon* derived, neut. of perf. pass. ptp. of *parágein* to bring side by side, derive. See PAR-, PARAGON]

par•e•gor•ic (par′i gôr′ik, -gor′-), *n. Pharm.* **1.** a camphorated tincture of opium, containing benzoic acid, anise oil, etc., used chiefly to stop diarrhea in children. **2.** any soothing medicine; anodyne. —*adj.* **3.** *Archaic.* assuaging pain; soothing. [1675–85; < LL *parēgoricus* < Gk *parēgorikós* soothing, equiv. to *parēgor(os)* pertaining to consolatory speech (equiv. to *par-* PAR- + *-ēgor-,* comb. form of *agorá* AGORA + *-os* adj. suffix) + *-ikos* -IC]

pa•rei•ra (pə râr′ə), *n.* the root of a South American vine, *Chondodendron tomentosum,* used as a source of curare, a diuretic, etc. [1705–15; short for PAREIRA BRAVA]

parei′ra bra′va (brä′və, brā′-), pareira. [1705–15; < Pg *parreira brava* lit., wild vine]

paren., parenthesis.

pa•ren•chy•ma (pə reng′kə mə), *n.* **1.** *Bot.* the fundamental tissue of plants, composed of thin-walled cells able to divide. **2.** *Anat., Zool.* the specific tissue of an animal organ as distinguished from its connective or supporting tissue. **3.** *Zool.* a type of soft, spongy connective tissue of certain invertebrates, as the flatworms. **4.** *Pathol.* the functional tissue of a morbid growth. [1645–55; < NL < Gk *parénchyma* lit., something poured in beside, equiv. to *par-* PAR- + *énchyma* infusion; see EN-[2], CHYME] —**pa•ren′chy•mal, par•en•chym•a•tous** (par′əng kim′ə təs), *adj.*

pa•rens (pə renz′), *n.pl. Informal.* parentheses: *The entire sentence should be in parens.* [by shortening]

parens., parentheses.

par•ent (pâr′ənt, par′-), *n.* **1.** a father or a mother. **2.** an ancestor, precursor, or progenitor. **3.** a source, origin, or cause. **4.** a protector or guardian. **5.** *Biol.* any organism that produces or generates another. **6.** *Physics.* the first nuclide in a radioactive series. —*adj.* **7.** being the original source: *a parent organization.* **8.** *Biol.* pertaining to an organism, cell, or complex molecular structure that generates or produces another: *parent cell; parent DNA.* —*v.t.* **9.** to be or act as parent of: *to parent children with both love and discipline.* [1375–1425; late ME (< MF) < L *parent-* (s. of *parēns*), n. use of prp. of *parere* to bring forth, breed] —**par′ent•less,** *adj.* —**par′ent•like′,** *adj.*

par•ent•age (pâr′ən tij, par′-), *n.* **1.** derivation or descent from parents or ancestors; birth, origin, or lineage: *a man of distinguished parentage.* **2.** the state or relation of a parent; parenthood. [1480–90; < MF; see PARENT, -AGE]
—**Syn. 1.** ancestry, extraction, stock.

pa•ren•tal (pə ren′tl), *adj.* **1.** of or pertaining to a parent. **2.** proper to or characteristic of a parent: *parental feelings.* **3.** having the relation of a parent. **4.** *Genetics.* pertaining to the sequence of generations preceding the filial generation, each generation being designated by a P followed by a subscript number indicating its place in the sequence. [1615–25; < L *parentālis* of, belonging to parents, equiv. to *parent-* PARENT + *-ālis* -AL[1]] —**pa•ren′tal•ly,** *adv.*

paren′tal home′, a school for problem children. Also called **paren′tal school′.**

paren′tal leave′, a leave of absence from a job for a parent to care for a new baby.

par′ent com′pany, a corporation or other business enterprise that owns controlling interests in one or more subsidiary companies (distinguished from *holding company*). [1865–70]

par′ent com′pound, *Chem.* a compound from which derivatives may be obtained.

par•en•ter•al (pa ren′tər əl), *adj. Anat., Med., Physiol.* **1.** taken into the body in a manner other than through the digestive canal. **2.** not within the intestine; not intestinal. [1905–10; PAR- + ENTER- + -AL[1]] —**par•en′ter•al•ly,** *adv.*

pa•ren•the•sis (pə ren′thə sis), *n., pl.* **-ses** (-sēz′). **1.** either or both of a pair of signs ( ) used in writing to mark off an interjected explanatory or qualifying remark, to indicate separate groupings of symbols in mathematics and symbolic logic, etc. **2.** Usually, **parentheses.** the material contained within these marks. **3.** *Gram.* a qualifying, explanatory, or appositive word, phrase, clause, or sentence that interrupts a syntactic construction without otherwise affecting it, having often a characteristic intonation and indicated in writing by commas, parentheses, or dashes, as in *William Smith —you must know him—is coming tonight.* **4.** an interval. [1560–70; < LL < Gk *parénthesis* a putting in beside. See PAR-, EN-[2], THESIS]

pa•ren•the•size (pə ren′thə sīz′), *v.t.,* **-sized, -siz•ing. 1.** to insert (a word, phrase, etc.) as a parenthesis. **2.** to put between marks of parenthesis: *to parenthesize the pronunciation of a word.* **3.** to interlard with parenthetic remarks, as a speech. Also, *esp. Brit.,* **pa•ren′the•sise′.** [1830–40; PARENTHES(IS) + -IZE]

par•en•thet•ic (par′ən thet′ik), *adj.* **1.** of, pertaining to, noting, or of the nature of a parenthesis: *several unnecessary parenthetic remarks.* **2.** characterized by the use of parentheses. Also, **par′en•thet′i•cal.** [1770–80; back formation from *parenthetical* < Gk *parénthet(os)* interpolated (verbid of *parentithénai,* equiv. to *par-* PAR- + *en-* EN-[2] + *the-,* var. s. of *tithénai* to put + *-tos* v. adj. suffix) + -IC + -AL[1]] —**par′en•thet′i•cal′i•ty, par′en•thet′i•cal•ness,** *n.* —**par′en•thet′i•cal•ly,** *adv.*

par•ent•hood (pâr′ənt hŏŏd′, par′-), *n.* the state, position, or relation of a parent. [1855–60; PARENT + -HOOD]

pa•ren•ti•cide (pə ren′tə sīd′), *n.* **1.** a person who kills one or both of his or her parents. **2.** the act of killing one's parent or parents. [1650–60; PARENT + -I- + -CIDE]

par•ent•ing (pâr′ən ting, par′-), *n.* **1.** the rearing of children: *The schedule allows her very little time for parenting.* **2.** the methods, techniques, etc., used or required in the rearing of children: *a course in parenting.* **3.** the state of being a parent; parenthood. —*adj.* **4.** of or concerned with the rearing of children: *good parenting skills.* [1955–60; PARENT + -ING[1]]
—**Usage.** PARENTING has come to be favored over *parenthood, rearing,* and *bringing up* in sociological and educational literature and in popular writing.

par•ent-in-law (pâr′ənt in lô′, par′-), *n., pl.* **par•ents-in-law.** the father or mother of one's wife or husband. [1895–1900]

Par′ent-Teach′er Associa′tion (pâr′ənt tē′chər, par′-), an organization of teachers and the parents of their students, as within a public school, to promote mutual understanding and to increase the effectiveness of the educational program. *Abbr.:* PTA, P.T.A.

pa•re•o (pär′ā ō′, -ā ōō′), *n., pl.* **-re•os.** pareu (def. 2).

par•er•gon (pa rûr′gon), *n., pl.* **-ga** (-gə). **1.** something that is an accessory to a main work or subject; embellishment. **2.** work undertaken in addition to one's principal work. [1595–1605; < Gk *párergon,* n. use of neut. of *párergos* beside the main subject, subordinate, equiv. to *par-* PAR- + *érg(on)* WORK + *-os* adj. suffix]

pa•re•sis (pə rē′sis, par′ə sis), *n. Pathol.* **1.** partial motor paralysis. **2.** a late manifestation of syphilis, characterized by progressive dementia and paralysis. [1685–95; < NL < Gk *páresis* paralysis, a letting go, equiv. to *pare-* (var. s. of *pariénai* to let go) + *-sis* -SIS] —**pa•ret•ic** (pə ret′ik, -rē′tik), *n., adj.* —**pa•ret′i•cal•ly,** *adv.*

par•es•the•sia (par′əs thē′zhə, -zhē ə, -zē ə), *n. Pathol.* an abnormal sensation, as prickling, itching, etc. Also, **paraesthesia.** [1855–60; < NL; see PAR-, ESTHESIA] —**par•es•thet•ic** (par′is thet′ik), *adj.*

Pa•re•to (pä RE′tô), *n.* **Vil•fre•do** (vēl FRE′dô), 1848–1923, Italian sociologist and economist in Switzerland.

pa•re•u (pär′ā ōō′), *n.* **1.** lavalava. **2.** Also, **pareo.** a length of cloth, esp. of a brightly colored print, wrapped on the body like a lavalava and worn by women as a cover-up, skirt, dress, or the like. [1855–60; < Tahitian]

pa•re•ve (pär′ə və, pär′və), *adj. Judaism.* having no meat or milk in any form as an ingredient and being permissible for use with both meat and dairy meals as stated in the dietary laws: *a pareve bread; pareve soup.* Also, **parve.** Cf. **fleishig, milchig.** [1940–45; < Yiddish *parev(e)*]

par ex•cel•lence (pär ek′sə läns′, ek′sə lans′; *Fr.* PA REK sE läns′), being an example of excellence; superior; preeminent: *a chef par excellence.* [< F]

par•fait (pär fā′), *n.* **1.** a dessert of ice cream and fruit or ice cream and syrup in alternate layers, often topped with whipped cream and served in a tall, narrow, short-stemmed glass. **2.** any frozen dessert in which fruit, nuts, etc., have been folded into whipped cream or egg custard. [1890–95; < F: lit., perfect < L *perfectus.* See PERFECT]

par•fleche (pär′flesh, pär flesh′), *n.* **1.** a rawhide that has been dried after having been soaked in a solution of lye and water to remove the hair. **2.** an article or object, as a case, pouch, etc., made of such rawhide. [1820–30; < CanF *parflèche,* equiv. to F *par(er)* to parry (see PARA-[2]) + *flèche* arrow]

par•fo•cal (pär fō′kəl), *adj. Optics.* of or pertaining to different eyepieces (of telescopes or microscopes) that all focus their images in the same plane, so that they can be interchanged without readjusting the instrument. [1885–90; PAR[1] + FOCAL]

par•fum (PAR fœN′), *n. French.* perfume.

par•gas•ite (pär′gə sīt′), *n. Mineral.* a green or blue-green variety of hornblende. [1810–20; named after *Pargas,* town in Finland; see -ITE[1]]

par•get (pär′jit), *n., v.,* **-get•ed, -get•ing** or (*esp. Brit.*) **-get•ted, -get•ting.** —*n.* **1.** any of various plasters or roughcasts for covering walls or other surfaces, esp. a mortar of lime, hair, and cow dung for lining chimney flues. **2.** gypsum. **3.** pargeting (defs. 2, 3). —*v.t.* **4.** to cover or decorate with parget or pargeting. [1300–50; ME < MF *pargeter,* equiv. to *par-* PER- + *geter,* sp. var. of *jeter* to throw; see JET[1]]

par•get•ing (pär′ji ting), *n.* **1.** the act of a person who pargets. **2.** ornamental or fine plasterwork, esp. exterior plasterwork bearing designs in low relief. **3.** a lining of mortar or plaster for a chimney flue or the like. Also, *esp. Brit.,* **par′get•ting; parget** (for defs. 2, 3). [1350–1400; ME; see PARGET, -ING[1]]

parg•ing (pär′jing), *n.* a thin coat of plaster or mortar for giving a relatively smooth surface to rough masonry or for sealing it against moisture. [1895–1900; *parge* (by shortening from PARGET) + -ING[1]]

parhe′lic cir′cle, *Meteorol.* a white, horizontal band passing through the sun, either incomplete or extending around the horizon, produced by the reflection of the sun's rays from the vertical faces of ice prisms in the atmosphere. Also called **par′heli′acal ring′.** [1885–90; PARHEL(ION) + -IC]

par•he•li•on (pär hē′lē ən, -hēl′yən), *n., pl.* **-he•li•a** (-hē′lē ə, -hēl′yə). *Meteorol.* a bright circular spot on a solar halo; a mock sun: usually one of two or more such spots seen on opposite sides of the sun, and often accompanied by additional luminous arcs and bands. Also called **sundog.** Cf. **paraselene.** [1640–50; alter. of L *parēlion* < Gk *parḗlion,* n. use of neut. of *parḗlios* beside the sun. See PAR-, HELIO-] —**par•he′lic, par•he•li•a•cal** (pär′hi lī′ə kəl), *adj.*

pari-, a combining form meaning "equal," used in the formation of compound words: *paripinnate.* [< LL *pari-* comb. form of *pār* PAR[1]]

pa•ri•ah (pə rī′ə), *n.* **1.** an outcast. **2.** any person or animal that is generally despised or avoided. **3.** (*cap.*) a member of a low caste in southern India and Burma. [1605–15; < Tamil *paṟaiyar,* pl. of *paṟaiyan* lit., drummer (from a hereditary duty of the caste), deriv. of *paṟai* a festival drum] —**pa•ri′ah•dom,** *n.* —**pa•ri′ah•ism,** *n.*

Par•i•an (pâr′ē ən, par′-), *adj.* **1.** of or pertaining to Paros, noted for its white marble. **2.** noting or pertaining to a fine, unglazed porcelain resembling this marble. **3.** of, pertaining to, or resembling a native or inhabitant of Paros. —*n.* **4.** a native or inhabitant of Paros. **5.** See **Parian ware.** [1630–40; < L *Pari(us)* of PAROS + -AN]

Par′ian ware′, an English and American hardpaste porcelain ware introduced c1850, having a white, hard surface and used mainly for biscuit figures. [1890–95]

par•i•ca (par′i kä′, -kə), *n.* a snuff used by certain Indians of South America containing dimethyltryptamine and other hallucinogenic agents, obtained from the seeds of the tree *Piptadenia peregrina.* Also called **cohoba.** [< Pg *paricá* the name of the tree < Tupi]

Pa•ri•cu•tín (pä RE′kōō tēn′), *n.* a volcano in W central Mexico: formed by an eruption 1943–52. 8200 ft. (2500 m).

par•i•es (pâr′ē ēz′), *n., pl.* **pa•ri•e•tes** (pə rī′i tēz′). Usually, **parietes.** *Biol.* a wall, as of a hollow organ; an investing part. [1720–30; < NL, special use of L *pariēs* a wall, partition]

pa•ri•e•tal (pə rī′i tl), *adj.* **1.** *Anat.* of, pertaining to, or situated near the side and top of the skull or the parietal bone. **2.** *Biol.* of or pertaining to parietes or structural walls. **3.** *Bot.* pertaining to or arising from a wall: usually applied to ovules when they proceed from or are borne on the walls or sides of the ovary. **4.** pertaining to or having authority over residence, and esp. visitation regulations between the sexes, within the walls or buildings of a college or university: *a listing of the parietal regulations for the law students' dormitory.* —*n.* **5.** *Anat.* any of several parts in the parietal region of the skull, esp. the parietal bone. **6. parietals.** Also called **pari′etal rules′.** campus regulations governing visits between members of opposite sexes to each other's dormitories or rooms. [1590–1600; < LL *parietālis* of, belonging to walls, equiv. to L *pariet-* (s. of *pariēs*) wall + *-ālis* -AL[1]]

pari′etal bone′, *Anat.* either of a pair of membrane bones forming, by their union at the sagittal suture, part of the sides and top of the skull. See diag. under **skull.** [1695–1705]

pari′etal cell′, *Anat.* any of the cells in the mucous membranes of the stomach that secrete hydrochloric acid. Also called **acid cell.** [1870–75]

pari′etal eye′, *Zool.* a median outgrowth of the diencephalon anterior to the pineal apparatus, having visual adaptations in many anamniotes and lizards. [1885–90]

pari′etal lobe′, *Anat.* the middle part of each cerebral hemisphere behind the central sulcus. [1900–05]

par•i•mu•tu•el (par′i myōō′chōō əl), *n.* **1.** a form of betting and of handling the betting on horse races at racetracks, in which those holding winning tickets divide the total amount bet in proportion to their wagers, less a percentage for the management, taxes, etc. **2.** Also called **parimu′tuel machine′.** an electronic machine that registers bets in parimutuel betting as they are made and calculates and posts the changing odds and final payoffs. [1880–85; < F: lit., mutual bet]

par•ing (pâr′ing), *n.* **1.** the act of a person or thing that pares. **2.** a piece or part pared off: *apple parings.* [1350–1400; ME (ger.); see PARE, -ING[1]]

par′ing chis′el, a woodworking chisel moved by steady hand pressure to make long, light cuts. [1695–1705]

par′ing gouge′, a woodworker's gouge having the bezel on the concave face. [1905–10]

par′ing knife′, a short-bladed kitchen knife for paring fruits and vegetables. [1585–95]

pa•ri pas•su (pä′RE päs′sōō; *Eng.* pâr′ī pas′ōō, pâr′-ē), *Latin.* **1.** with equal pace or progress; side by side. **2.** without partiality; equably; fairly.

par•i•pin•nate (par′i pin′āt, -it), *adj. Bot.* **1.** evenly pinnate. **2.** pinnate without an odd terminal leaflet. [1855–60; PARI- + PINNATE]

Par•is (par′is; *for 2 also Fr.* PA RE′), *n.* **1. Matthew.** See **Matthew of Paris. 2.** Ancient, **Lutetia Parisiorum, Pa•ris•i•i** (pə riz′ē ī′). a city in and the capital of France and capital of Ville-de-Paris Department, in the N part, on the Seine. 2,317,227. **3.** a city in NE Texas. 25,498. **4.** a town in NW Tennessee. 10,728. **5. Treaty of, a.** a treaty signed in 1763 by France, Spain, and Great Britain that ended the Seven Years' War and the French and Indian War. **b.** a treaty signed in 1783 by the United States and Great Britain that ended the American Revolution. **c.** a treaty signed in 1898 by the United States and Spain that ended the Spanish-American War.

Par•is (par′is), *n. Class. Myth.* a Trojan prince, son of Priam and Hecuba and brother of Cassandra, who awarded the apple of discord to Aphrodite and was by her help enabled to abduct Helen. Also called **Alexander, Alexandros.**

Par′is Com′mune, commune[3] (def. 8). [1960–65]

Par′is dai′sy, marguerite (def. 1). [1880–85]

Par′is green′, **1.** *Chem.* an emerald-green, poisonous, water-insoluble powder produced from arsenic trioxide and copper acetate: used chiefly as a pigment, insecticide, and wood preservative. **2.** (*sometimes l.c.*) a variable hue ranging from light to vivid yellow green in color. [1870–75]

par•ish (par′ish), *n.* **1.** an ecclesiastical district having its own church and member of the clergy. **2.** a local church with its field of activity. **3.** (in Louisiana) a county. **4.** the people of an ecclesiastical or civil parish. **5.** *Curling.* house (def. 20). **6. on the parish,** *Brit.* **a.** receiving charity from local authorities. **b.** *Informal.* meagerly or inadequately supplied. [1250–1300; ME, var. of *parosshe* < MF *paroisse* < LL *parochia,* alter. of *paroecia* < LGk *paroikía,* deriv. of Gk *pároikos* neighbor, (in Christian usage) sojourner (see PAROICOUS); see -IA]

par′ish house′, **1.** a building used by a church chiefly for administrative and social purposes. **2.** (esp. in the Roman Catholic Church) the residence of a cleric. [1755–65]

pa•rish•ion•er (pə rish′ə nər), *n.* one of the community or inhabitants of a parish. [1425–75; late ME; earlier *parishion,* ME *paroschian, -ien, -en* < OF *paroissien.* See PARISH, -IAN, -ER[1]] —**pa•rish′ion•er•ship′,** *n.*

par′ish reg′ister, *Eccles.* the register of the christenings, marriages, and burials in a parish. Also called **church register.** [1645–55]

Pa•ri•sian (pə rizh′ən, -rē′zhən, -riz′ē ən), *n.* **1.** a native or inhabitant of Paris, France. —*adj.* **2.** of, pertaining to, or characteristic of Paris, France. [1520–30; < F *parisien.* See PARIS, -IAN] —**Pa•ri′sian•ly,** *adv.*

Pa•ri•si•enne (pə rē′zē en′), *n.* a girl or woman who is a native or inhabitant of Paris, France. [1885–90; < F *parisienne,* fem. of *parisien* PARISIAN]
—**Usage.** See **-enne.**

par•i•son (par′ə sən), *n.* **1.** a partially shaped mass of molten glass. **2.** a hollow tube of plastic to be formed into a hollow object, as a bottle, by blow molding. Also, **paraison.** [1825–35; < F *paraison,* deriv. of *parer* to PREPARE < L *parāre*] —**par•i•son•ic** (par′ə son′ik), *adj.*

par•i•ty[1] (par′i tē), *n.* **1.** equality, as in amount, status, or character. **2.** equivalence; correspondence; similarity; analogy. **3.** *Finance.* **a.** equivalence in value in the currency of another country. **b.** equivalence in value at a fixed ratio between moneys of different metals. **4.** *Physics.* **a.** a property of a wave function, expressed as +1 or −1 and noting the relation of the given function to the function formed when each variable is replaced by its negative, +1 indicating that the functions are identical and −1 that the second function is the negative of the first. **b.** Also called **intrinsic parity.** a number +1 or −1 assigned to each kind of elementary particle in such a way that the product of the parities of the particles in a system of particles multiplied by the parity of the wave function describing the system is unchanged when particles are created or annihilated. **5.** a system of regulating prices of farm commodities, usually by government price supports, to provide farmers with the same purchasing power they had in a selected base period. **6.** *Computers.* the condition of the number of items in a set, particularly the number of bits per byte or word, being either even or odd: used as a means for detecting certain errors. [1565–75; < LL *paritās.* See PAR[1], -ITY]

par•i•ty[2] (par′i tē), *n. Obstet.* **1.** the condition or fact of having borne offspring. **2.** para[5] (def. 1). [1875–80; < L *par(ere)* to bring forth (cf. PARENT) + -ITY]

par′ity check′, *Computers.* a method for detecting errors in data communications or within a computer system by counting the number of ones or zeros per byte or per word, including a special check bit (**par′ity bit′**), to see if the value is even or odd. Also called **odd-even check, redundant check.** [1945–50]

par′ity opera′tion, *Physics.* See **space inversion.**

park (pärk), *n.* **1.** an area of land, usually in a largely natural state, for the enjoyment of the public, having facilities for rest and recreation, often owned, set apart, and managed by a city, state, or nation. **2.** an enclosed area or a stadium used for sports: *a baseball park.* **3.** a considerable extent of land forming the grounds of a country house. **4.** *Brit.* a tract of land reserved for wild animals; game preserve. **5.** *Western U.S.* a broad valley in a mountainous region. **6.** a space where vehicles, esp. automobiles, may be assembled or stationed. **7.** See **amusement park. 8.** See **theme park. 9.** any area set aside for public recreation. **10.** *Mil.* **a.** the space occupied by the assembled guns, tanks, or vehicles of a military unit. **b.** the assemblage so formed. **c.** (formerly) the ammunition trains and reserve artillery of an army. **11.** *Auto.* a setting in an automatic transmission in which the transmission is in neutral and the brake is engaged. —*v.t.* **12.** to place or leave (a vehicle) in a certain place for a period of time. **13.** *Informal.* to put, leave, or settle: *Park your coat on the chair. Park yourself over there for a moment.* **14.** to assemble (equipment or supplies) in a military park. **15.** to enclose in or as in a park. **16.** *Informal.* to invest (funds) in a stock, bond, etc., considered to be a safe investment with little chance of depreciation, as during a recession or an unstable economic period, or until one finds a more profitable investment. **17.** *Aerospace.* to place (a satellite) in orbit. —*v.i.* **18.** to park a car, bicycle, etc. **19.** *Informal.* to engage in kissing and caressing in a parked car. [1225–75; ME (n.) < OF *parc* enclosure < LL **parricus* < WGmc **parruk* (see PADDOCK[1])] —**park′er,** *n.* —**park′like′,** *adj.*

Park (pärk), *n.* **1. Mun•go** (mung′gō), 1771–1806?, Scottish explorer in Africa. **2. Robert E.,** 1864–1944, U.S. sociologist.

par•ka (pär′kə), *n.* **1.** a fur coat, shirtlike and hooded, for wear in the arctic and other regions of extreme cold. **2.** a hip-length jacket or overshirt with an attached hood, often of wool or of a windproof, water-repellent material lined or trimmed with wool, used by skiers, hunters, the military, etc. **3.** any coat or jacket with a hood, as a hooded raincoat or windbreaker. [1770–80; (< Aleut or Yupik) < dial. Russ *párka* (< Komi) < Nenets]

par•kade (pär kād′), *n. Canadian.* a building or other construction designed for the parking of motor vehicles. [b. PARK (v.) and ARCADE]

park-and-ride (pärk′ən rīd′), *n.* **1.** a municipal system that provides free parking for suburban commuters at an outlying terminus of a bus or rail line. —*adj.* **2.** of or pertaining to such a system: *park-and-ride lots.* [1965–70]

Park′ Av′enue, a wide street in New York City traditionally associated with luxurious residential and professional buildings, fashionable living, and high society.

Par•ker (pär′kər), *n.* **1. Charles Christopher, Jr.** ("Bird"), 1920–55, U.S. jazz saxophonist and composer. **2. Dorothy (Rothschild),** 1893–1967, U.S. author. **3. Sir Gilbert,** 1862–1932, Canadian novelist and politician in England. **4. Horatio William,** 1863–1919, U.S. composer, organist, and teacher. **5. John,** 1729–75, American Revolutionary patriot. **6. Matthew,** 1504–75, English theologian. **7. Quanah.** See **Quanah** (def. 1). **8. Theodore,** 1810–60, U.S. preacher, theologian, and reformer. **9.** a male given name.

Par′ker House′ roll′, a soft dinner roll made by folding a flat disk of dough in half. [1870–75, *Amer.;* after the *Parker House* hotel in Boston, which originally served the rolls]

Par•kers•burg (pär′kərz bûrg′), *n.* a city in NW West Virginia, on the Ohio River. 39,967.

park•ette (pär ket′), *n. Canadian.* a small park, usually open to the public and containing amenities like benches and children's play facilities. [PARK + -ETTE]

Park′ For′est, a city in NE Illinois. 26,222.

park•ing (pär′king), *n.* **1.** the act of a person or thing that parks, esp. a vehicle. **2.** space in which to park vehicles, as at a place of business or a public event: *There's plenty of free parking at the stadium.* **3.** permission to park vehicles: *Is there parking on this side of the street?* **4.** the activity or occupation of a person who operates or works in a parking lot, garage, or the like. **5.** See **parking strip. 6.** *Informal.* the act of kissing and caressing in a parked car: *Some of the couples went parking on their way home from the dance.* —*adj.* **7.** of, pertaining to, used for, or engaged in parking, esp. of vehicles: *parking regulations; a parking ticket; a parking space; a parking attendant.* [1520–30; PARK + -ING[1], -ING[2]]

park′ing brake′, *Auto.* See **emergency brake.** [1940–45]

park′ing lot′, an area, usually divided into individual spaces, intended for parking motor vehicles. [1920–25, *Amer.*]

park′ing me′ter, a mechanical device for registering and collecting payment for the length of time that a vehicle occupies a parking space, consisting typically of a timer, actuated by a coin that a driver deposits upon parking, set in a headpiece mounted on a pole. [1930–35]

park′ing or′bit, *Aerospace.* a temporary orbit in which a spacecraft awaits the next phase of its mission. [1955–60]

park′ing ramp′, apron (def. 6).

park′ing strip′, *Chiefly Upper Midwest and Western U.S.* parkway (def. 2). Also called **parking.**

Par·kin·son (pär′kin sən), *n.* **C(yril) North·cote** (nôrth′kət), 1909–93, English author and historian.

par·kin·so·ni·an (pär′kin sō′nē ən), *adj. Pathol.* of, related to, or resembling parkinsonism. [1905–10; see PARKINSONISM, -IAN]

par·kin·son·ism (pär′kin sə niz′əm), *n. Pathol.* a common neurologic disease believed to be caused by deterioration of the brain cells that produce dopamine, occurring primarily after the age of 60, characterized by tremors, esp. of the fingers and hands, muscle rigidity, shuffling gait, slow speech, and a masklike facial expression. Also called **Parkinson's disease.** [1920–25; named after James *Parkinson* (1755–1824), English physician who first described it]

Par′kinson's disease′, *Pathol.* parkinsonism.

Par′kinson's law′, the statement, expressed facetiously as if a law of physics, that work expands to fill the time allotted for its completion. Also, **Par′kinson's Law′.** [1950–55; after C. N. PARKINSON]

Par′kinson's syn′drome, a complex of symptoms indistinguishable from parkinsonism, commonly affecting boxers or sometimes occurring as a result of substance abuse or an encephalitic infection. [1950–55; see PARKINSONISM]

park·land (pärk′land′), *n.* **1.** a grassland region with isolated or grouped trees, usually in temperate regions. **2.** wooded or verdant land for recreational use by the public; parklike terrain. [1905–10; PARK + LAND]

Park·man (pärk′mən), *n.* **Francis,** 1823–93, U.S. historian.

Park′ Range′, a range of the Rocky Mountains in central Colorado. Highest peak, Mt. Lincoln, 14,287 ft. (4355 m).

Park′ Ridge′, a city in NE Illinois. 38,704.

Parks (pärks), *n.* **Gordon (Alexander Buchanan),** born 1912, U.S. photojournalist and film director.

Park·ville (pärk′vil), *n.* a city in N Maryland, near Baltimore. 35,159.

park·way (pärk′wā′), *n.* **1.** a broad thoroughfare with a dividing strip or side strips planted with grass, trees, etc. **2.** *Chiefly New York State and Western New Eng.* a strip of grass, sometimes planted with trees or shrubs, between a sidewalk and curb. [1885–90, *Amer.*; PARK + WAY[1]]

Parl., **1.** Parliament. **2.** Parliamentary. Also, **parl.**

par·lance (pär′ləns), *n.* **1.** a way or manner of speaking; vernacular; idiom: *legal parlance.* **2.** speech, esp. a formal discussion or debate. **3.** talk; parley. [1570–80; < AF; see PARLE, -ANCE]

par·lan·do (pär län′dō), *adj. Music.* sung or played as though speaking or reciting (a musical direction). [1875–80; < It, prp. of *parlare* to speak; see PARLE]

par·la·ry (pə lär′ē, pär-), *n.* Polari.

par·lay (pär′lā, -lē), —*v.t.* **1.** to bet or gamble (an original amount and its winnings) on a subsequent race, contest, etc. **2.** *Informal.* to use (one's money, talent, or other assets) to achieve a desired objective, as spectacular wealth or success: *He parlayed a modest inheritance into a fortune.* —*n.* **3.** a bet of an original sum and the subsequent winnings. [1820–30, *Amer.*; alter. of earlier *paroli* < F < Neapolitan It, pl. of *parolo*, perh. deriv. of *paro* equal < L *pār*; see PAIR]

parle (pärl), *n., v.i.,* **parled, parl·ing.** *Archaic.* talk; parley. [1350–1400; ME *parlen* < MF *parler* to speak < LL *parabolāre*; see PARABLE]

par·le·ment (pär′lə mənt), *n. Obs.* parliament.

par·ley (pär′lē), *n., pl.* **-leys,** *v.,* **-leyed, -ley·ing.** —*n.* **1.** a discussion or conference. **2.** an informal conference between enemies under a truce, esp. to discuss terms, conditions of surrender, etc. —*v.i.* **3.** to hold an informal conference with an enemy under a truce, as between active hostilities. **4.** to speak, talk, or confer. [1400–50; late ME *parlai* < MF *parlee*, n. use of fem. of *parle*, ptp. of *parler* to speak; see PARLE] —**par′ley·er,** *n.*
—**Syn. 1.** talk, conversation. **4.** discuss, converse.

Par·ley (pär′lē), *n.* **Peter,** pen name of Samuel Griswold Goodrich.

par·lia·ment (pär′lə mənt *or, sometimes,* pärl′yə-), *n.* **1.** (*usually cap.*) the legislature of Great Britain, historically the assembly of the three estates, now composed of Lords Spiritual and Lords Temporal, forming together the House of Lords, and representatives of the counties, cities, boroughs, and universities, forming the House of Commons. **2.** (*usually cap.*) the legislature of certain British colonies and possessions. **3.** a legislative body in any of various other countries. **4.** *Fr. Hist.* any of several high courts of justice in France before 1789. **5.** a meeting or assembly for conference on public or national affairs. **6.** *Cards.* fan-tan (def. 1). [1250–1300; ME: discourse, consultation, Parliament < AL *parliamentum*, alter. of ML *parlāmentum* < OF *parlement* a speaking, conference (see PARLE, -MENT); r. ME *parlement* < OF]

par·lia·men·tar·i·an (pär′lə men târ′ē ən, -mən- *or, sometimes,* pärl′yə-), *n.* **1.** a person who is expert in the formal rules and procedures of deliberative assemblies and other formal organizations. **2.** (*sometimes cap.*) *Brit.* a member of Parliament. **3.** (*cap.*) a partisan of the British Parliament in opposition to Charles I. [1605–15; PARLIAMENT + -ARIAN]

par·lia·men·tar·i·an·ism (pär′lə men târ′ē ə niz′əm, -mən- *or, sometimes,* pärl′yə-), *n.* advocacy of a parliamentary system of government. [1875–80; PARLIAMENTARIAN + -ISM]

par·lia·men·ta·ry (pär′lə men′tə rē, -trē *or, sometimes,* pärl′yə-), *adj.* **1.** of or pertaining to a parliament or any of its members. **2.** enacted or established by a parliament. **3.** having a parliament. **4.** of the nature of a parliament. **5.** in accordance with the formal rules governing the methods of procedure, discussion, and debate in deliberative bodies and organized assemblies: *parliamentary order.* [1610–20; PARLIAMENT + -ARY] —**par′lia·men′ta·ri·ly,** *adv.*

par′liamen′tary gov′ernment, government by a body of cabinet ministers who are chosen from and responsible to the legislature and act as advisers to a nominal chief of state. Also called **cabinet government.** [1855–60]

par′liamen′tary law′, the body of rules, usages, and precedents that governs proceedings of legislative and deliberative assemblies. [1905–10]

Par′liament clock′, a pendulum wall clock of the late 18th century, usually having a black dial with gilt numbers: originally installed in English taverns because a burdensome tax prevented many homes from having private clocks. Also called **Act of Parliament clock.**

par′liament hinge′, a butt hinge the knuckle of which protrudes from the door so that the door when fully opened stands away from the wall. [1835–45]

par·lor (pär′lər), *n.* **1.** *Older Use.* a room for the reception and entertainment of visitors to one's home; living room. **2.** a room, apartment, or building serving as a place of business for certain businesses or professions: *funeral parlor; beauty parlor.* **3.** a somewhat private room in a hotel, club, or the like for relaxation, conversation, etc.; lounge. **4.** Also called **locutorium.** a room in a monastery or the like where the inhabitants may converse with visitors or with each other. —*adj.* **5.** advocating something, as a political view or doctrine, at a safe remove from actual involvement in or commitment to action: *parlor leftism; parlor pink.* Also, *esp. Brit.,* **parlour.** [1175–1225; ME *parlur* < AF; OF *parleor*, equiv. to *parl(er)* to speak (see PARLE) + *-eor* -OR[2]]

par′lor car′, a railroad passenger car that has individual reserved seats and is more comfortable than a day coach. [1855–60]

par′lor game′, any game usually played indoors, esp. in the living room or parlor, as a word game or a quiz, requiring little or no physical activity. [1890–95]

par′lor grand′, a grand piano smaller than a concert grand but larger than a baby grand. [1855–60, *Amer.*]

par′lor house′, (esp. in the 19th and early 20th centuries) a brothel with a comfortable, often elaborately decorated parlor for the reception of clients. [1860–65]

par·lor·maid (pär′lər mād′), *n.* a maid who takes care of a parlor, answers the door, waits on guests, etc. [1830–40; PARLOR + MAID]

par′lor palm′, a small palm, *Chamaedorea elegans*, native to Central America, having a reedlike stem and long, pointed leaflets, widely cultivated as a houseplant. Also called **dwarf fan palm.** [1900–05]

par·lour (pär′lər), *n., adj. Chiefly Brit.* parlor.
—**Usage.** See **-or**[1].

par·lous (pär′ləs), *adj.* **1.** perilous; dangerous. **2.** *Obs.* clever; shrewd. —*adv.* **3.** to a large extent; greatly. [1350–1400; ME, var. of *perlous*, syncopated var. of PERILOUS] —**par′lous·ly,** *adv.* —**par′lous·ness,** *n.*

parl. proc., parliamentary procedure.

par·lya·ree (pəl yär′ē, pärl-), *n.* Polari.

Par·ma (pär′mə; *for 1 also It.* pär′mä), *n.* **1.** a city in N Italy, SE of Milan. 177,934. **2.** a city in NE Ohio. 92,548.

Par′ma Heights′ (pär′mə), a city in NE Ohio, near Cleveland. 23,112.

Par′ma vi′olet, a variety of the sweet violet, *Viola odorata*, that is the source of an essential oil used in perfumery. [1855–60; after PARMA, Italy]

Par·men·i·des (pär men′i dēz′), *n.* fl. c450 B.C., Greek Eleatic philosopher. —**Par·me·nid·e·an** (pär′mə-nid′ē ən), *adj.*

Par·men·tier (pär′men tyā′; *Fr.* PAR MÄN TYĀ′), *adj.* (*sometimes l.c.*) (of food) prepared or served with potatoes: *potage Parmentier.* Also, **Par·men·tière** (pär′-men tyâr′; *Fr.* PAR MÄN TYER′). [1905–10; named after A. A. *Parmentier* (1737–1813), French promoter of economic botany]

Par·me·san (pär′mə zän′, -zan′, -zən; pär′mə zän′, -zan′), *adj.* **1.** of or from Parma, in northern Italy. —*n.* **2.** (*sometimes l.c.*) Also called **Par′mesan cheese′.** a hard, dry variety of Italian cheese made from skim milk, usually grated and sprinkled over pasta dishes and soups. [1510–20; < MF < It *parmigiano* pertaining to Parma]

par·mi·gia·na (pär′mə zhä′nə, -zhan′; *It.* pär′mē jä′-nä), *adj. Italian Cookery.* cooked with Parmesan cheese: *veal parmigiana; eggplant parmigiana.* Also, **par·mi·gia·no** (pär′mə zhä′nō; *It.* pär′mē jä′nô). [1940–45; < It, fem. of *parmigiano* PARMESAN]

Par·na·í·ba (pär′nä ē′bä), *n.* **1.** a seaport in NE Brazil. 57,000. **2.** a river in NE Brazil, flowing NE to the Atlantic. 900 mi. (1450 km) long. Also, **Par′na·hi′ba, Par′na·hy′ba.**

Par·nas·si·an (pär nas′ē ən), *adj.* **1.** pertaining to Mount Parnassus. **2.** pertaining to poetry. **3.** of, pertaining to, or noting a school of French poets of the latter half of the 19th century, characterized chiefly by a belief in art for art's sake, by an emphasis on metrical form, and by the repression of emotive elements: so called from *Le Parnasse Contemporain*, the title of their first collection of poems, published in 1866. —*n.* **4.** a member of the Parnassian school of French poets. [1635–45; < L *Parnassi(us)* of PARNASSUS + -AN] —**Par·nas′si·an·ism, Par·nas′sism,** *n.*

Par·nas·sus (pär nas′əs), *n.* **1. Mount.** Modern, **Liakoura.** a mountain in central Greece, N of the Gulf of Corinth and near Delphi. ab. 8000 ft. (2440 m). **2.** a collection of poems or of elegant literature. **3.** the world of poetry or poets collectively: *a rhymester striving to enter Parnassus.* **4.** any center of poetry or artistic activity: *Greenwich Village was once the Parnassus of the U.S.*

Par·nell (pär nel′, pär′nl), *n.* **Charles Stewart,** 1846–91, Irish political leader. —**Par·nell′ism,** *n.* —**Par·nell′ite,** *n.*

Par·nis (pär′nis), *n.* **Mollie** (*Mollie Parnis Livingston*), born 1905, U.S. fashion designer.

pa·ro·cheth (*Seph.* pô RÔ′KHet; *Ashk.* pə RŌ′KHes), *n. Hebrew.* parokheth. Also, ***pa·ro′chet.***

pa·ro·chi·al (pə rō′kē əl), *adj.* **1.** of or pertaining to a parish or parishes. **2.** of or pertaining to parochial schools or the education they provide. **3.** very limited or narrow in scope or outlook; provincial: *parochial views; a parochial mentality.* [1350–1400; late ME *parochialle* < LL *parochiālis* (see PARISH, -AL[1]); r. ME *parochiele* < AF *parochiel* < LL as above] —**pa·ro′chi·al·ly,** *adv.* —**pa·ro′chi·al·ness,** *n.*

Paro′chial Church′ Coun′cil, *Anglican Ch.* the ruling body of a parish, composed of the vicar, the churchwardens, and elected laypersons.

pa·ro·chi·al·ism (pə rō′kē ə liz′əm), *n.* a parochial character, spirit, or tendency; excessive narrowness of interests or view; provincialism. [1840–50; PAROCHIAL + -ISM] —**pa·ro′chi·al·ist,** *n.* —**pa·ro′chi·al·i·za′tion,** *n.*

pa·ro·chi·al·ize (pə rō′kē ə līz′), *v.,* **-ized, -iz·ing.** —*v.t.* **1.** to make parochial. —*v.i.* **2.** to work in or for a parish. Also, *esp. Brit.,* **pa·ro′chi·al·ise′.** [1840–50; PAROCHIAL + -IZE]

paro′chial school′, a primary or secondary private school supervised by a religious organization, esp. a Roman Catholic day school affiliated with a parish or a holy order. Cf. **church school.** [1745–55]

pa·rod·ic (pə rod′ik), *adj.* having or of the nature of a parody. Also, **pa·rod′i·cal.** [1820–30; PAROD(Y) + -IC]

par·o·dist (par′ə dist), *n.* a writer of parodies, esp. of a literary subject, work, or style. [1735–45; < F *parodiste.* See PARODY, -IST]

par·o·dis·tic (par′ə dis′tik), *adj.* parodic. [1880–85; PARODIST + -IC] —**par′o·dis′ti·cal·ly,** *adv.*

par·o·don·tium (par′ə don′shəm; -shē əm), *n., pl.* **-tia** (-shə, -shē ə). periodontium. [< NL; see PAR-, PERIODONTIUM]

par·o·dos (par′ə dos′), *n., pl.* **-doi** (-doi′). (in ancient Greek drama) an ode sung by the chorus at their entrance, usually beginning the play and preceding the *proagōn* in comedy or the alteration of epeisodia and stasima in tragedy. [< Gk *párodos* way by, passage, equiv. to *par-* PAR- + *(h)odós* way, road]

par·o·dy (par′ə dē), *n., pl.* **-dies,** *v.,* **-died, -dy·ing.** —*n.* **1.** a humorous or satirical imitation of a serious piece of literature or writing: *his hilarious parody of Hamlet's soliloquy.* **2.** the genre of literary composition represented by such imitations. **3.** a burlesque imitation of a musical composition. **4.** any humorous, satirical, or burlesque imitation, as of a person, event, etc. **5.** the use in the 16th century of borrowed material in a musical setting of the Mass (**par′ody Mass′**). **6.** a poor or feeble imitation or semblance; travesty: *His acting is a parody of his past greatness.* —*v.t.* **7.** to imitate (a composition, author, etc.) for purposes of ridicule or satire. **8.** to imitate poorly or feebly; travesty. [1590–1600; < L *parōdia* a parody < Gk *parōidía* a burlesque song or poem. See PAR-, ODE, -Y[3]] —**par′o·di·a·ble,** *adj.*
—**Syn. 1, 2.** See **burlesque.**

pa·roi·cous (pə roi′kəs), *adj. Bot.* (of certain mosses) having the male and female reproductive organs beside or near each other. Also, **parecious, pa·roe·cious** (pə rē′shəs). [1885–90; < Gk *pároikos* dwelling beside, equiv. to *par-* PAR- + *oîk(os)* house + *-os* adj. suffix; see -OUS]

pa·ro·kheth (*Seph.* pô RÔ′KHET; *Ashk.* pə RŌ′KHes), *n. Hebrew.* a richly embroidered curtain that hangs in front of the Holy Ark in a synagogue. Also, ***pa·ro′khet, parocheth, parochet.*** [*pārokheth* curtain, deriv. of *pārakh* seperate, set off]

pa·rol (pə rōl′, par′əl), *Law.* —*n.* **1.** something stated or declared. **2. by parol,** by word of mouth; orally. —*adj.* **3.** given by word of mouth; oral; not contained in documents: *parol evidence.* [1470–80; earlier *parole* < AF, OF < VL **paraula*, syncopated var. of **paravola*; L *parabola* PARABLE; cf. PARLEY]

pa·role (pə rōl′), *n., v.,* **-roled, -rol·ing,** *adj.* —*n.* **1.** *Penol.* **a.** the conditional release of a person from prison prior to the end of the maximum sentence imposed. **b.** such release or its duration. **c.** an official document authorizing such a release. **2.** *Mil.* **a.** the promise, usually written, of a prisoner of war, that if released he or she either will return to custody at a specified time or will not again take up arms against his or her captors. **b.** (formerly) any password given by authorized personnel in passing by a guard. **3.** word of honor given or pledged. **4.** (in U.S. immigration laws) the temporary admission of aliens into the U.S. for emergency reasons or on grounds considered in the public interest, as au-

CONCISE ETYMOLOGY KEY: <, descended or borrowed from; >, whence; b., blend of; c., cognate with; cf., compare; deriv., derivative; equiv., equivalent; imit., imitative; obl., oblique; r., replacing; s., stem; sp., spelling, spelled; resp., respelling, respelled; trans., translation; ?, origin unknown; *, unattested; ‡, probably earlier than. See the full key inside the front cover.

thorized by and at the discretion of the attorney general. **5.** *Law.* parol. —*v.t.* **6.** to place or release on parole. **7.** to admit (an alien) into the U.S. under the parole provision: *An increased number of Hungarian refugees were paroled into the United States.* —*adj.* **8.** of or pertaining to parole or parolees: *a parole record.* [1610–20; < MF, short for *parole d'honneur* word of honor. See PAROL] —**pa·rol′a·ble,** *adj.*

pa·role (pa rôl′), *n. French.* language as manifested in the actual utterances produced by speakers of a language (contrasted with *langue*).

pa·rol·ee (pə rō lē′, -rō′lē), *n.* a person who is released from prison on parole. [1915–20; PAROLE + -EE]

par·o·no·ma·sia (par′ə nō mā′zhə, -zhē ə, -zē ə), *n. Rhet.* **1.** the use of a word in different senses or the use of words similar in sound to achieve a specific effect, as humor or a dual meaning; punning. **2.** a pun. [1570–80; < L < Gk *paronomasía* a play on words, assonance, deriv. of *paronomázein* to make a slight name-change (*par-* PAR- + *onomázein* to name, deriv. of *ónoma* NAME); see -IA] —**par·o·no·mas·tic** (par′ə nō mas′tik), *adj.* —**par′o·no·mas′ti·cal·ly,** *adv.*

par·o·nych·i·a (par′ə nik′ē ə), *n. Pathol.* inflammation of the folds of skin bordering a nail of a finger or toe, usually characterized by infection and pus formation; felon. [1590–1600; < L *parōnychia* < Gk *parōnychía* whitlow, equiv. to *par-* PAR- + *onych-* (s. of *ónyx*) claw, nail + *-ia* -IA] —**par′o·nych′i·al,** *adj.*

par·o·nym (par′ə nim), *n. Gram.* a paronymous word. [1840–50; < Gk *parṓnymon,* neut. of *parṓnymos* formed by a slight change in name, derivative, equiv. to *par-* PAR- + *-ōnymos,* adj. deriv. of *ónyma* NAME] —**par′o·nym′ic,** *adj.*

pa·ron·y·mous (pə ron′ə məs), *adj. Gram.* containing the same root or stem, as the words *wise* and *wisdom.* [1655–65; < Gk *parṓnymos.* See PARONYM, -OUS]

par·o·quet (par′ə ket′), *n.* parakeet.

Par·os (pâr′os; *Gk.* pä′rôs), *n.* a Greek island of the Cyclades, in the S Aegean: noted for its white marble. 6776; 77 sq. mi. (200 sq. km).

pa·ros·mi·a (pə roz′mē ə), *n. Pathol.* a disorder of the sense of smell, esp. the perception of odors that are not present. [1815–25; PAR- + Gk *osm(ḗ)* smell + -IA]

pa·ro·tic (pə rō′tik, -rot′ik), *adj. Anat., Zool.* situated about or near the ear. [1855–60; < NL *parōticus* < Gk *par-* PAR- + *ōtikós* of the ear; see OTO-, IC]

pa·rot·id (pə rot′id), *Anat.* —*n.* **1.** Also called **parot′id gland′.** a salivary gland situated at the base of each ear. —*adj.* **2.** of, pertaining to, or situated near either parotid. [1680–90; < NL *parōtid-* (s. of *parōtis*) parotid gland; L: tumor near the ear < Gk *parōtís.* See PAR-, OTO-] —**pa·rot′i·de′an,** *adj.*

par·o·tit·ic (par′ə tit′ik), *adj.* of or pertaining to parotitis. [1855–60; PAROTIT(IS) + -IC]

par·o·ti·tis (par′ə tī′tis), *n. Pathol.* **1.** inflammation of a parotid. **2.** mumps. Also, **pa·rot·i·di·tis** (pə rot′i-dī′tis). [1815–25; PAROT(ID) + -ITIS]

pa·ro·toid (pə rō′toid), *Zool.* —*n.* **1.** Also called **paro′toid gland′.** any of certain cutaneous glands forming warty masses near the ear in certain toads. —*adj.* **2.** of or pertaining to a parotoid. **3.** resembling a parotid. [1870–75; PAROT(ID) + -OID]

-parous, a combining form meaning "bearing," "producing" that specified by the initial element: *oviparous; viviparous.* [< L *-parus* bearing, equiv. to *par(ere)* to bear, bring forth + *-us* adj. suffix; see -OUS]

Par·ou·si·a (pə rōō′zē ə, -sē ə, pär′ōō sē′ə), *n.* **1.** advent (def. 4). **2.** (*l.c.*) *Platonism.* the presence in any thing of the idea after which it was formed. [1870–75; < Gk *parousía* a being present, presence, equiv. to *par-* PAR- + *ous-* (s. of *ōn,* prp. of *eînai* to be) + *-ia* -IA]

par·ox·ysm (par′ək siz′əm), *n.* **1.** any sudden, violent outburst; a fit of violent action or emotion: *paroxysms of rage.* **2.** *Pathol.* a severe attack or a sudden increase in intensity of a disease, usually recurring periodically. [1570–80; earlier *paroxismos* < Gk *paroxysmós* irritation, deriv. of *paroxýnein* to irritate. See PAR-, OXY-[1], -ISM] —**par′ox·ys′mal, par′ox·ys′mic,** *adj.* —**par′ox·ys′mal·ly,** *adv.*

paroxys′mal tachycar′dia, *Pathol.* tachycardia that begins and subsides suddenly.

par·ox·y·tone (pə rok′si tōn′), *Class. Gk. Gram.* —*adj.* **1.** having an acute accent on the next to the last syllable. —*n.* **2.** a paroxytone word. [1755–65; < NL *paroxytonus* < Gk *paroxýtonos.* See PAR-, OXYTONE] —**par·ox·y·ton·ic** (par′ok si ton′ik, pə rok′-), *adj.*

par·pen (pär′pən), *n.* perpend[1].

par·quet (pär kā′), *n., v.,* **-queted** (-kād′), **-quet·ing** (-kā′ing). —*n.* **1.** a floor composed of short strips or blocks of wood forming a pattern, sometimes with inlays of other woods or other materials. **2.** the part of the main floor of a theater, opera house, etc., that is between the musicians' area and the parterre or rear division or, esp. in the U.S., the entire floor space for spectators. —*v.t.* **3.** to construct (a floor) of parquetry. [1670–80; < F, dim. of *parc* PARK; see -ET]

par′quet cir′cle, parterre (def. 1). [1850–55, *Amer.*]

par·quet·ry (pär′ki trē), *n.* mosaic work of wood used for floors, wainscoting, etc.; marquetry. [1835–45; < F *parqueterie.* See PARQUET, -ERY]

parquetry

parr (pär), *n., pl.* **parrs,** (*esp. collectively*) **parr. 1.** a young salmon, having dark crossbars on its sides. **2.** the young of certain other fishes, as the codfish. [1705–15; orig. uncert.]

Parr (pär), *n.* **Catherine.** See **Catherine Parr.**

par·ra·keet (par′ə kēt′), *n.* parakeet.

par·ra·mat·ta (par′ə mat′ə), *n.* paramatta.

Par·ran (par′ən), *n.* **Thomas, Jr.,** 1892–1968, U.S. public health official.

par·rel (par′əl), *n. Naut.* a sliding ring or collar of rope, wood, or metal that confines a yard or the jaws of a gaff to the mast but allows vertical movement. Also, **par′ral.** [1425–75; late ME *perell,* var. of ME *parail,* aph. var. of *aparail* APPAREL]

par·ri·cide (par′ə sīd′), *n.* **1.** the act of killing one's father, mother, or other close relative. **2.** a person who commits such an act. [1545–55; < L *parricīdium* act of kin-murder, *parricīda* kin-killer, equiv. to *pāri-* (akin to Gk *pāós,* Attic *pēós* kinsman) + *-cīdum, -cīda* -CIDE] —**par′ri·cid′al,** *adj.*

Par·ring·ton (par′ing tən), *n.* **Vernon Louis,** 1871–1929, U.S. literary historian and critic.

Par·rish (par′ish), *n.* **1. Anne,** 1888–1957, U.S. novelist and author of books for children. **2. (Frederick) Max·field** (maks′fēld′), 1870–1966, U.S. painter and illustrator.

Par′ris Is′land (par′is), a U.S. Marine Corps base, recruit depot, and training station in SE South Carolina, SW of Beaufort and S of Port Royal Island.

par·ro·ket (par′ə ket′), *n.* parakeet. Also, **par′ro·quet′.**

par·rot (par′ət), *n.* **1.** any of numerous hook-billed, often brilliantly colored birds of the order Psittaciformes, as the cockatoo, lory, macaw, or parakeet, having the ability to mimic speech and often kept as pets. **2.** a person who, without thought or understanding, merely repeats the words or imitates the actions of another. —*v.t.* **3.** to repeat or imitate without thought or understanding. **4.** to teach to repeat or imitate in such a fashion. [1515–25; appar. < MF *P(i)errot,* dim. of *Pierre* (see PARAKEET), though a comparable sense of the F word is not known until the 18th century] —**par′rot·like′,** *adj.* —**par′rot·y,** *adj.*

par′rot fe′ver, *Pathol.* psittacosis. Also called **par′rot disease′.** [1950–55]

par·rot·fish (par′ət fish′), *n., pl.* (*esp. collectively*) **-fish,** (*esp. referring to two or more kinds or species*) **-fish·es.** any of various chiefly tropical marine fishes, esp. of the family Scaridae: so called because of their brilliant coloring and the shape of their jaws. Also called **pollyfish.** [1705–15; PARROT + FISH]

par·rot's-bill (par′əts bil′), *n.* a showy, vinelike plant, *Clianthus puniceus,* of New Zealand, having clusters of eight white-streaked, crimson flowers. Also called **par·rot-beak** (par′ət bēk′), **red kowhai.** [1865–70; presumably trans. of the Maori name of the plant, *kōwhai ŋutukākā* lit., kaka-billed kowhai]

par·rot's-feath·er (par′əts feth′ər), *n.* a South American water milfoil, *Myriophyllum aquaticum,* having hairlike pinnate leaves, widely cultivated as an aquarium plant.

par′rot tu′lip, a variety of the cultivated tulip *Tulipa gesnerana,* having variously colored, often double flowers with fringed petals. [1855–60]

par·ry (par′ē), *v.,* **-ried, -ry·ing,** *n., pl.* **-ries.** —*v.t.* **1.** to ward off (a thrust, stroke, weapon, etc.), as in fencing; avert. **2.** to turn aside; evade or dodge: *to parry an embarrassing question.* —*v.i.* **3.** to parry a thrust, blow, etc. —*n.* **4.** an act or instance of parrying, as in fencing. **5.** a defensive movement in fencing. [1665–75; < F *parez,* impv. of *parer* to ward off, set off < L *parāre* to set. See PARADE] —**par′ri·a·ble,** *adj.* —**par′ri·er,** *n.*

—**Syn. 2.** avert; elude; prevent, obviate, preclude.

Par·ry (par′ē), *n.* **William Edward,** 1790–1855, English arctic explorer.

pars (pärz), *n., pl.* **par·tes** (pär′tēz). (in prescriptions) a part. [< L]

parse (pärs, pärz), *v.,* **parsed, pars·ing.** —*v.t.* **1.** to analyze (a sentence) in terms of grammatical constituents, identifying the parts of speech, syntactic relations, etc. **2.** to describe (a word in a sentence) grammatically, identifying the part of speech, inflectional form, syntactic function, etc. **3.** *Computers.* to analyze (a string of characters) in order to associate groups of characters with the syntactic units of the underlying grammar. —*v.i.* **4.** to admit of being parsed. [1545–55; < L *pars* part, as in *pars ōrātiōnis* part of speech] —**pars′a·ble,** *adj.* —**pars′er,** *n.*

par·sec (pär′sek′), *n. Astron.* a unit of distance equal to that required to cause a heliocentric parallax of one second of an arc, equivalent to 206,265 times the distance from the earth to the sun, or 3.26 light-years. [1910–15; PAR(ALLAX) + SEC(OND)[2]]

Par·see (pär′sē, pär sē′), *n.* **1.** an Indian Zoroastrian descended from Persian Zoroastrians who went to India in the 7th and 8th centuries to escape Muslim persecution. **2.** the Middle Persian dialect of the Parsee scriptures. Also, **Par′si.** [1605–15; < Pers *Pārsī* Persian, equiv. to *Pārs* PERSIA + *-ī* suffix of appurtenance]

Par·see·ism (par′sē iz′əm, pär sē′iz əm), *n.* the religion and customs of the Parsees. Also, **Par′si·ism.** [1835–45; PARSEE + -ISM]

Par·si·fal (pär′sə fəl, -fäl′), *n.* **1.** (*italics*) a music drama by Richard Wagner: composed 1877–82; première 1882. **2.** *Teutonic Legend.* Percival (def. 1).

par·si·mo·ni·ous (pär′sə mō′nē əs), *adj.* characterized by or showing parsimony; frugal or stingy. [1590–1600; PARSIMON(Y) + -IOUS] —**par′si·mo′ni·ous·ly,** *adv.* —**par′si·mo′ni·ous·ness,** *n.*

—**Syn.** tight, close, niggardly, miserly, illiberal, mean, penurious; avaricious, covetous. See **stingy.** —**Ant.** generous.

par·si·mo·ny (pär′sə mō′nē), *n.* extreme or excessive economy or frugality; stinginess; niggardliness. [1400–50; late ME *parcimony* < L *parsimōnia, parcimōnia* frugality, thrift, equiv. to *parsi-* (comb. form of *parsus,* ptp. of *parcere* to economize) or *parci-* (comb. form of *parcus* sparing) + *-mōnia* -MONY]

pars in·ter·me·di·a (pärz′ in′tər mē′dē ə), *Anat.* See under **pituitary gland.** [1905–10; < NL: intermediate part]

pars·ley (pär′slē), *n.* **1.** an herb, *Pertoselinum crispum,* native to the Mediterranean, having either curled leaf clusters **(French parsley)** or flat compound leaves **(Italian parsley),** widely cultivated for use in garnishing or seasoning food. Cf. **parsley family. 2.** the leaves of this plant, used to garnish or season food. **3.** any of certain allied or similar plants. —*adj.* **4.** Also, **pars′lied, pars′leyed.** cooked or garnished with parsley: *parsley potatoes.* [bef. 1000; ME *persely,* b. OE *petersilie* and OF *persil;* both < LL **petrosilium,* alter. of L *petroselinum* < Gk *petrosélinon* rock-parsley. See PETRO-, CELERY] —**pars′ley·like′,** *adj.*

pars′ley fam′ily, the plant family Umbelliferae (or Apiaceae), characterized by herbaceous plants having alternate, usually compound leaves, hollow stems, numerous small flowers borne in umbels, and dry, seedlike, often aromatic fruit, and including anise, caraway, carrot, celery, dill, parsley, parsnip, and Queen Anne's lace, as well as poisonous plants such as cowbane and water hemlock.

pars·nip (pär′snip), *n.* **1.** a plant, *Pastinaca sativa,* cultivated varieties of which have a large, whitish, edible root. **2.** the root of this plant. [1350–1400; earlier *pars(e)nep, pass(e)nep,* ME *pas(t)nep(e)* < L *past(ināca)* parsnip (deriv. of *pastinum* forked dibble) + ME *nep* turnip; see NEEP]

par·son (pär′sən), *n.* **1.** a member of the clergy, esp. a Protestant minister; pastor; rector. **2.** the holder or incumbent of a parochial benefice, esp. an Anglican. [1200–50; ME *persone* < ML *persōna* parish priest, L: personage. See PERSON] —**par·son·ic** (pär son′ik), **par·son′i·cal,** *adj.* —**par·son′i·cal·ly,** *adv.* —**par′son·ish, par′son·like′,** *adj.*

par·son·age (pär′sə nij), *n.* **1.** the residence of a member of the clergy, as provided by the parish or church. **2.** *Eng. Eccles. Law.* the benefice of a parson. [1250–1300; ME *personage* < AF, equiv. to ML *persōnāticum* benefice. See PARSON, -AGE]

par′son bird′, tui. [1855–60]

Par·sons (pär′sənz), *n.* **1. Tal·cott** (tôl′kot, tal′-), 1902–79, U.S. sociologist and author. **2. Theophilus,** 1750–1813, U.S. jurist. **3.** a town in SE Kansas. 12,898.

par′son's nose′, *Facetious.* See **pope's nose.** [1830–40]

Par′sons ta′ble, a square or rectangular table, often of lightweight material, with straight legs that are square in cross section and of the same thickness as the top extending from the corners flush with the top so as to appear jointless. [1965–70; named after the Parsons School of Design, New York City]

Parsons table

Pars·va (pärsh′və, pärs′-), *n. Jainism.* a semilegendary Tirthankara of the 8th century B.C., said to have been born after a series of pious incarnations in each of which he was killed by an antagonist who had originally been his elder brother: the twenty-third Tirthankara.

part (pärt), *n.* **1.** a portion or division of a whole that is separate or distinct; piece, fragment, fraction, or section; constituent: *the rear part of the house; to glue the two parts together.* **2.** an essential or integral attribute or quality: *a sense of humor is part of a healthy personality.* **3.** a section or division of a literary work. **4.** a portion, member, or organ of an animal body. **5.** any of a number of more or less equal quantities that compose a whole or into which a whole is divided: *Use two parts sugar to one part cocoa.* **6.** an allotted portion; share. **7.** Usually, **parts. a.** a region, quarter, or district: *a journey to foreign parts.* **b.** a quality or attribute establishing the possessor as a person of importance or superior worth: *Being both a diplomat and a successful businesswoman, she is widely regarded as a woman of parts.* **8.** either of the opposing sides in a contest, question, agreement, etc. **9.** the dividing line formed in separating the hair of the head and combing it in different directions. **10.** a constituent piece of a machine or tool either included at the time of manufacture or set in place as a replacement for the original piece. **11.** *Music.* **a.** the written or printed matter extracted from the score that a single performer or section uses in the performance of concerted music: *a horn part.* **b.** a section or division of a composition: *the allegro part of the first movement.* **12.** participation, interest, or concern in something; role: *The neighbors must have had some part in planning the surprise party.* **13.** a person's share in or contribution to some action; duty, function, or office: *You must do your part if we're to finish by tonight.* **14.** a character or role acted in a play or sustained in real life. **15. for one's part,** as far as concerns one: *For my part, you can do whatever you please.* **16. for the most part,** with respect to the

greatest part; on the whole; generally; usually; mostly: *They are good students, for the most part.* **17. in good part, a.** without offense; in a good-natured manner; amiably: *She was able to take teasing in good part.* **b.** to a great extent; largely: *His success is in good part ascribable to dogged determination.* **18. in part,** in some measure or degree; to some extent; partly; partially: *The crop failure was due in part to unusual weather conditions.* **19. on the part of, a.** so far as pertains to or concerns one: *He expressed appreciation on the part of himself and his colleagues.* **b.** as done or manifested by: *attention on the part of the audience.* Also, **on one's part. 20. part and parcel,** an essential, necessary, or integral part: *Her love for her child was part and parcel of her life.* **21. take part,** to participate; share or partake: *They refused to take part in any of the activities of the community.* **22. take someone's part,** to align oneself with; support; defend: *His parents took his part, even though he was obviously in the wrong.*
—*v.t.* **23.** to divide (a thing) into parts; break; cleave; divide. **24.** to comb (the hair) away from a dividing line. **25.** to divide into shares; distribute in parts; apportion. **26.** to put or keep apart; separate: *They parted the calves from the herd.* **27.** *Metall.* **a.** to separate (silver) from gold in refining. **b.** to cut (one part) away from a piece, as an end from a billet. **c.** to keep the surface of (a casting) separate from the sand of the mold. **28.** *Obs.* to leave.
—*v.i.* **29.** to be or become divided into parts; break or cleave: *The oil tanker parted amidships.* **30.** to go or come apart; separate, as two or more things. **31.** to go apart from or leave one another, as persons: *We'll part no more.* **32.** to be or become separated from something else (usually fol. by *from*). **33.** *Naut.* to break or become torn apart, as a cable. **34.** to depart. **35.** to die. **36. part company, a.** to bid farewell or go separate ways; leave one another. **b.** to dissolve a personal affiliation, relationship, etc., esp. because of irreconcilable differences. **c.** to disagree. **37. part with,** to give up (property, control, etc.); relinquish: *to part with one's money.*
—*adj.* **38.** partial; of a part: *part owner.*
—*adv.* **39.** in part; partly: *part black.* [bef. 1000; (n.) ME (< OF < L), OE < L *part-* (s. of *pars*) piece, portion; (v.) ME *parten* < OF *partir* < L *partire,* deriv. of *pars*]
—Syn. 1. component, ingredient, division, sector. PART, PIECE, PORTION, SEGMENT, SECTION, FRACTION, FRAGMENT refer to something that is less than the whole. PART is the general word: *part of a house.* A PIECE suggests a part which is itself a complete unit or it may mean an irregular fragment: *a piece of pie; a piece of a broken vase.* A PORTION is a part allotted or assigned to a person, purpose, etc.: *a portion of food.* A SEGMENT is often a part into which something separates naturally: *a segment of an orange.* SECTION suggests a relatively substantial, clearly separate part that fits closely with other parts to form a whole: *a section of a fishing rod, a book.* FRACTION suggests a less substantial but still clearly delimited part, often separate from other parts: *a fraction of his former income.* FRAGMENT suggests a broken, inconsequential, incomplete part, with irregular or imprecise outlines or boundaries: *a fragment of broken pottery, of information.* **6.** apportionment, lot. **13.** responsibility. **26.** sever, sunder, dissociate, disconnect, disjoin, detach. **—Ant. 1.** whole. **23.** join.

part., **1.** participial. **2.** participle. **3.** particular.

part. adj., participial adjective.

par•take (pär tāk′), *v.,* **-took, -tak•en, -tak•ing.** —*v.i.* **1.** to take or have a part or share along with others; participate (usually fol. by *in*): *He won't partake in the victory celebration.* **2.** to receive, take, or have a share or portion (usually fol. by *of*): *to partake of a meal.* **3.** to have something of the nature or character (usually fol. by *of*): *feelings partaking of both joy and regret.* —*v.t.* **4.** to take or have a part in; share. [1555–65; back formation from *partaking,* ME *part taking,* trans. of L *participātiō* PARTICIPATION] **—par•tak′a•ble,** *adj.* **—par•tak′er,** *n.*
—Syn. 1. See **share**[1].

par•tan (pär′tn), *n. Scot.* a crab. [1375–1425; late ME (Scots) < ScotGael: crab]

part•ed (pär′tid), *adj.* **1.** divided into parts; cleft. **2.** divided by a part: *parted hair.* **3.** set or kept apart; separated. **4.** *Bot.* (of a leaf) separated into rather distinct portions by incisions that extend nearly to the midrib or the base. **5.** *Heraldry.* party (def. 18). **6.** *Archaic.* dead; deceased. [1350–1400; ME; see PART, -ED[2]] **—part′ed•ness,** *n.*

part′ed per tierce′, *Heraldry.* tierced.

par•te•ra (pär te′rä), *n., pl.* ***-ras*** (-räs). *Spanish.* a midwife.

par•terre (pär târ′), *n.* **1.** Also called **parquet circle.** the rear section of seats, and sometimes also the side sections, of the main floor of a theater, concert hall, or opera house. **2.** an ornamental arrangement of flower beds of different shapes and sizes. [1630–40; < F, n. use of phrase *par terre* on the ground. See PER, TERRA] **—par•terred′,** *adj.*

Par•the•ni•a (pär thē′nē ə), *n. Class. Myth.* an epithet of Athena, meaning "virgin."

partheno-, a combining form meaning "without fertilization," used in the formation of compound words: *parthenogenesis.* [< Gk, comb. form repr. *parthénos* maiden]

par•the•no•car•py (pär′thə nō kär′pē), *n. Bot.* the production of fruit without fertilization of an egg in the ovary. [1910–15; PARTHENO- + *-carpy;* see -CARP, -Y[3]] **—par′the•no•car′pic,** *adj.*

par•the•no•gen•e•sis (pär′thə nō jen′ə sis), *n. Biol.* development of an egg without fertilization. [1840–50; PARTHENO- + GENESIS] **—par•the•no•ge•net•ic** (pär′thə nō jə net′ik), *adj.* **—par′the•no•ge•net′i•cal•ly,** *adv.*

Par•the•non (pär′thə non′, -nən), *n.* the temple of Athena Parthenos on the Acropolis at Athens, completed c438 B.C. by Ictinus and Callicrates and decorated by Phidias: regarded as the finest Doric temple.

Par•the•no•pae•us (pär′thə nə pē′əs), *n. Class. Myth.* a son of Hippomenes and Atalanta, and one of the Seven against Thebes.

Par•then•os (pär then′əs, pär′thə nos′), *n.* an epithet of Athena, meaning "virgin."

par•the•no•spore (pär′thə nə spôr′, -spōr′), *n. Biol.* a spore developed without fertilization. [1885–90; PARTHENO- + -SPORE]

Par•thi•a (pär′thē ə), *n.* an ancient country in W Asia, SE of the Caspian Sea: conquered by the Persians A.D. 226; now a part of NE Iran.

Par•thi•an (pär′thē ən), *n.* **1.** a native or inhabitant of Parthia. **2.** an Iranian language of ancient and medieval Parthia. —*adj.* **3.** of, pertaining to, or characteristic of Parthia, its inhabitants, or their language. [1520–30; PARTHI(A) + -AN]

Par′thian shot′, a sharp, telling remark, act, gesture, etc., made in departing. [1900–05; so called from the ancient Parthian cavalry's habit of shooting arrows rearward at the enemy while in real or feigned flight]

par-three (pär′thrē′), *adj.* of, pertaining to, or noting a small-scale golf course, usually having 18 holes of 150 yd. (137 m) in length from tee to cup on 7 to 40 acres (3 to 16 hectares) of land. Cf. **pitch-and-putt.**

par•ti (pär tē′, pär′tē), *n. Archit.* the basic scheme or concept of an architectural design. [1805–15; < F: task assigned, treatment, n. use of ptp. of *partir* to PART]

par•tial (pär′shəl), *adj.* **1.** being such in part only; not total or general; incomplete: *partial blindness; a partial payment of a debt.* **2.** biased or prejudiced in favor of a person, group, side, etc., over another, as in a controversy: *a partial witness.* **3.** pertaining to or affecting a part. **4.** being a part; component; constituent. **5.** *Bot.* secondary or subordinate: *a partial umbel.* **6. partial to,** having a liking or preference for; particularly fond of: *I'm partial to chocolate cake.* —*n.* **7.** *Bridge.* part-score. **8.** *Acoustics, Music.* See **partial tone.** [1375–1425; late ME *parcial* biased, particular < MF < LL *partiālis* pertaining to a part, equiv. to L *parti-* (s. of *pars*) PART + *-ālis* -AL[1]] **—par′tial•ly,** *adv.* **—par′tial•ness,** *n.*
—Syn. 1. unfinished, imperfect, limited. **2.** one-sided, unfair, unjust. **—Ant. 1, 3.** complete. **2.** unbiased, fair.

par′tial den′ture. See under **denture.** [1855–60]

par′tial deriv′ative, *Math.* the derivative of a function with respect to one of its variables with all other variables held constant. [1970–75]

par′tial differen′tial, *Math.* an expression obtained from a given function of several variables by taking the partial derivative with respect to one of the variables and multiplying by the increment in that variable. [1810–20]

par′tial differen′tial equa′tion, *Math.* a differential equation containing partial derivatives. Cf. **ordinary differential equation.** [1885–90]

par′tial frac′tions, *Algebra.* one of the fractions into which a given fraction can be resolved, the sum of such simpler fractions being equal to the given fraction: *Partial fractions of* $5/(x^2-x)$ *are* $5/(x-1)$ *and* $-5/x$. [1810–20]

par•ti•al•i•ty (pär′shē al′i tē, pär shal′-), *n., pl.* **-ties. 1.** the state or character of being partial. **2.** a favorable bias or prejudice: *the partiality of parents for their own children.* **3.** a special fondness, preference, or liking (usually fol. by *to* or *for*): *a partiality for country living.* [1375–1425; late ME *parcialite* < ML *partiālitās.* See PARTIAL, -ITY]
—Syn. 2. favoritism. **3.** leaning, inclination, bent, predilection. **—Ant. 3.** dislike.

par•tial•ize (pär′shə līz′), *v.t.,* **-ized, -iz•ing.** to bias. Also, *esp. Brit.,* **par′tial•ise′.** [1585–95; < F *partialiser.* See PARTIAL, -IZE]

par′tially or′dered set′, *Math.* a set in which a relation as "less than or equal to" holds for some pairs of elements of the set, but not for all. Cf. **totally ordered set, well-ordered set.** [1970–75]

par′tial or′dering, *Math.* a relation defined on a set, having the properties that each element is in relation to itself, the relation is transitive, and if two elements are in relation to each other, the two elements are equal. [1940–45]

par′tial pres′sure, *Physics, Chem.* the pressure that a gas in a mixture of gases would exert if it occupied the same volume as the mixture at the same temperature. Cf. **Dalton's law.** [1855–60]

par′tial score′, *Bridge.* part-score.

par′tial sum′, *Math.* one of a series of sums of elements of a given sequence, the first sum being the first element, the second sum being the first element added to the second element, the third sum being equal to the sum of the first three elements, and so on. [1925–30]

par′tial tone′, *Acoustics, Music.* one of the pure tones forming a part of a complex tone. Also called **partial.** [1875–80]

par′tial vac′uum, an enclosed space from which part of the air or another gas has been removed.

par•ti•ble (pär′tə bəl), *adj.* capable of being divided or separated; separable; divisible. [1350–1400; ME < LL *partibilis* divisible, equiv. to L *part(īrī)* to divide, PART + *-ibilis* -IBLE] **—par′ti•bil′i•ty,** *n.*

par•ti•ceps cri•mi•nis (pär′tə seps′ krim′ə nis), *Law.* an accomplice in a crime. [< L]

par•tic•i•pa•ble (pär tis′ə pə bəl), *adj.* capable of being shared. [1400–50; late ME (< OF) < LL *participābilis* which can be shared, equiv. to L *particip(āre)* to PARTICIPATE + *-ābilis* -ABLE]

par•tic•i•pance (pär tis′ə pəns), *n.* participation. Also, **par•tic′i•pan•cy.** [PARTICIP(ANT) + -ANCE]

par•tic•i•pant (pär tis′ə pənt), *n.* **1.** a person or group that participates; partaker. —*adj.* **2.** participating; sharing. [1520–30; < L *participant-* (s. of *participāns*), prp. of *participāre.* See PARTICIPATE, -ANT] **—par•tic′i•pant•ly,** *adv.*
—Syn. 1. participator, associate, contributor, colleague.

partic′ipant observa′tion, a technique of field research, used in anthropology and sociology, by which an investigator **(partic′ipant observ′er)** studies the life of a group by sharing in its activities. [1930–35]

par•tic•i•pate (pär tis′ə pāt′), *v.,* **-pat•ed, -pat•ing.** —*v.i.* **1.** to take or have a part or share, as with others; partake; share (usually fol. by *in*): *to participate in profits; to participate in a play.* —*v.t.* **2.** *Archaic.* to take or have a part or share in; partake in; share. [1525–35; < L *participātus* (ptp. of *participāre* to share), equiv. to *particip-* (s. of *particeps*) taking part, partner (see PARTICIPLE) + *-ātus* -ATE[1]] **—par•tic′i•pat′ing•ly,** *adv.* **—par•tic′i•pa′tive,** *adj.* **—par•tic′i•pa′tive•ly,** *adv.* **—par•tic′i•pa′tor,** *n.* **—par•tic•i•pa•to•ry** (pär tis′ə pə tôr′ē, -tōr′ē), *adj.*
—Syn. 1. See **share**[1].

partic′ipating insur′ance, insurance in which the policyholders receive dividends and share in the surplus earnings of the company. [1950–55]

partic′ipating preferred′, *Stock Exchange.* a preferred stock entitled to its fixed dividend and to additional ones on a specified basis after payment of dividends on common stock. [1925–30]

par•tic•i•pa•tion (pär tis′ə pā′shən), *n.* **1.** an act or instance of participating. **2.** the fact of taking part, as in some action or attempt: *participation in a celebration.* **3.** a sharing, as in benefits or profits: *participation in a pension plan.* —*adj.* **4.** of or pertaining to a venture characterized by more than one person, bank, or company participating in risk or profit: *a participation loan.* [1325–75; < LL *participātiōn-,* s. of *participātiō* (see PARTICIPATE, -ION); r. ME *participacioun* < AF < LL, as above]

partic′ipatory democ′racy, individual participation by citizens in political decisions and policies that affect their lives, esp. directly rather than through elected representatives. Also, **partic′ipant democ′racy.** [1965–70]

par•ti•cip•i•al (pär′tə sip′ē əl), *Gram.* —*adj.* **1.** of or pertaining to a participle. **2.** similar to or formed from a participle. —*n.* **3.** a participle. [1560–70; < L *participiālis,* equiv. to *participi(um)* PARTICIPLE + *-ālis* -AL[1]] **—par′ti•cip′i•al′i•ty,** *n.* **—par′ti•cip′i•al•ly,** *adv.*

par•ti•cip•i•al•ize (pär′tə sip′ē ə līz′), *v.t.,* **-ized, -iz•ing.** to form (a word) into a participle; make participial. Also, *esp. Brit.,* **par′ti•cip′i•al•ise′.** [1780–90; PARTICIPIAL + -IZE] **—par′ti•cip′i•al•i•za′tion,** *n.*

par•ti•ci•ple (pär′tə sip′əl, -sə pəl), *n. Gram.* an adjective or complement to certain auxiliaries that is regularly derived from the verb in many languages and refers to participation in the action or state of the verb; a verbal form used as an adjective. It does not specify person or number in English, but may have a subject or object, show tense, etc., as *burning,* in *a burning candle,* or *devoted* in *his devoted friend.* [1350–1400; ME < MF, var. of *participe* < L *participium,* deriv. of *particeps* taking part, equiv. to *parti-* (s. of *pars*) PART + *-cep-* (comb. form of *capere* to take) + *-s* nom. sing. ending]
—Usage. See **dangling participle, misplaced modifier.**

par•ti•cle (pär′ti kəl), *n.* **1.** a minute portion, piece, fragment, or amount; a tiny or very small bit: *a particle of dust; not a particle of supporting evidence.* **2.** *Physics.* **a.** one of the extremely small constituents of matter, as an atom or nucleus. **b.** an elementary particle, quark, or gluon. **c.** a body in which the internal motion is negligible. **3.** a clause or article, as of a document. **4.** *Gram.* **a.** (in some languages) one of the major form classes, or parts of speech, consisting of words that are neither nouns nor verbs, or of all uninflected words, or the like. **b.** such a word. **c.** a small word of functional or relational use, as an article, preposition, or conjunction, whether of a separate form class or not. **5.** *Rom. Cath. Ch.* a small piece of the Host given to each lay communicant in a Eucharistic service. [1350–1400; ME < L *particula.* See PART, -I-, -CLE[1]] **—par′ti•cled,** *adj.*
—Syn. 1. mite, whit, iota, jot, tittle, grain, speck.

par′ticle accel′erator, accelerator (def. 7). [1945–50]

par′ticle beam′, 1. *Physics.* a concentrated stream of particles, as electrons, neutrons, or protons, generated for studying particle interactions, nuclear structure, crystal structure, etc. **2.** *Mil.* a high-energy stream of such particles for use as a weapon or for antimissile defense.

par′ticle board′, any of various composition boards formed from small particles of wood, as flakes or shavings, tightly compressed and bonded together with a resin. [1955–60]

par′ticle phys′ics, the branch of physics that deals with the properties and behavior of elementary particles. Cf. **high-energy physics.** [1945–50]

par′ticle veloc′ity, *Physics.* the velocity of a point in a medium that is undergoing wave motion. Cf. **group velocity, phase velocity.**

par•ti•col•ored (pär′tē kul′ərd), *adj.* having different colors in different areas or patches; variegated: *a particolored dress.* Also, **party-colored.** [1525–35; *parti* variegated < MF << L *partītus* divided, ptp. of *partīre* to PART. See PARTY]

par•tic•u•lar (pər tik′yə lər, pə tik′-), *adj.* **1.** of or pertaining to a single or specific person, thing, group, class, occasion, etc., rather than to others or all; special

CONCISE ETYMOLOGY KEY: <, descended or borrowed from; >, whence; b., blend of, blended; c., cognate with; cf., compare; deriv., derivative; equiv., equivalent; imit., imitative; obl., oblique; r., replacing; s., stem; sp., spelling, spelled; resp., respelling, respelled; trans., translation; ?, origin unknown; *, unattested; ‡, probably earlier than. See the full key inside the front cover.

rather than general: *one's particular interests in books.* **2.** immediately present or under consideration; in this specific instance or place: *Look at this particular clause in the contract.* **3.** distinguished or different from others or from the ordinary; noteworthy; marked; unusual: *She sang with particular warmth at last evening's concert.* **4.** exceptional or especial: *Take particular pains with this job.* **5.** being such in an exceptional degree: *a particular friend of mine.* **6.** dealing with or giving details, as an account or description, of a person; detailed; minute. **7.** exceptionally selective, attentive, or exacting; fastidious; fussy: *to be particular about one's food.* **8.** *Logic.* **a.** not general; referring to an indefinite part of a whole class. **b.** (of a proposition) containing only existential quantifiers. **c.** partaking of the nature of an individual as opposed to a class. **9.** *Law.* **a.** noting an estate that precedes a future or ultimate ownership, as lands devised to a widow during her lifetime and after that to her children. **b.** noting the tenant of such an estate. —*n.* **10.** an individual or distinct part, as an item of a list or enumeration. **11.** Usually, **particulars.** specific points, details, or circumstances: *to give an investigator the particulars of a case.* **12.** *Logic.* an individual or a specific group within a general class. **13. in particular,** particularly; specifically; especially: *There is one book in particular that may help you.* [1350–1400; < LL *particulāris,* equiv. to L *particul(a)* PARTICLE + *-āris* -AR[1]; r. ME *particuler* < MF < LL, as above]
—**Syn. 1.** See **special. 1, 2.** specific. **2.** distinct; discrete. **3.** notable. **6.** scrupulous, careful, exact, precise. **7.** discriminating; finical, finicky. PARTICULAR, DAINTY, FASTIDIOUS imply great care, discrimination, and taste in choices, in details about one's person, etc. PARTICULAR implies esp. care and attention to details: *particular about one's clothes.* DAINTY implies delicate taste and exquisite cleanliness: *a dainty dress.* FASTIDIOUS implies being difficult to please and critical of small or minor points: *a fastidious taste in styles.* **10.** feature, particularity. —**Ant. 3.** ordinary. **6.** inexact. **7.** undiscriminating.

partic′ular affirm′ative, *Logic.* a proposition of the form "Some S is P." *Symbol:* I

partic′ular av′erage, *Marine Insurance.* a loss at sea, as through accident or negligence, that is borne solely by the owner of the lost property. *Abbr.:* P.A. Also called **partic′ular av′erage loss′.** Cf. **general average.** [1765–75]

par·tic·u·lar·ism (pər tik′yə lə riz′əm, pə tik′-), *n.* **1.** exclusive attention or devotion to one's own particular interests, party, etc. **2.** the principle of leaving each state of a federation free to retain its laws and promote its interests. **3.** *Theol.* the doctrine that divine grace is provided only for the elect. [1815–25; < F *particularisme.* See PARTICULAR, -ISM] —**par·tic′u·lar·ist,** *n.* —**par·tic′u·lar·is′tic,** *adj.* —**par·tic′u·lar·is′ti·cal·ly,** *adv.*

par·tic·u·lar·i·ty (pər tik′yə lar′i tē, pə tik′-), *n., pl.* **-ties. 1.** the quality or state of being particular. **2.** detailed, minute, or circumstantial character, as of description or statement. **3.** attention to details; special care. **4.** fastidiousness. **5.** an individual or characteristic feature or trait; peculiarity. [1520–30; < MF *particularite* < LL *particulāritāt-* (s. of *particulāritās*) state of being apart. See PARTICULAR, -ITY]

par·tic·u·lar·ize (pər tik′yə lə rīz′, pə tik′-), *v.,* **-ized, -iz·ing.** —*v.t.* **1.** to make particular. **2.** to mention or indicate specifically; specify. **3.** to state or treat in detail. —*v.i.* **4.** to speak or treat particularly or specifically. Also, *esp. Brit.,* **par·tic′u·lar·ise′.** [1580–90; < MF *particulariser.* See PARTICULAR, -IZE] —**par·tic′u·lar·i·za′tion,** *n.* —**par·tic′u·lar·iz′er,** *n.*

par·tic·u·lar·ly (pər tik′yə lər lē, pə tik′-), *adv.* **1.** in a particular or to an exceptional degree; especially: *He read it with particularly great interest.* **2.** in a particular manner; specifically; individually. **3.** in detail; minutely. [1350–1400; ME. See PARTICULAR, -LY]
—**Syn. 1.** exceptionally, specially. See **especially. 3.** scrupulously.

partic′ular neg′ative, *Logic.* a proposition of the form "Some S is not P." *Symbol:* O

partic′ular quan′tifier, *Logic.* See **existential quantifier.**

partic′ular solu′tion, *Math.* a solution of a differential equation containing no arbitrary constants. Cf. **general solution.** [1895–1900]

par·tic·u·late (pər tik′yə lit, -lāt′, pə tik′-, pär-), *adj.* **1.** of, pertaining to, or composed of distinct particles. —*n.* **2.** a separate and distinct particle. **3.** a material composed of such particles. **4. particulates, a.** the aggregate of such particles, esp. as produced by one source: *tests to analyze diesel particulates.* **b.** *Meteorol.* solid or liquid particles suspended in the atmosphere, esp. pollutants. [1870–75; < NL *particulātus,* equiv. to L *particul(a)* PARTICLE + *-ātus* -ATE[1]]

partic′ulate inher′itance, *Genetics.* the inheritance of discrete characters via genes that are independently expressed without the blending of characters from one generation to the next. Cf. **blending inheritance.** [1885–90]

par·ti·er (pär′tē ər), *n.* partyer.

part·ing (pär′ting), *n.* **1.** the act of a person or thing that parts. **2.** a division or separation. **3.** a place of division or separation. **4.** a departure or leave-taking. **5.** death. **6.** something that serves to part or separate things. **7.** *Mineral.* a fracture of a crystal along a plane determined by twinning or pressure rather than along a cleavage plane. **8.** *Metall.* See **parting line.** —*adj.* **9.** given, happening, taken, done, etc., at parting: *a parting glance.* **10.** of or pertaining to parting, leave-taking, departure, or death: *parting words.* **11.** ending or taking leave: *the parting day.* **12.** dying. **13.** dividing or separating. [1250–1300; ME *partyng* (ger.). See PART, -ING[1], -ING[2]]

part′ing line′, *Metall.* **1.** the line at which two closed dies or two halves of a mold meet. **2.** a corresponding line or seam appearing on a molded or cast object. [1870–75]

part′ing shot′, a threat, insult, condemnation, sarcastic retort, or the like, uttered upon leaving. [1890–95; perh. by folk etym. from PARTHIAN SHOT]

part′ing strip′, a strip, as of wood, used to keep two parts separated, as one in each side of the frame of a window to keep the sashes apart when lowered or raised. See diag. under **double-hung.**

par·ti pris (PAR tē PRĒ′), *French.* a position or attitude resolved upon or taken in advance.

par·tis (pär′tis), *adj.* (in prescriptions) of a part. [< L]

par·ti·san[1] (pär′tə zən, -sən; *Brit.* pär′tə zan′), *n.* **1.** an adherent or supporter of a person, group, party, or cause, esp. a person who shows a biased, emotional allegiance. **2.** *Mil.* a member of a party of light or irregular troops engaged in harassing an enemy, esp. a member of a guerrilla band engaged in fighting or sabotage against an occupying army. —*adj.* **3.** of, pertaining to, or characteristic of partisans; partial to a specific party, person, etc.: *partisan politics.* **4.** of, pertaining to, or carried on by military partisans or guerrillas. Also, **partizan.** [1545–55; < MF < Upper It *partežan* (Tuscan *partigiano*), equiv. to *part(e)* faction, PART + *-ežan* (< VL *-ēs- -ESE + L *-iānus* -IAN)] —**par′ti·san·ship′, par′ti·san·ry,** *n.*
—**Syn. 1.** See **follower. 3.** biased, prejudiced. —**Ant. 1.** opponent.

par·ti·san[2] (pär′tə zən, -sən), *n.* a shafted weapon of the 16th and 17th centuries, having as a head a long spear blade with a pair of curved lobes at the base. Also, **partizan.** Cf. **halberd.** [1550–60; < MF *partizane* < Upper It *partežana,* prob. by ellipsis from *arma partežana* weapon borne by members of a faction; see PARTISAN[1]]

partisan[2] (head)

par·ti·san·ism (pär′tə zə niz′əm, -sə-), *n.* partisan action or spirit. [1885–90; PARTISAN[1] + -ISM]

par·ti·ta (pär tē′tə; *It.* pär tē′tä), *n., pl.* **-tas, -te** (-tä; *It.* -te). *Music.* **1.** an instrumental suite common chiefly in the 18th century. **2.** a set of variations. [1875–80; < It, fem. of *partito* divided. See PARTY]

par·tite (pär′tīt), *adj.* **1.** divided into parts, usually into a specified number of parts (usually used in combination): *a tripartite agreement.* **2.** *Bot.* parted. [1560–70; < L *partītus* (ptp. of *partīrī* to divide). See PART, -ITE[2]]

par·ti·tion (pär tish′ən, pər-), *n.* **1.** a division into or distribution in portions or shares. **2.** a separation, as of two or more things. **3.** something that separates or divides. **4.** a part, division, or section. **5.** an interior wall or barrier dividing a room, area of a building, enclosure, etc., into separate areas. **6.** a septum or dissepiment, as in a plant or animal structure. **7.** *Law.* a division of property among joint owners or tenants in common or a sale of such property followed by a division of the proceeds. **8.** *Logic.* the separation of a whole into its integrant parts. **9.** *Math.* **a.** a mode of separating a positive whole number into a sum of positive whole numbers. **b.** the decomposition of a set into disjoint subsets whose union is the original set: *A partition of the set (1, 2, 3, 4, 5) is the collection of subsets (1), (2, 3), (4), and (5).* **10.** *Rhet.* (in a speech organized on classical principles) the second, usually brief section or part in which a speaker announces the chief lines of thought to be discussed in support of his or her theme. —*v.t.* **11.** to divide into parts or portions. **12.** to divide or separate by interior walls, barriers, or the like (sometimes fol. by *off*): *to partition off a dormitory into cubicles.* **13.** to divide (a country or territory) into separate, usually differing political entities. Cf. **Balkanize. 14.** *Law.* to divide property among several owners, either in specie or by sale and division of the proceeds. [1400–50; late ME < L *partītiōn-* (s. of *partītiō*) division, equiv. to *partīt(us)* ptp. of *partīrī* to divide (see PARTY) + *-iōn-* -ION] —**par·ti′tion·a·ble,** *adj.* —**par·ti′tion·ar′y,** *adj.* —**par·ti′tion·er, par·ti′tion·ist,** *n.* —**par·ti′tion·ment,** *n.*
—**Syn. 1.** See **division. 11.** portion, apportion. —**Ant. 2.** unity. **11.** unite.

parti′tion line′, *Heraldry.* a plain or figured edge between two adjacent areas of an escutcheon, between an ordinary and the field of an escutcheon, or between two adjacent ordinaries. Also called **boundary line.** [1710–20]

par·ti·tive (pär′ti tiv), *adj.* **1.** serving to divide into parts. **2.** *Gram.* noting part of a whole: *the Latin partitive genitive.* —*n.* **3.** *Gram.* a partitive word or formation, as *of the men* in *half of the men.* [1510–20; < ML *partītīvus* divisive, equiv. to L *partīt(us),* ptp. of *partīrī* to divide (see PARTY) + *-īvus* -IVE] —**par′ti·tive·ly,** *adv.*

par·ti·zan[1] (pär′tə zən; *Brit.* pär′tə zan′), *n., adj.* partisan[1].

par·ti·zan[2] (pär′tə zən), *n.* partisan[2].

part·let (pärt′lit), *n.* a garment for the neck and shoulders, usually ruffled and having a collar, worn in the 16th century. [1510–20; unexplained var. of late ME *patelet* < MF *patelette* strip of cloth, band, lit., little paw, equiv. to OF *pate* paw + *-lete* -LET]

part·ly (pärt′lē), *adv.* in part; to some extent or degree; partially; not wholly: *His statement is partly true.* [1515–25; PART + -LY]

part′ mu′sic, music, esp. vocal music, with parts for two or more independent performers. [1875–80]

part·ner (pärt′nər), *n.* **1.** a person who shares or is associated with another in some action or endeavor; sharer; associate. **2.** *Law.* **a.** a person associated with another or others as a principal or a contributor of capital in a business or a joint venture, usually sharing its risks and profits. **b.** See **special partner. 3.** See **silent partner. 4.** a husband or a wife; spouse. **5.** either of two people who dance together: *my favorite partner in the waltz.* **6.** a player on the same side or team as another: *My tennis partner was an excellent player.* **7. partners,** *Naut.* a framework of timber round a hole in a ship's deck, to support a mast, capstan, pump, etc. —*v.t.* **8.** to associate as a partner or partners with. **9.** to serve as the partner of. [1250–1300; ME *partener,* alter. of PARCENER by assoc. with PART] —**part′ner·less,** *adj.*
—**Syn. 1.** colleague, accessory, accomplice.

part′ners' desk′, a desk constructed so that two people may work at it face-to-face, as one having a kneehole and drawers on two fronts. [‡1945–50]

part·ner·ship (pärt′nər ship′), *n.* **1.** the state or condition of being a partner; participation; association; joint interest. **2.** *Law.* **a.** the relation subsisting between partners. **b.** the contract creating this relation. **c.** an association of persons joined as partners in business. [1570–80; PARTNER + -SHIP]

Part′ of For′tune, *Astrol.* the celestial longitude of the moon plus the celestial longitude of the ascendant minus the celestial longitude of the sun: said to connote an area of life through which one achieves emotional satisfaction. [1690–1700]

part′ of speech′, *Gram.* any of the classes into which words in some languages, as Latin and English, have traditionally been divided on the basis of their meaning, form, or syntactic function, as, in English, noun, pronoun, verb, adverb, adjective, preposition, conjunction, and interjection. [1500–10]

par·ton (pär′ton), *n. Physics.* a constituent of the nucleon originally postulated in the theoretical analysis of high-energy scattering of electrons by nucleons and subsequently identified with quarks and gluons. [1965–70; PART(ICLE) + -ON[1]; coined by R. P. Feynman]

par·took (pär to͝ok′), *v.* pt. of **partake.**

par·tridge (pär′trij), *n., pl.* **-tridg·es,** (*esp. collectively*) **-tridge. 1.** any of several Old World gallinaceous game birds of the subfamily Perdicinae, esp. *Perdix perdix.* **2.** *Chiefly Northern U.S.* the ruffed grouse. **3.** *Chiefly South Midland and Southern U.S.* bobwhite. **4.** any of several other North American gallinaceous game birds. **5.** any of various South and Central American tinamous. [1250–1300; ME *partrich,* var. of *pertrich* < MF *pertris,* var. of *perdris,* OF *perd(r)iz* < L *perdix* < Gk *pérdix*] —**par′tridge·like′,** *adj.*

gray partridge,
Perdix perdix,
length 1 to 1½ ft.
(0.3 to 0.5 m)

Par·tridge (pär′trij), *n.* **Eric (Hon·ey·wood)** (hun′ē wo͝od′), 1894–1979, British lexicographer, born in New Zealand.

par·tridge·ber·ry (pär′trij ber′ē), *n., pl.* **-ries.** a North American trailing plant, *Mitchella repens,* of the madder family, having roundish evergreen leaves, fragrant white flowers, and scarlet berries. [1705–15; PARTRIDGE + BERRY]

par′tridge pea′, a North American plant, *Cassia fasciculata,* of the legume family, having yellow flowers and feathery compound leaves that fold shut when touched. [1780–90, *Amer.*; prob. so called because its fruit provides food for partridges]

par′tridge wood′, the rotted condition of the wood of certain trees, esp. oaks, caused by a parasitic fungus, *Xylobolus frustulatus.* [1820–30]

part-score (pärt′skôr′, -skōr′), *n. Bridge.* **1.** a contract to make less than the number of tricks required for game: *to bid a part-score of three diamonds.* **2.** the number of points gained by making such a contract: *a part-score of 60 points.* Also called **partial, partial score.**

part′ song′, a song with parts for several voices, esp. one meant to be sung without accompaniment. —**part′ sing′ing.** [1590–1600]

part′ time′, a period of time that is less than the usual or full time. Cf. **full time.** [1890–95]

part-time (*adj.* pärt′tīm′; *adv.* pärt′tīm′), *adj.* **1.** employed to work, used, expected to function, etc., less than the usual or full time: *a part-time clerk.* **2.** lasting, requiring, or being in force only a part of the time: *part-time employment; part-time jobs.* —*adv.* **3.** on a part-time basis: *to work part-time.* Cf. **full-time.** [1890–95; adj., adv. use of PART TIME]

CONCISE PRONUNCIATION KEY: act, cāpe, dâre, pärt; set, ēqual; if, īce; ox, ōver, ôrder, oil, bo͝ok, bo͞ot, out; up, ûrge; child; sing; shoe; thin, *th*at; zh as in *treasure.* ə = *a* as in *alone, e* as in *system, i* as in *easily, o* as in *gallop, u* as in *circus;* ə as in *fire* (fīər), *hour* (ouər). l and n can serve as syllabic consonants, as in *cradle* (krād′l), and *button* (but′n). See the full key inside the front cover.

part-tim·er (pärt′tī′mər), *n.* a person who works, attends school, etc., less than full time. [1925–30; PART-TIME + -ER[1]]

par·tu·ri·ent (pär to͝or′ē ənt, -tyo͝or′-), *adj.* **1.** bearing or about to bear young; travailing. **2.** pertaining to parturition. **3.** bringing forth or about to produce something, as an idea. [1585–95; < L *parturient-* (s. of *parturiēns*) being in labor, lit., desiring to bring forth (prp. of *parturīre* to be about to give birth), equiv. to *part(us)* (ptp. of *parere* to bring forth, bear) + *-uri-* desiderative suffix + *-ent-* -ENT] **—par·tu′ri·en·cy,** *n.*

par·tu·ri·fa·cient (pär to͝or′ə fā′shənt, -tyo͝or′-), *Med.* **—adj. 1.** inducing or accelerating labor, or childbirth; oxytocic. **—n. 2.** a parturifacient agent. [1850–55; < L *parturi-* (s. of *parturīre* to be in labor; see PARTURIENT) + -FACIENT]

par·tu·ri·tion (pär′to͞o rish′ən, -tyo͞o-, -cho͞o-), *n. Biol.* the process of bringing forth young. [1640–50; < LL *parturītiōn-* (s. of *parturītiō*) travail, equiv. to L *parturīt(us)* (ptp. of *parturīre;* see PARTURIENT) + *-iōn-* -ION]

part. vic., (in prescriptions) in divided doses. [< L *partibus vicibus*]

part·way (pärt′wā′, -wā′), *adv.* **1.** at or to a part of the way or distance: *Shall I walk you partway? I'm already partway home.* **2.** in some degree or part; partly; partially: *hopes that were only partway realized.* [1855–60; PART + WAY[1]]

par·ty (pär′tē), *n., pl.* **-ties,** *adj., v.,* **-tied, -ty·ing.** **—n. 1.** a social gathering, as of invited guests at a private home, for conversation, refreshments, entertainment, etc.: *a cocktail party.* **2.** a group gathered for a special purpose or task: *a fishing party; a search party.* **3.** a detachment, squad, or detail of troops assigned to perform some particular mission or service. **4.** a group of persons with common purposes or opinions who support one side of a dispute, question, debate, etc. **5.** a group of persons with common political opinions and purposes organized for gaining political influence and governmental control and for directing government policy: *the Republican party; the Democratic party.* **6.** the system of taking sides on public or political questions or the like. **7.** attachment or devotion to one side or faction; partisanship: *to put considerations of party first.* **8.** *Law.* **a.** one of the litigants in a legal proceeding; a plaintiff or defendant in a suit. **b.** a signatory to a legal instrument. **c.** a person participating in or otherwise privy to a crime. **9.** a person or group that participates in some action, affair, plan, etc.; participant: *He was a party to the merger deal.* **10.** the person under consideration; a specific individual: *Look at the party in the green velvet shorts.* **11.** a person or, usually, two or more persons together patronizing a restaurant, attending a social or cultural function, etc.: *The headwaiter asked how many were in our party; a party of 12 French physicists touring the labs; a party of one at the small table.* **12.** a person participating in a telephone conversation: *I have your party on the line.* **13.** any occasion or activity likened to a social party, as specified; session: *The couple in the next apartment are having their usual dish-throwing party.* **14.** an advantageous or pleasurable situation or combination of circumstances of some duration and often of questionable character; period of content, license, exemption, etc.: *The police broke in and suddenly the party was over for the nation's most notorious gunman.* **—adj. 15.** of or pertaining to a party or faction; partisan: *party leaders.* **16.** of or for a social gathering: *her new party dress.* **17.** being shared by or pertaining to two or more persons or things. **18.** *Heraldry.* (of an escutcheon) having the field divided into a number of parts, usually two; parted. **—v.i.** *Informal.* **19.** to go to or give parties, esp. a series of parties. **20.** to enjoy oneself thoroughly and without restraint; indulge in pleasure. [1250–1300; ME *partie* < OF, n. use of fem. of *parti,* ptp. of *partir* < L *partīre* to share. See PART] **—par′ty·less,** *adj.*

—Syn. 1. meeting, assemblage. See **company. 4.** faction, circle, coterie, ring.

—Usage. PARTY meaning "a specific individual" is old in the language, going back to the 15th century, and was formerly in common use. Today, it remains standard in limited senses, chiefly the legal, and is often used humorously or condescendingly: *the party holding the balloon. Person* is the neutral and common term.

par′ty boat′, a boat that takes paying passengers for a day or several hours of fishing, as in coastal waters or a bay, and usually rents fishing tackle and sells or provides bait. [1935–40]

par·ty-col·ored (pär′tē kul′ərd), *adj.* parti-colored.

par′ty-col·umn bal′lot (pär′tē kol′əm). See **Indiana ballot.**

par·ty·er (pär′tē ər), *n.* a person who parties, esp. regularly or habitually: *New Year's Eve always brings out the partyers.* Also, **partier.** [PARTY + -ER[1]]

par′ty girl′, 1. a girl or woman who is interested in little else besides attending parties. **2.** a physically attractive young woman hired to attend parties and entertain men. **3.** a prostitute. [1905–10]

par·ty·go·er (pär′tē gō′ər), *n.* a person who enjoys or frequently attends parties and celebrations. [PARTY + GOER]

par·ty·ism (pär′tē iz′əm), *n.* **1.** adherence to a political party or organization. **2.** the organization of political affairs into parties; the political system of a state, region, etc. (often used in combination): *Two-partyism was never significant in continental politics.* [1835–45; PARTY + -ISM] **—par′ty·ist,** *n.*

par·ty line (pär′tē līn′ *for 1, 2;* pär′tē līn′ *for 3, 4*), **1.** the authorized, prescribed policies and practices of a group, esp. of the Communist party, usually followed by the members without deviation; official philosophy or credo. **2.** the guiding policy, tenets, or practices of a political party: *The judge was chosen on party lines.* **3.** a telephone line connecting the telephones of a number of subscribers by one circuit to a central office, used in some rural areas. **4.** the boundary line separating adjoining properties. [1825–35, *Amer.*] **—par′ty-line′,** *adj.*

CONCISE ETYMOLOGY KEY: <, descended or borrowed from; >, whence; b., blend of, blended; c., cognate with; cf., compare; deriv., derivative; equiv., equivalent; imit., imitative; obl., oblique; r., replacing; s., stem; sp., spelling, spelled; resp., respelling, respelled; trans., translation; ?, origin unknown; *, unattested; ‡, probably earlier than. See the full key inside the front cover.

par′ty lin′er, a person who follows a party line, esp. the Communist party line. [1935–40; PARTY LINE + -ER[1]]

par′ty man′, a person belonging to a political party, esp. one who adheres strictly or blindly to its principles and policies. [1685–95]

par′ty pol′itics, politics based on strict adherence to the policies and principles of a political party regardless of the public interest; partisan loyalism. [1765–75]

par′ty poop′, *Slang.* **1.** to behave like a party pooper. **2.** a party pooper.

par′ty poop′er (po͞o′pər), *Slang.* a person who hasn't the interest or vitality to participate actively in a social party and whose mood, attitude, or personality lessens others' enjoyment; killjoy. Also called **poop.** [1940–45; POOP[2] + -ER[1]]

par′ty wall′, a wall used, or usable, as a part of contiguous structures. [1660–70] **—par′ty-walled′,** *adj.*

par′ty whip′, *Politics.* whip (def. 24). [1875–80, *Amer.*]

par·u·la (par′yə lə, -ə lə), *n.* any of several American wood warblers of the genus *Parula,* esp. *P. americana* **(northern parula),** having bluish plumage with a yellow throat and breast. Also called **par′ula war′bler.** [< NL *Parula* a genus name, alter. of *Parulus* an earlier genus name, equiv. to LL *pār(us)* titmouse (akin to L *parra* a bird whose cry was considered a bad omen) + L *-ulus* -ULE]

pa·ru·lis (pə ro͞o′lis), *n. Pathol.* gumboil. [< NL < Gk *paroulís,* equiv. to *par-* PAR- + *-oulis,* deriv. of *oûlon* gum]

pa·rure (pə ro͝or′; *Fr.* PA RYR′), *n., pl.* **-rures** (-ro͝orz′; *Fr.* -RYR′). a matching set of jewels or ornaments. [1200–50; ME < OF *pareure* peeling < L *parātūra* (*parāt-,* ptp. s. of *parāre* to PREPARE (see PARE) + *-ūra* -URE)]

par′ val′ue. See **face value** (def. 1). [1800–10]

Pār·va·tī (pär′və tē), *n. Hinduism.* the wife of Shiva and the benevolent form of the Mother Goddess. Cf. **Kālī.**

par·ve (pär′və), *adj. Judaism.* pareve.

par·ve·nu (pär′və no͞o′, -nyo͞o′, pär′və no͞o′, -nyo͞o′), *n.* **1.** a person who has recently or suddenly acquired wealth, importance, position, or the like, but has not yet developed the conventionally appropriate manners, dress, surroundings, etc. **—adj. 2.** being or resembling a parvenu. **3.** characteristic of a parvenu. [1795–1805; < F: upstart, n. use of ptp. of *parvenir* to arrive, reach < L *pervenīre,* equiv. to *per-* PER- + *venīre* to COME] **—par′·ve·nu′dom,** *n.* **—par′ve·nu·ism,** *n.*

par·vis (pär′vis), *n.* **1.** a vacant enclosed area in front of a church. **2.** a colonnade or portico in front of a church. Also called **paradise.** [1350–1400; ME < MF; OF *pare(v)is* < LL *paradīsus* church courtyard, orig. the one before St. Peter's, Rome. See PARADISE]

par·vo (pär′vō), *n., pl.* **-vos.** parvovirus. [by shortening]

par·vo·vi·rus (pär′vō vī′rəs), *n., pl.* **-vi·rus·es. 1.** *Vet. Pathol.* a highly contagious, often fatal viral disease of dogs, characterized by vomiting, severe diarrhea, and depression and accompanied by high fever and loss of appetite. **2.** any of several small DNA-containing viruses belonging to the genus *Parvovirus,* of the family Parvoviridae, esp. the virus that causes the disease parvovirus in dogs or distemper in cats. [1960–65; < L *parv(us)* small + -o- + VIRUS]

Par·zi·val (pär′tsi fäl′), *n. Teutonic Legend.* Percival. Also, **Par′zi·fal′.**

pas (pä), *n., pl.* **pas. 1.** a step or series of steps in ballet. **2.** right of precedence. [1695–1705; < F < L *passus.* See PACE[1]]

Pas·a·de·na (pas′ə dē′nə), *n.* **1.** a city in SW California, near Los Angeles. 119,374. **2.** a city in SE Texas, near Houston. 112,560.

pas al·lé (*Fr.* pä ZA lā′), *pl.* **pas al·lés** (*Fr.* pä ZA lā′). *Ballet.* a simple walking step in which the whole foot is put down softly on the ground. [< F: lit., walking step]

Pa·sar·ga·dae (pə sär′gə dē′), *n.* an ancient ruined city in S Iran, NE of Persepolis: an early capital of ancient Persia; tomb of Cyrus the Great.

Pa·say (pä′sī), *n.* a city in E Philippines, on Manila Bay, on E Luzon. 287,770.

Pas·ca·gou·la (pas′kə go͞o′lə), *n.* a city in SE Mississippi, on the Gulf of Mexico. 29,318.

pas·cal (pa skal′, pä skäl′), *n. Physics.* the SI unit of pressure or stress, equal to one newton per square meter. *Abbr.:* Pa [1955–60; after PASCAL]

Pas·cal (pa skal′, pä skäl′; *Fr.* PAS KAL′), *n.* **Blaise** (blāz; *Fr.* blez), 1623–62, French philosopher and mathematician.

PASCAL (pa skal′), *n. Computers.* a high-level programming language, a descendant of ALGOL, designed to facilitate structured programming.

Pascal's′ law′, *Physics.* the law that an external pressure applied to a fluid in a closed vessel is uniformly transmitted throughout the fluid. [named after PASCAL]

Pascal's′ lim′açon, *Geom.* limaçon. [1950–55; after Blaise PASCAL, who studied and named it]

Pascal's′ the′orem, *Geom.* the theorem that the lines joining adjacent vertices of a hexagon intersect the same straight line if alternate vertices lie on two intersecting straight lines. [named after PASCAL]

Pascal's′ tri′angle, *Math.* a triangular arrangement of the binomial coefficients of the expansion $(x + y)^n$ for positive integral values of n. [named after PASCAL]

Pasch (pask), *n.* **1.** the Jewish festival of Passover. **2.** Easter. [bef. 1150; ME, OE < LL *Pascha* < Gk *Páscha* < Aram: Passover; cf. Heb *Pesaḥ* PESACH]

pas·chal (pas′kəl), *adj.* **1.** of or pertaining to Easter. **2.** of or pertaining to Passover. **—n. 3.** a paschal candle or candlestick. [1400–50; late ME *paschall* < LL *paschālis.* See PASCH, -AL[1]]

Pas·chal I (pas′kəl), died A.D. 824, pope 817–824.

Paschal II, (*Ranieri*) died 1118, Italian ecclesiastic: pope 1099–1118.

pas′chal can′dle, a tall candle, symbolizing Christ, that is sometimes blessed and placed on the gospel side of an altar on Holy Saturday and kept burning until Ascension Day. Also called **Easter candle.**

pas′chal lamb′, 1. *Jewish Hist.* a lamb slaughtered and eaten on the eve of the first day of Passover. Ex. 12:3–11. **2.** (*caps.*) Christ. **3.** (*caps.*) any of several symbolic representations of Christ, as the Agnus Dei. **4.** (*caps.*) Also called **Holy Lamb.** *Heraldry.* a representation of a lamb passant having around its head a nimbus and supporting on the dexter shoulder a crosslike staff bearing a flag argent charged with a cross gules. [1400–50; late ME]

pas′chal let′ter, (in the early Christian church) a letter, written by a patriarch, archbishop, or bishop to a cleric under his authority, announcing the date of the next Easter festival.

Pa′schen-Back′ effect′ (pä′shən bäk′), *Physics.* a splitting of spectral lines observed when the source of a radiation is subjected to a strong magnetic field, caused when the vectors associated with the spin and orbital angular momentum exhibit individual rather than common precession. Cf. **Zeeman effect.** [1920–25; named after Friedrich *Paschen* (1865–1947) and Ernst *Back* (1881–1959), German physicists]

Pa′schen se′ries (pä′shən), *Physics.* a series of lines in the infrared spectrum of hydrogen. [1920–25; see PASCHEN-BACK EFFECT]

Pas·cin (pä skaN′), *n.* **Jules** (zhYl), (*Julius Pincas*), 1885–1930, French painter, born in Bulgaria.

Pas·co (pas′kō), *n.* a city in S Washington, on the Columbia River. 17,944.

pas d'ac·tion (*Fr.* pä dAk syôN′), *pl.* **pas d'ac·tion.** *Ballet.* a dramatic, pantomimic dance sequence serving to advance the plot. [1950–55; < F: step of action]

pas d'âne (pä dän′), *pl.* **pas d'âne.** a pair of rings set below and at right angles to the quillons of a sword as a guard for the forefinger. [< F: a guard on a hilt, lit., ass's step]

pas de basque (*Fr.* päd[ə] bAsk′), *pl.* **pas de basque.** *Ballet.* a step in which the dancer swings one foot to the side, springs onto it, and swings the other foot against it. [1810–20; < F: Basque step]

pas de bour·rée (*Fr.* päd[ə] bo͞o RĀ′), *pl.* **pas de bourrée.** *Ballet.* a short running step. [1910–15; < F: lit., bourrée step]

Pas de Ca·lais (päd[ə] kA le′). French name of the Strait of Dover.

Pas-de-Ca·lais (päd[ə] kA le′), *n.* a department in N France. 1,403,035; 2607 sq. mi. (6750 sq. km). *Cap.:* Arras.

pas de chat (*Fr.* päd[ə] shA′), *pl.* **pas de chat.** *Ballet.* a jump of one foot over the other. [1910–15; < F: cat step]

pas de che·val (*Fr.* päd[ə] shə vAl′), *pl.* **pas de cheval.** *Ballet.* a step in which the dancer hops on one foot and paws the ground with the other. [1915–20; < F: horse step]

pas de cô·té (*Fr.* päd[ə] kō tā′), *Dressage.* a two-track. [< F: sideways step]

pas de deux (*Fr.* päd[ə] dœ′), *pl.* **pas de deux.** *Ballet.* **1.** a dance by two persons. **2.** (in classical ballet) a set dance for a ballerina and a danseur noble, consisting typically of an entrée, an adagio, a variation for each dancer, and a coda. [1755–65; < F: lit., step for two]

pas de trois (*Fr.* päd[ə] tRwä′), *pl.* **pas de trois.** *Ballet.* a dance for three dancers. [1755–65; < F: lit., step for three]

pas du tout (pä dY to͞o′), *French.* not at all.

pa·se (pä′sā), *n.* (in bullfighting) a maneuver by a bullfighter with the capa or muleta to gain the attention of the bull and to guide the course of its attack. [1935–40; < Sp: lit., a pass, n. use of *pase* let him pass, 3rd person sing. pres. subj. of *pasar* to PASS]

pa·se·o (pä sā′ō; *Sp.* pä se′ô), *n., pl.* **-se·os** (-sā′ōz; *Sp.* -se′ôs). **1.** a slow, idle, or leisurely walk or stroll. **2.** a public place or path designed for walking; promenade. **3.** (esp. in Spanish-speaking countries) a usually tree-lined thoroughfare; avenue. [1825–35; < Sp]

pash (pash), *n. Slang.* **1.** an infatuation for another person; crush. **2.** the object of such a passion. [1910–15; shortening and resp. of PASSION]

pa·sha (pä′shə, pash′ə, pə shä′, -shô′), *n.* a title, placed after the name, formerly held by high officials in countries under Turkish rule. Also, **pacha.** [1640–50; < Turk *paşa;* see BASHAW] **—pa′sha·dom,** *n.*

pa·sha·lik (pə shä′lik, -shô′-), *n.* the territory governed by a pasha. Also, **pachalic, pa·sha′lic.** [1735–45; < Turk, equiv. to *paşa* PASHA + *-lık* suffix of appurtenance]

pashm (push′əm), *n.* the fine woolly underhair of goats raised in northern India. Also, **pash·im** (push′ĕm), **pash·mi·na** (push mē′nə), **pushmina.** [1875–80; < Pers: wool]

Pash·to (push′tō), *n.* an Indo-European, Iranian language that is the official language of Afghanistan and the chief vernacular of the eastern part of the nation. Also, **Pushtu, Pushto.** Also called **Afghan, Afghani.**

Pa·siph·a·ë (pə sif′ə ē′), *n.* **1.** *Class. Myth.* the wife of Minos, mother of Ariadne, and mother of the Minotaur by the Cretan bull. **2.** *Astron.* a small moon of the planet Jupiter. [1775–85]

Pa·sith·e·a (pə sith′ē ə), *n. Class. Myth.* one of the Graces.

pas·kha (päs′KHə), *n. Russian Cookery.* an Easter dessert of pot cheese mixed with sugar, butter, cream, raisins, nuts, etc., and pressed into a pyramidal mold: usually served with kulich. [< Russ *páskha,* special use of *Páskha* Easter < Gk *páscha;* see PASCH]

pas mar·ché (*Fr.* pä MAR shā′), *pl.* **pas mar·chés** (*Fr.* pä MAR shā′). *Ballet.* **1.** a marching step. **2.** a walking step in which the turned-out pointed toe reaches the ground first, then the heel is lowered before the weight is transferred to the whole foot on the ground. [< F: lit., marching step]

pa·so do·ble (pä′sō dō′blā; *Sp.* pä′sô dô′vle), *pl.* **pa·so do·bles,** *Sp.* ***pa·sos do·bles*** (pä′sôs dô′vles). **1.** a quick, light march often played at bullfights. **2.** a two-step, esp. one done to Latin-American rhythms. [1925–30; < Sp: lit., double step]

Pas·qua·le (pə skwä′lē; *It.* päs kwä′le), *n.* a male given name.

pasque·flow·er (pask′flou′ər), *n.* **1.** an Old World plant, *Anemone pulsatilla,* of the buttercup family, having purple, crocuslike flowers blooming about Easter. **2.** a related plant, *A. patens,* having similar flowers: the state flower of South Dakota. [*Pasque* (var. sp. of PASCH) + FLOWER (so named by the herbalist Gerarde in 1597); r. *passeflower* < MF *passefleur;* see PASS]

pas·quil (pas′kwil), *n.* a pasquinade. [1525–35; < NL *pasquillus* < It *pasquillo,* dim. of *Pasquino;* see PASQUINADE] —**pas·quil′ic, pas·quil′lic,** *adj.*

pas·quin·ade (pas′kwə nād′), *n., v.,* **-ad·ed, -ad·ing.** —*n.* **1.** a satire or lampoon, esp. one posted in a public place. —*v.t.* **2.** to assail in a pasquinade or pasquinades. [1585–95; *Pasquin* (< It *Pasquino,* name given an antique Roman statue unearthed in 1501 that was annually decorated and posted with verses) + -ADE[1]; r. *pasquinata* < It] —**pas′quin·ad′er,** *n.* —**pas·quin·i·an** (pas-kwin′ē ən), *adj.*

pass (pas, päs), *v.t.* **1.** to move past; go by: *to pass another car on the road.* **2.** to let go without notice, action, remark, etc.; leave unconsidered; disregard; overlook: *Pass chapter two and go on to chapter three.* **3.** to omit the usual or regular payment of: *The company decided to pass its dividend in the third quarter of the year.* **4.** to cause or allow to go through or beyond a gate, barrier, etc.: *The guard checked the identification papers and then passed the visitor.* **5.** to go across or over (a stream, threshold, etc.); cross. **6.** to endure or undergo: *They passed the worst night of their lives.* **7.** to undergo or complete successfully: *to pass an examination.* **8.** to cause or permit to complete successfully (an investigation, examination, course of study, etc.): *I am passing the whole class this term.* **9.** to go beyond (a point, degree, stage, etc.); transcend; exceed; surpass. **10.** to cause to go or extend farther: *to pass a rope through a hole.* **11.** to cause to go, move, or march by: *to pass troops in review.* **12.** to allot to oneself (a portion of time); spend: *He decided to pass a year abroad.* **13.** to live through, utilize, or fill; occupy oneself during: *How to pass the time?* **14.** to cause to circulate or spread; disseminate: *to pass rumors.* **15.** to cause to be accepted or received: *to pass a worthless check.* **16.** to convey, transfer, or transmit; deliver (often fol. by *on*): *Pass this memo on after reading it.* **17.** to convey from one person, hand, etc., to another: *Please pass the salt.* **18.** to pledge: *to pass one's word of honor to remain loyal.* **19.** to utter, pronounce, or speak: *She passed a remark about every passerby.* **20.** to cause to go through something, as a process or agency: *to pass returning travelers through customs.* **21.** to discharge or void from the body, as excrement or a kidney stone. **22.** to sanction or approve, esp. by vote: *Congress passed the bill.* **23.** to obtain the approval or sanction of (a legislative body, committee, etc.), esp. by a vote: *The bill passed Congress on the second vote.* **24.** to express or pronounce, as an opinion: *to pass judgment without knowing the facts.* **25.** *Law.* to place legal title or interest in (another) by a conveyance, a will, or other transfer. **26.** (in feats of magic) to perform a pass on. **27.** *Tennis.* to make a passing shot against (an opponent). **28.** *Sports.* to transfer (the ball or puck) to a teammate. **29.** *Bullfighting.* (of a bullfighter) to provoke and guide the charge of (a bull) with the capa or esp. the muleta.
—*v.i.* **30.** to go or move onward; proceed. **31.** to come to or toward, then go beyond: *to pass by a shop; to pass through town.* **32.** to go away; depart: *The dizzy feeling will pass in a minute.* **33.** to elapse or slip by; be spent: *The day passed very quickly for him.* **34.** to come to an end: *The crisis soon passed.* **35.** to die. **36.** to take place; happen; occur: *What passed while I was on vacation?* **37.** to go by or move past: *The funeral procession passed slowly.* **38.** to go about or circulate; be current. **39.** to serve as a marginally acceptable substitute: *The facsimile isn't very good but it will pass.* **40.** to live or be known as a member of a racial, religious, or ethnic group other than one's own, esp. to live and be known as a white person although of black ancestry. **41.** to be transferred or conveyed: *The crown passed to the king's nephew.* **42.** to be interchanged, as between two persons: *Sharp words passed between them.* **43.** to undergo transition or conversion: *to pass from a solid to a liquid state.* **44.** to go or get through a barrier, test, course of study, etc., successfully: *Of the twenty who took the exam, only twelve passed.* **45.** to go unheeded, unchallenged, or unremarked on: *He decided to let the insult pass.* **46.** to express or pronounce an opinion, judgment, verdict, etc. (usually fol. by *on* or *upon*): *Will you pass on the authenticity of this drawing?* **47.** to be voided, as excrement or a kidney stone. **48.** to obtain the vote of approval or sanction of a legislative body, official committee, or the like: *The new tax bill finally passed.* **49.** *Law.* **a.** (of a member of an inquest or other deliberative body) to sit (usually fol. by *on* or *upon*): *to pass on a case of manslaughter.* **b.** to adjudicate. **c.** to vest title or other legal interest in real or personal property in a new owner. **50.** to throw a ball from one person to another, as in a game of catch. **51.** *Sports.* to make a pass, as in football or ice hockey. **52.** *Cards.* **a.** to forgo one's opportunity to bid, play, etc. **b.** to throw in one's hand. **53.** *Fencing Obs.* to thrust or lunge. **54. bring to pass,** to cause to happen; bring about: *His wife's death brought to pass a change in his attitude toward religion.* **55. come to pass,** to occur; happen: *Strange things came to pass.* **56. pass along** or **through,** to add (incurred extra costs or expenses) to the amount charged a client or customer: *Airlines were passing along the sudden increase in fuel prices.* **57. pass away, a.** to cease; end: *All this trouble will pass away.* **b.** to die: *He passed away during the night.* **58. pass for,** to be accepted as; be considered: *material that passed for silk.* **59. pass muster.** See **muster** (def. 11). **60. pass off, a.** to present or offer (something) under false pretenses; dispose of deceptively: *to pass off a spurious de Kooning on a gullible buyer.* **b.** to cause to be accepted or received under a false identity: *He passed himself off as a doctor.* **c.** to cease gradually; end: *The headache passed off in the late afternoon.* **d.** to disregard or ignore. **e.** to continue to completion; occur: *The meeting passed off without incident.* **61. pass on,** to die: *The patient passed on after a long illness.* **62. pass out,** *Informal.* **a.** to lose consciousness; faint. **b.** to die; pass away. **c.** to distribute, esp. individually by hand: *to pass out discount coupons on a street corner.* **d.** to walk or march out or through; leave or exit by means of: *The graduates will pass out the center aisle after receiving their diplomas. Pass out this door and turn left.* **e.** to be exempted or promoted from: *Jerry passed out of freshman composition on the basis of his entering essay.* **63. pass over, a.** to disregard; ignore: *Just pass over the first part of his letter.* **b.** to fail to take notice of or consider: *He was passed over for the promotion.* **64. pass up,** to refuse or neglect to take advantage of; reject: *The opportunity may not come again, so don't pass it up.*
—*n.* **65.** an act of passing. **66.** a narrow route across a relatively low notch or depression in a mountain barrier. **67.** a road, channel, or other way providing a means of passage, as through an obstructed region or other barrier. **68.** a navigable channel, as at the mouth or in the delta of a river. **69.** a permission or license to pass, go, come, or enter. **70.** *Mil.* **a.** a military document granting the right to cross lines or to enter or leave a military or naval base or building. **b.** written authority given a soldier to leave a station or duty for a specified period of time. **71.** a free ticket or permit: *two passes to a concert; a railroad pass.* **72.** *South African.* See **reference book** (def. 2). **73.** *Chiefly Brit.* the act of passing a university or school examination or course without honors or distinction. **74.** *Sports.* the transfer of a ball or puck from one teammate to another. **75.** *Baseball.* See **base on balls.** **76.** *Fencing.* a thrust or lunge. **77.** a single movement, effort, maneuver, etc.: *He made a pass at the control tower of the enemy airfield.* **78.** *Informal.* **a.** a gesture, action, or remark that is intended to be sexually inviting; amorous overture. **b.** a jab or poke with the arm, esp. one that misses its mark. **79.** *Cards.* the act or statement of not bidding or raising another bid: *There have been two passes and now it's your bid.* **80.** (in feats of magic) **a.** a passing of the hand over, along, or before anything. **b.** the transference or changing of objects by or as by sleight of hand; a manipulation, as of a juggler. **81.** a particular stage or state of affairs: *The economic situation had come to a dreadful pass.* **82.** *Bullfighting.* a pase. **83.** one passage of a tool over work or one passage of work through a machine. **84.** *Archaic.* a witty remark or thrust. **85.** *Mining.* an opening for delivering coal or ore to a lower level underground. [1175–1225; (v.) ME *passen* < OF *passer* < VL **passāre,* deriv. of L *passus* step, PACE[1]; (n.) ME; in part < MF *passe* (n. deriv. of *passer*), in part n. deriv. of *passen*] —**pass′less,** *adj.*
—**Syn. 2.** ignore. **9.** excel. **22.** enact. **32.** leave. **34.** expire, cease, terminate, vanish, fade, disappear. **57b.** See **die**[1]. **66.** saddle, col. **81.** juncture, situation, condition.

pass., 1. passenger. **2.** passim. **3.** passive.

pass·a·ble (pas′ə bəl, pä′sə-), *adj.* **1.** capable of being passed through, beyond, or over; fit to be traversed, penetrated, crossed, etc., as a road, forest, or stream. **2.** adequate; acceptable: *a passable knowledge of French.* **3.** capable of being circulated legally or having a valid currency, as a coin. **4.** capable of being or liable to be ratified or enacted: *passable legislation.* [1375–1425; late ME < MF; see PASS, -ABLE] —**pass′a·ble·ness,** *n.*
—**Syn. 2.** presentable, respectable, allowable, tolerable, fair.

pass·a·bly (pas′ə blē, pä′sə-), *adv.* fairly; moderately: *a passably good novel.* [1600–10; PASSABLE + -LY]

pas·sa·ca·glia (pä′sə käl′yə, pas′ə kal′-), *n.* **1.** a slow, dignified dance of Spanish origin. **2.** the music for this dance, based on an ostinato figure. **3.** a musical form based on continuous variations over a ground bass. [1650–60; pseudo-It sp. of earlier *passacalle* < Sp *pasacalle* lit., step (i.e., dance) in the street (*pasa* 3d sing. pres. of *pasar* to step, PACE[1] + *calle* street < L *callem,* acc. of *callis* path)]

pas·sade (pə sād′), *n. Manège.* a turn or course of a horse backward or forward on the same ground. [1650–60; < F < It *passata.* See PASS, -ADE[1]]

pas·sa·do (pə sä′dō), *n., pl.* **-dos, -does.** *Fencing.* a forward thrust with the weapon while advancing with one foot. [1580–90; alter. of Sp *pasada* or It *passata.* See PASSADE]

pas·sage[1] (pas′ij), *n., v.,* **-saged, -sag·ing.** —*n.* **1.** a portion or section of a written work; a paragraph, verse, etc.: *a passage of Scripture.* **2.** a phrase or other division of a musical work. **3.** *Fine Arts.* an area, section, or detail of a work, esp. with respect to its qualities of execution: *passages of sensitive brushwork.* **4.** an act or instance of passing from one place, condition, etc., to another; transit. **5.** the permission, right, or freedom to pass: *to refuse passage through a territory.* **6.** the route or course by which a person or thing passes or travels. **7.** a hall or corridor; passageway. **8.** an opening or entrance into, through, or out of something: *the nasal passages.* **9.** a voyage by water from one point to another: *a rough passage across the English Channel.* **10.** the privilege of conveyance as a passenger: *to book passage on an ocean liner.* **11.** the price charged for accommodation on a ship; fare. **12.** a lapse or passing, as of time. **13.** a progress or course, as of events. **14.** the enactment into law of a legislative measure. **15.** an interchange of communications, confidences, etc., between persons. **16.** an exchange of blows; altercation or dispute: *a passage at arms.* **17.** the act of causing something to pass; transference; transmission. **18.** an evacuation of the bowels. **19.** an occurrence, incident, or event. —*v.i.* **20.** to make a passage; cross; pass; voyage. [1250–1300; ME < OF, equiv. to *pass(er)* to PASS + *-age* -AGE]

pas·sage[2] (pas′ij, pə säzh′), *n., v.,* **-saged, -sag·ing.** *Manège.* —*n.* **1.** a slow, cadenced trot executed with great elevation of the feet and characterized by a moment of suspension before the feet strike the ground. —*v.i.* **2.** (of a horse) to execute such a movement. **3.** (of a rider) to cause a horse to execute such a movement. —*v.t.* **4.** to cause (a horse) to passage. [1790–1800; < F *passager* (v.), var. of *passéger* < It *passeggiare* to walk; see PACE[1]]

pas′sage grave′, *Archaeol.* a megalithic tomb of the Neolithic and Copper or early Bronze ages found in the British Isles and Europe, consisting of a roofed burial chamber and narrow entrance passage covered by a round mound and containing human remains and funerary offerings. Cf. **chamber tomb.** [1930–35]

pas′sage hawk′, 1. a young hawk during its first migration. **2.** *Falconry.* a hawk captured during its migration. [1820–30]

Pas′sage to In′dia, A, a novel (1924) by E. M. Forster.

pas·sage·way (pas′ij wā′), *n.* **1.** a way for passing into, through, or out of something, as within a building or between buildings; a corridor, hall, alley, catwalk, or the like. **2.** a corridor on a ship. [1640–50; PASSAGE[1] + WAY]
—**Syn. 1.** passage, access, path, walk.

pas·sage·work (pas′ij wûrk′), *n. Music.* **1.** writing that is often extraneous to the thematic material of a work and is typically of a virtuosic or decorative character: *passagework consisting of scales, arpeggios, trills, and double octaves.* **2.** the performance of such writing: *The pianist's passagework is brilliantly clear and smooth.* [1860–65; PASSAGE[1] + WORK]

Pas·sa·ic (pə sā′ik), *n.* a city in NE New Jersey. 52,463.

pass·a·long (pas′ə lông′, -long′, päs′-), *n.* **1.** the act of giving or conveying something to another person for additional use: *Readership passalong means that three people read every copy of the magazine.* **2.** the act, policy, etc., of compensating for increased costs by incorporating them in the price charged a customer or client: *a passalong to hotel guests of rising energy costs.* **3.** the additional amount charged; surcharge: *a passalong of thirty cents per gallon of gas.* —*adj.* **4.** pertaining to or being a passalong. [1975–80; n. use of v. phrase *pass along*]

Pas·sa·ma·quod·dy (pas′ə mə kwod′ē), *n., pl.* **-dies,** (*esp. collectively*) **-dy** for 1. **1.** a member of a small tribe of North American Indians formerly of coastal Maine and New Brunswick and now living in Maine. **2.** the Eastern Algonquian language of the Passamaquoddy, mutually intelligible with Malecite.

Pas′samaquod′dy Bay′, an inlet of the Bay of Fundy, between Maine and New Brunswick, at the mouth of the St. Croix River.

pas·sa·ment (pas′ə mənt), *n.* passement.

pas·sant (pas′ənt), *adj. Heraldry.* (of a beast) represented as in the act of walking, with one forepaw raised. [1375–1425; late ME < MF, prp. of *passer* to PASS; see -ANT]

pass·band (pas′band′, päs′-), *n. Radio and Television.* the range of frequencies that pass with a minimum of attenuation through an electronic filter. [1920–25; PASS + BAND[2]]

pass·book (pas′bo͝ok′, päs′-), *n.* **1.** a bankbook. **2.** (formerly) a small book or ledger for each customer in which a merchant keeps a record of goods sold on credit and the amounts owed and paid. **3.** *South African.* See **reference book** (def. 2). [1820–30; PASS + BOOK]

pass′book sav′ings account′, a type of savings account in which transactions are entered into a passbook in the possession of the account holder. Cf. **statement savings account.**

pass′ degree′, (in English universities) an ordinary bachelor's degree conferred without honors. Also called **poll, poll degree.** [1910–15]

passe (päs), *n. French.* the numbers 19 through 36 in roulette. Cf. ***manque.*** [lit., passing, pass]

pas·sé (pa sā′; *for 4 also Fr.* pä sā′), *adj., n., pl.* **pas·sés** (pa sāz′; *Fr.* pä sā′). —*adj.* **1.** no longer fashionable, in wide use, etc.; out-of-date; outmoded: *There were many photographs of passé fashions. I thought hand-cranked pencil sharpeners were passé.* **2.** past: *time passé.* **3.** past the prime of one's life. —*n.* **4.** *Ballet.* a

CONCISE PRONUNCIATION KEY: *act, cāpe, dâre, pärt; set, ēqual; if, īce; ox, ōver, ôrder, oil, bo͝ok, bo͞ot, out; up, ûrge; child; sing; shoe; thin, that;* zh as in *treasure.* ə = *a* as in *alone, e* as in *system, i* as in *easily, o* as in *gallop, u* as in *circus;* ə as in *fire* (fīər), *hour* (ouər). l and n can serve as syllabic consonants, as in *cradle* (krād′l), and *button* (but′n). See the full key inside the front cover.

movement in which one leg passes behind or in front of the other. [1765–75; < F, ptp. of *passer* to PASS]
—**Syn.** **1.** old-fashioned, démodé, quaint.

pas·sé com·po·sé (pä sā kôN pō zā′), *French.* a grammatical construction of French consisting of the present tense of an auxiliary, either *avoir* or *être,* followed by a past participle and corresponding in function to both the English present perfect and the English simple past tenses. [lit., compound past]

passed (past, päst), *adj.* **1.** having completed the act of passing. **2.** having received a passing grade on an examination or test or successfully completed a school course, year, or program of study. **3.** *Finance.* noting a dividend not paid at the usual dividend date. **4.** *U.S. Navy.* having successfully completed an examination for promotion, and awaiting a vacancy in the next grade: *a passed chief engineer.* [1400–50; late ME; see PASS, -ED²]

passed′ ball′, *Baseball.* a pitched ball that the catcher can reasonably be expected to catch but misses, resulting in a base runner's or runners' advancing one or more bases or in the batter's reaching first base safely. Cf. **wild pitch.** [1860–65, *Amer.*]

passed′ pawn′, *Chess.* a pawn with no opposing pawn either on an adjacent file or on its own file. [1790–1800]

pas·sel (pas′əl), *n.* a group or lot of indeterminate number: *a passel of dignitaries.* [1825–35; alter. of PARCEL]

passe·ment (pas′mənt), *n.* a garment trimming of gold, silver, linen, or silk thread. Also, **passament.** [1530–40; < F, for *passeman* < Sp *pasamano* railing (so called because one passes one's hand along it in going up and down stairs), hence edging for clothes. See PASS, MANUAL]

passe·men·terie (pas men′trē; *Fr.* päs mäN trē′), *n.* trimming of braid, cord, bead, etc., in any of various forms. [1850–55; < F; see PASSEMENT, -ERY]

pas·sen·ger (pas′ən jər), *n.* **1.** a person who is traveling in an automobile, bus, train, airplane, or other conveyance, esp. one who is not the driver, pilot, or the like. **2.** a wayfarer; traveler. [1300–50; ME *passager* < MF, n. use of *passag(i)er* (adj.) passing, temporary; see PASSAGE, -IER²; for *-n-* cf. MESSENGER, HARBINGER, SCAVENGER, POPINJAY]

pas′senger mile′, a unit of measurement, consisting of one mile traveled by a passenger, that airlines, railroads, and other public transportation facilities use in recording volume of traffic. Also, **pas′sen·ger-mile′.** [1900–05] —**pas′senger mile′age.**

pas′senger pi′geon, an extinct pigeon, *Ectopistes migratorius,* once found in great numbers in North America, noted for its sustained migratory flights. [1795–1805, *Amer.*]

passe-par·tout (pas′pär to͞o′; *Fr.* päs PAR to͞o′), *n., pl.* **-touts** (-to͞oz′; *Fr.* -to͞o′). **1.** something that passes everywhere or provides a universal means of passage. **2.** a master key; skeleton key. **3.** an ornamental mat for a picture. **4.** a method of framing in which a piece of glass is placed over a picture and is affixed to a backing by means of adhesive strips of paper or other material pasted over the edges. **5.** paper prepared for this purpose. [1635–45; < F: lit., (it) passes everywhere]

passe·pied (päs pyā′), *n., pl.* **-pieds** (-pyā′, -pyāz′). **1.** a lively dance in triple meter popular in France in the 17th and 18th centuries. **2.** a dance form in moderately fast 3/8 or 6/8 meter, occasionally constituting part of the 17th- and 18th-century instrumental suite. [1685–95; < F: lit., pass (the) foot, i.e., move it, dance. See PASS, -PED]

pass·er (pas′ər, pä′sər), *n.* **1.** a person or thing that passes or causes something to pass. **2.** a passerby. [1350–1400; ME; see PASS, -ER¹]

pass·er·by (pas′ər bī′, -bī′, pä′sər-), *n., pl.* **pass·ers·by** (pas′ərz bī′, -bī′, pä′sərz-), a person passing by. Also, **pass′er-by′.** [1560–70; *pass by* + -ER¹, with postposing of the particle]

pas·ser·i·form (pas′ər ə fôrm′, pə ser′ə-), *adj.* of or pertaining to the order Passeriformes; passerine. [< NL *Passeriformes,* equiv. to L *passer* sparrow + *-iformes* -IFORMES]

pas·ser·ine (pas′ər in, -ə rīn′, -ə rēn′), *adj.* **1.** of, belonging, or pertaining to the order Passeriformes, comprising more than half of all birds and typically having the feet adapted for perching. **2.** oscine (def. 1). —*n.* **3.** any bird of the order Passeriformes. [1770–80; < L *passerinus* of a sparrow, equiv. to *passer* sparrow + *-inus* -INE¹]

pas seul (*Fr.* pä sœl′), *pl.* **pas seuls** (*Fr.* pä sœl′). *Ballet.* a dance performed by one person; dance solo. [1805–15; < F: lit., solo step]

pass-fail (pas′fāl′, päs′-), *n. Educ.* a system of grading in some educational institutions in which a student simply passes or fails instead of receiving a letter or numerical grade. [1955–60]

pas·si·ble (pas′ə bəl), *adj.* capable of feeling, esp. suffering; susceptible of sensation or emotion; impressionable. [1300–50; ME < ML *passibilis.* See PASSION, -IBLE] —**pas′si·bil′i·ty,** *n.*

pas·sim (pas′im), *adv. Latin.* here and there: used in bibliographic references to indicate that the writer has drawn upon material scattered throughout the source cited.

pass·ing (pas′ing, pä′sing), *adj.* **1.** going by or past; elapsing: *He was feeling better with each passing day.* **2.** brief, fleeting, or fortuitous; transitory: *to take a passing fancy to something.* **3.** done, given, etc., in passing; cursory: *a passing mention.* **4.** surpassing, preeminent, or extreme. **5.** indicating satisfactory performance in a course, on a paper, in a test, etc.: *a passing grade on a test.* —*adv.* **6.** surpassingly; exceedingly; very. —*n.* **7.** the act of a person or thing that passes or causes something to pass. **8.** a means or place of passage. **9. in passing,** by the way; incidentally: *The speaker mentioned his latest book in passing.* [1275–1325; ME; see PASS, -ING², -ING¹] —**pass′ing·ly,** *adv.* —**pass′ing·ness,** *n.*

CONCISE ETYMOLOGY KEY: <, descended or borrowed from; >, whence; b., blend of, blended; c., cognate with; cf., compare; deriv., derivative; equiv., equivalent; imit., imitative; obl., oblique; r., replacing; s., stem; sp., spelling, spelled; resp., respelling, respelled; trans., translation; ?, origin unknown; *, unattested; ‡, probably earlier than. See the full key inside the front cover.

pass′ing bell′, **1.** a bell tolled to announce a death or funeral. **2.** a portent or sign of the passing away of anything. [1520–30]

pass′ing lane′, **1.** a highway lane in which a driver may pass other vehicles legally. **2.** *Basketball.* any open space through which players attempt to pass the ball.

pass′ing modula′tion, *Music.* See **transient modulation.**

pass′ing note′, *Music.* a note that is foreign to a harmony and is introduced between two successive chord tones in order to produce a melodic transition. Also called **pass′ing tone′.** [1720–30]

pass′ing shot′, *Tennis.* a shot played to one side of and beyond the reach of an opponent coming to or stationed at the net. [1945–50]

pas·sion (pash′ən), *n.* **1.** any powerful or compelling emotion or feeling, as love or hate. **2.** strong amorous feeling or desire; love; ardor. **3.** strong sexual desire; lust. **4.** an instance or experience of strong love or sexual desire. **5.** a person toward whom one feels strong love or sexual desire. **6.** a strong or extravagant fondness, enthusiasm, or desire for anything: *a passion for music.* **7.** the object of such a fondness or desire: *Accuracy became a passion with him.* **8.** an outburst of strong emotion or feeling: *He suddenly broke into a passion of bitter words.* **9.** violent anger. **10.** the state of being acted upon or affected by something external, esp. something alien to one's nature or one's customary behavior (contrasted with *action*). **11.** (*often cap.*) *Theol.* **a.** the sufferings of Christ on the cross or His sufferings subsequent to the Last Supper. **b.** the narrative of Christ's sufferings as recorded in the Gospels. **12.** *Archaic.* the sufferings of a martyr. [1125–75; ME (< OF) < ML *passiōn-* (s. of *passiō*) Christ's sufferings on the cross, any of the Biblical accounts of these (> late OE *passiōn*), special use of LL *passiō* suffering, submission, deriv. of L *passus,* ptp. of *patī* to suffer, submit; see -ION] —**pas′sion·ful,** *adj.* —**pas′sion·ful·ly,** *adv.* —**pas′sion·ful·ness,** *n.* —**pas′sion·like′,** *adj.*
—**Syn.** **1.** See **feeling. 6.** fervor, zeal, ardor. **9.** ire, fury, wrath, rage. —**Ant. 1.** apathy.

pas·sion·al (pash′ə nl), *adj.* **1.** of, pertaining to, or marked by passion. **2.** caused or accompanied by passion: *a passional crime.* —*n.* **3.** a book containing descriptions of the sufferings of saints and martyrs, for reading on their festivals. [1400–50; late ME < ML *passiōnālis,* equiv. to LL *passiōn-* PASSION + L *-ālis* -AL¹; (n.) < ML *passiōnāle,* n. use of neut. of *passiōnālis*]

pas·sion·ar·y (pash′ə ner′ē), *n., pl.* **-ar·ies.** passional (def. 3). [1490–1500; < ML *passiōnārium,* equiv. to LL *passiōn-* PASSION + L *-ārium* -ARY]

pas·sion·ate (pash′ə nit), *adj.* **1.** having, compelled by, or ruled by intense emotion or strong feeling; fervid: *a passionate advocate of socialism.* **2.** easily aroused to or influenced by sexual desire; ardently sensual. **3.** expressing, showing, or marked by intense or strong feeling; emotional: *passionate language.* **4.** intense or vehement, as emotions or feelings: *passionate grief.* **5.** easily moved to anger; quick-tempered; irascible. [1375–1425; late ME < ML *passiōnātus,* equiv. to LL *passiōn-* PASSION + L *-ātus* -ATE¹] —**pas′sion·ate·ly,** *adv.* —**pas′sion·ate·ness,** *n.*
—**Syn. 1.** excitable, emotional, impulsive, zealous. **1, 3, 4.** ardent, impassioned, excited, fervent, warm, enthusiastic, earnest, glowing, burning, fiery; animated, impetuous, violent. **5.** testy, choleric, hasty, short-tempered, fiery, hotheaded. —**Ant. 1, 3–5.** cool, calm.

Pas′sion cross′, *Heraldry.* See **Latin cross.** [1770–80]

pas·sion·flow·er (pash′ən flou′ər), *n.* any chiefly American climbing vine or shrub of the genus *Passiflora,* having showy flowers and a pulpy berry or fruit that in some species is edible. [1605–15; trans. of NL *flōs passiōnis* flower of the Passion; so named because the parts of the flower were imagined as symbolic of the objects and events of Christ's Passion]

passionflower, *Passiflora incarnata*

pas·sion·fruit (pash′ən fro͞ot′), *n.* any edible fruit of a passionflower, as the maypop. [1745–55; PASSION + FRUIT]

Pas·sion·ist (pash′ə nist), *n. Rom. Cath. Ch.* a member of the "Congregation of Barefooted Clerks of the Most Holy Cross and Passion of Our Lord Jesus Christ," founded in 1720 and engaged chiefly in missionary work. [1840–50; < It *passionista.* See PASSION, -IST]

pas·sion·less (pash′ən lis), *adj.* not feeling or moved by passion; cold or unemotional; calm or detached. [1605–15; PASSION + -LESS] —**pas′sion·less·ly,** *adv.* —**pas′sion·less·ness,** *n.*

pas′sion pit′, *Older Slang.* a drive-in movie theater. [1935–40, *Amer.*; so called from its use by adolescents as a place for unobserved sexual intimacy]

pas′sion play′, a dramatic representation of the passion of Christ, as that given every ten years at the Bavarian village of Oberammergau. Also, **Pas′sion Play′.** [1865–70]

Pas′sion Sun′day, the fifth Sunday in Lent, being the second week before Easter. [1350–1400; ME]

Pas·sion·tide (pash′ən tīd′), *n.* the two-week period from Passion Sunday to Holy Saturday. [1840–50; PASSION + TIDE¹]

Pas′sion Week′, **1.** the week preceding Easter; Holy Week. **2.** the week before Holy Week, beginning with Passion Sunday. [1350–1400; ME]

pas·si·vate (pas′ə vāt′), *v.t.,* **-vat·ed, -vat·ing.** *Metall.* to treat (a metal) to render the surface less reactive chemically. [1910–15; PASSIVE + -ATE¹]

pas·sive (pas′iv), *adj.* **1.** not reacting visibly to something that might be expected to produce manifestations of an emotion or feeling. **2.** not participating readily or actively; inactive: *a passive member of a committee.* **3.** not involving visible reaction or active participation: *to play a passive role.* **4.** inert or quiescent. **5.** influenced, acted upon, or affected by some external force, cause, or agency; being the object of action rather than causing action (opposed to *active*). **6.** receiving or characterized by the reception of impressions or influences from external sources. **7.** produced or caused by an external agency. **8.** receiving, enduring, or submitting without resistance: *a passive hypnotic subject.* **9.** *Gram.* **a.** noting a voice in the inflection of the verb in some languages which is used to indicate that the subject undergoes the action of the verb. Latin *portātur,* "he, she, or it is carried," is in the passive voice. **b.** noting or pertaining to a construction similar to this in meaning, as English *He is carried* (opposed to *active*). **10.** *Chem.* inactive, esp. under conditions in which chemical activity is to be expected. **11.** *Metall.* (of a metal) treated so as to impart impassivity. **12.** *Med.* of or pertaining to certain unhealthy but dormant conditions; inactive, as opposed to active or spontaneous. **13.** *Telecommunications.* designed to relay signals without electronic devices: *a passive communications satellite.* **14.** (of a solar heating system) accumulating and distributing solar heat without the aid of machinery. —*n. Gram.* **15.** the passive voice. **16.** a passive form or construction. [1350–1400; ME < L *passīvus* lit., submissive, equiv. to *pass(us)* (ptp. of *patī* to experience, undergo, submit) + *-īvus* -IVE] —**pas′sive·ly,** *adv.*
—**Syn. 8.** submissive, unresisting. —**Ant. 1–3.** active. **8.** recalcitrant.

pas′sive-ag·gres′sive personal′ity (pas′iv ə gres′iv), *Psychiatry.* a personality disorder characterized by aggressive behavior expressed in passive ways, as procrastination, stubbornness, or pouting.

pas′sive-de·pend′ent personal′ity (pas′iv di pen′dənt), *Psychiatry.* a personality disorder characterized by a lack of self-confidence and self-reliance and consequent surrender to and dependence on others to take responsibility for major areas of one's life. [1965–70]

pas′sive immu′nity, *Immunol.* immunity resulting from the injection of antibodies or sensitized lymphocytes from another organism or, in infants, from the transfer of antibodies through the placenta or from colostrum. [1890–95]

pas′sive noun′, *Gram.* a noun whose referent is the recipient of an action, as *trainee, multiplicand.*

pas′sive rea′son, *Aristotelianism.* the reasoning faculty existing only within an individual mind, limited in scope and perishing with the body. Cf. **active reason.**

pas′sive resist′ance, opposition to a government or to specific governmental laws by the use of noncooperation and other nonviolent methods, as economic boycotts and protest marches. Cf. **civil disobedience, noncooperation** (def. 2). [1880–85] —**pas′sive re·sist′er.**

pas′sive restraint′, a safety device, as an air bag or special seat belt, that is activated automatically to protect an automobile passenger at the moment of impact when a collision occurs. [1965–70]

pas′sive smok′ing, the inhaling of cigarette, cigar, and pipe smoke of others, esp. by a nonsmoker in an enclosed area. [1970–75]

pas′sive trans′fer, *Immunol.* injection of lymphocytes or antibody from an immune or sensitized donor to a nonimmune host in order to impart immunity or test for allergic reactions. [1940–45]

pas·siv·ism (pas′ə viz′əm), *n.* **1.** the quality of being passive. **2.** the principle or practice of passive resistance. [1900–05; PASSIVE + -ISM] —**pas′siv·ist,** *n.*

pas·siv·i·ty (pa siv′i tē), *n.* **1.** Also, **pas·sive·ness** (pas′iv nis). the state or condition of being passive. **2.** chemical inactivity, esp. the resistance to corrosion of certain metals when covered with a coherent oxide layer. [1650–60; PASSIVE + -ITY]

pass·key (pas′kē′, päs′-), *n., pl.* **-keys. 1.** See **master key. 2.** See **skeleton key. 3.** a private key. **4.** a latchkey. [1810–20; PASS + KEY¹]

Pas·so Fun·do (pä′so͝o fo͞oN′do͝o), a city in S Brazil. 76,452.

Pass·o·ver (pas′ō′vər, päs′-), *n.* **1.** Also called **Pesach, Pesah.** a Jewish festival that commemorates the exodus of the Jews from Egypt and is marked chiefly by the Seder ritual and the eating of matzoth. It begins on the 14th day of Nisan and is celebrated for eight days by Orthodox and Conservative Jews outside of Israel and for seven days by Reform Jews and Jews in Israel. **2.** (*l.c.*) See **paschal lamb** (def. 1). [1520–30; n. use of v. phrase *pass over,* as trans. of Heb *pesaḥ*]

pass′ point′, *Survey.* a point located photogrammetrically and used as a reference point in orienting other photographs.

pass·port (pas′pôrt, -pōrt, päs′-), *n.* **1.** an official document issued by the government of a country to one of its citizens and, varying from country to country, authorizing travel to foreign countries and authenticating the bearer's identity, citizenship, right to protection while abroad, and right to reenter his or her native country. **2.** anything that ensures admission or acceptance: *A good education can be your passport to success.* **3.** any authorization to pass or go somewhere. **4.** a document issued to a ship, esp. to a neutral merchant ship in time of war, granting or requesting permission to proceed without molestation in certain waters. **5.** a certificate intended to secure admission. [1490–1500; earlier *passeport* < MF, equiv. to *passe-* (s. of *passer* to PASS) + *port* PORT[1]] —**pass′port·less,** *adj.*

pass-through (pas′thro͞o′, päs′-), *n.* **1.** a windowlike opening, as one for passing food or dishes between a kitchen and a dining area. **2.** a place through which one passes or is obliged to pass: *Motorists used the park as a pass-through. The new gate will be a pass-through for security clearance.* **3.** passalong. —*adj.* **4.** denoting a pass-through; passalong. Also, **pass′through′.** [1950–55, *Amer.*; n. and adj. use of v. phrase *pass through*]

pas·sus (pas′əs), *n., pl.* **-sus, -sus·es.** a section or division of a story, poem, etc.; canto. [1565–75; < ML, L: step. See PACE[1]]

pass·word (pas′wûrd′, päs′-), *n.* **1.** a secret word or expression used by authorized persons to prove their right to access, information, etc. **2.** a word or other string of characters, sometimes kept secret or confidential, that must be supplied by a user in order to gain full or partial access to a multiuser computer system or its data resources. Cf. **countersign.** [1810–20; PASS + WORD]
—**Syn. 1.** watchword.

Pas·sy (pa sē′), *n.* **1. Fré·dé·rick** (frā dā rēk′), 1822–1912, French economist and statesman: Nobel peace prize 1901. **2.** his son, **Paul É·douard** (pôl ā dwar′), 1859–1940, French phonetician.

past (past, päst), *adj.* **1.** gone by or elapsed in time: *It was a bad time, but it's all past now.* **2.** of, having existed in, or having occurred during a time previous to the present; bygone: *the past glories of the Incas.* **3.** gone by just before the present time; just passed: *during the past year.* **4.** ago: *six days past.* **5.** having formerly been or served as; previous; earlier: *three past presidents of the club.* **6.** *Gram.* designating a tense, or other verb formation or construction, that refers to events or states in time gone by. —*n.* **7.** the time gone by: *He could remember events far back in the past.* **8.** the history of a person, nation, etc.: *our country's glorious past.* **9.** what has existed or has happened at some earlier time: *Try to forget the past, now that your troubles are over.* **10.** the events, phenomena, conditions, etc., that characterized an earlier historical period: *That hat is something out of the past.* **11.** an earlier period of a person's life, career, etc., that is thought to be of a shameful or embarrassing nature: *When he left prison, he put his past behind him.* **12.** *Gram.* **a.** the past tense, as *he ate, he smoked.* **b.** another verb formation or construction with past meaning. **c.** a form in the past tense. —*adv.* **13.** so as to pass by or beyond; by: *The troops marched past.* —*prep.* **14.** beyond in time; later than; after: *past noon; half past six.* **15.** beyond in space or position; farther on than: *the house just past the church.* **16.** in a direction so as to pass by or go beyond: *We went past the house by mistake.* **17.** beyond in amount, number, etc.: *past the maximum age for enlisting in the army.* **18.** beyond the reach, scope, influence, or power of: *He is past hope of recovery.* [1250–1300; ME; var. sp. of *passed,* ptp. of PASS]

pas·ta (pä′stə; *esp. Brit.* pas′tə), *n.* any of various flour-and-egg food preparations of Italian origin, made of thin, unleavened dough and produced in a variety of forms, usually served with a sauce and sometimes stuffed. [1870–75; < It < LL. See PASTE]

past′ contin′uous. See **past progressive.** [1920–25]

paste (pāst), *n., v.,* **past·ed, past·ing.** —*n.* **1.** a mixture of flour and water, often with starch or the like, used for causing paper or other material to adhere to something. **2.** any soft, smooth, and plastic material or preparation. **3.** dough, esp. when prepared with shortening, as for making pie crust and other pastry: *puff paste.* **4.** any of various semisoft fruit confections of pliable consistency: *almond paste; guava paste.* **5.** a preparation of fish, tomatoes, or other food reduced to a smooth, soft mass, as for a relish or for seasoning. **6.** pasta. **7.** a mixture of clay, water, etc., for making pottery or porcelain. **8.** *Jewelry.* **a.** a brilliant, heavy glass, as strass, used for making artificial gems. **b.** an artificial gem of this material. **9.** *Slang.* a hard smack, blow, or punch, esp. on the face. —*v.t.* **10.** to fasten or stick with paste or the like. **11.** to cover with something applied by means of paste. **12.** *Slang.* to hit (a person) hard, esp. on the face. [1350–1400; ME < MF < LL *pasta* dough < Gk *pastá* barley porridge, n. use of neut. pl. of *pastós,* verbid of *pássein* to strew, sprinkle; a *pasta* was orig. a kind of gruel sprinkled with salt; (defs. 9, 12) prob. by assoc. with BASTE[3]]

paste·board (pāst′bôrd′, -bōrd′), *n.* **1.** a stiff, firm board made of sheets of paper pasted or layers of paper pulp pressed together. **2.** *Older Slang.* a card, as a visiting card or a playing card. **3.** *Older Slang.* a ticket, as for the theater. —*adj.* **4.** made of pasteboard. **5.** unsubstantial, flimsy, or sham. [1540–50; PASTE + BOARD] —**paste′board′y,** *adj.*

pas·tel[1] (pa stel′; *esp. Brit.* pas′tl), *n.* **1.** a color having a soft, subdued shade. **2.** a kind of dried paste made of pigments ground with chalk and compounded with gum water. **3.** a chalklike crayon made from such paste. **4.** the art of drawing with such crayons. **5.** a drawing so made. **6.** a short, light prose study or sketch. —*adj.* **7.** having a soft, subdued shade. **8.** drawn with pastels: *a pastel portrait.* [1655–65; < F < It *pastello* < LL *pastellus,* var. of L *pastillus* (see PASTILLE)]

pas·tel[2] (pas′tel), *n.* **1.** the woad plant. **2.** the dye made from it. [1570–80; < MF < Pr < ML *pastellum* (neut.) woad (orig. woad paste), for LL *pastellus* (masc.), dim. of *pasta* PASTE; change of gender by influence of L *glastum* woad]

pas·tel·ist (pa stel′ist; *esp. Brit.* pas′tl ist), *n.* an artist who draws with pastels. Also, *esp. Brit.,* **pas′tel·list.** [1880–85; PASTEL[1] + -IST]

pa·stel′ or′ange (pa stel′; *esp. Brit.* pas′tl), suntan (def. 3).

paste′ mold′, *Glassmaking.* a mold lined with a moist carbonized paste, for shaping glass as it is blown.

paste-on (pāst′on′, -ôn′), *adj.* that can be pasted or stuck on: *canning jars with paste-on labels.*

past·er (pā′stər), *n.* **1.** a slip of paper gummed on the back, to be pasted on or over something, as over a name on a ballot. **2.** a person or thing that pastes. [1730–40; PASTE + -ER[1]]

pas·tern (pas′tərn), *n.* **1.** the part of the foot of a horse, cow, etc., between the fetlock and the hoof. See diag. under **horse. 2.** either of the two bones of this part, the upper or first phalanx **(great pastern bone)** and the lower or second phalanx **(small pastern bone),** between which is a joint **(pas′tern joint′).** [1300–50; ME *pastron* shackle, prob. same word as MF *pasturon,* *pastern* < VL **pastōria* herding (see PASTOR, -IA) + MF *-on* n. suffix]

Pas·ter·nak (pas′tər nak′; *Russ.* pə styir näk′), *n.* **Bo·ris Le·o·ni·do·vich** (bôr′is, bōr′-, bor′-; *Russ.* bu ryēs′ lyi u nyē′də vyich), 1890–1960, Russian poet, novelist, and translator: declined 1958 Nobel prize.

paste-up (pāst′up′), *n. Print.* mechanical (def. 14). [1925–30; n. use of v. phrase *paste up*]

Pas·teur (pa stûr′; *Fr.* pä stœr′), *n.* **Louis** (lo͞o′ē; *Fr.* lwē), 1822–95, French chemist and bacteriologist. —**Pas·teur′i·an,** *adj.*

Pasteur′ effect′, the inhibiting of fermentation by oxygen. [1930–35; named after L. PASTEUR]

pas·teu·rel·la (pas′tə rel′ə), *n., pl.* **-rel·lae** (-rel′ē), **-rel·las.** *Bacteriol.* any of several rod-shaped bacteria of the genus *Pasturella,* certain species of which are parasitic and pathogenic for humans and animals. [< NL (1887), after L. PASTEUR; see -ELLA]

pas·teu·rel·lo·sis (pas′tər ə lō′sis), *n. Vet. Pathol.* See **hemorrhagic septicemia.** [1900–05; < NL; see PASTEURELLA, -OSIS]

pas·teur·ize (pas′chə rīz′, pas′tə-), *v.t.,* **-ized, -iz·ing.** to expose (a food, as milk, cheese, yogurt, beer, or wine) to an elevated temperature for a period of time sufficient to destroy certain microorganisms, as those that can produce disease or cause spoilage or undesirable fermentation of food, without radically altering taste or quality. Also, *esp. Brit.,* **pas′teur·ise′.** [1880–85; PASTEUR + -IZE] —**pas′teur·i·za′tion,** *n.*

pas·teur·iz·er (pas′chə rī′zər, pas′tə-), *n.* an apparatus for pasteurizing milk and other liquids. [1895–1900; PASTEURIZE + -ER[1]]

pas·tic·cio (pa stē′chō; *It.* päs tēt′chô), *n., pl.* **-ci** (-chē). a pastiche. [1700–10; < It < VL *pasticium* pasty, pie, deriv. of LL *pasta;* see PASTE]

pas·tiche (pa stēsh′, pä-), *n.* **1.** a literary, musical, or artistic piece consisting wholly or chiefly of motifs or techniques borrowed from one or more sources. **2.** an incongruous combination of materials, forms, motifs, etc., taken from different sources; hodgepodge. [1700–10; < F < It *pasticcio* PASTICCIO]

pas·ti·cheur (pas tē shœr′), *n., pl.* ***-cheurs*** (-shœr′). *French.* **1.** a person who makes, composes, or concocts a pastiche. **2.** a person who imitates the work of others.

pas·ti·cheuse (pas tē shœz′), *n., pl.* ***-cheuses*** (-shœz′). *French.* a woman who makes or composes a pastiche.

pas·ti·glia (pä stēl′yə; *It.* päs tē′lyä), *n.* a plaster used during the Italian Renaissance for bas-relief ornament of furniture, being applied in layers, molded, carved, and gilded. [1925–30; < It < Sp *pastilla.* See PASTILLE]

pas·tille (pa stēl′, -stil′), *n.* **1.** a flavored or medicated lozenge; troche. **2.** a roll or cone of paste containing aromatic substances, burned as a disinfectant or deodorant. **3.** pastel for crayons. **4.** a crayon made of pastel. Also, **pas·til** (pas′til). [1610–20; < F < Sp *pastilla;* akin to L *pastillus* lump of meal, lozenge, akin to *pānis* bread]

pas·time (pas′tīm′, päs′-), *n.* something that serves to make time pass agreeably; a pleasant means of amusement, recreation, or sport: *to play cards as a pastime.* [1480–90; earlier *pas(s)e tyme,* trans. of MF *passetemps*]
—**Syn.** entertainment, hobby, diversion, avocation.

past·i·ness (pā′stē nis), *n.* the quality of being pasty. [1600–10; PASTY[1] + -NESS]

pas·tis (pa stēs′; *Fr.* pas tēs′), *n.* a yellowish, anise-based liqueur originally made in Marseilles and similar to absinthe but containing no wormwood. [1925–30; < F < Pr; OPr *pastitz* pastry, pâté < VL **pasticius;* see PASTICCIO, PATISSERIE]

past′ mas′ter, 1. a person who is thoroughly experienced or exceptionally skilled in a profession, art, etc.: *a past master at chess.* **2.** a person who has held the office of master in a guild, lodge, etc. [1755–65]

past′ mis′tress, a woman who is thoroughly experienced or exceptionally skilled in a profession, art, etc. [1865–70]

past·ness (past′nis), *n.* the state or fact of being past. [1820–30; PAST + -NESS]

Pas·to (päs′tô), *n.* **1.** a city in SW Colombia. 119,339; ab. 8350 ft. (2545 m) above sea level. **2.** a volcanic peak near this city. 13,990 ft. (4265 m).

pas·tor (pas′tər, pä′stər), *n.* **1.** a minister or priest in charge of a church. **2.** a person having spiritual care of a number of persons. **3.** *Ornith.* any of various starlings, esp. *Sturnus roseus* **(rosy pastor)** of Europe and Asia. —*v.t.* **4.** to serve as the pastor of: *He pastored the church here for many years.* [1325–75; < L *pāstor* shepherd, lit., feeder, equiv. to *pās-,* base of *pāscere* to put to PASTURE, feed + *-tor* -TOR; r. ME *pastour* < AF] —**pas′tor·less,** *adj.* —**pas′tor·like′, pas′tor·ly,** *adj.*

pas·tor·age (pas′tər ij, pä′stər-), *n.* pastorate. [1655–65; PASTOR + -AGE]

pas·to·ral (pas′tər əl, pä′stər-), *adj.* **1.** having the simplicity, charm, serenity, or other characteristics generally attributed to rural areas: *pastoral scenery; the pastoral life.* **2.** pertaining to the country or to life in the country; rural; rustic. **3.** portraying or suggesting idyllically the life of shepherds or of the country, as a work of literature, art, or music: *pastoral poetry; a pastoral symphony.* **4.** of, pertaining to, or consisting of shepherds. **5.** of or pertaining to a pastor or the duties of a pastor: *pastoral visits to a hospital.* **6.** used for pasture, as land. —*n.* **7.** a poem, play, or the like, dealing with the life of shepherds, commonly in a conventional or artificial manner, or with simple rural life generally; a bucolic. **8.** a picture or work of art representing the shepherds' life. **9.** *Music.* pastorale. **10.** a treatise on the duties of a pastor. **11.** a letter to the people from their spiritual pastor. **12.** a letter to the clergy or people of an ecclesiastical district from its bishop. **13.** Also called **pas′toral staff′.** crosier (def. 1). [1350–1400; ME < L *pāstōrālis,* equiv. to *pāstōr-,* s. of *pāstor* (see PASTOR) + *-ālis* -AL[1]] —**pas′to·ral·ly,** *adv.*
—**Syn. 1.** rustic, rural, simple. **3.** bucolic, idyllic. **7.** eclogue, idyll; georgic.

pas′toral coun′seling, the use of psychotherapeutic techniques by trained members of the clergy to assist parishioners who seek help for personal or emotional problems.

pas·to·rale (pas′tə räl′, -ral′, -rä′lē, pä′stə-; *It.* päs′tô rä′le), *n., pl.* **-rales, -ra·li** (-rä′lē, -ral′ē; *It.* -rä′lē). *Music.* **1.** an opera, cantata, or the like, with a pastoral subject. **2.** a piece of music suggestive of pastoral life. [1715–25; < It, n. use of *pastorale* PASTORAL]

Pas′toral Epis′tles, the New Testament books of I and II Timothy and Titus that stress pastoral and ecclesiastical concerns.

pas·to·ral·ism (pas′tər ə liz′əm, pä′stər-), *n.* the practice of herding as the primary economic activity of a society. [1850–55; PASTORAL + -ISM]

pas·to·ral·ize (pas′tər ə līz′, pä′stər-), *v.t.,* **-ized, -iz·ing. 1.** to make pastoral or rural. **2.** to celebrate in a pastoral or set in a pastoral form. Also, *esp. Brit.,* **pas′to·ral·ise′.** [1815–25; PASTORAL + -IZE] —**pas′to·ral·i·za′tion,** *n.*

pas′toral let′ter, pastoral (defs. 11, 12).

pas′toral prayer′ (prâr), the main prayer in a church service.

Pas′toral Sym′phony, The, (French, *La Symphonie Pastorale*), the Symphony No. 6 in F major (1807–08) by Ludwig van Beethoven.

pas′toral theol′ogy, the branch of theology dealing with the responsibilities of members of the clergy to the people under their care. Also called **poimenics.**

pas·tor·ate (pas′tər it, pä′stər-), *n.* **1.** the office or term of office of a pastor. **2.** a body of pastors. **3.** parsonage (def. 1). [1785–95; < ML *pāstōrātus,* equiv. to L *pāstōr-,* s. of *pāstor* (see PASTOR) + *-ātus* -ATE[3]]

pas·to·ri·um (pa stôr′ē əm, -stōr′-, pä-), *n. Southern U.S.* a Baptist parsonage. [1895–1900; < NL, equiv. to *pās(tor)* PASTOR + *-tōrium* -TORY[2]]

pas·tor·ship (pas′tər ship′, pä′stər-), *n.* the position, authority, or office of a pastor. [1555–65; PASTOR + -SHIP]

pas·tose (pa stōs′), *adj.* having a heavy impasto. [1775–85; < It *pastoso* doughy. See PASTE, -OSE[1]] —**pas·tos·i·ty** (pa stos′i tē), *n.*

past′ par′ticiple, *Gram.* a participle with past, perfect, or passive meaning, as *fallen, sung, defeated;* perfect participle: used in English and other languages in forming the present perfect, pluperfect, and passive and as an adjective. [1790–1800]

past′ per′fect, *Gram.* pluperfect. [1885–90]

past′ progres′sive, *Gram.* (in English) a verb form consisting of an auxiliary *be* in the past tense followed by a present participle and used esp. to indicate that an action or event was incomplete or in progress at a point of reference in the past, as *was sleeping* in *I was sleeping when the phone rang.* Also called **past continuous.**

pas·tra·mi (pə strä′mē), *n.* a brisket of beef that has been cured in a mixture of garlic, peppercorns, sugar, coriander seeds, etc., then smoked before cooking. [1935–40; < Yiddish *pastrame* < Rum *pastramă* pressed, cured meat; a Balkanism of uncert. orig. (cf. ModGk *pastramâs,* Serbo-Croatian *pàstrma*), perh. ult. < Turk *pastırma,* taken as var. of *bastırma,* equiv. to *bastır-,* causative s. of *bas-* press, squeeze + *-ma* verbal n. suffix]

pas·try (pā′strē), *n., pl.* **-tries. 1.** a sweet baked food made of dough, esp. the shortened paste used for pie crust and the like. **2.** any item of food of which such dough forms an essential part, as a pie, tart, or napoleon. [1530–40; PASTE + -RY]

pas′try blend′er, a kitchen utensil having several parallel wires bent in a semicircle and secured by a handle, used esp. for mixing pastry dough.

pas′try brush′, a small, flat brush for coating pastry with butter, egg, etc. [1945–50]

pas′try tube′, a conical tube with a patterned hole at one end, fitted over the opening of a cloth funnel **(pas′·**

try bag′), for shaping icings, food pastes, etc., as they are forced through by squeezing the bag.

pas·tur·a·ble (pas′chər ə bəl, päs′-), *adj.* capable of providing pasture, as land. [1570–80; PASTURE + -ABLE] **—pas/tur·a·bil′i·ty,** *n.*

pas·tur·age (pas′chər ij, päs′-), *n.* **1.** pasture. **2.** the activity or business of pasturing livestock. [1525–35; PASTURE + -AGE]

pas·ture (pas′chər, päs′-), *n., v.,* **-tured, -tur·ing.** *—n.* **1.** Also called **pas·ture·land** (pas′chər land′, päs′-). an area covered with grass or other plants used or suitable for the grazing of livestock; grassland. **2.** a specific area or piece of such ground. **3.** grass or other plants for feeding livestock. **4. put out to pasture, a.** to put in a pasture to graze. **b.** to dismiss, retire, or use sparingly as being past one's or its prime: *Most of our older employees don't want to be put out to pasture.* *—v.t.* **5.** to feed (livestock) by putting them out to graze on pasture. **6.** (of land) to furnish with pasture. **7.** (of livestock) to graze upon. *—v.i.* **8.** (of livestock) to graze in a pasture. [1250–1300; ME < MF < LL *pāstūra,* equiv. to L *pās-t(us),* ptp. of *pāscere* to feed, pasture (cf. PASTOR) + *-ūra* -URE] **—pas′tur·al,** *adj.* **—pas′ture·less,** *adj.* **—pas′tur·er,** *n.*

Pas·ture (*Fr.* pä tyʀ′), *n.* **Ro·gi·er** (*Fr.* rô zhē ā′) or **Ro·ger** (*Fr.* rô zhā′) **de la** (*Fr.* də lᴀ). See **Weyden, Rogier van der.**

pas′ture rose′, a bristly-stemmed rose, *Rosa carolina,* of the eastern U.S., having slender, straight thorns and large, solitary, rose-pink flowers. [1930–35, *Amer.*]

past·y[1] (pā′stē), *adj.,* **past·i·er, past·i·est,** *n., pl.* **past·ies.** *—adj.* **1.** of or like paste in consistency, texture, color, etc. *—n.* **2. pasties,** a pair of small, cuplike coverings for the nipples of a striptease dancer, nude model, etc. [1650–60 for def. 1; 1950–55 for def. 2; PASTE + -Y[1] (def. 1), -Y[2] (def. 2)]
—Syn. 1. pale, ashen, ashy, wan, sallow.

pas·ty[2] (pas′tē), *n., pl.* **-ties.** *Chiefly Brit.* a pie filled with game, fish, or the like. [1250–1300; ME *pastee* < MF. See PÂTÉ]

past·y-faced (pā′stē fāst′), *adj.* having a pale, unhealthy, sallow complexion: *an awkward, pasty-faced youth.* [1600–10]

PA system. See **public-address system.** Also, **P.A. system, p.a. system.** [1935–40]

pat[1] (pat), *v.,* **pat·ted, pat·ting,** *n. —v.t.* **1.** to strike lightly or gently with something flat, as with a paddle or the palm of the hand, usually in order to flatten, smooth, or shape: *to pat dough into flat pastry forms.* **2.** to stroke or tap gently with the palm or fingers as an expression of affection, approbation, etc. **3.** to strike (the floor, ground, etc.) with light footsteps. *—v.i.* **4.** to strike lightly or gently. **5.** to walk or run with light footsteps. **6. pat down,** to pat or pass the hands over the body of (a clothed person) to detect concealed weapons, drugs, etc. **7. pat on the back,** to praise, congratulate, or encourage: *The boss patted him on the back for the deal he made yesterday.* *—n.* **8.** a light stroke, tap, or blow with the palm, fingers, or a flat object. **9.** the sound of a light stroke or of light footsteps. **10.** a small piece or mass, usually flat and square, formed by patting, cutting, etc.: *a pat of butter.* **11. a pat on the back,** a word of praise, congratulations, or encouragement: *Everyone needs a pat on the back now and then.* [1375–1425; late ME *pat* blow, stroke, appar. of expressive orig.]
—Syn. 10. square, cake, dab.

pat[2] (pat), *adj.* **1.** exactly to the point or purpose; apt; opportune: *a pat solution to a problem.* **2.** excessively glib; unconvincingly facile: *His answers were too pat to suit the examining board.* **3.** learned, known, or mastered perfectly or exactly: *to have something pat.* *—adv.* **4.** exactly or perfectly. **5.** aptly; opportunely. **6. down pat.** See **down**[1] (def. 37). **7. stand pat, a.** to cling or hold firm to one's decision, policy, or beliefs: *The government must stand pat in its policy.* **b.** *Poker.* to play a hand as dealt, without drawing other cards. [1570–80; orig. adverbial use of PAT[1], as obs. *to hit pat* to strike accurately] **—pat′ness,** *n.* **—pat′ter,** *n.*

Pat (pat), *n.* **1.** a male given name, form of **Patrick. 2.** a female given name, form of **Patricia.**

PAT, 1. *Football.* point after touchdown; points after touchdown. **2.** *Banking.* preauthorized automatic transfer.

pat., 1. patent. **2.** patented.

pa·ta·ca (pə tä′kə), *n.* a nickel, silver, or cupronickel coin and monetary unit of Macao, equal to 100 avos. [1575–85; < Pg << Ar *abū ṭāqah* a kind of coin]

pat-a-cake (pat′ə kāk′), *n.* a children's game in which a child claps hands alone and with another child while chanting a nursery rhyme. Also, **patty-cake.** [1870–75; after the opening words of a rhyme that accompanies such play]

pa·ta·gi·um (pə tā′jē əm), *n., pl.* **-gi·a** (-jē ə). **1.** a wing membrane, as of a bat. **2.** the extensible fold of skin of certain insects or of a gliding mammal or reptile, as a flying squirrel. **3.** either of two small processes on the anterior thorax, found esp. among butterflies and moths. [1820–30; < NL, special use of L *patagium* tunic border]

Pat·a·go·ni·a (pat′ə gō′nē ə, -gōn′yə), *n.* **1.** a tableland region of southern Argentina. **2.** a region in S South America, in S Argentina and S Chile, extending from the Andes to the Atlantic. **—Pat′a·go′ni·an,** *adj., n.*

CONCISE ETYMOLOGY KEY: <, descended or borrowed from; >, whence; b., blend of, blended; c., cognate with; cf., compare; deriv., derivative; equiv., equivalent; imit., imitative; obl., oblique; r., replacing; s., stem; sp., spelling, spelled; resp., respelling, respelled; trans., translation; ?, origin unknown; *, unattested; ‡, probably earlier than. See the full key inside the front cover.

Pa·tan (pä′tun), *n.* Lalitpur.

Pa·tan·ja·li (pə tun′jə lē), *n.* fl. late 2nd century B.C., Indian scholar and philosopher: sometimes regarded as the founder of yoga.

patch[1] (pach), *n.* **1.** a small piece of material used to mend a tear or break, to cover a hole, or to strengthen a weak place: *patches at the elbows of a sports jacket.* **2.** a piece of material used to cover or protect a wound, an injured part, etc.: *a patch over the eye.* **3.** any of the pieces of cloth sewed together to form patchwork. **4.** a small piece, scrap, or area of anything: *a patch of ice on the road.* **5.** a piece or tract of land; plot. **6.** a small field, plot, or garden, esp. one in which a specific type of plant grows or is cultivated: *a cabbage patch; a bean patch.* **7.** See **beauty spot** (def. 1). **8.** *Mil.* a cloth emblem worn on the upper uniform sleeve to identify the military unit of the wearer. **9.** a small organizational or affiliational emblem of cloth sewn to one's jacket, shirt, cap, etc. **10.** a connection or hookup, as between radio circuits or telephone lines: *The patch allowed shut-ins to hear the game by telephone.* *—v.t.* **11.** to mend, cover, or strengthen with or as if with a patch or patches. **12.** to repair or restore, esp. in a hasty or makeshift way (usually fol. by *up*). **13.** to make by joining patches or pieces together: *to patch a quilt.* **14.** to settle or smooth over (a quarrel, difference, etc.) (often fol. by *up*): *They patched up their quarrel before the company arrived.* **15.** (esp. in radio and telephone communications) to connect or hook up (circuits, programs, conversations, etc.) (often fol. by *through, into,* etc.): *The radio show was patched through to the ship. Patch me through to the mainland.* *—v.i.* **16.** to make a connection between radio circuits, telephone lines, etc. (often fol. by *in* or *into*): *We patched into the ship-to-shore conversation.* [1350–1400; ME *pacche;* perh. akin to OPr *pedas* piece to cover a hole < VL **pedaceum* lit., something measured; cf. ML *pedāre* to measure in feet; see PED-] **—patch′a·ble,** *adj.* **—patch′er,** *n.* **—patch′less,** *adj.*
—Syn. 11. See **mend. 12.** fix. **—Ant. 11.** break.

patch[2] (pach), *n.* a clown, fool, or booby. [1540–50; perh. < It *pazzo* fool]

Patch (pach), *n.* **Alexander Mc·Car·rell** (mə kar′əl), 1889–1945, U.S. World War II general.

patch′ cord′, *Teleph., Electronics.* a short cord with a plug at each end, or a plug at one end and a pair of clips at the other, used for temporarily connecting two pieces of equipment or signal paths. Also, **patch′cord′.** [1925–30]

Patch·en (pach′ən), *n.* **Kenneth,** 1911–72, U.S. poet and novelist.

Pat·chogue (pach′ôg, -og), *n.* a town on S Long Island, in SE New York. 11,291.

patch·ou·li (pach′o͝o lē, pə cho͞o′lē), *n.* **1.** a plant, *Pogostemon cablin,* of tropical Asia, that yields a fragrant oil **(patchouli oil)** used in the manufacture of perfumes. **2.** a penetrating perfume made from this oil. Also, **pachouli, patch′ou·ly.** [1835–45; < Tamil *paccuḷi*]

patch′ pock′et, a pocket formed by sewing a piece of shaped material to the outside of a garment. [1890–95]

patch′ reef′, an isolated coral growth forming a small platform in a lagoon, barrier reef, or atoll.

patch·stand (pach′stand′), *n.* a small tazza. [PATCH[1] + STAND]

patch′ test′, *Med.* a test for suspected allergy by application to the skin of a patch impregnated with an allergen: allergic reaction is indicated by redness at the site of application. [1930–35]

patch-up (pach′up′), *n.* **1.** an act or instance of patching or repair. *—adj.* **2.** done by patching or fixing: *a quick patch-up job.* [1900–05; n., adj. use of v. phrase *patch up*]

patch·work (pach′wûrk′), *n.* **1.** something made up of an incongruous variety of pieces or parts; hodgepodge: *a patchwork of verse forms.* **2.** work made of pieces of cloth or leather of various colors or shapes sewed together, used esp. for covering quilts, cushions, etc. *—adj.* **3.** resembling a patchwork, esp. in being makeshift, irregular, or improvised: *a patchwork policy of dispensing foreign aid.* *—v.t.* **4.** to make as patchwork: *She specializes in patchworking skirts.* **5.** to assemble or connect in making patchwork: *to patchwork neckties into bedspreads.* [1685–95; PATCH[1] + WORK] **—patch′work′y,** *adj.*
—Syn. 1. medley, jumble, mélange.

patch·y (pach′ē), *adj.,* **patch·i·er, patch·i·est. 1.** characterized by or made up of patches. **2.** occurring in, forming, or like patches. **3.** of inconsistent or irregular quality, texture, etc.; not uniform: *patchy acting; patchy areas of fog.* [1790–1800; PATCH[1] + -Y[1]] **—patch′i·ly,** *adv.* **—patch′i·ness,** *n.*

patd., patented.

pat-down (pat′doun′), *n.* an act or instance of passing the hands over the body of a clothed person to detect concealed weapons, drugs, etc.; frisking. Also, **pat′ down′.** [n. use of v. phrase *pat down*]

pate (pāt), *n.* **1.** the crown or top of the head. **2.** the head. **3.** the brain. [1275–1325; ME < ?]

pâte (pät), *n.* porcelain paste used in ceramic work. [1860–65; < F; see PASTE]

pâ·té (pä tā′, pa-; *Fr.* pä tā′), *n., pl.* **-tés** (-tāz′; *Fr.* -tā′). **1.** *French Cookery.* a paste or spread made of puréed or finely chopped liver, meat, fish, game, etc., served as an hors d'oeuvre. **2.** See **foie gras.** [1695–1705; < F; see PASTE, -EE]

pâte à chou (pä tᴀ sho͞o′), *French Cookery.* See **cream puff paste.** [< F: lit., cabbage paste]

-pated, a combining form of **pate:** *addlepated.* [PATE + -ED[3]]

pâ·té de foie gras (pä tā′ də fwä′ grä′, pa tā′; *Fr.* pä tādᵊ fwᴀ grä′), *pl.* **pâ·tés de foie gras** (pä tāz′ də fwä′ grä′, pa tāz′; *Fr.* pä tādᵊ fwᴀ grä′). See under **foie gras.** [1820–30; < F: goose-liver pâté]

pâte de verre (pät də vᴇʀ′), *French.* a decorative glass made in a mold in which powdered glass of various hues is mixed, blended, and fused. [lit., glass paste]

pâte dure (*Fr.* pät dʏʀ′). See **hard paste.** [1860–65; < F: lit., hard paste]

pa·tel·la (pə tel′ə), *n., pl.* **-las, -tel·lae** (-tel′ē). **1.** *Anat.* the flat, movable bone at the front of the knee; kneecap. See diag. under **skeleton. 2.** *Biol.* a panlike or cuplike formation. **3.** *Zool.* any limpet of the family Patellidae. **4.** *Archaeol.* a small pan or shallow vessel. [1665–75; < L, dim. of *patina, patena* pan, lit., something wide open. See PATEN, -ELLE] **—pa·tel′lar,** *adj.*

patel′lar re′flex. See **knee jerk.** [1890–95]

pa·tel·late (pə tel′it, -āt), *adj.* **1.** having a patella. **2.** patelliform. [1820–30; PATELL(A) + -ATE[1]]

pa·tel·li·form (pə tel′ə fôrm′), *adj.* having the form of a patella; shaped like a saucer, kneecap, or limpet shell. [1810–20; PATELL(A) + -I- + -FORM]

pat·en (pat′n), *n.* a metal plate on which the bread is placed in the celebration of the Eucharist. [1250–1300; ME *pateyn(e)* < OF *patene* < ML *patena, patina* Eucharistic plate (L: pan); akin to Gk *patánē* flat dish, L *patēre* to be open (see PATENT)]

pa·ten·cy (pāt′n sē, pat′-), *n.* **1.** the state of being patent. **2.** *Med.* the condition of not being blocked or obstructed. **3.** *Phonet.* openness of articulation, found more or less in all phonemes except stops. [1650–60; PAT(ENT) + -ENCY]

pat·ent (pat′nt *or, for 10, 12–15,* pāt′-; *esp. Brit.* pāt′nt), *n.* **1.** the exclusive right granted by a government to an inventor to manufacture, use, or sell an invention for a certain number of years. **2.** an invention or process protected by this right. **3.** an official document conferring such a right; letters patent. **4.** the instrument by which the government of the United States conveys the legal fee-simple title to public land. **5.** patent leather. *—adj.* **6.** protected by a patent; patented: *a patent cooling device.* **7.** pertaining to, concerned with, or dealing with patents, esp. on inventions: *a patent attorney; patent law.* **8.** conferred by a patent, as a right or privilege. **9.** holding a patent, as a person. **10.** readily open to notice or observation; evident; obvious: *a patent breach of good manners.* **11.** made of patent leather: *patent shoes.* **12.** lying open; not enclosed or shut in: *a patent field.* **13.** *Chiefly Bot.* expanded or spreading. **14.** open, as a doorway or a passage. **15.** *Phonet.* open, in various degrees, to the passage of the breath stream. *—v.t.* **16.** to take out a patent on; obtain the exclusive rights to (an invention, process, etc.) by a patent. **17.** to originate and establish as one's own. **18.** *Metall.* to heat and quench (wire) so as to prepare for cold-drawing. **19.** to grant (public land) by a patent. [1250–1300; (adj.) ME < L *patent-* (s. of *patēns*) open, orig. prp. of *patēre* to stand wide open; (n.) ME, short for *letters patent,* trans. of ML *litterae patentēs* open letters] **—pat′ent·a·ble,** *adj.* **—pat′ent·a·bil′i·ty,** *n.* **—pat′ent·a·bly,** *adv.* **—pat′ent·ly,** *adv.*
—Syn. 10. clear, palpable, conspicuous, unconcealed. See **apparent. —Ant. 10.** dim, obscure, hidden.

pat′ent ambigu′ity, *Law.* uncertainty of meaning created by the obscure or ambiguous language appearing on the face of a written instrument.

pat·ent·ee (pat′n tē′ *or, esp. Brit.,* pāt′-), *n.* a person, group, or company that has been granted a patent. [1400–50; late ME; see PATENT, -EE]

pat′ent flour′, a fine grade of flour, consisting chiefly of the inner part of the endosperm.

pat′ent fora′men ova′le, *Pathol.* a congenital heart defect resulting from failure of the foramen ovale to close shortly after birth.

pat′ent ham′mer, a hammer for dressing stone, having a head with two faces formed of a number of broad, thin chisels bolted side by side. [1895–1900]

pat′ent leath′er (pat′nt, pat′n *or, esp. Brit.,* pāt′nt), a hard, glossy, smooth leather, used esp. in shoes and accessories. [1820–30, *Amer.*]

pat′ent log′, *Naut.* any of various devices for determining the speed of a ship by means of a vaned rotor streamed at the end of a log line upon which it exerts a torsion transmitted to a registering device on board. Also called **screw log.** [1875–80]

pat′ent med′icine, 1. a medicine sold without a prescription in drugstores or by sales representatives, and usually protected by a trademark. **2.** a medicine distributed by a company having a patent on its manufacture. [1760–70]

pat′ent of′fice, (*often caps.*) a governmental agency that administers and regulates patents and trademarks, in the U.S. forming a division of the Department of Commerce. [1690–1700]

pat·en·tor (pat′n tər, pat′n tôr′ *or, esp. Brit.,* pāt′-, păt′-), *n.* a person or official agency that grants patents. [1885–90; PATENT + -OR²]

pat′ent right′, the exclusive right granted by a patent, as on an invention. [1795–1805]

pat′ent slip′, *Brit.* See **marine railway.**

pa·ter (pä′tər; *also for 2, 3* pat′ər), *n.* **1.** *Brit. Informal.* father. **2.** (*often cap.*) the paternoster; Lord's Prayer. **3.** a recitation of it. [1300–50; ME < L: FATHER]

Pa·ter (pā′tər), *n.* **Walter Horatio,** 1839–94, English critic, essayist, and novelist.

pa·ter·fa·mil·i·as (pä′tər fə mil′ē əs, pä′-, pat′ər-), *n., pl.* **pa·ter·fa·mil·i·as·es** for 1, **pa·tres·fa·mil·i·as** (pä′trēz fə mil′ē əs, pä′-, pa′-) for 2. **1.** the male head of a household or family, usually the father. **2.** *Roman Law.* **a.** the head of the Roman family; a juridical entity who holds the patria potestas. **b.** a person who is not under the patria potestas of another. [1425–75; late ME < L: lit., FATHER (i.e., master) of the household, with archaic genitive form *familiās* of *familia;* see FAMILY] **—pa′ter·fa·mil′iar,** *adj.* **—pa′ter·fa·mil′iar·ly,** *adv.*

pa·ter·nal (pə tûr′nl), *adj.* **1.** characteristic of or befitting a father; fatherly: *a kind and paternal reprimand.* **2.** of or pertaining to a father. **3.** related on the father's side: *one's paternal grandfather.* **4.** derived or inherited from a father: *paternal traits.* [1400–50; late ME < LL *paternālis,* equiv. to L *patern(us)* paternal (*pater* FATHER + *-nus* adj. suffix) + *-ālis* -AL¹] **—pa·ter′nal·ly,** *adv.*
—Syn. 1. See **fatherly.**

pa·ter·nal·ism (pə tûr′nl iz′əm), *n.* the system, principle, or practice of managing or governing individuals, businesses, nations, etc., in the manner of a father dealing benevolently and often intrusively with his children: *The employees objected to the paternalism of the old president.* [1880–85; PATERNAL + -ISM] **—pa·ter′nal·ist,** *n., adj.* **—pa·ter′nal·is′tic,** *adj.* **—pa·ter′nal·is′ti·cal·ly,** *adv.*

pa·ter·ni·ty (pə tûr′ni tē), *n.* **1.** the state of being a father; fatherhood. **2.** derivation or acquirement from a father. **3.** origin or authorship. **—***adj.* **4.** noting or pertaining to a legal dispute in which an unwed mother accuses a man of being the father of her child: *a paternity suit.* [1400–50; late ME *paternite* < LL *paternitās.* See PATERNAL, -ITY]

pater′nity leave′, a leave of absence from a job for a father to care for a new baby. [1970–75]

pater′nity test′, an assessment of possible paternity based on a comparison of the genetic markers of the offspring and those of the putative father. [1925–30]

pa·ter·nos·ter (pā′tər nos′tər, pä′-, pat′ər-), *n.* **1.** (*often cap.*) Also, **Pa′ter Nos′ter.** the Lord's Prayer, esp. in the Latin form. **2.** a recitation of this prayer as an act of worship. **3.** one of certain beads in a rosary, regularly every 11th bead, differing in size or material from the rest and indicating that the Lord's Prayer is to be said. **4.** any fixed recital of words used as a prayer or magical charm. **5.** a doorless, continuously moving elevator for passengers or goods, having numerous platforms or compartments that rise or descend on a moving chain. **6.** (*cap.*) *Archit.* See **pearl molding.** [bef. 1000; ME, OE: Lord's prayer < L *pater noster* our father, its first two words in the Vulgate (Matthew VI: 9)]

Pa·ter Pa·tri·ae (pä′ter pä′trē ī′; *Eng.* pā′tər pā′trē ē′, pä′tər pä′trē ī′, pat′ər pa′trē ē′), *Latin.* father of his country.

Pat·er·son (pat′ər sən), *n.* a city in NE New Jersey. 137,970.

pâte ten·dre (*Fr.* pät täN′drᵊ). See **soft paste.** [1860–65; < F]

path (path, päth), *n., pl.* **paths** (pat͟hz, pät͟hz, paths, päths). **1.** a way beaten, formed, or trodden by the feet of persons or animals. **2.** a narrow walk or way: *a path through a garden; a bicycle path.* **3.** a route, course, or track along which something moves: *the path of a hurricane.* **4.** a course of action, conduct, or procedure: *the path of righteousness.* **5.** *Math.* a continuous curve that connects two or more points. **6.** *Computers.* the sequence of steps that a computer follows in carrying out a routine, as in storing and retrieving a file at a specific location. **7. cross one's path,** to encounter or meet unexpectedly: *Tragedy crossed our path again.* [bef. 900; ME; OE *pæth;* c. G *Pfad*]
—Syn. 1. footpath, pathway. PATH, LANE, TRAIL are passages or routes not as wide as a way or road. A PATH is a way for passing on foot; a track, beaten by feet, not specially constructed, is often along the side of a road: *a path through a field.* A LANE is a narrow road or track, generally between fields, often enclosed with fences or trees; sometimes it is an alley or narrow road between buildings in towns: *a lane leading to a farmhouse; Drury Lane.* A TRAIL is a rough way made or worn through woods, or across mountains, prairies, or other untraveled regions: *an Indian trail.*

path-, var. of **patho-** before a vowel: *pathosis.*

-path, a combining form occurring in personal nouns corresponding to abstract nouns ending in **-pathy,** with the general sense "one practicing such a treatment" (*osteopath*) or "one suffering from such an ailment" (*psychopath*).

path., **1.** pathological. **2.** pathology.

Pa·than (pə tän′, pət hän′), *n.* **1.** Afghan (def. 1). **2.** an Afghan dwelling in India.

pa·thet·ic (pə thet′ik), *adj.* **1.** causing or evoking pity, sympathetic sadness, sorrow, etc.; pitiful; pitiable: *a pathetic letter; a pathetic sight.* **2.** affecting or moving the feelings. **3.** pertaining to or caused by the feelings. **4.** miserably or contemptibly inadequate: *In return for our investment we get a pathetic three percent interest.* Also, **pa·thet′i·cal.** [1590–1600; < LL *patheticus* < Gk *pathētikós* sensitive, equiv. to *pathēt(ós)* made or liable to suffer (verbal of *páschein* to suffer) + *-ikos* -IC] **—pa·thet′i·cal·ly,** *adv.* **—pa·thet′i·cal·ness,** *n.*
—Syn. 1. plaintive. **2.** touching, tender. **3.** emotional.

pathet′ic fal′lacy, the endowment of nature, inanimate objects, etc., with human traits and feelings, as in *the smiling skies; the angry sea.* [coined by John Ruskin in *Modern Painters* Vol. III, Part IV (1856)]

Pa′thet Lao′ (pä′tet), the Communist nationalist group that took over the government of Laos in 1975 after two decades of civil war.

path·find·er (path′fīn′dər, päth′-), *n.* **1.** a person who finds or makes a path, way, route, etc., esp. through a previously unexplored or untraveled wilderness. **2.** an airplane, or a person dropped from a plane, sent into a target area to illuminate the area for succeeding aircraft. **3.** a radar beacon beamed into a target area to provide guidance for missiles seeking the target. [1830–40, *Amer.*; PATH + FINDER] **—path′find′ing,** *n.*

Pathfinder, The, a historical novel (1840) by James Fenimore Cooper. Cf. ***Leather-Stocking Tales.***

-pathia, an obsolete var. of **-pathy:** *psychopathia.* [< NL; see -PATH, -IA]

-pathic, a combining form occurring in adjectives that correspond to nouns ending in **-pathy:** *psychopathic.* [< NL; see -PATHY, -IC]

path·less (path′lis, päth′-), *adj.* trackless; untrodden: *a pathless forest.* [1585–95; PATH + -LESS]

patho-, a combining form meaning "suffering," "disease," "feeling," used in the formation of compound words: *pathology.* Also, *esp. before a vowel,* **path-.** Cf. **-path, -pathia, -pathic, -pathy.** [comb. form repr. Gk *páthos;* see PATHOS]

path·o·cure (path′ə kyŏŏr′), *n. Psychiatry.* cessation of a neurosis with the appearance of an organic disease. [PATHO- + CURE]

path·o·for·mic (path′ə fôr′mik), *adj. Pathol.* pertaining to the beginning of a disease, esp. to symptoms that occur in the preliminary stages of mental disease. [PATHO- + -FORM + -IC]

path·o·gen (path′ə jən, -jen′), *n.* any disease-producing agent, esp. a virus, bacterium, or other microorganism. [1940–45; PATHO- + -GEN]

path·o·gen·e·sis (path′ə jen′ə sis), *n.* the production and development of disease. Also, **pa·thog·e·ny** (pə thoj′ə nē). [1875–80; < NL; see PATHO-, -GENESIS] **—path·o·ge·net·ic** (path′ō jə net′ik), *adj.*

path·o·gen·ic (path′ə jen′ik), *adj. Pathol.* capable of producing disease: *pathogenic bacteria.* [1850–55; PATHO- + -GENIC]

path·o·ge·nic·i·ty (path′ō jə nis′i tē), *n.* the disease-producing capacity of a pathogen. [1895–1900; PATHOGENIC + -ITY]

pa·thog·no·mon·ic (pə thog′nə mon′ik), *adj. Med.* characteristic or diagnostic of a specific disease: *a pathognomonic sign of pneumonia.* [1615–25; < Gk *pathognōmonikós* skilled in judging disease. See PATHO-, GNOMON, -IC] **—pa·thog′no·mon′i·cal·ly,** *adv.*

pa·thog·no·my (pə thog′nə mē), *n. Med.* the study of the symptoms or characteristics of a disease; diagnosis. [1785–95; PATHOGNOM(IC) + -Y³]

pathol., **1.** pathological. **2.** pathology.

path·o·log·i·cal (path′ə loj′i kəl), *adj.* **1.** of or pertaining to pathology. **2.** caused by or involving disease; morbid. **3.** caused by or evidencing a mentally disturbed condition: *a pathological liar.* **4.** dealing with diseases: *a pathological casebook.* Also, **path′o·log′ic.** [1680–90; < Gk *pathologik(ós)* (see PATHOLOGY, -IC) + -AL¹] **—path′o·log′i·cal·ly,** *adv.*

patholog′ic anat′omy, the branch of pathology dealing with the morphologic changes in tissues.

pa·thol·o·gy (pə thol′ə jē), *n., pl.* **-gies.** **1.** the science or the study of the origin, nature, and course of diseases. **2.** the conditions and processes of a disease. **3.** any deviation from a healthy, normal, or efficient condition. [1590–1600; earlier *pathologia* < L < Gk *pathología.* See PATHO-, -LOGY] **—pa·thol′o·gist,** *n.*

path·o·morph·ism (path′ə môr′fiz əm), *n.* abnormal morphology. [PATHO- + -MORPH + -ISM]

path·o·phys·i·ol·o·gy (path′ō fiz′ē ol′ə jē), *n. Pathol.* the physiology of abnormal or diseased organisms or their parts; the functional changes associated with a disease or syndrome. [1950–55; PATHO- + PHYSIOLOGY]

pa·thos (pā′thos, -thōs, -thôs), *n.* **1.** the quality or power in an actual life experience or in literature, music, speech, or other forms of expression, of evoking a feeling of pity or compassion. **2.** pity. **3.** *Obs.* suffering. [1570–80; < Gk *páthos* suffering, sensation, akin to *páschein* to suffer]

pa·tho·sis (pə thō′sis), *n.* a diseased condition. [< NL; see PATH-, -OSIS]

path·way (path′wā′, päth′-), *n.* **1.** a path, course, route, or way. **2.** *Biochem.* a sequence of reactions, usually controlled and catalyzed by enzymes, by which one organic substance is converted to another. [1530–40; PATH + WAY¹] **—path′wayed′,** *adj.*

-pathy, a combining form occurring in loanwords from Greek, where it meant "suffering," "feeling" (*antipathy; sympathy*); in compound words of modern formation, often used with the meaning "morbid affection," "disease" (*arthropathy; deuteropathy; neuropathy; psychopathy*), and hence used also in names of systems or methods of treating disease (*allopathy; homeopathy; hydropathy; osteopathy*). Cf. **-path, -pathia.** [comb. form repr. Gk *pátheia* suffering, feeling, equiv. to *páth(os)* PATHOS + *-eia* -Y³]

Pa·ti·a·la (put′ē ä′lə), *n.* **1.** an important state of the former Punjab States: now part of Punjab in NW India. **2.** a city in E Punjab, in N India. 151,903.

pa·tience (pā′shəns), *n.* **1.** the quality of being patient, as the bearing of provocation, annoyance, misfortune, or pain, without complaint, loss of temper, irritation, or the like. **2.** an ability or willingness to suppress restlessness or annoyance when confronted with delay: *to have patience with a slow learner.* **3.** quiet, steady perseverance; even-tempered care; diligence: *to work with patience.* **4.** *Cards. Chiefly Brit.* solitaire (def. 1). **5.** Also called **pa′tience dock′.** a European dock, *Rumex patientia,* of the buckwheat family, whose leaves are often used as a vegetable. **6.** *Obs.* leave; permission; sufferance. [1175–1225; ME *pacience* < OF < L *patientia.* See PATIENT, -ENCE]
—Syn. 1. composure, stability, self-possession; submissiveness, sufferance. PATIENCE, ENDURANCE, FORTITUDE, STOICISM imply qualities of calmness, stability, and persistent courage in trying circumstances. PATIENCE may denote calm, self-possessed, and unrepining bearing of pain, misfortune, annoyance, or delay; or painstaking and untiring industry or (less often) application in the doing of something: *to bear afflictions with patience.* ENDURANCE denotes the ability to bear exertion, hardship, or suffering (without implication of moral qualities required or shown): *Running in a marathon requires great endurance.* FORTITUDE implies not only patience but courage and strength of character in the midst of pain, affliction, or hardship: *to show fortitude in adversity.* STOICISM is calm fortitude, with such repression of emotion as to seem almost like indifference to pleasure or pain: *The American Indians were noted for stoicism under torture.* **3.** indefatigability, persistence, assiduity.

Pa·tience (pā′shəns), *n.* a female given name.

pa·tient (pā′shənt), *n.* **1.** a person who is under medical care or treatment. **2.** a person or thing that undergoes some action. **3.** *Archaic.* a sufferer or victim. **—***adj.* **4.** bearing provocation, annoyance, misfortune, delay, hardship, pain, etc., with fortitude and calm and without complaint, anger, or the like. **5.** characterized by or expressing such a quality: *a patient smile.* **6.** quietly and steadily persevering or diligent, esp. in detail or exactness: *a patient worker.* **7.** undergoing the action of another (opposed to *agent*). **8. patient of, a.** having or showing the capacity for endurance: *a man patient of distractions.* **b.** susceptible of: *This statement is patient of criticism.* [1275–1325; ME *pacient* (adj. and n.) < MF < L *patient-* (s. of *patiēns*), prp. of *patī* to undergo, suffer, bear; see -ENT] **—pa′tient·less,** *adj.* **—pa′tient·ly,** *adv.* **—pa′tient·ness,** *n.*
—Syn. 1. invalid. **4.** uncomplaining, long-suffering, forbearing, resigned, passive, calm. **5.** quiet, serene, unruffled, unexcited, self-possessed, composed. **6.** sedulous, assiduous, untiring. **—Ant. 4.** hostile. **5.** impatient, agitated.

pat·i·na (pat′n ə, pə tē′nə), *n.* **1.** a film or incrustation, usually green, produced by oxidation on the surface of old bronze and esteemed as being of ornamental value. **2.** a similar film or coloring on some other substance. **3.** a surface calcification of implements, usually indicating great age. Also, **patine.** [1740–50; < It: coating < L: pan. See PATEN]

pat·i·nate (pat′n āt′), *v.t.,* **-nat·ed, -nat·ing.** to cover or encrust with a patina. [1875–80; PATIN(A) + -ATE¹] **—pat′i·na′tion,** *n.*

pa·tine (pə tēn′ *for 1;* pa tēn′ *for 2, 3*), *n., v.,* **-tined, -tin·ing.** **—***n.* **1.** patina. **—***v.t.* **2.** to patinate. [< F; see PATINA]

pat·i·nous (pat′n əs), *adj.* patinated. [1840–50; PATIN(A) + -OUS]

pat·i·o (pat′ē ō′, pä′tē ō′), *n., pl.* **-i·os.** **1.** an area, usually paved, adjoining a house and used as an area for outdoor lounging, dining, etc. **2.** a courtyard, esp. of a house, enclosed by low buildings or walls. [1820–30, *Amer.*; < Sp, OSp: courtyard, perh. orig. open area; cf. ML *patium* meadow, pasturage, perh. deriv. of L **patitus,* ptp. of *patēre* to lie open. See PATENT]

pa·tis·se·rie (pə tis′ə rē; *Fr.* pä tēsᵊ rē′), *n., pl.* **-ries** (-rēz; *Fr.* -rē′). **1.** a shop where pastry, esp. French pastry, is made and sold. **2.** See **French pastry.** [1760–70; < F *pâtisserie,* MF *pastiserie,* equiv. to *pastis-,* presumed OF **pastitz* pastry (< VL **pasticium;* see PASTICCIO) + *-erie* -ERY]

Pat·more (pat′môr, -mōr), *n.* **Cov·en·try (Ker·sey Digh·ton)** (kov′ən trē kûr′zē dīt′n, kuv′ən-), 1823–96, English poet and essayist.

Pat·mos (pat′mos, -mōs, -məs; *Gk.* pät′môs), *n.* one of the Dodecanese Islands, off the SW coast of Asia Minor: St. John is supposed to have been exiled here (Rev. 1:9). 2432; 13 sq. mi. (34 sq. km). Italian, **Pat·mo** (pät′mô). **—Pat′mi·an,** *adj.*

Pat·na (put′nə, pat′-, put′nä′), *n.* a city in and the capital of Bihar, in NE India, on the Ganges. 490,265.

pa·to (pä′tō; *Sp.* pä′tō), *n.* an Argentine game played by two teams of four on horseback, resembling a cross between polo and basketball, using a ball with six large leather handles, the object of which is to place or throw the ball through the opponent's net that hangs from a 9 ft. (2.7 m) high pole. [< AmerSp; Sp: duck (of obscure orig.; perh. orig. a nursery word, akin to *pata* leg, foot (of an animal); cf. PAW¹); the game was allegedly first played with a duck in a skin or leather bag]

Pat. Off., Patent Office.

pat·ois (pa′twä, pä′-; *Fr.* pa twa′), *n., pl.* **pat·ois** (pa′twäz, pä′-; *Fr.* pa twa′). **1.** a regional form of a language, esp. of French, differing from the standard, literary form of the language. **2.** a rural or provincial form of speech. **3.** jargon; cant; argot. [1635–45; < F: lit., clumsy speech; akin to OF *patoier* to handle clumsily, deriv. of *pate* paw]

Pa·ton (pāt′n), *n.* **Alan (Stewart),** 1903–88, South African novelist.

pat. pend., patent pending.

Pa·tras (pə tras′, pa′trəs), *n.* **1.** Greek, **Pa·trai** (pä′tre). a seaport in the Peloponnesus, in W Greece, on the Gulf of Patras. 112,000. **2. Gulf of,** an inlet of the Ionian

Sea in the NW Peloponnesus, 10 mi. (16 km) long; 25 mi. (40 km) wide.

pa·tres con·scrip·ti (pä′tres kōn skrip′tē; *Eng.* pā′trēz kən skrip′tī, -tē, pä′-, pa′-), *Latin.* See **conscript fathers.**

pa·tres·fa·mil·i·as (pā′trēz fə mil′ē əs, pä′-, pa′-), *n.* a pl. of **paterfamilias.**

Pa·tri (pä′trē), *n.* **An·ge·lo** (an′jə lō′), 1877–1965, U.S. educator and writer, born in Italy.

patri-, a combining form meaning "father," occurring originally in loanwords from Greek and Latin (*patriarch; patrician*), and used in the formation of new compounds (*patrilineal*). [comb. form repr. L *pater,* Gk *patḗr* FATHER]

pa·tri·al (pā′trē əl), *n. Brit.* a native of any country who, by virtue of the birth of a parent or grandparent in Great Britain, has citizenship and residency rights there. [1620–30; lit., pertaining to one's own country < L *patri(a)* native land (fem. n. from *patrius,* adj. deriv. of *pater* FATHER) + -AL[1]]

pa·tri·a po·tes·tas (pā′trē ə pō tes′təs, pä′-, pa′-; *Lat.* pä′tri ä′ pō tes′täs), *Roman Law.* the power vested in the paterfamilias or head of the Roman family with respect to his wife, natural or adopted children, and agnatic descendants: title to family property is vested exclusively in the paterfamilias. Property acquired by a family member becomes family property, and no family member can enter into a transaction in his or her own right. [< L: lit., paternal power]

pa·tri·arch (pā′trē ärk′), *n.* **1.** the male head of a family or tribal line. **2.** a person regarded as the father or founder of an order, class, etc. **3.** any of the very early Biblical personages regarded as the fathers of the human race, comprising those from Adam to Noah (**antediluvian patriarchs**) and those between the Deluge and the birth of Abraham. **4.** any of the three great progenitors of the Israelites: Abraham, Isaac, or Jacob. **5.** any of the sons of Jacob (the **twelve patriarchs**), from whom the tribes of Israel were descended. **6.** (in the early Christian church) any of the bishops of any of the ancient sees of Alexandria, Antioch, Constantinople, Jerusalem, or Rome having authority over other bishops. **7.** *Gk. Orth. Ch.* the head of any of the ancient sees of Alexandria, Antioch, Constantinople, or Jerusalem, and sometimes including other sees of chief cities. Cf. **ecumenical patriarch. 8.** the head of certain other churches in the East, as the Coptic, Nestorian, and Armenian churches, that are not in full communication with the ecumenical patriarch of Constantinople. **9.** *Rom. Cath. Ch.* **a.** the pope as patriarch of the West. **b.** any of certain bishops of the Eastern rites, as a head of an Eastern rite or a bishop of one of the ancient sees. **c.** the head of a Uniate church. **10.** *Mormon Ch.* any of the high dignitaries who pronounce the blessing of the church; Evangelist. **11.** one of the elders or leading older members of a community. **12.** a venerable old man. [1175–1225; ME *patriark(e)* (< OF) < LL *patriarcha* < LGk *patriárchēs* high-ranking bishop, Gk: family head, equiv. to *patri(á)* family (deriv. of *patḗr* FATHER) + *-archēs* -ARCH] **—pa′tri·ar′chal, pa′tri·ar′chic, pa′tri·ar′chi·cal,** *adj.* **—pa′tri·ar′chal·ly, pa′tri·ar′chi·cal·ly,** *adv.* **—pa′tri·arch′dom, pa′tri·arch·ship′,** *n.*

pa′triar′chal cross′, a Latin cross having a shorter crosspiece above the customary one. See illus. under **cross.** [1675–85]

pa·tri·ar·chal·ism (pā′trē är′kə liz′əm), *n.* a philosophy, form, or system of patriarchal government. [1840–50; PATRIARCHAL + -ISM]

pa·tri·arch·ate (pā′trē är′kit, -kāt), *n.* **1.** the office, dignity, jurisdiction, province, or residence of an ecclesiastical patriarch. **2.** a patriarchy. [1610–20; < ML *patriarchātus,* equiv. to LL *patriarch(a)* (see PATRIARCH) + L *-ātus* -ATE[3]]

pa·tri·arch·y (pā′trē är′kē), *n., pl.* **-ies. 1.** a form of social organization in which the father is the supreme authority in the family, clan, or tribe and descent is reckoned in the male line, with the children belonging to the father's clan or tribe. **2.** a society, community, or country based on this social organization. [1555–65; < Gk *patriarchía.* See PATRIARCH, -Y[3]]

pa·tri·ate (pā′trē āt′; *esp. Brit.* pa′-), *v.t.,* **-at·ed, -at·ing.** *Canadian.* to transfer (legislation) to the authority of an autonomous country from its previous mother country. [1965–70; back formation from REPATRIATE] **—pa′tri·a′tion,** *n.*

Pa·tri·cia (pə trish′ə, -trē′shə), *n.* a female given name: from a Latin word meaning "patrician."

pa·tri·cian (pə trish′ən), *n.* **1.** a person of noble or high rank; aristocrat. **2.** a person of very good background, education, and refinement. **3.** a member of the original senatorial aristocracy in ancient Rome. **4.** (under the later Roman and Byzantine empires) a title or dignity conferred by the emperor. **5.** a member of an influential and hereditary ruling class in certain medieval German, Swiss, and Italian free cities. *—adj.* **6.** of high social rank or noble family; aristocratic. **7.** befitting or characteristic of persons of very good background, education, and refinement: *patrician tastes.* **8.** of or belonging to the patrician families of ancient Rome. [1400–50; < L *patrici(us)* patrician (*pat(e)r* FATHER + *-icius* adj. suffix) + -AN; r. late ME *patricion* < OF *patricien*] **—pa·tri′cian·hood′, pa·tri′cian·ship′,** *n.* **—pa·tri′cian·ism,** *n.* **—pa·tri′cian·ly,** *adv.*
—Syn. 7. dignified, genteel, stately.

pa·tri·ci·ate (pə trish′ē it, -āt′), *n.* **1.** the patrician class. **2.** patrician rank. [1650–60; < ML *patriciātus,* equiv. to L *patrici(us)* (see PATRICIAN) + *-ātus* -ATE[1]]

pat·ri·cide (pa′trə sīd′, pā′-), *n.* **1.** the act of killing one's own father. **2.** a person who commits such an act. [1585–95; PATRI- + -CIDE] **—pat′ri·cid′al,** *adj.*

Pat·rick (pa′trik), *n.* **1. Saint,** A.D. 389?–461?, English missionary and bishop in Ireland: patron saint of Ireland. **2. (Curtis) Lester,** 1883–1960, Canadian ice-hockey player and manager, in the U.S. after 1926. **3.** a male given name: from a Latin word meaning "patrician."

pat·ri·cli·ny (pa′tri klī′nē, pā′-), *n. Genetics.* patrocliny.

pat·ri·fo·cal (pa′trə fō′kəl, pā′-), *adj.* focused or centered on the father. [PATRI- + FOCAL]

pat·ri·lat·er·al (pa′trə lat′ər əl, pā′-), *adj.* related through the father. Cf. **matrilateral.** [1945–50; PATRI- + LATERAL]

pat·ri·lin·e·age (pa′trə lin′ē ij, pā′-), *n.* lineal descent traced through the male line. [1945–50; PATRI- + LINEAGE[1]]

pat·ri·lin·e·al (pa′trə lin′ē əl, pā′-), *adj.* inheriting or determining descent through the male line. Cf. **matrilineal.** [1900–05; PATRI- + LINEAL] **—pat′ri·lin′e·al·ly,** *adv.*

pat·ri·lin·e·ar (pa′trə lin′ē ər, pā′-), *adj.* patrilineal. [1910–15; PATRI- + LINEAR] **—pat′ri·lin′e·ar·ly,** *adv.*

pat·ri·li·ny (pa′trə lī′nē, pā′-), *n., pl.* **-nies.** the tracing of descent exclusively through the male members of a family. [1905–10; PATRILIN(EAL) + -Y[3]]

pat·ri·lo·cal (pa′trə lō′kəl, pā′-), *adj. Anthropol.* virilocal. [1905–10; PATRI- + LOCAL] **—pat′ri·lo·cal′i·ty,** *n.*

pat·ri·mo·ny (pa′trə mō′nē), *n., pl.* **-nies. 1.** an estate inherited from one's father or ancestors. **2.** any quality, characteristic, etc., that is inherited; heritage. **3.** the aggregate of one's property. **4.** the estate or endowment of a church, religious house, etc. [1300–50; ME *patrimonie* < MF < L *patrimōnium.* See PATRI-, -MONY] **—pat′ri·mo′ni·al,** *adj.* **—pat′ri·mo′ni·al·ly,** *adv.*
—Syn. 1. inheritance.

pa·tri·ot (pā′trē ət, -ot′ *or, esp. Brit.,* pa′trē ət), *n.* **1.** a person who loves, supports, and defends his or her country and its interests with devotion. **2.** (*cap.*) *Mil.* a U.S. Army antiaircraft missile with a range of 37 mi. (60 km) and a 200-lb. (90 kg) warhead, launched from a tracked vehicle with radar and computer guidance and fire control. [1590–1600; < MF *patriote* < LL *patriōta* < Gk *patriṓtēs* fellow-countryman, lineage member, equiv. to *patri(á)* lineage, clan (deriv. of *patḗr* FATHER) + *-ōtēs,* var. of *-tēs* suffix of personal nouns, with nouns ending in *-ia*]

pa·tri·ot·ic (pā′trē ot′ik *or, esp. Brit.,* pa′-), *adj.* **1.** of, like, suitable for, or characteristic of a patriot. **2.** expressing or inspired by patriotism: *a patriotic ode.* [1645–55; < LL *patriōticus* < Gk *patriōtikós.* See PATRIOT, -IC] **—pa′tri·ot′i·cal·ly,** *adv.*

pa·tri·ot·ism (pā′trē ə tiz′əm *or, esp. Brit.,* pa′-), *n.* devoted love, support, and defense of one's country; national loyalty. [1720–30; PATRIOT + -ISM]

Pa′triots' Day′, the anniversary of the battles of Lexington and Concord (1775), celebrated the third Monday in April: a legal holiday in Massachusetts and Maine.

pat·ri·po·tes·tal (pa′trə pō tes′tl, pā′-), *adj. Anthropol.* of or pertaining to the authority exercised by a father or a father's blood relatives. [1905–10; PATRI- + POTESTAL]

pa·tris·tic (pə tris′tik), *adj.* of or pertaining to the fathers of the Christian church or their writings. Also, **pa·tris′ti·cal.** [1830–40; PATR(I)- + -ISTIC] **—pa·tris′ti·cal·ly,** *adv.* **—pa·tris′ti·cal·ness,** *n.*

pa·tris·tics (pə tris′tiks), *n.* (*used with a singular v.*) patrology (def. 1). [1840–50; see PATRISTIC, -ICS]

pa·trix (pā′triks, pa′-), *n., pl.* **-tri·ces** (-trə sēz′), **-trix·es.** *Print.* a mold of a Linotype for casting right-reading type for use in dry offset. [1880–85; b. PATRI- and MATRIX]

pat·ro·cli·ny (pa′trə klī′nē, pā′-), *n. Genetics.* inheritance in which the traits of the offspring are derived primarily from the paternal parent (opposed to *matrocliny*). Also, **patricliny.** [1915–20; *patro-* (var. of PATRI- with -O-) + *-cliny* (see MATROCLINY)] **—pat′ro·cli′nous, pat′ro·clin′al, pat·ro·clin·ic** (pa′trə klin′ik, pā′-), *adj.*

Pa·tro·clus (pə trō′kləs), *n. Class. Myth.* a friend of Achilles who was slain by Hector at Troy.

pa·trol (pə trōl′), *v.,* **-trolled, -trol·ling,** *n.* *—v.i.* **1.** (of a police officer, soldier, etc.) to pass along a road, beat, etc., or around or through a specified area in order to maintain order and security. *—v.t.* **2.** to maintain the order and security of (a road, beat, area, etc.) by passing along or through it. *—n.* **3.** a person or group of persons assigned to patrol an area, road, etc. **4.** an automobile, ship, plane, squadron, fleet, etc., assigned to patrol an area. **5.** *Mil.* a detachment of two or more persons, often a squad or platoon, detailed for reconnaissance or combat. **6.** the act of patrolling. **7.** See **patrol wagon. 8.** (in the Boy Scouts and Girl Scouts) a subdivision of a troop, usually consisting of about eight members. [1655–65; < F *patrouille* (n.), *patrouiller* (v.) patrol, orig. a pawing (n.), to paw (v.) in mud; deriv. (with suffixal *-ouille*) of *patte* paw; *-r-* unexplained] **—pa·trol′ler,** *n.*

patrol′ car′. See **squad car.** [1930–35]

pa·trol·man (pə trōl′mən), *n., pl.* **-men. 1.** a police officer who is assigned to patrol a specific district, route, etc. **2.** a person who patrols. [1840–50, *Amer.*]
—Usage. See **-man.**

pa·trol·o·gist (pə trol′ə jist), *n.* a student of patrology. [1710–20; PATROLOG(Y) + -IST]

pa·trol·o·gy (pə trol′ə jē), *n., pl.* **-gies. 1.** Also called **patristics.** the branch of theology dealing with the teachings of the church fathers. **2.** a collection of the writings of the early church fathers. [1590–1600; < NL *patrologia.* See PATRI-, -O-, -LOGY] **—pat·ro·log·ic** (pa′trə loj′ik), **pat′ro·log′i·cal,** *adj.*

patrol′ wag′on, an enclosed truck or van used by the police to transport prisoners. Also called **police wagon.**

pa·trol·wom·an (pə trōl′wo͝om′ən), *n., pl.* **-wom·en.** *n.* a policewoman who is assigned to patrol a specific district, route, etc. [PATROL(MAN) + -WOMAN]
—Usage. See **-woman.**

pa·tron (pā′trən), *n.* **1.** a person who is a customer, client, or paying guest, esp. a regular one, of a store, hotel, or the like. **2.** a person who supports with money, gifts, efforts, or endorsement an artist, writer, museum, cause, charity, institution, special event, or the like: *a patron of the arts; patrons of the annual Democratic dance.* **3.** a person whose support or protection is solicited or acknowledged by the dedication of a book or other work. **4.** See **patron saint. 5.** *Rom. Hist.* the protector of a dependent or client, often the former master of a freedman still retaining certain rights over him. **6.** *Eccles.* a person who has the right of presenting a member of the clergy to a benefice. [1250–1300; ME < ML, L *patrōnus* legal protector, advocate (ML: lord, master) deriv. of *pater* FATHER. See PATTERN] **—pa′tron·al, pa′tron·ly,** *adj.* **—pa′tron·dom, pa′tron·ship′,** *n.* **—pa′tron·less,** *adj.*

pa·trón (pä trôn′) *n., pl.* **-tro·nes** (-trô′nes). *Spanish.* (in Mexico and the southwestern U.S.) a boss; employer.

pa·tron·age (pā′trə nij, pa′-), *n.* **1.** the financial support or business provided to a store, hotel, or the like, by customers, clients, or paying guests. **2.** patrons collectively; clientele. **3.** the control of or power to make appointments to government jobs or the power to grant other political favors. **4.** offices, jobs, or other favors so controlled. **5.** the distribution of jobs and favors on a political basis, as to those who have supported one's party or political campaign. **6.** a condescending manner or attitude in granting favors, in dealing with people, etc.; condescension: *an air of patronage toward his business subordinates.* **7.** the position, encouragement, influence, or support of a patron, as toward an artist, institution, etc. **8.** the right of presentation to an ecclesiastical benefice; advowson. [1350–1400; ME < MF; see PATRON, -AGE]
—Syn. 1. custom, commerce, trade.

pa·tron·ess (pā′trə nis), *n.* a woman who protects, supports, or sponsors someone or something. [1375–1425; late ME *patronesse* female patron saint < OF]
—Usage. See **-ess.**

pa·tron·ize (pā′trə nīz′, pa′-), *v.t.,* **-ized, -iz·ing. 1.** to give (a store, restaurant, hotel, etc.) one's regular patronage; trade with. **2.** to behave in an offensively condescending manner toward: *a professor who patronizes his students.* **3.** to act as a patron toward (an artist, institution, etc.); support. Also, *esp. Brit.,* **pa′tron·ise′.** [1580–90; PATRON + -IZE] **—pa′tron·iz′a·ble,** *adj.* **—pa′tron·i·za′tion,** *n.* **—pa′tron·iz′er,** *n.*

pa·tron·iz·ing (pā′trə nī′zing, pa′-), *adj.* displaying or indicative of an offensively condescending manner: *a patronizing greeting, accompanied by a gentle pat on the back.* [1720–30; PATRONIZE + -ING[2]] **—pa′tron·iz′ing·ly,** *adv.*

pa′tron saint′, a saint regarded as the special guardian of a person, group, trade, place, etc. [1710–20]

pat·ro·nym (pa′trə nim), *n.* patronymic (defs. 3, 4). [1825–35; < Gk *patrṓnymos* (adj.) patronymic. See PATRI-, -ONYM]

pat·ro·nym·ic (pa′trə nim′ik), *adj.* **1.** (of family names) derived from the name of a father or ancestor, esp. by the addition of a suffix or prefix indicating descent. **2.** (of a suffix or prefix) indicating such descent. *—n.* **3.** a patronymic name, as *Williamson* (son of William) or *Macdonald* (son of Donald). **4.** a family name; surname. [1605–15; < LL *patrōnymicus* < Gk *patrōnymikós,* equiv. to *patrṓnym(os)* (see PATRONYM) + *-ikos* -IC] **—pat′ro·nym′i·cal·ly,** *adv.*

pa·troon (pə tro͞on′), *n.* a person who held an estate in land with certain manorial privileges granted under the old Dutch governments of New York and New Jersey. [1655–65; < D < F < L *patrōnus.* See PATRON, -OON] **—pa·troon′ship,** *n.*

pat·sy (pat′sē), *n., pl.* **-sies.** *Slang.* **1.** a person who is easily swindled, deceived, coerced, persuaded, etc.; sucker. **2.** a person upon whom the blame for something falls; scapegoat; fall guy. **3.** a person who is the object of a joke, ridicule, or the like. [1900–05, *Amer.*]

Pat·sy (pat′sē), *n.* **1.** a male given name, form of **Patrick. 2.** a female given name, form of **Patricia.**

pat·ten (pat′n), *n.* **1.** any of various kinds of footwear, as a wooden shoe, a shoe with a wooden sole, a chopine, etc., to protect the feet from mud or wetness. **2.** a separate sole attached to a shoe or boot for this purpose. **3.** *Building Trades.* any stand or support, esp. one of a number resting on unbroken ground as a substitute for a foundation. [1350–1400; ME *paten* < MF *patin* wooden shoe, perh. deriv. of *pate* paw] **—pat′tened,** *adj.*

Pat·ten (pat′n), *n.* **Gilbert** (*"Burt L. Standish"*), 1866–1945, U.S. writer of adventure stories.

pat·ter[1] (pat′ər), *v.i.* **1.** to make a rapid succession of light taps: *Raindrops patter on the windowpane.* **2.** to move or walk lightly or quickly: *The child pattered across the room.* *—v.t.* **3.** to cause to patter. **4.** to spatter with something. *—n.* **5.** a rapid succession of light tapping sounds: *the steady patter of rain on the tin roof.* **6.** the act of pattering. [1605–15; PAT[1] + -ER[6]]
—Syn. 1. pat, beat, rap, pelt.

pat·ter[2] (pat′ər), *n.* **1.** meaningless, rapid talk; mere chatter; gabble. **2.** the usually glib and rapid speech or talk used by a magician while performing, a barker at a circus or sideshow, a comedian or other entertainer, a vendor of questionable wares, or the like; stylized or rehearsed talk used to attract attention, entertain, etc. **3.** amusing lines delivered rapidly by an entertainer or performer, as in a comic routine or in a song. **4.** the jargon or cant of any class, group, etc. *—v.i.* **5.** to talk glibly or rapidly, esp. with little regard to meaning; chatter. **6.** to repeat a paternoster or other prayer in a rapid, mechanical way. *—v.t.* **7.** to recite or repeat (prayers, verses, etc.) in a rapid, mechanical way. **8.** to repeat or say rapidly or glibly. [1350–1400; ME; var. of PATER] **—pat′ter·er, pat′ter·ist,** *n.*

pat·ter[3] (pat′ər), *n.* a person or thing that pats. [PAT[1] + -ER[1]]

pat·tern (pat′ərn; *Brit.* pat′n), *n.* **1.** a decorative design, as for wallpaper, china, textile fabrics, etc. **2.** decoration or ornament having such a design. **3.** a natural or chance marking, configuration, or design: *patterns of frost on the window.* **4.** a distinctive style, model, or form: *a new pattern of army helmet.* **5.** a combination of qualities, acts, tendencies, etc., forming a consistent or characteristic arrangement: *the behavior patterns of teenagers.* **6.** an original or model considered for or deserving of imitation: *Our constitution has been a pattern for those of many new republics.* **7.** anything fashioned or designed to serve as a model or guide for something to be made: *a paper pattern for a dress.* **8.** a sufficient quantity of material for making a garment. **9.** the path of flight established for an aircraft approaching an airport at which it is to land. **10.** a diagram of lines transmitted occasionally by a television station to aid in adjusting receiving sets; test pattern. **11.** *Metall.* a model or form, usually of wood or metal, used for giving the shape of the interior of a mold. **12.** *Numis.* a coin, either the redesign of an existing piece or the model for a new one, submitted for authorization as a regular issue. **13.** an example, instance, sample, or specimen. **14.** *Gunnery, Aerial Bombing.* **a.** the distribution of strikes around a target at which a shotgun or a number of rifle or artillery rounds have been fired or on which bombs have been dropped. **b.** a diagram showing such distribution. *—v.t.* **15.** to make or fashion after or according to a pattern. **16.** to cover or mark with a pattern. **17.** *Chiefly Brit. Dial.* **a.** to imitate. **b.** to attempt to match or duplicate. *—v.i.* **18.** to make or fall into a pattern. [1325–75; ME *patron* < ML *patrōnus* model, special use of L *patrōnus* PATRON] **—pat′tern·a·ble,** *adj.* **—pat′terned,** *adj.* **—pat′tern·er,** *n.* **—pat′tern·less,** *adj.* **—pat′tern·like′,** *adj.* **—pat′tern·y,** *adj.*
—Syn. 1. figure. **4.** kind, sort. **6.** example, exemplar.

pat′tern bar′gaining, a collective bargaining technique in which contract terms in one settlement are used as models to be imposed on other negotiating parties within an industry.

pat′tern bomb′ing, aerial bombing in which bombs are dropped on a target in a predetermined pattern. Also called **saturation bombing.** Cf. **area bombing, precision bombing.** [1935–40]

pat·tern·ing (pat′ər ning), *n.* **1.** a design or decoration formed by the creative arrangement or formation of patterns. **2.** the following of a specific pattern of movement, as in a dance or exercise: *the floor patterning of a folk dance.* **3.** a system of physical therapy in which a pattern of specific movements is practiced or imposed regularly as a way of improving, restoring, or stimulating muscular coordination, esp. in brain-damaged or handicapped persons. [1860–65; PATTERN + -ING[1]]

pat·tern·mak·er (pat′ərn mā′kər *or, Brit.,* pat′n-), *n.* a person who makes patterns, as for clothing or metal castings. Also, **pat′tern mak′er.** [1810–20; PATTERN + MAKER] **—pat′tern·mak′ing,** *n.*

pat′tern prac′tice, **1.** (in foreign-language learning) a technique for practicing a linguistic structure in which students repeat a sentence or other structure, each time substituting a new element, such as a new verb, as directed by the teacher, or transforming the original structure, as in changing a statement to a question. **2.** Also called **pat′tern drill′.** a drill using this technique.

pat′tern recogni′tion, *Computers.* the automated identification of shapes or forms or patterns of speech.

Pat·ter·son (pat′ər sən), *n.* **1. Eleanor Medill** ("Cissy"), 1884–1948, U.S. newspaper editor and publisher. **2. Floyd,** born 1935, U.S. boxer: world heavyweight champion 1956–59, 1960–62. **3. Frederick Douglass,** born 1901, U.S. educator.

pat′ter song′, a comic song depending for its humorous effect on rapid enunciation of the words, occurring most commonly in comic opera and operetta. [1815–25]

Pat·ti (pat′ē; *for 1 also It.* pät′tē), *n.* **1. A·de·li·na** (ä′de lē′nä), (*Adela Juana Maria Patti*), 1843–1919, Italian operatic soprano, born in Spain. **2.** a female given name.

pat·tle (pat′l, pät′l), *n. Brit. Dial.* paddle[1] (def. 11).

Pat·ton (pat′n), *n.* **George Smith,** 1885–1945, U.S. general.

pat·ty (pat′ē), *n., pl.* **-ties. 1.** any item of food covered with dough, batter, etc., and fried or baked: *oyster patties.* **2.** a thin, round piece of ground or minced food, as of meat or the like: *hamburger patty.* **3.** a thin, round piece, as of candy: *peppermint patties.* **4.** a little pie; pasty. [1700–10; alter. of PÂTÉ, conformed to E words with the suffix -Y[2]]

Pat·ty (pat′ē), *n.* a female given name, form of **Patience** or **Patricia.**

pat·ty-cake (pat′i kāk′), *n.* pat-a-cake.

pat′ty pan′, a small pan for baking patties. [1685–95]

pat′ty·pan squash′ (pat′i pan′), a flat, whitish variety of squash, *Cucurbita pepo melopepo,* having a scalloped edge. Also called **cymling, scallop squash.** [1905–10]

pat′ty shell′, a cup-shaped shell of light, flaky pastry, for serving vegetable, fish, or meat mixtures, usually with a sauce. [1905–10, *Amer.*]

Pa·tu·ca (pä to͞o′kä), *n.* a river rising in E central Honduras and flowing NE to the Caribbean Sea. ab. 300 mi. (485 km) long.

pat·u·lin (pat′yo͝o lin, pach′o͝o-), *n. Pharm.* a toxic antibiotic, $C_7H_6O_4$, derived from various fungi, as *Penicillium patulum* and *Aspergillus clavatus.* Also called **clavacin.** [1940–45; < NL *patul(um)* specific epithet of the fungus (L: neut. of *patulus* PATULOUS) + -IN[2]]

pat·u·lous (pach′ə ləs), *adj.* **1.** open; gaping; expanded. **2.** *Bot.* **a.** spreading, as a tree or its boughs. **b.** spreading slightly, as a calyx. **c.** bearing the flowers loose or dispersed, as a peduncle. [1610–20; < L *patulus* standing wide-open. See PATENT, -ULOUS] **—pat′u·lous·ly,** *adv.* **—pat′u·lous·ness,** *n.*

Pat·win (pat′win), *n., pl.* **-wins,** (*esp. collectively*) **-win** for 1. **1.** a member of a North American Indian people of the western Sacramento River valley in California. **2.** the Wintun language of the Patwin.

pat·y (pat′ē), *adj. Heraldry.* (of a cross) having arms of equal length, each expanding outward from the center; formée: *a cross paty.* [1480–90; var. of *pattee* < MF, equiv. to *patte* paw + *-ee;* see -EE, -ATE[1]]

pat·zer (pät′sər, pat′-), *n.* a casual, amateurish chess player. [1955–60; prob. < G *Patzer* bungler, equiv. to *patz(en)* to bungle (cf. Austrian dial. *Patzen* stain, blot, *patzen* to make a stain) + *-er* -ER[1]]

Pau (pō), *n.* a city in and the capital of Pyrénées-Atlantiques department, in SW France: winter resort. 85,860.

P.A.U., Pan American Union.

pau·a (pou′ə), *n.* a large, edible abalone of New Zealand, *Haliotis iris,* the shell of which is used in making jewelry. [1810–20; < Maori]

pau·cis ver·bis (pou′kis weʀ′bis; *Eng.* pô′sis vûr′-bis), *Latin.* in or by few words; with brevity.

pau·ci·ty (pô′si tē), *n.* **1.** smallness of quantity; scarcity; scantiness: *a country with a paucity of resources.* **2.** smallness or insufficiency of number; fewness. [1375–1425; late ME *paucite* < L *paucitās* fewness, deriv. of *paucus* few; see -ITY]

Paul (pôl *for 1–3, 5;* poul *for 4*), *n.* **1. Saint,** died A.D. c67, a missionary and apostle to the gentiles: author of several of the Epistles. Cf. **Saul** (def. 2). **2. Alice,** 1885–1977, U.S. women's-rights activist. **3. Elliot (Harold),** 1891–1958, U.S. novelist. **4. Jean** (zhäɴ), pen name of Jean Paul Friedrich Richter. **5.** a male given name: from a Latin word meaning "little".

Paul I, **1.** died A.D. 767, pope 757–767. **2.** Russian, **Pavel Petrovich,** 1754–1801, emperor of Russia 1796–1801 (son of Peter III). **3.** 1901–64, king of Greece 1947–64.

Paul II, (*Pietro Barbo*) 1417–71, Italian ecclesiastic: pope 1464–71.

Paul III, (*Alessandro Farnese*) 1468–1549, Italian ecclesiastic: pope 1534–49.

Paul IV, (*Gian Pietro Caraffa*) 1476–1559, Italian ecclesiastic: pope 1555–59.

Paul V, (*Camillo Borghese*) 1552–1621, Italian ecclesiastic: pope 1605–21.

Paul VI, (*Giovanni Batista Montini*) 1897–1978, Italian ecclesiastic: pope 1963–78.

Pau·la (pô′lə), *n.* a female given name: derived from *Paul.*

Paul-Bon·cour (pôl bôɴ ko͞oʀ′), *n.* **Jo·seph** (zhô zef′), 1873–1972, French lawyer and statesman: premier 1932–33.

Paul′ Bun′yan, a legendary giant lumberjack, an American folk hero.

paul·dron (pôl′drən), *n. Armor.* a piece of plate armor for the shoulder and the uppermost part of the arm, often overlapping the adjacent parts of the chest and back. Also called **epaulière.** Cf. **spaulder.** See diag. under **armor.** [1400–50; earlier *paleron, poleron,* late ME *polron, pollerons* (pl.) < MF *espalleron* shoulder. See EPAULET]

Pau·lette (pô let′), *n.* a female given name: derived from *Paul.*

Pau·li (pô′lē; *Ger.* pou′lē), *n.* **Wolf·gang** (wo͝olf′gang; *Ger.* vôlf′gäng), 1900–58, Austrian physicist in the U.S.: Nobel prize 1945.

Pau′li exclu′sion prin′ciple, *Physics.* See **exclusion principle.** [1925–30; named after W. PAULI]

Paul·ine (pô′lin, -lēn), *adj.* of or pertaining to the apostle Paul or to his doctrines or writings. [1325–75; < ML *Paulīnus.* See PAUL, -INE[1]]

Pau·line (pô lēn′), *n.* a female given name.

Paul′ine priv′ilege, *Rom. Cath. Ch.* (in canon law) the privilege given to converts to dissolve a marriage with an unbaptized spouse if either obstructs the religious practices of the other.

Paul·ing (pô′ling), *n.* **Li·nus Carl** (lī′nəs), 1901–94, U.S. chemist: Nobel prize in chemistry 1954, Nobel prize for peace 1962.

Paul·in·ism (pô′lə niz′əm), *n.* the body of theological doctrine taught by or attributed to the apostle Paul. [1855–60; PAULINE + -ISM] **—Paul′in·ist,** *n.* **—Paul′in·is′tic,** *adj.* **—Paul′in·is′ti·cal·ly,** *adv.*

Pau·li·nus (pô lī′nəs), *n.* **Saint,** died A.D. 644, Roman missionary in England with Augustine: 1st archbishop of York 633–644.

Paul·ist (pô′list), *n. Rom. Cath. Ch.* a member of the "Missionary Society of St. Paul the Apostle," a community of priests founded in New York in 1858. [1880–85; PAUL + -IST]

pau·low·ni·a (pô lō′nē ə), *n.* **1.** a Japanese tree, *Paulownia tomentosa,* of the bignonia family, having showy clusters of pale-violet or blue flowers blossoming in early spring. **2.** any other tree of the genus *Paulownia.* [1835–45; < NL; named after Anna *Pavlovna,* daughter of Paul I of Russia; see -IA]

Paul′ Pry′, an inquisitive, meddlesome person. [from name of title character of *Paul Pry* (1853) by John Poole (1786–1872), English dramatist]

Paum·gart·ner (poum′gärt′nəʀ), *n.* **Bern·hard** (beʀn′härt), 1887–1971, Austrian composer, conductor, and musicologist.

Pau·mo′tu Archipel′ago (pou mō′to͞o). See **Tuamotu Archipelago.**

paunch (pônch, pänch), *n.* **1.** a large and protruding belly; potbelly. **2.** the belly or abdomen. **3.** the rumen. [1325–75; ME *paunche* < AF, for MF *pance* < L *panticēs* (pl.) bowels] **—paunched,** *adj.*

paunch·y (pôn′chē, pän′-), *adj.,* **paunch·i·er, paunch·i·est.** having a large and protruding belly; potbellied: *a paunchy middle-aged man.* [1590–1600; PAUNCH + -Y[1]] **—paunch′i·ness,** *n.*

pau·per (pô′pər), *n.* **1.** a person without any means of support, esp. a destitute person who depends on aid from public welfare funds or charity. **2.** a very poor person. [1485–95; < L: poor] **—pau′per·age, pau′per·dom,** *n.*

pau·per·ism (pô′pə riz′əm), *n.* the state or condition of utter poverty. [1805–15; PAUPER + -ISM]

pau·per·ize (pô′pə rīz′), *v.t.,* **-ized, -iz·ing.** to make a pauper of: *His extravagance pauperized him.* Also, *esp. Brit.,* **pau′per·ise′.** [1825–35; PAUPER + -IZE] **—pau′per·i·za′tion,** *n.* **—pau′per·iz′er,** *n.*

pau·piette (pō pyet′), *n., pl.* **-piettes** (-pyets′; *Fr.* -pyet′). *French Cookery.* bird (def. 6). [1885–90; earlier *po(u)piette,* prob. deriv. of MF *poulpe* fleshy part of the body or of an animal, OF *polpe* < L *pulpa* PULP; see -ETTE]

Paur (pouᵊr, pou′ər; *Ger.* pouʀ), *n.* **E·mil** (ā′mēl), 1855–1932, Austrian violinist and conductor.

pau·ra·que (pou rä′kā; *Sp.* pou ʀä′ke), *n., pl.* **-ques** (-kāz; *Sp.* -kes). a large, tropical American goatsucker, *Nyctidromus albicollis.* [1905–10; presumably Hispanicized sp. of a word < a language of tropical America]

Pau·sa·ni·as (pô sā′nē əs), *n.* fl. A.D. c175, Greek traveler, geographer, and author.

pause (pôz), *n., v.,* **paused, paus·ing.** *—n.* **1.** a temporary stop or rest, esp. in speech or action: *a short pause after each stroke of the oar.* **2.** a cessation of activity because of doubt or uncertainty; a momentary hesitation. **3.** any comparatively brief stop, delay, wait, etc.: *I would like to make a pause in my talk and continue after lunch.* **4.** a break or rest in speaking or reading to emphasize meaning, grammatical relation, metrical division, etc., or in writing or printing by the use of punctuation. **5.** *Pros.* a break or suspension, as a caesura, in a line of verse. **6.** *Music.* a fermata. **7. give pause,** to cause to hesitate or be unsure, as from surprise or doubt: *These frightening statistics give us pause.* *—v.i.* **8.** to make a brief stop or delay; wait; hesitate: *He paused at the edge of the pool for a moment. I'll pause in my lecture so we can all get some coffee.* **9.** to dwell or linger (usually fol. by *on* or *upon*): *to pause upon a particular point.* [1400–50; (n.) ME < L *pausa* < Gk *paûsis* a halt, equiv. to *paú(ein)* to stop + *-sis* -SIS; (v.) deriv. of the n.] **—paus′al,** *adj.* **—pause′ful,** *adj.* **—pause′ful·ly,** *adv.* **—pause′less,** *adj.* **—pause′less·ly,** *adv.* **—paus′er,** *n.* **—paus′ing·ly,** *adv.*
—Syn. 1–3. suspension, interruption, break, halt; hiatus, lacuna. **8.** rest. **9.** tarry, delay.

pa·vane (pə vän′, -van′; *Fr.* pᴀ vᴀɴ′), *n., pl.* **pa·vanes** (pə vänz′, -vanz′; *Fr.* pᴀ vᴀɴ′). **1.** a stately dance dating from the 16th century. **2.** the music for this dance. Also, **pav·an** (pav′ən, pə vän′, -van′), **pavin.** [1525–35; < MF < It *pavana,* contr. of *padovana* (fem.) of Padua (It *Padova*)]

Pa·va·rot·ti (pav′ə rot′ē; *It.* pä′vä rôt′tē), *n.* **Lu·cia·no** (lo͞o′chē ä′nō; *It.* lo͞o chä′nō), born 1935, Italian operatic tenor.

pave (pāv), *v.t.,* **paved, pav·ing. 1.** to cover or lay (a road, walk, etc.) with concrete, stones, bricks, tiles, wood, or the like, so as to make a firm, level surface. **2. pave the way to** or **for,** to prepare for and facilitate the entrance of; lead up to: *His analysis of the college market paved the way for their entry into textbook publishing.* *—n.* **3.** *Southern Louisiana.* a paved road. [1275–1325; ME *paven* < MF *paver* < VL **pavare,* for L *pavīre* to beat, ram, tread down]

pa·vé (pə vā′, pav′ā; *Fr.* pᴀ vā′), *n., pl.* **pa·vés** (pə vāz′, pav′āz; *Fr.* pᴀ vā′), *adv., adj.* *—n.* **1.** a pavement. **2.** *Jewelry.* a setting of stones placed close together so as to show no metal between them. *—adv.* **3.** *Jewelry.* in the manner of a pavé; as a pavé: *diamonds set pavé.* *—adj.* **4.** Also, **pa·véd′, pa·véed′.** being set pavé: *pavé rubies.* [1755–65; < F, ptp. of *paver.* See PAVE]

Pa·vel Pe·tro·vich (*Russ.* pä′vyil pyi tʀô′vyich). See **Paul I** (def. 2).

pave·ment (pāv′mənt), *n.* **1.** a paved road, highway, etc. **2.** a paved surface, ground covering, or floor. **3.** a material used for paving. **4.** *Atlantic States and Brit.* sidewalk. **5. pound the pavement,** *Informal.* to walk the streets in order to accomplish something: *If you're going to find work you'd better start pounding the pavement.* [1250–1300; ME < OF < L *pavīmentum.* See PAVE, -MENT] **—pave·men·tal** (pāv men′tl), *adj.*

pave′ment art′ist, *Chiefly Brit.* See **sidewalk artist.** [1895–1900]

pave′ment light′. See **vault light.**

pav·er (pā′vər), *n.* **1.** a person or thing that paves. **2.** a brick, tile, stone, or block used for paving. [1375–1425; late ME; see PAVE, -ER[1]]

Pa·vi·a (pä vē′ä), *n.* a city in N Italy, S of Milan: Charles V captured Francis I here. 87,804.

pav·id (pav′id), *adj.* timid; afraid; fearful; frightened. [1650–60; < L *pavidus* trembling, timid, deriv. of *pavēre* to quake; see -ID[4]]

pa·vil·ion (pə vil′yən), *n.* **1.** a light, usually open building used for shelter, concerts, exhibits, etc., as in a park or fair. **2.** any of a number of separate or attached buildings forming a hospital or the like. **3.** *Archit.* a projecting element of a façade, used esp. at the center or at each end and usually treated so as to suggest a tower. **4.** a tent, esp. a large and elaborate one. **5.** a small, ornamental building in a garden. **6.** Also called **base.** *Jewelry.* the part of a cut gem below the girdle. —*v.t.* **7.** to shelter in or as if in a pavilion. **8.** to furnish with pavilions. [1250–1300; ME *pavilon* < OF *paveillon* < L *pāpiliōn-* (s. of *pāpiliō*) butterfly]

pavil′ion roof′, a pyramidal hip roof. [1875–80]

pa•vil•lon (*Fr.* pa vē yôɴ′), *n., pl.* **-vil•lons** (*Fr.* -vē yôɴ′). *Music.* the bell of a wind instrument. [1875–80; < F: lit., pavilion]

pa•vil•lon Chi•nois (*Fr.* pa vē yôɴ′ shē nwa′), *pl.* **pa•vil•lons Chi•nois** (*Fr.* pa vē yôɴ′ shē nwa′). crescent (def. 6). [< F: lit., Chinese pavillon]

pav•in (pav′ən), *n.* pavane.

pav•ing (pā′ving), *n.* **1.** a pavement. **2.** material for paving. **3.** the laying of a pavement. [1400–50; late ME; see PAVE, -ING[1]]

pav•ior (pāv′yər), *n.* **1.** a person that paves; paver. **2.** a material used for paving. Also, *esp. Brit.,* **pav′iour.** [1375–1425; alter. of late ME *pavier;* see PAVE, -IER[1]]

Pa•vi•o•tso (pä′vē ôt′sō), *n., pl.* **-tsos,** (*esp. collectively*) **-tso.** See **Northern Paiute** (def. 1).

pav•is (pav′is), *n.* a large oblong shield of the late 14th through the early 16th centuries, often covering the entire body and used esp. by archers and soldiers of the infantry. Also, **pav′ise.** [1350–1400; ME *paveys* < MF *pavais* < OIt *pavese* lit., of PAVIA; see -ESE]

Pa•vlo•dar (pav′lə där′; *Russ.* pə vlu där′), *n.* a city in NE Kazakhstan. 331,000.

Pa•vlo•grad (pav′lə grad′; *Russ.* pə vlu grät′), *n.* a city in the SE Ukraine, in the W central Soviet Union in Europe, S of Kharkov. 107,000.

Pa•vlov (pav′lov, -lôf; *Russ.* pä′vləf), *n.* **I•van Pe•tro•vich** (ē vän′ pyi trô′vyich), 1849–1936, Russian physiologist: Nobel prize for medicine 1904.

Pa•vlo•va (pav′lə və, päv lō′və, pav-; *Russ.* pä′vlə və), *n.* **An•na** (ä′nə), 1885–1931, Russian ballet dancer.

Pav•lov•i•an (pav lō′vē ən, -lô′-, -lov′ē-), *adj.* of, pertaining to, or characteristic of Pavlov or his work, esp. of experiments in which he elicited predictable responses from laboratory animals. [1925–30; PAVLOV + -IAN]

Pavlov′ian condi′tioning, conditioning (def. 2). [1930–35]

Pa•vo (pā′vō), *n., gen.* **Pa•vo•nis** (pə vō′nis). *Astron.* the Peacock, a southern constellation between Triangulum Australe and Indus. [< L *pāvō* PEACOCK]

pav•o•nine (pav′ə nīn′, -nin), *adj.* **1.** of or like a peacock. **2.** resembling the feathers of a peacock, as in coloring. [1650–60; < L *pāvōnīnus,* deriv. of *pāvō* (s. *pāvōn-*) PEACOCK; see -INE[1]]

paw[1] (pô), *n.* **1.** the foot of an animal having claws. **2.** the foot of any animal. **3.** *Informal.* the human hand, esp. one that is large, rough, or clumsy: *Keep your paws off my property.* —*v.t.* **4.** to strike or scrape with the paws or feet: *a dog pawing the door.* **5.** *Informal.* to handle or caress clumsily, rudely, or with unwelcome familiarity. —*v.i.* **6.** to beat or scrape the floor, ground, etc., with the paws or feet. **7.** *Informal.* to handle or caress someone or something in a clumsy or rude manner or with unwelcome familiarity. [1300–50; ME *pawe,* var. of *powe* < MF *poue* (c. Pr *pauta*) < Gmc; cf. D *poot,* G *Pfote*] —**paw′er,** *n.*

paw[2] (pô), *n. Informal.* father; pa. [1900–05, *Amer.*; earlier and dial. pron. of PA, reflecting the now lapsed constraint against a maximally open back vowel in an open stressed final syll.]

pawk•y (pô′kē), *adj.,* **pawk•i•er, pawk•i•est.** *Chiefly Brit.* cunning; sly. [1670–80; Scots *pawk* trick + -Y[1]] —**pawk′i•ly,** *adv.* —**pawk′i•ness,** *n.*

pawl (pôl), *n.* **1.** a pivoted bar adapted to engage with the teeth of a ratchet wheel or the like so as to prevent movement or to impart motion. —*v.t.* **2.** to check or hold with a pawl. [1620–30; < D *pal* ratchet]

pawn[1] (pôn), *v.t.* **1.** to deposit as security, as for money borrowed, esp. with a pawnbroker: *He raised the money by pawning his watch.* **2.** to pledge; stake; risk: *to pawn one's life.* —*n.* **3.** the state of being deposited or held as security, esp. with or by a pawnbroker: *jewels in pawn.* **4.** something given or deposited as security, as for money borrowed. **5.** a person serving as security; hostage. **6.** the act of pawning. [1490–1500; (n.) < MF *pan;* OF *pan(d), pant,* appar. < WGmc; cf. OFris *pand,* OS, MD *pant,* G *Pfand;* (v.) deriv. of the n.] —**pawn′a•ble,** *adj.* —**pawn•er** (pô′nər), **paw•nor** (pô′nər, -nôr), *n.*
—**Syn. 4.** pledge.

pawn[2] (pôn), *n.* **1.** *Chess.* one of eight men of one color and of the lowest value, usually moved one square at a time vertically and capturing diagonally. **2.** someone who is used or manipulated to further another person's purposes. [1325–75; ME *poun* < AF, equiv. to MF *poon,* var. of *paon,* earlier *pe(h)on* lit., walker; see PEON[1]]
—**Syn. 2.** puppet, tool, dupe.

pawn•age (pô′nij), *n.* the act of pawning. [1615–25; PAWN[1] + -AGE]

pawn•bro•ker (pôn′brō′kər), *n.* a person whose business is lending money at interest on personal, movable property deposited with the lender until redeemed. [1680–90; PAWN[1] + BROKER]

pawn•bro•king (pôn′brō′king), *n.* the business of a pawnbroker. Also, **pawn′bro′ker•age, pawn′bro′ker•y.** [1805–15; PAWNBROK(ER) + -ING[1]]

Paw•nee (pô nē′), *n., pl.* **-nees,** (*esp. collectively*) **-nee** for 1. **1.** a member of a confederacy of North American Plains Indians of Caddoan stock formerly located along the Platte River valley, Nebraska, and now living in northern Oklahoma. **2.** the Caddoan language of the Pawnee Indians.

pawn•shop (pôn′shop′), *n.* the shop of a pawnbroker, esp. one where unredeemed items are displayed and sold. [1840–50; PAWN[1] + SHOP]

pawn′ tick′et, a receipt given for goods left with a pawnbroker. [1855–60]

paw•paw (pô′pô′), *n.* **1.** a tree, *Asimina triloba,* of the annona family, native to the eastern U.S., having large, oblong leaves and purplish flowers. **2.** the fleshy, edible fruit of this tree. **3.** papaya. Also, **papaw.** [unexplained var. of *papaye* PAPAYA]

Paw•tuck•et (pô tuk′it), *n.* a city in NE Rhode Island. 71,204.

pax (paks, päks), *n.* **1.** *Eccles.* See **kiss of peace. 2.** (*cap.*) a period in history marked by the absence of major wars, usually imposed by a predominant nation. [1325–75; ME < L: PEACE]

Pax (paks, päks), *n.* the Roman goddess of peace.

PAX, private automatic exchange.

Pax′ Bri•tan′ni•ca (bri tan′i kə), a peace imposed by Great Britain upon hostile nations, esp. in the 19th century. [1895–1900; < L: British peace]

Pax•os (pak′sos, -sōs), *n.* one of the Ionian Islands, off the NW coast of Greece. 7 sq. mi. (18 sq. km). Greek, **Pa•xoi** (pä ksē′).

Pax Ro•ma•na (paks′ rō mä′nə, -mā′-, päks′; *Lat.* päks′ rō mä′nä), **1.** the terms of peace imposed by ancient Rome on its dominions. **2.** any state of peace imposed by a strong nation on weaker or defeated nations. **3.** an uneasy or hostile peace. [1880–85; < L: Roman peace]

Pax•ton (pak′stən), *n.* **Sir Joseph,** 1801–65, English horticulturist and architect.

pax vo•bis•cum (päks′ wō bis′ko͝om; *Eng.* paks′ vō bis′kəm, päks′), *Latin.* peace be with you.

pax•wax (paks′waks′), *n. Brit. Dial.* the neck ligament; nuchal ligament. [1400–50; late ME, alter. of ME *fax wax* lit., hair growth (cf. OE *feax* hair, *weaxan* to grow; see WAX[2]); cf. G *Haarwachs* sinew, lit., hair growth]

pay[1] (pā), *v.,* **paid** or (*Obs. except for def. 12*) **payed; pay•ing;** *n., adj.* —*v.t.* **1.** to settle (a debt, obligation, etc.), as by transferring money or goods, or by doing something: *Please pay your bill.* **2.** to give over (a certain amount of money) in exchange for something: *He paid twenty dollars for the shirt.* **3.** to transfer money as compensation or recompense for work done or services rendered; to satisfy the claims of (a person, organization, etc.), as by giving money due: *He paid me for my work.* **4.** to defray (cost or expense). **5.** to give compensation for. **6.** to yield a recompense or return to; be profitable to: *Your training will pay you well in the future.* **7.** to yield as a return: *The stock paid six percent last year.* **8.** to requite, as for good, harm, or an offense: *How can I pay her for her kindness and generosity?* **9.** to give or render (attention, respects, compliments, etc.), as if due or fitting. **10.** to make (a call, visit, etc.). **11.** to suffer in retribution; undergo: *You'll pay the penalty for your stubbornness!* **12.** *Naut.* to let (a ship) fall off to leeward.
—*v.i.* **13.** to transfer money, goods, etc., as in making a purchase or settling a debt. **14.** to discharge a debt or obligation. **15.** to yield a return, profit, or advantage; be worthwhile: *It pays to be courteous.* **16.** to give compensation, as for damage or loss sustained. **17.** to suffer or be punished for something: *The murderer paid with his life.* **18. pay as you go, a.** to pay for (goods, services, etc.) at the time of purchase, as opposed to buying on credit. **b.** to spend no more than income permits; keep out of debt. **c.** to pay income tax by regular deductions from one's salary or wages. **19. pay back, a.** to repay or return: *to pay back a loan.* **b.** to retaliate against or punish: *She paid us back by refusing the invitation.* **c.** to requite. **20. pay down, a.** to pay (part of the total price) at the time of purchase, with the promise to pay the balance in installments: *On this plan you pay only ten percent down.* **b.** to pay off or back; amortize: *The company's debt is being paid down rapidly.* **21. pay for,** to suffer or be punished for: *to pay for one's sins.* **22. pay off, a.** to pay (someone) everything that is due that person, esp. to do so and discharge from one's employ. **b.** to pay (a debt) in full. **c.** *Informal.* to bribe. **d.** to retaliate upon or punish. **e.** *Naut.* to fall off to leeward. **f.** to result in success or failure: *The risk paid off handsomely.* **23. pay one's** or **its way, a.** to pay one's portion of shared expenses. **b.** to yield a return on one's investment sufficient to repay one's expenses: *It will take time for the restaurant to begin paying its way.* **24. pay out, a.** to distribute (money, wages, etc.); disburse. **b.** to get revenge upon for an injury; punish. **c.** to let out (a rope) by slackening. **25. pay up, a.** to pay fully. **b.** to pay on demand: *The gangsters used threats of violence to force the shopkeepers to pay up.*
—*n.* **26.** the act of paying or being paid; payment. **27.** wages, salary, or a stipend. **28.** a person with reference to solvency or reputation for meeting obligations: *The bank regards him as good pay.* **29.** paid employment: *in the pay of the enemy.* **30.** reward or punishment; requital. **31.** a rock stratum from which petroleum is obtained.
—*adj.* **32.** requiring subscribed or monthly payment for use or service: *pay television.* **33.** operable or accessible on deposit of a coin or coins: *a pay toilet.* **34.** of or pertaining to payment. [1150–1200; ME *payen* < OF *paier* < ML *pācāre* to satisfy, settle (a debt), L: to pacify (by force of arms). See PEACE]
—**Syn. 1.** discharge, liquidate. **3.** reward, reimburse, indemnify. **27.** remuneration, emolument, fee, honorarium, income, allowance. PAY, WAGE or WAGES, SALARY, STIPEND are terms for amounts of money or equivalent benefits, usually given at a regular rate or at regular intervals, in return for services. PAY is the general term: *His pay went up every year.* WAGE usually designates the pay given at an hourly, daily, or weekly rate, often for manual or semiskilled work; WAGES usually means the cumulative amount paid at regular intervals for such work: *an hourly wage; weekly wages.* SALARY designates a fixed, periodic payment for regular work or services, usually computed on a monthly or yearly basis: *an annual salary paid in twelve equal monthly installments.* STIPEND designates a periodic payment, either as a professional salary or, more commonly, as a salary in return for special services or as a grant in support of creative or scholarly work: *an annual stipend for work as a consultant; a stipend to cover living expenses.*

pay[2] (pā), *v.t.,* **payed, pay•ing.** *Naut.* to coat or cover (seams, a ship's bottom, etc.) with pitch, tar, or the like. [1620–30; < MF *peier,* OF < L *picāre* to smear with pitch, deriv. of *pix* (s. *pic-*) PITCH[2]]

pay•a•ble (pā′ə bəl), *adj.* **1.** to be paid; due: *a loan payable in 30 days.* **2.** capable of being or liable to be paid. **3.** profitable. **4.** *Law.* imposing an immediate obligation on the debtor. —*n.* **5.** an amount, bill, etc., that is to be paid. **6. payables,** the accounts payable of a business: *Payables are now handled by our computer.* [1400–50; late ME; see PAY[1], -ABLE] —**pay′a•bil′i•ty, pay′a•ble•ness,** *n.* —**pay′a•bly,** *adv.*

pay-as-you-go (pā′əz yo͞o gō′), *n.* **1.** the principle or practice of paying for goods and services at the time of purchase, rather than relying on credit. —*adj.* **2.** of, pertaining to, or based on such a principle or practice: *a pay-as-you-go budget.* [1830–40, *Amer.*]

pay•back (pā′bak′), *n.* **1.** the period of time required to recoup a capital investment. **2.** the return on an investment: *a payback of 15 percent tax-free.* **3.** the act or fact of paying back; repayment. **4.** something done in retaliation: *a really vicious payback for years of being snubbed.* [1955–60; n. use of v. phrase *pay back*]

pay•box (pā′boks′), *n. Brit.* See **box office** (def. 1). [1850–55; PAY[1] + BOX[1]]

pay′ ca′ble. See **cable television.** [1970–75]

pay•check (pā′chek′), *n.* **1.** a bank check given as salary or wages. **2.** salary or wages: *One can stretch the paycheck only just so far.* [1900–05; PAY[1] + CHECK]

pay•day (pā′dā′), *n.* **1.** the day on which wages are given, payment is made, etc. **2.** *Informal.* a day or period during which a great deal of money, success, fame, etc., is won or obtained: *Payday came when she was given a screen test by a big Hollywood studio.* [1520–30; PAY[1] + DAY]

pay′ dirt′, 1. soil, gravel, or ore that can be mined profitably. **2.** *Informal.* any source of success or wealth; a fortunate discovery or profitable venture: *After months of experimentation, the scientists finally hit pay dirt.* **3.** *Football.* See **end zone** (def. 1). [1855–60, *Amer.*]

PAYE, pay as you earn.

pay•ee (pā ē′), *n.* a person to whom a check, money, etc., is payable. [1750–60; PAY[1] + -EE]

pay′ en′velope, 1. an envelope containing a paycheck or wages. **2.** *Informal.* wages or salary; paycheck.

pay•er (pā′ər), *n.* **1.** a person who pays. **2.** the person named in a bill or note who has to pay the holder. [1325–75; ME; see PAY[1], -ER[1]]

pay′ grade′, the grade of a member of the armed services established according to a scale of increasing amounts of base pay and related to but not identical with official rank.

pay-in (pā′in′), *n.* a deposit in an account. [n. use of the v. phrase *pay in*]

pay•load (pā′lōd′), *n.* **1.** the part of a cargo producing revenue or income, usually expressed in weight. **2.** the number of paying passengers, as on an airplane. **3.** *Aerospace, Mil.* **a.** the bomb load, warhead, cargo, or passengers of an aircraft, a rocket, missile, etc., for delivery at a target or destination. **b.** the total complement of equipment carried by a spacecraft for the performance of a particular mission in space. **c.** the explosive energy of the warhead of a missile or of the bomb load of an aircraft: *a payload of 50 megatons.* [1925–30; PAY[1] + LOAD]

pay′load assist′ mod′ule, a U.S. solid-propellant rocket used to boost a medium-weight spacecraft from a circular low-earth orbit to an elliptical transfer orbit for later insertion into a geosynchronous orbit. *Abbr.:* PAM Cf. **inertial upper stage.** [1980–85]

pay′load bay′. See **cargo bay.**

pay•load•er (pā′lō′dər), *n.* a heavy, wheeled vehicle with a large, movable blade or scoop at the front. Cf. **bulldozer.** [1950–55; PAYLOAD + -ER[1]]

pay′load spe′cialist, 1. an astronaut trained to handle highly complex or classified equipment carried aboard a space shuttle and to conduct experiments in space. **2.** a specialist in transporting cargo. [1970–75]

pay•mas•ter (pā′mas′tər, -mä′stər), *n.* a person authorized by a company, government, etc., to pay out wages or salaries, esp. in the military. [1540–50; PAY[1] + MASTER] —**pay′mas′ter•ship′,** *n.*

pay•ment (pā′mənt), *n.* **1.** something that is paid; an amount paid; compensation; recompense. **2.** the act of paying. **3.** reward or punishment; requital. [1300–50; ME, var. of *paiement* < MF. See PAY[1], -MENT]

pay′ment bond′. See under **contract bond.**

Payne (pān), *n.* **John Howard,** 1791–1852, U.S. actor and dramatist.

pay•nim (pā′nim), *n. Archaic.* **1.** a pagan or heathen. **2.** a Muslim. **3.** pagandom; heathendom. [1200–50; ME: pagan (n. and adj.), pagan countries, heathendom < OF *pai(e)nime* < LL *pāgānismus* PAGANISM] —**pay′nim•hood′,** *n.*

pay•off (pā′ôf′, -of′), *n.* **1.** the payment of a salary, debt, wager, etc. **2.** the time at which such payment is made. **3.** the consequence, outcome, or final sequence in a series of events, actions, or circumstances: *The payoff was when they fired him.* **4.** *Informal.* the climax of

CONCISE ETYMOLOGY KEY: <, descended or borrowed from; >, whence; b., blend of, blended; c., cognate with; cf., compare; deriv., derivative; equiv., equivalent; imit., imitative; obl., oblique; r., replacing; s., stem; sp., spelling, spelled; resp., respelling, respelled; trans., translation; ?, origin unknown; *, unattested; ‡, probably earlier than. See the full key inside the front cover.

something, esp. a story or joke. **5.** a settlement or reckoning, as in retribution or reward. **6.** *Informal.* a bribe. —*adj.* **7.** yielding results, esp. rewarding or decisive results: *The payoff play was the long pass into the end zone.* [1910–15; n., adj. use of v. phrase *pay off*]
—Syn. 3. climax, upshot, finale.

pay·o·la (pā ō′lə), *n. Informal.* a secret or private payment in return for the promotion of a product, service, etc., through the abuse of one's position, influence, or facilities. [1935–40, *Amer.*; PAY[1] + -OLA]

pay·out (pā′out′), *n.* **1.** an act or instance of paying, expending, or disbursing. **2.** money paid, expended, or disbursed, as a dividend or winning: *He went to the betting window to collect his payout.* [1900–05; n. use of v. phrase *pay out*]

pay′out ra′tio, the ratio between dividends paid out and earnings per share of common stock within a time period.

pay-per-view (pā′pûr′vyo͞o′, -pər-), *Television.* —*n.* **1.** a system requiring that a subscriber pay for each program viewed. —*adj.* **2.** noting or pertaining to such a system. *Abbr.:* ppv

pay′ phone′, a public telephone requiring that the caller deposit coins or use a credit card to pay for a call. Also called **pay′ sta′tion.** [1935–40]

pay·roll (pā′rōl′), *n.* **1.** a list of employees to be paid, with the amount due to each. **2.** the sum total of these amounts. **3.** the actual money on hand for distribution: *The bandits got away with the payroll.* **4.** the total number of people employed by a business firm or organization. —*v.t.* **5.** to fund or subsidize: *to be payrolled by the State Department.* [1765–75; PAY[1] + ROLL]

pay·roll·er (pā′rō′lər), *n. Informal.* a wage earner, esp. a government employee. [PAYROLL + -ER[1]]

pay′roll tax′, a tax levied against the amount of wages and salaries paid workers. [1980–85]

Pay·san·dú (pī′sän do͞o′), *n.* a city in W Uruguay, on the Uruguay River. 80,000.

payt., payment.

pay′ tel′evision, **1.** a commercial service that broadcasts or provides television programs to viewers who pay a monthly charge or a per-program fee. **2.** the programming provided. Also called **pay-TV** (pā′tē′vē′), **subscription television.** [1955–60]

Paz (päz; *Sp.* päs), *n.* **Oc·ta·vio** (ok tā′vē ō′; *Sp.* ôk tä-vyô), born 1914, Mexican poet and essayist: Nobel prize 1990.

pa·zazz (pə zaz′), *n.* pizazz.

Paz Es·tens·so·ro (päs′ es′tens sô′rô), *n.* **Víc·tor** (bēk′tôr), born 1907, Bolivian economist and statesman: president 1952–56, 1960–64.

Paz·y·ryk (paz′ə rik), *n.* the site of 40 wood-lined pit tombs c500–c300 B.C. in the Altai Mountains of central Asia, containing the tattooed bodies of nomadic chieftains of the eastern Steppes and grave goods all well-preserved in a frozen state.

PB, power brakes.

Pb, *Symbol, Chem.* lead. [< L *plumbum*]

P.B., **1.** British Pharmacopoeia. [< L *Pharmacopoeia Britannica*] **2.** Prayer Book.

p.b., *Baseball.* passed ball; passed balls.

PBA, **1.** Professional Bowlers Association. **2.** Public Buildings Administration.

P.B.A., Patrolmen's Benevolent Association.

PBB, *Chem.* any of the highly toxic and possibly carcinogenic aromatic compounds consisting of two benzene rings in which bromine takes the place of two or more hydrogen atoms: used as a fire retardant and additive for plastics. Also called **polybrominated biphenyl.** [*p*(*oly*)*b*(*rominated*) *b*(*iphenyl*)]

PBS, Public Broadcasting Service: a network of noncommercial television stations devoted to educational and other quality programming and funded by members' contributions, government allocations, and grants from private industry.

PBX, a manually or automatically operated telephone facility that handles communications within an office, office building, or organization and that is connected to the public telephone network. Cf. **PABX** [*P*(*rivate*) *B*(*ranch*) *Ex*(*change*)]

PC, **1.** See **Peace Corps.** **2.** See **personal computer.** **3.** See **politically correct.** **4.** See **printed circuit.** **5.** See **professional corporation.**

pc, picocurie; picocuries.

pc., **1.** *pl.* **pcs.** piece. **2.** prices.

P/C, **1.** petty cash. **2.** price current. Also, **p/c**

P.C., **1.** Past Commander. **2.** *Brit.* Police Constable. **3.** See **politically correct.** **4.** Post Commander. **5.** *Brit.* Prince Consort. **6.** *Brit.* Privy Council. **7.** See **professional corporation.**

p.c., **1.** percent. **2.** petty cash. **3.** postal card. **4.** (in prescriptions) after eating; after meals. [< L *post cibōs*] **5.** price current. **6.** See **printed circuit.**

PCB, a family of highly toxic chemical compounds consisting of two benzene rings in which chlorine takes the place of two or more hydrogen atoms: known to cause skin diseases and suspected of causing birth defects and cancer. Also called **polychlorinated biphenyl.** [*p*(*oly*)-*c*(*hlorinated*) *b*(*iphenyl*)]

PC board, *Electronics.* See under **printed circuit.**

P-Celt·ic (pē′sel′tik, -kel′-), *n.* **1.** the subbranch of Celtic in which the Proto-Indo-European *kw*-sound became a *p*-sound. Welsh, Breton, Cornish, and Gaulish belong to P-Celtic. —*adj.* **2.** of or belonging to P-Celtic.

pcf, pounds per cubic foot.

pci, pounds per cubic inch.

PCM, **1.** plug-compatible manufacturer. **2.** *Telecommunications.* pulse-code modulation.

PCNB, pentachloronitrobenzene.

PCP, **1.** *Slang.* phencyclidine. [perh. *p*(*hen*)*c*(*yclidine*) + (*peace*) *p*(*ill*), an earlier designation] **2.** See **pneumocystis pneumonia.**

pct., percent.

PCT theorem, *Physics.* See **CPT theorem.**

PCV, *Auto.* See **positive crankcase ventilation.**

PCV valve, *Auto.* a valve used to control and direct the flow of gases during positive crankcase ventilation.

Pd, *Symbol, Chem.* palladium.

pd., paid.

P.D., **1.** per diem. **2.** Police Department. **3.** *Insurance.* property damage.

p.d., **1.** per diem. **2.** potential difference.

PDB, para-dichlorobenzene.

Pd.B., Bachelor of Pedagogy.

Pd.D., Doctor of Pedagogy.

pdl, poundal.

Pd.M., Master of Pedagogy.

P.D.Q., *Informal.* immediately; at once: *You'd better get started P.D.Q.* Also, **PDQ** [1870–75; *p*(*retty*) *d*(*amn*) *q*(*uick*)]

PDT, Pacific Daylight Time.

pe (pā), *n.* **1.** the 17th letter of the Hebrew alphabet. **2.** either of the consonant sounds represented by this letter. Also, **peh.** [1895–1900; < Heb *pē*, akin to *peh* mouth]

p/e, See **price-earnings ratio.** Also, **P/E, PE, P-E, p-e**

P.E., **1.** Petroleum Engineer. **2.** physical education. **3.** Presiding Elder. **4.** See **printer's error.** **5.** *Statistics.* probable error. **6.** Professional Engineer. **7.** Protestant Episcopal.

p.e., See **printer's error.**

pea[1] (pē), *n., pl.* **peas,** (*Archaic or Brit. Dial.*) **pease;** *adj.* —*n.* **1.** the round, edible seed of a widely cultivated plant, *Pisum sativum*, of the legume family. **2.** the plant itself. **3.** the green, somewhat inflated pod of this plant. **4.** any of various related or similar plants or their seed, as the chickpea. **5.** something resembling a pea, esp. in being small and round. —*adj.* **6.** pertaining to, growing, containing, or cooked with peas: *We cultivated some tomato vines and a pea patch.* **7.** small or small and round (usually used in combination). **8.** See **pea coal.** Also called **English pea, garden pea, green pea** (for defs. 1, 2). [1275–1325; ME; back formation from PEASE, taken as pl.] **—pea′like′,** *adj.*

pea[2] (pē), *n. Naut.* bill[3] (def. 4). [1825–35; perh. short for PEAK[1]]

pea′ a′phid, a large green aphid, *Acyrthosiphon pisum*, that is a pest of peas, clovers, alfalfa, and similar plants and occurs throughout North America. [1920–25]

pea′ bean′, *Chiefly New Eng. and New York State.* a variety of kidney bean having a small, white seed, used dried for food. [1885–90]

Pea·bod·y (pē′bod′ē, -bə dē), *n.* **1. Elizabeth Palmer,** 1804–94, U.S. educator and reformer: founded the first kindergarten in the U.S. **2. Endicott,** 1857–1944, U.S. educator. **3. George,** 1795–1869, U.S. merchant, banker, and philanthropist in England. **4.** a city in NE Massachusetts. 45,976.

pea′body bird′, *Chiefly New Eng.* the white-throated sparrow. [1860–65, *Amer.*; prob. imit.]

peace (pēs), *n., interj., v.,* **peaced, peac·ing.** —*n.* **1.** the normal, nonwarring condition of a nation, group of nations, or the world. **2.** (*often cap.*) an agreement or treaty between warring or antagonistic nations, groups, etc., to end hostilities and abstain from further fighting or antagonism: *the Peace of Ryswick.* **3.** a state of mutual harmony between people or groups, esp. in personal relations: *Try to live in peace with your neighbors.* **4.** the normal freedom from civil commotion and violence of a community; public order and security: *He was arrested for being drunk and disturbing the peace.* **5.** cessation of or freedom from any strife or dissension. **6.** freedom of the mind from annoyance, distraction, anxiety, an obsession, etc.; tranquillity; serenity. **7.** a state of tranquillity or serenity: *May he rest in peace.* **8.** a state or condition conducive to, proceeding from, or characterized by tranquillity: *the peace of a mountain resort.* **9.** silence; stillness: *The cawing of a crow broke the afternoon's peace.* **10.** (*cap., italics*) a comedy (421 B.C.) by Aristophanes. **11. at peace, a.** in a state or relationship of nonbelligerence or concord; not at war. **b.** untroubled; tranquil; content. **c.** deceased. **12. hold** or **keep one's peace,** to refrain from or cease speaking; keep silent: *He told her to hold her peace until he had finished.* **13. keep the peace,** to maintain order; cause to refrain from creating a disturbance: *Several officers of the law were on hand to keep the peace.* **14. make one's peace with,** to become reconciled with: *He repaired the fence he had broken and made his peace with the neighbor on whose property it stood.* **15. make peace,** to ask for or arrange a cessation of hostilities or antagonism. —*interj.* **16.** (used to express greeting or farewell or to request quietness or silence). —*v.i.* **17.** *Obs.* to be or become silent. [1125–75; ME *pes* < OF, var. of *pais* < L *pax* (s. *pāc-*); akin to PACT] **—peace′·less,** *adj.* **—peace′less·ness,** *n.* **—peace′like′,** *adj.*
—Syn. 2. armistice, truce, pact, accord. **3.** rapport, concord, amity. **6.** calm, quiet. **—Ant. 6.** insecurity, disturbance.

peace·a·ble (pē′sə bəl), *adj.* **1.** inclined or disposed to avoid strife or dissension; not argumentative or hostile: *a peaceable person; a peaceable disposition.* **2.** peaceful; tranquil: *in peaceable periods; a peaceable adjustment of a dispute.* [1300–50; ME *pesible* < MF *paisible.* See PEACE, -ABLE] **—peace′a·ble·ness,** *n.* **—peace′a·bly,** *adv.*

—Syn. 1. amicable, friendly, amiable. **—Ant. 1.** quarrelsome, hostile.

Peace′ Corps′, a civilian organization, sponsored by the U.S. government, that sends volunteers to instruct citizens of underdeveloped countries in the execution of industrial, agricultural, educational, and health programs.

peace′ div′idend, money cut by a government from its defense budget as a result of the cessation of hostilities with other countries. [1985–90]

peace′ dove′, dove[1] (def. 5).

peace·ful (pēs′fəl), *adj.* **1.** characterized by peace; free from war, strife, commotion, violence, or disorder: *a peaceful reign; a peaceful demonstration.* **2.** of, pertaining to, or characteristic of a state or time of peace. **3.** peaceable; not argumentative, quarrelsome, or hostile: *a peaceful disposition.* [1250–1300; ME *pesful.* See PEACE, -FUL] **—peace′ful·ly,** *adv.* **—peace′ful·ness,** *n.*
—Syn. 1. PEACEFUL, PLACID, SERENE, TRANQUIL refer to what is characterized by lack of strife or agitation. PEACEFUL today is rarely applied to persons; it refers to situations, scenes, and activities free of disturbances or, occasionally, of warfare: *a peaceful life.* PLACID, SERENE, TRANQUIL are used mainly of persons; when used of things (usually elements of nature) there is a touch of personification. PLACID suggests an unruffled calm that verges on complacency: *a placid disposition; a placid stream.* SERENE is a somewhat nobler word; when used of persons it suggests dignity, composure, and graciousness: *a serene old man;* when applied to nature there is a suggestion of mellowness: *the serene landscapes of autumn.* TRANQUIL implies a command of emotions, often because of strong faith, which keeps one unagitated even in the midst of excitement or danger.

peace′ful coexist′ence, competition without war, or a policy of peace between nations of widely differing political systems and ideologies, esp. between Communist and non-Communist nations: *peaceful coexistence between the U.S. and the Soviet Union.* [1915–20; often as trans. of Russ *mírnoe sosushchestvovánie*]

peace·keep·er (pēs′kē′pər), *n.* **1.** a person who maintains or restores peace and amity; mediator. **2.** a soldier, military force, etc., deployed to maintain or restore peace. [1570–80; PEACE + KEEPER]

peace·keep·ing (pēs′kē′ping), *n.* **1.** the maintenance of international peace and security by the deployment of military forces in a particular area: *the United Nations' efforts toward peacekeeping.* **2.** an instance of this. —*adj.* **3.** for or pertaining to peacekeeping: *peacekeeping forces.* [1960–65; PEACE + KEEPING]

peace′ lil′y, spathiphyllum.

peace·mak·er (pēs′mā′kər), *n.* a person, group, or nation that tries to make peace, esp. by reconciling parties who disagree, quarrel, or fight. [1375–1425; late ME; see PEACE, MAKER] **—peace′mak′ing,** *n., adj.*
—Syn. intermediary, conciliator, mediator, arbitrator.

peace·nik (pēs′nik), *n. Slang* (*often disparaging*). an activist or demonstrator who opposes war and military intervention; pacifist. [1960–65, *Amer.*; PEACE + -NIK]

peace′ offen′sive, an active program, policy, propaganda campaign, etc., by a national government for the purpose of terminating a war or period of hostility, lessening international tensions, or promoting peaceful cooperation with other nations. [1915–20]

peace′ of′fering, **1.** any offering made to procure peace. **2.** a sacrificial offering made in order to assure communion with God. Ex. 20:24; Lev. 7:11–18. [1525–35]

peace′ of′ficer, a civil officer appointed to preserve the public peace, as a sheriff or constable. [1705–15]

peace′ pipe′, calumet. [1770–80]

Peace′ Riv′er, a river in W Canada, flowing NE from the Rocky Mountains in E British Columbia through Alberta to the Slave River. 1050 mi. (1690 km) long.

peace′ sign′, a sign representing "peace," made by extending the forefinger and middle finger upward in a V-shape with the palm turned outward. [1965–70]

peace·time (pēs′tīm′), *n.* **1.** a time or period of peace. —*adj.* **2.** of or for such a period: *peacetime uses of atomic energy.* [1545–55; PEACE + TIME]

peach[1] (pēch), *n.* **1.** the subacid, juicy, drupaceous fruit of a tree, *Prunus persica*, of the rose family. **2.** the tree itself, cultivated in temperate climates. **3.** a light pinkish yellow, as of a peach. **4.** *Informal.* a person or thing that is especially attractive, liked, or enjoyed. —*adj.* **5.** made or cooked with peaches or a flavor like that of a peach: *peach pie.* **6.** of the color peach. [1325–75; ME *peche* < MF < VL **pess*(*i*)*ca*, neut. pl. (taken as fem. sing.) of L *Persicum*, *mālum Persicum* peach, lit., Persian apple; cf. OE *persoc*, G *Pfirsich*, D *perzik* peach, all << L; cf. APRICOT] **—peach′like′,** *adj.*

peach[2] (pēch), *Slang.* —*v.i.* **1.** to inform against an accomplice or associate. —*v.t.* **2.** to inform against; betray. [1425–75; late ME *peche*, aph. var. of ME *apeche* < AF *apecher* < LL *impedicāre* to hold up. See IMPEACH] **—peach′er,** *n.*

peach′ bark′ bee′tle, a bark beetle, *Phloeotribus liminaris*, that feeds on and nests in peach and other drupaceous trees.

peach′ blos′som, the flower of the peach tree: the state flower of Delaware. [1655–65]

peach·blow (pēch′blō′), *n.* a delicate purplish pink. [1820–30, *Amer.*; PEACH[1] + BLOW[3]]

peach′blow glass′, an American art glass made in various pale colors and sometimes having an underlayer of milk glass. [1885–90]

peach′ bran′dy, brandy distilled from the fermented juice of peaches. [1705–15, *Amer.*]

peach•er•i•no (pē′chə rē′nō), *n., pl.* **-nos.** *Informal (older use).* peach[1] (def. 4). [1895–1900; PEACH[1] + *-erino,* alter. of -EROO, after Sp or It words ending in *-ino*]

peach′ Mel′ba, a dessert consisting of cooked peach halves served with vanilla ice cream and Melba sauce. Also, **peach′ mel′ba, pêche Melba.** [1925–30, *Amer.*]

peach′ moth′. See **Oriental fruit moth.**

peach′ tree′ bor′er, the larva of any of several clearwing moths, as *Sanninoidea exitiosa,* that bore into the wood of the peach and other drupaceous trees. [1840–50, *Amer.*]

peach•y (pē′chē), *adj.,* **peach•i•er, peach•i•est. 1.** resembling a peach, as in color or appearance. **2.** *Informal.* excellent; wonderful; fine. [1590–1600; PEACH[1] + -Y[1]] **—peach′i•ness,** *n.*

peach•y-keen (pē′chē kēn′), *adj. Informal.* peachy (def. 2). [1955–60, *Amer.*]

pea′ coal′, 1. anthracite in sizes ranging from under 13/16 in. (2.1 cm) to over 3/8 in. (1 cm). **2.** bituminous in sizes ranging from under 3/4 in. (1.9 cm) to over 3/8 in. (1 cm). [1880–85]

pea•coat (pē′kōt′), *n.* See **pea jacket.** Also, **pea′ coat′.** [1780–90, *Amer.*; *pea* (see PEA JACKET) + COAT]

pea•cock (pē′kok′), *n., pl.* **-cocks,** (*esp. collectively*) **-cock.** *v.* **—***n.* **1.** the male of the peafowl distinguished by its long, erectile, greenish, iridescent tail coverts that are brilliantly marked with ocellated spots and that can be spread in a fan. **2.** any peafowl. **3.** a vain, self-conscious person. **4.** (*cap.*) *Astron.* the constellation Pavo. **—***v.i.* **5.** to make a vainglorious display; strut like a peacock. [1250–1300; ME *pecok,* equiv. to *pe-* (OE *pēa* peafowl < L *pāvōn-* PAVO) + *cok* (OE *coc* COCK[1])] **—pea′•cock′er•y, pea′cock′ism,** *n.* **—pea′cock′ish, pea′•cock′y,** *adj.* **—pea′cock′ish•ly,** *adv.* **—pea′cock′•ish•ness,** *n.*

peacock (peafowl), *Pavo cristatus,* head and body 2½ ft. (0.8 m); train 5 ft. (1.5 m)

Pea•cock (pē′kok′), *n.* **Thomas Love,** 1785–1866, English poet and novelist.

pea′cock blue′, a lustrous greenish blue, as of certain peacock feathers. [1880–85]

pea′cock chair′, a wicker armchair with a high, circular back.

pea•cock-flow•er (pē′kok′flou′ər), *n.* See **royal poinciana.** [1880–85]

pea′cock ore′, *Mineral.* bornite. [1855–60]

pea′cock plant′, a plant, *Calathea makoyana,* native to Brazil, having leaves that are spotted on the upper surface and purple on the lower surface.

pea′cock worm′. See **feather-duster worm.**

pea′ crab′, any of several tiny crabs of the family Pinnotheridae, the female of which lives as a commensal in the shells of bivalve mollusks. [1830–40]

pea•fowl (pē′foul′), *n., pl.* **-fowls,** (*esp. collectively*) **-fowl.** any of several gallinaceous birds of the genera *Pavo,* of India, Sri Lanka, southeastern Asia, and the East Indies, and *Afropavo,* of Africa. Cf. **peacock, peahen.** [1795–1805; *pea* (see PEACOCK) + FOWL]

peag (pēg), *n.* wampum (def. 1). [1640–50, *Amer.*; shortening of WAMPUMPEAG]

pea′ green′, a medium or yellowish green. [1745–55]

pea•hen (pē′hen′), *n.* the female peafowl. [1375–1425; late ME *pehenne.* See PEACOCK, HEN]

pea′ jack′et, 1. a short coat of thick wool, usually double-breasted and navy in color, worn by seamen, fishermen, etc. **2.** a jacket or short coat styled like this, worn by adults and children. Also called **peacoat, pea coat.** [1715–25, *Amer.*; *pea,* var. sp. of *pay, pee, pie* coat of coarse woolen cloth (late ME *pee, pey, pie;* akin to D *pij,* dial. Fris *pey,* dial. Sw *paje*) + JACKET; perh. modeled on Fris (N dial.) *pijekkat*]

peak[1] (pēk), *n.* **1.** the pointed top of a mountain or ridge. **2.** a mountain with a pointed summit. **3.** the pointed top of anything. **4.** the highest or most important point or level: *the peak of her political career.* **5.** the maximum point, degree, or volume of anything: *Oil prices reached their peak last year.* **6.** a time of the day or year when traffic, use, demand, etc., is greatest and charges, fares, or the like are at the maximum: *Early evening is the peak on commuter railroads.* **7.** the higher fare, charges, etc., during such a period: *If you fly during the Christmas holidays, you'll have to pay peak.* **8.** *Physics.* **a.** the maximum value of a quantity during a specified time interval: *a voltage peak.* **b.** the maximum power consumed or produced by a unit or group of units in a stated period of time. **9.** a projecting point: *the peak of a man's beard.* **10.** See **widow's peak. 11.** a projecting front piece, or visor, of a cap. **12.** *Phonet.* nucleus (def. 8a). **13.** *Naut.* **a.** the contracted part of a ship's hull at the bow or the stern. **b.** the upper after corner of a sail that is extended by a gaff. See diag. under **sail. c.** the outer extremity of a gaff. **—***v.i.* **14.** to project in a peak. **15.** to attain a peak of activity, development, popularity, etc.: *The artist peaked in the 1950's.* **—***v.t.* **16.** *Naut.* to raise the after end of (a yard, gaff, etc.) to or toward an angle above the horizontal. **—***adj.* **17.** being at the point of maximum frequency, intensity, use, etc.; busiest or most active: *Hotel rooms are most expensive during the peak travel seasons.* **18.** constituting the highest or maximum level, volume, etc.; optimal; prime: *a machine running at peak performance.* [1520–30; perh. < MLG *pēk* pick, pike] **—peak′less,** *adj.* **—peak′like′,** *adj.*
—Syn. 2, 4. pinnacle. **4.** acme, zenith. **—Ant. 4.** abyss, nadir.

CONCISE ETYMOLOGY KEY: <, descended or borrowed from; >, whence; b., blend of, blended; c., cognate with; cf., compare; deriv., derivative; equiv., equivalent; imit., imitative; obl., oblique; r., replacing; s., stem; sp., spelling, spelled; resp., respelling, respelled; trans., translation; ?, origin unknown; *, unattested; ‡, probably earlier than. See the full key inside the front cover.

peak[2] (pēk), *v.i.* to become weak, thin, and sickly. [1500–10; orig. uncert.] **—peak′ish,** *adj.* **—peak′ish•ly,** *adv.* **—peak′ish•ness,** *n.*

peaked[1] (pēkt, pē′kid), *adj.* having a peak: *a peaked cap.* [1400–50; late ME *pekyd.* See PEAK[1], -ED[3]]

peak•ed[2] (pē′kid), *adj.* pale and drawn in appearance so as to suggest illness or stress; wan and sickly. [PEAK[2] + -ED[2]] **—peak′ed•ly,** *adv.* **—peak′ed•ness,** *n.*

peak′ expe′rience, *Psychol.* a high point in the life of a self-actualizer, during which the person feels ecstatic and more alive and whole than is usual. [1960–65]

peak′ time′. See **prime time.** [1965–70]

peak•y (pē′kē), *adj.,* **peak•i•er, peak•i•est.** peaked[2]. [1870–75; PEAK(ED)[2] + -Y[1]] **—peak′i•ly,** *adv.* **—peak′i•ness,** *n.*

peal (pēl), *n.* **1.** a loud, prolonged ringing of bells. **2.** a set of bells tuned to one another. **3.** a series of changes rung on a set of bells. **4.** any loud, sustained sound or series of sounds, as of cannon, thunder, applause, or laughter. **—***v.t.* **5.** to sound loudly and sonorously: *to peal the bells of a tower.* **6.** *Obs.* to assail with loud sounds. **—***v.i.* **7.** to sound forth in a peal; resound. [1350–1400; ME *pele,* akin to *peal* to beat, strike (now dial.)]
—Syn. 4. reverberation, resounding, clangor.

Peale (pēl), *n.* **1. Charles Will•son** (wil′sən), 1741–1827, and his brother **James,** 1749–1831, U.S. painters. **2. Norman Vincent,** born 1898, U.S. Protestant clergyman and author. **3. Raph•a•elle** (raf′ā el′, -ē el′, rā′-fē-), 1774–1825, and his brother **Rem•brandt** (rem′-brant), 1778–1860, U.S. painters (sons of Charles Willson Peale).

pea•mouth (pē′mouth′), *n., pl.* **-mouths** (-mouths′, -mouthz′). a minnow, *Mylocheilus caurinus,* of northwestern U.S. and British Columbian waters. [PEA[1] + MOUTH]

pe•an (pē′ən), *n.* paean.

Pe•a•no (pē ä′nō; *It.* pe ä′nô), *n.* **Giu•sep•pe** (jo͞o zep′-pe), 1858–1932, Italian mathematician.

Pea′no curve′, *Math.* a curve that passes through every point of a two-dimensional region. [named after G. PEANO]

Pea′no's pos′tulates, *Math.* a collection of axioms concerning the properties of the set of all positive integers, including the principle of mathematical induction. Also called **Pea′no's ax′ioms.** Cf. **principle of mathematical induction.** [named after G. PEANO]

pea•nut (pē′nut′, -nət), *n.* **1.** the pod or the enclosed edible seed of the plant, *Arachis hypogaea,* of the legume family: the pod is forced underground in growing, where it ripens. **2.** the plant itself. **3.** any small or insignificant person or thing. **4. peanuts, a.** *Informal.* a very small amount of money: *working for peanuts.* **b.** *Slang.* barbiturates. **c.** small pieces of Styrofoam used as a packing material. **—***adj.* **5.** of or pertaining to the peanut or peanuts. **6.** made with or from peanuts. **7.** *Informal.* small, insignificant, or petty. [1790–1800, *Amer.*; PEA[1] + NUT]

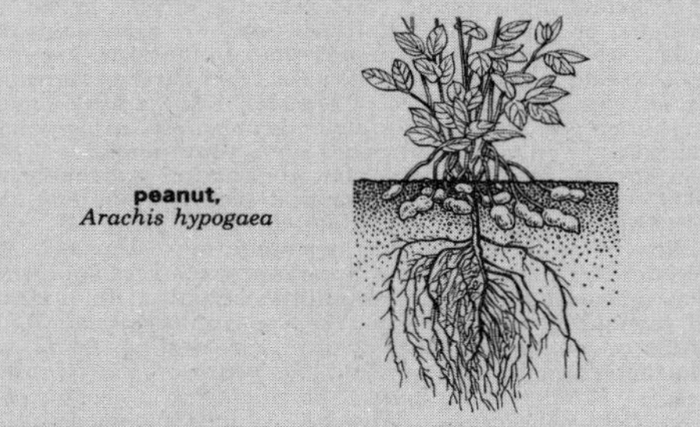
peanut, *Arachis hypogaea*

pea′nut but′ter, a paste made from ground roasted peanuts, used as a spread or in cookery. [1885–90, *Amer.*]

pea′nut gal′lery, 1. *Informal.* the rearmost and cheapest section of seats in the balcony or the uppermost balcony of a theater. **2.** *Slang.* a source of insignificant criticism: *No remarks from the peanut gallery!* [1885–90, *Amer.*]

pea′nut heav′en, *North Midland U.S.* See **peanut gallery** (def. 1).

pea′nut oil′, a yellow to greenish oil expressed or extracted from peanuts, used in cookery, as a vehicle for medicines, and in the manufacture of margarine and soap. Also called **arachis oil.** [1880–85]

pea′nut worm′, any small, unsegmented, marine worm of the phylum Sipuncula, that when disturbed retracts its anterior portion into the body, giving the appearance of a peanut seed. Also called **sipunculid.**

pear (pâr), *n.* **1.** the edible fruit, typically rounded but elongated and growing smaller toward the stem, of a tree, *Pyrus communis,* of the rose family. **2.** the tree itself. [bef. 1000; ME *pe(e)re,* OE *peru* < LL *pira,* fem. sing. use of pl. of L of *pirum* (neut.) pear] **—pear′like′,** *adj.*

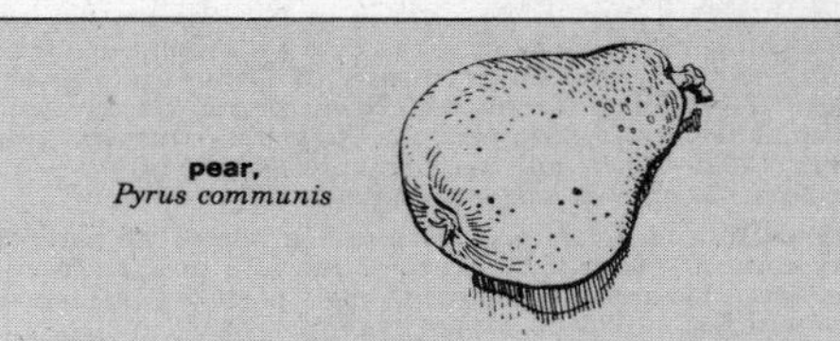
pear, *Pyrus communis*

pear′ haw′, a shrub or small tree, *Crataegus uniflora,* of the eastern and southern coastal areas of the U.S., having pear-shaped, orange-red fruit. Also called **blackthorn.**

pearl[1] (pûrl), *n.* **1.** a smooth, rounded bead formed within the shells of certain mollusks and composed of the mineral aragonite or calcite in a matrix, deposited in concentric layers as a protective coating around an irritating foreign object: valued as a gem when lustrous and finely colored. Cf. **cultured pearl. 2.** something resembling this, as various synthetic substances for use in costume jewelry. **3.** something similar in form, luster, etc., as a dewdrop or a capsule of medicine. **4.** something precious or choice; the finest example of anything: *pearls of wisdom.* **5.** a very pale gray approaching white but commonly with a bluish tinge. **6.** mother-of-pearl: *a pearl-handled revolver.* **7.** *Print.* a 5-point type. **8.** Also called **epithelial pearl.** *Pathol.* a rounded mass of keratin occurring in certain carcinomas of the skin. **9. cast pearls before swine,** to offer or give something of great value to those incapable of appreciating it: *She read them Shakespeare but it was casting pearls before swine.* **—***v.t.* **10.** to adorn or stud with or as with pearls. **11.** to make like pearls, as in form or color. **—***v.i.* **12.** to dive, fish, or search for pearls. **13.** to assume a pearl-like form or appearance. **—***adj.* **14.** resembling a pearl in form or color. **15.** of or pertaining to pearls: *pearl diving.* **16.** set with a pearl or pearls or covered or inlaid with pearls or mother-of-pearl: *a pearl necklace.* **17.** having or reduced to small, rounded grains. [1300–50; ME *perle* < MF < It or assumed VL **perla* (> G *Perle,* OE *pærl*), for L **pernula* (> Pg *perola,* perh. OS *pĕrula*), dim. of L *perna* sea mussel] **—pearl′er,** *n.* **—pearl′ish,** *adj.* **—pearl′like′,** *adj.*

pearl[2] (pûrl), *v.t., v.i., n.* purl[1].

Pearl (pûrl), *n.* **1.** a town in central Mississippi. 20,778. **2.** a female given name.

Pear•land (pâr′land′, -lənd), *n.* a town in SE Texas. 13,248.

pearl•ash (pûrl′ash′), *n.* commercial potassium carbonate. [1720–30; PEARL[1] + ASH[1]]

pearl′ bar′ley, barley milled into small, round grains, used in cooking, esp. in soups. [1700–10]

pearl′ blue′, a light bluish gray. **—pearl′ blu′ish.**

Pearl′ Cit′y, a city on S Oahu, in central Hawaii. 42,575.

pearl′ cot′ton, a two-ply mercerized cotton thread used chiefly in handweaving and needlework. Also, **perle cotton.**

pearl′ da′nio, a slender iridescent tropical cyprinid, *Brachydanio albolineatus,* from parts of southeast Asia: a popular freshwater aquarium fish.

pearl′ div′er, a person who dives for pearl oysters or other pearl-bearing mollusks. [1660–70]

pearl•es•cent (pər les′ənt), *adj.* having an iridescent luster resembling that of pearl; nacreous: *healthy skin with a pearlescent glow.* [1945–50; PEARL[1] + -ESCENT, on the model of IRIDESCENT, OPALESCENT, etc.]

pearl′ es′sence, a lustrous, silvery-white substance obtained from the scales of certain fishes or derived synthetically, as from mercuric chloride: used chiefly in the manufacture of simulated pearls and as a pigment in lacquer **(pearl′ lac′quer).** [1920–25]

pearl•eye (pûrl′ī′), *n., pl.* **-eyes,** (*esp. collectively*) **-eye.** any of several deep-sea fishes of the family Scopelarchidae, having large, hooked teeth on the tongue, telescopic eyes, and an iridescent patch on each eye tube. [1835–45; PEARL[1] + EYE] **—pearl′eyed′,** *adj.*

pearl•fish (pûrl′fish′), *n., pl.* **-fish•es,** (*esp. collectively*) **-fish.** any of several small fishes of the family Carapidae, living within pearl oysters, sea cucumbers, starfishes, etc. [1585–95; PEARL[1] + FISH]

pearl′ gray′, a very pale bluish gray. [1790–1800]

Pearl′ Har′bor, 1. a harbor near Honolulu, on S Oahu, in Hawaii: surprise attack by Japan on the U.S. naval base and other military installations December 7, 1941. **2.** any significant or crippling defeat, betrayal, loss, etc., that comes unexpectedly.

pearl′ hom′iny. See under **hominy.**

pearl•ite (pûr′līt), *n.* **1.** *Metall.* a microscopic lamellar structure found in iron or steel, composed of alternating layers of ferrite and cementite. **2.** *Petrog.* perlite. [1885–90; PEARL[1] + -ITE[1]] **—pearl•it•ic** (pûr lit′ik), *adj.*

pearl•ized (pûr′līzd), *adj.* resembling or made to resemble mother-of-pearl; iridescent: *pearlized buttons.* [1950–55; PEARL[1] + -IZE + -ED[2]]

pearl′ light′ning. See **bead lightning.**

pearl′ mil′let, a tall grass, *Pennisetum americanum* (or *P. glaucum*), cultivated in Africa, the Orient, and the southern U.S. for its edible seeds and as a forage plant. Also called **African millet, Indian millet.** [1885–90]

pearl′ mold′ing, *Archit.* a molding having the form of a row of pearls. Also called **bead molding, Paternoster.**

pearl′ on′ion, a small white onion, often pickled and used as an appetizer or garnish. [1885–90]

pearl′ oys′ter, any of several marine bivalve mollusks of the family Pteriidae, some of which form pearls of great value, inhabiting waters of eastern Asia and off the coasts of Panama and Lower California. [1685–95]

pearl′ perch′, an edible marine fish, *Glaucosoma scapulare,* of eastern Australian coastal waters.

Pearl′ Riv′er, **1.** a river flowing from central Mississippi into the Gulf of Mexico. 485 mi. (780 km) long. **2.** See **Zhu Jiang.**

pearl′ tapio′ca. See under **tapioca.**

pearl·y (pûr′lē), *adj.,* **pearl·i·er, pearl·i·est. 1.** like a pearl, esp. in being white or lustrous; nacreous: *her pearly teeth.* **2.** adorned with or abounding in pearls or mother-of-pearl. [1400–50; late ME *peerly.* See PEARL[1], -Y[1]] **—pearl′i·ness,** *n.*

Pearl′y Gates′, the entrance to heaven.

pearl′y nau′tilus, nautilus (def. 1). [1770–80]

pearl′y ra′zorfish. See under **razorfish.**

pearl′y white′, **1.** white and lustrous as a pearl. **2. pearly whites,** *Slang.* teeth. [1890–95]

pear′ psyl′la, a small jumping plant louse, *Psylla pyricola,* originally of Europe, that is a major pest of pears in the eastern U.S. [1900–05; < NL *Psylla,* genus name < Gk: flea]

Pears (pârz), *n.* **Peter,** 1910–86, British tenor.

pear-shaped (pâr′shāpt′), *adj.* **1.** having the shape of a pear; tapering near the top and bulging toward the base or bottom: *a pear-shaped vase.* **2.** (of a vocal tone) clear, resonant, and without harshness; full-bodied. [1750–60]

Pear·son (pēr′sən), *n.* **1. Drew** (*Andrew Russell Pearson*), 1897–1969, U.S. journalist. **2. Karl,** 1857–1936, English statistician. **3. Lester Bowles** (bōlz), 1897–1972, Canadian diplomat and politician: Nobel prize for peace 1957; prime minister 1963–68.

peart (pērt, pyert), *adj. Dial.* lively; brisk; cheerful. [1590–1600; var. of PERT] **—peart′ly,** *adv.* **—peart′·ness,** *n.*

pear·wood (pâr′wo͝od′), *n.* the hard, fine-grained, reddish wood of the pear tree, used for ornamentation, small articles of furniture, and musical instruments. [1910–15; PEAR + WOOD[1]]

Pea·ry (pēr′ē), *n.* **Robert Edwin,** 1856–1920, U.S. admiral and arctic explorer.

peas·ant (pez′ənt), *n.* **1.** a member of a class of persons, as in Europe, Asia, and Latin America, who are small farmers or farm laborers of low social rank. **2.** a coarse, unsophisticated, boorish, uneducated person of little financial means. *—adj.* **3.** of, pertaining to, or characteristic of peasants or their traditions, way of life, crafts, etc. **4.** of or designating a style of clothing modeled on the folk costumes of Western cultures, esp. women's full-sleeved, round-necked blouses and long, full skirts. [1375–1425; late ME *paissaunt* < AF *paisant,* OF *païsant,* earlier *païsenc,* equiv. to *païs* country (< LL *pāgēnsis,* equiv. to L *pāg(us)* country district + *-ēnsis* -ENSIS) + *-enc* < Gmc (see -ING[3])] **—peas′ant·like′,** *adj.*

peas′ant propri′etor, a peasant who owns land, esp. the land he or she tills. [1785–95] **—peas′ant propri′·etorship.**

peas·ant·ry (pez′ən trē), *n.* **1.** peasants collectively. **2.** the status or character of a peasant. [1545–55; PEASANT + -RY]

pease (pēz), *n., pl.* **pease.** *Archaic.* **1.** a pea. **2.** pl. of **pea.** [bef. 900; ME *pese,* OE *peose, pise* < LL *pisa* fem. sing. use of pl. of L *pisum* (neut.) < Gk *píson* pea, pulse] **—pease′like′,** *adj.*

pease·cod (pēz′kod′), *n.* **1.** the pod of the pea. **2.** the front of a 16th-century doublet, quilted or stuffed to form a pointed bulge over the stomach and abdomen. [1325–75; ME *pesecodde.* See PEASE, COD[2]]

pease′cod breast′plate, *Armor.* a breastplate having a long central ridge terminating in a raised area overhanging the waistline.

pease′ pud′ding, *Chiefly Brit.* a pudding of strained split peas mixed with egg. [1750–60]

pea·shoot·er (pē′sho͞o′tər), *n.* a tube through which dried peas, beans, or small pellets are blown, used as a toy. Also called **beanshooter.** [1860–65; PEA[1] + SHOOTER]

pea′ shrub′. See **pea tree.**

pea′ soup′, **1.** a thick soup made from split peas. **2.** *Informal.* a dense, yellow fog. [1705–15]

pea-soup·er (pē′so͞o′pər), *n.* **1.** *Chiefly Brit. Informal.* See **pea soup** (def. 2). **2.** *Canadian Slang* (*disparaging and offensive*). a French Canadian. [1885–90; PEA SOUP + -ER[1]]

peat[1] (pēt), *n.* **1.** a highly organic material found in marshy or damp regions, composed of partially decayed vegetable matter: it is cut and dried for use as fuel. **2.** such vegetable matter used as fertilizer or fuel. [1300–50; ME *pete* (cf. AL *peta*) < ?]

peat[2] (pēt), *n. Obs.* a merry young girl; darling (used as a term of endearment). [1560–70; orig. uncert.]

peat′ bog′, a swamp in which peat has accumulated. [1765–75]

peat·land (pēt′land′), *n.* an extensive tract of land where peat has formed. [1905–10; PEAT[1] + -LAND]

peat′ moss′, **1.** Also called **bog moss.** any moss, esp. of the genus *Sphagnum,* from which peat may form. **2.** such moss after it has been dried, used chiefly as a mulch or seedbed, for acidification. [1225–75 for earlier sense; 1870–80 for def. 1; ME *petemos* (in placename) peat bog]

peat′ pot′, a small flowerpot formed of peat in which a plant can be grown and transplanted without having to be removed. [1375–1425, late ME]

pea′ tree′, any of various small trees or shrubs belonging to the genus *Caragana,* of the legume family, native to central Asia, having showy, usually yellow flowers, cultivated as an ornamental. Also called **pea shrub.** [1815–25]

peat·y (pē′tē), *adj.,* **peat·i·er, peat·i·est.** of, pertaining to, resembling, or containing the substance peat. [1755–65; PEAT[1] + -Y[1]]

peau de soie (pō′ də swä′, pō′ də swä′), a soft, satin-weave cloth of silk or rayon, grainy and having a dull luster, used to make dresses, coats, trimmings, etc. [1865–70; < F: lit., pelt of silk]

pea·vey (pē′vē), *n., pl.* **-veys.** a cant hook with a sharply pointed end, used in handling logs. [1865–70, *Amer.*; named after Joseph *Peavey,* its inventor]

pea·vy (pē′vē), *n., pl.* **-vies.** peavey.

pea′ wee′vil, a seed beetle, *Bruchus pisorum,* the larvae of which live in and feed on the seeds of the pea plant. [1835–45, *Amer.*]

peb·a (peb′ə), *n.* See **nine-banded armadillo.** [1825–35; short for Tupi *tatu-peba,* equiv. to *tatu* armadillo + *peba* low]

peb·ble (peb′əl), *n., v.,* **-bled, -bling.** *—n.* **1.** a small, rounded stone, esp. one worn smooth by the action of water. **2.** Also called **peb′ble leath′er.** leather that has been given a granulated surface. **3.** any granulated or crinkled surface, esp. of a textile. **4.** a transparent colorless rock crystal used for the lenses of eyeglasses. **5.** a lens made from this crystal. *—v.t.* **6.** to prepare (leather) so as to have a granulated surface. **7.** to pelt with or as with pebbles. [1250–1300; ME *pibbil, puble, pobble;* cf. OE *pæbbel* (in place names), *papel-, popel-* (in compounds); phonological relations unclear]

peb′ble dash′, an exterior wall finish composed of mortar against which, while still wet, small pebbles have been thrown and pressed in. Cf. **roughcast.** [1900–05] **—peb′ble-dash′, peb′ble-dashed′,** *adj.*

peb′ble heat′er, a heat exchanger utilizing refractory pellets to store and give off heat.

peb·bly (peb′lē), *adj.* **1.** having or covered with pebbles: *the pebbly beach at Nice.* **2.** (of a texture, design, etc.) having a granular or pebbled surface: *shoes with a pebbly finish.* [1590–1600; PEBBLE + -Y[1]]

pe·brine (pā brēn′), *n.* an infectious disease of silkworms, characterized by a black spotting of the integument and by stunted growth, caused by the protozoan *Nosema bomycis.* [1865–70; < F < Pr *pebrino* lit., peppery, with reference to the black spots. See PEPPER, -INE[1]]

pe·can (pi kän′, -kan′, pē′kan), *n.* **1.** a tall hickory tree, *Carya illinoinensis,* of the southern U.S. and Mexico, cultivated for its oval, smooth-shelled, edible nuts: the state tree of Texas. **2.** a nut of this tree. [1765–75, *Amer.*; < Mississippi Valley F *pacane* < Illinois *pakani* < Proto-Algonquian **paka·n-* nut (deriv. of **pake·* crack nuts)]

pecan′ pat′ty, *Southeastern U.S.* a praline made with pecans.

pec·ca·ble (pek′ə bəl), *adj.* liable to sin or error. [1595–1605; < ML *peccābilis.* See PECCAVI, -BLE] **—pec′ca·bil′i·ty,** *n.*

pec·ca·dil·lo (pek′ə dil′ō), *n., pl.* **-loes, -los.** a very minor or slight sin or offense; a trifling fault. [1585–95; < Sp *pecadillo,* dim. of *pecado* sin < L *peccātum* transgression, n. use of neut. of ptp. of *peccāre* to err, offend] **—Syn.** lapse, slip, faux pas, indiscretion.

pec·cant (pek′ənt), *adj.* **1.** sinning; guilty of a moral offense. **2.** violating a rule, principle, or established practice; faulty; wrong. [1595–1605; < L *peccant-* (s. of *peccāns*), prp. of *peccāre* to err, offend; see -ANT] **—pec′can·cy, pec′cant·ness,** *n.* **—pec′cant·ly,** *adv.*

collared peccary, *Tayassu tajacu,* about 2 ft. (0.6 m) high at shoulder; length 3 ft. (0.9 m)

pec·ca·ry (pek′ə rē), *n., pl.* **-ries,** (*esp. collectively*) **-ry.** any of several piglike hoofed mammals of the genus *Tayassu,* of North and South America, as *T. tajacu* (**collared peccary,** or **javelina**), having a dark gray coat with a white collar. [1605–15; < Carib]

pec·ca·to·pho·bi·a (pə kä′tə fō′bē ə, -kä′-), *n. Psychiatry.* an abnormal fear of sinning. [< L *peccāt(um)* sin + -o- + -PHOBIA]

pec·ca·vi (pe kā′vī, -vē, -kä′vē), *n., pl.* **-vis.** a confession of guilt or sin. [1500–10; < L: lit., I have sinned, perf. 1st person sing. of *peccāre* to go wrong]

pêche′ Mel′ba (pēch, pesh), *pl.* **pêch·es Mel·ba** (pē′chiz, pesh). See **peach Melba.**

Pe·chen·ga (pə cheng′gə; *Russ.* pyi chyen′gə), *n.* a village in the NW Soviet Union in Europe, on the Arctic Ocean: ice-free all year; ceded by Finland 1944. Finnish, **Petsamo.**

Pe·cho·ra (pə chôr′ə, -chōr′ə; *Russ.* pyi chyô′rə), *n.* a river in the NE Russian Federation in Europe, flowing from the Ural Mountains to the Arctic Ocean. 1110 mi. (1785 km) long.

peck[1] (pek), *n.* **1.** a dry measure of 8 quarts; the fourth part of a bushel, equal to 537.6 cubic inches (8.81 liters). **2.** a container for measuring this quantity. *Abbr.:* pk, pk. **3.** a considerable quantity: *a peck of trouble.* [1250–1300; ME *pek* < OF < ?]

peck[2] (pek), *v.t.* **1.** to strike or indent with the beak, as a bird does, or with some pointed instrument, esp. with quick, repeated movements. **2.** to make (a hole, puncture, etc.) by such strokes; pierce. **3.** to take (food) bit by bit, with or as with the beak. *—v.i.* **4.** to make strokes with the beak or a pointed instrument. **5. peck at, a.** to nibble indifferently or unenthusiastically at (food). **b.** to nag or carp at: *Stop pecking at me, I'm doing the best I can.* *—n.* **6.** a quick stroke, as in pecking. **7.** a hole or mark made by or as by pecking. **8.** a quick, almost impersonal kiss: *a peck on the cheek.* **9.** (in timber) incipient decay from fungi, occurring in isolated spots. **10. pecks.** Also, **peck′ings.** *Slang.* food. [1300–50; ME *pecke* < MD *pecken;* akin to PICK[1]] **—Syn. 5a.** pick at, poke at.

peck·er (pek′ər), *n.* **1.** a person or thing that pecks. **2.** a bird's bill. **3.** a woodpecker. **4.** *Slang* (*vulgar*). penis. **5.** *Brit. Slang.* one's spirits or courage. [1580–90; PECK[2] + -ER[1]]

peck·er·wood (pek′ər wo͝od′), *n.* **1.** *Midland and Southern U.S.* woodpecker. **2.** *Southern U.S. Slang* (*disparaging and offensive*). See **poor white.** *—adj.* **3.** *Southern U.S.* small or insignificant: *He makes a living farming and running a peckerwood sawmill.* [1825–35, *Amer.*; PECKER + WOOD[1]; inversion of WOODPECKER]

peck′ing or′der, **1.** *Animal Behav.* a dominance hierarchy, seen esp. in domestic poultry, that is maintained by one bird pecking another of lower status. **2.** a sequence or hierarchy of authority in an organization or social group. Also, **peck′ or′der.** [1925–30]

peck·ish (pek′ish), *adj. Chiefly Brit. Informal.* **1.** somewhat hungry: *By noon we were feeling a bit peckish.* **2.** rather irritable: *He's always a bit peckish after his nap.* [1775–85; PECK[2] + -ISH[1]]

Peck's′ Bad′ Boy′, **1.** the mischievous boy in a series of newspaper stories and collected volumes by the American newspaperman and humorist George Wilbur Peck (1840–1916). **2.** Usually, **Peck's bad boy. a.** any mischievous boy. **b.** a recalcitrant person or organization.

peck·sniff (pek′snif), *n.* a person of Pecksniffian attitudes or behavior: *a virtuousness that only a pecksniff could aspire to.* [1910–15; see PECKSNIFFIAN]

Peck·sniff·i·an (pek snif′ē ən), *adj.* (*often l.c.*) hypocritically and unctuously affecting benevolence or high moral principles. Also, **Peck′sniff·ish.** [1850–55; named after Seth *Pecksniff,* character in *Martin Chuzzlewit,* a novel (1843) by Dickens; see -IAN] **—Peck′sniff·er·y, Peck·sniff′i·an·ism, Peck′sniff·ism,** *n.*

peck·y (pek′ē), *adj.,* **peck·i·er, peck·i·est.** (of timber) spotted with fungi. [1840–50, *Amer.*; PECK[2] + -Y[1]]

Pe·cos (pā′kəs, -kōs), *n.* **1.** a river flowing SE from N New Mexico through W Texas to the Rio Grande. 735 mi. (1183 km) long. **2.** a town in W Texas, near the Pecos River. 12,855.

Pe′cos Bill′, a legendary cowboy of the American frontier who performed such fabulous feats as digging the Rio Grande.

pecs (peks), *n.pl. Informal.* pectoral muscles. [1965–70; by shortening]

Pécs (pāch), *n.* a city in SW Hungary. 163,000. German, **Fünfkirchen.**

pec·tase (pek′tās, -tāz), *n. Biochem.* an enzyme occurring in various fruits and involved in the formation of pectic acid from pectin. [1865–70; PECT(IN) + -ASE]

pec·tate (pek′tāt), *n. Chem.* a salt or ester of pectic acid. [1825–35; PECT(IC ACID) + -ATE[2]]

pec·ten (pek′tən), *n., pl.* **-tens, -ti·nes** (-tə nēz′). **1.** *Zool., Anat.* **a.** a comblike part or process. **b.** a pigmented vascular membrane with parallel folds suggesting the teeth of a comb, projecting into the vitreous humor of the eye in birds and reptiles. **2.** any bivalve mollusk of the genus *Pecten;* scallop. [1350–1400; ME < L *pecten* comb, rake, scallop, pubes, akin to *pectere,* Gk *pékein* to comb, card]

pec·tic (pek′tik), *adj.* pertaining to pectin. [1825–35; < Gk *pēktikós* congealing, equiv. to *pēkt(ós)* congealed (verbid of *pēgnýnai* to fix in, make solid) + *-ikos* -IC]

pec′tic ac′id, *Chem.* any of several water-insoluble products of the hydrolysis of pectin esters. [1825–35]

pec·tin (pek′tin), *n. Biochem.* a white, amorphous, colloidal carbohydrate of high molecular weight occurring in ripe fruits, esp. in apples, currants, etc., and used in fruit jellies, pharmaceuticals, and cosmetics for its thickening and emulsifying properties and its ability to solidify to a gel. [1830–40; < Gk *pēkt(ós)* fixed, congealed (see PECTIC) + -IN[2]] **—pec·ti·na·ceous** (pek′tə nā′shəs), **pec′tin·ous,** *adj.*

pec·ti·nate (pek′tə nāt′), *adj.* formed into or having closely parallel, toothlike projections; comblike. Also, **pec′ti·nat′ed.** [1785–95; < L *pectinātus* ptp. of *pectināre* to comb, equiv to *pectin-,* s. of *pecten* (see PECTEN) + *-ātus* -ATE[1]] **—pec′ti·nate′ly,** *adv.* **—pec′ti·na′·tion,** *n.*

pec·tin·o·gen (pek tin′ə jən, -jen′), *n. Biochem.* protopectin. [PECTIN + -O- + -GEN]

pec·tin·ose (pek′tə nōs′), *n. Chem.* arabinose. Also called **pec′tin sug′ar.** [PECTIN + -OSE[2]]

pec·tize (pek′tīz), *v.t., v.i.,* **-tized, -tiz·ing.** to change into a jelly; jellify; gel; gelatinize; gelatinate. Also, *esp. Brit.,* **pec′tise.** [1880–85; < Gk *pēkt(ós)* fixed, congealed (see PECTIC) + -IZE] **—pec′tiz·a·ble,** *adj.* **—pec′ti·za′tion,** *n.*

pec·to·lite (pek′tə līt′), *n.* a mineral, hydrous calcium sodium silicate, usually occurring in radiating groups of crystals in rock cavities. [1820–30; < Gk *pēktó(s)* made solid (see PECTIC) + -LITE]

pec·to·ral (pek′tər əl), *adj.* **1.** of, in, on, or pertaining to the chest or breast; thoracic. **2.** worn on the breast or chest. **3.** proceeding from the heart or inner consciousness. **4.** *Speech.* (of a vocal quality) appearing to come from resonance in the chest; full or deep. **5.** of or for diseases of the lungs. **—***n.* **6.** *Anat.* a pectoral part or organ, as a pectoral muscle. **7.** See **pectoral fin. 8.** something worn on the breast for ornament, protection, etc., as a breastplate. [1400–50; (n.) late ME < L *pectorāle,* n. use of neut. of *pectorālis* of the breast (*pector-,* s. of *pectus* breast + *-ālis* -AL[1]); (adj.) < L *pectorālis*] **—pec′to·ral·ly,** *adv.*

pec′toral cross′, *Eccles.* a cross worn on the breast by various prelates, as a designation of office. [1720–30]

pec′toral fin′, (in fishes) either of a pair of fins usually situated behind the head, one on each side, and corresponding to the forelimbs of higher vertebrates. See illus. under **fish.** [1760–70]

pec′toral gir′dle, 1. (in vertebrates) a bony or cartilaginous arch supporting the forelimbs. **2.** Also called **shoulder girdle.** (in humans) the bony arch formed by the clavicles, or collarbones, and scapulas, or shoulder blades. Also called **pec′toral arch′.** [1885–90]

pec·to·ral·is (pek′tə ral′is, -rā′lis, -rä′-), *n., pl.* **-ral·es** (-ral′ēz, -rā′lēz, -rä′-). *Anat.* either of two muscles on each side of the upper and anterior part of the thorax, the action of the larger (**pec′toral′is ma′jor**) assisting in drawing the shoulder forward and rotating the arm inward, and the action of the smaller (**pec′toral′is mi′nor**) assisting in drawing the shoulder downward and forward. [< L *pectorālis;* see PECTORAL]

pec′toral sand′piper, an American sandpiper, *Calidris melanotos,* the male of which, when courting, inflates its chest conspicuously. [1820–30, *Amer.*]

pec·tose (pek′tōs), *n. Biochem.* protopectin. [1855–60; PECT(IC) + -OSE[2]]

pec·tous (pek′təs), *adj. Biochem.* of, pertaining to, or consisting of pectin or protopectin. [1860–65; *pect-* (repr. PECTIC, PECTIN, PECTOSE) + -OUS]

pec·u·late (pek′yə lāt′), *v.t., v.i.,* **-lat·ed, -lat·ing.** to steal or take dishonestly (money, esp. public funds, or property entrusted to one's care); embezzle. [1740–50; v. use of *peculate* embezzlement (now obs.) < L *pecūlātus,* equiv. to *pecūlā(rī)* to embezzle, lit., to make public property private + *-tus* suffix of v. action. See PECULIAR, -ATE[1]] **—pec′u·la′tion,** *n.* **—pec′u·la′tor,** *n.*

pe·cu·liar (pi kyōōl′yər), *adj.* **1.** strange; queer; odd: *peculiar happenings.* **2.** uncommon; unusual: *the peculiar hobby of stuffing and mounting bats.* **3.** distinctive in nature or character from others. **4.** belonging characteristically (usually fol. by *to*): *an expression peculiar to Canadians.* **5.** belonging exclusively to some person, group, or thing: *the peculiar properties of a drug.* **6.** *Astron.* designating a star or galaxy with special properties that deviates from others of its spectral type or galaxy class. **—***n.* **7.** a property or privilege belonging exclusively or characteristically to a person. **8.** *Brit.* a particular parish or church that is exempted from the jurisdiction of the ordinary or bishop in whose diocese it lies and is governed by another. **9. peculiars.** Also called **arbitraries.** *Brit. Print.* special characters not generally included in standard type fonts, as phonetic symbols, mathematical symbols, etc. [1400–50; late ME; < L *pecūliāris* as one's own, equiv. to *pecūli(um)* property (deriv. of *pecū* flock, farm animals; akin to *pecus* cattle (see FEE)) + *-āris* -AR[1]] **—pe·cu′liar·ly,** *adv.*
—Syn. 1. eccentric, bizarre. See **strange. 2.** extraordinary, singular, exceptional. **5.** individual, personal, particular, special, unique. **—Ant. 2, 5.** common.

pecu′liar institu′tion, black slavery in the southern U.S. before the Civil War. [1835–45, *Amer.*]

pe·cu·li·ar·i·ty (pi kyōō′lē ar′i tē, -kyōōl yar′-), *n., pl.* **-ties. 1.** a trait, manner, characteristic, or habit that is odd or unusual. **2.** oddity; singularity; eccentricity. **3.** a distinguishing quality or characteristic. **4.** the quality or condition of being peculiar. [1600–10; < LL *pecūliāritās.* See PECULIAR, -ITY]
—Syn. 1. idiosyncrasy. See **eccentricity. 2.** irregularity. **3.** See **feature.**

pe·cu·liar·ize (pi kyōōl′yə rīz′), *v.t.,* **-ized, -iz·ing.** to make peculiar, unusual, distinguished, etc. Also, *esp. Brit.,* **pe·cu′liar·ise′.** [1615–25; PECULIAR + -IZE]

pecu′liar peo′ple, 1. the Jews as being God's chosen people. Deut. 14:2. **2.** a name adopted by certain fundamentalist Christian sects, signifying their refusal to conform to any rule of conduct that is contrary to the letter or spirit of the Bible. [1485–95]

pe·cu·ni·ar·y (pi kyōō′nē er′ē), *adj.* **1.** of or pertaining to money: *pecuniary difficulties.* **2.** consisting of or given or exacted in money or monetary payments: *pecuniary tributes.* **3.** (of a crime, violation, etc.) involving a money penalty or fine. [1495–1505; < L *pecūniārius,* deriv. of *pecūnia* property, money (*pecūn-,* deriv. of *pecū* flock (see PECULIAR), with *-ūn-* as in *tribūna* TRIBUNE[1], *fortūna* FORTUNE, etc. + *-ia* -IA); see -ARY] **—pe·cu·ni·ar·i·ly** (pi kyōō′nē âr′i lē), *adv.*
—Syn. 1, 2. See **financial.**

CONCISE ETYMOLOGY KEY: <, descended or borrowed from; >, whence; b., blend of, blended; c., cognate with; cf., compare; deriv., derivative; equiv., equivalent; imit., imitative; obl., oblique; r., replacing; s., stem; sp., spelling, spelled; resp., respelling, respelled; trans., translation; ?, origin unknown; *, unattested; ‡, probably earlier than. See the full key inside the front cover.

ped, pedestrian. [by shortening]

ped-[1], var. of **pedo-**[1] before a vowel: *pedagogic.* Also, **paed-.**

ped-[2], var. of **pedi-** before a vowel.

ped-[3], var. of **pedo-**[2] before a vowel: *pedalfer.*

-ped, a combining form with the meaning "having a foot" of the kind specified by the initial element: *pinnatiped.* Also, **-pede.** Cf. **-pod.** [< L *-ped-,* s. of *-pēs* -footed, adj. deriv. of *pēs* FOOT]

ped., 1. pedal. **2.** pedestal.

ped·a·gog·ic (ped′ə goj′ik, -gō′jik), *adj.* of or pertaining to a pedagogue or pedagogy. Also, **ped′a·gog′i·cal.** [1775–85; < Gk *paidagōgikós* of a child's tutor. See PEDAGOGUE, -IC] **—ped′a·gog′i·cal·ly,** *adv.*

ped·a·gog·ics (ped′ə goj′iks, -gō′jiks), *n.* (*used with a singular v.*) the science or art of teaching or education; pedagogy. [1860–65; PEDAGOG(Y) + -ICS]

ped·a·gog·ism (ped′ə gog′iz əm, -gô′giz-), *n.* the principles, manner, method, or characteristics of pedagogues. Also, **ped·a·gogu·ism** (ped′ə gog′iz əm, -gô′giz-). [1635–45; PEDAGOG(Y) + -ISM]

ped·a·gogue (ped′ə gog′, -gôg′), *n.* **1.** a teacher; schoolteacher. **2.** a person who is pedantic, dogmatic, and formal. Also, **ped′a·gog′.** [1350–1400; ME *pedagoge* < L *paedagōgus* < Gk *paidagōgós* a boy's tutor. See PED-[1], -AGOGUE] **—ped′a·gogu′er·y, ped′a·gog′er·y,** *n.* **—ped′a·gogu′ish, ped′a·gog′ish,** *adj.*

ped·a·go·gy (ped′ə gō′jē, -goj′ē), *n., pl.* **-gies. 1.** the function or work of a teacher; teaching. **2.** the art or science of teaching; education; instructional methods. [1575–85; < Gk *paidagōgía* office of a child's tutor. See PEDAGOGUE, -Y[3]]

ped·al (ped′l *or, for 6–8,* pēd′l), *n., v.,* **-aled, -al·ing** or (*esp. Brit.*) **-alled, -al·ling,** *adj.* **—***n.* **1.** a foot-operated lever used to control certain mechanisms, as automobiles, or to play or modify the sounds of certain musical instruments, as pianos, organs, or harps. **2.** a leverlike part worked by the foot to supply power in various mechanisms, as the bicycle. **3.** *Music.* **a.** a foot-operated keyboard, as on an organ or harpsichord. **b.** any of the keys of such a keyboard. **c.** See **pedal point. —***v.i.* **4.** to work or use the pedals, as in playing an organ or propelling a bicycle. **—***v.t.* **5.** to work the pedals of (an organ, bicycle, etc.). **—***adj.* **6.** of or pertaining to a foot or the feet. **7.** of or pertaining to a pedal or pedals. **8.** using pedals: *a pedal mechanism.* [1605–15; (< F *pédale*) < L *pedālis* of the feet. See PED-[2], -AL[1]]

ped′al boat′, a recreational water vehicle, consisting of two pontoons with a transverse seat and propelled by a pedal-operated paddle wheel. Also, **ped′al·boat′, paddle boat.** [1950–55]

ped′al disk′. See **basal disk.**

pe·dal·fer (pi dal′fər), *n.* a soil rich in alumina and iron, with few or no carbonates. Cf. **pedocal.** [1925–30; PED-[3] + L *al(ūmen)* ALUM + *fer(rum)* iron]

ped′al key′board, pedal (def. 3a).

ped′al point′, *Music.* **1.** a tone sustained by one part, usually the bass, while other parts progress without reference to it. **2.** a passage containing it. Also called **organ point, ped′al note′.** [1875–80]

ped′al push′ers, slacks that extend to about the midpoint of the calf, worn by girls and women, originally used when cycling. [1940–45, *Amer.*]

ped′al steel′ guitar′, an oblong, floor-mounted electrified guitar, usually having ten strings, fretted with a steel bar and producing a wailing sound that is modulated by use of a foot pedal. Also called **ped′al steel′.** [1965–70, *Amer.*]

ped·ant (ped′nt), *n.* **1.** a person who makes an excessive or inappropriate display of learning. **2.** a person who overemphasizes rules or minor details. **3.** a person who adheres rigidly to book knowledge without regard to common sense. **4.** *Obs.* a schoolmaster. [1580–90; < It *pedante* teacher, pedant; appar. akin to PEDAGOGUE; see -ANT] **—ped′ant·esque′,** *adj.* **—ped′ant·hood′,** *n.*
—Syn. 2. hairsplitter.

pe·dan·tic (pə dan′tik), *adj.* **1.** ostentatious in one's learning. **2.** overly concerned with minute details or formalisms, esp. in teaching. Also, **pe·dan′ti·cal.** [1590–1600; PEDANT + -IC] **—pe·dan′ti·cal·ly,** *adv.* **—pe·dan′ti·cal·ness,** *n.*
—Syn. 2. didactic, doctrinaire.

pe·dan·ti·cism (pə dan′tə siz′əm), *n.* pedantry. Also, **ped·ant·ism** (ped′n tiz′əm). [1840–50; PEDANTIC + -ISM]

ped·ant·ry (ped′n trē), *n., pl.* **-ries. 1.** the character, qualities, practices, etc., of a pedant, esp. undue display of learning. **2.** slavish attention to rules, details, etc. **3.** an instance of being pedantic: *the pedantries of modern criticism.* [1575–85; It *pedanteria.* See PEDANT, -RY]

ped·ate (ped′āt), *adj.* **1.** having a foot or feet. **2.** resembling a foot. **3.** having divisions like toes. **4.** *Bot.* (of a leaf) palmately parted or divided with the lateral lobes or divisions cleft or divided. [1745–55; < L *pedātus.* See PED-[2], -ATE[1]] **—ped′ate·ly,** *adv.*

pedate leaf

Ped.D., Doctor of Pedagogy.

ped·dle (ped′l), *v.,* **-dled, -dling. —***v.t.* **1.** to carry (small articles, goods, wares, etc.) from place to place for sale at retail; hawk. **2.** to deal out, distribute, or dispense, esp. in small quantities: *to peddle radical ideas.* **3.** to sell (drugs) illicitly. **—***v.i.* **4.** to go from place to place with goods, wares, etc., for sale at retail. **5.** to occupy oneself with trifles; trifle. [1525–35; appar. back formation from PEDDLER; in def. 4, reinforced by PIDDLE]

ped·dler (ped′lər), *n.* **1.** a person who sells from door to door or in the street. **2.** a person who tries to promote some cause, candidate, viewpoint, etc. Also, **pedlar, pedler.** [1350–1400; ME *pedlere,* unexplained var. of *peder,* deriv. of *ped(de)* basket]

ped·dler·y (ped′lə rē), *n., pl.* **-dler·ies. 1.** the business of a peddler. **2.** peddlers' wares. **3.** trumpery. Also, **pedlary, pedlery.** [1520–30; PEDDLER + -Y[3]]

ped·dling (ped′ling), *adj.* trifling; paltry; piddling. [1590–1600; PEDDLE + -ING[2]] **—ped′dling·ly,** *adv.*

-pede, var. of **-ped:** *centipede.*

ped·er·ast (ped′ə rast′, pē′də-), *n.* a person who engages in pederasty. [1720–30; < Gk *paiderastḗs* lover of boys, equiv. to *paid-* (s. of *paîs*) boy, child + *erastḗs* lover, equiv. to *eras-,* s. of *erân* to love + *-tēs* agent n. suffix]

ped·er·as·ty (ped′ə ras′tē, pē′də-), *n.* sexual relations between two males, esp. when one of them is a minor. [1605–15; < NL *pederastia* < Gk *paiderastía* love of boys. See PEDERAST, -Y[3]] **—ped′er·as′tic,** *adj.* **—ped′er·as′ti·cal·ly,** *adv.*

Ped·er·nal·es (pûr′dn al′əs), *n.* a river in central Texas, flowing E to the Colorado river. ab. 105 mi. (169 km) long.

ped·es·tal (ped′ə stl), *n., v.,* **-taled, -tal·ing** or (*esp. Brit.*) **-talled, -tal·ling. —***n.* **1.** an architectural support for a column, statue, vase, or the like. See diag. under **column. 2.** a supporting structure or piece; base. **3.** *Furniture.* **a.** a support for a desk, consisting of a boxlike frame containing drawers one above the other. **b.** a columnar support for a tabletop. **4.** *Building Trades.* a bulge cast at the bottom of a concrete pile. **5. set** or **put on a pedestal,** to glorify; idealize: *When we first became engaged each of us set the other on a pedestal.* **—***v.t.* **6.** to put on or supply with a pedestal. [1555–65; alter. of MF *piedestal* < It *piedestallo,* var. of *piedistallo* lit., foot of stall. See PED-[2], DE, STALL[1]]

ped′estal ta′ble, a table supported upon a central shaft, or upon several shafts along its centerline, each resting upon a spreading foot or feet. [1935–40]

pe·des·tri·an (pə des′trē ən), *n.* **1.** a person who goes or travels on foot; walker. **—***adj.* **2.** going or performed on foot; walking. **3.** of or pertaining to walking. **4.** lacking in vitality, imagination, distinction, etc.; commonplace; prosaic or dull: *a pedestrian commencement speech.* [1710–20; < L *pedestri-* (s. of *pedester* on foot, deriv. of *pēs* (s. *ped-*); see PEDI-[1]) + -AN]

pe·des·tri·an·ism (pə des′trē ə niz′əm), *n.* **1.** the exercise or practice of walking. **2.** commonplace or prosaic manner, quality, etc. [1800–10; PEDESTRIAN + -ISM]

pe·des·tri·an·ize (pə des′trē ə nīz′), *v.i.,* **-ized, -iz·ing.** to go on foot; walk. Also, *esp. Brit.,* **pe·des′tri·an·ise′.** [1805–15; PEDESTRIAN + -IZE]

pedes′trian way′, pedway.

pedi-, a combining form meaning "foot," used in the formation of compound words: *pediform.* Also, *esp. before a vowel,* **ped-.** [comb. form of L *ped-* (s. of *pēs*) FOOT]

pe·di·a·tri·cian (pē′dē ə trish′ən, ped′ē-), *n.* a physician who specializes in pediatrics. Also, **pe·di·at·rist** (pē′dē a′trist, ped′ē-). [1900–05; PEDIATR(IC) + -ICIAN]

pe·di·at·rics (pē′dē a′triks, ped′ē-), *n.* (*used with a singular v.*) the branch of medicine concerned with the development, care, and diseases of babies and children. [1880–85; *pediatr(ic)* (see PED-[1], -IATRIC) + -ICS] **—pe′di·at′ric,** *adj.*

ped·i·cab (ped′i kab′), *n.* (esp. in Southeast Asia) a three-wheeled public conveyance operated by pedals, typically one having a hooded cab for two passengers mounted behind the driver. Also called **trishaw.** [1945–50; PEDI- + CAB[1]]

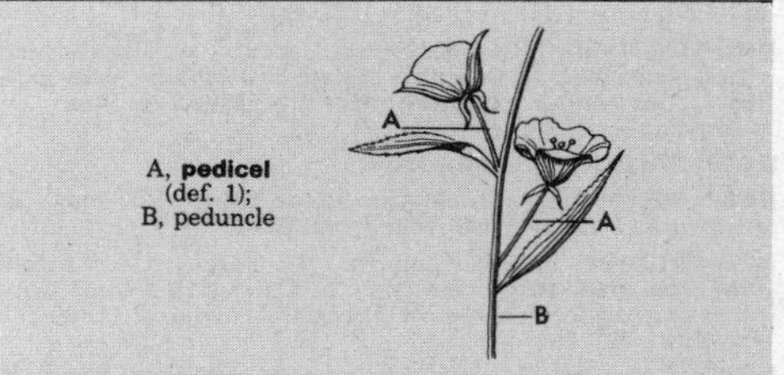

A, **pedicel** (def. 1); B, peduncle

ped·i·cel (ped′ə səl, -sel′), *n.* **1.** *Bot.* **a.** a small stalk. **b.** an ultimate division of a common peduncle. **c.** one of the subordinate stalks in a branched inflorescence, bearing a single flower. **2.** *Zool.* a pedicle or peduncle. [1670–80; < NL *pedicellus,* dim. of L *pediculus* a little foot. See PEDICLE] **—ped·i·cel·lar** (ped′ə sel′ər), *adj.*

ped·i·cel·lar·i·a (ped′ə sə lâr′ē ə), *n., pl.* **-i·ae** (-ē ē′). *Zool.* one of the minute pincerlike structures common to starfish and sea urchins, used for cleaning and to capture tiny prey. [1870–75; < NL; see PEDICEL, -ARIA]

ped·i·cel·late (ped′ə sel′it, -āt, ped′ə sə lit, -lāt′), *adj.* having a pedicel or pedicels. [1820–30; PEDICEL + -ATE[1]] **—ped′i·cel·la′tion,** *n.*

ped·i·cle (ped′i kəl), *n. Zool.* a small stalk or stalklike support, as the connection between the cephalothorax and abdomen in certain arachnids. [1555–65; < L *pediculus,* dim. of *pēs* (s. *ped-*) FOOT. See PEDI-, -CLE[1]]

pe·dic·u·lar (pə dik′yə lər), *adj.* of or pertaining to lice. [1650–60; < L *pēdiculāris,* deriv. of *pēdiculus,* dim. of *pēdis* louse; see -CULE[1], -AR[1]]

pe·dic·u·late (pə dik′yə lit, -lāt′), *adj.* **1.** of or related to the Pediculati, a group of teleost fishes, characterized by the elongated base of their pectoral fins, simulating an arm or peduncle. —*n.* **2.** a pediculate fish. [1855–60; < NL *Pediculati.* See PEDICLE, -ATE[1]]

pe·dic·u·li·cide (pə dik′yə lə sīd′), *adj.* **1.** Also, **pe·dic′u·li·cid′al.** destructive to lice. —*n.* **2.** a pediculicide agent. [< L *pēdicul(us)* louse (see PEDICULAR) + -I- + -CIDE]

pe·dic·u·lo·sis (pə dik′yə lō′sis), *n. Pathol.* the state of being infested with lice. [1885–90; < L *pēdicul(us)* louse (see PEDICULAR) + -OSIS] —**pe·dic·u·lous** (pə dik′yə ləs), *adj.*

ped·i·cure (ped′i kyŏŏr′), *n.* **1.** professional care and treatment of the feet, as removal of corns and trimming of toenails. **2.** a single treatment of the feet. **3.** a podiatrist. [1835–45; < F *pédicure.* See PEDI-, CURE] —**ped′i·cur′ist,** *n.*

ped·i·form (ped′ə fôrm′), *adj.* in the form of a foot; footlike. [1820–30; PEDI- + -FORM]

ped·i·gree (ped′i grē′), *n.* **1.** an ancestral line; line of descent; lineage; ancestry. **2.** a genealogical table, chart, list, or record, esp. of a purebred animal. **3.** distinguished, excellent, or pure ancestry. **4.** derivation, origin, or history: *the pedigree of a word.* [1375–1425; late ME *pedegru* < AF, equiv. to MF *pie de grue* lit., foot of crane, a fanciful way of describing the appearance of the lines of a genealogical chart] —**ped′i·gree′less,** *adj.*
—**Syn. 2.** PEDIGREE, GENEALOGY refer to an account of ancestry. A PEDIGREE is a table or chart recording a line of ancestors, either of persons or (more especially) of animals, as horses, cattle, and dogs; in the case of animals, such a table is used as proof of superior qualities: *a detailed pedigree.* A GENEALOGY is an account of the descent of a person or family traced through a series of generations, usually from the first known ancestor: *a genealogy that includes a king.*

ped·i·greed (ped′i grēd′), *adj.* having established purebred ancestry: *a pedigreed collie.* [1810–20; PEDIGREE + -ED[3]]

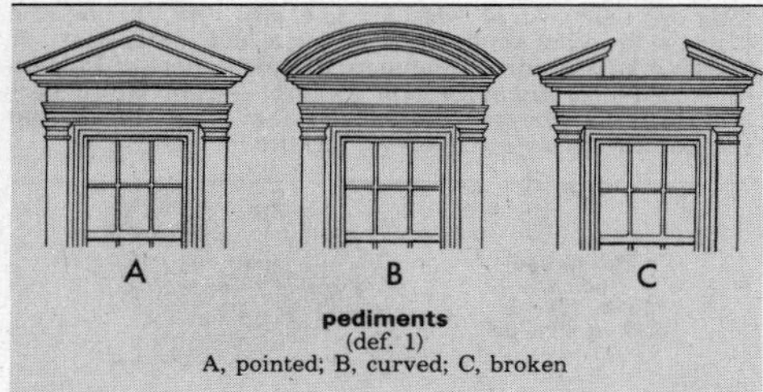

pediments
(def. 1)
A, pointed; B, curved; C, broken

ped·i·ment (ped′ə mənt), *n.* **1.** (in classical architecture) a low gable, typically triangular with a horizontal cornice and raking cornices, surmounting a colonnade, an end wall, or a major division of a façade. **2.** any imitation of this, often fancifully treated, used to crown an opening, a monument, etc., or to form part of a decorative scheme. **3.** *Geol.* a gently sloping rock surface at the foot of a steep slope, as of a mountain, usually thinly covered with alluvium. [1655–65; earlier *pedament, pedement,* alter., by assoc. with L *pēs* (s. *ped-*) FOOT, of earlier *periment,* perh. an unlearned alter. of PYRAMID; (def. 3) by construal as PEDI- + -MENT] —**ped·i·men·tal** (ped′ə men′tl), *adj.* —**ped·i·ment·ed** (ped′ə men′tid, -mən-), *adj.*

ped·i·o·coc·cus (ped′ē ə kok′əs), *n., pl.* **-coc·ci** (-kok′sī, -sē). *Bacteriol.* any of several spherical, facultatively anaerobic bacteria of the genus *Pediococcus,* producing acid and clouding in beer and wort. [< NL; see PEDI-[1], -O-, COCCUS] —**ped·i·o·coc·cal** (ped′ē ə-kok′əl), **ped·i·o·coc·cic** (ped′ē ə kok′sik), *adj.*

ped·i·on (ped′ē ən, pē′dē-), *n., pl.* **ped·i·a** (ped′ē ə, pē′dē ə). *Crystall.* a crystal form having only a single face, without a symmetrical equivalent: unique to the triclinic system. [1885–90; < NL < Gk *pedíon* plain, level ground, dim. of *pédon* ground, earth]

ped·i·palp (ped′ə palp′), *n.* **1.** (in arachnids) one member of the usually longer pair of appendages immediately behind the chelicerae. **2.** any member of the arachnid order Pedipalpida. [1820–30; < NL *Pedipalpus.* See PEDI-, PALP] —**ped′i·pal′pal, ped·i·pal·pate** (ped′-ə pal′pāt), *adj.*

P.E.Dir., Director of Physical Education.

ped·lar (ped′lər), *n.* peddler. Also, **ped′ler.**

ped·lar·y (ped′lə rē), *n., pl.* **-lar·ies.** peddlery.

ped·ler·y (ped′lə rē), *n., pl.* **-ler·ies.** peddlery.

pedo-[1], a combining form meaning "child," used in the formation of compound words: *pedophilia.* Also, **paedo-;** *esp. before a vowel,* **ped-.** [var. sp. of *paedo-* < Gk *paido-,* comb. form of *paid-* (s. of *paîs*) child]

pedo-[2], a combining form meaning "soil," used in the formation of compound words: *pedocal.* Also, *esp. before a vowel,* **ped-.** [< Gk, comb. form of *pédon*]

pe·do·bap·tism (pē′dō bap′tiz əm), *n.* the baptism of infants. [1630–40; PEDO-[1] + BAPTISM]

pe·do·bap·tist (pē′dō bap′tist), *n.* a person who advocates or practices pedobaptism. [1645–55; PEDOBAPT(ISM) + -IST]

ped·o·cal (ped′ə kal′), *n.* a soil rich in carbonates, esp. those of lime. Cf. **pedalfer.** [1925–30; PEDO-[2] + *-cal* < L *calc-* (s. of *calx*) lime]

pe·do·don·tics (pē′də don′tiks), *n.* (*used with a singular v.*) the branch of dentistry dealing with the care and treatment of children's teeth. Also, **pe·do·don·tia** (pē′də don′shə, -shē ə). [PED-[1] + -ODONT + -ICS] —**pe′do·don′tic,** *adj.*

pe·do·don·tist (pē′də don′tist), *n.* a specialist in pedodontics. [PEDODONT(ICS) + -IST]

pe·do·gen·e·sis[1] (pē′də jen′ə sis), *n.* neoteny (def. 1). [1870–75; PEDO-[1] + -GENESIS] —**pe·do·ge·net·ic** (pē′dō-jə net′ik), **pe′do·gen′ic,** *adj.*

ped·o·gen·e·sis[2] (ped′ə jen′ə sis), *n.* the process of soil formation. [1935–40; PEDO-[2] + -GENESIS] —**ped′o·gen′ic, ped·o·ge·net·ic** (ped′ə jə net′ik), *adj.*

ped·o·graph (ped′ə graf′, -gräf′), *n.* an imprint on paper of the foot. [PED-[2] + -O- + -GRAPH]

pe·dol·o·gy[1] (pi dol′ə jē), *n.* the science that deals with the study of soils. Also called **soil science.** [1920–25; PEDO-[2] + -LOGY] —**ped·o·log·i·cal** (ped′l oj′i kəl), **ped′o·log′ic,** *adj.* —**pe·dol′o·gist,** *n.*

pe·dol·o·gy[2] (pi dol′ə jē), *n.* **1.** the scientific study of the nature and development of children. **2.** pediatrics. [PEDO-[1] + -LOGY] —**pe·do·log·i·cal** (pēd′l oj′i kəl), **pe′do·log′ic,** *adj.* —**pe·dol′o·gist,** *n.*

pe·dom·e·ter (pə dom′i tər), *n.* an instrument worn by a walker or runner for recording the number of steps taken, thereby showing approximately the distance traveled. [1723; < F *pédomètre,* equiv. to *péd-* (learned use of L *ped-* foot (s. of *pēs*); see PEDI-) + *-omètre* (see -O-, -METER)] —**ped·o·met·ri·cal** (ped′ə me′tri kəl), *adj.* —**ped′o·met′ri·cal·ly,** *adv.* —**pe·dom′e·trist,** *n.*

pe·do·mor·phism (pē′də môr′fiz əm), *n. Biol.* a speeding up of the rate of development, resulting in an adult form that has the appearance of its larval or juvenile ancestor. Cf. **neoteny** (def. 2). [PEDO-[1] + -MORPHISM] —**pe′do·mor′phic,** *adj.*

pe·do·phile (pē′də fīl′), *n. Psychiatry.* an adult who is sexually attracted to young children. Also, **pedophiliac.** [1950–55; PEDO-[1] + -PHILE, or directly < Gk *paidóphilos* loving children]

pe·do·phil·i·a (pē′də fil′ē ə), *n. Psychiatry.* sexual desire in an adult for a child. [1905–10; < NL; see PEDO-[1], -PHILIA]

pe·do·phil·i·ac (pē′də fil′ē ak), *n.* **1.** pedophile. —*adj.* **2.** Also, **pe′do·phil′ic.** of or pertaining to pedophilia. [PEDOPHILI(A) + -AC]

pe·dro (pē′drō, pā′-), *n., pl.* **-dros.** *Cards.* **1.** any of several varieties of all fours in which the five of trumps counts at its face value. **2.** the five of trumps. [1870–75; < Sp: lit., Peter]

Pe·dro Juan Ca·ba·lle·ro (pe′thrô hwän′ kä′vä-ye′rô), a city in E central Paraguay. 20,901.

Peds (pedz), *Trademark.* a brand of footlet.

pe·dun·cle (pi dung′kəl, pē′dung-), *n.* **1.** *Bot.* **a.** a flower stalk, supporting either a cluster or a solitary flower. **b.** the stalk bearing the fruiting body in fungi. **2.** *Zool.* a stalk or stem; a stalklike part or structure. **3.** *Anat.* **a.** a stalklike structure composed of white matter, connecting various regions of the brain. **b.** an attachment process, as in the brachiopods. [1745–55; < NL *pedunculus,* equiv. to L *ped-,* s. of *pēs* FOOT + *-unculus* dim. suffix, orig. of n-stems; cf. CARBUNCLE, HOMUNCULUS] —**pe·dun′cled, pe·dun·cu·lar** (pi dung′kyə lər), *adj.*

P, **peduncle**
(def. 1a)

pe·dun·cu·late (pi dung′kyə lit, -lāt′), *adj.* **1.** having a peduncle. **2.** growing on a peduncle. Also, **pe·dun′cu·lat′ed.** [1750–60; < NL *pedunculātus.* See PEDUNCLE, -ATE[1]] —**pe·dun′cu·la′tion,** *n.*

ped·way (ped′wā′), *n.* a walkway, usually enclosed, permitting pedestrians to go from building to building, as in an urban center, without passing through traffic. Also called **pedestrian way.** [PED(ESTRIAN) + WAY[1]]

ped-Xing, pedestrian crossing.

pee[1] (pē), *n., pl.* **pees** for 1; **pee** for 2. **1.** the letter *p.* **2.** *Brit.* penny (def. 2). [ME *pe* (< OF) < L *pē* < Gk *peî* PI[1]]

pee[2] (pē), *v.,* **peed, pee·ing,** *n. Slang* (*sometimes vulgar*). —*v.i.* **1.** to urinate. —*n.* **2.** urine. **3.** the act of urinating. [1875–80; euphemism for *piss,* using initial letter]

Pee·bles (pē′bəlz), *n.* a historic county in S Scotland. Also called **Pee·bles·shire** (pē′bəlz shēr′, -shər, -bəl-), **Tweeddale.**

Pee Dee (pē′ dē′), a river flowing through central North Carolina and NE South Carolina into the Atlantic. 435 mi. (700 km) long. Cf. **Yadkin.**

pee′gee hydran′gea (pē′jē), a widely cultivated hydrangea, *Hydrangea paniculata grandiflora,* having pyramidal clusters of persistent flowers that are white on opening and turn pinkish as they mature. [sp. of initials of NL *paniculata grandiflora,* the specific and varietal epithets]

peek (pēk), *v.i.* **1.** to look or glance quickly or furtively, esp. through a small opening or from a concealed location; peep; peer. —*n.* **2.** a quick or furtive look or glance; peep. [1325–75; ME *piken* (v.); perh. dissimilated var. of *kiken* to KEEK]
—**Syn. 1.** See **peep**[1].

peek·a·boo (pēk′ə bōō′), *n.* **1.** Also called **bo-peep.** a game played by or with very young children, typically in which one covers the face or hides and then suddenly uncovers the face or reappears, calling "Peekaboo!" —*adj.* **2.** *Clothing.* **a.** decorated with openwork. **b.** made of a sheer and revealing material, as some blouses for women. **3.** appearing briefly and then vanishing, or promising to appear but failing to do so: *the fluctuating response of the stock market to a peekaboo economic recovery.* [1590–1600; PEEK + *-a-* connective + BOO[1]]

peek·a·poo (pē′kə pōō′), *n., pl.* **-poos.** one of a variety of dogs crossbred from a Pekingese and a miniature poodle. Also, **pekepoo.** [PEK(INGESE) + (COCK)APOO; sp. copies PEEKABOO]

Peeks·kill (pēk′skil), *n.* a city in SE New York, on the Hudson. 18,236.

peel[1] (pēl), *v.t.* **1.** to strip (something) of its skin, rind, bark, etc.: *to peel an orange.* **2.** to strip (the skin, rind, bark, paint, etc.) from something: *to peel paint from a car.* **3.** *Croquet.* to cause (another player's ball) to go through a wicket. —*v.i.* **4.** (of skin, bark, paint, etc.) to come off; become separated. **5.** to lose the skin, rind, bark, paint, etc. **6.** *Informal.* to undress. **7.** *Metall.* (of a malleable iron casting) to lose, or tend to lose, the outer layer. **8. keep one's eyes peeled,** *Informal.* to watch closely or carefully; be alert: *Keep your eyes peeled for a gas station.* **9. peel off, a.** to remove (the skin, bark, etc.) or be removed: *The old skin peeled off.* **b.** *Aeron.* to leave a flying formation of aircraft with a banking turn, usually from one end of an echelon. **c.** *Informal.* to turn off or leave (a road): *We peeled off the highway onto a dirt road.* **d.** to remove (clothing) in a swift upward or downward motion. —*n.* **10.** the skin or rind of a fruit, vegetable, etc. **11.** *Metall.* the presence of a brittle outer layer on a malleable iron casting. [bef. 1100; ME *pelen,* OE *pilian* to strip, skin < L *pilāre* to remove hair, deriv. of *pilus* hair. See PILL[2]] —**peel′a·ble,** *adj.*
—**Syn. 1.** PEEL, PARE agree in meaning to remove the skin or rind from something. PEEL means to pull or strip off the natural external covering or protection of something: *to peel an orange, a potato.* PARE is used of trimming off chips, flakes, or superficial parts from something, as well as of cutting off the skin or rind: *to pare the nails; to pare a potato.*

peel[2] (pēl), *n.* **1.** a shovellike implement for putting bread, pies, etc., into the oven or taking them out. **2.** *Metall.* a long, shovellike iron tool for charging an open-hearth furnace. [1350–1400; ME *pele* < MF < L *pāla* spade. See PALETTE]

peel[3] (pēl), *n.* a small fortified tower for residence or for use during an attack, common in the border counties of England and Scotland in the 16th century. Also, **pele.** [1250–1300; ME *pele* fortress < AF *pel* stockade, MF *pel* stake < L *pālus* stake. See PALE[2]]

Peel (pēl), *n.* **1. Sir Robert,** 1788–1850, British political leader: founder of the London constabulary; prime minister 1834–35; 1841–46. **2.** a seaport on W Isle of Man: castle; resort. 3295.

peel-and-stick (pēl′ən stik′), *adj.* ready to be applied after peeling off the backing to expose an adhesive surface: *peel-and-stick labels.*

Peele (pēl), *n.* **George,** 1558?–97?, English dramatist.

peel·er[1] (pē′lər), *n.* **1.** a person or thing that peels. **2.** a kitchen implement, often having a swiveling, protected blade, for removing the peel or outer skin of a vegetable or fruit. **3.** a long-staple cotton raised originally in the regions along the Yazoo River and the Mississippi River delta. **4.** a yarn made from this cotton. **5.** *Slang.* a striptease dancer. **6.** a log, esp. of a Douglas fir, suitable for rotary cutting into veneers. [1325–75; ME *peler.* See PEEL[1], -ER[1]]

peel·er[2] (pē′lər), *n. Brit. Archaic.* a police officer. [1810–20; named after Sir R. PEEL; see -ER[1]]

peel·ing (pē′ling), *n.* **1.** the act of a person or thing that peels. **2.** that which is peeled from something, as a piece of the skin or rind of a fruit. [1555–65; PEEL[1] + -ING[1]]

peel-off (pēl′ôf′, -of′), *adj.* designed to be peeled off from a backing or large sheet, usually of paper, before use; readied for use by peeling off: *peel-off labels.* [1935–40; adj. use of v. phrase *peel off*]

peen (pēn), *n.* **1.** a wedgelike, spherical, or other striking end of a hammer head opposite the face. —*v.t.* **2.** to enlarge, straighten, or smooth with a peen. **3.** to strengthen (a metal surface) by light hammering or by bombardment with steel balls or shot. [1505–15; earlier *pen* < Scand; cf. Sw, Norw *pen* (n.) in same sense (perh. < G *Pinne* peen). See PIN]

Pee·ne (pā′nə), *n.* a river in N East Germany, flowing E to the Baltic Sea. ab. 97 mi. (155 km) long.

Pee·ne·mün·de (pā′nə myn′də), *n.* a village in NE East Germany: German center for missile and rocket research and manufacture in World War II.

peep[1] (pēp), *v.i.* **1.** to look through a small opening or from a concealed location. **2.** to look slyly, pryingly, or furtively. **3.** to look curiously or playfully. **4.** to come partially into view; begin to appear: *the first crocuses peeping through the snow-covered ground.* —*v.t.* **5.** to show or protrude slightly. —*n.* **6.** a quick or furtive look or glance. **7.** the first appearance, as of dawn. **8.** an aperture for looking through. [1425–75; late ME *pepe;* assimilated var. of PEEK]
—**Syn. 1, 2.** PEEP, PEEK, PEER mean to look through, over, or around something. To PEEP or PEEK is usually to give a quick look through a narrow aperture or small opening, often furtively, slyly, or pryingly, or to look over or around something curiously or playfully: *to peep over a wall; to peek into a room.* PEEK is often associated with children's games. To PEER is to look continuously and narrowly for some time, esp. in order to penetrate obscurity or to overcome some obstacle in the way of vision: *The firefighter peered through the smoke.*

peep[2] (pēp), *n.* **1.** a short, shrill little cry or sound, as of a young bird; cheep; squeak. **2.** any of various small sandpipers. **3.** a slight sound or remark, esp. in com-

CONCISE PRONUNCIATION KEY: act, cāpe, dâre, pärt; set, ēqual; if, īce; ox, ōver, ôrder, oil, bŏŏk, bōōt, out; up, ûrge; child; sing; shoe; thin, *th*at; zh as in *treasure.* ə = *a* as in *alone, e* as in *system, i* as in *easily, o* as in *gallop, u* as in *circus;* ᵊ as in *fire* (fīᵊr), *hour* (ouᵊr). l and n can serve as syllabic consonants, as in *cradle* (krād′l), and *button* (but′n). See the full key inside the front cover.

plaint: *I don't want to hear a peep out of any of you!* —*v.i.* **4.** to utter the short, shrill little cry of a young bird, a mouse, etc.; cheep; squeak. **5.** to speak in a thin, weak voice. [1400–50; late ME *pepen, pipen;* cf. D, G *piepen,* OF *piper,* L *pīpāre,* Gk *pippízein,* Czech *pípat,* Lith *pýpti,* all ult. of imit. orig.]

peep[3] (pēp), *n.* jeep. [1940–45, *Amer.*; appar. alter. of JEEP]

pee•pee (pē′pē′), *v.i.,* **-peed, -pee•ing,** *n. Baby Talk.* pee[2]. [1840–50]

peep•er[1] (pē′pər), *n.* **1.** a person or thing that emits or utters a peeping sound. **2.** *Northeastern U.S.* any of several frogs having a peeping call, esp. the spring peeper. [1585–95; PEEP[2] + -ER[1]]

peep•er[2] (pē′pər), *n.* **1.** a person who peeps in an abnormally prying manner; a voyeur. **2. peepers,** *Slang.* the eyes. [1645–55; PEEP[1] + -ER[1]]

peep•hole (pēp′hōl′), *n.* a small hole or opening through which to peep or look, as in a door. [1675–85; PEEP[1] + HOLE]

Peep′ing Tom′, a person who obtains sexual gratification by observing others surreptitiously, esp. a man who looks through windows at night. [1910–15; allusion to the legendary man who peeped at Lady Godiva as she rode naked through Coventry]

peep′ show′, **1.** a display of objects or pictures viewed through a small opening that is usually fitted with a magnifying lens. **2.** a short, usually erotic or titillating film shown in a coin-operated viewing machine equipped with a projector. [1850–55]

peep′ sight′, a plate containing a small hole through which a gunner peeps in sighting. [1880–85]

pee•pul (pē′pəl), *n.* pipal.

peer[1] (pēr), *n.* **1.** a person of the same legal status: *a jury of one's peers.* **2.** a person who is equal to another in abilities, qualifications, age, background, and social status. **3.** something of equal worth or quality: *a skyscraper without peer.* **4.** a nobleman. **5.** a member of any of the five degrees of the nobility in Great Britain and Ireland (duke, marquis, earl, viscount, and baron). **6.** *Archaic.* a companion. [1175–1225; ME *per* < OF *per* < L *pār* equal]

peer[2] (pēr), *v.i.* **1.** to look narrowly or searchingly, as in the effort to discern clearly. **2.** to peep out or appear slightly. **3.** to come into view. [1585–95; perh. aph. var. of APPEAR] —**peer′ing•ly,** *adv.*
—**Syn. 1.** See **peep**[1].

peer•age (pēr′ij), *n.* **1.** the body of peers of a country or state. **2.** the rank or dignity of a peer. **3.** a book listing the peers and giving their genealogies. [1425–75; late ME *perage.* See PEER[1], -AGE]

Peerce (pērs), *n.* **Jan** (*Jacob Pincus Perelmuth*), 1904–84, U.S. opera singer.

peer•ess (pēr′is), *n.* **1.** the wife or widow of a peer. **2.** a woman having in her own right the rank of a peer. [1680–90; PEER[1] + -ESS]
—**Usage.** See **-ess.**

peer′ group′, a group of people, usually of similar age, background, and social status, with whom a person associates and who are likely to influence the person's beliefs and behavior. [1940–45]

Peer Gynt (pēr′ gint′; *Norw.* pâr′ gynt′), a play (1867) by Henrik Ibsen.

peer•less (pēr′lis), *adj.* having no equal; matchless; unrivaled. [1275–1325; ME *pereles.* See PEER[1], -LESS] —**peer′less•ly,** *adv.* —**peer′less•ness,** *n.*
—**Syn.** unmatched, unequaled; unique, unsurpassed.

peer′ of the realm′, *pl.* **peers of the realm.** any of a class of peers in Great Britain and Ireland entitled by heredity to sit in the House of Lords. [1585–95]

peer′ pres′sure, social pressure by members of one's peer group to take a certain action, adopt certain values, or otherwise conform in order to be accepted.

peer′ review′, evaluation of a person's work or performance by a group of people in the same occupation, profession, or industry. [1970–75]

peet•weet (pēt′wēt), *n.* the spotted sandpiper. [1830–40, *Amer.*; imit. rhyming compound; cf. PEWEE, PEWIT]

peeve (pēv), *v.,* **peeved, peev•ing,** *n.* —*v.t.* **1.** to render peevish; annoy. —*n.* **2.** a source of annoyance or irritation: *Tardiness is one of my greatest peeves.* **3.** an annoyed or irritated mood: *to be in a peeve.* [1905–10, *Amer.*; back formation from PEEVISH]
—**Syn. 2.** vexation, affliction, grievance.

peeved (pēvd), *adj.* annoyed; irritated; vexed. [1905–10, *Amer.*; PEEVE + -ED[2]] —**peev•ed•ly** (pē′vid lē, pēvd′-), *adv.* —**peev′ed•ness,** *n.*

pee•vish (pē′vish), *adj.* **1.** cross, querulous, or fretful, as from vexation or discontent: *a peevish youngster.* **2.** showing annoyance, irritation, or bad mood: *a peevish reply; a peevish frown.* **3.** perverse or obstinate. [1350–1400; ME *pevysh* < ?] —**pee′vish•ly,** *adv.* —**pee′vish•ness,** *n.*
—**Syn. 1.** petulant, irritable, snappish. See **cross.**

pee•wee (pē′wē′), *Informal.* —*adj.* **1.** very small; tiny. **2.** insignificant or inconsequential: *a player sent to the peewee leagues.* —*n.* **3.** a person or thing that is unusually small. **4.** an animal that is small for its kind; runt. **5.** *Marbles.* a small playing marble, often one made of clay rather than glass. [1885–90; rhyming compound based on WEE]

pee•wit (pē′wit, pyōō′it), *n.* pewit.

P.E.F., *Insurance.* personal effects floater.

CONCISE ETYMOLOGY KEY: <, descended or borrowed from; >, whence; b., blend of, blended; c., cognate with; cf., compare; deriv., derivative; equiv., equivalent; imit., imitative; obl., oblique; r., replacing; s., stem; sp., spelling, spelled; resp., respelling, respelled; trans., translation; ?, origin unknown; *, unattested; ‡, probably earlier than. See the full key inside the front cover.

peg (peg), *n., v.,* **pegged, peg•ging,** *adj.* —*n.* **1.** a pin of wood or other material driven or fitted into something, as to fasten parts together, to hang things on, to make fast a rope or string on, to stop a hole, or to mark some point. **2.** *Informal.* a leg, either real or wooden: *still on his pegs at 99.* **3.** a notch or degree: *to come down a peg.* **4.** an occasion, basis, or reason: *a peg to hang a grievance on.* **5.** Also called **pin.** *Music.* a pin of wood or metal in the neck of a stringed instrument that may be turned in its socket to adjust a string's tension. **6.** *Informal.* a throw, esp. in baseball: *The peg to the plate was late.* **7.** See **news peg. 8.** *Econ.* the level at which some price, exchange rate, etc., is set. **9.** *Brit., Anglo-Indian.* an alcoholic drink, esp. a whiskey or brandy and soda. **10.** *Brit.* clothespin. **11. take down a peg,** to reduce the pride or arrogance of; humble: *I guess that'll take him down a peg!* —*v.t.* **12.** to drive or insert a peg into. **13.** to fasten with or as with pegs. **14.** to mark with pegs. **15.** to strike or pierce with or as with a peg. **16.** to keep (the commodity price, exchange rate, etc.) at a set level, as by manipulation or law. **17.** *Informal.* to throw (a ball). **18.** *Journalism.* to base (an article, feature story, etc.) upon; justify by (usually fol. by *on*): *The feature on the chief of police was pegged on the riots.* **19.** *Informal.* to identify: *to peg someone as a good prospect.* —*v.i.* **20.** to work or continue persistently or energetically: *to peg away at a homework assignment.* **21.** *Informal.* to throw a ball. **22.** *Croquet.* to strike a peg, as in completing a game. —*adj.* **23.** Also, **pegged.** tapered toward the bottom of the leg: *peg trousers.* [1400–50; late ME *pegge* (n.), *peggen* (v.) < MD] —**peg′less,** *adj.* —**peg′like′,** *adj.*

Peg (peg), *n.* a female given name, form of **Peggy.**

Pegasus (def. 1)

Peg•a•sus (peg′ə səs), *n., gen.* **-si** (-sī′) for 2. **1.** *Class. Myth.* a winged horse, created from the blood of Medusa, that opened the spring of Hippocrene with a stroke of its hoof, and that carried Bellerophon in his attack on the Chimera. **2.** *Astron.* the Winged Horse, a northern constellation between Cygnus and Aquarius. —**Pe•ga•si•an** (pə gā′sē ən), *adj.*

Peg-Board (peg′bôrd′, -bōrd′), *Trademark.* a brand name for perfboard.

peg•board (peg′bôrd′, -bōrd′), *n.* a board having holes into which pegs are placed in specific patterns, used for playing or scoring certain games. [1895–1900; PEG + BOARD]

peg•box (peg′boks′), *n.* the widened end of the neck of a stringed instrument, to which the tuning pegs are fixed. [1880–85; PEG + BOX[1]]

Peg•gy (peg′ē), *n.* a female given name, form of **Margaret.**

peg′ leg′, **1.** an artificial leg, esp. a wooden one. **2.** a person with an artificial leg. [1760–70] —**peg′legged′,** *adj.*

Peg•ler (peg′lər), *n.* **(James) Westbrook,** 1894–1969, U.S. journalist.

peg•ma•tite (peg′mə tīt′), *n. Petrol.* a coarsely crystalline granite or other high-silica rock occurring in veins or dikes. [1825–35; < Gk *pēgmat-* (s. of *pēgma*) anything fastened together, a bond (cf. *pēgnýein* to stick) + -ITE[1]] —**peg•ma•tit•ic** (peg′mə tit′ik), *adj.*

peg′ top′, **1.** a child's wooden top that spins on a metal peg. **2. peg tops,** peg-top trousers. [1730–40]

peg-top (peg′top′), *adj.* wide at the hips and narrowing to the ankle: *peg-top trousers; peg-top skirts.* [1730–40; adj. use of PEG TOP (def. 1)]

Pe•gu (pe gōō′), *n.* a city in central Burma: pagodas. 50,000. —**Pe•gu′an,** *adj., n.*

peg•wood (peg′wo͝od′), *n.* a rod of boxwood of about ⅛ in. (3 mm) diameter, cut in various ways at the end and used by watchmakers for cleaning jewels. [1800–85; PEG + WOOD[1]]

peh (pā), *n.* pe.

Peh•le•vi (pā′lə vē′), *n.* the Pahlavi language.

Pei (pā), *n.* **I(eoh) M(ing)** (yō ming), born 1917, U.S. architect, born in China.

P.E.I., Prince Edward Island.

Pei•ching (*Chin.* bā′jing′), *n. Wade-Giles.* Beijing.

peign•oir (pān wär′, pen-, pān′wär, pen′-), *n.* **1.** a woman's dressing gown. **2.** a cloak or gown of terry cloth for wear after swimming or, esp. in France, after the bath. [1825–35; < F: lit., comber, i.e., something worn while one's hair is being combed, equiv. to *peign(er)* to comb (< LL *pectināre;* see PECTEN) + *-oir* < L *-ōrium* -ORY[1]]

Pei•ping (*Chin.* bā′ping′), *n. Wade-Giles.* former name of **Beijing.**

Pei•pus (pī′pəs), *n.* a lake in N Europe, on the border between Estonia and the W Russian Federation. 93 mi. (150 km) long; 356 sq. mi. (920 sq. km). Russian, **Chudskoye Ozero.** Estonian, **Peip•si** (pāp′sē).

Pei•rae•us (pī rē′əs, pi rā′-), *n.* Piraeus.

Pei•rai•evs (pē′ʀe efs′), *n.* Greek name of **Piraeus.**

Peirce (pûrs, pērs), *n.* **1. Benjamin,** 1809–80, U.S. mathematician. **2. Charles San•ders** (san′dərz), 1839–1914, U.S. philosopher, mathematician, and physicist. **3.** a male given name.

pej•o•ra•tion (pej′ə rā′shən, pē′jə-), *n.* **1.** depreciation; a lessening in worth, quality, etc. **2.** *Historical Ling.* semantic change in a word to a lower, less approved, or less respectable meaning. Cf. **melioration** (def. 1). [1650–60; < ML *pējōrātiōn-* (s. of *pējōrātiō*) a making worse, equiv. to LL *pējōrāt(us)* (ptp. of *pējōrāre* to make worse, deriv. of *pējor* worse) + *-iōn-* -ION]

pe•jo•ra•tive (pi jôr′ə tiv, -jor′-, pej′ə rā′-, pē′jə-), *adj.* **1.** having a disparaging, derogatory, or belittling effect or force: *the pejorative affix* -ling *in* princeling. —*n.* **2.** a pejorative form or word, as *poetaster.* [1880–85; < L *pējōrāt(us)* (see PEJORATION) + -IVE] —**pe•jo′•ra•tive•ly,** *adv.*
—**Syn. 1.** deprecatory.

pek•an (pek′ən), *n.* the fisher, *Martes pennanti.* [1710–20, *Amer.*; < CanF *pécan, pécant, pékan* < Eastern Abenaki (F sp.) *pékané*]

peke (pēk), *n. Informal.* Pekingese (def. 1). [1910–15; by shortening]

pe•ke•poo (pē′kə pōō′), *n., pl.* **-poos.** peekapoo.

pe•kin (pē′kin′), *n.* (*often cap.*) a silk fabric in which broad stripes of equal width and in various colors or weaves are alternated. [1775–85; < F *pékin;* after PEKING]

Pe•kin (pē′kin′), *n.* one of a hardy breed of yellowish-white domestic ducks, raised originally in China. [1880–85; after PEKING]

Pe•kin (pē′kin), *n.* a city in central Illinois. 33,967.

Pe•king (pē′king′, pā′-; *Chin.* bā′jing′), *n. Older Spelling.* Beijing.

Pe′king duck′, *Chinese Cookery.* a roasted duck prized for its crisp skin, prepared by forcing air between skin and meat, brushing with sugar water, and hanging up to dry before final cooking. Also called **Beijing duck.** [1875–80]

Pe•king•ese (pē′kə nēz′, -nēs′; *esp. for 2–5 also* pē′king ēz′, -ēs′), *n., pl.* **-ese** for 1, 4, *adj.* —*n.* **1.** one of a Chinese breed of small dogs having a long, silky coat. **2.** the standard Chinese language. **3.** the dialect of Peking. **4.** a native or inhabitant of Peking. —*adj.* **5.** of, pertaining to, or characteristic of Peking. Also, **Pe•kin•ese** (pē′kə nēz′, -nēs′). [1840–50; PEKING + -ESE]

Pekingese (def. 1), 11 in. (28 cm) high at shoulder

Pe′king′ man′, the skeletal remains of *Homo erectus,* formerly classified as *Sinanthropus pekinensis,* found at Zhoukoudian, near Peking, China, in the late 1930's and early 1940's and subsequently lost during World War II.

pe•koe (pē′kō), *n.* a superior kind of black tea from Sri Lanka, India, and Java, made from leaves coarser than those used for orange pekoe. [1705–15; < dial. Chin (Xiamen) *pek-ho,* akin to Chin *báu* white + *hòu* empress]

pel•age (pel′ij), *n.* the hair, fur, wool, or other soft covering of a mammal. [1820–30; < F, deriv. of *poil* (OF *peil, pel;* see POILU); see -AGE] —**pe•la•gi•al** (pə lā′jē əl), *adj.*

Pe•la•gi•an (pə lā′jē ən, -jən), *n.* **1.** a follower of Pelagius, who denied original sin and believed in freedom of the will. —*adj.* **2.** of or pertaining to Pelagius or Pelagianism. [1525–35; < LL *Pelagiānus;* see -AN] —**Pe•la′gi•an•ism,** *n.*

Pe•la•gi•an•ize (pə lā′jē ə nīz′, -jə nīz′), *v.i., v.t.,* **-ized, -iz•ing.** to become or make Pelagian. Also, *esp. Brit.,* **Pe•la′gi•an•ise′.** [1615–25; PELAGIAN + -IZE] —**Pe•la′gi•an•iz′er,** *n.*

pe•lag•ic (pə laj′ik), *adj.* **1.** of or pertaining to the open seas or oceans. **2.** living or growing at or near the surface of the ocean, far from land, as certain organisms. Cf. **neritic, oceanic.** [1650–60; < L *pelagicus* < Gk *pelagikós,* equiv. to *pélag(os)* the sea + *-ikos* -IC]

pelag′ic divi′sion, the biogeographic realm or zone that comprises the open seas and oceans, including water of all depths. Cf. **benthos.** [1890–95]

Pe•la•gi•us (pə lā′jē əs), *n.* 360?–420?, English monk and theologian who lived in Rome: teachings opposed by St. Augustine.

Pelagius I, died A.D. 561, pope 556–561.

Pelagius II, died A.D. 590, pope 579–590.

pel•ar•gon•ic (pel′är gon′ik, -gō′nik, -ər-), *adj. Chem.* of or derived from a pelargonium or pelargonic acid. [1855–60; PELARGON(IUM) + -IC]

pel′argon′ic ac′id, *Chem.* a colorless, oily, water-immiscible liquid, $C_9H_{18}O_2$, occurring as an ester in a volatile oil in species of pelargonium: used chiefly in organic synthesis and in the manufacture of lacquers and plastics. Also called **nonanoic acid.** [1855–60]

pel•ar•go•ni•um (pel′är gō′nē əm, -ər-), *n.* any plant of the genus *Pelargonium,* the cultivated species of which are usually called geraniums. Cf. **geranium** (def. 2). [1810–20; < NL < Gk *pelargó(s)* stork + *(gerá)nion* GERANIUM]

Pe•las•gi (pə laz′jē), *n.pl.* the Pelasgians. [< L *Pelasgī* < Gk *Pelasgoí*]

Pe•las•gi•an (pə laz′jē ən, -jən, -gē ən), *adj.* **1.** of or pertaining to the Pelasgians. —*n.* **2.** a member of a prehistoric people inhabiting Greece, Asia Minor, and the islands of the eastern Mediterranean. [1480–90; << Gk *Pelásgi(os)* Pelasgian (*Pelasg(oí)* PELASGI + *-ios* adj. suffix) + -AN]

Pe·las·gic (pə laz′jik, -gik), *adj.* Pelasgian. [1775–85; << Gk *Pelasgikós.* See PELASGI, -IC]

pele (pēl), *n.* peel³.

Pe·lé (pā lā′, pā′lā), *n.* (*Edson Arantes do Nascimento*), born 1940, Brazilian soccer player.

pe·lec·y·pod (pə les′ə pod′), *n.* **1.** any mollusk of the class Pelecypoda (Lamellibranchiata), characterized by a bivalve shell enclosing the headless body and lamellate gills, comprising the oysters, clams, mussels, and scallops. —*adj.* **2.** Also, **pel·e·cyp·o·dous** (pel′ə sip′ə dəs). belonging or pertaining to the Pelecypoda. [1855–60; < NL *Pelecypoda* < Gk *péleky(s)* hatchet + NL *-poda;* see -POD]

Pe·lée (pə lā′), *n.* **Mount,** a volcano in the West Indies, on the island of Martinique: eruption 1902. 4428 ft. (1350 m).

pel·er·ine (pel′ə rēn′, pel′ər in), *n.* a woman's cape of fur or cloth, usually waist-length in back with long descending ends in front. [1735–45; < F *pèlerine,* fem. of *pèlerin* pilgrim]

Pe′le's hair′ (pā′lāz, pē′lēz), volcanic glass thread, usually basaltic, caused by the solidification of exploding or ejected lava in the open air. [1840–50; trans. of Hawaiian *lauoho-o-Pele* hair of Pele (goddess of the volcano Kilauea)]

Pe′le's tears′, drops of volcanic glass, often with pendent threads, thrown out during a volcanic eruption. [named after *Pele;* see PELE'S HAIR]

Pe·le·us (pē′lē əs, pēl′yo͞os), *n. Class. Myth.* a king of the Myrmidons, the son of Aeacus and father of Achilles.

Pe·lew′ Is′lands (pē lo͞o′). a former name of the Republic of **Belau.**

pelf (pelf), *n.* money or wealth, esp. when regarded with contempt or acquired by reprehensible means. [1300–50; ME < OF *pelfre* booty]

Pel·ham (pel′əm), *n.* a bit that is used with two pairs of reins, designed to serve the purpose of a full bridle. [after the proper name *Pelham*]

Pel·ham (pel′əm), *n.* **Henry,** 1696–1754, British statesman: prime minister 1743–54 (brother of Thomas Pelham-Holles).

Pel·ham-Hol·les (pel′əm hol′is), *n.* **Thomas, 1st Duke of Newcastle,** 1693–1768, British statesman: prime minister 1754–56, 1757–62 (brother of Henry Pelham).

pelican, *Pelecanus erythrorhynchos,* length 5 ft. (1.5 m)

pel·i·can (pel′i kən), *n.* **1.** any of several large, totipalmate, fish-eating birds of the family Pelecanidae, having a large bill with a distensible pouch. **2.** a still or retort with two tubes that leave the body from the neck, curve in opposite directions, and reenter the body through the belly. [bef. 1000; ME *pellican,* OE < LL *pelicānus,* var. of *pelecān* < Gk *pelekā́n*]

pel·i·can-flow·er (pel′i kən flou′ər), *n.* a woody vine, *Aristolochia grandiflora,* of the West Indies, having heart-shaped leaves and purple-spotted, purple-veined flowers from 18 to 24 in. (46 to 61 cm) wide with a long, taillike structure at the tip of the corolla. [1895–1900]

pel′ican hook′, a hooklike device for holding the link of a chain or the like, consisting of a long shackle with a hinged rod held closed with a sliding ring. Also called **slip hook.**

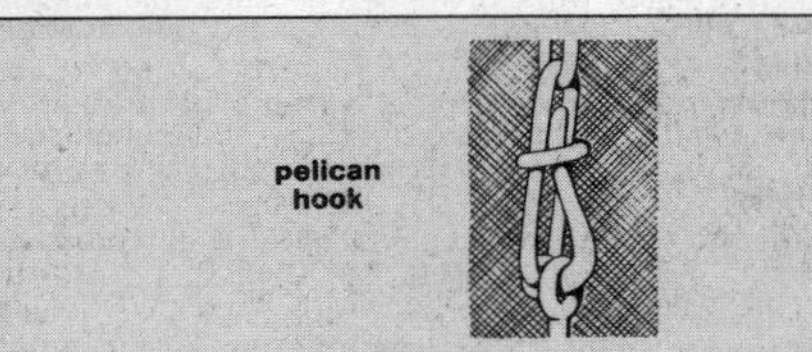
pelican hook

Pel′ican State′, Louisiana (used as a nickname).

pel·i·ke (pel′i kē′), *n., pl.* **-kai** (-kī′). *Gk. and Rom. Antiq.* a storage jar with two handles extending from the lip to the shoulder, characterized by an oval body that is wider at the base than at the neck and rests on a foot. Cf. **amphora, stamnos.** [1870–75; < Gk *pelíkē* pitcher]

Pe·li·on (pē′lē ən; *Gk.* pē′lē ôn), *n.* **Mount,** a mountain near the E coast of Greece, in Thessaly. 5252 ft. (1600 m).

pe·lisse (pə lēs′), *n.* **1.** an outer garment lined or trimmed with fur. **2.** a woman's long cloak with slits for the arms. [1710–20; < F < LL *pellicia* mantle, n. use of fem. of L *pellicius* of skin, deriv. of *pellis* skin]

pe·lite (pē′līt), *n. Geol.* any clayey rock, as mudstone or shale. [1875–80; < Gk *pēl(ós)* clay, earth + -ITE¹] —**pe·lit·ic** (pi lit′ik), *adj.*

Pel·la (pel′ə), *n.* a ruined city in N Greece, NW of Salonika: the capital of ancient Macedonia; birthplace of Alexander the Great.

pel·la·gra (pə lag′rə, -lā′grə, -lä′-), *n. Pathol.* a disease caused by a deficiency of niacin in the diet, characterized by skin changes, severe nerve dysfunction, mental symptoms, and diarrhea. [1805–15; < It < NL: skin disease, equiv. to *pell(is)* skin + *-agra* < Gk *ágra* seizure] —**pel·la′grose, pel·la′grous,** *adj.*

pel·la′gra-pre·ven′tive fac′tor (pə lag′rə pri-ven′tiv, -lā′grə-, -lä′-), *Biochem.* nicotinic acid or its amide, nicotinamide, being the vitamin-B-complex members that serve to prevent pellagra. Also called **P.P. factor.**

pel·la·grin (pə lag′rin, -lā′grin, -lä′-), *n. Pathol.* a person affected with pellagra. [1860–65; PELLAGR(A) + -IN¹]

Pel·lan (*Fr.* pe läɴ′), *n.* **Al·fred** (*Fr.* al fʀed′), born 1906, Canadian painter.

pel·le·kar (pel′i kär′), *n.* palikar.

pel·let (pel′it), *n.* **1.** a small, rounded or spherical body, as of food or medicine. **2.** a small wad or ball of wax, paper, etc., for throwing, shooting, or the like. **3.** one of a charge of small shot, as for a shotgun. **4.** a bullet. **5.** a ball, usually of stone, formerly used as a missile. **6.** Also called **cast.** *Ornith.* a small, roundish mass of matter regurgitated by certain predatory birds, consisting of the indigestible remains, as the fur, feathers, and bones, of the prey. **7.** (in Romanesque architecture) a hemispherical or disklike carved ornament. **8.** *Heraldry.* ogress². —*v.t.* **9.** to form into pellets; pelletize. **10.** to hit with pellets. [1325–75; ME *pelet* < MF *pelote* < VL **pilotta,* dim. of L *pila* ball. See PILL¹, -ET] —**pel′let·like′,** *adj.*

Pel·le·tier (pel′i tēr′; *Fr.* pelᵊ tyā′), *n.* **Wilfrid,** 1896–1982, Canadian orchestra conductor.

pel·let·ize (pel′i tīz′), *v.,* **-ized, -iz·ing.** —*v.t.* **1.** to make or form (concentrated ore) into pellets. —*v.i.* **2.** to make or manufacture pellets. Also, *esp. Brit.,* **pel′let·ise′.** [1940–45; PELLET + -IZE] —**pel′let·i·za′tion,** *n.* —**pel′let·i′zer,** *n.*

pel·li·cle (pel′i kəl), *n.* **1.** a thin skin or membrane; film; scum. **2.** *Photog.* a thin, partially reflective coating, as on a beam splitter or pellicle mirror. [1535–45; < L *pellicul(a),* equiv. to *pelli(s)* skin + *-cula* -CLE¹] —**pel·lic·u·lar** (pə lik′yə lər), **pel·lic·u·late** (pə lik′yə-lit, -lāt′), *adj.*

pel′licle mir′ror, *Photog.* a fixed mirror in a single-lens reflex camera that reflects some of the light entering the lens to the ground-glass view screen while permitting most of the light to pass through to the film. [in reference to the thin, partially reflective coating covering such mirrors]

pell-mell (pel′mel′), *adv.* **1.** in disorderly, headlong haste; in a recklessly hurried manner. **2.** in a confused or jumbled mass, crowd, manner, etc.: *The crowd rushed pell-mell into the store when the doors opened.* —*adj.* **3.** indiscriminate; disorderly; confused: *a pell-mell dash after someone.* **4.** overhasty or precipitate; rash: *pell-mell spending.* —*n.* **5.** a confused or jumbled mass, crowd, etc. **6.** disorderly, headlong haste. Also, **pell′-mell′.** [1570–80; < MF *pelemele,* OF *pesle mesle,* rhyming compound based on *mesler* to mix. See MEDDLE]

pel·lu·cid (pə lo͞o′sid), *adj.* **1.** allowing the maximum passage of light, as glass; translucent. **2.** clear or limpid: *pellucid waters.* **3.** clear in meaning, expression, or style: *a pellucid way of writing.* [1610–20; < L *pellūcidus,* var. of *perlūcidus.* See PER-, LUCID] —**pel·lu·cid·i·ty** (pel′o͞o sid′i tē), **pel·lu′cid·ness,** *n.* —**pel·lu′cid·ly,** *adv.*
—**Syn. 2.** transparent. —**Ant. 1, 2.** opaque. **3.** obscure.

pel·me·ny (pel′mə nē; *Russ.* pyil mye′nyi), *n.pl. Russian Cookery.* a Siberian dish of small pockets of dough filled with seasoned, minced beef, lamb, or pork and served boiled, fried, or in a soup. Also, **pel′me·ni.** [1940–45; < Russ *pel′méni,* pl. of *pel′mén′,* dissimilated form of dial. *pel′nyán′* < Komi, Udmurt *pel′ńań,* equiv. to *pel′* ear + *ńań* bread, pastry (so called from their earlike shape]

pel·met (pel′mit), *n.* a decorative cornice or valance at the head of a window or doorway, used to cover the fastenings from which curtains are hung. [1900–05; perh. alter. of PALMETTE (or < F *palmette*), employed as an ornament on wood or plaster window cornices]

pel·oid (pel′oid), *n. Med.* mud used therapeutically. [< Gk *pēl(ós)* mud, clay + -OID]

Pe·lop·i·das (pə lop′i dəs), *n.* died 364 B.C., Greek general and statesman of Thebes.

Pel′oponne′sian War′, a war between Athens and Sparta, 431–404 B.C., that resulted in the transfer of hegemony in Greece from Athens to Sparta.

Pel·o·pon·ne·sus (pel′ə pə nē′səs), *n.* a peninsula forming the S part of Greece: seat of the early Mycenaean civilization and the powerful city-states of Argos, Sparta, etc. 986,912; 8356 sq. mi. (21,640 sq. km). Also, **Pel·o·pon·nese** (pel′ə pə nēz′, -nēs′), **Pel·o·pon·ne·sos** (pel′ə pə nē′sos, -sōs, -səs). Also called **Morea.** [< L < Gk *Pelopónnēsos* (repr. phrase *Pélopos nêsos* lit., island of PELOPS with *sn* > *nn*)] —**Pel·o·pon·ne·sian** (pel′ə-pə nē′zhən, -shən), *adj., n.*

Pel·ops (pē′lops, pel′ops), *n. Class. Myth.* a son of Tantalus and Dione, slaughtered by his father and served to the Olympians as food; Hermes restored him to life and he later ruled over southern Greece, which was called Peloponnesus after him.

pe·lo·ri·a (pə lôr′ē ə, -lōr′-), *n. Bot.* regularity of structure occurring abnormally in flowers normally irregular. [1855–60; < NL < Gk *pélōr(os)* monstrous (*pélōr* monster + *-os* adj. suffix) + *-ia* -IA] —**pe·lor·ic** (pə lôr′ik, -lor′-), *adj.*

pel·o·rize (pel′ə rīz′), *v.t.,* **-rized, -riz·ing.** *Bot.* to affect with peloria. Also, *esp. Brit.,* **pel′o·rise′.** [1865–70; PELOR(IA) + -IZE] —**pel′o·ri·za′tion,** *n.*

pe·lo·rus (pə lôr′əs, -lōr′-), *n., pl.* **-rus·es.** *Navig.* a device for measuring in degrees the relative bearings of observed objects. Also called **dumb compass.** [1850–55; perh. < L *Pelōrus,* now Faro in Sicily, a cape which requires skill in navigation]

pe·lo·ta (pə lō′tə; *Sp.* pe lô′tä), *n., pl.* **-tas** (-təz; *Sp.* -täs). **1.** a Basque and Spanish game from which jai alai was developed. **2.** the game of jai alai. **3.** the ball used in pelota and jai alai. [1890–95; < Sp: ball < MF *pelote;* see PELLET]

Pe·lo·tas (pə lō′təs; *Port.* pi lô′täs), *n.* a city in S Brazil. 150,278.

pel·o·ton (pel′ə ton′, pel′ə ton′; *Fr.* plô tôɴ′), *n.* an ornamental glass made in Bohemia in the late 19th century, usually having a striated overlay of glass filaments in a different color. Also called **pel′oton glass′.** [1710–20; < F: lit., ball, ball of string, equiv. to *pelote* ball (see PELLET) + *-on* dim. suffix]

pelt¹ (pelt), *v.t.* **1.** to attack or assail with repeated blows or with missiles. **2.** to throw (missiles). **3.** to drive by blows or missiles: *The child pelted the cows home from the fields.* **4.** to assail vigorously with words, questions, etc. **5.** to beat or rush against with repeated forceful blows: *The wind and rain pelted the roofs and walls of the houses for four days.* —*v.i.* **6.** to strike blows; beat with force or violence. **7.** to throw missiles. **8.** to hurry. **9.** to beat or pound unrelentingly: *The wind, rain, and snow pelted against the castle walls.* **10.** to cast abuse. —*n.* **11.** the act of pelting. **12.** a vigorous stroke; whack. **13.** a blow with something thrown. **14.** speed. **15.** an unrelenting or repeated beating, as of rain or wind. [1490–1500; orig. uncert.]

pelt² (pelt), *n.* **1.** the untanned hide or skin of an animal. **2.** *Facetious.* the human skin. **3. in one's pelt,** *Facetious.* naked. [1275–1325; ME; perh. back formation from PELTRY; cf. OF *pelete,* deriv. of L *pellis* skin] —**pelt′ish,** *adj.* —**pelt′less,** *adj.*
—**Syn. 1.** See **skin.**

pel·tate (pel′tāt), *adj. Bot.* having the stalk or support attached to the lower surface at a distance from the margin, as a leaf; shield-shaped. [1745–55; < L *peltātus,* equiv. to *pelt(a)* small shield (< Gk *péltē*) + *-ātus* -ATE¹] —**pel′tate·ly,** *adv.* —**pel·ta′tion,** *n.*

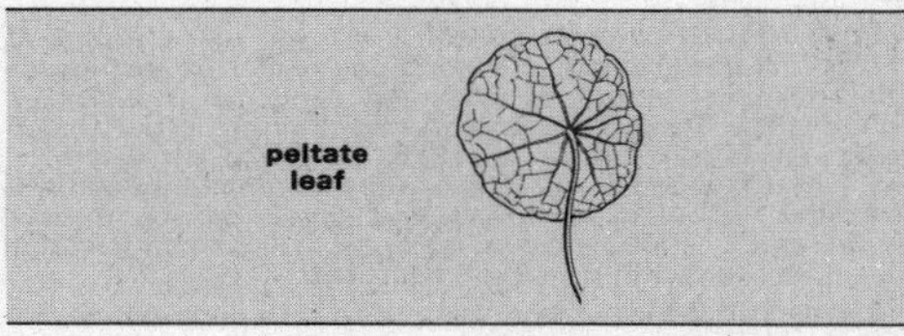
peltate leaf

pelt·er (pel′tər), *n.* **1.** a person or thing that pelts. **2.** *Poker.* skeet². [1820–30; PELT¹ + -ER¹]

Pel′tier effect′ (pel′tyā), *Physics.* the change in temperature of either junction of a thermocouple when a current is maintained in the thermocouple and after allowance is made for a temperature change due to resistance. [1855–60; named after Jean C. A. Peltier (1785–1845), French physicist who discovered it]

Pel′tier heat′, *Physics.* the heat gained or lost at a junction of a thermocouple due to the Peltier effect. [1915–20; see PELTIER EFFECT]

pelt·ing (pel′ting), *adj. Archaic.* paltry; petty; mean. [1530–40; perh. dial. *pelt* rags, rubbish (akin to Dan *pjalt* rag) + -ING². See PALTRY] —**pelt′ing·ly,** *adv.*

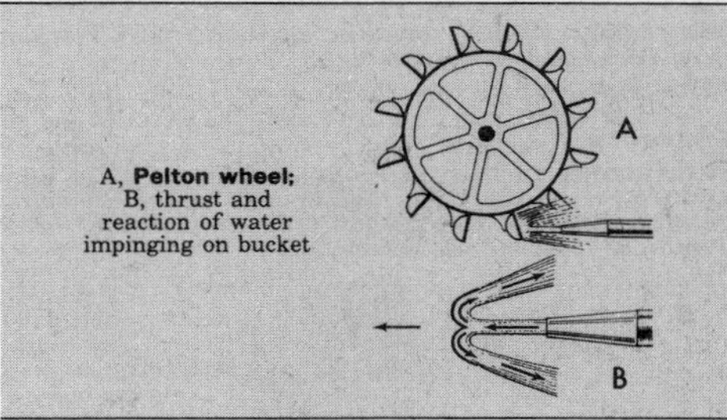

A, **Pelton wheel;** B, thrust and reaction of water impinging on bucket

Pel′ton wheel′ (pel′tn), a high-pressure impulse water turbine in which one or more free jets of water are directed against the buckets of the rotor. [1880–85; named after L. A. Pelton (d. 1908), U.S. engineer, its inventor]

pelt·ry (pel′trē), *n., pl.* **-ries. 1.** fur skins; pelts collectively. **2.** a pelt. [1400–50; late ME < AF *pelterie,* OF *peleterie* furrier's wares, equiv. to *peleter* furrier (deriv. of L *pellis* skin; see -ER²) + *-ie* -Y³]

CONCISE PRONUNCIATION KEY: act, cāpe, dâre, pärt; set, ēqual; if, īce; ox, ōver, ôrder, oil, bo͝ok, bo͞ot, out; up, ûrge; child; sing; shoe; thin, *th*at; zh as in *treasure.* ə = *a* as in *alone, e* as in *system, i* as in *easily, o* as in *gallop, u* as in *circus;* ᵊ as in *fire* (fīᵊr), *hour* (ouᵊr). l and n can serve as syllabic consonants, as in *cradle* (krād′l), and *button* (but′n). See the full key inside the front cover.

pel•vic (pel′vik), *adj.* of or pertaining to the pelvis. [1820–30; PELV(IS) + -IC]

pel′vic fin′, (in fishes) either of a pair of fins on the lower surface of the body, corresponding to the hind limbs of a land vertebrate; ventral fin. [1905–10]

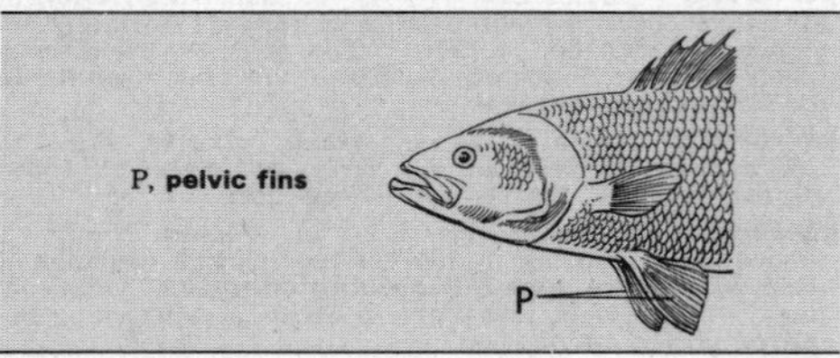

P, pelvic fins

pel′vic gir′dle, **1.** (in vertebrates) a bony or cartilaginous arch supporting the hind limbs or analogous parts. **2.** (in humans) the arch formed by the ilium, ischium, and pubis. See illus. under **pelvis.** Also called **pel′vic arch′.** [1885–90]

pel′vic inflam′matory disease′, *Pathol.* an inflammation of the female pelvic organs, most commonly the fallopian tubes, usually as a result of bacterial infection. *Abbr.:* PID [1980–85]

pel•vim•e•try (pel vim′i trē), *n., pl.* **-tries.** measurement of the diameters of the female pelvis, esp. the birth canal. [1860–65; PELVI(S) + -METRY]

pel•vis (pel′vis), *n., pl.* **-vis•es, -ves** (-vēz). *Anat., Zool.* **1.** the basinlike cavity in the lower part of the trunk of many vertebrates, formed in humans by the innominate bones, sacrum, etc. **2.** the bones forming this cavity. **3.** the cavity of the kidney that receives the urine before it is passed into the ureter. See diag. under **kidney.** [1605–15; < NL; L: basin; akin to Gk *pellís* bowl]

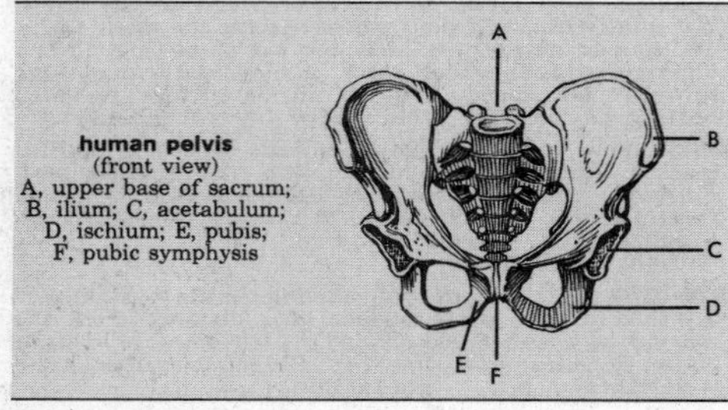

human pelvis (front view) A, upper base of sacrum; B, ilium; C, acetabulum; D, ischium; E, pubis; F, pubic symphysis

pel•y•co•saur (pel′i kə sôr′), *n.* any of a group of large primitive reptiles belonging to the extinct order Pelycosauria, abundant in North America and Europe during the Permian Period, often having a tall spinal sail. [< NL *Pelycosauria* (1878), equiv. to Gk *pelyk-*, s. of *pélyx* wooden bowl, cup (taken as meaning PELVIS, parallel to the NL sense of L *pelvis*) + *-o-* -O- + *saû-r(os)* -SAUR + NL *-ia* -IA; so named from the peculiar form of the ischium in such reptiles]

Pe•ma•tang•sian•tar (pə mä′täng syän′tär), *n.* a city on NE Sumatra, in Indonesia. 129,232.

Pem•ba (pem′bə), *n.* **1.** an island near the E coast of equatorial Africa: formerly part of Zanzibar protectorate; now a part of Tanzania. 164,321; 380 sq. mi. (984 sq. km). **2.** Formerly, **Pôrto Amélia.** a seaport in NE Mozambique. 7520.

pem•bi•na (pem′bə nə, pem bē′-), *n. Canadian (chiefly the Prairie Provinces).* highbush cranberry. [1750–60; earlier *panbina, pemine* < CanF (now sp. *pimbina*) < Cree *ni·pimina·na,* pl. of *ni·pimina·n,* a deriv. with *-min-* berry]

Pem•broke (pem′brŏŏk *or, esp. for 4,* -brōk), *n.* **1.** a borough in Dyfed, in SW Wales: birthplace of King Henry VII. 14,092. **2.** Pembrokeshire. **3.** one of a variety of Welsh corgi having a short or docked tail. Cf. **Cardigan** (def. 2). **4.** a city in SE Massachusetts. 13,487.

Pem′broke Pines′ (pem′brōk), a city in SE Florida, near Fort Lauderdale. 35,776.

Pem•broke•shire (pem′brŏŏk shēr′, -shər, -brōk-), *n.* a historic county in Dyfed, in SW Wales. Also called **Pembroke.**

Pem′broke ta′ble, a drop-leaf table with fly rails and with a drawer at one end or each end of the skirt. Also, **pem′broke ta′ble.** [1770–80; perh. named after *Pembroke,* English aristocratic family]

Pembroke table

CONCISE ETYMOLOGY KEY: <, descended or borrowed from; >, whence; b., blend of, blended; c., cognate with; cf., compare; deriv., derivative; equiv., equivalent; imit., imitative; obl., oblique; r., replacing; s., stem; sp., spelling, spelled; resp., respelling, respelled; trans., translation; ?, origin unknown; *, unattested; ‡, probably earlier than. See the full key inside the front cover.

pem•mi•can (pem′i kən), *n.* dried meat pounded into a powder and mixed with hot fat and dried fruits or berries, pressed into a loaf or into small cakes, originally prepared by North American Indians. Also, **pem′i•can.** [1735–45; < Cree *pimihka·n,* deriv. of *pimihke·w* he makes pemmican (mixing together the grease and other ingredients), he makes grease < Proto-Algonquian **pemihke·wa,* equiv. to **pemy-* grease + *-*ehke·* make]

pem•o•line (pem′ə lēn′, -lin), *n. Pharm.* a synthetic, weak, central nervous system stimulant, $C_9H_8N_2O_2$, with sympathomimetic activity, used as an adjunct in the management of hyperkinetic behavior disorders. [1960–65; perh. *p(h)e(nyl)* + *(i)m(ino)-* + *(oxaz)ol(id)ine,* components of its chemical name]

pem•phi•gus (pem′fi gəs, pem fī′-), *n. Pathol.* any of several diseases, often fatal, characterized by blisters on the skin and mucous membranes. [1770–80; < NL < Gk *pemphig-* (s. of *pémphix*) bubble + L *-us* n. suffix] —**pem•phi•goid** (pem′fi goid′), *adj.* —**pem′phi•gous,** *adj.*

pen[1] (pen), *n., v.,* **penned, pen•ning.** —*n.* **1.** any of various instruments for writing or drawing with ink or a similar substance. **2.** a detachable metal penpoint, filled by dipping or with a quill; nib. **3.** such a penpoint with its penholder. **4.** fountain pen. **5.** ball-point pen. **6.** the pen as the instrument of writing or authorship: *The pen is mightier than the sword.* **7.** a person's style or quality of writing: *He writes with a witty, incisive pen.* **8.** a writer: *I leave this story to abler pens.* **9.** the profession of writing: *a master of the pen.* **10.** *Ornith.* **a.** a quill. **b.** a pinfeather. **11.** something resembling or suggesting a feather or quill. **12.** *Zool.* an internal, corneous or chitinous, feather-shaped structure in certain cephalopods, as the squid. —*v.t.* **13.** to write with or as with a pen; put down in writing: *to pen an essay.* **14.** to draw with or as with a pen: *to pen a sketch.* [1250–1300; ME *penne* < OF *penne* pen, feather << LL *penna,* L: feather] —**pen′like′,** *adj.* —**pen′ner,** *n.*

pen[2] (pen), *n., v.,* **penned** or **pent, pen•ning.** —*n.* **1.** a small enclosure for domestic animals. **2.** animals so enclosed: *We have a pen of twenty sheep.* **3.** an enclosure used for confinement or safekeeping: *We have built several pens to hold our harvest of corn.* **4.** playpen. **5.** See **bull pen. 6.** a dock having a protective concrete structure overhead, used to service and repair submarines. —*v.t.* **7.** to confine in or as in a pen. [bef. 1000; (n.) ME *penne,* OE *penn* (in compounds); perh. akin to PIN; (v.) ME *pennen,* deriv. of the n.]

pen[3] (pen), *n. Slang.* penitentiary (def. 1). [1880–85; *Amer.*; shortened form]

pen[4] (pen), *n.* a female swan. [1540–50; orig. uncert.]

pen-, var. of **pene-** before a vowel: *penannular.*

Pen., peninsula. Also, **pen.**

P.E.N., International Association of Poets, Playwrights, Editors, Essayists, and Novelists.

pe•nal (pēn′l), *adj.* **1.** of, pertaining to, or involving punishment, as for crimes or offenses. **2.** prescribing punishment: *penal laws.* **3.** constituting punishment: *He survived the years of penal hardship.* **4.** used as a place of confinement and punishment: *a penal colony.* **5.** subject to or incurring punishment: *a penal offense.* **6.** payable or forfeitable as a penalty: *a penal sum.* [1400–50; late ME < L *poenālis,* equiv. to *poen(a)* penalty (< Gk *poinḗ* fine) + *-ālis* -AL[1]] —**pe•nal•i•ty** (pi nal′i tē), *n.* —**pe′nal•ly,** *adv.*

pe′nal code′, *Law.* the aggregate of statutory enactments dealing with crimes and their punishment. [1880–85]

pe•nal•ize (pēn′l īz′, pen′-), *v.t.,* **-ized, -iz•ing. 1.** to subject to a penalty, as a person. **2.** to declare (an action, deed, etc.) punishable by law or rule. **3.** to put under a disadvantage or handicap. Also, *esp. Brit.,* **pe′nal•ise′.** [1865–70; PENAL + -IZE] —**pe′nal•iz′a•ble,** *adj.* —**pe′nal•i•za′tion,** *n.*

pe′nal ser′vitude, *Eng. Criminal Law.* imprisonment together with hard labor. [1855–60]

pen•al•ty (pen′l tē), *n., pl.* **-ties. 1.** a punishment imposed or incurred for a violation of law or rule. **2.** a loss, forfeiture, suffering, or the like, to which one subjects oneself by nonfulfillment of some obligation. **3.** something that is forfeited, as a sum of money. **4.** a disadvantage imposed upon one of the competitors or upon one side for infraction of the rules of a game, sport, etc. **5.** consequence or disadvantage attached to any action, condition, etc. [1505–15; << ML *poenālitās.* See PENAL, -TY[2]]

pen′alty ar′ea, *Soccer.* the area, 44 yd. (40 m) wide and 18 yd. (16 m) deep, centered on the goal line and extending in front of the goal, where a foul by a defensive player results in a penalty kick for the offensive team. [1900–05]

pen′alty box′, *Ice Hockey.* an enclosed space adjacent to the rink for penalized players, the penalty timekeeper, the game timekeeper, and the official scorer.

pen′alty dou′ble, *Bridge.* See **business double.**

pen′alty kick′, *Soccer.* a free kick awarded for an infraction committed by a defensive player in the penalty area and taken by the offensive player who has been fouled from a point 12 yd. (11 m) directly in front of the goal. [1885–90]

pen′alty kill′er, *Ice Hockey.* a player used when the player's team is short-handed as a result of a penalty, esp. a player skilled at defense and employed regularly in such situations. [1960–65]

pen′alty shot′, *Ice Hockey.* a free shot at the goal defended only by the goalkeeper, awarded to an offensive player for certain defensive violations. [1945–50]

pen′alty stroke′, *Golf.* a stroke added to a score for a rule infraction. [1890–95]

pen•ance (pen′əns), *n.* **1.** a punishment undergone in token of penitence for sin. **2.** a penitential discipline imposed by church authority. **3.** a sacrament, as in the Roman Catholic Church, consisting in a confession of sin, made with sorrow and with the intention of amendment, followed by the forgiveness of the sin. [1250–1300; ME *penaunce* < AF; OF *peneance* < L *paenitentia* PENITENCE] —**pen′ance•less,** *adj.*

Pe•nang (pi nang′, -näng′, pē′näng′), *n.* **1.** an island in SE Asia, off the W coast of the Malay Peninsula. 110 sq. mi. (285 sq. km). **2.** a state including this island and parts of the adjacent mainland: now part of Malaysia; formerly one of the Straits Settlements and part of the former Federation of Malaya. 911,586; 400 sq. mi. (1036 sq. km). *Cap.:* Georgetown. Malay, **Pinang.**

pen•an•nu•lar (pen an′yə lər), *adj.* having the shape or design of an incomplete circle. [1850–55; PEN- + ANNULAR]

Pe•na•tes (pə nā′tēz, -nä′-), *n.pl. Rom. Religion.* gods who watched over the home or community to which they belonged: originally, two deities of the storeroom. Also, **pe•na′tes.** Cf. **Lares.** [1505–15; < L *Penātēs,* akin to *penus* stock of provisions]

pen-based (pen′bāst′), *adj.* (of a computer) having an electronic stylus rather than a keyboard as the primary input device. [1991]

pence (pens), *n. Brit.* a pl. of **penny;** used in referring to a sum of money rather than to the coins themselves (often used in combination): *sixpence; The fare was 15 pence.* [1275–1325; ME *pens, pans*] —**pence′less,** *adj.*

pen•cel (pen′səl), *n.* a small pennon, as at the head of a lance. Also, **pensil, pennoncel, penoncel.** [1225–75; ME < AF, syncopated var. of *penoncel* PENNONCEL]

pen•chant (pen′chənt; *Fr.* päɴ shäɴ′), *n.* a strong inclination, taste, or liking for something: *a penchant for outdoor sports.* [1665–75; < F, n. use of prp. of *pencher* to incline, lean < VL **pendicāre,* deriv. of L *pendēre* to hang]

pen•ché (*Fr.* päɴ shā′), *adj. Ballet.* performed or executed while leaning forward. [< F: leaned, ptp. of *pencher* to incline, bend, lean; see PENCHANT]

Pen•chi (*Chin.* bun′chē′), *n. Wade-Giles.* Benxi.

pen•cil (pen′səl), *n., v.,* **-ciled, -cil•ing** or (*esp. Brit.*) **-cilled, -cil•ling.** —*n.* **1.** a slender tube of wood, metal, plastic, etc., containing a core or strip of graphite, a solid coloring material, or the like, used for writing or drawing. **2.** a stick of cosmetic coloring material for use on the eyebrows, eyelids, etc. **3.** anything shaped or used like a pencil, as a stick of medicated material: *a styptic pencil.* **4.** a narrow set of lines, light rays, or the like, diverging from or converging to a point: *a pencil of sunlight.* **5.** a slender, pointed piece of a substance used for marking. **6.** style or skill in drawing or delineation: *He favored the late products of the artist's pencil.* **7.** *Math.* the collection of lines, planes, or surfaces passing through a given point or set of points and satisfying a given equation or condition. **8.** *Archaic.* an artist's paintbrush, esp. for fine work. —*v.t.* **9.** to write, draw, mark, or color with, or as if with, a pencil. **10.** to use a pencil on. **11. pencil in,** to schedule or list tentatively, as or as if by writing down in pencil rather than in ink: *I'll pencil you in for ten o'clock.* [1350–1400; ME *pencel* < MF *pincel* << L *pēnicillus* painter's brush or pencil, dim. of *pēniculus* little tail. See PENIS, -CULE[1]] —**pen′•cil•er;** *esp. Brit.,* **pen′cil•ler,** *n.* —**pen′cil•like′,** *adj.*

pen′cil beam′, a cone-shaped radar beam. [1945–50]

pen′cil box′, a shallow covered box, usually of pasteboard, for holding pencils and crayons: used by children as an item of school equipment. [1905–10]

pen′cil ce′dar, the red cedar, *Juniperus virginiana,* or its wood. [1865–70]

pen′cil gate′, *Metall.* any of a large number of narrow gates used for rapid distribution of metal in large castings.

pen•cil•i•form (pen sil′ə fôrm′, pen′sə lə-), *adj.* **1.** having a pencillike shape. **2.** (of a set of lines, rays, or the like) parallel or nearly parallel. [PENCIL + -I- + -FORM]

pen•cil•ing (pen′sə ling), *n.* **1.** work or markings done with or as if with a pencil or brush, esp. fine or delicate work done with a pencil or brush on a painting or drawing. **2.** a drawing or sketch made with a pencil. [1700–10; PENCIL + -ING[1]]

pen′cil push′er, *Informal.* a person, as a clerk or bookkeeper, whose work involves a considerable amount of writing, record-keeping, etc. Also called **pen pusher.** [1880–85, *Amer.*]

pen′cil stripe′, **1.** a stripe of varying widths, esp. a dark stripe on a light ground. **2.** a pattern of such stripes. **3.** a fabric or garment having such stripes. [1895–1900]

pend (pend), *v.i.* **1.** to remain undecided or unsettled. **2.** to hang. **3.** *Obs.* to depend. [1490–1500; << L *pendēre* to be suspended, hang, depend]

pend•ant (pen′dənt), *n.* Also **pendent. 1.** a hanging ornament, as an earring or the main piece suspended from a necklace. **2.** an ornament suspended from a roof, vault, or ceiling. **3.** a hanging electrical lighting fixture; chandelier. **4.** that by which something is suspended, as the ringed stem of a watch. **5.** a match, parallel, companion, or counterpart. **6.** Also, **pennant.** *Naut.* a length of rope attached to a masthead, the end of a yardarm, etc., and having a block or thimble secured to its free end. —*adj.* **7.** pendent. [1300–50; ME *pendaunt* < AF; MF *pendant,* n. use of prp. of *pendre* to hang < VL **pendere* for L *pendēre.* See PEND, -ANT] —**pend′ant•ed,** *adj.* —**pend′ant•like′,** *adj.*

pend′ant cloud′. See **funnel cloud.**

Pen•del•i•kon (pen del′i kon′; *Gk.* pen′de lē kôn′), *n.* a mountain in SE Greece, near Athens: noted for its fine marble. 3640 ft. (1110 m). Also, **Pentelikon.** Latin, **Pentelicus.**

pen•den•cy (pen′dən sē), *n., pl.* **-cies.** the state or time of being pending, undecided, or undetermined, as of a lawsuit awaiting settlement. [1630–40 PEND(ENT) + -ENCY]

pend•ent (pen′dənt), *adj.* Also, **pendant. 1.** hanging or suspended: *a pendent lamp.* **2.** overhanging; jutting;

projecting: *pendent cliffs.* **3.** undecided; undetermined; pending: *a lawsuit that is still pendent.* **4.** impending. —*n.* **5.** pendant. [1275–1325; < L *pendent-* (s. of *pendēns*), prp. of *pendēre* to hang; r. ME *pendaunt* < AF (OF *pendant*), prp. of *pendre* < L *pendēre;* see PENDANT] —**pend′ent·ly,** *adv.*

pen·den·te li·te (pen den′tē lī′tē), *Law.* during litigation; while a suit is in progress. [1720–30; < L: lit., with a lawsuit pending]

pen·den·tive (pen den′tiv), *n. Archit.* **1.** any of several spandrels, in the form of spherical triangles, forming a transition between the circular plan of a dome and the polygonal plan of the supporting masonry. **2.** any of several masonry devices, as squinches or trompes, for forming a transition between a circular or polygonal construction, as a dome or lantern, and supporting masonry of a different plan. —*adj.* **3.** functioning as, or substituting for, a pendentive: *pendentive corbeling.* [1720–30; PENDENT + -IVE, modeled on F *pendentif*]

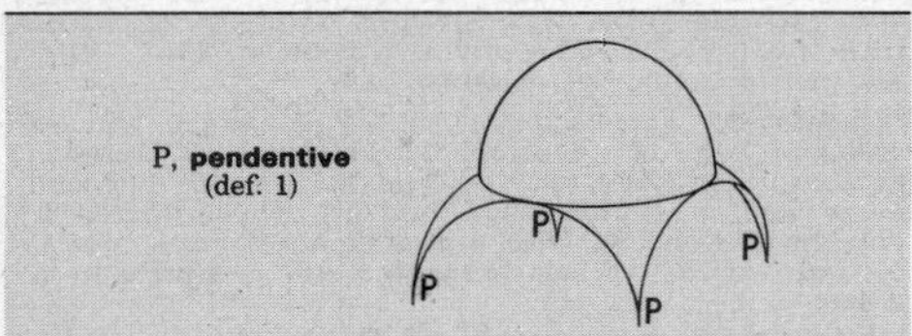

P, **pendentive** (def. 1)

Pen·de·rec·ki (pen′də ret′skē; *Pol.* pen′de rets′kē), *n.* **Krzysz·tof** (kshish′tôf), born 1933, Polish composer.

pend·ing (pen′ding), *prep.* **1.** while awaiting; until: *pending his return.* **2.** in the period before the decision or conclusion of; during: *pending the negotiations.* —*adj.* **3.** remaining undecided; awaiting decision or settlement; unfinished: *pending business; pending questions; pending litigation.* **4.** about to take place; impending. [1635–45; PEND + -ING[2], on the model of F *pendant* (see PENDENT)]

Pen·dle·ton (pen′dl tən), *n.* **1.** a city in N Oregon. 14,521. **2.** a male given name.

pen·drag·on (pen drag′ən), *n.* the supreme leader: the title of certain ancient British chiefs. [1470–80; < ML (Geoffrey of Monmouth) *Uthyrpendragun* Uther Pendragon, taken as Medieval Welsh *pen(n)* head + **dragun* < LL *dracōnēs,* pl. of *dracō* military standard, L: serpent, DRAGON (hence, chief or head standard), though the compound is unattested in Welsh sources outside of translations of Geoffrey of Monmouth] —**pen·drag′on·ish,** *adj.* —**pen·drag′on·ship′,** *n.*

Pen·drag·on (pen drag′ən), *n.* either of two kings of ancient Britain. Cf. **Arthur** (def. 2), **Uther.**

pen·du·lar (pen′jə lər, pen′də-), *adj.* **1.** of or pertaining to a pendulum. **2.** of or resembling the motion of a pendulum: *a pendular vibration.* [1875–80; PENDUL(UM) + -AR[1]]

pen·du·lous (pen′jə ləs, pen′də-), *adj.* **1.** hanging down loosely: *pendulous blossoms.* **2.** swinging freely; oscillating. **3.** vacillating or undecided; wavering. [1595–1605; < L *pendulus* hanging, swinging. See PEND, -ULOUS] —**pen′du·lous·ly,** *adv.* —**pen′du·lous·ness,** *n.*
—**Syn. 1.** dangling, drooping, pendent, sagging.

pen·du·lum (pen′jə ləm, pen′də-), *n.* **1.** a body so suspended from a fixed point as to move to and fro by the action of gravity and acquired momentum. **2.** *Horol.* a swinging lever, weighted at the lower end, for regulating the speed of a clock mechanism. [1650–60; < NL, n. use of neut. of L *pendulus* PENDULOUS] —**pen′du·lum·like′,** *adj.*

pen′dulum watch′, (formerly) a watch having a balance wheel, esp. a balance wheel bearing a fake pendulum bob oscillating behind a window in the dial. [1655–65]

pene-, a combining form meaning "almost," used in the formation of compound words: *penecontemporaneous.* Also, *esp. before a vowel,* **pen-.** [< L *paene-,* comb. form of *paene*]

pe·ne·con·tem·po·ra·ne·ous (pē′nē kən tem′pə rā′nē əs), *adj. Geol.* formed during or shortly after the formation of the containing rock stratum: *penecontemporaneous minerals.* [1900–05; PENE- + CONTEMPORANEOUS]

Pe·nei·os (pē nyôs′), *n.* Modern Greek name of **Salambria.**

Pe·nel·o·pe (pə nel′ə pē), *n.* **1.** *Class. Myth.* the wife of Odysseus, who remained faithful to him during his long absence at Troy. **2.** a faithful wife. **3.** a female given name: from a Greek word meaning "weaver."

pe·ne·plain (pē′nə plān′, pē′nə plān′), *n. Geol.* an area reduced almost to a plain by erosion. Also, **pe′ne·plane′.** [1885–90; PENE- + PLAIN[1]] —**pe·ne·pla·na·tion** (pē′nə plə nā′shən), *n.*

pen·e·tra·ble (pen′i trə bəl), *adj.* capable of being penetrated. [1375–1425; late ME < L *penetrābilis,* equiv. to *penetrā(re)* to PENETRATE + *-bilis* -BLE] —**pen′e·tra·bil′i·ty, pen′e·tra·ble·ness,** *n.* —**pen′e·tra·bly,** *adv.*

pen·e·tra·li·a (pen′i trā′lē ə), *n.pl.* **1.** the innermost parts or recesses of a place or thing. **2.** the most private or secret things. [1660–70; < L, n. use of neut. pl. of *penetrālis* inner, equiv. to *penetr(āre)* to PENETRATE + *-ālis* -AL[1]] —**pen′e·tra′li·an,** *adj.*

pen·e·trance (pen′i trəns), *n. Genetics.* the frequency, expressed as a percentage, with which a particular gene produces its effect in a group of organisms. Cf. **expressivity** (def. 2). [1635–45; PENETR(ANT) + -ANCE]

pen·e·trant (pen′i trənt), *n.* **1.** a person or thing that penetrates. **2.** a compound that penetrates the skin, as a lotion or cream. **3.** a substance that lowers the surface tension of water; wetting agent. **4.** *Zool.* a large nematocyst discharging a barbed thread that penetrates the body of the prey and injects a toxic fluid. —*adj.* **5.** penetrating. [1535–45; < L *penetrant-* (s. of *penetrāns*), prp. of *penetrāre* to PENETRATE; see -ANT]

pen·e·trate (pen′i trāt′), *v.,* **-trat·ed, -trat·ing.** —*v.t.* **1.** to pierce or pass into or through: *The bullet penetrated the wall. The fog lights penetrated the mist.* **2.** to enter the interior of: *to penetrate a forest.* **3.** to enter and diffuse itself through; permeate. **4.** to arrive at the truth or meaning of; understand; comprehend: *to penetrate a mystery.* **5.** to obtain a share of (a market): *to penetrate the Canadian coffee market.* **6.** to affect or impress (the mind or feelings) deeply. **7.** to extend influence, usually peacefully, into the affairs of (another country). —*v.i.* **8.** to enter, reach, or pass through something, as by piercing: *We penetrated to the interior of the Kasbah.* **9.** to be diffused through something. **10.** to understand or read the meaning of something. **11.** to have a deep effect or impact on someone. [1520–30; < L *penetrātus* (ptp. of *penetrāre*), equiv. to *penet-,* var. s. of *penitus* deep down + *-r-* (prob. by analogy with *intus* inside: *intrāre* to ENTER) + *-ātus* + -ATE[1]] —**pen′e·tra′tor,** *n.*
—**Syn. 1.** See **pierce. 4.** fathom, discern. **6.** touch.

pen·e·trat·ing (pen′i trā′ting), *adj.* **1.** able or tending to penetrate; piercing; sharp: *a penetrating shriek; a penetrating glance.* **2.** acute; discerning: *a penetrating observation.* **3.** *Surg.* noting a wound that pierces the skin, esp. a deep wound entering an organ or body cavity. Also, **penetrant.** [1590–1600; PENETRATE + -ING[2]] —**pen′e·trat′ing·ly,** *adv.* —**pen′e·trat′ing·ness,** *n.*
—**Syn. 2.** keen, sharp. See **acute.** —**Ant. 1.** blunt. **2.** obtuse.

pen·e·tra·tion (pen′i trā′shən), *n.* **1.** the act or power of penetrating. **2.** mental acuteness, discernment, or insight: *a scholar of rare penetration.* **3.** the obtaining of a share of a market for some commodity or service. **4.** the extension, usually peaceful, of the influence of one nation or culture into the affairs of another. **5.** a military attack that penetrates into enemy territory. **6.** *Gunnery.* the depth to which a projectile goes into the target. **7.** the measure of relative depth of field of a telescope or microscope, esp. a binocular microscope. [1595–1605; < LL *penetrātiōn-* (s. of *penetrātiō*). See PENETRATE, -ION]
—**Syn. 2.** understanding, perception, discrimination, depth, profundity.

penetra′tion aid′, *Mil.* a device or tactic, as the use of chaff or decoys or the maintaining of a low flight level, that helps an aircraft or missile to enter hostile air space. [1965–70]

pen·e·tra·tive (pen′i trā′tiv), *adj.* **1.** tending to penetrate; piercing. **2.** acute; keen. [1375–1425; late ME < ML *penetrātīvus.* See PENETRATE, -IVE] —**pen′e·tra′tive·ly,** *adv.* —**pen′e·tra′tive·ness, pen·e·tra·tiv·i·ty** (pen′i trə tiv′i tē), *n.*

pen·e·trom·e·ter (pen′i trom′i tər), *n.* **1.** a device for measuring the penetrating power of x-ray or other radiations. **2.** a device for measuring the penetrability of a solid. [1900–05; PENETR(ATE) + -O- + -METER]

Pe·ne·us (pə nē′əs), *n.* ancient name of **Salambria.**

Peng De·huai (peng′ du′hwī′), 1898–1974, Chinese Communist military leader: defense minister 1954–59. Also, **P'eng Te-huai** (pung′ du′hwī′).

Peng·hu (*Chin.* pung′hōō′), *n.* a group of small islands off the coast of SE China, in the Taiwan Strait: controlled by Taiwan. 115,613; ab. 50 sq. mi. (130 sq. km). Also, *Wade-Giles,* **P'eng'hu′.** Also called, *Wade-Giles,* **P'eng'hu′ Ch'ün'tao′** (chyn′dou′); **Pescadores, Pescadores Islands.**

pen·gö (peng′gœ′), *n., pl.* **-gö, -gös** (-gœz′). a former silver coin and monetary unit of Hungary, equal to 100 fillér: replaced by the forint in 1946. [1925–30; < Hungarian: lit., sounding; prp. of *pengeni* to sound, jingle]

Peng·pu (*Chin.* pung′pōō′), *n.* Bengbu.

pen·guin (peng′gwin, pen′-), *n. Ornith.* **1.** any of several flightless, aquatic birds of the family Spheniscidae, of the Southern Hemisphere, having webbed feet and wings reduced to flippers. **2.** *Obs.* See **great auk.** [1570–80; orig. uncert.; perh. < Welsh *pen gwyn* lit., white head (referring to the great auk in its winter plumage); later misapplied to the Spheniscidae]

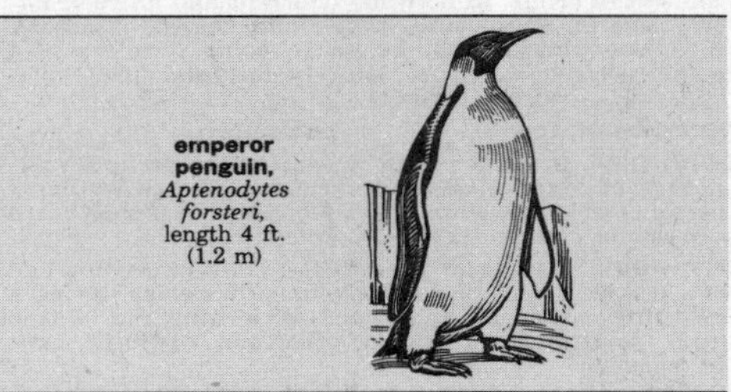
emperor penguin, *Aptenodytes forsteri,* length 4 ft. (1.2 m)

pen·hold·er (pen′hōl′dər), *n.* **1.** a holder in which a penpoint is placed. **2.** a rack for a pen or pens. [1805–15; PEN[1] + HOLDER]

Pen·hsi (*Chin.* bun′shē′), *n. Wade-Giles.* Benxi.

-penia, a combining form used in the formation of compound words that have the general sense "lack, deficiency," as specified by the initial element: *leukopenia.* [< NL, comb. form repr. Gk *penía* poverty, need]

pen·i·cil (pen′ə sil), *n.* a small, brushlike tuft of hairs, as on a caterpillar. [1820–30; < L *pēnicillus* painter's brush or pencil. See PENCIL]

pen·i·cil·la·mine (pen′ə sil′ə mēn′, -min), *n. Pharm.* a chelating agent, $C_5H_{11}NO_2S$, produced by the degradation of penicillin, used in the treatment of severe rheumatoid arthritis and in heavy metal poisoning. [1940–45; PENICILL(IN) + -AMINE]

pen·i·cil·late (pen′ə sil′it, -āt), *adj.* having a penicil or penicils. [1810–20; < L *pēnicill(us)* (see PENCIL) + -ATE[1]] —**pen′i·cil′late·ly,** *adv.* —**pen′i·cil·la′tion,** *n.*

pen·i·cil·lin (pen′ə sil′in), *n. Pharm.* any of several antibiotics of low toxicity, produced naturally by molds of the genus *Penicillium* and also semisynthetically, having a bactericidal action on many susceptible Gram-positive or Gram-negative cocci and bacilli, some also being effective against certain spirochetes. [1925–30; PENICILL(IUM) + -IN[2]]

pen·i·cil·li·um (pen′ə sil′ē əm), *n., pl.* **-cil·li·ums, -cil·li·a** (-sil′ē ə). any fungus of the genus *Penicillium,* certain species of which are used in cheesemaking and as the source of penicillin. [1925–30; < NL, equiv. to L *pēnicill(us)* brush (see PENCIL) + *-ium* -IUM]

pen·in·su·la (pə nin′sə lə, -nins′yə lə), *n.* **1.** an area of land almost completely surrounded by water except for an isthmus connecting it with the mainland. **2. the Peninsula, a.** Spain and Portugal together; Iberian Peninsula; Iberia. **b.** a district in SE Virginia between the York and James rivers: Civil War battles. [1530–40; < L *paenīnsula,* equiv. to *paen-* PEN- + *īnsula* island] —**pen·in′su·lar,** *adj.* —**pen·in′su·lar·ism, pen·in·su·lar·i·ty** (pə nin′sə lar′i tē, -nins′yə-), *n.*

Penin′sular State′, Florida (used as a nickname).

Penin′sula War′, a war (1808–14) in Spain and Portugal, with British, Spanish, and Portuguese troops opposing the French.

pe·nis (pē′nis), *n., pl.* **-nis·es, -nes** (-nēz). *Anat., Zool.* the male organ of copulation and, in mammals, of urinary excretion. [1685–95; < L *pēnis* tail, penis] —**pe·nile** (pēn′l, pē′nīl), **pe·ni·al** (pē′nē əl), *adj.*

pe′nis en′vy, *Psychoanal.* the repressed wish of a female to possess a penis. [1920–25]

pen·i·tence (pen′i təns), *n.* the state of being penitent; regret for one's wrongdoing or sinning; contrition; repentance. [1150–1200; ME (< OF) < ML *pēnitentia,* L *paenitentia* a regretting. See PENITENT, -ENCE]
—**Syn.** See **regret.**

pen·i·tent (pen′i tənt), *adj.* **1.** feeling or expressing sorrow for sin or wrongdoing and disposed to atonement and amendment; repentant; contrite. —*n.* **2.** a penitent person. **3.** *Rom. Cath. Ch.* a person who confesses sin and submits to a penance. [1325–75; ME < ML *pēnitent-,* L *paenitent-* (s. of *paenitēns*), prp. of *paenitēre* to regret; r. ME *penaunt* < AF; see PENANCE] —**pen′i·tent·ly,** *adv.*
—**Syn. 1.** remorseful, rueful, sorrowful. —**Ant. 1.** unrepentant, impenitent.

Pen·i·ten·te (pen′i ten′tā, -tē), *n.* a member of a religious order, chiefly in Spanish-American communities in New Mexico, known for their practice of self-flagellation, esp. during Holy Week. [1830–40, *Amer.;* < Sp, sing. of *Penitentes,* short for *Los Hermanos Penitentes* the penitent brothers]

pen·i·ten·tial (pen′i ten′shəl), *adj.* **1.** of, pertaining to, proceeding from, or expressive of penitence or repentance. —*n.* **2.** a penitent. **3.** a book or code of canons relating to penance, its imposition, etc. [1500–10; < ML *pēnitentiālis,* LL *paenitentiālis.* See PENITENT, -IAL] —**pen′i·ten′tial·ly,** *adv.*

pen′iten′tial Psalm′, any of the Psalms (the 6th, 32nd, 38th, 51st, 102nd, 130th, and 143rd) that give expression to feelings of penitence and that are used in various Christian liturgical services.

pen·i·ten·tia·ry (pen′i ten′shə rē), *n., pl.* **-ries,** *adj.* —*n.* **1.** a place for imprisonment, reformatory discipline, or punishment, esp. a prison maintained in the U.S. by a state or the federal government for serious offenders. **2.** *Rom. Cath. Ch.* a tribunal in the Curia Romana, presided over by a cardinal **(grand penitentiary),** having jurisdiction over certain matters, as penance, confession, dispensation, absolution, and impediments, and dealing with questions of conscience reserved for the Holy See. —*adj.* **3.** (of an offense) punishable by imprisonment in a penitentiary. **4.** of, pertaining to, or intended for imprisonment, reformatory discipline, or punishment. **5.** penitential. [1375–1425; late ME *penitenciarie* priest who administers penance, prison < ML *pēnitentiārius* of penance. See PENITENCE, -ARY]

Pen·ki (*Chin.* bun′jē′), *n.* Benxi.

pen·knife (pen′nīf′), *n., pl.* **-knives.** a small pocketknife, formerly one used for making and sharpening quill pens. [1400–50; late ME; see PEN[1], KNIFE]

pen·light (pen′līt′), *n.* a flashlight similar in size and shape to a fountain pen. Also, **pen′lite′.** [1955–60; PEN[1] + LIGHT[1]]

pen·man (pen′mən), *n., pl.* **-men. 1.** a person who writes or copies; scribe; copyist. **2.** an expert in penmanship. **3.** a writer or author. [1585–95; PEN[1] + -MAN]

pen·man·ship (pen′mən ship′), *n.* **1.** the art of handwriting; the use of the pen in writing. **2.** a person's style or manner of handwriting: *clear penmanship; poor penmanship.* [1685–95; PENMAN + -SHIP]

Penn (pen), *n.* **1. Sir William,** 1621–70, English admiral. **2.** his son, **William,** 1644–1718, English Quaker: founder of Pennsylvania 1682.

Penn., Pennsylvania. Also, **Penna.**

pen·na (pen′ə), *n., pl.* **pen·nae** (pen′ē). *Ornith.* a contour feather, as distinguished from a down feather, plume, etc. [< L: feather. See PEN[1]]

pen·na·ceous (pə nā′shəs), *adj.* having the texture of

a penna; not downy. [1855–60; < NL *pennāceus.* See PENNA, -ACEOUS]

pen′ name′, a pseudonym used by an author; nom de plume. [1840–50]

pen•nant (pen′ənt), *n.* **1.** a long, tapering flag or burgee of distinctive form and special significance, borne on naval or other vessels and used in signaling or for identification. **2.** any relatively long, tapering flag. **3.** a flag serving as an emblem of victory or championship, esp. in baseball. **4.** *Music.* hook (def. 12a). **5.** *Naut.* pendant (def. 6). [1605–15; b. PENNON and PENDANT]

pen•nate (pen′āt), *adj.* winged; feathered. Also, **pen′•nat•ed.** [1695–1705; < L *pennātus.* See PENNA, -ATE[1]]

Pen•nell (pen′l), *n.* **Joseph,** 1860–1926, U.S. etcher, illustrator, and writer.

Pen•ney (pen′ē), *n.* **J(ames) C(ash),** 1875–1971, U.S. retail merchant.

Penn′ Hills′, a town in W Pennsylvania. 57,632.

pen•ni (pen′ē), *n., pl.* **pen•ni•a** (pen′ē ə), **pen•nis.** an aluminum coin of Finland, the 100th part of a markka. [1890–95; < Finnish < LG *pennig* PENNY]

Pen•nie (pen′ē), *n.* a female given name, form of **Penelope.**

pen•ni•less (pen′i lis), *adj.* without any money whatsoever; totally impoverished; destitute. [1275–1325; ME *peniles.* See PENNY, -LESS] **—pen′ni•less•ly,** *adv.* **—pen′ni•less•ness,** *n.*
—Syn. indigent. See **poor.** **—Ant.** rich.

Pen′nine Alps′ (pen′īn), a mountain range on the border between Switzerland and Italy: part of the Alps. Highest peak, Monte Rosa, 15,217 ft. (4640 m).

Pen′nine Chain′, a range of hills in N England, extending from the S Midlands to the Cheviot Hills.

pen•ning (pen′ing), *n.* pitching. [1620–30; PEN[2] + -ING[1]]

pen′ning gate′, a sluice gate that opens by lifting upward.

pen•ni•nite (pen′ə nīt′), *n. Mineral.* a member of the chlorite group, rhombohedral in habit. Also, **pen•nine** (pen′in, -īn). [1865–70; < G *Pennin* (after the PENNINE ALPS) + -ITE[1]]

pen•non (pen′ən), *n.* **1.** a distinctive flag in any of various forms, as tapering, triangular, or swallow-tailed, formerly one borne on the lance of a knight. **2.** a pennant. **3.** any flag or banner. **4.** a wing or pinion. [1325–75; ME *penon* < MF, aug. of OF *pene* < L *penna* or *pinna* feather. See PEN[1]] **—pen′noned,** *adj.*

pen•non•cel (pen′ən sel′), *n.* pencel. Also, **penoncel.** [1350–1400; ME *penonceal* < MF *penoncel,* dim. of *penon* PENNON]

Penn•sau•ken (pen sô′kin), *n.* a township in W New Jersey, on the Delaware River. 33,775.

Penn•syl•va•nia (pen′səl vān′yə, -vā′nē ə), *n.* a state in the E United States. 11,886,728; 45,333 sq. mi. (117,410 sq. km). *Cap.:* Harrisburg. *Abbr.:* PA (for use with zip code), Pa., Penn., Penna.

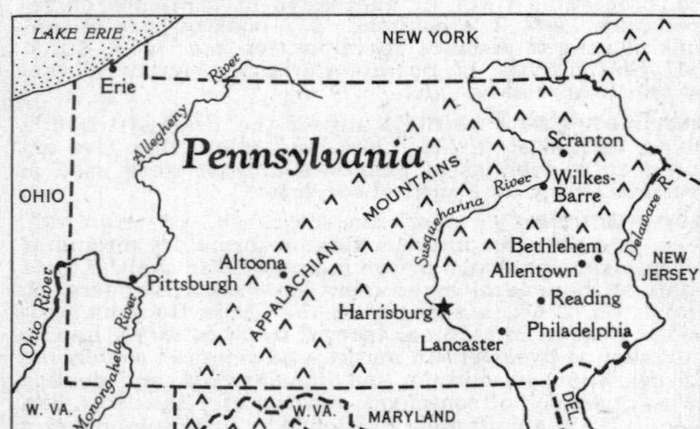

Penn′sylva′nia Dutch′, **1.** the descendants of 17th- and 18th-century settlers in Pennsylvania from southwest Germany and Switzerland. **2.** Also called **Penn′•sylva′nia Ger′man.** a dialect of High German with an admixture of English spoken mainly in eastern Pennsylvania, developed from the language of these settlers. **3.** the folk style of applied and decorative art developed by the Pennsylvania Dutch. [1815–25] **—Penn′syl•va′•nia-Dutch′,** *adj.*

Penn•syl•va•nian (pen′səl vān′yən, -vā′nē ən), *adj.* **1.** of or pertaining to the state of Pennsylvania. **2.** *Geol.* noting or pertaining to a period of the Paleozoic Era, occurring from about 310 to 280 million years ago and characterized by warm climates, swampy land areas, and the development of insects and reptiles: sometimes considered as an epoch of the Carboniferous Period. See table under **geologic time.** **—***n.* **3.** a native or inhabitant of Pennsylvania. **4.** *Geol.* the Pennsylvanian Period or System. [1675–85; PENNSYLVANI(A) + -AN]

Penn′sylva′nia ri′fle. See **Kentucky rifle.**

pen•ny (pen′ē), *n., pl.* **pen•nies,** (*esp. collectively for* 2, 3) **pence,** *adj.* **—***n.* **1.** a bronze coin, the 100th part of the dollars of various nations, as Australia, Canada, New Zealand, and the United States; one cent. **2.** Also called **new penny.** a bronze coin and monetary unit of the United Kingdom and various other nations, the 100th part of a pound. *Abbr.:* p **3.** a former bronze coin and monetary unit of the United Kingdom and various other nations, the 12th part of a shilling: use phased out in 1971. *Abbr.:* d. **4.** a sum of money: *He spent every penny he ever earned.* **5.** the length of a nail in terms of certain standard designations from twopenny to sixtypenny. **6. a bad penny,** someone or something undesirable. **7. a pretty penny,** *Informal.* a considerable sum of money: *Their car must have cost them a pretty penny.* **8.** *Chiefly Brit. Slang.* **spend a penny,** to urinate: from the former cost of using a public lavatory. **9. turn an honest penny,** to earn one's living honestly; make money by fair means: *He's never turned an honest penny in his life.* **—***adj.* **10.** *Stock Exchange.* of, pertaining to, or being penny stock: *frenzied speculation in the penny market.* [bef. 900; ME *peni,* OE *penig, pænig, pen(n)ing, pending,* c. OFris *penning, panning,* OS, D *penning,* OHG *pfenning, phantinc, phenting* (G *Pfennig*), ON *penningr* (perh. < OE); < WGmc or Gmc **pandingaz,* prob. equiv. to **pand-* PAWN[2] + *-*ingaz* -ING[3]] **—pen′nied,** *adj.*

Pen•ny (pen′ē), *n.* a female given name, form of **Penelope.**

pen•ny-a-lin•er (pen′ē ə lī′nər), *n. Chiefly Brit. Archaic.* a hack writer. [1825–35; *penny-a-line* (of writing) paid for at the rate of a penny per line + -ER[1]]

pen′ny an′te, **1.** *Cards.* a game of poker in which the ante or basic bet is one cent. **2.** *Informal.* any business arrangement or transaction involving a trifling or paltry sum of money. [1850–55, *Amer.*]

pen•ny-an•te (pen′ē an′tē), *adj. Informal.* **1.** involving a trifling sum of money; small in amount: *a penny-ante investment.* **2.** inconsiderable; minor; small-time. [1930–35, *Amer.*]

pen′ny arcade′, an amusement hall or area that contains coin-operated entertainment devices, originally operated for a penny a play. [1905–10]

pen•ny•cress (pen′ē kres′), *n.* any of several plants belonging to herbs of the genus *Thlaspi,* of the mustard family, esp. *T. arvense,* of Europe, bearing somewhat round, flat pods. Also, **penny′ cress′, pen′ny-cress′.** [1705–15; PENNY + CRESS]

pen′ny dread′ful, *pl.* **penny dreadfuls.** *Chiefly Brit.* a cheap, sensational novel of adventure, crime, or violence; dime novel. [1870–75]

pen′ny loaf′er, a loafer with a slot on the vamp that can hold a coin, usually a penny. [1965–70]

pen′ny pinch′er, a miserly, niggardly, or stingy person. [1920–25] **—pen′ny-pinch′ing,** *n., adj.*

pen′ny post′, (formerly) any of various postal systems delivering mail for a penny a letter. [1670–80]

pen•ny•roy•al (pen′ē roi′əl), *n.* **1.** an aromatic Old World plant, *Mentha pulegium,* of the mint family, having clusters of small purple flowers and yielding a pungent essential oil used medicinally and as an insect repellent. **2.** Also called **mock pennyroyal.** a similar, related plant, *Hedeoma pulegioides,* of eastern North America, having bluish flowers growing from the leaf axils. **3.** any of several other aromatic plants of the mint family. [1520–30; PENNY + ROYAL; r. late ME *puliol real* < AF; MF *poliol* (< L **pūlēgiōlum,* dim. of *pūlēgium* pennyroyal) + *real,* earlier form of *royal*]

pen′ny stock′, *Stock Exchange.* common stock, usually highly speculative, selling for less than a dollar a share. [1930–35, *Amer.*]

pen•ny•weight (pen′ē wāt′), *n.* (in troy weight) a unit of 24 grains or 1/20 of an ounce (1.555 grams). *Abbr.:* dwt, pwt [1350–1400; ME *penyweight,* OE *penega gewihte.* See PENNY, WEIGHT]

pen•ny•wort (pen′ē wûrt′, -wôrt′), *n.* any of several plants having round or roundish leaves, as the navelwort. [1275–1325; ME *penywort.* See PENNY, WORT[2]]

pen•ny•worth (pen′ē wûrth′), *n.* **1.** as much as may be bought for a penny. **2.** a small quantity. **3.** a bargain. [bef. 1000; ME *penyworth,* OE *penigweorth.* See PENNY, WORTH[1]]

Pe•nob•scot (pə nob′skot, -skət), *n., pl.* **-scots,** (*esp. collectively*) **-scot** *for* 2. **1.** a river flowing S from N Maine into Penobscot Bay. 350 mi. (565 km) long. **2.** a member of a North American Indian people of the Penobscot River valley. **3.** the Eastern Algonquian language of the Penobscot, a dialect of Abenaki.

Penob′scot Bay′, an inlet of the Atlantic in S Maine. 30 mi. (48 km) long.

pe•nol•o•gy (pē nol′ə jē), *n.* **1.** the study of the punishment of crime, in both its deterrent and its reformatory aspects. **2.** the study of the management of prisons. Also, **poenology.** [1830–40; *peno-* (comb. form repr. Gk *poinḗ* penalty) + -LOGY] **—pe•no•log•i•cal** (pēn′l oj′i kəl), *adj.* **—pe•nol′o•gist,** *n.*

pen•on•cel (pen′ən sel′), *n.* pennoncel.

pen′ pal′, a person with whom one keeps up an exchange of letters, usually someone so far away that a personal meeting is unlikely: *My niece in Texas has a pen pal in France.* [1935–40, *Amer.*]

pen•point (pen′point′), *n.* **1.** the point or writing end of a pen, esp. a small, tapering, metallic device having a split tip for drawing up ink and for writing; nib. **2.** the tip or point of a ball-point or other pen. [1880–85; PEN[1] + POINT]

pen′ push′er, *Informal.* See **pencil pusher.** [1910–15]

Pen•sa•co•la (pen′sə kō′lə), *n.* a seaport in NW Florida, on Pensacola Bay. 57,619.

Pen′saco′la Bay′, an inlet of the Gulf of Mexico, in NW Florida. ab. 30 mi. (48 km) long.

pen•sée (pän sā′), *n., pl.* ***-sées*** (-sā′). *French.* a reflection or thought.

Pen•sées (pän sāz′, pän-; *Fr.* pän sā′), *n.* a collection of notes, essays, etc., dealing with religious and philosophical matters by Blaise Pascal, published posthumously in 1670.

pen•sil (pen′səl), *n.* pencel.

pen•sile (pen′sīl, -sil), *adj.* **1.** hanging, as the nests of certain birds. **2.** building a hanging nest. [1595–1605; < L *pēnsilis* hanging down, equiv. to *pēns(us)* ptp. of *pendēre* to hang (equiv. to *pend-* v. s. + *-tus* ptp. suffix, with *dt* > *s*) + *-ilis* -ILE]

pen•sion (pen′shən; *Fr.* pän syôN′ *for* 3), *n., pl.* **-sions** (-shənz; *Fr.* -syôN′ *for* 3), *v.* **—***n.* **1.** a fixed amount, other than wages, paid at regular intervals to a person or to the person's surviving dependents in consideration of past services, age, merit, poverty, injury or loss sustained, etc.: *a retirement pension.* **2.** an allowance, annuity, or subsidy. **3.** (in France and elsewhere in continental Europe) **a.** a boardinghouse or small hotel. **b.** room and board. **—***v.t.* **4.** to grant or pay a pension to. **5.** to cause to retire on a pension (usually fol. by *off*). [1325–75; ME (< OF *pensïon*) < L *pēnsiōn-* (s. of *pēnsiō*) a weighing out, hence, a paying out, installment paying, equiv. to *pēns(us)* (ptp. of *pendere* to weigh out, pay by weight, equiv. to *pend-* v. s. + *-tus* ptp. suffix, with *dt* > *s*) + *-iōn-* -ION] **—pen′sion•a•ble,** *adj.* **—pen′•sion•a•bly,** *adv.* **—pen′sion•less,** *adj.*

pen•sion•ar•y (pen′shə ner′ē), *n., pl.* **-ar•ies,** *adj.* **—***n.* **1.** a pensioner. **2.** a hireling. **—***adj.* **3.** of the nature of a pension. **4.** receiving a pension. [1530–40; < ML *pēnsiōnārius.* See PENSION, -ARY]

pen•sion•er (pen′shə nər), *n.* **1.** a person who receives or lives on a pension. **2.** a hireling. **3.** a student at Cambridge University who pays for his or her commons and other expenses, and is not supported by any foundation. **4.** *Obs.* a gentleman-at-arms. [1400–50; late ME < AF; see PENSION, -ER[2]] **—pen′sion•er•ship′,** *n.*

pen′sion fund′, a fund created and maintained, as by a corporation, to provide benefits under a pension plan. [1865–70]

pen′sion plan′, **1.** a systematic plan created and maintained, as by a corporation, to make regular payments of benefits to retired or disabled employees, either on a contributory or a noncontributory basis. **2.** See **retirement plan** (def. 1). [1955–60]

pen•sive (pen′siv), *adj.* **1.** dreamily or wistfully thoughtful: *a pensive mood.* **2.** expressing or revealing thoughtfulness, usually marked by some sadness: *a pensive adagio.* [1325–75; < F (fem.); r. ME *pensif* < MF (masc.), deriv. of *penser* to think < L *pēnsāre* to weigh, consider, deriv. of *pēnsus,* ptp. of *pendere.* See PENSION, -IVE] **—pen′sive•ly,** *adv.* **—pen′sive•ness,** *n.*
—Syn. 1. PENSIVE, MEDITATIVE, REFLECTIVE suggest quiet modes of apparent or real thought. PENSIVE, the weakest of the three, suggests dreaminess or wistfulness, and may involve little or no thought to any purpose: *a pensive, faraway look.* MEDITATIVE involves thinking of certain facts or phenomena, perhaps in the religious sense of "contemplation," without necessarily having a goal of complete understanding or of action: *meditative but unjudicial.* REFLECTIVE has a strong implication of orderly, perhaps analytic, processes of thought, usually with a definite goal of understanding: *a careful and reflective critic.* **—Ant. 1.** thoughtless.

pen•ste•mon (pen stē′mən, pen′stə mən), *n.* any of numerous chiefly North American plants belonging to the genus *Penstemon,* of the figwort family, some species of which are cultivated for their showy, variously colored flowers. Also, **pentstemon.** [1750–60; var. of PENTSTEMON (> NL *Penstemon* genus name)]

pen•stock (pen′stok′), *n.* **1.** a pipe conducting water from a head gate to a waterwheel. **2.** a conduit for conveying water to a power plant. See diag. under **dam**[1]. **3.** a sluicelike contrivance used to control the flow of water. [1600–10; PEN[2] + STOCK]

pent[1] (pent), *v.* **1.** a pt. and pp. of **pen**[2]. **—***adj.* **2.** shut in; confined. [ptp. of late ME *pend* (now obs.), var. of PEN[2] (v.); cf. SPEND]

pent[2] (pent), *n.* penthouse (def. 4). [by shortening]

Pent., Pentecost.

penta-, a combining form occurring in loanwords from Greek, meaning "five" (*Pentateuch*); on this model, used in the formation of compound words (*pentavalent*). Also, *esp. before a vowel,* **pent-.** [< Gk *pent-, penta-,* comb. forms repr. *pénte* FIVE]

pen•ta•chlo•ro•ni•tro•ben•zene (pen′tə klôr′ō nī′trō ben′zēn, -ben zēn′, -klōr′-), *n. Chem.* a crystalline compound, $C_6Cl_5NO_2$, used as an herbicide and insecticide. *Abbr.:* PCNB Also called **terrachlor.** [PENTA- + CHLORO-[2] + NITROBENZENE]

pen•ta•chlo•ro•phe•nol (pen′tə klôr′ə fē′nôl, -nol, -klōr′-), *n. Chem.* a white, crystalline, water-insoluble powder, C_6Cl_5OH, used chiefly in fungicides, disinfectants, and wood preservatives. [1875–80; PENTA- + CHLORO-[2] + PHENOL]

pen•ta•cle (pen′tə kəl), *n.* **1.** pentagram. **2.** a similar figure, as a hexagram. [1585–95; < It *pentacolo* five-cornered object. See PENTA-, -CLE[1]]

pen•tad (pen′tad), *n.* **1.** a period of five years. **2.** a group of five. **3.** the number five. **4.** *Chem.* a pentavalent element or group. **5.** *Climatol.* a period of five consecutive days. [1645–55; < Gk *pentad-* (s. of *pentás*) group of five. See PENT-, -AD[1]]

pen•ta•dac•tyl (pen′tə dak′tl, -til), *adj.* **1.** having five digits on each hand or foot. **2.** having five finger-like projections or parts. [1655–65; < L *pentadactylus* < Gk *pentadáktylos.* See PENTA-, -DACTYL] **—pen′ta•dac′•tyl•ism,** *n.*

pen•ta•dec•a•gon (pen′tə dek′ə gon′), *n. Geom.* a polygon having 15 angles and 15 sides. [PENTA- + DECAGON]

pen•ta•e•ryth•ri•tol (pen′tə i rith′ri tôl′, -tol′), *n. Chem.* a white, crystalline, water-soluble powder, $C_5H_{12}O_4$, used chiefly in the manufacture of alkyd resins, varnishes, plasticizers, and explosives. [1890–95; PENTA- + ERYTHRITOL]

pentaeryth′ritol tetrani′trate, *Chem., Pharm.* a white, crystalline, water-insoluble, explosive solid, $C_5H_8N_4O_{12}$, used chiefly as a high explosive and as a vasodilator in treating angina pectoris. Also called **PETN** [1920–25]

pen·ta·gon (pen′tə gon′), *n.* **1.** a polygon having five angles and five sides. **2. the Pentagon, a.** a building in Arlington, Virginia, having a plan in the form of a regular pentagon, containing most U.S. Defense Department offices. **b.** the U.S. Department of Defense; the U.S. military establishment. [1560–70; < LL *pentagōnum* < Gk *pentágōnon,* n. use of neut. of *pentágōnos* five-angled. See PENTA-, -GON] **—pen·tag·o·nal** (pen tag′ə nl), *adj.* **—pen·tag′o·nal·ly,** *adv.*

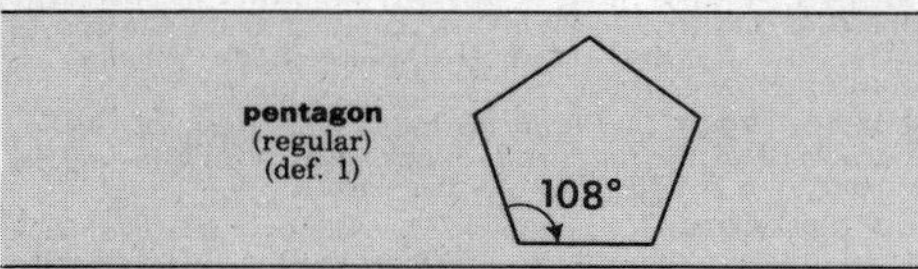

pentag′onal dodecahe′dron, *Crystall.* pyritohedron. [1850–55]

Pen·ta·gon·ese (pen′tə gə nēz′, -nēs′), *n.* a style of language characterized by the use of euphemisms, technical jargon, acronyms, and circumlocutions, used esp. by people working in the U.S. military establishment. [1950–55, *Amer.*; PENTAGON + -ESE]

pen·tag·o·noid (pen tag′ə noid′), *adj.* like a pentagon in shape. [1880–85; PENTAGON + -OID]

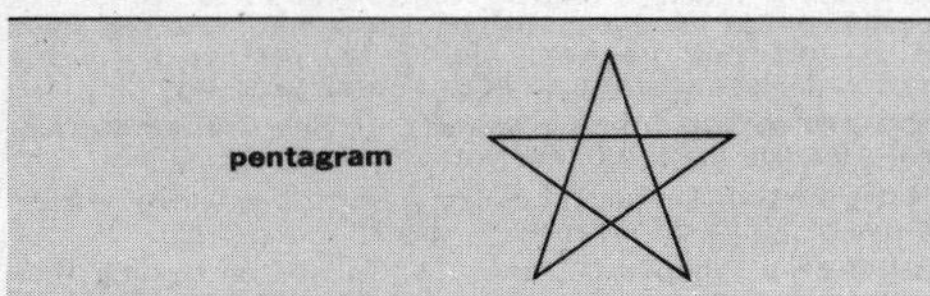

pen·ta·gram (pen′tə gram′), *n.* a five-pointed, star-shaped figure made by extending the sides of a regular pentagon until they meet, used as an occult symbol by the Pythagoreans and later philosophers, by magicians, etc. Also called **pentacle, pentangle, pentalpha.** [1825–35; < Gk *pentágrammon.* See PENTA-, -GRAM[1]] **—pen·ta·gram·mat·ic** (pen′tə grə mat′ik), *adj.*

pen·ta·he·dron (pen′tə hē′drən), *n., pl.* **-drons, -dra** (-drə). a solid figure having five faces. [1655–65; PENTA- + -HEDRON] **—pen′ta·he′dral,** *adj.*

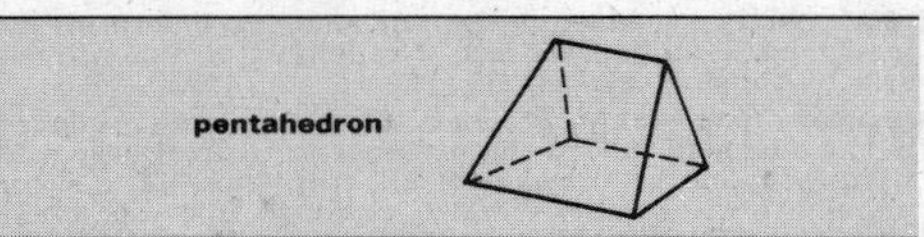

pen·ta·hy·drate (pen′tə hī′drāt), *n. Chem.* a hydrate that contains five molecules of water, as potassium molybdate, $KMoO_4 \cdot 5H_2O$. [1915–20; PENTA- + HYDRATE] **—pen′ta·hy′drat·ed,** *adj.*

pen·ta·hy·dric (pen′tə hī′drik), *adj. Chem.* (esp. of alcohols and phenols) pentahydroxy. [1890–95; PENTA- + -HYDRIC]

pen·ta·hy·drox·y (pen′tə hī drok′sē), *adj. Chem.* (of a molecule) containing five hydroxyl groups. [PENTA- + HYDROXY]

pen·tal·pha (pen tal′fə), *n.* pentagram. [1810–20; < Gk *péntalpha* (see PENT-, ALPHA); so called from the A represented at each point]

pen·tam·er·ous (pen tam′ər əs), *adj.* **1.** consisting of or divided into five parts. **2.** *Bot.* (of flowers) having five members in each whorl. [1820–30; < NL *pentamerus.* See PENTA-, -MEROUS] **—pen·tam′er·ism, pen·tam′er·y,** *n.*

pen·tam·e·ter (pen tam′i tər), *Pros.* **—***n.* **1.** a line of verse consisting of five metrical feet. **2.** Also called **elegiac pentameter.** *Class. Pros.* a verse consisting of two dactyls, one long syllable, two more dactyls, and another long syllable. **3.** unrhymed verse of five iambic feet; heroic verse. **—***adj.* **4.** consisting of five metrical feet. [1540–50; < L *pentametrus* < Gk *pentámetros.* See PENTA-, METER[2]] **—pen·tam′e·trist,** *n.*

pen·ta·meth·yl·ene (pen′tə meth′ə lēn′), *n. Chem.* cyclopentane. [PENTA- + METHYLENE]

pen·ta·meth·yl·ene·di·a·mine (pen′tə meth′ə lēn dī′ə mēn′, -min, -dī′ə mēn′), *n. Biochem.* cadaverine. [PENTA- + METHYLENE + DIAMINE]

pen·tam·i·dine (pen tam′i dēn′, -din), *n. Pharm.* an antiprotozoal substance, $C_{19}H_{24}N_4O_2$, used in the treatment of leishmaniasis, trypanosomiasis, and pneumonia due to *Pneumocystis carinii.* [1941; PENT(ANE) + AMIDINE]

pen·tane (pen′tān), *n. Chem., Pharm.* **1.** a hydrocarbon of the methane series, existing in three liquid isomeric forms. **2.** Also called **normal pentane.** the most important isomer of pentane, a colorless, flammable, water-insoluble, very volatile liquid, C_5H_{12}, obtained from petroleum by distillation: used chiefly as a solvent and in medicine as an anesthetic. [1875–80; PENT- + -ANE]

pen·tan·gle (pen′tang gəl), *n.* pentagram. [1350–1400; ME; see PENT-, ANGLE[1]]

pen·tan·gu·lar (pen tang′gyə lər), *adj.* having five angles and five sides; pentagonal. [1655–65; PENT- + ANGULAR]

pen·ta·ploid (pen′tə ploid′), *adj.* **1.** having a chromosome number that is five times the haploid number. **—***n.* **2.** a pentaploid cell or organism. [1920–25; PENTA- + -PLOID] **—pen′ta·ploi′dy,** *n.*

pen·tap·o·dy (pen tap′ə dē), *n., pl.* **-dies.** *Pros.* a measure consisting of five feet. [1860–65; PENTA- + -POD + -Y[3]] **—pen·ta·pod·ic** (pen′tə pod′ik), *adj.*

pen·ta·prism (pen′tə priz′əm), *n.* a prism that has five faces, a pair of which are at 90° to each other; a ray entering one of the pair emerges from the other at an angle of 90° to its original direction: used esp. in single-lens reflex cameras to reverse images laterally and reflect them to the viewfinder. Also, **pen′ta prism′.** [1935–40; PENTA- + PRISM]

pen·tap·tych (pen′tap tik), *n.* a work of art consisting of five panels or sections. [1850–55; PENTA- + Gk *ptychḗ* a fold]

pen·tar·chy (pen′tär kē), *n., pl.* **-chies. 1.** a government by five persons. **2.** a governing body of five persons. **3.** a federation of five nations, each under its own government or ruler. [1580–90; < Gk *pentarchía.* See PENT-, -ARCHY] **—pen′tarch,** *n.* **—pen·tar′chi·cal,** *adj.*

pen·ta·stich (pen′tə stik′), *n. Pros.* a strophe, stanza, or poem consisting of five lines or verses. [1650–60; < NL *pentastichus* < Gk *pentástichos.* See PENTA-, STICH[1]]

pen·ta·sto·mid (pen′tə stō′mid), *n. Zool.* See **tongue worm.** [1905–10; < NL *Pentastomida* name of the class of tongue worms, equiv. to *Pentastom(um)* a genus name (*penta-* PENTA- + *-stomum* < Gk *-stomon,* neut. of *-stomos* -STOMOUS) + *-ida* -IDA]

pen·ta·style (pen′tə stīl′), *adj. Archit.* **1.** having five columns. **2.** (of a classical temple or a building in the style of one) having five columns on one or each front. [1720–30; PENTA- + -STYLE[2]]

pen·ta·sty·los (pen′tə stī′los), *n.* a pentastyle building, as a classical temple. [< NL; see PENTASTYLE]

pen·ta·syl·la·ble (pen′tə sil′ə bəl), *n.* a word or line of verse of five syllables. [1810–20; PENTA- + SYLLABLE] **—pen·ta·syl·lab·ic** (pen′tə si lab′ik), *adj.* **—pen′ta·syl′la·bism,** *n.*

Pen·ta·teuch (pen′tə to͞ok′, -tyo͞ok′), *n.* the first five books of the Old Testament: Genesis, Exodus, Leviticus, Numbers, and Deuteronomy. [< LL *Pentateuchus* < LGk *pentáteuchos,* equiv. to Gk *penta-* PENTA- + *teû-chos* tool, vessel (LGk: scroll case book)] **—Pen′ta·teuch′al,** *adj.*

pen·tath·lete (pen tath′lēt), *n.* an athlete participating or specializing in the pentathlon. [1820–30; b. PENTATHLON and ATHLETE]

pen·tath·lon (pen tath′lən, -lon), *n.* **1.** an athletic contest comprising five different track and field events and won by the contestant gaining the highest total score. **2.** See **modern pentathlon.** [1700–10; < Gk *pénthāthlon,* equiv. to *pent-* PENT- + *âthlon* contest]

pen′ta·ton′ic scale′ (pen′tə ton′ik, pen′-), *Music.* a scale having five tones to an octave, as one having intervals that correspond to the five black keys of a piano octave. [1860–65; PENTA- + TONIC]

pen·ta·ton·ism (pen′tə tō niz′əm, -to-), *n. Music.* the use of a five-tone scale. Also, **pen·ta·ton·i·cism** (pen′tə-ton′ə siz′əm). [1965–70; PENTATON(IC) + -ISM]

pen·ta·va·lent (pen′tə vā′lənt, pen tav′ə-), *adj. Chem.* **1.** having a valence of 5: *pentavalent arsenic.* **2.** quinquevalent (def. 2). [1870–75; PENTA- + -VALENT]

pen·taz·o·cine (pen taz′ə sēn′), *n. Pharm.* a synthetic narcotic analgesic, $C_{19}H_{27}NO$, used chiefly for the relief of moderate to severe pain. [1960–65; PENTA- + (*benz*)*azocine,* a component of its chemical name]

Pen·te·cost (pen′ti kôst′, -kost′), *n.* **1.** a Christian festival celebrated on the seventh Sunday after Easter, commemorating the descent of the Holy Ghost upon the apostles; Whitsunday. **2.** Shavuoth. [bef. 1000; ME *pentecoste,* OE *pentecosten* < LL *pentēcostē* < Gk *pentēkostḗ* (*hēmérā*) fiftieth (day)]

Pen·te·cos·tal (pen′ti kô′stəl, -stl, -kos′təl, -tl-), *adj.* **1.** of or pertaining to Pentecost. **2.** noting or pertaining to any of various Christian groups, usually fundamentalist, that emphasize the activity of the Holy Spirit, stress holiness of living, and express their religious feelings uninhibitedly, as by speaking in tongues. **—***n.* **3.** Also called **Pen′te·cos′tal·ist.** a member of any Pentecostal denomination. [1540–50; < LL *pentēcostālis.* See PENTECOST, -AL[1]]

pen·te·cos·ta·ri·on (pen′dē kôs tä′rē ôn; *Eng.* pen′-ti ko stâr′ē on′), *n., pl.* **-cos·ta·ri·a** (-kôs tä′rē ä; *Eng.* -ko stâr′ē ə), **-cos·ta·ri·ons.** *Gk. Orth. Ch.* a service book of offices for the period from Easter to the Sunday after Pentecost. [< LGk *pentēkostárion,* equiv. to Gk *pentēkost(ḗ)* PENTECOST + *-arion* < L *-ārium* -ARY]

Pen·tel·i·cus (pen tel′i kəs), *n.* Latin name of **Pendelikon.** **—Pen·tel′ic, Pen·tel′i·can,** *adj.*

Pen·tel·i·kon (pen tel′i kon′; *Gk.* pen′de lē kôn′), *n.* Pendelikon.

pent·house (pent′hous′), *n., pl.* **-hous·es** (-hou′ziz). **1.** an apartment or dwelling on the roof of a building, usually set back from the outer walls. **2.** any specially designed apartment on an upper floor, esp. the top floor, of a building. **3.** a structure on a roof for housing elevator machinery, a water tank, etc. **4.** Also called **pent, pen·tice** (pen′tis). a shed with a sloping roof, or a sloping roof, projecting from a wall or the side of a building, as to shelter a door. **5.** any rooflike shelter or overhanging part. **6.** See **shed roof. 7.** *Court Tennis.* a corridor having a slanted roof and projecting from three walls of the court. [1520–30; alter. (by folk etymology) of ME *pentis* < OF *apentiz,* equiv. to *apent* ptp. of *apendre* to hang against (see APPENDANT) + *-iz* (F *-is*) < VL **-āticium,* n. use of neut. of **-āticius,* equiv. to L *-āt(us)* -ATE[1] + *-icius* adj. suffix] **—pent′house′like′,** *adj.*

Pen·tic·ton (pen tik′tən), *n.* a city in S British Columbia, in SW Canada. 21,344.

pen·ti·men·to (pen′tə men′tō), *n., pl.* **-ti** (-tē). *Painting.* the presence or emergence of earlier images, forms, or strokes that have been changed and painted over. [1900–05; < It, equiv. to *penti(re)* to repent (< L *paenitēre* to regret) + *-mento* -MENT]

pent·land·ite (pent′lən dīt′), *n.* a mineral, sulfide of nickel, occurring in the form of bronze-colored granular aggregates, found with pyrrhotite: the principal source of nickel. [1855–60; < F; named after Joseph B. *Pentland* (d. 1873), Irish scientist; see -ITE[1]]

pen·to·bar·bi·tal (pen′tə bär′bi tôl′, -tal′), *n. Pharm.* a barbiturate, $C_{11}H_{17}N_2O_3$, used as a hypnotic and as a sedative. [1930–35; PENT- + -O- + BARBITAL]

pen·tode (pen′tōd), *n. Electronics.* a vacuum tube having five electrodes, usually a plate, three grids, and a cathode, within the same envelope. [1915–20; PENT- + -ODE[2]]

pen·to·lite (pen′tl īt′), *n.* a high explosive consisting of pentaerythritol tetranitrate and TNT. [PENT- + -OL[1] + -ITE[1]]

pen·tom·ic (pen tom′ik), *adj. Mil.* pertaining to or characterizing the organization of an army division into five groups, each with supporting units, geared to maneuver in keeping with the requirements of atomic warfare. [1955–60; PENT- + (AT)OMIC]

pen·to·san (pen′tə san′), *n. Biochem.* any of a class of polysaccharides that occur in plants, humus, etc., and form pentoses upon hydrolysis. [< G (1892), equiv. to *Pentos(e)* PENTOSE + *-an* -ANE]

pen·tose (pen′tōs), *n. Chem.* a monosaccharide containing five atoms of carbon, as xylose, $C_5H_{10}O_5$, or produced from pentosans by hydrolysis. [< G (1890); see PENT-, -OSE[2]]

pen′tose nucle′ic ac′id, *Biochem.* **1.** a nucleic acid containing a pentose. **2.** See **RNA.** [1825–35]

Pen·to·thal (pen′tə thôl′), *Pharm., Trademark.* a brand of thiopental sodium.

pent·ox·ide (pen tok′sīd), *n. Chem.* an oxide containing five atoms of oxygen, as phosphorus pentoxide, P_2O_5. [1860–65; PENT- + OXIDE]

pent·ste·mon (pent stē′mən, pent′stə-), *n.* penstemon. [1750–60; < NL, equiv. to *pent-* PENT- + Gk *stḗmōn* warp, thread]

pent-up (pent′up′), *adj.* confined; restrained; not vented or expressed; curbed: *pent-up emotions; pent-up rage.* [1705–15; adj. use of v. phrase *pent up*]
—Syn. repressed, suppressed, bottled-up.

pen·tyl (pen′tl), *adj. Chem.* containing a pentyl group; amyl. [1875–80; PENT- + -YL]

pen·tyl·ene·tet·ra·zol (pen′tl ēn te′trə zôl′, -zol′), *n. Pharm.* a white, crystalline, bitter-tasting, water-soluble powder, $C_6H_{10}N_4$, used as a respiratory and circulatory stimulant, esp. in the treatment of barbiturate poisoning, and to induce a convulsive state in the treatment of certain mental diseases. [PENT- + (METH)YLENE + TETR(A)- + AZ- + -OL[2]]

pen′tyl group′, *Chem.* any of the univalent, isomeric groups having the formula $C_5H_{11}-$.

pe·nu·che (pə no͞o′chē), *n.* **1.** Also, **panocha.** *Northern, North Midland, and Western U.S.* a fudgelike candy made of brown sugar, butter, and milk, usually with nuts. **2.** panocha (def. 1). [1840–50, *Amer.*; var. of PANOCHA]

pe·nuch·le (pē′nuk əl), *n.* pinochle. Also, **pe′nuck·le.**

pe·nult (pē′nult, pi nult′), *n.* the next to the last syllable in a word. Also, **pe·nul·ti·ma** (pi nul′tə mə). [1530–40; < L *paenultima (syllaba),* contr. of *paene ultima* almost the last; see PEN-, ULTIMA]

pe·nul·ti·mate (pi nul′tə mit), *adj.* **1.** next to the last: *the penultimate scene of the play.* **2.** of or pertaining to a penult. **—***n.* **3.** a penult. [1670–80; see PENULT, ULTIMATE]

pe·num·bra (pi num′brə), *n., pl.* **-brae** (-brē), **-bras. 1.** *Astron.* **a.** the partial or imperfect shadow outside the complete shadow of an opaque body, as a planet, where the light from the source of illumination is only partly cut off. Cf. **umbra** (def. 3a). **b.** the grayish marginal portion of a sunspot. Cf. **umbra** (def. 3b). **2.** a shadowy, indefinite, or marginal area. [1660–70; < NL, equiv. to L *paen-* PEN- + *umbra* shade] **—pe·num′bral, pe·num′brous,** *adj.*

pe·nu·ri·ous (pə no͝or′ē əs, -nyo͝or′-), *adj.* **1.** extremely stingy; parsimonious; miserly. **2.** extremely poor; destitute; indigent. **3.** poorly or inadequately supplied; lacking in means or resources. [1590–1600; < ML *pēnūriōsus.* See PENURY, -OUS] **—pe·nu′ri·ous·ly,** *adv.* **—pe·nu′ri·ous·ness,** *n.*
—Syn. 1. tight, close, niggardly. **—Ant. 1.** generous.

pen·u·ry (pen′yə rē), *n.* **1.** extreme poverty; destitution. **2.** scarcity; dearth; inadequacy; insufficiency. [1400–50; late ME < L *pēnūria;* akin to Gk *peîna* hunger, *penía* poverty]
—Syn. 1. indigence, need, want. **—Ant. 1.** wealth.

Pe·nu·ti·an (pə no͞o′tē ən, -shən), *n.* **1.** a group of American Indian language families of central and coastal California, including Wintu, Maidu, Yokuts, Miwok, and Costanoan, thought to be descendants of a single protolanguage spoken at a remote period. **2.** any of several other hypothesized genetic groupings of languages that include these languages and, in addition, otherwise unclassified languages of the Pacific Northwest, Columbia River plateau, Mexico, and Central America. **—***adj.* **3.** of or pertaining to Penutian. [1913; *pen* + *uti,* schematized bases for "two" in Maidu-Wintu-Yokuts and Miwok-Costanoan, respectively + -AN]

Pen·za (pen′zə; *Russ.* pyen′zə), *n.* a city in the W Russian Federation in Europe. 543,000.

Pen·zance (pen zans′), *n.* a seaport in SW Cornwall, in the SW extremity of England: resort. 19,352.

Pen·zi·as (pent′sē əs, pen′zē-), *n.* **Arno Allan,** born

CONCISE PRONUNCIATION KEY: *act, cāpe, dâre, pärt; set, ēqual; if, īce; ox, ōver, ôrder, oil, bo͝ok, bo͞ot, out; up, ûrge; child; sing; shoe; thin,* t͟h*at;* zh as in *treasure.* ə = *a* as in *alone, e* as in *system, i* as in *easily, o* as in *gallop, u* as in *circus;* ᵊ as in *fire* (fīᵊr), *hour* (ouᵊr). l and n can serve as syllabic consonants, as in *cradle* (krād′l), and *button* (but′n). See the full key inside the front cover.

1933, U.S. astrophysicist, born in Germany: Nobel prize for physics 1978.

pe·on[1] (pē′ən, pē′on), *n.* **1.** (in Spanish America) a farm worker or unskilled laborer; day laborer. **2.** (formerly, esp. in Mexico) a person held in servitude to work off debts or other obligations. **3.** any person of low social status, esp. one who does work regarded as menial or unskilled; drudge. [1820–30; < Sp *peón* peasant, day laborer < VL **pedōn-* (s. of **pedō*) walker (whence ML *pedōnēs* infantry, OF *peon* PAWN[2]), deriv. of L *ped-* (s. of *pēs*) foot]

pe·on[2] (pē′ən, pē′on), *n.* (in India and Sri Lanka) **1.** a messenger, attendant, or orderly. **2.** a foot soldier or police officer. [1600–10; < Pg *peão,* F *pion* foot soldier, pedestrian, day laborer. See PEON[1]]

pe·on·age (pē′ə nij), *n.* **1.** the condition or service of a peon. **2.** the practice of holding persons in servitude or partial slavery, as to work off a debt or to serve a penal sentence. [1840–50, *Amer.*; PEON[1] + -AGE]

pe·o·ny (pē′ə nē), *n., pl.* **-nies.** any of various plants or shrubs of the genus *Paeonia,* having large, showy flowers, as the widely cultivated species *P. lactiflora:* the state flower of Indiana. [bef. 1000; ME < LL *peōnia,* L *paeōnia* < Gk *paiōnía* peony, akin to *Paiā́n* PAEAN; r. ME *pione* < AF < OF *peone* < L; r. OE *peonie* < LL, L, as above]

peo·ple (pē′pəl), *n., pl.* **-ples** for 4, *v.,* **-pled, -pling.** —*n.* **1.** persons indefinitely or collectively; persons in general: *to find it easy to talk to people; What will people think?* **2.** persons, whether men, women, or children, considered as numerable individuals forming a group: *Twenty people volunteered to help.* **3.** human beings, as distinguished from animals or other beings. **4.** the entire body of persons who constitute a community, tribe, nation, or other group by virtue of a common culture, history, religion, or the like: *the people of Australia; the Jewish people.* **5.** the persons of any particular group, company, or number (sometimes used in combination): *the people of a parish; educated people; salespeople.* **6.** the ordinary persons, as distinguished from those who have wealth, rank, influence, etc.: *a man of the people.* **7.** the subjects, followers, or subordinates of a ruler, leader, employer, etc.: *the king and his people.* **8.** the body of enfranchised citizens of a state: *representatives chosen by the people.* **9.** a person's family or relatives: *My grandmother's people came from Iowa.* **10.** (used in the possessive in Communist or left-wing countries to indicate that an institution operates under the control of or for the benefit of the people, esp. under Communist leadership): *people's republic; people's army.* **11.** animals of a specified kind: *the monkey people of the forest.* —*v.t.* **12.** to furnish with people; populate. **13.** to supply or stock as if with people: *a meadow peopled with flowers.* [1225–75; ME *peple* < AF *poeple,* OF *pueple* < L *populus.* See POPULAR] —**peo′ple·less,** *adj.* —**peo′pler,** *n.*
—**Syn. 4.** See **race**[2].
—**Usage.** PEOPLE is usually followed by a plural verb and referred to by a plural pronoun: *People are always looking for a bargain. The people have made their choice.* The possessive is formed regularly, with the apostrophe before the *-s: people's desire for a bargain; the people's choice.* When PEOPLE means "the entire body of persons who constitute a community or other group by virtue of a common culture, history, etc.," it is used as a singular, with the plural PEOPLES: *This people shares characteristics with certain inhabitants of central Asia. The aboriginal peoples of the Western Hemisphere speak many different languages.* The formation of the possessive is regular; the singular is PEOPLE'S and the plural is PEOPLES'.
At one time, some usage guides maintained that PEOPLE could not be preceded by a number, as in *Fewer than 30 people showed up.* This use is now unquestionably standard in all contexts.

peo·ple·hood (pē′pəl ho͝od′), *n.* **1.** the state or condition of being a people. **2.** the consciousness of certain beliefs or characteristics that make one part of a people; sense of belonging to a people. [1905–10; PEOPLE + -HOOD]

peo′ple mov′er, 1. any of various forms of mass transit, as moving sidewalks or automated driverless vehicles, used for transporting people along limited, fixed routes, as around airports or congested urban areas. **2.** any vehicle that transports people quickly from one destination to another. [1965–70]

Peo′ple's Char′ter. See under **Chartism.**

peo′ple's com′mune, a usually rural, Communist Chinese social and administrative unit of from 2000 to 4000 families combined for collective farming, fishing, mining, or industrial projects. Also called **commune.** [1970–75]

peo′ple's court′, *Informal.* See **small-claims court.**

peo′ple's front′. See **popular front.** [1935–40]

Peo′ple's Libera′tion Ar′my, 1. See under **Huk** (def. 1). **2.** the name of the armed forces of the People's Republic of China. **3.** a rebel army or army of liberation in any of various other countries.

Peo′ple's par′ty, *U.S. Politics.* a political party (1891–1904), advocating expansion of currency, state control of railroads, the placing of restrictions upon ownership of land, etc.; Populist party.

Peo′ple's Repub′lic of Chi′na. See **China, People's Republic of.**

Pe·o·ri·a (pē ôr′ē ə, -ōr′-), *n.* **1.** a city in central Illinois, on the Illinois River. 124,160. **2.** a town in central Arizona. 12,251. —**Pe·o′ri·an,** *adj., n.*

CONCISE ETYMOLOGY KEY: <, descended or borrowed from; >, whence; b., blend of, blended; c., cognate with; cf., compare; deriv., derivative; equiv., equivalent; imit., imitative; obl., oblique; r., replacing; s., stem; sp., spelling, spelled; resp., respelling, respelled; trans., translation; ?, origin unknown; *, unattested; ‡, probably earlier than. See the full key inside the front cover.

pep (pep), *n., v.,* **pepped, pep·ping.** *Informal.* —*n.* **1.** lively spirits or energy; vigor; animation. —*v.t., v.i.* **2. pep up,** to make or become spirited, vigorous, or lively; animate: *We need something to pep up this party.* [1840–50; short for PEPPER] —**pep′ful,** *adj.*

pep·er·o·mi·a (pep′ə rō′mē ə), *n.* any of numerous tropical and subtropical plants belonging to the genus *Peperomia,* of the pepper family, cultivated as houseplants for their ornamental foliage. [< NL < Gk *péper(i)* PEPPER + *(h)om(ós)* same (see HOMO-; the intended sense is prob. that of *hómoios* like, similar) + NL *-ia* -IA]

pep·er·o·ni (pep′ə rō′nē), *n.* pepperoni.

Pep·in (pep′in), *n.* ("*Pepin the Short*") died A.D. 768, king of the Franks 751–768 (father of Charlemagne).

pe·pi·no (pə pē′nō), *n., pl.* **-nos. 1.** a rounded, cone-shaped hill in a karstic area. **2.** Also called **melon pear, melon shrub.** a Peruvian plant, *Solanum muricatum,* of the nightshade family, having spiny foliage, bright blue flowers, and edible purple, egg-shaped fruit. [1895–1900; < Sp: cucumber, ult. < L *pepō;* see PEPO, -INE[1]]

pe·pi·ta (pə pē′tə, pe-), *n.* the edible seed of a pumpkin or squash, used in cooking and often dried or toasted and eaten as a snack food. [< AmerSp, Sp: seed, pip, prob. deriv. of the same Rom base **pep-* as OF *pepin* PIPPIN]

Pe·pi·ta (pə pē′tə, pe-; *Sp.* pe pē′tä), *n.* a female given name.

pep·los (pep′ləs), *n., pl.* **-los·es.** a loose-fitting outer garment worn, draped in folds, by women in ancient Greece. Also, **peplus.** [1770–80; < Gk *péplos* (masc.)] —**pep·losed** (pep′ləst), *adj.*

pep·lum (pep′ləm), *n., pl.* **-lums, -la** (-lə). **1.** a short full flounce or an extension of a garment below the waist, covering the hips. **2.** a short skirt attached to a bodice or jacket. **3.** *Obs.* a peplos. [1670–80; < L < Gk **péplon* (neut.; only pl. *pépla* occurs). See PEPLOS]

pep·lus (pep′ləs), *n., pl.* **-lus·es.** peplos.

pe·po (pē′pō), *n., pl.* **-pos.** the characteristic fruit of plants of the gourd family, having a fleshy, many-seeded interior and a hard or firm rind, as the gourd, melon, and cucumber. [1700–10; < L *pepō* large melon, pumpkin < Gk *pépōn,* short for *pépōn (síkyos)* ripe (gourd)]

pep·per (pep′ər), *n.* **1.** a pungent condiment obtained from various plants of the genus *Piper,* esp. from the dried berries, used whole or ground, of the tropical climbing shrub *P. nigrum.* **2.** any plant of the genus *Piper.* Cf. **pepper family. 3.** any of several plants of the genus *Capsicum,* esp. *C. annuum,* cultivated in many varieties, or *C. frutescens.* **4.** the usually green or red fruit of any of these plants, ranging from mild to very pungent in flavor. **5.** the pungent seeds of several varieties of *C. annuum* or *C. frutescens,* used ground or whole as a condiment. **6.** *Baseball.* See **pepper game.** —*v.t.* **7.** to season with or as if with pepper. **8.** to sprinkle or cover, as if with pepper; dot. **9.** to sprinkle like pepper. **10.** to hit with rapidly repeated short jabs. **11.** to pelt with or as if with shot or missiles: *They peppered the speaker with hard questions.* **12.** to discharge (shot or missiles) at something. [bef. 1000; ME *peper, piper,* OE *pipor* (> ON *pipari, piparr*) < L *piper* < Gk *péperi;* cf. OFris *piper,* D *peper,* OHG *pfeffar* (G *Pfeffer*); these and OE *pipor* perh. < a common WGmc borrowing < L] —**pep′per·er,** *n.* —**pep′per·ish,** *adj.* —**pep′per·ish·ly,** *adv.*

pep·per-and-salt (pep′ər ən sôlt′), *adj.* **1.** composed of a fine mixture of black with white: *pepper-and-salt hair.* —*n.* **2.** an apparel fabric having a pepper-and-salt effect. **3.** the harbinger-of-spring. [1765–75]

pep·per·box (pep′ər boks′), *n.* a small box with perforations in the top, for sprinkling pepper. Also called **pepper pot.** [1540–50; PEPPER + BOX[1]]

pep·per·bush (pep′ər bo͝osh′), *n.* See **sweet pepperbush.** [1775–85, *Amer.*; PEPPER + BUSH[1]]

pep·per·corn (pep′ər kôrn′), *n.* **1.** the berry of the pepper plant, *Piper nigrum,* dried and used as a condiment, in pickling, etc. **2.** anything very small or insignificant. —*adj.* **3.** (of hair) growing in tight spirals. [bef. 1000; ME *pepercorn;* OE *piporcorn.* See PEPPER, CORN[1]] —**pep′per·corn′ish, pep′per·corn′y,** *adj.*

pep′per fam′ily, the plant family Piperaceae, characterized by tropical woody vines and herbaceous plants having simple leaves, dense spikes of very small flowers, and fleshy, berrylike fruit, and including peperomia and peppers of the genus *Piper.*

pep′per game′, *Baseball.* a pregame warm-up performed at a brisk rate, in which one batter bunts back balls tossed by fielders stationed a short distance away.

pep·per·grass (pep′ər gras′, -gräs′), *n.* any pungent plant belonging to the genus *Lepidium,* of the mustard family, used as a potherb or salad vegetable. Cf. **garden cress.** [1425–75; late ME; see PEPPER, GRASS]

pep·per·idge (pep′ər ij), *n.* See **sour gum.** [1815–25; orig. uncert.]

pep′per mill′, a small hand-held device for storing and grinding peppercorns. [1855–60]

pep·per·mint (pep′ər mint′, -mənt), *n.* **1.** an herb, *Mentha piperita,* of the mint family, cultivated for its aromatic, pungent oil. **2.** Also called **pep′permint oil′.** this oil, or a preparation made from it. **3.** a lozenge or confection flavored with peppermint. [1690–1700; PEPPER + MINT[1]]

pep′permint cam′phor, menthol. [1860–65]

pep′permint spir′it, a green or colorless alcoholic solution of the volatile oil produced by the peppermint leaf, used as a carminative and flavoring agent.

pep·per·o·ni (pep′ə rō′nē), *n.* a highly seasoned, hard sausage of beef and pork. Also, **peperoni.** [1920–25, *Amer.*; < It *peperoni,* pl. of *peperone* cayenne pepper plant, aug. of *pepe* PEPPER]

pep′per pot′, 1. Also called **Philadelphia pepper pot.** a highly seasoned, thick soup made of tripe or other meat, vegetables, and sometimes dumplings. **2.** a West Indian stew of meat or fish and vegetables, flavored with cassareep. **3.** pepperbox. [1670–80]

pep′per rat′. See **spiny dormouse.**

pep·per·root (pep′ər ro͞ot′, -ro͝ot′), *n.* toothwort (def. 2). [1805–15, *Amer.*; PEPPER + ROOT[1]]

pep·per·shrike (pep′ər shrīk′), *n.* either of two large vireos of the genus *Cyclarhis,* ranging from Mexico to Chile, and having heavy shrikelike bills. [PEPPER + SHRIKE]

pep′per spot′, *Plant Pathol.* a disease of clover, characterized by numerous black specks on the leaves, caused by a fungus, *Pseudoplea trifolii.*

pep′per steak′, 1. strips of beefsteak sautéed with strips of green pepper and onion, and often flavored with soy sauce. **2.** beefsteak patted with crushed peppercorns, sautéed, and served with a sauce containing butter and cognac. [1950–55]

pep′per tree′, any of several chiefly South American, evergreen trees belonging to the genus *Schinus,* of the cashew family, cultivated in subtropical regions as an ornamental. [1685–95]

pep·per-up·per (pep′ər up′ər), *n.* *Informal.* **1.** something, as a food, beverage, or pill, that provides a quick but temporary period of energy and alertness. **2.** something added to food to relieve blandness. **3.** an experience that increases enthusiasm or zeal, as a pep talk. Also, **pep′per up′per.** [1935–40; *pep up* + -ER[1], suffixed pleonastically to both v. and particle]

pep·per·wood (pep′ər wo͝od′), *n.* See **California laurel** (def. 1). [1855–60; PEPPER + WOOD[1]]

pep·per·wort (pep′ər wûrt′, -wôrt′), *n.* See **water clover.** [1555–65; PEPPER + WORT[2]]

pep·per·y (pep′ə rē), *adj.* **1.** full of or tasting like pepper; hot; pungent. **2.** of, pertaining to, or resembling pepper. **3.** sharp or stinging: *a peppery speech.* **4.** easily angered; bad-tempered; irritable; irascible: *the peppery leader of a political faction.* [1690–1700; PEPPER + -Y[1]] —**pep′per·i·ly,** *adv.* —**pep′per·i·ness,** *n.*
—**Syn. 1.** spicy. **3.** biting. **4.** hot-tempered, hot-headed, testy, choleric.

pep′ pill′, a pill, tablet, or capsule that contains a stimulant drug, esp. amphetamine. [1935–40, *Amer.*]

pep·py (pep′ē), *adj.,* **-pi·er, -pi·est.** *Informal.* energetic; vigorous; lively. [1920–25; PEP + -Y[1]] —**pep′pi·ly,** *adv.* —**pep′pi·ness,** *n.*

pep′ ral′ly, a meeting, esp. of students before an interscholastic athletic contest, to stimulate group enthusiasm by rousing talks, songs, cheers, etc. [1920–25]

pep·sin (pep′sin), *n. Biochem.* **1.** an enzyme, produced in the stomach, that in the presence of hydrochloric acid splits proteins into proteoses and peptones. **2.** a commercial form of this substance, obtained from the stomachs of hogs, used as a digestive, as a ferment in the manufacture of cheese, etc. Also, **pep′sine.** [1835–45; < Gk *péps(is)* digestion (*pep-,* base of *péptein* to digest + *-sis* -SIS) + -IN[2]]

pep·sin·ate (pep′sə nāt′), *v.t.,* **-at·ed, -at·ing.** to treat, prepare, or mix with pepsin. [1880–85; PEPSIN + -ATE[1]]

pep·sin·o·gen (pep sin′ə jən, -jen′), *n. Biochem.* crystals, occurring in the gastric glands, that during digestion are converted into pepsin. [1875–80; PEPSIN + -O- + -GEN] —**pep·si·no·gen·ic** (pep′sə nō jen′ik), **pep·si·nog·e·nous** (pep′sə noj′ə nəs), *adj.*

pep′ talk′, a vigorous, emotional talk, as to a person or group, intended to arouse enthusiasm, increase determination to succeed, etc.: *The coach gave the team a pep talk before the game.* [1920–25]

pep·talk (pep′tôk′), *v.t.* **1.** to give a pep talk to (a person, group, etc.). —*v.i.* **2.** to deliver a pep talk. [v. use of PEP TALK]

pep·tic (pep′tik), *adj.* **1.** pertaining to or associated with digestion; digestive. **2.** promoting digestion. **3.** of or pertaining to pepsin. —*n.* **4.** a substance promoting digestion. [1645–55; < Gk *peptikós* conducive to digestion, equiv. to *pept(ós)* digested (verbid of *péptein*) + *-ikos* -IC]

pep′tic ul′cer, *Pathol.* an erosion of the mucous membrane of the lower esophagus, stomach, or duodenum, caused in part by the corrosive action of the gastric juice. [1895–1900]

pep·ti·dase (pep′ti dās′, -dāz′), *n. Biochem.* any of the class of enzymes that catalyze the hydrolysis of peptides or peptones to amino acids. [1915–20; PEPTIDE + -ASE]

pep·tide (pep′tīd), *n. Biochem.* a compound containing two or more amino acids in which the carboxyl group of one acid is linked to the amino group of the other. [1905–10; PEPT(IC) + -IDE]

pep′tide bond′, *Biochem.* a covalent bond formed by joining the carboxyl group of one amino acid to the amino group of another, with the removal of a molecule of water. Also called **pep′tide link′age.** [1930–35]

pep·ti·do·lyt·ic (pep′ti dō lit′ik), *adj. Biochem.* causing the hydrolysis of peptides. [1965–70; PEPTIDE + -O- + -LYTIC]

pep·tize (pep′tīz), *v.t.,* **-tized, -tiz·ing.** to disperse (a substance) into colloidal form, usually in a liquid. Also, *esp. Brit.,* **pep′tise.** [1860–65; PEPT(ONE) + -IZE] —**pep·tiz′a·ble,** *adj.* —**pep′ti·za′tion,** *n.* —**pep′tiz·er,** *n.*

pep·to·lyt·ic (pep′tə lit′ik), *adj. Biochem.* causing the hydrolysis of peptones. [1900–05; PEPTO(NE) + -LYTIC] —**pep·tol·y·sis** (pep tol′ə sis), *n.*

pep·tone (pep′tōn), *n. Biochem.* any of a class of diffusible, soluble substances into which proteins are converted by partial hydrolysis. [1855–60; < G *Pepton* < Gk *peptón,* neut. of *peptós* cooked, digested, verbid of *péptein*] —**pep′tone·like′,** *adj.* —**pep·ton·ic** (pep ton′ik), *adj.* —**pep·to·noid** (pep′tə noid′), *n.*

pep•to•nize (pep′tə nīz′), *v.t.*, **-nized, -niz•ing. 1.** to subject (food) to an artificial, partial digestion by pepsin or pancreatic extract in order to aid digestion. **2.** to hydrolyze or dissolve by a proteolytic enzyme, as pepsin. Also, *esp. Brit.*, **pep′to•nise′.** [1875–80; PEPTONE + -IZE] **—pep′to•ni•za′tion,** *n.* **—pep′to•niz′er,** *n.*

Pepys (pēps, peps, pē′pis, pep′is), *n.* **Samuel,** 1633–1703, English diarist and naval official. **—Pepys•i•an** (pēp′sē ən, pep′-), *adj.*

Pepys′ Di′ary, a diary kept by Samuel Pepys from January 1, 1660 to May 31, 1669, in which are recorded his impressions of contemporary London life, the life of the court, and the administration of the navy.

Pe•quot (pē′kwot), *n., pl.* **-quots,** (*esp. collectively*) **-quot.** a member of a powerful tribe of Algonquian-speaking Indians of Connecticut that was essentially destroyed in the Pequot War. [1625–35, *Amer.*; < Narragansett (E sp.) *Peguttôog* (pl.), and the cognate in other SE New England languages, e.g., (D sp.) *Pequat*(*s*), *Pequatoo*(*s*), prob. lit., people of the shoals]

Pe′quot War′, *Amer. Hist.* a war in 1637 between Connecticut colonists, aided by British soldiers and friendly Indian tribes, and the Pequot Indians under their chief, Sassacus, that resulted in the defeat and dispersion of the Pequot tribe.

per (pûr; *unstressed* pər), *prep.* **1.** for each; for every: *Membership costs ten dollars per year. This cloth is two dollars per yard.* **2.** by means of; by; through: *I am sending the recipe per messenger.* **3.** according to; in accordance with: *I delivered the box per your instructions.* —*adv.* **4.** *Informal.* each; for each one: *The charge for window-washing was five dollars per.* [1580–90; < L: through, by, for, for each. See FOR]
—Usage. PER for *a* or *an* or *for each* occurs chiefly in technical or statistical contexts: *miles per gallon; work-hours per week; feet per second; gallons of beer per person per year.* It is also common in sports commentary: *He averaged 16 points per quarter.* PER is sometimes criticized in business writing in the sense "according to" and is rare in literary writing.

per-, **1.** a prefix meaning "through," "thoroughly," "utterly," "very": *pervert; pervade; perfect.* **2.** *Chem.* a prefix used in the names of inorganic acids and their salts that possess the maximum amount of the element specified in the base word: *percarbonic* ($H_2C_2O_5$), *permanganic* ($HMnO_4$), *persulfuric* ($H_2S_2O_8$), *acids; potassium permanganate* ($KMnO_4$); *potassium persulfate* ($K_2S_2O_8$). [< L, comb. form of *per* PER, and used as an intensive]

Per., **1.** Persia. **2.** Persian.

per., **1.** percentile. **2.** period. **3.** person.

Pe•ra (pe′rä), *n.* former name of **Beyoğlu.**

per•ac•id (pər as′id), *n. Chem.* an oxyacid, the primary element of which is in its highest possible oxidation state, as perchloric acid, $HClO_4$, and permanganic acid, $HMnO_4$. [1895–1900; PER- + ACID]

per•ad•ven•ture (pûr′əd ven′chər, per′-), *n.* **1.** chance, doubt, or uncertainty. **2.** surmise. —*adv.* **3.** *Archaic.* it may be; maybe; possibly; perhaps. [1250–1300; ME *per aventure* < OF. See PER, ADVENTURE]

Pe•rae•a (pə rē′ə), *n.* a region in ancient Palestine, E of the Jordan and the Dead Sea.

Pe•ra•hia (pə rī′ə), *n.* **Murray,** born 1947, U.S. pianist.

Pe•rak (pā′rak, -räk, per′ə, pēr′ə), *n.* a state in Malaysia, on the SW Malay Peninsula. 1,569,139; 7980 sq. mi. (20,668 sq. km). *Cap.:* Ipoh.

per•am•bu•late (pər am′byə lāt′), *v.*, **-lat•ed, -lat•ing.** —*v.t.* **1.** to walk through, about, or over; travel through; traverse. **2.** to traverse in order to examine or inspect. —*v.i.* **3.** to walk or travel about; stroll. [1560–70; < L *perambulātus* ptp. of *perambulāre* to walk through. See PER-, AMBULATE] **—per•am′bu•la′tion,** *n.* **—per•am•bu•la•to•ry** (pər am′byə lə tôr′ē, -tōr′ē), *adj.*
—Syn. 3. saunter, promenade, amble, mosey, meander, ramble.

per•am•bu•la•tor (pər am′byə lā′tər), *n.* **1.** See **baby carriage. 2.** an odometer pushed by a person walking. **3.** a person who makes a tour of inspection on foot. [1605–15; < ML: inspector, surveyor; see PERAMBULATE, -TOR]

per an., per annum.

per an•num (pər an′əm), by the year; yearly. [1595–1605; < L]

per•bo•rate (pər bôr′āt, -bōr′-), *n. Chem.* a salt of perboric acid, as sodium perborate, $NaBO_3 \cdot 4H_2O$, used for bleaching, disinfecting, etc. Also, **peroxyborate.** [1880–85; PER- + BORATE]

per•bo•rax (pər bôr′əks, -aks, -bōr′-), *n. Chem.* See **sodium perborate.** [PER- + BORAX]

per•bo′ric ac′id (pər bôr′ik, -bōr′-), *Chem.* a hypothetical acid, HBO_3, known only in the form of its salts. [1880–85; PER- + BORIC ACID]

Per•bu•nan (pûr byōō′nən), *Trademark.* a brand of synthetic rubber made by copolymerizing acrylonitrile with butadiene.

perc (pûrk), *n.* perk[3].

per•cale (pər kāl′), *n.* a closely woven, smooth-finished, plain or printed cotton cloth, used for bed sheets, clothing, etc. [1615–25; < F < Pers *pargāla* rag; r. *percalla* < Pers]

per•ca•line (pûr′kə lēn′), *n.* a fine, lightweight cotton fabric, usually finished with a gloss and dyed in one color, used esp. for linings. [1855–60; < F; see PERCALE, -INE[2]]

per cap•i•ta (pər kap′i tə), **1.** by or for each individual person: *income per capita.* **2.** *Law.* noting or pertaining to a method of dividing an estate by which all those equally related to the decedent take equal shares individually without regard to the number of lines of descent. Cf. **per stirpes.** [1675–85; < L: lit., by heads]

per•ceiv•a•ble (pər sē′və bəl), *adj.* capable of being perceived; perceptible. [1400–50; late ME *perceyvable.* See PERCEIVE, -ABLE] **—per•ceiv′a•bil′i•ty, per•ceiv′a•ble•ness,** *n.* **—per•ceiv′a•bly,** *adv.*

per•ceive (pər sēv′), *v.t.*, **-ceived, -ceiv•ing. 1.** to become aware of, know, or identify by means of the senses: *I perceived an object looming through the mist.* **2.** to recognize, discern, envision, or understand: *I perceive a note of sarcasm in your voice. This is a nice idea but I perceive difficulties in putting it into practice.* [1250–1300; ME *perceiven* < AF **perceivre,* for *perçoivre* < L *percipere* to lay hold of, grasp, equiv. to *per-* PER- + *-cipere,* comb. form of *capere* to take] **—per•ceiv•ed•ly** (pər sē′vid lē, -sēvd′-), *adv.* **—per•ceiv′ed•ness,** *n.* **—per•ceiv′er,** *n.* **—per•ceiv′ing•ness,** *n.*
—Syn. 1. note, discover, observe, descry, distinguish. See **notice.**

per•cent (pər sent′), *n.* **1.** Also called **per centum.** one one-hundredth part; 1⁄100. **2.** percentage (defs. 1, 3.). **3.** *Brit.* stocks, bonds, etc., that bear an indicated rate of interest. —*adj.* **4.** figured or expressed on the basis of a rate or proportion per hundred (used in combination with a number in expressing rates of interest, proportions, etc.): *to get three percent interest. Symbol:* % Also, **per cent′.** [1560–70; short for ML *per centum* by the hundred. See PER, CENT] **—per•cent′al,** *adj.*
—Usage. PERCENT is from the Latin adverbial phrase *per centum* meaning "by the hundred." The Latin phrase entered English in the 16th century. Later, it was abbreviated *per cent.* with a final period. Eventually, the period was dropped and the two parts merged to produce the modern one-word form PERCENT. The two-word form PER CENT is still used occasionally, but its use is diminishing. The percent sign (%) is used chiefly in scientific, tabular, or statistical material and only with numerals preceding it: *58%.*
In the senses "rate or proportion per hundred" and "proportion in general" PERCENT and PERCENTAGE are frequently interchangeable. With a preceding number, only PERCENT occurs (*a 16 percent decline*); with no preceding number, either occurs, but PERCENTAGE is much more common: *a certain percentage* (or *percent*) *of the land.*

per•cent•age (pər sen′tij), *n.* **1.** a rate or proportion per hundred. **2.** an allowance, commission, or rate of interest calculated by percent. **3.** a proportion in general: *Only a small percentage of the class will graduate with honors.* **4.** gain; benefit; profit; advantage. [1780–90; PERCENT + -AGE] **—per•cent′aged,** *adj.*
—Usage. See **percent.**

per•cent•er (pər sen′tər), *n.* a person or thing that charges or pays a certain percentage, cooperates to a specified degree, etc. (used in combination): *agents and other ten-percenters.* [1860–65; PERCENT + -ER[1]]

per•cen•tile (pər sen′tīl, -til), *Statistics.* —*n.* **1.** one of the values of a variable that divides the distribution of the variable into 100 groups having equal frequencies: *Ninety percent of the values lie at or below the ninetieth percentile, ten percent above it.* —*adj.* **2.** of or pertaining to a percentile or a division of a distribution by percentiles. [1880–85; PERCENT + -ILE]

percent′ sign′, a symbol (%) for "percent": *a 10% drop in population.*

per cent•um (pər sen′təm), percent (def. 1). [1555–65; < L: lit., by the hundred]

per•cept (pûr′sept), *n.* **1.** the mental result or product of perceiving, as distinguished from the act of perceiving; an impression or sensation of something perceived. **2.** something that is perceived; the object of perception. [1830–40; < L *perceptum* something perceived, n. use of neut. of *perceptus,* ptp. of *percipere* to PERCEIVE]

per•cep•ti•ble (pər sep′tə bəl), *adj.* capable of being perceived; recognizable; appreciable: *a perceptible change in his behavior.* [1545–55; < LL *perceptibilis.* See PERCEPT, -IBLE] **—per•cep′ti•bil′i•ty, per•cep′ti•ble•ness,** *n.* **—per•cep′ti•bly,** *adv.*
—Syn. discernible, apparent.

per•cep•tion (pər sep′shən), *n.* **1.** the act or faculty of apprehending by means of the senses or of the mind; cognition; understanding. **2.** immediate or intuitive recognition or appreciation, as of moral, psychological, or aesthetic qualities; insight; intuition; discernment: *an artist of rare perception.* **3.** the result or product of perceiving, as distinguished from the act of perceiving; percept. **4.** *Psychol.* a single unified awareness derived from sensory processes while a stimulus is present. **5.** *Law.* the taking into possession of rents, crops, profits, etc. [1350–1400; ME *percepcioun* (< OF *percepcion*) < L *perceptiōn-* (s. of *perceptiō*) comprehension, lit., a taking in. See PERCEPT, -ION] **—per•cep′tion•al,** *adj.*
—Syn. 1. awareness, sense, recognition.

per•cep•tive (pər sep′tiv), *adj.* **1.** having or showing keenness of insight, understanding, or intuition: *a perceptive analysis of the problems involved.* **2.** having the power or faculty of perceiving. **3.** of, pertaining to, or showing perception. [1650–60; < L *percept*(*us*) (see PERCEPT) + -IVE] **—per•cep′tive•ly,** *adv.* **—per′cep•tiv′i•ty, per•cep′tive•ness,** *n.*
—Syn. 1. discerning, sensitive, keen, astute.

per•cep•tu•al (pər sep′chōō əl), *adj.* of, pertaining to, or involving perception. [1875–80; PERCEPT + *-ual,* on the model of CONCEPT, CONCEPTUAL] **—per•cep′tu•al•ly,** *adv.*

Per•ce•val (pûr′sə vəl), *n.* **1. Spencer,** 1762–1812, British statesman: prime minister 1809–12. **2.** *Arthurian Romance.* Percival.

perch[1] (pûrch), *n.* **1.** a pole or rod, usually horizontal, serving as a roost for birds. **2.** any place or object, as a sill, fence, branch, or twig, for a bird, animal, or person to alight or rest upon. **3.** a high or elevated position, resting place, or the like. **4.** a small, elevated seat for the driver of any of certain vehicles. **5.** a pole connecting the fore and hind running parts of a spring carriage or other vehicle. **6.** a post set up as a navigational aid on a navigational hazard or on a buoy. **7.** *Brit.* **a.** a linear or square rod. **b.** a measure of volume for stone, about 24 cubic feet (0.7 cubic meters). **8.** *Textiles.* an apparatus consisting of two vertical posts and a horizontal roller, used for inspecting cloth after it leaves the loom. **9.** *Obs.* any pole, rod, or the like. —*v.i.* **10.** to alight or rest upon a perch. **11.** to settle or rest in some elevated position, as if on a perch. —*v.t.* **12.** to set or place on or as if on a perch. **13.** to inspect (cloth) for defects and blemishes after it has been taken from the loom and placed upon a perch. [1250–1300; ME *perche* < OF < L *pertica* pole, staff, measuring rod] **—perch′a•ble,** *adj.*

perch[2] (pûrch), *n., pl.* (*esp. collectively*) **perch,** (*esp. referring to two or more kinds or species*) **perch•es. 1.** any spiny-finned, freshwater food fish of the genus *Perca,* as *P. flavescens* **(yellow perch),** of the U.S., or *P. fluviatilis,* of Europe. **2.** any of various other related, spiny-finned fishes. **3.** any of several embiotocid fishes, as *Hysterocarpus traski* **(tule perch)** of California. [1350–1400; ME *perche* < MF < L *perca* < Gk *pérkē*]

yellow perch,
Perca flavescens,
length 1 ft. (0.3 m)

per•chance (pər chans′, -chäns′), *adv.* **1.** *Literary.* perhaps; maybe; possibly. **2.** *Archaic.* by chance. [1300–50; ME, var. of *par chance* by chance < AF. See PER, CHANCE]

Perche (pârsh; *Fr.* peʀsh), *n.* a former division of N France.

perch•er (pûr′chər), *n.* **1.** a person or thing that perches. **2.** a bird whose feet are adapted for perching. [1575–85; PERCH[1] + -ER[1]]

Per•che•ron (pûr′chə ron′, -shə-), *n.* one of a French breed of draft horses, having a gray or black coat. Also called **Per′cheron Nor′man.** [1870–75; < F; named after *Perche,* French district where first bred]

perch′ing bird′, any member of the avian order Passeriformes. [1815–25]

per•chlo•rate (pər klôr′āt, -klōr′-), *n. Chem.* a salt or ester of perchloric acid, as potassium perchlorate, $KClO_4$. [1820–30; PER- + CHLORATE]

per•chlo•ric (pər klôr′ik, -klōr′-), *adj. Chem.* of or derived from perchloric acid. [1810–20; PER- + CHLORIC]

perchlo′ric ac′id, *Chem.* a colorless, syrupy hygroscopic liquid, $HClO_4$, an acid of chlorine containing one more oxygen atom than chloric acid: used chiefly as a reagent in analytical chemistry. [1810–20]

per•chlo•ride (pər klôr′īd, -id, -klōr′-), *n. Chem.* the chloride of any particular element or group with the maximum proportion of chlorine. [1810–20; PER- + CHLORIDE]

per•chlo•ri•nate (pər klôr′ə nāt′, -klōr′-), *v.t.*, **-nat•ed, -nat•ing.** *Chem.* to combine with the maximum proportion of chlorine. [1855–60; PER- + CHLORINATE] **—per•chlo′ri•na′tion,** *n.*

perchloro-, a combination of **per-** and **chloro-**[2]: *perchloromethane.* Also, **perchlor-.**

per•chlo•ro•eth•ane (pər klôr′ō eth′ān, -klōr′-), *n. Chem.* hexachloroethane. [PERCHLORO- + ETHANE]

per•chlo•ro•eth•yl•ene (pər klôr′ō eth′ə lēn′, -klōr′-), *n. Chem.* tetrachloroethylene. [1870–75; PERCHLORO- + ETHYLENE]

per•chlo•ro•meth•ane (pər klôr′ō meth′ān, -klōr′-), *n. Chem.* See **carbon tetrachloride.** [PERCHLORO- + METHANE]

Perch•ta (peʀкн′tä), *n. Germanic Myth.* the goddess of death and of fertility: sometimes identified with Holle. Also, **Berchta.**

per•cip•i•ent (pər sip′ē ənt), *adj.* **1.** perceiving or capable of perceiving. **2.** having perception; discerning; discriminating: *a percipient choice of wines.* —*n.* **3.** a person or thing that perceives. [1655–65; < L *percipient-* (s. of *percipiēns*) prp. of *percipere* to take in, equiv. to *per-* PER- + *-cipi-* comb. form of pres. s. of *capere* to take + *-ent-* -ENT] **—per•cip′i•ence, per•cip′i•en•cy,** *n.*

Per•ci•val (pûr′sə vəl), *n.* **1.** Also, **Perceval, Per′ci•vale.** *Arthurian Romance.* a knight of King Arthur's court who sought the Holy Grail: comparable to Parzival or Parsifal in Teutonic legend. **2.** a male given name: from Old French words meaning "pierce" and "valley."

per•close (pûr′klōz′), *n.* parclose.

Per•co•dan (pûr′kə dan′), *Pharm., Trademark.* a brand name for a preparation containing aspirin, oxycodone, caffeine, and other ingredients, used for the relief of pain.

per•coid (pûr′koid), *adj.* **1.** belonging to the Percoidea, a group of acanthopterygian fishes comprising the true perches and related families, and constituting one of the largest natural groups of fishes. **2.** resembling a perch. Also, **per•coi•de•an** (pər koi′dē ən). [1830–40; < L *perc*(*a*) PERCH[2] + -OID]

per•co•late (*v.* pûr′kə lāt′; *n.* pûr′kə lit, -lāt′), *v.*, **-lat•ed, -lat•ing,** *n.* —*v.t.* **1.** to cause (a liquid) to pass through a porous body; filter. **2.** (of a liquid) to filter through; permeate. **3.** to brew (coffee) in a percolator. —*v.i.* **4.** to pass through a porous substance; filter; ooze; seep; trickle. **5.** to become percolated: *The coffee is starting to percolate.* **6.** to become active, lively, or spirited. **7.** to show activity, movement, or life; grow or spread gradually; germinate: *Interest in the idea has begun to percolate.* —*n.* **8.** a percolated liquid. [1620–30; < L *percōlātus,* ptp. of *percōlāre* to filter. See PER-, COLANDER, -ATE[1]] —**per′co·la·ble,** *adj.* —**per′co·la′·tive,** *adj.*

—**Pronunciation.** The pronunciation of PERCOLATE as (pûr′kyə lāt′), with an intrusive *y*-glide, results from analogy with words like *circulate* and *matriculate,* where the unstressed vowel following the *k*-sound is symbolized by a *u* spelling, making the *y*-glide mandatory. In similar words where (k) is followed by some other vowel, the (y) represents a hypercorrection. The pronunciation of *escalate* as (es′kyə lāt′) is another such example. See **coupon, new.**

per·co·la·tion (pûr′kə lā′shən), *n.* **1.** the act or state of percolating or of being percolated. **2.** *Pharm.* the extraction of the soluble principles of a crude drug by the passage of a suitable liquid through it. **3.** *Geol.* the slow movement of water through the pores in soil or permeable rock. [1605–15; < L *percōlātiōn-* (s. of *percōlātiō*). See PERCOLATE, -ION]

per·co·la·tor (pûr′kə lā′tər), *n.* **1.** a kind of coffeepot in which boiling water in a repeated process is forced up a hollow stem, filters down through ground coffee in a sievelike container, and returns to the pot below. **2.** something that percolates. [1835–45; PERCOLATE + -OR[2]]

per con·tra (pər kon′trə; *Lat.* peʀ kōn′trä), on the other hand; on the contrary. [1545–55; < L *per contrā*]

per cu·ri·am (pər kyo͝or′ē am′), *Law.* noting an action taken by the court as a whole, esp. an anonymous opinion of the whole court, as contrasted with an opinion delivered in the name of a particular judge. [< ML: lit., through the court]

per·cur·rent (pər kûr′ənt, -kur′-), *adj. Bot.* extending through the entire length, as a midrib through a leaf. [1570–80; < L *percurrent-* (s. of *percurrēns*), prp. of *percurrere* to run through. See PER-, CURRENT]

per·cuss (pər kus′), *v.t.* **1.** *Med.* to strike or tap for diagnostic or therapeutic purposes. **2.** to strike (something) so as to shake or cause a shock to. —*v.i.* **3.** *Med.* to strike the surface of a part of the body for diagnostic purposes. [1550–60; < L *percussus,* ptp. of *percutere* to strike hard, beat, equiv. to *per-* PER- + *-cut(ere),* comb. form of *quatere* to shake (see QUASH) + *-tus* ptp. suffix, with *tt* > *ss*]

per·cus·sion (pər kush′ən), *n.* **1.** the striking of one body against another with some sharpness; impact; blow. **2.** *Med.* the striking or tapping of the surface of a part of the body for diagnostic or therapeutic purposes. **3.** the striking of a musical instrument to produce tones. **4.** *Music.* **a.** the section of an orchestra or band comprising the percussion instruments. **b.** the percussion instruments themselves. **5.** a sharp blow for detonating a percussion cap or the fuze of an artillery shell. **6.** the striking of sound on the ear. **7.** the act of percussing. [1535–45; < L *percussiōn-* (s. of *percussiō*) a beating. See PERCUSS, -ION] —**per·cus′sion·al,** *adj.*

percus′sion cap′, a small metallic cap or cup containing fulminating powder, formerly exploded by percussion to fire the charge of small arms. [1815–25]

percus′sion flak′ing, a method of forming a flint tool by striking flakes from a stone core with another stone or a piece of bone or wood.

percus′sion in′strument, a musical instrument, as the drum, cymbal, triangle, xylophone, or piano, that is struck to produce a sound, as distinguished from string or wind instruments. [1870–75]

per·cus·sion·ist (pər kush′ə nist), *n.* a musician who plays percussion instruments. [1810–20; PERCUSSION + -IST]

percus′sion lock′, a gunlock on a firearm that fires by striking a percussion cap. Cf. **flintlock.** [1820–30]

percus′sion weld′ing, a form of resistance welding in which the required pressure is provided by a hammerlike blow.

per·cus·sive (pər kus′iv), *adj.* of, pertaining to, or characterized by percussion. [1785–95; PERCUSS(ION) + -IVE] —**per·cus′sive·ly,** *adv.* —**per·cus′sive·ness,** *n.*

per·cus·sor (pər kus′ər), *n. Med.* plexor. [1885–90; < NL, L: one that beats, equiv. to *percut-,* s. of *percutere* to beat (see PERCUSS) + *-tor* -TOR, with *tt* > *ss*]

per·cu·ta·ne·ous (pûr′kyo͞o tā′nē əs), *adj.* administered, removed, or absorbed by way of the skin, as an injection, needle biopsy, or transdermal drug. [1885–90; PER- + CUTANEOUS]

Per·cy (pûr′sē), *n.* **1. Sir Henry** (*"Hotspur"*), 1364–1403, English military and rebel leader. **2. Thomas,** 1729–1811, English poet and antiquary: bishop of Dromore 1782–1811. **3.** a male given name, form of Percival.

Per·di·do (*Sp.* peʀ ᵺē′ᵺô), *n.* **Mon·te** (*Sp.* môn′te), a mountain in NE Spain, a peak of the Pyrenees. 10,994 ft. (3350 m). French, **Mont Perdu** (môɴ peʀ dʏ′).

per·die (pər dē′), *adv., interj. Archaic.* pardi.

per di·em (pər dē′əm, dī′əm), **1.** by the day; for each day. **2.** a daily allowance, usually for living expenses while traveling in connection with one's work or being employed at a distance from one's home: *a per diem for lawmakers while the legislature is in session.* **3.** paid by the day. [1510–20; < L]

per·di·tion (pər dish′ən), *n.* **1.** a state of final spiritual ruin; loss of the soul; damnation. **2.** the future state of the wicked. **3.** hell (def. 1). **4.** utter destruction or ruin. **5.** *Obs.* loss. [1300–50; < L *perditiōn-* (s. of *perditiō*) destruction, equiv. to *perdit(us)* (ptp. of *perdere* to do in, ruin, lose, equiv. to *per-* PER- + *di-,* comb. form of *dare* to give + *-tus* ptp. suffix) + *-iōn* -ION; r. ME *perdiciun* < OF < L, as above]

per·du (pər do͞o′, -dyo͞o′, per-), *adj.* **1.** hidden; concealed; obscured. —*n.* **2.** *Obs.* a soldier assigned to a very dangerous mission or position. Also, **per·due′.** [1585–95; < F: lost, ptp. of *perdre* < L *perdere* to lose]

per·dur·a·ble (pər do͝or′ə bəl, -dyo͝or′-), *adj.* **1.** very durable; permanent; imperishable. **2.** *Theol.* eternal; everlasting. [1200–50; ME < LL *perdūrābilis.* See PER-, DURE[2], -ABLE] —**per·dur′a·bil′i·ty, per·dur′a·ble·ness,** *n.* —**per·dur′a·bly,** *adv.*

per·dure (pər do͝or′, -dyo͝or′), *v.i.,* **-dured, -dur·ing.** to continue or last permanently; endure. [1350–1400; ME *perduren* < L *perdūrāre.* See PER-, DURE[2]]

père (peʀ; *Eng.* pâr), *n., pl.* **pères** (peʀ; *Eng.* pârz). *French.* **1.** father. **2.** senior: *Dumas père.*

Père′ Da·vid′s deer′ (pâr′ dä vēdz′, pâr′ dā′vidz), a medium-sized, reddish-gray deer, *Elaphurus davidianus,* of which stocks were obtained in Peking in 1865 and brought to parks in Europe before the remaining Chinese deer were killed in 1900: the species is sustained in captivity. [1895–1900; named after *Père* Armand *David* (1826–1900), French missionary, the deer's first European observer]

per·e·gri·nate (per′i grə nāt′), *v.,* **-nat·ed, -nat·ing.** —*v.i.* **1.** to travel or journey, esp. to walk on foot. —*v.t.* **2.** to travel or walk over; traverse. [1585–95; < L *peregrīnātus,* ptp. of *peregrīnārī* to travel abroad. See PEREGRINE, -ATE[1]] —**per′e·gri·na′tor,** *n.*

per·e·gri·na·tion (per′i grə nā′shən), *n.* **1.** travel from one place to another, esp. on foot. **2.** a course of travel; journey. [1425–75; late ME *peregrinacioun* (< MF *peregrinacion*) < L *peregrīnātiōn-* (s. of *peregrīnātiō*) a traveling abroad. See PEREGRINATE, -ION]

per·e·grine (per′i grin, -grēn′, -grīn′), *adj.* **1.** foreign; alien; coming from abroad. **2.** wandering, traveling, or migrating. —*n.* **3.** See **peregrine falcon.** [1350–1400; ME < L *peregrīnus* foreign, deriv. of *peregrē* abroad, lit., through (i.e., beyond the borders of) the field, equiv. to *per-* PER- + *-egr-,* comb. form of *ager* field + *-ē* adv. suffix; see -INE[1]] —**per·e·grin·i·ty** (per′i grin′i tē), *n.*

per′egrine fal′con, a globally distributed falcon, *Falco peregrinus,* much used in falconry because of its swift flight: several subspecies are endangered. See illus. under **falcon.** [1350–1400; ME]

per·ei·on (pə rī′on, -rā′-, -rē′-), *n., pl.* **-rei·a** (-rī′ə, -rā′ə, -rē′ə). (in a crustacean) the thorax. [1850–55; < NL, repr. Gk *peraiôn* (prp. of *peraioûn* to carry about, transport); so called from the location of the legs on the thorax]

pe·rei·o·pod (pə rī′ə pod′, -rā′-, -rē′-), *n.* (in a crustacean) an appendage of the thorax. [1850–55; < NL; see PEREION, -POD]

Pe·rei·ra (pe ʀā′ʀä), *n.* a city in W Colombia. 211,965.

pe·rei′ra bark′ (pə râr′ə), the bark of any of several South American trees belonging to the genus *Geissospermum,* of the dogbane family, esp. that of *G. vellosii,* used in Brazil to allay fever. [*pereira* < NL, named after J. *Pereira* (1804–53), English professor of medicine]

pe·rei·rine (pə râr′ēn), *n. Chem. Pharm.* an alkaloid, $C_{19}H_{24}ON_2$, obtained from pereira bark and formerly used as a quinine substitute. [PEREIR(A BARK) + -INE[2]]

Perel·man (per′əl mən, pûrl′-), *n.* **S(idney) J(oseph),** 1904–79, U.S. author.

per·emp·to·ry (pə remp′tə rē, per′əmp tôr′ē, -tōr′ē), *adj.* **1.** leaving no opportunity for denial or refusal; imperative: *a peremptory command.* **2.** imperious or dictatorial. **3.** positive or assertive in speech, tone, manner, etc. **4.** *Law.* **a.** that precludes or does not admit of debate, question, etc.: *a peremptory edict.* **b.** decisive or final. **c.** in which a command is absolute and unconditional: *a peremptory writ.* [1505–15; < L *peremptōrius* final, decisive, lit., deadly, destructive (deriv. of *perimere* to take away fully, destroy, slay), equiv. to *per-* PER- + *em-,* base of *emere* to buy, orig. to take + *-tōrius* -TORY[1], with intrusive *p*] —**per·emp′to·ri·ly,** *adv.* —**per·emp′to·ri·ness,** *n.*

—**Syn. 2.** arbitrary, dogmatic, domineering.

peremp′tory chal′lenge, *Law.* a formal objection to the service of a juror by a party to a criminal prosecution or a civil action that requires no showing of cause. [1520–30]

peremp′tory excep′tion, *Law.* a plea in bar of an action. Also, **peremp′tory plea′.** [1590–1600]

per·en·nate (per′ə nāt′, pə ren′āt), *v.i.,* **-nat·ed, -nat·ing.** *Bot.* to survive from season to season for an indefinite number of years. [1615–25; < L *perennātus,* ptp. of *perennāre* to continue for a long time, deriv. of *perennis;* see PERENNIAL, -ATE[1]] —**per′en·na′tion,** *n.*

per·en·ni·al (pə ren′ē əl), *adj.* **1.** lasting for an indefinitely long time; enduring: *her perennial beauty.* **2.** (of plants) having a life cycle lasting more than two years. **3.** lasting or continuing throughout the entire year, as a stream. **4.** perpetual; everlasting; continuing; recurrent. —*n.* **5.** a perennial plant. **6.** something that is continuing or recurrent. [1635–45; < L *perenni(s)* lasting the whole year through (*per-* PER- + *-enn-,* comb. form of *annus* year + *-is* adj. suffix) + -AL[1]] —**per·en′ni·al′i·ty,** *n.* —**per·en′ni·al·ly,** *adv.*

—**Syn. 1.** perdurable; constant, incessant, continual. **4.** imperishable, undying, eternal, immortal.

peren′nial pea′. See **everlasting pea.**

peren′nial rye′grass. See under **ryegrass.**

Per·es (per′ez), *n.* **Shi·mon** (shi mōn′), born 1923, Israeli political leader: prime minister 1984–86.

pe·re·stroi·ka (per′ə stroi′kə; *Russ.* pyi ʀyi stʀoi′kə), *n. Russian.* the program of economic and political reform in the Soviet Union initiated by Mikhail Gorbachev in 1986. [*perestróĭka* lit., rebuilding, reorganization]

Per·etz (per′its; *Yiddish.* pe′ʀets), *n.* **I(saac) L(oeb)** or **Yitz·chok Lei·bush** (yits′ᴋʜôk lā′bo͝osh), 1852–1915, Polish author: writer of plays, poems, and short stories in Yiddish. Also, **Per′ez.**

Pé·rez de Cué·llar (per′ez də kwā′yär; *Sp.* pe′ʀes ᵺe kwe′yäʀ), **Ja·vier** (hä vyeʀ′), born 1920, Peruvian diplomat: secretary-general of the United Nations 1982–91.

perf., **1.** perfect. **2.** perforated. **3.** performance.

perf·board (pûrf′bôrd′, -bōrd′), *n.* hardboard with perforations into which pegs or hooks can be inserted for hanging or displaying objects. [PERF(ORATED) + BOARD]

per·fect (*adj., n.* pûr′fikt; *v.* pər fekt′), *adj.* **1.** conforming absolutely to the description or definition of an ideal type: *a perfect sphere; a perfect gentleman.* **2.** excellent or complete beyond practical or theoretical improvement: *There is no perfect legal code. The proportions of this temple are almost perfect.* **3.** exactly fitting the need in a certain situation or for a certain purpose: *a perfect actor to play Mr. Micawber; a perfect saw for cutting out keyholes.* **4.** entirely without any flaws, defects, or shortcomings: *a perfect apple; the perfect crime.* **5.** accurate, exact, or correct in every detail: *a perfect copy.* **6.** thorough; complete; utter: *perfect strangers.* **7.** pure or unmixed: *perfect yellow.* **8.** unqualified; absolute: *He has perfect control over his followers.* **9.** expert; accomplished; proficient. **10.** unmitigated; out-and-out; of an extreme degree: *He made a perfect fool of himself.* **11.** *Bot.* **a.** having all parts or members present. **b.** monoclinous. **12.** *Gram.* **a.** noting an action or state brought to a close prior to some temporal point of reference, in contrast to imperfect or incomplete action. **b.** designating a tense or other verb formation or construction with such meaning. **13.** *Music.* **a.** applied to the consonances of unison, octave, and fifth, as distinguished from those of the third and sixth, which are called imperfect. **b.** applied to the intervals, harmonic or melodic, of an octave, fifth, and fourth in their normal form, as opposed to augmented and diminished. **14.** *Math.* (of a set) equal to its set of accumulation points. **15.** *Obs.* assured or certain. —*n. Gram.* **16.** the perfect tense. **17.** a verb form or construction in the perfect tense. Cf. **future perfect, pluperfect, present perfect.** —*v.t.* **18.** to bring to completion; finish. **19.** to bring to perfection; make flawless or faultless. **20.** to bring nearer to perfection; improve. **21.** to make fully skilled. **22.** *Print.* to print the reverse of (a printed sheet). [1250–1300; < L *perfectus,* ptp. of *perficere* to finish, bring to completion (*per-* PER- + *-fec-,* comb. form of *facere* to DO[1] + *-tus* ptp. suffix); r. ME *parfit* < OF < L as above] —**per·fect′ed·ly,** *adv.* —**per·fect′er,** *n.* —**per′fect·ness,** *n.*

—**Syn. 1, 2.** See **complete. 4.** unblemished; faultless.

—**Usage.** A few usage guides still object to the use of comparison words such as *more, most, nearly, almost,* and *rather* with PERFECT on the grounds that PERFECT describes an absolute, yes-or-no condition that cannot logically be said to exist in varying degrees. The English language has never agreed to this limitation. Since its earliest use in the 13th century, PERFECT has, like almost all adjectives, been compared, first in the now obsolete forms PERFECTER and PERFECTEST, and more recently with *more, most,* and similar comparison words: *the most perfect arrangement of color and line imaginable.* PERFECT is compared in most of its general senses in all varieties of speech and writing. After all, one of the objectives of the writers of the U.S. Constitution was "to form a more perfect union." See also **complete, unique.**

per·fec·ta (pər fek′tə), *n.* exacta. [1965–70; ellipsis of AmerSp *quiniela perfecta* perfect quinella]

per′fect bind′ing, *Bookbinding.* a technique for binding books by a machine that cuts off the backs of the sections and glues the leaves to a cloth or paper backing. Also called **adhesive binding.** [1925–30] —**per′·fect-bound′,** *adj.*

per′fect ca′dence, *Music.* a cadence in which the tonic chord has its root in both bass and soprano. [1720–30]

per′fect contin′uous. See **perfect progressive.** [1920–25]

per′fect contri′tion. See under **contrition** (def. 2).

per′fect game′, **1.** a baseball game in which the same player pitches throughout the full game without allowing any player of the opposing team to reach first base by a base hit, base on balls, error, or any other means. Cf. **no-hitter. 2.** a game in bowling of 12 consecutive strikes. [1945–50]

per′fect gas′, *Physics.* See **ideal gas.** [1840–50]

per·fect·i·ble (pər fek′tə bəl), *adj.* capable of becoming or of being made perfect; improvable. [1625–35; < F < ML *perfectibilis.* See PERFECT, -IBLE] —**per·fect′i·bil·ist,** *n.* —**per·fect′i·bil′i·ty,** *n.*

perfect′ing press′, *Print.* a rotary press for printing both sides of a sheet or web in one operation. [1855–60, *Amer.*]

per·fec·tion (pər fek′shən), *n.* **1.** the state or quality of being or becoming perfect. **2.** the highest degree of proficiency, skill, or excellence, as in some art. **3.** a perfect embodiment or example of something. **4.** a quality, trait, or feature of the highest degree of excellence. **5.** the highest or most nearly perfect degree of a quality or trait. **6.** the act or fact of perfecting. [1175–1225; < L *perfectiōn-* (s. of *perfectiō*) a finishing (see PERFECT, -ION); r. ME *perfectiun, perfeccioun* < AF < L, as above]

per·fec·tion·ism (pər fek′shə niz′əm), *n.* **1.** any of various doctrines holding that religious, moral, social, or political perfection is attainable. **2.** a personal standard, attitude, or philosophy that demands perfection and rejects anything less. [1830–40, *Amer.*; PERFECTION + -ISM]

per·fec·tion·ist (pər fek′shə nist), *n.* **1.** a person who adheres to or believes in perfectionism. **2.** a person who demands perfection of himself, herself, or others. —*adj.* **3.** of, pertaining to, or distinguished by perfection or perfectionism. [1650–60; PERFECTION + -IST] —**per·fec′tion·is′tic,** *adj.*

per·fec·tive (pər fek′tiv), *adj.* **1.** tending to make perfect; conducive to perfection. **2.** *Gram.* noting an aspect of verbal inflection, as in Russian, that indicates completion of the action or state denoted by the verb. —*n. Gram.* **3.** the perfective aspect. **4.** a form in the perfective. [1590–1600; < ML *perfectīvus.* See PERFECT, -IVE] —**per·fec′tive·ly,** *adv.* —**per·fec′tive·ness, per·fec·tiv·i·ty** (pûr′fek tiv′i tē), *n.*

per·fec·tiv·ize (pər fek′tə vīz′), *v.t.,* **-ized, -iz·ing.** to make perfective. Also, *esp. Brit.,* **per·fec′tiv·ise′.** [1900–05; PERFECTIVE + -IZE]

per·fect·ly (pûr′fikt lē), *adv.* **1.** in a perfect manner or to a perfect degree: *to sing an aria perfectly.* **2.** completely; fully; adequately: *This will suit my purpose perfectly.* [1275–1325; PERFECT + -LY; r. ME *parfitly,* deriv. of *parfit* (see PERFECT)]
—**Syn. 1.** flawlessly, superbly, ideally.

per′fect num′ber, *Math.* a positive number that is equal to the sum of all positive integers that are submultiples of it, as 6, which is equal to the sum of 1, 2, and 3. Cf. **abundant number, deficient number.** [1350–1400; ME]

per·fec·to (pər fek′tō), *n., pl.* **-tos.** a rather thick, medium-sized cigar tapering almost down to a point at each end. [1890–95, *Amer.;* < Sp: lit., perfect]

per·fec′tor press′ (pər fek′tər), *Print.* a flatbed press for printing both sides of a sheet in one operation. [*perfector* < L. See PERFECT, -TOR]

per′fect par′ticiple. See **past participle.** [1860–65]

per′fect pitch′. See **absolute pitch** (def. 2). [1945–50]

per′fect progres′sive, *Gram.* (in English) a verb form including the auxiliary *have* followed by *been* and a present participle, noting the continuation of an activity or event, its incompleteness or interruption, and its connection to the temporal point of reference, as in *I've been waiting for over an hour, They had been talking about her before she came into the room,* or *In July, he will have been living here for two years.* Also called **perfect continuous.**

per′fect ra′diator, *Physics.* blackbody.

per′fect ream′. See under **ream**[1] (def. 1). [1885–90]

per′fect rhyme′, 1. rhyme of two words spelled or pronounced identically but differing in meaning, as *rain, reign;* rich rhyme. **2.** See **full rhyme.**

per′fect square′, *Math.* **1.** a rational number that is equal to the square of another rational number. **2.** a polynomial that is the square of another polynomial. [1935–40]

per′fect stage′, *Mycol.* a phase in the life cycle of certain fungi in which sexual spores are formed, as the asci in the sexual stage of the ascomycete.

per′fect year′. See under **Jewish calendar.** [1905–10]

per·fer·vid (pər fûr′vid), *adj.* very fervent; extremely ardent; impassioned: *perfervid patriotism.* [1855–60; < NL *perfervidus.* See PER-, FERVID] —**per′fer·vid′i·ty, per·fer′vid·ness,** *n.* —**per·fer′vid·ly,** *adv.* —**per·fer′vor;** *esp. Brit.,* **per·fer′vour,** *n.*

per·fid·i·ous (pər fid′ē əs), *adj.* deliberately faithless; treacherous; deceitful: *a perfidious lover.* [1590–1600; < L *perfidiōsus* faithless, dishonest. See PERFIDY, -OUS] —**per·fid′i·ous·ly,** *adv.* —**per·fid′i·ous·ness,** *n.*
—**Syn.** false, disloyal; unfaithful, traitorous. —**Ant.** faithful.

per·fi·dy (pûr′fi dē), *n., pl.* **-dies. 1.** deliberate breach of faith or trust; faithlessness; treachery: *perfidy that goes unpunished.* **2.** an act or instance of faithlessness or treachery. [1585–95; < L *perfidia* faithlessness, equiv. to *perfid(us)* faithless, lit., through (i.e., beyond the limits of) faith (*per-* PER- + *fid(ēs)* faith + *-us* adj. suffix) + *-ia* -Y[3]]
—**Syn.** See **disloyalty.**

perf·in (pûrf′in′), *n.* a postage stamp having perforated initials punched into the paper: used by businesses to prevent unauthorized use of stamps. [*perf(orated) in(itial)*]

per·fo·li·ate (pər fō′lē it, -āt′), *adj. Bot.* having the stem apparently passing through the leaf, owing to congenital union of the basal edges of the leaf round the stem. [1540–50; < NL *perfoliātus* (see PER-, FOLIATE), the fem. of which, *perfoliāta,* was formerly used as the name of a plant with a stalk that seemed to grow through (pierce) its leafage] —**per·fo′li·a′tion,** *n.*

perfoliate leaves

perfo′liate bell′wort, a slender plant, *Uvularia perfoliata,* of the lily family, of eastern North America, having pale yellow, bell-shaped flowers.

per·fo·rate (*v.* pûr′fə rāt′; *adj.* pûr′fər it, -fə rāt′), *v.,* **-rat·ed, -rat·ing,** *adj.* —*v.t.* **1.** to make a hole or holes through by boring, punching, piercing, or the like. **2.** to pierce through or to the interior of; penetrate. —*v.i.* **3.** to make a way through or into something; penetrate. —*adj.* **4.** perforated. [1530–40; < L *perforātus,* ptp. of *perforāre* to BORE[1] through; see PER-] —**per′for·a·ble,** *adj.* —**per′fo·ra′tive,** *adj.* —**per′fo·ra′tor,** *n.*

per·fo·rat·ed (pûr′fə rā′tid), *adj.* **1.** pierced with a hole or holes: *Punch out along the perforated line.* **2.** *Philately.* (of a number of stamps joined together) having rows of closely spaced perforations dividing each stamp from the others. **3.** marked by or having perforation: *a perforated ulcer.* Also, **perforate.** [1480–90; PERFORATE + -ED[2]]

per′forated trac′ery. See **plate tracery.**

per·fo·ra·tion (pûr′fə rā′shən), *n.* **1.** a hole, or one of a series of holes, bored or punched through something, as those between individual postage stamps of a sheet to facilitate separation. **2.** a hole made or passing through a thing. **3.** the act of perforating. **4.** the condition or state of being perforated. [1400–50; late ME < ML *perforātiōn-* (s. of *perforātiō*) a boring through. See PERFORATE, -ION]

perfora′tion gauge′, *Philately.* a marked ruler used to measure the number of perforations per unit length along the borders of a stamp. [1890–95]

per·force (pər fôrs′, -fōrs′), *adv.* of necessity; necessarily; by force of circumstance: *The story must perforce be true.* [1300–50; PER + FORCE; r. ME *par force* < MF]

per·form (pər fôrm′), *v.t.* **1.** to carry out; execute; do: *to perform miracles.* **2.** to go through or execute in the proper, customary, or established manner: *to perform the marriage ceremony.* **3.** to carry into effect; fulfill: *Perform what you promise.* **4.** to act (a play, part, etc.), as on the stage, in movies, or on television. **5.** to render (music), as by playing or singing. **6.** to accomplish (any action involving skill or ability), as before an audience: *to perform a juggling act.* **7.** to complete. —*v.i.* **8.** to fulfill a command, promise, or undertaking. **9.** to execute or do something. **10.** to act in a play: *to perform in the role of Romeo.* **11.** to perform music. **12.** to go through any performance. **13.** (of loans, investments, etc.) to yield a profit; earn income. [1250–1300; ME *parformen* < AF *parformer,* alter. (by assoc. with *forme* FORM) of MF, OF *parfournir* to accomplish. See PER-, FURNISH] —**per·form′a·ble,** *adj.* —**per·form′er,** *n.*
—**Syn. 1.** PERFORM, DISCHARGE, EXECUTE, TRANSACT mean to carry to completion a prescribed course of action. PERFORM is the general word, often applied to ordinary activity as a more formal expression than DO, but usually implying regular, methodical, or prolonged application or work: *to perform an exacting task.* DISCHARGE implies carrying out an obligation, often a formal or legal one: *to discharge one's duties as a citizen.* EXECUTE means either to carry out an order or to carry through a plan or program: *to execute a maneuver.* TRANSACT, meaning to conduct or manage, has commercial connotations: *to transact business.* **3.** accomplish, achieve, effect.

per·for·mance (pər fôr′məns), *n.* **1.** a musical, dramatic, or other entertainment presented before an audience. **2.** the act of performing a ceremony, play, piece of music, etc. **3.** the execution or accomplishment of work, acts, feats, etc. **4.** a particular action, deed, or proceeding. **5.** an action or proceeding of an unusual or spectacular kind: *His temper tantrum was quite a performance.* **6.** the act of performing. **7.** the manner in which or the efficiency with which something reacts or fulfills its intended purpose. **8.** *Ling.* the actual use of language in real situations, which may or may not fully reflect a speaker's competence, being subject to such nonlinguistic factors as inattention, distraction, memory lapses, fatigue, or emotional state. Cf. **competence** (def. 6). [1485–95; PERFORM + -ANCE]

perfor′mance art′, a collaborative art form originating in the 1970's as a fusion of several artistic media, as painting, film, video, music, drama, and dance, and deriving in part from the 1960's performance happenings. [1970–75] —**perfor′mance art′ist.**

perfor′mance bond′. See **contract bond.** [1935–40]

perfor′mance test′, *Psychol.* a test requiring little or no use of language, the test materials being designed to elicit manual or behavioral responses rather than verbal ones. [1915–20]

per·for·ma·tive (pər fôr′mə tiv), *adj. Philos., Ling.* **1.** (of an expression or statement) performing an act by the very fact of being uttered, as with the expression "I promise," that performs the act of promising. —*n.* **2.** a performative utterance. Cf. **constative.** [1950–55; PERFORM + -ATIVE]

perform′ing arts′, arts or skills that require public performance, as acting, singing, or dancing. [1945–50]

perf. part., perfect participle.

per·fume (*n.* pûr′fyo͞om, pər fyo͞om′; *v.* pər fyo͞om′, pûr′fyo͞om), *n., v.,* **-fumed, -fum·ing.** —*n.* **1.** a substance, extract, or preparation for diffusing or imparting an agreeable or attractive smell, esp. a fluid containing fragrant natural oils extracted from flowers, woods, etc., or similar synthetic oils. **2.** the scent, odor, or volatile particles emitted by substances that smell agreeable. —*v.t.* **3.** (of substances, flowers, etc.) to impart a pleasant fragrance to. **4.** to impregnate with a sweet odor; scent. [1525–35; earlier *parfume* (n.) < MF *parfum,* n. deriv. of *parfumer* (v.) < obs. It *parfumare* (mod. *profumare*). See PER-, FUME] —**per′fume·less,** *adj.* —**per′fum·y,** *adj.*
—**Syn. 1.** essence, attar, scent; incense. **2.** PERFUME, AROMA, FRAGRANCE all refer to agreeable odors. PERFUME often indicates a strong, rich smell, natural or manufactured: *the perfume of flowers.* FRAGRANCE is usually applied to fresh, delicate, and delicious odors, esp. from growing things: *fragrance of new-mown hay.* AROMA is restricted to a somewhat spicy smell: *the aroma of coffee.* —**Ant. 2.** stench.

per·fum·er (pər fyo͞o′mər, pûr′fyo͞o-), *n.* **1.** a person or thing that perfumes. **2.** a maker or seller of perfumes. [1565–75; PERFUME + -ER[1]]

per·fum·er·y (pər fyo͞o′mə rē), *n., pl.* **-er·ies. 1.** perfumes collectively. **2.** a perfume. **3.** the art or business of a perfumer. **4.** the place of business of a perfumer. **5.** the preparation of perfumes. [1790–1800; PERFUMER + -Y[3]; see -ERY]

per·func·to·ry (pər fungk′tə rē), *adj.* **1.** performed merely as a routine duty; hasty and superficial: *perfunctory courtesy.* **2.** lacking interest, care, or enthusiasm; indifferent or apathetic: *In his lectures he reveals himself to be merely a perfunctory speaker.* [1575–85; < LL *perfūnctōrius* negligent, superficial, deriv. of *perfungī* to do one's job, be done, equiv. to *per-* PER- + *fung-,* base of *fungī* to perform, FUNCTION + *-tōrius* -TORY[1]] —**per·func′to·ri·ly,** *adv.* —**per·func′to·ri·ness,** *n.*
—**Syn. 1, 2.** negligent, heedless, thoughtless, uninterested. —**Ant. 1, 2.** careful, diligent.

per·fus·ate (pər fyo͞o′zāt, -zit), *n. Med., Surg.* a fluid pumped or flowing through an organ or tissue. [1910–15; PERFUSE + -ATE[1], prob. on the model of FILTRATE, PRECIPITATE]

per·fuse (pər fyo͞oz′), *v.t.,* **-fused, -fus·ing. 1.** to overspread with moisture, color, etc.; suffuse. **2.** to diffuse (a liquid, color, etc.) through or over something. **3.** *Surg.* to pass (fluid) through blood vessels or the lymphatic system. [1520–30; < L *perfūsus,* ptp. of *perfundere* to drench, flood. See PER-, FUSE[2]] —**per·fu·sive** (pər fyo͞o′siv), *adj.*

per·fu·sion (pər fyo͞o′zhən), *n.* **1.** the act of perfusing. **2.** *Surg.* the passage of fluid through the lymphatic system or blood vessels to an organ or a tissue. [1565–75; < L *perfūsiōn-* (s. of *perfūsiō*) a drenching. See PERFUSE, -ION]

Per·ga·mum (pûr′gə məm), *n.* **1.** an ancient Greek kingdom on the coast of Asia Minor: later a Roman province. **2.** the ancient capital of this kingdom; now the site of Bergama, in W Turkey. **3.** ancient name of **Bergama.** Also, **Per·ga·mon** (pûr′gə mən, -mon′), **Per·ga·mus** (pûr′gə məs), **Per·ga·mos** (pûr′gə məs, -mos′). —**Per·ga·mene** (pûr′gə mēn′), **Per·gam·ic** (pər gam′ik), *adj.* —**Per′ga·me′ni·an,** *adj., n.*

per·gel·i·sol (pər jel′ə sôl′, -sol′), *n.* permafrost. [1945–50; PER(MANENT) + L *gel(āre)* to freeze + -I- + -SOL]

per·go·la (pûr′gə lə), *n.* **1.** an arbor formed of horizontal trelliswork supported on columns or posts, over which vines or other plants are trained. **2.** a colonnade having the form of such an arbor. [1645–55; < It < L *pergula* projecting roof, arbor]

pergola (def. 1)

Per·go·le·si (peʀ′gô le′zē), *n.* **Gio·van·ni Bat·tis·ta** (jô vän′nē bät tēs′tä), 1710–36, Italian composer.

Per·go·nal (pûr′gə nal′), *Pharm., Trademark.* a brand name for a preparation containing FSH and LH obtained from the urine of postmenopausal women, prepared for injection in both men and women in the treatment of certain kinds of infertility.

perh., perhaps.

per·haps (pər haps′), *adv.* maybe; possibly: *Perhaps the package will arrive today.* [1520–30; earlier *per-happes, perhapis* by haps. See PER, HAP[1], -S[1]]

per·hy·dro·gen·ate (pər hī′drə jə nāt′, pûr′hī-droj′ə-), *v.t.,* **-at·ed, -at·ing.** to hydrogenate as completely as possible. [PER- + HYDROGENATE] —**per·hy′dro·gen·a′tion,** *n.*

per·hy·dro·gen·ize (pər hī′drə jə nīz′, pûr′hī-droj′ə-), *v.t.,* **-ized, -iz·ing.** perhydrogenate. Also, *esp. Brit.,* **per·hy′dro·gen·ise′.** [PER- + HYDROGENIZE]

pe·ri (pēr′ē), *n., pl.* **-ris. 1.** one of a large group of beautiful, fairylike beings of Persian mythology, represented as descended from fallen angels and excluded from paradise until their penance is accomplished. **2.** any lovely, graceful person. [1770–80; < Pers *perī,* var. of *parī* fairy, MPers *parik,* Avestan *pairikā* witch]

Pe·ri (pe′ʀē), *n.* **Ja·co·po** (yä′kô pô), 1561–1633, Italian composer.

peri-, a prefix meaning "about" or "around" (*perimeter, periscope*), "enclosing" or "surrounding" (*pericardium*), and "near" (*perigee, perihelion*), appearing in loanwords from Greek (*peripeteia*); on this model, used in the formation of compound words (*perimorph*). [< Gk, prefixal use of *perí* (adv. and prep.)]

Per·i·an·der (per′ē an′dər), *n.* died 585 B.C., tyrant of Corinth.

per·i·anth (per′ē anth′), *n. Bot.* the envelope of a flower, whether calyx or corolla or both. [1700–10; earlier *perianthium* < NL. See PERI-, ANTH-, -IUM] —**per′i·an′thi·al,** *adj.*

per·i·a·pi·cal (per′ē ā′pi kəl, -ap′i-), *adj.* encompassing or surrounding the tip of the root of a tooth. [1915–20; PERI- + APICAL]

per·i·apt (per′ē apt′), *n.* an amulet. [1575–85; < Gk *períapton* amulet, n. use of neut. of *períaptos* hung around, equiv. to *peri-* PERI- + *(h)aptós,* verbal of *háptein* to fasten]

per·i·ar·te·ri·tis (per′ē är′tə rī′tis), *n. Pathol.* in-

CONCISE PRONUNCIATION KEY: *act, cāpe, dâre, pärt; set, ēqual; if, īce; ox, ōver, ôrder, oil, bo͝ok, bo͞ot, out; up, ûrge; child; sing; shoe; thin, that;* zh as in *treasure.* ə = *a* as in *alone, e* as in *system, i* as in *easily, o* as in *gallop, u* as in *circus;* ᵊ as in *fire* (fīᵊr), *hour* (ouᵊr). l and n can serve as syllabic consonants, as in *cradle* (krād′l), and *button* (but′n). See the full key inside the front cover.

flammation of the outer coat and tissues surrounding an artery. [1875–80; < NL; see PERI-, ARTERITIS]

periarteri′tis no·do′sa (nō dō′sə), *Pathol.* polyarteritis. [1890–95; *nodosa* < L *nōdōsa,* fem. of *nōdōsus* NODOSE]

per·i·as·tron (per′ē as′trən, -tron), *n., pl.* **-tra** (-trə). *Astron.* the point at which the stars of a binary system are closest (opposed to *apastron*). [1850–55; < PERI- + Gk *ástron* star; modeled on *perihelion*] —**per′i·as′tral,** *adj.*

per·i·blem (per′ə blem′), *n. Bot.* the histogen in plants that gives rise to the cortex. [1870–75; < Gk *períblēma* a cloak, covering, akin to *peribállein* to throw about, put on. See PERI-, PROBLEM]

per·i·car·di·al (per′i kär′dē əl), *adj.* of or pertaining to the pericardium. Also, **per′i·car′di·ac′.** [1645–55; PERICARDI(UM) + -AL[1]]

per·i·car·di·tis (per′i kär dī′tis), *n. Pathol.* inflammation of the pericardium. [1790–1800; PERICARD(IUM) + -ITIS] —**per·i·car·dit·ic** (per′i kär dit′ik), *adj.*

per·i·car·di·um (per′i kär′dē əm), *n., pl.* **-di·a** (-dē ə). *Anat.* the membranous sac enclosing the heart. [1570–80; < NL < Gk *perikárdion,* n. use of neut. of *perikárdios* surrounding the heart, equiv. to *peri-* PERI- + *kardios,* adj. deriv. of *kardía* HEART; cf. -CARDIUM]

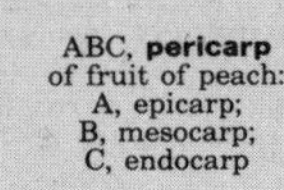
ABC, **pericarp** of fruit of peach: A, epicarp; B, mesocarp; C, endocarp

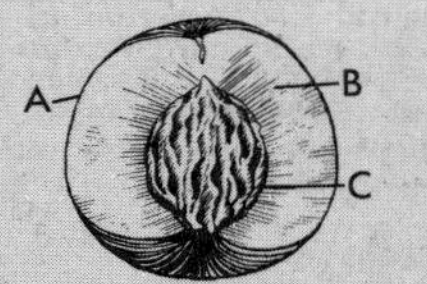

per·i·carp (per′i kärp′), *n. Bot.* **1.** the walls of a ripened ovary or fruit, sometimes consisting of three layers, the epicarp, mesocarp, and endocarp. **2.** a membranous envelope around the cystocarp of red algae. [1750–60; < NL *pericarpium* < Gk *perikárpion* pod. See PERI-, -CARP] —**per′i·car′pi·al, per′i·car′pic,** *adj.* —**per′i·car·poi′dal,** *adj.*

per·i·ce·men·tum (per′ē si men′təm), *n. Dentistry.* See **periodontal membrane.** [1895–1900; < NL; see PERI-, CEMENTUM] —**per′i·ce·men′tal,** *adj.*

per·i·cen·ter (per′ə sen′tər), *n. Astron.* the point at which a heavenly body orbiting around a primary other than the earth or sun is closest to the primary. Cf. **apocenter.** [1900–05; PERI- + CENTER] —**per′i·cen′tral, per′i·cen′tric,** *adj.*

per·i·chon·dri·um (per′i kon′drē əm), *n., pl.* **-dri·a** (-drē ə). *Anat.* the membrane of fibrous connective tissue covering the surface of cartilages except at the joints. [1735–45; < NL < Gk *peri-* PERI- + *chondríon,* dim. of *chóndros* cartilage] —**per′i·chon′dral, per′i·chon′dri·al,** *adj.*

per·i·clase (per′i klās′, -klāz′), *n.* a cubic mineral, native magnesia, MgO, occurring usually in metamorphosed dolomite. [1835–45; < G *Periklas* < NL *periclasia,* equiv. to *peri-* PERI- + Gk *klás(is)* a breaking (cf. -CLASE) + *-ia* -IA]

Per·i·cle·an (per′i klē′ən), *adj.* of or pertaining to Pericles or to the period **(Per′icle′an Age′)** when Athens was intellectually, artistically, and materially preeminent. [1815–25; PERICLE(S) + -AN]

Per·i·cles (per′i klēz′), *n.* c495–429 B.C., Athenian statesman.

per·i·cline (per′i klīn′), *n. Mineral.* a variety of albite occurring in large, white opaque crystals. [1825–35; < Gk *periklinḗs* sloping on all sides]

pe·ric·o·pe (pə rik′ə pē′), *n., pl.* **-pes, -pae** (-pē′). **1.** a selection or extract from a book. **2.** lection (def. 2). [1650–60; < LL *pericopē* section < Gk *perikopḗ* a cutting, equiv. to *peri-* PERI- + *kopḗ* a cutting] —**pe·ric′o·pal, per·i·cop·ic** (per′i kop′ik), *adj.*

per·i·cra·ni·um (per′i krā′nē əm), *n., pl.* **-ni·a** (-nē ə). *Anat.* the outer periosteum of the cranium. [1515–25; < NL < Gk *perikránion,* n. use of neut. of *perikránios* surrounding the skull, equiv. to *peri-* PERI- + *kraní(on)* CRANIUM + *-os* adj. suffix] —**per′i·cra′ni·al,** *adj.*

per·i·cy·cle (per′ə sī′kəl), *n. Bot.* the outermost cell layer of the stele in a plant, frequently becoming a multilayered zone. [1890–95; < Gk *perikyklos.* See PERI-, CYCLE]

per·i·den·tal (per′i den′tl), *adj. Dentistry.* periodontal. [PERI- + DENTAL]

per′iden′tal mem′brane, *Dentistry.* See **periodontal membrane.**

per·i·derm (per′i dûrm′), *n.* **1.** *Bot.* the cork-producing tissue of stems together with the cork layers and other tissues derived from it. **2.** *Embryol.* epitrichium. [1830–40; < NL *peridermis.* See PERI-, -DERM] —**per′i·der′mal, per′i·der′mic,** *adj.*

pe·rid·i·um (pə rid′ē əm), *n., pl.* **-rid·e·a** (-rid′ē ə). *Mycol.* the outer enveloping coat of the fruit body in many fungi. [1815–25; < NL < G *perídion,* dim. of *pḗra* wallet; see -IDIUM] —**pe·rid′i·al,** *adj.* —**pe·rid·i·i·form** (pə rid′ē ə fôrm′), *adj.*

per·i·dot (per′i dō′, -dot′), *n. Mineral.* a green transparent variety of olivine, used as a gem. [1300–50; < F *péridot;* r. ME *peritot* < MF] —**per·i·dot·ic** (per′i dot′ik, -dō′tik), *adj.*

per·i·do·tite (per′i dō′tīt, pə rid′ə tīt′), *n.* a coarsely granular igneous rock composed chiefly of olivine with an admixture of various other minerals. [1895–1900; < F; see PERIDOT, -ITE[1]] —**per·i·do·tit·ic** (per′i dō tit′ik, pə rid′ə-), *adj.*

per′idot of Ceylon′, *Jewelry.* a honey-colored tourmaline, used as a gem: not a true peridot.

per′ige′an tide′, an ocean tide that occurs in the spring, when the moon is at its perigee.

per·i·gee (per′i jē′), *n. Astron.* the point in the orbit of a heavenly body, esp. the moon, or of an artificial satellite at which it is nearest to the earth. See diag. under **apogee.** [1585–95; < F *perigée* < NL *perigēum, perigaeum* < Gk *perígeion* (*sēmeîon* limit), neut. of *perígeios* near, of the earth, equiv. to *peri-* PERI- + *-geios,* adj. deriv. of *gaîa, gê* the earth] —**per′i·ge′al, per′i·ge′an,** *adj.*

per·i·gla·cial (per′i glā′shəl), *adj. Geol.* occurring or operating adjacent to the margin of a glacier. [1925–30; PERI- + GLACIAL]

per·i·gon (per′i gon′), *n.* an angle of 360°. Also called **round angle.** [1865–70; PERI- + -GON]

per·i·go·ni·um (per′i gō′nē əm), *n., pl.* **-ni·a** (-nē ə). *Bot.* the envelope of modified leaves surrounding the antheridia in mosses. Also, **per·i·gone** (per′i gōn′). [1810–20; < NL; see PERI-, -GONIUM] —**per′i·go′ni·al, per′i·go′nal,** *adj.*

Pé·ri·gord (pā rᴇ gôr′), *n.* a division of the former province of Guienne, in SW France.

Per·i·gor·di·an (per′i gôr′dē ən), *adj.* of, pertaining to, or characteristic of an Upper Paleolithic cultural epoch in southern France, esp. of the Périgord region. [1935–40; PÉRIGORD + -IAN]

pe·rig·y·nous (pə rij′ə nəs), *adj. Bot.* **1.** situated around the pistil on the edge of a cuplike receptacle, as stamens or petals. **2.** having stamens, petals, etc., so arranged. [1800–10; < NL *perigynus.* See PERI-, -GYNOUS]

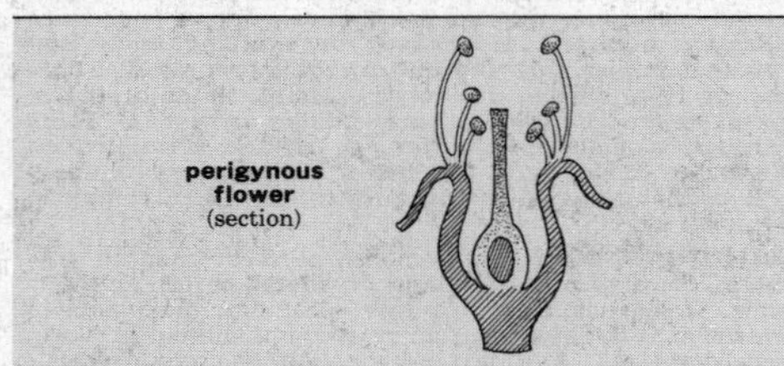
perigynous flower (section)

pe·rig·y·ny (pə rij′ə nē), *n. Bot.* a perigynous condition. [1875–80; PERIGYN(OUS) + -Y[3]]

per·i·he·li·on (per′ə hē′lē ən, -hēl′yən), *n., pl.* **-he·li·a** (-hē′lē ə, -hēl′yə). *Astron.* the point in the orbit of a planet or comet at which it is nearest to the sun. Cf. **aphelion.** See diag. under **aphelion.** [1660–70; < Gk *peri-* PERI- + *hḗli(os)* sun + *-on* neut. n. suffix, on the model of PERIGEE; earlier in the NL form *perihelium*] —**per′i·he′li·al, per′i·he′li·an,** *adj.*

per·i·kar·y·on (per′i kar′ē on′, -ən), *n., pl.* **-kar·y·a** (-kar′ē ə). *Biol.* See **cell body.** [1895–1900; PERI- + Gk *káryon* nut, kernel]

per·il (per′əl), *n., v.,* **-iled, -il·ing** or (*esp. Brit.*) **-illed, -il·ling.** —*n.* **1.** exposure to injury, loss, or destruction; grave risk; jeopardy; danger: *They faced the peril of falling rocks.* **2.** something that causes or may cause injury, loss, or destruction. —*v.t.* **3.** to expose to danger; imperil; risk. [1175–1225; ME < OF < L *perīculum* trial, test, danger, equiv. to *perī-,* verb base meaning "try" (found in the compound *experīrī;* see EXPERIENCE) + *-culum* -CLE[2]] —**per′il·less,** *adj.*
—**Syn. 1.** See **danger.**

pe·ril·la (pə ril′ə), *n.* any of several aromatic Asian plants belonging to the genus *Perilla,* of the mint family, esp. *P. frutescens,* which has become naturalized in the eastern U.S. and from which perilla oil is obtained. [< NL (Linnaeus), of uncert. orig.]

peril′la oil′, a light yellow oil, obtained from the seeds of mints of the genus *Perilla,* used in the Orient as a cooking oil and elsewhere in the manufacture of varnish, printing ink, and artificial leather. [1915–20]

per·il·ous (per′ə ləs), *adj.* involving or full of grave risk or peril; hazardous; dangerous: *a perilous voyage across the Atlantic in a small boat.* [1250–1300; ME < AF *perillous* < L *perīculōsus.* See PERIL, -OUS] —**per′il·ous·ly,** *adv.* —**per′il·ous·ness,** *n.*
—**Syn.** risky. —**Ant.** safe.

per′il point′, the lower limit of a tariff on a commodity at which import of that commodity would have a seriously adverse effect on the local producers. [1945–50]

per·i·lune (per′i lo͞on′), *n.* the point in a lunar orbit that is nearest to the moon. Cf. **apolune.** [1955–60; PERI- + *-lune* < L *lūna* moon, on the model of PERIGEE]

per·i·lymph (per′i limf′), *n. Anat.* the fluid between the bony and membranous labyrinths of the ear. [1830–40; PERI- + LYMPH] —**per′i·lym·phat′ic,** *adj.*

pe·rim·e·ter (pə rim′i tər), *n.* **1.** the border or outer boundary of a two-dimensional figure. **2.** the length of such a boundary. **3.** a line bounding or marking off an area. **4.** the outermost limits. **5.** *Mil.* a fortified boundary that protects a troop position. **6.** *Ophthalm.* an instrument for determining the peripheral field of vision. [1585–95; < F *périmètre* < L *perimetros* (fem.) < Gk *perímetron* (neut.). See PERI-, -METER] —**pe·rim′e·ter·less,** *adj.* —**pe·rim′e·tral, per·i·met·ric** (per′ə me′trik), **per′i·met′ri·cal,** *adj.* —**per′i·met′ri·cal·ly,** *adv.* —**pe·rim′e·try,** *n.*

per·i·morph (per′ə môrf′), *n.* a crystal of one mineral enclosing that of another mineral. Cf. **endomorph** (def. 1). [1880–85; PERI- + -MORPH] —**per′i·mor′phic, per′i·mor′phous,** *adj.* —**per′i·mor′phism,** *n.*

per·i·my·si·um (per′ə miz′ē əm, -mizh′-), *n., pl.* **-my·si·a** (-miz′ē ə, -mizh′-). *Anat.* the connective tissue surrounding bundles of skeletal muscle fibers. [1835–45; irreg. from PERI- + Gk *mŷs* mouse, muscle (cf. MYO-) + -IUM] —**per′i·my′si·al,** *adj.*

per·i·na·tal (per′ə nāt′l), *adj.* occurring during or pertaining to the phase surrounding the time of birth, from the twentieth week of gestation to the twenty-eighth day of newborn life. [1950–55; PERI- + NATAL] —**per′i·na′tal·ly,** *adv.*

per·i·na·tol·o·gy (per′ə nā tol′ə jē), *n.* a field of medicine focusing on problems emerging during the perinatal period. [1975–80; PERI- + NAT(AL) + -O- + -LOGY] —**per′i·na·tol′o·gist,** *n.*

per·in·de (pər in′dē), *adv.* (in prescriptions) in the same manner as before. [< L]

per·i·neph·ri·um (per′ə nef′rē əm), *n., pl.* **-neph·ri·a** (-nef′rē ə). *Anat.* the capsule of connective tissue that envelops the kidney. [< NL; see PERI-, NEPHR-, -IUM] —**per′i·neph′ral, per′i·neph′ri·al, per′i·neph′ric,** *adj.*

per·i·ne·um (per′ə nē′əm), *n., pl.* **-ne·a** (-nē′ə). *Anat.* **1.** the area in front of the anus extending to the fourchette of the vulva in the female and to the scrotum in the male. **2.** the diamond-shaped area corresponding to the outlet of the pelvis, containing the anus and vulva or the roots of the penis. [1625–35; < NL < Gk *perineon, perineos, perinaios,* appar. equiv. to *per(i)-* PERI- + *ine-, ina-,* stems of *ineîn, inân* to evacuate, empty + *-(i)os, -(i)on* n. suffix] —**per′i·ne′al,** *adj.*

per·i·neu·ri·um (per′ə no͝or′ē əm, -nyo͝or′-), *n., pl.* **-neu·ri·a** (-no͝or′ē ə, -nyo͝or′-). *Anat.* the sheath of connective tissue that encloses a bundle of nerve fibers. [1835–45; < NL; see PERI-, NEUR-, -IUM] —**per′i·neu′ri·cal,** *adj.*

per·i·nu·cle·ar (per′ə no͞o′klē ər, -nyo͞o′- *or, by metathesis,* -kyə lər), *adj. Cell Biol.* **1.** situated near or occurring around the nucleus. **2.** pertaining to the narrow space between the inner and outer layers of the nuclear membrane. [1895–1900; PERI- + NUCLEAR]
—**Pronunciation.** See **nuclear.**

pe·ri·od (pēr′ē əd), *n.* **1.** a rather large interval of time that is meaningful in the life of a person, in history, etc., because of its particular characteristics: *a period of illness; a period of great profitability for a company; a period of social unrest in Germany.* **2.** any specified division or portion of time: *poetry of the period from 1603 to 1660.* **3.** a round of time or series of years by which time is measured. **4.** a round of time marked by the recurrence of some phenomenon or occupied by some recurring process or action. **5.** the point of completion of a round of time or of the time during which something lasts or happens. **6.** *Educ.* a specific length of time during school hours that a student spends in a classroom, laboratory, etc., or has free. **7.** any of the parts of equal length into which a game is divided. **8.** the time during which something runs its course. **9.** the present time. **10.** the point or character (.) used to mark the end of a declarative sentence, indicate an abbreviation, etc.; full stop. **11.** a full pause, as is made at the end of a complete sentence; full stop. **12.** a sentence, esp. a well-balanced, impressive sentence: *the stately periods of Churchill.* **13.** a periodic sentence. **14.** an occurrence of menstruation. **15.** a time of the month during which menstruation occurs. **16.** *Geol.* the basic unit of geologic time, during which a standard rock system is formed: comprising two or more epochs and included with other periods in an era. See table under **geologic time. 17.** *Physics.* the duration of one complete cycle of a wave or oscillation; the reciprocal of the frequency. **18.** *Music.* a division of a composition, usually a passage of eight or sixteen measures, complete or satisfactory in itself, commonly consisting of two or more contrasted or complementary phrases ending with a conclusive cadence. **19.** *Astron.* **a.** Also called **period of rotation.** the time in which a body rotates once on its axis. **b.** Also called **period of revolution.** the time in which a planet or satellite revolves once about its primary. **20.** *Math.* See under **periodic** (def. 5). **21.** *Class. Pros.* a group of two or more cola. —*adj.* **22.** noting, pertaining to, evocative of, imitating, or representing a historical period or the styles current during a specific period of history: *period costumes; a period play.* —*interj.* **23.** (used by a speaker or writer to indicate that a decision is irrevocable or that a point is no longer discussable): *I forbid you to go, period.* [1375–1425; late ME *periode* (< MF) < ML *periodus,* L < Gk *períodos* circuit, period of time, period in rhetoric, lit., way around. See PERI-, -ODE[2]]
—**Syn. 1.** See **age. 2.** term.

per·i·o·date (pə rī′ə dāt′), *n. Chem.* a salt of a periodic acid, as sodium periodate, $Na_2H_3IO_6$. [1830–40; PERIOD(IC ACID) + -ATE[2]]

pe·ri·od·ic[1] (pēr′ē od′ik), *adj.* **1.** recurring at intervals of time: *periodic revivals of an interest in handicrafts.* **2.** occurring or appearing at regular intervals: *periodic visits of a mail steamer to an island.* **3.** repeated at irregular intervals; intermittent: *periodic outbreaks of the disease.* **4.** *Physics.* recurring at equal intervals of time. **5.** *Math.* (of a function) having a graph that repeats after a fixed interval **(period)** of the independent variable. **6.** *Astron.* **a.** characterized by a series of successive circuits or revolutions, as the motion of a planet or satellite. **b.** of or pertaining to a period, as of the revolution of a heavenly body. **7.** pertaining to or characterized by rhetorical periods, or periodic sentences. [1635–45; < L *periodicus* < Gk *periodikós.* See PERIOD, -IC] —**pe′ri·od′i·cal·ly,** *adv.*

per·i·od·ic[2] (pûr′ī od′ik), *adj. Chem.* of or derived from a periodic acid. [1830–40; PER- + IODIC]

per′i·od′ic ac′id (pûr′ī od′ik, pûr′-), *Chem.* any of a series of acids derived from I_2O_7 by the addition of water molecules, as HIO_4 or H_5IO_6. [1830–40]

pe·ri·od·i·cal (pēr′ē od′i kəl), *n.* **1.** a magazine or other journal that is issued at regularly recurring intervals. —*adj.* **2.** published at regularly recurring intervals. **3.** of or pertaining to such publications. **4.** periodic[1]. [1595–1605; PERIODIC[1] + -AL[1]] —**pe′ri·od′·**

CONCISE ETYMOLOGY KEY: <, descended or borrowed from; >, whence; b., blend of, blended; c., cognate with; cf., compare; deriv., derivative; equiv., equivalent; imit., imitative; obl., oblique; r., replacing; s., stem; sp., spelling, spelled; resp., respelling, respelled; trans., translation; ?, origin unknown; *, unattested; ‡, probably earlier than. See the full key inside the front cover.

i·cal·ism, *n.* **—pe′ri·od′i·cal·ist,** *n.* **—pe′ri·od′i·cal·ness,** *n.*

period′ical cica′da. See **seventeen-year locust.** [1885–90]

pe′ri·od′ic dec′imal (pēr′ē od′ik, pēr′-), *Math.* See **repeating decimal.**

per′i·od′ic func′tion (pēr′ē od′ik, pēr′-), *Math.* a function of a real or complex variable that is periodic. Cf. **periodic**[1] (def. 5).

pe·ri·o·dic·i·ty (pēr′ē ə dis′i tē), *n.* the character of being periodic; the tendency to recur at regular intervals. [1825–35; < F *périodicité.* See PERIODIC[1], -ITY]

pe′ri·od′ic law′ (pēr′ē od′ik, pēr′-), *Chem.* **1.** the law that the properties of the elements are periodic functions of their atomic numbers. **2.** Also called **Mendeleev's law.** (originally) the statement that the chemical and physical properties of the elements recur periodically when the elements are arranged in the order of their atomic weights. [1870–75]

pe′ri·od′ic mo′tion (pēr′ē od′ik, pēr′-), *Physics.* any motion that recurs in identical forms at equal intervals of time.

pe′ri·od′ic sen′tence (pēr′ē od′ik, pēr′-), a sentence that, by leaving the completion of its main clause to the end, produces an effect of suspense, as in *Unable to join the others at the dance because of my sprained ankle, I went to a movie.* Cf. **loose sentence.** [1895–1900]

pe′ri·od′ic sys′tem (pēr′ē od′ik, pēr′-), *Chem.* a system of classification of the elements based on the periodic law. [1870–75]

pe′ri·od′ic ta′ble (pēr′ē od′ik, pēr′-), *Chem.* a table illustrating the periodic system, in which the chemical elements, formerly arranged in the order of their atomic weights and now according to their atomic numbers, are shown in related groups. See table below. [1890–95]

per·i·o·dide (pə rī′ə dīd′, -did), *n. Chem.* an iodide with the maximum proportion of iodine. [1810–20; PERI-OD(IC ACID) + -IDE]

pe·ri·od·i·za·tion (pēr′ē ə də zā′shən), *n.* an act or instance of dividing a subject into historical eras for purposes of analysis and study. [1935–40; PERIOD + -IZATION]

pe′ri·od-lu·mi·nos′i·ty rela′tion (pēr′ē əd lo͞o′mə-nos′i tē), *Astron.* the relationship between the period of light variation and of the absolute magnitude of Cepheid variable stars. [1945–50]

pe′riod of revolu′tion, *Astron.* period (def. 19b).

pe′riod of rota′tion, *Astron.* period (def. 19a).

per·i·o·don·tal (per′ē ə don′tl), *adj. Dentistry.* **1.** of or pertaining to the periodontium. **2.** of or pertaining to periodontics. **3.** of or pertaining to the periodontal membrane. Also, **peridental.** [1850–55; PERI- + -ODONT + -AL[1]]

periodon′tal disease′, any of various mixed bacterial infections that affect the soft tissues and bones supporting the teeth. Cf. **pyorrhea.**

per′iodon′tal mem′brane, *Dentistry.* the collagenous, fibrous connective tissue between the cementum of the tooth and the alveolus. Also, **pericementum.** [1895–1900]

per·i·o·don·tics (per′ē ə don′tiks), *n.* (*used with a singular v.*) the branch of dentistry dealing with the study and treatment of diseases of the periodontium. Also, **per·i·o·don·tia** (per′ē ə don′shə, -shē ə). [1945–50; < NL *periodont(ia)* (see PERI-, -ODONT, -IA) + -ICS] **—per′i·o·don′tic,** *adj.*

per·i·o·don·tist (per′ē ə don′tist), *n.* a specialist in periodontics. [1915–20; PERIODONT(ICS) + -IST]

per·i·o·don·ti·tis (per′ē ō don tī′tis), *n. Dentistry.* inflammation of the periodontium caused by bacteria that infect the roots of teeth and the surrounding gum crevices, producing bleeding, pus formation, and gradual loss of bone and the tissues that support the teeth. Cf. **pyorrhea** (def. 2). [1870–75; PERIODONT(IUM) + -ITIS]

per·i·o·don·tium (per′ē ə don′shəm, -shē əm), *n., pl.* **-tia** (-shə, -shē ə). the bone, connective tissue, and gum surrounding and supporting a tooth. Also, **parodontium.** [1955–60; < NL; see PERI-, -ODONT, -IUM]

per·i·o·don·tol·o·gy (per′ē ō don tol′ə jē), *n.* periodontics. [1910–15; PERIODONT(IA) + -O- + -LOGY]

per·i·o·don·to·sis (per′ē ō don tō′sis), *n. Dentistry.* (no longer in technical use) See **rapidly advancing juvenile periodontitis.** [1935–40; PERIODONT(IUM) + -OSIS]

pe′riod piece′, something, as a novel, painting, or building, of interest or value primarily because it evokes or epitomizes a particular period of history. [1925–30]

Per·i·oe·ci (per′ē ē′sī), *n.pl., sing.* **-cus** (-kəs). the inhabitants of ancient Laconia, constituting a dependent people of Sparta, who governed themselves and had a monopoly on trade and manufacture. Cf. **Helot** (def. 1), **Spartiate.** [1585–95; < ML *perioeci* < Gk *períoikoi* countryside dwellers, n. use of pl. of *períoikos* neighboring, equiv. to *peri-* PERI- + *-oikos,* adj. deriv. of *oîkos* house] **—per′i·oe′cic, per′i·oe′cid,** *adj.*

per·i·o·nych·i·a[1] (per′ē ō nik′ē ə), *n. Pathol.* inflammation of the perionychium. [1875–80; < NL < Gk *peri-* PERI- + *onych-* (s. of *ónyx*) nail (see ONYX) + *-ia* -IA]

per·i·o·nych·i·a[2] (per′ē ō nik′ē ə), *n.* pl. of **perionychium.**

per·i·o·nych·i·um (per′ē ō nik′ē əm), *n., pl.* **-nych·i·a** (-nik′ē ə). *Anat.* the epidermis surrounding the base and sides of a fingernail or toenail. [1900–05; < NL; see PERIONYCHIA[1], -IUM]

per·i·os·te·um (per′ē os′tē əm), *n., pl.* **-te·a** (-tē ə). *Anat.* the normal investment of bone, consisting of a dense, fibrous outer layer, to which muscles attach, and a more delicate, inner layer capable of forming bone. [1590–1600; < NL, var. of LL *periosteon,* n. use of neut. of Gk *periósteos* around the bones. See PERI-, OSTEO-] **—per′i·os′te·al, per′i·os′te·ous,** *adj.* **—per′i·os′te·al·ly,** *adv.*

per·i·os·ti·tis (per′ē o stī′tis), *n. Pathol.* inflammation of the periosteum. [1835–45; PERIOST(EUM) + -ITIS] **—per·i·os·tit·ic** (per′ē o stit′ik), *adj.*

per·i·os·tra·cum (per′ē os′trə kəm), *n., pl.* **-ca** (-kə). the external, chitinlike covering of the shell of certain mollusks that protects the limy portion from acids. [1830–40; < NL, equiv. to *peri-* PERI- + *ostracum* a shell < Gk *óstrakon.* See OYSTER] **—per′i·os′tra·cal,** *adj.*

per·i·o·tic (per′ē ō′tik, -ot′ik), *adj. Anat.* **1.** surrounding the ear. **2.** noting or pertaining to certain bones or bony elements that form or help to form a protective capsule for the internal ear. [1865–70; PERI- + OTIC]

per·i·pa·tet·ic (per′ə pə tet′ik), *adj.* **1.** walking or traveling about; itinerant. **2.** (*cap.*) of or pertaining to Aristotle, who taught philosophy while walking in the Lyceum of ancient Athens. **3.** (*cap.*) of or pertaining to the Aristotelian school of philosophy. **—***n.* **4.** a person who walks or travels about. **5.** (*cap.*) a member of the Aristotelian school. [1400–50; late ME < L *peripatēticus* < Gk *peripatētikós* of Aristotle and his school, lit., walking about, equiv. to *peripatē-* (verbid s. of *peripateîn* to walk about, equiv. to *peri-* PERI- + *pateîn* to walk; akin to PATH) + *-tikos* -TIC] **—per′i·pa·tet′i·cal·ly,** *adv.* **—per·i·pa·tet·i·cism** (per′ə pə tet′ə siz′əm), *n.*
—Syn. 1. wandering, roving; vagrant.

per·i·pe·tei·a (per′ə pi tī′ə, -tē′ə), *n.* a sudden turn of events or an unexpected reversal, esp. in a literary work. Also, **per′i·pe·ti′a, pe·rip·e·ty** (pə rip′i tē). [1585–95; < Gk *peripéteia* sudden change, equiv. to *peripet(ḗs)* lit., falling round (*peri-* PERI- + *pet-,* base of *píptein* to fall) + *-eia* -Y[3]]

pe·riph·er·al (pə rif′ər əl), *adj.* **1.** pertaining to, situated in, or constituting the periphery: *peripheral resistance on the outskirts of the battle area.* **2.** concerned with relatively minor, irrelevant, or superficial aspects of the subject in question. **3.** *Anat.* near the surface or outside of; external. **4.** *Computers.* of or pertaining to a peripheral. **—***n.* **5.** *Computers.* a device or unit that operates separately from the CPU but is connected to it, as a magnetic disk or tape unit or a printer. Also, **peripheric** (for defs. 1–3). [1800–10; 1965–70 for def. 4; < Gk *peripher(ḗs)* (see PERIPHERY) + -AL[1]] **—pe·riph′er·al·ly,** *adv.*

pe·riph·er·al·ism (pə rif′ər ə liz′əm), *n. Psychol.* the explanation of psychological events emphasizing peripheral human functions, as those of skeletal muscles or the sex organs, rather than cognition or other processes of the central nervous system. [PERIPHERAL + -ISM]

periph′eral nerv′ous sys′tem, the portion of the nervous system lying outside the brain and spinal cord. [1930–35]

periph′eral vi′sion, all that is visible to the eye outside the central area of focus; side vision.

per·i·pher·ic (per′ə fer′ik), *adj.* peripheral (defs. 1–3). [1800–10] **—per′i·pher′i·cal·ly,** *adv.*

pe·riph·er·y (pə rif′ə rē), *n., pl.* **-er·ies. 1.** the external boundary of any surface or area. **2.** the external surface of a body. **3.** the edge or outskirts, as of a city or urban area. **4.** the relatively minor, irrelevant, or superficial aspects of the subject in question: *The preliminary research did not, of course, take me beyond the periphery of my problem.* **5.** *Anat.* the area in which nerves end. [1350–1400; < LL *peripherīa* < Gk *periphéreia* circumference, lit., a bearing round, equiv. to *peri-* PERI- + *phér(ein)* to BEAR[1] + *-eia* -Y[3]; r. ME *periferie* < ML *periferīa,* var. sp. of LL *peripherīa*]
—Syn. 1. circumference, perimeter. **—Ant. 1, 2.** center.

pe·riph·ra·sis (pə rif′rə sis), *n., pl.* **-ses** (-sēz′). **1.** the use of an unnecessarily long or roundabout form of expression; circumlocution. **2.** an expression phrased in such fashion. Also, **per·i·phrase** (per′ə frāz′). [1525–35; < L < Gk *períphrasis.* See PERI-, PHRASE, -SIS]

per·i·phras·tic (per′ə fras′tik), *adj.* **1.** circumlocutory; roundabout. **2.** *Gram.* noting a construction of two or more words having the same syntactic function as an inflected word, as *of Mr. Smith* in *the son of Mr. Smith,*

CONCISE PRONUNCIATION KEY: *act, cāpe, dâre, pärt; set, ēqual; if, īce; ox, ōver, ôrder, oil, bo͝ok, bo͞ot, out; up, ûrge; child; sing; shoe; thin, that;* zh as in *treasure.* ə = *a* as in *alone, e* as in *system, i* as in *easily, o* as in *gallop, u* as in *circus;* ᵊ as in *fire* (fīᵊr), *hour* (ouᵊr). l and n can serve as syllabic consonants, as in *cradle* (krād′l), and *button* (but′n). See the full key inside the front cover.

PERIODIC TABLE OF THE ELEMENTS

Key: 1A — Group; 1 — Atomic number; H — Symbol; 1.00797 — Atomic mass (Approx. values in parentheses)

1A	2A	3B	4B	5B	6B	7B	8B	8B	8B	1B	2B	3A	4A	5A	6A	7A	8A
1 H 1.00797																	2 He 4.0026
3 Li 6.939	4 Be 9.0122											5 B 10.811	6 C 12.011	7 N 14.0067	8 O 15.9994	9 F 18.9984	10 Ne 20.183
11 Na 22.9898	12 Mg 24.312											13 Al 26.9815	14 Si 28.086	15 P 30.9738	16 S 32.064	17 Cl 35.453	18 Ar 39.948
19 K 39.102	20 Ca 40.08	21 Sc 44.956	22 Ti 47.90	23 V 50.942	24 Cr 51.996	25 Mn 54.938	26 Fe 55.847	27 Co 58.933	28 Ni 58.71	29 Cu 63.54	30 Zn 65.37	31 Ga 69.72	32 Ge 72.59	33 As 74.922	34 Se 78.96	35 Br 79.909	36 Kr 83.80
37 Rb 85.47	38 Sr 87.62	39 Y 88.905	40 Zr 91.22	41 Nb 92.906	42 Mo 95.94	43 Tc (98)	44 Ru 101.07	45 Rh 102.905	46 Pd 106.4	47 Ag 107.870	48 Cd 112.40	49 In 114.82	50 Sn 118.69	51 Sb 121.75	52 Te 127.60	53 I 126.904	54 Xe 131.30
55 Cs 132.905	56 Ba 137.34	57 La 138.91	72 Hf 178.49	73 Ta 180.948	74 W 183.85	75 Re 186.2	76 Os 190.2	77 Ir 192.2	78 Pt 195.09	79 Au 196.967	80 Hg 200.59	81 Tl 204.37	82 Pb 207.19	83 Bi 208.980	84 Po (210)	85 At (210)	86 Rn (222)
87 Fr (223)	88 Ra (226)	89 Ac (227)	104 Unq (257)	105 Unp (260)	106 Unh (263)	107 Uns (262)											

58 Ce 140.12	59 Pr 140.907	60 Nd 144.24	61 Pm (147)	62 Sm 150.35	63 Eu 151.96	64 Gd 157.25	65 Tb 158.924	66 Dy 162.50	67 Ho 164.930	68 Er 167.26	69 Tm 168.934	70 Yb 173.04	71 Lu 174.97
90 Th 232.038	91 Pa (231)	92 U 238.03	93 Np (237)	94 Pu (242)	95 Am (243)	96 Cm (247)	97 Bk (247)	98 Cf (249)	99 Es (254)	100 Fm (253)	101 Md (256)	102 No (254)	103 Lw (257)

which is equivalent to *Mr. Smith's* in *Mr. Smith's son.* [1795–1805; < Gk *periphrastikós,* deriv. of *periphrázein* to use periphrasis. See PERI-, PHRASE, -TIC] —**per′i·phras′ti·cal·ly,** *adv.*

pe·riph·y·ton (pə rif′i ton′), *n. Ecol.* the community of tiny organisms, as protozoans, hydras, insect larvae, and snails, that lives on the surfaces of rooted aquatic plants. [1940–45; prob. PERI- + Gk *phytón* plant, -PHYTE, on the model of PLANKTON] —**per·i·phyt·ic** (per′ə fit′ik), *adj.*

per·i·plasm (per′ə plaz′əm), *n.* an outer cytoplasmic layer that surrounds the oosphere in certain fungi. [1885–90; PERI- + -PLASM]

per·i·proct (per′ə prokt′), *n.* (in certain echinoids) that part of the body surface bordering the anus. [1875–80; PERI- + *-proct* < Gk *prōktós* anus] —**per′i·proc′tal, per′i·proc′tic, per′i·proc′tous,** *adj.*

pe·rip·ter·al (pə rip′tər əl), *adj.* (of a classical temple or other structure) surrounded by a single row of columns. [1820–30; < L *peripter(on)* (< Gk, n. use of neut. of *perípteros* encompassed round with columns, lit., flying around; see PERI-, -PTEROUS) + -AL[1]]

pe·rip·ter·y (pə rip′tə rē), *n., pl.* **-ter·ies.** a peripteral building. [< Gk *perípter(os)* (see PERIPTERAL) + -Y[3]]

pe·rique (pə rēk′), *n.* a strong, rich-flavored tobacco produced in Louisiana, usually blended with other tobaccos. [1880–85, *Amer.*; allegedly after *Périque,* nickname of Pierre Chenet, Louisiana grower who first developed it]

per·i·sarc (per′ə särk′), *n. Zool.* the horny or chitinous outer case or covering protecting the soft parts of hydrozoans. [1870–75; PERI- + *-sarc* < Gk *sárx* (gen. *sarkós*) flesh] —**per′i·sar′cal, per′i·sar′cous,** *adj.*

per·i·scope (per′ə skōp′), *n.* **1.** an optical instrument for viewing objects that are above the level of direct sight or in an otherwise obstructed field of vision, consisting essentially of a tube with an arrangement of prisms or mirrors and, usually, lenses: used esp. in submarines. **2.** a periscopic lens. [1815–25; back formation from PERISCOPIC]

periscope (def. 1)

per·i·scop·ic (per′ə skop′ik), *adj.* **1.** *Optics.* (of certain lenses in special microscopes, cameras, etc.) giving distinct vision obliquely, or all around, as well as, or instead of, in a direct line. **2.** pertaining to periscopes or their use. Also, **per′i·scop′i·cal.** [1795–1805; < Gk *periskop(eîn)* to look about (see PERI-, -SCOPE) + -IC]

per·ish (per′ish), *v.i.* **1.** to die or be destroyed through violence, privation, etc.: *to perish in an earthquake.* **2.** to pass away or disappear: *an age of elegance that has forever perished.* **3.** to suffer destruction or ruin: *His valuable paintings perished in the fire.* **4.** to suffer spiritual death: *Save us, lest we perish.* **5. perish the thought,** may it never happen: used facetiously or as an afterthought of foreboding. [1200–50; ME *perissen* < OF *periss-,* long s. of *perir* < L *perīre* to perish, lit., go through, spend fully, equiv. to *per-* PER- + *īre* to go] —**per′ish·less,** *adj.* —**per′ish·ment,** *n.*
—**Syn. 1.** expire. See **die**[1]. **2.** wither, shrivel, rot, molder, vanish. —**Ant. 2.** appear.

per·ish·a·ble (per′i shə bəl), *adj.* **1.** subject to decay, ruin, or destruction: *perishable fruits and vegetables.* —*n.* **2.** Usually, **perishables.** something perishable, esp. food. [1605–15; PERISH + -ABLE] —**per′ish·a·bil′i·ty, per′ish·a·ble·ness,** *n.* —**per′ish·a·bly,** *adv.*

per·ish·ing (per′i shing), *adj.* causing destruction, ruin, extreme discomfort, or death: *lost in the perishing cold.* [1400–50; late ME; see PERISH, -ING[2]] —**per′ish·ing·ly,** *adv.*

per·i·spore (per′ə spôr′, -spōr′), *n. Mycol.* a membrane surrounding a spore. [1840–50; PERI- + -SPORE]

pe·ris·so·dac·tyl (pə ris′ō dak′til), *adj.* **1.** having an uneven number of toes or digits on each foot. —*n.* **2.** any mammal of the order Perissodactyla, comprising the odd-toed hoofed quadrupeds and including the tapirs, rhinoceroses, and horses. Also, **pe·ris·so·dac·tyle** (pə ris′ō dak′til, -tīl). Cf. **artiodactyl.** [1840–50; < NL *perissodactylus* < Gk *perissó(s)* uneven, lit., beyond the norm, strange (deriv. of *périx* (prep. and adv.) round about, akin to *perí;* see PERI-) + *-daktylos* -DACTYLOUS] —**pe·ris′so·dac′ty·lous,** *adj.*

pe·ris·ta·lith (pə ris′tl ith), *n.* a group of stones encircling a mound, dolmen, or the like. [1880–85; < Gk *perísta(tos)* surrounded (verbid of *periístanai* to stand round, equiv. to *peri-* PERI- + *sta-,* base of *histánai* to STAND + *-tos* verbal adj. suffix) + -LITH]

per·i·stal·sis (per′ə stôl′sis, -stal′-), *n., pl.* **-ses** (-sēz). *Physiol.* the progressive wave of contraction and relaxation of a tubular muscular system, esp. the alimentary canal, by which the contents are forced through the system. [1855–60; < NL < Gk *peri-* PERI- + *stálsis* contraction, equiv. to *stal-* (var. s. of *stéllein* to set, bring together, compress) + *-sis* -SIS]

per·i·stal·tic (per′ə stôl′tik, -stal′-), *adj. Physiol.* of, pertaining to, or resembling peristalsis. [1645–55; < Gk *peristaltikós* compressing, equiv. to *peri-* PERI- + *stal-* (see PERISTALSIS) + *-tikos* -TIC] —**per′i·stal′ti·cal·ly,** *adv.*

Pe·ri·sté·ri (pe′Rē ste′Rē), *n.* a city in SE Greece, constituting part of Greater Athens. 118,413.

pe·ris·te·rite (pə ris′tə rīt′), *n.* a whitish, iridescent variety of albite, used as a gem. [1835–45; < Gk *peristér(a)* pigeon, dove + -ITE[1]]

per·i·stome (per′ə stōm′), *n.* **1.** *Bot.* the one or two circles of small, pointed, toothlike appendages around the orifice of a capsule or urn of mosses, appearing when the lid is removed. **2.** *Zool.* any of various structures or sets of parts that surround or form the walls of a mouth or mouthlike opening. [1790–1800; < NL *peristoma.* See PERI-, -STOME] —**per′i·sto′mal, per·i·sto·mat·ic** (per′ə stə mat′ik), **per′i·sto′mi·al,** *adj.*

per·i·style (per′ə stīl′), *n. Archit.* **1.** a colonnade surrounding a building or an open space. **2.** an open space, as a courtyard, surrounded by a colonnade. [1605–15; < L *peristȳlum* < Gk *perístȳlon,* n. use of neut. of *perístȳlos* surrounded with columns, equiv. to *peri-* PERI- + *-stȳlos* -STYLE[2]] —**per′i·sty′lar,** *adj.*

per·i·sty·li·um (per′ə stī′lē əm, -stil′ē-), *n., pl.* **-sty·li·a** (-stī′lē ə, -stil′ē ə). a peristyle. [1665–75; < L *peristȳlium* < Gk *peristȳ́lion,* dim. of *perístȳlon* PERISTYLE]

per·i·tec·tic (per′i tek′tik), *adj. Physical Chem.* of or noting the phase intermediate between a solid and the liquid that results from the melting of the solid. [1920–25; PERI- + Gk *tēktikós* able to dissolve, akin to *tḗkein* to melt]

per·i·the·ci·um (per′ə thē′shē əm, -sē əm), *n., pl.* **-ci·a** (-shē ə, -sē ə). *Mycol.* the fruiting body of ascomycetous fungi, typically a minute, more or less completely closed, globose or flask-shaped body enclosing the asci. [1825–35; < NL; see PERI-, THECIUM] —**per′i·the′ci·al,** *adj.*

per·i·the·li·um (per′ə thē′lē əm), *n., pl.* **-li·a** (-lē ə). *Anat.* the connective tissue surrounding certain small vessels, as capillaries. [1875–80; < NL, equiv. to Gk *peri-* PERI- + *thēl(ḗ)* nipple + L *-ium* -IUM] —**per′i·the′li·al,** *adj.*

per·i·to·ne·al·ize (per′i tn ē′ə līz′), *v.t.,* **-ized, -iz·ing.** *Surg.* to cover with peritoneum. Also, *esp. Brit.,* **per′i·to·ne′al·ise′.** [PERITONEAL + -IZE]

per·i·to·ne·um (per′i tn ē′əm), *n., pl.* **-to·ne·ums, -to·ne·a** (-tn ē′ə). *Anat.* the serous membrane lining the abdominal cavity and investing its viscera. [1535–45; < LL, var. sp. of *peritonaeum* < Gk *peritónaion,* n. use of neut. of *peritónaios,* synonymous deriv. of *perítonos* stretched round. See PERI-, TONE, -EOUS] —**per′i·to·ne′al,** *adj.* —**per′i·to·ne′al·ly,** *adv.*

per·i·to·ni·tis (per′i tn ī′tis), *n. Pathol.* inflammation of the peritoneum, often accompanied by pain and tenderness in the abdomen, vomiting, constipation, and moderate fever. [1770–80; PERITON(EUM) + -ITIS] —**per·i·to·nit·ic** (per′i tn it′ik), **per′i·to·nit′al,** *adj.*

Per·i·trate (per′i trāt′), *Pharm., Trademark.* a brand of pentaerythritol tetranitrate.

pe·rit·ri·chate (pə ri′tri kit, -kāt′), *adj.* (of bacteria) having flagella on the entire surface. Also, **per·i·trich·ic** (per′i trik′ik). [PERI- + TRICH- + -ATE[1]] —**per′i·trich, pe·rit·ri·chan** (pə ri′trə kin), *n.*

pe·rit·ri·chous (pə ri′tri kəs), *adj.* **1.** (of bacteria) having a uniform distribution of flagella over the body surface. **2.** (of certain protozoans) having cilia arranged spirally around the mouth. [1875–80; PERI- + *-trichous* < Gk *-trichos* -haired; see -TRICHA, -OUS]

per·i·vis·cer·al (per′ə vis′ər əl), *adj. Anat.* surrounding or situated about the viscera. [1865–70; PERI- + VISCERAL]

per·i·wig (per′i wig′), *n.* a wig, esp. a peruke. [1520–30; earlier *perwyke,* alter. of MF *perruque* PERUKE]

per′iwig chair′, a chair of c1700 having a high, caned back with an elaborately carved cresting.

per·i·win·kle[1] (per′i wing′kəl), *n.* **1.** any of various marine gastropods or sea snails, esp. *Littorina littorea,* used for food in Europe. **2.** the shell of any of these animals. [1520–30; perh. reflecting (through assimilation to PERIWINKLE[2]) OE *pinewincle,* equiv. to *pine* (< L *pīna* < Gk *pína,* var. of *pínna* kind of mollusk) + *wincle,* c. dial. Dan *vinkel* snail shell]

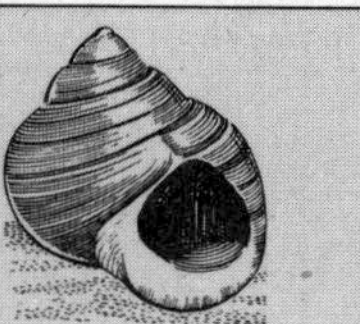
periwinkle[1], *Littorina littorea,* length to 1 in. (2.5 cm)

per·i·win·kle[2] (per′i wing′kəl), *n.* **1.** Also called **myrtle.** a trailing plant, *Vinca minor,* of the dogbane family, having glossy, evergreen foliage and usually blue-violet flowers. **2.** any of several similar plants of the genus *Vinca* or *Catharanthus.* [bef. 1000; earlier *pervinkle, perwinkle,* alter. (see -LE) of ME *perwinke, pervinke* < AF *pervenke* (OF *pervenche*) < LL *pervinca,* L *vi(n)capervi(n)ca;* cf. OE *peruince,* MHG *ber(e)winke* < LL *pervinca*] —**per′i·win′kled,** *adj.*

per·jure (pûr′jər), *v.t.,* **-jured, -jur·ing.** to render (oneself) guilty of swearing falsely or of willfully making a false statement under oath or solemn affirmation: *The witness perjured herself when she denied knowing the defendant.* [1475–85; < L *perjūrāre* to swear falsely, equiv. to *per-* through, i.e., beyond the limits (see PER-) + *jūrāre* to swear, lit., to be at law, deriv. of *jūs* JUS] —**per′jure·ment,** *n.* —**per′jur·er,** *n.*

per·jured (pûr′jərd), *adj.* **1.** guilty of perjury. **2.** characterized by or involving perjury: *perjured testimony.* [1425–75; late ME; see PERJURE, -ED[2]] —**per′jured·ly,** *adv.* —**per′jured·ness,** *n.*

per·ju·ry (pûr′jə rē), *n., pl.* **-ries.** *Law.* the willful giving of false testimony under oath or affirmation, before a competent tribunal, upon a point material to a legal inquiry. [1250–1300; ME *perjurie* < AF < L *perjūrium,* equiv. to *perjūr(us)* swearing falsely (see PERJURE) + *-ium* -IUM; r. *parjure* < OF < L as above] —**per·ju·ri·ous** (pər jŏŏr′ē əs), *adj.* —**per·ju′ri·ous·ly,** *adv.* —**per·ju′ri·ous·ness,** *n.*

perk[1] (pûrk), *v.i.* **1.** to become lively, cheerful, or vigorous, as after depression or sickness (usually fol. by *up*): *The patients all perked up when we played the piano for them.* **2.** to act, or carry oneself, in a jaunty manner. **3.** to put oneself forward briskly or presumptuously. —*v.t.* **4.** to make smart, trim, or jaunty (sometimes fol. by *up* or *out*): *to perk up a suit with a new white blouse.* **5.** to raise smartly or briskly (often fol. by *up* or *out*): *to perk one's head up.* —*adj.* **6.** perky; jaunty: *a perk manner.* [1350–1400; ME *perken;* perh. akin to PEER[2]] —**perk′ing·ly,** *adv.* —**perk′ish,** *adj.*

perk[2] (pûrk), *v.i., v.t. Informal.* to percolate: *Has the coffee perked yet? The research team is perking with new ideas.* [1930–35, *Amer.*; by shortening and resp. of PERCOLATE]

perk[3] (pûrk), *n. Informal.* perquisite. [1815–25; by shortening and resp.]

Per·kin (pûr′kin), *n.* **Sir William Henry,** 1838–1907, English chemist.

Per·kins (pûr′kinz), *n.* **1. Frances,** 1882–1965, U.S. sociologist: Secretary of Labor 1933–45. **2. Maxwell (Evarts),** 1884–1947, U.S. editor.

perk·y (pûr′kē), *adj.,* **perk·i·er, perk·i·est.** jaunty; cheerful; brisk; pert. [1850–55; PERK[1] + -Y[1]] —**perk′i·ly,** *adv.* —**perk′i·ness,** *n.*

perle (pûrl), *n.* a medicinal capsule that resembles a pearl in shape. [1885–90; < F: lit., PEARL[1]]

Per·le·a (per′lā ə), *n.* **Jo·nel** (zhō′nel), 1900–70, U.S. conductor and composer, born in Rumania.

perle′ cot′ton. See **pearl cotton.**

Per·lis (pûr′lis), *n.* a state in Malaysia, on the SW Malay Peninsula. 121,062; 310 sq. mi. (803 sq. km). *Cap.:* Kangar.

per·lite (pûr′lit), *n. Petrog.* a volcanic glass in which concentric fractures impart a distinctive structure resembling masses of small spheroids, used as a plant growth medium. Also, **pearlite.** [1825–35; < F; see PEARL[1], -ITE[1]] —**per·lit·ic** (pûr lit′ik), *adj.*

per·lo·cu·tion·ar·y (pûr′lə kyōō′shə ner′ē), *adj. Philos., Ling.* (of a speech act) producing an effect upon the listener, as in persuading, frightening, amusing, or causing the listener to act. Cf. **illocutionary, locutionary.** [1950–55; PER- + LOCUTION + -ARY] —**per′lo·cu′tion,** *n.*

per·lu·ci·dus (pər lōō′si dəs), *adj. Meteorol.* (of a cloud) having transparent spaces between the elements. [< NL; see PER-, LUCID]

perm (pûrm), *Informal.* —*n.* **1.** permanent (def. 4). —*v.t.* **2.** to give (the hair) a permanent. —*v.i.* **3.** to apply a permanent to the hair. [1925–30; by shortening]

Perm (pûrm, pârm; *Russ.* pyerm), *n.* a city in the E Russian Federation in Europe, on the Kama River. 1,091,000. Formerly, **Molotov.**

per·ma·frost (pûr′mə frôst′, -frost′), *n.* (in arctic or subarctic regions) perennially frozen subsoil. Also called **pergelisol.** [1943; PERMA(NENT) + FROST]

per′mafrost ta′ble, the variable surface constituting the upper limit of permafrost. Cf. **frostline** (def. 2).

Perm·al·loy (pûrm′al′oi, pûr′mə loi′), *Trademark.* a brand name for any of a class of alloys of high magnetic permeability, containing from 30 to 90 percent nickel. [1920–25; PERM(ANENT) + ALLOY]

per·ma·nence (pûr′mə nəns), *n.* the condition or quality of being permanent; perpetual or continued existence. [1400–50; late ME < ML *permanentia.* See PERMANENT, -ENCE]

per·ma·nen·cy (pûr′mə nən sē), *n., pl.* **-cies** for 2. **1.** permanence. **2.** something that is permanent. [1545–55; < ML *permanentia.* See PERMANENT, -ENCY]

per·ma·nent (pûr′mə nənt), *adj.* **1.** existing perpetually; everlasting, esp. without significant change. **2.** intended to exist or function for a long, indefinite period without regard to unforeseeable conditions: *a permanent employee; the permanent headquarters of the United Nations.* **3.** long-lasting or nonfading: *permanent pleating; permanent ink.* —*n.* **4.** Also called **per′manent wave′.** a wave or curl that is set into the hair by the application of a special chemical preparation and that remains for a number of months. [1400–50; late ME < L *permanent-* (s. of *permanēns*), prp. of *permanēre* to remain. See PER-, REMAIN, -ENT] —**per′ma·nent·ly,** *adv.* —**per′ma·nent·ness,** *n.*
—**Syn. 1.** stable, invariable, constant. —**Ant. 1.** temporary; inconstant.

Per′manent Court′ of Arbitra′tion, official name of the **Hague Tribunal.**

Per′manent Court′ of Interna′tional Jus′tice, official name of the **World Court.**

per′manent ech′o, *Electronics.* a radar signal reflected to a radar station on the ground by a building or other fixed object.

per′manent lens′. See **intraocular lens.**

per′manent mag′net, a magnet that retains its magnetism after being removed from an external magnetic field. [1820–30] **—per′manent mag′netism.**

per′manent mold′, *Metalworking.* a reusable metal mold used for making a large number of identical castings.

per′manent press′, **1.** a process in which a fabric is chemically treated to make it wrinkle-resistant so as to require little or no ironing after washing. **2.** the condition of a fabric so treated. [1960–65] **—per′manent-press′,** *adj.*

per′manent tooth′, any of the 32 adult teeth that replace the 20 milk teeth. [1830–40]

per′manent way′, *Brit.* the roadbed and track of a railroad. [1830–40]

per•man•ga•nate (pər mang′gə nāt′), *n. Chem.* a salt of permanganic acid, as potassium permanganate. [1835–45; PERMANGAN(IC ACID) + -ATE[2]]

per•man•gan•ic (pûr′man gan′ik), *adj. Chem.* of or derived from permanganic acid. [1830–40; PER- + MANGANIC]

per′mangan′ic ac′id, *Chem.* an acid, $HMnO_4$, known only in solution. [1830–40]

per•ma-press (pûr′mə pres′), *adj.* permanent-press. [by shortening]

per•me•a•bil•i•ty (pûr′mē ə bil′i tē), *n.* **1.** the property or state of being permeable. **2.** Also called **magnetic permeability.** *Elect.* a measure of the change in magnetic induction produced when a magnetic material replaces air, expressed as a coefficient or a set of coefficients that multiply the components of magnetic intensity to give the components of magnetic induction. **3.** *Geol.* the capability of a porous rock or sediment to permit the flow of fluids through its pore spaces. **4.** *Aeron.* the rate at which gas is lost through the envelope of an aerostat, usually expressed as the number of liters thus diffused in one day through a square meter. **5.** *Naut.* the capacity of a space in a vessel to absorb water, measured with reference to its temporary or permanent contents and expressed as a percentage of the total volume of the space. [1750–60; PERMEA(BLE) + -BILITY]

per•me•a•ble (pûr′mē ə bəl), *adj.* capable of being permeated. [1400–50; late ME < LL *permeābilis,* equiv. to *permeā(re)* to PERMEATE + *-bilis* -BLE] **—per′me•a•ble•ness,** *n.* **—per′me•a•bly,** *adv.*

per•me•am•e•ter (pûr′mē ə mē′tər, pûr′mē am′i tər), *n.* an instrument for measuring magnetic permeability. [1885–90; PERMEA(BILITY) + -METER]

per•me•ance (pûr′mē əns), *n.* **1.** the act of permeating. **2.** the conducting power of a magnetic circuit for magnetic flux; the reciprocal of magnetic reluctance. [1835–45; PERME(ANT) + -ANCE]

per•me•ant (pûr′mē ənt), *adj.* permeating; pervading. [1640–50; < L *permeant-* (s. of *permeāns*), prp. of *permeāre* to PERMEATE; see -ANT]

per•me•ase (pûr′mē ās′, -āz′), *n. Biochem.* any of the proteins that mediate the transport of various molecules across biological membranes. [< F *perméase* (1956), equiv. to *permé(able)* PERMEABLE + *-ase* -ASE]

per•me•ate (pûr′mē āt′), *v.,* **-at•ed, -at•ing.** —*v.t.* **1.** to pass into or through every part of: *Bright sunshine permeated the room.* **2.** to penetrate through the pores, interstices, etc., of. **3.** to be diffused through; pervade; saturate: *Cynicism permeated his report.* —*v.i.* **4.** to become diffused; penetrate. [1650–60; < L *permeātus* ptp. of *permeāre* to pass through. See PER-, MEATUS] **—per′me•a′tion,** *n.* **—per′me•a′tive,** *adj.* **—per′me•a′tor,** *n.*

per men•sem (pᴇʀ men′sem; *Eng.* pər men′səm), *Latin.* by the month.

Per•mi•an (pûr′mē ən), *adj.* **1.** *Geol.* noting or pertaining to a period of the Paleozoic Era occurring from about 280 to 230 million years ago and characterized by a profusion of amphibian species. See table under **geologic time.** —*n.* **2.** *Geol.* the Permian Period or System. **3.** Permic. [1835–45; PERM + -IAN]

Per•mic (pûr′mik), *n.* a subfamily of Finnic, comprising the modern languages Udmurt and Komi, spoken in northeastern European Russia, and fragmentary attestations of an earlier language (**Old Permic**), dating from the 15th century. [PERM (Russ *Perm′*) + -IC, as trans. of Russ *pérmskiĭ*]

per mill (pûr′ mil′, pər), per thousand. Also, **per mil′.** [1900–05]

per•mil•lage (pər mil′ij), *n.* a rate or proportion per thousand. Cf. **percentage** (def. 1). [1885–90; PER MILL + -AGE]

per•mis•si•ble (pər mis′ə bəl), *adj.* that can be permitted; allowable: *a permissible amount of sentimentality under the circumstances; Such behavior is not permissible!* [1400–50; late ME < ML *permissibilis.* See PERMISSION, -IBLE] **—per•mis′si•bil′i•ty, per•mis′si•ble•ness,** *n.* **—per•mis′si•bly,** *adv.*

—Syn. allowed, sanctioned, lawful, legal, tolerated.

permis′sible yield′, *Ecol.* See **allowable cut.**

per•mis•sion (pər mish′ən), *n.* **1.** authorization granted to do something; formal consent: *to ask permission to leave the room.* **2.** the act of permitting. [1400–50; late ME < L *permissiōn-* (s. of *permissiō*) a yielding, giving leave, equiv. to *permiss(us)* (ptp. of *permittere* to PERMIT) + *-iōn-* -ION] **—per•mis′sioned,** *adj.* **—per•mis•so•ry** (pər mis′ə rē), *adj.*

—Syn. 1. leave, sanction. **—Ant. 1.** restraint, refusal.

per•mis•sive (pər mis′iv), *adj.* **1.** habitually or characteristically accepting or tolerant of something, as social behavior or linguistic usage, that others might disapprove or forbid. **2.** granting or denoting permission: *a permissive nod.* **3.** optional. **4.** *Genetics.* (of a cell) permitting replication of a strand of DNA that could be lethal, as a viral segment or mutant gene. [1425–75; late ME; see PERMISSION, -IVE; cf. F *permissif*] **—per•mis′sive•ly,** *adv.* **—per•mis′sive•ness,** *n.*

—Syn. 1. indulgent, lenient, lax.

per•mis•siv•ism (pər mis′ə viz′əm), *n.* lenience toward or indulgence of a wide variety of social behavior. [1965–70; PERMISSIVE + -ISM] **—per•mis′siv•ist,** *n.*

per•mit[1] (*v.* pər mit′; *n.* pûr′mit, pər mit′), *v.,* **-mit•ted, -mit•ting,** *n.* —*v.t.* **1.** to allow to do something: *Permit me to explain.* **2.** to allow to be done or occur: *The law does not permit the sale of such drugs.* **3.** to tolerate; agree to: *a law permitting Roman Catholicism in England.* **4.** to afford opportunity for, or admit of: *vents to permit the escape of gases.* —*v.i.* **5.** to grant permission; allow liberty to do something. **6.** to afford opportunity or possibility: *Write when time permits.* **7.** to allow or admit (usually fol. by *of*): *statements that permit of no denial.* —*n.* **8.** an authoritative or official certificate of permission; license: *a fishing permit.* **9.** a written order granting special permission to do something. **10.** permission. [1425–75; late ME < L *permittere* to let go through, give leave, equiv. to *per-* PER- + *mittere* to let or make (someone) go. See ADMIT, COMMIT, etc.] **—per•mit′ted•ly,** *adv.* **—per•mit•tee** (pûr′mi tē′), *n.* **—per•mit′ter,** *n.*

—Syn. 1. See **allow. 8.** franchise. **—Ant. 1.** refuse.

per•mit[2] (pûr′mit), *n.* a pompano, *Trachinotus falcatus,* of the waters off the West Indies. [1880–85, *Amer.*; appar. by folk etym. < Sp *palometa* PALOMETA]

per•mit•tiv•i•ty (pûr′mi tiv′i tē), *n., pl.* **-ties.** *Elect.* the ratio of the flux density produced by an electric field in a given dielectric to the flux density produced by that field in a vacuum. Also called **dielectric constant, relative permittivity, specific inductive capacity.** [1885–90; PERMIT + -IVE + -ITY]

per•mon′o•sul•fu′ric ac′id (pər mon′ō sul fyŏŏr′ik), *Chem.* See **persulfuric acid** (def. 1). [PER- + MONO- + SULFURIC ACID]

per•mu•tate (pûr′myŏŏ tāt′, pər myōō′tāt), *v.t.,* **-tat•ed, -tat•ing. 1.** to cause (something) to undergo permutation. **2.** to arrange (items) in a different sequence. [1590–1600; < L *permūtātus,* ptp. of *permūtāre* to PERMUTE; see -ATE[1]]

per•mu•ta•tion (pûr′myŏŏ tā′shən), *n.* **1.** the act of permuting or permutating; alteration; transformation. **2.** *Math.* **a.** the act of changing the order of elements arranged in a particular order, as *abc* into *acb, bac,* etc., or of arranging a number of elements in groups made up of equal numbers of the elements in different orders, as *a* and *b* in *ab* and *ba;* a one-to-one transformation of a set with a finite number of elements. **b.** any of the resulting arrangements or groups. Cf. **combination** (def. 8b). [1325–75; ME *permutacioun* (< MF *permutacion*) < L *permūtātiōn-* (s. of *permūtātiō*) thoroughgoing change. See PER-, MUTATION, PERMUTE] **—per′mu•ta′tion•al,** *adj.* **—per′mu•ta′tion•ist,** *n.*

—Syn. 1. modification, transmutation, change.

permuta′tion group′, a mathematical group whose elements are permutations and in which the product of two permutations is the same permutation as is obtained by performing them in succession. [1900–05]

per•mute (pər myōōt′), *v.t.,* **-mut•ed, -mut•ing. 1.** to alter; change. **2.** *Math.* to subject to permutation. [1350–1400; ME < L *permūtāre* to change throughout. See PER-, MUTATE] **—per•mut′a•ble,** *adj.* **—per•mut′a•bil′i•ty, per•mut′a•ble•ness,** *n.* **—per•mut′a•bly,** *adv.* **—per•mut′er,** *n.*

Per•nam•bu•co (pûr′nəm byōō′kō, -bōō′-; *Port.* pᴇʀ′nām bōō′kŏŏ), *n.* **1.** a state in NE Brazil. 6,240,836; 38,000 sq. mi. (98,420 sq. km). *Cap.:* Recife. **2.** former name of **Recife.**

per•nan•cy (pûr′nən sē), *n. Law.* a taking or receiving, as of the rents or profits of an estate. [1635–45; alter. of AF *pernance,* metathetic var. of OF *prenance* lit., a taking, equiv. to *pren-,* pretonic s. of *prendre* to take (< L *pre(he)ndere;* see APPREHEND) + *-ance* -ANCE; see -ANCY]

per•ni•cious (pər nish′əs), *adj.* **1.** causing insidious harm or ruin; ruinous; injurious; hurtful: *pernicious teachings; a pernicious lie.* **2.** deadly; fatal: *a pernicious disease.* **3.** *Obs.* evil; wicked. [1515–25; < L *perniciōsus* ruinous, equiv. to *pernici(ēs)* ruin (*per-* PER- + *-nici-,* comb. form of *nex* death, murder (s. *nec-*) + *-iēs* n. suffix) + *-ōsus* -OUS] **—per•ni′cious•ly,** *adv.* **—per•ni′cious•ness,** *n.*

—Syn. 1. harmful, detrimental, deleterious, destructive, damaging, baneful, noxious, malicious. **2.** lethal.

perni′cious ane′mia, *Pathol.* a severe anemia caused by the diminution or absence of stomach acid secretion, with consequent failure of the gastric mucosa to secrete the intrinsic factor necessary for the absorption of vitamin B_{12}, characterized by a great reduction in the number of red blood cells and an increase in their size. [1870–75]

per•nick•et•y (pər nik′i tē), *adj.* persnickety. [1800–10; orig. Scots; of uncert. orig.; the prefix *per-* occurs in a number of other expressive words in Scots, e.g. *pergaddus* thump, clatter, *perskeet* fastidious, *perjink* trim, neat] **—per•nick′et•i•ness,** *n.*

Per•nik (*Bulg.* pᴇʀ′nik), *n.* former name of **Dimitrovo.**

per•ni•o (pûr′nē ō′), *n. Pathol.* chilblain. [1670–80; < L *perniō* chilblain on the foot, deriv. of *pern(a)* haunch of the leg; see -ION]

Per•nod (pâr nō′; *Fr.* pᴇʀ nô′), *Trademark.* a brand of green, aromatic anise- and licorice-flavored liqueur, originally from France.

per•nor (pûr′nər, -nôr), *n. Law.* a person who takes or receives the rents, profits, or other benefit of an estate, lands, etc. [1300–50; ME *pernour* < AF, metathetic var. of OF *preneor* taker, equiv. to *pren-* (see PERNANCY) + *-eor* -OR[2]]

Pe•rón (pə rōn′; *Sp.* pe ʀôn′), *n.* **1. E•va Duar•te de** (ē′və dwär′tā də; *Sp.* e′vä dwär′te ᵺe), 1919–52, Argentine political figure (wife of Juan Perón). **2. Juan (Do•min•go)** (wän də ming′gō; *Sp.* hwän dô mēng′gô), 1895–1974, Argentine military and political leader: president 1946–55, 1973–74.

per•o•ne•al (per′ə nē′əl), *adj. Anat.* pertaining to or situated near the fibula. [1825–35; < NL *peronē* the fibula (< Gk *peróne* orig., linchpin, pin of a buckle or brooch) + -AL[1]]

per•o•ne•us (per′ə nē′əs), *n., pl.* **-ne•i** (-nē′ī). *Anat.* any of several muscles on the outer side of the leg, the action of which assists in extending the foot and in turning it outward. [1695–1705; < NL: lit., of the fibula, equiv. to *peronē* the fibula (see PERONEAL) + *-us* -OUS]

Pe•ro•nism (pə rō′niz əm), *n.* (*sometimes l.c.*) the principles or policies of Juan Perón. Also, **Pe•ro•nis•mo** (per′ə niz′mō; *Sp.* pe′ʀô nēz′mô). [1945–50; < Sp *peronismo;* see PERÓN, -ISM]

Pe•ro•nist (pə rō′nist), *n.* (*sometimes l.c.*) **1.** a supporter of Juan Perón or of his principles and policies. —*adj.* **2.** of or pertaining to Juan Perón or Peronism. [1945–50; < Sp *peronista.* See PERÓN, -IST]

Pe•ro•nis•ta (per′ə nis′tə; *Sp.* pe′ʀô nēs′tä), *n., pl.* **-tas** (-təz; *Sp.* -täs). Peronist.

per•o•ral (pə rôr′əl, -rōr′-), *adj.* administered or performed through the mouth, as surgery or administration of a drug. [1905–10; PER- + ORAL] **—per•o′ral•ly,** *adv.*

per•o•rate (per′ə rāt′), *v.i.,* **-rat•ed, -rat•ing. 1.** to speak at length; make a long, usually grandiloquent speech. **2.** to bring a speech to a close with a formal conclusion. [1595–1605; < L *perōrātus* ptp. of *perōrāre.* See PER-, ORATE] **—per′o•ra′tor,** *n.*

per•o•ra•tion (per′ə rā′shən), *n.* **1.** a long speech characterized by lofty and often pompous language. **2.** *Rhet.* the concluding part of a speech or discourse, in which the speaker or writer recapitulates the principal points and urges them with greater earnestness and force. [1400–50; late ME < L *perōrātiōn-* (s. of *perōrātiō*) the closing of a speech. See PERORATE, -ION] **—per′o•ra′tion•al, per′o•ra′tive,** *adj.* **—per•o•ra•tor•i•cal** (pə rôr′ə tôr′i kəl, -ror′ə tor′-), *adj.* **—per•or′a•tor′i•cal•ly,** *adv.* **—per•or•a•to•ry** (pə rôr′ə tôr′ē, -tōr′ē, -ror′-), *n.*

Per•o•ti•nus (per′ə tī′nəs, -tē′-), *n.* (*"Magnus Magister"*), fl. late 12th to early 13th century, French composer. Also called **Per•o•tin** (per′ə tēn′), **Pé•ro•tin** (*Fr.* pā rô taɴ′).

Pe•ro•vo (pə rō′və; *Russ.* pyi ʀô′və), *n.* a former city in the W RSFSR, in the central Soviet Union in Europe, incorporated into Moscow.

pe•rovsk•ite (pə rof′skīt, -rov′-), *n. Mineral.* a naturally occurring titanate of calcium, $CaTiO_3$, found as yellow, brown, or black cubic crystals, usually in metamorphic rocks. [1835–45; < G *Perowskit,* named after Count Lev Alekseevich *Perovskiĭ* (1792–1856), Russian statesman; see -ITE[1]]

per•ox•i•dase (pə rok′si dās′, -dāz′), *n. Biochem.* any of a class of oxidoreductase enzymes that catalyze the oxidation of a compound by the decomposition of hydrogen peroxide or an organic peroxide. [1900–05; PEROXIDE + -ASE]

per•ox•i•date (pə rok′si dāt′), *v.t., v.i.,* **-dat•ed, -dat•ing.** *Chem.* peroxidize. [1855–60; PER- + OXIDATE] **—per•ox′i•da′tion,** *n.*

per•ox•ide (pə rok′sīd), *n., v.,* **-id•ed, -id•ing.** —*n.* **1.** *Chem.* **a.** hydrogen peroxide, H_2O_2 or H–O–O–H. **b.** a compound containing the bivalent group $-O_2-$, derived from hydrogen peroxide, as sodium peroxide, Na_2O_2, or dimethyl peroxide, $C_2H_6O_2$. **c.** the oxide of an element that contains an unusually large amount of oxygen. —*v.t.* **2.** to use peroxide as a bleaching agent on (esp. the hair). [1795–1805; PER- + OXIDE] **—per•ox•id•ic** (pûr′ok sid′ik), *adj.*

per•ox•i•dize (pə rok′si dīz′), *v.t., v.i.,* **-dized, -diz•ing.** *Chem.* to convert into a peroxide, esp. of the highest oxidation potential. Also, *esp. Brit.,* **per•ox′i•dise′.** [1820–30; PEROXIDE + -IZE]

per•ox•y (pə rok′sē), *adj. Chem.* containing the peroxy group. [1955–60; PER- + OXY-[2]]

peroxy-, a combining form used in the names of chemical compounds in which the peroxy group is present: *peroxyborate.*

per•ox•y•ac•id (pə rok′sē as′id), *n. Chem.* an acid derived from hydrogen peroxide and containing the –O–O– group, as peroxysulfuric acid, $H_2S_2O_8$. [1960–65; PEROXY- + ACID]

per•ox•y•bo•rate (pə rok′sē bôr′āt, -it, -bōr′-), *n. Chem.* perborate. [PEROXY- + BORATE]

per•ox′y•di•sul•fu′ric ac′id (pə rok′sē dī′sul fyŏŏr′ik, -rok′-), *Chem.* See **persulfuric acid** (def. 2). [PEROXY- + DI-[1] + SULFURIC ACID]

perox′y group′, *Chem.* the bivalent group $-O_2-$, derived from hydrogen peroxide. Also called **perox′y rad′ical.** [1970–75]

per•ox′y•mon′o•sul•fu′ric ac′id (pə rok′sē mon′ō sul fyŏŏr′ik, -rok′sē mon′-), *Chem.* See **persulfuric acid** (def. 1). [PEROXY- + MONO- + SULFURIC ACID]

per•ox′y•sul•fu′ric ac′id (pə rok′sē sul fyŏŏr′ik, -rok′-), *Chem.* See **persulfuric acid** (def. 1). [PEROXY- + SULFURIC ACID]

perp (pûrp), *n. Police Slang.* the perpetrator of a crime.

perp., perpendicular.

CONCISE PRONUNCIATION KEY: *act, cāpe, dâre, pärt; set, ēqual; if, ice; ox, ōver, ôrder, oil, bŏŏk, bōōt, out; up, ûrge; child; sing; shoe; thin, ᵺat;* zh as in *treasure.* ə = *a* as in *alone, e* as in *system, i* as in *easily, o* as in *gallop, u* as in *circus;* ə as in *fire* (fīər), *hour* (ouər). l and n can serve as syllabic consonants, as in *cradle* (krād′l), and *button* (but′n). See the full key inside the front cover.

per·pend[1] (pûr′pənd), *n.* a large stone passing through the entire thickness of a wall. Also, **parpen, perpent.** Also called **through stone.** [1225–75; var. of *parpen, parpend,* ME *perpein, parpein* (late ME *perpend-* in compound) a stone dressed on more than one side < OF *perpein, parpain,* perh. repr. ML *parpanus* < ?]

per·pend[2] (pər pend′), *v.t.* **1.** to consider. —*v.i.* **2.** to ponder; deliberate. [1520–30; < L *perpendere* to weigh carefully, ponder, equiv. to *per-* PER- + *pendere* to weigh]

per·pen·dic·u·lar (pûr′pən dik′yə lər), *adj.* **1.** vertical; straight up and down; upright. **2.** *Geom.* meeting a given line or surface at right angles. **3.** maintaining a standing or upright position; standing up. **4.** having a sharp pitch or slope; steep. **5.** (*cap.*) noting or pertaining to the last style of English Gothic architecture, prevailing from the late 14th through the early 16th century and characterized by the use of predominantly vertical tracery, an overall linear, shallow effect, and fine intricate stonework. —*n.* **6.** a perpendicular line or plane. **7.** an instrument for indicating the vertical line from any point. **8.** an upright position. **9.** a sharply pitched or precipitously steep mountain face. **10.** moral virtue or uprightness; rectitude. **11.** *Naut.* either of two lines perpendicular to the keel line, base line, or designed water line of a vessel. [1350–1400; < L *perpendiculāris* vertical, equiv. to *perpendicul(um)* plumb line (see PERPEND[2], -I-, -CULE[2]) + *-āris* -AR[1]; r. ME *perpendiculer(e)* (adj. and adv.) < OF *perpendiculiere*] —**per′pen·dic′u·lar′i·ty, per′pen·dic′u·lar·ness,** *n.* —**per′pen·dic′u·lar·ly,** *adv.*
—**Syn. 1.** standing. See **upright.**

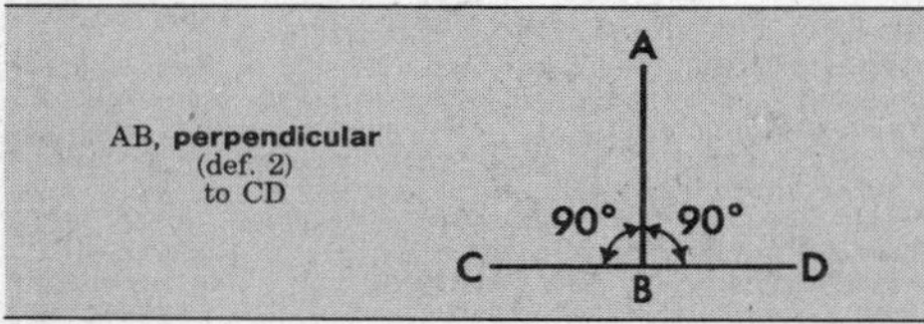

AB, **perpendicular** (def. 2) to CD

per·pent (pûr′pənt), *n.* perpend[1].

per·pe·trate (pûr′pi trāt′), *v.t.,* **-trat·ed, -trat·ing. 1.** to commit: *to perpetrate a crime.* **2.** to present, execute, or do in a poor or tasteless manner: *Who perpetrated this so-called comedy?* [1540–50; < L *perpetrātus* (ptp. of *perpetrāre* to carry out, execute, perform), equiv. to *per-* PER- + *-petr-* (comb. form of *patrāre* to father, bring about; see PATER) + *-ā-* theme vowel + *-tus* ptp. suffix; see -ATE[1]] —**per·pe·tra·ble** (pûr′pi trə bəl), *adj.* —**per′pe·tra′tion,** *n.* —**per′pe·tra′tor,** *n.*

per·pet·u·al (pər pech′o͞o əl), *adj.* **1.** continuing or enduring forever; everlasting. **2.** lasting an indefinitely long time: *perpetual snow.* **3.** continuing or continued without intermission or interruption; ceaseless: *a perpetual stream of visitors all day.* **4.** blooming almost continuously throughout the season or the year. —*n.* **5.** a hybrid rose that is perpetual. **6.** a perennial plant. [1300–50; late ME *perpetuall* < L *perpetuālis* permanent, equiv. to *perpetu(us)* uninterrupted (*per-* PER- + *pet-,* base of *petere* to seek, reach for + *-uus* deverbal adj. suffix) + *-ālis* -AL[1]; r. ME *perpetuel* < MF (< L as above] —**per·pet′u·al′i·ty, per·pet′u·al·ness,** *n.* —**per·pet′u·al·ly,** *adv.*
—**Syn. 1.** permanent, enduring. See **eternal. 3.** continuous, incessant, constant, unending, uninterrupted. —**Ant. 1.** temporary. **3.** discontinuous.

perpet′ual adora′tion, *Rom. Cath. Ch.* uninterrupted adoration of the Blessed Sacrament.

perpet′ual cal′endar, 1. a calendar devised to be used for many years, as in determining the day of the week on which a given date falls. **2.** a desk calendar with months, days, and dates that can be changed, as by adjusting various dials, so that it may be used over and over for many years. [1890–95]

perpet′ual check′, *Chess.* **1.** a continuing series of checks resulting in a drawn game because they cannot be halted or evaded without resulting in checkmate or a serious disadvantage. **2.** the situation in which this occurs. [1810–20]

perpet′ual mo′tion, *Mech.* the motion of a theoretical mechanism that, without any losses due to friction or other forms of dissipation of energy, would continue to operate indefinitely at the same rate without any external energy being applied to it. [1585–95]

per·pet·u·ate (pər pech′o͞o āt′), *v.t.,* **-at·ed, -at·ing. 1.** to make perpetual. **2.** to preserve from extinction or oblivion: *to perpetuate one's name.* [1520–30; < L *perpetuātus* (ptp. of *perpetuāre,* deriv. of *perpetuus* uninterrupted). See PERPETUAL, -ATE[1]] —**per·pet′u·a·ble,** *adj.* —**per·pet′u·a′tion, per·pet·u·ance** (pər pech′o͞o əns), *n.* —**per·pet′u·a′tor,** *n.*
—**Syn. 2.** save, maintain, sustain.

per·pe·tu·i·ty (pûr′pi to͞o′i tē, -tyo͞o′-), *n., pl.* **-ties. 1.** the state or character of being perpetual (often prec. by *in*): *to desire happiness in perpetuity.* **2.** endless or indefinitely long duration or existence; eternity. **3.** something that is perpetual. **4.** an annuity paid for life. **5.** *Law.* an interest under which property is less than completely alienable for longer than the law allows. [1375–1425; late ME *perpetuite* < L *perpetuitās.* See PERPETUAL, -ITY]

per·phen·a·zine (pər fen′ə zēn′, -zin), *n. Pharm.* a crystalline, water-insoluble powder, $C_{21}H_{26}ClN_3OS$, used chiefly as a tranquilizer and in the treatment of intractable hiccoughs and nausea and vomiting. [1955–60; PER- + PHEN(OTHI)AZINE]

CONCISE ETYMOLOGY KEY: <, descended or borrowed from; >, whence; b., blend of, blended; c., cognate with; cf., compare; deriv., derivative; equiv., equivalent; imit., imitative; obl., oblique; r., replacing; s., stem; sp., spelling, spelled; resp., respelling, respelled; trans., translation; ?, origin unknown; *, unattested; ‡, probably earlier than. See the full key inside the front cover.

Per·pi·gnan (per pē nyäN′), *n.* a city in and the capital of Pyrénées-Orientales, in the S extremity of France. 107,971.

per·plex (pər pleks′), *v.t.* **1.** to cause to be puzzled or bewildered over what is not understood or certain; confuse mentally: *Her strange response perplexed me.* **2.** to make complicated or confused, as a matter or question. **3.** to hamper with complications, confusion, or uncertainty. [1585–95; back formation from PERPLEXED] —**per·plex′er,** *n.* —**per·plex′ing·ly,** *adv.*
—**Syn. 1.** mystify, confound. **2.** tangle, snarl. **3.** vex, annoy, bother.

per·plexed (pər plekst′), *adj.* **1.** bewildered; puzzled: *a perplexed state of mind.* **2.** complicated; involved; entangled. [1350–1400; ME *perplex* confused (< L *perplexus;* see PER-, COMPLEX) + -ED[2]] —**per·plex·ed·ly** (pər plek′sid lē), *adv.* —**per·plex′ed·ness,** *n.*

per·plex·i·ty (pər plek′si tē), *n., pl.* **-ties. 1.** the state of being perplexed; confusion; uncertainty. **2.** something that perplexes: *a case plagued with perplexities.* **3.** a tangled, involved, or confused condition or situation. [1350–1400; ME *perplexite* < OF < LL *perplexitās,* equiv. to L *perplex(us)* (see PERPLEXED) + *-itās* -ITY]

per pro., per procurationem. Also, **per proc.**

per proc·u·ra·ti·o·nem (pər prok′yə rä′shē ō′nem, per prok′ə rä′tē ō′nem), *Chiefly Law.* by one acting as an agent; by proxy. Also, **per proc·u·ra·tion** (pər prok′yə rā′shən). [1810–20; < L *per prōcūrātiōnem*]

per·qui·site (pûr′kwə zit), *n.* **1.** an incidental payment, benefit, privilege, or advantage over and above regular income, salary, or wages: *Among the president's perquisites were free use of a company car and paid membership in a country club.* **2.** a gratuity or tip. **3.** something demanded or due as a particular privilege: *homage that was once the perquisite of royalty.* [1400–50; late ME < ML *perquīsītum* something acquired, n. use of neut. of L *perquīsītus* (ptp. of *perquīrere* to search everywhere for, inquire diligently). See PER-, INQUISITIVE]

Per·rault (pə rō′, pe-; *Fr.* pe rō′), *n.* **1. Charles** (chärlz; *Fr.* sharl), 1628–1703, French poet, critic, and author of fairy tales. **2.** his brother, **Claude** (klôd; *Fr.* klōd), 1613–88, French architect, scientist, and physician.

Per·ret (pe rā′), *n.* **Au·guste** (ō gyst′), 1874–1954, French architect.

Per·rin (pe raN′), *n.* **Jean Bap·tiste** (zhäN ba tēst′), 1870–1942, French physicist and chemist: Nobel prize for physics 1926.

Per·rine (pûr′īn), *n.* a town in S Florida. 16,129.

per·ron (per′ən; *Fr.* pe rôN′), *n., pl.* **per·rons** (per′ənz; *Fr.* pe rôN′). *Archit.* an outside platform upon which the entrance door of a building opens, with steps leading to it. [1350–1400; ME < MF, OF, deriv. of *pierre* stone < L *petra* < Gk *pétra*]

Per·ron·et (pe rô ne′), *n.* **Jean Ro·dolphe** (zhäN rô dôlf′), 1708–94, French engineer.

Per·rot (pə rō′, pe-; *Fr.* pe rō′), *n.* **Ni·co·las** (nik′ə ləs; *Fr.* nē kô lä′), 1644–1717, North American fur trader and explorer in the Great Lakes region, born in France.

per·ry (per′ē), *n., pl.* **-ries.** a fermented beverage similar to cider, made from the juice of pears. [1275–1325; ME *pereye* < MF *perey,* var. of *pere* << VL **pirātum* (L *pir(a)* PEAR + *-ātum,* neut. of *-ātus* -ATE[1])]

Per·ry (per′ē), *n.* **1. Antoinette,** 1888–1946, U.S. actress, theatrical manager, and producer. **2. Bliss,** 1860–1954, U.S. educator, literary critic, and editor. **3. Frederick John** (*Fred*), born 1909, British tennis player. **4. Matthew Cal·braith** (kal′brāth), 1794–1858, U.S. commodore. **5.** his brother, **Oliver Hazard,** 1785–1819, U.S. naval officer. **6. Ralph Barton,** 1876–1957, U.S. philosopher and educator. **7.** a male given name: from a Middle English word meaning "pear tree."

Per·rys·burg (per′ēz bûrg′), *n.* a town in NW Ohio. 10,215.

Pers, Persian.

Pers., 1. Persia. **2.** Persian.

pers., 1. person. **2.** personal.

per·salt (pûr′sôlt′), *n. Chem.* **1.** (in a series of salts of a given metal or group) the salt in which the metal or group has a high, or the highest apparent, valence. **2.** (loosely) the salt of a peroxy acid. [1810–20; PER- + SALT[1]]

per se (pûr sā′, sē′, pər), by, of, for, or in itself; intrinsically. [1565–75; < L *per sē* by itself, trans. of Gk *kath' autó*]

perse (pûrs), *adj.* of a very deep shade of blue or purple. [1325–75; ME *pers* < ML *persus,* perh. var. of *perseus* kind of blue, itself alter. of L *Persicus* Persian]

Perse (pers, pûrs), *n.* **St.-John** (sin′jən). See **St.-John Perse.**

per·se·cute (pûr′si kyo͞ot′), *v.t.,* **-cut·ed, -cut·ing. 1.** to pursue with harassing or oppressive treatment, esp. because of religion, race, or beliefs; harass persistently. **2.** to annoy or trouble persistently. [1400–50; late ME; back formation from *persecutour* persecutor << LL *persecūtor* orig. prosecutor, equiv. to *persecū-,* var. s. of *persequī* to prosecute, pursue closely (see PER-, SEQUENCE) + *-tor* -TOR] —**per′se·cut′ing·ly,** *adv.* —**per′se·cu′tive,** *adj.* —**per′se·cu′tive·ness,** *n.* —**per′se·cu′tor,** *n.* —**per·se·cu·to·ry** (pûr′si kyo͞o′tə rē, -kyə tôr′ē, -tōr′ē), *adj.*
—**Syn. 1.** afflict, torture, torment. **2.** worry, badger, vex, bother, pester.

per·se·cu·tion (pûr′si kyo͞o′shən), *n.* **1.** the act of persecuting. **2.** the state of being persecuted. **3.** a program or campaign to exterminate, drive away, or subjugate a people because of their religion, race, or beliefs: *the persecutions of Christians by the Romans.* [1300–50; ME *persecucio(u)n* < LL *persecūtiōn-* (s. of *persecūtiō*), L: prosecution, equiv. to *persecūt(us)* ptp. of *persequī* (see PERSECUTE) + *-iōn-* -ION] —**per′se·cu′tion·al,** *adj.*

Per·se·id (pûr′sē id), *n. Astron.* any of a shower of meteors appearing in August and radiating from a point in the constellation Perseus. [1875–80; PERSE(US) + -ID[1], or directly < Gk *Perseídēs* offspring of Perseus]

per·se·i·ty (pər sā′i tē, -sē′-), *n.* (in medieval philosophy) the quality of those things having substance independently of any real object. [1685–95; < ML *perseitās,* equiv. to L *per sē* PER SE + *-itās* -ITY]

Per·seph·o·ne (pər sef′ə nē), *n.* **1.** Also, **Proserpina, Proserpine.** *Class. Myth.* a daughter of Zeus and Demeter, abducted by Pluto to be queen of Hades, but allowed to return to the surface of the earth for part of the year. **2.** a female given name.

Per·sep·o·lis (pər sep′ə lis), *n.* an ancient capital of Persia: its imposing ruins are in S Iran, ab. 30 mi. (48 km) NE of Shiraz. —**Per·se·pol·i·tan** (pûr′sə pol′i tn), *adj., n.*

Per·ses (pûr′sēz), *n. Class. Myth.* **1.** a son of Perseus and Andromeda and the ancestor of the kings of Persia. **2.** brother of King Aeëtes of Colchis. Having murdered Aeëtes and seized the throne, Perses was killed by his niece Medea and her son Medus.

Per·se·us (pûr′sē əs, -syo͞os), *n., gen.* **-se·i** (-sē ī′) for 3. **1.** *Class. Myth.* a hero, the son of Zeus and Danaë, who slew the Gorgon Medusa, and afterward saved Andromeda from a sea monster. **2.** *Astron.* a northern constellation between Cassiopeia and Taurus, containing the variable star Algol.

Per′seus clus′ter, *Astron.* a cluster of about 500 galaxies in the direction of the constellation Perseus, grouped around a particular Seyfert galaxy that is an intense radio source (**Perseus A**).

per·se·ver·ance (pûr′sə vēr′əns), *n.* **1.** steady persistence in a course of action, a purpose, a state, etc., esp. in spite of difficulties, obstacles, or discouragement. **2.** *Theol.* continuance in a state of grace to the end, leading to eternal salvation. [1300–50; ME *perseveraunce* < MF *perseverance* < L *persevērantia.* See PERSEVERE, -ANCE] —**per′se·ver′ant,** *adj.*
—**Syn. 1.** doggedness, steadfastness. PERSEVERANCE, PERSISTENCE, TENACITY, PERTINACITY imply resolute and unyielding holding on in following a course of action. PERSEVERANCE commonly suggests activity maintained in spite of difficulties or steadfast and long-continued application: *Endurance and perseverance combined to win in the end.* It is regularly used in a favorable sense. PERSISTENCE, which may be used in either a favorable or an unfavorable sense, implies unremitting (and sometimes annoying) perseverance: *persistence in a belief; persistence in talking when others wish to study.* TENACITY, with the original meaning of adhesiveness, as of glue, is a dogged and determined holding on. Whether used literally or figuratively it has favorable implications: *a bulldog quality of tenacity; the tenacity of one's memory.* PERTINACITY, unlike its related word, is used chiefly in an unfavorable sense, that of overinsistent tenacity: *the pertinacity of the social climber.*

per·sev·er·ate (pər sev′ə rāt′), *v.i.,* **-at·ed, -at·ing.** to repeat something insistently or redundantly: *to perseverate in reminding children of their responsibilities.* [1910–15; back formation from PERSEVERATION] —**per·sev′er·a′tive,** *adj.*

per·sev·er·a·tion (pər sev′ə rā′shən), *n.* **1.** the act or process of perseverating. **2.** *Psychiatry.* the pathological, persistent repetition of a word, gesture, or act, often associated with brain damage or schizophrenia. [1605–15 in sense "perseverance"; PERSEVERE + -ATION, or < L *persevērātiōn-,* s. of *persevērātiō*]

per·se·vere (pûr′sə vēr′), *v.,* **-vered, -ver·ing.** —*v.i.* **1.** to persist in anything undertaken; maintain a purpose in spite of difficulty, obstacles, or discouragement; continue steadfastly. **2.** to persist in speech, interrogation, argument, etc.; insist. —*v.t.* **3.** to bolster, sustain, or uphold: *unflagging faith that had persevered him.* [1325–75; ME *perseveren* < MF *perseverer* < L *persevērāre* to persist, deriv. of *persevērus* very strict. See PER-, SEVERE]
—**Syn. 1.** See **continue.**

per·se·ver·ing (pûr′sə vēr′ing), *adj.* displaying perseverance; resolutely persistent; steadfast: *a persevering student.* [1640–50; PERSEVERE + -ING[2]] —**per′se·ver′ing·ly,** *adv.*

Per·shing (pûr′shing *or, for* 2, -zhing), *n.* **1. John Joseph** (*"Blackjack"*), 1860–1948, U.S. general: commander of the American Expeditionary Forces in World War I. **2.** *Mil.* **a.** a 46-ton (42 m ton) U.S. heavy tank of 1944–52, with a five-man crew and a 90mm gun. **b.** a two-stage surface-to-surface ballistic missile.

Pershing II, a 38-ft. (12 m) U.S. Army surface-to-surface nuclear missile with a single warhead and range of more than 1000 mi. (1609 km).

Per·sia (pûr′zhə, -shə), *n.* **1.** Also called **Persian Empire.** an ancient empire located in W and SW Asia: at its height it extended from Egypt and the Aegean to India; conquered by Alexander the Great 334–331 B.C. **2.** former official name (until 1935) of **Iran.**

Per·sian (pûr′zhən, -shən), *adj.* **1.** of or pertaining to ancient and recent Persia (now Iran), its people, or their language. —*n.* **2.** a member of the native peoples of Iran, descended in part from the ancient Iranians. **3.** a citizen of ancient Persia. **4.** an Iranian language, the principal language of Iran and western Afghanistan, in its historical and modern forms. Cf. **Old Persian, Pahlavi, Farsi. 5.** *Archit.* a figure of a man used as a column. **6. Persians.** See **Persian blinds.** [1325–75; PERSI(A) + -AN; r. ME *Persien* < MF; r. OE *Persisc* (see -ISH[1])]

Per′sian blinds′, 1. outside window shutters made of thin, movable horizontal slats. **2.** (loosely) venetian blinds.

Per′sian car′pet, a handwoven carpet or rug produced in Iran and characterized by fine warp and filling yarns, a usually tight, even pile made with the Sehna knot, and a variety of floral, foliate, animal, and avian designs woven in rich, harmonious colors. Also called **Persian rug.** [1610–20]

Persian cat

Per′sian cat′, a long-haired variety of the domestic cat, originally raised in Persia and Afghanistan. [1815–25]

Per′sian Em′pire, Persia (def. 1).

Per′sian Gulf′, an arm of the Arabian Sea, between SW Iran and Arabia. 600 mi. (965 km) long. Also called **Arabian Gulf.**

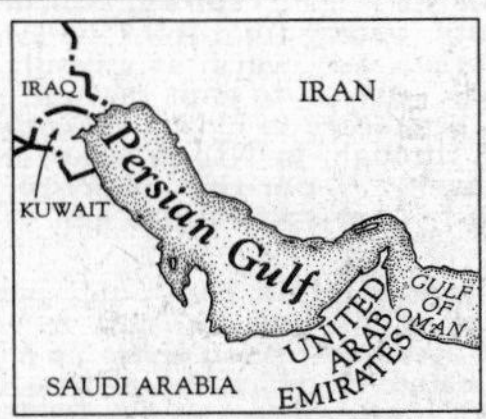

Per′sian Gulf′ States′. See **Gulf States** (def. 2).

Per′sian knot′. See **Sehna knot.**

Per′sian lamb′, **1.** the young lamb of the Karakul sheep. **2.** the lustrous, tightly curled fur of this animal, used to make coats and hats and as a trimming on various kinds of apparel and accessories. [1885–90]

Per′sian li′lac, an Asian lilac, *Syringa persica,* having pale reddish-purple flowers. [1630–40]

Per′sian mel′on, **1.** a round variety of muskmelon having a green, reticulate, unribbed rind and orange flesh. **2.** the plant bearing this fruit.

Per′sian rug′. See **Persian carpet.**

Persians, The, a tragedy (472 B.C.) by Aeschylus.

Per′sian vi′olet, any of several plants belonging to the genus *Exacum,* native to the Old World, as *E. affine,* having glossy, ovate leaves, and fragrant, bluish flowers: cultivated as a houseplant.

Per′sian wal′nut. See **English walnut.**

Per•si•chet•ti (pûr′si ket′ē), *n.* **Vincent,** born 1915, U.S. composer.

per•si•ennes (pûr′zē enz′; *Fr.* per syen′), *n.* **1.** (*used with a plural v.*) See **Persian blinds. 2.** (*used with a singular v.*) a printed or painted fabric of cotton or silk. [1835–45; < F, n. use of pl. of *persienne,* fem. of *persien,* obs. var. of *persan* PERSIAN]

per•si•flage (pûr′sə fläzh′, pâr′-), *n.* **1.** light, bantering talk or writing. **2.** a frivolous or flippant style of treating a subject. [1750–60; < F, deriv. of *persifler* to banter, equiv. to *per-* PER- + *siffler* to whistle, hiss < LL *sifilāre,* for L *sībilāre;* see SIBILANT, -AGE]
—Syn. 1. banter, badinage, jesting.

per•sim•mon (pər sim′ən), *n.* **1.** any of several trees of the genus *Diospyros,* esp. *D. virginiana,* of North America, bearing astringent, plumlike fruit that is sweet and edible when ripe, and *D. kaki,* of Japan and China, bearing soft, red or orange fruit. **2.** the fruit itself. [1605–15, *Amer.;* < Virginia Algonquian (E sp.) *pessemmins, pichamins, pushemins, putchamins* (unidentified initial element + reflex of Proto-Algonquian **-min-* fruit, berry)]

per•sist (pər sist′, -zist′), *v.i.* **1.** to continue steadfastly or firmly in some state, purpose, course of action, or the like, esp. in spite of opposition, remonstrance, etc.: *to persist in working for world peace; to persist in unpopular political activities.* **2.** to last or endure tenaciously: *The legend of King Arthur has persisted for nearly fifteen centuries.* **3.** to be insistent in a statement, request, question, etc. [1530–40; < L *persistere* lit., to stand firm permanently, equiv. to *per-* PER- + *-sistere,* akin to *stāre* to STAND] **—per•sist′er,** *n.* **—per•sist′ing•ly,** *adv.* **—per•sis′tive,** *adj.* **—per•sis′tive•ly,** *adv.* **—per•sis′tive•ness,** *n.*
—Syn. 1, 2. See **continue. 3.** insist.

per•sist•ence (pər sis′təns, -zis′-), *n.* **1.** the act or fact of persisting. **2.** the quality of being persistent: *You have persistence, I'll say that for you.* **3.** continued existence or occurrence: *the persistence of smallpox.* **4.** the continuance of an effect after its cause is removed. Also, **per•sist′en•cy.** [1540–50; PERSIST + -ENCE]
—Syn. 1. See **perseverance.**

persist′ence of vi′sion, the retention of a visual image for a short period of time after the removal of the stimulus that produced it: the phenomenon that produces the illusion of movement when viewing motion pictures. [1900–05]

per•sist•ent (pər sis′tənt, -zis′-), *adj.* **1.** persisting, esp. in spite of opposition, obstacles, discouragement, etc.; persevering: *a most annoyingly persistent young man.* **2.** lasting or enduring tenaciously: *the persistent aroma of verbena; a persistent cough.* **3.** constantly repeated; continued: *persistent noise.* **4.** *Biol.* **a.** continuing or permanent. **b.** having continuity of phylogenetic characteristics. **5.** *Bot.* remaining attached beyond the usual time, as flowers, flower parts, or leaves. [1820–30; < L *persistent-* (s. of *persistēns*), prp. of *persistere* to PERSIST; see -ENT] **—per•sist′ent•ly,** *adv.*
—Syn. 1. indefatigable, pertinacious, tenacious. See **stubborn. 3.** steady. **—Ant. 3.** sporadic.

Per•sius (pûr′shəs, -shē əs), *n.* (*Aulus Persius Flaccus*), A.D. 34–62, Roman satirist.

per•snick•et•y (pər snik′i tē), *adj. Informal.* **1.** overparticular; fussy. **2.** snobbish or having the aloof attitude of a snob. **3.** requiring painstaking care. Also, **pernickety.** [1885–90; orig. Scots, var. of PERNICKETY] **—per•snick′et•i•ness,** *n.*
—Syn. 1. nitpicking, finicky.

per•son (pûr′sən), *n.* **1.** a human being, whether man, woman, or child: *The table seats four persons.* **2.** a human being as distinguished from an animal or a thing. **3.** *Sociol.* an individual human being, esp. with reference to his or her social relationships and behavioral patterns as conditioned by the culture. **4.** *Philos.* a self-conscious or rational being. **5.** the actual self or individual personality of a human being: *You ought not to generalize, but to consider the person you are dealing with.* **6.** the body of a living human being, sometimes including the clothes being worn: *He had no money on his person.* **7.** the body in its external aspect: *an attractive person to look at.* **8.** a character, part, or role, as in a play or story. **9.** an individual of distinction or importance. **10.** a person not entitled to social recognition or respect. **11.** *Law.* a human being **(natural person)** or a group of human beings, a corporation, a partnership, an estate, or other legal entity **(artificial person** or **juristic person)** recognized by law as having rights and duties. **12.** *Gram.* a category found in many languages that is used to distinguish between the speaker of an utterance and those to or about whom he or she is speaking. In English there are three persons in the pronouns, the first represented by *I* and *we,* the second by *you,* and the third by *he, she, it,* and *they.* Most verbs have distinct third person singular forms in the present tense, as *writes;* the verb *be* has, in addition, a first person singular form *am.* **13.** *Theol.* any of the three hypostases or modes of being in the Trinity, namely the Father, the Son, and the Holy Ghost. **14. be one's own person,** to be free from restrictions, control, or dictatorial influence: *Now that she's working, she feels that she's her own person.* **15. in person,** in one's own bodily presence; personally: *Applicants are requested to apply in person.* [1175–1225; ME *persone* < L *persōna* role (in life, a play, or a tale) (LL: member of the Trinity), orig. actor's mask < Etruscan *phersu* (< Gk *prósōpa* face, mask) + *-na* a suffix]
—Syn. 1. PERSON, INDIVIDUAL, PERSONAGE are terms applied to human beings. PERSON is the most general and common word: *the average person.* INDIVIDUAL views a person as standing alone or as a single member of a group: *the characteristics of the individual;* its implication is sometimes derogatory: *a disagreeable individual.* PERSONAGE is used (sometimes ironically) of an outstanding or illustrious person: *We have a distinguished personage visiting us today.*
—Usage. See **individual, party, people, they.**

-person, a combining form of **person,** replacing in existing compound words such paired, sex-specific forms as **-man** and **-woman** or **-er**[1] and **-ess:** *chairperson; salesperson; waitperson.*
—Usage. The -PERSON compounds are increasingly used, especially in the press, on radio and television, and in government and corporate communications, with the object of avoiding sex discrimination in language. Earlier practice was to use *-man* as the final element in such compounds regardless of the sex of the person referred to (*anchorman; businessman*) or to use *-woman* when referring to a woman (*anchorwoman; businesswoman*). Some object to these new -PERSON compounds on the grounds that they are awkward or unnecessary, insisting that the equivalent and long-used compounds in *-man* are generic, not sex-marked. Others reject the *-man* compounds as discriminatory when applied to women or to persons whose sex is unknown or irrelevant. See also **chairperson, -ess, lady, -man, -woman.**

per•so•na (pər sō′nə), *n., pl.* **-nae** (-nē), **-nas. 1.** a person. **2. personae,** the characters in a play, novel, etc. **3.** the narrator of or a character in a literary work, sometimes identified with the author. **4.** (in the psychology of C. G. Jung) the mask or façade presented to satisfy the demands of the situation or the environment and not representing the inner personality of the individual; the public personality (contrasted with *anima*). **5.** a person's perceived or evident personality, as that of a well-known official, actor, or celebrity; personal image; public role. [1905–10; < L *persōna* mask, character. See PERSON]

per•son•a•ble (pûr′sə nə bəl), *adj.* **1.** of pleasing personal appearance; handsome or comely; attractive. **2.** having an agreeable or pleasing personality; affable; amiable; sociable. [1400–50; late ME; see PERSON, -ABLE] **—per′son•a•ble•ness,** *n.* **—per′son•a•bly,** *adv.*

Per•so•nae (pər sō′nē), *n.* a collection of poems (1926) by Ezra Pound.

per•son•age (pûr′sə nij), *n.* **1.** a person of distinction or importance. **2.** any person. **3.** a character in a play, story, etc. [1425–75; late ME: body or image (statue, portrait) of a person (< OF) < ML *persōnāgium.* See PERSON, -AGE]
—Syn. 1. See **person.**

per•so•na gra•ta (per sō′nä grä′tä; *Eng.* pər sō′nə grä′tə, grā′tə, grat′ə), *pl.* ***per•so•nae gra•tae*** (per sō′ni grä′ti; *Eng.* pər sō′nē grä′tē, grā′-, grat′ē). *Latin.* an acceptable person, esp. a diplomatic representative acceptable to the government to which he or she is accredited.

per•son•al (pûr′sə nl), *adj.* **1.** of, pertaining to, or coming as from a particular person; individual; private: *a personal opinion.* **2.** relating to, directed to, or intended for a particular person: *a personal favor; one's personal life; a letter marked "Personal."* **3.** intended for use by one person: *a personal car.* **4.** referring or directed to a particular person in a disparaging or offensive sense or manner, usually involving character, behavior, appearance, etc.: *personal remarks.* **5.** making personal remarks or attacks: *to become personal in a dispute.* **6.** done, carried out, held, etc., in person: *a personal interview.* **7.** pertaining to or characteristic of a person or self-conscious being: *That is my personal belief.* **8.** of the nature of an individual rational being. **9.** pertaining to the body, clothing, or appearance: *personal cleanliness.* **10.** provided for one's discretionary use: *Employees are allowed 15 vacation days and two personal days.* **11.** *Gram.* **a.** noting person: *In Latin* portō *"I carry," -ō is a personal ending.* **b.** of, pertaining to, or characteristic of the personal pronoun. **12.** *Law.* of or pertaining to personal property: *personal interests.* **—n. 13.** *Journalism.* **a.** a short news paragraph in a newspaper concerning a particular person, as one who is socially prominent, or a group of particular persons who are socially prominent. **b.** a brief, private notice in a newspaper or magazine, often addressed to a particular person and typically bearing an abbreviated salutation and signature to preserve its confidentiality, usually printed in a special part of the classified advertising section. **c.** a similar notice placed by a person seeking companionship, a spouse, etc. **d.** Usually, **personals.** a column, page, or section of a newspaper, magazine, etc., featuring such notices or items. [1350–1400; ME < LL *persōnālis.* See PERSON, -AL[1]] **—per′son•al•ness,** *n.*

per′sonal comput′er, a microcomputer designed for individual use, as by a person in an office or at home or school, for such applications as word processing, data management, financial analysis, or computer games. *Abbr.:* PC [1975–80]

per′sonal dis′tance. See **personal space.** [1965–70]

per′sonal effects′, privately owned articles consisting chiefly of clothing, toilet items, etc., for intimate use by an individual. Cf. **household effects.** [1835–45]

per′sonal equa′tion, the tendency to personal bias that accounts for variation in interpretation or approach and for which allowance must be made. [1835–45]

per′sonal flota′tion device′, a life preserver, life jacket, or other device for keeping a person afloat in the water: esp. in Coast Guard use. *Abbr.:* PFD [1970–75]

per′sonal foul′, *Sports.* a foul called in certain games, as basketball or football, for illegal body contact or rough, unsportsmanlike play. [1820–30]

per•so•na•li•a (pûr′sə nā′lē ə, -nāl′yə), *n.pl.* **1.** personal belongings. **2.** biographical data, personal reminiscences, or the like: *He could never keep the personalia out of his essays.* [1900–05; < LL, neut. pl. of L *persōnālis* PERSONAL]

per′sonal identifica′tion num′ber, *Computers.* See **PIN.**

per•son•al•ism (pûr′sə nl iz′əm), *n.* **1.** Also called **per′sonal ide′alism.** a modern philosophical movement locating ultimate value and reality in persons, human or divine. **2.** *Psychol.* an approach stressing individual personality as the central concern of psychology. [1840–50; PERSONAL + -ISM] **—per′son•al•ist,** *n.* **—per′son•al•is′tic,** *adj.*

per•son•al•i•ty (pûr′sə nal′i tē), *n., pl.* **-ties. 1.** the visible aspect of one's character as it impresses others: *He has a pleasing personality.* **2.** a person as an embodiment of a collection of qualities: *He is a curious personality.* **3.** *Psychol.* **a.** the sum total of the physical, mental, emotional, and social characteristics of an individual. **b.** the organized pattern of behavioral characteristics of the individual. **4.** the quality of being a person; existence as a self-conscious human being; personal identity. **5.** the essential character of a person. **6.** something apprehended as reflective of or analogous to a distinctive human personality, as the atmosphere of a place or thing: *This house has a warm personality.* **7.** a famous, notable, or prominent person; celebrity. **8.** application or reference to a particular person or particular persons, often in disparagement or hostility. **9.** a disparaging or offensive statement referring to a particular person: *The political debate deteriorated into personalities.* [1350–1400; ME *personalite* (< MF) < LL *persōnālitās.* See PERSONAL, -ITY]
—Syn. 1. See **character.**

personal′ity disor′der, *Psychiatry.* any of a group of mental disorders characterized by deeply ingrained maladaptive patterns of behavior and personality style, which are usually recognizable as early as adolescence and are often lifelong in duration. [1935–40]

personal′ity in′ventory, *Psychol.* a questionnaire designed to measure personality types or characteristics. [1930–35]

personal′ity test′, *Psychol.* an instrument, as a questionnaire or series of standardized tasks, used to measure personality characteristics or to discover personality disorders. [1910–15]

per•son•al•ize (pûr′sə nl īz′), *v.t.,* **-ized, -iz•ing. 1.** to have marked with one's initials, name, or monogram: *to personalize stationery.* **2.** to make personal, as by applying a general statement to oneself. **3.** to ascribe personal qualities to; personify. Also, *esp. Brit.,* **per′son•al•ise′.** [1720–30; PERSONAL + -IZE] **—per′son•al•i•za′tion,** *n.*

per′sonal lib′erty, the liberty of an individual to do his or her will freely except for those restraints imposed

CONCISE PRONUNCIATION KEY: *act, cāpe, dâre, pärt; set, ēqual; if, īce; ox, ōver, ôrder, oil, bo͝ok, bo͞ot, out; up, ûrge; child; sing; shoe; thin, that;* zh as in *treasure.* ə = *a* as in *alone, e* as in *system, i* as in *easily, o* as in *gallop, u* as in *circus;* ᵊ as in *fire* (fīᵊr), *hour* (ouᵊr). l and n can serve as syllabic consonants, as in *cradle* (krād′l), and *button* (but′n). See the full key inside the front cover.

by law to safeguard the physical, moral, political, and economic welfare of others. [1840–50]

per·son·al·ly (pûr′sə nl ē), *adv.* **1.** through direct contact; in person; directly: *I will thank him personally.* **2.** as if intended for or directed at one's own person: *to take someone's comments personally.* **3.** as regards oneself: *Personally, I don't care to go.* **4.** as an individual: *to like someone personally, but not as an employer.* [1350–1400; ME; see PERSONAL, -LY]

per′son·al-o·pin′ion tel′egram (pûr′sə nl ə pin′yən), **1.** a type of domestic telegram sent at the lowest rate with a minimum charge for 20 words or less to elected federal or state officials on a subject of national or regional interest. **2.** the service offering such a telegram. Cf. **fast telegram, overnight telegram.**

per′sonal pro′noun, *Gram.* any one of the pronouns used to refer to the speaker, or to one or more to or about whom or which he or she is speaking, as, in English, *I, we, you, he, she, it, they.* [1660–70]

per′sonal prop′erty, *Law.* an estate or property consisting of movable articles both corporeal, as furniture or jewelry, or incorporeal, as stocks or bonds (distinguished from *real property*). [1830–40] —**Syn.** chattels, effects.

per′sonal rap′id tran′sit, a short system of small, self-propelled, automated, rubber-tired vehicles that usually run on elevated concrete tracks and allow a passenger a limited selection of routes, as in an amusement park or at an airport. *Abbr.:* PRT

per′sonal space′, the variable and subjective distance at which one person feels comfortable talking to another. Also called **personal distance.**

per′sonal staff′, *Mil.* the aides of a general officer or a flag officer. Cf. **general staff, special staff.**

per·son·al·ty (pûr′sə nl tē), *n., pl.* **-ties.** *Law.* personal estate or property. [1600–10; < AF *personalte* < LL *persōnālitās* PERSONALITY]

per·so·na non gra·ta (peʀ sō′nä nōn grä′tä; *Eng.* pər sō′nə non grä′tə, grā′-, grat′ə), *pl.* **per·so·nae non gra·tae** (peʀ sō′nī nōn grä′tī; *Eng.* pər sō′nē non grä′tē, grā′-, grat′ē). *Latin.* **1.** a person who is not welcome: *He has become persona non grata in our club since his angry outburst.* **2.** a diplomatic representative unacceptable to an accrediting government.

per·son·ate[1] (pûr′sə nāt′), *v.,* **-at·ed, -at·ing.** —*v.t.* **1.** to act or portray (a character in a play, a part, etc.). **2.** to assume the character or appearance of; pass oneself off as, esp. with fraudulent intent; impersonate. **3.** to represent in terms of personal properties or characteristics; personify. —*v.i.* **4.** to act or play a part. [1590–1600; v. use of L *persōnātus* PERSONATE[2]] —**per′son·a′tion,** *n.* —**per′son·a′tive,** *adj.* —**per′son·a′tor,** *n.*

per·son·ate[2] (pûr′sə nit, -nāt′), *adj.* **1.** *Bot.* **a.** (of a bilabiate corolla) masklike. See illus. under **corolla. b.** having the lower lip pushed upward so as to close the gap between the lips, as in the snapdragon. **2.** *Zool.* **a.** having a masked or disguised form, as the larvae of certain insects. **b.** having masklike markings. [1750–60; < NL, L *persōnātus* masked; see PERSONA, -ATE[1]] —**per′son·ate·ly,** *adv.*

per·son-day (pûr′sən dā′), *n.* a unit of measurement, esp. in accountancy, based on an ideal amount of work done by one person in one working day. [1965–70]

per·son·hood (pûr′sən ho͝od′), *n.* **1.** the state or fact of being a person. **2.** the state or fact of being an individual or having human characteristics and feelings: *a harsh prison system that deprives prisoners of their personhood.* [1955–60; PERSON + -HOOD]

per·son·i·fi·ca·tion (pər son′ə fi kā′shən), *n.* **1.** the attribution of a personal nature or character to inanimate objects or abstract notions, esp. as a rhetorical figure. **2.** the representation of a thing or abstraction in the form of a person, as in art. **3.** the person or thing embodying a quality or the like; an embodiment or incarnation: *He is the personification of tact.* **4.** an imaginary person or creature conceived or figured to represent a thing or abstraction. **5.** the act of personifying. **6.** a character portrayal or representation in a dramatic or literary work. [1745–55; PERSONI(FY) + -FICATION] —**per·son′i·fi·ca′tor,** *n.*

per·son·i·fy (pər son′ə fī′), *v.t.,* **-fied, -fy·ing.** **1.** to attribute human nature or character to (an inanimate object or an abstraction), as in speech or writing. **2.** to represent (a thing or abstraction) in the form of a person, as in art. **3.** to embody (a quality, idea, etc.) in a real person or a concrete thing. **4.** to be an embodiment or incarnation of; typify: *He personifies the ruthless ambition of some executives.* **5.** to personate. [1720–30; PERSON + -IFY; cf. F *personnifier,* It *personificare*] —**per·son′i·fi′a·ble,** *adj.* —**per·son′i·fi′ant,** *adj.* —**per·son′i·fi′er,** *n.* —**Syn. 4.** represent, exemplify, incorporate.

per·son·nel (pûr′sə nel′), *n.* **1.** a body of persons employed in an organization or place of work. **2.** (*used with a plural v.*) persons: *All personnel are being given the day off.* **3.** See **personnel department.** [1825–35; < F, n. use of *personnel* (adj.) PERSONAL < LL *persōnāle,* neut. of *persōnālis;* r. *personal* (n.), Anglicized form of F *personnel;* cf. G *Personal,* var. of *Personale,* It *personale.* See MATÉRIEL] —**Usage. 2.** Some usage guides object to the use of PERSONNEL as a plural. However, this use is well established and standard in all varieties of speech and writing. The use of PERSONNEL with a preceding number is largely restricted to business and government communications: *Six personnel were transferred.*

CONCISE ETYMOLOGY KEY: <, descended or borrowed from; >, whence; b., blend of, blended; c., cognate with; cf., compare; deriv., derivative; equiv., equivalent; imit., imitative; obl., oblique; r., replacing; s., stem; sp., spelling, spelled; resp., respelling, respelled; trans., translation; ?, origin unknown; *, unattested; ‡, probably earlier than. See the full key inside the front cover.

personnel′ a′gency, an agency for placing employable persons in jobs; employment agency.

personnel′ depart′ment, the department in an organization dealing with matters involving employees, as hiring, training, labor relations, and benefits. Also called **human resources department.** [1940–45]

per·son-to-per·son (pûr′sən tə pûr′sən), *adj.* **1.** (of a long-distance telephone call) chargeable only upon speaking with a specified person at the number called: *a person-to-person call to her brother in California.* Cf. **station-to-station. 2.** involving personal or intimate contact between persons: *person-to-person diplomacy; a disease contracted through person-to-person contacts.* —*adv.* **3.** (in making a long-distance telephone call) to a specified person: *I telephoned him person-to-person.* Cf. **station-to-station. 4.** face-to-face; in person: *They interviewed her person-to-person.* [1915–20]

per·son-year (pûr′sən yēr′), *n.* a unit of measurement, esp. in accountancy, based on an ideal amount of work done by one person in a year consisting of a standard number of person-days.

per·sorp·tion (pər sôrp′shən, -zôrp′-), *n. Physical Chem.* the deep penetration of a liquid into a highly porous solid, resulting in an intimate mixture. [1925–30; PER- + (AD)SORPTION]

per·spec·tive (pər spek′tiv), *n.* **1.** a technique of depicting volumes and spatial relationships on a flat surface. Cf. **aerial perspective, linear perspective. 2.** a picture employing this technique, esp. one in which it is prominent: *an architect's perspective of a house.* **3.** a visible scene, esp. one extending to a distance; vista: *a perspective on the main axis of an estate.* **4.** the state of existing in space before the eye: *The elevations look all right, but the building's composition is a failure in perspective.* **5.** the state of one's ideas, the facts known to one, etc., in having a meaningful interrelationship: *You have to live here a few years to see local conditions in perspective.* **6.** the faculty of seeing all the relevant data in a meaningful relationship: *Your data is admirably detailed but it lacks perspective.* **7.** a mental view or prospect: *the dismal perspective of terminally ill patients.* —*adj.* **8.** of or pertaining to the art of perspective, or represented according to its laws. [1350–1400; ME < ML *perspectīva* (*ars*) optical (science), *perspectīvum* optical glass, n. uses of fem. and neut. of *perspectīvus* optical, equiv. to L *perspect-,* ptp. s. of *perspicere* to look at closely (see PER-, INSPECT) + *-īvus* -IVE] —**per·spec′tiv·al,** *adj.* —**per·spec′tived,** *adj.* —**per·spec′tive·less,** *adj.* —**per·spec′tive·ly,** *adv.*

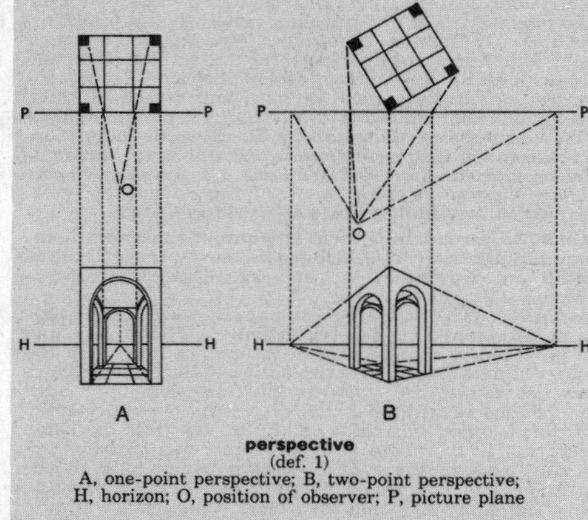

perspective
(def. 1)
A, one-point perspective; B, two-point perspective; H, horizon; O, position of observer; P, picture plane

per·spec·tiv·ism (pər spek′tə viz′əm), *n. Philos.* the doctrine that reality is known only in terms of the perspectives of it seen by individuals or groups at particular moments. [1905–10; < G *Perspektivismus.* See PERSPECTIVE, -ISM] —**per·spec′tiv·ist,** *n., adj.*

per·spi·ca·cious (pûr′spi kā′shəs), *adj.* **1.** having keen mental perception and understanding; discerning: *to exhibit perspicacious judgment.* **2.** *Archaic.* having keen vision. [1610–20; PERSPICACI(TY) + -OUS] —**per′spi·ca′cious·ly,** *adv.* —**per′spi·ca′cious·ness,** *n.* —**Syn. 1.** perceptive, acute, shrewd, penetrating. —**Ant. 1.** dull, stupid.

per·spi·cac·i·ty (pûr′spi kas′i tē), *n.* **1.** keenness of mental perception and understanding; discernment; penetration. **2.** *Archaic.* keen vision. [1540–50; earlier *perspicacite* < LL *perspicācitās* sharpness of sight, equiv. to *perspicāci-* (s. of *perspicāx* sharp-sighted; see PERSPICUOUS) + *-tās* -TY[2]] —**Syn. 1.** shrewdness, acuity, astuteness, insight, acumen. See **perspicuity.** —**Ant. 1.** obtuseness.

per·spi·cu·i·ty (pûr′spi kyo͞o′i tē), *n.* **1.** clearness or lucidity, as of a statement. **2.** the quality of being perspicuous. [1470–80; < L *perspicuitās.* See PERSPICUOUS, -ITY] —**Syn. 1.** clarity, plainness, intelligibility. **2.** transparency. **3.** PERSPICUITY, PERSPICACITY are both derived from a Latin word meaning "to see through." PERSPICACITY refers to the power of seeing clearly, to clearness of insight or judgment: *a person of acute perspicacity; the perspicacity of his judgment.* PERSPICUITY refers to something that can be seen through, i.e., to lucidity, clearness of style or exposition, freedom from obscurity: *the perspicuity of her argument.* —**Ant. 2.** dimness, opacity.

per·spic·u·ous (pər spik′yo͞o əs), *adj.* **1.** clearly expressed or presented; lucid. **2.** perspicacious. [1470–80; < L *perspicuus* transparent, equiv. to *perspic-,* s. of *perspicere* to look or see through (*per-* PER- + *-spicere,* comb. form of *specere* to look; see INSPECT) + *-uus* deverbal adj. suffix] —**per·spic′u·ous·ly,** *adv.* —**per·spic′u·ous·ness,** *n.* —**Syn. 1.** intelligible, plain, distinct, explicit. —**Ant. 1.** obscure, indistinct.

per·spi·ra·tion (pûr′spə rā′shən), *n.* **1.** a salty, watery fluid secreted by the sweat glands of the skin, esp. when very warm as a result of strenuous exertion; sweat. **2.** the act or process of perspiring. [1605–15, in sense "a breathing through"; 1620–30 for current senses; < NL *perspīrātiōn-* (s. of *perspīrātiō*) imperceptible sweating, lit., a breathing through. See PERSPIRE, -ATION] —**Syn. 1.** PERSPIRATION, SWEAT refer primarily to moisture exuded by animals and people from the pores of the skin. PERSPIRATION is often regarded as the more polite word, and is often used overfastidiously by those who consider SWEAT coarse; but SWEAT is a strong word and in some cases obviously more appropriate: *a light perspiration; the sweat of his brow.* SWEAT is always used when referring to animals or objects: *Sweat drips from a horse's flanks.* It may also be used metaphorically of objects: *Sweat forms on apples after they are gathered.*

per·spir·a·to·ry (pər spī′rə tôr′ē, -tōr′ē, pûr′spər ə-), *adj.* of, pertaining to, or stimulating perspiration. [1715–25; PERSPIRAT(ION) + -ORY[1]]

per·spire (pər spīər′), *v.,* **-spired, -spir·ing.** —*v.i.* **1.** to secrete a salty, watery fluid from the sweat glands of the skin, esp. when very warm as a result of strenuous exertion; sweat. —*v.t.* **2.** to emit through pores; exude. [1640–50; < L *perspīrāre* to blow constantly (said of the wind), breathe through; in NL: to sweat imperceptibly. See PER-, INSPIRE] —**per·spir′a·bil′i·ty,** *n.* —**per·spir′a·ble,** *adj.* —**per·spir′ing·ly,** *adv.* —**per·spir′y,** *adj.*

per stir·pes (pûr stûr′pēz, pər), *Law.* pertaining to or noting a method of dividing an estate in which the descendants of a deceased person share as a group in the portion of the estate to which the deceased would have been entitled. Cf. **per capita** (def. 2). [1675–85; < L *per stirpēs* lit., by stocks]

per·suade (pər swād′), *v.t.,* **-suad·ed, -suad·ing.** **1.** to prevail on (a person) to do something, as by advising or urging: *We could not persuade him to wait.* **2.** to induce to believe by appealing to reason or understanding; convince: *to persuade the judge of the prisoner's innocence.* [1505–15; < L *persuādēre.* See PER-, DISSUADE, SUASION] —**per·suad′a·ble,** *adj.* —**per·suad′a·bil′i·ty, per·suad′a·ble·ness,** *n.* —**per·suad′a·bly,** *adv.* —**per·suad′ing·ly,** *adv.* —**Syn. 1.** urge, influence, move, entice, impel. PERSUADE, INDUCE imply influencing someone's thoughts or actions. They are used today mainly in the sense of winning over a person to a certain course of action: *It was I who persuaded him to call a doctor. I induced him to do it.* They differ in that PERSUADE suggests appealing more to the reason and understanding: *I persuaded him to go back to his wife* (although it is often lightly used: *Can't I persuade you to stay to supper?*); INDUCE emphasizes only the idea of successful influence, whether achieved by argument or by promise of reward: *What can I say that will induce you to stay at your job?* Owing to this idea of compensation, INDUCE may be used in reference to the influence of factors as well as of persons: *The prospect of a raise in salary was what induced him to stay.* —**Ant. 1.** dissuade. —**Usage.** See **convince.**

per·suad·er (pər swā′dər), *n.* **1.** a person or thing that persuades: *The cool lake was a most enticing persuader for those who liked to swim.* **2.** *Slang.* **a.** (in underworld use) a gun, blackjack, or other weapon. **b.** something that persuades, as by coercing or threatening: *Sometimes the teacher used a hickory persuader to get our attention.* [1530–40; PERSUADE + -ER[1]]

per·sua·si·ble (pər swā′sə bəl, -zə-), *adj.* capable of being persuaded; open to or yielding to persuasion. [1350–1400; ME < L *persuāsibilis* convincing, equiv. to *persuās(us)* (ptp. of *persuādēre* to PERSUADE; see SUASION) + *-ibil(is)* -IBLE] —**per·sua′si·bil′i·ty,** *n.*

per·sua·sion (pər swā′zhən), *n.* **1.** the act of persuading or seeking to persuade. **2.** the power of persuading; persuasive force. **3.** the state or fact of being persuaded or convinced. **4.** a deep conviction or belief. **5.** a form or system of belief, esp. religious belief: *the Quaker persuasion.* **6.** a sect, group, or faction holding or advocating a particular belief, idea, ideology, etc.: *Several of the people present are of the socialist persuasion.* **7.** *Facetious.* kind or sort. [1350–1400; late ME < L *persuāsiōn-* (s. of *persuāsiō;* see PER-, SUASION); r. ME *persuacioun* < MF *persuacion* < L, as above] —**Syn. 1.** See **advice.**

per·sua·sive (pər swā′siv, -ziv), *adj.* **1.** able, fitted, or intended to persuade: *a very persuasive argument.* —*n.* **2.** something that persuades; inducement. [1580–90; ML *persuāsīvus.* See PERSUASIBLE, -IVE] —**per·sua′sive·ly,** *adv.* —**per·sua′sive·ness,** *n.* —**Syn. 1.** convincing, compelling, forceful.

per·sul·fate (pər sul′fāt), *n. Chem.* a salt of persulfuric acid, as potassium persulfate, $K_2S_2O_5$ or $K_2S_2O_8$. [1805–15; PER- + SULFATE]

per′sul·fu′ric ac′id (pûr′sul fyo͝or′ik, pûr′-), *Chem.* **1.** Also called **Caro's acid, permonosulfuric acid, peroxymonosulfuric acid, peroxysulfuric acid.** a white, crystalline solid, H_2SO_5, used as an oxidizing agent for certain organic compounds. **2.** Also called **peroxydisulfuric acid.** a white, crystalline solid, $H_2S_2O_8$, used in the manufacture of hydrogen peroxide. [1880–85; PER- + SULFURIC]

pert (pûrt), *adj.,* **-er, -est.** **1.** boldly forward in speech or behavior; impertinent; saucy. **2.** jaunty and stylish; chic; natty. **3.** lively; sprightly; in good health. **4.** *Obs.* clever. [1200–50; ME, aph. var. of *apert* < OF < L *apertus* open (ptp. of *aperīre;* see APERIENT); in ME and OF, influenced by OF *aspert* < L *expertus* EXPERT] —**pert′ly,** *adv.* —**pert′ness,** *n.* —**Syn. 1.** presumptuous, impudent.

PERT (pûrt), *n.* a management method of controlling and analyzing a system or program using periodic time and money reports, often computer generated, to determine dollar and labor status at any given time. [*P*(*rogram*) *E*(*valuation and*) *R*(*eview*) *T*(*echnique*)]

pert., pertaining.

per·tain (pər tān′), *v.i.* **1.** to have reference or relation; relate: *documents pertaining to the lawsuit.* **2.** to belong or be connected as a part, adjunct, possession, or attribute. **3.** to belong properly or fittingly; be appropriate. [1300–50; ME *pertenen, partenen, perteinen* < MF *partein-,* tonic s. of *partenir* < L *pertinēre* to be applicable, lit., to hold through, reach, equiv. to *per-* PER- + *-tinēre,* comb. form of *tenēre* to hold]

Perth (pûrth), *n.* **1.** Also called **Perthshire.** a historic county in central Scotland. **2.** a city in this county: a port on the Tay River. 42,438. **3.** a city in and the capital of Western Australia, in SW Australia. 809,035.

Perth′ Am′boy (am′boi), a seaport in E New Jersey. 38,951.

perth·ite (pûr′thit), *n. Mineral* a variety of feldspar containing irregular bands of albite in microcline. [1832; named after *Perth,* Ontario, Canada; see -ITE[1]] —**per·thit·ic** (pər thit′ik), *adj.* —**per·thit′i·cal·ly,** *adv.*

Perth·shire (pûrth′shēr, -shər), *n.* Perth (def. 1).

per·ti·na·cious (pûr′tn ā′shəs), *adj.* **1.** holding tenaciously to a purpose, course of action, or opinion; resolute. **2.** stubborn or obstinate. **3.** extremely or objectionably persistent: *a pertinacious salesman from whom I could not escape.* [1620–30; PERTINACI(TY) + -OUS] —**per′ti·na′cious·ly,** *adv.* —**per′ti·na′cious·ness,** *n.*
—**Syn. 1.** persevering. **2.** dogged.

per·ti·nac·i·ty (pûr′tn as′i tē), *n.* the quality of being pertinacious; persistence. [1495–1505; < LL *pertinācitās,* for L *pertinācia* stubbornness, perseverance (> obs. *pertinacy*), equiv. to *pertināci-* (s. of *pertināx*) steadfast, stubborn + *-tās* -TY[2]. See PER-, TENACITY]
—**Syn.** firmness, determination, resolution. See **perseverance.**

per·ti·nent (pûr′tn ənt), *adj.* pertaining or relating directly and significantly to the matter at hand; relevant: *pertinent details.* [1350–1400; ME < L *pertinent-* (s. of *pertinēns*), prp. of *pertinēre* to PERTAIN; see -ENT] —**per′ti·nence, per′ti·nen·cy,** *n.* —**per′ti·nent·ly,** *adv.*
—**Syn.** appropriate, fitting, fit, suitable, applicable. See **apt.** —**Ant.** irrelevant.

per·turb (pər tûrb′), *v.t.* **1.** to disturb or disquiet greatly in mind; agitate. **2.** to throw into great disorder; derange. **3.** *Astron.* to cause perturbation in the orbit of (a celestial body). [1325–75; ME *perturben* (< OF *perturber*) < L *perturbāre* to throw into confusion, equiv. to *per-* PER- + *turbāre* to disturb; see TURBID] —**per·turb′a·ble,** *adj.* —**per·turb′a·bil′i·ty,** *n.* —**per·tur·ba·tious** (pûr′tər bā′shəs), *adj.* —**per·turb·ed·ly** (pər tûr′bid lē), *adv.* —**per·turb′ed·ness,** *n.* —**per·turb′er, per·tur·ba·tor** (pûr′tər bā′tər), *n.* —**per·turb′ing·ly,** *adv.* —**per·turb′ment,** *n.*
—**Syn. 1.** trouble. **2.** confuse, addle, muddle. —**Ant. 1.** pacify.

per·tur·ba·tion (pûr′tər bā′shən), *n.* **1.** the act of perturbing. **2.** the state of being perturbed. **3.** mental disquiet, disturbance, or agitation. **4.** a cause of mental disquiet, disturbance, or agitation. **5.** *Astron.* deviation of a celestial body from a regular orbit about its primary, caused by the presence of one or more other bodies that act upon the celestial body. [1325–75; < L *perturbātiōn-* (s. of *perturbātiō;* see PERTURB, -ATION); r. ME *perturbacioun* < AF < L, as above] —**per′tur·ba′tion·al,** *adj.*

per·tur·ba·tive (pûr′tər bā′tiv, pər tûr′bə tiv), *adj.* having a tendency to perturb; disturbing. [1630–40; < LL *perturbātīvus.* See PERTURBATION, -IVE]

per·tus·sis (pər tus′is), *n. Pathol.* See **whooping cough.** [1790–1800; < NL, equiv. to L *per-* PER- + *tussis* a cough] —**per·tus′sal,** *adj.*

Pe·ru (pə rōō′), *n.* **1.** Spanish, **Pe·rú** (pe rōō′). a republic in W South America. 15,500,000; 496,222 sq. mi. (1,285,215 sq. km). *Cap.:* Lima. **2.** a city in N central Indiana. 13,764. **3.** a city in N Illinois. 10,886. —**Pe·ru·vi·an** (pə rōō′vē ən), *adj., n.*

Peru′ bal′sam, a dark, molasseslike, aromatic, water-insoluble liquid having a warm, bitter taste, obtained from the leguminous tree, *Myroxylon pereirae,* of Central America: used in medicine, perfumery, and in the manufacture of chocolate. Also called **balsam of Peru, Peruvian balsam, black balsam, China oil, Indian balsam.**

Peru′ Cur′rent, a cold Pacific Ocean current flowing N along the coasts of Chile and Peru. Also called **Humboldt Current.**

Pe·ru·gia (pe rōō′jä; *Eng.* pə rōō′jə, -jē ə), *n.* **1.** a city in central Umbria, in central Italy. 136,933. **2. Lake of.** See **Trasimeno.** —**Pe·ru·gian** (pə rōō′jən, -jē ən), *adj., n.*

Pe·ru·gi·no (per′ōō jē′nō; *It.* pe′rōō jē′nô), (*Pietro Vannucci*), 1446–1524, Italian painter. —**Pe·ru·gin·esque** (pə rōō′jə nesk′, per′ōō-), *adj.*

pe·ruke (pə rōōk′), *n.* a man's wig of the 17th and 18th centuries, usually powdered and gathered at the back of the neck with a ribbon; periwig. [1540–50; < MF *perruque* head of hair, wig, of disputed orig.] —**pe·ruked′,** *adj.* —**pe·ruke′less,** *adj.*

pe·rus·al (pə rōō′zəl), *n.* **1.** a reading: *a perusal of the current books.* **2.** the act of perusing; survey; scrutiny: *A more careful perusal yields this conclusion.* [1590–1600; PERUSE + -AL[2]]

pe·ruse (pə rōōz′), *v.t.,* **-rused, -rus·ing. 1.** to read through with thoroughness or care: *to peruse a report.* **2.** to read. **3.** to survey or examine in detail. [1470–80 in sense "use up, go through"; 1525–35 for current senses; PER- + USE] —**pe·rus′a·ble,** *adj.* —**pe·rus′er,** *n.*

Per·utz (per′əts, pə rōōts′), *n.* **Max Ferdinand,** born 1914, English chemist, born in Austria: Nobel prize 1962.

Peru′vian bal′sam. See **Peru balsam.** [1740–50]

Peru′vian bark′, cinchona (def. 2). [1655–65]

Peru′vian mas′tic tree′, a pepper tree, *Schinus molle.* [1810–20]

Peru′vian rhat′any. See under **rhatany** (def. 1).

Pe·ruz·zi (pe rōōt′tsē), *n.* **Bal·das·sa·re Tom·ma·so** (bäl′däs sä′re tôm mä′zô), 1481–1536, Italian architect and painter.

per·vade (pər vād′), *v.t.,* **-vad·ed, -vad·ing.** to become spread throughout all parts of: *Spring pervaded the air.* [1645–55; < L *pervādere* to pass through, equiv. to *per-* PER- + *vādere* to go, walk] —**per·vad′er,** *n.* —**per·vad′ing·ly,** *adv.* —**per·vad′ing·ness,** *n.* —**per·va·sion** (pər vā′zhən), *n.* —**per·va·sive** (pər vā′siv), *adj.* —**per·va′sive·ly,** *adv.* —**per·va′sive·ness,** *n.*
—**Syn.** diffuse, fill.

per·verse (pər vûrs′), *adj.* **1.** willfully determined or disposed to go counter to what is expected or desired; contrary. **2.** characterized by or proceeding from such a determination or disposition: *a perverse mood.* **3.** wayward or cantankerous. **4.** persistent or obstinate in what is wrong. **5.** turned away from or rejecting what is right, good, or proper; wicked or corrupt. [1325–75; ME < L *perversus* facing the wrong way, askew, orig. ptp. of *pervertere.* See PERVERT] —**per·verse′ly,** *adv.* —**per·verse′ness,** *n.*
—**Syn. 1.** contumacious, disobedient. **4.** stubborn, headstrong. See **willful. 5.** evil, bad, sinful. —**Ant. 1.** agreeable. **4.** tractable.

per·ver·sion (pər vûr′zhən, -shən), *n.* **1.** the act of perverting. **2.** the state of being perverted. **3.** a perverted form of something. **4.** any of various means of obtaining sexual gratification that are generally regarded as being abnormal. **5.** *Pathol.* a change to what is unnatural or abnormal: *a perversion of function or structure.* [1350–1400; ME < L *perversiōn-* (s. of *perversiō*). See PERVERSE, -ION]

per·ver·si·ty (pər vûr′si tē), *n., pl.* **-ties** for 2. **1.** the state or quality of being perverse. **2.** an instance of this. [1520–30; < L *perversitās.* See PERVERSE, -ITY]

per·ver·sive (pər vûr′siv), *adj.* tending to pervert. [1685–95; < L *pervers(us)* PERVERSE + -IVE]

per·vert (*v.* pər vûrt′; *n.* pûr′vərt), *v.t.* **1.** to affect with perversion. **2.** to lead astray morally. **3.** to turn away from the right course. **4.** to lead into mental error or false judgment. **5.** to turn to an improper use; misapply. **6.** to misconstrue or misinterpret, esp. deliberately; distort: *to pervert someone's statement.* **7.** to bring to a less excellent state; vitiate; debase. **8.** *Pathol.* to change to what is unnatural or abnormal. **9.** to convert or persuade to a religious belief regarded as false or wrong. —*n.* **10.** a person who practices sexual perversion. **11.** *Pathol.* a person affected with perversion. **12.** a person who has been perverted, esp. to a religious belief regarded as erroneous. [1300–50; (v.) ME *perverten* < L *pervertere* to overturn, subvert, equiv. to *per-* PER- + *vertere* to turn; (n.) n. use of obs. *pervert* perverted] —**per·vert′er,** *n.* —**per·vert′i·ble,** *adj.* —**per·vert′i·bil′i·ty,** *n.* —**per·vert′i·bly,** *adv.*
—**Syn. 2.** seduce, corrupt, demoralize. **3.** divert. **4.** mislead, misguide. **7.** pollute, defile; impair, degrade.

per·vert·ed (pər vûr′tid), *adj.* **1.** *Pathol.* changed to or being of an unnatural or abnormal kind: *a perverted interest in death.* **2.** turned from what is right; wicked; misguided; distorted. **3.** affected with or caused by perversion. [1660–70; PERVERT + -ED[2]] —**per·vert′ed·ly,** *adv.* —**per·vert′ed·ness,** *n.*

per·vi·ca·cious (pûr′vi kā′shəs), *adj.* extremely willful; obstinate; stubborn. [1625–35; < L *pervicāc-,* s. of *pervicāx* stubborn, willful (*per-* PER- + *vic-,* var. s. of *vincere* to conquer (see VICTOR) + *-āx* adj. suffix denoting tendency or ability) + -IOUS] —**per′vi·ca′cious·ly,** *adv.* —**per′vi·ca′cious·ness,** *n.*

per·vi·ous (pûr′vē əs), *adj.* **1.** admitting of passage or entrance; permeable: *pervious soil.* **2.** open or accessible to reason, feeling, argument, etc. [1605–15; < L *pervius* passable, equiv. to *per-* PER- + *vi(a)* way, road + *-us* adj. suffix; see -OUS] —**per′vi·ous·ness,** *n.*

Per·vo·u·ralsk (pûr′və yŏŏ ralsk′; *Russ.* pyir və ōō-rälsk′), *n.* a city in the central RSFSR, in the Ural Mountains in Asia. 129,000.

pes (pēs, pās), *n., pl.* **pe·des** (pē′dēz, ped′ēz). *Anat., Zool.* a foot or footlike part. [1835–45; < L *pēs*]

Pe·sach (*Seph. Heb.* pe′säkh; *Ashk. Heb.* pā′säkh), *n. Judaism.* Passover (def. 1). Also, **Pe′sah.** [< Heb *pesaḥ*]

pe·sade (pə säd′, -zäd′, -zäd′), *n. Dressage.* a maneuver in which the horse is made to rear, keeping its hind legs stationary and its forelegs drawn in. [1720–30; < F, earlier *posade* < It *posata* a halt (see POSE[1], -ADE[1]); *pes-* by assoc. with *peser* to weigh. See POISE]

Pe·sa·ro (pe′zä rô), *n.* a seaport in E Italy, on the Adriatic Sea. 89,908.

Pes·ca·do·res (pes′kə dôr′is, -ēz, -dōr′-), *n.* (*used with a plural v.*) Penghu. Also called **Pes′cado′res Is′lands.**

Pe·sca·ra (pes kä′rä), *n.* a city in E Italy, on the Adriatic Sea. 135,612.

pe·se·ta (pə sā′tə; *Sp.* pe se′tä), *n., pl.* **-tas** (-təz; *Sp.* -täs). **1.** a bronze coin and monetary unit of Spain and Spanish territories, equal to 100 centimos. *Abbr.:* P., Pta. **2.** a former silver coin of Spain and Spanish America, equal to two reals; pistareen. **3.** a former monetary unit of Equatorial Guinea: replaced by the ekuele in 1973. [1805–15; < Sp, dim. of *pesa* a weight. See PESO]

pe·se·wa (pā sä′wä), *n., pl.* **-wa, -was.** a bronze coin and monetary unit of Ghana, the 100th part of a cedi.

Pe·sha·war (pe shä′wər), *n.* a city in N Pakistan, near the Khyber Pass: capital of the former North-West Frontier province. 555,000.

Pe·shit·ta (pə shē′tə), *n.* the principal Syriac version of the Bible. Also, **Pe·shi·to** (pə shē′tō).

pes·ky (pes′kē), *adj.,* **-ki·er, -ki·est.** *Informal.* annoyingly troublesome: *bothered by a pesky fly.* [1765–75; alter. of *pesty* (PEST + -Y[1])] —**pesk′i·ly,** *adv.* —**pesk′i·ness,** *n.*
—**Syn.** vexatious, irksome, bothersome, pestiferous.

pe·so (pā′sō; *Sp.* pe′sô), *n., pl.* **-sos** (-sōz; *Sp.* -sôs). **1.** a coin and monetary unit of Chile, Colombia, Cuba, the Dominican Republic, Guinea-Bissau, Mexico, and the Philippines, equal to 100 centavos. **2.** a coin and monetary unit of Uruguay, equal to 100 centesimos. **3.** a former monetary unit of Argentina, equal to 100 centavos: replaced by the austral in 1985. **4.** a former silver coin of Spain and Spanish America, equal to eight reals; dollar; piece of eight; piaster. [< Sp: lit., weight < L *pēnsum* something weighed, n. use of neut. of *pēnsus,* ptp. of *pendere* to weigh]

pe′so bolivia′no, *pl.* **pesos bolivianos.** a nickel-clad steel coin, paper money, and monetary unit of Bolivia, equal to 100 centavos: replaced the boliviano in 1963. [< Sp: Bolivian peso]

pes·sa·ry (pes′ə rē), *n., pl.* **-ries.** *Med.* **1.** a device worn in the vagina to support a displaced uterus. **2.** a vaginal suppository. **3.** diaphragm (def. 4). [1350–1400; ME *pessarie* < LL *pessārium* a suppository, equiv. to L *pess(um), pess(us)* (< Gk *pessós* oval stone used in a game) + *-ārium* -ARY]

pes·si·mism (pes′ə miz′əm), *n.* **1.** the tendency to see, anticipate, or emphasize only bad or undesirable outcomes, results, conditions, problems, etc.: *His pessimism about the future of our country depresses me.* **2.** the doctrine that the existing world is the worst of all possible worlds, or that all things naturally tend to evil. **3.** the belief that the evil and pain in the world are not compensated for by goodness and happiness. [1785–95; < L *pessim(us),* suppletive superl. of *malus* bad + -ISM; modeled on *optimism*]

pes·si·mist (pes′ə mist), *n.* **1.** a person who habitually sees or anticipates the worst or is disposed to be gloomy. **2.** an adherent of the doctrine of pessimism. [1830–40; PESSIM(ISM) + -IST]

pes·si·mis·tic (pes′ə mis′tik), *adj.* pertaining to or characterized by pessimism; gloomy: *a pessimistic outlook.* [1865–70; PESSIMIST + -IC] —**pes′si·mis′ti·cal·ly,** *adv.*
—**Syn.** despairing, hopeless. See **cynical.**

pest (pest), *n.* **1.** an annoying or troublesome person, animal, or thing; nuisance. **2.** an insect or other small animal that harms or destroys garden plants, trees, etc. **3.** a deadly epidemic disease, esp. a plague; pestilence. [1545–55; < L *pestis* plague]
—**Syn. 1.** annoyance. **3.** pandemic, scourge, epidemic.

Pest (pest; *Hung.* pesht), *n.* See under **Budapest.**

Pes·ta·loz·zi (pes′tl ot′sē; *It.* pes′tä lôt′tsē), *n.* **Jo·hann Hein·rich** (*Ger.* yō′hän hīn′rikh), 1746–1827, Swiss educational reformer. —**Pes′ta·loz′zi·an,** *adj., n.* —**Pes′ta·loz′zi·an·ism,** *n.*

pes·ter (pes′tər), *v.t.* **1.** to bother persistently with petty annoyances; trouble: *Don't pester me with your trivial problems.* **2.** *Obs.* to overcrowd. [1530–40; perh.

aph. var. of *empester, impester* to tangle, encumber (though *pester* is found earlier than these 2 words) < MF *empestrer* to hobble, entangle < VL **impāstōriāre* to hobble, equiv. to *im-* IM-[1] + *pāstōri(a)* a hobble, n. use of L *pāstōrius* of a herdsman or shepherd + *-āre* inf. suffix (see PASTOR); aph. form appar. reinforced by PEST (cf. -ER[6])] **—pes′ter·er,** *n.* **—pes′ter·ing·ly,** *adv.* **—pes′ter·some,** *adj.*

—Syn. 1. annoy, vex, tease, disturb; irritate, provoke, plague; badger, harry, hector. **—Ant. 1.** delight, entertain.

pest·hole (pest′hōl′), *n.* a place infested with or especially liable to epidemic disease. [1900–05; PEST + HOLE]

pest·house (pest′hous′), *n., pl.* **-hous·es** (-hou′ziz). a house or hospital for persons infected with pestilential disease. [1605–15; PEST + HOUSE]

pes·ti·cide (pes′tə sīd′), *n.* a chemical preparation for destroying plant, fungal, or animal pests. Also called **biocide.** [1935–40; PEST + -I- + -CIDE] **—pes′ti·cid′al,** *adj.*

pes·tif·er·ous (pe stif′ər əs), *adj.* **1.** bringing or bearing disease. **2.** pestilential. **3.** pernicious; evil. **4.** *Informal.* mischievous; troublesome or annoying. [1425–75; late ME < L *pestiferus* plague-bringing, equiv. to *pesti-* (s. of *pestis*) PEST + *-ferus* -FEROUS] **—pes·tif′er·ous·ly,** *adv.* **—pes·tif′er·ous·ness,** *n.*

pes·ti·lence (pes′tl əns), *n.* **1.** a deadly or virulent epidemic disease. **2.** See **bubonic plague. 3.** something that is considered harmful, destructive, or evil. [1275–1325; ME < MF < L *pestilentia.* See PESTILENT, -ENCE]

pes·ti·lent (pes′tl ənt), *adj.* **1.** producing or tending to produce infectious or contagious, often epidemic, disease; pestilential. **2.** destructive to life; deadly; poisonous. **3.** injurious to peace, morals, etc.; pernicious. **4.** troublesome, annoying, or mischievous. [1350–1400; ME < L *pestilent-* (s. of *pestilēns*) unhealthy, noxious, alter. of *pestilentus,* equiv. to *pesti-* (s. of *pestis*) PEST + *-lentus* -LENT] **—pes′ti·lent·ly,** *adv.*

pes·ti·len·tial (pes′tl en′shəl), *adj.* **1.** producing or tending to produce pestilence. **2.** pertaining to or of the nature of pestilence, esp. bubonic plague. **3.** pernicious; harmful. **4.** annoyingly troublesome. [1350–1400; ME < ML *pestilentiālis.* See PESTILENT, -IAL] **—pes′ti·len′tial·ly,** *adv.* **—pes′ti·len′tial·ness,** *n.*

pes·tle (pes′əl, pes′tl), *n., v.,* **-tled, -tling.** **—n. 1.** a tool for pounding or grinding substances in a mortar. See illus. under **mortar**[1]. **2.** any of various appliances for pounding, stamping, etc. **—v.t. 3.** to pound or grind with or as if with a pestle. **—v.i. 4.** to work with a pestle. [1300–50; ME *pestel* < MF < L *pistillum,* deriv. of *pistus,* ptp. of *pīnsere* to pound, crush]

pes·to (pes′tō), *n. Italian Cookery.* a sauce typically made with basil, pine nuts, olive oil, and grated Parmesan blended together and served hot or cold over pasta, fish, or meat. [1935–40; < Upper It (cf. Genoese dial. *pésto* pesto), It: n. deriv. of *pestare* to pound, crush; see PISTE, PESTLE]

pet[1] (pet), *n., adj., v.,* **pet·ted, pet·ting.** **—n. 1.** any domesticated or tamed animal that is kept as a companion and cared for affectionately. **2.** a person especially cherished or indulged; favorite: *He was the teacher's pet.* **3.** a thing particularly cherished. **—adj. 4.** kept or treated as a pet: *a pet lamb.* **5.** especially cherished or indulged, as a child or other person. **6.** favorite; most preferred: *a pet theory.* **7.** showing fondness or affection: *to address someone with pet words.* **—v.t. 8.** to treat as a pet; fondle or indulge. **9.** *Informal.* to fondle or caress amorously. **—v.i. 10.** *Informal.* to engage in amorous fondling and caressing. [1500–10; (n.) perh. back formation from *pet lamb* cade lamb, shortened var. of *petty lamb* little lamb (see PETTY); (v.) deriv. of the n.] **—pet′ta·ble,** *adj.*

—Syn. 8. baby, humor, pamper, favor.

pet[2] (pet), *n.* **1.** a fit of peevishness, sulking, or bad mood. **—v.i. 2.** to be peevish; sulk. [1580–90; orig. uncert.; cf. PETTISH]

PET (pet), positron emission tomography. Cf. **PET scan.**

Pet., Peter.

pet., petroleum.

Pe·tach Tik·va (pe′täkн tik′vä), a city in W Israel, NE of Tel Aviv. 119,800. Also, **Pe′tah Tiq′wa.**

Pé·tain (pā taɴ′), *n.* **Hen·ri Phi·lippe O·mer** (äɴ rē′ fē lēp′ ô mer′), 1856–1951, marshal of France: premier of the Vichy government 1940–44.

pet·al (pet′l), *n.* one of the often colored segments of the corolla of a flower. See diag. under **flower.** [1695–1705; < NL *petalum* petal, L: metal plate < Gk *pétalon* a thin plate, leaf, n. use of neut. of *pétalos* spread out, akin to *petannýnai* to be open, L *patēre* to stand open (see PATENT)] **—pet′al·age,** *n.* **—pet′aled, pet′alled,** *adj.* **—pet′al·less,** *adj.* **—pet′al·like′,** *adj.*

-petal, a combining form meaning "seeking, moving toward" that specified by the initial element, used in the formation of compound words: *acropetal.* [< NL *-pet(us)* seeking, deriv. of L *petere* to seek + -AL[1]]

pet·al·ine (pet′l in, -īn′), *adj.* pertaining to or resembling a petal. [1785–95; < NL *petalinus.* See PETAL, -INE[1]]

pet·al·ite (pet′l īt′), *n.* a mineral, lithium aluminum silicate, $Li(AlSi_4O_{10})$, occurring in colorless or white foliated masses: an important source of lithium. [1800–10; < G *Petalit.* See PETAL, -ITE[1]]

CONCISE ETYMOLOGY KEY: <, descended or borrowed from; >, whence; b., blend of, blended; c., cognate with; cf., compare; deriv., derivative; equiv., equivalent; imit., imitative; obl., oblique; r., replacing; s., stem; sp., spelling, spelled; resp., respelling, respelled; trans., translation; ?, origin unknown; *, unattested; ‡, probably earlier than. See the full key inside the front cover.

pet·a·lo·dy (pet′l ō′dē), *n. Bot.* a condition in flowers, in which certain organs, as the stamens in most double flowers, assume the appearance of or become metamorphosed into petals. [1880–85; < Gk *petalṓdēs* leaflike (see PETAL, -ODE[1]) + -Y[3]] **—pet·a·lod·ic** (pet′l od′ik), *adj.*

pet·al·oid (pet′l oid′), *adj.* having the form or appearance of a petal. [1720–30; PETAL + -OID]

pet·al·ous (pet′l əs), *adj.* having petals. [1720–30; PETAL + -OUS]

Pet·a·lu·ma (pet′l o͞o′mə), *n.* a city in W California, N of San Francisco. 33,834.

pé·tanque (pā tängk′; *Fr.* pe täɴk′), *n.* a form of lawn bowling originating in France, usually played on rough ground using steel balls. Also called **boule.** [1950–55; < F < Pr *pé* foot (< L *ped-,* s. of *pēs*) + *tanco* post, stake (deriv. of *tancar* to close, bar < VL **stanticāre;* see STANCH[1]); so called because the feet are to be planted firmly on the ground, as if staked, when the ball is released]

pe·tard (pi tärd′), *n.* **1.** an explosive device formerly used in warfare to blow in a door or gate, form a breach in a wall, etc. **2.** a kind of firecracker. **3.** (*cap.*) Also called **Flying Dustbin.** a British spigot mortar of World War II that fired a 40-pound (18 kg) finned bomb, designed to destroy pillboxes and other concrete obstacles. **4. hoist by** or **with one's own petard,** hurt, ruined, or destroyed by the very device or plot one had intended for another. [1590–1600; < MF, equiv. to *pet(er)* to break wind (deriv. of *pet* < L *pēditum* a breaking wind, orig. neut. of ptp. of *pēdere* to break wind) + *-ard* -ARD]

pet·a·sus (pet′ə səs), *n., pl.* **-sus·es.** a broad-brimmed hat worn by ancient Greek travelers and hunters, often represented in art as a winged hat worn by Hermes or Mercury. Also, **pet·a·sos** (pet′ə səs, -sos′). [1590–1600; < L < Gk *pétasos,* akin to *petannýnai* to spread out]

Pe·ta·vi·us (pi tä′vē əs), *n.* a walled plain in the fourth quadrant of the face of the moon: about 100 miles (160 km) in diameter from crest to crest.

pet·cock (pet′kok′), *n.* a small valve or faucet, as for draining off excess or waste material from the cylinder of a steam engine or an internal-combustion engine. Also, **pet′ cock′.** [1860–65; *pet,* perh. < F *pet* (see PETARD) + COCK[1]]

Pet.E., Petroleum Engineer.

pe·te·chi·a (pi tē′kē ə, -tek′ē ə), *n., pl.* **-te·chi·ae** (-tē′kē ē′, -tek′ē ē′). *Pathol.* a minute, round, nonraised hemorrhage in the skin or in a mucous or serous membrane. [1575–85; < NL < It *petecchia* (in pl.) rash, spots on skin < VL **(im)peticula,* equiv. to L *impetīc-,* s. of *impetīx,* var. of *impetīgō* IMPETIGO + *-ula* -ULE]

pe·te·chi·al (pi tē′kē əl, -tek′ē-), *adj. Pathol.* pertaining to, resembling, or characterized by petechiae. [1700–10; < NL *petechiālis.* See PETECHIA, -AL[1]]

pe·te·chi·ate (pi tē′kē it, -āt′, -tek′ē-), *adj. Pathol.* having or marked with petechiae. [1885–90; PETECHI(A) + -ATE[1]]

pete·man (pēt′mən), *n., pl.* **-men.** *Slang.* peterman. [1910–15; by shortening]

Pe·tén-It·zá (pe ten′ēt sä′, -ēt′sə), *n.* **Lake,** a lake in N central Guatemala: nearby site of Mayan ruins. ab. 38 sq. mi. (98 sq. km).

pe·ter[1] (pē′tər), *v.i.* **peter out, 1.** to diminish gradually and stop; dwindle to nothing: *The hot water always peters out in the middle of my shower.* **2.** to tire; exhaust (usually used as a past participle): *I'm petered out after that walk.* [1805–15, in sense "put an end to"; 1860–65 for def. 1; orig. uncert.]

pe·ter[2] (pē′tər), *n. Slang (vulgar).* penis. [1900–05; generic use of the proper name]

pe·ter[3] (pē′tər), *n. Whist.* a signal for an echo. [1935–40; from BLUE PETER]

Pe·ter (pē′tər), *n.* **1.** Also called **Simon Peter.** died A.D. 67?, one of the 12 apostles and the reputed author of two of the Epistles. **2.** either of these two Epistles in the New Testament, I Peter or II Peter. **3.** a word formerly used in communications to represent the letter *P.* **4.** a male given name. [ME; OE *Petrus* < L < Gk *Pétros* stone, trans. of Syriac *kēfā*]

Peter I, 1. (*"the Great"*), 1672–1725, czar of Russia 1682–1725. **2.** (*Peter Karageorgevich*), 1844–1921, king of Serbia 1903–21.

Peter II, 1923–70, king of Yugoslavia 1934–45.

Peter III, 1728–62, czar of Russia 1762 (husband of Catherine II; father of Paul I).

Pe·ter·bor·ough (pē′tər bûr′ō, -bur′ō, -bər ə), *n.* **1.** a city in Cambridgeshire, in central England. 115,000. **2.** a city in SE Ontario, in SE Canada. 59,683. **3. Soke of** (sōk), a former administrative division in Cambridgeshire, in central England. 84 sq. mi. (218 sq. km).

pe·ter·man (pē′tər mən), *n., pl.* **-men.** *Slang.* a safecracker. Also, **peteman.** [1805–15; *peter* a safe or cash box, orig. a portmanteau or trunk, as an object to be stolen or rifled (of obscure orig.) + -MAN]

Pe′ter·mann Peak′ (pā′tər män′), a mountain in E Greenland. 9645 ft. (2940 m).

Pe′ter of Am′iens. See **Peter the Hermit.**

Pe′ter Pan′, 1. the hero of Sir James M. Barrie's play about a boy who never grew up. **2.** (*italics*) the play itself (1904).

Pe′ter Pan′ col′lar, a close-fitting flat or rolled collar with rounded ends that meet in front of a high, round neckline. [1920–25]

Pe′ter Prin′ciple, any of several satirical "laws" concerning organizational structure, esp. one that holds that people tend to be promoted until they reach their level of incompetence. [from the title of a book by Laurence J. Peter (b. 1919), Canadian educator]

Pe·ters·burg (pē′tərz bûrg′), *n.* a city in SE Virginia: besieged by Union forces 1864–65. 41,055.

pe·ter·sham (pē′tər shəm, -sham′), *n.* **1.** a heavy woolen cloth for men's overcoats and other bulky outerwear. **2.** a coat or jacket made of this cloth. **3.** a corded material for hatbands, the insides of belts, etc. **4.** a narrow belting for the tops of skirts. [1805–15; named after Viscount *Petersham* (1780–1851)]

Pe·ter·son (pē′tər sən), *n.* **Roger Tory,** born 1908, U.S. ornithologist, author, and artist.

Pe′ter's pence′, 1. an annual tax or tribute, originally of a penny, paid by certain English property owners to the papal see until the Reformation. **2.** a voluntary contribution to the pope, made by Roman Catholics. Also, **Pe′ter pence′.** [1175–1225; ME *Peteres peni* (sing.)]

Pe′ter the Her′mit, c1050–1115, French monk: preacher of the first Crusade 1095–99. Also called **Peter of Amiens.**

pé·til·lant (pā tē yäɴ′), *adj. French.* (of wine) slightly sparkling.

pet·i·o·lar (pet′ē ə lər, pet′ē ō′lər), *adj. Bot.* of, pertaining to, or growing from a petiole. [1750–60; PETIOLE + -AR[1]]

pet·i·o·late (pet′ē ə lāt′), *adj. Bot., Zool.* having a petiole or peduncle. Also, **pet′i·o·lat′ed.** [1745–55; < NL *petiolātus.* See PETIOLE, -ATE[1]]

pet·i·ole (pet′ē ōl′), *n.* **1.** *Bot.* the slender stalk by which a leaf is attached to the stem; leafstalk. See diag. under **leaf. 2.** *Zool.* a stalk or peduncle, as that connecting the abdomen and thorax in wasps. [1745–55; < NL *petiolus* leafstalk, special use of L *petiolus,* scribal var. of *peciolus,* prob. for **pediciolus,* dim. of *pediculus* PEDICLE]

pet·i·o·lule (pet′ē əl yo͞ol′, -ə lo͞ol′, pet′ē ol′yo͞ol), *n. Bot.* a small petiole, as of a leaflet in a compound leaf. [1825–35; < NL *petiolulus.* See PETIOLE, -ULE] **—pet·i·ol·u·lar** (pet′ē ol′yə lər), **pet·i·ol·u·late** (pet′ē ol′yə lāt′, -lit), *adj.*

Pe·ti·pa (pet′ē pä′, pet′ē pä′; *Fr.* pə tē pä′), *n.* **Mar·i·us** (mâr′ē əs, mar′-; *Fr.* ᴍᴀ ʀʏs′), 1819–1910, French ballet dancer and choreographer in Russia.

pet·it (pet′ē; *Fr.* pə tē′), *adj. Law.* small; petty; minor. [1325–75; ME < MF; see PETTY]

pe·tit beurre (pə tē bœʀ′), *pl.* **pe·tits beurre** (pə tē bœʀ′). *French Cookery.* a small, usually oblong butter cookie. [1905–10; < F: lit., little butter]

pe·tit bour·geois (pə tē′ bo͝or zhwä′; pet′ē bo͝or′-zhwä, bo͝or zhwä′; *Fr.* pə tē bo͞oʀ zhwᴀ′), *pl.* **pe·tits bour·geois** (pə tē′ bo͝or zhwäz′; pet′ē bo͝or′zhwäz, bo͝or zhwäz′; *Fr.* pə tē bo͞oʀ zhwᴀ′). a person who belongs to the petite bourgeoisie. [1855–60; < F] **—pe·tit′-bour·geois′,** *adj.*

pe·tit dé·jeu·ner (pə tē dā zhœ nā′), *pl.* ***pe·tits dé·jeu·ners*** (pə tē dā zhœ nā′). *French.* breakfast.

pe·tite (pə tēt′), *adj.* **1.** (of a woman) short and having a small, trim figure; diminutive. **—n. 2.** a category of clothing sized for women or girls of less than average height and with average or diminutive figures. **3.** a garment in such a size: *The petites are on that rack.* **4.** a woman or girl who wears clothing of such a size. [1705–15; < F; fem. of PETIT] **—pe·tite′ness,** *n.*

pe·tite bour·geoise (pə tēt′ bo͝or zhwäz′; *Fr.* pə tēt bo͞oʀ zhwᴀz′), *pl.* **pe·tites bour·geoises** (pə tēt′ bo͝or-zhwäz′; *Fr.* pə tēt bo͞oʀ zhwᴀz′). a woman who belongs to the petite bourgeoisie. [1850–55; < F; fem. of PETIT BOURGEOIS]

pe·tite bour·geoi·sie (pə tēt′ bo͝or′zhwä zē′; *Fr.* pə tēt bo͞oʀ zhwᴀ zē′), the portion of the bourgeoisie having the least wealth and lowest social status; the lower middle class. [1915–20; < F]

pe·tite mar·mite (pə tēt′ mär′mit, mär mēt′), **1.** an aromatic broth made from meat, vegetables, and seasonings, served in the pot in which it has cooked. **2.** a small marmite for cooking and serving this soup. [1905–10; < F: lit., little pot]

pe·tit feu (*Fr.* pə tē fœ′), *Ceram.* **1.** a firing of ceramics at a low temperature. **2.** the category of ceramic colors fired in a muffle kiln at low temperature. Cf. **grand feu.** [< F: lit., small fire]

pet·it four (pet′ē fôr′, fōr′; *Fr.* pə tē fo͞oʀ′), *pl.* **pet·its fours** (pet′ē fôrz′, fōrz′; *Fr.* pə tē fo͞oʀ′). a small teacake, variously frosted and decorated. [1880–85; < F: lit., small oven]

pe·ti·tion (pə tish′ən), *n.* **1.** a formally drawn request, often bearing the names of a number of those making the request, that is addressed to a person or group of persons in authority or power, soliciting some favor, right, mercy, or other benefit: *a petition for clemency; a petition for the repeal of an unfair law.* **2.** a request made for something desired, esp. a respectful or humble request, as to a superior or to one of those in authority; a supplication or prayer: *a petition for aid; a petition to God for courage and strength.* **3.** something that is sought by request or entreaty: *to receive one's full petition.* **4.** *Law.* an application for a court order or for some judicial action. **—v.t. 5.** to beg for or request (something). **6.** to address a formal petition to (a sovereign, a legislative body, etc.): *He received everything for which he had petitioned the king.* **7.** to ask by petition for (something). **—v.i. 8.** to present a petition. **9.** to address or present a formal petition. **10.** to request or solicit, as by a petition: *to petition for redress of grievances.* [1300–50; ME *peticioun* (< MF *peticion*) < L *petītiōn-* (s. of *petītiō*) a seeking out, equiv. to *petīt(us)* (ptp. of *petere* to seek) + *-iōn-* -ION] **—pe·ti′tion·a·ble,** *adj.* **—pe·ti′tion·er, pe·ti′tion·ist,** *n.*

—Syn. 1. suit. **2.** entreaty, solicitation, appeal. **9.** solicit, sue. See **appeal.**

pe·ti·tion·ar·y (pə tish′ə ner′ē), *adj.* **1.** of the nature of or expressing a petition. **2.** *Archaic.* petitioning; suppliant. [1570–80; PETITION + -ARY]

pe·ti·ti·o prin·ci·pi·i (pi tish′ē ō′ prin sip′ē ī′; *Lat.* pe tē′ti ō′ pring kip′i ē′), *Logic.* a fallacy in reasoning resulting from the assumption of that which in the beginning was set forth to be proved; begging the question. [1525–35; < ML *petītiō prīncipiī,* trans. of Gk *tò en archêi aiteîsthai* the assumption at the outset]

pet′it ju′ry (pet′ē), *Law.* See **petty jury.** [1490–1500] **—pet′it ju′ror.**

pet′it lar′ceny (pet′ē), *Law.* See **petty larceny.** [1580–90]

pe·tit mal (pet′ē mäl′, mal′; *Fr.* pə tē mal′), *Pathol.* See under **epilepsy.** [1870–75; < F: lit., small illness]

pet·i·tor (pet′i tər, pə tī′tər), *n. Obs.* a seeker; an applicant or candidate. [1605–15; < L *petītor,* equiv. to *petī-,* var. s. of *petere* to seek + *-tor* -TOR] **—pet·i·to·ry** (pet′i tôr′e, -tōr′ē), *adj.*

pet′it point′ (pet′ē), **1.** a small stitch used in embroidery. Cf. **gros point** (def. 1), **tent stitch. 2.** embroidery done on a canvas backing and resembling woven tapestry. [1880–85; < F: lit., small stitch]

pet′it ser′jeanty (pet′ē), *Medieval Eng. Law.* serjeanty in which the tenant renders services of an impersonal nature to the king, as providing him annually with an implement of war, as a lance or bow. Cf. **grand serjeanty.** [1515–25; < AF]

pe·tits pois (pə tē pwa′; *Eng.* pet′ē pwä′), *French.* small green peas.

pet′it trea′son (pet′ē), *Eng. Law.* the killing of a husband by his wife, of a lord by his servant, or of an ecclesiastic by a subordinate ecclesiastic. Also, **petty treason.** [1490–1500; < AF]

PETN, See **pentaerythritol tetranitrate.**

pet′ name′, a name or a term of address used to express affection for a person, thing, etc. [1910–15]

pet·nap·ping (pet′nap′ing), *n.* the stealing of a pet, as for resale or ransom. Also, **pet′nap′ing.** [1965–70, *Amer.*; PET[1] + -NAP + -ING[1]] **—pet′nap′per, pet′·nap′er,** *n.*

pe·to (pā′tō), *n., pl.* **-tos,** (*esp. collectively*) **-to.** wahoo[3]. [1955–60; < AmerSp; Sp: breastplate < It *petto* breast, breastplate < L *pectus* breast]

Pe·tö·fi (pe′tœ fē), *n.* **Sán·dor** (shän′dôr), (*Sándor Petrovics*), 1823–49, Hungarian poet and patriot.

pet′ peeve′, a particular and often continual annoyance; personal bugbear: *This train service is one of my pet peeves.* [1915–20, *Amer.*]

petr-, var. of **petro-**[1] before a vowel: *petrous.*

Pe·tra (pē′trə, pe′-), *n.* an ancient city in SW Jordan: ruined structures carved out of varicolored stratified rock; capital of the Nabataeans and Edomites.

Pe·trarch (pē′trärk, pe′-), *n.* (*Francesco Petrarca*), 1304–74, Italian poet and scholar.

Pe·trar·chan (pi trär′kən), *adj.* Also, **Pe·trar·chi·an** (pi trär′kē ən). **1.** of, pertaining to, or characteristic of the works of Petrarch. **2.** characteristic or imitative of the style of Petrarch. **—***n.* **3.** Petrarchist. [1820–30; PETRARCH + -AN]

Petrar′chan son′net, a sonnet form popularized by Petrarch, consisting of an octave with the rhyme scheme *abbaabba* and of a sestet with one of several rhyme schemes, as *cdecde* or *cdcdcd.* Also called **Italian sonnet.** [1905–10]

Pe·trarch·ism (pē′trär kiz′əm, pe′-), *n.* the poetic style introduced by Petrarch and characteristic of his work, marked by complex grammatical structure, elaborate conceits, and conventionalized diction. Also, **Pe·trar·chi·an·ism** (pi trär′kē ə niz′əm). [1880–85; PETRARCH + -ISM]

Pe·trarch·ist (pē′trär kist, pe′-), *n.* a person who imitates the literary style employed by Petrarch, esp. the poets of the English Renaissance who employed the Petrarchan sonnet style. Also, **Petrarchan.** [1815–25; PETRARCH + -IST]

pet·rel (pe′trəl), *n.* any of numerous tube-nosed seabirds of the families Procellariidae, Hydrobatidae, and Pelecanoididae. Cf. **storm petrel, diving petrel.** [1670–80; earlier *pitteral,* of uncert. orig.; perh. altered by assoc. with St. *Peter* (who attempted to walk on the water of Lake Gennesareth), alluding to the bird's habit of flying close to the ocean surface]

petri-, var. of **petro-**[1] before elements of Latin origin: *petrifaction.*

pe′tri dish′ (pē′trē), a shallow, circular, glass or plastic dish with a loose-fitting cover over the top and sides, used for culturing bacteria and other microorganisms. [1890–95; named after J. R. Petri (d. 1921), German bacteriologist]

petri dish

Pe·trie (pē′trē), *n.* **Sir (William Matthew) Flin·ders** (flin′dərz), 1853–1942, English Egyptologist and archaeologist.

pet·ri·fac·tion (pe′trə fak′shən), *n.* **1.** the act or process of petrifying; the state of being petrified. **2.** something petrified. Also, **pet·ri·fi·ca·tion** (pe′trə fi kā′shən). [1640–50; PETRI- + *-faction* < L *factiōn-* (s. of *factiō*) a making. See PETRIFY, FACTION] **—pet′ri·fac′·tive,** *adj.*

Pet′rified For′est Na′tional Park′, a national park in E Arizona: buried tree trunks turned to stone by the action of mineral-laden water. 147 sq. mi. (381 sq. km).

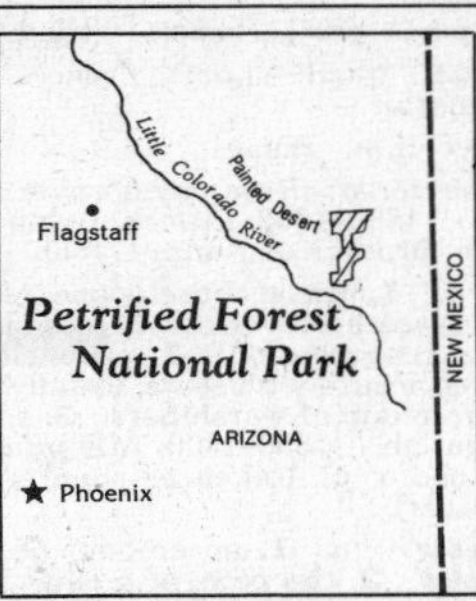

pet·ri·fy (pe′trə fī′), *v.,* **-fied, -fy·ing.** **—***v.t.* **1.** to convert into stone or a stony substance. **2.** to benumb or paralyze with astonishment, horror, or other strong emotion: *I was petrified with fear.* **3.** to make rigid or inert; harden; deaden: *The tragedy in his life petrified his emotions.* **—***v.i.* **4.** to become petrified. [1585–95; < MF *petrifier.* See PETRI-, -FY] **—pet′ri·fi′a·ble,** *adj.* **—pe·trif·i·cant** (pi trif′i kənt), *adj.* **—pet′ri·fi′er,** *n.* **—Syn. 2.** immobilize, dumbfound, daze.

Pe·tril·lo (pi tril′ō), *n.* **James Caesar,** 1892–1984, U.S. labor leader: president of the American Federation of Musicians 1940–58.

Pe·trine (pē′trīn, -trin), *adj.* of or pertaining to the apostle Peter or the Epistles bearing his name. [1840–50; < LL *Petr(us)* PETER + -INE[1]]

Pe·trin·ism (pē′trə niz′əm), *n.* the body of theological doctrine taught by, or attributed to, the apostle Peter. [PETRINE + -ISM] **—Pe′trin·ist,** *n.*

pet·ro (pe′trō), *adj.* **1.** of or pertaining to petroleum or the petroleum industry **—***n.* **2.** *Canadian.* the federally owned petroleum industry. [1970–75; independent use of PETRO-[2]]

petro-[1], a combining form meaning "rock," "stone," used in the formation of compound words: *petrology.* Also, **petri-;** *esp. before a vowel,* **petr-.** [< Gk, comb. form of *pétra* rock, *pétros* a stone]

petro-[2], a combining form meaning "petroleum," "the extraction and export of petroleum," used in the formation of compound words: *petrochemistry; petropower.* [extracted from PETROLEUM]

Pet·ro·bru·sian (pe′trō brōō′zhən, -shən), *n.* a member of a 12th-century sect in S France that rejected the Mass, infant baptism, prayers for the dead, sacerdotalism, the veneration of the cross, and the building of churches. [1550–60; < ML *petrobrusiānus,* named after *Petrus Brusius* Pierre de Bruys, 12th-century Frenchman who founded the sect; see -AN]

pet·ro·chem·i·cal (pe′trō kem′i kəl), *n.* **1.** a chemical substance obtained from petroleum or natural gas, as gasoline, kerosene, or petrolatum. **—***adj.* **2.** of or pertaining to petrochemistry or a petrochemical. [1910–15; PETRO-[2] + CHEMICAL]

pet·ro·chem·is·try (pe′trō kem′ə strē), *n.* **1.** the branch of chemistry dealing with petroleum or its products. **2.** the chemistry of rocks. [1935–40; PETRO-[2] or PETRO-[1] + CHEMISTRY]

pet·ro·dol·lars (pe′trō dol′ərz), *n.pl.* surplus revenues in dollars accumulated by petroleum-exporting countries, as those of the Middle East, esp. when then used for foreign loans or investments. [1970–75; PETRO-[2] + DOLLARS]

petrog., petrography.

pet·ro·gen·e·sis (pe′trō jen′ə sis), *n.* **1.** the branch of petrology dealing with the origin and formation of rocks. **2.** the origin and formation of rocks. Also called **pe·trog·e·ny** (pi troj′ə nē). [1900–05; PETRO-[1] + -GENESIS] **—pet·ro·ge·net·ic** (pe′trō jə net′ik), *adj.*

pet·ro·glyph (pe′trə glif′), *n.* a drawing or carving on rock, made by a member of a prehistoric people. Also called **petrograph.** [1865–70; < F *pétroglyphe.* See PETRO-[1], GLYPH] **—pet′ro·glyph′ic,** *adj.* **—pe·trog·ly·phy** (pi trog′lə fē), *n.*

Pet·ro·grad (pe′trə grad′; *Russ.* pyi tru grät′), *n.* former name (1914–24) of **St. Petersburg** (def. 2).

pet·ro·gram (pe′trə gram′), *n.* a drawing or painting on rock, esp. one made by a member of a prehistoric people. [PETRO-[1] + -GRAM[1]]

pet·ro·graph (pe′trə graf′, -gräf′), *n.* petroglyph. [1805–15; PETRO-[1] + -GRAPH]

pe·trog·ra·phy (pi trog′rə fē), *n.* the branch of petrology dealing with the description and classification of rocks, esp. by microscopic examination. [1645–55; < NL *petrographia.* See PETRO-[1], -GRAPHY] **—pe·trog′ra·pher,** *n.* **—pet·ro·graph·ic** (pe′trə graf′ik), **pet′ro·graph′i·cal,** *adj.* **—pet′ro·graph′i·cal·ly,** *adv.*

pet·rol (pe′trəl), *n., v.,* **-rolled, -rol·ling.** **—***n.* **1.** *Brit.* gasoline. **2.** *Archaic.* petroleum. **—***v.t.* **3.** *Brit.* to clean with gasoline. [1590–1600; < MF *petrole* < ML *petroleum* PETROLEUM]

petrol., petrology.

pet·ro·la·tum (pe′trə lā′təm, -lä′-), *n.* a yellowish or whitish, translucent, gelatinous, oily, semisolid, amorphous mass obtained from petroleum: used as a lubricant, rust preventive, in the manufacture of cosmetics, and in medicine as a protective dressing, emollient, and ointment base. Also called **petro′leum jel′ly.** [1885–90, *Amer.*; < NL; see PETROLEUM, -ATE[2]]

pet′rol bomb′, *Brit.* See **Molotov cocktail.** [1955–60]

pet·ro·lene (pe′trə lēn′), *n.* any of the constituents of a bitumen, as asphalt, that are soluble in pentane, hexane, or naphthalene. Also called **malthene.** Cf. **asphaltene.** [1830–40; PETROL(EUM) + -ENE]

pe·tro·le·um (pə trō′lē əm), *n.* an oily, thick, flammable, usually dark-colored liquid that is a form of bitumen or a mixture of various hydrocarbons, occurring naturally in various parts of the world and commonly obtained by drilling: used in a natural or refined state as fuel, or separated by distillation into gasoline, naphtha, benzene, kerosene, paraffin, etc. [1520–30; < ML: lit., rock oil, equiv. to L *petr(a)* rock (< Gk *pétra*) + *oleum* OIL] **—pe·tro′le·ous,** *adj.*

petro′leum e′ther, a flammable, low-boiling hydrocarbon mixture produced by the fractional distillation of petroleum, used as a solvent. [1865–70]

pe·trol·ic (pi trol′ik), *adj.* of, pertaining to, or produced from petroleum. [1895–1900; PETROL(EUM) + -IC]

pet·ro·lif·er·ous (pe′trə lif′ər əs), *adj.* (of a rock or geologic formation) containing or yielding petroleum. [1885–90; PETROL(EUM) + -I- + -FEROUS]

Pe·tro·li·na (pi trōō lē′nä), *n.* a city in NE Brazil. 37,800.

pe·trol·o·gy (pi trol′ə jē), *n.* the scientific study of rocks, including petrography and petrogenesis. [1805–15; PETRO-[1] + -LOGY] **—pet·ro·log·ic** (pe′trə loj′ik), **pet′ro·log′i·cal,** *adj.* **—pet′ro·log′i·cal·ly,** *adv.* **—pe·trol′o·gist,** *n.*

pet·ro·nel (pe′trə nl), *n.* a firearm of large caliber, used from the 15th to the 17th century, that fired with its butt resting against the chest. [1570–80; < MF *petrinal,* dial. var. of *poitrinal,* equiv. to *poitrine* chest (< VL **pectorīna,* n. use of fem. of **pectorīnus* of the breast; see PECTORAL, -INE[1]) + *-al* -AL[1]]

Pe·tro·ni·us (pi trō′nē əs), *n.* **Ga·ius** (gā′əs), (*Gaius Petronius Arbiter*) ("*Arbiter Elegantiae*"), died A.D. 66?, Roman satirist.

Pe·tro·pa·vlovsk (pe′trə pav′lôfsk, -lofsk; *Russ.* pyi tru pä′vləfsk), *n.* a city in N Kazakhstan. 233,000.

Pe·tro·pa·vlovsk-Kam·chat·ski (pe′trə pav′lôfsk kam chät′skē; *Russ.* pyi tru pä′vləfsk kum chyät′skyē), *n.* a city in SE Kamchatka, in the E Russian Federation in Asia. 215,000.

Pe·tró·po·lis (pi trô′pōō lis), *n.* a city in SE Brazil, NE of Rio de Janeiro. 116,080.

pet·ro·pow·er (pe′trō pou′ər), *n.* the economic or political power of a nation resulting from its petroleum reserves needed by other nations. [1975–80; PETRO-[2] + POWER]

pe·tro·sal (pi trō′səl), *adj.* **1.** petrous; hard. **2.** *Anat.* of or pertaining to the petrous portion of the temporal bone. [1735–45; < L *petrōs(us)* rocky (see PETRO-[1], -OSE[1]) + -AL[1]]

Pe·trouch·ka (pə trōōsh′kə), *n.* a ballet suite (1911) by Stravinsky.

pet·rous (pe′trəs, pē′-), *adj.* **1.** *Anat.* noting or pertaining to the hard dense portion of the temporal bone, containing the internal auditory organs; petrosal. **2.** like stone, esp. in hardness; stony; rocky. [1350–1400; ME (< MF *petros*) < L *petrōsus* rocky. See PETR-, -OUS]

Pe·tro·za·vodsk (pe′trə zə votsk′; *Russ.* pyi trə zuvôtsk′), *n.* a city in and the capital of the Karelian Autonomous Republic, in the NW Russian Federation in Europe. 270,000.

pe-tsai (bā′tsī′), *n.* See **Chinese cabbage.** [1785–95; < Chin (Wade-Giles) *pai*[2]*ts'ai*[4], (pinyin) *báicài* (literary *bócài*) lit., white vegetable; cf. BOK CHOY]

Pet·sa·mo (*Fin.* pet′sä mô), *n.* Finnish name of **Pechenga.**

PET′ scan′, **1.** an image obtained by positron emission tomography, using a PET scanner. **2.** an examination performed with a PET scanner. [*P(ositron) E(mission) T(omography)*]

PET′ scan′ner, a tomographic imaging device that yields visual information about the ongoing activity of the brain: positron-emitting isotopes, incorporated into biologically important compounds, are injected intravenously or administered by inhalation, and the resultant gamma radiation is sensed by detectors and converted into computer-generated images of blood flow, oxygen utilization, glucose uptake, etc.

pet·ti (pet′ē), *n. Informal.* **1.** petticoat (def. 1). **2.** pettislip. [by shortening]

pet·ti·coat (pet′ē kōt′), *n.* **1.** Also called **pettiskirt.** an underskirt, esp. one that is full and often trimmed and ruffled and of a decorative fabric. **2.** any skirtlike part or covering. **3.** a flounce or valance fitting around the sides of a bed, couch, or chair, as to conceal the legs. **4.** *Informal.* a woman or girl. **—***adj.* **5.** of, pertaining to, or controlled by women; female; feminine: *petticoat government.* [1375–1425; late ME *petycote.* See PETTY, COAT] **—pet′ti·coat′less,** *adj.*

pet′ticoat breech′es, men's breeches, often ornate, having loose, skirtlike legs, worn in France and England from about 1650 to 1680. Also called **Rhinegrave breeches.** [1650–60]

pet·ti·coat·ed (pet′ē kō′tid), *adj.* having or wearing a petticoat. [1740–50; PETTICOAT + -ED[3]]

pet′ticoat in′sulator, *Elect.* a bell-shaped insulator used for high-voltage insulation.

pet′ticoat narcis′sus, a narcissus, *Narcissus bulbocodium,* of southern France and Morocco, having solitary, yellow or white flowers with an enlarged cup. Also called **hoop-petticoat narcissus.**

pet·ti·fog (pet′ē fog′, -fôg′), *v.i.,* **-fogged, -fog·ging.** **1.** to bicker or quibble over trifles or unimportant mat-

CONCISE PRONUNCIATION KEY: act, cāpe, dâre, pärt; set, ēqual; if, īce; ox, ōver, ôrder, oil, bŏŏk, bōōt, out; up, ûrge; child; sing; shoe; thin, *th*at; zh as in *treasure.* ə = *a* as in *alone, e* as in *system, i* as in *easily, o* as in *gallop, u* as in *circus;* ə as in *fire* (fīər), *hour* (ouər). l and n can serve as syllabic consonants, as in *cradle* (krād′l), and *button* (but′n). See the full key inside the front cover.

ters. **2.** to carry on a petty, shifty, or unethical law business. **3.** to practice chicanery of any sort. [1605–15; back formation from *pettifogger,* equiv. to PETTY + *fogger* < MLG *voger* or MD *voeger* one who arranges things; akin to OE *gefōg* a joining] **—pet′ti·fog′ger,** *n.* **—pet′ti·fog′ger·y,** *n.*

pet·ti·fog·ging (pet′ē fog′ing, -fô′ging), *adj.* **1.** insignificant; petty: *pettifogging details.* **2.** dishonest or unethical in insignificant matters; meanly petty. [1570–80; see PETTIFOG, -ING[2]]

pet·ting (pet′ing), *n.* amorous caressing and kissing. [1870–75; PET[1] + -ING[1]]

pet′ting zoo′, a zoo, or a special part of a larger zoo, where children may hold and stroke and sometimes feed small or young animals.

pet·ti·pants (pet′ē pants′), *n.* (*used with a plural v.*) close-fitting, dress-length panties, sometimes trimmed with lace or ruffles on the legs. [1960–65; PETTI(COAT) + PANTS]

pet·tish (pet′ish), *adj.* petulantly peevish: *a pettish refusal.* [1585–95; see PET[2], -ISH[1]] **—pet′tish·ly,** *adv.* **—pet′tish·ness,** *n.*

pet·ti·skirt (pet′ē skûrt′), *n.* petticoat (def. 1). [1940–45; PETTI(COAT) + SKIRT]

pet·ti·slip (pet′ē slip′), *n.* a half-slip. [PETTI(COAT) + SLIP[1]]

pet·ti·toes (pet′ē tōz′), *n.pl.* **1.** the feet of a pig, esp. used as food. **2.** the human toes or feet, esp. those of a child. [1545–55; pl. of obs. *pettytoe* offal < MF *petite oye* giblets of a goose, equiv. to *petite* PETITE + *oye* goose < LL *avica;* see OCARINA]

pet·tle (pet′l), *v.t.,* **-tled, -tling.** *Scot. and North Eng.* to fondle; pet. [1710–20; PET[1] + -LE]

pet·ty (pet′ē), *adj.,* **-ti·er, -ti·est.** **1.** of little or no importance or consequence: *petty grievances.* **2.** of lesser or secondary importance, merit, etc.; minor: *petty considerations.* **3.** having or showing narrow ideas, interests, etc.: *petty minds.* **4.** mean or ungenerous in small or trifling things: *a petty person.* **5.** showing or caused by meanness of spirit: *a petty revenge.* **6.** of secondary rank, esp. in relation to others of the same class or kind: *petty states; a petty tyrant.* [1325–75; ME *peti(t)* small, minor < OF *petit* < Gallo-Romance **pittittus,* of expressive orig.] **—pet′ti·ly,** *adv.* **—pet′ti·ness,** *n.*
—Syn. 1. nugatory, negligible, inconsiderable, slight. PETTY, PALTRY, TRIFLING, TRIVIAL apply to something that is so insignificant as to be almost unworthy of notice. PETTY implies contemptible insignificance and littleness, inferiority and small worth: *petty quarrels.* PALTRY is applied to something that is beneath one's notice, even despicable: *a paltry amount.* Something that is TRIFLING is so unimportant and inconsiderable as to be practically negligible: *a trifling error.* Something that is TRIVIAL is slight, insignificant, and even in incongruous contrast to something that is significant or important: *a trivial remark; a trivial task.* **3.** small. **4.** stingy, miserly.
—Ant. 1. important. **4.** generous.

Pet·ty (pet′ē), *n.* **1. Richard,** born 1937, U.S. racing-car driver. **2. William, 2nd Earl of Shelburne, 1st Marquis of Lansdowne.** See **Lansdowne, 1st Marquis of.**

pet′ty bourgeois′. See **petit bourgeois.** [1885–90]

pet′ty bourgeoisie′. See **petite bourgeoisie.** [1840–50]

pet′ty cash′, a cash fund for paying small charges, as for minor office supplies or deliveries. [1825–35]

Pet·ty-Fitz·mau·rice (pet′ē fits môr′is, -mor′-), *n.* **Henry Charles Keith, 5th Marquis of Lansdowne.** See **Lansdowne, 5th Marquis of.**

pet′ty ju′ry, (in a civil or criminal proceeding) a jury, usually of 12 persons, impaneled to determine the facts and render a verdict pursuant to the court's instructions on the law. Also, **petit jury.** Also called **traverse jury.** Cf. **grand jury.** [1680–90] **—pet′ty ju′ror.**

pet′ty lar′ceny, *Law.* larceny in which the value of the goods taken is below a certain legally specified amount. Also, **petit larceny.** Cf. **grand larceny.** [1810–20]

pet′ty of′ficer, 1. a noncommissioned U.S. Navy rank with three grades. **2.** one of the minor officers on a merchant ship, as a boatswain or carpenter. [1570–80]

pet′ty ses′sions, *Eng. Law.* a court of summary jurisdiction for minor offenses that is held without a jury.

pet′ty trea′son, *Eng. Law.* See **petit treason.**

pet·u·lance (pech′ə ləns), *n.* **1.** the state or quality of being petulant. **2.** a petulant speech or action. [1600–10; < L *petulantia* impudence. See PETULANT, -ANCE]

pet·u·lan·cy (pech′ə lən sē), *n., pl.* **-cies.** *Rare.* petulance. [1550–60; < L *petulantia.* See PETULANCE, -ANCY]

pet·u·lant (pech′ə lənt), *adj.* moved to or showing sudden, impatient irritation, esp. over some trifling annoyance: *a petulant toss of the head.* [1590–1600; < L *petulant-* (s. of *petulāns*) impudent, akin to *petere* to seek, head for] **—pet′u·lant·ly,** *adv.*
—Syn. irritable, peevish, fretful, pettish, touchy.

pe·tu·nia (pi to͞o′nyə, -nē ə, -tyo͞o′-), *n.* **1.** any garden plant belonging to the genus *Petunia,* of the nightshade family, native to tropical America, having funnel-shaped flowers of various colors. **2.** a deep, reddish purple. [1815–25; < NL < obs. F *petun* tobacco < Tupi *petyn;* see -IA]

pe·tun·tse (pi to͝on′tse; *Chin.* bô′dun′dzu′), *n.* a type of feldspar, used in certain porcelains. Also, **pe·tun′tze.** [1720–30; < Chin (Wade-Giles) *pai²tun¹tzŭ⁰,* (pinyin) *báidùnzi* white mound]

CONCISE ETYMOLOGY KEY: <, descended or borrowed from; >, whence; b., blend of, blended; c., cognate with; cf., compare; deriv., derivative; equiv., equivalent; imit., imitative; obl., oblique; r., replacing; s., stem; sp., spelling, spelled; resp., respelling, respelled; trans., translation; ?, origin unknown; *, unattested; ‡, probably earlier than. See the full key inside the front cover.

peu à peu (pœ A pœ′), *French.* little by little.

peu de chose (pœd[a] shōz′), *French.* a trifling or unimportant matter.

Peul (po͞ol, pyo͞ol), *n.* Fulani.

Pevs·ner (pevz′nər; *Russ.* pyef′snyir), *n.* **An·toine** (*Fr.* äN twAN′), 1886–1962, French sculptor and painter, born in Russia (brother of Naum Gabo).

pew (pyo͞o), *n.* **1.** (in a church) one of a number of fixed, benchlike seats with backs, accessible by aisles, for the use of the congregation. **2.** an enclosed seat in a church, or an enclosure with seats, usually reserved for a family or other group of worshipers. **3.** those occupying pews; congregation. [1350–1400; ME *puwe* < MF *puie* balcony < L *podia,* pl. (taken as sing.) of *podium* balcony. See PODIUM]

pew·age (pyo͞o′ij), *n.* **1.** an amount or the dues paid for a church pew. **2.** the pews of a church; pews collectively. [1675–85; PEW + -AGE]

pe·wee (pē′wē), *n.* **1.** any of several New World flycatchers of the genus *Contopus.* Cf. **wood pewee. 2.** the phoebe. [1790–1800, *Amer.;* imit.]

pew′ hinge′, a rising hinge for a small door.

pew·hold·er (pyo͞o′hōl′dər), *n.* a person who rents or owns a pew. [1835–45; PEW + HOLDER]

pe·wit (pē′wit, pyo͞o′it), *n.* **1.** the lapwing, *Vanellus vanellus.* **2.** the phoebe. Also, **peewit.** [1520–30; imit.]

pew·ter (pyo͞o′tər), *n.* **1.** any of various alloys in which tin is the chief constituent, originally one of tin and lead. **2.** a container or utensil made of such an alloy. **3.** such utensils collectively: *a revival of interest in pewter.* **4.** *Brit. Slang.* **a.** a cup awarded as a prize or trophy, as in a sporting event. **b.** See **prize money** (def. 2). *—adj.* **5.** consisting or made of pewter: *a pewter mug.* [1325–75; ME *pewtre* < MF *peutre* < VL **piltrum;* perh. akin to SPELTER]

pew·ter·er (pyo͞o′tər ər), *n.* a maker of pewter utensils or containers. [1300–50; ME *peuterer* < MF *peutrier.* See PEWTER, -ER[2]]

pe·yo·te (pā ō′tē; *Sp.* pe yô′te), *n., pl.* **-tes** (-tēz; *Sp.* -tes). **1.** mescal (def. 3). **2.** See **mescal button. 3.** mescaline. **4.** (in Mexico) any of several cacti related to or resembling mescal. [1840–50, *Amer.;* < MexSp < Nahuatl *peyotl*]

Pey·ton (pāt′n), *n.* a male given name, form of **Payton.**

pF, picofarad; picofarads.

pf., 1. perfect. **2.** pfennig. **3.** pianoforte; piano. **4.** (of stock) preferred. **5.** proof.

p.f., *Music.* louder. [< It *più forte*]

Pfalz (pfälts), *n.* German name of the Palatinate.

Pfc., *Mil.* private first class. Also, **PFC**

PFD, See **personal flotation device.**

pfd., (of stock) preferred.

pfen·nig (fen′ig; *Ger.* pfen′iKH), *n., pl.* **pfen·nigs, pfen·ni·ge** (*Ger.* pfen′i gə). **1.** a copper-coated iron coin and monetary unit of Germany, the 100th part of a Deutsche mark. **2.** (formerly) a minor coin and monetary unit of East Germany, the 100th part of an ostmark. [1540–50; < G: PENNY]

pfft (ft), *interj.* (used to express or indicate a dying or fizzling out.) Also, **phfft.** [1920–25]

pfg., pfennig.

Pfitz·ner (pfits′nər), *n.* **Hans E·rich** (häns′ ā′riKH), 1869–1949, German composer and conductor.

Pforz·heim (fôrts′hīm′; *Ger.* pfôrts′hīm′), *n.* a city in W Baden-Württemberg, in SW Germany. 106,600.

pfu·i (fo͞o′ē), *interj.* phooey.

Pfund′ se′ries (fund, pfo͝ont), *Spectroscopy.* a series of lines in the infrared spectrum of hydrogen.

PG, *Informal.* pregnant.

PG, parental guidance: a rating assigned to a motion picture by the Motion Picture Association of America indicating that children of all ages may attend but that some material may be deemed unsuitable and that parental guidance is advised. Cf. **G** (def. 7), **PG-13, R** (def. 5), **X** (def. 8). [1965–70, *Amer.*]

PG-13 (pē′jē′thûr′tēn′), a motion-picture rating advising parents that a film contains material deemed unsuitable for children under the age of 13. Cf. **PG**

Pg., 1. Portugal. **2.** Also, **Pg** Portuguese.

pg, picogram; picograms.

pg., page.

P.G., 1. Past Grand. **2.** paying guest. **3.** Postgraduate. **4.** Also, **p.g.** *Informal.* pregnant.

PGA, Professional Golfers' Association. Also, **P.G.A.**

PGA, *Biochem.* See **folic acid.** [*p*(*teroyl*) + *g*(*lutamic*) *a*(*cid*)]

Ph, *Chem.* phenyl.

pH, *Chem.* the symbol for the logarithm of the reciprocal of hydrogen ion concentration in gram atoms per liter, used to express the acidity or alkalinity of a solution on a scale of 0 to 14, where less than 7 represents acidity, 7 neutrality, and more than 7 alkalinity.

ph, *Optics.* phot; phots.

ph., 1. phase. **2.** phone.

P.H., Public Health.

PHA, Public Housing Administration.

pha·ce·li·a (fə sē′lē ə), *n.* any of numerous plants belonging to the genus *Phacelia,* of the waterleaf family, chiefly of the western U.S. and Mexico, having clusters of violet, blue, or white flowers. [< NL (1789), equiv. to Gk *phákel(os)* bundle (referring to the clustered flowers) + NL *-ia* -IA]

phac·o·e·mul·si·fi·ca·tion (fak′ō i mul′sə fi kā′shən), *n. Surg.* the removal of a cataract by first liquefying the affected lens with ultrasonic vibrations and then extracting it by suction. Also, **phakoemulsification.** [*phaco-* (< Gk *phako-,* comb. form of *phakós* lentil; see LENS) + EMULSIFICATION]

phac·o·lite (fak′ə līt′), *n. Mineral.* a colorless variety of chabazite. [1835–45; < Gk *phakó(s)* lentil plant + -LITE]

Phae·a·cia (fē ā′shə), *n. Class. Myth.* an island nation on the shores of which Odysseus was shipwrecked and discovered by Nausicaä. **—Phae·a′cian,** *n., adj.*

Phae·do (fē′dō), *n.* a philosophical dialogue (4th century B.C.) by Plato, purporting to describe the death of Socrates, dealing with the immortality of the soul, and setting forth the theory of Ideas.

Phae·dra (fē′drə, fed′rə), *n. Class. Myth.* the wife of Theseus who fell in love with Hippolytus, her stepson, and eventually hanged herself after causing his death.

Phae·drus (fē′drəs, fed′rəs), *n.* fl. A.D. c40, Roman writer of fables.

Pha·ën·na (fā en′ə), *n. Class. Myth.* one of the Graces worshiped at Sparta.

Phaes·tus (fē′stəs, fes′təs), *n.* Phaistos.

Pha·ë·thon (fā′ə thən, -thon′), *n. Class. Myth.* a son of Helios who borrowed the chariot of the sun and drove it so close to earth that Zeus struck him down to save the world. [< Gk *Phaéthōn,* special use of prp. of *phaéthein* to shine]

pha·e·ton (fā′i tn *or, esp. Brit.,* fāt′n), *n.* **1.** any of various light, four-wheeled carriages, with or without a top, having one or two seats facing forward, used in the 19th century. **2.** a vintage automobile of the touring-car type. [1585–95; special use of L *Phaetōn,* var. of *Phaethōn* PHAETHON]

phaeton (def. 1)

phage (fāj), *n.* bacteriophage. [by shortening, or independent use of -PHAGE]

-phage, a combining form meaning "a thing that devours," used in the formation of compound words, esp. the names of phagocytes: *macrophage.* Also, **-phag.** Cf. **phago-, -phagous, -phagy.** [n. use of Gk *-phagos* -PHAGOUS]

phag·e·de·na (faj′i dē′nə), *n. Pathol.* a severe, destructive, eroding ulcer. Also, **phag′e·dae′na.** [1650–60; < NL *phagedaena* < Gk *phagédaina* an ulcer, akin to *phageîn* to eat] **—phag·e·den·ic** (faj′i den′ik, -dē′nik), *adj.*

-phagia, var. of **-phagy.** [< NL < Gk]

phago-, a combining form meaning "eating, devouring," used in the formation of compound words: *phagocyte.* Cf. **-phage, -phagous, -phagy.** [< Gk, comb. form akin to *phageîn* to eat, devour]

phag·o·cyte (fag′ə sīt′), *n. Cell Biol.* any cell, as a macrophage, that ingests and destroys foreign particles, bacteria, and cell debris. [1880–85; PHAGO- + -CYTE] **—phag·o·cyt·ic** (fag′ə sit′ik), *adj.*

phag′ocyt′ic in′dex, the average number of bacteria ingested per phagocyte in an incubated mixture of bacteria, phagocytes, and blood serum: used in determining the opsonic index. [1900–05]

phag·o·cyt·ize (fag′ə sī′tiz, -si tīz′), *v.t.,* **-ized, -iz·ing.** (of a phagocyte) to devour (material). Also, *esp. Brit.,* **phag′o·cyt·ise′.** [1920–25; PHAGOCYTE + -IZE]

phag·o·cy·tose (fag′ə sī′tōs, -tōz), *v.t.,* **-tosed, -tos·ing.** phagocytize. [1930–35; back formation from PHAGOCYTOSIS]

phag·o·cy·to·sis (fag′ə sī tō′sis), *n. Physiol.* the ingestion of a smaller cell or cell fragment, a microorganism, or foreign particles by means of the local infolding of a cell's membrane and the protrusion of its cytoplasm around the fold until the material has been surrounded and engulfed by closure of the membrane and formation of a vacuole: characteristic of amebas and some types of white blood cells. Cf. **endocytosis, exocytosis, pinocytosis.** [1890–95; PHAGOCYTE + -OSIS]

phag·o·some (fag′ə sōm′), *n.* a vacuole within a phagocyte that contains bacteria or other ingested particles and that becomes fused with a lysosome. [1955–60; PHAGO- + -SOME[3]]

-phagous, a combining form meaning "eating," "feeding on," "devouring" that specified by the initial element: *creophagous; hylophagous; rhizophagous.* [< Gk *-phagos,* adj. deriv. of *phágein* to eat; see -OUS]

-phagy, a combining form meaning "eating," "devouring" that specified by the initial element, esp. as a practice or habit: *allotriophagy; anthropophagy.* Also, **-phagia.** [< Gk *-phagia;* see -PHAGE, -Y[3]]

pha·i·no·pep·la (fā ī′nō pep′lə, fā′ə-), *n.* a crested passerine bird, *Phainopepla nitens,* of the southwestern U.S. and Mexico. [< NL, equiv. to Gk *phaín(ein)* to give light, shine + *-o-* -O- + NL *-pepla,* fem. deriv. of Gk *péplos* PEPLOS; see -A[2]]

Phais·tos (fī′stəs), *n.* an ancient city in S central Crete: site of Minoan palace; Linear A tablets and important pottery objects unearthed here. Also, **Phaestus.**

phak·o·e·mul·si·fi·ca·tion (fak′ō i mul′sə fi kā′shən), *n. Surg.* phacoemulsification.

phal·ae·nop·sis (fal′ə nop′sis), *n., pl.* **-sis.** any of various epiphytic orchids of the genus *Phalaenopsis*, native to tropical Asia, having clusters of showy, variously colored flowers. Also called **moth orchid.** [< NL (1825), equiv. to Gk *phál(l)ain(a)* moth + *-opsis* -OPSIS; reflecting the popular name *moth orchid*]

phal•ange (fal′ənj, fə lanj′, fā′lanj), *n., pl.* **pha•lan•ges** (fə lan′jēz). *Anat., Zool.* a phalanx. [1550–60; back formation from PHALANGES]

pha•lan•ge•al (fə lan′jē əl), *adj.* **1.** of or pertaining to a phalanx. **2.** *Anat., Zool.* of or pertaining to a phalanx or the phalanges. [1825–35; < NL *phalange(us)* + -AL[1]]

pha•lan•ger (fə lan′jər), *n.* any of numerous arboreal marsupials of the family Phalangeridae, of Australia, having foxlike ears and a long, bushy tail. [1765–75; < F (Buffon) or < NL (1780) < Gk *phalang-*, s. of *phálanx* PHALANX + NL *-er*, of unclear orig.; the name refers to the syndactylous 2d and 3d digits of the hind feet]

pha•lan•ges (fə lan′jēz), *n.* **1.** a pl. of **phalanx. 2.** pl. of **phalange.** [< L < Gk *phálanges*]

phal•an•ste•ri•an (fal′ən stēr′ē ən), *adj.* **1.** of or pertaining to a phalanstery. **2.** of or pertaining to phalansterianism. —*n.* **3.** a member of a phalanstery. **4.** an advocate of phalansterianism; a Fourierist. [1835–45; PHALANSTERY + -AN]

phal•an•ste•ri•an•ism (fal′ən stēr′ē ə niz′əm), *n.* a system by which society would be reorganized into units comprising their own social and industrial elements; Fourierism. [1840–50; PHALANSTERIAN + -ISM]

phal•an•ster•y (fal′ən ster′ē), *n., pl.* **-ster•ies. 1.** (in Fourierism) **a.** the buildings occupied by a phalanx. **b.** the community itself. **2.** any similar association, or the buildings they occupy. [1840–50; < F *phalanstère*, b. *phalange* PHALANX and *monastère* MONASTERY]

pha•lanx (fā′langks, fal′angks), *n., pl.* **pha•lanx•es** or, for 7, **pha•lan•ges** (fə lan′jēz), *v.* —*n.* **1.** (in ancient Greece) a group of heavily armed infantry formed in ranks and files close and deep, with shields joined and long spears overlapping. **2.** any body of troops in close array. **3.** a number of individuals, esp. persons united for a common purpose. **4.** a compact or closely massed body of persons, animals, or things. **5.** *Mil.* (*cap.*) a radar-controlled U.S. Navy 20mm Gatling-type gun deployed on ships as a last line of defense against antiship cruise missiles. **6.** (in Fourierism) a group of about 1800 persons, living together and holding their property in common. **7.** *Anat., Zool.* any of the bones of the fingers or toes. See diag. under **skeleton.** —*v.i.* **8.** *Print.* to arrange the distribution of work in a shop as evenly as possible. [1545–55; < L < Gk *phálanx* military formation, bone of finger or toe, wooden roller]

phal•a•rope (fal′ə rōp′), *n.* any of three species of small, aquatic birds of the family Phalaropodidae, resembling sandpipers but having lobate toes. [1770–80; < F < NL *Phalaropus* genus name < Gk *phalār(ís)* coot + -o- -o- + *-pous* -footed; see -POD]

phal•er•a (fal′ər ə), *n., pl.* **phal•er•ae** (fal′ə rē′). a metal disk or boss worn on a man's breast as an ornament or as a military decoration or used to adorn the harness of a horse. [1600–10; < L, sing. use of Gk *phálara* (pl.) cheek-pieces]

phal•lic (fal′ik), *adj.* **1.** of, pertaining to, or resembling a phallus. **2.** of or pertaining to phallicism. **3.** genital (def. 2b). Also, **phal′li•cal.** [1780–90; < Gk *phallikós*. See PHALLUS, -IC]

phal•li•cism (fal′ə siz′əm), *n.* worship of the phallus, esp. as symbolic of power or of the generative principle of nature. Also, **phal•lism** (fal′iz əm). [1880–85; PHALLIC + -ISM] —**phal′li•cist, phal′list,** *n.*

phal′lic phase′, *Psychoanal.* the time from about age three to five when the genitals become the focus of a child's sensual pleasure. Also called **phal′lic stage′.**

phal′lic sym′bol, *Psychoanal.* any object, as a cigar or skyscraper, that may broadly resemble or represent the penis, esp. such an object that symbolizes power, as an automobile. [1905–10]

phal•lo•cen•trism (fal′ō sen′triz əm), *n.* a doctrine or belief centered on the phallus, esp. a belief in the superiority of the male sex. [1925–30] —**phal′lo•cen′tric,** *adj.*

phal•lo•tox•in (fal′ə tok′sin), *n. Mycol.* any of a group of potent mycotoxins produced by certain mushroom species of the genus *Amanita.* [1965–70; < NL (*Amanita*) *phallo(ides)* one such species (see PHALLUS, -OID) + TOXIN]

phal•lus (fal′əs), *n., pl.* **phal•li** (fal′ī), **phal•lus•es. 1.** an image of the male reproductive organ, esp. that carried in procession in ancient festivals of Dionysus, or Bacchus, symbolizing the generative power in nature. **2.** *Anat.* the penis, the clitoris, or the sexually undifferentiated embryonic organ out of which either of these develops. [1605–15; < L < Gk *phallós* penis]

Pham Van Dong (fäm′ vän′ dông′), born 1906, Vietnamese political leader: prime minister of North Vietnam 1955–76 and of unified Vietnam 1976–86.

phan•er•ite (fan′ə rīt′), *n.* any igneous rock whose grains are visible to the naked eye. [1855–60; < Gk *phaner(ós)* manifest, visible + -ITE[1]]

phan•e•ro•crys•tal•line (fan′ə rō kris′tl in, -īn′), *adj. Petrog.* (of a rock) having the principal constituents in the form of crystals visible to the naked eye. Also, **phan•er•it•ic** (fan′ə rit′ik). [1860–65; < Gk *phaneró(s)* visible, manifest + CRYSTALLINE]

phan•er•o•gam (fan′ər ə gam′), *n. Bot.* any of the Phanerogamia, a former primary division of plants comprising those having reproductive organs; a flowering plant or seed plant (opposed to *cryptogam*). [1860–65; < NL *phanerogamus*, equiv. to Gk *phaneró(s)* visible + *-gamos* -GAMOUS] —**phan′er•o•gam′ic, phan•er•og•a•mous** (fan′ə rog′ə məs), **phan•er•o•ga•mi•an** (fan′ər ə gā′mē ən), *adj.* —**phan′er•og′a•my,** *n.*

Phan•er•o•zo•ic (fan′ər ə zō′ik), *Geol.* —*n.* **1.** the eon comprising the Paleozoic, Mesozoic, and Cenozoic eras. —*adj.* **2.** of or pertaining to this eon. [1925–30; < Gk *phaneró(s)* manifest, visible + zo- + -IC]

phan•o (fan′ō), *n., pl.* **phan•os.** fanon.

phan•o•tron (fan′ə tron′), *n. Electronics.* a hot-cathode gas diode. [1930–35; perh. < Gk *phan(ázein)* to appear + -o- -o- + -TRON]

phan•ta•size (fan′tə sīz′), *v.i., v.t.,* **-sized, -siz•ing.** fantasize. Also, *esp. Brit.,* **phan′ta•sise′.**

phan•tasm (fan′taz əm), *n.* **1.** an apparition or specter. **2.** a creation of the imagination or fancy; fantasy. **3.** a mental image or representation of a real object. **4.** an illusory likeness of something. Also, **fantasm.** [1175–1225; < L *phantasma* < Gk *phántasma* image, vision (akin to *phantázein* to bring before the mind); r. ME *fantesme* < OF < L as above]
—**Syn. 1.** ghost, vision. See **apparition. 4.** hallucination, illusion.

phan•tas•ma (fan taz′mə), *n., pl.* **-ma•ta** (-mə tə). phantasm (defs. 1, 2). [1590–1600; < L]

phan•tas•ma•go•ri•a (fan taz′mə gôr′ē ə, -gōr′-), *n.* **1.** a shifting series of phantasms, illusions, or deceptive appearances, as in a dream or as created by the imagination. **2.** a changing scene made up of many elements. **3.** an optical illusion produced by a magic lantern or the like in which figures increase or diminish in size, pass into each other, dissolve, etc. [1795–1805; < F *fantasmagorie*, compound based on *fantasme* PHANTASM; second element perh. repr. Gk *agorá* assembly, gathering; see -IA] —**phan•tas′ma•go′ri•al, phan•tas•ma•gor•ic** (fan taz′mə gôr′ik, -gor′-), **phan•tas′ma•gor′i•cal, phan•tas′ma•go′ri•an,** *adj.* —**phan•tas′ma•go′ri•al•ly, phan•tas′ma•gor′i•cal•ly, phan•tas′ma•go′ri•an•ly,** *adv.* —**phan•tas′ma•gor′ist,** *n.*

phan•tas•ma•go•ry (fan taz′mə gôr′ē, -gōr′ē), *n., pl.* **-ries.** phantasmagoria.

phan•tas•mal (fan taz′məl), *adj.* pertaining to or of the nature of a phantasm; unreal; illusory; spectral: *phantasmal creatures of nightmare.* Also, **phan•tas′•mic, phan•tas′mi•cal, phan•tas•mat•ic** (fan′taz mat′ik), **phan′tas•mat′i•cal.** [1805–15; PHANTASM + -AL[1]] —**phan′tas•mal′i•ty,** *n.* —**phan•tas′mal•ly, phan•tas′mi•cal•ly, phan′tas•mat′i•cal•ly,** *adv.*

phan•tast (fan′tast), *n.* fantast.

phan•ta•sy (fan′tə sē, -zē), *n., pl.* **-sies.** fantasy.

phan•tom (fan′təm), *n.* **1.** an apparition or specter. **2.** an appearance or illusion without material substance, as a dream image, mirage, or optical illusion. **3.** a person or thing of merely illusory power, status, efficacy, etc.: *the phantom of fear.* **4.** an illustration, part of which is given a transparent effect so as to permit representation of details otherwise hidden from view, as the inner workings of a mechanical device. —*adj.* **5.** of, pertaining to, or of the nature of a phantom; illusory: *a phantom sea serpent.* **6.** *Elect.* noting or pertaining to a phantom circuit. **7.** named, included, or recorded but nonexistent; fictitious: *Payroll checks were made out and cashed for phantom employees.* Also, **fantom.** [1250–1300; ME *fantosme* < MF, OF < L *phantasma* PHANTASM] —**phan′tom•like′,** *adj.*
—**Syn. 1, 2.** See **apparition. 5.** imaginary. —**Ant. 5.** real, material.

phan′tom cir′cuit, *Elect.* a circuit derived from two suitably arranged pairs of wires, each pair being a circuit (**side circuit**) and also acting as one half of an additional derived circuit, the entire system providing the capabilities of three circuits while requiring wires for only two. [1880–85]

phan′tom limb′ pain′, *Pathol.* a phenomenon characterized by the experience of pain, discomfort, or other sensation in the area of a missing limb or other body part, as a breast. Also called **pseudesthesia.**

phan′tom stock′, an employee bonus expressed as the cash value of a specified amount of company stock to be received at a future date, meant to create employee interest in raising stock prices without giving any stock away.

-phany, a combining form occurring in loanwords from Greek, meaning "appearance," "manifestation" (*epiphany*); used in the formation of compound words (*Christophany; Satanophany*). [< Gk *-phania*, akin to *phaínesthai* to appear]

Phar., **1.** pharmaceutical. **2.** pharmacology. **3.** pharmacopoeia. **4.** pharmacy. Also, **phar.**

Phar•aoh (fâr′ō, far′ō, fā′rō), *n.* **1.** a title of an ancient Egyptian king. **2.** (*l.c.*) any person who uses power or authority to oppress others; tyrant. [bef. 900; ME *Pharao*, OE *Pharaon* < L *pharaō* < Gk *pharaṓ* (s. *pharaōn-*) < Heb *phar'ōh* < Egyptian *pr* house + ʿ great; orig. a designation for the palace, but used to refer to the king from the time of Akhenaton (14th cent. B.C.); *-h* restored from Heb]

Phar′aoh ant′, a red or yellow ant, *Monomorium pharaonis*, introduced from Europe into North America: a common household pest. Also, **Phar′aoh's ant′.**

phar′aoh hound′ (fâr′ō, far′ō, fā′rō), one of a breed of medium-sized gazehounds with a smooth coat, red to tan in color with white markings, and erect ears.

Phar•a•on•ic (fâr′ā on′ik, far′-), *adj.* **1.** (*sometimes l.c.*) of or like a Pharaoh: *living in Pharaonic splendor.* **2.** (*usually l.c.*) impressively or overwhelmingly large, luxurious, etc.: *a construction project of pharaonic proportions.* **3.** (*l.c.*) cruelly oppressive; tyrannical: *pharaonic tax laws.* [1850–55; < Gk *Pharaōn-* (s. of *Pharaṓ* PHARAOH) + -IC]

Phar.B., Bachelor of Pharmacy.

Phar.D., Doctor of Pharmacy.

Phar•i•sa•ic (far′ə sā′ik), *adj.* **1.** of or pertaining to the Pharisees. **2.** (*l.c.*) practicing or advocating strict observance of external forms and ceremonies of religion or conduct without regard to the spirit; self-righteous; hypocritical. Also, **Phar′i•sa′i•cal.** [1610–20; < LL *Pharisaicus* < Gk *Pharisaikós.* See PHARISEE, -IC] —**Phar′i•sa′i•cal•ly,** *adv.* —**Phar′i•sa′i•cal•ness,** *n.*

Phar•i•sa•ism (far′ə sā iz′əm), *n.* **1.** the principles and practices of the Pharisees. **2.** (*l.c.*) rigid observance of external forms of religion or conduct without genuine piety; hypocrisy. Also, **Phar•i•see•ism** (far′ə sē iz′əm). [1595–1605; < NL *Pharisaismus.* See PHARISAIC, -ISM] —**Phar′i•sa•ist,** *adj.*

Phar•i•see (far′ə sē′), *n.* **1.** a member of a Jewish sect that flourished during the 1st century B.C. and 1st century A.D. and that differed from the Sadducees chiefly in its strict observance of religious ceremonies and practices, adherence to oral laws and traditions, and belief in an afterlife and the coming of a Messiah. **2.** (*l.c.*) a sanctimonious, self-righteous, or hypocritical person. [bef. 900; ME *Pharise, Farise,* OE *Farisēus* < LL *Pharisēus,* var. of *Pharisaeus* < Gk *Pharisaîos* < Aram *pərīshayyā,* pl. of *pərīshā* lit., separated]

pharm., **1.** pharmaceutical. **2.** pharmacology. **3.** pharmacopoeia. **4.** pharmacy.

phar•ma•ceu•ti•cal (fär′mə sōō′ti kəl), *adj.* **1.** pertaining to pharmacy or pharmacists. —*n.* **2.** a pharmaceutical preparation or product. Also, **phar′ma•ceu′tic.** [1640–50; PHARMACEUTIC(S) + -AL[1]] —**phar′ma•ceu′ti•cal•ly,** *adv.*

phar•ma•ceu•tics (fär′mə sōō′tiks), *n.* (*used with a singular v.*) pharmacy (def. 1). [1535–45; < LL *pharmaceuticus* < Gk *pharmakeutikós*, equiv. to *pharmakeu(tḗs)* druggist, orig. poisoner (deriv. of *phármakon*; see PHARMACO-) + *-ikos* -IC; see -ICS]

phar•ma•cist (fär′mə sist), *n.* a person licensed to prepare and dispense drugs and medicines; druggist; apothecary; pharmaceutical chemist. Also, **phar•ma•ceu•tist** (fär′mə sōō′tist). [1825–35; PHARMAC(Y) + -IST]
—**Syn.** chemist.

pharmaco-, a combining form meaning "drug," used in the formation of compound words: *pharmacology.* [comb. form repr. Gk *phármakon* drug]

phar•ma•co•dy•nam•ics (fär′mə kō dī nam′iks), *n.* (*used with a singular v.*) the branch of pharmacology dealing with the course of action, effect, and breakdown of drugs within the body. [1835–45; PHARMACO- + DYNAMICS] —**phar′ma•co•dy•nam′ic, phar′ma•co•dy•nam′i•cal,** *adj.*

phar•ma•co•ge•net•ics (fär′mə kō jə net′iks), *n.* (*used with a singular v.*) *Pharm.* the branch of pharmacology that examines the relation of genetic factors to variations in response to drugs. [1955–60; PHARMACO- + GENETICS] —**phar•ma•co•ge•net•ic** (fär′mə kō jə net′ik), *adj.*

phar•ma•cog•no•sy (fär′mə kog′nə sē), *n.* See **materia medica** (def. 2). [1835–45; PHARMACO- + -GNOS(IS) + -Y[3]] —**phar′ma•cog′no•sist,** *n.* —**phar•ma•cog•nos•tic** (fär′mə kog nos′tik), *adj.*

phar•ma•co•ki•net•ics (fär′mə kō ki net′iks, -kī-), *n.* (*used with a singular v.*) *Pharm.* the branch of pharmacology that studies the fate of pharmacological substances in the body, as their absorption, distribution, metabolism, and elimination. [1955–60; PHARMACO- + KINETICS]

phar•mac•o•lite (fär mak′ə līt′, fär′mə kə-), *n.* hydrous calcium arsenate, $2CaO \cdot As_2O_5 \cdot 5H_2O$, formed by natural alteration of mineral deposits containing arsenopyrite and arsenical ores of cobalt and silver. [1795–1805; PHARMACO- + -LITE; modeled on G *Pharmakolith*]

phar•ma•col•o•gy (fär′mə kol′ə jē), *n.* the science dealing with the preparation, uses, and esp. the effects of drugs. [1715–25; < NL *pharmacologia.* See PHARMACO-, -LOGY] —**phar•ma•co•log•i•cal** (fär′mə kə loj′i kəl), **phar′ma•co•log′ic,** *adj.* —**phar′ma•co•log′i•cal•ly,** *adv.* —**phar′ma•col′o•gist,** *n.*

phar•ma•co•poe•ia (fär′mə kə pē′ə), *n. Pharm.* **1.** a book published usually under the jurisdiction of the government and containing a list of drugs, their formulas, methods for making medicinal preparations, requirements and tests for their strength and purity, and other related information. **2.** a stock of drugs. Also, **phar′•ma•co•pe′ia.** [1615–25; < NL < Gk *pharmakopoiïa* drug-maker's art, equiv. to *phármako(n)* drug + *-poi(os)* making (*poi(eîn)* to make + *-os* adj. suffix) + *-ia* -IA] —**phar′ma•co•poe′ial, phar′ma•co•poe′ic,** *adj.* —**phar′ma•co•poe′ist,** *n.*

phar•ma•co•ther•a•py (fär′mə kō ther′ə pē), *n.* the treatment of disease through the administration of drugs. [1905–10; PHARMACO- + THERAPY]

phar•ma•cy (fär′mə sē), *n., pl.* **-cies. 1.** Also called **pharmaceutics.** the art and science of preparing and dispensing drugs and medicines. **2.** a drugstore. [1645–55; earlier *pharmacia* < ML < Gk *pharmakeía* druggist's work. See PHARMACO-, -Y[3]]

Pharm.D., Doctor of Pharmacy.

Pharm.M., Master of Pharmacy.

Pha•ros (fâr′os), *n.* **1.** a small peninsula in N Egypt, near Alexandria: site of ancient lighthouse built by Ptolemy. **2.** the lighthouse on this peninsula. Cf. **Seven Wonders of the World. 3.** any lighthouse or beacon to direct sailors.

Pharr (fär), *n.* a city in S Texas. 21,381.

Phar•sa•li•a (fär sā′lē ə, -sāl′yə), *n.* a district in ancient Greece whose chief city was Pharsalus. —**Phar•sa′li•an,** *adj.*

Phar•sa•lus (fär sā′ləs), *n.* an ancient city in central Greece, in Thessaly: site of Caesar's victory over Pompey 48 B.C.

pharyng-, var. of **pharyngo-** before a vowel: *pharyngitis.*

pha•ryn•ge•al (fə rin′jē əl, -jəl, far′in jē′əl), *adj.* **1.** of, pertaining to, or situated near the pharynx. **2.** *Pho-*

net. articulated with retraction of the root of the tongue and constriction of the pharynx. —*n.* **3.** *Phonet.* a pharyngeal speech sound. Also, **pha•ryn•gal** (fə ring′gəl). [1820–30; < NL *pharynge(us)* pharyngeal (see PHARYNG-, -EOUS) + -AL[1]]

pha•ryn•ge•al•ize (fə rin′jē ə līz′, -jə līz′, far′ən jē′ə-līz′), *v.t.,* **-ized, -iz•ing.** *Phonet.* to pronounce with pharyngeal coarticulation. Also, **pha•ryn•gal•ize** (fə ring′gə līz′); *esp. Brit.,* **pha•ryn′ge•al•ise′, pha•ryn′gal•ise′.** [1930–35; PHARYNGEAL + -IZE] —**pha•ryn′ge•al•i•za′tion,** *n.*

pharyn′geal pouch′. See **branchial pouch.**

phar•yn•gec•to•my (far′in jek′tə mē), *n., pl.* **-mies.** *Surg.* excision of part or all of the pharynx. [1885–90; PHARYNG- + -ECTOMY]

phar•yn•gi•tis (far′in jī′tis), *n. Pathol.* inflammation of the mucous membrane of the pharynx; sore throat. [1835–45; PHARYNG- + -ITIS]

pharyngo-, a combining form representing **pharynx** in compound words: *pharyngology.* Also, *esp. before a vowel,* **pharyng-.** [< Gk, comb. form of *phárynx* throat]

phar•yn•gol•o•gy (far′ing gol′ə jē), *n.* the science of the pharynx and its diseases. [1835–45; PHARYNGO- + -LOGY]

pha•ryn•go•scope (fə ring′gə skōp′), *n.* an instrument for inspecting the pharynx. [1865–70; PHARYNGO- + -SCOPE] —**pha•ryn•go•scop•ic** (fə ring′gə skop′ik), *adj.* —**phar•yn•gos•co•pist** (far′ing gos′kə pist), *n.*

phar•yn•gos•co•py (far′ing gos′kə pē), *n., pl.* **-pies.** an examination by means of a pharyngoscope. [PHARYNGOSCOPE + -Y[3]; see -SCOPY]

phar•ynx (far′ingks), *n., pl.* **pha•ryn•ges** (fə rin′jēz), **phar•ynx•es.** *Anat.* the tube or cavity, with its surrounding membrane and muscles, that connects the mouth and nasal passages with the esophagus. See diag. under **mouth.** [1685–95; < NL < Gk *phárynx* throat, akin to *pháranx* gulf, chasm]

phase (fāz), *n., v.,* **phased, phas•ing.** —*n.* **1.** any of the major appearances or aspects in which a thing of varying modes or conditions manifests itself to the eye or mind. **2.** a stage in a process of change or development: *Each phase of life brings its own joys.* **3.** a side, aspect, or point of view: *This is only one phase of the question.* **4.** a state of synchronous operation: *to put two mechanisms in phase.* **5.** *Astron.* **a.** the particular appearance presented by the moon or a planet at a given time. **b.** one of the recurring appearances or states of the moon or a planet in respect to the form, or the absence, of its illuminated disk: *the phases of the moon.* See diag. under **moon.** **6.** *Zool.* See **color phase.** **7.** *Chem.* a mechanically separate, homogeneous part of a heterogeneous system: *the solid, liquid, and gaseous phases of a system.* **8.** *Physics.* a particular stage or point of advancement in a cycle; the fractional part of the period through which the time has advanced, measured from some arbitrary origin often expressed as an angle **(phase angle),** the entire period being taken as 360°. —*v.t.* **9.** to schedule or order so as to be available when or as needed. **10.** to put in phase; synchronize: *to phase one mechanism with another.* **11. phase down,** to reduce by gradual stages. **12. phase in,** to put or come into use gradually; incorporate by degrees: *to phase in new machinery.* **13. phase out,** to bring or come to an end gradually; ease out of service: *to phase out obsolescent machinery.* [1805–15; (n.) back formation from *phases,* pl. of PHASIS] —**phase′less,** *adj.* —**pha′sic, pha′se•al,** *adj.*
—**Syn. 1.** form, shape; facet, side.

phase′ an′gle, *Physics.* See under **phase** (def. 8). [1885–90]

phased′ array′, a radar antenna consisting of an array of dipoles that are excited in or out of phase with each other to control beam direction and radiation pattern without moving the antenna. Cf. **dipole** (def. 3). [1930–35]

phase′ di′agram, *Chem.* a graph, usually using temperature, pressure, and composition as coordinates, indicating the regions of stability of the various phases of a system. [1910–15]

phase•down (fāz′doun′), *n.* an act or instance of phasing down; gradual reduction. Also, **phase′-down′.** [1965–70; n. use of v. phrase *phase down*]

phase-in (fāz′in′), *n.* an act or instance of phasing in; gradual introduction or implementation. [n. use of v. phrase *phase in*]

phase′ mi′croscope, a microscope that utilizes the phase differences of light rays transmitted by different portions of an object to create an image in which the details of the object are distinct despite their near-uniformity of refractive index. Also called **phase′-con′trast mi′croscope** (fāz′kon′trast). [1945–50]

phase′ modula′tion, *Electronics.* radio transmission in which the carrier wave is modulated by changing its phase to transmit the amplitude and pitch of the signal. [1925–30]

phase•out (fāz′out′), *n.* an act or instance of phasing out; planned discontinuation or expiration. Also, **phase′-out′.** [1955–60; n. use of v. phrase *phase out*]

phase′ rule′, *Physical Chem.* a law that the number of degrees of freedom in a system in equilibrium is equal to two plus the number of components less the number of phases. Thus, a system of ice, melted ice, and water vapor, being one component and three phases, has no degrees of freedom. Cf. **variance** (def. 4). [1895–1900]

phase′ space′, *Physics.* a hypothetical space constructed so as to have as many coordinates as are necessary to define the state of a given substance or system. [1925–30]

phase′ veloc′ity, *Physics.* the velocity with which a simple harmonic wave is propagated, equal to the wavelength divided by the period of vibration. Cf. **group velocity, particle velocity.** [1930–35]

-phasia, a combining form used in the names of speech disorders, as specified by the initial element: *aphasia.* Also, **-phasy.** [< Gk, comb. form akin to *phánai* to speak]

pha•sis (fā′sis), *n., pl.* **-ses** (-sēz). a manner, stage, or aspect of being; phase. [1650–60; < NL < Gk *phásis* appearance, equiv. to *pha-* (base of *phaínein* to show) + *-sis* -SIS]

phas•mid (faz′mid), *n.* **1.** any insect of the order Phasmida, comprising the walking sticks and leaf insects. —*adj.* **2.** of or pertaining to the phasmids. [1870–75; < NL *Phasmida* the order name, equiv. to *Phasm(a)* the type genus (< Gk *phásma* apparition, so named from their extremely close resemblance to surrounding plants) + *-ida* -ID[2]]

pha•sor (fā′zər), *n. Physics.* a vector that represents a sinusoidally varying quantity, as a current or voltage, by means of a line rotating about a point in a plane, the magnitude of the quantity being proportional to the length of the line and the phase of the quantity being equal to the angle between the line and a reference line. [1940–45; PHASE + (VECT)OR]

phat (fat), *n. Typesetting.* fat (def. 25). [by resp.]

phat•ic (fat′ik), *adj.* denoting speech used to express or create an atmosphere of shared feelings, goodwill, or sociability rather than to impart information: *phatic communion.* [1923; prob. < Gk *phat(ós)* spoken, capable of being spoken (verbid of *phánai* to speak; cf. PROPHET) + -IC; coined (in phrase *phatic communion*) by Bronislaw Malinowski]

Ph.B., Bachelor of Philosophy. [< L *Philosophiae Baccalaureus*]

Ph. C., Pharmaceutical Chemist.

Ph.D., See **Doctor of Philosophy.** [< L *Philosophiae Doctor*]

Phe, *Biochem.* phenylalanine. [by shortening]

P.H.E., Public Health Engineer.

pheas•ant (fez′ənt), *n.* **1.** any of numerous large, usually long-tailed, Old World gallinaceous birds of the family Phasianidae, widely introduced. **2.** any of various other birds that resemble or suggest a pheasant. **3.** *Southern U.S.* the ruffed grouse. [1250–1300; ME *fesaunt* < AF; OF *fesan* < L *phāsiānus* < Gk *phāsiānós* (*órnis*) (bird) of the Phasis, river in the Caucasus]

ring-necked pheasant, *Phasianus colchicus,* length to 3 ft. (0.9 m)

pheas′ant cou′cal, a brown and black, red-eyed Australian bird, *Centropus phasianinus,* with a pheasantlike tail. [1870–75]

Phe•ba (fē′bä, fib′ä), *n.* a female day name for Friday. See under **day name.** Also, **Phibbi.**

Phe•be (fē′bē), *n.* a female given name.

Phè•dre (*Fr.* fe′drᵊ), *n.* a tragedy (1677) by Racine.

Phei•dip•pi•des (fī dip′i dēz′), *n.* the Athenian runner who secured aid from Sparta in the struggle between the Athenians and the Persians 490 B.C. Also, **Philippides.**

phel•lem (fel′əm, -em), *n. Bot.* cork (def. 6). [1885–90; < Gk *phell(ós)* cork + (PHLO)EM]

phel•lo•gen (fel′ə jən), *n. Bot.* cork cambium, a layer of tissue or secondary meristem external to the true cambium, giving rise to cork tissue. [1870–75; < Gk *pheló(s)* cork + -GEN] —**phel•lo•ge•net•ic** (fel′ə jə-net′ik), **phel•lo•gen•ic** (fel′ə jen′ik), *adj.*

phe•lo•ni•on (fe lô′nē ôn; *Eng.* fə lō′nē ən), *n., pl.* **-ni•a** (-nē ä; *Eng.* -nē ə), **-ni•ons.** *Gk. Orth. Ch.* a liturgical vestment resembling a chasuble. Also called **phenolion.** [< LGk *phelónion* a kind of mantle, alter. of *phainólis;* akin to *phaínein* to shine]

Phelps (felps), *n.* **1. William Ly•on** (lī′ən), 1865–1943, U.S. educator and literary critic. **2.** a male given name.

phen-, var. of **pheno-** esp. before a vowel: *phenazine.*

phe•na•caine (fē′nə kān′, fen′ə-), *n. Pharm.* a compound, $C_{18}H_{22}N_2O_2$, usually used in the form of its hydrochloride as a local anesthetic for the eye. [1905–10; PHEN- + A(CET-) + (CO)CAINE]

phe•nac•e•tin (fə nas′i tin), *n. Pharm.* a white, slightly water-soluble, crystalline solid, $C_{10}H_{13}NO_2$, used in medicine chiefly as an agent for checking or preventing fever or for relieving pain: withdrawn because of unfavorable side effects. Also called **acetophenetidin.** [1885–90; PHEN(ETIDINE) + ACET(YL) + -IN[2]]

phen•a•cite (fen′ə sīt′), *n.* a rare vitreous mineral, beryllium silicate, Be_2SiO_4, occurring in crystals, sometimes used as a gem. Also, **phen•a•kite** (fen′ə kīt′). [1825–35; < Gk *phenak-* (s. of *phénax*) a cheat, quack + -ITE[1]]

phe•nan•threne (fə nan′thrēn), *n. Chem.* a colorless, shiny, crystalline, water-insoluble isomer of anthracene, $C_{14}H_{10}$, derived from coal tar: used chiefly in dyestuffs and in the synthesis of drugs. [1880–85; PHEN- + ANTHR- + -ENE]

phe•nan•threne•qui•none (fə nan′thrēn kwə nōn′, -kwin′ōn), *n. Chem.* a yellowish-orange, crystalline, water-insoluble solid, $C_{14}H_8O_2$, used chiefly in organic synthesis and the manufacture of dyes. Also, **phe•nan•thra•qui•none** (fə nan′thrə kwə nōn′, -kwin′ōn). [1880–85; PHENANTHRENE + QUIN(INE) + -ONE]

phen•ar′sa•zine chlo′ride (fə när′sə zēn′), *Chem.* adamsite. [PHEN- + ARS(ENIC) + AZINE]

phen•a•zine (fen′ə zēn′, -zin), *n. Chem.* a yellow, crystalline, slightly water-soluble solid, $C_{12}H_8N_2$, used in organic synthesis chiefly in the manufacture of dyes. Also called **azophenylene.** [1895–1900; PHEN- + AZINE]

phen•a•zo•pyr•i•dine (fen′ə zō pir′i dēn′, -din), *n. Pharm.* a substance, $C_{11}H_{12}ClN_5$, used as a lower urinary tract analgesic. [PHEN- + AZO- + PYRIDINE]

phen•cy•cli•dine (fen sī′kli dēn′, -sik′li-), *n. Pharm.* an anesthetic drug, $C_{17}H_{25}N$, used as an animal tranquilizer: also widely used in several forms as an illicit hallucinogen. Also called **angel dust, PCP** [1955–60; PHEN- + CYCL(IC) + -ID[3] + -INE[2]]

phene (fēn), *n. Biol.* any characteristic of an individual organism that is genetically determined. [extracted from PHENOTYPE, or directly < Gk *phaínein* to show, (pass.) to appear]

phen•el•zine (fen′l zēn′), *n. Pharm.* a potent monoamine oxidase inhibitor, $C_8H_{12}N_2$, used to treat certain kinds of depression. [1955–60; PHEN- + E(THY)L + (HYDRA)ZINE]

phen•eth′yl al′cohol (fen eth′əl), *Chem.* a colorless, viscous, slightly water-soluble liquid, $C_8H_{10}O$, having a faint roselike odor: used chiefly in perfumery. Also, **phenylethyl alcohol.** [PHEN- + ETHYL]

phe•net•ic (fi net′ik), *adj. Biol.* pertaining to or based on the observable similarities and differences between organisms without regard to assumed genealogy. [1960; *phen-* (extracted from PHENOTYPE, or directly from Gk *phaínein* to show; cf. PHENO-) + -ETIC, perh. on the model of PHYLETIC or PHYLOGENETIC]

phe•net•ics (fi net′iks), *n.* (*used with a singular v.*) *Biol.* classification of organisms based on measurable similarities and differences rather than genetic makeup and evolutionary descent. [see PHENETIC, -ICS] —**phe•net•i•cist** (fi net′ə sist), *n.*
—**Usage.** See **-ics.**

phe•net•i•dine (fə net′i dēn′, -din), *n. Chem.* a colorless organic liquid, $C_8H_{11}NO$, used chiefly in its para form **(para-phenetidine)** in the synthesis of phenacetin, dyes, and other compounds. Also, **phe•net•i•din** (fə net′i din). [1860–65; PHENET(OLE) + -ID[3] + -INE[2]]

phen•e•tole (fen′i tōl′), *n. Chem.* a colorless, volatile, aromatic, water-insoluble liquid, $C_8H_{10}O$. Also called **phenyl ethyl ether.** [1855–60; PHEN- + ET(HYL) + -OLE]

Phe•ni•cia (fi nish′ə, -nē′shə), *n.* Phoenicia.

phe•nix (fē′niks), *n.* phoenix.

Phe′nix Cit′y (fē′niks), a city in E Alabama, on the Chattahoochee River. 26,928.

phen•met•ra•zine (fen me′trə zēn′), *n. Pharm.* a compound, $C_{11}H_{15}NO$, used chiefly to control the appetite in the treatment of obesity. [1955–60; PHEN(YL) + ME(THYL) + (TE)TRA- + (OXA)ZINE]

pheno-, 1. a combining form meaning "shining," "appearing, seeming," used in the formation of compound words: *phenocryst.* **2.** a combining form used in the names of chemical compounds that contain phenol or the phenyl group, are related to aromatic compounds, or derive from benzene: *phenobarbital.* Also, *esp. before a vowel,* **phen-.** [< NL *phaeno-* < Gk *phaino-* shining, comb. form of *phaínein* to shine, appear; in chemical senses, used orig. with reference to products from the manufacture of illuminating gas]

phe•no•bar•bi•tal (fē′nō bär′bi tôl′, -tal′, -nə-), *n. Pharm.* a white, crystalline powder, $C_{12}H_{12}N_2O_3$, used as a sedative, a hypnotic, and as an antispasmodic in epilepsy. Also, *esp. Brit.,* **phe•no•bar•bi•tone** (fē′nō bär′bi-tōn′, -nə-). Also called **phenylethylbarbituric acid.** [1915–20; PHENO- + BARBITAL]

phe•no•cop•y (fē′nə kop′ē), *n., pl.* **-cop•ies.** *Genetics.* the observed result of an environmentally induced, nongenetic alteration of a phenotype to a form that resembles the expression of a known genetic mutation. [< G *Phänokopie* (1935); see PHENOTYPE, COPY]

phe•no•cryst (fē′nə krist, fen′ə-), *n. Petrol.* any of the conspicuous crystals in a porphyritic rock. [1890–95; PHENO- + CRYST(AL)]

phe•no•gram (fē′nə gram′), *n. Biol.* a diagram depicting taxonomic relationships among organisms based on overall similarity of many characteristics without regard to evolutionary history or assumed significance of specific characters: usually generated by computer. Cf. **cladogram, dendrogram.** [PHENO- + -GRAM[1]]

phe•nol (fē′nôl, -nol), *n. Chem.* **1.** Also called **carbolic acid, hydroxybenzene, oxybenzene, phenylic acid.** a white, crystalline, water-soluble, poisonous mass, C_6H_5OH, obtained from coal tar, or a hydroxyl derivative of benzene: used chiefly as a disinfectant, as an antiseptic, and in organic synthesis. **2.** any analogous hydroxyl derivative of benzene. [1850–55; PHEN- + -OL[1]] —**phe•no•lic** (fi nō′lik, -nol′ik), *adj.*

phe•no•late (fēn′l āt′), *n., v.,* **-lat•ed, -lat•ing.** —*n.* **1.** Also called **phenoxide.** a salt of phenol, as sodium phenolate, C_6H_5ONa. —*v.t.* **2.** to treat, impregnate, or disinfect with phenol; carbolize. [1880–85; PHENOL + -ATE[2], -ATE[1]]

phe•no•lat•ed (fēn′l ā′tid), *adj. Chem.* containing phenol; carbolated. [1920–25; PHENOL + -ATE[1] + -ED[2]]

phe′nol coeffi′cient, *Chem.* the number indicating the effectiveness of a disinfectant as a germicide relative to phenol, which is arbitrarily assigned the number 1:

CONCISE ETYMOLOGY KEY: <, descended or borrowed from; >, whence; b., blend of, blended; c., cognate with; cf., compare; deriv., derivative; equiv., equivalent; imit., imitative; obl., oblique; r., replacing; s., stem; sp., spelling, spelled; resp., respelling, respelled; trans., translation; ?, origin unknown; *, unattested; ‡, probably earlier than. See the full key inside the front cover.

based on the time required to kill a given quantity of a specific type of bacteria.

pheno′lic res′in, *Chem.* any of the class of thermosetting resins formed by the condensation of phenol, or of a phenol derivative, with an aldehyde, esp. formaldehyde: used chiefly in the manufacture of paints and plastics and as adhesives for sandpaper and plywood. Also called **phenolic, phenoplast.** [1915–20; PHENOL + -IC]

phe•no•li•on (fe nô′lē ôn; *Eng.* fə nō′lē ən), *n., pl.* **-li•a** (-lē ä; *Eng.* -lē ə), **-li•ons.** *Gk. Orth. Ch.* phelonion.

phe•nol•o•gy (fi nol′ə jē), *n.* the science dealing with the influence of climate on the recurrence of such annual phenomena of animal and plant life as budding and bird migrations. [1880–85; syncopated var. of PHENOMENOLOGY, with restriction to climatic phenomena] **—phe•no•log•i•cal** (fēn′l oj′i kəl), *adj.* **—phe′no•log′i•cal•ly,** *adv.* **—phe•nol′o•gist,** *n.*

phe•nol•phthal•ein (fē′nôl thal′ēn, -ē in, -fthal′-, -nol-), *n. Chem., Pharm.* a white, crystalline compound, $C_{20}H_{14}O_4$, used as an indicator in acid-base titration and as a laxative. [1870–75; PHENOL + PHTHALEIN]

phe•nol•sul•fone•phthal•ein (fē′nôl sul′fōn thal′ēn, -ē in, -fthal′-, -nol-), *n. Chem.* a bright to dark red crystalline compound, $C_{19}H_{14}O_5S$, slightly soluble in water, alcohol, and acetone: used as an acid-base indicator and as a diagnostic reagent in medicine. Also called **phe′nol red′.** [PHENOL + SULFONE + PHTHALEIN]

phe•nom (fi nom′), *n. Slang.* a phenomenon: *a tennis phenom.* [by shortening]

phe•nom•e•na (fi nom′ə nə), *n.* a pl. of **phenomenon.**

phe•nom•e•nal (fi nom′ə nl), *adj.* **1.** highly extraordinary or prodigious; exceptional: *phenomenal speed.* **2.** of or pertaining to phenomena. **3.** of the nature of a phenomenon; cognizable by the senses. [1815–25; PHENOMEN(ON) + -AL[1]] **—phe•nom′e•nal′i•ty,** *n.* **—phe•nom′e•nal•ly,** *adv.*
—Syn. 1. uncommon, outstanding, surpassing, unprecedented.

phe•nom•e•nal•ism (fi nom′ə nl iz′əm), *n. Philos.* **1.** the doctrine that phenomena are the only objects of knowledge or the only form of reality. **2.** the view that all things, including human beings, consist simply of the aggregate of their observable, sensory qualities. [1860–65; PHENOMENAL + -ISM] **—phe•nom′e•nal•ist,** *n.* **—phe•nom′e•nal•is′tic,** *adj.* **—phe•nom′e•nal•is′ti•cal•ly,** *adv.*

phe•nom•e•nal•ize (fi nom′ə nl īz′), *v.t.,* **-ized, -iz•ing.** *Philos.* to regard or interpret as a phenomenon. Also, **phe•nom•e•nize** (fi nom′ə nīz′); *esp. Brit.,* **phe•nom′e•nal•ise′, phe•nom′e•nise′.** [1865–70; PHENOMENAL + -IZE]

phe•nom•e•nol•o•gy (fi nom′ə nol′ə jē), *n. Philos.* **1.** the study of phenomena. **2.** the system of Husserl and his followers stressing the description of phenomena. [1790–1800; PHENOMEN(ON) + -O- + -LOGY] **—phe•nom•e•no•log•i•cal** (fi nom′ə nl oj′i kəl), **phe•nom′e•no•log′ic,** *adj.* **—phe•nom′e•no•log′i•cal•ly,** *adv.* **—phe•nom′e•nol′o•gist,** *n.*

phe•nom•e•non (fi nom′ə non′, -nən), *n., pl.* **-na** (-nə) or, esp. for 3, **-nons. 1.** a fact, occurrence, or circumstance observed or observable: *to study the phenomena of nature.* **2.** something that is impressive or extraordinary. **3.** a remarkable or exceptional person; prodigy; wonder. **4.** *Philos.* **a.** an appearance or immediate object of awareness in experience. **b.** *Kantianism.* a thing as it appears to and is constructed by the mind, as distinguished from a noumenon, or thing-in-itself. [1595–1605; < LL *phaenomenon* < Gk *phainómenon* appearance, n. use of neut. of *phainómenos,* prp. of *phaínesthai* to appear, pass. of *phaínein* to show]
—Syn. 1. event, incident. **2, 3.** marvel, miracle.
—Usage. As with other plurals of Latin or Greek origin, like *media* and *criteria,* there is a tendency to use the plural PHENOMENA as a singular (*This phenomena will not be seen again*), but such use occurs infrequently in edited writing. The plural form PHENOMENAS, though occasionally seen, has even less currency.

phe•no•plast (fē′nə plast′), *n. Chem.* See **phenolic resin.** [PHENO- + -PLAST]

phe•no•saf•ra•nine (fē′nə saf′rə nēn′, -nin), *n. Chem.* safranine (def. 2). [1880–85; PHENO- + SAFRANINE]

phe•no•thi•a•zine (fē′nə thī′ə zēn′, -zin), *n.* **1.** *Chem.* a grayish-green to greenish-yellow, crystalline, water-insoluble solid, $C_{12}H_9NS$, used chiefly as an insecticide and vermifuge, and in the synthesis of pharmaceuticals. **2.** *Pharm.* any of a class of medications used principally to treat psychotic symptoms, as delusions or hallucinations, and excessive excitability. [1890–95; PHENO- + THIAZINE]

phe•no•type (fē′nə tīp′), *n. Genetics.* **1.** the observable constitution of an organism. **2.** the appearance of an organism resulting from the interaction of the genotype and the environment. Cf. **genotype.** [< G *Phänotypus* (1909); see PHENO-, -TYPE] **—phe•no•typ•ic** (fē′nə tip′ik), **phe′no•typ′i•cal,** *adj.* **—phe′no•typ′i•cal•ly,** *adv.*

phe•nox•ide (fi nok′sīd), *n. Chem.* phenolate (def. 1). [1885–90; PHEN- + OXIDE]

phe•nox•y•ben•za•mine (fi nok′sē ben′zə mēn′), *n. Pharm.* an alpha blocker, $C_{18}H_{22}ClNO$, used to dilate vascular peripheral blood vessels in the treatment of Raynaud's disease and in pheochromocytoma. [PHEN- + OXY-[2] + BENZAMINE]

phen•tol•a•mine (fen tol′ə mēn′, -min), *n. Pharm.* an alpha blocker, $C_{17}H_{19}N_3O$, used to reduce hypertensive states caused by a catecholamine excess, as in the treatment of pheochromocytoma. [1950–55; PHEN- + TOL(UIDINE) + -AMINE; see TOLU]

phen•yl (fen′l, fēn′l), *adj. Chem.* containing the phenyl group. [1840–50; PHEN- + -YL]

phen•yl•ac•et•al•de•hyde (fen′l as′i tal′də hīd′, fēn′-), *n. Chem.* a colorless, oily, water-insoluble liquid, C_8H_8O, having a hyacinthlike odor: used chiefly in perfumery. Also, **phen′yl•a•ce′tic al′dehyde** (fen′l ə sē′tik, -set′ik, fēn′-, fen′-, fēn′-). Also called **hyacinthin.** [PHENYL + ACET- + ALDEHYDE]

phen′yl ac′etate, *Chem.* a colorless, water-insoluble liquid, $C_8H_8O_2$, having a phenolic odor: used chiefly as a solvent.

phen′ylace′tic ac′id, *Chem.* a white crystalline, aromatic acid, $C_8H_8O_2$, used in the manufacture of penicillin and in perfumes. [1875–80; PHENYL + ACETIC ACID]

phen•yl•al•a•nine (fen′l al′ə nēn′, -nin, fēn′-), *n. Biochem.* a crystalline, water-soluble, essential amino acid, $C_6H_5CH_2CH(NH_2)COOH$, necessary to the nutrition of humans and most animals, obtained chiefly from egg white or skim milk. *Abbr.:* Phe; *Symbol:* F Also called **phen′yl•a•mi′no•pro•pi•on′ic ac′id** (fen′l ə mē′nō prō pē on′ik, -am′ə nō-, fēn′-, fen′l ə mē′nō-, -am′ə-nō-, fēn′-). [1880–85; PHENYL + ALANINE]

phen•yl•a•mine (fen′l ə mēn′, -am′in, fēn′-), *n. Chem.* aniline. [1865–70; PHENYL + AMINE]

phen•yl•ben•zene (fen′l ben′zēn, -ben zēn′, fēn′-), *n. Chem.* biphenyl. [PHENYL + BENZENE]

phen•yl•bu•ta•zone (fen′l byo͞o′tə zōn′, fēn′-), *n. Pharm.* a potent substance, $C_{19}H_{20}N_2O_2$, used to reduce pain and inflammation in rheumatic diseases and gout, and used in veterinary medicine for musculoskeletal disorders. [1950–55; PHENYL + BUT(YRIC) + *(pyr)az(olidinedi)one,* a component of its chemical name; see AZO-, -ONE]

phen•yl•car•bi•nol (fen′l kär′bə nôl′, -nol′, fēn′-), *n. Chem.* See **benzyl alcohol.** [PHENYL + CARBINOL]

phen•yl•di•eth•a•nol•a•mine (fen′l dī eth′ə nôl′ə-mēn′, -nol′ə-, fēn′-), *n. Chem.* a white, crystalline, slightly water-soluble substance, $C_{10}H_{15}NO_2$, used in the manufacture of dyes and in organic synthesis. [PHENYL + DI-[1] + ETHANOL + AMINE]

phen•yl•ene (fen′l ēn′, fēn′-), *adj. Chem.* containing a phenylene group. [1885–90; PHENYL + -ENE]

phen′ylene group′, *Chem.* any of three bivalent, isomeric groups having the formula $-C_6H_4-$, derived from benzene by the removal of two hydrogen atoms. Also called **phen′ylene rad′ical.**

phen•yl•eph•rine (fen′l ef′rēn, -rin, fēn′-), *n. Pharm.* an alpha-adrenergic stimulant, $C_9H_{13}NO_2$, used chiefly as a nasal decongestant. [1945–50; PHENYL + (EPIN)EPHRINE]

phen′yl•eth′yl al′cohol (fen′l eth′əl, fēn′-, fen′-, fēn′-), *Chem.* See **phenethyl alcohol.** [PHENYL + ETHYL]

phen′yl•eth•yl•bar•bi•tu′ric ac′id (fen′l eth′əl-bär′bi to͝or′ik, -tyo͝or′-, fēn′-, fen′-, fēn′-), *Pharm.* phenobarbital. [PHENYL + ETHYL + BARBITURIC ACID]

phen•yl•eth•yl•ene (fen′l eth′ə lēn′, fēn′-), *n. Chem.* styrene. [PHENYL + ETHYLENE]

phen′yl eth′yl e′ther, *Chem.* phenetole.

phen′yl•for′mic ac′id (fen′l fôr′mik, fēn′-, fen′-, fēn′-), *Chem., Pharm.* See **benzoic acid.** [PHENYL + FORMIC ACID]

phen′yl group′, *Chem.* the univalent group C_6H_5-, derived from benzene. Also called **phenyl radical.**

phen•yl•hy•dra•zine (fen′l hī′drə zēn′, -zin, fēn′-), *n. Chem.* a yellow, poisonous liquid or low-melting solid, $C_6H_8N_2$, used in chemical analysis and organic synthesis. [1895–1900; < G *Phenylhydrazin;* see PHENYL, HYDRAZINE]

phe•nyl′ic ac′id (fə nil′ik), *Chem.* phenol (def. 1). [1855–60; PHENYL + -IC]

phen′yl isocy′anate, *Chem.* a liquid reagent, C_7H_5NO, having an unpleasant, irritating odor: used chiefly for identifying alcohols and amines. Also called **carbanil.**

phen•yl•ke•to•nu•ri•a (fen′l kē′tō no͝or′ē ə, -nyo͝or′-, fēn′-), *n. Pathol.* an inherited disease due to faulty metabolism of phenylalanine, characterized by phenylketones in the urine and usually first noted by signs of mental retardation in infancy. Also called **phenylpyruvic oligophrenia.** [1930–35; < NL; see PHENYL, KETONE, -URIA] **—phen′yl•ke′to•nu′ric,** *adj.*

phen•yl•meth•ane (fen′l meth′ān, fēn′-), *n. Chem.* toluene. [PHENYL + METHANE]

phen′yl•meth•yl•car′bi•nyl ac′etate (fen′l-meth′əl kär′bə nil, fēn′-, fen′-, fēn′-), *Chem.* See **methylphenylcarbinyl acetate.** [PHENYL + METHYL + *carbinyl* (perh. < obs. G *Karbin* + -YL)]

phen′yl meth′yl ke′tone, *Chem.* acetophenone.

phen•yl•pro•pan•ol•a•mine (fen′l prō′pə nol′ə-mēn′, -min), *n. Pharm.* a substance, $C_9H_{13}NO$, related to ephedrine and amphetamine, available in various popular nonprescription diet aids as an appetite suppressant. Also called **PPA** [1945–50; PHENYL + PROPANE + -OL[1] + -AMINE]

phen′yl•pro′pyl ac′etate (fen′l prō′pil, fēn′-, fen′-, fēn′-), *Chem.* a colorless, water-insoluble liquid, $C_{11}H_{14}O_2$, used chiefly in perfumery. Also, **propylphenyl acetate.** [PHENYL + PROPYL]

phen•yl•py•ru•vic oligophre′nia (fen′l pī ro͞o′vik, -pi-, fēn′-), *Pathol.* phenylketonuria. [PHENYL + PYRUVIC (ACID)]

phen′yl rad′ical, *Chem.* See **phenyl group.**

phen′yl salic′ylate, *Chem.* salol.

phen•yl•thi•o•u•re•a (fen′l thī′ō yo͞o rē′ə, -yo͝or′ē ə, -fēn′-), *n. Biochem.* a crystalline, slightly water-soluble solid, $C_6H_5NHCSNH_2$, that is either tasteless or bitter, depending upon the heredity of the taster, and is used in medical genetics and as a diagnostic. Also called **phenyl•thi•o•car•bam•ide** (fen′l thī′ō kär bam′īd, -id, -kär′-bə mīd′, -mid, fēn′-). [1895–1900; PHENYL + THIOUREA]

phen′yl val′er•ate (val′ə rāt′), *Chem.* a colorless, slightly water-soluble liquid, $C_{11}H_{14}O_2$, used chiefly in flavoring and perfumery. [VALER(IC ACID) + -ATE[2]]

phen•y•to•in (fen′i tō′in, fə nit′ō-), *n. Pharm.* a barbiturate-related substance, $C_{15}H_{12}N_2O_2$, used as an anticonvulsant in the treatment of grand mal epilepsy and in focal seizures. [1940–45; *(di)pheny(lhydan)toin,* its full chemical name; see DI-[1], PHENYL, HYDANTOIN]

phe•o•chro•mo•cy•to•ma (fē′ō krō′mō sī tō′mə), *n., pl.* **-mas, -ma•ta** (-mə tə). *Pathol.* a tumor of the sympathetic nervous system or adrenal medulla, that produces excess norepinephrine and epinephrine and causes hypertension, headaches, nausea, etc. [1925–30; *pheochromocyte* a chromaffin cell of the adrenal medulla (*pheochrome* chromaffin (< Gk *phai(ós)* dusky + -O- + -CHROME) + -O- + -CYTE) + -OMA; cf. G *Phäochromocytom* (1912)]

phe•on (fē′on), *n. Heraldry.* a charge representing an arrowhead with widely spread barbs. Also called **broad arrow.** [1480–90; earlier *feon,* of uncert. orig.]

Phe•rae (fēr′ē), *n.* (in ancient geography) a town in SE Thessaly: the home of Admetus and Alcestis.

phe•re•sis (fə rē′sis, fer′ə-), *n. Med. Informal.* apheresis, esp. plasmapheresis. [prob. by construal of PLASMAPHERESIS as PLASMA + *-pheresis*]

pher•o•mone (fer′ə mōn′), *n. Animal Behav.* any chemical substance released by an animal that serves to influence the physiology or behavior of other members of the same species. [1959; < Gk *phér(ein)* to bear, bring + -O- + (HOR)MONE] **—pher′o•mo′nal,** *adj.*

phew (fyo͞o, pfyo͞o, whyo͞o), *interj.* (used as an exclamation to express disgust, exhaustion, surprise, impatience, relief, etc.): *Phew, it's hot!* [1595–1605]

phfft (ft), *interj.* pfft.

Ph. G., Graduate in Pharmacy.

phi (fī), *n., pl.* **phis. 1.** the 21st letter of the Greek alphabet (Φ,φ). **2.** the consonant sound represented by this letter.

phi•al (fī′əl), *n.* vial. [1350–1400; ME < L *phiala* saucer < Gk *phiálē;* r. ME *phiole, fiole* < MF *fiole* < L, as above] **—phi•al•ine** (fī′ə lin, -līn′), *adj.*

phi•a•le (fī′ə lē), *n., pl.* **-lae** (-lē′), **-lai** (-lī′). *Gk. and Rom. Antiq.* a shallow cup resembling a saucer, having a central boss and sometimes set upon a foot, used as a drinking vessel or to pour libations. [< Gk *phiálē* PHIAL]

Phib•bi (fib′ē, fē′bē), *n.* a female day name for Friday. See under **day name.** Also, **Pheba.**

Phi Be•ta Kap•pa (fī′ bā′tə kap′ə, bē′tə), **1.** a national honor society, founded in 1776, whose members are chosen, for lifetime membership, usually from among college undergraduates of high academic distinction. **2.** a member of Phi Beta Kappa.

Phi Bete (fī′ bāt′), *Informal.* **1.** a member of Phi Beta Kappa. **2.** Phi Beta Kappa.

Phi•chol (fī′kol), *n.* the commander of Abimelech's army. Gen. 26:26. Also, *Douay Bible,* **Phi′col.**

Phid•i•an (fid′ē ən), *adj.* of, associated with, or following the style of Phidias, as exemplified in the Parthenon. [1800–10; PHIDI(AS) + -AN]

Phid•i•as (fid′ē əs), *n.* c500–432? B.C., Greek sculptor.

Phi•dip•pi•des (fī dip′i dēz′), *n.* Pheidippides.

phi-func•tion (fī′fungk′shən), *n. Math.* See **Euler's phi-function.**

Phil (fil), *n.* a male given name, form of **Philip.**

phil-, var. of **philo-** before a vowel: *philanthropy.*

-phil, var. of **-phile:** *eosinophil.*

Phil., 1. Philemon. **2.** Philip. **3.** Philippians. **4.** Philippine.

phil., 1. philosophical. **2.** philosophy.

Phila., Philadelphia.

phil•a•beg (fil′ə beg′), *n.* filibeg.

Phil•a•del•phi•a (fil′ə del′fē ə), *n.* a city in SE Pennsylvania, on the Delaware River: Declaration of Independence signed here July 4, 1776. 1,688,210.

Phil′adel′phia law′yer, a lawyer of outstanding ability at exploiting legal fine points and technicalities. [1780–90, *Amer.*]

Philadel′phia pep′per pot′. See **pepper pot** (def. 1). [1925–30]

Philadel′phia scrap′ple, a superior variety of scrapple made with pork shoulder and other cuts of pork rather than with pork scraps. [1810–20]

Phi•lae (fī′lē), *n.* an island in the Nile, in Upper Egypt: the site of ancient temples; now submerged by the waters of Lake Nasser.

phi•lan•der (fi lan′dər), *v.i.* (of a man) to make love with a woman one cannot or will not marry; carry on flirtations. [1675–85; < Gk *philandros* one who loves (of a woman, loving her husband); see PHILO-, ANDRO-; later used in fiction as a proper name for a lover, and appar. mistaken as "a man who loves"] **—phi•lan′der•er,** *n.*
—Syn. trifle, dally, womanize.

phil•an•throp•ic (fil′ən throp′ik), *adj.* of, pertaining to, engaged in, or characterized by philanthropy; benevolent: *a philanthropic foundation.* Also, **phil′an•throp′i•cal.** [1780–90; PHILANTHROP(Y) + -IC] **—phil′an•throp′i•cal•ly,** *adv.*

phi•lan•thro•pist (fi lan′thrə pist), *n.* a person who practices philanthropy. [1720–30; PHILANTHROP(Y) + -IST] **—phi•lan′thro•pis′tic,** *adj.*

phi·lan·thro·pize (fi lan′thrə pīz′), *v.*, **-pized, -piz·ing.** —*v.t.* **1.** to treat (persons) in a philanthropic manner. —*v.i.* **2.** to practice philanthropy. Also, *esp. Brit.,* **phi·lan′thro·pise′.** [1820–30; PHILANTHROP(Y) + -IZE]

phi·lan·thro·py (fi lan′thrə pē), *n., pl.* **-pies. 1.** altruistic concern for human welfare and advancement, usually manifested by donations of money, property, or work to needy persons, by endowment of institutions of learning and hospitals, and by generosity to other socially useful purposes. **2.** the activity of donating to such persons or purposes in this way: *to devote one's later years to philanthropy.* **3.** a particular act, form, or instance of this activity: *The art museum was their favorite philanthropy.* **4.** a philanthropic organization. [1600–10; earlier *philanthropia* < LL < Gk *philanthrōpía* love for mankind. See PHIL-, ANTHROPO-, -Y³]

phi·lat·e·ly (fi lat′l ē), *n.* **1.** the collecting of stamps and other postal matter as a hobby or an investment. **2.** the study of postage stamps, revenue stamps, stamped envelopes, postmarks, postal cards, covers, and similar material relating to postal or fiscal history. [1860–65; < F *philatélie* < Gk *phil-* PHIL- + *atéleia* freedom from charges (taken to mean recipient's freedom from delivery charges by virtue of the stamp which sender affixed to the letter), lit., want of taxation, equiv. to *a-* A-⁶ + *tél(os)* tax + *-eia* -Y³] —**phil·a·tel·ic** (fil′ə tel′ik), **phil′·a·tel′i·cal,** *adj.* —**phil′a·tel′i·cal·ly,** *adv.* —**phi·lat·e·list** (fi lat′l ist), *n.*

Phil·by (fil′bē), *n.* **Harold Adrian Russell** (*"Kim"*), born 1912, British double agent: defected to U.S.S.R. 1963.

-phile, a combining form meaning "lover of," "enthusiast for" that specified by the initial element: *Anglophile; bibliophile; demophile.* Also, **-phil.** [< L *-philus, -phila* < Gk *-philos* dear, beloved (occurring in proper names). Cf. F *-phile*]

Philem., Philemon.

Phi·le·mon (fi lē′mən, fī-), *n.* **1.** an Epistle written by Paul. *Abbr.:* Phil. **2.** a person who was probably a convert of Paul and to whom this Epistle is addressed.

phil·har·mon·ic (fil′här mon′ik, fil′ər-), *adj.* **1.** fond of or devoted to music; music-loving: used esp. in the name of certain musical societies that sponsor symphony orchestras (**Philharmon′ic Soci′eties**) and hence applied to their concerts (**phil′harmon′ic con′certs**). **2.** of, noting, or presented by a symphony orchestra or the society sponsoring it. —*n.* **3.** a symphony orchestra or the society sponsoring it. [1755–65; PHIL- + HARMONIC; modeled on F *philharmonique* or It *filarmonico*]

phil′harmon′ic pitch′, *Music.* a standard of pitch in which A above middle C is established at 440 vibrations per second. Cf. **diapason normal pitch.**

phil·hel·lene (fil hel′ēn), *n.* a friend or supporter of the Greeks. Also, **phil·hel·len·ist** (fil hel′ə nist, fil′helē′nist). [1815–25; < Gk *philéllēn* Greek-loving. See PHIL-, HELLENE] —**phil·hel·len·ic** (fil′he len′ik, -lē′nik), *adj.* —**phil·hel·len·ism** (fil hel′ə niz′əm), *n.*

Phil. I., Philippine Islands.

-philia, a combining form used in the formation of compound words that have the general sense "unnatural attraction" (*necrophilia*), "tendency" (*hemophilia*); also forming abstract nouns that correspond to adjectives ending in **-philic** or **-philous** or nouns ending in **-phile.** Also, **-phily.** [< Gk *philía* friendship, affinity; see -PHILE, -IA]

-philiac, a combining form occurring in personal nouns that correspond to nouns ending in **-philia:** *hemophiliac; necrophiliac.* [< Gk *-philiakos;* see -PHILIA, -AC]

phil·i·beg (fil′ə beg′), *n.* filibeg.

-philic, 1. a combining form occurring in adjectives that correspond to nouns ending in **-phile:** *francophilic.* **2.** a combining form used to form adjectives that characterize classes of substances or organisms with an affinity for a chemical, environment, etc., as specified by the initial element: *acidophilic; cryophilic.* [-PHILE + -IC]

Phil·ip (fil′ip), *n.* **1.** one of the 12 apostles. Mark 3:18; John 1:43–48; 6:5–7. **2.** one of the leaders of the Christian Hellenists in the early church in Jerusalem who afterwards became an evangelist and missionary. Acts 6; 8:26–40. **3. King** (*Metacomet*), died 1676, North American Indian chief: sachem of the Wampanoag tribe 1662–76; leader of the Indians in King Philip's War. **4. Prince, Duke of Edinburgh,** born 1921, consort of Elizabeth II. **5.** a male given name: from a Greek word meaning "lover of horses."

Philip I, 1052–1108, king of France 1060–1108 (son of Henry I of France).

Philip II, 1. (*"Philip of Macedon"*) 382–336 B.C., king of Macedonia 359–336 (father of Alexander the Great). **2.** (*"Philip Augustus"*) 1165–1223, king of France 1180–1223. **3.** 1527–98, king of Spain 1556–98 (husband of Mary I).

Philip III, 1578–1621, king of Spain 1598–1621 (son of Philip II of Spain).

Philip IV, 1. (*"Philip the Fair"*) 1268–1314, king of France 1285–1314. **2.** 1605–65, king of Spain 1621–65 (son of Philip III).

Philip V, 1683–1746, king of Spain 1700–46.

Philip VI, 1293–1350, king of France 1328–50: first ruler of the house of Valois.

Philip., Philippians.

Phil′ip of Swa′bia, 1180?–1208, king of Germany and uncrowned emperor of the Holy Roman Empire 1198–1208 (son of Frederick I).

CONCISE ETYMOLOGY KEY: <, descended or borrowed from; >, whence; b., blend of, blended; c., cognate with; cf., compare; deriv., derivative; equiv., equivalent; imit., imitative; obl., oblique; r., replacing; s., stem; sp., spelling, spelled; resp., respelling, respelled; trans., translation; ?, origin unknown; *, unattested; ‡, probably earlier than. See the full key inside the front cover.

Phi·lip·pa (fi lip′ə), *n.* a female given name: derived from *Philip.*

Phi·lippe·ville (*Fr.* fē lēp vēl′; *Eng.* fil′ip vil′), *n.* former name of **Skikda.**

Phi·lip·pi (fi lip′ī, fil′ə pī′), *n.* a ruined city in NE Greece, in Macedonia: Octavian and Mark Antony defeated Brutus and Cassius here, 42 B.C.; the site of one of the first Christian churches in Europe, founded by St. Paul. —**Phi·lip·pi·an** (fi lip′ē ən), *adj., n.*

Phi·lip·pi·ans (fi lip′ē ənz), *n.* (*used with a singular v.*) an Epistle written by Paul to the Christian community in Philippi. *Abbr.:* Phil.

Phi·lip·pic (fi lip′ik), *n.* **1.** any of the orations delivered by Demosthenes, the Athenian orator, in the 4th century B.C., against Philip, king of Macedon. **2.** (*l.c.*) any speech or discourse of bitter denunciation. [1585–95; < L *Philippicus* < Gk *Philippikós.* See PHILIP, -IC]

Phil·ip·pine (fil′ə pēn′, fil′ə pēn′), *adj.* of or pertaining to the Philippines or their inhabitants; Filipino.

Phil′ippine mahog′any, 1. any of several Philippine trees of the genus *Shorea* and related genera, having brown or reddish wood used as lumber and in cabinetry. **2.** the wood of any of these trees. Also called **lauan.** [1920–25]

Phil·ip·pines (fil′ə pēnz′, fil′ə pēnz′), *n.* (*used with a plural v.*) an archipelago of 7083 islands in the Pacific, SE of China: formerly (1898–1946) under the guardianship of the U.S.; now an independent republic. 48,098,460; 114,830 sq. mi. (297,410 sq. km). *Cap.:* Manila. Also called **Phil′ippine Is′lands.** Formerly (1935–46), **Commonwealth of the Philippines.** Official name, **Republic of the Philippines.**

Phil·ip·pop·o·lis (*Eng.* fil′ə pop′ə lis), *n.* Greek name of **Plovdiv.**

phi·lip·pus (fi lip′əs), *n., pl.* **-lip·pi** (-lip′ī). a gold coin of ancient Greece, originally issued by Philip II of Macedon. [< L < Gk *philippeios*]

Phil·ips (fil′ips), *n.* **Ambrose,** 1675?–1749, English poet and dramatist.

Phil′ip the Good′, 1396–1467, duke of Burgundy 1419–67.

-philism, a combining form used to form abstract nouns corresponding to nouns ending in **-phile:** *bibliophilism.* [-PHILE + -ISM]

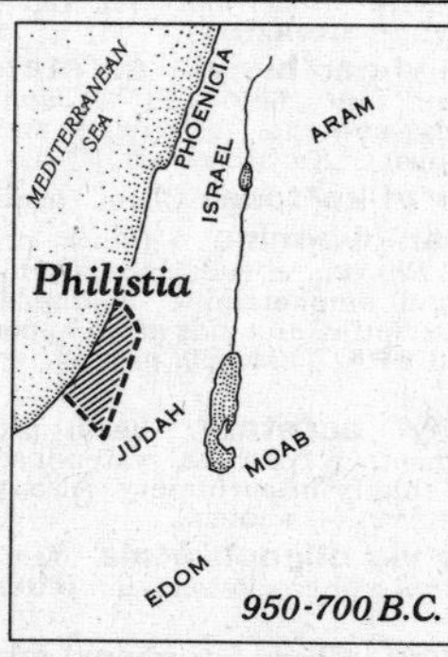

Phi·lis·ti·a (fi lis′tē ə), *n.* an ancient country on the E coast of the Mediterranean. —**Phi·lis′ti·an,** *adj.*

phil·is·tine (fil′ə stēn′, -stīn′, fi lis′tin, -tēn), *n.* **1.** (*sometimes cap.*) a person who is lacking in or hostile or smugly indifferent to cultural values, intellectual pursuits, aesthetic refinement, etc., or is contentedly commonplace in ideas and tastes. **2.** (*cap.*) a native or inhabitant of ancient Philistia. —*adj.* **3.** (*sometimes cap.*) lacking in or hostile to culture. **4.** smugly commonplace or conventional. **5.** (*cap.*) of or belonging to the ancient Philistines. [1350–1400; ME < LL *Philistīnī* (pl.) < LGk *Philistînoi* < Heb *pəlishtīm*] —**phil·is·tin·ism** (fil′ə stē niz′əm, -stī-, fi lis′tə niz′əm, -tē-), *n.*
—**Syn. 1.** Babbitt, vulgarian. **3.** lowbrow.

Phil·lip (fil′ip), *n.* a male given name.

Phil·lips (fil′ips), *n.* **1. David Graham,** 1867–1911, U.S. novelist. **2. Stephen,** 1868–1915, English poet and playwright. **3. Wendell,** 1811–84, U.S. orator and reformer.

Phil·lips·burg (fil′ips bûrg′), *n.* a city in NW New Jersey, on the Delaware River. 16,647.

Phil′lips head′, a screw head having two partial slots crossed at right angles, driven by a special screwdriver (**Phil′lips screw′driver**). See illus. under **screw.** [1930–35; after trademark *Phillips Screws*] —**Phil′·lips-head′,** *adj.*

phil·lips·ite (fil′ip sīt′), *n.* a zeolite mineral, similar to stilbite but with potassium replacing some of the calcium. [1815–25; named after J. W. *Phillips* (1775–1828), English mineralogist; see -ITE¹]

phil·lu·men·ist (fi lo͞o′mə nist), *n.* a collector of matchbooks and matchboxes. [1940–45; PHIL- + L *lūmen* light + -IST]

Phil·ly (fil′ē), *n.* Philadelphia (used as a nickname).

philo-, a combining form appearing in loanwords from Greek, where it meant "loving" (*philology*); on this model, used in the formation of compound words (*philoprogenitive*). Also, *esp. before a vowel,* **phil-.** [< Gk, comb. of *philos* loving, dear]

Phil·oc·te·tes (fil′ək tē′tēz), *n.* **1.** *Class. Myth.* a noted archer and squire of Hercules. Bitten by a snake and abandoned on an island because of his festering wound, he was at length brought by the Greeks to Troy, where he recovered and later killed Paris. **2.** (*italics*) a tragedy (408? B.C.) by Sophocles.

phil·o·den·dron (fil′ə den′drən), *n.* a tropical American climbing plant belonging to the genus *Philodendron,* of the arum family, usually having smooth, shiny, evergreen leaves, often used as an ornamental houseplant. [1875–80; < NL < Gk, n. use of neut. of *philódendros* fond of trees, in reference to its climbing habit. See PHILO-, -DENDRON]

phi·log·ra·phy (fi log′rə fē), *n.* the collecting of autographs, esp. those of famous persons. [PHILO- + -GRAPHY] —**phi·log′ra·pher,** *n.*

phi·log·y·ny (fi loj′ə nē), *n.* love of or liking for women. [1745–55; < Gk *philogynía.* See PHILO-, GYNY] —**phi·log′y·nist,** *n.* —**phi·log′y·nous,** *adj.*

Phi·lo Ju·dae·us (fī′lō jo͞o dē′əs), c20 B.C.–A.D. c50, Alexandrian Jewish theologian and philosopher.

philol., 1. philological. **2.** philology.

phil·o·lo·gi·an (fil′ə lō′jē ən), *n.* a philologist. [1820–30; < L *philologi(a)* (see PHILOLOGY) + -AN]

phi·lol·o·gy (fi lol′ə jē), *n.* **1.** the study of literary texts and of written records, the establishment of their authenticity and their original form, and the determination of their meaning. **2.** (esp. in older use) linguistics, esp. historical and comparative linguistics. **3.** *Obs.* the love of learning and literature. [1350–1400; ME *philologie* < L *philologia* < Gk *philologia* love of learning and literature, equiv. to *philólog(os)* literary, studious, argumentative + *-ia* -Y³. See PHILO-, -LOGY] —**phil·o·log·i·cal** (fil′ə loj′i kəl), **phil′o·log′ic,** *adj.* —**phil′o·log′i·cal·ly,** *adv.* —**phi·lol′o·gist, phi·lol′o·ger,** *n.*

phil·o·mel (fil′ə mel′), *n. Literary.* the nightingale. Also, **philomela.** [1350–1400; earlier *Philomele, Philomela* (< MF *philomèle*) < L *Philomēla* < Gk *Philómēla* PHILOMELA; r. ME *Philomene* < ML *Philomēna,* dissimilated var. of *Philomēla*]

Phil·o·me·la (fil′ə mē′lə), *n.* **1.** *Class. Myth.* an Athenian princess who was raped by her brother-in-law Tereus and was subsequently avenged and transformed into a nightingale. **2.** (*l.c.*) philomel.

Phil·o·me·li·des (fil′ə mə lī′dēz), *n. Class. Myth.* a king of Lesbos who wrestled and killed every opponent until he himself was defeated by Odysseus.

phil·o·pe·na (fil′ə pē′nə), *n.* **1.** a custom, presumably of German origin, in which two persons share the kernels of a nut and determine that one shall receive a forfeit from the other at a later time upon the saying of a certain word or the performance of a certain action. **2.** the thing shared. **3.** the forfeit paid. Also, **fillipeen.** [1830–40, *Amer.;* earlier *philippina* < D *philippine* < G *Vielliebchen,* dim. of *viellieb* very dear; in earlier form *viellieb* was taken as proper name *Philippe* Philip and *-chen* was made into fem. suffix *-ina,* giving a woman's name; in later form the word was Anglicized along pseudo-classical lines (cf. PHILO-, PENAL)]

phil·o·pro·gen·i·tive (fil′ō prō jen′i tiv), *adj.* **1.** producing offspring, esp. abundantly; prolific. **2.** of, pertaining to, or characterized by love for offspring, esp. one's own. [1860–65; PHILO- + PROGENITIVE]

philos., 1. philosopher. **2.** philosophical. **3.** philosophy.

phi·los·o·phas·ter (fi los′ə fas′tər, fi los′ə fas′tər), *n.* a person who has only a superficial knowledge of philosophy or who feigns a knowledge he or she does not possess. [1605–15; < LL: a bit of a philosopher. See PHILOSOPHER, -ASTER¹]

phil·o·sophe (fil′ə sof′, fil′ə zof′; *Fr.* fē lô zôf′), *n., pl.* **-sophes** (-sofs′, -zofs′; *Fr.* -zôf′). **1.** any of the popular French intellectuals or social philosophers of the 18th century, as Diderot, Rousseau, or Voltaire. **2.** a philosophaster. [1770–80; < F]

phi·los·o·pher (fi los′ə fər), *n.* **1.** a person who offers views or theories on profound questions in ethics, metaphysics, logic, and other related fields. **2.** a person who is deeply versed in philosophy. **3.** a person who establishes the central ideas of some movement, cult, etc. **4.** a person who regulates his or her life, actions, judgments, utterances, etc., by the light of philosophy or reason. **5.** a person who is rationally or sensibly calm, esp. under trying circumstances. **6.** *Obs.* an alchemist or occult scientist. [bef. 900; ME, var. of *philosophre* < AF (MF *philosophe* < L *philosophus*); r. OE *philosoph* < L *philosophus* < Gk *philósophos* philosopher, equiv. to *philo-* PHILO- + *soph(ía)* wisdom (see -SOPHY) + *-os* n. suffix] —**phi·los′o·pher·ship′,** *n.*

philos′opher king′, the Platonic ideal of a ruler, philosophically trained and enlightened. [1920–25]

philos′ophers' stone′, *Alchemy.* a substance sought by alchemists that would be capable of transmuting baser metals into gold or silver and of prolonging life. Also, **philos′opher's stone′.** [1350–1400; ME]

phil·o·soph·i·cal (fil′ə sof′i kəl), *adj.* **1.** of or pertaining to philosophy: *philosophical studies.* **2.** versed in or occupied with philosophy. **3.** proper to or befitting a philosopher. **4.** rationally or sensibly calm, patient, or composed. **5.** *Rare.* of or pertaining to natural philosophy or physical science. Also, **phil′o·soph′ic.** [1350–1400; ME: learned, pertaining to alchemy < L *philosophic(us)* (< Gk *philosophikós*; see PHILOSOPHER, -IC) + -AL[1]] —**phil′o·soph′i·cal·ly,** *adv.* —**phil′o·soph′i·cal·ness,** *n.*

philosoph′ical anal′ysis. See **linguistic analysis.** [1940–45]

philosoph′ical anthropol′ogy, anthropology (def. 4).

phi·los·o·phism (fi los′ə fiz′əm), *n.* **1.** spurious or deceitful philosophy. **2.** a false or contrived argument, esp. one designed to deceive. [1785–95; PHILOSOPH(Y) + -ISM]

phi·los·o·phize (fi los′ə fīz′), *v.i.*, **-phized, -phiz·ing. 1.** to speculate or theorize, usually in a superficial or imprecise manner. **2.** to think or reason as a philosopher. Also, *esp. Brit.,* **phi·los′o·phise′.** [1585–95; PHILOSOPH(Y) + -IZE] —**phi·los′o·phi·za′tion,** *n.* —**phi·los′o·phiz′er,** *n.*

phi·los·o·phy (fi los′ə fē), *n., pl.* **-phies. 1.** the rational investigation of the truths and principles of being, knowledge, or conduct. **2.** any of the three branches, namely natural philosophy, moral philosophy, and metaphysical philosophy, that are accepted as composing this study. **3.** a system of philosophical doctrine: *the philosophy of Spinoza.* **4.** the critical study of the basic principles and concepts of a particular branch of knowledge, esp. with a view to improving or reconstituting them: *the philosophy of science.* **5.** a system of principles for guidance in practical affairs. **6.** a philosophical attitude, as one of composure and calm in the presence of troubles or annoyances. [1250–1300; ME *philosophie* < L *philosophia* < Gk *philosophía.* See PHILO-, -SOPHY]

philos′ophy of life′, any philosophical view or vision of the nature or purpose of life or of the way that life should be lived. [1850–55]

-philous, a combining form meaning "liking," "having an affinity for" that specified by the initial element: *dendrophilous.* Cf. **-philic.** [< L *-philus* < Gk *-philos.* See -PHILE, -OUS]

phil·ter (fil′tər), *n., v.,* **-tered, -ter·ing.** —*n.* **1.** a potion, charm, or drug supposed to cause the person taking it to fall in love, usually with some specific person. **2.** a magic potion for any purpose. —*v.t.* **3.** to enchant or bewitch with a philter. [1580–90; < F *philtre* < L *philtrum;* see PHILTRUM] —**phil′ter·er,** *n.*

phil·tre (fil′tər), *n., v.t.,* **-tred, -tring.** *Chiefly Brit.* philter.

phil·trum (fil′trəm), *n., pl.* **-tra** (-trə). **1.** *Anat.* the vertical groove on the surface of the upper lip, below the septum of the nose. **2.** a philter. [1600–10; < L: love philter < Gk *philtron* love philter, dimple in upper lip. See PHIL-, -TRON]

-phily, var. of **-philia.**

phi·mo·sis (fī mō′sis, fi-), *n., pl.* **-ses** (-sēz). *Pathol.* **1.** constriction of the orifice of the prepuce so as to prevent the foreskin from being drawn back to uncover the glans penis. **2.** a similar condition involving the clitoris. **3.** narrowness of the vagina. [1665–75; < NL *phimōsis* < Gk *phímōsis* lit., a muzzling, equiv. to *phīmō-,* verbid s. of *phimoûn* to muzzle + *-sis* -SIS] —**phi·mot·ic** (fī mot′ik, fi-), *adj.*

Phin·e·as (fin′ē əs), *n.* a male given name: from a Hebrew word meaning "serpent's mouth or oracle."

Phin·e·us (fin′ē əs, fī′nyo͞os), *n. Class. Myth.* a brother of Cepheus who was not brave enough to rescue his betrothed Andromeda from a sea monster and who was eventually turned to stone.

phi-phe·nom·e·non (fī′fī nom′ə non′, -nən), *n., pl.* **-na** (-nə). *Psychol.* motion perceived by a subject, esp. the illusion of movement produced when stationary stimuli, as pictures or lights, are presented in rapid succession and are sometimes in slightly different positions. [1925–30]

Phit·sa·nu·lok (pēt′sä no͝o′lōk), *n.* a city in central Thailand. 33,883.

phiz (fiz), *n. Slang.* face. [abbr. of PHYSIOGNOMY]

Ph.L., Licentiate in Philosophy.

phle·bi·tis (flə bī′tis), *n. Pathol.* inflammation of a vein, often occurring in the legs and involving the formation of a thrombus, characterized by swelling, pain, and change of skin color. [1815–25; < NL; see PHLEB-, -ITIS] —**phle·bit·ic** (flə bit′ik), *adj.*

phlebo-, a combining form meaning "vein," used in the formation of compound words: *phlebosclerosis.* Also, *esp. before a vowel,* **phleb-.** [< Gk, comb. form of *phléps* vein]

phleb·o·gram (fleb′ə gram′), *n. Med.* **1.** venogram. **2.** the tracing made by a phlebograph. [1880–85; PHLEBO- + -GRAM[1]]

phleb·o·graph (fleb′ə graf′, -gräf′), *n.* an instrument for recording the venous pulse. [1900–05; PHLEBO- + -GRAPH]

phle·bog·ra·phy (flə bog′rə fē), *n., pl.* **-phies.** venography. [1890–95; PHLEBO- + -GRAPHY]

phleb·oid (fleb′oid), *adj. Anat.* pertaining to or resembling a vein. [PHLEB- + -OID]

phle·bol·o·gy (flə bol′ə jē), *n.* the study of the anatomy, physiology, and diseases of veins. Also called **venology.** [1890–95; PHLEBO- + -LOGY] —**phle·bol′o·gist,** *n.*

phleb·o·scle·ro·sis (fleb′ō skli rō′sis), *n. Pathol.* sclerosis, or hardening, of the walls of veins. [1895–1900; PHLEBO- + SCLEROSIS]

phleb·o·throm·bo·sis (fleb′ō throm bō′sis), *n. Pathol.* the presence of a thrombus in a vein. Cf. **thrombophlebitis.** [1890–95; < NL; see PHLEBO-, THROMBOSIS]

phleb·o·tome (fleb′ə tōm′), *n.* a cutting instrument used for phlebotomy. [PHLEBO- + -TOME]

phleb·o·tom·ic (fleb′ə tom′ik), *adj.* **1.** of or noting phlebotomy. **2.** (of insects) bloodsucking. Also, **phleb′o·tom′i·cal.** [1790–1800; PHLEBOTOM(Y) + -IC] —**phleb′o·tom′i·cal·ly,** *adv.*

phle·bot·o·mist (flə bot′ə mist), *n. Surg.* **1.** a specialist in phlebotomy. **2.** a nurse or other health worker trained in drawing venous blood for testing or donation. [1650–60; PHLEBOTOM(Y) + -IST]

phle·bot·o·mize (flə bot′ə mīz′), *v.t.,* **-mized, -miz·ing.** to subject to phlebotomy; bleed. Also, *esp. Brit.,* **phle·bot′o·mise′.** [1590–1600; < MF *phlebotomiser* (cf. ML *flebotomizāre*). See PHLEBOTOMY, -IZE] —**phle·bot′o·mi·za′tion,** *n.*

phle·bot′o·mus fe′ver (flə bot′ə məs), *Pathol.* See **sandfly fever.** [1920–25; < NL *Phlebotomus* genus name of the sandfly < Gk *phlebotómos* vein-cutting (referring to instruments for letting blood); see PHLEBO-, -TOME]

phle·bot·o·my (flə bot′ə mē), *n., pl.* **-mies.** *Med.* the act or practice of opening a vein for letting blood as a therapeutic measure; venesection; bleeding. [1350–1400; earlier *flebotomye, phlebothomy* (< MF *flebotomie*) < ML *phlebotomia,* LL < Gk *phlebotomía* (see PHLEBO-, -TOMY); r. ME *fleobotomie* < ML *fleobotomia,* var. of *phlebotomia*]

Phleg·e·thon (fleg′ə thon′, flej′-), *n.* **1.** Also called **Pyriphlegethon.** *Class. Myth.* a river of fire, one of five rivers surrounding Hades. **2.** (*often l.c.*) a stream of fire or fiery light. [< L < Gk, n. use of *phlegéthōn* blazing, prp. of *phlegéthein* to blaze. See PHLEGM] —**Phleg′e·thon′tal, Phleg′e·thon′tic,** *adj.*

phlegm (flem), *n.* **1.** the thick mucus secreted in the respiratory passages and discharged through the mouth, esp. that occurring in the lungs and throat passages, as during a cold. **2.** one of the four elemental bodily humors of medieval physiology, regarded as causing sluggishness or apathy. **3.** sluggishness, indifference, or apathy. **4.** self-possession, calmness, or composure. [1350–1400; ME *fleem* < MF *flemme* < LL *phlegma* < Gk *phlégma* flame, phlegmatic humor, equiv. to *phlég(ein)* to burn + *-ma* resultative n. suffix] —**phlegm′less,** *adj.*
—**Syn. 3.** impassivity. —**Ant. 3.** animation, concern.

phleg·mat·ic (fleg mat′ik), *adj.* **1.** not easily excited to action or display of emotion; apathetic; sluggish. **2.** self-possessed, calm, or composed. **3.** of the nature of or abounding in the humor phlegm. Also, **phleg·mat′i·cal.** [1300–50; < LL *phlegmaticus* < Gk *phlegmatikós* pertaining to phlegm, equiv. to *phlegmat-* (s. of *phlégma* PHLEGM) + *-ikos* -IC; r. ME *fleumatik* < MF *fleumatique* < LL, as above] —**phleg·mat′i·cal·ly,** *adv.* —**phleg·mat′i·cal·ness, phleg·mat′ic·ness,** *n.*
—**Syn. 1.** stoical, cool, cold, uninterested, dull, torpid. **2.** cool, collected, unruffled, placid, quiet.

phlegm·y (flem′ē), *adj.,* **phlegm·i·er, phlegm·i·est.** of, pertaining to, or characterized by phlegm. [1540–50; PHLEGM + -Y[1]]

phlo·em (flō′em), *n.* the part of a vascular bundle consisting of sieve tubes, companion cells, parenchyma, and fibers and forming the food-conducting tissue of a plant. [< G (1858), irreg. < Gk *phló(os)* bark (var. of *phloiós*) + *-ēma* deverbal n. ending]

phlo′em necro′sis, *Plant Pathol.* a disease of the American elm caused by a mycoplasmalike organism, characterized by yellowing and necrosis of the foliage and yellowish-brown discoloration of the phloem. [1920–25]

phlo′em ray′, *Bot.* a vascular ray extending into or located entirely within the secondary phloem. [1870–75]

phlo·gis·tic (flō jis′tik), *adj.* **1.** *Pathol.* inflammatory. **2.** pertaining to or consisting of phlogiston. [1725–35; < Gk *phlogist(ós)* inflammable (verbid of *phlogízein* to set on fire; akin to PHLOX, PHLEGM) + -IC]

phlo·gis·ton (flō jis′ton, -tən), *n.* a nonexistent chemical that, prior to the discovery of oxygen, was thought to be released during combustion. [1720–30; < NL: inflammability, n. use of Gk *phlogistón,* neut. of *phlogistós* inflammable, burnt up; see PHLOGISTIC]

phlog·o·pite (flog′ə pīt′), *n.* a magnesium-rich mica mineral, usually yellowish-brown, but sometimes red-dish-brown. [1840–50; < Gk *phlogōp(ós)* fiery-looking (*phlog-,* s. of *phlóx* flame + *ōp(ē)* view, look + *-os* adj. suffix) + -ITE[1]]

phlor·i·zin (flôr′ə zin, flor′-, flə rī′zin), *n. Chem.* a bitter, crystalline glucoside, $C_{21}H_{24}O_{10}$, obtained from the root bark of the apple, pear, cherry, etc.: formerly used as a tonic and in the treatment of malaria; now used chiefly in biochemical research. Also, **phlo·rid·zin** (flə rid′zin), **phlo′rhi·zin, phlor′rhi·zin.** [1830–40; < Gk *phló(os)* bark (var. of *phloiós*) + *rhíz(a)* ROOT[1] + -IN[2]]

phlor·o·glu·cin·ol (flôr′ə glo͞o′sə nôl′, -nol′, flor′-), *n. Chem.* a white to yellow, crystalline, slightly water-soluble powder, $C_6H_3(OH)_3 \cdot 2H_2O$, used chiefly in analytical chemistry and in the preparation of pharmaceuticals. Also, **phlor·o·glu·cin** (flôr′ə glo͞o′sin, flor′-), **phlor·o·glu·cine** (flôr′ə glo͞o′sēn, -sin, flor′-). [1875–80; PHLOR(IZIN) + -O- + GLUC- + -IN[2] + -OL[1]]

phlox (floks), *n.* **1.** any plant of the genus *Phlox,* of North America, certain species of which are cultivated for their showy flowers of various colors. Cf. **phlox family. 2.** the flower of this plant. [1595–1605; < ML, special use of L *phlox* < Gk *phlóx* a flame-colored plant, lit., FLAME. See PHLEGM, PHLOGISTIC]

phlox′ fam′ily, the plant family Polemoniaceae, characterized by herbaceous or sometimes shrubby plants having simple or compound leaves, flowers with a five-lobed corolla, and capsular fruit, and including gilia, Jacob's-ladder, moss pink, and phlox.

phlyc·te·na (flik tē′nə), *n., pl.* **-nae** (-nē). *Pathol.* a small vesicle, blister, or pustule. Also, **phlyctaena.** [1685–95; < NL, var. of *phlyctaena* < Gk *phlýktaina* a blister, akin to *phlýein, phlýzein* to swell, boil over]

Ph.M., Master of Philosophy.

Phnom Penh (nom′ pen′, pə nôm′ pen′), a city in and the capital of Cambodia, in the S part. 400,000. Also, **Pnom Penh, Pnom-penh, Pnompenh.**

-phobe, a combining form used to form personal nouns corresponding to nouns ending in **-phobia:** *Anglophobe.* Also, **-phobiac.** [< Gk *-phobos,* adj. deriv. of *phóbos* fear, panic]

pho·bi·a (fō′bē ə), *n.* a persistent, irrational fear of a specific object, activity, or situation that leads to a compelling desire to avoid it. [1780–90; extracted from nouns ending in -PHOBIA]
—**Syn.** aversion, hatred.

-phobia, a combining form meaning "fear," occurring in loanwords from Greek (*hydrophobia*); on this model, used in the names of mental disorders that have the general sense "dread of, aversion toward" that specified by the initial element: *agoraphobia.* [< L < Gk, equiv. to *-phob(os)* -PHOBE + *-ia* -IA]

pho·bic (fō′bik), *adj.* **1.** of or pertaining to a phobia or phobias. —*n.* **2.** a person suffering from a phobia. [1895–1900; PHOB(IA) + -IC, or by abstraction from adjectives ending in -PHOBIC]

-phobic, a combining form used to form adjectives corresponding to nouns ending in **-phobe:** *acrophobic; photophobic.* [-PHOBE + -IC]

Pho·bos (fō′bəs, -bos), *n.* **1.** Also, **Pho·bus** (fō′bəs). *Class. Myth.* a son and attendant of Ares and the personification of a fear held to possess armies and cause their defeat. **2.** *Astron.* one of the two moons of Mars. Cf. **Deimos.**

Pho·cae·a (fō sē′ə), *n.* an ancient seaport in Asia Minor: northernmost of the Ionian cities; later an important maritime state.

pho·cine (fō′sīn, -sin), *adj. Zool.* of or pertaining to seals. [1840–50; < L *phōc(a)* seal (< Gk *phṓkē*) + -INE[1]]

Pho·ci·on (fō′shē ən, -on′), *n.* 402?–317 B.C., Athenian statesman and general.

Pho·cis (fō′sis), *n.* an ancient district in central Greece, N of the Gulf of Corinth: site of Delphic oracle.

pho·co·me·li·a (fō′kō mē′lē ə, -mēl′yə), *n. Pathol.* a usually congenital deformity of the extremities in which the limbs are abnormally short. Also, **phokomelia, pho·com·e·ly** (fō kom′ə lē). [1890–95; < NL, equiv. to *phōco-,* comb. form repr. Gk *phṓkē* seal + *-melia* -MELIA]

phoe·be (fē′bē), *n.* any of several small American flycatchers of the genus *Sayornis,* esp. *S. phoebe,* of eastern North America. [1690–1700, *Amer.*; imit.; sp. by influence of PHOEBE]

Phoe·be (fē′bē), *n.* **1.** *Class. Myth.* a Titan, daughter of Uranus and Gaea and mother of Leto, later identified with Artemis and with the Roman goddess Diana. **2.** *Astron.* one of the moons of Saturn. **3.** *Literary.* the moon personified. **4.** a female given name.

Phoe·bus (fē′bəs), *n.* **1.** *Class. Myth.* Apollo as the sun god. **2.** *Literary.* the sun personified. [< L < Gk *Phoîbos* lit., bright, akin to *pháos* light; r. ME *Phebus* < ML; L, as above] —**Phoe·be·an** (fi bē′ən, fē′bē-), *adj.*

Phoe·ni·cia (fi nish′ə, -nē′shə), *n.* an ancient kingdom on the Mediterranean, in the region of modern Syria, Lebanon, and Israel. Also, **Phenicia.** See map under **Tyre.**

Phoe·ni·cian (fi nish′ən, -nē′shən), *n.* **1.** a native or inhabitant of Phoenicia. **2.** the extinct Semitic language of the Phoenicians. —*adj.* **3.** of or pertaining to Phoenicia, its people, or their language. **4.** noting or pertaining to the script used for the writing of Phoenician from the 11th century B.C. or earlier and from which were derived the Greek, Roman, and all other Western alphabets. [1350–1400; ME; see PHOENICIA, -AN]

phoe·nix (fē′niks), *n., gen.* **Phoe·ni·cis** (fē nī′sis, -nē′-) for 2. **1.** (*sometimes cap.*) a mythical bird of great beauty fabled to live 500 or 600 years in the Arabian wilderness, to burn itself on a funeral pyre, and to rise from its ashes in the freshness of youth and live through another cycle of years: often an emblem of immortality or of reborn idealism or hope. **2.** (*cap.*) *Astron.* a southern constellation between Hydrus and Sculptor. **3.** a person or thing of peerless beauty or excellence; paragon. **4.** a person or thing that has become renewed or restored after suffering calamity or apparent annihilation. Also, **phenix.** [bef. 900; < L < Gk *phoînix* a mythical bird, purple-red color, Phoenician, date palm; r. ME, OE *fēnix* < ML; L as above]

CONCISE PRONUNCIATION KEY: *act, cāpe, dâre, pärt; set, ēqual; if, īce; ox, ōver, ôrder, oil, bo͝ok, bo͞ot, out; up, ûrge; child; sing; shoe; thin, that;* zh as in *treasure.* ə = *a* as in *alone, e* as in *system, i* as in *easily, o* as in *gallop, u* as in *circus;* ə as in *fire* (fīər), *hour* (ouər). l and n can serve as syllabic consonants, as in *cradle* (krād′l), and *button* (but′n). See the full key inside the front cover.

Phoe•nix (fē′niks), *n.* **1.** *Class. Myth.* **a.** the brother of Cadmus and Europa, and eponymous ancestor of the Phoenicians. **b.** a son of Amyntor and Cleobule who became the foster father of Achilles and who fought with the Greek forces in the Trojan War. **2.** a city in and the capital of Arizona, in the central part. 764,911. **3.** *Mil.* a 13-ft. (4 m), 989-lb. (445 kg), U.S. Navy air-to-air missile with radar guidance and a range of over 120 nautical mi.

Phoe′nix Is′lands, a group of eight coral islands in the central Pacific: part of Kiribati (formerly Gilbert Islands). 11 sq. mi. (28 sq. km).

Phoe•nix•ville (fē′niks vil′), *n.* a city in SE Pennsylvania. 14,165.

pho•ko•me•li•a (fō′kō mē′lē ə, -mēl′yə), *n. Pathol.* phocomelia.

Phol•i•do•ta (fol′i dō′tə), *n.* the order comprising the pangolins. [< NL < Gk *pholidōt(ós)* clad in scales + NL *-a* neut. pl. ending]

phon (fon), *n.* a unit for measuring the apparent loudness of a sound, equal in number for a given sound to the intensity in decibels of a sound having a frequency of 1000 cycles per second when, in the judgment of a group of listeners, the two sounds are of equal loudness. [1930–35; < Gk *phōnḗ* voice]

phon-, var. of **phono-** before a vowel: *phonic.*

phon., phonetics.

phon•as•the•ni•a (fō′nas thē′nē ə), *n. Med.* difficult or abnormal voice production; vocal weakness. [PHON- + ASTHENIA]

pho•nate (fō′nāt), *v.t., v.i.,* **-nat•ed, -nat•ing. 1.** *Phonet.* to provide (a sound source, and hence the pitch) for a given voiced continuant or vowel, through rapid, periodic glottal action. **2.** to vocalize. [1875–80]

phon•a•thon (fō′nə thon′), *n.* a campaign to solicit funds or support in which volunteers make phone calls to prospective donors or supporters. [PHONE[1] + -ATHON]

pho•na•tion (fō nā′shən), *n. Phonet.* **1.** rapid, periodic opening and closing of the glottis through separation and apposition of the vocal cords that, accompanied by breath under lung pressure, constitutes a source of vocal sound. **2.** (not in technical use) voice; vocalization. Cf. **voice** (defs. 15, 16). [1835–45; PHON- + -ATION] **—pho•na•to•ry** (fō′nə tôr′ē, -tōr′ē), *adj.*

phone[1] (fōn), *n., v.t., v.i.,* **phoned, phon•ing.** telephone. [1880–85; by shortening]

phone[2] (fōn), *n. Phonet.* a speech sound: *There are three phonetically different "t" phones in an utterance of "titillate," and two in an utterance of "tattletale."* Cf. **allophone, phoneme.** [1865–70; < Gk *phōnḗ* voice] **—pho′nal,** *adj.*

-phone, a combining form meaning "speech sound" (*homophone*), "an instrument of sound transmission or reproduction" (*telephone*), "a musical instrument" (*saxophone; xylophone*). [see PHONE[2]]

phone′ book′. See **telephone book.** [1900–05]

phone-in (fōn′in′), *n., adj.* call-in. [1965–70]

pho•ne•mat•ic (fō′nə mat′ik), *adj.* phonemic. [1935–40; < Gk *phōnēmat-* (s. of *phṓnēma*) utterance + -IC]

pho•ne•mat•ics (fō′nə mat′iks), *n.* (*used with a singular v.*) *Chiefly Brit.* phonemics. [1935–40; see PHONEMATIC, -ICS]

pho•neme (fō′nēm), *n. Ling.* any of a small set of units, usually about 20 to 60 in number, and different for each language, considered to be the basic distinctive units of speech sound by which morphemes, words, and sentences are represented. They are arrived at for any given language by determining which differences in sound function to indicate a difference in meaning, so that in English the difference in sound and meaning between *pit* and *bit* is taken to indicate the existence of different labial phonemes, while the difference in sound between the unaspirated *p* of *spun* and the aspirated *p* of *pun,* since it is never the only distinguishing feature between two different words, is not taken as ground for setting up two different *p* phonemes in English. Cf. **distinctive feature** (def. 1). [1890–95; < F *phonème* < Gk *phṓnēma* sound, equiv. to *phōnē-,* verbid s. of *phōneîn* to make a sound (deriv. of *phōnḗ* sound, voice) + *-ma* n. suffix denoting result of action]

pho•ne•mic (fə nē′mik, fō-), *adj.* **1.** of or pertaining to phonemes: *a phonemic system.* **2.** of or pertaining to phonemics. **3.** concerning or involving the discrimination of distinctive speech elements of a language: *a phonemic contrast.* [1930–35; PHONEME + -IC] **—pho•ne′•mi•cal•ly,** *adv.*

pho•ne•mi•cize (fə nē′mə sīz′, fō-), *v.t.,* **-cized, -ciz•ing. 1.** to transcribe into phonemic symbols. **2.** to analyze (a word, the sound structure of a language, etc.) by establishing its phonemes. Also, *esp. Brit.,* **pho•ne′mi•cise′.** [1935–40] **—pho•ne′mi•ci•za′tion,** *n.*

pho•ne•mics (fə nē′miks, fō-), *n.* (*used with a singular v.*) **1.** the study of phonemes and phonemic systems. **2.** the phonemic system of a language, or a discussion of this: *English phonemics.* [1935–40; PHONEME + -ICS] **—pho•ne•mi•cist** (fə nē′mə sist, fō-), *n.*

phone′ phreak′, a person who uses computers or other electronic devices to place long-distance telephone calls without paying toll charges. Also called **phreak.** [1975–80]

pho•nes•the•mic (fō′nəs thē′mik), *adj. Ling.* (of a speech sound) shared by a set of echoic or symbolic words, as the *sn-* of *sneer, snarl, snatch, snide, snitch, snoop,* etc. [*phonestheme* such a sound or group of sounds (coined by J. R. Firth in 1930; appar. PHON- + ESTH(ETIC) + -EME) + -IC]

phonet., phonetics.

phone′ tag′. See **telephone tag.**

pho•net•ic (fə net′ik, fō-), *adj.* **1.** Also, **pho•net′i•cal.** of or pertaining to speech sounds, their production, or their transcription in written symbols. **2.** corresponding to pronunciation: *phonetic transcription.* **3.** agreeing with pronunciation: *phonetic spelling.* **4.** concerning or involving the discrimination of nondistinctive elements of a language. In English, certain phonological features, as length and aspiration, are phonetic but not phonemic. *—n.* **5.** (in Chinese writing) a written element that represents a sound and is used in combination with a radical to form a character. [1820–30; < NL *phōnēticus* < Gk *phōnētikós* vocal, equiv. to *phōnēt(ós)* to be spoken (verbid of *phōneîn* to speak) + *-ikos* -IC] **—pho•net′i•cal•ly,** *adv.*

phonet′ic al′phabet, an alphabet containing a separate character for each distinguishable speech sound. See table below. [1860–65]

pho•ne•ti•cian (fō′ni tish′ən), *n.* **1.** a specialist in phonetics or in some aspect of phonetics. **2.** a dialectologist. [1840–50; PHONETIC + -IAN]

pho•net•i•cize (fə net′ə sīz′, fō-), *v.t.,* **-cized, -ciz•ing. 1.** to represent (speech) in writing by means of a system in which individual symbols correspond regularly with speech sounds. **2.** to increase the regularity of correspondence between sound and symbol in (a writing system): *a proposal for a new system of phoneticized English spelling.* Also, *esp. Brit.,* **pho•net′i•cise′.** [PHONETIC + -IZE] **—pho•net′i•ci•za′tion,** *n.*

phonet′ic law′, *Historical Ling.* a statement of some regular pattern of sound change in a specific language, as Grimm's law or Verner's law.

pho•net•ics (fə net′iks, fō-), *n.* (*used with a singular v.*) **1.** the science or study of speech sounds and their production, transmission, and reception, and their analysis, classification, and transcription. Cf. **acoustic phonetics, articulatory phonetics, auditory phonetics, physiological phonetics. 2.** the phonetic system or the body of phonetic facts of a particular language. **3.** the symbols used to represent the speech sounds of a language. [1835–45; see PHONETIC, -ICS]

pho•ne•tist (fō′ni tist), *n.* a person who uses or advocates phonetic spelling. [1860–65; < Gk *phōnēt(ós)* (see PHONETIC) + -IST]

Phone•vi•sion (fōn′vizh′ən), *Trademark.* a brand name for a system of transmitting television signals over telephone lines so that callers can see each other on small television receivers.

pho•ney (fō′nē), *adj.,* **-ni•er, -ni•est,** *n., pl.* **-neys,** *v.t.,* **-neyed, -ney•ing.** phony. **—pho′ney•ness,** *n.*

pho•ni•at•rics (fō′nē a′triks), *n.* (*used with a singular v.*) *Speech Pathol.* the study and treatment of voice disorders. Also, **pho•ni•a•try** (fō nī′ə trē). [1945–50; PHON- + -IATRIC; see -ICS] **—pho′ni•at′ric,** *adj.*

phon•ic (fon′ik, fō′nik), *adj.* of or pertaining to speech sounds. [1815–25; PHON- + -IC] **—phon′i•cal•ly,** *adv.*

phon•ics (fon′iks *or, for 2,* fō′niks), *n.* (*used with a singular v.*) **1.** a method of teaching reading and spelling based upon the phonetic interpretation of ordinary spelling. **2.** *Obs.* phonetics. [1675–85; PHON- + -ICS]

pho•no (fō′nō), *n., pl.* **-nos.** *Informal.* phonograph.

phono-, a combining form meaning "sound," "voice," used in the formation of compound words: *phonology.* Also, *esp. before a vowel,* **phon-.** Cf. **-phone, -phony.** [1945–50; < Gk, comb. form repr. *phōnḗ* voice]

pho•no•car•di•o•gram (fō′nə kär′dē ə gram′), *n. Med.* the graphic record produced by a phonocardiograph. [1910–15; PHONO- + CARDIOGRAM]

pho•no•car•di•o•graph (fō′nə kär′dē ə graf′, -gräf′), *n. Med.* an instrument for graphically recording the sound of the heartbeat. [1925–30; PHONO- + CARDIOGRAPH] **—pho•no•car•di•og•ra•phy** (fō′nə kär′dē og′rə fē), *n.*

pho•no•gram (fō′nə gram′), *n.* a unit symbol of a phonetic writing system, standing for a speech sound, syllable, or other sequence of speech sounds without reference to meaning. [1855–60; PHONO- + -GRAM[1]] **—pho′no•gram′ic, pho′no•gram′mic,** *adj.* **—pho′no•gram′i•cal•ly, pho′no•gram′mi•cal•ly,** *adv.*

pho•no•graph (fō′nə graf′, -gräf′), *n.* any sound-reproducing machine using records in the form of cylinders or discs. [1825–35 in sense "phonogram"; 1877 for the "talking phonograph" invented by T. A. Edison; PHONO- + -GRAPH]

pho•no•graph•ic (fō′nə graf′ik), *adj.* **1.** of, pertaining to, or characteristic of a phonograph. **2.** of, pertaining to, or noting phonography. Also, **pho′no•graph′i•cal.** [1830–40 in sense "pertaining to phonograms"; 1878 for current senses; PHONOGRAPH, PHONOGRAPH(Y) + -IC] **—pho′no•graph′i•cal•ly,** *adv.*

pho•nog•ra•phy (fō nog′rə fē), *n., pl.* **-phies** for 2. **1.** phonetic spelling, writing, or shorthand. **2.** a system of

THE INTERNATIONAL PHONETIC ALPHABET (revised to 1989)

CONSONANTS Where symbols appear in pairs, the one to the right represents a voiced consonant. Shaded areas denote articulations judged impossible.

	Bilabial	Labiodental	Dental	Alveolar	Postalveolar	Retroflex	Palatal	Velar	Uvular	Pharyngeal	Glottal
Plosive	p b			t d		ʈ ɖ	c ɟ	k ɡ	q ɢ		ʔ
Nasal	m	ɱ		n		ɳ	ɲ	ŋ	ɴ		
Trill	ʙ			r					ʀ		
Tap or Flap				ɾ		ɽ					
Fricative	ɸ β	f v	θ ð	s z	ʃ ʒ	ʂ ʐ	ç ʝ	x ɣ	χ ʁ	ħ ʕ	h ɦ
Lateral fricative				ɬ ɮ							
Approximant		ʋ		ɹ		ɻ	j	ɰ			
Lateral approximant				l		ɭ	ʎ	ʟ			
Ejective stop	p'			t'		ʈ'	c'	k'	q'		
Implosive	ɓ ɓ̥			ɗ̥ ɗ			ʄ̊ ʄ	ɠ̊ ɠ	ʛ̥ ʛ		

DIACRITICS

̥ Voiceless	n̥ d̥	̹ More rounded	ɔ̹	ʷ Labialized	tʷ dʷ	̃ Nasalized	ẽ
̬ Voiced	s̬ t̬	̜ Less rounded	ɔ̜	ʲ Palatalized	tʲ dʲ	ⁿ Nasal release	dⁿ
ʰ Aspirated	tʰ dʰ	̟ Advanced	u̟	ˠ Velarized	tˠ dˠ	ˡ Lateral release	dˡ
̤ Breathy voiced	b̤ a̤	̠ Retracted	i̠	ˤ Pharyngealized	tˤ dˤ	̚ No audible release	d̚
̰ Creaky voiced	b̰ a̰	̈ Centralized	ë	̴ Velarized or pharyngealized	ɫ		
̼ Linguolabial	t̼ d̼	̽ Mid-centralized	e̽	̝ Raised	e̝ (ɹ̝ = voiced alveolar fricative)		
̪ Dental	t̪ d̪	̩ Syllabic	ɹ̩	̞ Lowered	e̞ (β̞ = voiced bilabial approximant)		
̺ Apical	t̺ d̺	̯ Non-syllabic	e̯	̘ Advanced Tongue Root	e̘		
̻ Laminal	t̻ d̻	˞ Rhoticity	ə˞	̙ Retracted Tongue Root	e̙		

VOWELS

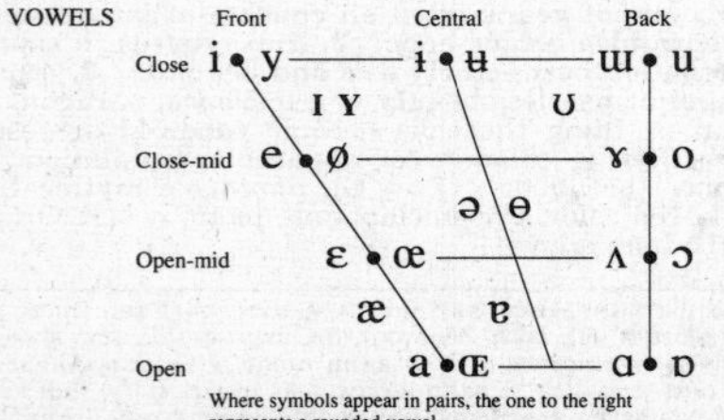

	Front	Central	Back
Close	i • y	ɨ • ʉ	ɯ • u
	ɪ ʏ		ʊ
Close-mid	e • ø		ɤ • o
		ə ɵ	
Open-mid	ɛ • œ		ʌ • ɔ
	æ	ɐ	
Open	a • ɶ		ɑ • ɒ

Where symbols appear in pairs, the one to the right represents a rounded vowel.

OTHER SYMBOLS

ʍ	Voiceless labial-velar fricative	ʘ	Bilabial click
w	Voiced labial-velar approximant	ǀ	Dental click
ɥ	Voiced labial-palatal approximant	!	(Post)alveolar click
ʜ	Voiceless epiglottal fricative	ǂ	Palatoalveolar click
ʢ	Voiced epiglottal fricative	ǁ	Alveolar lateral click
ʡ	Epiglottal plosive	ɺ	Alveolar lateral flap
ɕ ʑ	Alveolo-palatal fricatives	ɧ	Simultaneous ʃ and x
ɜ	Additional mid central vowel		

Affricates and double articulations can be represented by two symbols joined by a tie bar if necessary. k͡p t͡s

SUPRASEGMENTALS

ˈ	Primary stress	ˌfoʊnəˈtɪʃən
ˌ	Secondary stress	
ː	Long	eː
ˑ	Half-long	eˑ
̆	Extra-short	ĕ
.	Syllable break	ɹi.ækt
|	Minor (foot) group	
‖	Major (intonation) group	
‿	Linking (absence of a break)	
↗	Global rise	
↘	Global fall	

TONES & WORD ACCENTS

LEVEL		CONTOUR	
e̋ or ˥	Extra high	ě or ˩˥	Rising
é ˦	High	ê ˥˩	Falling
ē ˧	Mid	e᷄ ˦˥	High rising
è ˨	Low	e᷅ ˩˨	Low rising
ȅ ˩	Extra low	e᷈ ˧˦˧	Rising-falling etc.
↓ Downstep			
↑ Upstep			

phonetic shorthand, as that invented by Sir Isaac Pitman in 1837. [1695–1705; PHONO- + -GRAPHY] **—pho•nog′ra•pher, pho•nog′ra•phist,** *n.*

phonol., phonology.

pho•no•lite (fōn′l īt′), *n.* a fine-grained volcanic rock composed chiefly of alkali feldspar and nepheline, some varieties of which split into pieces that ring on being struck. [1820–30; < F < G *Phonolith.* See PHONO-, -LITE] **—pho•no•lit•ic** (fōn′l it′ik), *adj.*

phonolog′ical rule′, *Ling.* an operation in generative phonology that substitutes one sound or class of sounds for another in a phonological derivation.

pho•nol•o•gist (fə nol′ə jist, fō-), *n.* a specialist in phonology. [1840–50; PHONOLOG(Y) + -IST]

pho•nol•o•gy (fə nol′ə jē, fō-), *n., pl.* **-gies. 1.** the study of the distribution and patterning of speech sounds in a language and of the tacit rules governing pronunciation. **2.** the phonological system or the body of phonological facts of a language. [1790–1800; PHONO- + -LOGY] **—pho•no•log•i•cal** (fōn′l oj′i kəl), **pho′no•log′ic,** *adj.* **—pho′no•log′i•cal•ly,** *adv.*

pho•nom•e•ter (fə nom′i tər, fō-), *n.* a device for measuring the intensity of a sound. [1815–25; PHONO- + -METER] **—pho•no•met•ric** (fō′nə me′trik), *adj.* **—pho•nom′e•try,** *n.*

pho•non (fō′non), *n. Physics.* a quantum of sound or vibratory elastic energy, being the analogue of a photon of electromagnetic energy. [1930–35; PHON- + -ON[1]]

pho•no•re•cep•tion (fō′nō ri sep′shən), *n.* the physiological perception of sound. [PHONO- + RECEPTION]

pho•no•re•cep•tor (fō′nō ri sep′tər), *n. Physiol., Biol.* a receptor stimulated by sound waves. [PHONO- + RECEPTOR]

pho•no•scope (fō′nə skōp′), *n.* **1.** an instrument for making visible the motions or properties of a sounding body. **2.** a device for testing the quality of strings for musical instruments. [1880–85; PHONO- + -SCOPE]

pho•no•tac•tic (fō′nə tak′tik), *adj. Ling.* of or pertaining to phonotactics: *Phonotactic constraints in English prevent the occurrence of the consonant clusters (sr) and (dl) at the beginning of words.* [1955–60; PHONO- + TACTIC]

pho•no•tac•tics (fō′nə tak′tiks), *n.* (*used with a singular v.*) *Ling.* **1.** the patterns in which the phonemes of a language may combine to form sequences. **2.** the study and description of such patterns. [1955–60; see PHONOTACTIC, -ICS]

pho•no•type (fō′nə tīp′), *n. Print.* a piece of type bearing a phonetic character or symbol. [1835–45; PHONO- + -TYPE] **—pho•no•typ•ic** (fō′nə tip′ik), **pho′no•typ′i•cal,** *adj.* **—pho′no•typ′i•cal•ly,** *adv.*

pho•no•typ•y (fō′nə tī′pē), *n., pl.* **-typ•ies.** phonography (def. 2). [1875–80; PHONOTYPE + -Y[3]] **—pho′no•typ′ist, pho′no•typ′er,** *n.*

pho•ny (fō′nē), *adj.,* **-ni•er, -ni•est,** *n., pl.* **-nies,** *v.,* **-nied, -ny•ing.** *—adj.* **1.** not real or genuine; fake; counterfeit: *a phony diamond.* **2.** false or deceiving; not truthful; concocted: *a phony explanation.* **3.** insincere or deceitful; affected or pretentious: *a phony sales representative.* *—n.* **4.** something that is phony; a counterfeit or fake. **5.** an insincere, pretentious, or deceitful person: *He thought my friends were a bunch of phonies.* *—v.t.* **6.** to falsify; counterfeit; fabricate (often fol. by *up*): *to phony up a document.* Also, **phoney.** [1895–1900; perh. alter. and resp. of *fawney* (slang) finger ring (< Ir *fáinne*), if taken to mean "false" in the phrase *fawney rig* a confidence game in which a brass ring is sold as a gold one] **—pho′ni•ly,** *adv.* **—pho′ni•ness,** *n.*
—Syn. 4. fraud, imitation, hoax.

-phony, a combining form used in the formation of abstract nouns corresponding to nouns ending in **-phone:** *telephony.* [< Gk *-phōnia;* see -PHONE, -Y[3]]

pho•ny-ba•lo•ney (fō′nē bə lō′nē), *Slang.* *—n.* **1.** nonsense; baloney. *—adj.* **2.** nonsensical; foolish.

pho′ny disease′, *Plant Pathol.* a disease of peaches, characterized by dwarfing, dark-green leaves, premature leafing and flowering, and the production of reduced numbers of small fruit, caused by a virus, *Nanus mirabilis.* Also called **pho′ny peach′.**

phoo•ey (fo͞o′ē), *interj. Informal.* (an exclamation indicating rejection, contempt, or disgust): *Phooey on all those political promises!* [1925–30, *Amer.*; perh. < G *pfui!* expression of disgust, conflated with E *phoo!* with similar force]

pho•rate (fôr′āt, fōr′-), *n. Chem.* a systemic insecticide, $C_7H_{17}O_2PS_3$, used esp. as a soil treatment for the control of numerous crop-damaging insects. [1955–60; prob. by shortening of the name of one of its chemical components, *(phos)phor(odithio)ate;* see PHOSPHORO-, DITHIONOUS, -ATE[2]]

phor•bol (fôr′bōl, -bol), *n. Biochem.* the parent alcohol, $C_{20}H_{28}O_6$, of certain carcinogenic compounds in croton oil. [< G *Phorbol* (1927) < Gk *phorb(ḗ)* forage (see FORB) + G *-ol* -OL[1]]

Phor•cys (fôr′sis), *n. Class. Myth.* a sea god who fathered the Gorgons.

-phore, a combining form meaning "bearer of," "thing or part bearing" that specified by the initial element: *gonophore.* Cf. **-phorous.** [< NL *-phorus* < Gk *-phoros* bearing, verbid of *phérein;* see BEAR[1]]

phor•e•sy (fôr′ə sē), *n. Zool.* (among insects and arachnids) a nonparasitic relationship in which one species is carried about by another. [1920–25; < NL *phoresia* < Gk *phórēs(is)* a wearing (*phorē-,* verbid s. of *phoreîn,* durative of *phérein* to BEAR[1] + *-sis* -SIS) + *-ia* -Y[3]]

pho•ro•nid (fə rō′nid), *n.* **1.** any member of the invertebrate phylum Phoronida, wormlike marine animals living in a chitinous tube and having an anterior structure bearing ciliated tentacles for feeding. *—adj.* **2.** belonging or pertaining to the phoronids. [< NL *Phoronida,* equiv. to *Phoron(is)* name of genus (< L: a name of Io) + *-ida* neut. pl. n. suffix; see -ID[2]]

-phorous, a combining form occurring in adjectives that correspond to nouns ending in **-phore:** *gonophorous.* [< NL *-phorus* < Gk *-phoros* bearing. See -PHORE, -OUS]

phos•gene (fos′jēn, foz′-), *n. Chem.* a poisonous, colorless, very volatile liquid or suffocating gas, $COCl_2$, a chemical-warfare compound: used chiefly in organic synthesis. Also called **carbon oxychloride, carbonyl chloride, chloroformyl chloride.** [1805–15; < Gk *phôs* light (contr. of *pháos*) + *-genēs* -GEN]

phos•ge•nite (fos′jə nīt′, foz′-), *n.* a mineral, lead chlorocarbonate, $Pb_2Cl_2CO_3$, occurring in crystals. [1840–50; < G *Phosgenit.* See PHOSGENE, -ITE[1]]

phosph-, var. of **phospho-** before a vowel: *phosphate.*

phos•pha•gen (fos′fə jən, -jen′), *n. Biochem.* a high-energy phosphoric ester that serves as a reservoir of phosphate-bond energy, as phosphocreatine in vertebrates and phosphoarginine in invertebrates. [1925–30; PHOSPHA(TE) + -GEN]

phos•pham•i•don (fos fam′i don′), *n. Chem.* a systemic and contact insecticide, $C_{10}H_{19}ClNO_5P$, used against beetles, aphids, mites, and other crop pests. [1955–60; perh. PHOSPH(ATE) + AMIDE + -ON[1]]

phos•pha•tase (fos′fə tās′, -tāz′), *n. Biochem.* any of several classes of esterases of varying specificity that catalyze the hydrolysis of phosphoric esters. [1910–15; PHOSPHATE + -ASE]

phos•phate (fos′fāt), *n.* **1.** *Chem.* **a.** (loosely) a salt or ester of phosphoric acid. **b.** a tertiary salt of orthophosphoric acid, as sodium phosphate. **2.** *Agric.* a fertilizing material containing compounds of phosphorus. **3.** a carbonated drink of water and fruit syrup containing a little phosphoric acid. [1785–95; PHOSPH- + -ATE[2]]

phos′phate group′, *Chem.* the group or radical obtained by removal of one or more hydrogen atoms from phosphoric acid. [1950–55]

phos′phate rock′, phosphorite. [1865–70]

phos•phat•ic (fos fat′ik, -fā′tik), *adj.* of, pertaining to, or containing phosphates: *phosphatic slag.* [1820–30; PHOSPHATE + -IC]

phos•pha•tide (fos′fə tīd′, -tid), *n. Biochem.* phospholipid. [1884; PHOSPHATE + -IDE]

phos•pha•tize (fos′fə tīz′), *v.t.,* **-tized, -tiz•ing. 1.** to treat with phosphates. **2.** to change to phosphate. Also, *esp. Brit.,* **phos′pha•tise′.** [1880–85; PHOSPHATE + -IZE] **—phos′pha•ti•za′tion, phos•pha•tion** (fos fā′shən), *n.*

phos•pha•tu•ri•a (fos′fə to͝or′ē ə, -tyo͝or′-), *n. Pathol.* the presence of an excessive quantity of phosphates in the urine. [1875–80; PHOSPHATE + -URIA] **—phos′pha•tu′ric,** *adj.*

phos•phene (fos′fēn), *n. Physiol.* a luminous image produced by mechanical stimulation of the retina, as by pressure applied to the eyeball by the finger when the lid is closed. [1870–75; < F *phosphène,* irreg. < Gk *phôs* light (contr. of *pháos*) + *phaínein* to show, shine]

phos•phide (fos′fīd, -fid), *n. Chem.* a binary compound of phosphorus with a basic element or group. [1840–50; PHOSPH- + -IDE]

phos•phine (fos′fēn, -fin), *n. Chem.* **1.** a colorless, poisonous, ill-smelling, flammable gas, PH_3. **2.** any of certain organic derivatives of this compound. [1870–75; PHOSPH- + -INE[1]]

phos•phite (fos′fīt), *n. Chem.* (loosely) a salt of phosphorous acid. [1790–1800; PHOSPH- + -ITE[1]]

phospho-, a combining form representing **phosphorus** in compound words: *phosphoprotein.* Also, *esp. before a vowel,* **phosph-.** Cf. **phosphoro-.**

phos•pho•cre•a•tine (fos′fō krē′ə tēn′, -tin), *n. Biochem.* a compound, $C_4H_{10}O_5N_3P$, found chiefly in muscle, formed by the enzymatic interaction of an organic phosphate and creatine, the breakdown of which provides energy for muscle contraction. Also called **creatine phosphate.** [1925–30; PHOSPHO- + CREATINE]

phos•pho•li•pase (fos′fō lī′pās, -pāz), *n. Biochem.* any of a group of enzymes that catalyze the breaking down of phospholipids. [< G (1935); see PHOSPHOLIPID, -ASE]

phos•pho•lip•id (fos′fō lip′id), *n. Biochem.* any of a group of fatty compounds, as lecithin, composed of phosphoric esters, and occurring in living cells. Also called **phosphatide, phos•pho•lip•ide** (fos′fō lip′īd), **phos•pho•lip•in** (fos′fō lip′in). [1925–30; PHOSPHO- + LIPID]

phos′pholip′id bi′layer, a two-layered arrangement of phosphate and lipid molecules that form a cell membrane, the hydrophobic lipid ends facing inward and the hydrophilic phosphate ends facing outward. Also called **lipid bilayer.**

phos•pho•ni•um (fos fō′nē əm), *n. Chem.* the positively charged group PH_4^+. [1865–70; PHOSPH(ORUS) + (AMM)ONIUM]

phospho′nium i′odide, *Chem.* a colorless to slightly yellowish, crystalline, water-soluble solid, PH_4I, used in chemical synthesis. [1870–75]

phos•pho•pro•tein (fos′fō prō′tēn, -tē in), *n. Biochem.* a protein, as casein or ovalbumin, in which one or more hydroxyl groups of serine, threonine, or tyrosine are hydroxylated. [1905–10; PHOSPHO- + PROTEIN]

phos•phor (fos′fər, -fôr), *n.* **1.** any of a number of substances that exhibit luminescence when struck by light of certain wavelengths, as by ultraviolet. **2.** *Literary.* a phosphorescent substance. *—adj.* **3.** *Archaic.* phosphorescent. [1625–35; < F *phosphore* < L *Phōsphorus* PHOSPHOR]

Phos•phor (fos′fər, -fôr), *n.* the morning star, esp. Venus. Also, **Phos•phore** (fos′fôr, -fōr), **Phosphorus.** [1625–35; < L *Phōsphorus* < Gk *Phōsphóros* the morning star, lit., the light-bringing one, equiv. to *phôs* light + *-phoros* bringing; see -PHOROUS]

phosphor-, var. of **phosphoro-** before a vowel: *phosphorate.*

phos•pho•rate (fos′fə rāt′), *v.t.,* **-rat•ed, -rat•ing. 1.** Also, **phosphorize.** *Chem.* to combine or impregnate with phosphorus. **2.** to cause to have phosphorescence. [1780–90; PHOSPHOR- or PHOSPHOR + -ATE[1]]

phos′phor bronze′, a bronze, composed of about 80 percent copper, 10 percent tin, 9 percent antimony, and 1 percent phosphorus, having great hardness and resistance to corrosion. [1870–75]

phos•pho•resce (fos′fə res′), *v.i.,* **-resced, -resc•ing.** to be luminous without sensible heat, as phosphorus. [1785–95; PHOSPHOR(US) + -ESCE]

phos•pho•res•cence (fos′fə res′əns), *n.* **1.** the property of being luminous at temperatures below incandescence, as from slow oxidation in the case of phosphorus or after exposure to light or other radiation. **2.** a luminous appearance resulting from this. **3.** any luminous radiation emitted from a substance after the removal of the exciting agent. [1790–1800; PHOSPHORESC(ENT) + -ENCE]

phos•pho•res•cent (fos′fə res′ənt), *adj.* exhibiting phosphorescence. [1760–70; PHOSPHOR(US) + -ESCENT] **—phos′pho•res′cent•ly,** *adv.*

phos•pho•ret•ed (fos′fə ret′id), *adj. Chem.* phosphureted. Also, **phos′pho•ret′ted.**

phos•phor•ic (fos fôr′ik, -for′-), *adj. Chem.* of or containing phosphorus, esp. in the pentavalent state. [1775–85; PHOSPHOR- + -IC]

phosphor′ic ac′id, *Chem.* any of three acids, orthophosphoric acid, H_3PO_4, metaphosphoric acid, HPO_3, or pyrophosphoric acid, $H_4P_2O_7$, derived from phosphorus pentoxide, P_2O_5, and various amounts of water. [1785–95]

phosphor′ic anhy′dride, *Chem.* See **phosphorus pentoxide.** [1875–80]

phos•pho•rism (fos′fə riz′əm), *n. Pathol.* chronic phosphorus poisoning. [1780–90; PHOSPHOR- + -ISM]

phos•pho•rite (fos′fə rīt′), *n.* a sedimentary rock sufficiently rich in phosphate minerals to be used as a source of phosphorus for fertilizers. [1790–1800; PHOSPHOR- + -ITE[1]] **—phos•pho•rit•ic** (fos′fə rit′ik), *adj.*

phos•pho•rize (fos′fə rīz′), *v.t.,* **-rized, -riz•ing.** phosphorate (def. 1). Also, *esp. Brit.,* **phos′pho•rise′.** [1790–1800; PHOSPHOR- + -IZE] **—phos′pho•ri•za′tion,** *n.*

phosphoro-, a combining form representing **phosphorus** in compound words: *phosphoroscope.* Also, *esp. before a vowel,* **phosphor-.** Cf. **phospho-.**

phos•phor•o•scope (fos fôr′ə skōp′, -for′-), *n.* an instrument for measuring the duration of evanescent phosphorescence in different substances. [1855–60; PHOSPHORO- + -SCOPE]

phos•pho•rous (fos′fər əs, fos fôr′əs, -fōr′-), *adj. Chem.* containing trivalent phosphorus. [1770–80; PHOSPHOR- + -OUS]

phos′phorous ac′id, *Chem.* a colorless, crystalline, water-soluble acid of phosphorus, H_3PO_3, from which phosphites are derived. [1785–95]

phos•pho•rus (fos′fər əs), *n., pl.* **-pho•ri** (-fə rī′). **1.** *Chem.* a solid, nonmetallic element existing in at least three allotropic forms, one that is yellow, poisonous, flammable, and luminous in the dark, one that is red, less poisonous, and less flammable, and another that is black, insoluble in most solvents, and the least flammable. The element is used in forming smoke screens, its compounds are used in matches and phosphate fertilizers, and it is a necessary constituent of plant and animal life in bones, nerves, and embryos. *Symbol:* P; *at. wt.:* 30.974; *at. no.:* 15; *sp. gr.:* (yellow) 1.82 at 20°C, (red) 2.20 at 20°C, (black) 2.25–2.69 at 20°C. **2.** any phosphorescent substance. **3.** phosphor. [1620–30; < NL *phōsphorus;* L: morning star; see PHOSPHOR]

Phos•pho•rus (fos′fər əs), *n.* Phosphor.

phosphorus 32, *Chem.* a radioactive isotope of phosphorus, used as a chemotherapeutic agent. Also called **radiophosphorus.**

phos′phorus pent•ox′ide (pen tok′sīd, -sid), *Chem.* a white, deliquescent, crystalline powder, P_2O_5, that, depending upon the amount of water it absorbs, forms orthophosphoric acid, metaphosphoric acid, or pyrophosphoric acid, produced by the burning of phosphorus in dry air: used in the preparation of phosphoric acids, as a drying and dehydrating agent, and in organic synthesis. Also called **phosphoric anhydride.**

phos′phorus ses•qui•sul′fide (ses′kwi sul′fīd), (not in scientific use) a yellow, crystalline, flammable substance, P_4S_3, insoluble in cold water and decomposed by hot water: used chiefly in organic synthesis and in the manufacture of matches. [SESQUI- + SULFIDE]

phos′phorus trichlo′ride, *Chem.* a clear, colorless, fuming liquid, PCl_3, used chiefly in organic synthesis as a chlorinating agent.

phos•pho•ryl•ase (fos′fər ə lās′, -lāz′, fos fôr′ə-, -for′-), *n. Biochem.* any enzyme, occurring widely in animal and plant tissue, that in the presence of an inorganic phosphate catalyzes the conversion of glycogen into sugar phosphate. [1935–40; PHOSPHOR- + -YL + -ASE]

phos•pho•ryl•ate (fos′fər ə lāt′, fos fôr′ə-, -for′-), *v.t.,* **-at•ed, -at•ing.** *Chem.* to introduce the phosphoryl group into (an organic compound). [1930–35; PHOSPHOR- + -YL + -ATE[1]] **—phos′pho•ryl•a′tion,** *n.*

phos′pho•ryl group′ (fos′fə ril), *Chem.* the triva-

CONCISE PRONUNCIATION KEY: *act, cāpe, dâre, pärt; set, ēqual; if, īce; ox, ōver, ôrder, oil, bo͝ok, bo͞ot, out; up, ûrge; child; sing; shoe; thin, that;* zh as in *treasure.* ə = *a* as in *alone, e* as in *system, i* as in *easily, o* as in *gallop, u* as in *circus;* ə as in *fire* (fīər), *hour* (ouər). l and n can serve as syllabic consonants, as in *cradle* (krād′l), and *button* (but′n). See the full key inside the front cover.

lent group ≡P≡O. Also called **phos′phoryl rad′ical.** [PHOSPHOR- + -YL]

phos•phu•ret•ed (fos′fyə ret′id), *adj. Chem.* combined with phosphorus, esp. in its lowest valence state. Also, **phosphoreted, phosphoretted, phos′phu•ret′•ted.** [*phosphuret* phosphide (see PHOSPH-, -URET) + -ED[3]]

Phos•vel (fos′vel), *Chem., Trademark.* a brand of leptophos.

phot (fot, fōt), *n. Optics.* a unit of illumination, equal to 1 lumen per square centimeter. *Abbr.:* ph [1915–20; < Gk *phōt-*, s. of *phôs* (contr. of *pháos*) light]

phot-, var. of **photo-** before a vowel: *photalgia.*

phot., 1. photograph. **2.** photographer. **3.** photographic. **4.** photography.

pho•tal•gia (fō tal′jə, -jē ə), *n. Pathol.* pain, as in an eye, that is caused by intensity of light. [PHOT- + -ALGIA]

pho•tic (fō′tik), *adj.* **1.** of or pertaining to light. **2.** pertaining to the generation of light by organisms, or their excitation by means of light. [1835–45; < Gk *phōt-* (see PHOT) + -IC]

pho•tics (fō′tiks), *n.* (*used with a singular v.*) the science of light. [1855–60; see PHOTIC, -ICS]

pho′tic zone′, *Biol.* the upper layer of a body of water delineated by the depth to which enough sunlight can penetrate to permit photosynthesis. [1970–75]

pho•tin•i•a (fō tin′ē ə), *n.* any of various trees or shrubs belonging to the genus *Photinia,* of the rose family, having clusters of small white flowers and red, berrylike fruit. [< NL (1821) < Gk *phōtein(ós)* shining, bright, (deriv. of *phôs,* s. *phōt-* light) + NL *-ia* -IA; so named in reference to the glossy evergreen leaves and white flowers]

pho•tism (fō′tiz əm), *n. Psychol.* a form of synesthesia in which a visual sensation, as of color or form, is produced by the sense of touch, hearing, etc. [1890–95; < Gk *phōtismós* illumination, equiv. to *phōt(ízein)* to give light + *-ismos* -ISM]

Pho•ti•us (fō′shē əs), *n.* A.D. c820–891, patriarch of Constantinople 858–867, 877–882.

pho•to (fō′tō), *n., pl.* **-tos. 1.** photograph. **2.** *Informal.* See **photo finish.** [1855–60; shortened form of PHOTOGRAPH]

photo-, a combining form meaning "light" (*photobiology*); also used to represent "photographic" or "photograph" in the formation of compound words: *photocopy.* Also, *esp. before a vowel,* **phot-.** [< Gk, comb. form of *phôs* (gen. *phōtós*)]

pho•to•ac•tin•ic (fō′tō ak tin′ik), *adj.* emitting radiation having the chemical effects of light and ultraviolet rays, as on a photographic film. [PHOTO- + ACTINIC]

pho•to•ac•ti•va•tion (fō′tō ak′tə vā′shən), *n. Chem.* the activation or control of a chemical, chemical reaction, or organism by light, as the activation of chlorophyll by sunlight during photosynthesis. [1920–25; PHOTO- + ACTIVATION] **—pho′to•ac′tive,** *adj.* **—pho′to•ac•tiv′•i•ty,** *n.*

pho•to•ag•ing (fō′tō ā′jing), *n.* damage to the skin, as wrinkles or discoloration, caused by prolonged exposure to sunlight. [1985–90]

pho•to•al•ler•gic (fō′tō ə lûr′jik), *adj.* photosensitive. Cf. **photosensitivity.** [1935–40; PHOTO- + ALLERGIC]

pho•to•an•a•lyst (fō′tō an′l ist), *n.* a person who interprets photographs, esp. a military specialist in aerial or satellite photography. [PHOTO- + ANALYST]

pho•to•au•to•troph (fō′tō ô′tə trof′, -trōf′), *n. Biol.* any organism that derives its energy for food synthesis from light and is capable of using carbon dioxide as its principal source of carbon. [1945–50; PHOTO- + AUTOTROPH] **—pho′to•au′to•troph′ic,** *adj.*

pho•to•bi•ol•o•gy (fō′tō bī ol′ə jē), *n.* the study of the effects of light on biological systems. [1930–35; PHOTO- + BIOLOGY] **—pho•to•bi•o•log•i•cal** (fō′tō bī′ə loj′i kəl), **pho′to•bi′o•log′ic,** *adj.* **—pho′to•bi•ol′o•gist,** *n.*

pho•to•bi•ot•ic (fō′tō bī ot′ik, -bē-), *adj. Bot., Zool.* living or thriving only in the presence of light. [PHOTO- + BIOTIC]

pho•to•ca•tal•y•sis (fō′tō kə tal′i sis), *n., pl.* **-ses** (-sēz′). *Chem.* the acceleration or retardation of the reaction rate in chemical reactions by light. [1910–15; PHOTO- + CATALYSIS] **—pho•to•cat•a•lyt•ic** (fō′tō kat′l-it′ik), *adj.*

pho•to•cath•ode (fō′tō kath′ōd), *n.* a cathode, typically of a cesium or sodium compound, having the property of emitting electrons when activated by light or other radiation. [1925–30; PHOTO- + CATHODE]

pho•to•cell (fō′tō sel′), *n. Electronics.* a solid-state device that converts light into electrical energy by producing a voltage, as in a photovoltaic cell, or uses light to regulate the flow of current, as in a photoconductive cell: used in automatic control systems for doors, lighting, etc. Also called **electric eye, photoelectric cell.** [1890–95; PHOTO- + CELL[1]]

pho′tochem′ical smog′, *Meteorol.* air pollution containing ozone and other reactive chemical compounds formed by the action of sunlight on nitrogen oxides and hydrocarbons, esp. those in automobile exhaust. Also called **oxidant smog, smog.** [1957; PHOTO- + CHEMICAL]

pho•to•chem•is•try (fō′tō kem′ə strē), *n.* the branch of chemistry that deals with the chemical action of light. [1865–70; PHOTO- + CHEMISTRY] **—pho•to•chem•i•cal** (fō′tō kem′i kəl), **pho′to•chem′ic,** *adj.* **—pho′to•chem′i•cal•ly,** *adv.* **—pho′to•chem′ist,** *n.*

pho•to•chro•mic (fō′tə krō′mik), *adj.* (of chemically treated glass or plastic) capable of darkening or changing color when exposed to light. [1950–55; PHOTO- + CHROM- + -IC] **—pho′to•chro′mism,** *n.*

pho•to•chro•my (fō′tə krō′mē), *n.* a former technique of color photography. [1885–90; PHOTO- + -CHROME + -Y[3]]

pho•to•chron•o•graph (fō′tə kron′ə graf′, -gräf′), *n.* **1.** a device formerly used for taking a series of instantaneous photographs of a rapidly moving object. **2.** a picture taken by such a device. **3.** a chronograph in which the tracing or record is made by a pencil of light on a sensitized surface. **4.** an instrument for measuring small intervals of time by the photographic trace of a pencil of light. [1885–90; PHOTO- + CHRONOGRAPH] **—pho•to•chro•nog•ra•phy** (fō′tō krə nog′rə fē), *n.*

pho•to•co•ag•u•la•tion (fō′tō kō ag′yə lā′shən), *n.* a surgical technique using an intense beam of light from a laser or a xenon-arc bulb to seal blood vessels or coagulate tissue, used primarily in ophthalmology to repair detached retinas or to treat certain kinds of retinopathy. [1960–65; PHOTO- + COAGULATION] **—pho•to•co•ag•u•la•tive** (fō′tō kō ag′yə lā′tiv, -lə tiv), *adj.*

pho•to•com•pose (fō′tō kəm pōz′), *v.t.,* **-posed, -pos•ing.** to set (type) on a photocomposer. [1925–30; PHOTO- + COMPOSE]

pho•to•com•pos•er (fō′tō kəm pō′zər), *n.* a machine for setting type photographically. [1925–30; PHOTO- + COMPOSER]

pho•to•com•po•si•tion (fō′tō kom′pə zish′ən), *n. Print.* any method of composition using photography, as composition by means of a photocomposer. Also called **phototypesetting, phototypography.** [1925–30; PHOTO- + COMPOSITION]

pho•to•con•duc•tive (fō′tō kən duk′tiv), *adj.* of, pertaining to, or exhibiting photoconductivity. [1925–30; PHOTO- + CONDUCTIVE] **—pho′to•con•duc′tion,** *n.* **—pho′to•con•duc′tor,** *n.*

pho′toconduc′tive cell′, *Electronics.* a photocell whose resistance varies according to the intensity of light falling on it. [1930–35]

pho•to•con•duc•tiv•i•ty (fō′tō kon′duk tiv′i tē), *n. Physics.* the increase in the electrical conductivity of a substance, often nonmetallic, caused by the absorption of electromagnetic radiation. [1925–30; PHOTO- + CONDUCTIVITY]

pho•to•cop•i•er (fō′tə kop′ē ər), *n.* any electrically operated machine using a photographic method, as the electrostatic process, for making instant copies of written, drawn, or printed material. Also called **copier, copy machine, pho′tocopying machine′.** [1930–35; PHOTO- + COPIER]

pho•to•cop•y (fō′tə kop′ē), *n., pl.* **-cop•ies,** *v.,* **-cop•ied, -cop•y•ing.** *—n.* **1.** a photographic reproduction of a document, print, or the like. *—v.t.* **2.** to reproduce (a document, print, or the like) photographically. [1920–25; PHOTO- + COPY]

pho•to•cur•rent (fō′tō kûr′ənt, -kur′-), *n. Physics.* an electric current produced by a photoelectric effect. Also called **photoelectric current.** [1910–15; PHOTO- + CURRENT]

pho•to•de•com•po•si•tion (fō′tō dē′kom pə zish′ən), *n. Chem.* the breaking down of molecules by radiant energy. [1885–90; PHOTO- + DECOMPOSITION]

pho•to•de•grad•a•ble (fō′tō di grā′də bəl), *adj.* (of a substance) capable of being broken down by light. [1970–75; PHOTO- + DEGRADABLE]

pho•to•de•tec•tor (fō′tō di tek′tər), *n.* **1.** photosensor. **2.** *Electronics.* any device, as a photodiode, phototube, or photovoltaic cell, that uses the photoelectric effect to convert radiant energy into an electrical signal. [1945–50; PHOTO- + DETECTOR]

pho•to•di•ode (fō′tō dī′ōd), *n. Electronics.* a photosensitive semiconductor diode. [1940–45; PHOTO- + DIODE]

pho•to•dis•in•te•gra•tion (fō′tō di sin′ti grā′shən), *n. Physics.* the disintegration of a nucleus, induced by its absorption of a photon. [1930–35; PHOTO- + DISINTEGRATION]

pho•to•dis•so•ci•a•tion (fō′tō di sō′sē ā′shən, -shē-), *n.* the dissociation or breakdown of a chemical compound by radiant energy. [1920–25; PHOTO- + DISSOCIATION]

pho•to•dra•ma (fō′tə drä′mə, -dram′ə), *n.* photoplay. [1915–20; PHOTO- + DRAMA] **—pho•to•dra•mat•ic** (fō′tō drə mat′ik), *adj.* **—pho•to•dram•a•tist** (fō′tə-dram′ə tist, -drä′mə-), *n.*

pho•to•du•pli•cate (*n.* fō′tō do͞o′pli kit, -dyo͞o′-; *v.* fō′tō do͞o′pli kāt′, -dyo͞o′-), *n., v.,* **-cat•ed, -cat•ing.** *—n.* **1.** photocopy. *—v.t.* **2.** to photocopy. [1950–55; PHOTO- + DUPLICATE] **—pho′to•du′pli•ca′tion,** *n.*

pho•to•dy•nam•ics (fō′tō dī nam′iks), *n.* (*used with a singular v.*) the science dealing with light and its effects on living organisms. [1885–90; PHOTO- + DYNAMICS] **—pho′to•dy•nam′ic, pho′to•dy•nam′i•cal,** *adj.* **—pho′•to•dy•nam′i•cal•ly,** *adv.*

pho•to•e•las•tic•i•ty (fō′tō i la stis′i tē, -ē′la stis′-), *n. Physics.* the phenomenon of double refraction of polarized light by a transparent substance under elastic stress, used to measure strain in elastic, transparent materials. [1910–15; PHOTO- + ELASTICITY] **—pho•to•e•las•tic** (fō′tō i las′tik), *adj.*

pho•to•e•lec•tric (fō′tō i lek′trik), *adj.* pertaining to the electronic or other electric effects produced by light. Also, **pho′to•e•lec′tri•cal.** [1860–65; PHOTO- + ELECTRIC] **—pho′to•e•lec′tri•cal•ly,** *adv.*

pho′toelec′tric cell′, *Electronics.* photocell. [1890–95]

pho′toelec′tric cur′rent, *Physics.* photocurrent. [1875–80]

pho′toelec′tric effect′, *Physics.* the phenomenon in which the absorption of electromagnetic radiation, as light, of sufficiently high frequency by a surface, usually metallic, induces the emission of electrons from the surface. Also called **photoemission.** [1890–95]

pho•to•e•lec•tric•i•ty (fō′tō i lek tris′i tē, -ē′lek-), *n. Physics.* **1.** electricity induced by electromagnetic radiation, as in certain processes, as the photoelectric and photovoltaic effects, photoconductivity, and photoionization. **2.** the branch of physics that deals with these phenomena. [1875–80; PHOTO- + ELECTRICITY]

pho′toelec′tric me′ter, *Photog.* an exposure meter using a photocell for the measurement of light intensity.

pho′toelec′tric thresh′old, *Physics.* the minimum frequency or maximum wavelength of incident radiation necessary to release photons from a given surface.

pho′toelec′tric tube′, *Electronics.* phototube.

pho•to•e•lec•tron (fō′tō i lek′tron), *n. Physics.* an electron emitted from a system by the photoelectric effect. [1910–15; PHOTO- + ELECTRON]

pho•to•e•lec•tro•type (fō′tō i lek′trə tīp′), *n.* an electrotype made by photographic means. [1870–75; PHOTO- + ELECTROTYPE]

pho•to•e•mis•sion (fō′tō i mish′ən), *n. Physics.* See **photoelectric effect.** [1915–20; PHOTO- + EMISSION] **—pho•to•e•mis•sive** (fō′tō i mis′iv), *adj.*

photoeng., photoengraving.

pho•to•en•grave (fō′tō en grāv′), *v.t.,* **-graved, -grav•ing.** to make a photoengraving of. [1870–75; PHOTO- + ENGRAVE] **—pho′to•en•grav′er,** *n.*

pho•to•en•grav•ing (fō′tō en grā′ving), *n.* **1.** a photographic process of preparing printing plates for letterpress printing. **2.** a plate so produced. **3.** a print made from it. [1870–75; PHOTO- + ENGRAVING]

pho′to es′say, a group of photographs, usually with supplementary text, that conveys a unified story and is published as a book or as a feature in a magazine or newspaper. Also called **photo story.** [1975–80] **—pho′•to es′sayist.**

pho′to fin′ish, *Sports.* a finish of a race in which two or more contestants are so close to the finish line that reference to a photograph of the finish is necessary to determine the winner. [1935–40] **—pho′to-fin′ish,** *adj.*

pho•to•fin•ish•ing (fō′tō fin′i shing), *n.* the act or occupation of developing films, printing photographs, etc. [PHOTO + FINISHING] **—pho′to•fin′ish•er,** *n.*

pho•to•fis•sion (fō′tə fish′ən, fō′tə fish′-), *n. Physics.* nuclear fission induced by the absorption of a high-energy photon. [1935–40; PHOTO- + FISSION]

pho•to•flash (fō′tə flash′), *n.* **1.** flashbulb. *—adj.* **2.** of or pertaining to flash photography. [1925–30; PHOTO- + FLASH]

pho•to•flight (fō′tə flīt′), *adj.* pertaining to a flight made for the purpose of aerial photography. [PHOTO- + FLIGHT[1]]

pho′to•flood lamp′ (fō′tə flud′), an incandescent tungsten lamp in which high intensity is obtained by overloading voltage: used in photography, television, etc. Also, **pho′to•flood′.** [PHOTO- + FLOOD]

pho•to•fluor•o•gram (fō′tō flo͝or′ə gram′, -flôr′-, -flōr′-), *n.* a recording on photographic film of images produced by a fluoroscopic examination. [1940–45; PHOTO- + FLUORO- + -GRAM[1]]

pho•to•fluo•rog•ra•phy (fō′tō flo͝o rog′rə fē, -flô-, -flō-), *n.* photography of images produced by a fluoroscopic examination, used in x-ray examination of the lungs of large groups of people. Also called **fluorography.** [1940–45; PHOTO- + FLUORO- + -GRAPHY]

pho•tog (fə tog′), *n. Informal.* a photographer. [by shortening]

photog., 1. photographer. **2.** photographic. **3.** photography.

pho•to•gel•a•tin (fō′tə jel′ə tin, -ə tn), *adj.* pertaining to any photographic process in which gelatin is used to receive or transfer a print. [1870–75; PHOTO- + GELATIN]

photogel′atin proc′ess, collotype (def. 1).

pho•to•gen (fō′tə jən, -jen′), *n.* **1.** a light oil obtained by the distillation of bituminous shale, coal, or peat: once commercially produced chiefly as an illuminant and as a solvent. **2.** *Biol.* a photogenic organ, organism, or substance. [1855–60; PHOTO- + -GEN]

pho•to•gene (fō′tə jēn′), *n. Ophthalm.* an afterimage on the retina. [1850–55; PHOTO- + *-gene,* var. of -GEN]

pho•to•gen•ic (fō′tə jen′ik), *adj.* **1.** forming an attractive subject for photography or having features that look well in a photograph: *a photogenic face.* **2.** *Biol.* producing or emitting light, as certain bacteria; luminiferous; phosphorescent. **3.** *Med.* produced or caused by light, as a skin condition. [1830–40; PHOTO- + -GENIC] **—pho′to•gen′i•cal•ly,** *adv.*

pho•to•ge•ol•o•gy (fō′tō jē ol′ə jē), *n.* the technique of interpreting geology from aerial photographs or compiling geologic maps therefrom. [1940–45; PHOTO- + GEOLOGY] **—pho•to•ge•o•log•ic** (fō′tō jē′ə loj′ik), **pho′to•ge′o•log′i•cal,** *adj.* **—pho′to•ge′o•log′i•cal•ly,** *adv.*

pho•to•gram (fō′tə gram′), *n.* a silhouette photograph made by placing an object directly on sensitized paper and exposing it to light. [1855–60; PHOTO- + -GRAM[1]]

pho•to•gram•me•try (fō′tə gram′i trē), *n.* the process of making surveys and maps through the use of photographs, esp. aerial photographs. [1870–75; PHOTO- + -GRAM[1] + -METRY] **—pho•to•gram•met•ric** (fō′tō-grə me′trik), **pho′to•gram•met′ri•cal,** *adj.* **—pho′to•gram•met′ri•cal•ly,** *adv.* **—pho′to•gram′me•trist,** *n.*

pho•to•graph (fō′tə graf′, -gräf′), *n.* **1.** a picture produced by photography. *—v.t.* **2.** to take a photograph of. *—v.i.* **3.** to practice photography. **4.** to be photographed or be suitable for being photographed in

CONCISE ETYMOLOGY KEY: <, descended or borrowed from; >, whence; b., blend of, blended; c., cognate with; cf., compare; deriv., derivative; equiv., equivalent; imit., imitative; obl., oblique; r., replacing; s., stem; sp., spelling, spelled; resp., respelling, respelled; trans., translation; ?, origin unknown; *, unattested; ‡, probably earlier than. See the full key inside the front cover.

some specified way: *The children photograph well.* [1839; PHOTO- + -GRAPH] **—pho′to·graph′a·ble,** *adj.*

pho·tog·ra·pher (fə tog′rə fər), *n.* a person who takes photographs, esp. one who practices photography professionally. [1840–50; PHOTOGRAPH + -ER[1]]

pho·to·graph·ic (fō′tə graf′ik), *adj.* **1.** of or pertaining to photography. **2.** used in, or produced by means of, photography: *photographic equipment; the photographic coverage of a newspaper.* **3.** suggestive of a photograph; extremely realistic and detailed: *photographic accuracy.* **4.** remembering, reproducing, or functioning with the precision of a photograph: *a photographic memory.* Also, **pho′to·graph′i·cal.** [1839; PHOTOGRAPH + -IC] **—pho′to·graph′i·cal·ly,** *adv.*

pho·tog·ra·phy (fə tog′rə fē), *n.* **1.** the process or art of producing images of objects on sensitized surfaces by the chemical action of light or of other forms of radiant energy, as x-rays, gamma rays, or cosmic rays. **2.** cinematography. [1839; PHOTO- + -GRAPHY]

pho·to·gra·vure (fō′tə grə vyŏŏr′, -grā′vyər), *n.* **1.** any of various processes, based on photography, by which an intaglio engraving is formed on a metal plate, from which ink reproductions are made. **2.** the plate. **3.** a print made from it. [1875–80; PHOTO- + GRAVURE] **—pho′to·gra·vure′ist,** *n.*

pho·to·he·li·o·graph (fō′tə hē′lē ə graf′, -gräf′), *n. Astron.* an instrument for photographing the sun, consisting of a camera and a specially adapted telescope. Also called **heliograph.** [1860–65; PHOTO- + HELIOGRAPH] **—pho·to·he·li·o·graph·ic** (fō′tə hē′lē ə graf′ik), *adj.* **—pho·to·he·li·og·ra·phy** (fō′tə hē′lē og′rə fē), *n.*

pho·to·in·duced (fō′tō in do͞ost′, -dyo͞ost′), *adj.* induced by light. [1945–50; PHOTO- + INDUCE + -ED[2]]

pho·to·i·o·ni·za·tion (fō′tō ī′ə nə zā′shən), *n. Physics.* the phenomenon in which the absorption of electromagnetic radiation by an atom in a gas induces the atom to emit a bound electron and thereby become ionized. [1910–15; PHOTO- + IONIZATION]

pho·to·i·som·er·i·za·tion (fō′tō ī som′ər ə zā′shən), *n. Chem.* isomerization induced by light. [1925–30; PHOTO- + ISOMERIZATION]

pho·to·jour·nal·ism (fō′tō jûr′nl iz′əm), *n.* **1.** journalism in which photography dominates written copy, as in certain magazines. **2.** news photography, whether or not for primarily pictorial media, publications, or stories. [1940–45; PHOTO- + JOURNALISM] **—pho′to·jour′nal·ist,** *n.*

pho·to·ki·ne·sis (fō′tō ki nē′sis, -kī-), *n. Physiol.* movement occurring upon exposure to light. [1900–05; PHOTO- + -KINESIS] **—pho·to·ki·net·ic** (fō′tō ki net′ik, -kī-), *adj.*

pho′to lay′out, a picture spread. See under **spread** (def. 34).

pho·to·lith·o (fō′tə lith′ō), *n., pl.* **-lith·os,** *adj.* **—***n.* **1.** photolithography. **2.** photolithograph. **—***adj.* **3.** photolithographic. [1855–60; PHOTO- + LITHO-]

pho·to·lith·o·graph (fō′tə lith′ə graf′, -gräf′), *n.* **1.** Also, **pho·to·lith·o·print** (fō′tə lith′ə print′). a lithograph printed from a stone or the like upon which a picture or design has been formed by photography. **—***v.t.* **2.** to make a photolithograph of. [1850–55; PHOTO- + LITHOGRAPH]

pho·to·li·thog·ra·phy (fō′tō li thog′rə fē), *n.* **1.** the technique or art of making photolithographs. **2.** *Electronics.* a process whereby integrated and printed circuits are produced by photographing the circuit pattern on a photosensitive substrate and chemically etching away the background. [1855–60; PHOTO- + LITHOGRAPHY] **—pho·to·lith·o·graph·ic** (fō′tə lith′ə graf′ik), *adj.* **—pho′to·li·thog′ra·pher,** *n.*

pho·to·lu·mi·nes·cence (fō′tə lo͞o′mə nes′əns), *n. Physics.* luminescence induced by the absorption of infrared radiation, visible light, or ultraviolet radiation. [1885–90; PHOTO- + LUMINESCENCE] **—pho′to·lu′mi·nes′cent,** *adj.*

pho·tol·y·sis (fō tol′ə sis), *n.* the chemical decomposition of materials under the influence of light. [1910–15; PHOTO- + -LYSIS] **—pho·to·lyt·ic** (fōt′l it′ik), *adj.*

pho·to·lyze (fōt′l īz′), *v.,* **-lyzed, -lyz·ing.** *Chem.* **—***v.t.* **1.** to break down molecules with light. **—***v.i.* **2.** to experience photolysis. Also, *esp. Brit.,* **pho′to·lyse′.** [1935–40; PHOTO(LYSIS) + *-lyze,* on the model of ANALYSIS, ANALYZE] **—pho′to·ly·za′tion,** *n.*

photom., photometry.

pho·to·mac·ro·graph (fō′tə mak′rə graf′, -gräf′), *n.* **1.** a photograph showing a subject at actual size or somewhat larger. **2.** a photograph made through a microscope of low power. [1945–50; PHOTO- + MACROGRAPH] **—pho·to·ma·crog·ra·phy** (fō′tə ma krog′rə fē), *n.*

pho·to·map (fō′tə map′), *n., v.,* **-mapped, -map·ping.** **—***n.* **1.** a mosaic of aerial photographs marked as a map, with grid lines, place-names, etc. **—***v.t.* **2.** to map by means of aerial photography. [1865–70; PHOTO- + MAP]

pho·to·me·chan·i·cal (fō′tō mə kan′i kəl), *adj.* noting or pertaining to any of various processes for printing from plates or surfaces prepared by the aid of photography. [1885–90; PHOTO- + MECHANICAL] **—pho′to·me·chan′i·cal·ly,** *adv.*

pho·tom·e·ter (fō tom′i tər), *n. Optics.* an instrument that measures luminous intensity or brightness, luminous flux, light distribution, color, etc., usually by comparing the light emitted by two sources, one source having certain specified standard characteristics. [1770–80; < NL *photometrum.* See PHOTO-, -METER]

pho·tom·e·try (fō tom′i trē), *n.* **1.** the measurement of the intensity of light or of relative illuminating power. **2.** the science dealing with such measurements. [1815–25; < NL *photometria.* See PHOTO-, -METRY] **—pho·to·met·ric** (fō′tə me′trik), **pho′to·met′ri·cal,** *adj.* **—pho·tom′e·trist, pho·to·me·tri·cian** (fō′tə me trish′ən), *n.*

pho·to·mi·cro·graph (fō′tə mī′krə graf′, -gräf′), *n.* a photograph taken through a microscope. Cf. **cinemicrograph.** [1855–60; PHOTO- + MICROGRAPH] **—pho·to·mi·crog·ra·phy** (fō′tə mī krog′rə fē), *n.*

pho·to·mi·cro·scope (fō′tə mī′krə skōp′), *n.* a microscope having an illuminator and a camera mechanism for producing a photomicrograph. [1905–10; PHOTO- + MICROSCOPE] **—pho·to·mi·cros·co·py** (fō′tə mī kros′kə pē), *n.*

pho·to·mon·tage (fō′tə mon täzh′), *n. Photog.* a combination of several photographs joined together for artistic effect or to show more of the subject than can be shown in a single photograph. Also called **montage.** [1930–35; PHOTO- + MONTAGE]

pho·to·mor·pho·gen·e·sis (fō′tə môr′fə jen′ə sis), *n.* plant development that is controlled by light. [1955–60; PHOTO- + MORPHOGENESIS] **—pho′to·mor′pho·gen′ic,** *adj.*

pho·to·mo·sa·ic (fō′tō mō zā′ik), *n. Survey.* mosaic (def. 4). [1955–60; PHOTO- + MOSAIC]

pho·to·mount (fō′tō mount′), *n.* a heavy paper or board suitable for mounting photographs.

pho·to·mul·ti·pli·er (fō′tə mul′tə plī′ər), *n.* an extremely sensitive detector of light and of other radiation, consisting of a tube in which the electrons released by radiation striking a photocathode are accelerated, greatly amplifying the signal obtainable from small quantities of radiation. [1935–40; PHOTO- + MULTIPLIER]

pho·to·mu·ral (fō′tə myŏŏr′əl), *n.* a wall decoration consisting of a very large photograph or photographs. [1930–35; PHOTO- + MURAL] **—pho′to·mu′ral·ist,** *n.*

pho·ton (fō′ton), *n.* a quantum of electromagnetic radiation, usually considered as an elementary particle that is its own antiparticle and that has zero rest mass and charge and a spin of one. *Symbol:* γ Also called **light quantum.** [1900–05; PHOT- + -ON[1]]

pho·to·neg·a·tive (fō′tə neg′ə tiv), *adj. Physics.* pertaining to a substance, as selenium, having a conductivity that decreases upon absorption of electromagnetic radiation. [1910–15; PHOTO- + NEGATIVE]

pho·to·neu·tron (fō′tə no͞o′tron, -nyo͞o′-), *n. Physics.* a neutron emitted from a nucleus during photodisintegration. [1930–35; PHOTO- + NEUTRON]

pho·ton·ic (fō ton′ik), *adj.* of or pertaining to processes involving photons. [PHOTON + -IC]

pho·ton·ics (fō ton′iks), *n.* (*used with a singular v.*) the study and technology of the use of light for the transmission of information. [1950–55; see PHOTONIC, -ICS; perh. on the model of ELECTRONICS]

pho·to·nov·el (fō′tō nov′əl), *n.* a novel published as a series of sequential photographs coupled with dialogue enclosed in balloons. [1975–80; trans. of AmerSp *fotonovela;* see PHOTO-, NOVEL[1]]

pho·to·nu·cle·ar (fō′tō no͞o′klē ər, -nyo͞o′- *or, by metathesis,* -kyə lər), *adj. Physics.* of, pertaining to, or caused by the collision of high-energy photons with the nucleus of an atom. [1940–45; PHOTO- + NUCLEAR] **—Pronunciation.** See **nuclear.**

pho·to-off·set (fō′tō ôf′set′, -of′-), *n., v.,* **-set, -set·ting.** **—***n.* **1.** a method of printing, based on photolithography, in which the inked image is transferred from the metal plate to a rubber surface and then to the paper. **—***v.t., v.i.* **2.** to print by photo-offset. [1925–30]

pho′to opportu′nity, a brief period set aside for the media to take photographs of a high government official or celebrity, usually immediately before or after a newsworthy event. [1975–80]

pho·to·ox·i·da·tion (fō′tō ok′si dā′shən), *n. Chem.* oxidation induced by light. [1885–90]

pho·top·a·thy (fō top′ə thē), *n.* **1.** movement of an organism in response to the intensity of light, esp. away from the source of light. **2.** any condition or disease produced by the effect of light, esp. in excessive amounts. [1895–1900; PHOTO- + -PATHY] **—pho·to·path·ic** (fō′tə path′ik), *adj.*

pho·to·pe·ri·od (fō′tə pēr′ē əd), *n. Biol.* the interval in a 24-hour period during which a plant or animal is exposed to light. [1915–20; PHOTO- + PERIOD] **—pho·to·pe·ri·od·ic** (fō′tə pēr′ē od′ik), **pho′to·pe′ri·od′i·cal,** *adj.* **—pho′to·pe′ri·od′i·cal·ly,** *adv.*

pho·to·pe·ri·od·ism (fō′tə pēr′ē ə diz′əm), *n. Biol.* the response, as affecting growth or reproduction, of an organism to the length of exposure to light in a 24-hour period. Also called **pho·to·pe·ri·o·dic·i·ty** (fō′tō pēr′ē ə dis′i tē). [1915–20; PHOTOPERIOD + -ISM]

pho·to·phil·ic (fō′tə fil′ik), *adj.* of or pertaining to an organism, as a plant, that is receptive to, seeks, or thrives in light. Also, **pho·toph·i·lous** (fō tof′ə ləs). [1895–1900; PHOTO- + -PHILIC]

pho·to·pho·bi·a (fō′tə fō′bē ə), *n. Pathol.* **1.** an abnormal sensitivity to or intolerance of light, as in iritis. **2.** an abnormal fear of light. [1790–1800; PHOTO- + -PHOBIA]

pho·to·pho·bic (fō′tə fō′bik), *adj.* of or pertaining to an organism that avoids light. [1855–60; PHOTO- + -PHOBIC]

pho·to·phore (fō′tə fôr′, -fōr′), *n. Zool.* a luminous organ found in certain fishes and crustaceans. [1880–85; PHOTO- + -PHORE]

pho·to·phos·pho·ryl·a·tion (fō′tə fos′fər ə lā′shən), *n. Biochem.* phosphorylation that utilizes light as a source of energy, as in the formation of ATP from ADP and phosphorus during photosynthesis. [1955–60; PHOTO- + PHOSPHORYLATION]

pho·to·pi·a (fō tō′pē ə), *n. Ophthalm.* vision in bright light (opposed to *scotopia*). Cf. **light adaptation.** [1910–15; PHOT- + -OPIA] **—pho·top·ic** (fō top′ik, -tō′pik), *adj.*

pho·to·play (fō′tə plā′), *n.* a motion-picture scenario; screenplay. [1910–15; *Amer.;* PHOTO- + PLAY] **—pho′·to·play′er,** *n.*

pho·to·po·lar·im·e·ter (fō′tō pō′lə rim′i tər), *n. Optics.* a polarimeter that uses a photocell. [PHOTO(ELECTRIC) + POLARIMETER]

pho·to·pol·y·mer (fō′tō pol′ə mər), *n. Chem.* a polymer or plastic that undergoes a change in physical or chemical properties when exposed to light. [PHOTO- + POLYMER]

pho·to·po·lym·er·i·za·tion (fō′tō pə lim′ər ə zā′shən, -pol′ə mər-), *n. Chem.* polymerization induced by light. [1915–20; PHOTO- + POLYMERIZATION]

pho·to·pos·i·tive (fō′tə poz′i tiv), *adj. Physics.* pertaining to a substance whose conductivity increases upon absorption of electromagnetic radiation. [1910–15; PHOTO- + POSITIVE]

pho·to·print (fō′tə print′), *n.* **1.** a photographic print. **2.** a print made by a photomechanical process; a photocopy. [1885–90; PHOTO- + PRINT] **—pho′to·print′er,** *n.* **—pho′to·print′ing,** *n.*

pho·to·pro·ton (fō′tō prō′ton), *n. Physics.* a proton emitted from a nucleus during photodisintegration. [1930–35; PHOTO- + PROTON]

pho·to·re·ac·tion (fō′tō rē ak′shən), *n. Chem.* a chemical reaction that involves or requires light. [1905–10; PHOTO- + REACTION]

pho·to·re·ac·ti·va·tion (fō′tō rē ak′tə vā′shən), *n. Biochem.* a process that repairs DNA damaged by ultraviolet light using an enzyme that requires visible light. [1945–50; PHOTO- + REACTIVATION]

pho·to·re·al·ism (fō′tō rē′ə liz′əm), *n.* (*sometimes cap.*) a style of painting flourishing in the 1970's, esp. in the U.S., England, and France, and depicting commonplace scenes or ordinary people, with a meticulously detailed realism, flat images, and barely discernible brushwork that suggests and often is based on or incorporates an actual photograph. Also, **pho′to re′alism.** Also called **sharp-focus realism, superrealism.** [1960–65; PHOTO- + REALISM] **—pho′to·re′al·ist,** *n., adj.* **—pho′to·re′·al·is′tic,** *adj.*

pho·to·re·cep·tion (fō′tō ri sep′shən), *n.* the physiological perception of light. [1905–10; PHOTO- + RECEPTION] **—pho′to·re·cep′tive,** *adj.*

pho·to·re·cep·tor (fō′tō ri sep′tər), *n. Physiol., Biol.* a receptor stimulated by light. [1905–10; PHOTO- + RECEPTOR]

pho·to·re·con (fō′tō ri kon′), *n., adj. Informal.* photoreconnaissance. Also, **pho′to·re·con′.** [PHOTO- + RECON]

pho·to·re·con·nais·sance (fō′tō ri kon′ə səns, -zəns), *n.* reconnaissance using aerial photography. Also, **pho′to·re·con′nais·sance.** [1940–45; PHOTO- + RECONNAISSANCE]

pho·to·re·cord·er (fō′tō ri kôr′dər), *n.* a device for making photographic records. [PHOTO- + RECORDER]

pho·to·re·cord·ing (fō′tō ri kôr′ding), *n.* **1.** the act of making photographic records, esp. of documents. **2.** such a photographic record. [PHOTO- + RECORD + -ING[1]]

pho·to·re·duc·tion (fō′tō ri duk′shən), *n. Chem.* a reduction reaction induced by light. [PHOTO- + REDUCTION]

pho·to·re·sist (fō′tō ri zist′), *n. Electronics.* a photosensitive liquid polymer, used in photolithography to produce integrated circuits. [1950–55; PHOTO- + RESIST]

pho·to·scan (fō′tə skan′), *v.t.,* **-scanned, -scan·ning.** to study the distribution of a radioactive isotope or radiopaque dye in (a body organ or part) through the use of x-rays. [1955–60; PHOTO- + SCAN]

Pho·to-Se·ces·sion (fō′tō si sesh′ən), *n.* an association of photographers founded in New York City in 1902 by Alfred Stieglitz and Edward Steichen that advocated the development and public recognition of photography as a fine art. **—Pho′to-Se·ces′sion·ist,** *n.*

pho·to·sen·si·tive (fō′tə sen′si tiv), *adj.* sensitive to light or similar radiation. [PHOTO- + SENSITIVE]

pho·to·sen·si·tiv·i·ty (fō′tə sen′si tiv′i tē), *n.* **1.** the quality of being photosensitive. **2.** abnormal sensitivity of the skin to ultraviolet light, usually following exposure to certain oral or topical drugs or to other sensitizing chemicals and resulting in accelerated burning and blistering of the skin. [1915–20; PHOTO- + SENSITIVITY]

pho·to·sen·si·tize (fō′tə sen′si tīz′), *v.t.,* **-tized, -tiz·ing.** to make (a material) photosensitive, as by the application of a photosensitive emulsion. Also, *esp. Brit.,* **pho′to·sen′si·tise′.** [1920–25; PHOTOSENSIT(IVE) + -IZE] **—pho′to·sen′si·ti·za′tion,** *n.*

pho·to·sen·sor (fō′tə sen′sər, -sôr), *n.* a photocell used to detect light. Also called **photodetector.** [1960–65; PHOTO- + SENSOR]

pho·to·sphere (fō′tə sfēr′), *n.* **1.** a sphere of light or radiance. **2.** *Astron.* the luminous visible surface of the sun, being a shallow layer of strongly ionized gases. [1655–65; PHOTO- + -SPHERE] **—pho·to·spher·ic** (fō′tə sfer′ik, -sfēr′-), *adj.*

pho′to spread′, a picture spread. See under **spread** (def. 34).

Pho·to·stat (fō′tə stat′), **1.** *Trademark.* a brand of camera for making facsimile copies of documents, drawings, etc., in the form of paper negatives on which the positions of lines, objects, etc., in the originals are maintained. **—***n.* **2.** (*often l.c.*) a copy made with this camera. **—***v.t., v.i.* **3.** (*l.c.*) to copy with this camera. **—pho′to·**

stat′er, pho′to·stat′ter, *n.* **—pho′to·stat′ic,** *adj.* **—pho′to·stat′i·cal·ly,** *adv.*

pho′to sto′ry. See **photo essay.** Also **pho′to·sto′ry.**

pho·to·syn·thate (fō′tə sin′thāt), *n. Biochem.* a compound formed by photosynthesis. [1910–15; PHOTO-SYNTH(ESIS) + -ATE[2]]

pho·to·syn·the·sis (fō′tə sin′thə sis), *n. Biol., Biochem.* (esp. in plants) the synthesis of complex organic materials, esp. carbohydrates, from carbon dioxide, water, and inorganic salts, using sunlight as the source of energy and with the aid of chlorophyll and associated pigments. [1895–1900; PHOTO- + SYNTHESIS] **—pho·to·syn·thet·ic** (fō′tə sin thet′ik), *adj.* **—pho′to·syn·thet′i·cal·ly,** *adv.*

pho·to·tax·is (fō′tə tak′sis), *n. Biol.* movement of an organism toward or away from a source of light. Also, **pho′to·tax′y.** [1900–05; PHOTO- + -TAXIS] **—pho·to·tac·tic** (fō′tə tak′tik), *adj.* **—pho′to·tac′ti·cal·ly,** *adv.*

pho·to·te·leg·ra·phy (fō′tō tə leg′rə fē), *n.* facsimile (def. 2a). [1885–90; PHOTO- + TELEGRAPHY]

pho·to·the·od·o·lite (fō′tō thē od′l īt′), *n.* an optical tracking instrument consisting of a camera and theodolite mounted on a single tripod, used in photogrammetry and in tracking rockets. Cf. **theodolite.** [1890–95; PHOTO- + THEODOLITE]

pho·to·ther·a·peu·tics (fō′tə ther′ə pyōō′tiks), *n.* (*used with a singular v.*) the branch of therapeutics that deals with the curative use of light rays. [1900–05; PHOTO- + THERAPEUTICS] **—pho′to·ther′a·peu′tic,** *adj.*

pho·to·ther·a·py (fō′tə ther′ə pē), *n.* **1.** treatment of disease, esp. of the skin, by means of light rays. **2.** See **light therapy.** [1895–1900; PHOTO- + THERAPY] **—pho·to·the·rap·ic** (fō′tō thə rap′ik), *adj.* **—pho′to·ther′a·pist,** *n.*

pho·to·ther·mic (fō′tə thûr′mik), *adj.* **1.** pertaining to the thermal effects of light. **2.** pertaining to or involving both light and heat. [1890–95; PHOTO- + THERMIC]

pho·tot·o·nus (fō tot′n əs), *n. Biol.* **1.** the normal condition of sensitiveness to light in organisms or their organs. **2.** the irritability exhibited by cytoplasm when exposed to light of a certain intensity. [1870–75; PHOTO- + TONUS] **—pho·to·ton·ic** (fō′tə ton′ik), *adj.*

pho·to·to·pog·ra·phy (fō′tō tə pog′rə fē), *n.* topographical surveying employing photogrammetric methods. [1890–95; PHOTO- + TOPOGRAPHY] **—pho·to·top·o·graph·ic** (fō′tə top′ə graf′ik), **pho′to·top′o·graph′i·cal,** *adj.*

pho·to·tox·in (fō′tə tok′sin), *n. Biochem.* a plant toxin causing an allergic reaction when touched or eaten by a susceptible person or animal subsequently exposed to sunlight. [PHOTO- + TOXIN]

pho·to·tran·sis·tor (fō′tō tran zis′tər), *n. Electronics.* a transistor that amplifies current induced by photoconductivity. [1945–50; PHOTO- + TRANSISTOR]

pho·to·troph (fō′tə trof′, -trōf′), *n. Biol.* any organism that uses light as its principal source of energy. [1940–45; PHOTO- + -TROPH] **—pho′to·troph′ic,** *adj.*

phototroph′ic bacte′ria, *Bacteriol.* a group of bacteria, including the green bacteria and purple bacteria, whose energy for growth is derived from sunlight and whose carbon is derived from carbon dioxide or organic carbon.

pho·to·trop·ic (fō′tə trop′ik, -trō′pik), *adj. Bot.* **1.** growing toward or away from the light. **2.** taking a particular direction under the influence of light. [1895–1900; PHOTO- + -TROPIC] **—pho′to·trop′i·cal·ly,** *adv.*

pho·tot·ro·pism (fō to′trə piz′əm, fō′tō trō′piz əm), *n. Bot.* phototropic tendency or growth. [1895–1900; PHOTO- + -TROPISM]

pho·to·tube (fō′tə tōōb′, -tyōōb′), *n. Electronics.* an electron tube with a photosensitive cathode, used like a photocell. Also called **photoelectric tube.** [1925–30; PHOTO- + TUBE]

pho·to·type (fō′tə tīp′), *n. Print.* **1.** a plate with a relief printing surface produced by photography. **2.** any process for making such a plate. **3.** a print made from it. [1855–60; PHOTO- + -TYPE] **—pho·to·typ·ic** (fō′tə-tip′ik), *adj.* **—pho′to·typ′i·cal·ly,** *adv.*

pho·to·type·set·ting (fō′tō tīp′set′ing), *n. Print.* photocomposition. [1930–35; PHOTO- + TYPESETTING] **—pho′to·type′set′ter,** *n.*

pho·to·ty·pog·ra·phy (fō′tō tī pog′rə fē), *n.* **1.** (formerly) the art or technique of making printing surfaces by light or photography, by any of a large number of processes. **2.** photocomposition. [1885–90; PHOTO- + TYPOGRAPHY] **—pho·to·ty·po·graph·ic** (fō′tə tī′pə-graf′ik), *adj.*

pho·to·vol·ta·ic (fō′tō vol tā′ik, -vōl-), *adj. Elect.* of or pertaining to the photovoltaic effect. [1920–25; PHOTO- + VOLTAIC]

pho′tovolta′ic cell′, *Elect.* a photocell in which an electromotive force is generated by a photovoltaic effect.

pho′tovolta′ic effect′, *Physics.* the phenomenon in which the incidence of light or other electromagnetic radiation upon the junction of two dissimilar materials, as a metal and a semiconductor, induces the generation of an electromotive force. [1955–60]

pho·to·vol·ta·ics (fō′tō vōl tā′iks), *n.* **1.** (*used with a singular v.*) a field of semiconductor technology involving the direct conversion of electromagnetic radiation as sunlight, into electricity. **2.** (*used with a plural v.*) devices designed to perform such conversion. [1975–80; see PHOTOVOLTAIC, -ICS]

CONCISE ETYMOLOGY KEY: <, descended or borrowed from; >, whence; b., blend of, blended; c., cognate with; cf., compare; deriv., derivative; equiv., equivalent; imit., imitative; obl., oblique; r., replacing; s., stem; sp., spelling, spelled; resp., respelling, respelled; trans., translation; ?, origin unknown; *, unattested; ‡, probably earlier than. See the full key inside the front cover.

pho·to·zin·cog·ra·phy (fō′tō zing kog′rə fē), *n. Obs.* a type of photoengraving using a sensitized zinc plate. [1855–60; PHOTO- + ZINCOGRAPHY]

phr., phrase.

phrag·mi·tes (frag mī′tēz), *n.* any of several tall grasses of the genus *Phragmites,* having plumed heads, growing in marshy areas, esp. the common reed *P. australis* (or *P. communis*). [< NL (1820) < Gk *phragmī́tēs* growing in hedges, equiv. to *phrágm(a)* fence, breastwork, screen (n. deriv. of *phrássein* (Attic *phráttein*) to fence in, hedge around) + *-ītēs* -ITE[1]]

phrag·mo·plast (frag′mə plast′), *n. Bot.* the cytoplasmic structure that forms at the equator of the spindle after the chromosomes have divided during the anaphase of plant mitosis, and that initiates cell division. Also called **cell plate.** [1910–15; < Gk *phrágm(a)* fence (see PHRAGMITES) + -O- + -PLAST]

phras·al (frā′zəl), *adj.* of, consisting of, or of the nature of a phrase or phrases: *phrasal construction.* [1870–75; PHRASE + -AL[1]] **—phras′al·ly,** *adv.*

phras′al verb′, *Gram.* a combination of verb and one or more adverbial or prepositional particles, as *catch on, take off, bring up,* or *put up with,* functioning as a single semantic unit and often having an idiomatic meaning that could not be predicted from the meanings of the individual parts. [1875–80]

phrase (frāz), *n., v.,* **phrased, phras·ing.** —*n.* **1.** *Gram.* **a.** a sequence of two or more words arranged in a grammatical construction and acting as a unit in a sentence. **b.** (in English) a sequence of two or more words that does not contain a finite verb and its subject or that does not consist of clause elements such as subject, verb, object, or complement, as a preposition and a noun or pronoun, an adjective and noun, or an adverb and verb. **2.** *Rhet.* a word or group of spoken words that the mind focuses on momentarily as a meaningful unit and is preceded and followed by pauses. **3.** a characteristic, current, or proverbial expression: *a hackneyed phrase.* **4.** *Music.* a division of a composition, commonly a passage of four or eight measures, forming part of a period. **5.** a way of speaking, mode of expression, or phraseology: *a book written in the phrase of the West.* **6.** a brief utterance or remark: *In a phrase, he's a dishonest man.* **7.** *Dancing.* a sequence of motions making up part of a choreographic pattern. —*v.t.* **8.** to express or word in a particular way: *to phrase an apology well.* **9.** to express in words: *to phrase one's thoughts.* **10.** *Music.* **a.** to mark off or bring out the phrases of (a piece), esp. in execution. **b.** to group (notes) into a phrase. —*v.i.* **11.** *Music.* to perform a passage or piece with proper phrasing. [1520–30; (n.) back formation from *phrases,* pl. of earlier *phrasis* < L *phrasis* diction, style (pl. *phrasēs*) < Gk *phrásis* diction, style, speech, equiv. to *phrá(zein)* to speak + *-sis* -SIS; (v.) deriv. of the n.]
—Syn. 1. PHRASE, EXPRESSION, IDIOM, LOCUTION all refer to grammatically related groups of words. A PHRASE is a sequence of two or more words that make up a grammatical construction, usually lacking a finite verb and hence not a complete clause or sentence: *shady lane* (a noun phrase); *at the bottom* (a prepositional phrase); *very slowly* (an adverbial phrase). In general use, PHRASE refers to any frequently repeated or memorable group of words, usually of less than sentence length or complexity: *a case of feast or famine—to use the well-known phrase.* EXPRESSION is the most general of these words and may refer to a word, a phrase, or even a sentence: *prose filled with old-fashioned expressions.* An IDIOM is a phrase or larger unit of expression that is peculiar to a single language or a variety of a language and whose meaning, often figurative, cannot easily be understood by combining the usual meanings of its individual parts, as *to go for broke.* LOCUTION is a somewhat formal term for a word, a phrase, or an expression considered as peculiar to or characteristic of a regional or social dialect: *a unique set of locutions heard only in the mountainous regions of the South.*

phrase′ book′, a small book containing everyday phrases and sentences and their equivalents in a foreign language, written esp. for travelers. [1585–95]

phrase·mak·er (frāz′mā′kər), *n.* **1.** a person who is skilled in coining phrases; phraseologist. **2.** a person who makes catchy but often empty statements. [1815–25; PHRASE + MAKER] **—phrase′mak′ing,** *n.*

phrase′ mark′er, *Ling.* (in generative grammar) a representation of the constituent structure of a sentence, using a tree diagram or labeled bracketing. Also, **phrase′-mark′er.** [1960–65]

phrase·mon·ger (frāz′mung′gər, -mong′-), *n.* phrasemaker (def. 2). [1805–15; PHRASE + MONGER] **—phrase′mon′ger·ing,** *n.*

phra·se·o·gram (frā′zē ə gram′), *n.* a written symbol or combination of symbols, as in shorthand, used to represent a phrase. [1840–50; PHRASE + -O- + -GRAM[1]]

phra·se·o·graph (frā′zē ə graf′, -gräf′), *n.* a phrase for which there is a phraseogram. [1835–45; PHRASE + -O- + -GRAPH]

phra·se·ol·o·gist (frā′zē ol′ə jist), *n.* **1.** a person who treats of or is concerned with phraseology. **2.** a person who affects a particular phraseology or is skilled in coining phrases. [1705–15; PHRASEOLOG(Y) + -IST]

phra·se·ol·o·gy (frā′zē ol′ə jē), *n.* **1.** manner or style of verbal expression; characteristic language: *legal phraseology.* **2.** expressions; phrases: *obscure phraseology.* [1655–65; < NGk *phraseología* (erroneously for **phrasiología*), coined by German humanist Michael Neander (1525–95); see PHRASE, -O-, -LOGY] **—phra·se·o·log·i·cal** (frā′zē ə loj′i kəl), **phra′se·o·log′ic,** *adj.* **—phra′se·o·log′i·cal·ly,** *adv.*
—Syn. 1. See **diction.**

phrase′ struc′ture, *Ling.* the hierarchical arrangement of the constituent words and phrases of a sentence. Also called **constituent structure.** [1955–60]

phrase′-struc·ture gram′mar (frāz′struk′chər), *Ling.* a grammar that consists of phrase-structure rules. [1965–70]

phrase′-structure rule′, *Ling.* a rule that generates a sentence or other syntactic construction from words and phrases and identifies its constituent structure. Cf. **rewrite rule.**

phrase′ struc′ture tree′, *Ling.* a structural representation of a sentence in the form of an inverted tree, with each node of the tree labeled according to the phrasal constituent it represents. Cf. **tree diagram.**

phras·ing (frā′zing), *n.* **1.** the act of forming phrases. **2.** a manner or method of forming phrases; phraseology. **3.** *Music.* the grouping of the notes of a musical line into distinct phrases. [1605–15; PHRASE + -ING[1]]

phra·try (frā′trē), *n., pl.* **-tries. 1.** a grouping of clans or other social units within a tribe. **2.** (in ancient Greece) a subdivision of a phyle. [1745–55; < Gk *phratría,* equiv. to *phrātr-,* s. of *phrātēr* clansman (akin to BROTHER) + *-ia* -Y[3]] **—phra′tric, phra′tral, phra′·tri·ac′, phra′tri·al,** *adj.*

phreak (frēk), *n., v.,* **phreaked, phreak·ing.** —*n.* **1.** See **phone phreak.** —*v.i.* **2.** to act as a phone phreak. —*v.t.* **3.** to tamper with (telephones) as a phone phreak does. [1970–75; altered sp. of FREAK[1], copying *ph-* of PHONE[1]]

phre·at·ic (frē at′ik), *adj. Geol.* **1.** noting or pertaining to ground water. **2.** noting or pertaining to explosive volcanic activity involving steam derived from ground water: *a phreatic explosion.* [1890–95; < Gk *phreat-* (s. of *phréar*) artificial well + -IC]

phre·at·o·phyte (frē at′ə fīt′), *n.* a long-rooted plant that absorbs its water from the water table or the soil above it. [1915–20; < Gk *phreat-* (see PHREATIC) + -O- + -PHYTE] **—phre·at·o·phyt·ic** (frē at′ə fit′ik), *adj.*

phren-, var. of **phreno-** before a vowel: *phrenic.*

phren., 1. phrenological. **2.** phrenology.

phre·net·ic (fri net′ik), *adj.* Also, **phre·net′i·cal. 1.** frenetic. **2.** filled with extreme excitement; fanatic; frenzied. —*n.* **3.** a phrenetic person. [1325–75; < L *phrenēticus* < LGk *phrenētikós,* Gk *phrenitikós* frenzied (see PHRENITIS, -IC); r. ME *frenetike* < AF < L as above; cf. FRENETIC] **—phre·net′i·cal·ly,** *adv.* **—phre·net′ic·ness,** *n.*

-phrenia, a combining form used in the names of mental disorders: *schizophrenia.* [< NL < Gk *phren-* (s. of *phrḗn*) mind + *-ia* -IA]

phren·ic (fren′ik), *adj.* **1.** *Anat.* of or pertaining to the diaphragm. **2.** *Physiol.* relating to the mind or mental activity. [1695–1705; < NL *phrenicus.* See PHREN-, -IC]

phre·ni·tis (fri nī′tis), *n. Pathol.* (formerly) **1.** inflammation of the brain; encephalitis. **2.** delirium; frenzy. [1615–25; < LL *phrenītis* delirium, frenzy < Gk *phrenī́tis.* See PHREN-, -ITIS]

phreno-, a combining form meaning "mind," "diaphragm," used in the formation of compound words: *phrenology.* Also, *esp. before a vowel,* **phren-.** [< Gk *phreno-,* comb. form repr. *phrḗn* mind, diaphragm]

phrenol., 1. phrenological. **2.** phrenology.

phre·nol·o·gy (fri nol′ə jē, fre-), *n.* a psychological theory or analytical method based on the belief that certain mental faculties and character traits are indicated by the configurations of the skull. [1795–1805, *Amer.*; PHRENO- + -LOGY] **—phren·o·log·ic** (fren′l oj′ik), **phren′o·log′i·cal,** *adj.* **—phren′o·log′i·cal·ly,** *adv.* **—phre·nol′o·gist,** *n.*

Phrix·us (frik′səs), *n. Class. Myth.* a child who escaped on the back of a ram with his sister Helle from a plot against them. The fleece of the ram, which he sacrificed, was the Golden Fleece.

phro·ne·sis (frō nē′sis), *n. Philos.* wisdom in determining ends and the means of attaining them. [1885–90; < Gk *phrónēsis* thinking, equiv. to *phronē-* (verbid s. of *phroneîn* to think; akin to *phrḗn* mind) + *-sis* -SIS]

Phryg·i·a (frij′ē ə), *n.* an ancient country in central and NW Asia Minor.

Phryg·i·an (frij′ē ən), *adj.* **1.** of or pertaining to Phrygia, its people, or their language. —*n.* **2.** a native or inhabitant of Phrygia. **3.** an Indo-European language that was the language of Phrygia. [1570–80; < L *Phrygiānus.* See PHRYGIA, -AN]

Phryg′ian cap′, a soft, conical cap represented in ancient Greek art as part of Phrygian or oriental dress and associated, since the late 18th and early 19th centuries, with the liberty cap. [1840–50]

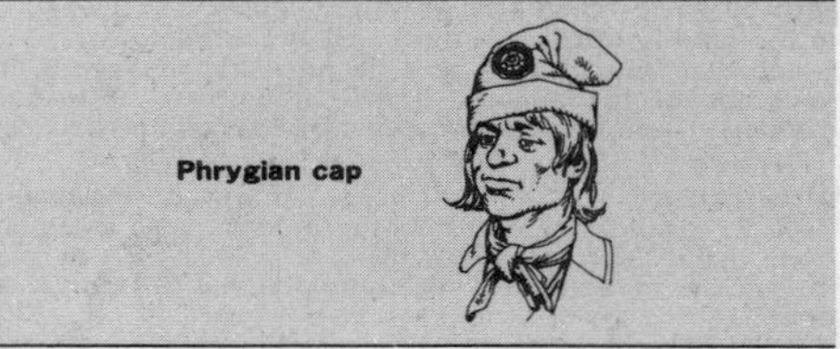
Phrygian cap

Phryg′ian mode′, *Music.* an authentic church mode represented on the white keys of a keyboard instrument by an ascending scale from E to E. [1800–10]

PHS, Public Health Service. Also, **P.H.S.**

phthal·ein (thal′ēn, -ē in, fthal′-), *n. Chem.* any of a group of compounds formed by treating phthalic anhydride with phenols, from which certain important dyes are derived. [1900–05; (NA)PHTHALE(NE) + -IN[2]]

phthal·ic (thal′ik, fthal′-), *adj. Chem.* of or derived from phthalic acid. [1855–60; (NA)PHTHAL(ENE) + -IC]

phthal′ic ac′id, 1. *Chem.* any of three isomeric acids having the formula $C_8H_6O_4$, esp. the ortho isomer (**orthophthalic acid**), a colorless, crystalline, slightly water-soluble solid used chiefly in the manufacture of dyes, medicine, and perfume. **2.** See **isophthalic acid. 3.** See **terephthalic acid.** [1855–60]

phthal′ic anhy′dride, *Chem.* a white, crystalline, slightly water-soluble solid, $C_8H_4O_3$, used chiefly in the manufacture of dyes, alkyd resins, and plasticizers. [1850–55]

phthal·in (thal′in, fthal′-), *n. Chem.* any of a group of compounds obtained by the reduction of the phthaleins. [1870–75; (NA)PHTHAL(ENE) + -IN[2]]

phthal·o·cy·a·nine (thal′ə sī′ə nēn′, -nin, fthal′-), *n. Chem.* **1.** Also called **metal-free phthalocyanine.** a blue-green pigment, $C_{32}H_{18}N_8$, derived from phthalic anhydride. **2.** any of the group of blue or green pigments produced by the interaction of metal-free phthalocyanine and a metal, esp. copper: used chiefly in the manufacture of enamels, printing inks, and automotive finishes. [1930–35; (NA)PHTHAL(ENE) + -O- + CYANINE]

phthal′ocy′anine blue′, a pigment used in painting, derived from copper phthalocyanine and characterized chiefly by its brilliant, dark-blue color and by permanence. [1945–50]

phthal′ocy′anine green′, a pigment used in painting, derived from chlorinated copper phthalocyanine and characterized chiefly by its intense green color and permanence. [1940–45]

phthi·o·col (thī′ə kôl′, -kol′), *n. Biochem.* a yellow crystalline substance, $C_{11}H_8O_3$, produced by the human tubercle bacillus, *Mycobacterium tuberculosis,* having antibiotic and blood-clotting properties. [1930–35; PHTHI(SIS) + -O- + intrusive -c- + -OL[1]]

phthi·ri·a·sis (thi rī′ə sis, thi-), *n.* crab lice infestation. [1590–1600; < Gk *phtheiríāsis,* equiv. to *phtheír* louse + *-iāsis* -IASIS]

phthis·ic (tiz′ik, thiz′-), *Pathol.* —*n.* **1.** a wasting disease of the lungs; phthisis. **2.** asthma. **3.** a person who suffers from phthisis. —*adj.* **4.** pertaining to phthisis; phthisical. [1300–50; < L *phthisicus* < Gk *phthisikós* (see PHTHISIS, -IC); r. ME *tisike* < ML *(p)tisicus;* L, as above]

phthis·i·cal (tiz′i kəl, thiz′-), *adj.* pertaining to, of the nature of, or affected by phthisis. Also, **phthis′ick·y.** [1605–15; PHTHISIC + -AL[1]]

phthi·sis (thī′sis, tī′-), *n. Pathol.* **1.** a wasting away. **2.** pulmonary tuberculosis; consumption. [1515–25; < Gk *phthísis* lung disease, lit., a wasting away, equiv. to *phthí(ein)* to decay + *-sis* -SIS]

phu·goid (fyōō′goid), *adj. Aerospace.* of or pertaining to long-period oscillation in the longitudinal motion of an aircraft, rocket, or missile. [1905–10; irreg. < Gk *phyg(ḗ)* flight + -OID]

Phu·ket (pōō′ket′), *n.* an island near the W coast of Thailand. 75,652; 294 sq. mi. (761 sq. km).

Phu·mi·phon A·dul·det (pōō mi′pôn ä dōōl′det). See **Rama IX.**

phyco-, a combining form meaning "seaweed," "algae," used in the formation of compound words: *phycochrome.* [< Gk *phŷko-,* comb. form repr. *phŷkos* seaweed]

phy·co·bi·ont (fī′kō bī′ont), *n.* the algae component of a lichen. [1957; PHYCO- + *-biont;* see MYCOBIONT]

phy·co·cy·an·in (fī′kō sī′ə nin), *n. Biochem.* a blue protein pigment, found in algae, involved in the process of photosynthesis. [1870–75; PHYCO- + CYAN-[1] + -IN[2]]

phy·co·e·ryth·rin (fī′kō i rith′rin, -er′ə thrin), *n.* a red protein pigment occurring in red algae. [1865–70; PHYCO- + ERYTHR- + -IN[2]]

phy·col·o·gy (fī kol′ə jē), *n.* the branch of botany dealing with algae. [1875–80; PHYCO- + -LOGY] —**phy·co·log·i·cal** (fī′kə loj′i kəl), *adj.* —**phy·col′o·gist,** *n.*

phy·co·my·cete (fī′kō mī′sēt, -mī sēt′), *n.* any of various fungi that resemble algae, as downy mildew. [1930–35; < NL *Phycomycetes* name of a class; see PHYCO-, -MYCETE] —**phy′co·my·ce′tous,** *adj.*

Phyfe (fīf), *n.* **Duncan,** 1768–1854, U.S. cabinetmaker, born in Scotland.

phyl-, var. of **phylo-** before a vowel: *phylic.*

-phyl, var. of **-phyll.**

phy·la (fī′lə), *n.* pl. of **phylum.**

phy·lac·ter·y (fi lak′tə rē), *n., pl.* **-ter·ies. 1.** *Judaism.* either of two small, black, leather cubes containing a piece of parchment inscribed with verses 4–9 of Deut. 6, 13–21 of Deut. 11, and 1–16 of Ex. 13: one is attached with straps to the left arm and the other to the forehead during weekday morning prayers by Orthodox and Conservative Jewish men. **2.** (in the early Christian church) a receptacle containing a holy relic. **3.** an amulet, charm, or safeguard against harm or danger. [1350–1400; < LL *phylactērium* < Gk *phylaktḗrion* outpost, safeguard, amulet, equiv. to *phylak-,* s. of *phylássein* to protect, guard + *-tērion* n. suffix denoting place; r. ME *philaterie* < ML *philatērium,* for LL, as above] —**phyl·ac·ter·ic** (fil′ak ter′ik), **phyl′ac·ter′i·cal,** *adj.* —**phy·lac′ter·ied,** *adj.*

phylactery (def. 1)

phy·lac·tic (fi lak′tik), *adj.* defending or protecting, esp. from disease. [1700–10; < Gk *phylaktikós* preservative, equiv. to *phylakt(ós)* guarding (verbal of *phylássein* to guard) + *-ikos* -IC. See PROPHYLACTIC]

Phy·la·ko·pi (fē lä kô pē′), *n.* an archaeological site on the Greek island of Melos, in the Cyclades group: excavations have revealed the remains of three successive ancient cities erected on a primitive Cycladic settlement.

phy·le (fī′lē), *n., pl.* **-lae** (-lē). (in ancient Greece) a tribe or clan, based on supposed kinship. [1860–65; < Gk *phȳlḗ,* akin to *phŷlon* PHYLON] —**phy′lic,** *adj.*

phy·let·ic (fī let′ik), *adj. Biol.* of, pertaining to, or based on the evolutionary history of a group of organisms; phylogenetic. [1880–85; Gk *phȳletikós* pertaining to a tribesman, equiv. to *phȳlét(ēs)* tribesman (deriv. of *phȳlḗ* PHYLE) + *-ikos* -IC] —**phy·let′i·cal·ly,** *adv.*

phylet′ic classifica′tion. See **phylogenetic classification.**

phy·let·ics (fī let′iks), *n.* (*used with a singular v.*) *Biol.* See **phylogenetic classification.** [see PHYLETIC, -ICS]

phyll-, var. of **phyllo-** before a vowel: *phyllite.*

-phyll, var. of **-phyllo** as final element of compound words: *sporophyll.* Also, **-phyl.**

phyl·la·ry (fil′ə rē), *n., pl.* **-ries.** *Bot.* one of the bracts forming the involucre or the head or inflorescence of a composite plant. [1855–60; < NL *phyllarium* < Gk *phyllárion,* dim. of *phýllon* leaf]

Phyl·lis (fil′is), *n.* **1.** a name used in pastoral literature, as the *Eclogues* of Vergil, for a country girl or sweetheart. **2.** Also, **Phyl′iss.** a female given name: from a Greek word meaning "green leaf."

phyl·lite (fil′īt), *n.* a slaty rock, the cleavage planes of which have a luster imparted by minute scales of mica. [1820–30; PHYLL- + -ITE[1]] —**phyl·lit·ic** (fi lit′ik), *adj.*

phyl·lo (fē′lō), *n. Greek and Middle Eastern Cookery.* flaky, tissue-thin layers of pastry used in baked desserts and appetizers. Also, **filo.** [1945–50; < ModGk *phýllo(n)* lit., leaf; see PHYLLO-]

phyllo-, a combining form meaning "leaf," used in the formation of compound words: *phyllopod.* Also, **phyll-, -phyll.** [< Gk, comb. form of *phýllon*]

phyl·lo·clade (fil′ə klād′), *n. Bot.* **1.** a flattened stem or branch having the function of a leaf. **2.** a cladophyll. [1855–60; < NL *phyllocladium.* See PHYLLO-, CLAD-, -IUM] —**phyl′lo·cla′di·oid′,** *adj.*

phyl·loc·la·dous (fi lok′lə dəs), *adj. Bot.* having phylloclades. [PHYLLOCLADE + -OUS]

phyl·lode (fil′ōd), *n. Bot.* an expanded petiole resembling and having the function of a leaf, but without a true blade. [1840–50; < Gk *phyllṓdēs* leaflike. See PHYLL-, -ODE[1]] —**phyl·lo′di·al,** *adj.*

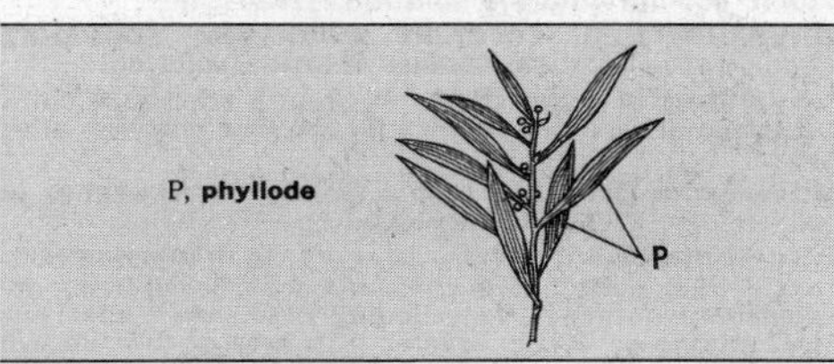

P, phyllode

phyl·lo·di·um (fi lō′dē əm), *n., pl.* **-di·a** (-dē ə). phyllode. [1840–50; < NL, equiv. to Gk *phyllṓd(ēs)* leaflike (see PHYLLODE) + NL *-ium* -IUM]

phyl·lo·dy (fil′ə dē), *n. Bot.* the abnormal transformation of a floral structure into a foliage leaf. [1885–90; PHYLLODE + -Y[3]]

phyl·lo·ge·net·ic (fil′ō jə net′ik), *adj. Bot.* of or pertaining to the development of leaves. [1895–1900; PHYLLO- + GENETIC]

phyl·loid (fil′oid), *adj.* leaflike. [1855–60; < NL *phylloīdēs.* See PHYLL-, -OID]

phyl·lo·ma·ni·a (fil′ə mā′nē ə, -mān′yə), *n. Bot.* the production of leaves in abnormal numbers or places. [1660–70; PHYLLO- + -MANIA] —**phyl′lo·ma′ni·ac′,** *adj.*

phyl·lome (fil′ōm), *n. Bot.* **1.** a leaf of a plant. **2.** a structure corresponding to a plant leaf. [1855–60; < NL *phyllōma* < Gk *phýllōma* foliage. See PHYLL-, -OMA] —**phyl·lom·ic** (fi lom′ik, -lō′mik), *adj.*

phyl·loph·a·gous (fi lof′ə gəs), *adj. Zool.* (of an organism) feeding on leaves. [1865–70; PHYLLO- + -PHAGOUS, prob. on the model of NL *Phyllophaga*]

phyl·lo·phore (fil′ə fôr′, -fōr′), *n. Bot.* the terminal bud of a stem, esp. of the stem of a palm. [1840–50; PHYLLO- + -PHORE]

phyl·lo·pod (fil′ə pod′), *n.* **1.** any crustacean of the order Phyllopoda, having leaflike swimming appendages. —*adj.* **2.** belonging or pertaining to the Phyllopoda. Also, **phyl·lop·o·dan** (fi lop′ə dən). [1860–65; < NL *Phyllopoda.* See PHYLLO-, -POD]

phyl·lo·qui·none (fil′ō kwi nōn′, -kwin′ōn), *n. Biochem.* See **vitamin K_1.** [1935–40; PHYLLO- + QUINONE]

phyl·lo·sil·i·cate (fil′ō sil′i kit, -kāt′), *n.* any silicate mineral having the tetrahedral silicate groups linked in sheets, each group containing four oxygen atoms, three of which are shared with other groups so that the ratio of silicon atoms to oxygen atoms is two to five. [1945–50; PHYLLO- + SILICATE]

phyl·lo·tax·is (fil′ə tak′sis), *n., pl.* **-tax·es** (-tak′sēz). *Bot.* phyllotaxy. [1870–75; PHYLLO- + -TAXIS]

phyl·lo·tax·y (fil′ə tak′sē), *n., pl.* **-tax·ies.** *Bot.* **1.** the arrangement of leaves on a stem or axis. **2.** the study of such arrangement. [1855–60; PHYLLOTAX(IS) + -Y[3]] —**phyl·lo·tac·tic** (fil′ə tak′tik), —**phyl′lo·tac′ti·cal, phyl′lo·tax′ic,** *adj.*

-phyllous, a combining form meaning "having leaves" of the kind or number specified by the initial element: *diphyllous; monophyllous.* [< Gk *-phyllos,* deriv. of *phýllon* leaf]

phyl·lox·e·ra (fil′ək sēr′ə, fi lok′sər ə), *n., pl.* **phyl·lox·e·rae** (fil′ək sēr′ē, fi lok′sə rē′), **phyl·lox·e·ras.** any of several plant lice of the genus *Phylloxera,* esp. *P. vitifoliae* **(grape phylloxera),** which attacks the leaves and roots of grapevines. [1865–70; < NL (1834) < Gk *phyllo-* PHYLLO- + *xērá,* fem. of *xērós* dry; so named in reference to the dessication of leaves caused by some species]

phylo-, a combining form meaning "race," "tribe," "kind": *phylogeny.* Also, *esp. before a vowel,* **phyl-.** [< Gk, comb. form of *phŷlon* PHYLON]

phylogenet′ic classifica′tion, *Biol.* classification of organisms based on their assumed evolutionary histories and relationships. Also called **phyletic classification, phyletics.** [1880–85]

phy·log·e·ny (fī loj′ə nē), *n.* **1.** the development or evolution of a particular group of organisms. **2.** the evolutionary history of a group of organisms, esp. as depicted in a family tree. Also, **phy·lo·gen·e·sis** (fī′lə jen′ə sis). Cf. **ontogeny.** [1865–70; PHYLO- + -GENY] —**phy·lo·ge·net·ic** (fī′lə jə net′ik), **phy′lo·ge·net′i·cal, phy′lo·gen′ic,** *adj.* —**phy′lo·ge·net′i·cal·ly,** *adv.* —**phy·log′e·nist,** *n.*

phy·lon (fī′lon), *n., pl.* **-la** (-lə). a group that has genetic relationship, as a race. [< NL < Gk *phŷlon* race, tribe, class, akin to *phŷein* to bring forth, produce, BE]

phy·lum (fī′ləm), *n., pl.* **-la** (-lə). **1.** *Biol.* the primary subdivision of a taxonomic kingdom, grouping together all classes of organisms that have the same body plan. **2.** *Ling.* a category consisting of language stocks that, because of cognates in vocabulary, are considered likely to be related by common origin. Cf. **stock** (def. 13). [1875–80; < NL < Gk *phŷlon* tribe, stock; see PHYLON] —**phy′lar,** *adj.*

phy·ma (fī′mə), *n., pl.* **-mas, -ma·ta** (-mə tə). *Pathol.* a nodule, swelling, or small, rounded tumor of the skin. [1685–95; < L < Gk *phŷma* a swelling, tumor, equiv. to *phý(esthai)* to grow (akin to *phŷlon* PHYLON) + *-ma* n. suffix denoting result] —**phy·mat·ic** (fī mat′ik), *adj.*

-phyre, a combining form representing **porphyry** in compound words: *granophyre.* [< F, extracted from *porphyre* PORPHYRY]

phys., 1. physical. **2.** physician. **3.** physics. **4.** physiological. **5.** physiology.

phys. chem., physical chemistry.

phys ed (fiz′ ed′), *Informal.* physical education. Also, **phys. ed.** [1950–55; by shortening]

phys. geog., physical geography.

phys·i·at·rics (fiz′ē a′triks), *n.* (*used with a singular v.*) **1.** See **physical medicine. 2.** See **physical therapy.** [1855–60; PHYS(I)- + -IATRICS] —**phys′i·at′ric, phys′i·at′ri·cal,** *adj.*

phys·i·at·rist (fiz′ē a′trist, fi zī′ə trist′), *n.* a physician specializing in physical medicine. [1945–50; PHYSIATR(ICS) + -IST]

phy·si·a·try (fi zī′ə trē, fiz′ē a′-), *n.* **1.** See **physical medicine. 2.** See **physical therapy.** [PHYS(I)- + -IATRY]

phys·ic (fiz′ik), *n., v.,* **-icked, -ick·ing.** —*n.* **1.** a medicine that purges; cathartic; laxative. **2.** any medicine; a drug or medicament. **3.** *Archaic.* the medical art or profession. **4.** *Obs.* See **natural science.** —*v.t.* **5.** to treat with or act upon as a physic or medicine. **6.** to work upon as a medicine does; relieve or cure. [1250–1300; (n.) ME *fisyk(e), phisik(e)* (< OF *fisique*) < L *physica* natural science (ML: medical science) < Gk *physikḗ* science of nature, n. use of fem. adj.: pertaining to nature (akin to *phŷlon* tribe, PHYLON); (v.) ME, deriv. of the n.]

phys·i·cal (fiz′i kəl), *adj.* **1.** of or pertaining to the body: *physical exercise.* **2.** of or pertaining to that which is material: *the physical universe; the physical sciences.* **3.** noting or pertaining to the properties of matter and energy other than those peculiar to living matter. **4.** pertaining to the physical sciences, esp. physics. **5.** carnal; sexual: *a physical attraction.* **6.** tending to touch, hug, pat, etc.; physically demonstrative: *a physical person.* **7.** requiring, characterized by, or liking rough physical contact or strenuous physical activity: *Football is a physical sport.* —*n.* **8.** See **physical examination.** [1400–50; late ME < ML *physicālis* concerning medicine. See PHYSIC, -AL[1]] —**phys′i·cal·ly,** *adv.* —**phys′i·cal·ness,** *n.*

—**Syn. 1.** somatic; fleshly. PHYSICAL, BODILY, CORPOREAL, CORPORAL agree in pertaining to the body. PHYSICAL indicates connected with, pertaining to, the animal or human body as a material organism: *physical strength, exercise.* BODILY means belonging to, concerned with, the human body as distinct from the mind or spirit: *bodily pain or suffering.* CORPOREAL, a more poetic and philosophical word than BODILY, refers esp. to the mortal substance of which the human body is composed as opposed to spirit: *this corporeal habitation.* CORPORAL is now usually reserved for reference to whippings and other punishments inflicted on the human body. **2.** tangible, palpable.

phys′ical anthropol′ogy, the branch of anthropology dealing with the evolutionary changes in human bodily structure and the classification of modern races, using mensurational and descriptive techniques. Cf. **cultural anthropology.** [1870–75] —**phys′ical anthropol′ogist.**

phys′ical chem′istry, the branch of chemistry dealing with the relations between the physical properties of substances and their chemical composition and transformations. [1890–95]

phys′ical dou′ble star′. See under **double star.**

phys′ical educa′tion, systematic instruction in sports, exercises, and hygiene given as part of a school or college program. [1830–40]

phys′ical examina′tion, an examination, usually by a physician, of a person's body in order to determine his or her state of health or physical fitness, as for military service or participation in a sport. [1880–85]

phys′ical geog′raphy, the branch of geography concerned with natural features and phenomena of the earth's surface, as landforms, drainage features, climates, soils, and vegetation. [1800–10]

phys•i•cal•ism (fiz′i kə liz′əm), *n.* a doctrine associated with logical positivism and holding that every meaningful statement, other than the necessary statements of logic and mathematics, must refer directly or indirectly to observable properties of spatiotemporal things or events. [1930–35; < G *Physikalismus.* See PHYSICAL, -ISM] —**phys′i•cal•ist,** *n., adj.*

phys•i•cal•is•tic (fiz′i kə lis′tik), *adj. Philos.* **1.** of or pertaining to physicalism. **2.** (of a statement) capable of being interpreted quantitatively in terms of space and time. [1930–35; PHYSICALIST + -IC]

phys•i•cal•i•ty (fiz′i kal′i tē), *n., pl.* **-ties. 1.** the physical attributes of a person, esp. when overdeveloped or overemphasized. **2.** preoccupation with one's body, physical needs, or appetites. [1585–95; PHYSICAL + -ITY]

phys•i•cal•ize (fiz′i kə līz′), *v.t.,* **-ized, -iz•ing.** to express in physical terms; give form or shape to: *The dancers physicalized the mood of the music.* Also, *esp. Brit.,* **phys′i•cal•ise′.** [1945–50; PHYSICAL + -IZE] —**phys′i•cal•i•za′tion,** *n.*

phys′ical jerks′, *Brit.* physical conditioning exercises, as push-ups and knee bends. Also called **jerks.**

phys′ical med′icine, the branch of medicine dealing with the diagnosis and treatment of disease and injury by means of physical agents, as manipulation, massage, exercise, heat, or water. Also called **physiatrics, physiatry.** [1935–40]

phys′ical meteorol′ogy, the branch of meteorology dealing with the study of optical, electrical, acoustical, and thermodynamic phenomena in the atmosphere, including the physics of clouds and precipitation. Cf. **dynamic meteorology.**

phys′ical op′tics, the branch of optics concerned with the wave properties of light, the superposition of waves, the deviation of light from its rectilinear propagation in a manner other than that considered by geometrical optics, the interaction of light with matter, and the quantum, corpuscular aspects of light. Cf. **diffraction, interference, quantum optics.** [1825–35]

phys′ical pen′dulum, *Physics.* any apparatus consisting of a body of possibly irregular shape allowed to rotate freely about a horizontal axis on which it is pivoted (distinguished from *simple pendulum*). Also called **compound pendulum.**

phys′ical sci′ence, 1. any of the natural sciences dealing with inanimate matter or with energy, as physics, chemistry, and astronomy. **2.** these sciences collectively. [1835–45] —**phys′ical sci′entist.**

phys′ical ther′apy, 1. the treatment or management of physical disability, malfunction, or pain by exercise, massage, hydrotherapy, etc., without the use of medicines, surgery, or radiation. **2.** the health profession that provides such care. [1920–25] —**phys′ical ther′apist.**

phy•si•cian (fi zish′ən), *n.* **1.** a person who is legally qualified to practice medicine; doctor of medicine. **2.** a person engaged in general medical practice, as distinguished from one specializing in surgery. **3.** a person who is skilled in the art of healing. [1175–1225; PHYSIC + -IAN (see -ICIAN); r. ME *fisicien* < OF] —**phy•si′•cian•ly,** *adj.*

physi′cian's assis′tant, a person trained to perform under the supervision of a physician many clinical procedures traditionally performed by a physician, as diagnosing and treating minor ailments. *Abbr.:* PA Also, **physi′cian assis′tant.** Cf. **nurse-practitioner.**

phy•si•cian•ship (fi zish′ən ship′), *n.* the position, function, or office of a physician. [1725–35; PHYSICIAN + -SHIP]

phys•i•cist (fiz′ə sist), *n.* a scientist who specializes in physics. [1710–20; PHYSIC(S) + -IST]

phys′ic nut′, 1. an ornamental, tropical American tree, *Jatropha curcas,* of the spurge family, having ivy-like leaves, small, yellow or greenish-yellow flowers, and olive-shaped fruit yielding a purgative, poisonous oil. **2.** the fruit itself. Also called **Barbados nut, purging nut.** [1775–85]

phys•i•co•chem•i•cal (fiz′i kō kem′i kəl), *adj. Chem.* **1.** physical and chemical: *the physicochemical properties of an isomer.* **2.** pertaining to physical chemistry. [1655–65; PHYSIC(AL) + -O- + CHEMICAL] —**phys′i•co•chem′i•cal•ly,** *adv.*

phys•ics (fiz′iks), *n.* (*used with a singular v.*) the science that deals with matter, energy, motion, and force. [1580–90; see PHYSIC, -ICS]

physio-, a combining form representing **physical** or **physiological** in compound words: *physiotherapy.* [< Gk *physio-* comb. form of *phýsis* origin, form, natural order. See PHYSIS, -O-]

phys•i•o•crat (fiz′ē ə krat′), *n.* one of a school of political economists who followed Quesnay in holding that an inherent natural order properly governed society, regarding land as the basis of wealth and taxation, and advocating a laissez-faire economy. [1790–1800; < F *physiocrate.* See PHYSIO-, -CRAT] —**phys′i•o•crat′ic,** *adj.*

phys•i•og•no•my (fiz′ē og′nə mē, -on′ə mē), *n., pl.* **-mies. 1.** the face or countenance, esp. when considered as an index to the character: *a fierce physiognomy.* **2.** Also called **anthroposcopy.** the art of determining character or personal characteristics from the form or features of the body, esp. of the face. **3.** the outward appearance of anything, taken as offering some insight into its character: *the physiognomy of a nation.* [1350–1400; earlier *phisognomie, phisiognomie,* late ME *phisonomie* < ML *physionomia, physonomia* < LGk *physiognōmía,* syncopated var. of Gk *physiognōmonía* art of judging a person by his features (see PHYSIO-, GNOMON, -Y[3]); r. ME *fisenamie, fisnamie, fisnomie* < MF *fisonomie* < ML, as above; cf. PHIZ] —**phys•i•og•nom•ic** (fiz′ē og nom′ik, -ē ə nom′-), **phys′i•og•nom′i•cal, phys•i•og•no•mon•ic** (fiz′ē og′nə mon′ik, -on′ə-), **phys′i•og′no•mon′i•cal,** *adj.* —**phys′i•og•nom′i•cal•ly, phys′i•og′no•mon′i•cal•ly,** *adv.* —**phys′i•og′no•mist,** *n.*

phys′iograph′ic prov′ince, a geographic region in which climate and geology have given rise to an array of landforms different from those of surrounding regions. [1910–15]

phys•i•og•ra•phy (fiz′ē og′rə fē), *n.* **1.** the science of physical geography. **2.** (formerly) geomorphology. **3.** the systematic description of nature in general. [1820–30; PHYSIO- + -GRAPHY] —**phys′i•og′ra•pher,** *n.* —**phys•i•o•graph•ic** (fiz′ē ə graf′ik), **phys′i•o•graph′i•cal,** *adj.*

physiol., 1. physiological. **2.** physiologist. **3.** physiology.

phys•i•o•log•i•cal (fiz′ē ə loj′i kəl), *adj.* **1.** of or pertaining to physiology. **2.** consistent with the normal functioning of an organism. Also, **phys′i•o•log′ic.** [1600–10; PHYSIOLOG(Y) + -ICAL] —**phys′i•o•log′i•cal•ly,** *adv.*

physiolog′ical at′mosphere, ecosphere.

physiolog′ical phonet′ics, the branch of phonetics that deals with the motive processes, anatomical measurements, spirometric properties, muscle and membrane tone, and kinetic aspects of the production of speech and with related aspects of the reception of speech.

physiolog′ical psychol′ogy, the branch of psychology concerned with the relationship between the physical functioning of an organism and its behavior. [1885–90]

physiolog′ical salt′ solu′tion, *Pharm.* See **isotonic sodium chloride solution.** [1920–25]

physiolog′ical so′dium chlo′ride solu′tion, *Pharm.* See **isotonic sodium chloride solution.**

physiolog′ic jaun′dice, *Pathol.* a transitory jaundice that affects some infants for the first few days after birth.

phys•i•ol•o•gist (fiz′ē ol′ə jist), *n.* a specialist in physiology. [1655–65; PHYSIOLOG(Y) + -IST]

phys•i•ol•o•gy (fiz′ē ol′ə jē), *n.* **1.** the branch of biology dealing with the functions and activities of living organisms and their parts, including all physical and chemical processes. **2.** the organic processes or functions in an organism or in any of its parts. [1555–65; < L *physiologia* < Gk *physiología* science of natural causes and phenomena. See PHYSIO-, -LOGY]

phys•i•om•e•try (fiz′ē om′i trē), *n.* measurement of the physiological functions of the body. [PHYSIO- + -METRY]

phys•i•o•pa•thol•o•gy (fiz′ē ō pə thol′ə jē), *n.* the science dealing with the disturbances of bodily function resulting from disease. [1900–05; PHYSIO- + PATHOLOGY] —**phys•i•o•path•o•log•i•cal** (fiz′ē ō path′ə loj′i kəl), **phys′i•o•path′o•log′ic,** *adj.*

phys•i•o•ther•a•py (fiz′ē ō ther′ə pē), *n.* See **physical therapy.** [1900–05; PHYSIO- + THERAPY] —**phys′i•o•ther′a•pist,** *n.*

phy•sique (fi zēk′), *n.* physical or bodily structure, appearance, or development: *the physique of an athlete.* [1820–30; < F < L *physicus.* See PHYSIC]

phy•sis (fī′sis), *n., pl.* **-ses** (-sēz). **1.** the principle of growth or change in nature. **2.** nature as the source of growth or change. **3.** something that grows, becomes, or develops. [< Gk *phýsis* origin, natural form of a thing; akin to *phŷlon* race (see PHYLON)]

physo-, a combining form meaning "bladder," used in the formation of compound words: *physogastric.* [comb. form repr. Gk *phŷsa* bladder, bellows]

phy•so•clis•tous (fī′sə klis′təs), *adj. Ichthyol.* having the air bladder closed off from the mouth. Cf. **physostomous.** [1885–90; < NL *Physoclist(i)* genus name (< Gk *phŷso-* PHYSO- + *kleistoí,* pl. of *kleistós* shut, verbal of *kleíein* to shut) + -OUS]

phy•so•gas•tric (fī′sə gas′trik), *adj.* pertaining to the swollen, membranous abdomen of certain insects, esp. termite and ant queens. [1910–15; PHYSO- + GASTRIC] —**phy′so•gas′trism, phy′so•gas′try,** *n.*

phy•so•stig•mine (fī′sō stig′mēn, -min), *n. Pharm.* an alkaloid, $C_{15}H_{21}N_3O_2$, used in the treatment of Alzheimer's disease to raise the level of the neurotransmitter acetylcholine and also as a miotic in glaucoma. [1860–65; < NL *Physostigm(a)* genus of plants yielding the alkaloid (see PHYSO-, STIGMA) + -INE[2]]

phy•sos•to•mous (fī sos′tə məs), *adj. Ichthyol.* having the mouth and air bladder connected by an air duct. Cf. **physoclistous.** [1885–90; PHYSO- + -STOMOUS]

phy•tate (fī′tāt), *n. Chem., Biochem.* a salt or ester of phytic acid, occurring in plants, esp. cereal grains, capable of forming insoluble complexes with calcium, zinc, iron, and other nutrients and interfering with their absorption by the body. [PHYT(IC ACID) + -ATE[2]]

-phyte, var. of **phyto-** as final element of compound words: *lithophyte.*

phy′tic ac′id (fī′tik, fit′ik), *Chem.* a white to pale-yellow, water-soluble liquid, $C_6H_{18}O_{24}P_6$, found in cereal grains: used chiefly to chelate heavy metals during the manufacture of animal fats and vegetable oils and as a water-softening agent. [1905–10; *phyt(in)* a salt of phytic acid (< G *Phytin* < Gk *phyt(ón)* plant + G *-in* -IN[2]) + -IC]

Phy•tin (fī′tin), *Trademark.* a brand of white, powdered calcium-magnesium salt, obtained from seeds, tubers, and rhizomes: used in the synthesis of inositol and as a calcium supplement.

phyto-, a combining form meaning "plant," used in the formation of compound words: *phytogenesis.* Also, **-phyte.** [< Gk *phyt(ón)* a plant + -O-]

phy•to•a•lex•in (fī′tō ə lek′sin), *n. Biochem.* any of a class of plant compounds that accumulate at the site of invading microorganisms and confer resistance to disease. [1945–50; PHYTO- + ALEXIN]

phy•to•bi•ol•o•gy (fī′tō bī ol′ə jē), *n.* the branch of biology dealing with plants. [1885–90; PHYTO- + BIOLOGY]

phy•to•chem•is•try (fī′tə kem′ə strē), *n.* the branch of biochemistry dealing with plants and plant processes. [1830–40; PHYTO- + CHEMISTRY] —**phy•to•chem•i•cal** (fī′tə kem′i kəl), *adj.* —**phy′to•chem′i•cal•ly,** *adv.* —**phy′to•chem′ist,** *n.*

phy•to•chrome (fī′tə krōm′), *n. Bot.* a plant pigment that is associated with the absorption of light in the photoperiodic response and that may regulate various types of growth and development. [1890–95; PHYTO- + -CHROME]

phy•to•cide (fī′tə sīd′), *n.* a substance or preparation for killing plants. [1935–40; PHYTO- + -CIDE] —**phy′to•cid′al,** *adj.*

phy•to•cli•mate (fī′tō klī′mit), *n.* See under **microclimate.** [1945–50; PHYTO- + CLIMATE]

phy•to•coe•no•sis (fī′tō sē nō′sis), *n., pl.* **-ses** (-sēz). the plants of a given area considered as a whole. [1925–30; < NL; see PHYTO-, COENO-, -SIS]

phy•to•flag•el•late (fī′tə flaj′ə lit, -lāt′), *n.* any microscopic flagellate that is photosynthetic. [1930–35; PHYTO- + FLAGELLATE]

phy•to•gen•e•sis (fī′tə jen′ə sis), *n.* the origin and development of plants. Also, **phy•tog•e•ny** (fī toj′ə nē). [1850–55; PHYTO- + GENESIS] —**phy•to•ge•net•ic** (fī′tō jə net′ik), **phy′to•ge•net′i•cal,** *adj.* —**phy′to•ge•net′i•cal•ly,** *adv.*

phy•to•gen•ic (fī′tə jen′ik), *adj.* of plant origin. [1855–60; PHYTO- + -GENIC]

phy•to•ge•og•ra•phy (fī′tō jē og′rə fē), *n.* the science dealing with the geographical relationships of plants. [1840–50; PHYTO- + GEOGRAPHY] —**phy′to•ge•og′ra•pher,** *n.* —**phy•to•ge•o•graph•i•cal** (fī′tō jē′ə graf′i kəl), **phy′to•ge′o•graph′ic,** *adj.* —**phy′to•ge′o•graph′i•cal•ly,** *adv.*

phy•tog•ra•phy (fī tog′rə fē), *n.* the branch of botany dealing with the description of plants. [1690–1700; < NL *phytographia.* See PHYTO-, -GRAPHY] —**phy•tog′ra•pher, phy•tog′ra•phist,** *n.* —**phy•to•graph•ic** (fī′tə graf′ik), **phy′to•graph′i•cal,** *adj.*

phy•to•hor•mone (fī′tə hôr′mōn), *n.* hormone (def. 3). [1930–35; PHYTO- + HORMONE]

phy•tol (fī′tôl, -tol), *n. Biochem.* a hydrophobic alcohol, $C_{20}H_{40}O$, that occurs esterified as a side chain in the chlorophyll molecule. [< G (1907); see PHYTO-, -OL]

phy•tol•o•gy (fī tol′ə jē), *n.* botany. [1650–60; < NL *phytologia.* See PHYTO-, -LOGY] —**phy•to•log•ic** (fīt′l-oj′ik), **phy′to•log′i•cal,** *adj.* —**phy′to•log′i•cal•ly,** *adv.*

phy•ton (fī′ton), *n. Bot.* the smallest part of a stem, root, or leaf, that, when removed from a plant, may grow into a new plant. [1840–50; < NL < Gk *phytón* a plant] —**phy•ton′ic,** *adj.*

phy•to•na•di•one (fī′tō nə dī′ōn), *n. Biochem.* See **vitamin K_1.** [PHYT(IC ACID) + -O- + NA(PHTHOQUINONE) + DIONE]

phy•to•pa•thol•o•gy (fī′tō pə thol′ə jē), *n.* See **plant pathology.** [1860–65; PHYTO- + PATHOLOGY] —**phy•to•path•o•log•i•cal** (fī′tō path′ə loj′i kəl), **phy′to•path′o•log′ic,** *adj.* —**phy′to•pa•thol′o•gist,** *n.*

phy•toph•a•gous (fī tof′ə gəs), *adj.* herbivorous. [1820–30; PHYTO- + -PHAGOUS]

phy•toph•tho•ra (fī tof′thər ə), *n.* any of a group of fungi of the genus *Phytophthora,* which cause a serious plant disease, esp. affecting apple and pear trees and potatoes. [< NL (1876), equiv. to Gk *phyto-* PHYTO- + *-phthora,* fem. of *-phthoros,* verbid of *phtheírein* to destroy]

phy•to•plank•ton (fī′tə plangk′tən), *n.* the aggregate of plants and plantlike organisms in plankton. Cf. **zooplankton.** [1895–1900; PHYTO- + PLANKTON]

phy•to•plasm (fī′tə plaz′əm), *n.* protoplasm of a plant or plants. [PHYTO- + -PLASM]

phy•to•saur (fī′tə sôr′), *n.* any armored, semiaquatic reptile of the extinct order Phytosauria, of the Mesozoic Era, resembling the crocodile but unrelated, having the nostrils high on the snout and with well-developed hind limbs suggestive of bipedal ancestors. [< NL *Phytosauria* (see PHYTO-, -SAUR, -IA)]

phy•to•so•ci•ol•o•gy (fī′tō sō′sē ol′ə jē, -shē-), *n.* the branch of ecology dealing with the origin, composition, structure, and classification of plant communities. [1925–30; PHYTO- + SOCIOLOGY] —**phy•to•so•ci•o•log•ic** (fī′tə sō′sē ə loj′ik, -sō′shē-), **phy′to•so′ci•o•log′i•cal,** *adj.* —**phy′to•so′ci•o•log′i•cal•ly,** *adv.* —**phy′to•so′ci•ol′o•gist,** *n.*

phy·tos·te·rol (fī tos′tə rôl′, -rol′), *n. Biochem.* any of various sterols obtained from plants. [1895–1900; PHYTO- + STEROL]

phy·to·suc·civ·o·rous (fī′tō sək siv′ər əs), *adj.* feeding on sap, as certain sucking insects. [PHYTO- + *succi-*, comb. form of L *succus* juice (see SUCCULENT) + -VOROUS]

phy·to·tox·ic (fī′tə tok′sik), *adj.* **1.** of or pertaining to phytotoxin. **2.** inhibitory to the growth of or poisonous to plants. [1930–35; PHYTO- + TOXIC] —**phy·to·tox·ic·i·ty** (fī′tō tok sis′i tē), *n.*

phy·to·tox·in (fī′tə tok′sin), *n.* any toxin, as ricin or crotin, produced by a plant. [1905–10; PHYTO- + TOXIN]

pi[1] (pī), *n., pl.* **pis. 1.** the 16th letter of the Greek alphabet (Π, π). **2.** the consonant sound represented by this letter. **3.** *Math.* **a.** the letter π, used as the symbol for the ratio of the circumference of a circle to its diameter. **b.** the ratio itself: 3.141592+. [1835–45; < Gk *pî, peî*; used in mathematics to represent Gk *periphérion* periphery]

pi[2] (pī), *n., pl.* **pies,** *v.,* **pied, pi·ing.** —*n.* **1.** printing types mixed together indiscriminately. **2.** any confused mixture; jumble. —*v.t.* **3.** to reduce (printing types) to a state of confusion. **4.** to jumble. Also, **pie.** [1650–60; orig. uncert.]

PI, 1. *Law.* personal injury. **2.** principal investigator. **3.** private investigator.

Pi., piaster. Also, **pi.**

P.I., 1. Philippine Islands. **2.** Also, **p.i.** private investigator.

Pi·a (pē′ə), *n.* a female given name.

Pia·cen·za (pyä chen′tsä), *n.* a city in N Italy, on the Po River. 109,302. Ancient, **Placentia.**

pi·ac·u·lar (pī ak′yə lər), *adj.* **1.** expiatory; atoning; reparatory. **2.** requiring expiation; sinful or wicked. [1600–10; < L *piāculāris* atoning, equiv. to *piācul(um)* a means of atoning (*piā(re)* to appease, deriv. of *pius* PIOUS + *-culum* -CULE[2]) + *-āris* -AR[1]] —**pi·ac′u·lar·ly,** *adv.* —**pi·ac′u·lar·ness,** *n.*

Pi·af (pē äf′, pē′äf), *n.* **Edith** (*Edith Giovanna Gassion*), 1914–63, French singer.

piaffe (pyaf), *n., v.,* **piaffed, piaff·ing.** *Dressage.* —*n.* **1.** a cadenced trot executed on one spot, with a well-elevated leg action. —*v.i.* **2.** (of a horse) to execute such a movement. **3.** (of a rider) to cause a horse to piaffe. —*v.t.* **4.** to cause (a horse) to piaffe. [1755–65; < F *piaffer*; imit.]

Pia·get (pē′ə zhä′, py′ä-; *Fr.* pyA zhe′), *n.* **Jean** (zhäN), 1896–1980, Swiss psychologist: studied cognitive development of children.

Pi·a·get·ian (pē′ə zhä′ən, pyä-), *adj.* of or pertaining to the theories developed by Jean Piaget. [PIAGET + -IAN]

pi·al (pī′əl, pē′-), *adj.* of or pertaining to the pia mater. [1885–90; PI(A MATER) + -AL[1]]

pi·a ma·ter (pī′ə mā′tər, pē′ə), *Anat.* the delicate, fibrous, and highly vascular membrane forming the innermost of the three coverings of the brain and spinal cord. Cf. **arachnoid** (def. 6), **dura mater.** [1350–1400; ME < ML: lit., pious mother, erroneous trans. of Ar *umm raqīqah* tender mother]

pi·an (pē an′, -än′, pyän), *n. Pathol.* yaws. [1795–1805; < F *pians,* said to be < Tupi] —**pi·an′ic,** *adj.*

pi·a·nette (pē′ə net′), *n.* a small upright piano. [1875–80; PIAN(O)[1] + -ETTE]

pi·a·nism (pē′ə niz′əm, pē an′iz-, pyan′-), *n.* **1.** the artistry and technique of a pianist. **2.** performance by a pianist: *an evening of first-rate pianism.* [1835–45; PIAN(O)[1] + -ISM]

pi·a·nis·si·mo (pē′ə nis′ə mō′; *It.* pyä nēs′sē mô′), *adj., adv., n., pl.* **-mos.** *Music.* —*adj.* **1.** very soft. —*adv.* **2.** very softly. —*n.* **3.** a passage or movement played in this way. [1715–25; < It, superl. of *piano* PIANO[2]]

pi·an·ist (pē an′ist, pyan′-, pē′ə nist), *n.* a person who plays the piano, esp. one who performs expertly or professionally. [1830–40; < F *pianiste* < It *pianista.* See PIANO[1], -IST]

pi·a·nis·tic (pē′ə nis′tik), *adj.* relating to, characteristic of, or adaptable for the piano. [1880–85; PIANIST + -IC] —**pi′a·nis′ti·cal·ly,** *adv.*

pi·an·o[1] (pē an′ō, pyan′ō), *n., pl.* **-an·os.** a musical instrument in which felt-covered hammers, operated from a keyboard, strike the metal strings. Cf. **baby grand, concert grand, grand piano, spinet, square piano, upright piano.** [1795–1805; short for PIANOFORTE]

grand piano

pi·a·no[2] (pē ä′nō; *It.* pyä′nô), *Music.* —*adj.* **1.** soft; subdued. —*adv.* **2.** softly. *Abbr.:* p, p. [1675–85; < It: soft, low (of sounds), plain, flat < L *plānus* PLAIN[1]]

pian′o accor′dion, accordion (def. 1). [1855–60]

pian′o bar′, a cocktail lounge featuring live piano music.

pian′o duet′, a musical composition for two pianists playing two pianos or together at one piano.

pi·an·o·forte (pē an′ə fôrt′, -fōrt′; pē an′ə fôr′tē, -tä, -fōr′-), *n.* a piano. [1760–70; < It (*gravecembalo col*) *piano e forte* lit., (harpsicord with) soft and loud, equiv. to *piano* soft (see PIANO[2]) + *forte* loud (see FORTE[2])]

pian′o hinge′, a long narrow hinge that runs the full length of the two surfaces to which its leaves are joined. Also called **continuous hinge.** [1925–30]

Pi·a·no·la (pē′ə nō′lə), **1.** *Trademark.* a brand of player piano. —*n.* **2.** (*l.c.*) *Bridge.* a hand, as a laydown, that is very easy to play. **3.** (*l.c.*) something that is very easy to do or accomplish.

pia·no no·bi·le (pyä′nô nô′bē le), *pl.* ***pia·ni no·bi·li*** (pyä′nē nô′bē lē). *Italian.* the principal story of a large building, as of a palace or villa.

pian′o play′er, 1. pianist. **2.** a mechanical device that actuates the keys of a player piano. [1895–1900]

pian′o quartet′, 1. a musical composition scored for piano and three other instruments, typically violin, viola, and cello. **2.** an instrumental group consisting of a pianist and three other musicians, typically a violinist, violist, and cellist. **3.** a group of four pianists playing music written or arranged for four pianos. [1930–35]

pian′o quintet′, 1. a musical composition scored for a string quartet, or other combination of four instruments, and piano. **2.** a group of five musicians playing a piano quintet. [1920–25]

pian′o reduc′tion, a musical score having the parts condensed or simplified in two staves, to render the music playable on the piano by one person. Also called **pian′o score′.** [1940–45]

pian′o roll′, a roll of paper containing perforations such that air passing through them actuates the keys of a player piano. [1925–30]

pia′no tun′er, a person who tunes pianos and sometimes other keyboard instruments. [1855–60]

pian′o wire′, a very thin steel wire of high tensile strength. [1865–70]

Pi·a·rist (pī′ər ist), *n.* a member of a Roman Catholic teaching congregation founded in Rome in 1597. [1835–45; < NL *piār(um),* in phrase (*patrēs scholārum*) *piārum* (fathers) of religious (schools) + -IST]

pias., piaster.

pi·as·sa·va (pē′ə sä′və), *n.* **1.** Also called **monkey grass.** a coarse, woody fiber obtained from either of two palms, *Leopoldina piassaba* or *Attalea funifera,* of South America, used in making brooms, mats, etc. **2.** either of these trees. Also, **pi·as·sa·ba** (pē′ə sä′və, -bə). [1825–35; < Pg < Tupi *piaçaba*]

pi·as·ter (pē as′tər, -ä′stər), *n.* **1.** a former coin of Turkey, the 100th part of a lira: replaced by the kurus in 1933. **2.** a monetary unit of Egypt, Lebanon, Sudan, and Syria, the 100th part of a pound. **3.** a former monetary unit of South Vietnam: replaced by the dong in 1976. **4.** the former peso or dollar of Spain and Spanish America. Also, **pi·as′tre.** [1605–15; < F *piastre* < It *piastra* thin sheet of metal, silver coin (short for *piastra d'argento,* lit., plate of silver), akin to *piastro* PLASTER]

Pi·at (pē′at, -ät), *n.* a spring-powered British antitank weapon of World War II, mounted on a tripod and capable of firing a 2½-lb. (1-kg) bomb up to 350 yd. (320 m). [*P*(*rojector*) *i*(*nfantry*) *a*(*nti*)*t*(*ank*)]

Pia·ti·gorsk (pyä′ti gôrsk′; *Russ.* pyi tyi gôRsk′), *n.* Pyatigorsk.

Pia·ti·gor·sky (pyä′ti gôr′skē, pyat′i-), *n.* **Greg·or** (greg′ər), 1903–76, U.S. cellist, born in Russia.

Piau·í (pyou ē′), *n.* a state in NE Brazil. 2,188,148; 96,860 sq. mi. (250,870 sq. km). *Cap.:* Teresina.

Pia·ve (pyä′ve), *n.* a river in NE Italy, flowing S and SE into the Adriatic. 137 mi. (220 km) long.

pi·az·za (pē az′ə, -ä′zə *or, for 1, 3 esp. Brit.,* pē at′sə, -ät′-; *for 1 also It.* pyät′tsä), *n., pl.* **pi·az·zas,** *It.* **piaz·ze** (pyät′tse). **1.** an open square or public place in a city or town, esp. in Italy. **2.** *Chiefly New Eng. and Inland South.* a large porch on a house; veranda. **3.** *Chiefly Brit.* an arcade or covered walk or gallery, as around a public square or in front of a building. [1575–85; < It < L *platēa* courtyard, orig., street < Gk *plateîa,* n. use of fem. of *platýs* FLAT[1]. See PLACE] —**pi·az′zaed,** *adj.* —**pi·az′zi·an,** *adj.*

Pi·az·zi (pē ät′sē, -ä′zē; *It.* pyät′tsē), *n.* **Giuseppe,** 1746–1826, Italian astronomer.

pi·bal (pī′bəl), *n. Meteorol.* the measurement and computation of the speed and direction of winds by theodolitic tracking of a pilot balloon. Cf. **rabal.** [*pi*(*lot*) *bal*(*loon*)]

pib·gorn (pib′gôrn), *n.* an ancient wind instrument of Wales resembling the hornpipe. Also, **pib·corn** (pib′kôrn′). Also called **stockhorn.** [1760–70; < Welsh *pib gorn,* equiv. to *pib* PIPE[1] + *gorn,* lenited form of *corn* HORN]

pi·blok·to (pi blok′tō), *n., pl.* **-tos.** *Psychol.* a culture-specific syndrome occurring among traditional Eskimo women, characterized by an outburst of cries or screams, the removal of clothing, and seeming possession by a bird or animal spirit. Also, **pi·block′to.** [1955–60; < Inuit *pibloktoq*]

pi·broch (pē′brokH), *n.* (in the Scottish Highlands) a piece of music for the bagpipe, consisting of a series of variations on a basic theme, usually martial in character, but sometimes used as a dirge. [1710–20; < ScotGael *piobaireachd* piper music, equiv. to *piobair* piper (*piob* PIPE[1] + *-air* agent suffix << L *-ārius* -ARY) + *-eachd* n. suffix denoting quality or state]

pic[1] (pik), *n., pl.* **pix** (piks), **pics.** *Slang.* **1.** a movie. **2.** a photograph. Also, **pix.** [1880–85; by shortening from PICTURE]

pic[2] (pēk), *n. Piquet.* **1.** the scoring of 30 points in the declaration of hands and in the play before one's opponent scores a point. **2.** the bonus of 30 points won for so scoring. Cf. **repic.** Also, **pique.** [< F: lit., prick]

pi·ca[1] (pī′kə), *n. Print.* **1.** a 12-point type of a size between small pica and English. **2.** the depth of this type size as a unit of linear measurement for type, pages containing type, etc.; one sixth of an inch. **3.** a 12-point type, widely used for typewriters, having 10 characters to the inch. Cf. **elite** (def. 4). [1580–90; appar. < ML *pīca* PIE[4], on the model of BREVIER, CANON[1] (def. 14)]

pi·ca[2] (pī′kə), *n. Pathol.* an abnormal appetite or craving for substances that are not fit to eat, as chalk or clay, common in malnutrition, pregnancy, etc. [1555–65; < NL, special use of L *pīca* jay, MAGPIE, with ref. to its omnivorous feeding]

pic·a·dor (pik′ə dôr′; *Sp.* pē′kä ᵺôR′), *n., pl.* **-dors,** *Sp.* **-do·res** (-ᵺô′Res). one of the mounted assistants to a matador, who opens the bullfight by enraging the bull and weakening its shoulder muscles with a lance. [1790–1800; < Sp: lit., pricker, equiv. to *pic(ar)* to prick (see PIQUE[1]) + *-ador* < L *-ātor* -ATOR]

pic·a·nin·ny (pik′ə nin′ē), *n., pl.* **-nies.** pickaninny.

pi·can·te (pi kän′tā; *Sp.* pē kän′te), *adj., n., pl.* **-tes** (tāz; *Sp.* -tes). *Spanish and Latin American Cookery.* —*adj.* **1.** prepared so as to be very hot and spicy, esp. with a hot and spicy sauce. —*n.* **2.** any food that is very hot and spicy, esp. a hot sauce. [< Sp: spicy, hot, ptp. of *picar* to prick, bite; see PIQUE, PIQUANT]

pic·a·ra (pik′ər ə, pē′kə-), *n.,* a woman who is a rogue or vagabond. [1925–30; < Sp; fem. of PICARO]

Pi·card (pē kAR′), *n.* **1. Charles É·mile** (shARl ā mēl′), 1856–1941, French mathematician. **2. Jean** (zhäN), 1620–82, French astronomer.

Pic·ar·dy (pik′ər dē), *n.* a region in N France: formerly a province.

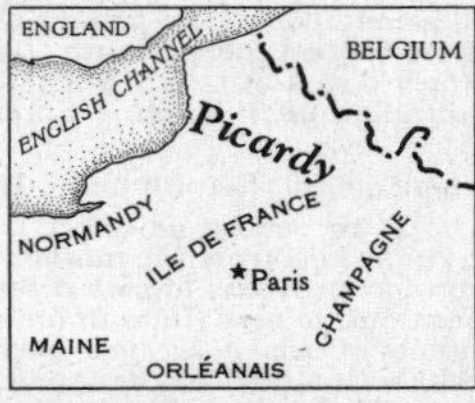

Pic′ardy third′, *Music.* a major third in the final tonic chord of a composition written in a minor key. [trans. of F *tierce de Picardy*]

pic·a·resque (pik′ə resk′), *adj.* **1.** pertaining to, characteristic of, or characterized by a form of prose fiction, originally developed in Spain, in which the adventures of an engagingly roguish hero are described in a series of usually humorous or satiric episodes that often depict, in realistic detail, the everyday life of the common people: *picaresque novel; picaresque hero.* **2.** of, pertaining to, or resembling rogues. [1800–10; < Sp *picaresco.* See PICARO, -ESQUE]
—**Syn. 2.** prankish, rascally, devilish, raffish.

pic·a·ro (pik′ə rō′, pē′kə-), *n., pl.* **-ros.** a rogue or vagabond. [1615–25; < Sp *pícaro* rogue]

pic·a·roon (pik′ə ro͞on′), *n.* **1.** a rogue, vagabond, thief, or brigand. **2.** a pirate or corsair. —*v.i.* **3.** to act or operate as a pirate or brigand. Also, **pickaroon.** [1615–25; < Sp *picarón,* aug. of *pícaro* PICARO]

Pi·cas·so (pi kä′sō, -kas′ō; *Sp.* pē kä′sô), *n.* **Pa·blo** (pä′blō; *Sp.* pä′vlô), 1881–1973, Spanish painter and sculptor in France.

pic·a·yune (pik′ē yo͞on′, pik′ə-), *adj.* Also, **pic′a·yun′ish.** *Informal.* **1.** of little value or account; small; trifling: *a picayune amount.* **2.** petty, carping, or prejudiced: *I didn't want to seem picayune by criticizing.* —*n.* **3.** (formerly, in Louisiana, Florida, etc.) a coin equal to half a Spanish real. **4.** any small coin, as a five-cent piece. **5.** *Informal.* an insignificant person or thing. [1780–90; < Pr *picaioun* small copper coin (< F *picaillons*), deriv. of an onomatopoetic base **pikk-* beat, here referring to the coining of coppers] —**pic′a·yun′ish·ly,** *adv.* —**pic′a·yun′ish·ness,** *n.*
—**Syn. 1.** trivial, insignificant. **2.** narrow-minded.

Pic·a·yune (pik′ə yo͞on′, pik′ē-), *n.* a town in SE Mississippi. 10,361.

Pic′cadilly Cir′cus, a traffic circle and open square in W London, England: theater and amusement center.

pic·ca·lil·li (pik′ə lil′ē), *n., pl.* **-lis.** a pungent relish of East Indian origin, made of chopped vegetables, mustard, vinegar, and hot spices. [1760–70; earlier *piccalillo* Indian pickle; obscurely akin to PICKLE[1]]

pic·ca·nin·ny (pik′ə nin′ē), *n., pl.* **-nies.** pickaninny. [1650–60]

Pic·card (*Fr.* pē kAR′), *n.* **1. Au·guste** (*Fr.* ō gYst′), 1884–1962, Swiss physicist, aeronaut, inventor, and deep-sea explorer: designer of bathyscaphes. **2.** his son **Jacques** (zhäk), born 1922, Swiss oceanographer and bathyscaphe designer, born in Belgium. **3. Jean Fé·lix** (zhäN fā lēks′), 1884–1963, U.S. chemist and aeronautical engineer, born in Switzerland (brother of Auguste).

pic·ca·ta (pi kä′tə; *It.* pēk kä′tä), *adj. Italian Cookery.* cooked, served, or sauced with lemon and parsley: *veal piccata.* [< It: a slice of veal cooked in this manner < F *piqué,* ptp. of *piquer* to lard (meat), attach (ingredients) by pricking or puncturing, lit., to prick; see PIQUE[1], -ATE[1]]

Pic·cin·ni (pēt chēn′ē), *n.* **Nic·co·lò** (nēk′kô lô′) (or

CONCISE PRONUNCIATION KEY: act, cāpe, dâre, pärt; set, ēqual; *if,* ice; ox, ōver, ôrder, oil, bo͝ok, bo͞ot, out; up, ûrge; child; sing; shoe; thin, *that*; zh as in *treasure.* ə = *a* as in *alone, e* as in *system, i* as in *easily, o* as in *gallop, u* as in *circus;* ᵊ as in *fire* (fīᵊr), *hour* (ouᵊr). l and n can serve as syllabic consonants, as in *cradle* (krād′l), and *button* (but′n). See the full key inside the front cover.

Ni·co·la) (nē kô′lä), 1728–1800, Italian composer. Also, **Pic·ci·ni** (pēt chē′nē), **Picinni.**

pic·co·lo (pik′ə lō′), *n., pl.* **-los.** a small flute sounding an octave higher than the ordinary flute. [1855–60; < It: lit., small]

piccolo

pic·co·lo·ist (pik′ə lō′ist), *n.* a person who plays the piccolo. [1880–85; PICCOLO + -IST]

pice (pīs), *n., pl.* **pice.** **1.** a former bronze coin of British India, one quarter of an anna. Cf. **pie**[5]. **2.** paisa (def. 1). [1605–15; < Marathi *paisā*]

pic·e·ous (pis′ē əs, pī′sē əs), *adj.* **1.** of, pertaining to, or resembling pitch. **2.** inflammable; combustible. **3.** *Zool.* black or nearly black as pitch. [1640–50; < L *piceus* made of pitch, equiv. to *pice-* (s. of *pix*) PITCH[2] + *-us* adj. suffix; see -OUS]

pich (pich), *n.* a West Indian shrub or small tree, *Calliandra portoricensis,* of the legume family, having numerous leaflets and white, night-blooming, flowers. [< AmerSp]

pich·i·ci·a·go (pich′ə sē ä′gō, -ā′gō), *n., pl.* **-gos.** any of several small armadillos of the genera *Chalmyphorus* and *Burmeisteria,* of southern South America. Also, **pich·i·ci·e·go** (pich′ə sē ā′gō). [1815–25; < AmerSp *pichiciego* < Araucanian *pichi* small + Sp *ciego* blind (< L *caecus*)]

Pi·cin·ni (pē chēn′nē), *n.* See **Piccinni, Niccolò.**

pick[1] (pik), *v.t.* **1.** to choose or select from among a group: *to pick a contestant from the audience.* **2.** to seek and find occasion for; provoke: *to pick a fight.* **3.** to attempt to find; seek out: *to pick flaws in an argument.* **4.** to steal the contents of: *Her pocket was picked yesterday.* **5.** to open (a lock) with a device other than the key, as a sharp instrument or wire, esp. for the purpose of burglary. **6.** to pierce, indent, dig into, or break up (something) with a pointed instrument: *to pick rock; to pick ore.* **7.** to form (a hole) by such action: *to pick a hole in asphalt.* **8.** to use a pointed instrument, the fingers, the teeth, the beak, etc., on (a thing), in order to remove or loosen something, as a small part or adhering matter: *to pick one's teeth.* **9.** to prepare for use by removing a covering piece by piece, as feathers, hulls, or other parts: *to pick a fowl.* **10.** to detach or remove piece by piece with the fingers: *She picked the meat from the bones.* **11.** to pluck or gather one by one: *to pick flowers.* **12.** (of birds or other animals) to take up (small bits of food) with the bill or teeth. **13.** to eat daintily or in small morsels. **14.** to separate, pull apart, or pull to pieces: *to pick fibers.* **15.** *Music.* **a.** to pluck (the strings of an instrument). **b.** to play (a stringed instrument) by plucking with the fingers. —*v.i.* **16.** to strike with or use a pick or other pointed instrument on something. **17.** (of birds or other animals) to take up small bits of food with the bill or teeth: *The hens were busily picking about in their coop.* **18.** to select carefully or fastidiously. **19.** to pilfer; steal. **20.** to pluck or gather fruit, flowers, etc. **21.** *Basketball.* to execute a pick. **22. pick and choose,** to be very careful or particular in choosing: *With such a limited supply of fresh fruit, you won't be able to pick and choose.* **23. pick apart,** to criticize severely or in great detail: *They picked her apart the moment she left the room.* **24. pick at, a.** to find fault with unnecessarily or persistently; nag. **b.** to eat sparingly or daintily: *As he was ill, he only picked at his food.* **c.** to grasp at; touch; handle: *The baby loved to pick at her mother's glasses.* **25. pick it up,** *Informal.* to move, work, etc., at a faster rate. **26. pick off, a.** to remove by pulling or plucking off. **b.** to single out and shoot: *The hunter picked off a duck rising from the marsh.* **c.** *Baseball.* to put out (a base runner) in a pick-off play. **27. pick on, a.** *Informal.* to criticize or blame; tease; harass. **b.** to single out; choose: *The professor always picks on me to translate long passages.* **28. pick one's way** or **steps,** to walk with care and deliberation: *She picked her way across the muddy field.* **29. pick out, a.** to choose; designate: *to pick out one's successor.* **b.** to distinguish from that which surrounds or accompanies; recognize: *to pick out a well-known face in a crowd.* **c.** to discern (sense or meaning); discriminate. **d.** to play (a melody) by ear; work out note by note. **e.** to extract by picking. **30. pick over,** to examine (an assortment of items) in order to make a selection: *Eager shoppers were picking over the shirts on the bargain tables.* **31. pick someone's brains.** See **brain** (def.10). **32. pick up, a.** to lift or take up: *to pick up a stone.* **b.** to collect, esp. in an orderly manner: *Pick up the tools when you're finished.* **c.** to recover (one's courage, health, etc.); regain. **d.** to gain by occasional opportunity; obtain casually: *to pick up a livelihood.* **e.** to learn, as by experience: *I've picked up a few Japanese phrases.* **f.** to claim: *to pick up one's bags at an airport.* **g.** to take (a person or thing) into a car or ship, etc., or along with one. **h.** to bring into range of reception, observation, etc.: *to pick up Rome on one's radio.* **i.** to accelerate; gain (speed). **j.** to put in good order; tidy: *to pick up a room.* **k.** to make progress; improve: *Business is beginning to pick up.* **l.** to catch or contract, as a disease. **m.** *Informal.* to become acquainted with informally or casually, often in hope of a sexual relationship: *Let's pick up some dates tonight.* **n.** to resume or continue after being left off: *Let's pick up the discussion in our next meeting.* **o.** *Informal.* to take into custody; arrest: *They picked him up for vagrancy.* **p.** *Informal.* to obtain; find; purchase: *She picked up some nice shoes on sale.* **q.** *Slang.* to steal: *to pick up jewels and silver.* **r.** to accept, as in order to pay: *to pick up the check.* **33. pick up on,** *Informal.* **a.** become aware or cognizant of; be perceptive about; notice: *to pick up on the hostess's hostility.* **b.** to pay special attention to; keep an eye on: *to pick up on a troubled student.*
—*n.* **34.** the act of choosing or selecting; choice; selection: *to take one's pick.* **35.** a person or thing that is selected: *He is our pick for president.* **36.** the choicest or most desirable part, example, or examples: *This horse is the pick of the stable.* **37.** the right of selection: *He gave me my pick of the litter.* **38.** the quantity of a crop picked, as from trees, bushes, etc., at a particular time: *The pick was poor this season.* **39.** *Print.* **a.** a speck of dirt, hardened ink, or extra metal on set type or a plate. **b.** a small area removed from the surface of a coated paper by ink that adheres to the form. **40.** a stroke with something pointed: *The rock shattered at the first pick of the ax.* **41.** *Basketball.* an offensive maneuver in which a player moves into a position between a defender and a teammate with the ball so as to prevent the defender from interfering with the shot. [1250–1300; v. ME *pyken, pikken, pekken,* c. D *pikken,* G *picken,* ON *pikka* to pick; akin to PECK[2], PIKE[5]; (n.) deriv. of the v.] —**pick′a·ble,** *adj.*
—**Syn. 1.** See **choose. 4.** rob, pilfer. **12.** reap, collect.

pick[2] (pik), *n.* **1.** a heavy tool consisting of an iron or steel head, usually curved, tapering to a point at one or both ends, mounted on a wooden handle, and used for loosening and breaking up soil, rock, etc.; pickax. **2.** a hammerlike tool for the rough dressing of stone, having two sharp, pyramidal faces. **3.** any pointed or other tool or instrument for picking (often used in combination): *a toothpick; an ice pick.* **4.** *Music.* plectrum. **5.** *Slang.* a large pocket comb having long, widely spaced teeth. [1300–50; ME *pikk(e);* perh. var. of PIKE[5]]

pick[3] (pik), *Textiles.* —*v.t.* **1.** to cast (a shuttle). —*n.* **2.** (in a loom) one passage of the shuttle. **3.** filling (def. 5). [var. of PITCH[1]]

pick·a·back (pik′ə bak′), *adv., adj.* piggyback (defs. 1, 2). [1555–65; earlier *a pickback;* see PICK[1], BACK[1]]

pick′aback plane′, a powered airplane designed to be carried aloft by another airplane and released in flight.

pick′aback plant′. See **piggyback plant.** [1945–50]

pick-and-roll (pik′ən rōl′), *n. Basketball.* an offensive maneuver in which a player interposes himself or herself between a teammate with the ball and a defender, then cuts quickly toward the basket for a pass from the same teammate. Cf. **pick** (def. 41).

pick-and-shov·el (pik′ən shuv′əl), *adj.* marked by drudgery; laborious: *the pick-and-shovel work necessary to get a political campaign underway.* [1890–95]

pick·a·nin·ny (pik′ə nin′ē), *n., pl.* **-nies.** *Offensive.* a black child. Also, **picaninny, piccaninny.** [1645–55; prob. ult. < Pg *pequenino,* dim. of *pequeno* small; as a word for "small child," *pickaninny* and its variants are widespread in English-based creoles of the New World and West Africa; cf. Jamaican E *pickney,* West African E *pickin* small child]

pick·a·roon (pik′ə ro͞on′), *n., v.i.* picaroon.

pick·ax (pik′aks′), *n., pl.* **-ax·es,** *v.,* **-axed, -ax·ing.** —*n.* **1.** a pick, esp. a mattock. —*v.t.* **2.** to cut or clear away with a pickax. —*v.i.* **3.** to use a pickax. Also, **pick′axe′.** [1275–1325; PICK[2] + AX; r. ME *picois* < MF, OF; akin to F *pic* PICK[2]. See PIQUE[1]]

picked[1] (pikt), *adj.* **1.** specially chosen or selected, usually for special skill: *a crew of picked men.* **2.** cleared or cleaned by or as if by picking: *picked fruit.* [1300–50; ME; see PICK[1], -ED[2]]

pick·ed[2] (pik′id, pikt), *adj. Chiefly Dial.* having or coming to a sharp point; peaked; pointed. [1400–50; late ME; see PICK[2], -ED[3]]

pick·eer (pik ēr′), *v.i. Obs.* **1.** to engage in skirmishes in advance of troops of an army. **2.** to reconnoiter; scout; survey. [1635–45; < D *pikeeren,* var. of *pikereien* < F *picorée* < Sp *pecorea* pillaging, lit., cattle-raiding, verbid of *pecorear* to carry off cattle, deriv. of L *pecus* cattle]

Pick·ens (pik′ənz), *n.* **1. Andrew,** 1739–1817, American Revolutionary general. **2. Fort.** See **Fort Pickens.**

pick·er (pik′ər), *n.* **1.** someone or something that picks. **2.** a special tool or machine for picking fruit, vegetables, etc., from their plants. **3.** a machine that picks fibers. **4.** a person who gathers fruit, flowers, etc. **5.** *Slang.* a player of a stringed instrument, esp. a banjo. **6.** *Metall.* a pointed rod for removing a pattern from a half mold. [1520–30; PICK[1] + -ER[1]]

pick·er·el (pik′ər əl, pik′rəl), *n., pl.* (*esp. collectively*) **-el,** (*esp. referring to two or more kinds or species*) **-els.** **1.** any of several small species of pike, as *Esox niger* **(chain pickerel)** and *E. americanus americanus* **(redfin pickerel),** of eastern North America. **2.** the walleye or pikeperch, *Stizostedion vitreum.* **3.** *Brit.* a young pike. [1300–50; ME *pickerel.* See PIKE[1], -EREL]

pick′erel frog′, a meadow frog, *Rana palustris,* common in eastern North America, similar to the leopard frog but with squarish dark spots on the back. [1830–40, *Amer.*]

pick·er·el·weed (pik′ər əl wēd′, pik′rəl-), *n.* any American plant of the genus *Pontederia,* esp. *P. cordata,* having spikes of blue flowers, common in shallow fresh water. [1645–55; PICKEREL + WEED[1]]

Pick·er·ing (pik′ər ing, pik′ring), *n.* **Edward Charles,** 1846–1919, and his brother, **William Henry,** 1858–1938, U.S. astronomers.

pick·er·ing·ite (pik′ər ing īt′, pik′ring-), *n.* a mineral, magnesia alum, occurring usually in the form of white fibrous masses. [1835–45; named after John *Pickering* (1777–1846), American linguist; see -ITE[1]]

pick·er-up·per (pik′ər up′ər), *n. Informal.* something that restores one's depleted energy or depressed spirits; pick-me-up. [1935–40; *pick up* + -ER[1], joined pleonastically to both v. and particle]

pick·et (pik′it), *n.* **1.** a post, stake, pale, or peg that is used in a fence or barrier, to fasten down a tent, etc. **2.** a person stationed by a union or the like outside a factory, store, mine, etc., in order to dissuade or prevent workers or customers from entering it during a strike. **3.** a person engaged in any similar demonstration, as against a government's policies or actions, before an embassy, office building, construction project, etc. **4.** *Mil.* a soldier or detachment of soldiers placed on a line forward of a position to warn against an enemy advance. **5.** *Navy, Air Force.* an aircraft or ship performing similar sentinel duty. —*v.t.* **6.** to enclose within a picket fence or stockade, as for protection, imprisonment, etc.: *to picket a lawn; to picket captives.* **7.** to fasten or tether to a picket. **8.** to place pickets in front of or around (a factory, store, mine, embassy, etc.), as during a strike or demonstration. **9.** *Mil.* **a.** to guard, as with pickets. **b.** to post as a picket. —*v.i.* **10.** to stand or march as a picket. [1680–90; < F *piquet.* See PIKE[2], -ET] —**pick′et·er,** *n.*

pick′et boat′, a vessel used to patrol a harbor. [1865–70]

pick′et fence′, a fence consisting of pickets or pales nailed to horizontal stringers between upright posts. Also called **paling, paling fence.** [1790–1800, *Amer.*]

pick′et line′, a line of strikers or other demonstrators serving as pickets. [1855–60]

Pick·ett (pik′it), *n.* **George Edward,** 1825–75, Confederate general in the American Civil War.

Pick·ford (pik′fərd), *n.* **Mary** (*Gladys Marie Smith*), 1893–1979, U.S. motion-picture actress, born in Canada.

pick·ing (pik′ing), *n.* **1.** the act of a person or thing that picks. **2.** something that is or may be picked or picked up. **3.** the amount picked. **4. pickings, a.** scraps or gleanings: *the pickings of a feast.* **b.** profits or gains; spoils. [bef. 900; ME; OE *picung* (once) a mark made by picking; see PICK[1], -ING[1]]

pick·le[1] (pik′əl), *n., v.,* **-led, -ling.** —*n.* **1.** a cucumber that has been preserved in brine, vinegar, or the like. **2.** Often, **pickles.** any other vegetable, as cauliflower, celery, etc., preserved in vinegar and eaten as a relish. **3.** something preserved in a brine or marinade. **4.** a liquid usually prepared with salt or vinegar for preserving or flavoring fish, meat, vegetables, etc.; brine or marinade. **5.** *Metall.* an acid or other chemical solution in which metal objects are dipped to remove oxide scale or other adhering substances. **6.** *Informal.* a troublesome or awkward situation; predicament: *I was in a pickle after the check bounced.* **7.** *Informal.* a sour, disagreeable person. —*v.t.* **8.** to preserve or steep in brine or other liquid. **9.** to treat with a chemical solution, as for the purpose of cleaning. **10.** to give a pale, streaked finish to (wood) by applying and partly removing paint or by bleaching, as to give an appearance of age. **11.** *Slang.* to store; prepare for long-range storage: *Let's pickle these old cars for a few years.* [1400–50; late ME *pikkyll, pekille* < MD, MLG *pekel* (> G *Pökel*) brine, pickle]
—**Syn. 6.** plight, quandary; fix, bind, scrape, jam.

pick·le[2] (pik′əl), *n. Scot. and North Eng.* **1.** a single grain or kernel, as of barley or corn. **2.** a small amount; a little. [1545–55; perh. n. use of *pickle* to take tiny bits of food in eating, freq. of PICK[1]; see -LE]

pick·led (pik′əld), *adj.* **1.** preserved or steeped in brine or other liquid. **2.** *Slang.* drunk; intoxicated. **3.** (of wood) given an antique appearance by applying and partly removing paint or by bleaching. [1545–55; PICKLE[1] + -ED[2]]

pick′led pigs′′ feet′. See **pigs' feet.**

pick·le·worm (pik′əl wûrm′), *n.* the larva of a pyralid moth, *Diaphania nitidalis,* that bores into the stem and fruit of squash, cucumber, and other cucurbitaceous plants. [1865–70, *Amer.;* PICKLE[1] + WORM]

pick·lock (pik′lok′), *n.* **1.** a person who picks locks, esp. a burglar. **2.** a thief. **3.** an instrument for picking locks; lock pick. [1545–55; PICK[1] + LOCK[1]]

pick-me-up (pik′mē up′), *n. Informal.* **1.** an alcoholic drink taken to restore one's energy or good spirits. **2.** any restorative, as a snack or coffee. Also called **pickup.** [1865–70; n. use of v. phrase *pick me up*]

pick-off (pik′ôf′, -of′), *n.* **1.** *Baseball.* a play in which a base runner, caught off base, is tagged out by an infielder on a quick throw, usually from the pitcher or catcher. **2.** *Electronics.* a mechanism that senses mechanical motion and produces a corresponding electric signal. [1935–40; n. use of v. phrase *pick off*]

pick·pock·et (pik′pok′it), *n.* **1.** a person who steals money, wallets, etc., from the pockets of people, as in crowded public places. —*v.t.* **2.** to steal (a wallet, money, etc.) in the manner of a pickpocket. **3.** to steal from (a person) in the manner of a pickpocket. [1585–95; PICK[1] + POCKET]

pick·proof (pik′pro͞of′), *adj.* (of a lock) designed so that it cannot be picked. [1930–35; PICK[1] + -PROOF]

pick·thank (pik′thangk′), *n. Archaic.* a person who seeks favor by flattery or gossip; sycophant. [1490–1500; n. use of v. phrase *pick a thank, pick thanks*]

pick·up (pik′up′), *n.* **1.** an improvement, as in health, business conditions, work, production, etc. **2.** *Informal.* pick-me-up. **3.** *Informal.* a casual, usually unintroduced acquaintance, often one made in hope of a sexual relationship. **4.** an instance of stopping for or taking aboard passengers or freight, as by a train, ship, taxicab, etc., esp. an instance of taking freight or a shipment of goods onto a truck. **5.** the person, freight, or shipment so taken aboard: *The cab driver had a pickup at the airport who wanted to be driven to the docks.* **6.** *Auto.* **a.** capacity for rapid acceleration. **b.** acceleration; increase in speed. **c.** Also called **pick′up truck′.** a small truck with a low-sided open body, used for deliveries and light hauling. **7.** *Baseball.* the act of fielding a ball after it hits the ground. **8.** Also called **cartridge.** a small device attached to the end of a phonograph tone arm that contains a stylus and the mechanism that translates the movement of the stylus in a record groove into a changing electrical voltage. **9.** *Radio.* **a.** the act of receiving sound waves in the transmitting set in order to change them into electrical waves. **b.** a receiving or recording device. **c.** the place from which a broadcast is being transmitted. **d.** interference (def. 4). **10.** *Television.* **a.** the change of light energy into electrical energy in a television camera. **b.** See **camera tube. c.** a telecast made directly from the scene of an action. **11.** a hitchhiker. **12.** *Metalworking.* (in the cold-drawing of metal) the adhesion of particles of the metal to the die or plug. —*adj.* **13.** composed of or employing whatever persons are available on a more or less impromptu basis: *a pickup game of baseball; a pickup dance band.* **14.** using whatever ingredients are handy or available: *a Sunday night pickup supper.* [1855–60; n. use of v. phrase *pick up*]

pick′up arm′. See **tone arm.** [1935–40]

pick′up camp′er, camper (def. 3). [1970–75]

pick-up-sticks (pik′up′stiks′), *n.* jackstraws played with sticks.

pick′up tube′, *Television.* See **camera tube.** Also, **pickup.** [1930–35]

pick•wick (pik′wik), *n.* a picklike implement for catching up and raising a short wick of an oil lamp. [1860–65; PICK[1] + WICK[1]]

Pick•wick•i•an (pik wik′ē ən), *adj.* **1.** of, pertaining to, or characteristic of Mr. Pickwick, central character of *The Pickwick Papers.* **2.** (of the use or interpretation of an expression) intentionally or unintentionally odd or unusual. **3.** (of words or ideas) meant or understood in a sense different from the apparent or usual one. [1830–40; *Pickwick* + -IAN] —**Pick•wick′i•an•ly,** *adv.*

Pick•wick•i•an•ism (pik wik′ē ə niz′əm), *n.* a Pickwickian statement, expression, word, or the like. [1890–95; PICKWICKIAN + -ISM]

Pickwick′ian syn′drome, *Pathol.* an abnormality characterized by extreme obesity accompanied by sleepiness, hypoventilation, and polycythemia. Also, **Pick′•wick syn′drome.** [1955–60; named for Joe, a character in Dickens' *The Pickwick Papers* who exhibited symptoms of the disorder]

Pick′wick Pa′pers, The, (*The Posthumous Papers of the Pickwick Club*) a novel (1837) by Charles Dickens.

pick•y (pik′ē), *adj.,* **pick•i•er, pick•i•est.** extremely fussy or finicky, usually over trifles. [1865–70; PICK[1] + -Y[1]] —**pick′i•ness,** *n.*

pic•lo•ram (pik′lə ram′, pī′klə-), *n. Chem.* a colorless powder, $C_6H_3Cl_3N_2O_2$, used as a systemic herbicide for controlling annual weeds and deep-rooted perennials on noncrop land. [1960–65; reverse compound from *am(i-notrich)lor(o)pic(olinic acid)*; see AMINO-, TRI-, CHLORO-, PICOLINIC]

pic•nic (pik′nik), *n., v.,* **-nicked, -nick•ing.** —*n.* **1.** an excursion or outing in which the participants carry food with them and share a meal in the open air. **2.** the food eaten on such an excursion. **3.** Also called **pic′nic ham′, pic′nic shoul′der.** a section of pork shoulder, usually boned, smoked, and weighing 4–6 pounds. Cf. **daisy** (def. 2). **4.** *Informal.* an enjoyable experience or time, easy task, etc.: *Being laid up in a hospital is no picnic.* —*v.i.* **5.** to go on or take part in a picnic. [1740–50; < G *Pic-nic* (now *Picknick*) < F *pique-nique,* rhyming compound < ?] —**pic′nick•er,** *n.*

pico-, a combining form meaning "one trillionth" (10^{-12}): *picogram.* [< Sp *pico* peak, beak, bit. See PIC[2]]

Pi•co del•la Mi•ran•do•la (pē′kō del′ə mə ran′dl ə; *It.* pē′kô del′lä mē RÄN′dô lä′), **Count Gio•van•ni** (jô-vän′nē), 1463–94, Italian humanist and writer.

Pi•co de São To•mé (pē′ko͝o də soun′ to͞o me′). See **São Tomé** (def. 3).

Pi•co de Tei•de (*Sp.* pē′kô t͟he tā′t͟he). See **Teide, Pico de.**

pi•co•far•ad (pē′kō far′əd, -ad, pī′-), *n. Elect.* one trillionth of a farad. *Abbr.:* pF Also called **micromicrofarad.** [1925–30; PICO- + FARAD]

pi•co•gram (pē′kə gram′, pī′-), *n.* one trillionth of a gram. *Abbr.:* pg [1950–55; PICO- + -GRAM[2]]

pic•o•line (pik′ə lēn′, -lin), *n. Chem.* any of three isomeric methyl derivatives of pyridine having the formula C_6H_7N, obtained from coal tar as a colorless oily liquid with a strong odor. [1850–55; < L *pic-* (s. of *pix*) PITCH[2] + -OL[2] + -INE[2]] —**pic•o•lin•ic** (pik′ə lin′ik), *adj.*

Pi•co Ri•ve•ra (pē′kō ri vâr′ə, -vēr′ə), a city in SW California, near Los Angeles. 53,459.

pi•cor•na•vi•rus (pi kôr′nə vī′rəs, -kôr′nə vī′-), *n., pl.* **-rus•es.** any of a group of small, RNA-containing viruses of the family Picornaviridae, infectious to humans and other animals, and including the poliovirus and the rhinoviruses that cause the common cold. [1960–65; PICO- (in the sense "very small") + RNA + VIRUS]

pi•co•sec•ond (pē′kə sek′ənd, pī′-), *n.* one trillionth of a second. *Abbr.:* ps, psec [1965–70; PICO- + SECOND[2]]

pi•cot (pē′kō), *n.* one of a number of ornamental loops in embroidery, or along the edge of lace, ribbon, etc. [1880–85; < F: a purl, lit., a splinter, dim. of *pic* prick < Gmc; see PIC[2], PIKE[2]]

pic•o•tee (pik′ə tē′), *n.* a variety of carnation, tulip, etc., having an outer margin of another color. [1720–30; < F *picoté* marked, pricked, ptp. of *picoter* to mark with tiny points, deriv. of *picot* PICOT; see -EE]

pi′cot stitch′, a stitch that produces picots, or loops, of thread that extend beneath a row of connecting or finishing stitches. [1890–95]

pi•co•wave (pē′kə wāv′, pī′-), *v.t.,* **-waved, -wav•ing.** to irradiate (food) with gamma rays in order to retard spoilage. [1981–86; PICO- + WAVE; cf. MICROWAVE]

pic•quet (pi kā′, -ket′), *n.* piquet.

pic•ram′ic ac′id (pi kram′ik), *Chem.* a red, crystalline substance, $C_6H_5N_3O_5$, soluble in alcohol, used chiefly in the manufacture of azo dyes. [PICR(IC) + AMIC]

pic•rate (pik′rāt), *n. Chem.* a salt or ester of picric acid. [1865–70; PICR(IC ACID) + -ATE[2]] —**pic•rat′ed,** *adj.*

pic•ric (pik′rik), *adj. Chem.* of or derived from picric acid. [1850–55; < Gk *pikr(ós)* bitter + -IC]

pic′ric ac′id, *Chem.* a yellow, crystalline, water-soluble, intensely bitter, poisonous acid, $C_6H_3N_3O_7$, used chiefly in explosives. Also called **carbazotic acid, nitroxanthic acid, pi′cro•ni′tric ac′id** (pī′krō nī′trik, pī′krō-), **trinitrophenol.** [1850–55]

pic•rite (pik′rīt), *n.* a granular igneous rock composed chiefly of olivine and augite, but containing small amounts of feldspar. [1805–15; < Gk *pikr(ós)* bitter + -ITE[1]]

pic•ro•tox•in (pik′rə tok′sin), *n. Pharm.* a white, crystalline, bitter, poisonous, central nervous system stimulant, $C_{30}H_{34}O_{13}$, obtained from the seeds of *Anamirta cocculus:* used chiefly in the treatment of barbiturate poisoning. [1865–70; < Gk *pikr(ós)* bitter + -O- + TOXIN] —**pic′ro•tox′ic,** *adj.*

Pict (pikt), *n.* a member of an ancient people of uncertain origin who inhabited parts of northern Britain, fought against the Romans, and in the 9th century A.D. united with the Scots. [bef. 900; back formation from ME *Pictes* (pl.) < L *Pictī* lit., painted ones, pl. of *pictus,* ptp. of *pingere* to PAINT; r. ME *Peghttes,* OE *Peohtas, Pihtas* << L, as above]

Pict•ish (pik′tish), *n.* **1.** the language of the Picts, apparently a Celtic language. —*adj.* **2.** of or pertaining to the Picts. [1700–10; PICT + -ISH[1]]

pic•to•gram (pik′tə gram′), *n.* pictograph. [1960–65; < L *pict(us)* painted (see PICTURE) + -O- + -GRAM[1]]

pic•to•graph (pik′tə graf′, -gräf′), *n.* **1.** a pictorial sign or symbol. **2.** a record consisting of pictorial symbols, as a prehistoric cave drawing or a graph or chart with symbolic figures representing a certain number of people, cars, factories, etc. [1850–55; < L *pict(us)* painted (see PICTURE) + -O- + -GRAPH] —**pic•to•graph•ic** (pik′tə graf′ik), *adj.* —**pic′to•graph′i•cal•ly,** *adv.*

pic•tog•ra•phy (pik tog′rə fē), *n.* the use of pictographs; picture writing. [1850–55; PICTOGRAPH + -Y[3]; see -GRAPHY]

Pic•tor (pik′tər), *n., gen.* **Pic•to•res** (pik tôr′is, -tōr′-). *Astron.* the Painter, a southern constellation between Dorado and Carina.

pic•to•ri•al (pik tôr′ē əl, -tōr′ē əl), *adj.* **1.** pertaining to, expressed in, or of the nature of a picture. **2.** illustrated by or containing pictures: *a pictorial history.* **3.** of or pertaining to the art of painting and drawing pictures, the pictures themselves, or their makers: *the pictorial masterpieces of the Renaissance.* **4.** having or suggesting the visual appeal or imagery of a picture: *a pictorial metaphor.* —*n.* **5.** a periodical in which pictures constitute an important feature. **6.** a magazine feature that is primarily photographic. [1640–50; < L *pictōri(us)* of painting (*pic-,* var. s. of *pingere* to PAINT + *-tōrius* -TORY[1]) + -AL[1]] —**pic•to′ri•al•ly,** *adv.* —**pic•to′ri•al•ness,** *n.*

—**Syn. 4.** picturesque, vivid, striking, telling.

pic•to•ri•al•ism (pik tôr′ē ə liz′əm, -tōr′-), *n.* **1.** *Fine Arts.* the creation or use of pictures or visual images, esp. of recognizable or realistic representations. **2.** emphasis on purely photographic or scenic qualities for its own sake, sometimes with a static or lifeless effect: *The movie's self-conscious pictorialism makes it little more than a travelogue.* Cf. **representationalism.** [1865–70; PICTORIAL + -ISM] —**pic•to′ri•al•ist,** *n.*

pic•to•ri•al•ize (pik tôr′ē ə līz′, -tōr′-), *v.t.,* **-ized, -iz•ing.** to make pictorial; illustrate or represent with or as if with pictures. Also, *esp. Brit.,* **pic•to′ri•al•ise′.** [1865–70; PICTORIAL + -IZE] —**pic•to′ri•al•i•za′tion,** *n.*

pic•ture (pik′chər), *n., v.,* **-tured, -tur•ing.** —*n.* **1.** a visual representation of a person, object, or scene, as a painting, drawing, photograph, etc.: *I carry a picture of my grandchild in my wallet.* **2.** any visible image, however produced: *pictures reflected in a pool of water.* **3.** a mental image: *a clear picture of how he had looked that day.* **4.** a particular image or reality as portrayed in an account or description; depiction; version. **5.** a tableau, as in theatrical representation. **6.** See **motion picture. 7. pictures,** *Informal* (*older use*). movies. **8.** a person, thing, group, or scene regarded as resembling a work of pictorial art in beauty, fineness of appearance, etc.: *She was a picture in her new blue dress.* **9.** the image or perfect likeness of someone else: *He is the picture of his father.* **10.** a visible or concrete embodiment of some quality or condition: *the picture of health.* **11.** a situation or set of circumstances: *the economic picture.* **12.** the image on a computer monitor, the viewing screen of a television set, or a motion-picture screen. —*v.t.* **13.** to represent in a picture or pictorially, as by painting or drawing. **14.** to form a mental picture of; imagine: *He couldn't picture himself doing such a thing.* **15.** to depict in words; describe graphically: *He pictured Rome so vividly that you half-believed you were there.* **16.** to present or create as a setting; portray: *His book pictured the world of the future.* [1375–1425; late ME < L *pictūra* the act of painting, a painting, equiv. to *pict(us)* (ptp. of *pingere* to PAINT) + *-ūra* -URE] —**pic′tur•a•ble,** *adj.* —**pic′tur•a•ble•ness,** *n.* —**pic′tur•a•bly,** *adv.* —**pic′tur•er,** *n.*

—**Syn. 13, 15.** delineate, paint, draw, represent.

pic′ture book′, a book consisting mainly or entirely of pictures, esp. one for children who have not yet learned to read. [1850–55]

pic′ture hat′, a woman's hat having a very broad, flexible brim, often decorated with feathers, flowers, or the like. [1885–90]

pic′ture lay′out, a picture spread. See under **spread** (def. 34).

pic′ture mold′, a molding near a ceiling from which pictures can be suspended. Also called **pic′ture rail′.**

Pic′ture of Do′ri•an Gray′, The (dôr′ē ən, dōr′-), a novel (1891) by Oscar Wilde.

Pic•ture•phone (pik′chər fōn′), *Trademark.* a brand of videophone that enables telephone users to see each other while talking.

pic′ture plane′, the plane of a painting, drawing, or the like, that is in the extreme foreground of a picture, is coextensive with but not the same as the material surface of the work, is the point of visual contact between the viewer and the picture, and is conceived as a major structural element in the production of abstract or illusionistic forms. See diag. under **perspective.** [1790–1800]

pic′ture post′card, postcard (def. 1). [1905–10]

pic′ture puz′zle. See **jigsaw puzzle** (def. 1). [1895–1900]

pic′ture sash′, a large window sash, as for a picture window.

pic′ture show′, *Older Use.* **1.** See **motion picture. 2.** a motion-picture theater. [1865–70, in sense "exhibition of pictures"; 1910–15 for current senses]

pic′ture spread′. See under **spread** (def. 34).

pic•tur•esque (pik′chə resk′), *adj.* **1.** visually charming or quaint, as if resembling or suitable for a painting: *a picturesque fishing village.* **2.** (of writing, speech, etc.) strikingly graphic or vivid; creating detailed mental images: *a picturesque description of the Brazilian jungle.* **3.** having pleasing or interesting qualities; strikingly effective in appearance: *a picturesque hat.* [1695–1705; < F *pittoresque* < It *pittoresco* (*pittor(e)* PAINTER + *-esco* -ESQUE), with assimilation to PICTURE] —**pic′•tur•esque′ly,** *adv.* —**pic′tur•esque′ness,** *n.*

—**Syn. 2.** PICTURESQUE, GRAPHIC, VIVID apply to descriptions that produce a strong, especially a visual, impression. PICTURESQUE is a less precise term than the other two. A PICTURESQUE account, though striking and interesting, may be inaccurate or may reflect personal ideas: *He called the landscape picturesque.* A GRAPHIC account is more objective and factual: it produces a clear, definite impression, and carries conviction. A VIVID account is told with liveliness and intenseness; the description is so interesting, or even exciting, that the reader or hearer may be emotionally stirred.

pic′ture tube′, a cathode-ray tube with a screen at one end on which televised images are reproduced. [1935–40]

pic′ture win′dow, a large window in a house, usually dominating the room or wall in which it is located, and often designed or placed to present an attractive view. [1935–40]

pic′ture writ′ing, 1. the art of recording events or expressing ideas by pictures, or pictorial symbols, as practiced by preliterate peoples. **2.** pictorial symbols forming a record or communication. [1735–45]

pic•tur•ize (pik′chə rīz′), *v.t.,* **-ized, -iz•ing.** to represent in a picture, esp. in a motion picture; make a picture of. Also, *esp. Brit.,* **pic′tur•ise′.** [1840–50; PICTURE + -IZE] —**pic′tur•i•za′tion,** *n.*

pic•ul (pik′əl), *n.* (in China and southeast Asia) a weight equal to 100 catties, or from about 133 to about 143 pounds avoirdupois (60–64 kg). [1580–90; < Malay *pikull* the maximum load a man can carry]

pic•u•let (pik′yə lit), *n.* any of numerous small, tropical woodpeckers, chiefly of the genus *Picumnus,* that lack stiffened shafts in the tail feathers. [1840–50; < L *pīcu(s)* woodpecker + -LET]

Pi•cum•nus (pi kum′nəs), *n.* one of two ancient Roman fertility gods. Cf. **Pilumnus.**

Pi•cus (pī′kəs), *n.* an ancient Italian god of agriculture.

PID, See **pelvic inflammatory disease.**

pid•dle (pid′l), *v.,* **-dled, -dling.** —*v.i.* **1.** to spend time in a wasteful, trifling, or ineffective way; dawdle (often fol. by *around*): *He wasted the day piddling around.* **2.** *Informal.* (esp. of children and pets) to urinate. —*v.t.* **3.** to waste (time, money, etc.); fail to utilize (usually fol. by *away*). [1535–45; orig. uncert.] —**pid′dler,** *n.*

pid•dling (pid′ling), *adj.* amounting to very little; trifling; negligible: *a piddling sum of money.* [1550–60; PIDDLE + -ING[2]]

—**Syn.** trivial, insignificant, paltry, picayune.

pid•dock (pid′ək), *n.* any bivalve mollusk of the genus *Pholas* or the family Pholadidae, having long, ovate shells and burrowing in soft rock, wood, etc. [1850–55; perh. akin to OE *puduc* wart]

Pid•geon (pij′ən), *n.* **Walter,** 1898–1984, U.S. actor, born in Canada.

pidg•in (pij′ən), *n.* **1.** an auxiliary language that has come into existence through the attempts by the speakers of two different languages to communicate and that is primarily a simplified form of one of the languages, with a reduced vocabulary and grammatical structure and considerable variation in pronunciation. **2.** (loosely) any simplified or broken form of a language, esp. when used for communication between speakers of different languages. [1875–80; extracted from PIDGIN ENGLISH]

pidg′in Eng′lish, **1.** a pidgin language based on English formerly used in commerce in Chinese ports. **2.** a similar language used in other areas, such as Papua New Guinea (where it has semiofficial status) and parts of West Africa. Also, **Pidg′in Eng′lish.** [1820–30; *pidgin, pigeon* < Chin Pidgin E: business, affair; etym. uncert., but often alleged to be Chin pron. of *business*]

pidg•in•ize (pij′ə nīz′), *v.t.,* **-ized, -iz•ing.** to develop (a language) into a pidgin. Also, *esp. Brit.,* **pidg′in•ise′.** [1935–40; PIDGIN + -IZE] —**pidg′in•i•za′tion,** *n.*

Pidg′in Sign′ Eng′lish, an auxiliary language formed by using the signs and fingerspelling, but not the grammar, of American Sign Language in the word order of English, often used in communication between deaf signers and speakers of English. *Abbr.:* PSE

pid•yon ha•ben (*Seph. Heb.* pēd yôn′ hä ben′; *Ashk. Heb., Eng.* pid′yən hä ben′), *Judaism.* the rite of relieving the first male child born to parents not descended from Aaron or Levi of certain religious obligations by redeeming him from a member of the priestly class, celebrated 30 days after the child's birth. Also, **Pid•yon′ ha-Ben′.** [< Heb *pidyōn habbēn* lit., redemption of the son]

pie[1] (pī), *n.* **1.** a baked food having a filling of fruit, meat, pudding, etc., prepared in a pastry-lined pan or dish and often topped with a pastry crust: *apple pie; meat pie.* **2.** a layer cake with a filling of custard, cream jelly, or the like: *chocolate cream pie.* **3.** a total or whole that can be divided: *They want a bigger part of the profit pie.* **4.** an activity or affair: *He has his finger in the political pie too.* **5.** pizza. **6. easy as pie,** extremely easy or simple. **7. nice as pie,** extremely well-behaved, agreeable, or the like: *The children were nice as pie.* **8. pie in the sky, a.** the illusory prospect of future benefits: *Political promises are often pie in the sky.* **b.** a state of perfect happiness; utopia: *to promise pie in the sky.* [1275–1325; ME, of obscure orig.] —**pie′like′,** *adj.*

pie[2] (pī), *n.* magpie. [1200–50; ME < OF < L *pīca,* akin to *picus* woodpecker]

pie[3] (pī), *n., v.t.,* **pied, pie•ing.** pi[2].

pie[4] (pī), *n.* (in England before the Reformation) a book of ecclesiastical rules for finding the particulars of the service for the day. Also, **pye.** [1470–80; trans. of L *pīca* PIE[2]; the allusion is obscure; cf. PICA[1]]

pie[5] (pī), *n.* a former bronze coin of India, the 12th part of an anna. Cf. **naya paisa, paisa, pice.** [1855–60; < Marathi *pā′ī* lit., a fourth]

PIE, Proto-Indo-European.

pie•bald (pī′bôld′), *adj.* **1.** having patches of black and white or of other colors; parti-colored. —*n.* **2.** a piebald animal, esp. a horse. [1580–90; PIE[2] (see PIED) + BALD] —**pie′bald′ly,** *adv.* —**pie′bald′ness,** *n.*
—**Syn. 1.** dappled, mottled.

pie′bald skin′, *Pathol.* vitiligo.

pie′ bed′. See **apple-pie bed.**

piece (pēs), *n., v.,* **pieced, piec•ing.** —*n.* **1.** a separate or limited portion or quantity of something: *a piece of land; a piece of chocolate.* **2.** a quantity of some substance or material forming a single mass or body: *a nice piece of lumber.* **3.** a more or less definite portion or quantity of a whole: *to cut a blueberry pie into six pieces.* **4.** a particular length, as of certain goods prepared for the market: *cloth sold by the piece.* **5.** an amount of work forming a single job: *to be paid by the piece and not by the hour.* **6.** an example of workmanship, esp. of artistic production, as a picture or a statue: *The museum has some interesting pieces by Picasso.* **7.** a literary composition, usually short, in prose or verse. **8.** a literary selection for recitation: *Each child had a chance to recite a piece.* **9.** a musical composition. **10.** one of the parts that, when assembled, form a whole: *the pieces of a clock.* **11.** an individual article of a set or collection: *a set of dishes containing 100 pieces.* **12.** *Chess, Checkers.* **a.** one of the figures, disks, blocks, or the like, of wood, ivory, or other material, used in playing, as on a board or table. **b.** (in chess) a superior man, as distinguished from a pawn: *to take a rook, a bishop, and other pieces.* **13.** a token, charm, or amulet: *a good-luck piece.* **14.** an individual thing of a particular class or kind: *a piece of furniture; a piece of drawing paper.* **15.** an example, specimen, or instance of something: *a fine piece of workmanship.* **16.** one of the parts into which a thing is destructively divided or broken; a part, fragment, or shred: *to tear a letter into pieces.* **17.** *Mil.* **a.** a soldier's rifle, pistol, etc. **b.** a cannon or other unit of ordnance: *field piece.* **18.** a coin: *a five-cent piece.* **19.** *Midland and Southern U.S.* a distance: *I'm going down the road a piece.* **20.** *Chiefly North Midland U.S.* a snack. **21.** Also called **piece′ of ass′.** *Slang (vulgar).* **a.** coitus. **b.** a person considered as a partner in coitus. **22. give someone a piece of one's mind.** See **mind** (def. 20). **23. go to pieces, a.** to break into fragments. **b.** to lose control of oneself; become emotionally or physically upset: *When he flunked out of medical school he went to pieces.* **24. of a piece,** of the same kind; harmonious; consistent. Also, **of one piece. 25. piece of the action.** See **action** (def. 22). **26. speak one's piece,** to express one's opinion; reveal one's thoughts upon a subject: *I decided to speak my piece whether they liked it or not.* —*v.t.* **27.** to mend (a garment, article, etc.) by adding, joining, or applying a piece or pieces; patch. **28.** to complete, enlarge, or extend by an added piece or something additional (often fol. by *out*): *to piece out a library with new books.* **29.** to make by or as if by joining pieces (often fol. by *together*): *to piece a quilt; to piece together a musical program.* **30.** to join together, as pieces or parts: *to piece together the fragments of a broken dish.* **31.** to join as a piece or addition to something: *to piece new wire into the cable.* **32.** to assemble into a meaningful whole by combining available facts, information, details, etc.: *He pieced the story together after a lot of effort.* —*v.i.* **33.** *Chiefly North Midland U.S.* to eat small portions of food between meals; snack. [1175–1225; ME *pece* < OF < Gaulish **pettia;* akin to Breton *pez* piece, Welsh, Cornish *peth* thing]
—**Syn. 1.** section, segment, scrap, fragment. See **part. 28.** augment. —**Ant. 1.** whole.

pièce de ré•sis•tance (pyes də ʀā zē stäɴs′; *Eng.* pē es′ də ri zē stäns′), *pl.* ***pièces de ré•sis•tance*** (pyes də ʀā zē stäɴs′; *Eng.* pē es′ də ri zē stäns′). *French.* **1.** the principal dish of a meal. **2.** the most noteworthy or prized feature, aspect, event, article, etc., of a series or group; special item or attraction.

pièce d'oc•ca•sion (pyes dô kä zyôɴ′), *pl.* ***pièces d'oc•ca•sion*** (pyes dô kä zyôɴ′). *French.* something prepared or used for a special occasion.

piece-dyed (pēs′dīd′), *adj.* dyed after weaving (opposed to *yarn-dyed*). [1835–45]

piece′ goods′, goods, esp. fabrics, sold at retail by linear measure. Also called **yard goods.** [1655–65]

piece•meal (pēs′mēl′), *adv.* **1.** piece by piece; one piece at a time; gradually: *to work piecemeal.* **2.** into pieces or fragments: *to tear a letter piecemeal.* —*adj.* **3.** done piecemeal. [1250–1300; ME *pecemele;* r. OE *styccemǣlum.* See PIECE, -MEAL]

piece′ of busi′ness, business (def. 10).

piece′ of eight′, peso (def. 4). [1600–10]

piece′ of exchange′, a piece of plate armor for reinforcing or replacing a piece ordinarily used in a suit. Also called **double piece.**

piec•er (pē′sər), *n.* a person whose occupation is the joining together of pieces or threads, as in textile work. [1815–25; PIECE + -ER[1]]

piece′ rate′, compensation based on a worker's quantitative output or production, usually an agreed sum per article of work turned out. [1890–95]

piece•wise (pēs′wīz′), *adv. Math.* denoting that a function has a specified property, as smoothness or continuity, on each of a finite number of pieces into which its domain is divided: *a piecewise continuous function; a piecewise differentiable curve.* [1665–75; PIECE + -WISE]

piece•work (pēs′wûrk′), *n.* work done and paid for by the piece. Cf. **timework.** [1540–50; PIECE + WORK] —**piece′work′er,** *n.*

pie′ chart′, a graphic representation of quantitative information by means of a circle divided into sectors, in which the relative sizes of the areas (or central angles) of the sectors correspond to the relative sizes or proportions of the quantities. Also called **circle graph, pie graph.** [1920–25]

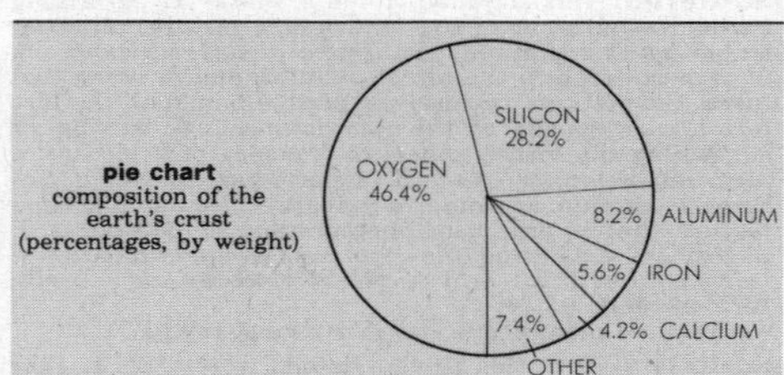

pie chart
composition of the earth's crust (percentages, by weight)

pie•crust (pī′krust′), *n.* **1.** the crust or shell of a pie. **2.** dough prepared with shortening for making the crust or shell of a pie; paste. [1575–85; PIE[1] + CRUST]

pie′crust ta′ble, *U.S. Furniture.* a table having a top, usually round, with a raised and intricately carved edge. [1900–05]

pied (pīd), *adj.* **1.** having patches of two or more colors, as various birds and other animals: *a pied horse.* **2.** wearing pied clothing. [1350–1400; ME; PIE[2] (with reference to the black and white plumage of the magpie) + -ED[3]]

pied-à-terre (pē ā′də târ′, -dä-, pyā′-), *n., pl.* **pieds-à-terre** (pē ā′də târ′, -dä-, pyā′-), a residence, as an apartment, for part-time or temporary use. [1820–30; < F: lit., foot on ground]

pied′-billed grebe′ (pīd′bild′), an American grebe, *Podilymbus podiceps,* having a whitish bill with a black band around it. [1830–40, *Amer.*]

pied-de-biche (pē ā′də bēsh′; *Fr.* pyādᵊ bēsh′), *n., pl.* **pieds-de-biche** (pē āz′də bēsh′; *Fr.* pyādᵊ bēsh′). *Furniture.* a termination to a leg, consisting of a slight outward curve ending in the semblance of a cloven hoof. Also called **hoof foot.** [< F: lit., doe's foot]

pied-de-biche′ spoon′, a spoon having a handle with a trifid end.

pied•fort (pē ā′fôr′; *Fr.* pyā fôʀ′), *n. Coining.* a coin or pattern struck on a blank thicker than that used for the regular issue. Also, **piefort.** [< F, equiv. to *pied* FOOT + *fort* strong]

pied′ goose′. See **magpie goose.** [1895–1900]

Pied•mont (pēd′mont), *n.* **1.** a plateau between the coastal plain and the Appalachian Mountains, including parts of Virginia, North Carolina, South Carolina, Georgia, and Alabama. **2.** Italian, **Piemonte.** a region in NW Italy. 4,540,822; 11,335 sq. mi. (29,360 sq. km). **3.** a city in W California, near Oakland. 10,498. **4.** (*l.c.*) a district lying along or near the foot of a mountain range. —*adj.* **5.** (*l.c.*) lying along or near the foot of a mountain range. [< It *Piemonte* lit., foothill]

Pied•mon•tese (pēd′mon tēz′, -tēs′), *n., pl.* **-tese,** *adj.* —*n.* **1.** a native or inhabitant of Piedmont, Italy. —*adj.* **2.** of, pertaining to, or characteristic of the people or region of Piedmont, Italy. [1635–45; PIEDMONT + -ESE]

pied•mont•ite (pēd′mon tīt′), *n.* a mineral, similar to epidote but containing manganese: found in schists and manganese ores. [1850–55; < G; see PIEDMONT, -ITE[1]]

pied noir (pē ā′ nwär′, pyā′; *Fr.* pyā nwaʀ′), *pl.* **pieds noirs** (pē āz′ nwär′, pyāz′; *Fr.* pyā nwaʀ′). *Often Disparaging.* **1.** an Algerian-born French person. **2.** formerly, a person of French origin living in French-ruled Algeria. Also, **pied′-noir′.** [1960–65; < F: lit., black foot]

Pied′ Pip′er, *n.* **1.** the hero of a German folk legend, popularized in *The Pied Piper of Hamelin* (1842) by Robert Browning. **2.** (*sometimes l.c.*) a person who induces others to follow or imitate him or her, esp. by means of false or extravagant promises.

Pie•dras Ne•gras (pye′thräs ne′gräs), a city in N Mexico, on the Rio Grande. 65,883.

pie-eyed (pī′īd′), *adj. Slang.* drunk; intoxicated. [1880–85, *Amer.*]

pie-faced (pī′fāst′), *adj. Informal.* having a broad, flat face and, sometimes, a vacuous or stupid expression. [1910–15]

pi•e•fort (pē ā fôr′, pyā-), *n.* piedfort.

pie′ graph′. See **pie chart.**

pie′ in the sky′, pie[1] (def. 8). [1910–15, *Amer.*]

Pie•mon•te (pye môn′te), *n.* Italian name of **Piedmont.**

piend (pēnd), *n.* arris. Also, **pien** (pēn). [1835–45; perh. var. of PEEN]

pie•plant (pī′plant′, -plänt′), *n.* the edible rhubarb, *Rheum rhabarbarum.* [1840–50, *Amer.;* PIE[1] + PLANT]

pier (pēr), *n.* **1.** a structure built on posts extending from land out over water, used as a landing place for ships, an entertainment area, a strolling place, etc.; jetty. **2.** (in a bridge or the like) a support for the ends of adjacent spans. **3.** a square pillar. **4.** a portion of wall between doors, windows, etc. **5.** a pillar or post on which a gate or door is hung. **6.** a support of masonry, steel, or the like for sustaining vertical pressure. See diag. under **arch**[1]. **7.** a long passageway or corridor that extends from a central area of a building, esp. one at an airport that leads to boarding gates. [bef. 1150; ME *pere,* earlier (perh. late OE) *per* < AL *pera, pēra* pier of a bridge]

pierce (pērs), *v.,* **pierced, pierc•ing.** —*v.t.* **1.** to penetrate into or run through (something), as a sharp, pointed dagger, object, or instrument does. **2.** to make a hole or opening in. **3.** to bore into or through; tunnel. **4.** to perforate. **5.** to make (a hole, opening, etc.) by or as by boring or perforating. **6.** to make a way or path into or through: *a road that pierces the dense jungle.* **7.** to penetrate with the eye or mind; see into or through: *She couldn't pierce his thoughts.* **8.** to affect sharply with some sensation or emotion, as of cold, pain, or grief: *The wind pierced her body. Her words pierced our hearts.* **9.** to sound sharply through (the air, stillness, etc.): *A pistol shot pierced the night.* —*v.i.* **10.** to force or make a way into or through something; penetrate: *to pierce to the heart.* [1250–1300; ME *percen* < OF *perc(i)er* < VL **pertūsiāre,* v. deriv. of L *pertūsus,* ptp. of *pertundere* to bore a hole through, perforate, equiv. to *per-* PER- + *tundere* to strike, beat] —**pierce′a•ble,** *adj.* —**pierc′•er,** *n.*
—**Syn. 1.** enter, puncture. PIERCE, PENETRATE suggest the action of one object passing through another or making a way through and into another. The terms are used both concretely and figuratively. To PIERCE is to perforate quickly, as by stabbing; it suggests the use of a sharp, pointed instrument which is impelled by force: *to pierce the flesh with a knife; a scream pierces one's ears.* PENETRATE suggests a slow or difficult movement: *No ordinary bullet can penetrate an elephant's hide; to penetrate the depths of one's ignorance.* **8.** touch, move, strike, thrill.

Pierce (pērs), *n.* **1. Franklin,** 1804–69, 14th president of the U.S. 1853–57. **2. John Robinson,** born 1910, U.S. electrical engineer: helped develop communications satellites. **3.** a male given name, form of **Peter.**

pierced (pērst), *adj.* **1.** punctured or perforated, as to form a decorative design: *a pendant in pierced copper.* **2.** (of the ear) having the lobe punctured, as for earrings. **3.** (of an earring) made to be attached, as by a post or wire, through the hole in a pierced ear lobe. **4.** *Heraldry.* (of a charge) open at the center to reveal the field: *a lozenge pierced.* [1300–50; ME; see PIERCE, -ED[2]]

Pierce′'s disease′, *Plant Pathol.* a disease of grapes caused by a rickettsialike organism, characterized by dwarfing of vines, mottling of woody tissues, and plant death. [named after N. B. *Pierce* (d. 1917), American plant pathologist]

pierc•ing (pēr′sing), *adj.* **1.** loud or shrill, as the quality of a voice. **2.** extremely cold or bitter: *a piercing wind.* **3.** appearing to gaze deeply or penetratingly into something: *piercing eyes.* **4.** perceptive or aware; acute: *a piercing mind.* **5.** sarcastic or caustic; cutting: *piercing remarks.* [1375–1425; late ME; see PIERCE, -ING[2]] **—pierc′ing·ly,** *adv.* **—pierc′ing·ness,** *n.* **—Syn. 1.** grating, strident, screeching.

pierc′ing saw′, *Jewelry.* a small, fine-gauge saw blade with uniformly spaced, angled teeth, inserted in a jeweler's saw frame and used to cut precious metal and such soft materials as ivory and shell. [1870–75]

pier′ glass′, a tall mirror, often full-length, intended to be set between windows. [1695–1705]

pier·head (pēr′hed′), *n.* **1.** the outermost end of a pier or wharf. **2.** (in the Great Lakes area) a breakwater. [1675–85; PIER + HEAD]

Pi·e·ri·a (pī ēr′ē ə), *n.* a coastal region in NE Greece, W of the Gulf of Salonika.

Pi·e·ri·an (pī ēr′ē ən), *adj.* **1.** of or pertaining to the Muses. **2.** of or pertaining to poetry or poetic inspiration. **3.** of or pertaining to Pieria. [1585–95; < L *Pieri(us)* of Pieria + -AN]

Pie′rian Spring′, *Class. Myth.* a fountain in Pieria, sacred to the Muses and supposedly conferring inspiration or learning on anyone who drank from it.

pi·er·id (pī er′id, pī′ər-), *adj.* **1.** belonging or pertaining to the Pieridae, a family of butterflies comprising the whites, sulfurs, etc. —*n.* **2.** Also called **pi·er·i·dine** (pī er′i dīn′, -din). any member of the butterfly family Pieridae. [1880–85; < NL *Pieridae,* appar. by haplology from **Pierididae,* equiv. to *Pierid-,* s. of *Pieris* a genus (< Gk *Pierís,* sing. of *Pierídes* a name for the Muses; see PIERIDES) + *-idae* -ID[2]]

Pi·e·ri·des (pī er′i dēz′), *n.pl. Class. Myth.* **1.** the Muses. **2.** nine Thessalian maidens who challenged the Muses to a singing contest, lost, and were changed into magpies for insulting the victors.

Pie·ro del·la Fran·ce·sca (pē âr′ō del′ə fran-ches′kə, frän-; *It.* pye′RÔ del′lä frän che′skä), (*Piero de' Franceschi*). See **Francesca, Piero della.** Also called **Pie′ro.**

Pie·ro di Co·si·mo (pē âr′ō di kō′zə mō′; *It.* pye′RÔ dē kô′zē mô), (*Piero di Lorenzo*), 1462–1521, Italian painter.

Pierre (pēr *for 1;* pē âr′ *or, Fr.,* pyeR *for 2*), *n.* **1.** a city in and the capital of South Dakota, in the central part, on the Missouri River. 11,973. **2.** a male given name, form of **Peter.**

Pi·er·rette (pē′ə ret′; *Fr.* pye RET′), *n., pl.* **-rettes** (-rets′; *Fr.* -RET′). (*sometimes l.c.*) the female counterpart of a Pierrot, usually accompanying him, as in an entertainment or masquerade. [1885–90]

Pi·er·rot (pē′ə rō′; *Fr.* pye RŌ′), *n., pl.* **-rots** (-rōz′; *Fr.* -RŌ′). **1.** a male character in certain French pantomime, having a whitened face and wearing a loose, white, fancy costume. **2.** (*l.c.*) an actor, masquerader, or buffoon so made up. [1735–45; < F, dim. of *Pierre* Peter]

Pier·rot Lu·naire (pē′ə rō′ lōō nâr′; *Fr.* pye RŌ LY-NER′), a cycle of 21 songs (1912) for voice and instruments, by Arnold Schönberg, written in *Sprechgesang* style and set to poems of Albert Giraud in German translation.

pier·shed (pēr′shed′), *n.* See under **transit shed.** [PIER + SHED[1]]

Piers Plow·man (pērz′ plou′mən), (*The Vision Concerning Piers Plowman*) an alliterative poem written in three versions (1360–99), ascribed to William Langland.

pier′ ta′ble, a low table or console intended to be set between two windows, often beneath a pier glass. [1825–35]

pies (pīz), *n.* **1.** pl. of **pi[2]**. **2.** pl. of **pie.**

pi·et (pī′it), *n.* **1.** *Scot.* a magpie. **2.** *Scot. and North Eng.* a talkative person; one who chatters. [1175–1225; PIE[2] + -ET; r. ME *piot* < OF, equiv. to *pie* PIE[2] + *-ot* dim. suffix]

Pie·tà (pē′ā tä′, pyā tä′, pē ā′tə, pyā′-), *n.* (*sometimes l.c.*) *Fine Arts.* a representation of the Virgin Mary mourning over the body of the dead Christ, usually shown held on her lap. [1635–45; < It: lit., pity < L *pietās* PIETY; cf. PITY]

Pi·e·tas (pī′i tas′), *n.* the ancient Roman personification of familial affection, patriotism, and piety.

Pie·ter·mar·itz·burg (pē′tər mar′its bûrg′), *n.* a city in and the capital of Natal province, in the E Republic of South Africa. 158,921.

Pi·e·tism (pī′i tiz′əm), *n.* **1.** a movement, originating in the Lutheran Church in Germany in the 17th century, that stressed personal piety over religious formality and orthodoxy. **2.** the principles and practices of the Pietists. **3.** (*l.c.*) intensity of religious devotion or feeling. **4.** (*l.c.*) exaggeration or affectation of piety. [1690–1700; < G *Pietismus* < L *piet(ās)* PIETY + G *-ismus* -ISM] **—Pi′e·tist,** *n.* **—pi′e·tis′tic, pi′e·tis′ti·cal,** *adj.* **—pi′e·tis′ti·cal·ly,** *adv.* **—Syn. 4.** sanctimony.

pi·e·ty (pī′i tē), *n., pl.* **-ties. 1.** reverence for God or devout fulfillment of religious obligations: *a prayer full of piety.* **2.** the quality or state of being pious: *saintly piety.* **3.** dutiful respect or regard for parents, homeland, etc.: *filial piety.* **4.** a pious act, remark, belief, or the like: *the pieties and sacrifices of an austere life.* [1275–1325; ME *piete* < MF < L *pietās,* equiv. to *pi(us)* + *-etās,* var. (after *i*) of *-itās;* see PIOUS, -ITY] **—Syn. 1.** respect, veneration, awe. **2.** godliness, devotion, devoutness, sanctity, holiness. **—Ant.** irreverence.

piezoelec′tric ceram′ic, any ceramic that exhibits piezoelectric properties.

piezoelec′tric effect′, the property exhibited by some nonconducting crystals of becoming electrically polarized when mechanically strained and of becoming mechanically strained when an electric field is applied.

pi·e·zo·e·lec·tric·i·ty (pī ē′zō i lek tris′i tē, -ē′lek-, pē ā′zō-), *n.* electricity, or electric polarity, produced by the piezoelectric effect. [1890–95; < Gk *piéz(ein)* to press + -o- + ELECTRICITY] **—pi·e·zo·e·lec·tric** (pī ē′zō i lek′trik, pē ā′-), *adj.* **—pi·e′zo·e·lec′tri·cal·ly,** *adv.*

pi·e·zom·e·ter (pī′ə zom′i tər, pē′ə-), *n.* any of several instruments for measuring the pressure of a fluid or the compressibility of a substance when subjected to such a pressure. [1810–20; < Gk *piéz(ein)* to press + -o- + -METER] **—pi·e·zo·met·ric** (pī ē′zə me′trik, pē ā′-), **pi·e′zo·met′ri·cal,** *adj.*

pi·e·zom·e·try (pī′ə zom′i trē, pē′ə-), *n.* the measurement of pressure or compressibility. [< Gk *piéz(ein)* to press + -o- + -METRY]

pif·fle (pif′əl), *n., v.,* **-fled, -fling.** *Informal.* —*n.* **1.** nonsense, as trivial or senseless talk. —*v.i.* **2.** to talk nonsense. [1840–50; perh. akin to PUFF]

pif·fling (pif′ling), *adj.* of little worth; trifling; piddling: *piffling efforts.* [1890–95; PIFFLE + -ING[2]]

pig[1] (pig), *n., v.,* **pigged, pig·ging.** —*n.* **1.** a young swine of either sex, esp. a domestic hog, *Sus scrofa,* weighing less than 120 lb. (220 kg.) **2.** any wild or domestic swine. **3.** the flesh of swine; pork. **4.** a person of piglike character, behavior, or habits, as one who is gluttonous, very fat, greedy, selfish, or filthy. **5.** *Slang.* a slatternly, sluttish woman. **6.** *Disparaging.* a police officer. **7.** *Mach.* any tool or device, as a long-handled brush or scraper, used to clear the interior of a pipe or duct. **8.** *Metall.* **a.** an oblong mass of metal that has been run while still molten into a mold of sand or the like, esp. such a mass of iron from a blast furnace. **b.** one of the molds for such masses of metal. **c.** metal in the form of such masses. **d.** pig iron. **9. on the pig's back,** *Australian Slang.* in a fortunate position. —*v.t.* **10.** to mold (metal) into pigs. **11.** *Informal.* to eat (something) quickly; gulp: *He pigged three doughnuts and ran off to school.* —*v.i.* **12.** to bring forth pigs; farrow. **13. pig it, a.** to live like a pig, esp. in dirt. **b.** to lead a disorganized, makeshift life; live without plan or pattern. **14. pig out,** *Slang.* to overindulge in eating: *We pigged out on pizza last night.* [1175–1225; ME *pigge* young pig, with doubled consonant appropriate to terms for smaller animals (cf. DOG, FROG[1]) but with no obvious relations; almost certainly not akin to LG, D *big(ge),* MD *vigghe* young pig, which involve further obscurities; if Dan *pige,* Sw *piga* maid, young girl are compared, perh. < ON word meaning "young, small," applied in Scand to girls but in OE to swine]

pig[1] (def. 1), *Sus scrofa*

pig[2] (pig), *n. Scot. and North Eng.* **1.** an earthenware crock, pot, pitcher, or jar. **2.** potter's clay; earthenware as a material. [1400–50; late ME *pygg* < ?]

Pi·galle (*Fr.* pē GAL′), *n.* See **Place Pigalle.**

pig′ bed′, *Metall.* a bed of sand for molding pigs into which molten metal is poured. [1815–25]

pig·boat (pig′bōt′), *n. Older Slang.* a submarine. [1920–25, *Amer.;* PIG[1] + BOAT]

pig′ boil′ing, *Metall.* See **wet puddling.** [1855–60]

pi·geon[1] (pij′ən), *n.* **1.** any bird of the family Columbidae, having a compact body and short legs, esp. the larger species with square or rounded tails. Cf. **dove[1]** (def. 1). **2.** a domesticated member of this family, as one of the varieties of the rock dove. **3.** *Slang.* **a.** a young, usually attractive, girl. **b.** a person who is easily fooled or cheated; dupe. **4.** *Poker Slang.* a card, acquired in the draw, that greatly improves a hand or makes it a winner. [1350–1400; ME *pejon* young dove < MF *pijon* < LL *pipiōn-* (s. of *pipiō*) squab, akin to *pipire, pipāre* to chirp]

pi·geon[2] (pij′ən), *n.* (not in technical use) pidgin; pidgin English.

pi′geon blood′, dark red. Also, **pi′geon's blood′.** [1890–95]

pi′geon breast′, *Pathol.* See **chicken breast.** Also called **pi′geon chest′.** [1840–50] **—pi′geon-breast′·ed,** *adj.* **—pi′geon-breast′ed·ness,** *n.*

pi′geon clock′. See **pigeon timer.**

pi′geon drop′, a confidence game or sleight-of-hand swindle whereby cash is extracted from the victim as collateral for a supposed share in a large sum of discovered money, dishonest profits, or gambling winnings, which in fact are nonexistent. [1935–40, *Amer.;* so called because such swindles orig. began with the dropping of a wallet in front of the intended victim, the *pigeon*]

pi′geon grape′. See **summer grape.**

pi′geon guil′lemot. See under **guillemot** (def. 1).

pi′geon hawk′, merlin. [1720–30, *Amer.*]

pi·geon-heart·ed (pij′ən här′tid), *adj.* timid; meek. [1615–25]

pi·geon·hole (pij′ən hōl′), *n., v.,* **-holed, -hol·ing.** —*n.* **1.** one of a series of small, open compartments, as in a desk, cabinet, or the like, used for filing or sorting papers, letters, etc. **2.** a hole or recess, or one of a series of recesses, for pigeons to nest in. **3.** Also called **pi′geon hole′, white hole.** *Print.* white space created by setting words or lines too far apart. —*v.t.* **4.** to assign to a definite place or to definite places in some orderly system: *to pigeonhole new ideas.* **5.** to lay aside for use or reference at some later, indefinite time: *We must pigeonhole this excellent plan until the time is ripe.* **6.** to put aside for the present, esp. with the intention of ignoring or forgetting, often indefinitely: *to pigeonhole an unwanted invitation.* **7.** to place in or as if in a pigeonhole or pigeonholes: *to pigeonhole papers.* **8.** to fit or provide with pigeonholes: *The desk must be pigeonholed for all my papers.* [1570–80; PIGEON[1] + HOLE] **—Syn. 4.** categorize, catalog. **5.** file. **6.** postpone, shelve.

pi·geon·ite (pij′ə nīt′), *n. Mineral.* a monoclinic variety of pyroxene consisting mainly of a mixture of $(MgFe)SiO_3$ and $CaMg(SiO_3)_2$. [1895–1900; named after *Pigeon* Point, NE Minnesota; see -ITE[1]]

pi·geon-liv·ered (pij′ən liv′ərd), *adj.* meek-tempered; spiritless; mild. [1595–1605]

pi′geon milk′. See **crop milk.** [1885–90]

pi′geon pea′, **1.** a tropical shrub, *Cajanus cajan,* having showy yellow flowers. **2.** the brown, edible seed of this plant. [1715–25]

pi′geon pox′, *Vet. Pathol.* a disease affecting pigeons, similar to fowl pox. Also, **pi·geon·pox** (pij′ən-poks′).

pi′geon tim′er, a device for timing the arrivals of pigeons being raced, consisting of a magazine for holding the identification bands of the contestants in the order in which they are inserted and a recording clock to register the times of insertion. Also called **pigeon clock.**

pi·geon-toed (pij′ən tōd′), *adj.* having the toes or feet turned inward. [1795–1805]

pi·geon·wing (pij′ən wing′), *n.* **1.** a particular figure in skating, outlining the spread wing of a pigeon. **2.** a similar fancy step or evolution in dancing. [1775–85; PIGEON[1] + WING]

pig·fish (pig′fish′), *n., pl.* **-fish·es,** (*esp. collectively*) **-fish.** a grunt, *Orthopristis chrysoptera,* living in waters off the Atlantic coast of the southern U.S. [1800–10, *Amer.;* PIG[1] + FISH]

pig·ger·y (pig′ə rē), *n., pl.* **-ger·ies.** *Chiefly Brit.* a pigsty or pig breeder's establishment. [1795–1805; PIG[1] + -ERY]

pig·gie (pig′ē), *n., adj.,* **-gi·er, -gi·est.** piggy.

pig·gin (pig′in), *n.* **1.** *Dial.* a small wooden pail or tub with a handle formed by continuing one of the staves above the rim. **2.** See **cream pail.** [1545–55; perh. akin to PIG[2]]

pig′ging string′, (in rodeo calf roping) a short length of rope used to bind a calf's legs after it is lassoed. Also, **pig′gin′ string′** (pig′in). [1925–30, *Amer.;* appar. PIG[1] + -ING[1]]

pig·gish (pig′ish), *adj.* **1.** resembling a pig, esp. in being slovenly, greedy, or gluttonous: *piggish table manners.* **2.** (of food portions) indecently large. **3.** stubborn. [1810–20; PIG[1] + -ISH[1]] **—pig′gish·ly,** *adv.* **—pig′gish·ness,** *n.*

pig·gy (pig′ē), *n., pl.* **-gies,** *adj.,* **-gi·er, -gi·est.** —*n.* **1.** a small or young pig. —*adj.* **2.** *Informal.* piggish. **3.** (of a sow) in an advanced state of pregnancy. Also, **piggie.** [1790–1800; (def. 1) PIG[1] + -Y[2]; (defs. 2 and 3) PIG[1] + -Y[1]] **—pig′gi·ness,** *n.*

pig·gy·back (pig′ē bak′), *adv.* **1.** on the back or shoulders: *The little girl rode piggyback on her father.* —*adj.* **2.** astride the back or shoulders: *a piggyback ride.* **3.** sharing commercial time, space, etc.: *piggyback advertising.* **4.** carryable or attachable: *a piggyback turbine unit.* **5.** added or tacked on; supplementary: *a piggyback clause.* **6.** noting or pertaining to the carrying of one vehicle or the like by another, as the carrying of loaded truck trailers on flatcars. —*v.t.* **7.** to attach or ally to as or as if a part of the same thing: *to piggyback human rights agreements with foreign aid.* **8.** to carry (somebody) on the back or shoulders. **9.** to carry (truck trailers) by railroad on flatcars. **10.** *Radio and Television Slang.* to advertise (two or more products) in the same commercial. —*v.i.* **11.** to be transported aboard or atop another carrier: *The space shuttle piggybacked on the airplane.* **12.** to use, appropriate, or exploit the availability, services, or facilities of another: *private clinics piggybacking on federal health-care facilities.* **13.** to carry truck trailers by railroad on flatcars. —*n.* **14.** a house trailer designed to fit over a pickup truck. **15.** a truck trailer carried on a flatcar. **16.** anything that operates in connection with or as part of another. Also, **pickaback** (for defs. 1, 2). [1580–90; alter. of PICKABACK]

pig′gyback car′, *Railroads.* a flatcar designed to accommodate containers or highway truck trailers.

pig′gyback plant′, a plant, *Tolmiea menziesii,* of the saxifrage family, native to western North America, that produces new plants at the base of its broad, hairy leaves and that is popular as a houseplant. Also called **pickaback plant.**

pig′gy bank′, **1.** a small bank, having the shape of a pig, provided with a slot at the top to receive small coins. **2.** any small bank in which coins are kept. [1940–45]

pig·head·ed (pig′hed′id), *adj.* stupidly obstinate; stubborn: *pigheaded resistance.* [1610–20; PIG[1] + -HEADED] **—pig′head′ed·ly,** *adv.* **—pig′head′ed·ness,** *n.* **—Syn.** bullheaded, mulish.

pig′ in a poke′, something not adequately appraised or of undetermined value, as an offering or purchase. [1520–30]

pig′ i′ron, **1.** iron tapped from a blast furnace and cast into pigs in preparation for conversion into steel, cast iron, or wrought iron. **2.** iron in the chemical state in which it exists when tapped from the blast furnace, without alloying or refinement. [1655–65]

pig′ Lat′in, a form of language, used esp. by children, that is derived from ordinary English by moving the first consonant or consonant cluster of each word to the end of the word and adding the sound (ā), as in *Eakspay igpay atinlay* for "Speak Pig Latin." [1935–40]

pig′ lead′ (led), lead molded in pigs. [1785–95]

pig·let (pig′lit), *n.* a little pig. [1880–85; PIG[1] + -LET]

pig·ling (pig′ling), *n.* a young or small pig; piglet. [1705–15; PIG[1] + -LING[1]]

pig·ment (pig′mənt), *n.* **1.** a dry insoluble substance, usually pulverized, which when suspended in a liquid vehicle becomes a paint, ink, etc. **2.** a coloring matter or substance. **3.** *Biol.* any substance whose presence in the tissues or cells of animals or plants colors them. —*v.t.* **4.** to color; add pigment to. —*v.i.* **5.** to become pigmented; acquire color; develop pigmentation: *a poor quality of paper that doesn't pigment well.* [1350–1400; ME < L *pigmentum* paint, equiv. to *pig-* (s. of *pingere* to PAINT) + *-mentum* -MENT]

pig·men·tar·y (pig′mən ter′ē), *adj.* of, pertaining to, having, or producing pigment. [1425–75; late ME: a dyer < L *pigmentārius.* See PIGMENT, -ARY]

pig·men·ta·tion (pig′mən tā′shən), *n.* **1.** coloration, esp. of the skin. **2.** *Biol.* coloration with or deposition of pigment. [1865–70; < LL *pigmentāt(us)* painted, colored (see PIGMENT, -ATE[1]) + -ION]

Pig·my (pig′mē), *n., pl.* **-mies,** *adj.* Pygmy.

pi·gno·li·a (pēn yō′lē ə), *n.* See **pine nut** (def. 1). [1895–1900; < It *pignol(o)* + *-ia* -IA; cf. L *pīneus* of PINE]

pi·gnon (pēn′yon), *n.* the edible seed of the cones of certain pines, as the nut pine, *Pinus pinea,* of southern Europe. [1595–1605; < Sp *piñón;* cf. L *pīneus* of PINE]

pig·nus (pig′nəs), *n., pl.* **-no·ra** (-nər ə). *Roman and Civil Law.* **1.** property held as security for a debt. **2.** the contract containing such a pledge. [< L: lit., pledge]

pig·nut (pig′nut′), *n.* **1.** the nut of the brown hickory, *Carya glabra,* of North America. **2.** the tree itself. **3.** the tuber of a European plant, *Conopodium denudatum.* [1600–10; PIG[1] + NUT]

pig-out (pig′out′), *n. Slang.* an instance of overindulging in eating; food binge. [1975–80; n. use of v. phrase *pig out*]

pig·pen (pig′pen′), *n.* **1.** a pen for keeping pigs. **2.** a filthy or untidy place: *This kitchen is a pigpen.* [1795–1805; PIG[1] + PEN[2]]

Pigs (pigz), *n.* **Bay of.** See **Bay of Pigs.**

pig's′ ears′, either of two common edible North American fungi, *Peziza badia* and *Discina perlata.*

pigs′ feet′, *Cookery.* the feet of swine cooked and marinated. Also called **pickled pigs' feet.**

pigs′ in blan′kets, *sing.* **pig in a blanket. 1.** frankfurters or small sausages wrapped in dough and baked or broiled. **2.** oysters, chicken livers, etc., wrapped in bacon, skewered, and broiled or sautéed.

pig·skin (pig′skin′), *n.* **1.** the skin of a pig. **2.** leather made from it. **3.** *Informal.* a saddle. **4.** *Informal.* a football. [1850–55; PIG[1] + SKIN]

pigs·ney (pigz′nē), *n. Obs.* **1.** a darling. **2.** an eye. [1350–1400; ME *piggesnye,* earlier *piggesneyge,* equiv. to *pigges* pig's (see PIG[1], 's[1]) + *n-* (prob. extracted from *an,* indefinite article) + *-ye, eyge* EYE]

pig·stick (pig′stik′), *v.i.* to hunt for wild boar, usually on horseback and using a spear. [1890–95; PIG[1] + STICK[1]] —**pig′stick′er,** *n.*

pig·sty (pig′stī′), *n., pl.* **-sties.** pigpen. [1585–95; PIG[1] + STY[1]]

pig·tail (pig′tāl′), *n.* **1.** a braid of hair hanging down the back of the head. **2.** tobacco in a thin, twisted roll. **3.** *Elect.* **a.** a short, flexible wire used in connecting a stationary terminal with a terminal having a limited range of motion. **b.** a short wire connected to an electric device, as a lead or ground. [1680–90; PIG[1] + TAIL[1]]

pig′-tailed macaque′ (pig′tāld′), a forest-dwelling southeast Asian macaque, *Macaca nemestrina,* having a short, curled tail, colonized for animal behavior studies. Also, **pig′tailed′ macaque′.** [1930–35]

pig′tail hook′, a screw hook having an eye in the form of a spiral for holding a loop, chain link, etc., at any angle.

pig·weed (pig′wēd′), *n.* **1.** any goosefoot of the genus *Chenopodium,* esp. *C. album.* **2.** any of certain amaranths, as *Amaranthus retroflexus.* [1795–1805; PIG[1] + WEED[1]]

PIK, *n.* payment in kind. Also, **p.i.k.**

pi·ka (pī′kə), *n.* any of several small, brown to gray tailless mammals of the genus *Ochotona,* resembling rabbits with short ears and legs and inhabiting western mountains of North America and parts of eastern Europe and Asia. [1820–30; recorded by the German naturalist P.S. Pallas (1741–1811) as the name for the animal in Evenki; cf. Evenki (N Baikal dial.) *pikačān* a name for the tree creeper (*Certhia familiaris*), appar. based on Russ *pikat'* to squeak, peep (cf. Russ *pishchúkha* a name for both the tree creeper and the pika, which emits a shrill sound)]

pi·ka·ke (pē′kä kā′), *n.* a climbing vine, *Jasminium sambac,* of the olive family, probably of Asian origin, having fragrant white flowers used to flavor jasmine tea and, in Hawaii, to make leis. [1935–40; < Hawaiian *pīkake* lit., PEACOCK, allegedly a name given to the plant by the Hawaiian princess Ka'iu-lani (1875–99)]

pike[1] (pīk), *n., pl.* (*esp. collectively*) **pike,** (*esp. referring to two or more kinds or species*) **pikes. 1.** any of several large, slender, voracious freshwater fishes of the genus *Esox,* having a long, flat snout: the blue pike of the Great Lakes is now extinct. **2.** any of various superficially similar fishes, as the walleye or pikeperch. [1275–1325; ME; so called from its pointed snout (see PIKE[5])] —**pike′like′,** *adj.*

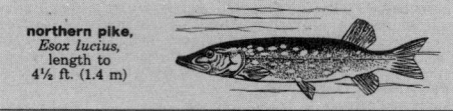

northern pike, *Esox lucius,* length to 4½ ft. (1.4 m)

pike[2] (pīk), *n., v.,* **piked, pik·ing.** —*n.* **1.** a shafted weapon having a pointed head, formerly used by infantry. —*v.t.* **2.** to pierce, wound, or kill with or as with a pike. [1505–15; < MF *pique,* fem. var. of *pic* PICK[2] < Gmc. See PIKE[5], PIQUE[1]]

pike[3] (pīk), *n.* **1.** a toll road or highway; turnpike road. **2.** a turnpike or tollgate. **3.** the toll paid at a tollgate. **4. come down the pike,** *Informal.* to appear or come forth: *the greatest idea that ever came down the pike.* [1820–30, *Amer.;* short for TURNPIKE]

pike[4] (pīk), *n. Chiefly Brit.* a hill or mountain with a pointed summit. [1350–1400; ME; special use of PIKE[5]; cf. OE *hornpīc* pinnacle]

pike[5] (pīk), *n.* **1.** a sharply pointed projection or spike. **2.** the pointed end of anything, as of an arrow or a spear. [bef. 900; ME *pik* pick, spike, (pilgrim's) staff, OE *pīc* pointed tool. See PICK[2]]

pike[6] (pīk), *v.i.,* **piked, pik·ing.** *Older Slang.* to go, leave, or move along quickly. [1425–75; late ME *pyke* (reflexive); perh. orig. to equip oneself with a walking stick. See PIKE[5]]

pike[7] (pīk), *n. Diving, Gymnastics.* a body position, resembling a V shape, in which the back and head are bent forward and the legs lifted and held together, with the hands touching the feet or backs of the knees or the arms extended sideways. Cf. **layout** (def. 10), **tuck[1]** (def. 14). [1955–60; perh. special use of PIKE[1]]

Pike (pīk), *n.* **1. James Albert,** 1913–69, U.S. Protestant Episcopal clergyman, lawyer, and author. **2. Zeb·u·lon Montgomery** (zeb′yo͝o lən), 1779–1813, U.S. general and explorer.

pike·blen·ny (pīk′blen′ē), *n., pl.* (*esp. collectively*) **-ny,** (*esp. referring to two or more kinds or species*) **-nies.** any of several tropical American clinid fishes of the genus *Chaenopsis,* as *C. ocellata* **(bluethroat pikeblenny),** the male of which is noted for its aggressive behavior in defending its territory. [PIKE[1] + BLENNY]

piked′ dog′fish, *Brit.* the spiny dogfish. [1870–75]

pike·man (pīk′mən), *n., pl.* **-men.** a soldier armed with a pike. [1540–50; PIKE[2] + -MAN]

pike·perch (pīk′pûrch′), *n., pl.* (*esp. collectively*) **-perch,** (*esp. referring to two or more kinds or species*) **-perch·es.** any of several pikelike fishes of the perch family, esp. the walleye, *Stizostedion vitreum.* [1835–45, *Amer.;* PIKE[1] + PERCH[2]]

pike′ pole′, (in lumbering) a long pole with a metal point and a fixed hook, for catching and guiding logs. [1820–30, *Amer.*]

pik·er (pī′kər), *n. Informal.* **1.** a person who does anything in a contemptibly small or cheap way. **2.** a stingy, tight-fisted person; tightwad. **3.** a person who gambles, speculates, etc., in a small, cautious way. [1275–1325; ME: petty thief, equiv. to *pik(en)* to PICK[1] + -ER[1]; cf. dial. (N England, Scots, Hiberno-E) *pike* to PICK[1]]
—**Syn. 2.** cheapskate, penny pincher, skinflint.

Pikes′ Peak′, a mountain in central Colorado: a peak of the Rocky Mountains. 14,108 ft. (4300 m).

pike·staff (pīk′staf′, -stäf′), *n., pl.* **-staves** (-stāvz′). **1.** the shaft of an infantry pike. **2.** a foot traveler's staff with a metal point or spike at the lower end. [1325–75; ME *pykstaf.* See PIKE[5], STAFF[1]]

Pikes·ville (pīks′vil), *n.* a town in central Maryland, near Baltimore. 22,555.

Pik Po·be·dy (pyēk′ pu bye′di), Russian name of **Pobeda Peak.**

pil., (in prescriptions) pill. [< L *pilula*]

pi·laf (pi läf′, pē′läf), *n.* **1.** a Middle Eastern dish consisting of sautéed, seasoned rice steamed in bouillon, sometimes with poultry, meat or shellfish. **2.** rice cooked in a meat or poultry broth. Also, **pi·laff′, pilau, pilaw.** [1925–30; < Turk *pilâv* < Pers *pilāw*]

pi·lar (pī′lər), *adj.* of, pertaining to, or covered with hair. [1855–60; < NL *pilāris* of hair. See PILE[3], -AR[1]]

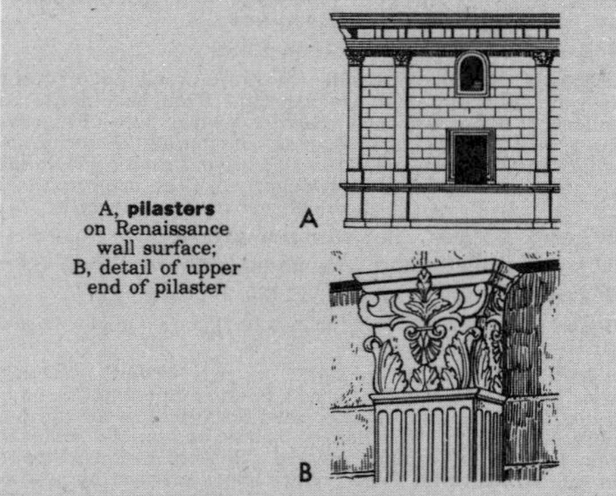

A, pilasters on Renaissance wall surface; B, detail of upper end of pilaster

pi·las·ter (pi las′tər), *n. Archit.* a shallow rectangular feature projecting from a wall, having a capital and base and usually imitating the form of a column. [1565–75; PILE[1] (in obs. sense "pillar") + -ASTER[1], modeled on It *pilastro* or ML *pīlastrum*]

pi·las·tered (pi las′tərd), *adj.* having, or supported by, pilasters. [1680–90; PILASTER + -ED[3]]

pilas′ter mass′, *Archit.* an engaged pier, usually plain, used as a buttress.

pilas′ter strip′, *Archit.* a pilaster mass of relatively slight projection. [1870–75]

pil·as·trade (pil′ə strād′, pil′ə strād′), *n.* a row of pilasters. [1720–30; < It *pilastrata.* See PILASTER, -ADE[1]]

Pi·late (pī′lət), *n.* **Pon·tius** (pon′shəs, -tē əs), fl. early 1st century A.D., Roman procurator of Judea A.D. 26–36?: the final authority concerned in the condemnation and execution of Jesus Christ.

Pi·la·tus (*Ger.* pē lä′to͝os), *n.* a mountain in central Switzerland, near Lucerne: a peak of the Alps; cable railway. 6998 ft. (2130 m).

pi·lau (pi läf′, pē′läf, pi lô′, -lou′, pē′lô, -lou), *n.* pilaf. Also, **pi·law′.**

pilch (pilch), *n.* an infant's wrapper worn over a diaper. [bef. 1000; ME *pilche* a kind of outer garment, OE *pylece* < ML *pellicia* a furred garment, L *pellicea,* fem. of *pelliceus* of skins, hides, deriv. of *pellis* a skin]

pil·chard (pil′chərd), *n.* **1.** a small, southern European, marine fish, *Sardina pilchardus,* related to the herring but smaller and rounder. **2.** any of several related fishes, as *Sardinops caeruleus,* common off the California coast. [1520–30; earlier *pilcher;* orig. uncert.]

Pil·co·ma·yo (pēl′kô mä′yô), *n.* a river in S central South America, flowing SE from S Bolivia along the boundary between Paraguay and Argentina to the Paraguay River at Asunción. 1000 mi. (1610 km) long.

pil·crow (pil′krō), *n.* a paragraph mark. [1400–50; appar. alter. (perh. conformed to CROW[1]) of late ME *pylcraft(e),* perh. < OF *paragrafe, pelagraphe* PARAGRAPH]

pile[1] (pīl), *n., v.,* **piled, pil·ing.** —*n.* **1.** an assemblage of things laid or lying one upon the other: *a pile of papers; a pile of bricks.* **2.** *Informal.* a large number, quantity, or amount of anything: *a pile of work.* **3.** a heap of wood on which a dead body, a living person, or a sacrifice is burned; pyre. **4.** a lofty or large building or group of buildings: *the noble pile of Windsor Castle.* **5.** *Informal.* a large accumulation of money: *They made a pile on Wall Street.* **6.** a bundle of pieces of iron ready to be welded and drawn out into bars; fagot. **7.** reactor (def. 4). **8.** *Elect.* See **voltaic pile.** —*v.t.* **9.** to lay or dispose in a pile (often fol. by *up*): *to pile up the fallen autumn leaves.* **10.** to accumulate or store (often fol. by *up*): *to pile up money; squirrels piling up nuts against the winter.* **11.** to cover or load with a pile: *He piled the wagon with hay.* —*v.i.* **12.** to accumulate, as money, debts, evidence, etc. (usually fol. by *up*). **13.** *Informal.* to move as a group in a more or less confused, disorderly cluster: *to pile off a train.* **14.** to gather, accumulate, or rise in a pile or piles (often fol. by *up*): *The snow is piling up on the roofs.* [1350–1400; ME < MF < L *pīla* pillar, mole of stone]
—**Syn. 1.** collection, heap, mass, accumulation, stack.

pile[2] (pīl), *n., v.,* **piled, pil·ing.** —*n.* **1.** a cylindrical or flat member of wood, steel, concrete, etc., often tapered or pointed at the lower end, hammered vertically into soil to form part of a foundation or retaining wall. **2.** *Heraldry.* an ordinary in the form of a wedge or triangle coming from one edge of the escutcheon, from the chief unless otherwise specified. **3.** *Archery.* the sharp head or striking end of an arrow, usually of metal and of the form of a wedge or conical nub. **4. in pile,** *Heraldry.* (of a number of charges) arranged in the manner of a pile. —*v.t.* **5.** to furnish, strengthen, or support with piles. **6.** to drive piles into. [bef. 1000; ME; OE *pīl* shaft < L *pīlum* javelin]

pile[3] (pīl), *n.* **1.** hair. **2.** soft, fine hair or down. **3.** wool, fur, or pelage. **4.** a fabric with a surface of upright yarns, cut or looped, as corduroy, Turkish toweling, velvet, and velveteen. **5.** such a surface. **6.** one of the strands in such a surface. [1300–50; ME *piles* hair, plumage < L *pilus* hair; *-i-* short in L but long in Anglicized school pronunciation]

pile[4] (pīl), *n.* Usually, **piles. 1.** a hemorrhoid. **2.** the condition of having hemorrhoids. [1375–1425; late ME *pyles* (pl.) < L *pilae* lit., balls. See PILL[1]]

pile[5] (pīl), *n.* the lower of two dies for coining by hand. [1350–1400; ME *pyl* reverse of a coin < ML *pīla,* special use of L *pīla* PILE[1]]

pi·le·a (pī′lē ə, pil′ē ə), *n.* any of numerous plants belonging to the genus *Pilea,* of the nettle family, many species of which are cultivated for their ornamental foliage. [< NL (1821), coinage based on L *pileus, pilleus* skullcap (see PILEUS, -A[2]); orig. so called because one of the three sepals forms a hood over the fruit]

pi·le·ate (pī′lē it, -āt′, pil′ē-), *adj. Bot., Zool.* having a pileus. [1820–30; < L *pileātus* capped. See PILEUS, -ATE[1]]

pi·le·at·ed (pī′lē ā′tid, pil′ē-), *adj. Ornith.* crested. [1720–30; PILEATE + -ED[2]]

pi′leated wood′pecker, a large, black-and-white American woodpecker, *Dryocopus pileatus,* having a prominent red crest. [1775–85, *Amer.*]

pileated woodpecker, *Dryocopus pileatus,* length 17 to 19½ in. (43 to 50 cm)

CONCISE ETYMOLOGY KEY: <, descended or borrowed from; >, whence; b., blend of, blended; c., cognate with; cf., compare; deriv., derivative; equiv., equivalent; imit., imitative; obl., oblique; r., replacing; s., stem; sp., spelling, spelled; resp., respelling, respelled; trans., translation; ?, origin unknown; *, unattested; ‡, probably earlier than. See the full key inside the front cover.

piled (pīld), *adj.* having a pile, as velvet and other fabrics. [1400–50; late ME: covered with hair; see PILE[3], -ED[3]]

pile′ driv′er, **1.** a machine for driving piles, usually composed of a tall framework in which either a weight is raised and dropped on a pile head or in which a steam hammer drives the pile. **2.** a person who operates such a machine. **3.** a person who hits or attacks forcefully or powerfully. **4.** *Wrestling.* a move whereby an opponent is turned upside down and slammed headfirst to the mat. **5.** *Brit. Sports.* a powerful stroke, hit, kick, etc. [1765–75]

pile′ fend′er. See **fender pile.**

pi·le·o·lat·ed (pī′lē ə lā′tid, pil′ē-), *adj.* pileated.

pi′leolated war′bler, either of two western subspecies of Wilson's warbler.

pi·le·ous (pī′lē əs, pil′ē-), *adj.* hairy or furry. [1835–45; PILE[3] + -OUS]

pi·le·um (pī′lē əm, pil′ē-), *n., pl.* **pi·le·a** (pī′lē ə, pil′ē ə). the top of the head of a bird, from the base of the bill to the nape. [1870–75; < NL, special use of L *pīleum*, var. of *pīleus* skullcap]

pile·up (pīl′up′), *n.* **1.** a massive collision of several or many moving vehicles. **2.** an accumulation, as of work, chores, or bills. **3.** a rough or disorderly falling of people upon one another, as in a football game. [1825–35; n. use of v. phrase *pile up*]

pi·le·us (pī′lē əs, pil′ē-), *n., pl.* **pi·le·i** (pī′lē ī′, pil′ē ī′) for 1, 2, 4, **pi·le·us** for 3. **1.** *Mycol.* the horizontal portion of a mushroom, bearing gills, tubes, etc., on its underside; a cap. See diag. under **mushroom. 2.** *Zool.* **a.** the umbrella or bell of a jellyfish. **b.** pileum. **3.** Also called **cap cloud, scarf cloud.** *Meteorol.* a small, thin cloud just above or attached to a growing cumulus cloud. **4.** a felt skullcap worn by the ancient Romans and Greeks. [1750–60; < NL, special use of L *pileus* skullcap; akin to Gk *pîlos* felt, felt cap]

pile·wort (pīl′wûrt′, -wôrt′), *n.* **1.** Also called **fireweed.** a weedy composite plant, *Erechtites hieracifolia*, having narrow flower heads enclosed in green bracts. **2.** a North American figwort, *Scrophularia marilandica*, having small, greenish flowers. **3.** See **lesser celandine.** [1570–80; PILE[4] + WORT[1], so called from its use in medicine]

pil·fer (pil′fər), *v.i., v.t.* to steal, esp. in small quantities. [1540–50; v. use of late ME *pilfre* booty < MF *pelfre.* See PELF] —**pil′fer·er,** *n.*
—**Syn.** thieve, purloin, filch, appropriate.

pil·fer·age (pil′fər ij), *n.* **1.** the act or practice of pilfering; petty theft. **2.** something that is pilfered. [1620–30; PILFER + -AGE]

pil·gar·lic (pil gär′lik), *n.* **1.** a person regarded with mild or pretended contempt or pity. **2.** *Obs.* a baldheaded man. [1520–30; earlier *pyllyd garleke* lit., peeled garlic, orig. metaphor for a bald man, whose head is compared to a peeled garlic bulb. See PILL[2], GARLIC] —**pil·gar′lick·y,** *adj.*

pil·grim (pil′grim, -grəm), *n.* **1.** a person who journeys, esp. a long distance, to some sacred place as an act of religious devotion: *pilgrims to the Holy Land.* **2.** a traveler or wanderer, esp. in a foreign place. **3.** an original settler in a region. **4.** (*cap.*) one of the band of Puritans who founded the colony of Plymouth, Mass., in 1620. **5.** a newcomer to a region or place, esp. to the western U.S. [1150–1200; ME *pilegrim, pelegrim,* c. OFris *pilegrim,* MLG *pelegrim,* OHG *piligrim,* ON *pīlagrīmr,* all < ML *pelegrīnus,* dissimilated var. of L *peregrīnus* PEREGRINE] —**pil′gri·mat′ic, pil′gri·mat′i·cal,** *adj.*

pil·grim·age (pil′grə mij), *n., v.,* **-aged, -ag·ing.** —*n.* **1.** a journey, esp. a long one, made to some sacred place as an act of religious devotion: *a pilgrimage to Lourdes.* **2.** *Islam.* **a. the Pilgrimage,** hajj. **b.** ʿumrah. **3.** any long journey, esp. one undertaken as a quest or for a votive purpose, as to pay homage: *a pilgrimage to the grave of Shakespeare.* —*v.i.* **4.** to make a pilgrimage. [1200–50; ME *pilegrimage* (see PILGRIM, -AGE); r. earlier *pelrimage,* alter. of OF *pelerinage*]
—**Syn. 3.** excursion, tour. See **trip.**

pil′grim bot′tle, a flat-sided water bottle having two loops at the side of a short neck for a suspending cord or chain. Also, **pil′grim's bot′tle.** [1870–75]

Pil′grim's Prog′ress, an allegory (1678) by John Bunyan.

pi·li[1] (pē lē′), *n., pl.* **-lies. 1.** a Philippine tree, *Canarium ovatum,* the edible seeds of which taste like a sweet almond. **2.** Also called **pili′ nut′.** the seed of this tree. [< Tagalog]

pi·li[2] (pī′lī), *n. Biol.* pl. of **pilus.**

pili-, a combining form meaning "hair," used in the formation of compound words: *piliform.* [comb. form repr. L *pilus;* see -I-]

pi·lif·er·ous (pī lif′ər əs), *adj.* having or producing hair. [1840–50; PILI- + -FEROUS]

pil·i·form (pil′ə fôrm′), *adj.* having the form of a hair; resembling hair. [1820–30; < NL *piliformis.* See PILI-, -FORM]

pi·li·ki·a (pē′lē kē′ä), *n. Hawaiian.* trouble.

pil·ing (pī′ling), *n.* **1.** a mass of building piles considered collectively. **2.** a structure composed of piles. [1400–50; late ME *pylyng.* See PILE[2], -ING[1]]

Pil·i·pi·no (pil′ə pē′nō), *n.* a language essentially the same as Tagalog that has been adopted as the official national language of the Philippines. Also called **Filipino.**

pill[1] (pil), *n.* **1.** a small globular or rounded mass of medicinal substance, usually covered with a hard coating, that is to be swallowed whole. **2.** something unpleasant that has to be accepted or endured: *Ingratitude is a bitter pill.* **3.** *Slang.* a tiresomely disagreeable person. **4.** *Sports Slang.* a ball, esp. a baseball or golf ball. **5. the pill.** See **birth-control pill. 6. pills,** *Brit. Slang.* billiards. —*v.t.* **7.** to dose with pills. **8.** to form or make into pills. **9.** *Slang.* to blackball. —*v.i.* **10.** to form into small, pill-like balls, as the fuzz on a wool sweater. [1375–1425; late ME *pille* < MLG, MD *pille* << L *pilula,* dim. of *pila* ball; see -ULE]

pill[2] (pil), *v.t., v.i.* **1.** *Brit. Dial.* to peel. **2.** *Obs.* to become or cause to become bald. [bef. 1100; ME *pilen,* OE *pilian* to skin, peel < L *pilāre* to strip (said of hair). See PILE[3]]

pill[3] (pil), *v.t. Archaic.* to rob, plunder, or pillage. [1150–1200; ME; prob. conflation of PILL[2] with MF *piller* (see PILLAGE)]

pil·lage (pil′ij), *v.,* **-laged, -lag·ing,** *n.* —*v.t.* **1.** to strip ruthlessly of money or goods by open violence, as in war; plunder: *The barbarians pillaged every conquered city.* **2.** to take as booty. —*v.i.* **3.** to rob with open violence; take booty: *Soldiers roamed the countryside, pillaging and killing.* —*n.* **4.** the act of plundering, esp. in war. **5.** booty or spoil. [1350–1400; ME *pilage* (see PILL[3], -AGE), modeled on MF *pillage* (deriv. of *piller* to pillage, orig., to abuse, mistreat, tear, of uncert. orig.)] —**pil′lag·er,** *n.*
—**Syn. 1.** rob, sack, spoil, despoil, rape. **4.** rapine, depredation, spoliation. **5.** plunder.

pil·lar (pil′ər), *n.* **1.** an upright shaft or structure, of stone, brick, or other material, relatively slender in proportion to its height, and of any shape in section, used as a building support, or standing alone, as for a monument: *Gothic pillars; a pillar to commemorate Columbus.* **2.** a natural formation resembling such a construction: *a pillar of rock; a pillar of smoke.* **3.** any upright, supporting part; post: *the pillar of a table.* **4.** a person who is a chief supporter of a society, state, institution, etc.: *a pillar of the community.* **5.** *Horol.* any of several short parts for spacing and keeping in the proper relative positions two plates holding the bearings of a watch or clock movement. **6.** *Mining.* an isolated mass of rock or ore in a mine, usually serving as a roof support in early operations and later removed, wholly or in part. **7.** *Naut.* mast[1] (def. 2). **8. from pillar to post, a.** aimlessly from place to place. **b.** uneasily from one bad situation or predicament to another. —*v.t.* **9.** to provide or support with pillars. [1175–1225; ME *pillare* < ML *pīlāre* (see PILE[1], -AR[2]); r. earlier *piler* < OF < ML, as above] —**pil′lared,** *adj.* —**pil′lar·like′,** *adj.*
—**Syn. 1.** pilaster, pier. See **column.**

pil·lar-and-breast (pil′ər ən brest′), *adj. Mining.* room-and-pillar.

pil′lar box′, *Brit.* a pillarlike box in which letters are deposited for collection by mail carriers; mailbox. Also called **pil′lar post′.** [1855–60]

pil·lar·et (pil′ə ret′), *n.* a small pillar. [1655–65; PILLAR + -ET]

Pil′lars of Her′cules, the two promontories on either side of the eastern end of the Strait of Gibraltar: the Rock of Gibraltar in Europe and the Jebel Musa in Africa; fabled to have been raised by Hercules. Also called **Hercules' Pillars.**

Pil′lars of Is′lam, the five bases of the Islamic faith: shahada (confession of faith), salat (prayer), zakat (almsgiving), sawm (fasting, esp. during the month of Ramadan), and hajj (the pilgrimage to Mecca). Also called **Pil′lars of the Faith′.** Cf. **din**[2], **Ibada.**

pill·box (pil′boks′), *n.* **1.** a box, usually shallow and often round, for holding pills. **2.** a small, low structure of reinforced concrete, enclosing machine guns, and employed as a minor fortress in warfare. **3.** a small, round, brimless hat with straight sides and a flat top, worn esp. by women. [1720–30; PILL[1] + BOX[1]]

pill′ bug′, any of various small terrestrial isopods, esp. of the genera *Armadillidium* and *Oniscus,* which can roll themselves up into a spherical shape. [1835–45, *Amer.*]

pill·head (pil′hed′), *n. Slang.* a person who habitually takes pills, esp. amphetamines or barbiturates. [1960–65; PILL[1] + HEAD]

pil·lion (pil′yən), *n.* **1.** a pad or cushion attached behind a saddle, esp. as a seat for a woman. **2.** a pad, cushion, saddle, or the like, used as a passenger seat on a bicycle, motor scooter, etc. **3.** a passenger's saddle or seat behind the driver's seat on a motorcycle. [1495–1505; < ScotGael *pillinn* or Ir *pillín,* dim. of *peall* skin, rug blanket, MIr *pell* < L *pellis* skin]

pil·li·winks (pil′ə wingks′), *n.* (*used with a singular or plural v.*) an old instrument of torture similar to the thumbscrew. [1350–1400; Scots var. of late ME *pyrwykes, pyrewinkes* < ?]

pil·lo·ry (pil′ə rē), *n., pl.* **-ries,** *v.,* **-ried, -ry·ing.** —*n.* **1.** a wooden framework erected on a post, with holes for securing the head and hands, formerly used to expose an offender to public derision. —*v.t.* **2.** to set in the pillory. **3.** to expose to public derision, ridicule, or abuse: *The candidate mercilessly pilloried his opponent.* [1225–75; ME *pyllory* < OF *pilori,* perh. < ML *pīlōrium,* equiv. to L *pīl(a)* pillar (see PILE[1]) + *-ōrium* -ORY[2], though Rom vars. such as Pr *espillori* suggest a less transparent source]

pillory (def. 1)

pil·low (pil′ō), *n.* **1.** a bag or case made of cloth that is filled with feathers, down, or other soft material, and is used to cushion the head during sleep or rest. **2.** anything used to cushion the head; headrest: *a pillow of moss.* **3.** Also called **lace pillow.** a hard cushion or pad that supports the pattern and threads in the making of bobbin lace. **4.** a supporting piece or part, as the block on which the inner end of a bowsprit rests. —*v.t.* **5.** to rest on or as on a pillow. **6.** to support with pillows. **7.** to serve as a pillow for: *She pillowed the child with her body.* —*v.i.* **8.** to rest as on a pillow. [bef. 900; ME *pilwe,* OE *pylu* < L *pulvīnus* cushion (whence also G *Pfühl*)] —**pil′low·less,** *adj.* —**pil′low·like′,** *adj.*
—**Syn. 1.** See **cushion.**

pil′low block′, *Mach.* a cast-iron or steel block for supporting a journal or bearing. [1835–45]

pil·low·case (pil′ō kās′), *n.* a removable sacklike covering, usually of cotton, drawn over a pillow. Also called **pil·low·slip** (pil′ō slip′). [1715–25; PILLOW + CASE[1]]

pil′low lace′. See **bobbin lace.** [1855–60]

pil′low la′va, *Geol.* lava in the form of an agglomeration of rounded, pillow-shaped masses, the result of subaqueous or subglacial volcanic eruption. [1900–05]

pil′low sham′, an ornamental cover laid over a bed pillow. [1870–75]

pil′low sword′, a straight sword of the 17th century.

pil′low talk′, private conversation, endearments, or confidences exchanged in bed or in intimate circumstances between spouses or lovers. [1935–40]

pil·low·y (pil′ō ē), *adj.* pillowlike; soft; yielding: *a pillowy carpet.* [1790–1800; PILLOW + -Y[1]]

pill′ pop′per, *Informal.* a person who takes pills regularly and in quantity. [1960–65]

pill′ push′er, *Slang* (*usually disparaging*). **1.** a medical doctor, esp. one who too readily prescribes medication. **2.** a pharmacist. [1905–10]

Pills·bur·y (pilz′ber′ē, -bə rē), *n.* **Charles Alfred,** 1842–99, U.S. businessman.

pi·lo·car·pine (pī′lə kär′pēn, -pin, pil′ə-), *n. Pharm.* an oil or crystalline alkaloid, $C_{11}H_{16}N_2O_2$, obtained from jaborandi, and used chiefly to produce sweating, promote the flow of saliva, contract the pupil of the eye, and for glaucoma. [1870–75; < NL *Pilocarp(us)* name of the genus of shrubs which includes jaborandi (< Gk *pîlo(s)* felt, wool or hair made into felt + -o- -o- + *-karpos* -CARP) + -INE[1]]

pi·lon (pē lōn′), *n. Southwestern U.S.* (*chiefly Texas*). something extra; lagniappe. [1880–85; *Amer.;* < MexSp *pilón* lit., trough, mortar, Sp: deriv. of *pila* basin, trough < L *pīla* mortar]

pi·lo·ni·dal (pī′lə nīd′l), *adj. Pathol.* noting or pertaining to a growth of hair in a dermoid cyst or in the deeper layers of the skin. [1875–80; < NL; see PILE[3], -O-, NIDUS, -AL[1]]

Pi·los (pē′lôs), *n.* Greek name of **Navarino.**

pi·lose (pī′lōs), *adj.* covered with hair, esp. soft hair; furry. Also, **pilous.** [1745–55; < L *pilōsus* shaggy. See PILE[3], -OSE[1]] —**pi·los·i·ty** (pī los′i tē), *n.*

pi·lot (pī′lət), *n.* **1.** a person duly qualified to steer ships into or out of a harbor or through certain difficult waters. **2.** a person who steers a ship. **3.** *Aeron.* a person duly qualified to operate an airplane, balloon, or other aircraft. **4.** a guide or leader: *the pilot of the expedition.* **5.** See **coast pilot** (def. 1). **6.** See **pilot light** (def. 1). **7.** *Mach.* a guide for centering or otherwise positioning two adjacent parts, often consisting of a projection on one part fitting into a recess in the other. **8.** *Railroads.* cowcatcher. **9.** Also called **pilot film, pilot tape.** *Television.* a prototypical filmed or taped feature, produced with hopes of network adoption as a television series and aired to test potential viewer interest and attract sponsors. **10.** a preliminary or experimental trial or test: *The school will offer a pilot of its new computer course.* —*v.t.* **11.** to steer. **12.** to lead, guide, or conduct, as through unknown places, intricate affairs, etc. **13.** to act as pilot on, in, or over. **14.** to be in charge of or responsible for: *We're looking for someone to pilot the new project.* —*adj.* **15.** serving as an experimental or trial undertaking prior to full-scale operation or use: *a pilot project.* [1520–30; earlier *pylotte* < MF *pillotte* < It *pilota,* dissimilated var. of *pedota* < MGk **pēdṓtēs* steersman, equiv. to *pēd(á)* rudder (pl. of *pēdón* oar) + *-ōtēs* agent suffix]
—**Syn. 2.** helmsman. **13.** maneuver, manage.

pi·lot·age (pī′lə tij), *n.* **1.** act, occupation, or skill of piloting. **2.** the fee paid to a pilot for his or her services. **3.** See **pilot station** (def. 1). **4.** the process of directing the movement of a ship or aircraft by visual or electronic observations of recognizable landmarks. [1610–20; < F; see PILOT, -AGE]

pi′lot balloon′, a balloon for the visual observation of upper-atmosphere wind currents. [1840–50]

pi′lot bis′cuit, hardtack. Also called **pi′lot bread′.** [1830–40, *Amer.*]

pi′lot boat′, a boat carrying pilots to or from large ships. [1580–90]

pi′lot burn′er. See **pilot light** (def. 1). [1900–05]

pi′lot chart′, **1.** any of a number of charts issued to mariners by the U.S. Hydrographic Office and showing meteorological, hydrographic, and navigational conditions prevailing, or likely to prevail, subsequent to the date of issue in some part of the world: issued monthly for most areas. **2.** a chart giving information on atmospheric conditions at various altitudes.

pi′lot en′gine, a locomotive sent on ahead of a railroad train to see that the way is clear and the track safe. [1830–40]

pi′lot film′, *Television.* pilot (def. 9). [1950–55]

pi•lot•fish (pī′lət fish′), *n., pl.* (*esp. collectively*) **-fish,** (*esp. referring to two or more kinds or species*) **-fish•es.** **1.** a small, marine fish, *Naucrates ductor,* often swimming with sharks. **2.** any of various other fishes having similar habits. [1625–35; PILOT + FISH]

pi′lot flag′, *Naut.* **1.** the flag symbolizing the letter *G* in the International Code of Signals, flown by itself to request a pilot from a pilot service: a flag of three yellow and three blue vertical stripes. **2.** the flag symbolizing the letter *H* in the International Code of Signals, flown by itself to indicate that a pilot is on board: a flag with one white and one red vertical stripe.

pi•lot•house (pī′lət hous′), *n., pl.* **-hous•es** (-hou′ziz). *Naut.* an enclosed structure on the deck of a ship from which it can be navigated. Also called **wheelhouse.** [1840–50, *Amer.*; PILOT + HOUSE]

pi•lo•ti (pi lot′ē), *n.* a column of iron, steel, or reinforced concrete supporting a building above an open ground level. [1945–50; < F *pilotis,* equiv. to *pilot* (aug. of *pile* PILE[1]) + *-is* collective suffix]

pi•lot•ing (pī′lə ting), *n.* the determination of the course or position of a ship or airplane by any of various navigational methods or devices. [1710–20]

pi′lot lad′der, *Naut.* See **Jacob's ladder** (def. 2a).

pi′lot lamp′, an electric lamp, used in association with a control, which by means of position or color indicates the functioning of the control; an indicator light or a control light. Also called **pilot light.** [1880–85]

pi•lot•less (pī′lət lis), *adj.* **1.** lacking a pilot or needing no pilot: *pilotless aircraft.* **2.** having no pilot light: *a pilotless furnace.* [1595–1605; PILOT + -LESS]

pi′lotless air′craft, an aircraft equipped for operation by radio or by robot control, without a human pilot aboard; drone. [1940–45; PILOT + -LESS]

pi′lotless igni′tion, a system for igniting a gas burner, as in a gas range, furnace, or boiler, without the use of a pilot light.

pi′lot light′, **1.** Also called **pilot, pilot burner.** a small flame kept burning continuously, as in a gas stove or furnace, to relight the main gas burners whenever necessary or desired. **2.** See **pilot lamp.** [1885–90]

pi′lot plant′, an experimental industrial plant in which processes or techniques planned for use in full-scale operation are tested in advance. [1935–40]

pi′lot raise′, *Mining.* a small raise intended to be enlarged later.

pi′lot sig′nal, *Naut.* **1.** a signal, as a flag or light, used to request a pilot. **2.** a signal to indicate that a pilot is on board.

pi′lot sta′tion, *Naut.* **1.** Also called **pilotage.** an onshore office or headquarters for pilots. **2.** an area in which pilot boats cruise.

pi′lot tape′, *Television.* pilot (def. 9).

pi′lot wa′ters, *Naut.* waters in which the services of a pilot are available or required by law. [1780–90]

pi•lot•weed (pī′lət wēd′), *n.* the compass plant, *Silphium laciniatum.* [1840–50, *Amer.*; PILOT + WEED[1]]

pi′lot whale′, a small, common whale, *Globicephala sieboldii,* of tropical and temperate seas, having a bulbous head. [1865–70]

pi•lous (pī′ləs), *adj.* pilose. [1650–60; < L *pilōsus.* See PILOSE, -OUS]

pil•pul (pil′po͝ol), *n.* a method of disputation among rabbinical scholars regarding the interpretation of Talmudic rules and principles or Scripture that involves the development of careful and often excessively subtle distinctions. [1890–95; < Aram, Heb *pilpūl,* akin to *pilpēl* to search, debate] **—pil′pul•ist,** *n.* **—pil′pul•is′tic,** *adj.*

Pil•sen (pil′zən), *n.* German name of **Plzeň.**

Pil•sner (pilz′nər, pils′-), *n.* (*sometimes l.c.*) **1.** a pale, light lager beer. **2.** any lager beer of high quality. **3.** Also called **pil′sner glass′.** a tall glass that is tapered to a short stem at the bottom, used esp. for beer. Also, **Pil•sen•er** (pil′zə nər, -sə-, pilz′nər, pils′-). [1875–80; < G *Pilsener* lit., of PILSEN; see -ER[1]]

Pil•sud•ski (pil so͞ot′skē), *n.* **Jó•zef** (yo͞o′zef), 1867–1935, Polish marshal and statesman: president 1918–22; premier 1926–28, 1930.

Pilt′down man′ (pilt′doun′), a hypothetical early modern human, assigned to the genus *Eoanthropus,* whose existence was inferred from skull fragments that were allegedly found at Piltdown, England, in 1912 but were exposed as fraudulent through chemical analysis in 1953.

pil•u•lar (pil′yə lər), *adj.* of, pertaining to, or resembling pills. [1795–1805; < L *pilul(a)* PILULE + -AR[1]]

pil•ule (pil′yo͞ol), *n.* a small pill (contrasted with *bolus*). [1535–45; < L *pilula.* See PILE[4], -ULE]

pi•lum (pī′ləm), *n., pl.* **-la** (-lə). a javelin used in ancient Rome by legionaries, consisting of a three-foot-long shaft with an iron head of the same length. [< L *pīlum* dart, javelin]

Pi•lum•nus (pi lum′nəs), *n.* one of two ancient gods of fertility. Cf. **Picumnus.**

pi•lus (pī′ləs), *n., pl.* **-li** (-lī). *Biol.* a hair or hairlike structure. [1955–60; < L]

PIM, *pl.* **PIMs, PIM's.** personal information manager.

CONCISE ETYMOLOGY KEY: <, descended or borrowed from; >, whence; b., blend of, blended; c., cognate with; cf., compare; deriv., derivative; equiv., equivalent; imit., imitative; obl., oblique; r., replacing; s., stem; sp., spelling, spelled; resp., respelling, respelled; trans., translation; ?, origin unknown; *, unattested; ‡, probably earlier than. See the full key inside the front cover.

Pi•ma (pē′mə), *n., pl.* **-mas,** (*esp. collectively*) **-ma** for 1. **1.** a member of an Indian people of southern Arizona and northern Mexico. **2.** the Uto-Aztecan language of the Pima Indians, closely related to Papago. [< AmerSp, earlier *Pimahitos* < 16th-cent. Pima (Sp sp.) *pimahaitu* nothing]

Pi′ma cot′ton, (*often l.c.*) a variety of fine cotton developed from Egyptian cotton, produced in the southwestern U.S., used chiefly in the manufacture of shirts, ties, etc. Also called **Pima.** [1935–40, *Amer.*; after *Pima* Co., Arizona]

Pi•man (pē′mən), *n.* **1.** any of various groupings of Uto-Aztecan languages, of varying degrees of inclusiveness, comprising Pima and its closest relatives. *—adj.* **2.** pertaining or belonging to such a language grouping. **3.** of or pertaining to the Pima or their language. [PIM(A) + -AN]

pi•mel′ic ac′id (pə mel′ik, -mē′lik), *Chem.* a crystalline compound, $C_7H_{12}O_4$, soluble in alcohol and ether: used in polymers and as a plasticizer. Also called **heptanedioic acid.** [1830–40; < Gk *pimel(ḗ)* soft fat + -IC]

pi•men•to (pi men′tō), *n., pl.* **-tos. 1.** pimiento. **2.** allspice. **3.** Also called **Chinese vermilion, Harrison red, signal red.** a vivid red color. [1665–75; alter. of Sp *pimiento* pepper plant, masc. deriv. of *pimienta* pepper fruit < LL *pigmenta* spiced drink, spice, pepper, pl. (taken as sing.) of L *pigmentum* PIGMENT]

pimen′to cheese′, a processed cheese made from Neufchâtel, cream cheese, Cheddar, or other cheese, flavored with chopped pimientos. Also, **pimien′to cheese′.** [1915–20]

pi′ me′son, *Physics.* pion. [1945–50]

pi•mien•to (pi myen′tō, -men′-), *n., pl.* **-tos. 1.** the ripe, red, mild-flavored fruit of the sweet or bell pepper, *Capsicum annuum,* used as a vegetable, relish, to stuff olives, etc. **2.** the plant itself. Also, **pimento.** [1835–45; see PIMENTO]

pim•o•la (pi mō′lə), *n.* an olive stuffed with red sweet pepper; stuffed olive. [PIM(IENTO) + OL(IVE) + *-a* (cf. -OLA)]

pimp (pimp), *n.* **1.** a person, esp. a man, who solicits customers for a prostitute or a brothel, usually in return for a share of the earnings; pander; procurer. **2.** a despicable person. **3.** *Australia and New Zealand.* an informer; stool pigeon. *—v.i.* **4.** to act as a pimp. *—v.t.* **5.** to act as a pimp for. **6.** to exploit. [1630–40; orig. uncert.]

pim•per•nel (pim′pər nel′, -nl), *n.* a plant belonging to the genus *Anagallis,* of the primrose family, esp. *A. arvensis* **(scarlet pimpernel),** having scarlet or white flowers that close at the approach of bad weather. [1400–50; late ME *pympernele* < MF *pimprenelle,* nasalized var. of OF *piprenelle* < LL **piperīnella,* equiv. to *piper* PEPPER + *-īn-* -INE[1] + *-ella* dim. suffix; r. OE *pipeneale* < LL *pipinella,* syncopated var. of **piperīnella*]

pimp•ing (pim′ping), *adj.* **1.** petty; insignificant; trivial. **2.** *Brit. Dial.* puny; weak; sickly. [1680–90; orig. uncert.]

pim•ple (pim′pəl), *n. Pathol.* a small, usually inflammatory swelling or elevation of the skin; papule or pustule. [1350–1400; ME, nasalized var. of OE **pypel* (whence *pyplian* to break out in pimples) < L *papula* pimple]

pim′ple cop′per, *Metall.* a form of copper matte about 80 percent pure, somewhat less refined than blister copper. Also called **pim′ple met′al.** [1865–70]

pim•ply (pim′plē), *adj.* **-pli•er, -pli•est.** having many pimples. Also, **pim•pled** (pim′pəld). [1740–50; PIMPLE + -Y[1]]

pimp•mo•bile (pimp′mō bēl′, -mə-), *n. Slang.* a large, expensive, and ostentatious or vulgarly ornate automobile, typically one painted in bright colors and fitted out with a lavish or overelaborate interior. [1970–75, *Amer.*; PIMP + -MOBILE]

pin (pin), *n., v.,* **pinned, pin•ning.** *—n.* **1.** a small, slender, often pointed piece of wood, metal, etc., used to fasten, support, or attach things. **2.** a short, slender piece of wire with a point at one end and a head at the other, for fastening things together. **3.** any of various forms of fasteners or ornaments consisting essentially or partly of a pointed or penetrating wire or shaft (often used in combination): *a jeweled pin.* **4.** a badge having a pointed bar or pin attached, by which it is fastened to the clothing: *a fraternity pin.* **5.** *Mach.* **a.** a short metal rod, as a linchpin, driven through holes in adjacent parts, as a hub and an axle, to keep the parts together. **b.** a short cylindrical rod or tube, as a wrist pin or crankpin, joining two parts so as to permit them to move in one plane relative to each other. **c.** a short axle, as one on which a pulley rotates in a block. **6.** the part of a cylindrical key stem entering a lock. **7.** a clothespin. **8.** a hairpin. **9.** See **rolling pin. 10.** a peg, nail, or stud marking the center of a target. **11.** *Bowling.* any one of the rounded wooden clubs set up as the target in tenpins, ninepins, duckpins, etc. **12.** *Golf.* the flag staff which identifies a hole. **13.** any of the projecting knobs or rails on a pinball machine that serve as targets for the ball. **14.** *Informal.* a human leg. **15.** *Music.* peg (def. 5). **16.** *Wrestling.* a fall. **17.** *Naut.* **a.** an axle for a sheave of a block. **b.** See **belaying pin. 18.** *Carpentry.* a tenon in a dovetail joint; dovetail. **19.** a very small amount; a trifle: *Such insincere advice isn't worth a pin.* **20.** *Chess.* the immobilization of an enemy piece by attacking with one's queen, rook, or bishop. **21.** *Electronics.* a pin-shaped connection, as the terminals on the base of an electron tube or the connections on an integrated circuit. **22. pull the pin,** *Informal.* to end a relationship, project, program, or the like, because of lack of continuing interest, success, funds, etc. *—v.t.* **23.** to fasten or attach with or as with a pin or pins: *to pin two pieces of cloth together.* **24.** to hold fast in a spot or position (sometimes fol. by *down*): *The debris pinned him down.* **25.** to transfix or mount with a pin or the like: *to pin a flower as a botanical specimen.* **26.** *Chess.* to immobilize (an enemy piece) by placing one's queen, rook, or bishop in a position to check the exposed king or capture a valuable piece if the pinned piece were moved. **27.** *Wrestling.* to secure a fall over one's opponent. **28. get pinned, a.** (of a young woman) to receive a male student's fraternity pin as a symbol of his affection and fidelity, usually symbolizing that the couple is going steady or plans to become engaged. **b.** (of a young couple) to become formally pledged to one another, though not yet engaged, by the bestowing of such a pin or the exchange of pins. **29. pin down, a.** to bind or hold to a course of action, a promise, etc. **b.** to force (someone) to deal with a situation or to come to a decision: *We tried to pin him down for a definite answer, but he was too evasive for us.* **30. pin in,** to fill (gaps in a rubble wall, etc.) with spalls. **31. pin something on someone,** *Informal.* to ascribe the blame or guilt for something to a person; show someone to be culpable: *They pinned the crime on him.* **32. pin up,** to make (a piece of masonry) level or plumb with wedges. [bef. 1100; (n.) ME *pinne,* OE *pinn* peg; c. D *pin,* G *Pinne,* ON *pinni;* perh. < L *pinna* feather, quill (see PINNA); (v.) ME *pinnen,* deriv. of the n.]
—Syn. 1. bolt, peg. **3.** brooch.

PIN (pin), *n. Computers.* a number assigned to an individual, used to establish identity in order to gain access to a computer system via an automatic teller machine, a point-of-sale terminal, or other device. [*p(ersonal) i(dentification) n(umber)*]

pi•ña (pē′nyä; *Eng.* pēn′yə), *n., pl.* **pi•ñas** (pē′nyäs; *Eng.* pēn′yəz). *Spanish.* pineapple.

pi•na•ceous (pī nā′shəs), *adj.* belonging to the plant family Pinaceae. Cf. **pine family.** [1870–75; < NL *Pinace(ae)* (see PINE[1], -ACEAE) + -OUS]

pi′ña cloth′, a fine, sheer fabric of pineapple-leaf fiber, used esp. for lingerie. [1855–60]

pin•a•coid (pin′ə koid′), *n. Crystall.* a form whose faces are parallel to two of the axes. [1875–80; < Gk *pinak-* (s. of *pínax*) slab, board + -OID] **—pin′a•coi′dal,** *adj.*

pi•ña co•la•da (pēn′yə kō lä′də, kə lä′-), **1.** a tall mixed drink of rum, cream of coconut, pineapple juice, and ice usually frappéed in a blender. **2.** a flavor of ice cream, soft drinks, etc., made with coconut milk and pineapple juice. [1920–25; < Sp: lit., strained pineapple]

pin•a•fore (pin′ə fôr′, -fōr′), *n.* **1.** a child's apron, usually large enough to cover the dress and sometimes trimmed with flounces. **2.** a woman's sleeveless garment derived from it, low-necked, tying or buttoning in the back, and worn as an apron or as a dress, usually over a blouse, a sweater, or another dress. **3.** *Chiefly Brit.* **a.** a large apron worn by adults. **b.** a sleeveless smock. [1775–85; PIN + AFORE]

pinafore (def. 1)

pi•nang (pi nang′), *n.* the betel palm or its nut. [1655–65; < Malay]

Pi•nang (pi nang′, -näng′), *n.* Penang.

pi•nard (pē NAR′; *Eng.* pē När′), *n., pl.* **-nards** (-NAR′; *Eng.* -närz′). *French Informal.* wine.

Pi•nar del Rí•o (pē när′ *th*el rē′ô), a city in W Cuba. 73,206.

pi•ña•ta (pēn yä′tə, pin yä′-; *Sp.* pē nyä′tä), *n., pl.* **-tas** (-təz; *Sp.* -täs). (in Mexico and Central America) a gaily decorated crock or papier-mâché figure filled with toys, candy, etc., and suspended from above, esp. during Christmas or birthday festivities, so that children, who are blindfolded, may break it or knock it down with sticks and release the contents. [1885–90; < Sp: lit., pot < It *pignatta,* prob. deriv. of dial. *pigna* pinecone (from the pot's shape) < L *pinea,* n. use of fem. of *pineus* of the pine tree; see PINE[1], -EOUS]

pin•ball (pin′bôl′), *n.* any of various games played on a sloping, glass-topped table presenting a field of colorful, knoblike target pins and rails, the object usually being to shoot a ball, driven by a spring, up a side passage and cause it to roll back down against these projections and through channels, which electrically flash or ring and record the score. [1880–85, *Amer.*; PIN + BALL[1]]

pin•ball•er (pin′bô′lər), *n.* a person who plays pinball machines, esp. regularly or habitually. [PINBALL + -ER[1]]

pin′ball machine′, the tablelike, usually coin-operated machine on which pinball is played. [1935–40]

pin•bone (pin′bōn′), *n.* the hipbone, esp. in a four-footed animal. [1630–40; PIN + BONE]

pin′ boy′, (formerly) a person stationed in the sunken area of a bowling alley behind the pins who places the pins in the proper positions, removes pins that have been knocked down, and returns balls to the bowlers. Also called **pinsetter.** [1890–95]

pince-nez (pans′nā′, pins′-; *Fr.* paNs nā′), *n., pl.* **pince-nez** (pans′nāz′, pins′-; *Fr.* paNs nā′). a pair of glasses held on the face by a spring that grips the nose. [1875–80; < F: lit., (it) pinches (the) nose]

pin•cers (pin′sərz), *n.* (*usually used with a plural v.*) **1.** a gripping tool consisting of two pivoted limbs forming a pair of jaws and a pair of handles (usually used with *pair of*). **2.** *Zool.* a grasping organ or pair of organs resembling this, as the claw of a lobster. Also, **pinchers.** [1300–50; ME *pinsers,* earlier *pynceours,* pl. of **pinceour* < AF *pince(r)* to PINCH + *-our* -OR[2]]

pin′cers move′ment, a military maneuver in which both flanks of an enemy force are attacked with the aim of attaining complete encirclement. Also, **pin′cer move′ment.** [1935–40]

pinch (pinch), *v.t.* **1.** to squeeze or compress between the finger and thumb, the teeth, the jaws of an instrument, or the like. **2.** to constrict or squeeze painfully, as a tight shoe does. **3.** to cramp within narrow bounds or quarters: *The crowd pinched him into a corner.* **4.** to render (the face, body, etc.) unnaturally constricted or drawn, as pain or distress does: *Years of hardship had pinched her countenance beyond recognition.* **5.** *Hort.* to remove or shorten (buds or shoots) in order to produce a certain shape of the plant, improve the quality of the bloom or fruit, or increase the development of buds (often fol. by *out, off,* or *back*). **6.** to affect with sharp discomfort or distress, as cold, hunger, or need does. **7.** to straiten in means or circumstances: *The depression pinched them.* **8.** to stint (a person, family, etc.) in allowance of money, food, or the like: *They were severely pinched by the drought.* **9.** to hamper or inconvenience by the lack of something specified: *The builders were pinched by the shortage of good lumber.* **10.** to stint the supply or amount of (a thing). **11.** to put a pinch or small quantity of (a powder, spice, etc.) into something. **12.** *Slang.* **a.** to steal. **b.** to arrest. **13.** to roll or slide (a heavy object) with leverage from a pinch bar. **14.** *Naut.* to sail (a ship) so close to the wind that the sails shake slightly and the speed is reduced. **15.** *Horse Racing, Brit.* to press (a horse) to the point of exhaustion. —*v.i.* **16.** to exert a sharp or painful constricting force: *This shoe pinches.* **17.** to cause sharp discomfort or distress: *Their stomachs were pinched with hunger.* **18.** to economize unduly; stint oneself: *They pinched and scraped for years to save money for a car.* **19.** *Mining.* (of a vein of ore or the like) **a.** to diminish. **b.** to diminish to nothing (sometimes fol. by *out*). **20.** *Naut.* to trim a sail too flat when sailing to windward. **21. pinch pennies,** to stint on or be frugal or economical with expenditures; economize: *I'll have to pinch pennies if I'm going to get through school.* —*n.* **22.** the act of pinching; nip; squeeze. **23.** as much of anything as can be taken up between the finger and thumb: *a pinch of salt.* **24.** a very small quantity of anything: *a pinch of pungent wit.* **25.** sharp or painful stress, as of hunger, need, or any trying circumstances: *the pinch of conscience; to feel the pinch of poverty.* **26.** a situation or time of special stress, esp. an emergency: *A friend is someone who will stand by you in a pinch.* **27.** See **pinch bar. 28.** *Slang.* a raid or an arrest. **29.** *Slang.* a theft. **30. with a pinch of salt.** See **grain** (def. 22). [1250–1300; ME *pinchen* < AF **pinchier* (equiv. to OF *pincier,* Sp *pinchar*) < VL **pīnctiāre,* var. of **pūnctiāre* to prick (cf. PIQUE[1])] —**pinch′a·ble,** *adj.*

Pinch·back (pinch′bak′), *n.* **Pinckney Benton Stewart,** 1837–1921, U.S. politician.

pinch′ bar′, a kind of crowbar or lever with a projection that serves as a fulcrum. Also called **ripping bar, wrecking bar.** [1830–40]

pinch·beck (pinch′bek), *n.* **1.** an alloy of copper and zinc, used in imitation of gold. **2.** something sham, spurious, or counterfeit. —*adj.* **3.** made of pinchbeck. **4.** sham, spurious, or counterfeit: *pinchbeck heroism.* [1725–35; named after Christopher *Pinchbeck* (d. 1732), English watchmaker and its inventor]

pinch·bot·tle (pinch′bot′l), *n.* a bottle with concave sides, as for containing liquor. [1935–40, *Amer.;* PINCH + BOTTLE[1]]

pinch·cock (pinch′kok′), *n.* a clamp for compressing a flexible pipe, as a rubber tube, in order to regulate or stop the flow of a fluid. [1870–75; PINCH + COCK[1]]

pin·check (pin′chek′), *n.* **1.** a very small check woven into fabric, much used in the manufacture of men's and women's suits. **2.** a strong cotton cloth having a vertical and horizontal design of white dots on a blue ground, used in the manufacture of work clothes. —*adj.* **3.** of or pertaining to a fabric having a pincheck design. [PIN + CHECK]

pinch′ effect′, *Physics.* the tendency of an electric conductor or stream of charged particles to constrict, caused by the action of a magnetic field that is produced by a flow of electricity. [1905–10]

pinch·er (pin′chər), *n.* **1.** a person or thing that pinches. **2. pinchers,** (*usually used with a plural v.*) pincers. [1400–50; late ME *pynchar* niggard. See PINCH, -ER[2]]

pin′ cher′ry, 1. a wild, often shrubby cherry, *Prunus pensylvanica,* having white flowers. **2.** the red, acid fruit of this tree. [1895–1900]

pinch′ hit′, *Baseball.* a hit made by a pinch hitter. [1910–15]

pinch-hit (pinch′hit′), *v.i.,* **-hit, -hit·ting. 1.** *Baseball.* to serve as a pinch hitter. **2.** *Informal.* to substitute for someone, esp. in an emergency. —*v.t.* **3.** *Baseball.* to get, or make (a hit) in pinch-hitting. [1930–35, *Amer.;* back formation from PINCH HITTER]

pinch′ hit′ter, 1. *Baseball.* a substitute who bats for a teammate, often at a critical moment of the game. **2.** any substitute for another, esp. in an emergency. [1910–15, *Amer.*]

Pin·chot (pin′shō), *n.* **Gifford,** 1863–1946, U.S. political leader, forester, and teacher.

pinch·pen·ny (pinch′pen′ē), *n., pl.* **-nies,** *adj.* —*n.* **1.** a miser or niggard. —*adj.* **2.** stingy; miserly; niggardly. [1375–1425; late ME; see PINCH, PENNY]

pinch′ pleat′, a narrow pleat that is usually part of a series at the top of curtains. [1955–60]

pinch′ roll′er, a flexible device that presses magnetic tape against the capstan in a tape recorder. [1945–50]

pinch′ run′ner, *Baseball.* a player sent into a game to replace a base runner. [1960–65] —**pinch′ run′ning.**

Pinck·ney (pingk′nē), *n.* **1. Charles,** 1757–1824, American Revolutionary leader and politician: senator 1798–1801. **2. Charles Cotes·worth** (kōts′wûrth), 1746–1825, and his brother **Thomas,** 1750–1828, American patriots and statesmen.

Pinck′ney's Trea′ty, an agreement in 1795 between Spain and the U.S. by which Spain recognized the 31st parallel as the southern boundary of the U.S. and permitted free navigation of the Mississippi to American ships.

pin′ clo′ver, alfilaria. [1880–85, *Amer.*]

pin′ curl′, a dampened curl that is kept in place by a clip or hairpin. [1895–1900]

pin-curl (pin′kûrl′), *v.t.* to curl (the hair) by using clips or hairpins. [v. use of PIN CURL]

pin·cush·ion (pin′ko͝osh′ən), *n.* a small cushion into which pins are stuck until needed. [1625–35; PIN + CUSHION]

pin′cushion cac′tus, any of various low-growing, spiny cacti of the genus *Mammillaria.* [1915–20, *Amer.*]

pin′cushion distor′tion, *Optics.* a distortion produced by a lens in which the magnification increases toward the edge of the field. Cf. **barrel distortion.** [1890–95]

pin′cushion flow′er, 1. scabious[2] (def. 1). **2.** any of various shrubs of the genus *Leucospermum,* native to southern Africa, having yellow or reddish flowers. [1855–60]

pin·dan (pin′dən, -dan), *n. Australian.* **1.** semiarid country; scrubland. **2.** the scrubs, grasses, and small trees covering scrublands. [1930–35; perh. < an Australian Aboriginal language]

Pin·dar (pin′dər), *n.* 522?–443? B.C., Greek poet.

Pin·dar·ic (pin dar′ik), *adj.* **1.** of, pertaining to, or in the style of Pindar. **2.** of elaborate form and metrical structure, as an ode or verse. —*n.* **3.** See **Pindaric ode.** [1630–40; < L *Pindaricus* < Gk *Pindarikós.* See PINDAR, -IC] —**Pin·dar′i·cal·ly,** *adv.*

Pindar′ic ode′, *Pros.* an ode consisting of several units, each of which is composed of a strophe and an antistrophe of identical form followed by a contrasting epode. Also called **regular ode.** [1630–40]

pin·der (pin′dər), *n. Southern U.S.* (*chiefly South Carolina*). peanut. [1690–1700; < Kongo *mpinda,* or a cognate Bantu word]

pind·ling (pind′ling), *adj. Older Use.* puny; sickly; frail; weak. [1860–65, *Amer.;* PINE[2] + -LING[1], on the model of *dwindling*]

Pind·ling (pind′ling), *n.* **Lynden Oscar,** born 1930, Bahamian political leader: prime minister since 1967.

pin·do·lol (pin′də lôl′, -lol′), *n. Pharm.* a synthetic beta blocker, $C_{14}H_{20}N_2O_2$, used in the management of hypertension. [1970–75; P(ROPANE) or P(ROPYL) + INDOLE + -OL]

pin′do palm′ (pin′dō), a feather palm, *Butia capitata,* of Brazil, having long, arching leaves, grayish beneath, and small, egg-shaped fruit. [*pindo* < AmerSp < Guarani *pindo* palm, perh. reinforced by Tupi *píndoba* palm]

Pin·dus (pin′dəs), *n.* a mountain range in central Greece: highest peak, 7665 ft. (2335 m).

pine[1] (pīn), *n.* **1.** any evergreen, coniferous tree of the genus *Pinus,* having long, needle-shaped leaves, certain species of which yield timber, turpentine, tar, pitch, etc. Cf. **pine family. 2.** any of various similar coniferous trees. **3.** the wood of the pine tree. **4.** *Informal.* the pineapple. [bef. 1000; ME; OE *pīn* < L *pinus*] —**pine′like′,** *adj.*

pine[2] (pīn), *v.,* **pined, pin·ing,** *n.* —*v.i.* **1.** to yearn deeply; suffer with longing; long painfully (often fol. by *for*): *to pine for one's home and family.* **2.** to fail gradually in health or vitality from grief, regret, or longing (often fol. by *away*): *Separated by their families, the lovers pined away.* **3.** *Archaic.* to be discontented; fret. —*v.t.* **4.** *Archaic.* to suffer grief or regret over. —*n.* **5.** *Archaic.* painful longing. [bef. 900; ME *pinen* to torture, torment, inflict pain, be in pain; OE *pīnian* to torture, deriv. of *pīn* torture (ME *pine*) < LL *pēna,* L *poena* punishment. See PAIN]
—**Syn. 1.** See **yearn. 2.** dwindle, decline, languish, droop, waste.

pin·e·al (pin′ē əl, pī′nē-, pī nē′-), *adj.* **1.** resembling a pine cone in shape. **2.** of or pertaining to the pineal body. [1675–85; < NL *pineālis,* equiv. to L *pīne(a)* pine cone, n. use of fem. of *pineus* of a pine tree (*pīn(us)* PINE[1] + *-eus* -EOUS) + *-ālis* -AL[1]]

pin′eal apparat′us, 1. a median outgrowth of the roof of the diencephalon in vertebrates that in some develops into the pineal eye and in others into the pineal gland. **2.** See **parietal eye.**

pin′eal bod′y, (formerly) the pineal gland. [1830–40]

pin′eal eye′, an eyelike structure that develops from the pineal apparatus in certain cold-blooded vertebrates. Also called **third eye.** [1885–90]

pin′eal gland′, a small, cone-shaped endocrine organ in the posterior forebrain, secreting melatonin and involved in biorhythms and gonadal development. Also called **epiphysis.** See diag. under **brain.** [1705–15]

pine·ap·ple (pī′nap′əl), *n.* **1.** the edible, juicy, collective fruit of a tropical, bromeliaceous plant, *Ananas comosus,* that develops from a spike or head of flowers and is surmounted by a crown of leaves. **2.** the plant itself, having a short stem and rigid, spiny-margined, recurved leaves. **3.** *Mil. Slang.* a fragmentation hand grenade. [1350–1400 for earlier sense; 1655–65 for def. 1; ME *pinappel* pine cone; see PINE[1], APPLE]

pineapple, *Ananas comosus*

pine′apple gua′va, feijoa.

pine′ bar′ren, a tract of sandy or peaty soil in which pine trees are the principal growth, as in low-lying areas near the Atlantic and Gulf coasts of the U.S. [1725–35, *Amer.*]

Pine′ Bar′rens, the, an extensive coastal region in S and SE New Jersey, composed chiefly of pine stands, sandy soils, and swampy streams. ab. 2000 sq. mi. (5180 sq. km). Official name, **the Pinelands.**

Pine′ Bluff′, a city in central Arkansas, on the Arkansas River. 56,576.

pine′ cone′, the cone or strobile of a pine tree. [1685–95]

pine·drops (pīn′drops′), *n., pl.* **-drops. 1.** a slender, leafless, parasitic North American plant, *Pterospora andromedea,* having nodding white to red flowers, found growing under pines. **2.** beechdrops. [1855–60, *Amer.;* PINE[1] + DROP + -S[3]]

pine′ fam′ily, the plant family Pinaceae, characterized by mostly evergreen, resinous trees having narrow, often needlelike leaves, male flowers in catkinlike clusters, and scaly female flowers that develop into fruit in the form of a woody cone, and including cedar (genus *Cedrus*), fir, hemlock, larch, pine, and spruce.

pine′ finch′. See **pine siskin.** [1800–10, *Amer.*]

pine′ gros′beak, a large grosbeak, *Pinicola enucleator,* of coniferous forests of northern North America and Eurasia, the male of which has rose and gray plumage. [1765–75, *Amer.*]

Pi·nel (pē nel′), *n.* **Phil·ippe** (fē lēp′), 1745–1826, French physician: reformer in the treatment and care of the mentally ill.

pine·land (pīn′land′, -lənd), *n.* Often, **pinelands.** an area or region covered largely with pine forest: *He longed for the pinelands of his home state.* [1650–60, *Amer.;* PINE[1] + LAND]

Pine·lands (pīn′ləndz), *n.* **the,** official name of **the Pine Barrens.**

pine′ leaf′ a′phid. See under **adelgid.**

Pi·nel′las Park′ (pī nel′əs), a city in W central Florida. 32,811.

pine′ mar′ten, 1. a marten, *Martes martes,* of Europe and western Asia. **2.** Also called **American marten.** a marten, *Martes americana,* inhabiting forests of the U.S. and Canada. [1760–70]

pine′ mouse′, any of a widespread genus of voles, *Pitymys,* having small ears and a short tail; esp. the American forest-dwelling mouse *P. pinetorum.* Also called **pine vole.** [1850–55, *Amer.*]

pi·nene (pī′nēn), *n. Chem.* a liquid terpene, $C_{10}H_{16}$, the principal constituent of oil of turpentine, found in other essential oils: used chiefly in the manufacture of camphor. [1880–85; PINE[1] + -ENE]

pine′ nee′dle, the needlelike leaf of a pine tree. [1865–70]

pine′ nut′, 1. Also, **pignolia.** the seed of any of several pine trees, as the piñon, eaten roasted or salted or used in making candy, pastry, etc., after removing the hard seed coat. **2.** See **pine cone.** [bef. 1000; ME; OE]

Pi·ne·ro (pə nēr′ō, -nâr′ō), *n.* **Sir Arthur Wing,** 1855–1934, English playwright and actor.

pin·er·y (pī′nə rē), *n., pl.* **-er·ies. 1.** a place in which pineapples are grown. **2.** a forest or grove of pine trees. [1750–60; PINE[1] + -ERY]

Pines (pīnz), *n.* **Isle of,** an island in the Caribbean, south of and belonging to Cuba. 1182 sq. mi. (3060 sq. km).

pine·sap (pīn′sap′), *n.* either of two parasitic or saprophytic plants of the genus *Monotropa,* esp. the tawny or reddish *M. hypopithys* **(false beechdrops),** of eastern North America. Cf. **Indian pipe.** [1830–40, *Amer.;* PINE[1] + SAP[1]]

pine′ sis′kin, a small, North American finch, *Carduelis pinus,* of coniferous forests, having yellow markings on the wings and tail. Also called **pine finch.** [1885–90, *Amer.*]

pine′ snake′, any of several subspecies of bullsnake of the eastern and southeastern U.S., chiefly in pine woods: now threatened. [1785–95, *Amer.*]

pine′ tar′, a very viscid, blackish-brown liquid having an odor resembling that of turpentine, obtained by the destructive distillation of pine wood, used in paints, roofing, soaps, and, medicinally, for skin infections. [1875–80]

pine′ tree′ shil′ling, a silver coin minted in Massachusetts in the mid to late 17th century, named for the pine tree within a circle shown on the obverse side. [1820–30, *Amer.*]

Pine′ Tree′ State′, Maine (used as a nickname).

CONCISE PRONUNCIATION KEY: *act, cāpe, dâre, pärt; set, ēqual; if, ice; ox, ōver, ôrder, oil, bo͝ok, bo͞ot, out; up, ûrge; child; sing; shoe; thin, that;* zh as in *treasure.* ə = *a* as in *alone, e* as in *system, i* as in *easily, o* as in *gallop, u* as in *circus;* ə as in *fire* (fīər), *hour* (ouər). l and n can serve as syllabic consonants, as in *cradle* (krād′l), and *button* (but′n). See the full key inside the front cover.

pi•ne•tum (pī nē′təm), *n., pl.* **-ta** (-tə). an arboretum of pines and coniferous trees. [1835–45; < L *pinētum* a pine wood, equiv. to *pīn(us)* PINE[1] + *-ētum* suffix denoting a grove (of the plant specified)]

Pine•ville (pīn′vil), *n.* a town in central Louisiana. 12,034.

pine′ vole′. See **pine mouse.**

pine′ war′bler, a warbler, *Dendroica pinus,* inhabiting pine forests of the southeastern U.S. [1830–40, *Amer.*]

pine•wood (pīn′wo͝od′), *n.* **1.** the wood of a pine. **2.** Often, **pinewoods.** a forest consisting chiefly of pines. [1665–75; PINE[1] + WOOD[1]]

pine•y (pī′nē), *adj.,* **pin•i•er, pin•i•est.** piny.

pin•feath•er (pin′feth′ər), *n. Ornith.* **1.** an undeveloped feather before the web portions have expanded. **2.** a feather just coming through the skin. [1765–75; PIN + FEATHER]

pin•fire (pin′fīᵊr′), *adj.* **1.** of or pertaining to a cartridge fitted with a pin that, when struck by the hammer of the firearm, causes the cartridge to explode. **2.** of or pertaining to a firearm that uses such a cartridge. [1850–55; PIN + FIRE]

pin•fish (pin′fish′), *n., pl.* **-fish•es,** (*esp. collectively*) **-fish.** a small fish, *Lagodon rhomboides,* of the porgy family, inhabiting bays of the South Atlantic and Gulf coasts of the U.S. [1875–80, *Amer.*; PIN + FISH]

pin•fold (pin′fōld′), *n.* **1.** a pound for stray animals. **2.** a fold, as for sheep or cattle. **3.** a place of confinement or restraint. —*v.t.* **4.** to confine in or as in a pinfold. [1150–1200; late ME *pynfold* for **pindfold,* equiv. to OE *pynd(an)* to impound (deriv. of *pund* POUND[3]) + FOLD[2]; r. ME *po(u)n(d)fold(e),* late OE *pundfald*]

ping (ping), *v.i.* **1.** to produce a sharp sound like that of a bullet striking a sheet of metal. —*n.* **2.** a pinging sound. [1850–55; imit.]

Ping Hsin (*Chin.* bing′ shin′), *Wade-Giles.* (*Hsieh Wan-ying*) See **Bing Xin.**

pin•go (ping′gō), *n., pl.* **-gos.** *Geol.* **1.** a hill of soil-covered ice pushed up by hydrostatic pressure in an area of permafrost. **2.** a hill of similar origin remaining after the melting of permafrost. [1925–30; < Inuit *pinguq*]

ping-pong (ping′pong′, -pông′), *Informal.* —*v.t.* **1.** to move back and forth or transfer rapidly from one locale, job, etc., to another; switch: *The patient was ping-ponged from one medical specialist to another.* —*v.i.* **2.** to go back and forth; change rapidly or regularly; shift; bounce: *For ten years the foreign correspondent ping-ponged between London and Paris.* [1900–05]

Ping-Pong (ping′pong′, -pông′), *Trademark.* See **table tennis.**

pin•guid (ping′gwid), *adj.* fat; oily. [1625–35; < L *pingu(is)* fat (cf. Gk *píōn*) + -ID[4]] —**pin•guid′i•ty,** *n.*

pin•head (pin′hed′), *n.* **1.** the head of a pin. **2.** something very small or insignificant. **3.** *Slang.* a stupid person; nitwit. [1655–65; PIN + HEAD]

pin•head•ed (pin′hed′id), *adj.* stupid or foolish. [1860–65; PIN + HEADED] —**pin′head′ed•ness,** *n.*

pin•hole (pin′hōl′), *n.* **1.** a small hole made by or as by a pin. **2.** a hole for a pin to go through; tiny aperture. [1670–80; PIN + HOLE]

pin′hole cam′era, a simple camera in which an aperture provided by a pinhole in an opaque diaphragm is used in place of a lens. [1890–95]

pin•ion[1] (pin′yən), *n.* **1.** *Mach.* **a.** a gear with a small number of teeth, esp. one engaging with a rack or larger gear. See diag. under **rack**[1]. **b.** a shaft or spindle cut with teeth engaging with a gear. **2.** *Metalworking.* a gear driving a roll in a rolling mill. [1650–60; < F *pignon* cogwheel, MF *peignon,* deriv. of *peigne* comb, var. of *pigne* < L *pectin-* (s. of *pecten*) comb; see PECTEN] —**pin′ion•less,** *adj.* —**pin′ion•like′,** *adj.*

pin•ion[2] (pin′yən), *n.* **1.** the distal or terminal segment of the wing of a bird consisting of the carpus, metacarpus, and phalanges. **2.** the wing of a bird. **3.** a feather. **4.** the flight feathers collectively. —*v.t.* **5.** to cut off the pinion of (a wing) or bind (the wings), as in order to prevent a bird from flying. **6.** to disable or restrain (a bird) in such a manner. **7.** to bind (a person's arms or hands) so they cannot be used. **8.** to disable (someone) in such a manner; shackle. **9.** to bind or hold fast, as to a thing: *to be pinioned to one's bad habits.* [1400–50; late ME *pynyon* < MF *pignon* wing, pinion < VL **pinniōn* (s. of *pinniō*), deriv. of L *pinna* feather, wing, fin]

pin•ite (pin′īt, pē′nīt), *n.* a micaceous mineral, similar in composition to muscovite, formed by chemical alteration of various other minerals. [1795–1805; < G *Pinit,* named after *Pini,* mine in Germany; see -ITE[1]]

pi•ni•tol (pī′ni tôl′, -tol′, pin′i-), *n. Chem.* a white, crystalline, inositol derivative, $C_7H_{14}O_6$, obtained from the resin of the sugar pine. [obs. *pinite* pinitol (< F; see PINE[1], -ITE[1]) + -OL[1]]

pink[1] (pingk), *n., adj.,* **-er, -est.** —*n.* **1.** a color varying from light crimson to pale reddish purple. **2.** any of several plants of the genus *Dianthus,* as the clove pink or carnation. Cf. **pink family. 3.** the flower of such a plant; carnation. **4.** the highest form or degree; prime: *a runner in the pink of condition.* **5.** (*often cap.*) Also, **pinko.** *Slang (disparaging).* a person with left-wing, but not extreme, political opinions. **6.** *Business Informal.* a carbon copy, as of a sales slip or invoice, made on pink tissue paper. **7. pinks,** *a. Fox Hunting.* See **pink coat. b.** pinkish-tan gabardine trousers formerly worn by military officers as part of the dress uniform. **8.** the scarlet color of hunting pinks. —*adj.* **9.** of the color pink: *pink marble.* **10.** *Slang (disparaging).* holding, or regarded as holding, mildly leftist views, esp. in politics. **11. tickled pink.** See **tickle** (def. 8). [1565–75; orig. uncert.] —**pink′ness,** *n.*

pink[2] (pingk), *v.t.* **1.** to pierce with a rapier or the like; stab. **2.** to finish at the edge with a scalloped, notched, or other ornamental pattern. **3.** to punch (cloth, leather, etc.) with small holes or figures for ornament. **4.** *Chiefly Brit. Dial.* to adorn or ornament, esp. with scalloped edges or a punched-out pattern. [1275–1325; ME *pynken* to prick, deriv. of OE *pinca* point, itself deriv. of *pinn* PIN]

pink[3] (pingk), *n.* a vessel with a pink stern. Also, **pinky.** Cf. **pink stern.** [1425–75; late ME *pinck* < MD *pinke* fishing boat]

pink′ boll′worm, the larva of a gelechiid moth, *Pectinophora gossypiella,* that feeds on the seeds of the bolls of cotton and was introduced into cotton-growing regions of the world from Asia. Also called **bollworm.** [1905–10]

pink′ champagne′, a sparkling white wine, esp. of the Champagne district of France, colored slightly by the grape skins during fermentation or the addition of a small amount of red wine just before the second fermentation. [1830–40]

pink′ coat′, *Fox Hunting.* the coat, usually scarlet, of the hunt uniform worn by the staff and by male members of the hunt. Also called **pinks.** [1855–60]

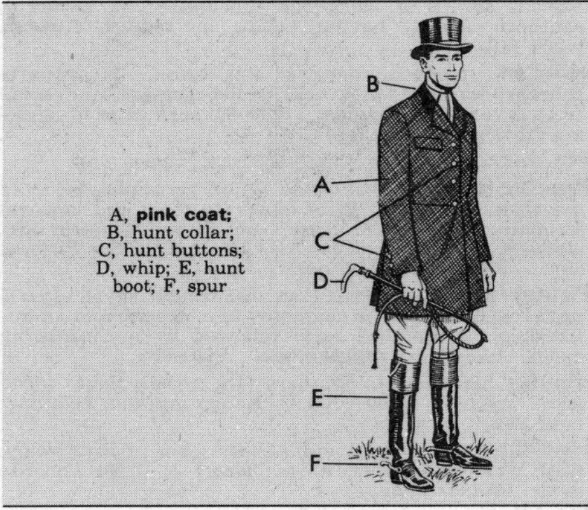

A, **pink coat;** B, hunt collar; C, hunt buttons; D, whip; E, hunt boot; F, spur

pink-col•lar (pingk′kol′ər), *adj.* of or pertaining to a type of employment traditionally held by women, esp. relatively low-paying work: *secretaries, phone operators, and other pink-collar workers.* [1975–80; on the model of BLUE-COLLAR and WHITE-COLLAR]

pink′ el′ephants, any of various visual hallucinations sometimes experienced as a withdrawal symptom after sustained alcoholic drinking. [1905–10]

pink•en (ping′kən), *v.i.* to grow or turn pink. [1885–90; PINK[1] + -EN[1]]

Pink•er•ton (ping′kər tən), *n.* **Allan,** 1819–84, U.S. detective, born in Scotland.

pink•eye (pingk′ī′), *n. Pathol.* a contagious, epidemic form of acute conjunctivitis occurring in humans and certain animals: so called from the color of the inflamed eye. [1785–95; PINK[1] + EYE]

pink′ fam′ily, the plant family Caryophyllaceae, characterized by herbaceous plants having opposite leaves, usually swollen-jointed stems, flowers with petals notched at the tips, and fruit generally in the form of a many-seeded capsule, and including baby's-breath, carnation, chickweed, pink, and sweet william.

pink′ gin′ (jin), a cocktail of gin and bitters usually made and served without ice. [1925–30]

Pink•ham (ping′kəm), *n.* **Lydia (Estes),** 1819–83, U.S. businesswoman: manufactured patent medicine.

Pin•kiang (*Chin.* bin′gyäng′), *n. Older Spelling.* former name of **Harbin.**

pink•ie[1] (ping′kē), *n. Informal.* the little finger. Also, **pinky.** [1585–95; < D *pinkie,* dial. var. of *pinkje,* dim. of *pink* little finger]

pink•ie[2] (ping′kē), *n. Australian Informal.* inferior or cheap wine, esp. red wine. [1895–1900; PINK[1] + -IE]

pink′ing i′ron, a tool for perforating, or for notching or scalloping the edge of fabric, leather, etc. [1755–65]

pink′ing shears′, shears that have notched blades, for cutting and simultaneously pinking fabric or for finishing garments with a notched, nonfraying edge. [1960–65]

pink•ish (ping′kish), *adj.* somewhat pink: *The sky at sunset has a pinkish glow.* [1775–85; PINK[1] + -ISH[1]]

pink′ la′dy, 1. a cocktail made with gin, grenadine, and the white of eggs, shaken and strained before serving. **2.** (*often caps.*) a female volunteer in a hospital, usually wearing a pink uniform or pinafore. Cf. **candy striper.** [1940–45, *Amer.*]

pink′ noise′, a random signal within the audible frequency range whose amplitude decreases as frequency increases, maintaining constant audio power per frequency increment. [1960–65]

pin′ knot′, a knot in lumber less than ½ in. (1.3 cm) in diameter. [1905–10]

pink•o (ping′kō), *n., pl.* **-os, -oes.** *U.S. Slang.* pink[1] (def. 5). [1935–40; PINK[1] + -O]

pink′ rhododen′dron. See **coast rhododendron.**

pink′ root′, *Plant Pathol.* a disease of onions and other plants, characterized by pink, withered roots, caused by a fungus, *Pyrenochaeta terrestris.*

pink•root (pingk′ro͞ot′, -ro͝ot′), *n.* **1.** the root of any of various plants belonging to the genus *Spigelia,* of the logania family, esp. that of *S. marilandica* of the U.S., that is used as a vermifuge. **2.** any of these plants. [1755–65, *Amer;* PINK[1] + ROOT[1]]

pink′ salm′on, a small Pacific salmon, *Oncorhynchus gorbuscha,* distinguished by its small scales and long anal fin and by the bright red spawning coloration of males, occurring from California to Alaska and in waters of Japan: fished commercially and for sport. Also called **humpback salmon.** [1930–35]

pink′ slip′, notice of dismissal from one's job. [1910–15]

pink-slip (pingk′slip′) *v.t.,* **-slipped, -slip•ping.** to dismiss from a job: *He will be pink-slipped next month.* [1950–55]

Pink•ster (pingk′stər), *n. Hudson Valley (older use).* Whitsuntide. Also, **Pinxter.** [1790–1800, *Amer.*; < D *Pinksteren* << Gk *pentēkostḗ* PENTECOST]

pink′ster flow′er. See **pinxter flower.** [1865–70, *Amer.*]

pink′ stern′, *Naut.* a sharp stern having a narrow, overhanging, raking transom. [1885–60] —**pink′-sterned′,** *adj.*

pink′ tea′, *Informal.* a formal tea or reception. [1885–90, *Amer.*]

pink•y[1] (ping′kē), *n., pl.* **pink•ies.** pink[3]. [1830–40; < D *pinkie,* dial. var. of *pinkje,* dim. of *pink* PINK[3]]

pink•y[2] (ping′kē), *n., pl.* **pink•ies.** pinkie[1].

pin′ mark′, the circular indentation on the upper part of a type body, made by the pin that ejects the type from the caster. See diag. under **type.** [1885–90]

pin′ mon′ey, 1. any small sum set aside for nonessential minor expenditures. **2.** (formerly) an allowance of money given by a husband to his wife for her personal expenditures. [1535–45] —**pin′-mon′ey,** *adj.*

pin•na (pin′ə), *n., pl.* **pin•nae** (pin′ē), **pin•nas. 1.** *Bot.* one of the primary divisions of a pinnate leaf. **2.** *Zool.* **a.** a feather, wing, or winglike part. **b.** a fin or flipper. **3.** *Anat.* auricle (def. 1a). [1660–70; < L: feather, wing, fin] —**pin′nal,** *adj.*

pin•nace (pin′is), *n.* **1.** a light sailing ship, esp. one formerly used in attendance on a larger ship. **2.** any of various kinds of ship's boats. **3.** a small 17th-century ship having two or three masts and a flat stern, used in northern Europe as a warship and merchant ship and as a tender. [1540–50; < MF *pinace* < OSp *pinaza* lit., something made of *pino* PINE[1]]

pin•na•cle (pin′ə kəl), *n., v.,* **-cled, -cling.** —*n.* **1.** a lofty peak. **2.** the highest or culminating point, as of success, power, fame, etc.: *the pinnacle of one's career.* **3.** any pointed, towering part or formation, as of rock. **4.** *Archit.* a relatively small, upright structure, commonly terminating in a gable, a pyramid, or a cone, rising above the roof or coping of a building, or capping a tower, buttress, or other projecting architectural member. See illus. under **imbrication.** —*v.t.* **5.** to place on or as on a pinnacle. **6.** to form a pinnacle on; crown. [1300–50; ME *pinacle* < MF < LL *pinnāculum* gable, equiv. to L *pinn(a)* raised part of a parapet, lit., wing, feather (see PINNA) + *-āculum;* see TABERNACLE] —**Syn. 2.** apex, acme, summit, zenith. **3.** needle. —**Ant. 2.** base.

pin•nate (pin′āt, -it), *adj.* **1.** resembling a feather, as in construction or arrangement; having parts arranged on each side of a common axis: *a pinnate branch; pinnate trees.* **2.** *Bot.* (of a leaf) having leaflets or primary divisions arranged on each side of a common stalk. Also, **pin′nat•ed.** [1695–1705; < L *pinnātus* feathered, winged. See PINNA, -ATE[1]] —**pin′nate•ly, pin′nat•ed•ly,** *adv.*

pinnati-, a combining form representing **pinnate** in compound words: *pinnatipartite.* [repr. L *pinnātus;* see -I-]

pin•nat•i•fid (pi nat′ə fid), *adj. Bot.* (of a leaf) pinnately cleft, with clefts reaching halfway or more to the midrib. [1745–55; < NL *pinnātifidus.* See PINNATI-, -FID]

pin•na•tion (pi nā′shən), *n. Bot.* pinnate condition or formation. [1870–75; PINNATE + -ION]

pin•nat•i•ped (pi nat′ə ped′), *adj. Ornith.* having lobate feet. [1820–30; < NL *pinnātiped-* (s. of *pinnātipēs*). See PINNATI-, -PED]

pin•nat•i•sect (pi nat′ə sekt′), *adj. Bot.* (of a leaf) divided in a pinnate manner. [1855–60; PINNATI- + -SECT]

pin•ner (pin′ər), *n.* **1.** a person or thing that pins. **2.** a headdress with a long hanging flap pinned on at each side. **3.** a small apron fastened on by pins. [1645–55; PIN + -ER[1]]

pin•ni•grade (pin′i grād′), *adj.* **1.** moving by means of finlike parts or flippers, as the seals and walruses. —*n.* **2.** a pinnigrade animal. [1840–50; < NL *pinnigradus.* See PINNA, -I-, -GRADE]

pin•ni•ped (pin′ə ped′), *adj.* **1.** belonging to the Pinnipedia, a suborder of carnivores with limbs adapted to an aquatic life, including the seals and walruses. —*n.* **2.** a pinniped animal. [1835–45; < NL *Pinnipedia.* See PINNA, -I-, -PED, -IA] —**pin•ni•pe•di•an** (pin′ə pē′dē ən), *adj., n.*

pin•nu•la (pin′yə lə), *n., pl.* **-lae** (-lē′). **1.** a pinnule. **2.** a barb of a feather. [1740–50; < L, dim. of *pinna* PINNA; see -ULE]

pin•nu•late (pin′yə lāt′), *adj.* having pinnules. Also, **pin′nu•lat′ed.** [1820–30; PINNULE + -ATE[1]]

pin•nule (pin′yo͞ol), *n.* **1.** *Zool.* **a.** a part or organ resembling a barb of a feather, a fin, or the like. **b.** a finlet. **2.** *Bot.* a secondary pinna, one of the pinnately disposed divisions of a bipinnate leaf. **3.** a metal plate

CONCISE ETYMOLOGY KEY: <, descended or borrowed from; >, whence; b., blend of, blended; c., cognate with; cf., compare; deriv., derivative; equiv., equivalent; imit., imitative; obl., oblique; r., replacing; s., stem; sp., spelling, spelled; resp., respelling, respelled; trans., translation; ?, origin unknown; *, unattested; ‡, probably earlier than. See the full key inside the front cover.

with a small hole in it, used as a sight in a quadrant. [1585–95; < L *pinnula* PINNULA] —**pin·nu·lar** (pin′yə lər), *adj.*

pin′ oak′, an oak, *Quercus palustris,* characterized by the pyramidal manner of growth of its branches and deeply pinnatifid leaves. [1805–15, *Amer.*]

Pi·no·cchi·o (pi nō′kē ō′), *n.* the hero of Carlo Collodi's children's story, *The Adventures of Pinocchio* (1883), a wooden puppet who comes to life as a boy and whose nose grows longer whenever he tells a lie. [< It: lit., pine seed, pine cone, equiv. to *pin(o)* PINE[1] + *-occhio* < VL *-*uc(u)lu(m),* L *-i-culum;* see -I-, -CULE[1]]

Pi·no·chet U·gar·te (pē′nô chet′ ōō gär′te), **Au·gus·to** (ou gōōs′tô), born 1915, Chilean army general and political leader: president 1973–90.

pi·noch·le (pē′nuk əl, -nok-), *n.* **1.** a popular card game played by two, three, or four persons, with a 48-card deck. **2.** a meld of the queen of spades and the jack of diamonds in this game. Also, **penuchle, penuckle, pi′noc·le.** [1860–65, *Amer.*; < Swiss G *Binokel, Binoggel* < Swiss F *binocle* lit., pince-nez (see BINOCLE[1]), prob. adopted as synonym of the less current F *besicles* spectacles, folk-etymological alter. of *bezigue* BEZIQUE]

pi′nochle rum′my, *Cards.* See **five hundred rummy.**

pi·no·cy·tose (pin′ə sī tōs′, -tōz′, pī′nə-), *v.i.*, **-tosed, -tos·ing.** (of a cell) to take within by means of pinocytosis. [1955–60; back formation from PINOCYTOSIS]

pin·o·cy·to·sis (pin′ə sī tō′sis, pī′nə-), *n. Physiol.* the transport of fluid into a cell by means of local infoldings by the cell membrane so that a tiny vesicle or sac forms around each droplet, which is then taken into the interior of the cytoplasm. [1931; < Gk *pín(ein)* to drink + -O- + -CYTE + -OSIS, on the model of PHAGOCYTOSIS] —**pin·o·cy·tot·ic** (pin′ə sī tot′ik, pī′nə-), *adj.*

pi·no·le (pi nō′lē; *Sp.* pē nô′le), *n.* corn or wheat, dried, ground, and sweetened, usually with the flour of mesquite beans. [1835–45, *Amer.*; < MexSp < Nahuatl *pinolli* flour, something ground]

Pi·nole (pi nōl′), *n.* a town in W California. 14,253.

pi·ñon (pin′yən, pēn′yōn, pēn yōn′; *Sp.* pē nyôn′), *n., pl.* **pi·ñons,** *Sp.* ***pi·ño·nes*** (pē nyô′nes). **1.** Also, **pinyon.** Also called **pinyon pine, nut pine.** any of several pines of southwestern North America, as *Pinus monophylla* or *P. edulis,* bearing edible, nutlike seeds. **2.** Also called **pi′ñon nut′.** the seed. [1825–35, *Amer.*; < Sp *piñón,* deriv. of *piña* pine cone]

pi′ñon jay′. See **pinyon jay.** [1885–90]

Pi·not (pē nō′), *n.* **1.** any of several varieties of purple or white vinifera grapes yielding a red or white wine, used esp. in making burgundies and champagnes. **2.** a red **(Pinot Noir)** or white **(Pinot Blanc)** wine made from this grape. [1910–15; < F, equiv. to *pine* pine cone + *-ot* n. suffix]

Pi·not Blanc (pē′nō bläN′, pē nō′; *Fr.* pē nō bläN′). See under **Pinot** (def. 2). [1965–70]

Pi·not Char·don·nay (pē nō′ shär′dn ā′; *Fr.* pē nō shar dô ne′), Chardonnay.

Pi·not Noir (pē′nō nwär′, pē nō′; *Fr.* pē nō nwar′). See under **Pinot** (def. 2). Also, **pi′not noir′.** [1960–65]

pin′ plate′, *Building Trades.* a bearing plate having a projection for fixing into masonry. [1890–95]

pin·point (pin′point′), *n.* **1.** the point of a pin. **2.** a trifle; pinhead. **3.** a tiny spot or sharp point. —*v.t.* **4.** to locate or describe exactly or precisely: *to pinpoint the problem.* —*adj.* **5.** exact; precise: *pinpoint accuracy.* [1840–50; PIN + POINT]
—**Syn. 4.** spot, localize, identify, define.

pin′point bomb′ing. See **precision bombing.** [1940–45]

pin·prick (pin′prik′), *n.* **1.** any minute puncture made by a pin or the like. **2.** a negligible irritation or annoyance. [1745–55; PIN + PRICK]

pin′ rail′, **1.** *Theat.* a rail on a fly gallery, wall, etc., holding two rows of pins or cleats for securing lines attached to scenery. **2.** *Naut.* a strong rail at the side of the deck of a vessel, for holding the pins to which some of the running rigging is belayed. Cf. **fife rail.** [1875–80]

PINS (pinz), *n.* a person of less than 16 years of age placed under the jurisdiction of a juvenile court because of habitual disobedience, intractability, or antisocial but noncriminal behavior. [*P(erson) I(n) N(eed of) S(upervision)*]

pins′ and nee′dles, **1.** a tingly, prickly sensation in a limb that is recovering from numbness. **2. on pins and needles,** in a state of nervous anticipation: *The father-to-be was on pins and needles.* [1800–10]

pin·scher (pin′shər), *n.* one of a group of related dogs including the Doberman pinscher, miniature pinscher, and affenpinscher. [1925–30; by shortening]

pin′ seal′, leather made of the skin of young seals. [1925–30]

pin·set·ter (pin′set′ər), *n.* **1.** a mechanical apparatus in a bowling alley that places all of the pins into position at one time and removes pins that have been knocked down. **2.** See **pin boy.** [1915–20; PIN + SETTER]

Pinsk (pinsk; *Russ.* pyĕnsk), *n.* a city in SW Byelorussia (Belarus), E of Brest. 106,000.

pin′ spot′, *Theat.* **1.** a spotlight that produces a narrow beam of light illuminating a very small part of a stage, used esp. to focus attention on a detail. **2.** the beam of light so produced. [1945–50]

pin-spot (pin′spot′), *v.t.*, **-spot·ted, -spot·ting.** *Theat.* to illuminate with a pin spot. [v. use of PIN SPOT]

pin·spot·ter (pin′spot′ər), *n.* pinsetter. [1955–60; PIN + SPOTTER]

pin·stripe (pin′strīp′), *n.* **1.** a very thin stripe, esp. in fabrics. **2.** a pattern of such stripes. **3.** a fabric or garment having such stripes. [1895–1900; PIN + STRIPE[1]]

pin·striped (pin′strīpt′), *adj.* **1.** (of a fabric or garment) having a pattern of pin stripes. **2.** *Informal.* having or conveying the attitudes, policies, etc., often associated with persons who typically wear such garments in their work, as bankers or lawyers: *a pinstriped mind.* Also, **pin′-striped′.** [1895–1900; PINSTRIPE + -ED[3]]

pin·strip·ing (pin′strī′ping), *n.* a design, as on a fabric or surface, consisting of pinstripes: *There's a surcharge if the car has pinstriping.* [PINSTRIPE + -ING[1]]

pint (pīnt), *n.* a liquid and also dry measure of capacity, equal to one half of a liquid and dry quart respectively, approximately 35 cubic inches (0.6 liter). *Abbr.:* pt, pt. [1350–1400; ME *pynte* < OF *pinte* or MD, MLG *pinte*]

pin·ta (pin′tə; *Sp.* pēn′tä), *n. Pathol.* a nonvenereal treponematosis occurring chiefly in Central and South America, caused by *Treponema carateum,* characterized by spots of various colors on the skin. [1815–25; < AmerSp, special use of Sp *pinta* spot < VL **pincta,* fem. of **pinctus,* nasalized var. of L *pictus,* ptp. of *pingere* to PAINT]

Pin·ta (pin′tə; *Sp.* pēn′tä), *n.* one of the three ships under the command of Columbus during his first voyage to America in 1492.

pin·ta·do (pin tä′dō), *n., pl.* **-dos, -does.** cero (def. 1). Also, **pin·ta·da** (pin tä′də). [1595–1605; < Pg, ptp. of *pintar* to paint < VL **pinctus* painted. See PINTA]

pin·tail (pin′tāl′), *n., pl.* **-tails,** (*esp. collectively*) **-tail. 1.** a long-necked river duck, *Anas acuta,* of the Old and New Worlds, having long and narrow middle tail feathers. **2.** See **sharp-tailed grouse.** [1760–70; PIN + TAIL[1]]

pin-tailed (pin′tāld′), *adj. Ornith.* **1.** having a tapered tail with long, pointed central feathers. **2.** having the feathers of the tail stiff, narrow, and pointed. [1870–75]

pin·ta·no (pin tä′nō), *n., pl.* **-nos.** See **sergeant major** (def. 3). [< Cuban Sp]

Pin·ter (pin′tər), *n.* **Harold,** born 1930, English playwright.

pin′ the tail′ on the don′key, a children's party game in which a blindfolded player, holding a paper tail, is turned around several times before a large picture of a tailless donkey that the player then attempts to locate in order to pin the tail in place. Also, **pin′-the-tail′-on-the-don′key.**

pin·tle (pin′tl), *n.* **1.** a pin or bolt, esp. one on which something turns, as the gudgeon of a hinge. **2.** a pin, bolt, or hook by which a gun or the like is attached to the rear of a towing vehicle. **3.** a cast iron or steel base for a wooden post, often cast in a single piece with a cap for a lower post. [bef. 1100; ME *pintel* penis, OE; c. ODan *pintel*]

pintle (def. 1)

pin·to (pin′tō, pēn′-), *adj., n., pl.* **-tos.** —*adj.* **1.** marked with spots of white and other colors; mottled; spotted: *a pinto horse.* —*n.* **2.** *Western U.S.* a pinto horse. **3.** See **pinto bean.** [1855–60, *Amer.*; < AmerSp (obs. Sp) < VL **pinctus* painted; see PINTA]

pin′to bean′, a variety of the common bean, *Phaseolus vulgaris,* having mottled or spotted seeds: grown chiefly in the southern U.S. [1915–20, *Amer.*]

Pintsch′ gas′ (pinch), gas with high illuminating power made from shale oil or petroleum, used in buoys, lighthouses, and railroad cars. [named after Richard *Pintsch* (1840–1919), German inventor]

pint-size (pīnt′sīz′), *adj. Informal.* comparatively small in size: *a pint-size typewriter.* Also, **pint′-sized′.** [1935–40]

pin·up (pin′up′), *n.* **1.** a large photograph, as of a sexually attractive person, suitable for pinning on a wall. **2.** a person in such a photograph. **3.** a device or fixture that is fastened to a wall, as a lamp. —*adj.* **4.** of, pertaining to, or appearing in a pinup: *a pinup girl.* **5.** designed or suitable for hanging or fastening on a wall: *a pinup lamp.* Also, **pin′-up′.** [1670–80 for general senses; 1940–45 as photograph of a pretty woman; n., adj. use of *pin up*]

pin′wale cor′duroy (pin′wāl′), a lightweight corduroy with very thin wales. [PIN + WALE[1]]

pin·wheel (pin′hwēl′, -wēl′), *n.* **1.** a child's toy consisting of a wheel or leaflike curls of paper or plastic loosely attached by a pin to a stick, designed to revolve when blown by or as by the wind. **2.** Also called **catherine wheel.** a kind of firework supported on a pin which, when ignited, revolves rapidly and gives a dazzling display of light. **3.** a wheel having pins at right angles to its rim for engaging the teeth of a gear. —*v.i.* **4.** to revolve rapidly like a pinwheel: *Images of the past pinwheeled through his mind.* Also, **pin′ wheel′.** [1695–1705; PIN + WHEEL]

pin′wheel escape′ment, a clock escapement in which two pallets, usually of unequal length, alternately engage and release pins set on the escape wheel perpendicular to its plane of rotation. [1880–85]

pin·wheel·ing (pin′hwē′ling, -wē′-), *n. U.S. Naut.* the act of turning a multiple-screw ship within a minimum radius by having some engines going forward and others going in reverse. [PINWHEEL + -ING[1]]

pin·work (pin′wûrk′), *n.* (in the embroidery of needlepoint lace) crescent-shaped stitches raised from the surface of the design. [1885–90; PIN + WORK]

pin·worm (pin′wûrm′), *n.* a small nematode worm, *Enterobius vermicularis,* infesting the intestine and migrating to the rectum and anus, esp. in children. [1905–10; PIN + WORM]

pin′ wrench′, a wrench having a pin for insertion into the heads of certain bolts to drive them. Cf. **spanner** (def. 2).

pinx., pinxit.

pinx·it (pingk′sit), *v. Latin.* he or she painted (it): formerly used on paintings as part of the artist's signature.

Pinx·ter (pingk′stər), *n.* Pinkster.

pinx′ter flow′er, a wild azalea, *Rhododendron periclymenoides,* of the U.S., having pink or purplish flowers. Also, **pinkster flower.** Also called **wild honeysuckle.** [1865–70, *Amer.*]

pin·y (pī′nē), *adj.*, **pin·i·er, pin·i·est. 1.** abounding in or covered with pine trees: *piny hillsides.* **2.** pertaining to or suggestive of pine trees: *a piny fragrance.* Also, **piney.** [1620–30; PINE[1] + -Y[1]]

COMPARATIVE SPELLINGS OF PINYIN AND TRADITIONAL FORMS

Traditional Name or Form*	Pinyin
chiao (dime)	jiao
Chou En-lai	Zhou Enlai
Hunan	Hunan
jên-min-pi	renminbi
Kweilin	Guilin
Mao Tse-tung	Mao Zedong
Nanching	Nanjing
Peking	Beijing
Sian	Xian
Soochow	Suzhou
Szechwan, Szechuan	Sichuan
t'ai chi ch'uan	tai ji quan
Teng Hsiao-ping	Deng Xiaoping

*This column includes the Wade-Giles transliterations and other older forms.

pin·yin (pin′yin′), *n.* (*sometimes cap.*) a system for transliterating Chinese into the Latin alphabet: introduced in 1958 and adopted as the official system of romanization by the People's Republic of China in 1979. Cf. **Wade-Giles system.** [< Chin *pīnyīn* lit., phonetic spelling (*pīn* arrange, classify + *yīn* sound, pronunciation)]

pin·yon (pin′yən, pēn′yōn, pēn yōn′), *n.* piñon (def. 1). Also called **pin′yon pine′.**

pin′yon jay′, a grayish-blue, uncrested jay, *Gymnorhinus cyanocephalus,* found in mountainous parts of the western U.S. Also called **piñon jay.** [1885–90, *Amer.*]

Pin·za (pin′zə; *It.* pēn′dzä), *n.* **E·zi·o** (et′sē ō′, ā′zē ō′; *It.* e′tsyô), 1895–1957, Italian basso, in the U.S.

Pin·zón (pēn thôn′), *n.* **Mar·tín A·lon·zo** (mär tēn′ ä lôn′thô), c1440–93?, and his brother, **Vi·cen·te Yá·ñez** (bē then′te yä′nyeth), c1460–1524?, Spanish navigators with Christopher Columbus.

PIO, *U.S. Mil.* **1.** public information office. **2.** public information officer.

pi·o·let (pē′ə lā′), *n.* an ice ax used in mountaineering. [1865–70; < F < Franco-Provencal; cf. *piolet, pioula,* derivs. of *apia* << Gmc; see HATCHET]

pi·on (pī′on), *n. Physics.* the first meson to be discovered: it has spin 0 and may be positively or negatively charged or neutral; charged pions decay into a muon and a neutrino or antineutrino. *Symbol:* π Also called **pi meson.** [1950–55; PI (MESON) + -ON[1]]

pi·o·neer (pī′ə nēr′), *n.* **1.** a person who is among those who first enter or settle a region, thus opening it for occupation and development by others. **2.** one who is first or among the earliest in any field of inquiry, enterprise, or progress: *pioneers in cancer research.* **3.** one of a group of foot soldiers detailed to make roads, dig intrenchments, etc., in advance of the main body. **4.** *Ecol.* an organism that successfully establishes itself in a barren area, thus starting an ecological cycle of life. **5.** (*cap.*) *Aerospace.* one of a series of U.S. space probes that explored the solar system and transmitted scientific information to earth. **6.** (*cap.*) a member of a Communist organization in the Soviet Union for children ranging in age from 10 to 16. Cf. **Komsomol, Octobrist.** —*v.i.* **7.** to act as a pioneer. —*v.t.* **8.** to be the first to open or prepare (a way, settlement, etc.). **9.** to take part in the beginnings of; initiate: *to pioneer an aid program.* **10.** to lead the way for (a group); guide. —*adj.* **11.** being the earliest, original, first of a particular kind, etc.: *a pioneer method of adult education.* **12.** of, pertaining to, or characteristic of pioneers: *pioneer justice.* **13.** being a pioneer: *a pioneer fur trader.* [1515–25; < MF *pionier,* OF *peonier* foot soldier. See PEON, -EER]
—**Syn. 2.** leader, trailblazer, forerunner, pathfinder.

Pioneer′ Day′, *U.S. Hist.* a legal holiday in Utah on July 24 to commemorate Brigham Young's founding of Salt Lake City in 1847.

CONCISE PRONUNCIATION KEY: *act, cāpe, dâre, pärt; set, ēqual; if, īce; ox, ōver, ôrder, oil, bŏŏk, bōōt, out; up, ûrge; child; sing; shoe; thin, that;* zh *as in treasure.* ə = *a* as in *alone, e* as in *system, i* as in *easily, o* as in *gallop, u* as in *circus;* ᵊ as in *fire* (fīᵊr), *hour* (ouᵊr). l and n can serve as syllabic consonants, as in *cradle* (krād′l), and *button* (but′n). See the full key inside the front cover.

Pioneers, The, a historical novel (1823) by James Fenimore Cooper. Cf. **Leather-Stocking Tales.**

pi·os·i·ty (pī os′i tē), *n., pl.* **-ties. 1.** an excessive or obvious show of piety; sanctimoniousness. **2.** an act or instance of such piety: *the piosities of our Puritan forefathers.* [1920–25; PIOUS + -ITY; modeled on *religious, religiosity*]

pi·ous (pī′əs), *adj.* **1.** having or showing a dutiful spirit of reverence for God or an earnest wish to fulfill religious obligations. **2.** characterized by a hypocritical concern with virtue or religious devotion; sanctimonious. **3.** practiced or used in the name of real or pretended religious motives, or for some ostensibly good object; falsely earnest or sincere: *a pious deception.* **4.** of or pertaining to religious devotion; sacred rather than secular: *pious literature.* **5.** having or showing appropriate respect or regard for parents or others. [1595–1605; < L *pius,* akin to *piāre* to propitiate] **—pi′ous·ly,** *adv.* **—pi′ous·ness,** *n.*
—Syn. 1. devout, godly, reverent. See **religious.**

Pi·oz·zi (pē ot′sē; *It.* pyôt′tsē), *n.* **Hester Lynch.** See **Thrale, Hester Lynch.**

pip[1] (pip), *n.* **1.** one of the spots on dice, playing cards, or dominoes. **2.** each of the small segments into which the surface of a pineapple is divided. **3.** *Informal.* metal insigne of rank on the shoulders of commissioned officers. **4.** *Hort.* **a.** an individual rootstock of a plant, esp. of the lily of the valley. **b.** a portion of the rootstock or root of several other plants, as the peony. [1590–1600; earlier *peep;* orig. uncert.]

pip[2] (pip), *n.* **1.** *Vet. Pathol.* a contagious disease of birds, esp. poultry, characterized by the secretion of a thick mucus in the mouth and throat. **2.** *Facetious.* any minor or unspecified ailment in a person. [1375–1425; late ME *pippe* < MD < VL **pipita,* for L *pītuīta* phlegm, pip]

pip[3] (pip), *n.* **1.** a small seed, esp. of a fleshy fruit, as an apple or orange. **2.** Also called **pipperoo.** *Informal.* someone or something wonderful: *Last night's party was a pip.* [1590–1600; 1910–15 for def. 2; short for PIPPIN]

pip[4] (pip), *v.,* **pipped, pip·ping.** *—v.i.* **1.** to peep or chirp. **2.** (of a young bird) to break out from the shell. *—v.t.* **3.** to crack or chip a hole through (the shell), as a young bird. [1650–60; var. of PEEP[2]]

pip[5] (pip), *n. Electronics.* blip (def. 1). [1940–45; imit.]

pip[6] (pip), *v.t.,* **pipped, pip·ping.** *Brit. Slang.* **1.** to blackball. **2.** to defeat (an opponent). **3.** to shoot, esp. to wound or kill by a gunshot. [1875–80; perh. special use of PIP[1], in metaphorical sense of a small ball]

Pip (pip), *n.* a male given name, form of **Philip.**

pi·pa (pē′pä′), *n.* a short-necked fretted lute of Chinese origin. [1840–50; < Chin *píba* or *pípa* lute (lit., loquat, which it resembles in shape)]

pip·age (pī′pij), *n.* **1.** conveyance, as of water, gas, or oil, by means of pipes. **2.** the pipes so used. **3.** the sum charged for the conveyance. [1605–15; PIPE[1] + -AGE]

pi·pal (pī′pəl, pē′-), *n.* a fig tree, *Ficus religiosa,* of India, somewhat resembling the banyan. Also, **peepul.** [1780–90; < Hindi *pīpal* < Skt *pippala*]

pipe[1] (pīp), *n., v.,* **piped, pip·ing.** *—n.* **1.** a hollow cylinder of metal, wood, or other material, used for the conveyance of water, gas, steam, petroleum, etc. **2.** a tube of wood, clay, hard rubber, or other material, with a small bowl at one end, used for smoking tobacco, opium, etc. **3.** a quantity, as of tobacco, that fills the bowl of such a smoking utensil. **4.** *Music.* **a.** a tube used as, or to form an essential part of, a musical wind instrument. **b.** a musical wind instrument consisting of a single tube of straw, reed, wood, or other material, as a flute, clarinet, or oboe. **c.** one of the wooden or metal tubes from which the tones of an organ are produced. **d.** a small end-blown flute played with one hand while the other beats a small drum. **5.** *Naut.* **a.** See **boatswain's pipe. b.** the sound of a boatswain's pipe. **6.** the call or utterance of a bird, frog, etc. **7. pipes,** *Informal.* the human vocal cords or the voice, esp. as used in singing. **8.** Usually, **pipes. a.** *Music.* bagpipe. **b.** a set of flutes, as a panpipe. **c.** *Informal.* a tubular organ or passage of a human or animal body, esp. a respiratory passage: *to complain of congested pipes.* **9.** any of various tubular or cylindrical objects, parts, or formations, as an eruptive passage of a volcano or geyser. **10.** *Mining.* **a.** a cylindrical vein or body of ore. **b.** (in South Africa) a vertical, cylindrical matrix, of intrusive igneous origin, in which diamonds are found. **11.** *Metall.* a depression occurring at the center of the head of an ingot as a result of the tendency of solidification to begin at the bottom and sides of the ingot mold. **12.** *Bot.* the stem of a plant. *—v.i.* **13.** to play on a pipe. **14.** *Naut.* to signal, as with a boatswain's pipe. **15.** to speak in a high-pitched or piercing tone. **16.** to make or utter a shrill sound like that of a pipe: *songbirds piping at dawn.* *—v.t.* **17.** to convey by or as by pipes: *to pipe water from the lake.* **18.** to supply with pipes. **19.** to play (music) on a pipe or pipes. **20.** to summon, order, etc., by sounding the boatswain's pipe or whistle: *all hands were piped on deck.* **21.** to bring, lead, etc., by or as by playing on a pipe: *to pipe dancers.* **22.** to utter in a shrill tone: *to pipe a command.* **23.** to trim or finish with piping, as an article of clothing. **24.** *Cookery.* to force (dough, frosting, etc.) through a pastry tube onto a baking sheet, cake or pie, etc. **25.** *Informal.* to convey by an electrical wire or cable: *to pipe a signal from the antenna.* **26.** *Slang.* to look at; notice: *Pipe the cat in the hat.* **27. pipe down,** *Slang.* to stop talking; be quiet: *He shouted at us to pipe down.* **28. pipe up, a.** to begin to play (a musical instrument) or to sing. **b.** to make oneself heard; speak up, esp. as to assert oneself. **c.** to increase in velocity, as the wind. [bef. 1000; (n.) ME, OE *pipe* musical pipe, tube (c. D *pijp,* LG *pipe,* G *Pfeife,* ON *pīpa*) < VL **pīpa,* deriv. of L *pīpāre* to chirp, play a pipe; (v.) ME *pipen;* in part continuing OE *pīpian* to play a pipe < L *pīpāre;* in part < OF *piper* to make a shrill sound < L *pīpāre* (cf. PEEP[2])] **—pipe′less,** *adj.* **—pipe′like′,** *adj.*
—Syn. 16. cheep, chitter, whistle, chirp, peep, trill, twitter, tweet.

pipe[2] (pīp), *n.* **1.** a large cask, of varying capacity, esp. for wine or oil. **2.** such a cask as a measure of liquid capacity, equal to 4 barrels, 2 hogsheads, or half a tun, and containing 126 wine gallons. **3.** such a cask with its contents. [1350–1400; ME < MF, ult. same as PIPE[1]]

pipe′ bat′ten, batten[2] (def. 5a).

pipe′ bomb′, a small homemade bomb typically contained in a metal pipe. [1965–70]

pipe′ clay′, a fine, white clay used for making tobacco pipes, whitening parts of military or other dress, etc. [1750–60]

pipe-clay (pīp′klā′), *v.t.* to whiten with pipe clay. [1825–35]

pipe′ clean′er, a short length of twisted flexible wires covered with tufted fabric, used to clean the stem of a smoker's pipe and for various handicrafts. [1865–70]

pipe′ cut′ter, a machine or tool used for cutting pipe. [1885–90]

pipe′ dream′, any fantastic notion, hope, or story: *Her plans for a movie career are just a pipe dream.* [1895–1900, *Amer.*]

pipe-dream (pīp′drēm′), *v.i.,* **-dreamed** or **-dreamt, -dream·ing.** to indulge in pipe dreams; fantasize.

pipe·fish (pīp′fish′), *n., pl.* (*esp. collectively*) **-fish,** (*esp. referring to two or more kinds or species*) **-fish·es.** any elongated, marine and sometimes freshwater fish species of the family Syngnathidae, having a tubular snout and covered with bony plates. [1760–70; PIPE[1] + FISH]

pipe′ fit′ter, a person who installs and repairs pipe systems. [1885–90]

pipe′ fit′ting, 1. a joint or connector, as an elbow, union, or tee, used in a pipe system. **2.** the work performed by a pipe fitter. [1885–90; PIPE[1] + FIT[1] + -ING[1]]

pipe·ful (pīp′fo͝ol), *n., pl.* **-fuls.** a quantity sufficient to fill the bowl of a pipe: *a pipeful of tobacco.* [1595–1605; PIPE[1] + -FUL]
—Usage. See **-ful.**

pipe-lay·er (pīp′lā′ər), *n.* a worker employed in laying a pipeline or one experienced in such work. Also, **pipe′lay′er.** [1830–40]

pipe·line (pīp′līn′), *n., v.,* **-lined, -lin·ing.** *—n.* **1.** a long tubular conduit or series of pipes, often underground, with pumps and valves for flow control, used to transport crude oil, natural gas, water, etc., esp. over great distances. **2.** a route, channel, or process along which something passes or is provided at a steady rate; means, system, or flow of supply or supplies: *Freighters and cargo planes are a pipeline for overseas goods.* **3.** a channel of information, esp. one that is direct, privileged, or confidential; inside source; reliable contact. **4. in the pipeline, a.** *Informal.* in the process of being developed, provided, or completed; in the works; under way. **b.** *Govt. Informal.* (of funds) authorized but not spent. *—v.t.* **5.** to convey by or as if by pipeline: *to pipeline oil from the far north to ice-free ports; to pipeline graduates into the top jobs.* [1855–60; PIPE[1] + LINE[1]]

pipe·lin·er (pīp′lī′nər), *n.* a person or company that specializes in laying pipelines. [1925–30, *Amer.;* PIPELINE + -ER[1]]

pipe·lin·ing (pīp′lī′ning), *n.* the act, technique, or business of installing pipelines. [1885–90; PIPELINE + -ING[1]]

pip em·ma (pip′ em′ə), *Brit.* in, on, or during the afternoon. [1910–15; phrase repr. *P.M.,* used by signalmen]

pipe′ of peace′, a calumet; peace pipe. [1685–95, *Amer.*]

pipe′ or′gan, organ (def. 1). [1880–85, *Amer.*]

pip·er (pī′pər), *n.* **1.** a person who plays on a pipe. **2.** a bagpiper. **3. pay the piper, a.** to pay the cost of something. **b.** to bear the unfavorable consequences of one's actions or pleasures: *Someday he'll have to pay the piper for all that gambling.* [bef. 1000; ME; OE *pīpere.* See PIPE[1], -ER[1]]

pip·er·a·ceous (pip′ə rā′shəs, pī′pə-), *adj.* belonging to the Piperacae, the pepper family of plants. Cf. **pepper family.** [1665–75; < NL *Piperac(ae)* (*Piper* the type genus (L: PEPPER) + *-aceae* -ACEAE) + -OUS]

pi·per·a·cil·lin (pī per′ə sil′in), *n. Pharm.* a broad-spectrum semisynthetic penicillin, $C_{23}H_{26}N_5NaO_7$, used against certain susceptible Gram-positive and Gram-negative bacteria and certain anaerobes, esp. *P. aeruginosa.* [*pipera(zinyl),* a component of its chemical name (see PIPERAZINE, -YL) + *-cillin,* as in PENICILLIN]

pipe′ rack′, 1. a usually wheeled rack of metal piping on which to hang clothing, as in a store. **2.** a small rack, usually of wood, for holding a smoker's pipes.

pipe-rack (pīp′rak′), *adj. Informal.* offering services or goods at low cost because of avoidance of expensive interior decoration, as by displaying clothing for sale on plain pipe racks. [1945–50]

pi·per·a·zine (pi per′ə zēn′, -zin, pī-, pip′ər ə-), *n. Chem.* **1.** Also called **pip·er·az·i·dine** (pip′ə raz′i dēn′, -din, pī′pə-). a colorless, crystalline, deliquescent ring compound, $C_4H_{10}N_2$, prepared by the reaction of ethylene bromide or ethylene chloride with ammonia: used chiefly in veterinary medicine as an anthelmintic, and as an insecticide. **2.** any derivative of this compound. [1885–90; < L *piper* PEPPER + -AZINE]

pi·per·i·dine (pi per′i dēn′, -din, pī-, pip′ər i-), *n. Chem.* a colorless, water-soluble liquid, $C_5H_{11}N$, obtained from the alkaloid piperine or from pyridine: used chiefly as a solvent. [1850–55; < L *piper* PEPPER + -ID[3] + -INE[1]]

pip·er·ine (pip′ə rēn′, -ər in), *n. Chem.* a white, crystalline alkaloid, $C_{17}H_{19}NO_3$, obtained from pepper and other piperaceous plants and also prepared synthetically: used as an insecticide. [1810–20; < L *piper* PEPPER + -INE[1]]

pi·per·o·nal (pi per′ə nal′, pī-, pip′ər ə-), *n. Chem.* a white, crystalline, water-insoluble aldehyde, $C_8H_6O_3$, which darkens on exposure to light: used chiefly in perfumery and organic synthesis. Also called **piper′onyl al′dehyde, heliotropin.** [1865–70; PIPER(INE) + -ONE + -AL[1]]

pi·per′o·nyl butox′ide (pi per′ə nl, pī-, pip′ər ə-nil), *Chem.* a light-brown liquid, $C_{19}H_{30}O_5$, used chiefly as a synergist in certain insecticides. [1940–45; PIPERON(AL) + -YL; *but-* (from BUTYRIC) + OXIDE]

pipe′ snake′, any of several nonvenomous, burrowing snakes of the genus *Cylindrophis,* of southeastern Asia and the Malay Archipelago, having an evenly cylindrical body.

pipe·stem (pīp′stem′), *n.* **1.** the stem of a tobacco pipe. **2.** something resembling this in slenderness, as an unusually thin arm or leg. [1720–30, *Amer.;* PIPE[1] + STEM[1]]

pipe·stone (pīp′stōn′), *n.* a reddish argillaceous stone used by North American Indians for making tobacco pipes. [1755–65; PIPE[1] + STONE]

pi·pet (pī pet′, pi-), *n., v.t.,* **-pet·ted, -pet·ting.** pipette.

pi·pette (pī pet′, pi-), *n., v.,* **-pet·ted, -pet·ting.** *—n.* **1.** a slender graduated tube used in a laboratory for measuring and transferring quantities of liquids from one container to another. *—v.t.* **2.** to measure or transfer a quantity of a liquid with a pipette. [1830–40; < F; see PIPE[1], -ETTE]

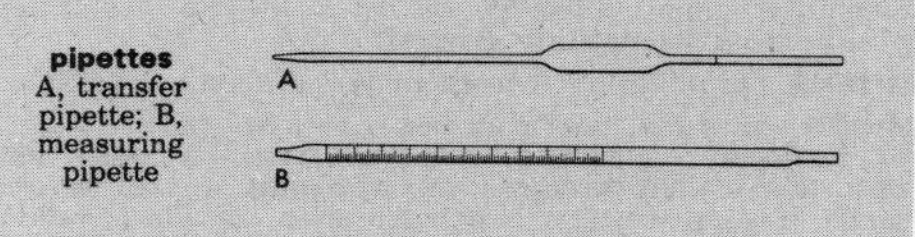

pipettes A, transfer pipette; B, measuring pipette

pipe′ vine′, the Dutchman's-pipe. [1805–15]

pipe′ wrench′, a tool having two toothed jaws, one fixed and the other free to grip pipes and other tubular objects when the tool is turned in one direction only. [1885–90]

pi·pi (pē′pē), *n., pl.* **-pi, -pis. 1.** an edible bivalve of eastern Australia, *Plebidonax deltoides.* **2.** an edible bivalve of New Zealand, *Mesodesma novae-zelandiae.* [1810–20; < Maori]

pip·ing (pī′ping), *n.* **1.** pipes collectively; a system or network of pipes. **2.** material formed into a pipe or pipes. **3.** the act of a person or thing that pipes. **4.** the sound of pipes. **5.** a shrill sound. **6.** the music of pipes. **7.** a cordlike ornamentation made of icing, used on pastry. **8.** a tubular band of ornamental material, sometimes containing a cord, used for trimming the edges and seams of clothing, upholstery, etc. *—adj.* **9.** characterized by the peaceful music of the pipe. **10.** playing on a musical pipe. **11.** that pipes. **12.** emitting a shrill sound: *a piping voice.* **13. piping hot,** (of food or drink) very hot. [1200–50; ME (ger.); see PIPE[1], -ING[1], -ING[2]] **—pip′ing·ly,** *adv.*

pip·i·strelle (pip′ə strel′, pip′ə strel′), *n.* any of numerous insectivorous bats of the genus *Pipistrellus,* esp. *P. pipistrellus* of Europe and Asia. [1775–85; < F < It *pipistrello,* var. of *vipistrello* << L *vespertīliōn-* (s. of *vespertīliō*) bat. See VESPERTILIONINE]

pip·it (pip′it), *n.* any of several small songbirds of the genus *Anthus,* of the family Motacillidae, resembling the larks in coloration, structure, and habits. [1760–70; imit.]

pip·kin (pip′kin), *n.* **1.** a small, earthen pot. **2.** *Brit. Dial.* a piggin. [1555–65; perh. PIPE[2] + -KIN]

Pip·pa (pip′ə; *It.* pēp′pä), *n.* a female given name, Italian form of **Philippa.**

pip·per (pip′ər), *n.* the center of the reticule of a gunsight. [PIP[1] + -ER[1]]

pip·per·oo (pip′ə ro͞o′), *n., pl.* **-oos.** *Slang.* pip[3] (def. 2). [PIP[3] + -EROO]

pip·pin (pip′in), *n.* **1.** any of numerous roundish or oblate varieties of apple. **2.** *Bot.* a seed. [1250–1300; ME *pipin,* var. of *pepin* < OF]

pip·sis·se·wa (pip sis′ə wə, -wô′), *n.* any evergreen plant of the genus *Chimaphila,* esp. *C. umbellata,* the leaves of which are used medicinally for their tonic, diuretic, and astringent properties. Also called **prince's-pine.** [1780–90, *Amer.;* perh. < Eastern Abenaki *kpi-psk*ʷ*áhsawe* lit., flower of the woods]

pip·squeak (pip′skwēk′), *n. Informal.* a contemptibly small or unimportant person; a twerp. [1895–1900; PIP[4] + SQUEAK]

pip·y (pī′pē), *adj.,* **pip·i·er, pip·i·est. 1.** pipelike; tubular. **2.** piping; shrill: *a pipy voice.* [1715–25; PIPE[1] + -Y[1]]

Piq·ua (pik′wä, -wə), *n.* a city in W Ohio. 20,480.

pi·quant (pē′kənt, -känt, pē känt′), *adj.* **1.** agreeably pungent or sharp in taste or flavor; pleasantly biting or tart: *a piquant aspic.* **2.** agreeably stimulating, interesting, or attractive: *a piquant glance.* **3.** of an interestingly provocative or lively character: *a piquant wit.* **4.** *Archaic.* sharp or stinging, esp. to the feelings. [1515–25; < F: lit., pricking (see PIQUE[1], -ANT); r. *pickante* < It *piccante*] **—pi′quan·cy, pi′quant·ness,** *n.* **—pi′quant·ly,** *adv.*
—Syn. 1. spicy. **2.** intriguing. **3.** sharp, clever.
—Ant. 1. insipid.

pique[1] (pēk), *v.,* **piqued, piqu•ing,** *n.* —*v.t.* **1.** to affect with sharp irritation and resentment, esp. by some wound to pride: *She was greatly piqued when they refused her invitation.* **2.** to wound (the pride, vanity, etc.). **3.** to excite (interest, curiosity, etc.): *Her curiosity was piqued by the gossip.* **4.** to arouse an emotion or provoke to action: *to pique someone to answer a challenge.* **5.** *Archaic.* to pride (oneself) (usually fol. by *on* or *upon*). —*v.i.* **6.** to arouse pique in someone: *an action that piqued when it was meant to soothe.* —*n.* **7.** a feeling of irritation or resentment, as from a wound to pride or self-esteem: *to be in a pique.* **8.** *Obs.* a state of irritated feeling between persons. [1525–35; < MF *pique* (n.), *piquer* (v.) < VL **piccare* to PICK[1]; see PICKAX, PIKE[2], PIQUÉ]
—Syn. 1. offend, sting, nettle, vex, irritate, chafe. **2.** affront. **3.** stimulate, stir, prick, incite, goad. **—Ant. 1.** please. **2.** compliment.

pique[2] (pēk), *n. Piquet.* pic[2].

pi•que[3] (pi kā′, pē-), *n., adj.* piqué.

pi•qué (pi kā′, pē-; *Fr.* pē kā′), *n., pl.* **-qués** (-kāz′; *Fr.* -kā′) for 2, *adj.* —*n.* **1.** a fabric of cotton, spun rayon, or silk, woven lengthwise with raised cords. **2.** *Ballet.* a step in which the dancer steps onto the tip of the toe without bending the knee. **3.** ornamentation by means of punched or stippled patterns, sometimes inlaid with metal, ivory, tortoise shell, etc. —*adj.* **4.** (of glove seams and gloves) stitched through lapping edges. **5.** decorated with inlay: *a piqué box.* Also, **pique.** [1830–40; < F, ptp. of *piquer* to quilt, prick; see PIQUE[1]]

pi•quet (pi kā′, -ket′), *n.* a card game played by two persons with a pack of 32 cards, the cards from deuces to sixes being excluded. Also, **picquet.** [1640–50; < F; see PIC[2], -ET]

pir (pēr), *n. Islam.* **1.** a term of respect for the head of a religious group, esp. in Pakistan and various areas of the Middle and Near East. **2.** a religious instructor, esp. in mystical sects. [1665–75; < Hindi, Urdu *pīr* old man < Pers]

Pi•ra•ci•ca•ba (pē′rä si kä′bä), *n.* a city in SE Brazil, NW of São Paulo. 125,490.

pi•ra•cy (pī′rə sē), *n., pl.* **-cies. 1.** practice of a pirate; robbery or illegal violence at sea. **2.** the unauthorized reproduction or use of a copyrighted book, recording, television program, patented invention, trademarked product, etc.: *The record industry is beset with piracy.* **3.** Also called **stream capture.** *Geol.* diversion of the upper part of one stream by the headward growth of another. [1545–55; earlier *pyracie* < ML *pirātia* < LGk *peirāteia.* See PIRATE, -ACY]

Pi•rae•us (pī rē′əs, pi rā′-), *n.* a seaport in SE Greece: the port of Athens. 186,223. Also, **Peiraeus.** Greek, **Peiraievs.**

pi•ra•gua (pi rä′gwə, -rag′wə), *n.* **1.** Also, **pirogue.** a canoe made by hollowing out a tree trunk. **2.** a flat-bottomed sailing vessel having two masts. [1525–35; < Sp < Carib: dugout]

Pi•ran•del•lo (pir′ən del′ō; *It.* pē′rän del′lō), *n.* **Lu•i•gi** (lo͞o ē′jē), 1867–1936, Italian dramatist, novelist, and poet: Nobel prize 1934.

Pi•ra•ne•si (pē′rä ne′zē), *n.* **Giam•bat•tis•ta** (jäm′bät-tēs′tä) or **Gio•van•ni Bat•tis•ta** (jô vän′nē bät tēs′tä), 1720–78, Italian architect and engraver.

pi•ra•nha (pi rän′yə, -ran′- or, *often,* -rä′nə, -ran′ə), *n., pl.* **-nhas,** (*esp. collectively*) **-nha.** any of several small South American freshwater fishes of the genus *Serrasalmus* that eat other fish and sometimes plants but occasionally also attack humans and other large animals that enter the water. Also called **caribe.** [1865–70; < Pg < Tupi]

piranha, *Serrasalmus rhombeus,* length to 1½ ft. (0.5 m)

Pi•ra•pó•ra (pē′rä pô′rä), *n.* a city in E Brazil. 16,889.

pi•ra•ru•cu (pi rär′ə ko͞o′), *n.* the arapaima. [1830–40; < Pg < Tupi *pirá-rucú* lit., red fish]

pi•rate (pī′rət), *n., v.,* **-rat•ed, -rat•ing.** —*n.* **1.** a person who robs or commits illegal violence at sea or on the shores of the sea. **2.** a ship used by such persons. **3.** any plunderer, predator, etc.: *confidence men, slumlords, and other pirates.* **4.** a person who uses or reproduces the work or invention of another without authorization. **5.** Also called **pi′rate stream′.** *Geol.* a stream that diverts into its own flow the headwaters of another stream, river, etc. —*v.t.* **6.** to commit piracy upon; plunder; rob. **7.** to take by piracy: *to pirate gold.* **8.** to use or reproduce (a book, an invention, etc.) without authorization or legal right: *to pirate hit records.* **9.** to take or entice away for one's own use: *Our competitor is trying to pirate our best salesman.* —*v.i.* **10.** to commit or practice piracy. [1250–1300; ME < L *pīrāta* < Gk *peirātḗs,* equiv. to *peirā-,* var. s. of *peirân* to attack + *-tēs* agent n. suffix] **—pi′rate•like′,** *adj.* **—pi•rat•i•cal** (pī rat′i kəl, pi-), **pi•rat′ic,** *adj.* **—pi•rat′i•cal•ly,** *adv.*
—Syn. 1. freebooter, buccaneer, corsair, plunderer.

Pi′rate Coast′. See under **United Arab Emirates.**

pi′rate perch′, a purplish North American freshwater fish, *Aphredoderus sayanus,* the adult of which has the vent located in back of the lower jaw. [1865–70, *Amer.*]

Pi′rates of Penzance′, an operetta (1879) by Sir William S. Gilbert and Sir Arthur Sullivan.

Pire (*Fr.* pēʀ), *n.* **Do•mi•nique Georges Hen•ri** (*Fr.* dô-mē nēk′ zhôʀzh äɴ ʀē′), 1910–69, Belgian priest: Nobel peace prize 1958.

Pir•ke A•voth (*Seph. Heb.* pēʀ ke′ ä vôt′; *Ashk. Heb.* piʀ′kä ô′vōs), *Judaism.* a treatise of the Mishnah that comprises six chapters and consists chiefly of proverbs, aphorisms, and principles of ethics, law, and religion. Also, **Pir•ke′ A•vot′, Pir•ke′ A•both′, Pir•ke′ A•bot′.** Also called **Ethics of the Fathers.** [Heb *pirqē ăbhōth* chapters of the fathers]

pirn (pûrn, pirn), *n. Brit. Dial.* **1.** a weaver's bobbin, spool, or reel. **2.** a fishing reel. [1400–50; late ME *pyrne* < ?]

pir•o (pir′ō), *n. Informal.* piroplasmosis. [by shortening]

pi•ro•gen (pi rō′gən), *n.* (*used with a plural v.*) *Jewish Cookery.* small baked pastries filled with chopped chicken livers, onion, etc. [1950–55; < Yiddish *pirogn,* pl. of *pirog* < East Slavic; see PIROSHKI]

pi•rogue (pi rōg′, pē′rōg), *n.* **1.** piragua (def. 1). **2.** a native boat, esp. an American dugout. [1655–65; < F < Sp *piragua* PIRAGUA]

pir•o•plasm (pir′ə plaz′əm), *n.* babesia. [1890–95; < NL *Piroplasma* a genus of the family, equiv. to L *pi-r(um)* PEAR + -o- -o- + Gk *plásma* PLASMA] **—pir′o•plas′mic,** *adj.*

pir•o•plas•mo•sis (pir′ə plaz mō′sis), *n., pl.* **-ses** (-sēz). *Vet. Pathol.* babesiosis. [1900–05; PIROPLASM + -OSIS]

pi•rosh•ki (pi rôsh′kē, -rosh′-), *n.* (*used with a plural v.*) *Russian Cookery.* small turnovers or dumplings with a filling, as of meat or fruit. [1910–15; < Russ *pirozhki,* pl. of *pirozhók,* dim. of *piróg* stuffed pastry]

pir•ou•ette (pir′o͞o et′), *n., v.,* **-et•ted, -et•ting.** —*n.* **1.** a whirling about on one foot or on the points of the toes, as in ballet dancing. **2.** *Dressage.* a complete turn in which the horse uses its hind legs as a pivot. —*v.i.* **3.** to perform a pirouette; whirl, as on the toes. [1700–10; < F: a whirl, top, fem. of MF *pirouet,* equiv. to *pirou-* (c. It *pirolo,* dim. of *piro* peg) + *-et* -ET]

pi•rox•i•cam (pī rok′si kam′), *n. Pharm.* a white crystalline solid substance, $C_{15}H_{13}N_3O_4S$, used in the symptomatic treatment of osteoarthritis and rheumatoid arthritis and other musculoskeletal disorders. [by rearrangement and alter. of parts of its chemical name]

Pi•sa (pē′zə; *It.* pē′zä), *n.* a city in NW Italy, on the Arno River: leaning tower. 384,878. **—Pi′san,** *adj., n.*

pis al•ler (pē zᴀ lā′), *French.* the last resort or the final resource.

Pi•sa•nel•lo (pē′zä nel′lō), *n.* **An•to•nio** (än tô′nyô), (*Antonio Pisano*), 1397–1455?, Italian painter and medalist.

Pi•sa•no (pē zä′nô), *n.* **1. An•dre•a** (än dʀe′ä), c1270–c1348, Italian sculptor. **2. Gio•van•ni** (jô vän′nē), c1245–c1320, and his father, **Ni•co•la** (nē kô′lä), c1220–78, Italian sculptors and architects.

pi•say (pē′zā), *n.* pisé.

pis•ca•ry (pis′kə rē), *n., pl.* **-ries. 1.** *Law.* the right or privilege of fishing in particular waters. **2.** a place for fishing. [1425–75; late ME < ML *piscāria,* neut. pl. (fishing rights) and fem. sing. (fishing place) of L *piscārius* of fishing or fish. See PISCI-, -ARY]

pis•ca•tol•o•gy (pis′kə tol′ə jē), *n. Now Rare.* the art or science of fishing. [1865–70; PISCAT(OR) or PISCAT(ORY) + -O- + -LOGY]

pis•ca•tor (pi skā′tər, pis′kə-), *n.* fisherman. [1645–55; < L *piscātor,* equiv. to *piscā(rī)* to fish (v. deriv. of *piscis* FISH) + *-tor* -TOR]

pis•ca•to•ry (pis′kə tôr′ē, -tōr′ē), *adj.* **1.** of or pertaining to fishermen or fishing: *a piscatory treaty.* **2.** devoted to or dependent upon fishing: *a piscatory people; piscatory birds.* Also, **pis•ca•to•ri•al** (pis′kə tôr′ē əl, -tōr′-). [1625–35; < L *piscātōrius,* equiv. to *piscā(rī)* to fish (see PISCATOR) + *-tōrius* -TORY[1]]

Pis•ces (pī′sēz, pis′ēz), *n., gen.* **Pis•ci•um** (pish′ē əm), for 1. **1.** *Astron.* the Fishes, a zodiacal constellation between Aries and Aquarius. **2.** *Astrol.* **a.** the twelfth sign of the zodiac: the mutable water sign. See illus. under **zodiac. b.** a person born under this sign, usually between February 19th and March 20th. **3.** the class of vertebrates comprising the fish and sometimes including, in certain classifications, the cyclostomes. [< NL, L *piscēs,* pl. of *piscis* FISH]

pisci-, a combining form meaning "fish," used in the formation of compound words: *piscivorous.* [comb. form repr. L *piscis;* c. FISH]

pis•ci•cul•ture (pis′i kul′chər, pī′si-), *n.* the breeding, rearing, and transplantation of fish by artificial means. [1855–60; PISCI- + CULTURE] **—pis′ci•cul′tur•al,** *adj.* **—pis′ci•cul′tur•al•ly,** *adv.* **—pis′ci•cul′tur•ist,** *n.*

pis•ci•form (pis′ə fôrm′, pī′sə-), *adj.* shaped like a fish. [1820–30; PISCI- + FORM]

pis•ci•na (pi sī′nə, pi sē′-), *n., pl.* **-nae** (-nē). *Eccles.* a basin with a drain used for certain ablutions, now generally in the sacristy. [1590–1600; < ML, special use of L *piscīna* a fish pond, swimming pool, equiv. to *pisc(is)* FISH + *-īna,* fem. of *-īnus* -INE[1]]

pis•cine (pī′sēn, pis′īn, -ēn, -in), *adj.* of, pertaining to, or resembling a fish or fishes. [1790–1800; < L *piscīnus,* equiv. to *pisc(is)* FISH + *-īnus* -INE[1]]

Pis•cis Aus•tri•nus (pī′sis ô strī′nəs, pis′is), *gen.* **Pis•cis Aus•tri•ni** (pī′sis ô strī′nī, pis′is). *Astron.* the Southern Fish, a southern constellation between Aquarius and Grus, containing the bright star Fomalhaut.

pis•civ•o•rous (pi siv′ər əs), *adj.* fish-eating. [1660–70; PISCI- + -VOROUS]

pis•co (pis′kō, pē′skō; *Sp.* pē′skô), *n.* a brandy made in the district near Pisco, a seaport in Peru. [1840–50, *Amer.;* < Sp]

pi•sé (pē zā′), *n.* See **rammed earth.** Also, **pisay.** Also called **pisé′ de terre′** (də târ′). [1790–1800; < F, n. use of ptp. of *piser* to beat down (earth) < L *pīsāre, pinsere* to pound, stamp down]

Pis•gah (piz′gə), *n.* **Mount,** a mountain ridge of ancient Moab, now in Jordan, NE of the Dead Sea: from its summit **(Mt. Nebo)** Moses viewed the Promised Land. Deut. 34:1.

pish (psh; *spelling pron.* pish), *interj.* **1.** (used as an exclamation of mild contempt or impatience.) —*n.* **2.** an exclamation of "pish!" —*v.i.* **3.** to say "pish." —*v.t.* **4.** to say "pish" at or to. [1585–95; imit.]

pi•shogue (pi shōg′), *n. Irish Eng.* **1.** sorcery; witchcraft; black magic. **2.** an evil spell; hex. [1820–30; < Ir *piseog* charm, spell]

Pish•pek (pish pek′; *Russ.* pyi shpyek′), *n.* former name (until 1926) of **Bishkek.**

Pi•sid•i•a (pi sid′ē ə, pī-), *n.* an ancient country in S Asia Minor: later a Roman province.

Pi•sid•i•an (pi sid′ē ən, pī-), *n.* the extinct language of Pisidia, not known to be related to any other language, written in a script derived from the Greek alphabet. [PISIDI(A) + -AN]

pi•si•form (pī′sə fôrm′), *adj.* pea-shaped. [1760–70; < NL *pisiformis,* equiv. to *pisi-* (comb. form repr. L *pisum* PEA) + *-formis* -FORM]

Pi•sis•trat•i•dae (pī′sə strat′i dē′, pis′ə-), *n.pl.* Hippias and Hipparchus, the sons of Pisistratus.

Pi•sis•tra•tus (pī sis′trə təs, pi-), *n.* c605–527 B.C., tyrant of Athens 560–527 (father of Hipparchus and Hippias).

pis•mire (pis′mīᵊr′, piz′-), *n.* an ant. [1350–1400; ME *pissemyre,* equiv. to *pisse* to urinate + obs. *mire* ant, perh. < Scand (cf. Dan *myre,* Sw *myra*), c. D *mier;* pejorative name from stench of formic acid proper to ants]

pis′mo clam′ (piz′mō), a large edible clam, *Tivela stultorum,* of sandy shores of California and Mexico. [1910–15; after *Pismo* Beach, California]

pis•o•lite (pis′ə līt′, piz′-, pī′sə-), *n.* limestone composed of rounded concretions about the size of a pea. [1700–10; < NL *pisolithus* < Gk *píso(s)* PEA + *lithos* -LITE] **—pis•o•lit•ic** (pis′ə lit′ik, piz′-, pī′sə-), *adj.*

pis•o•lith (pis′ə lith, piz′-, pī′sə-), *n.* a pea-size calcareous concretion, larger than an oolith, aggregates of which constitute a pisolite. [1790–1800; see PISOLITE, -LITH]

piss (pis), *n., v.* **pissed, piss•ing.** *Vulgar.* —*n.* **1.** urine. **2. take a piss,** to urinate. —*v.i.* **3.** to urinate. **4. piss away,** *Slang.* to squander; fritter away: **5. piss off,** *Slang.* **a.** to anger. **b.** to go away; leave (often used imperatively). [1250–1300; ME *pissen* < OF *pissier* < VL **pissāre* (imit.)]

piss•ant (pis′ant′), *n.* **1.** *Slang* (*vulgar*). a person or thing of no value or consequence; a despicable person or thing. **2.** *Obs.* an ant. —*adj.* **3.** *Slang* (*vulgar*). insignificant or worthless. Also, **piss′-ant′.** [1655–65, in sense "ant"; PISS + ANT, prob. orig. on the model of PISMIRE]

Pis•sar•ro (pi sär′ō; *Fr.* pē sᴀ ʀō′), *n.* **Ca•mille** (kᴀ-mē′yᵊ), 1830–1903, French painter.

pissed (pist), *adj. Slang* (*vulgar*). **1.** drunk; intoxicated. **2.** See **pissed off.** [1840–50; PISS + -ED[2]]

pissed′ off′, *Slang* (*vulgar*). angry or annoyed. [1935–40]

piss•er (pis′ər), *n. Slang* (*vulgar*). **1.** something extremely difficult or unpleasant. **2.** something or someone that is extraordinary. [1350–1400; ME: one who urinates; see PISS, -ER[1]]

pis•soir (pē swᴀʀ′), *n., pl.* **-soirs** (-swᴀʀ′). *French.* a street urinal for public use, esp. one enclosed by a low wall, screen, or the like.

piss-poor (pis′po͝or′), *adj. Slang* (*vulgar*). of extremely inferior or disappointing quality or rating. [1945–50]

piss•pot (pis′pot′), *n. Vulgar.* **1.** a chamber pot. **2.** *Slang.* a despicable person. [1400–50; late ME; see PISS, POT[1]]

piss•y (pis′ē), *adj.,* **piss•i•er, piss•i•est.** *Slang* (*vulgar*). **1.** soiled with or reeking of urine. **2.** inferior, nasty, or disagreeable. [1981–86; PISS + -Y[1]]

pis•tach•i•o (pi stash′ē ō′, -stä′shē ō′), *n., pl.* **-chi•os. 1.** the nut of a Eurasian tree, *Pistacia vera,* of the cashew family, containing an edible, greenish kernel. **2.** the kernel itself, used for flavoring. **3.** the tree itself. **4.** pistachio nut flavor. **5.** See **pistachio green.** Also, **pistache** (pi stash′), **pistach′io nut′** (for defs. 1, 2). [1375–1425; < It *pistacchio* < L *pistācium* < Gk *pistákion* pistachio nut, dim. of *pistákē* pistachio tree < MPers **pistak* (Pers *pista*); r. late ME *pistace* < MF < L, as above]

pistach′io green′, a light or medium shade of yellow green. [1790–1800]

pis•ta•reen (pis′tə rēn′), *n.* **1.** peseta (def. 2). —*adj.* **2.** of little value or worth. [1735–45, *Amer.;* perh. alter. of Sp *peseta* PESETA]

piste (pēst), *n.* **1.** a track or trail, as a downhill ski run or a spoor made by a wild animal. **2.** (in fencing) a regulation-size strip, usually 2 meters wide and 14 meters long, on which fencers compete. [1720–30; < F: animal track < It *pista, pesta,* n. deriv. of *pestare* to pound, crush < VL, freq. of L *pī(n)sere;* cf. PESTLE]

pis•til (pis′tl), *n. Bot.* **1.** the ovule-bearing or seed-bearing female organ of a flower, consisting when complete of ovary, style, and stigma. See diag. under **flower. 2.** such organs collectively, where there are more than one in a flower. **3.** a gynoecium. [1570–80; earlier *pistillum,* special use of L *pistillum* PESTLE]

pis•til•late (pis′tl it, -āt′), *adj. Bot.* **1.** having a pistil or pistils. **2.** having a pistil or pistils but no stamens. See illus. under **monoecious.** [1820–30; PISTIL + -ATE[1]]

Pis·to·ia (pē stô′yä), *n.* a city in N Tuscany, in N Italy. 263,752.

pis·tol (pis′tl), *n., v.,* **-toled, -tol·ing** or (*esp. Brit.*) **-tolled, -tol·ling.** —*n.* **1.** a short firearm intended to be held and fired with one hand. —*v.t.* **2.** to shoot with a pistol. [1560–70; < MF *pistole* < G; earlier *pitschal, pitschole, petsole* < Czech *píšťala* lit., pipe, fife, whistle (presumably a slang term for a type of light harquebus employed during the Hussite wars), akin to *pištět* to squeak, peep] —**pis′tol·like′,** *adj.*

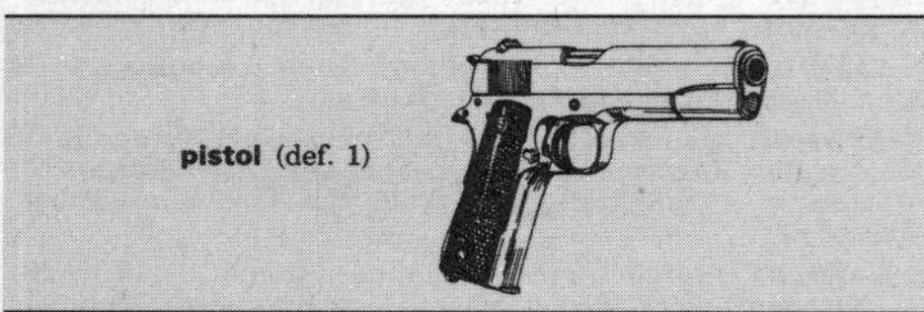
pistol (def. 1)

pis·tole (pi stōl′), *n.* **1.** a former gold coin of Spain, equal to two escudos. **2.** any of various former gold coins of Europe, as the louis d'or. [1585–95; < MF, back formation from *pistolet* the coin]

pis·to·leer (pis′tl ēr′), *n. Archaic* a person, esp. a soldier, who uses or is armed with a pistol. Also, **pis′to·lier′.** [1825–35; PISTOL + -EER]

pis·to·le·ro (pis′tl âr′ō; *Sp.* pēs′tô le′rô), *n., pl.* **-to·le·ros** (-tl âr′ōz; *Sp.* -tô le′rôs). (esp. in Mexico and Central America) **1.** a member of an armed band of roving mounted bandits. **2.** a gunman or hired killer. [1935–40; < Sp, equiv. to *pistol(a)* PISTOL + *-ero* < L *-ārius* -ARY]

pis′tol grip′, a handle or grip, as of a rifle or saw, shaped like the butt of a pistol. [1870–75] —**pis′·tol-grip′,** *adj.*

pis′tol-han·dle knife′ (pis′tl han′dl), a table knife, esp. of the 18th century, having a slightly curved handle resembling the grip of a flintlock pistol.

pis·tol·o·gy (pi stol′ə jē), *n.* the branch of theology dealing with faith. [< Gk *píst(is)* faith (akin to *peíthein* to persuade) + -o- + -LOGY]

pis′tol shrimp′. See **snapping shrimp.**

pis·tol-whip (pis′tl hwip′, -wip′), *v.t.,* **-whipped, -whip·ping.** to beat or hit (someone) repeatedly with a pistol, esp. in the head and shoulder area. [1940–45, *Amer.*]

pis·ton (pis′tən), *n.* **1.** a disk or cylindrical part tightly fitting and moving within a cylinder, either to compress or move a fluid collected in the cylinder, as air or water, or to transform energy imparted by a fluid entering or expanding inside the cylinder, as compressed air, explosive gases, or steam, into a rectilinear motion usually transformed into rotary motion by means of a connecting rod. **2.** a pumplike valve used to change the pitch in a cornet or the like. [1695–1705; < F < It *pistone* piston, a learned alter. of *pestone* large PESTLE, equiv. to *pest(are)* to pound (var. of ML *pistare,* deriv. of L *pistus* ptp. of *pinsere* to pound) + *-one* aug. suffix] —**pis′ton·like′,** *adj.*

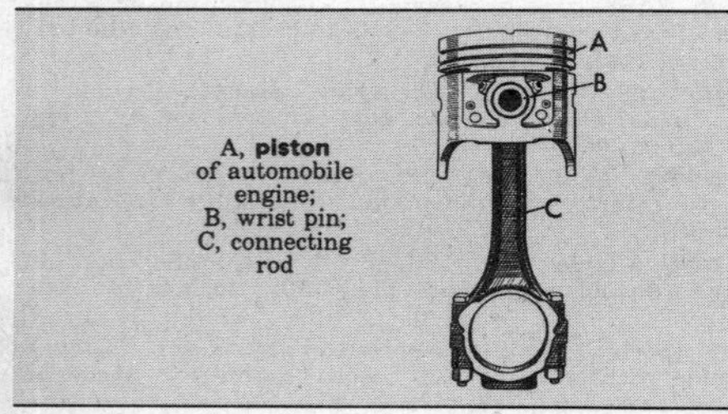

A, **piston** of automobile engine; B, wrist pin; C, connecting rod

Pis·ton (pis′tən), *n.* **Walter,** 1894–1976, U.S. composer.

pis′ton en′gine. See **reciprocating engine.** [1905–10]

pis′ton pin′. See **wrist pin.** [1895–1900]

pis′ton ring′, a metallic ring, usually one of a series, and split so as to be expansible, placed around a piston in order to maintain a tight fit, as inside the cylinder of an engine. Also called **packing ring, ring.** [1865–70]

pis′ton rod′, a rod communicating the rectilinear motion of a piston to the small end of a connecting rod or elsewhere. [1780–90]

pit[1] (pit), *n., v.,* **pit·ted, pit·ting.** —*n.* **1.** a naturally formed or excavated hole or cavity in the ground: *pits caused by erosion; clay pits.* **2.** a covered or concealed excavation in the ground, serving as a trap. **3.** *Mining.* **a.** an excavation made in exploring for or removing a mineral deposit, as by open-cut methods. **b.** the shaft of a coal mine. **c.** the mine itself. **4.** the abode of evil spirits and lost souls; hell: *an evil inspiration from the pit.* **5. the pits,** *Slang.* an extremely unpleasant, boring, or depressing place, condition, person, etc.; the absolute worst: *When you're alone, Christmas is the pits.* **6.** a hollow or indentation in a surface: *glass flawed by pits.* **7.** a natural hollow or depression in the body: *the pit of the back.* **8. pits,** *Informal.* the armpits: *up to my pits in work.* **9.** a small, depressed scar, as one of those left on the skin after smallpox or chicken pox. **10.** an enclosure, usually below the level of the spectators, as for staging fights between dogs, cocks, or, formerly, bears. **11.** (in a commodity exchange) a part of the floor of the exchange where trading in a particular commodity takes place: *the corn pit.* **12.** *Archit.* **a.** all that part of the main floor of a theater behind the musicians. **b.** *Brit.* the main floor of a theater behind the stalls. **c.** orchestra (def. 2a). **13.** (in a hoistway) a space below the level of the lowest floor served. **14.** *Auto Racing.* an area at the side of a track, for servicing and refueling the cars. **15.** *Bowling.* the sunken area of a bowling alley behind the pins, for the placement or recovery of pins that have been knocked down. **16.** *Track.* the area forward of the takeoff point in a jumping event, as the broad jump or pole vault, that is filled with sawdust or soft earth to lessen the force of the jumper's landing. **17.** the area or room of a casino containing gambling tables. —*v.t.* **18.** to mark or indent with pits or depressions: *ground pitted by erosion.* **19.** to scar with pockmarks: *His forehead was pitted by chicken pox.* **20.** to place or bury in a pit, as for storage. **21.** to set in opposition or combat, as one against another. **22.** to put (animals) in a pit or enclosure for fighting. —*v.i.* **23.** to become marked with pits or depressions. **24.** (of body tissue) to retain temporarily a mark of pressure, as by a finger, instrument, etc. [bef. 900; (n.) ME; OE *pytt* < L *puteus* well, pit, shaft; (v.) deriv. of the n.]
—**Syn. 21.** match, oppose.

pit[2] (pit), *n., v.,* **pit·ted, pit·ting.** *Chiefly Northern U.S.* —*n.* **1.** the stone of a fruit, as of a cherry, peach, or plum. —*v.t.* **2.** to remove the pit from (a fruit or fruits): *to pit cherries for a pie.* [1835–45, *Amer.*; < D: kernel; c. PITH]

pi·ta[1] (pē′tə), *n.* **1.** a fiber obtained from plants of the genera *Agave, Aechmea,* etc., used for cordage, mats, etc. **2.** any of these plants. [1690–1700; < AmerSp < Quechua *pita* or Aymara *p'ita*]

pi·ta[2] (pē′tä, -tə), *n.* a round, flat Middle Eastern bread that is often filled with meat, peppers, etc., to make a sandwich. Also called **pi′ta bread′.** [1950–55, *Amer.*; < ModGk *pēta, pitta* bread, cake, pie]

pit·a·ha·ya (pit′ə hi′ə), *n.* **1.** any of several cacti of the genus *Lemaireocereus* and related genera, of the southwestern U.S. and Mexico, bearing edible fruit. **2.** the fruit of such a cactus. Also, **pi·ta·ya** (pi tī′ə). [1750–60, *Amer.*; < AmerSp < Taino]

Pit·a·ka (pit′ə kə), *n. Buddhism.* See under **Pali Canon.** [< Pali: lit., basket]

pi·tan·ga (pi tang′gə), *n.* See **Surinam cherry.** [< Pg < Tupi *pïtanga* yellowish]

pit·a·pat (pit′ə pat′), *adv., n., v.,* **-pat·ted, -pat·ting.** —*adv.* **1.** with a quick succession of beats or taps: *Her heart beat pitapat with excitement.* —*n.* **2.** the movement or the sound of something going pitapat: *the pitapat of hail on a roof.* —*v.i.* **3.** to go pitapat. [1515–25; imit. gradational compound]

Pi·ta·tus (pi tä′təs), *n.* a walled plain in the third quadrant of the face of the moon: about 50 miles (80 km) in diameter.

pit′ boss′, a casino employee who supervises gambling-table activity. [1915–20, for an earlier sense; *Amer.*]

pit′ bull′ ter′rier. See **American Staffordshire terrier.** [1940–45]

Pit′cairn Is′land, a small British island in the S Pacific, SE of Tuamotu Archipelago: settled 1790 by mutineers of the *Bounty.* 74; 2 sq. mi. (5 sq. km).

pitch[1] (pich), *v.t.* **1.** to erect or set up (a tent, camp, or the like). **2.** to put, set, or plant in a fixed or definite place or position. **3.** to throw, fling, hurl, or toss. **4.** *Baseball.* **a.** to deliver or serve (the ball) to the batter. **b.** to fill the position of pitcher in (a game): *He pitched a no-hitter. He pitched a good game.* **c.** to choose or assign as a pitcher for a game: *The manager pitched Greene the next night.* **5.** to set at a certain point, degree, level, etc.: *He pitched his hopes too high.* **6.** *Music.* to set at a particular pitch, or determine the key or keynote of (a melody). **7.** *Cards.* **a.** to lead (a card of a particular suit), thereby fixing that suit as trump. **b.** to determine (the trump) in this manner. **8.** to pave or revet with small stones. **9.** *Masonry.* **a.** to square (a stone), cutting the arrises true with a chisel. **b.** to cut with a chisel. **10.** *Informal.* to attempt to sell or win approval for; promote; advertise: *to pitch breakfast foods at a sales convention.* **11.** *Informal.* to approach or court (as a person, company, or the public) in hope of a sale, approval, or interest; make an appeal to. **12.** to cause to pitch. **13.** *Obs.* to set in order; to arrange, as a field of battle. **14.** *Obs.* to fix firmly as in the ground; embed. —*v.i.* **15.** to plunge or fall forward or headlong. **16.** to lurch. **17.** to throw or toss. **18.** *Baseball.* **a.** to deliver or serve the ball to the batter. **b.** to fill the position of pitcher: *He pitched for the Mets last year.* **19.** to slope downward; dip. **20.** to plunge with alternate fall and rise of bow and stern, as a ship (opposed to *roll*). **21.** (of a rocket or guided missile) to deviate from a stable flight attitude by oscillations of the longitudinal axis in a vertical plane about the center of gravity. **22.** to fix a tent or temporary habitation; encamp: *They pitched by a mountain stream.* **23.** *Golf.* to play a pitch shot. **24.** *Informal.* to attempt to sell or win approval for something or someone by advertising, promotion, etc.: *politicians pitching on TV.* **25.** *Rare.* to become established; settle down. **26. pitch in,** *Informal.* **a.** to begin to work in earnest and vigorously: *If I really pitch in, I may be able to finish the paper before the deadline.* **b.** to contribute to a common cause; join in: *When they took up a collection for the annual dinner, he promised to pitch in.* **27. pitch into,** *Informal.* **a.** to attack verbally or physically: *He apologized for pitching into me yesterday.* **b.** to begin to work on vigorously. **28. pitch on** or **upon,** to choose, esp. casually or without forethought; decide on: *We pitched on a day for our picnic.*
—*n.* **29.** relative point, position, or degree: *a high pitch of excitement.* **30.** the degree of inclination or slope; angle: *the pitch of an arch; the pitch of a stair.* **31.** the highest point or greatest height: *enjoying the pitch of success.* **32.** (in music, speech, etc.) the degree of height or depth of a tone or of sound, depending upon the relative rapidity of the vibrations by which it is produced. **33.** *Music.* the particular tonal standard with which given tones may be compared in respect to their relative level. **34.** *Acoustics.* the apparent predominant frequency sounded by an acoustical source. **35.** act or manner of pitching. **36.** a throw or toss. **37.** *Baseball.* the serving of the ball to the batter by the pitcher, usually preceded by a windup or stretch. **38.** a pitching movement or forward plunge, as of a ship. **39.** upward or downward inclination or slope: *a road descending at a steep pitch.* **40.** a sloping part or place: *to build on the pitch of a hill.* **41.** a quantity of something pitched or placed somewhere. **42.** *Cricket.* the central part of the field; the area between the wickets. **43.** *Informal.* **a.** a high-pressure sales talk: *The salesman made his pitch for the new line of dresses.* **b.** a specific plan of action; angle: *to tackle a problem again, using a new pitch.* **44.** the specific location in which a person or object is placed or stationed; allotted or assigned place. **45.** *Chiefly Brit.* the established location, often a street corner, of a beggar, street peddler, newspaper vendor, etc. **46.** *Aeron.* **a.** the nosing of an airplane or spacecraft up or down about a transverse axis. **b.** the distance that a given propeller would advance in one revolution. **47.** (of a rocket or guided missile) **a.** the motion due to pitching. **b.** the extent of the rotation of the longitudinal axis involved in pitching. **48.** Also called **plunge.** *Geol.* the inclination of a linear feature, as the axis of a fold or an oreshoot, from the horizontal. **49.** *Mach.* **a.** the distance between the corresponding surfaces of two adjacent gear teeth measured either along the pitch circle (**circular pitch**) or between perpendiculars to the root surfaces (**normal pitch**). **b.** the ratio of the number of teeth in a gear or splined shaft to the pitch circle diameter, expressed in inches. **c.** the distance between any two adjacent things in a series, as screw threads, rivets, etc. **50.** (in carpet weaving) the weftwise number of warp ends, usually determined in relation to 27 inches (68.6 cm). **51.** *Cards.* **a.** See **all fours** (def. 2). **b.** See **auction pitch. 52.** *Masonry.* a true or even surface on a stone. **53.** (of typewriter type) a unit of measurement indicating the number of characters to a horizontal inch: *Pica is a 10-pitch type.* [1175–1225; (v.) ME *picchen* to thrust, pierce, set, set up (a tent, etc.), array, throw; perh. akin to PICK[1]; (n.) deriv. of the v.] —**pitch′a·ble,** *adj.*
—**Syn. 3.** See **throw.**

pitch[2] (pich), *n.* **1.** any of various dark, tenacious, and viscous substances for caulking and paving, consisting of the residue of the distillation of coal tar or wood tar. **2.** any of certain bitumens, as asphalt: *mineral pitch.* **3.** any of various resins. **4.** the sap or crude turpentine that exudes from the bark of pines. —*v.t.* **5.** to smear or cover with pitch. [bef. 900; ME *pich,* OE *pic* < L *pic-* (s. of *pix*), whence also D *pek,* G *Pech;* akin to Gk *píssa* pitch] —**pitch′like′,** *adj.*

pitch-and-putt (pich′ən put′), *adj.* of or pertaining to a small-scale golf course, 5 to 20 acres, and usually having 9 holes of 50 yards in length from tee to cup. Cf. **par-three.**

pitch′-and-run′ shot′ (pich′ən run′), *Golf.* See **chip shot.** Also called **pitch′-and-run′.**

pitch-and-toss (pich′ən tôs′, -tos′), *n.* a game in which players toss coins at a mark, the person whose coin hits closest to the mark tossing all the coins in the air and winning all those that come down heads up. [1800–10]

pitch-black (pich′blak′), *adj.* extremely black or dark as pitch: *a pitch-black night.* [1590–1600]

pitch·blende (pich′blend′), *n. Mineral.* a massive variety of uraninite, occurring in black pitchlike masses: a major ore of uranium and radium. [1760–70; half trans., half adoption of G *Pechblende.* See PITCH[2], BLENDE]

pitch′ chain′, *Mach.* See **power chain.** [1835–45]

pitch′ chis′el, *Masonry.* a broad-edged chisel for cutting plane surfaces on stones.

pitch′ cir′cle, *Mach.* an imaginary circle within the profiles of the teeth of a gear, such that it rotates against a similar circle rotating at the same rate on a meshing gear. Also called **pitch line.** [1810–20]

pitch′ cone′, *Mach.* See under **pitch surface.**

pitch′ cyl′inder, *Mach.* See under **pitch surface.**

pitch-dark (pich′därk′), *adj.* dark or black as pitch: *a pitch-dark night.* [1820–30] —**pitch′-dark′ness,** *n.*

pitched′ bat′tle, **1.** a battle in which the orderly arrangement of armed forces and the location have been predetermined. **2.** an encounter in which the antagonists are completely and intensely engaged: *The dispute evolved into a pitched battle between management and labor.* [1600–10]

pitch·er[1] (pich′ər), *n.* **1.** a container, usually with a handle and spout or lip, for holding and pouring liquids. **2.** *Bot.* **a.** a pitcherlike modification of the leaf of certain plants. **b.** an ascidium. [1250–1300; ME *picher* < OF *pichier* < ML *picārium,* var. of *bicārium* BEAKER] —**pitch′er·like′,** *adj.*

pitch·er[2] (pich′ər), *n.* **1.** a person who pitches. **2.** *Baseball.* the player who throws the ball to the opposing batter. **3.** Also called **number seven iron.** *Golf.* a club with an iron head the face of which has more slope than a mashie but less slope than a pitching niblick. **4.** sett (def. 1). [1700–10; PITCH[1] + -ER[1]]

Pitch·er (pich′ər), *n.* **Molly** (*Mary Ludwig Hays McCauley*), 1754–1832, American Revolutionary heroine.

pitch·er·ful (pich′ər fo͝ol′), *n., pl.* **-fuls.** the amount held by a pitcher. [1685–95; PITCHER[1] + -FUL]
—**Usage.** See **-ful.**

pitch′er plant′, **1.** any of various insectivorous New World bog plants of the genera *Sarracenia, Darlingtonia,* and *Heliamphora,* having tubular or trumpet-shaped leaves containing a liquid in which insects are

CONCISE ETYMOLOGY KEY: <, descended or borrowed from; >, whence; b., blend of, blended; c., cognate with; cf., compare; deriv., derivative; equiv., equivalent; imit., imitative; obl., oblique; r., replacing; s., stem; sp., spelling, spelled; resp., respelling, respelled; trans., translation; ?, origin unknown; *, unattested; ‡, probably earlier than. See the full key inside the front cover.

trapped. **2.** the common pitcher plant, *S. purpurea,* having red or green leaves and a large, nodding, globular dull-red flower. **3.** any of various insectivorous Old World plants of the genus *Nepenthes,* having leathery leaves each ending in a tendril that bears a lidded, pitcherlike receptacle. [1810–20]

pitcher plant, *Sarracenia purpurea*

pitch-faced (pich′fāst′), *adj. Masonry.* (of a stone) having all arrises in the same plane and the faces roughly dressed with a pick. [1880–85]

pitch•fork (pich′fôrk′), *n.* **1.** a large, long-handled fork for manually lifting and pitching hay, stalks of grain, etc. **2. pitchforks,** *Northern U.S.* beggar's-lice, esp. the achenes of Spanish needles. —*v.t.* **3.** to pitch or throw with or as if with a pitchfork. [1425–75; late ME; see PITCH[1], FORK]

pitch•ing (pich′ing), *n.* **1.** the act of revetting or paving with small stones. **2.** stones so used. Also called **penning, soling.** [1685–95; PITCH[1] + -ING[1]]

pitch′ing nib′lick, *Golf.* a club with an iron head the face of which has more slope than a pitcher but less slope than a niblick. Also called **number eight iron.**

pitch′ing pen′nies, a gambling game in which pennies are tossed to a mark or against a wall, the winner being the person whose penny lands closest to the mark or wall.

pitch′ing piece′, *Carpentry.* See **apron piece.** [1815–25]

pitch′ing rota′tion, *Baseball.* the regular, scheduled succession of starting pitchers designated by a manager: *a four-man pitching rotation in September.* Also called **rotation.**

Pitch′ Lake′, a deposit of natural asphalt in SW Trinidad, West Indies. 114 acres. (47 hectares).

pitch′ line′, *Mach.* **1.** See **pitch circle. 2.** an imaginary line within the profiles of the teeth of a rack, such that it moves against, and at the same rate as, the pitch circle of an engaging pinion. [1790–1800]

pitch•man (pich′mən), *n., pl.* **-men. 1.** an itinerant vendor of small wares that are usually carried in a case with collapsible legs, allowing it to be set up or removed quickly. **2.** any high-pressure salesperson, as one at a concession at a fair or carnival. **3.** a person who delivers a message on radio or television, as for a product, cause, etc. [1925–30, *Amer.*; PITCH[1] + -MAN]

pitch•out (pich′out′), *n.* **1.** *Baseball.* a ball purposely thrown by a pitcher too far outside of the plate for the batter to hit, esp. in anticipation of an attempted steal by a base runner. **2.** *Football.* a lateral pass thrown behind the line of scrimmage by one back, esp. a T-formation quarterback, to another. [1910–15, *Amer.*; n. use of v. phrase *pitch out*]

pitch′ pine′, any of several pines from which pitch or turpentine is obtained. [1670–80, *Amer.*]

pitch′ pipe′, a small flute or reed pipe producing one or more pitches when blown into, used chiefly for establishing the proper pitch in singing or in tuning a musical instrument. Also called **tuning pipe.** [1705–15]

pitch′ plane′, *Mach.* See under **pitch surface.**

pitch•pole (pich′pōl′), *v.i.,* **-poled, -pol•ing.** (of a boat) to capsize end over end, as in heavy surf. [1655–65; PITCH[1] + *pole,* alter. of POLL[1]]

pitch•pot (pich′pot′), *n.* a pot used by sailors for heating pitch. [1710–20; PITCH[2] + POT[1]]

pitch′ shot′, *Golf.* a shot in which the ball is hit high into the air and with backspin to ensure little roll upon landing, used in approaching the green. Cf. **chip shot.**

pitch•stone (pich′stōn′), *n.* a glassy volcanic rock having a resinous luster and resembling hardened pitch. [1775–85; trans. of G *Pechstein.* See PITCH[2], STONE]

pitch′ sur′face, (in a gear or rack) an imaginary surface forming a plane **(pitch plane),** a cylinder **(pitch cylinder),** or a cone or frustrum **(pitch cone)** that moves tangentially to a similar surface in a meshing gear so that both surfaces travel at the same speed. [1885–90]

pitch•y (pich′ē), *adj.,* **pitch•i•er, pitch•i•est. 1.** full of or abounding in pitch. **2.** smeared with pitch. **3.** resembling pitch, as in color, consistency, etc.: *pitchy mud.* **4.** dark or black as pitch. [1505–15; PITCH[2] + -Y[1]] —**pitch′i•ness,** *n.*

pit′ dwell′ing, a primitive dwelling consisting of a pit excavated in the earth and roofed over. Also called **pit house.** [1895–1900]

pit•e•ous (pit′ē əs), *adj.* **1.** evoking or deserving pity; pathetic: *piteous cries for help.* **2.** *Archaic.* compassionate. [1250–1300; ME; r. *pitous* < OF < ML *pietōsus.* See PITY, -OUS] —**pit′e•ous•ly,** *adv.* —**pit′e•ous•ness,** *n.*
—**Syn. 1.** affecting, moving, distressing, lamentable, woeful, sad, wretched, sorrowful. See **pitiful.**

pit•fall (pit′fôl′), *n.* **1.** a lightly covered and unnoticeable pit prepared as a trap for people or animals. **2.** any trap or danger for the unwary: *the pitfall of excessive pride.* [1275–1325; ME *pittefalle,* equiv. to *pitte* PIT[1] + *falle* (OE *fealle*) trap]
—**Syn. 1, 2.** See **trap**[1].

pit′ grave′, *Archaeol.* a shallow grave hollowed out of a bed of rock or the floor of a tholos. [1895–1900]

pith (pith), *n.* **1.** *Bot.* the soft, spongy central cylinder of parenchymatous tissue in the stems of dicotyledonous plants. **2.** *Zool.* the soft inner part of a feather, a hair, etc. **3.** the important or essential part; essence; core; heart: *the pith of the matter.* **4.** significant weight; substance; solidity: *an argument without pith.* **5.** *Archaic.* spinal cord or bone marrow. **6.** *Archaic.* strength, force, or vigor; mettle: *men of pith.* —*v.t.* **7.** to remove the pith from (plants). **8.** to destroy the spinal cord or brain of. **9.** to slaughter, as cattle, by severing the spinal cord. [bef. 900; ME; OE *pitha;* c. D *pit.* See PIT[2]]

pit•head (pit′hed′), *n.* a mine entrance and the surrounding area. [1830–40; PIT[1] + HEAD]

pith•e•can•thrope (pith′i kan′thrōp, pith′i kən thrōp′), *n.* (*sometimes cap.*) a member of the former genus *Pithecanthropus.* [1875–80; short for PITHECANTHROPUS] —**pith•e•can•throp•ic** (pith′i kən throp′ik), **pith•e•can•thro•pine** (pith′i kan′thrə pīn′), *adj.* —**pith•e•can•thro•pid** (pith′i kan′thrə pid, -kən thrō′pid, -throp′id), *n., adj.*

pith•e•can•thro•poid (pith′i kan′thrə poid′, -kən thrō′poid), *adj.* of, pertaining to, or resembling the former genus *Pithecanthropus* or one of its members. [1885–90; PITHECANTHROP(US) + -OID]

Pith•e•can•thro•pus (pith′i kan′thrə pəs, -kən thrō′pəs), *n.* a former genus of extinct hominids whose members have now been assigned to the proposed species *Homo erectus.* [< NL (1891) < Gk *píthēk(os)* ape + *ánthrōpos* man]

pith•e•coid (pith′i koid′, pi thē′koid), *adj.* **1.** belonging or pertaining to the genus *Pithecia* and related genera, including the saki monkeys. **2.** (loosely) apelike; monkeylike. [1860–65; < NL *pithēc(us)* ape (< Gk *píthēkos*) + -OID]

Pi•thom (pī′thəm), *n.* one of the two cities built by Israelite slaves in Egypt. Ex. 1:11. Cf. **Raamses.**

pi•thos (pith′os, pī′thos), *n., pl.* **pi•thoi** (pith′oi, pī′thoi). a very large earthenware jar having a wide mouth, used by the ancient Greeks for storing liquids, as wine, or for holding food, as grain, or for the burial of the dead. [1875–80; < Gk *píthos*]

pit′ house′. See **pit dwelling.**

pith′ ray′. See **medullary ray.** [1900–05]

pith•y (pith′ē), *adj.,* **pith•i•er, pith•i•est. 1.** brief, forceful, and meaningful in expression; full of vigor, substance, or meaning; terse; forcible: *a pithy observation.* **2.** of, like, or abounding in pith. [1300–50; ME; see PITH, -Y[1]] —**pith′i•ly,** *adv.* —**pith′i•ness,** *n.*
—**Syn. 1.** succinct, pointed, meaty, concise.

pit•i•a•ble (pit′ē ə bəl), *adj.* **1.** evoking or deserving pity; lamentable: *pitiable, homeless children.* **2.** evoking or deserving contemptuous pity; miserable; contemptible: *a pitiable lack of character.* [1425–75; late ME < OF *piteable,* equiv. to *pite(er)* to PITY + *-able* -ABLE] —**pit′i•a•ble•ness,** *n.* —**pit′i•a•bly,** *adv.*
—**Syn. 1, 2.** See **pitiful.**

pit•i•er (pit′ē ər), *n.* a person who pities. [1595–1605; PITY + -ER[1]]

pit•i•ful (pit′i fəl), *adj.* **1.** evoking or deserving pity: *a pitiful fate.* **2.** evoking or deserving contempt by smallness, poor quality, etc.: *pitiful attempts.* **3.** *Archaic.* full of pity; compassionate. [1400–50; late ME; see PITY, -FUL] —**pit′i•ful•ly,** *adv.* —**pit′i•ful•ness,** *n.*
—**Syn. 1.** lamentable, deplorable, woeful, pathetic. **1, 2.** PITIFUL, PITIABLE, PITEOUS apply to that which excites pity (with compassion or with contempt). That which is PITIFUL is touching and excites pity or is mean and contemptible: *a pitiful leper; a pitiful exhibition of cowardice.* PITIABLE may mean lamentable, or wretched and paltry: *a pitiable hovel.* PITEOUS refers only to that which exhibits suffering and misery, and is therefore heart-rending: *piteous poverty.* **2.** deplorable, mean, low, base, vile, despicable. —**Ant. 1.** delightful. **2.** honorable.

pit•i•less (pit′i lis, pit′ē-), *adj.* feeling or showing no pity; merciless: *pitiless criticism of his last novel.* [1375–1425; late ME *piteles.* See PITY, -LESS] —**pit′i•less•ly,** *adv.* —**pit′i•less•ness,** *n.*
—**Syn.** unmerciful, implacable, relentless. See **cruel.**
—**Ant.** merciful.

pit•man (pit′mən), *n., pl.* **-men** for 1, **-mans** for 2. **1.** a person who works in a pit, as in coal mining. **2.** *Mach.* any of certain types of connecting rods. [1600–10; PIT[1] + -MAN]

Pit•man (pit′mən), *n.* **Sir Isaac,** 1813–97, English inventor of a system of shorthand.

Pi•to•cin (pi tō′sin), *Pharm., Trademark.* a brand of oxytocin.

pi•ton (pē′ton), *n. Mountain Climbing.* a metal spike with an eye through which a rope may be passed. [1895–1900; < F: ringbolt, peak (of a mountain)]

Pi′tot-stat′ic tube′ (pē′tō stat′ik, pē tō′-), (*often l.c.*) *Aeron.* a device combining a Pitot tube with a static tube: used to measure airspeed. [1970–75; see PITOT TUBE]

Pi′tot tube′ (pē′tō, pē tō′), (*often l.c.*) an instrument for measuring fluid velocity, consisting of a narrow tube, one end of which is open and faces upstream, the other end being connected to a manometer. [1880–85; named after Henri Pitot (1695–1771), French physicist, who invented it]

Pi•tri (pi′trē), *n., pl.* **-tris, -tri.** *Hinduism.* the legendary progenitor of any family. [< Skt *pitṛ* FATHER]

pit′ sam′ple, *Metall.* a sample of new steel taken for chemical analysis during teeming.

pit•saw (pit′sô′), *n.* a two-handed saw used in pit sawing. Also, **pit′ saw′.** [1670–80; PIT[1] + SAW[1]] —**pit′ saw′yer.**

pit′ saw′ing, a method of sawing logs or timbers, as into boards, in which the piece to be cut is laid horizontally across a pit and cut by a saw operated vertically by two people, one above and one in the pit below the piece. [1905–10]

pit′ scale′, any of various small oval-shaped homopterous insects of the family Asterolecaniidae, the female members of which have their bodies embedded in a waxy mass, as in the destructive *Cerococcus quercus* **(oak wax scale** or **oak scale),** or covered with a waxy film.

pit′ stop′, 1. *Auto Racing.* a stop in the pits during a race, in which a competing car receives gasoline, a change of tires, or other servicing or repair. **2.** *Informal.* any brief stop, as during an automobile ride, so that one may eat, get a drink, use a rest room, etc. **3.** a place where one makes such stops. [1930–35]

Pitt (pit), *n.* **1. William, 1st Earl of Chatham,** 1708–78, British statesman. **2.** his son **William,** 1759–1806, British statesman: prime minister 1783–1801, 1804–06.

pit•ta (pit′ə), *n.* any of several brilliantly colored, passerine birds of the family Pittidae, inhabiting dark, Old World, tropical forests. [1830–40; < Telugu *piṭṭa* bird]

Pit•ta•cus (pit′ə kəs), *n.* c650–570 B.C., democratic statesman and reformer from Mytilene.

pit•tance (pit′ns), *n.* **1.** a small amount or share. **2.** a small allowance or sum, as of money for living expenses. **3.** a scanty income or remuneration. [1175–1225; ME *pitaunce* < OF *pitance,* var. of *pietance* piety, pity, allowance of food (in a monastery). See PITY, -ANCE]

pit•ted[1] (pit′id), *adj.* marked or scarred with pits: *a pitted complexion.* [bef. 1050; OE *pytted* (not found in ME); see PIT[1], -ED[3]]

pit•ted[2] (pit′id), *adj.* (of fruit) having the pit removed: *a pitted olive.* [PIT[2] + -ED[2]]

pit•ter-pat•ter (pit′ər pat′ər), *n.* **1.** the sound of a rapid succession of light beats or taps, as of rain, footsteps, etc. —*v.i.* **2.** to produce or move with this sound: *She pitter-pattered along the hallway.* —*adv.* **3.** with such a sound: *to run pitter-patter through the house.* [1400–50; late ME: a babbled prayer; perh. imit.]

pit•ting[1] (pit′ing), *n.* **1.** the act or operation of digging a pit or pits. **2.** the act or operation of placing in a pit or pits. **3.** arranging or staging cockfights. [1655–65; PIT[1] + -ING[1]]

pit•ting[2] (pit′ing), *n.* the act of removing a pit or pits. [PIT[2] + -ING[1]]

pit•tos•po•rum (pi tos′pər əm, pit′ə spôr′əm, -spōr′-), *n.* any of various shrubs or trees of the genus *Pittosporum,* native to warm regions of the Old World, many species of which are cultivated as ornamentals for their attractive foliage, flowers, or fruit. [< NL, equiv. to Gk (Attic) *pitto-* (comb. form of *pítta, píssa* PITCH[2]) + *spór(os)* seed (see SPORE) + NL *-um* neut. n. ending; so called from the resinous coating of the seeds]

Pitts•burg (pits′bûrg), *n.* **1.** a city in W California. 33,034. **2.** a city in SE Kansas. 18,770.

Pitts•burgh (pits′bûrg), *n.* a port in SW Pennsylvania, at the confluence of the Allegheny and Monongahela rivers that forms the Ohio River: steel industry. 423,938.

Pitts′burg Land′ing, a village in SW Tennessee, on the Tennessee River: battle of Shiloh in 1862.

Pitts•field (pits′fēld′), *n.* a city in W Massachusetts. 51,974.

pi•tu•i•tar•y (pi to͞o′i ter′ē, -tyo͞o′-), *n., pl.* **-tar•ies,** *adj.* —*n.* **1.** See **pituitary gland. 2.** *Pharm.* the extract obtained from the lobes of the pituitary glands of hogs, sheep, and other domestic animals: the posterior lobe constituent increases blood pressure, contracts stomach muscles, etc., and the anterior lobe constituent regulates growth of the skeleton. —*adj.* **3.** of, pertaining to, or involving the pituitary gland. **4.** noting a physical type of abnormal size with overgrown extremities resulting from excessive pituitary secretion. [1605–15; < L *pituitārius* pertaining to or secreting phlegm. See PIP[2], -ARY]

pitu′itary bod′y, (formerly) the pituitary gland.

pitu′itary gland′, *Anat.* a small, somewhat cherry-shaped double structure attached by a stalk to the base of the brain and constituting the master endocrine gland affecting all hormonal functions in the body, consisting of an anterior region **(anterior pituitary** or **adenohypophysis)** that develops embryonically from the roof of the mouth and that secretes growth hormone, LH, FSH, ACTH, TSH, and MSH, a posterior region **(posterior pituitary** or **neurohypophysis)** that develops from the back of the forebrain and that secretes the hormones vasopressin and oxytocin, and an intermediate part **(pars intermedia),** derived from the anterior region but joined to the posterior region, that secretes the hormone MSH in lower vertebrates. Also called **hypophysis.** See diag. under **brain.** [1605–15]

pi•tu•i•tous (pi to͞o′i təs, -tyo͞o′-), *adj. Archaic.* mucous. [1600–10; < L *pituitōsus* full of phlegm. See PIP[2], -OUS] —**pi•tu′i•tous•ness,** *n.*

pit•u•ri (pich′ə rē), *n.* **1.** a solanaceous shrub or small tree, *Duboisia hopwoodi,* of Australia. **2.** a stimulant made from the dried leaves and twigs of this plant, used by the aborigines as a narcotic. [1860–65; < Wiradjuri *pi-ju-ri*]

pit′ vi′per, any of numerous venomous snakes of the family Crotalidae, of the New World, Asia, and the Malay Archipelago, as the rattlesnake, water moccasin, and copperhead, having a heat-sensitive pit on each side of the head between the eye and nostril. [1880–85]

pit•y (pit′ē), *n., pl.* **pit•ies,** *v.,* **pit•ied, pit•y•ing.** —*n.* **1.** sympathetic or kindly sorrow evoked by the suffering, distress, or misfortune of another, often leading one to give relief or aid or to show mercy: *to feel pity for a*

starving child. **2.** a cause or reason for pity, sorrow, or regret: *What a pity you could not go!* **3. have** or **take pity.** to show mercy or compassion. —*v.t.* **4.** to feel pity or compassion for; be sorry for; commiserate with. —*v.i.* **5.** to have compassion; feel pity. [1175–1225; ME *pite* < OF *pite,* earlier *pitet* < L *pietāt-* (s. of *pietās*) PIETY]
—Syn. 1. commiseration, compassion. See **sympathy.**

pit•y•ing (pit′ē ing), *adj.* full of or expressing pity: *a pitying look.* [1640–50; PITY + -ING[2]] **—pit′y•ing•ly,** *adv.*

pit•y•ri•a•sis (pit′ə rī′ə sis), *n.* **1.** *Pathol.* any of various skin diseases marked by the shedding of branlike scales of epidermis. **2.** *Vet. Pathol.* a skin disease in various domestic animals marked by dry scales. [1685–95; < NL < Gk *pityríāsis* branlike eruption, equiv. to *pítyr(on)* bran, scale + *-iāsis* -IASIS]

pit•y•roid (pit′ə roid′), *adj. Med.* scaly; resembling bran. [1840–50; < Gk *pítyr(on)* bran, scale + -OID]

più (pyo͞o), *adv. Music.* more: *più allegro.* [1715–25; < It < L *plus;* see PLUS]

Piu•ra (pyo͞o′rä), *n.* a city in N Peru. 126,010.

Pi•us I (pī′əs), **Saint,** pope A.D. 140–155?.

Pius II, (*Enea Silvio de Piccolomini*) 1405–64, Italian ecclesiastic: pope 1458–64. Literary name, **Aeneas Silvius.**

Pius III, (*Francesco Nanni Todeschini Piccolomini*) 1439–1503, Italian ecclesiastic: pope 1503.

Pius IV, (*Giovanni Angelo Medici*) 1499–1565, Italian ecclesiastic: pope 1559–65.

Pius V, **Saint** (*Michele Ghislieri*), 1504–72, Italian ecclesiastic: pope 1566–72.

Pius VI, (*Giovanni Angelo,* or *Giannangelo, Braschi*) 1717–99, Italian ecclesiastic: pope 1775–99.

Pius VII, (*Luigi Barnaba Chiaramonti*) 1740–1823, Italian ecclesiastic: pope 1800–23.

Pius VIII, (*Francesco Saverio Castiglioni*) 1761–1830, Italian ecclesiastic: pope 1829–30.

Pius IX, (*Giovanni Maria Mastai-Ferretti*) 1792–1878, Italian ecclesiastic: pope 1846–78.

Pius X, **Saint** (*Giuseppe Sarto*), 1835–1914, Italian ecclesiastic: pope 1903–14.

Pius XI, (*Achille Ratti*) 1857–1939, Italian ecclesiastic: pope 1922–39.

Pius XII, (*Eugenio Pacelli*) 1876–1958, Italian ecclesiastic: pope 1939–58.

Pi•ute (pī o͞ot′, pī′o͞ot), *n., pl.* **-utes,** (*esp. collectively*) **-ute.** Paiute.

piv•ot (piv′ət), *n.* **1.** a pin, point, or short shaft on the end of which something rests and turns, or upon and about which something rotates or oscillates. **2.** the end of a shaft or arbor, resting and turning in a bearing. **3.** any thing or person on which something or someone functions or depends vitally: *He is the pivot of my life.* **4.** the person in a line, as of troops on parade, whom the others use as a point about which to wheel or maneuver. **5.** a whirling about on one foot. **6.** *Basketball.* the act of keeping one foot in place while holding the ball and moving the other foot one step in any direction, so as not to be charged with walking. **7.** *Basketball.* **a.** an offensive position in the front court, usually played by the center, in which the player stands facing away from the offensive basket and serves as the pivot of the offense by setting up plays through passing, making screens, and taking shots. **b.** Also called **pivotman.** the player who plays in the pivot position. **8.** *Dentistry.* (formerly) dowel (def. 4). —*v.i.* **9.** to turn on or as on a pivot. **10.** *Basketball.* to keep one foot in place while holding the ball and moving the other foot one step in any direction. —*v.t.* **11.** to mount on, attach by, or provide with a pivot or pivots. [1605–15; < F *pivot* (n.), *pivoter* (v.), OF < ?]

piv•ot•al (piv′ə tl), *adj.* **1.** of, pertaining to, or serving as a pivot. **2.** of vital or critical importance: *a pivotal event.* [1835–45; PIVOT + -AL[1]] **—piv′ot•al•ly,** *adv.*

piv•ot•ing (piv′ə ting), *n. Dentistry.* (formerly) the attaching of an artificial crown to the root of a tooth with a metal dowel. [1850–55; PIVOT (v.) + -ING[1]]

piv•ot•man (piv′ət man′), *n., pl.* **-men** (-men′). *Basketball.* a pivot (def. 7b). [1810–15; PIVOT + MAN[1]]

piv′ot tooth′, *Dentistry.* (formerly) an artificial crown attached to the root of a tooth by pivoting. [1835–45, *Amer.*]

pix[1] (piks), *n.* pyx.

pix[2] (piks), *n., pl.* **pix** for 2. **1.** a pl. of **pic**[1]. **2.** pic[2].

pix•el (pik′səl, -sel), *n. Computers, Television.* the smallest element of an image that can be individually processed in a video display system. [1965–70; PIX[2] (def. 1) + EL(EMENT)]

pix•ie (pik′sē), *n.* **1.** a fairy or sprite, esp. a mischievous one. **2.** a small, pert, or mischievous person. —*adj.* **3.** Also, **pix′ie•ish, pix′y•ish.** playfully impish or mischievous; prankish: *pixie mood; a pixie sense of humor.* [1620–30; orig. dial. (SW England) *pixy, pigsy, pisky;* orig. uncert.]

pix•i•lat•ed (pik′sə lā′tid), *adj.* **1.** slightly eccentric or mentally disordered. **2.** amusingly whimsical, prankish, silly, or the like. [1840–50, *Amer.;* PIX(IE) + (TIT)ILLATED]

pix•i•la•tion (pik′sə lā′shən), *n.* **1.** the state or quality of being pixilated. **2.** *Motion Pictures.* animation of people, where performers change their positions slightly between exposures of one or two frames each, to obtain a comic effect of jerky movement when the film is projected at normal speed. [1945–50; (in def. 1) PIXILATE + -ION; (in def. 2) PIXIL(ATED) + (ANIM)ATION]

pix•y (pik′sē), *n., pl.* **pix•ies,** *adj.* pixie.

Piy•yut (*Seph. Heb.* pē yo͞ot′; *Ashk. Heb.* pē′yo͝ot), *n., pl.* **Piy•yut•im** (*Seph. Heb.* pē yo͞o tēm′; *Ashk. Heb.* pi yo͞o′tim). *Judaism.* a liturgical poem included in the services on holidays and special Sabbaths in addition to the established prayers.

pi•zaine (pē′zān), *n. Armor.* a mail collar of the 14th century, worn with a hauberk. [1895–1900; appar. < OF, equiv. to *piz* breast (< L *pectus*) + *-aine* n. suffix < L *āna* -AN]

Pi•zar•ro (pi zär′ō; *Sp.* pē thär′rô, -sär′-), *n.* **Fran•cis•co** (fran sis′kō; *Sp.* frän thēs′kô, -sēs′-), c1470–1541, Spanish conqueror of Peru.

pi•zazz (pə zaz′), *n. Informal.* **1.** energy; vitality; vigor. **2.** attractive style; dash; flair. Also, **piz•zazz′.** [1935–40, *Amer.;* orig. obscure] **—pi•zazz′y,** *adj.*

pizz., *Music.* pizzicato.

piz•za (pēt′sə), *n.* a flat, open-faced baked pie of Italian origin, consisting of a thin layer of bread dough topped with spiced tomato sauce and cheese, often garnished with anchovies, sausage slices, mushrooms, etc. Also called **piz′za pie′.** [1930–35; < It *pizza* (var. *pitta*), perh. ult. < Gk; cf. *pḗtea* bran, *petítēs* bran bread]

piz•ze•ri•a (pēt′sə rē′ə), *n.* a restaurant, bakery, or the like, where pizzas are made and sold. [1940–45; < It, equiv. to *pizz(a)* PIZZA + *-eria* -ERY]

piz•zi•ca•to (pit′si kä′tō; *It.* pēt′tsē kä′tô), *adj., n., pl.* **-ti** (-tē). *Music.* —*adj.* **1.** played by plucking the strings with the finger instead of using the bow, as on a violin. —*n.* **2.** a note or passage so played. [1835–45; < It, ptp. of *pizzicare* to pluck, pick, twang (a stringed instrument)]

piz•zle (piz′əl), *n.* **1.** the penis of an animal, esp. a bull. **2.** a whip made from a bull's pizzle. [1515–25; prob. < dial. D *pezel* or LG *pēsel,* equiv. to MD, MLG *pēs(e)* (D *pees*) tendon, sinew + *-el* dim. suffix; see -LE]

p.j.'s (pē′jāz′), *n.* (*used with a plural v.*) *Informal.* pajamas. Also, **P.J.'s** [1950–55]

PK, **1.** personal knowledge **2.** psychokinesis.

pk, peck; pecks.

pk., *pl.* **pks. 1.** pack. **2.** park. **3.** peak. **4.** peck.

pkg., *pl.* **pkgs.** package.

pkt., **1.** packet. **2.** pocket.

PKU, phenylketonuria.

pkwy., parkway.

PL, Public Law: *PL #480.*

pl., **1.** place. **2.** plate. **3.** plural.

P/L, profit and loss.

P.L., Poet Laureate.

PL/1 (pē′el′wun′), *n. Computers.* a high-level programming language that is designed for solving problems in science and engineering as well as in business data processing. [*P(rogramming) L(anguage)/1*]

PLA, See **People's Liberation Army.**

plac•a•ble (plak′ə bəl, plā′kə-), *adj.* capable of being placated, pacified, or appeased; forgiving. [1490–1500; < OF < L *plācābilis.* See PLACATE[1], -ABLE] **—plac′a•bil′i•ty, plac′a•ble•ness,** *n.*

plac•age (plak′ij), *n.* a thin facing on a building. [1765–75; < F; see PLAQUE, -AGE]

plac•ard (plak′ärd, -ərd), *n.* **1.** a paperboard sign or notice, as one posted in a public place or carried by a demonstrator or picketer. **2.** *Armor.* placate[2]. —*v.t.* **3.** to display placards on or in: *The square was placarded by peace marchers.* **4.** to publicize, announce, or advertise by means of placards. **5.** to post as a placard. [1475–85; < MF. See PLAQUE, -ARD] **—plac′ard•er,** *n.*

pla•cas (plä′kəz; *Sp.* plä′käs), *n.pl., sing.* **-ca** (-kə; *Sp.* -kä). (esp. in the southwestern U.S.) graffiti, as of initials or slogans, spray-painted on an outdoor wall, esp. in the lettering style and colors identified with an individual or a street gang. [< AmerSp; Sp: pl. of *placa* plate, tablet, slab < F *plaque* PLAQUE]

pla•cate[1] (plā′kāt, plak′āt), *v.t.,* **-cat•ed, -cat•ing.** to appease or pacify, esp. by concessions or conciliatory gestures: *to placate an outraged citizenry.* [1670–80; < L *plācātus* ptp. of *plācāre* to quiet, calm, appease, akin to *placēre* to PLEASE; see -ATE[1]] **—pla′cat•er,** *n.* **—pla•ca•tion** (plā kā′shən), *n.*
—Syn. conciliate, satisfy.

plac•ate[2] (plak′āt, -it), *n. Armor.* a piece of plate armor of the 15th to the 18th century protecting the lower part of the torso in front: used esp. as a reinforcement over a breastplate. Also, **placard, plac′cate, plackart.** [1625–35; appar. var. of PLACARD]

pla•ca•tive (plā′kā tiv, -kə-, plak′ā tiv, plak′ə-), *adj.* placatory. [1930–35; PLACATE[1] + -IVE]

pla•ca•to•ry (plā′kə tôr′ē, -tōr′ē, plak′ə-), *adj.* serving, tending, or intended to placate: *a placatory reply.* [1630–40; < LL *plācātōrius.* See PLACATE[1], -TORY[1]]

place (plās), *n., v.,* **placed, plac•ing.** —*n.* **1.** a particular portion of space, whether of definite or indefinite extent. **2.** space in general: *time and place.* **3.** the specific portion of space normally occupied by anything: *The vase is in its place. Every item on the shelf had its place.* **4.** a space, area, or spot, set apart or used for a particular purpose: *a place of worship; a place of entertainment.* **5.** any part or spot in a body or surface: *a decayed place in a tree.* **6.** a particular passage in a book or writing: *to find the place where one left off reading.* **7.** a space or seat for a person, as in a theater, train, etc.: *Please save my place for me.* **8.** position, situation, or circumstances: *I would complain if I were in your place.* **9.** a proper or appropriate location or position: *A restaurant is not the place for an argument.* **10.** a job, post, or office: *persons in high places.* **11.** a function or duty: *It is not your place to offer criticism.* **12.** proper sequence or relationship, as of ideas, details, etc.: *My thoughts began to fall into place.* **13.** high position or rank: *aristocrats of power and place.* **14.** a region or area: *to travel to distant places.* **15.** an open space, or square, as in a city or town. **16.** a short street, a court, etc. **17.** a portion of space used for habitation, as a city, town, or village: *Trains rarely stop in that place anymore.* **18.** a building, location, etc., set aside for a specific purpose: *He will soon need a larger place for his expanding business.* **19.** a part of a building: *The kitchen is the sunniest place in the house.* **20.** a residence, dwelling, or house: *Please come and have dinner at my place.* **21.** lieu; substitution (usually fol. by *of*): *Use yogurt in place of sour cream.* **22.** a step or point in order of proceeding: *in the first place.* **23.** a fitting or promising opportunity: *There's a place in this town for a man of his talents.* **24.** a reasonable ground or occasion: *This is no place for such an outburst.* **25.** *Arith.* **a.** the position of a figure in a series, as in decimal notation. **b.** Usually, **places.** the figures of the series. **26.** *Drama.* one of the three unities. Cf. **unity** (def. 8). **27.** *Sports.* **a.** a position among the leading competitors, usually the first, second, or third at the finish line. **b.** the position of the competitor who comes in second in a horse race, harness race, etc. Cf. **show** (def. 29), **win** (def. 17). **28. places,** *Theat.* a call summoning performers for the beginning of a performance or an act. **29.** room or space for entry or passage: *to make place for the gentry.* **30. give place to, a.** to give precedence or priority to: *The old gives place to the new.* **b.** to be succeeded or replaced by: *Travel by trains has given place to travel by airplanes.* **31. go places,** *Informal.* to succeed or advance in one's career: *He'll never go places if he stays in his hometown.* **32. in place, a.** in the correct or usual position or order: *Dinner is ready and everything is in place.* **b.** in the same spot, without advancing or retreating: *Stand by your desk and jog in place for a few minutes of exercise.* **33. know** or **keep one's place,** to recognize one's position or rank, esp. if inferior, and behave or act accordingly: *They treated their servants well but expected them always to know their place.* **34. out of place, a.** not in the correct or usual position or order: *The library books are all out of place.* **b.** unsuitable to the circumstances or surroundings; inappropriate: *He had always felt out of place in an academic environment. A green suit was out of place at the funeral.* **35. put someone in his** or **her place,** to lower someone's self-esteem; humble, esp. an arrogant person: *She put me in my place by reminding me who was boss.* **36. take place,** to happen; occur: *The commencement exercises will take place outdoors unless it rains.*
—*v.t.* **37.** to put in the proper position or order; arrange; dispose: *Place the silverware on the table for dinner.* **38.** to put or set in a particular place, position, situation, or relation. **39.** to put in a suitable place for some purpose: *to place an advertisement in the newspaper.* **40.** to put into particular or proper hands: *to place some incriminating evidence with the district attorney.* **41.** to give (an order or the like) to a supplier: *She placed the order for the pizza an hour ago.* **42.** to appoint (a person) to a post or office: *The president placed him in the Department of Agriculture.* **43.** to find a place, situation, etc., for (a person): *The agency had no trouble placing him with a good firm.* **44.** to determine or indicate the place or value of: *to place health among the greatest gifts in life.* **45.** to assign a certain position or rank to: *The army placed him in the infantry.* **46.** to succeed in attaining a position for in an athletic or other contest: *to place players on the all-American team; to place students in the finals of the interscholastic chess tournament.* **47.** to identify by connecting with the proper place, circumstances, etc.: *to be unable to place a person; to place a face; to place an accent.* **48.** to employ (the voice) for singing or speaking with consciousness of the bodily point of emphasis of resonance of each tone or register. —*v.i.* **49.** *Sports.* **a.** to finish among the first three competitors in a race. **b.** to finish second in a horse race, harness race, etc. **50.** to earn a specified standing with relation to others, as in an examination, competition, etc.: *He placed fifth in a graduation class of 90.* [bef. 950; (n.) ME, conflation of OE *plæce* and MF *place,* both < L *platea,* var. of *platēa* street, courtyard, area < Gk *plateîa* broad street, n. use of fem. of *platýs* broad, FLAT[1]; (v.) late ME, deriv. of the n.; see PLATY-] **—place′a•ble,** *adj.* **—place′less,** *adj.* **—place′less•ly,** *adv.*
—Syn. 1. location, locale, locality, site. **10.** rank, employment. See **position. 11.** charge, responsibility. **14.** section, sector. **37.** situate, station. See **put. 39.** locate, set, deposit, lay, seat. **42.** hire.

pla•ce•bo (plə sē′bō *for 1;* plä chā′bō *for 2*), *n., pl.* **-bos, -boes. 1.** *Med., Pharm.* **a.** a substance having no pharmacological effect but given merely to satisfy a patient who supposes it to be a medicine. **b.** a substance having no pharmacological effect but administered as a control in testing experimentally or clinically the efficacy of a biologically active preparation. **2.** *Rom. Cath. Ch.* the vespers of the office for the dead: so called from the initial word of the first antiphon, taken from Psalm 114:9 of the Vulgate. [1175–1225 for def. 2; 1775–85 for def. 1; ME < L *placēbō* I shall be pleasing, acceptable]

pla•ce′bo effect′ (plə sē′bō), a reaction to a placebo manifested by a lessening of symptoms or the production of anticipated side effects. [1945–50]

place′ card′, a small card with the name of a guest on it, placed on the table, to indicate where he or she is to sit. [1920–25]

place•hold•er (plās′hōl′dər), *n.* **1.** *Math, Logic.* a symbol in an expression that may be replaced by the name of any element of the set. **2.** a person who holds a government office, esp. one appointed to the position in return for political support or favors. [1550–60; PLACE + HOLDER]

place′ kick′, *Football.* a kick in which the ball is held nearly upright on the ground either by means of a tee or by a teammate, as in a kickoff, an attempt at a field goal, etc. Cf. **drop kick, punt**[1] (def. 1). [1855–60]

place-kick (plās′kik′), *Football.* —*v.t.* **1.** to make (a field goal or point after touchdown) by a place kick. **2.** to kick (the ball) as held for a place kick. —*v.i.* **3.** to make a place kick. Also, **place′kick′.** [1855–60; v. use of PLACE KICK] —**place′-kick′er, place′kick′er,** *n.*

place•man (plās′mən), *n., pl.* **-men.** *Brit.* a person appointed to a position, esp. one in the government, as a reward for political support of an elected official. [1735–45; PLACE + -MAN] —**place′man•ship′,** *n.*

place′ mat′, a mat set on a dining table beneath a place setting. [1950–55]

place•ment (plās′mənt), *n.* **1.** the act of placing. **2.** the state of being placed. **3.** the act of an employment office or employer in filling a position. **4.** location; arrangement: *the placement of furniture.* **5.** *Football.* **a.** the placing of the ball on the ground in attempting a place kick. **b.** the position of the ball. **c.** a place kick. **d.** a score made by a place kick: *Jones made 43 consecutive placements last season.* **6.** (in tennis, badminton, handball, etc.) a winning shot in which the ball or shuttlecock is so hit that one's opponent is unable to return it. [1835–45; PLACE + -MENT]

place′ment test′, *Educ.* a test to determine a student's level of ability in one or more subjects in order to place the student with others of the same approximate ability. [1925–30]

place•name (plās′nām′), *n.* the name given to or held by a geographical location, as a town, city, village, etc. Also, **place′-name′, place′ name′.** [1865–70; PLACE + NAME]

pla•cen•ta (plə sen′tə), *n., pl.* **-tas, -tae** (-tē). **1.** *Anat., Zool.* the organ in most mammals, formed in the lining of the uterus by the union of the uterine mucous membrane with the membranes of the fetus, that provides for the nourishment of the fetus and the elimination of its waste products. **2.** *Bot.* **a.** the part of the ovary of flowering plants that bears the ovules. **b.** (in ferns and related plants) the tissue giving rise to sporangia. [1670–80; < NL: something having a flat, circular form, L: a cake < Gk *plakóenta,* acc. of *plakóeis* flat cake, deriv. of *pláx* (gen. *plakós*) flat] —**pla•cen′tal, plac•en•tar•y** (plas′ən ter′ē, plə sen′tə rē), *adj.*

pla•cen•tate (plə sen′tāt), *adj.* having a placenta. [1885–90; PLACENT(A) + -ATE[1]]

plac•en•ta•tion (plas′ən tā′shən), *n.* **1.** *Anat., Zool.* **a.** the formation of a placenta. **b.** the manner of placement or construction of a placenta. **2.** *Bot.* the disposition or arrangement of a placenta or placentas. [1750–60; < F; see PLACENTA, -ATION]

Pla•cen•tia (plə sen′shə, -shē ə), *n.* **1.** a town in S California. 35,041. **2.** ancient name of **Piacenza.**

place′ of arms′, **1.** an area in a fortress or a fortified town where troops could assemble for defense. **2.** an enlarged part of the covered way in a fortification. [1590–1600]

place′ of articula′tion, *Phonet.* the location at which two speech organs approach or come together in producing a speech sound, as in the contact of the tongue and the teeth to form a dental sound. Also called **point of articulation.** Cf. **articulator** (def. 2).

Place Pi•galle (plas pē gal′), a square in Paris, France: noted for its night clubs. Also called **Pigalle.**

plac•er[1] (plas′ər), *n. Mining.* **1.** a surficial mineral deposit formed by the concentration of small particles of heavy minerals, as gold, rutile, or platinum, in gravel or small sands. **2.** the site of a form of mining (**plac′er min′ing**) in which a placer deposit is washed to separate the gold or other valuable minerals. [1835–45, *Amer.;* < AmerSp; Sp: sandbank < Catalan *placel,* deriv. of *plaza* open place; see PLAZA]

plac•er[2] (plā′sər), *n.* **1.** a person who sets things in their place or arranges them. **2.** a person or animal that is among the winners of a race or other contest. [1570–80; PLACE + -ER[1]]

Plac•er•ville (plas′ər vil′), *n.* a town in central California; 19th-century gold-mining center. 6739.

place′ set′ting, **1.** the group of dishes, silverware, glasses, etc., set at the place of each person at a meal. **2.** a single group of such dishes or eating utensils sold as a unit. [1945–50]

pla•cet (plā′sit), *n.* an expression or vote of assent or sanction, indicated by the use of the Latin word *placet* (it pleases). [1580–90]

plac•id (plas′id), *adj.* pleasantly calm or peaceful; unruffled; tranquil; serenely quiet or undisturbed: *placid waters.* [1620–30; < L *placidus* calm, quiet, akin to *placēre* to PLEASE (orig., to calm); see -ID[4]] —**pla•cid•i•ty** (plə sid′i tē), **plac′id•ness,** *n.* —**plac′id•ly,** *adv.* —**Syn.** See **peaceful.**

Plá′ci•do's disk′ (plä′si dōz′), *Ophthalm.* a device marked with concentric black rings, used to detect corneal irregularities. [after A. *Plácido* da Costa (1848–1916), Portuguese ophthalmologist, who devised it]

Plac•i•dyl (plas′i dil, plä′si-), *Pharm. Trademark.* a brand of ethchlorvynol.

plack (plak), *n.* a very small copper coin used in Scotland in the 15th and 16th centuries as a four-penny piece. [1425–75; late ME *placke* < MD: name of a coin]

plack•art (plak′ərt), *n. Armor.* placate[2].

plack•et (plak′it), *n.* **1.** the opening or slit at the top of a skirt, or in a dress or blouse, that facilitates putting it on and taking it off. **2.** a pocket, esp. one in a woman's skirt. **3.** *Archaic.* **a.** a petticoat. **b.** a woman. [1595–1605; var. of *placard* breastplate < OF, deriv. of *plaquier* to plate < MD *placken* to patch; cf. PLAQUE]

plac•ode (plak′ōd), *n. Embryol.* a local thickening of the endoderm in the embryo, that usually constitutes the primordium of a specific structure or organ. [1905–10; < Gk *plak-* (s. of *pláx*) something flat, tablet + -ODE[1]]

plac•o•derm (plak′ə dûrm′), *n.* any of various extinct jawed fishes of the class Placodermi, dominant in seas and rivers during the Devonian Period and characterized by bony armored plates on the head and upper trunk. [1855–60; < NL *Placodermi* name of the class, pl. of *placodermus,* equiv. to *placo-* (< Gk; see PLACOID, -O-) + *-dermus* -DERM]

plac•oid (plak′oid), *adj.* platelike, as the scales or dermal investments of sharks. [1835–45; < Gk *plak-* (s. of *pláx*) something flat, tablet + -OID]

pla•fond (plə fon′; *Fr.* pla fôn′), *n., pl.* **-fonds** (-fonz′; *Fr.* -fôn′). *Archit.* a ceiling, whether flat or arched, esp. one of decorative character. [1655–65; < F; MF *platfond* ceiling, lit., flat bottom, i.e., underside. See PLATE[1], FUND]

pla•gal (plā′gəl), *adj. Music.* (of a Gregorian mode) having the final in the middle of the compass. Cf. **authentic** (def. 5a). [1590–1600; < ML *plagālis,* equiv. to *plag(a)* plagal mode (appar. back formation from *plagius* plagal; see PLAGE) + *-ālis* -AL[1]]

pla′gal ca′dence, *Music.* a cadence in which the chord of the tonic is preceded by that of the subdominant. [1870–75]

plage (pläzh), *n.* **1.** a sandy bathing beach at a seashore resort. **2.** *Astron.* a luminous area in the sun's chromosphere that appears in the vicinity of a sunspot. [1885–90; < F < It *piaggia* < LL *plagia* shore, n. use of fem. of *plagius* horizontal < Gk *plágios* slanting, sideways; see PLAGIO-]

pla•gia•rism (plā′jə riz′əm, -jē ə riz′-), *n.* **1.** the unauthorized use or close imitation of the language and thoughts of another author and the representation of them as one's own original work. **2.** something used and represented in this manner. [1615–25; PLAGIAR(Y) + -ISM] —**pla′gia•rist,** *n.* —**pla′gia•ris′tic,** *adj.*

pla•gia•rize (plā′jə rīz′, -jē ə rīz′-), *v.,* **-rized, -riz•ing.** —*v.t.* **1.** to take and use by plagiarism. **2.** to take and use ideas, passages, etc., from (another's work) by plagiarism. —*v.i.* **3.** to commit plagiarism. Also, *esp. Brit.,* **pla′gia•rise′.** [1710–20; PLAGIAR(ISM) + -IZE] —**pla′•gia•riz′er,** *n.*

pla•gia•ry (plā′jə rē, -jē ə rē), *n., pl.* **-ries.** **1.** plagiarism. **2.** a plagiarist. [1590–1600; < L *plagiārius* kidnapper, equiv. to *plagi(um)* kidnapping (akin to *plaga* snare) + *-ārius* -ARY]

plagio-, a combining form meaning "oblique," used in the formation of compound words: *plagioclase.* [comb. form repr. Gk *plágios* slanting, sideways, equiv. to *plá-g(os)* side + *-ios* adj. suffix]

pla•gi•o•ceph•a•ly (plā′jē ə sef′ə lē), *n. Med.* a deformity of the skull in which one side is more developed in the front, and the other side is more developed in the rear. Also, **pla′gi•o•ceph′a•lism.** [1885–90; PLAGIO- + -CEPHALY] —**pla•gi•o•ce•phal•ic** (plā′jē ō sə fal′ik), **pla′gi•o•ceph′a•lous,** *adj.*

pla•gi•o•clase (plā′jē ə klās′), *n.* any of the feldspar minerals varying in composition from acidic albite, $NaAlSi_3O_8$, to basic anorthite, $CaAl_2Si_2O_8$, found in most igneous rocks: shows twinning striations on good cleavage surfaces. Also called **soda-lime feldspar.** [1865–70; PLAGIO- + -CLASE] —**pla•gi•o•clas•tic** (plā′jē ə klas′-tik), *adj.*

pla•gi•o•he•dral (plā′jē ə hē′drəl), *adj.* (of a crystal) having faces arranged obliquely in a helix. Also, **pla•gi•he•dral** (plā′jə hē′drəl). [PLAGIO- + -HEDRAL]

pla•gi•o•trop•ic (plā′jē ə trop′ik, -trō′pik), *adj. Bot.* growing more or less divergent from the vertical. [1880–85; PLAGIO- + -TROPIC] —**pla′gi•o•trop′i•cal•ly,** *adv.*

pla•gi•ot•ro•pism (plā′jē o′trə piz′əm), *n. Bot.* plagiotropic tendency or growth. [1885–90; PLAGIOTROP(IC) + -ISM]

plague (plāg), *n., v.,* **plagued, pla•guing.** —*n.* **1.** an epidemic disease that causes high mortality; pestilence. **2.** an infectious, epidemic disease caused by a bacterium, *Yersinia pestis,* characterized by fever, chills, and prostration, transmitted to humans from rats by means of the bites of fleas. Cf. **bubonic plague, pneumonic plague, septicemic plague.** **3.** any widespread affliction, calamity, or evil, esp. one regarded as a direct punishment by God: *a plague of war and desolation.* **4.** any cause of trouble, annoyance, or vexation: *Uninvited guests are a plague.* —*v.t.* **5.** to trouble, annoy, or torment in any manner: *The question of his future plagues him with doubt.* **6.** to annoy, bother, or pester: *Ants plagued the picnickers.* **7.** to smite with a plague, pestilence, death, etc.; scourge: *those whom the gods had plagued.* **8.** to infect with a plague; cause an epidemic in or among: *diseases that still plague the natives of Ethiopia.* **9.** to afflict with any evil: *He was plagued by allergies all his life.* [1350–1400; ME *plage* < L *plāga* stripe, wound, LL: pestilence] —**pla′guer,** *n.*
—**Syn. 4.** nuisance, bother, torment. **6.** harass, vex, harry, hector, fret, worry, badger, irritate, disturb. See **bother.**

Plague, The, (French, *La Peste*), a novel (1947) by Albert Camus.

plague•some (plāg′səm), *adj.* vexatious or troublesome. [1820–30; PLAGUE + -SOME[1]] —**plague′some•ness,** *n.*

pla•guy (plā′gē), *Chiefly Northern U.S.* —*adj.* **1.** such as to plague, torment, or annoy; vexatious: *a plaguy pile of debts.* —*adv.* **2.** vexatiously or excessively: *The room is plaguy hot.* Also, **pla′guey.** [1565–75; PLAGUE + -Y[1]]

plaice (plās), *n., pl.* **plaice.** **1.** a European flatfish, *Pleuronectes platessa,* used for food. **2.** any of various American flatfishes or flounders. [1250–1300; ME, var. of *plais* < OF < LL *platessa* flatfish < Gk *platýs* FLAT[1], broad]

plaid (plad), *n.* **1.** any fabric woven of differently colored yarns in a crossbarred pattern. **2.** a pattern of this kind. **3.** a long, rectangular piece of cloth, usually with such a pattern and worn across the left shoulder by Scottish Highlanders. —*adj.* **4.** having the pattern of a plaid. [1505–15; < ScotGael *plaide* blanket, plaid (def. 3)]

plaid•ed (plad′id), *adj.* **1.** made of plaid, or having a similar pattern. **2.** wearing a plaid. [1795–1805; PLAID + -ED[3]]

plain[1] (plān), *adj.,* **-er, -est,** *adv., n.* —*adj.* **1.** clear or distinct to the eye or ear: *a plain trail to the river; to stand in plain view.* **2.** clear to the mind; evident, manifest, or obvious: *to make one's meaning plain.* **3.** conveying the meaning clearly and simply; easily understood: *plain talk.* **4.** downright; sheer; utter; self-evident: *plain folly; plain stupidity.* **5.** free from ambiguity or evasion; candid; outspoken: *the plain truth of the matter.* **6.** without special pretensions, superiority, elegance, etc.; ordinary: *plain people.* **7.** not beautiful; physically unattractive or undistinguished: *a plain face.* **8.** without intricacies or difficulties. **9.** ordinary, simple, or unostentatious: *Although she was a duchess, her manners were attractively plain.* **10.** with little or no embellishment, decoration, or enhancing elaboration: *a plain blue suit.* **11.** without a pattern, figure, or device: *a plain fabric.* **12.** not rich, highly seasoned, or elaborately prepared, as food: *a plain diet.* **13.** flat or level: *plain country.* **14.** unobstructed, clear, or open, as ground, a space, etc. **15.** *Cards.* being other than a face card or a trump. —*adv.* **16.** clearly and simply: *He's just plain stupid.* —*n.* **17.** an area of land not significantly higher than adjacent areas and with relatively minor differences in elevation, commonly less than 500 ft. (150 m), within the area. **18. The Plains.** See **Great Plains.** [1250–1300; ME (adj., adv., and n.) < OF (adj. and n.) < L *plānus* flat, level, *plānum* flat country] —**plain′ly,** *adv.* —**plain′ness,** *n.*
—**Syn. 1, 2.** lucid, understandable, intelligible, unmistakable, apparent, perspicuous. **2. 3.** unambiguous, unequivocal, patent, transparent; direct. **5.** unreserved, straightforward, blunt, frank, ingenuous, open, sincere. **6.** unpretentious. **10.** unadorned. See **homely.** —**Ant. 1.** indistinct. **2.** obscure. **13.** hilly.

plain[2] (plān), *v.i. Brit. Dial.* to complain. [1250–1300; ME *plei(g)nen* < OF *plaign-,* s. of *plaindre* < L *plangere* to beat (the breast, etc.), lament; akin to Gk *plḗssein* to strike]

plain′ bear′ing, *Mach.* any of various bearings, not containing rolling elements, that present to the shaft or axle they support broad areas of corresponding form, usually segments of a cylinder. Cf. **rolling-element bearing.** [1915–20]

plain•chant (plān′chant′, -chänt′), *n.* plainsong (defs. 1, 2). [1720–30; PLAIN[1] + CHANT, modeled on F *plain-chant*]

plain′ clothes′, clothing other than one's uniform, esp. civilian clothes worn on duty by a police officer. Also, **plain′clothes′.** [1815–25] —**plain′-clothes′,** *adj.*

plain•clothes•man (plān′klōz′mən, -man′, -klōthz′-), *n., pl.* **-men** (-mən, -men′). a police officer, esp. a detective, who wears ordinary civilian clothes while on duty. Also, **plain′clothes′ man′.** [1925–30; PLAIN CLOTHES + MAN[1]]

plain′ deal′ing, direct and honest conduct in one's relations and transactions with others. [1560–70]

Plain•field (plān′fēld′), *n.* **1.** a city in N New Jersey. 45,555. **2.** a town in NE Connecticut. 12,774.

plain′ Jane′, *Informal.* a drab, unattractive, and generally uninteresting girl or woman. [1910–15]

plain-Jane (plān′jān′), *adj. Informal.* simple and modest; unadorned; basic: *a plain-Jane car dressed up with leather upholstery.* Also, **plain′-jane′.** [1935–40]

plain′ knit′, the simplest knitted construction, consisting of vertical ribs visible on the front of the fabric and horizontal rows of stitches visible on the back, used in the production of hosiery and jersey fabrics. Also called **flat knit.** [1965–70]

plain-laid (plān′lād′), *adj. Ropemaking.* noting a rope laid right-handed with three left-handed strands, without a heart; hawser-laid. [1885–90]

plain′ lap′. See **lap joint.**

Plain′ Peo′ple, members of the Amish, the Mennonites, or the Dunkers: so named because they stress simple living. [1870–75, *Amer.*]

plain′ rail′, (in a double-hung window) a meeting rail equal in thickness to its sash. Cf. **check rail.**

plain′ sail′, *Naut.* **1.** any of the ordinary working sails of a vessel. **2.** all these sails, taken collectively. [1820–30]

plain′ sail′ing, **1.** *Navig.* sailing on waters that are free of hazards or obstructions. Cf. **plane sailing.** **2.** an easy and unobstructed way, course, or plan: *As an heir to a large fortune, he looked forward to financial plain sailing.* [1800–10]

plain-saw (plān′sô′), *v.t.,* **-sawed, -sawed** or **-sawn, -saw•ing.** to reduce (a squared log) to boards with evenly spaced parallel cuts; bastard-saw. [1950–55]

plains′ grass′hopper, a large, destructive short-horned grasshopper, *Brachystola magna,* of the western U.S., marked by pinkish hind wings. Also called **lubber grasshopper.**

Plains′ In′dian, a member of any of the American Indian tribes, as those of the Algonquian, Athabascan, Caddoan, Kiowa, Siouan, or Uto-Aztecan linguistic families, that formerly inhabited the Great Plains. All were more or less nomadic, following the buffalo, and were often in touch with one another so that the development among them of common culture traits is noticeable. Also called **Buffalo Indian.**

plains•man (plānz′mən), *n., pl.* **-men.** an inhabitant of the plains. [1795–1805; PLAIN[1] + -S[3] + -MAN]

Plains′ of A′braham, a high plain adjoining the city of Quebec, Canada: battlefield where the English under Wolfe defeated the French under Montcalm in 1759.

plain•song (plān′sông′, -song′), *n.* **1.** the unisonous vocal music used in the Christian church from the earliest times. **2.** modal liturgical music; Gregorian chant. **3.** a cantus firmus or theme chosen for contrapuntal development. **4.** any simple and unadorned melody or air. Also, **plain′ song′.** Also called **plainchant** (for defs. 1, 2). [1505–15; trans. of ML *cantus plānus*]

plain-spo•ken (plān′spō′kən), *adj.* **1.** candid; frank; blunt. **2.** using simple, direct language: *a plain-spoken politician.* [1670–80]
—**Syn. direct, open, forthright.**

plain•stones (plān′stōnz′), *n.pl. Scot.* **1.** flagstones. **2.** (*used with a singular v.*) a flagstone walk or passageway. Also, **plain•stanes** (plān′stānz′). [1765–75; PLAIN[1] + STONE + -S[3]]

plain′ suit′, *Cards.* a suit other than the trump suit. Also called **side suit.**

plaint (plānt), *n.* **1.** a complaint. **2.** *Law.* a statement of grievance made to a court for the purpose of asking redress. **3.** a lament; lamentation. [1175–1225; ME < MF < L *planctus* a striking or beating (the breast) in grief, equiv. to *plang(ere)* to beat, strike, mourn for + *-tus*, suffix of v. action]

plain′ ta′ble, *Survey.* See **plane table.**

plain•text (plān′tekst′), *n.* the intelligible original message of a cryptogram, as opposed to the coded or enciphered version. Also called **clear text.** Cf. **cryptography.** [1915–20; PLAIN[1] + TEXT]

plain•tiff (plān′tif), *n. Law.* a person who brings suit in a court (opposed to *defendant*). [1350–1400; ME *plaintif* complaining person, n. use of the adj.: PLAINTIVE] —**plain′tiff•ship′,** *n.*

plain•tive (plān′tiv), *adj.* expressing sorrow or melancholy; mournful: *a plaintive melody.* [1350–1400; PLAINT + -IVE; r. ME *plaintif* < MF] —**plain′tive•ly,** *adv.* —**plain′tive•ness,** *n.*
—**Syn.** wistful, sorrowful, sad. —**Ant.** happy, joyful.

plain′ tripe′, the fatty, inner lining of the first stomach (the rumen) of a steer, calf, hog, or sheep, having a bland taste and used as a food, esp. in the preparation of such dishes as haggis, head cheese, etc. Cf. **honeycomb tripe.**

plain-va•nil•la (plān′və nil′ə), *adj. Informal.* having no embellishments, extra equipment, elaborate packaging, etc.; plain; simple; down-to-earth: *I want a plain-vanilla car without a lot of chrome trim.* [in allusion to vanilla ice cream, taken to be the most basic flavor]

Plain•view (plān′vyōō′), *n.* **1.** a town on W Long Island, in SE New York. 28,037. **2.** a city in N Texas. 22,187.

Plain•ville (plān′vil), *n.* a town in N Connecticut. 16,401.

plain′ weave′, the most common and tightest of basic weave structures in which the filling threads pass over and under successive warp threads and repeat the same pattern with alternate threads in the following row, producing a checkered surface. Cf. **satin weave, twill weave.** [1935–40]

plain weave

plain-wrap (plān′rap′), *adj.* packaged in a plain wrapper, esp. one displaying no brand name; no-frills: *the growing popularity of plain-wrap products.*

plais•ter (plā′stər), *n., v.t. Archaic.* plaster.

plait (plāt, plat), *n.* **1.** a braid, esp. of hair or straw. **2.** a pleat or fold, as of cloth. —*v.t.* **3.** to braid, as hair or straw. **4.** to make, as a mat, by braiding. **5.** to pleat. [1350–1400; ME *pleyt* < MF *pleit* < L *plicitum,* neut. of *plicitus,* ptp. of *plicāre* to fold; see PLY[2]]

plait•ing (plā′ting, plat′ing), *n.* **1.** anything that is braided or pleated. **2.** plaits collectively. [1375–1425; late ME *pleyting.* See PLAIT, -ING[1]]

plan (plan), *n., v.,* **planned, plan•ning.** —*n.* **1.** a scheme or method of acting, doing, proceeding, making, etc., developed in advance: *battle plans.* **2.** a design or scheme of arrangement: *an elaborate plan for seating guests.* **3.** a specific project or definite purpose: *plans for the future.* **4.** Also called **plan view.** a drawing made to scale to represent the top view or a horizontal section of a structure or a machine, as a floor layout of a building. **5.** a representation of a thing drawn on a plane, as a map or diagram: *a plan of the dock area.* **6.** (in perspective drawing) one of several planes in front of a represented object, and perpendicular to the line between the object and the eye. **7.** a formal program for specified benefits, needs, etc.: *a pension plan.* —*v.t.* **8.** to arrange a method or scheme beforehand for (any work, enterprise, or proceeding): *to plan a new recreation center.* **9.** to make plans for: *to plan one's vacation.* **10.** to draw or make a diagram or layout of, as a building. —*v.i.* **11.** to make plans: *to plan ahead; to plan for one's retirement.* [1670–80; < F: ground, plan, groundwork, scheme, n. use of the adj.: flat, PLANE[1], learned borrowing of L *plānus* level (cf. PLAIN[1])] —**plan′less,** *adj.* —**plan′less•ly,** *adv.* —**plan′less•ness,** *n.*
—**Syn. 1.** plot, formula, system. PLAN, PROJECT, DESIGN, SCHEME imply a formulated method of doing something. PLAN refers to any method of thinking out acts and purposes beforehand: *What are your plans for today?* A PROJECT is a proposed or tentative plan, often elaborate or extensive: *an irrigation project.* DESIGN suggests art, dexterity, or craft (sometimes evil and selfish) in the elaboration or execution of a plan, and often tends to emphasize the purpose in view: *a misunderstanding brought about by design.* A SCHEME is apt to be either a speculative, possibly impracticable, plan, or a selfish or dishonest one: *a scheme to swindle someone.* **4.** sketch, draft, diagram, chart. **8.** design, devise, plot.

plan-, var. of **plano-**[1] before a vowel: *planate.*

pla•nar (plā′nər), *adj.* **1.** of or pertaining to a geometric plane. **2.** flat or level. [1840–50; < LL *plānāris* flat, of a level surface, equiv. to L *plān(um)* PLANE[1] + *-āris* -AR[1]] —**pla•nar•i•ty** (plə nâr′i tē), *n.*

pla•nar•i•an (plə nâr′ē ən), *n. Zool.* any of various free-swimming, mostly freshwater flatworms of the class Turbellaria, having an undulating or sluglike motion: popular in laboratory studies for the ability to regenerate lost parts. [1885–60; < NL *Planari(a)* a flatworm genus (n. use of fem. of LL *plānārius* level, on level ground; taken to mean "flat"; see PLANE[1], -ARY + -AN]

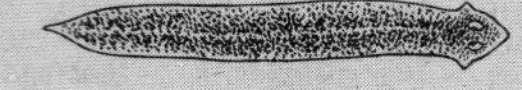
planarian, *Dugesia tigrina,* length 1¼ in. (3.2 cm)

pla•nate (plā′nāt), *adj.* having a plane or flat surface. [< LL *plānātus,* ptp. of *plānāre* to make smooth. See PLANE[2], -ATE[1]]

pla•na•tion (plā nā′shən, plə-), *n. Geol.* the process whereby an irregular land surface is made flat or level by erosion. [1875–80; PLANE[1] + -ATION]

plan•cer (plan′sər), *n.* the soffit of a cornice, esp. one of wood. Also, **plan•ceer** (plan sēr′), **plan•cher** (plan′chər), **plan•cier** (plan sēr′), **plansheer.** [1655–65; < obs. F, equiv. to MF *plancher.* See PLANCH, -ER[2]]

planch (planch, plänch), *n.* **1.** a flat piece of metal, stone, or baked clay, used as a tray in an enameling oven. **2.** *Brit. Dial.* **a.** a floor. **b.** a plank. Also, **planche.** [1300–50; ME *plaunche* < MF *planche* < L *planca* PLANK]

planch•et (plan′chit), *n.* a flat piece of metal for stamping as a coin; a coin blank. [1605–15; PLANCH + -ET]

plan•chette (plan shet′, -chet′), *n.* a small, heart-shaped board supported by two casters and a pencil or stylus that, when moved across a surface by the light, unguided pressure of the fingertips, is supposed to trace meaningful patterns or written messages revealing subconscious thoughts, psychic phenomena, clairvoyant messages, etc. Cf. **Ouija.** [1855–60; < F; see PLANCH, -ETTE]

Planck (plängk), *n.* **Max Karl Ernst** (mäks kärl ernst), 1858–1947, German physicist: Nobel prize 1918.

Planck's′ con′stant, *Physics.* the fundamental constant of quantum mechanics, expressing the ratio of the energy of one quantum of radiation to the frequency of the radiation and approximately equal to 6.624×10^{-27} erg-seconds. *Symbol:* h Also, **Planck′ con′stant.** [1905–10; named after M. K. E. PLANCK]

Planck's′ radia′tion law′, *Physics.* **1.** the law that energy associated with electromagnetic radiation, as light, is composed of discrete quanta of energy, each quantum equal to Planck's constant times the corresponding frequency of the radiation: the fundamental law of quantum mechanics. **2.** the law giving the spectral distribution of radiation from a blackbody. Also called **Planck′ radia′tion for′mula, Planck's′ law′.** [1905–10; named after M. K. E. PLANCK]

plane[1] (plān), *n., adj., v.,* **planed, plan•ing.** —*n.* **1.** a flat or level surface. **2.** *Geom.* a surface generated by a straight line moving at a constant velocity with respect to a fixed point. **3.** *Fine Arts.* an area of a two-dimensional surface having determinate extension and spatial direction or position: *oblique plane; horizontal plane.* **4.** a level of dignity, character, existence, development, or the like: *a high moral plane.* **5.** *Aeron.* **a.** an airplane or a hydroplane: *to take a plane to Dallas.* **b.** a thin, flat or curved, extended section of an airplane or a hydroplane, affording a supporting surface. **6.** *Archit.* a longitudinal section through the axis of a column. —*adj.* **7.** flat or level, as a surface. **8.** of or pertaining to planes or plane figures. —*v.i.* **9.** to glide or soar. **10.** (of a boat) to rise partly out of the water when moving at high speed. **11.** *Informal.* to fly or travel in an airplane: *We'll drive to Detroit and plane to Los Angeles.* [1400–50 for sense "to soar"; 1640–50 for n. and adj. senses; (n.) < L *plānum* flat surface (n. use of *plānus* flat); (adj.) < L *plānus;* first used to distinguish the geometrical senses formerly belonging to PLAIN[1]; in def. 5, shortened form of AIRPLANE, AEROPLANE, or HYDROPLANE; (v.) late ME *planen* (of a bird) to soar (cf. MF *planer*); akin to PLAIN[1]] —**plane′ness,** *n.*
—**Syn. 4.** stratum, stage. **7.** smooth, even, flush.

plane[2] (plān), *n., v.,* **planed, plan•ing.** —*n.* **1.** *Carpentry.* any of various woodworking instruments for paring, truing, or smoothing, or for forming moldings, chamfers, rabbets, grooves, etc., by means of an inclined, adjustable blade moved along and against the piece being worked. **2.** a trowellike tool for smoothing the surface of clay in a brick mold. —*v.t.* **3.** to smooth or dress with or as if with a plane or a planer. **4.** to remove by or as if by means of a plane (usually fol. by *away* or *off*). —*v.i.* **5.** to work with a plane. **6.** to function as a plane. [1275–1325; (n.) ME (< MF) < LL *plāna,* deriv. of *plānāre* to smooth, itself deriv. of L *plānus* PLAIN[1]; (v.) ME *planen* (< MF *planer*) < LL *plānāre*]

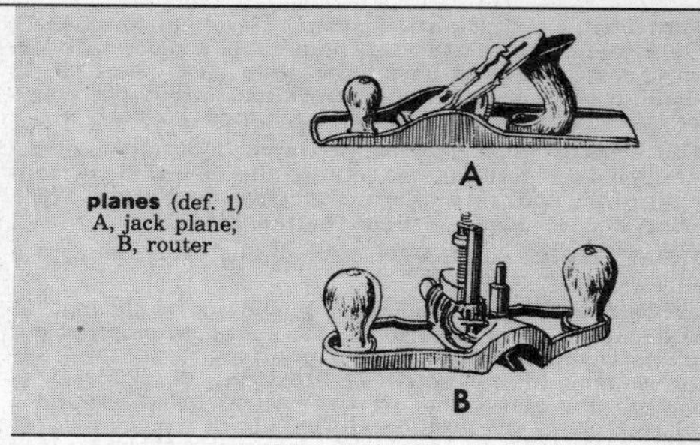

planes (def. 1) A, jack plane; B, router

plane[3] (plān), *n.* See **plane tree.** [1350–1400; ME < MF < L *platanus* < Gk *plátanos,* deriv. of *platýs* broad, FLAT[1] (with reference to the leaves)]

plane′ an′gle, *Math.* an angle between two intersecting lines. [1820–30]

plane′ geom′etry, *Math.* the geometry of figures whose parts all lie in one plane. [1740–50]

plane′ i′ron, *Carpentry.* the blade of a plane. [1575–85]

plane′ of in′cidence, *Optics.* a plane determined by a given ray, incident on a surface, and the normal at the point where the incident ray strikes the surface. [1825–35]

plane′ polariza′tion, *Optics.* polarization of light in which the vibrations are confined to a single plane, that of the wave front. Also called **linear polarization.** —**plane-po•lar•ized** (plān′pō′lə rīzd′), *adj.*

plan•er (plā′nər), *n.* **1.** *Carpentry.* a power machine for removing the rough or excess surface from a board. **2.** *Metalworking.* a machine for cutting flat surfaces, having a cutting tool supported by an overhead frame beneath which the work slides back and forth. Cf. **shaper** (def. 2). **3.** *Typesetting.* a block of smooth, hard wood for leveling the type in a chase by tapping with a mallet. [1375–1425; late ME; see PLANE[2], -ER[1]]

plan′er saw′, *Carpentry.* a hollow-ground circular saw for ripping and cutting across grain, having raker teeth for clearing away the chips cut by the cutting teeth.

pla′ner tree′ (plā′nər), a small tree, *Planera aquatica,* of the elm family, growing in moist ground in the southern U.S., bearing a small, ovoid, nutlike fruit and yielding a compact light-brown wood. Also called **water elm.** [1800–10, *Amer.*; named after I. J. *Planer,* 18th-century German botanist]

plane′ sail′ing, *Navig.* sailing on a course plotted without reference to the curvature of the earth. Cf. **plain sailing, spherical sailing.** [1690–1700]

plan•et (plan′it), *n.* **1.** *Astron.* **a.** Also called **major planet.** any of the nine large heavenly bodies revolving about the sun and shining by reflected light: Mercury, Venus, Earth, Mars, Jupiter, Saturn, Uranus, Neptune, or Pluto in the order of their proximity to the sun. See table on next page. **b.** a similar body revolving about a star other than the sun. **c.** (formerly) a celestial body moving in the sky, as distinguished from a fixed star, applied also to the sun and moon. **2.** *Astrol.* the sun, moon, Mercury, Venus, Mars, Jupiter, Saturn, Uranus, Neptune, or Pluto: considered sources of energy or consciousness in the interpretation of horoscopes. [1250–1300; ME *planete* (< OF *planète*) < LL *planēta, planētēs* (found only in pl. *planētae*) < Gk (*astéres*) *planētai* lit., wandering (stars)]

plane′ ta′ble, *Survey.* a drawing board mounted on a tripod, used in the field, with an alidade, for surveying tracts of land. Also, **plain table.** [1600–10]

plane-ta•ble (plān′tā′bəl), *v.t., v.i.,* **-bled, -bling.** to survey with a plane table. [1870–75]

plan•e•tar•i•um (plan′i târ′ē əm), *n., pl.* **-tar•i•ums, -tar•i•a** (-târ′ē ə). **1.** an apparatus or model representing the planetary system. **2.** a device that produces a representation of the heavens by the use of a number of moving projectors. **3.** the building or room in which such a device is housed. [1765–75; < NL, n. use of neut. of L *planētārius* PLANETARY; cf. -ARIUM]

plan•e•tar•y (plan′i ter′ē), *adj.* **1.** of, pertaining to, or resembling a planet or the planets. **2.** wandering; erratic. **3.** terrestrial; global. **4.** *Mach.* noting or pertaining to an epicyclic gear train in which a sun gear is linked to one or more planet gears also engaging with an encircling ring gear. —*n.* **5.** *Mach.* a planetary gear train. [1585–95; < L *planētārius.* See PLANET, -ARY]

plan′etary neb′ula, *Astron.* an expanding shell of thin ionized gas that is ejected from and surrounds a hot, dying star of about the same mass as the sun; the gas absorbs ultraviolet radiation from the central star and reemits it as visible light by the process of fluorescence. [1850–55; so named for its resemblance to the planets Uranus and Neptune]

plan′etary preces′sion, *Astron.* the small component of the precession of the equinoxes contributed by the motion of the ecliptic, the change in orientation of the plane of the earth's orbit being produced by the gravitational attraction of the planets. [1860–65]

plan•e•tes•i•mal (plan′i tes′ə məl), *Astron.* —*n.* **1.** one of the small celestial bodies that, according to one theory **(planetes′imal hypoth′esis),** were fused together to form the planets of the solar system. —*adj.* **2.** of or pertaining to a planetesimal or planetesimals. [1900–05; PLANET + (INFINIT)ESIMAL]

plan′et gear′, *Mach.* any of the gears in an epicyclic train surrounding and engaging with the sun gear. Also called **plan′et wheel′.** [1915–20]

PLANETS

Name	Mean Distance from Sun*		Period of Revolution around Sun**		Equatorial Diameter	
	Million Miles	Million Km			Miles	Km
Mercury	36.0	57.9	87.96	days	3031	4878
Venus	67.2	108.2	224.68	days	7521	12,104
Earth	93.0	149.6	365.26	days	7926	12,756
Mars	141.6	227.9	686.95	days	4222	6794
Jupiter	483.6	778.3	11.862	years	88,729	142,796
Saturn	886.7	1427.0	29.456	years	74,600	120,000
Uranus	1784.0	2871.0	84.07	years	32,600	52,460
Neptune	2794.4	4497.1	164.81	years	30,200	48,600
Pluto	3674.5	5913.5	248.53	years	2100†	3300†

*Semimajor axis (def. 2)
**Length of year
†Approximate

plan·et·oid (plan′i toid′), *n. Astron.* an asteroid. [1795–1805; PLANET + -OID] —**plan′et·oi′dal,** *adj.*

plan·e·tol·o·gy (plan′i tol′ə jē), *n.* the branch of astronomy that deals with the physical features of the planets. [1905–10; PLANET + -O- + -LOGY] —**plan·e·to·log·i·cal** (plan′i tl oj′i kəl), *adj.* —**plan′e′tol′o·gist,** *n.*

plane′ tree′, any tree of the genus *Platanus,* esp. *P. occidentalis,* the buttonwood or sycamore of North America, having palmately lobed leaves and bark that sheds. [1400–50; late ME]

plane′ trigonom′etry, *Math.* the branch of trigonometry dealing with plane triangles. [1800–10]

plan·et-struck (plan′it struk′), *adj.* **1.** affected adversely by the supposed influence of a planet. **2.** stricken with terror; panic-stricken. Also, **plan·et-strick·en** (plan′it strik′ən). [1605–15]

planet X (eks), *Astron.* a tenth planet beyond the orbit of Pluto whose existence has been hypothesized but not confirmed.

plan·form (plan′fôrm′), *n.* the outline of an object viewed from above. [1905–10; PLAN + FORM]

plan·gent (plan′jənt), *adj.* resounding loudly, esp. with a plaintive sound, as a bell. [1815–25; < L *plangent-* (s. of *plangēns*), prp. of *plangere* to beat, lament. See PLAIN², -ENT] —**plan′gen·cy,** *n.* —**plan′gent·ly,** *adv.*

planh (plä′nyᵊ), *n.* a Provençal elegiac poem. [1835–45; < Pr < L *planctus* a striking, beating, lamentation. See PLAINT]

plani-, var. of **plano-**¹: *planigraph.*

pla·ni·form (plā′nə fôrm′, plan′ə-), *adj.* having a flattened shape, as an anatomical joint. [1820–30; PLANI- + -FORM]

plan·i·fy (plan′ə fī′), *v.t., v.i.,* **-fied, -fy·ing.** *Informal.* to plan in great detail. [1970–75; < F *planifier* to organize (economic activity) according to a plan; see PLAN, -IFY] —**plan′i·fi·ca′tion,** *n.*

pla·ni·graph (plā′ni graf′, -gräf′, plan′i-), *n. Med.* an x-ray photograph in which a given plane of the body is well defined and those above and below it purposely out of focus. Also, **pla·ni·gram** (plā′ni gram′, plan′i-). [1880–85; PLANI- + -GRAPH] —**pla·nig·ra·phy** (plə nig′rə fē), *n.*

pla·nim·e·ter (plə nim′i tər), *n.* an instrument for measuring mechanically the area of plane figures. [1855–60; PLANI- + -METER]

pla·nim·e·try (plə nim′i trē), *n.* the measurement of plane areas. [1350–1400; ME *planemetrie* < ML *planimetria;* see PLANI-, -METRY] —**plan·i·met·ric** (plan′ə me′trik, plā′nə-), **plan′i·met′ri·cal,** *adj.*

plan′ing hull′, *Naut.* a hull that tends to rise from the water when under way so that no significant amount of water is displaced beyond a certain speed. Cf. **displacement hull.**

plan·ish (plan′ish), *v.t.* **1.** to give a smooth finish to (metal) by striking lightly with a smoothly faced hammer or die. **2.** to give a smooth finish to (metal, paper, etc.) by passing through rolls. [1350–1400; ME *planyssyng* (ger.) < OF *planiss-,* long s. of *planir* to smooth, deriv. of *plan* level < L *plānus* PLAIN¹] —**plan′ish·er,** *n.*

plan·i·sphere (plan′ə sfēr′, plā′nə-), *n.* **1.** a map of half or more of the celestial sphere with a device for indicating the part of a given location visible at a given time. **2.** a projection or representation of the whole or a part of a sphere on a plane. [1350–1400; PLANI- + SPHERE; r. ME *planisperie* < ML *plānisphaerium*] —**plan·i·spher·i·cal** (plan′ə sfer′i kəl, -sfēr′-, plā′nə-), **plan′i·spher′ic, plan·i·spher·al** (plan′i sfēr′əl, plā′nə-), *adj.*

plank (plangk), *n.* **1.** a long, flat piece of timber, thicker than a board. **2.** lumber in such pieces; planking. **3.** something to stand on or to cling to for support. **4.** any one of the stated principles or objectives comprising the political platform of a party campaigning for election: *They fought for a plank supporting a nuclear freeze.* **5. walk the plank, a.** to be forced, as by pirates, to walk to one's death by stepping off a plank extending from the ship's side over the water. **b.** to relinquish something, as a position, office, etc., under compulsion: *We suspect that the new vice-president walked the plank because of a personality clash.* —*v.t.* **6.** to lay, cover, or furnish with planks. **7.** to bake or broil and serve (steak, fish, chicken, etc.) on a wooden board. **8.** plunk (def. 2). [1275–1325; ME *planke* < ONF < L *planca* board, plank. See PLANCH] —**plank′less,** *adj.* —**plank′like′,** *adj.*

plank′ floor′, *Shipbuilding.* a floor made from sawed, straight-grained timber.

plank·ing (plang′king), *n.* **1.** planks collectively, as in a floor. **2.** the act of laying or covering with planks. [1485–95; PLANK + -ING¹]

plank·ter (plangk′tər), *n.* any organism that is an element of plankton. [1935–40; < Gk *plankter* roamer. See PLANKTON]

plank·ton (plangk′tən), *n.* the aggregate of passively floating, drifting, or somewhat motile organisms occurring in a body of water, primarily comprising microscopic algae and protozoa. [1890–95; < G, special use of neut. of Gk *planktós* drifting, equiv. to *plang-,* var. s. of *plázesthai* to drift, roam, wander + *-tos* verbid suffix] —**plank·ton·ic** (plangk ton′ik), *adj.*

planned′ econ′omy, an economic system in which the government controls and regulates production, distribution, prices, etc. Cf. **free enterprise.** [1930–35]

planned′ obsoles′cence, a method of stimulating consumer demand by designing products that wear out or become outmoded after limited use. Also called **built-in obsolescence.** [1965–70]

Planned′ Par′enthood, *Trademark.* an organization offering counseling and health-care services for family planning and for venereal disease and other reproductive problems.

plan·ner (plan′ər), *n.* **1.** a person who plans. **2.** a book, similar to a desk calendar, for recording appointments, things to be done, etc. [1710–20; PLAN + -ER¹]

plan·ning (plan′ing), *n.* the act or process of making a plan or plans. [1740–50; PLAN + -ING¹]

pla·no (plā′nō), *adj.* pertaining to eyeglasses that do not contain a curvature for correcting vision defects: *plano sunglasses.* [1945–50; independent use of PLANO-¹]

Pla·no (plā′nō), *n.* a town in N Texas. 72,331.

plano-¹, a combining form meaning "flat," "plane," used in the formation of compound words: *planography.* Also, **plani-;** *esp. before a vowel,* **plan-.** [comb. form repr. L *plānus* level, *plānum* level ground]

plano-², a combining form meaning "moving," "capable of movement," used in the formation of compound words: *planogamete.* [comb. form repr. Gk *plános* wandering, roaming. See PLANET]

plan·o·blast (plan′ə blast′), *n. Zool.* the medusa of a hydroid. [1870–75; PLANO-² + -BLAST] —**plan′o·blas′·tic,** *adj.*

pla·no-con·cave (plā′nō kon′kāv, -kon kāv′), *adj. Optics.* pertaining to or noting a lens that is plane on one side and concave on the other. See diag. under **lens.** [1685–95; PLANO-¹ + CONCAVE]

pla·no-con·vex (plā′nō kon′veks, -kon veks′, -kən-), *adj. Optics.* pertaining to or noting a lens that is plane on one side and convex on the other. See diag. under **lens.** [1655–65; PLANO-¹ + CONVEX]

plan·o·gam·ete (plan′ō gam′ēt, plan′ə gə mēt′), *n. Biol.* a motile gamete. [1885–90; PLANO-² + GAMETE]

pla·no·graph (plā′nə graf′, -gräf′, plan′ə-), *Print.* —*v.t.* **1.** (formerly) to print from a flat surface. —*n.* **2.** (formerly) an impression so produced. [PLANO-¹ + -GRAPH]

pla·nog·ra·phy (plə nog′rə fē), *n. Print.* the art or technique of printing from a flat surface directly or by offset. Also called **surface-printing.** [1840–50; PLANO-¹ + -GRAPHY] —**pla·no·graph·ic** (plā′nə graf′ik, plan′ə-), *adj.* —**pla′no·graph′i·cal·ly,** *adv.*

pla·nom·e·ter (plə nom′i tər), *n. Mach.* See **surface plate.** [1860–65, *Amer.;* PLANO-¹ + -METER] —**pla·nom′e·try,** *n.*

plan·o·spore (plan′ə spôr′, -spōr′), *n. Biol.* a zoospore. [1945–50; PLANO-² + SPORE]

plan′ posi′tion in′dicator, a radarscope on which an object reflecting radar waves shows its bearing and distance from the radar detector by causing a spot of light to appear on a screen that represents a map of the area around the detector. *Abbr.:* PPI [1940–45]

plan·sheer (plan′shēr), *n.* plancer.

plant (plant, plänt), *n.* **1.** any member of the kingdom Plantae, comprising multicellular organisms that typically produce their own food from inorganic matter by the process of photosynthesis and that have more or less rigid cell walls containing cellulose, including vascular plants, mosses, liverworts, and hornworts: some classification schemes may include fungi, algae, bacteria, blue-green algae, and certain single-celled eukaryotes that have plantlike qualities, as rigid cell walls or photosynthesis. **2.** an herb or other small vegetable growth, in contrast with a tree or a shrub. **3.** a seedling or a growing slip, esp. one ready for transplanting. **4.** the equipment, including the fixtures, machinery, tools, etc., and often the buildings, necessary to carry on any industrial business: *a manufacturing plant.* **5.** the complete equipment or apparatus for a particular mechanical process or operation: *the heating plant for a home.* **6.** the buildings, equipment, etc., of an institution: *the sprawling plant of the university.* **7.** *Slang.* something intended to trap, decoy, or lure, as criminals. **8.** *Slang.* a scheme to trap, trick, swindle, or defraud. **9.** a person, placed in an audience, whose rehearsed or prepared reactions, comments, etc., appear spontaneous to the rest of the audience. **10.** a person placed secretly in a group or organization, as by a foreign government, to obtain internal or secret information, stir up discontent, etc. **11.** *Theat.* a line of dialogue, or a character, action, etc., introducing an idea or theme that will be further developed at a later point in the play: *Afterward we remembered the suicide plant in the second act.*
—*v.t.* **12.** to put or set in the ground for growth, as seeds, young trees, etc. **13.** to furnish or stock (land) with plants: *to plant a section with corn.* **14.** to establish or implant (ideas, principles, doctrines, etc.): *to plant a love for learning in growing children.* **15.** to introduce (a breed of animals) into a country. **16.** to deposit (young fish, or spawn) in a river, lake, etc. **17.** to bed (oysters). **18.** to insert or set firmly in or on the ground or some other body or surface: *to plant posts along a road.* **19.** *Theat.* to insert or place (an idea, person, or thing) in a play. **20.** to place; put. **21.** to place with great force, firmness, or determination: *He planted himself in the doorway as if daring us to try to enter. He planted a big kiss on his son's cheek.* **22.** to station; post: *to plant a police officer on every corner.* **23.** to locate; situate: *Branch stores are planted all over.* **24.** to establish (a colony, city, etc.); found. **25.** to settle (persons), as in a colony. **26.** to say or place (something) in order to obtain a desired result, esp. one that will seem spontaneous: *The police planted the story in the newspaper in order to trap the thief.* **27.** *Carpentry.* to nail, glue, or otherwise attach (a molding or the like) to a surface. **28.** to place (a person) secretly in a group to function as a spy or to promote discord. **29.** *Slang.* to hide or conceal, as stolen goods. [bef. 900; (n.) ME *plaunte;* in part continuing OE *plante* sapling, young plant (< L *planta*); in part (< OF *plante*) < L *planta* a shoot, sprig, scion (for planting), plant; (v.) ME *plaunten;* in part continuing OE *plantian* (< L *plantāre*); in part (< OF *planter*) < L *plantāre* to plant] —**plant′a·ble,** *adj.* —**plant′less,** *adj.* —**plant′like′,** *adj.*

Plan·tae (plan′tē), *n.* (*used with a plural v.*) *Biol.* the taxonomic kingdom comprising all plants. [< NL, L: pl. of *planta* PLANT]

Plan·tag·e·net (plan taj′ə nit), *n.* a member of the royal house that ruled England from the accession of Henry II in 1154 to the death of Richard III in 1485.

plan′ta genis′ta (plan′tə), *Heraldry.* a representation of a sprig of broom: used as a badge of the Plantagenets. [< NL: broom plant; see PLANT, GENISTA]

plan·tain¹ (plan′tin, -tn), *n.* **1.** a tropical plant, *Musa paradisiaca,* of the banana family, resembling the banana. **2.** its fruit, eaten cooked as a staple food in tropical regions. [1545–55; earlier *pla(n)tan* < Sp *plá(n)tano* plantain, also plane tree < ML *pla(n)tanus,* L *platanus* PLANE³]

plan·tain² (plan′tin, -tn), *n.* any plant of the genus *Plantago,* esp. *P. major,* a weed with large, spreading leaves close to the ground and long, slender spikes of small flowers. [1350–1400; ME *plauntein* < OF *plantein* < L *plantāgin-* (s. of *plantāgō*), deriv. of *planta* sole of the foot, lit., something flat and spread out, like the broad leaf of the plantain; akin to Gk *platýs* FLAT¹; see PLATY-]

plan·tain-eat·er (plan′tin ē′tər, -tn-), *n.* any of various touracos, erroneously believed to feed chiefly on plantains and bananas. [1795–1805]

plan′tain lil′y, any Japanese or Chinese plant of the genus *Hosta,* of the lily family, having large leaves and spikes or one-sided clusters of white, lilac, or blue flowers. [1880–85]

plan·tar (plan′tər), *adj. Anat., Zool.* of or pertaining to the sole of the foot. [1700–10; < L *plantāris,* equiv. to *plant(a)* sole of the foot + *-āris* -AR¹]

plan′tar re′flex, a normal reflex flexion of the toes, esp. in persons above one year of age, resulting from stroking the sole of the foot. Cf. **Babinski's reflex.**

plan·ta·tion (plan tā′shən), *n.* **1.** a usually large farm or estate, esp. in a tropical or semitropical country, on which cotton, tobacco, coffee, sugar cane, or the like is cultivated, usually by resident laborers. **2.** a group of planted trees or plants. **3.** *Hist.* **a.** a colony or new settlement. **b.** the establishment of a colony or new settlement. **4.** *Archaic.* the planting of seeds, young trees, etc. —*adj.* **5.** (of clothing, furnishings, etc.) suitable for a plantation or for a tropical or semitropical country. [1400–50; late ME *plantacioune* < L *plantātiōn-* (s. of *plantātiō*) a planting. See PLANT (v.), -ATION] —**plan·ta′tion·like′,** *adj.*

Plan·ta·tion (plan tā′shən), *n.* a town in S Florida. 48,501.

Planta′tion walk′ing horse′. See **Tennessee walking horse.**

plant′ bug′, any of numerous, often brightly colored hemipterous insects of the family Miridae that feed on the juices of plants. Also called **capsid, leaf bug.** [1855–60, *Amer.*]

Plant′ Cit′y, a city in W Florida. 19,270.

plant-cut·ter (plant′kut′ər, plänt′-), *n.* any of several South American, passerine birds of the family Phytotomidae, superficially resembling grosbeaks but

CONCISE PRONUNCIATION KEY: act, cāpe, dâre, pärt; set, ēqual; if, ice; ox, ōver, ôrder, oil, bŏŏk, bōōt, out; up, ûrge; child; sing; shoe; thin, *th*at; zh as in *treasure.* ə = *a* as in *alone, e* as in *system, i* as in *easily, o* as in *gallop, u* as in *circus;* ᵊ as in *fire* (fīᵊr), *hour* (ouᵊr). l and n can serve as syllabic consonants, as in *cradle* (krād′l), and *button* (but′n). See the full key inside the front cover.

having serrated edges on the bill that aid in cutting leaves and other plant food. [1795–1805]

Plante (plänt; *Fr.* pläɴt), *n.* **Jacques** (zhäk), 1929–86, Canadian ice-hockey player.

plant•er (plan′tər, plän′-), *n.* **1.** a person who plants. **2.** an implement or machine for planting seeds in the ground. **3.** the owner or manager of a plantation. **4.** *Hist.* a colonist or new settler. **5.** a decorative container, of a variety of sizes and shapes, for growing flowers or ornamental plants. [1350–1400; ME *plaunter.* See PLANT, -ER¹]

plant′er's punch′, a punch made with rum, lime juice, sugar, and water or soda. [1840–50]

plant′ food′, nourishment, as fertilizer or chemicals, for plants. [1865–70]

plant•hop•per (plant′hop′ər, plänt′-), *n.* any member of a large and varied group of homopterous insects that are related to the leafhoppers and the spittlebugs but rarely damage cultivated plants. [PLANT + HOPPER]

plan•ti•grade (plan′ti gräd′), *adj.* **1.** walking on the whole sole of the foot, as humans, and bears. —*n.* **2.** a plantigrade animal. [1825–35; < NL *plantigradus,* equiv. to L *plant(a)* sole + *-i-* -I- + *-gradus* -GRADE]

Plan•tin (pläɴ taɴ′), *n.* **Chris•tophe** (krē stôf′), c1520–1589, French typographer.

plant′ king′dom, the plants of the world collectively. Also called **vegetable kingdom.** Cf. **animal kingdom, mineral kingdom.** [1880–85]

plant•let (plant′lit, plänt′-), *n.* a little plant, as one produced on the leaf margins of a kalanchoe or the aerial stems of a spider plant. [1810–20; PLANT + -LET]

plant′ louse′, **1.** aphid. **2.** any of various related insects having similar habits. [1795–1805]

plant′ pathol′ogy, the branch of botany dealing with diseases of plants. Also, **phytopathology.** [1890–95]

plants•man (plants′mən, plänts′-), *n., pl.* **-men.** **1.** a nurseryman. **2.** a horticulturist. **3.** a person with a keen interest in and wide knowledge of plants and their cultivation. [1880–85; PLANT + -S³ + -MAN, on the model of GAMESMAN, MARKSMAN, etc.]
—Usage. See **-man.**

plants•wom•an (plants′wo͝om′ən, plänts′-), *n., pl.* **-wom•en.** **1.** a nurserywoman. **2.** a horticulturist. **3.** a woman with a keen interest in and wide knowledge of plants and their cultivation. [PLANT + -S³ + -WOMAN]
—Usage. See **-woman.**

plan•u•la (plan′yə lə), *n., pl.* **-lae** (-lē′). *Zool.* the ciliate, free-swimming larva of a coelenterate. [1865–70; < NL, dim. of L *plānum* something flat. See PLANE¹, -ULE] **—plan′u•lar, plan•u•late** (plan′yə lāt′), *adj.*

plan′ view′, plan (def. 4). [1840–50]

plaque (plak), *n.* **1.** a thin, flat plate or tablet of metal, porcelain, etc., intended for ornament, as on a wall, or set in a piece of furniture. **2.** an inscribed commemorative tablet, usually of metal placed on a building, monument, or the like. **3.** a platelike brooch or ornament, esp. one worn as the badge of an honorary order. **4.** *Anat., Pathol.* a flat, often raised, patch on the skin or other organ, as on the inner lining of arterial walls in atherosclerosis. **5.** *Dentistry.* a soft, sticky, whitish matlike film attached to tooth surfaces, formed largely by the growth of bacteria that colonize the teeth. **6.** *Bacteriol.* a cleared region in a bacterial culture, resulting from lysis of bacteria by bacteriophages. [1848–50; < F, n. deriv. of *plaquer* to plate < MD *placken* to patch; cf. PLACKET]

plash¹ (plash), *n.* **1.** a gentle splash. **2.** a pool or puddle. —*v.t., v.i.* **3.** to splash gently. [bef. 1000; ME *plasch* pool, puddle, OE *plæsc;* c. D, LG *plas,* prob. of imit. orig.] **—plash′ing•ly,** *adv.*

plash² (plash), *v.t.* pleach. [1375–1425; late ME < MF *plaissier,* deriv. of *plais* hedge < VL **plaxum* < ?] **—plash′er,** *n.*

plash•y (plash′ē), *adj.,* **plash•i•er, plash•i•est.** **1.** marshy; wet. **2.** splashing. [1545–55; PLASH¹ + -Y¹]

-plasia, a combining form with the meaning "growth, cellular multiplication," of the kind specified by the initial element: *hypoplasia.* Also, **-plasy.** [< NL < Gk *plá-s(is)* a molding + *-ia* -IA]

plasm-, var. of **plasmo-** before a vowel: *plasmapheresis.*

-plasm, a combining form with the meanings "living substance," "tissue," "substance of a cell," used in the formation of compound words: *endoplasm; neoplasm; cytoplasm.* [comb. form repr. Gk *plásma.* See PLASMA]

plas•ma (plaz′mə), *n.* **1.** *Anat., Physiol.* the liquid part of blood or lymph, as distinguished from the suspended elements. **2.** *Cell Biol.* cytoplasm. **3.** whey. **4.** a green, faintly translucent chalcedony. **5.** *Physics.* a highly ionized gas containing an approximately equal number of positive ions and electrons. Also, **plasm** (plaz′əm) for defs. 1–3. [1705–15; < LL < Gk *plásma* something molded or formed, akin to *plássein* to form, mold. See PLASTIC] **—plas•mat•ic** (plaz mat′ik), **plas′mic,** *adj.*

plas′ma cell′, *Anat.* an antibody-secreting cell, derived from B cells, that plays a major role in antibody-mediated immunity. Also called **plas•ma•cyte** (plaz′mə-sīt′). [1885–90]

plas•ma•gel (plaz′mə jel′), *n.* the gelatinous outer layer of cytoplasm of the pseudopod of an ameba, beneath the cell membrane. [1920–25; PLASMA + GEL]

plas•ma•lem•ma (plaz′mə lem′ə), *n., pl.* **-mas.** *Cell Biol.* See **cell membrane.** [1920–25; PLASMA + Gk *lémma* husk (see LEMMA²)]

CONCISE ETYMOLOGY KEY: <, descended or borrowed from; >, whence; b., blend of, blended; c., cognate with; cf., compare; deriv., derivative; equiv., equivalent; imit., imitative; obl., oblique; r., replacing; s., stem; sp., spelling, spelled; resp., respelling, respelled; trans., translation; ?, origin unknown; *, unattested; ‡, probably earlier than. See the full key inside the front cover.

plas•mal•o•gen (plaz mal′ə jin, -jen′), *n. Biochem.* any of the class of phosphatides that contain an aldehyde of a fatty acid, found in heart and skeletal muscle, the brain, the liver, and in eggs. [1920–25; PLASM- + AL(KALAI) + -O- + -GEN]

plas′ma mem′brane, *Cell Biol.* See **cell membrane.** [1895–1900]

plas•ma•pause (plaz′mə pôz′), *n. Astron.* the boundary of the plasmasphere, where the particle density decreases very rapidly. [1965–70; PLASMA + PAUSE]

plas•ma•pher•e•sis (plaz′mə fə rē′sis), *n. Med.* a type of apheresis in which blood cells are returned to the bloodstream of the donor and the plasma is used, as for tranfusion. [1915–20; PLASM- + APHERESIS]

plas′ma phys′ics, the branch of physics that deals with plasmas and their interactions with electric and magnetic fields.

plas•ma•sol (plaz′mə sôl′, -sol′), *n.* the relatively fluid, inner cytoplasm of a pseudopod of an ameba. [1920–25; PLASMA + SOL⁴]

plas•ma•sphere (plaz′mə sfēr′), *n. Astron.* a region of cool plasma surrounding the earth, extending 8000–25,000 mi. (13,000–40,000 km) into space, and bounded by the plasmapause. [1965–70; PLASMA + -SPHERE]

plas′ma thromboplas′tic compo′nent, *Biochem.* See **Christmas factor.**

plas•mid (plaz′mid), *n. Microbiol.* a segment of DNA independent of the chromosomes and capable of replication, occurring in bacteria and yeast: used in recombinant DNA procedures to transfer genetic material from one cell to another. [1950–55; PLASM- + -ID³]

plas•min (plaz′min), *n. Biochem.* fibrinolysin (def. 1). [1865–70; PLASM- + -IN²]

plas•min•o•gen (plaz min′ə jən, -jen′), *n. Biochem.* the blood substance that when activated forms plasmin. [1940–45; PLASMIN + -O- + -GEN]

plasmo-, a combining form representing **plasma** or **cytoplasm** in compound words: *plasmolysis.* Also, *esp. before a vowel,* **plasm-.** [comb. form, repr. Gk *plásma.* See PLASMA, -O-]

plas•mo•des•ma (plaz′mə des′mə), *n., pl.* **-ma•ta** (-mə tə). *Bot.* any of many minute strands of cytoplasm that extend through plant cell walls and connect adjoining cells. [< G (1901) < Gk *plasmo-* PLASMO- + *désma* bond, fetter]

plas•mo•di•o•carp (plaz mō′dē ə kärp′), *n. Mycol.* a fruiting body of certain myxomycetes. [1875–80; PLASMODI(UM) + -O- + -CARP]

plas•mo•di•um (plaz mō′dē əm), *n., pl.* **-di•a** (-dē ə). **1.** *Biol.* an ameboid, multinucleate mass or sheet of cytoplasm characteristic of some stages of organisms, as of myxomycetes or slime molds. **2.** any parasitic protozoan of the genus *Plasmodium,* causing malaria in humans. [1870–75; < NL; see PLASM-, -ODE¹, -IUM] **—plas•mo′di•al,** *adj.*

plas•mog•a•my (plaz mog′ə mē), *n. Biol.* the fusion of the protoplasts of cells. Cf. **karyogamy.** [1910–15; PLASMO- + -GAMY]

plas•mol•y•sis (plaz mol′ə sis), *n. Bot.* contraction of the protoplasm in a living cell when water is removed by exosmosis. [1880–85; PLASMO- + -LYSIS] **—plas•mo•lyt•ic** (plaz′mə lit′ik), *adj.* **—plas′mo•lyt′i•cal•ly,** *adv.*

plas•mo•some (plaz′mə sōm′), *n. Cell Biol.* a true nucleolus, as distinguished from a karyosome. [1885–90; PLASMO- + -SOME³]

Plas•sey (plä′sē, plas′ē), *n.* a village in NE India, about 80 miles (128 km) north of Calcutta: Clive's victory over a Bengal army here (1757) led to the establishment of British power in India.

-plast, a combining form meaning "living substance," "organelle," "cell," used in the formation of compound words: *chloroplast; chromoplast; protoplast.* [comb. form repr. Gk *plastós* formed, molded, equiv. to *plath-,* base of *plássein* to form, mold + *-tos* verbal adj. suffix, with *tht* > *st.* See PLASTIC]

plas•ter (plas′tər, plä′stər), *n.* **1.** a composition, as of lime or gypsum, sand, water, and sometimes hair or other fiber, applied in a pasty form to walls, ceilings, etc., and allowed to harden and dry. **2.** powdered gypsum. **3.** See **plaster of Paris.** **4.** a solid or semisolid preparation spread upon cloth, plastic, or other material and applied to the body, esp. for some healing purpose. —*v.t.* **5.** to cover (walls, ceilings, etc.) with plaster. **6.** to treat with gypsum or plaster of Paris. **7.** to lay flat like a layer of plaster. **8.** to daub or fill with plaster or something similar. **9.** to apply a plaster to (the body, a wound, etc.). **10.** to overspread with something, esp. thickly or excessively: *a wall plastered with posters.* **11.** *Informal.* **a.** to defeat decisively; trounce; drub. **b.** to knock down or injure, as by a blow or beating. **c.** to inflict serious damage or injury on by heavy bombing, shelling, or other means of attack. [bef. 1000; ME, OE < ML *plastrum* plaster (both medical and building senses), aph. var. of L *emplastrum* < Gk *émplastron* salve, alter. of *émplaston,* neut. of *émplastos* daubed; see EM-², -PLAST] **—plas′ter•er,** *n.* **—plas′ter•i•ness,** *n.* **—plas′ter•like′, plas′ter•y,** *adj.*

plas•ter•board (plas′tər bôrd′, -bōrd′, plä′stər-), *n.* a material used for insulating or covering walls, or as a lath, consisting of paper-covered sheets of gypsum and felt. [1905–10; PLASTER + BOARD]

plas′ter cast′, any piece of sculpture reproduced in plaster of Paris. [1815–25]

plas•tered (plas′tərd, plä′stərd), *adj. Slang.* drunk. [1910–15; PLASTER + -ED²]

plas•ter•ing (plas′tər ing, plä′stər-), *n.* **1.** the process of working with plaster. **2.** a coating of plaster. **3.** a decisive defeat; drubbing. [1375–1425; late ME (ger.). See PLASTER, -ING¹]

plas′ter of Par′is, calcined gypsum in white, powdery form, used as a base for gypsum plasters, as an additive of lime plasters, and as a material for making fine and ornamental casts: characterized by its ability to set rapidly when mixed with water. Also, **plas′ter of par′is.** [1375–1425; late ME; so called because prepared from the gypsum of *Paris,* France]

plas•ter•work (plas′tər wûrk′, plä′stər-), *n. Building Trades.* finish or ornamental work done in plaster. [1590–1600; PLASTER + WORK]

plas•tic (plas′tik), *n.* **1.** Often, **plastics.** any of a group of synthetic or natural organic materials that may be shaped when soft and then hardened, including many types of resins, resinoids, polymers, cellulose derivatives, casein materials, and proteins: used in place of other materials, as glass, wood, and metals, in construction and decoration, for making many articles, as coatings, and, drawn into filaments, for weaving. They are often known by trademark names, as *Bakelite, Vinylite,* or *Lucite.* **2.** a credit card, or credit cards collectively, usually made of plastic: *He had a whole pocketful of plastic.* **3.** money, payment, or credit represented by the use of a credit card or cards. **4.** something, or a group of things, made of or resembling plastic: *The entire meal was served on plastic.* —*adj.* **5.** made of plastic. **6.** capable of being molded or of receiving form: *clay and other plastic substances.* **7.** produced by molding: *plastic figures.* **8.** having the power of molding or shaping formless or yielding material: *the plastic forces of nature.* **9.** being able to create, esp. within an art form; having the power to give form or formal expression: *the plastic imagination of great poets and composers.* **10.** *Fine Arts.* **a.** concerned with or pertaining to molding or modeling; sculptural. **b.** relating to three-dimensional form or space, esp. on a two-dimensional surface. **c.** pertaining to the tools or techniques of drawing, painting, or sculpture: *the plastic means.* **d.** characterized by an emphasis on formal structure: *plastic requirements of a picture.* **11.** pliable; impressionable: *the plastic mind of youth.* **12.** giving the impression of being made or of furnished with plastic: *We stayed at one of those plastic motels.* **13.** artificial or insincere; synthetic; phony: *jeans made of cotton, not some plastic substitute; a plastic smile.* **14.** lacking in depth, individuality, or permanence; superficial, dehumanized, or mass-produced: *a plastic society interested only in material acquisition.* **15.** of or pertaining to the use of credit cards: *plastic credit; plastic money.* **16.** *Biol., Pathol.* formative. **17.** *Surg.* concerned with or pertaining to the remedying or restoring of malformed, injured, or lost parts: *a plastic operation.* [1625–35; 1900–10 for def. 1; < L *plasticus* that may be molded < Gk *plastikós.* See -PLAST, -IC] **—plas′ti•cal•ly, plas′tic•ly,** *adv.*
—Syn. 11. pliant, flexible, amenable.

-plastic, a combining form occurring in *chloroplastic; protoplastic.* [see PLASTIC]

plas′tic art′, **1.** an art, as sculpture, in which forms are carved or modeled. **2.** an art, as painting or sculpture, in which forms are rendered in or as if in three dimensions. [1630–40]

plas′tic bomb′, a bomb made of plastic explosive. [1950–55]

plas′tic explo′sive, a puttylike substance that contains an explosive charge, and is detonated by fuse or by remote control: used esp. by terrorists and in guerrilla warfare. Also called **plastique.** [1905–10]

plas′tic flow′, deformation of a material that remains rigid under stresses of less than a certain intensity but that behaves under severer stresses approximately as a Newtonian fluid. Also called **plas′tic deforma′tion.** [1875–80]

plas′tic foam′. See **expanded plastic.** [1940–45]

Plas•ti•cine (plas′tə sēn′), *Trademark.* a brand name for a synthetic material used as a substitute for clay or wax in modeling.

plas•tic•i•ty (pla stis′i tē), *n.* **1.** the quality or state of being plastic. **2.** the capability of being molded, receiving shape, or being made to assume a desired form: *the plasticity of social institutions; the great plasticity of clay.* [1775–85; PLASTIC + -ITY]

plas•ti•cize (plas′tə sīz′), *v.t., v.i.,* **-cized, -ciz•ing.** to render or become plastic. Also, *esp. Brit.,* **plas′ti•cise′.** [1925–30; PLASTIC + -IZE] **—plas′ti•ci•za′tion,** *n.*

plas•ti•ciz•er (plas′tə sī′zər), *n.* **1.** any of a group of substances that are used in plastics or other materials to impart viscosity, flexibility, softness, or other properties to the finished product. **2.** an admixture for making mortar or concrete workable with little water. [1920–25; PLASTICIZE + -ER¹]

plas•tics (plas′tiks), *adj.* of or pertaining to a plastic or plastics: *a plastics firm; plastics research.* [1920–25; see PLASTIC, -ICS]

plas′tic sur′gery, the branch of surgery dealing with the repair or replacement of malformed, injured, or lost organs or tissues of the body, chiefly by the transplant of living tissues. [1830–40] **—plas′tic sur′geon.**

plas•tic•ware (plas′tik wâr′), *n.* knives, forks, spoons, cups, etc., made of plastic: *a picnic hamper with plasticware for six.* [PLASTIC + WARE¹]

Plas′tic Wood′, *Trademark.* a brand name for a compound used for patching and filling woodwork.

plas′tic wrap′, a very thin, transparent sheet of plastic, usually packaged in rolls and often having the ability to cling to other substances, used esp. to wrap and store food and for microwave cooking.

plas•tid (plas′tid), *n. Cell Biol.* a small, double-membraned organelle of plant cells and certain protists, occurring in several varieties, as the chloroplast, and containing ribosomes, prokaryotic DNA, and, often, pigment. [1875–80; < G *Plastide* < Gk *plastid-,* s. of *plástis,* fem. deriv. of *plástēs* modeler, creator, deriv. of *plássein* to form]

plas•tique (pla stēk′; *Fr.* plA stēk′), *n.* **1.** a ballet technique for mastering the art of slow, controlled movement and statuelike posing. **2.** See **plastic explosive.** [1795–1805; < F: PLASTIC]

plas•ti•queur (plA stē kœr′), *n., pl.* ***-queurs*** (-kœr′).

French. a person, esp. a terrorist, who makes, places, or detonates plastic bombs.

plas·ti·sol (plas′tə sôl′, -sol′), *n. Chem.* a dispersion of resin in a plasticizer, forming a liquid or paste that gels when heated. [1945–50; PLAST(IC)- + -I- + SOL[4]]

plas·tom·e·ter (pla stom′i tər), *n.* an instrument for measuring the plasticity of a substance. [1915–20; PLAST(IC) + -O- + -METER] —**plas·to·met·ric** (plas′tə me′trik), *adj.* —**plas·tom′e·try,** *n.*

plas·to·qui·none (plas′tō kwə nōn′, -kwin′ōn), *n. Biochem.* a quinone that occurs in the chloroplasts of plants and functions as an electron carrier during photosynthesis. [1955–60; (CHLORO)PLAST or PLAST(ID) + -O- + QUINONE]

plas·to·type (plas′tə tīp′), *n.* a casting of a type specimen, esp. of a fossil. [< Gk *plast(ós)* molded (see -PLAST) + -O- + -TYPE]

plas·tral (plas′trəl), *adj. Zool.* of or pertaining to a plastron. [1885–90; PLASTR(ON) + -AL[1]]

plas·tron (plas′trən), *n.* **1.** a piece of plate armor for the upper part of the torso in front. **2.** *Fencing.* a quilted pad worn over part of the torso, for protection. **3.** an ornamental front piece of a woman's bodice. **4.** the starched front of a shirt. **5.** *Zool.* the ventral part of the shell of a turtle. [1500–10; < MF < It *piastrone,* aug. of *piastra* metal plate, PIASTER. See PLASTER]

-plasty, a combining form with the meanings "molding, formation" "surgical repair, plastic surgery," used in the formation of compound words: *angioplasty; galvanoplasty; heteroplasty.* [< Gk *-plastia.* See -PLAST, -Y[3]]

-plasy, var. of **-plasia.**

plat[1] (plat), *n., v.,* **plat·ted, plat·ting.** —*n.* **1.** a plot of ground. **2.** a plan or map, as of land. —*v.t.* **3.** to make a plat of; plot. [1400–50; late ME; var. of PLOT, reinforced by ME *plat* flat of a sword < OF: something flat (see PLATE[1])]

plat[2] (plat), *n., v.,* **plat·ted, plat·ting.** —*n.* **1.** a plait or braid. —*v.t.* **2.** to plait; braid. [1350–1400; ME; var. of PLAIT]

plat-, var. of **platy-.**

plat., **1.** plateau. **2.** platoon.

Pla·ta (plä′tä), *n.* **Ri·o de la** (rē′ô thə lä), an estuary on the SE coast of South America between Argentina and Uruguay, formed by the Uruguay and Paraná rivers, ab. 185 mi. (290 km) long. Also, **La Plata.** Also called **Pla′ta Riv′er;** *Brit.* **River Plate.**

Pla·tae·a (plə tē′ə), *n.* an ancient city in Greece, in Boeotia: Greeks defeated Persians here 479 B.C.

plat·band (plat′band′), *n. Archit.* **1.** a flat structural member, as a lintel or flat arch. **2.** any shallow molding having a flat face. [1690–1700; < MF *platebande,* equiv. to *plate* flat (see PLATE[1]) + *bande* BAND[2]]

plat du jour (plä′ də zhŏŏr′; *Fr.* plA dʏ zhōōr′), *pl.* **plats du jour** (pläz′ də zhŏŏr′; *Fr.* plA dʏ zhōōr′). the special or featured dish of the day on a restaurant menu. [1905–10; < F: dish of the day]

plate[1] (plāt), *n., v.,* **plat·ed, plat·ing.** —*n.* **1.** a shallow, usually circular dish, often of earthenware or porcelain, from which food is eaten. **2.** the contents of such a dish; plateful. **3.** an entire course of a meal served on such a dish: *I had the vegetable plate for lunch.* **4.** the food and service for one person, as at a banquet, fund-raising dinner, or the like: *The wedding breakfast cost $20 a plate.* **5.** household dishes, utensils, etc., of metal plated with gold or silver. **6.** household dishes, utensils, etc., made of gold or silver. **7.** a dish, as of metal or wood, used for collecting offerings, as in a church. **8.** a thin, flat sheet or piece of metal or other material, esp. of uniform thickness. **9.** metal in such sheets. **10.** a flat, polished piece of metal on which something may be or is engraved. **11.** See **license plate. 12.** a flat or curved sheet of metal, plastic, glass, or similar hard material, on which a picture or text has been engraved, etched, molded, photographically developed, or drawn, that is inked, as in a press, for printing impressions on other surfaces. **13.** a printed impression from such a piece or from some similar piece, as a woodcut. **14.** a full-page illustration in a book, esp. an insert on paper different from the text pages. **15.** a piece of armor made from a thin, flat piece or several such pieces of tough material, esp. wrought iron or steel. **16.** armor composed of thin, flat pieces; plate armor. **17.** *Dentistry.* **a.** the part of a denture that conforms to the mouth and contains the teeth. **b.** the entire denture. **18.** *Baseball.* **a. the plate.** See **home plate. b.** rubber[1] (def. 14). **19.** See **plate glass. 20.** *Photog.* a sheet of glass, metal, etc., coated with a sensitized emulsion, used for taking a photograph. **21.** *Anat., Zool.* a platelike part, structure, or organ. **22.** a thin piece or cut of beef from the lower end of the ribs. See diag. under **beef. 23.** *Geol.* See **crustal plate. 24.** *Electronics.* one of the interior elements of a vacuum tube, toward which electrons are attracted by virtue of its positive charge; anode. *Abbr.:* P **25.** *Carpentry.* any of various horizontal timbers or boards laid flat across the heads of studding, upon floors, etc., to support joists, rafters, or studs at or near their ends. **26.** a gold or silver cup or the like awarded as the prize in a horse race or some other contest. **27.** a horse race or some other contest for such a prize. **28.** *Heraldry.* a rounded argent. **29. have on one's plate,** *Informal.* to have as an immediate task, obligation, or prospect: *I had too much on my plate already to take on another task.* —*v.t.* **30.** to coat (metal) with a thin film of gold, silver, nickel, etc., by mechanical or chemical means. **31.** to cover or overlay with metal plates for protection. **32.** *Metalworking.* **a.** to forge (a bloom or the like) into a broad piece. **b.** to hammer (cutlery) gently to produce an even surface. **33.** *Print.* to make a stereotype or electrotype plate from (type). **34.** *Papermaking.* to give a high gloss to (paper), as on supercalendered paper. [1250–1300; ME < OF: lit., something flat, n. use of fem. of *plat* FLAT[1] < VL **plattus,* akin to Gk *platýs* broad, flat] —**plate′less,** *adj.* —**plate′like′,** *adj.*

plate[2] (plāt), *n. Obs.* a coin, esp. of silver. [1200–50; ME < OF; special use of *plate* PLATE[1]]

plate′ ar′mor, **1.** armor made of thin, flat, shaped pieces of wrought iron or steel. **2.** any armor composed of, or having as an exterior surface, tough, stiff, flat pieces, large or small, of various materials, as iron, steel, or horn. [1795–1805]

pla·teau (pla tō′ *or, esp. Brit.,* plat′ō), *n., pl.* **-teaus, -teaux** (-tōz′, -tōz), *v.,* **-teaued, -teau·ing·** —*n.* **1.** a land area having a relatively level surface considerably raised above adjoining land on at least one side, and often cut by deep canyons. **2.** a period or state of little or no growth or decline: *to reach a plateau in one's career.* **3.** *Psychol.* a period of little or no apparent progress in an individual's learning, marked by an inability to increase speed, reduce number of errors, etc., and indicated by a horizontal stretch in a learning curve or graph. **4.** a flat stand, as for a centerpiece, sometimes extending the full length of a table. —*v.i.* **5.** to reach a state or level of little or no growth or decline, esp. to stop increasing or progressing; remain at a stable level of achievement; level off: *After a period of uninterrupted growth, sales began to plateau.* —*v.t.* **6.** to cause to remain at a stable level, esp. to prevent from rising or progressing: *Rising inflation plateaued sales income.* [1785–95; < F; OF *platel* flat object, dim. of *plat* PLATE[1]]

Pla·teau's′ prob′lem (pla tōz′), *Math.* the problem in the calculus of variations of finding the surface with the least area bounded by a given closed curve in space. [1910–15; named after J. A. F. *Plateau* (1801–83), Belgian physicist]

plate′ block′, *Philately.* a block of four or more stamps containing the number or numbers of the printing plate or plates in the margin of the sheet.

plat·ed (plā′tid), *adj.* **1.** coated with a thin film of gold, silver, etc., as for ornamental purposes. **2.** covered or overlaid with metal plates for protection. **3.** (of a knitted fabric) made of two yarns, as wool on the face and cotton on the back. [1475–85; PLATE[1] + -ED[3]]

plate-dog (plāt′dôg′, -dog′), *n. Print.* a heavy metal plate on which plates, stereos, etc., are locked into position for printing on a rotary press.

plate·ful (plāt′fo͝ol), *n., pl.* **-fuls. 1.** the amount that a plate will hold. **2.** a large portion or quantity: *a plateful of contracts to negotiate.* [1760–70; PLATE[1] + -FUL] —**Usage.** See **-ful.**

plate′ gird′er, an iron or steel beam built up from plates and shapes welded or riveted together, usually including a plate or plates for a web, four angle irons forming two flanges, and a pair of plates to reinforce the flanges. [1840–50]

plate′ glass′, a soda-lime-silica glass formed by rolling the hot glass into a plate that is subsequently ground and polished, used in large windows, mirrors, etc. [1720–30] —**plate′-glass′, plate′glass′,** *adj.*

plate·hold·er (plāt′hōl′dər), *n.* a lightproof container for a photographic plate, loaded into the camera with the plate and having a slide that is removed before exposing. [1870–75; PLATE[1] + HOLDER]

plate·let (plāt′lit), *n. Cell Biol.* a small platelike body, esp. a blood platelet. [1890–95; PLATE[1] + -LET]

plate·mak·er (plāt′mā′kər), *n. Print.* **1.** a machine that makes plates used for reproducing illustrations or printed matter, esp. halftone or etched illustrations. **2.** the operator of such a machine. [1250–1300; ME, as surname meaning "armorer"; see PLATE[1], MAKER]

plate′ mark′, **1.** hallmark. **2.** a mark made on paper by the edge of an intaglio plate during printing. [1855–60]

plat·en (plat′n), *n.* **1.** a flat plate in a printing press for pressing the paper against the inked type or plate to produce an impression. **2.** a rotating cylinder used for the same purpose. **3.** the roller of a typewriter. **4.** (on a planing machine or the like) the bed to which the work is fastened. **5.** (on a testing machine) a plate for applying compression to a sample. [1400–50; earlier *platyne,* late ME *plateyne* chalice cover < MF *platine.* See PLATE[1], -INE[1]]

plate′ proof′, *Print.* proof taken from a plate ready for printing.

plat·er (plā′tər; *for 2 also* plat′ər), *n.* **1.** a person or thing that plates. **2.** an inferior race horse. [1710–20; PLATE[1] + -ER[1]]

plate′ rail′, a rail or narrow shelf fixed along a wall to hold plates, esp. for ornament or display. [1815–25]

plate′ resist′ance, *Electronics.* See **anode resistance.**

plat·er·esque (plat′ə resk′), *adj.* (*sometimes cap.*) noting or pertaining to a 16th-century style of Spanish architecture characterized by profuse applications of delicate low-relief Renaissance ornament to isolated parts of building exteriors. [1835–45; < Sp *plateresco,* equiv. to *plater(o)* silversmith (*plat(a)* silver; see PLATINA + *-ero* < L *-ārius* -ARY) + *-esco* -ESQUE; so called because the heavy ornamentation of the style suggested decorated silverwork]

plate′ shop′, *Shipbuilding.* a shop for cold-forming metal plates. Also called **structural shop.**

plate′ tecton′ics, *Geol.* a theory of global tectonics in which the lithosphere is divided into a number of crustal plates, each of which moves on the plastic asthenosphere more or less independently to collide with, slide under, or move past adjacent plates. [1965–70] —**plate′-tec·ton′ic,** *adj.*

plate′ trac′ery, tracery, as in early Gothic architecture, formed of cut or pierced slabs of stone set on edge with the flat side outward. Also called **perforated tracery.** [1850–55]

plate·ware (plāt′wâr′), *n.* household dishes, esp. ones made of or plated with gold or silver. [PLATE[1] + WARE[1]]

plat·form (plat′fôrm), *n.* **1.** a horizontal surface or structure with a horizontal surface raised above the level of the surrounding area. **2.** a raised flooring or other horizontal surface, such as, in a hall or meeting place, a stage for use by public speakers, performers, etc. **3.** the raised area between or alongside the tracks of a railroad station, from which the cars of the train are entered. **4.** the open entrance area, or the vestibule, at the end of a railroad passenger car. **5.** a landing in a flight of stairs. **6.** a public statement of the principles, objectives, and policy of a political party, esp. as put forth by the representatives of the party in a convention to nominate candidates for an election: *The platform contained the usual platitudes.* **7.** a body of principles on which a person or group takes a stand in appealing to the public; program: *The Fabians developed an all-embracing platform promising utopia.* **8.** a set of principles; plan. **9.** a place for public discussion; forum. **10.** a decklike construction on which the drill rig of an offshore oil or gas well is erected. **11.** *Building Trades.* a relatively flat member or construction for distributing weight, as a wall plate, grillage, etc. **12.** *Mil.* **a.** solid ground on which artillery pieces are mounted. **b.** a metal stand or base attached to certain types of artillery pieces. **13.** *Naut.* flat[1] (def. 44a). **14.** a flat, elevated piece of ground. **15.** *Geol.* a vast area of undisturbed sedimentary rocks that, together with a shield, constitutes a craton. **16.** a thick insert of leather, cork, or other sturdy material between the uppers and the sole of a shoe, usually intended for stylish effect or to give added height. **17. platforms,** platform shoes. **18. a.** See **hardware platform. b.** See **software platform. 19.** a scheme of religious principles or doctrines. [1540–50; earlier *platte forme* < MF: lit., flat form, plane figure. See PLATE[1], FORM] —**plat′·form·less,** *adj.*
—**Syn. 2.** stage, dais, rostrum, pulpit.

plat′form bed′, a bed, originating in Scandinavia in the 1930's, consisting of a simple shallow box for holding a mattress situated on a slightly recessed pedestal.

plat′form car′, a railroad freight car having no enclosing sides or top; a flatcar. [1835–45, *Amer.*]

plat′form frame′, *Carpentry.* a building frame having studs only one story high, regardless of the number of stories built, each story having a box sill. Also called **western frame.**

plat′form scale′, a scale with a platform for holding the items to be weighed. Also called **plat′form bal′·ance.**

plat′form shoe′, a shoe with a platform. [1965–70]

plat′form ten′nis, a variation of tennis played on a wooden platform enclosed with chicken wire in which the players hit a rubber ball with wooden paddles following the same basic rules as tennis except that only one serve is permitted and balls can be played off the back and side fences. [1950–55, *Amer.*]

plat′form tick′et, *Brit.* a pass allowing a visitor to enter upon a railroad platform from which those not traveling are ordinarily excluded. [1900–05]

Plath (plath), *n.* **Sylvia,** 1932–63, U.S. poet.

plat·i·na (plat′n ə, plə tē′nə), *n.* a native alloy of platinum with palladium, iridium, osmium, etc. [1740–50; < Sp: lit., silverlike element, equiv. to *plat(a)* silver (< Pr: lit., silver plate; see PLATE[1]) + *-ina* -INE[1]. See PLATINUM]

plat·i·nate[1] (plat′n āt′), *n. Chem.* a salt of platinic acid. [1855–60; PLATIN(IC ACID) + -ATE[2]]

plat·i·nate[2] (plat′n āt′), *v.t.,* **-nat·ed, -nat·ing.** to platinize. [1885–90; PLATIN(UM) + -ATE[1]]

plat·ing (plā′ting), *n.* **1.** a thin coating of gold, silver, etc. **2.** an external layer of metal plates. **3.** the act of a person or thing that plates. [1535–45; PLATE[1] + -ING[1]]

pla·tin·ic (plə tin′ik), *adj. Chem.* of or containing platinum, esp. in the tetravalent state. [1835–45; PLATIN(UM) + -IC]

platin′ic ac′id, *Chem.* a white, crystalline, water-insoluble powder, H_2PtO_3, used chiefly in platinization.

platin′ic chlo′ride, *Chem.* See **chloroplatinic acid.** [1865–70]

plat·in·i·rid·i·um (plat′n i rid′ē əm, -ī rid′-), *n.* a natural alloy composed chiefly of platinum and iridium. [1865–70; PLATIN(UM) + IRIDIUM]

Plat·in·ite (plat′n īt′), *Trademark.* a brand name for an alloy of about 55 percent iron and 45 percent nickel, having the same coefficient of expansion as platinum and used as a substitute for platinum in electrical work.

plat·i·nize (plat′n īz′), *v.t.,* **-nized, -niz·ing.** to coat or plate with metallic platinum. Also, *esp. Brit.,* **plat′i·nise′.** [1815–25; PLATIN(UM) + -IZE] —**plat′i·ni·za′·tion,** *n.*

plat·i·no·cy·an·ic (plat′n ō sī an′ik), *adj. Chem.* of or derived from platinocyanic acid. [PLATIN(UM) + -O- + -CYANIC]

CONCISE PRONUNCIATION KEY: *act, cāpe, dâre, pärt; set, ēqual; if, īce; ox, ōver, ôrder, oil, bo͝ok, bo͞ot, out; up, ûrge; child; sing; shoe; thin, that;* zh as in *treasure.* ə = *a* as in *alone, e* as in *system, i* as in *easily, o* as in *gallop, u* as in *circus;* ᵊ as in *fire* (fīᵊr), *hour* (ouᵊr). l and n can serve as syllabic consonants, as in *cradle* (krād′l), and *button* (but′n). See the full key inside the front cover.

plat′inocyan′ic ac′id, *Chem.* the hypothetical acid containing platinum and the cyano group, $H_2Pt(CN)_4$.

plat·i·no·cy·a·nide (plat′n ō sī′ə nīd′, -nid), *n. Chem.* a salt of platinocyanic acid. Also called **cyanoplatinite.** [1835–45; PLATINOCYAN(IC ACID) + -IDE]

plat·i·noid (plat′n oid′), *adj.* **1.** resembling platinum: *the platinoid elements.* —*n.* **2.** any of the metals, as palladium or iridium, with which platinum is commonly associated. **3.** an alloy of copper, zinc, and nickel, to which small quantities of such elements as tungsten or aluminum have been added. [1860–65; PLATIN(UM) + -OID]

plat·i·no·type (plat′n ō tīp′), *n. Photog.* **1.** a process of printing positives in which a platinum salt is used, rather than the usual silver salts, in order to make a more permanent print. **2.** Also called **plat′inum print′.** a print made by this process. [1875–80; PLATIN(UM) + -O- + -TYPE]

plat·i·nous (plat′n əs), *adj. Chem.* containing bivalent platinum. [1835–45; PLATIN(UM) + -OUS]

plat·i·num (plat′n əm, plat′nəm), *n.* **1.** *Chem.* a heavy, grayish-white, highly malleable and ductile metallic element, resistant to most chemicals, practically unoxidizable except in the presence of bases, and fusible only at extremely high temperatures: used for making chemical and scientific apparatus, as a catalyst in the oxidation of ammonia to nitric acid, and in jewelry. *Symbol:* Pt; *at. wt.:* 195.09; *at. no.:* 78; *sp. gr.:* 21.5 at 20°C. **2.** a light, metallic gray with very slight bluish tinge when compared with silver. —*adj.* **3.** made of platinum. **4.** *Music Slang.* (of a recording or record album) having sold a minimum of two million single records or one million LPs. [1805–15; < NL, alter. of earlier *platina* < Sp; see PLATINA]

plat′inum black′, *Chem.* a black powder consisting of very finely divided metallic platinum, used as a catalyst, esp. in organic synthesis. [1850–55]

plat′inum blonde′, **1.** a person, esp. a girl or woman, whose hair is of a pale blond or silver color, usually colored artificially by bleaching or dyeing. **2.** a pale blond or silver color. [1930–35]

plat·i·tude (plat′i to͞od′, -tyo͞od′), *n.* **1.** a flat, dull, or trite remark, esp. one uttered as if it were fresh or profound. **2.** the quality or state of being flat, dull, or trite: *the platitude of most political oratory.* [1805–15; < F: lit., flatness, equiv. to *plat* flat (see PLATE[1]) + *-itude,* as in F *latitude, altitude, magnitude,* etc.]
—**Syn. 1.** cliché, truism.

plat·i·tu·di·nal (plat′i to͞od′n əl, -tyo͞od′-), *adj.* platitudinous. [1865–70; PLATITUDE + *-inal* (see -AL[1]), on the model of L derivatives of abstract nouns in *-tūdō,* s. *-tūdin-* (cf. LATITUDINAL)]

plat·i·tu·di·nar·i·an (plat′i to͞od′n âr′ē ən, -tyo͞od′-), *n.* a person who frequently or habitually utters platitudes. [1850–55; PLATITUDIN(OUS) + -ARIAN, perh. on the model of LATITUDINARIAN]

plat·i·tu·di·nize (plat′i to͞od′n īz, -tyo͞od′-), *v.i.,* **-nized, -niz·ing.** to utter platitudes. Also, *esp. Brit.,* **plat′i·tu′di·nise′.** [1880–85; PLATITUDIN(OUS) + -IZE] —**plat′i·tu′di·ni·za′tion,** *n.* —**plat′i·tu′di·niz′er,** *n.*

plat·i·tu·di·nous (plat′i to͞od′n əs, -tyo͞od′-), *adj.* **1.** characterized by or given to platitudes. **2.** of the nature of or resembling a platitude. [1855–60; PLATITUDE + *-inous* (see PLATITUDINAL, -OUS)] —**plat′i·tu′di·nous·ly,** *adv.* —**plat′i·tu′di·nous·ness,** *n.*

Pla·to (plā′tō), *n.* **1.** 427–347 B.C., Greek philosopher. **2.** a walled plain in the second quadrant of the face of the moon, having a dark floor: about 60 miles (96 km) in diameter.

Pla·ton·ic (plə ton′ik, plā-), *adj.* **1.** of, pertaining to, or characteristic of Plato or his doctrines: *the Platonic philosophy of ideal forms.* **2.** pertaining to, involving, or characterized by Platonic love as a striving toward love of spiritual or ideal beauty. **3.** (*usually l.c.*) purely spiritual; free from sensual desire, esp. in a relationship between two persons of the opposite sex. **4.** (*usually l.c.*) feeling or professing platonic love: *He insisted that he was completely platonic in his admiration.* [1525–35; < L *Platōnicus* < Gk *Platōnikós,* equiv. to *Platōn-,* s. of *Plátōn* PLATO + *-ikos,* -IC] —**Pla·ton′i·cal·ly,** *adv.*

Platon′ic love′, **1.** *Platonism.* love of the Idea of beauty, seen as terminating an evolution from the desire for an individual and the love of physical beauty to the love and contemplation of spiritual or ideal beauty. **2.** (*usually l.c.*) an intimate companionship or relationship, esp. between two persons of the opposite sex, that is characterized by the absence of sexual involvement; a spiritual affection. [1635–45]

Platon′ic sol′id, *Geom.* one of the five regular polyhedrons: tetrahedron, octahedron, hexahedron, icosahedron, or dodecahedron. [1950–55]

Platon′ic year′, *Astron.* a period of about 26,000 years, equal to the time required for a complete revolution of the equinoxes. Also called **great year.** Cf. **precession of the equinoxes.** [1630–40]

Pla·to·nism (plāt′n iz′əm), *n.* **1.** the philosophy or doctrines of Plato or his followers. **2.** a Platonic doctrine or saying. **3.** the belief that physical objects are impermanent representations of unchanging Ideas, and that the Ideas alone give true knowledge as they are known by the mind. **4.** (*sometimes l.c.*) the doctrine or practice of platonic love. [1560–70; < NL *Platōnismus.* See PLATONIC, -ISM] —**Pla′to·nist,** *n., adj.*

Pla·to·nize (plāt′n īz′), *v.,* **-nized, -niz·ing.** —*v.i.* **1.** to follow or adopt the doctrines of Plato. **2.** to think or reason in the manner of Plato. —*v.t.* **3.** to give a Platonic character to. **4.** to explain in accordance with Platonic principles. Also, *esp. Brit.,* **Pla′to·nise′.** [1600–10; < Gk *platōnízein.* See PLATONIC, -IZE] —**Pla′to·ni·za′tion,** *n.* —**Pla′to·niz′er,** *n.*

pla·toon (plə to͞on′), *n.* **1.** a military unit consisting of two or more squads or sections and a headquarters. **2.** a small unit of a police force. **3.** a company or group of persons: *a platoon of visitors.* **4.** *Football.* a group of players specially trained in one aspect of the game, as offense or defense, and used as a unit: *a halfback on the offensive platoon.* —*v.t.* **5.** *Sports.* **a.** to use (a player) at a position in a game alternately with another player or players. **b.** to alternate (two different teams or units), as separate offensive and defensive squads. —*v.i.* **6.** *Sports.* **a.** to alternate at a position with another player or players. **b.** to use players alternately at the same position. **c.** to alternate different teams. [1630–40; earlier *plotton* < F *peloton* little ball, group, platoon, dim. of *pelote* ball. See PELLET, -OON]

Platt·deutsch (plät′doich′), *n.* the Low German vernacular dialects spoken in northern Germany. Also called **Low German.** [1825–35; < G: lit., flat (i.e., lowland) German]

Platte (plat), *n.* a river flowing E from the junction of the North and South Platte rivers in central Nebraska to the Missouri River S of Omaha. 310 mi. (500 km) long.

Plat·ten·see (plät′n zā′), *n.* German name of **Balaton.**

plat·ter (plat′ər), *n.* **1.** a large, shallow dish, usually elliptical in shape, for holding and serving food, esp. meat or fish. **2.** a course of a meal, usually consisting of a variety of foods served on the same plate. **3.** *Slang.* a phonograph record. **4.** *Motion Picture Slang.* a part of a motion-picture projector, consisting of a large, horizontally rotating disk that houses a feature film. [1250–1300; ME *plater* < AF, deriv. of *plat* dish. See PLATE[1], -ER[2]]

Platts·burgh (plats′bûrg), *n.* a city in NE New York, on Lake Champlain: battle, 1814. 21,057.

plat·y[1] (plā′tē), *adj.,* **plat·i·er, plat·i·est.** (of an igneous rock) split into thin, flat sheets, often resembling strata, as a result of uneven cooling. [1525–35; PLATE[1] + -Y[1]]

plat·y[2] (plat′ē), *n., pl.* (*esp. collectively*) **plat·y,** (*esp. referring to two or more kinds or species*) **plat·ys, plat·ies.** platyfish. [1930–35; by shortening of NL *Platypoecilus* genus name, equiv. to *platy-* PLATY- + *-poecilus* < Gk *poikílos* mottled]

platy-, a combining form meaning "flat," "broad," used in the formation of compound words: *platyhelminth.* Also, **plat-.** [comb. form repr. Gk *platýs;* see FLAT[1]]

plat·y·ce·phal·ic (plat′ē sə fal′ik), *adj. Cephalom.* having a head whose cranial vault is broad or flat. Also, **plat·y·ceph·a·lous** (plat′i sef′ə ləs). [1860–65; PLATY- + -CEPHALIC]

plat·yc·ne·mi·a (plat′ik nē′mē ə, plat′i nē′-), *n.* (in the shinbone) the state of being laterally flattened. [1875–80; < NL; see PLATY-, CNEMIS, -IA]

plat·y·fish (plat′ē fish′), *n., pl.* (*esp. collectively*) **-fish,** (*esp. referring to two or more kinds or species*) **-fish·es.** any of several small, yellow-gray freshwater fishes of the genus *Xiphophorus,* esp. *X. variatus,* of Mexico: popular in home aquariums, in which the color varies widely. Also called **moon platy.** [see PLATY[2], FISH]

plat·y·hel·minth (plat′i hel′minth), *n.* any worm of the phylum Platyhelminthes; a flatworm. [1875–80; < NL *Platyhelmintha* flatworm. See PLATY-, HELMINTH] —**plat′y·hel·min′thic,** *adj.*

Plat·y·hel·min·thes (plat′ē hel min′thēz), *n.* a phylum of worms having bilateral symmetry and a soft, usually flattened body, comprising the flatworms. [1900–05; < NL (pl.); see PLATYHELMINTH]

plat·y·kur·tic (plat′i kûr′tik), *adj. Statistics.* **1.** (of a frequency distribution) less concentrated about the mean than the corresponding normal distribution. **2.** (of a frequency distribution curve) having a wide, rather flat distribution about the mode. [1900–05; PLATY- + *kurt-* (irreg. < Gk *kyrtós* bulging, swelling) + -IC]

plat·y·kur·to·sis (plat′ē kûr tō′sis), *n. Statistics.* the state of being platykurtic. [1935–40; PLATYKURT(IC) + -OSIS]

plat·y·pod (plat′i pod′), *adj.* **1.** Also, **pla·typ·o·dous** (plə tip′ə dəs). having a broad foot, as certain gastropod mollusks. —*n.* **2.** a platypod animal. [1840–50; PLATY- + -POD]

platypus, *Ornithorhynchus anatinus,* head and body 1½ ft. (0.5 m); tail 6 in. (15 cm)

plat·y·pus (plat′i pəs, -po͝os′), *n., pl.* **-pus·es, -pi** (-pī′). a small, aquatic, egg-laying monotreme, *Ornithorhynchus anatinus,* of Australia and Tasmania, having webbed feet, a tail like that of a beaver, a sensitive bill resembling that of a duck, and, in adult males, venom-injecting spurs on the ankles of the hind limbs, used primarily for fighting with other males during the breeding season. Also called **duckbill, duckbilled platypus.** [1790–1800; < NL < Gk *platýpous* flat-footed, equiv. to *platy-* PLATY- + *-pous,* adj. deriv. of *poús* FOOT]

plat·yr·rhine (plat′i rīn′, -rin), *adj.* **1.** *Anthropol.* having a broad, flat-bridged nose. **2.** belonging or pertaining to the primate group or superfamily Platyrrhini, comprising the New World monkeys, having a broad, flat nose and usually a long, prehensile tail. —*n.* **3.** a platyrrhine animal. Also, **plat·yr·rhin·i·an** (plat′i rin′ē ən). [1835–45; < NL *Platyrrhini,* pl. of *platyrrhinus* < Gk *platy-* PLATY- + *-rhīn-* -nosed, adj. deriv. of *rhís,* s. *rhīn-* nose, snout; cf. CATARRHINE]

pla·tys·ma (plə tiz′mə), *n., pl.* **-mas, -ma·ta** (-mə tə), *Anat.* a broad, thin muscle on each side of the neck, extending from the upper part of the shoulder to the corner of the mouth, the action of which wrinkles the skin of the neck and depresses the corner of the mouth. [1685–95; < NL < Gk *plátysma* a plate, lit., something wide and flat, equiv. to *platý(nein)* to widen (deriv. of *platýs;* see PLATY-) + *-sma,* var. of *-ma* resultative suffix]

plau·dit (plô′dit), *n.* Usually, **plaudits. 1.** an enthusiastic expression of approval: *Her portrayal of Juliet won the plaudits of the critics.* **2.** a demonstration or round of applause, as for some approved or admired performance. [1615–25; earlier *plaudite* (3 syllables) < L, 2nd person pl. impv. of *plaudere* to APPLAUD]

Plau·en (plou′ən), *n.* a city in E Germany. 78,632.

plau·si·ble (plô′zə bəl), *adj.* **1.** having an appearance of truth or reason; seemingly worthy of approval or acceptance; credible; believable: *a plausible excuse; a plausible plot.* **2.** well-spoken and apparently, but often deceptively, worthy of confidence or trust: *a plausible commentator.* [1535–45; < L *plausibilis* deserving applause, equiv. to *plaus(us)* (ptp. of *plaudere* to APPLAUD) + *-ibilis* -IBLE] —**plau′si·bil′i·ty, plau′si·ble·ness,** *n.* —**plau′si·bly,** *adv.*
—**Syn. 1.** PLAUSIBLE, SPECIOUS describe that which has the appearance of truth but might be deceptive. The person or thing that is PLAUSIBLE strikes the superficial judgment favorably; it may or may not be true: *a plausible argument* (one that cannot be verified or believed in entirely). SPECIOUS definitely implies deceit or falsehood; the surface appearances are quite different from what is beneath: *a specious pretense of honesty; a specious argument* (one deliberately deceptive, probably for selfish or evil purposes). —**Ant. 1.** honest, sincere.

plau·sive (plô′ziv, -siv), *adj.* **1.** applauding. **2.** *Obs.* plausible. [1590–1600; < L *plaus(us)* (ptp. of *plaudere* to APPLAUD) + -IVE]

Plau·tus (plô′təs), *n.* **Ti·tus Mac·ci·us** (tī′təs mak′sē-əs), c254–c184 B.C., Roman dramatist.

play (plā), *n.* **1.** a dramatic composition or piece; drama. **2.** a dramatic performance, as on the stage. **3.** exercise or activity for amusement or recreation. **4.** fun or jest, as opposed to seriousness: *I said it merely in play.* **5.** a pun. **6.** the playing, action, or conduct of a game: *The pitcher was replaced in the fourth inning of play.* **7.** the manner or style of playing or of doing something: *We admired his fine play throughout the game.* **8.** an act or instance of playing or of doing something: *a stupid play that cost us the match.* **9.** one's turn to play: *Whose play is it?* **10.** a playing for stakes; gambling. **11.** an attempt to accomplish something, often in a manner showing craft or calculation; maneuver: *They tried to buy up the stock in a takeover play.* **12.** an enterprise or venture; deal: *an oil and drilling play.* **13.** action, conduct, or dealing of a specified kind: *fair play; foul play.* **14.** action, activity, or operation: *the play of fancy.* **15.** brisk, light, or changing movement or action: *a fountain with a leaping play of water.* **16.** elusive change or movement, as of light or colors: *the play of a searchlight against the night sky.* **17.** a space in which something, as a part of a mechanism, can move. **18.** freedom of movement within a space, as of a part of a mechanism. **19.** freedom for action, or scope for activity: *full play of the mind.* **20.** attention in the press or other media; coverage; dissemination as news: *The birth of the panda got a big play in the papers.* **21.** an act or instance of being broadcast: *The governor's speech got two plays on our local station.* **22. bring into play,** to put into motion; cause to be introduced: *New evidence has been brought into play in this trial.* **23. in** or **out of play,** in or not in the state of being played during a game: *The umpire says the ball was not in play.* **24. make a play for,** *Informal.* **a.** to try to attract, esp. sexually: *He made a play for his friend's girlfriend.* **b.** to attempt to gain by impressing favorably: *This ad will make a play for new consumer markets.*
—*v.t.* **25.** to act the part of (a person or character) in a dramatic performance; portray: *to play Lady Macbeth.* **26.** to perform (a drama, pantomime, etc.) on or as if on the stage. **27.** to act or sustain (a part) in a dramatic performance or in real life: *to play the role of benefactor.* **28.** to act the part or character of in real life: *to play the fool; to play God.* **29.** to give performances in, as a theatrical company does: *to play the larger cities.* **30.** to engage in (a game, pastime, etc.). **31.** to contend against in a game. **32.** to function or perform as (a specified player) in a game or competition: *He usually plays left end.* **33.** to employ (a piece of equipment, a player, etc.) in a game: *I played my highest card.* **34.** to use as if in playing a game, as for one's own advantage: *He played his brothers against each other.* **35.** to stake or wager, as in a game. **36.** to lay a wager or wagers on (something). **37.** to represent or imitate, as for recreation or in jest: *to play cowboys and Indians.* **38.** to perform on (a musical instrument). **39.** to perform (music) on an instrument. **40.** to cause (a phonograph, radio, recording, etc.) to produce sound or pictures: *to play a tape; to play the radio.* **41.** to do or perform: *You shouldn't play tricks. Compromise plays an important part in marriage.* **42.** to carry or put into operation; act upon: *to play a hunch.* **43.** to cause to move or change lightly or quickly: *to play colored lights on a fountain.* **44.** to operate or cause to operate, esp. continuously or with repeated action: *to play a hose on a fire.* **45.** to allow (a hooked fish) to exhaust itself by pulling on the line. **46.** to display or feature (a news story, photograph, etc.), esp. prominently: *Play the flood photos on page one.* **47.** to exploit or trade in (an investment, business opportunity, stock, etc.).
—*v.i.* **48.** to exercise or employ oneself in diversion, amusement, or recreation. **49.** to do something in sport that is not to be taken seriously. **50.** to amuse oneself; toy; trifle (often fol. by *with*). **51.** to take part or engage in a game. **52.** to take part in a game for stakes; gamble. **53.** to conduct oneself or act in a specified way: *to play fair.* **54.** to act on or as if on the stage; perform. **55.** to perform on a musical instrument. **56.** (of an instrument or music) to sound in performance: *The strings are playing well this evening.* **57.** (of a phonograph,

CONCISE ETYMOLOGY KEY: <, descended or borrowed from; >, whence; b., blend of, blended; c., cognate with; cf., compare; deriv., derivative; equiv., equivalent; imit., imitative; obl., oblique; r., replacing; s., stem; sp., spelling, spelled; resp., respelling, respelled; trans., translation; ?, origin unknown; *, unattested; ‡, probably earlier than. See the full key inside the front cover.

radio, recording, etc.) to give forth sound: *The radio played all night.* **58.** to be performed or shown: *What's playing at the movie theater around the corner?* **59.** to be capable of or suitable for performance, as a television or dramatic script: *We hope this scene will play well.* **60.** *Informal.* to be accepted or effective; fare: *How will the senator's proposal play with the public?* **61.** to move freely within a space, as a part of a mechanism. **62.** to move about lightly or quickly: *The water of the fountain played in the air.* **63.** to present the effect of such motion, as light or the changing colors of an iridescent substance: *The lights played strangely over the faces of the actors.* **64.** to operate continuously or with repeated action. **65.** *Informal.* to comply or cooperate: *They wanted her to tell them what she knew about the plans, but she refused to play.* **66. come to play,** *Informal.* to be disposed to play or participate in a manner reflecting a determination to win or succeed: *We're a small new business, but we came to play.* **67. play along, a.** to cooperate or concur; go along. **b.** to pretend to cooperate or concur. **68. play around,** *Informal.* **a.** to behave in a playful or frivolous manner; fool around. **b.** to be sexually promiscuous. **c.** to be sexually unfaithful. **69. play at, a.** to pretend interest in: *It's obvious that you're just playing at fishing for my sake.* **b.** to do something without seriousness: *He is merely playing at being a student.* **70. play back,** to play (a recording, esp. one newly made): *Play it back and let's hear how I sound.* **71. play ball.** See **ball**[1] (def. 17). **72. play both ends against the middle,** to maneuver opposing groups in order to benefit oneself. **73. play by ear,** to play (music or a musical instrument) without printed music, as by memory of what one has heard or by unschooled musical instinct. **74. play down,** to treat as of little importance; belittle: *He has consistently played down his own part in the successful enterprise.* **75. played out, a.** exhausted; weary. **b.** out of fashion; hackneyed: *New styles in clothing are soon played out in New York.* **c.** used up; finished: *The original tires were played out and had to be replaced.* **76. play fast and loose,** to act in an irresponsible or inconsiderate manner, esp. to employ deception to gain one's ends: *to play fast and loose with someone's affections.* **77. play for time,** to prolong something in order to gain an advantage; forestall an event or decision: *Their maneuvering at the conference was obviously calculated to play for time.* **78. play hardball.** See **hardball** (def. 2). **79. play into the hands of,** to act in such a way as to give an advantage to (someone, esp. an opponent): *If you lose your temper when he insults you, you will be playing right into his hands.* Also, **play into (someone's) hands. 80. play it by ear,** to improvise, esp. in a challenging situation when confronted by unknown factors: *If you can't come up with a plan, we'll just have to play it by ear.* **81. play off, a.** *Sports.* to play an extra game or round in order to settle a tie. **b.** *Sports.* to engage in an elimination game or games after the regular season is over in order to determine the champion. **c.** to set (one person or thing) against another, usually for one's own gain or advantage: *The children could usually get what they wanted by playing one parent off against the other.* **82. play one's cards.** See **card**[1] (def. 17). **83. play on** or **upon,** to exploit, as the feelings or weaknesses of another; take selfish advantage of: *She would never think of playing on the good nature of others.* **84. play out, a.** to bring to an end; finish. **b.** to use up; exhaust: *to play out one's supplies.* **c.** to reel or pay out, as a rope, line, etc. **85. play politics.** See **politics** (def. 8). **86. play possum.** See **possum** (def. 2). **87. play second fiddle.** See **second fiddle** (def. 1). **88. play the field.** See **field** (def. 26). **89. play the game.** See **game**[1] (def. 18). **90. play up,** to emphasize the importance of; highlight or publicize: *The schools are playing up their science programs.* **91. play up to,** *Informal.* to attempt to impress in order to gain someone's favor: *Students who too obviously play up to their teachers are usually disliked by their classmates.* **92. play with a full deck.** See **deck** (def. 19). **93. play with fire.** See **fire** (def. 27). **94. play with oneself,** *Informal.* to masturbate. [bef. 900; (n.) ME *pleye,* OE *plega;* (v.) ME *pleyen,* OE *pleg(i)an* (c. MD *pleien* to leap for joy, dance, rejoice, be glad)] **—play′ing·ly,** *adv.* **—play′less,** *adj.* **—play′like′,** *adj.*

—Syn. 2. show. **3.** diversion, pastime. PLAY, GAME, SPORT refer to forms of diverting activity. PLAY is the general word for any such form of activity, often undirected, spontaneous, or random: *Childhood should be a time for play.* GAME refers to a recreational contest, mental or physical, usually governed by set rules: *a game of chess.* Besides referring to an individual contest, GAME may refer to a pastime as a whole: *Golf is a good game.* If, however, the pastime is one (usually an outdoor one) depending chiefly on physical strength, though not necessarily a contest, the word SPORT is applied: *Football is a vigorous sport.* **18, 19.** liberty. **26.** enact. **28.** personate, impersonate. **33.** use. **35.** bet. **36.** back. **48.** sport, frolic, romp, revel. **50.** dally. **—Ant. 3, 48.** work.

pla·ya (plī′ə), *n. Western U.S.* the sandy, salty, or mud-caked flat floor of a desert basin having interior drainage, usually occupied by a shallow lake during or after prolonged, heavy rains. Cf. **dry lake.** [1850–55, *Amer.;* < Sp: shore < LL *plagia;* see PLAGE]

play·a·ble (plā′ə bəl), *adj.* **1.** capable of or suitable for being played. **2.** (of ground) fit to be played on, as for a soccer game. [1475–85; PLAY + -ABLE] **—play′a·bil′i·ty,** *n.*

play·act (plā′akt′), *v.i.* **1.** to engage in make-believe. **2.** to be insincere or affected in speech, manner, etc.: *It's hard to get away with playacting with members of one's own family.* **3.** to perform in a play. *—v.t.* **4.** to dramatize (something): *They playacted the movements of a burglar.* [1895–1900; back formation from *playacting;* see PLAY, ACT, -ING[1]] **—play′act′ing,** *n.* **—play′ac′tor,** *n.*

play′-ac·tion pass′ (plā′ak′shən), *Football.* a pass play designed to deceive the defense by appearing to be a running play, in which the quarterback fakes a hand-off to a back before throwing a forward pass. [1960–65, *Amer.*]

play′ a′gent, a broker representing a playwright in dealings with theater managers, producers, etc. Also called **playbroker.**

play·back (plā′bak′), *n.* **1.** the act of reproducing a sound or video recording, esp. in order to check a recording that is newly made. **2.** (in a recording device) the apparatus used in producing playbacks. **3.** the recording so played, esp. the first time it is heard or viewed after being recorded. **4.** the response to a suggestion, act, product, venture, etc.; feedback: *The playback on the speech has been very favorable.* [1925–30; n. use of v. phrase *play back*]

play′back head′, the part of a tape recorder that is used to pick up the magnetic pattern on tape in order to play back material previously recorded. Also called **reproduce head.** [1945–50]

play·bill (plā′bil′), *n.* a program or announcement of a play. [1665–75; PLAY + BILL[1]]

play·book (plā′bo͝ok′), *n.* **1.** (in Elizabethan drama) the script of a play, used by the actors as an acting text. **2.** a book containing the scripts of one or more plays. **3.** *Football.* a notebook containing descriptions of all the plays and strategies used by a team, often accompanied by diagrams, issued to players for them to study and memorize before the season begins. **4.** *Informal.* any plan or set of strategies, as for outlining a campaign in business or politics. [1525–35; PLAY + BOOK]

play·boy (plā′boi′), *n.* a man who pursues a life of pleasure without responsibility or attachments, esp. one who is of comfortable means. [1620–30; PLAY + BOY]

Play′boy of the West′ern World′, The, a satiric comedy (1907) by John Millington Synge.

play·bro·ker (plā′brō′kər), *n.* See **play agent.** [1905–10, *Amer.;* PLAY + BROKER]

play-by-play (plā′bī plā′), *adj.* **1.** pertaining to or being a detailed account of each incident or act of an event, as in sports: *a play-by-play broadcast of a baseball game.* *—n.* **2.** a detailed and sequential description of a sports contest or other event, as by a sportscaster, usually as it is taking place. [1925–30]

play·clothes (plā′klōz′, -klōthz′), *n. pl.* casual, functional clothing worn for sports, games, and other recreational activities, when relaxing at home, for informal occasions, etc. Also called **playwear.** [PLAY + CLOTHES]

play′ date′, an appointment made by several parents to have their young children play together. [1985–90]

play·day (plā′dā′), *n.* a day for relaxation or for participation in sports contests; a holiday. [1595–1605; PLAY + DAY]

play′ doc′tor, *Theat.* a person, usually a professional playwright, employed to improve a script, esp. shortly before the play's opening. [1920–25]

Play-Doh (plā′dō′), *Trademark.* a brand name for a soft, nontoxic modeling compound made in bright colors and marketed for children.

play·down (plā′doun′), *n. Chiefly Canadian.* a play-off. Also, **play′-down′.** [1935–40; PLAY + DOWN[1]]

play·er (plā′ər), *n.* **1.** a person or thing that plays. **2.** a person who takes part or is skilled in some game or sport. **3.** a person who plays parts on the stage; an actor. **4.** a performer on a musical instrument. **5.** *Informal.* a participant, as in a conference or business deal. **6.** a sound- or image-reproducing machine: *a record player; a cassette player; a videodisc player.* **7.** a gambler. **8.** *Slang.* a person engaged in illicit or illegal activity, esp. a pimp. **9.** a mechanical device by which a musical instrument, as a player piano, is played automatically. [bef. 1000; ME *pleyer,* OE *plegere.* See PLAY, -ER[1]]

Play·er (plā′ər), *n.* **Gary,** born 1935, South African golfer.

play′er pian′o, a piano that can play automatically when the keys are activated electronically or by a pneumatic device controlled by a piano roll. [1900–05, *Amer.*]

play·fel·low (plā′fel′ō), *n.* a playmate. [1505–15; PLAY + FELLOW]

play·ful (plā′fəl), *adj.* **1.** full of play or fun; sportive; frolicsome. **2.** pleasantly humorous or jesting: *a playful remark.* [1200–50; ME *pleiful.* See PLAY, -FUL] **—play′ful·ly,** *adv.* **—play′ful·ness,** *n.*

play·girl (plā′gûrl′), *n.* a woman who pursues a life of pleasure without responsibility or attachments, esp. one who is of comfortable means. [1930–35; PLAY + GIRL]

play·go·er (plā′gō′ər), *n.* a person who attends the theater often or habitually. [1815–25; PLAY + GOER]

play·ground (plā′ground′), *n.* **1.** an area used for outdoor play or recreation, esp. by children, and often containing recreational equipment such as slides and swings. **2.** *Informal.* any place, environment, or facility used for recreation or amusement, as a resort: *The tropical island is an international playground for the rich.* **3.** an arena of operation or activity. [1770–80; PLAY + GROUND[1]]

play·group (plā′gro͞op′), *n.* a group of small children, esp. preschoolers, organized for play or play activities and supervised by adult volunteers. [1905–10; PLAY + GROUP]

play·house (plā′hous′), *n., pl.* **-hous·es** (-hou′ziz). **1.** a theater. **2.** a small house for children to play in. **3.** a toy house. [1590–1600; PLAY + HOUSE; cf. OE *pleghūs,* as gloss of L *theātrum* THEATER]

play′ing card′, **1.** one of the conventional set of 52 cards in four suits, as diamonds, hearts, spades, and clubs, used in playing various games of chance and skill. **2.** one of any set or pack of cards used in playing games. [1535–45]

play′ing field′, an expanse of level ground, as in a park or stadium, where athletic events are held. [1575–85]

play′ing trick′, *Bridge.* a card in a hand considered as likely to take a trick, assuming that the player who holds the hand or that player's partner is the declarer. [1955–60]

play·land (plā′land′), *n.* **1.** an area used for recreation or amusement; playground or amusement park. **2.** a town or city that relies heavily on its tourist trade to bolster its economy. [1945–50; PLAY + -LAND]

play·let (plā′lit), *n.* a short play. [1880–85; PLAY + -LET]

play·list (plā′list′), *n.* a list of the recordings to be played on the radio during a particular program or time period, often including their sequence, duration, etc. [1960–65; PLAY + LIST[1]]

play·mak·er (plā′mā′kər), *n. Sports.* **1.** an offensive player, as in basketball or ice hockey, who executes plays designed to put one or more teammates in a position to score. **2.** *Archaic.* a playwright; dramatist. [1520–30; PLAY + MAKER] **—play′mak′ing,** *n.*

play·mate (plā′māt′), *n.* **1.** a companion, esp. of a child, in play or recreation. **2.** *Informal.* a social companion or lover; girlfriend or boyfriend: *He showed up at the nightclub with his new playmate.* [1635–45; PLAY + MATE[1]]

play′ mon′ey, **1.** paper that is cut and printed to resemble paper money, often used in playing board games. **2.** *Informal.* worthless or counterfeit currency.

play-off (plā′ôf′, -of′), *n.* **1.** (in competitive sports) the playing of an extra game, round, innings, etc., in order to settle a tie. **2.** a series of games or matches, as between the leading teams of two leagues, in order to decide a championship: *In America the most exciting play-off is the World Series.* [1890–95; n. use of v. phrase *play off*]

play′ on words′, a pun or the act of punning.

play·pen (plā′pen′), *n.* **1.** a small enclosure, usually portable, in which a young child can play safely alone without constant supervision. **2.** playground (defs. 2, 3). [1930–35; PLAY + PEN[2]]

play·read·er (plā′rē′dər), *n.* a person who reads and evaluates plays, as for a publisher, producer, or theatrical company. Also called **script reader.** [PLAY + READER]

play·room (plā′ro͞om′, -ro͝om′), *n.* a room set aside for children's play or adult recreation. [1810–20; PLAY + ROOM]

play·script (plā′skript′), *n.* the manuscript of a play, esp. as prepared for use by actors in rehearsals. [PLAY + SCRIPT]

play·street (plā′strēt′), *n.* an urban street closed to traffic during specified times and sometimes equipped with recreational facilities, for use by children as a play area. [1935–40; PLAY + STREET]

play·suit (plā′so͞ot′), *n.* a sports costume for women and children, usually consisting of shorts and a shirt, worn as beachwear, for tennis, etc. [1905–10; PLAY + SUIT]

play′ ther′apy, a form of psychotherapy used chiefly with children, in which patients act out situations in play that are expressive of their emotional problems, conflicts, etc. [1935–40]

play·thing (plā′thing′), *n.* **1.** a thing to play with; toy. **2.** a person who is used capriciously and selfishly by another. [1665–75; PLAY + THING[1]]

play·time (plā′tīm′), *n.* time for play or recreation. [1610–20; PLAY + TIME]

play·wear (plā′wâr′), *n.* playclothes. [1960–65; PLAY + WEAR]

play·wright (plā′rīt′), *n.* a writer of plays; dramatist. [1680–90; PLAY + WRIGHT]

play·writ·ing (plā′rī′ting), *n.* the art or technique of writing plays; the work or profession of a playwright. [1895–1900; PLAY + WRITING]

pla·za (plä′zə, plaz′ə), *n.* **1.** a public square or open space in a city or town. **2.** See **shopping plaza. 3.** an area along an expressway where public facilities, as service stations and rest rooms, are available. [1675–85; < Sp < L *platea* street < Gk *plateîa* broad street. See PLACE]

pla·za de to·ros (*Sp.* plä′sä t͟he tô′rôs, plä′thä; *Eng.* plä′zə dä tôr′ōs, tōr′-, plaz′ə), *pl.* ***pla·zas de to·ros*** (*Sp.* plä′säs t͟he tô′rôs, plä′thäs; *Eng.* plä′zəz dä tôr′ōs, tōr′-, plaz′əz). *Spanish.* a bullring.

Pla·za Las·so (plä′sä lä′sô), **Ga·lo** (gä′lô), 1906–87, Ecuadorian statesman and diplomat, born in the U.S.: president 1948–52.

PLC, *Brit.* public limited company.

plea (plē), *n.* **1.** an appeal or entreaty: *a plea for mercy.* **2.** something that is alleged, urged, or pleaded in defense or justification. **3.** an excuse; pretext: *He begged off on the plea that his car wasn't working.* **4.** *Law.* **a.** an allegation made by, or on behalf of, a party to a legal suit, in support of his or her claim or defense. **b.** a defendant's answer to a legal declaration or charge. **c.** (in courts of equity) a plea that admits the truth of the declaration, but alleges special or new matter in avoidance. **d.** *Obs.* a suit or action. **5. cop a plea,** *Slang.* See **cop**[1] (def. 4b). [1175–1225; ME *ple,* earlier *plaid* < OF < early ML *placitum* law-court, suit, decision, decree, L: opinion (lit., that which is pleasing or agreeable), n. use of neut. of ptp. of *placēre* to please]

—Syn. 1. request, petition, supplication, solicitation, suit. **3.** justification.

plea-bar·gain (plē′bär′gin), *v.i.* **1.** to engage in plea

CONCISE PRONUNCIATION KEY: *act, cāpe, dâre, pärt; set, ēqual; if, ice; ox, ōver, ôrder, oil, bo͝ok, bo͞ot, out; up, ûrge; child; sing; shoe; thin, that;* zh as in *treasure.* ə = *a* as in *alone, e* as in *system, i* as in *easily, o* as in *gallop, u* as in *circus;* ° as in *fire* (fī°r), *hour* (ou°r). l and n can serve as syllabic consonants, as in *cradle* (krād′l), and *button* (but′n). See the full key inside the front cover.

bargaining. —*v.t.* **2.** to deal with or achieve by plea bargaining: *to plea-bargain a reduced sentence.* —*n.* **3.** the agreement arrived at as a result of plea bargaining. [1965–70] —**plea′-bar′gain·er,** *n.*

plea′ bar′gaining, an agreement between a prosecutor and a defendant whereby the defendant is allowed to plead guilty to a lesser charge rather than risk conviction for a graver crime in order to avoid a protracted trial or to win the defendant's cooperation as a witness. [1960–65, *Amer.*]

pleach (plēch), *v.t.* **1.** to interweave (branches, vines, etc.), as for a hedge or arbor. **2.** to make or renew (a hedge, arbor, etc.) by such interweaving. **3.** to braid (hair). [1350–1400; ME *plechen,* var. of *plashen* to PLASH[2]]

plead (plēd), *v.,* **plead·ed** or **pled; plead·ing.** —*v.i.* **1.** to appeal or entreat earnestly: *to plead for time.* **2.** to use arguments or persuasions, as with a person, for or against something: *She pleaded with him not to take the job.* **3.** to afford an argument or appeal: *His youth pleads for him.* **4.** *Law.* **a.** to make any allegation or plea in an action at law. **b.** to put forward an answer on the part of a defendant to a legal declaration or charge. **c.** to address a court as an advocate. **d.** *Obs.* to prosecute a suit or action at law. —*v.t.* **5.** to allege or urge in defense, justification, or excuse: *to plead ignorance.* **6.** *Law.* **a.** to maintain (a cause) by argument before a court. **b.** to allege or set forth (something) formally in an action at law. **c.** to allege or cite in legal defense: *to plead a statute of limitations.* [1200–50; ME *plaiden* < OF *plaid(i)er* to go to law, plead < early ML *placitāre* to litigate, deriv. of L *placitum* opinion. See PLEA]
—**Syn. 1.** beg, supplicate. **2.** reason. **5.** claim.

plead·a·ble (plē′də bəl), *adj.* capable of being pleaded, as a case in court. [1250–1300; ME < AF *pledable.* See PLEAD, -ABLE]

plead·er (plē′dər), *n.* a person who pleads, esp. at law. [1225–75; ME *pleder, plaidour;* see PLEAD, -ER[1]]

plead·ing (plē′ding), *n.* **1.** the act of a person who pleads. **2.** *Law.* **a.** the advocating of a cause in a court of law. **b.** the art or science of setting forth or drawing pleas in legal causes. **c.** a formal statement, usually written, setting forth the cause of action or defense of a case. **d. pleadings,** the successive statements delivered alternately by plaintiff and defendant until the issue is joined. [1250–1300; ME *pledynge* (ger.). See PLEAD, -ING[1]] —**plead′ing·ly,** *adv.* —**plead′ing·ness,** *n.*

pleas·ance (plez′əns), *n.* **1.** a place laid out as a pleasure garden or promenade. **2.** *Archaic.* pleasure. [1300–50; ME *plesaunce* < MF *plaisance.* See PLEASANT, -ANCE]

pleas·ant (plez′ənt), *adj.* **1.** pleasing, agreeable, or enjoyable; giving pleasure: *pleasant news.* **2.** (of persons, manners, disposition, etc.) socially acceptable or adept; polite; amiable; agreeable. **3.** fair, as weather: *a pleasant summer day.* **4.** *Archaic.* gay, sprightly, or merry. **5.** *Obs.* jocular or facetious. [1325–75; ME *plesaunt* < MF *plaisant,* orig. prp. of *plaisir* to PLEASE; see -ANT] —**pleas′ant·ly,** *adv.* —**pleas′ant·ness,** *n.*
—**Syn. 1.** welcome, gratifying. **2.** delightful, congenial, friendly.

Pleas′ant Grove′, a town in central Utah. 10,669.

Pleas′ant Hill′, a city in W California, near San Francisco Bay. 25,124.

Pleas′ant Is′land, former name of **Nauru.**

Pleas·an·ton (plez′ən tən), *n.* a town in W California. 35,160.

pleas·ant·ry (plez′ən trē), *n., pl.* **-ries. 1.** good-humored teasing; banter. **2.** a humorous or jesting remark. **3.** a courteous social remark used to initiate or facilitate a conversation: *to exchange pleasantries.* **4.** a humorous action. [1645–55; < F *plaisanterie,* OF *plesanterie.* See PLEASANT, -RY]

Pleas·ant·ville (plez′ənt vil′), *n.* a city in SE New Jersey. 13,435.

please (plēz), *adv., v.,* **pleased, pleas·ing.** —*adv.* **1.** (used as a polite addition to requests, commands, etc.) if you would be so obliging; kindly: *Please come here. Will you please turn the radio off?* —*v.t.* **2.** to act to the pleasure or satisfaction of: *to please the public.* **3.** to be the pleasure or will of: *May it please your Majesty.* —*v.i.* **4.** to like, wish, or feel inclined: *Go where you please.* **5.** to give pleasure or satisfaction; be agreeable: *manners that please.* **6. if you please, a.** if it be your pleasure; if you like or prefer. **b.** (used as an exclamation expressing astonishment, indignation, etc.): *The missing letter was in his pocket, if you please!* [1275–1325; (v.) ME *plesen, plaisen* < MF *plaisir* << L *placēre* to please, seem good (see PLACID); the use of *please* with requests, etc., is presumably a reduction of the clause *(it) please you* may it please you, later reinforced by imper. use of intransit. *please* to be pleased, wish] —**pleas′a·ble,** *adj.* —**pleas·ed·ly** (plē′zid lē, plēzd′-), *adv.* —**pleas′ed·ness,** *n.* —**pleas′er,** *n.*
—**Syn. 4.** choose, desire, prefer.

pleas·ing (plē′zing), *adj.* giving pleasure; agreeable; gratifying: *a pleasing performance.* [1350–1400; ME *plesing.* See PLEASE, -ING[2]] —**pleas′ing·ly,** *adv.* —**pleas′ing·ness,** *n.*
—**Syn.** pleasant, charming, delightful, engaging. See **interesting.**

pleas·ur·a·ble (plezh′ər ə bəl), *adj.* such as to give pleasure; enjoyable; agreeable; pleasant: *a pleasurable experience.* [1570–80; PLEASURE + -ABLE] —**pleas′ur·a·ble·ness,** *n.* —**pleas′ur·a·bly,** *adv.*

pleas·ure (plezh′ər), *n., v.,* **-ured, -ur·ing.** —*n.* **1.** the state or feeling of being pleased. **2.** enjoyment or satisfaction derived from what is to one's liking; gratification; delight. **3.** worldly or frivolous enjoyment: *the pursuit of pleasure.* **4.** recreation or amusement; diversion; enjoyment: *Are you traveling on business or for pleasure?* **5.** sensual gratification. **6.** a cause or source of enjoyment or delight: *It was a pleasure to see you.* **7.** pleasurable quality: *the pleasure of his company.* **8.** one's will, desire, or choice: *to make known one's pleasure.* —*v.t.* **9.** to give pleasure to; gratify; please. —*v.i.* **10.** to take pleasure; delight: *I pleasure in your company.* **11.** to seek pleasure, as by taking a holiday. [1325–75; late ME (see PLEASE, -URE); r. ME *plaisir* < MF (n. use of inf.) < L *placēre* to please] —**pleas′ure·ful,** *adj.* —**pleas′ure·less,** *adj.* —**pleas′ure·less·ly,** *adv.*
—**Syn. 1.** happiness, gladness, delectation. PLEASURE, ENJOYMENT, DELIGHT, JOY refer to the feeling of being pleased and happy. PLEASURE is the general term: *to take pleasure in beautiful scenery.* ENJOYMENT is a quiet sense of well-being and pleasurable satisfaction: *enjoyment at sitting in the shade on a warm day.* DELIGHT is a high degree of pleasure, usually leading to active expression of it: *delight at receiving a hoped-for letter.* JOY is a feeling of delight so deep and so lasting that one radiates happiness and expresses it spontaneously: *joy at unexpected good news.* **5.** voluptuousness. **8.** preference, wish, inclination, predilection.

pleas′ure dome′, a large building, facility, or place used for recreation. [1797; phrase appar. coined by S. T. Coleridge in his poem "Kubla Khan"]

pleas′ure prin′ciple, *Psychoanal.* an automatic mental drive or instinct seeking to avoid pain and to obtain pleasure. [1910–15]

pleat (plēt), *n.* **1.** a fold of definite, even width made by doubling cloth or the like upon itself and pressing or stitching it in place. —*v.t.* **2.** to fold or arrange in pleats. Also, **plait.** [1325–75; ME; var. of PLAIT] —**pleat′er,** *n.* —**pleat′less,** *adj.*

pleb (pleb), *n.* **1.** a member of the plebs; a plebeian or commoner. **2.** plebe (def. 1). [1850–55, *Amer.*; short for PLEBEIAN]

plebe (plēb), *n.* **1.** Also, **pleb.** (at the U.S. Military and Naval academies) a member of the freshman class. **2.** *Obs.* plebeian (def. 4). [1605–15; short for PLEBEIAN]

ple·be·ian (pli bē′ən), *adj.* **1.** belonging or pertaining to the common people. **2.** of, pertaining to, or belonging to the ancient Roman plebs. **3.** common, commonplace, or vulgar: *a plebeian joke.* —*n.* **4.** a member of the common people. **5.** a member of the ancient Roman plebs. [1525–35; < L *plēbēi(us)* of the plebs (*plēbē(s)* PLEBS + *-ius* adj. suffix) + -AN] —**ple·be′ian·ism,** *n.* —**ple·be′ian·ly,** *adv.* —**ple·be′ian·ness,** *n.*
—**Syn. 3.** lowbrow, low, ordinary, popular.

pleb·i·scite (pleb′ə sīt′, -sit), *n.* **1.** a direct vote of the qualified voters of a state in regard to some important public question. **2.** the vote by which the people of a political unit determine autonomy or affiliation with another country. [1525–35; < F < L *plēbiscītum* decree of the plebs, equiv. to *plēbi* (for *plēbis, plēbēī* gen. sing. of *plēbs, plēbēs* PLEBS) + *scītum* resolution, decree, n. use of neut. of *scītus,* ptp. of *scīscere* to enact, decree, orig., to seek to know, learn, inchoative of *scīre* to know]

plebs (plebz), *n.* (*used with a plural v.*) **1.** (in ancient Rome) the common people, as contrasted with the patricians and later with the senatorial nobility or the equestrian order. **2.** the common people; the populace. [1640–50; < L *plēbs, plēbēs*]

ple·cop·ter·an (pli kop′tər ən), *adj.* **1.** Also, **ple·cop′ter·ous.** belonging or pertaining to the insect order Plecoptera, comprising the stoneflies. —*n.* **2.** a plecopteran insect; stonefly. [1885–90; < NL *Plecopter(a)* the order (< Gk *plék(ein)* to twine, twist + -o- -o- + *-ptera,* neut. pl. of *-pteros* -PTEROUS) + -AN; so named in reference to the reticulated wings, which twist back upon themselves when the insect is resting]

plec·tog·nath (plek′tog nath′), *adj.* **1.** belonging to the Plectognathi, a group or order of fishes having the teeth fused into a beak and thick, often spiny, scaleless skin, and including the filefish, globefish, puffer, and triggerfish. —*n.* **2.** a plectognath fish. [1825–35; < NL *Plectognathi,* pl. of *Plectognathus,* equiv. to *plecto-* (< Gk *plektós* plaited, twisted; see -O-) + *-gnathus* -GNATHOUS] —**plec′tog·nath′ic, plec·tog·na·thous** (plek tog′nə thəs), *adj.*

plec·tron (plek′tron), *n., pl.* **-tra** (-trə). plectrum.

plec·trum (plek′trəm), *n., pl.* **-tra** (-trə), **-trums. 1.** a small piece of plastic, metal, ivory, etc., for plucking the strings of a guitar, lyre, mandolin, etc. **2.** *Anat., Zool.* an anatomical part resembling a plectrum in shape. [1620–30; < L *plēctrum* < Gk *plêktron*]

pled (pled), *v.* a pt. and pp. of **plead.**

pledge (plej), *n., v.,* **pledged, pledg·ing.** —*n.* **1.** a solemn promise or agreement to do or refrain from doing something: *a pledge of aid; a pledge not to wage war.* **2.** something delivered as security for the payment of a debt or fulfillment of a promise, and subject to forfeiture on failure to pay or fulfill the promise. **3.** the state of being given or held as security: *to put a thing in pledge.* **4.** *Law.* **a.** the act of delivering goods, property, etc., to another for security. **b.** the resulting legal relationship. **5.** something given or regarded as a security. **6.** a person accepted for membership in a club, fraternity, or sorority, but not yet formally approved. **7.** an assurance of support or goodwill conveyed by drinking a person's health; a toast. **8.** *Obs.* **a.** a hostage. **b.** a person who becomes bail or surety for another. **9. take the pledge,** to make a solemn, formal vow to abstain from intoxicating drink. —*v.t.* **10.** to bind by or as if by a pledge: *to pledge hearers to secrecy.* **11.** to promise solemnly: *to pledge one's support.* **12.** to give or deposit as a pledge; pawn. **13.** to stake, as one's honor. **14.** to secure by a pledge; give a pledge for. **15.** to accept as a pledge for club, fraternity, or sorority membership. **16.** to drink a health or toast to. —*v.i.* **17.** to make or give a pledge: *to pledge for someone.* **18.** to drink a pledge; toast someone's health, success, etc. [1275–1325; ME *plege* < AF < early ML *plevium, plebium,* deriv. of *plebīre* to pledge < Gmc; cf. OE *plēon* to risk, G *pflegen* to look after. See PLIGHT[2]] —**pledge′a·ble,** *adj.* —**pledg′er,** *n.* —**pledge′less,** *adj.*
—**Syn. 2.** warranty, surety, guaranty.

pledg·ee (plej ē′), *n.* a person to whom a pledge is made or with whom something is deposited as a pledge. [1760–70; PLEDGE + -EE]

Pledge′ of Alle′giance, a solemn oath of allegiance or fidelity to the U.S., beginning, "I pledge allegiance to the flag," and forming part of many flag-saluting ceremonies in the U.S.

pledg·et (plej′it), *n.* a small, flat mass of lint, absorbent cotton, or the like, for use on a wound, sore, etc. [1530–40; orig. uncert.]

pledg·or (plej ôr′), *n. Law.* a person who deposits personal property as a pledge. [PLEDGE + -OR[2]]

-plegia, a combining form meaning "paralysis, cessation of motion," in the limbs or region of the body specified by the initial element: *cardioplegia; hemiplegia; quadriplegia.* [< Gk *-plēgia,* comb. form repr. *plēgḗ* blow, stroke; see -IA]

Ple·iad (plē′əd, plī′əd), *n.* **1.** any of the Pleiades. **2.** French, **Plé·iade** (plā yad′). a group of seven French poets of the latter half of the 16th century. **3.** (*usually l.c.*) any group of eminent or brilliant persons or things, esp. when seven in number.

Ple·ia·des (plē′ə dēz′, plī′-), *n.pl.* **1.** *Class. Myth.* seven daughters of Atlas and half sisters of the Hyades, placed among the stars to save them from the pursuit of Orion. One of them (the **Lost Pleiad**) hides, either from grief or shame. **2.** *Astron.* a conspicuous group or cluster of stars in the constellation Taurus, commonly spoken of as seven, though only six are visible. [1350–1400; ME *Pliades* < L *Plīades* < Gk *Pleiades* (sing. *Pleiás*); akin to *pleîn* to sail]

plein air (plān′ âr′; *Fr.* ple neʀ′), **1.** the open air, esp. the daylight of outdoors. **2.** *Fine Arts.* the quality of light and atmosphere out of doors, esp. this quality as rendered in painting. [1890–95; < F: lit., full air]

plein-air (plān′âr′; *Fr.* ple neʀ′), *adj.* **1.** pertaining to a manner or style of painting developed chiefly in France in the mid-19th century, characterized by the representation of the luminous effects of natural light and atmosphere as contrasted with the artificial light and absence of the sense of air or atmosphere associated with paintings produced in the studio. **2.** designating a painting executed out of doors and representing a direct response to the scene or subject in front of the artist. **3.** (of a painting) having the qualities of air and natural light. [1890–95; adj. use of PLEIN AIR] —**plein′-air′ism,** —**plein′-air′ist,** *n.*

pleio-, var. of **pleo-.**

plei·o·tax·y (plī′ə tak′sē), *n. Bot.* an increase in the normal number of parts. Also, **plei′o·tax′is.** [1885–90; PLEIO- + -TAXY]

plei·ot·ro·py (plī o′trə pē), *n. Genetics.* the phenomenon of one gene being responsible for or affecting more than one phenotypic characteristic. [1935–40; PLEIO- + -TROPY] —**plei·o·trop·ic** (plī′ə trop′ik, -trō′pik), *adj.* —**plei′o·trop′i·cal·ly,** *adv.*

Pleis·to·cene (plī′stə sēn′), *Geol.* —*adj.* **1.** noting or pertaining to the epoch forming the earlier half of the Quaternary Period, beginning about two million years ago and ending 10,000 years ago, characterized by widespread glacial ice and the advent of modern humans. See table under **geologic time.** —*n.* **2.** the Pleistocene Epoch or Series. [1830–40; < Gk *pleîsto(s)* most (superl. of *polýs* much) + -CENE]

Ple·kha·nov (pli kä′nôf, -nof; *Russ.* plyi ᴋʜä′nəf), *n.* **Ge·or·gi** (or **Ge·or·gy**) **Va·len·ti·no·vich** (gyi ôʀ′gyē və lyin tyē′nə vyich), 1857–1918, Russian philosopher and leader of the Mensheviks.

ple·na·ry (plē′nə rē, plen′ə-), *adj., n., pl.* **-ries.** —*adj.* **1.** full; complete; entire; absolute; unqualified: *plenary powers.* **2.** attended by all qualified members; fully constituted: *a plenary session of Congress.* —*n.* **3.** a plenary session, meeting, or the like. [1375–1425; < LL *plēnārius* (see PLENUM, -ARY); r. late ME *plener* < AF < LL *plēnāris* (see -AR[1])] —**ple′na·ri·ly,** *adv.*

ple′nary indul′gence, *Rom. Cath. Ch.* a remission of the total temporal punishment that is still due to sin after absolution. Cf. **indulgence** (def. 6). [1665–75]

plench (plench), *n.* a tool combining pliers and wrench: used esp. by astronauts. [PL(IERS) + (WR)ENCH]

ple·nip·o·tent (plə nip′ə tənt), *adj.* invested with or possessing full power. [1650–60; < ML *plēnipotent-* (s. of *plēnipotēns*). See PLENUM, -I-, POTENT]

plen·i·po·ten·ti·ar·y (plen′ə pə ten′shē er′ē, -shə rē), *n., pl.* **-ar·ies,** *adj.* —*n.* **1.** a person, esp. a diplomatic agent, invested with full power or authority to transact business on behalf of another. —*adj.* **2.** invested with full power or authority, as a diplomatic agent. **3.** conferring or bestowing full power, as a commission. **4.** absolute or full, as power. [1635–45; < ML *plēnipotentiārius.* See PLENIPOTENT, -I-, -ARY]

plen·ish (plen′ish), *v.t. Chiefly Scot.* to fill up; stock; furnish. [1425–75; late ME *plenyss* < MF *pleniss-,* long s. of *plenir* to fill, ult. < L *plēnus* full. See PLENUM, -ISH[2]] —**plen′ish·er,** *n.* —**plen′ish·ment,** *n.*

plen·i·tude (plen′i to͞od′, -tyo͞od′), *n.* **1.** fullness or adequacy in quantity, measure, or degree; abundance: *a plenitude of food, air, and sunlight.* **2.** state of being full or complete. [1375–1425; late ME < L *plēnitūdō.* See PLENUM, -I-, TUDE]
—**Syn. 1.** profusion, quantity.

plen·i·tu·di·nous (plen′i to͞od′n əs, -tyo͞od′-), *adj.* **1.** characterized or marked by plenitude. **2.** stout or portly. [1805–15; < L *plēnitūdin-* (s. of *plēnitūdō* PLENITUDE) + -OUS]

ple·no ju·re (plā′nō yo͞o′ʀe; *Eng.* plē′nō jo͝or′ē), *Latin.* with full authority.

CONCISE ETYMOLOGY KEY: <, descended or borrowed from; >, whence; b., blend of, blended; c., cognate with; cf., compare; deriv., derivative; equiv., equivalent; imit., imitative; obl., oblique; r., replacing; s., stem; sp., spelling, spelled; resp., respelling, respelled; trans., translation; ?, origin unknown; *, unattested; ‡, probably earlier than. See the full key inside the front cover.

plen·te·ous (plen′tē əs), *adj.* **1.** plentiful; copious; abundant: *a plenteous supply of food.* **2.** yielding abundantly; fruitful: *a plenteous harvest.* [1250–1300; ME *plenteus* (see PLENTY, -OUS); r. ME *plentivous* < OF *plentivos,* equiv. to *plentif* abundant (*plent(e)* PLENTY + *-if* -IVE) + *-os* -OUS] —**plen′te·ous·ly,** *adv.* —**plen′te·ous·ness,** *n.*

plen·ti·ful (plen′ti fəl), *adj.* **1.** existing in great plenty: *Coal was plentiful, and therefore cheap, in that region.* **2.** yielding abundantly: *a plentiful source of inspiration.* [1425–75; late ME; see PLENTY, -FUL] —**plen′ti·ful·ly,** *adv.* —**plen′ti·ful·ness,** *n.*
—**Syn. 1.** PLENTIFUL, AMPLE, ABUNDANT, BOUNTIFUL describe a more than adequate supply of something. PLENTIFUL suggests an over-adequate quantity: *a plentiful supply.* AMPLE suggests a more than adequate quality as well: *to give ample praise.* ABUNDANT implies a greater degree of plenty, and BOUNTIFUL a still more ample quality as well: *an abundant, even a bountiful, harvest.* **2.** fruitful, bounteous, productive; luxuriant. —**Ant. 1.** sparse, scanty. **2.** barren, fruitless, sterile.

plen·ty (plen′tē), *n., pl.* **-ties,** *adj., adv.* —*n.* **1.** a full or abundant supply or amount: *There is plenty of time.* **2.** the state or quality of being plentiful; abundance: *resources in plenty.* **3.** an abundance, as of goods or luxuries, or a time of such abundance: *the plenty of a rich harvest; the plenty that comes with peace.* —*adj.* **4.** existing in ample quantity or number; plentiful; abundant: *Food is never too plenty in the area.* **5.** more than sufficient; ample: *That helping is plenty for me.* —*adv.* **6.** *Informal.* fully; quite: *plenty good enough.* [1175–1225; ME *plente* < OF; r. ME *plenteth* < OF *plented, plentet* < L *plēnitāt-* (s. of *plēnitās*) fullness. See PLENUM, -ITY]
—**Syn. 2.** plenteousness, copiousness, luxuriance, affluence. PLENTY, ABUNDANCE, PROFUSION refer to a large quantity or supply. PLENTY suggests a supply that is fully adequate to any demands: *plenty of money.* ABUNDANCE implies a great plenty, an ample and generous oversupply: *an abundance of rain.* PROFUSION applies to such a lavish and excessive abundance as often suggests extravagance or prodigality: *luxuries in great profusion.*
—**Usage.** The construction PLENTY OF is standard in all varieties of speech and writing: *plenty of room in the shed.* The use of PLENTY preceding a noun, without an intervening OF, first appeared in the late 19th century: *plenty room in the shed.* It occurs today chiefly in informal speech. As an adverb, a use first recorded in the mid-19th century, PLENTY is also informal and is found chiefly in speech or written representations of speech.

ple·num (plē′nəm, plen′əm), *n., pl.* **ple·nums, ple·na** (plē′nə, plen′ə). **1.** the state or a space in which a gas, usually air, is contained at a pressure greater than atmospheric pressure. **2.** a full assembly, as a joint legislative assembly. **3.** a space, usually above a ceiling or below a floor, that can serve as a receiving chamber for air that has been heated or cooled to be distributed to inhabited areas. **4.** the whole of space regarded as being filled with matter (opposed to *vacuum*). [1670–80; < L, neut. of *plēnus* FULL, in the phrase *plēnum* (*spatium*) FULL (space)]

ple′num ventila′tion, a system of mechanical ventilation in which fresh air is forced into the spaces to be ventilated from a chamber (**ple′num cham′ber**) at a pressure slightly higher than atmospheric pressure, so as to expel foul air. [1835–45]

pleo-, a combining form meaning "more," used in the formation of compound words: *pleomorphism.* Also, **pleio-, plio-.** [comb. form repr. Gk *pleíōn* more (comp. of *polýs;* see POLY-); see -O-]

ple·o·chro·ic (plē′ə krō′ik), *adj.* (of a biaxial crystal) characterized by pleochroism. [1860–65; PLEO- + -CHROIC]

ple·och·ro·ism (plē ok′rō iz′əm), *n.* the property of certain crystals of exhibiting different colors when viewed from different directions under transmitted light. Cf. **dichroism** (def. 1), **trichroism.** [1855–60; PLEOCHRO(IC) + -ISM]

ple·o·mor·phic (plē′ə môr′fik), *adj.* of, pertaining to, or characterized by pleomorphism; polymorphous. Also, **ple′o·mor′phous.** [1885–90; PLEOMORPH(ISM) + -IC]

ple·o·mor·phism (plē′ə môr′fiz əm), *n. Biol.* existence of an organism in two or more distinct forms during the life cycle; polymorphism. Also, **ple′o·mor′phy.** [1860–65; PLEO- + -MORPH + -ISM]

ple·on (plē′on), *n.* the abdomen of a crustacean. [1850–55; n. use of Gk *pléōn,* prp. of *pleîn* to swim, sail; see PLEOPOD] —**ple·on·al** (plē′ə nl), **ple·on′ic,** *adj.*

ple·o·nasm (plē′ə naz′əm), *n.* **1.** the use of more words than are necessary to express an idea; redundancy. **2.** an instance of this, as *free gift* or *true fact.* **3.** a redundant word or expression. [1580–90; < LL *pleonasmus* < Gk *pleonasmós* redundancy, surplus, deriv. of *pleonázein* to be or have more than enough, itself deriv. of *pleíōn* more (see PLEO-)] —**ple′o·nas′tic,** *adj.* —**ple′o·nas′ti·cal·ly,** *adv.*

ple·o·pod (plē′ə pod′), *n. Zool.* a swimmeret. [1850–55; PLEO(N) + -POD]

ple·op·tics (plē op′tiks) *n.* (*used with a singular v.*) *Ophthalmol.* the practice of treating the vision defect amblyopia. [< G *Pleoptik* (1953), equiv. to *ple(o)-* PLEO- + *Optik* OPTICS]

ple·ro·cer·coid (plēr′ō sûr′koid), *n. Zool.* the wormlike larval stage of some tapeworms, intermediate between the first parasitic larval stage and adult. Cf. **procercoid.** [1905–10; < Gk *plḗr(ēs)* full + *-o-* + Gk *kérk(os)* tail + -OID]

ple·si·o·saur (plē′sē ə sôr′), *n.* any marine reptile of the extinct genus *Plesiosaurus,* from the Jurassic and Cretaceous periods, having a small head, a long neck, four paddlelike limbs, and a short tail. [< NL *Plesiosaurus* (1821), equiv. to Gk *plēsí(os)* near, close to + *-o-* -O- + *saûros* -SAUR; orig. so named because of its conjectured nearness to modern reptiles, relative to the ichthyosaurs] —**ple′si·o·sau′roid,** *adj.*

ples·sor (ples′ər), *n. Med.* plexor. [< Gk *plḗss(ein)* to strike + -OR²]

pleth·o·ra (pleth′ər ə), *n.* **1.** overabundance; excess: *a plethora of advice and a paucity of assistance.* **2.** *Pathol. Archaic.* a morbid condition due to excess of red corpuscles in the blood or increase in the quantity of blood. [1535–45; < NL < Gk *plēthṓra* fullness]

ple·thor·ic (ple thôr′ik, -thor′-, pleth′ə rik), *adj.* **1.** overfull; turgid; inflated: *a plethoric, pompous speech.* **2.** of, pertaining to, or characterized by plethora. [1610–20; PLETHOR(A) + -IC] —**ple·thor′i·cal·ly,** *adv.*

ple·thys·mo·gram (plə thiz′mə gram′), *n.* the recording of a plethysmograph. [1890–95; see PLETHYSMOGRAPH, -GRAM¹]

ple·thys·mo·graph (plə thiz′mə graf′, -gräf′), *n.* a device for measuring and recording changes in the volume of the body or of a body part or organ. [1870–75; < Gk *plēthysm(ós)* increase, multiplication (*plēthý(nein)* to increase, deriv. of *plêthos* large number, crowd + *-smos,* var. of *-mos* n. suffix) + *-o-* + -GRAPH; first coined in It as *pletismografo*] —**ple·thys·mo·graph·ic** (plə thiz′mə-graf′ik), *adj.* —**pleth·ys·mog·ra·phy** (pleth′iz mog′rə-fē), *n.*

pleur-, var. of **pleuro-** before a vowel: *pleurite.*

pleu·ra (plŏŏr′ə), *n., pl.* **pleu·rae** (plŏŏr′ē) for 1. **1.** *Anat., Zool.* a delicate serous membrane investing each lung in mammals and folded back as a lining of the corresponding side of the thorax. **2.** pl. of **pleuron.** [1655–65; < NL < Gk *pleurá* (sing.) side, rib]

pleu·ral (plŏŏr′əl), *adj.* **1.** *Anat.* of or pertaining to the pleura. **2.** *Entomol.* of or pertaining to a pleuron. [1835–45; PLEUR(A), PLEUR(ON) + -AL¹]

pleu′ral cav′ity, a narrow, fluid-filled space between the pleural membranes of the lung and the inner chest wall. [1835–45]

pleu·ri·sy (plŏŏr′ə sē), *n. Pathol.* inflammation of the pleura, with or without a liquid effusion in the pleural cavity, characterized by a dry cough and pain in the affected side. [1350–1400; ME *pluresy* < OF *pleurisie* < LL *pleurīsis,* alter. of L *pleurītis* < Gk *pleurîtis.* See PLEURA, -ITIS] —**pleu·rit·ic** (plŏŏ rit′ik), *adj.*

pleu′risy root′, **1.** a North American milkweed, *Asclepias tuberosa,* whose root was used as a remedy for pleurisy. **2.** the root. [1775–85, *Amer.*]

pleuro-, a combining form meaning "side," "rib," "lateral," "pleura," used in the formation of compound words: *pleuropneumonia.* Also, *esp. before a vowel,* **pleur-.** [see PLEURA, -O-]

pleu·ro·car·pous (plŏŏr′ə kär′pəs), *adj.* (of certain mosses) bearing the fructifications along the main stem or lateral branches. Also, **pleu′ro·car′pic.** [1860–65; PLEURO- + -CARPOUS]

pleu·ro·dont (plŏŏr′ə dont′), *adj.* **1.** fused or attached to the inner edge of the jaw, as a tooth. **2.** having teeth so fused or attached, as certain lizards. —*n.* **3.** a pleurodont animal. [1830–40; PLEUR- + -ODONT]

pleu·ro·dyn·i·a (plŏŏr′ə din′ē ə), *n. Pathol.* **1.** pain in the chest or side. **2.** Also called **epidemic pleurodynia, devil's grip.** an epidemic disease caused by a coxsackievirus, characterized by sudden chest pain, mild fever, and recurrence on the third day of these symptoms. [1795–1805; < NL; see PLEUR-, -ODYNIA]

pleu·rog·e·nous (plŏŏ roj′ə nəs), *adj.* **1.** *Anat.* pertaining to or originating from the pleura. **2.** *Bot.* occurring on the side of a structure or body. [1890–95; PLEURO- + -GENOUS]

pleu·ron (plŏŏr′on), *n., pl.* **pleu·ra** (plŏŏr′ə). *Entomol.* the lateral plate or plates of a thoracic segment of an insect. [1700–10; < Gk *pleurón* rib, (pl.) side]

pleu·ro·pneu·mo·nia (plŏŏr′ō nŏŏ mōn′yə, -mō′nē ə, -nyŏŏ-), *n. Pathol.* pleurisy conjoined with pneumonia. [1715–25; PLEURO- + PNEUMONIA] —**pleu·ro·pneu·mon·ic** (plŏŏr′ō nŏŏ mon′ik, -nyŏŏ-), *adj.*

pleu′ro·pneu·mo′nia·like or′ganism (plŏŏr′ō-nŏŏ mōn′yə lik′, -mō′nē ə-, -nyŏŏ-, plŏŏr′-), any antibiotic-resistant mycoplasma causing a form of pneumonia in humans. *Abbr.:* PPLO [1930–35]

pleus·ton (plōō′stən, -ston), *n. Biol.* a buoyant mat of weeds, algae, and associated organisms that floats on or near the surface of a lake, river, or other body of fresh water. [1940–45; *pleus-* (< Gk *pleûs(is)* sailing, or *pleusaorist* s. of *pleîn* to sail, go by sea) + *-ton,* on the model of NEKTON, PLANKTON] —**pleus·ton·ic** (plōō ston′ik), *adj.*

Plev·en (plev′en), *n.* a city in N Bulgaria: siege of 143 days 1877. 108,180. Also, **Plev·na** (plev′nä).

plew (plōō), *n. Older Use* (in Western U.S. and Canada) a beaver skin, esp. one of prime quality. Also, **plu.** [1790–1800; < CanF *pelu;* F: n. use of *pelu* haired, hairy (now obs. or dial.); see POILU]

-plex, a combining form meaning "having parts or units" of the number specified by the initial element, occurring originally in loanwords from Latin (*duplex; quadruplex*); recent English coinages ending in *-plex,* esp. denoting structures with a given number of dwelling units, are probably in part new formations with this suffix and in part based on the noun *complex: fourplex; eightplex; Cineplex; Metroplex.* [< L *-plex, -plic-* (akin to *plicāre* to fold, bend, *plectere* to plait, braid; see -FOLD) + *-s* nom. sing. ending]

plex·al (plek′səl), *adj.* of or pertaining to a plexus. [1885–90; PLEX(US) + -AL¹]

plex·i·form (plek′sə fôrm′), *adj.* **1.** of, pertaining to, or resembling a plexus. **2.** intricate; complex. [1820–30; PLEX(US) + -I- + -FORM]

Plex·i·glas (plek′si glas′, -gläs′), *Trademark.* a brand name for a thermoplastic polymer of methyl methacrylate that is light in weight, resistant to weathering, capable of being bent when hot but returning to its original shape when reheated, used for signs, windows, furniture, etc.

plex·im·e·ter (plek sim′i tər), *n. Med.* a small, thin plate, as of ivory, placed against the body to mediate the blow of a plexor. [1835–45; < Gk *plêxi(s)* stroke, percussion + -METER] —**plex·i·met·ric** (plek′sə me′trik), *adj.* —**plex·im′e·try,** *n.*

plex·or (plek′sər), *n. Med.* a small hammer with a soft rubber head or the like, used in percussion for diagnostic purposes. Also, **percussor, plessor.** [1835–45; < Gk *plêx(is)* stroke, percussion + -OR²]

plex·us (plek′səs), *n., pl.* **-us·es, -us.** **1.** a network, as of nerves or blood vessels. **2.** any complex structure containing an intricate network of interrelated parts: *the plexus of international relations.* [1675–85; < NL: an interweaving, twining, equiv. to L *plect(ere)* to plait, twine + *-tus* suffix of v. action; akin to *plicāre* to fold]

plf, pounds per linear foot.

plf., plaintiff. Also, **plff.**

pli, pounds per linear inch.

pli·a·ble (plī′ə bəl), *adj.* **1.** easily bent; flexible; supple: *pliable leather.* **2.** easily influenced or persuaded; yielding: *the pliable mind of youth.* **3.** adjusting readily to change; adaptable. [1425–75; late ME < F, equiv. to *pli(er)* to PLY² + *-able* -ABLE] —**pli′a·bil′i·ty, pli′a·ble·ness,** *n.* —**pli′a·bly,** *adv.*

pli·ant (plī′ənt), *adj.* **1.** bending readily; flexible; supple; adaptable: *She manipulated the pliant clay.* **2.** easily influenced; yielding to others; compliant: *He has a pliant nature.* [1300–50; ME < OF, prp. of *plier* to PLY²; see -ANT] —**pli′an·cy, pli′ant·ness,** *n.* —**pli′ant·ly,** *adv.*
—**Syn. 1, 2.** pliable, flexile. See **flexible. 2.** manageable, tractable, docile.

pli·ca (plī′kə), *n., pl.* **pli·cae** (plī′sē, -kē). **1.** *Zool., Anat.* a fold or folding. **2.** Also called **pli′ca po·lon′i·ca** (pə lon′i kə). *Pathol.* a matted, filthy condition of the hair, caused by disease, vermin, etc. **3.** (in medieval music) a vertical mark attached to a neume, standing for an interpolated melodic ornament. [1675–85; < ML: a fold, back formation from L *plicāre* to fold, PLY²] —**pli′cal,** *adj.*

pli·cate (*adj.* plī′kāt, -kit; *v.* plī′kāt), *adj., v.,* **-cat·ed, -cat·ing.** —*adj.* **1.** Also, **pli′cat·ed.** folded like a fan; pleated. —*v.t.* **2.** *Surg.* to perform plication on. [1690–1700; < L *plicātus,* ptp. of *plicāre* to fold, PLY²; see -ATE¹] —**pli′cate·ly,** *adv.* —**pli′cate·ness,** *n.*

plicate leaf

pli·ca·tion (plī kā′shən, pli-), *n.* **1.** the act or procedure of folding. **2.** the state or quality of being folded; a fold. **3.** *Surg.* **a.** the folding in and suturing of tucks, so as to tighten weakened or stretched tissue. **b.** the folding of an organ, as a section of the intestine, and the attaching of it to another organ or tissue. Also, **plic·a·ture** (plik′ə chər). [1375–1425; late ME *plicacioun* < ML *plicātiōn-* (s. of *plicātiō*) a folding. See PLICATE, -ION]

pli·é (plē ā′), *n., pl.* **pli·és** (plē āz′; *Fr.* plē ā′). *Ballet.* a movement in which the knees are bent while the back is held straight. [1890–95; < F, n. use of ptp. of *plier* to bend; see PLY²]

pli·er (plī′ər), *n.* **1. pliers,** (*sometimes used with a singular v.*) small pincers with long jaws, for bending wire, holding small objects, etc. (usually used with *pair of*). **2.** a person or thing that plies. Also, *esp. Brit.,* **plyer.** [1560–70; PLY² + -ER¹]

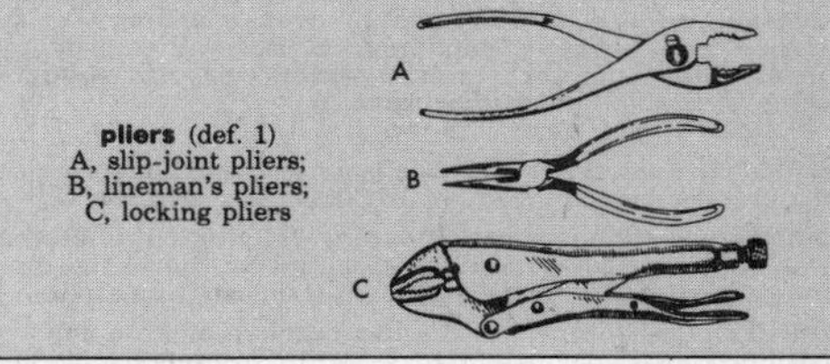

pliers (def. 1)
A, slip-joint pliers;
B, lineman's pliers;
C, locking pliers

plight¹ (plīt), *n.* a condition, state, or situation, esp. an unfavorable or unfortunate one: *to find oneself in a sorry plight.* [1350–1400; ME *plit* fold, condition, bad condition < AF (c. MF *pleit* PLAIT) fold, manner of folding, condition; sp. appar. influenced by PLIGHT² in obs. sense "danger"]
—**Syn.** case. See **predicament.**

plight² (plīt), *v.t.* **1.** to pledge (one's troth) in engagement to marry. **2.** to bind (someone) by a pledge, esp. of marriage. **3.** to give in pledge, as one's word, or to pledge, as one's honor. —*n.* **4.** *Archaic.* pledge. [bef. 1000; (n.) ME; OE *pliht* danger, risk; c. D *plicht,* G *Pflicht* duty, obligation; (v.) ME *plighten,* OE *plihtan* (deriv. of the n.) to endanger, risk, pledge; c. OHG *phlihten* to engage oneself, MD *plihten* to guarantee] —**plight′er,** *n.*

plim·soll (plim′səl, -sōl), *n. Brit.* a canvas shoe with a rubber sole; gym shoe; sneaker. Also, **plim′sol, plim′·sole.** [1905–10; perh. so called from fancied resemblance of the sole to a *Plimsoll* mark]

Plim′soll line′ (plim′səl, -sōl), *Naut.* See **load line** (def. 1). [1890–95; see PLIMSOLL MARK]

Plim′soll mark′, *Naut.* See **load-line mark.** Also called **Plim′soll.** [1880–85; named after Samuel *Plimsoll* (1824–98), English member of Parliament who brought about its adoption]

plink (plingk), *v.i.* **1.** to shoot, as with a rifle, at targets selected at whim: *to plink at coins tossed in the air.* **2.** to make a series of short, light, ringing sounds. —*v.t.* **3.** to shoot at for practice or amusement, as with a rifle: *to plink bottles set along a fence railing.* **4.** to cause to make a series of short, light, ringing sounds. —*n.* **5.** a plinking sound. [1965–70; imit.] —**plink′er,** *n.*

plinth (plinth), *n. Archit.* **1.** a slablike member beneath the base of a column or pier. See diag. under **column.** **2.** a square base or a lower block, as of a pedestal. **3.** Also called **plinth′ course′.** a projecting course of stones at the base of a wall; earth table. **4.** (in joinery) a flat member at the bottom of an architrave, dado, baseboard, or the like. [1555–65; earlier *plinthus* < L < Gk *plínthos* plinth, squared stone, brick, tile] —**plinth′less,** *adj.* —**plinth′like′,** *adj.*

plinth′ block′, a plinth interrupting a door or window architrave at the floor or ground level. [1890–95]

Plin·y (plin′ē), *n.* **1.** (*"the Elder," Gaius Plinius Secundus*) A.D. 23–79, Roman naturalist, encyclopedist, and writer. **2.** his nephew (*"the Younger," Gaius Plinius Caecilius Secundus*) A.D. 62?–c113, Roman writer, statesman, and orator. —**Plin′i·an,** *adj.*

plio-, var. of **pleo-.**

Pli·o·cene (plī′ə sēn′), *Geol.* —*adj.* **1.** noting or pertaining to an epoch of the Tertiary Period, occurring from 10 to 2 million years ago, and characterized by increased size and numbers of mammals, by the growth of mountains, and by global climatic cooling. See table under **geologic time.** —*n.* **2.** the Pliocene Epoch or Series. [1825–35; PLIO- + -CENE]

Pli·o·film (plī′ə film′), *Trademark.* a brand of resinlike rubber hydrochloride that forms a clear, flexible, water-resistant, heat-sealable plastic, used for packaging, raincoats, etc.

pli·o·tron (plī′ə tron′), *n. Electronics.* any hot-cathode vacuum tube having an anode and one or more grids. [1910–15; formerly a trademark]

plique-à-jour (plēk′ä zhŏŏr′; *Fr.* plē KA zhōōR′), *Fine Arts.* an enameling technique in which unbacked wirework is filled with transparent enamel, resulting in a stained-glass effect. [1875–80; < F: lit., braid that lets in the daylight]

Pli·set·ska·ya (pli set′skä yə; *Russ.* plyi syet′skə yə), *n.* **Ma·ya (Mi·khai·lov·na)** (mä′yə myi KHĪ′ləv nə), born 1925, Soviet ballet dancer.

plis·ky (plis′kē), *n., pl.* **-kies,** *adj. Scot. and North Eng.* —*n.* **1.** a mischievous trick; practical joke; prank. —*adj.* **2.** mischievous; playful. Also, **plis′kie.** [1780–90; orig. uncert.]

plis·sé (plē sā′, pli-), *n.* **1.** a textile finish characterized by a puckered or blistered effect, produced by chemical treatment. **2.** a usually lightweight fabric having this finish. Also, **plis·se′.** [1870–75; < F *plissé,* n. use of ptp. of *plisser* to pleat; see PLY[2]]

PLO, See **Palestine Liberation Organization.**

plo·ce (plō′sē), *n. Rhet.* the repetition of a word or phrase to gain special emphasis or to indicate an extension of meaning, as in Ex. 3:14: "I am that I am." [1580–90; earlier *ploche* < LL *plocē* < Gk *plokḗ* plaiting, akin to *plékein* to plait]

plod (plod), *v.,* **plod·ded, plod·ding,** *n.* —*v.i.* **1.** to walk heavily or move laboriously; trudge: *to plod under the weight of a burden.* **2.** to proceed in a tediously slow manner: *The play just plodded along in the second act.* **3.** to work with constant and monotonous perseverance; drudge. —*v.t.* **4.** to walk heavily over or along. —*n.* **5.** the act or a course of plodding. **6.** a sound of a heavy tread. [1555–65; perh. imit.] —**plod′der,** *n.* —**plod′·ding·ly,** *adv.* —**plod′ding·ness,** *n.*
—**Syn. 1.** See **pace**[1]. **3.** toil, moil, labor.

Plo·eș·ti (plô yesht′), *n.* a city in S Rumania: center of a rich oil-producing region. 207,009. Also, **Plo·ieș′ti.**

-ploid, a combining form meaning "having chromosome sets" of the kind or number specified by the initial element: *hexaploid.* [extracted from HAPLOID, DIPLOID, etc.]

ploi·dy (ploi′dē), *n. Biol.* the number of homologous chromosome sets present in a cell or organism. [1935–40; see -PLOID, -Y[3]]

plomb (plum), *n. Surg.* any inert material inserted into a body cavity for therapeutic purposes. [1900–05; var. of PLUMB]

plonk (plongk), *n. Chiefly Brit.* inferior or cheap wine. [1925–30; perh. alter. of F (*vin*) *blanc* white (wine)]

plop (plop), *v.,* **plopped, plop·ping,** *n., adv.* —*v.i.* **1.** to make a sound like that of something falling or dropping into water: *A frog plopped into the pond.* **2.** to fall with such a sound: *Big raindrops plopped against the window.* **3.** to drop or fall with full force or direct impact: *He plopped into a chair.* —*v.t.* **4.** to drop or set down heavily: *She plopped her books on the desk.* **5.** to cause to plop: *The fisherman plopped the bait into the river.* —*n.* **6.** a plopping sound or fall. **7.** the act of plopping. —*adv.* **8.** with a plop: *The stone fell plop into the water.* [1815–25; imit.]

plo·sion (plō′zhən), *n. Phonet.* the forced release of the occlusive phase of a plosive, whether voiceless or unvoiced, either audible due to frication or inaudible due to a contiguous following consonant. Also called **explosion.** Cf. **implosion** (def. 2). [1915–20; shortened form of EXPLOSION]

plo·sive (plō′siv), *Phonet.* —*adj.* **1.** (of a stop consonant or occlusive) characterized by release in a plosion; explosive. —*n.* **2.** Also called **explosive.** a plosive speech sound. [1895–1900; shortened form of EXPLOSIVE]

plot (plot), *n., v.,* **plot·ted, plot·ting.** —*n.* **1.** a secret plan or scheme to accomplish some purpose, esp. a hostile, unlawful, or evil purpose: *a plot to overthrow the government.* **2.** Also called **storyline.** the plan, scheme, or main story of a literary or dramatic work, as a play, novel, or short story. **3.** a small piece or area of ground: *a garden plot; burial plot.* **4.** a measured piece or parcel of land: *a house on a two-acre plot.* **5.** a plan, map, diagram, or other graphic representation, as of land, a building, etc. **6.** a list, timetable, or scheme dealing with any of the various arrangements for the production of a play, motion picture, etc.: *According to the property plot, there should be a lamp stage left.* **7.** a chart showing the course of a craft, as a ship or airplane. **8.** *Artillery.* a point or points located on a map or chart: *target plot.* —*v.t.* **9.** to plan secretly, esp. something hostile or evil: *to plot mutiny.* **10.** to mark on a plan, map, or chart, as the course of a ship or aircraft. **11.** to draw a plan or map of, as a tract of land or a building. **12.** to divide (land) into plots. **13.** to determine and mark (points), as on plotting paper, by means of measurements or coordinates. **14.** to draw (a curve) by means of points so marked. **15.** to represent by means of such a curve. **16.** to devise or construct the plot of (a play, novel, etc.). **17.** to prepare a list, timetable, or scheme of (production arrangements), as for a play or motion picture: *The stage manager hadn't plotted the set changes until one day before the dress rehearsal.* **18.** to make (a calculation) by graph. —*v.i.* **19.** to plan or scheme secretly; form a plot; conspire. **20.** to devise or develop a literary or dramatic plot. **21.** to be marked or located by means of measurements or coordinates, as on plotting paper. [bef. 1100; (n.) of multiple orig.: in sense "piece of ground," ME: small area, patch, stain, piece of ground, OE: piece of ground (orig. obscure); in senses "ground plan, outline, map, scheme," var. (since the 16th century) of PLAT[1], itself partly a var. of ME, OE *plot;* sense "secret plan" (from 16th century) by assoc. with COMPLOT, in pejorative sense; (v.) deriv. of the n.] —**plot′ful,** *adj.* —**plot′·less,** *adj.* —**plot′less·ness,** *n.*
—**Syn. 1.** intrigue, cabal. See **conspiracy. 9.** brew, hatch, frame. **19.** PLOT, CONSPIRE, SCHEME imply secret, cunning, and often unscrupulous planning to gain one's own ends. To PLOT is to contrive a secret plan of a selfish and often treasonable kind: *to plot against someone's life.* To CONSPIRE is to unite with others in an illicit or illegal machination: *to conspire to seize a government.* To SCHEME is to plan ingeniously, subtly, and often craftily for one's own advantage: *to scheme how to gain power.*

Plo·tin·i·an (plō tin′ē ən), *adj.* of, pertaining to, or in accordance with Plotinus or his philosophy. [1785–95; PLOTIN(US) + -IAN]

Plo·ti·nism (plō tī′niz əm, plōt′n iz′-), *n.* the Neoplatonism of Plotinus. [PLOTIN(US) + -ISM] —**Plo·ti′nist,** *n., adj.*

Plo·ti·nus (plō tī′nəs), *n.* A.D. 205?–270?, Roman philosopher, born in Egypt.

plot′ line′, Usually, **plot lines.** dialogue that advances the plot, as in a play or motion-picture script. [1955–60]

plot·tage (plot′ij), *n.* the area within or comprising a plot of land. [1935–40; PLOT + -AGE]

plot·ter (plot′ər), *n.* **1.** a person or thing that plots. **2.** an instrument, as a protractor, for plotting lines and measuring angles on a chart. **3.** *Computers.* an output device that produces a graphical representation by drawing on paper, as with one or more attached pens. [1580–90; PLOT + -ER[1]]

Plott′ hound′ (plot), an American hound having a brindled coat, used esp. in hunting bears and wild boars. [prob. named after J. *Plott,* 18th-century American who bred dogs]

plot′ting board′, **1.** *Navig.* a transparent table on a ship, used as a plotting sheet. **2.** *Mil.* a device based on a map or other scale representation of a region against which artillery fire is to be directed, for use in directing artillery fire against a fixed or moving target. [1900–05]

plot′ting sheet′, *Navig.* a blank chart having only a compass rose and latitude lines, longitude lines, or both, marked and annotated, as required, by a navigator. [1925–30]

plot·ty (plot′ē), *adj.,* **-ti·er, -ti·est.** characterized by the intricacies or complications of a plot or intrigue: *a plotty novel whose narrative is hard to follow.* [1895–1900; PLOT + -Y[1]] —**plot′ti·ness,** *n.*

plotz (plots), *v.i. Slang.* to collapse or faint, as from surprise, excitement, or exhaustion. [1940–45, *Amer.;* < Yiddish *platsn* lit., to crack, split, burst < MHG *blatzen, platzen*]

plotzed (plotst), *adj. Slang.* **1.** drunk; intoxicated. **2.** exhausted; worn out. [1960–65, *Amer.;* PLOTZ + -ED[2]]

plough (plou), *n., v.t., v.i. Chiefly Brit.* plow.

plough′man's lunch′, *Brit.* a light lunch consisting of bread and cheese, and sometimes pickled onions.

Plov·div (plôv′dif), *n.* a city in S Bulgaria, on the Maritsa River. 309,242. Greek, **Philippopolis.**

plov·er (pluv′ər, plō′vər), *n.* **1.** any of various shorebirds of the family Charadriidae. Cf. **dotterel** (def. 1), **killdeer, lapwing. 2.** any of various similar shorebirds, as the upland plover and other sandpipers. [1275–1325; ME < AF; OF *plovier* rainbird < VL **pluviārius.* See PLUVIAL, -ER[2]]

plow (plou), *n.* **1.** an agricultural implement used for cutting, lifting, turning over, and partly pulverizing soil. **2.** any of various implements resembling or suggesting this, as a kind of plane for cutting grooves or a contrivance for clearing away snow from a road or track. **3.** *Type Founding.* (formerly) an instrument for cutting the groove in the foot of type. **4.** *Bookbinding.* a device for trimming the edges of the leaves by hand. **5.** (*cap.*) *Astron.* **a.** the constellation Ursa Major. **b.** the Big Dipper. —*v.t.* **6.** to turn up (soil) with a plow. **7.** to make (a furrow) with a plow. **8.** to tear up, cut into, or make a furrow, groove, etc. in (a surface) with or as if with a plow (often fol. by *up*): *The tractor plowed up an acre of trees.* **9.** to clear by the use of a plow, esp. a snowplow (sometimes fol. by *out*): *The city's work crews were busily plowing the streets after the blizzard.* **10.** to invest, as capital (often fol. by *into*): *to plow several hundred million into developing new oil fields.* **11.** to reinvest or reutilize (usually fol. by *back*): *to plow profits back into new plants and equipment.* **12.** (of a ship, boat, animal, etc.) **a.** to cleave the surface of (the water): *beavers plowing the pond.* **b.** to make (a way) or follow (a course) in this manner: *The yacht plowed an easterly course through the choppy Atlantic.* **13.** *Slang* (*vulgar*). to have sexual intercourse with. —*v.i.* **14.** to till the soil or work with a plow. **15.** to take plowing in a specified way: *land that plows easily.* **16.** to move forcefully through something in the manner of a plow (often fol. by *through, into, along,* etc.): *The cop plowed through the crowd, chasing after the thief. The car plowed into our house.* **17.** to proceed in a slow, laborious, and steady manner (often fol. by *through*): *The researcher plowed through a pile of reports.* **18.** to move through water by cleaving the surface: *a ship plowing through a turbulent sea.* **19. plow under, a.** to bury under soil by plowing. **b.** to cause to disappear; force out of existence; overwhelm: *Many mom-and-pop groceries have been plowed under by the big chain stores.* Also, *esp. Brit.,* **plough.** [bef. 1100; ME *plouh, plugh(e), plough(e),* OE *plōh;* c. G *Pflug* plow] —**plow′a·ble,** *adj.* —**plow′a·bil′i·ty,** *n.* —**plow′er,** *n.*

plow·back (plou′bak′), *n.* **1.** a reinvestment of earnings or profits in a business enterprise. **2.** the money thus reinvested. [1945–50; n. use of v. phrase *plow back*]

plow·boy (plou′boi′), *n.* **1.** a boy who leads or guides a team drawing a plow. **2.** a country boy. [1560–70; PLOW + BOY]

plow·man (plou′mən), *n., pl.* **-men. 1.** a man who plows. **2.** a farm laborer or a rustic. [1225–75; ME; see PLOW, -MAN] —**plow′man·ship′,** *n.*

plow·share (plou′shâr′), *n.* the cutting part of the moldboard of a plow; share. [1350–1400; ME *ploughschare.* See PLOW, SHARE[2]]

plow′ steel′, steel that contains 0.5 to 0.95 percent carbon. [perh. from the quality of the strong wire rope made from it, used to attach a plow to a steam engine]

plow′ wind′ (wind), *Informal.* a wind squall with a narrow, straight path of advance.

ploy (ploi), *n.* **1.** a maneuver or stratagem, as in conversation, to gain the advantage. —*v.t.* **2.** *Mil. Archaic.* to move (troops) from a line into a column. Cf. **deploy.** —*v.i.* **3.** *Mil. Archaic.* to move from a line into a column. [1475–85; earlier *ploye* to bend < MF *ployer* (F *plier*) < L *plicāre* to fold, PLY[2]; see DEPLOY]
—**Syn. 1.** tactic, ruse, subterfuge, wile, gambit.

PLR, Public Lending Right.

PLSS, portable life support system.

plu (plōō), *n.* plew.

plu., plural.

pluck (pluk), *v.t.* **1.** to pull off or out from the place of growth, as fruit, flowers, feathers, etc.: *to pluck feathers from a chicken.* **2.** to give a pull at; grasp: *to pluck someone's sleeve.* **3.** to pull with sudden force or with a jerk. **4.** to pull or move by force (often fol. by *away, off,* or *out*). **5.** to remove the feathers, hair, etc., from by pulling: *to pluck a chicken.* **6.** *Slang.* to rob, plunder, or fleece. **7.** to sound (the strings of a musical instrument) by pulling at them with the fingers or a plectrum. —*v.i.* **8.** to pull or tug sharply (often fol. by *at*). **9.** to snatch (often fol. by *at*). **10. pluck up, a.** to eradicate; uproot. **b.** to summon up one's courage; rouse one's spirits: *He always plucked up at the approach of danger. She was a stranger in the town, but, plucking up her courage, she soon made friends.* —*n.* **11.** act of plucking; a tug. **12.** the heart, liver, and lungs, esp. of an animal used for food. **13.** courage or resolution in the face of difficulties. [bef. 1000; ME *plukken* (v.), OE *pluccian,* c. MLG *plucken;* akin to D *plukken,* G *pflücken*] —**pluck′er,** *n.*
—**Syn. 2.** tug. **3.** yank, tear, rip. **13.** bravery, boldness, determination, mettle, nerve.

pluck·y (pluk′ē), *adj.,* **pluck·i·er, pluck·i·est.** having or showing pluck or courage; brave: *The drowning swimmer was rescued by a plucky schoolboy.* [1820–30; PLUCK + -Y[1]] —**pluck′i·ly,** *adv.* —**pluck′i·ness,** *n.*
—**Syn.** courageous, determined; cheerful; spunky, spirited.

plug (plug), *n., v.,* **plugged, plug·ging.** —*n.* **1.** a piece of wood or other material used to stop up a hole or aperture, to fill a gap, or to act as a wedge. **2.** a core or interior segment taken from a larger matrix. **3.** *Elect.* a device to which may be attached the conductors of a cord and which by insertion in a jack, or screwing into a receptacle, establishes contact. **4.** See **spark plug** (def. 1). **5.** a fireplug or hydrant. **6.** a cake of pressed tobacco. **7.** a piece of tobacco cut off for chewing. **8.** *Informal.* the favorable mention of something, as in a lecture, radio show, etc.; advertisement; recommendation: *The actress was happy to give her new show a plug.* **9.** *Angling.* an artificial lure made of wood, plastic, or metal, and fitted with one or more gang hooks, used chiefly in casting. **10.** *Geol.* neck (def. 14). **11.** *Slang.* a worn-out or inferior horse. **12.** *Informal.* a shopworn or unsalable article. **13.** a small piece of sod used esp. for seeding a lawn. **14.** a patch of scalp with viable hair follicles that is used as a graft for a bald part of the head. Cf. **hair transplant. 15.** *Slang.* punch[1] (def. 1). **16.** *Metalworking.* **a.** a mandrel on which tubes are formed. **b.** a punch on which a cup is drawn. **c.** a protrusion on a forging die for forming a recess in the work. **d.** a false bottom on a die. **17.** Also called **dook.** a small piece of wood inserted into masonry as a hold for a nail. **18.** *Masonry.* See under **plug and feathers. 19.** Also called

CONCISE ETYMOLOGY KEY: <, descended or borrowed from; >, whence; b., blend of, blended; c., cognate with; cf., compare; deriv., derivative; equiv., equivalent; imit., imitative; obl., oblique; r., replacing; s., stem; sp., spelling, spelled; resp., respelling, respelled; trans., translation; ?, origin unknown; *, unattested; ‡, probably earlier than. See the full key inside the front cover.

plug hat. a man's tall silk hat. **20. pull the plug on,** *Informal.* **a.** to discontinue or terminate: *The government has threatened to pull the plug on further subsidies.* **b.** to disconnect life-sustaining equipment from (a moribund patient). —*v.t.* **21.** to stop or fill with or as if with a plug (often fol. by *up*): *to plug up a leak; plug a gap.* **22.** to insert or drive a plug into. **23.** to secure with or as if with a plug. **24.** to insert (something) as a plug. **25.** to remove a core or a small plug-shaped piece from. **26.** to remove the center of (a coin) and replace it with a baser metal: *a plugged nickel.* **27.** *Informal.* to mention (something) favorably, as in a lecture, radio show, etc.: *He says he will appear if he can plug his new TV series.* **28.** *Slang.* to punch with the fist. **29.** *Slang.* to shoot or strike with a bullet. —*v.i.* **30.** to work with stubborn persistence (often fol. by *along* or *away*): *You're doing a fine job—just keep plugging. Some writers will plug away at the same novel for several years.* **31.** *Informal.* to publicize insistently: *Whenever he gets the chance, he's plugging for his company.* **32.** *Slang.* to shoot or fire shots. **33. plug in, a.** to connect to an electrical power source: *Plug the TV set in over there.* **b.** *Informal.* to add or include; incorporate: *They still have to plug in more research data.* **34. plug into, a.** to connect or become connected by or as if by means of a plug: *The device will plug into any convenient wall outlet. The proposed new departments would eventually plug into the overall organizational plan.* **b.** *Informal.* to feel an affinity for; like; understand: *Some kids just don't plug into sports in school.* **35. plug up,** to become plugged: *The drain in the sink plugs up every so often.* [1620–30; < D; c. G *Pflock*] —**plug′ga·ble,** *adj.* —**plug′ging·ly,** *adv.* —**plug′less,** *adj.* —**plug′like′,** *adj.*

plug′ and feath′ers, an apparatus for splitting stone, consisting of two tapered bars **(feathers),** inserted into a hole drilled into the stone, between which a narrow wedge **(plug)** is hammered to spread them. [1835–45]

plug·board (plug′bôrd′, -bōrd′), *n.* **1.** *Elect.* an electric switchboard with plugs for telephones and the like. **2.** Also called **control panel.** *Computers.* a removable panel containing manually wired electrical terminals into which plugs or pins are inserted: formerly used to control operation of peripheral equipment, as a keyboard. [1885–90; PLUG + BOARD]

plug′ cast′ing, *Angling.* bait casting in which a plug is used as the lure.

plug-com·pat·i·ble (plug′kəm pat′ə bəl), *adj. Computers.* of or relating to computers or peripheral devices that are functionally equivalent to, and may be substituted for, other models.

plugged-in (plugd′in′), *adj. Informal.* closely connected; in touch with what is going on; informed; involved: *He's one of the more plugged-in advisers at State House.* [1955–60, for literal sense]

plug·ger (plug′ər), *n.* **1.** a person or thing that plugs. **2.** any of various machines or tools that insert, remove, or manipulate plugs or pluglike materials, as a dental instrument used to pack and mold the filling in a tooth cavity.

plug′ hat′, plug (def. 19).

plug-in (plug′in′), *adj.* **1.** capable of or designed for being connected to an electrical power source by plugging in or inserting: *a plug-in hair dryer; a plug-in transistor.* —*n.* **2.** plug (def. 3). **3.** jack[1] (def. 3). **4.** a plug-in appliance. [1920–25; adj., n. use of v. phrase *plug in*]

plug·o·la (plu gō′lə), *n. Slang.* **1.** payment or favor given to people in media or motion pictures for favorable mention or display of a particular product or brand name. **2.** promotional mention or praise of someone or something on radio or television. [1955–60; PLUG + -OLA]

plug·ug·ly (plug′ug′lē), *n., pl.* **-lies.** *Informal.* a ruffian; rowdy; tough. [1855–60, *Amer.*; PLUG + UGLY]

plum[1] (plum), *n., adj.,* **plum·mer, plum·mest.** —*n.* **1.** the drupaceous fruit of any of several trees belonging to the genus *Prunus,* of the rose family, having an oblong stone. **2.** the tree itself. **3.** any of various other trees bearing a plumlike fruit. **4.** the fruit itself. **5.** a sugarplum. **6.** a raisin, as in a cake or pudding. **7.** a deep purple varying from bluish to reddish. **8.** *Informal.* an excellent or desirable thing, as a fine position: *The choicest plums went to his old cronies.* **9.** *Informal.* an unanticipated large increase in money or property, as an unexpected legacy; a windfall: *The company offered bonuses and other plums.* **10.** Also called **displacer.** a large stone used in massive concrete construction. —*adj.* **11.** extremely desirable, rewarding, profitable, or the like: *a plum job in the foreign service.* [bef. 900; ME; OE *plūme* (c. G *Pflaume*) << Gk *proûmnon* plum, *proúmnē* plum tree; cf. PRUNE[1]] —**plum′like′,** *adj.*

plum[2] (plum), *adj., adv.* plumb (defs. 3–7).

Plum (plum), *n.* a city in SW Pennsylvania. 25,390.

plum·age (plo͞o′mij), *n.* **1.** the entire feathery covering of a bird. **2.** feathers collectively. [1375–1425; late ME < MF. See PLUME, -AGE] —**plum′aged,** *adj.*

plu·mate (plo͞o′māt, -mit), *adj. Zool.* resembling a feather, as a hair or bristle that bears smaller hairs. [1820–30; < L *plūmātus* feathered. See PLUME, -ATE[1]]

plumb (plum), *n.* **1.** a small mass of lead or other heavy material, as that suspended by a line and used to measure the depth of water or to ascertain a vertical line. Cf. **plumb line. 2. out of** or **off plumb,** not corresponding to the perpendicular; out of true. —*adj.* **3.** true according to a plumb line; perpendicular. **4.** *Informal.* downright or absolute. —*adv.* **5.** in a perpendicular or vertical direction. **6.** exactly, precisely, or directly. **7.** *Informal.* completely or absolutely: *She was plumb mad. You're plumb right.* —*v.t.* **8.** to test or adjust by a plumb line. **9.** to make vertical. **10.** *Shipbuilding.* horn (def. 35). **11.** to sound with or as with a plumb line. **12.** to measure (depth) by sounding. **13.** to examine closely in order to discover or understand: *to plumb someone's thoughts.* **14.** to seal with lead. **15.** to weight with lead. **16.** to provide (a house, building, apartment, etc.) with plumbing. —*v.i.* **17.** to work as a plumber. Also, **plum** (for defs. 3–7). [1250–1300; ME *plumbe,* prob. < AF **plombe* < VL **plumba,* for L *plumbum* lead] —**plumb′a·ble,** *adj.* —**plumb′less,** *adj.* —**plumb′ness,** *n.*
—**Syn. 3.** vertical, straight, square.

Plumb (plum), *n.* **J(ohn) H(arold),** born 1911, British historian.

plum·bag·i·na·ceous (plum baj′ə nā′shəs), *adj.* belonging to the Plumbaginaceae, the leadwort family of plants. Cf. **leadwort family.** [< NL *Plumbaginace(ae)* the family (*Plumbagin-,* s. of *Plumbago* genus of leadworts (see PLUMBAGO) + *-aceae* -ACEAE) + -OUS]

plum·bag·i·nous (plum baj′ə nəs), *adj.* containing graphite. [1790–1800; < L *plumbāgin-* (s. of *plumbāgō*) PLUMBAGO + -OUS]

plum·ba·go (plum bā′gō), *n., pl.* **-gos. 1.** graphite. **2.** a drawing made by an instrument with a lead point. [1595–1605; < L *plumbāgō,* trans. of Gk *molýbdaina* lead ore, deriv. of *mólybdos* lead]

plumb′ bob′, plummet (def. 1). [1825–35]

plum·be·ous (plum′bē əs), *adj.* resembling or containing lead; leaden. [1570–80; < L *plumbeus,* equiv. to *plumb(um)* lead + *-eus* -EOUS]

plumb·er (plum′ər), *n.* **1.** a person who installs and repairs piping, fixtures, appliances, and appurtenances in connection with the water supply, drainage systems, etc., both in and out of buildings. **2.** *Slang.* an undercover operative or spy hired to detect or stop leaks of news or secret information, often using questionable or illegal methods, as illegal entry or wiretapping. **3.** *Obs.* a worker in lead or similar metals. [1375–1425; 1965–70 for def. 2; late ME, sp. var. of ME *plowber* << LL *plumbārius* leadworker; r. ME *plummer* < AF; OF *plummier* < L, as above. See PLUMB, -ER[2]]

plumb′er's help′er, plunger (def. 3). Also called **plumb′er's friend′.** [1950–55, *Amer.*]

plumb′er's snake′, snake (def. 3a). [1935–40]

plumb·er·y (plum′ə rē), *n., pl.* **-er·ies. 1.** a plumber's workshop. **2.** the work or trade of a plumber. [1400–50; late ME < OF *plommerie.* See PLUMBER, -RY]

plum·bic (plum′bik), *adj. Chem.* containing lead, esp. in the tetravalent state. [1790–1800; < L *plumb(um)* lead + -IC]

plum·bif·er·ous (plum bif′ər əs), *adj.* yielding or containing lead. [1790–1800; < L *plumb(um)* lead + -I- + -FEROUS]

plumb·ing (plum′ing), *n.* **1.** the system of pipes and other apparatus for conveying water, liquid wastes, etc., as in a building. **2.** the work or trade of a plumber. **3.** act of a person who plumbs, as in ascertaining depth. [1660–70; PLUMB + -ING[1]]

plum·bism (plum′biz əm), *n. Pathol.* See **lead poisoning** (def. 1b). [1875–80; < L *plumb(um)* lead + -ISM]

plumb′ joint′, (in sheet metal work) a soldered lap joint. [1870–75]

plumb′ line′, 1. a cord with a lead bob attached to one end, used to determine perpendicularity, the depth of water, etc. Cf. **plumb** (def. 1). **2.** See **plumb rule.** [1530–40]

plum·bous (plum′bəs), *adj. Chem.* containing bivalent lead. [1675–85; < L *plumbōsus.* See PLUMB, -OUS]

plum′bous ox′ide, *Chem.* litharge. [1880–85]

plumb′ rule′, a device for determining perpendicularity, consisting of a narrow board with a plumb line and bob suspended from an upper edge. [1350–1400; ME *plomreule*]

plum·bum (plum′bəm), *n. Chem.* lead. [1910–15; < L]

plum·cot (plum′kot), *n.* **1.** a hybrid tree produced by crossing the apricot and the plum. **2.** the fruit of this tree. [PLUM[1] + (APRI)COT]

plum′ curcu′lio. See under **curculio.** [1885–90]

plum′ duff′, a duff containing raisins. [1830–40]

plume (plo͞om), *n., v.,* **plumed, plum·ing.** —*n.* **1.** a feather. **2.** a large, long, or conspicuous feather: *the brilliant plume of a peacock.* **3.** a soft, fluffy feather: *the plume of an egret.* **4.** any plumose part or formation. **5.** a feather, a tuft of feathers, or some substitute, worn as an ornament, as on a hat, helmet, etc. **6.** a feather or featherlike token of honor or distinction, esp. one worn on a helmet. **7.** plumage. **8.** a vertically or longitudinally moving, rising, or expanding fluid body, as of smoke or water. **9.** a visible pattern of smoke resulting from emissions from a stack, flue, or chimney. **10.** Also called **mantle plume.** *Geol.* a deep-seated upwelling of magma within the earth's mantle. Cf. **diapir.** —*v.t.* **11.** to furnish, cover, or adorn with plumes or feathers. **12.** (of a bird) to preen (itself or its feathers). **13.** to feel complacent satisfaction with (oneself); pride (oneself) (often fol. by *on* or *upon*): *She sat before the mirror, pluming herself upon her beauty.* [1350–1400; earlier *plome, plume,* ME *plume* < MF < L *plūma* soft feather (> OE *plūm-,* in *plūmfether* downy feather)] —**plume′less,** *adj.* —**plume′like′,** *adj.*

plumed (plo͞omd), *adj.* having or appearing to have a plume or plumes. [1520–30; PLUME + -ED[3]]

plume·let (plo͞om′lit), *n.* a small plume. [1810–20; PLUME + -LET]

plum·met (plum′it), *n.* **1.** Also called **plumb bob.** a piece of lead or some other weight attached to a line, used for determining perpendicularity, for sounding, etc.; the bob of a plumb line. **2.** something that weighs down or depresses. —*v.i.* **3.** to plunge. [1350–1400; (n.) ME *plommet* < MF, dim. of *plomb* lead; (v.) deriv. of the n. See PLUMB, -ET]
—**Syn. 3.** fall, dive, drop, swoop.

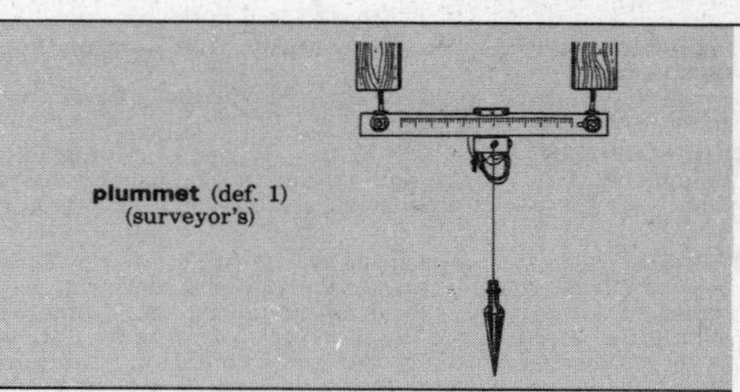
plummet (def. 1)
(surveyor's)

plum·my (plum′ē), *adj.,* **-mi·er, -mi·est. 1.** containing or resembling plums. **2.** good or desirable: *a plummy part for a good actress.* **3.** richly or mellowly resonant: *a plummy speaking voice.* [1750–60; PLUM[1] + -Y[1]]

plu·mose (plo͞o′mōs), *adj.* **1.** having feathers or plumes; feathered. **2.** feathery or plumelike. [1720–30; < L *plūmōsus.* See PLUME, -OSE[1]] —**plu′mose·ly,** *adv.* —**plu·mos·i·ty** (plo͞o mos′i tē), **plu′mose·ness,** *n.*

plump[1] (plump), *adj.,* **-er, -est,** *v.* —*adj.* **1.** well filled out or rounded in form; somewhat fleshy or fat. —*v.i.* **2.** to become plump (often fol. by *up* or *out*). —*v.t.* **3.** to make plump (often fol. by *up* or *out*): *to plump up the sofa pillows.* [1475–85; earlier *plompe* dull, rude < MD *plomp* blunt, not pointed; c. MLG *plump*] —**plump′ly,** *adv.* —**plump′ness,** *n.*
—**Syn. 1.** portly, round. See **stout. 2, 3.** fatten.
—**Ant. 1.** thin.

plump[2] (plump), *v.i.* **1.** to drop or fall heavily or suddenly; come down abruptly or with direct impact. **2.** *Chiefly Brit.* to vote exclusively for one candidate in an election, instead of distributing or splitting one's votes among a number. —*v.t.* **3.** to drop or throw heavily or suddenly (often fol. by *down*): *He plumped himself down and fell asleep.* **4.** to utter or say bluntly (often fol. by *out*): *She plumps out the truth at the oddest times.* **5.** to praise or extol: *road signs plumping the delights of a new candy bar.* **6. plump for,** to support enthusiastically; be wholeheartedly in favor of: *to plump for a team.* —*n.* **7.** a heavy or sudden fall. **8.** the sound resulting from such a fall. —*adv.* **9.** with a heavy or sudden fall or drop. **10.** directly or bluntly, as in speaking. **11.** in a vertical direction; straight down. **12.** with sudden encounter. **13.** with direct impact. —*adj.* **14.** direct; downright; blunt. [1300–50; ME *plumpen* (v.), c. D *plompen;* prob. imit.]

plump[3] (plump), *n. Chiefly Brit. Dial.* **1.** a group or cluster. **2.** a flock: *a plump of ducks.* [1375–1425; late ME *plumpe* < ?]

plump·en (plum′pən), *v.t., v.i.* to make or become plump. [1680–90; PLUMP[1] + -EN[1]]

plump·er[1] (plum′pər), *n.* **1.** an act of falling heavily; a plumping. **2.** *Chiefly Brit.* the vote of a person who plumps. [PLUMP[2] + -ER[1]]

plump·er[2] (plum′pər), *n.* something carried in the mouth to fill out hollow cheeks. [1755–65; PLUMP[1] + -ER[1]]

plump·ish (plum′pish), *adj.* somewhat plump; tending to plumpness. [1750–60; PLUMP[1] + -ISH[1]] —**plump′ish·ly,** *adv.*

plum′ pud′ding, a rich steamed or boiled pudding containing raisins, currants, citron, spices, etc. [1640–50]

plum′ toma′to, an egg-shaped or oblong variety of tomato.

plu·mu·la·ceous (plo͞om′yə lā′shəs), *adj.* having the texture of down. [1875–80; PLUMULE + -ACEOUS]

plu·mule (plo͞om′yo͞ol), *n.* **1.** *Bot.* the bud of the ascending axis of a plant while still in the embryo. **2.** *Ornith.* a down feather. [1720–30; < NL, L *plūmula.* See PLUME, -ULE] —**plu·mu·lar** (plo͞om′yə lər), *adj.*

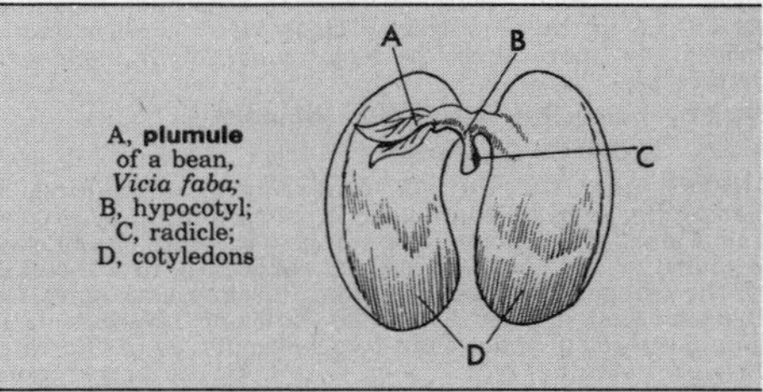

A, **plumule** of a bean, *Vicia faba;* B, hypocotyl; C, radicle; D, cotyledons

plu·mu·lose (plo͞om′yə lōs′), *adj. Zool.* shaped like a downy feather or plumule. [1820–30; < NL *plūmulōsus.* See PLUMULE, -OSE[1]]

plum·y (plo͞o′mē), *adj.,* **plum·i·er, plum·i·est. 1.** having plumes or feathers. **2.** adorned with a plume or plumes: *a plumy helmet.* **3.** plumelike or feathery. [1575–85; PLUME + -Y[1]]

plun·der (plun′dər), *v.t.* **1.** to rob of goods or valuables by open force, as in war, hostile raids, brigandage, etc.: *to plunder a town.* **2.** to rob, despoil, or fleece: *to plunder the public treasury.* **3.** to take wrongfully, as by pillage, robbery, or fraud: *to plunder a piece of property.* —*v.i.* **4.** to take plunder; pillage. —*n.* **5.** plundering, pillage, or spoliation. **6.** that which is taken in plundering; loot. **7.** anything taken by robbery, theft, or fraud. [1620–30; < D *plunderen*] —**plun′der·a·ble,** *adj.*

CONCISE PRONUNCIATION KEY: *act, cāpe, dâre, pärt; set, ēqual; if, ice; ox, ōver, ôrder, oil, bo͝ok, bo͞ot, out; up, ûrge; child; sing; shoe; thin, that;* zh as in *treasure.* ə = *a* as in *alone, e* as in *system, i* as in *easily, o* as in *gallop, u* as in *circus;* ′ as in *fire* (fī′r), *hour* (ou′r). l and n can serve as syllabic consonants, as in *cradle* (krād′l), and *button* (but′n). See the full key inside the front cover.

—**plun′der·er,** *n.* —**plun′der·ing·ly,** *adv.* —**plun′der·ous,** *adj.*
—**Syn. 1.** rape, ravage, sack, devastate. **5.** rapine, robbery. **6.** booty, spoils.

plun·der·age (plun′dər ij), *n.* **1.** act of plundering; pillage. **2.** *Law.* **a.** the embezzlement of goods on board a ship. **b.** the goods embezzled. [1790–1800; PLUNDER + -AGE]

plunge (plunj), *v.,* **plunged, plung·ing,** *n.* —*v.t.* **1.** to cast or thrust forcibly or suddenly into something, as a liquid, a penetrable substance, a place, etc.; immerse; submerge: *to plunge a dagger into one's heart.* **2.** to bring suddenly or forcibly into some condition, situation, etc.: *to plunge a country into war; to pull a switch and plunge a house into darkness.* **3.** *Hort.* to place (a potted plant) up to its rim in soil or in certain other materials, as sand or moss. **4.** *Survey.* to transit (the telescope of a transit or theodolite). —*v.i.* **5.** to cast oneself, or fall as if cast, into water, a hole, etc. **6.** to rush or dash with headlong haste: *to plunge through a crowd.* **7.** to bet or speculate recklessly: *to plunge on the stock market.* **8.** to throw oneself impetuously or abruptly into some condition, situation, matter, etc.: *to plunge into debt.* **9.** to descend abruptly or precipitously, as a cliff, road, etc. **10.** to pitch violently forward, as a horse, ship, etc. —*n.* **11.** act of plunging. **12.** a leap or dive, as into water. **13.** a headlong or impetuous rush or dash: *a plunge into danger.* **14.** a sudden, violent pitching movement. **15.** a place for plunging or diving, as a swimming pool. **16.** *Geol.* pitch (def. 48). **17. take the plunge,** to enter with sudden decision upon an unfamiliar course of action, as after hesitation or deliberation: *She took the plunge and invested her entire savings in the plan.* [1325–75; ME < MF *plung(i)er* << VL **plumbicāre* to heave the lead. See PLUMB]
—**Syn. 1.** See **dip**[1]. **5.** dive. **6.** hasten. **9.** drop.

plunge′ ba′sin, a cavity at the base of a falls or cataract, formed by the action of the falling water. [1900–05]

plunge′ pool′, the water in a plunge basin. [1915–20]

plung·er (plun′jər), *n.* **1.** *Mach.* a pistonlike reciprocating part moving within the cylinder of a pump or hydraulic device. **2.** *Auto.* a pistonlike part in the valve of a pneumatic tire. **3.** Also called **force cup, plumber's friend, plumber's helper.** a device consisting of a handle with a rubber suction cup at one end, used as a force pump to free clogged drains and toilet traps. **4.** a person or thing that plunges. **5.** a reckless bettor or speculator. [1605–15; PLUNGE + -ER[1]]

plung′ing fire′, *Mil.* artillery or other fire that strikes the ground at a steep angle, as from high ground overlooking the target or from a weapon fired at a high angle of elevation. [1870–75]

plunk (plungk), *v.t.* **1.** to pluck (a stringed instrument or its strings); twang: *to plunk a guitar.* **2.** to throw, push, put, drop, etc., heavily or suddenly; plump (often fol. by *down*): *Plunk down your money. She plunked herself down on the seat.* **3.** to push, shove, toss, etc. (sometimes fol. by *in, over,* etc.): *to plunk the ball over the net; to plunk a pencil into a drawer.* —*v.i.* **4.** to give forth a twanging sound. **5.** to drop heavily or suddenly; plump (often fol. by *down*): *to plunk down somewhere and take a nap.* —*n.* **6.** act or sound of plunking. **7.** *Informal.* a direct, forcible blow. **8.** *Slang.* a dollar. —*adv.* **9.** *Informal.* with a plunking sound. **10.** *Informal.* squarely; exactly: *The tennis ball landed plunk in the middle of the net.* [1760–70; expressive word akin to PLUCK]

plunk·er (plung′kər), *n.* **1.** a person or thing that plunks. **2.** *Angling.* a casting lure that makes a plunking sound upon hitting the surface of the water. [PLUNK + -ER[1]]

plu·per·fect (plo͞o pûr′fikt), —*adj.* **1.** *Gram.* **a.** perfect with respect to a point of reference in past time, as *had done* in *He had done it when I came.* **b.** designating a tense or other verb formation or construction with such meaning, as Latin *portāveram* "I had carried." **2.** more than perfect: *He spoke the language with pluperfect precision.* —*n. Gram.* **3. a.** the pluperfect tense, or other verb formation or construction with such meaning. **b.** a form in the pluperfect. [1520–30; < L *plū(s quam) perfectum* (more than) perfect, trans. of Gk *hypersyntelikós*]

plupf., pluperfect. Also, **plup., pluperf.**

plur., **1.** plural. **2.** plurality.

plu·ral (plo͝or′əl), *adj.* **1.** consisting of, containing, or pertaining to more than one. **2.** pertaining to or involving a plurality of persons or things. **3.** being one of such a plurality. **4.** *Gram.* noting or pertaining to a member of the category of number, found in many languages, indicating that a word has more than one referent, as in English *men,* or more than two referents, as in Old English *ge,* meaning "you." —*n. Gram.* **5.** the plural number. **6.** a form in the plural. [1350–1400; ME < L *plūrālis,* equiv. to *plūr-,* s. of *plūs* PLUS + *-ālis* -AL[1]]

plu·ral·ism (plo͝or′ə liz′əm), *n.* **1.** *Philos.* **a.** a theory that there is more than one basic substance or principle. Cf. **dualism** (def. 2), **monism** (def. 1a). **b.** a theory that reality consists of two or more independent elements. **2.** *Eccles.* **a.** the holding by one person of two or more offices at the same time. **b.** plurality (def. 7a). **3.** *Sociol.* See **cultural pluralism. 4.** state or quality of being plural. [1810–20; PLURAL + -ISM] —**plu′ral·ist,** *n., adj.* —**plu′ral·is′tic,** *adj.* —**plu′ral·is′ti·cal·ly,** *adv.*

plu·ral·i·ty (plo͞o ral′i tē), *n., pl.* **-ties. 1.** the excess of votes received by the leading candidate, in an election in which there are three or more candidates, over those received by the next candidate (distinguished from *majority*). **2.** more than half of the whole; the majority. **3.** a number greater than one. **4.** fact of being numerous. **5.** a large number; multitude. **6.** state or fact of being plural. **7.** *Eccles.* **a.** the holding by one person of two or more benefices at the same time; pluralism. **b.** any of the benefices so held. [1325–75; ME *pluralite* < OF < LL *plūrālitās.* See PLURAL, -ITY]
—**Syn. 1.** See **majority.**

plu·ral·ize (plo͝or′ə līz′), *v.,* **-ized, -iz·ing.** —*v.t.* **1.** to express in the plural form; make plural: *to pluralize a noun.* —*v.i.* **2.** to receive or take a plural form. Also, *esp. Brit.,* **plu′ral·ise′.** [1795–1805; PLURAL + -IZE] —**plu′ral·iz′a·ble,** *adj.* —**plu′ral·i·za′tion,** *n.* —**plu′·ral·iz′er,** *n.*

plu·ral·ly (plo͝or′ə lē), *adv.* as a plural; in a plural sense. [1350–1400; ME *pluraliche.* See PLURAL, -LY]

plur′al mar′riage, polygamy (def. 1). [1865–70]

plus (plus), *prep.* **1.** more by the addition of; increased by: *ten plus two is twelve.* **2.** with the addition of; with: *He had wealth plus fame.* —*adj.* **3.** involving or noting addition. **4.** positive: *a plus quantity.* **5.** more (by a certain amount). **6.** *Elect.* pertaining to or characterized by positive electricity: *the plus terminal.* **7.** *Mycol.* (in heterothallic fungi) designating, in the absence of morphological differentiation, one of the two strains of mycelia that unite in the sexual process. **8.** having a certain quality to an unusual degree: *He has personality plus.* —*n.* **9.** a plus quantity. **10.** *Arith.* See **plus sign. 11.** something additional. **12.** a surplus or gain. —*conj.* **13.** *Informal.* also; and; furthermore: *A bicycle is cheaper than a car, plus it doesn't pollute the air.* —*adv.* **14.** in addition; besides. [1570–80; < L *plūs* more; akin to Gk *pleíōn,* ON *fleiri* more, OE *feolu, fela,* G *viel,* Goth *filu,* OIr *il,* Gk *polý* many]
—**Usage.** Since PLUS as a preposition has long had the meanings "more by the addition of" and "with the addition of," it was but a short step to a newer use, mainly in informal writing and speech, as a conjunction meaning "also, and, furthermore." Although this use is increasing, many object to it, and it is rare in more formal writing. AND PLUS is likewise objected to, especially for being redundant: *The paper was delivered two hours late, and plus it was soaking wet.*

plus′ fours′, long, baggy knickers for men, introduced before World War I and worn until the 1930's for sports activities, esp. golf. [1915–20; so called because four inches are added to the length of ordinary knickers to give the desired looseness] —**plus′-foured′,** *adj.*

plush (plush), *n., adj.,* **-er, -est.** —*n.* **1.** a fabric, as of silk, cotton, or wool, whose pile is more than ⅛ inch (0.3 cm) high. —*adj.* **2.** expensively or showily luxurious: *the plushest hotel in town* **3.** abundantly rich; lush; luxuriant: *plush, rolling lawns.* [1585–95; 1920–25 for def. 2; < F *pluche,* syncopated var. of *peluche* << L *pilus* hair] —**plushed,** *adj.* —**plush′like′,** *adj.* —**plush′ly,** *adv.* —**plush′ness,** *n.*
—**Syn. 2.** opulent, lavish, palatial.

plush·y (plush′ē), *adj.,* **plush·i·er, plush·i·est. 1.** of, pertaining to, or resembling plush. **2.** *Informal.* characterized by luxury, wealth, or ease: *a plushy resort.* [1605–15; PLUSH + -Y[1]] —**plush′i·ness,** *n.*

plus′ junc′ture, *Phonet.* See **open juncture.**

plus·sage (plus′ij), *n.* a surplus amount. [1920–25; PLUS + -AGE]

plus′ sight′, *Survey.* a backsight used in leveling.

plus′ sign′, *Arith.* the symbol (+) indicating summation or a positive quality. [1645–55]

plus′ tick′, *Stock Exchange.* uptick (def. 2).

Plu·tarch (plo͞o′tärk), *n.* A.D. c46–c120, Greek biographer.

Plu·tarch·i·an (plo͞o tär′kē ən), *adj.* **1.** of or pertaining to the biographer Plutarch. **2.** characteristic of or resembling a biography by Plutarch or its subject: *a life worthy of Plutarchian description; a deed of Plutarchian splendor.* [1855–60; PLUTARCH + -IAN]

Plu′tarch's Lives′, (*Parallel Lives*) a collection (A.D. 105–15) by Plutarch of short biographies of the leading political figures of ancient Greece and Rome.

plu·te·us (plo͞o′tē əs), *n., pl.* **-te·i** (-tē ī′), **-te·us·es.** the free-swimming, bilaterally symmetrical larva of an echinoid or ophiuroid. [1825–35; < NL; L: breastwork, movable shelter] —**plu′te·al, plu′te·an,** *adj.*

Plu·to (plo͞o′tō), *n.* **1.** *Class. Myth.* a name given to Hades, under which he is identified by the Romans with Orcus. **2.** *Astron.* the planet ninth in order from the sun, having an equatorial diameter of about 2100 miles (3300 km), a mean distance from the sun of 3.674 billion miles (5.914 billion km), a period of revolution of 248.53 years, and one known moon, Charon. See table under **planet.**

plu·toc·ra·cy (plo͞o tok′rə sē), *n., pl.* **-cies. 1.** the rule or power of wealth or of the wealthy. **2.** a government or state in which the wealthy class rules. **3.** a class or group ruling, or exercising power or influence, by virtue of its wealth. [1645–55; < Gk *ploutokratía,* equiv. to *ploûto(s)* wealth + *-kratia* -CRACY]

plu·to·crat (plo͞o′tə krat′), *n.* a member of a plutocracy. [1840–50; PLUTO(CRACY) + -CRAT]

plu·to·crat·ic (plo͞o′tə krat′ik), *adj.* of, pertaining to, or characterized by a plutocracy or plutocrats. Also, **plu′to·crat′i·cal.** [1865–70; PLUTOCRAT + -IC] —**plu′·to·crat′i·cal·ly,** *adv.*

plu·ton (plo͞o′ton), *n. Geol.* any body of igneous rock that solidified far below the earth's surface. [1935–40; < G *Pluton,* back formation from *plutonisch* PLUTONIC]

Plu·to·ni·an (plo͞o tō′nē ən), *adj.* Also, **Plu·ton·ic** (plo͞o ton′ik). of, pertaining to, or resembling Pluto or the lower world; infernal. [1660–70; < L *Plūtōni(us)* (< Gk *Ploutṓnios,* deriv. of *Ploútōn* PLUTO) + -AN]

plu·ton·ic (plo͞o ton′ik), *adj. Geol.* noting or pertaining to a class of igneous rocks that have solidified far below the earth's surface. [1790–1800; < L *Plūtōn-* (s. of *Plūtō* Pluto < Gk *Ploútōn*) + -IC; orig. referring to the Plutonic theory (see PLUTONISM)]

plu·to·nism (plo͞ot′n iz′əm), *n. Geol.* **1.** the intrusion of magma and associated deep-seated processes within the earth's crust. **2.** (*often cap.*) the disproven theory that all rocks formed by solidification of a molten mass, promulgated by Scottish geologist James Hutton (1726–97). [1840–50; PLUTON(IC) + -ISM] —**plu′to·nist,** *n.*

plu·to·ni·um (plo͞o tō′nē əm), *n. Chem., Physics.* a transuranic element with a fissile isotope of mass number 239 **(plutonium 239)** that can be produced from non-fissile uranium 238, as in a breeder reactor. *Symbol:* Pu; *at. no.:* 94. [1940–45; < Gk *Ploútōn* PLUTO + -IUM]

plu·vi·al (plo͞o′vē əl), *adj.* **1.** of or pertaining to rain, esp. much rain; rainy. **2.** *Geol.* occurring through the action of rain. —*n.* **3.** *Geol.* a rainy period formerly regarded as coeval with a glacial age, but now recognized as episodic and, in the tropics, as characteristic of interglacial ages. [1650–60; < L *pluviālis,* equiv. to *pluvi(a)* rain + *-ālis* -AL[1]]

plu·vi·om·e·ter (plo͞o′vē om′i tər), *n.* See **rain gauge.** [1785–95; < L *pluvi(a)* rain + -O- + -METER] —**plu·vi·o·met·ric** (plo͞o′vē ə me′trik), **plu′vi·o·met′ri·cal,** *adj.* —**plu′vi·om′e·try,** *n.*

Plu·vi·ôse (plo͞o′vē ōs′; *Fr.* ply vyōz′), *n.* (in the French Revolutionary calendar) the fifth month of the year, extending from January 20 to February 18. [1790–1800; < F < L *pluviōsus* rainy. See PLUVIOUS]

plu·vi·ous (plo͞o′vē əs), *adj.* of or pertaining to rain; rainy. [1400–50; late ME < L *pluviōsus.* See PLUVIAL, -OUS] —**plu·vi·os·i·ty** (plo͞o′vē os′i tē), *n.*

ply[1] (plī), *v.,* **plied, ply·ing.** —*v.t.* **1.** to work with or at diligently; employ busily; use: *to ply the needle.* **2.** to carry on, practice, or pursue busily or steadily: *to ply a trade.* **3.** to treat with or apply to (something) repeatedly (often fol. by *with*): *to ply a fire with fresh fuel.* **4.** to assail persistently: *to ply horses with a whip.* **5.** to supply with or offer something pressingly to: *to ply a person with drink.* **6.** to address (someone) persistently or importunately, as with questions, solicitations, etc.; importune. **7.** to pass over or along (a river, stream, etc.) steadily or on a regular basis: *boats that ply the Mississippi.* —*v.i.* **8.** to run or travel regularly over a fixed course or between certain places, as a boat, bus, etc. **9.** to perform one's work or office busily or steadily: *to ply with the oars; to ply at a trade.* [1300–50; ME *plien,* aph. var. of *aplien* to APPLY] —**ply′ing·ly,** *adv.*
—**Syn. 2.** follow, exercise.

ply[2] (plī), *n., pl.* **plies,** *v.,* **plied, ply·ing.** —*n.* **1.** a thickness or layer. **2.** *Auto.* a layer of reinforcing fabric for a tire. **3.** a unit of yarn: *single ply.* **4.** one of the sheets of veneer that are glued together to make plywood. **5.** *Informal.* plywood. **6.** bent, bias, or inclination. —*v.t.* **7.** *Brit. Dial.* to bend, fold, or mold. —*v.i.* **8.** *Obs.* to bend, incline, or yield. [1300–50; ME *plien* (v.) < MF *plier* to fold, bend, var. of *ployer,* OF *pleier* < L *plicāre* to fold; see FOLD[1]]

ply·er (plī′ər), *n. Chiefly Brit.* plier.

ply′ met′al, a composition of dissimilar metals bonded together in sheet form. Also, **ply′met′al.**

Plym·outh (plim′əth), *n.* **1.** a seaport in SW Devonshire, in SW England, on the English Channel: naval base; the departing point of the *Mayflower* 1620. 257,900. **2.** a city in SE Massachusetts: the oldest town in New England, founded by the Pilgrims 1620. 35,913. **3.** a town in SE Minnesota. 31,615. **4.** a town in NW Connecticut. 10,732. **5.** a town in and the capital of Montserrat, West Indies. 3200.

Plym′outh Breth′ren, a loosely organized body of Christians founded in Plymouth, England, about 1830, having no ordained ministry, no formal creed or ritual, and accepting the Bible as the only guide. [1835–45]

Plym′outh Col′ony, the colony established in SE Massachusetts by the Pilgrims in 1620.

Plym′outh Com′pany, a company, formed in England in 1606 to establish colonies in America and that founded a colony in Maine in 1607.

Plym′outh Rock′, **1.** a rock at Plymouth, Massachusetts, on which the Pilgrims who sailed on the *Mayflower* are said to have stepped ashore when they landed in America in 1620. **2.** one of an American breed of medium-sized chickens, raised for meat and eggs.

ply′ roll′ing, *Metalworking.* See **pack rolling.**

ply·wood (plī′wo͝od′), *n.* a material used for various building purposes, consisting usually of an odd number of veneers glued over each other, usually at right angles. [1905–10; PLY[2] + WOOD[1]]

Pl·zeň (pl′zen′yə), *n.* a city in Bohemia, in the W Czech Republic. 175,000. German, **Pilsen.**

Pm, *Symbol, Chem.* promethium.

pm., premium.

P.M., **1.** Past Master. **2.** Paymaster. **3.** See **p.m. 4.** Police Magistrate. **5.** Postmaster. **6.** post-mortem. **7.** Prime Minister. **8.** Provost Marshal.

p.m., **1.** after noon. **2.** the period between noon and midnight. [< L *post merīdiem*]
—**Usage.** See **a.m.**

P marker. See **phrase marker.** Also, **P-marker.**

P.M.G., **1.** Paymaster General. **2.** Postmaster General. **3.** Provost Marshal General.

pmk., postmark.

P.M.L., *Insurance.* probable maximum loss.

PMLA, Publications of the Modern Language Association of America. Also, **P.M.L.A.**

PMS, See **premenstrual syndrome.**

pmt., payment.

PN, **1.** please note. **2.** promissory note. **3.** psychoneurotic.

pn, **1.** please note. **2.** promissory note.

P/N, promissory note. Also, **p.n.**

-pnea, a combining form meaning "breath, respiration," used in the formation of compound words that denote a

CONCISE ETYMOLOGY KEY: <, descended or borrowed from; >, whence; b., blend of, blended; c., cognate with; cf., compare; deriv., derivative; equiv., equivalent; imit., imitative; obl., oblique; r., replacing; s., stem; sp., spelling, spelled; resp., respelling, respelled; trans., translation; ?, origin unknown; *, unattested; ‡, probably earlier than. See the full key inside the front cover.

kind of breathing or condition of the respiratory system, as specified by the initial element: *dyspnea; hyperpnea.* Also, **-pnoea.** [< Gk *-pnoia,* akin to *pneîn* to breathe; cf. PNEUMA]

pneu•drau•lic (no͞o drô′lik, -drol′ik, nyo͞o-), *adj.* of or pertaining to a mechanism involving both pneumatic and hydraulic action. [PNEU(MATIC) + (HY)DRAULIC]

pneum., **1.** pneumatic. **2.** pneumatics.

pneu•ma (no͞o′mə, nyo͞o′-), *n.* **1.** the vital spirit; the soul. **2.** *Theol.* the Spirit of God; the Holy Ghost. [1875–80; < Gk *pneûma* lit., breath, wind, akin to *pneîn* to blow, breathe]

pneu•mat•ic (no͝o mat′ik, nyo͝o-), *adj.* **1.** of or pertaining to air, gases, or wind. **2.** of or pertaining to pneumatics. **3.** operated by air or by the pressure or exhaustion of air: *a pneumatic drill.* **4.** filled with or containing compressed air, as a tire. **5.** equipped with pneumatic tires. **6.** *Theol.* of or pertaining to the spirit; spiritual. **7.** *Zool.* containing air or air cavities. —*n.* **8.** a pneumatic tire. **9.** a vehicle having wheels with such tires. [1650–60; < L *pneumaticus* < Gk *pneumatikós* pertaining to air, breath or wind, spiritual, equiv. to *pneumat-* (s. of *pneûma;* see PNEUMA) + *-ikos* -IC] —**pneu•mat′i•cal•ly,** *adv.* —**pneu•ma•tic•i•ty** (no͞o′mə-tis′i tē, nyo͞o′-), *n.*

pneumat′ic duct′, the duct joining the air bladder and alimentary canal of a physostomous fish.

pneumat′ic pile′, *Building Trades.* a hollow pile, used under water, in which a vacuum is induced so that air and water pressure force it into place. [1855–60]

pneu•mat•ics (no͝o mat′iks, nyo͝o-), *n.* (*used with a singular v.*) the branch of physics that deals with the mechanical properties of air and other gases. Also called **pneumodynamics.** [1650–60; see PNEUMATIC, -ICS]

pneumat′ic trough′, *Chem.* a trough filled with liquid, esp. water, for collecting gases in bell jars or the like by displacement. [1820–30]

pneumato-, a combining form meaning "air," "breath," "spirit," used in the formation of compound words: *pneumatology; pneumatophore.* Also, **pneumo-.** [< Gk, comb. form of *pneûma;* see PNEUMA]

pneu•mat•o•cyst (no͝o mat′ə sist, nyo͝o-, no͞o′mə tə-, nyo͞o′-), *n. Biol.* **1.** the cavity of a pneumatophore. **2.** pneumatophore. [1855–60; PNEUMATO- + -CYST]

pneu•mat•o•graph (no͝o mat′ə graf′, -gräf′, nyo͝o-, no͞o′mə tə-, nyo͞o′-), *n. Med.* pneumograph.

pneu•ma•tol•o•gy (no͞o′mə tol′ə jē, nyo͞o′-), *n.* **1.** *Theol.* **a.** doctrine concerning the Holy Spirit. **b.** the belief in intermediary spirits between humans and God. **2.** the doctrine or theory of spiritual beings. **3.** *Archaic.* psychology. **4.** *Obs.* pneumatics. [1670–80; PNEUMATO- + -LOGY] —**pneu•mat•o•log•ic** (no͝o mat′l oj′ik, nyo͝o-, no͞o′mə tl-, nyo͞o′-), **pneu′ma•to•log′i•cal,** *adj.* —**pneu′ma•tol′o•gist,** *n.*

pneu•ma•tol•y•sis (no͞o′mə tol′ə sis, nyo͞o′-), *n. Geol.* the process by which rocks are altered or minerals and ores are formed by the action of vapors given off by magma. [1895–1900; PNEUMATO- + -LYSIS] —**pneu•mat•o•lyt•ic, pneu•mat•o•lit•ic** (no͝o mat′l it′ik, nyo͝o-, no͞o′mə tl-, nyo͞o′-), *adj.*

pneu•ma•tom•e•ter (no͞o′mə tom′i tər, nyo͞o′-), *n.* an instrument for measuring either the quantity of air inhaled or exhaled during a single inspiration or expiration or the force of inspiration or expiration. [1825–35; PNEUMATO- + -METER]

pneu•mat•o•phore (no͝o mat′ə fôr′, -fōr′, nyo͝o-, no͞o′mə tə-, nyo͞o′-), *n.* **1.** *Bot.* a specialized structure developed from the root in certain plants growing in swamps and marshes, serving as a respiratory organ. **2.** *Zool.* the air sac of a siphonophore, serving as a float. [1855–60; PNEUMATO- + -PHORE] —**pneu•ma•toph•or•ous** (no͞o′mə tof′ər əs, nyo͞o′-), *adj.*

pneu•mat•o•ther•a•py (no͝o mat′ō ther′ə pē, nyo͝o-, no͞o′mə tō-, nyo͞o′-), *n.* the use of compressed or rarefied air in treating disease. [1930–35; PNEUMATO- + THERAPY]

pneu•mec•to•my (no͝o mek′tə mē, nyo͝o-), *n., pl.* **-mies.** *Surg.* pneumonectomy.

pneumo-, var. of **pneumato-** or **pneumono-:** *pneumococcus.*

pneu•mo•ba•cil•lus (no͞o′mō bə sil′əs, nyo͞o′-), *n., pl.* **-cil•li** (-sil′ī). a bacterium, *Klebsiella pneumoniae,* causing a type of pneumonia and associated with certain other diseases, esp. of the respiratory tract. [< NL; see PNEUMO-, BACILLUS]

pneu•mo•coc•cus (no͞o′mə kok′əs, nyo͞o′-), *n., pl.* **-coc•ci** (-kok′sī, -sē). a bacterium, *Diplococcus pneumoniae,* causing lobar pneumonia and associated with certain other diseases, as pericarditis and meningitis. [1885–90; < NL; see PNEUMO-, -COCCUS] —**pneu•mo•coc•cal** (no͞o′mə kok′əl, nyo͞o′-), **pneu•mo•coc•cic** (no͞o′mə kok′sik, nyo͞o′-), **pneu•mo•coc•cous** (no͞o′mə-kok′əs, nyo͞o′-), *adj.*

pneu•mo•co•ni•o•sis (no͞o′mə kō′nē ō′sis, nyo͞o′-), *n. Pathol.* any chronic lung disease, including anthracosis, asbestosis, and silicosis, caused by the inhalation of particles of coal, asbestos, silica, or similar substances and leading to fibrosis and loss of lung function. Also, **pneumonoconiosis.** [1880–85; syncopated var. of PNEUMONOCONIOSIS]

pneu•mo•cys′tis pneumo′nia (no͞o′mə sis′tis, nyo͞o′-), *Pathol.* a pulmonary infection caused by the protozoan *Pneumocystis carinii,* occurring as an opportunistic disease in persons with impaired immune systems, as AIDS victims. *Abbr.:* PCP Also called **pneumocys′tis ca•ri′ni•i pneumo′nia** (kə rī′nē ī′). [1980–85; *pneumocystis* < NL: genus name; see PNEUMO-, CYST]

pneu•mo•dy•nam•ics (no͞o′mō dī nam′iks, -di-, nyo͞o′-), *n.* (*used with a singular v.*) *Physics.* pneumatics. [1830–40; PNEUMO- + DYNAMICS]

pneu•mo•en•ceph•a•lo•gram (no͞o′mō en sef′ə lə-gram′, nyo͞o′-), *n. Med.* an encephalogram made after the replacement of the cerebrospinal fluid by air or gas, rarely used since the development of the CAT scanner. [1930–35; PNEUMO- + ENCEPHALOGRAM]

pneu•mo•en•ceph•a•log•ra•phy (no͞o′mō en sef′ə-log′rə fē, nyo͞o′-), *n. Med.* encephalography. [1930–35; PNEUMO- + ENCEPHALOGRAPHY]

pneu•mo•gas•tric (no͞o′mə gas′trik, nyo͞o′-), *Anat.* —*adj.* **1.** of or pertaining to the lungs and stomach. —*n.* **2.** See **pneumogastric nerve.** [1825–35; PNEUMO- + GASTRIC]

pneu′mogas′tric nerve′, *Anat.* (formerly) the vagus nerve. [1825–35]

pneu•mo•graph (no͞o′mə graf′, -gräf′, nyo͞o′-), *n. Med.* a device for recording graphically the respiratory movements of the thorax. Also, **pneumatograph.** [1875–80; PNEUMO- + -GRAPH] —**pneu•mo•graph•ic** (no͞o′mə graf′ik, nyo͞o′-), *adj.*

pneu•mog•ra•phy (no͝o mog′rə fē, nyo͝o-), *n. Med.* **1.** the process of recording the movements of the thorax in respiration. **2.** the production of x-ray photographs of the lungs. [1835–45; PNEUMO- + -GRAPHY]

pneumon-, var. of **pneumono-** before a vowel: *pneumonectomy.*

pneu•mo•nec•to•my (no͞o′mə nek′tə mē, nyo͞o′-), *n., pl.* **-mies.** *Surg.* excision of part or all of a lung. Also, **pneumectomy.** [1885–90; PNEUMON- + -ECTOMY]

pneu•mo•nia (no͝o mōn′yə, -mō′nē ə, nyo͝o-), *n. Pathol.* **1.** inflammation of the lungs with congestion. **2.** Also called **lobar pneumonia.** an acute disease of the lungs, caused by the bacterium *Streptococcus pneumoniae* and characterized by fever, a cough with blood-tinged phlegm, and difficult breathing. [1595–1605; < NL < Gk *pneumonía.* See PNEUMON-, -IA]

pneu•mon•ic (no͝o mon′ik, nyo͝o-), *adj.* **1.** of, pertaining to, or affecting the lungs; pulmonary. **2.** pertaining to or affected with pneumonia. [1665–75; < NL *pneumonicus* < Gk *pneumonikós.* See PNEUMON-, -IC]

pneumon′ic plague′, *Pathol.* a form of plague characterized by lung involvement. Cf. **plague.**

pneu•mo•ni•tis (no͞o′mə nī′tis, nyo͞o′-), *n. Pathol.* inflammation of the lung caused by a virus or exposure to irritating substances. [1815–25; < NL; see PNEUMON-, -ITIS]

pneumono-, a combining form meaning "lung," used in the formation of compound words: *pneumonoconiosis.* Also, **pneumo-;** *esp. before a vowel,* **pneumon-.** [comb. form repr. Gk *pneúmōn* lung]

pneu•mo•no•co•ni•o•sis (no͞o′mə nō kō′nē ō′sis, nyo͞o′-), *n. Pathol.* pneumoconiosis. [1865–70; PNEUMONO- + Gk *kóni(s)* dust + -OSIS]

pneu•mo•no•ul•tra•mi•cro•scop•ic•sil•i•co•vol•ca•no•co•ni•o•sis (no͞o′mə nō ul′trə mī′krə skop′ik sil′-i kō′vol kā′nō kō′nē ō′sis, nyo͞o′-), *n.* an obscure term ostensibly referring to a lung disease caused by silica dust, sometimes cited as one of the longest words in the English language. [< NL; see PNEUMONO-, ULTRAMICROSCOPIC, SILICA, VOLCANO, (PNEUMONO)CONIOSIS]

pneu•mo•tho•rax (no͞o′mə thôr′aks, -thōr′-, nyo͞o′-), *n. Pathol.* the presence of air or gas in the pleural cavity. [1815–25; < NL; see PNEUMO-, THORAX]

pneu•mo•trop•ic (no͞o′mə trop′ik, -trō′pik, nyo͞o′-), *adj. Pathol.* directed toward or having an affinity for lung tissue. [1925–30; PNEUMO- + -TROPIC]

pnld, paneled.

pnlg, paneling.

-pnoea, var. of **-pnea.**

Pnom Penh (nom′ pen′, pə nôm′ pen′). See **Phnom Penh.** Also, **Pnom′-penh′, Pnom′penh′.**

pnxt., pinxit.

Pnyx (niks, pə niks), *n.* a hill in Athens, Greece, near the Acropolis: the place of assembly in ancient Athens.

po (pō), *n., pl.* **pos.** *Australia and New Zealand.* a chamber pot. [1875–80; prob. < F *pot (de chambre)* chamber pot]

Po (pō), *n.* a river in Italy, flowing E from the Alps in the NW to the Adriatic. 418 mi. (669 km) long. Ancient, **Padus.**

Po, *Symbol, Chem.* polonium.

po., *Baseball.* put-out; put-outs.

P.O., **1.** parole officer. **2.** petty officer. **3.** postal (money) order. **4.** post office.

p.o., (in prescriptions) by mouth. [< L *per ōs*]

POA, See **primary optical area.**

po•a•ceous (pō ā′shəs), *adj.* belonging to the Poaceae, an alternate name for the plant family Gramineae. Cf. **grass family.** [< NL *Po(a)* the type genus (< Gk *póa* grass) + -ACEOUS]

poach[1] (pōch), *v.i.* **1.** to trespass, esp. on another's game preserve, in order to steal animals or to hunt. **2.** to take game or fish illegally. **3.** (of land) to become broken up or slushy by being trampled. **4.** (in tennis, squash, handball, etc.) to play a ball hit into the territory of one's partner that is properly the partner's ball to play. **5.** *Informal.* to cheat in a game or contest. —*v.t.* **6.** to trespass on (private property), esp. in order to hunt or fish. **7.** to steal (game or fish) from another's property. **8.** to take without permission and use as one's own: *to poach ideas.* **9.** to break up by trampling. **10.** to mix with water and reduce to a uniform consistency, as clay. [1520–30; earlier: to shove, thrust < MF *pocher* to gouge < Gmc; akin to POKE[1]] —**poach′a•ble,** *adj.*

poach[2] (pōch), *v.t.* to cook (eggs, fish, fruits, etc.) in a hot liquid that is kept just below the boiling point. [1350–1400; ME *poche* < MF *pocher* lit., to bag (the yolk inside the white), deriv. of *poche* bag (F *poche* pocket) < MD *poke* POKE[2]] —**poach′a•ble,** *adj.*

poach•er[1] (pō′chər), *n.* **1.** a person who trespasses on private property, esp. to catch fish or game illegally. **2.** Also called **sea-poacher.** any of several slender, marine fishes of the family Agonidae, found chiefly in deeper waters of the North Pacific, having the body covered with bony plates. [1660–70; POACH[1] + -ER[1]]

poach•er[2] (pō′chər), *n.* **1.** a pan having a tight-fitting lid and metal cups for steaming or poaching eggs. **2.** any dish or pan used for poaching food, esp. a baking dish for poaching fish. [1860–65; POACH[2] + -ER[1]]

poach•ing (pō′ching), *n.* **1.** the illegal practice of trespassing on another's property to hunt or steal game without the landowner's permission. **2.** any encroachment on another's property, rights, ideas, or the like. [1605–15; POACH[1] + -ING[1]]

poach•y (pō′chē), *adj.,* **poach•i•er, poach•i•est.** (of land) slushy; swampy. [1700–10; POACH[1] + -Y[1]] —**poach′i•ness,** *n.*

POB, See **post-office box.** Also, **P.O.B.**

Po•be′da Peak′ (pə bed′ə), *n.* a mountain in central Asia, on the boundary between Kirghizia (Kyrgyzstan) and China; highest peak of the Tien Shan range. 24,406 ft. (7439 m). Russian, **Pik Pobedy.**

POC, port of call.

Po•ca•hon•tas (pō′kə hon′təs), *n.* (*Rebecca Rolfe*) 1595?–1617, American Indian woman who is said to have prevented the execution of Captain John Smith.

Po•ca•tel•lo (pō′kə tel′ō), *n.* a city in SE Idaho. 46,340.

po•chard (pō′chərd, -kərd), *n., pl.* **-chards,** (*esp. collectively*) **-chard.** **1.** an Old World diving duck, *Aythya ferina,* having a chestnut-red head. **2.** any of various related ducks, as the American redhead. [1545–55; orig. uncert.]

po•ché (pō shā′), *n.* the walls, columns, and other solids of a building or the like, as indicated on an architectural plan, usually in black. [< F, ptp. of *pocher* to make a rough sketch, POACH[2]]

po•chette (pō shet′), *n.* kit[2]. [1910–15; < F, dim. of *poche* POCKET]

po•chis•mo (pô chē′zmô; *Eng.* pō chēz′mō), *n., pl.* ***-chis•mos*** (-chē′zmôs; *Eng.* -chēz′mōz) for 1. *Mexican Spanish.* **1.** an English word or expression borrowed into Spanish; a Spanish word showing U.S. influence. **2.** a form of speech employing many such words. **3.** an adopted U.S. custom, attitude, etc.

po•cho (pô′chô; *Eng* pō′chō), *n., pl.* ***-chos*** (-chôs; *Eng.* -chōz). *Mexican Spanish* (*usually disparaging*). an American of Mexican parentage, esp. one who has adopted U.S. customs and attitudes; an Americanized Mexican.

Po Chü-i (bô′ jy′ē′), A.D. 772–846, Chinese poet.

pocill., (in prescriptions) a little cup. [< L *pōcillum*]

pock (pok), *n.* **1.** a pustule on the body in an eruptive disease, as smallpox. **2.** a mark or spot left by or resembling such a pustule. **3.** a small indentation, pit, hole, or the like. **4.** *Scot.* poke[2]. [bef. 1000; ME *pokke,* OE *poc;* c. G *Pocke;* perh. akin to OE *pocca.* See POKE[2]]

pocked (pokt), *adj.* marked with pustules or with pits left by them; pitted. [POCK + -ED[3]]

pock•et (pok′it), *n.* **1.** a shaped piece of fabric attached inside or outside a garment and forming a pouch used esp. for carrying small articles. **2.** a bag or pouch. **3.** means; financial resources: *a selection of gifts to fit every pocket.* **4.** any pouchlike receptacle, compartment, hollow, or cavity. **5.** an envelope, receptacle, etc., usually of heavy paper and open at one end, used for storing or preserving photographs, stamps, phonograph records, etc.: *Each album has 12 pockets.* **6.** a recess, as in a wall, for receiving a sliding door, sash weights, etc. **7.** any isolated group, area, element, etc., contrasted, as in status or condition, with a surrounding element or group: *pockets of resistance; a pocket of poverty in the central city.* **8.** *Mining.* **a.** a small orebody or mass of ore, frequently isolated. **b.** a bin for ore or rock storage. **c.** a raise or small slope fitted with chute gates. **9.** *Billiards, Pool.* any of the pouches or bags at the corners and sides of the table. **10.** a position in which a competitor in a race is so hemmed in by others that his or her progress is impeded. **11.** *Football.* the area from which a quarterback throws a pass, usually a short distance behind the line of scrimmage and protected by a wall of blockers. **12.** *Bowling.* the space between the headpin and the pin next behind to the left or right, taken as the target for a strike. **13.** *Baseball.* the deepest part of a mitt or glove, roughly in the area around the center of the palm, where most balls are caught. **14.** *Naut.* a holder consisting of a strip of sailcloth sewed to a sail, and containing a thin wooden batten that stiffens the leech of the sail. **15.** *Anat.* any saclike cavity in the body: *a pus pocket.* **16.** See **stage pocket.** **17.** an English unit of weight for hops equivalent to 168 pounds (76.4 kg). **18. in one's pocket,** in one's possession; under one's influence: *He has the audience in his pocket.* **19. line one's pockets,** to profit, esp. at the expense of

CONCISE PRONUNCIATION KEY: act, cāpe, dâre, pärt; set, ēqual; if, īce; ox, ōver, ôrder, oil, bo͝ok, bo͞ot, out; up, ûrge; child; sing; shoe; thin, *th*at; zh as in *treasure.* ə = *a* as in *alone, e* as in *system, i* as in *easily, o* as in *gallop, u* as in *circus;* ᵊ as in *fire* (fīᵊr), *hour* (ouᵊr). l and n can serve as syllabic consonants, as in *cradle* (krād′l), and *button* (but′n). See the full key inside the front cover.

others: *While millions were fighting and dying, the profiteers were lining their pockets.* **20. out of pocket,** having suffered a financial loss; poorer: *He had made unwise land purchases, and found himself several thousand dollars out of pocket.* —*adj.* **21.** small enough or suitable for carrying in the pocket: *a pocket watch.* **22.** relatively small; smaller than usual: *a pocket war; a pocket country.* —*v.t.* **23.** to put into one's pocket: *to pocket one's keys.* **24.** to take possession of as one's own, often dishonestly: *to pocket public funds.* **25.** to submit to or endure without protest or open resentment: *to pocket an insult.* **26.** to conceal or suppress: *to pocket one's pride.* **27.** to enclose or confine in or as if in a pocket: *The town was pocketed in a small valley.* **28.** *Billiards, Pool.* to drive (a ball) into a pocket. **29.** pocket-veto. **30.** so as to hem in (a contestant) so as to impede progress, as in racing. [1250–1300; ME *poket* < ONF (Picard) *poquet* (OF *pochet, pochette*), dim. of *poque* < MD *poke* POKE[2]; see -ET] —**pock′et·less,** *adj.* —**pock′et·like′,** *adj.*
—**Syn. 24.** steal, pilfer, appropriate, filch.

pock·et·a·ble (pok′i tə bəl), *adj.* small enough to be carried in one's pocket; pocket-size. [1690–1700; POCKET + -ABLE] —**pock′et·a·bil′i·ty, pock′et·a·ble·ness,** *n.*

pock′et bat′tleship, a small heavily armed and armored warship serving as a battleship because of limitations imposed by treaty. [1925–30]

pock′et bil′liards, pool[2] (def. 1). [1910–15]

pock·et·book (pok′it bo͝ok′), *n.* **1.** a woman's purse or handbag. **2.** a person's financial resources or means: *The price was out of reach of his pocketbook.* **3.** Also, **pock′et book′.** a book, usually paperback, that is small enough to carry in one's coat pocket. **4.** *Brit.* **a.** a notebook for carrying in one's pocket. **b.** a wallet or billfold. [1610–20; POCKET + BOOK]

pock′et bor′ough, 1. (before the Reform Bill of 1832) any English borough whose representatives in Parliament were controlled by an individual or family. **2.** an election district under the control of an individual, family, or group. [1855–60]

pock′et cal′culator, an electronic calculator small enough to be carried on one's person.

pock′et chis′el, any woodworking chisel having a blade of medium length.

pock′et door′, a door, usually one of a communicating pair, that slides into and out of a recess in a doorway wall.

pock′et edi′tion, 1. pocketbook (def. 3). **2.** *Informal.* a small or smaller form of something; miniature version. [1705–15]

pock·et·ful (pok′it fo͝ol′), *n., pl.* **-fuls.** the amount that a pocket will hold. [1605–15; POCKET + -FUL]
—**Usage.** See **-ful.**

pock′et go′pher, any of numerous burrowing rodents of the family Geomyidae, of western and southern North America and Central America, having large, external, fur-lined cheek pouches. Also called **gopher, pock′et rat′, pouched rat.** See illus. under **gopher**[1]. [1870–75, Amer.]

pock·et-hand·ker·chief (pok′it hang′kər chif, -chēf′), *n.* handkerchief (def. 1). [1635–45]

pock·et·ing (pok′i ting), *n.* any of various fabrics for making the insides of pockets. [1605–15; POCKET + -ING[1]]

pock·et·knife (pok′it nīf′), *n., pl.* **-knives.** a knife with one or more blades that fold into the handle, suitable for carrying in the pocket. [1720–30; POCKET + KNIFE]

pock′et mon′ey, money for small, current expenses.

pock′et mouse′, any of numerous burrowing rodents, esp. of the genus *Perognathus,* chiefly inhabiting arid regions of the southwestern U.S. and northern Mexico, having fur-lined cheek pouches and a long tail. [1880–85, *Amer.*]

pock′et park′, a very small park or outdoor area for public leisure, esp. an urban plaza or courtyard with benches and fountains. Also called **vest-pocket park.** [1965–70]

pock′et piece′, (in a window frame) a removable part of a pulley stile permitting access to sash weights. [1700–10]

pock′et sec′retary, a long, narrow walletlike case, usually of leather and containing pockets for credit and business cards, paper money, etc., and sometimes a notepad and pencil.

pock·et-size (pok′it sīz′), *adj.* small enough to fit conveniently into one's pocket. Also, **pock′et-sized′.** [1905–10]

pock·et-square (pok′it skwâr′), *n.* a handkerchief, often colored or figured, worn in the breast pocket of a suit or blazer as a fashion accessory.

pock′et ve′to, 1. a veto of a bill brought about by the president's failure to sign it within ten days of the adjournment of Congress. **2.** a similar action on the part of any legislative executive. [1835–45, *Amer.*]

pock·et-ve·to (pok′it vē′tō), *v.t.,* **-ve·toed, -ve·to·ing.** to veto (a bill) by exercising a pocket veto.

pock·mark (pok′märk′), *n.* **1.** Usually, **pockmarks.** scars or pits left by a pustule in smallpox or the like. **2.** a small pit or scar: *a tabletop full of pockmarks.* —*v.t.* **3.** to mark or scar with or as with pockmarks: *gopher holes pockmarking the field.* [1665–75; POCK + MARK[1]] —**pock′marked′,** *adj.*

pock·y (pok′ē), *adj.,* **pock·i·er, pock·i·est.** of, pertaining to, characterized by, or covered with pocks. [1300–50; ME *pokky.* See POCK, -Y[1]] —**pock′i·ly,** *adv.*

po·co (pō′kō; *It.* pô′kô), *adv. Music.* somewhat; rather: *poco presto.* [1715–25; < It: little < L *paucus* few]

po·co a po·co (pō′kō ä pō′kō; *It.* pô′kô ä pô′kô), *Music.* gradually; little by little: *poco a poco accelerando.* [1850–55; < It]

po·co·cu·ran·te (pō′kō ko͞o ran′tē, -rän′-, -kyo͞o-; *It.* pô′kô ko͞o rän′te), *n., pl.* **-ti** (-tē), *adj.* —*n.* **1.** a careless or indifferent person. —*adj.* **2.** caring little; indifferent; nonchalant. [1755–65; < It: lit., caring little. See POCO, CURE, -ANT] —**po·co·cu·ran·tism** (pō′kō ko͞o ran′tiz-əm, -rän′-, -kyo͞o-), **po′co·cu·ran′te·ism,** *n.*

Po′co·no Moun′tains (pō′kə nō′), a mountain range in NE Pennsylvania: resort area. ab. 2000 ft. (610 m) high. Also called **Po′co·nos′.**

Po·ços de Cal·das (pô′so͞os di kôl′däs), a city in E Brazil. 44,504.

po·co·sin (pə kō′sən, pō′kə sən), *n. Southeastern U.S.* a swamp or marsh in an upland coastal region. Also, **po·co′son, po·co′sen.** [1625–35, *Amer.*; prob. < an unattested form in a southern Eastern Algonquian language]

pocul., (in prescriptions) a cup. [< L *pōculum*]

poc·u·li·form (pok′yə lə fôrm′), *adj.* cup-shaped. [1825–35; < L *pōcul(um)* cup + -I- + -FORM]

pod[1] (pod), *n., v.,* **pod·ded, pod·ding.** —*n.* **1.** a somewhat elongated, two-valved seed vessel, as that of the pea or bean. **2.** a dehiscent fruit or pericarp having several seeds. **3.** *Entomol.* **a.** an insect egg case. **b.** a compact mass of insect eggs. **4.** a streamlined enclosure, housing, or detachable container of some kind: *an engine pod under the wing of an aircraft.* **5.** a protective compartment, as for an automobile's instrument gauges. **6.** *Mining.* an orebody that has an elongated or lenticular shape. **7.** *Radio and Television Slang.* a cluster of brief commercials or spot announcements. —*v.i.* **8.** to produce pods. **9.** to swell out like a pod. [1680–90; appar. back formation from *podder* peasecod gatherer; cf. *podder,* var. of *podware,* unexplained var. of *codware* bagged vegetables (COD[2] + *-ware* crops, vegetables)] —**pod′like′,** *adj.*

pod[2] (pod), *n.* **1.** a small herd or school, esp. of seals or whales. **2.** a small flock of birds. [1825–35, *Amer.*; perh. special (orig. facetious) use of POD[1]]

pod[3] (pod), *n.* **1.** the straight groove or channel in the body of certain augers or bits. **2.** *Carpentry.* pad[1] (def. 15b). [1565–75; orig. uncert.; perh. a continuation of OE *pād* covering, cloak, the socket being thought of as something that covers or hides from view what is held in it (though the phonology is irregular)]

pod-, a learned borrowing from Greek meaning "foot," used in the formation of compound words: *pododynia.* Also, *esp. before a consonant,* **podo-.** [comb. form repr. Gk *poús* (gen. *podós*) FOOT]

-pod, a combining form meaning "one having a foot" of the kind or number specified by the initial element; often corresponding to Neo-Latin class names ending in **-poda,** with **-pod** used in English to name a single member of such a class: *cephalopod.* Cf. **-ped.** [< NL < Gk *-pod-,* s. of *-pous,* adj. deriv. of *poús* FOOT]

POD, port of debarkation.

p.o.'d (pē′ōd′), *adj. Slang.* See **pissed off.**

P.O.D., 1. pay on delivery. **2.** Post Office Department.

-poda, a combining form meaning "those having feet" of the kind or number specified by the initial element, used in the names of classes in zoology: *Cephalopoda.* Cf. **-pod.** [< NL, neut. pl. of Gk *-pous;* see -POD]

po·dag·ra (pō dag′rə, pod′ə grə), *n. Pathol.* gouty inflammation of the great toe. [1250–1300; ME < L < Gk *podágra* lit., foot-trap, equiv. to *pod-* POD- + *ágra* a catching, seizure] —**po·dag′ral, po·dag′ric, po·dag′rous,** *adj.*

po·dal·gia (pō dal′jə, -jē ə), *n. Med.* pain in the foot. [1835–45; POD- + -ALGIA]

po·dal·ic (pō dal′ik), *adj. Med.* pertaining to the feet. [1885–90; *podal* of the feet (see POD-, -AL[1]) + -IC]

pod·dy (pod′ē), *n., pl.* **-dies.** *Australian.* **1.** a newborn or unweaned calf. **2.** any young animal. **3.** maverick. [1890–95; orig. uncert.]

-pode, var. of **-podium:** *pseudopode.*

po·des·ta (pō des′tə, pō′də stä′), *n.* **1.** any of certain magistrates in Italy, as a chief magistrate in medieval towns and republics. **2.** a person appointed to serve as mayor of an Italian city during the Fascist regime. [1540–50; < It *podestà* power < L *potestās* power, command]

po·de·ti·i·form (pə dē′shē ə fôrm′, -shə fôrm′), *adj.* shaped like a podetium. [1895–1900; PODETI(UM) + -I- + -FORM]

po·de·ti·um (pə dē′shē əm, -shəm), *n., pl.* **-ti·a** (-shē ə, -shə). *Bot., Mycol.* **1.** (in certain lichens) a stalk bearing an apothecium. **2.** any stalklike elevation. [1855–60; < NL, equiv. to Gk *pod-* POD- + NL *-etium* (appar. arbitrarily < Gk *-et-* or *-ēt-* + L *-ium*)]

Pod·go·ri·ca (*Serbo-Croatian.* pôd′gô ʀē′tsä), *n.* the capital of Montenegro, in SW Yugoslavia. 132,290. Formerly (1945–92), **Titograd.**

Pod·gor·ny (pod gôr′nē; *Russ.* pud gôʀ′nē), *n.* **Ni·ko·lai Vik·to·ro·vich** (nyi ku lī′ vyēk′tə ʀə vyich), 1903–83, Russian government official: president of the Soviet Union 1965–77.

podg·y (poj′ē), *adj.,* **podg·i·er, podg·i·est.** *Chiefly Brit.* pudgy. —**podg′i·ly,** *adv.* —**podg′i·ness,** *n.*

po·di·a·trist (pə dī′ə trist, pō-), *n.* a person qualified to diagnose and treat foot disorders. Also called **chiropodist.** [1910–15; PODIATR(Y) + -IST]

po·di·a·try (pə dī′ə trē, pō-), *n.* the care of the human foot, esp. the diagnosis and treatment of foot disorders. Also called **chiropody.** [1910–15; POD- + -IATRY]

pod·ite (pod′īt), *n.* **1.** an arthropod limb. **2.** a podomere. [1870–75; POD- + -ITE[1]] —**po·dit·ic** (pə dit′ik), *adj.*

po·di·um (pō′dē əm), *n., pl.* **-di·ums, -di·a** (-dē ə). **1.** a small platform for the conductor of an orchestra, for a public speaker, etc. **2.** *Archit.* **a.** a low wall forming a base for a construction, as a colonnade or dome. **b.** a stereobate for a classical temple, esp. one with perpendicular sides. **c.** the masonry supporting a classical temple. **d.** a raised platform surrounding the arena of an ancient Roman amphitheater having on it the seats of privileged spectators. **3.** lectern. **4.** a counter or booth, as one at an airport for handling tickets or dispensing information. **5.** *Zool., Anat.* a foot. **6.** *Bot.* a footstalk or stipe. [1605–15; < L: elevated place, balcony < Gk *pódion* little foot, equiv. to *pod-* POD- + *-ion* dim. suffix. See PEW]

-podium, a combining form meaning "footlike part" of an organism, used in the formation of compound words: *monopodium; pseudo-podium.* Also, **-pode.** [< NL; see PODIUM]

podo-, var. of **pod-** before a consonant: *podotheca.*

pod·o·car·pus (pod′ə kär′pəs), *n.* any of various coniferous evergreen trees of the genus *Podocarpus,* of tropical and semitropical regions, esp. *P. macrophyllus,* which is cultivated as an ornamental. [1880–85; < NL; see PODO-, -CARPOUS]

pod·o·dyn·i·a (pod′ə din′ē ə), *n. Med.* pain in the sole of the foot. [1895–1900; POD- + -ODYNIA]

Po·dolsk (pu dôlsk′), *n.* a city in the W Russian Federation in Europe, S of Moscow. 209,000.

pod·o·mere (pod′ə mēr′), *n. Zool.* any segment of a limb of an arthropod. [PODO- + -MERE]

pod·o·phyl·lin (pod′ə fil′in), *n.* a resin, occurring as a light brown to greenish amorphous powder, obtained from podophyllum, and used in medicine chiefly as a cathartic and, locally, in the treatment of genital warts. Also called **pod′ophyl′lin res′in.** [1850–55; PODOPHYL-L(UM) + -IN[2]] —**pod′o·phyl′lic,** *adj.*

pod·o·phyl·lum (pod′ə fil′əm), *n.* the dried rhizome of the May apple, *Podophyllum peltatum,* from which podophyllin is derived. [1750–60; < NL; see PODO-, -PHYLL]

pod·o·the·ca (pod′ə thē′kə), *n., pl.* **-cae** (-sē). *Ornith.* the horny integument covering unfeathered portions of the legs and toes of most birds. [1870–75; < NL; see PODO-, THECA] —**pod′o·the′cal,** *adj.*

-podous, a combining form meaning "footed, having a foot" of the kind or number specified by the initial element; often occurring in adjectives corresponding to nouns ending in **-pod:** *cephalopodous.* [-POD + -OUS]

pod·sol (pod′sol, -sôl), *n.* spodosol. Also, **pod·zol** (pod′zol, -zôl). [1905–10; < Russ *podzól,* equiv. to *pod-* under + *zol(á)* ash; *-s-* perh. by assoc. with -SOL] —**pod·sol′ic,** *adj.*

pod·sol·ize (pod′sə līz′), *v.,* **-ized, -iz·ing.** —*v.t.* **1.** to make into podsol. —*v.i.* **2.** to become podsol. Also, *esp. Brit.,* **pod′sol·ise′.** [1925–30; PODSOL + -IZE] —**pod′·sol·i·za′tion,** *n.*

Po·dunk (pō′dungk), *n.* any small and insignificant or inaccessible town or village: *After a year in the big city, I was ready to move back to Podunk.* [1660–70, *Amer.*; generic use of *Podunk,* village near Hartford, Conn.]

Poe (pō), *n.* **Edgar Allan,** 1809–49, U.S. poet, short-story writer, and critic.

POE, 1. port of embarkation. **2.** See **port of entry.** Also, **P.O.E.**

poe·cil·i·id (pē sil′ē id), *n.* **1.** any small New World fish of the family Poeciliidae, of fresh or brackish tropical and temperate waters, including the mosquitofish, guppies, and mollies. —*adj.* **2.** belonging or pertaining to the family Poeciliidae. [< NL *Poeciliidae,* equiv. to *Poecili(a)* name of genus (< Gk *poikilía* striped, marked with various colors) + *-idae* -ID[2]]

po·em (pō′əm), *n.* **1.** a composition in verse, esp. one that is characterized by a highly developed artistic form and by the use of heightened language and rhythm to express an intensely imaginative interpretation of the subject. **2.** composition that, though not in verse, is characterized by great beauty of language or expression: *a prose poem from the Scriptures; a symphonic poem.* **3.** something having qualities that are suggestive of or likened to those of poetry: *Marcel, that chicken cacciatore was an absolute poem.* [1540–50; < L *poēma* < Gk *poíēma* poem, something made, equiv. to *poiē-,* var. s. of *poieîn* to make + *-ma* suffix denoting result]

poe·nol·o·gy (pē nol′ə jē), *n.* penology.

po·e·sy (pō′ə sē, -zē), *n., pl.* **-sies. 1.** the work or the art of poetic composition. **2.** *Archaic.* **a.** poetry in general. **b.** verse or poetry in metrical form. **3.** *Obs.* **a.** a poem or verse used as a motto. Cf. **posy** (def. 2). **b.** a poem. [1300–50; ME *poesie* < MF < L *poēsis* < Gk *poíēsis* poetic art, poetry, lit., a making, equiv. to *poiē-,* var. s. of *poieîn* to make + *-sis* -SIS]

po·et (pō′it), *n.* **1.** a person who composes poetry. **2.** a person who has the gift of poetic thought, imagination, and creation, together with eloquence of expression. [1250–1300; ME *poete* < L *poēta* < Gk *poiētḗs* poet, lit., maker, equiv. to *poiē-,* var. s. of *poieîn* to make + *-tēs* agent n. suffix] —**po′et·less,** *adj.* —**po′et·like′,** *adj.*
—**Syn. 1.** versifier, bard.

poet., 1. poetic. **2.** poetical. **3.** poetry.

po·et·as·ter (pō′it as′tər), *n.* an inferior poet; a writer of indifferent verse. [1590–1600; < ML or NL; see POET, -ASTER[1]] —**po′et·as′ter·ing, po′et·as′ter·y, po′et·as′try, po′et·as′ter·ism,** *n.* —**po′et·as′tric, po′et·as′tri·cal,** *adj.*
—**Syn.** rhymester.

po·et·ess (pō′i tis), *n.* a woman who writes poetry. [1520–30; POET + -ESS]
—**Usage.** See **-ess.**

po•et•ic (pō et′ik), *adj.* Also, **po•et′i•cal.** **1.** possessing the qualities or charm of poetry: *poetic descriptions of nature.* **2.** of or pertaining to a poet or poets. **3.** characteristic of or befitting a poet: *poetic feeling; poetic insight.* **4.** endowed with the faculty or feeling of a poet: *a poetic eulogist.* **5.** having or showing the sensibility of a poet: *a poetic lover.* **6.** of or pertaining to poetry: *poetic literature.* **7.** of the nature of or resembling poetry: *a poetic composition; poetic drama; poetic imagination.* **8.** celebrated in poetry, as a place. **9.** providing a subject for poetry. **10.** of or pertaining to literature in verse form. —*n.* **11.** poetics. [1520–30; < L *poēticus* < Gk *poiētikós.* See POET, -IC] —**po•et′i•cal•ly,** *adv.*

Poet′ic Ed′da. See under ***Edda.***

po•et•i•cism (pō et′ə siz′əm), *n.* a poetic expression that has become hackneyed, forced, or artificial. [1840–50; POETIC + -ISM]

po•et•i•cize (pō et′ə sīz′), *v.,* **-cized, -ciz•ing.** —*v.t.* **1.** to make (thoughts, feelings, etc.) poetic; express in poetry. **2.** to write poetry about (an event, occasion, etc.). —*v.i.* **3.** to speak or write poetry. Also, *esp. Brit.,* **po•et′i•cise′.** [1795–1805; POETIC + -IZE]

poet′ic jus′tice, an ideal distribution of rewards and punishments such as is common in some poetry and fiction. [1720–30]

poet′ic li′cense, license or liberty taken by a poet, prose writer, or other artist in deviating from rule, conventional form, logic, or fact, in order to produce a desired effect. [1780–90]

po•et•ics (pō et′iks), *n.* (*used with a singular v.*) **1.** literary criticism treating of the nature and laws of poetry. **2.** the study of prosody. **3.** a treatise on poetry. **4.** (*cap., italics*) a treatise or collection of notes on aesthetics (4th century B.C.) by Aristotle. [1720–30; see POETIC, -ICS]

po•et•ize (pō′i tīz′), *v.,* **-ized, -iz•ing.** —*v.i.* **1.** to write poetry. —*v.t.* **2.** to express poetically: *to poetize a story.* **3.** to make or treat as poetic; poeticize: *to poetize reality.* Also, *esp. Brit.,* **po′et•ise′.** [1575–85; POET + -IZE] —**po′et•iz′er,** *n.*

po′et lau′reate, *pl.* **poets laureate.** **1.** (in Great Britain) a poet appointed for life as an officer of the royal household, formerly expected to write poems in celebration of court and national events. **2.** a poet recognized or acclaimed as the most eminent or representative of a country or locality. **3.** (in the U.S.) a poet appointed for a term of one year as the national laureate poet, in recognition of previous work. [1350–1400; ME]

po•et•ry (pō′i trē), *n.* **1.** the art of rhythmical composition, written or spoken, for exciting pleasure by beautiful, imaginative, or elevated thoughts. **2.** literary work in metrical form; verse. **3.** prose with poetic qualities. **4.** poetic qualities however manifested: *the poetry of simple acts and things.* **5.** poetic spirit or feeling: *The pianist played the prelude with poetry.* **6.** something suggestive of or likened to poetry: *the pure poetry of a beautiful view on a clear day.* [1350–1400; ME *poetrie* < ML *poētria* poetic art, deriv. of *poēta* POET, but formation is unclear; prob. not < Gk *poiētria* poetess] —**po′et•ry•less,** *adj.*
—**Syn.** **2.** POETRY, VERSE agree in referring to the work of a poet. The difference between POETRY and VERSE is usually the difference between substance and form. POETRY is lofty thought or impassioned feeling expressed in imaginative words: *Elizabethan poetry.* VERSE is any expression in words which simply conforms to accepted metrical rules and structure: *the differences between prose and verse.* —**Ant.** **2.** prose.

pog•a•mog•gan (pog′ə mog′ən), *n.* a club with a knobbed head, used by various American Indian peoples. [1780–90; < Ojibwa *pakama·kan,* equiv. to Proto-Algonquian **pakama·-* hit (someone) + **-kan* instrument for]

Po•ga•ny (pō gä′nē), *n.* **Willy** (*William Andrew*), 1882–1955, U.S. painter, stage designer, and illustrator; born in Hungary.

po•gey (pō′gē), *n., pl.* **-geys,** *adj.* **1.** *Slang.* Also, **pogy.** **a.** a package of food, candy, or other treats sent to a child at boarding school, a person in an institution, etc. **b.** candy or a treat. —*n.* **2.** *Canadian Slang.* **a.** an institution maintained by private charities or government funds for the housing of the aged, sick, orphaned, or feeble-minded; an old-age home, charity hospital, orphanage, or the like. **b.** any form of charity or government relief. **c.** unemployment insurance provided by the government. —*adj. Canadian Slang.* **3.** of, pertaining to, or obtained through charity or government relief: *pogey shoes.* [1890–95; earlier *pogie* workhouse < ?]

po′gey bait′, *Slang.* **1.** candy or a treat used to lure a child into a sexual situation. **2.** See **jail bait.** [1915–20, *Amer.*]

pogge (pog), *n.* a poacher, *Agonus cataphractus,* common near the British Isles and ranging north to Greenland and Iceland. Also called **armed bullhead.** [1665–75; orig. uncert.]

POGO (pō′gō), *n.* Polar Orbiting Geophysical Observatory.

po•go•ni•a (pə gō′nē ə, -gōn′yə), *n.* a terrestrial orchid of the genus *Pogonia,* of North America. [< NL < Gk *pōgōniās* bearded (with reference to the lip which is frequently fringed)]

pog•o•nip (pog′ə nip), *n.* an ice fog that forms in the mountain valleys of the western U.S. [1860–65, *Amer.*; < Shoshone *payinappih* thunder cloud; cf. *soyovayinappih* fog (with *soyo-* earth), *yayumpayinappih* fog (with *yayun-* valley)]

po•go•noph•o•ran (pō′gə nof′ər ən), *n.* any member of the small phylum Pogonophora, slender tentacled animals having a tubelike outer covering, living on the deep ocean bottom. Also called **beard worm.** [< NL *Pogonophor(a)* phylum name (Gk *pōgōno-,* comb. form repr. *pṓgōn* beard (see -O-) + *-phora,* neut. pl. of *-phoros* bearing, -PHOROUS; so named from the beardlike appearance of their shorter tentacles) + -AN]

po′go stick′ (pō′gō), a long stick having a pair of handles at the top and, near the bottom, a pair of footrests attached to a powerful spring, so that by standing on the footrests while grasping the handles, one can propel oneself along in a series of leaps. Also, **po′go-stick′.** [1920–25; *pogo,* formerly a trademark]

pogo stick

po•grom (pə grum′, -grom′, pō-), *n.* an organized massacre, esp. of Jews. [1880–85; (< Yiddish) < Russ *pogróm* lit., destruction, devastation (of a town, country, etc., as in war), n. deriv. of *pogromít′,* equiv. to *po-* perfective prefix + *gromít′* to destroy, devastate, deriv. of *grom* thunder]
—**Syn.** slaughter, butchery.

po•gy[1] (pō′gē, pog′ē), *n., pl.* (*esp. collectively*) **-gy,** (*esp. referring to two or more kinds or species*) **-gies.** **1.** a porgy. **2.** a viviparous perch, *Amphistichus rhodoterus,* found in the shallow waters off the Pacific coast of the U.S. **3.** the menhaden. [1855–60, *Amer.*; shortening of *poghaden, paughagen* (a Maine dial. term, perh. < Eastern Abenaki) + -Y[2]]

po•gy[2] (pō′gē), *n., pl.* **-gies.** *Slang.* pogey (def. 1).

Po•hai (pō′hī′; *Chin.* bô′hī′), *n. Wade-Giles.* Bohai.

Po•hjo•la (pô′hyô lä), *n. Finnish Legend.* a region to the north of Finland, ruled by the sorceress Louhi: often identified with Lapland.

poi (poi, pō′ē), *n.* a Hawaiian dish made of the root of the taro baked, pounded, moistened, and fermented. [1815–25; < Hawaiian]

-poiesis, a combining form meaning "making, formation," used in the formation of compound words: *hematopoiesis.* [< Gk *-poiēsis;* see POESY, -SIS]

-poietic, a combining form occurring in adjectives that correspond to nouns ending in **-poiesis:** *hematopoietic.* [< Gk *-poiētikos.* See POETIC]

poign•an•cy (poin′yən sē, poin′ən-), *n., pl.* **-cies** for 2. **1.** the state or condition of being poignant. **2.** a poignant moment, event, situation, or the like. [1680–90; POIGN(ANT) + -ANCY]

poign•ant (poin′yənt, poi′nənt), *adj.* **1.** keenly distressing to the feelings: *poignant regret.* **2.** keen or strong in mental appeal: *a subject of poignant interest.* **3.** affecting or moving the emotions: *a poignant scene.* **4.** pungent to the smell: *poignant cooking odors.* [1350–1400; ME *poynaunt* < MF *poignant,* prp. of *poindre* < L *pungere* to prick, pierce. See PUNGENT, -ANT] —**poign′•ant•ly,** *adv.*
—**Syn.** **1.** intense, sincere, heartfelt. **4.** piquant, sharp. —**Ant.** **1, 2.** mild.

poi•ki•lit•ic (poi′kə lit′ik), *adj. Petrog.* (of igneous rocks) having small crystals of one mineral scattered irregularly in larger crystals of another mineral. [1830–40; < Gk *poikíl(os)* various + -ITE[1] + -IC]

poi•kil•o•blas•tic (poi kil′ə blas′tik, poi′kə lə-), *adj. Petrog.* (of metamorphic rocks) having small grains of one mineral embedded in metacrysts of another mineral. [1915–20; < Gk *poikiló(s)* various + -BLASTIC]

poi•ki•lo•ther•mal (poi′kə lō thûr′məl, poi kil′ə-), *adj. Zool.* cold-blooded (def. 3) (opposed to *homoiothermal*). [1880–85; < Gk *poikílo(s)* various + THERMAL] —**poi′ki•lo•ther′mism, poi′ki•lo•ther′my,** *n.*

poil (poil), *n.* a yarn or thread made from silk, used for ribbon, velvet, and as the core of gold, silver, and tinsel yarn. [< F < L *pilus* hair]

poi•lu (pwä′lo͞o; *Fr.* pwa ly′), *n., pl.* **-lus** (-lo͞oz; *Fr.* -ly′). a French common soldier. [1910–15; < F, in earlier slang: tough individual, tough, brave, lit., hairy, haired; MF, OF *pelu* (cf. PLEW) < VL **pilūtus,* equiv. to L *pil(us)* hair + VL *-*ūtus,* for L -*ātus* -ATE[1] (*e* > *oi* by influence of *poil* hair < L *pilus*)]

poi•men•ics (poi men′iks), *n.* (*used with a singular v.*) See **pastoral theology.** [1880–85; < Gk *poimenikós* of a shepherd, equiv. to *poimen-,* s. of *poimḗn* shepherd + *-ikos* -IC; see -ICS]

Poin•ca•ré (pwan ka rā′), *n.* **1. Jules Hen•ri** (zhyl än rē′), 1854–1912, French mathematician. **2.** his cousin **Ray•mond** (re môn′), 1860–1934, French statesman: president of France 1913–20.

Poincaré′ conjec′ture, *Math.* the question of whether a compact, simply connected three-dimensional manifold is topologically equivalent to a three-dimensional sphere. [named after J. H. POINCARÉ]

poin•ci•an•a (poin′sē an′ə), *n.* **1.** See **royal poinciana.** **2.** any of several other tropical trees of the legume family, with showy flowers, as *Caesalpina pulcherrima* **(dwarf poinciana)** or *Peltophorum pterocarpum* **(yellow poinciana).** [1725–35; < NL; named after M. de *Poinci,* 17th-century governor of the French Antilles; see -AN, -A[2]]

poin•set•ti•a (poin set′ē ə, -set′ə), *n.* a plant, *Euphorbia (Poinsettia) pulcherrima,* of the spurge family, native to Mexico and Central America, having variously lobed leaves and brilliant scarlet, pink, or white petallike bracts. [1830–40; < NL, named after J. R. *Poinsett* (1799–1851), American minister to Mexico, who discovered the plant there in 1828; see -IA]

poinsettia, *Euphorbia pulcherrima*

point (point), *n.* **1.** a sharp or tapering end, as of a dagger. **2.** a projecting part of anything: *A point of land juts into the bay.* **3.** a tapering extremity: *the points of the fingers.* **4.** something having a sharp or tapering end: *a pen point.* **5.** a pointed tool or instrument, as an etching needle. **6.** a stone implement with a tapering end found in some Middle and Upper Paleolithic and Mesolithic cultures and used primarily for hunting. **7.** a mark made with or as if with the sharp end of something: *Her sharp heels left points in the carpet.* **8.** a mark of punctuation. **9.** period (def. 15). **10.** See under **decimal fraction.** **11.** *Phonet.* a diacritic indicating a vowel or other modification of sound. **12.** one of the embossed dots used in certain systems of writing and printing for the blind. **13.** something that has position but not extension, as the intersection of two lines. **14.** a place of which the position alone is considered; spot: *We're leaving for Chicago and points west.* **15.** any definite position, as in a scale, course, etc.: *the boiling point.* **16.** (in acupuncture) a particular spot on the body at which a needle may be inserted, as to relieve pain. **17.** *Navig.* any of 32 separate horizontal directions, 11° 15′ apart, as indicated on the card of a compass or gauged with reference to the heading of a vessel. **18.** *Naut.* See **point of sailing.** **19.** a degree or stage: *frankness to the point of insult.* **20.** a particular instant of time: *It was at that point that I told him he'd said enough.* **21.** a critical position in a course of affairs: *Morale had reached a low point.* **22.** a decisive state of circumstances: *He reached the point where he could no longer pay his debts.* **23.** the important or essential thing: *the point of the matter.* **24.** the salient feature of a story, epigram, joke, etc.: *to miss the point.* **25.** a particular aim, end, or purpose: *He carried his point.* **26.** a hint or suggestion: *points on getting a job.* **27.** a single or separate article or item, as in an extended whole; a detail or particular: *the fine points of a contract.* **28.** an individual part or element of something: *noble points in her character.* **29.** a distinguishing mark or quality, esp. one of an animal, used as a standard in stockbreeding, judging, etc. **30.** **points, a.** the extremities of an animal, esp. a horse or dog. **b.** *Railroads, Brit.* a switch. **31.** a single unit, as in counting. **32.** a unit of count in the score of a game: *Our team won by five points.* **33.** (in craps) the number that must be thrown to win but not including 7 or 11 on the first roll: *Your point is 4.* **34.** *Ice Hockey.* either of two positions, to the right or left of the goal, to which an attacking defenseman is assigned, usually in the execution of a power play, to help keep the puck in the attacking zone. **35.** *Basketball.* a position in the front court, usually taken by the guard in charge of setting up the team's offense. **36.** *Cricket.* **a.** the position of the fielder who plays a short distance in front of and to the offside of the batsman. **b.** the fielder playing this position. **37.** *Chiefly Boxing.* the end or tip (of the chin). **38.** *Hunting.* **a.** the action of a hunting dog that indicates the presence and location of game by standing rigid and directing its head toward the game. **b.** the position taken by a hunting dog in pointing game. **39.** a branch of an antler of a deer: *an eight-point buck.* **40.** *Sports.* a cross-country run. **41.** one of the narrow tapering spaces marked on a backgammon board. **42.** *Educ.* a single credit, usually corresponding to an hour's class work per week for one semester. **43.** *Elect.* **a.** Also called **breaker point.** either of a pair of contacts tipped with tungsten or platinum that make or break current flow in a distributor, as in an automobile. **b.** *Brit.* an outlet or socket. **44.** *Com.* **a.** a unit of price quotation, as in the U.S., one dollar in stock transactions, one hundredth of a cent in cotton and coffee, or one cent in oil, grain, pork, etc.: *The price of stock went up two points today.* **b.** (esp. in motion pictures) a percentage point, usually of the gross profits, granted to someone who agrees to invest or otherwise participate in a business project: *The star of the movie received a million dollar guarantee and five points.* **45.** one percent of the face value of a loan, esp. a mortgage loan, added on as a placement fee or a service charge and paid in advance or upon closing of the loan. **46.** *Jewelry.* a unit of weight equal to ¹⁄₁₀₀ of a carat. **47.** *Mil.* **a.** a patrol or reconnaissance unit that goes ahead of the advance party of an advance guard, or follows the rear party of the rear guard. **b.** the stroke in bayonet drill or combat. **48.** *Print.* **a.** a unit of type measurement equal to 0.013835 inch (¹⁄₇₂ inch), or ¹⁄₁₂ pica. Cf. **Didot point system.** **b.** Also called **press-point.** (in a press) one of several metal prongs for perforating the sheet so that it will be in register when the reverse is printed. **49.** a unit of measure of paper or card thickness, equal to 0.001 inch. **50.** See **vaccine point.** **51.** See **point lace.** **52.** any lace made by hand. **53.** *Heraldry.* one of the pendent parts of a label. **54.** *Railroads.* **a.** the vertex of the angle formed at a frog by two rails; the intersection of gauge lines in a switch or frog. **b.** *Brit.* a tapering movable rail, as in a railroad switch. **55.** (in the game of go) any place where lines intersect or meet. **56.** act of pointing. **57.** *Archaic.* a tagged ribbon or cord, formerly much used in dress, as for tying or fastening parts. **58.** *Obs.* an end or

conclusion. **59.** *Obs.* a pointed weapon, as a dagger. **60.** *Obs.* condition. **61. at, on,** or **upon the point of,** on the verge of; close to: *on the point of death.* **62. at this point in time,** now; at this precise moment in history: *At this point in time the President believes peace has been achieved.* **63. in point,** that is pertinent; applicable: *a case in point.* **64. in point of,** as regards; in reference to: *in point of fact.* **65. make a point of,** to regard as important; insist upon: *She made a point of complimenting her friend's apartment.* **66. make points with,** *Informal.* to curry favor with: *to make points with one's boss.* Also, **make Brownie points with. 67. strain** or **stretch a point,** to depart from the usual procedure or rule because of special circumstances; make a concession or exception: *Though the position required three years of previous experience, and he had only two, they stretched a point because of his outstanding record.* **68. to the point,** pertinent; fitting: *The reply was to the point.*
—*v.t.* **69.** to direct (the finger, a weapon, the attention, etc.) at, to, or upon something. **70.** to indicate the presence or position of (usually fol. by *out*): *to point out an object in the sky.* **71.** to direct attention to (usually fol. by *out*): *to point out the advantages of a proposal.* **72.** to furnish with a point or points; sharpen: *to point a lead pencil.* **73.** to mark with one or more points, dots, or the like. **74.** *Sculpture.* to transfer measurements of depth from a clay, wax, or plaster model to (a block of stone) by means of an apparatus that drills holes to the required depth prior to carving. **75.** to punctuate, as writing. **76.** *Phonet.* to mark (letters) with points. **77.** to separate (figures) by dots or points (usually fol. by *off*). **78.** to give greater or added force to (often fol. by *up*): *to point up the necessity for caution.* **79.** *Hunting.* (of a hunting dog) to indicate the presence and location of (game) by standing rigid and facing toward the game. **80.** *Masonry.* **a.** to fill the joints of (brickwork, stonework, etc.) with mortar or cement treated in various ways with tools after application. **b.** to dress the surface of (a stone) with a pointed tool. **81.** to dress (a stone) with a point. **82.** *Metalworking.* **a.** to narrow the end of (a rod) for passing through the dies of a drawbench. **b.** to narrow the end of (a tube) over the head of a pin that is gripped to pull the tube through the dies of a drawbench.
—*v.i.* **83.** to indicate position or direction, as with the finger. **84.** to direct the mind or thought in some direction; call attention to: *Everything points to his guilt.* **85.** to aim. **86.** to have a tendency toward something: *Economic conditions point to further inflation.* **87.** to have a specified direction: *The sign pointed west.* **88.** to face in a particular direction, as a building. **89.** *Hunting.* (of a hunting dog) to point game. **90.** *Naut.* to sail close to the wind. **91.** (of an abscess) to come to a head. [1175–1225; (n.) ME *point(e)*; partly < OF *point* dot, mark, place, moment < L *pūnctum,* n. use of neut. ptp. of *pungere* to prick, stab (cf. PUNGENT); partly < OF *pointe* sharp end < ML *pūncta,* n. use of L: fem. of ptp. of *pungere;* (v.) ME *pointen;* partly deriv. of the n., partly < MF *pointer,* deriv. of *pointe* (n.)]

poin•tal (poin′tl), *n.* pointel.

point′-bear•ing pile′ (point′bâr′ing), *Engin., Building Trades.* a pile depending on the soil or rock beneath its foot for support. Cf. **friction pile.**

point-blank (point′blangk′), *adj.* **1.** aimed or fired straight at the mark esp. from close range; direct. **2.** straightforward, plain, or explicit: *a point-blank denial.* —*adv.* **3.** with a direct aim; directly; straight. **4.** bluntly; frankly: *She told him point-blank that he was not welcome.* [1565–75]

point′ charge′, an electric charge considered to exist at a single point, and thus having neither area nor volume. [1900–05]

point′ count′, *Bridge.* **1.** a method of evaluating the strength of a hand by assigning a numerical value to high cards and to certain combinations and distributions of cards in the hand. **2.** the total number of points in one player's hand. [1955–60]

point cou•pé (*Fr.* pwaN ko͞o pā′), **1.** Also called **cutwork.** a process for producing lace in which predetermined threads in the ground material are cut and removed in order to provide open areas for the insertion of ornamental patterns. **2.** Also called **cutwork lace.** the lace produced by this process. [1860–65; < F: cut point]

point d'Al•en•çon (*Fr.* pwaN dA län sôN′). See **Alençon lace** (def. 1). [1840–50; < F: Alençon stitch]

point d'An•gle•terre (*Fr.* pwaN dän glə teR′), a bobbin lace in which the design is worked out with either a needle or bobbin. [1860–65; < F: English stitch]

point de gaze (*Fr.* pwaN də gäz′). a needlepoint lace in which delicate floral designs are sewn onto a net ground. [1900–05; < F: gauze stitch]

point de Hon•grie (*Fr.* pwaN də ôN gRē′). See **flame stitch.** [< F: Hungarian stitch]

point d'es•prit (*Fr.* pwaN de spRē′), a bobbinet or tulle with oval or square dots woven in an irregular pattern. [1860–65; < F: spirit (i.e., Holy Ghost) stitch]

point-de•vice (point′di vīs′), *Archaic.* —*adv.* **1.** completely; perfectly; exactly. —*adj.* **2.** perfect; precise; scrupulously nice or neat. [1325–75; ME *at point devis* arranged to a point, i.e., to a nicety, to perfection; see DEVICE]

pointe (*Fr.* pwaNt), *n., pl.* **pointes** (*Fr.* pwaNt). *Ballet.* **1.** the tip of the toe. **2.** a position on the extreme tips of the toes. [1820–30; < F: *pointe (du pied)* tiptoe, lit., extremity of the foot]

Pointe-à-Pi•tre (*Fr.* pwaN tA pē′tRᵊ), *n.* a seaport on central Guadeloupe, in the E West Indies. 50,000.

Pointe-aux-Trem•bles (*Fr.* pwaN tō tRäN′blᵊ), *n.* a city in S Quebec, in E Canada, N of Montreal, on the St. Lawrence. 36,270.

CONCISE ETYMOLOGY KEY: <, descended or borrowed from; >, whence; b., blend of, blended; c., cognate with; cf., compare; deriv., derivative; equiv., equivalent; imit., imitative; obl., oblique; r., replacing; s., stem; sp., spelling, spelled; resp., respelling, respelled; trans., translation; ?, origin unknown; *, unattested; ‡, probably earlier than. See the full key inside the front cover.

Pointe Claire (point′ klâr′; *Fr.* pwaNt kleR′), a city in S Quebec, in E Canada, near Montreal, on the St. Lawrence. 24,571.

point•ed (poin′tid), *adj.* **1.** having a point or points: *a pointed arch.* **2.** sharp or piercing: *pointed wit.* **3.** having direct effect, significance, or force: *pointed criticism.* **4.** directed; aimed: *a pointed gun.* **5.** directed particularly, as at a person: *a pointed remark.* **6.** marked; emphasized. **7.** *Heraldry.* (of a cross) having parallel sides with points formed by two inclined sides on each end: *a cross pointed.* [1250–1300; ME; see POINT, -ED², -ED³] —**point′ed•ly,** *adv.* —**point′ed•ness,** *n.*
—**Syn. 2.** penetrating; epigrammatic. —**Ant. 2.** blunt, dull.

point′ed arch′, an arch having a pointed apex. [1740–50]

poin•tel (poin′tl), *n.* a pavement of tile mosaic forming an abstract design. Also, **pointal, poyntell, poyntill.** [1250–1300; ME: stylus, pencil, pointed instrument < OF: point of a spear (F *pointeau*); c. It *puntello,* dim. of *punto* POINT; see -ELLE]

Pointe-Noire (*Fr.* pwaNt nwAR′), *n.* a seaport in the S Republic of Congo. 141,700.

point•er (poin′tər), *n.* **1.** a person or thing that points. **2.** a long, tapering stick used by teachers, lecturers, etc., in pointing things out on a map, blackboard, or the like. **3.** the hand on a watch dial, clock face, scale, etc. **4.** *Mil.* the member of an artillery crew who aims the weapon. **5.** one of a breed of short-haired hunting dogs trained to point game. **6.** a piece of advice, esp. on how to succeed in a specific area: *The food expert gave some good pointers on making better salads.* **7.** *Computers.* an identifier giving the location in storage of something of interest, as a data item, table, or subroutine. **8. Pointers,** *Astron.* the two outer stars of the Big Dipper that lie on a line that passes very near Polaris and are used for finding it. [1490–1500; POINT + -ER¹]
—**Syn. 6.** tip, hint, suggestion, caution.

pointer (def. 5), 26 in. (66 cm) high at shoulder

point′ estima′tion, *Statistics.* the process of determining a single estimated value **(point′ es′timate)** of a parameter of a given population. Cf. **interval estimation.** [1960–65]

point′ group′, *Crystall.* a class of crystals determined by a combination of their symmetry elements, all crystals left unchanged by a given set of symmetry elements being placed in the same class. Also called **symmetry class.** [1900–05]

point′ guard′, *Basketball.* the guard who directs the team's offense from the point.

poin•til•lé (*Fr.* pwaN tē yā′), *adj.* (of book covers) decorated with a tooled pattern of dots. [1900–05; < F, ptp. of *pointiller* to dot, POINT]

poin•til•lism (pwan′tl iz′əm, -tē iz′-, poin′tl iz′-), *n.* (*sometimes cap.*) a theory and technique developed by the neo-impressionists, based on the principle that juxtaposed dots of pure color, as blue and yellow, are optically mixed into the resulting hue, as green, by the viewer. [1900–05; < F *pointillisme,* equiv. to *pointill(er)* to mark with points + *-isme* -ISM] —**poin′til•list,** *n., adj.*

poin•til•list•ic (pwan′tl is′tik, -tē is′-, poin′tl is′-), *adj.* **1.** pertaining to or characteristic of pointillism or pointillists. **2.** made up of or using minute details; particularized; itemized: *a pointillistic style of acting.* [1920–25; < F *pointilliste* (see POINTILLISM, -IST) + -IC]

point•ing (poin′ting), *n.* (in masonry) mortar used as a finishing touch to brickwork. [1835–45; POINT + -ING¹]

point′ lace′, lace made with a needle rather than with bobbins; needlepoint. [1655–65] —**point′-laced′,** *adj.*

point•less (point′lis), *adj.* **1.** without a point: *a pointless pen.* **2.** blunt, as an instrument. **3.** without force, meaning, or relevance: *a pointless remark.* **4.** without a point scored, as in a game: *a pointless inning.* [1300–50; ME *point les.* See POINT, -LESS] —**point′less•ly,** *adv.* —**point′less•ness,** *n.*
—**Syn. 3.** meaningless, unproductive, futile, ineffectual.

point′ man′, **1.** the lead soldier of an infantry patrol on combat operations. **2.** a person who serves in the forefront, as of an economic or political issue. [1900–05, *Amer.*]

point′ muta′tion, *Genetics.* a change in a single base in a nucleotide sequence. [1920–25]

point′ of articula′tion, *Phonet.* See **place of articulation.**

point′ of depar′ture, **1.** *Naut.* the precise location of a vessel, established in order to set a course, especially in beginning a voyage in open water. **2.** a place to begin, as in a discussion, argument, etc. Also called **departure.** [1855–60]

point′ of hon′or, an issue that affects one's honor, reputation, etc.: *It was a point of honor with him to avenge any insult to his family.* [1605–15]

point′ of inflec′tion, *Math.* See **inflection point.** [1735–45]

point′ of no′ return′, **1.** *Aviation.* the point in a flight at which an aircraft will lack sufficient fuel to return to its starting point. **2.** the critical point in an undertaking, decision-making process, etc., where one has committed oneself irrevocably to a course of action or policy. [1940–45]

point′ of or′der, *Parl. Proc.* a question raised as to whether proceedings are in order, or in conformity with parliamentary law. [1745–55]

point-of-pur•chase (point′əv pûr′chəs), *adj.* designating or in use at a retail outlet where an item can be purchased; point-of-sale: *point-of-purchase displays to entice the buyer.*

point′ of sail′ing, *Naut.* the bearing of a sailing vessel, considered with relation to the direction of the wind.

point-of-sale (point′əv sāl′), *n., pl.* **points-of-sale,** *adj.* —*n.* **1.** the store, dealer, or other retail outlet where an item is sold: *from manufacturer to point-of-sale.* —*adj.* **2.** designating or in use at a point-of-sale, cashier's desk, or check-out counter; point-of-purchase. **3.** (in retailing) of or pertaining to a customer-checkout system that uses automated devices linked to a computer, as a terminal **(point′-of-sale′ ter′minal)** that directly transmits sales data as part of a computerized system for accounting and inventory control. *Abbr.:* P.O.S., POS [1950–55]

point′ of view′, **1.** a specified or stated manner of consideration or appraisal; standpoint: *from the point of view of a doctor.* **2.** an opinion, attitude, or judgment: *He refuses to change his point of view in the matter.* **3.** the position of the narrator in relation to the story, as indicated by the narrator's outlook from which the events are depicted and by the attitude toward the characters. [1720–30]

Point′ Pleas′ant, a borough in E New Jersey. 17,747.

Point′ Reyes′ li′lac (rāz), a prostrate shrub, *Ceanothus gloriosus,* of southern California, having leathery, roundish leaves and purplish or deep-blue flowers. [named after *Point Reyes,* Marin Co., California]

point-set (point′set′), *adj. Typesetting.* (of spaces) cast in widths that conform to standard point measure.

point′ set′ topol′ogy, *Math.* topology (def. 2). [1955–60]

point′ shav′ing, *Sports.* (esp. in basketball) the illegal practice, by one or more bribed players, of deliberately limiting the number of points scored to conform to the desires of corrupt gamblers.

points•man (points′mən), *n., pl.* **-men.** *Brit.* **1.** a railway switchman. **2.** a police officer who directs traffic, as at an intersection. [1840–50; POINT + -S³ + MAN¹]

point′ source′, *Physics, Optics.* a source of radiation sufficiently distant compared to its length and width that it can be considered as a point. [1900–05]

point′ spread′, a betting device, established by oddsmakers and used to attract bettors for uneven competitions, indicating the estimated number of points by which a stronger team can be expected to defeat a weaker team, the point spread being added to the weaker team's actual points in the game and this new figure then compared to the stronger team's points to determine winning bets. Also called **spread.**

point′ sys′tem, **1.** *Print.* a system for grading the sizes of type bodies, leads, etc., that employs the point as a unit of measurement. Cf. **point** (def. 48a). **2.** any of certain systems of writing and printing for the blind that employ embossed symbols for letters. **3.** a system of promoting students by an evaluation of their work on the basis of points representing quality of achievement. **4.** See **Bedaux system.**

point ti•ré (*Fr.* pwaN tē RĀ′). See **drawn work.** [< F: drawn stitch]

point-to-point (point′tə point′), *n.* a cross-country horse race between specified points, in which each rider is often free to select his or her own course between the points. [1880–85]

point•wise (point′wīz′), *adj. Math.* occurring at each point of a given set: *pointwise convergence.* [1535–45; POINT + -WISE]

point•y (poin′tē), *adj.,* **point•i•er, point•i•est.** having a comparatively sharp point: *The elf had pointy little ears.* [1635–45; POINT + -Y¹]

point•y-head•ed (poin′tē hed′id), *adj. Slang* (*disparaging*). **1.** stupid; idiotic. **2.** intellectual, esp. in a self-important or impractical way. [1970–75, *Amer.*] —**point′y-head′,** *n.*

Poi•ret (pwä rā′; *Fr.* pwA Re′), *n.* **Paul** (pôl), 1879–1944, French fashion designer.

poise¹ (poiz), *n., v.,* **poised, pois•ing.** —*n.* **1.** a state of balance or equilibrium, as from equality or equal distribution of weight; equipoise. **2.** a dignified, self-confident manner or bearing; composure; self-possession: *to show poise in company.* **3.** steadiness; stability: *intellectual poise.* **4.** suspense or wavering, as between rest and motion or two phases of motion: *the poise of the tides.* **5.** the way of being poised, held, or carried. **6.** the state or position of hovering: *the poise of a bird in the air.* —*v.t.* **7.** to adjust, hold, or carry in equilibrium; balance evenly. **8.** to hold supported or raised, as in position for casting, using, etc.: *to poise a spear.* **9.** to hold or carry in a particular manner: *She walked, carefully poising a water jug on her head.* **10.** *Obs.* to weigh. —*v.i.* **11.** to rest in equilibrium; be balanced. **12.** to hover, as a bird in the air. [1350–1400; (n.) ME *pois(e)* weight < OF (F *poids*) < LL *pēnsum,* n. use of neut. ptp. of L *pendere* to weigh; (v.) ME *poisen* to weigh < OF *poiser,* var., based on tonic s., of *peser* < L *pēnsāre,* freq. of *pendere*]
—**Syn. 2.** self-assurance; polish, grace, refinement. —**Ant. 1, 3.** instability.

poise² (pwäz), *n. Physics.* a centimeter-gram-second unit of viscosity, equal to the viscosity of a fluid in which a stress of one dyne per square centimeter is required to maintain a difference of velocity of one centimeter per second between two parallel planes in the fluid that lie in the direction of flow and are separated by a distance of one centimeter. *Symbol:* P [1910–15; < F; named after Jean Louis Marie *Poiseuille* (1799–1869), French physician]

poised (poizd), *adj.* **1.** (of a person) composed, dignified, and self-assured. **2.** being in balance or equilibrium: *a balloon poised on the nose of a seal.* **3.** teetering or wavering: *to be poised on the brink of disaster.* **4.** hovering or suspended in or as in midair: *a bird poised in flight; a helicopter poised overhead.* [1635–45; POISE[1] + -ED[2], -ED[3]]

pois·er (poi′zər), *n.* **1.** a person or thing that poises. **2.** *Obs.* halter[2]. [1375–1425 late ME; see POISE[1], -ER[1]]

Poi·seuille's′ law′ (pwä zwēz′), *Physics, Mech.* the law that the velocity of a liquid flowing through a capillary is directly proportional to the pressure of the liquid and the fourth power of the radius of the capillary and is inversely proportional to the viscosity of the liquid and the length of the capillary. [1880–85; see POISE[2]]

poi·sha (poi′shə), *n., pl.* **-sha.** an aluminum coin and monetary unit of Bangladesh, the 100th part of a taka. Also called **paisa.**

poi·son (poi′zən), *n.* **1.** a substance with an inherent property that tends to destroy life or impair health. **2.** something harmful or pernicious, as to happiness or well-being: *the poison of slander.* **3.** *Slang.* any variety of alcoholic liquor: *Name your poison!* —*v.t.* **4.** to administer poison to (a person or animal). **5.** to kill or injure with or as if with poison. **6.** to put poison into or upon; saturate with poison: *to poison food.* **7.** to ruin, vitiate, or corrupt: *Hatred had poisoned his mind.* **8.** *Chem.* to destroy or diminish the activity of (a catalyst or enzyme). —*adj.* **9.** causing poisoning; poisonous: *a poison shrub.* [1200–50; ME *puisun* < OF < L *pōtiōn-* (s. of *pōtiō*) drink, POTION, poisonous draught] —**poi′son·er,** *n.* —**poi′son·less,** *adj.* —**poi′son·less·ness,** *n.*
—**Syn. 1.** POISON, TOXIN, VENOM are terms for any substance that injures the health or destroys life when absorbed into the system, esp. of a higher animal. POISON is the general word: *a poison for insects.* A TOXIN is a poison produced by an organism; it is esp. used in medicine in reference to disease-causing bacterial secretions: *A toxin produces diphtheria.* VENOM is esp. used of the poisons secreted by certain animals, usually injected by bite or sting: *the venom of a snake.* **7.** contaminate, pollute, taint.

poi′son bean′, **1.** Also called **bladderpod.** a tall plant, *Glottidium vesicaria,* of the legume family, native to the southeastern U.S., having clusters of yellow flowers and pods containing highly poisonous seeds. **2.** a seed of this plant.

poi′son dog′wood. See **poison sumac.** [1805–15, *Amer.*]

poi′son gas′, any of various toxic gases, esp. those used in chemical warfare to kill or incapacitate on inhalation or contact, as phosgene, chlorine, etc. [1910–15]

poi′son haw′, a shrub, *Viburnum molle,* of the central U.S., having white flowers and bluish-black fruit.

poi′son hem′lock, hemlock (defs. 1, 3). [1810–20, *Amer.*]

poi·son·ing (poi′zə ning), *n. Pathol.* the condition produced by a poison or by a toxic substance. [1400–50; late ME *poisenynge.* See POISON, -ING[1]]

poi′son i′vy, **1.** a vine or shrub, *Rhus radicans,* having trifoliate leaves and whitish berries and causing severe dermatitis when touched by persons sensitive to it. **2.** See **poison oak. 3.** the rash caused by touching poison ivy. [1775–85, *Amer.*]

poison ivy, *Rhus radicans*

poi′son oak′, either of two shrubs, *Rhus toxicodendron,* of the eastern U.S., or *R. diversiloba,* of the Pacific coast of North America, resembling poison ivy and causing severe dermatitis when touched by persons sensitive to them. Also called **poison ivy.** [1735–45, *Amer.*]

poi·son·ous (poi′zə nəs), *adj.* **1.** full of or containing poison: *poisonous air; a poisonous substance.* **2.** harmful; destructive: *poisonous to animals; poisonous rumors.* **3.** deeply malicious; malevolent: *poisonous efforts.* [1565–75; POISON + -OUS] —**poi′son·ous·ly,** *adv.* —**poi′son·ous·ness,** *n.*

poi·son-pen (poi′zən pen′), *adj.* **1.** composed or sent maliciously, as a letter, usually anonymously and for the purpose of damaging another's reputation or happiness: *The newspaper received a poison-pen letter alleging that the mayor was misusing city funds.* **2.** characterized by or given to the sending of poison-pen letters: *a poison-pen campaign; a poison-pen writer.* [1910–15]

poi′son pill′, **1.** a pellet of a quick-acting poison, as cyanide, for a spy to carry in order to commit suicide when faced with capture or torture. **2.** *Financial Slang.* any of various business devices created to prevent a company from being taken over by another, as issuing a new class of stock or stock warrants that would become costly to the buyer in the event of a takeover. [1945–50]

poi′son su′mac, a shrub or small tree, *Rhus vernix* (or *Toxicodendron vernix*), of swampy areas of the eastern U.S., having pinnate leaves and causing severe dermatitis when touched by persons sensitive to it. Also called **poison dogwood.** [1810–20]

poi·son·wood (poi′zən wo͝od′), *n.* a tree, *Metopium toxiferum,* of southern Florida, that has compound leaves and yellowish, berrylike fruits and is poisonous to touch. Also called **poi′son tree′.** [1715–25, *Amer.*; POISON + WOOD[1]]

Pois·son′ distribu′tion (pwä sōn′; *Fr.* PWA SÔN′), *Statistics.* a limiting form of the binomial probability distribution for small values of the probability of success and for large numbers of trials: particularly useful in industrial quality-control work and in radiation and bacteriological problems. [1920–25; named after S. D. *Poisson* (1781–1840), French mathematician and physicist]

Poisson's′ ra′tio, *Physics.* the ratio, in an elastic body under longitudinal stress, of the transverse strain to the longitudinal strain. Also, **Poisson′ ra′tio.** [1925–30; see POISSON DISTRIBUTION]

Poi·tiers (pwA tyā′), *n.* a city in and the capital of Vienne, in W France: Roman ruins; battles A.D. 507, 732, 1356. 85,466.

Poi·tou (pwA to͞o′), *n.* **1.** a region and former province in W France. **2. Gate of,** a wide pass near Poitiers.

po·kal (pō käl′), *n.* a large German standing cup of silver, glass, or other material. [1865–70; < G < It *boccale* drinking-vessel < LL *baucalis* vessel used to cool wine < Gk *baúkalis*]

poke[1] (pōk), *v.,* **poked, pok·ing,** *n.* —*v.t.* **1.** to prod or push, esp. with something narrow or pointed, as a finger, elbow, stick, etc.: *to poke someone in the ribs.* **2.** to make (a hole, one's way, etc.) by or as by prodding or pushing. **3.** to thrust or push: *She poked her head out of the window.* **4.** to force, drive, or stir by or as by pushing or thrusting: *He poked the fire up.* **5.** to thrust obtrusively: *The prosecutor kept poking his finger at the defendant.* —*v.i.* **6.** to make a pushing or thrusting movement with the finger, a stick, etc. **7.** to extend or project (often fol. by *out*): *His handkerchief is poking out of his back pocket.* **8.** to thrust oneself obtrusively: *to poke into something that is not one's affair.* **9.** to search curiously; pry (often fol. by *around* or *about*). **10.** to go or proceed in a slow or aimless way (often fol. by *along*). **11. poke fun at,** to ridicule or mock, esp. covertly or slyly: *In her novel, she pokes fun at her ex-husband.* **12. poke one's nose into,** *Informal.* to meddle in; pry into: *We felt as if half the people in town were poking their noses into our lives.* —*n.* **13.** a thrust or push. **14.** *Informal.* a slow or dawdling person; slowpoke. [1300–50; ME < MD, MLG *poken* to thrust. See POACH[1]] —**pok′a·ble,** *adj.*

poke[2] (pōk), *n.* **1.** *Chiefly Midland U.S. and Scot.* a bag or sack, esp. a small one. **2.** a wallet or purse. **3.** *Archaic.* a pocket. [1250–1300; ME < MD, whence also ONF *poque,* F *poche* bag, pocket; cf. POACH[2], POCKET, POUCH]

poke[3] (pōk), *n.* **1.** a projecting brim at the front of a bonnet, framing the face. **2.** Also called **poke′ bon′net.** a bonnet or hat with such a brim. [1760–70; appar. special use of POKE[1]]

poke[3] (def. 2)

poke[4] (pōk), *n.* pokeweed. [1590–1600; perh. shortening of obs. *pocan* pokeweed, perh. var. of PUCCOON (pokeberries and puccoon roots were both sources of red dye)]

poke·ber·ry (pōk′ber′ē, -bə rē), *n., pl.* **-ries. 1.** the berry of the pokeweed. **2.** the plant. [1765–75, *Amer.*; POKE[4] + BERRY]

poke′ check′, *Ice Hockey.* an attempt to deprive an opponent of the puck by pushing it away with one's stick. Cf. **check[1]** (def. 42). [1940–45]

poke·lo·gan (pōk′lō′gən), *n. Northeastern U.S.* marshy or stagnant water that has branched off from a stream or lake. Also, **poke·lo·ken** (pōk′lō′kən). Also called **logan.** [1840–50 (earlier as placename); orig. uncert.; no AmerInd source substantiated; cf. BOGAN]

pok·er[1] (pō′kər), *n.* **1.** a person or thing that pokes. **2.** a metal rod for poking or stirring a fire. [1525–35; POKE[1] + -ER[1]]

pok·er[2] (pō′kər), *n.* a card game played by two or more persons, in which the players bet on the value of their hands, the winner taking the pool. [1825–35, *Amer.*; perh. orig. braggart, bluffer; cf. MLG *poken* to brag, play, MD *poken* to bluff, brag]

pok′er dice′, **1.** dice that, instead of being marked with spots, carry on their faces a picture or symbol representing the six highest playing cards: ace, king, queen, jack, ten, nine. **2.** any of various gambling games played with from three to six such dice. [1870–75, *Amer.*]

pok′er face′, **1.** an expressionless face: *He can tell a funny story with a poker face.* **2.** a person who has or deliberately assumes a poker face: *It is impossible to tell what that poker face is really thinking.* [1880–85, *Amer.*] —**pok′er-faced′,** *adj.*

pok′er plant′, tritoma.

poke·weed (pōk′wēd′), *n.* a tall herb, *Phytolacca americana,* of North America, having juicy purple berries and a purple root used in medicine, and young edible shoots resembling asparagus. Also called **poke·root** (pōk′ro͞ot′, -ro͝ot′), **scoke, garget.** [1745–55, *Amer.*; POKE[4] + WEED[1]]

pok·ey (pō′kē), *adj.* **pok·i·er, pok·i·est,** *n., pl.* **pok·eys.** poky.

pok·y (pō′kē), *adj.,* **pok·i·er, pok·i·est,** *n., pl.* **pok·ies.** —*adj. Informal.* **1.** puttering; slow; dull: *poky drivers.* **2.** (of a place) small and cramped: *a poky little room.* **3.** (of dress) dowdy. —*n.* **4.** *Slang.* a jail: *They put him in the poky for carrying a concealed weapon.* [1840–50; POKE[1] + -Y[1]] —**pok′i·ly,** *adv.* —**pok′i·ness,** *n.*

pol (pol), *n. Informal.* a politician, esp. one experienced in making political deals, exchanging political favors, etc. [1940–45; by shortening]

POL, petroleum, oil, and lubricants.

Pol., 1. Poland. **2.** Also, **Pol** Polish.

pol., 1. political. **2.** politics.

Po·la (pō′lə; *It.* pô′lä), *n.* **1.** Pula. **2.** a female given name.

Po·la·bi·an (pō lä′bē ən, -lā′-), *n.* **1.** a member of a Slavic people who once lived in the Elbe River basin and on the Baltic coast of northern Germany. **2.** the extinct Slavic language of this people. Also, **Po·lab** (pō läb′). [1865–70; *Polab* + -IAN; cf. G *polabisch,* NL *Polabicus;* ult. from tribal name, formed with common W Slavic *po-* along, bordering + *Lab(a)* Elbe River (cf. Czech *Labe*)]

Po·lack (pō′läk, -lak), *n. Slang (disparaging and offensive).* a Pole or person of Polish descent. [1590–1600; < Pol *polak* a Pole]

Po·land (pō′lənd), *n.* a republic in E central Europe, on the Baltic Sea. 37,800,000; ab. 121,000 sq. mi. (313,400 sq. km). *Cap.:* Warsaw. Polish, **Polska.**

Po′land Chi′na, one of an American breed of black hogs having white markings. [1875–80, *Amer.*]

po·lar (pō′lər), *adj.* **1.** of or pertaining to the North or South Pole. **2.** of or pertaining to the pole of any sphere, a magnet, an electric cell, etc. **3.** opposite in character or action: *The two have personalities that are polar.* **4.** capable of ionizing, as NaCl, HCl, or NaOH; electrolytic; heteropolar. **5.** central; pivotal: *the polar provision of the treaty.* **6.** analogous to the polestar as a guide; guiding: *a polar precept.* [1545–55; < ML *polāris.* See POLE[2], -AR[1]]

po′lar an′gle, *Math.* See under **polar coordinates.**

po′lar ax′is, *Math.* the fixed line, usually horizontal, from which the angle made by the radius vector is measured in a polar coordinate system. [1890–95]

po′lar bear′, a large white bear, *Ursus maritimus,* of the arctic regions. [1775–85]

polar bear, *Ursus maritimus,* 4 ft. (1.2 m) high at shoulder; length 7½ ft. (2.3 m)

po′lar bod′y, *Cell Biol.* one of the minute cells arising from the unequal meiotic divisions of the ovum at or near the time of fertilization. [1885–90]

po′lar cap′, **1.** *Geol.* the icecap situated at either end of the earth's poles. **2.** *Astron.* either of the two bright areas around the poles of the planet Mars, consisting of water ice and frozen carbon dioxide. [1890–95]

po′lar cir′cle, either the Arctic or the Antarctic Circle. [1545–55]

po′lar coor′dinates, *Math.* a system of coordinates for locating a point in a plane by the length of its radius vector and the angle this vector makes with the polar axis (**polar angle**). [1810–20]

po′lar dis′tance, *Astron.* codeclination. [1810–20]

po′lar equa′tion, *Math.* an equation in which the variables are polar coordinates. [1840–50]

po′lar front′, *Meteorol.* the variable frontal zone of middle latitudes separating air masses of polar and tropical origin. [1915–20]

Po·la·ri (pə lär′ē, pô-), *n.* a distinctive English argot in use since at least the 18th century among groups of theatrical and circus performers and in certain homosexual communities, derived largely from Italian, directly or through Lingua Franca. Also, **parlyaree, parlary.** [ult. < It *parlare* to speak, talk; see PARLE]

po•lar•im•e•ter (pō′lə rim′i tər), *n. Optics.* **1.** an instrument for measuring the amount of light received from a given source as a function of its state of polarization. **2.** a form of polariscope for measuring the angular rotation of the plane of polarization. [1860–65; < ML *polāri(s)* POLAR + -METER]

Po•lar•is (pō lâr′is, -lar′-, pə-), *n.* **1.** *Astron.* the polestar or North Star, a star of the second magnitude situated close to the north pole of the heavens, in the constellation Ursa Minor: the outermost star in the handle of the Little Dipper. **2.** a two-stage U.S. ballistic missile, usually fired from a submerged submarine. [1955–60; short for ML *stella polāris* polar star]

po•lar•i•scope (pō lar′ə skōp′, pə-), *n. Optics.* an instrument for measuring or exhibiting the polarization of light or for examining substances in polarized light, often to determine stress and strain in glass and other substances. [1820–30; < ML *polāri(s)* POLAR + -SCOPE] **—po•lar•i•scop•ic** (pō lar′ə skop′ik, pə-), *adj.* **—po•lar′i•scop′i•cal•ly,** *adv.*

po•lar•i•ty (pō lar′i tē, pə-), *n.* **1.** *Physics.* **a.** the property or characteristic that produces unequal physical effects at different points in a body or system, as a magnet or storage battery. **b.** the positive or negative state in which a body reacts to a magnetic, electric, or other field. **2.** the presence or manifestation of two opposite or contrasting principles or tendencies. **3.** *Ling.* **a.** (of words, phrases, or sentences) positive or negative character. **b.** polar opposition. [1640–50; POLAR + -ITY]

po•lar•i•za•tion (pō′lər ə zā′shən), *n.* **1.** a sharp division, as of a population or group, into opposing factions. **2.** *Optics.* a state, or the production of a state, in which rays of light or similar radiation exhibit different properties in different directions. Cf. **circular polarization, elliptical polarization, plane polarization. 3.** *Elect.* **a.** the deposit of gases, produced during electrolysis, on the electrodes of a cell, increasing the resistance of the cell. **b.** a vector quantity indicating the electric dipole moment per unit of volume of a dielectric. **c.** the induction of polarity in a ferromagnetic substance. **4.** the production or acquisition of polarity. [1805–15; POLARIZE + -ATION]

polariza′tion charge′, *Elect.* any electric charge that is bound to an atom or molecule (opposed to *free charge*). Also called **bound charge.**

po•lar•ize (pō′lə rīz′), *v.*, **-ized, -iz•ing.** **—***v.t.* **1.** to cause polarization in. **2.** to divide into sharply opposing factions, political groups, etc.: *The controversy has polarized voters into proabortion and antiabortion groups.* **3.** to give polarity to. **—***v.i.* **4.** to become polarized. Also, *esp. Brit.,* **po′lar•ise′.** [1805–15; POLAR + -IZE] **—po′lar•iz′a•ble,** *adj.* **—po′lar•iz′a•bil′i•ty,** *n.*

po•lar•ized (pō′lə rīzd′), *adj.* **1.** of or pertaining to a medium that exhibits polarization. **2.** (of an electric plug or outlet) designed so that the plug and outlet fit together in only one way. [1920–25; POLARIZE + -ED[2]]

po•lar•iz•er (pō′lə rī′zər), *n.* **1.** a person or thing that polarizes. **2.** *Optics.* a device, often a crystal or prism, that polarizes light. [1850–55; POLARIZE + -ER[1]]

po′larizing an′gle, *Optics.* See under **Brewster's law.** [1820–30]

po′larizing fil′ter, *Photog.* a camera lens filter used to control the plane of polarization of light entering the lens.

po′larizing mi′croscope, a microscope that utilizes polarized light to reveal detail in an object, used esp. to study crystalline and fibrous structures.

po′lar lights′, the aurora borealis in the Northern Hemisphere or the aurora australis in the Southern Hemisphere.

po′lar mol′ecule, a molecule in which the centroid of the positive charges is different from the centroid of the negative charges. Also called **dipole.**

po′lar nu′cleus, *Bot.* either of two female haploid nuclei, in the embryo sac of flowers, that fuse to produce a diploid nucleus, which combines with a male nucleus to form the endosperm. [1880–85]

po•lar•o•gram (pō lar′ə gram′), *n.* the record produced by the action of a Polarograph. [1920–25; POLAR + -O- + -GRAM[1]]

Po•lar•o•graph (pō lar′ə graf′, -gräf′, pə-), *Trademark.* a brand name for an instrument that automatically registers the current in electrolysis at a dropping mercury electrode.

po•lar•og•ra•phy (pō′lə rog′rə fē), *n. Chem.* the use of a Polarograph to perform qualitative or quantitative analyses. Also called **polarograph′ic anal′ysis.** [1935–40; POLARO(GRAPH) + -GRAPHY] **—po•lar•o•graph•ic** (pō lar′ə graf′ik, pə-), *adj.*

Po•lar•oid (pō′lə roid′), *Trademark.* **1.** a brand of material for producing polarized light from unpolarized light by dichroism, consisting typically of a stretched sheet of colorless plastic treated with an iodine solution so as to have long, thin, parallel chains of polymeric molecules containing conductive iodine atoms. It is used widely in optical and lighting devices to reduce glare. **2.** Also called **Po′laroid Cam′era, Po′laroid Land′ Cam′era.** the first brand of instant camera, developed by Edwin H. Land and marketed since 1948. **3.** Also called **Po′laroid print′.** a print made by such a camera.

po′lar opposi′tion, *Ling.* the relation between a pair of antonyms that denote relatively higher and lower degrees of a quality with respect to an explicit or implicit norm rather than absolute values, as the relation between *tall* and *short* or *light* and *dark,* but not between *true* and *false.*

po′lar or′bit, a spacecraft orbit that passes over, or close to, the geographic poles of the earth or some other celestial body. [1960–65]

po′lar out′break, *Meteorol.* a vigorous thrust of cold, polar air across temperate regions.

Po′lar Re′gions, the regions within the Arctic and Antarctic circles.

po′lar va′lence, *Chem.* electrovalence (def. 1).

pol•der (pōl′dər), *n.* a tract of low land, esp. in the Netherlands, reclaimed from the sea or other body of water and protected by dikes. [1595–1605; < D]

pole[1] (pōl), *n., v.,* **poled, pol•ing.** **—***n.* **1.** a long, cylindrical, often slender piece of wood, metal, etc.: *a telephone pole; a fishing pole.* **2.** *Northeastern U.S.* a long, tapering piece of wood or other material that extends from the front axle of a vehicle between the animals drawing it. **3.** *Naut.* **a.** a light spar. **b.** that part of a mast between the uppermost standing rigging and the truck. **4.** the lane of a racetrack nearest to the infield; the inside lane. Cf. **post**[1] (def. 5). **5.** a unit of length equal to 16½ feet (5 m); a rod. **6.** a square rod, 30¼ square yards (25.3 sq. m). **7. under bare poles, a.** *Naut.* (of a sailing ship) with no sails set, as during a violent storm. **b.** stripped; naked; destitute: *The thugs robbed him and left him under bare poles.* **—***v.t.* **8.** to furnish with poles. **9.** to push, strike, or propel with a pole: *to pole a raft.* **10.** *Baseball.* to make (an extra-base hit) by batting the ball hard and far: *He poled a triple to deep right-center.* **11.** *Metall.* to stir (molten metal, as copper, tin, or zinc) with poles of green wood so as to produce carbon, which reacts with the oxygen present to effect deoxidation. **—***v.i.* **12.** to propel a boat, raft, etc., with a pole: *to pole down the river.* [bef. 1050; ME; OE *pāl* < L *pālus* stake. See PALE[2]] **—pole′less,** *adj.*

pole[2] (pōl), *n.* **1.** each of the extremities of the axis of the earth or of any spherical body. **2.** *Astron.* See **celestial pole. 3.** one of two opposite or contrasted principles or tendencies: *His behavior ranges between the poles of restraint and abandon.* **4.** a point of concentration of interest, attention, etc.: *The beautiful actress was the pole of everyone's curiosity.* **5.** *Elect., Magnetism.* either of the two regions or parts of an electric battery, magnet, or the like, that exhibits electrical or magnetic polarity. **6.** *Cell Biol.* **a.** either end of an ideal axis in a nucleus, cell, or ovum, about which parts are more or less symmetrically arranged. **b.** either end of a spindle-shaped figure formed in a cell during mitosis. **c.** the place at which a cell extension or process begins, as a nerve cell axon or a flagellum. **7.** *Math.* **a.** a singular point at which a given function of a complex variable can be expanded in a Laurent series beginning with a specified finite, negative power of the variable. **b.** origin (def. 6b). **8.** *Crystall.* a line perpendicular to a crystal face and passing through the crystal center. **9. poles apart** or **asunder,** having widely divergent or completely opposite attitudes, interests, etc.: *In education and background they were poles apart.* [1350–1400; ME < L *polus* < Gk *pólos* pivot, axis, pole]

Pole (pōl), *n.* a native or inhabitant of Poland.

Pole (pōl), *n.* **Reginald,** 1500–58, English cardinal and last Roman Catholic archbishop of Canterbury.

pole•ax (pōl′aks′), *n., pl.* **-ax•es** (-ak′siz), *v.,* **-axed, -ax•ing.** **—***n.* **1.** a medieval shafted weapon with blade combining ax, hammer, and apical spike, used for fighting on foot. **2.** an ax, usually with a hammer opposite the cutting edge, used in stunning and slaughtering animals. **3.** an ax with both a blade and a hook, formerly used in naval warfare to assist sailors in boarding vessels. **—***v.t.* **4.** to strike down or kill with or as if with a poleax. [1300–50; ME *pollax* battle-ax, lit., head-ax (see POLL[1], AX); akin to MLG *polexe*]

pole•axe (pōl′aks′), *n., pl.* **-ax•es** (-ak′siz), *v.t.,* **-axed, -ax•ing.** poleax.

pole′ bean′, any vinelike variety of bean that is trained to grow upright on a pole, trellis, fence, etc. [1760–70, *Amer.*]

pole•cat (pōl′kat′), *n., pl.* **-cats,** (*esp. collectively*) **-cat. 1.** a European mammal, *Mustela putorius,* of the weasel family, having a blackish fur and ejecting a fetid fluid when attacked or disturbed. Cf. **ferret**[1] (def. 1). **2.** any of various North American skunks. [1275–1325; ME *polcat,* perh. equiv. to MF *pol, poul* chicken (< L *pullus*) + CAT[1]]

pole′ com′pass, (formerly) a ship's compass elevated on a wooden pole to isolate it as much as possible from local magnetism.

Pol. Econ., political economy. Also, **pol. econ.**

pole′ ham′mer, a shafted weapon having a spiked hammer head. Also called **war hammer.** [1870–75]

pole′ horse′, a horse harnessed to the tongue of a vehicle; poler; wheeler. [1815–25, *Amer.*]

pole′ jump′. See **pole vault.** [1895–1900]

pole-jump (pōl′jump′), *v.i.* pole-vault. [1895–1900] **—pole′-jump′er,** *n.*

pole′ mast′, *Naut.* a mast on a sailing vessel, consisting of a single piece without separate upper masts. [1760–70]

po•lem•ic (pə lem′ik, pō-), *n.* **1.** a controversial argument, as one against some opinion, doctrine, etc. **2.** a person who argues in opposition to another; controversialist. **—***adj.* **3.** Also, **po•lem′i•cal.** of or pertaining to a polemic; controversial. [1630–40; < Gk *polemikós* of or for war, equiv. to *pólem(os)* war + *-ikos* -IC] **—po•lem′i•cal•ly,** *adv.*

po•lem•i•cize (pə lem′ə sīz′, pō-), *v.i.,* **-cized, -ciz•ing.** to practice the art of disputation; to engage in polemics or controversy. Also, *esp. Brit.,* **po•lem′i•cise′.** [1945–50; POLEMIC + -IZE]

po•lem•ics (pə lem′iks, pō-), *n.* (*used with a singular v.*) **1.** the art or practice of disputation or controversy: *a master of polemics.* **2.** the branch of theology dealing with the history or conduct of ecclesiastical disputation and controversy. Cf. **irenics.** [1630–40; see POLEMIC, -ICS]

pol•e•mist (pol′ə mist, pə lem′ist, pō-), *n.* a person who is engaged or versed in polemics. Also, **po•lem•i•cist** (pə lem′ə sist, pō-). [1815–25; < Gk *polemistḗs* warrior, equiv. to *pólem(os)* war + *-istēs* -IST]

pol•e•mize (pol′ə mīz′), *v.i.,* **-mized, -miz•ing.** polemicize. Also, *esp. Brit.,* **pol′e•mise′.** [< Gk *pólem(os)* war + -IZE]

po•le•mol•o•gy (pō′lə mol′ə jē), *n.* the analysis of human conflict and war, particularly international war. [1935–40; < Gk *pólemo(s)* war + -LOGY] **—po•lem•o•log•i•cal** (pə lem′ə loj′i kəl), *adj.* **—po′le•mol′o•gist,** *n.*

pol•e•mo•ni•a•ceous (pol′ə mō′nē ā′shəs), *adj.* belonging to the Polemoniaceae, the phlox family of plants. Cf. **phlox family.** [1855–60; < NL *Polemoniac(ae)* family name (see POLEMONIUM, -ACEAE) + -OUS]

po•len•ta (pō len′tə), *n.* (esp. in Italian cooking) a thick mush of cornmeal. [1555–65; < It < L: hulled and crushed grain, esp. barley]

pole′ of cold′. See **cold pole.**

pole′ piece′, *Elect.* a piece of magnetic material at a pole of a permanent magnet or of an electromagnet, shaped to control the magnetic flux distribution in the vicinity of the pole. [1880–85]

pole′ plate′, *Carpentry.* (in a trussed roof) a plate resting upon the beams and supporting common rafters near their lower ends. [1815–25]

pole′ posi′tion, 1. a position on the inside of the track in any race. **2.** (in auto racing) a starting position on the inside of the front row. **3.** an advantageous position.

pol•er (pō′lər), *n.* **1.** a person or thing that poles. **2.** See **pole horse.** [1680–90; POLE[1] + -ER[1]]

pole•star (pōl′stär′), *n.* **1.** Polaris. **2.** something that serves as a guiding principle. **3.** something that is the center of attention or attraction. [1545–55; POLE[2] + STAR]

pole′ vault′, *Track.* **1.** a field event in which a leap or vault over a crossbar is performed with the aid of a long pole. **2.** a leap or vault so performed. [1890–95]

pole vault (def. 1)

pole-vault (pōl′vôlt′), *v.i.* to execute a pole vault. [1890–95] **—pole′-vault′er,** *n.*

pole•ward (pōl′wərd), *adv.* **1.** Also, **pole′wards.** toward a pole of the earth; toward the North or South Pole. **—***adj.* **2.** facing or moving toward the North or South Pole. [1870–75; POLE[2] + -WARD]

po•leyn (pō′lān), *n. Armor.* a piece for the knee, made of plate or leather. Also called **knee cop.** See diag. under **armor.** [1350–1400; ME *poleyn, polayne* < OF *po(u)lain* < ?]

po•li•a•nite (pō′lē ə nīt′), *n. Mineral.* a variety of pyrolusite, MnO_2, having well-developed crystals. [1840–50; < G *Polianit,* irreg. < Gk *polaínesthai* to grow white (with sea foam), deriv. of *poliós* gray; see -ITE[1]]

po•lice (pə lēs′), *n., v.,* **-liced, -lic•ing.** **—***n.* **1.** Also called **police force.** an organized civil force for maintaining order, preventing and detecting crime, and enforcing the laws. **2.** (*used with a plural v.*) members of such a force: *Several police are patrolling the neighborhood.* **3.** the regulation and control of a community, esp. for the maintenance of public order, safety, health, morals, etc. **4.** the department of the government concerned with this, esp. with the maintenance of order. **5.** any body of people officially maintained or employed to keep order, enforce regulations, etc. **6.** *Mil.* (in the U.S. Army) **a.** the cleaning and keeping clean of a camp, post, station, etc. **b.** the condition of a camp, post, station, etc., with reference to cleanliness. **—***v.t.* **7.** to regulate, control, or keep in order by or as if by means of police. **8.** *Mil.* to clean and keep clean (a camp, post, etc.) [1520–30; < MF: government, civil administration, police < LL *polītia* citizenship, government, for L *polītīa;* see POLITY]

—Pronunciation. Many English words exemplify the original stress rule of Old English and other early Germanic languages, according to which all parts of speech except unprefixed verbs were stressed on the first syllable, and prefixed verbs were stressed on the syllable immediately following the prefix. Although the scope of this rule has been greatly restricted by the incorporation into English of loanwords that exhibit other stress patterns, the rule has always remained operative to some degree, and many loanwords have been conformed to it throughout the history of English. For South Midland and Midland U.S. speakers in particular, shifting the stress in borrowed nouns from a noninitial syllable to the first syllable is still an active process, yielding (pō′lēs)

CONCISE ETYMOLOGY KEY: <, descended or borrowed from; >, whence; b., blend of, blended; c., cognate with; cf., compare; deriv., derivative; equiv., equivalent; imit., imitative; obl., oblique; r., replacing; s., stem; sp., spelling, spelled; resp., respelling, respelled; trans., translation; ?, origin unknown; *, unattested; ‡, probably earlier than. See the full key inside the front cover.

for POLICE and (dē′troit) for *Detroit,* as well as *cement, cigar, guitar, insurance, umbrella,* and *idea* said as (sē′-ment), (sē′gär), (git′är), (in′sho͝or əns), (um′brel ə), and (ī′dē^{ə}).

police′ ac′tion, a relatively localized military action undertaken by regular armed forces, without a formal declaration of war. [1880–85]

police′ car′. See **squad car.** [1920–25]

police′ court′, an inferior court with summary jurisdiction for the trial of persons accused of any of certain minor offenses, and with power to examine those charged with more serious offenses and hold them for trial in a superior court or for a grand jury. Also called **magistrate's court.** [1815–25]

police′ dog′, **1.** a dog trained to assist the police. **2.** See **German shepherd.** [1905–10]

police dog, German shepherd, 2 ft. (0.6 m) high at shoulder

police′ force′, police (def. 1). [1830–40]

po·lice·man (pə lēs′mən), *n., pl.* **-men. 1.** a member of a police force or body. **2.** *Ice Hockey.* enforcer (def. 4). [1795–1805; POLICE + -MAN] **—po·lice′man·like′,** *adj.*
—Usage. See **-man.**

police′ of′ficer, 1. any policeman or policewoman; patrolman or patrolwoman. **2.** a person having officer rank on a police force. [1790–1800]

po·lice·per·son (pə lēs′pûr′sən), *n.* a member of a police force. [1965–70; POLICE + -PERSON]
—Usage. See **-person.**

police′ pow′er, the power of a nation, within the limits of its constitution, to regulate the conduct of its citizens in the interest of the common good. [1820–30, *Amer.*]

police′ proce′dural, a mystery novel, film, or television drama that deals realistically with police work. Also called **procedural.** [1965–70]

police′ report′er, a news reporter assigned to cover a police department for newsworthy events. [1825–35]

police′ state′, a nation in which the police, esp. a secret police, summarily suppresses any social, economic, or political act that conflicts with governmental policy. [1860–65]

police′ sta′tion, police headquarters for a particular district, from which police officers are dispatched and to which persons under arrest are brought. Also called **station house.** [1840–50]

police′ vil′lage, *Canadian (chiefly Ontario).* a village lacking corporate status as a municipality, its affairs being administered by an elected board of trustees. [1850–55]

police′ wag′on. See **patrol wagon.**

po·lice·wom·an (pə lēs′wo͝om′ən), *n., pl.* **-wom·en.** a female member of a police force or body. [1850–55]
—Usage. See **-woman.**

pol·i·clin·ic (pol′ē klin′ik), *n.* a department of a hospital at which outpatients are treated. [1820–30; < G *Poliklinik,* equiv. to Gk *póli(s)* city + G *Klinik* CLINIC]

pol·i·cy[1] (pol′ə sē), *n., pl.* **-cies. 1.** a definite course of action adopted for the sake of expediency, facility, etc.: *We have a new company policy.* **2.** a course of action adopted and pursued by a government, ruler, political party, etc.: *our nation's foreign policy.* **3.** action or procedure conforming to or considered with reference to prudence or expediency: *It was good policy to consent.* **4.** sagacity; shrewdness: *Showing great policy, he pitted his enemies against one another.* **5.** *Rare.* government; polity. [1350–1400; ME *policie* government, civil administration < MF < L *polītia* POLITY]
—Syn. 1. strategy, principle, rule. **4.** acumen, astuteness, skill, art. **—Ant. 4.** ingenuousness, naiveté.

pol·i·cy[2] (pol′ə sē), *n., pl.* **-cies. 1.** a document embodying a contract of insurance. **2.** a method of gambling in which bets are made on numbers to be drawn by lottery. **3.** See **numbers pool** (def. 2). [1555–65; < MF *police* (< It *polizza* < ML *apodixa* receipt << Gk *apódeixis* a showing or setting forth; see APODICTIC, -SIS) + -Y[3]]

pol·i·cy·hold·er (pol′ə sē hōl′dər), *n.* the individual or firm in whose name an insurance policy is written; an insured. [1850–55, *Amer.*; POLICY[2] + HOLDER]

pol′icy loan′, *Insurance.* a loan made by a life-insurance company to a policyholder with the cash value of the policy serving as security.

pol·i·cy·mak·er (pol′ə sē mā′kər), *n.* a person responsible for making policy, esp. in government. [1945–50; POLICY[1] + MAKER] **—pol′i·cy·mak′ing,** *adj., n.*

pol·i·cy·own·er (pol′ə sē ō′nər), *n.* policyholder. [POLICY[2] + OWNER]

po·li·o (pō′lē ō′), *n.* poliomyelitis. [1930–35, *Amer.*; shortened form]

po·li·o·en·ceph·a·li·tis (pō′lē ō en sef′ə lī′tis), *n. Pathol.* **1.** a disease characterized by inflammation of the gray matter of the brain. **2.** poliomyelitis affecting the cerebrum. Also, **po·li·en·ceph·a·li·tis** (pō′lē en sef′ə lī′tis). [1880–85; < NL < Gk *poliό(s)* gray + NL *encephalitis* ENCEPHALITIS]

po·li·o·my·e·li·tis (pō′lē ō mī′ə lī′tis), *n. Pathol.* an acute viral disease, usually affecting children and young adults, caused by any of three polioviruses, characterized by inflammation of the motor neurons of the brain stem and spinal cord, and resulting in a motor paralysis, followed by muscular atrophy and often permanent deformities. Also called **acute anterior poliomyelitis, infantile paralysis, polio.** [1875–80; < NL < Gk *poliό(s)* gray + NL *myelitis* MYELITIS] **—po·li·o·my·e·lit·ic** (pō′lē ō mī′ə lit′ik), *adj.*

po′lio vaccine′, a vaccine administered to induce specific active immunity to poliomyelitis. Also called **poliomyeli′tis vaccine′.** Cf. **Sabin vaccine, Salk vaccine.**

po·li·o·vi·rus (pō′lē ō vī′rəs, pō′lē ō vī′-), *n., pl.* **-rus·es.** any of three picornaviruses of the genus *Enterovirus,* having a spherical capsid, infectious to humans and the cause of poliomyelitis. [1950–55; POLIO + VIRUS]

po·lis (pō′lis), *n., pl.* **-leis** (-līs). an ancient Greek city-state. [1890–95; < Gk *pólis,* pl. (Ionic) *póleis*]

-polis, a combining form, meaning "city," appearing in loanwords from Greek (*metropolis*), and used in the formation of placenames (*Annapolis*). [comb. form repr. Gk *pólis* POLIS]

Po·li·sa·ri·o (pō li sär′ē ō′), *n.* an independence movement opposing Moroccan control of the Western Sahara, a former Spanish territory that Morocco annexed in stages beginning in 1976. Also called **Polisa′rio Front′.** [< Sp *(Frente) Po(pular para la) Li(beración de) Sa(gnia el-Hamra y) Rí(o de) O(ro)* Popular Front for the Liberation of Sagnia El-Hamra and Río de Oro]

pol·i sci (pol′ē sī′), *Informal.* political science: *to major in poli sci.* Also, **poly sci.** [by shortening]

pol·ish (pol′ish), *v.t.* **1.** to make smooth and glossy, esp. by rubbing or friction: *to polish a brass doorknob.* **2.** to render finished, refined, or elegant: *His speech needs polishing.* **—***v.i.* **3.** to become smooth and glossy through polishing: *a flooring that polishes easily.* **4.** *Archaic.* to become refined or elegant. **5. polish off,** *Informal.* **a.** to finish or dispose of quickly: *They polished off a gallon of ice cream between them.* **b.** to subdue or get rid of someone: *The fighter polished off his opponent in the first round.* **6. polish up,** to improve; refine: *She took lessons to polish up her speech.* **—***n.* **7.** a substance used to give smoothness or gloss: *shoe polish.* **8.** the act of polishing. **9.** state of being polished. **10.** smoothness and gloss of surface. **11.** superiority of manner or execution; refinement; elegance: *the polish of a professional singer.* [1250–1300; ME *polishen* < MF *poliss-,* long s. of *polir* < L *polīre* to polish; see -ISH[2]] **—pol′ish·er,** *n.*
—Syn. 1. shine, brighten, burnish, buff, smooth. **10.** shine, gleam. POLISH, GLOSS, LUSTER, SHEEN refer to a smooth, shining, or bright surface from which light is reflected. POLISH suggests the smooth, bright reflection often produced by friction: *rubbed to a high polish.* GLOSS suggests a superficial, hard smoothness characteristic of lacquered, varnished, or enameled surfaces: *a gloss on oilcloth, on paper.* LUSTER denotes the characteristic quality of the light reflected from the surfaces of certain materials (pearls, silk, wax, freshly cut metals, etc.): *a pearly luster.* SHEEN, sometimes poetical, suggests a glistening brightness such as that reflected from the surface of silk or velvet, or from furniture oiled and hand-polished: *a rich velvety sheen.*

Po·lish (pō′lish), *adj.* **1.** of, pertaining to, or characteristic of Poland, its inhabitants, or their language. **—***n.* **2.** a Slavic language, the principal language of Poland. *Abbr.:* Pol [1695–1705; POLE + -ISH[1]]

Po′lish Cor′ridor, a strip of land near the mouth of the Vistula River: formerly separated Germany from East Prussia; given to Poland in the Treaty of Versailles 1919 to provide it with access to the Baltic.

pol·ished (pol′isht), *adj.* **1.** made smooth and glossy: *a figurine of polished mahogany.* **2.** naturally smooth and glossy: *polished pebbles on the beach.* **3.** refined, cultured, or elegant: *a polished manner.* **4.** flawless; skillful; excellent: *a polished conversationalist.* [1325–75; ME *polist.* See POLISH, -ED[2]]

pol′ished rice′, white rice polished or buffed by leather-covered cylinders during processing. [1920–25]

Po′lish Peo′ple's Repub′lic, former name of **Poland.**

Po′lish sau′sage, (*sometimes l.c.*) kielbasa.

Po′lish wheat′, a wheat, *Triticum polonicum,* grown chiefly in S Europe, N Africa, and Turkestan. [1825–35]

polit., 1. political. **2.** politics.

Po·lit·bu·ro (pol′it byo͝or′ō, pō′lit-, pə lit′-), *n.* **1.** the executive committee and chief policymaking body of the Communist party in the Soviet Union and in certain other Communist countries. **2.** (*often l.c.*) (in most Communist countries) the highest policymaking body of a Communist party. Also, **Po′lit·bu′reau.** [< Russ *politbyuró,* shortening of *politícheskoe byuró* political bureau]

po·lite (pə līt′), *adj.,* **-lit·er, -lit·est. 1.** showing good manners toward others, as in behavior, speech, etc.; courteous; civil: *a polite reply.* **2.** refined or cultured: *polite society.* **3.** of a refined or elegant kind: *polite learning.* [1400–50; late ME < L *polītus,* ptp. of *polīre* to POLISH] **—po·lite′ly,** *adv.* **—po·lite′ness,** *n.*
—Syn. 1. well-bred, gracious. See **civil. 2.** urbane, polished, poised, courtly, cultivated. **—Ant. 1, 2.** rude.

polit. econ., political economy.

pol·i·tesse (pol′i tes′; *Fr.* pô lē tes′), *n.* formal politeness; courtesy. [1710–20; < F: orig. clean or polished state < It *politezza,* var. of *pulitezza* (deriv. of *polito* POLITE)]

Po·li·tian (pō lish′ən), *n.* (*Angelo Poliziano*) 1454–94, Italian classical scholar, teacher, and poet.

pol·i·tic (pol′i tik), *adj.* **1.** shrewd or prudent in practical matters; tactful; diplomatic. **2.** contrived in a shrewd and practical way; expedient: *a politic reply.* **3.** political: *the body politic.* [1375–1425; late ME *politik* < MF *politique* < L *polīticus* < Gk *politikós* civic, equiv. to *polīt(ēs)* citizen (see POLITY) + *-ikos* -IC] **—pol′i·tic·ly,** *adv.*
—Syn. 1. astute, ingenius; wary, discreet. See **diplomatic. —Ant. 1.** imprudent; indiscreet, tactless.

po·lit·i·cal (pə lit′i kəl), *adj.* **1.** of, pertaining to, or concerned with politics: *political writers.* **2.** of, pertaining to, or connected with a political party: *a political campaign.* **3.** exercising or seeking power in the governmental or public affairs of a state, municipality, etc.: *a political machine; a political boss.* **4.** of, pertaining to, or involving the state or its government: *a political offense.* **5.** having a definite policy or system of government: *a political community.* **6.** of or pertaining to citizens: *political rights.* [1545–55; < L *polītic(us)* civic (see POLITIC) + -AL[1]] **—po·lit′i·cal·ly,** *adv.*

polit′ical asy′lum, asylum provided by one nation to refugees, esp. political refugees, from another nation. [1950–55]

polit′ical econ′omy, 1. a social science dealing with political policies and economic processes, their interrelations, and their influence on social institutions. **2.** (in the 17th–18th centuries) the art of management of communities, esp. as affecting the wealth of a government. **3.** (in the 19th century) a social science similar to modern economics but dealing chiefly with governmental policies. **4.** economics (def. 1). [1605–15] **—polit′ical econ′omist.**

po·lit·i·cal·ize (pə lit′i kə līz′), *v.t.,* **-ized, -iz·ing.** to cause to be political; color with politics. Also, *esp. Brit.,* **po·lit′i·cal·ise′.** [1865–70; POLITICAL + -IZE] **—po·lit′i·cal·i·za′tion,** *n.*

polit′ical lib′erty, the right to express oneself freely and effectually regarding the conduct, makeup, and principles of the government under which one lives.

polit′ically correct′, marked by or adhering to a typically progressive orthodoxy on issues involving esp. race, gender, sexual affinity, or ecology. *Abbr.:* PC, P.C. **—polit′ical correct′ness.**

polit′ical ques′tion, *Law.* a question regarded by the courts as being a matter to be determined by another department of government rather than of law and therefore one with which they will not deal, as the recognition of a foreign state.

polit′ical refugee′, a person who has fled from a homeland because of political persecution.

polit′ical sci′ence, a social science dealing with political institutions and with the principles and conduct of government. [1770–80] **—polit′ical sci′entist.**

pol·i·ti·cian (pol′i tish′ən), *n.* **1.** a person who is active in party politics. **2.** a seeker or holder of public office, who is more concerned about winning favor or retaining power than about maintaining principles. **3.** a person who holds a political office. **4.** a person skilled in political government or administration; statesman or stateswoman. **5.** an expert in politics or political government. **6.** a person who seeks to gain power or advancement within an organization in ways that are generally disapproved. [1580–90; < F *politicien.* See POLITIC, -IAN]
—Syn. 4. POLITICIAN, STATESMAN refer to one skilled in politics. These terms differ particularly in their connotations; POLITICIAN is more often derogatory, and STATESMAN laudatory. POLITICIAN suggests the schemes and devices of a person who engages in (esp. small) politics for party ends or for one's own advantage: *a dishonest politician.* STATESMAN suggests the eminent ability, foresight, and unselfish patriotic devotion of a person dealing with (esp. important or great) affairs of state: *a distinguished statesman.*

po·lit·i·cize (pə lit′ə sīz′), *v.,* **-cized, -ciz·ing. —***v.t.* **1.** to bring a political character or flavor to; make political: *to politicize a private dispute.* **—***v.i.* **2.** to engage in or discuss politics. Also, *esp. Brit.,* **po·lit′i·cise′.** [1750–60; POLITIC(AL) + -IZE] **—po·lit′i·ci·za′tion,** *n.*

pol·i·tick (pol′i tik), *v.i.* **1.** to engage in politicking. **—***v.t.* **2.** to influence, accomplish, or promote by politicking: *Somehow he politicked the bill through both houses of Congress.* [1915–20; earlier *politic,* v. deriv. of POLITIC; later as back formation from POLITICKING]

pol·i·tick·ing (pol′i tik′ing), *n.* activity undertaken for political reasons or ends, as campaigning for votes before an election, making speeches, etc., or otherwise promoting oneself or one's policies. [1925–30; POLITIC (as v.) + -ING[1], resp. to show non-assibilation of -c-]

po·lit·i·co (pə lit′i kō′), *n., pl.* **-cos.** a politician. [1620–30; < It or Sp]

politico-, a combining form representing **political** in compound words: *politico-religious.*

CONCISE PRONUNCIATION KEY: *act, cāpe, dâre, pärt; set, ēqual; if, īce; ox, ōver, ôrder, oil, bo͝ok, bo͞ot, out; up, ûrge; child; sing; shoe; thin,* t͟h*at; zh as in treasure.* ə = *a as in alone, e as in system, i as in easily, o as in gallop, u as in circus;* ^{ə} *as in fire* (fī^{ə}r), *hour* (ou^{ə}r). l *and* n *can serve as syllabic consonants, as in cradle* (krād′l), *and button* (but′n). *See the full key inside the front cover.*

pol•i•tics (pol′i tiks), *n.* (*used with a singular or plural v.*) **1.** the science or art of political government. **2.** the practice or profession of conducting political affairs. **3.** political affairs: *The advocated reforms have become embroiled in politics.* **4.** political methods or maneuvers: *We could not approve of his politics in winning passage of the bill.* **5.** political principles or opinions: *We avoided discussion of religion and politics. His politics are his own affair.* **6.** use of intrigue or strategy in obtaining any position of power or control, as in business, university, etc. **7.** (*cap., italics*) a treatise (4th century B.C.) by Aristotle, dealing with the structure, organization, and administration of the state, esp. the city-state as known in ancient Greece. **8. play politics. a.** to engage in political intrigue, take advantage of a political situation or issue, resort to partisan politics, etc.; exploit a political system or political relationships. **b.** to deal with people in an opportunistic, manipulative, or devious way, as for job advancement. [1520–30; see POLITIC, -ICS]

pol•i•ty (pol′i tē), *n., pl.* **-ties. 1.** a particular form or system of government: *civil polity; ecclesiastical polity.* **2.** the condition of being constituted as a state or other organized community or body: *The polity of ancient Athens became a standard for later governments.* **3.** government or administrative regulation: *The colonists demanded independence in matters of internal polity.* **4.** a state or other organized community or body. [1530–40; < L *polītia* < Gk *polīteía* citizenship, government, form of government, commonwealth, equiv. to *polītē-*, var. s. of *polī́tēs* citizen (see POLIS, -ITE[1]) + *-ia* -IA]

Polk (pōk), *n.* **James Knox,** 1795–1849, the 11th president of the U.S. 1845–49.

pol•ka (pōl′kə, pō′kə), *n., pl.* **-kas,** *v.,* **-kaed, -ka•ing.** —*n.* **1.** a lively couple dance of Bohemian origin, with music in duple meter. **2.** a piece of music for such a dance or in its rhythm. —*v.i.* **3.** to dance the polka. [1835–45; < Czech: lit., Polish woman or girl; cf. Pol *polka* Polish woman, *polak* Pole]

pol′ka dot′ (pō′kə), *Textiles.* **1.** a dot or round spot (printed, woven, or embroidered) repeated to form a pattern on a textile fabric. **2.** a pattern of or a fabric with such dots. [1880–85, *Amer.*] **—pol′ka-dot′ted, pol′ka-dot′,** *adj.*

poll[1] (pōl), *n.* **1.** a sampling or collection of opinions on a subject, taken from either a selected or a random group of persons, as for the purpose of analysis. **2.** Usually, **polls.** the place where votes are taken. **3.** the registering of votes, as at an election. **4.** the voting at an election. **5.** the number of votes cast. **6.** the numerical result of the voting. **7.** an enumeration or a list of individuals, as for purposes of taxing or voting. **8.** See **poll tax. 9.** a person or individual in a number or list. **10.** the head, esp. the part of it on which the hair grows. **11.** the back of the head. **12.** the rear portion of the head of a horse; the nape. See diag. under **horse. 13.** the part of the head between the ears of certain animals, as the horse and cow. **14.** the broad end or face of a hammer. —*v.t.* **15.** to take a sampling of the attitudes or opinions of. **16.** to receive at the polls, as votes. **17.** to enroll (someone) in a list or register, as for purposes of taxing or voting. **18.** to take or register the votes of (persons). **19.** to deposit or cast at the polls, as a vote. **20.** to bring to the polls, as voters. **21.** to cut short or cut off the hair, wool, etc., of (an animal); crop; clip; shear. **22.** to cut short or cut off (hair, wool, etc.). **23.** to cut off the top of (a tree); pollard. **24.** to cut off or cut short the horns of (cattle). —*v.i.* **25.** to vote at the polls; give one's vote. [1250–1300; ME *polle* (hair of the) head < MLG: hair of the head, top of a tree or other plant; akin to Dan *puld,* Sw *pull* crown of the head] **—poll′a•ble,** *adj.* **—poll′er,** *n.*

poll[2] (pol), *n.* (esp. at Cambridge University, England) **1.** the body of students who read for or obtain a degree without honors. **2.** Also called **poll′ degree′.** See **pass degree.** [1785–95; appar. < Gk *polloí,* in *hoi polloí* the many; see POLY-]

poll[3] (pol), *n.* polly.

pol•lack (pol′ək), *n., pl.* **-lacks,** (*esp. collectively*) **-lack. 1.** a food fish, *Pollachius pollachius,* of the cod family, inhabiting coastal North Atlantic waters from Scandinavia to northern Africa. **2.** pollock. [1495–1505; assimilated var. of *podlok* (Scots); akin to Scots *paddle* lumpfish; see -OCK]

Pol•lai•uo•lo (pō′lī wō′lō; *It.* pôl′lī wô′lô), *n.* **1. Antonio** (än tô′nyô), 1429–98, Italian sculptor, painter, and goldsmith. **2.** his brother **Pie•ro** (pye′rô), 1443–96, painter, sculptor, and goldsmith. Also, **Pol•lai•o•lo** (pō′lī-ō′lō; *It.* pôl′lī ô′lô), **Pol•laj•uo•lo** (pō′lī wō′lō; *It.* pôl′lī-wô′lô).

pol•la•ki•u•ri•a (pol′ə kē yŏŏr′ē ə, -kī-), *n. Med.* abnormally frequent urination. [< Gk *polláki, pollákis* many times + -URIA]

pol•lard (pol′ərd), *n.* **1.** a tree cut back nearly to the trunk, so as to produce a dense mass of branches. **2.** an animal, as a stag, ox, or sheep, having no horns. —*v.t.* **3.** to convert into a pollard. [1515–25; POLL[1] + -ARD]

poll•book (pōl′bŏŏk′), *n.* the official list of the registered voters in a given area. [1675–85; POLL[1] + BOOK]

polled (pōld), *adj.* **1.** hornless, esp. genetically hornless, as the Aberdeen Angus. **2.** *Obs.* having the hair cut off. [1300–50; ME; see POLL[1], -ED[2]]

poll•ee (pō lē′), *n.* a person who is asked questions in a poll. [1935–40; POLL[1] + -EE]

pol•len (pol′ən), *n.* **1.** the fertilizing element of flowering plants, consisting of fine, powdery, yellowish grains or spores, sometimes in masses. —*v.t.* **2.** to pollinate. [1515–25; < NL, special use of L: fine flour, mill dust] **—pol′len•less,** *adj.* **—pol′len•like′,** *adj.* **—pol•lin•ic** (pə lin′ik), **pol•lin′i•cal,** *adj.*

CONCISE ETYMOLOGY KEY: <, descended or borrowed from; >, whence; b., blend of, blended; c., cognate with; cf., compare; deriv., derivative; equiv., equivalent; imit., imitative; obl., oblique; r., replacing; s., stem; sp., spelling, spelled; resp., respelling, respelled; trans., translation; ?, origin unknown; *, unattested; ‡, probably earlier than. See the full key inside the front cover.

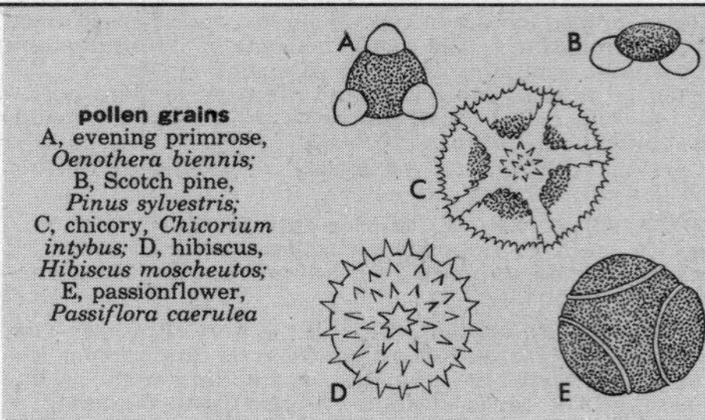

pollen grains A, evening primrose, *Oenothera biennis;* B, Scotch pine, *Pinus sylvestris;* C, chicory, *Chicorium intybus;* D, hibiscus, *Hibiscus moscheutos;* E, passionflower, *Passiflora caerulea*

pol′len bas′ket, (of bees) a smooth area on the hind tibia of each leg fringed with long hairs and serving to transport pollen. Also called **corbicula.** [1855–60]

pol′len brush′, the mass of stiff hairs on the legs or abdomen of an insect, for collecting pollen. Also called **scopa.** [1895–1900]

pol′len count′, a count of the amount of pollen in the air, based on the average of the number of pollen grains that collect on slides exposed to the air for a given period of time. [1925–30]

poll′ end′ (pōl), the hub holding the sail arms of a windmill.

pol′len grain′, a single granule of pollen. [1825–35]

pol•len•o•sis (pol′ə nō′sis), *n. Pathol.* See **hay fever.** [POLLEN + -OSIS]

pol′len sac′, *Bot.* one of the cavities in an anther in which pollen is produced. [1870–75]

pol′len tube′, *Bot.* the protoplasmic tube that is extruded from a germinating pollen grain and grows toward the ovule. [1825–35]

pol•le•ra (pə yâr′ə; *Sp.* pô ye′rä), *n., pl.* **pol•le•ras** (pə yâr′əz; *Sp.* pô ye′räs). a gaily colored costume worn by women during fiestas in Latin-American countries. [< AmerSp, special use of *pollera* poultry yard, chicken coop, deriv. of *pollo* chicken]

pol•le•ro (pô ye′rô; *Eng.* pō yâr′ō), *n., pl.* ***pol•le•ros*** (pô ye′rôs; *Eng.* pō yâr′ōz). *Mexican Spanish.* a smuggler of Mexican workers into the U.S.

poll′ e′vil (pōl), *Vet. Pathol.* an acute swelling on the top of the head of a horse originating in an inflamed bursa that underlies the great neck ligament there. [1600–10]

pol•lex (pol′eks), *n., pl.* **pol•li•ces** (pol′ə sēz′). the innermost digit of the forelimb; thumb. [1825–35; < L]

pol•li•ce ver•so (pōl′li ke′ wer′sō; *Eng.* pol′ə sē vûr′sō), *Latin.* with thumbs turned downward: the sign made by spectators calling for the death of a defeated gladiator in the ancient Roman circus.

pol•lic•i•ta•tion (pə lis′i tā′shən), *n. Civil Law.* an offer or promise made by one party to another before the latter's consent or acceptance. [1520–30; < L *pollicitātiōn-* (s. of *pollicitātiō*) a promising, equiv. to *pollicitāt(us)* (ptp. of *pollicitārī* to promise, freq. of *pollicērī* to promise, lit., bid for, equiv. to *pol-* (assimilated var. of *por-* forth, forward, akin to PER-) + *licērī* to bid) + *-iōn-* -ION]

pol•li•nate (pol′ə nāt′), *v.t.,* **-nat•ed, -nat•ing.** *Bot.* to convey pollen to the stigma of (a flower). [1870–75; < NL *pollin-* (s. of *pollen*) POLLEN + -ATE[1]] **—pol′li•na′tor,** *n.*

pol•li•na•tion (pol′ə nā′shən), *n. Bot.* the transfer of pollen from the anther to the stigma. [1870–75; POLLINATE + -ION]

poll′ing booth′, a booth in which voters cast their votes. [1850–55]

poll′ing place′, a place at or in which votes in an election are cast. [1825–35]

pol•li•nif•er•ous (pol′ə nif′ər əs), *adj.* **1.** *Bot.* producing or bearing pollen. **2.** *Zool.* fitted for carrying pollen. [1820–30; < NL *pollin-* (s. of *pollen*) POLLEN + -I- + -FEROUS]

pol•lin•i•um (pə lin′ē əm), *n., pl.* **-lin•i•a** (-lin′ē ə). *Bot.* an agglutinated mass or body of pollen grains, characteristic of plants of the orchid and milkweed families. [1860–65; < NL, equiv. to *pollin-* (s. of *pollen*) POLLEN + *-ium* -IUM]

pol•li•nize (pol′ə nīz′), *v.t.,* **-nized, -niz•ing.** pollinate. Also, *esp. Brit.,* **pol′li•nise′.** [1840–50; < NL *pollin-* (s. of *pollen*) POLLEN + -IZE] **—pol′li•ni•za′tion,** *n.*

pol•li•no•sis (pol′ə nō′sis), *n. Pathol.* See **hay fever.** [1920–25; < NL, equiv. to *pollin-* (s. of *pollen*) POLLEN + -OSIS]

pol•li•wog (pol′ē wog′), *n.* a tadpole. Also, **pollywog.** [1400–50; var. of *polliwig,* earlier *polwigge,* late ME *polwygle.* See POLL[1], WIGGLE]

pol•lo (pô′yô, -lyô), *n., pl.* ***pol•los*** (pô′yôs, -lyôs). *Spanish.* **1.** chicken. **2.** *Slang.* (in Mexico) a laborer who pays to be smuggled or guided over the border into the U.S. illegally.

pol•lock (pol′ək), *n., pl.* **-locks,** (*esp. collectively*) **-lock.** *Chiefly Brit.* **1.** Also called **saithe.** a North Atlantic food fish, *Pollachius virens,* of the cod family. **2.** pollack. [var. of POLLACK]

Pol•lock (pol′ək), *n.* **1. Sir Frederick,** 1845–1937, English legal scholar and author. **2. Jackson,** 1912–56, U.S. painter.

poll′ par′rot, (pol), polly.

poll•ster (pōl′stər), *n.* a person whose occupation is the taking of public-opinion polls. [1935–40, *Amer.*; POLL[1] + -STER]

poll•tak•er (pōl′tā′kər), *n.* a person or organization that conducts polls; pollster. [1955–60; POLL[1] + TAKER]

poll′ tax′ (pōl), a capitation tax, the payment of which is sometimes a prerequisite to exercise the right of suffrage. Also called **head tax.** [1685–95]

pol•lu•tant (pə lo͞ot′nt), *n.* **1.** something that pollutes. **2.** any substance, as certain chemicals or waste products, that renders the air, soil, water, or other natural resource harmful or unsuitable for a specific purpose. [1890–95; POLLUTE + -ANT]

pol•lute (pə lo͞ot′), *v.t.,* **-lut•ed, -lut•ing. 1.** to make foul or unclean, esp. with harmful chemical or waste products; dirty: *to pollute the air with smoke.* **2.** to make morally unclean; defile. **3.** to render ceremonially impure; desecrate: *to pollute a house of worship.* **4.** *Informal.* to render less effective or efficient: *The use of inferior equipment has polluted the company's service.* [1325–75; ME *polute* < L *pollūtus* ptp. of *polluere* to soil, defile, equiv. to *pol-,* assimilated var. of *por-* (see POLLICITATION; here marking the action as complete) + *-lū-* base of *-luere* (akin to *lutum* mud, dirt, *lustrum* muddy place) + *-tus* ptp. suffix] **—pol•lut′er,** *n.* **—pol•lu′tive,** *adj.*
—Syn. 1. soil, befoul. **2.** taint, contaminate, vitiate, corrupt, debase, deprave. **—Ant. 1, 2.** purify.

pol•lut•ed (pə lo͞o′tid), *adj.* **1.** made unclean or impure; contaminated; tainted: *swimming in polluted waters.* **2.** *Slang.* drunk. [1350–1400; ME; see POLLUTE, -ED[2]] **—pol•lut′ed•ness,** *n.*

pol•lu•tion (pə lo͞o′shən), *n.* **1.** the act of polluting or the state of being polluted. **2.** the introduction of harmful substances or products into the environment: *air pollution.* [1350–1400; ME *pollucioun* (< OF) < LL *pollūtiōn-,* s. of *pollūtiō* defilement; see POLLUTE, -ION]

Pol•lux (pol′əks), *n.* **1.** Greek, **Polydeuces.** *Class. Myth.* the brother of Castor. Cf. **Castor and Pollux. 2.** *Astron.* a first-magnitude star in the constellation Gemini.

poll′ watch′er (pōl), a representative of a political party or of an organization running a candidate who is assigned to the polls on an election day to watch for violations of the laws that regulate voting, campaigning, etc. Also, **poll′-watch′er.**

pol•ly (pol′ē), *n., pl.* **-lies.** a tame parrot. Also called **poll, poll parrot.** [generic use of POLLY]

Pol•ly (pol′ē), *n.* **1.** a female given name, form of **Mary. 2.** a common name for a parrot.

Pol•ly•an•na (pol′ē an′ə), *n.* **1.** an excessively or blindly optimistic person. —*adj.* **2.** (*often l.c.*) Also, **Pol′ly•an′na•ish.** unreasonably or illogically optimistic: *some pollyanna notions about world peace.* [from the name of the child heroine created by Eleanor Porter (1868–1920), American writer] **—Pol′ly•an′na•ism,** *n.*

pol•ly•fish (pol′ē fish′), *n., pl.* (*esp. collectively*) **-fish,** (*esp. referring to two or more kinds or species*) **-fish•es.** parrotfish. [POLLY + FISH]

pol•ly•wog (pol′ē wog′), *n.* polliwog.

po•lo (pō′lō), *n.* **1.** a game played on horseback between two teams, each of four players, the object being to score points by driving a wooden ball into the opponents' goal using a long-handled mallet. **2.** any game broadly resembling this, esp. water polo. **3.** See **polo shirt.** [1835–45; < Balti (Tibetan language of Kashmir): ball] **—po′lo•ist,** *n.*

Po•lo (pō′lō), *n.* **Mar•co** (mär′kō), c1254–1324, Venetian traveler.

po′lo coat′, a double-breasted, often belted overcoat made of camel's hair or a similar fabric. [1905–10]

pol•o•naise (pol′ə nāz′, pō′lə-), *n.* **1.** a slow dance of Polish origin, in triple meter, consisting chiefly of a march or promenade in couples. **2.** a piece of music for, or in the rhythm of, such a dance. **3.** Also, **pol•o•nese** (pol′ə nēz′, -nēs′, pō′lə-). a coatlike outer dress, combining bodice and cutaway overskirt, worn in the late 18th century over a separate skirt. [1765–75; < F, fem. of *polonais* Polish, equiv. to *Polon-* (< ML *Polonia* Poland) + *-ais* -ESE]

po•lo•ni•um (pə lō′nē əm), *n. Chem.* a radioactive element discovered by Pierre and Marie Curie in 1898; *Symbol:* Po; *at. no.:* 84; *at. wt.:* about 210. [1895–1900; < NL, equiv. to *polon-* (< ML *Polonia* Poland) + *-ium* -IUM]

Po•lo•ni•us (pə lō′nē əs), *n.* the sententious father of Ophelia in Shakespeare's *Hamlet.*

Po•lo•nize (pō′lə nīz′), *v.t.,* **-nized, -niz•ing. 1.** to make Polish; cause or force to take on ways, customs, viewpoints, etc., that are characteristically Polish. **2.** to alter (a word or phrase) so that it becomes Polish in form or character. Also, *esp. Brit.,* **Po′lo•nise′.** [1885–90; < ML *Polon(ia)* Poland + -IZE] **—Po′lo•ni•za′tion,** *n.*

Po•lon•na•ru•wa (pō lun′ə ro͞o′və), *n.* a town in E central Sri Lanka: Buddhist ruins.

po′lo po′ny, a small, swift, agile horse specially trained for use in polo. [1880–85]

pol•os (pol′os), *n., pl.* **pol•oi** (pol′oi). a tall, cylindrical headdress represented, esp. on statues, as worn by women in ancient Greece. [1840–50; < Gk *pólos* axis]

po′lo shirt′, a short-sleeved, pullover sport shirt, usually of cotton or cottonlike knit, with a round neckband or a turnover collar. Also called **polo.** [1915–20]

Pol•ska (pôl′skä), *n.* Polish name of **Poland.**

Pol•ta•va (pul tä′və), *n.* a city in E Ukraine, SW of Kharkov: Russian defeat of Swedes 1709. 309,000.

pol•ter•geist (pōl′tər gīst′), *n.* a ghost or spirit supposed to manifest its presence by noises, knockings, etc. [1840–50; < G *Poltergeist,* equiv. to *polter(n)* to make noise, knock, rattle + *Geist* GHOST]

Pol•to•ratsk (pol′tə rätsk′; *Russ.* pəl tu rätsk′), *n.* former name of **Ashkhabad.**

pol•troon (pol tro͞on′), *n.* **1.** a wretched coward; craven. —*adj.* **2.** marked by utter cowardice. [1520–30;

earlier *pultrowne, pultron, poultroone* < MF *poultron* < OIt *poltrone* idler, coward, deriv. of *poltro* foal < VL **pulliter,* deriv. of L *pullus* young animal; see FOAL] —**pol·troon′er·y,** *n.* —**pol·troon′ish,** *adj.* —**pol·troon′ish·ly,** *adv.*
—**Syn. 1.** dastard.

pol·y (pol′ē), *n., pl.* **pol·ies,** *adj.* —*n.* **1.** *Informal.* polyester (def. 2): *a blend of poly and cotton.* **2.** a fabric or garment made of polyester. —*adj.* **3.** made of or containing polyester: *a poly swimsuit.* [by shortening]

poly-, a combining form with the meanings "much, many" and, in chemistry, "polymeric," used in the formation of compound words: *polyandrous; polyculture; polyethylene.* [< Gk, comb. form repr. *polýs;* akin to OE *fela* many. See PLUS]

poly., polytechnic.

pol·y·ac·id (pol′ē as′id), *Chem.* —*adj.* **1.** having more than one replaceable hydrogen atom. **2.** capable of reacting with more than one equivalent weight of an acid. —*n.* **3.** an acid having more than one replaceable hydrogen atom. **4.** an oxyacid containing the equivalent of extra molecules of its anhydride, as the polysulfuric acids, $H_2S_2O_7$ or $H_2SO_4{\cdot}SO_3$, and $H_2S_3O_{10}$ or $H_2SO_4{\cdot}2SO_3$. [1855–60; POLY- + ACID]

pol·y·a·cryl·a·mide (pol′ē ə kril′ə mīd′, -mid, -ak′rə lam′īd, -id), *n. Chem.* a white, solid, water-soluble polymer of acrylamide, used in secondary oil recovery, as a thickening agent, a flocculant, and an absorbent, and to separate macromolecules of different molecular weights. [1940–45; POLY- + ACRYLAMIDE]

pol′y·a·cryl′ic ac′id (pol′ē ə kril′ik, pol′-), *Chem.* a polymer of acrylic acid used as a sizing agent in the manufacture of nylon and other synthetic textiles. [1925–30; POLY- + ACRYLIC]

pol·y·ac·ry·lo·ni·trile (pol′ē ak′rə lō nī′tril, -trēl, -tril), *n. Chem.* a polymer of acrylonitrile used in the manufacture of Orlon and other synthetic textiles. [1930–35; POLY- + ACRYLONITRILE]

pol·y·a·del·phous (pol′ē ə del′fəs), *adj. Bot.* (of stamens) united by the filaments into three or more sets or bundles. [1855–60; < Gk *polyádelphos* having many siblings; see POLY-, -ADELPHOUS]

pol′y·ad·e·nyl′ic ac′id (pol′ē ad′n il′ik, pol′-), *Biochem.* a homopolymer of adenylic acid enzymatically added to messenger RNA in eukaryotic cells to inhibit the hydrolytic breakdown of messenger RNA. [1955–60; POLY- + ADENYLIC ACID]

pol·y·al·co·hol (pol′ē al′kə hôl′, -hol′), *n. Chem.* polyol. [1895–1900; POLY- + ALCOHOL]

pol′y·al·pha·bet′ic substitu′tion (pol′ē al′fə bet′ik, pol′ē-), *Cryptography.* a system of substitution that mixes together a number of cipher alphabets in a cryptogram so that each plaintext letter is represented by a cipher that repeatedly changes. Cf. **monoalphabetic substitution.** [1935–40; POLY- + ALPHABETIC]

pol·y·am·ide (pol′ē am′īd, -id), *n. Chem.* a polymer in which the monomer units are linked together by the amide group –CONH–. [1925–30; POLY- + AMIDE]

pol·y·a·mine (pol′ē ə mēn′, -am′in), *n. Chem.* a compound containing more than one amino group. [1860–65; POLY- + -AMINE]

pol·y·an·dric (pol′ē an′drik), *adj.* polyandrous. [1865–70; POLYANDR(Y) + -IC]

pol·y·an·drist (pol′ē an′drist, pol′ē an′-), *n.* a woman who practices or favors polyandry. [1825–35; POLYANDR(Y) + -IST]

pol·y·an·drous (pol′ē an′drəs), *adj.* **1.** of, pertaining to, characterized by, or practicing polyandry; polyandric. **2.** *Bot.* having an indefinite number of stamens. [1820–30; < Gk *polyándros* having many husbands. See POLY-, -ANDROUS]

pol·y·an·dry (pol′ē an′drē, pol′ē an′-), *n.* **1.** the practice or condition of having more than one husband at one time. Cf. **monandry** (def. 1). **2.** (among female animals) the habit or system of having two or more mates, either simultaneously or successively. **3.** *Bot.* the state of being polyandrous. [1770–80; < Gk *polyandría.* See POLY-, -ANDRY]

pol·y·an·gu·lar (pol′ē ang′gyə lər), *adj.* multangular; multiangular. [1680–90; POLY- + ANGULAR]

pol·y·an·thus (pol′ē an′thəs), *n., pl.* **-thus·es. 1.** a hybrid primrose, *Primula polyantha.* **2.** a narcissus, *Narcissus tazetta,* having small white or yellow flowers. [1620–30; < NL < Gk *polyánthos* having many flowers. See POLY-, -ANTHOUS]

pol·y·ar·chy (pol′ē är′kē), *n., pl.* **-chies.** a form of government in which power is vested in three or more persons. [1600–10; POLY- + -ARCHY] —**pol′y·ar′chic, pol′y·ar′chi·cal,** *adj.*

pol·y·ar·te·ri·tis (pol′ē är′tə rī′tis), *n. Pathol.* inflammation of the layers of an artery or of many arteries, usually caused by a severe hypersensitivity reaction, and characterized by nodules and hemorrhage along the involved vessels. Also called **periarteritis nodosa.** [1905–10; < NL; see POLY-, ARTERITIS]

pol·y·ar·thri·tis (pol′ē är thrī′tis), *n. Pathol.* arthritis occurring in more than one joint. [1895–1900; POLY- + ARTHRITIS]

pol·y·ar·tic·u·lar (pol′ē är tik′yə lər), *adj. Anat.* pertaining to or affecting many joints. [1870–75; POLY- + ARTICULAR]

pol·y·a·tom·ic (pol′ē ə tom′ik), *adj. Chem.* pertaining to a molecule containing more than two atoms. [1855–60; POLY- + ATOMIC]

pol·y·ba·sic (pol′ē bā′sik), *adj. Chem.* (of an acid) having two or more atoms of replaceable hydrogen. [1835–45; POLY- + BASIC] —**pol·y·ba·sic·i·ty** (pol′ē bā sis′i tē), *n.*

pol·y·ba·site (pol′ē bā′sīt, pə lib′ə sīt′), *n.* a blackish mineral, Ag_9SbS_6: a minor ore of silver. [1820–30; < G *Polybasit.* See POLY-, BASE[1], -ITE[1]]

Po·lyb·i·us (pə lib′ē əs), *n.* c205–c123 B.C., Greek historian.

pol·y·bro′min·at·ed biphen′yl (pol′ē brō′mə nā′tid), *Chem.* See **PBB.** [1970–75; POLY- + BROMINATED]

Pol·y·bus (pol′ə bəs), *n. Class. Myth.* a Corinthian king who was the foster father of Oedipus.

pol·y·bu·ta·di·ene (pol′ē byōō′tə dī′ēn, -dī ēn′), *n. Chem.* a rubberlike polymer of butadiene blended with other synthetics to replace natural rubber in tires. [1930–35; POLY- + BUTADIENE]

pol·y·bu·tyl·ene (pol′ē byōōt′l ēn′), *n. Chem.* any of several polymers of butylene, used chiefly in the manufacture of lubricants and synthetic rubber. Also, **pol·y·bu·tene** (pol′ē byōō′tēn). [POLY- + BUTYLENE]

pol·y·car·bon·ate (pol′ē kär′bə nāt′, -nit), *n. Chem.* a synthetic thermoplastic resin, a linear polymer of carbonic acid, used for molded products, films, and nonbreakable windows. Cf. **Lexan.** [POLY- + CARBONATE]

Pol·y·carp (pol′ē kärp′), *n.* **Saint,** A.D. 69?–155, bishop of Smyrna and a Christian martyr.

pol·y·car·pel·lar·y (pol′ē kär′pə ler′ē), *adj. Bot.* consisting of two or more carpels. [1855–60; POLY- + CARPELLARY]

pol·y·car·pic (pol′ē kär′pik), *adj. Bot.* **1.** producing fruit many times, as a perennial plant. **2.** having a gynoecium composed of two or more distinct ovaries. Also, **pol′y·car′pous.** [1840–50; < NL *polycarpicus.* See POLY-, -CARPIC] —**pol′y·car′py,** *n.*

pol·y·cen·tric (pol′ē sen′trik), *adj.* having many centers, esp. of power or importance: *the polycentric world of banking.* [1885–90; POLY- + -CENTRIC]

pol·y·cen·trism (pol′ē sen′triz əm), *n.* **1.** the doctrine that a plurality of independent centers of leadership, power, or ideology may exist within a single political system, esp. Communism. **2.** the fact of having many centers of authority or importance: *the polycentrism of American intellectual life.* [1955–60; POLYCENTR(IC) + -ISM] —**pol′y·cen′tric,** *adj.* —**pol′y·cen′trist,** *n., adj.*

pol·y·chaete (pol′i kēt′), *n.* **1.** any annelid of the class Polychaeta, having unsegmented swimming appendages with many setae or bristles. —*adj.* **2.** Also, **pol′y·chae′tous.** belonging or pertaining to the Polychaeta. [1885–90; < NL *Polychaeta* < Gk *polychaítēs* having much hair. See POLY-, CHAETA]

pol·y·cha·si·um (pol′ē kā′zhē əm, -zhəm, -zē əm), *n., pl.* **-si·a** (-zhē ə, -zhə, -zē ə). *Bot.* a form of cymose inflorescence in which each axis produces more than two lateral axes. [< NL; see POLY-, DICHASIUM] —**pol′y·cha′si·al,** *adj.*

pol·y·chlo′rin·at·ed biphen′yl (pol′ē klôr′ə nā′tid, -klōr′-), *Chem.* See **PCB.** [1960–65; POLY- + CHLORINATED]

pol·y·chro·mat·ic (pol′ē krō mat′ik, -krə-), *adj.* having or exhibiting a variety of colors. Also, **pol·y·chro·mic** (pol′ē krō′mik). [1840–50; POLY- + CHROMATIC] —**pol·y·chro·ma·tism** (pol′ē krō′mə tiz′əm), *n.*

pol·y·chro·ma·to·phil·ic (pol′ē krō′mə tə fil′ik), *adj. Cell Biol.* having an affinity for more than one kind of stain, esp. for acid, neutral, and basic stains, as polychromatophilic erythroblasts characteristic of pernicious anemia. [1895–1900; POLYCHROMAT(IC) + -O- + -PHILIC]

pol·y·chrome (pol′ē krōm′), *adj., v.,* **-chromed, -chrom·ing,** *n.* —*adj.* **1.** being of many or various colors. **2.** decorated or executed in many colors, as a statue, vase, or mural. —*v.t.* **3.** to paint in many or various colors. —*n.* **4.** a polychrome object or work. [1795–1805; earlier *polychrom* < G < Gk *polýchrōmos* many-colored. See POLY-, -CHROME]

pol·y·chro·my (pol′ē krō′mē), *n.* the art of employing many colors in decoration, as in painting or architecture. [1855–60; POLYCHROME + -Y[3]] —**pol′y·chro′mous,** *adj.*

pol·y·cis·tron·ic (pol′ē si stron′ik), *adj. Genetics.* of or pertaining to the transcription of two or more adjacent cistrons into a single messenger RNA molecule. [1960–65; POLY- + CISTRON + -IC]

pol·y·clad (pol′ē klad′), *n.* any free-swimming, marine flatworm of the order Polycladida, having a broad, flat body and a many-branched gastrovascular cavity. [1885–90; < NL *Polycladus* genus name < Gk *polýklados* many-branched. See POLY-, CLADO-]

pol·y·clin·ic (pol′ē klin′ik), *n.* a clinic or a hospital dealing with various diseases. [1885–90; alter. of POLICLINIC by assoc. with POLY-]

Pol·y·cli·tus (pol′i klī′təs), *n.* fl. c450–c420 B.C., Greek sculptor. Also, **Pol′y·clei′tus, Pol·y·cle·tus** (pol′i klē′təs).

pol·y·clo·nal (pol′ē klōn′l), *adj.* **1.** *Biol.* pertaining to cells or cell products derived from several lines of clones. —*n.* **2.** *Immunol.* See **polyclonal antibody.** [1960–65; POLY- + CLONAL]

pol′yclo′nal an′tibody, a mixture of antibodies of different specificities, as in the serum of a person immunized to various antigens. Also called **polyclonal.**

pol·y·con·den·sa·tion (pol′ē kon′den sā′shən), *n. Chem.* formation of a polymer by chemical condensation with the elimination of a small molecule, such as water. [1935–40; POLY- + CONDENSATION]

pol·y·con·ic (pol′ē kon′ik), *adj.* pertaining to or utilizing two or more cones. [1860–65; POLY- + CONIC]

polycon′ic projec′tion, *Cartog.* a conic projection in which the parallels are arcs of circles that are not concentric but are equally spaced along the central straight meridian, all other meridians being curves equally spaced along the parallels. [1900–05]

pol·y·cot (pol′ē kot′), *n. Bot.* a polycotyledon. [by shortening]

pol·y·cot·y·le·don (pol′ē kot′l ēd′n), *n.* a plant having more than two cotyledons, as certain gymnosperms. [1750–60; POLY- + COTYLEDON] —**pol′y·cot′y·le′don·ous,** *adj.*

Po·lyc·ra·tes (pə lik′rə tēz′), *n.* died 522? B.C., Greek tyrant of Samos.

pol·y·crys·tal·line (pol′ē kris′tl in, -īn′, -ēn′), *adj.* **1.** (of a rock or metal) composed of aggregates of individual crystals. **2.** having or consisting of crystals that are variously oriented. [1920–25; POLY- + CRYSTALLINE]

pol·y·cul·ture (pol′ē kul′chər), *n.* **1.** the raising at the same time and place of more than one species of plant or animal. **2.** a place where this is done. [1910–15; POLY- + CULTURE]

pol·y·cy·clic (pol′ē sī′klik, -sik′lik), *adj. Chem.* pertaining to an organic compound containing several atomic rings, usually fused. [1865–70; POLY- + CYCLIC]

pol·y·dac·tyl (pol′ē dak′til), *adj.* Also, **pol′y·dac′tylous. 1.** having many or several digits. **2.** having more than the normal number of fingers or toes. —*n.* **3.** a polydactyl animal. [1860–65; < Gk *polydáktylos.* See POLY-, -DACTYL]

pol·y·dac·ty·ly (pol′ē dak′tə lē), *n. Pathol.* the condition of being polydactyl. Also, **pol′y·dac′tyl·ism.** [1885–90; POLYDACTYL + -Y[3]]

pol·y·dae·mon·ism (pol′ē dē′mə niz′əm), *n.* the belief in many evil spirits. Also, **pol′y·de′mon·ism.** [1705–15; POLY- + DAEMON + -ISM] —**pol′y·dae′mon·ist,** *n., adj.* —**pol′y·dae′mon·is′tic,** *adj.*

Pol·y·deu·ces (pol′i dōō′sēz, -dyōō′-), *n.* Greek name of **Pollux.**

pol·y·dip·si·a (pol′ē dip′sē ə), *n. Med.* excessive thirst. [1650–60; < NL < Gk *polydíps(ios)* very thirsty (*poly-* POLY- + *díps(a)* thirst + *-ios* adj. suffix) + *-ia* -IA]

pol·y·dis·perse (pol′ē di spûrs′), *adj. Physical Chem.* of or noting a sol that contains particles of different sizes. [1910–15; POLY- + DISPERSE]

po·lyd·o·mous (pə lid′ə məs), *adj.* living in more than one nest, as certain ant colonies. Cf. **monodomous.** [POLY- + Gk *dóm(os)* house + -OUS]

pol·y·don·tia (pol′ē don′shə, -shē ə), *n. Dentistry.* the condition of having more than the normal number of teeth. [POLY- + -(O)DONT + -IA]

Pol·y·do·rus (pol′i dôr′əs, -dōr′-), *n.* fl. 1st century B.C., Greek sculptor who, with Agesander and Athenodorus, carved the Laocoön group.

pol·y·drug (pol′ē drug′), *adj.* being or pertaining to several drugs used simultaneously, esp. narcotics or addictive drugs: *a center for dealing with polydrug abuse.* [1970–75; POLY- + DRUG]

pol·y·e·lec·tro·lyte (pol′ē i lek′trə līt′), *n. Chem.* an electrolyte of high molecular weight, usually polymeric, either natural or synthetic. [1945–50; POLY- + ELECTROLYTE]

pol·y·em·bry·o·ny (pol′ē em′brē ə nē, -ō′nē, -em bri′ə nē), *n. Embryol.* the production of more than one embryo from one egg. [1840–50; POLY- + Gk *émbryon* EMBRYO + -Y[3]]

pol·y·ene (pol′ē ēn′), *n. Chem.* a hydrocarbon containing two or more double bonds, often conjugated. [1925–30; POLY- + -ENE]

pol·y·es·ter (pol′ē es′tər, pol′ē es′tər), *n.* **1.** *Chem.* a polymer in which the monomer units are linked together by the group –COO–, usually formed by polymerizing a polyhydric alcohol with a polybasic acid: used chiefly in the manufacture of resins, plastics, and textile fibers. **2.** Also called **poly.** a fabric made from such textile fibers. [1925–30; POLY- + ESTER] —**pol·y·es·ter·i·fi·ca·tion** (pol′ē es′tər ə fi kā′shən), *n.*

pol·y·es·trous (pol′ē es′trəs), *adj.* having several estrus cycles annually or during a breeding season. Also, **polyoestrous.** [1895–1900; POLY- + ESTROUS]

pol·y·e·ther (pol′ē ē′thər) *n. Chem.* a polymeric ether. [1920–25; POLY- + ETHER]

pol·y·eth·nic (pol′ē eth′nik), *adj.* inhabited by or consisting of people of many ethnic backgrounds. [1885–90; POLY- + ETHNIC]

pol·y·eth·yl·ene (pol′ē eth′ə lēn′), *n. Chem.* a plastic polymer of ethylene used chiefly for containers, electrical insulation, and packaging. Also called, *Brit.,* **polythene.** [1935–40; POLY- + ETHYLENE]

polyeth′ylene gly′col, *Chem.* any of a series of polymers of ethylene glycol, having a molecular weight of from about 200 to 6000, obtained by condensation of ethylene glycol or of ethylene oxide and water, used as an emulsifying agent and lubricant in ointments, creams, etc. [1885–90]

pol·y·foam (pol′ē fōm′), *n.* a rigid, semirigid, or rubbery foam composed of minute bubbles of air or carbon dioxide embedded in a polymer matrix, often polyurethane: used in mattresses, padding, insulation, etc. [POLY- + FOAM]

pol·y·func·tion·al (pol′ē fungk′shə nl), *adj. Chem.* containing more than one functional group. [1925–30; POLY- + FUNCTIONAL]

po·lyg·a·la (pə lig′ə lə), *n.* any plant of the genus *Polygala,* comprising the milkworts. [1570–80; < NL, genus name, special use of L *polygala,* for Gk *polýgalon* milkwort, lit., something very milky, equiv. to *poly-* POLY- + *-galon,* deriv. of *gála* milk; see GALACTO-] —**pol·y·ga·la·ceous** (pol′ē gə lā′shəs, pə lig′ə-), *adj.*

pol·y·gam·ic (pol′ē gam′ik), *adj.* polygamous. [1810–20; POLYGAM(Y) + -IC]

po·lyg·a·mist (pə lig′ə mist), *n.* a person who prac-

CONCISE PRONUNCIATION KEY: *act, cāpe, dâre, pärt; set, ēqual; if, īce; ox, ōver, ôrder, oil, bŏŏk, bōōt, out; up, ûrge; child; sing; shoe; thin, that;* zh as in *treasure.* ə = *a* as in *alone, e* as in *system, i* as in *easily, o* as in *gallop, u* as in *circus;* ᵊ as in *fire* (fīᵊr), *hour* (ouᵊr). l and n can serve as syllabic consonants, as in *cradle* (krād′l), and *button* (but′n). See the full key inside the front cover.

tices or favors polygamy. [1630–40; POLYGAM(Y) + -IST] —**po·lyg′a·mis′tic,** *adj.*

pol·y·gam·o·phile (pol′ē gam′ə fīl′), *n.* a person who approves of or countenances polygamy, esp. as practiced by others. [1705–15; POLYGAM(Y) + -O- + -PHILE]

po·lyg·a·mous (pə lig′ə məs), *adj.* **1.** of, pertaining to, characterized by, or practicing polygamy; polygamic. **2.** *Bot.* bearing both unisexual and hermaphrodite flowers on the same or on different plants of the same species. [1605–15; < Gk *polýgamos.* See POLY-, -GAMOUS] —**po·lyg′a·mous·ly,** *adv.*

po·lyg·a·my (pə lig′ə mē), *n.* **1.** the practice or condition of having more than one spouse, esp. wife, at one time. Cf. **bigamy** (def. 1), **monogamy** (def. 1). **2.** *Zool.* the habit or system of mating with more than one individual, either simultaneously or successively. [1585–95; < Gk *polygamía.* See POLY-, -GAMY]

pol·y·gene (pol′ē jēn′), *n.* one of a group of nonallelic genes that together control a quantitative characteristic in an organism. [1940–45; back formation from *polygenic;* see POLY-, GENE, -IC] —**pol·y·gen·ic** (pol′ē jen′ik), *adj.*

pol·y·gen·e·sis (pol′ē jen′ə sis), *n. Biol., Anthropol.* origin from more than one ancestral species or line. [1860–65; POLY- + -GENESIS]

pol·y·ge·net·ic (pol′ē jə net′ik), *adj.* **1.** *Biol.* relating to or exhibiting polygenesis. **2.** having many or several different sources of origin. [1860–65; POLY- + -GENETIC] —**pol′y·ge·net′i·cal·ly,** *adv.*

polygen′ic inher′itance, *Genetics.* the heredity of complex characters that are determined by a large number of genes, each one usually having a relatively small effect. Cf. **quantitative inheritance.** [1960–65; POLY- + -GENIC]

po·lyg·e·nism (pə lij′ə niz′əm), *n.* the theory that the human race has descended from two or more ancestral types. [1875–80; POLY- + -GEN(Y) + -ISM] —**po·lyg′e·nist,** *n., adj.* —**po·lyg′e·nis′tic,** *adj.*

pol·y·glot (pol′ē glot′), *adj.* **1.** able to speak or write several languages; multilingual. **2.** containing, composed of, or written in several languages: *a polyglot Bible.* —*n.* **3.** a mixture or confusion of languages. **4.** a person who speaks, writes, or reads a number of languages. **5.** a book, esp. a Bible, containing the same text in several languages. [1635–45; < ML *polyglōttus* < Gk *polýglōttos* many-tongued. See POLY-, -GLOT] —**pol′y·glot′ism,** *n.*

Pol·yg·no·tus (pol′ig nō′təs), *n.* fl. c450 B.C., Greek painter.

pol·y·gon (pol′ē gon′), *n.* a figure, esp. a closed plane figure, having three or more, usually straight, sides. See illus. under **heptagon, hexagon, octagon, pentagon, quadrilateral, triangle.** [1560–70; < L *polygōnum* < Gk *polýgōnon,* n. use of neut. of *polýgōnos* many-angled. See POLY-, -GON] —**po·lyg·o·nal** (pə lig′ə nl), *adj.* —**po·lyg′o·nal·ly,** *adv.*

pol·y·go·na·ceous (pol′ē gə nā′shəs, pə lig′ə nā′-), *adj.* belonging to the Polygonaceae, the buckwheat family of plants. Cf. **buckwheat family.** [1870–75; < NL *Polygonace(ae)* (*Polygon(um)* the type genus (< Gk *polýgonon* knotgrass, lit., something with many joints; see POLY-, KNEE, -GON) + *-aceae* -ACEAE) + -OUS]

pol·y·graph (pol′i graf′, -gräf′), *n.* **1.** an instrument for receiving and recording simultaneously tracings of variations in certain body activities. **2.** a test using such an instrument to determine if a person is telling the truth. **3.** See **lie detector. 4.** an apparatus for producing copies of a drawing or writing. **5.** a prolific or versatile author. —*v.t.* **6.** to test (a person) with a polygraph. [1795–1805 for def. 1; 1920–25 for def. 3; < Gk *polýgraphos* writing much. See POLY-, -GRAPH] —**pol·y·graph·ic** (pol′i graf′ik), *adj.* —**po·lyg·ra·phist** (pə lig′rə fist), **po·lyg′ra·pher,** *n.*

po·lyg·y·nist (pə lij′ə nist), *n.* a person who practices or favors polygyny. [1875–80; POLYGYN(Y) + -IST]

po·lyg·y·nous (pə lij′ə nəs), *adj.* **1.** of, pertaining to, characterized by, or practicing polygyny. **2.** *Bot.* having many pistils or styles. [1840–50; POLYGYN(Y) + -OUS]

po·lyg·y·ny (pə lij′ə nē), *n.* **1.** the practice or condition of having more than one wife at one time. **2.** (among male animals) the habit or system of having two or more mates, either simultaneously or successively. **3.** (among social insects) the condition of having two or more functioning queens in a colony. **4.** *Bot.* the state or condition of having many pistils or styles. Cf. **monogyny.** [1770–80; < Gk *polygýn(aios)* having many wives (see POLY-, GYN-) + -Y[3]]

pol·y·he·dral (pol′ē hē′drəl), *adj.* of, pertaining to, or having the shape of a polyhedron. [1805–15; < Gk *polýedr(os)* many-based (see POLYHEDRON) + -AL[1]]

pol′yhe′dral an′gle, *Geom.* a configuration consisting of the lateral faces of a polyhedron around one of its vertices. The portion of a pyramid including one of its points is such a configuration. See illus. under **pyramid.** [1860–65]

pol·y·he·dron (pol′ē hē′drən), *n., pl.* **-drons, -dra** (-drə). a solid figure having many faces. See illus. under **dodecahedron, icosahedron, octahedron, pentahedron, tetrahedron.** [1560–70; < Gk *polýedron,* neut. of *polýedros* having many bases. See POLY-, -HEDRON]

pol·y·his·tor (pol′ē his′tər), *n.* a person of great and varied learning. Also, **pol·y·his·to·ri·an** (pol′ē hi stôr′ē ən, -stōr′-). [1565–75; < L *polyhistōr* < Gk *polyístōr* very learned. See POLY-, HISTORY] —**pol·y·his·tor·ic** (pol′ē hi stôr′ik, -stor′-), *adj.* —**pol′y·his′to·ry,** *n.*

CONCISE ETYMOLOGY KEY: <, descended or borrowed from; >, whence; b., blend of, blended; c., cognate with; cf., compare; deriv., derivative; equiv., equivalent; imit., imitative; obl., oblique; r., replacing; s., stem; sp., spelling, spelled; resp., respelling, respelled; trans., translation; ?, origin unknown; *, unattested; ‡, probably earlier than. See the full key inside the front cover.

pol·y·hy·dric (pol′ē hī′drik), *adj. Chem.* (esp. of alcohols and phenols) polyhydroxy. [1875–80; POLY- + HYDRIC[1]]

pol·y·hy·drox·y (pol′ē hī drok′sē), *adj. Chem.* containing two or more hydroxyl groups. [1890–95; POLY- + HYDROXY]

Pol·y·hym·ni·a (pol′i him′nē ə), *n. Class. Myth.* the Muse of sacred music and dance. [< L, alter. of Gk *Polýmnia.* See POLY-, HYMN, -IA]

pol·y·im·ide (pol′ē im′īd, -id), *n.* any of a class of polymers with an imido group: resistant to high temperatures, wear, radiation, and many chemicals. [1940–45; POLY- + -IMIDE]

pol·y·i·so·bu·tyl·ene (pol′ē ī′sə byo͞ot′l ēn′), *n. Chem.* a polymer of isobutylene, used chiefly in the manufacture of synthetic rubber. Also, **pol·y·i·so·bu·tene** (pol′ē ī′sə byo͞o′tēn). [1930–35; POLY- + ISOBUTYLENE]

pol·y·i·so·prene (pol′ē ī′sə prēn′), *n. Chem.* a thermoplastic polymer, $(C_5H_8)_n$, the major constituent of natural rubber and also obtained synthetically. [1930–35; POLY- + ISOPRENE]

pol·y·math (pol′ē math′), *n.* a person of great learning in several fields of study; polyhistor. [1615–25; < Gk *polymathḗs* learned, having learned much, equiv. to *poly-* POLY- + *-mathēs,* adj. deriv. of *manthánein* to learn] —**pol′y·math′ic,** *adj.*

po·lym·a·thy (pə lim′ə thē), *n.* learning in many fields; encyclopedic knowledge. [1635–45; < Gk *polymathía;* see POLYMATH, -Y[3]]

pol·y·mer (pol′ə mər), *n. Chem.* **1.** a compound of high molecular weight derived either by the addition of many smaller molecules, as polyethylene, or by the condensation of many smaller molecules with the elimination of water, alcohol, or the like, as nylon. **2.** a compound formed from two or more polymeric compounds. **3.** a product of polymerization. Cf. **monomer.** [1865–70; < Gk *polymerḗs* having many parts. See POLY-, -MER]

pol·y·mer·ase (pol′ə mə rās′, -rāz′), *n. Biochem.* any of several enzymes that catalyze the formation of a long-chain molecule by linking smaller molecular units, as nucleotides with nucleic acids. Cf. **DNA polymerase, RNA polymerase.** [1955–60; POLYMER + -ASE]

pol·y·mer·ic (pol′ə mer′ik), *adj. Chem.* **1.** of or relating to a polymer. **2.** (of compounds) having the same elements combined in the same proportion but different molecular weights. [1840–50; POLYMER + -IC]

po·lym·er·ism (pə lim′ə riz′əm, pol′ə mə-), *n.* **1.** *Chem.* a polymeric state. **2.** *Biol., Bot.* a polymerous state. [1825–35; POLYMER + -ISM]

po·lym·er·i·za·tion (pə lim′ər ə zā′shən, pol′ə mər-), *n. Chem.* **1.** the act or process of forming a polymer or polymeric compound. **2.** the combination of many like or unlike molecules to form a more complex product of higher molecular weight, with elimination of water, alcohol, or the like **(condensation polymerization),** or without such elimination **(addition polymerization). 3.** the conversion of one compound into another by such a process. [1875–80; POLYMERIZE + -ATION]

po·lym·er·ize (pə lim′ə rīz′, pol′ə mə-), *v.,* **-ized, -iz·ing.** *Chem.* —*v.t.* **1.** to subject to polymerization. —*v.i.* **2.** to undergo polymerization. Also, *esp. Brit.,* **po·lym′er·ise′.** [1860–65; POLYMER + -IZE]

po·lym·er·ous (pə lim′ər əs), *adj.* **1.** *Biol.* composed of many parts. **2.** *Bot.* having numerous members in each whorl. [1855–60; POLYMER + -OUS]

pol·y·meth·yl methac′rylate (pol′ē meth′əl), *Chem.* polymerized methyl methacrylate. [1930–35; POLY- + METHYL]

pol·y·morph (pol′ē môrf′), *n.* **1.** *Biol.* an organism having more than one adult form, as the different castes in social ants. **2.** *Crystall.* any of the crystal forms assumed by a substance that exhibits polymorphism. **3.** *Anat.* granulocyte. [1820–30; < Gk *polýmorphos;* see POLY-, -MORPH] —**pol′y·mor′phic,** *adj.*

pol·y·mor·phism (pol′ē môr′fiz əm), *n.* **1.** the state or condition of being polymorphous. **2.** *Crystall.* crystallization into two or more chemically identical but crystallographically distinct forms. **3.** *Biol.* the existence of an organism in several form or color varieties. **4.** *Genetics.* the presence of two or more distinct phenotypes in a population due to the expression of different alleles of a given gene, as human blood groups O, A, B, and AB. [1830–40; POLYMORPH + -ISM] —**pol′y·mor·phis′tic,** *adj.*

pol·y·mor·pho·nu·cle·ar (pol′ē môr′fə no͞o′klē ər, -nyo͞o′- *or, by metathesis,* -kyə lər), *adj. Cell Biol.* (of a leukocyte) having a lobulate nucleus. [1895–1900; POLY- + MORPHO- + NUCLEAR]
—**Pronunciation.** See **nuclear.**

pol·y·mor·phous (pol′ē môr′fəs), *adj.* **1.** having, assuming, or passing through many or various forms, stages, or the like. **2.** polymorphic. [1775–85; < Gk *polýmorphos* multiform. See POLY-, -MORPHOUS]

pol·y·my·al·gi·a rheu·mat·i·ca (pol′ē mī al′jē ə ro͞o mat′i kə, -al′jə), *Pathol.* a chronic inflammatory disease, common among older persons, characterized by recurrent episodes of muscle pain and stiffness, sometimes leading to cardiovascular complications or blindness. Also called **pol′y·my·al′gi·a.** [1955–60; < NL; see POLY-, MYALGIA, RHEUMATIC]

pol·y·myx·in (pol′ē mik′sin), *n. Pharm.* any of various polypeptide antibiotics derived from *Bacillus polymyxa.* [1945–50; < NL *polymyx(a)* specific epithet (< Gk *poly-* POLY- + *mýxa* mucus, slime) + -IN[2]]

Pol·y·ne·sia (pol′ə nē′zhə, -shə), *n.* one of the three principal divisions of Oceania, comprising those island groups in the Pacific lying E of Melanesia and Micronesia and extending from the Hawaiian Islands S to New Zealand.

Pol·y·ne·sian (pol′ə nē′zhən, -shən), *adj.* **1.** of or pertaining to Polynesia, its inhabitants, or their languages. —*n.* **2.** a member of any of a number of brown-skinned peoples, variously classified as to race, of distinctive customs, speaking closely related Austronesian languages, who inhabit Polynesia. **3.** the easternmost group of Austronesian languages, including Maori, Tahitian, Samoan, Hawaiian, and the language of Easter Island. [1805–15; POLYNESI(A) + -AN]

pol·y·neu·ri·tis (pol′ē no͞o rī′tis, -nyo͞o-), *n. Pathol.* inflammation of several nerves at the same time; multiple neuritis. [1885–90; POLY- + NEURITIS] —**pol·y·neu·rit·ic** (pol′ē no͞o rit′ik, -nyo͞o-), *adj.*

Pol·y·ni·ces (pol′ə nī′sēz), *n. Class. Myth.* a son of Oedipus and Jocasta and brother of Eteocles and Antigone on whose behalf the Seven against Thebes were organized.

pol·y·no·mi·al (pol′ə nō′mē əl), *adj.* **1.** consisting of or characterized by two or more names or terms. —*n.* **2.** *Algebra.* **a.** (in one variable) an expression consisting of the sum of two or more terms each of which is the product of a constant and a variable raised to an integral power: $ax^2 + bx + c$ is a polynomial, where *a, b,* and *c* are constants and *x* is a variable. **b.** a similar expression in more than one variable, as $4x^2y^3 - 3xy + 5x + 7$. **c.** *Now Rare.* Also called **multinomial.** any expression consisting of the sum of two or more terms, as $4x^3 + \cos x$. **3.** a polynomial name or term. **4.** *Biol.* a species name containing more than two terms. [1665–75; POLY- + (BI)NOMIAL]

pol′yno′mial ring′, *Math.* the set of all polynomials in an indeterminate variable with coefficients that are elements of a given ring.

pol·y·nu·cle·ar (pol′ē no͞o′klē ər, -nyo͞o′- *or, by metathesis,* -kyə lər), *adj.* having many nuclei. Also, **pol·y·nu·cle·ate** (pol′ē no͞o′klē it, -āt′, -nyo͞o′-). [1875–80; POLY- + NUCLEAR]
—**Pronunciation.** See **nuclear.**

pol·y·nu·cle·o·tide (pol′ē no͞o′klē ə tīd′, -nyo͞o′-), *n. Biochem.* a sequence of nucleotides, as in DNA or RNA, bound into a chain. [1910–15; POLY- + NUCLEOTIDE]

po·lyn·ya (pə lin′yə), *n.* an area of unfrozen sea water surrounded by ice. [1850–55; < Russ *polyn′yá,* ORuss *polynĭi* equiv. to *pol(ŭ)* empty, open + *-ynĭi* n. suffix]

pol·y·oes·trous (pol′ē es′trəs, -ē′strəs), *adj.* polyestrous.

pol·y·ol (pol′ē ôl′, -ol′), *n. Chem.* an alcohol containing three or more hydroxyl groups; a polyhydric alcohol. Also called **polyalcohol.** [POLY- + -OL[1]]

pol·y·o·le·fin (pol′ē ō′lə fin), *n. Chem.* any of a group of thermoplastic, stiff, light, and hard polymers obtained from the polymerization of simple olefins like propylene, used for injection molding, mostly in the automotive and appliance industries. [POLY- + OLEFIN]

pol·y·o′ma vi′rus (pol′ē ō′mə), a small DNA-containing virus, of the papovavirus group, that can produce a variety of tumors in mice, hamsters, rabbits, and rats. [1955–60; POLY- + -OMA]

pol·y·on·y·mous (pol′ē on′ə məs), *adj.* having or known by several or many names. [1670–80; < Gk *polyṓnymos,* equiv. to *poly-* POLY- + *-ōnymos* -named, adj. deriv. of *ónyma, ónoma* NAME; see -OUS] —**pol′y·on′y·my,** *n.*

pol·yp (pol′ip), *n.* **1.** *Zool.* **a.** a sedentary type of animal form characterized by a more or less fixed base, columnar body, and free end with mouth and tentacles, esp. as applied to coelenterates. **b.** an individual zooid of a compound or colonial organism. **2.** *Pathol.* a projecting growth from a mucous surface, as of the nose, being either a tumor or a hypertrophy of the mucous membrane. [1350–1400; ME *polip,* short for *polipus* nasal tumor (later, also cephalopod, now obs.) < ML, L *pōlypus* < dial. Gk *poulýpous* octopus, nasal tumor (Attic *polýpous,* gen. *polýpodos;* see POLY-, -POD)] —**pol′yp·ous,** *adj.*

pol·y·par·y (pol′ə per′ē), *n., pl.* **-par·ies.** the common supporting structure of a colony of polyps, as corals. [1740–50; < NL *polypārium.* See POLYP, -ARY] —**pol·y·par·i·an** (pol′ə pâr′ē ən), *adj.*

pol·y·ped (pol′ē ped′), *n.* **1.** a being or object having many legs: *Her favorite toy is a bug-shaped polyped.* —*adj.* **2.** having many legs: *a polyped table.* [1815–25; POLY- + -PED, perh. on the model of QUADRUPED]

pol·y·pep·tide (pol′ē pep′tīd, -tid), *n. Biochem.* a chain of amino acids linked together by peptide bonds and having a molecular weight of up to about 10,000. [1900–05; POLY- + PEPTIDE]

pol·y·pet·al·ous (pol′ē pet′l əs), *adj. Bot.* having a corolla of separate petals. [1695–1705; POLY- + PETALOUS] —**pol′y·pet′al·y,** *n.*

pol·y·pha·gi·a (pol′ē fā′jē ə, -jə), *n.* **1.** *Pathol.* excessive desire to eat. **2.** *Zool.* the habit of subsisting on many different kinds of food. [1685–95; < NL < Gk *polyphagía;* see POLY-, -PHAGY] —**pol′y·pha′gi·an,** *n., adj.* —**po·lyph·a·gist** (pə lif′ə jist), *n.* —**po·lyph·a·gous** (pə lif′ə gəs), **pol·y·phag·ic** (pol′ē faj′ik, -fā′jik), *adj.*

pol·y·phar·ma·cy (pol′ē fär′mə sē), *n. Pharm.* the use of two or more drugs together, usually to treat a single condition or disease. [1755–65; POLY- + PHARMACY]

pol·y·phase (pol′ē fāz′), *adj. Elect.* **1.** having more than one phase. **2.** of or pertaining to a set of alternating currents that have the same frequency but different phases and that enter a specified region at more than two points. [1890–95; POLY- + PHASE]

pol·y·pha·sic (pol′ē fā′zik), *adj.* **1.** having more than two phases. **2.** habitually doing more than one thing at a time: *a polyphasic personality.* [1920–25; POLYPHASE + -IC]

Pol·y·phe·mus (pol′ə fē′məs), *n. Class. Myth.* a Cyclops who was blinded by Odysseus.

Pol′yphe′mus moth′, a large, yellowish-brown American silkworm moth, *Antheraea polyphemus,* having a prominent eyespot on each hind wing and feeding on cherry, apple, and other trees.

pol•y•phe•nol (pol′ē fē′nôl, -nol), *n. Chem.* a polymeric phenol. [1895–1900; POLY- + PHENOL]

pol•y•phone (pol′ē fōn′), *n. Phonet.* a polyphonic letter or symbol. [1645–55; < Gk *polýphōnos.* See POLY-, -PHONE]

pol•y•phon•ic (pol′ē fon′ik), *adj.* **1.** consisting of many voices or sounds. **2.** *Music.* **a.** having two or more voices or parts, each with an independent melody, but all harmonizing; contrapuntal (opposed to *homophonic*). **b.** pertaining to music of this kind. **c.** capable of producing more than one tone at a time, as an organ or a harp. **3.** *Phonet.* having more than one phonetic value, as the letter *s*, that is voiced (z) in *nose* and unvoiced (s) in *salt.* [1775–85; POLYPHONE + -IC] **—pol′y•phon′i•cal•ly,** *adv.*

pol′yphon′ic prose′, prose characterized by the use of poetic devices, as alliteration, assonance, rhyme, etc., and esp. by an emphasis on rhythm not strictly metered. [1915–20]

po•lyph•o•ny (pə lif′ə nē), *n.* **1.** *Music.* polyphonic composition; counterpoint. **2.** *Phonet.* representation of different sounds by the same letter or symbol. [1820–30; < Gk *polyphōnía* variety of tones. See POLY-, -PHONY] **—po•lyph′o•nous,** *adj.* **—po•lyph′o•nous•ly,** *adv.*

pol•y•phy•let•ic (pol′ē fī let′ik), *adj.* developed from more than one ancestral type, as a group of animals. [1870–75; POLY- + PHYLETIC] **—pol′y•phy•let′i•cal•ly,** *adv.*

pol•y•ploid (pol′ē ploid′), *Biol.* **—***adj.* **1.** having a chromosome number that is more than double the basic or haploid number. **—***n.* **2.** a polyploid cell or organism. [1915–20; POLY- + -PLOID] **—pol′y•ploi′dic,** *adj.* **—pol′y•ploi′dy,** *n.*

pol•yp•ne•a (pol′ip nē′ə), *n. Med.* rapid breathing; panting. Also, **pol′yp•noe′a.** [1885–90; POLY- + -PNEA]

pol•y•pod (pol′ē pod′), *adj.* (of insect larvae) having many feet. [< It (1913) < Gk, s. of *polýpous* many-footed; see POLYP]

pol•y•po•dy (pol′ē pō′dē), *n., pl.* **-dies.** any fern of the genus *Polypodium,* as *P. vulgare,* having creeping rootstocks, deeply pinnatifid evergreen fronds, and round, naked sori. [1400–50; late ME *polypodye* < L *polypodion* < Gk *polypódion* (> NL *Polypodium*); see POLY-, -POD, -IUM]

pol•yp•oid (pol′ə poid′), *adj. Pathol.* resembling a polyp. [1835–45; POLYP + -OID]

pol•y•pore (pol′ē pôr′, -pōr′), *n.* a woody pore fungus, *Laetiporus* (*Polyporus*) *sulphureus,* that forms large, brightly colored, shelflike growths on old logs and tree stumps. [1900–05; < NL *Polyporus;* see POLY-, PORE²]

pol•yp•o•sis (pol′ə pō′sis), *n. Pathol.* the development of numerous polyps on a hollow internal organ, seen esp. in the intestinal tract. [1910–15; POLYP + -OSIS]

pol•yp•ous (pol′ə pəs), *adj.* polypoid. [1740–50; POLYP + -OUS]

pol•y•pro•pyl•ene (pol′ē prō′pə lēn′), *n. Chem.* a plastic polymer of propylene, $(C_3H_5)_n$, used chiefly for molded parts, electrical insulation, packaging, and fibers for wearing apparel. [1930–35; POLY- + PROPYLENE]

pol•y•prot•ic (pol′ē prot′ik), *adj. Chem.* (of an acid) having two or more transferable protons. [1940–45; POLY- + PROT(ON) + -IC]

pol•yp•tych (pol′ip tik), *n.* a work of art composed of several connected panels. Cf. **diptych, pentaptych, triptych.** [1855–60; special use of LL *polyptychum* < Gk *polýptychon* a register, roll, n. use of neut. of *polýptychos* having many folds. See POLY-, DIPTYCH, TRIPTYCH]

pol•y•rhythm (pol′ē rith′əm), *n. Music.* the simultaneous occurrence of sharply contrasting rhythms within a composition. [1925–30; POLY- + RHYTHM] **—pol′y•rhyth′mic,** *adj.* **—pol′y•rhyth′mi•cal•ly,** *adv.*

pol•y•ri•bo•some (pol′ē rī′bə sōm′), *n. Biol.* polysome. [1960–65; POLY- + RIBOSOME]

pol•y•sac•cha•ride (pol′ē sak′ə rīd′, -rid), *n. Chem.* a carbohydrate, as starch, inulin, or cellulose, containing more than three monosaccharide units per molecule, the units being attached to each other in the manner of acetals, and therefore capable of hydrolysis by acids or enzymes to monosaccharides. Also, **pol•y•sac•cha•rose** (pol′ē sak′ə rōs′). [1890–95; POLY- + SACCHARIDE]

pol′y sci′, *Informal.* See **poli sci.**

pol•y•se•my (pol′ē sē′mē, pə lis′ə mē), *n.* diversity of meanings. [1895–1900; < NL *polysēmia,* equiv. to LL *polysēm*(*us*) with many significations (< Gk *polýsēmos,* equiv. to *poly-* POLY- + *sêm*(*a*) sign + *-os* adj. suffix) + *-ia* -Y³] **—pol′y•se′mous,** *adj.*

pol•y•sep•al•ous (pol′ē sep′ə ləs), *adj. Bot.* having a calyx of separate or unconnected sepals. [1820–30; POLY- + -SEPALOUS]

pol•y•some (pol′ē sōm′), *n. Biol.* a complex of ribosomes strung along a single strand of messenger RNA that translates the genetic information coded in the messenger RNA during protein synthesis. Also called **polyribosome.** [1960–65; POLY- + (RIBO)SOME]

pol•y•som•no•gram (pol′ē som′nə gram′), *n.* a record of a person's sleep pattern, breathing, heart activity, and limb movements during sleep. *Abbr.:* PSG [POLY- + L *somn*(*um*) sleep + -o- + -GRAM¹; for sense of POLY-, cf. POLYGRAPH] **—pol•y•som•nog•ra•phy** (pol′ē som nog′rə fē, -səm-), *n.*

pol•y•spûr•mi•a (pol′ē spûr′mē ə), *n. Med.* the secretion of an excessive amount of semen. [< Gk *polyspermía* abundance of seed. See POLY-, SPERM, -IA]

pol•y•sper•my (pol′ē spûr′mē), *n.* the fertilization of an ovum by several spermatozoa. Cf. **dispermy, monospermy.** [1885–90; see POLYSPERMIA, -Y³] **—pol•y•sper•mic** (pol′ē spûr′mik), *adj.*

po•lys•ti•chous (pə lis′ti kəs), *adj.* arranged in rows or series. [1885–90; < Gk *polýstichos* having many lines or verses; see POLY-, -STICHOUS]

pol•y•style (pol′ē stīl′), *adj.* having many columns. [1835–45; < Gk *polýstylos* with many columns. See POLY-, -STYLE²]

pol•y•sty•rene (pol′ē stī′rēn, -stēr′ēn), *n. Chem.* a clear plastic or stiff foam, a polymer of styrene, used chiefly as an insulator in refrigerators and air conditioners. [1925–30; POLY- + STYRENE]

pol•y•sul•fide (pol′ē sul′fīd), *n. Chem.* a sulfide whose molecules contain two or more atoms of sulfur. [1840–50; POLY- + SULFIDE]

pol•y•sus•pen•soid (pol′ē sə spen′soid), *n. Physical Chem.* a suspensoid in which the solid particles are polydisperse. [POLY- + SUSPENSOID]

pol•y•syl•lab•ic (pol′ē si lab′ik), *adj.* **1.** consisting of several, esp. four or more, syllables, as a word. **2.** characterized by such words, as a language, piece of writing, etc. Also, **pol′y•syl•lab′i•cal.** [1650–60; < ML *polysyllab*(*us*) of many syllables (< Gk *polysýllabos*) + -IC. See POLY-, SYLLABIC] **—pol′y•syl•lab′i•cal•ly,** *adv.*

pol•y•syl•la•ble (pol′ē sil′ə bəl, pol′ē sil′-), *n.* a polysyllabic word. [1560–70; POLY- + SYLLABLE]

pol•y•syl•lo•gism (pol′ē sil′ə jiz′əm), *n. Logic.* an argument made up of a chain of syllogisms, the conclusion of each being a premise of the one following, until the last one. [1830–40; POLY- + SYLLOGISM] **—pol′y•syl′lo•gis′tic,** *adj.*

pol•y•syn•ap•tic (pol′ē si nap′tik), *adj. Physiol.* having or involving more than one synapse. [1960–65; POLY- + SYNAPTIC] **—pol′y•syn•ap′ti•cal•ly,** *adv.*

pol•y•syn•de•ton (pol′ē sin′di ton′, -tən), *n. Rhet.* the use of a number of conjunctions in close succession. Cf. **asyndeton.** [1580–90; < NL; see POLY-, ASYNDETON]

pol•y•syn•the•sism (pol′i sin′thə siz′əm), *n.* **1.** the synthesis of various elements. **2.** the combining of several words of a sentence into one word. [1880–85; POLY- + SYNTHES(IS) + -ISM]

pol•y•syn•thet•ic (pol′ē sin thet′ik), *adj.* **1.** (of a language) characterized by a prevalence of relatively long words containing a large number of affixes to express syntactic relationships and meanings. Many American Indian languages are polysynthetic. Cf. **analytic** (def. 3), **synthetic** (def. 3). **2.** of or pertaining to polysynthesism. Also, **pol′y•syn•thet′i•cal.** [1795–1805; < LGk *polysýnthet*(*os*) much compounded + -IC. See POLY-, SYNTHETIC]

pol•y•tech•nic (pol′ē tek′nik), *adj.* **1.** of, pertaining to, or offering instruction in a variety of industrial arts, applied sciences, or technical subjects: *a polytechnic institute.* **—***n.* **2.** a school or other institution in which instruction in technical subjects is given. [1795–1805; POLY- + TECHNIC, modeled on F *polytechnique*]

pol′y•tene chro′mosome (pol′ē tēn′), *Genetics.* a giant, cross-banded chromosome that results from multiple replication of its genetic material with the duplicated chromatin strands remaining closely associated. [1970–75; POLY- + -TENE]

pol•y•tet•ra•fluor•o•eth•y•lene (pol′ē te′trə flŏŏr′ō eth′ə lēn′, -flôr′-, -flōr′-), *n. Chem.* any polymer, plastic, or resin having the formula $(C_2F_4)_n$, prepared from tetrafluoroethylene, noted for its slippery, nonsticking properties, and used in the manufacture of gaskets, electrical insulation, tubing, candy molds, container linings, frying-pan coatings, etc. [1945–50; POLY- + TETRAFLUOROETHYLENE]

pol•y•the•ism (pol′ē thē iz′əm, pol′ē thē′iz əm), *n.* the doctrine of or belief in more than one god or in many gods. [1605–15; POLY- + THEISM; cf. F *polythéisme*] **—pol′y•the′ist,** *n.* **—pol′y•the•is′tic, pol′y•the•is′ti•cal,** *adj.* **—pol′y•the•is′ti•cal•ly,** *adv.*

pol•y•thene (pol′ə thēn′), *n. Chem. Brit.* polyethylene. [1935–40; by shortening]

pol•y•thi•a•zide (pol′ē thī′ə zīd′), *n. Pharm.* a substance, $C_{11}H_{13}ClF_3N_3O_4S_3$, used as a diuretic in the management of edema and hypertension. [POLY- + THIAZIDE]

po•lyt•o•my (pə lit′ə mē), *n., pl.* **-mies. 1.** the act or process of dividing into more than three parts. **2.** the state or condition of being so divided. [1860–65; POLY- + -TOMY] **—po•lyt′o•mous,** *adj.*

pol•y•ton•al (pol′ē tōn′l), *adj. Music.* marked by or using polytonality. [1920–25; POLY- + TONAL] **—pol′y•ton′al•ly,** *adv.*

pol•y•to•nal•i•ty (pol′ē tō nal′i tē), *n. Music.* the use of more than one key at the same time. Also, **pol•y•ton•al•ism** (pol′ē tōn′l iz′əm). [1920–25; POLY- + TONALITY] **—pol•y•ton•al•ist** (pol′ē tōn′l ist), *n.*

pol•y•tri•glyph (pol′ē trī′glif′), *n.* (in classical architecture) an intercolumniation of at least four triglyphs. [POLY- + TRIGLYPH]

pol•y•troph•ic (pol′ē trof′ik, -trō′fik), *adj.* (of certain bacteria) deriving nourishment from many organic substances. [1655–65; POLY- + -TROPHIC]

pol•y•typ•ic (pol′ē tip′ik), *adj.* having or involving many or several types. Also, **pol′y•typ′i•cal.** [1885–90; POLY- + TYPIC]

pol•y•un•sat•u•rate (pol′ē un sach′ər it, -ə rāt′), *n.* a polyunsaturated fat or fatty acid. [1945–50; back formation from POLYUNSATURATED]

pol•y•un•sat•u•rat•ed (pol′ē un sach′ə rā′tid), *adj. Nutrition.* of or noting a class of animal or vegetable fats, esp. plant oils, whose molecules consist of carbon chains with many double bonds unsaturated by hydrogen atoms and that are associated with a low cholesterol content of the blood. [1930–35; POLY- + UNSATURATED]

pol•y•u•re•thane (pol′ē yŏŏr′ə thān′, -yŏŏ reth′ān), *n. Chem.* a thermoplastic polymer containing the group NHCOO: used for padding and insulation in furniture, clothing, and packaging, and in the manufacture of resins for adhesives, elastomers, and fillers. Also, **pol•y•u•re•than** (pol′ē yŏŏr′ə than′). [1940–45; POLY- + URETHANE]

pol•y•u•ri•a (pol′ē yŏŏr′ē ə), *n. Pathol.* the passing of an excessive quantity of urine, as in diabetes, in certain nervous diseases, etc. [1875–80; < NL; see POLY-, -URIA] **—pol′y•u′ric,** *adj.*

pol•y•va•lent (pol′ē vā′lənt, pə liv′ə lənt), *adj.* **1.** *Chem.* having more than one valence. **2.** *Bacteriol.* (of an immune serum) containing several antibodies, each capable of reacting with a specific antigen. [1880–85; POLY- + -VALENT] **—pol′y•va′lence,** *n.*

pol•y•vi•nyl (pol′ē vīn′l), *adj. Chem.* pertaining to or derived from a vinyl polymer. [1930–35; POLY- + VINYL]

pol′yvi′nyl ac′etal, *Chem.* **1.** any of the class of thermoplastic resins derived by the condensation of an aldehyde with polyvinyl alcohol. **2.** the slightly yellow, water-insoluble resin produced from partially hydrolyzed polyvinyl acetate and formaldehyde: used chiefly in the manufacture of lacquers, photographic film, and adhesives. [1930–35]

pol′yvi′nyl ac′etate, *Chem.* a colorless, odorless, nontoxic, transparent, thermoplastic, water-insoluble resin used as an adhesive in certain paints and as an intermediate in the synthesis of polyvinyl acetal and polyvinyl alcohol. Also called **PVA** [1925–30]

pol′yvi′nyl al′cohol, *Chem.* a colorless, water-soluble, thermoplastic resin, derived by the hydrolysis of polyvinyl acetate: used chiefly as an adhesive and as a sizing agent in the manufacture of textiles, paper, and plastics. [1925–30]

pol′yvi′nyl bu′tyral, *Chem.* a white, water-insoluble, polyvinyl acetal made with butyraldehyde, used chiefly as an interlayer in the manufacture of safety glass. [1940–45]

pol′yvi′nyl chlo′ride, *Chem.* a white, water-insoluble, thermoplastic resin, derived by the polymerization of vinyl chloride: used chiefly for thin coatings, insulation, and pipings. Also called **PVC.** [1930–35]

pol′yvi′nyl for′mal (fôr′mal), *Chem.* a colorless, water-insoluble, polyvinyl acetal produced from partially hydrolyzed polyvinyl acetate and formaldehyde, used chiefly in the manufacture of lacquers.

pol•y•vi•nyl•i•dene (pol′ē vī nil′i dēn′), *adj. Chem.* pertaining to or derived from a polymer of a vinylidene compound. [1935–40; POLYVINYL + -ID³ + -ENE]

pol′yvinyl′idene chlo′ride, *Chem.* a polymer of vinylidene chloride, used chiefly in the manufacture of saran. [1935–40]

pol′yvinyl′idene res′in, *Chem.* See **vinylidene resin.**

pol•y•vi•nyl•pyr•rol•i•done (pol′ē vīn′l pi rō′li dōn′, -rol′i-), *n. Chem.* a white, amorphous, water-soluble powder, $(C_6H_9NO)_n$, used chiefly as a vehicle in the manufacture of pharmaceuticals. Also called **PVP** [1940–45; POLYVINYL + PYRROLE + -ID³ + -ONE]

pol′yvi′nyl res′in, *Chem.* any of the class of thermoplastic resins derived by the polymerization or copolymerization of a vinyl compound: used chiefly as adhesives, sizing agents, and coatings. Also called **vinyl resin.** [1930–35]

pol•y•vol•tine (pol′ē vōl′tēn, -tn), *adj.* multivoltine. [1885–90; POLY- + *-voltine* < F *voltin,* equiv. to It *volt*(*a*) turn, time (see VOLT²) + F *-in* -INE¹]

pol•y•wa•ter (pol′ē wô′tər, -wot′ər), *n. Chem.* a substance mistakenly identified as a polymeric form of water, now known to be water containing ions from glass or quartz. [1965–70; POLY(MERIC) + WATER]

Pol•y•zo•a (pol′ē zō′ə), *n. Zool. Brit.* Bryozoa. [1820–30; < NL; see POLY-, -ZOA]

pol•y•zo•an (pol′ē zō′ən), *adj., n. Brit.* bryozoan. [1855–60; < NL *Polyzo*(*a*) POLYZOA + -AN]

pol•y•zo•ar•i•um (pol′ē zō âr′ē əm), *n., pl.* **-ar•i•a** (-âr′ē ə). *Zool.* a bryozoan colony, or its supporting skeleton. [1875–80; < NL; see POLY-, -ZOA, -ARIUM] **—pol′y•zo•ar′i•al,** *adj.*

pol•y•zo•ic (pol′ē zō′ik), *adj.* **1.** (of a bryozoan colony) composed of many zooids. **2.** (of a spore) producing many sporozoites. **3.** (of a habitat) containing many animals or many different kinds of animals. [1850–55; POLY- + ZO- + -IC]

pom (pom), *n.* pommy. [prob. by back formation]

pom•ace (pum′is, pom′-), *n.* **1.** the pulpy residue from apples or similar fruit after crushing and pressing, as in cider making. **2.** any crushed or ground, pulpy substance. [1545–55; perh. < ML *pōmācium* cider, deriv. of L *pōmum* fruit; see POME]

pom′ace fly′. See **vinegar fly.** [1890–95]

po•ma•ceous (pō mā′shəs), *adj.* of, pertaining to, or of the nature of pomes. [1700–10; < NL *pōmāceus.* See POME, -ACEOUS]

po•made (po mād′, -mäd′, pō-), *n., v.,* **-mad•ed, -mad•ing.** **—***n.* **1.** a scented ointment, esp. one used for the scalp or for dressing the hair. **—***v.t.* **2.** to dress with pomade; apply pomade to. [1555–65; earlier *pommade* < F < It *pomata* (so called because apples were orig. an ingredient), equiv. to *pom*(*a*) apple (< L, pl. (taken in VL as fem. sing.) of *pōmum* fruit) + *-ata* -ADE¹. See POMATUM]

Pom′a lift′ (pom′ə), *Trademark.* a ski lift having a disklike support, placed between the legs, against which a skier leans while being pulled uphill. Also, **Pom′a•lift′.**

po•man•der (pō′man dər, pō man′dər), *n.* **1.** a mixture of aromatic substances, often in the form of a ball, formerly carried on the person as a supposed guard against infection but now placed in closets, dressers, etc. **2.** the ball, box, or other case in which it was formerly carried. [1425–75; earlier *pomaundre, pomemandre,* late

CONCISE PRONUNCIATION KEY: act, cāpe, dâre, pärt; set, ēqual; if, īce; ox, ōver, ôrder, oil, bŏŏk, bōōt, out; up, ûrge; child; sing; shoe; thin, *th*at; zh as in *treasure.* ə = *a* as in *alone, e* as in *system, i* as in *easily, o* as in *gallop, u* as in *circus;* ᵊ as in *fire* (fīᵊr), *hour* (ouᵊr). l and n can serve as syllabic consonants, as in *cradle* (krād′l), and *button* (but′n). See the full key inside the front cover.

ME *pomendambre* < MF *pome d'ambre* (cf. obs. E *pom(e)amber*) < ML *pōmum ambrē* (L *ambrae*) lit., apple of amber. See POME, AMBER]

po•ma•tum (pō mā′təm, -mä′-, pə-), *n.* pomade. [1555–65; < NL, Latinization of POMADE; neut. (for fem.) to agree with L *pōmum* fruit; see POME]

pome (pōm), *n. Bot.* the characteristic fruit of the apple family, as an apple, pear, or quince, in which the edible flesh arises from the greatly swollen receptacle and not from the carpels. [1350–1400; ME < MF < L *pōma*, pl. (taken as sing.) of *pōmum* fruit] **—pome′•like′**, *adj.*

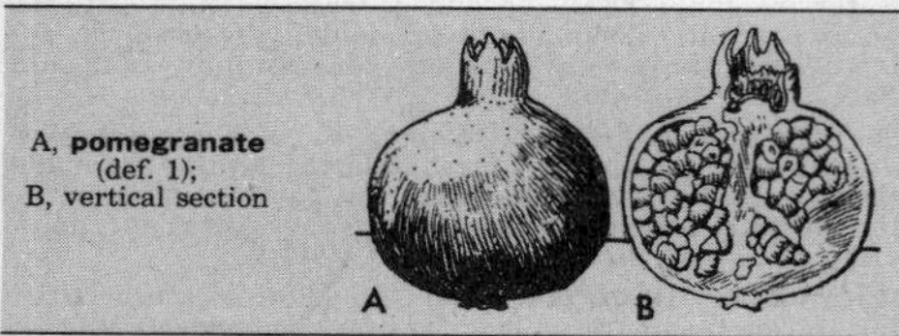

A, **pomegranate** (def. 1); B, vertical section

pome•gran•ate (pom′gran′it, pom′i-, pum′-), *n.* **1.** a chambered, many-seeded, globose fruit, having a tough, usually red rind and surmounted by a crown of calyx lobes, the edible portion consisting of pleasantly acid flesh developed from the outer seed coat. **2.** the shrub or small tree, *Punica granatum*, that bears it, native to southwestern Asia but widely cultivated in warm regions. [1275–1325; ME *poumgarnet, pomegarnade* (< OF *pome grenate, pome gernete*), repr. ML *pōmum grānātum* lit., seedy apple. See POME, GRENADE]

pom•e•lo (pom′ə lō′), *n., pl.* **-los. 1.** the very large, yellow or orange citrus fruit of a tree, *Citrus maxima*, of southeastern Asia. **2.** the tree itself. Also, **pommelo, pumelo, pummelo.** Also called **shaddock.** [1855–60; pseudo-Spanish alter. of *pomplemoose* < D *pompelmoes* shaddock, perh. b. *pompoen* PUMPKIN and Pg *limões*, pl. of *limão* LEMON]

Pom•er•a•ni•a (pom′ə rā′nē ə, -rān′yə), *n.* a former province of NE Germany, now mostly in NW Poland. German, **Pommern.**

Pom•er•a•ni•an (pom′ə rā′nē ən, -rān′yən), *adj.* **1.** of, pertaining to, or characteristic of Pomerania. *—n.* **2.** one of a breed of small dogs having long, straight hair, erect ears, and a tail carried over the back. **3.** a native or inhabitant of Pomerania. [1750–60; POMERANI(A) + -AN]

Pomeranian (def. 2), 7 in. (18 cm) high at shoulder

pom•fret (pom′frit, pum′-), *n., pl.* (*esp. collectively*) **-fret,** (*esp. referring to two or more kinds or species*) **-frets. 1.** any of several scombroid fishes of the family Bramidae, found in the North Atlantic and Pacific. **2.** any of several East Indian stromateid fishes, esp. *Stromateoides argenteus*, valued as food. [1720–30; earlier *pamplee, pamflet, pomphlet;* cf. F *pample*, Pg *pampo*]

po•mif•er•ous (pō mif′ər əs), *adj. Bot.* bearing pomes or pomelike fruits. [1650–60; < L *pōmifer* fruit-bearing (see POME, -I-, -FER) + -OUS]

Pom•mard (pō märd′; *Fr.* pô MAR′), *n.* a dry, red wine from the Pommard parish in Burgundy. [1825–35]

pomme blanche (*Fr.* pôm bläNsh′), *pl.* **pommes blanches** (*Fr.* pôm bläNsh′). breadroot. [< F: lit., white apple]

pom•mée (po mā′, pə-, pō-; *Fr.* pô mā′), *adj. Heraldry.* (of a cross) having arms with knoblike ends: *a cross pommée.* [1715–25; < F: lit., balled, equiv. to *pomme* apple, ball (see POME) + *-ée* -EE]

pom•mel (pum′əl, pom′-), *n., v.,* **-meled, -mel•ing** or (*esp. Brit.*) **-melled, -mel•ling.** *—n.* **1.** a knob, as on the hilt of a sword. **2.** the protuberant part at the front and top of a saddle. See illus. under **saddle. 3.** *Archit.* a spherical ornament or finial. **4.** *Gymnastics.* either of the two curved handles on the top surface of a side horse. *—v.t.* **5.** to beat or strike with or as if with the fists or a pommel. Also, **pummel.** [1300–50; (n.) ME *pomel* < MF, deriv. of OF *pom* hilt of a sword < L *pōmum* fruit; see POME, -ELLE]

pom′mel horse′, *Gymnastics.* a padded, somewhat cylindrical floor-supported apparatus, similar to a vaulting horse but having two graspable pommels on top, used by men for hand-supported balancing, rotating, and swinging maneuvers. Also called **side horse.** [1905–10]

pom•me•lo (pom′ə lō), *n., pl.* **-los.** pomelo.

Pom•mern (pôm′əRN), *n.* German name of **Pomerania.**

pommes frites (pôm fRēt′), *French Informal.* See **French fries.** [short for *pommes de terre frites* fried potatoes]

pom•my (pom′ē), *n., pl.* **-mies.** (*often cap.*) *Usually Disparaging.* (in Australia and New Zealand) a British person, esp. one who is a recent immigrant. Also, **pom′•mie, pom.** [1910–15; orig. obscure; corroborating evidence for any of the numerous fanciful etymologies proposed for the word is so far lacking]

po•mo (pō′mō), *Informal.* *—adj.* **1.** postmodern. *—n.* **2.** the postmodern movement; postmodernism. [1985–90]

Po•mo (pō′mō), *n., pl.* **-mos,** (*esp. collectively*) **-mo. 1.** a member of an American Indian people of northern California. **2.** any of several related languages of the Pomo Indians.

po•mol•o•gy (pō mol′ə jē), *n.* the science that deals with fruits and fruit growing. [1810–20; < NL *pōmologia.* See POME, -O-, -LOGY] **—po•mo•log•i•cal** (pō′mə loj′i kəl), *adj.* **—po′mo•log′i•cal•ly,** *adv.* **—po•mol′o•gist,** *n.*

Po•mo•na (pə mō′nə), *n.* **1.** the ancient Roman goddess of the fruit of trees. **2.** a city in SW California, E of Los Angeles, 92,742. **3.** Also called **Mainland.** the largest of the Orkney Islands, N of Scotland. 6502; 190 sq. mi. (490 sq. km)

Pomo′na glass′, an American art glass having one of its surfaces stained a pale amber color and the other surface etched.

pomp (pomp), *n.* **1.** stately or splendid display; splendor; magnificence. **2.** ostentatious or vain display, esp. of dignity or importance. **3. pomps,** pompous displays, actions, or things: *The official was accompanied by all the pomps of his high position.* **4.** *Archaic.* a stately or splendid procession; pageant. [1275–1325; ME < L *pompa* display, parade, procession < Gk *pompḗ* orig., a sending, akin to *pémpein* to send] **—pomp′less,** *adj.* **—Syn. 1.** See **show.**

pom•pa•dour (pom′pə dôr′, -dōr′, -do͝or′), *n.* **1.** an arrangement of a man's hair in which it is brushed up high from the forehead. **2.** an arrangement of a woman's hair in which it is raised over the forehead in a roll, sometimes over a pad. **3.** a pink or crimson color. **4.** *Textiles.* **a.** any fabric, as cotton or silk, having a design of small pink, blue, and sometimes gold flowers or bouquets on a white background. **b.** a fabric of the color pompadour, used for garments. [1745–55; named after the Marquise de POMPADOUR]

Pom•pa•dour (pom′pə dôr′, -dōr′, -do͝or′; *Fr.* pôN PA-DO͞OR′), *n.* **Marquise de** (*Jeanne Antoinette Poisson Le Normant d'Étioles*), 1721–64, mistress of Louis XV of France.

pom•pa•no (pom′pə nō′), *n., pl.* (*esp. collectively*) **-no,** (*esp. referring to two or more kinds or species*) **-nos. 1.** a deep-bodied food fish, *Trachinotus carolinus*, inhabiting waters off the South Atlantic and Gulf states. **2.** a food fish, *Peprilus simillimus*, of California. **3.** coquina. [1770–80; < Sp *pámpano* kind of fish]

Pom′pano Beach′, a city in SE Florida. 52,618.

Pom•pe•ia (pom pē′ə, -pā′ə), *n.* fl. 1st century B.C., second wife of Julius Caesar, divorced in 62 B.C. Cf. **Calpurnia, Cornelia** (def. 2).

Pom•pe•ian (pom pā′ən, -pē′-), *adj.* **1.** of or pertaining to Pompeii, or its culture. **2.** pertaining to or designating a style of mural painting, examples of which have been found in or near Pompeii, Herculaneum, etc., dating from about the beginning of the 1st century B.C. to A.D. 79, characterized chiefly by the illusion of three-dimensional form organized in an architectonic structure. *—n.* **3.** a native or inhabitant of Pompeii. Also, **Pom•pei′ian.** [1825–35; < L *Pompeiānus.* See POMPEII, -AN]

Pompe′ian red′, a dull, grayish red. Also, **pompe′•ian red′.** Also called **dragon's blood.** [1880–85]

Pom•peii (pom pā′, -pā′ē), *n.* an ancient city in SW Italy, on the Bay of Naples: it was buried along with Herculaneum by an eruption of nearby Mount Vesuvius in A.D. 79; much of the city has been excavated.

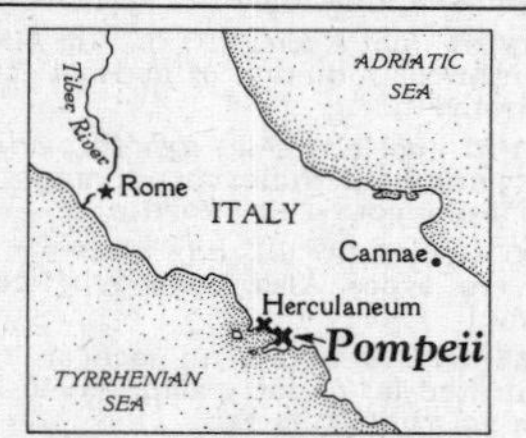

pom•pel•mous (pom′pəl mo͞os′), *n., pl.* **-mous, -mous•es.** shaddock. [1670–80; < D *pompelmoes.* See POMELO]

Pom•pey (pom′pē), *n.* (*Gnaeus Pompeius Magnus*) ("*the Great*") 106–48 B.C., Roman general and statesman: a member of the first triumvirate.

Pom•pi•dou (pom′pi do͞o′; *Fr.* pôN pē do͞o′), *n.* **Georges Jean Raymond** (zhôRzh zhäN RA môN′), 1911–74, French political leader: prime minister 1962–68; president 1969–74.

pom•pom[1] (pom′pom′), *n.* an automatic antiaircraft cannon. Also, **pom′-pom′.** [1895–1900; imit.]

pom•pom[2] (pom′pom′), *n.* **1.** Also, **pompon.** an ornamental tuft or ball of feathers, wool, or the like, used on hats, slippers, etc. **2.** pompon (def. 3). Also, **pom′-pom′.** [1740–50; var. of POMPON, with assimilation of final *n*]

pom′pom girl′, a female cheerleader, as for a football team, whose routines often include the waving of flowerlike clusters resembling pompoms. [1975–80]

pom•pon (pom′pon), *n.* **1.** pompom[2] (def. 1). **2.** the high plume at the front of a shako. **3.** *Hort.* a form of small, globe-shaped flower head that characterizes a class or type of various flowering plants, esp. chrysanthemums and dahlias. **4.** See **black margate.** [1740–50; < F; repetitive formation, appar. based on *pompe* POMP]

pom•pos•i•ty (pom pos′i tē), *n., pl.* **-ties** for 3. **1.** the quality of being pompous. **2.** pompous parading of dignity or importance. **3.** an instance of being pompous, as by ostentatious loftiness of language, manner, or behavior. Also, **pomp•ous•ness** (pom′pəs nis) (for defs. 1, 2). [1400–50; late ME *pomposite* < LL *pompōsitās.* See POMPOUS, -ITY]

pomp•ous (pom′pəs), *adj.* **1.** characterized by an ostentatious display of dignity or importance: *a pompous minor official.* **2.** ostentatiously lofty or high-flown: *a pompous speech.* **3.** characterized by pomp, stately splendor, or magnificence. [1325–75; ME < LL *pompōsus.* See POMP, -OUS] **—pomp′ous•ly,** *adv.*
—Syn. 1. pretentious. **2.** inflated, turgid, bombastic.

Pomp′ton Lakes′ (pomp′tən, pom′-), a town in NE New Jersey. 10,660.

Po•na•pe (pō′nə pā′, pon′ə-), *n.* an island in the W Pacific: part of the Federated States of Micronesia. 21,187 including adjacent islands; 134 sq. mi. (347 sq. km).

Pon•ca (pong′kə), *n., pl.* **-cas,** (*esp. collectively*) **-ca** for 1. **1.** a member of a North American Indian people formerly of northern Nebraska, now living mostly in northern Oklahoma. **2.** the Siouan language of the Ponca, mutually intelligible with Omaha.

Pon′ca Cit′y, a city in N Oklahoma. 26,238.

ponce (pons), *n. Brit. Slang.* **1.** a pimp. **2.** a campily effeminate male. [1870–75; of obscure orig.]

Pon•ce (pôn′se), *n.* a seaport in S Puerto Rico. 161,739.

pon•ceau (pon sō′), *n.* **1.** a vivid red to reddish-orange color. *—adj.* **2.** having the color ponceau. [1825–35; < F (cf. OF *pouncel* poppy), perh. dim. of *paon* peacock < L *pāvōn-* (s. of *pāvō*)]

Ponce de Le•ón (pons′ də lē′ən; *Sp.* pôn′the the le ôn′, pôn′se), **Juan** (hwän), c1460–1521, Spanish explorer.

Pon•ce•let (pôNsᵊ le′), *n.* **Jean Vic•tor** (zhäN vēk tôr′), 1788–1867, French mathematician.

Pon•chiel•li (pông kyel′lē), *n.* **A•mil•ca•re** (ä mēl′kä re), 1834–86, Italian composer.

pon•cho (pon′chō), *n., pl.* **-chos.** a blanketlike cloak with a hole in the center to admit the head, originating in South America, now often worn as a raincoat. [1710–20; < AmerSp < Araucanian] **—pon′choed,** *adj.*

poncho

pond (pond), *n.* **1.** a body of water smaller than a lake, sometimes artificially formed, as by damming a stream. *—v.i.* **2.** (esp. of water) to collect into a pond or large puddle: *to prevent rainwater from ponding on the roof.* [1250–1300; ME *ponde, pande,* akin to OE *pynding* dam, *gepyndan* to impound. See POUND[3]]

pond-ap•ple (pond′ap′əl), *n.* a tropical American, evergreen tree, *Annona glabra*, of the annona family, having yellowish-red flowers, grown as a grafting stock. [1880–85, *Amer.*]

pon•der (pon′dər), *v.i.* **1.** to consider something deeply and thoroughly; meditate (often fol. by *over* or *upon*). *—v.t.* **2.** to weigh carefully in the mind; consider thoughtfully: *He pondered his next words thoroughly.* [1300–50; ME *pondren* < MF *ponderer* < L *ponderāre* to ponder, weigh; akin to *pendere* to be suspended, hang (see PEND)] **—pon′der•er,** *n.*
—Syn. 1. reflect, cogitate, deliberate, ruminate.

pon•der•a•ble (pon′dər ə bəl), *adj.* **1.** capable of being considered carefully or deeply. **2.** capable of being weighed; having appreciable weight. [1640–50; < LL *ponderābilis.* See PONDER, -ABLE] **—pon′der•a•bil′i•ty, pon′der•a•ble•ness,** *n.*

pon′der•o′sa pine′ (pon′də rō′sə, pon′-), **1.** Also called **western yellow pine.** a large pine, *Pinus ponderosa*, of western North America, having yellowish-brown bark: the state tree of Montana. **2.** the light, soft wood of this tree, used for the construction of furniture, houses, ships, etc. [1875–80, *Amer.*; < NL *Pinus ponderosa* (1836) lit., heavy pine; see PONDEROUS]

pon•der•ous (pon′dər əs), *adj.* **1.** of great weight; heavy; massive. **2.** awkward or unwieldy: *He carried a ponderous burden on his back.* **3.** dull and labored: *a ponderous dissertation.* [1375–1425; late ME (< MF *pondereus, pondereuse*) < L *ponderōsus.* See PONDER, -OUS] **—pon′der•ous•ly,** *adv.* **—pon′der•ous•ness, pon•der•os•i•ty** (pon′də ros′i tē), *n.*

—**Syn.** **3.** heavy, boring, dreary, plodding, tedious. —**Ant.** **3.** lively, exciting.

Pon·di·cher·ry (pon′di cher′ē, -sher′ē), *n.* **1.** a union territory of India, on the Coromandel Coast: formerly the chief settlement of French India; territory includes Mahé (on the Malabar Coast), Karikal, and Yanaon. 471,707; 181 sq. mi. (469 sq. km). **2.** a seaport in and the capital of this territory. 90,639. Also, **Pon·di·ché·ry** (pôɴ dē shā ʀē′). Cf. **French India.**

pond′ lil′y, any of several water lilies, as the common water lily, *Nymphaea odorata,* or the spatterdock. [1740–50, *Amer.*]

pon·dok (pon′dok), *n. South African.* a crudely built hut or shelter formed of sheets of corrugated iron, tin, etc.; shanty. Also, **pon′dok·kie.** [1805–15; of uncert. orig.]

pond′ scum′, any free-floating freshwater alga that forms a green scum on water. [1885–90]

pond·weed (pond′wēd′), *n.* any aquatic plant of the genus *Potamogeton,* most species of which grow in ponds and quiet streams. [1570–80; POND + WEED[1]]

pone[1] (pōn), *n. South Midland and Southern U.S.* **1.** Also called **pone′ bread′.** a baked or fried bread usually made of cornmeal. **2.** a loaf or oval-shaped cake of any type of bread, esp. corn bread. [1605–15, *Amer.*; < Virginia Algonquian (E sp.) *apones, appoans, poan* < Proto-Algonquian **apwa·n-* thing roasted or baked, deriv. of **apwe-* to roast, bake]

pone[2] (pōn), *n. Cards.* **1.** the player on the dealer's right. Cf. **eldest hand.** **2.** the player who opposes the dealer in a game with two players. [1885–90; < L *pōne,* 2nd person sing. impv. of *pōnere* to place]

pong (pong, pông), *Brit. Informal.* *n.* **1.** an unpleasant smell; stink. —*v.i.* **2.** to have a disagreeable smell; stink. [1915–20; of obscure orig.]

pon·gee (pon jē′, pon′jē), *n.* **1.** silk of a slightly uneven weave made from filaments of wild silk woven in natural tan color. **2.** a cotton or rayon fabric imitating it. Cf. **Shantung** (def. 2), **tussah** (def. 1). [1705–15; < Chin *běnjī* homewoven, lit., one's own loom]

pon·gid (pon′jid), *n.* **1.** any anthropoid primate of the family Pongidae, comprising the gorilla, chimpanzee, and orangutan; a great ape. —*adj.* **2.** pertaining to or being a great ape. [1950–55; < NL *Pongidae* family name, equiv. to *Pong(o)* type genus (said to be < Kongo *mpongi, mpungu* ape) + *-idae* -ID[2]]

pon·iard (pon′yərd), *n.* **1.** a small, slender dagger. —*v.t.* **2.** to stab with a poniard. [1580–90; < F *poignard,* deriv. of *poing* fist < L *pugnus;* see -ARD]

po·no·graph (pō′nə graf′, -gräf′), *n. Med.* an instrument for graphically recording pain or muscular fatigue. [< Gk *pónο(s)* pain, work + -GRAPH]

pons (ponz), *n., pl.* **pon·tes** (pon′tēz). *Anat.* **1.** Also called **pons Varolii.** a band of nerve fibers in the brain connecting the lobes of the midbrain, medulla, and cerebrum. See diag. under **brain.** **2.** any tissue connecting two parts of a body organ or structure. [1685–95; < L *pōns* bridge (see PUNT[1])]

Pons (ponz; *Fr.* pôɴs), *n.* **Lil·y** (lil′ē; *Fr.* lē lē′), 1904–76, U.S. operatic soprano, born in France.

pons′ as·i·no′rum (as′ə nôr′əm, -nōr′-), a geometric proposition that if a triangle has two of its sides equal, the angles opposite these sides are also equal: so named from the difficulty experienced by beginners in mastering it. Euclid, 1:5. [1745–55; < L *pōns asinōrum* bridge of asses]

Pon·selle (pon sel′), *n.* **Rosa (Melba),** 1897–1981, U.S. soprano.

pons′ Va·ro′li·i (və rō′lē ī′), *pl.* **pontes Varolii.** pons (def. 1). [1685–95; < NL: lit., Varoli's bridge; named after *Varoli,* Italian anatomist (1543–75)]

Pon·ta Del·ga·da (*Port.* pôɴ′tə del gä′də), a seaport on SW São Miguel island, in the E Azores. 69,930.

Pon·ta Gros·sa (pôɴ′tä gʀô′sä), a city in S Brazil. 152,581.

Pont·char·train (pon′chər trān′), *n.* **Lake,** a shallow extension of the Gulf of Mexico in SE Louisiana, N of New Orleans. 41 mi. (66 km) long; 25 mi. (40 km) wide.

Pon·te·fract (pon′tə frakt′; *locally also* pum′frit, pom′-), *n.* a city in West Yorkshire, in N central England, SE of Leeds: ruins of a 12th-century castle. 31,335.

Pon·ti·ac (pon′tē ak′), *n.* **1.** c1720–69, North American Indian, chief of the Ottawa tribe: commander during the Pontiac War 1763–64. **2.** a city in SE Michigan. 76,715. **3.** a town in central Illinois. 11,227.

Pon·tian (pon′shən, -shē ən), *n.* pope A.D. 230–235. Also, **Pon·ti·a·nus** (pon′shē ā′nəs).

pon·ti·a·nak (pon′tē ä′näk), *n.* jelutong (def. 2). [1910–15; orig., jelutong from the region around PONTIANAK]

Pon·ti·a·nak (pon′tē ä′näk), *n.* a seaport on W Kalimantan (Borneo), in central Indonesia. 150,000.

pon·tic (pon′tik), *n. Dentistry.* an artificial tooth in a bridge. Also called **dummy.** [1930–35; < L *pont-* (s. of *pōns*) bridge + -IC]

Pon·tic (pon′tik), *adj.* pertaining to the Pontus Euxinus or to Pontus. [1470–80; < Gk *Pontikós.* See PONTUS, -IC]

Pon′tic Moun′tains, a mountain range in N Turkey, running parallel to the Black Sea coast for ab. 700 mi. (1125 km): highest peak, 12,917 ft. (3937 m).

pon·ti·fex (pon′tə feks′), *n., pl.* **pon·tif·i·ces** (pon tif′ə sēz′). *Rom. Relig.* a member of the Pontifical College, which was presided over by a chief priest **(Pon′tifex Max′imus).** [1570–80; < L: appar. lit., path-maker, equiv. to *ponti-* (s. of *pōns*) bridge, prob. orig., path (see PONS) + *-fec-* (comb. form of *facere* to make) + *-s* nom. sing. ending; the literal application is unclear]

pon·tiff (pon′tif), *n.* **1.** any pontifex. **2.** any high or chief priest. **3.** *Eccles.* **a.** a bishop. **b.** the Roman Catholic pope, the Bishop of Rome. [1600–10; earlier *pontife* < F, short for L *pontifex* PONTIFEX]

pon·tif·ic (pon tif′ik), *adj. Archaic.* pontifical. [1635–45; PONTIFF + -IC]

pon·tif·i·cal (pon tif′i kəl), *adj.* **1.** of, pertaining to, or characteristic of a pontiff; papal. **2.** pompous, dogmatic, or pretentious: *to resent someone's pontifical manner.* —*n.* **3.** (in the Western Church) a book containing the forms for the sacraments and other rites and ceremonies to be performed by bishops. **4. pontificals,** the vestments and other insignia of a pontiff, esp. a bishop. [1350–1400; ME < L *pontificālis,* equiv. to *pontific-* (s. of *pontifex*) PONTIFEX + *-ālis* -AL[1]] —**pon·tif′i·cal·ly,** *adv.*

Pontif′ical Col′lege, the chief body of priests in ancient Rome.

Pontif′ical Mass′, (*sometimes l.c.*) *Rom. Cath. Ch.* a High Mass celebrated by a bishop or other prelate.

pon·tif·i·cate (*n.* pon tif′i kit, -kāt′; *v.* pon tif′i kāt′), *n., v.,* **-cat·ed, -cat·ing.** —*n.* **1.** the office or term of office of a pontiff. —*v.i.* **2.** to perform the office or duties of a pontiff. **3.** to speak in a pompous or dogmatic manner: *Did he pontificate about the responsibilities of a good citizen?* **4.** to serve as a bishop, esp. in a Pontifical Mass. [1575–85; (n.) < L *pontificātus;* see PONTIFICAL, -ATE[3]; (v.) < ML *pontificātus* ptp. of *pontificāre* to be an ecclesiastic; see -ATE[1]]

pon·tif·i·ces (pon tif′ə sēz′), *n.* pl. of **pontifex.**

pon·til (pon′til), *n.* punty. [1825–35; < F; see POINT, -IL]

pon·tine (pon′tīn, -tēn), *adj. Anat.* of or pertaining to the pons. [1885–90; < L *pont-* (s. of *pōns*) PONS + -INE[1]]

Pon·tine (pon′tēn, -tīn), *adj.* of or pertaining to the Pontine Marshes.

Pon′tine Marsh′es, an area in W Italy, SE of Rome: formerly marshy, now drained.

Pon′tius Pi′late (pon′shəs, -tē əs). See **Pilate, Pontius.**

Pont l'É·vêque (pont lə vek′; *Fr.* pôɴ lā vek′), a strongly flavored, pale-yellow cheese with a soft center, made from whole or skimmed milk. [1895–1900; after the town of the same name in NW France]

pont·lev·is (pont lev′is), *n.* a drawbridge. [1480–90; < F, equiv. to *pont* bridge (< L *pont-,* s. of *pōns*) + *levis* (< VL **levāticius* liftable, adj. deriv. of L *levāre* to lift]

Pon·to·caine (pon′tə kān′), *Pharm., Trademark.* a brand of tetracaine.

Pon·toise (pôɴ twaz′), *n.* a city in and the capital of Val-d'Oise, in N France, on the Oise River, NW of Paris. 28,241.

pon·to·nier (pon′tn ēr′), *n. Mil.* an officer or soldier in charge of bridge equipment or the construction of pontoon bridges. [1820–30; < F *pontonnier.* See PONTOON[1], -IER[2]]

pon·toon[1] (pon to͞on′), *n.* **1.** *Mil.* a boat or some other floating structure used as one of the supports for a temporary bridge over a river. **2.** a float for a derrick, landing stage, etc. **3.** *Naut.* a float for raising a sunken or deeply laden vessel in the water; a camel or caisson. **4.** a seaplane float. Also, **pon·ton** (pon′tn). [1585–95; < F *ponton* < L *pontōn-* (s. of *pontō*) flat-bottomed boat, punt]

pon·toon[2] (pon to͞on′), *n. Brit.* the card game twenty-one. [1915–20; alter. of F *vingt-et-un* twenty-one]

pon′toon bridge′, a bridge supported by pontoons. [1695–1705]

pontoon bridge

Pon·top·pi·dan (pon top′i dän′), *n.* **Hen·rik** (hen′-ʀĕk), 1857–1943, Danish novelist: Nobel prize 1917.

Pon·tus (pon′təs), *n.* **1.** an ancient country in NE Asia Minor, bordering on the Black Sea: later a Roman province. **2.** Also, **Pon·tos** (pon′tos). the ancient Greek personification of the sea.

Pon′tus Eux·i′nus (yo͝ok sī′nəs), ancient name of the **Black Sea.**

po·ny (pō′nē), *n., pl.* **-nies,** *v.,* **-nied, -ny·ing.** —*n.* **1.** a small horse of any of several breeds, usually not higher at the shoulder than 14½ hands (58 in./146 cm). **2.** a horse of any small type or breed. **3.** *Slang.* a literal translation or other text, used illicitly as an aid in schoolwork or while taking a test; crib. **4.** something small of its kind. **5.** a small glass for liquor. **6.** the amount of liquor it will hold, usually one ounce (29.6 ml). **7.** a small beverage bottle, often holding seven ounces (196 g): *We bought a dozen ponies of Mexican beer.* **8.** *Older Slang.* a diminutive chorus girl. **9.** See **pony pack.** **10.** *Brit. Slang.* the sum of 25 pounds. —*v.t.* **11.** *Slang.* to prepare (lessons) by means of a pony. **12.** *Racing Slang.* **a.** to be the outrider for (a racehorse). **b.** to exercise (a racehorse) by having a rider mounted on another horse lead it at a gallop around a track. —*v.i.* **13.** to prepare a lesson or lessons with the aid of a pony. **14. pony up,** *Informal.* to pay (money), as in settling an account: *Next week you'll have to pony up the balance of the loan.* [1650–60; earlier *powney* < obs. F *poulenet,* dim. of *poulain* colt < ML *pullānus* (L *pull(us)* FOAL + *-ānus* -AN); see -ET]

po′ny express′, a former system in the American West of carrying mail and express by relays of riders mounted on ponies, esp. the system operating (1860–61) between St. Joseph, Missouri, and Sacramento, California. [1840–50, *Amer.*]

Po′ny League′, a baseball league similar to a Little League and having teams whose players are from 13 to 14 years of age.

po′ny pack′, a tray of usually one dozen growing plants that can be bought from a nursery for transplanting: *a pony pack of tomato plants.*

po·ny·tail (pō′nē tāl′), *n.* an arrangement of the hair in a long lock drawn tightly against the back of the head and cinched so as to hang loosely. [1870–75; PONY + TAIL[1]]

po′ny truss′, a through bridge truss having its deck between the top and bottom chords and having no top lateral bracing. [1930–35]

Pon·zi (pon′zē), *n.* a swindle in which a quick return, made up of money from new investors, on an initial investment lures the victim into much bigger risks. Also called **Pon′zi game′, Pon′zi scheme′.** [after Charles *Ponzi* (died 1949), the organizer of such a scheme in the U.S., 1919–20]

poo·bah (po͞o′bä′), *n.* See **Pooh Bah.**

pooch (po͞och), *n. Informal.* a dog. [1895–1900; orig. uncert.]

pood (po͞od; *Russ.* po͞ot), *n.* a Russian weight equal to about 36 pounds avoirdupois (16 kg). [1545–55; < Russ *pud* < LG or ON *pund* POUND[1]]

poo·dle (po͞od′l), *n.* one of a breed of very active dogs, probably originating in Germany but regarded as the national dog of France, having long, thick, frizzy or curly hair usually trimmed in standard patterns, occurring in three varieties (standard, miniature, and toy) differing only in size, and originally used as a water retriever. [1815–25; < G *Pudel,* short for *Pudelhund,* equiv. to *pudel(n)* to splash (see PUDDLE) + *Hund* HOUND[1]]

poodle, 13 in. (33 cm) high at shoulder

poof[1] (po͝of, po͞of), *interj.* **1.** (used to express or indicate a sudden disappearance): *Poof! The magician made the rabbit disappear.* **2.** pooh[1] (def. 1). [1815–25]

poof[2] (po͞of, po͝of), *n. Brit. Slang* (*disparaging and offensive*). **1.** a male homosexual. **2.** an effeminate male. Also **pooff, pouf, poove.** [1840–50; < F *pouffe* POUF[1]]

pooh[1] (po͞o, po͝o), *interj.* **1.** (used as an exclamation of disdain or contempt.) —*n.* **2.** an exclamation of "pooh." [1595–1605]

pooh[2] (po͞o), *v.t.* poop[2].

Pooh Bah (po͞o′ bä′), (*often l.c.*) **1.** a person who holds several positions, esp. ones that give him or her bureaucratic importance. **2.** a leader, authority, or other important person: *one of the pooh bahs of the record industry.* **3.** a pompous, self-important person. Also, **Pooh′-Bah′, poobah.** [1880–85; after a character in Gilbert and Sullivan's *The Mikado,* who holds all of the high offices of state simultaneously and uses them for personal gain]

pooh-pooh (po͞o′po͞o′), *v.t.* **1.** to express disdain or contempt for; dismiss lightly: *He pooh-poohed all their superstitious fears.* —*v.i.* **2.** to express disdain or contempt. Also, **poo-poo.** [1820–30; v. use of redupl. of POOH[1]] —**pooh′-pooh′er,** *n.*

poo·ka (po͞o′kə), *n.* puca.

pool[1] (po͞ol), *n.* **1.** a small body of standing water; pond. **2.** a still, deep place in a stream. **3.** any small collection of liquid on a surface: *a pool of blood.* **4.** a puddle. **5.** See **swimming pool.** **6.** a subterranean accumulation of oil or gas held in porous and permeable sedimentary rock **(reservoir).** —*v.i.* **7.** to form a pool. **8.** (of blood) to accumulate in a body part or organ. —*v.t.* **9.** to cause pools to form in. **10.** to cause (blood) to form pools. —*adj.* **11.** of or for a pool: *pool filters.* **12.** taking place or occurring around or near a pool: *a pool party.* [bef. 900; ME; OE *pōl;* c. D *poel,* G *Pfuhl*]

pool[2] (po͞ol), *n.* **1.** Also called **pocket billiards.** any of various games played on a pool table with a cue ball and 15 other balls that are usually numbered, in which the object is to drive all the balls into the pockets with the cue ball. **2.** the total amount staked by a combination of bettors, as on a race, to be awarded to the successful bettor or bettors. **3.** the combination of such bettors. **4.** an association of competitors who agree to control the production, market, and price of a commodity for mutual benefit, although they appear to be rivals. **5.** *Finance.* a combination of persons or organizations for the purpose of manipulating the prices of securities. **6.** a combination of resources, funds, etc., for common advantage. **7.** the combined interests or funds. **8.** a facility, resource, or service that is shared by a group of people: *a car pool; a typing pool.* **9.** the persons or parties involved. **10.**

the stakes in certain games. **11.** *Brit.* a billiard game. **12.** *Fencing.* a match in which each teammate successively plays against each member of the opposing team. —*v.t.* **13.** to put (resources, money, etc.) into a pool, or common stock or fund, as for a financial venture, according to agreement. **14.** to form a pool of. **15.** to make a common interest of. —*v.i.* **16.** to enter into or form a pool. —*adj.* **17.** of or belonging to a pool: *a pool typist; a pool reporter.* [1685–95; < F *poule* stakes, lit., hen. See PULLET] —**pool′er,** *n.*
—**Syn. 4.** corner, monopoly. **13.** combine, merge, consolidate.

pool′ hall′, poolroom (def. 1). Also, **pool′hall′.** [1925–30, *Amer.*]

pool•room (po͞ol′ro͞om′, -ro͝om′), *n.* **1.** an establishment or room for the playing of pool or billiards. **2.** a place where betting is carried on, esp. illegally; a bookmaker's establishment. [1860–65; POOL[2] + ROOM]

pool•side (po͞ol′sīd′), *n.* **1.** the lounging area around a swimming pool. —*adj.* **2.** located or occurring at or near the side of a swimming pool: *a poolside luncheon.* [1705–15; POOL[1] + SIDE[1]]

pool′ ta′ble, a billiard table with six pockets, on which pool is played. [1855–60]

pool′ train′, *Canadian.* a train operating over a track owned by two or more railway companies. Also **pooled′ train′.** [1955–60]

poon (po͞on), *n.* **1.** any of several East Indian trees of the genus *Calophyllum,* that yield a light, hard wood used for masts, spars, etc. **2.** the wood of these trees. [1690–1700; cf. Tamil *punnai, pinnai,* Malayalam *punna* name for *Calophyllum inophyllum*]

Poo•na (po͞o′nə), *n.* a city in W Maharashtra, W India, SE of Bombay. 1,135,034.

poon•tang (po͞on′tang), *n. Slang* (*vulgar*). **1.** sexual intercourse with a woman. **2.** *Offensive.* a woman regarded as a sexual object. [1925–30, *Amer.*; said to be < Limba (West Atlantic language of Sierra Leone) *puntuŋ* vagina, though the late documentation of the E word makes such an orig. questionable; F *putain* prostitute, often cited as the source, accounts precisely for neither the phonetics nor the sense]

poop[1] (po͞op), *n.* **1.** a superstructure at the stern of a vessel. **2.** See **poop deck.** —*v.t.* **3.** (of a wave) to break over the stern of (a ship). **4.** to take (seas) over the stern. [1375–1425; late ME *pouppe* < MF < L *puppis* stern of a ship]

poop[1] (def. 1)

poop[2] (po͞op), *v.t. Slang.* **1.** to cause to become out of breath or fatigued; exhaust: *Climbing that mountain pooped the whole group.* **2. poop out, a.** to cease from or fail in something, as from fear or exhaustion: *When the time for action came, they all pooped out and went home instead.* **b.** to break down; stop functioning: *The heater has pooped out again.* [1885–90; perh. to be identified with POOP[4]]

poop[3] (po͞op), *n. Slang.* relevant information, esp. a candid or pertinent factual report; low-down: *Send a reporter to get the real poop on that accident.* [1945–50, *Amer.*; appar. extracted from POOP SHEET; cf. POOP[4]]

poop[4] (po͞op), *Slang.* —*n.* **1.** excrement. —*v.i.* **2.** to defecate. [1735–45; earlier "to break wind," prob. the same word as ME *powpen, popen* to sound or blow a horn; uncert. if POOP[2], POOP[3] are sense developments or parallel expressive coinages]

poop[5] (po͞op), *n. Slang.* **1.** See **party pooper. 2.** a stupid, fussy, or boring person. [1910–15; perh. shortening of NINCOMPOOP]

poop′ cab′in, *Naut.* a cabin situated immediately beneath the poop deck of a ship. [1830–40]

poop′ deck′, a weather deck on top of a poop. See illus. under **quarterdeck.** [1830–40]

pooped (po͞opt), *adj. Informal.* fatigued; exhausted: *I'm too pooped to go shopping today.* Also, **pooped′ out′.** [1930–35, *Amer.*; POOP[2] + -ED[2]]

poop•er-scoop•er (po͞o′pər sko͞o′pər), *n.* **1.** Also called **poop′ scoop′er.** a small shovel or scooping device designed for use in cleaning up after a dog or other pet that has defecated on a street or sidewalk. —*adj.* **2.** of or pertaining to laws, city ordinances, or the like, that require a person to use a pooper-scooper. [1970–75; rhyming compound based on POOP[4], SCOOP, -ER[1]]

Po•o•pó (pô′ô pô′), *n.* a lake in SW Bolivia, in the Andes. 60 mi. (95 km) long; 12,000 ft. (3660 m) above sea level.

poo-poo (po͞o′po͞o′ *for 1, 2;* po͞o′po͞o′ *for 3*), *n. Baby Talk.* **1.** excrement; feces. **2. make poo-poo,** to defecate. —*v.t., v.i.* **3.** pooh-pooh. [1970–75; expressive formation; cf. POOP[4]]

poop′ sheet′, *n. Slang.* a circular, list of instructions, press release, etc., providing information about a particular subject. [1930–35, *Amer.*]

poop′ staff′. See **ensign staff.** [1840–50]

poor (po͝or), *adj.,* **-er, -est,** *n.* —*adj.* **1.** having little or no money, goods, or other means of support: *a poor family living on welfare.* **2.** *Law.* dependent upon charity or public support. **3.** (of a country, institution, etc.) meagerly supplied or endowed with resources or funds. **4.** characterized by or showing poverty. **5.** deficient or lacking in something specified: *a region poor in mineral deposits.* **6.** faulty or inferior, as in construction: *poor workmanship.* **7.** deficient in desirable ingredients, qualities, or the like: *poor soil.* **8.** excessively lean or emaciated, as cattle. **9.** of an inferior, inadequate, or unsatisfactory kind: *poor health.* **10.** lacking in skill, ability, or training: *a poor cook.* **11.** deficient in moral excellence; cowardly, abject, or mean. **12.** scanty, meager, or paltry in amount or number: *a poor audience.* **13.** humble; modest: *They shared their poor meal with a stranger.* **14.** unfortunate; hapless: *The poor dog was limping.* **15. poor as a church mouse,** extremely poor. **16. poor as Job's turkey,** extremely poor; impoverished. —*n.* **17.** (*used with a plural v.*) poor persons collectively (usually prec. by *the*): *sympathy for the poor.* [1150–1200; ME *pov(e)re* < OF *povre* < L *pauper.* See PAUPER] —**poor′ness,** *n.*
—**Syn. 1.** needy, indigent, necessitous, straitened, destitute, penniless, poverty-stricken. POOR, IMPECUNIOUS, IMPOVERISHED, PENNILESS refer to those lacking money. POOR is the simple term for the condition of lacking means to obtain the comforts of life: *a very poor family.* IMPECUNIOUS often suggests that the poverty is a consequence of unwise habits: *an impecunious actor.* IMPOVERISHED often implies a former state of greater plenty, from which one has been reduced: *the impoverished aristocracy.* PENNILESS may mean destitute, or it may apply simply to a temporary condition of being without funds: *The widow was left penniless with three small children.* **5.** meager. **6.** unsatisfactory, shabby. **7.** sterile, barren, unfruitful, unproductive. **8.** thin, skinny, meager, gaunt. **14.** miserable, unhappy, pitiable. —**Ant. 1, 5, 7.** rich. **1, 3, 4.** wealthy.
—**Pronunciation.** In the North and North Midland U.S., the vowel of POOR is most often (o͝o). POOR and *sure* thus contrast with *pour* and *shore:* (po͝or), (sho͝or) versus (pôr), (shôr) or (pōr), (shōr). In the South Midland and South, the vowel of POOR is generally (ô) or (ō) (often with the final (r) dropped), which means that in these areas, POOR and *pour* are homophones, as are *sure* and *shore.* Both types of pronunciation exist in the British Isles.

poor′ box′, a box, esp. in a church, into which contributions for the poor can be dropped. [1615–25]

poor′ boy′, *Chiefly New Orleans.* a hero sandwich. [1875–80, *Amer.*]
—**Regional Variation.** See **hero sandwich.**

poor′ boy′ sweat′er, a snug-fitting, pullover sweater with ribbing on both the body and sleeves, worn by girls and women.

poor-do (po͝or′do͞o′), *n. Chiefly Midland and Central Atlantic States.* scrapple. [1905–10, *Amer.*; of unclear derivation]

poor′ farm′, a farm maintained at public expense for the housing and support of paupers. [1850–55, *Amer.*]

poor•house (po͝or′hous′), *n., pl.* **-hous•es** (-hou′ziz). (formerly) an institution in which paupers were maintained at public expense. [1735–45; POOR + HOUSE]

poor•ish (po͝or′ish), *adj.* somewhat poor; rather poor. [1650–60; POOR + -ISH[1]]

Poor′ Joe′, *Coastal Georgia, South Carolina, and the Bahamas.* a heron. [1730–40, *Amer.*; prob. < a West African source; cf. Vai (Mande language of Liberia and Sierra Leone) *podžo* heron]

poor′ law′, a law or system of laws providing for the relief or support of the poor at public expense. [1745–55]

poor•ly (po͝or′lē), *adv.* **1.** in a poor manner or way: *The team played poorly.* —*adj.* **2.** in poor health; somewhat ill: *I hear she's been poorly.* [1250–1300; ME *pourely.* See POOR, -LY]

poor′ mouth′, *Informal.* **1.** a person who continually complains about a lack of money. **2.** a plea or complaint of poverty, often as an excuse for not contributing to charities, paying bills, etc. **3. cry poor mouth.** to complain, esp. habitually, about a lack of money. Also, **talk a poor mouth.** [1815–25]

poor-mouth (po͝or′mouth′), *v.,* **-mouthed** (-moutht′, -mouthd′), **-mouth•ing.** *Informal.* —*v.i.* **1.** to lament or argue that one is too poor; plead poverty. —*v.t.* **2.** to declare (one's ability, power, position, etc.) to be inadequate or disappointing, sometimes as an intentional understatement; downplay: *We know you're just poor-mouthing your skill at playing bridge—you're a good player.* **3.** bad-mouth. [1965–70; *Amer.*; orig. in v. phrases *put up a poor mouth, make a poor mouth*]

Poor′ Rich′ard's Al′manac, an almanac (1732–58) written and published by Benjamin Franklin.

Poor′ Rob′in's plan′tain, the rattlesnake weed, *Hieracium venosum.* Also called **Robin's plantain.** [1770–80, *Amer.*; orig. uncert.]

poor-spir•it•ed (po͝or′spir′i tid), *adj.* having or showing a poor, cowardly, or abject spirit. [1655–65]

poor′ white′, *Usually Disparaging and Offensive.* a white person, esp. of the southern U.S., having low social status and little or no money, property, or education. [1810–20, *Amer.*]

poor′ white′ trash′, *Disparaging and Offensive.* poor whites collectively. [1825–35, *Amer.*]

poor-will (po͝or′wil′), *n.* a goatsucker, *Phalaenoptilus nuttallii,* of western North America. [1875–80, *Amer.*; imit.]

poove (po͞ov), *n. Brit. Slang* (*disparaging and offensive*). poof[2].

pop[1] (pop), *v.,* **popped, pop•ping,** *n., adv., adj.* —*v.i.* **1.** to make a short, quick, explosive sound: *The cork popped.* **2.** to burst open with such a sound, as chestnuts or corn in roasting. **3.** to come or go quickly, suddenly, or unexpectedly: *She popped into the kitchen to check the stove.* **4.** to shoot with a firearm: *to pop at a mark.* **5.** to protrude from the sockets: *The news made her eyes pop.* **6.** *Baseball.* **a.** to hit a pop fly (often fol. by *up*). **b.** to pop out. —*v.t.* **7.** to cause to make a sudden, explosive sound. **8.** to cause to burst open with such a sound. **9.** to open suddenly or violently: *to pop the hood on a car; to pop the tab on a beer can.* **10.** to put or thrust quickly, suddenly, or unexpectedly: *He popped the muffins into the oven.* **11.** *Informal.* to cause to fire; discharge: *He popped his rifle at the bird.* **12.** to shoot (usually fol. by *at, off,* etc.): *He popped off bottles with a slingshot.* **13.** *Brit. Slang.* to pawn. **14.** *Informal.* **a.** to take or swallow (pills), esp. in excess or habitually; take orally in a compulsive or addictive way: *Popping all those pills will land him in the hospital.* **b.** to eat in a continual or thoughtless manner, as snack foods: *popping peanuts at the movies.* **15. pop for,** *Slang.* to pay or buy for oneself or another, esp. as a gift or treat; spring for: *I'll pop for the first round of drinks.* **16. pop in,** *Informal.* to visit briefly and unexpectedly; stop in; drop by: *Maybe we'll pop in after the movie.* **17. pop off,** *Informal.* **a.** to die, esp. suddenly. **b.** to depart, esp. abruptly. **c.** to express oneself volubly or excitedly and sometimes irately or indiscreetly: *He popped off about the injustice of the verdict.* **18. pop out,** *Baseball.* to be put out by hitting a pop fly caught on the fly by a player on the opposing team. **19. pop the question,** *Informal.* to propose marriage: *They dated for two years before he popped the question.* **20. pop up,** *Baseball.* to hit a pop fly. —*n.* **21.** a short, quick, explosive sound. **22.** a popping. **23.** a shot with a firearm. **24.** *Informal.* See **soda pop. 25.** a drink or portion of an alcoholic beverage, as a drink of whiskey or a glass of beer: *We had a couple of pops on the way home.* **26.** *Baseball.* See **pop fly. 27. a pop,** *Slang.* each; apiece: *five orchids at $30 a pop.* —*adv.* **28.** with an explosive sound: *The balloon went pop.* **29.** quickly, suddenly, or unexpectedly: *Pop, the door flew open!* —*adj.* **30.** *Informal.* unexpected; without prior warning or announcement: *The teacher gave us a pop quiz.* [1375–1425; late ME (n.) *poppe* a blow; (v.) *poppen* to strike; of expressive orig.]
—**Syn. 3.** appear, burst.
—**Regional Variation. 24.** See **soda pop.**

pop[2] (pop), *adj.* **1.** of or pertaining to popular songs: *pop music; pop singers.* **2.** of or pertaining to pop art. **3.** reflecting or aimed at the tastes of the general masses of people: *pop culture; pop novels.* —*n.* **4.** popular music: *It's the first time she's sung pop.* **5.** See **pop art.** [1860–65; shortening of POPULAR]

pop[3] (pop), *n. Informal.* father. [1820–30; short form of POPPA]

pop[4] (pop), *n.* a frozen ice or ice-cream confection on a stick. [prob. shortening of POPSICLE]

POP, proof-of-purchase.

pop., **1.** popular. **2.** popularly. **3.** population.

P.O.P., **1.** See **printout paper. 2.** point-of-purchase.

p.o.p., point-of-purchase.

pop′ art′, an art movement that began in the U.S. in the 1950's and reached its peak of activity in the 1960's, chose as its subject matter the anonymous, everyday, standardized, and banal iconography in American life, as comic strips, billboards, commercial products, and celebrity images, and dealt with them typically in such forms as outsize commercially smooth paintings, mechanically reproduced silkscreens, large-scale facsimiles, and soft sculptures. Also **Pop′ Art′.** [1960–65] —**pop′ ar′tist.**

Po•pa•yán (pô′pä yän′), *n.* a city in SW Colombia. 82,100.

pop′ con′cert, a concert of popular and light classical music played by a symphony orchestra. Also, **pops concert.** [1875–80]

pop•corn (pop′kôrn′), *n.* **1.** any of several varieties of corn whose kernels burst open and puff out when subjected to dry heat. **2.** popped corn. **3.** peanut (def. 4c). [1810–20, *Amer.*; short for *popped corn.* See POP[1], -ED[2], CORN[1]]

pop′corn flow′er, a plant, *Plagiobothrys nothofulvus,* of the borage family, native to the western U.S., having coiled clusters of small white flowers. [1900–05, *Amer.*]

pope (pōp), *n.* **1.** (*often cap.*) the bishop of Rome as head of the Roman Catholic Church. **2.** (in the early Christian church) a bishop. **3.** a person considered as having or assuming authority or a position similar to that of the Roman Catholic pope. **4.** the title of the Coptic patriarch of Alexandria. **5.** *Eastern Ch.* **a.** the Orthodox patriarch of Alexandria. **b.** (in certain churches) a parish priest. [bef. 900; ME; OE *pāpa* < LL: bishop, pope < LGk *pápas* bishop, priest, var. of *páppas* father; see PAPA] —**pope′less,** *adj.* —**pope′like′,** *adj.*

Pope (pōp), *n.* **1. Alexander,** 1688–1744, English poet. **2. John,** 1822–92, Union general in the U.S. Civil War. **3. John Russell,** 1874–1937, U.S. architect.

Po•pé (pō pā′), *n.* died 1690?, Pueblo medicine man: led rebellion against the Spanish 1680.

pope•dom (pōp′dəm), *n.* **1.** the office or dignity of a pope. **2.** the tenure of office of a pope. **3.** the papal government. [bef. 1150; ME *pape dom;* OE *pāpdōm.* See POPE, -DOM]

pop•e•line (pop′ə lēn′, pop′ə lēn′), *n.* a fabric, resembling broadcloth, rep, or poplin and made with silk or rayon warp and wool filling, used in the manufacture of dress goods. [< F: POPLIN]

pop•er•y (pō′pə rē), *n. Usually Disparaging.* the Roman Catholic Church, esp. its doctrines, ceremonies, and system of government. [1525–35; POPE + -ERY]

CONCISE ETYMOLOGY KEY: <, descended or borrowed from; >, whence; b., blend of, blended; c., cognate with; cf., compare; deriv., derivative; equiv., equivalent; imit., imitative; obl., oblique; r., replacing; s., stem; sp., spelling, spelled; resp., respelling, respelled; trans., translation; ?, origin unknown; *, unattested; ‡, probably earlier than. See the full key inside the front cover.

pope's′ nose′, *Slang.* the fleshy protuberance at the posterior end of a dressed fowl, esp. the tailpiece of a cooked chicken. Also called **parson's nose.** [1740–50]

pop′eye catalu′fa. See under **catalufa.**

pop·eyed (pop′īd′), *adj.* marked by bulging, staring eyes: *a young boy popeyed with excitement.* [1815–25, *Amer.*; POP[1] + EYED]

pop′ fly′, *Baseball.* a high fly ball hit to the infield or immediately beyond it that can easily be caught before reaching the ground. Also called **pop-up.** [1885–90, *Amer.*]

pop·gun (pop′gun′), *n.* a child's toy gun from which a pellet is shot by compressed air, producing a loud pop. [1655–65; POP[1] + GUN[1]]

pop-in (pop′in′), *adj.* requiring only a quick insertion into a receptacle to be ready for use: *pop-in film cassettes; a pop-in frozen dinner.* [adj. use of v. phrase *pop in*]

pop·i·nac (pop′ə nak′), *n.* huisache. [1895–1900, *Amer.*; alter. of L *opopanax* < Gk *opopánax* gum (of *Opopanax hispidus*), equiv. to *opo-*, comb. form of *opós* juice + *pánax* PANACEA]

pop·in·jay (pop′in jā′), *n.* **1.** a person given to vain, pretentious displays and empty chatter; coxcomb; fop. **2.** *Brit. Dial.* a woodpecker, esp. the green woodpecker. **3.** *Archaic.* the figure of a parrot usually fixed on a pole and used as a target in archery and gun shooting. **4.** *Archaic.* a parrot. [1275–1325; ME *papejay, popingay, papinjai(e)* < MF *papegai, papingay* parrot < Sp *papagayo* < Ar *bab(ba)ghā′*]

pop·ish (pō′pish), *adj. Usually Disparaging.* of, pertaining to, or characteristic of the Roman Catholic Church. [1520–30; POPE + -ISH[1]] **—pop′ish·ly,** *adv.* **—pop′ish·ness,** *n.*

Pop′ish Plot′, an imaginary conspiracy against the crown of Great Britain on the part of English Roman Catholics, fabricated in 1678 by Titus Oates as a means of gaining power.

pop-it (pop′it), *n.* poppit.

pop·lar (pop′lər), *n.* **1.** any of the rapidly growing, salicaceous trees of the genus *Populus,* usually characterized by the columnar or spirelike manner of growth of its branches. **2.** the light, soft wood of any of these trees, used for pulp. **3.** any of various similar trees, as the tulip tree. **4.** the wood of any such tree. [1350–1400; ME *popler(e),* var. of *populer,* equiv. to ME, OE *popul* POPPLE[2] (< L *pōpulus* poplar) + *-er* -ER[2]; suffix appar. added on model of MF *pouplier,* equiv. to *pouple* poplar + *-ier* -IER[2]] **—pop′lared,** *adj.*

Pop′lar Bluff′, a city in SE Missouri. 17,139.

pop·lin (pop′lin), *n.* a finely corded fabric of cotton, rayon, silk, or wool, for dresses, draperies, etc [1700–10; < F *popeline,* earlier *papeline* < It *papalina,* fem. of *papalino* papal; so called from being made at the papal city of Avignon. See PAPAL, -INE[1]]

pop·lit·e·al (pop lit′ē əl, pop′li tē′-), *adj. Anat.* of or pertaining to the ham, or part of the leg back of the knee. [1780–90; POPLITE(US) + -AL[1]]

pop·lit·e·us (pop lit′ē əs, pop′li tē′-), *n., pl.* **-lit·e·i** (-lit′ē ī′, -li tē′ī). *Anat.* a thin, flat, triangular muscle in back of the knee, the action of which assists in bending the knee and in rotating the leg toward the body. [1695–1705; < NL, equiv. to L *poplit-* (s. of *poples*) knee joint, back of the knee + *-eus* -EOUS]

Po·po·cat·e·petl (pō′pô kä te′pet/l, pō′pə kat′ə-pet′l), *n.* a volcano in S central Mexico, SE of Mexico City. 17,887 ft. (5450 m).

pop·off (pop′ôf′, -of′), *Slang.* **—***n.* **1.** a person who generally speaks loudly or irately; indiscreet arguer or complainer. **—***adj.* **2.** pertaining to or characteristic of such a person: *His popoff remarks cost him many friends.* [1940–45; n., adj. use of v. phrase *pop off*]

pop-out (pop′out′), *n.* pop-up (def. 6). Also, **pop′out′.** [1960–65; n. use of v. phrase *pop out*]

pop·o·ver (pop′ō′vər), *n.* a puffed muffin with a hollow center, made with a batter of flour, salt, egg, and milk. [1875–80, *Amer.*; POP[1] + OVER]

pop·pa (pop′ə), *n. Informal.* father. [1765–75; var. of PAPA]

Pop·pae·a Sa·bi·na (po pē′ə sə bī′nə, -bē′-), died A.D. 65?, second wife of the Roman emperor Nero.

pop·per (pop′ər), *n.* **1.** a person or thing that pops. **2.** a utensil, as a covered pan, used for popping corn. **3.** *Angling.* chugger. **4.** a vial of amyl or butyl nitrite abused as a vasodilator for the effect of exhilaration. [1740–50; POP[1] + -ER[1]; cf. ME *poppere* a small dagger]

Pop·per (pop′ər), *n.* **Sir Karl (Rai·mund)** (rā′mənd), born 1902, British philosopher, born in Austria.

pop·pet (pop′it), *n.* **1.** Also called **pop′pet valve′.** *Mach.* a rising and falling valve consisting of a disk at the end of a vertically set stem, used in internal-combustion and steam engines. **2.** *Brit. Dial.* a term of endearment for a girl or child. **3.** *Naut.* any of the vertical timbers bracing the bow or stern of a vessel about to be launched. **4.** poppit. **5.** poppethead. [1300–50; ME; earlier form of PUPPET]

pop·pet·head (pop′it hed′), *n.* a tailstock or headstock of a lathe. Also called **poppet, puppet.** [1655–65; POPPET + HEAD]

pop·pied (pop′ēd), *adj.* **1.** covered or adorned with poppies: *poppied fields.* **2.** affected by or as if by opium; listless. [1795–1805; POPPY + -ED[3]]

pop′ping crease′ (pop′ing), *Cricket.* a line parallel to and in advance of a bowling crease, marking the limit of a batsman's approach in hitting the ball. [1765–75; POP[1] + -ING[1]]

pop·pit (pop′it), *n.* a usually plastic bead that can be connected to or detached from others of the same kind without hooks or clasps, used to form necklaces, bracelets, etc. Also, **poppet, pop-it.** [1955–60; from the v. phrase *pop it*]

pop·ple[1] (pop′əl), *v.,* **-pled, -pling,** *n.* **—***v.i.* **1.** to move in a tumbling, irregular manner, as boiling water. **—***n.* **2.** a poppling motion. [1300–50; ME *poplen;* imit.; see -LE]

pop·ple[2] (pop′əl), *n. Northern U.S.* a poplar of the genus *Populus.* [bef. 1000; ME; OE *popul* < L *pōpulus*]

pop′ psych′, psychological or pseudopsychological counseling, interpretations, concepts, terminology, etc., often simplistic or superficial, popularized by certain personalities, magazine articles, television shows, advice columns, or the like, that influence the general public. Also called **pop′ psychol′ogy.** [1960–65] **—pop′-psych′,** *adj.* **—pop′ psychol′ogist.**

pop·py (pop′ē), *n., pl.* **-pies** for 1, 2, 4–7. **1.** any plant of the genus *Papaver,* having showy, usually red flowers. Cf. **poppy family. 2.** any of several related or similar plants, as the California poppy or the prickly poppy. **3.** an extract, as opium, from such a plant. **4.** Also called **poppy red.** an orangish red resembling scarlet. **5.** *Archit.* poppyhead. **6.** an artificial flower resembling a poppy, esp. one received as evidence of a contribution to a fund for disabled war veterans. **7. tall poppy,** *Australian.* someone of preeminence or with a large income; important and powerful person. [bef. 900; ME; OE *popæg, papig* << VL **papāvum,* for L *papāver*] **—pop′py·like′,** *adj.*

poppy, *Papaver orientale*

pop′py anem′one, a southern European plant, *Anemone coronaria,* of the buttercup family, having tuberous roots and solitary, poppylike, red, blue, or white flowers, grown as an ornamental. [1865–70]

pop·py·cock (pop′ē kok′), *n.* nonsense; bosh. [1840–50, *Amer.*; perh. < D *pappekak,* equiv. to *pappe-* PAP[1] + *kak* excrement] **—pop′py·cock′ish,** *adj.*
—Syn. balderdash, bunk, hogwash, rubbish.

pop′py fam′ily, the plant family Papaveraceae, characterized by chiefly herbaceous plants having white, yellow, or reddish juice, alternate and often lobed or dissected leaves, showy, usually solitary flowers, and capsular fruit, and including bloodroot, creamcups, greater celandine, and poppies of the genera *Papaver, Eschscholzia, Argemone,* and others.

pop·py·head (pop′ē hed′), *n. Archit.* a finial or other ornament, often richly carved, as the top of the upright end of a bench or pew. [1575–85; POPPY + HEAD]

pop′py red′, poppy (def. 4). [1825–35]

pop′py seed′, seed of the poppy plant, used as an ingredient or topping for breads, rolls, cakes, and cookies. [1375–1425; late ME]

pops (pops), *adj.* **1.** of or pertaining to a symphony orchestra specializing in popular or light classical music: *Thursday is pops night on the concert series.* **—***n.* **2.** (*often cap.*) (*used with a singular v.*) a symphony orchestra specializing in popular and light classical music: *When you're in Boston be sure to hear the Pops.* [1955–60; see POP[2]]

pops′ con′cert. See **pop concert.**

pop-shop (pop′shop′), *n. Brit. Slang.* pawnshop. [1765–75; POP[1] + SHOP]

Pop·si·cle (pop′si kəl, -sik′əl), *Trademark.* a brand of flavored ice on a stick.

pop·sy (pop′sē), *n., pl.* **-sies.** *Brit. Informal.* a girl or young woman. [1860–65; generic use of a term of endearment, prob. POP(PET) + -SY]

pop-top (pop′top′), *adj.* **1.** (of a can) having a top with a tab or ring that when pulled up or off exposes a precut hole or peels off the entire lid. **—***n.* **2.** Also, **pop′ top′.** a can having such a top: *drinking beer from a pop-top.* **3.** the top itself. **4.** the tab or ring fastener, esp. when removed from such a can: *a vest made entirely of pop-tops.* Also called **pull-top, flip-top.** [1965–70, *Amer.*]

pop·u·lace (pop′yə ləs), *n.* **1.** the common people of a community, nation, etc., as distinguished from the higher classes. **2.** all the inhabitants of a place; population. [1565–75; < F < It *popolaccio,* equiv. to *popol(o)* PEOPLE + *-accio* pejorative suffix]

pop·u·lar (pop′yə lər), *adj.* **1.** regarded with favor, approval, or affection by people in general: *a popular preacher.* **2.** regarded with favor, approval, or affection by an acquaintance or acquaintances: *He's not very popular with me just now.* **3.** of, pertaining to, or representing the people, esp. the common people: *popular discontent.* **4.** of the people as a whole, esp. of all citizens of a nation or state qualified to participate in an election: *popular suffrage; the popular vote; popular representation.* **5.** prevailing among the people generally: *a popular superstition.* **6.** suited to or intended for the general masses of people: *popular music.* **7.** adapted to the ordinary intelligence or taste: *popular lectures on science.* **8.** suited to the means of ordinary people; not expensive: *popular prices on all tickets.* [1375–1425; late ME *populer* < L *populāris.* See PEOPLE, -AR[1]]
—Syn. 1. favorite, approved, liked. **5.** common, current. See **general.**

pop′ular etymol′ogy. See **folk etymology.** [1875–80]

pop′ular front′, 1. a coalition, usually temporary, of leftist and sometimes centrist political parties, formed against a common opponent, as fascism, and promoting social reform. **2.** any similar political coalition formed to achieve short-term goals. Also called **people's front.** [1935–40; cf. Sp. *frente popular,* F *front populaire*]

pop·u·lar·i·ty (pop′yə lar′i tē), *n.* **1.** the quality or fact of being popular. **2.** the favor of the general public or of a particular group of people: *His popularity with television audiences is unrivaled.* [1540–50; < L *populāritās* a courting of popular favor. See POPULAR, -ITY]
—Syn. 1, 2. acclaim, vogue, fashion, fame, repute.

pop·u·lar·ize (pop′yə lə rīz′), *v.t.,* **-ized, -iz·ing.** to make popular: *to popularize a dance.* Also, *esp. Brit.,* **pop′u·lar·ise′.** [1585–95; POPULAR + -IZE] **—pop′u·lar·i·za′tion,** *n.* **—pop′u·lar·iz′er,** *n.*

pop·u·lar·ly (pop′yə lər lē), *adv.* **1.** by the people as a whole; generally; widely: *a fictitious story popularly accepted as true.* **2.** for popular taste; for the general masses of people: *He writes popularly on many subjects.* [1570–80; POPULAR + -LY]

pop′ular sing′er, a professional singer who specializes in popular songs. Cf. **jazz singer.**

pop′ular song′, a song that is written to have an immediate and wide appeal and is usually popular for only a short time, but that sometimes is of a sufficiently high quality to become part of the permanent repertoire of popular music and jazz. Cf. **standard** (def. 12). [1835–45]

pop′ular sov′ereignty, 1. the doctrine that sovereign power is vested in the people and that those chosen to govern, as trustees of such power, must exercise it in conformity with the general will. **2.** *Amer. Hist.* (before the Civil War) a doctrine, held chiefly by the opponents of the abolitionists, that the people living in a territory should be free of federal interference in determining domestic policy, esp. with respect to slavery. [1840–50, *Amer.*]

pop′ular vote′, 1. the vote for a U.S. presidential candidate made by the qualified voters, as opposed to that made by the electoral college. Cf. **electoral vote. 2.** the vote for a candidate, issue, etc., made by the qualified voters, as opposed to a vote made by elected representatives. [1830–40, *Amer.*]

pop·u·late (pop′yə lāt′), *v.t.,* **-lat·ed, -lat·ing. 1.** to inhabit; live in; be the inhabitants of. **2.** to furnish with inhabitants, as by colonization; people. [1570–80; < ML *populātus,* ptp. of *populāre* to inhabit. See PEOPLE, -ATE[1]]

pop·u·la·tion (pop′yə lā′shən), *n.* **1.** the total number of persons inhabiting a country, city, or any district or area. **2.** the body of inhabitants of a place: *The population of the city opposes the addition of fluorides to the drinking water.* **3.** the number or body of inhabitants of a particular race or class in a place: *the native population; the working-class population.* **4.** *Statistics.* any finite or infinite aggregation of individuals, not necessarily animate, subject to a statistical study. **5.** *Ecol.* **a.** the assemblage of a specific type of organism living in a given area. **b.** all the individuals of one species in a given area. **6.** the act or process of populating: *Population of the interior was hampered by dense jungles.* [1570–80; < LL *populātiōn-* (s. of *populātiō*). See POPULATE, -ION] **—pop′u·la′tion·al,** *adj.* **—pop′u·la′tion·less,** *adj.*

popula′tion explo′sion, the rapid increase in numbers of a particular species, esp. in the world's human population since the end of World War II, attributed to an accelerating birthrate, a decrease in infant mortality, and an increase in life expectancy. [1950–55, *Amer.*]

popula′tion genet′ics, 1. the branch of genetics concerned with the hereditary makeup of populations. **2.** the study of changes in gene frequencies in population of organisms and the effects of such changes on evolution and adaptation. Also called **quantitative genetics.** [1945–50]

popula′tion inver′sion, *Physics.* a condition of matter in which more electrons are in a high energy state than in a lower energy state, as is required for the operation of a laser. [1960–65]

popula′tion param′eter, *Statistics.* a quantity or statistical measure that, for a given population, is fixed and that is used as the value of a variable in some general distribution or frequency function to make it descriptive of that population: *The mean and variance of a population are population parameters.*

popula′tion pres′sure, *Ecol.* the force exerted by a growing population upon its environment, resulting in dispersal or reduction of the population. [1930–35]

popula′tion pyr′amid, *Sociol.* a graph showing the distribution of a population by sex, age, etc. [1945–50]

Pop·u·lism (pop′yə liz′əm), *n.* **1.** the political philosophy of the People's party. **2.** (*l.c.*) any of various, often antiestablishment or anti-intellectual political movements or philosophies that offer unorthodox solutions or policies and appeal to the common person rather than according with traditional party or partisan ideologies. **3.** (*l.c.*) grass-roots democracy; working-class activism; egalitarianism. **4.** (*l.c.*) representation or extolling of the common person, the working class, the underdog, etc.: *populism in the arts.* [1890–95, *Amer.*; < L *popul(us)* PEOPLE + -ISM]

Pop·u·list (pop′yə list), *n.* **1.** a member of the People's party. **2.** (*l.c.*) a supporter or adherent of populism. **—***adj.* **3.** Also, **Pop′u·lis′tic.** of or pertaining to the People's party. **4.** Also, **pop′u·lis′tic.** (*l.c.*) of, pertaining to, or characteristic of populism or its adherents. [1890–95, *Amer.*; < L *popul(us)* PEOPLE + -IST]

pop·u·lous (pop′yə ləs), *adj.* **1.** full of residents or inhabitants, as a region; heavily populated. **2.** jammed or crowded with people: *There's no more populous place*

than Times Square on New Year's Eve. **3.** forming or comprising a large number or quantity: *Because of epidemics the tribes are not nearly so populous as they once were.* [1400–50; late ME *populus* < L *populōsus.* See PEOPLE, -OUS] —**pop′u·lous·ly,** *adv.* —**pop′u·lous·ness,** *n.*
—**Syn. 2.** swarming, packed, teeming.

pop-up (pop′up′), *adj.* **1.** (of books, usually children's books) having pieces of artwork fastened to the pages so that when the page is opened, a three-dimensional cutout or object is formed and, sometimes, movement of a picture element, such as a door opening, can be activated by pulling a tab. **2.** of or being a device that ejects or raises a finished or used item from the top: *a pop-up toaster.* **3.** of or pertaining to a device, mechanism, or object that rises or pivots from a concealed or recessed position to its operating position: *a camera with a pop-up electronic flash; a car with pop-up headlights.* **4.** popping up, as from an appliance or object: *pop-up waffles heated in the toaster; a pop-up gauge for indicating when the turkey is done.* —*n.* **5.** a pop-up book. **6.** something, as a partially cut out or spring-mounted illustration in a children's book, that unfolds or springs up when opened or otherwise activated; pop-out: *a Christmas card with a pop-up of Santa Claus.* **7.** *Baseball.* See **pop fly.** Also, **pop′up′.** [1860–65 for def. 7; n., adj. use of v. phrase *pop up*]

pop′ wine′, an inexpensive wine having a low alcohol content and artificial fruit flavoring.

p.o.r., pay on return.

Por·ban·dar (pôr bun′dər), *n.* a seaport in SW Gujarat, in W India. 96,756.

por·bea·gle (pôr′bē′gəl), *n.* a shark of the genus *Lamna,* esp. *L. nasus,* a large, voracious species of the North Atlantic and North Pacific oceans. [1750–60; < Cornish *porghbugel*]

por·ce·lain (pôr′sə lin, pōr′-; pôrs′lin, pōrs′-), *n.* **1.** a strong, vitreous, translucent ceramic material, biscuit-fired at a low temperature, the glaze then fired at a very high temperature. **2.** ware made from this. [1520–30; < F *porcelaine* < It *porcellana* orig., a type of cowry shell, appar. likened to the vulva of a sow, n. use of fem. of *porcellano* of a young sow, equiv. to *porcell(a),* dim. of *porca* sow (see PORK, -ELLE) + *-ano* -AN] —**por·ce·la·ne·ous, por·cel·la·ne·ous** (pôr′sə lā′nē əs, pōr′-), *adj.*

por′celain enam′el, a glass coating, made to adhere to a metal or another enamel by fusion. [1880–85]

por·ce·lain·ite (pôr′sə lə nīt′, pōr′-, pôrs′lə-, pōrs′-), *n. Mineral.* mullite. [PORCELAIN + -ITE[1]]

por·ce·lain·ize (pôr′sə lə nīz′, pōr′-, pôrs′lə-, pōrs′-), *v.t.,* **-ized, -iz·ing.** to make into or coat with porcelain or something resembling porcelain. Also, *esp. Brit.,* **por′ce·lain·ise′.** [1860–65; PORCELAIN + -IZE] —**por′ce·lain·i·za′tion,** *n.*

porch (pôrch, pōrch), *n.* **1.** an exterior appendage to a building, forming a covered approach or vestibule to a doorway. **2.** a veranda. **3. the Porch,** the portico or stoa in the agora of ancient Athens, where the Stoic philosopher Zeno of Citium and his followers met. **4.** *Obs.* a portico. [1250–1300; ME *porche* < OF < L *porticus* porch, portico] —**porch′less,** *adj.* —**porch′like′,** *adj.*

por·cine (pôr′sīn, -sin), *adj.* **1.** of or pertaining to swine. **2.** resembling swine; hoggish; piggish. [1650–60; < L *porcīnus;* see PORK, -INE[1]]

por·cu·pine (pôr′kyə pīn′), *n.* any of several rodents covered with stiff, sharp, erectile spines or quills, as *Erethizon dorsatum* of North America. [1375–1425; late ME *porcupyne,* var. of *porcapyne;* r. *porke despyne* < MF *porc d'espine* thorny pig. See PORK, SPINE]

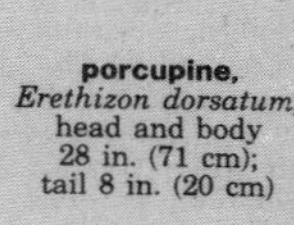

porcupine, *Erethizon dorsatum,* head and body 28 in. (71 cm); tail 8 in. (20 cm)

por′cupine ant′eater, an echidna or spiny anteater. [1865–70]

por·cu·pine·fish (pôr′kyə pīn′fish′), *n., pl.* (*esp. collectively*) **-fish,** (*esp. referring to two or more kinds or species*) **-fish·es.** any of several fishes of the family Diodontidae, esp. *Diodon hystrix,* of tropical seas, capable of inflating the body with water or air until it resembles a globe, with erection of the long spines covering the skin. [1675–85; PORCUPINE + FISH]

pore[1] (pôr, pōr), *v.i.,* **pored, por·ing. 1.** to read or study with steady attention or application: *a scholar poring over a rare old manuscript.* **2.** to gaze earnestly or steadily: *to pore over a painting.* **3.** to meditate or ponder intently (usually fol. by *over, on,* or *upon*): *He pored over the strange events of the preceding evening.* [1250–1300; ME *pouren* < ?]

pore[2] (pôr, pōr), *n.* **1.** a minute opening or orifice, as in the skin or a leaf, for perspiration, absorption, etc. **2.** a minute interstice, as in a rock. [1350–1400; ME *poore* < LL *porus* < Gk *póros* passage; see EMPORIUM, FORD] —**pore′like′,** *adj.*

pore′ fun′gus, *n.* any fungus of the families Boletaceae and Polyporaceae, bearing spores in tubes or pores. [1920–25]

CONCISE ETYMOLOGY KEY: <, descended or borrowed from; >, whence; b., blend of, blended; c., cognate with; cf., compare; deriv., derivative; equiv., equivalent; imit., imitative; obl., oblique; r., replacing; s., stem; sp., spelling, spelled; resp., respelling, respelled; trans., translation; ?, origin unknown; *, unattested; ‡, probably earlier than. See the full key inside the front cover.

por fa·vor (pôr′ fä vôr′), *Spanish.* please; if you please.

por·gy (pôr′gē), *n., pl.* (*esp. collectively*) **-gy,** (*esp. referring to two or more kinds or species*) **-gies. 1.** a sparid food fish, *Pagrus pagrus,* found in the Mediterranean and off the Atlantic coasts of Europe and America. **2.** any of several other sparid fishes, as the scup. [1715–25; *porg(o),* var. of *pargo* (< Sp or Pg < L *pag(a)rus* kind of fish < Gk *págros,* var. of *phágros*) + -Y[2]]

Por′gy and Bess (pôr′gē ən bes′), an opera (1935) with music by George Gershwin and lyrics by Ira Gershwin.

Po·ri (pôr′ē; *Fin.* pô′RĒ), *n.* a seaport in W Finland, on the Gulf of Bothnia. 80,242.

Po·rif·er·a (pô rif′ər ə, pō-, pə-), *n.* an animal phylum comprising the sponges. [1835–45; < NL equiv. to LL *porus* PORE[2] + -I- -I- + *-fera,* neut. pl. of *-ferus* -FEROUS]

po·rif·er·an (pô rif′ər ən, pō-, pə-), *n.* **1.** any animal of the phylum Porifera, comprising the sponges. —*adj.* **2.** belonging or pertaining to the Porifera. [1860–65; PORIFER(A) + -AN]

po·rif·er·ous (pô rif′ər əs, pō-, pə-), *adj.* bearing or having pores. [1860–65; < L *por(us)* PORE[2] + -I- + -FEROUS]

po·ri·form (pôr′ə fôrm′, pōr′-), *adj.* resembling a pore in form. [1840–50; < LL *por(us)* PORE[2] + -I- + -FORM]

po·ri·on (pôr′ē on′, pōr′-), *n., pl.* **po·ri·a** (pôr′ē ə, pōr′-), **po·ri·ons.** *Craniom.* the most lateral point in the roof of the bony external auditory meatus. [1905–10; < NL < Gk *pór(os)* passage, way (see PORE[2]) + *-ion* dim. suffix]

pork (pôrk, pōrk), *n.* **1.** the flesh of hogs used as food. **2.** *Informal.* appropriations, appointments, etc., made by the government for political reasons rather than for public benefit, as for public buildings or river improvements. [1250–1300; ME *porc* < OF < L *porcus* hog, pig; c. FARROW[1]] —**pork′ish, pork′like′,** *adj.* —**pork′less,** *adj.*

pork′ bar′rel, *Informal.* a government appropriation, bill, or policy that supplies funds for local improvements designed to ingratiate legislators with their constituents. [1905–10, *Amer.*] —**pork′-bar′rel,** *adj.* —**pork′-bar′rel·ing,** *adj., n.*

pork-bar·rel·er (pôrk′bar′ə lər, pōrk′-), *n. Informal.* a politician, esp. a senator or member of Congress who is party to or benefits from a pork barrel. [PORK BARREL + -ER[1]]

pork′ bel′ly, a side of fresh pork. [1945–50]

pork·chop (pôrk′chop′, pōrk′-), *n.* **1.** a chop of pork. **2.** *Journ., Print.* thumbnail (def. 4). [1855–60]

pork·chop·per (pôrk′chop′ər, pōrk′-), *n. Informal.* **1.** a labor official put on the union payroll as a reward for past loyalty or services. **2.** any legislator, political appointee, official, etc., who is primarily interested in personal gain or the perquisites of power. [1945–50, *Amer.;* PORKCHOP + -ER[1]; prob. from the use of "pork-chop" as a metaphor for livelihood, esp. one acquired with little effort]

pork·er (pôr′kər, pōr′-), *n.* a pig, esp. one being fattened for its meat. [1635–45; PORK + -ER[1]]

pork·fish (pôrk′fish′, pōrk′-), *n., pl.* **-fish·es,** (*esp. collectively*) **-fish.** a black and gold grunt, *Anisotremus virginicus,* of West Indian waters. [1725–35, *Amer.;* PORK + FISH]

pork·pie (pôrk′pī′, pōrk′-), *n.* a snap-brimmed hat with a round, flat crown, usually made of felt. [1725–35]

pork·y[1] (pôr′kē, pōr′-), *adj.,* **pork·i·er, pork·i·est. 1.** of, pertaining to, or resembling pork. **2.** fat: *a porky child.* [1850–55; PORK + -Y[1]] —**pork′i·ness,** *n.*

pork·y[2] (pôr′kē, pōr′-), *n. pl.* **pork·ies.** *Chiefly Inland North and Western U.S.* a porcupine. [1900–05, *Amer.;* PORC(UPINE) + -Y[2]]

porn (pôrn), *Informal.* —*n.* **1.** pornography. —*adj.* **2.** Also, **porn·y** (pôr′nē). pertaining to or dealing in pornography; pornographic: *porn shops.* Also, **por·no** (pôr′nō) [1960–65; by shortening]

por·nog·ra·pher (pôr nog′rə fər), *n.* a person who writes or sells pornography. [1840–50; PORNOGRAPH(Y) + -ER[1]]

por·nog·ra·phy (pôr nog′rə fē), *n.* obscene writings, drawings, photographs, or the like, esp. those having little or no artistic merit. [1840–50; < Gk *pornográph(os)* writing about harlots (*porno-,* comb. form of *pórnē* harlot + *-graphos* -GRAPH) + -Y[3]] —**por·no·graph·ic** (pôr′nə graf′ik), *adj.* —**por′no·graph′i·cal·ly,** *adv.*

po·ros·i·ty (pô ros′i tē, pō-, pə-), *n., pl.* **-ties** for 2. **1.** the state or quality of being porous. **2.** *Geol., Engin.* the ratio, expressed as a percentage, of the volume of the pores or interstices of a substance, as a rock or rock stratum, to the total volume of the mass. [1350–1400; ME *porosytee* < ML *porōsitās.* See POROUS, -ITY]

po·rous (pôr′əs, pōr′-), *adj.* **1.** full of pores. **2.** permeable by water, air, etc. [1350–1400; ME, var. of *porose* < ML *porōsus.* See PORE[2], -OUS] —**po′rous·ly,** *adv.* —**po′rous·ness,** *n.*
—**Syn. 2.** penetrable, pervious, sievelike, riddled.

por·phyr·i·a (pôr fēr′ē ə, -fī′rē ə), *n. Pathol.* a defect of blood pigment metabolism in which porphyrins are produced in excess, are present in the blood, and are found in the urine. Also called **hematoporphyria.** [1920–25; PORPHYR(IN) + -IA]

por·phy·rin (pôr′fə rin), *n. Biochem.* a dark red, photosensitive pigment consisting of four pyrrole rings linked by single carbon atoms: a component of chlorophyll, heme, and vitamin B_{12}. [1905–10; < Gk *porphýr(a)* PURPLE + -IN[2]]

por·phy·rit·ic (pôr′fə rit′ik), *adj. Petrol.* of, pertaining to, containing, or resembling porphyry, its texture, or its structure. [1375–1425; late ME *porphiritike* < ML *porphyriticus* < Gk *porphyrītikós* of PORPHYRY; see -IC]

por·phy·ri·za·tion (pôr′fə rə zā′shən), *n.* reduction to a powder, formerly done on a slab of porphyry. [1825–35; PORPHYRIZE + -ATION]

por·phy·rize (pôr′fə rīz′), *v.t.,* **-rized, -riz·ing.** to subject to porphyrization. Also, *esp. Brit.,* **por′phy·rise′.** [1740–50; PORPHYR(Y) + -IZE]

por·phy·roid (pôr′fə roid′), *n.* **1.** a rock resembling porphyry. **2.** a sedimentary rock that has been metamorphosed so as to leave some original crystals in a fine-textured, layered matrix. [1790–1800; PORPHYR(Y) + -OID]

por·phy·ry (pôr′fə rē), *n., pl.* **-ries. 1.** a very hard rock, anciently quarried in Egypt, having a dark, purplish-red groundmass containing small crystals of feldspar. **2.** *Petrol.* any igneous rock containing coarse crystals, as phenocrysts, in a finer-grained groundmass. [1350–1400; ME *porfurie, porfirie* < ML *porphyreum,* alter. of L *porphyrītēs* < Gk *porphyrī́tēs* porphyry, short for *porphyrī́tēs líthos* porphyritic (i.e., purplish) stone, equiv. to *pórphyr(os)* PURPLE + *-ītēs;* see -ITE[1]]

Por·phy·ry (pôr′fə rē), *n.* (*Malchus*) A.D. c233–c304, Greek philosopher. —**Por·phyr·e·an** (pôr fēr′ē ən), *adj.* —**Por·phyr′i·an,** *adj., n.* —**Por·phyr′i·an·ist,** *n.*

por·poise (pôr′pəs), *n., pl.* (*esp. collectively*) **-poise,** (*esp. referring to two or more kinds or species*) **-pois·es,** *v.,* **-poised, -pois·ing.** —*n.* **1.** any of several small, gregarious cetaceans of the genus *Phocoena,* usually blackish above and paler beneath, and having a blunt, rounded snout, esp. the common porpoise, *P. phocoena,* of both the North Atlantic and Pacific. **2.** any of several other small cetaceans, as the common dolphin, *Delphinus delphis.* —*v.i.* **3.** (of a speeding motorboat) to leap clear of the water after striking a wave. **4.** (of a torpedo) to appear above the surface of the water. **5.** to move forward with a rising and falling motion in the manner of a porpoise: *The car has a tendency to porpoise when overloaded.* [1275–1325; ME *porpoys* < MF *porpois* < VL **porcopiscis* hog fish, for L *porcus marinus* sea hog] —**por′poise·like′,** *adj.*

porpoise, *Phocoena phocoena,* length 5 to 8 ft. (1.5 to 2.4 m)

por·rect (pə rekt′, pô-), *adj.* extending horizontally; projecting. [1810–20; < L *porrēctus* (ptp. of *porrigere* to stretch out), equiv. to *por-* forth, forward (see PER, PRO-[1]) + *reg-,* comb. form of *regere* to rule, guide, DIRECT + *-tus* ptp. suffix]

por·ridge (pôr′ij, por′-), *n.* a food made of oatmeal, or some other meal or cereal, boiled to a thick consistency in water or milk. [1525–35; var. of earlier *poddidge,* akin to POTTAGE] —**por′ridge·like′,** *adj.*

por·rin·ger (pôr′in jər, por′-), *n.* a low dish or cup, often with a handle, from which soup, porridge, or the like is eaten. [1515–25; var. of earlier *poddinger,* akin to late ME *potinger,* nasalized var. of *potager* < MF. See POTTAGE, -ER[2]]

Por′ro prism′ (pôr′ō), *Optics.* an isosceles, right-triangular prism in which light entering one half of the hypotenuse face is reflected at the two short sides and is reversed in orientation when it leaves the other half of the hypotenuse: used in 90°-oriented pairs in binoculars to increase the length of the optical path and to erect the final image. [named after Ignazio *Porro* (1801–75), Italian engineer]

port[1] (pôrt, pōrt), *n.* **1.** a city, town, or other place where ships load or unload. **2.** a place along a coast in which ships may take refuge from storms; harbor. **3.** Also called **port of entry.** *Law.* any place where persons and merchandise are allowed to pass, by water or land, into and out of a country and where customs officers are stationed to inspect or appraise imported goods. **4.** a geographical area that forms a harbor: *the largest port on the eastern seaboard.* **5.** *Informal.* an airport. [bef. 900; ME, OE < L *portus* harbor, haven; akin to FORD] —**port′less,** *adj.*
—**Syn. 2.** anchorage. See **harbor.**

port[2] (pôrt, pōrt), *n.* **1.** the left-hand side of a vessel or aircraft, facing forward. —*adj.* **2.** pertaining to or designating port. **3.** located on the left side of a vessel or aircraft. —*v.t., v.i.* **4.** to turn or shift to the port, or left, side. [1570–80; special use of PORT[4]]

port[3] (pôrt, pōrt), *n.* any of a class of very sweet wines, mostly dark-red, originally from Portugal. [1695–95; earlier *Oporto,* (*Port*) *O Port* < Pg *Oporto* OPORTO, the main port of shipment for the wines of Portugal]

port[4] (pôrt, pōrt), *n., v.,* **port·ed, port·ing.** —*n.* **1.** an opening in the side or other exterior part of a ship for admitting air and light or for taking on cargo. Cf. **porthole** (def. 1). **2.** *Mach.* an aperture in the surface of a cylinder, for the passage of steam, air, water, etc. **3.** a small aperture in an armored vehicle, aircraft, or fortification through which a gun can be fired or a camera directed. **4.** *Computers.* a data connection in a computer to which a peripheral device or a transmission line from a remote terminal can be attached. **5.** the raised center portion on a bit for horses. **6.** *Chiefly Scot.* a gate or portal, as to a town or fortress. —*v.t.* **7.** *Computers.* to create a new version of (an application program) to run on a different hardware platform (sometimes fol. by *over*). [bef. 950; ME, OE < L *porta* gate; akin to *portus* PORT[1]]

port[5] (pôrt, pōrt), *v.t.* **1.** *Mil.* to carry (a rifle or other weapon) with both hands, in a slanting direction across the front of the body, with the barrel or like part near the left shoulder. —*n.* **2.** *Mil.* the position of a rifle or other weapon when ported. **3.** *Archaic.* manner of bearing oneself; carriage or deportment. [1560–70; < F *porter* < L *portāre* to carry; see FARE]

Port., 1. Portugal. 2. Portuguese.

port•a•bil•i•ty (pôr′tə bil′i tē, pōr′-), *n., pl.* **-ties** for 2. 1. the state or quality of being portable. 2. a plan or system under which employees may accumulate pension rights under any employer who is a participant in the plan negotiated with their union. [1965–70; PORT(ABLE) + -ABILITY]

port•a•ble (pôr′tə bəl, pōr′-), *adj.* 1. capable of being transported or conveyed: *a portable stage.* 2. easily carried or conveyed by hand: *a portable typewriter.* 3. *Computers.* (of data sets, software, etc.) capable of being used on different computer systems. 4. *Obs.* endurable. —*n.* 5. something that is portable, esp. as distinguished from a nonportable counterpart: *Of their three television sets, one is a portable.* [1375–1425; late ME < LL *portābilis.* See PORT[5], -ABLE] —**port′a•bly,** *adv.*

por•tage (pôr′tij, pōr′-, *or, for 2, 3, 5, 6,* pôr täzh′), *n., v.,* **-taged, -tag•ing.** —*n.* 1. the act of carrying; carriage. 2. the carrying of boats, goods, etc., overland from one navigable water to another. 3. the route over which this is done. 4. the cost of carriage. —*v.i.* 5. to make a portage: *On this stretch of the river, we have to portage for a mile.* —*v.t.* 6. to carry (something) over a portage; make a portage with: *We portaged our canoe around the rapids.* [1375–1425; late ME < MF; see PORT[5], -AGE]

Por•tage (pôr′tij, pōr′-), *n.* 1. a city in SW Michigan. 38,157. 2. a town in NW Indiana. 27,409.

Por•tage la Prai•rie (pôr′tij lə prâr′ē, pōr′-), a city in S Manitoba, in S central Canada, W of Winnipeg. 13,086.

por•tal[1] (pôr′tl, pōr′-), *n.* 1. a door, gate, or entrance, esp. one of imposing appearance, as to a palace. 2. an iron or steel bent for bracing a framed structure, having curved braces between the vertical members and a horizontal member at the top. 3. an entrance to a tunnel or mine. [1300–50; ME *portale* < ML, n. use of neut. of *portālis* of a gate. See PORTAL[2]] —**por′taled, por′talled,** *adj.*
—**Syn.** 1. entranceway, doorway, entry, threshold.

por•tal[2] (pôr′tl, pōr′-), *Anat.* —*adj.* 1. noting or pertaining to the transverse fissure of the liver. —*n.* 2. See **portal vein.** [1605–15; < ML *portālis* of a gate. See PORT[4], -AL[1]]

Port′ Al•ber′ni (al bûr′nē), a port in SW British Columbia, in SW Canada, on the E central part of Vancouver Island, on an inlet of the Pacific Ocean. 19,982.

por′tal circula′tion, *Physiol.* blood flow in a portal system. [1870–75]

por′tal sys′tem, *Anat.* 1. a vascular arrangement in which blood from the capillaries of one organ is transported to the capillaries of another organ by a connecting vein or veins. 2. (loosely) the hepatoportal system. [1850–55]

por′tal-to-por′tal pay′ (pôr′tl tə pôr′tl, pōr′tl tə-pōr′tl), payment, as to a miner or factory worker, that includes compensation for time spent on the employer's premises in preparation for a work shift, in travel from the entrance to the assigned work area and back, etc.: *Because workers must change their clothes and pick up tools prior to the work shift, they are demanding portal-to-portal pay.* [1940–45, *Amer.*]

por′tal vein′, *Anat.* the large vein conveying blood to the liver from the veins of the stomach, intestine, spleen, and pancreas. [1835–45]

por•ta•men•to (pôr′tə men′tō, pōr′-; *It.* pôr′tä men′tô), *n., pl.* **-ti** (-tē), **-tos.** *Music.* a passing or gliding from one pitch or tone to another with a smooth progression. [1765–75; < It: fingering, lit., a bearing, carrying. See PORT[5], -MENT]

port•ance (pôr′tns, pōr′-), *n. Archaic.* bearing; behavior. [1580–90; < MF; see PORT[5], -ANCE]

Port′ An′ge•les (an′jə ləs), a city in NW Washington, on the Juan de Fuca Strait. 17,311.

port′ arms′, a position in military drill in which one's rifle is held diagonally in front of the body, with the muzzle pointing upward to the left. [1795–1805]

Port′ Ar′thur, 1. Lüshun. 2. a seaport in SE Texas, on Sabine Lake. 61,195. 3. See under **Thunder Bay.**

por•ta•tive (pôr′tə tiv, pōr′-), *adj.* 1. capable of being carried; portable. 2. having or pertaining to the power or function of carrying. —*n.* 3. Also called **por′tative or′gan.** a small portable pipe organ used esp. during the Middle Ages and the Renaissance. [1350–1400; ME *portatif* < MF. See PORT[5], -ATIVE]

Port-au-Prince (pôrt′ō prins′, pōrt′-; *Fr.* pôʀ tō-pʀaNs′), *n.* a seaport in and the capital of Haiti, in the S part. 550,000.

port′ author′ity, a government commission that manages bridges, tunnels, airports, and other such facilities of a port or city.

Port′ Blair′ (blâr), a seaport in and the capital of the Andaman and Nicobar Islands, on S Andaman. 26,212.

port′ cap′tain, *Naut.* 1. an official in charge of the harbor activities of a seaport. 2. See **marine superintendent.**

Port′ Char′lotte, a town in SW Florida. 25,770.

Port′ Ches′ter, a city in SE New York, on Long Island Sound. 23,565.

Port′ Col′borne (kōl′bərn), a city in SE Ontario, in S Canada. 20,536.

Port′ Co•quit′lam (kō kwit′ləm), a city in SW British Columbia, in SW Canada, E of Vancouver. 27,535.

port•cul•lis (pôrt kul′is, pōrt-), *n.* (esp. in medieval castles) a strong grating, as of iron, made to slide along vertical grooves at the sides of a gateway of a fortified place and let down to prevent passage. [1300–50; ME *portecolys* < MF *porte coleice,* equiv. to *porte* PORT[4] + *coleice,* fem. of *coleis* flowing, sliding < VL **cōlāticius;* see COULEE, -ITIOUS]

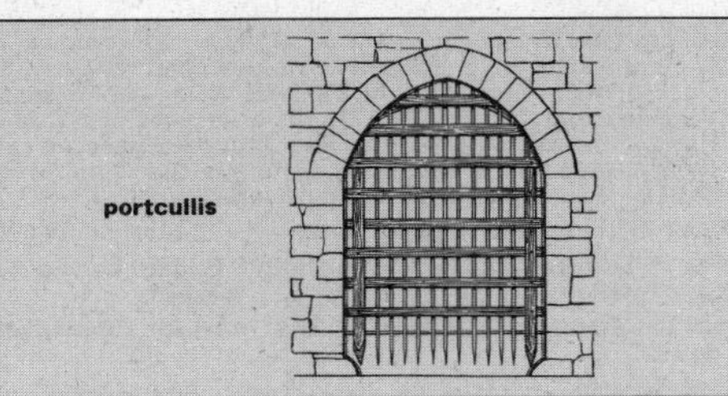
portcullis

port de bras (*Fr.* pôʀ də bʀä′), *Ballet.* 1. the technique of moving the arms properly. 2. the exercises for developing this technique. [1910–15; < F: carriage of arm]

Port du Sa•lut (pôrt′ də sə lo͞o′, pōrt′; *Fr.* pôʀ dʏ sa lʏ′), Port-Salut.

Porte (pôrt, pōrt), *n.* the former Ottoman court or government in Turkey. Official name, **Sublime Porte.** [short for *Sublime Porte* High Gate, F trans. of the Turkish official title *Babıâli,* with reference to the palace gate at which justice was administered]

porte-co•chere (pôrt′kō shâr′, -kə-, pōrt′-), *n.* 1. a covered carriage entrance leading into a courtyard. 2. a porch at the door of a building for sheltering persons entering and leaving carriages. Also, **porte′-co•chère′.** [1690–1700; < F: gate for coaches]

Port′ Eliz′abeth, a seaport in the SE Cape of Good Hope province, in the S Republic of South Africa. 406,000.

por•tend (pôr tend′, pōr-), *v.t.* 1. to indicate in advance; to foreshadow or presage, as an omen does: *The street incident may portend a general uprising.* 2. to signify; mean. [1400–50; late ME < L *portendere* to point out, indicate, portend, var. of *prōtendere* to extend. See PRO-[1], TEND[1]]
—**Syn.** 1. foretell, forecast, augur, promise, forebode.

port′ engineer′, a person who is responsible for the maintenance and repair of the machinery of the vessels of a shipping line and for the supervision of its engineering personnel. Also called **superintendent engineer.**

por•tent (pôr′tent, pōr′-), *n.* 1. an indication or omen of something about to happen, esp. something momentous. 2. threatening or disquieting significance: *an occurrence of dire portent.* 3. a prodigy or marvel. [1555–65; < L *portentum* sign, token, n. use of neut. of *portentus,* ptp. of *portendere* to PORTEND]
—**Syn.** 1. augury, warning. See **sign.** 2. import.

por•ten•tous (pôr ten′təs, pōr-), *adj.* 1. of the nature of a portent; momentous. 2. ominously significant or indicative: *a portentous defeat.* 3. marvelous; amazing; prodigious. [1530–40; < L *portentōsus.* See PORTENT, -OUS] —**por•ten′tous•ly,** *adv.* —**por•ten′tous•ness,** *n.*
—**Syn.** 1, 2. See **ominous.** 2. unpropitious, inauspicious, threatening.

por•ter[1] (pôr′tər, pōr′-), *n.* 1. a person hired to carry burdens or baggage, as at a railroad station or a hotel. 2. a person who does cleaning and maintenance work in a building, factory, store, etc. 3. an attendant in a railroad parlor car or sleeping car. [1350–1400; ME, var. of *portour* < MF *porteour* < LL *portātōr-* (s. of *portātor*). See PORT[5], -OR[2]]

por•ter[2] (pôr′tər, pōr′-), *n.* 1. a person who has charge of a door or gate; doorkeeper. 2. *Rom. Cath. Ch.* ostiary (def. 1). [1250–1300; ME < AF < LL *portārius* gatekeeper. See PORT[4], -ER[2]]

por•ter[3] (pôr′tər, pōr′-), *n.* a heavy, dark-brown ale made with malt browned by drying at a high temperature. [1720–30; short for *porter's ale,* appar. orig. brewed for porters]

Por•ter (pôr′tər, pōr′-), *n.* 1. **Cole,** 1893–1964, U.S. composer. 2. **David,** 1780–1843, U.S. naval officer. 3. his son, **David Dix•on** (dik′sən), 1813–91, Union naval officer in the Civil War. 4. **Gene** (*Gene Stratton Porter*), 1868–1924, U.S. novelist. 5. **Sir George,** born 1920, British chemist: Nobel prize 1967. 6. **Katherine Anne,** 1890–1980, U.S. writer. 7. **Noah,** 1811–92, U.S. educator, writer, and lexicographer. 8. **Rodney Robert,** 1917–85, British biochemist: Nobel prize for medicine 1972. 9. **William Sydney** ("*O. Henry*"), 1862–1910, U.S. short-story writer. 10. a male given name.

por•ter•age (pôr′tər ij, pōr′-), *n.* 1. the work of a porter or carrier. 2. the charge for such work. [1400–50; late ME; see PORTER[1], -AGE]

por′ter chair′, *Eng. Furniture.* a chair of the 18th century having deep wings continued to form an arch over the seat. Also called **page chair.** [1935–40]

por•ter•ess (pôr′tər is, pōr′-), *n.* portress.
—**Usage.** See **-ess.**

por•ter•house (pôr′tər hous′, pōr′-), *n., pl.* **-hous•es** (-hou′ziz). 1. Also called **por′terhouse steak′.** a choice cut of beef from between the prime ribs and the sirloin. 2. *Archaic.* a house at which porter and other liquors are retailed. [1750–60; PORTER[3] + HOUSE]

Por•ter•ville (pôr′tər vil′, pōr′-), *n.* a town in central California. 19,707.

Port-É•tienne (*Fr.* pôʀ tā tyen′), *n.* former name of **Nouadhibou.**

port•fo•li•o (pôrt fō′lē ō′, pōrt-), *n., pl.* **-li•os.** 1. a flat, portable case for carrying loose papers, drawings, etc. 2. such a case for carrying documents of a government department. 3. the total holdings of the securities, commercial paper, etc., of a financial institution or private investor. 4. the office or post of a minister of state or member of a cabinet. Cf. **minister without portfolio.** [1715–25; < It *portafoglio,* equiv. to *porta-,* s. of *portare* to carry (< L *portāre*) + *foglio* leaf, sheet (< L *folium;* see FOIL[2])]

Port Gen•til (*Fr.* pôʀ zhäN tē′), a seaport in W Gabon. 77,111.

Port′ Har′court (här′kərt, -kôrt, -kōrt), a seaport in S Nigeria. 220,000.

port•hole (pôrt′hōl′, pōrt′-), *n.* 1. a round, window-like opening with a hinged, watertight glass cover in the side of a vessel for admitting air and light. Cf. **port**[4] (def. 1). 2. an opening in a wall, door, etc., as one through which to shoot. [1585–95; PORT[4] + HOLE]

port′hole die′, *Metalworking.* a die having several openings for the extrusion of separate parts of an object later formed by the welding or fusing together of these parts.

Port′ Hud′son, a village in SE Louisiana, on the Mississippi, N of Baton Rouge: siege during the U.S. Civil War 1863.

Port′ Hue•ne′me (wī nē′mē), a city in S California. 17,803.

Port′ Hu′ron, a port in SE Michigan, on the St. Clair River, at the S end of Lake Huron. 33,981.

Por•tia (pôr′shə, -shē ə, pōr′-), *n.* 1. the heroine of Shakespeare's *Merchant of Venice,* who, in one scene, disguises herself as a lawyer. 2. a woman lawyer. 3. a female given name.

por•ti•co (pôr′ti kō′, pōr′-), *n., pl.* **-coes, -cos.** a structure consisting of a roof supported by columns or piers, usually attached to a building as a porch. [1595–1605; < It < L *porticus* porch, portico. See PORT[4]]

portico

por•ti•coed (pôr′ti kōd′, pōr′-), *adj.* provided with a portico or porticoes. [1655–65; PORTICO + -ED[3]]

por•tiere (pôr tyâr′, -tēr′, pōr-, pôr′tē âr′, pōr′-), *n.* a curtain hung in a doorway, either to replace the door or for decoration. Also, **por•tière′.** [1835–45; < F *portière* < ML *portāria,* n. use of fem. of LL *portārius;* see PORTER[2]] —**por•tiered′,** *adj.*

Por•ti•na•ri (pôʀ tē nä′ʀē), *n.* **Cân•di•do** (käN′dē do͝o), 1903–62, Brazilian painter.

port•ing (pôr′ting, pōr′-), *n. Auto., Mach.* the changing of the size, shape, or location of the intake and exhaust ports in an internal-combustion engine, generally to improve performance. [1955–60; PORT[4] + -ING[1]]

por•tion (pôr′shən, pōr′-), *n.* 1. a part of any whole, either separated from or integrated with it: *I read a portion of the manuscript.* 2. an amount of food served for one person; serving; helping: *He took a large portion of spinach.* 3. the part of a whole allotted to or belonging to a person or group; share. 4. the part of an estate that goes to an heir or a next of kin. 5. *Literary.* something that is allotted to a person by God or fate. 6. (esp. formerly) the money, goods, or estate that a woman brings to her husband at marriage; dowry. —*v.t.* 7. to divide into or distribute in portions or shares (often fol. by *out*). 8. to furnish with a portion, as with an inheritance or a dowry: *All of his children have been amply portioned.* 9. to provide with a lot or fate: *She was portioned with sorrow throughout her life.* [1250–1300; ME *porcion* < OF < L *portiōn-* (s. of *portiō*) share, part, akin to *pars* PART] —**por′tion•a•ble,** *adj.* —**por′tion•less,** *adj.*
—**Syn.** 1. section, segment. See **part.** 2. ration. 3. allotment, quota, lot, dividend. 4. inheritance. 5. fortune, lot, destiny, doom. 7. allot, apportion. 8. endow.
—**Ant.** 1. whole.

por•tion-con•trolled (pôr′shən kən trōld′, pōr′-), *adj.* being a standardized portion of food: *The restaurant uses frozen, portion-controlled entrées.*

por•tion•er (pôr′shə nər, pōr′-), *n.* a person who receives or holds a portion, or who divides something into portions. [1545–55; PORTION + -ER[1]]

Port′ Jack′son, an inlet of the Pacific in SE Australia: the harbor of Sydney.

Port•land (pôrt′lənd, pōrt′-), *n.* 1. a seaport in NW Oregon, at the confluence of the Willamette and Columbia rivers. 366,383. 2. a seaport in SW Maine, on Casco Bay. 61,572. 3. a town in S Texas. 12,023.

Port′land cement′, a type of hydraulic cement usually made by burning a mixture of limestone and clay in a kiln. Also, **port′land cement′.** [1815–25; named after the Isle of *Portland,* Dorsetshire, England]

Port′ La•vac′a (lə vak′ə), a town in S Texas. 10,911.

Port′ Lou′is (lo͞o′is, lo͞o′ē), a seaport in and the capital of Mauritius, in the Indian Ocean, E of Madagascar. 136,000.

port•ly (pôrt′lē, pōrt′-), *adj.,* **-li•er, -li•est.** 1. rather heavy or fat; stout; corpulent. 2. *Archaic.* stately, dignified, or imposing. [1520–30; PORT[5] (n.) + -LY] —**port′li•ness,** *n.*

port•man•teau (pôrt man′tō, pōrt-; pôrt′man tō′, pōrt′-), *n., pl.* **-teaus, -teaux** (-tōz, -tō, -tōz′, -tō′). *Chiefly Brit.* a case or bag to carry clothing in while traveling, esp. a leather trunk or suitcase that opens into

CONCISE PRONUNCIATION KEY: *act, cāpe, dâre, pärt; set, ēqual; if, īce; ox, ōver, ôrder, oil, bo͝ok, bo͞ot, out; up, ûrge; child; sing; shoe; thin, that;* zh as in *treasure.* ə = *a* as in *alone, e* as in *system, i* as in *easily, o* as in *gallop, u* as in *circus;* ᵊ as in *fire* (fīᵊr), *hour* (ouᵊr). l and n can serve as syllabic consonants, as in *cradle* (krād′l), and *button* (but′n). See the full key inside the front cover.

two halves. [1575–85; < F *portemanteau* lit., (it) carries (the) cloak; see PORT⁵, MANTLE]

portman′teau word′, blend (def. 9). [1880–85]

Port′ Moo′dy, a city in SW British Columbia, in SW Canada, E of Vancouver, on an inlet of the Strait of Georgia. 14,917.

Port′ Mores′by (môrz′bē, mōrz′-), a seaport in and the capital of Papua New Guinea: important Allied base in World War II. 76,507.

Port′ Nech′es (nech′iz), a town in SE Texas. 13,944.

Pôr·to (pôr′to͞o), *n.* Portuguese name of **Oporto.**

Pôr·to A·le·gre (pôʀ′to͞o ä le′gʀə), a seaport in S Brazil. 1,158,709.

Pôr·to A·mé·lia (*Port.* pôʀ′to͞o ə me′lyə), former name of **Pemba** (def. 2).

Por·to·bel·lo (pôr′tō bel′ō, pōr′-), *n.* a small seaport on the Caribbean coast of Panama, NE of Colón: harbor discovered and named by Columbus 1502; a principal city of Spanish colonial America.

port′ of call′, a port visited briefly by a ship, usually to take on or discharge passengers and cargo or to undergo repairs. [1880–85]

port′ of en′try, port¹ (def. 3). [1830–40]

Por·to·fi·no (pôr′tə fē′nō, pōr′-; *It.* pôr′tô fē′nô), *n.* a village in NW Italy, SE of Genoa: tourist resort. 923.

Port-of-Spain (pôrt′əv spān′, pōrt′-), *n.* a seaport on NW Trinidad, in the SE West Indies: the national capital of Trinidad and Tobago. 67,867.

por·to·la·no (pôr′tl ä′nō, pōr′-), *n., pl.* **-nos, -ni** (-nē). a descriptive atlas of the Middle Ages, giving sailing directions and providing charts showing rhumb lines and the location of ports and various coastal features. Also called **rutter.** [1855–60; < It: shipmaster's guidebook; earlier, harbor master < ML *portulānus.* See PORT¹, -ULE, -AN]

Por·to No·vo (pôr′tō nō′vō, pōr′-), a seaport in and the capital of Benin. 120,000.

Port′ Or′ange, a city in E Florida. 18,756.

Port′ Or′ford ce′dar (ôr′fərd), **1.** a tall tree, *Chamaecyparis lawsoniana,* of coastal Oregon, having flattened, scalelike foliage and wood highly valued as timber. **2.** the fragrant wood of this tree. Also called **Lawson cypress, Oregon cedar.** [1870–75, *Amer.*; named after *Port Orford,* Oregon]

Por·to Ri·co (pôr′tə rē′kō, pōr′-), former official name (until 1932) of **Puerto Rico.** —**Por′to Ri′can.**

Pôr·to Ve·lho (pôr′to͞o ve′lyo͞o), a city in and the capital of Rondônia, in W Brazil, on the Madeira River. 83,178.

Port′ Phil′lip Bay′, a bay in SE Australia: the harbor of Melbourne. 31 mi. (50 km) long; 25 mi. (40 km) wide.

Port′ Pir′ie (pir′ē), a city in S Australia. 14,695.

por·trait (pôr′trit, -trāt, pōr′-), *n.* **1.** a likeness of a person, esp. of the face, as a painting, drawing, or photograph: *a gallery of family portraits.* **2.** a verbal picture or description, usually of a person: *a biography that provides a fascinating portrait of an 18th-century rogue.* [1560–70; < MF: a drawing, image, etc., n. use of ptp. of *portraire* to PORTRAY] —**por′trait·like′,** *adj.*

por′trait flask′, a glass flask of the 19th century having a portrait molded onto the side.

por·trait·ist (pôr′tri tist, -trā-, pōr′-), *n.* a person who makes portraits. [1865–70; PORTRAIT + -IST]

por′trait lens′, *Photog.* a lens of moderately long focal length that is used, esp. in portrait photography, to produce soft-focus images. [1860–65]

Por′trait of a La′dy, The, a novel (1881) by Henry James.

Por′trait of the Art′ist as a Young′ Man′, a novel (1916) by James Joyce.

por·trai·ture (pôr′tri chər, pōr′-), *n.* **1.** the art or an instance of making portraits. **2.** a pictorial representation; portrait. **3.** a verbal picture. [1325–75; ME < MF; see PORTRAIT, -URE]

por·tray (pôr trā′, pōr-), *v.t.* **1.** to make a likeness of by drawing, painting, carving, or the like. **2.** to depict in words; describe graphically. **3.** to represent dramatically, as on the stage: *He portrayed Napoleon in the play.* [1300–50; ME *portrayen* < MF *portraire* < LL *prōtrahere* to depict, L: to draw forth, equiv. to *prō-* PRO-¹ + *trahere* to draw] —**por·tray′a·ble,** *adj.* —**por·tray′er,** *n.*
—**Syn. 1, 2.** picture, delineate, limn. See **depict.**

por·tray·al (pôr trā′əl, pōr-), *n.* **1.** the act of portraying. **2.** a portrait. [1840–50; PORTRAY + -AL²]

por·tress (pôr′tris, pōr′-), *n.* a woman who has charge of a door or gate; a female doorkeeper. Also, **porteress.** [1375–1425; late ME; see PORTER², -ESS]
—**Usage.** See **-ess.**

Port′ Roy′al, 1. a village in S South Carolina, on Port Royal island: colonized by French Huguenots 1562. 2977. **2.** a historic town on SE Jamaica at the entrance to Kingston harbor: a former capital of Jamaica. **3.** former name of **Annapolis Royal.**

Port′ Sa·id′ (sä ēd′), a seaport in NE Egypt at the Mediterranean end of the Suez Canal. 310,000. Also, **Port′ Sa·ïd′.**

Port-Sa·lut (pôr′sə lo͞o′, pōr′-; *Fr.* pôʀ sa lʏ′), *n.* a yellow, whole-milk cheese, esp. that made at the monastery of Port du Salut near the town of Laval, France.

CONCISE ETYMOLOGY KEY: <, descended or borrowed from; >, whence; b., blend of, blended; c., cognate with; cf., compare; deriv., derivative; equiv., equivalent; imit., imitative; obl., oblique; r., replacing; s., stem; sp., spelling, spelled; resp., respelling, respelled; trans., translation; ?, origin unknown; *, unattested; ‡, probably earlier than. See the full key inside the front cover.

Ports·mouth (pôrts′məth, pōrts′-), *n.* **1.** a seaport in S Hampshire, in S England, on the English Channel: chief British naval station. 200,900. **2.** a seaport in SE Virginia: navy yard. 104,577. **3.** a seaport in SE New Hampshire: naval base; Russian-Japanese peace treaty 1905. 26,254. **4.** a city in S Ohio, on the Ohio River. 25,943. **5.** a town in SE Rhode Island. 14,257.

Port St. Lu·cie (lo͞o′sē), a town in E Florida. 14,690.

Port′ Sudan′, a seaport in the NE Sudan, on the Red Sea. 123,000.

port′ superinten′dent. See **marine superintendent.**

Por·tu·gal (pôr′chə gəl, pōr′-; *Port.* pôʀ′to͞o gäl′), *n.* a republic in SW Europe, on the Iberian Peninsula, W of Spain. (Including the Azores and the Madeira Islands) 9,448,800; 35,414 sq. mi. (91,720 sq. km). *Cap.:* Lisbon.

Por·tu·guese (pôr′chə gēz′, -gēs′, pōr′-; pôr′chə gēz′, -gēs′, pōr′-), *adj., n., pl.* **-guese.** —*adj.* **1.** of, pertaining to, or characteristic of Portugal, its inhabitants, or their language. —*n.* **2.** a native or inhabitant of Portugal. **3.** a Romance language spoken in Portugal, Brazil, and a few countries of Africa. *Abbr.:* Pg, Pg. [1580–90; < Pg *português,* Sp *portugués;* see PORTUGAL, -ESE]

Por′tuguese East′ Af′rica, former name of **Mozambique** (def. 1).

Por′tuguese Guin′ea, former name of **Guinea-Bissau.**

Por′tuguese In′dia, a former Portuguese overseas territory on the W coast of India, consisting of the districts of Gôa, Daman, and Diu: annexed by India December 1961. *Cap.:* Gôa.

Por′tuguese man-of-war′, any of several large, oceanic hydrozoans of the genus *Physalia,* having a large, bladderlike structure with a saillike crest by which they are buoyed up and from which dangle tentacles with stinging cells. [1700–10]

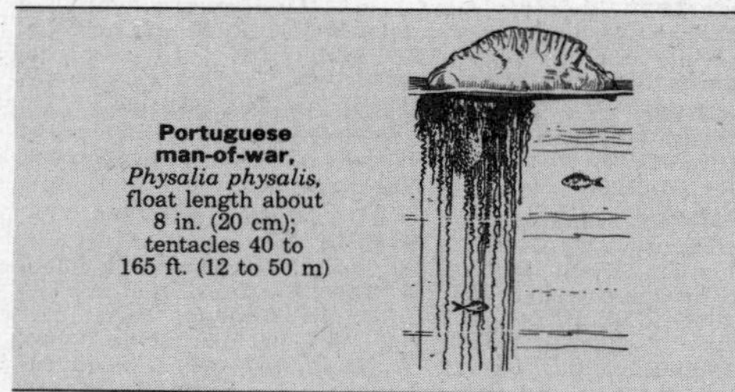
Portuguese man-of-war, *Physalia physalis,* float length about 8 in. (20 cm); tentacles 40 to 165 ft. (12 to 50 m)

Por′tuguese wa′ter dog′, one of a breed of medium-sized dogs originally developed to assist Portuguese fishermen and having a profuse black or brown coat with or without white markings and webbed feet.

Por′tuguese West′ Af′rica, former name of **Angola** (def. 1).

por·tu·lac·a (pôr′chə lak′ə, pōr′-), *n.* any of various fleshy-leaved plants of the genus *Portulaca,* esp. *P. grandiflora,* widely cultivated for its showy, variously colored flowers. [1540–50; < NL, genus name, L: PURSLANE]

por·tu·la·ca·ceous (pôr′chə lə kā′shəs, pōr′-), *adj.* belonging to the Portulacaceae, the purslane family of plants. Cf. **purslane family.** [< NL *Portulacac(ae)* family name (see PORTULACA, -ACEAE) + -OUS]

Port′ Wash′ington, a town on NW Long Island, in SE New York. 14,521.

port′-wine′ stain′ (pôrt′wīn′, pōrt′-), a large birthmark of purplish color, usually on the face or neck. [1885–90]

pos., 1. position. **2.** positive. **3.** possession. **4.** possessive.

P.O.S., point-of-sale; point-of-sales. Also, **POS**

po·sa·da (pō sä′də; *Sp.* pô sä′thä), *n., pl.* **-das** (-dəz; *Sp.* -thäs). *n.* (in some Spanish-speaking countries) a government-operated or -approved inn offering moderately priced rooms to tourists, esp. in a historic area. [1755–65; < Sp: inn, lodging, dwelling, equiv. to *pos(ar)* to lodge, rest (< LL *pausāre;* see POSE¹) + *-ada,* fem. of *-ado* -ATE¹]

Po·sa·das (pô sä′thäs), *n.* a city in NE Argentina, on the Paraná River. 97,514.

pose¹ (pōz), *v.,* **posed, pos·ing,** *n.* —*v.i.* **1.** to assume a particular attitude or stance, esp. with the hope of impressing others: *He likes to pose as an authority on literature.* **2.** to present oneself insincerely: *He seems to be posing in all his behavior.* **3.** to assume or hold a physical attitude, as for an artistic purpose: *to pose for a painter.* —*v.t.* **4.** to place in a suitable position or attitude for a picture, tableau, or the like: *to pose a group for a photograph.* **5.** to assert, state, or put forward: *That poses a difficult problem.* **6.** to put or place. —*n.* **7.** a bodily attitude or posture: *Her pose had a note of defiance in it.* **8.** a mental attitude or posture: *a pose cultivated by the upper classes.* **9.** the act or period of posing, as for a picture. **10.** a position or attitude assumed in posing, or exhibited by a figure in a picture, sculptural work, tableau, or the like. **11.** a moment in which a dancer remains motionless, usually in an assumed posture. **12.** a studied attitude; affectation: *His liberalism is merely a pose.* [1325–75; (v.) ME *posen* < MF *poser* < LL *pausāre* to stop, cease, rest, deriv. of L *pausa* PAUSE; F *poser* has taken over the basic sense of L *pōnere* "to put, place" and represents it in F borrowings of its prefixed derivatives (see COMPOSE, DEPOSE, etc.), prob. reinforced by the accidental resemblance of *poser* to *positum,* ptp. of *pōnere;* (n.) deriv. of the v.] —**pos′·ing·ly,** *adv.*
—**Syn. 3.** sit, model. **7.** See **position.**

pose² (pōz), *v.t.,* **posed, pos·ing. 1.** to embarrass or baffle, as by a difficult question or problem. **2.** *Obs.* to examine by putting questions. [1520–30; aph. var. of obs. *appose,* var. of OPPOSE, used in sense of L *appōnere* to put to]

po·sé (pō zā′; *Fr.* pô zā′), *n., pl.* **-sés** (-zāz′; *Fr.* -zā′). *Ballet.* a movement in which the dancer steps, in any desired position, from one foot to the other with a straight knee onto the flat foot, demi-pointe, or pointe. [1925–30; < F: poised, ptp. of *poser* to pose; see POSE¹]

Po·sei·don (pō sīd′n, pə-), *n.* **1.** the ancient Greek god of the sea, with the power to cause earthquakes, identified by the Romans with Neptune. **2.** *Mil.* a 34-foot (10-m), submarine-launched U.S. ballistic missile with up to 10 warheads and a range of 2800 miles (4502 km).

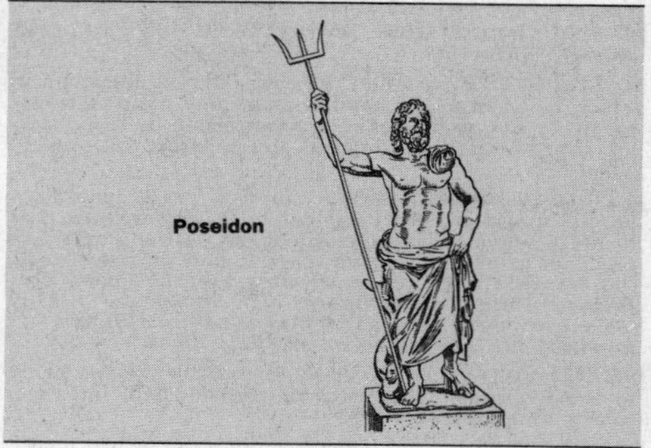
Poseidon

Po·sen (pō′zən), *n.* German name of **Poznań.**

pos·er¹ (pō′zər), *n.* a person who poses. [1885–90; POSE¹ + -ER¹]

pos·er² (pō′zər), *n.* a question or problem that is puzzling or confusing. [1580–90; POSE² + -ER¹]

po·seur (pō zûr′; *Fr.* pô zœʀ′), *n., pl.* **-seurs** (-zûrz′; *Fr.* -zœʀ′). a person who attempts to impress others by assuming or affecting a manner, degree of elegance, sentiment, etc., other than his or her true one. [1880–85; < F; see POSE¹, -EUR]

posh¹ (posh), *adj.* sumptuously furnished or appointed; luxurious: *a posh apartment.* [1915–20; of obscure orig.; cf. *posh* a dandy (recorded as British slang in 1890); the popular notion that the word is an acronym from *port out(ward), starboard home,* said to be the preferred accommodation on ships traveling between England and India, is without foundation]

posh² (posh), *interj.* (used as an exclamation of contempt or disgust.) [1920–25]

pos′i·grade rock′et (poz′i grād′), *Rocketry.* an auxiliary rocket used to separate the sections of a multistage rocket, fired in the direction of flight. [1960–65; POSI(TIVE) + -GRADE (perh. modeled on *retrograde*)]

pos·it (poz′it), *v.t.* **1.** to place, put, or set. **2.** to lay down or assume as a fact or principle; postulate. —*n.* **3.** something that is posited; an assumption; postulate. [1640–50; < L *positus,* ptp. of *pōnere* to place, put]

po·si·tion (pə zish′ən), *n.* **1.** condition with reference to place; location; situation. **2.** a place occupied or to be occupied; site: *a fortified position.* **3.** the proper, appropriate, or usual place: *out of position.* **4.** situation or condition, esp. with relation to favorable or unfavorable circumstances: *to be in an awkward position; to bargain from a position of strength.* **5.** status or standing: *He has a position to maintain in the community.* **6.** high standing, as in society; important status: *a person of wealth and position.* **7.** a post of employment: *a position in a bank.* **8.** manner of being placed, disposed, or arranged: *the relative position of the hands of a clock.* **9.** bodily posture or attitude: *to be in a sitting position.* **10.** mental attitude; stand: *one's position on a controversial topic.* **11.** the act of positing. **12.** something that is posited. **13.** *Ballet.* any of the five basic positions of the feet with which every step or movement begins and ends. Cf. **first position, second position, third position,**

fourth position, fifth position. 14. *Music.* **a.** the arrangement of tones in a chord, esp. with regard to the location of the root tone in a triad or to the distance of the tones from each other. Cf. **close position, inversion** (def. 8a), **open position, root position. b.** any of the places on the fingerboard of a stringed instrument where the fingers stop the strings to produce the various pitches. **c.** any of the places to which the slide of a trombone is shifted to produce changes in pitch. **15.** *Finance.* a commitment to buy or sell securities: *He took a large position in defense stocks.* **16.** *Class. Pros.* the situation of a short vowel before two or more consonants or their equivalent, making the syllable metrically long. —*v.t.* **17.** to put in a particular or appropriate position; place. **18.** to determine the position of; locate. [1325–75; ME *posicioun* a positing (< AF) < L *positiōn-* (s. of *positiō*) a placing, etc. See POSIT, -ION] **—po·si′tion·al,** *adj.* **—po·si′tion·less,** *adj.*
—Syn. 2. station, locality, spot. **5.** rank. **7.** POSITION, JOB, PLACE, SITUATION refer to a post of employment. POSITION is any employment, though usually above manual labor: *a position as clerk.* JOB is colloquial for POSITION, and applies to any work from lowest to highest in an organization: *a job as cook, as manager.* PLACE and SITUATION are both mainly used today in reference to a position that is desired or being applied for; SITUATION is the general word in the business world: *Situations Wanted;* PLACE is used rather of domestic employment: *He is looking for a place as a gardener.* **8.** placement, disposition, array, arrangement. **9.** POSITION, POSTURE, ATTITUDE, POSE refer to an arrangement or disposal of the body or its parts. POSITION is the general word for the arrangement of the body: *in a reclining position.* POSTURE is usually an assumed arrangement of the body, esp. when standing: *a relaxed posture.* ATTITUDE is often a posture assumed for imitative effect or the like, but may be one adopted for a purpose (as that of a fencer or a tightrope walker): *an attitude of prayer.* A POSE is an attitude assumed, in most cases, for artistic effect: *an attractive pose.* **12.** proposition, hypothesis, postulate, thesis; dictum, assertion, predication, contention; doctrine, principle. **17.** situate.

posi′tional astron′omy, astrometry.

posi′tional nota′tion, a type of numeration in which the position of a digit affects its value. [1940–45]

posi′tion effect′, *Genetics.* the alteration in the expression of a gene or genetic region due to its relocation within the genome as a result of inversion or translocation. [1925–30]

po·si·tion·er (pə zish′ə nər), *n.* **1.** a person or thing that positions. **2.** *Orthodontics.* a removable device of resilient plastic material worn in the mouth usually during sleep to produce minor adjustments in the position of teeth after straightening appliances have been taken off. [1930–35; POSITION + -ER[1]]

posi′tion i′somer, *Chem.* any of two or more isomers that differ only in the position occupied by a substituent.

posi′tion line′, *Navig.* See **line of position.** [1860–65]

posi′tion pa′per, a formal, usually detailed written statement, esp. regarding a single issue, that articulates a position, viewpoint, or policy, as of a government, organization, or political candidate. [1945–50]

pos·i·tive (poz′i tiv), *adj.* **1.** explicitly stated, stipulated, or expressed: *a positive acceptance of the agreement.* **2.** admitting of no question: *positive proof.* **3.** stated; express; emphatic: *a positive denial.* **4.** confident in opinion or assertion; fully assured: *He is positive that he will win the contest.* **5.** overconfident or dogmatic: *The less he knows, the more positive he gets.* **6.** without relation to or comparison with other things; not relative or comparative; absolute. **7.** *Informal.* downright; out-and-out: *She's a positive genius.* **8.** determined by enactment or convention; arbitrarily laid down: *positive law.* **9.** emphasizing what is laudable, hopeful, or to the good; constructive: *a positive attitude toward the future; positive things to say about a painting.* **10.** not speculative or theoretical; practical: *a positive approach to the problem.* **11.** possessing an actual force, being, existence, etc. **12.** *Philos.* **a.** constructive and sure, rather than skeptical. **b.** concerned with or based on matters of experience: *positive philosophy.* **13.** showing or expressing approval or agreement; favorable: *a positive reaction to the speech.* **14.** consisting in or characterized by the presence or possession of distinguishing or marked qualities or features (opposed to *negative*): *Light is positive, darkness negative.* **15.** noting the presence of such qualities, as a term. **16.** measured or proceeding in a direction assumed as beneficial, progressive, or auspicious: *a positive upturn in the stock market.* **17.** *Elect.* **a.** of, pertaining to, or characterized by positive electricity. **b.** indicating a point in a circuit that has a higher potential than that of another point, the current flowing from the point of higher potential to the point of lower potential. **18.** of, pertaining to, or noting the north pole of a magnet. **19.** *Chem.* (of an element or group) tending to lose electrons and become positively charged; basic. **20.** *Gram.* being, noting, or pertaining to the initial degree of the comparison of adjectives and adverbs, as the positive form *good.* Cf. **comparative** (def. 4), **superlative** (def. 2). **21.** *Med.* **a.** (of blood, affected tissue, etc.) showing the presence of disease. **b.** (of a diagnostic test) indicating disease. **22.** *Biochem.* See **Rh factor. 23.** *Math.* noting a quantity greater than zero. **24.** (of government) assuming control or regulation of activities beyond those involved merely with the maintenance of law and order. **25.** *Biol.* oriented or moving toward the focus of excitation: *a positive tropism.* **26.** *Photog.* denoting a print or transparency showing the brightness values as they are in the subject. **27.** *Mach.* noting or pertaining to a process or machine part having a fixed or certain operation, esp. as the result of elimination of play, free motion, etc.: *positive lubrication.* —*n.* **28.** something positive. **29.** a positive quality or characteristic. **30.** a positive quantity or symbol. **31.** *Gram.* **a.** the positive degree. **b.** a form in the positive, as *good* or *smooth.* **32.** *Photog.* a positive image, as on a print or transparency. [1250–1300; < L *positīvus;* r. ME *positif* < MF < L, as above. See POSIT, -IVE] **—pos′i·tive·ness,** *n.*
—Syn. 1. definite, unequivocal, categorical, clear, precise, sure. **2.** incontrovertible, indisputable. **4.** unquestioning. **4, 5.** See **sure. —Ant. 1.** indefinite. **2.** doubtful. **4.** unsure, unconfident, uncertain.

pos′itive cas′ter, *Auto.* See under **caster** (def. 6).

pos′itive col′umn, *Physics.* the luminous region between the Faraday dark space and the anode glow in a vacuum tube, occurring when the pressure is low.

pos′itive crank′case ventila′tion, *Auto.* a means of reducing air pollution by directing the fumes from the crankcase of an engine into the intake manifold, so that they will be channeled into the cylinders and burned. *Abbr.:* PCV

pos′itive def′inite, *Math.* **1.** (of a quadratic form) positive for all real values of the variables, where the values are not all zero. **2.** (of a matrix) displaying the coefficients of a positive definite quadratic form. [1905–10] **—pos′itive def′initeness.**

pos′itive electric′ity, *Elect.* the electricity present in a body or substance that has a deficiency of electrons, as the electricity developed on glass when rubbed with silk. Cf. **negative electricity.**

pos′itive elec′tron, *Physics.* positron. [1895–1900]

pos′itive eugen′ics. See under **eugenics.** [1905–10]

pos′itive feed′back, *Electronics.* See under **feedback** (def. 1).

pos′itive i′on, *Physics, Chem.* See under **ion** (def. 1).

pos′itive law′, customary law or law enacted by governmental authority (as distinguished from *natural law*). [1350–1400; ME]

pos′itive lens′, *Optics.* See **converging lens.**

pos·i·tive·ly (poz′i tiv lē *or, esp. for 3,* poz′i tiv′lē), *adv.* **1.** with certainty; absolutely: *The statement is positively true.* **2.** decidedly; unquestionably; definitely: *His conduct is positively shocking.* —*interj.* **3.** (used to express strong affirmation) yes: *Do you plan to go to the party? Positively!* [1585–95; POSITIVE + -LY]

pos′itive or′gan, 1. a small pipe organ of the Middle Ages. **2.** a section of a pipe organ having mostly flue stops. [1720–30]

pos′itive ray′, *Physics.* a stream of positive ions traveling from a metallic anode to the cathode in a gas-discharge tube. Also called **anode ray, canal ray.** [1900–05]

pos·i·tiv·ism (poz′i tə viz′əm), *n.* **1.** the state or quality of being positive; definiteness; assurance. **2.** a philosophical system founded by Auguste Comte, concerned with positive facts and phenomena, and excluding speculation upon ultimate causes or origins. [1850–55; POSITIVE + -ISM] **—pos′i·tiv·ist,** *adj., n.* **—pos′i·tiv·is′tic,** *adj.* **—pos′i·tiv·is′ti·cal·ly,** *adv.*

pos·i·tiv·i·ty (poz′i tiv′i tē), *n., pl.* **-ties. 1.** the state or character of being positive: a positivity that accepts the world as it is. **2.** something positive. [1650–60; POSITIVE + -ITY]

pos·i·tron (poz′i tron′), *n. Physics.* an elementary particle having the same mass and spin as an electron but having a positive charge equal in magnitude to that of the electron's negative charge; the antiparticle of the electron. Also called **antielectron, positive electron.** [1930–35; POSI(TIVE) + (ELEC)TRON]

pos′itron emis′sion tomog′raphy, the process of producing a PET scan. Cf. **PET scanner.**

pos·i·tro·ni·um (poz′i trō′nē əm), *n. Physics.* a short-lived atomic system consisting of a positron and an electron bound together. [1945; POSITRON + -IUM, coined by A. E. Ruark (b. 1899), U.S. physicist]

po·so·le (pō sō′lā, po-; *Sp.* pô sô′le), *n. Mexican Cookery.* a thick, stewlike soup of pork or chicken, hominy, mild chili peppers, and coriander leaves: traditionally served at Christmas and often favored as a hangover remedy. [< MexSp *posole, pozole* < Nahuatl *pozolli*]

po·sol·o·gy (pə sol′ə jē, pō-), *n.* the branch of pharmacology dealing with the determination of dosage. [1805–15; < Gk *póso(s)* how much + -LOGY] **—pos·o·log·ic** (pos′ə loj′ik), **pos′o·log′i·cal,** *adj.* **—po·sol′o·gist,** *n.*

poss., 1. possession. **2.** possessive. **3.** possible. **4.** possibly.

pos·se (pos′ē), *n.* **1.** See **posse comitatus. 2.** a body or force armed with legal authority. [1575–85; < ML *posse* power, force, n. use of L inf.: to be able, have power, equiv. to *pot-* (see POTENT) + *-se* inf. suffix]

pos·se co·mi·ta·tus (pos′ē kom′i tä′təs, -tā′-), **1.** the body of persons that a peace officer of a county is empowered to call upon for assistance in preserving the peace, making arrests, and serving writs. **2.** a body of persons so called into service. [1620–30; < ML: posse of the county]

pos·sess (pə zes′), *v.t.* **1.** to have as belonging to one; have as property; own: *to possess a house and a car.* **2.** to have as a faculty, quality, or the like: *to possess courage.* **3.** (of a spirit, esp. an evil one) to occupy, dominate, or control (a person) from within: *He thought he was possessed by devils.* **4.** (of a feeling, idea, etc.) to dominate or actuate in the manner of such a spirit: *He was possessed by envy.* **5.** (of a man) to succeed in having sexual intercourse with. **6.** to have knowledge of: *to possess a language.* **7.** to keep or maintain (oneself, one's mind, etc.) in a certain state, as of peace, patience, etc. **8.** to maintain control over (oneself, one's mind, etc.). **9.** to impart to; inform; familiarize (often fol. by *of* or *with*): *to possess someone of the facts of the case.* **10.** to cause to be dominated or influenced, as by an idea, feeling, etc. **11.** to make (someone) owner, holder, or master, as of property, information, etc.: *He possessed them of the facts.* **12.** to seize or take. **13.** to gain or win. **14.** to occupy or hold. [1425–75; late ME *possesen* < MF *possess(i)er,* n. deriv. of *possession* POSSESSION] **—pos·ses′sor,** *n.* **—pos·ses′sor·ship′,** *n.*
—Syn. 1. See **have.**

pos·sessed (pə zest′), *adj.* **1.** spurred or moved by a strong feeling, madness, or a supernatural power (often fol. by *by, of,* or *with*): *The army fought as if possessed. The village believed her to be possessed of the devil.* **2.** self-possessed; poised. **3. possessed of,** having; possessing: *He is possessed of intelligence and ambition.* [1525–35; POSSESS + -ED[2]] **—pos·sess·ed·ly** (pə zes′id lē, -zest′lē), *adv.* **—pos·sess′ed·ness,** *n.*

Possessed, The, a novel (1871) by Dostoevsky.

pos·ses·sion (pə zesh′ən), *n.* **1.** the act or fact of possessing. **2.** the state of being possessed. **3.** ownership. **4.** *Law.* actual holding or occupancy, either with or without rights of ownership. **5.** a thing possessed: *He packed all his possessions into one trunk.* **6. possessions,** property or wealth. **7.** a territorial dominion of a state. **8.** *Sports.* **a.** physical control of the ball or puck by a player or team: *He didn't have full possession when he was tackled.* **b.** the right of a team to put the ball into play: *They had possession after the other team sank a free throw.* **9.** control over oneself, one's mind, etc. **10.** domination, actuation, or obsession by a feeling, idea, etc. **11.** the feeling or idea itself. [1300–50; ME < L *possessiōn-* (s. of *possessiō*) occupancy, act of occupying, equiv. to *possess(us),* ptp. of *possidēre* to have in one's control, occupy (and, in active sense, ptp. of *posīdere* to seize upon) (**pots-,* akin to *posse* to be able + *-sidēre,* comb. form of *sedēre* to SIT[1]; cf. HOST[1]) + *-iōn-* -ION]
—Syn. 1. tenure, occupation. **1, 3.** See **custody.**

pos·ses·sive (pə zes′iv), *adj.* **1.** jealously opposed to the personal independence of, or to any influence other than one's own upon, a child, spouse, etc. **2.** desirous of possessing, esp. excessively so: *Young children are so possessive they will not allow others to play with their toys; a possessive lover.* **3.** of or pertaining to possession or ownership. **4.** *Gram.* **a.** indicating possession, ownership, origin, etc. *His* in *his book* is a possessive adjective. *His* in *The book is his* is a possessive pronoun. **b.** noting or pertaining to a case that indicates possession, ownership, origin, etc., as, in English, *John's* in *John's hat.* —*n. Gram.* **5.** the possessive case. **6.** a form in the possessive. [1520–30; < L *possessīvus.* See POSSESS, -IVE] **—pos·ses′sive·ly,** *adv.* **—pos·ses′sive·ness,** *n.*

pos·ses·so·ry (pə zes′ə rē), *adj.* **1.** of or pertaining to a possessor or to possession. **2.** arising from possession: *a possessory interest.* **3.** having possession. [1375–1425; late ME < LL *possessōrius,* equiv. to L *possed-,* s. of *possidēre* to possess (see POSSESSION) + *-tōrius* -TORY[1], with *dt* > *ss*] **—pos·ses′so·ri·ness,** *n.*

pos·set (pos′it), *n.* a drink made of hot milk curdled with ale, wine, or the like, often sweetened and spiced. [1400–50; late ME *poshote, possot* < ?]

pos·si·bil·i·ty (pos′ə bil′i tē), *n., pl.* **-ties** for 2. **1.** the state or fact of being possible: *the possibility of error.* **2.** something possible: *He had exhausted every possibility but one.* [1325–75; ME *possibilite* < LL *possibilitās.* See POSSIBLE, -ITY]
—Syn. 1. chance, prospect, likelihood, odds.

pos·si·ble (pos′ə bəl), *adj.* **1.** that may or can be, exist, happen, be done, be used, etc.: *a disease with no possible cure.* **2.** that may be true or may be the case, as something concerning which one has no knowledge to the contrary: *It is possible that he has already gone.* [1300–50; ME < L *possibilis* that may be done, equiv. to *poss(e)* to be able (see POSSE) + *-ibilis* -IBLE]
—Syn. 1. POSSIBLE, FEASIBLE, PRACTICABLE refer to that which may come about or take place without prevention by serious obstacles. That which is POSSIBLE is naturally able or even likely to happen, other circumstances being equal: *Discovery of a new source of plutonium may be possible.* FEASIBLE refers to the ease with which something can be done and implies a high degree of desirability for doing it: *This plan is the most feasible.* PRACTICABLE applies to that which can be done with the means that are at hand and with conditions as they are: *We ascended the slope as far as was practicable.*

pos·si·bly (pos′ə blē), *adv.* **1.** perhaps; maybe: *It may possibly rain today.* **2.** in a possible manner: *She has all the money she can possibly use.* **3.** by any possibility: *Could you possibly check this information for me?* [1350–1400; ME; see POSSIBLE, -LY]

pos·sie (pos′ē), *n. Australian.* a job; position. Also, **possy.** [1915–20; shortening and alter. of POSITION]

POSSLQ (pos′əl kyo͞o′), *n., pl.* **POSSLQs, POSSLQ's.** either of two persons, one of each sex, who share living quarters but are not related by blood, marriage, or adoption: a categorization used by the U.S. Census Bureau. [*p(erson of the) o(pposite) s(ex) s(haring) l(iving) q(uarters)*]

pos·sum (pos′əm), *n.* **1.** opossum. **2. play possum,** *Informal.* **a.** to feign sleep or death. **b.** to dissemble or pretend ignorance: *The baseball broke the window, but the children played possum when asked who had thrown it.* **3.** *Australian.* any of various phalangers, esp. of the genus *Trichosurus.* [1605–15, *Amer.;* short for OPOSSUM]

pos′sum haw′, a shrub, *Ilex decidua,* of the southeastern U.S., having leaves that are hairy on the upper surface and glossy, red fruit. Also called **bearberry.** [1855–60, *Amer.*]

pos·sy (pos′ē), *n., pl.* **-sies.** *Australian.* possie.

post[1] (pōst), *n.* **1.** a strong piece of timber, metal, or the like, set upright as a support, a point of attachment, a place for displaying notices, etc. **2.** *Furniture.* one of the principal uprights of a piece of furniture, as one supporting a chair back or forming one corner of a chest of drawers. Cf. **stump** (def. 11). **3.** *Papermaking.* a stack of 144 sheets of handmolded paper, interleaved with felt. **4.** *Horse Racing.* a pole on a racetrack indicating the point where a race begins or ends: *the starting post.* **5.** the lane of a racetrack farthest from the infield; the out-

CONCISE PRONUNCIATION KEY: act, cāpe, dâre, pärt; set, ēqual; if, ice; ox, ōver, ôrder, oil, bo͝ok, bo͞ot, out; up, ûrge; child; sing; shoe; thin, *that;* zh as in *treasure.* ə = *a* as in *alone, e* as in *system, i* as in *easily, o* as in *gallop, u* as in *circus;* ᵊ as in *fire* (fīᵊr), *hour* (ouᵊr). l and n can serve as syllabic consonants, as in *cradle* (krād′l), and *button* (but′n). See the full key inside the front cover.

side lane. Cf. **pole**[1] (def. 4). —*v.t.* **6.** to affix (a notice, bulletin, etc.) to a post, wall, or the like. **7.** to bring to public notice by or as by a poster or bill: *to post a reward.* **8.** to denounce by a public notice or declaration: *They were posted as spies.* **9.** to publish the name of in a list: *to post a student on the dean's list.* **10.** to publish the name of (a ship) as missing or lost. **11.** to placard (a wall, fence, etc.) with notices, bulletins, etc.: *The wall was posted with announcements.* **12.** to put up signs on (land or other property) forbidding trespassing:: *The estate has been posted by the owner.* [bef. 1000; ME, OE < L *postis* a post, doorpost, whence also D, LG *post,* G *Pfosten*] —**post′less,** *adv.* —**post′like′,** *adj.*

—**Syn. 1.** column, pillar, pile, pole. **6.** announce, advertise, publicize.

post[2] (pōst), *n.* **1.** a position of duty, employment, or trust to which one is assigned or appointed: *a diplomatic post.* **2.** the station or rounds of a person on duty, as a soldier, sentry or nurse. **3.** a military station with permanent buildings. **4.** a local unit of a veterans' organization. **5.** See **trading post. 6.** a place in the stock exchange where a particular stock is traded. **7.** (in the British military services) either of two bugle calls (**first post** and **last post**) giving notice of the time to retire for the night, similar in purpose to the U.S. taps. **8.** the body of troops occupying a military station. —*v.t.* **9.** to place or station at a post. **10.** to provide or put up, as bail. **11.** to appoint to a post of command. [1590–1600; < F *poste* < It *posto* < L *positum,* neut. of *positus,* ptp. of *pōnere* to place, put; cf. POSIT]

—**Syn. 1.** assignment. See **appointment.**

post[3] (pōst), *n.* **1.** *Chiefly Brit.* **a.** a single dispatch or delivery of mail. **b.** the mail itself. **c.** the letters and packages being delivered to a single recipient. **d.** an established mail system or service, esp. under government authority. **2.** *Brit.* See **post office** (def. 1). **3.** (formerly) one of a series of stations along a route, for furnishing relays of men and horses for carrying mail, currency, etc. **4.** (formerly) a person who traveled express, esp. over a fixed route, carrying mail, currency, etc. **5.** *Print.* a size of printing paper or, esp. in Britain, of drawing or writing paper, about 16 × 20 in. (41 × 51 cm). **6. post octavo,** a size of book, from about 5 × 8 in. to 5¼ × 8¼ in. (13 × 20 cm to 13⅓ × 21 cm), untrimmed, in America; 5 × 8 in. (13 × 20 cm), untrimmed, in England. *Abbr.:* post 8vo **7. post quarto,** *Chiefly Brit.* a size of book, about 8 × 10 in. (20 × 25 cm), untrimmed. *Abbr.:* post 4vo —*v.t.* **8.** *Chiefly Brit.* to place in a post office or a mailbox for transmission; mail. **9.** *Bookkeeping.* **a.** to transfer (an entry or item), as from the journal to the ledger. **b.** to enter (an item) in due place and form. **c.** to make all the requisite entries in (the ledger, etc.). **10.** to supply with up-to-date information; inform: *Keep me posted on his activities.* —*v.i.* **11.** *Manège.* to rise from and descend to the saddle in accordance with the rhythm of a horse at a trot. **12.** to travel with speed; go or pass rapidly; hasten. —*adv.* **13.** with speed or haste; posthaste. **14.** by post or courier. **15.** with post horses. [1500–10; < F *poste* < It *posta* < L *posita,* fem. of *positus,* ptp. of *pōnere* to place, put. See POST[2]]

—**Syn. 10.** notify, advise, apprise.

Post (pōst), *n.* **1. Charles William,** 1854–1914, U.S. businessman: developed breakfast foods. **2. Emily Price,** 1873?–1960, U.S. writer on social etiquette. **3. George Browne,** 1837–1913, U.S. architect. **4. Wiley,** 1899–1935, U.S. aviator.

post- a prefix, meaning "behind," "after," "later," "subsequent to," "posterior to," occurring originally in loanwords from Latin (*postscript*), but now used freely in the formation of compound words (*post-Elizabethan; postfix; postgraduate; postorbital*). [< L, comb. form repr. *post* (adv. and prep.)]

—**Note.** The lists at the bottom of this and following pages provide the spelling, syllabification, and stress for words whose meanings may be easily inferred by combining the meaning of POST- and an attached base word, or base word plus a suffix. Appropriate parts of speech are also shown. Words prefixed by POST- that have special meanings or uses are entered in their proper alphabetical places in the main vocabulary or as derived forms run on at the end of a main vocabulary entry.

post·age (pō′stij), *n.* the charge for the conveyance of a letter or other matter sent by mail, usually prepaid by means of a stamp or stamps. [1580–90; POST[3] + -AGE]

post′age due′ stamp′, a stamp that is affixed to mail at a post office when prepayment of postage is insufficient, to indicate the amount that must be collected from the addressee. [1890–95, *Amer.*]

post′age me′ter, an office machine used in bulk mailing that imprints prepaid postage and a dated postmark. [1925–30]

post′age stamp′, a small gummed label issued by postal authorities that can be affixed to an envelope, postcard, or package as evidence that postal charges have been paid. Also called **stamp.** [1830–40]

post·age-stamp (pō′stij stamp′), *adj. Informal.* of very small area or size: *a postage-stamp bikini.* [1960–65]

post·al (pōs′tl), *adj.* **1.** of or pertaining to the post office or mail service: *postal delivery; postal employees.* —*n.* **2.** *Informal.* See **postal card.** [1835–45; POST[3] + -AL[1]] —**post′al·ly,** *adv.*

post′al card′, 1. a card sold by the post office with a stamp already printed on it. **2.** postcard (def. 1). [1870–75, *Amer.*]

post′al car′rier. See **mail carrier.**

post′al code′, 1. *Brit.* postcode. **2.** *Canadian.* a mailing code system similar to the zip code in the U.S. and the postcode in Britain. [1965–70]

post′al deliv′ery zone′, zone (def. 10).

post′al or′der, *Chiefly Brit.* See **money order.** [1895–1900]

post′al sav′ings bank′, any of the savings banks formerly operated by local post offices and limited to small accounts. [1890–95]

post′al sta′tionery, *Philately.* an envelope, postal card, wrapper, or aérogramme, with the stamp printed directly on the paper.

post′al stor′age car′, a railroad car for transporting unsorted mail.

post′al un′ion, an international agreement on postal rates and services. Cf. **Universal Postal Union.** [1870–75]

post′-and-beam′ construc′tion (pōst′ən bēm′), *Building Trades.* wall construction in which beams rather than studs are used to support heavy posts.

post·a·tom·ic (pōst′ə tom′ik), *adj.* existing since or subsequent to the explosion of the first atomic bomb or the invention of atomic weapons: *the political tensions of the postatomic world.* [POST- + ATOMIC]

post·au·dit (pōst ô′dit), *n. Accounting.* an audit of accounting records, conducted at some interval of time after a transaction or a series of transactions has already occurred. Also, **post-au′dit.** Cf. **preaudit.** [POST- + AUDIT]

post·ax·i·al (pōst ak′sē əl), *adj. Anat., Zool.* pertaining to or situated behind the axis of the body, esp. the posterior side of the axis of a limb. [1870–75; POST- + AXIAL] —**post·ax′i·al·ly,** *adv.*

post-bag (pōst′bag′), *n. Brit.* **1.** mailbag. **2.** a batch of mail from a single delivery. [1805–15]

post·bel·lum (pōst bel′əm), *adj.* occurring after a war, esp. after the American Civil War: *postbellum reforms.* [1870–75; < L *post bellum* after the war]

post-boat (pōst′bōt′), *n. Brit.* mailboat. [1590–1600]

post·box (pōst′boks′), *n. Chiefly Brit.* a mailbox, esp. one for public deposit of mail. [1745–55; POST[3] + BOX[1]]

post·boy (pōst′boi′), *n.* **1.** (formerly) a boy or man who rode post or carried mail. **2.** a postilion. [1580–90; POST[3] + BOY]

post·ca·non·i·cal (pōst′kə non′i kəl), *adj.* written at a later date than the books belonging to a canon, esp. the Bible. [1895–1900; POST- + CANONICAL]

post·card (pōst′kärd′), *n.* **1.** Also called **picture postcard.** a small, commercially printed card, usually having a picture on one side and space for a short message on the other. **2.** See **postal card** (def. 1). Also, **post′ card′.** [1865–70; POST[3] + CARD[1]]

post·ca·va (pōst kā′və, -kä′-), *n., pl.* **-ca·vae** (-kā′vē, -kä′vī). See under **vena cava.** [1865–70; POST- + (VENA) CAVA] —**post·ca′val,** *adj.*

post′ chaise′, a four-wheeled coach for rapid transportation of passengers and mail, used in the 18th and early 19th centuries. [1705–15]

post·code (pōst′kōd′), *n. Brit.* an official post office code, similar to the U.S. zip code, that adds numbers and letters to addresses to expedite mail delivery. Also called **postal code.** [1965–70; POST[3] + CODE]

post·co·lo·ni·al (pōst′kə lō′nē əl), *adj.* of or pertaining to the period following a state of colonialism. [1930–35; POST- + COLONIAL]

post·com·mun·ion (pōst′kə myōōn′yən), *n. Eccles.* the part of a communion service that follows after the congregation has received communion. [1475–85; < ML *postcommūniōn-* (s. of *postcommūniō*). See POST-, COMMUNION]

post·con·cil·i·ar (pōst′kən sil′ē ər), *adj.* occurring or continuing after the Vatican ecumenical council of 1962–65. [1965–70; POST- + CONCILIAR]

post·con·so·nan·tal (pōst′kon sə nan′tl), *adj. Phonet.* immediately following a consonant. [1930–35; POST- + CONSONANTAL]

post·cra·ni·al (pōst krā′nē əl), *adj. Anat., Zool.* **1.** located posterior to the head. **2.** pertaining to or involving parts of the body that lie posterior to the head. [1910–15; POST- + CRANIAL]

post·date (pōst dāt′, pōst′-), *v.t.,* **-dat·ed, -dat·ing. 1.** to date (a check, invoice, letter, document) with a date later than the actual date. **2.** to follow in time: *His recognition as an artist postdated his death.* [1615–25; POST- + DATE[1]]

post·de·ter·min·er (pōst′di tûr′mə nər), *n. Gram.* a member of a subclass of English adjectival words, including ordinal and cardinal numbers, that may be placed after an article or other determiner and before a descriptive adjective, as *first* and *three* in *the first three new chapters.* [POST- + DETERMINER]

post·di·lu·vi·an (pōst′di lōō′vē ən), *adj.* **1.** existing or occurring after the Biblical Flood. —*n.* **2.** a person who lived after the Biblical Flood. [1670–80; POST- + DILUVIAN]

post·doc (pōst dok′), *Informal.* —*n.* **1.** a postdoctoral award or scholar. —*adj.* **2.** postdoctoral. [1965–70; by shortening]

post·doc·tor·al (pōst dok′tər əl), *adj.* of or pertaining to study or professional work undertaken after the receipt of a doctorate: *postdoctoral courses.* [1935–40; POST- + DOCTORAL]

post·em·bry·on·ic (pōst em′brē on′ik, pōst′em-), *adj.* occurring after the embryonic phase. [1890–95; POST- + EMBRYONIC]

post·e·mer·gence (pōst′i mûr′jəns), *adj.* occurring or applied after emergence of a plant from the soil and before full growth: *postemergence frost.* [1935–40; POST- + EMERGENCE]

post′ en′try, a late entry, as a horse in a horse show or race. [1655–65]

post·er[1] (pō′stər), *n.* **1.** a placard or bill posted or intended for posting in a public place, as for advertising. **2.** a person who posts bills, placards, etc. [1830–40; POST[1] + -ER[1]]

post·er[2] (pō′stər), *n.* **1.** See **post horse. 2.** *Archaic.* a person who travels rapidly. [1595–1605; POST[3] + -ER[1]]

post′er col′or. See **poster paint.** [1920–25]

poste res·tante (pōst′ re stänt′ or, esp. Brit., res′tänt; *Fr.* pôst RES tänt′), **1.** a direction written on mail to indicate that it should be held at the post office until called for by the addressee. **2.** *Chiefly Brit.* a department in charge of such mail. [1760–70; < F: lit., standing post]

pos·te·ri·ad (po stēr′ē ad′, pō-), *adv. Anat., Zool.* toward the posterior; posteriorly. [POSTERI(OR) + -AD[3]]

pos·te·ri·or (po stēr′ē ər, pō-), *adj.* **1.** situated behind or at the rear of; hinder (opposed to *anterior*). **2.** coming after in order, as in a series. **3.** coming after in time; later; subsequent (sometimes fol. by *to*). **4.** *Anat., Zool.* **a.** (in quadrupeds) pertaining to or toward the rear or caudal end of the body. **b.** (in humans and other primates) pertaining to or toward the back plane of the body, equivalent to the dorsal surface of quadrupeds. **5.**

CONCISE ETYMOLOGY KEY: <, descended or borrowed from; >, whence; b., blend of, blended; c., cognate with; cf., compare; deriv., derivative; equiv., equivalent; imit., imitative; obl., oblique; r., replacing; s., stem; sp., spelling, spelled; resp., respelling, respelled; trans., translation; ?, origin unknown; *, unattested; ‡, probably earlier than. See the full key inside the front cover.

post·ab′do·men, *n.*
post′ab·dom′i·nal, *adj.*
post′a·bor′tion, *adj.*
post·ac′ci·dent, *adj.*
post′ac·e·tab′u·lar, *adj.*
post′act′, *n.*
post′-A·dam′ic, *adj.*
post′ad·o·les′cent, *adj., n.*
post-Ad′vent, *adj.*
post′-Al·ex·an′drine, *adj.*
post′al·lan·to′ic, *adj.*
post′al·ve′o·lar, *adj.*
post′am·ni·ot′ic, *adj.*
post′am·pu·ta′tion, *adj.*
post·a′nal, *adj.*
post′an·es·thet′ic, *adj.*
post′an·ten′nal, *adj.*
post′a·or′tic, *adj.*
post′a·poc′a·lyp′tic, *adj.*
post′ap·o·plec′tic, *adj.*
post′ap·os·tol′ic, *adj.*
post′ap·os·tol′i·cal, *adj.*
post′ap·pen·dic′u·lar, *adj.*
post′-Ar·is·to·te′lian, *adj.*
post·ar′mi·stice, *n.*
post′ar·rest′, *adj.*
post′ar·te′ri·al, *adj.*
post′ar·thrit′ic, *adj.*
post′ar·tic′u·lar, *adj.*
post′ar·y·te′noid, *adj.*
post′asth·mat′ic, *adj.*
post′at·tack′, *adj.*
post·au′di·to′ry, *adj.*
post′-Au·gus′tan, *adj.*
post′-Au·gus·tin′i·an, *adj.*
post′au·ric′u·lar, *adj.*
post·ax′il·lar′y, *adj.*
post-Az′tec, *adj.*
post′-Bab·y·lo′ni·an, *adj.*
post′bac·ca·lau′re·ate, *adj.*
post′bap·tis′mal, *adj.*
post-Bib′li·cal, *adj.*
post′bour·geois′, *adj.*
post·bra′chi·al, *adj.*
post·bra′chi·um, *n., pl.* **-chi·a.**
post·break′fast, *adj.*
post·bron′chi·al, *adj.*
post·buc′cal, *adj.*
post·bulb′ar, *adj.*
post·bur′sal, *adj.*
post·cae′cal, *adj.*
post′-Cae·sar′e·an, *adj.*
post-Cam′bri·an, *adj.*
post′-Car·bon·if′er·ous, *adj.*
post·car′di·ac′, *adj.*
post·car′di·nal, *adj.*
post′-Car·o·lin′gi·an, *adj.*
post′ca·rot′id, *adj.*
post′-Car·te′sian, *adj.*
post′car·ti·lag′i·nous, *adj.*
post′ca·tarrh′al, *adj.*
post·cau′dal, *adj.*
post·cen′tral, *adj.*
post′ce·phal′ic, *adj.*
post′cer·e·bel′lar, *adj.*
post·ce·re′bral, *adj.*
post′-Ce·sar′e·an, *adj.*
post′-Chau·ce′ri·an, *adj.*
post′chlo·ri·na′tion, *adj.*
post-Chris′tian, *adj.*
post-Christ′mas, *adj.*
post′civ·i·li·za′tion, *adj.*
post-clas′si·cal, *adj.*
post·co′i·tal, *adj.;* **-ly,** *adv.*
post·col′lege, *n., adj.*
post′col·le′gian, *n.*
post′col·le′giate, *adj.*
post·co′lon, *adj.*
post′-Co·lum′bi·an, *adj.*
post′col·u·mel′lar, *adj.*
post′com·mu′ni·cant, *adj.*
post′con·cep′tion, *adj.*
post′con·cep′tu·al, *adj.*
post·con′cert, *adj.*
post·con′dy·lar, *adj.*
post′con·fine′ment, *n.*
post′-Con·fu′cian, *adj.*
post′con·nu′bi·al, *adj.*
post·con′quest, *adj.*
post′-Con·stan·tin′i·an, *adj.*
post′con·tem′po·rar′y, *adj.*
post·con′tract, *n.*
post′con·va·les′cent, *adj.*
post′con·ven′tion, *adj.*
post′con·vul′sive, *adj.*
post′-Co·per′ni·can, *adj.*
post·cor′o·nar′y, *adj.*
post·cos′tal, *adj.*
post·coup′, *adj.*
post·cox′al, *adj.*
post′cre·ta′ceous, *adj.*
post·cri′sis, *adj., n., pl.* **-ses.**
post·crit′i·cal, *adj.*
post·cru′ci·ate, *adj.*
post·cru′ral, *adj.*
post′-Cru·sade′, *adj.*
post′crys·tal·li·za′tion, *adj.*
post·cu′bi·tal, *adj.*
post′-Dar·win′i·an, *adj.*
post′-Da·vid′ic, *adj.*
post·dead′line′, *adj.*
post′de·bate′, *adj.*
post·deb′u·tante′, *n., adj.*
post′de·liv′er·y, *adj.*
post·den′tal, *adj., n.*
post′dep·o·si′tion·al, *adj.*
post′de·pres′sion, *adj.*
post′de·pres′sive, *adj.*
post′de·ter′mined, *adj.*
post′de·val′u·a′tion, *adj.*
post′de·vel′op·men′tal, *adj.*
post′-De·vo′ni·an, *adj.*
post′di·ag·nos′tic, *adj.*
post′di·a·phrag·mat′ic, *adj.*
post′di·as·tol′ic, *adj.*
post′di·ges′tive, *adj.*
post·dig′i·tal, *adj.*
post′-Di·o·cle′tian, *adj.*
post′diph·the′ri·al, *adj.*
post′diph·ther′ic, *adj.*
post′diph·the·rit′ic, *adj.*
post′dis·ap·proved′, *adj.*
post′dis·coi′dal, *adj.*
post·dive′, *adj.*
post′dys·en·ter′ic, *adj.*
post-Eas′ter, *adj.*
post′ed·u·ca′tion·al, *adj.*
post′e·lec′tion, *adj.*
post′el·e·men′tal, *adj.*
post′el·e·men′ta·ry, *adj.*
post′-E·liz′a·be′than, *adj.*
post′e·mer′gen·cy, *adj.*

Bot. toward the back and near the main axis, as the upper lip of a flower. —*n.* **6.** the hinder parts or rump of the body; buttocks. [1525–35; < L, comp. of *posterus* coming after, deriv. of *post* after] —**pos·te′ri·or·ly,** *adv.*
—**Syn. 1.** See **back**[1].

pos·te·ri·or·i·ty (po stēr′ē ôr′i tē, -or′-, pō-), *n.* the state or quality of being posterior. [1350–1400; ME *posteriorite* < ML *posteriōritās.* See POSTERIOR, -ITY]

poste′rior pitu′itary. See under **pituitary gland.**

pos·ter·i·ty (po ster′i tē), *n.* **1.** succeeding or future generations collectively: *Judgment of this age must be left to posterity.* **2.** all descendants of one person: *His fortune was gradually dissipated by his posterity.* [1350–1400; ME *posterite* < L *posteritās,* n. deriv. of *posterus* coming after. See POSTERIOR, -ITY]

post·er·i·za·tion (pō′stər ə zā′shən), *n. Print.* **1.** a process for producing a posterlike, high-contrast color reproduction from continuous-tone art by using separation negatives of various densities. **2.** *Photog.* a printing process in which all tone values of a negative are reduced to a few and the tonal separation negatives produced are printed at different exposure levels on a high-contrast film so that a set of flat tones results. [1945–50; POSTER[1] + -IZATION]

pos·tern (pō′stərn, pos′tərn), *n.* **1.** a back door or gate. **2.** a private entrance or any entrance other than the main one. —*adj.* **3.** of, pertaining to, or resembling a postern. [1250–1300; ME *posterne* < OF, var. of *posterle* < LL *posterula,* dim. of *postera* back door, n. use of fem. of *posterus* coming behind. See POSTERIOR, -ULE]

post′er paint′, an opaque, water-based, typically bright-colored paint with a glue-size or gum binder, that is suitable for use on posters and is usually packaged in jars. Also called **poster color.** [1935–40]

post′ exchange′, *U.S. Army.* a retail store on an army installation that sells goods and services to military personnel and their dependents and to certain authorized civilian personnel. *Abbr.:* PX [1890–95]

post·ex·il·ic (pōst′eg zil′ik, -ek sil′-), *adj.* being or occurring subsequent to the exile of the Jews in Babylonia 597–538 B.C. Also, **post′ex·il′i·an.** [1870–75; POST- + EXILIC]

post fac·tum (pōst fak′təm), after the fact; ex post facto: *She will announce her decision and then give us a post factum statement of the reasons for it.* [1685–95; < L: after (the) deed]

post·fem·i·nist (pōst fem′ə nist), *adj.* **1.** pertaining to or occurring in the period after the feminist movement of the 1970's. **2.** resulting from or incorporating the ideology of this movement: *a postfeminist household in which both partners share all tasks equally.* **3.** differing from or reflecting moderation of this ideology: *postfeminist thinking about motherhood and careers.* —*n.* **4.** a person who believes in, promotes, or embodies any of various ideologies springing from the feminism of the 1970's. [1980–85; POST- + FEMINIST] —**post·fem′i·nism,** *n.*

post·fix (*v.* pōst fiks′, pōst′fiks; *n.* pōst′fiks), *v.t.* **1.** to affix at the end of something; append; suffix. —*n.* **2.** something postfixed. **3.** a suffix. [1795–1805; POST- + *-fix,* modeled on PREFIX] —**post·fix′al, post·fix′i·al,** *adj.*

post-free (pōst′frē′), *adj.* **1.** that may be sent free of postal charges, as government mail. **2.** *Brit.* postpaid. —*adv.* **3.** *Brit.* postpaid. [1880–85]

post·gla·cial (pōst glā′shəl), *adj. Geol.* after a given glacial epoch, esp. the Pleistocene. [1850–55; POST- + GLACIAL]

post·grad (pōst grad′), *adj., n. Informal.* postgraduate. [1945–50; by shortening]

post·grad·u·ate (pōst graj′o͞o it, -āt′), *adj.* **1.** of, pertaining to, characteristic of, or consisting of postgraduates: *a postgraduate seminar.* —*n.* **2.** a student who is taking advanced work after graduation, as from a high school or college. [1855–60; POST- + GRADUATE]

post·haste (pōst′hāst′), *adv.* **1.** with the greatest possible speed or promptness: *to come to a friend's aid posthaste.* —*n.* **2.** *Archaic.* great haste. [1530–40; POST[3] + HASTE]

post·heat (pōst hēt′), *v.t.* to heat (a metal piece, as a weld) after working, so as to relieve stresses. [POST- + HEAT]

post hoc (pōst′ hōk′; *Eng.* pōst′ hok′), *Latin.* after this; afterward.

post hoc, er·go prop·ter hoc (pōst′ hōk′, er′gō prōp′ter hōk′; *Eng.* pōst′ hok′, ûr′gō prop′tər hok′, er′gō), *Latin.* after this, therefore because of it: a formula designating an error in logic that accepts as a cause something that merely occurred earlier in time.

post·hole (pōst′hōl′), *n.* **1.** a hole dug in the earth for setting in the end of a post, as for a fence. **2.** *Archaeol.* an excavated hole showing by its shape and by the remains of wood or other debris that it was once filled by a post. [1695–1705; POST[1] + HOLE]

post′hole dig′ger, a tool for digging a posthole.

post′ horn′, *n.* a straight or coiled copper or brass horn with no valves or slide, originally used to announce mail coaches. [1665–75]

post′ horse′, a horse kept, as at a station on a post road, for the use of persons riding post or for hire by travelers. Also called **poster.** [1520–30]

post′ house′, a house or inn keeping post horses. [1625–35]

post·hu·mous (pos′chə məs, -cho͝o-), *adj.* **1.** arising, occurring, or continuing after one's death: *a posthumous award for bravery.* **2.** published after the death of the author: *a posthumous novel.* **3.** born after the death of the father. [1600–10; < L *postumus* last-born, born after the death of the father (in form a superl. of *posterus;* see POSTERIOR); post-classical sp. with *h* by assoc. with *humus* ground, earth, as if referring to burial] —**post′·hu·mous·ly,** *adv.* —**post′hu·mous·ness,** *n.*

post·hyp·not·ic (pōst′hip not′ik), *adj.* **1.** of or pertaining to the period after hypnosis. **2.** (of a suggestion) made during hypnosis so as to be effective after awakening. [1885–90; POST- + HYPNOTIC] —**post′hyp·not′i·cal·ly,** *adv.*

pos·tiche (pô stēsh′, po-), *adj.* **1.** superadded, esp. inappropriately, as a sculptural or architectural ornament. **2.** artificial, counterfeit, or false. —*n.* **3.** an imitation or substitute. **4.** pretense; sham. **5.** a false hairpiece. [1850–55; < F < It *appostiecio* < VL **appositīcius* added to. See APPOSITE, -ITIOUS]

pos·ti·cous (po stī′kəs), *adj. Bot.* hinder; posterior. [1865–70; < L *posticus* behind, hinder, deriv. of *post* after; see -OUS]

pos·ti·cum (po stī′kəm), *n., pl.* **-ca** (-kə). **1.** epinaos. **2.** opisthodomos (def. 1). [1695–1705; < L *posticum* backdoor, back part (of a building), n. use of neut. of *posticus.* See POSTICOUS]

pos·til·ion (pō stil′yən, po-), *n.* a person who rides the left horse of the leading or only pair of horses drawing a carriage. Also, *esp. Brit.,* **pos·til′lion.** [1580–90; earlier *postillon* < MF < It *postiglione,* deriv. of *posta* POST[3]] —**pos·til′ioned,** *adj.*

Post-Im·pres·sion·ism (pōst′im presh′ə niz′əm), *n.* a varied development of Impressionism by a group of painters chiefly between 1880 and 1900 stressing formal structure, as with Cézanne and Seurat, or the expressive possibilities of form and color, as with Van Gogh and Gauguin. Also, **post′-im·pres′sion·ism.** [1905–10; POST- + IMPRESSIONISM] —**Post′-Im·pres′sion·ist,** *adj., n.* —**Post′-Im·pres′sion·is′tic,** *adj.*

post·in·dus·tri·al (pōst′in dus′trē əl), *adj.* of, pertaining to, or characteristic of an era following industrialization: *The economy of the postindustrial society is based on the provision of services rather than on the manufacture of goods.* [POST- + INDUSTRIAL] —**post′in·dus′tri·al·ist,** *n.*

post·ing[1] (pō′sting), *n.* assignment to a post, command, or particular location, esp. in a military or governmental capacity. [1790–1800; POST[2] + -ING[1]]

post·ing[2] (pō′sting), *n. Accounting.* **1. a.** the act or process of entering data in an accounts ledger. **b.** the record in a ledger after such entry. **2.** the act of mailing. **3.** an issuance or batch of mailed items. [1665–75; POST[3] + -ING[1]]

Post-it (pōst′it), *Trademark.* **1.** a small notepad with an adhesive strip on the back of each sheet that allows it to stick to smooth surfaces and be repositioned with ease. **2.** a sheet from such a pad.

post·lap·sar·i·an (pōst′lap sâr′ē ən), *adj.* occurring or being after the Fall. [1725–35; POST- + *-lapsarian,* as in INFRALAPSARIAN, SUPRALAPSARIAN]

post·li·min·i·um (pōst′lə min′ē əm), *n., pl.* **-min·i·a** (-min′ē ə). *Internat. Law.* postliminy. [< L; see POSTLIMINY]

post·lim·i·ny (pōst lim′ə nē), *n. Internat. Law.* the right by which persons and things taken in war are restored to their former status when coming again under the power of the nation to which they belonged. [1650–60; < L *postlīminium* resumption of rights or recovery of property after return from exile or captivity. See POST-, LIMINAL, -IUM]

post-loop·ing (pōst lo͞o′ping), *n. Motion Pictures, Television.* post-synchronization.

post·lude (pōst′lo͞od), *n. Music.* **1.** a concluding piece or movement. **2.** a voluntary at the end of a church service. [1850–55; POST- + *-lude* < L *lūdus* game, modeled on *prelude*]

post·man[1] (pōst′mən), *n., pl.* **-men. 1.** a postal employee who carries and delivers mail; mail carrier. **2.** *Archaic.* a courier. [1520–30; POST[3] + -MAN]
—**Usage.** See **-man.**

post·man[2] (pōst′mən), *n., pl.* **-men.** *Old Eng. Law.* a barrister in the Court of Exchequer who had precedence in motions. Cf. **tubman.** [1760–70; POST[1] + -MAN]

post·mark (pōst′märk′), *n.* **1.** an official mark stamped on letters and other mail, serving as a cancellation of the postage stamp and indicating the place, date, and sometimes time of sending or receipt. —*v.t.* **2.** to stamp with a postmark. [1670–80; POST[3] + MARK[1]]

post·mas·ter (pōst′mas′tər, -mä′stər), *n.* **1.** the official in charge of a post office. **2.** (formerly) the master of a station that furnished post horses to travelers. [1505–15; POST[3] + MASTER] —**post′mas′ter·ship′,** *n.*

post′master gen′eral, *pl.* **postmasters general.** the head of the postal system of a country. [1620–30]

post·me·rid·i·an (pōst′mə rid′ē ən), *adj.* **1.** of or pertaining to the afternoon. **2.** occurring after noon: *a postmeridian lull.* [1620–30; POST- + MERIDIAN]

post me·rid·i·em (pōst′ mə rid′ē əm, -em′). See **p.m.**

post·mill (pōst′mil′), *n.* a windmill with machinery mounted on a frame that turns in its entirety to face the wind. [1815–25; POST[1] + MILL[1]]

post·mil·le·nar·i·an·ism (pōst′mil ə nâr′ē ə niz′əm), *n.* postmillennialism. [1885–90; POST- + MILLENARIANISM] —**post′mil·le·nar′i·an,** *adj., n.*

post·mil·len·ni·al (pōst′mi len′ē əl), *adj.* of or pertaining to the period following the millennium. [1850–55; POST- + MILLENNIAL]

post·mil·len·ni·al·ism (pōst′mi len′ē ə liz′əm), *n.* the doctrine or belief that the second coming of Christ will follow the millennium. [1875–80; POSTMILLENNIAL + -ISM] —**post′mil·len′ni·al·ist,** *n.*

post·min·i·mal·ism (pōst min′ə mə liz′əm), *n.* (*sometimes cap.*) a style in painting and sculpture developing in the 1970's, retaining the formal simplifications of minimal art, but striving to imbue works with a broad range of meaning and reference and often demonstrating a concern with craft and a kinship with tribal art and sculpture. [POST- + MINIMALISM] —**post·min′i·mal,** *adj.* —**post·min′i·mal·ist,** *n., adj.*

post·mis·tress (pōst′mis′tris), *n.* a woman in charge of a post office. [1690–1700; POST[3] + MISTRESS]
—**Usage.** See **-ess.**

post·mod·ern (pōst mod′ərn), *adj.* noting or pertaining to architecture of the late 20th century, appearing in the 1960's, that consciously uses complex forms, fantasy, and allusions to historic styles, in contrast to the austere forms and emphasis on utility of standard modern architecture. [1945–50; POST- + MODERN]

post·mod·ern·ism (pōst mod′ər niz′əm), *n.* (*sometimes cap.*) any of a number of trends or movements in the arts and literature developing in the 1970's in reaction to or rejection of the dogma, principles, or practices of established modernism, esp. a movement in architecture and decorative arts running counter to the practice of the International Style and using elements from historical vernacular styles and often playful illusion, decoration, and complexity. [1970–75; POST- + MODERNISM] —**post·mod′ern·ist,** *n., adj.*

CONCISE PRONUNCIATION KEY: act, cāpe, dâre, pärt; set, ēqual; if, īce; ox, ōver, ôrder, oil, bo͝ok, bo͞ot, out; up, ûrge; child; sing; shoe; thin, *th*at; zh as in *treasure.* ə = *a* as in *alone, e* as in *system, i* as in *easily, o* as in *gallop, u* as in *circus;* ° as in *fire* (fī°r), *hour* (ou°r). l and n can serve as syllabic consonants, as in *cradle* (krād′l), and *button* (but′n). See the full key inside the front cover.

post′en·ceph′a·lit′ic, *adj.*
post-E′o·cene′, *adj.*
post′ep·i·lep′tic, *adj.*
post′e·rup′tive, *adj.*
post′e·soph′a·ge′al, *adj.*
post·eth′moid, *adj.*
post·ex′er·cise′, *adj.*
post′ex·ist′ence, *n.*
post′ex·pe′ri·ence, *adj.*
post′ex·per′i·men′tal, *adj.*
post′ex·plo′sion, *adj.*
post′ex·po′sure, *adj.*
post·fault′, *n.*
post·fe′brile, *adj.*
post·fem′o·ral, *adj.*
post·fe′tal, *adj.*
post·flight′, *adj.*
post·foe′tal, *adj.*
post·fo′ve·al, *adj.*
post·frac′ture, *adj., n.*
post·freeze′, *adj.*
post-Freud′i·an, *adj.*
post′-Gal·i·le′an, *adj.*
post·game′, *adj.*
post′gan·gli·on′ic, *adj.*
post·gas′tric, *adj.*
post′ge·ni′al, *adj.*
post·gen′i·tal, *adj.*
post-Goth′ic, *adj.*
post′grad·u·a′tion, *adj.*
post·grip′pal, *adj.*
post·har′vest, *adj.*
post′hem·i·ple′gic, *adj.*
post′hem·or·rhag′ic, *adj.*
post′he·pat′ic, *adj.*
post·hex′a·plar, *adj.*
post′hi·ber·na′tion, *adj.*
post′hip·po·cam′pal, *adj.*
post-Hit′tite, *adj.*
post′-Ho·mer′ic, *adj.*
post·hos′pi·tal, *adj.*
post·hu′mer·al, *adj.*
post·hy′oid, *adj.*
post′hys·ter′i·cal, *adj.*
post-Ib′sen, *adj.*
post′ic·ter′ic, *adj.*
post·im′pact, *adj.*
post′im·pe′ri·al, *adj.*
post′in·au′gu·ral, *adj.*
post′in·car·na′tion, *adj.*
post′in·cu·nab′u·la, *adj.*
post′in·de·pend′ence, *adj.*
post′in·farc′tion, *adj.*
post′in·fec′tion, *adj.*
post′in·fla′tion·ar′y, *adj.*
post′in·flu·en′zal, *adj.*
post′in·jec′tion, *adj.*
post′in·oc′u·la′tion, *adj.*
post′in·tes′ti·nal, *adj.*
post′ir·ra′di·a′tion, *adj.*
post′i·so·la′tion, *adj.*
post′-John·so′ni·an, *adj.*
post·jug′u·lar, *adj.*
post′-Ju·ras′sic, *adj.*
post′-Jus·tin′i·an, *adj.*
post-Jut′land, *adj.*
post-Kan′san, *adj.*
post-Kant′i·an, *adj.*
post·la′bi·al, *adj.;* **-ly,** *adv.*
post·lach′ry·mal, *adj.*
post·land′ing, *adj.*
post·lar′val, *adj.*
post′la·ryn′gal, *adj.*
post′la·ryn′ge·al, *adj.*
post·launch′, *adj.*
post·le′gal, *adj.*
post′le·git′i·ma′tion, *n.*
post′-Leib·nitz′i·an, *adj.*
post′-Leib·niz′i·an, *adj.*
post-Lent′, *adj.*
post′len·tic′u·lar, *adj.*
post′lib·er·a′tion, *adj.*
post′li·cen′ti·ate, *adj.*
post′-Lin·ne′an, *adj.*
post′ma·lar′i·al, *adj.*
post·mam′ma·ry, *adj.*
post·mam′mil·lar′y, *adj.*
post′man·dib′u·lar, *adj.*
post′ma·ni′a·cal, *adj.*
post·mar′i·tal, *adj.*
post·mar′riage, *n., adj.*
post-Marx′i·an, *adj.*
post′mas·tec′to·my, *adj.*
post·mas′toid, *adj.*
post·max′il·lar′y, *adj.*
post·max′i·mal, *adj.*
post′me·di·ae′val, *adj.*
post·me′di·al, *adj.*
post·me′di·an, *adj.*
post′me·di·e′val, *adj.*
post·med′ul·lar′y, *adj.*
post′mei·ot′ic, *adj.*
post′-Men·de′li·an, *adj.*
post′me·nin′ge·al, *adj.*
post′men·o·pau′sal, *adj.*
post·men′stru·al, *adj.*
post′mes·en·ter′ic, *adj.*
post′-Mes·o·zo′ic, *adj.*
post·mid′night, *adj.*
post-Mi′o·cene′, *adj.*
post′-Mish·na′ic, *adj.*
post-Mish′nic, *adj.*
post-Mish′ni·cal, *adj.*
post·mor′tal, *adj.;* **-ly,** *adv.*
post′-Mo·sa′ic, *adj.*
post′mun·dane′, *adj.*
post·mus′cu·lar, *adj.*
post′-My·ce·ne′an, *adj.*
post′my·cot′ic, *adj.*
post′myx·e·dem′a·tous, *adj.*
post′myx·e·dem′ic, *adj.*
post′-Na·po′le·on′ic, *adj.*
post′ne·crot′ic, *adj.*
post′ne·o·na′tal, *adj.*
post′ne·phrit′ic, *adj.*
post·neu′ral, *adj.*
post′neu·ral′gic, *adj.*
post′neu·rit′ic, *adj.*
post′neu·rot′ic, *adj.*
post′-New·to′ni·an, *adj.*
post·nod′al, *adj.*
post·nod′u·lar, *adj.*
post·nu′cle·ar, *adj.*
post-Ol′i·go·cene′, *adj.*
post·ol′i·var′y, *adj.*
post′o·men′tal, *adj.*
post·op′tic, *adj.*
post·o′ral, *adj.*
post′or·di·na′tion, *adj.*
post′-Or·do·vi′cian, *adj.*
post′or·gas′mic, *adj.*
post′or·gas′tic, *adj.*
post·os′se·ous, *adj.*
post′-Pa·le·o·zo′ic, *adj.*
post·pal′pe·bral, *adj.*
post′pa·lu′dal, *adj.*
post′par·a·lyt′ic, *adj.*
post′pa·ren′tal, *adj.*

post•mor•tem (pōst môr′təm), *adj.* **1.** of, pertaining to, or occurring in the time following death. **2.** of or pertaining to examination of the body after death. **3.** occurring after the end of something; after the event: *a postmortem criticism of a television show.* —*n.* **4.** *Med.* a postmortem examination; autopsy. **5.** an evaluation or discussion occurring after the end or fact of something: *to do a postmortem on the decision of a court.* **6.** *Cards.* a discussion of the bidding or playing of a previous hand. [1725–35; < L *post mortem* after death]

post•na•sal (pōst nā′zəl), *adj.* located or occurring behind the nose or in the nasopharynx, as a flow of mucus; nasopharyngeal: *a postnasal infection.* [1895–1900; POST- + NASAL[1]]

post′nasal drip′, a trickling of mucus onto the pharyngeal surface from the posterior portion of the nasal cavity, usually caused by a cold or allergy. [1945–50]

post•na•tal (pōst nāt′l), *adj.* subsequent to childbirth: *postnatal infection.* [1855–60; POST- + NATAL]

post•nup•tial (pōst nup′shəl, -chəl), *adj.* subsequent to marriage: *postnuptial adjustments.* [1800–10; POST- + NUPTIAL] —**post•nup′tial•ly,** *adv.*
—**Pronunciation.** See **nuptial.**

post′ oak′, any of several American oaks, esp. *Quercus stellata,* the wood of which is used for posts. [1755–65, *Amer.*]

post•o•bit (pōst ō′bit, -ob′it), *adj.* effective after a particular person's death. [1745–55; < L *post obitum* after death]

post-o′bit bond′, a bond paying a sum of money after the death of some specified person. [1780–90]

post o•bi•tum (pōst′ ō′bi to͝om′; *Eng.* pōst′ ob′i təm, ō′bi-), *Latin.* after death.

post′ of′fice, 1. an office or station of a government postal system at which mail is received and sorted, from which it is dispatched and distributed, and at which stamps are sold or other services rendered. **2.** (*often cap.*) the department of a government charged with the transportation of mail. **3.** a game in which one player is designated "postmaster" or "postmistress" and calls another player of the opposite sex into an adjoining room, ostensibly to receive a letter but actually to receive a kiss. [1625–35] —**post′-of′fice,** *adj.*

post′-office box′, (in a post office) a locked compartment into which the mail of a box renter is put to be called for. *Abbr.:* POB, P.O.B. [1825–35, *Amer.*]

Post′ Of′fice Depart′ment, former name of **United States Postal Service.**

post•op (pōst′op′), *Informal.* —*adj.* **1.** postoperative. —*adv.* **2.** postoperatively: *We'll have to see how he does postop.* Also, **post′-op′.** [1970–75; by shortening]

post•op•er•a•tive (pōst op′ər ə tiv, -ə rā′tiv, -op′rə tiv), *adj.* occurring after a surgical operation. [1885–90; POST- + OPERATIVE] —**post•op′er•a•tive•ly,** *adv.*

post•or•bit•al (pōst ôr′bi tl), *adj. Anat., Zool.* located behind the orbit or socket of the eye. [1825–35; POST- + ORBITAL]

post•paid (pōst′pād′), *adj., adv.* with the postage prepaid: *a postpaid reply card.* [1820–30; POST[3] + PAID]

post•par•tum (pōst pär′təm), *adj. Obstet.* of or noting the period of time following childbirth; after delivery. Cf. **antepartum.** [1840–50; < NL *post partum* after childbirth; *post* POST- + *partum,* acc. of *partus* a bringing forth, equiv. to *par(ere)* to bear (see PARTURIENT) + *-tus* suffix of v. action]

post-po′li•o syn′drome (pōst pō′lē ō′), *Pathol.* muscle weakness occurring several decades after recovery from a polio infection, caused by fatiguing of collateral nerve axons developed during physical rehabilitation.

post•pone (pōst pōn′, pōs-), *v.t.,* **-poned, -pon•ing. 1.** to put off to a later time; defer: *He has postponed his departure until tomorrow.* **2.** to place after in order of importance or estimation; subordinate: *to postpone private ambitions to the public welfare.* [1490–1500; < L *postpōnere* to put after, lay aside, equiv. to *post-* POST- + *pōnere* to put] —**post•pon′a•ble,** *adj.* —**post•pone′•ment,** *n.* —**post•pon′er,** *n.*
—**Syn. 1.** See **defer[1].**

post•pose (pōst pōz′), *v.t.,* **-posed, -pos•ing.** *Gram.* to place (a grammatical form) after a related grammatical form: *The adverb "out" in "put out the light" is postposed in "put the light out."* [1925–30; POST- + (PRE)POSE]

post•po•si•tion (pōst′pə zish′ən, pōst′pə zish′ən), *n.* **1.** the act of placing after. **2.** the state of being so placed. **3.** *Gram.* **a.** the use of words, particles, or affixes following the elements they modify or govern, as of the adjective *general* in *attorney general,* or of the particle *e* "to" in Japanese *Tokyo e* "to Tokyo." **b.** a word, particle, or affix so used. [1540–50; POST- + POSITION or (PRE)POSITION] —**post′po•si′tion•al,** *adj.*

post•pos•i•tive (pōst poz′i tiv), *Gram.* —*adj.* **1.** (of a word, particle, or affix) placed after a word to modify it or to show its relation to other elements of a sentence. —*n.* **2.** a postpositive word, particle, or affix; postposition. [1780–90; < L *postpositus* (ptp. of *postpōnere;* see POSTPONE, POSITION) + -IVE] —**post•pos′i•tive•ly,** *adv.*

post•pran•di•al (pōst pran′dē əl), *adj.* after a meal, esp. after dinner: *postprandial oratory; a postprandial brandy.* [1810–20; POST- + L *prandi(um)* meal + -AL[1]] —**post•pran′di•al•ly,** *adv.*

post•pro•duc•tion (pōst′prə duk′shən), *n.* (in motion pictures, recording, etc.) the technical processes, as cutting, editing, and post-synchronization, necessary to ready a filmed or recorded work for sale or exhibition. [1950–55; POST- + PRODUCTION]

post•pu•bes•cent (pōst′pyo͞o bes′ənt), *n.* **1.** a young person in his or her early teens. —*adj.* **2.** of, pertaining to, or characteristic of postpubescents. [POST- + PUBESCENT]

post′ race′, *Horse Racing.* a race in which each owner is allowed to list a number of possible entries and, at a stipulated time before the race, specify which horse will actually compete.

pos•tre•mo•gen•i•ture (po strē′mō jen′i chər, -cho͝or′), *n. Law.* a system of inheritance under which the estate of a deceased person goes to his youngest son. Also called **ultimogeniture.** Cf. **primogeniture** (def. 2). [< L *postrēm(us)* last (superl. of *posterus* coming after) + -o- + GENITURE]

post•rid•er (pōst′rī′dər), *n.* (formerly) a person who rode post; a mounted mail carrier. [1695–1705; POST[3] + RIDER]

post′ road′, 1. (formerly) a road with stations for furnishing horses for postriders, mail coaches, or travelers. **2.** a road or route over which mail is carried. [1650–60]

pos•trorse (pos′trôrs, po strôrs′), *adj.* directed backward. [1885–90; < L *post(erus)* behind + (RET)RORSE]

post•script (pōst′skript′, pōs′-), *n.* **1.** a paragraph, phrase, etc., added to a letter that has already been concluded and signed by the writer. **2.** any addition or supplement, as one appended by a writer to a book to supply further information. [1515–25; < L *postscrīptum,* neut. ptp. of *postscrībere* to write after]

post•sy•nap•tic (pōst′si nap′tik), *adj. Physiol.* being or occurring on the receiving end of a discharge across the synapse. [1905–10; POST- + SYNAPTIC]

post-syn•chro•ni•za•tion (pōst′sing krə nə zā′shən), *n. Motion Pictures, Television.* the recording of dialogue and sound effects in synchronization with the picture after the film has been shot. Also called **post-looping.** [1930–35]

post•ten•sion (pōst ten′shən), *v.t.* **1.** (in prestressed-concrete construction) to apply tension to (reinforcing strands) after the concrete has set. Cf. **pretension[2]** (def. 1). **2.** to make (a concrete member) with posttensioned reinforcement. [1970–75; POST- + TENSION]

post′ time′, *Horse Racing.* the time at which the entries in a race are required to be at the starting post. [1835–45]

post•ton•ic (pōst ton′ik), *adj.* immediately following a stressed syllable: *a posttonic syllable; a posttonic vowel.* [1880–85]

post•tran•scrip•tion•al (pōst′tran skrip′shə nl), *n. Genetics, Biochem.* occurring after the formation of RNA from DNA but before the RNA strand leaves the nucleus. [1965–70; POST- + TRANSCRIPTIONAL]

post•trans•la•tion•al (pōst′trans lā′shə nl, -tranz-), *n. Genetics, Biochem.* occurring after the synthesis of a polypeptide chain. [1970–75; POST- + TRANSLATIONAL]

post•trau•mat•ic (pōst′trə mat′ik, -trô-, -trou-), *adj.* occurring after physical or psychological trauma. [1900–05; POST- + TRAUMATIC]

post′traumat′ic stress′ disor′der, *Psychiatry.* a mental disorder, as battle fatigue, occurring after a traumatic event outside the range of usual human experience, and characterized by symptoms such as reliving the event, reduced involvement with others, and manifestations of autonomic arousal such as hyperalertness and exaggerated startle response. *Abbr.:* PTSD [1975–80]

post•ty•phoid (pōst tī′foid), *adj. Pathol.* occurring as a sequela of typhoid fever. [POST- + TYPHOID]

pos•tu•lan•cy (pos′chə lən sē), *n., pl.* **-cies.** the period or state of being a postulant, esp. in a religious order. Also, **pos′tu•lance.** [1880–85; POSTUL(ANT) + -ANCY]

pos•tu•lant (pos′chə lənt), *n.* **1.** a candidate, esp. for admission into a religious order. **2.** a person who asks or applies for something. [1750–60; < F < L *postulant-* (s. of *postulāns*), prp. of *postulāre* to ask for, claim, require] —**pos′tu•lant•ship′,** *n.*

pos•tu•late (*v.* pos′chə lāt′; *n.* pos′chə lit, -lāt′), *v.,* **-lat•ed, -lat•ing,** *n.* —*v.t.* **1.** to ask, demand, or claim. **2.** to claim or assume the existence or truth of, esp. as a basis for reasoning or arguing. **3.** to assume without proof, or as self-evident; take for granted. **4.** *Math., Logic.* to assume as a postulate. —*n.* **5.** something taken as self-evident or assumed without proof as a basis for reasoning. **6.** *Math., Logic.* a proposition that requires no proof, being self-evident, or that is for a specific purpose assumed true, and that is used in the proof of other propositions; axiom. **7.** a fundamental principle. **8.** a necessary condition; prerequisite. [1525–35; < L *postulātum* petition, thing requested, n. use of neut. of ptp. of *postulāre* to request, demand, akin to *pōscere* to request] —**pos′tu•la′tion,** *n.* —**pos′tu•la′tion•al,** *adj.*
—**Syn. 3.** hypothecate, presuppose, conjecture. **5.** hypothesis, theory; axiom; assumption, conjecture.

pos•tu•la•tor (pos′chə lā′tər), *n. Rom. Cath. Ch.* a priest who presents a plea for a beatification or the canonization of a beatus. Cf. **devil's advocate** (def. 2). [1860–65; < L *postulātor* claimant. See POSTULATE, -TOR]

pos′tural drain′age, a therapy for clearing congested lungs by placing the patient in a position for drainage by gravity, often accompanied by percussion with hollowed hands.

pos′tural hypoten′sion. See **orthostatic hypotension.**

pos•ture (pos′chər), *n., v.,* **-tured, -tur•ing.** —*n.* **1.** the relative disposition of the parts of something. **2.** the position of the limbs or the carriage of the body as a whole: *poor posture; a sitting posture.* **3.** an affected or unnatural attitude: *He struck a comic posture.* **4.** a mental or spiritual attitude: *His ideas reveal a defensive posture.* **5.** one's image or policy as perceived by the public, other nations, etc.: *The company wants to develop a more aggressive marketing posture.* **6.** position, condition, or state, as of affairs. —*v.t.* **7.** to place in a particular posture or attitude. **8.** to position, esp. strategically: *to posture troops along a border.* **9.** to develop a policy or stance for (oneself, a company, government, etc.): *The White House postured itself for dealing with the fuel crisis.* **10.** to adopt an attitude or take an official position on (a matter): *The company postured that the court's ruling could be interpreted as being in its favor.* —*v.i.* **11.** to assume a particular posture. **12.** to assume affected or unnatural postures, as by bending or contorting the body. **13.** to act in an affected or artificial manner, as to create a certain impression. [1595–1605; < F < It *postura* < L *positūra.* See POSIT, -URE] —**pos′tur•al,** *adj.* —**pos′tur•er,** *n.*
—**Syn. 2.** See **position.**

pos•tur•ize (pos′chə rīz′), *v.i.,* **-ized, -iz•ing.** to posture; pose. Also, *esp. Brit.,* **pos′tur•ise′.** [1700–10; POSTURE + -IZE]

post•vo•cal•ic (pōst′vō kal′ik), *adj. Phonet.* immediately following a vowel. [1890–95; POST- + VOCALIC] —**post′vo•cal′i•cal•ly,** *adv.*

post•war (pōst′wôr′), *adj.* of, pertaining to, or charac-

CONCISE ETYMOLOGY KEY: <, descended or borrowed from; >, whence; b., blend of, blended; c., cognate with; cf., compare; deriv., derivative; equiv., equivalent; imit., imitative; obl., oblique; r., replacing; s., stem; sp., spelling, spelled; resp., respelling, respelled; trans., translation; ?, origin unknown; *, unattested; ‡, probably earlier than. See the full key inside the front cover.

post′pa•rot′id, *adj.*
post′par•o•tit′ic, *adj.*
post′par•ox•ys′mal, *adj.*
post′par′tu•ri•ent, *adj.*
post′pa•tel′lar, *adj.*
post′path•o•log′ic, *adj.*
post′path•o•log′i•cal, *adj.*
post-Paul′ine, *adj.*
post•pec′to•ral, *adj.*
post′pe•dun′cu•lar, *adj.*
post′-Pen•te•cos′tal, *adj.*
post•per′fo•rat′ed, *adj.*
post′per•i•car′di•al, *adj.*
post-Per′mi•an, *adj.*
post-Pe′trine, *adj.*
post′pha•ryn′gal, *adj.*
post′pha•ryn′ge•al, *adj.*
post-Phid′i•an, *adj.*
post′phle•bit′ic, *adj.*
post′phlo•gis′tic, *adj.*
post•phren′ic, *adj.*
post•phthis′tic, *adj.*
post′pi•tu′i•tar′y, *adj.*
post′-Pla•ton′ic, *adj.*
post-Pleis′to•cene′, *adj.*
post-Pli′o•cene′, *adj.*
post′pneu•mon′ic, *adj.*
post′pol•li•na′tion, *adj.*
post•preg′nan•cy, *adj.*
post′pres•i•den′tial, *adj.*
post•pri′ma•ry, *adj.*
post•pris′on, *adj.*
post′pro•phet′ic, *adj.*
post′pro•phet′i•cal, *adj.*
post•pros′tate, *adj.*
post′psy•cho•an′a•lyt′ic, *adj.*
post•pu′ber•tal, *adj.*
post•pu′ber•ty, *adj.*
post′pu•er′per•al, *adj.*
post•pul′mo•nar′y, *adj.*
post•pu′pil•lar′y, *adj.*
post′py•lor′ic, *adj.*
post′py•ram′i•dal, *adj.*
post′py•ret′ic, *adj.*
post′-Py•thag′o•re′an, *adj.*
post′ra•chit′ic, *adj.*
post′re•ces′sion, *adj.*
post•rec′tal, *adj.*
post′re•demp′tion, *n.*
post′-Ref•or•ma′tion, *n.*
post-Ren′ais•sance′, *adj.*
post•re′nal, *adj.*
post′-Res•to•ra′tion, *n.*
post′res•ur•rec′tion, *n.*
post′res•ur•rec′tion•al, *adj.*
post•ret′i•nal, *adj.*
post′re•tire′ment, *adj.*
post′rev•o•lu′tion, *adj.*
post′-Rev•o•lu′tion•ar′y, *adj.*
post′rheu•mat′ic, *adj.*
post•rhi′nal, *adj.*
post-Ro′man, *adj.*
post′-Ro•man′tic, *adj.*
post′-Ro•man′ti•cism, *adj.*
post•ros′tral, *adj.*
post′ru•be′o•lar, *adj.*
post•sac′cu•lar, *adj.*
post′scar•la•ti′noid, *adj.*
post′scho•las′tic, *adj.*
post′scor•bu′tic, *adj.*
post•sea′son, *adj., n.*
post′-Shake•spear′e•an, *adj.*
post′-Shake•spear′i•an, *adj.*
post•sig′moid, *adj.*
post′sig•moi′dal, *adj.*
post•sign′, *v.t.*
post•sign′er, *n.*
post′-Si•lu′ri•an, *adj.*
post′-So•crat′ic, *adj.*
post′spas•mod′ic, *adj.*
post•sphe′noid, *adj.*
post•sphyg′mic, *adj.*
post•spi′nous, *adj.*
post•splen′ic, *adj.*
post•ster′nal, *adj.*
post•ster′to•rous, *adj.*
post′stim•u•la′tion, *adj.*
post•stim′u•lus, *adj.*
post•strike′, *adj.*
post•sup′pu•ra′tive, *adj.*
post•sur′gi•cal, *adj.*
post′sym•phys′i•al, *adj.*
post′syph•i•lit′ic, *adj.*
post′sys•tol′ic, *adj.*
post′ta•bet′ic, *adj.*
post′-Tal•mud′ic, *adj.*
post′-Tal•mud′i•cal, *adj.*
post•tar′sal, *adj.*
post•teen′, *n., adj.*
post•tem′po•ral, *adj.*
post-Ter′ti•ar′y, *adj.*
post′te•tan′ic, *adj.*
post′tha•lam′ic, *adj.*
post′tho•rac′ic, *adj.*
post′thy•roi′dal, *adj.*
post•tib′i•al, *adj.*
post•tox′ic, *adj.*
post•tra′che•al, *adj.*
post′-Tran•scen•den′tal, *adj.*
post•trap′e•zoid′, *adj.*
post•treat′ment, *adj.*
post•tri′al, *adj.*
post′-Tri•as′sic, *adj.*
post′-Tri•den′tine, *adj.*
post′tu•ber′cu•lar, *adj.*
post•tus′sive, *adj.*
post′tym•pan′ic, *adj.*
post•ul′nar, *adj.*
post′um•bil′i•cal, *adj.*
post•um′bo•nal, *adj.*
post′u•re′ter•al, *adj.*
post′u•re•ter′ic, *adj.*
post•u′ter•ine, *adj.*
post•vac′ci•nal, *adj.*
post′vac•ci•na′tion, *adj.*
post•var′i•o•loid′, *adj.*
post′vas•ec′to•my, *adj.*
post-Ve′dic, *adj.*
post•ve′lar, *adj.*
post′ve•ne′re•al, *adj.*
post•ve′nous, *adj.*
post•ven′tral, *adj.*
post•ver′te•bral, *adj.*
post•ves′i•cal, *adj.*
post′-Vic•to′ri•an, *adj.*
post-Vol′stead, *adj.*
post-Wa′ter•gate′, *adj.*
post•wean′ing, *adj.*
post•work′shop′, *adj.*
post•xiph′oid, *adj.*
post′zyg•ap•o•phys′e•al, *adj.*
post′zyg•ap•o•phys′i•al, *adj.*

teristic of a period following a war: *postwar problems; postwar removal of rationing.* [1905–10; POST- + WAR[1]]

po•sy (pō′zē), *n., pl.* **-sies.** **1.** a flower, nosegay, or bouquet. **2.** *Archaic.* a brief motto or the like, as one inscribed within a ring. [1400–50; late ME; syncopated var. of POESY]

pot[1] (pot), *n., v.,* **pot•ted, pot•ting.** —*n.* **1.** a container of earthenware, metal, etc., usually round and deep and having a handle or handles and often a lid, used for cooking, serving, and other purposes. **2.** such a container with its contents: *a pot of stew.* **3.** the amount contained in or held by a pot; potful. **4.** a flowerpot. **5.** a container of liquor or other drink: *a pot of ale.* **6.** liquor or other drink. **7.** a cagelike vessel for trapping fish, lobsters, eels, etc., typically made of wood, wicker, or wire. Cf. **lobster pot. 8.** a chamber pot. **9.** *Metall.* **a.** a vessel for melting metal; melting pot. **b.** an electrolytic cell for reducing certain metals, as aluminum, from fused salts. **10.** *Brit.* **a.** See **chimney pot. b.** *Dial.* a basket or box used for carrying provisions or the like; a pannier. **11.** *Slang.* a large sum of money. **12.** all the money bet at a single time; pool. **13.** *Brit. Slang.* (in horse racing) the favorite. **14.** See **pot shot. 15.** a liquid measure, usually equal to a pint or quart. **16.** *Armor.* **a.** an open, broad-brimmed helmet of the 17th century. **b.** any open helmet. **17.** *Slang.* a potbelly. **18. go to pot,** to become ruined; deteriorate: *With no one to care for it, the lovely old garden went to pot.* **19. sweeten the pot.** See **sweeten** (def. 8). —*v.t.* **20.** to put into a pot. **21.** to preserve (food) in a pot. **22.** to cook in a pot. **23.** to transplant into a pot: *We must pot the petunias.* **24.** *Hunting.* **a.** to shoot (game birds) on the ground or water, or (game animals) at rest, instead of in flight or running: *He can't even pot a sitting duck.* **b.** to shoot for food, not for sport. **25.** *Informal.* to capture, secure, or win. —*v.i.* **26.** *Informal.* to take a potshot; shoot. [1150–1200; ME *pott* (see POTTER[1]); c. D, LG *pot* (perh. > F *pot*)] —**pot′like′,** *adj.*

pot[2] (pot), *n. Slang.* marijuana. [1935–40, *Amer.*; said to be a shortening of MexSp *potiguaya* or *potaguaya*, appar. contr. of *potación de guaya* wine or brandy in which marijuana buds have been steeped (lit., drink of grief)]

pot[3] (pot), *n. Scot. and North Eng.* a deep hole; pit. [1325–75; ME; perh. identical with POT[1]]

pot., *Elect.* **1.** potential. **2.** potentiometer.

po•ta•ble (pō′tə bəl), *adj.* **1.** fit or suitable for drinking: *potable water.* —*n.* **2.** Usually, **potables.** drinkable liquids; beverages. [1565–75; < LL *pōtābilis* drinkable, equiv. to L *pōtā(re)* to drink + *-bilis* -BLE] —**po′ta•bil′i•ty, po′ta•ble•ness,** *n.*

po•tage (pō täzh′; *Fr.* pô tazh′), *n. French Cookery.* soup, esp. any thick soup made with cream. [< F; see POTTAGE]

po•tam•ic (pō tam′ik, pə-), *adj.* of or pertaining to rivers. [1880–85; < Gk *potam(ós)* river + -IC]

pot•a•mog•a•le (pot′ə mog′ə lē), *n.* See **otter shrew.** [1875–80; < NL < Gk *potamó(s)* river + *galê* weasel]

pot•a•mo•plank•ton (pot′ə mō plangk′tən), *n.* plankton living in freshwater streams. [1900–05; < Gk *potamó(s)* river + PLANKTON]

pot′ arch′, *Ceram.* an auxiliary furnace in which pots used in melting frit are preheated. [1830–40]

pot•ash (pot′ash′), *n.* **1.** potassium carbonate, esp. the crude impure form obtained from wood ashes. **2.** potassium hydroxide. **3.** the oxide of potassium, K_2O. **4.** potassium, as carbonate of potash. [1615–25; back formation from pl. *pot-ashes,* trans. of early D *potasschen.* See POT[1], ASH[1]]

pot′ash al′um, *Chem.* alum[1] (def. 1). [1830–40]

pot′ash feld′spar, any of the feldspar minerals having the composition $KAlSi_3O_8$, as orthoclase. [1860–65]

pot•ass (pot′as′), *n.* **1.** potash. **2.** potassium. [1790–1800; < F *potasse* < D *potasch* (now pronounced and spelled *potas*) POTASH]

po•tas•sa (pə tas′ə), *n. Chem.* potash [1805–15; < NL; see POTASS]

po•tas•sic (pə tas′ik), *adj.* of, pertaining to, or containing potassium. [1855–60; POTASS(IUM) + -IC]

po•tas•si•um (pə tas′ē əm), *n. Chem.* a silvery-white metallic element that oxidizes rapidly in the air and whose compounds are used as fertilizer and in special hard glasses. *Symbol:* K; *at. wt.:* 39.102; *at. no.:* 19; *sp. gr.:* 0.86 at 20°C. [1800–10; < NL; see POTASSA, -IUM]

potas′sium ac′etate, *Chem.* a white, crystalline, deliquescent, water-soluble powder, $KC_2H_3O_2$, used chiefly as a reagent in analytical chemistry.

potas′sium ac′id tar′trate, *Chem.* See **cream of tartar.**

potas′sium al′um, *Chem.* alum[1] (def. 1).

potas′sium an′timonate, *Chem.* a white, crystalline, slightly water-soluble powder, $KSbO_3$, used chiefly as a pigment in paints.

potas′sium an′timonyl tar′trate, *Chem.* See **tartar emetic.**

po•tas′si•um-ar′gon dat′ing, (pə tas′ē əm är′gon), *Geol.* a method for estimating the age of a mineral or rock, based on measurement of the rate of decay of radioactive potassium into argon. [1965–70]

potas′sium bicar′bonate, *Chem., Pharm.* a white, crystalline, slightly alkaline, salty-tasting, water-soluble powder, $KHCO_3$, produced by the passage of carbon dioxide through an aqueous potassium carbonate solution: used in cookery as a leavening agent and in medicine as an antacid. Also called **potas′sium ac′id car′bonate.**

potas′sium bichro′mate, *Chem.* See **potassium dichromate.**

potas′sium binox′alate, *Chem.* a white, crystalline, hygroscopic, poisonous solid, KHC_2O_4, that is usually hydrated: used chiefly for removing ink stains, cleaning metal and wood, and in photography. Also called **salt of sorrel, sorrel salt, potas′sium ac′id ox′alate.**

potas′sium bisul′fate, *Chem.* a colorless, crystalline, water-soluble solid, $KHSO_4$, used chiefly in the conversion of tartrates to bitartrates. Also called **potas′sium ac′id sul′fate.**

potas′sium bitar′trate, *Chem.* See **cream of tartar.**

potas′sium bro′mate, *Chem.* a white, crystalline, water-soluble powder, $KBrO_3$, used chiefly as an oxidizing agent and as an analytical reagent.

potas′sium bro′mide, *Chem.* a white, crystalline, water-soluble powder, KBr, having a bitter saline taste: used chiefly in the manufacture of photographic papers and plates, in engraving, and in medicine as a sedative. [1870–75]

potas′sium car′bonate, *Chem.* a white, granular, water-soluble powder, K_2CO_3, used chiefly in the manufacture of soap, glass, and potassium salts. [1880–85]

potas′sium chlo′rate, *Chem.* a white or colorless, crystalline, water-soluble, poisonous solid, $KClO_3$, used chiefly as an oxidizing agent in the manufacture of explosives, fireworks, matches, bleaches, and disinfectants. [1880–85]

potas′sium chlo′ride, *Chem.* a white or colorless, crystalline, water-soluble solid, KCl, used chiefly in the manufacture of fertilizers and mineral water, and as a source of other potassium compounds. [1880–85]

potas′sium co•bal•ti•ni′trite (kō′bôl tə nī′trīt), *Chem.* a yellow, crystalline, slightly water-soluble powder, $K_3Co(NO_2)_6$, used as a pigment in oil and watercolor paints, and for coloring surfaces of glass, porcelain, etc. Also called **cobalt yellow.** [COBALT + -I- + NITRATE]

potas′sium cy′anide, *Chem.* a white, granular, water-soluble, poisonous powder, KCN, having a faint almondlike odor, used chiefly in metallurgy and photography. [1880–85]

potas′sium dichro′mate, *Chem.* an orange-red, crystalline, water-soluble, poisonous powder, $K_2Cr_2O_7$, used chiefly in dyeing, photography, and as a laboratory reagent. Also called **potassium bichromate.** [1880–85]

potas′sium diphos′phate, *Chem.* See under **potassium phosphate.** Also called **monobasic potassium phosphate.**

potas′sium ferricy′anide, *Chem.* a bright-red, crystalline, water-soluble, poisonous solid, $K_3Fe(CN)_6$, used chiefly in the manufacture of pigments, as Prussian blue, and of paper, esp. blueprint paper. Also called **red prussiate of potash.**

potas′sium ferrocy′anide, *Chem.* a lemon-yellow, crystalline, water-soluble solid, $K_4Fe(CN)_6{\cdot}3H_2O$, used chiefly in casehardening alloys having an iron base and in dyeing wool and silk. Also called **yellow prussiate of potash.**

potas′sium fluor′ide, *Chem.* a white, crystalline, hygroscopic, toxic powder, KF, used chiefly as an insecticide, a disinfectant, and in etching glass.

potas′sium hydrox′ide, *Chem.* a white, deliquescent, water-soluble solid, KOH, usually in the form of lumps, sticks, or pellets, that upon solution in water generates heat: used chiefly in the manufacture of soap, as a laboratory reagent, and as a caustic. Also called **caustic potash, potas′sium hy′drate.** [1880–85]

potas′sium i′odide, *Chem., Pharm.* a white, crystalline, water-soluble powder, KI, having a bitter saline taste: used chiefly in the manufacture of photographic emulsions, as a laboratory reagent, in the preparation of Gram's solution for biological staining, and in medicine as an expectorant and to treat thyroid conditions.

potas′sium monophos′phate (mon′ə fos′fāt), *Chem.* See under **potassium phosphate.** Also called **dibasic potassium phosphate.**

potas′sium my′ron•ate (mī′rə nāt′), *Chem.* sinigrin. [1895–1900; < Gk *mýron* perfume + -ATE[2]]

potas′sium ni′trate, *Chem.* a crystalline compound, KNO_3, produced by nitrification in soil, and used in gunpowders, fertilizers, and preservatives; saltpeter; niter. [1880–85]

potas′sium ox′alate, *Chem.* a colorless, crystalline, water-soluble, poisonous solid, $K_2C_2O_4{\cdot}H_2O$, used chiefly as a bleaching agent and in medical tests as an anticoagulant.

potas′sium perman′ganate, *Chem.* a very dark purple, crystalline, water-soluble solid, $KMnO_4$, used chiefly as an oxidizing agent, disinfectant, laboratory reagent, and in medicine as an astringent and antiseptic. [1865–70]

potas′sium phos′phate, *Chem.* any of the three orthophosphates of potassium (**potassium monophosphate** (K_2HPO_4), **potassium diphosphate** (KH_2PO_4), and **tripotassium phosphate** (K_3PO_4)). [1880–85]

potas′sium so′dium tar′trate, *Chem.* See **Rochelle salt.**

potas′sium sul′fate, *Chem.* a crystalline, water-soluble solid, K_2SO_4, used chiefly in the manufacture of fertilizers, alums, and mineral water, and as a reagent in analytical chemistry. [1880–85]

potas′sium thiocy′anate, *Chem.* a colorless, crystalline, hygroscopic, water-soluble solid, KSCN, used chiefly in the manufacture of chemicals, dyes, and drugs. Also called **potas′sium rho′da•nide** (rōd′n īd′, rō dan′īd).

po•ta•tion (pō tā′shən), *n.* **1.** the act of drinking. **2.** a drink or draft, esp. of an alcoholic beverage. [1400–50; late ME *potacion* < L *pōtātiōn-* (s. of *pōtātiō*) a drinking, equiv. to *pōtāt(us)* (ptp. of *pōtāre* to drink) + *-iōn-* -ION]

po•ta•to (pə tā′tō, -tə), *n., pl.* **-toes. 1.** Also called **Irish potato, white potato.** the edible tuber of a cultivated plant, *Solanum tuberosum,* of the nightshade family. **2.** the plant itself. **3.** See **sweet potato** (defs. 1, 2). [1545–55; < Sp *patata* white potato, var. of *batata* sweet potato < Taino]

pota′to ap′ple, the green berry of the potato. [1790–1800]

pota′to bean′, groundnut (def. 1). [1795–1805]

po•ta•to•bug (pə tā′tō bug′, -tā′tə-), *n.* See **Colorado potato beetle.** Also, **pota′to bug′.** Also called **pota′to bee′tle.** [1790–1800, *Amer.*]

pota′to chip′, a thin slice of potato fried until crisp and usually salted. Also called **Saratoga chip.** [1835–45]

pota′to crisp′, *Brit.* See **potato chip.** [1925–30]

pota′to leaf′hopper, 1. any of various leafhoppers that are serious pests, damaging a wide variety of cultivated and wild plants, esp. potatoes. **2.** a small, light green, white-spotted leafhopper, *Empoasca fabae,* that is a pest of potatoes in the eastern U.S. and also attacks apple trees and numerous other cultivated plants. [1920–25]

pota′to moth′, a gelechiid moth, *Phthorimaea operculella,* the larvae of which feed on the leaves and bore into the tubers of potatoes and other solanaceous plants. [1890–95]

pota′to psyl′lid, a tiny homopterous insect, *Paratrioza cockerelli,* occurring in some areas of the western U.S., western Canada, and Mexico: a serious pest to potatoes, tomatoes, eggplants, and peppers, the nymphs acting as vectors in the transmission of psyllid yellows. Also called **tomato psyllid.** [1940–45]

pota′to race′, a novelty race in which each contestant must move a number of potatoes from one place to another, usually in a spoon, carrying one potato at a time. [1880–85]

po•ta•to•ry (pō′tə tôr′ē, -tōr′ē), *adj.* of, pertaining to, or given to drinking. [1820–30; < L *pōtātōrius.* See POTATION, -TORY[1]]

pota′to tu′ber•worm (to͞o′bər wûrm′, tyo͞o′-), the larva of the potato moth. [1935–40, *Amer.*; TUBER + WORM]

pota′to vine′, 1. a tender, woody Brazilian vine, *Solanum jasminoides,* of the nightshade family, having starlike, blue-tinged white flowers in clusters, grown as an ornamental. **2.** See **paradise flower.** [1765–75]

pota′to worm′. See **tomato hornworm.** [1835–45]

pot-au-feu (pô tō fœ′), *n. French Cookery.* a dish of boiled meat and vegetables, the broth of which is usually served separately. [1785–95; < F: lit., pot on the fire]

Pot•a•wat•o•mi (pot′ə wot′ə mē), *n., pl.* **-mis,** (*esp. collectively*) **-mi.** a member of an Algonquian Indian people originally of Michigan and Wisconsin.

pot•bel•ly (pot′bel′ē), *n., pl.* **-lies. 1.** a distended or protuberant belly. **2.** See **potbelly stove. 3.** See **potbelly wood.** [1705–15; POT[1] + BELLY] —**pot′bel′lied,** *adj.*

pot′belly stove′, a usually cast-iron wood- or coal-burning stove having a large, rounded chamber. Also, **pot′bellied stove′.** [1930–35]

pot′belly wood′, a load of firewood, approximately half a cord, cut in lengths of 16 in. (40 cm) or less for use in a potbelly stove.

pot•boil (pot′boil′), *v.i.* to create potboilers. [1865–70; back formation from POTBOILER]

pot•boil•er (pot′boi′lər), *n.* a mediocre work of literature or art produced merely for financial gain. [1860–65; POT[1] + BOILER]

pot•bound (pot′bound′), *adj. Hort.* (of a plant) having the roots so densely grown as to fill the container and require repotting. [1840–50; POT[1] + -BOUND[1]]

pot′ cheese′, *Chiefly Hudson Valley.* See **cottage cheese.** [1805–15, *Amer.*]
—Regional Variation. See **cottage cheese.**

po•teen (pə tēn′, -chēn′, -thēn′, pō-), *n.* **1.** the first distillation of a fermented mash in the making of whiskey. **2.** illicitly distilled whiskey. Also, **potheen.** [1805–15; < Ir *poitín* lit., small pot, dim. of *pota* POT[1]]

Po•tëm•kin (pō tem′kin, pə-; *Russ.* pu tyôm′kyin), *n.* **Prince Gri•go•ri A•le•ksan•dro•vich** (gri gôr′ē al′ig-zan′drə vich, -zän′-; *Russ.* gryi gô′ryē u lyi ksän′drə-vyich), 1739–91, Russian statesman and favorite of Catherine II.

Potem′kin vil′lage, a pretentiously showy or imposing façade intended to mask or divert attention from an embarrassing or shabby fact or condition. Also, **Potem′kin Vil′lage.** [1935–40; after Prince POTËMKIN, who allegedly had villages of cardboard constructed for Catherine II's visit to the Ukraine and the Crimea in 1787]

po•tence (pōt′ns), *n.* potency. [1375–1425; late ME < OF < L *potentia* POTENCY]

po•ten•cy (pōt′n sē), *n., pl.* **-cies** for 4–6. **1.** the state or quality of being potent. **2.** power; authority. **3.** efficacy; effectiveness; strength. **4.** capacity to be, become, or develop; potentiality. **5.** a person or thing exerting power or influence. **6.** *Math.* See **cardinal number** (def. 2). Also, **potence.** [1530–40; < L *potentia.* See POTENT[1], -ENCY]
—Syn. 1. strength, force, energy, capacity, potential.

po•tent[1] (pōt′nt), *adj.* **1.** powerful; mighty: *a potent fighting force.* **2.** cogent; persuasive: *Several potent arguments were in his favor.* **3.** producing powerful physical or chemical effects: *a potent drug.* **4.** having or exercising great power or influence: *a potent factor in the economy.* **5.** (of a male) capable of sexual intercourse. [1490–1500; < L *potent-* (s. of *potēns*), prp. of *posse* to be

able, have power; see -ENT] —**po′tent·ly,** *adv.* —**po′·tent·ness,** *n.*
—**Syn. 1.** strong, puissant. See **powerful. 4.** influential. —**Ant. 1.** weak. **4.** ineffectual.

po·tent[2] (pōt′nt), *Heraldry.* —*n.* **1.** a fur having a pattern of T-shaped forms, placed in alternate directions and having alternating tinctures, one metal and one color, so that all forms of one tincture face the same way and are between, above, and below forms of the other tincture facing the other way. **2.** a T-shaped form used in potent or counterpotent. —*adj.* **3.** (of a cross) having a crosspiece at the extremity of each arm: *a cross potent.* [1325–75; ME *potente* crutch, var. of *potence* < F crutch, support < ML *potentia,* L: power, POTENCY]

po·ten·tate (pōt′n tāt′), *n.* a person who possesses great power, as a sovereign, monarch, or ruler. [1350–1400; ME < LL *potentātus* potentate, L: power, dominion. See POTENT[1], -ATE[3]]

po·ten·tial (pə ten′shəl), *adj.* **1.** possible, as opposed to actual: *the potential uses of nuclear energy.* **2.** capable of being or becoming: *a potential danger to safety.* **3.** *Gram.* expressing possibility: *the potential subjunctive in Latin; the potential use of* can *in* I can go. **4.** *Archaic.* potent[1]. —*n.* **5.** possibility; potentiality: *an investment that has little growth potential.* **6.** a latent excellence or ability that may or may not be developed. **7.** *Gram.* **a.** a potential aspect, mood, construction, case, etc. **b.** a form in the potential. **8.** *Elect.* See **electric potential** (def. 1). **9.** *Math., Physics.* a type of function from which the intensity of a field may be derived, usually by differentiation. **10.** someone or something that is considered a worthwhile possibility: *The list of job applications has been narrowed to half a dozen potentials.* [1350–1400; ME *potencial* (< OF) < LL *potentiālis.* See POTENCY, -AL[1]]
—**Syn. 2.** See **latent. 5.** capacity, potency.

poten′tial dif′ference, *Elect.* the difference between the potentials of two points in an electric field. [1895–1900]

poten′tial divid′er, *Elect.* See **voltage divider.**

poten′tial en′ergy, *Physics.* the energy of a body or a system with respect to the position of the body or the arrangement of the particles of the system. Cf. **kinetic energy.** [1850–55]

poten′tial gra′dient, *Elect.* the rate of change of potential with respect to distance in the direction of greatest change. [1890–95]

po·ten·ti·al·i·ty (pə ten′shē al′i tē), *n., pl.* **-ties** for 2. **1.** the state or quality of being potential. **2.** something potential; a possibility: *Atomic destruction is a grim potentiality.* [1615–25; < ML *potentiālitās.* See POTENTIAL, -ITY]

po·ten·tial·ly (pə ten′shə lē), *adv.* possibly but not yet actually: *potentially useful information.* [1400–50; late ME; see POTENTIAL, -LY]

po·ten·ti·ate (pə ten′shē āt′), *v.t.,* **-at·ed, -at·ing. 1.** to cause to be potent; make powerful. **2.** to increase the effectiveness of; intensify. [1810–20; < L *potenti(a)* power (see POTENCY) + -ATE[1]] —**po·ten′ti·a′tion,** *n.* —**po·ten′ti·a′tor,** *n.*

po·ten·ti·om·e·ter (pə ten′shē om′i tər), *n. Elect.* **1.** a device for measuring electromotive force or potential difference by comparison with a known voltage. **2.** See **voltage divider.** [1880–85; POTENTI(AL) + -O- + -METER] —**po·ten·ti·o·met·ric** (pə ten′shē ə me′trik), *adj.*

poten′tiomet′ric titra′tion, *Chem.* titration in which the end point is determined by measuring the voltage of an electric current of given amperage passed through the solution. [1925–30]

po·tes·tas (pō tes′täs, -təs), *n.* (in Roman law) the authority of a paterfamilias over all members of his family and household. [1650–60; < L *potestās* lit., power, control, authority] —**po·tes′tal,** *adj.*

pot·ful (pot′fo͝ol), *n., pl.* **-fuls.** the amount that can be held by a pot. [1350–1400; ME. See POT[1], -FUL]
—**Usage.** See **-ful.**

pot·head (pot′hed′), *n. Slang.* a person who habitually smokes marijuana. [1965–70, *Amer.*; POT[2] + HEAD] —**pot′head′ed,** *adj.*

poth·e·car·y (poth′i ker′ē), *n., pl.* **-car·ies.** *Brit. Dial.* apothecary. [1350–1400; ME *potecarie,* aph. var. of *apothecarie* APOTHECARY]

po·theen (pə thēn′, -tēn′, -chēn′, pō-), *n.* poteen.

poth·er (poth′ər), *n.* **1.** commotion; uproar. **2.** a heated discussion, debate, or argument; fuss; to-do. **3.** a choking or suffocating cloud, as of smoke or dust. —*v.t., v.i.* **4.** to worry; bother. [1585–95; orig. uncert.]

pot·herb (pot′ûrb′, -hûrb′), *n.* any herb prepared as food by cooking in a pot, as spinach, or added as seasoning in cookery, as thyme. [1530–40; POT[1] + HERB]

pot·hold·er (pot′hōl′dər), *n.* a thick piece of material, as a quilted or woven pad, used in handling hot pots and dishes. [1940–45; POT[1] + HOLDER]

pot·hole (pot′hōl′), *n.* **1.** a deep hole; pit. **2.** a hole formed in pavement, as by excessive use or by extremes of weather. **3.** a more or less cylindrical hole formed in rock by the grinding action of the detrital material in eddying water. **4.** a cave opening vertically from the ground surface. [1820–30; POT[1] + HOLE]

pot·hol·er (pot′hō′lər), *n. Brit.* an explorer of caves; spelunker. [1895–1900; POTHOLE + -ER[1]]

pot·hook (pot′ho͝ok′), *n.* **1.** a hook for suspending a pot or kettle over an open fire. **2.** an iron rod, usually curved, with a hook at the end, used to lift hot pots, irons, stove lids, etc. **3.** an S-shaped stroke in writing, esp. as made by children in learning to write. [1425–75; late ME *pottehok.* See POT[1], HOOK]

po·thos (pō′thos, -thəs, poth′ōs, -əs), *n., pl.* **-thos, -thos·es.** any of various tropical climbing vines belonging to the genera *Pothos* and *Epipremnum,* of the arum family, esp. *E. aureum,* widely cultivated for its variegated foliage. [< NL (Linnaeus), said to be < Sinhalese]

pot·hunt·er (pot′hun′tər), *n.* **1.** a person who hunts for food or profit, ignoring the rules of sport. **2.** a person who takes part in contests merely to win prizes. [1585–95; POT[1] + HUNTER] —**pot′hunt′ing,** *n., adj.*

po·tiche (pō tēsh′; *Fr.* pô tēsh′), *n., pl.* **-tich·es** (-tē′shiz; *Fr.* -tēsh′). a vase or jar, as of porcelain, with a rounded or polygonal body narrowing at the top. [1890–95; < F; akin to POT[1]]

Pot·i·dae·a (pot′i dē′ə), *n.* a city on the Chalcidice Peninsula, whose revolt against Athens in 432 B.C. was one of the causes of the Peloponnesian War.

po·tion (pō′shən), *n.* a drink or draft, esp. one having or reputed to have medicinal, poisonous, or magical powers: *a love potion; a sleeping potion.* [1300–50; ME *pocion* < L *pōtiōn-* (s. of *pōtiō*) a drinking, equiv. to *pōt(us),* var. of *pōtātus,* ptp. of *pōtāre* to drink + *-iōn-* -ION; r. ME *pocioun* < AF < L, as above]
—**Syn.** elixir, brew, concoction, philter.

Pot·i·phar (pot′ə fər), *n.* the Egyptian officer whose wife tried to seduce Joseph. Gen. 39:1–20.

pot·latch (pot′lach), *n.* **1.** (among American Indians of the northern Pacific coast, esp. the Kwakiutl) a ceremonial festival at which gifts are bestowed on the guests and property is destroyed by its owner in a show of wealth that the guests later attempt to surpass. **2.** *Pacific Northwest.* a party or celebration. [1835–45; < Chinook Jargon *pátlač, pá˙ƛač* < Nootka *p̓aλ̓p̓a-* (redupl. of *p̓a-* make ceremonial gifts in potlatch) + *-č* suffix marking iterative aspect]

pot·lick·er (pot′lik′ər), *n.* **1.** *Midland and Southern U.S. Eye Dialect.* See **pot liquor. 2.** *Dial.* a worthless or disgusting person or animal. Also, **pot′lik′er, pot′lik′·ker.**

pot·line (pot′lin′), *n. Metall.* a row of electrolytic cells for reducing certain metals, as aluminum, from fused salts. [1940–45; POT[1] + LINE[1]]

pot′ liq′uor, *Midland and Southern U.S.* the broth in which meat or vegetables, as salt pork or greens, have been cooked. Also, **pot′-liq′uor.** [1735–45]

pot·luck (pot′luk′, -luk′), *n.* **1.** food or a meal that happens to be available without special preparation or purchase: *to take potluck with a friend.* **2.** Also called **pot′luck sup′per, pot′luck din′ner, pot′luck lunch′.** a meal, esp. for a large group, to which participants bring various foods to be shared. **3.** whatever is available or comes one's way: *With fluctuating interest rates, homebuyers are learning to take potluck with the banks.* [1585–95; POT[1] + LUCK]

pot′ mar′igold, calendula (def. 1). [1805–15]

pot′ mar′joram, oregano. [1630–40]

pot′ met′al, 1. an alloy of copper and lead, formerly used for making plumbing fixtures, bearings, etc. **2.** cast iron of a quality suitable for making pots. **3.** a low-grade nonferrous alloy used for die casting. **4.** *Glassmaking.* **a.** glass colored by being mixed with stained glass during fusion. **b.** glass melted in a pot. [1685–95]

pot′ of gold′, 1. the realization of all one's hopes and dreams; ultimate success, fulfillment, or happiness: *to find the pot of gold at the end of the rainbow.* **2.** a sudden, huge windfall; sudden wealth: *Your only chance for a pot of gold is to win the lottery.* [1890–95]

Po·to·mac (pə tō′mək), *n.* **1.** a river flowing SE from the Allegheny Mountains in West Virginia, along the boundary between Maryland and Virginia to the Chesapeake Bay. 287 mi. (460 km) long. **2.** a city in central Maryland, near Washington, D.C. 40,402.

Poto′mac fe′ver, the determination or fervor to share in the power and prestige of the U.S. government in Washington, D.C., esp. by being appointed or elected to a government position. [1965–70; after the POTOMAC River, on which Washington, D.C., is located]

po·tom·e·ter (pə tom′i tər), *n. Meteorol.* an instrument for measuring the amount of water that a plant loses through transpiration, consisting of a sealed vessel of water with a cutting inserted in such a way that moisture can escape only through absorption and transpiration. [1880–85; < Gk *potó(n)* drink + -METER]

po·too (pō to͞o′), *n., pl.* **-toos.** any of several nocturnal birds of the family Nyctibiidae, of Mexico and Central and South America, related to the goatsuckers. [1840–50; orig. Jamaican E *patoo;* cf. Twi *patú* owl]

po·to·roo (pō′tə ro͞o′), *n., pl.* **-roos.** any of several small, ratlike kangaroos of the genus *Potorous,* of Australia. [1790; perh. < Dharuk]

Po·to·sí (pô′tô sē′), *n.* a city in S Bolivia: formerly a rich silver-mining center. 209,850; 13,022 ft. (3970 m) above sea level.

pot·pie (pot′pī′, -pī′), *n.* **1.** a deep-dish pie containing meat, chicken, or the like, often combined with vegetables and topped with a pastry crust. **2.** a stew, as of chicken or veal, with dumplings, biscuits, or the like. [1785–95, *Amer.*; POT[1] + PIE[1]]

pot·pour·ri (pō′po͝o rē′, pō′po͝o rē′), *n.* **1.** a mixture of dried petals of roses or other flowers with spices, kept in a jar for their fragrance. **2.** a musical medley. **3.** a collection of miscellaneous literary extracts. **4.** any mixture, esp. of unrelated objects, subjects, etc. [1605–15; < F: lit., rotten pot, trans. of Sp *olla podrida* OLLA PODRIDA; see POT[1], PUTRID]
—**Syn. 4.** melange, pastiche, hodgepodge, mishmash.

pot′ roast′, a dish of meat, usually brisket of beef or chuck roast, stewed in one piece in a covered pot and served in its own gravy. [1880–85, *Amer.*]

Pots·dam (pots′dam; *for 1 also Ger.* pôts′däm), *n.* **1.** a city in and the capital of Brandenburg, in NE Germany, SW of Berlin: formerly the residence of German emperors; wartime conference July–August 1945 of Truman, Stalin, Churchill, and later, Attlee. 142,860. **2.** a town in N New York. 10,635.

pot·sherd (pot′shûrd′), *n.* a broken pottery fragment, esp. one of archaeological value. [1275–1325; ME; equiv. to *pot* POT[1] + *sherd,* var. of SHARD]

pot·shot (pot′shot′), *n., v.,* **-shot** or **-shot·ted, -shot·ting.** —*n.* **1.** a shot fired at game merely for food, with little regard to skill or the rules of sport. **2.** a shot at an animal or person within easy range, as from ambush. **3.** a casual or aimless shot. **4.** a random or incidental criticism: *to take a potshot at military spending in a speech on taxation.* —*v.i.* **5.** to fire or aim potshots: *critics potshotting at the administration.* [1855–60; POT[1] + SHOT[1]]

pot′ spin′ning, the spinning of rayon filaments in a centrifugal box. Also called **centrifugal spinning.**

pot′ still′, a simple and sometimes primitive type of still, used esp. in the making of cognac, corn liquor, and malt Scotch whisky. Also, **pot′-still′.** [1790–1800]

pot·stone (pot′stōn′), *n.* a kind of soapstone, sometimes used for making pots and other household utensils. [1765–75; POT[1] + STONE]

pot·sy (pot′sē), *n.* hopscotch. [1930–35; orig. uncert.]

pot·tage (pot′ij), *n.* a thick soup made of vegetables, with or without meat. [1175–1225; ME *potage* < OF: lit., something in or from a POT[1]; see -AGE]

pot·ted (pot′id), *adj.* **1.** placed or enclosed in a pot. **2.** transplanted into or grown in a pot. **3.** preserved or cooked in a pot: *potted beef.* **4.** *Slang.* drunk. **5.** *Brit. Slang.* (of the treatment of a subject) shallow; superficial. [1640–50; 1920–25 for def. 4; POT[1] + -ED[2]]

pot·ter[1] (pot′ər), *n.* a person who makes pottery. [bef. 1100; ME; late OE *pottere.* See POT[1], -ER[1]]

pot·ter[2] (pot′ər), *v.i., n. Chiefly Brit.* putter[1]. [1520–30; freq. of obs., dial. *pote* to push, poke, ME *poten,* OE *potian* to push, thrust. See PUT, -ER[6]] —**pot′ter·er,** *n.* —**pot′ter·ing·ly,** *adv.*

Pot·ter (pot′ər), *n.* **1. Be·a·trix** (bē′ə triks), 1866–1943, English writer and illustrator of children's books. **2. Paul,** 1625–54, Dutch painter.

Pot·ter·ies (pot′ə rēz), *n.* **the,** a district in central England famous for the manufacture of pottery and china. The towns comprising this district were combined in 1910 to form Stoke-on-Trent. Also called **Five Towns.** Cf. **Stoke-on-Trent.**

pot′ter's clay′, a clay, suitably plastic and free of iron and other impurities, for use by potters. [1610–20]

pot′ter's field′, (*sometimes caps.*) a piece of ground reserved as a burial place for strangers and the friendless poor. Matt. 27:7. [1520–30]

pot′ter's wheel′, a device with a rotating horizontal disk upon which clay is molded by a potter. [1720–30]

pot′ter wasp′, any of several mason wasps, esp. of the genus *Eumenes,* that construct a juglike nest of mud. [1875–80, *Amer.*]

pot·ter·y (pot′ə rē), *n., pl.* **-ter·ies. 1.** ceramic ware, esp. earthenware and stoneware. **2.** the art or business of a potter; ceramics. **3.** a place where earthen pots or vessels are made. [1475–85; POTTER[1] + -Y[3]]

pot′ting soil′, enriched topsoil for potting plants, esp. house plants. [1905–10]

pot·tle (pot′l), *n.* **1.** a former liquid measure equal to two quarts. **2.** a pot or tankard of this capacity. **3.** the wine or other liquid in it. [1250–1300; ME *potel* < MF, dim. of *pot* POT[1]; see -ELLE]

pot·to (pot′ō), *n., pl.* **-tos. 1.** any of several lorislike, African lemurs of the genera *Perodicticus* and *Arctocebus,* esp. *P. potto,* having a short tail and vestigial index fingers. **2.** the kinkajou. [1695–1705; < D, said to be < Wolof *pata* tailless monkey]

Pott's′ disease′ (pots), *Pathol.* caries of the bodies of the vertebrae, often resulting in marked curvature of the spine, and usually associated with a tuberculosis infection. [1825–35; named after Percival *Pott* (1714–88), British surgeon, who described it]

Pott's′ frac′ture, a fracture of the lower fibula and of the malleolus of the tibia, resulting in outward displacement of the foot. [see POTT'S DISEASE]

Potts·town (pots′toun′), *n.* a borough in SE Pennsylvania. 22,729.

Potts·ville (pots′vil), *n.* a city in E Pennsylvania. 18,195.

pot·ty[1] (pot′ē), *adj.,* **-ti·er, -ti·est. 1.** *Chiefly Brit. Informal.* slightly insane; eccentric. **2.** *Brit.* paltry; trifling; petty. [1855–60; POT[1] + -Y[1]]

pot·ty[2] (pot′ē), *n., pl.* **-ties. 1.** a seat of reduced size fitting over a toilet seat, for use by a small child. **2.** a small metal pot fitting under a potty-chair. **3.** *Baby Talk.* a toilet. [1840–50; POT[1] + -Y[2]]

pot·ty-chair (pot′ē châr′), *n.* a small chair with an

CONCISE ETYMOLOGY KEY: <, descended or borrowed from; >, whence; b., blend of, blended; c., cognate with; cf., compare; deriv., derivative; equiv., equivalent; imit., imitative; obl., oblique; r., replacing; s., stem; sp., spelling, spelled; resp., respelling, respelled; trans., translation; ?, origin unknown; *, unattested; ‡, probably earlier than. See the full key inside the front cover.

open seat over a removable pot, for use by a child during toilet training. [1960–65]

po·tus (pō′təs), *n., pl.* **-ti** (-tī). (in prescriptions) a drink. [< L *pōtus*]

pot-val·iant (pot′val′yənt), *adj.* brave only as a result of being drunk. [1635–45] **—pot′-val′iant·ly,** *adv.* **—pot-val·or** (pot′val′ər), **pot-val·ian·cy** (pot′val′yən-sē), *n.*

pot·wal·lop·er (pot′wol′ə pər, pot wol′-), *n. Eng. Hist.* (in some boroughs before the Reform Bill of 1832) a man who qualified as a householder, and therefore a voter, by virtue of ownership of his own fireplace at which to boil pots. Also, **pot′-wal′lop·er.** Also called **pot·wal·ler** (pot′wol′ər). [1715–25; POT[1] + WALLOPER; r. *potwaller* lit., potboiler (POT[1] + *wall,* OE *weallan* to boil + -ER[1])]

pouch (pouch), *n.* **1.** a bag, sack, or similar receptacle, esp. one for small articles or quantities: *a tobacco pouch.* **2.** a small moneybag. **3.** a bag for carrying mail. **4.** a bag or case of leather, used by soldiers to carry ammunition. **5.** something shaped like or resembling a bag or pocket. **6.** *Chiefly Scot.* a pocket in a garment. **7.** a baggy fold of flesh under the eye. **8.** *Anat., Zool.* a baglike or pocketlike part; a sac or cyst, as the sac beneath the bill of pelicans, the saclike dilation of the cheeks of gophers, or the receptacle for the young of marsupials. **9.** *Bot.* a baglike cavity. —*v.t.* **10.** to put into or enclose in a pouch, bag, or pocket; pocket. **11.** to arrange in the form of a pouch. **12.** (of a fish or bird) to swallow. —*v.i.* **13.** to form a pouch or a cavity resembling a pouch. [1350–1400; ME *pouche* < AF, var. of OF *poche;* also *poke, poque* bag. See POKE[2]]

pouched (poucht), *adj.* having a pouch, as the pelicans, gophers, and marsupials. [1815–25; POUCH + -ED[3]]

pouched′ mole′. See **marsupial mole.**

pouched′ rat′. See **pocket gopher.** [1820–30, *Amer.*]

pouch·y (pou′chē), *adj.,* **pouch·i·er, pouch·i·est.** possessing or resembling a pouch: *pouchy folds under the eyes.* [1820–30; POUCH + -Y[1]]

pou·drette (po͞o dret′), *n.* a fertilizer made from dried night soil mixed with other substances, as gypsum and charcoal. [1830–40; < F, equiv. to *poudre* POWDER + *-ette* -ETTE]

pou·dreuse (po͞o dro͞oz′; *Fr.* po͞o DRŒZ′), *n., pl.* **-dreus·es** (-dro͞o′ziz; *Fr.* -DRŒZ′). a small toilet table of the 18th century. [1925–30; < F, equiv. to *poudr(er)* to POWDER + *-euse* -EUSE]

pouf[1] (po͞of), *n.* **1.** a high headdress with the hair rolled in puffs, worn by women in the late 18th century. **2.** an arrangement of the hair over a pad; puff. **3.** a puff of material as an ornament on a dress or headdress. **4.** Also, **pouffe.** a broad, backless, usually round, cushionlike seat, often large enough for several people. [1810–20; < F; see PUFF]

pouf[2] (po͝of, po͞of), *n. Brit. Slang (disparaging and offensive).* poof[2].

Pough·keep·sie (pə kip′sē), *n.* a city in SE New York, on the Hudson. 29,757.

Pouil·ly (po͞o yē′), *n.* a village in central France: known for its wines. Also called **Pouil·ly-sur-Loire** (po͞o-yē SYR LWAR′).

Pouil·ly-Fuis·sé (po͞o yē′fwē sā′; *Fr.* po͞o yē fwē sā′), *n.* a dry, white wine from Burgundy. [1930–35]

Pouil·ly-Fu·mé (po͞o yē′fyo͞o mā′; *Fr.* po͞o yē fy mā′), *n.* a dry, white wine from the Loire Valley of France. [1930–35]

pou·laine (po͞o lān′), *n.* **1.** a shoe or boot with an elongated pointed toe, fashionable in the 15th century. **2.** the toe on such a shoe. Also called **crakow.** [1520–30; < MF *Poulaine* Poland (in the phrase *souliers à la Poulaine* shoes of Polish style); cf. AF *poleine*]

pou·lard (po͞o lärd′), *n.* a hen spayed to improve the flesh for use as food. Also, **pou·larde′.** [1725–35; < F, equiv. to *poule* hen (see PULLET) + *-ard* -ARD]

poulard′ wheat′, a Mediterranean wheat, *Triticum turgidum,* grown as a forage crop in the U.S. Also called **river wheat.**

Pou·lenc (po͞o laNk′), *n.* **Fran·cis** (frän sēs′), 1899–1963, French composer and pianist.

poult (pōlt), *n.* a young fowl, as of the turkey, the pheasant, or a similar bird. [1375–1425; late ME *pult(e)*; syncopated var. of PULLET]

poult-de-soie (*Fr.* po͞odᵊ swä′), *n.* a soft, ribbed silk fabric, used esp. for dresses. [1825–35; < F; see PADUASOY]

poul·ter·er (pōl′tər ər), *n. Brit.* a dealer in poultry, hares, and game; poultryman. [1525–35; obs. *poulter* poultry dealer (< MF *pouletier;* see PULLET, -IER[2]) + -ER[1]]

poul′ter's meas′ure (pōl′tərz), *Pros.* a metrical pattern using couplets having the first line in iambic hexameter, or 12 syllables, and the second in iambic heptameter, or 14 syllables. [1570–80; so called because *poulters* (see POULTERER) used to give extra eggs when counting by the dozen]

poul·tice (pōl′tis), *n., v.,* **-ticed, -tic·ing.** —*n.* **1.** a soft, moist mass of cloth, bread, meal, herbs, etc., applied hot as a medicament to the body. —*v.t.* **2.** to apply a poultice to. [1535–45; earlier *pultes,* pl. (taken as sing.) of L *puls* (s. *pult-*) thick pap. See PULSE[2]]

poul·try (pōl′trē), *n.* domesticated fowl collectively, esp. those valued for their meat and eggs, as chickens, turkeys, ducks, geese, and guinea fowl. [1350–1400; ME *pulletrie* < MF *pouleterie.* See PULLET, -ERY] **—poul′·try·less,** *adj.* **—poul′try·like′,** *adj.*

poul·try·man (pōl′trē mən), *n., pl.* **-men. 1.** a person who raises domestic fowls, esp. chickens, to sell as meat; a chicken farmer. **2.** a poultry dealer, esp. one who sells chickens at retail for cooking. [1565–75; POULTRY + -MAN]

pounce[1] (pouns), *v.,* **pounced, pounc·ing,** *n.* —*v.i.* **1.** to swoop down suddenly and grasp, as a bird does in seizing its prey. **2.** to spring, dash, or come suddenly: *Unexpectedly she pounced on the right answer.* —*v.t.* **3.** to seize (prey) suddenly: *The bird quickly pounced its prey.* —*n.* **4.** the claw or talon of a bird of prey. **5.** a sudden swoop, as on an object of prey. [1375–1425; late ME; perh. akin to PUNCH[1]] **—pounc′ing·ly,** *adv.*
—Syn. 5. leap, lunge, spring.

pounce[2] (pouns), *v.t.,* **pounced, pounc·ing.** to emboss (metal) by hammering on an instrument applied on the reverse side. [1350–1400; ME; perh. identical with POUNCE[1]]

pounce[3] (pouns), *n., v.,* **pounced, pounc·ing.** —*n.* **1.** a fine powder, as of cuttlebone, formerly used to prevent ink from spreading in writing, or to prepare parchment for writing. **2.** a fine powder, often of charcoal, used in transferring a design through a perforated pattern. **3.** Also, **pounce′ bag′.** a small bag filled with pounce and struck against a perforated design. —*v.t.* **4.** to sprinkle, smooth, or prepare with pounce. **5.** to trace (a design) with pounce. **6.** to finish the surface of (hats) by rubbing with sandpaper or the like. [1700–10; < F *ponce* << L *pūmicem,* acc. of *pūmex* PUMICE] **—pounc′er,** *n.*

poun′cet box′ (poun′sit), a small perfume box with a perforated lid. [1590–1600; POUNCE[2] or POUNCE[3] + -ET]

pound[1] (pound), *v.t.* **1.** to strike repeatedly with great force, as with an instrument, the fist, heavy missiles, etc. **2.** to produce or effect by striking or thumping, or in a manner resembling this (often fol. by *out*): *to pound out a tune on the piano.* **3.** to force (a way) by battering; batter (often fol. by *down*): *He pounded his way through the mob. He pounded the door down.* **4.** to crush into a powder or paste by beating repeatedly. —*v.i.* **5.** to strike heavy blows repeatedly: *to pound on a door.* **6.** to beat or throb violently, as the heart. **7.** to give forth a thumping sound: *The drums pounded loudly.* **8.** to walk or go with heavy steps; move along with force or vigor. —*n.* **9.** the act of pounding. **10.** a heavy or forcible blow. **11.** a thump. [bef. 1000; ME *pounen,* OE *pūnian;* akin to D *puin* rubbish] **—pound′er,** *n.*
—Syn. 1. See **beat.**

pound[2] (pound), *n., pl.* **pounds,** (*collectively*) **pound. 1.** a unit of weight and of mass, varying in different periods and countries. **2. a.** (in English-speaking countries) an avoirdupois unit of weight equal to 7000 grains, divided into 16 ounces (0.453 kg), used for ordinary commerce. *Abbr.:* lb., lb. av. **b.** a troy unit of weight, in the U.S. and formerly in Britain, equal to 5760 grains, divided into 12 ounces (0.373 kg), used for gold, silver, and other precious metals. *Abbr.:* lb. t. **c.** (in the U.S.) an apothecaries' unit of weight equal to 5760 grains, divided into 12 ounces (0.373 kg). *Abbr.:* lb. ap. **3.** Also called **pound sterling.** a paper money, nickel-brass coin, and monetary unit of the United Kingdom formerly equal to 20 shillings or 240 pence: equal to 100 new pence after decimalization in Feb. 1971. *Abbr.:* L; *Symbol:* £ **4.** Also called **pound Scots.** a former Scottish money of account, originally equal to the pound sterling but equal to only a twelfth of the pound sterling at the union of the crowns of England and Scotland in 1603. **5.** any of the monetary units of various countries, as Cyprus, Egypt, Ireland, Lebanon, Sudan, Syria, and of certain Commonwealth of Nations countries. **6.** (formerly) the Turkish lira. **7.** a former monetary unit of Israel, Libya, and Nigeria. **8. pounds,** *CB Slang.* a meter reading in units of five decibels: used as a measure of loudness for incoming signals. [bef. 900; ME; OE *pund* (c. D *pond,* G *Pfund,* Goth, ON *pund*) << L *pondō* pound (indeclinable n.), orig. abl. of *pondus* weight (see PONDER) in the phrase *libra pondō* a pound by weight; see LIBRA[1]]

pound[3] (pound), *n.* **1.** an enclosure maintained by public authorities for confining stray or homeless animals. **2.** an enclosure for sheltering, keeping, confining, or trapping animals. **3.** an enclosure or trap for fish. **4.** a place of confinement or imprisonment. **5.** a place or area where cars or other vehicles are impounded, as those towed away for being illegally parked. **6.** reach (def. 26). —*v.t.* **7.** *Archaic.* to shut up in or as in a pound; impound; imprison. [1350–1400; ME *poond;* cf. late OE *pund-* in *pundfald* PINFOLD; akin to POND]

Pound (pound), *n.* **1. Ezra Loo·mis** (lo͞o′mis), 1885–1972, U.S. poet. **2. Louise,** 1872–1958, U.S. scholar and linguist. **3.** her brother, **Roscoe,** 1870–1964, U.S. legal scholar and writer.

pound·age[1] (poun′dij), *n.* **1.** a tax, commission, rate, etc., of so much per pound sterling or per pound weight. **2.** weight in pounds. [1350–1400; ME; see POUND[2], -AGE]

pound·age[2] (poun′dij), *n.* **1.** confinement within an enclosure or within certain limits. **2.** the fee demanded to free animals from a pound. [1545–55; POUND[3] + -AGE]

pound·al (poun′dl), *n. Physics.* the foot-pound-second unit of force, equal to the force that produces an acceleration of one foot per second per second on a mass of one pound. *Abbr.:* pdl [1875–80; POUND[2] + -AL[2]]

pound′ cake′, a rich, sweet cake made originally with approximately a pound each of butter, sugar, and flour. [1740–50]

pound·er[1] (poun′dər), *n.* a person or thing that pounds, pulverizes, or beats. [bef. 1050; OE *pūnere* pestle (not found in ME); see POUND[1], -ER[1]]

pound·er[2] (poun′dər), *n.* **1.** a person or thing having or associated with a weight or value of a pound or a specified number of pounds (often used in combination): *He caught only one fish, but it was an eight-pounder.* **2.** a gun that discharges a missile of a specified weight in pounds: *a ten-pounder.* [1635–45; POUND[2] + -ER[1]]

pound-force (pound′fôrs′, -fōrs′), *n. Physics.* a foot-pound-second unit of force, equal to the force that produces an acceleration equal to the acceleration of gravity when acting on a mass of one pound. *Abbr.:* lbf [1895–1900]

pound′ net′, a trap for catching fish, consisting of a system of nets staked upright in the water and a rectangular enclosure or pound from which escape is impossible. [1855–60, *Amer.*]

pound′ Scots′, pound[2] (def. 4). [1605–15]

pound′ sign′, 1. a symbol (£) for "pound" or "pounds" as a monetary unit of the United Kingdom. **2.** a symbol (#) for "pound" or "pounds" as a unit of weight or mass: *20# bond paper stock.* Cf. **hash mark, number sign, space mark.**

pound′ ster′ling, pound[2] (def. 3). [1625–35]

pour (pôr, pōr), *v.t.* **1.** to send (a liquid, fluid, or anything in loose particles) flowing or falling, as from one container to another, or into, over, or on something: *to pour a glass of milk; to pour water on a plant.* **2.** to emit or propel, esp. continuously or rapidly: *The hunter poured bullets into the moving object.* **3.** to produce or utter in or as in a stream or flood (often fol. by *out*): *to pour out one's troubles to a friend.* —*v.i.* **4.** to issue, move, or proceed in great quantity or number: *Crowds poured from the stadium after the game.* **5.** to flow forth or along; stream: *Floodwaters poured over the embankments.* **6.** to rain heavily (often used impersonally with *it* as subject): *It was pouring, but fortunately we had umbrellas.* —*n.* **7.** the act of pouring. **8.** an abundant or continuous flow or stream: *a pour of invective.* **9.** a heavy fall of rain. [1300–50; ME *pouren;* orig. uncert.] **—pour′a·ble,** *adj.* **—pour′a·bil′i·ty,** *n.* **—pour′er,** *n.* **—pour′ing·ly,** *adv.*

pour·boire (po͝or bwar′; *Eng.* po͝or bwär′), *n., pl.* ***-boires*** (-BWAR′; *Eng.* -bwärz′). *French.* a gratuity; tip. [lit., for drinking]

pour′ing box′, *Metall.* tundish (def. 2). Also called **pour′ing bas′ket, pour′ing ba′sin.**

pour le mé·rite (po͞or lə mā RĕT′), *French.* for merit.

pour·par·ler (po͞or PAR lā′; *Eng.* po͝or′pär lā′), *n. pl.* ***-lers*** (-lā′; *Eng.* -lāz′). *French.* an informal preliminary conference. [lit., for talking]

pour·par·ty (po͝or′pär′tē), *n. Law.* purparty.

pour′ point′, *Chem.* the lowest temperature at which a substance will flow under given conditions. [1920–25]

pour·point (po͝or′point′, -pwant′), *n.* a stuffed and quilted doublet worn by men from the 14th to 17th centuries. [1350–1400; < F, n. use of ptp. of *pourpoindre* to quilt, perforate, equiv. to *pour-,* for *par-* (< L *per*) through + *poindre* (< L *pungere* to prick, pierce; see POINT); r. ME *purpont* < AL *purpunctus*]

pour·ri·ture no·ble (po͞o RĒ TYR nô′blᵊ), *French.* See **noble rot.**

pour′ test′, *Chem.* any test for determining the pour point of a substance.

pou·sa·da (pō sä′də), *n., pl.* **-das** (-dəz; *Port* -dəsh). a government-operated inn in Portugal. [1930–35; < Pg: inn, lodging, equiv. to *pous(ar)* to rest, halt (< LL *pausāre;* cf. POSE[1]) + *-ada,* fem. of *-ado* -ATE[1]; cf. POSADA]

pousse-ca·fé (po͞os′ka fā′; *Fr.* po͞os KA fā′), *n., pl.* **-fés** (-fāz′; *Fr.* -fā′). **1.** an after-dinner drink of liqueurs of various colors and specific gravities, carefully poured into a glass so as to remain floating in separate layers. **2.** a small glass of liqueur served after coffee. [1875–80; < F: lit., (it) pushes on (the) coffee]

pous·sette (po͞o set′), *n., v.,* **-set·ted, -set·ting.** —*n.* **1.** a dance step in which a couple or several couples dance around the ballroom, holding hands, as in country dances. —*v.i.* **2.** to perform a poussette, as a couple in a country dance. [1805–15; < F, equiv. to *pouss(er)* to PUSH + *-ette* -ETTE]

Pous·sin (po͞o SAN′), *n.* **Ni·co·las** (nē kô lä′), 1594–1655, French painter.

pout[1] (pout), *v.i.* **1.** to thrust out the lips, esp. in displeasure or sullenness. **2.** to look or be sullen. **3.** to swell out or protrude, as lips. —*v.t.* **4.** to protrude (the lips). **5.** to utter with a pout. —*n.* **6.** the act of pouting; a protrusion of the lips. **7.** a fit of sullenness: *to be in a pout.* [1275–1325; ME *pouten;* c. Sw (dial.) *puta* to be inflated] **—pout′ful,** *adj.* **—pout′ing·ly,** *adv.*
—Syn. 1, 2. brood, mope, glower, scowl, sulk.

pout[2] (pout), *n., pl.* (*esp. collectively*) **pout,** (*esp. referring to two or more kinds or species*) **pouts. 1.** See **horned pout. 2.** See **ocean pout. 3.** a northern, marine food fish, *Trisopterus luscus.* [bef. 1000; OE *-pūta,* in *ǣlepūta* eelpout (not recorded in ME); c. D *puit* frog]

pout·er (pou′tər), *n.* **1.** a person who pouts. **2.** one of a breed of long-legged domestic pigeons, characterized by the habit of puffing out the distensible crop. [1715–25; POUT[1] + -ER[1]]

pout·y (pou′tē), *adj.,* **pout·i·er, pout·i·est.** inclined to pout, or marked by pouting: *a sullen, pouty child; a pouty face.* [1860–65, *Amer.*; POUT[1] + -Y[1]]

POV, *Motion Pictures.* point of view: used esp. in describing a method of shooting a scene or film that expresses the attitude of the director or writer toward the material or of a character in a scene.

pov·er·ty (pov′ər tē), *n.* **1.** the state or condition of having little or no money, goods, or means of support; condition of being poor; indigence. **2.** deficiency of necessary or desirable ingredients, qualities, etc.: *poverty of the soil.* **3.** scantiness; insufficiency: *Their efforts to stamp out disease were hampered by a poverty of medical supplies.* [1125–75; ME *poverte* < OF < L *paupertāt-* (s. of *paupertās*) small means, moderate circumstances. See PAUPER, -TY[2]]
—Syn. 1. penury. POVERTY, DESTITUTION, NEED, WANT imply a state of privation and lack of necessities. POVERTY denotes serious lack of the means for proper existence: *living in a state of extreme poverty.* DESTITUTION, a somewhat more literary word, implies a state of having absolutely none of the necessities of life: *widespread destitution in countries at war.* NEED emphasizes the fact that help or relief is necessary: *Most of the people were*

CONCISE PRONUNCIATION KEY: act, cāpe, dâre, pärt; set, ēqual; if, ice; ox, ōver, ôrder, oil, bo͝ok, bo͞ot, out; up, ûrge; child; sing; shoe; thin, *th*at; zh as in *treasure.* ə = *a* as in *alone, e* as in *system, i* as in *easily, o* as in *gallop, u* as in *circus;* ᵊ as in *fire* (fīᵊr), *hour* (ouᵊr). l and n can serve as syllabic consonants, as in *cradle* (krād′l), and *button* (but′n). See the full key inside the front cover.

in great need. WANT emphasizes privations, esp. lack of food and clothing: *Families were suffering from want.* **3.** meagerness. **—Ant. 1.** riches, wealth, plenty.

pov′erty lev′el. See **poverty line.** [1975–80] **—pov′er·ty-lev′el,** *adj.*

pov′erty line′, a minimum income level used as an official standard for determining the proportion of a population living in poverty.

pov·er·ty-strick·en (pov′ər tē strik′ən), *adj.* suffering from poverty; extremely poor: *poverty-stricken refugees.* [1795–1805]

po·vi·done-i·o·dine (pō′vi dōn ī′ə dīn′, -din), *n. Pharm.* a complex of iodine and polyvinylpyrrolidone that has broad-spectrum antimicrobial activity: used as an antiseptic. [PO(LY)VI(NYLPYRROLI)DONE]

pow[1] (pou), *interj.* **1.** (used to express or indicate a heavy blow or a loud, explosive noise.) *—n.* **2.** a heavy blow or a loud, explosive noise. **3.** the power of exciting. *—adj.* **4.** exciting and appealing. [1880–85, *Amer.*]

pow[2] (pō, pou), *n. Scot. and North Eng.* the head; poll. [1715–25; var. of POLL[1]]

POW, prisoner of war. Also, **P.O.W.**

Pow·ay (pou′ā), *n.* a city in SW California. 32,263.

pow·der[1] (pou′dər), *n.* **1.** any solid substance reduced to a state of fine, loose particles by crushing, grinding, disintegration, etc. **2.** a preparation in this form, as gunpowder or face powder. **3.** Also, **powder snow.** *Skiing.* loose, usually fresh snow that is not granular, wet, or packed. *—v.t.* **4.** to reduce to powder; pulverize. **5.** to sprinkle or cover with powder: *She powdered the cookies with confectioners' sugar.* **6.** to apply powder to (the face, skin, etc.) as a cosmetic. **7.** to sprinkle or strew as if with powder: *A light snowfall powdered the landscape.* **8.** to ornament in this fashion, as with small objects scattered over a surface: *a dress lightly powdered with sequins.* *—v.i.* **9.** to use powder as a cosmetic. **10.** to become pulverized. [1250–1300; (n.) ME *poudre* < OF < L *pulver-* (s. of *pulvis*) dust, powder; akin to POLLEN; (v.) ME *poudren* < OF *poudrer,* deriv. of *poudre*] **—pow′der·er,** *n.*

pow·der[2] (pou′dər), *v.i.* **1.** *Brit. Dial.* to rush. *—n.* **2.** *Brit. Dial.* a sudden, frantic, or impulsive rush. **3. take a powder,** *Slang.* to leave in a hurry; depart without taking leave, as to avoid something unpleasant: *He took a powder and left his mother to worry about his gambling debts.* Also, **take a runout powder.** [1625–35; orig. uncert.]

pow′der blue′, a pale blue diluted with gray. [1700–10] **—pow′der-blue′,** *adj.*

pow′der boy′. See **powder monkey** (def. 1). [1795–1805]

pow′der burn′, a skin burn caused by exploding gunpowder. [1840–50, *Amer.*]

pow′der charge′, propellant (def. 2). [1930–35]

pow′der chest′, a small wooden box containing a charge of powder, old nails, scrap iron, etc., formerly secured over the side of a ship and exploded on the attempt of an enemy to board.

pow′der down′, modified down feathers that continually crumble at the tips, producing a fine powder that forms a bloom on the plumage of certain birds, as pigeons and herons.

pow′dered milk′. See **dry milk.** [1885–90]

pow′dered sug′ar, a sugar produced by pulverizing granulated sugar, esp. a coarser variety used for fruits or cold beverages. *Symbol:* XX Cf. **confectioners' sugar.** [1615–25]

pow′der flag′, *Naut.* See **red flag** (def. 4). [1870–75]

pow′der flask′, a small flask of gunpowder formerly carried by soldiers and hunters. [1745–55]

pow′der horn′, a powder flask made from the horn of a cow or ox. [1525–35]

pow′der keg′, **1.** a small, metal, barrellike container for gunpowder or blasting powder. **2.** a potentially dangerous situation, esp. one involving violent repercussions. [1850–55]

pow′der magazine′, a compartment for the storage of ammunition and explosives. [1755–65]

pow·der·man (pou′dər man′, -mən), *n., pl.* **-men** (-men′, -mən). **1.** a person in charge of explosives, esp. in a demolition crew. **2.** *Slang.* a safe-cracker who uses explosives to open safes. [1660–70; POWDER[1] + MAN[1]]

pow′der met′allurgy, the art or science of manufacturing useful articles by compacting metal and other powders in a die, followed by sintering. [1930–35]

pow′der meth′od, *Crystall.* a method of x-ray determination of crystal structure using a powdered sample. Cf. **x-ray crystallography.**

pow′der mill′, a mill in which gunpowder is made. [1640–50]

pow′der mon′key, **1.** (formerly) a boy employed on warships to carry gunpowder from the magazine to the guns. **2.** powderman (def. 1). [1675–85]

pow′der pa′per, *Pharm.* charta (def. 2). [1880–85]

pow′der puff′, a soft, feathery ball or pad, as of cotton or down, for applying powder to the skin. [1695–1705]

pow·der-puff (pou′dər puf′), *adj. Informal.* **1.** limited to participation by women or girls: *She plays on the powder-puff touch football team.* **2.** inconsequential; trifling; lightweight: *a powder-puff company with little financing and a weak sales effort.* [1935–40]

pow′der room′, **1.** a room containing a toilet and washing facilities for women; lavatory. **2.** such a room provided for the use of female guests, as in a restaurant or nightclub. [1905–10]

pow′der snow′, *Skiing.* powder[1] (def. 3). [1925–30]

pow·der·y (pou′də rē), *adj.* **1.** consisting of or resembling powder: *powdery sand; powdery clouds.* **2.** easily reduced to powder: *powdery plaster.* **3.** sprinkled or covered with or as with powder: *flowers powdery with pollen.* [1400–50; late ME *powdry.* See POWDER[1], -Y[1]]

pow′dery mil′dew, **1.** any of various parasitic fungi of the ascomycete order Erysiphales, which produce a powderlike film of mycelium on the surface of host plants. **2.** *Plant Pathol.* a disease caused by powdery mildew, characterized by yellowing and death of the foliage and a white mealy growth of fungus on the surface of above-ground parts. [1885–90, *Amer.*]

Pow·ell (pou′əl *for 1, 4, 5;* pō′əl, pou′- *for 2, 3*), *n.* **1. Adam Clayton, Jr.,** 1908–72, U.S. clergyman, politician, and civil-rights leader: congressman 1945–67, 1969–71. **2. Anthony,** born 1905, English author. **3. Cecil Frank,** 1903–69, English physicist: Nobel prize 1950. **4. John Wesley,** 1834–1902, U.S. geologist and ethnologist. **5. Lewis Franklin, Jr.,** born 1907, U.S. jurist: associate justice of the U.S. Supreme Court 1972–87.

pow·er (pou′ər), *n.* **1.** ability to do or act; capability of doing or accomplishing something. **2.** political or national strength: *the balance of power in Europe.* **3.** great or marked ability to do or act; strength; might; force. **4.** the possession of control or command over others; authority; ascendancy: *power over men's minds.* **5.** political ascendancy or control in the government of a country, state, etc.: *They attained power by overthrowing the legal government.* **6.** legal ability, capacity, or authority: *the power of attorney.* **7.** delegated authority; authority granted to a person or persons in a particular office or capacity: *the powers of the president.* **8.** a document or written statement conferring legal authority. **9.** a person or thing that possesses or exercises authority or influence. **10.** a state or nation having international authority or influence: *The great powers held an international conference.* **11.** a military or naval force: *The Spanish Armada was a mighty power.* **12.** Often, **powers.** a deity; divinity: *the heavenly powers.* **13. powers,** *Theol.* an order of angels. Cf. **angel** (def. 1). **14.** *Dial.* a large number or amount: *There's a power of good eatin' at the church social.* **15.** *Physics.* **a.** work done or energy transferred per unit of time. *Symbol:* P **b.** the time rate of doing work. **16.** mechanical energy as distinguished from hand labor: *a loom driven by power.* **17.** a particular form of mechanical or physical energy: *hydroelectric power.* **18.** energy, force, or momentum: *The door slammed shut, seemingly under its own power.* **19.** *Math.* **a.** the product obtained by multiplying a quantity by itself one or more times: *The third power of 2 is 8.* **b.** (of a number x) a number whose logarithm is a times the logarithm of x (and is called the ath power of x). Symbolically, $y = x^a$ is a number that satisfies the equation $\log y = a \log x$. **c.** the exponent of an expression, as a in x^a. **d.** See **cardinal number** (def. 2). **20.** *Optics.* **a.** the magnifying capacity of a microscope, telescope, etc., expressed as the ratio of the diameter of the image to the diameter of the object. Cf. **magnification** (def. 2). **b.** the reciprocal of the focal length of a lens. **21. the powers that be,** those in supreme command; the authorities: *The decision is in the hands of the powers that be.* *—v.t.* **22.** to supply with electricity or other means of power: *Atomic energy powers the new submarines.* **23.** to give power to; make powerful: *An outstanding quarterback powered the team in its upset victory.* **24.** to inspire; spur; sustain: *A strong faith in divine goodness powers his life.* **25.** (of a fuel, engine, or any source able to do work) to supply force to operate (a machine): *An electric motor powers this drill.* **26.** to drive or push by applying power: *She powered the car expertly up the winding mountain road.* **27. power down,** *Computers.* to shut off. **28. power up,** *Computers.* to turn on. *—adj.* **29.** operated or driven by a motor or electricity: *a power mower; power tools.* **30.** power-assisted: *His new car has power brakes and power windows.* **31.** conducting electricity: *a power cable.* **32.** *Informal.* expressing or exerting power; characteristic of those having authority or influence: *to host a power lunch.* [1250–1300; ME *pouer(e), poer(e)* < AF *poueir, poer,* n. use of inf.: to be able < VL **potēre* (r. L *posse* to be able, have power). See POTENT]
—Syn. 1. capacity. **3.** energy. See **strength. 4, 5.** sway, rule, sovereignty. **—Ant. 1.** incapacity. **3.** weakness.

pow′er am′plifier, *Elect.* an amplifier for increasing the power of a signal. [1915–20]

pow′er assist′, a procedure for supplementing or replacing the manual effort needed to operate a device or system, often by hydraulic, electrical, or mechanical means. **—pow′er-as·sist′ed, pow′er-as·sist′,** *adj.*

pow′er base′, a source of authority or influence, esp. in politics, founded on support by an organized body of voters, ethnic minority, economic class, etc.: *His election as governor gives him a power base for seeking the presidency.* [1965–70]

pow·er·boat (pou′ər bōt′), *n.* **1.** a boat propelled by mechanical power. **2.** motorboat. [1905–10; POWER + BOAT] **—pow′er·boat′ing,** *n.*

pow·er·boat·er (pou′ər bō′tər), *n.* a powerboat owner or operator. [1950–55; POWERBOAT + -ER[1]]

pow′er brake′, an automotive brake set by pressure from some power source, as a compressed-air reservoir, in proportion to a smaller amount of pressure on the brake pedal. [1895–1900]

pow·er·bro·ker (pou′ər brō′kər), *n.* a person who wields great political, governmental, or financial power. [1960–65, *Amer.*; POWER + BROKER]

pow′er ca′ble, *Elect.* cable for conducting electric power. [1900–05]

pow′er chain′, an endless chain for transmitting motion and power between sprockets on shafts with parallel axes. Also called **pitch chain.** Cf. **roller chain.**

pow′er dive′, *Aeron.* a dive, esp. a steep dive, by an aircraft in which the engine or engines are delivering thrust at or near full power. [1925–30]

pow·er-dive (pou′ər dīv′), *v.t., v.i.,* **-dived** or **-dove, -dived, -div·ing.** *Aeron.* to cause to perform or to perform a power dive. [1935–40]

pow′er drill′, a drill operated by a motor. [1960–65]

pow·ered (pou′ərd), *adj.* (of a machine, vehicle, etc.) having a specified fuel or prime mover: *a gasoline-powered engine; an engine-powered pump.* [1875–80; POWER + -ED[2]]

pow′er elite′, a closely knit alliance of military, government, and corporate officials perceived as the center of wealth and political power in the U.S. [1950–55]

pow′er for′ward, *Basketball.* a forward valued chiefly for aggressive rebounding capability, rather than scoring, and thus a big, physically strong player.

pow·er·ful (pou′ər fəl), *adj.* **1.** having or exerting great power or force. **2.** physically strong, as a person: *a large, powerful athlete.* **3.** producing great physical effects, as a machine or a blow. **4.** potent; efficacious: *a powerful drug.* **5.** having great effectiveness, as a speech, speaker, description, reason, etc. **6.** having great power, authority, or influence; mighty: *a powerful nation.* **7.** *Chiefly South Midland and Southern U.S.* great in number or amount: *a powerful lot of money.* [1350–1400; ME *powarfull.* See POWER, -FUL] **—pow′er·ful·ly,** *adv.* **—pow′er·ful·ness,** *n.*
—Syn. 1. forceful, strong. POWERFUL, MIGHTY, POTENT suggest great force or strength. POWERFUL suggests capability of exerting great force or overcoming strong resistance: *a powerful machine like a bulldozer.* MIGHTY, now chiefly rhetorical, implies uncommon or overwhelming strength of power: *a mighty army.* POTENT implies great natural or inherent power: *a potent influence.* **5.** influential, convincing, forcible, cogent, effective. **—Ant. 1.** weak.

pow·er·house (pou′ər hous′), *n., pl.* **-hous·es** (-hou′ziz). **1.** *Elect.* a generating station. **2.** a person, group, team, or the like, having great energy, strength, or potential for success. [1880–85; POWER + HOUSE]

pow·er·less (pou′ər lis), *adj.* **1.** unable to produce an effect: *a disease against which modern medicine is virtually powerless.* **2.** lacking power to act; helpless: *His legs crumpled, and he was powerless to rise.* [1545–55; POWER + -LESS] **—pow′er·less·ly,** *adv.* **—pow′er·less·ness,** *n.*
—Syn. 1. ineffective. **2.** feeble, impotent, prostrate, infirm.

pow′er line′, *Elect.* a line for conducting electric power. [1890–95]

pow′er load′ing, *Aeron.* See under **loading** (def. 4). [1915–20]

pow·er-loom (pou′ər lōōm′), *n.* a loom operated by mechanical or electrical power. [1800–10]

pow′er mow′er, a lawn mower that is powered and propelled by an electric motor or gasoline engine (distinguished from *hand mower*). [1935–40]

pow′er of appoint′ment, *Law.* the authority granted by a donor to a donee to select the person or persons who are to enjoy property rights or income upon the death of the donor or of the donee or after the termination of existing rights or interests. [1930–35]

pow′er of attor′ney, *Law.* a written document given by one person or party to another authorizing the latter to act for the former. [1740–50]

pow′er pack′, *Electronics.* a device for converting the voltage from a power line or battery to the various voltages required by the components of an electronic circuit. [1935–40]

pow′er plant′, **1.** a plant, including engines, dynamos, etc., and the building or buildings necessary for the generation of power, as electric or nuclear power. **2.** the machinery for supplying power for a particular mechanical process or operation. **3.** the engine, motor, or other power source along with related ignition, transmission, etc., components of a vehicle, aircraft, machine, etc. Also, **pow′er·plant′.** [1885–90]

pow′er play′, **1.** *Football.* an aggressive running play in which numerous offensive players converge and forge ahead to block and clear a path for the ball carrier. **2.** *Ice Hockey.* **a.** a situation in which one team has a temporary numerical advantage because an opposing player or players are in the penalty box, and hence has an opportunity for a concerted, swarming attack on the opponent's goal. **b.** the offensive strategy or effectiveness of the team having such an advantage. **3.** an action, stratagem, or maneuver, as in politics or business, by which power is concentrated or manipulated in order to subdue a rival or gain control of a situation. [1960–65]

pow′er pol′itics, **1.** political action characterized by the exercise or pursuit of power as a means of coercion. **2.** international diplomacy based on the use or threatened use of military or economic power. [1935–40]

pow′er press′, a press operated by a mechanical, hydraulic, or electrical device. [1835–45]

Pow·ers (pou′ərz), *n.* **Hiram,** 1805–73, U.S. sculptor.

pow′er saw′, a saw driven by a motor. [1955–60]

pow·er-saw (pou′ər sô′), *v.t.,* **-sawed, -sawed** or **-sawn, -saw·ing.** to cut with a power saw.

pow′er se′ries, *Math.* an infinite series in which the terms are coefficients times successive powers of a given variable, or times products of powers of two or more variables. [1890–95]

pow′er set′, *Math.* the collection of all subsets of a given set. [1950–55]

pow′er shov′el, any self-propelled shovel for excavating earth, ore, or coal with a dipper that is powered by a diesel engine or electric motor. Cf. **shovel** (def. 2). [1905–10]

pow′er sta′tion, *Elect.* a generating station. [1900–05]

CONCISE ETYMOLOGY KEY: <, descended or borrowed from; >, whence; b., blend of, blended; c., cognate with; cf., compare; deriv., derivative; equiv., equivalent; imit., imitative; obl., oblique; r., replacing; s., stem; sp., spelling, spelled; resp., respelling, respelled; trans., translation; ?, origin unknown; *, unattested; ‡, probably earlier than. See the full key inside the front cover.

pow′er steer′ing, *Auto.* an automotive steering system in which the engine's power is used to supplement the driver's effort in turning the steering wheel. [1930–35]

pow′er struc′ture, **1.** the system of authority or influence in government, politics, education, etc.: *The state elections threatened to upset the existing power structure.* **2.** the people who participate in such a system: *She hoped to become a part of the power structure.* [1945–50]

pow′er supply′, a device that provides power to electric machines, generators, etc.

pow′er take′off, an accessory unit or apparatus attached to an engine-powered machine and powered by the engine. *Abbr.:* PTO [1925–30]

pow′er tool′, a tool powered by an electric motor or a gasoline engine. [1955–60]

pow′er train′, a train of gears and shafting transmitting power from an engine, motor, etc., to a mechanism being driven. [1940–45]

Pow·ha·tan (pou′ə tan′, -hat′n), *n., pl.* **-tans,** (*esp. collectively*) **-tan** for 1. **1.** a member of any of the Indian tribes belonging to the Powhatan Confederacy. **2.** the Eastern Algonquian language spoken by the Powhatan people. **3.** c1550–1618, North American Indian chief in Virginia, father of Pocahontas and founder of the Powhatan Confederacy.

Pow′hatan Confed′eracy, a network of Algonquian-speaking Indian settlements in Virginia that was ruled by Powhatan.

pow·wow (pou′wou′), *n.* **1.** (among North American Indians) a ceremony, esp. one accompanied by magic, feasting, and dancing, performed for the cure of disease, success in a hunt, etc. **2.** a council or conference of or with Indians. **3.** (among North American Indians) a priest or shaman. **4.** *Informal.* any conference or meeting. —*v.i.* **5.** to hold a powwow. **6.** *Informal.* to confer. [1615–25, *Amer.*; < Narragansett (E sp.) *powwaw* Indian priest (and the identical word in Massachusett) < Proto-Algonquian **pawe·wa* he dreams (used as a derived agent n. meaning "he who dreams", i.e., one who derives his power from visions)]

Pow·ys (pō′is), *n.* **1. John Cowper,** 1872–1963, English author. **2.** his brother, **Llewelyn,** 1884–1939, English author. **3.** his brother, **Theodore Francis,** 1875–1953, English author. **4.** a county in E Wales. 100,800; 1960 sq. mi. (5077 sq. km).

pox (poks), *n. Pathol.* **1.** a disease characterized by multiple skin pustules, as smallpox. **2.** syphilis. **3.** Also called **soil rot.** *Plant Pathol.* a disease of sweet potatoes, characterized by numerous pitlike lesions on the roots, caused by a fungus, *Streptomyces ipomoea.* **4.** (used interjectionally to express distaste, rejection, aversion, etc.): *A pox on you and your bright ideas!* [1540–50 (earlier as surname); sp. var. of *pocks,* pl. of POCK]

pox·vi·rus (poks′vī′rəs), *n. pl.* **-rus·es.** any of a group of large, brick-shaped DNA-containing viruses that infect humans and other animals, including the viruses of smallpox and various other poxes. [1940–45; POX + VIRUS]

Po·yang (pō′yäng′), *n.* a lake in E China, in Kiangsi province. 90 mi. (145 km) long.

poyn·tell (poin′tel), *n.* pointel. Also, **poyn·till** (poin′til).

Poyn′ting-Rob′ert·son effect′ (poin′ting rob′ərt sən), *Astron.* the slowing down and consequent spiraling inward of small particles orbiting the sun, due to their interaction with solar radiation. [1955–60; after English physicist John H. *Poynting* (1852–1914) and U.S. physicist Howard P. *Robertson* (1903–61)]

Po·za Ri·ca de Hi·dal·go (pô′sä rē′kä the ē thäl′gô), a city in N Veracruz, in E Mexico. 160,682.

Poz·nań (pōz′nan, -nän; *Pol.* pôz′nän′yə), *n.* a city in W Poland, on the Warta River. 516,000. German, **Posen.**

Po·zsony (pô′zhôn′yə), *n.* Hungarian name of **Bratislava.**

poz·zo·la·na (pot′sə lä′nə; *It.* pôt′tsô lä′nä), *n.* a porous variety of volcanic tuff or ash used in making hydraulic cement. Also, **poz·zo·lan** (pot′sə lən), **poz·zuo·la·na** (pot′swə lä′nə; *It.* pôt′tswô lä′nä), **puzzolan, puzzolana.** [1905–10; < It < L *puteolāna,* fem. of *puteolānus* of POZZUOLI (< L *Puteolī* lit., little springs); see -AN]

poz·zo·lan·ic (pot′sə lan′ik, -lä′nik), *adj.* (of a cement admixture) having properties similar to those of pozzolana. Also, **poz·zuo·la·nic** (pot′swə lä′nik). [1925–30; POZZOLAN(A) + -IC]

Poz·zuo·li (pot swô′lē; *It.* pôt tswô′lē), *n.* a seaport in SW Italy, near Naples: Roman ruins. 67,787.

PP, prepositional phrase.

pp, *Radio.* push-pull.

pp., **1.** pages. **2.** past participle. **3.** pianissimo. **4.** privately printed.

P.P., **1.** parcel post. **2.** parish priest. **3.** past participle. **4.** postpaid. **5.** prepaid.

p.p., **1.** parcel post. **2.** past participle. **3.** per person. **4.** postpaid.

PPA, *Pharm.* phenylpropanolamine.

PPB, (in publishing) paper, printing, and binding. Also, **P.P.B.**

ppb, **1.** (in publishing) paper, printing, and binding. **2.** parts per billion. Also, **p.p.b.**

ppd., **1.** postpaid. **2.** prepaid.

p.p.d.o., per person, double occupancy.

PPE, *Brit.* philosophy, politics, and economics.

P.P.F., *Insurance.* personal property floater.

P.P. factor, *Biochem.* See **pellagra-preventive factor.**

PPH, paid personal holidays. Also, **P.P.H.**

pph., pamphlet.

PPI, **1.** patient package insert: a leaflet included with a prescription medication indicating its proper use. **2.** plan position indicator. **3.** producer price index.

ppl., participle.

PPLO, See **pleuropneumonialike organism.**

ppm, **1.** parts per million. **2.** pulse per minute.

p.p.m., parts per million. Also, **P.P.M., ppm, PPM**

PPO, See **preferred-provider organization.**

ppp, *Music.* pianississimo; double pianissimo.

ppr., present participle. Also, **p.pr.**

pps, pulse per second.

P.P.S., a second or additional postscript. Also, **p.p.s.** [< L *post postscrīptum*]

ppt., *Chem.* precipitate.

ppv, *Television.* pay-per-view. Also, **p.p.v., PPV, P.P.V.**

P.Q., Province of Quebec.

p.q., previous question.

PR, **1.** payroll. **2.** percentile rank. **3.** public relations. **4.** *Slang* (*often disparaging and offensive*). Puerto Rican. **5.** Puerto Rico (approved esp. for use with zip code).

Pr, Provençal.

Pr, *Symbol, Chem.* praseodymium.

Pr., **1.** (of stock) preferred. **2.** Priest. **3.** Prince. **4.** Provençal.

pr., **1.** pair; pairs. **2.** paper. **3.** power. **4.** preference. **5.** (of stock) preferred. **6.** present. **7.** price. **8.** priest. **9.** *Computers.* printer. **10.** printing. **11.** pronoun.

P.R., **1.** parliamentary report. **2.** Roman people. [< L *populus Rōmānus*] **3.** press release. **4.** prize ring. **5.** proportional representation. **6.** public relations. **7.** Puerto Rico.

p.r., public relations.

PRA, Public Roads Administration.

prac·tic (prak′tik), *adj.* practical. [1375–1425; late ME *practik* < L *prācticus* < Gk *prāktikós,* equiv. to *prāk-* (verbid s. of *prā́ssein* to do; see PRAGMATIC, PRAXIS) + *-tikos* -TIC]

prac·ti·ca·ble (prak′ti kə bəl), *adj.* **1.** capable of being done, effected, or put into practice, with the available means; feasible: *a practicable solution.* **2.** capable of being used: *a practicable gift.* **3.** *Theat.* (of a stage property or part of a set) designed or constructed for actual use; *a practicable window; practicable water faucets.* [1660–70; < ML *practic(āre)* to PRACTICE + -ABLE] **—prac′ti·ca·bil′i·ty, prac′ti·ca·ble·ness,** *n.* **—prac′·ti·ca·bly,** *adv.*
—Syn. 1. workable, achievable, attainable. See **possible.** **—Ant. 1.** unfeasible.

prac·ti·cal (prak′ti kəl), *adj.* **1.** of or pertaining to practice or action: *practical mathematics.* **2.** consisting of, involving, or resulting from practice or action: *a practical application of a rule.* **3.** of, pertaining to, or concerned with ordinary activities, business, or work: *practical affairs.* **4.** adapted or designed for actual use; useful: *practical instructions.* **5.** engaged or experienced in actual practice or work: *a practical politician.* **6.** inclined toward or fitted for actual work or useful activities: *a practical person.* **7.** mindful of the results, usefulness, advantages or disadvantages, etc., of action or procedure. **8.** matter-of-fact; prosaic. **9.** being such in practice or effect; virtual: *a practical certainty.* **10.** *Theat.* practicable (def. 3). [1375–1425; late ME. See PRACTIC, -AL[1]] **—prac′ti·cal′i·ty, prac′ti·cal·ness,** *n.*
—Syn. 1. pragmatic. **7.** PRACTICAL, JUDICIOUS, SENSIBLE refer to good judgment in action, conduct, and the handling of everyday matters. PRACTICAL suggests the ability to adopt means to an end or to turn what is at hand to account: *to adopt practical measures for settling problems.* JUDICIOUS implies the possession and use of discreet judgment, discrimination, and balance: *a judicious use of one's time.* SENSIBLE implies the possession and use of sound reason and shrewd common sense: *a sensible suggestion.* **—Ant. 7.** ill-advised, unwise, foolish.

prac′tical art′, an art or craft, as woodworking or needlework, that serves a utilitarian purpose. [1920–25]

prac′tical imper′ative, (in Kantian ethics) the dictum that one should treat oneself and all humanity as an end and never as a means.

prac·ti·cal·ism (prak′ti kə liz′əm), *n.* devotion to practical matters. [1835–45; PRACTICAL + -ISM] **—prac′ti·cal·ist,** *n.*

prac′tical joke′, a playful trick, often involving some physical agent or means, in which the victim is placed in an embarrassing or disadvantageous position. [1840–50] **—prac′tical jok′er.**

prac·ti·cal·ly (prak′tik lē), *adv.* **1.** in effect; virtually: *It is practically useless to protest.* **2.** in a practical manner: *to think practically.* **3.** from a practical point of view: *Practically speaking, the plan is not very promising.* **4.** almost; nearly: *Their provisions were practically gone.* [1615–25; PRACTICAL + -LY]
—Usage. A few usage guides object to the use of PRACTICALLY in the senses "in effect, virtually" and "almost, nearly." Both uses, however, are well established and standard in all varieties of speech and writing.

prac′tical nurse′, a person who has not graduated from an accredited school of nursing but whose vocation is caring for the sick. Cf. **licensed practical nurse.** [1920–25]

prac′tical rea′son, (in Kantian ethics) reason applied to the problem of action and choice, esp. in ethical matters. [1895–1900]

prac·tice (prak′tis), *n., v.,* **-ticed, -tic·ing.** —*n.* **1.** habitual or customary performance; operation: *office practice.* **2.** habit; custom: *It is not the practice here for men to wear long hair.* **3.** repeated performance or systematic exercise for the purpose of acquiring skill or proficiency: *Practice makes perfect.* **4.** condition arrived at by experience or exercise: *She refused to play the piano, because she was out of practice.* **5.** the action or process of performing or doing something: *to put a scheme into practice; the shameful practices of a blackmailer.* **6.** the exercise or pursuit of a profession or occupation, esp. law or medicine: *She plans to set up practice in her hometown.* **7.** the business of a professional person: *The doctor wanted his daughter to take over his practice when he retired.* **8.** *Law.* the established method of conducting legal proceedings. **9.** *Archaic.* plotting; intrigue; trickery. **10.** Usually, **practices.** *Archaic.* intrigues; plots. —*v.t.* **11.** to perform or do habitually or usually: *to practice a strict regimen.* **12.** to follow or observe habitually or customarily: *to practice one's religion.* **13.** to exercise or pursue as a profession, art, or occupation: *to practice law.* **14.** to perform or do repeatedly in order to acquire skill or proficiency: *to practice the violin.* **15.** to train or drill (a person, animal, etc.) in something in order to give proficiency. —*v.i.* **16.** to do something habitually or as a practice. **17.** to pursue a profession, esp. law or medicine. **18.** to exercise oneself by repeated performance in order to acquire skill: *to practice at shooting.* **19.** *Archaic.* to plot or conspire. Also, *Brit.,* **practise** (for defs. 11–19). [1375–1425; (v.) late ME *practisen, practizen* (< MF *pra(c)tiser*) < ML *prācticāre,* alter. of *prācticāre,* deriv. of *prāctica* practical work < Gk *prāktikḗ* n. use of fem. of *prāktikós* PRACTIC; see -IZE; (n.) late ME, deriv. of the v.] **—prac′tic·er,** *n.*
—Syn. 2. See **custom. 3.** application. See **exercise.**

prac·ticed (prak′tist), *adj.* **1.** skilled or expert; proficient through practice or experience: *a practiced hand at politics.* **2.** acquired or perfected through practice: *a practiced English accent.* Also, **prac′tised.** [1560–70; PRACTICE + -ED[2]]

prac·tice-teach (prak′tis tēch′), *v.i.,* **-taught, -teach·ing.** to work as a practice teacher. [1950–55]

prac′tice teach′er. See **student teacher.**

prac·tic·ing (prak′ti sing), *adj.* **1.** actively working at a profession, esp. medicine or law. **2.** actively following a specific way of life, religion, philosophy, etc.: *a practicing Catholic.* [PRACTICE + -ING[2]]

prac·ti·cum (prak′ti kəm), *n.* (in a college or university) the part of a course consisting of practical work in a particular field. [1900–05; < L, neut. of *prācticus* PRACTIC]

prac·tise (prak′tis), *v.t., v.i.,* **-tised, -tis·ing.** *Brit.* practice.

prac·ti·tion·er (prak tish′ə nər), *n.* **1.** a person engaged in the practice of a profession, occupation, etc.: *a medical practitioner.* **2.** a person who practices something specified. **3.** *Christian Science.* a person authorized to practice healing. [1535–45; alter. of *practician* (PRACTIC + -IAN) + -ER[1]]

prad (prad), *n. Australian Informal.* horse. [1790–1800; metathetic var. of D *paard* horse (c. G *Pferd*) << LL *paraverēdus* post horse for lesser highways. See PALFREY]

prae-, var. of **pre-.**

prae·ci·pe (prē′sə pē′, pres′ə-), *n. Law.* **1.** any of various legal writs commanding a defendant to do something or to appear and show why it should not be done. **2.** a written order addressed to the clerk of the court requesting that a writ be issued and specifying its contents. [1400–50; late ME *presepe* < L *praecipe,* 2d sing. impv. of *praecipere* to take in advance; see PRECEPT]

prae·cip·i·ta·ti·o (prē sip′i tā′shē ō′), *n. Meteorol.* precipitation from a cloud that reaches the surface of the earth (distinguished from *virga*). [< L; see PRECIPITATION]

prae·di·al (prē′dē əl), *adj.* **1.** of, pertaining to, or consisting of land or its products; real; landed. **2.** arising from or consequent upon the occupation of land. **3.** attached to land. Also, **predial.** [1425–75; late ME < ML *praediālis* landed, equiv. to L *praedi(um)* farm, estate + *-ālis* -AL[1]] **—prae′di·al′i·ty,** *n.*

prae·fect (prē′fekt), *n.* prefect.

prae·lect (pri lekt′), *v.i.* prelect.

prae·mu·ni·re (prē′myo͞o nī′rē), *n. Eng. Law.* **1.** a writ charging the offense of resorting to a foreign court or authority, as that of the pope, and thus calling in question the supremacy of the English crown. **2.** the offense. **3.** the penalty of forfeiture, imprisonment, outlawry, etc., incurred. [1375–1425; short for ML *praemūnīre faciās* (for L *praemonēre faciās* that you cause (the person specified) to be forewarned), the operative words of the writ; *praemūnīre* to warn (L: protect, lit., fortify); r. late ME *premunire facias* < ML, as above. See PRAE-, MUNIMENT]

Prae·nes·te (prē nes′tē), *n.* ancient name of **Palestrina.**

Prae·nes·tine (prē nes′tin), *adj.* of or pertaining to the ancient town of Praeneste in Italy, or to the Latin dialect spoken there. [1875–80; < L *Praenestīnus.* See PRAENESTE, -INE[1]]

prae·no·men (prē nō′mən), *n., pl.* **-nom·i·na** (-nom′ə nə, -nō′mə-), **-no·mens.** the first or personal name of a Roman citizen, as "Gaius" in "Gaius Julius Caesar." Also, **prenomen.** [1655–65; < L *praenōmen,* equiv. to *prae-* PRAE- + *nōmen* NAME] **—prae·nom·i·nal** (prē nom′ə nl), *adj.*

prae·pos·tor (prē pos′tər), *n.* a senior student at an English public school who is given authority over other students. Also, **prepositor, prepostor.** [1510–20; < ML *praepositor.* See PRAE-, POSIT, -TOR] **—prae·pos·to·ri·al** (prē′po stôr′ē əl, -stōr′-), *adj.*

CONCISE PRONUNCIATION KEY: act, cāpe, dâre, pärt; set, ēqual; if, īce; ox, ōver, ôrder, oil, bo͝ok, bo͞ot, out; up, ûrge; child; sing; shoe; thin, that; zh as in *treasure.* ə = *a* as in *alone, e* as in *system, i* as in *easily, o* as in *gallop, u* as in *circus;* ə as in *fire* (fīər), *hour* (ouər). l and n can serve as syllabic consonants, as in *cradle* (krād′l), and *button* (but′n). See the full key inside the front cover.

Prae•se•pe (pri sē′pē, prī′sə pē′), *n. Astron.* an open star cluster in the center of the constellation Cancer, visible to the naked eye. Also called **Beehive cluster, Manger.** [1650–60; < L *praesēpe* crib from which cattle or horses are fed, manger; the neighboring brighter stars Gamma and Delta Cancri (*Asellus Borealis* and *Asellus Australis*) were pictured as asses which fed from a manger]

prae•tex•ta (prē tek′stə), *n., pl.* **-tex•tae** (-tek′stē). **1.** (in ancient Rome) a white toga with a broad purple border, worn by priests and magistrates as an official costume, and by certain other Romans as ceremonial dress. **2.** a similar garment worn by a boy until he assumed the toga virilis, or by a girl until she married. Also, **pretexta.** [1595–1605; < L, short for *toga praetexta* lit., bordered toga. See PRETEXT]

prae•tor (prē′tər), *n.* (in the ancient Roman republic) one of a number of elected magistrates charged chiefly with the administration of civil justice and ranking next below a consul. Also, **pretor.** [1375–1425; late ME *pretor* < L *praetor,* for **praeitor* leader, lit., one going before, equiv. to **praei-,* var. s. of *praeire* to go before, lead (*prae-* PRAE- + *-i-,* base of *ire* to go) + *-tor* -TOR] —**prae•to•ri•al** (prē tôr′ē əl, -tōr′-), *adj.*

prae•to•ri•an (prē tôr′ē ən, -tōr′-), *adj.* **1.** of or pertaining to a praetor. **2.** (*often cap.*) noting or pertaining to the Praetorian Guard. —*n.* **3.** a person having the rank of praetor or ex-praetor. **4.** (*often cap.*) a soldier of the Praetorian Guard. [1375–1425; late ME < L *praetōriānus.* See PRAETOR, -IAN]

Praeto′rian Guard′, *Rom. Hist.* the bodyguard of a military commander, esp. the imperial guard stationed in Rome.

prae•to•ri•an•ism (prē tôr′ē ə niz′əm, -tōr′-), *n.* the control of a society by force or fraud, esp. when exercised through titular officials and by a powerful minority. [1865–70; PRAETORIAN + -ISM]

prae•tor•ship (prē′tər ship′), *n.* the office of a praetor. Also, **pretorship.** [1535–45; PRAETOR + -SHIP]

Prag (prāk), *n.* German name of **Prague.**

prag•mat•ic (prag mat′ik), *adj.* **1.** of or pertaining to a practical point of view or practical considerations. **2.** *Philos.* of or pertaining to pragmatism (def. 2). **3.** of or pertaining to pragmatics (defs. 1, 2). **4.** treating historical phenomena with special reference to their causes, antecedent conditions, and results. **5.** of or pertaining to the affairs of state or community. **6.** *Archaic.* **a.** busy; active. **b.** officious; meddlesome; interfering. **c.** dogmatic; opinionated. —*n.* **7.** See **pragmatic sanction. 8.** *Archaic.* an officious or meddlesome person. Also, **prag•mat′i•cal** (for defs. 1, 2, 5). [1580–90; < L *prāgmaticus* < Gk *prāgmatikós* practical, equiv. to *prāgmat-* (s. of *prâgma*) deed, state business (deriv. of *prássein* to do, fare; see PRACTIC) + *-ikos* -IC] —**prag•mat′i•cal′i•ty, prag•mat′i•cal•ness,** *n.* —**prag•mat′i•cal•ly,** *adv.*

prag•mat•i•cism (prag mat′ə siz′əm), *n.* the pragmatist philosophy of C. S. Peirce, chiefly a theory of meaning: so called by him to distinguish it from the pragmatism of William James. [1905; PRAGMATIC + -ISM]

prag•mat•ics (prag mat′iks), *n.* (*used with a singular v.*) **1.** *Logic, Philos.* the branch of semiotics dealing with the causal and other relations between words, expressions, or symbols and their users. **2.** *Ling.* the analysis of language in terms of the situational context within which utterances are made, including the knowledge and beliefs of the speaker and the relation between speaker and listener. **3.** practical considerations. [1935–40; see PRAGMATIC, -ICS]

pragmat′ic sanc′tion, 1. any one of various imperial decrees with the effect of fundamental law. **2.** (*caps.*) *Hist.* **a.** any of several imperial or royal decrees limiting the power or privilege of the papacy, as the decree of Charles VII of France in 1438 or that of the Diet of Mainz in 1439. **b.** the imperial decree of Charles VI of Austria in 1713, by which his daughter, Maria Theresa, inherited his dominions.

pragmat′ic the′ory, *Philos.* the theory of truth that the truth of a statement consists in its practical consequences, esp. in its agreement with subsequent experience. Cf. **coherence theory, correspondence theory.**

prag•ma•tism (prag′mə tiz′əm), *n.* **1.** character or conduct that emphasizes practicality. **2.** a philosophical movement or system having various forms, but generally stressing practical consequences as constituting the essential criterion in determining meaning, truth, or value. Cf. **pragmaticism, instrumentalism.** [1860–65; PRAGMAT(IC) + -ISM] —**prag′ma•tis′tic,** *adj.*

prag•ma•tist (prag′mə tist), *n.* **1.** a person who is oriented toward the success or failure of a particular line of action, thought, etc.; a practical person. **2.** an advocate or adherent of philosophical pragmatism. —*adj.* **3.** of, pertaining to, or characteristic of pragmatism. [1630–40; PRAGMAT(IC) + -IST]

Prague (präg), *n.* a city in and the capital of the Czech Republic, in the W central part, on the Vltava: formerly capital of Czechoslovakia. 1,211,000. Czech, **Pra•ha** (prä′hä). German, **Prag.**

Prague′ School′, a school of linguistics emphasizing structure, active in the 1920's and 1930's.

Prai•a (*Port.* prī′ä; *Eng.* prī′ə), *n.* the capital of Cape Verde, in the S Atlantic Ocean, on S São Tiago Island. 39,000.

prai•rie (prâr′ē), *n.* **1.** an extensive, level or slightly undulating, mostly treeless tract of land in the Mississippi valley, characterized by a highly fertile soil and originally covered with coarse grasses, and merging into drier plateaus in the west. Cf. **pampas, savanna, steppe. 2.** a tract of grassland; meadow. **3.** (in Florida) a low, sandy tract of grassland often covered with water. **4.** *Southern U.S.* wet grassland; marsh. **5.** (*cap.*) a steam locomotive having a two-wheeled front truck, six driving wheels, and a two-wheeled rear truck. See table under **Whyte classification.** [1675–85; < F: meadow < VL **prātāria,* equiv. to L *prāt(um)* meadow + *-āria,* fem. of *-ārius* -ARY] —**prai′rie•like′,** *adj.*

CONCISE ETYMOLOGY KEY: <, descended or borrowed from; >, whence; b., blend of, blended; c., cognate with; cf., compare; deriv., derivative; equiv., equivalent; imit., imitative; obl., oblique; r., replacing; s., stem; sp., spelling, spelled; resp., respelling, respelled; trans., translation; ?, origin unknown; *, unattested; ‡, probably earlier than. See the full key inside the front cover.

Prairie, The, a historical novel (1827) by James Fenimore Cooper. Cf. ***Leather-Stocking Tales.***

prai′rie break′er, breaker[1] (def. 6). [1865–70, *Amer.*]

prai′rie but′ton snake′root, a stout composite plant, *Liatris pycnostachya,* of prairies in the central U.S., having showy, rose-purple flower heads in dense spikes. Also called **Kansas gay-feather.**

prai′rie chick′en, 1. either of two North American gallinaceous birds of western prairies, *Tympanuchus cupido* (**greater prairie chicken**), or *T. pallidicinctus* (**lesser prairie chicken**), having rufous, brown, black, and white plumage. **2.** See **sharp-tailed grouse.** Also called **prairie fowl, prairie grouse.** [1685–95, *Amer.*]

prai′rie clo′ver, any plant belonging to the genus *Petalostemon,* of the legume family, common in western North America, having pinnately compound leaves and spikes of white, purple, or pink flowers. [1855–60, *Amer.*]

prai′rie crab′ ap′ple, a tree, *Malus ioensis,* of the rose family, native to the central U.S., having downy branchlets, white or rose-tinted flowers, and round, waxy, greenish fruit.

prai′rie dog′, any of several burrowing rodents of the genus *Cynomys,* of North American prairies, having a barklike cry: some are endangered. [1765–75, *Amer.*]

prairie dog, *Cynomys ludovicianus,* head and body 1½ ft. (0.5 m); tail 3½ in. (8.9 cm)

prai′rie fal′con, a North American falcon, *Falco mexicanus,* grayish-brown above and white barred with brown below. [1870–75, *Amer.*]

prai′rie fowl′. See **prairie chicken.** Also called **prai′rie grouse′.** [1795–1805, *Amer.*]

prai′rie lil′y. See **sand lily.** [1905–10, *Amer.*]

prai′rie owl′, 1. See **burrowing owl. 2.** See **short-eared owl.** [1840–50, *Amer.*]

prai′rie oys′ter, 1. a raw egg, or the yolk of a raw egg, often mixed with seasonings, as salt, pepper, Worcestershire sauce, and used as a hangover remedy. **2.** the testis of a calf used as food. Cf. **mountain oyster.** [1880–85]

prai′rie point′er. See **shooting star** (def. 2).

Prai′rie Prov′inces, the provinces of Manitoba, Saskatchewan, and Alberta, in W Canada.

prai′rie rat′tlesnake, a rattlesnake, *Crotalus viridis viridis,* of the prairies of western North America. [1810–20, *Amer.*]

prai′rie rose′, a climbing rose, *Rosa setigera,* of the central U.S., having pinkish to white flowers: the state flower of North Dakota. [1815–25, *Amer.*]

Prai′rie School′, a group of early 20th-century architects of the Chicago area who designed houses and other buildings with emphasized horizontal lines responding to the flatness of the Midwestern prairie; the best-known member was Frank Lloyd Wright.

prai′rie schoon′er, a type of covered wagon, similar to but smaller than the Conestoga wagon, used by pioneers in crossing the prairies and plains of North America. [1835–45]

prai′rie skirt′, a full, dirndl-style skirt with a flounce on the bottom edge that is sometimes trimmed or lined to suggest a petticoat underneath.

prai′rie smoke′, a plant *Geum triflorum,* of the rose family, native to North America, having purplish flowers and silky-plumed fruit. Also called **Johnny smokers.** [1890–95, *Amer.*]

prai′rie soil′, a soil that forms in subhumid, temperate regions with tall grass as native vegetation. [1810–20, *Amer.*]

Prai′rie State′, Illinois (used as a nickname).

prai′rie tur′nip, breadroot. [1805–15, *Amer.*]

Prai′rie Vil′lage, a city in E Kansas. 24,657.

prai′rie wake′-robin, a woodland trillium, *Trillium recurvatum,* of the central U.S., having purple-mottled leaves and brown-purple flowers.

prai′rie war′bler, an eastern North American wood warbler, *Dendroica discolor,* olive-green above, yellow below, and striped with black on the face and sides. [1805–15, *Amer.*]

prai′rie wolf′, coyote (def. 1). [1795–1805, *Amer.*]

prai•ril•lon (prā ril′yən, prə ril′ən), *n. Obs.* a small prairie. [1795–1805, *Amer.*; prob. < North American F, dim. of F *prairie* PRAIRIE]

praise (prāz), *n., v.,* **praised, prais•ing.** —*n.* **1.** the act of expressing approval or admiration; commendation; laudation. **2.** the offering of grateful homage in words or song, as an act of worship: *a hymn of praise to God.* **3.** the state of being approved or admired: *The king lived in praise for many years.* **4.** *Archaic.* a ground for praise, or a merit. **5. sing someone's praises,** to praise someone publicly and enthusiastically: *He is always singing his wife's praises.* —*v.t.* **6.** to express approval or admiration of; commend; extol. **7.** to offer grateful homage to (God or a deity), as in words or song. [1175–1225; (v.) ME *preisen* < OF *preisier* to value, prize < LL *pretiāre,* deriv. of L *pretium* PRICE, worth, reward; (n.) ME, deriv. of the v.; see PRIZE[2]] —**praise′ful,** *adj.* —**praise′ful•ly,** *adv.* —**praise′less,** *adj.* —**prais′er,** *n.*
—**Syn. 1.** acclamation, plaudit, applause, approbation, compliment. **2.** encomium, eulogy, panegyric. **6.** laud, applaud, eulogize. See **approve. 7.** glorify, exalt, honor.
—**Ant. 1.** condemnation. **6.** depreciate.

praise•wor•thy (prāz′wûr′thē), *adj.* deserving of praise; laudable: *a praiseworthy motive.* [1530–40; PRAISE + -WORTHY] —**praise′wor′thi•ly,** *adv.* —**praise′wor′thi•ness,** *n.*

Pra•ja•dhi•pok (prə chä′ti pok′), *n.* 1893–1941, king of Siam 1925–35.

Pra•ja•pa•ti (prə jä′put′ē), *n. Hindu Myth.* a Vedic god personifying a creative force that evolves all things from itself.

praj•na (pruj′nyä, -nə), *n. Buddhism, Hinduism.* pure and unqualified knowledge. Also called **Enlightenment.** [< Skt *prajñā*]

Praj•nā•Pa•ra•mi•ta (pruj′nyä pä rum′i tə, pruj′nə-), *n. Buddhism.* **1.** a series of sutras dealing with the perfection of wisdom: systematized by the Madhyamikas. **2.** (*pl.*) the 10 perfections of the Bodhisattva. **3.** (in Mahayana Buddhism) a female deity, the personification of transcendental wisdom.

Pra•krit (prä′krit, -krēt), *n.* any of the vernacular Indic languages of the ancient and medieval periods, as distinguished from Sanskrit. [1780–90; < Skt *prākṛta,* deriv. of *prakṛti;* see PRAKRITI] —**Pra•krit′ic,** *adj.*

pra•kri•ti (pruk′ri tē), *n. Hinduism.* (in Sankhya philosophy) primal matter or substance from which the physical and mental universe evolves under the influence of purusha. Cf. **guna, purusha.** [< Skt *prakṛti* original nature]

pra•line (prä′lēn, prā′-, prä lēn′), *n.* **1.** a French confection consisting of a caramel-covered almond or, sometimes, a hazelnut. **2.** a cookie-size confection made esp. of butter, brown sugar, and pecans: developed in New Orleans in the early 19th century. **3.** a similar confection of nuts mixed or covered with chocolate, coconut, maple sugar or syrup, etc. [1715–25; < F; named after Marshall César du Plessis-*Praslin* (1598–1675), whose cook invented them]

prall•tril•ler (präl′tril′ər), *n. Music.* See **inverted mordent.** [1835–45; < G: lit., rebounding trill]

pram[1] (pram), *n. Chiefly Brit. Informal.* perambulator. [1880–85; by shortening]

pram[2] (präm), *n.* a flat-bottomed, snub-nosed boat used as a fishing vessel or tender for larger vessels. [1540–50 (late 14th century in AL); < D *praam,* MD *prame, praem* (cf. MLG *pram(e),* OFris *pram,* G *Prahm*) < Slavic; cf. Czech *prám,* Pol *prom,* Russ *paróm,* Serbo-Croatian *prām* ferryboat, raft, c. OHG *farm* boat, raft, ON *farmr* freight, cargo; akin to FARE, FERRY]

pra•na (prä′nə), *n.* **1.** *Yoga, Jainism.* the vital principle. **2.** *Yoga.* one of five vital breaths moving in the body. [1820–30; < Skt *prāṇa* breath]

pra•na•va (prun′ə və), *n. Hinduism.* the word "Om." [< Skt *praṇava*]

prance (prans, präns), *v.,* **pranced, pranc•ing,** *n.* —*v.i.* **1.** to spring from the hind legs; to move by springing, as a horse. **2.** to ride on a horse doing this. **3.** to ride gaily, proudly, or insolently. **4.** to move or go in an elated manner; cavort. **5.** to dance or move in a lively or spirited manner; caper. —*v.t.* **6.** to cause to prance. —*n.* **7.** the act of prancing; a prancing movement. [1325–75; ME *prauncen, praunsen* (v.); akin to Dan (dial.) *pransk* spirited, said of a horse] —**pranc′er,** *n.* —**pranc′ing•ly,** *adv.*
—**Syn. 4, 5.** gambol, leap, skip, romp, frolic, frisk.

prand., (in prescriptions) dinner. [< L *prandium*]

pran•di•al (pran′dē əl), *adj.* of or pertaining to a meal, esp. dinner. [1810–20; < L *prandi(um)* luncheon, meal + -AL[1]] —**pran′di•al•ly,** *adv.*

Prand′tl num′ber (prän′tl), *Physics, Thermodynam.* the ratio of the fluid viscosity to the thermal conductivity of a substance, a low number indicating high convection. [1930–35; named after Ludwig *Prandtl* (1875–1953), German physicist]

prang (prang), *v.t. Brit. Slang.* **1.** to collide with; bump into. **2.** to destroy or severely damage by a bombing raid; bomb (an enemy target). **3.** to destroy or shoot down (an enemy aircraft). [1930–35; imit.]

pra•ni•dha•na (prun′i dä′nə), *n.* (in Mahayana Buddhism) the resolution not to enter nirvana until all beings are ready to enter. [< Skt *praṇidhāna*]

prank[1] (prangk), *n.* a trick of an amusing, playful, or sometimes malicious nature. [1520–30; orig. uncert.]
—**Syn.** caper, escapade, antic, shenanigan.

prank[2] (prangk), *v.t.* **1.** to dress or adorn in an ostentatious manner: *They were all pranked out in their fanciest clothes.* —*v.i.* **2.** to make an ostentatious show or display. [1540–50; akin to D *pronken* to show off, strut, *pronk* show, finery, MLG *prank* pomp]

prank•ish (prang′kish), *adj.* **1.** of the nature of a prank: *a prankish plan.* **2.** full of pranks; playful: *a prankish child; a prankish kitten.* [1820–30; PRANK[1] + -ISH[1]] —**prank′ish•ly,** *adv.* —**prank′ish•ness,** *n.*

prank•ster (prangk′stər), *n.* a mischievous or malicious person who plays tricks, practical jokes, etc., at the expense of another. [1925–30, *Amer.*; PRANK[1] + -STER]

prao (prou), *n., pl.* **praos.** [see PROA]

Pra•sad (prə säd′), *n.* **Ra•jen•dra** (rä jen′drə), 1884–1963, first president of the Republic of India 1950–62.

prase (prāz), *n. Mineral.* a leek-green cryptocrystalline variety of chalcedony. [1350–1400; < F < L *prasius* leek-green stone < Gk *prásios* leek-green, deriv. of *práson* leek; r. ME *prassius* < L, as above]

pra·se·o·dym·i·um (prā′zē ō dim′ē əm, prā′sē-), *n. Chem.* a rare-earth, metallic, trivalent element, named from its green salts. *Symbol:* Pr; *at. wt.:* 140.91; *at. no.:* 59; *sp. gr.:* 6.77 at 20°C. [1880–85; < NL, equiv. to *praseo-* (comb. form repr. Gk *prásios* leek-green; see PRASE) + (DI)DYMIUM]

prat (prat), *n. Slang.* the buttocks. [1560–70; orig. uncert.]

prate (prāt), *v.,* **prat·ed, prat·ing,** *n.* —*v.i.* **1.** to talk excessively and pointlessly; babble: *They prated on until I was ready to scream.* —*v.t.* **2.** to utter in empty or foolish talk: *to prate absurdities with the greatest seriousness.* —*n.* **3.** act of prating. **4.** empty or foolish talk. [1375–1425; late ME *praten* (v.) < MD *praeten.* See PRATTLE] —**prat′er,** *n.* —**prat′ing·ly,** *adv.*

prat·fall (prat′fôl′), *n.* **1.** a fall in which one lands on the buttocks, often regarded as comical or humiliating. **2.** a humiliating blunder or defeat. [1935–40; PRAT + FALL]

prat·in·cole (prat′ing kōl′, prat′n-), *n.* any of several limicoline birds of the genus *Glareola,* of the Eastern Hemisphere, having a short bill, long, narrow, pointed wings, and a forked tail. [< NL *Pratincola* (1756) genus name, equiv. to L *prāt(um)* meadow + *incola* inhabitant (see IN-[2], -COLOUS)]

pra·tin·co·lous (prə ting′kə ləs), *adj. Zool.* living in a meadow. [< NL *pratincol(a)* (see PRATINCOLE) + -OUS]

pra·tique (pra tēk′, prat′ik; *Fr.* PRA tēk′), *n.* license or permission to use a port, given to a ship after quarantine or on showing a clean bill of health. [1600–10; < F: practice < ML *practica.* See PRACTICE]

Pra·to (prä′tô), *n.* a city in central Italy, near Florence. 154,848. Also called **Pra′to in To·sca′na** (ēn tō-skä′nä).

Pratt (prat), *n.* **Edwin John,** 1883–1964, Canadian poet.

prat·tle (prat′l), *v.,* **-tled, -tling,** *n.* —*v.i.* **1.** to talk in a foolish or simple-minded way; chatter; babble. —*v.t.* **2.** to utter by chattering or babbling. —*n.* **3.** the act of prattling. **4.** chatter; babble: *the prattle of children.* **5.** a babbling sound: *the prattle of water rushing over stones.* [1525–35; < MLG *pratelen* to chatter, freq. of *praten* to PRATE; see -LE] —**prat′tler,** *n.* —**prat′tling·ly,** *adv.*
—**Syn. 1.** gab, jabber, gabble, blab.

Pratt·ville (prat′vil), *n.* a town in central Alabama. 18,647.

pra·tya·ha·ra (prə tyä här′ə), *n.* the Yogic practice of turning the mind to introspection by voluntarily shutting out distractions provided by the senses. Also, **pra·thya·ha′ra.** [1880–85; < Skt *pratyāhāra*]

Prat·ye·ka (prut yā′kə), *n.* (in Mahayana Buddhism) a buddha who enters into nirvana without teaching others. Pali, ***Pacceka.*** [shortening of Skt *pratyekabuddha,* equiv. to *pratyeka* alone, by oneself + *buddha* BUDDHA]

Prav·da (präv′də), *n.* (formerly) the official newspaper of the Communist party in the U.S.S.R. Cf. ***Izvestia.***

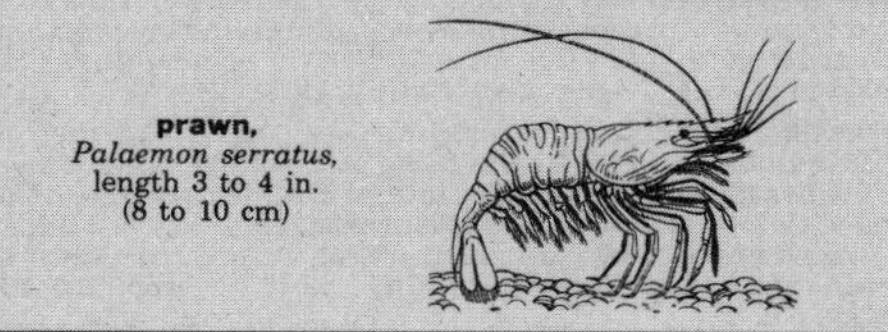
prawn, *Palaemon serratus,* length 3 to 4 in. (8 to 10 cm)

prawn (prôn), *n.* **1.** any of various shrimplike decapod crustaceans of the genera *Palaemon, Penaeus,* etc., certain of which are used as food. **2. come the raw prawn,** *Australian Slang.* to try to impose on or deceive someone (fol. by *with*). —*v.t.* **3.** to catch prawns, as for food. [1400–50; late ME *prane,* of uncert. orig.] —**prawn′er,** *n.*

prax·e·ol·o·gy (prak′sē ol′ə jē), *n.* the study of human conduct. Also, **prax′i·ol′o·gy.** [1900–05; < Gk *prâxe-* (taken as s. of *prâxis* PRAXIS) + -O- + -LOGY; perh. via. F *praxéologie*] —**prax·e·o·log·i·cal, prax·i·o·log·i·cal** (prak′sē ə loj′i kəl), *adj.*

prax·is (prak′sis), *n., pl.* **prax·is·es, prax·es** (prak′sēz). **1.** practice, as distinguished from theory; application or use, as of knowledge or skills. **2.** convention, habit, or custom. **3.** a set of examples for practice. [1575–85; < ML < Gk *prâxis* deed, act, action, equiv. to *prāk-,* base of *prâssein* to do, fare + *-sis* -SIS]

Prax·it·e·les (prak sit′l ēz′), *n.* fl. c350 B.C., Greek sculptor. —**Prax·it′e·le′an,** *adj.*

pray (prā), *v.t.* **1.** to offer devout petition, praise, thanks, etc., to (God or an object of worship). **2.** to offer (a prayer). **3.** to bring, put, etc., by praying: *to pray a soul into heaven.* **4.** to make earnest petition to (a person). **5.** to make petition or entreaty for; crave: *She prayed his forgiveness.* **6.** to offer devout petition, praise, thanks, etc., to God or to an object of worship. **7.** to enter into spiritual communion with God or an object of worship through prayer. —*v.i.* **8.** to make entreaty or supplication, as to a person or for a thing. [1250–1300; ME *preien* < OF *preier* << L *precārī* to beg, pray, deriv. of *prex* (s. *prec-*) prayer; akin to OE *fricgan,* D *vragen,* G *fragen,* Goth *fraihnan* to ask] —**pray′ing·ly,** *adv.*
—**Syn. 4.** importune, entreat, supplicate, beg, beseech, implore.

prayer[1] (prâr), *n.* **1.** a devout petition to God or an object of worship. **2.** a spiritual communion with God or an object of worship, as in supplication, thanksgiving, adoration, or confession. **3.** the act or practice of praying to God or an object of worship. **4.** a formula or sequence of words used in or appointed for praying: *the Lord's Prayer.* **5. prayers,** a religious observance, either public or private, consisting wholly or mainly of prayer. **6.** that which is prayed for. **7.** a petition; entreaty. **8.** the section of a bill in equity, or of a petition, that sets forth the complaint or the action desired. **9.** a negligible hope or chance: *Do you think he has a prayer of getting that job?* [1250–1300; ME *preiere* < OF < ML *precāria,* n. use of fem. of *precārius* obtained by entreaty, equiv. to *prec-* (s. of *prex*) prayer + *-ārius* -ARY; cf. PRECARIOUS] —**prayer′less,** *adj.* —**prayer′less·ly,** *adv.* —**prayer′less·ness,** *n.*

pray·er[2] (prā′ər), *n.* a person who prays. [1400–50; late ME *preyare.* See PRAY, -ER[1]]

prayer′ beads′ (prâr), a rosary. [1620–30]

prayer′ book′ (prâr), **1.** a book containing formal prayers to be used in public or private religious devotions. **2.** (*usually caps.*) See **Book of Common Prayer. 3.** *Naut.* a small holystone. [1590–1600]

prayer′ flag′ (prâr), a flag stamped with printed prayers, used by Himalayan Buddhists, who believe that its fluttering sends out the prayers inscribed on it. [1880–85]

prayer·ful (prâr′fəl), *adj.* given to, characterized by, or expressive of prayer; devout. [1620–30; PRAYER + -FUL] —**prayer′ful·ly,** *adv.* —**prayer′ful·ness,** *n.*
—**Syn.** pious, godly, reverent.

prayer′ meet′ing (prâr), **1.** a meeting chiefly for prayer. **2.** (in certain Protestant churches) a meeting in midweek, chiefly for individual prayer and the offering of testimonies of faith. Also called **prayer′ serv′ice.** [1810–20]

Prayer′ of Manas′ses (prâr), a book of the Apocrypha.

prayer′ plant′ (prâr), a plant, *Maranta leuconeura,* native to Brazil, that is widely cultivated for its variegated leaves that close up at night. [1950–55]

prayer′ rug′ (prâr), a small rug upon which a Muslim kneels and prostrates himself during his devotions. [1900–05]

prayer′ shawl′ (prâr), *Judaism.* a tallith. [1900–05]

prayer′ wheel′ (prâr), a wheel or cylinder inscribed with or containing prayers, used chiefly by Buddhists of Tibet. [1805–15]

pray-in (prā′in′), *n.* a form of social protest in which demonstrators engage in passive resistance and prayer: popular esp. in the 1970's. [1960–65; PRAY + -IN[3]]

pray′ing man′tis, mantis. [1700–10]

pra·zo·sin (prā′zō sin), *n. Pharm.* a white crystalline substance, $C_{19}H_{21}N_5O_4$, used in the treatment of hypertension. [1965–70; prob. by rearrangement and alter. of parts of its chemical name]

PRC, 1. Also, **P.R.C.** People's Republic of China. **2.** Postal Rate Commission.

pre-, a prefix occurring originally in loanwords from Latin, where it meant "before" (*preclude; prevent*); applied freely as a prefix, with the meanings "prior to," "in advance of," "early," "beforehand," "before," "in front of," and with other figurative meanings (*preschool; prewar; prepay: preoral; prefrontal*). Also, **prae-.** [< L *prae-,* prefixal use of *prae* (prep. and adv.); akin to FIRST, FORE, PRIOR, PRO[1]]
—**Note.** The lists at the bottom of this and following pages provide the spelling, syllabification, and stress for words whose meanings may be easily inferred by combining the meaning of PRE- and an attached base word, or base word plus a suffix. Appropriate parts of speech are also shown. Words prefixed by PRE- that have special meanings or uses are entered in their proper alphabetical places in the main vocabulary or as derived forms run on at the end of a main entry.

P.R.E., Petroleum Refining Engineer.

preach (prēch), *v.t.* **1.** to proclaim or make known by sermon (the gospel, good tidings, etc.). **2.** to deliver (a sermon). **3.** to advocate or inculcate (religious or moral truth, right conduct, etc.) in speech or writing. —*v.i.* **4.** to deliver a sermon. **5.** to give earnest advice, as on religious or moral subjects or the like. **6.** to do this in an obtrusive or tedious way. [1175–1225; ME *prechen* < OF *pre(ë)chier* < LL *praedicāre* to preach (L: to assert publicly, proclaim). See PREDICATE]
—**Syn. 5.** advocate, profess, pronounce, expound.

preach·er (prē′chər), *n.* **1.** a person whose occupation or function it is to preach the gospel. **2.** a person who preaches. **3.** See **Friar Preacher.** [1175–1225; ME *precho(u)r* < OF *prech(e)or,* earlier *preëch(e)or* < LL *praedicātor.* See PREACH, -OR[2]]

preach′er bird′. See **red-eyed vireo.**

preach·i·fy (prē′chə fī′), *v.i.,* **-fied, -fy·ing.** to preach in an obtrusive or tedious way. [1765–75; PREACH + -IFY] —**preach′i·fi·ca′tion,** *n.*

preach·ing (prē′ching), *n.* **1.** the act or practice of a person who preaches. **2.** the art of delivering sermons. **3.** a sermon. **4.** a public religious service with a sermon. —*adj.* **5.** of, pertaining to, or resembling preaching: *a preaching tone of voice.* [1225–75; ME *preching* (ger.); see PREACH, -ING[1], -ING[2]] —**preach′ing·ly,** *adv.*

preach·ment (prēch′mənt), *n.* **1.** the act of preaching. **2.** a sermon or other discourse, esp. when obtrusive or tedious. [1300–50; ME *prechement* < OF *preë(s)chement* < ML *praedicāmentum* speech; see PREDICAMENT]

preach·y (prē′chē), *adj.,* **preach·i·er, preach·i·est.** tediously or pretentiously didactic. [1810–20; PREACH + -Y[1]] —**preach′i·ly,** *adv.* —**preach′i·ness,** *n.*

pre-Ad·am·ite (prē ad′ə mīt′), *n.* **1.** a person supposed to have existed before Adam. **2.** a person who believes that there were people in existence before Adam. —*adj.* Also, **pre-A·dam·ic** (prē′ə dam′ik). **3.** existing before Adam. **4.** of or pertaining to the pre-Adamites. [1655–65; PRE- + ADAM + -ITE[1]]

pre·a·dapt (prē′ə dapt′), *v.i. Biol.* to undergo preadaptation. [1840–50; PRE- + ADAPT] —**pre′a·dapt′a·ble,** *adj.*

pre·ad·ap·ta·tion (prē′ad əp tā′shən), *n. Biol.* a structure or property that developed in an ancestral stock and was useful in a descendant in a changed environment. [1885–90; PRE- + ADAPTATION]

pre·ad·mis·sion (prē′ad mish′ən), *n.* (in a reciprocating engine) admission of steam or the like to the head of the cylinder near the end of the stroke, as to cushion the force of the stroke or to allow full pressure at the beginning of the return stroke. [1885–90; PRE- + ADMISSION]

pre·ad·o·les·cence (prē′ad l es′əns), *n.* the period preceding adolescence, usually designated as the years from 10 to 13. [1925–30; PRE- + ADOLESCENCE]

pre·ad·o·les·cent (prē′ad l es′ənt), *adj.* **1.** of or pertaining to preadolescence or a preadolescent. —*n.* **2.** a person who is in the preadolescent years. [1905–10; PRE- + ADOLESCENT]

pre·a·dult (prē′ə dult′, prē ad′ult), *adj.* of or pertain-

CONCISE PRONUNCIATION KEY: *act, cāpe, dâre, pärt; set, ēqual; if, īce; ox, ōver, ôrder, oil, bŏŏk, bōōt, out; up, ûrge; child; sing; shoe; thin, that;* zh as in *treasure.* ə = *a* as in *alone, e* as in *system, i* as in *easily, o* as in *gallop, u* as in *circus;* ᵊ as in *fire* (fīᵊr), *hour* (ouᵊr). l and n can serve as syllabic consonants, as in *cradle* (krād′l), and *button* (but′n). See the full key inside the front cover.

pre′ab·sorb′, *v.*
pre′ab·sorb′ent, *adj., n.*
pre′ab·stract′, *adj.*
pre′a·bun′dance, *n.*
pre′a·bun′dant, *adj.;* **-ly,** *adv.*
pre′ac·cept′, *v.*
pre′ac·cept′ance, *n.*
pre·ac′cess, *n.*
pre′ac·ces′si·ble, *adj.*
pre′ac·ci·den′tal, *adj.;* **-ly,** *adv.*
pre′ac·com′mo·date′, *v.t.,* **-dat·ed, -dat·ing.**
pre′ac·com′mo·dat′ing·ly, *adv.*
pre′ac·com′mo·da′tion, *n.*
pre′ac·com′plish, *v.t.*
pre′ac·com′plish·ment, *n.*
pre′ac·cord′, *n., v.i.*
pre′ac·cord′ance, *n.*
pre′ac·count′, *v.*
pre′ac·cred′it, *v.t.*
pre′ac·cu′mu·late′, *v.t.,* **-lat·ed, -lat·ing.**
pre′ac·cu′mu·la′tion, *n.*
pre′ac·cu·sa′tion, *n.*
pre′ac·cuse′, *v.t.,* **-cused, -cus·ing.**
pre′ac·cus′tom, *v.t.*
pre′ac·e·tab′u·lar, *adj.*
pre′a·chieved′, *adj.*
pre·ac′id, *adj.;* **-ness,** *n.*
pre′a·cid′i·ty, *n.*
pre′ac·knowl′edge, *v.t.,* **-edged, -edg·ing.**
pre′ac·knowl′edge·ment, *n.*
pre′ac·knowl′edg·ment, *n.*
pre′ac·quaint′, *v.t.*
pre′ac·quaint′ance, *n.*
pre′ac·quire′, *v.,* **-quired, -quir·ing.**
pre′ac·qui·si′tion, *n.*
pre′ac·quis′i·tive, *adj.;* **-ly,** *adv.;* **-ness,** *n.*
pre′ac·quit′, *v.t.,* **-quit·ted, -quit·ting.**
pre′ac·quit′tal, *n.*
pre·act′, *v.t.*
pre·ac′tion, *n.*
pre·ac′tive, *adj.;* **-ly,** *adv.;* **-ness,** *n.*
pre′ac·tiv′i·ty, *n., pl.* **-ties.**
pre′ad·di′tion, *n.*
pre′ad·di′tion·al, *adj.*
pre′ad·dress′, *n., v.t.*
pre·ad′e·qua·cy, *n.*
pre·ad′e·quate, *adj.;* **-ly,** *adv.;* **-ness,** *n.*
pre′ad·here′, *v.i.,* **-hered, -her·ing.**
pre′ad·her′ence, *n.*
pre′ad·her′ent, *adj.;* **-ly,** *adv.*
pre′ad·jec·ti′val, *adj.;* **-ly,** *adv.*
pre·ad′jec·tive, *adj.*
pre′ad·journ′, *v.*
pre′ad·journ′ment, *n.*
pre′ad·just′, *v.t.*
pre′ad·just′a·ble, *adj.*
pre′ad·just′ment, *n.*
pre′ad·min′is·tra′tion, *n.*
pre′ad·min′is·tra′tive, *adj.*
pre′ad·min′is·tra′tor, *n.*
pre′ad·mire′, *v.t.,* **-mired, -mir·ing.**
pre′ad·mir′er, *n.*
pre′ad·mit′, *v.t.,* **-mit·ted, -mit·ting.**
pre′ad·mon′ish, *v.t*
pre′ad·mo·ni′tion, *n.*
pre′a·dopt′, *v.t*
pre′a·dop′tion, *n.*
pre′a·dorn′, *v.t*
pre′a·dorn′ment, *n.*
pre′ad·ver·tise′, *v.,* **-tised, -tis·ing.**
pre′ad·ver·tise′ment, *n.*
pre′ad′ver·tis′er, *n.*
pre′ad·vice′, *n.*
pre′ad·vis′a·ble, *adj.*
pre′ad·vise′, *v.t.,* **-vised, -vis·ing.**
pre′ad·vi′so·ry, *adj.*
pre·ad′vo·ca·cy, *n.*
pre·ad′vo·cate, *n.*
pre·ad′vo·cate′, *v.t.,* **-cat·ed, -cat·ing.**
pre′aes′ti·val, *adj.*
pre′af·fect′, *v.t.*
pre′af·fec′tion, *n.*
pre′af·fi·da′vit, *n.*
pre′af·fil′i·ate, *n.*
pre′af·fil′i·ate′, *v.,* **-at·ed, -at·ing.**
pre′af·fil′i·a′tion, *n.*
pre′af·firm′, *v.*
pre′af·fir·ma′tion, *n.*
pre′af·firm′a·tive, *adj.*
pre′af·flict′, *v.t*
pre′af·flic′tion, *n.*
pre′af·ter·noon′, *n., adj.*
pre·age′, *v.,* **-aged, -ag·ing.**
pre·aged′, *adj.*
pre·ag′gra·vate′, *v.t.,* **-vat·ed, -vat·ing.**
pre′ag·gra·va′tion, *n.*
pre′ag·gres′sion, *n.*
pre′ag·gres′sive, *adj.;* **-ly,** *adv.;* **-ness,** *n.*
pre·ag′i·tate′, *v.t.,* **-tat·ed, -tat·ing.**
pre′ag·i·ta′tion, *n.*
pre′a·gree′, *v.i.,* **-greed, -gree·ing.**
pre′a·gree′ment, *n.*
pre′ag·ri·cul′tur·al, *adj.*
pre·ag′ri·cul′ture, *n.*
pre′a·larm′, *v.t., n.*
pre′al·co·hol′ic, *adj.*
pre·al′ge·bra, *n., adj.*
pre′al·ge·bra′ic, *adj.*
pre′al·le·ga′tion, *n.*
pre′al·lege′, *v.t.,* **-leged, -leg·ing.**
pre′al·li′ance, *n.*
pre′al·lied′, *adj.*
pre′al·lot′, *v.t.,* **-lot·ted, -lot·ting.**
pre′al·low′, *v.t*
pre′al·low′a·ble, *adj.;* **-bly,** *adv.*
pre′al·low′ance, *n.*
pre′al·lude′, *v.i.,* **-lud·ed, -lud·ing.**

ing to the period prior to adulthood: *preadult strivings for independence.* [1900–05; PRE- + ADULT] **—pre·a·dult′hood,** *n.*

pre-AIDS (prē ādz′), *n.* (not in technical use) See **AIDS-related complex.**

pre·al·lot·ment (prē′ə lot′mənt), *n.* an allotment given in advance. [PRE- + ALLOTMENT]

pre·al·tar (prē ôl′tər), *adj.* in front of the altar. [PRE- + ALTAR]

pre·al′ter·nate molt′ (prē ôl′tər nit), *Ornith.* the molt by which many birds replace only some and rarely all of the feathers assumed at the prebasic molt, usually occurring prior to breeding. [PRE- + ALTERNATE]

pre·am·ble (prē′am′bəl, prē am′-), *n.* **1.** an introductory statement; preface; introduction. **2.** the introductory part of a statute, deed, or the like, stating the reasons and intent of what follows. **3.** a preliminary or introductory fact or circumstance: *His childhood in the slums was a preamble to a life of crime.* **4.** (*cap.*) the introductory statement of the U.S. Constitution, setting forth the general principles of American government and beginning with the words, "We the people of the United States, in order to form a more perfect union . . . ." [1350–1400; ME < ML *praeambulum,* n. use of neut. of LL *praeambulus* walking before. See PRE-, AMBLE] **—pre′am′bled,** *adj.*
—Syn. 1. opening, beginning; foreword, prologue, prelude.

pre·amp (prē′amp′), *n. Informal.* a preamplifier. Also, **pre′-amp′.** [1955–60; by shortening]

pre·am·pli·fi·er (prē am′plə fī′ər), *n.* a device in the amplifier circuit of a radio or phonograph that increases the strength of a weak signal for detection and further amplification. [1930–35; PRE- + AMPLIFIER]

pre·an·es·thet·ic (prē an′əs thet′ik, prē′an-), *n.* **1.** a substance that produces a preliminary or light anesthesia. *—adj.* **2.** given prior to an anesthetic that induces total insensibility. [1890–95; PRE- + ANESTHETIC]

pre·an·ti·sep·tic (prē′an tə sep′tik), *adj. Med.* (esp. of surgery) noting that period of time before the adoption of the principles of antisepsis (about 1867). [PRE- + ANTISEPTIC]

pre·ap·point (prē′ə point′), *v.t.* to appoint beforehand. [1625–35; PRE- + APPOINT] **—pre′ap·point′·ment,** *n.*

pre·ar·range (prē′ə rānj′), *v.t.,* **-ranged, -rang·ing.** to arrange in advance or beforehand. [1805–15; PRE- + ARRANGE] **—pre′ar·range′ment,** *n.*

pre·a·sep·tic (prē′ə sep′tik), *adj. Med.* pertaining to the period before the use of aseptic practices in surgery. [PRE- + ASEPTIC]

pre·a·tom·ic (prē′ə tom′ik), *adj.* of or pertaining to the period of history preceding the atomic age. [1910–15; PRE- + ATOMIC]

pre·au·dit (prē ô′dit), *n. Accounting.* an examination of vouchers, contracts, etc., in order to substantiate a transaction or a series of transactions before they are paid for and recorded. Also, **pre-au′dit.** Cf. **postaudit.** [1935–40; PRE- + AUDIT]

pre·ax·i·al (prē ak′sē əl), *adj. Anat., Zool.* situated before the body axis; pertaining to the radial side of the upper limb and the tibial side of the lower limb. [1870–75; PRE- + -AXIAL] **—pre·ax′i·al·ly,** *adv.*

pre·ba′sic molt′ (prē bā′sik), *Ornith.* the molt by which most birds replace all of their feathers, usually occurring annually after the breeding season. [PRE- + BASIC]

preb·end (preb′ənd), *n.* **1.** a stipend allotted from the revenues of a cathedral or a collegiate church to a canon or member of the chapter. **2.** the land yielding such a stipend. **3.** a prebendary. [1375–1425; late ME *prebende* < ML *prēbenda,* var. of *praebenda* prebend, LL: allowance, neut. pl. gerundive of L *prae(hi)bēre* to offer, furnish, equiv. to *prae-* PRE- + *-hibēre,* comb. form of *habēre* to have, hold] **—pre·ben·dal** (pri ben′dl, preb′-ən-), *adj.*

CONCISE ETYMOLOGY KEY: <, descended or borrowed from; >, whence; b., blend of, blended; c., cognate with; cf., compare; deriv., derivative; equiv., equivalent; imit., imitative; obl., oblique; r., replacing; s., stem; sp., spelling, spelled; resp., respelling, respelled; trans., translation; ?, origin unknown; *, unattested; ‡, probably earlier than. See the full key inside the front cover.

preb·en·dar·y (preb′ən der′ē), *n., pl.* **-dar·ies. 1.** a canon or member of the clergy who is entitled to a prebend for special services at a cathedral or collegiate church. **2.** *Ch. of Eng.* an honorary canon having the title of a prebend but not receiving a stipend. [1375–1425; late ME < ML *praebendārius.* See PREBEND, -ARY]

pre·bi·o·log·i·cal (prē′bī ə loj′i kəl), *adj.* of or pertaining to chemicals or environmental conditions existing before the development of the first living things. Also, **pre·bi·ot·ic** (prē′bī ot′ik). [1950–55; PRE- + BIOLOGICAL]

pre·birth (prē bûrth′), *n.* **1.** the period, usually six months, preceding a child's birth. *—adj.* **2.** pertaining to or occurring during such a period. [PRE- + BIRTH]

Pre·ble (preb′əl), *n.* **Edward,** 1761–1807, U.S. naval officer.

pre·board (prē bôrd′, -bōrd′), *v.t.* **1.** to put or allow to go aboard in advance of the usual time or before others: *Handicapped passengers will be preboarded.* *—v.i.* **2.** to go aboard in advance. [PRE- + BOARD]

prec., **1.** preceded. **2.** preceding.

pre·cal·cu·lus (prē kal′kyə ləs), *Math.* *—adj.* **1.** pertaining to the mathematical prerequisites for the study of calculus, as algebra, analytical geometry, and trigonometry. *—n.* **2.** the course of study leading to calculus. [1960–65; PRE- + CALCULUS]

Pre·cam·bri·an (prē kam′brē ən, -kām′-), *Geol.* *—adj.* **1.** noting or pertaining to the earliest era of earth history, ending 570 million years ago, during which the earth's crust formed and life first appeared in the seas. See table under **geologic time.** *—n.* **2.** the Precambrian Era. Also, **Pre-Cam′bri·an.** [1860–65; PRE- + CAMBRIAN]

pre·can·cel (prē kan′səl), *v.,* **-celed, -cel·ing** or (*esp. Brit.*) **-celled, -cel·ling,** *n. Philately.* *—v.t.* **1.** to cancel (a stamp) before placing it on a piece of postal matter. *—n.* **2.** a precanceled stamp. [1920–25; PRE- + CANCEL] **—pre′can·cel·la′tion,** *n.*

pre·can·cer·ous (prē kan′sər əs), *adj.* showing pathological changes that may be preliminary to malignancy. [1880–85; PRE + CANCEROUS]

pre·car·i·ous (pri kâr′ē əs), *adj.* **1.** dependent on circumstances beyond one's control; uncertain; unstable; insecure: *a precarious livelihood.* **2.** dependent on the will or pleasure of another; liable to be withdrawn or lost at the will of another: *He held a precarious tenure under an arbitrary administration.* **3.** exposed to or involving danger; dangerous; perilous; risky: *the precarious life of an underseas diver.* **4.** having insufficient, little, or no foundation: *a precarious assumption.* [1640–50; < L *precārius* obtained by entreaty or mere favor, hence uncertain. See PRAYER[1]] **—pre·car′i·ous·ly,** *adv.* **—pre·car′i·ous·ness,** *n.*
—Syn. 1. unsure, unsteady. See **uncertain. 2.** doubtful, dubious, unreliable, undependable. **3.** hazardous. **4.** groundless, baseless, unfounded. **—Ant. 1.** secure. **2.** reliable. **3.** safe. **4.** well-founded.

pre·cast (prē kast′, -käst′), *v.,* **-cast, -cast·ing,** *adj. Building Trades.* *—v.t.* **1.** to cast (a concrete block or slab, etc.) in a place other than where it is to be installed in a structure. *—adj.* **2.** (of a building or section) cast before being transported to the site of installation: *a precast concrete roof.* [1860–65; PRE- + CAST]

prec·a·to·ry (prek′ə tôr′ē, -tōr′ē), *adj.* of, pertaining to, characterized by, or expressing entreaty or supplication: *precatory overtures.* Also, **prec·a·tive** (prek′ə tiv). [1630–40; < LL *precātōrius,* equiv. to L *precā(rī)* to PRAY, entreat + *-tōrius* -TORY[1]]

pre·cau·tion (pri kô′shən), *n.* **1.** a measure taken in advance to avert possible evil or to secure good results. **2.** caution employed beforehand; prudent foresight. *—v.t.* **3.** to forewarn; put on guard. [1595–1605; < LL *praecautiōn-* (s. of *praecautiō*). See PRE-, CAUTION]
—Syn. 2. forethought, prudence, circumspection.

pre·cau·tion·ar·y (pri kô′shə ner′ē), *adj.* **1.** of, pertaining to, or characterized by precaution: *precautionary measures.* **2.** expressing or advising precaution: *precautionary warnings against possible tornadoes.* Also, **pre·cau′tion·al.** [1740–50; PRECAUTION + -ARY]

pre·cau·tious (pri kô′shəs), *adj.* using or displaying precaution: *a precautious reply; a precautious person.* [1705–15; PRECAUTI(ON) + -OUS]

pre·ca·va (prē kā′və, -kä′-), *n., pl.* **-ca·vae** (-kā′vē, -kä′vī). **1.** See under **vena cava. 2.** (in squids) either of a pair of veins that pass through the kidney to the branchial heart. [1865–70; PRE- + (VENA) CAVA] **—pre·ca′val,** *adj.*

pre·cede (pri sēd′), *v.,* **-ced·ed, -ced·ing,** *n.* *—v.t.* **1.** to go before, as in place, order, rank, importance, or time. **2.** to introduce by something preliminary; preface: *to precede one's statement with a qualification.* *—v.i.* **3.** to go or come before. *—n.* **4.** *Journalism.* copy printed at the beginning of a news story presenting late bulletins, editorial notes, or prefatory remarks. [1325–75; ME *preceden* < L *praecēdere.* See PRE-, CEDE] **—pre·ced′a·ble,** *adj.*

prec·e·dence (pres′i dəns, pri sēd′ns), *n.* **1.** act or fact of preceding. **2.** the right to precede in order, rank, or importance; priority. **3.** the fact of preceding in time; antedating. **4.** the right to precede others in ceremonies or social formalities. **5.** the order to be observed in ceremonies by persons of different ranks, as by diplomatic protocol. [1475–85; PRECED(ENT) + -ENCE]

prec·e·den·cy (pres′i dən sē, pri sēd′n sē), *n., pl.* **-cies.** precedence. [1590–1600; PRECED(ENCE) + -ENCY]

prec·e·dent (*n.* pres′i dənt; *adj.* pri sēd′nt, pres′i-dənt), *n.* **1.** *Law.* a legal decision or form of proceeding serving as an authoritative rule or pattern in future similar or analogous cases. **2.** any act, decision, or case that serves as a guide or justification for subsequent situations. *—adj.* **3.** preceding; anterior. [1350–1400; (adj.) ME < L *praecēdent-* (s. of *praecēdēns*) prp. of *praecēdere* to go before, PRECEDE (see -ENT); (n.) late ME, deriv. of the adj.] **—prec′e·dent·less,** *adj.*
—Syn. 2. example, model, pattern, standard.

prec·e·den·tial (pres′i den′shəl), *adj.* **1.** of the nature of or constituting a precedent. **2.** having precedence. [1635–45; PRECEDENT + -IAL]

pre·ced·ing (pri sē′ding), *adj.* that precedes; previous: *Refer back to the footnote on the preceding page.* [1485–95; PRECEDE + -ING[2]]
—Syn. foregoing, prior, former, earlier. **—Ant.** succeeding, following.

pre·cent (pri sent′), *v.t.* **1.** to lead as a precentor in singing. *—v.i.* **2.** to act as a precentor. [1725–35; back formation from PRECENTOR]

pre·cen·tor (pri sen′tər), *n.* a person who leads a church choir or congregation in singing. [1605–15; < LL *praecentor* leader in music, equiv. to L *praecen-,* var. s. of *praecinere* to lead in singing (*prae-* PRE- + *-cinere,* comb. form of *canere* to sing; see CANTO) + *-tor* -TOR] **—pre·cen·to·ri·al** (prē′sen tôr′ē əl, -tōr′-), *adj.* **—pre·cen′tor·ship′,** *n.*

pre·cept (prē′sept), *n.* **1.** a commandment or direction given as a rule of action or conduct. **2.** an injunction as to moral conduct; maxim. **3.** a procedural directive or rule, as for the performance of some technical operation. **4.** *Law.* **a.** a writ or warrant. **b.** a written order issued pursuant to law, as a sheriff's order for an election. [1300–50; ME < L *praeceptum* piece of advice, rule, n. use of neut. of *praeceptus,* ptp. of *praecipere* to direct, foresee, lit., to take beforehand, equiv. to *prae-* PRE- + *-cep-,* comb. form of *capere* to take + *-tus* ptp. suffix]
—Syn. 1. directive, order, guide, instruction, prescription.

pre·cep·tive (pri sep′tiv), *adj.* **1.** of the nature of or expressing a precept; mandatory. **2.** giving instructions; instructive. [1425–75; late ME < L *praeceptīvus.* See PRECEPT, -IVE] **—pre·cep′tive·ly,** *adv.*

pre·cep·tor (pri sep′tər, prē′sep-), *n.* **1.** an instructor; teacher; tutor. **2.** the head of a school. **3.** the head of a preceptory. [1400–50; late ME < L *praeceptor.* See PRECEPT, -TOR] **—pre·cep·tor·ate** (pri sep′tər it), *n.* **—pre·cep·to·ri·al** (prē′sep tôr′ē əl, -tōr′-), **pre·cep′to·ral,** *adj.* **—pre′cep·to′ri·al·ly,** *adv.* **—pre·cep′tor·ship′,** *n.*

pre·cep·to·ry (pri sep′tə rē, prē′sep-), *n., pl.* **-ries.** a subordinate house or community of the Knights Templars; commandery. [1530–40; < ML *praeceptōria.* See PRECEPTOR, -Y[3]]

pre·cep·tress (pri sep′tris, prē′sep-), *n.* **1.** a woman who is an instructor; teacher; tutor. **2.** a woman who is the head of a school. [PRECEPT(O)R + -ESS]
—Usage. See **-ess.**

pre·cess (prē ses′), *v.i. Mech.* to undergo precession (def. 2). [1890–95; back formation from PRECESSION]

pre·ces·sion (prē sesh′ən), *n.* **1.** the act or fact of preceding; precedence. **2.** *Mech.* the motion of the rota-

pre′al·lu′sion, *n.*
pre·al′ly, *n., pl.* **-lies.**
pre′al·ly′, *v.,* **-lied, -ly·ing.**
pre·al′pha·bet′, *adj., n.*
pre′al·pha·bet′i·cal, *adj.;* **-ly,** *adv.*
pre·al′ter, *v.t.*
pre′al·ter·a′tion, *n.*
pre′a·mal′ga·ma′tion, *n.*
pre′am·bas′sa·do′ri·al, *adj.*
pre′am·bi′tion, *n.*
pre′am·bi′tious, *adj.;* **-ly,** *adv.*
pre-Am′mon·ite′, *adj., n.*
pre·a′nal, *adj.*
pre′a·naph′o·ral, *adj.*
pre′an·nex′, *v.t.*
pre′an·nounce′, *v.t.,* **-nounced, -nounc·ing.**
pre′an·nounce′ment, *n., adj.*
pre′an·nounc′er, *n.*
pre′an·te·pe′nult, *adj.*
pre′an·te·pe·nul′ti·mate, *adj.*
pre′an·tic′i·pate′, *v.t.,* **-pat·ed, -pat·ing.**
pre′an·tiq′ui·ty, *n., pl.* **-ties.**
pre′a·or′tic, *adj.*
pre′ap·pear′ance, *n.*
pre′ap·per·cep′tion, *n.*
pre′ap·pli·ca′tion, *n.*
pre′ap·ply′, *v.t.,* **-plied, -ply·ing.**
pre′ap·pre·hen′sion, *n.*
pre′ap·prize′, *v.t.,* **-prized, -priz·ing.**
pre′ap·pro·ba′tion, *n.*
pre′ap·prov′al, *n.*
pre′ap·prove′, *v.,* **-proved, -prov·ing.**
pre·ap′ti·tude′, *n.*
pre·arm′, *v.t.*
pre′ar·rest′, *v.t.*
pre′ar·rest′ment, *n.*
pre′-Ar·thu′ri·an, *adj.*
pre′ar·tic′u·late, *adj.*
pre′ar·tis′tic, *adj.*
pre-Ar′y·an, *adj.*
pre′as·cer·tain′, *v.t.*
pre′as·cer·tain′ment, *n.*
pre′as·cet′ic, *adj.*
pre′as·sem′ble, *v.t.,* **-bled, -bling.**
pre′as·sem′bly, *n., pl.* **-blies.**
pre′as·sert′, *v.t*
pre′as·sign′, *v.t*
pre′as·signed′, *adj.*
pre′as·sume′, *v.t.,* **-sumed, -sum·ing.**
pre′as·sump′tion, *n.*
pre′as·sur′ance, *n.*
pre′as·sure′, *v.t.,* **-sured, -sur·ing.**
pre′-As·syr′i·an, *adj.*
pre′a·tax′ic, *adj.*
pre′at·tach′ment, *n.*
pre′at·tune′, *v.t.,* **-tuned, -tun·ing.**
pre·au′di·to′ry, *adj.*
pre′-Au·gus′tan, *adj.*
pre-Au′gus·tine′, *adj.*
pre′au·ric′u·lar, *adj.*
pre′au·thor·i·za′tion, *n.*
pre·au′thor·ize′, *v.t.,* **-ized, -iz·ing.**
pre′a·ver′, *v.t.,* **-verred, -ver·ring.**
pre′a·vow′al, *n.*
pre′-Bab·y·lo′ni·an, *adj.*
pre·bach′e·lor, *adj., n.*
pre′-Ba·co′ni·an, *adj.*
pre·bake′, *v.,* **-baked, -bak·ing.**
pre·bal′ance, *v.,* **-anced, -anc·ing.**
pre·bal′lot, *v.t.,* **-lot·ed, -lot·ing.**
pre·bank′rupt·cy, *n., pl.* **-cies.**
pre′bar·bar′ic, *adj.*
pre·bar′ba·rous, *adj.;* **-ly,** *adv.;* **-ness,** *n.*
pre·bar′gain, *v.t.*
pre·ba′sal, *adj.*
pre·bas′i·lar, *adj.*
pre′be·lief′, *n.*
pre′be·lieve′, *v.,* **-lieved, -liev·ing.**
pre′be·liev′er, *n.*
pre′be·lov′ed, *adj., n.*
pre′ben·e·dic′tion, *n.*
pre′ben·e·fi′ci·ar′y, *n., pl.* **-ar·ies.**
pre·ben′e·fit, *v.,* **-fit·ed, -fit·ing.**
pre′be·set′, *v.t.,* **-set, -set·ting.**
pre′be·stow′, *v.t*
pre′be·stow′al, *n.*
pre′be·tray′, *v.t*
pre′be·tray′al, *n.*
pre′be·troth′al, *adj.*
pre·bid′, *n., v.,* **-bade** or **-bad** or **-bid, -bid·den** or **-bid, -bid·ding.**
pre·bill′, *n., v.t.*
pre·bless′, *v.t*
pre′block·ade′, *n., v.t.,* **-ad·ed, -ad·ing.**
pre·bloom′ing, *adj.*
pre·board′ing, *adj., n.*
pre·boast′, *n., v.*
pre·bod′ing, *adj.*
pre·boil′, *v.t.*
pre·book′, *v.*
pre·boom′, *n.*
pre·born′, *adj.*
pre·bor′row·ing, *n.*
pre·boy′hood, *n.*
pre·bra′chi·al, *adj.*
pre·bran′chi·al, *adj.*
pre·breathe′, *v.t.,* **-breathed, -breath·ing.**
pre·brid′al, *adj.*
pre-Brit′ish, *adj.*
pre·broad′cast′ing, *adj.*
pre′bro·mid′ic, *adj.*
pre·bron′chi·al, *adj.*
pre·bronze′, *adj.*
pre·brute′, *adj.*
pre·buc′cal, *adj.*
pre-Bud′dhist, *adj.*
pre·budg′et, *n., adj.*
pre·budg′et·ar′y, *adj.*
pre·build′, *v.t.,* **-built, build·ing.**
pre′bur·lesque′, *adj.*
pre·burn′, *v.t*
pre·buy′, *v.t.,* **-bought, -buy·ing.**

tion axis of a rigid body, as a spinning top, when a disturbing torque is applied while the body is rotating such that the rotation axis describes a cone, with the vertical through the vertex of the body as axis of the cone, and the motion of the rotating body is perpendicular to the direction of the torque. **3.** *Astron.* **a.** the slow, conical motion of the earth's axis of rotation, caused by the gravitational attraction of the sun and moon, and, to a smaller extent, of the planets, on the equatorial bulge of the earth. **b.** See **precession of the equinoxes.** [1300–50; < LL *praecessiōn-* (s. of *praecessiō*) a going before, advance, equiv. to L *praecess(us)* (ptp. of *praecēdere* to PRECEDE) + *-iōn-* -ION; see CESSION] **—pre·ces′sion·al,** *adj.*

preces′sion of the e′quinoxes, 1. the earlier occurrence of the equinoxes in each successive sidereal year because of the slow retrograde motion of the equinoctial points along the ecliptic, caused by the precession of the earth's axis of rotation; a complete precession of the equinoxes requires about 25,800 years. **2.** the resulting drift of celestial coordinates with respect to the positions of celestial objects. [1615–25]

pre-Chris·tian (prē kris′chən), *adj.* of, pertaining to, or belonging to a time or period before the Christian Era. [1820–30; PRE- + CHRISTIAN]

pré·cieuse (prā′sē o͞oz′; *Fr.* prā syœz′), *n., pl.* **-cieus·es** (-sē o͞o′ziz; *Fr.* -syœz′), *adj.* **—***n.* **1.** one of the 17th-century literary women of France who affected an extreme care in the use of language. **2.** an affected or pretentious woman, esp. one marked by preciosity in manner or speech. **—***adj.* **3.** (of a woman) marked by affectation or preciosity. [1720–30; < F; fem. of PRÉCIEUX; see -EUSE]

pré·cieux (prā′sē o͞o′; *Fr.* prā syœ′), *adj., n., pl.* **-cieux** (-sē o͞oz′; *Fr.* -syœ′). **—***adj.* **1.** (of a man) overly fastidious or refined; precious; affected. **—***n.* **2.** an affected or excessively fastidious man, as in dress, manner, or speech. [1890–95; < F; lit., PRECIOUS]

pre·cinct (prē′singkt), *n.* **1.** a district, as of a city, marked out for governmental or administrative purposes, or for police protection. **2.** Also called **pre′cinct house′.** the police station in such a district. **3.** Also called **election district.** one of a fixed number of districts, each containing one polling place, into which a city, town, etc., is divided for voting purposes. **4.** a space or place of definite or understood limits. **5.** Often, **precincts.** an enclosing boundary or limit. **6. precincts,** the parts or regions immediately surrounding a place; environs: *the precincts of a town.* **7.** *Chiefly Brit.* the ground immediately surrounding a church, temple, or the like. **8.** a walled or otherwise bounded or limited space within which a building or place is situated. [1350–1400; ME < ML *praecinctum,* n. use of neut. of L *praecinctus,* ptp. of *praecingere* to gird about, surround, equiv. to *prae-* PRE- + *cing-* (s. of *cingere* to surround; cf. CINCH[1]) + *-tus* ptp. suffix]
—Syn. 1. ward. **4.** territory. **8.** compound.

pre·ci·os·i·ty (presh′ē os′i tē), *n., pl.* **-ties.** fastidious or carefully affected refinement, as in language, style, or taste. [1350–1400; ME *preciousite* < MF *preciosite* < L *pretiōsitās.* See PRECIOUS, -ITY]

pre·cious (presh′əs), *adj.* **1.** of high price or great value; very valuable or costly: *precious metals.* **2.** highly esteemed for some spiritual, nonmaterial, or moral quality: *precious memories.* **3.** dear; beloved: *a precious child.* **4.** affectedly or excessively delicate, refined, or nice: *precious manners.* **5.** flagrant; gross: *a precious fool.* **—***n.* **6.** a dearly beloved person; darling. **—***adv.* **7.** extremely; very: *She wastes precious little time.* [1250–1300; ME *preciose* (< OF *precios*) < L *pretiōsus* costly, valuable, equiv. to *preti(um)* PRICE, value + *-ōsus* -OUS] **—pre′cious·ly,** *adv.* **—pre′cious·ness,** *n.*
—Syn. 1. See **valuable. 3.** darling, cherished.

pre′cious cor′al. See **red coral.** [1905–10]

pre′cious met′al, a metal of the gold, silver, or platinum group.

pre′cious moon′stone, moonstone (def. 1).

pre′cious o′pal, any opal having a play of colors, used as a gemstone. Also called **noble opal.**

pre′cious stone′, a gem distinguished for its beauty and rarity, used in jewelry. [1250–1300; ME]

prec·i·pice (pres′ə pis), *n.* **1.** a cliff with a vertical, nearly vertical, or overhanging face. **2.** a situation of great peril: *on the precipice of war.* [1590–1600; < MF < L *praecipitium* steep place, equiv. to *praecipit-* (s. of *praeceps*) steep, headlong (*prae-* PRE- + *-cipit-,* comb. form of *caput* head; see CAPUT) + *-ium* -IUM] **—prec′i·piced,** *adj.*

pre·cip·i·ta·ble (pri sip′i tə bəl), *adj. Chem.* capable of being precipitated. [1660–70; PRECIPIT(ATE) + -ABLE]

precip′itable wa′ter the total water vapor contained in a unit vertical column of the atmosphere. [1925–30]

pre·cip·i·tan·cy (pri sip′i tən sē), *n., pl.* **-cies. 1.** the quality or state of being precipitant. **2.** headlong or rash haste. **3. precipitancies,** hasty or rash acts. Also, **pre·cip′i·tance.** [1610–20; PRECIPIT(ANT) + -ANCY]

pre·cip·i·tant (pri sip′i tənt), *adj.* **1.** falling headlong. **2.** rushing headlong, rapidly, or hastily onward. **3.** hasty; rash. **4.** unduly sudden or abrupt. **—***n.* **5.** *Chem.* anything that causes precipitation. [1600–10; < L *praecipitant-* (s. of *praecipitāns*), prp. of *praecipitāre* to cast down headlong. See PRECIPITATE, -ANT] **—pre·cip′i·tant·ly,** *adv.*

pre·cip·i·tate (*v.* pri sip′i tāt′; *adj., n.* pri sip′i tit, -tāt′), *v.,* **-tat·ed, -tat·ing,** *adj., n.* **—***v.t.* **1.** to hasten the occurrence of; bring about prematurely, hastily, or suddenly: *to precipitate an international crisis.* **2.** to cast down headlong; fling or hurl down. **3.** to cast, plunge, or send, esp. violently or abruptly: *He precipitated himself into the struggle.* **4.** *Chem.* to separate (a substance) in solid form from a solution, as by means of a reagent. **—***v.i.* **5.** *Meteorol.* to fall to the earth's surface as a condensed form of water; to rain, snow, hail, drizzle, etc. **6.** to separate from a solution as a precipitate. **7.** to be cast or thrown down headlong. **—***adj.* **8.** headlong: *a precipitate fall down the stairs.* **9.** rushing headlong or rapidly onward. **10.** proceeding rapidly or with great haste: *a precipitate retreat.* **11.** exceedingly sudden or abrupt: *a precipitate stop; a precipitate decision.* **12.** done or made without sufficient deliberation; overhasty; rash: *a precipitate marriage.* **—***n.* **13.** *Chem.* a substance precipitated from a solution. **14.** moisture condensed in the form of rain, snow, etc. [1520–30; (v. and adj.) < L *praecipitātus* (ptp. of *praecipitāre* to cast down headlong), equiv. to *praecipit-* (s. of *praeceps* steep; see PRECIPICE) + *-ātus* -ATE[1]; (n.) < NL *praecipitātum* a precipitate, n. use of neut. of *praecipitātus*] **—pre·cip′i·tate·ly,** *adv.* **—pre·cip′i·tate·ness,** *n.* **—pre·cip′i·ta′tive,** *adj.* **—pre·cip′i·ta′tor,** *n.*
—Syn. 1. accelerate. **4.** crystallize. **12.** reckless, impetuous. **—Ant. 1.** retard. **12.** careful.

pre·cip·i·ta·tion (pri sip′i tā′shən), *n.* **1.** the act of precipitating; state of being precipitated. **2.** a casting down or falling headlong. **3.** a hastening or hurrying in movement, procedure, or action. **4.** sudden haste. **5.** unwise or rash rapidity. **6.** *Meteorol.* **a.** falling products of condensation in the atmosphere, as rain, snow, or hail. **b.** the amount of rain, snow, hail, etc., that has fallen at a given place within a given period, usually expressed in inches or centimeters of water. **7.** *Chem., Physics.* the precipitating of a substance from a solution. [1425–75; late ME < L *praecipitātiōn-* (s. of *praecipitātiō*) a falling headlong. See PRECIPITATE, -ION]

pre·cip·i·tin (pri sip′i tin), *n. Immunol.* an antibody that reacts with its specific antigen to form an insoluble precipitate. [1895–1900; PRECIPIT(ATE) + -IN[2]]

pre·cip·i·tin·o·gen (pri sip′i tin′ə jən, -jen′), *n. Immunol.* an antigen that stimulates precipitin production or that reacts with antibody in an immunoprecipitation reaction. [1900–05; PRECIPITIN + -O- + -GEN]

pre·cip·i·tous (pri sip′i təs), *adj.* **1.** of the nature of or characterized by precipices: *a precipitous wall of rock.* **2.** extremely or impassably steep: *precipitous mountain trails.* **3.** precipitate. [1640–50; < obs. F *précipiteux;* see PRECIPITATE, -OUS] **—pre·cip′i·tous·ly,** *adv.* **—pre·cip′i·tous·ness,** *n.*
—Syn. 2. abrupt, sheer, perpendicular. **—Ant. 1, 2.** flat, level.

pré·cis (prā sē′, prā′sē), *n., pl.* **-cis** (-sēz′, -sēz), *v.* **—***n.* **1.** a concise summary. **—***v.t.* **2.** to make a précis of. [1750–60; < F, n. use of adj., lit., cut short. See PRECISE]
—Syn. 1. digest, condensation, abstract.

pre·cise (pri sīs′), *adj.* **1.** definitely or strictly stated, defined, or fixed: *precise directions.* **2.** being exactly that and neither more nor less: *a precise temperature; a precise amount.* **3.** being just that and no other: *the precise dress she had wanted.* **4.** definite or exact in statement, as a person. **5.** carefully distinct: *precise articulation.* **6.** exact in measuring, recording, etc.: *a precise instrument.* **7.** excessively or rigidly particular: *precise observance of regulations; precise grooming.* [1350–1400; ME < L *praecīsus* curtailed, brief, orig. ptp. of *praecīdere* to cut off, cut short, equiv. to *prae-* PRE- + *-cīsus,* comb. form of *caesus,* ptp. of *caedere* to cut] **—pre·cise′ly,** *adv.* **—pre·cise′ness,** *n.*
—Syn. 1. explicit. See **correct. —Ant. 1.** indefinite, vague.

pre·ci·sian (pri sizh′ən), *n.* **1.** a person who adheres punctiliously to the observance of rules or forms, esp. in matters of religion. **2.** one of the English Puritans of the 16th and 17th centuries. [1565–75; PRECISE + -IAN] **—pre·ci′sian·ism,** *n.*

pre·ci·sion (pri sizh′ən), *n.* **1.** the state or quality of being precise. **2.** accuracy; exactness: *to arrive at an estimate with precision.* **3.** mechanical or scientific exactness: *a lens ground with precision.* **4.** punctiliousness; strictness: *precision in one's business dealings.* **5.** *Math.* the degree to which the correctness of a quantity is expressed. Cf. **accuracy** (def. 3). **6.** *Chem., Physics.* the extent to which a given set of measurements of the same sample agree with their mean. Cf. **accuracy** (def. 2). **—***adj.* **7.** of, pertaining to, or characterized by precision: *precision swimming; precision instruments for aircraft.* [1630–40; < L *praecīsiōn-* (s. of *praecīsiō*) a cutting off. See PRECISE, -ION] **—pre·ci′sion·al,** *adj.*
—Syn. 2. preciseness, meticulousness, rigor.

preci′sion bomb′ing, aerial bombing in which bombs are dropped, as accurately as possible, on a specific, usually small, target. Also called **pinpoint bombing.** Cf. **area bombing, pattern bombing.** [1935–40]

preci′sion cast′ing, *Metall.* See **investment casting.** [1940–45]

pre·ci·sion·ism (pri sizh′ə niz′əm), *n.* (*sometimes cap.*) a style of painting developed to its fullest in the U.S. in the 1920's, associated esp. with Charles Demuth, Georgia O'Keeffe, and Charles Sheeler, and characterized by clinically precise, simple, and clean-edged rendering of architectural, industrial, or urban scenes usually devoid of human activity or presence. [1955–60; PRECISION + -ISM] **—pre·ci′sion·ist,** *n., adj.* **—pre·ci′·sion·is′tic,** *adj.*

pre·ci·sive[1] (pri sī′siv), *adj.* separating or distinguishing (a person or thing) from another or others: *precisive imputation of guilt.* [1670–80; < L *praecīs(us)* (see PRECISE) + -IVE]

pre·ci·sive[2] (pri sī′siv), *adj.* characterized by accuracy or exactness: *a precisive method of expressing oneself.* [1800–10; PRECIS(ION) + -IVE]

pre·cli·max (prē klī′maks), *n. Ecol.* a stable community that precedes the full development of the climax community of a given area and that results from local variations in soil and water. [1915–20; PRE- + CLIMAX]

pre·clin·i·cal (prē klin′i kəl), *adj. Med.* of or pertaining to the period prior to the appearance of the symptoms. [1930–35; PRE- + CLINICAL] **—pre·clin′i·cal·ly,** *adv.*

pre·clude (pri klo͞od′), *v.t.,* **-clud·ed, -clud·ing. 1.** to prevent the presence, existence, or occurrence of; make impossible: *The insufficiency of the evidence precludes a conviction.* **2.** to exclude or debar from something: *His physical disability precludes an athletic career for him.* [1610–20; < L *praeclūdere* to shut off, close, equiv. to *prae-* PRE- + *-clūdere,* comb. form of *claudere* to shut, CLOSE] **—pre·clud′a·ble,** *adj.* **—pre·clu·sion** (pri klo͞o′zhən), *n.* **—pre·clu·sive** (pri klo͞o′siv), *adj.* **—pre·clu′sive·ly,** *adv.*
—Syn. 1. forestall; eliminate.

pre·co·cial (pri kō′shəl), *adj. Biol.* (of an animal species) active and able to move freely from birth or hatching and requiring little parental care (opposed to *altricial*). [1870–75; PRECOCI(OUS) + -AL[1]]

pre·co·cious (pri kō′shəs), *adj.* **1.** unusually advanced or mature in development, esp. mental development: *a precocious child.* **2.** prematurely developed, as the mind, faculties, etc. **3.** of or pertaining to premature development. **4.** *Bot.* **a.** flowering, fruiting, or ripening early, as plants or fruit. **b.** bearing blossoms before leaves, as plants. **c.** appearing before leaves, as flowers.

CONCISE PRONUNCIATION KEY: *act, cāpe, dâre, pärt; set, ēqual; if, īce; ox, ōver, ôrder, oil, bo͝ok, bo͞ot, out; up, ûrge; child; sing; shoe; thin, that;* zh as in *treasure.* ə = *a* as in *alone, e* as in *system, i* as in *easily, o* as in *gallop, u* as in *circus;* ᵊ as in *fire* (fīᵊr), *hour* (ouᵊr). l and n can serve as syllabic consonants, as in *cradle* (krād′l), and *button* (but′n). See the full key inside the front cover.

pre-Byz′an·tine′, *adj.*
pre·cal′cu·la·ble, *adj.*
pre·cal′cu·late′, *v.t.,* **-lat·ed, -lat·ing.**
pre′cal·cu·la′tion, *n.*
pre-Cam′bridge, *adj.*
pre′cam·paign′, *n., adj.*
pre-Ca′naan·ite′, *n., adj.*
pre′-Ca·naan·it′ic, *adj.*
pre·can′di·da·cy, *n.*
pre·can′di·da·ture, *n.*
pre·can′ning, *n., adj.*
pre·can′vass, *v.t., n.*
pre·cap′i·tal·ist, *n., adj.*
pre·cap′i·tal·is′tic, *adj.*
pre′cap·tiv′i·ty, *n.*
pre·cap′ture, *adj., v.t.,* **-tured, -tur·ing.**
pre′-Car·bon·if′er·ous, *adj.*
pre·car′di·ac′, *adj.*
pre·car′ni·val, *adj.*
pre′-Car·o·lin′gi·an, *adj.*
pre′car·ti·lag′i·nous, *adj.*
pre·cau′dal, *adj.*
pre·cel′e·brant, *n.*
pre·cel′e·brate′, *v.,* **-brat·ed, -brat·ing.**
pre′cel·e·bra′tion, *n.*
pre-Celt′ic, *adj.*
pre·cen′sor, *v.t.*
pre·cen′sor·ship′, *n.*
pre·cen′sure, *v.t.,* **-sured, -sur·ing.**
pre·cen′sus, *n.*
pre′cen·ten′ni·al, *adj.*
pre′cer·e·bel′lar, *adj.*
pre′ce·re′bral, *adj.*
pre′ce·re′broid, *adj.*
pre·cer′e·mo′ni·al, *adj.*
pre·cer′e·mo′ny, *n., pl.* **-nies.**
pre′cer·ti·fi·ca′tion, *n.*
pre·cer′ti·fy′, *v.t.,* **-fied, -fy·ing.**
pre·chal′lenge, *v.t.,* **-lenged, -leng·ing.**
pre·cham′pi·oned, *adj.*
pre·cham′pi·on·ship′, *n.*
pre·charge′, *v.t.,* **-charged, -charg·ing,** *n.*
pre·chart′, *v.t.*
pre·chart′ed, *adj.*
pre′-Chau·ce′ri·an, *adj.*
pre·check′, *v.t., n.*
pre·chem′i·cal, *adj.*
pre·child′hood, *n.*
pre·chill′, *v.t.*
pre′-Chi·nese′, *adj., n., pl.* **-nese.**
pre·chlo′ric, *adj.*
pre·chlo′ro·form′, *v.t.*
pre·choice′, *n.*
pre·choose′, *v.t.,* **-chose, -cho·sen, -choos·ing.**
pre·chord′al, *adj.*
pre·cho′roid, *adj.*
pre-Christ′mas, *adj.*
pre·cir′cu·late′, *v.,* **-lat·ed, -lat·ing.**
pre′cir·cu·la′tion, *n.*
pre′ci·ta′tion, *n.*
pre·cite′, *v.t.,* **-cit·ed, -cit·ing.**
pre′civ·i·li·za′tion, *n.*
pre·claim′, *v.t., n.*
pre·claim′ant, *n.*
pre·claim′er, *n.*
pre·clas′sic, *adj.*
pre·clas′si·cal, *adj.;* **-ly,** *adv.*
pre′clas·si·fi·ca′tion, *n.*
pre·clas′si·fy′, *v.t.,* **-fied, -fy·ing.**
pre·clean′, *v.t.*
pre·clean′er, *n.*
pre·clear′, *v.t.*
pre·clear′ance, *n., adj.*
pre·cler′i·cal, *adj.*
pre·clo′a·cal, *adj.*
pre·close′, *v.t.,* **-closed, -clos·ing.**
pre·clo′sure, *n.*
pre·clothe′, *v.t.,* **-clothed, -cloth·ing.**
pre′coc·cyg′e·al, *adj.*
pre·code′, *v.t.,* **-cod·ed, -cod·ing.**
pre·cog′i·tate′, *v.,* **-tat·ed, -tat·ing.**
pre′cog·i·ta′tion, *n.*
pre·cog′ni·za·ble, *adj.*
pre·cog′ni·zant, *adj.*
pre·cog′nize, *v.t.,* **-nized, -niz·ing.**
pre·coil′, *v.i.*
pre′co·in′ci·dence, *n.*
pre′co·in′ci·dent, *adj.;* **-ly,** *adv.*
pre·co′i·tal, *adj.*
pre′col·laps′a·bil′i·ty, *n.*
pre′col·laps′a·ble, *adj.*
pre′col·lapse′, *v.,* **-lapsed, -laps·ing.**
pre′col·laps′i·bil′i·ty, *n.*
pre′col·laps′i·ble, *adj.*
pre′col·lect′, *v.t.*
pre′col·lect′a·ble, *adj.*
pre′col·lect′i·ble, *adj.*
pre′col·lec′tion, *n.*
pre′col·lec′tor, *n.*
pre·col′lege, *n., adj.*
pre′col·le′giate, *adj.*
pre′col·lude′, *v.i.,* **-lud·ed, -lud·ing.**
pre′col·lu′sion, *n.*
pre′col·lu′sive, *adj.*
pre·col′or, *n., v.*
pre·col′or·a·ble, *adj.*
pre′col·or·a′tion, *n.*
pre·com′bat, *n., v.,* **-bat·ed, -bat·ing** or (*esp. Brit.*) **-bat·ted, -bat·ting.**
pre′com·bat′ant, *n.*
pre′com·bi·na′tion, *n.*
pre′com·bine′, *v.,* **-bined, -bin·ing.**
pre′com·bus′tion, *n.*
pre′com·mand′, *n., v.*
pre·com′ment, *n., v.*
pre′com·mer′cial, *adj.*
pre′com·mit′, *v.t.,* **-mit·ted, -mit·ting.**
pre′com·mit′ment, *adj.*

[1640–50; L *praecoci-,* s. of *praecox* (see PRECOCITY) + -OUS] **—pre·co′cious·ly,** *adv.* **—pre·co′cious·ness,** *n.*

pre·coc·i·ty (pri kos′i tē), *n.* the state of being or tendency to be precocious. [1630–40; < F *précosité,* equiv. to *précose* (< L *praecoci-,* s. of *praecox* early ripening, adj. deriv. of *praecoquere* to bake or ripen early; see PRE-, COOK[1]) + *-ité* -ITY]

pre·cog·ni·tion (prē′kog nish′ən), *n.* **1.** knowledge of a future event or situation, esp. through extrasensory means. **2.** *Scot. Law.* **a.** the examination of witnesses and other parties before a trial in order to supply a legal ground for prosecution. **b.** the evidence established in such an examination. [1400–50; late ME < LL *praecognitiōn-,* s. of *praecognitiō;* see PRE-, COGNITION] **—pre·cog·ni·tive** (prē kog′ni tiv), *adj.*

pre·co·lo·ni·al (prē′kə lō′nē əl), *adj.* of or pertaining to the time before a region or country became a colony. [1960–65; PRE- + COLONIAL]

pre-Co·lum·bi·an (prē′kə lum′bē ən), *adj.* of or pertaining to the Americas before the arrival of Columbus: *pre-Columbian art; pre-Columbian Indians.* [1885–90]

pre·com·pose (prē′kəm pōz′), *v.t.,* **-posed, -pos·ing.** to compose beforehand: *to precompose a reply to a possible question.* [1640–50; PRE- + COMPOSE]

pre·con·ceive (prē′kən sēv′), *v.t.,* **-ceived, -ceiv·ing.** to form a conception or opinion of beforehand, as before seeing evidence or as a result of previously held prejudice. [1570–80; PRE- + CONCEIVE]

pre·con·cep·tion (prē′kən sep′shən), *n.* **1.** a conception or opinion formed beforehand. **2.** bias. [1615–25; PRE- + CONCEPTION] **—pre′con·cep′tion·al,** *adj.*

pre·con·cert (*adj.* prē kon′sûrt, -sərt; *v.* prē′kən-sûrt′), *adj.* **1.** preceding a concert: *a preconcert reception for sponsors.* —*v.t.* **2.** to arrange in advance or beforehand, as by a previous agreement. [1740–50; PRE- + CONCERT] **—pre′con·cert′ed·ly,** *adv.*

pre·con·demn (prē′kən dem′), *v.t.* to condemn beforehand, as before a legitimate trial. [1625–35; PRE- + CONDEMN] **—pre·con·dem·na·tion** (prē′kon dem nā′-shən, -dəm-), *n.*

pre·con·di·tion (prē′kən dish′ən), *n.* **1.** something that must come before or is necessary to a subsequent result; condition: *a precondition for a promotion.* —*v.t.* **2.** to subject (a person or thing) to a special treatment in preparation for a subsequent experience, process, test, etc.: *to precondition a surface to receive paint.* [1910–15; PRE- + CONDITION]

pre·co·nize (prē′kə nīz′), *v.t.,* **-nized, -niz·ing. 1.** to proclaim or commend publicly. **2.** to summon publicly. **3.** *Rom. Cath. Ch.* (of the pope) to declare solemnly in consistory the appointment of (a new bishop or other high ecclesiastic). Also, *esp. Brit.,* **pre′co·nise′.** [1400–50; late ME < ML *praecōnizāre* to herald, announce, equiv. to L *praecōn-* (s. of *praecō*) crier, herald + *-izāre* -IZE] **—pre′co·ni·za′tion,** *n.* **—pre′co·niz′er,** *n.*

pre·con·quest (prē kon′kwest, -kong′-), *adj.* of or pertaining to the time before the conquest of one people, region, or country by another. [PRE- + CONQUEST]

pre-Con·quest (prē kon′kwest, -kong′-), of or pertaining to the time before the Norman conquest of England in 1066.

pre·con·scious (prē kon′shəs), *adj.* **1.** *Psychoanal.* absent from but capable of being readily brought into consciousness. **2.** occurring prior to the development of consciousness. —*n.* **3.** the preconscious portion of the mind; foreconscious. [1855–60; PRE- + CONSCIOUS] **—pre·con′scious·ly,** *adv.*

pre·con·so·nan·tal (prē kon′sə nan′tl, prē′kon-), *adj.* *Phonet.* immediately preceding a consonant. [1950–55; PRE- + CONSONANTAL]

pre·con·tract (*n.* prē kon′trakt; *v.* prē′kən trakt′, -kon′trakt), *n.* **1.** a preexisting contract that legally prevents a person from making another contract of the same nature. **2.** (formerly) such an agreement constituting a legally binding betrothal. —*v.t.* **3.** to bind by means of a precontract. **4.** to contract for or agree to do (something) by means of a precontract. —*v.i.* **5.** to make a precontract. [1375–1425; late ME (n.); see PRE-, CONTRACT] **—pre′con·trac′tive,** *adj.* **—pre·con·trac·tu·al** (prē′kən trak′cho͞o əl), *adj.*

CONCISE ETYMOLOGY KEY: <, descended or borrowed from; >, whence; b., blend of, blended; c., cognate with; cf., compare; deriv., derivative; equiv., equivalent; imit., imitative; obl., oblique; r., replacing; s., stem; sp., spelling, spelled; resp., respelling, respelled; trans., translation; ?, origin unknown; *, unattested; ‡, probably earlier than. See the full key inside the front cover.

pre·cook (prē ko͝ok′), *v.t.* to cook (food) partly or completely beforehand, so that it may be cooked or warmed and served quickly at a later time. [1945–50; PRE- + COOK[1]] **—pre·cook′er,** *n.*

pre·cool (prē ko͞ol′), *v.t.* to cool in advance; cool artificially, as meat or fresh produce, before shipping. [1900–05; PRE- + COOL] **—pre·cool′er,** *n.*

pre·crit·i·cal (prē krit′i kəl), *adj. Med.* anteceding a crisis. [1880–85; PRE- + CRITICAL]

pre·cur·sor (pri kûr′sər, prē′kûr-), *n.* **1.** a person or thing that precedes, as in a job, a method, etc.; predecessor. **2.** a person, animal, or thing that goes before and indicates the approach of someone or something else; harbinger: *The first robin is a precursor of spring.* **3.** *Chem., Biochem.* a chemical that is transformed into another compound, as in the course of a chemical reaction, and therefore precedes that compound in the synthetic pathway: *Cholesterol is a precursor of testosterone.* **4.** *Biol.* a cell or tissue that gives rise to a variant, specialized, or more mature form. [1375–1425; late ME < L *praecursor* forerunner. See PRE-, CURSOR]
—Syn. 1. forerunner. **2.** herald.

pre·cur·so·ry (pri kûr′sə rē), *adj.* **1.** of the nature of a precursor; preliminary; introductory: *precursory remarks.* **2.** indicative of something to follow: *precursory indications of disease.* Also, **pre·cur·sive** (pri kûr′siv). [1590–1600; < L *praecursōrius.* See PRECURSOR, CURSORY]

pre·cut (prē kut′), *adj., v.,* **-cut, -cut·ting.** —*adj.* **1.** cut to a specific shape or size before being assembled or used: *a kit with precut parts.* —*v.t.* **2.** to cut or cut out in advance: *The logs were precut to size.* [1940–45; PRE- + CUT]

pred., predicate.

pre·da·cious (pri dā′shəs), *adj.* predatory; rapacious. Also, *esp. Biol.,* **pre·da′ceous.** [1705–15; PRED(ATORY) + -ACIOUS] **—pre·da′cious·ness, pre·dac·i·ty** (pri das′i-tē); *esp. Biol.,* **pre·da′ceous·ness,** *n.*

pre·date (prē dāt′), *v.t.,* **-dat·ed, -dat·ing. 1.** to date before the actual time; antedate: *He predated the check by three days.* **2.** to precede in date: *a house that predates the Civil War.* [1860–65; PRE- + DATE[1]]

pre·da·tion (pri dā′shən), *n.* **1.** depredation; plundering. **2.** act of plundering or robbing. **3.** predatory behavior. **4.** a relation between animals in which one organism captures and feeds on others. [1425–75; late ME < L *praedātiōn-* (s. of *praedātiō*) a taking of booty, plundering, equiv. to *praedāt(us),* ptp. of *praedārī* to plunder, catch (see PREDATOR) + *-iōn-*]

preda′tion pres′sure, *Ecol.* the effect of predation upon a population, resulting in the decrease in size of that population. [1940–45]

pre·dat·ism (pri dā′tiz əm, pred′ə tiz′əm), *n.* the state of living as a predator or by predation. [1925–30; PREDAT(ION) + -ISM]

pred·a·tor (pred′ə tər, -tôr′), *n.* **1.** *Zool.* any organism that exists by preying upon other organisms. **2.** a predatory person. [1920–25; < L *praedātor* plunderer, equiv. to *praedā(rī)* to plunder (deriv. of *praeda* PREY) + *-tor* -TOR]

pred·a·to·ry (pred′ə tôr′ē, -tōr′ē), *adj.* **1.** *Zool.* preying upon other organisms for food. **2.** of, pertaining to, or characterized by plunder, pillage, robbery, or exploitation: *predatory tactics.* **3.** engaging in or living by these activities: *predatory bands of brigands.* **4.** excessive or exploitive in amount or cost, as out of greed or to take advantage of consumers or patrons: *predatory pricing.* **5.** acting with or possessed by overbearing, rapacious, or selfish motives: *He was cornered at the party by a predatory reporter.* [1580–90; < L *praedātōrius.* See PREDATOR, -TORY[1]] **—pred′a·to′ri·ly,** *adv.* **—pred′a·to′ri·ness,** *n.*
—Syn. 2, 3. rapacious.

pre·dawn (prē dôn′, prē′-), *n.* **1.** the period immediately preceding dawn. —*adj.* **2.** noting the time immediately prior to dawn. [1945–50; PRE- + DAWN]

pre·de·cease (prē′di sēs′), *v.t.,* **-ceased, -ceas·ing.** to die before (another person, the occurrence of an event, etc.). [1585–95; PRE- + DECEASE]

pred·e·ces·sor (pred′ə ses′ər, pred′ə ses′ər *or, esp. Brit.,* prē′də ses′ər), *n.* **1.** a person who precedes another in an office, position, etc. **2.** something succeeded or replaced by something else: *The new monument in the park is more beautiful than its predecessor.* **3.** *Archaic.* an ancestor; forefather. [1250–1300; ME *predecessour* < AF < LL *praedēcessor,* equiv. to L *prae-* PRE- + *dēcessor* retiring official, itself equiv. to *dēced-,* var. s. of *dēcēdere* to withdraw (*dē-* DE- + *cēdere* to yield; see CEDE) + *-tor* -TOR, with *dt* > ss]

pre·del·la (pri del′ə; *It.* pre del′lä), *n., pl.* **-le** (-lē; *It.* -le). *Fine Arts.* the base of an altarpiece, often decorated with small paintings or reliefs. [1840–50; < It < Langobardic **predel,* **pretel,* deriv. of **pret-* board < Gmc **bret-* (> OHG *brët* (G *Brett*), OE, OS *bred* board, plank; akin to BOARD); conformed in It to the dim. suffix *-ella* -ELLE]

pre·des·ig·nate (prē dez′ig nāt′), *v.t.,* **-nat·ed, -nat·ing.** to designate beforehand. [1815–25; PRE- + DESIGNATE] **—pre′des·ig·na′tion,** *n.* **—pre·des·ig·na·to·ry** (prē dez′ig nə tôr′ē, -tōr′ē, prē′dez ig nā′tə rē), *adj.*

pre·des·ti·nar·i·an (pri des′tə nâr′ē ən, prē′des-), *adj.* **1.** of or pertaining to predestination. **2.** believing in predestination. —*n.* **3.** a person who believes in predestination. [1630–40; PREDESTIN(ATION) + -ARIAN] **—pre·des′ti·nar′i·an·ism,** *n.*

pre·des·ti·nate (*v.* pri des′tə nāt′; *adj.* pri des′tə nit, -nāt′), *v.,* **-nat·ed, -nat·ing,** *adj.* —*v.t.* **1.** *Theol.* to foreordain by divine decree or purpose. **2.** *Obs.* to foreordain; predetermine. —*adj.* **3.** predestined; foreordained. [1350–1400; ME *predestinaten* (v.) < L *praedestinātus,* ptp. of *praedestināre* to appoint beforehand. See PRE-, DESTINE, -ATE[1]] **—pre·des′ti·nate·ly,** *adv.*

pre·des·ti·na·tion (pri des′tə nā′shən, prē′des-), *n.* **1.** an act of predestinating or predestining. **2.** the state of being predestinated or predestined. **3.** fate; destiny. **4.** *Theol.* **a.** the action of God in foreordaining from eternity whatever comes to pass. **b.** the decree of God by which certain souls are foreordained to salvation. Cf. **election** (def. 4), **double predestination.** [1300–50; ME *predestinacioun* < LL *praedestinātiōn-* (s. of *praedestinātiō*). See PREDESTINATE, -ION]

pre·des·ti·na·tor (pri des′tə nā′tər), *n.* **1.** a person or thing that predestinates something. **2.** *Archaic.* a predestinarian. [1570–80; PREDESTINATE + -OR[2]]

pre·des·tine (pri des′tin), *v.t.,* **-tined, -tin·ing.** to destine in advance; foreordain; predetermine: *He seemed predestined for the ministry.* [1350–1400; ME *predestinen* < L *praedestināre.* See PRE-, DESTINE] **—pre·des′ti·na·ble,** *adj.*

pre·de·ter·mi·nate (prē′di tûr′mə nit), *adj.* determined beforehand; predetermined. [1625–35; PRE- + DETERMINATE] **—pre′de·ter′mi·nate·ly,** *adv.*

pre·de·ter·mine (prē′di tûr′min), *v.t.,* **-mined, -min·ing. 1.** to settle or decide in advance: *He had predetermined his answer to the offer.* **2.** to ordain in advance; predestine: *She believed that God had predetermined her sorrow.* **3.** to direct or impel; influence strongly: *His sympathy for the poor predetermined his choice of a career.* [1615–25; PRE- + DETERMINE] **—pre′de·ter′mi·na′tion,** *n.* **—pre·de·ter·mi·na·tive** (prē′di tûr′mə-nā′tiv, -nə tiv), *adj.*

pre·de·ter·min·er (prē′di tûr′mə nər), *n. Gram.* a member of a subclass of English adjectival words, often quantitative in meaning, that may be placed before an article or other determiner, as *all* in *all the paintings* or *half* in *half her salary.* [1670–80; PRE- + DETERMINER]

pre·di·a·be·tes (prē dī′ə bē′tis, -tēz, prē′dī-), *n. Pathol.* **1.** a condition in which carbohydrate metabolism is mildly abnormal but other criteria indicating diabetes mellitus are absent. **2.** a condition in which the development of diabetes mellitus is expected. [1935–40; PRE- + DIABETES] **—pre·di·a·bet·ic** (prē dī′ə bet′ik, prē′dī-), *adj., n.*

pre·di·al (prē′dē əl), *adj.* praedial.

pred·i·ca·ble (pred′i kə bəl), *adj.* **1.** that may be predicated or affirmed; assertable. —*n.* **2.** that which may be predicated; an attribute. **3.** *Logic.* any one of the various kinds of predicate that may be used of a subject. [1545–55; < L *praedicābilis* assertable, L: praiseworthy, equiv. to *praedicā(re)* to declare publicly (see PREDICATE) + *-bilis* -BLE] **—pred′i·ca·bil′i·ty, pred′i·ca·ble·ness,** *n.* **—pred′i·ca·bly,** *adv.*

pre·dic·a·ment (pri dik′ə mənt *for 1, 3;* pred′i kə-mənt *for 2*), *n.* **1.** an unpleasantly difficult, perplexing, or dangerous situation. **2.** a class or category of logical or philosophical predication. **3.** *Archaic.* a particular state, condition, or situation. [1350–1400; 1580–90 for

pre′com·mune′, *v.i.,* **-muned, -mun·ing.**
pre′com·mu′ni·cate′, *v.,* **-cat·ed, -cat·ing.**
pre′com·mu′ni·ca′tion, *n.*
pre′com·pare′, *v.t.,* **-pared, -par·ing.**
pre′com·par′i·son, *n.*
pre·com′pass, *v.t., n.*
pre′com·pel′, *v.t.,* **-pelled, -pel·ling.**
pre·com′pen·sate′, *v.t.,* **-sat·ed, -sat·ing.**
pre′com·pen·sa′tion, *n.*
pre′com·pi·la′tion, *n.*
pre′com·pile′, *v.t.,* **-piled, -pil·ing.**
pre′com·pil′er, *n.*
pre′com·plete′ness, *n.*
pre′com·ple′tion, *n.*
pre′com·pli′ance, *n.*
pre′com·pli′ant, *adj.*
pre·com′pli·cate′, *v.t.,* **-cat·ed, -cat·ing.**
pre′com·pli·ca′tion, *n.*
pre′com·pound′, *v.*
pre′com·pre·hend′, *v.t.*
pre′com·pre·hen′sion, *n.*
pre′com·pre·hen′sive, *adj.;* **-ly,** *adv.;* **-ness,** *n.*
pre′com·press′, *v.t.*
pre′com·pres′sion, *n.*
pre′com·pul′sion, *n.*
pre′com·pute′, *v.,* **-put·ed, -put·ing.**
pre·com′rade·ship′, *n.*
pre′con·ceal′, *v.t.*
pre′con·ceal′ment, *n.*
pre′con·cede′, *v.t.,* **-ced·ed, -ced·ing.**
pre·con′cen·trate′, *n., v.,* **-trat·ed, -trat·ing.**
pre′con·cen·tra′tion, *n.*
pre′con·cern′, *n., v.t.*
pre′con·cern′ment, *n.*
pre′con·ces′sion, *n.*
pre′con·ces′sive, *adj.*
pre′con·cil′i·ar, *adj.*
pre′con·clude′, *v.t.,* **-clud·ed, -clud·ing.**
pre′con·clu′sion, *n.*
pre′con·cur′, *v.i.,* **-curred, -cur·ring.**
pre′con·cur′rence, *n.*
pre′con·cur′rent, *adj.;* **-ly,** *adv.*
pre′con·den·sa′tion, *n.*
pre′con·dense′, *v.,* **-densed, -dens·ing.**
pre′con·duct′, *v.t.*
pre′con·duc′tion, *n.*
pre′con·duc′tor, *n.*
pre·con′dy·lar, *adj.*
pre·con′dy·loid′, *adj.*
pre′con·fer′, *v.i.,* **-ferred, -fer·ring.**
pre·con′fer·ence, *n.*
pre′con·fess′, *v.t.*
pre′con·fes′sion, *n.*
pre′con·fide′, *v.,* **-fid·ed, -fid·ing.**
pre′con·fig′u·ra′tion, *n.*
pre′con·fig′ure, *v.t.,* **-ured, -ur·ing.**
pre′con·fine′, *v.t.,* **-fined, -fin·ing.**
pre′con·fin′ed·ly, *adv.*
pre′con·fine′ment, *n.*
pre′con·firm′, *v.t.*
pre′con·fir·ma′tion, *n.*
pre′con·flict′, *v.i.*
pre·con′flict, *n.*
pre′con·form′, *v.*
pre′con·form′i·ty, *n.*
pre′con·found′, *v.t.*
pre′con·fuse′, *v.t.,* **-fused, -fus·ing.**
pre′con·fus′ed·ly, *adv.*
pre′con·fu′sion, *n.*
pre′con·gen′ial, *adj.*
pre′con·gest′ed, *adj.*
pre′con·ges′tion, *n.*
pre′con·ges′tive, *adj.*
pre′con·grat′u·late′, *v.t.,* **-lat·ed, -lat·ing.**
pre′con·grat′u·la′tion, *n.*
pre′-Con·gre·ga′tion·al·ist, *n., adj.*
pre-Con′gress, *n.*
pre′con·gres′sion·al, *adj.*
pre′con·jec′ture, *v.t.,* **-tured, -tur·ing.**
pre′con·nec′tion, *n.*
pre′con·nec′tive, *adj.*
pre′con·nu′bi·al, *adj.*
pre·con′quer, *v.t.*
pre·con′se·crate′, *v.t.,* **-crat·ed, -crat·ing.**
pre′con·se·cra′tion, *n.*
pre′con·sent′, *n., v.i.*
pre′con·sid′er, *v.t.*
pre′con·sid′er·a′tion, *n.*
pre′con·sign′, *v.t.*
pre′con·sol′i·date′, *v.,* **-dat·ed, -dat·ing.**
pre′con·sol′i·da′tion, *n.*
pre′con·spir′a·cy, *n., pl.* **-cies.**
pre′con·spir′a·tor, *n.*
pre′con·spire′, *v.,* **-spired, -spir·ing.**
pre·con·stit′u·ent, *n.*
pre·con′sti·tute′, *v.t.,* **-tut·ed, -tut·ing.**
pre′con·struct′, *v.t.*
pre′con·struc′tion, *n.*
pre′con·sult′, *v.*
pre′con·sul·ta′tion, *n.*
pre′con·sul′tor, *n.*
pre′con·sume′, *v.t.,* **-sumed, -sum·ing.**
pre′con·sum′er, *n.*
pre′con·sump′tion, *n.*
pre′con·tain′, *v.t.*
pre′con·temn′, *v.t.*
pre′con·tem·plate′, *v.,* **-plat·ed, -plat·ing.**
pre′con·tem·pla′tion, *n.*
pre′con·tem′po·ra·ne′i·ty, *n.*
pre′con·tem′po·ra′ne·ous, *adj.;* **-ly,** *adv.*
pre′con·tend′, *v.i.*

def. 1; ME < LL *praedicāmentum* something predicated, asserted, deriv. of *praedicāre*. See PREDICATE, -MENT] —**pre·dic·a·men·tal** (pri dik′ə men′tl, pred′i kə-), *adj.* —**pre·dic′a·men′tal·ly,** *adv.*
—**Syn. 1.** PREDICAMENT, DILEMMA, PLIGHT, QUANDARY refer to unpleasant or puzzling situations. PREDICAMENT and PLIGHT stress more the unpleasant nature, QUANDARY and DILEMMA the puzzling nature of the situation. PREDICAMENT and PLIGHT are sometimes interchangeable; PLIGHT, however, though originally meaning peril or danger, is seldom used today except laughingly: *When his suit wasn't ready at the cleaners, he was in a terrible plight.* PREDICAMENT, though likewise capable of being used lightly, may also refer to a really crucial situation: *Stranded in a strange city without money, he was in a predicament.* DILEMMA, in popular use, means a position of doubt or perplexity in which one is faced by two equally undesirable alternatives: *the dilemma of a hostess who must choose between offending her anti-drinking guests or disappointing those who expected cocktails.* QUANDARY is the state of mental perplexity of one faced with a difficult situation: *There seemed to be no way out of the quandary.*

pred·i·cant (pred′i kənt), *adj.* **1.** preaching: *a predicant religious order.* —*n.* **2.** a preacher. [1580–90; < L *praedicant-* (s. of *praedicāns*), prp. of *praedicāre* to PREACH; see -ANT]

pred·i·cate (*v.* pred′i kāt′; *adj., n.* pred′i kit), *v.*, **-cat·ed, -cat·ing,** *adj.*, *n.* —*v.t.* **1.** to proclaim; declare; affirm; assert. **2.** *Logic.* **a.** to affirm or assert (something) of the subject of a proposition. **b.** to make (a term) the predicate of such a proposition. **3.** to connote; imply: *His retraction predicates a change of attitude.* **4.** to found or derive (a statement, action, etc.); base (usually fol. by *on*): *He predicated his behavior on his faith in humanity.* —*v.i.* **5.** to make an affirmation or assertion. —*adj.* **6.** predicated. **7.** *Gram.* belonging to the predicate: *a predicate noun.* —*n.* **8.** *Gram.* (in many languages, as English) a syntactic unit that functions as one of the two main constituents of a simple sentence, the other being the subject, and that consists of a verb, which in English may agree with the subject in number, and of all the words governed by the verb or modifying it, the whole often expressing the action performed by or the state attributed to the subject, as *is here* in *Larry is here.* **9.** *Logic.* that which is affirmed or denied concerning the subject of a proposition. [1400–50; (n.) late ME (< MF *predicat*) < ML *praedicātum*, n. use of neut. of L *praedicātus*, ptp. of *praedicāre* to declare publicly, assert, equiv. to *prae-* PRE- + *dicā(re)* to show, INDICATE, make known + *-tus* ptp. suffix; (v. and adj.) < L *praedicātus*; cf. PREACH] —**pred′i·ca′tion,** *n.* —**pred′i·ca′tion·al,** *adj.* —**pred·i·ca·tive** (pred′i kā′tiv, -kə-; *Brit.* pri dik′ə tiv), *adj.* —**pred′i·ca′tive·ly,** *adv.*

pred′icate ad′jective, *Gram.* an adjective used in the predicate, esp. with a copulative verb and attributive to the subject, as in *He is dead*, or attributive to the direct object, as in *It made him sick.* [1880–85]

pred′icate cal′culus, *Logic.* See **functional calculus.** Also called **pred′icate log′ic.** [1945–50]

pred′icate nom′inative, (in Latin, Greek, and certain other languages) a predicate noun or adjective in the nominative case. [1885–90]

pred′icate noun′, *Gram.* a noun used in the predicate with a copulative verb or a factitive verb and having the same referent as the subject of the copulative verb or the direct object of the factitive verb, as in *She is the mayor* or *They elected her mayor.*

pred′icate objec′tive, *Gram.* See **objective complement.**

pred·i·ca·tor (pred′i kā′tər), *n. Gram.* the verbal element of a clause or sentence. [1425–75 for an earlier sense; late ME: preacher < L *praedicātor* publicizer; see PREDICATE, -TOR]

pred·i·ca·to·ry (pred′i kə tôr′ē, -tōr′ē), *adj.* of or pertaining to preaching. [1605–15; < L *praedicātōrius* prophetic; see PREDICATE, -TORY[1]]

pre·dict (pri dikt′), *v.t.* **1.** to declare or tell in advance; prophesy; foretell: *to predict the weather; to predict the fall of a civilization.* —*v.i.* **2.** to foretell the future; make a prediction. [1540–50; < L *praedictus*, ptp. of *praedīcere* to foretell, equiv. to *prae-* PRE- + *dic-*, var. s. of *dīcere* to say + *-tus* ptp. suffix; see DICTUM] —**pre·dict′a·ble,** *adj.* —**pre·dict′a·bil′i·ty,** *n.* —**pre·dict′a·bly,** *adv.*
—**Syn. 1, 2.** presage, divine, augur, project, prognosticate, portend. PREDICT, PROPHESY, FORESEE, FORECAST mean to know or tell (usually correctly) beforehand what will happen. To PREDICT is usually to foretell with precision of calculation, knowledge, or shrewd inference from facts or experience: *The astronomers can predict an eclipse;* it may, however, be used without the implication of underlying knowledge or expertise: *I predict she'll be a success at the party.* PROPHESY usually means to predict future events by the aid of divine or supernatural inspiration: *Merlin prophesied the two knights would meet in conflict;* this verb, too, may be used in a more general, less specific sense. *I prophesy he'll be back in the old job.* To FORESEE refers specifically not to the uttering of predictions but to the mental act of seeing ahead; there is often (but not always) a practical implication of preparing for what will happen: *He was clever enough to foresee this shortage of materials.* FORECAST has much the same meaning as PREDICT; it is used today particularly of the weather and other phenomena that cannot easily be accurately predicted: *Rain and snow are forecast for tonight. Economists forecast a rise in family income.*

pre·dic·tion (pri dik′shən), *n.* **1.** an act of predicting. **2.** an instance of this; prophecy. [1555–65; < L *praedictiōn-* (s. of *praedictiō*) a foretelling. See PREDICT, -ION]
—**Syn. 2.** forecast, augury, prognostication, divination, projection.

pre·dic·tive (pri dik′tiv), *adj.* **1.** of or pertaining to prediction: *losing one's predictive power.* **2.** used or useful for predicting or foretelling the future: *to look for predictive signs among the stars.* **3.** being an indication of the future or of future conditions: *a cold wind predictive of snow.* [1650–60; < LL *praedictīvus* foretelling. See PREDICT, -IVE] —**pre·dic′tive·ly,** *adv.* —**pre·dic′tive·ness,** *n.*

pre·dic·tor (pri dik′tər), *n.* **1.** a person or thing that predicts. **2.** *Math.* a formula for determining additional values or derivatives of a function from the relationship of its given values. [1645–55; < ML *praedictor.* See PREDICT, -TOR]

pre·dic·to·ry (pri dik′tə rē), *adj. Archaic.* predictive. [1645–55; PREDICT + -ORY[1]]

pre·di·gest (prē′di jest′, -dī-), *v.t.* **1.** to treat (food) by an artificial process analogous to digestion so that, when taken into the body, it is more easily digestible. **2.** to make simpler or plainer, as for easier understanding. [1655–65; PRE- + DIGEST] —**pre′di·ges′tion,** *n.*

pre·di·lec·tion (pred′l ek′shən, prēd′-), *n.* a tendency to think favorably of something in particular; partiality; preference: *a predilection for Bach.* [1735–45; < ML *praedilect(us)* beloved, ptp. of *praediligere* to prefer (see PRE-, DILIGENT) + -ION]
—**Syn.** bias, inclination, leaning, liking, weakness, predisposition, prepossession.

pre·dis·pose (prē′di spōz′), *v.*, **-posed, -pos·ing.** —*v.t.* **1.** to give an inclination or tendency to beforehand; make susceptible: *Genetic factors may predispose human beings to certain metabolic diseases.* **2.** to render subject, susceptible, or liable: *The evidence predisposes him to public censure.* **3.** to dispose beforehand. **4.** *Archaic.* to dispose of beforehand, as in a will, legacy, or the like. —*v.i.* **5.** to give or furnish a tendency or inclination: *an underground job that predisposes to lung infection.* [1640–50; PRE- + DISPOSE] —**pre′dis·pos′al,** *n.* —**pre·dis·pos·ed·ly** (prē′di spō′zid lē, -spōzd′-), *adv.* —**pre′dis·pos′ed·ness,** *n.*
—**Syn. 1.** prearrange, prepare. **3.** bias, incline.

pre·dis·po·si·tion (prē dis′pə zish′ən, prē′dis-), *n.* **1.** the fact or condition of being predisposed: *a predisposition to think optimistically.* **2.** *Med.* tendency to a condition or quality, usually based on the combined effects of genetic and environmental factors. [1615–25; PRE- + DISPOSITION] —**pre·dis′po·si′tion·al,** *adj.*

pre·dis·tor·tion (prē′di stôr′shən), *n. Electronics.* preemphasis. Also, **pre′-dis·tor′tion.** [PRE- + DISTORTION]

pred·nis·o·lone (pred nis′ə lōn′), *n. Pharm.* a synthetic glucocorticoid, $C_{21}H_{28}O_5$, used in various forms to treat inflammation and allergies and in the treatment of acute leukemia, Hodgkin's disease, and lymphomas. [1950–55; alter. of PREDNISONE by insertion of -OL[1]]

pred·ni·sone (pred′nə sōn′, -zōn′), *n. Pharm.* an analogue of cortisone, $C_{21}H_{26}O_5$, used as an anti-inflammatory, immunosuppressive, and antineoplastic in the treatment of various diseases. [1950–55; *pre(gna)-d(ie)n(e)*, a component of its chemical name + (CORT)ISONE]

pre·dom·i·nance (pri dom′ə nəns), *n.* the state, condition, or quality of being predominant: *the predominance of the rich over the poor.* Also, **pre·dom′i·nan·cy.** [1595–1605; PREDOMIN(ANT) + -ANCE]

pre·dom·i·nant (pri dom′ə nənt), *adj.* **1.** having ascendancy, power, authority, or influence over others; preeminent. **2.** preponderant; prominent: *a predominant trait; the predominant color of a painting.* [1570–80; < ML *praedominant-* (s. of *praedominans*), prp. of *praedominārī* to predominate. See PRE-, DOMINANT] —**pre·dom′i·nant·ly,** *adv.*
—**Syn. 1, 2.** See **dominant.**

pre·dom·i·nate (pri dom′ə nāt′), *v.*, **-nat·ed, -nat·ing.** —*v.i.* **1.** to be the stronger or leading element or force. **2.** to have numerical superiority or advantage: *The radicals predominate in the new legislature.* **3.** to surpass others in authority or influence; be preeminent: *He predominated in the political scene.* **4.** to have or exert controlling power (often fol. by *over*): *Good sense predominated over the impulse to fight.* **5.** to appear more noticeable or imposing than something else: *Blues and greens predominated in the painting.* —*v.t.* **6.** to dominate or prevail over. [1585–95; < ML *praedominātus*, ptp. of *praedominārī* to predominate. See PRE-, DOMINATE] —**pre·dom·i·nate·ly** (pri dom′ə nit lē), *adv.* —**pre·dom′i·nat′ing·ly,** *adv.* —**pre·dom′i·na′tion,** *n.* —**pre·dom′i·na′tor,** *n.*
—**Syn. 4.** overrule, dominate.

pre·dy·nas·tic (prē′dī nas′tik), *adj.* of, pertaining to, or belonging to a time or period before the first dynasty of a nation, esp. the period in Egypt before c3200 B.C. [1895–1900; PRE- + DYNASTIC]

pree (prē), *n.*, *v.*, **preed, pree·ing.** *Scot. and North Eng.* —*n.* **1.** a test, trial, or taste; a test by sampling. —*v.t.* **2.** to try, test, or taste. **3. pree the mouth of,** *Scot.* to kiss. Also, **prie.** [1690–1700; shortened form of *preive*, ME *preve* (n.), *preven* (v.) < OF *pr(o)eve, preuver;* see PROVE]

pre·e·clamp·si·a (prē′i klamp′sē ə), *n. Pathol.* a form of toxemia of pregnancy, characterized by hypertension, fluid retention, and albuminuria, sometimes progressing to eclampsia. Also, **pre′-e·clamp′si·a.** [1920–25; PRE- + ECLAMPSIA]

pre·e·lec·tion (prē′i lek′shən), *n.* **1.** a choice or selection made beforehand. —*adj.* **2.** coming before an election: *preelection promises.* Also, **pre′-e·lec′tion.** [1890–95; PRE- + ELECTION]

pre-E·liz·a·be·than (prē′i liz′ə bē′thən, -beth′ən), *adj.* (of English culture, history, traditions, etc.) before the reign of Queen Elizabeth I; before the second half of the 16th century.

pre·e·mer·gence (prē′i mûr′jəns), *adj.* occurring or applied before the emergence of a plant from the soil: *preemergence herbicide.* Also, **pre′-e·mer′gence.** [1930–35; PRE- + EMERGENCE]

pre·e·mer·gent (prē′i mûr′jənt), *adj. Hort.* **1.** of or pertaining to seedlings before they emerge or appear above ground: *a preemergent weed-killer.* —*n.* **2.** a preemergence chemical, as a herbicide. Also, **pre′-e·mer′gent.** [1955–60; PRE- + EMERGENT]

pree·mie (prē′mē), *n. Informal.* an infant born prematurely; a preterm. [1925–30; PREM(ATURE), respelled to represent the pron. unambiguously + -IE]

pre·em·i·nence (prē em′ə nəns), *n.* the state or character of being preeminent. Also, **pre-em′i·nence.** [1175–1225; ME < LL *praeēminentia.* See PREEMINENT, -ENCE]

pre·em·i·nent (prē em′ə nənt), *adj.* eminent above or before others; superior; surpassing: *He is preeminent in his profession.* Also, **pre-em′i·nent.** [1400–50; late ME < L *praeēminent-* (s. of *praeēminēns*), prp. of *praeēminēre* to project forward, be prominent. See PRE-, EMINENT] —**pre·em′i·nent·ly,** *adv.*
—**Syn.** distinguished, peerless, supreme. See **dominant.**

pre·em·pha·sis (prē em′fə sis), *n. Electronics.* a process of increasing the amplitude of certain frequencies relative to others in a signal in order to help them override noise, complemented by deemphasis before final

CONCISE PRONUNCIATION KEY: act, cāpe, dâre, pärt; set, ēqual; *if*, īce; ox, ōver, ôrder, oil, bo͝ok, bo͞ot, out; up, ûrge; child; sing; shoe; thin, *th*at; zh as in *treasure.* ə = *a* as in *alone*, *e* as in *system*, *i* as in *easily*, *o* as in *gallop*, *u* as in *circus*; ᵊ as in *fire* (fīᵊr), *hour* (ouᵊr). l and n can serve as syllabic consonants, as in *cradle* (krād′l), and *button* (but′n). See the full key inside the front cover.

pre′con·ten′tion, *n.*
pre′con·tent′ment, *n.*
pre′con·test′, *v.t.*
pre·con′test, *n.*
pre′con·ti·nen′tal, *adj.*
pre′con·trib′ute, *v.t.*, **-ut·ed, -ut·ing.**
pre′con·tri·bu′tion, *n.*
pre′con·trib′u·tive, *adj.*
pre′con·triv′ance, *n.*
pre′con·trive′, *v.*, **-trived, -triv·ing.**
pre′con·trol′, *n.*, *v.t.*, **-trolled, -trol·ling.**
pre′con·tro·ver′sial, *adj.*
pre·con′tro·ver′sy, *n.*, *pl.* **-sies.**
pre′con·ven′tion, *n.*
pre′con·ver·sa′tion, *n.*
pre′con·ver·sa′tion·al, *adj.*
pre′con·ver′sion, *n.*
pre′con·vert′, *v.t.*
pre′con·vey′, *v.t.*
pre′con·vey′ance, *n.*
pre′con·vict′, *v.t.*
pre′con·vic′tion, *n.*
pre′con·vince′, *v.t.*, **-vinced, -vinc·ing.**
pre′-Co·per′ni·can, *adj.*
pre′-Co·per′ni·can·ism, *n.*
pre·cop′y, *n.*, *pl.* **-cop·ies,** *v.t.*, **-cop·ied, -cop·y·ing.**
pre·cor′a·coid′, *adj.*
pre·cor′dial, *adj.*
pre·cor′ne·al, *adj.*
pre′cor·o·na′tion, *n.*
pre′cor·rect′, *v.t.*; **-ly,** *adv.*; **-ness,** *n.*
pre′cor·rec′tion, *n.*
pre′cor·re·spond′, *v.i.*
pre′cor·re·spond′ence, *n.*
pre′cor·re·spond′ent, *adj.*
pre·cor′ri·dor, *n.*
pre′cor·rupt′, *v.t.*; **-ly,** *adv.*; **-ness,** *n.*
pre′cor·rup′tion, *n.*
pre′cor·rup′tive, *adj.*
pre·cos′mic, *adj.*
pre·cos′mi·cal, *adj.*; **-ly,** *adv.*
pre·cos′tal, *adj.*
pre·coun′sel, *n.*, *v.*, **-seled, -sel·ing** or (*esp. Brit.*) **-selled, -sel·ling.**
pre·coun′sel·lor, *n.*
pre·coup′, *adj.*
pre·cov′er, *v.t.*
pre·cra′ni·al, *adj.*; **-ly,** *adv.*
pre·crash′, *v.*, *adj.*
pre·crease′, *v.t.* **-creased, -creas·ing.**
pre′cre·a′tion, *n.*
pre·cred′it, *v.t.*
pre·cred′i·tor, *n.*
pre·creed′, *n.*
pre·crit′i·cism, *n.*
pre·crit′i·cize′, *v.t.*, **-cized, -ciz·ing.**
pre·cru′cial, *adj.*
pre·cru′ral, *adj.*
pre′-Cru·sade′, *adj.*
pre·crys′tal·line, *adj.*
pre·cul′ti·vate′, *v.t.*, **-vat·ed, -vat·ing.**
pre′cul·ti·va′tion, *n.*
pre·cul′tur·al, *adj.*; **-ly,** *adv.*
pre·cul′ture, *n.*
pre·cure′, *n.*, *v.t.*, **-cured, -cur·ing.**
pre·cur′rent, *adj.*
pre′cur·ric′u·lar, *adj.*
pre′cur·ric′u·lum, *n.*, *pl.* **-lums, -la.**
pre·cy′clone, *n.*
pre′cy·clon′ic, *adj.*
pre·cys′tic, *adj.*
pre·dam′age, *n.*, *v.t.*, **-aged, -ag·ing.**
pre·damn′, *v.t.*
pre′dam·na′tion, *n.*
pre-Dan′te·an, *adj.*
pre·dark′, *adj.*
pre·dark′ness, *n.*
pre′-Dar·win′i·an, *adj.*
pre·da′ta, *n.*
pre·day′, *n.*
pre·day′light′, *n.*
pre·day′time′, *n.*
pre·deal′er, *n.*
pre·deal′ing, *n.*
pre·death′, *n.*
pre·death′ly, *adj.*
pre′de·bate′, *n.*
pre′de·bat′er, *n.*
pre·deb′it, *n.*, *v.t.*
pre·debt′or, *n.*
pre′de·ceive′, *v.t.*, **-ceived, -ceiv·ing.**
pre′de·ceiv′er, *n.*
pre′de·cep′tion, *n.*
pre′de·cide′, *v.t.*, **-cid·ed, -cid·ing.**
pre′de·cid′ed, *adj.*
pre′de·ci′sion, *n.*
pre′de·ci′sive, *adj.*; **-ly,** *adv.*
pre′dec·la·ra′tion, *n.*
pre′de·clare′, *v.t.*, **-clared, -clar·ing.**
pre′dec·li·na′tion, *n.*
pre′de·cline′, *v.t.*, **-clined, -clin·ing.**
pre′de·cree′, *v.t.*, **-creed, -cree·ing.**
pre·ded′i·cate′, *v.t.*, **-cat·ed, -cat·ing.**
pre′ded·i·ca′tion, *n.*
pre′de·duct′, *v.t.*
pre′de·duc′tion, *n.*
pre′de·fault′, *n.*, *v.*
pre′de·feat′, *n.*, *v.*
pre·de′fect, *n.*
pre′de·fec′tive, *adj.*
pre′de·fence′, *n.*
pre′de·fend′, *v.t.*
pre′de·fense′, *n.*
pre′de·fi′ance, *n.*
pre′de·fi′cien·cy, *n.*, *pl.* **-cies.**
pre′de·fi′cient, *adj.*; **-ly,** *adv.*
pre′de·fine′, *v.t.*, **-fined, -fin·ing.**
pre′def·i·ni′tion, *n.*
pre′de·fray′, *v.t.*

reproduction of the signal being received. Also, **pre·em′pha·sis.** Also called **emphasis, predistortion, preequalization.** [1940–45; PRE- + EMPHASIS]

pre·em·ploy·ment (prē′em ploi′mənt), *adj.* **1.** being required or accomplished before an employee begins a new job: *a preemployment medical exam.* —*n.* **2.** the period of testing, processing, etc., before the start of employment. Also, **pre′-em·ploy′ment.** [1940–45; PRE- + EMPLOYMENT]

pre·empt (prē empt′), *v.t.* **1.** to occupy (land) in order to establish a prior right to buy. **2.** to acquire or appropriate before someone else; take for oneself; arrogate: *a political issue preempted by the opposition party.* **3.** to take the place of because of priorities, reconsideration, rescheduling, etc.; supplant: *The special newscast preempted the usual television program.* —*v.i.* **4.** *Bridge.* to make a preemptive bid. **5.** to forestall or prevent (something anticipated) by acting first; preclude; head off: *an effort to preempt inflation.* —*n.* **6.** *Bridge.* a preemptive bid. Also, **pre-empt′.** [1840–50, *Amer.*; back formation from PREEMPTION] —**pre·emp′ti·ble,** *adj.* —**pre·emp·tor** (prē emp′tôr, -tər), *n.* —**pre·emp·to·ry** (prē emp′tə rē), *adj.*
—**Syn. 1.** claim, appropriate, usurp.

pre·emp·tion (prē emp′shən), *n.* the act or right of claiming or purchasing before or in preference to others. Also, **pre-emp′tion.** [1595–1605; < ML *praeëmpt(us)* bought beforehand (ptp. of *praeëmere*) + -ION. See PRE-, EMPTOR]

pre·emp·tive (prē emp′tiv), *adj.* **1.** of or pertaining to preemption. **2.** taken as a measure against something possible, anticipated, or feared; preventive; deterrent: *a preemptive tactic against a ruthless business rival.* **3.** preempting or possessing the power to preempt; appropriative; privileged: *a commander's preemptive authority.* **4.** *Bridge.* pertaining to, involving, or noting an opening bid or an overcall in a suit that is at an unnecessarily high level and that is essentially a defensive maneuver designed to make communication between one's opponents more difficult: *a preemptive bid; to give a preemptive response.* Also, **pre-emp′tive.** [1785–95, *Amer.*; PREEMPT + -IVE] —**pre·emp′tive·ly,** *adv.*

preemp′tive right′, a privilege given to an existing shareholder to buy a portion of a new stock issue at the offering price on a pro-rata per-share basis. [1850–55]

preemp′tive strike′. See **preventive war.** [1955–60]

preen[1] (prēn), *v.t.* **1.** (of animals, esp. birds) to trim or dress (feathers, fur, etc.) with the beak or tongue: *The peacock preened itself on the lawn.* **2.** to dress (oneself) carefully or smartly; primp: *The king preened himself in his elaborate ceremonial robes.* **3.** to pride (oneself) on an achievement, personal quality, etc.: *He preened himself on having been graduated with honors.* —*v.i.* **4.** to make oneself appear striking or smart in dress or appearance: *No amount of careful preening will compensate for poor posture.* **5.** to be exultant or proud. [1480–90; late ME *prene,* var. of ME *prunen, proynen* (see PRUNE[3]), perh. by assoc. with *prenen,* to stab, pierce (v. use, now dial., of *prene* PREEN[2]), from the pricking action of a bird's beak in preening] —**preen′er,** *n.*

preen[2] (prēn), *n. Chiefly Brit. Dial.* a pin or brooch. [bef. 1000; ME *prene,* OE *prēon* a pin; c. ON *prjōnn* pin; akin to D *priem,* G *Pfriem* awl]

pre·en·gage (prē′en gāj′), *v.t., v.i.,* **-gaged, -gag·ing.** **1.** to engage beforehand. **2.** to put under obligation, esp. to marry, by a prior engagement. **3.** to win the favor or attention of beforehand: *Other matters preengaged him.* Also, **pre′-en·gage′.** [1640–50; PRE- + ENGAGE]

preen′ gland′. See **uropygial gland.** [1920–25]

pre·e·qual·i·za·tion (prē ē′kwə lə zā′shən), *n. Electronics.* preemphasis. Also, **pre-e′qual·i·za′tion.** [PRE- + EQUALIZATION]

pre·es·tab·lish (prē′i stab′lish), *v.t.* to establish beforehand. Also, **pre′-es·tab′lish.** [1635–45; PRE- + ESTABLISH]

pre′estab′lished har′mony, (in the philosophy of Leibnitz) synchronous operation of all monads, since their simultaneous creation, in accordance with the preexisting plan of God. [1720–30]

pre·ex·il·i·an (prē′eg zil′ē ən, -zil′yən, -ek sil′-), *adj.* being or occurring prior to the exile of the Jews in Babylonia 597–538 B.C. Also, **pre′-ex·il′i·an, pre′ex·il′ic, pre′-ex·il′ic.** [1860–65; PRE- + L *exili(um)* EXILE + -AN]

pre·ex·ist (prē′ig zist′), *v.i.* **1.** to exist beforehand. **2.** to exist in a previous state. —*v.t.* **3.** to exist prior to (something or someone else); precede: *primitive artifacts that preexisted sophisticated tools.* Also, **pre′-ex·ist′.** [1590–1600; PRE- + EXIST] —**pre′ex·ist′ence,** *n.* —**pre′ex·ist′ent,** *adj.*

pre·ex·po·sure (prē′ik spō′zhər), *n.* **1.** exposure beforehand. **2.** *Photog.* the exposing of a film to even light, before photographing a subject, to increase its sensitivity. Also, **pre′-ex·po′sure.** [1935–40; PRE- + EXPOSURE]

pref., 1. preface. **2.** prefaced. **3.** prefatory. **4.** preference. **5.** preferred. **6.** prefix. **7.** prefixed.

pre·fab (*adj., n.* prē′fab′; *v.* prē fab′), *adj., n., v.,* **-fabbed, -fab·bing.** —*adj.* **1.** prefabricated. —*n.* **2.** something that is prefabricated, as a building or fixture: *You would never know that such an attractive house is a prefab.* —*v.t.* **3.** to prefabricate. [1935–40; by shortening]

pre·fab·ri·cate (prē fab′ri kāt′), *v.t.,* **-cat·ed, -cat·ing.** **1.** to fabricate or construct beforehand. **2.** to manufacture in standardized parts or sections ready for quick assembly and erection, as buildings. [1930–35; PRE- + FABRICATE] —**pre′fab·ri·ca′tion,** *n.* —**pre·fab′ri·ca′tor,** *n.*

pref·ace (pref′is), *n., v.,* **-aced, -ac·ing.** —*n.* **1.** a preliminary statement in a book by the book's author or editor, setting forth its purpose and scope, expressing acknowledgment of assistance from others, etc. **2.** an introductory part, as of a speech. **3.** something preliminary or introductory: *The meeting was the preface to an alliance.* **4.** *Eccles.* a prayer of thanksgiving, the introduction to the canon of the Mass, ending with the *Sanctus.* —*v.t.* **5.** to provide with or introduce by a preface. **6.** to serve as a preface to. [1350–1400; ME < MF < ML *prēfātia,* for L *praefātiō* a saying beforehand, equiv. to *praefāt(us)* (ptp. of *praefārī* to say beforehand; see PRE-, FATE) + *-iōn-* -ION] —**pref′ac·er,** *n.*
—**Syn. 1.** See **introduction. 2, 3.** preamble, prologue, prolegomena. —**Ant. 1.** appendix. **2, 3.** epilogue.

pref·a·to·ry (pref′ə tôr′ē, -tōr′ē), *adj.* of, pertaining to, or of the nature of a preface: *prefatory explanations.* Also, **pref′a·to′ri·al.** [1665–75; < L *praefāt(iō)* PREFACE + -ORY[1]] —**pref′a·to′ri·ly,** *adv.*

pre·fect (prē′fekt), *n.* **1.** a person appointed to any of various positions of command, authority, or superintendence, as a chief magistrate in ancient Rome or the chief administrative official of a department of France or Italy. **2.** *Rom. Cath. Ch.* **a.** the dean of a Jesuit school or college. **b.** a cardinal in charge of a congregation in the Curia Romana. **3.** *Chiefly Brit.* a praeposter. Also, **praefect.** [1300–50; ME < L *praefectus* overseer, director (n. use of ptp. of *praeficere* to make prior, i.e., put in charge), equiv. to *prae-* PRE- + *-fectus* (comb. form of *factus,* ptp. of *facere* to make, DO[1]); see FACT]

pre′fect apostol′ic, *pl.* **prefects apostolic.** *Rom. Cath. Ch.* the administrator, usually below the rank of bishop, in charge of a prefecture apostolic. [1905–10]

pre·fec·to·ri·al (prē′fek tôr′ē əl, -tōr′-), *adj.* of, pertaining to, or characteristic of a prefect: *prefectorial powers.* [1860–65; < LL *praefectōri(us)* (see PREFECT, -TORY) + -AL[1]]

pre·fec·ture (prē′fek chər), *n.* the office, jurisdiction, territory, or official residence of a prefect. [1570–80; < L *praefectūra.* See PREFECT, -URE] —**pre·fec·tur·al** (pri fek′chər əl), *adj.*

prefec′ture apostol′ic, *pl.* **prefectures apostolic.** *Rom. Cath. Ch.* a territory in the early stage of missionary development. [1910–15]

pre·fer (pri fûr′), *v.t.,* **-ferred, -fer·ring.** **1.** to set or hold before or above other persons or things in estimation; like better; choose rather than: *to prefer beef to chicken.* **2.** *Law.* to give priority, as to one creditor over another. **3.** to put forward or present (a statement, suit, charge, etc.) for consideration or sanction. **4.** to put forward or advance, as in rank or office; promote: *to be preferred for advancement.* [1350–1400; ME *preferre* < L *praeferre* to bear before, set before, prefer, equiv. to *prae-* PRE- + *ferre* to BEAR[1]] —**pre·fer′red·ly** (pri fûr′id lē, -fûrd′lē), *adv.* —**pre·fer′red·ness,** *n.* —**pre·fer′rer,** *n.*
—**Syn. 1.** favor, fancy. See **choose. 3.** offer, proffer, tender. —**Ant. 1.** reject. **3.** retract.

pref·er·a·ble (pref′ər ə bəl, pref′rə- *or, often,* pri fûr′-), *adj.* **1.** more desirable. **2.** worthy to be preferred. [1640–50; < F *préférable.* See PREFER, -ABLE] —**pref′er·a·bil′i·ty, pref′er·a·ble·ness,** *n.* —**pref′er·a·bly,** *adv.*

pref·er·ence (pref′ər əns, pref′rəns), *n.* **1.** the act of preferring. **2.** the state of being preferred. **3.** that which is preferred; choice: *His preference is vanilla, not chocolate.* **4.** a practical advantage given to one over others. **5.** a prior right or claim, as to payment of dividends or to assets upon dissolution. **6.** the favoring of one country or group of countries by granting special advantages over others in international trade. [1595–1605; < ML *praeferentia.* See PREFER, -ENCE]
—**Syn. 3.** selection, pick. See **choice.**

pref′erence share′, *Brit.* a share of preferred stock. [1835–45]

pref′erence stock′, *Brit.* See **preferred stock.** [1855–60]

pref·er·en·tial (pref′ə ren′shəl), *adj.* **1.** of, pertaining to, or of the nature of preference: *preferential policies.* **2.** showing or giving preference: *a preferential hiring system.* **3.** receiving or enjoying preference, as a country in trade relations; favored. [1840–50; < ML *praeferenti(a)* PREFERENCE + -AL[1]] —**pref′er·en′tial·ism,** *n.* —**pref′er·en′tial·ist,** *n.* —**pref′er·en′tial·ly,** *adv.*

pref′eren′tial shop′, a shop in which union members are preferred, usually by agreement of an employer with a union.

pref′eren′tial vot′ing, a system of voting designed to permit the voter to indicate an order of preference for the candidates on the ballot. [1865–70]

pre·fer·ment (pri fûr′mənt), *n.* **1.** the act of preferring. **2.** the state of being preferred. **3.** advancement or promotion, esp. in the church. **4.** a position or office affording social or pecuniary advancement. [1425–75; late ME; see PREFER, -MENT]

preferred′ lie′, *Golf.* a nearby position for a ball preferable to that where it actually landed and to which repositioning is sometimes allowed without loss of a stroke or strokes to the player.

preferred′ posi′tion, especially desirable advertising space for which, if it is specifically requested by the advertiser, a publication charges a premium rate. Cf. **R.O.P.**

pre·ferred′-pro·vid′er organiza′tion (pri fûrd′-prə vī′dər), a comprehensive health-care plan offered to corporate employees that allows them to choose their own physicians and hospitals within certain limits. *Abbr.:* PPO

preferred′ stock′, stock that has a superior claim to that of common stock with respect to dividends and often to assets in the event of liquidation. [1840–50, *Amer.*]

pre·fig·u·ra·tion (prē fig′yə rā′shən, prē′fig-), *n.* **1.** the act of prefiguring. **2.** that in which something is prefigured. [1350–1400; ME *prefiguracioun* < LL *praefigūrātiōn-* (s. of *praefigūrātiō*), equiv. to *praefigūrāt(us)* (ptp. of *praefigūrāre* to PREFIGURE) + *-iōn-* -ION]

pre·fig·ure (prē fig′yər), *v.t.,* **-ured, -ur·ing.** **1.** to show or represent beforehand by a figure or type; foreshadow. **2.** to picture or represent to oneself beforehand; imagine. [1400–50; late ME < LL *praefigūrāre.* See PRE-, FIGURE (v.)] —**pre·fig·ur·a·tive** (prē fig′yər ə tiv), *adj.* —**pre·fig′ur·a·tive·ly,** *adv.* —**pre·fig′ur·a·tive·ness,** *n.* —**pre·fig′ure·ment,** *n.*

pre·fix (*n.* prē′fiks; *v.* prē fiks′, prē fiks′), *n.* **1.** *Gram.* an affix placed before a base or another prefix, as *un-* in *unkind, un-* and *re-* in *unrewarding.* **2.** something prefixed, as a title before a person's name. —*v.t.* **3.** to fix or put before or in front: *to prefix an impressive title to one's name.* **4.** *Gram.* to add as a prefix. **5.** to fix, settle, or appoint beforehand. [1375–1425; (v.) late ME *prefixen* < MF *prefixer* < L *praefixus,* ptp. of *praefigere* to set up in front; see PRE-, FIX; (n.) < NL *praefixum,* neut. of *praefixus*] —**pre·fix′a·ble,** *adj.* —**pre·fix·al** (prē′fik səl, prē fik′-), *adj.* —**pre′fix·al·ly,** *adv.* —**pre·fix·ion** (prē fik′shən), *n.*

pre·flight (prē flīt′), *adj.* **1.** occurring or done before a flight: *a preflight briefing of the plane's crew.* —*n.* **2.**

CONCISE ETYMOLOGY KEY: <, descended or borrowed from; >, whence; b., blend of, blended; c., cognate with; cf., compare; deriv., derivative; equiv., equivalent; imit., imitative; obl., oblique; r., replacing; s., stem; sp., spelling, spelled; resp., respelling, respelled; trans., translation; ?, origin unknown; *, unattested; ‡, probably earlier than. See the full key inside the front cover.

pre′de·fray′al, *adj.*
pre′de·fy′, *v.t.,* **-fied, -fy·ing.**
pre′de·gen′er·a·cy, *n.*
pre′de·gen′er·ate, *adj.*
pre′de·gree′, *n.*
pre′de·lay′, *n., v.*
pre·del′e·gate′, *n., v.,* **-gat·ed, -gat·ing.**
pre′del·e·ga′tion, *n.*
pre′de·lib′er·ate′, *v.t.,* **-at·ed, -at·ing.**
pre′de·lib′er·ate, *adj.;* **-ly,** *adv.*
pre′de·lib′er·a′tion, *n.*
pre′de·lin′e·ate′, *v.t.,* **-at·ed, -at·ing.**
pre′de·lin′e·a′tion, *n.*
pre′de·lin′quen·cy, *n., pl.* **-cies.**
pre′de·lin′quent, *adj.;* **-ly,** *adv.*
pre′de·liv′er, *v.t.*
pre′de·liv′er·y, *n., pl.* **-er·ies.**
pre′de·lude′, *v.t.,* **-lud·ed, -lud·ing.**
pre′de·lu′sion, *n.*
pre′de·mand′, *v.t.*
pre′de·moc′ra·cy, *n., pl.* **-cies.**
pre′dem·o·crat′ic, *adj.*
pre·dem′on·strate′, *v.t.,* **-strat·ed, -strat·ing.**
pre′dem·on·stra′tion, *n.*
pre′de·mon′stra·tive, *adj.*
pre′de·ni′al, *adj.*
pre′de·ny′, *v.t.,* **-nied, -ny·ing.**
pre′de·part·men′tal, *adj.*
pre′de·par′ture, *n.*
pre′de·pend′a·ble, *adj.*
pre′de·pend′ence, *n.*
pre′de·pend′ent, *adj.*
pre′de·plete′, *v.t.,* **-plet·ed, -plet·ing.**
pre′de·ple′tion, *n.*
pre′de·pos′it, *n., v.*
pre′de·pos′i·to′ry, *n., pl.* **-ries.**
pre′de·pre′ci·ate′, *v.,* **-at·ed, -at·ing.**
pre′de·pre′ci·a′tion, *n.*
pre′de·pres′sion, *n., adj.*
pre′dep·ri·va′tion, *n.*
pre′de·prive′, *v.t.,* **-prived, -priv·ing.**
pre′der·i·va′tion, *n.*
pre′de·rive′, *v.t.,* **-rived, -riv·ing.**
pre′de·scend′, *v.*
pre′de·scent′, *n.*
pre′de·scribe′, *v.t.,* **-scribed, -scrib·ing.**
pre′de·scrip′tion, *n.*
pre′de·sert′, *v.t.*
pre′de·sert′er, *n.*
pre′de·ser′tion, *n.*
pre′de·serve′, *v.t.,* **-served, -serv·ing.**
pre′de·sign′, *v.t.*
pre′de·signed′, *adj.*
pre′de·sir′ous, *adj.;* **-ly,** *adv.*
pre′de·spond′en·cy, *n.*
pre′de·spond′ent, *adj.*
pre·des′ti·tute′, *adj.*
pre′des·ti·tu′tion, *n.*
pre′de·stroy′, *v.t.*
pre′de·struc′tion, *n.*
pre′de·tach′, *v.t.*
pre′de·tach′ment, *n.*
pre′de·tail′, *v.t.*
pre′de·tain′, *v.t.*
pre′de·tain′er, *n.*
pre′de·tect′, *v.t.*
pre′de·tec′tion, *n.*
pre′de·ten′tion, *n.*
pre′det·ri·men′tal, *adj.*
pre′de·val′u·a′tion, *n., adj.*
pre′de·vel′op, *v.*
pre′de·vel′op·ment, *n.*
pre′de·vise′, *v.t.,* **-vised, -vis·ing.**
pre′de·vo′tion, *n.*
pre′de·vour′, *v.t.*
pre′di·ag·no′sis, *n., pl.* **-ses.**
pre′di·ag·nos′tic, *adj.*
pre′di·as·tol′ic, *adj.*
pre′di·crot′ic, *adj.*
pre·dic′tate, *v.t.,* **-tat·ed, -tat·ing.**
pre·di′et, *n.*
pre·di′e·tar′y, *adj.*
pre·dif′fi·cul′ty, *n., pl.* **-ties.**
pre·dig′i·tal, *adj.*
pre·dil′i·gent, *adj.;* **-ly,** *adv.*
pre′di·lu′vi·al, *adj.*
pre′di·min′ish, *v.t.*
pre′di·min′ish·ment, *n.*
pre′dim·i·nu′tion, *n.*
pre·dine′, *v.i.,* **-dined, -din·ing.**
pre·din′ner, *n., adj.*
pre′diph·the·rit′ic, *adj.*
pre′di·plo′ma, *n.*
pre′di·plo′ma·cy, *n.*
pre′dip·lo·mat′ic, *adj.*
pre′di·rect′, *v.t.*
pre′di·rec′tion, *n.*
pre′di·rec′tor, *n.*
pre′dis·a·gree′, *v.i.,* **-greed, -gree·ing.**
pre′dis·a·gree′ment, *n.*
pre′dis·ap·point′ment, *n.*
pre′dis·as′ter, *n.*
pre′dis·as′trous, *adj.;* **-ly,** *adv.*
pre′dis·cern′, *v.t.*
pre′dis·cern′ment, *n.*
pre·dis′charge, *n.*
pre′dis·charge′, *v.t.,* **-charged, -charg·ing.**
pre·dis′ci·pline, *n., v.t.,* **-plined, -plin·ing.**
pre′dis·close′, *v.t.,* **-closed, -clos·ing.**
pre′dis·clo′sure, *n.*
pre′dis·con·tent′, *n.*
pre′dis·con·tent′ed, *adj.*
pre′dis·con·tent′ment, *n.*
pre·dis′count, *n., v.t.*
pre·dis′count·a·ble, *adj.*
pre′dis·cour′age, *v.t.,* **-aged, -ag·ing.**
pre′dis·cour′age·ment, *n.*
pre·dis′course, *n.*
pre′dis·cov′er, *v.t.*
pre′dis·cov′er·er, *n.*

a preflight briefing or a ground check, as of an airplane. [1920–25; PRE- + FLIGHT[1]]

pre•form (*v.* prē′fôrm′; *n.* prē′fôrm′), *v.t.* **1.** to form beforehand. **2.** to determine or decide beforehand: *to preform an opinion.* **3.** to shape or fashion beforehand: *to preform a mold.* —*n.* **4.** biscuit (def. 5). **5.** any of various uncompleted objects of manufacture after preliminary shaping. [1595–1605; < L *praefōrmāre.* See PRE-, FORM]

pre•for•ma•tion (prē′fôr mā′shən), *n.* **1.** previous formation. **2.** *Biol.* (formerly) the theory that the individual, with all its parts, preexists in the germ cell and grows from microscopic to normal proportions during embryogenesis (opposed to *epigenesis*). [1725–35; PRE- + FORMATION] —**pre′for•ma′tion•ar•y,** *adj.*

pre•fron•tal (prē frun′tl), *adj. Anat.* anterior to, situated in, or pertaining to the anterior part of a frontal structure. [1850–55; PRE- + FRONTAL]

prefron′tal lobot′omy, *Surg.* a psychosurgical procedure in which the frontal lobes are separated from the rest of the brain by cutting the connecting nerve fibers. Also called **frontal lobotomy, lobotomy.** [1935–40]

preg•gers (preg′ərz), *adj. Chiefly Brit. Informal.* pregnant[1]. (def. 1). [1940–45; PREG(NANT) + -ERS]

Pregl (prā′gəl), *n.* **Fritz** (frits), 1869–1930, Austrian chemist: Nobel prize 1923.

pre•gla•cial (prē glā′shəl), *adj. Geol.* prior to a given glacial epoch, esp. the Pleistocene. [1850–55; PRE- + GLACIAL]

preg•na•ble (preg′nə bəl), *adj.* **1.** capable of being taken or won by force: *a pregnable fortress.* **2.** open to attack; assailable: *a pregnable argument.* [1400–50; late ME *prenable* < MF *prenable, pregnable,* equiv. to *pren-* (weak s. of *prendre* to seize, take < L *pre(he)ndere;* see PREHENSION) + *-able* -ABLE; *-g-* perh. from obs. *expugnable* (in same sense)] —**preg′na•bil′i•ty,** *n.*

preg•nan•cy (preg′nən sē), *n., pl.* **-cies.** the state, condition, or quality of being pregnant. [1520–30; PREGN(ANT) + -ANCY]

preg•nant[1] (preg′nənt), *adj.* **1.** having a child or other offspring developing in the body; with child or young, as a woman or female mammal. **2.** fraught, filled, or abounding (usually fol. by *with*): *a silence pregnant with suspense.* **3.** teeming or fertile; rich (often fol. by *in*): *a mind pregnant in ideas.* **4.** full of meaning; highly significant: *a pregnant utterance.* **5.** of great importance or potential; momentous: *a pregnant moment in the history of the world.* [1375–1425; late ME < L *praegnant-* (s. of *praegnāns*), var. of *praegnās,* equiv. to *prae-* PRE- + *gnāt- (akin to *(g)nātus* born, *gignere* to bring into being) + *-s* nom. sing. ending] —**preg′nant•ly,** *adv.* —**preg′nant•ness,** *n.*

preg•nant[2] (preg′nənt), *adj. Archaic.* convincing; cogent: *a pregnant argument.* [1350–1400; ME *preignant* < OF, prp. of *preindre,* earlier *priembre* to PRESS[1] < L *premere.* Cf. PRINT]

pre•heat (prē hēt′), *v.t.* to heat before using or before subjecting to some further process: *to preheat an oven before baking a cake.* [1895–1900; PRE- + HEAT] —**pre•heat′er,** *n.*

pre•hen•si•ble (pri hen′sə bəl), *adj.* able to be seized or grasped. [1825–35; < L *prehēns(us)* (see PREHENSION) + -IBLE]

pre•hen•sile (pri hen′sil, -sīl), *adj.* **1.** adapted for seizing, grasping, or taking hold of something: *a prehensile tail.* **2.** able to perceive quickly; having keen mental grasp. **3.** greedy; grasping; avaricious. [1781–85; < F *préhensile* (coined by Buffon), equiv. to L *prehens(us)* (see PREHENSION) + F *-ile* -ILE] —**pre•hen•sil•i•ty** (prē′hen sil′i tē), *n.*

pre•hen•sion (pri hen′shən), *n.* **1.** the act of seizing or grasping. **2.** mental apprehension. [1525–35; < L *prehēnsiōn-* (s. of *prehēnsiō*) a taking hold, equiv. to *prehēns(us)* (ptp. of *prehendere* to seize, equiv. to *pre-* PRE- + *-hendere* to grasp; akin to GET) + *-iōn-* -ION]

pre•his•tor•ic (prē′hi stôr′ik, -stor′-, prē′i-), *adj.* **1.** of or pertaining to the time or a period prior to recorded history: *The dinosaur is a prehistoric beast.* **2.** *Slang.* outdated; passé: *My mom has these prehistoric ideas about proper dress.* Also, **pre′his•tor′i•cal.** [1850–55; PRE- + HISTORIC] —**pre′his•tor′i•cal•ly,** *adv.*

pre•his•to•ry (prē his′tə rē, -his′trē), *n., pl.* **-ries.** **1.** human history in the period before recorded events, known mainly through archaeological discoveries, study, research, etc.; history of prehistoric humans. **2.** a history of the events or incidents leading to a crisis, situation, or the like. [1870–75; PRE- + HISTORY] —**pre•his•to•ri•an** (prē′hi stôr′ē ən, -stor′-), *n.*

prehn•ite (prā′nīt, pren′īt), *n.* a mineral, hydrous calcium aluminum silicate, $Ca_2Al_2Si_3O_{10}(OH)_2$, occurring in light-green reniform aggregates or tabular crystals. [1785–95; named after Col. Van *Prehn,* 18th-century Dutchman who brought it from South Africa to Europe; see -ITE[1]]

pre•hom•i•nid (prē hom′ə nid), *n.* **1.** any of the extinct humanlike primates classified in the former family Prehominidae. **2.** any extinct form that is thought to be an ancestor of the hominids. [1935–40; PRE- + HOMINID]

pre•hu•man (prē hyōō′mən *or, often,* -yōō′-), *adj.* **1.** preceding the appearance or existence of human beings: *the prehuman ages.* **2.** of or pertaining to a human prototype. —*n.* **3.** a prehuman animal. [1835–45; PRE- + HUMAN]

pre•ig•ni•tion (prē′ig nish′ən), *n.* ignition of the charge in an internal-combustion engine earlier in the cycle than is compatible with proper operation. [1895–1900; PRE- + IGNITION]

pre-In•can (prē ing′kən), *adj.* of or pertaining to the period preceding the Incan empire in Peru.

pre•in•car•na•tion (prē in′kär nā′shən, prē′in-), *n.* a previous incarnation or an existence before incarnation. [1900–05; PRE- + INCARNATION]

pre•in•cline (prē′in klīn′), *v.t.,* **-clined, -clin•ing.** to dispose or prepare beforehand: *Their experiences had preinclined them to think pessimistically.* [1665–75; PRE- + INCLINE] —**pre•in•cli•na•tion** (prē in′klə nā′shən, prē′in-), *n.*

pre•in•di•cate (prē in′di kāt′), *v.t.,* **-cat•ed, -cat•ing.** to indicate in advance; presage: *The early thaw preindicated an avalanche.* [1795–1805; PRE- + INDICATE] —**pre•in′di•ca′tion,** *n.*

pre•in•form (prē′in fôrm′), *v.t.* to supply with information beforehand: *He preinformed the newspapers of his decision.* [1785–95; PRE- + INFORM[1]]

pre•in•va•sive (prē′in vā′siv), *adj. Pathol.* of or pertaining to a stage preceding invasion of the tissues; in situ. [PRE- + INVASIVE]

pre-Is•lam•ic (prē′is lam′ik, -lä′mik, -iz-), *adj.* existing prior to the ascendancy of Islam; pre-Muslim. [1875–80]

pre•judge (prē juj′), *v.t.,* **-judged, -judg•ing.** **1.** to judge beforehand. **2.** to pass judgment on prematurely or without sufficient reflection or investigation. [1555–65; < F *préjuger* < L *praejūdicāre.* See PRE-, JUDGE] —**pre•judg′er,** *n.* —**pre•judg′ment;** *esp. Brit.,* **pre•judge′ment,** *n.*

pre•judg•ing (prē juj′ing), *n.* a preliminary round of judging, as in a contest where a certain number or percentage of the entrants are eliminated before the final judging. [1660–70; PRE- + JUDGE + -ING[1]]

prej•u•dice (prej′ə dis), *n., v.,* **-diced, -dic•ing.** —*n.* **1.** an unfavorable opinion or feeling formed beforehand or without knowledge, thought, or reason. **2.** any preconceived opinion or feeling, either favorable or unfavorable. **3.** unreasonable feelings, opinions, or attitudes, esp. of a hostile nature, regarding a racial, religious, or national group. **4.** such attitudes considered collectively: *The war against prejudice is never-ending.* **5.** damage or injury; detriment: *a law that operated to the prejudice of the majority.* **6. without prejudice,** *Law.* without dismissing, damaging, or otherwise affecting a legal interest or demand. —*v.t.* **7.** to affect with a prejudice, either favorable or unfavorable: *His honesty and sincerity prejudiced us in his favor.* [1250–1300; ME < OF < L *praejūdicium* prejudgment, orig. preliminary or previous judicial inquiry, equiv. to *prae-* PRE- + *jūdicium* legal proceedings, judging (*jūdic-,* s. of *jūdex* JUDGE + *-ium* -IUM)] —**prej′u•diced•ly,** *adv.* —**prej′u•dice•less,** *adj.*
—**Syn. 2.** preconception, partiality, predilection, predisposition. See **bias. 7.** bias, influence.

prej•u•di•cial (prej′ə dish′əl), *adj.* causing prejudice or disadvantage; detrimental. [1375–1425; late ME < LL *praejūdiciālis;* see PREJUDICE, -AL[1]] —**prej′u•di′cial•ly,** *adv.* —**prej′u•di′cial•ness,** *n.*

prel•a•cy (prel′ə sē), *n., pl.* **-cies.** **1.** the office or dignity of a prelate. **2.** the order of prelates. **3.** the body of prelates collectively. **4.** *Sometimes Disparaging.* the system of church government by prelates. [1275–1325; ME *prelacie* < AF < ML *praelātia.* See PRELATE, -Y[3]]

pre•lap•sar•i•an (prē′lap sâr′ē ən), *adj.* **1.** *Theol.* occurring before the Fall: *the prelapsarian innocence of Eden.* **2.** characteristic of or pertaining to any innocent or carefree period: *a prelapsarian youth.* **3.** supralapsarian. —*n.* **4.** supralapsarian. [1875–80; PRE- + *-lapsarian,* as in INFRALAPSARIAN, SUPRALAPSARIAN]

prel•ate (prel′it), *n.* an ecclesiastic of a high order, as an archbishop, bishop, etc.; a church dignitary. [1175–1225; ME *prelat* < ML *praelātus* a civil or ecclesiastical dignitary, n. use of L *praelātus* (ptp. of *praeferre* to PREFER), equiv. to *prae-* PRE- + *lātus,* suppletive ptp. of *ferre* to BEAR[1]] —**prel′ate•ship′,** *n.* —**pre•lat•ic** (pri lat′ik), *adj.*

prel′ate nul•li′us (nŏŏ lē′əs), *pl.* **prelates nullius.** *Rom. Cath. Ch.* a prelate having independent jurisdiction over a district not under a diocesan bishop. [< NL or ML *nullīus dioecēsis* of no diocese]

prel•a•tism (prel′ə tiz′əm), *n.* prelacy; episcopacy. [1605–15; PRELATE + -ISM] —**prel′a•tist,** *n.*

prel•a•ture (prel′ə chər, -chŏŏr′), *n.* **1.** the office of a prelate. **2.** the order of prelates. **3.** prelates collectively. [1600–10; < ML *praelātūra.* See PRELATE, -URE]

pre•launch (prē lônch′, -länch′), *adj.* preparatory to launch, as of a spacecraft. [PRE- + LAUNCH[1]]

pre•lease (prē lēs′), *v.,* **-leased, -leas•ing,** *n.* —*v.t.* **1.** to sign or grant a lease on (a building, apartment, etc.) in advance of construction: *Agents have preleased more than 60 percent of the new building.* —*n.* **2.** a lease on a building, apartment, etc., that is offered or signed before construction has begun. [PRE- + LEASE[1]]

pre•lect (pri lekt′), *v.i.* to lecture or discourse publicly. Also, **praelect.** [1610–20; < L *praelectus,* ptp. of *praelegere* to lecture, equiv. to *prae-* PRE- + *legere* to read aloud; see LECTION] —**pre•lec•tion** (pri lek′shən), *n.* —**pre•lec′tor,** *n.*

pre•li•ba•tion (prē′lī bā′shən), *n.* a foretaste. [1520–30; < LL *praelībātiōn-* (s. of *praelībātiō*) a foretaste, anticipation, equiv. to *praelībāt(us)* (ptp. of *praelībāre* to taste beforehand) + *-iōn-* -ION. See PRE-, LIBATION]

pre•lim (prē′lim, pri lim′), *n. Informal.* preliminary. [1880–85; by shortening]

prelim., preliminary.

pre•lim•i•nar•y (pri lim′ə ner′ē), *adj., n., pl.* **-nar•ies.** —*adj.* **1.** preceding and leading up to the main part, matter, or business; introductory; preparatory: *preliminary examinations.* —*n.* **2.** something preliminary, as an introductory or preparatory step, measure, contest, etc.: *He passed the preliminary and went on to the finals.* **3.** a boxing match or other athletic contest that takes place before the main event on the program: *A preliminary was fought at 8:00.* **4.** a preliminary examination, as of a candidate for an academic degree. **5. preliminaries,** *Print.* See **front matter.** [1650–60; < F *prélimin(aire)* and NL *praelimin(āris)* (see PRE-, LIMINAL) + -ARY] —**pre•lim′i•nar′i•ly,** *adv.*
—**Syn. 1.** prefatory. PRELIMINARY, INTRODUCTORY both refer to that which comes before the principal subject of consideration. That which is PRELIMINARY is in the nature of preparation or of clearing away details which would encumber the main subject or problem; it often deals with arrangements and the like, which have to do only incidentally with the principal subject: *preliminary negotiations.* That which is INTRODUCTORY leads with natural, logical, or close connection directly into the main subject of consideration: *introductory steps.*
—**Ant. 1.** concluding.

Prelim′inary Scholas′tic Ap′titude Test′, a standardized multiple-choice aptitude test administered by the College Entrance Examination Board, and usually taken by eleventh graders, to help secondary-school students prepare for the Scholastic Aptitude Test. *Abbr.:* PSAT

pre•lim•it (prē lim′it), *v.t.* to limit within bounds beforehand: *The chairman prelimited his speech to 10 minutes.* [1630–40; PRE- + LIMIT] —**pre•lim′i•ta′tion,** *n.*

pre•lit•er•ate (prē lit′ər it), *adj. Anthropol.* **1.** lack-

CONCISE PRONUNCIATION KEY: act, cāpe, dâre, pärt; set, ēqual; if, īce; ox, ōver, ôrder, oil, bŏŏk, bōōt, out; up, ûrge; child; sing; shoe; thin, *th*at; zh as in *treasure.* ə = *a* as in *alone, e* as in *system, i* as in *easily, o* as in *gallop, u* as in *circus;* ᵊ as in *fire* (fīᵊr), *hour* (ouᵊr). l and n can serve as syllabic consonants, as in *cradle* (krād′l), and *button* (but′n). See the full key inside the front cover.

pre′dis•cov′er•y, *n., pl.* **-er•ies.**
pre′dis•crim′i•nate′, *v.t.,* **-nat•ed, -nat•ing.**
pre′dis•crim′i•na′tion, *n.*
pre′dis•cuss′, *v.t.*
pre′dis•cus′sion, *n.*
pre′dis•grace′, *n.*
pre′dis•guise′, *n., v.t.,* **-guised, -guis•ing.**
pre′dis•gust′, *n.*
pre′dis•like′, *n., v.t.,* **-liked, -lik•ing.**
pre′dis•miss′, *v.t.*
pre′dis•miss′al, *n.*
pre′dis•or′der, *n.*
pre′dis•or′dered, *adj.*
pre′dis•patch′, *n., v.t.*
pre′dis•patch′er, *n.*
pre′dis•perse′, *v.t.,* **-persed, -pers•ing.**
pre′dis•per′sion, *n.*
pre′dis•place′, *v.t.,* **-placed, -plac•ing.**
pre′dis•place′ment, *n.*
pre′dis•play′, *n., v.t.*
pre′dis•pu′tant, *n.*
pre′dis•pu•ta′tion, *n.*
pre′dis•pute′, *n., v.,* **-put•ed, -put•ing.**
pre′dis•rupt′, *v.t.*
pre′dis•rup′tion, *n.*
pre′dis•sat′is•fac′tion, *n.*
pre′dis•so•lu′tion, *n.*
pre′dis•solve′, *v.t.,* **-solved, -solv•ing.**
pre′dis•suade′, *v.t.,* **-suad•ed, -suad•ing.**
pre′dis•tin′guish, *v.t.*
pre′dis•tress′, *n., v.t.*
pre′dis•trib′ute, *v.t.,* **-ut•ed, -ut•ing.**
pre′dis•tri•bu′tion, *n.*
pre•dis′trict, *n.*
pre′dis•trust′, *n., v.t.*
pre′dis•trust′ful, *adj.*
pre′dis•turb′, *v.t.*
pre′dis•turb′ance, *n.*
pre′di•ver′sion, *n.*
pre•dive′, *adj.*
pre′di•vert′, *v.t.*
pre′di•vide′, *v.t.,* **-vid•ed, -vid•ing.**
pre′di•vid′er, *n.*
pre′di•vin′a•ble, *adj.*
pre′di•vin′i•ty, *n.*
pre′di•vi′sion, *n.*
pre′di•vorce′, *n., adj.*
pre′di•vorce′ment, *n.*
pre•doc′tor•ate, *n.*
pre′doc•u•men′ta•ry, *adj.*
pre′do•mes′tic, *adj.*
pre′do•mes′ti•cal•ly, *adv.*
pre•do′nate, *v.t.,* **-nat•ed, -nat•ing.**
pre′do•na′tion, *n.*
pre•do′nor, *n.*
pre•doom′, *v.t.*
pre-Do′ri•an, *adj.*
pre-Dor′ic, *adj.*
pre•dor′sal, *adj.*
pre•doubt′, *n., v.*
pre•doubt′er, *n.*
pre•doubt′ful, *adj.;* **-ly,** *adv.*
pre•draft′, *n., v.t.*
pre′dra•mat′ic, *adj.*
pre′-Dra•vid′i•an, *adj.*
pre′-Dra•vid′ic, *adj.*
pre•draw′, *v.,* **-drew, -drawn, -draw•ing;** *n.*
pre•draw′er, *n.*
pre•dread′, *n., v.t.*
pre•drill′, *v.t.*
pre•drive′, *v.,* **-drove, -driv•en, -driv•ing.**
pre•dry′, *v.t.,* **-dried, -dry•ing.**
pre•du′pli•cate′, *v.t.,* **-cat•ed, -cat•ing.**
pre′du•pli•ca′tion, *n.*
pre•dusk′, *n.*
pre-Dutch′, *adj.*
pre•dwell′, *v.i.*
pre•earth′quake′, *adj.*
pre-Eas′ter, *n.*
pre′ec•o•nom′ic, *adj.*
pre′ec•o•nom′i•cal, *adj.;* **-ly,** *adv.*
pre•ed′it, *v.t.*
pre′e•di′tion, *n.*
pre•ed′i•tor, *n.*
pre′ed•i•to′ri•al, *adj.;* **-ly,** *adv.*
pre•ed′u•cate′, *v.t.,* **-cat•ed, -cat•ing.**
pre′ed•u•ca′tion, *n.*
pre′ed•u•ca′tion•al, *adj.;* **-ly,** *adv.*
pre′ef•fect′, *n., v.t.*
pre′ef•fec′tive, *adj.;* **-ly,** *adv.*
pre′ef•fec′tu•al, *adj.;* **-ly,** *adv.*
pre•ef′fort, *n.*
pre′e•lect′, *v.t.*
pre′e•lec′tive, *adj.*
pre′e•lec′tric, *adj.*
pre′e•lec′tri•cal, *adj.;* **-ly,** *adv.*
pre′e•lec•tron′ic, *adj.*
pre′el•e•men′tal, *adj.*
pre′el•e•men′ta•ry, *adj.*
pre′el•i•gi•bil′i•ty, *n.*
pre•el′i•gi•ble, *adj.;* **-ble•ness,** *n.;* **-bly,** *adv.*
pre′e•lim′i•nate′, *v.t.,* **-nat•ed, -nat•ing.**
pre′e•lim′i•na′tion, *n.*
pre′e•lim′i•na′tor, *n.*
pre′e•man′ci•pa′tion, *n.*
pre′em•bar′go, *adj.*
pre′em•bar′rass, *v.t.*
pre′em•bar′rass•ment, *n.*
pre′em•bod′i•ment, *n.*
pre′em•bod′y, *v.t.,* **-bod•ied, -bod•y•ing.**
pre′e•mer′gen•cy, *adj., n., pl.* **-cies.**
pre′e•mo′tion, *n.*
pre′e•mo′tion•al, *adj.;* **-ly,** *adv.*
pre•em′per•or, *n.*
pre-Em′pire, *adj.*
pre′em•ploy′, *v.t.*
pre′em•ploy•ee′, *n.*
pre′em•ploy′er, *n.*
pre′en•a′ble, *v.t.,* **-bled, -bling.**

ing a written language; nonliterate: *a preliterate culture.* **2.** occurring before the development or use of writing. [1920–25; PRE- + LITERATE]

Pre·log (prel′ôg, -og), *n.* **Vlad·i·mir** (vlad′ə mēr′), born 1906, Swiss chemist, born in Yugoslavia: Nobel prize 1975.

prel·ude (prel′yo͞od, prāl′-, prā′lo͞od, prē′-), *n., v.,* **-ud·ed, -ud·ing.** —*n.* **1.** a preliminary to an action, event, condition, or work of broader scope and higher importance. **2.** any action, event, comment, etc. that precedes something else. **3.** *Music.* **a.** a relatively short, independent instrumental composition, free in form and resembling an improvisation. **b.** a piece that precedes a more important movement. **c.** the overture to an opera. **d.** an independent piece, of moderate length, sometimes used as an introduction to a fugue. **e.** music opening a church service; an introductory voluntary. —*v.t.* **4.** to serve as a prelude or introduction to. **5.** to introduce by a prelude. **6.** to play as a prelude. —*v.i.* **7.** to serve as a prelude. **8.** to give a prelude. **9.** to play a prelude. [1555–65; (n.) < ML *praelūdium,* equiv. to *prae-* PRE- + *-lūdium* play; cf. L *lūdus* play; (v.) < L *praelūdere* to play beforehand] —**prel′ud·er,** *n.* —**pre·lu·di·al** (pri lo͞o′dē əl), **pre·lu′di·ous,** *adj.* —**pre·lu′di·ous·ly,** *adv.*
—**Syn. 1.** introduction, opening, beginning.

Pre·lu·din (pri lo͞od′n, prā-), *Pharm., Trademark.* a brand of phenmetrazine.

pre·lu·sion (pri lo͞o′zhən), *n.* a prelude. [1590–1600; < L *praelūsiōn-* (s. of *praelūsiō*) a prelude, equiv. to *praelūs(us)* (ptp. of *praelūdere;* see PRELUDE) + *-iōn-* -ION]

pre·lu·sive (pri lo͞o′siv), *adj.* introductory. Also, **pre·lu·so·ry** (pri lo͞o′sə rē). [1595–1605; < L *praelūs(us)* (see PRELUSION) + -IVE] —**pre·lu′sive·ly, pre·lu′so·ri·ly,** *adv.*

prem., premium.

Prem·a·rin (prem′ə rin), *Pharm., Trademark.* a brand name for a mixture of conjugated natural estrogens used to treat menopausal symptoms, dysfunctional uterine bleeding, and certain cancers.

pre·mar·i·tal (prē mar′i tl), *adj.* preceding marriage. [1885–90; PRE- + MARITAL]

pre·ma·ture (prē′mə cho͝or′, -to͝or′, -tyo͝or′, prē′mə-cho͝or′ *or, esp. Brit.,* prem′ə-, prem′ə-), *adj.* **1.** occurring, coming, or done too soon: *a premature announcement.* **2.** mature or ripe before the proper time. —*n.* **3.** a premature infant. [1520–30; < L *praemātūrus.* See PRE-, MATURE] —**pre′ma·ture′ly,** *adv.* —**pre′ma·tu′ri·ty, pre′ma·ture′ness,** *n.*

pre′mature beat′, *Med.* extrasystole.

pre′mature contrac′tion, *Med.* extrasystole.

premature′ ejacula′tion, a male psychosexual disorder in which ejaculation occurs soon after the commencement of sexual intercourse. [1905–10]

pre·max·il·la (prē′mak sil′ə), *n., pl.* **-max·il·lae** (-mak sil′ē). *Anat., Zool.* one of a pair of bones of the upper jaw of vertebrates, situated in front of and between the maxillary bones. [1865–70; < NL *praemaxilla.* See PRE-, MAXILLA] —**pre·max·il·lar·y** (prē mak′sə ler′ē), *adj.*

pre·med (prē med′), *n.* **1.** a program of premedical study or training. **2.** a student enrolled in such a program. —*adj.* **3.** of or pertaining to premedical studies. [1960–65; short for PREMEDICAL]

pre·med·i·cal (prē med′i kəl), *adj.* of or pertaining to studies in preparation for the formal study of medicine: *a premedical course.* [1900–05; PRE- + MEDICAL]

pre·med·i·e·val (prē mē′dē ē′vəl, -med′ē-, -mid′ē-, prē′mē dē-, prē′med ē-, -mid ē-, prē′mid ē′vəl), *adj.* prior to the Middle Ages. Also, **pre·me′di·ae′val.** [1855–60; PRE- + MEDIEVAL]

pre·med·i·tate (pri med′i tāt′), *v.t., v.i.,* **-tat·ed, -tat·ing.** to meditate, consider, or plan beforehand: *to premeditate a murder.* [1540–50; < L *praemeditātus* ptp. of *praemeditārī* to contemplate in advance. See PRE-, MEDITATE] —**pre·med′i·ta′tive,** *adj.* —**pre·med′i·ta′tor,** *n.*
—**Syn.** See **deliberate.**

CONCISE ETYMOLOGY KEY: <, descended or borrowed from; >, whence; b., blend of, blended; c., cognate with; cf., compare; deriv., derivative; equiv., equivalent; imit., imitative; obl., oblique; r., replacing; s., stem; sp., spelling, spelled; resp., respelling, respelled; trans., translation; ?, origin unknown; *, unattested; ‡, probably earlier than. See the full key inside the front cover.

pre·med·i·tat·ed (pri med′i tā′tid), *adj.* done deliberately; planned in advance: *a premeditated murder.* [1580–90; PRE- + MEDITATE + -ED[2]] —**pre·med′i·tat′·ed·ly,** *adv.*

pre·med·i·ta·tion (pri med′i tā′shən), *n.* **1.** an act or instance of premeditating. **2.** *Law.* sufficient forethought to impute deliberation and intent to commit the act. [1400–50; late ME < L *praemeditātiōn-* (s. of *praemeditātiō*) a considering beforehand. See PREMEDITATE, -ION]

premen′strual syn′drome, *Pathol.* a complex of physical and emotional changes, including depression, irritability, appetite changes, bloating and water retention, breast soreness, and changes in muscular coordination, one or more of which may be experienced in the several days before the onset of menstrual flow. *Abbr.:* PMS Also called **premen′strual ten′sion.** [1980–85; PRE- + MENSTRUAL]

pre·mi·ate (prē′mē āt′), *v.t.,* **-at·ed, -at·ing.** to grant a prize or an award to. [1530–40; < ML *praemiātus,* ptp. of *praemiāre* to reward (L: stipulate for a reward). See PREMIUM, -ATE[1]]

pre·mier (pri mēr′, -myēr′, prē′mēr), *n.* **1.** the head of the cabinet in France or Italy or certain other countries; first minister; prime minister. **2.** a chief officer. —*adj.* **3.** first in rank; chief; leading. **4.** first in time; earliest; oldest. [1400–50; late ME *primer, primier, premer* (adj.) < AF *primer, premer* and MF *premier, primier* lit., first < L *primārius* of the first rank; see PRIMARY] —**pre·mier′ship,** *n.*

Pre·mier Cru (prə myā krʏ′), *pl.* **Pre·miers Crus** (prə myā krʏ′). *French.* See under **cru.**

pre·mier dan·seur (*Fr.* prə myā dän sœr′), *n., pl.* **pre·miers dan·seurs** (*Fr.* prə myā dän sœr′). the leading male dancer in a ballet company. [1820–30; < F: lit., first dancer (masc.)]

pre·miere (pri mēr′, -myâr′), *n., v.,* **-miered, -mier·ing,** *adj.* —*n.* **1.** a first public performance or showing of a play, opera, film, etc. **2.** the leading woman, as in a drama. —*v.t.* **3.** to present publicly for the first time: *to premiere a new foreign film.* —*v.i.* **4.** to have the first public showing: *It will premiere at the Arcadia Theater.* **5.** to perform publicly for the first time, as in a particular role, entertainment medium, etc.: *When does he premiere as Hamlet?* —*adj.* **6.** first; initial; principal: *a premiere showing; the premiere attraction of the evening.* [1890–95; < F *première* lit., first; fem. of *premier* PREMIER]

pre·mière (pri mēr′, -myâr′; *Fr.* prə myer′), *n., pl.* **-mières** (-mērz′, -myârz′; *Fr.* -myer′), *v.t., v.i.,* **-miered, -mier·ing,** *adj.* premiere.

pre·mière dan·seuse (*Fr.* prə myer dän sœz′), *pl.* **pre·mières dan·seuses** (*Fr.* prə myer dän sœz′). the leading female dancer in a ballet company. [1820–30; < F: lit., first dancer (fem.)]

pre·mière par·tie (pri mēr′ pär tē′, -myâr′; *Fr.* prə myer par tē′), *Furniture.* (in buhl) the primary inlay formed, in which the tortoise shell forms the ground for a design cut in brass. Cf. **contrepartie.** [< F: lit., the first part]

pre·mil·le·nar·i·an (prē′mil ə nâr′ē ən), *n.* **1.** a believer in premillennialism. —*adj.* **2.** of or pertaining to the doctrine of premillennialism or a believer in this doctrine. [1835–45; PRE- + MILLENARIAN] —**pre′mil·le·nar′i·an·ism,** *n.*

pre·mil·len·ni·al (prē′mi len′ē əl), *adj.* of or pertaining to the period preceding the millennium. [1840–50; PRE- + MILLENNIAL] —**pre′mil·len′ni·al·ly,** *adv.*

pre·mil·len·ni·al·ism (prē′mi len′ē ə liz′əm), *n.* the doctrine or belief that the Second Coming of Christ will precede the millennium. [1840–50; PREMILLENNIAL + -ISM] —**pre′mil·len′ni·al·ist,** *n.*

pre·mil·len·ni·al·ize (prē′mi len′ē ə līz′), *v.i.,* **-ized, -iz·ing.** to support or believe in premillennialism. Also, *esp. Brit.,* **pre′mil·len′ni·al·ise′.** [1840–50; PREMILLENNIAL + -IZE]

Prem·in·ger (prem′in jər), *n.* **Otto (Ludwig),** 1906–86, U.S. motion-picture actor, director, and producer, born in Austria.

prem·ise (prem′is), *n., v.,* **-ised, -is·ing.** —*n.* **1.** Also, **prem′iss.** *Logic.* a proposition supporting or helping to support a conclusion. **2. premises, a.** a tract of land including its buildings. **b.** a building together with its grounds or other appurtenances. **c.** the property forming the subject of a conveyance or bequest. **3.** *Law.* **a.** a basis, stated or assumed, on which reasoning proceeds. **b.** an earlier statement in a document. **c.** (in a bill in equity) the statement of facts upon which the complaint is based. —*v.t.* **4.** to set forth beforehand, as by way of introduction or explanation. **5.** to assume, either explicitly or implicitly, (a proposition) as a premise for a conclusion. —*v.i.* **6.** to state or assume a premise. [1325–75; ME *premiss* < ML *praemissa,* n. use of fem. of L *praemissus* ptp. of *praemittere* to send before, equiv. to *prae-* PRE- + *mittere* to send. See DISMISS, REMISS]
—**Syn. 1.** assumption, postulate. **5.** postulate, hypothesize.

pre·mi·um (prē′mē əm), *n.* **1.** a prize, bonus, or award given as an inducement, as to purchase products, enter competitions initiated by business interests, etc. **2.** a bonus, gift, or sum additional to price, wages, interest, or the like. **3.** *Insurance.* the amount paid or to be paid by the policyholder for coverage under the contract, usually in periodic installments. **4.** *Econ.* the excess value of one form of money over another of the same nominal value. **5.** a sum above the nominal or par value of a thing. **6.** the amount paid to the lender of stock by the borrower, typically a short seller. **7.** the amount the buyer of a call or put option pays to the seller, quoted in dollars per share of stock. **8.** a fee paid for instruction in a trade or profession. **9.** a sum additional to the interest paid for the loan of money. **10. at a premium, a.** at an unusually high price. **b.** in short supply; in demand: *Housing in that area is at a premium.* —*adj.* **11.** of exceptional quality or greater value than others of its kind; superior: *a wine made of premium grapes.* **12.** of higher price or cost. **13.** of or pertaining to premiums: *to work in premium sales.* [1595–1605; < L *praemium* profit, reward]
—**Syn. 2.** reward. See **bonus.**

pre′mium loan′, *Insurance.* a loan made by a life-insurance company in order that a policyholder may pay the due premium, the cash value on the policy serving as security.

pre·mix (prē miks′), *n., adj., v.,* **-mixed** or **-mixt, -mix·ing.** —*n.* **1.** Also, **pre·mix·ture** (prē miks′chər). a mixture of ingredients, made before selling, using, etc.: *The chain saw runs on a premix of oil and gasoline.* —*adj.* **2.** mixed prior to using, marketing, etc.; premixed: *premix concrete.* —*v.t.* **3.** to mix beforehand, as in advance of selling or using. [1930–35; PRE- + MIX] —**pre·mix′·er,** *n.*

pre·mo·lar (prē mō′lər), *adj.* **1.** situated in front of the molar teeth. **2.** pertaining to a milk tooth that will later be supplanted by a permanent molar. —*n.* **3.** a premolar tooth. **4.** Also called **bicuspid.** (in humans) any of eight teeth located in pairs on each side of the upper and lower jaws between the cuspids and molar teeth. See illus. under **tooth.** [1835–45; PRE- + MOLAR[1]]

pre·mon·ish (pri mon′ish), *v.t., v.i.* to warn beforehand. [1520–30; PRE- + (AD)MONISH]

pre·mo·ni·tion (prē′mə nish′ən, prem′ə-), *n.* **1.** a feeling of anticipation of or anxiety over a future event; presentiment: *He had a vague premonition of danger.* **2.** a forewarning. [1425–75; late ME *premunicioun* (cf. PRAEMUNIRE) < LL *praemonitiōn-* (s. of *praemonitiō*) forewarning. See PRE-, MONITION]
—**Syn. 1.** foreboding, portent, omen, sign.

pre·mon·i·to·ry (pri mon′i tôr′ē, -tōr′ē), *adj.* giving premonition; serving to warn beforehand. [1640–50; < LL *praemonitōrius.* See PRE-, MONITORY]

pre·morse (pri môrs′), *adj. Biol.* having the end irregularly truncate, as if bitten or broken off. [1745–55; < L *praemorsus* bitten off in front (ptp. of *praemordēre*), equiv. to *prae-* PRE- + *morsus* bitten; see MORSEL]

pre·mun·dane (prē mun′dān, prē′mən dān′), *adj.* before the creation of the world; antemundane. [PRE- + MUNDANE]

pre·mu·ni·tion (prē′myo͞o nish′ən), *n. Immunol.* a state of balance between host and infectious agent, as a bacterium or parasite, such that the immune defense of the host is sufficient to resist further infection but insufficient to destroy the agent. Also called **coinfectious immunity.** [1920–35; < F *prémunition* < L *praemūnītiōn-,* s. of *praemūnītiō* advance provisions for defense; see PRE-, MUNITION] —**pre·mu·ni·tive** (prē myo͞o′ni tiv), *adj.*

pre·na·tal (prē nāt′l), *adj.* previous to birth or to giving birth: *prenatal care for mothers.* [1820–30; PRE- + NATAL] —**pre·na′tal·ly,** *adv.*

pre′en·act′, *v.t.*
pre′en·ac′tion, *n.*
pre′en·close′, *v.t.,* **-closed, -clos·ing.**
pre′en·clo′sure, *n.*
pre′en·coun′ter, *n., v.t.*
pre′en·cour′age, *v.t.,* **-aged, -ag·ing.**
pre′en·cour′age·ment, *n.*
pre′en·deav′or, *n.*
pre′en·dorse′, *v.t.,* **-dorsed, -dors·ing.**
pre′en·dorse′ment, *n.*
pre′en·force′, *v.t.,* **-forced, -forc·ing.**
pre′en·force′ment, *n.*
pre′en·gi·neer′ing, *adj.*
pre-Eng′lish, *adj.*
pre′en·joy′, *v.t.*
pre′en·joy′a·ble, *adj.*
pre′en·joy′ment, *n.*
pre′en·large′, *v.t.,* **-larged, -larg·ing.**
pre′en·large′ment, *n.*
pre′en·light′en, *v.t.*
pre′en·light′en·er, *n.*
pre′en·light′en·ment, *n.*
pre′en·list′, *v.*
pre′en·list′ment, *n.*
pre′en·roll′, *v.*
pre′en·roll′ment, *n.*
pre′en·tail′, *v.t.*
pre′en·tail′ment, *n.*
pre·en′ter, *v.i.*
pre′en·ter·tain′, *v.t.*
pre′en·ter·tain′er, *n.*
pre′en·ter·tain′ment, *n.*
pre′en·thu′si·asm, *n.*
pre·en·ti′tle, *v.t.,* **-tled, -tling.**
pre·en′trance, *n.*
pre·en′try, *n., pl.* **-tries.**
pre′e·nu′mer·ate′, *v.t.,* **-at·ed, -at·ing.**
pre′e·nu′mer·a′tion, *n.*
pre′en·vel′op, *v.t.*
pre′en·vel′op·ment, *n.*
pre′en·vi′ron·men′tal, *adj.*
pre′ep·i·dem′ic, *n., adj.*
pre·ep′och·al, *adj.*
pre′e·quip′, *v.t.,* **-quipped, -quip·ping.**
pre′e·quip′ment, *n.*
pre·eq′ui·ty, *n., pl.* **-ties.**
pre′e·rect′, *v.t.*
pre′e·rec′tion, *n.*
pre′e·rupt′, *v.i.*
pre′e·rup′tion, *n.*
pre′e·rup′tive, *adj.;* **-ly,** *adv.*
pre′es·cape′, *n., v.i.,* **-caped, -cap·ing.**
pre′e·soph′a·ge′al, *adj.*
pre′es·say′, *v.i.*
pre′es·sen′tial, *n., adj.;* **-ly,** *adv.*
pre′es·teem′, *v.t.*
pre·es′ti·mate′, *v.t.,* **-mat·ed, -mat·ing.**
pre·es′ti·mate, *n.*
pre′es·ti·ma′tion, *n.*
pre′es·ti′val, *adj.*
pre′e·ter′nal, *adj.*
pre′e·ter′ni·ty, *n.*
pre′e·vade′, *v.t.,* **-vad·ed, -vad·ing.**
pre′e·vap′o·rate′, *v.,* **-rat·ed, -rat·ing.**
pre′e·vap′o·ra′tion, *n.*
pre′e·vap′o·ra′tor, *n.*
pre′e·va′sion, *n.*
pre·ev′i·dence, *n.*
pre·ev′i·dent, *adj.;* **-ly,** *adv.*
pre′ev·o·lu′tion·al, *adj.*
pre′ev·o·lu′tion·ar′y, *adj.*
pre′ev·o·lu′tion·ist, *n.*
pre′ex·act′, *adj., v.t.*
pre′ex·am′i·na′tion, *n.*
pre′ex·am′ine, *v.t.,* **-ined, -in·ing.**
pre′ex·am′in·er, *n.*
pre′ex·cept′, *v.t.*
pre′ex·cep′tion, *n.*
pre′ex·cep′tion·al, *adj.;* **-ly,** *adv.*
pre′ex·change′, *v.t.,* **-changed, -chang·ing.**
pre′ex·ci·ta′tion, *n.*
pre′ex·cite′, *v.t.,* **-cit·ed, -cit·ing.**
pre′ex·clude′, *v.t.,* **-clud·ed, -clud·ing.**
pre′ex·clu′sion, *n.*
pre′ex·clu′sive, *adj.;* **-ly,** *adv.*
pre′ex·cur′sion, *n.*
pre′ex·cuse′, *v.t.,* **-cused, -cus·ing.**
pre·ex′e·cute′, *v.t.,* **-cut·ed, -cut·ing.**
pre′ex·e·cu′tion, *n.*
pre′ex·ec′u·tor, *n.*
pre′ex·empt′, *v.t.*
pre′ex·emp′tion, *n.*
pre′ex·haust′, *v.t.*
pre′ex·haus′tion, *n.*
pre′ex·hib′it, *n., v.t.*
pre′ex·hi·bi′tion, *n.*
pre′ex·pand′, *v.t.*
pre′ex·pan′sion, *n.*
pre′ex·pect′, *v.t.*
pre′ex·pect′ant, *n.*
pre′ex·pec·ta′tion, *n.*
pre′ex·pe·di′tion, *n.*
pre′ex·pe·di′tion·ar′y, *adj.*
pre′ex·pend′, *v.t.*
pre′ex·pend′i·ture, *n.*
pre′ex·pense′, *n.*
pre′ex·pe′ri·ence, *n., v.t.,* **-enced, -enc·ing.**
pre′ex·per′i·ment, *n.*
pre′ex·per′i·men′tal, *adj.*
pre′ex·pi·ra′tion, *n.*
pre′ex·plain′, *v.*
pre′ex·pla·na′tion, *n.*
pre′ex·plan′a·to′ry, *adj.*
pre′ex·plode′, *v.,* **-plod·ed, -plod·ing.**
pre′ex·plo′sion, *n.*
pre′ex·pose′, *v.t.,* **-posed, -pos·ing.**
pre′ex·po·si′tion, *n.*
pre′ex·pound′, *v.t.*

Pren·der·gast (pren′dər gast′, -gäst′), *n.* **Maurice Braz·il** (braz′əl), 1859–1924, U.S. painter.

pre·no·men (prē nō′mən), *n., pl.* **-nom·i·na** (-nom′ə nə, -nō′mə-), **-no·mens.** praenomen.

pre·nom·i·nate (*adj.* pri nom′ə nit; *v.* pri nom′ə nāt′), *adj., v.,* **-nat·ed, -nat·ing.** *Obs.* —*adj.* **1.** mentioned beforehand. —*v.t.* **2.** to mention beforehand. [1540–50; < L *praenōminātus* ptp. of *praenōmināre* to name beforehand. See PRE-, NOMINATE] —**pre·nom′i·na′tion,** *n.*

pre·no·ti·fi·ca·tion (prē′nō tə fi kā′shən), *n.* notice that is given or served prior to a specific date; advance notice. [1755–65; PRE- + NOTIFICATION]

pre·no·tion (prē nō′shən), *n.* a preconception. [1580–90; < L *praenōtiōn-* (s. of *praenōtiō*) an innate idea. See PRE-, NOTION]

pren·tice (pren′tis), *n., v. Informal.* apprentice. [1250–1300; ME; aph. form of APPRENTICE]

Pren·tice (pren′tis), *n.* a male given name.

pre·nu·cle·ar (prē nōō′klē ər, -nyōō′- *or, by metathesis,* -kyə lər), *adj.* of or pertaining to the era before the development of nuclear weapons. [1950–55; PRE- + NUCLEAR]
—**Pronunciation.** See **nuclear.**

pre·nup·tial (prē nup′shəl, -chəl), *adj.* before marriage: *a prenuptial agreement.* [1865–70; PRE- + NUPTIAL]
—**Pronunciation.** See **nuptial.**

pre·oc·cu·pan·cy (prē ok′yə pən sē), *n.* **1.** the act, right, or instance of prior occupancy. **2.** the state of being absorbed in thought; preoccupation. [1745–55; PRE- + OCCUPANCY]

pre·oc·cu·pa·tion (prē ok′yə pā′shən, prē′ok-), *n.* **1.** the state of being preoccupied. **2.** an act of preoccupying. [1530–40; < L *praeoccupātiōn-* (s. of *praeoccupātiō*) a taking possession beforehand. See PRE-, OCCUPATION]

pre·oc·cu·pied (prē ok′yə pīd′), *adj.* **1.** completely engrossed in thought; absorbed. **2.** previously occupied; taken; filled. **3.** *Biol.* already used as a name for some species, genus, etc., and not available as a designation for any other. [1835–45; PREOCCUPY + -ED²] —**pre·oc′cu·pied′ly,** *adv.* —**pre·oc′cu·pied′ness,** *n.*
—**Syn. 1.** busy; concentrating.

pre·oc·cu·py (prē ok′yə pī′), *v.t.,* **-pied, -py·ing. 1.** to absorb or engross to the exclusion of other things. **2.** to occupy beforehand or before others. [1560–70; PRE- + OCCUPY] —**pre·oc′cu·pi′er,** *n.*

pre·op (prē′op′), *adj., adv. Informal.* preoperative; preoperatively. Also, **pre′-op′.** [by shortening]

pre·op·er·a·tive (prē op′ər ə tiv, -ə rā′tiv, -op′rə tiv), *adj.* occurring or related to the period or preparations before a surgical operation. [1900–05; PRE- + OPERATIVE] —**pre·op′er·a·tive·ly,** *adv.*

pre·o·ral (prē ôr′əl, -ōr′-), *adj. Zool.* situated in front of or before the mouth. [1865–70; PRE- + ORAL] —**pre·o′ral·ly,** *adv.*

pre·or·dain (prē′ôr dān′), *v.t.* to ordain beforehand; foreordain. [1525–35; PRE- + ORDAIN] —**pre·or·di·na·tion** (prē′ôr dn ā′shən), *n.*

pre·owned (prē ōnd′), *adj.* previously owned; used; secondhand: *a sale of preowned furs.* Also, **pre-owned′.** [1960–65; PRE- + OWN + -ED²]

prep (prep), *n., adj., v.,* **prepped, prep·ping.** —*n.* **1.** See **preparatory school. 2.** a preliminary or warm-up activity or event; trial run: *The race is a good prep for the Kentucky Derby.* **3.** preparation: *dealer prep on the car included.* **4.** the act of preparing a patient for a medical or surgical procedure. —*adj.* **5.** preparatory: *a prep school.* **6.** involving or used for preparation: *the mortuary's prep room.* —*v.t.* **7.** to prepare (a person) for a test, debate, etc. **8.** to prepare (a patient) for a medical or surgical procedure, as by shaving and washing the skin with an antibacterial soap. **9.** to prepare (a vehicle or craft) for sale, use, a test drive, or a race. —*v.i.* **10.** to prepare; get ready: *to prep for the game.* **11.** to attend a preparatory school. [1860–65; by shortening]

prep., 1. preparation. **2.** preparatory. **3.** prepare. **4.** preposition.

pre·pack (*n.* prē′pak′; *v.* prē pak′), *n.* **1.** a package assembled by a manufacturer, distributor, or retailer and containing a specific number of items or a specific assortment of sizes, colors, flavors, etc., of a product. —*v.t.* **2.** prepackage. [1955–60; PRE- + PACK¹]

pre·pack·age (prē pak′ij), *v.t.,* **-aged, -ag·ing. 1.** to package (foodstuffs or manufactured goods) before retail distribution or sale. **2.** to combine various elements into a single unit that is offered for sale, usually at an all-inclusive price: *The travel agency prepackages tours to the Middle East.* [1940–45; PRE- + PACKAGE]

prep·a·ra·tion (prep′ə rā′shən), *n.* **1.** a proceeding, measure, or provision by which one prepares for something: *preparations for a journey.* **2.** any proceeding, experience, or the like considered as a mode of preparing for the future. **3.** an act of preparing. **4.** the state of being prepared. **5.** something prepared, manufactured, or compounded: *a special preparation for sunbathers.* **6.** a specimen, as an animal body, prepared for scientific examination, dissection, etc. **7.** *Music.* **a.** the preparing of a dissonance, by introducing the dissonant tone as a consonant tone in the preceding chord. **b.** the tone so introduced. **8.** *New Testament.* the day before the Sabbath or a feast day. **9.** *Brit.* work done by students in preparation for class; homework. **10. the Preparation,** the introductory prayers of the Mass or other divine service. [1350–1400; ME *preparacion* < L *praeparātiōn-* (s. of *praeparātiō*), a preparing, equiv. to *praeparāt(us)* (ptp. of *praeparāre* to PREPARE) + *-iōn-* -ION]

pre·par·a·tive (pri par′ə tiv, -pâr′-), *adj.* **1.** preparatory. —*n.* **2.** something that prepares. **3.** a preparation. [1400–50; late ME *preparatif* < MF < ML *praeparātīvus.* See PREPARATION, -IVE] —**pre·par′a·tive·ly,** *adv.*

pre·par·a·tor (pri par′ə tər, -pâr′-), *n.* a person who prepares a specimen, as an animal, for scientific examination or exhibition. [1755–65; < LL *praeparātor* preparer, equiv. to *praeparā(re)* to PREPARE + *-tor* -TOR]

pre·par·a·to·ry (pri par′ə tôr′ē, -tōr′ē, -pâr′-, prep′ər ə-), *adj.* **1.** serving or designed to prepare: *preparatory arrangements.* **2.** preliminary; introductory: *preparatory remarks.* **3.** of or pertaining to training that prepares for more advanced education. —*adv.* **4. preparatory to,** in advance of; before: *The astronauts met with the press preparatory to lifting off.* [1375–1425; late ME < ML *praeparātōrius.* See PREPARE, -TORY¹] —**pre·par′a·to′ri·ly,** *adv.*

prepar′atory school′, 1. a private or parochial secondary school, esp. one boarding its students and providing a college-preparatory education. **2.** *Brit.* a private elementary school, esp. one preparing its students for public school. Also called **prep school.** [1815–25]

pre·pare (pri pâr′), *v.,* **-pared, -par·ing.** —*v.t.* **1.** to put in proper condition or readiness: *to prepare a patient for surgery.* **2.** to get (a meal) ready for eating, as by proper assembling, cooking, etc. **3.** to manufacture, compound, or compose: *to prepare a cough syrup.* **4.** *Music.* to lead up to (a discord, an embellishment, etc.) by some preliminary tone or tones. —*v.i.* **5.** to put things or oneself in readiness; get ready: *to prepare for war.* [1520–30; < L *praeparāre* to make ready beforehand, equiv. to *prae-* PRE- + *parāre* to set, get ready (akin to PARENT)] —**pre·par′er,** *n.*
—**Syn. 1.** provide, arrange, order. PREPARE, CONTRIVE, DEVISE imply planning for and making ready for something expected or thought possible. To PREPARE is to make ready beforehand for some approaching event, need, and the like: *to prepare a room, a speech.* CONTRIVE and DEVISE emphasize the exercise of ingenuity and inventiveness. The first word suggests a shrewdness that borders on trickery, but this is absent from DEVISE: *to contrive a means of escape; to devise a time-saving method.* **3.** make. —**Ant. 1.** disorganize.

pre·pared (pri pârd′), *adj.* **1.** properly expectant, organized, or equipped; ready: *prepared for a hurricane.* **2.** (of food) processed by the manufacturer or seller, by cooking, cleaning, or the like, so as to be ready to serve or use with little or no further preparation. [1520–30; PREPARE + -ED²] —**pre·par·ed·ly** (pri pâr′id lē, -pârd′lē), *adv.*

pre·par·ed·ness (pri pâr′id nis, -pârd′nis), *n.* **1.** the state of being prepared; readiness. **2.** possession of adequate armed forces, industrial resources and potential, etc., esp. as a deterrent to enemy attack. [1580–90; PREPARED + -NESS]

prepared′ pian′o, a grand piano that has been altered for some modern compositions by having various objects attached to its strings to change the sound and pitch, and performance on which typically involves playing the keys, plucking the strings, slapping the body of the instrument, and slamming the keyboard lid. [1955–60]

pre·pa·ren·tal (prē′pə ren′tl), *adj.* prior to becoming a parent: *preparental instruction.* [PRE- + PARENTAL]

pre·pay (prē pā′), *v.t.,* **-paid, -pay·ing.** to pay or arrange to pay beforehand or before due: *to prepay the loan.* [1830–40; PRE- + PAY¹] —**pre·pay′a·ble,** *adj.* —**pre·pay′ment,** *n.*

pre·pense (pri pens′), *adj.* planned or intended in advance; premeditated. [1695–1705; PRE- + *-pense* < L *pēnsus,* ptp. of *pendere* to weigh, consider; see PENSIVE]

pre·pol·lex (pri pol′eks), *n., pl.* **-pol·li·ces** (-pol′ə sēz′). a rudimentary additional digit on the preaxial side of the thumb of certain amphibians and mammals. [1885–90; < NL; see PRE-, POLLEX]

pre·pon·der·ance (pri pon′dər əns), *n.* the fact or quality of being preponderant; superiority in weight, power, numbers, etc.: *The preponderance of votes is against the proposal.* Also, **pre·pon′der·an·cy.** [1675–85; PREPONDER(ANT) + -ANCE]
—**Syn.** predominance, majority, mass, bulk.

pre·pon·der·ant (pri pon′dər ənt), *adj.* superior in weight, force, influence, numbers, etc.; prevailing: *a preponderant misconception.* [1650–60; < L *praeponderant-* (s. of *praeponderāns*), prp. of *praeponderāre* to outweigh. See PRE-, PONDER, -ANT] —**pre·pon′der·ant·ly,** *adv.*
—**Syn.** overpowering, overruling, major, dominant.

pre·pon·der·ate (pri pon′də rāt′), *v.i.,* **-at·ed, -at·ing. 1.** to exceed something else in weight; be the heavier. **2.** to incline downward or descend, as one scale or end of a balance, because of greater weight; be weighed down. **3.** to be superior in power, force, influence, number, amount, etc.; predominate: *Evidence for the accused preponderated at the trial.* [1615–25; < L *praeponderātus,* ptp. of *praeponderāre* to outweigh. See PRE-, PONDER, -ATE¹] —**pre·pon′der·a′tion,** *n.*

pre·por·tion (prē pôr′shən, pōr′-), *v.t.* to divide into portions before packaging, selling, etc.: *to preportion meals for schools and hospitals.* [PRE- + PORTION]

pre·pose (prē pōz′), *v.t.,* **-posed, -pos·ing.** *Gram.* to place (a grammatical form) before a related grammatical form: *The adverb "out" of "put the light out" is preposed in "put out the light."* [1655–65; prob. back formation from PREPOSITION¹; cf. obs. *prepose* to set over < MF *preposer;* see PRE-, POSE¹]

prep·o·si·tion¹ (prep′ə zish′ən), *n. Gram.* any member of a class of words found in many languages that are used before nouns, pronouns, or other substantives to form phrases functioning as modifiers of verbs, nouns, or adjectives, and that typically express a spatial, temporal, or other relationship, as *in, on, by, to, since.* [1350–1400; ME *preposicioun* < L *praepositiōn-* (s. of *praepositiō*) a putting before, a prefix, preposition. See PRE-, POSITION] —**prep′o·si′tion·al,** *adj.* —**prep′o·si′tion·al·ly,** *adv.*
—**Usage.** The often heard but misleading "rule" that a sentence should not end with a preposition is transferred from Latin, where it is an accurate description of practice. But English grammar is different from Latin grammar, and the rule does not fit English. In speech, the final preposition is normal and idiomatic, especially in questions: *What are we waiting for? Where did he come from? You didn't tell me which floor you worked on.* In writing, the problem of placing the preposition arises most when a sentence ends with a relative clause in which the relative pronoun (*that; whom; which; whomever; whichever; whomsoever*) is the object of a preposition. In edited writing, especially more formal writing, when a pronoun other than *that* introduces a final relative clause, the preposition usually precedes its object: *He abandoned the project to which he had devoted his whole life. I finally telephoned the representative with whom I had been corresponding.* If the pronoun is *that,* which cannot be preceded by a preposition, or if the pronoun is omitted, then the preposition must occur at the end: *The librarian found the books that the child had scribbled in. There is the woman he spoke of.*

pre·po·si·tion² (prē′pə zish′ən), *v.t.* to position in advance or beforehand: *to preposition troops in anticipated trouble spots.* Also, **pre′-po·si′tion.** [1960–65; PRE- + POSITION]

preposi′tional phrase′, *Gram.* a phrase consisting

CONCISE PRONUNCIATION KEY: *act, cāpe, dâre, pärt; set, ēqual; if, īce; ox, ōver, ôrder, oil, bŏŏk, bōōt, out; up, ûrge; child; sing; shoe; thin, that;* zh as in *treasure.* ə = *a* as in *alone, e* as in *system, i* as in *easily, o* as in *gallop, u* as in *circus;* ᵊ as in *fire* (fīᵊr), *hour* (ouᵊr). l and n can serve as syllabic consonants, as in *cradle* (krād′l), and *button* (but′n). See the full key inside the front cover.

pre′ex·press′, *v.t.*
pre′ex·pres′sion, *n.*
pre′ex·pres′sive, *adj.*
pre′ex·tend′, *v.*
pre′ex·ten′sive, *adj.;* **-ly,** *adv.*
pre′ex·tent′, *n.*
pre′ex·tinc′tion, *n.*
pre′ex·tin′guish, *v.t.*
pre′ex·tin′guish·ment, *n.*
pre′ex·tract′, *v.t.*
pre′ex·trac′tion, *n.*
pre·fade′, *v.t.,* **-fad·ed, -fad·ing.**
pre′fa·mil′iar, *adj.;* **-ly,** *adv.*
pre′fa·mil′i·ar′i·ty, *n.*
pre·fa′mous, *adj.;* **-ly,** *adv.*
pre·fas′cist, *adj., n.*
pre·fash′ion, *v.t., n.*
pre·fash′ioned, *adj.*
pre·fa′vor, *n., v.t.*
pre·fa′vor·a·ble, *adj.;* **-bly,** *adv.*
pre·fa′vor·ite, *n., adj.*
pre·fear′ful, *adj.;* **-ly,** *adv.*
pre·feast′, *n.*
pre′fe·cun·da′tion, *n.*
pre′fer·men·ta′tion, *n.*
pre·fer′rous, *adj.*
pre·fer′tile, *adj.*
pre′fer·til′i·ty, *n.*
pre′fer·ti·li·za′tion, *n.*
pre·fer′ti·lize′, *v.t.,* **-lized, -liz·ing.**
pre·fes′ti·val, *n.*
pre·feu′dal, *adj.*
pre·feu′dal·ism, *n.*
pre·fight′, *adj.*
pre·file′, *v.t.,* **-filed, -fil·ing.**
pre·fill′er, *n.*
pre·fil′ter, *n.*
pre′fi·nance′, *v.t.,* **-nanced, -nanc·ing.**
pre′fi·nan′cial, *adj.*
pre·fin′ish, *v.t., n.*
pre·flag′el·late′, *adj.*
pre·flag′el·lat′ed, *adj.*
pre·flame′, *adj.*
pre·fla′vor, *n., v.t.*
pre·flood′, *adj.*
pre·flow′er·ing, *adj.*
pre′for·bid′den, *adj.*
pre′for·give′, *v.t.* **-gave, -giv·en, -giv·ing.**
pre′for·give′ness, *n.*
pre·for′mat, *v.t.,* **-mat·ted, -mat·ting.**
pre·for′mu·late′, *v.t.,* **-lat·ed, -lat·ing.**
pre′for·mu·la′tion, *n.*
pre′foun·da′tion, *n.*
pre·found′er, *n.*
pre·frank′ness, *n.*
pre′fra·ter′nal, *adj.;* **-ly,** *adv.*
pre·fraud′, *n.*
pre′free′-trade′, *adj.*
pre·freeze′, *v.t.,* **-froze, -fro·zen, -freez·ing.**
pre-French′, *adj.*
pre·fresh′man, *n., pl.* **-men.**
pre·friend′ly, *adj.*
pre·friend′ship, *n.*
pre·fro′zen, *adj.*
pre′ful·fill′, *v.t.*
pre′ful·fill′ment, *n.*
pre·func′tion, *n.*
pre·func′tion·al, *adj.*
pre·fund′, *v.t.*
pre·fu′ner·al, *adj.*
pre·fur′lough, *n.*
pre·fur′nish, *v.t.*
pre·gain′, *v.t.*
pre·gain′er, *n.*
pre·gal′va·nize′, *v.t.,* **-nized, -niz·ing.**
pre·game′, *adj.*
pre′gan·gli·on′ic, *adj.*
pre·gas′tru·lar, *adj.*
pre·gath′er, *v.i.*
pre·gen′er·ate′, *v.t.,* **-at·ed, -at·ing.**
pre′gen·er·a′tion, *n.*
pre·gen′i·tal, *adj.*
pre′ge·o·log′i·cal, *adj.*
pre-Geor′gian, *adj.*
pre-Ger′man, *adj., n.*
pre′-Ger·man′ic, *adj., n.*
pre·girl′hood, *n.*
pre-Goth′ic, *adj., n.*
pre·grade′, *v.t.,* **-grad·ed, -grad·ing,** *n.*
pre′grad·u·a′tion, *n.*
pre·gran′ite, *n.*
pre·gra·nit′ic, *adj.*
pre′grat·i·fi·ca′tion, *n.*
pre·grat′i·fy′, *v.t.,* **-fied, -fy·ing.**
pre-Greek′, *adj., n.*
pre·greet′, *v.t.*
pre·griev′ance, *n.*
pre·growth′, *n.*
pre′guar·an·tee′, *n., v.t.,* **-teed, -tee·ing.**
pre·guar′an·tor′, *n.*
pre·guard′, *v.t.*
pre·guess′, *n., v.*
pre·guid′ance, *n.*
pre·guide′, *v.t.,* **-guid·ed, -guid·ing.**
pre·guilt′, *n.*
pre-Han′, *adj.*
pre·hand′i·cap′, *n., v.t.,* **-capped, -cap·ping.**
pre·han′dle, *v.t.,* **-dled, -dling.**
pre·hard′en, *v.t.*
pre′har·mo′ni·ous, *adj.;* **-ly,** *adv.;* **-ness,** *n.*
pre·har′mo·ny, *n.*
pre·har′vest, *n.*
pre·ha′tred, *n.*
pre·haz′ard, *adj.*
pre·heal′, *v.t.*
pre·hear′ing, *n.*
pre-He′brew, *adj., n.*
pre′-Hel·len′ic, *adj.*
pre′hem·i·ple′gic, *adj.*
pre·hes′i·tan·cy, *n., pl.* **-cies.**
pre·hes′i·tate′, *v.i.,* **-tat·ed, -tat·ing.**
pre′hes·i·ta′tion, *n.*
pre′hex·am′er·al, *adj.*
pre′-Hi·er·o·nym′i·an, *adj.*
pre′-Hi·er·o·nym′ic, *adj.*
pre·hir′ing, *adj.*

of a preposition, its object, which is usually a noun or a pronoun, and any modifiers of the object, as *in the gray desk I use.* [1960–65]

preposi′tional verb′, *Gram.* a combination of verb and preposition, often with idiomatic meaning, differing from other phrasal verbs in that an object must always follow the preposition, as *take after* in *The children take after their mother.* Cf. **phrasal verb.** [1960–65]

pre•pos•i•tive (prē poz′i tiv), *Gram.* —*adj.* **1.** (of a word) placed before another word to modify it or to show its relation to other parts of the sentence. In *red book, red* is a prepositive adjective. *John's* in *John's book* is a prepositive genitive. —*n.* **2.** a word placed before another as a modifier or to show its relation to other parts of the sentence. [1575–85; < LL *praepositīvus* prefixed. See PREPOSITION, -IVE] —**pre•pos′i•tive•ly,** *adv.*

pre•pos•i•tor (prē poz′i tər), *n.* praepostor. Also, **pre•pos•tor** (prē pos′tər).

pre•pos•sess (prē′pə zes′), *v.t.* **1.** to possess or dominate mentally beforehand, as a prejudice does. **2.** to prejudice or bias, esp. favorably. **3.** to impress favorably beforehand or at the outset. [1605–15; PRE- + POSSESS]

pre•pos•sess•ing (prē′pə zes′ing), *adj.* that impresses favorably; engaging or attractive: *a confident and prepossessing young man.* [1635–45; PREPOSSESS + -ING[2]] —**pre′pos•sess′ing•ly,** *adv.* —**pre′pos•sess′•ing•ness,** *n.*

pre•pos•ses•sion (prē′pə zesh′ən), *n.* **1.** the state of being prepossessed. **2.** a prejudice, esp. one in favor of a person or thing. [1640–50; PRE- + POSSESSION] —**pre′pos•ses′sion•ar′y,** *adj.*
—**Syn. 2.** predilection, liking, bias, interest.

pre•pos•ter•ous (pri pos′tər əs, -trəs), *adj.* completely contrary to nature, reason, or common sense; absurd; senseless; utterly foolish: *a preposterous tale.* [1535–45; < L *praeposterus* with the hinder part foremost. See PRE-, POSTERIOR, -OUS] —**pre•pos′ter•ous•ly,** *adv.* —**pre•pos′ter•ous•ness,** *n.*
—**Syn.** unreasonable, excessive, ridiculous. See **absurd.**

pre•po•ten•cy (prē pōt′n sē), *n. Genetics.* the ability of one parent to impress its hereditary characters on its progeny because it possesses more homozygous, dominant, or epistatic genes. [1640–50 for general sense "predominance"; < L *praepotentia.* See PREPOTENT, -ENCY]

pre•po•tent (prē pōt′nt), *adj.* **1.** preeminent in power, authority, or influence; predominant: *a prepotent name in the oil business.* **2.** *Genetics.* noting, pertaining to, or having prepotency. [1375–1425; late ME < L *praepotent-* (s. of *praepotēns*), prp. of *praeposse* to have greater power. See PRE-, POTENT[1]] —**pre•po′tent•ly,** *adv.*

prep•py (prep′ē), *n., pl.* **-pies,** *adj.,* **-pi•er, -pi•est.** —*n.* **1.** a person who is a student at or a graduate of a preparatory school. **2.** a person who favors or is viewed as favoring clothing style or behavior associated with traditional preparatory schools. —*adj.* **3.** of, pertaining to, or characteristic of preparatory schools or their students. **4.** of, pertaining to, characteristic of, or being a style in dress or mode of behavior of a preppy. Also **prep′pie.** [1895–1900, *Amer.*; PREP + -Y[1], -Y[2]]

pre•pran•di•al (prē pran′dē əl), *adj.* before a meal, esp. before dinner; anteprandial: *a preprandial apéritif.* [1815–25; PRE- + PRANDIAL]

pre•pref•er•ence (prē pref′ər əns, -pref′rəns), *adj. Brit.* taking precedence over preference shares in dividends or in capital distribution at the time of dissolution or liquidation of a business. [1880–85; PRE- + PREFERENCE]

pre•press (prē′pres′), *adj. Print.* **1.** of or pertaining to all operations other than the preparation of the press that are required in preparing a job for printing. **2.** (of a proof) pulled from a finished plate prior to or in lieu of a press proof. [PRE- + PRESS[1]]

pre•pri•ma•ry (prē prī′mer ē, -mə rē), *adj. Politics.* preceding a primary election: *preprimary endorsement.* [PRE- + PRIMARY]

CONCISE ETYMOLOGY KEY: <, descended or borrowed from; >, whence; b., blend of, blended; c., cognate with; cf., compare; deriv., derivative; equiv., equivalent; imit., imitative; obl., oblique; r., replacing; s., stem; sp., spelling, spelled; resp., respelling, respelled; trans., translation; ?, origin unknown; *, unattested; ‡, probably earlier than. See the full key inside the front cover.

pre•print (*n.* prē′print′; *v.* prē print′), *n.* **1.** an advance printing, usually of a portion of a book or of an article in a periodical. —*v.t.* **2.** to print for future use. **3.** to print a preprint. [1885–90; PRE- + PRINT]

pre•proc•es•sor (prē′pros′es ər, -ə sər *or, esp. Brit.,* -prō′ses ər, -sə sər), *n. Computers.* a program that performs some type of processing, as organization of data or preliminary computation, in advance of another program that will perform most of the processing. [1965–70; PRE- + PROCESSOR]

pre•pro•duc•tion (prē′prə duk′shən), *n.* **1.** *Motion Pictures.* the steps necessary to prepare a film for production, as casting, choosing locations, and designing sets and costumes. —*adj.* **2.** occurring before production. [1935–40; PRE- + PRODUCTION]

pre•pro•fes•sion•al (prē′prə fesh′ə nl), *adj.* of or pertaining to the time preceding one's concentrated study or practice of a profession: *preprofessional training.* [1945–50; PRE- + PROFESSIONAL]

pre•pro•gram (prē prō′gram, -grəm), *v.t.,* **-grammed** or **-gramed, -gram•ming** or **-gram•ing.** to program in advance: *to preprogram a manufacturing process.* [1960–65; PRE- + PROGRAM]

prep′ school′. See **preparatory school.** [1890–95]

pre•psy•chot•ic (prē′sī kot′ik), *adj.* exhibiting behavior that indicates the approach of a psychotic reaction. [1925–30; PRE- + PSYCHOTIC]

pre•pu•ber•ty (prē pyōō′bər tē), *n. Physiol.* the period of life just prior to sexual maturation. [1920–25; PRE- + PUBERTY] —**pre•pu′ber•tal, pre•pu′ber•al,** *adj.* —**pre•pu′ber•tal•ly, pre•pu′ber•al•ly,** *adv.*

pre•pu•bes•cent (prē′pyōō bes′ənt), *adj.* **1.** of or pertaining to the years immediately preceding puberty, prepubertal. —*n.* **2.** a prepubescent boy or girl. [1900–05; PRE- + PUBESCENT] —**pre′pu•bes′cence,** *n.*

pre•pub•li•ca•tion (prē′pub li kā′shən), *n.* **1.** the period immediately preceding the publication of a book. —*adj.* **2.** of, pertaining to, or characteristic of such a period: *a prepublication party for the author.* [1920–25; PRE- + PUBLICATION]

pre•pub•lish (prē pub′lish), *v.t.* to publish in advance of a scheduled date. [1970–75; PRE- + PUBLISH]

pre•puce (prē′pyōōs), *n. Anat.* **1.** the fold of skin that covers the head of the penis; foreskin. **2.** a similar covering of the clitoris. [1350–1400; ME < MF < L *praepūtium*] —**pre•pu•tial** (pri pyōō′shəl), *adj.*

pre•pu•pa (prē pyōō′pə), *n., pl.* **-pae** (-pē), **-pas.** an insect in the nonfeeding, inactive stage between the larval period and the pupal period. [1920–25; < NL; see PRE-, PUPA] —**pre•pu′pal,** *adj.*

pre•quel (prē′kwəl), *n.* a literary, dramatic, or filmic work that prefigures a later work, as by portraying the same characters at a younger age. [1970–75; PRE- + (SE)QUEL]

Pre-Raph•a•el•ite (prē raf′ē ə līt′, -rā′fē-), *n.* **1.** any of a group of English artists (**Pre-Raph′aelite Broth′erhood**) formed in 1848, and including Holman Hunt, John Everett Millais, and Dante Gabriel Rossetti, who aimed to revive the style and spirit of the Italian artists before the time of Raphael. —*adj.* **2.** of, pertaining to, or characteristic of the Pre-Raphaelites. [1840–50; PRE- + RAPHAEL + -ITE[1]] —**Pre-Raph′a•el•it′ism,** *n.*

pre•re•cord (prē′ri kôrd′), *v.t.* **1.** to record beforehand or in advance. **2.** to record (a radio show, television program, etc.) prior to an actual broadcast or showing. **3.** *Motion Pictures.* to record (music, sound effects, etc.) before filming begins, as to facilitate synchronization. [1935–40; PRE- + RECORD]

pre•re•cord•ed (prē′ri kôr′did), *adj.* containing previously recorded information: *a prerecorded audiotape; a prerecorded videocassette.* Cf. **blank** (def. 5). [1955–60; PRERECORD + -ED[2]]

pre•re•lease (prē′ri lēs′), *n.* **1.** something released beforehand, as a movie shown before its scheduled premiere. —*adj.* **2.** of or pertaining to a period prior to an official release: *prerelease photos of a new car; convicts housed in a prerelease center.* [1925–30; PRE- + RELEASE]

pre•req•ui•site (pri rek′wə zit, prē-), *adj.* **1.** required beforehand: *a prerequisite fund of knowledge.* —*n.* **2.** something prerequisite: *A visa is still a prerequisite for travel in many countries.* [1625–35; PRE- + REQUISITE]
—**Syn. 2.** requirement, requisite, essential, precondition.

pre•rog•a•tive (pri rog′ə tiv, pə rog′-), *n.* **1.** an exclusive right, privilege, etc., exercised by virtue of rank, office, or the like: *the prerogatives of a senator.* **2.** a right, privilege, etc., limited to a specific person or to persons of a particular category: *It was the teacher's prerogative to stop the discussion.* **3.** a power, immunity, or the like restricted to a sovereign government or its representative: *The royal prerogative exempts the king from taxation.* **4.** *Obs.* precedence. —*adj.* **5.** having or exercising a prerogative. **6.** pertaining to, characteristic of, or existing by virtue of a prerogative. [1350–1400; ME < L *praerogātīvus* (adj.) voting first, *praerogātīva* (n. use of fem. of adj.) tribe or century with right to vote first. See PRE-, INTERROGATIVE]
—**Syn. 1.** See **privilege.**

prerog′ative court′, **1.** a former ecclesiastical court in England and Ireland for the trial of certain testamentary cases. **2.** (formerly) the court of probate in New Jersey. [1595–1605]

Pres (pres, prez), *n.* a male given name, form of **Presley.**

Pres., **1.** Presbyterian. **2.** President.

pres., **1.** present. **2.** presidency. **3.** president.

pre•sa (prā′sə; *It.* pre′zä), *n., pl.* **-se** (-sā; *It.* -ze). a mark, as :S:, +, or ※, used in a canon, round, etc., to indicate where the successive voice parts are to take up the theme. [1715–25; < It: lit., a taking up, fem. of *preso,* ptp. of *prendere* to take < L *prehendere* to seize; see PREHENSION]

pres•age (*n.* pres′ij; *v.* pres′ij, pri sāj′), *n., v.,* **-aged, -ag•ing.** —*n.* **1.** a presentiment or foreboding. **2.** something that portends or foreshadows a future event; an omen, prognostic, or warning indication. **3.** prophetic significance; augury. **4.** foresight; prescience. **5.** *Archaic.* a forecast or prediction. —*v.t.* **6.** to have a presentiment of. **7.** to portend, foreshow, or foreshadow: *The incidents may presage war.* **8.** to forecast; predict. —*v.i.* **9.** to make a prediction. **10.** *Archaic.* to have a presentiment. [1350–1400; ME (n.) < MF *presage* < L *praesāgium* presentiment, forewarning, equiv. to *praesāg(us)* having a foreboding (*prae-* PRE- + *sāgus* prophetic; cf. SAGACIOUS) + *-ium* -IUM] —**pres′age•ful,** *adj.* —**pres′age•ful•ly,** *adv.* —**pres′ag•er,** *n.*
—**Syn. 1.** foreshadowing, indication, premonition. **2.** portent, sign, token.

pre•sale (prē′sāl′), *n.* a sale held in advance of an advertised sale, as for select customers. [PRE- + SALE]

pre•sanc•ti•fied (prē sangk′tə fīd′), *adj.* (of the Eucharistic elements) consecrated at a previous Mass. [1850–55; trans. of ML *praesanctificātus.* See PRE-, SANCTIFIED] —**pre•sanc′ti•fi•ca′tion,** *n.*

Presb., Presbyterian.

pres•by•cu•sia (prez′bi kyōō′zhə, -zhē ə, -zē ə, pres′-), *n. Med.* impaired hearing due to old age. [1885–90; < NL < Gk *presby-* (comb. form of *présbys* old, old man) + (*á*)*kous(is)* hearing (*akoú(ein)* to hear + *-sis* -SIS) + *-ia* -IA]

pres•by•o•pi•a (prez′bē ō′pē ə, pres′-), *n. Ophthalm.* farsightedness due to ciliary muscle weakness and loss of elasticity in the crystalline lens. [1785–95; < Gk *presby-* (comb. form of *présbys* old, old man) + -OPIA] —**pres•by•op•ic** (prez′bē op′ik, pres′-), *adj.*

Presbyt., Presbyterian.

pres•by•ter (prez′bi tər, pres′-), *n.* **1.** (in the early Christian church) an office bearer who exercised teaching, priestly, and administrative functions. **2.** (in hierarchical churches) a priest. **3.** an elder in a Presbyterian church. [1590–1600; < LL, n. use of the adj.: older < Gk *presbýteros,* equiv. to *présby(s)* old + *-teros* comp. suffix] —**pres•byt•er•al** (prez bit′ər əl, pres-), *adj.*

pres•byt•er•ate (prez bit′ər it, -ə rāt′, pres-), *n.* **1.** the office of a presbyter or elder. **2.** a body of presbyters or elders. [1635–45; < ML *presbyterātus.* See PRESBYTER, -ATE[3]]

pres•by•te•ri•al (prez′bi tēr′ē əl, pres′-), *adj.* **1.** of or pertaining to a presbytery. **2.** presbyterian (def. 1). [1585–95; PRESBYTERY + -AL[1]]

pres•by•te•ri•an (prez′bi tēr′ē ən, pres′-), *adj.* **1.** pertaining to or based on the principle of ecclesiastical government by presbyters or presbyteries. **2.** (*cap.*) designating or pertaining to various churches having this form of government and professing more or less modified forms of Calvinism. —*n.* **3.** (*cap.*) a member of

pre′-His•pan′ic, *adj.*
pre•hold′er, *n.*
pre•hold′ing, *n.*
pre•hol′i•day′, *adj.*
pre′-Ho•mer′ic, *adj.*
pre•hos′tile, *adj.*
pre′hos•til′i•ty, *n., pl.* **-ties.**
pre•hu′mor, *n., v.t.*
pre•hun′ger, *n.*
pre′hyp•not′ic, *adj.*
pre′i•de′a, *n.*
pre′i•den′ti•fi•ca′tion, *n.*
pre′i•den′ti•fy′, *v.t.,* **-fied, -fy•ing.**
pre•il′i•um, *n., pl.* **-i•a.**
pre′il•lu′mi•nate′, *v.t.*
pre′il•lu′mi•na′tion, *n.*
pre•il′lus•trate′, *v.t.,* **-trat•ed, -trat•ing.**
pre′il•lus•tra′tion, *n.*
pre•im′age, *n.*
pre′im•ag′i•nar′y, *adj.*
pre′im•ag′ine, *v.t.,* **-ined, -in•ing.**
pre′im•bibe′, *v.t.,* **-bibed, -bib•ing.**
pre′im•bue′, *v.t.,* **-bued, -bu•ing.**
pre•im′i•tate′, *v.t.,* **-tat•ed, -tat•ing.**
pre′im•i•ta′tion, *n.*
pre•im′i•ta′tive, *adj.*
pre′im•mi•gra′tion, *n.*
pre′im•pair′, *v.t.*
pre′im•pair′ment, *n.*
pre′im•part′, *v.t.*
pre′im•pe′ri•al, *adj.*
pre′im•port′, *v.t.*
pre•im′port, *n.*
pre′im•por′tance, *n.*
pre′im•por′tant, *adj.;* **-ly,** *adv.*
pre′im•por•ta′tion, *n.*
pre′im•pose′, *v.t.,* **-posed, -pos•ing.**
pre′im•po•si′tion, *n.*
pre′im•press′, *v.t.*
pre′im•pres′sion, *n.*
pre′im•pres′sive, *adj.*
pre′im•prove′, *v.t.,* **-proved, -prov•ing.**
pre′im•prove′ment, *n.*
pre′in•au′gu•ral, *adj.*
pre′in•au′gu•rate′, *v.t.,* **-rat•ed, -rat•ing.**
pre′in•cen′tive, *n.*
pre′in•clude′, *v.t.,* **-clud•ed, -clud•ing.**
pre′in•clu′sion, *n.*
pre′in•cor′po•rate′, *v.t.,* **-rat•ed, -rat•ing.**
pre′in•cor′po•rate, *adj.*
pre′in•cor′po•ra′tion, *n.*
pre•in′crease, *n.*
pre′in•crease′, *v.t.,* **-creased, -creas•ing.**
pre′in•debt′ed, *adj.;* **-ness,** *n.*
pre′in•dem′ni•fi•ca′tion, *n.*
pre′in•dem′ni•fy′, *v.t.,* **-fied, -fy•ing.**
pre′in•dem′ni•ty, *n., pl.* **-ties.**
pre′in•de•pend′ence, *n.*
pre′in•de•pend′ent, *adj.;* **-ly,** *adv.*
pre-In′di•an, *n., adj.*
pre′in•dis•pose′, *v.t.,* **-posed, -pos•ing.**
pre′in•dis•po•si′tion, *n.*
pre′in•duce′, *v.t.,* **-duced, -duc•ing.**
pre′in•duce′ment, *n.*
pre′in•duc′tion, *n.*
pre′in•duc′tive, *adj.*
pre′in•dulge′, *v.t.,* **-dulged, -dulg•ing.**
pre′in•dul′gence, *n.*
pre′in•dul′gent, *adj.*
pre′in•dus′tri•al, *adj.*
pre•in′dus•try, *n., adj.*
pre′in•fect′, *v.t.*
pre′in•fec′tion, *n.*
pre′in•fer′, *v.t.,* **-ferred, -fer•ring.**
pre•in′fer•ence, *n.*
pre′in•fla′tion•ar′y, *adj.*
pre′in•flec′tion, *n.*
pre′in•flec′tion•al, *adj.*
pre′in•flict′, *v.t.*
pre′in•flic′tion, *n.*
pre•in′flu•ence, *n.*
pre′in•hab′it, *v.t.*
pre′in•hab′it•ant, *n.*
pre′in•hab′i•ta′tion, *n.*
pre′in•here′, *v.i.,* **-hered, -her•ing.**
pre′in•her′it, *v.t.*
pre′in•her′it•ance, *n.*
pre′in•i′tial, *v.t.*
pre′in•i′ti•ate′, *v.t.,* **-at•ed, -at•ing.**
pre′in•i′ti•ate, *n.*
pre′in•i′ti•a′tion, *n.*
pre′in•ju′ri•ous, *adj.*
pre′in•qui•si′tion, *n.*
pre′in•scribe′, *v.t.,* **-scribed, -scrib•ing.**
pre′in•scrip′tion, *n.*
pre′in•sert′, *v.t.*
pre′in•ser′tion, *n.*
pre′in•sin′u•ate′, *v.,* **-at•ed, -at•ing.**
pre′in•sin′u•at′ing•ly, *adv.*
pre′in•sin′u•a′tion, *n.*
pre′in•sin′u•a′tive, *adj.*
pre′in•spect′, *v.t.*
pre′in•spec′tion, *n.*
pre′in•spec′tor, *n.*
pre′in•spire′, *v.t.,* **-spired, -spir•ing.**
pre′in•stall′, *v.t.*
pre′in•stal•la′tion, *n.*
pre′in•still′, *v.t.*
pre′in•stil•la′tion, *n.*
pre′in•struct′, *v.t.*
pre′in•struc′tion, *n.*
pre•in′su•late′, *v.t.,* **-lat•ed, -lat•ing.**
pre′in•su•la′tion, *n.*
pre′in•sult′, *v.t.*
pre′in•sur′ance, *n.*
pre′in•sure′, *v.t.,* **-sured, -sur•ing.**

a Presbyterian church; a person who supports Presbyterianism. [1635–45; PRESBYTERY + -AN]

Pres·by·te·ri·an·ism (prez′bi tēr′ē ə niz′əm, pres′-), *n.* **1.** church government by presbyters or elders, equal in rank and organized into graded administrative courts. **2.** the doctrines of Presbyterian churches. [1635–45; PRESBYTERIAN + -ISM]

pres·by·ter·y (prez′bi ter′ē, pres′-), *n., pl.* **-ter·ies.** **1.** a body of presbyters or elders. **2.** (in Presbyterian churches) an ecclesiastical court consisting of all the ministers and one or two presbyters from each congregation in a district. **3.** the churches under the jurisdiction of a presbytery. **4.** the part of a church appropriated to the clergy. **5.** *Rom. Cath. Ch.* a rectory. [1375–1425; late ME *presbetory, presbitory* priests' bench, for LL *presbyterium* group of elders < Gk *presbytérion.* See PRESBYTER, -Y[3]]

pre·school (*adj.* prē′skōōl′; *n.* prē′skōōl′), *adj.* **1.** of, pertaining to, or intended for a child between infancy and school age: *new methods of preschool education.* —*n.* **2.** a school or nursery for preschool children. [1920–25; PRE- + SCHOOL[1]]

pre·school·er (prē′skōō′lər), *n.* a child below the official school starting age, usually a child up to age five. [1945–50; PRESCHOOL + -ER[1]]

pre·science (presh′əns, -ē əns, prē′shəns, -shē əns), *n.* knowledge of things before they exist or happen; foreknowledge; foresight. [1325–75; ME < LL *praescientia* foreknowledge. See PRE-, SCIENCE] —**pre′scient,** *adj.* —**pre′scient·ly,** *adv.*

pre·scind (pri sind′), *v.t.* **1.** to separate or single out in thought; abstract. **2.** to cut off, terminate, or remove. —*v.i.* **3.** to withdraw one's attention (usually fol. by *from*). **4.** to turn aside in thought. [1630–40; < L *praescindere* to cut off in front. See PRE-, RESCIND]

pre·score (prē skôr′, -skōr′), *v.t.,* **-scored, -scor·ing.** to record the sound of (a motion picture) before filming. [1935–40; PRE- + SCORE]

Pres·cott (pres′kət, -kot), *n.* **1. William,** 1726–95, American Revolutionary military leader. **2. William Hick·ling** (hik′ling), 1796–1859, U.S. historian (grandson of William Prescott). **3.** a city in central Arizona. 20,055.

pre·screen (prē skrēn′), *v.t.* to screen in advance; select before a more detailed selecting process. [1965–70; PRE- + SCREEN]

pre·scribe (pri skrīb′), *v.,* **-scribed, -scrib·ing.** —*v.t.* **1.** to lay down, in writing or otherwise, as a rule or a course of action to be followed; appoint, ordain, or enjoin. **2.** *Med.* to designate or order the use of (a medicine, remedy, treatment, etc.). —*v.i.* **3.** to lay down rules; direct; dictate. **4.** *Med.* to designate remedies, treatment, etc., to be used. **5.** *Law.* to claim a right or title by virtue of long use and enjoyment; make a prescriptive claim. (usually fol. by *for* or *to*). [1425–75; late ME < L *praescrībere* to direct in writing, lit., to write before or above, equiv. to *prae-* PRE- + *scrībere* to write; see SCRIBE[1], PRESCRIPTION] —**pre·scrib′a·ble,** *adj.* —**pre·scrib′er,** *n.*
—**Syn. 1.** direct, dictate, decree.

prescribed′ cut′, *Ecol.* See **allowable cut.**

pre·script (*adj.* pri skript′, prē′skript; *n.* prē′skript), *adj.* **1.** prescribed. —*n.* **2.** that which is prescribed or laid down, as a rule, precept, or order. [1425–75; late ME (adj.) < L *praescrīptus* ptp. of *praescrībere* to PRESCRIBE. See PRE-, SCRIPT]

pre·scrip·ti·ble (pri skrip′tə bəl), *adj.* **1.** subject to or suitable for prescription. **2.** depending on or derived from prescription, as a claim or right. [1535–45; < ML *prescriptibilis.* See PRESCRIPTION, -IBLE] —**pre·scrip′ti·bil′i·ty,** *n.*

pre·scrip·tion (pri skrip′shən), *n.* **1.** *Med.* **a.** a direction, usually written, by the physician to the pharmacist for the preparation and use of a medicine or remedy. **b.** the medicine prescribed: *Take this prescription three times a day.* **2.** an act of prescribing. **3.** that which is prescribed. **4.** *Law.* **a.** a long or immemorial use of some right with respect to a thing so as to give a right to continue such use. **b.** the process of acquiring rights by uninterrupted assertion of the right over a long period of time. —*adj.* **5.** (of drugs) sold only upon medical prescription; ethical. Cf. **over-the-counter** (def. 2). [1250–1300; ME < ML *praescrīptiōn-* (s. of *praescrīptiō*) legal possession (of property), law, order, lit., a writing before, hence, a heading on a document. See PRESCRIPT, -ION]

pre·scrip·tive (pri skrip′tiv), *adj.* **1.** that prescribes; giving directions or injunctions: *a prescriptive letter from an anxious father.* **2.** depending on or arising from effective legal prescription, as a right or title established by a long unchallenged tenure. [1740–50; PRESCRIPT + -IVE, modeled on *descriptive,* etc.] —**pre·scrip′tive·ly,** *adv.* —**pre·scrip′tive·ness,** *n.*

prescrip′tive gram′mar, 1. an approach to grammar that is concerned with establishing norms of correct and incorrect usage and formulating rules based on these norms to be followed by users of the language. **2.** a set of grammatical rules based on such an approach. [1930–35]

pre·scrip·tiv·ist (pri skrip′tə vist), *n.* **1.** a writer, teacher, or supporter of prescriptive grammar. —*adj.* **2.** of, pertaining to, or based on prescriptive grammar. [1950–55; PRESCRIPTIVE + -IST] —**pre·scrip′tiv·ism,** *n.*

pre·scu·tum (prē skyōō′təm), *n., pl.* **-ta** (-tə), **-tums.** the anterior dorsal sclerite of a thoracic segment of an insect. [< NL; see PRE-, SCUTUM]

pre·se·lect (prē′si lekt′), *v.t.* to select in advance; choose beforehand. [1860–65; PRE- + SELECT] —**pre′se·lec′tion,** *n.*

pre·se·lec·tor (prē′si lek′tər), *n. Radio.* a preamplifier between the antenna and receiving circuit, used to improve reception. [1925–30; PRESELECT + -OR[2]]

pre·sell (prē sel′), *v.t.,* **-sold, -sell·ing.** to sell in advance, as before manufacture or construction: *to presell a planned house.* [1945–50; PRE- + SELL[1]]

pres·ence (prez′əns), *n.* **1.** the state or fact of being present, as with others or in a place. **2.** attendance or company: *Your presence is requested.* **3.** immediate vicinity; proximity: *in the presence of witnesses.* **4.** the military or economic power of a country as reflected abroad by the stationing of its troops, sale of its goods, etc.: *the American military presence in Europe; the Japanese presence in the U.S. consumer market.* **5.** *Chiefly Brit.* the immediate personal vicinity of a great personage giving audience or reception: *summoned to her presence.* **6.** the ability to project a sense of ease, poise, or self-assurance, esp. the quality or manner of a person's bearing before an audience: *The speaker had a good deal of stage presence.* **7.** personal appearance or bearing, esp. of a dignified or imposing kind: *a man of fine presence.* **8.** a person, esp. of noteworthy appearance or compelling personality: *He is a real presence, even at a private party.* **9.** a divine or supernatural spirit felt to be present: *He felt a presence with him in the room.* **10.** *Brit. Obs.* See **presence chamber.** [1300–50; ME < MF < L *praesentia.* See PRESENT[1], -ENCE]
—**Syn. 3.** neighborhood. **6.** carriage, mien. —**Ant. 1.** absence.

pres′ence cham′ber, *Chiefly Brit.* the special room in which a great personage, as a sovereign, receives guests, holds audiences, etc. [1555–65]

pres′ence of mind′, a calm state of mind that allows one to think clearly or act effectively in an emergency. [1655–65]

pre·se·nile (prē sē′nīl, -nil, -sen′il), *adj.* pertaining to or exhibiting the characteristics of presenility; prematurely old. [1895–1900; PRE- + SENILE]

pre·se·nil·i·ty (prē′si nil′i tē), *n.* premature old age. [1895–1900; PRE- + SENILITY]

pres·ent[1] (prez′ənt), *adj.* **1.** being, existing, or occurring at this time or now; current: *the present ruler.* **2.** at this time; at hand; immediate: *articles for present use.* **3.** *Gram.* **a.** noting an action or state occurring at the moment of speaking. *Knows* is a present form in *He knows that.* **b.** noting or pertaining to a tense or other verb formation with such meaning. **4.** being with one or others or in the specified or understood place: *to be present at the wedding.* **5.** being here: *Is everyone present?* **6.** existing or occurring in a place, thing, combination, or the like: *Carbon is present in many minerals.* **7.** being actually here or under consideration: *the present document; the present topic.* **8.** being before the mind. **9.** *Obs.* mentally alert and calm, esp. in emergencies. **10.** *Obs.* immediate or instant. —*n.* **11.** the present time. **12.** *Gram.* **a.** the present tense. **b.** a verb formation or construction with present meaning. **c.** a form in the present. **13. presents,** *Law.* the present writings, or this document, used in a deed of conveyance, a lease, etc., to denote the document itself: *Know all men by these presents.* **14.** *Obs.* the matter in hand. **15. at present,** at the present time or moment; now: *There are no job openings here at present.* **16. for the present,** for now; temporarily: *For the present, we must be content with matters as they stand.* [1250–1300; (adj.) ME < OF < L *praesent-* (s. of *praesēns*) prp. of *praeësse* to be present, before others, i.e., to preside, be in charge; (n.) ME: presence, spatial or temporal present; partly deriv. of the adj., partly < OF. See PRE-, IS, -ENT] —**pres′ent·ness,** *n.*
—**Syn. 1.** extant. See **current.** —**Ant. 1.** absent.

pre·sent[2] (*v.* pri zent′; *n.* prez′ənt), *v.t.* **1.** to furnish or endow with a gift or the like, esp. by formal act: *to present someone with a gold watch.* **2.** to bring, offer, or give, often in a formal or ceremonious way: *to present one's card.* **3.** afford or furnish (an opportunity, possibility, etc.). **4.** to hand over or submit, as a bill or a check, for payment: *The waiter presented our bill for lunch.* **5.** to introduce (a person) to another, esp. in a formal manner: *Mrs. Smith, may I present Mr. Jones?* **6.** to bring before or introduce to the public: *to present a new play.* **7.** to come to show (oneself) before a person, in or at a place, etc. **8.** to show or exhibit: *This theater will present films on a larger screen.* **9.** to bring forth or render for or before another or others; offer for consideration: *to present an alternative plan.* **10.** to set forth in words; frame or articulate: *to present arguments.* **11.** to represent, impersonate, or act, as on the stage. **12.** to direct, point, or turn (something) to something or someone: *He presented his back to the audience.* **13.** to level or aim (a weapon, esp. a firearm). **14.** *Law.* **a.** to bring against, as a formal charge against a person. **b.** to bring formally to the notice of the proper authority, as an offense. **15.** *Eccles. Brit.* to offer or recommend (a member of the clergy) to the bishop for institution to a benefice. —*n.* **pres·ent 16.** a thing presented as a gift; gift: *Christmas presents.* [1175–1225; (n.) ME < OF, orig. in phrase *en present* in presence (see PRESENT[1]); (v.) ME *presenten* < OF *presenter* < ML *praesentāre* to give, show, present for approval, L: to exhibit (to the mind or senses), deriv. of *praesēns* PRESENT[1]]
—**Syn. 1.** bestow, donate. See **give. 2.** proffer. **3.** yield. **5.** See **introduce. 9.** introduce. **11.** enact. **16.** benefaction, grant, tip, gratuity. PRESENT, GIFT, DONATION, BONUS refer to something freely given. PRESENT and GIFT are both used of something given as an expression of affection, friendship, interest, or respect. PRESENT is the less formal; GIFT is generally used of something conferred (esp. with ceremony) on an individual, a group, or an institution: *a birthday present; a gift to a bride.* DONATION applies to an important gift, most often of money and usually of considerable size, though the term is often used to avoid the suggestion of charity in speaking of small gifts to or for the needy: *a donation to an endowment fund, to the Red Cross.* BONUS applies to something, again usually money, given in addition to what is due, esp. to employees who have worked for a long time or particularly well: *a bonus at the end of the year.*

pre·sent·a·ble (pri zen′tə bəl), *adj.* **1.** that may be presented. **2.** suitable or socially acceptable in appearance, dress, manners, etc., as for being introduced into society: *a presentable young man.* **3.** of sufficiently good, clothed, or clean appearance; fit to be seen: *Are you presentable now?* [1400–50; late ME; see PRESENT[2], -ABLE] —**pre·sent′a·bil′i·ty, pre·sent′a·ble·ness,** *n.* —**pre·sent′a·bly,** *adv.*
—**Syn. 2.** becoming, proper, acceptable.

present′ arms′, *Mil.* **1.** a position of salute in the manual of arms in which the rifle is held in both hands vertically in front of the body, with the muzzle upward and the trigger side forward. **2.** (for troops in formation not under arms) the hand salute. [1750–60]

pres·en·ta·tion (prez′ən tā′shən, prē′zen-), *n.* **1.** an act of presenting. **2.** the state of being presented. **3.** a social introduction, as of a person at court. **4.** an exhibition or performance, as of a play or film. **5.** offering, delivering, or bestowal, as of a gift. **6.** a gift. **7.** a demonstration, lecture, or welcoming speech. **8.** a manner or style of speaking, instructing, or putting oneself forward: *His presentation was very poor.* **9.** *Com.* the presentment of a bill, note, or the like. **10.** *Obstet.* **a.** the position of the fetus in the uterus during labor. **b.** the appearance of a particular part of the fetus at the cervix during labor: *a breech presentation.* **11.** *Eccles.* the act or the right of presenting a member of the clergy to the

CONCISE PRONUNCIATION KEY: act, cāpe, dâre, pärt; set, ēqual; *if,* ice; ox, ōver, ôrder, oil, bŏŏk, bōōt, out; up, ûrge; child; sing; shoe; thin, *that;* zh as in *treasure.* ə = *a* as in *alone, e* as in *system, i* as in *easily, o* as in *gallop, u* as in *circus;* ᵊ as in *fire* (fīᵊr), *hour* (ouᵊr). l and n can serve as syllabic consonants, as in *cradle* (krād′l), and *button* (but′n). See the full key inside the front cover.

pre′in·tel·lec′tu·al, *adj.;* **-ly,** *adv.*
pre′in·tel′li·gence, *n.*
pre′in·tel′li·gent, *adj.;* **-ly,** *adv.*
pre′in·tend′, *v.t.*
pre′in·ten′tion, *n.*
pre′in·ter·cede′, *v.i.,* **-ced·ed, -ced·ing.**
pre′in·ter·ces′sion, *n.*
pre·in′ter·change′, *n.*
pre·in′ter·course′, *n.*
pre·in′ter·est, *n., v.*
pre·in′ter′pret, *v.t.*
pre′in·ter′pre·ta′tion, *n.*
pre′in·ter′pre·ta′tive, *adj.*
pre·in′ter·view′, *n., v.t.*
pre·in′ti·mate, *adj.;* **-ly,** *adv.*
pre·in′ti·mate′, *v.t.,* **-mat·ed, -mat·ing.**
pre′in·ti·ma′tion, *n.*
pre′in·va′sion, *adj.*
pre′in·vent′, *v.t.*
pre′in·ven′tion, *n.*
pre′in·ven′tive, *adj.*
pre·in′ven·to′ry, *n., pl.* **-ries.**
pre′in·vest′, *v.t.*
pre′in·ves′ti·gate′, *v.,* **-gat·ed, -gat·ing.**
pre′in·ves′ti·ga′tion, *n.*
pre′in·ves′ti·ga′tor, *n.*
pre′in·vest′ment, *n.*
pre′in·vi·ta′tion, *n.*
pre′in·vite′, *v.t.,* **-vit·ed, -vit·ing.**
pre′in·vo·ca′tion, *n.*
pre′in·volve′, *v.t.,* **-volved, -volv·ing.**
pre′in·volve′ment, *n.*
pre·I′rish, *adj.*
pre′ir·ri·ga′tion, *n.*
pre′ir·ri·ga′tion·al, *adj.*
pre·Is′ra·el·ite′, *adj., n.*
pre·is′su·ance, *n.*
pre·is′sue, *n., v.t.,* **-sued, -su·ing.**
pre-Jew′ish, *adj.*
pre′jour·nal·is′tic, *adj.*
pre′ju·di′ci·a·ble, *adj.*
pre·jun′ior, *adj.*
pre′ju·ris·dic′tion, *n.*
pre′jus·ti·fi·ca′tion, *n.*
pre·jus′ti·fy, *v.t.,* **-fied, -fy·ing.**
pre′-Jus·tin′i·an, *adj.*
pre·ju′ve·nile, *adj.*
pre-Kant′i·an, *adj.*
pre·kin′der·gar′ten, *n., adj.*
pre·kin′dle, *v.t.,* **-dled, -dling.**
pre·knit′, *v.t.,* **-knit·ted** or **-knit, -knit·ting.**
pre·know′, *v.t.,* **-knew, -known, -know·ing.**
pre·knowl′edge, *n.*
pre′-Ko·ran′ic, *adj.*
pre·la′bel, *n., v.t.,* **-beled, -bel·ing** or (*esp. Brit.*) **-belled, -bel·ling.**
pre·la′bi·al, *adj.*
pre·la′bor, *n., v.i.*
pre·lac′te·al, *adj.*
pre·lan′guage, *adj.*
pre′la·ryn′go·scop′ic, *adj.*
pre-Lat′in, *adj., n.*
pre·law′ful, *adj.;* **-ly,** *adv.;* **-ness,** *n.*
pre·lec′ture, *n., adj., v.,* **-tured, -tur·ing.**
pre·le′gal, *adj.*
pre·leg′end, *n., adj.*
pre·leg′end·ar′y, *adj.*
pre·leg′is·la′tive, *adj.*
pre′li·a·bil′i·ty, *n., pl.* **-ties.**
pre·li′a·ble, *adj.*
pre·lib′er·al, *adj., n.;* **-ly,** *adv.*
pre′lib·er·al′i·ty, *n.*
pre·lib′er·ate′, *v.t.,* **-at·ed, -at·ing.**
pre′lib·er·a′tion, *n.*
pre·li′cense, *n., v.t.,* **-censed, -cens·ing.**
pre·life′, *adj.*
pre·lin′gual, *adj.;* **-ly,** *adv.*
pre′-Lin·nae′an, *adj.*
pre′-Lin·ne′an, *adj.*
pre·liq′ui·date′, *v.t.,* **-dat·ed, -dat·ing.**
pre′liq·ui·da′tion, *n.*
pre·lit′er·ar′y, *adj.*
pre·lit′er·a·ture, *n.*
pre·lith′ic, *adj.*
pre′lit·i·ga′tion, *n.*
pre·loan′, *n., v.*
pre·lo′cate, *v.,* **-cat·ed, -cat·ing.**
pre·log′i·cal, *adj.;* **-ly,** *adv.*
pre·loss′, *n.*
pre·lum′bar, *adj.*
pre·lunch′, *adj., n.*
pre-Lu′ther·an, *adj.*
pre′lux·u′ri·ous, *adj.;* **-ly,** *adv.;* **-ness,** *n.*
pre·mad′ness, *n.*
pre′main·tain′, *v.t.*
pre·main′te·nance, *n.*
pre·make′, *v.t.,* **-made, -mak·ing.**
pre·mak′er, *n.*
pre-Ma′lay, *adj.*
pre′-Ma·lay′an, *adj.*
pre′-Ma·lay′sian, *adj.*
pre′man·dib′u·lar, *adj.*
pre·man′hood, *n.*
pre′ma·ni′a·cal, *adj.*
pre·man′i·fest′, *v.*
pre′man·i·fes·ta′tion, *n.*
pre′man′kind′, *n.*
pre′man·u·fac′ture, *v.t.,* **-tured, -tur·ing.**
pre·mar′ket, *v.*
pre·mar′ket·ing, *adj.*
pre·mar′riage, *n.*
pre·mar′ry, *v.t.,* **-ried, -ry·ing.**
pre-Marx′i·an, *adj.*
pre·mas′ter·y, *n.*
pre·match′, *n., v.t.*
pre·mate′, *n., v.t.,* **-mat·ed, -mat·ing.**
pre′ma·te′ri·al, *adj.*
pre′ma·ter′ni·ty, *n.*
pre′mat·ri·mo′ni·al, *adj.;* **-ly,** *adv.*
pre·meas′ure, *v.t.,* **-ured, -ur·ing.**

bishop for institution to a benefice. [1350–1400; ME < LL *praesentātiōn-* (s. of *praesentātiō*) nomination (of a priest) to a benefice, religious dedication (of a person) by bringing him before God. See PRESENT², -ATION]

pres•en•ta•tion•al (prez′ən tā′shə nl, prē′zen-), *adj.* **1.** of or pertaining to presentation. **2.** pertaining to or characterized by presentationalism. **3.** notional (def. 7). [1885–90; PRESENTATION + -AL¹]

pres•en•ta•tion•al•ism (prez′ən tā′shə nl iz′əm, prē′zen-), *n. Theat.* a style of production in which the audience is addressed directly with songs, skits, exposition, etc., and no attempt is made at realism. [1885–90; PRESENTATIONAL + -ISM]

pres•en•ta•tion•ism (prez′ən tā′shə niz′əm, prē′-zen-), *n. Epistemology.* the doctrine that in perception, or in all forms of knowledge, there is an immediate awareness of the things perceived. Also called **presentative realism.** [1835–45; PRESENTATION + -ISM] **—pres′en•ta′tion•ist,** *n., adj.*

pre•sen•ta•tive (pri zen′tə tiv), *adj.* **1.** (of an image, idea, etc.) presented, known, or capable of being known directly. **2.** *Eccles.* admitting of or pertaining to presentation. **3.** *Philos.* immediately knowable; capable of being known without thought or reflection. [1550–60; PRESENT² + -ATIVE]

presen′tative re′alism, *Epistemology.* presentationism. **—presen′tative re′alist.**

pres′ent contin′uous. See **present progressive.**

pres•ent-day (prez′ənt dā′), *adj.* current; modern: *present-day techniques; present-day English.* [1885–90]

pres•en•tee (prez′ən tē′), *n.* **1.** a person to whom something is presented. **2.** a person who is presented, as to a benefice. **3.** a debutante. [1490–1500; < AF; see PRESENT², -EE]

pre•sent•er (pri zen′tər), *n.* **1.** a person or thing that presents. **2.** a person who presents an award, as at a formal ceremony. [1535–45; PRESENT² + -ER¹]

pre•sen•tient (prē sen′shənt), *adj.* having a presentiment. [1805–15; < L *praesentient-* (s. of *praesentiēns*), prp. of *praesentire.* See PRE-, SENTIENT]

pre•sen•ti•ment (pri zen′tə mənt), *n.* a feeling or impression that something is about to happen, esp. something evil; foreboding. [1705–15; < F, now obs. spelling of *pressentiment.* See PRE-, SENTIMENT] **—pre•sen′ti•ment′al,** *adj.*

pres•en•tist (prez′ən tist), *n. Theol.* a person who maintains that the prophecies in the Apocalypse are now being fulfilled. Cf. **futurist, preterist** (def. 1). [1875–80; PRESENT¹ + -IST]

pre•sen•tive (pri zen′tiv), *adj. Semantics.* notional (def. 7). [1870–75; PRESENT² + -IVE] **—pre•sen′tive•ly,** *adv.* **—pre•sen′tive•ness,** *n.*

pres•ent•ly (prez′ənt lē), *adv.* **1.** in a little while; soon: *They will be here presently.* **2.** at the present time; now: *He is presently out of the country.* **3.** *Archaic.* immediately. [1350–1400; ME; see PRESENT¹, -LY]
—Syn. 1. shortly, forthwith. **—Ant. 1.** later.
—Usage. The two apparently contradictory meanings of PRESENTLY, "in a little while, soon" and "at the present time, now," are both old in the language. In the latter meaning PRESENTLY dates back to the 15th century. It is currently in standard use in all varieties of speech and writing in both Great Britain and the United States. The sense "soon" arose gradually during the 16th century. Strangely, it is the older sense "now" that is sometimes objected to by usage guides. The two senses are rarely if ever confused in actual practice. PRESENTLY meaning "now" is most often used with the present tense (*The professor is presently on sabbatical leave*) and PRESENTLY meaning "soon" often with the future tense (*The supervisor will be back presently*). The semantic development of PRESENTLY parallels that of *anon,* which first had the meaning, now archaic, of "at once, immediately," but later came to mean "soon."

pre•sent•ment (pri zent′mənt), *n.* **1.** an act of presenting, esp. to the mind, as an idea, view, etc. **2.** the state of being presented. **3.** a presentation. **4.** the manner or mode in which something is presented. **5.** a representation, picture, or likeness. **6.** *Com.* the presenting of a bill, note, or the like, as for acceptance or payment. **7.** *Law.* the written statement of an offense by a grand jury, of their own knowledge or observation, when no indictment has been laid before them. **8.** a theatrical or dramatic presentation. [1275–1325; ME *presentement* < MF. See PRESENT², -MENT]

pres′ent par′ticiple, *Gram.* a participle form, in English having the suffix *-ing,* denoting repetition or duration of an activity or event: used as an adjective, as in *the growing weeds,* and in forming progressive verb forms, as in *The weeds are growing.*

pres′ent per′fect, **1.** (in English) the tense form consisting of the present tense of *have* with a past participle and noting that the action of the verb was completed prior to the present, as *I have finished.* **2.** a tense of similar construction found in certain other languages. **3.** a form in this tense. [1570–80]

pres′ent progres′sive, *Gram.* (in English) a verb form consisting of an auxiliary *be* in the present tense followed by a present participle and used esp. to indicate that a present action or event is in progress, being repeated, or of a temporary nature or to express the future. Also called **present continuous.**

pres•er•va•tion•ist (prez′ər vā′shə nist), *n.* a person who advocates or promotes preservation, esp. of wildlife, natural areas, or historical places. [1925–30; PRESERVATION + -IST] **—pres′er•va′tion•ism,** *n.*

pre•serv•a•tive (pri zûr′və tiv), *n.* **1.** something that preserves or tends to preserve. **2.** a chemical substance used to preserve foods or other organic materials from decomposition or fermentation. **—***adj.* **3.** tending to preserve. [1350–1400; ME (adj. and n.) < MF *preservatif* (adj.) < ML *praeservātīvus.* See PRESERVE, -ATIVE]

pre•serve (pri zûrv′), *v.,* **-served, -serv•ing,** *n.* **—***v.t.* **1.** to keep alive or in existence; make lasting: *to preserve our liberties as free citizens.* **2.** to keep safe from harm or injury; protect or spare. **3.** to keep up; maintain: *to preserve historical monuments.* **4.** to keep possession of; retain: *to preserve one's composure.* **5.** to prepare (food or any perishable substance) so as to resist decomposition or fermentation. **6.** to prepare (fruit, vegetables, etc.) by cooking with sugar, pickling, canning, or the like. **7.** to maintain and reserve (game, fish, etc.) for continued survival or for private use, as in hunting or fishing. **—***v.i.* **8.** to preserve fruit, vegetables, etc.; make preserves. **9.** to maintain a preserve for game or fish, esp. for sport. **—***n.* **10.** something that preserves. **11.** that which is preserved. **12.** Usually, **preserves.** fruit, vegetables, etc., prepared by cooking with sugar. **13.** a place set apart for protection and propagation of game or fish, esp. for sport. [1325–75; ME *preserven* < ML *praeservāre* to guard (LL: to observe), equiv. to L *prae-* PRE- + *servāre* to watch over, keep, preserve, observe] **—pre•serv′a•ble,** *adj.* **—pre•serv′a•bil′i•ty,** *n.* **—pres•er•va•tion** (prez′ər vā′shən), *n.* **—pre•serv′er,** *n.*
—Syn. 1. conserve. **2.** safeguard, shelter, shield. See **defend. 3.** continue, uphold, sustain. **—Ant. 1.** destroy.

pre•set (*v., adj.* prē set′; *n.* prē′set′), *v.,* **-set, -set•ting,** *adj., n.* **—***v.t.* **1.** to set beforehand. **2.** to set (an electric or electronic appliance) to become activated at a designated time: *We preset the coffeemaker to go on at 6 A.M.* **3.** to adjust (a connector, switch, or the like) so that when activated it will perform a designated function: *The tuning buttons on the radio are preset to my favorite FM stations.* **—***adj.* **4.** set in advance: *a preset radio adjusted to receive certain stations.* **5.** (of the guidance system of a missile or the course of flight it determines) set before launching to reach a specific destination without any alteration in response to signals from the ground. **—***n.* **6.** a knob or button that activates a preset appliance: *Just push the preset and coffee will be ready when you get up.* **7.** a similar device on a radio that can be activated to tune in a preselected station. [1930–35; PRE- + SET] **—pre•set′ta•ble,** *adj.*

pre′set board′, a control board for setting up theatrical lighting switches and dimmer readings in advance so that during a performance the lights can be automatically operated for one or several scenes. Also called **pre′set control′ board′, multi-scene control board, pre′set switch′board.**

pre•shave (prē′shāv′), *n.* **1.** a liquid preparation, usually containing alcohol, for applying to the face to dry the skin and beard before shaving with an electric razor. **—***adj.* **2.** used before shaving: *preshave lotions.* [PRE- + SHAVE, on the model of AFTERSHAVE]

pre•shrink (prē shringk′), *v.t.,* **-shrank** or, often, **-shrunk; -shrunk** or **-shrunk•en; -shrink•ing.** to subject (textiles, garments, etc.) to a shrinking process before marketing to minimize subsequent shrinkage. [1935–40; PRE- + SHRINK]

pre•shrunk (prē shrungk′), *adj.* of or pertaining to a fabric or garment that has been subjected to a shrinking process in order to reduce contraction when the apparel is washed or laundered. [1940–45; PRE- + SHRUNK]

pre•side (pri zīd′), *v.i.,* **-sid•ed, -sid•ing. 1.** to occupy the place of authority or control, as in an assembly or meeting; act as president or chairperson. **2.** to exercise management or control (usually fol. by *over*): *The lawyer presided over the estate.* [1605–15; < L *praesidēre* to preside over, lit., sit in front of, equiv. to *prae-* PRE- + *-sidēre,* comb. form of *sedēre* to SIT] **—pre•sid′er,** *n.*

Pre•si•den•cia Ro•que Sá•enz Pe•ña (pre′sē-then′syä rô′ke sä′ens pe′nyä), a city in N Argentina. 38,620.

pres•i•den•cy (prez′i dən sē), *n., pl.* **-cies. 1.** the office, function, or term of office of a president. **2.** (*often cap.*) the office of President of the United States. **3.** *Mormon Ch.* **a.** a local governing body consisting of a council of three. **b.** (*often cap.*) the highest administrative body, composed of the prophet and his two councilors. **4.** the former designation of any of the three original provinces of British India: Bengal, Bombay, and Madras. [1585–95; < ML *praesidentia.* See PRESIDENT, -ENCY]

pres•i•dent (prez′i dənt), *n.* **1.** (*often cap.*) the highest executive officer of a modern republic, as the Chief Executive of the United States. **2.** an officer appointed or elected to preside over an organized body of persons. **3.** the chief officer of a college, university, society, corporation, etc. **4.** a person who presides. See table of Presidents of the U.S. [1325–75; ME < L *praesident-* (s. of *praesidēns*), n. use of prp. of *praesidēre* to PRESIDE, govern; see -ENT]

pres•i•dent-e•lect (prez′i dənt i lekt′), *n.* a president after election but before induction into office. [1815–25, *Amer.*]

Pre•si•den•te Pru•den•te (pre′zi den′tə proo den′-tə), a city in central Brazil. 92,851.

pres•i•den•tial (prez′i den′shəl), *adj.* **1.** of or pertaining to a president or presidency. **2.** of the nature of a president. [1595–1605; < ML *praesidentiālis.* See PRESIDENCY, -AL¹] **—pres′i•den′tial•ly,** *adv.*

pres′iden′tial gov′ernment, a system of government in which the powers of the president are constitutionally separate from those of the legislature. [1900–05]

Presiden′tial Med′al of Free′dom, a medal awarded by the president of the U.S. to any citizen who has made an exceptionally meritorious contribution to the security or national interest of the U.S., to world peace, or to cultural or other significant endeavors.

pres′iden′tial pri′mary, a direct primary for the selection of state delegates to a national party convention and the expression of preference for a U.S. presidential nominee.

presiden′tial suite′, a suite of rooms, as in a hotel, suitable for a president or other head of state.

pres′ident pro tem′pore, *U.S. Govt.* a senator, usually a senior member of the majority party, who is chosen to preside over the Senate in the absence of the vice president. Also, **pres′ident pro tem′.**

Pres′idents′ Day′, the third Monday in February, a legal holiday in the U.S., commemorating the birthdays of George Washington and Abraham Lincoln.

pres•i•dent•ship (prez′i dənt ship′), *n. Chiefly Brit.* presidency. [1515–25; PRESIDENT + -SHIP]

pre•sid•i•o (pri sid′ē ō′; *Sp.* pre sē′thyô), *n., pl.* **-sid•i•os** (-sid′ē ōz′; *Sp.* -sē′thyôs). **1.** a garrisoned fort; military post. **2.** a Spanish penal settlement. [1755–65, *Amer.*; < Sp < L *praesidium* guard, garrison, post, lit., defense, protection. See PRESIDIUM] **—pre•sid′i•al, pre•sid•i•ar•y** (pri sid′ē er′ē), *adj.*

pre•sid•i•um (pri sid′ē əm), *n., pl.* **-sid•i•ums, -sid•i•a** (-sid′ē ə). (*often cap.*) (in the Soviet Union and other Communist countries) an administrative committee, usually permanent and governmental, acting when its parent body is in recess but exercising full powers: *the presidium of the Supreme Soviet.* [1815–25; < L *prae-*

CONCISE ETYMOLOGY KEY: <, descended or borrowed from; >, whence; b., blend of, blended; c., cognate with; cf., compare; deriv., derivative; equiv., equivalent; imit., imitative; obl., oblique; r., replacing; s., stem; sp., spelling, spelled; resp., respelling, respelled; trans., translation; ?, origin unknown; *, unattested; ‡, probably earlier than. See the full key inside the front cover.

pre•meas′ure•ment, *n.*
pre•me′di•an, *n., adj.*
pre•med′i•cate′, *v.t.,* **-cat•ed, -cat•ing.**
pre•meet′, *n., v.,* **-met, -meet•ing.**
pre′meg•a•lith′ic, *adj.*
pre′mem•o•ran′dum, *n., pl.* **-dums, -da.**
pre•men′ace, *n., v.t.,* **-aced, -ac•ing.**
pre′-Men•de′li•an, *adj.*
pre′men•o•pau′sal, *adj.*
pre•men′stru•al, *adj.;* **-ly,** *adv.*
pre•men′tion, *n., v.t.*
pre•merg′er, *adj.*
pre•mer′it, *v.t.*
pre′-Mes•si•an′ic, *adj.*
pre′met•a•mor′phic, *adj.*
pre′me•thod′i•cal, *adj.*
pre-Meth′od•ist, *adj., n.*
pre•mid′night′, *n.*
pre′mid•sum′mer, *n., adj.*
pre′mi•gra′tion, *adj.*
pre•mi′gra•to′ry, *adj.*
pre•mil′i•tar′y, *adj.*
pre•min′is•ter, *v.i.*
pre•min′is•try, *n., pl.* **-tries.**
pre′mis•rep′re•sent′, *v.t.*
pre′mis•rep′re•sen•ta′tion, *n.*
pre•mod′el, *v.i.,* **-eled, -el•ing** or (*esp. Brit.*) **-elled, -el•ling.**
pre•mod′ern, *adj.*
pre′mod•i•fi•ca′tion, *n.*
pre•mod′i•fy′, *v.t.,* **-fied, -fy•ing.**
pre•mois′tened, *adj.*
pre•mold′, *n., v.t.*
pre•mold′er, *n.*
pre′mo•nar′chal, *adj.*
pre′mo•nar′chi•al, *adj.*
pre′mo•nar′chi•cal, *adj.*
pre•mon′e•tar′y, *adj.*
pre′-Mon•go′li•an, *adj.*
pre′mo•nop′o•lize′, *v.t.,* **-lized, -liz•ing.**
pre′mo•nop′o•ly, *n., pl.* **-lies,** *adj.*
pre′mon•u•men′tal, *adj.*
pre•mor′al, *adj.;* **-ly,** *adv.*
pre′mo•ral′i•ty, *n.*
pre•mor′bid, *adj.;* **-ly,** *adv.;* **-ness,** *n.*
pre•morn′ing, *adj.*
pre•mor′tal, *adj.;* **-ly,** *adv.*
pre′mor•ti•fi•ca′tion, *n.*
pre•mor′ti•fy′, *v.t.,* **-fied, -fy•ing.**
pre•mor′tu•ar′y, *adj.*
pre•mor′u•lar, *adj.*
pre′mo•sa′ic, *adj.*
pre-Mos′lem, *adj., n.*
pre•mud′dle, *n., v.t.,* **-dled, -dling.**
pre′mu•nic′i•pal, *adj.*
pre•mu′si•cal, *adj.;* **-ly,** *adv.*
pre-Mus′lim, *adj., n.*
pre•mus′ter, *v.t.*
pre•mu′ti•ny, *n., pl.* **-nies;** *v.t.,* **-nied, -ny•ing.**
pre′-My•ce•nae′an, *adj.*
pre′my•cot′ic, *adj.*
pre•myth′i•cal, *adj.*
pre′-Na•po′le•on′ic, *adj.*
pre′nar•cot′ic, *adj.*
pre•nar′i•al, *adj.*
pre•na′sal, *adj.*
pre•na′tion•al, *adj.*
pre•nat′u•ral, *adj.*
pre•na′val, *adj.*
pre•neb′u•lar, *adj.*
pre′ne•ces′si•tate′, *v.t.,* **-tat•ed, -tat•ing.**
pre′ne•glect′, *v.t.*
pre′ne•glect′ful, *adj.*
pre•neg′li•gence, *n.*
pre•neg′li•gent, *adj.*
pre′ne•go′ti•ate′, *v.,* **-at•ed, -at•ing.**
pre′ne•go′ti•a′tion, *n.*
pre′ne•o•lith′ic, *adj.*
pre′ne•phrit′ic, *adj.*
pre•neu′ral, *adj.*
pre′neu•ral′gic, *adj.*
pre′-New•to′ni•an, *adj.*
pre•nom′i•nal, *adj.*
pre-Nor′man, *adj., n.*
pre-Norse′, *adj.*
pre•note′, *n., v.t.,* **-not•ed, -not•ing.**
pre•no′ti•fy′, *v.t.,* **-fied, -fy•ing.**
pre•num′ber, *v.t., n.*
pre•nurs′er•y, *adj., n., pl.* **-er•ies.**
pre′o•be′di•ence, *n.*
pre′o•be′di•ent, *adj.;* **-ly,** *adv.*
pre′ob•ject′, *v.i.*
pre′ob•jec′tion, *n.*
pre′ob•jec′tive, *adj.*
pre•ob′li•gate′, *v.t.,* **-gat•ed, -gat•ing.**
pre′ob•li•ga′tion, *n.*
pre′o•blige′, *v.t.,* **-bliged, -blig•ing.**
pre′ob•lon•ga′ta, *n., pl.* **-tas, -tae.**
pre′ob•serv′ance, *n.*
pre′ob•ser•va′tion, *n.*
pre′ob•ser•va′tion•al, *adj.*
pre′ob•serve′, *v.t.,* **-served, -serv•ing.**
pre′ob•struct′, *v.t.*
pre′ob•struc′tion, *n.*
pre′ob•tain′, *v.t.*
pre′ob•tain′a•ble, *adj.*
pre′ob•trude′, *v.t.,* **-trud•ed, -trud•ing.**
pre′ob•tru′sion, *n.*
pre′ob•tru′sive, *adj.*
pre•ob′vi•ate′, *v.t.,* **-at•ed, -at•ing.**
pre•ob′vi•ous, *adj.;* **-ly,** *adv.;* **-ness,** *n.*
pre′oc•ca′sioned, *adj.*
pre′oc•cip′i•tal, *adj.*
pre′oc•clu′sion, *n.*
pre′oc•cul•ta′tion, *n.*
pre•oc′cu•pant, *n.*
pre′oc•cur′, *v.i.,* **-curred, -cur•ring.**

PRESIDENTS AND VICE PRESIDENTS OF THE UNITED STATES

President	Born	Died	Birthplace	Residence	Religious Affiliation	Party	Dates in Office	Vice President	Dates in Office
1. GEORGE WASHINGTON	Feb. 22, 1732	Dec. 14, 1799	Westmoreland Co.,Va.	Va.	Episcopalian	Fed.	1789–1797	JOHN ADAMS	1789–1797
2. JOHN ADAMS	Oct. 30, 1735	July 4, 1826	Quincy, Mass.	Mass.	Unitarian	Fed.	1797–1801	THOMAS JEFFERSON	1797–1801
3. THOMAS JEFFERSON	Apr. 13, 1743	July 4, 1826	Shadwell, Va.	Va.	Episcopalian	Rep.*	1801–1809	AARON BURR	1801–1805
								GEORGE CLINTON	1805–1809
4. JAMES MADISON	Mar. 16, 1751	June 28, 1836	Port Conway, Va.	Va.	Episcopalian	Rep.*	1809–1817	GEORGE CLINTON†	1809–1812
								ELBRIDGE GERRY†	1813–1814
5. JAMES MONROE	Apr. 28, 1758	July 4, 1831	Westmoreland Co.,Va.	Va.	Episcopalian	Rep.*	1817–1825	DANIEL D. TOMPKINS	1817–1825
6. JOHN QUINCY ADAMS	July 11, 1767	Feb. 23, 1848	Quincy, Mass.	Mass.	Unitarian	Rep.*	1825–1829	JOHN C. CALHOUN	1825–1829
7. ANDREW JACKSON	Mar. 15, 1767	June 8, 1845	New Lancaster Co., S.C.	Tenn.	Presbyterian	Dem.	1829–1837	JOHN C. CALHOUN	1829–1832
								MARTIN VAN BUREN**	1833–1837
8. MARTIN VAN BUREN	Dec. 5, 1782	July 24, 1862	Kinderhook, N.Y.	N.Y.	Reformed Dutch	Dem.	1837–1841	RICHARD M. JOHNSON	1837–1841
9. WILLIAM HENRY HARRISON†	Feb. 9, 1773	Apr. 4, 1841	Berkeley, Va.	Ohio	Episcopalian	Whig	1841	JOHN TYLER**	1841
10. JOHN TYLER	Mar. 29, 1790	Jan. 18, 1862	Greenway, Va.	Va.	Episcopalian	Whig	1841–1845		
11. JAMES KNOX POLK	Nov. 2, 1795	June 15, 1849	Mecklenburg Co., N.C.	Tenn.	Methodist	Dem.	1845–1849	GEORGE M. DALLAS	1845–1849
12. ZACHARY TAYLOR†	Nov. 24, 1784	July 9, 1850	Orange Co., Va.	La.	Episcopalian	Whig	1849–1850	MILLARD FILLMORE**	1849–1850
13. MILLARD FILLMORE	Jan. 7, 1800	Mar. 8, 1874	Cayuga Co., N.Y.	N.Y.	Unitarian	Whig	1850–1853		
14. FRANKLIN PIERCE	Nov. 23, 1804	Oct. 8, 1869	Hillsboro, N.H.	N.H.	Episcopalian	Dem.	1853–1857	WILLIAM R. KING†	1853
15. JAMES BUCHANAN	Apr. 23, 1791	June 1, 1868	Mercersburg, Pa.	Pa.	Presbyterian	Dem.	1857–1861	JOHN C. BRECKINRIDGE	1857–1861
16. ABRAHAM LINCOLN†	Feb. 12, 1809	Apr. 15, 1865	Hardin Co., Ky.	Ill.	Nonaffiliated	Rep.‡	1861–1865	HANNIBAL HAMLIN	1861–1865
								ANDREW JOHNSON**	1865
17. ANDREW JOHNSON	Dec. 29, 1808	July 31, 1875	Raleigh, N.C.	Tenn.	Nonaffiliated	Dem.‡	1865–1869		
18. ULYSSES SIMPSON GRANT	Apr. 27, 1822	July 23, 1885	Point Pleasant, Ohio	Ill.	Methodist	Rep.	1869–1877	SCHUYLER COLFAX	1869–1873
								HENRY WILSON†	1873–1875
19. RUTHERFORD BIRCHARD HAYES	Oct. 4, 1822	Jan. 17, 1893	Delaware, Ohio	Ohio	Nonaffiliated	Rep.	1877–1881	WILLIAM A. WHEELER	1877–1881
20. JAMES ABRAM GARFIELD†	Nov. 19, 1831	Sept. 19, 1881	Orange, Ohio	Ohio	Disciples of Christ	Rep.	1881	CHESTER A. ARTHUR**	1881
21. CHESTER ALAN ARTHUR	Oct. 5, 1830	Nov. 18, 1886	Fairfield, Vt.	N.Y.	Episcopalian	Rep.	1881–1885		
22. GROVER CLEVELAND	Mar. 18, 1837	June 24, 1908	Caldwell, N.J.	N.Y.	Presbyterian	Dem.	1885–1889	THOMAS A. HENDRICKS†	1885
23. BENJAMIN HARRISON	Aug. 20, 1833	Mar. 13, 1901	North Bend, Ohio	Ind.	Presbyterian	Rep.	1889–1893	LEVI P. MORTON	1889–1893
24. GROVER CLEVELAND	See number 22						1893–1897	ADLAI E. STEVENSON	1893–1897
25. WILLIAM MCKINLEY†	Jan. 29, 1843	Sept. 14, 1901	Niles, Ohio	Ohio	Methodist	Rep.	1897–1901	GARRET A. HOBART†	1897–1899
								THEODORE ROOSEVELT**	1901
26. THEODORE ROOSEVELT	Oct. 27, 1858	Jan. 6, 1919	New York, N.Y.	N.Y.	Reformed Dutch	Rep.	1901–1909	CHARLES W. FAIRBANKS	1905–1909
27. WILLIAM HOWARD TAFT	Sept. 15, 1857	Mar. 8, 1930	Cincinnati, Ohio	Ohio	Unitarian	Rep.	1909–1913	JAMES S. SHERMAN†	1909–1912
28. WOODROW WILSON	Dec. 28, 1856	Feb. 3, 1924	Staunton, Va.	N.J.	Presbyterian	Dem.	1913–1921	THOMAS R. MARSHALL	1913–1921
29. WARREN GAMALIEL HARDING†	Nov. 2, 1865	Aug. 2, 1923	Bloomington Grove, Ohio	Ohio	Baptist	Rep.	1921–1923	CALVIN COOLIDGE**	1921–1923
30. CALVIN COOLIDGE	July 4, 1872	Jan. 5, 1933	Plymouth, Vt.	Mass.	Congregational	Rep.	1923–1929	CHARLES G. DAWES	1925–1929
31. HERBERT CLARK HOOVER	Aug. 10, 1874	Oct. 20, 1964	West Branch, Iowa	Calif.	Society of Friends	Rep.	1929–1933	CHARLES CURTIS	1929–1933
32. FRANKLIN DELANO ROOSEVELT†	Jan. 30, 1882	Apr. 12, 1945	Hyde Park, N.Y.	N.Y.	Episcopalian	Dem.	1933–1945	JOHN NANCE GARNER	1933–1941
								HENRY AGARD WALLACE	1941–1945
								HARRY S TRUMAN**	1945
33. HARRY S TRUMAN	May 8, 1884	Dec. 26, 1972	Lamar, Mo.	Mo.	Baptist	Dem.	1945–1953	ALBEN W. BARKLEY	1949–1953
34. DWIGHT DAVID EISENHOWER	Oct. 14, 1890	Mar. 28, 1969	Denison, Tex.	N.Y.	Presbyterian	Rep.	1953–1961	RICHARD M. NIXON	1953–1961
35. JOHN FITZGERALD KENNEDY†	May 29, 1917	Nov. 22, 1963	Brookline, Mass.	Mass.	Roman Catholic	Dem.	1961–1963	LYNDON B. JOHNSON**	1961–1963
36. LYNDON BAINES JOHNSON	Aug. 27, 1908	Jan. 22, 1973	Johnson City, Tex.	Tex.	Disciples of Christ	Dem.	1963–1969	HUBERT H. HUMPHREY	1965–1969
37. RICHARD MILHOUS NIXON§	Jan. 9, 1913		Yorba Linda, Calif.	Calif.	Society of Friends	Rep.	1969–1974	SPIRO T. AGNEW§	1969–1973
								GERALD R. FORD**	1973–1974
38. GERALD RUDOLPH FORD	July 14, 1913		Omaha, Nebr.	Mich.	Episcopalian	Rep.	1974–1977	NELSON A. ROCKEFELLER	1974–1977
39. JAMES EARL CARTER, JR.	Oct. 1, 1924		Plains, Ga.	Ga.	Baptist	Dem.	1977–1981	WALTER F. MONDALE	1977–1981
40. RONALD WILSON REAGAN	Feb. 6, 1911		Tampico, Ill.	Calif.	Disciples of Christ	Rep.	1981–1989	GEORGE H.W. BUSH	1981–1989
41. GEORGE H.W. BUSH	June 12, 1924		Milton, Mass.	Tex.	Episcopalian	Rep.	1989–1993	JAMES DANFORTH QUAYLE	1989–1993
42. WILLIAM JEFFERSON CLINTON	Aug. 19, 1946		Hope, Ark.	Ark.	Baptist	Dem.	1993–	ALBERT A. GORE, JR.	1993–

*Now the Democratic Party †Died in office ‡Elected on the Union party ticket **Succeeded to Presidency §Resigned

sidium, deriv. of *praes(es)* (s. *praesid-*) guardian, governor, lit., one sitting before. See PRESIDE, -IUM]

pre·sig·ni·fy (prē sig′nə fī′), *v.t.*, **-fied, -fy·ing.** to signify or indicate beforehand; foretell. [1580–90; < L *praesignificāre* to show beforehand. See PRE-, SIGNIFY]

pre·sin·ter (prē sin′tər), *v.t.* (in powder metallurgy) to heat (a compact) in preparation for sintering. [PRE- + SINTER]

Pres·ley (pres′lē, prez′-), *n.* **1. Elvis (Aron),** 1935–77, U.S. rock-'n'-roll singer. **2.** a male given name.

pre·soak (*v.* prē sōk′; *n.* prē′sōk′), *v.t.* **1.** to soak (laundry) in a liquid containing agents that loosen dirt, remove stains, etc., before washing. —*n.* **2.** a preparation in which laundry is presoaked. **3.** an act or instance of presoaking. [1915–20; PRE- + SOAK]

pre-So·crat·ic (prē′sə krat′ik, -sō-), *adj.* **1.** of or pertaining to the philosophers or philosophical systems of the period before the Socratic period. —*n.* **2.** any philosopher of this period. [1870–75]

pre·sort (prē sôrt′), *v.t.* to sort (letters, packages, etc.) by zip code or class before collection or delivery to a post office. [1965–70; PRE- + SORT]

Pres·pa (pres′pə), *n.* **Lake,** a lake on the borders of E Albania, SW Macedonia, and N Greece: drains underground NW to Lake Ohrid. 112 sq. mi. (290 sq. km). Serbo-Croatian, **Pre·span·sko Je·ze·ro** (pre′spän skô ye′ze rô; *Eng.* pres′pən skō′ yez′ə rō′).

pres. part., present participle.

Presque Isle (presk′ īl′), a city in NE Maine. 11,172.

press[1] (pres), *v.t.* **1.** to act upon with steadily applied weight or force. **2.** to move by weight or force in a certain direction or into a certain position: *The crowd pressed him into a corner.* **3.** to compress or squeeze, as to alter in shape or size: *He pressed the clay into a ball.* **4.** to weigh heavily upon; subject to pressure. **5.** to hold closely, as in an embrace; clasp: *He pressed her in his arms.* **6.** to flatten or make smooth, esp. by ironing: *to press clothes; to press flowers in the leaves of a book.* **7.** to extract juice, sugar, etc., from by pressure: *to press grapes.* **8.** to squeeze out or express, as juice: *to press the juice from grapes.* **9.** to beset or harass; afflict: *He was pressed by problems on all sides.* **10.** to trouble or oppress; put into a difficult position, as by depriving: *Poverty pressed them hard.* **11.** to urge or entreat strongly or insistently: *to press for payment of a debt; to press for an answer.* **12.** to emphasize or propound forcefully; insist upon: *He pressed his own ideas on us.* **13.** to plead with insistence: *to press a claim.* **14.** to urge onward; hasten: *He pressed his horse to go faster.* **15.** to push forward. —*v.i.* **16.** to manufacture (phonograph records, videodiscs, or the like), esp. by stamping from a mold or matrix. **17.** to exert weight, force, or pressure. **18.** *Weight Lifting.* to raise or lift, esp. a specified amount of weight, in a press. **19.** to iron clothing, curtains, etc. **20.** to bear heavily, as upon the mind. **21.** (of athletes and competitors) to perform tensely or overanxiously, as when one feels pressured or is determined to break out of a slump; strain because of frustration: *For days he hasn't seemed able to buy a hit, and he's been pressing.* **22.** to compel haste: *Time presses.* **23.** to demand immediate attention. **24.** to use urgent entreaty: *to press for an answer.* **25.** to push forward or advance with force, eagerness, or haste: *The army pressed to reach the river by dawn.* **26.** to crowd or throng. **27.** *Basketball.* to employ a press. **28. press the flesh,** *Informal.* See **flesh** (def. 15).
—*n.* **29.** an act of pressing; pressure. **30.** the state of being pressed. **31.** printed publications collectively, esp. newspapers and periodicals. **32.** all the media and agencies that print, broadcast, or gather and transmit news, including newspapers, newsmagazines, radio and television news bureaus, and wire services. **33.** the editorial employees, taken collectively, of these media and

CONCISE PRONUNCIATION KEY: *act, cāpe, dâre, pärt; set, ēqual; if, īce; ox, ōver, ôrder, oil, bŏŏk, bōōt, out; up, ûrge; child; sing; shoe; thin, that;* zh *as in treasure.* ə = *a* as in *alone, e* as in *system, i* as in *easily, o* as in *gallop, u* as in *circus;* ᵊ as in *fire* (fīᵊr), *hour* (ouᵊr). l and n can serve as syllabic consonants, as in *cradle* (krād′l), and *button* (but′n). See the full key inside the front cover.

pre′oc·cur′rence, *n.*
pre′o·ce·an′ic, *adj.*
pre·oc′u·lar, *adj.*
pre·o′dor·ous, *adj.*
pre′oe·soph′a·ge′al, *adj.*
pre′of·fend′, *v.t.*
pre′of·fen′sive, *adj.;* **-ly,** *adv.;* **-ness,** *n.*
pre·of′fer, *n., v.t.*
pre′of·fi′cial, *adj.;* **-ly,** *adv.*
pre′o·mis′sion, *n.*
pre′o·mit′, *v.t.,* **-mit·ted, -mit·ting.**
pre·o′pen, *v.t.*
pre·o′pen·ing, *adj.*
pre·op′er·ate′, *v.i.,* **-at·ed, -at·ing.**
pre′op·er·a′tion, *n.*
pre′op·er·a′tion·al, *adj.*
pre·op′er·a′tor, *n.*
pre′o·pin′ion, *n.*
pre′op·pose′, *v.t.,* **-posed, -pos·ing.**
pre′op·posed′, *adj.*
pre′op·po·si′tion, *n.*
pre′op·press′, *v.t.*
pre′op·pres′sion, *n.*
pre′op·pres′sor, *n.*
pre·op′tic, *adj.*
pre·op′ti·mis′tic, *adj.*
pre·op′tion, *n.*
pre·or′bit·al, *adj.*
pre·or′der, *n.*
pre·or′di·nance, *n.*
pre′or·gan′ic, *adj.*
pre′or·gan′i·cal·ly, *adv.*
pre·or′gan·i·za′tion, *n.*
pre·or′gan·ize′, *v.,* **-ized, -iz·ing.**
pre′o·rig′i·nal, *adj.;* **-ly,** *adv.*
pre′or·na·men′tal, *adj.*
pre·o′tic, *adj.*
pre·out′fit′, *v.t.,* **-fit·ted, -fit·ting.**
pre·out′line′, *n., v.t.,* **-lined, -lin·ing.**
pre·o′ver·throw′, *n.*
pre′o·ver·throw′, *v.t.,* **-threw, -thrown, -throw·ing.**
pre·ov′u·la·to′ry, *adj.*
pre′pa·lae·o·lith′ic, *adj.*
pre′-Pa·lae·o·zo′ic, *adj.*
pre·pal′a·tal, *adj.*
pre·pal′a·tine′, *adj.*
pre′pa·le·o·lith′ic, *adj.*
pre′-Pa·le·o·zo′ic, *adj.*
pre′par·lia·men′ta·ry, *adj.*
pre′par·ox·ys′mal, *adj.*
pre′par·take′, *v.i.,* **-took, -tak·en, -tak·ing.**
pre′par·tic′i·pa′tion, *n.*
pre·par′ti·san, *adj.*
pre′par·ti′tion, *n., v.t.*
pre·part′ner·ship′, *n.*
pre·paste′, *v.t.,* **-past·ed, -past·ing.**
pre·pat′ent, *n., v.t.*
pre′pa·tri′cian, *adj.*
pre-Paul′ine, *adj.*
pre·pave′, *v.t.,* **-paved, -pav·ing.**
pre·pave′ment, *n.*
pre·pec′to·ral, *adj.*
pre′pe·dun′cle, *n.*
pre′pen′e·trate′, *v.t.,* **-trat·ed, -trat·ing.**
pre′pen·e·tra′tion, *n.*
pre′per·i·to·ne′al, *adj.*
pre-Per′mi·an, *adj.*
pre-Per′sian, *adj., n.*
pre′per·suade′, *v.t.,* **-suad·ed, -suad·ing.**
pre′per·sua′sion, *n.*
pre′per·sua′sive, *adj.*
pre′pe·rus′al, *adj.*
pre′pe·ruse′, *v.t.,* **-rused, -rus·ing.**
pre′pe·ti′tion, *n., v.t.*
pre-Pe′trine, *adj.*
pre′-Phar·a·on′ic, *adj.*
pre-Phid′i·an, *adj.*
pre·phthis′i·cal, *adj.*
pre·pin′e·al, *adj.*
pre·pi′ous, *adj.;* **-ly,** *adv.*
pre′pi·tu′i·tar′y, *adj.*
pre·place′, *v.t.,* **-placed, -plac·ing.**
pre·place′ment, *n.*
pre′pla·cen′tal, *adj.*
pre·plan′, *v.,* **-planned, -plan·ning.**
pre·plant′, *v.t.*
pre·pledge′, *v.t.,* **-pledged, -pledg·ing;** *n.*
pre·plot′, *v.t.,* **-plot·ted, -plot·ting.**
pre′po·et′ic, *adj.*
pre′po·et′i·cal, *adj.*
pre′po·lice′, *adj.*
pre·pol′i·cy, *adj.*
pre·pol′ish, *n., v.t.*
pre-Pol′ish, *adj.*
pre′pol′i·tic, *adj.*
pre′po·lit′i·cal, *adj.;* **-ly,** *adv.*
pre′por·tray′, *v.t.*
pre′por·tray′al, *n.*
pre·prac′ti·cal, *adj.*
pre·prac′tice, *v.,* **-ticed, -tic·ing.**
pre·prac′tise, *v.,* **-tised, -tis·ing.**
pre′prep·a·ra′tion, *n.*
pre′pres·i·den′tial, *adj.*
pre·price′, *v.t.,* **-priced, -pric·ing;** *n.*
pre·prim′er, *n.*
pre·prim′i·tive, *adj.*
pre·proc′ess, *v.*
pre′pro·fess′, *v.t.*
pre′pro·hi·bi′tion, *n.*
pre·prom′ise, *n., v.t.,* **-ised, -is·ing.**
pre′pro·mote′, *v.t.,* **-mot·ed, -mot·ing.**
pre′pro·mo′tion, *n.*
pre′pro·nounce′, *v.t.,* **-nounced, -nounc·ing.**
pre′pro·nounce′ment, *n.*
pre′pro·phet′ic, *adj.*
pre′pro·stat′ic, *adj.*

agencies. **34.** (*often used with a plural v.*) a group of news reporters, or of news reporters and news photographers: *The press are in the outer office, waiting for a statement.* **35.** the consensus of the general critical commentary or the amount of coverage accorded a person, thing, or event, esp. in newspapers and periodicals (often prec. by *good* or *bad*): *The play received a good press. The minister's visit got a bad press.* **36.** See **printing press.** **37.** an establishment for printing books, magazines, etc. **38.** the process or art of printing. **39.** any of various devices or machines for exerting pressure, stamping, or crushing. **40.** a wooden or metal viselike device for preventing a tennis or other racket from warping when not in use. **41.** a pressing or pushing forward. **42.** a crowding, thronging, or pressing together; collective force: *The press of the crowd drove them on.* **43.** a crowd, throng, or multitude. **44.** the desired smooth or creased effect caused by ironing or pressing: *His suit was out of press.* **45.** pressure or urgency, as of affairs or business. **46.** an upright case or other piece of furniture for holding clothes, books, pamphlets, etc. **47.** *Basketball.* an aggressive form of defense in which players guard opponents very closely. **48.** *Weightlifting.* a lift in which the barbell, after having been lifted from the ground up to chest level, is pushed to a position overhead with the arms extended straight up, without moving the legs or feet. **49. go to press,** to begin being printed: *The last edition has gone to press.* [1175–1225; (n.) ME *press(e)* throng, company, trouble, machine for pressing, clothespress < OF, deriv. of *presser* to press < L *pressāre,* freq. of *premere* (ptp. *pressus*) to press (cf. rare OE *press* clothespress < ML *pressa,* n. use of fem. of *pressus*); (v.) ME *pressen* (< OF *presser*) < L *pressāre,* as above] **—press′a•ble,** *adj.*
—Syn. 9. annoy, worry, torment, assail, besiege. **11.** induce, persuade, beg, implore.

press[2] (pres), *v.t.* **1.** to force into service, esp. naval or military service; impress. **2.** to make use of in a manner different from that intended or desired: *French taxis were pressed into service as troop transports.* **—n. 3.** impressment into service, esp. naval or military service. [1535–45; back formation from *prest,* ptp. of obs. *prest* to take (men) for military service, v. use of PREST[2] in sense "enlistment money"]

Press (pres), *n.* a male given name.

press′ a′gent, a person employed to promote the interests of an individual, organization, etc., by obtaining favorable publicity through advertisements, mentions in columns, and the like. Also, **press′a′gent.** [1880–85]

press-a•gent•ry (pres′ā′jən trē), *n.* **1.** the vocation or responsibilities of a press agent. **2.** publicity produced by a press agent's work or skill, esp. in making a person or thing seem more desirable, admirable, or successful. [1910–15; PRESS AGENT + -RY]

press′ associa′tion, **1.** an organization formed for the purpose of gathering news for transmittal to its members. Cf. **news agency. 2.** an association of publishers in a particular area. [1875–80, *Amer.*]

press-back (pres′bak′), *n.* a wooden chair back having a design pressed, rather than carved, into its cross-rails.

press′ bar′on, an influential newspaper publisher or owner who usually controls more than one widely circulated newspaper. Also called **press lord.** [1955–60]

press′ bed′, a bed enclosed within a closet, cupboard, etc. Cf. **Murphy bed.** [1650–60]

press•board (pres′bôrd′, -bōrd′), *n.* **1.** a kind of millboard or pasteboard. **2.** sleeveboard. [1905–10; PRESS[1] + BOARD]

press′ box′, a press section, esp. at a sports event. [1885–90, *Amer.*]

press•box•er (pres′bok′sər), *n. Informal.* a sportswriter or sportscaster. [PRESS BOX + -ER[1]]

press′ brake′, brake[1] (def. 6).

press′ bu′reau, an organization or a department whose function is press-agentry.

CONCISE ETYMOLOGY KEY: <, descended or borrowed from; >, whence; b., blend of, blended; c., cognate with; cf., compare; deriv., derivative; equiv., equivalent; imit., imitative; obl., oblique; r., replacing; s., stem; sp., spelling, spelled; resp., respelling, respelled; trans., translation; ?, origin unknown; *, unattested; ‡, probably earlier than. See the full key inside the front cover.

Press•burg (pres′bŏŏrk′), *n.* German name of **Bratislava.**

press′ clip′ping, clipping (def. 2). [1900–05, *Amer.*]

press′ con′ference, a prearranged interview with news reporters, held to elicit publicity or, as granted by a dignitary, public official, research scientist, etc., to fulfill a request from the press. [1935–40]

press′ corps′, a group of journalists representing various publications who regularly cover the same beat: *the White House press corps.* [1935–40]

press′ cup′board, *Eng. Furniture.* a cupboard of the 16th and 17th centuries having an overhanging top above a recessed cabinet, beneath which is a section of drawers or cabinets. Cf. **court cupboard.**

pressed′ brick′, face brick molded under pressure to a desired finish. [1840–50]

pressed′ duck′, a cooked duck sprinkled with red wine and then pressed in a device **(duck press)** so that the juices can be collected and served as a sauce over the breast meat and legs.

pressed′ glass′, molded glass that has been shaped or given its pattern, while molten, by the action of a plunger thrust into the mold. [1865–70]

press•er (pres′ər), *n.* **1.** a person or thing that presses or applies pressure. **2.** a person whose occupation is pressing or ironing clothes in a laundry or dry-cleaning establishment. [1535–45; PRESS[1] + -ER[1]]

press′er foot′, a forked, metal device on a sewing machine used for holding the fabric in place while stitching. [1890–95]

press′ fas′tener, *Brit.* See **snap fastener.** [1925–30]

press′ fit′, *Mach.* assembly of two tightly fitting parts, as a hub on a shaft, made by a press or the like. Also called **drive fit, force fit.** [1885–90] **—press-fit′,** *adj.*

press′ gal′lery, **1.** a press section, esp. in a legislative chamber. **2.** the group of news reporters present or qualified to be present in this section. [1880–85]

press′ gang′, a body of persons under the command of an officer, formerly employed to impress others for service, esp. in the navy or army. Also, **press′gang′.** [1685–95]

press-gang (pres′gang′), *v.t.* **1.** to force (a person) into military or naval service. **2.** to coerce (a person) into taking a certain action, political stand, etc.: *to be press-ganged into endorsing a candidate.*

press•ing (pres′ing), *adj.* **1.** urgent; demanding immediate attention: *a pressing need.* **—n. 2.** any phonograph record produced in a record-molding press from a master or a stamper. **3.** a number of such records produced at one time: *The fifth pressing of his hit song has sold out.* [1300–50; ME *presing* (ger.); see PRESS[1], -ING[2], -ING[1]] **—press′ing•ly,** *adv.* **—press′ing•ness,** *n.*
—Syn. 1. crucial, vital, critical, imperative.

press′ing plant′, a manufacturing plant where phonograph records are produced by pressing in a mold or by stamping. [1955–60]

press′ kit′, a packet of promotional materials, as background information, photographs, or samples, for distribution to the press, as at a press conference. [1965–70]

press′ lord′. See **press baron.** [1925–30]

press•man (pres′mən), *n., pl.* **-men. 1.** a person who operates or has charge of a printing press. **2.** *Brit.* a writer or reporter for the press. [1590–1600; PRESS[1] + -MAN]

press•mark (pres′märk′), *n. Chiefly Brit. Library Science.* a symbol indicating the location of a book in the library. [1675–85; PRESS[1] + MARK[1]]

press′ mon′ey, *Brit. Obs.* See **prest money.** [1550–60]

press′ of sail′, *Naut.* as much sail as the wind or other conditions will permit a ship to carry. Also called **press′ of can′vas.** [1585–95]

pres•sor (pres′ər), *adj. Physiol.* causing an increase in blood pressure; causing vasoconstriction. [1885–90; attributive use of LL *pressor* presser, equiv. to L **pret-,* var. s. of *premere* to press + *-tor* -TOR, with *-tt-* > *-ss-*]

pres•so•re•cep•tor (pres′ō ri sep′tər), *n. Physiol.* a proprioceptor responding to changes of blood pressure. [1940–45; PRESS(URE) + -O- + RECEPTOR]

press′ par′ty, a party given for reporters and photographers exclusively or particularly to get publicity, as for the introduction of a new product, the maiden voyage of a liner, or the like. Cf. **press conference.**

press-point (pres′point′), *n. Print.* point (def. 48b).

press′ proof′, *Print.* the last proof examined before matter goes to press. [1835–45]

press′ release′, a statement prepared and distributed to the press by a public relations firm, governmental agency, etc. Also called **news release, release.** [1955–60]

press•room (pres′ro͞om′, -rŏŏm′), *n.* the room in a printing or newspaper publishing establishment where the printing presses are installed. [1675–85; PRESS[1] + ROOM]

press•run (pres′run′), *n.* **1.** the running of a printing press for a specific job: *The pressrun will take about an hour.* **2.** the quantity that is run: *a pressrun of more than 5000.* Also called **run.** [1955–60; PRESS[1] + RUN]

press′ sec′retary, a person officially responsible for press and public relations for a prominent figure or organization and who often holds press conferences to answer journalists' questions. [1955–60]

press′ sec′tion, a section or part of an area, as at the scene of a public event, reserved for reporters.

press′ stud′, *Chiefly Brit.* See **snap fastener.** [1915–20]

press′ time′, the time at which a pressrun begins, esp. that of a newspaper. Also, **press′time′.** [1925–30]

press-up (pres′up′), *n. Brit.* push-up. [1945–50; n. use of v. phrase *press up*]

pres•sure (presh′ər), *n., v.,* **-sured, -sur•ing. —n. 1.** the exertion of force upon a surface by an object, fluid, etc., in contact with it: *the pressure of earth against a wall.* **2.** *Physics.* force per unit area. *Symbol:* P Cf. **stress** (def. 6). **3.** *Meteorol.* See **atmospheric pressure. 4.** *Elect.* See **electromotive force. 5.** the state of being pressed or compressed. **6.** harassment; oppression: *the pressures of daily life.* **7.** a constraining or compelling force or influence: *the social pressures of city life; financial pressure.* **8.** urgency, as of affairs or business: *He works well under pressure.* **9.** *Obs.* that which is impressed. **—v.t. 10.** to force (someone) toward a particular end; influence: *They pressured him into accepting the contract.* **11.** pressurize. [1350–1400; ME (n.) < L *pressūra.* See PRESS[1], -URE] **—pres′sure•less,** *adj.*

pres′sure altim′eter, *Meteorol.* an aneroid barometer adapted for measuring altitude by converting the indicated atmospheric pressure to altitude according to a standard relationship. Cf. **standard atmosphere.**

pres′sure al′titude, *Meteorol.* the altitude for a given pressure in a standard atmosphere, such as that registered by a pressure altimeter.

pres′sure cab′in, *Aeron.* a pressurized cabin. [1930–35]

pres′sure cen′ter, *Meteorol.* the central point of an atmospheric high or low.

pres′sure cone′, *Geol.* See **shatter cone.**

pres•sure-cook (presh′ər ko͝ok′), *v.t.* to cook in a pressure cooker. [1935–40]

pres′sure cook′er, **1.** a reinforced pot, usually of steel or aluminum, in which soups, meats, vegetables, etc., may be cooked quickly in heat above boiling point by steam maintained under pressure. **2.** any situation, job, assignment, etc., in which a person is faced with urgent responsibilities or demands by other people, constant deadlines, or a hectic work schedule. Also, **pres′sure-cook′er.** [1910–15]

pres′sure flak′ing, a method of manufacturing a flint tool by pressing flakes from a stone core with a pointed implement, usually of wood tipped with antler or copper. [1925–30]

pres′sure gauge′, **1.** an instrument for measuring the pressure of a gas or liquid. **2.** an instrument used to determine the pressure in the bore or chamber of a gun when the charge explodes. [1860–65]

pres′sure gra′dient, *Meteorol.* the change in atmospheric pressure per unit of horizontal distance in the

pre•prove′, *v.t.,* **-proved, -proved** or **-prov•en, -prov•ing.**
pre′pro•vide′, *v.t.,* **-vid•ed, -vid•ing.**
pre′pro•vi′sion, *n.*
pre′prov•o•ca′tion, *n.*
pre′pro•voke′, *v.t.,* **-voked, -vok•ing.**
pre•pru′dent, *adj.;* **-ly,** *adv.*
pre′psych•e•del′ic, *adj.*
pre′psy•cho•log′i•cal, *adj.*
pre′psy•chol′o•gy, *n.*
pre•pu′bis, *n., pl.* **-bes.**
pre•pueb′lo, *adj.*
pre•punch′, *v.t.*
pre•pun′ish, *v.t.*
pre•pun′ish•ment, *n.*
pre•pur′chase, *n., v.t.,* **-chased, -chas•ing.**
pre•pur′chas•er, *n.*
pre•pur′pose, *v.t.,* **-posed, -pos•ing.**
pre•pur′pos•ive, *adj.*
pre′py•lor′ic, *adj.*
pre′qual•i•fi•ca′tion, *n.*
pre•qual′i•fy′, *v.,* **-fied, -fy•ing.**
pre•quar′an•tine′, *n., v.t.,* **-tined, -tin•ing.**
pre•ques′tion, *v.t.*
pre′quo•ta′tion, *n.*
pre•quote′, *v.t.,* **-quot•ed, -quot•ing.**
pre•race′, *adj.*
pre•rac′ing, *adj.*
pre•ra′di•o′, *adj.*
pre•rail′road′, *adj.*
pre•rail′way′, *adj.*
pre•ra′tion•al, *adj.*
pre•read′i•ness, *n.*
pre•read′y, *adj.*
pre•re′al•i•za′tion, *n.*
pre•re′al•ize′, *v.t.,* **-ized, -iz•ing.**
pre′re•bel′lion, *adj.*
pre′re•ceipt′, *v.t.*
pre′re•ceive′, *v.t.,* **-ceived, -ceiv•ing.**
pre′re•ceiv′er, *n.*
pre′re•ces′sion, *adj.*
pre′re•cit′al, *n.*
pre′re•cite′, *v.t.,* **-cit•ed, -cit•ing.**
pre•reck′on, *v.t.*
pre•reck′on•ing, *n.*
pre•rec′og•ni′tion, *n.*
pre•rec′og•nize′, *v.t.,* **-nized, -niz•ing.**
pre′rec•om•mend′, *v.t.*
pre′rec•om•men•da′tion, *n.*
pre•rec′on•cile′, *v.t.,* **-ciled, -cil•ing.**
pre•rec′on•cile′ment, *n.*
pre•rec•on•cil′i•a′tion, *n.*
pre′-Re•con•struc′tion, *n., adj.*
pre•rec′tal, *adj.*
pre′re•deem′, *v.t.*
pre′re•demp′tion, *n.*
pre′re•fer′, *v.t.,* **-ferred, -fer•ring.**
pre•ref′er•ence, *n.*
pre′re•fine′, *v.t.,* **-fined, -fin•ing.**
pre′re•fine′ment, *n.*
pre′re•form′, *adj.*
pre′-Ref•or•ma′tion, *n.*
pre•ref•or•ma′tion, *adj.*
pre′re•form′a•to′ry, *adj.*
pre′re•fus′al, *n.*
pre′re•fuse′, *v.t.,* **-fused, -fus•ing.**
pre•re′gal, *adj.*
pre•reg′is•ter, *v.t., v.i.*
pre•reg•is•tra′tion, *n.*
pre•reg′u•late′, *v.t.,* **-lat•ed, -lat•ing.**
pre′re•hears′al, *adj.*
pre′re•ject′, *v.t.*
pre′re•jec′tion, *n.*
pre′re•joice′, *v.i.,* **-joiced, -joic•ing.**
pre′re•late′, *v.t.,* **-lat•ed, -lat•ing.**
pre′re•la′tion, *n.*
pre′re•la′tion•ship′, *n.*
pre′re•li′gious, *adj.*
pre′re•luc′tance, *n.*
pre′re•mit′, *v.t.,* **-mit•ted, -mit•ting.**
pre′re•mit′tance, *n.*
pre′re•morse′, *n.*
pre′re•mov′al, *n.*
pre′re•move′, *v.t.,* **-moved, -mov•ing.**
pre′re•mu′ner•ate′, *v.t.,* **-at•ed, -at•ing.**
pre′re•mu′ner•a′tion, *n.*
pre-Ren′ais•sance′, *adj.*
pre•re′nal, *adj.*
pre•rent′, *v.t.*
pre•rent′al, *n.*
pre′re•port′, *n., v.*
pre′rep•re•sent′, *v.t.*
pre′rep•re•sen•ta′tion, *n.*
pre′re•pub′li•can, *adj.*
pre′re•quest′, *n., v.t.*
pre′re•quire′, *v.t.,* **-quired, -quir•ing.**
pre′re•quire′ment, *n.*
pre′re•sem′blance, *n.*
pre′re•sem′ble, *v.,* **-bled, -bling.**
pre′res•o•lu′tion, *n.*
pre′re•solve′, *v.,* **-solved, -solv•ing.**
pre′re•sort′, *v.i.*
pre′re•spect′a•bil′i•ty, *n.*
pre′re•spect′a•ble, *adj.*
pre′res•pi•ra′tion, *n.*
pre′re•spire′, *v.t.,* **-spired, -spir•ing.**
pre′re•spon′si•bil′i•ty, *n., pl.* **-ties.**
pre′re•spon′si•ble, *adj.*
pre′-Res•to•ra′tion, *adj.*
pre′res•to•ra′tion, *adj.*
pre′re•strain′, *v.t.*
pre′re•straint′, *n.*
pre′re•strict′, *v.t.*
pre′re•stric′tion, *n.*
pre′re•tire′ment, *adj., n.*
pre′re•turn′, *n., v.i.*

direction in which pressure changes most rapidly. Also called **barometric gradient.** [1915–20]

pres′sure group′, an interest group that attempts to influence legislation through the use of lobbying techniques and propaganda. [1925–30]

pres′sure head′, *Physics.* head (def. 32). [1905–10]

pres′sure hull′, the inner, pressure-resistant hull of a submarine. [1920–25]

pres′sure ice′, a general term for ice broken and deformed by stresses generated by wind, currents, or waves.

pres′sure point′, 1. a point on the skin that is extremely sensitive to pressure because of the presence of pressure-sensing organs. **2.** a point on the body where relatively slight pressure serves to press an artery lying close to the surface against underlying bony tissue, so as to arrest the flow of blood into a part. **3.** a sensitive, crucial area or issue against which concerted persuasion or pressure tactics can be wielded to produce a desired result: *Lobbyists attempt to find the pressure points of government.* [1875–80]

pres′sure ridge′, 1. a ridge produced on floating ice by buckling or crushing under lateral pressure of wind or ice. **2.** *Geol.* a ridge produced on a congealing lava flow by pressure from the still-liquid interior. [1895–1900]

pres′sure suit′, *Aerospace.* See **pressurized suit.** [1935–40]

pres•sure-treat•ed (presh′ər trē′tid), *adj.* (of wood) treated with a chemical or chemicals applied under pressure to reduce such problems as insect infestation, decay, and rotting. [1935–40]

pres′sure-vac′u•um valve′ (presh′ər vak′yo͞o əm, -yo͞om), a valve for relieving a sealed tank of any pressure or vacuum exceeding acceptable limits.

pres′sure weld′ing, the welding together of two objects by holding them together under pressure. [1925–30]

pres•sur•i•za•tion (presh′ər ə zā′shən), *n.* **1.** the process or act of pressurizing. **2.** the state of being pressurized. [1935–40; PRESSURIZE + -ATION]

pres•sur•ize (presh′ə rīz′), *v.t.,* **-ized, -iz•ing. 1.** to raise the internal atmospheric pressure of to the required or desired level: *to pressurize an astronaut's spacesuit before a walk in space.* **2.** to maintain normal air pressure in (the cockpit or cabin of an airplane) at high altitudes. **3.** to apply pressure to (a gas or liquid); supercharge. **4.** to pressure-cook. Also, *esp. Brit.,* **pres′•sur•ise′.** [1940–45; PRESSURE + -IZE] **—pres′sur•iz′•er,** *n.*

pres•sur•ized (presh′ə rīzd′), *adj.* **1.** brought to and maintained at an atmospheric pressure higher than that of the surroundings: *cooking with pressurized steam.* **2.** maintained at an air pressure comfortable for breathing: *a pressurized cabin and cockpit; a pressurized suit for diving.* **3.** *Informal.* subject or subjected to undue pressure or harassment: *the pressurized milieu of big business.* [1935–40; PRESSURIZE + -ED[2]]

pres′surized suit′, *Aerospace.* an airtight suit that can be inflated to maintain approximately normal atmospheric pressure on a person in space or at high altitudes. Also called **pressure suit.** [1955–60]

press•work (pres′wûrk′), *n.* **1.** the working or management of a printing press. **2.** the work done by it. [1765–75; PRESS[1] + WORK]

prest[1] (prest), *adj. Obs.* ready. [1250–1300; ME < OF < LL *praestus* ready. See PRESTO]

prest[2] (prest), *n. Obs.* **1.** a loan. **2.** an advance payment on wages. **3.** See **prest money.** [1400–50; late ME *prest(e)* < MF *prest,* OF, n. deriv. of *prester* to lend < L *praestāre* to perform, vouch for, excel (ML: to lend), lit., to stand in front. See PRE-, STAND]

Pres′ter John′ (pres′tər), a legendary Christian monk and potentate of the Middle Ages, supposed to have had a kingdom in some remote part of Asia or Africa and associated with fabulous narratives of travel.

pre•ster•num (prē stûr′nəm), *n., pl.* **-na** (-nə), **-nums.** *Anat.* manubrium. [1870–75; < NL; see PRE-, STERNUM] **—pre•ster′nal,** *adj.*

pres•ti•dig•i•ta•tion (pres′ti dij′i tā′shən), *n.* sleight of hand; legerdemain. [1855–60; < F: lit., ready-fingeredness, coinage perh. based on *prestigiateur* juggler, conjurer, deriv. of L *praestigiae* juggler's tricks (see PRESTIGE). See PREST[1], DIGIT, -ATION] **—pres′ti•dig′i•ta′•tor,** *n.* **—pres•ti•dig•i•ta•to•ry** (pres′ti dij′i tə tôr′ē, -tōr′ē), **pres′ti•dig′i•ta•to′ri•al,** *adj.*

pres•tige (pre stēzh′, -stēj′), *n.* **1.** reputation or influence arising from success, achievement, rank, or other favorable attributes. **2.** distinction or reputation attaching to a person or thing and thus possessing a cachet for others or for the public: *The new discothèque has great prestige with the jet set.* **—*adj.* 3.** having or showing success, rank, wealth, etc. [1650–60 for an earlier sense; < F (orig. pl.): deceits, delusions, juggler's tricks < L *praestigiae* juggler's tricks, var. of *praestrigiae,* deriv. from base of *praestringere* to blunt (sight or mind), lit., to tie up so as to constrict, equiv. to *prae-* PRE- + *stringere* to bind fast; see STRINGENT] **—pres•tige′ful,** *adj.*
—Syn. 1. weight, importance. **—Ant. 1.** disrepute.

pres•tig•ious (pre stij′əs, -stij′ē əs, -stē′jəs, -stē′jē-əs), *adj.* **1.** indicative of or conferring prestige: *the most prestigious address in town.* **2.** having a high reputation; honored; esteemed: *a prestigious author.* [1540–50; < L *praestigiōsus* full of tricks, deceitful, equiv. to *praestigi(um)* (see PRESTIGE) + *-ōsus* -OUS] **—pres•tig′ious•ly,** *adv.* **—pres•tig′ious•ness,** *n.*
—Syn. 1. distinguished. **2.** respected, illustrious, notable.

pres•tis•si•mo (pre stis′ə mō′; *It.* pre stēs′sē mô′), *adv.* (a musical direction) in the most rapid tempo. [1715–25; < It: most quickly, superl. of *presto* PRESTO]

prest′ mon′ey, *Brit. Obs.* a sum of money advanced to men enlisting in the navy or the army, given to bind the bargain and as an inducement. Also called **press money, prest.** [1400–50; late ME]

pres•to (pres′tō), *adv., adj., n., pl.* **-tos. —*adv.* 1.** quickly, rapidly, or immediately. **2.** at a rapid tempo (used as a musical direction). **—*adj.* 3.** quick or rapid. **4.** executed at a rapid tempo (used as a musical direction). **—*n.* 5.** *Music.* a movement or piece in quick tempo. [1590–1600; < It: quick, quickly < LL *praestus* (adj.) ready, L *praestō* (adv.) at hand]

pres′to chan′go (chān′jō), **1.** change at once (usually used imperatively, as in a magician's command). **2.** a change occurring suddenly and as if by magic: *There is always an element of presto chango in international relations.* [rhyming alter. of CHANGE]

Pres•ton (pres′tən), *n.* **1.** a seaport in W Lancashire, in NW England. 131,900. **2.** a male given name.

Pres•ton•pans (pres′tən panz′), *n.* a seaside resort in the Lothian region, in SE Scotland, E of Edinburgh: battle 1745. 3138.

pre•store (prē stôr′, -stōr′), *v.t.,* **-stored, -stor•ing.** *Computers.* to fix an opening value for (the address of an operand or of a cycle index). [PRE- + STORE]

pre•stress (prē stres′), *v.t.* **1.** (in certain concrete construction) to apply stress to (reinforcing strands) before subjecting to a load. **2.** to make (a concrete member) with prestressed reinforcing strands. [1930–35; PRE- + STRESS]

pre′stressed con′crete, concrete reinforced with wire strands, pretensioned or post-tensioned within their elastic limit to give an active resistance to loads. [1935–40]

Prest•wick (prest′wik), *n.* international airport in W Scotland.

pre•sum•a•ble (pri zo͞o′mə bəl), *adj.* capable of being taken for granted; probable. [1685–95; PRESUME + -ABLE]

pre•sum•a•bly (pri zo͞o′mə blē), *adv.* by assuming reasonably; probably: *Since he is a consistent winner, he is presumably a superior player.* [1640–50; PRESUMABLE + -LY]
—Syn. doubtless, likely, apparently.

pre•sume (pri zo͞om′), *v.,* **-sumed, -sum•ing. —*v.t.* 1.** to take for granted, assume, or suppose: *I presume you're tired after your drive.* **2.** *Law.* to assume as true in the absence of proof to the contrary. **3.** to undertake with unwarrantable boldness. **4.** to undertake (to do something) without right or permission: *to presume to speak for another.* **—*v.i.* 5.** to take something for granted; suppose. **6.** to act or proceed with unwarrantable or impertinent boldness. **7.** to go too far in acting unwarrantably or in taking liberties (usually fol. by *on* or *upon*): *Do not presume upon his tolerance.* [1300–50; ME *presumen* (< OF *presumer*) < L *praesūmere* to take beforehand (LL: take for granted, assume, dare), equiv. to *prae-* PRE- + *sūmere* to take up, suppose (see CONSUME)] **—pre•sum•ed•ly** (pri zo͞o′mid lē), *adv.* **—pre•sum′er,** *n.*
—Syn. 1. presuppose. **6.** overstep.

pre•sum•ing (pri zo͞o′ming), *adj.* presumptuous. [1575–85; PRESUME + -ING[2]] **—pre•sum′ing•ly,** *adv.*

pre•sump•tion (pri zump′shən), *n.* **1.** the act of presuming. **2.** assumption of something as true. **3.** belief on reasonable grounds or probable evidence. **4.** something that is presumed; an assumption. **5.** a ground or reason for presuming or believing. **6.** *Law.* an inference required or permitted by law as to the existence of one fact from proof of the existence of other facts. **7.** an assumption, often not fully established, that is taken for granted in some piece of reasoning. **8.** unwarrantable, unbecoming, or impertinent boldness. [1175–1225; ME: effrontery, supposition < L *praesūmptiōn-* (s. of *praesūmptiō*) anticipation, supposition, LL: presumptuousness, equiv. to *praesūmpt(us)* (ptp. of *praesūmere* to undertake beforehand; see PRESUME) + *-iōn-* -ION]
—Syn. 8. audacity, effrontery, arrogance, gall.

presump′tion of fact′, *Law.* a presumption based on experience or knowledge of the relationship between a known fact and a fact inferred from it. [1875–80]

presump′tion of in′nocence, *Law.* the rebuttable presumption of the innocence of the defendant in a criminal action in Anglo-Saxon jurisprudence, placing upon the prosecution the burden of proof of the defendant's guilt.

presump′tion of law′, *Law.* a presumption based upon a policy of law or a general rule and not upon the facts or evidence in an individual case. [1590–1600]

presump′tion of survi′vorship, *Law.* a presumption that one of two or more related persons was the last to die in a common disaster, made so that the estates may be settled and the final heirs determined.

pre•sump•tive (pri zump′tiv), *adj.* **1.** affording ground for presumption: *presumptive evidence.* **2.** based on presumption: *a presumptive title.* **3.** regarded as such by presumption; based on inference. **4.** *Embryol.* pertaining to the part of an embryo that, in the course of normal development, will predictably become a particular structure or region. [1555–65; < LL *praesūmptīvus.* See PRESUMPTION, -IVE] **—pre•sump′tive•ly,** *adv.*

presump′tive heir′, *Law.* See **heir presumptive.** [1620–30]

pre•sump•tu•ous (pri zump′cho͞o əs), *adj.* **1.** full of, characterized by, or showing presumption or readiness to presume in conduct or thought. **2.** unwarrantedly or impertinently bold; forward. **3.** *Obs.* presumptive. [1300–50; ME < LL *praesūmptuōsus,* var. of L *praesūmptiōsus.* See PRESUMPTION, -OUS] **—pre•sump′tu•ous•ly,** *adv.* **—pre•sump′tu•ous•ness,** *n.*
—Syn. 1, 2. impertinent, audacious; fresh; arrogant. See **bold. —Ant. 1, 2.** modest, unassuming.

pre•sup•pose (prē′sə pōz′), *v.t.,* **-posed, -pos•ing. 1.** to suppose or assume beforehand; take for granted in advance. **2.** (of a thing, condition, or state of affairs) to require or imply as an antecedent condition: *An effect presupposes a cause.* [1400–50; late ME < MF *presupposer.* See PRE-, SUPPOSE] **—pre•sup•po•si•tion** (prē′sup ə-zish′ən), *n.* **—pre′sup•po•si′tion•less,** *adj.*
—Syn. 1. presume.

pre•sup•pu•ra•tive (prē sup′yə rā′tiv), *adj. Pathol.* noting or pertaining to the stage of inflammation before the formation of pus. [PRE- + SUPPURATIVE]

pre•sur•mise (*n.* prē′sər mīz′, prē sûr′mīz; *v.* prē′sər-mīz′), *n., v.,* **-mised, -mis•ing. —*n.* 1.** a surmise previously formed. **—*v.t.* 2.** to surmise beforehand. [1655–65; PRE- + SURMISE]

pre•syn•ap•tic (prē′si nap′tik), *adj. Physiol.* being or occurring on the transmitting end of a discharge across a synapse. [1905–10; PRE- + SYNAPTIC] **—pre′syn•ap′ti•cal•ly,** *adv.*

pret., preterit.

pre•ta (prā′tə), *n. Hindu Myth.* a wandering or disturbed ghost. [< Skt: dead]

CONCISE PRONUNCIATION KEY: act, cāpe, dâre, pärt; set, ēqual; if, ice; ox, ōver, ôrder, oil, bo͝ok, bo͞ot, out; up, ûrge; child; sing; shoe; thin, *th*at; zh as in *treasure.* ə = *a* as in *alone, e* as in *system, i* as in *easily, o* as in *gallop, u* as in *circus;* ᵊ as in *fire* (fīᵊr), *hour* (ouᵊr). l and n can serve as syllabic consonants, as in *cradle* (krād′l), and *button* (but′n). See the full key inside the front cover.

pre′re•veal′, *v.t.*
pre′rev•e•la′tion, *n.*
pre′re•venge′, *n., v.t.,* **-venged, -veng•ing.**
pre′re•ver′sal, *n.*
pre′re•verse′, *n., v.t.,* **-versed, -vers•ing.**
pre′re•view′, *n., v.t.*
pre′re•vise′, *v.t.,* **-vised, -vis•ing.**
pre′re•vi′sion, *n.*
pre′re•viv′al, *n., adj.*
pre′-Rev•o•lu′tion, *adj.*
pre′rev•o•lu′tion•ar′y, *adj.*
pre′rheu•mat′ic, *adj.*
pre•right′eous, *adj.;* **-ly,** *adv.;* **-ness,** *n.*
pre•rinse′, *v.t.,* **-rinsed, -rins•ing.**
pre′rinse′, *n.*
pre-Ro′man, *adj., n.*
pre′ro•man′tic, *adj.*
pre′ro•man′ti•cism, *n.*
pre•route′, *v.t.,* **-rout•ed, -rout•ing.**
pre•roy′al, *adj.;* **-ly,** *adv.*
pre•roy′al•ty, *n., pl.* **-ties.**
pre•sa′cral, *adj.*
pre•sac′ri•fice′, *n., v.,* **-ficed, -fic•ing.**
pre′sac•ri•fi′cial, *adj.*
pre•sanc′ti•fy′, *v.t.,* **-fied, -fy•ing.**
pre•san′guine, *adj.*
pre•san′i•tar′y, *adj.*
pre′sar•to′ri•al, *adj.*
pre′sat•is•fac′tion, *n.*
pre′sat•is•fac′to•ry, *adj.*
pre•sat′is•fy′, *v.t.,* **-fied, -fy•ing.**
pre•sav′age, *adj.*
pre•sav′age•ry, *n.*
pre-Sax′on, *adj., n.*
pre•sched′ule, *v.t.,* **-uled, -ul•ing.**
pre′scho•las′tic, *adj.*
pre′sci•en•tif′ic, *adj.*
pre•scout′, *adj.*
pre•screen′ing, *n.*
pre•seal′, *n., v.t.*
pre•search′, *n., v.t.*
pre•sea′son, *n.*
pre•sea′son•al, *adj.*
pre•sec′u•lar, *adj.*
pre•se•cure′, *v.t.,* **-cured, -cur•ing.**
pre•sed′en•tar′y, *adj.*
pre•see′, *v.t.,* **-saw, -seen, -see•ing.**
pre′sem•i•lu′nar, *adj.*
pre•sem′i•nal, *adj.*
pre•sem′i•nar′y, *adj., n., pl.* **-nar•ies.**
pre′-Se•mit′ic, *adj., n.*
pre•sen′tence, *v.t.,* **-tenced, -tenc•ing.**
pre•sep′a•rate′, *v.t.,* **-rat•ed, -rat•ing.**
pre′sep•a•ra′tion, *n.*
pre•sep′a•ra′tor, *n.*
pre•sep′tal, *adj.*
pre•serv′ice, *adj.*
pre•ses′sion, *n.*
pre•set′tle, *v.t.,* **-tled, -tling.**
pre•set′tle•ment, *n.*
pre•shad′ow, *n., v.t.*
pre-Shake′speare, *adj.*
pre′-Shake•spear′e•an, *adj.*
pre′-Shake•spear′i•an, *adj.*
pre•shape′, *n., v.t.,* **-shaped, -shap•ing.**
pre•share′, *n., v.t.,* **-shared, -shar•ing.**
pre•sharp′en, *v.t.*
pre•ship′, *v.t.,* **-shipped, -ship•ping.**
pre•ship′ment, *n.*
pre•short′age, *n.*
pre•short′en, *v.t.*
pre•show′, *adj., n., v.t.,* **-showed, -shown** or **-showed, -show•ing.**
pre•sift′, *v.t.*
pre•sig′nal, *n., v.t.,* **-naled, -nal•ing** or (*esp. Brit.*) **-nalled, -nal•ling.**
pre′-Si•lu′ri•an, *adj., n.*
pre•slav′er•y, *adj., n.*
pre•slice′, *v.t.,* **-sliced, -slic•ing.**
pre•smooth′, *v.t.*
pre•so′cial, *adj.*
pre•so′cial•ism, *n.*
pre•so′cial•ist, *n.*
pre•so′lar, *adj.*
pre′so•lic′it, *v.t.*
pre′so•lic′i•ta′tion, *n.*
pre′-Sol•o•mon′ic, *adj.*
pre′-So•lo′ni•an, *adj.*
pre′so•lu′tion, *n.*
pre•solve′, *v.t.,* **-solved, -solv•ing.**
pre•soph′o•more′, *adj.*
pre•sound′, *n., v.*
pre-Span′ish, *adj.*
pre•spe′cial•ist, *n.*
pre•spe′cial•ize′, *v.i.,* **-ized, -iz•ing.**
pre′spe•cif′ic, *adj.*
pre′spe•cif′i•cal•ly, *adv.*
pre′spec•i•fi•ca′tion, *n.*
pre•spec′i•fy′, *v.t.,* **-fied, -fy•ing.**
pre•spec′u•late′, *v.i.,* **-lat•ed, -lat•ing.**
pre′spec•u•la′tion, *n.*
pre•sphe′noid, *adj.*
pre•spi′nal, *adj.*
pre′spi•rac′u•lar, *adj.*
pre•split′, *adj.*
pre•spread′, *v.t.,* **-spread, -spread•ing.**
pre•sprin′kle, *v.t.,* **-kled, -kling.**
pre•spur′, *v.t.,* **-spurred, -spur•ring.**
pre•stamp′, *n., v.t.*
pre•stand′ard, *n., adj.*
pre•stand′ard•i•za′tion, *n.*
pre•stand′ard•ize′, *v.t.,* **-ized, -iz•ing.**
pre′sta•tis′ti•cal, *adj.*
pre•steam′, *adj., v.t.*
pre•steel′, *n., adj.*

prêt-à-por·ter (pret′ä pôr tā′, -pōr-), *n.* ready-to-wear clothing. [1955–60; < F: trans. of READY-TO-WEAR]

pre·tar·sus (prē tär′səs), *n., pl.* **-si** (-sī). the terminal outgrowth of the tarsus of an arthropod. [< NL; see PRE-, TARSUS]

pre·tax (prē taks′), *adj., adv.* prior to the payment of taxes: *pretax income; bonds earning 12 percent pretax.* [1940–45; PRE- + TAX]

pre·teen (prē tēn′), *n.* **1.** Also called **pre·teen·ag·er** (prē tēn′ā′jər), **pre·teen′er.** a boy or girl under the age of 13, esp. one between the ages of 9 and 12. **2. preteens,** the years immediately preceding one's thirteenth birthday. **—*adj.*** **3.** designating or characteristic of a preteen or preteens: *two preteen daughters.* [1950–55; PRE- + TEEN[2]]

pre·tence (pri tens′, prē′tens), *n. Chiefly Brit.* pretense.

pre·tend (pri tend′), *v.t.* **1.** to cause or attempt to cause (what is not so) to seem so: *to pretend illness; to pretend that nothing is wrong.* **2.** to appear falsely, as to deceive; feign: *to pretend to go to sleep.* **3.** to make believe: *The children pretended to be cowboys.* **4.** to presume; venture: *I can't pretend to say what went wrong.* **5.** to allege or profess, esp. insincerely or falsely: *He pretended to have no knowledge of her whereabouts.* **—*v.i.*** **6.** to make believe. **7.** to lay claim to (usually fol. by *to*): *She pretended to the throne.* **8.** to make pretensions (usually fol. by *to*): *He pretends to great knowledge.* **9.** *Obs.* to aspire, as a suitor or candidate (fol. by *to*). **—*adj.*** **10.** *Informal.* make-believe; simulated; counterfeit: *pretend diamonds.* [1325–75; ME *pretenden* < L *praetendere* to stretch forth, put forward, pretend. See PRE-, TEND[1]]
—Syn. 1. simulate, fake, sham, counterfeit. PRETEND, AFFECT, ASSUME, FEIGN imply an attempt to create a false appearance. To PRETEND is to create an imaginary characteristic or to play a part: *to pretend sorrow.* To AFFECT is to make a consciously artificial show of having qualities that one thinks would look well and impress others: *to affect shyness.* To ASSUME is to take on or put on a specific outward appearance, often (but not always) with intent to deceive: *to assume an air of indifference.* To FEIGN implies using ingenuity in pretense, and some degree of imitation of appearance or characteristics: *to feign surprise.*

pre·tend·ed (pri ten′did), *adj.* **1.** insincerely or falsely professed: *a pretended interest in art.* **2.** feigned, fictitious, or counterfeit: *His pretended wealth was proved to be nonexistent.* **3.** alleged or asserted; reputed. [1425–75; late ME; see PRETEND, -ED[2]] **—pre·tend′ed·ly,** *adv.*

pre·tend·er (pri ten′dər), *n.* **1.** a person who pretends, esp. for a dishonest purpose. **2.** an aspirant or claimant (often fol. by *to*): *a pretender to the throne.* **3.** a person who makes unjustified or false claims, statements, etc., as about personal status, abilities, intentions, or the like: *a pretender to literary genius.* [1585–95; PRETEND + -ER[1]]

pre·tense (pri tens′, prē′tens), *n.* **1.** pretending or feigning; make-believe: *My sleepiness was all pretense.* **2.** a false show of something: *a pretense of friendship.* **3.** a piece of make-believe. **4.** the act of pretending or alleging falsely. **5.** a false allegation or justification: *He excused himself from the lunch on a pretense of urgent business.* **6.** insincere or false profession: *His pious words were mere pretense.* **7.** the putting forth of an unwarranted claim. **8.** the claim itself. **9.** any allegation or claim: *to obtain money under false pretenses.* **10.** pretension (usually fol. by *to*): *destitute of any pretense to wit.* **11.** pretentiousness. Also, *esp. Brit.,* **pretence.** [1375–1425; late ME < AF < ML **praetēnsa*, n. use of fem. of *praetēnsus*, ptp. (r. L *praetentus*) of *praetendere* to PRETEND] **—pre·tense′ful,** *adj.* **—pre·tense′less,** *adj.*
—Syn. 1. shamming. **2.** semblance. **3.** mask, veil.

pre·ten·sion[1] (pri ten′shən), *n.* **1.** the laying of a claim to something. **2.** a claim or title to something. **3.** Often, **pretensions.** a claim made, esp. indirectly or by implication, to some quality, merit, or the like: *They laughed at my pretensions to superior judgment.* **4.** a claim to dignity, importance, or merit. **5.** pretentiousness. **6.** the act of pretending or alleging. **7.** an allegation of doubtful veracity. **8.** a pretext. [1590–1600; < ML *praetēnsiōn-* (s. of *praetēnsiō*). See PRETENSE, -ION]

CONCISE ETYMOLOGY KEY: <, descended or borrowed from; >, whence; b., blend of, blended; c., cognate with; cf., compare; deriv., derivative; equiv., equivalent; imit., imitative; obl., oblique; r., replacing; s., stem; sp., spelling, spelled; resp., respelling, respelled; trans., translation; ?, origin unknown; *, unattested; ‡, probably earlier than. See the full key inside the front cover.

pre·ten·sion[2] (prē ten′shən), *v.t.* **1.** (in prestressed-concrete construction) to apply tension to (reinforcing strands) before the concrete is poured. Cf. **posttension** (def. 1). **2.** to make (a concrete member) with pretensioned reinforcement. [1935–40; PRE- + TENSION]

pre·ten·tious (pri ten′shəs), *adj.* **1.** full of pretense or pretension. **2.** characterized by assumption of dignity or importance. **3.** making an exaggerated outward show; ostentatious. [1835–45; earlier *pretensious.* See PRETENSE, -IOUS] **—pre·ten′tious·ly,** *adv.* **—pre·ten′tious·ness,** *n.*
—Syn. 2. pompous. See **bombastic. 3.** showy. See **grandiose.**

preter-, a prefix, meaning "beyond," "more than," "by," "past," occurring originally in loanwords from Latin (*preterit*), and used in the formation of compound words (*preterlegal*). [< L *praeter-*, prefixal use of *praeter* (adv. and prep.); akin to PRE-]

pre·ter·hu·man (prē′tər hyōō′mən *or, often,* -yōō′-), *adj.* beyond what is human: *preterhuman experience.* [1805–15; PRETER- + HUMAN]

pret·er·ist (pret′ər ist), *Theol.* **—*n.*** **1.** a person who maintains that the prophecies in the Apocalypse have already been fulfilled. Cf. **futurist** (def. 2), **presentist.** **—*adj.*** **2.** of or pertaining to the preterists. [1960–65; PRETER- + -IST]

pret·er·it (pret′ər it), *n. Gram.* **1.** past (def. 12). **2.** a preterit tense. **3.** a verb form in this tense. **—*adj.*** **4.** *Gram.* noting a past action or state. **5.** *Archaic.* bygone; past. Also, **pret′er·ite.** [1300–50; ME < L *praeteritus* past, ptp. of *praeterīre* to go by, equiv. to *praeter-* PRETER- + *-i-*, base of *īre* to go + *-tus* ptp. suffix; as tense name < L (*tempus*) *praeteritum*] **—pret′er·it·ness,** *n.*

pret·er·i·tion (pret′ə rish′ən), *n.* **1.** the act of passing by or over; omission; disregard. **2.** *Law.* the passing over by a testator of an heir otherwise entitled to a portion. **3.** *Calvinistic Theol.* the passing over by God of those not elected to salvation or eternal life. **4.** *Rhet.* paralipsis. [1600–10; < LL *praeteritiōn-* (s. of *praeteritiō*) a passing by. See PRETERIT, -ION]

pre·ter·i·tive (pri ter′i tiv), *adj. Gram.* (of verbs) limited to past tenses. [1830–40; PRETERIT + -IVE]

pre·ter·le·gal (prē′tər lē′gəl), *adj.* being beyond the scope or limits of law. [1640–50; PRETER- + LEGAL]

pre·term (prē tûrm′), *adj.* **1.** occurring earlier in pregnancy than expected; premature: *preterm labor.* **—*n.*** **2.** a baby born prematurely, esp. one born before the 37th week of pregnancy and weighing less than 5½ lb. (2.5 kg). [1925–30; PRE- + TERM]

pre·ter·mit (prē′tər mit′), *v.t.,* **-mit·ted, -mit·ting.** **1.** to let pass without notice; disregard. **2.** to leave undone; neglect; omit. **3.** to suspend or interrupt: *The government temporarily pretermitted its repayments of foreign aid.* [1505–15; < L *praetermittere* to let pass, equiv. to *praeter-* PRETER- + *mittere* to let go, send] **—pre·ter·mis·sion** (prē′tər mish′ən), *n.* **—pre′ter·mit′ter,** *n.*

pre·ter·nat·u·ral (prē′tər nach′ər əl, -nach′rəl), *adj.* **1.** out of the ordinary course of nature; exceptional or abnormal: *preternatural powers.* **2.** outside of nature; supernatural. [1570–80; < ML *praeternātūrālis*, adj. based on L phrase *praeter nātūram* beyond nature. See PRETER-, NATURAL] **—pre′ter·nat′u·ral·ism, pre·ter·nat·u·ral·i·ty** (prē′tər nach′ə ral′i tē), **pre′ter·nat′u·ral·ness,** *n.* **—pre′ter·nat′u·ral·ly,** *adv.*
—Syn. 1. unusual, extraordinary, unnatural. See **miraculous.** **—Ant. 1.** ordinary, usual.

pre·test (*n.* prē′test′; *v.* prē test′), *n.* **1.** an advance or preliminary testing or trial, as of a new product. **2.** a test given to determine if students are sufficiently prepared to begin a new course of study. **3.** a test taken for practice. **—*v.t.*** **4.** to give a pretest to (a student, product, etc.). **—*v.i.*** **5.** to conduct a pretest: *to pretest for consumer acceptance.* [1945–50; PRE- + TEST]

pre·text (prē′tekst), *n.* **1.** something that is put forward to conceal a true purpose or object; an ostensible reason; excuse: *The leaders used the insults as a pretext to declare war.* **2.** the misleading appearance or behavior assumed with this intention: *His many lavish compliments were a pretext for subtle mockery.* [1505–15; < L *praetextum* pretext, ornament, n. use of neut. ptp. of *praetexere* to pretend, lit., to weave in front, hence, adorn. See PRE-, TEXTURE]
—Syn. 2. subterfuge, evasion.

pre·tex·ta (prē tek′stə), *n., pl.* **-tex·tae** (-tek′stē). praetexta.

pre·tick·et·ed (prē tik′i tid), *adj.* having or furnished with a ticket beforehand: *preticketed passengers.* [PRE- + TICKET + -ED[2]]

pre·tor (prē′tər), *n.* praetor.

Pre·to·ri·a (pri tôr′ē ə, -tōr′-), *n.* a city in and the administrative capital of the Republic of South Africa, in the NE part: also the capital of Transvaal. 595,000.

Pre·to·ri·us (pri tôr′ē əs, -tōr′-; *Du.* prä tō′rē ōōs′), *n.* **An·dries Wil·hel·mus Ja·co·bus** (än′drēs vil hel′mōōs yä kô′bōōs), 1799–1853, and his son **Mar·thi·nus Wes·sels** (mär tē′nōōs ves′əls), 1819–1901, Boer soldiers and statesmen in South Africa.

pre·tor·ship (prē′tər ship′), *n.* praetorship.

pre·treat (prē trēt′), *v.t.* to treat in advance or as part of a preliminary treatment: *to pretreat wood before staining it.* [1930–35; PRE- + TREAT] **—pre·treat′·ment,** *n.*

pre·tri·al (prē trī′əl, -trīl′), *n.* **1.** a proceeding held by a judge, arbitrator, etc., before a trial to simplify the issues of law and fact and stipulate certain matters between the parties, in order to expedite justice and curtail costs at the trial. **—*adj.*** **2.** of or pertaining to such a proceeding. **3.** done, occurring, etc., prior to a trial: *pretrial publicity.* [1935–40; PRE- + TRIAL]

pret·ti·fy (prit′ə fī′), *v.t.,* **-fied, -fy·ing.** **1.** to make pretty, esp. in a small, petty way: *to prettify a natural beauty.* **2.** to minimize or gloss over (something unpleasant): *to prettify his rude behavior.* [1840–50; PRETT(Y) + -IFY] **—pret′ti·fi·ca′tion,** *n.* **—pret′ti·fi′·er,** *n.*

pret·ty (prit′ē), *adj.,* **-ti·er, -ti·est,** *n., pl.* **-ties,** *adv., v.,* **-tied, -ty·ing.** **—*adj.*** **1.** pleasing or attractive to the eye, as by delicacy or gracefulness: *a pretty face.* **2.** (of things, places, etc.) pleasing to the eye, esp. without grandeur. **3.** pleasing to the ear: *a pretty tune.* **4.** pleasing to the mind or aesthetic taste: *He writes pretty little stories.* **5.** (often used ironically) fine; grand: *This is a pretty mess!* **6.** *Informal.* considerable; fairly great: *This accident will cost him a pretty sum.* **7.** *Archaic* or *Scot.* brave; hardy. **—*n.*** **8.** Usually, **pretties.** pretty ornaments, clothes, etc. **9.** a pretty person: *Sit down, my pretty.* **—*adv.*** **10.** fairly or moderately: *Her work was pretty good.* **11.** quite; very: *The wind blew pretty hard.* **12.** *Informal.* prettily. **13. sitting pretty,** *Informal.* **a.** in an advantageous position. **b.** well-to-do; successful. **—*v.t.*** **14.** to make pretty; improve the appearance of (sometimes fol. by *up*): *to pretty oneself for a party; to pretty up a room.* [bef. 1000; ME *prati(e), pratte, prettie* cunning, gallant, fine, handsome, pretty; OE *prættig, pretti* cunning, deriv. of *prætt* a trick, wile (c. D *part, pret* trick, prank, ON *prettr* trick, *prettugr* tricky)] **—pret′·ti·ly,** *adv.* **—pret′ti·ness,** *n.* **—pret′ty·ish,** *adj.*
—Syn. 1. See **beautiful. 2–4.** pleasant. **10.** somewhat. **—Ant. 1.** ugly.
—Usage. The qualifying adverb PRETTY, meaning "fairly or moderately" has been in general use since the late 16th century. Although most common in informal speech and writing, it is far from restricted to them, and often is less stilted than alternatives such as *relatively, moderately,* and *quite.*

pre·typ·i·fy (prē tip′ə fī′), *v.t.,* **-fied, -fy·ing.** to foreshadow or prefigure the type of: *The father's personality pretypified his son's.* [1650–60; PRE- + TYPIFY]

pret·zel (pret′səl), *n.* **1.** a crisp, dry biscuit, usually in the form of a knot or stick, salted on the outside. **2.** a larger version of this, made of soft, chewy bread dough. [1815–25, *Amer.*; < G *Pretzel,* var. of *Bretzel;* OHG *brizzila* < ML *bracellus* BRACELET]

Preus·sen (proi′sən), *n.* German name of **Prussia.**

prev., 1. previous. **2.** previously.

pre·vail (pri vāl′), *v.i.* **1.** to be widespread or current; exist everywhere or generally: *Silence prevailed along the funeral route.* **2.** to appear or occur as the more important or frequent feature or element; predominate: *Green tints prevail in the upholstery.* **3.** to be or prove superior in strength, power, or influence (usually fol. by *over*): *They prevailed over their enemies in the battle.* **4.** to succeed; become dominant; win out: *to wish that the right side might prevail.* **5.** to use persuasion or inducement successfully: *He prevailed upon us to accompany*

pre·ster′i·lize′, *v.t.,* **-lized, -liz·ing.**
pre·stim′u·late′, *v.t.,* **-lat·ed, -lat·ing.**
pre′stim·u·la′tion, *n.*
pre·stim′u·lus, *n., pl.* **-li.**
pre·stock′, *n., v.t.*
pre·stor′age, *n.*
pre·straight′en, *v.t.*
pre·strain′, *n., v.t.*
pre·strength′en, *v.t.*
pre·stretch′, *v.t., n.*
pre·strike′, *adj., v.,* **-struck, -struck** or **-strick·en, -strik·ing.**
pre·struc′ture, *v.t.,* **-tured, -tur·ing.**
pre·strug′gle, *n., v.i.,* **-gled, -gling.**
pre·stub′born, *adj.*
pre·stu′di·ous, *adj.;* **-ly,** *adv.;* **-ness,** *n.*
pre·stud′y, *v.t.,* **-stud·ied, -stud·y·ing,** *n., pl.* **-stud·ies.**
pre′sub·due′, *v.t.,* **-dued, du·ing.**
pre′sub·ject′, *v.t.*
pre′sub·jec′tion, *n.*
pre′sub·mis′sion, *n.*
pre′sub·mit′, *v.t.,* **-mit·ted, -mit·ting.**
pre′sub·or′di·nate′, *v.t.,* **-nat·ed, -nat·ing.**
pre′sub·or′di·na′tion, *n.*
pre′sub·scribe′, *v.,* **-scribed, -scrib·ing.**
pre′sub·scrib′er, *n.*
pre′sub·scrip′tion, *n.*
pre′sub·sist′, *v.i.*
pre′sub·sist′ence, *n.*
pre′sub·sist′ent, *adj.*
pre′sub·stan′tial, *adj.*
pre·sub′sti·tute′, *v.t.,* **-tut·ed, -tut·ing.**
pre′sub·sti·tu′tion, *n.*
pre′suc·cess′, *n.*
pre′suc·cess′ful, *adj.;* **-ly,** *adv.*
pre·suf′fer, *v.*
pre′suf·fi′cien·cy, *n.*
pre′suf·fi′cient, *adj.;* **-ly,** *adv.*
pre·suf′frage, *n.*
pre′sug·gest′, *v.t.*
pre′sug·ges′tion, *n.*
pre′sug·ges′tive, *adj.*
pre′suit·a·bil′i·ty, *n.*
pre·suit′a·ble, *adj.;* **-bly,** *adv.*
pre′-Su·me′ri·an, *adj., n.*
pre·sum′mit, *adj., n.*
pre′su·per·in·tend′ence, *n.*
pre′su·per·in·tend′en·cy, *n.*
pre·su′per·vise′, *v.t.,* **-vised, -vis·ing.**
pre′su·per·vi′sion, *n.*
pre·su′per·vi′sor, *n.*
pre′sup·ple·men′tal, *adj.*
pre′sup·ple·men′ta·ry, *adj.*
pre·sup′pli·cate′, *v.t.,* **-cat·ed, -cat·ing.**
pre′sup·pli·ca′tion, *n.*
pre′sup·ply′, *n., pl.* **-plies,** *v.t.,* **-plied, -ply·ing.**
pre′sup·port′, *n., v.t.*
pre′sup·press′, *v.t.*
pre′su·prem′a·cy, *n.*
pre·sur′ger·y, *adj.*
pre·sur′gi·cal, *adj.*
pre′sur·ren′der, *n.*
pre′sur·round′, *v.t.*
pre·sur′vey, *n.*
pre′sur·vey′, *v.t.*
pre′sus·cep′ti·bil′i·ty, *n., pl.* **-ties.**
pre′sus·cep′ti·ble, *adj.*
pre′sus·pect′, *v.t.*
pre′sus·pend′, *v.t.*
pre′sus·pen′sion, *n.*
pre′sus·pi′cion, *n.*
pre′sus·pi′cious, *adj.;* **-ly,** *adv.;* **-ness,** *n.*
pre′sus·tain′, *v.t.*
pre·su′tur·al, *adj.*
pre·swal′low, *n., v.t.*
pre·sweet′en, *v.t.*
pre·sym′pa·thize′, *v.i.,* **-thized, -thiz·ing.**
pre·sym′pa·thy, *n.*
pre′sym·phon′ic, *adj.*
pre·sym′pho·ny, *n., pl.* **-nies.**
pre′sym·phys′i·al, *adj.*
pre·symp′tom, *n.*
pre′symp·to·mat′ic, *adj.*
pre′syn·sa′cral, *adj.*
pre-Syr′i·ac′, *adj., n.*
pre-Syr′i·an, *adj., n.*
pre′sys·tem·at′ic, *adj.*
pre′sys·tem·at′i·cal·ly, *adv.*
pre·sys′to·le′, *n.*
pre′sys·tol′ic, *adj.*
pre·tab′u·late′, *v.t.,* **-lat·ed, -lat·ing.**
pre′tab·u·la′tion, *n.*
pre·tan′gi·ble, *adj.;* **-bly,** *adv.*
pre·tape′, *v.t.,* **-taped, -tap·ing.**
pre·tar′iff, *n., adj.*
pre·taste′, *n., v.t.,* **-tast·ed, -tast·ing.**
pre·tast′er, *n.*
pre·teach′, *v.,* **-taught, -teach·ing.**
pre·tech′ni·cal, *adj.;* **-ly,** *adv.*
pre′tech·no·log′i·cal, *adj.;* **-ly,** *adv.*
pre·tel′e·graph′, *adj.*
pre′tel·e·graph′ic, *adj.*
pre·tel′e·phone′, *adj.*
pre′tel·e·phon′ic, *adj.*
pre·tel′e·vi′sion, *adj.*
pre·tell′, *v.,* **-told, -tell·ing.**
pre·tem′per·ate, *adj.;* **-ly,** *adv.*
pre·tempt′, *v.t.*
pre′temp·ta′tion, *n.*
pre·ten′ta·tive, *adj.*
pre·ter′mi·nal, *adj.*
pre′ter·res′tri·al, *adj.*
pre′ter·ri·to′ri·al, *adj.*
pre-Ter′ti·ar′y, *adj.*
pre·tes′ti·fy′, *v.t.,* **-fied, -fy·ing.**
pre·tes′ti·mo′ny, *n., pl.* **-nies.**
pre′-Thanks·giv′ing, *adj.*
pre·the′a·ter, *adj.*
pre′the·o·log′i·cal, *adj.*

him. [1350–1400; ME *prevayllen* to grow very strong < L *praevalēre* to be more able, equiv. to *prae-* PRE- + *valēre* to be strong; see PREVALENT] —**pre•vail′er,** *n.*
—**Syn. 2.** preponderate. **3.** overcome. —**Ant. 3.** lose.

pre•vail•ing (pri vā′ling), *adj.* **1.** predominant: *prevailing winds.* **2.** generally current: *the prevailing opinion.* **3.** having superior power or influence. **4.** effectual. [1580–90; PREVAIL + -ING²] —**pre•vail′ing•ly,** *adv.* —**pre•vail′ing•ness,** *n.*
—**Syn. 1.** preponderant, preponderating, dominant; prevalent. **2.** common. See **current. 4.** effective.
—**Ant. 2.** rare.

prev•a•lent (prev′ə lənt), *adj.* **1.** widespread; of wide extent or occurrence; in general use or acceptance. **2.** having the superiority or ascendancy. **3.** *Archaic.* effectual or efficacious. [1570–80; < L *praevalent-* (s. of *praevalēns*), prp. of *praevalēre* to PREVAIL. See PRE-, -VALENT] —**prev′a•lence, prev′a•lent•ness,** *n.* —**prev′a•lent•ly,** *adv.*
—**Syn. 1.** common, extensive. See **current.** —**Ant. 1.** rare.

pre•var•i•cate (pri var′i kāt′), *v.i.*, **-cat•ed, -cat•ing.** to speak falsely or misleadingly; deliberately misstate or create an incorrect impression; lie. [1575–85; < L *praevāricātus*, ptp. of *praevāricārī* to straddle something, (of an advocate) collude with an opponent's advocate, equiv. to *prae-* PRE- + *vāricāre* to straddle, deriv. of *vārus* bent outwards, bow-legged] —**pre•var′i•ca′tion,** *n.* —**pre•var′i•ca′tive, pre•var•i•ca•to•ry** (pri var′i kə tôr′ē, -tōr′ē), *adj.*
—**Syn.** evade, shift.

pre•var•i•ca•tor (pri var′i kā′tər), *n.* **1.** a person who speaks falsely; liar. **2.** a person who speaks so as to avoid the precise truth; quibbler; equivocator. [1535–45; < L *praevāricātor;* see PREVARICATE, -TOR]

pré•ve•nance (prāvᵊ näns′), *n., pl.* ***-nances*** (-näns′) for 2. *French.* **1.** assiduity in anticipating or catering to the pleasures of others. **2.** an instance of this.

pre•ve•nient (pri vēn′yənt), *adj.* **1.** coming before; antecedent. **2.** anticipatory. [1600–10; < L *praevenient-* (s. of *praeveniēns*) coming before, prp. of *praevenīre* to anticipate. See PRE-, CONVENIENT] —**pre•ve•nance** (prev′ə nəns), **pre•ven•ience** (pri vēn′yəns), *n.* —**pre•ven′ient•ly,** *adv.*

preven′ient grace′, divine grace operating on the human will prior to its turning to God. [1660–70]

pre•vent (pri vent′), *v.t.* **1.** to keep from occurring; avert; hinder: *He intervened to prevent bloodshed.* **2.** to hinder or stop from doing something: *There is nothing to prevent us from going.* **3.** *Archaic.* to act ahead of; forestall. **4.** *Archaic.* to precede. **5.** *Archaic.* to anticipate. —*v.i.* **6.** to interpose a hindrance: *He will come if nothing prevents.* [1375–1425; late ME < L *praeventus* (ptp. of *praevenīre* to anticipate), equiv. to *prae-* PRE- + *ven-* (s. of *venīre* to COME) + *-tus* ptp. suffix] —**pre•vent′a•ble, pre•vent′i•ble,** *adj.* —**pre•vent′a•bil′ty,** *n.* —**pre•vent′ing•ly,** *adv.*
—**Syn. 1.** obstruct, forestall, preclude, obviate, thwart. PREVENT, HAMPER, HINDER, IMPEDE refer to different degrees of stoppage of action or progress. To PREVENT is to stop something effectually by forestalling action and rendering it impossible: *to prevent the sending of a message.* To HAMPER is to clog or entangle or put an embarrassing restraint upon: *to hamper preparations for a trip.* To HINDER is to keep back by delaying or stopping progress or action: *to hinder the progress of an expedition.* To IMPEDE is to make difficult the movement or progress of anything by interfering with its proper functioning: *to impede a discussion by demanding repeated explanations.* —**Ant. 1.** help, assist.

pre•vent•er (pri ven′tər), *n.* **1.** a person or thing that prevents. **2.** *Naut.* **a.** any of various lines set up to reinforce or relieve ordinary running or standing rigging. **b.** a line for preventing a sail from jibbing. [1580–90; PREVENT + -ER¹]

pre•ven•tion (pri ven′shən), *n.* **1.** the act of preventing; effectual hindrance. **2.** a preventive: *This serum is a prevention against disease.* [1520–30; < LL *praeventiōn-* (s. of *praeventiō*) a forestalling. See PREVENT, -ION]

pre•ven•tive (pri ven′tiv), *adj.* **1.** *Med.* of or noting a drug, vaccine, etc., for preventing disease; prophylactic. **2.** serving to prevent or hinder: *preventive measures.* —*n.* **3.** *Med.* a drug or other substance for preventing disease. **4.** a preventive agent or measure. Also, **pre•vent•a•tive** (pri ven′tə tiv) (for defs. 2, 4). [1630–40; PREVENT + -IVE] —**pre•ven′tive•ly,** *adv.* —**pre•ven′tive•ness,** *n.*

preven′tive deten′tion, 1. the holding of someone in jail or in an institution because he or she is regarded as a danger to the community. **2.** *Eng. Law.* imprisonment of habitual criminals for periods ranging from 5 to 14 years during which they are given corrective training or placed under psychiatric and medical care. [1905–10]

preven′tive law′, *Law.* consultation, as between lawyer and client, to prevent future litigation by dispensing legal advice, clarifying the terms of a contract, etc.

preven′tive med′icine, 1. the branch of medical science that deals with prevention of disease. **2.** a medication or other agent used for prophylaxis. [1760–70]

preven′tive war′, *Mil.* an attack against a possible enemy to prevent an attack by that enemy at a later time. Also called **preemptive strike.** [1630–40]

pre•view (prē′vyōō′), *n.* **1.** an earlier or previous view. **2.** an advance showing of a motion picture, play, etc., before its public opening. **3.** an advance showing of brief scenes in a motion picture, television show, etc., for purposes of advertisement. **4.** anything that gives an advance idea or impression of something to come. —*v.t.* **5.** to view or show beforehand or in advance. Also, **prevue.** [1600–10; 1920–25 for def. 2; PRE- + VIEW]

pre•vi•ous (prē′vē əs), *adj.* **1.** coming or occurring before something else; prior: *the previous owner.* **2.** *Informal.* done, occurring, etc., before the proper time; premature: *Aren't you a little previous with that request?* **3. previous to,** before; prior to: *Previous to moving here she lived in Chicago.* [1615–25; < L *praevius* going before, equiv. to *prae-* PRE- + *vi(a)* way + *-us* adj. suffix] —**pre′vi•ous•ly,** *adv.* —**pre′vi•ous•ness,** *n.*
—**Syn. 1.** earlier, former, preceding, foregoing.

pre′vious ques′tion, *Parl. Proc.* a move that a vote be taken at once on a main question, used esp. as a means of cutting off further debate. [1690–1700]

pre•vise (pri vīz′), *v.t.*, **-vised, -vis•ing. 1.** to foresee. **2.** to forewarn. [1425–75; late ME < L *praevīsus* ptp. of *praevidēre* to foresee. See PRE-, VISA] —**pre•vi′sor,** *n.*

pre•vi•sion (pri vizh′ən), *n.* **1.** foresight, foreknowledge, or prescience. **2.** a prophetic or anticipatory vision or perception. [1605–15; PRE- + VISION] —**pre•vi′sion•al,** *adj.*

pre•vo•cal•ic (prē′vō kal′ik), *adj. Phonet.* immediately preceding a vowel. [1905–10; PRE- + VOCALIC] —**pre′vo•cal′i•cal•ly,** *adv.*

pre•vo•ca•tion•al (prē′vō kā′shə nl), *adj.* of, pertaining to, or constituting preliminary vocational training. [1910–15; PRE- + VOCATIONAL]

Pré•vost (prā vō′), *n.* **Mar•cel** (MAR sel′), 1862–1941, French novelist and dramatist.

Pré•vost d'Ex•iles (prā vō′ deg zēl′), **An•toine Fran•çois** (äN TWAN′ FRÄN SWA′), ("*Abbé Prévost*"), 1697–1763, French novelist.

pre•vue (prē′vyōō′), *n., v.t.*, **-vued, -vu•ing.** preview.

pre•war (prē′wôr′), *adj.* before the war: *prewar prices.* [1905–10; PRE- + WAR¹]

pre•washed (prē′wosht′, -wôsht′), *adj.* being washed before sale, esp. to produce a soft texture or a worn look: *prewashed blue jeans.* [PRE- + WASHED]

prex•y (prek′sē), *n., pl.* **prex•ies.** *Slang.* a president, esp. of a college or university. Also, **prex.** [1855–60; *prex* (by shortening and alter. of *president*) + -Y²]

prey (prā), *n.* **1.** an animal hunted or seized for food, esp. by a carnivorous animal. **2.** a person or thing that is the victim of an enemy, a swindler, a disease, etc.; gull. **3.** the action or habit of preying: *a beast of prey.* **4.** *Archaic.* booty or plunder. —*v.i.* **5.** to seize and devour prey, as an animal does (usually fol. by *on* or *upon*): *Foxes prey on rabbits.* **6.** to make raids or attacks for booty or plunder: *The Vikings preyed on coastal settlements.* **7.** to exert a harmful or destructive influence: *His worries preyed upon his mind.* **8.** to victimize another or others (usually fol. by *on* or *upon*): *loan sharks that prey upon the poor.* [1200–50; ME *preye* < OF < L *praeda* booty, prey; akin to *prehendere* to grasp, seize (see PREHENSION)] —**prey′er,** *n.*
—**Syn. 2.** dupe, target.

prez (prez), *n. Informal.* president. [by shortening and resp.]

PRF, *Telecommunications.* pulse repetition frequency.

prf., proof.

Pri•am (prī′əm), *n. Class. Myth.* **1.** a king of Troy, the son of Laomedon, husband of Hecuba, and father of Paris, Cassandra, Hector, Polyxena, and many others. He was killed during the capture of Troy. **2.** the grandson of King Priam. Also, **Pri•a•mus** (prī′ə məs).

pri•a•pe•an (prī′ə pē′ən), *adj.* priapic. [< F *priapéen* < L *Priāpē(us)* (< Gk *Priāpeios*) + -AN. See PRIAPUS, -AN]

pri•ap•ic (prī ap′ik), *adj.* **1.** (*sometimes cap.*) of or pertaining to Priapus; phallic. **2.** characterized by or emphasizing a phallus: *priapic figurines.* **3.** (of an image) suggestive of or resembling a phallus by its shape. **4.** exaggeratedly concerned with masculinity and male sexuality. [1780–90; PRIAP(US) + -IC]

pri•a•pism (prī′ə piz′əm), *n.* **1.** *Pathol.* continuous, usually nonsexual erection of the penis, esp. due to disease. **2.** prurient behavior or display. [1580–90; PRIAP(US) + -ISM] —**pri′a•pis′mic,** *adj.*

pri•a•pi•tis (prī′ə pī′tis), *n. Pathol.* inflammation of the penis. [PRIAP(US) + -ITIS]

Pri•a•pus (prī ā′pəs), *n.* **1.** *Class. Myth.* a god of male procreative power, the son of Dionysus and Aphrodite. **2.** (*l.c.*) a phallus.

Prib′i•lof Is′lands (prib′ə lôf′, -lof′), a group of islands in the Bering Sea, SW of Alaska, and belonging to the U.S.: the breeding ground of fur seals.

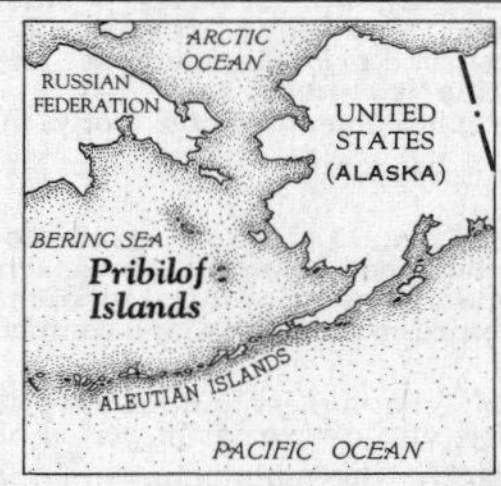

price (prīs), *n., v.*, **priced, pric•ing.** —*n.* **1.** the sum or amount of money or its equivalent for which anything is bought, sold, or offered for sale. **2.** a sum offered for the capture of a person alive or dead: *The authorities put a price on his head.* **3.** the sum of money, or other consideration, for which a person's support, consent, etc., may be obtained, esp. in cases involving sacrifice of integrity: *They claimed that every politician has a price.* **4.** that which must be given, done, or undergone in order to obtain a thing: *He gained the victory, but at a heavy price.* **5.** odds (def. 2). **6.** *Archaic.* value or worth. **7.** *Archaic.* great value or worth (usually prec. by *of*). **8. at any price,** at any cost, no matter how great: *Their orders were to capture the town at any price.* **9. beyond** or **without price,** of incalculable value; priceless: *The crown jewels are beyond price.* —*v.t.* **10.** to fix the price of. **11.** to ask or determine the price of: *We spent the day pricing furniture at various stores.* [1175–1225; (n.) ME *pris(e)* < OF < L *pretium* price, value, worth (cf. PRECIOUS); (v.) late ME *prisen* < MF *prisier*, deriv. of *pris*, OF as above; see PRIZE², PRAISE] —**price′a•ble,** *adj.*
—**Syn. 1, 4.** PRICE, CHARGE, COST, EXPENSE refer to outlay or expenditure required in buying or maintaining something. PRICE is used mainly of single, concrete objects offered for sale; CHARGE, of services: *What is the price of that coat? There is a small charge for mailing packages.* COST is mainly a purely objective term, often used in financial calculations: *The cost of building a new annex was estimated at $10,000.* EXPENSE suggests cost plus incidental expenditure: *The expense of the journey was more than the contemplated cost.* Only CHARGE is not used figuratively. PRICE, COST, and sometimes EXPENSE may be used to refer to the expenditure of mental energy, what one "pays" in anxiety, suffering, etc.

CONCISE PRONUNCIATION KEY: act, cāpe, dâre, pärt; set, ēqual; if, ice; ox, ōver, ôrder, oil, bŏŏk, bōōt, out; up, ûrge; child; sing; shoe; thin, *that;* zh as in *treasure.* ə = *a* as in *alone, e* as in *system, i* as in *easily, o* as in *gallop, u* as in *circus;* ᵊ as in *fire* (fīᵊr), *hour* (ouᵊr). l and n can serve as syllabic consonants, as in *cradle* (krād′l), and *button* (but′n). See the full key inside the front cover.

pre′tho•rac′ic, *adj.*
pre•threat′en, *v.t.*
pre•thrust′, *n., v.t.,* **-thrust, -thrust•ing.**
pre•thy′roid, *adj.*
pre•tib′i•al, *adj.*
pre•time′li•ness, *n.*
pre•time′ly, *adj.*
pre•tinc′ture, *n.*
pre•tire′, *v.t.,* **-tired, -tir•ing.**
pre•to′ken, *n., v.t.*
pre•ton′ic, *n., adj.*
pre•tor′ture, *n., v.t.,* **-tured, -tur•ing.**
pre•tour′na•ment, *n.*
pre•trace′, *n., v.t.,* **-traced, -trac•ing.**
pre•tra′che•al, *adj.*
pre′tra•di′tion•al, *adj.*
pre•train′, *v.t.*
pre•train′ing, *n.*
pre′trans•act′, *v.t.*
pre′trans•ac′tion, *n.*
pre′tran•scribe′, *v.t.,* **-scribed, -scrib•ing.**
pre′tran•scrip′tion, *n.*
pre′trans•late′, *v.t.,* **-lat•ed, -lat•ing.**
pre′trans•la′tion, *n.*
pre′trans•mis′sion, *n.*
pre′trans•mit′, *v.t.,* **-mit•ted, -mit•ting.**
pre′trans•port′, *v.t.*
pre′trans•por•ta′tion, *n.*
pre•trav′el, *n., v.,* **-eled, -el•ing** or (*esp. Brit.*) **-elled, -el•ling.**
pre•trib′al, *adj.*
pre′-Tri•den′tine, *adj.*
pre•trim′, *v.,* **-trimmed, -trim•ming.**
pre•tro′chal, *adj.*
pre•try′, *v.t.,* **tried, -try•ing.**
pre-Tu′dor, *adj.*
pre′tym•pan′ic, *adj.*
pre•type′, *v.t.,* **-typed, -typ•ing.**
pre•ty′phoid, *adj.*
pre′ty•po•graph′i•cal, *adj.*
pre′ty•ran′ni•cal, *adj.*
pre•tyr′an•ny, *n., pl.* **-nies.**
pre•um′bo•nal, *adj.*
pre′un•der•stand′, *v.,* **-stood, -stand•ing.**
pre′un•der•take′, *v.t.,* **-took, -tak•en, -tak•ing.**
pre′u•ni•fi•ca′tion, *adj.*
pre•un′ion, *adj.*
pre′u•nite′, *v.t.,* **-nit•ed, -nit•ing.**
pre•u•ni•ver′si•ty, *adj.*
pre•u′ti•liz′a•ble, *adj.*
pre•u′ti•li•za′tion, *n.*
pre•u′ti•lize′, *v.t.,* **-lized, -liz•ing.**
pre•va′cate, *v.t.,* **-cat•ed, -cat•ing.**
pre′va•ca′tion, *n., adj.*
pre′vac′ci•nate′, *v.t.,* **-nat•ed, -nat•ing.**
pre′vac•ci•na′tion, *n.*
pre•val′id, *adj.;* **-ly,** *adv.*
pre′va•lid′i•ty, *n.*
pre′val•u•a′tion, *n.*
pre•val′ue, *n., v.t.,* **-ued, -u•ing.**
pre′var•i•a′tion, *n.*
pre′veg•e•ta′tion, *n.*
pre•ven′tral, *adj.*
pre•ven′ture, *n., v.,* **-tured, -tur•ing.**
pre•ver′bal, *adj.*
pre′-Ver•gil′i•an, *adj.*
pre′ver•i•fi•ca′tion, *n.*
pre•ver′i•fy′, *v.t.,* **-fied, -fy•ing.**
pre•ver′sion, *n.*
pre•ver′te•bral, *adj.*
pre•ve′to, *n., pl.* **-toes,** *v.t.,* **-toed, -to•ing.**
pre′-Vic•to′ri•an, *adj.*
pre′vic•to′ri•ous, *adj.*
pre•vig′i•lance, *n.*
pre•vig′i•lant, *adj.;* **-ly,** *adv.*
pre•vi′o•late′, *v.t.,* **-lat•ed, -lat•ing.**
pre′vi•o•la′tion, *n.*
pre′-Vir•gil′i•an, *adj.*
pre•vis′i•bil′i•ty, *n.*
pre•vis′i•ble, *adj.;* **-bly,** *adv.*
pre•vis′it, *n., v.*
pre•vis′i•tor, *n.*
pre•vogue′, *n.*
pre•void′, *v.t.*
pre•void′ance, *n.*
pre′vo•li′tion•al, *adj.*
pre-Vol′stead, *adj.*
pre′vol•un•teer′, *n., v.*
pre•vote′, *n., v.,* **-vot•ed, -vot•ing.**
pre•warm′, *v.t.*
pre•warn′, *v.t.*
pre•war′rant, *n., v.t.*
pre•wash′, *n., v.t.*
pre•wean′ing, *adj.*
pre•weigh′, *v.t.*
pre•wel′come, *n., v.t.,* **-comed, -com•ing.**
pre•whip′, *v.t.,* **-whipped, -whip•ping.**
pre•will′ing, *adj.;* **-ly,** *adv.;* **-ness,** *n.*
pre•wire′, *v.t.,* **-wired, -wir•ing.**
pre•wire′less, *adj.*
pre•wit′ness, *n., v.t.*
pre•work′, *v.,* **-worked** or **-wrought, work•ing.**
pre•work′, *n., adj.*
pre•world′li•ness, *n.*
pre•world′ly, *adj.*
pre•wor′ship, *n., v.,* **-shiped, -ship•ing** or (*esp. Brit.*) **-shipped, -ship•ping.**
pre•wor′thi•ly, *adv.*
pre•wor′thi•ness, *n.*
pre•wor′thy, *adj.*
pre•wound′, *n., v.t.*
pre•wrap′, *v.t.,* **-wrapped, -wrap•ping.**
pre′wrap′, *n.*
pre•writ′ten, *adj.*
pre•youth′ful, *adj.*
pre′zy•go•mat′ic, *adj.*

Price (prīs), *n.* **1. Bruce,** 1845–1903, U.S. architect. **2. (Mary) Le·on·tyne** (lē′ən tēn′), born 1927, U.S. soprano. **3.** a male given name.

price′ control′, government regulation of prices by establishing maximum price levels for goods or services, as during a period of inflation. [1910–15]

price-cut (prīs′kut′), *v.t.,* **-cut, -cut·ting.** to reduce the price of, esp. to gain a competitive advantage. [1920–25] **—price′-cut′ter,** *n.*

price′ cut′ting, selling an article at a price under the usual or advertised price. Also, **price′-cut′ting.** [1895–1900]

price′ discrimina′tion, the practice of offering identical goods to different buyers at different prices, when the goods cost the same. [1955–60]

price′-earn′ings ra′tio (prīs′ûr′ningz), the current price of a share of common stock divided by earnings per share over a 12-month period, often used in stock evaluation. *Abbr.:* p/e Also called **price′-earn′ings mul′tiple.** [1960–65]

price′ fix′ing, the establishing of prices at a determined level, either by a government or by mutual consent among producers or sellers of a commodity. Also, **price′-fix′ing.** [1945–50]

price′ in′dex, an index of the changes in the prices of goods and services, based on the prices of the same goods and services at a period arbitrarily selected as a base, usually expressed as 100. [1885–90]

price·less (prīs′lis), *adj.* **1.** having a value beyond all price; invaluable: *a priceless artwork.* **2.** delightfully amusing or absurd: *a priceless anecdote.* [1905–10; PRICE + -LESS] **—price′less·ness,** *n.*
—Syn. 1. irreplaceable, precious, costly, incomparable.

price′ list′, a list giving the prices of items for sale. [1870–75]

pric·er (prī′sər), *n.* **1.** (esp. in retail stores) an employee who establishes prices at which articles will be sold, or one who affixes price tags to merchandise. **2.** a person who inquires prices, as from a competitor. [1875–80; PRICE + -ER[1]]

price′ range′, the highest and lowest price of a commodity, security, etc., over a given period of time.

price′ support′, the maintenance of the price of a commodity, product, etc., esp. by means of a public subsidy or government purchase of surpluses. [1945–50]

price′ tag′, a label or tag that shows the price of the item to which it is attached. [1880–85, *Amer.*]

price′ war′, intensive competition, esp. among retailers, in which prices are repeatedly cut in order to undersell competitors or sometimes to force smaller competitors out of business. [1925–30]

pric·ey (prī′sē), *adj.,* **pric·i·er, pric·i·est.** expensive or unduly expensive: *a pricey wine.* Also, **pricy.** [1930–35; PRICE + -Y[1]] **—pric′i·ly,** *adv.* **—pric′ey·ness,** *n.*

Prich·ard (prich′ərd), *n.* a city in S Alabama. 39,541.

prick (prik), *n.* **1.** a puncture made by a needle, thorn, or the like. **2.** a sharp point; prickle. **3.** the act of pricking: *the prick of a needle.* **4.** the state or sensation of being pricked. **5.** a sharp pain caused by or as if by being pricked; twinge. **6.** the pointed end of a prickspur. **7.** *Slang* (*vulgar*). **a.** penis. **b.** an obnoxious or contemptible person. **8.** *Archaic.* a goad for oxen. **9.** *Obs.* a small or minute mark, a dot, or a point. **10.** *Obs.* any pointed instrument or weapon. **11. kick against the pricks,** to resist incontestable facts or authority; protest uselessly: *In appealing the case again, you will just be kicking against the pricks.* —*v.t.* **12.** to pierce with a sharp point; puncture. **13.** to affect with sharp pain, as from piercing. **14.** to cause sharp mental pain to; sting, as with remorse, anger, etc.: *His conscience pricked him.* **15.** to urge on with or as if with a goad or spur: *My duty pricks me on.* **16.** to mark (a surface) with pricks or dots in tracing something. **17.** to mark or trace (something) on a surface by pricks or dots. **18.** to cause to stand erect or point upward (usually fol. by *up*): *The dog pricked his ears at the sound of the bell.* **19.** *Farriery.* **a.** to lame (a horse) by driving a nail improperly into its hoof. **b.** to nick: *to prick a horse's tail.* **20.** to measure (distance, the size of an area, etc.) on a chart with dividers (usually fol. by *off*). **21.** *Hort.* to transplant (a seedling) into a container that provides more room for growth (usually fol. by *out* or *off*). —*v.i.* **22.** to perform the action of piercing or puncturing something. **23.** to have a sensation of being pricked. **24.** to spur or urge a horse on; ride rapidly. **25.** to rise erect or point upward, as the ears of an animal (usually fol. by *up*). **26. prick up one's ears,** to become very alert; listen attentively: *The reporter pricked up his ears at the prospect of a scoop.* [bef. 1000; (n.) ME *prike;* OE *prica, price* dot, point; (v.) ME *priken,* OE *prician;* c. D, LG *prik* point] **—prick′er,** *n.* **—prick′ing·ly,** *adv.*

prick-eared (prik′ērd′), *adj.* **1.** having the ears upright and pointed: *a prick-eared dog.* **2.** *Brit.* **a.** *Informal.* (of a man) having the hair cut short. **b.** *Archaic.* following or sympathetic to the Puritans or Roundheads. **c.** *Archaic.* priggish. [1375–1425; late ME]

prick·et (prik′it), *n.* **1.** a sharp metal point on which to stick a candle. **2.** a candlestick with one or more such points. **3.** a buck in his second year. [1300–50; ME; see PRICK, -ET]

prick·ing (prik′ing), *n.* **1.** the act of a person or thing that pricks. **2.** a prickly or smarting sensation. [bef. 1000; ME; OE *pricung;* see PRICK, -ING[1]]

prick·le (prik′əl), *n., v.,* **-led, -ling.** —*n.* **1.** a sharp point. **2.** a small, pointed process growing from the bark of a plant. **3.** a sharp process or projection, as from the skin of an animal; a spine. **4.** a pricking sensation. —*v.t.* **5.** to prick lightly. **6.** to cause a pricking or tingling sensation in. —*v.i.* **7.** to tingle as if pricked. [bef. 950; ME *prykel* (n.), OE *pricel.* See PRICK, -LE]

prick·le·back (prik′əl bak′), *n.* **1.** any of several blennioid fishes of the family Stichaeidae, usually inhabiting cold waters, having spiny rays in the dorsal fin. **2.** stickleback. [1740–50; PRICKLE + BACK[1]]

prick·ly (prik′lē), *adj.,* **-li·er, -li·est. 1.** full of or armed with prickles. **2.** full of troublesome points: *a prickly problem.* **3.** prickling; smarting: *a prickly sensation.* [1570–80; PRICKLE + -Y[1]] **—prick′li·ness,** *n.*

prick′ly ash′, 1. Also called **toothache tree.** a citrus shrub or small tree, *Zanthoxylum americanum,* having aromatic leaves and usually prickly branches. **2.** Hercules-club (def. 2). [1700–10, *Amer.*]

prick′ly heat′, *Pathol.* a cutaneous eruption accompanied by a prickling and itching sensation, due to an inflammation of the sweat glands. Also called **heat rash.** [1730–40, *Amer.*]

prick′ly pear′, 1. any of numerous cacti of the genus *Opuntia,* having flattened, usually spiny stem joints, yellow, orange, or reddish flowers, and ovoid, often edible fruit. **2.** the usually prickly fruit of such a cactus. [1605–15]

prick′ly pop′py, any tropical American poppy of the genus *Argemone,* esp. *A. mexicana* **(Mexican poppy),** having prickly pods and leaves and yellow or white, poppylike flowers. [1715–25]

prick-post (prik′pōst′), *n.* (in a framed structure) a secondary post, as a queen post. [1580–90]

prick′ song′, *Archaic.* **1.** written music. **2.** descant (def. 1a). [1400–50; late ME, short for *pricked song*]

prick·spur (prik′spûr′), *n.* a spur having a single sharp goad or point. [1680–90; PRICK + SPUR[1]]

prick·y (prik′ē), *adj.,* **prick·i·er, prick·i·est.** prickly. [1540–50; PRICK + -Y[1]]

pric·y (prī′sē), *adj.,* **pric·i·er, pric·i·est.** pricey. **—pric′i·ness,** *n.*

pride (prīd), *n., v.,* **prid·ed, prid·ing.** —*n.* **1.** a high or inordinate opinion of one's own dignity, importance, merit, or superiority, whether as cherished in the mind or as displayed in bearing, conduct, etc. **2.** the state or feeling of being proud. **3.** a becoming or dignified sense of what is due to oneself or one's position or character; self-respect; self-esteem. **4.** pleasure or satisfaction taken in something done by or belonging to oneself or believed to reflect credit upon oneself: *civic pride.* **5.** something that causes a person or persons to be proud: *His art collection was the pride of the family.* **6.** the best of a group, class, society, etc.: *This bull is the pride of the herd.* **7.** the most flourishing state or period: *in the pride of adulthood.* **8.** mettle in a horse. **9.** *Literary.* splendor, magnificence, or pomp. **10.** a group of lions. **11.** sexual desire, esp. in a female animal. **12.** ornament or adornment. **13. pride and joy,** someone or something cherished, valued, or enjoyed above all others: *Their new grandchild is their pride and joy.* —*v.t.* **14.** to indulge or plume (oneself) in a feeling of pride (usually fol. by *on* or *upon*): *She prides herself on her tennis.* [bef. 1000; ME (n.); OE *prȳde* (c. ON *prȳthi* bravery, pomp), deriv. of *prūd* PROUD] **—pride′ful,** *adj.* **—pride′ful·ly,** *adv.* **—pride′ful·ness,** *n.* **—pride′less,** *adj.* **—pride′less·ly,** *adv.*
—Syn. 1. PRIDE, CONCEIT, SELF-ESTEEM, EGOTISM, VANITY, VAINGLORY imply an unduly favorable idea of one's own appearance, advantages, achievements, etc., and often apply to offensive characteristics. PRIDE is a lofty and often arrogant assumption of superiority in some respect: *Pride must have a fall.* CONCEIT implies an exaggerated estimate of one's own abilities or attainments, together with pride: *blinded by conceit.* SELF-ESTEEM may imply an estimate of oneself that is higher than that held by others: *a ridiculous self-esteem.* EGOTISM implies an excessive preoccupation with oneself or with one's own concerns, usually but not always accompanied by pride or conceit: *His egotism blinded him to others' difficulties.* VANITY implies self-admiration and an excessive desire to be admired by others: *His vanity was easily flattered.* VAINGLORY, somewhat literary, implies an inordinate and therefore empty or unjustified pride: *puffed up by vainglory.* **5.** boast. **—Ant. 1.** humility.

Pride (prīd), *n.* **Thomas,** died 1658, English soldier and regicide.

Pride′ and Prej′udice, a novel (1813) by Jane Austen (written 1796–97).

pride-of-Cal·i·for·nia (prīd′əv kal′ə fôr′nyə, -nē ə), *n.* a shrubby plant, *Lathyrus splendens,* of the legume family, native to southern California, having showy clusters of pale rose-pink, violet, or magenta flowers and large, smooth, beaked pods. [1890–95]

pride′ of Chi′na, the chinaberry, *Melia azedarach.* Also called **pride′ of In′dia.** [1775–85, *Amer.*]

pride′ of place′, the highest or most outstanding position; first place. [1615–25]

pride′ of the morn′ing, light mist or precipitation observed at sea in the morning and regarded as indicating a fine day.

Pride's′ Purge′, *Eng. Hist.* the forceful exclusion from the House of Commons, carried out by Col. Thomas Pride in December 1648, of about 100 members who favored compromise with the Royalist party.

prie (prē), *n., v.t. Scot. and North Eng.* pree.

prie-dieu (prē′dyŏŏ′; *Fr.* prē dyœ′), *n., pl.* **-dieus, -dieux** (-dyŏŏz′), *Fr.* **-dieu.** a piece of furniture for kneeling on during prayer, having a rest above, as for a book. [1750–60; < F: lit., pray God]

pri·er (prī′ər), *n.* a person who pries; a curious or inquisitive person. Also, **pryer.** [1545–55; PRY[1] + -ER[1]]

priest (prēst), *n.* **1.** a person whose office it is to perform religious rites, and esp. to make sacrificial offerings. **2.** (in Christian use) **a.** a person ordained to the sacerdotal or pastoral office; a member of the clergy; minister. **b.** (in hierarchical churches) a member of the clergy of the order next below that of bishop, authorized to carry out the Christian ministry. **3.** a minister of any religion. —*v.t.* **4.** to ordain as a priest. [bef. 900; ME *prest(e), priest,* OE *prēost,* ult. < LL *presbyter* PRESBYTER] **—priest′less,** *adj.* **—priest′like′,** *adj., adv.*

priest·craft (prēst′kraft′, -kräft′), *n.* the training, knowledge, and abilities necessary to a priest. [1475–85; PRIEST + CRAFT]

priest·ess (prē′stis), *n.* a woman who officiates in sacred rites. [1685–95; PRIEST + -ESS]
—Usage. See **-ess.**

priest·fish (prēst′fish′), *n., pl.* **-fish·es,** (*esp. collectively*) **-fish.** See **blue rockfish.** [PRIEST + FISH; so called from its dark color]

priest·hood (prēst′hŏŏd), *n.* **1.** the condition or office of a priest. **2.** priests collectively. [bef. 900; ME *presthed(e), presthod(e),* OE *prēosthād.* See PRIEST, -HOOD]

Priest·ley (prēst′lē), *n.* **1. J(ohn) B(oyn·ton)** (boin′tən, -tn), 1894–1984, English novelist. **2. Joseph,** 1733–1804, English chemist, author, and clergyman.

priest·ly (prēst′lē), *adj.,* **-li·er, -li·est. 1.** of or pertaining to a priest; sacerdotal: *priestly vestments.* **2.** characteristic of or befitting a priest. [bef. 1000; ME *prestli,* OE *prēostlic.* See PRIEST, -LY] **—priest′li·ness,** *n.*

prig[1] (prig), *n.* a person who displays or demands of others pointlessly precise conformity, fussiness about trivialities, or exaggerated propriety, esp. in a self-righteous or irritating manner. [1560–70; formerly, coxcomb; perh. akin to PRINK] **—prig′gish,** *adj.* **—prig′gish·ly,** *adv.* **—prig′gish·ness,** *n.*
—Syn. prude, puritan, bluenose.

prig[2] (prig), *v.,* **prigged, prig·ging,** *n.* —*v.t.* **1.** *Chiefly Brit.* to steal. —*v.i.* **2.** *Scot. and North Eng.* to haggle or argue over price. **3.** *Brit. Informal.* to beg or entreat; ask a favor. —*n.* **4.** *Chiefly Brit.* a thief. [1505–15; orig. thieves' cant; orig. uncert.]

prig·ger·y (prig′ə rē), *n., pl.* **-ger·ies** for 2. **1.** the conduct or character of a prig. **2.** an act or remark characteristic of a prig. [1735–45; PRIG[1] + -ERY]

prig·gism (prig′iz əm), *n.* priggish character or ideas; priggishness. [1735–45; PRIG[1] + -ISM]

Pri·go·gine (pri gō′zhin; *Fr.* prē gô zhēn′; *Russ.* pryi gô′zhin), *n.* **Il·ya** (il′yə, ēl′-; *Russ.* ē lyä′), born 1917, Belgian chemist, born in Russia: Nobel prize 1977.

prim[1] (prim), *adj.,* **prim·mer, prim·mest,** *v.,* **primmed, prim·ming.** —*adj.* **1.** formally precise or proper, as persons or behavior; stiffly neat. —*v.i.* **2.** to draw up the mouth in an affectedly nice or precise way. —*v.t.* **3.** to make prim, as in appearance. **4.** to draw (one's face, lips, etc.) into a prim expression. [1675–85; orig. uncert.] **—prim′ly,** *adv.* **—prim′ness,** *n.*
—Syn. 1. prissy, formal, rigid. **—Ant. 1.** flexible.

prim[2] (prim), *n.* privet (def. 1). [1565–75; shortening of earlier *primprint* privet < ?]

prim., 1. primary. **2.** primitive.

pri′ma balleri′na (prē′mə), the principal ballerina in a ballet company. [1895–1900; < It: lit., first ballerina]

pri·ma·cy (prī′mə sē), *n., pl.* **-cies** for 2, 3. **1.** the state of being first in order, rank, importance, etc. **2.** Also called **primateship.** *Eng. Eccles.* the office, rank, or dignity of a primate. **3.** *Rom. Cath. Ch.* the jurisdiction of a bishop, as a patriarch, over other bishoprics, or the supreme jurisdiction of the pope as supreme bishop. [1350–1400; ME *primacie* < ML *primātia,* alter. of L *primātus* (*prim*(*us*) PRIME + *-ātus* -ATE[3]); see -Y[3]]

pri·ma don·na (prē′mə don′ə, prim′ə; *It.* prē′mä dôn′nä), *pl.* **pri·ma don·nas,** *It.* **pri·me don·ne** (prē′me dôn′ne). **1.** a first or principal female singer of an opera company. **2.** a temperamental person; a person who takes adulation and privileged treatment as a right and reacts with petulance to criticism or inconvenience. [1760–70; < It: lit., first lady; see PRIME, DUENNA]

pri·mae·val (prī mē′vəl), *adj.* primeval.

pri·ma fa·ci·e (prī′mə fā′shē ē′, fā′shē, fā′shə, prē′-), **1.** at first appearance; at first view, before investigation. **2.** plain or clear; self-evident; obvious. [1425–75; late ME < L *prīmā faciē*]

pri′ma fa′cie case′, *Law.* a case in which the evidence produced is sufficient to enable a decision or verdict to be made unless the evidence is rebutted. [1890–95]

pri′ma fa′cie ev′idence, *Law.* evidence sufficient to establish a fact or to raise a presumption of fact unless rebutted. [1790–1800]

pri·mage (prī′mij), *n.* a small allowance formerly paid by a shipper to the master and crew of a vessel for the loading and care of the goods: now charged with the freight and retained by the shipowner. [1530–40; < AL *primāgium;* see PRIME, -AGE]

pri·ma in·ter pa·res (prē′mä in′ter pä′res; *Eng.* prī′mə in′tər pâr′ēz, prē′mə), *Latin.* (of a female) first among equals.

pri·mal (prī′məl), *adj.* **1.** first; original; primeval: *primal eras before the appearance of life on earth.* **2.** of first importance; fundamental: *the primal resources of a nation.* [1535–45; < ML *prīmālis.* See PRIME, -AL[1]]

pri′mal scene′, *Psychoanal.* a child's first real or imagined observation of parental sexual intercourse. [1920–25]

pri′mal scream′, a scream uttered by a person undergoing primal therapy. [1970–75, *Amer.*]

pri′mal ther′apy, *Psychiatry.* a form of psychotherapy in which the patient is encouraged to relive traumatic events, often screaming or crying, in order to achieve catharsis and a breakdown of psychological defenses. [1970–75, *Amer.*]

pri·ma·quine (prī′mə kwēn′), *n. Pharm.* a viscous liquid, $C_{15}H_{21}N_3O$, used in the treatment of malaria. [1945–50; < NL *prima* PRIME + QUIN(OLIN)E]

CONCISE ETYMOLOGY KEY: <, descended or borrowed from; >, whence; b., blend of, blended; c., cognate with; cf., compare; deriv., derivative; equiv., equivalent; imit., imitative; obl., oblique; r., replacing; s., stem; sp., spelling, spelled; resp., respelling, respelled; trans., translation; ?, origin unknown; *, unattested; ‡, probably earlier than. See the full key inside the front cover.

pri·ma·ri·ly (prī mâr′ə lē, -mer′-, prī′mer ə lē, -mər ə-), *adv.* **1.** essentially; mostly; chiefly; principally: *They live primarily from farming.* **2.** in the first instance; at first; originally: *Primarily a doctor, he later became a lawyer.* [1610–20; PRIMARY + -LY]

pri·ma·ry (prī′mer ē, -mə rē), *adj., n., pl.* **-ries.** **—*adj.*** **1.** first or highest in rank or importance; chief; principal: *his primary goals in life.* **2.** first in order in any series, sequence, etc. **3.** first in time; earliest; primitive. **4.** of, pertaining to, or characteristic of primary school: *the primary grades.* **5.** constituting or belonging to the first stage in any process. **6.** of the nature of the ultimate or simpler constituents of which something complex is made up: *Animals have a few primary instincts.* **7.** original; not derived or subordinate; fundamental; basic. **8.** immediate or direct, or not involving intermediate agency: *primary perceptions.* **9.** *Sociol.* (of social values or ideals) conceived as derived from the primary group and culturally defined as being necessary to the welfare of the individual and society. **10.** *Ornith.* pertaining to any of the set of flight feathers situated on the distal segment of a bird's wing. **11.** *Elect.* noting or pertaining to the circuit, coil, winding, or current that induces current in secondary windings in an induction coil, transformer, or the like. **12.** *Chem.* **a.** involving or obtained by replacement of one atom or group. **b.** noting or containing a carbon atom united to no other or to only one other carbon atom in a molecule. **13.** *Gram.* **a.** (of a derivative) having a root or other unanalyzable element as the underlying form. **b.** (of Latin, Greek, Sanskrit tenses) having reference to present or future time. Cf. **secondary** (def. 9). **—*n.*** **14.** something that is first in order, rank, or importance. **15.** *U.S. Politics.* **a.** Also called **primary election.** a preliminary election in which voters of each party nominate candidates for office, party officers, etc. Cf. **closed primary, direct primary, indirect primary, open primary. b.** a meeting of the voters of a political party in an election district for nominating candidates for office, choosing delegates for a convention, etc.; caucus. **16.** See **primary color. 17.** *Ornith.* a primary feather. **18.** *Elect.* a winding in a transformer or the like that carries a current and that induces a current in secondary windings. **19.** *Astron.* **a.** a body in relation to a smaller body or smaller bodies revolving around it, as a planet in relation to its satellites. **b.** the brighter of the two stars comprising a double star. Cf. **companion**[1] (def. 6). [1425–75; late ME (adj.) < L *prīmārius* of the first rank. See PRIME, -ARY] **—pri′ma·ri·ness,** *n.*
—Syn. 1. main, prime. **3.** original; primeval. **5.** beginning, opening. See **elementary. —Ant. 1, 2.** last. **2.** final.

pri′mary ac′cent, the principal or strongest stress of a word. Also called **primary stress.**

pri′mary beam′, *Physics.* See under **secondary beam.**

pri′mary care′ medical care by a physician, or other health-care professional, who is the patient's first contact with and who provides access to the health-care system. [1970–75] **—pri′mary-care′,** *adj.*

pri′mary cell′, *Elect.* a cell designed to produce electric current through an electrochemical reaction that is not efficiently reversible, so that the cell when discharged cannot be efficiently recharged by an electric current. [1900–05]

pri′mary col′or, **1.** *Art.* a color, as red, yellow, or blue, that in mixture yields other colors. Cf. **complementary color** (def. 1), **secondary color, tertiary color. 2.** *Optics.* any of a set of monochromatic colors, as red, green, and blue, that are added to match or specify the chromaticity of a stimulus or sample. [1605–15]

pri′mary con′tact, *Sociol.* a communication or relationship between people that is characterized by intimacy and personal familiarity. Cf. **secondary contact.**

pri′mary de′viance, *Sociol.* the violation of a norm or rule that does not result in the violator's being stigmatized as deviant. Cf. **secondary deviance.**

pri′mary elec′tion, primary (def. 15a). [1785–95]

pri′mary gain′, *Psychiatry.* the removal of emotional conflict or relief of anxiety that is the immediate benefit of a defense mechanism or neurotic symptom. Cf. **secondary gain.**

pri′mary group′, *Sociol.* a group of individuals living in close, intimate, and personal relationship. Cf. **secondary group.** [1890–95]

pri′mary in′dustry, an industry, as agriculture, forestry, or fishing, that deals in obtaining natural materials. [1945–50]

pri′mary inten′tion, *Logic.* See under **intention** (def. 5a).

pri′mary let′ter, *Print.* a lowercase character having neither a descender nor an ascender, as *a, c, e, i, m, n, o, r, s, u, v, w, x, z.*

pri′mary mem′ory, *Computers.* See **main storage.**

pri′mary met′al, metal derived directly from ore rather than from scrap. Also called **virgin metal.** Cf. **secondary metal.**

pri′mary op′tical a′rea, *Graphic Design.* a point in or toward the upper left-hand corner of a printed page, advertisement, or the like, looked at first in reading. *Abbr.:* POA

pri′mary phlo′em, *Bot.* phloem derived directly from the growth of an apical meristem.

pri′mary proc′ess, *Psychoanal.* the generally unorganized mental activity characteristic of the unconscious and occurring in dreams, fantasies, and related processes. Cf. **secondary process.**

pri′mary produc′er, *Biol.* any green plant or any of various microorganisms that can convert light energy or chemical energy into organic matter. [1925–30] **—pri′mary produc′tion.**

pri′mary qual′ity, *Epistemology.* any of the qualities inherent in an object, namely quantity, extent, figure, solidity, and motion or rest. Cf. **secondary quality.** [1650–60]

pri′mary rain′bow, the most commonly seen rainbow, formed by light rays that undergo a single internal reflection in a drop of water. Cf. **secondary rainbow.** [1785–95]

pri′mary root′, *Bot.* the first root produced by a germinating seed, developing from the radicle of the embryo. [1885–90]

pri′mary school′, **1.** a school usually covering the first three or four years of elementary school and sometimes kindergarten. **2.** See **elementary school.** [1795–1805]

pri′mary sex′ characteris′tic, *Anat.* any of the body structures directly concerned in reproduction, as the testes, ovaries, and external genitalia. Also called **primary sex′ char′acter.**

pri′mary spermat′ocyte, *Cell Biol.* See under **spermatocyte.** [1895–1900]

pri′mary stress′. See **primary accent.** [1950–55]

pri′mary syph′ilis, *Pathol.* the first stage of syphilis, characterized by the formation of a chancre at the site of infection. [1900–05]

pri′mary tis′sue, *Bot.* any tissue resulting directly from differentiation of an apical meristem. [1870–75]

pri′mary type′, *Biol.* a specimen used in the original description or illustration of a species.

pri′mary wave′. *Seismol.* See **P wave.** [1915–20]

pri′mary xy′lem, *Bot.* xylem derived directly from the growth of an apical meristem.

pri·mate (prī′māt *or, esp. for 1,* prī′mit), *n.* **1.** *Eccles.* an archbishop or bishop ranking first among the bishops of a province or country. **2.** any of various omnivorous mammals of the order Primates, comprising the three suborders Anthropoidea (humans, great apes, gibbons, Old World monkeys, and New World monkeys), Prosimii (lemurs, loris, and their allies), and Tarsioidea (tarsiers), esp. distinguished by the use of hands, varied locomotion, and by complex flexible behavior involving a high level of social interaction and cultural adaptability. **3.** *Archaic.* a chief or leader. [1175–1225; ME *primat* dignitary, religious leader < LL *prīmāt-* (s. of *prīmās*), n. use of L *prīmās* of first rank, deriv. of *prīmus* first (see PRIME); (def. 2) taken as sing. of NL *Primates* PRIMATES, as if ending in -ATE[1]] **—pri·ma′tal,** *adj., n.* **—pri·ma·tial** (prī mā′shəl), **pri·mat·i·cal** (prī mat′i kəl), *adj.*

Pri′mate of All′ Eng′land (prī′mit), *Ch. of Eng.* a title of the archbishop of Canterbury. [1350–1400; ME]

Pri′mate of Eng′land, *Ch. of Eng.* a title of the archbishop of York. [1350–1400; ME]

Pri·ma·tes (prī mā′tēz), *n.* the order comprising the primates. [1765–75; < NL, pl. of L *prīmās* one of the first, chief, principal. See PRIMATE]

pri·mate·ship (prī′mit ship′, -māt-), *n.* primacy (def. 2). [1625–35; PRIMATE + -SHIP]

pri·ma·tol·o·gy (prī′mə tol′ə jē), *n.* the branch of zoology dealing with the primates. [1940–45; PRIMATE + -O- + -LOGY] **—pri·ma·to·log·i·cal** (prī′mə tl oj′i kəl), *adj.* **—pri′ma·tol′o·gist,** *n.*

pri·ma·ve·ra[1] (prē′mə vâr′ə), *n.* **1.** a central American tree, *Cybistax donnell-smithii,* of the bignonia family, having showy, tubular yellow flowers. **2.** Also called **white mahogany.** the hard, yellowish-white wood of this tree, used for making furniture. [1890–95; < Sp: lit., spring; so called from its early flowering; see PRIMAVERAL]

pri·ma·ve·ra[2] (prē′mə vâr′ə; *It.* prē′mä ve′rä), *adj.* *Italian Cookery.* prepared with a variety of chopped or minced vegetables: *pasta primavera.* [appar. ellipsis from It *alla primavera* in the style of springtime; see PRIMAVERAL]

pri·ma·ve·ral (prī′mə vēr′əl), *adj.* of, in, or pertaining to the early springtime: *primaveral longings to sail around the world.* [1815–25; < Sp or It *primaver(a)* spring (also Pg, Pr, Catalan; cf. L *prīmō vēre* in the early spring; Rom *-vera* prob. orig. neut pl. construed as fem., or re-formation as fem. n.) + -AL[1]]

prime (prīm), *adj., n., v.,* **primed, prim·ing.** **—*adj.*** **1.** of the first importance; demanding the fullest consideration: *a prime requisite.* **2.** of the greatest relevance or significance: *a prime example.* **3.** of the highest eminence or rank: *the prime authority on Chaucer.* **4.** of the greatest commercial value: *prime building lots.* **5.** first-rate: *This ale is prime!* **6.** (of meat, esp. of beef) noting or pertaining to the first grade or best quality: *prime ribs of beef.* **7.** first in order of time, existence, or development; earliest; primitive. **8.** basic; fundamental: *the prime axioms of his philosophy.* **9.** *Math.* (of any two or more numbers) having no common divisor except unity: *The number 2 is prime to 9.*
—*n.* **10.** the most flourishing stage or state. **11.** the time of early manhood or womanhood: *the prime of youth.* **12.** the period or state of greatest perfection or vigor of human life: *a man in his prime.* **13.** the choicest or best part of anything. **14.** (esp. in the grading of U.S. beef) a grade, classification, or designation indicating the highest or most desirable quality. **15.** the beginning or earliest stage of any period. **16.** the spring of the year. **17.** the first hour or period of the day, after sunrise. **18.** *Banking.* See **prime rate. 19.** *Eccles.* the second of the seven canonical hours or the service for it, originally fixed for the first hour of the day. **20.** *Math.* **a.** See **prime number. b.** one of the equal parts into which a unit is primarily divided. **c.** the mark (′) indicating such a division: *a, a′.* **21.** *Fencing.* the first of eight defensive positions. **22.** *Music.* **a.** unison (def. 2). **b.** (in a scale) the tonic or keynote. **23.** *Ling.* any basic, indivisible unit used in linguistic analysis. **24.** *Metall.* a piece of tin plate free from visible defects.
—*v.t.* **25.** to prepare or make ready for a particular purpose or operation. **26.** to supply (a firearm) with powder for communicating fire to a charge. **27.** to lay a train of powder to (a charge, mine, etc.). **28.** to pour or admit liquid into (a pump) to expel air and prepare for action. **29.** to put fuel into (a carburetor) before starting an engine, in order to insure a sufficiently rich mixture at the start. **30.** to cover (a surface) with a preparatory coat or color, as in painting. **31.** to supply or equip with information, words, etc., for use: *The politician was primed by his aides for the press conference.* **32.** to harvest the bottom leaves from (a tobacco plant).
—*v.i.* **33.** (of a boiler) to deliver or discharge steam containing an excessive amount of water. **34.** to harvest the bottom leaves from a tobacco plant. [bef. 1000; 1910–15 for def. 5; (adj.) ME (< OF *prim*) < L *prīmus* FIRST (superl. corresponding to *prior* PRIOR[1]); (n.) in part deriv. of the adj.; in part continuing ME *prim(e)* first canonical hour, OE *prīm* < L *prīma* (*hōra*) first (hour); (v.) appar. deriv. of the adj.] **—prime′ness,** *n.*
—Syn. 1. primary. **7.** PRIME, PRIMEVAL, PRIMITIVE have reference to that which is first. PRIME means first in numerical order or order of development: *prime meridian; prime cause.* PRIMEVAL means belonging to the first or earliest ages: *the primeval forest.* PRIMITIVE suggests the characteristics of the origins or early stages of a development, and hence implies the simplicity of original things: *primitive tribes, conditions, ornaments, customs, tools.*

prime′ cost′, that part of the cost of a commodity deriving from the labor and materials directly utilized in its manufacture. [1710–20]

prime′ field′, *Math.* a field that contains no proper subset that is itself a field.

prime′ ide′al, *Math.* an ideal in a ring with a multiplicative identity, having the property that when the product of two elements of the ring results in an element of the ideal, at least one of the elements is an element of the ideal.

prime′ in′terest rate′, *Banking.* See **prime rate.** Also called **prime′ lend′ing rate′.**

prime·ly (prīm′lē), *adv.* excellently. [1605–15; PRIME + -LY]

prime′ merid′ian, the meridian running through Greenwich, England, from which longitude east and west is reckoned. [1860–65]

prime′ min′ister, the principal minister and head of government in parliamentary systems; chief of the cabinet or ministry: *the British prime minister.* [1640–50] **—prime-min·is·te·ri·al** (prīm′min ə stēr′ē əl), *adj.* **—prime′-min′is·ter·ship′,** *n.* **—prime′ min′istry.**

prime′ mov′er, **1.** *Mech.* **a.** the initial agent, as wind or electricity, that puts a machine in motion. **b.** a machine, as a water wheel or steam engine, that receives and modifies energy as supplied by some natural source. **2.** means of towing a cannon, as an animal, truck, or tractor. **3.** Also called **unmoved mover.** *Aristotelianism.* that which is the first cause of all movement and does not itself move. **4.** a person or thing that initiates or gives power and cohesion to something, as an idea, endeavor, or organization. [1935–40]

prime′ num′ber, *Math.* a positive integer that is not divisible without remainder by any integer except itself and 1, with 1 often excluded: *The integers 2, 3, 5, and 7 are prime numbers.* Also called **prime.** [1585–95]

prime′ num′ber the′orem, *Math.* the theorem that the number of prime numbers less than or equal to a given number is approximately equal to the given number divided by its natural logarithm. [1660–70]

prim·er[1] (prim′ər *or, esp. Brit.,* prī′mər), *n.* **1.** an elementary book for teaching children to read. **2.** any book of elementary principles: *a primer of phonetics.* **3.** See **great primer. 4.** See **long primer.** [1350–1400; ME < ML *prīmārium,* n. use of neut. of *prīmārius* PRIMARY]

prim·er[2] (prī′mər), *n.* **1.** a person or thing that primes. **2.** a cap, cylinder, etc., containing a compound that may be exploded by percussion or other means, used for firing a charge of powder. **3.** a first coat or layer of paint, size, etc., given to any surface as a base, sealer, or the like. [1490–1500; PRIME (v.) + -ER[1]]

prime′ rate′, *Banking.* the minimum interest rate charged by a commercial bank on short-term business loans to large, best-rated customers or corporations. Also called **prime, prime interest rate, prime lending rate.** [1955–60]

prime′ ribs′, a serving of the roasted ribs and meat from a prime cut of beef. Also, **prime′ rib′.** [1955–60]

pri·me·ro (pri mâr′ō), *n.* a card game fashionable in England in the 16th and 17th centuries. [1525–35; < Sp: lit., first < L *prīmārius* PRIMARY]

prime′ time′, *Radio and Television.* the hours, generally between 8 and 11 P.M., usually having the largest audience of the day. [1955–60]

pri·me·val (prī mē′vəl), *adj.* of or pertaining to the first age or ages, esp. of the world: *primeval forms of life.* Also, **primaeval.** [1765–75; < L *primaev(us)* young (*prīm(us)* PRIME + *aev(um)* AGE + *-us* adj. suffix) + -AL[1]] **—pri·me′val·ly,** *adv.*
—Syn. primary, primordial, pristine. See **prime.**

pri·mi·grav·i·da (prī′mi grav′i də), *n., pl.* **-das, -dae** (-dē′). *Obstet.* a woman pregnant for the first time. [1885–90; < NL, equiv. to L *prīmi-,* comb. form of *prīmus* first (see PRIME) + *gravida,* fem. of *gravidus* pregnant (see GRAVID), on the model of PRIMIPARA]

pri·mine (prī′min), *n. Bot.* the outer integument of an ovule. Cf. **secundine.** [1825–35; < L *prīm(us)* first (see PRIME) + -INE[2]]

prim·ing (prī′ming), *n.* **1.** the powder or other material used to ignite a charge. **2.** the act of a person or thing that primes. **3.** material used as a primer, or a first coat or layer of paint, size, etc. [1590–1600; PRIME + -ING[1]]

pri·mip·a·ra (prī mip′ər ə), *n., pl.* **-a·ras, -a·rae** (-ə rē′). *Obstet.* a woman who has borne but one child or who is parturient for the first time. [1835–45; < L *primipara,* equiv. to *prīmi-* (comb. form of *prīmus* first; see PRIME) + *-para,* fem. of *-parus* -PAROUS] —**pri·mi·par·i·ty** (prī′mi par′i tē), *n.* —**pri·mip′a·rous,** *adj.*

prim·i·tive (prim′i tiv), *adj.* **1.** being the first or earliest of the kind or in existence, esp. in an early age of the world: *primitive forms of life.* **2.** early in the history of the world or of humankind. **3.** characteristic of early ages or of an early state of human development: *primitive toolmaking.* **4.** *Anthropol.* of or pertaining to a preliterate or tribal people having cultural or physical similarities with their early ancestors: no longer in technical use. **5.** unaffected or little affected by civilizing influences; uncivilized; savage: *primitive passions.* **6.** being in its earliest period; early: *the primitive phase of the history of a town.* **7.** old-fashioned: *primitive ideas and habits.* **8.** simple; unsophisticated: *a primitive farm implement.* **9.** crude; unrefined: *primitive living conditions.* **10.** *Ling.* **a.** of or pertaining to a form from which a word or other linguistic form is derived; not derivative; original or radical. **b.** of or pertaining to a protolanguage. **c.** of or pertaining to a linguistic prime. **11.** primary, as distinguished from secondary. **12.** *Biol.* **a.** rudimentary; primordial. **b.** noting species, varieties, etc., only slightly evolved from early antecedent types. **c.** of early formation and temporary, as a part that subsequently disappears. —*n.* **13.** someone or something primitive. **14.** *Fine Arts.* **a.** an artist of a preliterate culture. **b.** a naive or unschooled artist. **c.** an artist belonging to the early stage in the development of a style. **d.** a work of art by a primitive artist. **15.** *Math.* **a.** a geometric or algebraic form or expression from which another is derived. **b.** a function of which the derivative is a given function. **16.** *Ling.* the form from which a given word or other linguistic form has been derived, by either morphological or historical processes, as *take* in *undertake.* [1350–1400; ME (n. and adj.) (< MF *primitif*) < L *prīmitīvus* first of its kind. See PRIME, -ITIVE] —**prim′i·tive·ly,** *adv.* —**prim′i·tive·ness, prim′i·tiv′i·ty,** *n.*
—**Syn. 1, 2.** prehistoric, primal, primary, primordial, original, aboriginal, antediluvian, pristine. See **prime.**

Prim′itive Bap′tist, (esp. in the Southern U.S.) one belonging to a highly conservative, loosely organized Baptist group, characterized by extreme fundamentalism and by opposition to missionary work, Sunday Schools, and the use of musical instruments in church. [1850–55, *Amer.*]

prim′itive cell′, *Crystall.* a unit cell containing no points of the lattice except at the corners of the cell. [1930–35]

prim′itive church′, **1.** the early Christian church, esp. in reference to its earliest form and organization. **2.** this church, esp. as representative of Christianity in its supposedly purest form. [1520–30]

Prim′itive Friends′, a group of Quakers, noted for their extreme conservatism, who withdrew from the Wilburites in 1861.

prim′itive gut′, archenteron.

Prim′itive Meth′odist, **1.** a member of a Protestant denomination **(Prim′itive Meth′odist Church′)** founded in England in 1812 and later established in the U.S., characterized by its adherence to the basic doctrines, principles, and practices taught by John Wesley. **2.** a member of a Protestant denomination **(Prim′itive Meth′odist Church′ in Great′ Brit′ain)** that united with other British Methodist groups in 1932 to form the Methodist Church. [1805–15] —**Prim′itive Meth′odism.**

prim′itive polyno′mial, *Math.* a polynomial that has content equal to 1. Cf. **content**[1] (def. 10).

prim·i·tiv·ism (prim′i ti viz′əm), *n.* **1.** a recurrent theory or belief, as in philosophy or art, that the qualities of primitive or chronologically early cultures are superior to those of contemporary civilization. **2.** the state of being primitive: *the primitivism of the Stone Age peoples.* **3.** the qualities or style characterizing primitive art. [1860–65; PRIMITIVE + -ISM] —**prim′i·tiv·ist,** *n.* —**prim′i·tiv·is′tic,** *adj.*

pri·mo (prē′mō; *for 1, 2 also It.* pʀē′mô), *n., pl.* **-mos, -mi** (-mē), *adj.* —*n. Music.* **1.** the part of a piano duet played on the upper half of the keyboard. **2.** the first or leading part in an ensemble. —*adj.* **3.** *Slang.* **a.** first-class: *dinner at a primo restaurant.* **b.** highly valuable or most essential: *the primo player on the team.* [1785–95; < It: lit., first < L *prīmus.* See PRIME]

Pri·mo de Ri·ve·ra (pʀē′mô the ʀē ve′ʀä), **Mi·guel** (mē gel′), **Mar·qués de Es·te·lla** (mäʀ kes′ the es te′lyä), (*Miguel Prima de Rivera y Orbaneja*), 1870–1930, Spanish general and political leader: dictator of Spain 1923–29.

pri·mo·gen·i·tor (prī′mə jen′i tər), *n.* **1.** a first parent or earliest ancestor: *Adam and Eve are the primogenitors of the human race.* **2.** a forefather or ancestor. [1645–55; < LL *prīmōgenitor* ancestor, equiv. to L *prīmō* at first + *genitor* GENITOR]

pri·mo·gen·i·ture (prī′mə jen′i chər, -cho͝or′), *n.* **1.** the state or fact of being the firstborn of children of the same parents. **2.** *Law.* the system of inheritance or succession by the firstborn, specifically the eldest son. Cf. **postremogeniture.** [1585–95; < ML *prīmōgenitūra* a first birth, equiv. to L *prīmō* at first + *genitūra,* equiv. to *genit(us)* (ptp. of *gignere* to beget; see KIN) + *-ūra* -URE] —**pri′mo·gen′i·tar′y, pri′mo·gen′i·tal,** *adj.* —**pri′mo·gen′i·ture·ship′,** *n.*

CONCISE ETYMOLOGY KEY: <, descended or borrowed from; >, whence; b., blend of, blended; c., cognate with; cf., compare; deriv., derivative; equiv., equivalent; imit., imitative; obl., oblique; r., replacing; s., stem; sp., spelling, spelled; resp., respelling, respelled; trans., translation; ?, origin unknown; *, unattested; ‡, probably earlier than. See the full key inside the front cover.

pri·mor·di·al (prī môr′dē əl), *adj.* **1.** constituting a beginning; giving origin to something derived or developed; original; elementary: *primordial forms of life.* **2.** *Embryol.* first formed. **3.** pertaining to or existing at or from the very beginning: *primordial matter.* [1350–1400; ME < LL *prīmōrdiālis* of the beginning. See PRIMORDIUM, -AL[1]] —**pri·mor·di·al·i·ty** (prī môr′dē al′i tē), *n.* —**pri·mor′di·al·ly,** *adv.*

primor′dial soup′, *Biol.* **1.** the seas and atmosphere as they existed on earth before the existence of life, consisting primarily of an oxygen-free gaseous mixture containing chiefly water, hydrogen, methane, ammonia, and carbon dioxide. **2.** a laboratory preparation containing the substances believed to have composed primordial soup, and used in experiments seeking to understand the origin of life. [1925–30]

pri·mor·di·um (prī môr′dē əm), *n., pl.* **-di·a** (-dē ə). *Embryol.* the first recognizable, histologically differentiated stage in the development of an organ. [1665–75; < L *prīmōrdium,* in pl.: beginnings, elementary stage, equiv. to *prīm(us)* first (see PRIME) + *ōrd(īrī)* to begin + *-ium* -IUM; cf. EXORDIUM]

primp (primp), *v.t.* **1.** to dress or adorn with care. —*v.i.* **2.** to groom oneself carefully: *The photographer waited while we primped.* [1795–1805; akin to PRIM[1]]
—**Syn. 1,2.** preen, prettify, prink.

prim·rose (prim′rōz′), *n.* **1.** any plant of the genus *Primula,* as *P. vulgaris* **(English primrose),** of Europe, having yellow flowers, or *P. sinensis* **(Chinese primrose),** of China, having flowers in a variety of colors. Cf. **primrose family. 2.** See **evening primrose. 3.** pale yellow. —*adj.* **4.** of or pertaining to the primrose. **5.** Also, **prim′rosed′.** abounding in primroses: *a primrose garden.* **6.** of a pale yellow. [1375–1425; late ME *primerose* < ML *prīma rosa* first rose]

Prim·rose (prim′rōz′), *n.* **Archibald Philip, 5th Earl of Rosebery.** See **Rosebery, Archibald Philip Primrose, 5th Earl of.**

prim′rose fam′ily, the plant family Primulaceae, characterized by herbaceous plants having simple, opposite, whorled, or basal leaves, flowers with a five-lobed corolla, and capsular fruit, and including cyclamen, loosestrife of the genus *Lysimachia,* pimpernel, primrose, and shooting star.

prim′rose jas′mine, an evergreen shrub, *Jasminum mesnyi,* of China, having thick, shiny leaflets and yellow flowers with a darker eye.

prim′rose path′, **1.** a way of life devoted to irresponsible hedonism, often of a sensual nature: *The evangelist exhorted us to avoid the primrose path and stick to the straight and narrow.* **2.** a course of action that is easy or tempting but hazardous: *the primrose path to insolvency.* [1595–1605]

prim′rose yel′low, primrose (def. 3). [1880–85]

prim·sie (prim′sē, -zē), *adj. Scot.* prim[1]. [1775–85; PRIM + *-sie,* sp. var. of -SY]

prim·u·la (prim′yə lə), *n.* primrose (def. 1). [1745–55; < ML *prīmula,* short for *prīmula vēris,* lit., first (flower) of spring. See PRIME, -ULE]

prim·u·la·ceous (prim′yə lā′shəs), *adj.* belonging to the plant family Primulaceae. Cf. **primrose family.** [1835–45; < NL *Primulace(ae)* family name (see PRIMULA, -ACEAE) + -OUS]

pri·mum mo·bi·le (pʀē′mo͞om mō′bi le′; *Eng.* prī′məm mob′ə lē′, prē′-), *Latin.* **1.** (in Ptolemaic astronomy) the outermost of the 10 concentric spheres of the universe, making a complete revolution every 24 hours and causing all the others to do likewise. **2.** See **prime mover.** [lit., first moving (thing)]

pri·mus[1] (prī′məs), *n., pl.* **-mus·es.** (*often cap.*) *Scot. Episc. Ch.* a bishop who is elected to represent the church body and to summon and preside at synods but who possesses no metropolitan power. [1855–60; < ML *prīmus,* n. use of L adj.; see PRIME]

pri·mus[2] (prī′məs), *adj.* (in prescriptions) first. [1790–1800; < L *prīmus;* see PRIME]

Pri·mus (prē′məs) *n.* **Pearl,** born 1919, U.S. dancer, born in Trinidad.

pri·mus in·ter pa·res (pʀē′mo͞os in′teʀ pä′ʀes; *Eng.* prī′məs in′tər pâr′ēz, prē′-), *Latin.* (of males) first among equals.

Pri′mus stove′ (prī′məs), *Trademark.* a brand of portable oil stove used by campers and the like.

prin., **1.** principal. **2.** principally. **3.** principle.

prince (prins), *n.* **1.** a nonreigning male member of a royal family. **2.** *Hist.* a sovereign or monarch; king. **3.** (in Great Britain) a son or grandson (if the child of a son) of a king or queen. **4.** the English equivalent of any of various titles of nobility in other countries. **5.** a holder of such a title. **6.** the ruler of a small state, as one actually or nominally subordinate to a suzerain: *Monaco is ruled by a prince.* **7.** a person or thing that is chief or preeminent in any class, group, etc.: *a merchant prince.* **8.** a person possessing admirably fine and genial characteristics: *He is a prince of a man.* [1175–1225; ME < OF < L *princip-* (s. of *princeps*) first, principal (adj.), principal person, leader (n.), equiv. to *prin-* for *prīmus* PRIME + *-cep-* (comb. form of *capere* to take) + *-s* nom. sing. ending] —**prince′less,** *adj.* —**prince′ship,** *n.*

Prince (prins), *n.* **1. Harold S.,** born 1928, U.S. stage director and producer. **2.** a male given name.

Prince, The, (Italian, *Il Principe*), a treatise on statecraft (1513) by Niccolò Machiavelli.

Prince′ Al′bert, **1.** a city in central Saskatchewan, in S Canada. 28,631. **2.** a long, double-breasted frock coat.

Prince′ Al′bert Na′tional Park′, a national park in W Canada, in central Saskatchewan. 1869 sq. mi.

Prince′ Charm′ing, **1.** (*sometimes l.c.*) a man who embodies a woman's romantic ideal. **2.** a man who avidly seeks the attention and affections of women; ladies' man. [1840–50; on the pattern of earlier *King Charming,* ult. trans. (with word order unchanged) of F *Roi Charmant,* the hero of a fairy tale by the Comtesse Marie-Catherine d'Aulnoy (ca. 1650–1705)]

prince′ con′sort, a prince who is the husband of a reigning female sovereign. [1860–65]

prince·dom (prins′dəm), *n.* **1.** the position, rank, or dignity of a prince. **2.** the territory of a prince; principality. **3. princedoms,** (in medieval angelology) principalities. Cf. **angel** (def. 1). [1550–60; PRINCE + -DOM]

Prince′ Ed′ward Is′land, an island in the Gulf of St. Lawrence, forming a province of Canada: 116,251; 2184 sq. mi. (5655 sq. km). *Cap.:* Charlottetown.

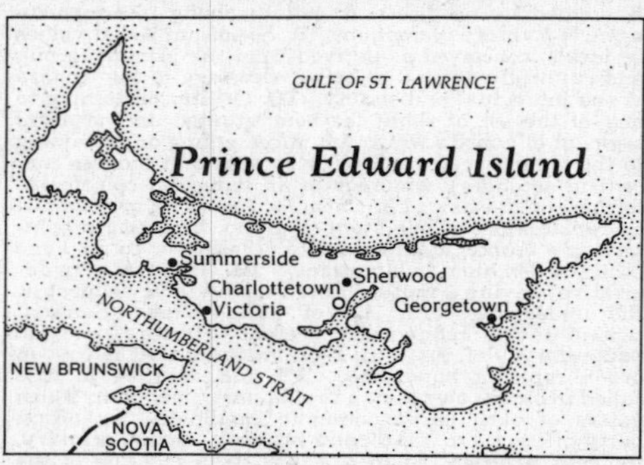

Prince′ George′, a city in central British Columbia, in W Canada. 59,929.

prince·kin (prins′kin), *n.* a small, young, or minor prince. Also, **prince·let** (prins′lit). [1850–55; PRINCE + -KIN]

prince·ling (prins′ling), *n.* **1.** a young prince. **2.** a subordinate, minor, or insignificant prince. [1610–20; PRINCE + -LING[1]]

prince·ly (prins′lē), *adj.,* **-li·er, -li·est. 1.** greatly liberal; lavish; magnificent: *a princely entertainment.* **2.** like or befitting a prince; magnificent: *princely manners.* **3.** of or pertaining to a prince; royal; noble: *princely blood.* **4.** that is a prince: *his princely self.* [1490–1500; PRINCE + -LY] —**prince′li·ness,** *n.*

Prince′ of Dark′ness, Satan. [1595–1605]

Prince′ of Peace′, Jesus Christ, regarded by Christians as the Messiah. Isa. 9:6. [1350–1400; ME]

Prince′ of Wales′, **1.** a title conferred on the eldest son, or heir apparent, of the British sovereign. **2. Cape,** a cape in W Alaska, on Bering Strait opposite the Soviet Union: the westernmost point of North America. [1275–1325; ME]

Prince′ of Wales′ Is′land, **1.** the largest island in the Alexander Archipelago, in SE Alaska. 1500 sq. mi. (3990 sq. km). **2.** an island in N Canada, in the Northwest Territories. ab. 14,000 sq. mi. (36,000 sq. km).

prince′ re′gent, a prince who is regent of a country. [1780–90]

prince′ roy′al, the eldest son of a king or queen. [1655–65]

Prince′ Ru′pert, a seaport and railway terminus in W British Columbia, in W Canada. 14,754.

Prince′ Ru′pert's met′al, a brass composed of from about 60 to 85 percent copper and about 15 to 40 percent zinc, used to imitate gold. Also called **Prince′'s met′al.** [1690–1700]

prince's-feath·er (prin′siz feth′ər), *n.* **1.** a tall, showy plant, *Amaranthus hybridus erythrostachys,* of the amaranth family, having reddish foliage and thick spikes of small, red flowers. **2.** a hairy, much-branched, plant, *Polygonum orientale,* of the buckwheat family, native to Asia and Australia, having pink or rose-colored flower spikes, naturalized in North America. [1620–30]

Prince′'s Is′land, former name of **Príncipe.**

prince's-pine (prin′siz pīn′), *n.* pipsissewa. [1810–20, *Amer.*]

prin·cess (prin′sis, -ses, prin ses′), *n.* **1.** a nonreigning female member of a royal family. **2.** *Hist.* a female sovereign or monarch; queen. **3.** the consort of a prince. **4.** (in Great Britain) a daughter or granddaughter (if the child of a son) of a king or queen. **5.** a woman considered to have the qualities or characteristics of a princess. —*adj.* **6.** Also, **prin′cesse.** (of a woman's dress, coat, or the like) styled with a close-fitting bodice and flared skirt, cut in single pieces, as gores, from shoulder to hem. [1350–1400; ME *princesse* < MF. See PRINCE, -ESS] —**prin′cess·like′,** *adj.* —**prin′cess·ly,** *adj.*
—**Usage.** See **-ess.**

prin′cess flow′er, a shrub, *Tibouchina urvilleana,* native to Brazil, having showy purple flowers, cultivated as an ornamental. Also called **glory bush.**

prin′cess post′, (in a queen truss) one of two vertical suspension members supplementing the queen posts nearer to the ends of the span.

prin′cess re′gent, **1.** a princess who is regent of a country. **2.** the wife of a prince regent. [1705–15]

prin′cess roy′al, **1.** the eldest daughter of a king or queen. **2.** (in Great Britain and, formerly, Prussia) an eldest princess to whom this title has been granted for life by the sovereign. [1640–50]

prin′cess tree′, a Chinese tree, *Paulownia tomentosa,* of the bignonia family, having hairy leaves and clusters of fragrant, violet flowers, naturalized in the eastern U.S. Also called **karri-tree, empress tree.** [1930–35, *Amer.*]

Prince·ton (prins′tən), *n.* a borough in central New Jersey: battle 1777. 12,035.

prin·ci·pal (prin′sə pəl), *adj.* **1.** first or highest in rank, importance, value, etc.; chief; foremost. **2.** of, of the nature of, or constituting principal or capital: *a principal investment.* **3.** *Geom.* (of an axis of a conic) passing through the foci. —*n.* **4.** a chief or head. **5.** the head or director of a school or, esp. in England, a college. **6.** a person who takes a leading part in any activity, as a play; chief actor or doer. **7.** the first player of a division of instruments in an orchestra (excepting the leader of the first violins). **8.** something of principal or chief importance. **9.** *Law.* **a.** a person who authorizes another, as an agent, to represent him or her. **b.** a person directly responsible for a crime, either as an actual perpetrator or as an abettor present at its commission. Cf. **accessory** (def. 3). **10.** a person primarily liable for an obligation, in contrast with an endorser, or the like. **11.** the main body of an estate, or the like, as distinguished from income. **12.** *Finance.* a capital sum, as distinguished from interest or profit. **13.** *Music.* **a.** an organ stop. **b.** the subject of a fugue. **14.** (in a framed structure) a member, as a truss, upon which adjacent or similar members depend for support or reinforcement. **15.** each of the combatants in a duel, as distinguished from the seconds. [1250–1300; ME < L *prīncipālis* first, chief, equiv. to *prīncip-* (see PRINCE) + *-ālis* -AL[1]] —**prin′ci·pal·ship′,** *n.*
—**Syn. 1.** prime, paramount, leading, main, cardinal, preeminent. See **capital**[1]. **4.** leader. **5.** headmaster, dean, master. —**Ant. 1.** secondary, ancillary.
—**Usage.** The noun PRINCIPLE and the noun and adjective PRINCIPAL are often confused. Although pronounced alike, the words are not interchangeable in writing. A PRINCIPLE is broadly "a rule of action or conduct" (*His overriding principle is greed*) or "a fundamental doctrine or tenet" (*Their principles do not permit the use of alcoholic beverages*). The adjective PRINCIPAL has the general sense "chief, first, foremost": *My principal objection is the cost of the project.* The noun PRINCIPAL has among other meanings "the head or director of a school" (*The faculty supported the principal in her negotiations with the board*) and "a capital sum, as distinguished from interest or profit" (*The monthly payments go mostly for interest, leaving the principal practically untouched*).

prin′cipal ar′gument, *Math.* the radian measure of the argument between $-\pi$ and π of a complex number. Cf. **argument** (def. 8c).

prin′cipal ax′is, 1. *Optics.* a line passing through the center of the surface of a lens or spherical mirror and through the centers of curvature of all segments of the lens or mirror. **2.** *Physics.* one of three mutually perpendicular axes of a body about which the moment of inertia is maximum or minimum. [1875–80]

prin′cipal clause′, the main clause.

prin′cipal diag′onal. *Math.* See under **diagonal** (def. 9). [1960–65]

prin′cipal fo′cus, *Optics.* See **focal point** (def. 1). [1825–35]

prin′cipal ide′al, *Math.* the smallest ideal containing a given element in a ring; an ideal in a ring with a multiplicative identity, obtained by multiplying each element of the ring by one specified element. [1935–40]

prin′cipal ide′al domain′, *Math.* a commutative integral domain with multiplicative identity in which every ideal is principal. Also called **prin′cipal ide′al ring′.** [1960–65]

prin·ci·pal·i·ty (prin′sə pal′i tē), *n., pl.* **-ties. 1.** a state ruled by a prince, usually a relatively small state or a state that falls within a larger state such as an empire. **2.** the position or authority of a prince or chief ruler; sovereignty; supreme power. **3.** the rule of a prince of a small or subordinate state. **4. the Principality,** *Brit.* Wales. **5. principalities,** *Theol.* **a.** an order of angels. Cf. **angel** (def. 1). **b.** supramundane powers often in conflict with God. Ephes. 6:12. **6.** *Obs.* preeminence. [1300–50; ME *principalite* < OF < LL *prīncipālitās* first place, superiority (ML: authority or territory of a prince). See PRINCIPAL, -ITY]

prin·ci·pal·ly (prin′sə pə lē, -sip lē), *adv.* chiefly; mainly. [1300–50; ME; see PRINCIPAL, -LY]
—**Syn.** primarily. See **especially.**

prin′cipal parts′, *Gram.* a set of inflected forms of a form class from which all the other inflected forms can be derived, as *sing, sang, sung; smoke, smoked.* [1865–70]

prin′cipal plane′, *Optics.* a plane that is perpendicular to the axis of a lens, mirror, or other optical system and at which rays diverging from a focal point are deviated parallel to the axis or at which rays parallel to the axis are deviated to converge to a focal point.

prin′cipal point′, *Optics.* the point where a principal plane intersects the axis. [1695–1705]

prin′cipal quan′tum num′ber, *Physics.* the nonnegative, integral quantum number that defines the stationary orbits in the Bohr model of the atom. Also called **total quantum number.** [1920–25]

prin′cipal raft′er, a diagonal member of a roof principal, usually forming part of a truss and supporting the purlins on which the common rafters rest. See diag. under **king post.** [1655–65]

prin′cipal se′ries, *Math.* See **composition series.**

prin′cipal sum′, *Insurance.* See **capital sum.**

prin′cipal val′ue, *Math.* a value selected at a point in the domain of a multiple-valued function, chosen so that the function has a single value at the point.

prin·ci·pate (prin′sə pāt′), *n.* supreme power or office. [1300–50; ME < L *prīncipātus,* equiv. to *prīncip-* (see PRINCE) + *-ātus* -ATE[3]]

Prín·ci·pe (prin′sə pə, -pā′; *Port.* prēN′sē pə), *n.* an island in the Gulf of Guinea, off the W coast of Africa: one of the two chief components of the Democratic Republic of São Tomé and Príncipe. 4305; 54 sq. mi. (140 sq. km). Also, **Prin′ci·pe.** Formerly, **Prince's Island.**

prin·cip·i·um (prin sip′ē əm), *n., pl.* **-cip·i·a** (-sip′ē ə). a principle. [1575–85; < L *prīncipium* lit., that which is first, equiv. to *prīncip-* (see PRINCE) + *-ium* -IUM]

prin·ci·ple (prin′sə pəl), *n.* **1.** an accepted or professed rule of action or conduct: *a person of good moral principles.* **2.** a fundamental, primary, or general law or truth from which others are derived: *the principles of modern physics.* **3.** a fundamental doctrine or tenet; a distinctive ruling opinion: *the principles of the Stoics.* **4. principles,** a personal or specific basis of conduct or management: *to adhere to one's principles; a kindergarten run on modern principles.* **5.** guiding sense of the requirements and obligations of right conduct: *a person of principle.* **6.** an adopted rule or method for application in action: *a working principle for general use.* **7.** a rule or law exemplified in natural phenomena, the construction or operation of a machine, the working of a system, or the like: *the principle of capillary attraction.* **8.** the method of formation, operation, or procedure exhibited in a given case: *a community organized on the patriarchal principle.* **9.** a determining characteristic of something; essential quality. **10.** an originating or actuating agency or force: *growth is the principle of life.* **11.** an actuating agency in the mind or character, as an instinct, faculty, or natural tendency: *the principles of human behavior.* **12.** *Chem.* a constituent of a substance, esp. one giving to it some distinctive quality or effect. **13.** *Obs.* beginning or commencement. **14. in principle,** in essence or substance; fundamentally: *to accept a plan in principle.* **15. on principle, a.** according to personal rules for right conduct; as a matter of moral principle: *He refused on principle to agree to the terms of the treaty.* **b.** according to a fixed rule, method, or practice: *He drank hot milk every night on principle.* [1350–1400; ME, alter. of MF *principe* or L *prīncipium,* on the analogy of MANCIPLE. See PRINCIPIUM]
—**Syn. 1, 2, 3.** PRINCIPLE, CANON, RULE imply something established as a standard or test, for measuring, regulating, or guiding conduct or practice. A PRINCIPLE is a general and fundamental truth that may be used in deciding conduct or choice: *to adhere to principle.* CANON, originally referring to an edict of the Church (a meaning that it still retains), is used of any principle, law, or critical standard that is officially approved, particularly in aesthetics and scholarship: *canons of literary criticism.* A RULE, usually something adopted or enacted, is often the specific application of a principle: *the golden rule.* **2.** theorem, axiom, postulate, proposition. **5.** integrity, probity, rectitude, honor.
—**Usage.** See **principal.**

prin·ci·pled (prin′sə pəld), *adj.* imbued with or having moral principles (often used in combination): *high-principled.* [1635–45; PRINCIPLE + -ED[3]]

prin′ciple of complementar′ity, *Physics.* See **complementarity principle.** [COMPLEMENTARY + -TY[2]]

prin′ciple of correspond′ence, *Physics.* See **correspondence principle.**

prin′ciple of dual′ity, *Math.* See **duality principle.**

prin′ciple of equiv′alence, *Physics.* See **equivalence principle.**

prin′ciple of mathemat′ical induc′tion, *Math.* a law in set theory which states that if a set is a subset of the set of all positive integers and contains 1, and if for each number in the given set the succeeding natural number is in the set, then the given set is identical to the set of all positive integers. Cf. **induction** (def. 5).

prin′ciple of superposi′tion, *Physics.* any of several physical laws that the resultant of similar vector quantities at a point is a function of the sum of the individual quantities, esp. the law that the displacement at a point in a medium undergoing simple harmonic motion is equal to the sum of the displacements of each individual wave. Also called **superposition principle.**

prin′ciple of vir′tual work′, *Mech.* the principle that the total work done by all forces on a system in static equilibrium is zero for a set of infinitesimally small displacements.

prin·cox (prin′koks, pring′-), *n. Archaic.* a self-confident young fellow; coxcomb. Also, **prin·cock** (prin′kok, pring′-). [1530–40; orig. uncert.]

prink (pringk), *v.t.* **1.** to deck or dress for show. —*v.i.* **2.** to deck oneself out. **3.** to fuss over one's dress, esp. before the mirror. [1570–80; appar. akin to PRANK[2]] —**prink′er,** *n.*

print (print), *v.t.* **1.** to produce (a text, picture, etc.) by applying inked types, plates, blocks, or the like, to paper or other material either by direct pressure or indirectly by offsetting an image onto an intermediate roller. **2.** to reproduce (a design or pattern) by engraving on a plate or block. **3.** to form a design or pattern upon, as by stamping with an engraved plate or block: *to print calico.* **4.** to cause (a manuscript, text, etc.) to be published in print. **5.** to write in letters like those commonly used in print: *Print your name on these forms.* **6.** *Computers.* to produce (data) in legible alphanumeric or graphic form. **7.** to indent or mark by pressing something into or upon (something). **8.** to produce or fix (an indentation, mark, etc.), as by pressure. **9.** to impress on the mind, memory, etc. **10.** to fingerprint. **11.** to apply (a thing) with pressure so as to leave an indentation, mark, etc.: *The horses printed their hoofs on the wet grass.* **12.** *Photog.* to produce a positive picture from (a negative) by the transmission of light. —*v.i.* **13.** to take impressions from type, an engraved plate, etc., as in a press. **14.** to produce by means of a reproduction process: *to print in color; to print unevenly.* **15.** to make an image by means of ink, chemical action, etc., as type, engraved plates, etc.: *This type is too worn to print cleanly.* **16.** to write in characters such as are used in print: *He'd rather print than use longhand.* **17.** to follow the vocation of a printer. **18. print in,** *Photog.* See **burn** (def. 36). **19. print out,** *Computers.* to make a printout of. —*n.* **20.** the state of being printed. **21.** printed lettering, esp. with reference to character, style, or size: *This print is too large for footnotes.* **22.** printed material. **23.** a printed publication, as a newspaper or magazine. **24.** newsprint. **25.** a picture, design, or the like, printed from an engraved or otherwise prepared block, plate, etc. **26.** an indentation, mark, etc., made by the pressure of one body or thing on another. **27.** something with which an impression is made; a stamp or die. **28.** a fingerprint. **29.** *Textiles.* **a.** a design or pattern on cloth made by dyeing, weaving, or printing with engraved rollers, blocks of wood, stencils, etc. **b.** a cloth so treated. **c.** an article of apparel made of this cloth. **30.** something that has been subjected to impression, as a pat of butter. **31.** *Photog.* a picture, esp. a positive made from a negative. **32.** any reproduced image, as a blueprint. **33.** *Motion Pictures, Television.* a positive copy of a completed film or filmed program ready for showing; release print. **34. in print, a.** in printed form; published. **b.** (of a book or the like) still available for purchase from the publisher. **35. out of print,** (of a book or the like) no longer available for purchase from the publisher. —*adj.* **36.** of, for, or comprising newspapers and magazines: *print media.* [1250–1300; (n.) ME *prent(e), print(e), prient(e)* < OF *priente* impression, print, n. use of fem. ptp. of *preindre* to PRESS[1] < L *premere;* (v.) ME *prenten,* deriv. of the n.]

print., printing.

print·a·ble (prin′tə bəl), *adj.* **1.** capable of being printed. **2.** suitable for publication; fit to print. [1830–40; PRINT + -ABLE] —**print′a·bil′i·ty, print′a·ble·ness,** *n.*

prin·ta·nier (*Fr.* pRAN tA nyā′), *adj.* (of food) prepared or garnished with mixed fresh vegetables. Also, **prin·ta·nière** (*Fr.* pRAN tA nyeR′). [1860–65; < F: lit., of spring, MF, equiv. to OF *prin(s)tan(s)* spring (< L *primum tempus* lit., first season; see PRIME, TEMPORAL) + *-ier* -IER[2]]

print·back (print′bak′), *n. Photog.* an enlarged print from a microfilm copy. [n. use of v. phrase *print back*]

print′ed cir′cuit, *Electronics.* a circuit in which the interconnecting conductors and some of the circuit components have been printed, etched, etc., onto a sheet or board of dielectric material (**PC board, print′ed-cir′·cuit board′**). [1945–50]

print′ed mat′ter, 1. any of various kinds of printed material that qualifies for a special postal rate. **2.** a classification of international mail consisting of such items, including catalogs and circulars. [1875–80]

print·er (prin′tər), *n.* **1.** a person or thing that prints, esp. a person whose occupation is printing. **2.** *Computers.* an output device that produces a paper copy of alphanumeric or graphic data. **3.** an instrument that automatically records telegraphic messages by means of a printing mechanism activated by incoming signals. **4.** *Motion Pictures.* a photographic machine through which either the negative or positive of a master print can be run, together with unexposed film, to make a duplicate. [1495–1505; PRINT + -ER[1]] —**print′er·like′,** *adj.*

print′er's dev′il, devil (def. 5). [1755–65]

print′er's er′ror, an error introduced into typeset copy by the compositor, so that the printer cannot charge for correcting it. *Abbr.:* P.E., p.e. Cf. **author's alteration.**

print′er's mark′, a stamp or device, usually found on the copyright page, that identifies a book as the work of a particular printer.

print′er's ream′. See under **ream**[1] (def. 1).

print·er·y (prin′tə rē), *n., pl.* **-er·ies. 1.** (formerly) an establishment for typographic printing. **2.** an establishment where printing, as of books or newspapers, etc., is done. [1630–40; PRINT + -ERY]

print·head (print′hed′), *n. Computers.* the printing element, as a daisy wheel or thimble, on a computer printer. Also, **print′ head′.** [PRINT + HEAD]

print·ing (prin′ting), *n.* **1.** the art, process, or business of producing books, newspapers, etc., by impression from movable types, plates, etc. **2.** the act of a person or thing that prints. **3.** words, symbols, etc., in printed form. **4.** printed material. **5.** the total number of copies of a book or other publication printed at one time: *The book had a first printing of 10,000.* **6.** writing in which the letters resemble printed ones. [1350–1400; ME; see PRINT, -ING[1]]

print′ing frame′, *Photog.* a shallow, boxlike device with a glass plate on one side and an opaque, removable back, for holding a negative firmly against printing paper in contact printing. [1870–75]

print′ing ink′, a type of ink that flows smoothly, dries quickly, and is of a consistency able to hold enough color to make printed matter legible: used to transfer the image on a press plate to the printing surface. [1670–80]

print′ing of′fice, a shop or factory in which printing is done. [1725–35]

print′ing pa′per, *Photog.* sensitized paper for printing positives. [1780–90]

print′ing press′, a machine, as a cylinder press or rotary press, for printing on paper or the like from type, plates, etc. [1580–90]

print′ jour′nalism, journalism as practiced in newspapers and magazines. [1970–75] —**print′ jour′nalist.**

print·less (print′lis), *adj.* making, retaining, or showing no print or impression. [1600–10; PRINT + -LESS]

print·mak·er (print′mā′kər), *n.* a person who makes prints, esp. an artist working in one of the graphic mediums. [1925–30; PRINT + MAKER]

print·mak·ing (print′mā′king), *n.* the art or technique of making prints, esp. as practiced in engraving, etching, drypoint, woodcut or serigraphy. [1925–30; PRINT + MAKING]

print·out (print′out′), *n. Computers.* output produced by a printer, generally on continuous sheets of paper. Also, **print′-out′.** [1950–55; n. use of v. phrase *print out*]

print′out pa′per, *Photog.* sensitized paper for prints that darkens under light and requires treatment to fix an image: largely supplanted at the turn of the century by developing-out paper. *Abbr.:* P.O.P. Also called **print′ing-out′ pa′per.** [1890–95]

print′ shop′, 1. a shop where prints or graphics are sold. **2.** a shop where printing is done. [1690–1700]

print·wheel (print′hwēl′, -wēl′), *n.* See **daisy wheel.** Also, **print′ wheel′.** [1940–45; PRINT + WHEEL]

print·works (print′wûrks′), *n., pl.* **-works.** (*used with a singular or plural v.*) a factory that prints textiles or other materials. [1825–35; PRINT + *works* (see WORK)]

pri·on[1] (prī′on), *n.* any of several petrels of the genus *Pachyptila,* located in the oceans of the Southern Hemisphere and having serrated edges on the bill. [1840–50; < NL < Gk *priṓn* a saw]

pri·on[2] (prī′on), *n. Microbiol.* a hypothetical infectious particle composed solely of protein and likened to viruses and viroids but having no genetic component. [1980–85; PR(OTEINACEOUS) + I(NFECTIOUS) + -ON[1]]

pri·or[1] (prī′ər), *adj.* **1.** preceding in time or in order; earlier or former; previous: *A prior agreement prevents me from accepting this.* **2.** preceding in importance or privilege. **3. prior to,** preceding; before: *Prior to that time, buffalo had roamed the Great Plains in tremendous numbers.* —*n.* **4.** *Informal.* a prior conviction. [1705–15; < L: former, elder, superior (adj.), before (adv.); akin to PRIME, PRE-] **—pri′or·ly,** *adv.*
—Syn. 1. anterior, antecedent.

pri·or[2] (prī′ər), *n.* **1.** an officer in a monastic order or religious house, sometimes next in rank below an abbot. **2.** a chief magistrate, as in the medieval republic of Florence. [bef. 1100; ME, late OE < ML, LL: one superior in rank; n. use of *prior* PRIOR[1]] **—pri′or·ship′,** *n.*

Pri·or (prī′ər), *n.* **Matthew,** 1664–1721, English poet.

pri·or·ate (prī′ər it), *n.* **1.** the office, rank, or term of office of a prior. **2.** a priory. [1350–1400; ME < LL *priōrātus* priority, preference (ML: office of a prior). See PRIOR[2], -ATE[3]]

pri·or·ess (prī′ər is), *n.* a woman holding a position corresponding to that of a prior, sometimes ranking next below an abbess. [1250–1300; ME *prioresse* < OF. See PRIOR[2], -ESS]
—Usage. See **-ess.**

pri·or·i·tize (prī ôr′i tīz′, -or′-), *v.,* **-tized, -tiz·ing.** —*v.t.* **1.** to arrange or do in order of priority: *learning to prioritize our assignments.* **2.** to give a high priority to. —*v.i.* **3.** to organize or deal with something according to its priority. Also, *esp. Brit.,* **pri·or′i·tise′.** [1970–75; PRIORIT(Y) + -IZE] **—pri·or′i·ti·za′tion,** *n.*
—Usage. See **-ize.**

pri·or·i·ty (prī ôr′i tē, -or′-), *n., pl.* **-ties** for 2–4. **1.** the state or quality of being earlier in time, occurrence, etc. **2.** the right to precede others in order, rank, privilege, etc.; precedence. **3.** the right to take precedence in obtaining certain supplies, services, facilities, etc., esp. during a shortage. **4.** something given special attention. —*adj.* **5.** highest or higher in importance, rank, privilege, etc.: *a priority task.* [1350–1400; ME < MF *priorite* < ML *priōritās.* See PRIOR[1], -ITY]

prior′ity mail′, (in the U.S. Postal Service) mail consisting of merchandise weighing more than 12 ounces sent at first-class rates.

pri′or lien′, a lien having priority over others attached to the same property. Also called **first lien.**

pri′or restraint′, a court order banning publication of unpublished material. [1970–75]

pri·o·ry (prī′ə rē), *n., pl.* **-ries.** a religious house governed by a prior or prioress, often dependent upon an abbey. [1250–1300; ME *priorie* < ML *priōria.* See PRIOR[2], -Y[3]]

Prip·et (prip′it, -et, prē′pet), *n.* a river in NW Ukraine and S Byelorussia (Belarus), flowing E through the Pripet Marshes to the Dnieper River in NW Ukraine. 500 mi. (800 km) long. Russian, **Pri·pyat** (pryē′pyit). Polish, **Prypeć.**

Prip′et Marsh′es, an extensive wooded marshland in S Byelorussia (Belarus) and NW Ukraine. 33,500 sq. mi. (86,765 sq. km).

pri·sage (prī′zij), *n. Old Eng. Law.* the right of the king to take a certain quantity of every cargo of wine imported. Cf. **butlerage.** [1495–1505; PRISE + -AGE; cf. ML *prisāgium*]

Pris·ci·an (prish′ē ən, prish′ən), *n.* fl. A.D. c500, Latin grammarian.

Pris·cil·la (pri sil′ə), *n.* a female given name: from a Roman family name.

prise (prīz), *v.t.,* **prised, pris·ing,** *n.* prize[3].

pri·siad·ka (pris yäd′kə), *n.* a step in Slavic folk dancing in which the dancer squats on the haunches and kicks out each foot alternately; the characteristic step of the kazachok. [1935–40; < Russ *prisyádka,* equiv. to *prisyad-,* var. s. of *prisést′* to squat (*pri-* v. prefix, here marking action done incompletely or temporarily + *sest′* to sit down, akin to SIT[1]) + *-ka* n. suffix; or < Ukrainian *prýsyadka,* formed in a parallel manner from *prysísty* to squat]

prism (priz′əm), *n.* **1.** *Optics.* a transparent solid body, often having triangular bases, used for dispersing light into a spectrum or for reflecting rays of light. **2.** *Geom.* a solid having bases or ends that are parallel, congruent polygons and sides that are parallelograms. **3.** *Crystall.* a form having faces parallel to the vertical axis and intersecting the horizontal axes. [1560–70; < LL *prīsma* < Gk *prîsma* lit., something sawed, akin to *prízein* to saw, *pristēs* sawyer]

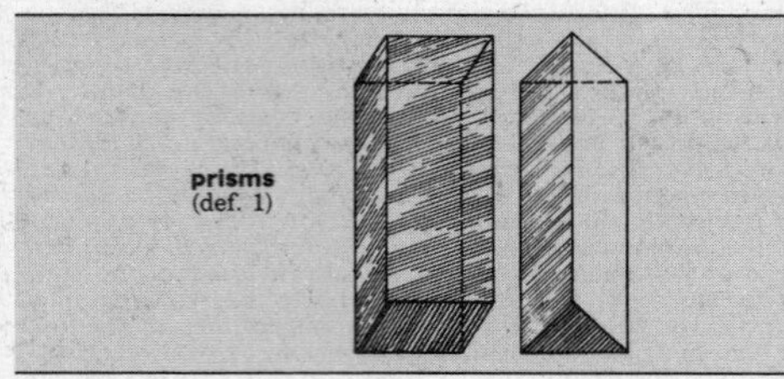
prisms
(def. 1)

pris·mat·ic (priz mat′ik), *adj.* **1.** of, pertaining to, or like a prism. **2.** formed by or as if by a transparent prism. **3.** spectral in color; brilliant: *prismatic colors.* **4.** highly varied or faceted: *a prismatic existence.* Also, **pris·mat′i·cal.** [1700–10; < Gk *prismat-* (s. of *prîsma*) PRISM + -IC] **—pris·mat′i·cal·ly,** *adv.*

prismat′ic coeffi′cient, *Naval Archit.* See **longitudinal coefficient.**

prismat′ic com′pass, a hand compass equipped with sights and prisms to permit aiming the instrument at a point and at the same time reading the compass direction of the point. [1850–55]

prismat′ic lay′er, the middle layer of the shell of certain mollusks, consisting chiefly of crystals of calcium carbonate.

prismat′ic tel′escope, *Survey.* a telescope having an eyepiece at the side or top equipped with a reflecting prism, used for taking sights at steep angles.

pris·ma·toid (priz′mə toid′), *n. Geom.* a polyhedron having its vertices lying on two parallel planes. [1855–60; < Gk *prismat-* (s. of *prîsma*) PRISM + -OID]

prism′ binoc′ular, Usually, **prism binoculars.** *Optics.* binocular (def. 1).

prism′ diop′ter, *Optics.* a unit of prismatic deviation, in which the number one represents a prism that deflects a beam of light a distance of one centimeter on a plane placed normal to the initial direction of the beam and one meter away from the prism.

pris·moid (priz′moid), *n. Geom.* a solid having sides that are trapezoids and bases or ends that are parallel and similar but not congruent polygons. Cf. **prism** (def. 2). [1695–1705; PRISM + -OID] **—pris·moi′dal,** *adj.*

prism′ spectrom′eter, *Optics.* See under **spectrometer.**

pris·on (priz′ən), *n.* **1.** a building for the confinement of persons held while awaiting trial, persons sentenced after conviction, etc. **2.** See **state prison. 3.** any place of confinement or involuntary restraint. **4.** imprisonment. [bef. 1150; ME *prison,* earlier *prisun* < OF, var. of *preson* imprisonment, a prison < L *pre(hē)nsiōn-* (s. of *prehēnsiō*) a seizure, arrest, equiv. to *prehēns(us)* (ptp. of *prehendere* to seize) + *-iōn-* -ION; doublet of PREHENSION] **—pris′on·like′,** *adj.*

pris′on camp′, 1. a camp for the confinement of prisoners of war or political prisoners. **2.** a camp for less dangerous prisoners assigned to outdoor work, usually for the government. [1905–10]

pris·on·er (priz′ə nər, priz′nər), *n.* **1.** a person who is confined in prison or kept in custody, esp. as the result of legal process. **2.** See **prisoner of war. 3.** a person or thing that is deprived of liberty or kept in restraint. [1300–50; ME < AF. See PRISON, -ER[2]]

pris′oner of war′, a person who is captured and held by an enemy during war, esp. a member of the armed forces. *Abbr.:* POW [1670–80]

pris′oner's base′, any of various children's games in which each of two teams has a home base where members of the opposing team are kept prisoner after being tagged or caught and from which they can be freed only in specified ways. Also called **pris′on base′.** [1590–1600; cf. late ME *bace* prisoner's base, perh. from the phrase *bringen bas* to lay low, cause to surrender; later taken as an assimilated form of *bars,* pl. of BAR[1], or as BASE[1] (though the sense "goal or starting point" originated with this game)]

pris′on fe′ver, typhus.

pris′on psycho′sis, *Psychiatry.* a state of mental confusion, transitory or permanent, brought on by incarceration or by the anticipation of imprisonment.

pris′on rus′tic work′, rustication having a deeply pitted surface.

priss (pris), *n. Informal.* a prissy person. [1920–25, *Amer.,* back formation from PRISSY]

Pris·sie (pris′ē), *n.* a female given name, form of **Priscilla.** Also, **Pris′sy.**

pris·sy (pris′ē), *adj.,* **-si·er, -si·est.** excessively proper; affectedly correct; prim. [1890–95, *Amer.*; b. PRIM[1] and SISSY] **—pris′si·ly,** *adv.* **—pris′si·ness,** *n.*

pris·tine (pris′tēn, pri stēn′; *esp. Brit.* pris′tin), *adj.* **1.** having its original purity; uncorrupted or unsullied. **2.** of or pertaining to the earliest period or state; primitive. [1525–35; < L *pristinus* early; akin to *primus* PRIME]
—Syn. 1. undefiled, unpolluted, untouched.

prith·ee (prith′ē), *interj. Archaic.* (I) pray thee. [1570–80; by shortening and alter.]

Pri·thi·vi (pri tē′vē), *n. Hindu Myth.* a Vedic goddess personifying the earth and fertility.

pri·us (prī′əs), *adj.* (in prescriptions) before; former. [1890–95; < L]

priv., 1. private. **2.** privative.

pri·va·cy (prī′və sē; *Brit. also* priv′ə sē), *n., pl.* **-cies. 1.** the state of being private; retirement or seclusion. **2.** the state of being free from intrusion or disturbance in one's private life or affairs: *the right to privacy.* **3.** secrecy. **4.** *Archaic.* a private place. [1400–50; late ME *privacе.* See PRIVATE, -ACY]

pri·vat·do·cent (prē vät′dō tsent′), *n.* (in German and certain other universities) a private teacher or lecturer recognized by the university but receiving no compensation from it, being remunerated by fees. Also, **pri·vat′do·zent′.** Also called **docent.** [1880–85; < G *Privatdocent;* see PRIVATE, DOCENT]

pri·vate (prī′vit), *adj.* **1.** belonging to some particular person: *private property.* **2.** pertaining to or affecting a particular person or a small group of persons; individual; personal: *for your private satisfaction.* **3.** confined to or intended only for the persons immediately concerned; confidential: *a private meeting.* **4.** personal and not publicly expressed: *one's private feelings.* **5.** not holding public office or employment: *private citizens.* **6.** not of an official or public character: *private life.* **7.** removed from or out of public view or knowledge; secret: *private papers.* **8.** not open or accessible to the general public: *a private beach.* **9.** undertaken individually or personally: *private research.* **10.** without the presence of others; alone. **11.** solitary; secluded. **12.** preferring privacy; retiring: *a very private person.* **13.** intimate; most personal: *private behavior.* **14.** of, having, or receiving special hospital facilities, privileges, and services, esp. a room of one's own and liberal visiting hours: *a private room; a private patient.* **15.** of lowest military rank. **16.** of, pertaining to, or coming from nongovernmental sources: *private funding.* —*n.* **17.** a soldier of one of the three lowest enlisted ranks. **18. privates.** See **private parts. 19. in private,** not publicly; secretly: *The hearing will be conducted in private.* [1350–1400; ME < L *prīvātus* private, lit., taken away (from public affairs), special use of ptp. of *prīvāre* to rob. See DEPRIVE, -ATE[1]] **—pri′vate·ly,** *adv.* **—pri′vate·ness,** *n.*
—Syn. 2. singular, particular, peculiar. **10.** sequestered, retired. **—Ant. 2.** general, public.

pri′vate bill′, a congressional or parliamentary bill involving the private interests of a particular individual, corporation, or local unit. Cf. **public bill.** [1670–80]

pri′vate brand′, a product marketed under a private label.

pri′vate com′pany, *Brit.* a company whose shareholders may not exceed 50 in number and whose shares may not be offered for public subscription. Cf. **public company.** [1905–10]

pri′vate detec′tive, a detective who is not a member of an official force but is employed by private parties. Also called **private investigator.** [1865–70]

pri′vate en′terprise. See **free enterprise** (def. 1). [1835–45]

pri·va·teer (prī′və tēr′), *n.* **1.** an armed ship that is privately owned and manned, commissioned by a government to fight or harass enemy ships. **2.** privateersman. —*v.i.* **3.** to cruise as a privateer. [1640–50; PRIVATE + -EER, modeled on *volunteer*]

pri·va·teers·man (prī′və tērz′mən), *n., pl.* **-men.** an officer or sailor of a privateer. [1770–80, *Amer.*; PRIVATEER + 'S[1] + -MAN]

pri′vate eye′, *Slang.* a private detective. [1935–40; *eye,* allusive phonetic rendering of *I,* abbr. of *investigator*]

pri′vate first′ class′, a soldier ranking above a private and below a corporal or specialist fourth class in the U.S. Army, and above a private and below a lance corporal in the U.S. Marine Corps. [1910–15, *Amer.*]

pri′vate interna′tional law′. See **conflict of laws** (def. 2). Cf. **public international law.** [1825–35]

pri′vate inves′tigator. See **private detective.** *Abbr.:* p.i., P.I. [1935–40]

pri′vate judg′ment, personal opinion formed independently of the expressed position of an institution, as in matters of religion or politics.

pri′vate la′bel, the label of a product, or the product itself, sold under the name of a wholesaler or retailer, by special arrangement with the manufacturer or producer.

pri′vate law′, 1. a branch of law dealing with the legal relationships of private individuals. Cf. **public law** (def. 2). **2.** a statute affecting only one person or a small number of persons directly. [1765–75]

pri′vate-line′ car′ (prī′vit līn′), a freight car owned by a company other than a railroad but operated over the tracks of railroads.

Pri′vate Mem′ber, (*sometimes l.c.*) *Brit.* a member of a legislative body, esp. of the House of Commons, who has no special duties and is not a member of the ministry. [1600–10]

pri′vate parts′, the external genital organs. [1765–75]

pri′vate place′ment, *Finance.* a sale of an issue of securities by the issuing company directly to a limited number of investors, often only one or two large institutional investors, such as a bank or an insurance company (opposed to *public offering*): required to be cleared but not registered with the Securities and Exchange Commission.

pri′vate prac′tice, the practice of one's profession as an independent rather than as an employee.

pri′vate school′, a school founded, conducted, and maintained by a private group rather than by the government, usually charging tuition and often following a particular philosophy, viewpoint, etc. [1820–30]

pri′vate sec′retary, a person who attends to the individual or confidential correspondence, files, etc., of a business executive, official, or the like. [1765–75]

pri′vate sec′tor, the area of the nation's economy under private rather than governmental control. Cf. **public sector.** [1950–55]

pri′vate trea′ty, a property sale based on terms resulting from a conference between buyer and seller. [1855–60]

pri′vate trust′, a trust designed for the benefit of a designated or known individual (opposed to *charitable trust*).

pri•va•tion (prī vā′shən), *n.* **1.** lack of the usual comforts or necessaries of life: *His life of privation began to affect his health.* **2.** an instance of this. **3.** the act of depriving. **4.** the state of being deprived. [1350–1400; ME (< MF *privacion*) < L *prīvātiōn-* (s. of *prīvātiō*) a taking away. See PRIVATE, -ION]
—Syn. 1. deprivation, want, need, distress. See **hardship.**

pri•va•tism (prī′və tiz′əm), *n.* concern with or pursuit of one's personal or family interests, welfare, or ideals to the exclusion of broader social issues or relationships. [1945–50; PRIVATE + -ISM] **—pri′va•tist,** *n., adj.* **—pri′•va•tis′tic,** *adj.*

priv•a•tive (priv′ə tiv), *adj.* **1.** causing, or tending to cause, deprivation. **2.** consisting in or characterized by the taking away, loss, or lack of something. **3.** *Gram.* indicating negation or absence. **—*n.* 4.** *Gram.* a privative element, as *a-* in *asymmetric.* **5.** something that is deprived. [1520–1400; ME *privatif* < L *prīvātīvus.* See PRIVATE, -IVE] **—priv′a•tive•ly,** *adv.*

pri•va•tize (prī′və tīz′), *v.t.,* **-tized, -tiz•ing. 1.** to transfer from public or government control or ownership to private enterprise: *a campaign promise to privatize some of the public lands.* **2.** to make exclusive; delimit or appropriate: *special-interest groups attempting to privatize social issues.* Also, *esp. Brit.,* **pri′va•tise′.** [1945–50; PRIVATE + -IZE] **—pri′va•ti•za′tion,** *n.*

priv•et (priv′it), *n.* any of various deciduous or evergreen shrubs of the genus *Ligustrum,* esp. *L. vulgare,* having clusters of small white flowers and commonly grown as a hedge. [1535–45; orig. uncert.]

priv′et androm′eda. See **swamp andromeda.**

priv•i•lege (priv′ə lij, priv′lij), *n., v.,* **-leged, -leg•ing.** **—*n.* 1.** a right, immunity, or benefit enjoyed only by a person beyond the advantages of most: *the privileges of the very rich.* **2.** a special right, immunity, or exemption granted to persons in authority or office to free them from certain obligations or liabilities: *the privilege of a senator to speak in Congress without danger of a libel suit.* **3.** a grant to an individual, corporation, etc., of a special right or immunity, under certain conditions. **4.** the principle or condition of enjoying special rights or immunities. **5.** any of the rights common to all citizens under a modern constitutional government: *We enjoy the privileges of a free people.* **6.** an advantage or source of pleasure granted to a person: *It's my privilege to be here.* **7.** *Stock Exchange.* an option to buy or sell stock at a stipulated price for a limited period of time, including puts, calls, spreads, and straddles. **—*v.t.* 8.** to grant a privilege to. **9.** to exempt (usually fol. by *from*). **10.** to authorize or license (something otherwise forbidden). [1125–75; (n.) ME; earlier *privilegie* (< OF *privilege*) < L *prīvilēgium* orig., a law for or against an individual, equiv. to *privi-* (comb. form of *prīvus* one's own) + *lēg-* (see LEGAL) + *-ium* -IUM; (v.) ME *privilegen* (< MF *privilegier*) < ML *prīvilēgiāre,* deriv. of *prīvilēgium*] **—priv′i•leg•er,** *n.*
—Syn. 1. PRIVILEGE, PREROGATIVE refer to a special advantage or right possessed by an individual or group. A PRIVILEGE is a right or advantage gained by birth, social position, effort, or concession. It can have either legal or personal sanction: *the privilege of paying half fare; the privilege of calling whenever one wishes.* PREROGATIVE refers to an exclusive right claimed and granted, often officially or legally, on the basis of social status, heritage, sex, etc.: *the prerogatives of a king; the prerogatives of management.* **4.** license, freedom, liberty.

priv•i•leged (priv′ə lijd, priv′lijd), *adj.* **1.** belonging to a class that enjoys special privileges; favored: *the privileged few.* **2.** entitled to or exercising a privilege. **3.** restricted to a select group or individual: *privileged information; a privileged position.* **4.** *Law.* (of utterances or communications) **a.** not rendering the person making them liable to prosecution for libel or slander, in view of the attendant circumstances. **b.** not requiring any testimony concerning them to be presented in court. **5.** *Navig.* (of a vessel) having the right of way. Cf. **burdened.** [1350–1400; ME; see PRIVILEGE, -ED[2], -ED[3]]

priv′ileged al′tar, *Rom. Cath. Ch.* an altar at which a plenary indulgence for a departed soul may be granted upon celebration of a Mass. [1880–85]

priv′ileged communica′tion, *Law.* See **confidential communication.**

priv•i•ly (priv′ə lē), *adv.* in a privy manner; secretly. [1250–1300; ME; see PRIVY, -LY]

priv•i•ty (priv′i tē), *n., pl.* **-ties. 1.** private or secret knowledge. **2.** participation in the knowledge of something private or secret, esp. as implying concurrence or consent. **3.** *Law.* the relation between privies. **4.** *Obs.* privacy. [1175–1225; ME *privete, privite* < OF. See PRIVY, -ITY]

priv. pr., privately printed.

priv•y (priv′ē), *adj.,* **priv•i•er, priv•i•est,** *n., pl.* **priv•ies. —*adj.* 1.** participating in the knowledge of something private or secret (usually fol. by *to*): *Many persons were privy to the plot.* **2.** private; assigned to private uses. **3.** belonging or pertaining to some particular person, esp. with reference to a sovereign. **4.** secret, concealed, hidden, or secluded. **5.** acting or done in secret. **—*n.* 6.** outhouse (def. 1). **7.** *Law.* a person participating directly in or having a derivative interest in a legal transaction. [1175–1225; ME *prive* < OF: private (adj.), close friend, private place (n.) < L *prīvātus* PRIVATE]

priv′y cham′ber, 1. a private apartment in a royal residence. **2.** *Archaic.* a room reserved for the private or exclusive use of some particular person. [1350–1400; ME]

priv′y coat′, a mail shirt worn under ordinary clothing as a defense against swords or daggers. [1525–35]

priv′y coun′cil, 1. a board or select body of personal advisers, as of a sovereign. **2.** (*caps.*) (in Great Britain) a body of persons who advise the sovereign in matters of state, the majority of members being selected by the prime minister. **3.** (*sometimes caps.*) any similar body, as one appointed to assist the governor of a British dominion. [1250–1300; ME *prive counseil* privy counsel] **—priv′y coun′cilor.**

priv′y purse′, *Brit.* **1.** a sum from the public revenues allotted to the sovereign for personal expenses. **2.** a member of the royal household in charge of paying these expenses. [1655–65]

priv′y seal′, (in Great Britain) the seal affixed to grants, documents, etc., that are to pass the great seal, and to documents of less importance that do not require the great seal. [1250–1300; ME]

prix fixe (prē′ fiks′; *Fr.* prē fēks′), *pl.* **prix fixes** (prē′ fiks′; *Fr.* prē fēks′). a fixed price charged for any meal chosen from the variety listed on the menu. Cf. **à la carte, table d'hôte.** [1880–85; < F]

Prix Gon•court (prē′ gon ko͝or′; *Fr.* prē gôn ko͞or′), Goncourt (def. 2).

prize[1] (prīz), *n.* **1.** a reward for victory or superiority, as in a contest or competition. **2.** something that is won in a lottery or the like. **3.** anything striven for, worth striving for, or much valued. **4.** something seized or captured, esp. an enemy's ship and cargo captured at sea in wartime. **5.** the act of taking or capturing, esp. a ship at sea. **6.** *Archaic.* a contest or match. **—*adj.* 7.** having won a prize: *a prize bull; a prize play.* **8.** worthy of a prize. **9.** given or awarded as a prize. [1250–1300; in senses referring to something seized, continuing ME *prise* something captured, a seizing < MF < L *pre(hē)nsa,* n. use of fem. ptp. of *pre(he)ndere* to take; in senses referring to something won, sp. var. of PRICE (ME *pris(e)*) since the late 16th century]
—Syn. 1. premium. See **reward.**

prize[2] (prīz), *v.t.,* **prized, priz•ing. 1.** to value or esteem highly. **2.** to estimate the worth or value of. [1325–75; ME *prisen* < MF *prisier,* var. of *preisier* to PRAISE]
—Syn. 1. See **appreciate.**

prize[3] (prīz), *v.,* **prized, priz•ing,** *n.* **—*v.t.* 1.** pry[2]. **—*n.* 2.** leverage. **3.** a lever. Also, **prise.** [1350–1400; ME *prise* < MF: a hold, grasp < L *pre(hē)nsa.* See PRIZE[1]]

prize′ court′, a court whose function it is to adjudicate on prizes taken in war. [1785–95, *Amer.*]

prize•fight (prīz′fīt′), *n.* a contest between boxers for a prize, a sum of money, etc.; a professional boxing match. Also, **prize′ fight′.** [1695–1705] **—prize′fight′•er,** *n.* **—prize′fight′ing,** *n.*

prize′ flag′, a flag hoisted by a yacht upon learning that it has won a prize in a race.

prize′ mon′ey, 1. money offered, won, or received in prizes. **2.** a portion of the money realized from the sale of a prize, esp. an enemy's vessel, divided among the captors. [1740–50]

priz•er (prī′zər), *n. Archaic.* a competitor for a prize. [1590–1600; PRIZE[1] + -ER[1]]

prize′ ring′, 1. a ring where prizefights take place; boxing ring. **2.** the sport of prizefighting. [1815–25]

prize•win•ner (prīz′win′ər), *n.* a person or thing that wins a prize or is deserving of a prize. [1890–95; PRIZE[1] + WINNER] **—prize′win′ning,** *adj.*

prize•wor•thy (prīz′wûr′thē), *adj.* deserving or qualified for a prize: *a prizeworthy performance.* [PRIZE[1] + -WORTHY]

p.r.n., (in prescriptions) as the occasion arises; as needed. [< L *prō rē nāta*]

pro[1] (prō), *adv., n., pl.* **pros. —*adv.* 1.** in favor of a proposition, opinion, etc. **—*n.* 2.** a proponent of an issue; a person who upholds the affirmative in a debate. **3.** an argument, consideration, vote, etc., for something. Cf. **con[1].** [1350–1400; ME < L *prō* (prep) in favor of, FOR; akin to PER-, Gk *pró,* Skt *pra*]

pro[2] (prō), *adj., n., pl.* **pros.** *Informal.* **—*adj.* 1.** professional. **—*n.* 2.** professional. **3. the pros,** the professional athletic leagues, as of football, baseball, or basketball: *He's sure to be signed by the pros.* [1840–50; shortened form]

pro[3] (prō), *n., pl.* **pros.** *Slang.* prophylactic (def. 5). [shortened form]

pro (prō; *Eng.* prō), *prep. Latin.* for.

PRO, public relations officer. Also, **P.R.O.**

Pro, *Biochem.* proline.

pro-[1], 1. a prefix indicating favor for some party, system, idea, etc., without identity with the group (*pro-British; pro-Communist; proslavery*), having *anti-* as its opposite. **2.** a prefix of priority in space or time having especially a meaning of advancing or projecting forward or outward, and also used to indicate substitution, attached widely to stems not used as words: *provision; prologue; proceed; produce; protract; procathedral; proconsul.* [< L *prō-, pro-,* comb. form repr. *prō* PRO[1]]
—Note. The lists at the bottom of this and following pages provide the spelling, syllabification, and stress for words whose meanings may be easily inferred by combining the meaning of PRO-[1] and an attached base word, or base word plus a suffix. Appropriate parts of speech are also shown. Words prefixed by PRO-[1] that have special meanings or uses are entered in their proper alphabetical places in the main vocabulary or as derived forms run on at the end of a main entry.

pro-[2], a prefix identical in meaning with **pro-[1],** occurring in words borrowed from Greek (*prodrome*) or formed of Greek (and occasionally Latin) elements. [< Gk, comb. form of *pró* for, before; see PRO[1]]

pro•a (prō′ə), *n.* any of various types of Indonesian boats, esp. a swift Malay sailing boat built with the lee side flat and balanced by a single outrigger. Also, **prao.** [1575–85; < Malay *pərahu, pərau* (sp. *perahu*) (< Kannada *paḍahu,* or a cognate Dravidian word); prob. influenced by Sp or Pg *proa* PROW[1], bow]

pro•a•bor•tion (prō′ə bôr′shən), *adj.* pro-choice. Also, **pro′-a•bor′tion.** [1975–80; PRO-[1] + ABORTION] **—pro′•a•bor′tion•ism,** *n.* **—pro′a•bor′tion•ist,** *n.*

pro•ac•tive (prō ak′tiv), *adj.* serving to prepare for, intervene in, or control an expected occurrence or situation, esp. a negative or difficult one; anticipatory: *proactive measures against crime.* [1930–35; PRO-[1] + ACTIVE]

pro•ag•on (prō ag′ōn, -on, prō′ä gōn′), *n., pl.* ***pro•a•go•nes*** (prō′ə gō′nēz). *Greek.* (in ancient Greek comedy) a disputatious exchange, sometimes of a slapstick nature, between the chorus and the characters, or among the characters themselves, usually following the *parodos* and preceding the *agon.*

pro-am (prō′am′), *adj.* **1.** including both professionals and amateurs. **—*n.* 2.** any sporting event in which professionals play with amateurs. [1945–50; *pro(fessional)-am(ateur)*]

prob (prob), *n. Chiefly Brit. Slang.* problem. [by shortening]

prob., 1. probable. **2.** probably. **3.** problem.

prob•a•bil•ism (prob′ə bə liz′əm), *n.* **1.** *Philos.* the doctrine, introduced by the Skeptics, that certainty is impossible and that probability suffices to govern faith and practice. **2.** *Rom. Cath. Theol.* a theory that in cases of doubt as to the lawfulness of an action, it is permissible to follow a sound opinion favoring its lawfulness. Cf. **equiprobabilism.** [1835–45; < F *probabilisme.* See PROBABLE, -ISM] **—prob′a•bi•list,** *n., adj.*

prob•a•bi•lis•tic (prob′ə bə lis′tik), *adj.* **1.** *Statistics.* of or pertaining to probability: *probabilistic forecasting.* **2.** of or pertaining to probabilism. [1650–60; PROBABIL(ISM) or PROBABIL(ITY) + -ISTIC; cf. F *probabiliste* believer in probabilism]

prob•a•bil•i•ty (prob′ə bil′i tē), *n., pl.* **-ties. 1.** the quality or fact of being probable. **2.** a strong likelihood or chance of something: *The probability of the book's success makes us optimistic.* **3.** a probable event, circumstance, etc.: *Our going to China is a probability.* **4.** *Statistics.* **a.** the relative possibility that an event will occur, as expressed by the ratio of the number of actual occurrences to the total number of possible occurrences. **b.** the relative frequency with which an event occurs or is likely to occur. **5. in all probability,** very probably; quite likely: *The factory will in all probability be relocated.* [1545–55; < L *probābilitās.* See PROBABLE, -ITY]

probabil′ity curve′, *Statistics.* **1.** a curve that describes the distribution of probability over the values of a random variable. **2.** See **normal curve.** [1890–95]

probabil′ity den′sity func′tion, *Statistics.* **1.** a function of a continuous variable whose integral over a region gives the probability that a random variable falls within the region. **2.** Also called **frequency function.** a function of a discrete variable whose sum over a discrete set gives the probability of occurrence of a specified value. [1935–40]

probabil′ity distribu′tion, *Statistics.* a distribution of all possible values of a random variable together with an indication of their probabilities. [1935–40]

probabil′ity the′ory, *Math., Statistics.* the theory of analyzing and making statements concerning the probability of the occurrence of uncertain events. Cf. **probability** (def. 4). [1830–40]

prob•a•ble (prob′ə bəl), *adj.* **1.** likely to occur or prove true: *He foresaw a probable business loss. He is the probable writer of the article.* **2.** having more evidence

CONCISE PRONUNCIATION KEY: *act, cāpe, dâre, pärt; set, ēqual; if, īce; ox, ōver, ôrder, oil, bo͝ok, bo͞ot, out; up, ûrge; child; sing; shoe; thin, that;* zh as in *treasure.* ə = *a* as in *alone, e* as in *system, i* as in *easily, o* as in *gallop, u* as in *circus;* ᵊ as in *fire* (fīᵊr), *hour* (ouᵊr). l and n can serve as syllabic consonants, as in *cradle* (krād′l), and *button* (but′n). See the full key inside the front cover.

pro′ab•o•li′tion, *adj.*
pro′ab•o•li′tion•ist, *n., adj.*
pro•ab′so•lut′ism, *n.*
pro•ab′so•lut′ist, *adj., n.*
pro•ab′sti•nence, *adj.*
pro′-Ab•ys•sin′i•an, *adj., n.*
pro′ac•a•dem′ic, *adj.*
pro′ac•cept′ance, *adj.*
pro′ac•qui•si′tion, *adj.*
pro′ac•quit′tal, *adj.*
pro•act′ing, *adj.*
pro•ac′tion, *adj.*
pro′ad•journ′ment, *adj.*
pro′ad•min′is•tra′tion, *adj.*
pro′ad•mis′sion, *adj.*
pro′a•dop′tion, *adj.*
pro•ad′ver•tis′ing, *adj.*
pro•ad′ver•tiz′ing, *adj.*
pro•Af′ri•can, *adj., n.*
pro′ag•i•ta′tion, adj.
pro′a•grar′i•an, *adj.*
pro′a•gree′ment, *adj.*
pro•air′plane′, *adj.*
pro′-Al•a•bam′an, *adj., n.*
pro′-A•las′kan, *adj., n.*
pro′-Al•ge′ri•an, *adj., n.*
pro•al′ien, *adj.*
pro′al•li′ance, *adj.*
pro′al•lot′ment, *adj.*
pro′-Al•sa′tian, *adj., n.*

for than against, or evidence that inclines the mind to belief but leaves some room for doubt. **3.** affording ground for belief. [1350–1400; ME < L *probābilis* likely, lit., capable of standing a test, equiv. to *probā(re)* to test (see PROBE) + *-bilis* -BLE]

prob′able cause′, *Law.* reasonable ground for a belief, as, in a criminal case, that the accused was guilty of the crime, or, in a civil case, that grounds for the action existed: used esp. as a defense to an action for malicious prosecution. [1670–80]

prob′able er′ror, *Statistics.* a quantity formerly used as a measure of variability: equal to 0.6745 times the standard deviation. A normally distributed population has half of its elements within one probable error of the mean. [1805–15]

prob•a•bly (prob′ə blē), *adv.* in all likelihood; very likely: *He will probably attend.* [1525–35; PROBABLE + -LY]

pro•band (prō′band), *n. Genetics.* a patient who is the initial member of a family to come under study. Also called **propositus.** [1925–30; < L *probandus,* gerundive of *probāre* to test, PROBE]

pro•bang (prō′bang), *n. Surg.* a long, slender, elastic rod with a sponge, ball, or the like, at the end, to be introduced into the esophagus or larynx, as for removing foreign bodies, or for introducing medication. [1650–60; alter. (by assoc. with PROBE) of *provang,* unexplained coinage of the inventor]

pro•bate (prō′bāt), *n., adj., v.,* **-bat•ed, -bat•ing.** —*n.* **1.** *Law.* the official proving of a will as authentic or valid in a probate court. **2.** an officially certified copy of a will so proved. —*adj.* **3.** of or pertaining to probate or a probate court. —*v.t.* **4.** to establish the authenticity or validity of (a will). **5.** *Law.* to put (an offender) on probation. [1400–50; late ME *probat* < L *probātum* a thing approved, n. use of neut. ptp. of *probāre* to test and find good; see PROBE, -ATE[1]]

pro′bate court′, a special court with power over administration of estates of deceased persons, the probate of wills, etc. [1720–30, *Amer.*]

pro•ba•tion (prō bā′shən), *n.* **1.** the act of testing. **2.** the testing or trial of a person's conduct, character, qualifications, or the like. **3.** the state or period of such testing or trial. **4.** *Law.* **a.** a method of dealing with offenders, esp. young persons guilty of minor crimes or first offenses, by allowing them to go at large under supervision of a probation officer. **b.** the state of having been conditionally released. **5.** *Educ.* a trial period or condition of students in certain educational institutions who are being permitted to redeem failures, misconduct, etc. **6.** the testing or trial of a candidate for membership in a religious body or order, for holy orders, etc. **7.** *Archaic.* proof. [1375–1425; late ME *probacion* < L *probātiōn-* (s. of *probātiō*). See PROBATE, -ION] —**pro•ba′tion•al, pro•ba•tion•ar•y** (prō bā′shə ner′ē), *adj.* —**pro•ba′•tion•ship′,** *n.*

pro•ba•tion•er (prō bā′shə nər), *n.* a person undergoing probation or trial. [1595–1605; PROBATION + -ER[1]] —**pro•ba′tion•er•ship′,** *n.*

proba′tion of′ficer, an officer who investigates and reports on the conduct of offenders who are free on probation. [1895–1900, *Amer.*]

pro•ba•tive (prō′bə tiv, prob′ə-), *adj.* **1.** serving or designed for testing or trial. **2.** affording proof or evidence. Also, **pro•ba•to•ry** (prō′bə tôr′ē, -tōr′ē). [1425–75; late ME < MF *probatif* < L *probātivus* of proof. See PROBATE, -IVE] —**pro′ba•tive•ly,** *adv.*

probe (prōb), *v.,* **probed, prob•ing,** *n.* —*v.t.* **1.** to search into or examine thoroughly; question closely: *to probe one's conscience.* **2.** to examine or explore with a probe. —*v.i.* **3.** to examine or explore with or as if with a probe. —*n.* **4.** the act of probing. **5.** a slender surgical instrument for exploring the depth or direction of a wound, sinus, or the like. **6.** an investigation, esp. by a legislative committee, of suspected illegal activity. **7.** *Aerospace.* See **space probe. 8.** a projecting, pipelike device on a receiving aircraft used to make connection with and receive fuel from a tanker aircraft during refueling in flight. **9.** a device, attached by cord to an oven, that can be inserted into roasts or other food so that the oven shuts off when the desired internal temperature of the food is reached. **10.** *Biol.* any identifiable substance that is used to detect, isolate, or identify another substance, as a labeled strand of DNA that hybridizes with its complementary RNA or a monoclonal antibody that combines with a specific protein. [1555–65; (n.) < ML *proba* examination, LL: test, deriv. of *probāre* (see PROVE); (v.) partly deriv. of the n., partly < L *probāre.* See PROOF] —**probe′a•ble,** *adj.* —**prob′er,** *n.*
—**Syn. 1.** investigate, scrutinize.

pro•ben•e•cid (prō ben′ə sid), *n. Pharm.* a white, crystalline, water-insoluble powder, $C_{13}H_{19}NO_4S$, used chiefly in the treatment of gout. [1945–50; PRO(PYL) + BEN(ZEN)E + (A)CID]

pro•bie (prō′bē), *n. Informal.* a probationer, esp. a firefighter who has recently joined a department. [1895–1900; PROB(ATIONARY) or PROB(ATION) + -IE]

prob•it (prob′it), *n. Statistics.* a normal equivalent deviate increased by five. [1930–35; PROB(ABILITY) + (UN)IT]

pro•bi•ty (prō′bi tē, prob′i-), *n.* integrity and uprightness; honesty. [1505–15; < L *probitās* uprightness, equiv. to *prob(us)* upright + *-itās* -ITY]
—**Syn.** rectitude. —**Ant.** dishonesty.

prob•lem (prob′ləm), *n.* **1.** any question or matter involving doubt, uncertainty, or difficulty. **2.** a question proposed for solution or discussion. **3.** *Math.* a statement requiring a solution, usually by means of a mathematical operation or geometric construction. **4. no problem,** (used as a conventional reply to a request or to express confirmation, affirmation, or gratitude). —*adj.* **5.** difficult to train or guide; unruly: *a problem child.* **6.** *Literature.* dealing with choices of action difficult either for an individual or for society at large: *a problem play.* [1350–1400; ME *probleme* < L *problēma* < Gk *próblēma* orig., obstacle, (akin to *probállein* to throw or lay before), equiv. to *pro-* PRO-[2] + *-blē-,* var. s. of *bállein* to throw (cf. PARABOLA) + *-ma* n. suffix of result]
—**Syn. 1, 2.** puzzle, riddle, enigma. —**Ant. 1.** certitude.

prob•lem•at•ic (prob′lə mat′ik), *adj.* of the nature of a problem; doubtful; uncertain; questionable. Also, **prob′lem•at′i•cal.** [1600–10; < LL *problēmaticus* < Gk *problēmatikós,* equiv. to *problēmat-* (s. of *próblēma*) PROBLEM + *-ikos* -IC] —**prob′lem•at′i•cal•ly,** *adv.*
—**Syn.** unsure, indeterminate, unsettled, dubious, ambiguous.

prob•lem•at•ics (prob′lə mat′iks), *n.pl.* the uncertainties or difficulties inherent in a situation or plan. [1955–60; see PROBLEMATIC, -ICS]

pro bo•no (prō′ bō′nō), done or donated without charge; free: *pro bono legal services.* Also, **pro′-bon′o.** [1720–30; < L *prō bonō* for (the) good, rightly, morally]

pro bo•no pu•bli•co (prō bō′nō pōō′bli kō′; *Eng.* prō bō′nō pub′li kō′), *Latin.* for the public good or welfare.

pro•bos•ci•date (prō bos′i dāt′), *adj.* having a proboscis. [1820–30; < L *proboscid-* (s. of *proboscis*) + -ATE[1]]

pro•bos•cid•e•an (prō′bə sid′ē ən, -bo-, prō bos′i-dē′ən), *adj.* **1.** pertaining to or resembling a proboscis. **2.** having a proboscis. **3.** belonging or pertaining to the mammals of the order Proboscidea, characterized by a flexible trunk formed of the nostrils and upper lip, large tusks, a massive body, and columnar legs, comprising the elephant and the now-extinct mammoth and mastodon. —*n.* **4.** a proboscidean animal. Also, **pro′bos•cid′i•an.** [1825–35; < NL *Proboscide(a)* order name (L *proboscid-* (s. of *proboscis* PROBOSCIS) + *-ea,* neut. pl. of *-eus* adj. suffix; see -EOUS) + -AN]

pro•bos•cis (prō bos′is, -kis), *n., pl.* **-bos•cis•es, -bos•ci•des** (-bos′i dēz′). **1.** the trunk of an elephant. **2.** any long flexible snout, as of the tapir. **3.** Also called **beak.** the elongate, protruding mouth parts of certain insects, adapted for sucking or piercing. **4.** any of various elongate feeding, defensive, or sensory organs of the oral region, as in certain leeches and worms. **5.** *Facetious.* the human nose, esp. when unusually long or prominent. [1570–80; < L < Gk *proboskís* elephant's trunk, lit., feeder, equiv. to *pro-* PRO-[2] + *bósk(ein)* to feed + *-is* (s. *-id-*) n. suffix]

probos′cis mon′key, a reddish, arboreal monkey, *Nasalis larvatus,* of Borneo, the male of which has a long, flexible nose: an endangered species. [1785–95]

pro-bus•ing (prō bus′ing), *adj.* favoring or advocating legislation that requires the busing of students from one school district to another to achieve racial balance in public schools. Also, **pro-bus′sing.**

proc., **1.** procedure. **2.** proceedings. **3.** process. **4.** proclamation. **5.** proctor.

pro•caine (prō kān′, prō′kān), *n. Pharm.* a compound, $C_{13}H_{20}N_2O_2$, used chiefly as a local and spinal anesthetic. [1915–20; PRO-[1] + (CO)CAINE]

procaine′ am′ide, *Pharm.* a white, crystalline compound, $C_{13}H_{21}ON_3$, used in the treatment of cardiac arrhythmias. [1945–50]

pro•cam•bi•um (prō kam′bē əm), *n. Bot.* the meristem from which vascular bundles are developed. Also called **provascular tissue.** [1870–75; < NL; see PRO-[1], CAMBIUM] —**pro•cam′bi•al,** *adj.*

pro•carp (prō′kärp), *n. Bot.* (in red algae) a carpogonium with its associated cells. [1885–90; < NL *procarpium* < Gk *pro-* PRO-[2] + *karpíon,* dim. of *karpós* fruit]

pro•car•y•ote (prō kar′ē ōt′, -ē ət), *n.* prokaryote. [1960–65] —**pro•car•y•ot•ic** (prō kar′ē ot′ik), *adj.*

pro•ca•the•dral (prō′kə thē′drəl), *n.* a church used temporarily as a cathedral. [1865–70; PRO-[1] + CATHEDRAL]

pro•ce•dur•al (prə sē′jər əl), *adj.* **1.** of or pertaining to a procedure or procedures, esp. of a court of law, legislative body, or law enforcement agency. —*n.* **2.** See **police procedural.** [1885–90; PROCEDURE + -AL[1]] —**pro•ce′dur•al•ly,** *adv.*

pro•ce•dure (prə sē′jər), *n.* **1.** an act or a manner of proceeding in any action or process; conduct. **2.** a particular course or mode of action. **3.** any given mode of conducting legal, parliamentary, or other business, esp. litigation and judicial proceedings. **4.** *Computers.* **a.** the sequence of actions or instructions to be followed in solving a problem or accomplishing a task. **b.** Also called **subprogram.** a group of statements that may be used at one or more points in a computer program. [1605–15; < F *procédure.* See PROCEED, -URE] *adj.*
—**Syn. 1.** management. **2.** operation, maneuver, transaction. See **process.**

pro•ceed (*v.* prə sēd′; *n.* prō′sēd), *v.i.* **1.** to move or go forward or onward, esp. after stopping. **2.** to carry on or continue any action or process. **3.** to go on to do something. **4.** to continue one's discourse. **5.** *Law.* **a.** to begin and carry on a legal action. **b.** to take legal action (usually fol. by *against*). **6.** to be carried on, as an action or process. **7.** to go or come forth; issue (often fol. by *from*). **8.** to arise, originate, or result (usually fol. by *from*). —*n.* **9. proceeds, a.** something that results or accrues. **b.** the total amount derived from a sale or other transaction: *The proceeds from the deal were divided equally among us.* **c.** the profits or returns from a sale, investment, etc. **10.** *Archaic.* proceeds. [1350–1400; ME *procede* < L *prōcēdere.* See PRO-[1], CEDE] —**pro•ceed′er,** *n.*
—**Syn. 1.** progress, continue, pass on. See **advance. 7.** emanate. **8.** spring, ensue. —**Ant. 1.** recede.

pro•ceed•ing (prə sē′ding), *n.* **1.** a particular action or course or manner of action. **2. proceedings,** a series of activities or events; happenings. **3.** the act of a person or thing that proceeds: *Our proceeding down the mountain was hindered by mud slides.* **4. proceedings,** a record of the doings or transactions of a fraternal, academic, etc., society. **5. proceedings,** *Law.* **a.** the instituting or carrying on of an action at law. **b.** a legal step or measure: *to institute proceedings against a person.* [1375–1425; late ME; see PROCEED, -ING[1]]
—**Syn. 1, 2, 4.** See **process.**

proc•e•leus•mat•ic (pros′ə lōōs mat′ik, prō′sə-), *adj.* **1.** inciting, animating, or inspiring. **2.** *Pros.* **a.** noting a metrical foot of four short syllables. **b.** pertaining to or consisting of feet of this kind. —*n.* **3.** *Pros.* a proceleusmatic foot. [1700–10; < LL *proceleusmaticus* < Gk *prokeleusmatikós* lit., calling for incitement, equiv. to *pro-* PRO-[2] + *keleusmat-* (s. of *kéleusma* summons, deriv. of *keleúein* to rouse to action) + *-ikos* -IC]

pro•cel•las (prō sel′əs), *n.* (*used with a singular v.*) pucellas. [said to be < It *procello*]

pro•cel•lous (prō sel′əs), *adj.* stormy, as the sea. [1640–50; < L *procellōsus* stormy, equiv. to *procell(a)* storm + *-ōsus* -OUS]

pro•cer•coid (prō sûr′koid), *n. Zool.* an elongate larval stage of some tapeworms that usually develops in the body of a freshwater copepod. Cf. **plerocercoid.** [1925–30; PRO-[2] + Gk *kérk(os)* tail + -OID]

proc•ess (pros′es *or, esp. Brit.,* prō′ses), *n., pl.* **proc•ess•es** (pros′es iz, -ə siz, -ə sēz′ *or, esp. Brit.,* prō′ses-, prō′sə-), *v., adj.* —*n.* **1.** a systematic series of actions directed to some end: *to devise a process for homogenizing milk.* **2.** a continuous action, operation, or series of changes taking place in a definite manner: *the process of decay.* **3.** *Law.* **a.** the summons, mandate, or writ by which a defendant or thing is brought before court for litigation. **b.** the whole course of the proceedings in an action at law. **4.** *Photog.* photomechanical or photoengraving methods collectively. **5.** *Biol., Anat.* a natural outgrowth, projection, or appendage: *a process of a bone.* **6.** the action of going forward or on. **7.** the condition of being carried on. **8.** course or lapse, as of time. **9.** conk[4] (defs. 1, 2). —*v.t.* **10.** to treat or prepare by some particular process, as in manufacturing. **11.** to handle (papers, records, etc.) by systematically organizing them, recording or making notations on them, following up with appropriate action, or the like: *to process mail.* **12.** to require (someone) to answer questionnaires, perform various tasks, and sometimes to undergo physical and aptitude classification examinations before the beginning or termination of a period of service: *The army processes all personnel entering or leaving the service.* **13.** to convert (an agricultural commodity) into marketable form by a special process, as pasteurization. **14.** to institute a legal process against. **15.** to serve a process or summons on. **16.** *Computers.* to carry out operations on (data or programs). **17.** conk[4] (def. 3). —*v.i.* **18.** to undergo the activities involved in processing personnel: *The recruits expected to process in four days.* —*adj.* **19.** prepared or modified by an artificial process: *process cheese.* **20.** noting, pertaining to, or involving photomechanical or photoengraving methods: *a process print.* **21.** *Informal.* of or pertaining to hair that has been conked. **22.** *Motion Pictures.* created by or used in process cinematography: *a moving background on a process screen.* [1275–1325; ME *proces* (n.) (< OF) < L *prōcessus* a going forward, equiv. to *prō-* PRO-[1] + *ced-,* var. s. of *cēdere* to yield (see CEDE) + *-tus* suffix of v. action; see CESSION] —**pro•ces•su•al** (prə sesh′ōō əl *or, esp. Brit,* prō-), *adj.*
—**Syn. 1.** operation. PROCESS, PROCEDURE, PROCEEDING apply to something that goes on or takes place. A PROCESS is a series of progressive and interdependent steps by which an end is attained: *a chemical process.* PROCEDURE usually implies a formal or set order of doing a thing, a method of conducting affairs: *parliamentary procedure.* PROCEEDING (usually pl.) applies to what goes on or takes place on a given occasion or to the records of the occasion: *Proceedings of the Royal Academy of Sciences.*
—**Pronunciation.** The word PROCESS, an early 14th century French borrowing, has a regularly formed plural that adds *-es* to the singular. This plural, as in similar words like *recesses* and *successes,* has traditionally been pronounced (-iz): (pros′es iz, prō′ses-) or (pros′ə siz, prō′sə-). Recent years have seen the increasing popularity of an (-ēz′) pronunciation for PROCESSES, perhaps by mistaken analogy with such plurals as *theses* and *hypotheses,* with which it has no connection. This newer pronunciation is common among younger educated speakers.

proc′ess cinematog′raphy, *Motion Pictures.* cinematography in which the main or foreground action or scene is superimposed on or combined with simulated or separately filmed background action or scenery to produce special visual effects.

proc′ess cost′ing, *Accounting.* a method of assigning costs to production processes where products must of

CONCISE ETYMOLOGY KEY: <, descended or borrowed from; >, whence; b., blend of, blended; c., cognate with; cf., compare; deriv., derivative; equiv., equivalent; imit., imitative; obl., oblique; r., replacing; s., stem; sp., spelling, spelled; resp., respelling, respelled; trans., translation; ?, origin unknown; *, unattested; ‡, probably earlier than. See the full key inside the front cover.

pro′al•ter•a′tion, *adj.*
pro•am′a•teur′, *adj.*
pro•a•mend′ment, *adj.*
pro′-A•mer′i•can, *adj., n.*
pro′-A•mer′i•can•ism, *n.*
pro′an•ar′chic, adj.
pro•an′ar•chism, *n.*
pro•an′ar•chy, *adj.*
pro-An′gli•can, *adj., n.*
pro′an•nex•a′tion, adj.
pro′ap•os•tol′ic, *adj.*
pro′ap•point′ment, *adj.*
pro′ap•por′tion•ment, *adj.*
pro′ap•pro′pri•a′tion, *adj.*
pro′ap•prov′al, *adj.*
pro-Ar′ab, *adj.*
pro′-A•ra′bi•an, *adj., n.*
pro-Ar′a•bic, *adj.*
pro′ar•bi•tra′tion, *adj.*
pro′ar•bi•tra′tion•ist, *n., adj.*
pro′-Ar•gen•ti′na, *adj.*
pro′-Ar•gen•tin′e•an, *adj., n.*
pro-Ar′i•an, *adj., n.*
pro′ar•is•toc′ra•cy, *adj.*
pro′a•ris′to•crat′ic, *adj.*
pro′-Ar•is•to•te′li•an, *adj.*
pro′-Ar•me′ni•an, *adj., n.*
pro•ar′my, *adj.*
pro•art′, *adj.*
pro-A′sian, *adj.*

necessity be produced in one continuous process, with unit cost arrived at by averaging units produced to the total cost of the process. Cf. **job-order costing.**

proc′essed cheese′, a mass-produced product made of one or more types of cheeses that have been heated and mixed with emulsifiers, colorings, flavorings, etc., primarily to retard spoilage and enhance spreadability at reduced cost. Also, **proc′ess cheese′.** [1915–20]

proc·ess·i·ble (pros′es ə bəl), *adj.* capable of being processed. Also, **proc′ess·a·ble.** [1955–60; PROCESS + -IBLE] —**proc′ess·i·bil′i·ty, proc′ess·a·bil′i·ty,** *n.*

proc′essing tax′, a tax levied by the government at an intermediate stage in the production of goods.

pro·ces·sion (prə sesh′ən), *n.* **1.** the act of moving along or proceeding in orderly succession or in a formal and ceremonious manner, as a line of people, animals, vehicles, etc. **2.** the line or body of persons or things moving along in such a manner. **3.** *Eccles.* an office, litany, etc., said or sung in a religious procession. **4.** *Theol.* the emanation of the Holy Spirit from the Father and later, in the Western Church, from the Son: distinguished from the "generation" of the Son and the "unbegottenness" of the Father. **5.** the act of coming forth from a source. —*v.i.* **6.** to go in procession. [bef. 1150; early ME (< OF) < LL *prōcessiōn-* (s. of *prōcessiō*) a religious procession, lit., a marching on. See PROCESS, -ION]

pro·ces·sion·al (prə sesh′ə nl), *adj.* **1.** of, pertaining to, or characteristic of a procession. **2.** of the nature of a procession; moving in an orderly or regular succession, sequence, or the like. **3.** of a style, design, etc., customarily used in processions: *processional regalia.* **4.** sung or played during a procession, as a hymn, march, etc. —*n.* **5.** a piece of music, as a hymn or slow march, suitable for accompanying a procession. **6.** a book containing hymns, litanies, etc., for use in religious processions. [1400–50; (n.) late ME: service book < ML *prōcessiōnāle,* n. use of neut. of *prōcessiōnālis* in a procession; (adj.) < ML *prōcessiōnālis;* see PROCESSION, -AL², -AL¹] —**pro·ces′sion·al·ly,** *adv.*

pro·ces·sive (prə ses′iv), *adj.* advancing or going forward; progressive: *the processive quality of language.* [1615–25; < L *prōcess(us)* (see PROCESS) + -IVE]

proc·es·sor (pros′es ər *or, esp. Brit.,* prō′ses-), *n.* **1.** a person or thing that processes. **2.** *Computers.* **a.** computer. **b.** controller (def. 5). **3.** See **food processor.** Also, **proc′ess·er.** [1905–10; PROCESS + -OR²]

proc′ess print′ing, a method of printing almost any color by using a limited number of separate color plates, as yellow, magenta, cyan, and black, in combination. [1930–35]

proc′ess serv′er, *Law.* a person who serves legal documents, as subpoenas, writs, or warrants, esp. those requiring appearance in court. [1605–15]

proc′ess theol′ogy, a form of theology that emphasizes the close relation of human beings, nature, and God. [1970–75]

pro·cès-ver·bal (prō sā′ver bäl′; *Fr.* prô se ver-bal′), *n., pl.* **-baux** (-bō′). **1.** a report of proceedings, as of an assembly. **2.** *Fr. Law.* an authenticated written account of facts in connection with a criminal or other charge. [1625–35; < F; see PROCESS, VERBAL]

pro·chein a·mi (prō′shen ə mē′), *Law.* See **next friend.** Also, **pro′chein a·my′.** [1425–75; late ME < AF]

pro·chlo·rite (prō klôr′īt, -klōr′-), *n. Mineral.* a dark green member of the chlorite group, usually foliated. [1865–70; PRO-¹ + CHLORITE¹]

pro·chlo·ron (prō klôr′on, -klōr′-), *n. Biol.* any spherical, photosynthetic, prokaryotic microorganism of the genus *Prochloron,* occurring in subtropical and tropical habitats in symbiosis with various invertebrates, esp. marine chordates, proposed as ancestral to the chloroplast of green algae and plants. [< NL < Gk *próchlō-ron,* neut. of *próchlōros* greenish (see PRO-², CHLORO-¹)]

pro-choice (prō chois′), *adj.* supporting or advocating legalized abortion. Also, **pro·choice′.** Cf. **pro-life.** [1970–75] —**pro-choic′er,** *n.*

pro·cho·os (prō′kō os′, prok′ō-), *n., pl.* **pro·cho·oi** (prō′kō oi′, prok′ō-). *Gk. and Rom. Antiq.* an elongated form of the oinochoe. [1840–50; < Gk *próchoos, próchous,* equiv. to *pro-* PRO-² + *choós, choûs* pitcher, akin to *cheîn* to pour. See OINOCHOE]

pro·chro·nism (prō′krə niz′əm, prok′rə-), *n.* a chronological error in which a person, event, etc., is assigned a date earlier than the actual one; prolepsis. Cf. **anachronism, parachronism.** [1640–50; PRO-² + Gk *chrón(os)* time + -ISM. See ANACHRONISM]

pro·claim (prō klām′, prə-), *v.t.* **1.** to announce or declare in an official or formal manner: *to proclaim war.* **2.** to announce or declare in an open or ostentatious way: *to proclaim one's opinions.* **3.** to indicate or make known publicly or openly. **4.** to extol or praise publicly: *Let them proclaim the Lord.* **5.** to declare (a territory, district, etc.) subject to particular legal restrictions. **6.** to declare to be an outlaw, evildoer, or the like. **7.** to denounce or prohibit publicly. —*v.i.* **8.** to make a proclamation. [1350–1400; ME < L *prōclāmāre* to cry out. See PRO-¹, CLAIM] —**pro·claim′er,** *n.*
—**Syn. 1.** advertise. See **announce. 2.** promulgate.

proc·la·ma·tion (prok′lə mā′shən), *n.* **1.** something that is proclaimed; a public and official announcement. **2.** the act of proclaiming. [1350–1400; ME *proclamacioun* (< MF *proclamacion*) < L *prōclāmātiōn-* (s. of *prōclāmātiō*), equiv. to *prōclāmāt(us)* (ptp. of *prōclāmāre* to PROCLAIM) + *-iōn-* -ION]

pro·cli·nate (prok′lə nāt′), *adj. Zool.* (of a part) directed or inclined forward. [< L *prōclīnātus* bent forward, ptp. of *prōclīnāre.* See PRO-¹, RECLINE, -ATE¹]

pro·clit·ic (prō klit′ik), *Gram.* —*adj.* **1.** (of a word) closely connected in pronunciation with the following word and not having an independent accent or phonological status. —*n.* **2.** a proclitic word. [1840–50; < NL *procliticus;* modeled on ENCLITIC; see PRO-²]

pro·cliv·i·ty (prō kliv′i tē), *n., pl.* **-ties.** natural or habitual inclination or tendency; propensity; predisposition: *a proclivity to meticulousness.* [1585–95; < L *prōclīvitās* tendency, lit., a steep descent, steepness, equiv. to *prōclīv(is)* sloping forward, steep (*prō-* PRO-¹ + *clīv(us)* slope + *-is* adj. suffix) + *-itās* -ITY]
—**Syn.** bent, leaning, disposition. —**Ant.** aversion.

Pro·clus (prō′kləs, prok′ləs), *n.* A.D. c411–485, Greek philosopher and theologian.

pro·con·sul (prō kon′səl), *n.* **1.** *Rom. Hist.* an official, usually a former consul, who acted as governor or military commander of a province, and who had powers similar to those of a consul. **2.** any appointed administrator over a dependency or an occupied area. [1350–1400; ME < L *prōconsul;* see PRO-¹, CONSUL] —**pro·con′su·lar,** *adj.* —**pro·con′su·lar·ly,** *adv.*

Pro·con·sul (prō kon′səl), *n.* an African subgenus of *Dryopithecus* that lived 17–20 million years ago and is possibly ancestral to modern hominoids. [< NL (1933), equiv. to *pro-* PRO-¹ + *Consul,* allegedly the name of a chimpanzee in a London zoo (with a pun on L *prōconsul* PROCONSUL); the genus was thought to be ancestral to the chimpanzee]

pro·con·su·late (prō kon′sə lit), *n. Hist.* the office or term of office of a proconsul. Also, **pro·con′sul·ship′.** [1650–60; < L *prōconsulātus.* See PROCONSUL, -ATE³]

Pro·co·pi·us (prō kō′pē əs, prə-), *n.* A.D. c490–c562, Greek historian.

pro·cras·ti·nate (prō kras′tə nāt′, prə-), *v.,* **-nat·ed, -nat·ing.** —*v.i.* **1.** to defer action; delay: *to procrastinate until an opportunity is lost.* —*v.t.* **2.** to put off till another day or time; defer; delay. [1580–90; < L *prōcrāstinātus* (ptp. of *prōcrāstināre* to put off until tomorrow, equiv. to *prō-* PRO-¹ + *-crāstināre,* deriv. of *crāstinus* of tomorrow; *crās* tomorrow + *-tinus* suffix forming adjs. from temporal advs.); see -ATE¹] —**pro·cras′ti·nat′ing·ly, pro·cras′ti·na′tive·ly,** *adv.* —**pro·cras′ti·na′tion,** *n.* —**pro·cras′ti·na′tive, pro·cras·ti·na·to·ry** (prō-kras′tə nə tôr′ē, -tōr′ē, prə-), *adj.* —**pro·cras′ti·na′tive·ness,** *n.* —**pro·cras′ti·na′tor,** *n.*
—**Syn. 2.** prolong, postpone.

pro·cre·ant (prō′krē ənt), *adj.* **1.** procreating or generating: *a sufficiently procreant breed of fish; a procreant cause.* **2.** pertaining to procreation. [1580–90; < L *prōcreant-* (s. of *prōcreāns*), prp. of *prōcreāre* to breed. See PROCREATE, -ANT]

pro·cre·ate (prō′krē āt′), *v.,* **-at·ed, -at·ing.** —*v.t.* **1.** to beget or generate (offspring). **2.** to produce; bring into being. —*v.i.* **3.** to beget offspring. **4.** to produce; bring into being. [1530–40; < L *prōcreātus,* ptp. of *prōcreāre* to breed. See PRO-¹, CREATE] —**pro′cre·a′tion,** *n.* —**pro′cre·a′tive,** *adj.* —**pro′cre·a′tive·ness,** *n.* —**pro′cre·a′tor,** *n.*

Pro·crus·te·an (prō krus′tē ən), *adj.* **1.** pertaining to or suggestive of Procrustes. **2.** (*often l.c.*) tending to produce conformity by violent or arbitrary means. [1840–50; PROCRUSTE(S) + -AN]

Pro·crus·tes (prō krus′tēz), *n. Class. Myth.* a robber who stretched or amputated the limbs of travelers to make them conform to the length of his bed. He was killed by Theseus. Also called **Damastes.**

pro·cryp·tic (prō krip′tik), *adj. Zool.* serving to conceal an animal from predators. Cf. **anticryptic.** [1890–95; PRO(TECTIVE) + CRYPTIC] —**pro·cryp′ti·cal·ly,** *adv.*

proc·ti·tis (prok tī′tis), *n. Pathol.* inflammation of the rectum and anus. [PROCT- + -ITIS]

proc·to (prok′tō), *n., pl.* **-tos.** *Informal.* proctosigmoidoscopy. [by shortening]

procto-, a combining form meaning "anus," "rectum," used in the formation of compound words: *proctoscope.* Also, *esp. before a vowel,* **proct-.** [< Gk *prōkto-,* comb. form of *prōktós*]

proc·toc·ly·sis (prok tok′lə sis), *n. Med.* the slow, continuous introduction of a solution into the rectum to improve fluid intake. [< NL; see PROCTO-, CLYSIS]

proc·to·dae·um (prok′tə dē′əm), *n., pl.* **-dae·a** (-dē′ə). proctodeum. —**proc′to·dae′al,** *adj.*

proc·to·de·um (prok′tə dē′əm), *n., pl.* **-de·a** (-dē′ə), **-de·ums.** *Embryol.* a depression in the ectoderm of the anal region of a young embryo, which develops into part of the anal canal. [1875–80; < NL < Gk *prōkt-* PROCT- + NL *-odeum* < Gk *hodaîon,* neut. of *hodaîos* on or by the way; see -ODE², -EUM] —**proc′to·de′al,** *adj.*

proc·tol·o·gy (prok tol′ə jē), *n.* the branch of medicine dealing with the rectum and anus. [1895–1900; PROCTO- + -LOGY] —**proc·to·log·ic** (prok′tl oj′ik), **proc′to·log′i·cal,** *adj.* —**proc·tol′o·gist,** *n.*

proc·tor (prok′tər), *n.* **1.** a person appointed to keep watch over students at examinations. **2.** an official charged with various duties, esp. with the maintenance of good order. —*v.t., v.i.* **3.** to supervise or monitor. [1350–1400; ME; contracted var. of PROCURATOR] —**proc·to·ri·al** (prok tôr′ē əl, -tōr′-), *adj.* —**proc·to′ri·al·ly,** *adv.* —**proc′tor·ship′,** *n.*

proc·to·scope (prok′tə skōp′), *n.* an instrument for visual examination of the interior of the rectum. [1895–1900; PROCTO- + -SCOPE] —**proc·to·scop·ic** (prok′tə-skop′ik), *adj.*

proc·tos·co·py (prok tos′kə pē), *n., pl.* **-pies.** examination by means of a proctoscope. [1895–1900; PROCTO- + -SCOPY] —**proc·tos′co·pist,** *n.*

proc·to·sig·moid·o·scope (prok′tō sig moi′də-skōp′), *n.* sigmoidoscope. [PROCTO- + SIGMOIDOSCOPE] —**proc·to·sig·moid·o·scop·ic** (prok′tō sig moi′də-skop′ik), *adj.* —**proc·to·sig·moid·os·co·pist** (prok′tō-sig′moi dos′kə pist), *n.*

proc·to·sig·moid·os·co·py (prok′tō sig′moi dos′kə-pē), *n., pl.* **-pies.** sigmoidoscopy. [PROCTO- + SIGMOIDOSCOPY]

pro·cum·bent (prō kum′bənt), *adj.* **1.** lying on the face; prone; prostrate. **2.** *Bot.* (of a plant or stem) lying along the ground, but not putting forth roots. [1660–70; < L *prōcumbent-* (s. of *prōcumbēns*) bending forward, prp. of *prōcumbere.* See PRO-, INCUMBENT]

pro·cur·a·ble (prō kyo͝or′ə bəl, prə-), *adj.* obtainable. [1605–15; PROCURE + -ABLE]

proc·u·ra·cy (prok′yər ə sē), *n., pl.* **-cies.** *Archaic.* the office of a proctor or procurator. [1250–1300; ME *procuracie* < ML *prōcūrātia,* for L *prōcūrātiō* PROCURATION; see -ACY]

pro·cur·ance (prō kyo͝or′əns, prə-), *n.* the act of bringing about or getting something; agency; procurement. [1545–55; PROCURE + -ANCE]

proc·u·ra·tion (prok′yə rā′shən), *n.* **1.** the act of obtaining or getting; procurement. **2.** the act of procuring prostitutes. **3.** the appointment of a procurator, agent, or attorney. **4.** the authority given. **5.** a document whereby the authority is given. **6.** *Archaic.* management for another; agency. [1375–1425; late ME *procuracion* < L *prōcūrātiōn-* (s. of *prōcūrātiō*) management, equiv. to *prōcūrāt(us)* (ptp. of *prōcūrāre* to take care of; see PROCURE) + *-iōn-* -ION]

proc·u·ra·tor (prok′yə rā′tər), *n.* **1.** *Rom. Hist.* any of various imperial officials with fiscal or administrative powers. **2.** a cellarer. **3.** a person, as a deputy, attorney, or agent, employed to manage the affairs of another. [1250–1300; ME < L *prōcūrātor* manager. See PROCURATION, -TOR] —**proc′u·ra′tor·ate, proc′u·ra′·tor·ship′,** *n.* —**proc·u·ra·to·ri·al** (prok′yər ə tôr′ē əl, -tōr′-), **proc′u·ra·to′ry,** *adj.*

pro·cure (prō kyo͝or′, prə-), *v.,* **-cured, -cur·ing.** —*v.t.* **1.** to obtain or get by care, effort, or the use of special means: *to procure evidence.* **2.** to bring about, esp. by unscrupulous and indirect means: *to procure secret documents.* **3.** to obtain (a person) for the purpose of prostitution. —*v.i.* **4.** to act as a procurer or pimp. [1250–1300; ME *procuren* < L *prōcūrāre* to take care of. See PRO-¹, CURE] —**pro·cure′ment,** *n.*
—**Syn. 1.** gain, win. See **get. 2.** contrive. **4.** pander, pimp. —**Ant. 1.** lose.

pro·cur·er (prō kyo͝or′ər, prə-), *n.* a person who procures, esp. a pander or pimp. [1350–1400; ME (see PROCURE, -ER¹); r. ME *procurour* < AF << L *prōcūrātōr-* (s. of *prōcūrātor*) PROCURATOR]

pro·cur·ess (prō kyo͝or′is, prə-), *n.* a woman who procures prostitutes. [1375–1425; late ME; see PROCURER, -ESS]
—**Usage.** See **-ess.**

Pro·cy·on (prō′sē on′), *n. Astron.* a first-magnitude star in the constellation Canis Minor. [1650–60; < L < Gk *Prokýōn* name of a star, equiv. to *pro-* PRO-² + *kýōn* dog (see HOUND); so called because it rises just before Sirius, the Dog Star]

prod (prod), *v.,* **prod·ded, prod·ding,** *n.* —*v.t.* **1.** to poke or jab with or as if with something pointed: *I prodded him with my elbow.* **2.** to rouse or incite as if by poking; nag; goad. —*n.* **3.** the act of prodding; a poke or jab. **4.** any of various pointed instruments used as a goad, esp. an electrified rod that administers a mild shock: *a cattle prod.* [1525–35; orig. uncert.] —**prod′·der,** *n.*
—**Syn. 2.** impel, stir, prompt, excite.

Prod (prod), *n. Chiefly Ulster Slang* (*often disparaging and offensive*). a Protestant, esp. an Anglo-Irish Protestant. [by shortening; *d* prob. reflects the voicing or flap characteristic of some Ulster accents]

prod., 1. produce. **2.** produced. **3.** producer. **4.** product. **5.** production.

prodd (prod), *n.* a crossbow for hurling stones or balls: used for sport. [perh. sp. var. of PROD]

prod·i·gal (prod′i gəl), *adj.* **1.** wastefully or recklessly extravagant: *prodigal expenditure.* **2.** giving or yielding profusely; lavish (usually fol. by *of* or *with*): *prodigal of smiles; prodigal with money.* **3.** lavishly abundant; profuse: *nature's prodigal resources.* —*n.* **4.** a person who spends, or has spent, his or her money or substance with wasteful extravagance; spendthrift. [1500–10; back formation from PRODIGALITY] —**prod′i·gal·ly,** *adv.*
—**Syn. 1.** profligate. See **lavish. 2, 3.** copious, bounteous. **4.** waster, wastrel. —**Ant. 1.** cautious, provident.

prod·i·gal·i·ty (prod′i gal′i tē), *n., pl.* **-ties** for 2, 3. **1.** the quality or fact of being prodigal; wasteful extravagance in spending. **2.** an instance of it. **3.** lavish abundance. [1300–50; ME *prodigalite* < L *prōdigālitās* wastefulness, equiv. to *prōdig(us)* extravagant + *-āl(is)* -AL¹ + *-itās* -ITY]

CONCISE PRONUNCIATION KEY: *act, cāpe, dâre, pärt; set, ēqual; if, ice; ox, ōver, ôrder, oil, bo͝ok, bo͞ot, out; up, ûrge; child; sing; shoe; thin, that;* zh as in *treasure.* ə = *a* as in *alone, e* as in *system, i* as in *easily, o* as in *gallop, u* as in *circus;* ᵊ as in *fire* (fīᵊr), *hour* (ouᵊr). l and n can serve as syllabic consonants, as in *cradle* (krād′l), and *button* (but′n). See the full key inside the front cover.

pro′-A·si·at′ic, *adj.*
pro′as·sess′ment, *adj.*
pro′as·so′ci·a′tion, adj.
pro·a′the·ism, *n.*
pro·a′the·ist, *n., adj.*
pro′-A·the′ni·an, *adj., n.*
pro′at·tack′, *adj.*
pro′at·tend′ance, *adj.*
pro′auc′tion, *adj.*
pro·au′di·ence, *adj.*
pro′-Aus·tral′ian, *adj., n.*
pro-Aus′tri·an, *adj., n.*
pro·au′thor, *adj.*
pro′au·to·ma′tion, adj.
pro-Ba·co′ni·an, *adj.*
pro·ban′ish·ment, *adj.*
pro-Bap′tist, *adj., n.*
pro·bar′gain·ing, *adj.*
pro·base′ball′, *adj.*
pro·bas′ket·ball′, *adj.*
pro-Bel′gian, *adj., n.*
pro-Bib′li·cal, *adj.*
pro·birth′-con·trol′, *adj.*
pro′block·ade′, *adj.*
pro′-Bo·he′mi·an, *adj., n.*
pro′-Bo·liv′i·an, *adj., n.*
pro-Bol′she·vik, *adj., n.*
pro-Bol′she·vism, *n.*
pro-Bol′she·vist, *n., adj.*
pro·box′ing, *adj.*

prod′igal son′, a figure in a parable of Jesus (Luke 15:11–32); a wayward son who squanders his inheritance but returns home to find that his father forgives him. [1545–55]

pro·di·gious (prə dij′əs), *adj.* **1.** extraordinary in size, amount, extent, degree, force, etc.: *a prodigious research grant.* **2.** wonderful or marvelous: *a prodigious feat.* **3.** abnormal; monstrous. **4.** *Obs.* ominous. [1545–55; < L *prōdigiōsus* marvelous. See PRODIGY, -OUS] **—pro·di′gious·ly,** *adv.* **—pro·di′gious·ness,** *n.*
—Syn. 1. enormous, immense, huge, gigantic, tremendous. **2.** amazing, stupendous, astounding, wondrous, miraculous. **—Ant. 1.** tiny. **2.** ordinary.

prod·i·gy (prod′i jē), *n., pl.* **-gies. 1.** a person, esp. a child or young person, having extraordinary talent or ability: *a musical prodigy.* **2.** a marvelous example (usually fol. by *of*). **3.** something wonderful or marvelous; a wonder. **4.** something abnormal or monstrous. **5.** *Archaic.* something extraordinary regarded as of prophetic significance. [1425–75; late ME *prodige* < L *prōdigium* prophetic sign]

pro·do·mos (prō dō′mos), *n., pl.* **-moi** (-moi). *Archit.* an open vestibule, as a pronaos. [< Gk *pródomos* lit., before-house, equiv. to *pro-* PRO-[2] + *dómos* house (see DOME)]

pro·drome (prō′drōm), *n. Pathol.* a premonitory symptom. [1635–45; < F < NL *prodromus,* n. use of Gk *pródromos* running before. See PRO-[2], -DROME] **—prod·ro·mal** (prod′rə məl, prə drō′-), *adj.*

pro·drug (prō′drug′), *n. Pharm.* an inactive substance that is converted to a drug within the body by the action of enzymes or other chemicals. [PRO-[1] + DRUG]

pro·duce (*v.* prə do͞os′, -dyo͞os′; *n.* prod′o͞os, -yo͞os, prō′do͞os, -dyo͞os), *v.,* **-duced, -duc·ing,** *n.* **—*v.t.* 1.** to bring into existence; give rise to; cause: *to produce steam.* **2.** to bring into existence by intellectual or creative ability: *to produce a great painting.* **3.** to make or manufacture: *to produce automobiles for export.* **4.** to bring forth; give birth to; bear: *to produce a litter of puppies.* **5.** to provide, furnish, or supply; yield: *a mine producing silver.* **6.** *Finance.* to cause to accrue: *stocks producing unexpected dividends.* **7.** to bring forward; present to view or notice; exhibit: *to produce one's credentials.* **8.** to bring (a play, movie, opera, etc.) before the public. **9.** to extend or prolong, as a line. **—*v.i.* 10.** to create, bring forth, or yield offspring, products, etc.: *Their mines are closed because they no longer produce.* **11.** *Econ.* to create economic value; bring crops, goods, etc., to a point at which they will command a price. **—*n.* prod·uce 12.** something that is produced; yield; product. **13.** agricultural products collectively, esp. vegetables and fruits. **14.** offspring, esp. of a female animal: *the produce of a mare.* [1375–1425; late ME *producen* < L *prōdūcere* to lead or bring forward, extend, prolong, produce, equiv. to *prō-* PRO-[1] + *dūcere* to lead] **—pro·duc′i·ble, pro·duce′a·ble, pro·duct′i·ble,** *adj.* **—pro·duc′i·bil′i·ty, pro·duct·i·bil·i·ty** (prə duk′tə bil′i tē), **pro·duc′i·ble·ness, pro·duce′a·ble·ness,** *n.*
—Syn. 1. generate, create. **5.** afford. **7.** show. **13.** See **crop. —Ant. 1.** destroy, ruin. **7.** conceal.

pro·duc·er (prə do͞o′sər, -dyo͞o′-), *n.* **1.** a person who produces. **2.** *Econ.* a person who creates economic value, or produces goods and services. **3.** a person responsible for the financial and administrative aspects of a stage, film, television, or radio production; the person who exercises general supervision of a production and is responsible chiefly for raising money, hiring technicians and artists, etc., required to stage a play, make a motion picture, or the like. Cf. **director** (def. 3). **4.** *Theat. Brit.* (formerly) a director of theatrical productions; stage director. **5.** an apparatus for making producer gas. **6.** *Ecol.* an organism, as a plant, that is able to produce its own food from inorganic substances. [1505–15; PRODUCE + -ER[1]]

prod′uce race′, *Horse Racing.* a race for the offspring of parents identified or characterized at the time of nomination.

produc′er gas′, a gas composed of carbon monoxide, hydrogen, and nitrogen, obtained by passing air and steam through incandescent coke: used as an industrial fuel, in certain gas engines, and in the manufacture of ammonia. Also called **air gas.** [1890–95]

produc′er goods′, *Econ.* goods, as machinery, raw materials, etc., that are used in the process of creating consumer goods. [1950–55]

prod·uct (prod′əkt, -ukt), *n.* **1.** a thing produced by labor: *products of farm and factory; the product of his thought.* **2.** a person or thing produced by or resulting from a process, as a natural, social, or historical one; result: *He is a product of his time.* **3.** the totality of goods or services that a company makes available; output: *a decrease in product during the past year.* **4.** *Chem.* a substance obtained from another substance through chemical change. **5.** *Math.* **a.** the result obtained by multiplying two or more quantities together. **b.** intersection (def. 3a). [1400–50; late ME < L *prōductum* (thing) produced, neut. of ptp. of *prōdūcere* to PRODUCE]

pro·duc·tile (prə duk′til), *adj.* capable of being lengthened out; extensile. [1720–30; < LL *prōductilis* prolongable, equiv. to L *prōduct(us)* (ptp. of *prōdūcere* to extend, PRODUCE) + *-ilis* -ILE]

pro·duc·tion (prə duk′shən), *n.* **1.** the act of producing; creation; manufacture. **2.** something that is produced; a product. **3.** *Econ.* the creation of value; the producing of articles having exchange value. **4.** the total amount produced: *Production is up this month.* **5.** a work of literature or art. **6.** the act of presenting for display; presentation; exhibition: *the production of evidence in support of the case.* **7.** *Informal.* an unnecessarily or exaggeratedly complicated situation or activity: *That child makes a production out of going to bed.* **8.** the organization and presentation of a dramatic entertainment. **9.** the entertainment itself: *an expensive production.* **—*adj.* 10.** regularly manufactured; not custom-made, specially produced, or experimental: *a production model.* [1400–50; late ME < L *prōductiōn-* (s. of *prōductiō*) a lengthening. See PRODUCT, -ION] **—pro·duc′tion·al,** *adj.*
—Syn. 6. introduction, appearance, display, materialization.

produc′tion control′, the planning and supervision of manufacturing activities to ensure that goods will be produced on time at the lowest possible cost. [1925–30]

produc′tion line′, an arrangement of machines or sequence of operations involved with a single manufacturing operation or production process. Cf. **assembly line, line**[1] (def. 29). [1930–35]

produc′tion num′ber, *Theat.* a specialty number or routine, usually performed by the entire cast consisting of musicians, singers, dancers, stars, etc., of a musical comedy, vaudeville show, or the like. [1935–40]

pro·duc·tive (prə duk′tiv), *adj.* **1.** having the power of producing; generative; creative: *a productive effort.* **2.** producing readily or abundantly; fertile: *a productive vineyard.* **3.** causing; bringing about (usually fol. by *of*): *conditions productive of crime and sin.* **4.** *Econ.* producing or tending to produce goods and services having exchange value. **5.** *Gram.* (of derivational affixes or patterns) readily used in forming new words, as the suffix *-ness.* **6.** (in language learning) of or pertaining to the language skills of speaking and writing (opposed to *receptive*). [1605–15; < ML *productīvus.* See PRODUCT, -IVE] **—pro·duc′tive·ly,** *adv.* **—pro·duc′tive·ness,** *n.* **—pro·duc·tiv·i·ty** (prō′duk tiv′i tē), *n.*
—Syn. 2. fecund. PRODUCTIVE, FERTILE, FRUITFUL, PROLIFIC apply to the generative aspect of something. PRODUCTIVE refers to a generative source of continuing activity: *productive soil; a productive influence.* FERTILE applies to that in which seeds, literal or figurative, take root: *fertile soil; a fertile imagination.* FRUITFUL refers to that which has already produced and is capable of further production: *fruitful soil, discovery, theory.* PROLIFIC means highly productive: *a prolific farm, writer.*

prod′uct liabil′ity, the responsibility of a manufacturer for injury or loss caused by its product. [1975–80]

prod′uct line′, **1.** all of the products carried by a manufacturer, wholesaler, or retailer. **2.** a group of products of the same manufacturer having similar or related characteristics and intended for similar or related markets. [1965–70]

prod′uct mark′, a trademark used on only one product. Cf. **house mark, line mark.**

pro·em (prō′em), *n.* an introductory discourse; introduction; preface; preamble. [1350–1400; < L *prooemium* < Gk *prooímion* prelude (*pro-* PRO-[2] + *oím(ē)* song + *-ion* dim. suffix); r. ME *proheme* < MF < L, as above] **—pro·e·mi·al** (prō ē′mē əl, -em′ē-), *adj.*

pro·en·zyme (prō en′zīm), *n. Biochem.* any of a group of proteins that are converted to active enzymes by partial breakdown, as by the action of an acid or other enzyme. Also called **zymogen.** [1895–1900; PRO-[1] + ENZYME]

pro·es·trus (prō es′trəs), *n.* the period immediately preceding estrus. Also, **pro·oestrus.** [1920–25; PRO-[1] + ESTRUS]

prof (prof), *n. Informal.* professor. [1830–40, *Amer.*; by shortening]

Prof., Professor.

pro·fam·i·ly (prō fam′ə lē, -fam′lē), *adj.* favoring or supporting laws against abortion; antiabortion; pro-life. Also, **pro-fam′i·ly.** [1980–85; PRO-[1] + FAMILY]

prof·a·na·tion (prof′ə nā′shən), *n.* the act of profaning; desecration; defilement; debasement. [1545–55; < LL *profānātiōn-* (s. of *profānātiō*) desecration, equiv. to L *profānāt(us)* (ptp. of *profānāre* to PROFANE) + *-iōn-* -ION; r. *prophanation* < MF < ML *prophānātiō,* for LL *profānātiō,* as above]
—Syn. sacrilege, blasphemy.

pro·fan·a·to·ry (prə fan′ə tôr′ē, -tōr′ē, prō-), *adj.* tending to desecrate; profaning. [1850–55; PROFANA-T(ION) + -ORY[1]]

pro·fane (prə fān′, prō-), *adj., v.,* **-faned, -fan·ing. —*adj.* 1.** characterized by irreverence or contempt for God or sacred principles or things; irreligious. **2.** not devoted to holy or religious purposes; unconsecrated; secular (opposed to *sacred*). **3.** unholy; heathen; pagan: *profane rites.* **4.** not initiated into religious rites or mysteries, as persons. **5.** common or vulgar. **—*v.t.* 6.** to misuse (anything that should be held in reverence or respect); defile; debase; employ basely or unworthily. **7.** to treat (anything sacred) with irreverence or contempt; violate the sanctity of: *to profane a shrine.* [1350–1400; (adj.) < L *profānus* lit., before (outside of) the temple; r. ME *prophane* < ML *prophānus* desecrated (see PRO-[1], FANE); (v.) < L *profānāre,* deriv. of *profānus;* r. ME *prophanen* < ML *prophānāre* to desecrate] **—pro·fane′ly,** *adv.* **—pro·fane′ness,** *n.* **—pro·fan′er,** *n.*
—Syn. 1. blasphemous, sacrilegious, impious, ungodly. **2.** temporal. **3.** unhallowed. **5.** low, mean, base. **7.** desecrate. **—Ant. 1.** sacred. **2.** spiritual. **3.** holy.

pro·fan·i·ty (prə fan′i tē, prō-), *n., pl.* **-ties** for 2. **1.** the quality of being profane; irreverence. **2.** profane conduct or language; a profane act or utterance. [1600–10; < LL *profānitās.* See PROFANE, -ITY]
—Syn. 1, 2. blasphemy, sacrilege. **2.** swearing, malediction; curse.

Prof. Eng., Professional Engineer.

pro·fert (prō′fərt), *n. Law.* an exhibition of a record or paper in open court. [1710–20; < L: lit., he brings forward]

pro·fess (prə fes′), *v.t.* **1.** to lay claim to, often insincerely; pretend to: *He professed extreme regret.* **2.** to declare openly; announce or affirm; avow or acknowledge: *to profess one's satisfaction.* **3.** to affirm faith in or allegiance to (a religion, God, etc.). **4.** to declare oneself skilled or expert in; claim to have knowledge of; make (a thing) one's profession or business. **5.** to teach as a professor: *She professes comparative literature.* **6.** to receive or admit into a religious order. **—*v.i.* 7.** to make a profession, avowal, or declaration. **8.** to take the vows of a religious order. [1400–50; late ME; back formation from PROFESSED]
—Syn. 1. claim, allege, purport, avow.

pro·fessed (prə fest′), *adj.* **1.** avowed; acknowledged. **2.** professing to be qualified; professional, rather than amateur. **3.** having taken the vows of, or been received into, a religious order. **4.** alleged; pretended. [1300–50; ME (in religious sense) < ML *profess(us)* (special use of L *professus,* ptp. of *profitērī* to declare publicly, equiv. to *pro-* PRO-[1] + *-fet-,* comb. form of *fatērī* to acknowledge + *-tus* ptp. suffix, with *tt* > *ss*) + -ED[2]]

pro·fess·ed·ly (prə fes′id lē), *adv.* **1.** allegedly; pretendedly: *He is only professedly poor.* **2.** avowedly; by open declaration: *She is professedly guilty of the crime.* [1560–70; PROFESSED + -LY]

pro·fes·sion (prə fesh′ən), *n.* **1.** a vocation requiring knowledge of some department of learning or science: *the profession of teaching.* Cf. **learned profession. 2.** any vocation or business. **3.** the body of persons engaged in an occupation or calling: *to be respected by the medical profession.* **4.** the act of professing; avowal; a declaration, whether true or false: *professions of dedication.* **5.** the declaration of belief in or acceptance of religion or a faith: *the profession of Christianity.* **6.** a religion or faith professed. **7.** the declaration made on entering into membership of a church or religious order. [1175–1225; ME < ML *professiōn-* (s. of *professiō*) the taking of the vows of a religious order. See PROFESSED, -ION] **—pro·fes′sion·less,** *n.*
—Syn. 1. calling, employment. See **occupation. 4.** asseveration, assertion, protestation.

pro·fes·sion·al (prə fesh′ə nl), *adj.* **1.** following an occupation as a means of livelihood or for gain: *a professional builder.* **2.** of, pertaining to, or connected with a profession: *professional studies.* **3.** appropriate to a profession: *professional objectivity.* **4.** engaged in one of the learned professions: *A lawyer is a professional person.* **5.** following as a business an occupation ordinarily engaged in as a pastime: *a professional golfer.* **6.** making a business or constant practice of something not properly to be regarded as a business: *"A salesman," he said, "is a professional optimist."* **7.** undertaken or engaged in as a means of livelihood or for gain: *professional baseball.* **8.** of or for a professional person or his or her place of business or work: *a professional apartment; professional equipment.* **9.** done by a professional; expert: *professional car repairs.* **—*n.* 10.** a person who belongs to one of the professions, esp. one of the learned professions. **11.** a person who earns a living in a sport or other occupation frequently engaged in by amateurs: *a golf professional.* **12.** an expert player, as of golf or tennis, serving as a teacher, consultant, performer, or contestant; pro. **13.** a person who is expert at his or her work: *You can tell by her comments that this editor is a real professional.* [1740–50; PROFESSION + -AL[1]] **—pro·fes′sion·al·ly,** *adv.*

profes′sional corpora′tion, a corporation formed by one or more licensed practitioners, esp. medical or legal, to operate their practices on a corporate plan. *Abbr.:* PC, P.C. [1965–70]

pro·fes·sion·al·ism (prə fesh′ə nl iz′əm), *n.* **1.** professional character, spirit, or methods. **2.** the standing, practice, or methods of a professional, as distinguished from an amateur. [1855–60; PROFESSIONAL + -ISM]

pro·fes·sion·al·ize (prə fesh′ə nl īz′), *v.,* **-ized, -iz·ing. —*v.t.* 1.** to give a professional character or status to; make into or establish as a profession. **—*v.i.* 2.** to become professional. Also, *esp. Brit.,* **pro·fes′sion·al·ise′.** [1855–60; PROFESSIONAL + -IZE] **—pro·fes′sion·al·ist,** *n.* **—pro·fes′sion·al·i·za′tion,** *n.*

Profes′sional Stand′ards Review′ Organiza′tion, a group of physicians and sometimes other health-care professionals that monitors the quality and cost of medical services in a particular region or community. *Abbr.:* PSRO

pro·fes·sor (prə fes′ər), *n.* **1.** a teacher of the highest academic rank in a college or university, who has been awarded the title *Professor* in a particular branch of learning; a full professor: *a professor of Spanish literature.* **2.** any teacher who has the rank of professor, associate professor, or assistant professor. **3.** a teacher. **4.** an instructor in some art or skilled sport: *a professor of singing; a professor of boxing.* **5.** a person who professes his or her sentiments, beliefs, etc. [1350–1400; ME < ML *professor* one who has taken the vows of a religious order, L: a public lecturer, equiv. to *prō-* PRO-[1] + *-fet-,* comb. form of *fatērī* to acknowledge, declare + *-tor* -TOR, with *tt* > *ss*] **—pro·fes·so·ri·al** (prō′fə sôr′ē-əl, -sōr′-, prof′ə-), *adj.* **—pro′fes·so′ri·al·ism,** *n.* **—pro′fes·so′ri·al·ly,** *adv.*

CONCISE ETYMOLOGY KEY: <, descended or borrowed from; >, whence; b., blend of, blended; c., cognate with; cf., compare; deriv., derivative; equiv., equivalent; imit., imitative; obl., oblique; r., replacing; s., stem; sp., spelling, spelled; resp., respelling, respelled; trans., translation; ?, origin unknown; *, unattested; ‡, probably earlier than. See the full key inside the front cover.

pro·boy′cott, *adj.*
pro′-Bra·zil′ian, *adj., n.*
pro-Brit′ish, *adj.*
pro-Bud′dhist, *n., adj.*
pro·budg′et·ing, *adj.*
pro′-Bul·gar′i·an, *adj., n.*
pro-Bur′man, *adj.*
pro·busi′ness, *adj.*
pro′-Cam·bo′di·a, *adj.*
pro′-Cam·bo′di·an, *adj., n.*
pro′-Cam·e·roon′, *adj., n.*
pro′-Ca·na′di·an, *adj., n.*
pro·cap′i·tal·ism, *n.*
pro·cap′i·tal·ist, *n., adj.*
pro-Cath′o·lic, *adj., n.*
pro′-Ca·thol′i·cism, *n.*
pro·cen′sor·ship′, *adj.*
pro·cen′sure, *adj.*
pro′cen·tral·i·za′tion, *adj.*
pro′ce·phal′ic, *adj.*
pro′-Cey·lon′, *adj.*
pro′-Cey·lo·nese′, *adj., n., pl.* **-nese.**
pro·char′i·ty, *adj.*
pro-Chil′e·an, *adj., n.*
pro′-Chi·nese′, *adj., n., pl.* **-nese.**
pro·church′, *adj.*
pro·cit′y, *adj.*

pro·fes·sor·ate (prə fes′ər it), *n.* **1.** the office or the period of service of a professor. **2.** a group of professors. [1855–60; PROFESSOR + -ATE[3]]

pro·fes·so·ri·ate (prō′fə sôr′ē it, -sōr′-, prof′ə-), *n.* **1.** a group of professors. **2.** the office or post of professor. **3.** all of the academicians in a given place, as at an educational institution or in a country. Also, **pro′fes·so′ri·at.** [1855–60; PROFESSORI(AL) + -ATE[3]]

pro·fes·sor·ship (prə fes′ər ship′), *n.* the office or post of a professor. [1635–45; PROFESSOR + -SHIP]

prof·fer (prof′ər), *v.t.* **1.** to put before a person for acceptance; offer. —*n.* **2.** the act of proffering. **3.** an offer or proposal. [1250–1300; ME *profren* < AF *profrer,* var. of OF *poroffrir,* equiv. to *por-* PRO-[1] + *offrir* to OFFER] —**prof′fer·er,** *n.*
—**Syn. 1.** volunteer, propose, suggest. See **offer.**

pro·fi·cien·cy (prə fish′ən sē), *n.* the state of being proficient; skill; expertness: *proficiency in music.* [1535–45; < L *prōfici(ēns)* PROFICIENT + -ENCY]

profi′ciency badge′, an insignia or device granted by the Girl Scouts and worn esp. on a uniform to indicate special achievement. Cf. **merit badge.** [1920–25]

pro·fi·cient (prə fish′ənt), *adj.* **1.** well-advanced or competent in any art, science, or subject; skilled: *a proficient swimmer.* —*n.* **2.** an expert. [1580–90; < L *prōficient-* (s. of *prōficiēns*) prp. of *prōficere* to advance, make progress, equiv. to *prō-* PRO-[1] + *-ficere,* comb. form of *facere* to make, DO[1]. See -ENT, EFFICIENT] —**pro·fi′·cient·ly,** *adv.* —**pro·fi′cient·ness,** *n.*
—**Syn. 1.** adept, competent, experienced, accomplished, able, finished. —**Ant. 1.** unskilled, inept.

pro·file (prō′fīl), *n., v.,* **-filed, -fil·ing.** —*n.* **1.** the outline or contour of the human face, esp. the face viewed from one side. **2.** a picture or representation of the side view of a head. **3.** an outlined view, as of a city or mountain. **4.** an outline of an object, as a molding, formed on a vertical plane passed through the object at right angles to one of its principal horizontal dimensions. **5.** a drawing or the like representing this. **6.** *Survey.* a vertical section of the ground surface taken parallel to a survey line. Cf. **cross section** (def. 6). See diagram under **contour map. 7.** a verbal, arithmetical, or graphic summary or analysis of the history, status, etc., of a process, activity, relationship, or set of characteristics: *a biochemical profile of a patient's blood; a profile of national consumer spending.* **8.** an informal biography or a concisely presented sketch of the life and character of a person. **9.** a set of characteristics or qualities that identify a type or category of person or thing: *a profile of a typical allergy sufferer.* **10.** the look, configuration, or lines of something: *cars with a modern profile.* **11.** degree of noticeability; visibility. **12.** *Psychol.* a description of behavioral and personality traits of a person compared with accepted norms or standards. **13.** *Theat.* a flat stage property or scenic piece cut from a firm, thin material, as of beaverboard or plywood, and having an irregular edge resembling the silhouette of a natural object. **14.** (in a gear) the outline of either end of a tooth. **15.** *Naval Archit.* a longitudinal elevation or section of a vessel. Cf. **outboard profile.** —*v.t.* **16.** to draw a profile of. **17.** to produce or present a history, description, or analysis of: *The magazine will profile the candidate.* [1650–60; (n.) < It *prof(f)ilo,* n. deriv. of *profilare* to delineate, outline, equiv. to *pro-* PRO-[1] + *-filare,* deriv. of *filo* line, thread < L *fīlum*] —**pro′fil·er,** *n.*
—**Syn. 1.** silhouette.

pro′file plan′, *Naval Archit.* See **sheer plan.**

pro·fil·er (prō′fī lər), *n.* any of several types of machine tools for reproducing shapes in metal or other materials from a master form. Also called **duplicating machine.** [1900–05; PROFILE + -ER[1]]

Pro·fi·lom·e·ter (prō′fə lom′i tər), *Trademark.* a brand name for a device that measures the roughness of a surface.

prof·it (prof′it), *n.* **1.** Often, **profits. a.** pecuniary gain resulting from the employment of capital in any transaction. Cf. **gross profit, net profit. b.** the ratio of such pecuniary gain to the amount of capital invested. **c.** returns, proceeds, or revenue, as from property or investments. **2.** the monetary surplus left to a producer or employer after deducting wages, rent, cost of raw materials, etc.: *The company works on a small margin of profit.* **3.** advantage; benefit; gain. —*v.i.* **4.** to gain an advantage or benefit: *to profit from schooling.* **5.** to make a profit. **6.** to take advantage: *to profit from the weaknesses of others.* **7.** to be of service or benefit. **8.** to make progress. —*v.t.* **9.** to be of advantage or profit to: *Nothing profits one so much as education.* [1250–1300; (n.) ME < MF < L *prōfectus* progress, profit, equiv. to *prō-* PRO-[1] + *-fec-,* comb. form of *facere* to make, DO[1] + *-tus* suffix of v. action; (v.) ME *profiten,* deriv. of the n.] —**prof′it·er,** *n.* —**prof′it·less,** *adj.* —**prof′it·less·ly,** *adv.* —**prof′it·less·ness,** *n.*
—**Syn. 1.** return. **2.** net income. **3.** good, welfare, advancement, improvement. See **advantage. 4, 9.** advance, improve. —**Ant. 1.** loss.

prof·it·a·ble (prof′i tə bəl), *adj.* **1.** yielding profit; remunerative: *a profitable deal.* **2.** beneficial or useful. [1275–1325; ME; see PROFIT, -ABLE] —**prof′it·a·bil′i·ty, prof′it·a·ble·ness,** *n.* —**prof′it·a·bly,** *adv.*
—**Syn. 2.** advantageous, valuable, helpful.

prof′it and loss′, the gain and loss arising from commercial or other transactions, applied esp. to an account or statement of account in bookkeeping showing gains and losses in business. [1580–90]

prof′it and loss′ account′. See **income account** (def. 2). [1720–30]

prof′it cen′ter, 1. a segment of a business organization that has a profitable base independent of the business as a whole. **2.** any source of profit.

prof·it·eer (prof′i tēr′), *n.* **1.** a person who seeks or exacts exorbitant profits, esp. through the sale of scarce or rationed goods. —*v.i.* **2.** to act as a profiteer. [1910–15; PROFIT + -EER]

pro·fit·er·ole (prə fit′ə rōl′), *n.* a small cream puff with a sweet or savory filling, as of cream and chocolate sauce. [1505–15; < F, said to be dim. of *profit* PROFIT]

prof′it mar′gin, the percentage that profit constitutes of total sales. [1925–30]

prof′it mo′tive, the desire for profit that motivates one to engage in business ventures. [1930–35]

prof′it shar′ing, the sharing of profits, as between employer and employee, esp. in such a way that the employee receives his or her share in addition to wages. [1880–85] —**prof′it-shar′ing,** *adj.*

prof′it squeeze′, a sharp narrowing of the gap between cost and revenue. [1955–60]

prof′it tak′ing, *Stock Exchange.* the selling of securities that have risen in price above costs; selling in order to realize a profit. [1895–1900]

prof·li·ga·cy (prof′li gə sē), *n.* **1.** shameless dissoluteness. **2.** reckless extravagance. **3.** great abundance. [1730–40; PROFLIG(ATE) + -ACY]

prof·li·gate (prof′li git, -gāt′), *adj.* **1.** utterly and shamelessly immoral or dissipated; thoroughly dissolute. **2.** recklessly prodigal or extravagant. —*n.* **3.** a profligate person. [1525–35; < L *prōflīgātus* broken down in character, degraded, orig. ptp. of *prōflīgāre* to shatter, debase, equiv. to *prō-* PRO-[1] + *-flīgāre,* deriv. of *flīgere* to strike; see INFLICT, -ATE[1]] —**prof′li·gate·ly,** *adv.* —**prof′li·gate·ness,** *n.*
—**Syn. 1.** abandoned, licentious.

prof·lu·ent (prof′lo͞o ənt), *adj.* flowing smoothly or abundantly forth. [1400–50; late ME < L *prōfluent-* (s. of *prōfluēns*), prp. of *prōfluere* to flow forth. See PRO-[1], FLUENT]

pro-form (prō′fôrm′), *n. Gram.* a word used to replace or substitute for a word, phrase, or clause belonging to a given grammatical class, as a pronoun used to replace a noun or noun phrase, *there* used to replace an adverb or adverbial phrase of place, as in *I parked the car near the entrance and left it there,* or *so* used to substitute for a clause, as in *Have they come? I think so.* [1960–65]

pro for·ma (prō fôr′mə), **1.** according to form; as a matter of form; for the sake of form. **2.** *Com.* provided in advance of shipment and merely showing the description and quantity of goods shipped without terms of payment: *a pro forma invoice.* **3.** *Accounting.* indicating hypothetical financial figures based on previous business operations for estimate purposes: *a pro forma balance sheet.* Also, **pro·for′ma** (for defs. 2, 3). [1565–75; < L *prō fōrmā*]

pro·found (prə found′), *adj.,* **-er, -est,** *n.* —*adj.* **1.** penetrating or entering deeply into subjects of thought or knowledge; having deep insight or understanding: *a profound thinker.* **2.** originating in or penetrating to the depths of one's being; *profound grief.* **3.** being or going far beneath what is superficial, external, or obvious: *profound insight.* **4.** of deep meaning; of great and broadly inclusive significance: *a profound book.* **5.** pervasive or intense; thorough; complete: *a profound silence.* **6.** extending, situated, or originating far down, or far beneath the surface: *the profound depths of the ocean.* **7.** low: *a profound bow.* **8.** deep. —*n. Literary.* **9.** something that is profound. **10.** the deep sea; ocean. **11.** depth; abyss. [1275–1325; ME < AF < L *profundus* deep, vast, equiv. to *pro-* PRO-[1] + *fundus* bottom (see FOUND[2])] —**pro·found′ly,** *adv.* —**pro·found′ness,** *n.*
—**Syn. 1.** deep, sagacious. —**Ant. 1.** shallow, superficial.

pro·fun·di·ty (prə fun′di tē), *n., pl.* **-ties** for 2, 3. **1.** the quality or state of being profound; depth. **2.** Usually, **profundities.** profound or deep matters. **3.** a profoundly deep place; abyss. [1375–1425; late ME *profundite* < LL *profunditās.* See PROFOUND, -ITY]

pro·fuse (prə fyo͞os′), *adj.* **1.** spending or giving freely and in large amount, often to excess; extravagant (often fol. by *in*): *profuse praise.* **2.** made or done freely and abundantly: *profuse apologies.* **3.** abundant; in great amount. [1375–1425; late ME < L *profūsus,* ptp. of *profundere* to pour out or forth. See PRO-[1], FUSE[2]] —**pro·fuse′ly,** *adv.* —**pro·fuse′ness,** *n.*
—**Syn. 1.** See **lavish. 3.** See **ample.** —**Ant. 1.** thrifty.

pro·fu·sion (prə fyo͞o′zhən), *n.* **1.** abundance; abundant quantity. **2.** a great quantity or amount (often fol. by *of*). **3.** lavish spending; extravagance. [1535–45; < L *profūsiōn-* (s. of *profūsiō*) a pouring out, extravagance, orig. libation; see PROFUSE, FUSION]
—**Syn. 1.** copiousness, bounty. See **plenty. 3.** prodigality, profligacy, excess, waste. —**Ant. 1.** scarcity.

pro·fu·sive (prə fyo͞o′siv), *adj.* profuse; lavish; prodigal: *profusive generosity.* [1630–40; PROFUSE + -IVE] —**pro·fu′sive·ly,** *adv.* —**pro·fu′sive·ness,** *n.*

prog (prog), *v.,* **progged, prog·ging,** *n. Brit. Slang.* —*v.i.* **1.** to search or prowl about, as for plunder or food; forage. —*n.* **2.** food or victuals. [1560–70; orig. uncert.]

Prog., Progressive.

prog., 1. progress. **2.** progressive.

pro·gam·e·tan·gi·um (prō′gam i tan′jē əm), *n., pl.* **-gi·a** (-jē ə). *Mycol.* the hyphal tip of certain fungi that produces the gametangium and subsequent gamete. [< NL; see PRO-[2], GAMETANGIUM]

pro·gam·ete (prō gam′ēt, prō′gə mēt′), *n. Biol.* a cell that is the precursor of one ovum or many spermatozoa; a spermatocyte or oocyte. [1890–95; PRO-[2] + GAMETE]

pro·gen·i·tive (prō jen′i tiv), *adj.* capable of having offspring; reproductive. [1830–40; PROGENIT(OR) + -IVE] —**pro·gen′i·tive·ness,** *n.*

pro·gen·i·tor (prō jen′i tər), *n.* **1.** a biologically related ancestor: *a progenitor of the species.* **2.** a person or thing that first indicates a direction, originates something, or serves as a model; predecessor; precursor: *the progenitor of modern painting.* [1350–1400; ME < L *prōgenitor* the founder of a family. See PRO-[1], GENITOR] —**pro·gen·i·to·ri·al** (prō jen′i tôr′ē əl, -tōr′-), *adj.* —**pro·gen′i·tor·ship′,** *n.*

prog·e·ny (proj′ə nē), *n., pl.* **-ny** or, for plants or animals, **-nies. 1.** a descendant or offspring, as a child, plant, or animal. **2.** such descendants or offspring collectively. **3.** something that originates or results from something else; outcome; issue. [1250–1300; ME *progenie* < MF < L *prōgeniēs* offspring, equiv. to *prō-* PRO-[1] + *gen-,* base of *gignere* to beget (akin to KIN) + *-iēs* fem. n. suffix]

pro·ge·ri·a (prō jēr′ē ə), *n. Pathol.* a rare congenital abnormality characterized by premature and rapid aging, the affected individual appearing in childhood as an aged person and having a shortened life span. [1900–05; < NL < Gk *progḗr(ōs)* prematurely old (*pro-* PRO-[2] + *gêr(as)* old age + *-ōs* adj. suffix) + NL *-ia* -IA]

pro·ges·ta·tion·al (prō′je stā′shə nl), *adj. Med.* **1.** prepared for pregnancy, as the lining of the uterus prior to menstruation or in the early stages of gestation itself; progravid. **2.** of, noting, or characteristic of the action of progesterone; inducing a progravid state. [1920–25; PRO-[1] + GESTATIONAL]

pro·ges·ter·one (prō jes′tə rōn′), *n.* **1.** *Biochem.* a hormone, $C_{21}H_{30}O_2$, that prepares the uterus for the fertilized ovum and maintains pregnancy. **2.** *Pharm.* a commercial form of this compound, obtained from the corpus luteum of pregnant sows or synthesized: used in the treatment of dysfunctional uterine bleeding, dysmenorrhea, threatened or recurrent abortion, etc. [1930–35; b. PROGESTIN and *luteosterone* (< G *Luteosteron,* synonymous with progestin, equiv. to *Luteo-* LUTEO- (repr. CORPUS LUTEUM) + *-steron* (see STEROL, -ONE))]

pro·ges·tin (prō jes′tin), *n. Pharm.* any substance having progesteronelike activity. Also called **progestogen.** [1925–30; PRO-[1] + GEST(ATION) + -IN[2]]

pro·ges·to·gen (prō jes′tə jən), *n. Pharm.* progestin. Also, **pro·ges′ta·gen.** [1940–45; PRO-[1] + GEST(ATION) + -O- + -GEN]

pro·glot·tis (prō glot′is), *n., pl.* **-glot·ti·des** (-glot′i-dēz′). *Zool.* one of the segments or joints of a tapeworm, containing complete reproductive systems, usually both male and female. Also, **pro·glot·tid** (prō glot′id). [1850–55; < NL, for Gk *proglōssís* point of the tongue. See PRO-[2], GLOTTIS] —**pro·glot′tic, pro′glot·tid′e·an,** *adj.*

prog·na·thous (prog′nə thəs, prog nā′-), *adj. Craniom.* having protrusive jaws; having a gnathic index over 103. Also, **prog·nath·ic** (prog nath′ik). [1830–40; PRO-[2] + -GNATHOUS] —**prog·na·thism** (prog′nə thiz′əm), **prog′na·thy,** *n.*

prog·nose (prog nōs′, -nōz′), *v.t., v.i.,* **-nosed, -nos·ing.** *Med.* to subject to or make a prognosis. [1895–1900; back formation from PROGNOSIS]

prog·no·sis (prog nō′sis), *n., pl.* **-ses** (-sēz). **1.** *Med.* a forecasting of the probable course and outcome of a disease, esp. of the chances of recovery. **2.** a forecast or prognostication. [1645–55; < LL < Gk *prógnōsis* foreknowledge. See PRO-[2], GNOSIS]

prog·nos·tic (prog nos′tik), *adj.* **1.** of or pertaining to prognosis. **2.** predictive of something in the future: *prognostic signs and symbols.* —*n.* **3.** a forecast or prediction. **4.** an omen or portent; sign. [1375–1425; (adj.) late ME *pronostik* < ML *prognōsticus* < Gk *prognōstikós* of foreknowledge, equiv. to *pro(gi)gnṓs(kein)* to KNOW[1] beforehand + *-tikos* -TIC (see PRO-[2], GNOSTIC); (n.) < L *prognōsticon* < Gk *prognōstikón,* neut. of *prognōstikós*] —**prog·nos′ti·ca·ble,** *adj.* —**prog·nos′ti·cal·ly,** *adv.*

prog·nos·ti·cate (prog nos′ti kāt′), *v.,* **-cat·ed, -cat·ing.** —*v.t.* **1.** to forecast or predict (something future) from present indications or signs; prophesy. **2.** to foretoken; presage: *birds prognosticating spring.* —*v.i.* **3.** to make a forecast; prophesy. [1375–1425; late ME < ML *prognōsticātus,* ptp. of *prognōsticāre.* See PROGNOSTIC, -ATE[1]] —**prog·nos′ti·ca′tive, prog·nos·ti·ca·to·ry** (prog nos′ti kə tôr′ē, -tōr′ē), *adj.* —**prog·nos′ti·ca′tor,** *n.*
—**Syn. 1.** foretell, foresee, project.

prog·nos·ti·ca·tion (prog nos′ti kā′shən), *n.* **1.** the act of prognosticating. **2.** a forecast or prediction. [1350–1400; ME *pronosticacion* < ML *prognōsticātiōn-* (s. of *prognōsticātiō*). See PROGNOSTICATE, -ION]

prognos′tic chart′, *Meteorol.* a chart showing the predicted state of the atmosphere for a given time in the future.

pro·gra·da·tion (prō′grā dā′shən), *n. Geol.* seaward growth of a beach, delta, fan, etc., by progressive deposition of sediment by rivers or shoreline processes. [1905–10; *prograde* (PRO-[1] + (RETRO)GRADE) + -ATION]

CONCISE PRONUNCIATION KEY: *act, cāpe, dâre, pärt; set, ēqual; if, īce; ox, ōver, ôrder, oil, bo͝ok, bo͞ot, out; up, ûrge; child; sing; shoe; thin, that;* zh as in *treasure.* ə = *a* as in *alone, e* as in *system, i* as in *easily, o* as in *gallop, u* as in *circus;* ᵊ as in *fire* (fīᵊr), *hour* (ouᵊr). l and n can serve as syllabic consonants, as in *cradle* (krād′l), and *button* (but′n). See the full key inside the front cover.

pro·civ′ic, *adj.*
pro′ci·vil′ian, *adj.*
pro·clas′si·cal, *adj.*
pro·cler′gy, *adj.*
pro·cler′i·cal, *adj.*
pro′co·er′cion, *adj.*
pro′col·lec′tiv·ism, *n.*
pro′col·lec′tiv·ist, *adj., n.*
pro′col·lec′tiv·is′tic, *adj.*
pro′col·le′giate, adj.
pro′-Co·lom′bi·an, *adj., n.*
pro′co·lo′ni·al, *adj., n.*
pro·com′e·dy, *adj.*
pro′com·mer′cial, *adj.*
pro·com′mun·ism, *n., adj.*
pro·com′mun·ist, *adj., n.*
pro′com·mu′nity, *adj.*
pro′com·mu·ta′tion, *adj.*
pro′com·pen·sa′tion, *adj.*
pro′com·pe·ti′tion, *adj.*
pro·com′pro·mise′, *adj.*
pro′con·ces′sion, *adj.*
pro′con·cil′i·a′tion, *adj.*
pro′-Con·fed′er·ate, *adj.*
pro′con·fis·ca′tion, *adj.*
pro′-Con·go·lese′, *adj., n., pl.* **-lese.**
pro′-Con·gres′sion·al, *adj.*
pro′con·scrip′tion, *adj.*
pro′con·ser·va′tion, *adj.*

pro•gram (prō′gram, -grəm), *n., v.,* **-grammed** or **-gramed, -gram•ming** or **-gram•ing.** —*n.* **1.** a plan of action to accomplish a specified end: *a school lunch program.* **2.** a plan or schedule of activities, procedures, etc., to be followed. **3.** a radio or television performance or production. **4.** a list of items, pieces, performers, etc., in a musical, theatrical, or other entertainment. **5.** an entertainment with reference to its pieces or numbers: *a program of American and French music.* **6.** a planned, coordinated group of activities, procedures, etc., often for a specific purpose, or a facility offering such a series of activities: *a drug rehabilitation program; a graduate program in linguistics.* **7.** a prospectus or syllabus: *a program of courses being offered.* **8.** *Computers.* **a.** a systematic plan for the automatic solution of a problem by a computer. **b.** the precise sequence of instructions enabling a computer to solve a problem. —*v.t.* **9.** to schedule as part of a program. **10.** *Computers.* to prepare a program for. **11.** to insert or encode specific operating instructions into (a machine or apparatus): *We'll program the bells to ring at ten-minute intervals.* **12.** to insert (instructions) into a machine or apparatus: *An automatic release has been programmed into the lock as a safety feature.* **13.** to cause to absorb or incorporate automatic responses, attitudes, or the like; condition: *Our parents programmed us to respect our elders.* **14.** to set, regulate, or modify so as to produce a specific response or reaction: *Program your eating habits to eliminate sweets.* —*v.i.* **15.** to plan or write a program. Also, *esp. Brit.,* **pro′gramme.** [1625–35; < LL *programma* < Gk *prógramma* public notice in writing. See PRO-[2], -GRAM[1]]

pro′gram direc′tor, *Radio and Television.* a chief executive responsible for selecting and scheduling programs. [1950–55]

pro•gram•ma•ble (prō′gram ə bəl, prō gram′-), *adj.* **1.** capable of being programmed. —*n.* **2.** an electronic device, as a calculator or telephone, that can be programmed to perform specific tasks. Also, **pro′gram•a•ble.** [1955–60; PROGRAM + -ABLE] —**pro′gram•ma•bil′i•ty,** *n.*

pro•gram•mat•ic (prō′grə mat′ik), *adj.* **1.** of, pertaining to, consisting of, or resembling program music. **2.** of, having, advocating, resembling, or following a plan, policy, or program: *programmatic art.* [1895–1900; < Gk *programmat-* (s. of *prógramma*) PROGRAM + -IC] —**pro′gram•mat′i•cal•ly,** *adv.*

pro′grammed instruc′tion, *Educ.* a progressively monitored, step-by-step teaching method, employing small units of information or learning material and frequent testing, whereby the student must complete or pass one stage before moving on to the next. Also called **pro′grammed learn′ing.** [1960–65]

pro•gram•mer (prō′gram ər), *n.* **1.** a person who writes computer programs; a person who programs a device, esp. a computer. **2.** a person who prepares program schedules, as for radio or television. **3.** a person who prepares instructional programs. Also, **pro′gram•er.** [1885–90; PROGRAM + -ER[1]]

pro•gram•ming (prō′gram ing, -grə ming), *n.* **1.** the act or process of planning or writing a program. **2.** *Radio and Television.* **a.** the selection and scheduling of programs for a particular period, station, or network. **b.** the programs scheduled. Also, **pro′gram•ing.** [1885–90; PROGRAM + -ING[1]]

pro′gramming lan′guage, a high-level language used to write computer programs, as COBOL or BASIC, or, sometimes, an assembly language. [1955–60]

pro′gram mu′sic, music intended to convey an impression of a definite series of images, scenes, or events. Cf. **absolute music.** [1880–85]

pro′gram pic′ture, a motion picture produced on a low budget, usually shown as the second film of a double feature. [1925–30]

pro•grav•id (prō grav′id), *adj. Med.* progestational (def. 1). [PRO-[1] + GRAVID]

Pro•gre•so (prô gre′sô), *n.* a city in NW Honduras. 22,100.

prog•ress (*n.* prog′res, -rəs *or, esp. Brit.,* prō′gres; *v.* prə gres′), *n.* **1.** a movement toward a goal or to a further or higher stage: *the progress of a student toward a degree.* **2.** developmental activity in science, technology, etc., esp. with reference to the commercial opportunities created thereby or to the promotion of the material well-being of the public through the goods, techniques, or facilities created. **3.** advancement in general. **4.** growth or development; continuous improvement: *He shows progress in his muscular coordination.* **5.** the development of an individual or society in a direction considered more beneficial than and superior to the previous level. **6.** *Biol.* increasing differentiation and perfection in the course of ontogeny or phylogeny. **7.** forward or onward movement: *the progress of the planets.* **8.** the forward course of action, events, time, etc. **9.** an official journey or tour, as by a sovereign or dignitary. **10. in progress,** going on; under way; being done; happening: *The meeting was already in progress.* —*v.i.* **pro•gress 11.** to go forward or onward in space or time: *The wagon train progressed through the valley. As the play progressed, the leading man grew more inaudible.* **12.** to grow or develop, as in complexity, scope, or severity; advance: *Are you progressing in your piano studies? The disease progressed slowly.* [1400–50; late ME *progresse* (n.) < L *prōgressus* a going forward, equiv. to *prōgred-,* s. of *prōgredī* to advance (*prō-* PRO-[1] + *-gredi,* comb. form of *gradi* to step; see GRADE) + *-tus* suffix of v. action]
—**Syn. 1.** advance, progression. **4.** increase; betterment. **12.** proceed; develop, improve, grow, increase.
—**Ant. 1.** regression. **12.** regress.

CONCISE ETYMOLOGY KEY: <, descended or borrowed from; >, whence; b., blend of, blended; c., cognate with; cf., compare; deriv., derivative; equiv., equivalent; imit., imitative; obl., oblique; r., replacing; s., stem; sp., spelling, spelled; resp., respelling, respelled; trans., translation; ?, origin unknown; *, unattested; ‡, probably earlier than. See the full key inside the front cover.

pro•gres•sion (prə gresh′ən), *n.* **1.** the act of progressing; forward or onward movement. **2.** a passing successively from one member of a series to the next; succession; sequence. **3.** *Math.* a succession of quantities in which there is a constant relation between each member and the one succeeding it. Cf. **arithmetic progression, geometric progression, harmonic progression.** **4.** *Music.* the manner in which chords or melodic tones follow one another; a succession of chords or tones. **5.** *Astrol.* any of a variety of methods of comparing the natal chart to subsequent planetary positions in order to establish an optimum time to accomplish things or to establish the probable time an event occurred or will occur. [1400–50; late ME < L *prōgressiōn-* (s. of *prōgressiō*). See PROGRESS, -ION] —**pro•gres′sion•al,** *adj.* —**pro•gres′•sion•al•ly,** *adv.*

pro•gres•sion•ist (prə gresh′ə nist), *n.* a person who believes in progress, as of humankind or society. [1840–50; PROGRESSION + -IST] —**pro•gres′sion•ism,** *n.*

prog•ress•ist (prog′res ist, -rə sist *or, esp. Brit.* prō′gres ist, -grə sist), *n.* a person favoring progress, as in politics; progressive. [1840–50; PROGRESS + -IST] —**prog′ress•ism,** *n.*

pro•gres•sive (prə gres′iv), *adj.* **1.** favoring or advocating progress, change, improvement, or reform, as opposed to wishing to maintain things as they are, esp. in political matters: *a progressive mayor.* **2.** making progress toward better conditions; employing or advocating more enlightened or liberal ideas, new or experimental methods, etc.: *a progressive community.* **3.** characterized by such progress, or by continuous improvement. **4.** (*cap.*) of or pertaining to any of the Progressive parties in politics. **5.** going forward or onward; passing successively from one member of a series to the next; proceeding step by step. **6.** noting or pertaining to a form of taxation in which the rate increases with certain increases in taxable income. **7.** of or pertaining to progressive education: *progressive schools.* **8.** *Gram.* noting a verb aspect or other verb category that indicates action or state going on at a temporal point of reference. **9.** *Med.* continuously increasing in extent or severity, as a disease. —*n.* **10.** a person who is progressive or who favors progress or reform, esp. in political matters. **11.** (*cap.*) a member of a Progressive party. **12.** *Gram.* **a.** the progressive aspect. **b.** a verb form or construction in the progressive, as *are thinking* in *They are thinking about it.* [1600–10; PROGRESS + -IVE] —**pro•gres′sive•ly,** *adv.* —**pro•gres′sive•ness, pro•gres•siv•i•ty** (prō′gre siv′i tē), *n.*
—**Syn. 1, 9.** liberal. **5.** successive.

progres′sive assimila′tion, *Phonet.* assimilation in which a preceding sound has an effect on a following one, as in shortening *captain* to *cap'm* rather than *cap'n.* Cf. **regressive assimilation.** [1910–15]

Progres′sive Conserv′ative, 1. a member of the Progressive Conservative party of Canada. **2.** of or pertaining to the Progressive Conservative party of Canada.

Progres′sive Conserv′ative par′ty, a political party in Canada characterized by conservatism.

progres′sive din′ner, a dinner party in which each successive course is prepared and eaten at the residence of a different participant.

progres′sive educa′tion, any of various reformist educational philosophies and methodologies since the late 1800's, applied esp. to elementary schools, that reject the rote recitation and strict discipline of traditional, single-classroom teaching, favoring instead more stimulation of the individual pupil as well as group discussion, more informality in the classroom, a broader curriculum, and use of laboratories, gymnasiums, kitchens, etc., in the school. Also called **progressivism.**

progres′sive jazz′, an experimental, nonmelodic, and often free-flowing style of modern jazz, esp. in the form of highly dissonant, rhythmically complex orchestral arrangements. Cf. **bop[1], cool jazz, hard bop, modern jazz.** [1945–50]

Progres′sive Ju′daism. See **Reform Judaism.**

progres′sive lens′, a multifocal eyeglass lens that provides a continuous range of focal power between near and far distances. [1975–80]

progres′sive par′ticiple. See **present participle.**

Progres′sive par′ty, 1. a political party formed in 1912 under the leadership of Theodore Roosevelt, advocating popular control of government, direct primaries, the initiative, the referendum, woman suffrage, etc. **2.** a similar party formed in 1924 under the leadership of Robert M. La Follette. **3.** a political party formed in 1948 under the leadership of Henry A. Wallace.

pro•gres′sive-re•sist′ance ex′ercise (prə gres′iv ri zis′təns), **1.** exercise or a program of exercises that builds physical strength, esp. in a weak or injured bodily part, through the lifting of progressively heavier weight according to a formula based on the subject's maximum strength at the starting point. **2.** any specific exercise of this type.

pro•gres•siv•ism (prə gres′ə viz′əm), *n.* **1.** the principles and practices of progressives. **2.** (*cap.*) the doctrines and beliefs of the Progressive party. **3.** See **progressive education.** [1890–95; PROGRESSIVE + -ISM] —**pro•gres′siv•ist,** *n., adj.*

pro-growth (prō′grōth′), *adj.* favoring or advocating the commercial development or exploitation of land and other natural resources, esp. with minimal government restriction and regulation. —**pro′-growth′er,** *n.*

pro•hib•it (prō hib′it), *v.t.* **1.** to forbid (an action, activity, etc.) by authority or law: *Smoking is prohibited here.* **2.** to forbid the action of (a person). **3.** to prevent; hinder. [1400–50; late ME < L *prohibitus* ptp. of *prohibēre* to hold before, hold back, hinder, forbid, equiv. to *pro-* PRO-[1] + *-hibēre,* comb. form of *habēre* to have, hold; see HABIT] —**pro•hib′it•er, pro•hib′i•tor,** *n.*
—**Syn. 1.** interdict. See **forbid. 3.** obstruct. —**Ant. 1.** permit.

pro•hi•bi•tion (prō′ə bish′ən), *n.* **1.** the act of prohibiting. **2.** the legal prohibiting of the manufacture and sale of alcoholic drinks for common consumption. **3.** (*often cap.*) the period (1920–33) when the Eighteenth Amendment was in force and alcoholic beverages could not legally be manufactured, transported, or sold in the U.S. **4.** a law or decree that forbids. [1275–1325; ME < L *prohibitiōn-* (s. of *prohibitiō*). See PROHIBIT, -ION] —**pro′hi•bi′tion•ar′y,** *adj.*
—**Syn. 4.** interdiction.

pro•hi•bi•tion•ist (prō′ə bish′ə nist), *n.* **1.** a person who favors or advocates prohibition. **2.** (*cap.*) a member of the Prohibition party. [1840–50; PROHIBITION + -IST]

Prohibi′tion par′ty, a U.S. political party organized in 1869, advocating the prohibition of the manufacture and sale of alcoholic beverages.

pro•hib•i•tive (prō hib′i tiv), *adj.* **1.** serving or tending to prohibit or forbid something. **2.** sufficing to prevent the use, purchase, etc., of something: *prohibitive prices.* [1595–1605; < ML *prohibitīvus.* See PROHIBIT, -IVE] —**pro•hib′i•tive•ly,** *adv.* —**pro•hib′i•tive•ness,** *n.*

pro•hib•i•to•ry (prō hib′i tôr′ē, -tōr′ē), *adj.* prohibitive. [1585–95; < L *prohibitōrius* restraining. See PROHIBIT, -TORY[1]] —**pro•hib′i•to′ri•ly,** *adv.*

pro•hor•mone (prō hôr′mōn), *n. Biochem.* the inactive precursor molecule from which a hormone is derived. [1930–35; PRO-[1] + HORMONE]

pro•in•su•lin (prō in′sə lin, -ins′yə-), *n. Biochem.* the prohormone of insulin, converted into insulin by enzymatic removal of part of the molecule. [1915–20; PRO-[1] + INSULIN]

proj•ect (*n.* proj′ekt, -ikt; *v.* prə jekt′), *n.* **1.** something that is contemplated, devised, or planned; plan; scheme. **2.** a large or major undertaking, esp. one involving considerable money, personnel, and equipment. **3.** a specific task of investigation, esp. in scholarship. **4.** *Educ.* a supplementary, long-term educational assignment necessitating personal initiative, undertaken by an individual student or a group of students. **5.** Often, **projects.** See **housing project.** —*v.t.* **pro•ject 6.** to propose, contemplate, or plan. **7.** to throw, cast, or impel forward or onward. **8.** to set forth or calculate (some future thing): *They projected the building costs for the next five years.* **9.** to throw or cause to fall upon a surface or into space, as a ray of light or a shadow. **10.** to cause (a figure or image) to appear, as on a background. **11.** to regard (something within the mind, as a feeling, thought, or attitude) as having some form of reality outside the mind: *He projected a thrilling picture of the party's future.* **12.** to cause to jut out or protrude. **13.** *Geom.* **a.** to throw forward an image of (a figure or the like) by straight lines or rays, either parallel, converging, or diverging, that pass through all its points and reproduce it on another surface or figure. **b.** to transform the points (of one figure) into those of another by a correspondence between points. **14.** to present (an idea, program, etc.) for consideration or action: *They made every effort to project the notion of world peace.* **15.** to use (one's voice, gestures, etc.) forcefully enough to be perceived at a distance, as by all members of the audience in a theater. **16.** to communicate clearly and forcefully (one's thoughts, personality, role, etc.) to an audience, as in a theatrical performance; produce a compelling image of. **17.** to cause (the voice) to appear to come from a source other than oneself, as in ventriloquism; throw. —*v.i.* **pro•ject 18.** to extend or protrude beyond something else. **19.** to use one's voice forcefully enough to be heard at a distance, as in a theater. **20.** to produce a clear impression of one's thoughts, personality, role, etc., in an audience; communicate clearly and forcefully. **21.** *Psychol.* to ascribe one's own feelings, thoughts, or attitudes to others. [1350–1400; (n.) ME *project(e)* design, plan < ML *prōjectum,* L: projecting part, n. use of neut. of L *prōjectus,* ptp. of *prōicere* to throw forward, extend, equiv. to *prō-* PRO-[1] + *-icere,* comb. form of *jacere* to throw; (v.) late ME *project(e)* (ptp.) extended, projected < L *prōjectus*] —**pro•ject′a•ble,** *adj.* —**pro•ject′ing•ly,** *adv.*
—**Syn. 1.** proposal. See **plan. 6.** contrive, scheme, plot, devise. **8.** predict. **18.** bulge, obtrude, overhang.

project′ed win′dow, a casement window in which the inner end of the sash slides along a track on the sill as the sash swings outward.

pro•jec•tile (prə jek′til, -tīl), *n.* **1.** an object fired from a gun with an explosive propelling charge, such as a bullet, shell, rocket, or grenade. **2.** a body projected or impelled forward, as through the air. —*adj.* **3.** impelling or driving forward, as a force. **4.** caused by impulse, as motion. **5.** capable of being impelled forward, as a missile. **6.** *Zool.* protrusile, as the jaws of a fish. [1655–65; < NL, neut. of *prōjectilis* (adj.) projecting. See PROJECT, -ILE]

pro•jec•tion (prə jek′shən), *n.* **1.** a projecting or protruding part. **2.** the state or fact of jutting out or protruding. **3.** a causing to jut or protrude. **4.** the act, process, or result of projecting. **5.** *Cartog.* a systematic construction of lines drawn on a plane surface representative of and corresponding to the meridians and parallels of the curved surface of the earth or celestial sphere. **6.** *Photog.* **a.** the act of reproducing on a surface, by optical

pro′con•ser•va′tion•ist, *adj., n.*
pro′con•sol′i•da′tion, *adj.*
pro′con•sti•tu′tion•al, *adj.*
pro′con•sti•tu′tion•al•ism, *n.*
pro′con•sul•ta′tion, *adj.*
pro′con•tin•u•a′tion, *adj.*
pro′con•ven′tion, *adj.*
pro′con•vic′tion, *adj.*
pro-Cu′ban, *adj., n.*
pro′cy′cli•cal, *adj.*
pro-Cyp′ri•ote′, *adj., n.*
pro-Cy′prus, *adj.*
pro-Czech′, *adj., n.*
pro′-Czech•o•slo•va′ki•an, *adj., n.*
pro-Dan′ish, *adj.*
pro-Dar′win, *adj.*
pro′-Dar•win′i•an, *adj., n.*
pro-Dar′win•ism, *n.*
pro′dem′o•crat′, *adj., n.*
pro′dem•o•crat′ic, *adj.*
pro′de•moc′ra•cy, *adj.*
pro-Den′mark, *adj.*
pro′de•por•ta′tion, *adj.*

means, a remote image on a film, slide, etc. **b.** an image so reproduced. **7.** the act of visualizing and regarding an idea or the like as an objective reality. **8.** something that is so visualized and regarded. **9.** calculation of some future thing: *They fell short of their projection for the rate of growth.* **10.** the act of communicating distinctly and forcefully to an audience. **11.** *Psychol.* **a.** the tendency to ascribe to another person feelings, thoughts, or attitudes present in oneself, or to regard external reality as embodying such feelings, thoughts, etc., in some way. **b.** *Psychoanal.* such an ascription relieving the ego of a sense of guilt or other intolerable feeling. **12.** the act of planning or scheming. **13.** *Alchemy.* the casting of the powder of philosophers' stone upon metal in fusion, to transmute it into gold or silver. [1470–80; < L *prōjectiōn-* (s. of *prōjectiō*) a throwing forward. See PROJECT, -ION] **—pro·jec·tion·al** (prə jek′shə nl), *adj.*
—Syn. 1. jut, overhang, protrusion. **9.** prediction.

projec′tion booth′, 1. a soundproof compartment in a theater where a motion-picture projector is housed and from which the picture is projected on the screen. **2.** a compartment at the rear of or above an auditorium, in which spotlights and other lighting units are operated. [1925–30]

pro·jec·tion·ist (prə jek′shə nist), *n.* **1.** an operator of a motion-picture or slide projector. **2.** a person who makes projections, esp. a cartographer. [1920–25; PROJECTION + -IST]

projec′tion machine′, an apparatus that projects motion pictures; projector.

projec′tion pa′per, *Photog.* sensitized paper for recording a projected image.

projec′tion print′, *Photog.* a print made by the projection of an image onto sensitized paper. Cf. **contact print.**

projec′tion print′er, *Photog.* enlarger. [1960–65]

projec′tion print′ing, *Photog.* the act or process of making projection prints. Cf. **contact printing.** [1935–40]

projec′tion room′, 1. See **projection booth** (def. 1). **2.** a room with a projector and screen for the private viewing of motion pictures. [1910–15]

projec′tion tel′evision, a television picture display system consisting of a special receiver and an optical system that projects an enlarged picture on a screen.

pro·jec·tive (prə jek′tiv), *adj.* **1.** of or pertaining to projection. **2.** produced, or capable of being produced, by projection. **3.** *Psychol.* of, pertaining to, or noting a test or technique for revealing the hidden motives or underlying personality structure of an individual by the use of ambiguous or unstructured test materials, as ink blots, cloud pictures, or cartoons, that encourage spontaneous responses. [1625–35; PROJECT + -IVE] **—pro·jec′tive·ly,** *adv.* **—pro·jec·tiv·i·ty** (prō′jek tiv′i tē), *n.*

projec′tive geom′etry, the geometric study of projective properties. [1880–85]

projec′tive prop′erty, a geometric property that is unaltered by projection; a property of relative position, as coincidence or length, but not of magnitude. [1880–85]

proj′ect note′, a short-term municipal note issued by a local government housing agency to finance a public housing project.

pro·jec·tor (prə jek′tər), *n.* **1.** an apparatus for throwing an image on a screen, as a motion-picture projector or magic lantern. **2.** a device for projecting a beam of light. **3.** a person who forms projects or plans; schemer. [1590–1600; PROJECT + -OR²]

pro·jet (prō zhā′; *Fr.* prô zhe′), *n., pl.* **-jets** (-zhāz′; *Fr.* -zhe′). **1.** a project. **2.** a draft of a proposed treaty or other instrument. [1800–10; < F < L *prōjectum.* See PROJECT]

pro·kar·y·ote (prō kar′ē ōt′, -ē ət), *n.* any cellular organism that has no nuclear membrane, no organelles in the cytoplasm except ribosomes, and has its genetic material in the form of single continuous strands forming coils or loops, characteristic of all organisms in the kingdom Monera, as the bacteria and blue-green algae. Also, **procaryote.** Cf. **eukaryote.** [taken as sing. of NL *Prokaryota,* earlier *Procaryotes* (1925); see PRO-¹, EUKARYOTE] **—pro·kar·y·ot·ic** (prō kar′ē ot′ik), *adj.*

Pro·kho·rov (prō′kə rôf′, -rof′; *Russ.* prô′khə rəf), *n.* **A·le·ksan·dr Mi·khai·lo·vich** (al′ig zan′dər mi kī′lə vich, -zän′-; *Russ.* u lyi ksän′dr myi khī′lə vyich), born 1916, Russian physicist: Nobel prize 1964.

Pro·ko·fiev (prə kô′fē əf, -ef′, -kō′-; *Russ.* pru kô′fyif), *n.* **Ser·gei Ser·ge·e·vich** (syir gyā′ syir gye′yi vyich), 1891–1953, Russian composer.

Pro·ko·pyevsk (prə kôp′yəfsk; *Russ.* pru kô′pyifsk), *n.* a city in the S central Russian Federation in Asia, NW of Novokuznetsk. 278,000.

pro·lac·tin (prō lak′tin), *n. Biochem.* an anterior pituitary polypeptide hormone that stimulates lactation by the mammary glands at parturition in mammals, the activity of the crop in birds, and in some mammalian species the production of progesterone by the corpus luteum. Also called **anterior pituitary hormone, lactogenic hormone, luteotropin.** [1930–35; PRO-¹ + LACT- + -IN²]

pro·lam·in (prō lam′in, prō′lə min), *n. Biochem.* any of the class of simple proteins, as gliadin, hordein, or zein, found in grains, soluble in dilute acids, alkalis, and alcohols, and insoluble in water, neutral salt solutions, and absolute alcohol. Also, **pro·lam·ine** (prō lam′in, -ēn, prō′lə min, -mēn′). [1905–10; PROL(INE) + AM(MONIA) + -IN²]

pro·lapse (*n.* prō laps′, prō′laps; *v.* prō laps′), *n., v.,* **-lapsed, -laps·ing.** **—n. 1.** *Pathol.* a falling down of an organ or part, as the uterus, from its normal position. **—v.i. 2.** to fall or slip down or out of place. [1555–65; < LL *prōlāpsus* a slipping forth. See PRO-¹, LAPSE]

pro·lap·sus (prō lap′səs), *n., pl.* **-sus·es.** prolapse.

pro·late (prō′lāt), *adj.* elongated along the polar diameter, as a spheroid generated by the revolution of an ellipse about its longer axis (opposed to *oblate*). [1685–95; < L *prōlātus,* ptp. of *prōferre* to bring forward, extend; see PRO-¹, OBLATE] **—pro′late·ly,** *adv.* **—pro′late·ness,** *n.*

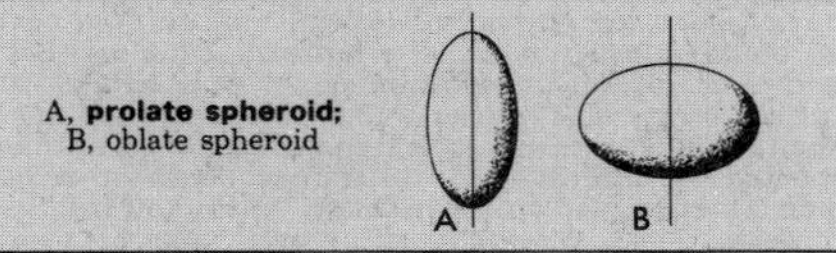

A, **prolate spheroid;** B, oblate spheroid

pro·la·tion (prō lā′shən), *n. Medieval Music.* the time relationship between a semibreve and a minim in mensural notation. [1325–75; ME *prolacion* < L *prōlātiōn-* (s. of *prōlātiō*) a bringing forward. See PROLATE, -ION]

prole (prōl, prō′lē), *n. Informal.* **1.** a member of the proletariat. **2.** a person who performs routine tasks in a society. **—adj. 3.** proletarian (def. 1). [1885–90; shortened form of PROLETARIAT]

pro·leg (prō′leg′), *n.* one of the abdominal ambulatory processes of caterpillars and other larvae, as distinct from the true or thoracic legs. [1810–20; PRO-¹ + LEG]

P, **prolegs** of larva of monarch butterfly, *Danaus plexippus*

pro·le·gom·e·non (prō′li gom′ə non′, -nən), *n., pl.* **-na** (-nə). **1.** a preliminary discussion; introductory essay, as prefatory matter in a book; a prologue. **2.** Usually, **prolegomena.** (*sometimes used with a singular v.*) a treatise serving as a preface or introduction to a book. [1645–55; < NL < Gk *prolegómenon,* neut. of pass. prp. of *prolégein* to say beforehand, equiv. to *pro-* PRO-² + *légein* to say (akin to *lógos* LOGOS)]

pro·le·gom·e·nous (prō′li gom′ə nəs), *adj.* **1.** prefatory; preliminary; introductory. **2.** characterized by unnecessary or lengthy prologizing. [1740–50; PROLEGOMEN(ON) + -OUS]

pro·lep·sis (prō lep′sis), *n., pl.* **-ses** (-sēz). **1.** *Rhet.* the anticipation of possible objections in order to answer them in advance. **2.** the assigning of a person, event, etc., to a period earlier than the actual one; the representation of something in the future as if it already existed or had occurred; prochronism. **3.** the use of a descriptive word in anticipation of its becoming applicable. **4.** a fundamental conception or assumption in Epicureanism or Stoicism arising spontaneously in the mind without conscious reflection; thought provoked by sense perception. **5.** *Pathol.* the return of an attack of a periodic disease or of a paroxysm before the expected time or at progressively shorter intervals. [1570–80; < LL *prolēpsis* < Gk *prólēpsis* anticipation, preconception, equiv. to *prolēp-* (verbid s. of *prolambánein* to anticipate (*pro-* PRO-² + *lambánein* to take)) + *-sis* -SIS] **—pro·lep·tic** (prō lep′tik), **pro·lep′ti·cal,** *adj.* **—pro·lep′ti·cal·ly,** *adv.*

pro·le·tar·i·an (prō′li târ′ē ən), *adj.* **1.** pertaining or belonging to the proletariat. **2.** (in ancient Rome) belonging to the lowest or poorest class of the people. **—n. 3.** a member of the proletariat. [1650–60; see PROLETARY, -AN] **—pro′le·tar′i·an·ly,** *adv.* **—pro′le·tar′i·an·ness,** *n.*

pro·le·tar·i·an·ism (prō′li târ′ē ə niz′əm), *n.* the practices, attitudes, or social status of a proletarian. [1860–65; PROLETARIAN + -ISM]

pro·le·tar·i·an·ize (prō′li târ′ē ə nīz′), *v.t.,* **-ized, -iz·ing. 1.** to convert or transform into a member or members of the proletariat: *to proletarianize the middle class.* **2.** to change to or adopt (the language, manners, etc.) of the proletariat. Also, *esp. Brit.,* **pro′le·tar′i·an·ise′.** [1885–90; PROLETARIAN + -IZE] **—pro′le·tar′i·an·i·za′tion,** *n.*

pro·le·tar·i·at (prō′li târ′ē ət), *n.* **1.** the class of wage earners, esp. those who earn their living by manual labor or who are dependent for support on daily or casual employment; the working class. **2.** (in Marxist theory) the class of workers, esp. industrial wage earners, who do not possess capital or property and must sell their labor to survive. **3.** the lowest or poorest class of people, possessing no property, esp. in ancient Rome. [1850–55; < F *prolétariat;* see PROLETARY, -ATE³]

pro·le·tar·ize (prō′li târ′īz), *v.t.,* **-ized, -iz·ing.** to proletarianize. Also, *esp. Brit.,* **pro′le·tar′ise.** **—pro′le·tar′i·za′tion,** *n.*

pro·le·tar·y (prō′li ter′ē), *adj., n., pl.* **-tar·ies.** proletarian. [1570–80; < L *prōlētārius* belonging to the lowest class of Roman citizens, i.e., those who contributed to the state only through their offspring, equiv. to *prōlēt-* (akin to *prōlēs* offspring; *pro-* PRO-¹ + *-olēs* (see ADULT)) + *-ārius* -ARY]

pro·li·cide (prō′lə sīd′), *n.* the killing of one's child. [1835–45; < ML *prōli-* (comb. form repr. L *prōlēs* offspring; see PROLETARY) + -CIDE] **—pro′li·cid′al,** *adj.*

pro-life (prō līf′), *adj.* opposed to legalized abortion; right-to-life. Cf. **pro-choice.** [1960–65] **—pro-lif′er,** *n.*

pro·lif·er·ate (prə lif′ə rāt′), *v.i., v.t.,* **-at·ed, -at·ing. 1.** to grow or produce by multiplication of parts, as in budding or cell division, or by procreation. **2.** to increase in number or spread rapidly and often excessively. [1870–75; PROLIFER(OUS) + -ATE¹] **—pro·lif′er·a′tive,** *adj.*

pro·lif·er·a·tion (prə lif′ə rā′shən), *n.* **1.** the growth or production of cells by multiplication of parts. **2.** a rapid and often excessive spread or increase: *nuclear proliferation.* [1855–60; PROLIFERATE + -ION]

pro·lif·er·ous (prə lif′ər əs), *adj.* **1.** proliferating. **2.** *Bot.* **a.** producing new individuals by budding or the like. **b.** producing an organ or shoot from an organ that is itself normally the last, as a shoot or a new flower from the midst of a flower. [1645–55; < ML *prōlifer* bearing offspring + -OUS. See PROLICIDE, -FEROUS]

pro·lif·ic (prə lif′ik), *adj.* **1.** producing offspring, young, fruit, etc., abundantly; highly fruitful: *a prolific pear tree.* **2.** producing in large quantities or with great frequency; highly productive: *a prolific writer.* **3.** profusely productive or fruitful (often fol. by *in* or *of*): *a bequest prolific of litigations.* **4.** characterized by abundant production: *a prolific year for tomatoes.* [1640–50; < ML *prōlificus* fertile. See PROLICIDE, -FIC] **—pro·lif·i·ca·cy** (prə lif′i kə sē), **pro·li·fic·i·ty** (prō′lə fis′i tē), **pro·lif′ic·ness,** *n.* **—pro·lif′i·cal·ly,** *adv.*
—Syn. 1, 2. teeming, fecund, abundant. See **productive.** **—Ant. 1.** barren.

pro·line (prō′lēn, -lin), *n. Biochem.* an alcohol-soluble amino acid, $C_4H_8NHCOOH$, occurring in high concentration in collagen. *Abbr.:* Pro; *Symbol:* P [1900–05; alter. of PYRROLIDINE]

pro·lix (prō liks′, prō′liks), *adj.* **1.** extended to great, unnecessary, or tedious length; long and wordy. **2.** (of a person) given to speaking or writing at great or tedious length. [1375–1425; late ME < L *prōlixus* extended, long, equiv. to *prō-* PRO-¹ + *-lixus,* akin to *liquī* to flow; see LIQUOR] **—pro·lix·i·ty** (prō lik′si tē), **pro·lix′ness,** *n.* **—pro·lix′ly,** *adv.*
—Syn. 1. prolonged, protracted. See **wordy. 1, 2.** verbose.

pro·loc·u·tor (prō lok′yə tər), *n.* **1.** a presiding officer of an assembly; chairperson. **2.** *Ch. of Eng.* the chairperson of the lower house of a convocation. [1400–50; late ME: one who speaks for another < L *prōlocūtor* one who speaks out, equiv. to *prōlocū-* (var. s. of *prōloquī* to speak forth; *prō-* PRO-¹ + *loquī* to speak) + *-tor* -TOR] **—pro·loc′u·tor·ship′,** *n.*

pro·logue (prō′lôg, -log), *n., v.,* **-logued, -logu·ing.** **—n. 1.** a preliminary discourse; a preface or introductory part of a discourse, poem, or novel. **2.** an introductory speech, often in verse, calling attention to the theme of a play. **3.** the actor or actress who delivers this. **4.** an introductory scene, preceding the first act of a play, opera, etc. **5.** any introductory proceeding, event, etc.: *Appetizing delicacies were the prologue to a long dinner.* **—v.t. 6.** to introduce with or as if with a prologue. Also, **pro′log.** [1250–1300; ME *prologe, prologue* (< OF *prologue*) < L *prologus* < Gk *prólogos.* See PRO-², -LOGUE] **—pro′logu·ist, pro′log·ist,** *n.* **—pro′logue·like′, pro′log·like′,** *adj.*
—Syn. 5. preamble; beginning, opening; prelude.

pro·logu·ize (prō′lô gīz′, -lo-), *v.i.,* **-ized, -iz·ing.** to compose or deliver a prologue. Also, **pro′log·ize′;** *esp. Brit.,* **pro′logu·ise′.** [1755–65; PROLOGUE + -IZE] **—pro′logu·iz′er,** *n.*

pro·long (prə lông′, -long′), *v.t.* **1.** to lengthen out in time; extend the duration of; cause to continue longer: *to prolong one's stay abroad.* **2.** to make longer in spatial extent: *to prolong a line.* [1375–1425; late ME *prolongen* < LL *prōlongāre* to lengthen, equiv. to *prō-* PRO-¹ + *long(us)* LONG¹ + *-ā-* theme vowel + *-re* inf. ending] **—pro·long′a·ble,** *adj.* **—pro·long′a·ble·ness,** *n.* **—pro·long′a·bly,** *adv.* **—pro·long′er,** *n.* **—pro·long′ment,** *n.*
—Syn. 1. See **lengthen.** **—Ant. 1.** abbreviate.

pro·lon·gate (prə lông′gāt, -long′-), *v.t.,* **-gat·ed, -gat·ing.** to prolong. [1590–1600; < LL *prōlongātus,* ptp. of *prōlongāre* to PROLONG; see -ATE¹]

pro·lon·ga·tion (prō′lông gā′shən, -long-), *n.* **1.** the act of prolonging: *the prolongation of a line.* **2.** the state of being prolonged. **3.** a prolonged or extended form. **4.** an added part. [1480–90; < LL *prōlongātiōn-* (s. of *prōlongātiō*) extension. See PROLONGATE, -ION]

pro·longe (prō lonj′; *Fr.* prô lônzh′), *n., pl.* **-long·es** (-lon′jiz; *Fr.* -lônzh′). *Mil.* a rope having a hook at one end and a toggle at the other, used for various purposes, as to draw a gun carriage. [1855–60; < F, n. deriv. of *prolonger* to PROLONG]

pro·longed-ac·tion (prə lôngd′ak′shən, -longd′-), *adj. Pharm.* sustained-release.

prolonge′ knot′, a knot consisting of three overlapping loops formed by a single rope passed alternately over and under itself at crossings. Also called **sailor's breastplate.** See illus. under **knot.**

pro·lu·sion (prō lo͞o′zhən), *n.* **1.** a preliminary written article. **2.** an essay of an introductory nature, prelimi-

CONCISE PRONUNCIATION KEY: act, cāpe, dâre, pärt; set, ēqual; if, īce; ox, ōver, ôrder, oil, bo͝ok, bo͞ot, out; up, ûrge; child; sing; shoe; thin, *th*at; zh as in *treasure.* ə = *a* as in *alone, e* as in *system, i* as in *easily, o* as in *gallop, u* as in *circus;* ᵊ as in *fire* (fīᵊr), *hour* (ouᵊr). l and n can serve as syllabic consonants, as in *cradle* (krād′l), and *button* (but′n). See the full key inside the front cover.

pro′dis·ar′ma·ment, *adj.*
pro′dis·so·lu′tion, *adj.*
pro′dis·tri·bu′tion, *adj.*
pro′di·vi′sion, *adj.*
pro′di·vorce′, *adj.*
pro′-Do·min′i·can, *adj., n.*
pro-East′, *adj.*
pro-East′ern, *adj.*
pro-Ec′ua·dor′, *adj.*
pro′ed·u·ca′tion, *adj.*
pro′-E·gyp′tian, *adj., n.*
pro′e·lec′tri·fi·ca′tion, *adj.*
pro′e·lim′i·na′tion, *adj.*
pro′-E·liz′a·be′than, *adj.*
pro′-Em·er·so′ni·an, *adj., n.*
pro′em′pire, *adj.*
pro′em·pir′i·cism, *n., adj.*
pro′em·pir′i·cist, *n.*
pro′em·ploy′ee, *adj.*
pro′em·ploy′er, *adj.*
pro′em·ploy′ment, *adj.*
pro′en·force′ment, *adj.*
pro-Eng′lish, *adj.*
pro′en·large′ment, *adj.*
pro′en·vi′ron·men′tal, *adj.*

nary to a more profound work. [1595–1605; < L *prōlūsiōn-* (s. of *prōlūsiō*) preliminary exercise, prelude, equiv. to *prōlūs(us)*, ptp. of *prōlūdere* (*prō-* PRO-¹ + *lūdere* to play; cf. PRELUDE) + *-iōn-* -ION]

pro·lu·so·ry (prō lo͞o′sə rē, -zə-), *adj.* **1.** serving for prolusion. **2.** of the nature of a prolusion. [1865–70; < ML *prōlūsōrius*, equiv. to *prōlūd-*, s. of *prōlūdere* (see PROLUSION) + *-tōrius* -TORY¹, with *dt > s*]

prom (prom), *n.* a formal dance, esp. one held by a high school or college class at the end of an academic year. [1890–95, *Amer.*; short for PROMENADE]

PROM (prom), *n. Computers.* a memory chip whose contents can be programmed by a user or manufacturer for a specific purpose. Cf. **EPROM.** [*p(rogrammable) r(ead)-o(nly) m(emory)*]

prom., promontory.

pro·ma·zine (prō′mə zēn′), *n. Pharm.* a compound, $C_{17}H_{20}N_2S$, used as a tranquilizer. [1955–60; PRO(PYL) + M(ETHYL) + (THI)AZINE, components of its chemical name]

Prome (prōm), *n.* a city in central Burma, on the Irrawaddy River: location of several noted pagodas. 40,000.

pro me·mo·ri·a (prō me mô′ri ä; *Eng.* prō′ mə môr′ē ə, -mōr′-), *Latin.* for memory (used in diplomacy to recall rights that have lapsed for a long time).

prom·e·nade (prom′ə nād′, -näd′), *n., v.,* **-nad·ed, -nad·ing.** —*n.* **1.** a stroll or walk, esp. in a public place, as for pleasure or display. **2.** an area used for such walking. **3.** a march of guests into a ballroom constituting the opening of a formal ball. **4.** a march of dancers in square dancing. **5.** a formal dance; prom. —*v.i.* **6.** to go for or take part in a promenade. **7.** to execute a promenade in square dancing. —*v.t.* **8.** to take a promenade through or about. **9.** to conduct or display in or as if in a promenade; parade: *They promenaded their prisoner before the townspeople.* [1560–70; < F, deriv. of *promener* to lead out, take for a walk or airing < L *prōmināre* to drive (beasts) forward (*prō-* PRO-¹ + *mināre* to drive); see -ADE¹] —**prom′e·nad′er,** *n.*

promenade′ deck′, an upper deck or part of a deck on a passenger ship where passengers can stroll, often covered with a light shade deck. [1820–30, *Amer.*]

promenade′ tile′. See **quarry tile.**

pro·meth·a·zine (prō meth′ə zēn′, -zin), *n. Pharm.* a phenothiaxine derivative, $C_{17}H_{20}N_2S$, used for the symptomatic relief of allergies and in the management of motion sickness. [1950–55; PROPYL + *(di)meth(ylamine)* + (PHENOTHI)AZINE, components of its chemical name]

Pro·me′the·a moth′ (prə mē′thē ə), a silkworm moth, *Callosamia promethea*, having reddish-brown wings, each with a border of white or yellow, the larvae of which feed on spicebush and other lauraceous plants. Also called **spicebush silk moth.** See illus. under **moth.** [1900–05, *Amer.*; < NL, fem. of L *Prometheus* PROMETHEUS]

Pro·me·the·an (prə mē′thē ən), *adj.* **1.** of or suggestive of Prometheus. **2.** creative; boldly original. —*n.* **3.** a person who resembles Prometheus in spirit or action. [1580–90; PROMETHE(US) + -AN]

Pro·me·the·us (prə mē′thē əs, -thyo͞os), *n. Class. Myth.* a Titan, the father of Deucalion and brother of Atlas and Epimetheus, who taught humankind various arts and was sometimes said to have shaped humans out of clay and endowed them with the spark of life. For having stolen fire from Olympus and given it to humankind in defiance of Zeus, he was chained to a rock where an eagle daily tore at his liver, until he was finally released by Hercules.

Prome′theus Bound′, a tragedy (c457 B.C.) by Aeschylus.

Prome′theus Unbound′, a drama in verse (1820) by Shelley.

pro·me·thi·um (prə mē′thē əm), *n. Chem.* a rare-earth, metallic, trivalent element. *Symbol:* Pm; *at. no.:* 61. [1945–50; < NL; see PROMETHEUS, -IUM]

prom·i·nence (prom′ə nəns), *n.* **1.** Also, **prom′i·nen·cy.** the state of being prominent; conspicuousness. **2.** something that is prominent; a projection or protuberance: *a prominence high over a ravine.* **3.** Also called **solar prominence.** *Astron.* an eruption of a flamelike tongue of relatively cool, high-density gas from the solar chromosphere into the corona where it can be seen during a solar eclipse or by observing strong spectral lines in its emission spectrum. [1590–1600; < L *prōminentia* a jutting out, protuberance. See PROMINENT, -ENCE]
—**Syn. 2.** promontory, height, precipice, peak.

prom·i·nent (prom′ə nənt), *adj.* **1.** standing out so as to be seen easily; conspicuous; particularly noticeable: *Her eyes are her most prominent feature.* **2.** standing out beyond the adjacent surface or line; projecting. **3.** leading, important, or well-known: *a prominent citizen.* [1535–45; < L *prōminent-* (s. of *prōminēns*), prp. of *prōminēre* to project, stand out, equiv. to *pro-* PRO-¹ + *-minēre;* see IMMINENT] —**prom′i·nent·ly,** *adv.*
—**Syn. 2.** protruding, jutting, protuberant. **3.** eminent, celebrated, famous, famed, distinguished. —**Ant. 1.** inconspicuous. **2.** recessed. **3.** unknown.

prom·is·cu·i·ty (prom′i skyo͞o′i tē, prō′mi-), *n., pl.* **-ties** for 3. **1.** the state of being promiscuous. **2.** promiscuous sexual behavior. **3.** an indiscriminate mixture. [1840–50; PROMISCU(OUS) + -ITY; cf. F *promiscuité*]

CONCISE ETYMOLOGY KEY: <, descended or borrowed from; >, whence; b., blend of, blended; c., cognate with; cf., compare; deriv., derivative; equiv., equivalent; imit., imitative; obl., oblique; r., replacing; s., stem; sp., spelling, spelled; resp., respelling, respelled; trans., translation; ?, origin unknown; *, unattested; ‡, probably earlier than. See the full key inside the front cover.

pro·mis·cu·ous (prə mis′kyo͞o əs), *adj.* **1.** characterized by or involving indiscriminate mingling or association, esp. having sexual relations with a number of partners on a casual basis. **2.** consisting of parts, elements, or individuals of different kinds brought together without order. **3.** indiscriminate; without discrimination. **4.** casual; irregular; haphazard. [1595–1605; < L *prōmiscuus* mixed up, equiv. to *prō-* PRO-¹ + *misc(ēre)* to MIX + *-uus* deverbal adj. suffix; see -OUS] —**pro·mis′cu·ous·ly,** *adv.* —**pro·mis′cu·ous·ness,** *n.*
—**Syn. 1.** unchaste. **2.** hodgepodge, confused, mixed, jumbled. See **miscellaneous. 3.** careless. —**Ant. 1, 2.** pure. **3.** selective.

prom·ise (prom′is), *n., v.,* **-ised, -is·ing.** —*n.* **1.** a declaration that something will or will not be done, given, etc., by one: *unkept political promises.* **2.** an express assurance on which expectation is to be based: *promises that an enemy will not win.* **3.** something that has the effect of an express assurance; indication of what may be expected. **4.** indication of future excellence or achievement: *a writer who shows promise.* **5.** something that is promised. —*v.t.* **6.** to engage or undertake by promise (usually used with an infinitive or a clause as object): *She promised to go tomorrow.* **7.** to make a promise of (some specified act, gift, etc.): *to promise help.* **8.** to make a promise of something to (a specified person): *Promise me that you will come.* **9.** to afford ground for expecting: *The sky promised a storm.* **10.** to engage to join in marriage. **11.** to assure (used in emphatic declarations): *I won't go there again, I promise you that!* —*v.i.* **12.** to afford ground for expectation (often fol. by *well* or *fair*): *His forthcoming novel promises well.* **13.** to make a promise. [1375–1425; (n.) late ME *promis(se)* < ML *prōmissa*, for L *prōmissum*, n. use of neut. ptp. of *prōmittere* to promise, lit., to send forth, equiv. to *prō-* PRO-¹ + *mittere* to send; (v.) late ME *promisen*, deriv. of the n.] —**prom′is·a·ble,** *adj.* —**prom′ise·ful,** *adj.* —**prom′is·er,** *n.*
—**Syn. 2.** word, pledge. **6.** pledge, covenant, agree.

Prom′ised Land′, 1. Heaven. **2.** Canaan, the land promised by God to Abraham and his descendants. Gen. 12:7. **3.** (*often l.c.*) a place or situation believed to hold ultimate happiness.

prom·is·ee (prom′ə sē′), *n. Law.* a person to whom a promise is made. [1725–35; PROMISE + -EE]

prom·is·ing (prom′ə sing), *adj.* giving favorable promise; likely to turn out well: *a promising young man; a promising situation.* [1505–15; PROMISE + -ING²] —**prom′is·ing·ly,** *adv.* —**prom′is·ing·ness,** *n.*
—**Syn.** favorable, reassuring, encouraging.

prom·i·sor (prom′ə sôr′, prom′ə sôr′), *n. Law.* a person who makes a promise. [1840–50; PROMISE + -OR²]

prom·is·so·ry (prom′ə sôr′ē, -sōr′ē), *adj.* **1.** containing or implying a promise. **2.** of the nature of a promise. **3.** *Insurance.* of or noting agreements or representations stipulating what is required to take place after the issuance of a policy. [1640–50; < ML *prōmissōrius.* See PROMISE, -TORY¹] —**prom′is·so′ri·ly,** *adv.*

prom′issory note′, 1. a written promise to pay a specified sum of money to a designated person or to his or her order, or to the bearer of the note, at a fixed time or on demand. **2.** a written promise to do or provide something, usually presented as a gift and claimable when or however the recipient chooses. [1700–10]

pro·mo (prō′mō), *n., pl.* **-mos,** *adj., v.,* **-moed, -mo·ing.** *Informal.* —*n.* **1.** promotion (def. 5). —*adj.* **2.** of, pertaining to, or involving the promotion of a product, event, etc.; promotional. —*v.t.* **3.** to promote (def. 5). [1960–65; by shortening; cf. -O]

prom·on·to·ry (prom′ən tôr′ē, -tōr′ē), *n., pl.* **-ries. 1.** a high point of land or rock projecting into the sea or other water beyond the line of coast; a headland. **2.** a bluff, or part of a plateau, overlooking a lowland. **3.** *Anat.* a prominent or protuberant part. [1540–50; < L *prōmontorium, prōmunturium,* of unclear derivation]

pro·mote (prə mōt′), *v.t.,* **-mot·ed, -mot·ing. 1.** to help or encourage to exist or flourish; further: *to promote world peace.* **2.** to advance in rank, dignity, position, etc. (opposed to *demote*). **3.** *Educ.* to put ahead to the next higher stage or grade of a course or series of classes. **4.** to aid in organizing (business undertakings). **5.** to encourage the sales, acceptance, etc., of (a product), esp. through advertising or other publicity. **6.** *Informal.* to obtain (something) by cunning or trickery; wangle. [1350–1400; ME *promoten* < L *prōmōtus,* ptp. of *prōmovēre* to move forward, advance. See PRO-¹, MOTIVE] —**pro·mot′able,** *adj.* —**pro·mot′a·bil′i·ty,** *n.*
—**Syn. 1.** abet, back, forward, advance, assist, help, support. **2.** elevate, raise, exalt. —**Ant. 1.** discourage, obstruct. **2.** demote, degrade, abase.

pro·mot·er (prə mō′tər), *n.* **1.** a person or thing that promotes, furthers, or encourages. **2.** a person who initiates or takes part in the organizing of a company, development of a project, etc. **3.** a person who organizes and provides financial backing for a sporting event or entertainment. **4.** *Chem.* any substance that in small amounts is capable of increasing the activity of a catalyst. **5.** Also called **collector.** *Metall.* a water-repellent reagent enhancing the ability of certain ores to float so that they can be extracted by the flotation process. **6.** *Genetics.* **a.** a site on a DNA molecule at which RNA polymerase binds and initiates transcription. **b.** a gene sequence that activates transcription. **7.** *Obs.* an informer. [1400–50; late ME; see PROMOTE, -ER¹; r. earlier *promotour* < AF]

promot′er of the faith′. See **devil's advocate** (def. 2).

pro·mo·tion (prə mō′shən), *n.* **1.** advancement in rank or position. **2.** furtherance or encouragement. **3.** the act of promoting. **4.** the state of being promoted. **5.** something devised to publicize or advertise a product, cause, institution, etc., as a brochure, free sample, poster, television or radio commercial, or personal appearance. **6.** Also called **queening.** *Chess.* the replacement of a pawn that has reached the enemy's first rank by a more powerful piece of the same color, usually a queen. [1400–50; late ME < LL *prōmōtiōn-* (s. of *prōmōtiō*). See PROMOTE, -ION] —**pro·mo′tion·al,** *adj.*

pro·mo·tive (prə mō′tiv), *adj.* tending to promote. [1635–45; PROMOTE + -IVE] —**pro·mo′tive·ness,** *n.*

prompt (prompt), *adj.,* **-er, -est,** *v., n.* —*adj.* **1.** done, performed, delivered, etc., at once or without delay: *a prompt reply.* **2.** ready in action; quick to act as occasion demands. **3.** quick or alert: *prompt to take offense.* **4.** punctual. —*v.t.* **5.** to move or induce to action: *What prompted you to say that?* **6.** to occasion or incite; inspire: *What prompted his resignation?* **7.** to assist (a person speaking) by suggesting something to be said. **8.** *Theat.* to supply (an actor, singer, etc.) from offstage with a missed cue or forgotten line. —*v.i.* **9.** *Theat.* to supply forgotten lines, lyrics, or the like to an actor, singer, etc. —*n.* **10.** *Com.* **a.** a limit of time given for payment for merchandise purchased, the limit being stated on a note of reminder **(prompt′ note′). b.** the contract setting the time limit. **11.** the act of prompting. **12.** something serving to suggest or remind. **13.** *Computers.* a message or symbol from a computer system to a user, generally appearing on a display screen, requesting more information or indicating that the system is ready for user instructions. **14. take a prompt,** (in acting) to move or speak in response to a cue. [1300–50; (v.) ME < ML *promptāre* to incite, L: to distribute, freq. of *prōmere* to bring out, equiv. to *prō-* PRO-¹ + *(e)mere* to take, buy; (adj.) late ME < L *promptus* ready, prompt, special use of ptp. of *prōmere*] —**prompt′ly,** *adv.* —**prompt′ness,** *n.*
—**Syn. 5.** urge, spur, instigate, impel.

prompt·book (prompt′bo͝ok′), *n. Theat.* a copy of the script of a play, containing cues and notes, used by the prompter, stage manager, etc. [1800–10; PROMPT + BOOK]

prompt·er (promp′tər), *n.* **1.** a person or thing that prompts. **2.** *Theat.* a person who is offstage and follows a play in progress from the book, repeating missed cues and supplying actors with forgotten lines. **3.** an electronic or mechanical device for prompting a speaker or performer. Cf. **TelePrompTer.** [1400–50; late ME; see PROMPT, -ER¹]

promp·ti·tude (promp′ti to͞od′, -tyo͞od′), *n.* promptness. [1400–50; late ME < LL *prōmptitūdō.* See PROMPT, -I-, -TUDE]

prompt′ side′, *Theat.* the part of the stage that in the U.S. is to the right and in Britain to the left as one faces the audience. *Abbr.:* P.S. Also, **prompt′-side′.** [1830–40]

prom·ul·gate (prom′əl gāt′, prō mul′gāt), *v.t.,* **-gat·ed, -gat·ing. 1.** to make known by open declaration; publish; proclaim formally or put into operation (a law, decree of a court, etc.). **2.** to set forth or teach publicly (a creed, doctrine, etc.). [1520–30; < L *prōmulgātus,* ptp. of *prōmulgāre* to PROMULGE; see -ATE¹] —**prom·ul·ga·tion** (prom′əl gā′shən, prō′məl-), *n.* —**prom′ul·ga′·tor,** *n.*
—**Syn. 1.** announce, issue, declare. **2.** advocate.

pro·mulge (prō mulj′), *v.t.,* **-mulged, -mulg·ing.** *Archaic.* to promulgate. [1480–90; < L *prōmulgāre* to make known, promulgate, equiv. to *prō-* PRO-¹ + *-mulgāre,* prob. akin to *mulgēre* to milk, extract] —**pro·mulg′er,** *n.*

pro·my·ce·li·um (prō′mī sē′lē əm), *n., pl.* **-li·a** (-lē ə). *Mycol.* a short filament produced in the germination of a spore that bears small spores and then dies. [1865–70; < NL; see PRO-¹, MYCELIUM] —**pro′my·ce′li·al,** *adj.*

pron., 1. pronominal. **2.** pronoun. **3.** pronounced. **4.** pronunciation.

pro·na·os (prō nā′os), *n., pl.* **-na·oi** (-nā′oi). (in a classical temple) an open vestibule before the cella. Also called **anticum.** Cf. **epinaos.** [1605–15; < Gk *prónāos.* See PRO-², NAOS]

pro·na·tal·ism (prō nāt′l iz′əm), *n.* the policy or practice of encouraging the bearing of children, esp. government support of a higher birthrate. [1935–40; PRO-¹ + NATAL (in a sense perh. influenced by F *natalité* birthrate) + -ISM] —**pro·na′tal·ist,** *n., adj.* —**pro·na′tal·is′tic,** *adj.*

pro·nate (prō′nāt), *v.,* **-nat·ed, -nat·ing.** —*v.t.* **1.** to turn into a prone position; to rotate (the hand or forearm) so that the surface of the palm is downward or toward the back; to turn (the sole of the foot) outward so that the inner edge of the foot bears the weight when standing. **2.** (in vertebrates) to rotate (any limb or joint) in a similar manner. —*v.i.* **3.** to become pronated. [1830–40; < LL *prōnātus,* ptp. of *prōnāre* to bend forward, deriv. of L *prōnus;* see PRONE¹, -ATE¹]

pro·na·tion (prō nā′shən), *n.* **1.** rotation of the hand or forearm so that the surface of the palm is facing downward or toward the back (opposed to *supination*). **2.** a comparable motion of the foot consisting of abduction followed by eversion. **3.** the position assumed as the result of this rotation. **4.** any similar motion of the limbs or feet of animals. [1660–70; PRONATE + -ION]

pro·na·tor (prō′nā tər, prō nā′-), *n. Anat., Zool.* any of several muscles that permit pronation of the hand, forelimb, or foot. [1720–30; PRONATE + -OR²]

prone¹ (prōn), *adj.* **1.** having a natural inclination or tendency to something; disposed; liable: *to be prone to anger.* **2.** having the front or ventral part downward; lying face downward. **3.** lying flat; prostrate. **4.** having a downward direction or slope. **5.** having the palm

pro′e·qual′i·ty, *adj.*
pro-Es′ki·mo′, *adj., n., pl.* **-mos, -mo.**
pro′-E·thi·o′pi·an, *adj., n.*
pro′-Eu·ro·pe′an, *adj., n.*
pro′eu·tha·na′sia, *adj.*
pro′ev·o·lu′tion, *adj.*
pro′ev·o·lu′tion·ar′y, *adj.*
pro′ev·o·lu′tion·ist, *adj., n.*
pro′ex·ec′u·tive, *adj.*
pro′ex·per′i·ment, *adj.*
pro′ex·per′i·men·ta′tion, *adj.*
pro·ex′pert, *adj.*
pro′ex·ten′sion, *adj.*
pro·fac′ul·ty, *adj.*
pro·farm′, *adj.*
pro·farm′er, *adj.*
pro·fas′cism, *n.*
pro·fas′cist, *adj., n.*
pro′fed·er·a′tion, *adj.*
pro·fem′i·nism, *n.*
pro·fem′i·nist, *n., adj.*
pro·fic′tion, *adj.*
pro-Finn′ish, *adj.*

downward, as the hand. [1350–1400; ME < L *prōnus* turned or leaning forward, inclined downward, disposed, prone] —**prone′ly,** *adv.* —**prone′ness,** *n.*
—**Syn. 1.** apt, subject, tending. **3.** recumbent.

prone[2] (prōn), *n.* a sermon or a brief hortatory introduction to a sermon, usually delivered at a service at which the Eucharist is celebrated. [1660–70; < F *prône* grill, grating (separating chancel from nave); so called because notices and addresses were delivered there]

prone′ float′. See **dead-man's float.**

pro•neph•ros (prō nef′ros, -rəs), *n., pl.* **-roi** (-roi), **-ra** (-rə). *Embryol.* one of the three embryonic excretory organs of vertebrates, which becomes the functional kidney of certain primitive fishes. Cf. **mesonephros, metanephros.** [1875–80; < NL < Gk *pro-* PRO-[2] + *nephrós* kidney] —**pro•neph•ric** (prō nef′rik), *adj.*

prone′ pres′sure meth′od, a method of artificial respiration in which the patient is placed face downward, pressure then being rhythmically applied with the hands to the lower part of the thorax. Also called **Schafer method, Schafer's method.**

prong (prông, prong), *n.* **1.** one of the pointed tines of a fork. **2.** any pointed, projecting part, as of an antler. **3.** a branch of a stream. **4.** *Jewelry.* a tapering metal projection, usually heavier than a claw, rising from the base of a jewelry setting and used to hold a stone in position as needed. Cf. **claw** (def. 7). —*v.t.* **5.** to pierce or stab with or as if with a prong. **6.** to supply with prongs. [1400–50; late ME *pronge, prange* pain, affliction, pointed instrument; akin to OSw *prang* gorge, narrow street, MLG *prange* stake, *prangen* to press, Goth *anaprangan* to oppress]
—**Syn. 2.** hook, tooth, spur.

pronged (prôngd, prongd), *adj.* having prongs (often used in combination): *a four-pronged fork.* [1760–70; PRONG + -ED[3]]

prong•horn (prông′hôrn′, prong′-), *n., pl.* **-horns,** (*esp. collectively*) **-horn.** a fleet, antelopelike ruminant, *Antilocapra americana,* of the plains of western North America: now greatly reduced in number and endangered in some areas. Also called **prong′horn an′telope.** [1805–15; PRONG + HORN]

pronghorn, *Antilocapra americana,* 3 ft. (0.9 m) high at shoulder; horns 12 to 15 in. (30 to 38 cm); length 5½ ft. (1.7 m)

pro•nom•i•nal (prō nom′ə nl), *adj.* **1.** *Gram.* pertaining to, resembling, derived from, or containing a pronoun: *"My" in "my book" is a pronominal adjective. "There" is a pronominal adverb.* **2.** *Heraldry.* noting the coat of arms on a quartered escutcheon: customarily occupying the first quarter and being the original coat of arms of the paternal line. —*n.* **3.** *Gram.* a pronominal word. [1635–45; < LL *prōnōminālis.* See PRONOUN, -AL[1]] —**pro•nom′i•nal•ly,** *adv.*

pro•nom•i•nal•ize (prō nom′ə nl īz′), *v.t.,* **-ized, iz•ing.** to replace (a noun or noun phrase) with a pronoun. Also, *esp. Brit.,* **pro•nom′i•nal•ise′.** [PRONOMINAL + -IZE] —**pro•nom′i•nal•i•za′tion.** *n.*

pro•no•tum (prō nō′təm), *n., pl.* **-ta** (-tə). the dorsal sclerite of the prothorax of an insect. [1830–40; < NL; see PRO-[1], NOTUM]

pro•noun (prō′noun′), *n. Gram.* any member of a small class of words found in many languages that are used as replacements or substitutes for nouns and noun phrases, and that have very general reference, as *I, you, he, this, who, what.* Pronouns are sometimes formally distinguished from nouns, as in English by the existence of special objective forms, as *him* for *he* or *me* for *I,* and by nonoccurrence with an article or adjective. [1520–30; < MF *pronom* < L *prōnōmen* (s. *prōnōmin-*). See PRO-[1], NOUN]

pro•nounce (prə nouns′), *v.,* **-nounced, -nounc•ing.** —*v.t.* **1.** to enunciate or articulate (sounds, words, sentences, etc.). **2.** to utter or sound in a particular manner in speaking: *He pronounces his words indistinctly.* **3.** to utter or articulate in the accepted or correct manner: *I can't pronounce this word.* **4.** to declare (a person or thing) to be as specified: *She pronounced it the best salmon she had ever tasted.* **5.** to utter or deliver formally or solemnly: *to pronounce sentence.* **6.** to announce authoritatively or officially: *The judge pronounced the defendant guilty.* **7.** to indicate the pronunciation of (words) by providing a phonetic transcription: *This dictionary pronounces most of the words entered.* —*v.i.* **8.** to pronounce words, phrases, etc. **9.** to make a statement or assertion, esp. an authoritative statement (often fol. by *on*): *He was required to pronounce on the findings of his research.* **10.** to give an opinion or decision (usually fol. by *on*): *to pronounce on an important matter.* **11.** to indicate the pronunciation of words: *a spelling book that pronounces.* [1300–50; ME *pronouncen* < MF *prononcier* < L *prōnūntiāre* to proclaim, announce, recite, utter. See PRO-[1], ANNOUNCE] —**pro•nounce′a•ble,** *adj.* —**pro•nounce′a•ble•ness,** *n.* —**pro•nounc′er,** *n.*

pro•nounced (prə nounst′), *adj.* **1.** strongly marked: *a pronounced fishy taste.* **2.** clearly indicated: *a pronounced contrast.* **3.** decided; unequivocal: *pronounced views.* [1570–80; PRONOUNCE + -ED[2]] —**pro•nounc•ed•ly** (prə noun′sid lē, -nounst′lē), *adv.* —**pro•nounc′ed•ness,** *n.*
—**Syn. 1.** distinct, unmistakable.

pro•nounce•ment (prə nouns′mənt), *n.* **1.** a formal or authoritative statement. **2.** an opinion or decision. **3.** act of pronouncing. [1585–95; PRONOUNCE + -MENT]

pron•to (pron′tō), *adv. Informal.* promptly; quickly. [1840–50, *Amer.*; < Sp (adj. and adv.) quick, quickly < L *promptus* PROMPT (adj.)]

pro•nu•cle•ar[1] (prō no͞o′klē ər, -nyo͞o′- *or, by metathesis,* -kyə lər), *adj.* **1.** advocating the building or use of nuclear power plants. **2.** advocating the building, stockpiling, or use of nuclear weapons. [1970–75; PRO-[1] + NUCLEAR]
—**Pronunciation.** See **nuclear.**

pro•nu•cle•ar[2] (prō no͞o′klē ər, -nyo͞o′- *or, by metathesis,* -kyə lər), *adj. Cell Biol.* of or pertaining to a pronucleus. [1885–90; PRONUCLE(US) + -AR[1]]

pro•nu•cle•us (prō no͞o′klē əs, -nyo͞o′-), *n., pl.* **-cle•i** (-klē ī′). *Cell Biol.* either of the gametic nuclei that unite in fertilization to form the nucleus of the zygote. [1875–80; < NL; see PRO-[1], NUCLEUS]

pro•nuke (prō no͝ok′, -nyo͝ok′), *Informal.* —*adj.* **1.** pronuclear[1]. —*n.* **2.** Also, **pro•nuk′er.** a person who advocates the building or use of nuclear power plants or nuclear weapons. [1975–80; PRO-[1] + NUKE]

pro•nun•ci•a•men•to (prə nun′sē ə men′tō, -shē ə-), *n., pl.* **-tos.** a proclamation; manifesto; edict. [1825–35; < Sp *pronunciamiento* < L *prōnūntiā(re)* to PRONOUNCE + *-mentum* -MENT]

pro•nun•ci•a•tion (prə nun′sē ā′shən), *n.* **1.** the act or result of producing the sounds of speech, including articulation, stress, and intonation, often with reference to some standard of correctness or acceptability. **2.** an accepted standard of the sound and stress patterns of a syllable, word, etc.: *He said the pronunciation of "curl" is* (kûrl), *not* (koil). **3.** the conventional patterns of treatment of the sounds of a language: *the pronunciation of French.* **4.** a phonetic transcription of a given word, sound, etc.: *The pronunciation of "pheasant" is* (fez′ənt). [1400–50; late ME *pronunciacion* < L *prōnūntiātiōn-* (s. of *prōnūntiātiō*) delivery (of a speech), equiv. to *prōnūntiāt(us)* (ptp. of *prōnūntiāre* to PRONOUNCE; see -ATE[1]) + *-iōn-* -ION] —**pro•nun′ci•a′tion•al, pro•nun•ci•a•to•ry** (prə nun′sē ə tôr′ē, -tōr′ē), **pro•nun′ci•a′tive,** *adj.*

pro′ny brake′ (prō′nē), a friction brake serving as a dynamometer for measuring torque. [named after G.C.F.M. Riche, Baron de *Prony* (d. 1839), French engineer]

pro•oes•trus (prō es′trəs, -ē′strəs), *n.* proestrus.

proof (pro͞of), *n.* **1.** evidence sufficient to establish a thing as true, or to produce belief in its truth. **2.** anything serving as such evidence: *What proof do you have?* **3.** the act of testing or making trial of anything; test; trial: *to put a thing to the proof.* **4.** the establishment of the truth of anything; demonstration. **5.** *Law.* (in judicial proceedings) evidence having probative weight. **6.** the effect of evidence in convincing the mind. **7.** an arithmetical operation serving to check the correctness of a calculation. **8.** *Math., Logic.* a sequence of steps, statements, or demonstrations that leads to a valid conclusion. **9.** a test to determine the quality, durability, etc., of materials used in manufacture. **10.** *Distilling.* **a.** the arbitrary standard strength, as of an alcoholic liquor. **b.** strength with reference to this standard: "100 proof" signifies a proof spirit, usually 50% alcohol. **11.** *Photog.* a trial print from a negative. **12.** *Print.* **a.** a trial impression, as of composed type, taken to correct errors and make alterations. **b.** one of a number of early and superior impressions taken before the printing of the ordinary issue: *to pull a proof.* **13.** (in printmaking) an impression taken from a plate or the like to show the quality or condition of work during the process of execution; a print pulled for examination while working on a plate, block, stone, etc. **14.** *Numis.* one of a limited number of coins of a new issue struck from polished dies on a blank having a polished or matte surface. **15.** the state of having been tested and approved. **16.** proved strength, as of armor. **17.** *Scot. Law.* the trial of a case by a judge alone, without a jury. —*adj.* **18.** able to withstand; successful in not being overcome: *proof against temptation.* **19.** impenetrable, impervious, or invulnerable: *proof against outside temperature changes.* **20.** used for testing or proving; serving as proof. **21.** of standard strength, as an alcoholic liquor. **22.** of tested or proven strength or quality: *proof armor.* **23.** noting pieces of pure gold and silver that the U.S. assay and mint offices use as standards. —*v.t.* **24.** to test; examine for flaws, errors, etc.; check against a standard or standards. **25.** *Print.* prove (def. 7). **26.** to proofread. **27.** to treat or coat for the purpose of rendering resistant to deterioration, damage, etc. (often used in combination): *to proof a house against termites; to shrink-proof a shirt.* **28.** *Cookery.* **a.** to test the effectiveness of (yeast), as by combining with warm water so that a bubbling action occurs. **b.** to cause (esp. bread dough) to rise due to the addition of baker's yeast or other leavening. [1175–1225; ME *prove, prooff, prof, proufe,* alter. (by assoc. with the vowel of PROVE) of *preove, proeve, prieve, pref* < MF *preve, proeve, prueve* < LL *proba* a test, akin to L *probāre* to test and find good; cf. PREE]
—**Syn. 1.** confirmation, demonstration, corroboration, support. See **evidence. 3.** examination, assay. **18.** firm, steadfast.

-proof, a combining form meaning "resistant, impervious to" that specified by the initial element: *burglarproof; childproof; waterproof.*

proof•ing (pro͞o′fing), *n.* **1.** the act or process of making a thing resistant, as in waterproof fabrics or fireproof material. **2.** any chemical used in the manufacture of a substance to make it proof against water, fire, etc. [1900–05; PROOF + -ING[1]]

proof-of-pur•chase (pro͞of′əv pûr′chəs), *n., pl.* **proofs-of-pur•chase.** a sales slip, label, box top, or other item associated with a product that is presentable as evidence of actual purchase, as for claiming a refund or rebate.

proof•read (pro͞of′rēd′), *v.,* **-read** (-red′), **-read•ing.** —*v.t.* **1.** to read (printers' proofs, copy, etc.) in order to detect and mark errors to be corrected. —*v.i.* **2.** to read printers' proofs, copy, etc., to detect and mark errors, esp. as an employee of a typesetting firm, newspaper office, or publishing house. See table of **Proofreader's Marks** in back matter. [1930–35; back formation from *proofreader* (see PROOF, READ)] —**proof′read′er,** *n.*

proof′ sheet′, **1.** a printer's proof. **2.** *Photog.* a contact print. Cf. **contact sheet.** [1615–25]

proof′ spir′it, an alcoholic liquor, or mixture of alcohol and water, containing a standard amount of alcohol. In the U.S. proof spirit has a specific gravity of .93353 (containing one half of its volume of alcohol of a specific gravity of .7939 at 60° F). In Britain proof spirit has a specific gravity of .91984. [1735–45]

proof′ stress′, the load per unit area that a structure can withstand without being permanently deformed by more than a specified amount. [1860–65]

prop[1] (prop), *v.,* **propped, prop•ping,** *n.* —*v.t.* **1.** to support, or prevent from falling, with or as if with a prop (often fol. by *up*): *to prop an old fence; to prop up an unpopular government.* **2.** to rest (a thing) against a support: *He propped his cane against the wall.* **3.** to support or sustain (often fol. by *up*). —*n.* **4.** a stick, rod, pole, beam, or other rigid support. **5.** a person or thing serving as a support or stay: *His father is his financial prop.* [1400–50; late ME *proppe* (n.); c. MD *proppe* bottle stopper]
—**Syn. 1.** brace, buttress, bolster.

prop[2] (prop), *n. Theat.* property (def. 8). [1910–15; by shortening] —**prop′less,** *adj.*

prop[3] (prop), *n.* a propeller. [1910–15; by shortening]

prop., **1.** properly. **2.** property. **3.** proposition. **4.** proprietary. **5.** proprietor.

pro•pae•deu•tic (prō′pi do͞o′tik, -dyo͞o′-), *adj.* Also, **pro′pae•deu′ti•cal. 1.** pertaining to or of the nature of preliminary instruction. **2.** introductory to some art or science. —*n.* **3.** a propaedeutic subject or study. **4.** **propaedeutics,** (*used with a singular v.*) the preliminary body of knowledge and rules necessary for the study of some art or science. [1830–40; PRO-[2] + Gk *paideutikós* pertaining to teaching, equiv. to *paideú(ein)* to teach (deriv. of *paîs* child; cf. PEDO-[1]) + *-tikos* -TIC]

prop•a•ga•ble (prop′ə gə bəl), *adj.* capable of being propagated. [1645–55; < ML *propāgābilis.* See PROPAGATE, -BLE] —**prop′a•ga•bil′i•ty, prop′a•ga•ble•ness,** *n.*

prop•a•gan•da (prop′ə gan′də), *n.* **1.** information, ideas, or rumors deliberately spread widely to help or harm a person, group, movement, institution, nation, etc. **2.** the deliberate spreading of such information, rumors, etc. **3.** the particular doctrines or principles propagated by an organization or movement. **4.** *Rom. Cath. Ch.* **a.** a committee of cardinals, established in 1622 by Pope Gregory XV, having supervision over foreign missions and the training of priests for these missions. **b.** a school **(College of Propaganda)** established by Pope Urban VIII for the education of priests for foreign missions. **5.** *Archaic.* an organization or movement for the spreading of propaganda. [1710–20; < NL, short for *congregātiō dē propāgandā fidē* congregation for propagating the faith; *propāgandā,* abl. sing. fem. gerundive of *propāgāre;* see PROPAGATE]

prop•a•gan•dist (prop′ə gan′dist), *n.* **1.** a person involved in producing or spreading propaganda. **2.** a member or agent of a propaganda. —*adj.* **3.** Also, **prop′a•gan•dis′tic.** pertaining to propaganda or propagandists. [1790–1800; PROPAGAND(A) + -IST] —**prop′a•gan′dism,** *n.* —**prop′a•gan•dis′ti•cal•ly,** *adv.*

prop•a•gan•dize (prop′ə gan′dīz), *v.,* **-dized, -diz•ing.** —*v.t.* **1.** to propagate or publicize (principles, dogma, etc.) by means of propaganda. **2.** to subject to propaganda: *to propagandize enemy countries.* —*v.i.* **3.** to carry on or disseminate propaganda. Also, *esp. Brit.,* **prop′a•gan′dise.** [1835–45; PROPAGAND(A) + -IZE]

prop•a•gate (prop′ə gāt′), *v.,* **-gat•ed, -gat•ing.** —*v.t.* **1.** to cause (an organism) to multiply by any process of natural reproduction from the parent stock. **2.** to reproduce (itself, its kind, etc.), as an organism does. **3.** to transmit (hereditary features or elements) to, or through, offspring. **4.** to spread (a report, doctrine, practice, etc.) from person to person; disseminate. **5.** to cause to increase in number or amount. **6.** to create (an effect) at a distance, as by electromagnetic waves, compression waves, etc., traveling through space or a physical medium; transmit: *to propagate sound.* —*v.i.* **7.** to multiply by any process of natural reproduction, as organisms; breed. **8.** to increase in extent, as a structural

CONCISE PRONUNCIATION KEY: act, cāpe, dâre, pärt; set, ēqual; if, īce; ox, ōver, ôrder, oil, bo͝ok, bo͞ot, out; up, ûrge; child; sing; shoe; thin, that; zh as in *treasure.* ə = *a* as in *alone, e* as in *system, i* as in *easily, o* as in *gallop, u* as in *circus;* ᵊ as in *fire* (fīᵊr), *hour* (ouᵊr). l and n can serve as syllabic consonants, as in *cradle* (krād′l), and *button* (but′n). See the full key inside the front cover.

pro-Flor′en•tine′, *adj.*
pro•for′eign, *adj.*
pro-France′, *adj.*
pro-French′, *adj.*
pro-Freud′, *adj.*
pro-Freud′i•an, *adj., n.*
pro-Gael′ic, *adj.*
pro•gam′bling, *adj.*
pro-Gen′tile, *adj., n.*
pro-Ger′man, *adj., n.*
pro-Gha′na, *adj.*
pro-Goth′ic, *adj.*
pro-gov′ern•ment, *adj.*
pro-Gre′cian, *adj.*
pro-Greek′, *adj., n.*
pro′-Gua•te•ma′lan, *adj., n.*
pro-Hai′tian, *adj.*
pro′-Ha•wai′ian, *adj.*
pro′-Hel•len′ic, *adj.*
pro-Hin′du, *adj.*
pro-Hit′ler, *adj.*
pro′-Hon•du′ran, *adj., n.*
pro′-Hun•gar′i•an, *adj., n.*
pro′-Ice•lan′dic, *adj.*

flaw: *The crack will propagate only to this joint.* **9.** (of electromagnetic waves, compression waves, etc.) to travel through space or a physical medium. [1560–70; < L *propāgātus* (ptp. of *propāgāre* to reproduce (a plant) by cuttings, spread for sprouting, propagate, enlarge), equiv. to *propāg(ēs)* something set out, scion, slip (*pro-* PRO-[1] + *pāg-*, base of *pangere* to fasten + *-ēs* n. suffix) + *-ātus* -ATE[1]] **—prop′a·ga′tive, prop·a·ga·to·ry** (prop′ə gə tôr′ē, -tōr′ē), *adj.* **—prop′a·ga′tor,** *n.*

prop·a·ga·tion (prop′ə gā′shən), *n.* **1.** the act of propagating. **2.** the fact of being propagated. **3.** multiplication by natural reproduction. **4.** transmission or dissemination. [1400–50; late ME *propagacyon* < L *propāgātiōn-* (s. of *propāgātiō*). See PROPAGATE, -ION] **—prop′a·ga′tion·al,** *adj.*
—Syn. 4. spreading, dispersion, diffusion.

prop·a·gule (prop′ə gyo͞ol′), *n. Bot., Mycol.* any structure capable of being propagated or acting as an agent of reproduction. Also, **pro·pag·u·lum** (prō pag′yə ləm). [1855–60; < NL *propāgulum*, deriv. of *propāgō* shoot, runner; see PROPAGATE, -ULE]

pro·pane (prō′pān), *n. Chem.* a colorless, flammable gas, C_3H_8, of the alkane series, occurring in petroleum and natural gas: used chiefly as a fuel and in organic synthesis. Also called **dimethylmethane.** [1866; PROP(IONIC) + -ANE]

pro·pane·di·o·ic (prō′pān dī ō′ik), *adj. Chem.* malonic. [PROPANE + DI-[1] + -O- + -IC]

pro·pa·nil (prō′pə nil), *n. Chem.* a postemergence herbicide, $C_9H_9Cl_2NO$, used for weed control on potatoes, rice, and other crop plants. [PROP(IONIC) + ANIL(IDE)]

pro′pa·no′ic ac′id (prō′pə nō′ik, prō′-), *Chem.* See **propionic acid.** [PROPANE + -O- + -IC]

pro·pan′the·line bro′mide (prō pan′thə lēn′, -lin), *n. Pharm.* a substance, $C_{23}H_{30}BrNO_3$, used in the treatment of peptic ulcers. [1950–55; by rearrangement of parts of its chemical name]

pro·par·ox·y·tone (prō′pa rok′si tōn′), *Class. Gk. Gram.* **—adj. 1.** having an accent or heavy stress on the antepenultimate syllable. **—n. 2.** a proparoxytone word. [1755–65; < Gk *proparoxýtonos.* See PRO-[2], PAROXYTONE] **—pro·par·ox·y·ton·ic** (prō′pa rok′si ton′ik), *adj.*

pro pa·tri·a (prō pä′tri ä′; *Eng.* prō pā′trē ə, pa′-), *Latin.* for one's country.

pro·pel (prə pel′), *v.t.,* **-pelled, -pel·ling. 1.** to drive, or cause to move, forward or onward: *to propel a boat by rowing.* **2.** to impel or urge onward: *Urgent need of money propelled him to take a job.* [1400–50; late ME *propellen* to expel < L *prōpellere* to drive forward, equiv. to *prō-* PRO-[1] + *pellere* to drive]
—Syn. 1, 2. push, prod.

pro·pel·lant (prə pel′ənt), *n.* **1.** a propelling agent. **2.** the charge of explosive used to propel the projectile from a gun. **3.** a substance, usually a mixture of fuel and oxidizer, for propelling a rocket. **4.** a compressed inert gas that serves to dispense the contents of an aerosol container when the pressure is released. [1915–20; PROPEL + -ANT]

pro·pel·lent (prə pel′ənt), *adj.* **1.** serving or tending to propel or drive forward. **—n. 2.** a propellant. [1635–45; < L *prōpellent-* (s. of *prōpellēns*), prp. of *prōpellere* to drive forward. See PROPEL, -ENT]

pro·pel·ler (prə pel′ər), *n.* **1.** a device having a revolving hub with radiating blades, for propelling an airplane, ship, etc. **2.** a person or thing that propels. **3.** the bladed rotor of a pump that drives the fluid axially. **4.** a wind-driven, usually three-bladed, device that provides mechanical energy, as for driving an electric alternator in wind plants. [1770–80; PROPEL + -ER[1]]

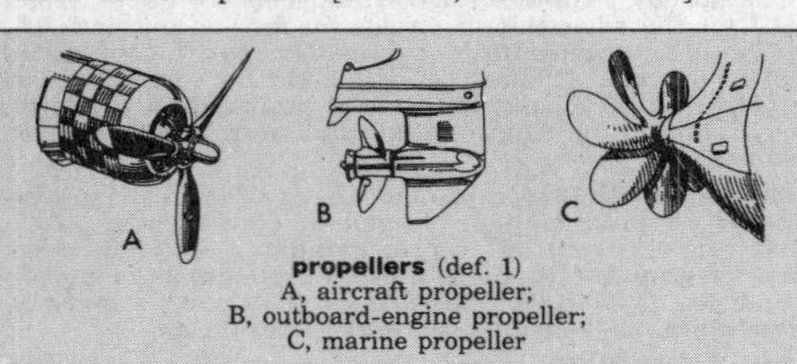

propellers (def. 1)
A, aircraft propeller;
B, outboard-engine propeller;
C, marine propeller

propel′ler horse′power, a measure of the power actually available for driving a propeller after all wasted energy is deducted.

propel′ler shaft′, 1. a shaft that transmits power from an engine to a propeller. **2.** a drive shaft. [1830–40]

propel′ler wash′, *Aeron.* the backwash from a propeller.

pro·pend (prō pend′), *v.i. Obs.* to incline or tend. [1535–45; < L *prōpendēre* to hang down, be inclined. See PRO-[1], PEND]

pro·pene (prō′pēn), *n. Chem.* propylene (def. 2). [1865–70; PROP(IONIC) + -ENE]

pro·pense (prō pens′), *adj. Archaic.* having a tendency toward; prone; inclined. [1520–30; < L *prōpēnsus,* ptp. of *prōpendēre* to PROPEND] **—pro·pense′ly,** *adv.* **—pro·pense′ness** *n.*

pro·pen·sion (prə pen′shən), *n. Archaic.* propensity. [1520–30; < L *prōpēnsiōn-* (s. of *prōpēnsiō*) inclination. See PROPENSE, -ION]

pro·pen·si·ty (prə pen′si tē), *n., pl.* **-ties. 1.** a natural inclination or tendency: *a propensity to drink too much.* **2.** *Obs.* favorable disposition or partiality. [1560–70; PROPENSE + -ITY]
—Syn. 1. bent, leaning, disposition, penchant, proclivity.

pro·pe·nyl (prō′pə nil), *adj. Chem.* containing the propenyl group. Also, **pro′pe·nyl′ic.** [1865–70; PROPENE + -YL]

pro′penyl al′cohol, *Chem.* See **allyl alcohol.**

pro′penyl group′, *Chem.* a univalent group derived from propylene, $CH_3CH{=}CH-$. Also called **pro′penyl rad′ical.**

prop·er (prop′ər), *adj.* **1.** adapted or appropriate to the purpose or circumstances; fit; suitable: *the proper time to plant strawberries.* **2.** conforming to established standards of behavior or manners; correct or decorous: *a very proper young man.* **3.** fitting; right: *It was only proper to bring a gift.* **4.** strictly belonging or applicable: *the proper place for a stove.* **5.** belonging or pertaining exclusively or distinctly to a person, thing, or group. **6.** strict; accurate. **7.** in the strict sense of the word (usually used postpositively): *Shellfish do not belong to the fishes proper. Is the school within Boston proper or in the suburbs?* **8.** *Gram.* **a.** (of a name, noun, or adjective) designating a particular person or thing and written in English with an initial capital letter, as *Joan, Chicago, Monday, American.* **b.** having the force or function of a proper name: *a proper adjective.* **9.** normal or regular. **10.** belonging to oneself or itself; own. **11.** *Chiefly Brit. Informal.* complete or thorough: *a proper thrashing.* **12.** *Eccles.* used only on a particular day or festival: *the proper introit.* **13.** *Heraldry.* (of a device) depicted in its natural colors: *an oak tree proper.* **14.** *Informal.* **a.** excellent; capital; fine. **b.** good-looking or handsome. **15.** *Math.* (of a subset of a set) not equal to the whole set. **16.** *Archaic.* of good character; respectable. **—adv. 17.** *Informal.* thoroughly; completely. **—n. 18.** *Eccles.* a special office or special parts of an office appointed for a particular day or time. [1250–1300; ME *propre* < OF < L *proprius* one's own] **—prop′er·ly,** *adv.* **—prop′er·ness,** *n.*
—Syn. 1. suited. **2, 3.** meet, befitting, becoming, decent, polite. **5.** special, individual, peculiar. **6.** precise, exact, just, formal.

prop′er ad′jective, *Gram.* an adjective formed from a proper noun, as *American* from *America.* [1900–05]

prop′er frac′tion, *Math.* a fraction having the numerator less, or lower in degree, than the denominator. [1665–75]

prop′er func′tion, *Math.* eigenfunction. [1930–35]

prop′er mo′tion, *Astron.* the angular motion of a star relative to a suitably defined frame of reference, expressed in seconds of arc per year. Cf. **tangential motion.** [1595–1605]

prop′er noun′, *Gram.* a noun that is not normally preceded by an article or other limiting modifier, as *any* or *some,* and that is arbitrarily used to denote a particular person, place, or thing without regard to any descriptive meaning the word or phrase may have, as *Lincoln, Beth, Pittsburgh.* Also called **prop′er name′.** Cf. **common noun.** [1490–1500]

prop·er·tied (prop′ər tēd), *adj.* owning property: *the propertied class.* [1600–10; PROPERTY + -ED[3]]

Pro·per·ti·us (prō pûr′shē əs, -shəs), *n.* **Sex·tus** (seks′təs), c50–c15 B.C., Roman poet.

prop·er·ty (prop′ər tē), *n., pl.* **-ties. 1.** that which a person owns; the possession or possessions of a particular owner: *They lost all their property in the fire.* **2.** goods, land, etc., considered as possessions: *The corporation is a means for the common ownership of property.* **3.** a piece of land or real estate: *property on Main Street.* **4.** ownership; right of possession, enjoyment, or disposal of anything, esp. of something tangible: *to have property in land.* **5.** something at the disposal of a person, a group of persons, or the community or public: *The secret of the invention became common property.* **6.** an essential or distinctive attribute or quality of a thing: *the chemical and physical properties of an element.* **7.** *Logic.* **a.** any attribute or characteristic. **b.** (in Aristotelian logic) an attribute not essential to a species but always connected with it and with it alone. **8.** Also called **prop.** a usually movable item, other than costumes or scenery, used on the set of a theater production, motion picture, etc.; any object handled or used by an actor in a performance. **9.** a written work, play, movie, etc., bought or optioned for commercial production or distribution. **10.** a person, esp. one under contract in entertainment or sports, regarded as having commercial value: *an actor who was a hot property at the time.* [1275–1325; ME *proprete* possession, attribute, what is one's own, equiv. to *propre* PROPER + *-te* -TY[2]. See PROPRIETY] **—prop′er·ty·less,** *n.*
—Syn. 1. belongings. PROPERTY, CHATTELS, EFFECTS, ESTATE, GOODS refer to what is owned. PROPERTY is the general word: *She owns a great deal of property. He said that the umbrella was his property.* CHATTELS is a term for pieces of personal property or movable possessions; it may be applied to livestock, automobiles, etc.: *a mortgage on chattels.* EFFECTS is a term for any form of personal property, including even things of the least value: *All his effects were insured against fire.* ESTATE refers to property of any kind that has been, or is capable of being, handed down to descendants or otherwise disposed of in a will: *He left most of his estate to his niece.* It may consist of personal estate (money, valuables, securities, chattels, etc.), or real estate (land and buildings). GOODS refers to household possessions or other movable property, esp. that comprising the stock in trade of a business: *The store arranged its goods on shelves.* **3.** acreage. **6.** feature. See **quality.**

prop′erty right′, a legal right to or in a particular property. [1940–45]

prop′erty tax′, a tax levied on real or personal property. [1800–10]

prop′er val′ue, *Math.* See **characteristic root.** [1925–30]

prop·fan (prop′fan′), *n. Aeron.* a turbojet having a turbine-driven propeller that operates completely outside the jet engine. Cf. **turbofan, turboprop.** [1965–70; PROP[3] + FAN[1]]

pro·phage (prō′fāj′), *n. Microbiol.* a stable, inherited form of bacteriophage in which the genetic material of the virus is integrated into, replicated, and expressed with the genetic material of the bacterial host. [1950–55; shortening of F *probactériophage;* see PRO-[1], BACTERIOPHAGE]

pro·phase (prō′fāz′), *n. Cell Biol.* the first stage of mitosis or meiosis in eukaryotic cell division, during which the nuclear envelope breaks down and strands of chromatin form into chromosomes. [1880–85; PRO-[1] + PHASE]

proph·e·cy (prof′ə sē), *n., pl.* **-cies. 1.** the foretelling or prediction of what is to come. **2.** something that is declared by a prophet, esp. a divinely inspired prediction, instruction, or exhortation. **3.** a divinely inspired utterance or revelation: *oracular prophecies.* **4.** the action, function, or faculty of a prophet. [1175–1225; ME *prophecie* < OF < LL *prophētia* < Gk *prophēteía.* See PROPHET, -Y[3]]

proph·e·sy (prof′ə sī′), *v.,* **-sied, -sy·ing. —v.t. 1.** to foretell or predict. **2.** to indicate beforehand. **3.** to declare or foretell by or as if by divine inspiration. **4.** to utter in prophecy or as a prophet. **—v.i. 5.** to make predictions. **6.** to make inspired declarations of what is to come. **7.** to speak as a mediator between God and humankind or in God's stead. **8.** *Archaic.* to teach religious subjects. [1350–1400; ME; v. use of var. of PROPHECY (fully distinguished in form and meaning in the 18th century)] **—proph′e·si′a·ble,** *adj.* **—proph′e·si′er,** *n.*
—Syn. 1. augur, prognosticate. See **predict. 3.** divine.

proph·et (prof′it), *n.* **1.** a person who speaks for God or a deity, or by divine inspiration. **2.** (in the Old Testament) **a.** a person chosen to speak for God and to guide the people of Israel: *Moses was the greatest of Old Testament prophets.* **b.** (*often cap.*) one of the Major or Minor Prophets. **c.** one of a band of ecstatic visionaries claiming divine inspiration and, according to popular belief, possessing magical powers. **d.** a person who practices divination. **3.** one of a class of persons in the early church, next in order after the apostles, recognized as inspired to utter special revelations and predictions. 1 Cor. 12:28. **4. the Prophet,** Muhammad, the founder of Islam. **5.** a person regarded as, or claiming to be, an inspired teacher or leader. **6.** a person who foretells or predicts what is to come: *a weather prophet; prophets of doom.* **7.** a spokesperson of some doctrine, cause, or movement. [1150–1200; ME *prophete* < LL *prophēta* < Gk *prophḗtēs,* equiv. to *pro-* PRO-[2] + *-phētēs* speaker, deriv. of *phánai* to speak] **—proph′et·hood′,** *n.* **—proph′et·less,** *adj.* **—proph′et·like′,** *adj.*

proph·et·ess (prof′i tis), *n.* **1.** a woman who speaks for God or a deity, or by divine inspiration. **2.** a woman who foretells future events. **3.** a woman who is a spokesperson of some doctrine, cause, or movement. **4.** the wife or female companion of a prophet. [1250–1300; ME *prophetesse* < OF < LL *prophētissa.* See PROPHET, -ESS]
—Usage. See **-ess.**

pro·phet·ic (prə fet′ik), *adj.* **1.** of or pertaining to a prophet: *prophetic inspiration.* **2.** of the nature of or containing prophecy: *prophetic writings.* **3.** having the function or powers of a prophet, as a person. **4.** predictive; presageful or portentous; ominous: *prophetic signs; prophetic warnings.* Also, **pro·phet′i·cal.** [1585–95; < LL *prophēticus* < Gk *prophētikós.* See PROPHET, -IC] **—pro·phet′i·cal′i·ty, pro·phet′i·cal·ness,** *n.* **—pro·phet′i·cal·ly,** *adv.*

Proph·ets (prof′its), *n.* (*used with a singular v.*) the canonical group of books that forms the second of the three Jewish divisions of the Old Testament, comprising Joshua, Judges, I and II Samuel, I and II Kings, Isaiah, Jeremiah, Ezekiel, Hosea, Joel, Amos, Obadiah, Jonah, Micah, Nahum, Habakkuk, Zephaniah, Haggai, Zechariah, and Malachi. Cf. **Law of Moses, Hagiographa.**

pro·phy·lac·tic (prō′fə lak′tik, prof′ə-), *adj.* **1.** defending or protecting from disease or infection, as a drug. **2.** preventive or protective. **—n. 3.** *Med.* a prophylactic medicine or measure. **4.** a preventive. **5.** a device, usually a rubber sheath, used to prevent conception or venereal infection; condom. [1565–75; < Gk *prophylaktikós* of guarding, equiv. to *prophylak-* (base of *prophylássein* to guard beforehand) + *-tikos* -TIC. See PROPHYLAXIS] **—pro′phy·lac′ti·cal·ly,** *adv.*

pro·phy·lax·is (prō′fə lak′sis, prof′ə-), *n.* **1.** *Med.* **a.** the preventing of disease. **b.** the prevention of a specific disease, as by studying the biological behavior, transmission, etc., of its causative agent and applying a series of measures against it. **2.** prophylactic treatment, as the cleaning of the teeth by a dentist or dental hygienist. [1835–45; < NL < Gk *pro-* PRO-[2] + *phýlaxis* a watching, guarding, equiv. to *phylak-* (base of *phylássein* to guard) + *-sis* -SIS]

CONCISE ETYMOLOGY KEY: <, descended or borrowed from; >, whence; b., blend of, blended; c., cognate with; cf., compare; deriv., derivative; equiv., equivalent; imit., imitative; obl., oblique; r., replacing; s., stem; sp., spelling, spelled; resp., respelling, respelled; trans., translation; ?, origin unknown; *, unattested; ‡, probably earlier than. See the full key inside the front cover.

pro′im·mi·gra′tion, *adj.*
pro·in′crease, *adj.*
pro-In′di·an, *adj.*
pro′-In·do·ne′sian, *adj.*
pro′in·dus′tri·al, *adj.*
pro′in·dus′tri·al·i·za′tion, *adj.*
pro·in′dus·try, *adj.*
pro′in·sur′ance, *adj.*
pro′in·te·gra′tion, *adj.*
pro′in·ter·ven′tion, *adj.*
pro′in·vest′ment, *adj.*
pro′-I·ra′ni·an, *adj., n.*
pro′-I·raq′, *adj.*
pro′-I·ra′qi, *n., adj.*
pro-I′rish, *adj.*
pro′ir·ri·ga′tion, *adj.*
pro-Is′ra·el, *adj.*
pro′-Is·rae′li, *n., adj.*
pro′-I·tal′ian, *adj., n.*
pro′-Jac·o·be′an, *adj.*
pro′-Jap·a·nese′, *adj., n., pl.* **-nese.**
pro′-Jef·fer·so′ni·an, *adj.*
pro-Jew′ish, *adj.*

pro•pine (*v.* prō pēn′; *n.* prō pēn′, -pīn′), *v.*, **-pined, -pin•ing,** *n. Scot.* —*v.t.* **1.** to offer as a present. —*n.* **2.** a present; gift. [1400–50; late ME *propinen* < MF *propiner* to give to drink, drink one's health < L *propināre* < Gk *propínein* to drink first, equiv. to *pro-* PRO-² + *pínein* to drink]

pro•pin•qui•ty (prō ping′kwi tē), *n.* **1.** nearness in place; proximity. **2.** nearness of relation; kinship. **3.** affinity of nature; similarity. **4.** nearness in time. [1350–1400; ME *propinquite* < L *propinquitās* nearness, equiv. to *propinqu(us)* near (*prop(e)* near (see PRO-¹) + *-inquus* adj. suffix) + *-itās* -ITY]

pro•pi•on•al•de•hyde (prō′pē on al′də hīd′), *n. Chem.* a colorless, water-soluble liquid, C_3H_6O, having a pungent odor: used chiefly in the manufacture of plastics. Also called **propyl aldehyde.** [PROPION(IC) + ALDEHYDE]

pro•pi•o•nate (prō′pē ə nāt′), *n. Chem.* an ester or salt of propionic acid. [1860–65; PROPION(IC ACID) + -ATE²]

pro•pi•on•i•bac•te•ri•um (prō′pē on′ə bak tēr′ē əm, -ō′nə-), *n., pl.* **-te•ri•a** (-tēr′ē ə). *Bacteriol.* any of several aerobic or anaerobic bacteria of the genus *Propionibacterium,* found in dairy products, esp. hard cheeses where certain species are associated with the ripening process. [< NL (1909); see PROPIONIC, BACTERIUM]

pro•pi•on•ic (prō′pē on′ik, -ō′nik), *adj. Chem.* of or derived from propionic acid. [1840–50; PRO-² + Gk *pīon-* (s. of *píōn*) fat + -IC]

pro′pion′ic ac′id, *Chem., Pharm.* a colorless, oily, water-soluble liquid, $C_3H_6O_2$, having a pungent odor: used in making bread-mold-inhibiting propionates, in perfumery, and in medicine as a topical fungicide. Also, **propanoic acid.** Also called **methylacetic acid.** [1850–55]

pro•pi•ti•ate (prə pish′ē āt′), *v.t.* **-at•ed, -at•ing.** to make favorably inclined; appease; conciliate. [1635–45; < L *propitiātus,* ptp. of *propitiāre* to appease. See PROPITIOUS, -ATE¹] —**pro•pi•ti•a•ble** (prə pish′ē ə bəl), *adj.* —**pro•pi′ti•at′ing•ly,** *adv.* —**pro•pi′ti•a′tive,** *adj.* —**pro•pi′ti•a′tor,** *n.*
—**Syn.** See **appease.** —**Ant.** anger, arouse.

pro•pi•ti•a•tion (prə pish′ē ā′shən), *n.* **1.** the act of propitiating; conciliation: *the propitiation of the wrathful gods.* **2.** something that propitiates. [1350–1400; ME *propiciacioun* < LL *propitiātiōn-* (s. of *propitiātiō*) appeasement. See PROPITIATE, -ION]

pro•pi•ti•a•to•ry (prə pish′ē ə tôr′ē, -tōr′ē), *adj.* **1.** serving or intended to propitiate. **2.** making propitiation; conciliatory. —*n.* **3.** See **mercy seat.** [1275–1325; (n.) ME *propiciatori* the mercy seat < LL *propitiātōrium* (see PROPITIATE, -TORY²); (adj.) < LL *propitiātōrius* (see -TORY¹)] —**pro•pi′ti•a•to′ri•ly,** *adv.*

pro•pi•tious (prə pish′əs), *adj.* **1.** presenting favorable conditions; favorable: *propitious weather.* **2.** indicative of favor; auspicious: *propitious omens.* **3.** favorably inclined; disposed to bestow favors or forgive: *propitious gods.* [1400–50; late ME *propicius* < L *propitius* favorably inclined, propitious, prob. equiv. to *pro-* PRO-¹ + *-pit-,* comb. form of *petere* to head for, resort to, solicit + *-ius* adj. suffix; see -OUS] —**pro•pi′tious•ly,** *adv.* —**pro•pi′tious•ness,** *n.*

prop•jet (prop′jet′), *n. Aeron.* an airplane equipped with turboprops. [1945–50; PROP³ + JET¹]

prop′jet en′gine. See **turbo-propeller engine.** [1960–65]

prop•man (prop′man′), *n., pl.* **-men.** a person responsible for securing, handling, and storing the properties used in a theatrical, motion-picture, or television production. [1930–35; PROP³ + MAN¹]
—**Usage.** See **-man.**

prop•o•lis (prop′ə lis), *n.* a reddish resinous cement collected by bees from the buds of trees, used to stop up crevices in the hives, strengthen the cells, etc. Also called **bee glue.** [1350–1400; < L < Gk *própolis* bee glue, lit., outskirts of a city (see PRO-², -POLIS), appar. orig. the name for a structure around the entrance to a hive, hence applied to the glue from which it was made; r. ME *propoleos* < ML, for L *propolis* as above]

pro•pone (prə pōn′), *v.t.,* **-poned, -pon•ing.** *Scot.* **1.** to suggest for consideration; propose. **2.** to present before a jury or judge; plead for or request (an official decision). [1325–75; ME *proponen* < L *prōpōnere* to set forth, PROPOUND. See PROPOSE]

pro•po•nent (prə pō′nənt), *n.* **1.** a person who puts forward a proposition or proposal. **2.** a person who argues in favor of something; an advocate. **3.** a person who supports a cause or doctrine; adherent. **4.** a person who propounds a legal instrument, such as a will for probate. [1580–90; < L *prōpōnent-* (s. of *prōpōnēns*). See PROPONE, -ENT]
—**Syn. 2, 3.** supporter, champion, enthusiast.

pro•por•tion (prə pôr′shən, -pōr′-), *n.* **1.** comparative relation between things or magnitudes as to size, quantity, number, etc.; ratio. **2.** proper relation between things or parts: *to have tastes way out of proportion to one's financial means.* **3.** relative size or extent. **4. proportions,** dimensions or size: *a rock of gigantic proportions.* **5.** a portion or part in its relation to the whole: *A large proportion of the debt remains.* **6.** symmetry, harmony, or balance: *an architect with a sense of proportion.* **7.** the significance of a thing or event that an objective view reveals: *You must try to see these mishaps in proportion.* **8.** *Math.* a relation of four quantities such that the first divided by the second is equal to the third divided by the fourth; the equality of ratios. Cf. **rule of three. 9.** *Archaic.* analogy; comparison. —*v.t.* **10.** to adjust in proper proportion or relation, as to size, quantity, etc. **11.** to balance or harmonize the proportions of. [1350–1400; ME *proporcio(u)n* < L *prōportiōn-* (s. of *prōportiō*) symmetry, analogy. See PRO-¹, PORTION] —**pro•por′tion•er,** *n.* —**pro•por′tion•less,** *adj.*
—**Syn. 1.** comparison. **5.** share. **6.** distribution, arrangement. See **symmetry. 10.** regulate, arrange, balance, harmonize.

pro•por•tion•a•ble (prə pôr′shə nə bəl, -pōr′-), *adj.* being in due proportion; proportional. [1350–1400; ME *proporcionable* < LL *prōportiōnābilis.* See PROPORTION, -ABLE] —**pro•por′tion•a•bil′i•ty, pro•por′tion•a•ble•ness,** *n.* —**pro•por′tion•a•bly,** *adv.*

pro•por•tion•al (prə pôr′shə nl, -pōr′-), *adj.* **1.** having due proportion; corresponding. **2.** being in or characterized by proportion. **3.** of, pertaining to, or based on proportion; relative. **4.** *Math.* **a.** (of two quantities) having the same or a constant ratio or relation: *The quantities* y *and* x *are proportional if* y/x = k, *where* k *is the constant of proportionality.* **b.** (of a first quantity with respect to a second quantity) a constant multiple of: *The quantity* y *is proportional to* x *if* y = kx, *where* k *is the constant of proportionality.* [1350–1400; ME *proporcional* < L *prōportiōnālis.* See PROPORTION, -AL¹] —**pro•por′tion•al′i•ty,** *n.* —**pro•por′tion•al•ly,** *adv.*
—**Syn. 1.** harmonious, comparative, accordant, consonant, proportionate.

propor′tional count′er, *Physics.* a radiation counter in which the strength of each electric pulse generated per count is proportional to the energy of the particle or photon producing the pulse, alpha particles producing a different electric pulse from beta rays. [1935–40]

propor′tional lim′it, *Physics.* See **elastic limit.** [1945–50]

propor′tional representa′tion, a method of voting by which political parties are given legislative representation in proportion to their popular vote. [1865–70]

pro•por•tion•ate (*adj.* prə pôr′shə nit, -pōr′-; *v.* prə-pôr′shə nāt′, -pōr′-), *adj., v.,* **-at•ed, -at•ing.** —*adj.* **1.** proportioned; being in due proportion; proportional. —*v.t.* **2.** to make proportionate. [1350–1400; ME *proporcionate* < LL *prōportiōnātus.* See PROPORTION, -ATE¹] —**pro•por′tion•ate•ly,** *adv.* —**pro•por′tion•ate•ness,** *n.*
—**Syn. 1.** according, accordant, consonant, harmonious, balanced.

pro•por•tioned (prə pôr′shənd, -pōr′-), *adj.* **1.** adjusted to proper proportion or relation. **2.** having proportions as specified: *a badly proportioned room.* [1350–1400; ME *proporcioned.* See PROPORTION, -ED²]

pro•por•tion•ment (prə pôr′shən mənt, -pōr′-), *n.* **1.** the act of proportioning. **2.** the state of being proportioned. [1690–1700; PROPORTION + -MENT]

pro•pos•al (prə pō′zəl), *n.* **1.** the act of offering or suggesting something for acceptance, adoption, or performance. **2.** a plan or scheme proposed. **3.** an offer or suggestion of marriage. [1645–55; PROPOSE + -AL²]
—**Syn. 1.** recommendation. **2.** suggestion, design. PROPOSAL, OVERTURE, PROPOSITION refer to something in the nature of an offer. A PROPOSAL is a plan, a scheme, an offer to be accepted or rejected: *to make proposals for peace.* An OVERTURE is a friendly approach, an opening move (perhaps involving a proposal) tentatively looking toward the settlement of a controversy or else preparing the way for a proposal or the like: *to make overtures to an enemy.* PROPOSITION, used in mathematics to refer to a formal statement of truth, and often including the proof or demonstration of the statement, has something of this same meaning when used nontechnically (particularly in business). A PROPOSITION is a PROPOSAL in which the terms are clearly stated and their advantageous nature emphasized: *His proposition involved a large discount to the retailer.*

pro•pose (prə pōz′), *v.,* **-posed, -pos•ing.** —*v.t.* **1.** to offer or suggest (a matter, subject, case, etc.) for consideration, acceptance, or action: *to propose a new method.* **2.** to offer (a toast). **3.** to suggest: *He proposed that a messenger be sent.* **4.** to present or nominate (a person) for some position, office, membership, etc. **5.** to put before oneself as something to be done; design; intend. **6.** to present to the mind or attention; state. **7.** to propound (a question, riddle, etc.). —*v.i.* **8.** to make an offer or suggestion, esp. of marriage. **9.** to form or consider a purpose or design. [1300–50; ME < MF *proposer* (see PRO-¹, POSE¹), by assoc. with derivatives of L *prōpositus,* ptp. of *prōpōnere* to set forth. See PROPOSITUS] —**pro•pos′a•ble,** *adj.* —**pro•pos′er,** *n.*
—**Syn. 1.** proffer, tender, suggest, recommend, present. **4.** name. **5.** plan. See **intend. 6.** pose, posit.
—**Ant. 1.** withdraw.

prop•o•si•tion (prop′ə zish′ən), *n.* **1.** the act of offering or suggesting something to be considered, accepted, adopted, or done. **2.** a plan or scheme proposed. **3.** an offer of terms for a transaction, as in business. **4.** a thing, matter, or person considered as something to be dealt with or encountered: *Keeping diplomatic channels open is a serious proposition.* **5.** anything stated or affirmed for discussion or illustration. **6.** *Rhet.* a statement of the subject of an argument or a discourse, or of the course of action or essential idea to be advocated. **7.** *Logic.* a statement in which something is affirmed or denied, so that it can therefore be significantly characterized as either true or false. **8.** *Math.* a formal statement of either a truth to be demonstrated or an operation to be performed; a theorem or a problem. **9.** a proposal of usually illicit sexual relations. —*v.t.* **10.** to propose sexual relations to. **11.** to propose a plan, deal, etc., to. [1300–50; ME *proposicio(u)n* < L *prōpositiōn-* (s. of *prōpositiō*) a setting forth. See PROPOSITUS, -ION] —**prop′o•si′tion•al,** *adj.* —**prop′o•si′tion•al•ly,** *adv.*
—**Syn. 2.** See **proposal.**

proposi′tional cal′culus, *Logic.* See **sentential calculus.** [1900–05]

proposi′tional func′tion, *Logic.* See **sentential function.** [1900–05]

pro•pos•i•tus (prə poz′i təs), *n., pl.* **-ti** (-tī′). **1.** *Law.* the person from whom a line of descent is derived on a genealogical table. **2.** *Genetics.* proband. [1925–30; < NL, special use of ptp. of L *prōpōnere* to set forth, PROPOUND]

pro•pound (prə pound′), *v.t.* to put forward or offer for consideration, acceptance, or adoption; set forth; propose: *to propound a theory.* [1545–55; later var. of ME *propone* (see PROPONE) < L *prōpōnere* to set forth, equiv. to *prō-* PRO-¹ + *pōnere* to put, place, set. See COMPOUND¹, EXPOUND] —**pro•pound′er,** *n.*

pro•pox•ur (prō pok′sər), *n. Chem.* a crystalline compound, $C_{11}H_{15}NO_3$, used as a nonsystemic insecticide against a wide variety of insects. [1960–65; PROP(YL) + OX(Y)-² + UR(ETHANE)]

pro•pox•y•phene (prō pok′sə fēn′), *n. Pharm.* a nonnarcotic analgesic, $C_{22}H_{29}NO_2$. [1950–55; PROP(IONATE) + OXY-² + (DI)PHEN(YL)]

propr., proprietor.

pro•prae•tor (prō prē′tər), *n. Rom. Hist.* an officer who, after having served as praetor in Rome, was sent to govern a province with praetorial authority. Also, **pro•pre′tor.** [1570–80; < L *prōpraetor;* see PRO-¹, PRAETOR] —**pro•prae•to•ri•al** (prō′pri tôr′ē əl, -tōr′-), **pro′prae•to′ri•an,** *adj.*

pro•pran•o•lol (prō pran′ə lôl′, -lol′), *n. Pharm.* a beta-blocking drug, $C_{16}H_{21}NO_2$, used in the treatment of hypertension, angina pectoris, and cardiac arrhythmias. [1960–65; PRO(PYL) + PR(OP)ANOL + -OL¹]

pro•pri•e•tar•y (prə prī′i ter′ē), *adj., n., pl.* **-tar•ies.** —*adj.* **1.** belonging to a proprietor. **2.** being a proprietor; holding property: *the proprietary class.* **3.** pertaining to property or ownership: *proprietary wealth.* **4.** belonging or controlled as property. **5.** manufactured and sold only by the owner of the patent, formula, brand name, or trademark associated with the product: *proprietary medicine.* **6.** privately owned and operated for profit: *proprietary hospitals.* —*n.* **7.** an owner or proprietor. **8.** a body of proprietors. **9.** *Amer. Hist.* the grantee or owner, or one of the grantees or owners, of a proprietary colony. **10.** ownership. **11.** something owned, esp. real estate. **12.** a proprietary medicine. **13.** Also called **propri′etary school′.** a school organized as a profit-making venture primarily to teach vocational skills or self-improvement techniques. [1400–50; late ME (n.) < ML *proprietārius* owner, n. use of LL: of an owner, of ownership. See PROPRIETY, -ARY] —**pro•pri•e•tar•i•ly** (prə prī′i târ′i lē, -prī′i ter′-), *adv.*

propri′etary col′ony, *Amer. Hist.* any of certain colonies, as Maryland and Pennsylvania, that were granted to an individual or group by the British crown and that were granted full rights of self-government. Cf. **charter colony, royal colony.**

pro•pri•e•tor (prə prī′i tər), *n.* **1.** the owner of a business establishment, a hotel, etc. **2.** a person who has the exclusive right or title to something; an owner, as of real property. **3.** a group of proprietors; proprietary. [1630–40; PROPRIET(ARY) + -OR²] —**pro•pri•e•to•ri•al** (prə prī′i tôr′ē əl, -tōr′-), *adj.* —**pro•pri′e•to′ri•al•ly,** *adv.* —**pro•pri′e•tor•ship′,** *n.*

pro•pri•e•tress (prə prī′i tris), *n.* **1.** a woman who owns a business establishment. **2.** a woman who has the exclusive right or title to something. [1685–95; PROPRIET(O)R + -ESS]
—**Usage.** See **-ess.**

pro•pri•e•trix (prə prī′i triks), *n.* proprietress. [1830–40; PROPRIE(TOR) + -TRIX]
—**Usage.** See **-trix.**

pro•pri•e•ty (prə prī′i tē), *n., pl.* **-ties.** **1.** conformity to established standards of good or proper behavior or manners. **2.** appropriateness to the purpose or circumstances; suitability. **3.** rightness or justness. **4. the proprieties,** the conventional standards of proper behavior; manners: *to observe the proprieties.* **5.** *Obs.* a property. **6.** *Obs.* a peculiarity or characteristic of something. [1425–75; late ME *propriete* ownership, something owned, one's own nature (cf. var. *proprete* PROPERTY) < MF *propriété* < L *proprietās* peculiarity, ownership, equiv. to *propri(us)* PROPER + *-etās,* var., after vowels, of *-itās* -ITY]
—**Syn. 1.** decency, modesty. See **etiquette. 2.** aptness, fitness, seemliness. **3.** correctness.

proprio-, a combining form meaning "one's own," used in the formation of compound words: *proprioceptive.* [comb. form repr. L *proprius* one's own, special, particular, PROPER]

pro•pri•o•cep•tion (prō′prē ə sep′shən), *n. Physiol.* perception governed by proprioceptors, as awareness of the position of one's body. [1905–10; PROPRIO- + (RE)CEPTION]

pro•pri•o•cep•tive (prō′prē ə sep′tiv), *adj. Physiol.* pertaining to proprioceptors, the stimuli acting upon them, or the nerve impulses initiated by them. [1905–10; PROPRIO- + (RE)CEPTIVE]

pro•pri•o•cep•tor (prō′prē ə sep′tər), *n. Physiol.* a receptor located in subcutaneous tissues, as muscles, tendons, and joints, that responds to stimuli produced within the body. [1905–10; PROPRIO- + (RE)CEPTOR]

pro•pri•o mo•tu (prô′pri ō′ mō′tōō; *Eng.* prō′prē ō′

CONCISE PRONUNCIATION KEY: act, cāpe, dâre, pärt; set, ēqual; if, īce; ox, ōver, ôrder, oil, bŏŏk, bōōt, out; up, ûrge; child; sing; shoe; thin, *th*at; zh as in *treasure.* ə = *a* as in *alone, e* as in *system, i* as in *easily, o* as in *gallop, u* as in *circus;* ᵊ as in *fire* (fīᵊr), *hour* (ouᵊr). l and n can serve as syllabic consonants, as in *cradle* (krād′l), and *button* (but′n). See the full key inside the front cover.

pro-Jor′dan, *adj.*
pro′-Ko•re′an, *adj., n.*
pro′-Ko•weit′, *adj.*
pro′-Ku•wait′, *adj.*
pro•la′bor, *adj.*
pro-La′os, *adj.*
pro′-La•o′tian, *adj., n.*
pro-Lat′in, *adj.*
pro′-Leb•a•nese′, *adj., n., pl.* **-nese.**
pro′-Li•be′ri•an, *adj., n.*
pro-Lib′y•an, *adj., n.*
pro′-Mad•a•gas′can, *adj., n.*
pro′-Ma•lay′an, *adj., n.*
pro′-Ma•lay′sian, *adj., n.*
pro•man′age•ment, *adj.*
pro•mar′riage, *adj.*
pro•merg′er, *adj.*
pro-Meth′od•ist, *adj., n.*
pro•met′ric, *adj.*
pro-Mex′i•can, *adj., n.*
pro•mil′i•ta•rism, *adj.*
pro•mil′i•ta•rist, *adj., n.*
pro•mil′i•tar′y, *adj.*
pro′mi•nor′i•ty, *adj.*

mō′tōō), *Latin.* by one's own volition; on one's own initiative.

prop′ root′, *Bot.* an adventitious root that supports the plant, as the aerial roots of the mangrove tree or of corn. Also called **brace root.** [1900–05]

prop·ter hoc (prôp′ter hôk′; *Eng.* prop′tər hok′), *Latin.* because of this. Cf. ***post hoc.***

prop·to·sis (prop tō′sis), *n. Pathol.* **1.** the forward displacement of an organ. **2.** exophthalmos. [1670–80; < NL < Gk *próptōsis* a fall forward. See PRO-², PTOSIS] **—prop·tosed** (prop′tōst), **prop·tot·ic** (prop tot′ik), *adj.*

pro·pul·sion (prə pul′shən), *n.* **1.** the act or process of propelling. **2.** the state of being propelled. **3.** a means of propelling; propelling force, impulse, etc. [1605–15; < L *prōpuls(us)* (ptp. of *prōpellere* to PROPEL) + -ION] **—pro·pul·sive** (prə pul′siv), **pro·pul′so·ry,** *adj.*

prop′ wash′, *Informal.* See **propeller wash.** Also, **prop′wash′.** [1940–45]

pro·pyl (prō′pil), *adj. Chem.* containing a propyl group. [1840–50; PROP(IONIC) + -YL]

prop·y·lae·um (prop′ə lē′əm), *n., pl.* **-lae·a** (-lē′ə). Often, **propylaea.** a vestibule or entrance to a temple area or other enclosure, esp. when elaborate or of architectural importance. Also, **propylon.** [1700–10; < L < Gk *propýlaion* gateway, n. use of neut. of *propýlaios* before the gate, equiv. to *pro-* PRO-² + *pýl(ē)* gate + *-aios* adj. suffix]

pro′pyl al′cohol, *Chem.* a colorless, water-soluble liquid, C_3H_8O, used chiefly in organic synthesis and as a solvent. [1865–70]

pro′pyl al′dehyde, *Chem.* propionaldehyde.

pro·pyl·ene (prō′pə lēn′), *Chem.* **—adj. 1.** containing the propylene group. **—n. 2.** Also, **propene.** a colorless, flammable gas, C_3H_6, of the olefin series: used chiefly in organic synthesis. [1840–50; PROPYL + -ENE]

pro′pylene gly′col, *Chem.* a colorless, viscous, hygroscopic liquid, $C_3H_8O_2$, used chiefly as a lubricant, as an antifreeze, as a heat transfer fluid, and as a solvent for fats, oils, waxes, and resins. [1880–85]

pro′pylene group′, *Chem.* the bivalent group $-CH(CH_3)CH_2-$, derived from propylene or propane. Also called **pro′pylene rad′ical.**

pro′pyl group′, *Chem.* any of two univalent, isomeric groups having the formula C_3H_7-. Also called **pro′pyl rad′ical.** Cf. **isopropyl group.**

pro·pyl·hex·e·drine (prō′pil hek′si drēn′), *n. Pharm.* a colorless, adrenergic, water-soluble liquid, $C_{10}H_{21}N$, used by inhalation as a nasal decongestant. [PROPYL + HEX- + (EPH)EDRINE]

pro·pyl·ic (prō pil′ik), *adj.* of, pertaining to, or characteristic of the propyl group. [1840–50; PROPYL + -IC]

prop·y·lite (prop′ə līt′), *n. Petrog.* a hydrothermally altered andesite or allied rock containing secondary minerals, as calcite, chlorite, serpentine, or epidote. [1867; PROPYL + -ITE¹]

prop·y·lon (prop′ə lon′), *n.* propylaeum. [1825–35; < Gk *própylon,* equiv. to *pro-* PRO-² + *pýl(ē)* gate + *-on* neut. sing. n. ending]

pro′pyl·phen′yl ac′etate (prō′pəl fen′l, -fēn′l, prō′-), *Chem.* See **phenylpropyl acetate.** [PROPYL + PHENYL]

pro·pyl·thi·o·u·ra·cil (prō′pil thī′ō yŏŏr′ə sil), *n. Pharm.* a white crystalline compound, $C_7H_{10}N_2OS$, that interferes with the synthesis of thyroid hormone by the thyroid gland: used in the treatment of hyperthyroidism. [PROPYL + THIOURACIL]

pro ra·ta (prō rā′tə, rä′-), in proportion; according to a certain rate. [1565–75; < ML *prō ratā*]

pro-ra·ta (prō rā′tə, -rä′-), *adj.* proportionately determined: *a pro-rata share of income.*

pro·rate (prō rāt′, prō′rāt′), *v.,* **-rat·ed, -rat·ing.** *—v.i.* **1.** to make an arrangement on a basis of proportional distribution. *—v.t.* **2.** to divide, distribute, or calculate proportionately. [1855–60, *Amer.*; partial trans. of PRO RATA] **—pro·rat′a·ble,** *adj.* **—pro·ra′tion,** *n.*

pro re na·ta (prō′ re′ nä′tä; *Eng.* prō′ rē′ nā′tə, rā′), *Latin.* for an unforeseen need or contingency. [lit., for a thing born]

pro·rogue (prō rōg′), *v.t.,* **-rogued, -ro·guing. 1.** to discontinue a session of (the British Parliament or a similar body). **2.** to defer; postpone. [1375–1425; late ME *proroge* < L *prōrogāre* to prolong, protract, defer, lit., to ask publicly, equiv. to *prō-* PRO-¹ + *rogāre* to ask, propose] **—pro·ro·ga·tion** (prō′rə gā′shən), *n.*
—Syn. 1. suspend.

pros., 1. proscenium. **2.** prosody.

pro·sa·ic (prō zā′ik), *adj.* **1.** commonplace or dull; matter-of-fact or unimaginative: *a prosaic mind.* **2.** of or having the character or form of prose rather than poetry. Also, **pro·sa′i·cal.** [1650–60; LL *prōsaicus.* See PROSE, -IC] **—pro·sa′i·cal·ly,** *adv.* **—pro·sa′ic·ness,** *n.*
—Syn. 1. ordinary, everyday; vapid, humdrum, tedious, tiresome, uninteresting.

pro·sa·ism (prō zā′iz əm), *n.* **1.** prosaic character or style. **2.** a prosaic expression. Also, **pro·sa·i·cism** (prō zā′ə siz′əm). [1780–90; < F *prosaïsme* see PROSE, -ISM]

CONCISE ETYMOLOGY KEY: <, descended or borrowed from; >, whence; b., blend of, blended; c., cognate with; cf., compare; deriv., derivative; equiv., equivalent; imit., imitative; obl., oblique; r., replacing; s., stem; sp., spelling, spelled; resp., respelling, respelled; trans., translation; ?, origin unknown; *, unattested; ‡, probably earlier than. See the full key inside the front cover.

pro·sa·ist (prō zā′ist), *n.* **1.** a person who writes prose. **2.** a prosaic, dull, or commonplace person. [1795–1805; < L *prōsa* PROSE + -IST]

pros′ and cons′, the favorable and the unfavorable factors or reasons; advantages and disadvantages.

pro·sa·teur (prō′zə tûr′), *n.* a person who writes prose, esp. as a livelihood. [1875–80; < F < It *prosatore;* see PROSE, -ATOR, -EUR]

Pros. Atty., prosecuting attorney.

pro·sce·ni·um (prō sē′nē əm, prə-), *n., pl.* **-ni·a** (-nē ə). *Theat.* **1.** Also called **prosce′nium arch′.** the arch that separates a stage from the auditorium. *Abbr.:* pros. **2.** (formerly) the apron or, esp. in ancient theater, the stage itself. [1600–10; < L *proscēnium, proscaenium* < Gk *proskḗnion* entrance to a tent, porch, stage (LGk: stage curtain), equiv. to *pro-* PRO-² + *skēn(ē)* (see SCENE) + *-ion* neut. n. suffix]

pro·sciut·to (prō shōō′tō), *n.* salted ham that has been cured by drying, always sliced paper-thin for serving. [1935–40; < It *prosciutto,* earlier *presciutto* < VL **perexsuctus* all dried up, equiv. to L *per-* PER- + *exsuctus* lacking juice]

pro·scribe (prō skrīb′), *v.t.,* **-scribed, -scrib·ing. 1.** to denounce or condemn (a thing) as dangerous or harmful; prohibit. **2.** to put outside the protection of the law; outlaw. **3.** to banish or exile. **4.** to announce the name of (a person) as condemned to death and subject to confiscation of property. [1375–1425; late ME < L *prōscrībere* to publish in writing, confiscate, outlaw. See PRO-¹, PRESCRIBE] **—pro·scrib′a·ble,** *adj.* **—pro·scrib′er,** *n.*
—Syn. 1. censure, disapprove, repudiate.

pro·scrip·tion (prō skrip′shən), *n.* **1.** the act of proscribing. **2.** the state of being proscribed. **3.** outlawry, interdiction, or prohibition. [1350–1400; ME *proscripcioun* < L *prōscrīptiōn-* (s. of *prōscrīptiō*) public notice of confiscation or outlawry, equiv. to *prōscrīpt(us)* (ptp. of *prōscrībere* to PROSCRIBE) + *-iōn-* -ION] **—pro·scrip·tive** (prō skrip′tiv), *adj.* **—pro·scrip′tive·ly,** *adv.*

prose (prōz), *n., adj., v.,* **prosed, pros·ing.** **—n. 1.** the ordinary form of spoken or written language, without metrical structure, as distinguished from poetry or verse. **2.** matter-of-fact, commonplace, or dull expression, quality, discourse, etc. **3.** *Liturgy.* a hymn sung after the gradual, originating from a practice of setting words to the jubilatio of the alleluia. **—adj. 4.** of, in, or pertaining to prose. **5.** commonplace; dull; prosaic. *—v.t.* **6.** to turn into or express in prose. *—v.i.* **7.** to write or talk in a dull, matter-of-fact manner. [1300–50; ME < MF < L *prōsa* (*ōrātiō*) lit., straightforward (speech), fem. of *prōsus,* for *prōrsus,* contr. of *prōversus,* ptp. of *prōvertere* to turn forward, equiv. to *prō-* PRO-¹ + *vertere* to turn] **—prose′like′,** *adj.*

pro·sect (prō sekt′), *v.t. Med.* to dissect (a cadaver or part) for anatomical demonstration. [1885–90; back formation from PROSECTOR]

pro·sec·tor (prō sek′tər), *n.* **1.** a person who dissects cadavers for the illustration of anatomical lectures or the like. **2.** a person who performs autopsies to establish the cause of death or the nature and seat of disease. [1855–60; < LL: anatomist, lit., one who cuts in public (or beforehand), equiv. to L *prōsec(āre)* to cut out (body organs) in public sacrifice (see PRO-¹, SECT) + *-tor* -TOR] **—pro·sec·to·ri·al** (prō′sek tôr′ē əl, -tōr′-), *adj.* **—pro·sec′tor·ship′,** *n.*

pros·e·cute (pros′i kyōōt′), *v.,* **-cut·ed, -cut·ing.** *—v.t.* **1.** *Law.* **a.** to institute legal proceedings against (a person). **b.** to seek to enforce or obtain by legal process. **c.** to conduct criminal proceedings in court against. **2.** to follow up or carry forward something undertaken or begun, usually to its completion: *to prosecute a war.* **3.** to carry on or practice. *—v.i.* **4.** *Law.* **a.** to institute and carry on a legal prosecution. **b.** to act as prosecutor. [1400–50; late ME *prosecuten* to follow up, go on with < L *prōsecūtus,* ptp. of *prōsequī* to pursue, proceed with, equiv. to *prō-* PRO-¹ + *secū-,* var. s. of *sequī* to follow + *-tus* ptp. suffix] **—pros′e·cut′a·ble,** *adj.* **—pros′e·cut′a·bil′i·ty,** *n.*
—Syn. 3. perform, discharge, execute, conduct.

pros′ecuting attor′ney, (*sometimes caps.*) the public officer in a county, district, or other jurisdiction charged with carrying on the prosecution in criminal proceedings. [1825–35]

pros·e·cu·tion (pros′i kyōō′shən), *n.* **1.** *Law.* **a.** the institution and carrying on of legal proceedings against a person. **b.** the body of officials by whom such proceedings are instituted and carried on. **2.** the following up of something undertaken or begun, usually to its completion. [1555–65; < LL *prōsecūtiōn-* (s. of *prōsecūtiō*) a following up. See PROSECUTE, -ION]

pros·e·cu·tor (pros′i kyōō′tər), *n.* **1.** *Law.* **a.** See **prosecuting attorney. b.** a person, as a complainant or chief witness, instigating prosecution in a criminal proceeding. **2.** a person who prosecutes. [1590–1600; < ML, LL *prōsecūtor* pursuer. See PROSECUTE, -TOR]

pros·e·cu·to·ri·al (pros′i kyŏŏ tôr′ē əl, -tōr′-), *adj.* of or pertaining to a prosecutor or prosecution: *prosecutorial zeal.* [1970–75; PROSECUTOR + -IAL]

pros·e·cu·to·ry (pros′ə kyŏŏ tôr′ē, -tōr′ē), *adj.* of, pertaining to, or concerned with prosecution. [PROSECUTE + -ORY¹]

Prose′ Ed′da. See under **Edda.**

pros·e·lyte (pros′ə līt′), *n., v.,* **-lyt·ed, -lyt·ing.** **—n. 1.** a person who has changed from one opinion, religious belief, sect, or the like, to another; convert. *—v.i., v.t.* **2.** proselytize. [1325–75; ME < LL *prosēlytus* < Gk (Septuagint) *prosḗlytos,* for **prosḗlythos* newcomer, proselyte, equiv. to *prosēlyth-* (suppletive s. of *prosérchesthai* to approach) + *-os* n. suffix] **—pros′e·lyt′er,** *n.*
—Syn. 1. neophyte, disciple.

pros·e·lyt·ism (pros′ə li tiz′əm, -lī-), *n.* **1.** the act or fact of becoming a proselyte; conversion. **2.** the state or condition of a proselyte. **3.** the practice of making proselytes. [1650–60; PROSELYTE + -ISM] **—pros·e·lyt·i·cal** (pros′ə lit′i kəl), *adj.*

pros·e·lyt·ize (pros′ə li tīz′), *v.t., v.i.,* **-ized, -iz·ing.** to convert or attempt to convert as a proselyte; recruit. Also, *esp. Brit.,* **pros′e·lyt·ise′.** [1670–80; PROSELYTE + -IZE] **—pros·e·lyt·is·tic** (pros′ə li tis′tik, -lī-), *adj.* **—pros′e·lyt·i·za′tion,** *n.* **—pros′e·lyt·iz′er,** *n.*

pro·sem·i·nar (prō sem′ə när′), *n. Educ.* a course conducted in the manner of a seminar for graduate students but often open to advanced undergraduates. [1920–25, *Amer.*; PRO-¹ + SEMINAR]

pros·en·ceph·a·lon (pros′en sef′ə lon′, -lən), *n., pl.* **-las, -la** (-lə). *Anat.* the forebrain. [1840–50; < NL < Gk *prós(ō)* forward (akin to *pró* PRO-²) + *enképhalon* ENCEPHALON] **—pros·en·ce·phal·ic** (pros′en sə fal′ik), *adj.*

pros·en·chy·ma (pros eng′kə mə), *n. Bot.* the tissue characteristic of the woody and bast portions of plants, consisting typically of long, narrow cells with pointed ends. [1825–35; < NL < Gk *pros-* toward, to + *énchyma* infusion; modeled on PARENCHYMA] **—pros·en·chym·a·tous** (pros′eng kim′ə təs), *adj.*

prose′ po′em, a composition written as prose but having the concentrated, rhythmic, figurative language characteristic of poetry. [1835–45]

pros·er (prō′zər), *n.* **1.** a person who talks or writes in prose. **2.** a person who talks or writes in a dull or tedious fashion. [1620–30; PROSE + -ER¹]

Pro·ser·pi·na (prō sûr′pə nə), *n.* Persephone. Also, **Pro·ser·pi·ne** (prō sûr′pə nē).

pro′ shop′, a shop that is operated in connection with a golf or tennis club, resort, etc., and has sports equipment and often recreational clothing for sale or rent and is usually supervised by a resident professional coach or instructor. [1935–40]

pro·sim·i·an (prō sim′ē ən), *adj.* **1.** belonging or pertaining to the primate suborder Prosimii, characterized by nocturnal habits, a long face with a moist snout, prominent whiskers, large mobile ears, and large, slightly sideways-facing eyes, comprising the lemur, loris, potto, bush baby, and aye-aye. Cf. **anthropoid, tarsioid.** **—n. 2.** a prosimian animal. [1855–60; < NL *Prosimi(i)* name of the suborder + -AN (see PRO-¹, SIMIAN)]

pro·sit (*Eng.* prō′sit, -zit), *interj.* (used as a toast to wish good health to one's drinking companions). Also, **prost.** [1840–50; < G < L: lit., may it benefit, 3rd person sing. pres. subj. of *prodesse* to be beneficial]

pros·ko·mi·de (prôs kô′mē thē′; *Eng.* pros′kə mīd′), *n. Gk. Orth. Ch.* prothesis (def. 2a). [< Gk *proskomidḗ* oblation, equiv. to *pros-* toward + *komidḗ* conveyance, a bringing to a place; cf. *komízein* to provide, bring]

Pro·sku·rov (*Russ.* pru skōō′rəf), *n.* former name of **Khmelnitsky.**

pro·slav·er·y (prō slā′və rē, -slāv′rē), *adj.* **1.** favoring slavery. **2.** *U.S. Hist.* favoring the continuance of the institution of slavery of blacks, or opposed to interference with it. **—n. 3.** the favoring or support of slavery. [1830–40, *Amer.*; PRO-¹ + SLAVERY] **—pro·slav′er,** *n.* **—pro·slav′er·y·ism,** *n.*

pros·o·dist (pros′ə dist), *n.* an expert in prosody. [1770–80; PROSOD(Y) + -IST]

pros·o·dy (pros′ə dē), *n.* **1.** the science or study of poetic meters and versification. **2.** a particular or distinctive system of metrics and versification: *Milton's prosody.* **3.** *Ling.* the stress and intonation patterns of an utterance. [1400–50; late ME < L *prosōdia* < Gk *prosōidía* tone or accent, modulation of voice, song sung to music, equiv. to *prós* toward + *ōid(ḗ)* ODE + *-ia* -Y³] **—pro·sod·ic** (prə sod′ik), **pro·sod′i·cal,** *adj.*

pro·so·ma (prō sō′mə), *n., pl.* **-mas, -ma·ta** (-mə tə). *Zool.* an anterior body region, esp. the arthropod cephalothorax. [1870–75; < NL; see PRO-², -SOMA] **—pro·so′·mal,** *adj.*

pro·so·po·poe·ia (prō sō′pə pē′ə), *n. Rhet.* **1.** personification, as of inanimate things. **2.** a figure of speech in which an imaginary, absent, or deceased person is represented as speaking or acting. Also, **pro·so′·po·pe′ia.** [1555–65; < L *prosōpopoeia* < Gk *prosōpopoiía* personification, equiv. to *prósōpo(n)* face, PERSON + *poi(eîn)* to make + *-ia* -IA] **—pro·so′po·poe′ial,** *adj.*

pros·o·pyle (pros′ə pīl′), *n.* (in sponges) a pore through which water is drawn from the outside into one of the saclike chambers formed by the evagination of the body wall. Cf. **apopyle.** [1885–90; < Gk *prósō* forward + *pýlē* gate]

pros·pect (pros′pekt), *n.* **1.** Usually, **prospects. a.** an apparent probability of advancement, success, profit, etc. **b.** the outlook for the future: *good business prospects.* **2.** anticipation; expectation; a looking forward. **3.** something in view as a source of profit. **4.** a potential or likely customer, client, etc. **5.** a potential or likely candidate. **6.** a view, esp. of scenery; scene. **7.** outlook or view over a region or in a particular direction. **8.** a mental view or survey, as of a subject or situation. **9.** *Mining.* **a.** an apparent indication of ore or native metal. **b.** a place giving such indications. **c.** a mine working or excavation undertaken in a search for additional ore. **10.** *Archaic.* sight; range of vision. **11. in prospect,** under consideration; expected; in view: *He had no other alternative in prospect.* *—v.t.* **12.** to search or explore (a region), as for gold. **13.** to work (a mine or claim) ex-

pro′mod·er·a′tion, *adj.*
pro′mod·er·a′tion·ist, *adj., n.*
pro·mod′ern, *adj.*
pro·mod′ern·ist, *adj., n.*
pro′mod·ern·is′tic, *adj.*
pro-Mon′a·co′, *adj.*
pro·mon′ar·chist, *n., adj.*
pro·mon′ar·chy, *adj.*
pro′mo·nop′o·lis′tic, *adj.*
pro′mo·nop′o·ly, *adj.*
pro′-Mo·roc′can, *adj., n.*
pro-Mos′lem, *adj., n.*
pro-Mus′lem, *adj., n.*
pro-Mus′lim, *adj., n.*
pro·na′tion·al, *adj.*
pro·na′tion·al·ism, *n.*
pro·na′tion·al·ist, *adj., n.*
pro′na·tion·al·is′tic, *adj.*
pro·na′tive, *adj.*
pro·na′val, *adj.*
pro·na′vy, *adj.*
pro′ne·go′ti·a′tion, *adj.*
pro-Ne′gro, *adj., n., pl.* **-groes.**
pro′-Ni·ge′ri·an, *adj., n.*

perimentally in order to test its value. —*v.i.* **14.** to search or explore a region for gold or the like. [1400–50; late ME *prospecte* < L *prōspectus* outlook, view. See PROSPECTUS] —**pros′pect·less,** *adj.* —**pros·pec·tor** (pros′pek tər, prə spek′tər), *n.*
—**Syn. 6, 7.** See **view. 7, 8.** perspective.

Pros′pect Heights′, a town in N Illinois. 11,808.

pro·spec·tive (prə spek′tiv), *adj.* **1.** of or in the future: *prospective earnings.* **2.** potential, likely, or expected: *a prospective partner.* [1580–90; < LL *prōspectīvus.* See PROSPECTUS, -IVE] —**pro·spec′tive·ly,** *adv.* —**pro·spec′tive·ness,** *n.*

pro·spec·tus (prə spek′təs), *n., pl.* **-tus·es. 1.** a document describing the major features of a proposed literary work, project, business venture, etc., in enough detail so that prospective investors, participants, or buyers may evaluate it: *Don't buy the new stock offering until you read the prospectus carefully.* **2.** a brochure or other document describing the major features, attractions, or services of a place, institution, or business to prospective patrons, clients, owners, or members. [1770–80; < L *prōspectus* outlook, view, equiv. to *prōspec-,* s. of *prōspicere* (*prō-* PRO-[1] + *-spicere,* comb. form of *specere* to look) + *-tus* suffix of v. action]

pros·per (pros′pər), *v.i.* **1.** to be successful or fortunate, esp. in financial respects; thrive; flourish. —*v.t.* **2.** *Archaic.* to make successful or fortunate. [1425–75; late ME *prosperen* < L *prosperāre* to make happy, deriv. of *prosperus* PROSPEROUS]
—**Syn. 1.** See **succeed.** —**Ant. 1.** fail.

pros·per·i·ty (pro sper′i tē), *n., pl.* **-ties. 1.** a successful, flourishing, or thriving condition, esp. in financial respects; good fortune. **2. prosperities,** prosperous circumstances. [1175–1225; ME *prosperite* < OF < L *prosperitās.* See PROSPEROUS, -ITY]

Pros·per·o (pros′pə rō′), *n.* (in Shakespeare's *The Tempest*) the exiled Duke of Milan, who is a magician.

pros·per·ous (pros′pər əs), *adj.* **1.** having or characterized by financial success or good fortune; flourishing; successful: *a prosperous business.* **2.** well-to-do or well-off: *a prosperous family.* **3.** favorable or propitious. [1400–50; late ME < L *prosperus*] —**pros′per·ous·ly,** *adv.* —**pros′per·ous·ness,** *n.*
—**Syn. 1.** thriving. **2.** wealthy, rich. **3.** fortunate, lucky, auspicious.

pros·pho·ra (*Gk.* prôs′fô rä; *Eng.* pros′fə rä′, -fər ə), *n. Eastern Ch.* antidoron. [1870–75; < Gk *prosphorá* an offering, lit., a bringing to, applying, equiv. to *pros-* toward + *phorá* something carried (verbid of *phérein* to bring)]

pros·pho·ron (*Gk.* prôs′fô rôn; *Eng.* pros′fə ron′, -fər ən), *n. Eastern Ch.* an uncut loaf of altar bread before it is consecrated. [< Gk *prósphoron,* n. use of neut. of *prósphoros* useful, fitting, deriv. of *prosphorá* PROSPHORA]

pross[1] (pros), *v.i. Scot. and North Eng.* to exhibit pride or haughtiness; put on airs. [perh. Scots var., in v. use, of PROWESS] —**pross′er,** *n.* —**pross′y,** *adj.*

pross[2] (pros), *n. Slang.* prostitute. [by shortening and resp.]

Pros·ser (pros′ər), *n.* **Gabriel,** 1775?–1800, U.S. leader of unsuccessful slave revolt.

'prost (prōst), *interj.* prosit. [by contr.]

pros·ta·cy·clin (pros′tə sī′klin), *n. Biochem.* a prostaglandin, $C_{20}H_{32}O_5$, that specifically inhibits the formation of blood clots. [1975–80; PROSTA(TE) + CYCL(IC) + -IN[2], on the model of PROSTAGLANDIN]

pros·ta·glan·din (pros′tə glan′din), *n.* **1.** *Biochem.* any of a class of unsaturated fatty acids that are involved in the contraction of smooth muscle, the control of inflammation and body temperature, and many other physiological functions. **2.** *Pharm.* any commercial preparation of this substance. [1935–40; PROSTA(TE) + GLAND[1] + -IN[2]]

pro·stas (prō′stas), *n., pl.* **pro·sta·des** (prō stä′dēz). **1.** (in classical architecture) an antechamber or vestibule. **2.** (in a classical temple) the area included between parastades. [< Gk *prostás* lit., that which stands before (cf. PROSTASIS)]

pro·sta·sis (prō stā′sis), *n., pl.* **-ses** (-sēz). (in a classical temple) a pronaos or prostas before a cella. [< Gk *próstasis;* see PRO-[2], STASIS]

pros·tate (pros′tāt), *Anat.* —*adj.* **1.** Also, **pros·tat·ic** (pro stat′ik). of or pertaining to the prostate gland. —*n.* **2.** See **prostate gland.** [1640–50; < NL *prostata* < Gk *prostátēs* one standing before. See PRO-[2], -STAT]

pros·ta·tec·to·my (pros′tə tek′tə mē), *n., pl.* **-mies.** *Surg.* excision of part or all of the prostate gland. [1885–90; PROSTATE + -ECTOMY]

pros′tate gland′, *Anat.* an organ that surrounds the urethra of males at the base of the bladder, comprising a muscular portion, which controls the release of urine, and a glandular portion, which secretes an alkaline fluid that makes up part of the semen and enhances the motility and fertility of sperm. [1830–40]

prostat′ic u′tricle, *Anat.* a small pouch near the prostate gland that opens into the urethra. [1920–25]

pros·ta·tism (pros′tə tiz′əm), *n.* symptoms of prostate disorder, esp. obstructed urination, arising from benign enlargement or chronic disease of the prostate gland. [1895–1900; PROSTATE + -ISM]

pros·ta·ti·tis (pros′tə tī′tis), *n. Pathol.* inflammation of the prostate gland. [PROSTATE + -ITIS]

pro·ster·num (prō stûr′nəm), *n., pl.* **-na** (-nə), **-nums.** the ventral sclerite of the prothorax of an insect. [1820–30; < NL; see PRO-[1], STERNUM] —**pro·ster′nal,** *adj.*

pros·the·sis (pros thē′sis *for 1;* pros′thə sis *for 2*), *n., pl.* **-ses** (-sēz *for 1;* -sēz′ *for 2*). **1.** a device, either external or implanted, that substitutes for or supplements a missing or defective part of the body. **2.** *Gram., Prosody.* the addition of one or more sounds or syllables to a word or line of verse, esp. at the beginning. [1545–55; < LL < Gk *prósthesis* a putting to, addition, equiv. to *prós* to + *thésis* a placing; see THESIS] —**pros·thet·ic** (pros thet′ik), *adj.* —**pros·thet′i·cal·ly,** *adv.*

prosthet′ic den′tistry, prosthodontics.

prosthet′ic group′, *Biochem.* the nonprotein acid constituent of a conjugate protein, as the heme group of hemoglobin. [1895–1900]

pros·thet·ics (pros thet′iks), *n.* (*used with a singular or plural v.*) **1.** the branch of surgery or of dentistry that deals with the replacement of missing parts with artificial structures. Cf. **prosthodontics. 2.** the fabrication and fitting of prosthetic devices, esp. artificial limbs. [1890–95; see PROSTHETIC, -ICS]

pros·the·tist (pros′thi tist), *n.* a person skilled in making or fitting prosthetic devices. [1900–05; PROSTHET(ICS) + -IST]

pros·thi·on (pros′thē on′), *n. Craniom.* the most forward projecting point of the anterior surface of the upper jaw, in the midsagittal plane. [1920–25; < Gk *prósthion,* neut. of *prósthios* frontal, akin to *prósthen* forward] —**pros′thi·on′ic,** *adj.*

pros·tho·don·tics (pros′thə don′tiks), *n.* (*used with a singular v.*) the branch of dentistry that deals with the restoration and maintenance of oral function by the replacement of missing teeth and other oral structures by artificial devices. Also, **pros·tho·don·tia** (pros′thə don′shə, -shē ə). [1945–50; PROSTH(ESIS) + -ODONT + -ICS]

pros·tho·don·tist (pros′thə don′tist), *n.* a specialist in prosthodontics. [1915–20; PROSTHODONT(ICS) + -IST]

pros·tie (pros′tē), *n. Slang.* a prostitute. [PROST(ITUTE) + -IE]

Pro·stig·min (prō stig′min), *Pharm., Trademark.* a brand of neostigmine.

pros·ti·tute (pros′ti to͞ot′, -tyo͞ot′), *n., v.,* **-tut·ed, -tut·ing.** —*n.* **1.** a woman who engages in sexual intercourse for money; whore; harlot. **2.** a man who engages in sexual acts for money. **3.** a person who willingly uses his or her talent or ability in a base and unworthy way, usually for money. —*v.t.* **4.** to sell or offer (oneself) as a prostitute. **5.** to put to any base or unworthy use: *to prostitute one's talents.* [1520–30; < L *prōstitūta,* n. use of fem. of *prōstitūtus,* ptp. of *prōstituere* to expose (for sale), equiv. to *prō-* PRO-[1] + *-stitū-,* comb. form of var. s. of *statuere* to cause to stand + *-tus* ptp. suffix; see STATUS] —**pros′ti·tu′tor,** *n.*
—**Syn. 1.** call girl, streetwalker, courtesan; trollop, strumpet.

pros·ti·tu·tion (pros′ti to͞o′shən, -tyo͞o′-), *n.* **1.** the act or practice of engaging in sexual intercourse for money. **2.** base or unworthy use, as of talent or ability. [1545–55; < LL *prōstitūtiōn-* (s. of *prōstitūtiō*). See PROSTITUTE, -ION]

pro·sto·mi·ate (prō stō′mē āt′), *adj.* having a prostomium. [1885–90; PROSTOMI(UM) + -ATE[1]]

pro·sto·mi·um (prō stō′mē əm), *n., pl.* **-mi·a** (-mē ə). the unsegmented, preoral portion of the head of certain lower invertebrates. [1865–70; < NL < Gk *prostómion* mouth. See PRO-[2], STOMA, -IUM] —**pro·sto′mi·al,** *adj.*

pro·sto·on (prō stō′on), *n., pl.* **-sto·a** (-stō′ə). (in classical architecture) a portico. [< Gk *próstoon;* see PRO-[2], STOA]

pros·trate (pros′trāt), *v.,* **-trat·ed, -trat·ing,** *adj.* —*v.t.* **1.** to cast (oneself) face down on the ground in humility, submission, or adoration. **2.** to lay flat, as on the ground. **3.** to throw down level with the ground. **4.** to overthrow, overcome, or reduce to helplessness. **5.** to reduce to physical weakness or exhaustion. —*adj.* **6.** lying flat or at full length, as on the ground. **7.** lying face down on the ground, as in token of humility, submission, or adoration. **8.** overthrown, overcome, or helpless: *a country left prostrate by natural disasters.* **9.** physically weak or exhausted. **10.** submissive. **11.** utterly dejected or depressed; disconsolate. **12.** *Bot.* (of a plant or stem) lying flat on the ground. [1350–1400; (adj.) ME *prostrat* < L *prōstrātus,* ptp. of *prōsternere* to throw prone, equiv. to *prō-* PRO-[1] + *strā-,* var. s. of *sternere* to stretch out + *-tus* ptp. suffix; (v.) ME *prostraten,* deriv. of the adj.] —**pros·tra·tive** (pros′trə tiv), *adj.* —**pros′tra·tor,** *n.*
—**Syn. 6.** prone, supine, recumbent.

pros·tra·tion (pro strā′shən), *n.* **1.** the act of prostrating. **2.** the state of being prostrated. **3.** extreme mental or emotional depression or dejection: *nervous prostration.* **4.** extreme physical weakness or exhaustion: *heat prostration.* [1520–30; < LL *prōstrātiōn-* (s. of *prōstrātiō*) a lying prone. See PROSTRATE, -ION]

pro·style (prō′stīl), *Archit.* —*adj.* **1.** (of a classical temple) having a portico on the front with the columns in front of the antae. —*n.* **2.** a prostyle building or portico. [1690–1700; (adj.) < L *prostȳlos* < Gk *próstȳlos* with pillars in front, equiv. to *pro-* PRO-[2] + *-stȳlos* -STYLE[2]; (n.) < Gk *próstȳlon,* n. use of neut. of *próstȳlos*]

pros·y (prō′zē), *adj.,* **pros·i·er, pros·i·est. 1.** of the nature of or resembling prose. **2.** prosaic; dull, tedious, wearisome, or commonplace. [1805–15; PROSE + -Y[1]] —**pros′i·ly,** *adv.* —**pros′i·ness,** *n.*

pro·syl·lo·gism (prō sil′ə jiz′əm), *n. Logic.* a syllogism the conclusion of which is used as a premise of another syllogism; any of the syllogisms included in a polysyllogism except the last. Cf. **episyllogism.** [1575–85; < ML *prosyllogismus* < Gk *prosyllogismós.* See PRO-[2], SYLLOGISM]

prot-, var. of **proto-** before a vowel: *protamine.*

Prot., Protestant.

prot·ac·tin·i·um (prō′tak tin′ē əm), *n. Chem.* a radioactive, metallic element. *Symbol:* Pa; *at. no.:* 91. Also, **protoactinium.** [1915–20; PROT- + ACTINIUM]

pro·tag·o·nist (prō tag′ə nist), *n.* **1.** the leading character, hero, or heroine of a drama or other literary work. **2.** a proponent for or advocate of a political cause, social program, etc. **3.** the leader or principal person in a movement, cause, etc. **4.** the first actor in ancient Greek drama, who played not only the main role, but also other roles when the main character was offstage. Cf. **deuteragonist, tritagonist. 5.** *Physiol.* agonist. [1665–75; < Gk *prōtagōnistḗs* actor who plays the first part, lit., first combatant, equiv. to *prôt(os)* first + *agōnistḗs* one who contends for a prize, combatant, actor. See PROTO-, ANTAGONIST] —**pro·tag′o·nism,** *n.*

Pro·tag·o·ras (prō tag′ər əs), *n.* c480–c421 B.C., Greek Sophist philosopher. —**Pro·tag·o·re·an** (prō tag′ə rē′ən), *adj.* —**Pro·tag′o·re′an·ism,** *n.*

prot·a·mine (prō′tə mēn′, pro tam′in), *n. Biochem.* any of a group of arginine-rich, strongly basic proteins that are not coagulated by heat, occurring primarily in the sperm of fish. [1870–75; PROT- + AMINE]

prot·a·nom·a·ly (prōt′n om′ə lē), *n. Ophthalm.* a defect of vision characterized by a diminished response of the retina to red. [1935–40; PROT- + ANOMALY] —**prot′·a·nom′a·lous,** *adj.*

pro·ta·no·pi·a (prōt′n ō′pē ə), *n. Ophthalm.* a defect of vision in which the retina fails to respond to red or green. [1900–05; < NL; see PROT-, AN-[1], -OPIA] —**pro·ta·nop·ic** (prōt′n op′ik), *adj.*

prot·a·sis (prot′ə sis), *n., pl.* **-ses** (-sēz′). **1.** the clause expressing the condition in a conditional sentence, in English usually beginning with *if.* Cf. **apodosis. 2.** the first part of an ancient drama, in which the characters are introduced and the subject is proposed. Cf. **catastasis, catastrophe** (def. 4), **epitasis. 3.** (in Aristotelian logic) a proposition, esp. one used as a premise in a syllogism. [1610–20; < LL: introduction in a drama < Gk *prótasis* proposition, lit., a stretching forward, equiv. to *pro-* PRO-[2] + *tásis* a stretching (*ta-,* verbid s. of *teínein* to stretch + *-sis* -SIS)]

pro·te·an (prō′tē ən, prō tē′-), *adj.* **1.** readily assuming different forms or characters; extremely variable. **2.** changeable in shape or form, as an amoeba. **3.** (of an actor or actress) versatile; able to play many kinds of roles. **4.** (*cap.*) of, pertaining to, or suggestive of Proteus. [1590–1600; PROTE(US) + -AN] —**pro′te·an·ism,** *n.*

pro·te·ase (prō′tē ās′, -āz′), *n. Biochem.* any of a group of enzymes that catalyze the hydrolytic degradation of proteins or polypeptides to smaller amino acid polymers. [1900–05; PROTE(IN) + -ASE]

pro·tect (prə tekt′), *v.t.* **1.** to defend or guard from attack, invasion, loss, annoyance, insult, etc.; cover or shield from injury or danger. **2.** *Econ.* to guard (the industry or an industry of a nation) from foreign competition by imposing import duties. **3.** to provide funds for the payment of (a draft, note, etc.). —*v.i.* **4.** to provide, or be capable of providing, protection: *a floor wax that protects as well as shines.* [1520–30; < L *prōtēctus,* ptp. of *prōtegere* to cover in front, equiv. to *prō-* PRO-[1] + *teg-,* s. of *tegere* to cover (akin to TOGA, THATCH) + *-tus* ptp. suffix] —**pro·tect′i·ble, pro·tect′a·ble,** *adj.* —**pro·tect′i·bil′i·ty, pro·tect′a·bil′i·ty,** *n.*
—**Syn. 1.** screen, shelter. See **defend.** —**Ant. 1.** attack.

pro·tect·ant (prə tek′tənt), *n.* a substance, as a chemical spray, that provides protection, as against insects, frost, rust, etc.; protective agent. [1660–70, for an earlier sense; PROTECT + -ANT]

pro·tec·tee (prō′tek tē′, prə tek-), *n.* a person, as a head of state, for whom official protection is provided. [1595–1605; PROTECT + -EE]

pro·tect·ing (prə tek′ting), *adj.* providing protection or shelter. [1620–30; PROTECT + -ING[2]] —**pro·tect′ing·ly,** *adv.* —**pro·tect′ing·ness,** *n.*

pro·tec·tion (prə tek′shən), *n.* **1.** the act of protecting or the state of being protected; preservation from injury or harm. **2.** a thing, person, or group that protects: *This vaccine is a protection against disease.* **3.** patronage. **4.** *Insurance.* coverage (def. 1). **5.** *Informal.* **a.** money paid to racketeers for a guarantee against threatened violence. **b.** bribe money paid to the police, politicians, or other authorities for overlooking criminal activity. **6.** *Econ.* protectionism. **7.** a document that assures safety from harm, delay, or the like, for the person, persons, or property specified in it. **8.** *Archaic.* a document given by the U.S. customs authorities to a sailor traveling abroad certifying that the holder is a citizen of the U.S. [1275–1325; ME *proteccio(u)n* < LL *prōtēctiōn-* (s. of *prōtēctiō*) a covering in front. See PROTECT, -ION] —**pro·tec′tion·al,** *adj.*
—**Syn. 1.** security, refuge, safety. **2.** guard, defense, shield, bulwark. See **cover. 3.** aegis, sponsorship. **7.** pass, permit.

pro·tec·tion·ism (prə tek′shə niz′əm), *n.* **1.** *Econ.* the theory, practice, or system of fostering or developing domestic industries by protecting them from foreign competition through duties or quotas imposed on importations. **2.** any program, policy, or system of laws that seeks to provide protection for property owners, wildlife,

pro-Nor′dic, *adj.*
pro-North′, *adj.*
pro-North′ern, *adj.*
pro′-Nor·we′gian, *adj., n.*
pro-op′er·a, *adj.*
pro′-O·ri·en′tal, *adj., n.*
pro-or′tho·dox′, *adj.*
pro-or′tho·dox′y, *adj.*
pro·pac′i·fism, *n.*
pro·pac′i·fist, *n., adj.*
pro-Pan′a·ma′, *adj.*
pro′-Pan·a·ma′ni·an, *adj., n.*
pro·pa′pist, *n., adj.*
pro-Par′a·guay′, *adj.*
pro′-Par·a·guay′an, *adj., n.*
pro·pa′tri·ot′ic, *adj.*
pro·pa′tri·ot·ism, *n.*
pro·pa′tron·age, *adj.*
pro·pay′ment, *adj.*
pro′-Pe·ru′vi·an, *adj., n.*
pro-Phil′ip·pine′, *adj.*
pro-Pol′ish, *adj.*
pro·pol′i·tics, *adj.*
pro′-Por·tu·guese′, *adj., n., pl.* **-guese.**

the environment, etc. [1855–60; PROTECTION + -ISM] **—pro·tec′tion·ist,** *n., adj.* **—pro·tec′tion·is′tic,** *adj.*

pro·tec·tive (prə tek′tiv), *adj.* **1.** having the quality or function of protecting: *a protective covering.* **2.** tending to protect. **3.** *Econ.* of, pertaining to, or designed to favor protectionism: *protective tariffs.* **4.** defensive (def. 4). [1655–65; PROTECT + -IVE] **—pro·tec′tive·ly,** *adv.* **—pro·tec′tive·ness,** *n.*

protec′tive col′loid, *Physical Chem.* a lyophilic colloid added to a lyophobic sol to lessen its sensitivity to the precipitating effect of an electrolyte. [1905–10]

protec′tive colora′tion, coloration or anything likened to it that eliminates or reduces visibility or conspicuousness. [1890–95]

protec′tive custody, detention of a person by the police solely as protection against a possible attack or reprisal by someone. [1935–40]

protec′tive slope′, a slope given to a yard or the like to drain surface water away from a building.

protec′tive sys′tem, *Econ.* protectionism (def. 1). [1810–20]

pro·tec·tor (prə tek′tər), *n.* **1.** a person or thing that protects; defender; guardian. **2.** *Eng. Hist.* **a.** a person in charge of the kingdom during the sovereign's minority, incapacity, or absence. **b.** (*cap.*) Also called **Lord Protector.** the title of the head of the government during the period of the Protectorate, held by Oliver Cromwell (1653–58) and by Richard Cromwell, his son (1658–59). [1325–75; < LL (see PROTECT, -TOR); r. ME *protectour* < MF] **—pro·tec′tor·al,** *adj.* **—pro·tec′·tor·less,** *adj.* **—pro·tec′tor·ship′,** *n.*

pro·tec·tor·ate (prə tek′tər it), *n.* **1.** the relation of a strong state toward a weaker state or territory that it protects and partly controls. **2.** a state or territory so protected. **3.** the office or position, or the term of office, of a protector. **4.** the government of a protector. **5.** (*cap.*) *Eng. Hist.* the period (1653–59) during which Oliver and Richard Cromwell held the title of Lord Protector, sometimes extended to include the period of the restoration of the Rump Parliament (1659–60). [1685–95; PROTECTOR + -ATE[3]]

pro·tec·to·ry (prə tek′tə rē), *n., pl.* **-ries.** an institution for the care of destitute or delinquent children. [1650–60; PROTECT + -ORY[2]]

pro·tect·ress (prō tek′tris), *n.* a woman who guards or defends someone or something; protector. [1560–70; PROTECT(O)R + -ESS]
—Usage. See **-ess.**

pro·té·gé (prō′tə zhā′, prō′tə zhā′), *n.* a person under the patronage, protection, or care of someone interested in his or her career or welfare. [1780–90; < F, n. use of ptp. of *protéger* to protect < L *prōtegere.* See PROTECT]

pro·té·gée (prō′tə zhā′, prō′tə zhā′), *n.* a woman under the patronage, protection, or care of someone interested in his or her career or welfare. [1770–80; < F, fem. of *protégé* PROTÉGÉ]

pro·tein (prō′tēn, -tē in), *n.* **1.** *Biochem.* any of numerous, highly varied organic molecules constituting a large portion of the mass of every life form and necessary in the diet of all animals and other nonphotosynthesizing organisms, composed of 20 or more amino acids linked in a genetically controlled linear sequence into one or more long polypeptide chains, the final shape and other properties of each protein being determined by the side chains of the amino acids and their chemical attachments: proteins include such specialized forms as collagen for supportive tissue, hemoglobin for transport, antibodies for immune defense, and enzymes for metabolism. **2.** the plant or animal tissue rich in such molecules, considered as a food source supplying essential amino acids to the body. **3.** (formerly) a substance thought to be the essential nitrogenous component of all organic bodies. **—***adj.* **4.** *Biochem.* of the nature of or containing protein. Also, **pro·teid** (prō′tēd, -tē id). [1835–45; < G *Protein* < Gk *prōte(îos)* primary + G *-in* -IN[2]; r. *proteine* < F] **—pro·tein·a·ceous** (prō′tē nā′shəs, -tē i nā′-), **pro·tein′ic, pro·tei′nous,** *adj.*

pro·tein·ase (prō′tē nās′, -nāz′, -tē i-), *n. Biochem.* any of a group of enzymes that are capable of hydrolyzing proteins. [1925–30; PROTEIN + -ASE]

pro′tein coat′, *Microbiol.* capsid.

pro·tein·oid (prō′tē noid′, -tē ə-), *n. Biochem.* a polymer of amino acids resembling a biological polypeptide but formed abiotically: suggested as a possible intermediate in protein development during primitive earth conditions. [1955–60; PROTEIN + -OID]

pro′tein syn′thesis, *Biochem.* the process by which amino acids are linearly arranged into proteins through the involvement of ribosomal RNA, transfer RNA, messenger RNA, and various enzymes.

pro·tein·u·ri·a (prō′tē no͝or′ē ə, -nyo͝or′-, -tē ə-), *n. Pathol.* the presence of abnormally large amounts of protein in the urine, usually resulting from kidney disease but sometimes from fever, excessive exercise, or other abnormal condition. [1910–15; < NL; see PROTEIN, -URIA]

pro tem (prō′ tem′). See ***pro tempore.***

pro tem·po·re (PRŌ′ tem′pô RE′; *Eng.* prō′ tem′pə rē′), *Latin.* **1.** temporarily; for the time being. **2.** temporary.

CONCISE ETYMOLOGY KEY: <, descended or borrowed from; >, whence; b., blend of, blended; c., cognate with; cf., compare; deriv., derivative; equiv., equivalent; imit., imitative; obl., oblique; r., replacing; s., stem; sp., spelling, spelled; resp., respelling, respelled; trans., translation; ?, origin unknown; *, unattested; ‡, probably earlier than. See the full key inside the front cover.

pro·tend (prō tend′), *Archaic.* **—***v.t.* **1.** to stretch forth. **2.** to extend in duration. **—***v.i.* **3.** to stretch forward. [1400–50; late ME *protenden* < L *protendere* to stretch out, extend, equiv. to *pro-* PRO-[1] + *tendere* to stretch; see TEND[1]]

pro·ten·sive (prō ten′siv), *adj. Archaic.* extended in dimension or extended in time. [1635–45; < L *protēn-s(us)* (ptp. of *protendere* to PROTEND) + -IVE, on the model of EXTENSIVE, INTENSIVE, etc.] **—pro·ten′sive·ly,** *adv.*

pro·te·o·gly·can (prō′tē ō glī′kan), *n. Biochem.* a macromolecule composed of a polysaccharide joined to a polypeptide and forming the ground substance of connective tissue. [1969; PROTE(IN) + -O- + GLYC- + *-an,* var. of -ANE]

pro·te·ol·y·sis (prō′tē ol′ə sis), *n. Biochem.* the breaking down of proteins into simpler compounds, as in digestion. [1875–80; *proteo-* (comb. form repr. PROTEIN) + -LYSIS] **—pro·te·o·lyt·ic** (prō′tē ə lit′ik), *adj.*

pro·te·ose (prō′tē ōs′), *n. Biochem.* any of a class of soluble compounds derived from proteins by the action of the gastric juices, pancreatic juices, etc. [1885–90; PROTE(IN) + -OSE[2]]

protero-, a combining form meaning "earlier," "before," "former," used in the formation of compound words: *proterotype.* Also, *esp. before a vowel,* **proter-.** Cf. **proto-.** [< Gk, comb. form repr. *próteros,* comp. formed from *pró;* see PRO-[2]]

prot·er·o·type (prot′ər ə tīp′, prō′tər-), *n.* a primary type. [PROTERO- + TYPE]

Prot·er·o·zo·ic (prot′ər ə zō′ik, prō′tər-), *Geol.* **—***adj.* **1.** noting or pertaining to the latter half of the Precambrian Era, from about 2.5 billion to 570 million years ago, characterized by the appearance of bacteria and marine algae; Algonkian. **—***n.* **2.** the Proterozoic division of geologic time or the rock systems formed then; Algonkian. See table under **geologic time.** [1905–10; PROTERO- + ZO- + -IC]

pro·test (*n.* prō′test; *v.* prə test′, prō′test), *n.* **1.** an expression or declaration of objection, disapproval, or dissent, often in opposition to something a person is powerless to prevent or avoid: *a protest against increased taxation.* **2.** *Com.* **a.** a formal notarial certificate attesting the fact that a check, note, or bill of exchange has been presented for acceptance or payment and that it has been refused. **b.** the action taken to fix the liability for a dishonored bill of exchange or note. **3.** *Law.* **a.** (upon one's payment of a tax or other state or city exaction) a formal statement disputing the legality of the demand. **b.** a written and attested declaration made by the master of a ship stating the circumstances under which some damage has happened to the ship or cargo, or other circumstances involving the liability of the officers, crew, etc. **4.** *Sports.* a formal objection or complaint made to an official. **—***v.i.* **5.** to give manifest expression to objection or disapproval; remonstrate. **6.** to make solemn or earnest declaration. **—***v.t.* **7.** to make a protest or remonstrance against; object to. **8.** to say in protest or remonstrance. **9.** to declare solemnly or earnestly; affirm; assert. **10.** to make a formal declaration of the nonacceptance or nonpayment of (a bill of exchange or note). **11.** *Obs.* to call to witness. [1350–1400; (n.) ME < MF (F *protêt*), deriv. of *protester* to protest < L *prōtestārī* to declare publicly, equiv. to *prō-* PRO-[1] + *testārī* to testify, deriv. of *testis* a witness; (v.) late ME *protesten* < MF *protester*] **—pro·test′a·ble,** *adj.* **—pro·test′er, pro·tes′tor,** *n.* **—pro·test′ing·ly,** *adv.* **—pro·test′ive,** *adj.*
—Syn. 5. complain. **6.** asseverate, avow, aver, attest. See **declare. —Ant. 1.** approval. **5.** approve.

Prot·es·tant (prot′ə stənt *or, for 4, 6,* prə tes′tənt), *n.* **1.** any Western Christian who is not an adherent of a Catholic, Anglican, or Eastern church. **2.** an adherent of any of those Christian bodies that separated from the Church of Rome during the Reformation, or of any group descended from them. **3.** (originally) any of the German princes who protested against the decision of the Diet of Speyer in 1529, which had denounced the Reformation. **4.** (*l.c.*) a person who protests. **—***adj.* **5.** belonging or pertaining to Protestants or their religion. **6.** (*l.c.*) protesting. [1530–40; < G or F, for L *prōtestantēs,* pl. of prp. of *prōtestārī* to bear public witness. See PROTEST, -ANT]

Prot′estant Epis′copal Church′. See **Episcopal Church in America.**

Prot′estant eth′ic. See **work ethic.** Also called **Prot′estant work′ eth′ic.** [1925–30]

Prot·es·tant·ism (prot′ə stən tiz′əm), *n.* **1.** the religion of Protestants. **2.** the Protestant churches collectively. **3.** adherence to Protestant principles. [1640–50; PROTESTANT + -ISM]

Prot·es·tant·ize (prot′ə stən tīz′), *v.t.,* **-ized, -iz·ing.** to convert or cause to conform to Protestantism. Also, *esp. Brit.,* **Prot′es·tant·ise′.** [1825–35; PROTESTANT + -IZE]

Prot′estant Reforma′tion, reformation (def. 2).

prot·es·ta·tion (prot′ə stā′shən, prō′tə-, -te-), *n.* **1.** the act of protesting or affirming. **2.** a solemn or earnest declaration or affirmation. **3.** formal expression or declaration of objection, dissent, or disapproval; protest. [1300–50; ME *protestacio(u)n* < LL *prōtestātiōn-* (s. of *prōtestātiō*) declaration. See PROTEST, -ATION]

pro′test flag′, a flag hoisted by a racing yacht to advise the judges of a violation of the rules by another yacht.

pro′test vote′, a ballot cast for a candidate with a minimal chance of winning, to register dislike for the other candidates. [1970–75]

Pro·te·us (prō′tē əs, -tyo͞os), *n.* **1.** *Class. Myth.* a sea god, son of Oceanus and Tethys, noted for his ability to assume different forms and to prophesy. **2.** a person or thing that readily changes appearance, character, principles, etc. **3.** (*l.c.*) *Bacteriol.* any of several rod-shaped, aerobic bacteria of the genus *Proteus,* sometimes found as pathogens in the gastrointestinal and genitourinary tracts of humans.

pro·tha·la·mi·on (prō′thə lā′mē on′, -ən), *n., pl.* **-mi·a** (-mē ə). a song or poem written to celebrate a marriage. [1597; PRO-[2] + (EPI)THALAMION; coined by Edmund Spenser]

pro·tha·la·mi·um (prō′thə lā′mē əm), *n., pl.* **-mi·a** (-mē ə). prothalamion.

pro·thal·li·um (prō thal′ē əm), *n., pl.* **-thal·li·a** (-thal′ē ə). **1.** *Bot.* the gametophyte of ferns and related plants. **2.** the analogous rudimentary gametophyte of seed-bearing plants. [1855–60; < NL < Gk *pro-* PRO-[2] + *thallíon,* dim. of *thallós* young shoot; see -IUM] **—pro·thal′li·al, pro·thal′lic, pro·thal·line** (prō thal′ēn, -in), *adj.* **—pro·thal′loid,** *adj.*

pro·thal·lus (prō thal′əs), *n., pl.* **-thal·li** (-thal′ī). *Bot.* prothallium. [1850–55; < NL; see PRO-, THALLUS]

proth·e·sis (proth′ə sis), *n., pl.* **-ses** (-sēz′) for 2b, c, 3. **1.** the addition of a sound or syllable at the beginning of a word, as in Spanish *escala* "ladder" from Latin *scala.* **2.** *Eastern Ch.* **a.** Also called **proskomide.** the preparation and preliminary oblation of the Eucharistic elements. **b.** the table on which this is done. **c.** the part of the sanctuary or bema where this table stands. **3.** (*often cap.*) *Gk. Antiq.* a representation of a dead person lying in state. [1665–75; < LL < Gk *próthesis* a putting before. See PRO-[2], THESIS] **—pro·thet·ic** (prə thet′ik), *adj.* **—pro·thet′i·cal·ly,** *adv.*

pro·thon·o·tar·y (prō thon′ə ter′ē, prō′thə nō′tə rē), *n., pl.* **-tar·ies.** **1.** a chief clerk or official in certain courts of law. **2.** *Rom. Cath. Ch.* **a.** any of the seven members of the college of prothonotaries apostolic, charged chiefly with the registry of pontifical acts and canonizations. **b.** an honorary title for certain other prelates. **3.** *Gk. Orth. Ch.* the chief secretary of the patriarch of Constantinople. Also, **protonotary.** [1400–50; late ME < ML *prōthonotārius,* LL *prōtonotārius* < Gk *prōtonotários.* See PROTO-, NOTARY] **—pro·thon·o·tar·i·al** (prō thon′ə târ′ē əl, prō′thə nō târ′-), *adj.*

prothon′otary apostol′ic, *pl.* **prothonotaries apostolic.** a member of the first college of prelates of the Roman Curia. [1545–55]

prothon′otary war′bler, a wood warbler, *Protonotaria citrea,* of the eastern U.S., having an orange-yellow head and underparts, and bluish-gray wings and tail. [1780–90, *Amer.*; so called because its coloration resembles the robes traditionally worn by prothonotaries]

prothorac′ic gland′, either of a pair of endocrine glands in the anterior thorax of some insects, functioning to promote the series of molts from hatching to adulthood. [1885–90]

pro·tho·rax (prō thôr′aks, -thōr′-), *n., pl.* **-tho·rax·es, -tho·ra·ces** (-thôr′ə sēz′, -thōr′-). the anterior division of the thorax of an insect, bearing the first pair of legs. [1820–30; < NL; see PRO-[1], THORAX] **—pro·tho·rac·ic** (prō′thô ras′ik, -thō-), *adj.*

pro·throm·bin (prō throm′bin), *n. Biochem.* a plasma protein involved in blood coagulation that on activation by factors in the plasma is converted to thrombin. Also called **thrombogen.** [1895–1900; PRO-[1] + THROMBIN]

pro·tist (prō′tist), *n.* any of various one-celled organisms, classified in the kingdom Protista, that are either free-living or aggregated into simple colonies and that have diverse reproductive and nutritional modes, including the protozoans, eukaryotic algae, and slime molds: some classification schemes also include the fungi and the more primitive bacteria and blue-green algae or may distribute the organisms between the kingdoms Plantae and Animalia according to dominant characteristics. [1885–90; < NL *Protista* (neut. pl.) name of the kingdom < Gk *prṓtistos* (masc. sing.) the very first, superl. of *prôtos* first; see PROTO-] **—pro·tis·tan** (prō tis′tən), *adj., n.* **—pro·tis′tic,** *adj.*

Pro·tis·ta (prō tis′tə), *n.* (*used with a plural v.*) *Biol.* a taxonomic kingdom comprising the protists. [1875–80; < NL; see PROTIST]

pro·tis·tol·o·gy (prō′ti stol′ə jē), *n.* the biology of the Protista. [1910–15; PROTIST + -O- + -LOGY] **—pro·tis·to·log·i·cal** (prō tis′tl oj′i kəl), *adj.* **—pro′tis·tol′o·gist,** *n.*

pro·ti·um (prō′tē əm, -shē əm), *n. Chem.* the lightest and most common isotope of hydrogen. *Symbol:* H^1 [1930–35; PROT- + -IUM]

proto-, a combining form meaning "first," "foremost," "earliest form of," used in the formation of compound words (*protomartyr; protolithic; protoplasm*), specialized in chemical terminology to denote the first of a series of compounds, or the one containing the minimum amount of an element. Also, *esp. before a vowel,* **prot-.** [< Gk, comb. form repr. *prôtos* FIRST, superl. formed from *pró;* see PRO[2]-]

pro·to·ac·tin·i·um (prō′tō ak tin′ē əm), *n. Chem.* protactinium.

Pro·to-Al·gon·qui·an (prō′tō al gong′kē ən, -kwē-ən), *n.* the unattested parent language from which the Algonquian languages are descended.

pro·to·a·vis (prō′tō ā′vis), *n.* a fossil bird of the genus *Protoavis,* from the Triassic Period, having a birdlike, partly toothless jaw structure, a tail and hind legs resembling those of the dinosaur, and the hollow bones and keellike breast that are characteristic of modern birds: the oldest known avian type, preceding the ar-

pro′-Pres·by·te′ri·an, *adj., n.*
pro·priv′i·lege, *adj.*
pro·prof′it, *adj.*
pro-Prot′es·tant, *adj., n.*
pro-Prus′sian, *adj., n.*
pro′pub·li·ca′tion, *adj.*
pro′pub·lic′i·ty, *adj.*
pro·pun′ish·ment, *adj.*
pro-Quak′er, *adj.*
pro·rac′ing, *adj.*
pro·rail′road′, *adj.*
pro·re′al·ism, *n.*
pro·re′al·ist, *adj., n.*
pro′re·al·is′tic, *adj.*
pro′re·al′i·ty, *n.*
pro·reb′el, *adj.*
pro′rec·on·cil′i·a′tion, *adj.*
pro′re·duc′tion, *adj.*
pro′re·form′, *adj.*
pro·ref′u·gee′, *adj.*
pro-Ren′ais·sance′, *adj.*
pro′re·pub′li·can, *adj., n.*
pro′re·search′, *adj.*
pro′res·ig·na′tion, *adj.*
pro′res·to·ra′tion, *adj.*

chaeopteryx by an estimated 75 million years. [< NL (1986), equiv. to Gk *proto-* PROTO- + L *avis* bird]

pro·to·chor·date (prō′tō kôr′dāt), *n. Zool.* any of the nonvertebrate chordates, as the tunicates, cephalochordates, and hemichordates. [1890–95; < NL *Protochordata* name of the group; see PROTO-, CHORDATE]

pro·to·col (prō′tə kôl′, -kol′, -kōl′), *n.* **1.** the customs and regulations dealing with diplomatic formality, precedence, and etiquette. **2.** an original draft, minute, or record from which a document, esp. a treaty, is prepared. **3.** a supplementary international agreement. **4.** an agreement between states. **5.** an annex to a treaty giving data relating to it. **6.** *Med.* the plan for carrying out a scientific study or a patient's treatment regimen. **7.** *Computers.* a set of rules governing the format of messages that are exchanged between computers. **8.** Also called **pro′tocol state′ment, pro′tocol sen′tence, pro′tocol proposi′tion.** *Philos.* a statement reporting an observation or experience in the most fundamental terms without interpretation: sometimes taken as the basis of empirical verification, as of scientific laws. —*v.i.* **9.** to draft or issue a protocol. [1535–45; earlier *protocoll* < ML *prōtocollum* < LGk *prōtókollon* orig., a leaf or tag attached to a rolled papyrus manuscript and containing notes as to contents. See PROTO-, COLLOID] —**pro·to·col·ar** (prō′tə kol′ər), **pro′to·col′a·ry, pro′to·col′ic,** *adj.*

pro·to·con·ti·nent (prō′tō kon′tn ənt), *n. Geol.* an actual or hypothetical landmass that might later be enlarged into a major continent or broken up into smaller ones. [1955–60; PROTO- + CONTINENT]

pro·to·dea·con (prō′tō dē′kən), *n.* a chief deacon in the Greek Church. [1690–1700; PROTO- + DEACON]

pro·to·derm (prō′tə dûrm′), *n. Bot.* a thin outer layer of the meristem in embryos and growing points of roots and stems, which gives rise to the epidermis. Also called **dermatogen.** [1930–35; PROTO- + -DERM]

pro·to-Dor·ic (prō′tō dôr′ik, -dor′-), *adj.* of or pertaining to architecture, as in certain Egyptian tombs, supposedly anticipating the Grecian Doric order. [1875–80]

pro·to-E·lam·ite (prō′tō ē′lə mīt′), *n.* the indigenous script of Elam, found on inscriptions and tablets from the fourth millennium B.C.

pro·to·form (prō′tō fôrm′), *n. Ling.* a hypothetical linguistic form reconstructed as an element of a protolanguage. [1960–65]

pro·to·gal·ax·y (prō′tō gal′ək sē, prō′tō gal′-), *n., pl.* **-ax·ies.** *Astron.* the large concentration of gas and dust from which a galaxy is formed. [1945–50; PROTO- + GALAXY]

Pro·to·ge·ni·a (prō′tə jə nī′ə), *n. Class. Myth.* the first woman born after the great flood of Zeus, daughter of Deucalion and Pyrrha. Also, **Pro·to·ge·ne·a** (prō′tə-jə nē′ə).

Pro·to·ge·o·met·ric (prō′tō jē′ə me′trik), *adj.* (*sometimes l.c.*) pertaining to or designating a style of vase painting developed in Greece chiefly during the 10th century B.C. and characterized by use of abstract geometrical motifs. Also, **Pro′to-ge′o·met′ric, pro′to-ge′o·met′ric, Pro′to-Ge′o·met′ric.** Cf. **geometric** (def. 4). [1925–30; PROTO- + GEOMETRIC]

Pro·to-Ger·man·ic (prō′tō jər man′ik), *n.* **1.** the unattested prehistoric parent language of the Germanic languages; Germanic. —*adj.* **2.** of or pertaining to Proto-Germanic.

pro·to·his·to·ry (prō′tō his′tə rē, -his′trē), *n., pl.* **-ries. 1.** a branch of study concerned with the transition period between prehistory and the earliest recorded history. **2.** the period in a culture immediately before its recorded history begins. [1915–20; PROTO- + HISTORY] —**pro·to·his·to·ri·an** (prō′tō hi stôr′ē ən, -stōr′-), *n.* —**pro·to·his·tor·ic** (prō′tō hi stôr′ik, -stor′-), **pro′to·his·tor′i·cal,** *adj.*

pro·to·hu·man (prō′tō hyōō′mən *or, often,* -yōō′-), *adj.* **1.** of, pertaining to, or resembling extinct hominid populations that had some but not all the features of modern *Homo sapiens.* —*n.* **2.** a protohuman animal. [1905–10; PROTO- + HUMAN]

Pro·to-In·do-Eu·ro·pe·an (prō′tō in′dō yŏŏr′ə pē′ən), *n.* **1.** the unattested prehistoric parent language of the Indo-European languages; Indo-European. —*adj.* **2.** of or pertaining to Proto-Indo-European.

pro·to-I·on·ic (prō′tō ī on′ik), *adj.* of or pertaining to architecture supposedly anticipating the Grecian Ionic order. [1885–90]

pro·to·lan·guage (prō′tō lang′gwij), *n. Ling.* the reconstructed or postulated parent form of a language or a group of related languages. [1945–50; PROTO- + LANGUAGE]

pro·to·lith·ic (prōt′l ith′ik), *adj. Anthropol.* noting or pertaining to stone implements selected according to suitability of the form to a particular purpose without definite shaping on the part of the user. [1895–1900; PROTO- + LITHIC]

pro·to·log (prōt′l ôg′, -og′), *n. Biol.* the original description of a species, genus, etc. Also, **pro′to·logue′.** [1900–05; PROTO- + (CATA)LOG]

pro·to·mar·tyr (prō′tō mär′tər), *n.* **1.** the first Christian martyr, Saint Stephen. **2.** the first martyr in any cause. [1400–50; late ME *prothomartyr* < LL *protomartyr* < LGk *prōtómartys.* See PROTO-, MARTYR]

pro·to·mor·phic (prō′tə môr′fik), *adj. Biol.* having a primitive character or structure. [1855–60; PROTO- + -MORPHIC[1]] —**pro′to·morph′,** *n.*

pro·ton (prō′ton), *n. Physics, Chem.* a positively charged elementary particle that is a fundamental constituent of all atomic nuclei. It is the lightest and most stable baryon, having a charge equal in magnitude to that of the electron, a spin of ½, and a mass of 1.673×10^{-27} kg. *Symbol:* P [1915–20; n. use of Gk *prôton,* neut. of *prôtos* FIRST] —**pro·ton′ic,** *adj.*

pro·to·ne·ma (prō′tə nē′mə), *n., pl.* **-ma·ta** (-mə tə). *Bot.* a primary, usually filamentous structure produced by the germination of the spore in mosses and certain related plants, and from which the leafy plant which bears the sexual organs arises as a lateral or terminal shoot. [1855–60; < NL < Gk *prōto-* PROTO- + *nêma* thread] —**pro′to·ne′mal,** *adj.*

pro′ton num′ber. See **atomic number.**

pro·ton·o·tar·y (prō ton′ə ter′ē, prōt′n ō′tə rē), *n., pl.* **-tar·ies.** prothonotary. —**pro·ton′o·tar′y·ship′,** *n.*

pro′ton-pro′ton chain′ (prō′ton prō′ton), *Physics., Astron.* a series of thermonuclear reactions, responsible for the energy production in stars like the sun, in which the nuclei of hydrogen atoms are transformed into helium nuclei by sequential addition of single hydrogen nuclei.

pro′ton syn′chrotron, *Physics.* a synchrotron used for accelerating protons. [1945–50]

pro·to·path·ic (prō′tə path′ik), *adj. Physiol.* **1.** noting or pertaining to a general, nondiscriminating responsiveness to pain or temperature stimuli (opposed to *epicritic*). **2.** primitive; primary. [1855–60; PROTO- + -PATHIC] —**pro·top·a·thy** (prə top′ə thē), *n.*

pro·to·pec·tin (prō′tə pek′tin), *n. Biochem.* any of the class of water-insoluble pectic substances that are found in the rind of citrus fruits or in apple peels and that are hydrolyzed to pectin or pectic acid. Also called **pectinogen, pectose.** [1905–10; PROTO- + PECTIN]

pro·to·phlo·em (prō′tə flō′em), *n. Bot.* the part of the primary phloem that develops first, consisting of narrow, thin-walled cells. [1880–85; PROTO- + PHLOEM]

pro·to·plan·et (prō′tō plan′it), *n. Astron.* the collection of matter, in the process of condensation, from which a planet is formed. [1945–50; PROTO- + PLANET]

pro·to·plasm (prō′tə plaz′əm), *n.* **1.** *Biol.* (no longer in technical use) the colloidal and liquid substance of which cells are formed, excluding horny, chitinous, and other structural material; the cytoplasm and nucleus. **2.** *Obs.* the living matter of organisms regarded as the physical basis of life, having the ability to sense and conduct stimuli. [1840–50; < NL *prōtoplasma.* See PROTO-, -PLASM] —**pro′to·plas′mic, pro′to·plas′mal, pro·to·plas·mat·ic** (prō′tō plaz mat′ik), *adj.*

pro·to·plast (prō′tə plast′), *n.* **1.** *Biol.* **a.** the contents of a cell within the cell membrane, considered as a fundamental entity. **b.** the primordial living unit or cell. **2.** a person or thing that is formed first; original; prototype. **3.** the hypothetical first individual or one of the supposed first pair of a species or the like. [1525–35; < LL *prōtoplastus* the first man, n. use of Gk *prōtóplastos* formed first. See PROTO-, -PLAST] —**pro′to·plas′tic,** *adj.*

pro·top·o·dite (prō top′ə dīt′), *n. Zool.* the basal portion of a two-branched crustacean leg or other appendage. Also, **pro·to·pod** (prō′tə pod′). Cf. **endopodite, exopodite.** [1865–70; PROTO- + POD- + -ITE[1]] —**pro·top·o·dit·ic** (prə top′ə dit′ik), *adj.*

pro·to·pope (prō′tə pōp′), *n.* the ranking priest in a cathedral of the Eastern Church. Also called **protopresbyter.** [1655–65; < Russ *protopóp* < LGk *protopapâs.* See PROTO-, POPE]

pro·to·pres·by·ter (prō′tō prez′bi tər, -pres′-), *n. Eastern Ch.* **1.** a title given to distinguished priests. **2.** protopope. [1880–85; < MGk *prōtopresbýteros.* See PROTO-, PRESBYTER]

pro·to·star (prō′tō stär′), *n. Astron.* an early stage in the evolution of a star, after the beginning of the collapse of the gas cloud from which it is formed, but before sufficient contraction has occurred to permit initiation of nuclear reactions at its core. [1945–50; PROTO- + STAR]

pro·to·stele (prō′tə stēl′, -stē′lē), *n. Bot.* the solid stele of most roots, having a central core of xylem enclosed by phloem. [1900–05; PROTO- + STELE] —**pro·to·ste·lic** (prō′tə stē′lik), *adj.*

pro·to·stome (prō′tə stōm′), *n. Zool.* any member of the lower invertebrate phyla in which the mouth appears before the anus during development, cleavage is spiral and determinate, and the coelom forms as a splitting of the mesoderm. Cf. **deuterostome.** [PROTO- + -STOME]

pro·to·the·ri·an (prō′tə thēr′ē ən), *adj.* **1.** belonging or pertaining to the group Prototheria, comprising the monotremes. —*n.* **2.** a prototherian animal. [1880–85; < NL *Prototheri(a)* (< Gk *prōto-* PROTO- + *thēría,* pl. of *thēríon* beast) + -AN]

pro·to·troph (prō′tə trof′, -trōf′), *n. Biol.* **1.** a microorganism that has the same nutritional requirements as the parent organism. Cf. **auxotroph. 2.** an organism or cell capable of synthesizing all its metabolites from inorganic material, requiring no organic nutrients. [1945–50; back formation from PROTOTROPHIC]

pro·to·troph·ic (prō′tə trof′ik, -trō′fik), *adj.* **1.** (esp. of certain bacteria) requiring only inorganic substances for growth. **2.** (of certain microorganisms) requiring no specific nutriments for growth. [1895–1900; PROTO- + -TROPHIC]

pro·to·type (prō′tə tīp′), *n., v.* **-typed, -typ·ing.** —*n.* **1.** the original or model on which something is based or formed. **2.** someone or something that serves to illustrate the typical qualities of a class; model; exemplar: *She is the prototype of a student activist.* **3.** something analogous to another thing of a later period: *a Renaissance prototype of our modern public housing.* **4.** *Biol.* an archetype; a primitive form regarded as the basis of a group. —*v.t.* **5.** to create the prototype or an experimental model of: *to prototype a solar-power car.* [1595–1605; < NL *prōtotypon* < Gk *prōtótypon,* n. use of neut. of *prōtótypos* original. See PROTO-, TYPE] —**pro′to·typ′·al, pro·to·typ·i·cal** (prō′tə tip′i kəl), **pro′to·typ′ic,** *adj.* —**pro′to·typ′i·cal·ly,** *adv.*
—**Syn. 1.** pattern.

pro·tox·ide (prō tok′sīd, -sid), *n. Chem.* the one of a series of oxides having the smallest proportion of oxygen. Also, **pro·tox·id** (prō tok′sid). [PROT- + OXIDE]

pro·to·xy·lem (prō′tə zī′ləm, -lem), *n. Bot.* the part of the primary xylem that develops first, consisting of narrow, thin-walled cells. [1895–1900; PROTO- + XYLEM]

Pro·to·zo·a (prō′tə zō′ə), *n.* a major grouping or superphylum of the kingdom Protista, comprising the protozoans. [1825–35; < NL; see PROTO-, -ZOA]

pro·to·zo·an (prō′tə zō′ən), *n., pl.* **-zo·ans,** (*esp. collectively*) **-zo·a** (-zō′ə), *adj. Biol.* —*n.* **1.** any of a diverse group of eukaryotes, of the kingdom Protista, that are primarily unicellular, existing singly or aggregating into colonies, are usually nonphotosynthetic, and are often classified further into phyla according to their capacity for and means of motility, as by pseudopods, flagella, or cilia. —*adj.* **2.** of, pertaining to, or characteristic of a protozoan. [1860–65; PROTOZO(A) + -AN]

pro·to·zo·on (prō′tə zō′on, -ən), *n., pl.* **-zo·a** (-zō′ə). protozoan. [sing. of PROTOZOA]

pro·tract (prō trakt′, prə-), *v.t.* **1.** to draw out or lengthen, esp. in time; extend the duration of; prolong. **2.** *Anat.* to extend or protrude. **3.** (in surveying, mathematics, etc.) to plot and draw (lines) with a scale and a protractor. [1540–50; < L *prōtractus* (ptp. of *prōtrahere* to draw forth, prolong). See PRO-[1], TRACT[1]] —**pro·tract′ed·ly,** *adv.* —**pro·tract′ed·ness,** *n.* —**pro·tract′i·ble,** *adj.* —**pro·trac′tive,** *adj.*
—**Syn. 1.** continue. See **lengthen.** —**Ant. 1.** curtail.

pro·trac·tile (prō trak′til, -tīl, prə-), *adj.* capable of being protracted, lengthened, or protruded. [1820–30; PROTRACT + -ILE] —**pro′trac·til′i·ty,** *n.*

pro·trac·tion (prō trak′shən, prə-), *n.* **1.** the act of protracting; prolongation; extension. **2.** protrusion. **3.** something that is protracted. **4.** a drawing or rendering to scale. [1525–35; < LL *prōtractiōn-* (s. of *prōtractiō*) prolongation. See PROTRACT, -ION]

pro·trac·tor (prō trak′tər, prə-), *n.* **1.** a person or thing that protracts. **2.** (in surveying, mathematics, etc.) an instrument having a graduated arc for plotting or measuring angles. **3.** *Anat.* a muscle that causes a part to protrude. [1605–15; < ML; see PROTRACT, -TOR]

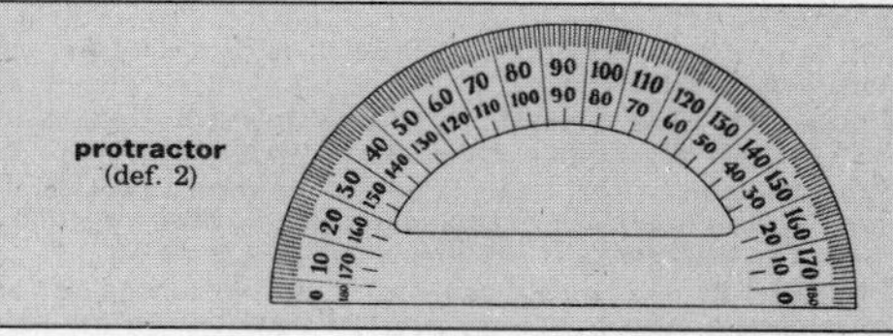

protractor (def. 2)

pro·trip·ty·line (prō trip′tl ēn′, -in), *n. Pharm.* a white to yellow powder, $C_{19}H_{21}N$, used for the treatment of depression. [1960–65; PRO(PYL) + TRI- + (*he*)*ptyl* (see HEPTANE, -YL) + -INE[2]]

pro·trude (prō trōōd′, prə-), *v.,* **-trud·ed, -trud·ing.** —*v.i.* **1.** to project. —*v.t.* **2.** to thrust forward; cause to project. [1610–20; < L *prōtrūdere* to thrust forward, equiv. to *prō-* PRO-[1] + *trūdere* to thrust] —**pro·trud′·ent,** *adj.* —**pro·tru·si·ble** (prō trōō′sə bəl, -zə-, prə-), **pro·trud′a·ble,** *adj.*
—**Syn. 1.** bulge, swell, belly.

pro·tru·sile (prō trōō′sil, -sīl, prə-), *adj.* capable of being thrust forth or extended, as the tongue of a hummingbird. [1840–50; < L *prōtrūs(us)* (ptp. of *prōtrūdere* to PROTRUDE) + -ILE]

pro·tru·sion (prō trōō′zhən, prə-), *n.* **1.** the act of protruding or the state of being protruded. **2.** something that protrudes or projects. [1640–50; < L *prōtrūs(us)* (ptp. of *prōtrūdere* to PROTRUDE) + -ION]
—**Syn. 2.** jut, projection, bulge, protuberance.

pro·tru·sive (prō trōō′siv, prə-), *adj.* **1.** projecting or protuberant; thrusting forward, upward, or outward. **2.** obtrusive. **3.** *Archaic.* pushing forward; having propulsive force. [1670–80; < L *prōtrūs(us)* (ptp. of *prōtrūdere* to PROTRUDE) + -IVE] —**pro·tru′sive·ly,** *adv.* —**pro·tru′sive·ness,** *n.*

pro·tu·ber·ance (prō tōō′bər əns, -tyōō′-, prə-), *n.* **1.** the condition, state, or quality of being protuberant. **2.** a protuberant part or thing; projection or bulge. [1640–50; PROTUBER(ANT) + -ANCE] —**pro·tu·ber·an·tial** (prō tōō′bə ran′shəl, -tyōō′-), *adj.*
—**Syn. 2.** protrusion, swelling.

pro·tu·ber·an·cy (prō tōō′bər ən sē, -tyōō′-, prə-), *n., pl.* **-cies.** protuberance. [1645–55; PROTUBER(ANT) + -ANCY]

CONCISE PRONUNCIATION KEY: act, cāpe, dâre, pärt; set, ēqual; if, īce; ox, ōver, ôrder, oil, bŏŏk, bōōt, out; up, ûrge; child; sing; shoe; thin, *th*at; zh as in *treasure.* ə = *a* as in *alone, e* as in *system, i* as in *easily, o* as in *gallop, u* as in *circus;* ᵊ as in *fire* (fīᵊr), *hour* (ouᵊr). l and n can serve as syllabic consonants, as in *cradle* (krād′l), and *button* (but′n). See the full key inside the front cover.

pro′re·stric′tion, *adj.*
pro′re·vi′sion, *adj.*
pro·rev·o·lu′tion, *adj.*
pro′rev·o·lu′tion·ar′y, *adj.*
pro′rev·o·lu′tion·ist, *adj., n.*
pro·rit′u·al, *adj.*
pro′ro·man′tic, *adj.*
pro′ro·man′ti·cism, *n.*
pro′-Ru·ma′ni·an, *adj., n.*
pro-Rus′sian, *adj., n.*
pro′-Scan·di·na′vi·an, *adj.*
pro′scho·las′tic, *adj.*
pro′scho·las′ti·cism, *n.*
pro·sci′ence, *adj.*
pro′sci·en·tif′ic, *adj.*
pro-Scrip′tur·al, *adj.*
pro-Scrip′ture, *adj.*
pro·se′cre·cy, *adj.*
pro·slave′, *adj.*
pro′-So·ma′li·a, *adj.*
pro-South′, *adj.*
pro-South′ern, *adj.*
pro-So′vi·et, *adj.*
pro-Spain′, *adj.*
pro-Span′ish, *adj.*

pro•tu•ber•ant (prō to͞o′bər ənt, -tyo͞o′-, prə-), *adj.* bulging out beyond the surrounding surface; protruding; projecting: *protuberant eyes.* [1640–50; < LL *prōtūberant-* (s. of *prōtūberāns*), prp. of *prōtūberāre* to swell. See PRO-[1], TUBER, -ANT] —**pro•tu′ber•ant•ly,** *adv.*

pro•tu•ber•ate (prō to͞o′bə rāt′, -tyo͞o′-, prə-), *v.i.*, **-at•ed, -at•ing.** to bulge out, forming a rounded projection. [1570–80; < LL *prōtūberātus,* ptp. of *prōtūberāre.* See PROTUBERANT, -ATE[1]]

pro•tu•ran (prə to͝or′ən, -tyo͝or′-), *n.* **1.** a proturan insect; telsontail. —*adj.* **2.** belonging or pertaining to the order Protura, compromising the telsontails. [< NL *Protur(a)* name of the order (see PROT-, URO-[2], -A[1]) + -AN]

proud (proud), *adj.*, **-er, -est,** *adv.* —*adj.* **1.** feeling pleasure or satisfaction over something regarded as highly honorable or creditable to oneself (often fol. by *of,* an infinitive, or a clause). **2.** having, proceeding from, or showing a high opinion of one's own dignity, importance, or superiority. **3.** having or showing self-respect or self-esteem. **4.** highly gratifying to the feelings or self-esteem: *It was a proud day for him when his son entered college.* **5.** highly honorable or creditable: *a proud achievement.* **6.** stately, majestic, or magnificent: *proud cities.* **7.** of lofty dignity or distinction: *a proud name; proud nobles.* **8.** *Chiefly South Midland and Southern U.S.* pleased; happy: *I'm proud to meet you.* **9.** full of vigor and spirit: *a proud young stallion.* **10.** *Obs.* brave. —*adv.* **11. do one proud, a.** to be a source of pride or credit to a person: *His conduct in such a difficult situation did him proud.* **b.** to treat someone or oneself generously or lavishly: *You really did us proud with this supper.* [bef. 1000; ME; late OE *prūd, prūt* arrogant (c. ON *prūthr* stately, fine), appar. < VL; cf. OF *prud, prod* gallant, LL *prōde* useful, L *prōdesse* to be of worth] —**proud′ly,** *adv.* —**proud′ness,** *n.*
—**Syn. 1.** contented, self-satisfied. **2.** overbearing, self-important, disdainful, imperious, presumptuous. PROUD, ARROGANT, HAUGHTY imply a consciousness of, or a belief in, one's superiority in some respect. PROUD implies sensitiveness, lofty self-respect, or jealous preservation of one's dignity, station, and the like. It may refer to an affectionate admiration of or a justifiable pride concerning someone else: *proud of his son.* ARROGANT applies to insolent or overbearing behavior, arising from an exaggerated belief in one's importance: *arrogant rudeness.* HAUGHTY implies lofty reserve and confident, often disdainful assumption of superiority over others: *the haughty manner of the butler in the play.* **6.** noble, imposing, splendid. —**Ant. 1.** dissatisfied. **2.** humble. **5.** dishonorable. **6.** mean; impoverished; lowly.

proud′ flesh′, *Pathol.* See **granulation tissue.** [1350–1400; ME]

proud•ful (proud′fəl′), *adj. Chiefly South Midland and Southern U.S.* proud; full of pride. [1300–50; ME; see PROUD, -FUL]

proud•heart•ed (proud′här′tid), *adj.* **1.** full of pride. **2.** haughty; disdainful. [1350–1400; ME *proude-herted.* See PROUD, HEARTED]

Prou•dhon (pro͞o dôN′), *n.* **Pierre Jo•seph** (pyer zhô zef′), 1809–65, French socialist and writer.

Proust (pro͞ost; *Fr.* pro͞ost), *n.* **1. Jo•seph Louis** (zhô zef′ lwē), 1754–1826, French chemist. **2. Mar•cel** (mär sel′; *Fr.* mar sel′), 1871–1922, French novelist.

Proust•i•an (pro͞o′stē ən), *adj.* of, pertaining to, or resembling Marcel Proust, his writings, or the middle-class and aristocratic worlds he described. [1925–30; PROUST + -IAN]

proust•ite (pro͞o′stit), *n. Mineral.* a mineral, silver arsenic sulfide, Ag_3AsS_3, occurring in scarlet crystals and masses: a minor ore of silver; ruby silver. [1825–35; named after J. L. PROUST; see -ITE[1]]

Prov (prov), *n.* Provo. [by shortening from PROVO or PROVISIONAL]

Prov., **1.** Provençal. **2.** Provence. **3.** Proverbs. **4.** Province. **5.** Provost.

prov., **1.** province. **2.** provincial. **3.** provisional. **4.** provost.

pro•vas′cu•lar tis′sue (prō vas′kyə lər), *Bot.* procambium. [PRO-[1] + VASCULAR]

prove (pro͞ov), *v.*, **proved, proved** or **prov•en, prov•ing.** —*v.t.* **1.** to establish the truth or genuineness of, as by evidence or argument: *to prove one's claim.* **2.** *Law.* to establish the authenticity or validity of (a will); probate. **3.** to give demonstration of by action. **4.** to subject to a test, experiment, comparison, analysis, or the like, to determine quality, amount, acceptability, characteristics, etc.: *to prove ore.* **5.** to show (oneself) to have the character or ability expected of one, esp. through one's actions. **6.** *Math.* to verify the correctness or validity of by mathematical demonstration or arithmetical proof. **7.** Also, **proof.** *Print.* to take a trial impression of (type, a cut, etc.). **8.** to cause (dough) to rise to the necessary lightness. **9.** *Archaic.* to experience. —*v.i.* **10.** to turn out: *The experiment proved to be successful.* **11.** to be found by trial or experience to be: *His story proved false.* **12.** (of dough) to rise to a specified lightness: *Leave covered until it has proved.* [1125–75; ME *proven* < OF *prover* < L *probāre* to try, test, prove, approve, deriv. of *probus* good. See PROBITY] —**prov′a•ble,** *adj.* —**prov′a•bil′i•ty, prov′a•ble•ness,** *n.* —**prov′a•bly,** *adv.* —**prov′en•ly,** *adv.* —**prov′er,** *n.*
—**Syn. 1.** demonstrate, confirm, substantiate, verify. —**Ant. 1.** disprove.
—**Usage.** Either PROVED or PROVEN is standard as the past participle of PROVE: *Events have proved* (or *proven*) *him wrong.* As a modifier, PROVEN is by far the more common: *a proven fact.*

prov•e•nance (prov′ə nəns, -näns′), *n.* place or source of origin: *The provenance of the ancient manuscript has never been determined.* [1860–65; < F, deriv. of *provenant,* prp. of *provenir* < L *prōvenīre* to come forth; see PRO-[1], CONVENE, -ANT]

Pro•ven•çal (prō′vən säl′, prov′ən-; *Fr.* prô vän sal′), *adj.* **1.** of or pertaining to Provence, its people, or their language. —*n.* **2.** a native or inhabitant of Provence. **3.** Also called **Occitan.** A Romance language once widely spoken in southern France, still in use in some rural areas. *Abbr.:* Pr, Pr., Prov. Cf. **langue d'oc. 4.** the dialect of Provençal used in Provence. [1580–90; < MF < L *prōvinciālis* PROVINCIAL. See PROVENCE, -AL[1]]

Pro•ven•çale (prō′vən säl′, -ven-, prov′ən-, -en-; *Fr.* prô vän sal′), *Cookery.* —*adj.* **1.** (*sometimes l.c.*) cooked, usually in olive oil, with garlic, tomatoes, onions, and herbs. —*n.* **2.** Also called **Provençale′ sauce′.** a thick sauce of tomatoes, garlic, and seasonings cooked in oil. [1835–45; < F (*à la*) *provençale* in the Provençal manner]

Pro•vence (prô väns′; *Eng.* prə väns′), *n.* a region in SE France, bordering on the Mediterranean: formerly a province; famous for medieval poetry and courtly traditions.

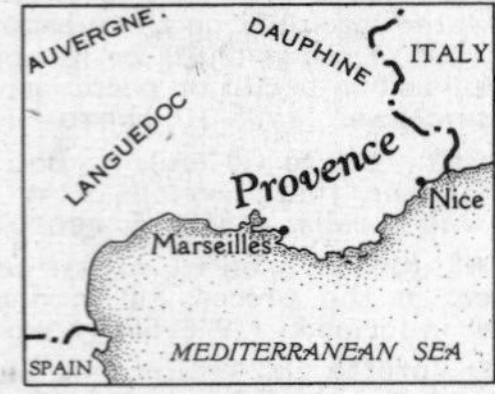

Provence′ rose′, an erect Eurasian shrub, *Rosa gallica,* of the rose family, having a creeping rootstock, densely prickly and bristly stems, and large, solitary, pink or crimson flowers. Also called **French rose.** [1570–80]

prov•en•der (prov′ən dər), *n.* **1.** dry food, as hay or oats, for livestock or other domestic animals; fodder. **2.** food; provisions. [1275–1325; ME *provendre* < OF, var. of *provende* prebend, provender < ML *prōbenda,* alter. of *praebenda* PREBEND, perh. by assoc. with L *prōvidēre* to look out for, PROVIDE]
—**Syn. 1.** See **feed.**

pro•ve•ni•ence (prō vē′nē əns, -vēn′yəns), *n.* provenance; origin; source. [1880–85; < L *prōveni(ent)-* (s. of *prōveniēns,* prp. of *prōvenīre* to come forth, arise) + -ENCE. See PROVENANCE]

pro•ven•tric•u•lus (prō′ven trik′yə ləs), *n., pl.* **-tric•u•li** (-trik′yə lī′). **1.** the glandular portion of the stomach of birds, in which food is partially digested before passing to the ventriculus or gizzard. **2.** a similar enlargement in the alimentary tract of several invertebrates, variously modified for maceration and digestion. [1825–35; PRO-[1] + VENTRICULUS] —**pro′ven•tric′u•lar,** *adj.*

pro-verb (prō′vûrb′), *n. Gram.* a word that can substitute for a verb or verb phrase, as *do* in *They never attend board meetings, but we do regularly.* [1905–10; by analogy with PRONOUN]

prov•erb (prov′ərb), *n.* **1.** a short popular saying, usually of unknown and ancient origin, that expresses effectively some commonplace truth or useful thought; adage; saw. **2.** a wise saying or precept; a didactic sentence. **3.** a person or thing that is commonly regarded as an embodiment or representation of some quality; byword. **4.** *Bible.* a profound saying, maxim, or oracular utterance requiring interpretation. —*v.t.* **5.** to utter in the form of a proverb. **6.** to make (something) the subject of a proverb. **7.** to make a byword of. [1275–1325; ME *proverbe* < MF < L *prōverbium* adage, equiv. to *prō-* PRO-[1] + *verb(um)* WORD + *-ium* -IUM] —**prov′erb•like′,** *adj.*
—**Syn. 1.** aphorism, apothegm. PROVERB, MAXIM are terms for short, pithy sayings. A PROVERB is such a saying popularly known and repeated, usually expressing simply and concretely, though often metaphorically, a truth based on common sense or the practical experience of humankind: *"A stitch in time saves nine."* A MAXIM is a brief statement of a general and practical truth, esp. one that serves as a rule of conduct or a precept: *"It is wise to risk no more than one can afford to lose."*

pro•ver•bi•al (prə vûr′bē əl), *adj.* **1.** of, pertaining to, or characteristic of a proverb: *proverbial brevity.* **2.** expressed in a proverb or proverbs: *proverbial wisdom.* **3.** of the nature of or resembling a proverb: *proverbial sayings.* **4.** having been made the subject of a proverb: *the proverbial barn door which is closed too late.* **5.** having become an object of common mention or reference: *your proverbial inability to get anywhere on time.* [1400–50; late ME < L *prōverbiālis.* See PROVERB, -AL[1]] —**pro•ver′bi•al•ly,** *adv.*

Prov•erbs (prov′ərbz), *n.* (*used with a singular v.*) a book of the Bible, containing the sayings of sages. *Abbr.:* Prov.

pro•vide (prə vīd′), *v.*, **-vid•ed, -vid•ing.** —*v.t.* **1.** to make available; furnish: *to provide employees with various benefits.* **2.** to supply or equip: *to provide the army with new fighter planes.* **3.** to afford or yield. **4.** *Law.* to arrange for or stipulate beforehand, as by a provision or proviso. **5.** *Archaic.* to prepare or procure beforehand. —*v.i.* **6.** to take measures with due foresight (usually fol. by *for* or *against*). **7.** to make arrangements for supplying means of support, money, etc. (usually fol. by *for*): *He provided for his children in his will.* **8.** to supply means of support (often fol. by *for*): *to provide for oneself.* [1375–1425; late ME *providen* < L *prōvidēre* to foresee, look after, provide for, equiv. to *prō-* PRO-[1] + *vidēre* to see] —**pro•vid′a•ble,** *adj.*
—**Syn. 1.** give, render. **3.** produce.

pro•vid•ed (prə vī′did), *conj.* on the condition or understanding (that); providing: *I'll go provided that the others go, too.* [1375–1425; late ME. See PROVIDE, -ED[2]]
—**Syn.** in case, granted. See **if.** —**Ant.** lest.
—**Usage.** The conjunctions PROVIDED and PROVIDING are interchangeable. Both mean "on the condition or understanding that," with *that* sometimes expressed: *Provided* (or *Providing*) *no further objections are raised, we will consider the matter settled.*

prov•i•dence (prov′i dəns), *n.* **1.** (*often cap.*) the foreseeing care and guidance of God or nature over the creatures of the earth. **2.** (*cap.*) God, esp. when conceived as omnisciently directing the universe and the affairs of humankind with wise benevolence. **3.** a manifestation of divine care or direction. **4.** provident or prudent management of resources; prudence. **5.** foresight; provident care. [1300–50; ME < L *prōvidentia* foresight, forethought. See PROVIDENT, -ENCE]

Prov•i•dence (prov′i dəns), *n.* a seaport in and the capital of Rhode Island, in the NE part, at the head of Narragansett Bay. 156,804.

prov•i•dent (prov′i dənt), *adj.* **1.** having or showing foresight; providing carefully for the future. **2.** characterized by or proceeding from foresight: *provident care.* **3.** mindful in making provision (usually fol. by *of*). **4.** economical; frugal; thrifty. [1400–50; ME < L *prōvident-* (s. of *prōvidēns*), prp. of *prōvidēre* to look out for, PROVIDE] —**prov′i•dent•ly,** *adv.* —**prov′i•dent•ness,** *n.*
—**Syn. 1.** cautious, prudent. —**Ant. 1.** careless.

prov•i•den•tial (prov′i den′shəl), *adj.* **1.** of, pertaining to, or resulting from divine providence: *providential care.* **2.** opportune, fortunate, or lucky: *a providential event.* [1640–50; < L *prōvidenti(a)* PROVIDENCE + -AL[1]] —**prov′i•den′tial•ly,** *adv.*
—**Syn. 2.** happy.

pro•vid•er (prə vī′dər), *n.* **1.** a person or thing that provides. **2.** a person who supports a family or another person. [1515–25; PROVIDE + -ER[1]]

pro•vid•ing (prə vī′ding), *conj.* on the condition or understanding (that); provided: *He can stay here providing he works.* [1375–1425; late ME *provydyng.* See PROVIDE, -ING[2]]
—**Syn.** See **if.**
—**Usage.** See **provided.**

prov•ince (prov′ins), *n.* **1.** an administrative division or unit of a country. **2. the provinces, a.** the parts of a country outside of the capital or the largest cities. **b.** (in England) all parts of the country outside of London. **3.** a country, territory, district, or region. **4.** *Geog.* See **physiographic province. 5.** a department or branch of learning or activity: *the province of mathematics.* **6.** sphere or field of activity or authority, as of a person; office, function, or business: *Such decisions do not lie within his province.* **7.** a major subdivision of British India. **8.** an ecclesiastical territorial division, as that within which an archbishop or a metropolitan exercises jurisdiction. **9.** *Hist.* **a.** any of the North American colonies now forming major administrative divisions of Canada. **b.** any of certain colonies of Great Britain which are now part of the U.S. **10.** *Rom. Hist.* a country or territory outside of Italy, brought under the ancient Roman dominion and administered by a governor sent from Rome. **11.** *Mining.* an individual mineral-producing area. [1300–50; ME < MF < L *prōvincia* province, official charge]
—**Syn. 5.** area.

Prov•ince•town (prov′ins toun′), *n.* a town at the tip of Cape Cod, in SE Massachusetts: resort. 3536.

Prov′incetown print′, a print made from a woodblock incised with grooves that serve to separate the colors being used and to leave white lines highlighting the design.

pro•vin•cial (prə vin′shəl), *adj.* **1.** belonging or peculiar to some particular province; local: *the provincial newspaper.* **2.** of or pertaining to the provinces: *provincial customs; provincial dress.* **3.** having or showing the manners, viewpoints, etc., considered characteristic of unsophisticated inhabitants of a province; rustic; narrow or illiberal; parochial: *a provincial point of view.* **4.** (*often cap.*) *Fine Arts.* noting or pertaining to the styles of architecture, furniture, etc., found in the provinces, esp. when imitating styles currently or formerly in fashion in or around the capital: *Italian Provincial.* **5.** *Hist.* of or pertaining to any of the American provinces of Great Britain. —*n.* **6.** a person who lives in or comes from the provinces. **7.** a person who lacks urban sophistication or broad-mindedness. **8.** *Eccles.* **a.** the head of an ecclesiastical province. **b.** a member of a religious order presiding over the order in a given district or province. [1300–50; ME (n. and adj.) < L *prōvinciālis.* See PROVINCE, -AL[1]] —**pro•vin′cial•ly,** *adv.*
—**Syn. 3.** rural, small-town.

pro•vin•cial•ism (prə vin′shə liz′əm), *n.* **1.** narrowness of mind, ignorance, or the like, considered as resulting from lack of exposure to cultural or intellectual activity. **2.** a trait, habit of thought, etc., characteristic of a provincial, a province, or the provinces. **3.** a word, ex-

CONCISE ETYMOLOGY KEY: <, descended or borrowed from; >, whence; b., blend of, blended; c., cognate with; cf., compare; deriv., derivative; equiv., equivalent; imit., imitative; obl., oblique; r., replacing; s., stem; sp., spelling, spelled; resp., respelling, respelled; trans., translation; ?, origin unknown; *, unattested; ‡, probably earlier than. See the full key inside the front cover.

pro•strike′, *adj.*
pro′sub•scrip′tion, *adj.*
pro′sub•sti•tu′tion, *adj.*
pro′-Su•da•nese′, *adj., n., pl.* **-nese.**
pro•suf′frage, *adj.*
pro′su•per•vi′sion, *adj.*
pro′sup•port′, *adj.*
pro•sur′gi•cal, *adj.*
pro′sur•ren′der, *adj.*
pro-Swe′den, *adj.*
pro-Swed′ish, *adj.*
pro-Swiss′, *adj.*
pro-Switz′er•land, *adj.*
pro•syn′di•cal•ism, *n.*
pro•syn′di•cal•ist, *n., adj.*
pro-Syr′i•an, *adj.*
pro•tar′iff, *adj.*
pro•tax′, *adj.*
pro′tax•a′tion, *adj.*
pro•trade′, *adj.*
pro′tra•di′tion, *adj.*
pro′tra•di′tion•al, *adj.*
pro•trag′e•dy, *adj.*
pro′-Tu•ni′sian, *adj., n.*

pression, or mode of pronunciation peculiar to a province. **4.** devotion to one's own province before the nation as a whole. [1760–70; PROVINCIAL + -ISM]

pro•vin•ci•al•i•ty (prə vin′shē al′i tē), *n., pl.* **-ties. 1.** provincial character. **2.** provincial characteristic: *Her provincialities reflect a refreshing naturalness.* [1775–85; PROVINCIAL + -ITY]

pro•vin•cial•ize (prə vin′shə līz′), *v.t.,* **-ized, -iz•ing.** to make provincial in character. Also, *esp. Brit.,* **pro•vin′cial•ise′.** [1795–1805; PROVINCIAL + -IZE] —**pro•vin′cial•i•za′tion,** *n.*

prov′ing ground′, any place, context, or area for testing something, as a piece of scientific equipment, a theory, etc. [1940–45]

pro•vi•rus (prō′vī′rəs, prō vī′-), *n., pl.* **-rus•es.** a viral form that is incorporated into the genetic material of a host cell. [1945–50; PRO-[1] + VIRUS, on the model of PROPHAGE]

pro•vi•sion (prə vizh′ən), *n.* **1.** a clause in a legal instrument, a law, etc., providing for a particular matter; stipulation; proviso. **2.** the providing or supplying of something, esp. of food or other necessities. **3.** arrangement or preparation beforehand, as for the doing of something, the meeting of needs, the supplying of means, etc. **4.** something provided; a measure or other means for meeting a need. **5.** a supply or stock of something provided. **6. provisions,** supplies of food. **7.** *Eccles.* **a.** an appointment to an ecclesiastical office. **b.** appointment by the pope to a see or benefice not yet vacant. —*v.t.* **8.** to supply with provisions. [1300–50; ME < L *prōvīsiōn-* (s. of *prōvīsiō*) a foreseeing, equiv. to *prōvīs(us)* (ptp. of *prōvidēre* to PROVIDE) + *-iōn-* -ION] —**pro•vi′sion•er,** *n.* —**pro•vi′sion•less,** *adj.*
—**Syn. 1.** condition. **2.** catering, purveying. **6.** store, provender, stock. See **food.**

pro•vi•sion•al (prə vizh′ə nl), *adj.* **1.** providing or serving for the time being only; existing only until permanently or properly replaced; temporary: *a provisional government.* **2.** accepted or adopted tentatively; conditional; probationary. **3.** (*usually cap.*) of or being the wing of the Irish Republican Army that follows a policy of violence. —*n.* **4.** *Philately.* a stamp that serves temporarily, pending the appearance of the regular issue, or during a temporary shortage of the regular stamps. **5.** a provisional member of a group. **6.** (*usually cap.*) a member of the Provisional wing of the Irish Republican Army. Also, **pro•vi•sion•ar•y** (prə vizh′ə ner′ē) (for defs. 1, 2). [1595–1605; PROVISION + -AL[1]] —**pro•vi′sion•al′i•ty, pro•vi′sion•al•ness,** *n.* —**pro•vi′sion•al•ly,** *adv.*

pro•vi•so (prə vī′zō), *n., pl.* **-sos, -soes. 1.** a clause in a statute, contract, or the like, by which a condition is introduced. **2.** a stipulation or condition. [1400–50; late ME < ML *prōvīsō,* for *prōvīsō (quod)* it being provided (that), abl. neut. sing. of L *prōvīsus,* ptp. of *prōvidēre* to PROVIDE]
—**Syn. 2.** restriction, limitation, qualification.

pro•vi•so•ry (prə vī′zə rē), *adj.* **1.** containing a proviso or condition; conditional. **2.** provisional (defs. 1, 2). [1605–15; < ML *prōvīsōrius,* equiv. to L *prōvīd-,* s. of *prōvidēre* to PROVIDE + *-tōrius* -TORY[1], with *dt* > *s*] —**pro•vi′so•ri•ly,** *adv.*

pro•vi•ta•min (prō vī′tə min; *Brit. also* prō vit′ə min), *n. Biochem.* a substance that an organism can transform into a vitamin, as carotene, which is converted to vitamin A in the liver. [1925–30; PRO-[1] + VITAMIN]

provitamin A, carotene. [1950–55]

pro•vo (prō′vō), *n., pl.* **-vos.** (*sometimes cap.*) a Dutch or German political agitator, esp. in the 1960's and 1970's. [1965–70; shortened from F *provocateur* PROVOCATEUR]

Pro•vo (prō′vō), *n.* a city in central Utah. 73,907.

Pro•vo (prō′vō), *n., pl.* **-vos.** (*sometimes l.c.*) *Informal.* a member of the Provisional wing of the Irish Republican Army. [1970–75; PROV(ISIONAL) + -O]

pro•vo•ca•teur (prə vok′ə tûr′, -to͝or′; *Fr.* prô vô ka tœr′), *n., pl.* **-teurs** (-tûrz′, -to͝orz′; *Fr.* -tœr′). **1.** a person who provokes trouble, causes dissension, or the like; agitator. **2.** (*italics*) *French.* See **agent provocateur.** [1915–20; < F < L *prōvocātor* challenger, appellant, equiv. to *provocā(re)* to PROVOKE + *-tor* -TOR]

prov•o•ca•tion (prov′ə kā′shən), *n.* **1.** the act of provoking. **2.** something that incites, instigates, angers, or irritates. **3.** *Crim. Law.* words or conduct leading to killing in hot passion and without deliberation. [1375–1425; late ME < L *prōvocātiōn-* (s. of *prōvocātiō*) a calling forth, equiv. to *prōvocāt(us)* (ptp. of *prōvocāre* to PROVOKE; see -ATE[1]) + *-iōn-* -ION] —**prov′o•ca′tion•al,** *adj.*

pro•voc•a•tive (prə vok′ə tiv), *adj.* **1.** tending or serving to provoke; inciting, stimulating, irritating, or vexing. —*n.* **2.** something provocative. [1375–1425; late ME < LL *prōvocātīvus.* See PROVOCATION, -IVE] —**pro•voc′a•tive•ly,** *adv.* —**pro•voc′a•tive•ness,** *n.*

pro•voke (prə vōk′), *v.t.,* **-voked, -vok•ing. 1.** to anger, enrage, exasperate, or vex. **2.** to stir up, arouse, or call forth (feelings, desires, or activity): *The mishap provoked a hearty laugh.* **3.** to incite or stimulate (a person, animal, etc.) to action. **4.** to give rise to, induce, or bring about: *What could have provoked such an incident?* **5.** *Obs.* to summon. [1400–50; late ME < L *prōvocāre* to call forth, challenge, provoke, equiv. to *prō-* PRO-[1] + *vocāre* to call; akin to *vōx* VOICE] —**pro•vok′er,** *n.*
—**Syn. 1.** irk, annoy, aggravate, exacerbate, infuriate. See **irritate. 2.** rouse, instigate. **2, 3.** See **incite.**

pro•vok•ing (prə vō′king), *adj.* serving to provoke; causing annoyance. [1520–30; PROVOKE + -ING[2]] —**pro•vok′ing•ly,** *adv.*

pro•vo•lo•ne (prō′və lō′nē), *n.* a mellow light-colored, Italian cheese, usually smoked after drying. Also called **pro′vo•lo′ne cheese′.** [1945–50; < It, equiv. to *provol(a)* kind of cheese (of debated origin) + *-one* aug. suffix]

pro•vost (prō′vōst, prov′əst *or, esp. in military usage,* prō′vō), *n.* **1.** a person appointed to superintend or preside. **2.** an administrative officer in any of various colleges and universities who holds high rank and is concerned with the curriculum, faculty appointments, etc. **3.** *Eccles.* the chief dignitary of a cathedral or collegiate church. **4.** the steward or bailiff of a medieval manor or an officer of a medieval administrative district. **5.** the mayor of a municipality in Scotland. **6.** *Obs.* a prison warden. [bef. 900; ME; OE *profost* < ML *prōpositus* abbot, prior, provost, lit., (one) placed before, L: ptp. of *prōpōnere.* See PRO-[1], POSIT] —**pro′vost•ship′,** *n.*

pro′vost court′ (prō′vō), a military court convened in occupied territory under military government, usually composed of one officer and empowered to try military personnel and civilians for minor offenses. [1860–65]

pro′vost guard′ (prō′vō), a detachment of soldiers assigned to police duties under the provost marshal. Cf. **military police.** [1770–80, *Amer.*]

pro′vost mar′shal (prō′vō), **1.** *Army.* an officer on the staff of a commander, charged with the maintaining of order and with other police functions within a command. **2.** *Navy.* an officer charged with the safekeeping of a prisoner pending trial by court-martial. [1525–35]

pro′vost ser′geant (prō′vō), *Mil.* the senior noncommissioned officer of a prison or other confinement facility whose chief duty is the supervision of prisoners and of the military police unit. [1865–70]

prow[1] (prou), *n.* **1.** the forepart of a ship or boat; bow. **2.** the front end of an airship. **3.** *Literary.* a ship. [1545–55; < MF *proue* < Upper It (Genoese) *prua* < L *prōra* < Gk *prōira*] —**prowed,** *adj.*

prow[2] (prou), *adj. Archaic.* valiant. [1350–1400; ME < OF *prou* < VL **prōdis.* See PROUD]

prow•ess (prou′is), *n.* **1.** exceptional valor, bravery, or ability, esp. in combat or battle. **2.** exceptional or superior ability, skill, or strength: *his prowess as a public speaker.* **3.** a valiant or daring deed. [1250–1300; ME < OF *proesse, proece* goodness, bravery, equiv. to *prou* PROW[2] + *-esse* < L *-itia* -ICE] —**prow′essed,** *adj.*

prow•fish (prou′fish′), *n., pl.* **-fish•es,** (*esp. collectively*) **-fish.** a fish, *Zaprora silenus,* of the North Pacific. [PROW[1] + FISH]

prowl (proul), *v.i.* **1.** to rove or go about stealthily, as in search of prey, something to steal, etc. —*v.t.* **2.** to rove over or through in search of what may be found: *The cat prowled the alleys in search of food.* —*n.* **3.** act of prowling. **4. on the prowl,** in the act of prowling; searching stealthily: *The cat is on the prowl for mice.* [1350–1400; ME *prollen* < ?] —**prowl′ing•ly,** *adv.*
—**Syn. 1.** roam. See **lurk.**

prowl′ car′. See **squad car.** [1935–40, *Amer.*]

prowl•er (prou′lər), *n.* **1.** a person or animal that prowls. **2.** a person who goes stealthily about with some unlawful intention, as to commit a burglary or theft. [1510–20; PROWL + -ER[1]]

prox., proximo.

prox•e•mics (prok sē′miks), *n.* (*used with a singular v.*) **1.** *Sociol., Psych.* the study of the spatial requirements of humans and animals and the effects of population density on behavior, communication, and social interaction. **2.** *Ling.* the study of the symbolic and communicative role in a culture of spatial arrangements and variations in distance, as in how far apart individuals engaged in conversation stand depending on the degree of intimacy between them. Cf. **personal space.** [1960–65; PROX(IMITY) + *-emics* (extracted from PHONEMICS); appar. coined by U.S. anthropologist Edward T. Hall (b. 1914)] —**prox•e′mic,** *adj.*

Prox′i•ma Centau′ri (prok′sə mə), the nearest star to the sun at a distance of 4.3 light-years, part of the Alpha Centauri triple-star system located in the constellation Centaurus. [< NL: nearest (star) of CENTAURUS]

prox•i•mal (prok′sə məl), *adj.* situated toward the point of origin or attachment, as of a limb or bone. Cf. **distal** (def. 1). [1720–30; < L *proxim(us)* next (superl. of *prope* near) + -AL[1]] —**prox′i•mal•ly,** *adv.*

prox•i•mate (prok′sə mit), *adj.* **1.** next; nearest; immediately before or after in order, place, occurrence, etc. **2.** close; very near. **3.** approximate; fairly accurate. **4.** forthcoming; imminent. [1590–1600; < LL *proximātus,* ptp. of *proximāre* to near, approach. See PROXIMAL, -ATE[1]] —**prox′i•mate•ly,** *adv.* —**prox′i•mate•ness,** *n.* —**prox•i•ma•tion** (prok′sə mā′shən), *n.*

prox•im•i•ty (prok sim′i tē), *n.* nearness in place, time, order, occurrence, or relation. [1475–85; < L *proximitās* nearness, vicinity. See PROXIMAL, -ITY]

proxim′ity fuze′, a design for detonating a charge, as in a projectile, within a predesignated radius of a target. Also called **variable time fuze, VT fuze.** [1940–45]

prox•i•mo (prok′sə mō′), *adv.* in, of, or during the next month: *on the 10th proximo.* Cf. **instant** (def. 11), **ultimo.** [1850–55; < L *proximō* abl. of *proximus* next. See PROXIMAL]

prox•y (prok′sē), *n., pl.* **prox•ies. 1.** the agency, function, or power of a person authorized to act as the deputy or substitute for another. **2.** the person so authorized; substitute; agent. **3.** a written authorization empowering another person to vote or act for the signer, as at a meeting of stockholders. **4.** an ally or confederate who can be relied upon to speak or act in one's behalf. [1400–50; late ME *prokesye, procusie,* contr. of *procuracy* procuration. See PROCURE, -ACY]

prox′y fight′, a contest between factions of stockholders in a company, in which each group attempts to gain control by soliciting signed proxy statements for sufficient votes. Also called **prox′y bat′tle.**

prox′y mar′riage, a marriage performed between one of the two contracting parties and a proxy who has been authorized to represent the other. [1895–1900]

prox′y state′ment, a statement containing information about a corporation, its officers, and any propositions to be voted on, sent to stockholders when their proxies are being solicited for a stockholders' meeting.

Pro•zac (prō′zak), *Trademark.* a drug that inhibits the release of serotonin and is used chiefly as an antidepressant. [1988]

prp., present participle.

prs., pairs.

PRT, See **personal rapid transit.**

prude (pro͞od), *n.* a person who is excessively proper or modest in speech, conduct, dress, etc. [1695–1705; < F *prude* a prude (n.), prudish (adj.), short for *prudefemme,* OF *prodefeme* worthy or respectable woman. See PROUD, FEME] —**prude′like′,** *adj.*

pru•dence (pro͞od′ns), *n.* **1.** the quality or fact of being prudent. **2.** caution with regard to practical matters; discretion. **3.** regard for one's own interests. **4.** provident care in the management of resources; economy; frugality. [1300–50; ME < MF < L *prūdentia.* See PRUDENT, -ENCE]
—**Syn. 1.** PRUDENCE, CALCULATION, FORESIGHT, FORETHOUGHT imply attempted provision against possible contingencies. PRUDENCE is care, caution, and good judgment, as well as wisdom in looking ahead: *sober prudence in handling one's affairs.* CALCULATION suggests a disposition to get a large return for as small an outlay as possible and willingness to benefit at the expense of others: *cold calculation.* FORESIGHT implies a prudent looking ahead rather far into the future: *clear foresight in planning.* FORETHOUGHT emphasizes the adequacy of preparation for the future: *Careful forethought helped him deal with the emergency.* —**Ant. 1.** rashness.

Pru•dence (pro͞od′ns), *n.* a female given name.

pru•dent (pro͞od′nt), *adj.* **1.** wise or judicious in practical affairs; sagacious; discreet or circumspect; sober. **2.** careful in providing for the future; provident: *a prudent decision.* [1350–1400; ME < L *prūdent-* (s. of *prūdēns*), contr. of *prōvidēns* PROVIDENT] —**pru′dent•ly,** *adv.*
—**Syn. 1.** sensible. **2.** economical, thrifty, frugal.

pru•den•tial (pro͞o den′shəl), *adj.* **1.** of, pertaining to, characterized by, or resulting from prudence. **2.** exercising prudence. **3.** having discretionary or advisory authority, as in business matters. [1635–45; < L *prūdenti(a)* PRUDENCE + -AL[1]] —**pru•den′tial•ly,** *adv.* —**pru•den′tial•ness, pru•den•ti•al•i•ty** (pro͞o den′shē al′i tē), *n.*

prud•er•y (pro͞o′də rē), *n., pl.* **-er•ies** for 2. **1.** excessive propriety or modesty in speech, conduct, etc. **2. pruderies,** prudish actions, phrases, or words. [1700–10; < F *pruderie.* See PRUDE, -ERY]

Prud′hoe Bay′ (pro͞o′dō), an inlet of the Beaufort Sea, N of Alaska: large oil and gas fields.

Pru•d'hon (prʀᴏᴏ dôɴ′), *n.* **Pierre Paul** (pyeʀ pôl), (*Pierre Prudon*), 1758–1823, French painter.

prud•ish (pro͞o′dish), *adj.* **1.** excessively proper or modest in speech, conduct, dress, etc. **2.** characteristic of a prude. [1710–20; PRUDE + -ISH[1]] —**prud′ish•ly,** *adv.* —**prud′ish•ness,** *n.*
—**Syn. 1.** reserved, coy. See **modest.**

pru•i•nose (pro͞o′ə nōs′), *adj. Bot., Zool.* covered with a frostlike bloom or powdery secretion, as a plant surface. [1820–30; < L *pruīnōsus* frosty, equiv. to *pruīn(a)* frost (akin to FREEZE) + *-ōsus* -OSE[1]]

prune[1] (pro͞on), *n.* **1.** a variety of plum that dries without spoiling. **2.** such a plum when dried. **3.** any plum. [1300–50; late ME < MF < L *prūna,* pl. (taken as fem. sing.) of *prūnum* plum < Gk *proû(m)non* PLUM[1]]

prune[2] (pro͞on), *v.t.,* **pruned, prun•ing. 1.** to cut or lop off (twigs, branches, or roots). **2.** to cut or lop superfluous or undesired twigs, branches, or roots from; trim. **3.** to rid or clear of (anything superfluous or undesirable). **4.** to remove (anything considered superfluous or undesirable). [1400–50; late ME *prouynen* < MF *proognier* to prune (vines), var. of *provigner,* deriv. of *provain* scion (< L *propāgin-,* s. of *propāgō*; see PROPAGATE)] —**prun′•a•ble,** *adj.* —**prun•a•bil′i•ty,** *n.* —**prun′er,** *n.*

prune[3] (pro͞on), *v.t.,* **pruned, prun•ing.** *Archaic.* to preen. [1350–1400; ME *prunen, pruynen, proy(g)nen* < OF *poroign-,* pres. s. of *poroindre,* equiv. to *por-* (< L *pro-* PRO-[1]) + *oindre* to anoint (< L *unguere*); see PREEN[1]] —**prun′a•ble,** *adj.*

pru•nel•la (pro͞o nel′ə), *n.* **1.** a strong, lightweight worsted constructed in a twill weave, used in the manufacture of women's and children's apparel. **2.** a smooth-faced fabric made of mixed fibers or wool, formerly used in the manufacture of women's dresses and of robes for clerics, scholars, and lawyers. Also, **prunelle, pru•nel•lo** (pro͞o nel′ō). [1650–60; perh. special use of PRUNELLE, from the dark color of the cloth]

pru•nelle (pro͞o nel′), *n.* **1.** a liqueur distilled from plums. **2.** prunella. [< F, dim. of *prune* PRUNE[1]]

prun′ing hook′, an implement with a hooked blade, used for pruning vines, branches, etc. [1605–15]

CONCISE PRONUNCIATION KEY: *act, cāpe, dâre, pärt; set, ēqual; if, īce; ox, ōver, ôrder, oil, bo͝ok, bo͞ot, out; up, ûrge; child; sing; shoe; thin, that;* zh as in *treasure.* ə = *a* as in *alone, e* as in *system, i* as in *easily, o* as in *gallop, u* as in *circus;* ᵊ as in *fire* (fīᵊr), *hour* (ouᵊr). l and n can serve as syllabic consonants, as in *cradle* (krād′l), and *button* (but′n). See the full key inside the front cover.

pro-Tur′key, *adj.*
pro-Turk′ish, *adj.*
pro′u•ni•form′i•ty, *adj.*
pro•un′ion, *adj.*
pro•un′ion•ism, *n.*
pro•un′ion•ist, *adj., n.*
pro′-U•ni•tar′i•an, *adj., n.*
pro′-U•nit′ed States′, *adj.*
pro′u•ni•ver′si•ty, *adj.*
pro′-U•ru•guay′an, *adj., n.*
pro′vac•ci•na′tion, *adj.*
pro′vac•cine′, *adj.*
pro′-Ven•e•zue′lan, *adj., n.*
pro′-Vi•et′nam•ese′, *adj., n., pl.* **-ese.**
pro•war′, *adj.*
pro-West′, *adj.*
pro-West′ern, *adj.*
pro-West′ern•er, *n.*
pro-Whig′, *adj.*
pro-Yu′go•slav′, *n., adj.*
pro′-Yu′go•sla′vi•an, *adj., n.*
pro-Zi′on•ism, *n.*
pro-Zi′on•ist, *n., adj.*

prun′ing shears′, small, sturdy shears used for pruning shrubbery. [1800–10]

prunt (prunt), *n.* a small mass of glass fused to the body of a glass piece. [1890–95; of obscure orig.] **—prunt′ed,** *adj.*

pru·ri·ent (pro͝or′ē ənt), *adj.* **1.** having, inclined to have, or characterized by lascivious or lustful thoughts, desires, etc. **2.** causing lasciviousness or lust. **3.** having a restless desire or longing. [1630–40; < L *prūrient-* (s. of *prūriēns*), prp. of *prūrīre* to itch] **—pru′ri·ence, pru′ri·en·cy,** *n.* **—pru′ri·ent·ly,** *adv.*

pru·rig·i·nous (pro͞o rij′ə nəs), *adj. Med.* of, pertaining to, or causing prurigo. [1600–10; < LL *prūrīginōsus* itchy, lascivious, equiv. to *prūrīgin-* (s. of *prūrīgō*) PRURIGO + *-ōsus* -OUS]

pru·ri·go (pro͞o rī′gō), *n. Pathol.* a skin condition characterized by itching papules. [1640–50; < L *prūrīgō* an itching; see PRURIENT]

pru·ri·tus (pro͞o rī′təs), *n. Pathol.* itching. [1375–1425; late ME < L *prūrītus* an itching, equiv. to *prūrī(re)* to itch + *-tus* suffix of v. action] **—pru·rit·ic** (pro͞o rit′ik), *adj.*

Prus., **1.** Prussia. **2.** Prussian. Also, **Pruss., Pruss**

Prus·sia (prush′ə), *n.* a former state in N Europe: became a military power in the 18th century and in 1871 led the formation of the German empire; formally abolished as an administrative unit in 1947. German, **Preussen.** Cf. **East Prussia, West Prussia.**

Prus·sian (prush′ən), *adj.* **1.** of or pertaining to Prussia or its inhabitants. **2.** characterized by, exemplifying, or resembling Prussianism. **—***n.* **3.** a native or inhabitant of Prussia. **4.** (originally) one of a Lettic people formerly inhabiting territory along and near the coast at the southeastern corner of the Baltic Sea. **5.** a Baltic language formerly spoken in Prussia; Old Prussian. *Abbr.:* Pruss [1555–65; PRUSSI(A) + -AN]

Prus′sian blue′, **1.** a moderate to deep greenish blue. **2.** one of the iron blues, a dark-blue, crystalline, water-insoluble pigment, $Fe_4[Fe(CN)_6]_3$, produced by reacting ferrocyanic acid or a ferrocyanide with a ferric compound: used in painting, fabric printing, and laundry bluing. [1715–25; trans. of F *bleu de Prusse,* so called because it was discovered and first reported in Berlin, capital of Prussia]

Prus·sian·ism (prush′ə niz′əm), *n.* the militaristic spirit, system, policy, or methods historically associated with the Prussians. [1855–60; PRUSSIAN + -ISM]

prus·sian·ize (prush′ə nīz′), *v.t.,* **-ized, -iz·ing.** (*sometimes cap.*) to make Prussian, as in character, method, organization, etc. Also, *esp. Brit.,* **prus′sian·ise′.** [1860–65; PRUSSIAN + -IZE] **—prus′sian·i·za′tion,** *n.* **—prus′sian·iz′er,** *n.*

prus·si·ate (prush′ē āt′, -it, prus′-), *n. Chem.* **1.** a ferricyanide or ferrocyanide. **2.** a salt of prussic acid; a cyanide. [1780–90; < F; see PRUSSIC ACID, -ATE[2]]

prus·sic (prus′ik), *adj. Chem.* of or derived from prussic acid. [1780–90; see PRUSSIC ACID]

prus′sic ac′id, *Chem.* See **hydrocyanic acid.** [1780–90; trans. of F *acide prussique* (equiv. to *Prusse* PRUSSIA + *-ique* -IC); so called because it was first obtained by heating Prussian blue with sulfuric acid]

Prusso-, a combining form of **Prussia** or **Prussian.**

Prus′so-Dan′ish War′ (prus′ō dā′nish), a war of 1864 between Prussia and Denmark by which Denmark lost Schleswig-Holstein.

Prut (pro͞ot), *n.* a river in E Europe, flowing SE from the Carpathian Mountains in Ukraine along the boundary between Moldavia (Moldova) and Rumania into the Danube. 500 mi. (800 km) long. German, **Pruth** (PRO͞OT).

pru·ta (pro͞o tä′), *n., pl.* **-toth, -tot** (-tôt′). prutah.

pru·tah (pro͞o tä′), *n., pl.* **-toth, -tot** (-tôt′). a former aluminum coin of Israel, the thousandth part of a pound. [1945–50; < ModHeb *pruta,* post-Biblical Heb *pərūṭāh* a small coin]

CONCISE ETYMOLOGY KEY: <, descended or borrowed from; >, whence; b., blend of, blended; c., cognate with; cf., compare; deriv., derivative; equiv., equivalent; imit., imitative; obl., oblique; r., replacing; s., stem; sp., spelling, spelled; resp., respelling, respelled; trans., translation; ?, origin unknown; *, unattested; ‡, probably earlier than. See the full key inside the front cover.

pry[1] (prī), *v.,* **pried, pry·ing,** *n., pl.* **pries.** **—***v.i.* **1.** to inquire impertinently or unnecessarily into something: *to pry into the personal affairs of others.* **2.** to look closely or curiously; peer; peep. **—***n.* **3.** an impertinently inquisitive person. **4.** an act of prying. [1275–1325; ME *pryen, prien* < ?]

pry[2] (prī), *v.,* **pried, pry·ing,** *n., pl.* **pries.** **—***v.t.* **1.** to move, raise, or open by leverage. **2.** to get, separate, or ferret out with difficulty: *to pry a secret out of someone; We finally pried them away from the TV.* **—***n.* **3.** a tool, as a crowbar, for raising, moving, or opening something by leverage. **4.** the leverage exerted. [1800–10; back formation from PRIZE[3], taken as a pl. n. or 3rd pers. sing. verb]

Pry·de·ri (pru dâr′ē), *n. Welsh Legend.* the son of Pwyll and Rhiannon who was stolen by Gwawl shortly after his birth and was restored to his parents a few years later. Cf. **Cigfa.**

pry·er (prī′ər), *n.* prier.

pry·ing (prī′ing), *adj.* **1.** that pries; looking or searching curiously. **2.** impertinently or unnecessarily curious or inquisitive. [1950–55; PRY[1] + -ING[2]] **—pry′ing·ly,** *adv.* **—pry′ing·ness,** *n.*

—Syn. **1.** peeping, peering, peeking. **2.** nosy. See **curious.**

Prynne (prin), *n.* **William,** 1600–69, English Puritan leader and pamphleteer.

Pry·peć (pʀɪ′pech), *n.* Polish name of the **Pripet.**

pryt·a·ne·um (prit′n ē′əm), *n.* a public building in ancient Greece, containing the symbolic hearth of the community and commonly resembling a private dwelling in plan, used as a community meeting place and as a lodging for guests of the community. [1590–1600; < L *prytanēum* < Gk *prytaneîon,* akin to *prýtanis* prince, ruler, chief]

pryth·ee (prith′ē), *interj. Archaic.* prithee.

Prze·myśl (pshe′mish əl), *n.* a city in SE Poland: occupied by the Russians 1915. 53,200.

Prze·wal′ski's horse′ (pshə väl′skēz, shə-), a wild horse, *Equus caballus przevalskii,* chiefly of Mongolia and Sinkiang, characterized by light yellow coloring and a stiff, upright black mane with no forelock: the only remaining breed of wild horse, it is now endangered and chiefly maintained in zoos. Also, **Prze·val′ski's horse′.** Cf. **tarpan.** [after Nikolaĭ Mikhaĭlovich *Przheval′skiĭ* (Pol *Przewalski*) (1839–88), Russian explorer, the animal's first European observer (1876)]

PS, **1.** phrase structure. **2.** power steering.

ps, picosecond; picoseconds.

Ps., Psalm; Psalms. Also, **Psa.**

ps., **1.** pieces. **2.** pseudonym.

P.S., **1.** passenger steamer. **2.** permanent secretary. **3.** postscript. **4.** Privy Seal. **5.** *Theat.* See **prompt side.** **6.** Public School.

p.s., postscript.

psalm (säm), *n.* **1.** a sacred song or hymn. **2.** (*cap.*) any of the songs, hymns, or prayers contained in the Book of Psalms. **3.** a metric version or paraphrase of any of these. **4.** a poem of a similar nature. [bef. 900; ME *psalm(e), s(e)alm(e), psame,* OE *ps(e)alm, sealm* < LL *psalmus* < Gk *psalmós* song sung to the harp, orig., a plucking, as of strings, akin to *psállein* to pluck, pull, play (the harp)] **—psalm′ic,** *adj.*

psalm·book (säm′bo͝ok′), *n.* a book containing psalms for liturgical or devotional use. [1150–1200; ME *salm boc.* See PSALM, BOOK]

psalm·ist (sä′mist), *n.* **1.** an author of psalms. **2. the Psalmist,** David, the traditional author of the Psalms. [1475–85; < LL *psalmista.* See PSALM, -IST]

psal·mo·dy (sä′mə dē, sal′mə-), *n., pl.* **-dies.** **1.** the act, practice, or art of setting psalms to music. **2.** psalms or hymns collectively. **3.** the act, practice, or art of singing psalms. [1300–50; ME < LL *psalmōdia* < Gk *psalmōidía* singing to the harp. See PSALM, ODE, -Y[3]] **—psal·mod·ic** (sä mod′ik, sal-), **psal·mod′i·cal, psal·mo·di·al** (sä mō′dē əl, sal-), *adj.* **—psal′mo·dist,** *n.*

Psalms (sämz), *n.* (*used with a singular v.*) a book of the Bible, composed of 150 songs, hymns, and prayers. *Abbr.:* Ps.

Psal·ter (sôl′tər), *n.* **1.** the Biblical book of Psalms. **2.** (*sometimes l.c.*) a psalmbook. [bef. 900; < LL *psaltērium* the Psalter, L: a psaltery < Gk *psaltḗrion* stringed instrument; r. ME *sauter* (< AF < LL) and OE *saltere* (< LL, as above)]

psal·te·ri·um (sôl tēr′ē əm), *n., pl.* **-te·ri·a** (-tēr′ē ə). *Zool.* the omasum. [1855–60; < LL *psaltērium* the PSALTER, the folds of the omasum being likened to the leaves of a book] **—psal·te′ri·al,** *adj.*

psal·ter·y (sôl′tə rē), *n., pl.* **-ter·ies.** **1.** an ancient musical instrument consisting of a flat sounding box with numerous strings which are plucked with the fingers or with a plectrum. **2.** (*cap.*) the Psalter. [1250–1300; < L *psaltērium* (see PSALTER, -Y[3]); r. ME *sautrie* < OF < L, as above]

psaltery (def. 1)

psam·mite (sam′īt), *n. Geol.* any sandstone. Also called **arenite.** [1880–85; < Gk *psámm(os)* sand + -ITE[1]] **—psam·mit·ic** (sa mit′ik), *adj.*

psam·mo·phyte (sam′ə fīt′), *n.* a plant that grows in sand or sandy soil. [1900–05; < Gk *psammo-* (comb. form of *psámmos* sand) + -PHYTE] **—psam·mo·phyt·ic** (sam′ə fit′ik), *adj.*

psam·mo·sere (sam′ə sēr′), *n. Ecol.* a sere originating on sand or sandy soil. [1915–20; < Gk *psammo-* (comb. form of *psámmos* sand) + SERE[2]]

Psam·tik I (sam′tik), king of Egypt 663–609 B.C. (son of Necho I).

p's and q's, manners; behavior; conduct (usually prec. by *mind* or *watch*): *The children were told to mind their p's and q's.* [1770–80; perh. from some children's difficulty in distinguishing the two letters]

PSAT, Preliminary Scholastic Aptitude Test.

PSC, Public Service Commission.

pschent (skent, pskent), *n.* the double crown worn by ancient Egyptian kings, symbolic of dominion over Upper and Lower Egypt, which had previously been separate kingdoms. [1805–15; < Gk *pschént* < Egyptian *p′-sḫmty,* equiv. to *p′-* deictic + *sḫm* powerful + *ty* fem. dual marker]

PSD, prevention of significant deterioration: used as a standard of measurement by the U.S. Environmental Protection Agency.

PSE, See **Pidgin Sign English.**

psec, picosecond; picoseconds. Also **ps**

psel·lism (sel′iz əm), *n. Pathol.* stuttering; stammering. [1790–1800; < Gk *psellismós* stammering, equiv. to *psell(ízein)* to stammer + *-ismos* -ISM]

pse·phite (sē′fīt), *n. Geol.* any coarse rock, as breccia or conglomerate. [< Gk *psêph(os)* pebble + -ITE[1]]

pse·phol·o·gy (sē fol′ə jē), *n.* the study of elections. [1950–55; < Gk *psêpho(s)* pebble + -LOGY; so called from the Athenian custom of casting votes by means of pebbles] **—pse·pho·log·i·cal** (sē′fə loj′i kəl), *adj.* **—pse·phol′o·gist,** *n.*

pseud (so͞od), *Informal.* **—***n.* **1.** a person of fatuously earnest intellectual, artistic, or social pretensions. **—***adj.* **2.** of, pertaining to, or characteristic of a pseud. [1960–65; by shortening of PSEUDOINTELLECTUAL or parallel compounds with PSEUDO-]

pseud-, var. of **pseudo-** before a vowel: *pseudaxis.*

pseud., pseudonym.

pseud·am·pho·ra (so͞o dam′fər ə), *n., pl.* **-pho·rae** (-fə rē′). a Mycenaean vase having a spherical body, a spout on the shoulder, and a handle, curving across the top, supported by a solid conical neck. Also called **stirrup jar, stirrup vase.** [PSEUD- + AMPHORA]

pseud·e·pig·ra·pha (so͞o′də pig′rə fə), *n.* (*used with a plural v.*) certain writings (other than the canonical books and the Apocrypha) professing to be Biblical in character. [1685–95; < NL < Gk, neut. pl. of *pseudepígraphos* falsely inscribed, bearing a false title. See PSEUD-, EPIGRAPH, -OUS] **—pseud·ep·i·graph·ic** (so͞o′dep i graf′ik), **pseud′ep·i·graph′i·cal, pseud′e·pig′ra·phous, pseud′e·pig′ra·phal,** *adj.*

pseud·e·pig·ra·phy (so͞o′də pig′rə fē), *n.* the false ascription of a piece of writing to an author. [1835–45; PSEUD- + Gk *epigraph(eús)* title, ascription to an author (see EPIGRAPH) + -Y[3]]

pseud·es·the·sia (so͞o′dəs thē′zhə, -zhē ə, -zē ə), *n.* See **phantom limb pain.** [1835–45; PSEUD- + ESTHESIA]

pseu·di·so·dom·ic (so͞o′dī sə dom′ik), *adj. Archit.* (of ashlar) composed of stones having the same length, laid in courses of different heights. [< Gk *pseudisódomos.* See PSEUD-, ISODOMIC]

pseu·do (so͞o′dō), *adj.* **1.** not actually but having the appearance of; pretended; false or spurious; sham. **2.** almost, approaching, or trying to be. [1940–45; independent use of PSEUDO-]

pseudo-, a combining form meaning "false," "pretended," "unreal," used in the formation of compound words (*pseudoclassic; pseudointellectual*): in scientific use, denoting close or deceptive resemblance to the following element (*pseudobulb; pseudocarp*), and used sometimes in chemical names of isomers (*pseudoephedrine*). Also, *esp. before a vowel,* **pseud-.** [< Gk, comb. form of *pseudḗs* false, *pseûdos* falsehood]

—Note. The lists at the bottom of this and following

pseu′do·ac′a·dem′ic, *adj.*
pseu′do·ac′a·dem′i·cal·ly, *adv.*
pseu′do·ac′ci·den′tal, *adj.;* **-ly,** *adv.*
pseu′do·ac·quaint′ance, *n.*
pseu′do·ac′ro·meg′a·ly, *n.*
pseu′do·aes·thet′ic, *adj.*
pseu′do·aes·thet′i·cal·ly, *adv.*
pseu′do·af·fec′tion·ate, *adj.;* **-ly,** *adv.*
pseu′do-Af′ri·can, *adj., n.*
pseu′do·ag·gres′sive, *adj.;* **-ly,** *adv.*
pseu′do·al′le·go·ris′tic, *adj.*
pseu′do·al·ve′o·lar, *adj.*
pseu′do·am′a·teur′ish, *adj.;* **-ly,** *adv.*
pseu′do·am′a·teur·ism, *n.*
pseu′do·am′a·to′ri·al, *adj.*
pseu′do·am′a·to′ry, *adj.*
pseu′do·am′bi·dex′trous, *adj.;* **-ly,** *adv.*
pseu′do-A·mer′i·can, *adj., n.*
pseu′do·a·nach′ro·nis′tic, *adj.*
pseu′do·a·nach′ro·nis′ti·cal, *adj.*
pseu′do·a·nae′mi·a, *n.*
pseu′do·a·nae′mic, *adj.*
pseu′do·an′a·phy·lac′tic, *adj.*
pseu′do·an′ar·chis′tic, *adj.*
pseu′do·an′a·tom′ic, *adj.*
pseu′do·an′a·tom′i·cal, *adj.;* **-ly,** *adv.*
pseu′do·an·ces′tral, *adj.;* **-ly,** *adv.*
pseu′do·a·ne′mi·a, *n.*
pseu′do·a·ne′mic, *adj.*
pseu′do·an·gel′ic, *adj.*
pseu′do·an·gel′i·cal, *adj.;* **-ly,** *adv.*
pseu′do·an′thro·poid′, *adj.*
pseu′do·an′thro·po·log′i·cal, *adj.*
pseu′do·an·tique′, *adj., n.*
pseu′do·a·pol′o·get′ic, *adj.*
pseu′do·a·pol′o·get′i·cal·ly, *adv.*
pseu′do·ap′o·plec′tic, *adj.*
pseu′do·ap′o·plec′ti·cal, *adj.;* **-ly,** *adv.*
pseu′do·ap·pen′di·ci′tis, *n.*
pseu′do·ap′pli·ca′tive, *adj.*
pseu′do·ap′pre·hen′sive, *adj.;* **-ly,** *adv.*
pseu′do·ar·cha′ic, *adj.*
pseu′do·ar·cha′i·cal·ly, *adv.*
pseu′do-Ar′gen·tin′e·an, *adj., n.*
pseu′do·a·ris′to·crat′ic, *adj.*
pseu′do·a·ris′to·crat′i·cal, *adj.;* **-ly,** *adv.*
pseu′do-Ar′is·to·te′lian, *adj., n.*
pseu′do·ar·tic′u·late, *adj.;* **-ly,** *adv.*
pseu′do·ar·tis′tic, *adj.*
pseu′do·ar·tis′ti·cal·ly, *adv.*
pseu′do-Ar′y·an, *adj., n.*
pseu′do·as·cet′ic, *adj.*

pages provide the spelling, syllabification, and stress for words whose meanings may be easily inferred by combining the meaning of PSEUDO- and an attached base word, or base word and suffix. Appropriate parts of speech are also shown. Words prefixed by PSEUDO- that have special meanings or uses are entered in their proper alphabetical places in the main vocabulary or as derived forms run on at the end of a main vocabulary entry.

pseu•do•a•quat•ic (so͞o′dō ə kwat′ik, -kwot′-), *adj.* not aquatic but indigenous to moist regions. [PSEUDO- + AQUATIC]

pseu•do•bulb (so͞o′də bulb′), *n. Bot.* an enlarged, aboveground portion of stem, present in many tropical orchids, in which moisture is stored. [1825–35; PSEUDO- + BULB]

pseu•do•carp (so͞o′də kärp′), *n.* See **accessory fruit.** [1825–35; PSEUDO- + -CARP] —**pseu′do•car′pous,** *adj.*

pseu•do•clas•sic (so͞o′dō klas′ik), *adj.* **1.** falsely or spuriously classic. **2.** imitating the classic: *the pseudoclassic style of some modern authors.* [1895–1900; PSEUDO- + CLASSIC] —**pseu•do•clas•si•cism** (so͞o′dō klas′ə siz′əm), **pseu′do•clas′si•cal′i•ty,** *n.*

pseu′do•cleft sen′tence (so͞o′dō kleft′, so͞o′dō-kleft′). See **cleft sentence** (def. 2).

pseu•do•code (so͞o′dō kōd′), *n. Computers.* a program code unrelated to the hardware of a particular computer and requiring conversion to the code used by the computer before the program can be used. Also called **symbolic code.** [1950–55]

pseu•do•coel (so͞o′dō sēl′), *n. Zool.* the body cavity of certain invertebrate metazoan animals between the body wall and the intestine, which is not lined with a mesodermal epithelium. Also, **pseu′do•cele′, pseu′do•coele′, pseu•do•coe•lom, pseu•do•ce•lom** (so͞o′dō sē′ləm). [1885–90; PSEUDO- + -COEL]

pseu•do•coe•lo•mate (so͞o′dō sē′lə māt′, -si lō′mit), *Zool.* —*adj.* **1.** having a pseudocoel. —*n.* **2.** an invertebrate having a pseudocoel. [1935–40; PSEUDO- + COELOM + -ATE[1]]

pseu•do•cy•e•sis (so͞o′dō sī ē′sis), *n., pl.* **-ses** (-sēz). *Pathol., Vet Pathol.* See **false pregnancy.** [1810–20; PSEUDO- + CYESIS]

Pseu•do-Di•o•ny•si•us (so͞o′dō dī′ə nish′ē əs, -nis′-), *n.* fl. c4th or 5th century A.D., author of a number of mystical works: identified, during the Middle Ages, with Dionysius the Areopagite.

pseu•do•dip•ter•al (so͞o′dō dip′tər əl), *adj. Archit.* having an arrangement of columns suggesting a dipteral structure but without the inner colonnade. [1690–1700; < Gk *pseudodípter(os)* (see PSEUDO-, DIPTERAL) + -AL[1]]

pseu•do•e•phed•rine (so͞o′dō i fed′rin, -ef′i drēn′, -drin), *n. Pharm.* a dextrorotatory, isomeric compound, $C_{10}H_{15}NO$, used as a nasal decongestant. [PSEUDO- + EPHEDRINE]

pseu•do-e•vent (so͞o′dō i vent′), *n.* an event that is staged primarily so that it can be reported in the media. [1960–65, *Amer.*]

pseu•do•he•mo•phil•i•a (so͞o′dō hē′mə fil′ē ə, -fēl′-yə, -hem′ə-), *n. Pathol.* a clotting disorder caused by abnormal factor VIII activity, and characterized by a prolonged bleeding time but without the delayed coagulation time of hemophilia. Also called **hemogenia.** [PSEUDO- + HEMOPHILIA]

pseu•do•her•maph•ro•dite (so͞o′dō hûr maf′rə dīt′), *n.* an individual having internal reproductive organs of one sex and external sexual characteristics resembling those of the other sex or being ambiguous in nature. Cf. **hermaphrodite** (def. 1). [1890–95; PSEUDO- + HERMAPHRODITE] —**pseu•do•her•maph•ro•dit•ic** (so͞o′dō-hər maf′rə dit′ik), *adj.* —**pseu•do•her•maph•ro•dit•ism** (so͞o′dō hûr maf′rə dī tiz′əm), **pseu•do•her•maph•ro•dism** (so͞o′dō hûr maf′rə diz′əm), *n.*

pseu•do•hi•er•o•glyph•ic (so͞o′dō hī′ər ə glif′ik, -hī′rə-), *adj.* noting or pertaining to a script dating from the second millennium B.C. that appears to be syllabic and to represent the Phoenician language and that is inscribed on objects found at Byblos.

pseu•do•in•tel•lec•tu•al (so͞o′dō in′tl ek′cho͞o əl), *n.* **1.** a person exhibiting intellectual pretensions that have no basis in sound scholarship. **2.** a person who pretends an interest in intellectual matters for reasons of status. —*adj.* **3.** of, pertaining to, or characterized by fraudulent intellectuality; unscholarly: *a pseudointellectual book.* [1935–40; PSEUDO- + INTELLECTUAL] —**pseu′do•in′tel•lec′tu•al•ly,** *adv.*

Pseu•do-Is•i•do•ri•an (so͞o′dō iz′i dôr′ē ən, -dōr′-), *adj.* of or pertaining to the collection of documents of the 9th century A.D. that consist chiefly of the Decretals, attributed to Isidore, archbishop of Seville, A.D. 600–36, and that were rejected as spurious in the 15th century.

pseu•dol•o•gy (so͞o dol′ə jē), *n. Facetious.* lying considered as an art. [1570–80; < Gk *pseudología* falsehood; see PSEUDO-, -LOGY; or E recoinage from same elements] —**pseu•do•log•i•cal** (so͞od′l oj′i kəl), *adj.* —**pseu•dol′o•gist,** *n.*

pseu•dom•o•nas (so͞o dom′ə nəs, -nas′), *n., pl.* **pseu•do•mon•a•des** (so͞o′də mon′ə dēz′). *Bacteriol.* any of several rod-shaped bacteria of the genus *Pseudomonas,* certain species of which are pathogenic for plants and animals. [< NL (1897); see PSEUDO-, MONAD]

pseu•do•morph (so͞o′də môrf′), *n.* **1.** an irregular or unclassifiable form. **2.** a mineral having the outward appearance of another mineral that it has replaced by chemical action. [1840–50; PSEUDO- + -MORPH] —**pseu′do•mor′phic, pseu′do•mor′phous,** *adj.* —**pseu′do•mor′phism,** *n.*

pseu•do•ne•phri•tis (so͞o′dō nə frī′tis), *n. Pathol.* a condition, thought to be benign, in which microscopic amounts of blood and protein are present in the urine, occurring commonly among athletes after strenuous exercise. [PSEUDO- + NEPHRITIS]

pseu•do•nym (so͞od′n im), *n.* a fictitious name used by an author to conceal his or her identity; pen name. Cf. **allonym** (def. 1). [1840–50; < Gk *pseudṓnymon* false name; see PSEUD-, -ONYM]
—**Syn.** alias, nom de plume.

pseu•do•nym•i•ty (so͞od′n im′i tē), *n.* **1.** pseudonymous character. **2.** use of a pseudonym. [1875–80; PSEUDONYM + -ITY]

pseu•don•y•mous (so͞o don′ə məs), *adj.* **1.** bearing a false or fictitious name. **2.** writing or written under a fictitious name. [1700–10; < Gk *pseudṓnymos;* see PSEUDONYM, -OUS] —**pseu•don′y•mous•ly,** *adv.* —**pseu•don′y•mous•ness,** *n.*

pseu•do•pa•ral•y•sis (so͞o′dō pə ral′ə sis), *n. Pathol.* the inability to move a part of the body owing to factors, as pain, other than those causing actual paralysis. [1885–90; PSEUDO- + PARALYSIS] —**pseu•do•par•a•lyt•ic** (so͞o′də par′ə lit′ik), *adj.*

pseu•do•pa•ren•chy•ma (so͞o′dō pə reng′kə mə), *n. Biol.* (in certain fungi and red algae) a compact mass of tissue, made up of interwoven hyphae or filaments, that superficially resembles plant tissue. [1870–75; PSEUDO- + PARENCHYMA] —**pseu′do•pa•ren′chy•mal, pseu•do•par•en•chym•a•tous** (so͞o′dō par′əng kim′ə təs), *adj.*

pseu•do•pe•rip•ter•al (so͞o′dō pə rip′tər əl), *adj. Archit.* having a freestanding colonnade at each end, with engaged columns at the sides. [1840–50; PSEUDO- + PERIPTERAL]

pseu•do•phone (so͞o′də fōn′), *n.* an instrument for producing illusory auditory localization by changing the relationship between the receptor and the actual direction of the sound. [1875–80; PSEUDO- + -PHONE]

pseu•do•pod (so͞o′də pod′), *n. Biol.* a temporary protrusion of the protoplasm, as of certain protozoans, usually serving as an organ of locomotion or prehension. Also called **pseudopodium.** See diag. under **ameba.** [1870–75; < NL *pseudopodium;* see PSEUDO-, -PODIUM] —**pseu•dop•o•dal** (so͞o dop′ə dl), **pseu•do•po•di•al** (so͞o′-də pō′dē əl), **pseu′do•pod′ic,** *adj.*

pseu•do•po•di•um (so͞o′də pō′dē əm), *n., pl.* **-di•a** (-dē ə). *Biol.* pseudopod. [1850–55]

pseu•do•preg•nan•cy (so͞o′dō preg′nən sē), *n., pl.* **-cies.** *Pathol., Vet. Pathol.* See **false pregnancy.** [1855–60; PSEUDO- + PREGNANCY] —**pseu′do•preg′•nant,** *adj.*

pseu•do•pro•style (so͞o′dō prō′stīl), *adj. Archit.* having a colonnade at each end, either very close to the front wall or engaged in it. [1880–85; PSEUDO- + PROSTYLE]

pseu•do•ra•bies (so͞o′dō rā′bēz), *n. Vet. Pathol.* a highly contagious, usually fatal disease of cattle, sheep, and other animals, caused by the herpesvirus *Herpes suis,* and characterized by severe pruritus and progressive central nervous system involvement sometimes including an aggressive excitement phase. [1895–1900; PSEUDO- + RABIES]

pseu•do•sca•lar (so͞o′də skā′lər), *adj. Physics, Math.* a scalar quantity that changes sign when the sense of the orientation of the coordinate system is changed. [1940–45; PSEUDO- + SCALAR]

pseu•do•sci•ence (so͞o′dō sī′əns), *n.* any of various methods, theories, or systems, as astrology, psychokinesis, or clairvoyance, considered as having no scientific basis. [1835–45; PSEUDO- + SCIENCE] —**pseu•do•sci•en•tif•ic** (so͞o′dō sī′ən tif′ik), *adj.* —**pseu′do•sci′en•tif′i•cal•ly,** *adv.* —**pseu′do•sci′en•tist,** *n.*

pseu•do•scope (so͞o′də skōp′), *n.* an optical instrument for producing an image in which the depth or relief of an object is reversed. Cf. **stereoscope.** [1850–55; PSEUDO- + -SCOPE]

pseu•dos•co•py (so͞o dos′kə pē), *n.* the use of a pseudoscope. [1950–55; PSEUDOSCOPE + -Y[3]]

pseu•do•scor•pi•on (so͞o′dō skôr′pē ən), *n.* any of several small arachnids of the order Chelonethida that resemble a tailless scorpion and that feed chiefly on small insects. Also called **book scorpion.** [1825–35; < NL *Pseudoscorpionidae* former name of the group; see PSEUDO-, SCORPION]

pseu•do•sen•tence (so͞o′dō sen′tns), *n. Logical Positivism.* a sentence rejected as meaningless because it does not express anything verifiable in experience. [PSEUDO- + SENTENCE]

pseu•do•so•lu•tion (so͞o′dō sə lo͞o′shən), *n. Physical Chem.* a colloidal suspension in which the finely divided particles appear to be dissolved because they are so widely dispersed in the surrounding medium. [1910–15; PSEUDO- + SOLUTION]

pseu•do•sphere (so͞o′də sfēr′), *n. Geom.* a surface generated by revolving a tractrix about its asymptote. [1885–90; PSEUDO- + SPHERE] —**pseu•do•spher•i•cal** (so͞o′də sfer′i kəl, -sfēr′-), *adj.*

pseu•do•sym•me•try (so͞o′dō sim′i trē), *n. Crystall.* an apparent symmetry different from that appropriate to a crystal of a given mineral. [1885–90; PSEUDO- + SYMMETRY]

pseu•do•trip•ter•al (so͞o′dō trip′tər əl), *adj. Archit.* having an arrangement of columns suggesting a tripteral structure but without the inner colonnades. [PSEUDO- + TRIPTERAL]

CONCISE PRONUNCIATION KEY: act, cāpe, dâre, pärt; set, ēqual; if, īce; ox, ōver, ôrder, oil, bo͝ok, bo͞ot, out; up, ûrge; child; sing; shoe; thin, that; zh as in treasure. ə = a as in *alone,* e as in *system,* i as in *easily,* o as in *gallop,* u as in *circus;* ᵊ as in *fire* (fīᵊr), *hour* (ouᵊr). l and n can serve as syllabic consonants, as in *cradle* (krād′l), and *button* (but′n). See the full key inside the front cover.

pseu′do•as•cet′i•cal, *adj.;* **-ly,** *adv.*
pseu′do•as•ser′tive, *adj.;* **-ly,** *adv.*
pseu′do•as•so′ci•a′tion•al, *adj.*
pseu′do-As•syr′i•an, *adj., n.*
pseu′do-Aus•tral′ian, *adj., n.*
pseu′do-Aus′tri•an, *adj., n.*
pseu′do-Bab′y•lo′ni•an, *adj., n.*
pseu′do•bank′rupt, *adj.*
pseu′do•bap•tis′mal, *adj.*
pseu′do-Bap′tist, *adj., n.*
pseu′do-Bel′gian, *adj., n.*
pseu′do•be•nev′o•lent, *adj.;* **-ly,** *adv.*
pseu′do•bi′o•graph′ic, *adj.*
pseu′do•bi′o•graph′i•cal, *adj.;* **-ly,** *adv.*
pseu′do•bi′o•log′i•cal, *adj.;* **-ly,** *adv.*
pseu′do-Bo•he′mi•an, *adj., n.*
pseu′do-Bo•liv′i•an, *adj., n.*
pseu′do•bra′chi•al, *adj.*
pseu′do•bra′chi•um, *n., pl.* **-chi•a.**
pseu′do-Brah′man, *adj., n.*
pseu′do-Bra•zil′ian, *adj., n.*
pseu′do•broth′er•ly, *adv.*
pseu′do-Bud′dhist, *adj., n.*
pseu′do-Bul•gar′i•an, *adj., n.*
pseu′do-Ca•na′di•an, *adj., n.*
pseu′do•can′did, *adj.;* **-ly,** *adv.*
pseu′do•cap′tive, *adj.*
pseu′do-Car′tha•gin′i•an, *adj., n.*
pseu′do•car′ti•lag′i•nous, *adj.*
pseu′do-Cath′o•lic, *adj., n.*
pseu′do•ca•thol′i•cal•ly, *adv.*
pseu′do•cer•car′i•a, *n., pl.* **-i•ae.**
pseu′do•char′i•ta•ble, *adj.;* **-bly,** *adv.*
pseu′do•chem′i•cal, *adj.*
pseu′do-Chil′e•an, *adj., n.*
pseu′do-Chi•nese′, *adj., n., pl.* **-nese.**
pseu′do-Chris′tian, *adj., n.*
pseu′do•chy′lous, *adj.*
pseu′do-Cic′e•ro′ni•an, *adj., n.*
pseu′do•cler′i•cal, *adj.;* **-ly,** *adv.*
pseu′do•col•le′giate, *adj.*
pseu′do•col′u•mel′lar, *adj.*
pseu′do•com•mis′su•ral, *adj.*
pseu′do•com•pet′i•tive, *adj.;* **-ly,** *adv.*
pseu′do•con′cha, *n., pl.* **-chae.**
pseu′do•con•fes′sion•al, *adj.*
pseu′do•con•glom′er•ate, *adj.*
pseu′do•con•serv′a•tive, *adj.;* **-ly,** *adv.*
pseu′do•cor′ne•ous, *adj.*
pseu′do•cos′ta, *n., pl.* **-tae.**
pseu′do•cot′y•le′don•al, *adj.*
pseu′do•cot′y•le′don•ar′y, *adj.*
pseu′do•cour′te•ous, *adj.;* **-ly,** *adv.*
pseu′do•crit′i•cal, *adj.;* **-ly,** *adv.*
pseu′do•crys′tal•line, *adj.*
pseu′do•cul′ti•vat′ed, *adj.*
pseu′do•cul′tur•al, *adj.;* **-ly,** *adv.*
pseu′do•cy•clo′sis, *n., pl.* **-ses.**
pseu′do•cy•phel′la, *n., pl.* **-lae.**
pseu′do-Dan•tesque′, *adj.*
pseu′do-Dem′o•crat′ic, *adj.*
pseu′do•dem′o•crat′ic, *adj.*
pseu′do•dem′o•crat′i•cal•ly, *adv.*
pseu′do•di′as•tol′ic, *adj.*
pseu′do•diph•the′ri•al, *adj.*
pseu′do•diph•ther′ic, *adj.*
pseu′do•diph′the•rit′ic, *adj.*
pseu′do•di•vine′, *adj.*
pseu′do•dra•mat′ic, *adj.*
pseu′do•dra•mat′i•cal•ly, *adv.*
pseu′do-Dutch′, *adj.*
pseu′do-East′In′di•an, *adj., n.*
pseu′do•ec′o•nom′i•cal, *adj.;* **-ly,** *adv.*
pseu′do•e•de′ma, *n., pl.* **-ma•ta.**
pseu′do•ed′i•to′ri•al, *adj.;* **-ly,** *adv.*
pseu′do•ed′u•ca′tion•al, *adj.;* **-ly,** *adv.*
pseu′do-E•gyp′tian, *adj., n.*
pseu′do•e•lec′tor•al, *adj.*
pseu′do-E•liz′a•be′than, *adj., n.*
pseu′do•em′bry•on′ic, *adj.*
pseu′do•e•mo′tion•al, *adj.;* **-ly,** *adv.*
pseu′do•en•ceph′a•lit′ic, *adj.*
pseu′do-Eng′lish, *adj.*
pseu′do•en•thu′si•as′tic, *adj.*
pseu′do•en•thu′si•as′ti•cal•ly, *adv.*
pseu′do•e•pis′co•pal, *adj.*
pseu′do-E•pis′co•pa′lian, *adj., n.*
pseu′do•e•qual′i•tar′i•an, *adj.*
pseu′do•e•rot′ic, *adj.*
pseu′do•e•rot′i•cal•ly, *adv.*
pseu′do•er′y•si•pel′a•tous, *adj.*
pseu′do•eth′i•cal, *adj.;* **-ly,** *adv.*
pseu′do•et′y•mo•log′i•cal, *adj.;* **-ly,** *adv.*
pseu′do-Eu′ro•pe′an, *adj., n.*
pseu′do•e′van•gel′ic, *adj.*
pseu′do•e′van•gel′i•cal, *adj.;* **-ly,** *adv.*
pseu′do•ex•per′i•men′tal, *adj.;* **-ly,** *adv.*
pseu′do•faith′ful, *adj.;* **-ly,** *adv.*
pseu′do•fa′mous, *adj.;* **-ly,** *adv.*
pseu′do•fa′ther•ly, *adv.*
pseu′do•fem′i•nine, *adj.*
pseu′do•fe′ver•ish, *adj.;* **-ly,** *adv.*
pseu′do•fi′nal, *adj.;* **-ly,** *adv.*
pseu′do-French′, *adj.*
pseu′do•gas′e•ous, *adj.*
pseu′do•gen′er•al, *adj.*
pseu′do•ge•ner′ic, *adj.*
pseu′do•ge•ner′i•cal, *adj.;* **-ly,** *adv.*
pseu′do•gen•teel′, *adj.*
pseu′do•gen′tle•man•ly, *adv.*
pseu′do•ge′nus, *n., pl.* **-gen•e•ra, -ge•nus•es.**
pseu′do-Geor′gian, *adj., n.*
pseu′do-Ger′man, *adj., n.*
pseu′do-Ger•man′ic, *adj.*
pseu′do-Goth′ic, *adj.*
pseu′do-Gre′cian, *adj.*
pseu′do-Greek′, *adj., n.*
pseu′do•gy′rate, *adj.*
pseu′do•he′mal, *adj.*
pseu′do•he•ro′ic, *adj.*
pseu′do•he•ro′i•cal, *adj.;* **-ly,** *adv.*
pseu′do•hex•ag′o•nal, *adj.;* **-ly,** *adv.*
pseu′do-Hin′du, *adj., n.*
pseu′do•his•tor′ic, *adj.*
pseu′do•his•tor′i•cal, *adj.;* **-ly,** *adv.*
pseu′do-Ho•mer′ic, *adj.*
pseu′do•hu′man, *adj.*
pseu′do•hu′man•is′tic, *adj.*
pseu′do-Hun•gar′i•an, *adj., n.*
pseu′do•hy′per•troph′ic, *adj.*
pseu′do•i•den′ti•cal, *adj.*
pseu′do•im•par′tial, *adj.;* **-ly,** *adv.*
pseu′do-In′can, *adj., n.*
pseu′do•in′de•pend′ent, *adj.;* **-ly,** *adv.*
pseu′do-In′di•an, *adj., n.*
pseu′do•in•sane′, *adj.*
pseu′do•in′spi•ra′tion•al, *adj.*
pseu′do•in•spir′ing, *adj.*
pseu′do•in′ter•na′tion•al, *adj.*
pseu′do•in′ter•na′tion•al•is′tic, *adj.*

pseu·do·tu·ber·cu·lo·sis (so͞o′dō to͞o bûr′kyə lō′sis, -tyo͞o-), *n. Pathol.* **1.** an acute, sometimes fatal disease of rodents, birds, and other animals, including humans, caused by the bacterium *Yersinia* (*Pasteurella*) *pseudotuberculosis,* and characterized by the formation of nodules resembling those that result from tuberculosis. **2.** any disease resembling tuberculosis but caused by an organism other than *Mycobacterium tuberculosis.* [1895–1900; PSEUDO- + TUBERCULOSIS; def. 1 after the specific epithet of the bacterium causing the disease]

psf, pounds per square foot. Also, **p.s.f.**

PSG, polysomnogram.

pshaw (shô), *interj.* **1.** (used to express impatience, contempt, disbelief, etc.) —*n.* **2.** an exclamation of "pshaw!" —*v.i.* **3.** to say "pshaw." —*v.t.* **4.** to say "pshaw" at or to. [1665–75]

psi[1] (sī, psī), *n., pl.* **psis. 1.** the 23rd letter of the Greek alphabet (Ψ, ψ). **2.** the group of consonant sounds represented by this letter. [1350–1400; ME < Gk *pseî*]

psi[2] (sī), *n.* any purportedly psychic phenomenon, as psychokinesis, telepathy, clairvoyance, or the like. Cf. **pseudoscience, parapsychology.** [1940–45; shortening of PSYCHIC or *parapsychic*]

psi, pounds per square inch. Also, **p.s.i.**

psia, pounds per square inch, absolute.

psid, pounds per square inch, differential.

psig, pounds per square inch, gauge.

psi·lan·thro·pism (sī lan′thrə piz′əm), *n.* the doctrine that Jesus Christ was only a human being. Also, **psi·lan′thro·py.** [1800–10; < Gk *psilánthrōp(os)* merely human (*psil(ós)* mere + *ánthrōp(os)* man + *-os* -OUS) + -ISM] —**psi·lan·throp·ic** (sī′lən throp′ik), *adj.* —**psi·lan′thro·pist,** *n.*

psi·lo·cin (sil′ə sin, sī′lə-), *n. Biochem.* a psilocybin metabolite with strong hallucinogenic potency, produced after ingestion of the mushroom *Psilocybe mexicana.* [1955–60; PSILOC(YBIN) + -IN[2]]

psil·o·cy·bin (sil′ə sī′bin, sī′lə-), *n. Pharm.* a hallucinogenic crystalline solid, $C_{12}H_{17}N_2O_4P$, obtained from the mushroom *Psilocybe mexicana.* [1955–60; < NL *Psilocyb(e)* genus of mushrooms (< Gk *psiló(s)* bare + *kýbē* head) + -IN[2]]

psi·lom·e·lane (sī lom′ə lān′), *n.* a common mineral consisting of a mixture of pyrolusite and other oxides of manganese, usually found in black, rounded masses: an ore of manganese. [1825–35; < Gk *psiló(s)* bare, smooth + *mélan,* neut. of *mélas* black]

Psi·lo·ri·ti (*Gk.* psē′lô rē′tē), *n.* **Mount,** modern name of Mount Ida.

psi·lo·sis (sī lō′sis), *n. Pathol.* **1.** a falling out of the hair. **2.** sprue[2]. [1835–45; < NL < Gk *psílōsis* lit., a stripping bare, equiv. to *psilō-,* var. s. of *psiloûn* to strip (deriv. of *psilós* bare, smooth) + *-sis* -SIS] —**psi·lot·ic** (sī lot′ik, -lō′tik), *adj.*

psi′ par′ticle, (sī, psī), *Physics.* **1.** any of a family of mesons consisting of a charmed quark and a charmed antiquark. **2.** an early name for the J/psi particle.

psit·ta·cine (sit′ə sīn′, -sin), *adj.* of or pertaining to parrots. [1870–75; < L *psittacinus* < Gk *psittákinos.* equiv. to *psittak(ós)* parrot + *-inos* -INE[1]]

psit·ta·cin·ite (sit′ə si nīt′), *n. Mineral.* mottramite. [1875–80; PSITTACINE + -ITE]

psit·ta·cism (sit′ə siz′əm), *n.* mechanical, repetitive, and meaningless speech. [1895–1900; < L *psittac(us)* parrot (see PSITTACOSIS) + -ISM] —**psit′ta·cis′tic,** *adj.*

CONCISE ETYMOLOGY KEY: <, descended or borrowed from; >, whence; b., blend of, blended; c., cognate with; cf., compare; deriv., derivative; equiv., equivalent; imit., imitative; obl., oblique; r., replacing; s., stem; sp., spelling, spelled; resp., respelling, respelled; trans., translation; ?, origin unknown; *, unattested; ‡, probably earlier than. See the full key inside the front cover.

psit·ta·co·sis (sit′ə kō′sis), *n. Pathol.* a rickettsial disease affecting birds of the parrot family, pigeons, and domestic fowl, caused by the chlamydia *Chlamydia psittaci* and transmissible to humans. Also called **ornithosis, parrot fever.** [1895–1900; < L *psittac(us)* parrot (< Gk *psittakós*) + -OSIS]

Pskov (pskôf), *n.* **1.** a lake in N Europe, between Estonia and the W Russian Federation, forming the S part of Lake Peipus. **2.** a city near this lake, in the NW Russian Federation. 202,000.

pso·as (sō′əs), *n., pl.* **pso·ai** (sō′ī), **pso·ae** (sō′ē). *Anat.* either of two muscles, one on each side of the loin, extending internally from the sides of the spinal column to the upper end of the femur, which assist in flexing and rotating the thigh and flexing the trunk on the pelvis. [1675–85; < NL < Gk *psóās,* acc. pl. (taken as nom. sing.) of *psóa* a muscle of the loins] —**pso·at·ic** (sō at′ik), *adj.*

pso·cid (sō′sid, sos′id), *n.* **1.** any of numerous minute winged insects of the family Psocidae (order Psocoptera), including most of the common barklice, having mouth parts adapted for chewing and feeding on fungi, lichens, algae, decaying plant material, etc., and occurring on the bark of trees and the leaves of plants. **2.** any member of the order Psocoptera, comprising the booklice and barklice. [1890–95; < NL *Psocidae,* equiv. to *Psoc(us)* name of a genus (< Gk *psôchos* dust) + *-idae* -ID[2]] —**pso·cine** (sō′sīn, sos′īn), *adj.*

pso·ra (sôr′ə, sōr′ə), *n. Pathol.* **1.** psoriasis. **2.** scabies. [1675–85; < L *psōra* < Gk *psṓra* itch] —**pso·ric** (sôr′ik, sor′-), *adj.*

pso·ra·len (sôr′ə lən, sōr′-), *n. Pharm.* a toxic substance, $C_{11}H_6O_3$, found in certain plants, including parsnips, used to increase the response to ultraviolet light in the treatment of severe cases of acne and psoriasis. Also called **furocoumarin.** [1930–35; < NL *Psoral(ea)* name of a genus of plants yielding the compound (< Gk *psōraléa,* neut. pl. of *psōraléos* mangy, in reference to the glandular dots on the plant; see PSORIASIS) + *-en,* var. of -ENE]

pso·ri·a·sis (sə rī′ə sis), *n. Pathol.* a common chronic, inflammatory skin disease characterized by scaly patches. Also called **psora.** [1675–85; < NL < Gk *psōríāsis,* equiv. to *psōriā-,* var. s. of *psōriân* to have the itch (deriv. of *psṓra* itch) + *-sis* -SIS] —**pso·ri·at·ic** (sôr′ē at′ik, sōr′-), *adj.*

pso·ro·sis (sə rō′sis), *n. Plant Pathol.* a disease of citrus trees, characterized by a scaly, rough bark, yellow-flecked leaves, and stunting, caused by a virus. [1895–1900; < NL; see PSORA, -OSIS]

PSRO, Professional Standards Review Organization. Also, **P.S.R.O.**

P.SS., postscripts. Also, **p.ss.** [< L *postscrīpta*]

psst (pst), *interj.* (used to attract someone's attention in an unobtrusive manner.) Also, **pst.** [1870–75]

PST, Pacific Standard Time. Also, **P.S.T., p.s.t.**

psych[1] (sīk), *v.t. Informal.* **1.** to intimidate or frighten psychologically, or make nervous (often fol. by *out*): *to psych out the competition.* **2.** to prepare psychologically to be in the right frame of mind or to give one's best (often fol. by *up*): *to psych oneself up for an interview.* **3.** to figure out psychologically; decipher (often fol. by *out*): *to psych out a problem.* Also, **psyche.** [1915–20 in earlier sense "to subject to psychoanalysis"; orig. a shortening of PSYCHOANALYZE; in later use (especially in defs. 1 and 2) perh. independent use of PSYCH-]

psych[2] (sīk), *n. Informal.* psychology, esp. as a course or field of study: *She took two semesters of psych in college.* [1890–95; by shortening]

psych-, var. of **psycho-** before some vowels: *psychasthenia.*

psych., 1. psychological. **2.** psychologist. **3.** psychology.

psy·chas·the·ni·a (sī′kəs thē′nē ə), *n. Psychiatry.* (no longer in technical use) a neurosis marked by fear, anxiety, phobias, etc. [1905–10; < NL; see PSYCH-, ASTHENIA] —**psy·chas·then·ic** (sī′kəs then′ik), *adj.*

psyche (sīk), *v.t.* **psyched, psych·ing.** psych[1].

Psy·che (sī′kē), *n.* **1.** *Class. Myth.* a personification of the soul, which in the form of a beautiful girl was loved by Eros. **2.** (*l.c.*) the human soul, spirit, or mind. **3.** (*l.c.*) *Psychol., Psychoanal.* the mental or psychological structure of a person, esp. as a motive force. **4.** *Neoplatonism.* the second emanation of the One, regarded as a universal consciousness and as the animating principle of the world. **5.** a female given name. [1650–60 for def. 2; < L *psȳchē* < Gk *psȳchḗ* lit., breath, deriv. of *psȳ́chein* to breathe, blow, hence, live (see PSYCHO-)]

psy·che·de·lia (sī′ki dēl′yə, -del′yə), *n.* the realm or artifacts of psychedelic drugs, art, writings, or the like. [1965–70, *Amer.*; PSYCHEDEL(IC) + -IA]

psy·che·del·ic (sī′ki del′ik), *adj.* **1.** of or noting a mental state characterized by a profound sense of intensified sensory perception, sometimes accompanied by severe perceptual distortion and hallucinations and by extreme feelings of either euphoria or despair. **2.** of, pertaining to, or noting any of various drugs producing this state, as LSD, mescaline, or psilocybin. **3.** resembling, characteristic of, or reproducing images, sounds, or the like, experienced while in such a state: *psychedelic painting.* —*n.* **4.** a psychedelic drug. **5.** a person who uses such a substance. Also, **psychodelic.** [1956; PSYCHE + Gk *dêl(os)* visible, manifest, evident + -IC] —**psy′·che·del′i·cal·ly,** *adv.*

Psy′che knot′, a woman's hairdo in which a knot or coil of hair projects from the back of the head. [1885–90]

psy·chi·a·trist (si kī′ə trist, sī-), *n.* a physician who practices psychiatry. [1885–90; PSYCHIATR(Y) + -IST]

psy·chi·a·try (si kī′ə trē, sī-), *n.* the practice or science of diagnosing and treating mental disorders. [1840–50; PSYCH- + -IATRY] —**psy·chi·at·ric** (sī′kē a′trik), **psy′chi·at′ri·cal,** *adj.* —**psy′chi·at′ri·cal·ly,** *adv.*

psy·chic (sī′kik), *adj.* Also, **psy′chi·cal. 1.** of or pertaining to the human soul or mind; mental (opposed to *physical*). **2.** *Psychol.* pertaining to or noting mental phenomena. **3.** outside of natural or scientific knowledge; spiritual. **4.** of or pertaining to some apparently nonphysical force or agency: *psychic research; psychic phenomena.* **5.** sensitive to influences or forces of a nonphysical or supernatural nature. —*n.* **6.** a person who is allegedly sensitive to psychic influences or forces; medium. [1855–60; < Gk *psȳchikós* of the soul. See PSYCHE, -IC] —**psy′chi·cal·ly,** *adv.*

psy′chic bid′, *Bridge.* a bid designed to mislead one's opponents that is not based on the strength of one's hand or of the suit named but rather on one's feeling that not bidding would be more costly. [1930–35]

psy′chic deter′minism, the theory that all aspects of a person's psychological makeup arise from specific causes or forces, as previous experiences or instinctual drives, which may be conscious or unconscious. [1875–80]

psy′chic dis′tance, the degree of emotional detachment maintained toward a person, group of people, event, etc. Also, **psy′chical dis′tance.**

psy′chic en′ergizer, *Pharm.* antidepressant (def. 2). [1955–60]

psy′chic en′ergy, *Psychoanal.* according to Freud, the force that lies behind all mental processes, having its basic source as the id. [1920–25]

psy′chic in′come, the personal or subjective benefits, rewards, or satisfactions derived from a job or undertaking as separate from its objective or financial ones. [1900–05]

psy·cho (sī′kō), *n., pl.* **-chos,** *adj. Slang.* —*n.* **1.** a psychopathic or neurotic person. —*adj.* **2.** psychopathic; psychoneurotic. [1935–40; shortened form]

psycho-, a combining form representing **psyche** (*psy-*

pseu′do·in′va·lid, *adj., n.*
pseu′do·in·val′id, *adj.;* **-ly,** *adv.*
pseu′do-I·ra′ni·an, *adj., n.*
pseu′do-I′rish, *adj.*
pseu′do·i′so·met′ric, *adj.*
pseu′do-I·tal′ian, *adj., n.*
pseu′do-Jap′a·nese′, *adj., n., pl.* **-nese.**
pseu′do·la′bi·al, *adj.*
pseu′do·la′bi·um, *n., pl.* **-bi·a.**
pseu′do·lat′er·al, *adj.*
pseu′do·le′gal, *adj.*
pseu′do·le·gal′i·ty, *n., pl.* **-ties.**
pseu′do·leg′end·ar′y, *adj.*
pseu′do·leg′is·la′tive, *adj.*
pseu′do·leu′cite, *n.*
pseu′do·lib′er·al, *adj., n.;* **-ly,** *adv.*
pseu′do·lin·guis′tic, *adj.*
pseu′do·lin·guis′ti·cal·ly, *adv.*
pseu′do·lit′er·ar′y, *adj.*
pseu′do·lo′bar, *adj.*
pseu′do·lu′nu·la, *n., pl.* **-lae.**
pseu′do·lu′nule, *n.*
pseu′do·ma·lar′i·a, *n.*
pseu′do·mas′cu·line, *adj.*
pseu′do-Ma′yan, *adj., n.*
pseu′do·me′di·ae′val, *adj.*
pseu′do·med′i·cal, *adj.;* **-ly,** *adv.*
pseu′do·me′di·e′val, *adj.;* **-ly,** *adv.*
pseu′do-Mes′si·an′ic, *adj.*
pseu′do-Meth′od·ist, *adj., n.*
pseu′do-Mex′i·can, *adj., n.*
pseu′do·mil′i·tar′i·ly, *adv.*
pseu′do·mil′i·ta·ris′tic, *adj.*
pseu′do·mil′i·tar′y, *adj.*
pseu′do-Mil·ton′ic, *adj.*
pseu′do·min′is·te′ri·al, *adj.*
pseu′do·min′is·try, *n., pl.* **-tries.**
pseu′do·mi·rac′u·lous, *adj.;* **-ly,** *adv.*
pseu′do·mod′ern, *adj.*
pseu′do·mod′est, *adj.;* **-ly,** *adv.*
pseu′do-Mo·ham′med·an, *adj., n.*
pseu′do·mo·nas′tic, *adj.*
pseu′do·mo·nas′ti·cal, *adj.;* **-ly,** *adv.*
pseu′do-Mon·go′li·an, *adj., n.*
pseu′do·mor′al, *adj.*
pseu′do·mor′al·is′tic, *adj.*
pseu′do·mor′u·lar, *adj.*
pseu′do-Mos′lem, *adj., n.*
pseu′do·mul′ti·loc′u·lar, *adj.*
pseu′do·mul′ti·sep′tate, *adj.*
pseu′do-Mus′lem, *adj., n.*
pseu′do-Mus′lim, *adj., n.*
pseu′do·myth′i·cal, *adj.;* **-ly,** *adv.*
pseu′do·nar·cot′ic, *adj., n.*
pseu′do·na′tion·al, *adj.;* **-ly,** *adv.*
pseu′do·no′ble, *adj.*
pseu′do-Nor·we′gian, *adj., n.*
pseu′do·oc′ci·den′tal, *adj.*
pseu′do·of·fi′cial, *adj., n.;* **-ly,** *adv.*
pseu′do·or·gan′ic, *adj.*
pseu′do·or·gan′i·cal·ly, *adv.*
pseu′do·o′ri·en′tal, *adj.;* **-ly,** *adv.*
pseu′do·or′tho·rhom′bic, *adj.*
pseu′do·o′val, *adj.;* **-ly,** *adv.*
pseu′do·pa′gan, *adj.*
pseu′do-Pan′a·ma′ni·an, *adj., n.*
pseu′do·pa′pal, *adj.*
pseu′do·par′a·sit′ic, *adj.*
pseu′do·pa′tri·ot′ic, *adj.*
pseu′do·pa′tri·ot′i·cal·ly, *adv.*
pseu′do·ped′i·form′, *adj.*
pseu′do·per′ma·nent, *adj.*
pseu′do-Per′sian, *adj., n.*
pseu′do·phal′lic, *adj.*
pseu′do·phil′an·throp′ic, *adj.*
pseu′do·phil′an·throp′i·cal, *adj.;* **-ly,** *adv.*
pseu′do·phil′o·soph′i·cal, *adj.*
pseu′do·pi′ous, *adj.;* **-ly,** *adv.*
pseu′do·po·et′ic, *adj.*
pseu′do·po·et′i·cal, *adj.*
pseu′do-Po′lish, *adj.*
pseu′do·pol′i·tic, *adj.*
pseu′do·po·lit′i·cal, *adj.*
pseu′do·pop′u·lar, *adj.*
pseu′do·por′phy·rit′ic, *adj.*
pseu′do-Pres′by·te′ri·an, *adj., n.*
pseu′do·priest′ly, *adj.*
pseu′do·prim′i·tive, *adj.*
pseu′do·prince′ly, *adv.*
pseu′do·pro·fes′sion·al, *adj.*
pseu′do·pro′fes·so′ri·al, *adj.*
pseu′do·pro·phet′ic, *adj.*
pseu′do·pro·phet′i·cal, *adj.*
pseu′do·pros′per·ous, *adj.;* **-ly,** *adv.*
pseu′do·psy′cho·log′i·cal, *adj.*
pseu′do·pyr′i·form′, *adj.*
pseu′do·re′al·is′tic, *adj.*
pseu′do·re·form′a·to′ry, *adj.*
pseu′do·re·formed′, *adj.*
pseu′do·re′gal, *adj.;* **-ly,** *adv.*
pseu′do·re·li′gious, *adj.;* **-ly,** *adv.*
pseu′do-Re·pub′li·can, *adj., n.*
pseu′do·re·pub′li·can, *adj.*
pseu′do·res′i·dent, *adj.*
pseu′do·res′i·den′tial, *adj.*
pseu′do·rheu·mat′ic, *adj.*
pseu′do-Ro′man, *adj., n.*
pseu′do·ro·man′tic, *adj.*
pseu′do·ro·man′ti·cal·ly, *adv.*
pseu′do·roy′al, *adj.;* **-ly,** *adv.*
pseu′do-Rus′sian, *adj., n.*
pseu′do·sa′cred, *adj.*
pseu′do·sac′ri·le′gious, *adj.;* **-ly,** *adv.*
pseu′do·sa·tir′i·cal, *adj.;* **-ly,** *adv.*
pseu′do·schol′ar·ly, *adj.*
pseu′do·scho·las′tic, *adj.*
pseu′do·scho·las′ti·cal·ly, *adv.*
pseu′do·se·man′tic, *adj.*
pseu′do·se·man′ti·cal·ly, *adv.*
pseu′do-Se·mit′ic, *adj.*
pseu′do·sen·sa′tion·al, *adj.*
pseu′do-Ser′bi·an, *adj., n.*
pseu′do·ser′vile, *adj.;* **-ly,** *adv.*
pseu′do·ses′sile, *adj.*
pseu′do-Shake·spear′e·an, *adj.*
pseu′do-Shake·spear′i·an, *adj.*
pseu′do·si′phon·al, *adj.*
pseu′do·si·phon′ic, *adj.*
pseu′do·skel′e·tal, *adj.*
pseu′do·so′cial, *adj.;* **-ly,** *adv.*
pseu′do·so′cial·is′tic, *adj.*
pseu′do-So·crat′ic, *adj.*
pseu′do-Span′ish, *adj.*
pseu′do·spir′i·tu·al, *adj.;* **-ly,** *adv.*
pseu′do·squa′mate, *adj.*
pseu′do·stig·mat′ic, *adj.*
pseu′do·stu′di·ous, *adj.;* **-ly,** *adv.*
pseu′do·sub′tle, *adj.;* **-tly,** *adv.*
pseu′do·su′i·ci′dal, *adj.*
pseu′do-Swed′ish, *adj.*
pseu′do·symp′to·mat′ic, *adj.*
pseu′do·syph′i·lit′ic, *adj.*
pseu′do·trib′al, *adj.;* **-ly,** *adv.*
pseu′do-Turk′ish, *adj.*
pseu′do·var′i·an, *adj.*
pseud·o′va·ry, *n., pl.* **-ries.**
pseu′do·ve′lar, *adj.*
pseu′do-Ver·gil′i·an, *adj.*
pseu′do-Vic·to′ri·an, *adj., n.*
pseu′do·vi′per·ine, *adj.*
pseu′do·vi′per·ous, *adj.;* **-ly,** *adv.*
pseu′do-Vir·gil′i·an, *adj.*
pseu′do·vis′cous, *adj.*
pseu′do·zeal′ous, *adj.;* **-ly,** *adv.*
pseu′do·zo′o·gloe′al, *adj.*
pseu′do·zo′o·log′i·cal, *adj.*

chological) and **psychological** (*psychoanalysis*) in compound words. Also, *esp. before a vowel,* **psych-.** [< Gk, comb. form of *psȳchḗ* breath, spirit, soul, mind; akin to *psȳ́chein* to blow (see PSYKTER)]

psy•cho•a•cous•tics (sī′kō ə ko͞o′stiks *or, esp. Brit.,* -ə kou′-), *n.* (*used with a singular v.*) the study of sound perception. [1945–50; PSYCHO- + ACOUSTICS] —**psy′cho•a•cous′tic, psy′cho•a•cous′ti•cal,** *adj.*

psy•cho•ac•tive (sī′kō ak′tiv), *adj.* of or pertaining to a substance having a profound or significant effect on mental processes: *a psychoactive drug.* [1960–65; PSYCHO- + ACTIVE]

psychoanal., psychoanalysis.

psy•cho•a•nal•y•sis (sī′kō ə nal′ə sis), *n.* **1.** a systematic structure of theories concerning the relation of conscious and unconscious psychological processes. **2.** a technical procedure for investigating unconscious mental processes and for treating psychoneuroses. [1905–10; < G *Psychoanalyse.* See PSYCHO-, ANALYSIS] —**psy•cho•an•a•lyt•ic** (sī′kō an′l it′ik), **psy′cho•an′a•lyt′i•cal,** *adj.* —**psy′cho•an′a•lyt′i•cal•ly,** *adv.*

psy•cho•an•a•lyst (sī′kō an′l ist), *n.* a person trained to practice psychoanalysis. [1910–15; PSYCHO- + ANALYST]

psy•cho•an•a•lyze (sī′kō an′l īz′), *v.t.,* **-lyzed, -lyz•ing.** to investigate or treat by psychoanalysis. Also, *esp. Brit.,* **psy′cho•an′a•lyse′.** [1910–15; PSYCHO- + ANALYZE] —**psy′cho•an′a•lyz′er,** *n.*

psy•cho•bab•ble (sī′kō bab′əl), *n.* writing or talk using jargon from psychiatry or psychotherapy without particular accuracy or relevance. [PSYCHO- + BABBLE; popularized by a book of the same title (1977) by U.S. journalist Richard D. Rosen (b. 1949)] —**psy′cho•bab′bler,** *n.*

psy•cho•bi•og•ra•phy (sī′kō bī og′rə fē, -bē-), *n., pl.* **-phies.** a biographical study focusing on psychological factors, as childhood traumas and unconscious motives. [1930–35; PSYCHO- + BIOGRAPHY] —**psy′cho•bi•og′ra•pher,** *n.*

psy•cho•bi•ol•o•gy (sī′kō bī ol′ə jē), *n.* **1.** the use of biological methods to study normal and abnormal emotional and cognitive processes, as the anatomical basis of memory or neurochemical abnormalities in schizophrenia. **2.** the branch of biology dealing with the relations or interactions between body and behavior, esp. as exhibited in the nervous system, receptors, effectors, or the like. [1900–05; < G *Psychobiologie.* See PSYCHO-, BIOLOGY] —**psy•cho•bi•o•log•i•cal** (sī′kō bī′ə loj′i kəl), **psy′cho•bi′o•log′ic,** *adj.* —**psy′cho•bi•ol′o•gist,** *n.*

psy•cho•chem•i•cal (sī′kō kem′i kəl), *adj.* **1.** pertaining to chemicals or drugs that affect the mind or behavior. —*n.* **2.** any such substance, esp. when used as a chemical warfare agent. [1955–60; PSYCHO- + CHEMICAL]

psy•cho•del•ic (sī′kə del′ik), *adj., n.* psychedelic.

psy•cho•di•ag•no•sis (sī′kō dī′əg nō′sis), *n.* a psychological examination using psychodiagnostic techniques. [1935–40; < NL; see PSYCHO-, DIAGNOSIS]

psy•cho•di•ag•nos•tics (sī′kō dī′əg nos′tiks), *n.* (*used with a singular v.*) the study and evaluation of character or personality in terms of behavioral and anatomical traits, as gesture, posture and physiognomy. [1930–35; see PSYCHODIAGNOSTIC, -ICS] —**psy′cho•di′ag•nos′tic,** *adj.*

psy•cho•dra•ma (sī′kō drä′mə, -dram′ə, sī′kō drä′mə, -dram′ə), *n.* a method of group psychotherapy in which participants take roles in improvisational dramatizations of emotionally charged situations. Cf. **sociodrama.** [1935–40; PSYCHO- + DRAMA] —**psy•cho•dra•mat•ic** (sī′kō drə mat′ik), *adj.*

psy•cho•dy•nam•ics (sī′kō dī nam′iks), *n.* (*used with a singular v.*) **1.** *Psychol.* any clinical approach to personality, as Freud's, that sees personality as the result of a dynamic interplay of conscious and unconscious factors. **2.** the aggregate of motivational forces, both conscious and unconscious, that determine human behavior and attitudes. Also called **dynamics.** [1870–75; PSYCHO- + DYNAMICS] —**psy′cho•dy•nam′ic,** *adj.* —**psy′cho•dy•nam′i•cal•ly,** *adv.*

psy•cho•en•do•cri•nol•o•gy (sī′kō en′dō kri nol′ə jē, -krī-), *n.* the study of the relationship between the endocrine system and various symptoms or types of mental illness. Also called **neuroendocrinology.** [1950–55; PSYCHO- + ENDOCRINOLOGY]

psy•cho•gal•van•ic (sī′kō gal van′ik), *adj. Med.* pertaining to or involving electric changes in the body resulting from reactions to mental or emotional stimuli. [1905–10; PSYCHO- + GALVANIC]

psy•cho•gal•va•nom•e•ter (sī′kō gal′və nom′i tər), *n. Med.* a type of galvanometer for detecting and measuring psychogalvanic currents. [1930–35; PSYCHO- + GALVANOMETER]

psy•cho•gen•e•sis (sī′kə jen′ə sis), *n.* **1.** genesis of the psyche. **2.** *Psychol.* the origin of physical or psychological states, normal or abnormal, out of the interplay of conscious and unconscious psychological forces. **3.** *Pathol.* the origin of symptoms as a result of emotional causes. [1830–40; < NL; see PSYCHO-, -GENESIS] —**psy•cho•ge•net•ic** (sī′kō jə net′ik), *adj.* —**psy′cho•ge•net′i•cal•ly,** *adv.*

psy•cho•gen•ic (sī′kə jen′ik), *adj. Psychol.* having origin in the mind or in a mental condition or process: *a psychogenic disorder.* [1900–05; PSYCHO- + -GENIC]

psy•cho•ger•i•at•rics (sī′kō jĕr′ē a′triks), *n.* (*used with a singular v.*) the psychology of old age. [1965–70; PSYCHO- + GERIATRICS] —**psy′cho•ger′i•at′ric,** *adj.*

psy•cho•graph (sī′kə graf′, -gräf′), *n.* **1.** *Psychol.* a graph indicating the relative strength of the personality traits of an individual. **2.** a psychologically oriented biography. [1880–85; PSYCHO- + -GRAPH] —**psy•cho•graph•ic** (sī′kə graf′ik), *adj.* —**psy′cho•graph′i•cal•ly,** *adv.*

psy•chog•ra•pher (sī kog′rə fər), *n.* a person who writes a psychograph; a psychological or psychographic biographer. [1850–55; PSYCHOGRAPH + -ER[1]]

psy•cho•graph•ics (sī′kə graf′iks), *n.* (*used with a singular v.*) the use of demographics to determine the attitudes and tastes of a particular segment of a population, as in marketing studies. [PSYCHO- + (DEMO)GRAPHICS]

psy•cho•his•to•ry (sī′kō his′tə rē, -his′trē), *n.* history or the writing of history employing the techniques of psychoanalysis to explore motivations, explain actions, etc. [1930–35; PSYCHO- + HISTORY] —**psy•cho•his•to•ri•an** (sī′kō hi stôr′ē ən, -stōr′-), *n.* —**psy•cho•his•tor•ic** (sī′kō hi stôr′ik, -stor′-), *adj.*

psy•cho•ki•ne•sis (sī′kō ki nē′sis, -kī-), *n.* the purported ability to move or deform inanimate objects, as metal spoons, through mental processes. Also called **telekinesis.** [1910–15; PSYCHO- + -KINESIS] —**psy•cho•ki•net•ic** (sī′kō ki net′ik, -kī-), *adj.*

psychol., **1.** psychological. **2.** psychologist. **3.** psychology.

psy•cho•lin•guis•tics (sī′kō ling gwis′tiks), *n.* (*used with a singular v.*) the study of the relationship between language and the cognitive or behavioral characteristics of those who use it. [1935–40; PSYCHO- + LINGUISTICS] —**psy′cho•lin′guist,** *n.* —**psy′cho•lin•guis′tic,** *adj.*

psy•cho•log•i•cal (sī′kə loj′i kəl), *adj.* **1.** of or pertaining to psychology. **2.** pertaining to the mind or to mental phenomena as the subject matter of psychology. **3.** of, pertaining to, dealing with, or affecting the mind, esp. as a function of awareness, feeling, or motivation: *psychological play; psychological effect.* Also, **psy′cho•log′ic.** [1785–95; PSYCHOLOG(Y) + -ICAL] —**psy′cho•log′i•cal•ly,** *adv.*

psycholog′ical mo′ment, the proper or critical time for achieving a desired result: *She found the right psychological moment to make her request.* [1870–75]

psycholog′ical nov′el, a novel that focuses on the complex mental and emotional lives of its characters and explores the various levels of mental activity. [1850–55]

psycholog′ical war′fare, the use of propaganda, threats, and other psychological techniques to mislead, intimidate, demoralize, or otherwise influence the thinking or behavior of an opponent. [1935–40]

psy•chol•o•gism (sī kol′ə jiz′əm), *n.* (often used pejoratively) **1.** emphasis upon psychological factors in the development of a theory, as in history or philosophy. **2.** a term or concept of psychology or psychoanalysis, esp. when used in ordinary conversation or a nontechnical context. [1855–60; PSYCHOLOG(Y) + -ISM]

psy•chol•o•gist (sī kol′ə jist), *n.* **1.** a specialist in psychology. **2.** *Philos.* an adherent to or advocate of psychologism. —*adj.* **3.** Also, **psy•chol′o•gis′tic.** of or pertaining to psychologism. [1720–30; PSYCHOLOG(Y) + -IST]

psy•chol•o•gize (sī kol′ə jīz′), *v.i.,* **-gized, -giz•ing.** to make psychological investigations or speculations, esp. those that are naive or uninformed. Also, *esp. Brit.,* **psy•chol′o•gise′.** [1820–30; PSYCHOLOG(Y) + -IZE] —**psy•chol′o•giz′er,** *n.*

psy•chol•o•gy (sī kol′ə jē), *n., pl.* **-gies.** **1.** the science of the mind or of mental states and processes. **2.** the science of human and animal behavior. **3.** the sum or characteristics of the mental states and processes of a person or class of persons, or of the mental states and processes involved in a field of activity: *the psychology of a soldier; the psychology of politics.* **4.** mental ploys or strategy: *He used psychology on his parents to get a larger allowance.* [1675–85; < NL *psȳchologia.* See PSYCHO-, -LOGY]

psy•cho•man•cy (sī′kō man′sē), *n.* occult communication between souls or with spirits. [1645–55; PSYCHO- + -MANCY]

psy•cho•met•rics (sī′kə me′triks), *n.* (*used with a singular v.*) *Psychol.* the measurement of mental traits, abilities, and processes. Also, **psychometry.** [1850–55; PSYCHO- + -METRICS]

psy•chom•e•try (sī kom′i trē), *n.* **1.** *Psychol.* psychometrics. **2.** the alleged art or faculty of divining facts concerning an object or a person associated with it, by contact with or proximity to the object. [1850–55; PSYCHO- + -METRY] —**psy′cho•met′ric, psy′cho•met′ri•cal,** *adj.* —**psy•chom•e•tri•cian** (sī kom′i trish′ən), **psy•chom′e•trist,** *n.*

psy•cho•mi•met•ic (sī′kō mi met′ik, -mī-), *adj.* psychotomimetic. [1965–70; PSYCHO- + MIMETIC]

psy•cho•mo•tor (sī′kō mō′tər), *adj.* of or pertaining to a response involving both motor and psychological components. [1875–80; PSYCHO- + MOTOR]

psychomo′tor agita′tion, agitation (def. 3).

psy′chomo′tor ep′ilepsy. See **temporal-lobe epilepsy.** [1935–40]

psychomo′tor retarda′tion, a generalized slowing of psychological and physical activity, frequently occurring as a symptom of severe depression.

psy•cho•neu•ro•sis (sī′kō no͝o rō′sis, -nyo͝o-), *n., pl.* **-ses** (-sēz). neurosis (def. 1). [1880–85; PSYCHO- + NEUROSIS]

psy•cho•neu•rot•ic (sī′kō no͝o rot′ik, -nyo͝o-), *adj., n.,* neurotic[1]. [1900–05; PSYCHO- + NEUROTIC]

psy•cho•path (sī′kə path′), *n.* a psychopathic person. [1880–85; PSYCHO- + -PATH]

psy•cho•path•ic (sī′kə path′ik), *adj.* of, pertaining to, or affected with psychopathy. [1840–50; PSYCHOPATH(Y) + -IC]

psy•cho•pa•thol•o•gy (sī′kō pə thol′ə jē), *n.* **1.** the science or study of mental disorders. **2.** the conditions and processes of a mental disorder. **3.** a pathological deviation from normal or efficient behavior; psychosis. [1840–50; PSYCHO- + PATHOLOGY] —**psy•cho•path•o•log•i•cal** (sī′kō path′ə loj′i kəl), **psy′cho•path′o•log′ic,** *adj.* —**psy′cho•pa•thol′o•gist,** *n.*

psy•chop•a•thy (sī kop′ə thē), *n. Psychiatry.* **1.** a mental disorder in which an individual manifests amoral and antisocial behavior, lack of ability to love or establish meaningful personal relationships, extreme egocentricity, failure to learn from experience, etc. **2.** any mental disease. [1840–50; PSYCHO- + -PATHY]

psy•cho•phar•ma•col•o•gy (sī′kō fär′mə kol′ə jē), *n.* the branch of pharmacology dealing with the psychological effects of drugs. [1915–20; PSYCHO- + PHARMACOLOGY] —**psy•cho•phar•ma•co•log•ic** (sī′kō fär′mə kə loj′ik), **psy′cho•phar′ma•co•log′i•cal,** *adj.*

psy•cho•phar•ma•co•ther•a•py (sī′kō fär′mə kō ther′ə pē), *n.* the use of psychoactive drugs in the symptomatic treatment or control of mental disorders or psychiatric disease. [PSYCHO- + PHARMACO- + THERAPY]

psy′chophys′ical par′allelism, *Philos.* the view that mental and bodily events occur in parallel series without causal interaction. Cf. **occasionalism.** [1890–95]

psy•cho•phys•ics (sī′kō fiz′iks), *n.* (*used with a singular v.*) the branch of psychology that deals with the relationships between physical stimuli and resulting sensations and mental states. [1875–80; < G *Psychophysik.* See PSYCHO-, PHYSICS] —**psy•cho•phys•i•cal** (sī′kō fiz′i kəl), **psy′cho•phys′ic,** *adj.* —**psy′cho•phys′i•cal•ly,** *adv.* —**psy•cho•phys•i•cist** (sī′kō fiz′ə sist), *n.*

psy•cho•phys•i•o•log•i•cal (sī′kō fiz′ē ə loj′i kəl), *adj.* of or pertaining to psychophysiology. Also, **psy′cho•phys′i•o•log′ic.** [1830–40; PSYCHOPHYSIOLOG(Y) + -ICAL] —**psy′cho•phys′i•o•log′i•cal•ly,** *adv.*

psy′chophysiolog′ic disor′der, any of a group of disorders, as tension headache, characterized by physical symptoms that are partly induced by emotional factors. [1975–80]

psy•cho•phys•i•ol•o•gy (sī′kō fiz′ē ol′ə jē), *n.* the branch of physiology that deals with the interrelation of mental and physical phenomena. [1830–40; PSYCHO- + PHYSIOLOGY] —**psy′cho•phys′i•ol′o•gist,** *n.*

psy•cho•pomp (sī′kō pomp′), *n.* a person who conducts spirits or souls to the other world, as Hermes or Charon. [1860–65; < Gk *psȳchopompós* conductor of souls. See PSYCHO-, POMP]

psy•cho•pro•phy•lax•is (sī′kō prō′fə lak′sis, -prof′ə-), *n.* See **Lamaze method.** [1955–60; PSYCHO- + PROPHYLAXIS] —**psy•cho•pro•phy•lac•tic** (sī′kō prō′fə lak′tik, -prof′ə-), *adj.*

psy•cho•sex•u•al (sī′kō sek′sho͞o əl *or, esp. Brit.,* -seks′yo͞o-), *adj.* of or pertaining to the relationship of psychological and sexual phenomena. [1895–1900; PSYCHO- + SEXUAL] —**psy′cho•sex′u•al′i•ty,** *n.* —**psy′cho•sex′u•al•ly,** *adv.*

psy•cho•sis (sī kō′sis), *n., pl.* **-ses** (-sēz). **1.** a mental disorder characterized by symptoms, such as delusions or hallucinations, that indicate impaired contact with reality. **2.** any severe form of mental disorder, as schizophrenia or paranoia. [1840–50; < LGk *psȳ́chōsis* animation, principle of life. See PSYCH-, -OSIS]

psy•cho•so•cial (sī′kō sō′shəl), *adj.* of or pertaining to the interaction between social and psychological factors. [1895–1900; PSYCHO- + SOCIAL] —**psy′cho•so′cial•ly,** *adv.*

psy•cho•so•ci•ol•o•gy (sī′kō sō′sē ol′ə jē, -sō′shē-), *n.* the study of subjects, issues, and problems common to psychology and sociology. [1905–10; PSYCHO- + SOCIOLOGY] —**psy•cho•so•ci•o•log•i•cal** (sī′kō sō′sē ə loj′i kəl, -sō′shē-), *adj.* —**psy′cho•so′ci•ol′o•gist,** *n.*

psy•cho•so•mat•ic (sī′kō sə mat′ik, -sō-), *adj.* **1.** of or pertaining to a physical disorder that is caused by or notably influenced by emotional factors. **2.** pertaining to or involving both the mind and the body. [1860–65; PSYCHO- + SOMATIC] —**psy′cho•so•mat′i•cal•ly,** *adv.*

psy•cho•sur•ger•y (sī′kō sûr′jə rē), *n.* treatment of mental disorders by means of brain surgery. Cf. **lobotomy.** [1935–40; PSYCHO- + SURGERY] —**psy•cho•sur•geon** (sī′kō sûr′jən), *n.* —**psy•cho•sur•gi•cal** (sī′kō sûr′ji kəl), *adj.*

psy•cho•syn•the•sis (sī′kō sin′thə sis), *n.* a theoretical effort to reconcile components of the unconscious, including dreams, with the rest of the personality. [1915–20; PSYCHO- + SYNTHESIS]

psy•cho•tech•nics (sī′kō tek′niks), *n.* (*used with a singular v.*) the use of psychological techniques for controlling and modifying human behavior, esp. for practical ends. Cf. **psychotechnology.** [1925–30; PSYCHO- + TECHNICS]

psy•cho•tech•nol•o•gy (sī′kō tek nol′ə jē), *n.* the body of knowledge, theories, and techniques developed for understanding and influencing individual, group, and societal behavior in specified situations. [1920–25; PSYCHO- + TECHNOLOGY] —**psy•cho•tech•no•log•i•cal** (sī′kō tek′nə loj′i kəl), *adj.* —**psy′cho•tech•nol′o•gist,** *n.*

psy•cho•ther•a•peu•tics (sī′kō ther′ə pyo͞o′tiks), *n.* (*used with a singular v.*) psychotherapy. [1870–75; PSYCHO- + THERAPEUTICS] —**psy′cho•ther′a•peu′tic,** *adj.* —**psy′cho•ther′a•peu′ti•cal•ly,** *adv.* —**psy′cho•ther′a•peu′tist,** *n.*

psy•cho•ther•a•py (sī′kō ther′ə pē), *n., pl.* **-pies.** the treatment of psychological disorders or maladjustments by a professional technique, as psychoanalysis, group therapy, or behavioral therapy. [1890–95; PSYCHO- + THERAPY] —**psy′cho•ther′a•pist,** *n.*

psy·chot·ic (sī kot′ik), *adj.* **1.** characterized by or afflicted with psychosis. —*n.* **2.** a person afflicted with psychosis. [1885–85; PSYCH(OSIS) + -OTIC] —**psy·chot′i·cal·ly,** *adv.*

psy·chot·o·gen (sī kot′ə jən, -jen′), *n.* a substance that causes a psychotic reaction. [1955–60; PSYCHOT(IC) + -O- + -GEN] —**psy·chot′o·gen′ic,** *adj.*

psy·chot·o·mi·met·ic (sī kot′ō mə met′ik, -mī-), *adj.* (of a substance or drug) tending to produce symptoms like those of a psychosis; hallucinatory. Also, **psychomimetic.** [1955–60; PSYCHOT(IC) + -O- + MIMETIC]

psy·cho·tox·ic (sī′kō tok′sik), *adj. Pharm.* toxic or harmful to the mind or personality. [1960–65; PSYCHO- + TOXIC] —**psy·cho·tox·ic·i·ty** (sī′kō tok sis′i tē), *n.*

psy·cho·tron·ic (sī′kə tron′ik), *adj.* of or pertaining to a genre of usu. low-budget movies that includes horror, fantasy, science-fiction, and underground films. [1985–90; appar. PSYCHO- + -TRON + -IC]

psy·cho·tro·pic (sī′kō trō′pik), *adj.* **1.** affecting mental activity, behavior, or perception, as a mood-altering drug. —*n.* **2.** a psychotropic drug, as a tranquilizer, sedative, or antidepressant. [1945–50; PSYCHO- + -TROPIC]

psych-out (sīk′out′), *n. Informal.* an act or instance of psyching out. [1960–65; n. use of v. phrase *psych out*]

psychro-, a combining form meaning "cold," used in the formation of compound words: *psychrometer.* [comb. form repr. Gk *psychrós* cold; akin to *psȳchein* to blow (see PSYKTER)]

psy·chrom·e·ter (sī krom′i tər), *n.* an instrument for determining atmospheric humidity by the reading of two thermometers, the bulb of one being kept moist and ventilated. [1720–30; PSYCHRO- + -METER] —**psy·chro·met·ric** (sī′krə me′trik), **psy′chro·met′ri·cal,** *adj.*

psy′chromet′ric chart′, a chart for calculating values of relative humidity, absolute humidity, and dew point from psychrometer readings.

psy·chrom·e·try (sī krom′i trē), *n.* **1.** the employment of the psychrometer. **2.** the science of measuring the water-vapor content of the air. [1860–65; PSYCHRO- + -METRY]

psyk·ter (sik′tər), *n., pl.* **-ters.** *Gk. and Rom. Antiq.* a wine jar with an ovoid body tapering at the neck, set on a high foot: used for cooling wine. Also, **psyc′ter.** [1840–50; < Gk *psyktḗr*, deriv. of *psȳ́chein* to blow (cool); cf. PSYCHE, PSYCHRO-]

psyl·la (sil′ə), *n.* See **jumping plant louse.** Also, **psyl′lid** (sil′id). [< NL (1811) *Psylla* genus name < Gk *psýlla* flea]

psyl′lid yel′lows, (*used with a singular or plural v.*) *Plant Pathol.* a viral disease transmitted by the potato psyllid, causing the young leaves of potatoes, tomatoes, eggplants, and peppers to curl and turn yellow or purplish.

psyl·li·um (sil′ē əm), *n.* **1.** fleawort. **2.** Also called **psyl′lium seed′.** the seeds of this plant, used as a laxative. [1595–1605; < NL < Gk *psyllion, psyllíon,* deriv. of *psýlla* flea]

psy·war (sī′wôr′), *Informal.* —*n.* **1.** See **psychological warfare.** —*adj.* **2.** of, pertaining to, or characteristic of psychological warfare: *to wage a psywar campaign against the enemy.* [1950–55, *Amer.*; by shortening]

Pt, *Symbol, Chem.* platinum.

pt, pint; pints.

Pt., **1.** point. **2.** port.

pt., **1.** part. **2.** payment. **3.** pint; pints. **4.** point. **5.** port. **6.** preterit.

P.T., **1.** Also, **PT** Pacific Time. **2.** physical therapy. **3.** physical training. **4.** postal telegraph. **5.** post town. **6.** pupil teacher.

p.t., **1.** Pacific Time. **2.** past tense. **3.** post town. **4.** pro tempore.

PTA, See **Parent-Teacher Association.** Also, **P.T.A.**

Pta., *pl.* **Ptas.** peseta.

Ptah (ptä, ptäKH), *n.* an ancient Egyptian deity, believed to be a universal creator, worshiped esp. at Memphis when it was the royal residence.

ptar·mi·gan (tär′mi gən), *n., pl.* **-gans,** (*esp. collectively*) **-gan.** any of several grouses of the genus *Lagopus,* of mountainous and cold northern regions, having feathered feet. [1590–1600; pseudo-Gk sp. of ScotGael *tarmarchan,* akin to Ir *tarmanach*]

ptarmigan, *Lagopus lagopus,* length 15 in. (38 cm)

PT boat, *U.S. Mil.* a small, fast, lightly armed, unarmored, and highly maneuverable boat used chiefly for torpedoing enemy shipping. Also called **mosquito boat, motor torpedo boat.** [1940–45; *p(atrol) t(orpedo)*]

PTC, *Biochem.* phenylthiocarbamide. Cf. **phenylthiourea.**

CONCISE ETYMOLOGY KEY: <, descended or borrowed from; >, whence; b., blend of, blended; c., cognate with; cf., compare; deriv., derivative; equiv., equivalent; imit., imitative; obl., oblique; r., replacing; s., stem; sp., spelling, spelled; resp., respelling, respelled; trans., translation; ?, origin unknown; *, unattested; ‡, probably earlier than. See the full key inside the front cover.

pter-, var. of **ptero-** before a vowel: *pteranodon.*

-pter, a combining form meaning "one with wings" of the kind specified: *hymenopter.* [see -PTEROUS]

pter·an·o·don (tə ran′ə don′), *n.* a flying reptile of the extinct order Pterosauria, from the Cretaceous Period, having a wingspread of about 25 feet (8 m). [< NL, equiv. to *pter-* PTER- + Gk *anódōn* toothless (see AN-¹, -ODONT)]

pterido-, a combining form meaning "fern," used in the formation of compound words: *pteridology.* [< NL, comb. form repr. Gk *pterís* (s. *pterid-*) fern, deriv. of *pterón* feather]

pter·i·dol·o·gy (ter′i dol′ə jē), *n.* the branch of botany dealing with ferns and related plants, as the horsetails and club mosses. [1850–55; PTERIDO- + -LOGY] —**pter·i·do·log·i·cal** (ter′i dl oj′i kəl), *adj.* —**pter′i·dol′o·gist,** *n.*

pte·rid·o·phyte (tə rid′ə fīt′, ter′i dō-), *n.* any plant of the division Pteridophyta, characterized by vascular tissue and differentiation into root, stem, and leaves, comprising the ferns, horsetails, and club mosses. [1875–80; < NL *Pteridophyta;* see PTERIDO-, -PHYTE] —**pte·rid·o·phyt·ic** (tə rid′ə fit′ik, ter′i dō-), **pter·i·doph·y·tous** (ter′i dof′i təs), *adj.*

pte·rid·o·sperm (tə rid′ə spûrm′, ter′i dō-), *n.* See **seed fern.** [1900–05; < NL *Pteridospermales* the order; see PTERIDO-, SPERM¹, -ALES]

pte·ri·on (tēr′ē on′, ter′-), *n. Craniom.* the craniometric point at the side of the sphenoidal fontanelle. [1875–80; < NL, alter. of Gk *pterón* wing, on model of INION]

ptero-, a combining form meaning "wing," "feather," used in the formation of compound words: *pterodactyl.* Also, **pter-.** [< NL, comb. form repr. Gk *pterón*]

pter·o·car·pous (ter′ə kär′pəs), *adj. Bot.* having winged fruit. [1865–70; < NL; see PTERO-, -CARPOUS]

pter·o·dac·tyl (ter′ə dak′til), *n.* any of a number of genera of flying reptiles of the extinct order Pterosauria, from the Jurassic and Cretaceous periods, having a highly reduced tail and teeth and a birdlike beak. [1820–30; < NL *Pterodactylus* genus name, equiv. to Gk *pteró(n)* wing + *-daktylos* -DACTYLOUS] —**pter′o·dac·tyl′ic, pter′o·dac′tyl·ous,** *adj.* —**pter′o·dac′tyl·id,** *adj., n.* —**pter′o·dac′tyl·oid′,** *adj.*

pterodactyl, genus *Pterodactylus,* wingspread to 20 ft. (0.3 to 6 m)

pte·ro·ma (tə rō′mə, te-), *n., pl.* **-ma·ta** (-mə tə). pteron. [< L *pterōma* < Gk *ptérōma*]

pte·ron (ter′on), *n. Archit.* **1.** (in a classical temple) a colonnade parallel to, but apart from, the cella. **2.** the space between this and the cella. [1840–50; < L < Gk *pterón* lit., wing]

pter·o·pod (ter′ə pod′), *adj.* **1.** belonging or pertaining to the Pteropoda, a group of mollusks having the lateral portions of the foot expanded into winglike lobes used in swimming. —*n.* **2.** a pteropod mollusk. [1825–35; < NL *Pteropoda* (pl.); see PTERO-, -POD]

pter·o·po·di·um (ter′ə pō′dē əm), *n., pl.* **-po·di·a** (-pō′dē ə). the foot of a pteropod. [1880–85; < NL; see PTEROPOD, -IUM]

pter·o·saur (ter′ə sôr′), *n.* any flying reptile of the extinct order Pterosauria, from the Jurassic and Cretaceous periods, having the outside digit of the forelimb greatly elongated and supporting a wing membrane. [1860–65; < NL *Pterosauria;* see PTERO-, -SAUR]

-pterous, a combining form meaning "having wings" of the kind or number specified: *dipterous.* [< Gk *-pteros,* adj. deriv. of *pterón* wing; see -OUS]

pte·ryg·i·um (tə rij′ē əm), *n., pl.* **-ryg·i·ums, -ryg·i·a** (-rij′ē ə). *Opthalm.* an abnormal triangular mass of thickened conjunctiva extending over the cornea and interfering with vision. [1650–60; < NL < Gk *pterýgion* little wing or fin, equiv. to *pteryg-* (s. of *ptéryx*) wing, fin + *-ion* dim. suffix] —**pte·ryg′i·al,** *adj.*

pter·y·gote (ter′i gōt′), *adj.* belonging or pertaining to the arthropod subclass Pterygota, comprising the winged insects. Also, **pte·ryg·o·tous** (tə rig′ə təs). [1875–80; < NL *Pterygota* < Gk *pterýgōta,* neut. pl. of *pterygōtós* winged, deriv. of *pteryg-* (s. of *ptéryx*) wing]

pter·y·la (ter′ə lə), *n., pl.* **-lae** (-lē′, -lī′). *Ornith.* one of the feathered areas on the skin of a bird. Also called **feather tract.** Cf. **apterium.** [1865–70; < NL < Gk *pter(ón)* feather + *hȳ́lē* woods]

ptg., printing.

PTH, See **parathyroid hormone.**

ptis·an (tiz′ən, ti zan′), *n.* a nourishing decoction, originally one made from barley, purported to have medicinal quality. [1350–1400; < L *ptisana* < Gk *ptisánē* peeled barley, barley water; r. ME *tisane* < F < L, as above]

PTM, *Telecommunications.* See **pulse-time modulation.**

PTO, **1.** Patent and Trademark Office. **2.** *Mach.* See **power takeoff.**

P.T.O., please turn over (a page or leaf). Also, **p.t.o.**

Ptol·e·mae·us (tol′ə mā′əs), *n.* a walled plain in the third quadrant of the face of the moon: about 90 miles (144 km) in diameter.

Ptol·e·ma·ic (tol′ə mā′ik), *adj.* **1.** of or pertaining to Ptolemy or his system of astronomy. **2.** of or pertaining to the dynastic house of the Ptolemies or the period of their rule in Egypt. [1665–75; < Gk *Ptolemaikós* of Ptolemy, equiv. to *Ptolema(îos)* PTOLEMY + *-ikos* -IC]

Ptol′ema′ic sys′tem, *Astron.* a system elaborated by Ptolemy and later modified by others, according to which the earth was the fixed center of the universe, with the heavenly bodies moving about it. [1765–75]

Ptol·e·ma·ist (tol′ə mā′ist), *n.* an adherent or advocate of the Ptolemaic system of astronomy. [1875–80; PTOLEMA(IC) + -IST]

Ptol·e·my (tol′ə mē), *n., pl.* **-mies** for 2. **1.** (*Claudius Ptolemaeus*) fl. A.D. 127–151, Hellenistic mathematician, astronomer, and geographer in Alexandria. **2.** any of the kings of the Macedonian dynasty that ruled Egypt 323–30 B.C.

Ptolemy I, (surnamed *Soter*) 367?–280 B.C., ruler of Egypt 323–285: founder of Macedonian dynasty in Egypt.

Ptolemy II, (surnamed *Philadelphus*) 309?–247? B.C., king of Egypt 285–247? (son of Ptolemy I).

pto·maine (tō′mān, tō mān′), *n.* any of a class of foul-smelling nitrogenous substances produced by bacteria during putrefaction of animal or plant protein: formerly thought to be toxic. [1875–80; < It *ptomaina* < Gk *ptôma* corpse + It *-ina* -INE[2]] —**pto·main′ic,** *adj.*

pto′maine poi′soning, (erroneously) food poisoning thought to be caused by ptomaine. [1890–95]

pto·sis (tō′sis), *n. Pathol.* **1.** a drooping of the upper eyelid. **2.** prolapse or drooping of any organ. [1735–45; < NL < Gk *ptôsis* a falling] —**pto·tic** (tō′tik), *adj.*

ptp., past participle.

pts., **1.** parts. **2.** payments. **3.** pints. **4.** points. **5.** ports.

PTSD, posttraumatic stress disorder.

PTT, Post, Telegraph, and Telephone (the government-operated system, as in France or Turkey).

ptu·i (to͞o′ē, pto͞o′ē), *interj.* (used to indicate the sound or act of spitting.)

PTV, public television.

pty·a·lec·ta·sis (tī′ə lek′tə sis), *n., pl.* **-ses** (-sēz′). spontaneous or surgical dilatation of a salivary duct. [< Gk *ptýal(on)* saliva + *éktasis* a stretching out, equiv. to *ek-* EC- + *ta-,* var. s. of *teínein* to stretch + *-sis* -SIS]

pty·a·lin (tī′ə lin), *n. Biochem.* an enzyme in the saliva that converts starch into dextrin and maltose. Also called **salivary amylase.** [1835–45; < Gk *ptýal(on)* spittle, saliva + -IN[2]]

pty·a·lism (tī′ə liz′əm), *n. Pathol.* excessive secretion of saliva. [1675–85; < Gk *ptyalismós* expectoration, equiv. to *ptýal(on)* spittle + *-ismos* -ISM]

Pu, *Symbol, Chem.* plutonium.

pub (pub), *n.* a bar or tavern. [1855–60; short for PUBLIC HOUSE]

pub., **1.** public. **2.** publication. **3.** published. **4.** publisher. **5.** publishing.

pub′ crawl′, an instance or period of pub-crawling. Also, **pub′-crawl′.** [1910–15]

pub-crawl (pub′krôl′), *v.i.* **1.** to have drinks at one bar after another. —*n.* **2.** See **pub crawl.** [1935–40] —**pub′-crawl′er,** *n.*

pub′ date′, *Informal.* See **publication date.** [by shortening]

pu·ber·tal (pyo͞o′bər tl), *adj.* of, pertaining to, or characteristic of puberty. Also, **pu·ber·al** (pyo͞o′bər əl). [1830–40; PUBERT(Y) + -AL[1]]

pu·ber·ty (pyo͞o′bər tē), *n.* the period or age at which a person is first capable of sexual reproduction of offspring: in common law, presumed to be 14 years in the male and 12 years in the female. [1350–1400; ME *puberte* < L *pūbertās* adulthood, equiv. to *pūber-,* s. of *pūbēs* grown-up + *-tās* -TY[2]]

pu·ber·u·lent (pyo͞o ber′yə lənt, -ber′ə-), *adj. Bot., Zool.* minutely pubescent. Also, **pu·ber·u·lous** (pyo͞o ber′yə ləs, -ber′ə-). [1860–65; < L *pūber-* (see PUBERTY) + -ULENT]

pu·bes[1] (pyo͞o′bēz), *n., pl.* **pu·bes.** *Anat.* **1.** the lower part of the abdomen, esp. the region between the right and left iliac regions. **2.** the hair appearing on the lower part of the abdomen at puberty. [1560–70; < L *pūbēs* adulthood, pubic hair, groin]

pu·bes[2] (pyo͞o′bēz), *n.* pl. of **pubis.**

pu·bes·cent (pyo͞o bes′ənt), *adj.* **1.** arriving or arrived at puberty. **2.** *Bot., Zool.* covered with down or fine short hair. [1640–50; < L *pūbēscent-* (s. of *pūbēscēns*), prp. of *pūbēscere* to attain puberty, reach puberty, become hairy or downy. See PUBES[1], -ESCENT] —**pu·bes′cence, pu·bes′cen·cy,** *n.*

pu·bic (pyo͞o′bik), *adj.* of, pertaining to, or situated near the pubes or the pubis. [1825–35; PUB(ES)[1] + -IC]

pu′bic louse′. See under **louse** (def. 1).

pu′bic sym′physis, *Anat.* the fixed joint at the front of the pelvic girdle where the halves of the pubis meet. See diag. under **pelvis.** [1930–35]

pu·bis (pyo͞o′bis), *n., pl.* **-bes** (-bēz). *Anat.* that part of either innominate bone that, with the corresponding part of the other, forms the front of the pelvis. See diag. under **pelvis.** [1590–1600; short for NL *os pūbis* bone of the PUBES[1]]

publ., **1.** public. **2.** publication. **3.** publicity. **4.** published. **5.** publisher.

pub·lic (pub′lik), *adj.* **1.** of, pertaining to, or affecting a population or a community as a whole: *public funds; a public nuisance.* **2.** done, made, acting, etc., for the community as a whole: *public prosecution.* **3.** open to all persons: *a public meeting.* **4.** of, pertaining to, or being in the service of a community or nation, esp. as a government officer: *a public official.* **5.** maintained at the public expense and under public control: *a public library; a public road.* **6.** generally known: *The fact became public.* **7.** familiar to the public; prominent: *public figures.* **8.** open to the view of all; existing or conducted in public: *a public dispute.* **9.** pertaining or devoted to the welfare or well-being of the community: *public spirit.* **10.** of or pertaining to all humankind; universal. **11. go public, a.** to issue stock for sale to the general public. **b.** to present private or previously concealed information, news, etc., to the public; make matters open to public view: *The Senator threatened to go public with his Congressional-reform plan.* **12. make public,** to cause to become known generally, as through the news media: *Her resignation was made public this morning.* —*n.* **13.** the people constituting a community, state, or nation. **14.** a particular group of people with a common interest, aim, etc.: *the book-buying public.* **15.** *Brit. Informal.* a tavern; public house. **16. in public,** not in private; in a situation open to public view or access; publicly: *It was the first time that she had sung in public.* [1400–50; < L *pūblicus* (earlier *pōblicus, pōplicus,* akin to *populus* PEOPLE); r. late ME *publique* < MF < L, as above]

pub′lic-ac·cess tel′evision (pub′lik ak′ses, -ak′-), **1.** a noncommercial system of broadcasting on television channels made available to independent or community groups for programs of general interest to the community. **2.** one or more channels on cable television that by law are reserved for noncommercial broadcasting by members of the public. Also called **public-access TV.** [1970–75]

pub′lic account′ant, an accountant whose services are available to the public at large, in contrast to one employed on a full-time basis by a company. —**pub′lic account′ing.**

pub′lic act′. See **public law** (def. 1).

pub′lic-ad·dress′ sys′tem (pub′lik ə dres′), a combination of electronic devices that makes sound audible via loudspeakers to many people, as in an auditorium or out of doors. Also called **PA system, P.A. system, p.a. system.** [1920–25]

pub′lic administra′tion, 1. the implementation of public policy, largely by the executive branch. **2.** a field of study preparing persons for careers in such work.

pub′lic admin′istrator, 1. an official of a city, county, or state government. **2.** a person appointed to administer the estate of a deceased person, esp. during the period when a will is being contested.

pub′lic affairs′, matters of general interest or concern, esp. those dealing with current social or political issues. [1605–15]

pub·li·can (pub′li kən), *n.* **1.** *Chiefly Brit.* a person who owns or manages a tavern; the keeper of a pub. **2.** *Rom. Hist.* a person who collected public taxes. **3.** any collector of taxes, tolls, tribute, or the like. [1150–1200; ME < L *pūblicānus.* See PUBLIC, -AN]

pub′lic assis′tance, government aid to the poor, disabled, or aged or to dependent children, as financial assistance or food stamps. [1900–05] —**pub′lic-as·sis′·tance,** *adj.*

pub·li·ca·tion (pub′li kā′shən), *n.* **1.** the act of publishing a book, periodical, map, piece of music, engraving, or the like. **2.** the act of bringing before the public; announcement. **3.** the state or fact of being published. **4.** something that is published, esp. a periodical. [1350–1400; ME *publicacioun* < L *pūblicātiōn-* (s. of *pūblicātiō*) a making public, confiscation, equiv. to *pūblicāt(us)* (ptp. of *pūblicāre* to make PUBLIC) + *-iōn-* -ION]

publica′tion date′, the date on which a book or periodical is or is planned to be published. [1930–35]

pub′lic bar′, *Brit.* (in a tavern or pub) the common section of a bar or barroom, not as exclusive, as quiet, or as comfortably furnished as the saloon section.

pub′lic bill′, a congressional or parliamentary bill involving the general interests of the people at large or of the whole community. Cf. **private bill.** [1670–80]

Pub′lic Broad′casting Serv′ice, a network of independent, noncommercial television stations that operate with public and government funding instead of with revenues from advertising. *Abbr.:* PBS [1965–70]

pub′lic charge′, a person who is in economic distress and is supported at government expense: *He assured the American consul that the prospective immigrant would not become a public charge.* [1880–85]

pub′lic com′pany, *Brit.* a company that has more than 50 shareholders and whose shares are offered for public subscription. Cf. **private company.**

pub′lic conven′ience, *Chiefly Brit.* a rest room, esp. at a large public place, as at a railroad station.

pub′lic corpora′tion, 1. a corporation, owned and operated by a government, established for the administration of certain public programs. **2.** See **municipal corporation. 3.** a large private corporation with many shares, which are sold to the public or traded on a stock exchange. [1820–30]

pub′lic debt′. See **national debt.** [1715–25]

pub′lic defend′er, a lawyer appointed or elected by a city or county as a full-time, official defender to represent indigents in criminal cases at public expense. Cf. **assigned counsel.** [1915–20]

pub′lic domain′, *Law.* **1.** the status of a literary work or an invention whose copyright or patent has expired or that never had such protection. **2.** land owned by the government. [1825–35, *Amer.*] —**pub′lic-do·main′,** *adj.*

pub′lic en′emy, 1. a person or thing considered a danger or menace to the public, esp. a wanted criminal widely sought by the F.B.I. and local police forces. **2.** a nation or government with which one's own is at war. [1750–60]

Pub′lic En′emy Num′ber One′, 1. (not in official use) a criminal at the top of the FBI's list of the ten most wanted criminals. **2.** a major menace to public safety, health, etc.: *Cancer is Public Enemy Number One.* Also **Public Enemy Number 1, Public Enemy No. 1.** [1930–35, *Amer.*]

pub′lic eye′, public attention or notice; limelight: *a politician who keeps out of the public eye.* [1890–95]

pub′lic health′, health services to improve and protect community health, esp. sanitation, immunization, and preventive medicine. [1610–20] —**pub′lic-health′,** *adj.*

pub′lic house′, 1. *Brit.* a tavern. **2.** an inn or hostelry. [1565–75]
—**Syn.** See **hotel.**

pub′lic hous′ing, housing owned or operated by a government and usually offered at low rent to the needy.

pub′lic in′terest, 1. the welfare or well-being of the general public; commonwealth: *health programs that directly affect the public interest.* **2.** appeal or relevance to the general populace: *a news story of public interest.* [1670–80] —**pub′lic-in′terest,** *adj.*

pub′lic-in′ter·est law′, a branch of law that often utilizes class-action suits to protect the interest of a large group or of the public at large, as in matters relating to racial discrimination, air pollution, etc. [1965–70]

pub′lic interna′tional law′, 1. Also called **public law.** the law governing the legal relations between independent states or nations and, increasingly, between these and individuals. **2.** See **conflict of laws** (def. 2).

pub·li·cist (pub′lə sist), *n.* **1.** a person who publicizes, esp. a press agent or public-relations consultant. **2.** an expert in current public or political affairs. **3.** an expert in public or international law. [1785–95; < G; see PUBLIC, -IST]

pub·lic·i·ty (pu blis′i tē), *n.* **1.** extensive mention in the news media or by word of mouth or other means of communication. **2.** public notice so gained. **3.** the measures, process, or business of securing public notice. **4.** information, articles, or advertisements issued to secure public notice or attention. **5.** the state of being public, or open to general observation or knowledge. [1785–95; < F *publicité* < ML *pūblicitās.* See PUBLIC, -ITY]

pub·li·cize (pub′lə sīz′), *v.t.,* **-cized, -ciz·ing.** to give publicity to; bring to public notice; advertise: *They publicized the meeting as best they could.* Also, *esp. Brit.,* **pub′li·cise′.** [1925–30; PUBLIC + -IZE]
—**Syn.** promote, sell, acclaim, announce.

pub′lic law′, 1. Also called **public act, public statute.** a law or statute of a general character that applies to the people of a whole state or nation. **2.** a branch of law dealing with the legal relationships between the state and individuals and with the relations among governmental agencies. Cf. **private law. 3.** See **public international law.** [1765–75]

Pub′lic Lend′ing Right′, (in Britain) an act of Parliament that directs compensation to an author for the library loan of his or her book.

pub′lic-li·a·bil′i·ty insur′ance (pub′lik lī′ə bil′i tē), insurance covering the insured against risks involving liability to the public for damages arising from negligence.

pub′lic li′brary, a nonprofit library established for the use of the general public and maintained chiefly by public funds. [1605–15]

pub′lic life′, public service as an elected or appointed government official. [1775–85]

pub·lic·ly (pub′lik lē), *adv.* **1.** in a public or open manner or place. **2.** by the public. **3.** in the name of the community. **4.** by public action or consent. [1925–30; PUBLIC + -LY]

pub·lic·ness (pub′lik nis), *n.* the quality or state of being public or being owned by the public. [1595–1605; PUBLIC + -NESS]

pú·bli·co (po͞o′bli kō′; *Sp.* po͞o′vlē kô′), *n., pl.* **-cos** (-kōz′; *Sp.* -kôs′). (esp. in Puerto Rico) a taxi that picks up and discharges passengers along a fixed route. [< AmerSp; Sp: lit., PUBLIC]

pub′lic of′fering, a sale of a new issue of securities to the general public through a managing underwriter (opposed to *private placement*): required to be registered with the Securities and Exchange Commission.

pub′lic of′ficer, a person appointed or elected to a governmental post. [1920–25]

pub′lic opin′ion, the collective opinion of many people on some issue, problem, etc., esp. as a guide to action, decision, or the like. [1560–70]

pub′lic-o·pin′ion poll′ (pub′lik ə pin′yən), a poll taken by sampling a cross section of the public in an effort to predict election results or to estimate public attitudes on issues. [1935–40]

pub′lic pol′icy, 1. the fundamental policy on which laws rest, esp. policy not yet enunciated in specific rules. **2.** *Law.* the principle that injury to the public good or public order constitutes a basis for setting aside, or denying effect to, acts or transactions. [1775–85]

pub′lic pros′ecutor, an officer charged with the conduct of criminal prosecution in the interest of the public.

pub′lic rela′tions, 1. the actions of a corporation, store, government, individual, etc., in promoting goodwill between itself and the public, the community, employees, customers, etc. **2.** the art, technique, or profession of promoting such goodwill. [1800–10]

pub′lic room′, a lounge or other room that is open to all, esp. in a hotel or on a ship. [1975–80]

pub′lic sale′, auction (def. 1). [1670–80]

pub′lic school′, 1. (in the U.S.) a school that is maintained at public expense for the education of the children of a community or district and that constitutes a part of a system of free public education commonly including primary and secondary schools. **2.** (in England) any of a number of endowed secondary boarding schools that prepare students chiefly for the universities or for public service. [1570–80] —**pub′lic-school′,** *adj.*

pub′lic sec′tor, the area of the nation's affairs under governmental rather than private control. Cf. **private sector.** [1950–55]

pub′lic serv′ant, a person holding a government office or job by election or appointment; person in public service. [1670–80]

pub′lic serv′ice, 1. the business of supplying an essential commodity, as gas or electricity, or a service, as transportation, to the general public. **2.** government employment; civil service. **3.** a service to the public rendered without charge by a profit-making organization: *This radio program has been brought to you as a public service.* [1560–70]

pub′lic-serv′ice corpora′tion (pub′lik sûr′vis), a private or quasi-private corporation chartered to provide an essential commodity or service to the public. [1900–05]

pub′lic speak′ing, 1. the act of delivering speeches in public. **2.** the art or skill of addressing an audience effectively. [1755–65]

pub·lic-spir·it·ed (pub′lik spir′i tid), *adj.* having or showing an unselfish interest in the public welfare: *a public-spirited citizen.* [1670–80] —**pub′lic-spir′it·ed·ness,** *n.*

pub′lic stat′ute. See **public law** (def. 1).

pub′lic trust′. See **charitable trust.**

pub′lic util′ity, 1. a business enterprise, as a public-service corporation, performing an essential public service and regulated by the federal, state, or local government. Cf. **utility** (def. 3). **2.** Usually, **public utilities.** stocks or bonds of public-utility companies, excluding railroads. [1900–05] —**pub′lic-u·til′i·ty,** *adj.*

pub′lic works′, structures, as roads, dams, or post offices, paid for by government funds for public use. [1670–80]

Pub′lic Works′ Administra′tion, the U.S. federal agency (1933–44) that instituted and administered projects for the construction of public works. *Abbr.:* PWA, P.W.A.

pub·lish (pub′lish), *v.t.* **1.** to issue (printed or otherwise reproduced textual or graphic material, computer software, etc.) for sale or distribution to the public. **2.** to issue publicly the work of: *Random House publishes Faulkner.* **3.** to announce formally or officially; proclaim; promulgate. **4.** to make publicly or generally known. **5.** *Law.* to communicate (a defamatory statement) to some person or persons other than the person defamed. —*v.i.* **6.** to issue newspapers, books, computer software, etc.; engage in publishing: *The new house will start to publish next month.* **7.** to have one's work published: *She has decided to publish with another house.* [1300–50; ME *publisshen* < AF **publiss-,* long s. of **publir,* for MF *publier* < L *pūblicāre* to make PUBLIC] —**pub′lish·a·ble,** *adj.*
—**Syn. 3.** disclose, reveal, declare. See **announce.**
—**Ant. 3.** conceal.

pub·lish·er (pub′li shər), *n.* **1.** a person or company whose business is the publishing of books, periodicals, engravings, computer software, etc. **2.** the business head of a newspaper organization or publishing house, commonly the owner or the representative of the owner. [1425–75; late ME: one who proclaims publicly; see PUBLISH, -ER[1]]

pub·lish·ing (pub′li shing), *n.* the activities or business of a publisher, esp. of books or periodicals: *He plans to go into publishing after college.* [1375–1425; late ME (ger.); see PUBLISH, -ING[1]]

pub′lishing house′, a company that publishes books, pamphlets, engravings, or the like: *a venerable publishing house in Boston.* [1820–30]

pub·lish·ment (pub′lish mənt), *n. Archaic.* publication. [1485–95; PUBLISH + -MENT]

PUC, Public Utilities Commission. Also, **P.U.C.**

pu·ca (po͞o′kə), *n.* (in folklore) an Irish spirit, mischievous but not malevolent, corresponding to the English Puck. Also, **pooka.** [< Ir *púca;* see PUCK]

Puc·ci·ni (po͞o chē′nē; *It.* po͞ot chē′nē), *n.* **Gia·co·mo** (jä′kô mô), 1858–1924, Italian operatic composer.

puc·coon (pə ko͞on′), *n.* **1.** any of certain plants that yield a red dye, as the bloodroot and certain plants belonging to the genus *Lithospermum,* of the borage family. **2.** the dye itself. [1605–15, *Amer.;* < Virginia Algonquian (E sp.) *poughkone* the herb *Lithospermum vulgare* and the red dye made from its root (c. Unami Delaware *pé·kə·n* bloodroot)]

puce (pyo͞os), *adj.* **1.** of a dark or brownish purple. —*n.* **2.** a dark or brownish purple. [1780–90; < F: lit., flea < L *pūlic-,* s. of *pūlex*]

pu·cel·las (pyə sel′əs), *n.* (*used with a singular v.*) a tool resembling tongs or shears for handling and shaping molten glass. Also, **procellas.** [1895–1900; appar. erroneously for PROCELLAS]

puck (puk), *n.* **1.** *Ice Hockey.* a black disk of vulcanized rubber that is to be hit into the goal. **2.** *Brit. Computers.* mouse (def. 4). [1890–95; alter. of POKE[1]]

Puck (puk), *n.* **1.** Also called **Hobgoblin, Robin Goodfellow.** a particularly mischievous sprite in English folklore who appears as a character in Shakespeare's *A Midsummer Night's Dream.* **2.** (*l.c.*) a malicious or mischievous demon or spirit; a goblin. [bef. 1000; ME *pouke,* OE *pūca;* c. ON *pūki* a mischievous demon]

puck·a (puk′ə), *adj.* pukka.

puck-car·ri·er (puk′kar′ē ər), *n. Ice Hockey.* the player who has the puck and moves it along. [1955–60]

CONCISE PRONUNCIATION KEY: act, cāpe, dâre, pärt; set, ēqual; *if,* īce; ox, ōver, ôrder, oil, bo͝ok, bo͞ot, out; up, ûrge; child; sing; shoe; thin, *th*at; zh as in *treasure.* ə = *a* as in *alone, e* as in *system, i* as in *easily, o* as in *gallop, u* as in *circus;* ᵊ as in *fire* (fīᵊr), *hour* (ouᵊr). l and n can serve as syllabic consonants, as in *cradle* (krād′l), and *button* (but′n). See the full key inside the front cover.

puck·er (puk′ər), *v.t., v.i.* **1.** to draw or gather into wrinkles or irregular folds, as material or a part of the face; constrict: *Worry puckered his brow.* —*n.* **2.** a wrinkle; an irregular fold. **3.** a puckered part, as of cloth tightly or crookedly sewn. **4.** *Archaic.* a state of agitation or perturbation. [1590–1600; appar. a freq. form connected with POKE[2]; see -ER[6] and for the meaning cf. PURSE] —**puck′er·er,** *n.*

puck·er·y (puk′ə rē), *adj.* **1.** puckered. **2.** puckering. **3.** tending to pucker. [1820–30, *Amer.*; PUCKER + -Y[1]]

puck·ish (puk′ish), *adj.* (*often cap.*) mischievous; impish. [1870–75; PUCK + -ISH[1]] —**puck′ish·ly,** *adj.* —**puck′ish·ness,** *n.*

pud (po͝od), *n. Chiefly Brit. Informal.* pudding. [by apocope]

pud·ding (po͝od′ing), *n.* **1.** a thick, soft dessert, typically containing flour or some other thickener, milk, eggs, a flavoring, and sweetener: *tapioca pudding.* **2.** a similar dish unsweetened and served with or as a main dish: *corn pudding.* **3.** *Brit.* the dessert course of a meal. **4.** *Naut.* a pad or fender for preventing scraping or chafing or for lessening shock between vessels or other objects. [1275–1325; ME *poding* kind of sausage; cf. OE *puduc* wen, sore (perh. orig. swelling), LG *puddewurst* black pudding] —**pud′ding·like′,** *adj.*

pud′ding-pipe tree′ (po͝od′ing pīp′). See **golden shower.** [1590–1600]

pud′ding stone′, *Brit. Geol.* conglomerate (def. 3). Also, **pud·ding·stone** (po͝od′ing stōn′). [1745–55]

pud·ding·wife (po͝od′ing wīf′), *n., pl.* **-wives** (-wīvz′). a bluish and bronze wrasse, *Halichoeres radiatus,* of the Atlantic coast from the Florida Keys to Brazil. [1725–35; cf. late ME *podyngwyf* a woman who sells sausages. See PUDDING, WIFE]

pud·dle (pud′l), *n., v.,* **-dled, -dling.** —*n.* **1.** a small pool of water, as of rainwater on the ground. **2.** a small pool of any liquid. **3.** clay or the like mixed with water and tempered, used as a waterproof lining for the walls of canals, ditches, etc. —*v.t.* **4.** to mark or scatter with puddles. **5.** to wet with dirty water, mud, etc. **6.** to make (water) muddy or dirty. **7.** to muddle or confuse. **8.** to make (clay or the like) into puddle. **9.** to cover with pasty clay or puddle. **10.** *Metall.* to subject (molten iron) to the process of puddling. **11.** to destroy the granular structure of (soil) by agricultural operations on it when it is too wet. **12.** *Hort.* to dip the roots of (a tree, shrub, etc.) into a thin mixture of loam and water to retard drying out during transplanting. —*v.i.* **13.** to wade in a puddle: *The children were puddling.* **14.** to be or become puddled: *The backyard was puddling.* [1300–50; (n.) ME *puddel, podel, pothel,* appar. dim. of OE *pudd* ditch, furrow (akin to LG *pudel* puddle); (v.) late ME *pothelen,* deriv. of the n.] —**pud′dler,** *n.* —**pud′dly,** *adj.*

pud·dle-jump·er (pud′l jum′pər), *n. Slang.* **1.** a light plane, esp. one traveling only short distances or making many stops. **2.** an old, rickety automobile; flivver. Also, **pud′dle-jump′er.** [1930–35; humorously so called because it is used on routes that include stopovers in small, insignificant places]

pud·dling (pud′ling), *n.* **1.** the act of a person or thing that puddles. **2.** *Metall.* the act or process of melting pig iron in a reverberatory furnace (**pud′dling fur′nace**) and converting it into wrought iron. **3.** the act or method of making puddle. **4.** puddle (def. 3). [1750–60; PUDDLE + -ING[1]]

pu·den·cy (pyo͞od′n sē), *n.* modesty; bashfulness; shamefacedness. [1605–15; < LL *pudentia* shame, equiv. to L *pudent-* (s. of *pudēns,* prp. of *pudēre* to be ashamed) + *-ia* -Y[3]; see -ENCY]

pu·den·dum (pyo͞o den′dəm), *n., pl.* **-da** (-də). Usually, **pudenda.** *Anat.* the external genital organs, esp. those of the female; vulva. [1350–1400; ME < LL, special use of neut. of L *pudendus,* gerundive of *pudēre* to be ashamed]

pudg·y (puj′ē), *adj.,* **pudg·i·er, pudg·i·est.** short and fat or thick: *an infant's pudgy fingers.* Also, *esp. Brit.,* **podgy.** [1830–40; orig. uncert.] —**pudg′i·ly,** *adv.* —**pudg′i·ness,** *n.*

Pu·dov·kin (po͞o dôf′kin, -dof′-, *Russ.* po͞o dôf′kyin), *n.* **Vse·vo·lod I·la·ri·o·no·vich** (fsye′və lət ē la ryi ô′nə vyich), 1893–1953, Russian motion-picture director.

pu·du (po͞o′do͞o), *n.* a small, hollow-toothed deer of the genus *Pudu,* native to the South American Andes, having a dark brown or gray coat, a small head, and spiked antlers: now greatly reduced in number; *P. pudu* may be at risk of extinction. [1885–90; < AmerSp < Araucanian]

Pue·bla (pwe′blä), *n.* **1.** a state in S central Mexico. 3,055,000; 13,124 sq. mi. (33,990 sq. km). **2.** the capital of this state, in the N part. 516,000.

pueb·lo (pweb′lō; *for 4, 5, also Sp.* pwe′blô), *n., pl.* **pueb·los** (pweb′lōz; *Sp.* pwe′blôs). **1.** a communal structure for multiple dwelling and defensive purposes of certain agricultural Indians of the southwestern U.S.: built of adobe or stone, typically many-storied and terraced, the structures were often placed against cliff walls, with entry through the roof by ladder. **2.** (*cap.*) a member of a group of Indian peoples living in pueblo villages in New Mexico and Arizona since prehistoric times. **3.** an Indian village. **4.** (in Spanish America) a town or village. **5.** (in the Philippines) a town or a township. [1800–10, *Amer.*; < AmerSp; Sp: town, people < L *populus* PEOPLE]

Pueb·lo (pweb′lō), *n.* a city in central Colorado. 101,106.

pu·er·ile (pyo͞o′ər il, -ə rīl′, pyo͝or′il, -īl), *adj.* **1.** of or pertaining to a child or to childhood. **2.** childishly foolish; immature or trivial: *a puerile piece of writing.* [1650–60; < L *puerīlis* boyish, equiv. to *puer* boy + *-īlis* -ILE] —**pu′er·ile·ly,** *adv.*
—**Syn. 1.** youthful, juvenile. **2.** juvenile, silly.

pu·er·il·ism (pyo͞o′ər ə liz′əm, pyo͝or′ə-), *n. Psychiatry.* childishness in the behavior of an adult. [1920–25; PUERILE + -ISM]

pu·er·il·i·ty (pyo͞o′ə ril′i tē, pyo͝o ril′-), *n., pl.* **-ties. 1.** the state or quality of being a child. **2.** the quality of being puerile; childish foolishness or triviality. **3.** a puerile act, idea, remark, etc.: *an inexcusable puerility.* [1425–75; late ME < L *puerīlitās.* See PUERILE, -ITY]

pu·er·per·a (pyo͞o ûr′pər ə), *n., pl.* **-per·ae** (-pə rē′). *Obstet.* a woman who has recently given birth to a child. [< L: woman in labor; akin to *puerperus;* see PUERPERIUM]

pu·er·per·al (pyo͞o ûr′pər əl), *adj.* **1.** of or pertaining to a woman in childbirth. **2.** pertaining to or connected with childbirth. [1760–70; < NL *puerperālis* of childbirth. See PUERPERA, -AL[1]]

puer′peral fe′ver, *Pathol.* a systemic bacterial infection of the endometrium characterized by fever, rapid heartbeat, uterine tenderness, and malodorous discharge, chiefly occurring in women after childbirth, usually as the result of unsterile obstetric procedures. [1760–70]

pu·er·pe·ri·um (pyo͞o′ər pēr′ē əm), *n. Obstet.* the four-week period following childbirth. [1885–90; < L: childbirth, childbed, equiv. to *puerper*(*us*) of a woman in labor (*puer* boy, child + *-perus* bringing forth, akin to *parere* to bear, breed) + *-ium* -IUM]

Puer·to A·ya·cu·cho (pweʀ′tô ä′yä ko͞o′chô), a city in S Venezuela, on the Orinoco River. 10,417.

Puer·to Bar·rios (pweʀ′tô väʀ′ʀyôs), a seaport in E Guatemala. 38,956.

Puer·to Ca·bel·lo (pweʀ′tô kä ve′yô), a seaport in N Venezuela. 70,598.

Puer·to Cor·tés (pweʀ′tô kôʀ tes′), a seaport in NW Honduras. 17,000.

Puer·to Li·món (*Sp.* pweʀ′tô lē môn′), Limón (def. 2).

Puer·to Montt (pweʀ′tô mônt′), a city in S Chile. 86,750.

Puer′to Ri′can cher′ry, acerola.

Puer′to Ri′can roy′al palm′, a feather palm, *Roystonea borinquena,* of Puerto Rico and St. Croix, having leaves about 10 ft. (3 m) long and egg-shaped, yellowish-brown fruit.

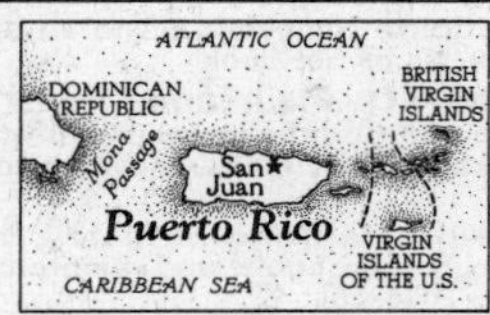

Puer·to Ri·co (pwer′tə rē′kō, pwer′tō, pôr′tə, pōr′-; *Sp.* pweʀ′tô ʀē′kô), an island in the central West Indies: a commonwealth associated with the U.S. 3,196,520; 3435 sq. mi. (8895 sq. km). *Cap.:* San Juan. Formerly (until 1932), **Porto Rico.** *Abbr.:* P.R., PR —**Puer′to Ri′can.**

Puer′to Ri′co Trench′, a depression in the ocean floor, N of Puerto Rico: includes deepest part of Atlantic Ocean, 28,374 ft. (8648 m). Also, **Puer′to Ri′co Trough′.**

puer·to·rri·que·ño (pweʀ′tô ʀē ke′nyô), *n., pl.* **-ños** (-nyôs). *Spanish.* a native or inhabitant of Puerto Rico.

Puer·to Val·lar·ta (pweʀ′tô vä yäʀ′tä), a city in W Mexico. 35,542.

Pu·fen·dorf (po͞o′fən dôrf′, -dôrf′), *n.* **Sa·mu·el von** (zä′mo͞o əl fən), ("*Severinus de Monzambano*"), 1632–94, German jurist and historian.

puff (puf), *n.* **1.** a short, quick blast, as of wind or breath. **2.** an abrupt emission of air, smoke, vapor, etc. **3.** an act of inhaling and exhaling, as on a cigarette or pipe; whiff. **4.** the sound of an abrupt emission of air, vapor, etc. **5.** a small quantity of vapor, smoke, etc., emitted at one blast. **6.** an inflated or distended part of a thing; swelling; protuberance. **7.** a form of light pastry with a filling of cream, jam, or the like. **8.** a portion of material gathered and held down at the edges but left full in the middle, as on a sleeve. **9.** a cylindrical roll of hair. **10.** a quilted bed covering, usually filled with down. **11.** a commendation, esp. an exaggerated one, of a book, an actor's performance, etc. **12.** See **powder puff. 13.** a ball or pad of soft material. **14.** puffball. **15.** *Chiefly Brit. Slang.* a male homosexual. —*v.i.* **16.** to blow with short, quick blasts, as the wind. **17.** to be emitted in a puff. **18.** to emit a puff or puffs; breathe quick and hard, as after violent exertion. **19.** to go with puffing or panting. **20.** to emit puffs or whiffs of vapor or smoke. **21.** to move with such puffs: *The locomotive puffed into the station.* **22.** to take puffs at a cigar, cigarette, etc. **23.** to become inflated, distended, or swollen (usually fol. by *up*). **24.** (esp. of an auctioneer's accomplice) to bid on an item at an auction solely to increase the price that the final bidder must pay. —*v.t.* **25.** to send forth (air, vapor, etc.) in short, quick blasts. **26.** to drive or impel by puffing, or with a short, quick blast. **27.** to extinguish by means of a puff (usually fol. by *out*): *to puff a match out.* **28.** to smoke (a cigar, cigarette, etc.). **29.** to inflate, distend, or swell, esp. with air. **30.** to make fluffy; fluff (often fol. by *up*): *to puff up a pillow.* **31.** to inflate with pride, vanity, etc. (often fol. by *up*): *Their applause puffed him up.* **32.** to praise unduly or with exaggeration. **33.** to apply powder to (the cheeks, neck, etc.) with a powder puff. **34.** to apply (powder) with a powder puff. **35.** to arrange in puffs, as the hair. [1175–1225; (v.) ME *puffen* (cf. MD *puffen,* LG *pof, puf*); (n.) ME *puf, puffe;* of imit. orig.] —**puff′ing·ly,** *adv.*
—**Syn. 11.** overpraise, exaggeration, puffery, flattery.

puff′ ad′der, 1. a large, thick-bodied, African viper, *Bitis arietans,* that inflates its body and hisses when disturbed. **2.** a similar viper, *B. inornata,* native to southern Africa. [1780–90]

puff·ball (puf′bôl′), *n.* any of various basidiomycetous fungi, esp. of the genus *Lycoperdon* and allied genera, characterized by a ball-like fruit body that emits a cloud of spores when broken. [1640–50; PUFF + BALL[1]]

puff·bird (puf′bûrd′), *n.* any of several tropical American birds of the family Bucconidae, related to the barbets, having a large head with the feathers often fluffed out. [1815–25; PUFF + BIRD]

puff·er (puf′ər), *n.* **1.** a person or thing that puffs. **2.** Also called **blowfish, globefish.** any of various fishes of the family Tetraodontidae, capable of inflating the body with water or air until it resembles a globe, the spines in the skin becoming erected: several species contain the potent nerve poison tetrodotoxin. [1620–30; PUFF + -ER[1]]

puff·er·y (puf′ə rē), *n., pl.* **-er·ies. 1.** undue or exaggerated praise. **2.** publicity, acclaim, etc., that is full of undue or exaggerated praise. [1775–85; PUFF + -ERY]

Atlantic puffin, *Fratercula arctica,* length 1 ft. (0.3 m)

puf·fin (puf′in), *n.* any of several alcidine sea birds of the genera *Fratercula* and *Lunda,* having a short neck and a large, compressed, grooved bill, as *F. arctica* (**Atlantic puffin**), of the North Atlantic. [1300–50; ME *poffoun, poffin, puffon* (cf. AL *poffo, puffo*); orig. uncert.]

puff′ paste′, a dough used in making very light, flaky, rich pastry for pies, tarts, and the like. [1595–1605]

puff′ piece′, *Informal.* a newspaper article, book, public-relations film, etc., whose purpose is to praise or flatter.

puff·y (puf′ē), *adj.,* **puff·i·er, puff·i·est. 1.** gusty. **2.** short-winded; panting. **3.** inflated, distended, or swollen. **4.** fat; plump. **5.** conceited. **6.** bombastic. [1590–1600; PUFF + -Y[1]] —**puff′i·ly,** *adv.* —**puff′i·ness,** *n.*

pug[1] (pug), *n.* **1.** one of a breed of small, short-haired dogs having a tightly curled tail, a deeply wrinkled face, and a smooth coat that is black or silver and fawn with black markings. **2.** See **pug nose.** [1560–70; orig. uncert.] —**pug′gi·ness,** *n.* —**pug′gish, pug′gy,** *adj.*

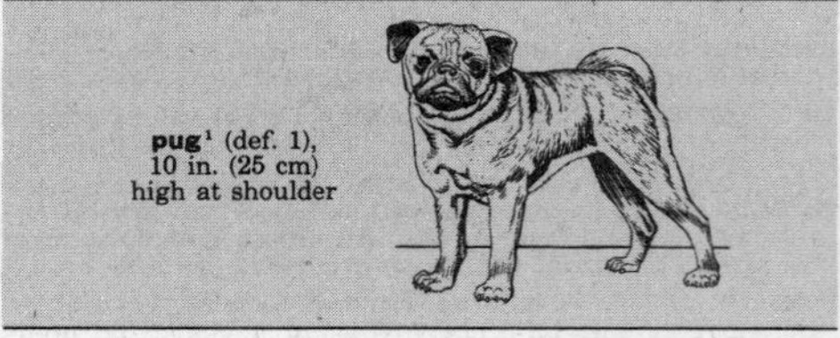
pug[1] (def. 1), 10 in. (25 cm) high at shoulder

pug[2] (pug), *v.t.,* **pugged, pug·ging. 1.** to knead (clay or the like) with water to make it plastic, as for brickmaking. **2.** to fill or stop with clay or the like. **3.** to pack or cover with mortar or the like, as to deaden sound. **4.** to mix with water so as to form a paste. [1800–10; orig. uncert.]

pug[3] (pug), *n. Slang.* a boxer; pugilist. [1855–60; short for PUGILIST]

pug[4] (pug), *n., v.,* **pugged, pug·ging.** —*n.* **1.** a footprint, esp. of a game animal. —*v.t.* **2.** to track (esp. game) by following footprints or another spoor. [1860–65; < Hindi *pag* footprint]

pug·a·ree (pug′ə rē), *n.* pugree.

pug·dog (pug′dôg′, -dog′), *n.* pug[1] (def. 1). [1740–50; PUG[1] + DOG]

Pu′get Sound′ (pyo͞o′jit), an arm of the Pacific, in NW Washington.

pug·ga·ree (pug′ə rē), *n.* pugree.

pug·ging (pug′ing), *n.* **1.** the act of a person who pugs. **2.** coarse mortar or the like for deadening sound. [1815–25; PUG[2] + -ING[1]]

pugh (po͞o, pyo͞o, pē′yo͞o′), *interj.* (used as an exclamation of disgust, as at an offensive odor.)

pu·gi·lism (pyo͞o′jə liz′əm), *n.* the art or practice of fighting with the fists; boxing. [1785–95; < L *pugil* boxer (akin to *pugnus* fist, *pugnāre* to fight; cf. Gk *pýx* with the fist, *pygmē* boxing) + -ISM]

pu·gi·list (pyo͞o′jə list), *n.* a person who fights with the fists; a boxer, usually a professional. [1780–90; < L *pugil* (see PUGILISM) + -IST] —**pu′gi·lis′tic,** *adj.* —**pu′gi·lis′ti·cal·ly,** *adv.*

Pu·gin (pyo͞o′jin), *n.* **1. Augustus Charles,** 1762–1832, French architectural draftsman and archaeologist in England. **2.** his son **Augustus Wel·by North·more** (wel′bē nôrth′môr, -mōr), 1812–52, English architect and designer.

Pu·glia (po͞o′lyä), *n.* Italian name of **Apulia.**

CONCISE ETYMOLOGY KEY: <, descended or borrowed from; >, whence; b., blend of, blended; c., cognate with; cf., compare; deriv., derivative; equiv., equivalent; imit., imitative; obl., oblique; r., replacing; s., stem; sp., spelling, spelled; resp., respelling, respelled; trans., translation; ?, origin unknown; *, unattested; ‡, probably earlier than. See the full key inside the front cover.

pug′ mill′, a mill for grinding and mixing materials, as clay or the ingredients of cement, to a desired condition. [1815–25]

pug•na•cious (pug nā′shəs), *adj.* inclined to quarrel or fight readily; quarrelsome; belligerent; combative. [1635–45; *pugnāci(ty)* (< L *pugnācitās* combativeness, equiv. to *pugnāci-,* s. of *pugnāx* combative (akin to *pugil;* see PUGILISM) + *-tās* -TY²) + -OUS] **—pug•na′•cious•ly,** *adv.* **—pug•nac•i•ty** (pug nas′i tē), **pug•na′•cious•ness,** *n.*
—Syn. argumentative, contentious, bellicose. **—Ant.** agreeable.

pug′ nose′, a short, broad, somewhat turned-up nose. [1770–80] **—pug-nosed** (pug′nōzd′), *adj.*

pug•ree (pug′rē), *n.* **1.** a light turban worn in India. **2.** a scarf of silk or cotton, usually colored or printed, wound round a hat or helmet and falling down behind as a protection against the sun. Cf. **havelock.** Also, **pugaree, puggaree.** [1655–65; < Hindi *pagṛī* turban]

P'u-i (po͞o′ē′), *n.* Pu-yi.

puir (po͝or, pyo͝or), *adj. Scot.* **1.** poor. **2.** pure.

puis•ne (pyo͞o′nē), *adj.* **1.** *Law.* younger; inferior in rank; junior, as in appointment. **—n. 2.** an associate judge as distinguished from a chief justice. [1590–1600; < AF, equiv. to OF *puis* after (< L *posteā*) + *ne* born, ptp. of *naistre* to be born (< L *nāscere*); cf. PUNY]

pu•is•sance (pyo͞o′ə səns, pyo͞o is′əns, pwis′əns), *n. Literary.* power, might, or force. [1375–1425; late ME < MF, equiv. to *puiss(ant)* PUISSANT + *-ance* -ANCE]

pu•is•sant (pyo͞o′ə sənt, pyo͞o is′ənt, pwis′ənt), *adj. Literary.* powerful; mighty; potent. [1400–50; late ME < MF < VL **possent-* (s. of **possēns*), for L *potent-* (s. of *potēns*), prp. of *posse* to be able, have power; see POTENT, -ANT] **—pu′is•sant•ly,** *adv.*

pu•ja (po͞o′jä), *n. Hinduism.* the worship of a particular god. [< Skt *pūjā*]

pu•ka (po͞o′kə), *n.* a small white shell found on Pacific, esp. Hawaiian, beaches and strung in clusters to make necklaces. [1970–75; of uncert. orig.]

puke (pyo͞ok), *v.,* **puked, puk•ing.** *n.* **—v.i., v.t.** *Slang.* **1.** to vomit. **—n. 2.** vomit. **3. a.** any food or drink that is repulsive. **b.** anything that is contemptible or worthless. [1590–1600; perh. imit.]

puk•ey (pyo͞o′kē), *adj.,* **puk•i•er, puk•i•est.** *Slang.* **—adj. 1.** on the verge of vomiting; nauseated. **2.** disgusting; repellent. Also, **puk′y.** [1860–65; PUKE + -Y¹]

puk•ka (puk′ə), *adj. Anglo-Indian.* genuine, reliable, or good; proper. Also, **pucka.** [1690–1700; < Hindi *pakkā* cooked, ripe, mature]

puk′ka sa′hib, (in British India) a term of respectful address used to British colonial authorities. Cf. **pukka, sahib.** [1935–40]

pu•ku (po͞o′ko͞o), *n.* an African antelope, *Adenota vardoni,* closely related to the waterbuck. [1880–85; of uncert. orig.]

pul (po͞ol), *n., pl.* **puls, pu•li** (po͞o′lē). a coin and monetary unit of Afghanistan, the 100th part of an afghani. [1925–30; < Pers *pūl* < Turk *pul*]

pu•la (po͞o′lä), *n.* a cupronickel coin, paper money, and monetary unit of Botswana, equal to 100 thebe: replaced the rand in 1976.

Pu•la (po͞o′lä), *n.* a seaport in W Croatia, on the Istrian Peninsula. 77,057. Also, **Pulj.** Italian, **Pola.**

Pu•las•ki (pə las′kē), *n.* **1. Count Cas•i•mir** (kaz′ə mēr′), 1748–79, Polish patriot; general in the American Revolutionary army. **2.** a town in SW Virginia. 10,106. **3. Fort.** See **Fort Pulaski.**

Pu•las•ki (pə las′kē), *n.* a double-edged hand tool having an ax blade on one side and a pickax or wide chisel on the opposite side, used esp. in clearing land and removing tree stumps. [1920–25, *Amer.*; after Edward C. *Pulaski* (1866–1931), U.S. forest ranger, its inventor]

pul•chri•tude (pul′kri to͞od′, -tyo͞od′), *n.* physical beauty; comeliness. [1350–1400; ME < L *pulchritūdō* beauty, equiv. to *pulchri-* (comb. form of *pulcher* beautiful) + *-tūdō* -TUDE]
—Syn. loveliness, beauteousness, fairness.

pul•chri•tu•di•nous (pul′kri to͞od′n əs, -tyo͞od′-), *adj.* physically beautiful; comely. [1910–15, *Amer.*; < L *pulchritūdin-* (s. of *pulchritūdō*) + -OUS]

pule (pyo͞ol), *v.i.,* **puled, pul•ing.** to cry in a thin voice; whine; whimper. [1525–35; perh. imit.] **—pul′er,** *n.*

Pu•le•sa•ti (po͞o′lə sä′tē, pyo͞o′-), *n.pl.* the ancient Assyrian name of the Philistines.

pu•li (po͝ol′ē, pyo͞o′lē), *n., pl.* **pu•lik** (po͝ol′ēk, pyo͞o′lēk), **pu•lis.** one of a Hungarian breed of medium-sized sheepdogs having long, fine hair that often mats, giving the coat a corded appearance. [1935–40; < Hungarian, alter. of *pudli* poodle, shortening of earlier *pudlikutya,* trans of G *Pudelhund;* see POODLE]

pul•ing (pyo͞o′ling), *adj.* whining; whimpering: *a puling child.* [1520–30; PULE + -ING²] **—pul′ing•ly,** *adv.*

Pu•litz•er (po͝ol′it sər, pyo͞o′lit-), *n.* **Joseph,** 1847–1911, U.S. journalist and publisher, born in Hungary.

Pu′litzer Prize′, one of a group of annual prizes in journalism, literature, music, etc., established by Joseph Pulitzer: administered by Columbia University; first awarded 1917.

Pulj (*Serbo-Croatian.* po͞ol′yᵊ), *n.* Pula.

pul•ka (pul′kə), *n.* a reindeer-drawn sleigh of Lapland, shaped like the front half of a canoe, in which a single rider sits with back against a vertical support and legs stretched forward. Also called **ahkio.** [1790–1800; < Finnish *pulkka* < Lappish]

pull (po͝ol), *v.t.* **1.** to draw or haul toward oneself or itself, in a particular direction, or into a particular position: *to pull a sled up a hill.* **2.** to draw or tug at with force. **3.** to rend or tear: *to pull a cloth to pieces.* **4.** to draw or pluck away from a place of growth, attachment, etc.: *to pull a tooth; to pull weeds.* **5.** to strip of feathers, hair, etc., as a bird or hide. **6.** to draw out (as a knife or gun) for ready use (usually fol. by *on*): *Do you know what to do when someone pulls a knife on you?* **7.** *Informal.* to perform successfully (often fol. by *off*): *They pulled a spectacular coup.* **8.** *Informal.* to carry out (esp. something deceitful or illegal): *Police believe the men pulled all three robberies. What kind of trick did she pull this time?* **9.** to put on or affect: *He pulled a long face when I reprimanded him.* **10.** to withdraw or remove: *to pull an ineffective pitcher.* **11.** to attract or win: *to pull many votes in the industrial areas.* **12.** to bring (a horse) to a stand by pulling on the reins. **13.** *Print., Graphics.* to take (an impression or proof) from type, a cut or plate, etc.: *to pull a print.* **14.** to be provided with or rowed with (a certain number of oars): *This boat pulls 12 oars.* **15.** to propel by rowing, as a boat. **16.** to strain (a muscle, ligament, or tendon). **17.** *Mil.* to be assigned (a specific task or duty): *I pulled guard duty our first night in port.* **18.** to hold in or check (a racehorse), esp. so as to prevent from winning. **19.** *Sports.* to hit (a ball) so that it travels in a direction opposite to the side from which it was struck, as when a right-handed batter hits into left field.
—v.i. 20. to exert a drawing, tugging, or hauling force (often fol. by *at*). **21.** to inhale through a pipe, cigarette, etc. **22.** to become or come as specified, by being pulled: *This rope will pull.* **23.** to row. **24.** to proceed by rowing. **25.** (of an advertisement) **a.** to have effectiveness, as specified: *The ad pulled badly.* **b.** to be effective: *That spot announcement really pulled!* **26. pull apart,** to analyze critically, esp. to point out errors: *The professor proceeded to pull the student's paper apart.* **27. pull away, a.** to move or draw back or away; withdraw. **b.** to free oneself with force: *He tried to pull away from his opponent's powerful grip.* **c.** to move or start to move ahead: *The car pulled away into traffic. The faster runners began to pull away from the others.* **28. pull down, a.** to draw downward: *to pull a shade down.* **b.** to demolish; wreck. **c.** to lower; reduce. **d.** *Informal.* to receive as a salary; earn: *It wasn't long before he was pulling down more than fifty thousand a year.* **29. pull for,** to support actively; encourage: *They were pulling for the Republican candidate.* **30. pull in, a.** to reach a place; arrive: *The train pulled in early.* **b.** to tighten; curb: *to pull in the reins.* **c.** *Informal.* to arrest (someone): *The police pulled her in for questioning.* **31. pull off,** *Informal.* to perform successfully, esp. something requiring courage, daring, or shrewdness: *We'll be rich if we can pull the deal off.* **32. pull oneself together,** to recover one's self-control; regain command of one's emotions: *It was only a minor accident, but the driver couldn't seem to pull himself together.* **33. pull out, a.** to leave; depart: *The ship pulled out of the harbor.* **b.** to abandon abruptly: *to pull out of an agreement.* **34. pull over,** to direct one's automobile or other vehicle to the curb; move out of a line of traffic: *The police officer told the driver to pull over.* **35. pull someone's leg.** See **leg** (def. 21). **36. pull the plug.** See **plug** (def. 20). **37. pull through,** to come safely through (a crisis, illness, etc.); survive: *The patient eventually pulled through after having had a close brush with death.* **38. pull up, a.** to bring or come to a halt. **b.** to bring or draw closer. **c.** to root up; pull out: *She pulled up all the crab grass in the lawn.*
—n. 39. the act of pulling or drawing. **40.** force used in pulling; pulling power. **41.** a drawing in of smoke or a liquid through the mouth: *He took a long, thoughtful pull on his pipe; I took a pull from the scout's canteen.* **42.** *Informal.* influence, as with persons able to grant favors. **43.** a part or thing to be pulled; a handle or the like: *to replace the pulls on a chest of drawers.* **44.** a spell, or turn, at rowing. **45.** a stroke of an oar. **46.** *Informal.* a pulled muscle: *He missed a week's work with a groin pull.* **47.** a pulling of the ball, as in baseball or golf. **48.** *Informal.* the ability to attract; drawing power. **49.** *Informal.* an advantage over another or others. [bef. 1000; ME *pullen* (v.), OE *pullian* to pluck, pluck the feathers of, pull, tug; cf. MLG *pūlen* to strip off husks, pick, ON *pūla* to work hard] **—pull′a•ble,** *adj.* **—pull′er,** *n.*
—Syn. 2. See **draw. —Ant. 2.** push.

pull•back (po͝ol′bak′), *n.* **1.** the act of pulling back, esp. a retreat or a strategic withdrawal of troops; pullout. **2.** that which pulls something back or impedes its forward movement. **3.** *Mach.* a device for pulling a moving part to its original position. [1585–95; n. use of v. phrase *pull back*]

pull′ date′, the last date on which perishable food should be sold, usually established with some allowance for home storage under refrigeration. Also called **sell date.** Cf. **shelf life.** [1970–75]

pull-down (po͝ol′doun′), *adj.* designed to be pulled down for use: *a pull-down bed; a desk with a pull-down front.* [1905–10; adj. use of v. phrase *pull down*]

pull•down (po͝ol′doun′), *n. Motion Pictures.* a mechanism that intermittently advances the film through the film gate of a camera or projector. [1950–55; n. use of v. phrase *pull down*]

pul•let (po͝ol′it), *n.* a young hen, less than one year old. [1325–75; ME *polet* < MF *poulet,* dim. of *poul* cock < L *pullus* chicken, young of an animal; akin to FOAL]

pul•ley (po͝ol′ē), *n., pl.* **-leys. 1.** a wheel, with a grooved rim for carrying a line, that turns in a frame or block and serves to change the direction of or to transmit force, as when one end of the line is pulled to raise a weight at the other end: one of the simple machines. **2.** a combination of such wheels in a block, or of such wheels or blocks in a tackle, to increase the force applied. **3.** a wheel driven by or driving a belt or the like, used to deliver force to a machine, another belt, etc., at a certain speed and torque. [1275–1325; ME *poley, puly* < MF *polie* << MGk **polídion* little pivot, equiv. to *pól(os)* POLE² + *-idion* dim. suffix] **—pul′ley•less,** *adj.*

pul′ley bone′, *South Midland and Inland South.* wishbone (def. 1). [1935–40, *Amer.*]

pul′ley stile′, (in a window frame) a stile against which a window sash slides. Also called **hanging stile.** [1815–25]

pull′ hit′ter, *Baseball.* a batter who tends to hit the ball to the same side of the field as that on which he or she stands at home plate. [1935–40]

pull-in (po͝ol′in′), *n., adj. Brit.* drive-in. [1935–40; n., adj. use of v. phrase *pull in*]

pull′ing boat′, a boat propelled by oars alone. [1910–15]

Pull•man (po͝ol′mən), *pl.* **-mans** for 1, 2. **1.** *Trademark.* a railroad sleeping car or parlor car. **—n. 2.** (*often l.c.*) Also called **Pull′man case′.** a large suitcase. **3. George Mortimer,** 1831–97, U.S. inventor and railroad car designer.

Pull•man (po͝ol′mən), *n.* a city in SE Washington. 23,579.

pull′man kitch′en, a kitchenette, often recessed into a wall and concealed by double doors or a screen. [1965–70, *Amer.*; so called because sinks and similar facilities were installed this way in Pullman-style railway cars]

pull-off (po͝ol′ôf′, -of′), *n.* **1.** an act of pulling off: *The inn is well worth a pull-off from the Interstate.* **2.** a rest area at the side of a road where vehicles may park. [1855–60; n. use of v. phrase *pull off*]

pull-on (*n.* po͝ol′on′, -ôn′; *adj.* po͝ol′on′, -ôn′), *n.* **1.** an item of apparel that is pulled on, as a sweater or glove. **—adj. 2.** designed to be put on by being pulled on: *a pull-on jersey.* [1915–20; n., adj. use of v. phrase *pull on*]

pul•lo′rum disease′ (pə lôr′əm, -lōr′-), *Vet. Pathol.* a highly contagious, frequently fatal disease of young poultry caused by the bacterium *Salmonella gallinarum* (*pullorum*), transmitted by the infected hen during egg production, and characterized by weakness, loss of appetite, and diarrhea. [1925–30; < NL (*Bacterium*) *pullorum* former name of the bacterium, L *pullōrum,* gen. pl. of *pullus* cockerel, chicken (see PULLET)]

pull•out (po͝ol′out′), *n.* **1.** an act or instance of pulling out; removal. **2.** a withdrawal, as of troops or funds; pullback. **3.** a maneuver by which an aircraft levels into horizontal flight after a dive. **4.** a section of a newspaper or magazine that is complete in itself and may be removed and retained: *a 24-page pullout of barbecue recipes.* **5.** an area at the side of a road where drivers may pull off for emergencies, to rest or view the scenery, etc.; pull-off. **—adj. 6.** designed to be pulled out or removed: *pullout compartments in a desk.* [1815–25; n., adj. use of v. phrase *pull out*]

pull•o•ver (po͝ol′ō′vər), *n.* **1.** Also called **slipover.** a garment, esp. a sweater, that must be drawn over the head to be put on. **—adj. 2.** designed to be put on by being drawn over the head. [1870–75; n., adj. use of v. phrase *pull over*]

pull-quote (po͝ol′kwōt′), *n.* (in a magazine or newspaper) an excerpted line or phrase, in a larger or display typeface, run at the top of a page or in a mid-column box to draw attention to the text of the article or story from which it is quoted; blurb.

pull-tab (po͝ol′tab′), *n.* **1.** a small metal tab or ring that is pulled up to uncover the precut opening in the top of a can or box. **2.** a ticket used for gambling, with winning amounts indicated on it, that players extract from a jar or other receptacle. **—adj. 3.** (of a can or box) equipped with a pull-tab. Also, **pull′ tab′, pull′tab′.** [1960–65]

pull-top (po͝ol′top′), *adj., n.* pop-top.

pul•lu•late (pul′yə lāt′), *v.i.,* **-lat•ed, -lat•ing. 1.** to send forth sprouts, buds, etc.; germinate; sprout. **2.** to breed, produce, or create rapidly. **3.** to increase rapidly; multiply. **4.** to exist abundantly; swarm; teem. **5.** to be produced as offspring. [1610–20; < L *pullulātus* (ptp. of *pullulāre* to sprout), deriv. of *pullulus* a sprout, young animal, dim. of *pullus;* see PULLET] **—pul′lu•la′tion,** *n.*

pull-up (po͝ol′up′), *n.* **1.** an exercise consisting of chinning oneself, as on a horizontal bar attached at each end to a doorpost. **2.** a flight maneuver in which an aircraft climbs sharply from level flight. Also, **pull′up′.** [1850–55; n. use of v. phrase *pull up*]

pul•lus (pul′əs), *n., pl.* **pul•li** (pul′ī). a young bird; a chick. [1765–75; < NL, L: a young animal (see PULLET)]

pul•mo•nar•y (pul′mə ner′ē, po͝ol′-), *adj.* **1.** of or pertaining to the lungs. **2.** of the nature of a lung; lunglike. **3.** affecting the lungs. **4.** having lungs or lunglike organs. **5.** pertaining to or affected with disease of the lungs. [1650–60; < L *pulmōnārius* of the lungs, equiv. to *pulmōn-* (s. of *pulmō* lung; akin to Gk *pleúmōn,* later *pneúmōn* lung; cf. PNEUMA) + *-ārius* -ARY]

pul′monary ar′tery, *Anat.* an artery conveying venous blood from the right ventricle of the heart to the lungs. See diag. under **heart.** [1695–1705]

pul′monary circula′tion, *Physiol.* the circulation of blood from the heart to the lungs for oxygenation and back to the heart.

pul′monary tree′, *Anat.* the trachea, bronchi, and bronchioles of the lungs, which together resemble an upside-down tree.

pul′monary tuberculo′sis, *Pathol.* tuberculosis of the lungs.

pul′monary valve′, *Anat.* a semilunar valve between the pulmonary artery and the right ventricle of the heart that prevents the blood from flowing back into the right ventricle.

pul′monary vein′, *Anat.* a vein conveying oxygenated blood from the lungs to the left atrium of the heart. See diag. under **heart.** [1695–1705]

pul•mo•nate (pul′mə nāt′, -nit, po͝ol′-), *adj.* **1.** *Zool.*

having lungs or lunglike organs. **2.** belonging to the Pulmonata, an order of gastropod mollusks usually breathing by means of a lunglike sac, and including most of the terrestrial snails and the slugs and certain aquatic snails. —*n.* **3.** a pulmonate gastropod. [1835–45; < NL *pulmōnātus.* See PULMONARY, -ATE[1]]

pul•mon•ic (pul mon′ik, po͝ol-), *adj.* pulmonary. [1655–65; < F *pulmonique.* See PULMONARY, -IC]

pulmon′ic air′stream, *Phonet.* a current of lung air set in motion by the respiratory muscles in the production of speech.

Pul•mo•tor (pul′mō′tər, po͝ol′-), *Trademark.* a mechanical device for artificial respiration that forces oxygen into the lungs when respiration has ceased because of asphyxiation, drowning, etc.

pulp (pulp), *n.* **1.** the soft, juicy, edible part of a fruit. **2.** the pith of the stem of a plant. **3.** a soft or fleshy part of an animal body. **4.** Also called **dental pulp.** the inner substance of the tooth, containing arteries, veins, and lymphatic and nerve tissue that communicate with their respective vascular, lymph, and nerve systems. See diag. under **tooth. 5.** any soft, moist, slightly cohering mass, as that into which linen, wood, etc., are converted in the making of paper. **6.** a magazine or book printed on rough, low-quality paper made of wood pulp or rags, and usually containing sensational and lurid stories, articles, etc. Cf. **slick**[1] (def. 9). **7.** *Mining.* **a.** ore pulverized and mixed with water. **b.** dry crushed ore. —*v.t.* **8.** to reduce to pulp. **9.** to reduce (printed papers, books, etc.) to pulp for use in making new paper. **10.** to remove the pulp from. —*v.i.* **11.** to become reduced to pulp. [1555–65; earlier *pulpe* < L *pulpa* flesh, pulp of fruit] —**pulp′er,** *n.* —**pulp′less,** *adj.* —**pulp′like′,** *adj.*

pulp•board (pulp′bôrd′, -bōrd′), *n.* a board made from pulpwood. [1900–05; PULP + BOARD]

pulp′ canal′, *Dentistry.* See **root canal.** [1835–45]

pulp′ canal′ ther′apy, endodontics. Also called **pulp′ canal′ treat′ment.**

pulp′ cav′ity, *Dentistry.* the entire space occupied by pulp, composed of the root canal and pulp chamber. [1830–40]

pulp′ cham′ber, *Dentistry.* the crown portion of the pulp cavity. [1870–75]

pulp•ec•to•my (pul pek′tə mē), *n., pl.* **-mies.** *Dentistry.* the removal of all the pulp tissue in a tooth in the course of endodontic therapy. [1920–25; PULP + -ECTOMY]

pulp′ fic′tion, fiction dealing with lurid or sensational subjects, often printed on rough, low-quality paper manufactured from wood pulp. [1950–55, *Amer.*]

pulp•ing (pul′ping), *n.* **1.** the process of making pulp, esp. from wood, for use in the manufacture of paper, cardboard, etc. —*adj.* **2.** of or involved in the making of pulp: *pulping facilities.* [1655–65; PULP + -ING[1]]

pul•pit (po͝ol′pit, pul′-), *n.* **1.** a platform or raised structure in a church, from which the sermon is delivered or the service is conducted. **2. the pulpit, a.** the clerical profession; the ministry. **b.** members of the clergy collectively: *In attendance were representatives of medicine, the pulpit, and the bar.* **3.** (esp. in Protestantism and Judaism) the position of pastor or rabbi: *He heard of a pulpit in Chicago that was about to be vacated.* **4.** preaching. **5.** (in small craft) **a.** a safety rail rising about 18 to 30 in. (48 to 76 cm) from the deck near the bow and extending around it. **b.** a similar rail at the stern. **6.** a control booth in a factory, usually elevated and glass-enclosed, from which an operator can observe and direct the manufacturing process. [1300–50; ME < LL *pulpitum* pulpit, L: platform, stage] —**pul′pit•al,** *adj.* —**pul′pit•less,** *adj.*

P, **pulpit**
(def. 5a)

pul•pit•eer (po͝ol′pi tēr′, pul′-), *n. Usually Disparaging.* a preacher by profession. Also, **pul•pit•er** (po͝ol′pi tər, pul′-). [1635–45; PULPIT + -EER]

pulp•ot•o•my (pul pot′ə mē), *n., pl.* **-mies.** *Dentistry.* the removal of infected portions of the pulp tissue in a tooth, used as a therapeutic measure to avoid pulpectomy. [1920–25; PULP + -O- + -TOMY]

pulp′ plas′ter, plaster containing shredded wood fiber.

pulp•wood (pulp′wo͝od′), *n.* spruce or other soft wood suitable for making paper. [1885–90; PULP + WOOD[1]]

pulp•y (pul′pē), *adj.,* **pulp•i•er, pulp•i•est. 1.** pertaining to, characteristic of, or resembling pulp; fleshy or soft. **2.** pertaining to, characteristic of, or resembling magazines or books considered pulp; sensationalistic; trashy. [1585–95; PULP + -Y[1]] —**pulp′i•ly,** *adv.* —**pulp′i•ness,** *n.*

pul•que (po͝ol′kē; *Sp.* po͞ol′ke), *n.* a fermented milky drink made from the juice of certain species of agave in Mexico. [1685–95; < MexSp]

CONCISE ETYMOLOGY KEY: <, descended or borrowed from; >, whence; b., blend of, blended; c., cognate with; cf., compare; deriv., derivative; equiv., equivalent; imit., imitative; obl., oblique; r., replacing; s., stem; sp., spelling, spelled; resp., respelling, respelled; trans., translation; ?, origin unknown; *, unattested; ‡, probably earlier than. See the full key inside the front cover.

pul•que•rí•a (po͞ol′ke rē′ä), *n. pl.* **-rí•as** (-rē′äs). *Mexican Spanish.* a tavern selling pulque.

pul•sar (pul′sär), *n. Astron.* one of several hundred known celestial objects, generally believed to be rapidly rotating neutron stars, that emit pulses of radiation, esp. radio waves, with a high degree of regularity. [1965–70; *puls(ating st)ar,* on the model of QUASAR]

pul•sate (pul′sāt), *v.i.,* **-sat•ed, -sat•ing. 1.** to expand and contract rhythmically, as the heart; beat; throb. **2.** to vibrate; quiver. [1785–95; < L *pulsātus,* ptp. of *pulsāre* to batter, strike, make (strings) vibrate. See PULSE[1], -ATE[1]]
—**Syn. 1.** pulse. PULSATE, BEAT, PALPITATE, THROB refer to the recurrent vibratory movement of the heart, the pulse, etc. To PULSATE is to move in a definite rhythm, temporarily or for a longer duration: *Blood pulsates in the arteries.* To BEAT is to repeat a vibration or pulsation regularly for some time: *One's heart beats many times a minute.* To PALPITATE is to beat at a rapid rate, often producing a flutter: *to palpitate with excitement.* To THROB is to beat with an unusual force that is often associated with pain or heightened emotion or sensation: *to throb with terror.*

pul•sa•tile (pul′sə til, -tīl′), *adj.* pulsating; throbbing. [1535–45; < ML *pulsātilis.* See PULSATE, -ILE] —**pul•sa•til•i•ty** (pul′sə til′i tē), *n.*

pul•sa•tion (pul sā′shən), *n.* **1.** the act of pulsating; beating or throbbing. **2.** a beat or throb, as of the pulse. **3.** vibration or undulation. **4.** a single vibration. [1375–1425; late ME *pulsacioun* < L *pulsātiōn-* (s. of *pulsātiō*). See PULSATE, -ION]

pul•sa•tive (pul′sə tiv), *adj.* throbbing; pulsating. [1350–1400; ME; see PULSATE, -IVE] —**pul′sa•tive•ly,** *adv.*

pul•sa•tor (pul′sā tər, pul sā′-), *n.* **1.** something that pulsates, beats, or throbs. **2.** pulsometer (def. 2). [1650–60; < L *pulsātor* one who strikes a lyre. See PULSATE, -TOR]

pul•sa•to•ry (pul′sə tôr′ē, -tōr′ē), *adj.* pulsating or throbbing. [1605–15; PULSAT(ION) + -ORY[1]]

pulse[1] (puls), *n., v.,* **pulsed, puls•ing.** —*n.* **1.** the regular throbbing of the arteries, caused by the successive contractions of the heart, esp. as may be felt at an artery, as at the wrist. **2.** a single pulsation, or beat or throb, of the arteries or heart. **3.** the rhythmic recurrence of strokes, vibrations, or undulations. **4.** a single stroke, vibration, or undulation. **5.** *Elect.* a momentary, sudden fluctuation in an electrical quantity, as in voltage or current. **6.** *Physics.* a single, abrupt emission of particles or radiation. **7.** a throb of life, emotion, etc. **8.** vitality. **9.** the general attitude, sentiment, preference, etc., as of the public. —*v.i.* **10.** to beat or throb; pulsate. **11.** to beat, vibrate, or undulate. **12.** *Physics.* to emit particles or radiation periodically in short bursts. —*v.t.* **13.** to cause to pulse. **14.** *Med.* to administer (medication) in interrupted, often concentrated dosages to avoid unwanted side effects. [1300–50; < L *pulsus* a beat, equiv. to **peld-,* base of *pellere* to set in motion by beating or striking (cf. IMPEL) + *-tus,* suffix of v. action, with *dt* < *s* and backing and raising of *e* before velar *l;* r. ME *pous* < MF < L, as above]

pulse[2] (puls), *n.* **1.** the edible seeds of certain leguminous plants, as peas, beans, or lentils. **2.** a plant producing such seeds. [1250–1300; ME *puls* < L: thick pap of meal, pulse. See POULTICE]

pulse′-am′pli•tude modula′tion (puls′am′pli to͞od′, -tyo͞od′), *Telecommunications.* modulation of the amplitude of a train of electric pulses used to carry signals **(pulse′ car′rier).** *Abbr.:* PAM [1945–50]

pulse•beat (puls′bēt′), *n.* **1.** pulse[1] (def. 1). **2.** a hint or intimation of feeling, desires, etc.: *the pulsebeat of a town.* [1835–45; PULSE[1] + BEAT]

pulse′-code modula′tion (puls′kōd′), *Telecommunications.* a form of modulation that transforms a wave-form, as an audio signal, into a binary signal in which information is conveyed by a coded order of pulses for transmission, storage on a disk, or processing by a computer. *Abbr.:* PCM [1945–50]

pulse′ di′aling, a system of calling telephone numbers wherein electrical pulses corresponding to the digits in the number called are generated by manipulating a rotary dial or push buttons (contrasted with *tone dialing*).

pulse′jet en′gine (puls′jet′), *Aeron.* a jet engine equipped with valves that continuously open to admit air, then close during combustion, giving a pulsating thrust: used to power the V-1, a German buzz bomb, in World War II. Also, **pulse′-jet en′gine.** Also called **pulse′jet′, pulse′-jet′, aeropulse.** [1945–50; PULSE[1] + JET[1]]

pulse′ pres′sure, the pressure of the pulse; the difference between the systolic and diastolic pressures. [1900–05]

pulse′ rate′, *Med.* the rate of the pulse: stated in pulsations per minute. [1875–80]

pulse′ repeti′tion fre′quency, *Telecommunications.* the number of pulses per second in a system of pulse transmission. Also, **pulse′-rep•e•ti′tion fre′quency.** *Abbr.:* PRF

pulse′-time modula′tion (puls′tīm′), *Electronics.* radio transmission in which the carrier is modulated to produce a series of pulses timed to transmit the amplitude and pitch of a signal. Abbr.: PTM [1940–45]

pul•sim•e•ter (pul sim′i tər), *n.* an instrument for measuring the strength or quickness of the pulse. [1835–45; PULSE[1] + -I- + -METER]

pul•som•e•ter (pul som′i tər), *n.* **1.** a pulsimeter. **2.** a pump without pistons, utilizing the pressure of steam and the partial vacuum caused by the condensation of steam alternately in two chambers. [1855–60; PULSE[1] + -O- + -METER]

pu•lu (po͞o′lo͞o), *n.* a soft, elastic vegetable fiber of yellow-brown hue obtained from the young fronds of Hawaiian tree ferns, used for mattress and pillow stuffing. Also called **pu′lu fi′ber.** [1825–35; < Hawaiian]

pulv., (in prescriptions) powder. [< L *pulvis*]

pul•ver•a•ble (pul′vər ə bəl), *adj.* capable of being pulverized; pulverizable. [1650–60; obs. *pulver* to PULVERIZE (< L *pulverāre*) + -ABLE]

pul•ver•ize (pul′və rīz′), *v.,* **-ized, -iz•ing.** —*v.t.* **1.** to reduce to dust or powder, as by pounding or grinding. **2.** to demolish or crush completely. **3.** *Slang.* to defeat, hurt badly, or, figuratively, render helpless: *The Kid pulverized Jackson with a series of brutal lefts. He's a veteran nightclub comic who can pulverize any audience in seconds.* —*v.i.* **4.** to become reduced to dust. Also, *esp. Brit.,* **pul′ver•ise′.** [1575–85; < LL *pulverizāre* to reduce to powder, equiv. to L *pulver-* (s. of *pulvis;* akin to POLLEN) dust + *-izāre* -IZE] —**pul′ver•iz′a•ble,** *adj.* —**pul′ver•i•za′tion,** *n.* —**pul′ver•iz′er,** *n.*

pul•ver•u•lent (pul ver′yə lənt, -ver′ə lənt), *adj.* **1.** consisting of dust or fine powder. **2.** crumbling to dust or powder. **3.** covered with dust or powder. [1650–60; < L *pulverulentus* dusty, equiv. to *pulver-* (s. of *pulvis*) dust + *-ulentus* -ULENT] —**pul•ver′u•lence,** *n.* —**pul•ver′u•lent•ly,** *adv.*

pul•vil•lus (pul vil′əs), *n., pl.* **-vil•li** (-vil′ī). *Entomol.* a soft, padlike structure located at the base of each claw on the feet of certain insects. [1685–95; < L, dim. of *pulvīnus* cushion]

pul•vi•nar (pul vī′nər), *n., pl.* **pul•vi•nar•i•a** (pul′və nâr′ē ə), *adj.* —*n.* **1.** (in ancient Rome) **a.** a cushioned couch kept in readiness for any visitation of a god. **b.** a cushioned seat at a circus. **2.** Also called **pulvinus.** (on an Ionic capital) either of two convex forms having on their ends two of the volutes. —*adj.* **3.** pulvinate (def. 3). [1590–1600; (n.) < L *pulvīnar* cushioned couch, equiv. to *pulvīn(us)* cushion + *-ar,* shortening of *-āre,* neut. of *āris* -AR[1]; (adj.) PULVIN(US) + -AR[1]]

pul•vi•nate (pul′və nāt′), *adj.* **1.** cushion-shaped. **2.** having a pulvinus. **3.** Also, **pulvinar.** *Archit.* (of a frieze or the like) having a convex surface from top to bottom. Also, **pul′vi•nat′ed.** [1815–25; < L *pulvīnātus* cushioned, equiv. to *pulvīn(us)* cushion + *-ātus* -ATE[1]] —**pul′vi•nate′ly,** *adv.*

pul•vi•nus (pul vī′nəs), *n., pl.* **-ni** (-nī). **1.** *Bot.* a cushionlike swelling at the base of a leaf or leaflet, at the point of junction with the axis. **2.** *Archit.* pulvinar (def. 2). [1855–60; < L *pulvīnus* cushion]

pu•ma (pyo͞o′mə, po͞o′-), *n.* **1.** cougar. **2.** the fur of a cougar. [1770–80; < Sp < Quechua]

pum•e•lo (pum′ə lō′), *n., pl.* **-los.** pomelo.

pum•ice (pum′is), *n., v.,* **-iced, -ic•ing.** —*n.* **1.** Also called **pum′ice stone′.** a porous or spongy form of volcanic glass, used as an abrasive. —*v.t.* **2.** to rub, smooth, clean, etc., with pumice. [bef. 1000; < L *pūmic-,* s. of *pūmex* pumice stone; r. ME *pomis(e), pomish(e), pomice* < MF *pomis* < L; cf. OE *pumic-* (< L), in *pumicstān* pumice stone; see POUNCE[3]] —**pu•mi•ceous** (pyo͞o mish′əs), *adj.* —**pum′ic•er,** *n.*

pum•mel (pum′əl), *v.t.,* **-meled, -mel•ing** or (*esp. Brit.*) **-melled, -mel•ling.** to beat or thrash with or as if with the fists. Also, **pommel.** [1540–50; alter. of POMMEL]

pum•me•lo (pum′ə lō′), *n., pl.* **-los.** pomelo.

pump[1] (pump), *n.* **1.** an apparatus or machine for raising, driving, exhausting, or compressing fluids or gases by means of a piston, plunger, or set of rotating vanes. **2.** *Engin., Building Trades.* a shore having a jackscrew in its foot for adjusting the length or for bearing more firmly against the structure to be sustained. **3.** *Biol.* an animal organ that propels fluid through the body; heart. **4.** *Cell Biol.* a system that supplies energy for transport against a chemical gradient, as the sodium pump for the transfer of sodium and potassium ions across a cell membrane. **5. prime the pump, a.** to increase government expenditure in an effort to stimulate the economy. **b.** to support or promote the operation or improvement of something. —*v.t.* **6.** to raise, drive, etc., with a pump. **7.** to free from water or other liquid by means of a pump. **8.** to inflate by pumping (often fol. by *up*): *to pump a tire up.* **9.** to operate or move by an up-and-down or back-and-forth action. **10.** to supply with air, as an organ, by means of a pumplike device. **11.** to drive, force, etc., as if from a pump: *He rapidly pumped a dozen shots into the bull's-eye.* **12.** to supply or inject as if by using a pump: *to pump money into a failing business.* **13.** to question artfully or persistently to elicit information: *to pump someone for confidential information.* **14.** to elicit (information) by questioning. —*v.i.* **15.** to work a pump; raise or move water, oil, etc., with a pump. **16.** to operate as a pump does. **17.** to move up and down like a pump handle. **18.** to exert oneself in a manner likened to pumping: *He pumped away at his homework all evening.* **19.** to seek to elicit information from a person. **20.** to come out in spurts. **21. pump iron.** See **iron** (def. 16). **22. pump up, a.** to inflate. **b.** to increase, heighten, or strengthen; put more effort into or emphasis on; intensify: *The store has decided to pump up its advertising.* **c.** to infuse with enthusiasm, competitive spirit, energy, etc.: *The contestants were all backstage pumping themselves up for their big moment.* [1400–50; late ME *pumpe* (n.); c. G *Pumpe,* D *pomp*] —**pump′a•ble,** *adj.* —**pump′less,** *adj.* —**pump′like′,** *adj.*

pump[2] (pump), *n.* **1.** a lightweight, low-cut shoe without fastenings for women. **2.** a slip-on black patent leather shoe for men, for wear with formal dress. [1720–30; orig. uncert.]

pump-ac•tion (pump′ak′shən), *adj.* (of a shotgun or rifle) having an action that extracts the empty case, loads, and cocks the piece by means of a hand-operated lever that slides backward and forward; slide-action. [1910–15, *Amer.*]

pump′ box′, a chamber of a pump in which a piston operates. [1690–1700]

pump•er (pum′pər), *n.* **1.** a person or thing that pumps. **2.** a fire truck specially equipped to pump water at the site of a fire. [1650–60; PUMP[1] + -ER[1]]

pum·per·nick·el (pum′pər nik′əl), *n.* a coarse, dark, slightly sour bread made of unbolted rye. [1750–60; < G *Pumpernickel* orig., an opprobrious name for anyone considered disagreeable, equiv. to *pumper(n)* to break wind + *Nickel* hypocoristic from of *Nikolaus* Nicholas (cf. NICKEL); presumably applied to the bread from its effect on the digestive system]

pump′ gun′, a shotgun or rifle having a pump-action mechanism. [1905–10]

pump·ing (pum′ping), *n.* **1.** the act or process of pumping or the action of a pump. **2.** *Meteorol.* rapid change in the height of the column in a mercury barometer, resulting from fluctuations in the surrounding air pressure. [1590–1600; PUMP[1] + -ING[1]]

pump·kin (pump′kin *or, commonly,* pung′kin), *n.* **1.** a large, edible, orange-yellow fruit borne by a coarse, decumbent vine, *Cucurbita pepo,* of the gourd family. **2.** the similar fruit of any of several related species, as *C. maxima* or *C. moschata.* **3.** a plant bearing such fruit. [1640–50; alter. of *pumpion* (see -KIN), var. of *pompon* < MF, nasalized var. of *popon* melon, earlier *pepon* < L *pepōn-* (s. of *pepō*) < Gk *pépōn* kind of melon]

pump′kin head′, a slow or dim-witted person; dunce. [1775–85, *Amer.*] —**pump′kin-head′ed,** *adj.*

pump·kin·seed (pump′kin sēd′ *or, commonly,* pung′-kin-), *n.* **1.** the seed of the pumpkin. **2.** a freshwater sunfish, *Lepomis gibbosus,* of eastern North America. [1775–85; PUMPKIN + SEED]

pump·man (pump′mən), *n., pl.* **-men.** a person who runs a power-operated pump. [1770–80; PUMP[1] + -MAN]

pump′ prim′ing, the spending of government funds in commercial enterprises, to stimulate the national economy. [1935–40, *Amer.*]

pump′ room′, a room at a spa for drinking mineral waters. [1735–45]

pun (pun), *n., v.,* **punned, pun·ning.** —*n.* **1.** the humorous use of a word or phrase so as to emphasize or suggest its different meanings or applications, or the use of words that are alike or nearly alike in sound but different in meaning; a play on words. **2.** the word or phrase used in this way. —*v.i.* **3.** to make puns. [1655–65; perh. special use of *pun,* var. (now dial.) of POUND[1], i.e., to mistreat (words)] —**pun′less,** *adj.*

pu·na (po͞o′nä), *n.* **1.** a high, cold, arid plateau, as in the Peruvian Andes. **2.** *Pathol.* See **altitude sickness.** [1605–15; < AmerSp < Quechua]

Pu·nan (po͞o nän′), *n., pl.* **-nans,** (*esp. collectively*) **-nan.** a member of a food-gathering people living in the forests of interior Borneo.

Pun·cak Ja·ya (po͝on′chäk jä′yä), a mountain in Irian Jaya, Indonesia, on W New Guinea: highest island point in the world. 16,503 ft. (5030 m). Also, **Puntjak Djaja.** Also called **Mount Carstensz.**

punch[1] (punch), *n.* **1.** a thrusting blow, esp. with the fist. **2.** forcefulness, effectiveness, or pungency in content or appeal; power; zest: *a letter to voters that needs more punch.* **3. pull punches, a.** to lessen deliberately the force of one's blows. **b.** *Informal.* to act with restraint or hold back the full force or implications of something: *He wasn't going to pull any punches when he warned them of what they would be up against.* **4. roll with the punches,** *Informal.* to cope with and survive adversity: *In the business world you quickly learn to roll with the punches.* —*v.t.* **5.** to give a sharp thrust or blow to, esp. with the fist. **6.** *Western U.S. and Western Canada.* to drive (cattle). **7.** to poke or prod, as with a stick. **8.** *Informal.* to deliver (lines in a play, a musical passage, or the like) with vigor. **9.** to strike or hit in operating: *to punch the typewriter keys.* **10.** to put into operation with or as if with a blow: *to punch a time clock.* **11.** *Baseball.* to hit (the ball) with a short, chopping motion rather than with a full swing: *He punched a soft liner just over third base for a base hit.* —*v.i.* **12.** to give a sharp blow to a person or thing, as with the fist: *The boxer punches well.* **13. punch away,** *Informal.* to keep trying or working, esp. in difficult or discouraging circumstances; persevere: *punching away at the same old job.* **14. punch in, a.** to record one's time of arrival at work by punching a time clock. **b.** to keyboard (information) into a computer: *to punch in the inventory figures.* **15. punch out, a.** to record one's time of departure from work by punching a time clock. **b.** *Slang.* to beat up or knock out with the fists. **c.** to extract (information) from a computer by the use of a keyboard: *to punch out data on last week's sales.* **d.** to bail out; eject from an aircraft. **16. punch up, a.** to call up (information) on a computer by the use of a keyboard: *to punch up a list of hotel reservations.* **b.** *Informal.* to enliven, as with fresh ideas or additional material: *You'd better punch up that speech with a few jokes.* [1350–1400; ME *punchen* (v.); appar. var. of POUNCE[1]] —**punch′er,** *n.*
—**Syn. 5.** strike, hit; drub, pummel.

punch[2] (punch), *n.* **1.** a tool or machine for perforating or stamping materials, driving nails, etc. **2.** the solid upper die of a punch press, used with a hollow die to blank out shaped pieces of sheet metal or the like. —*v.t.* **3.** to cut, stamp, pierce, perforate, form, or drive with a tool or machine that punches. —*v.i.* **4.** to work at or on something with or as if with a mechanical punch. [1495–1505; short for PUNCHEON[2], reinforced by PUNCH[1]] —**punch′a·ble,** *adj.*

punch[3] (punch), *n.* **1.** a beverage consisting of wine or spirits mixed with fruit juice, soda, water, milk, or the like, and flavored with sugar, spices, etc. **2.** a beverage of two or more fruit juices, sugar, and water, sometimes carbonated. [1625–35; of uncert. orig.]

Punch (punch), *n.* **1.** the chief male character in a Punch-and-Judy show. **2. pleased as Punch,** highly pleased; delighted: *They were pleased as Punch at having been asked to come along.* [short for PUNCHINELLO]

Punch′-and-Ju′dy show′ (punch′ən jo͞o′dē), a puppet show having a conventional plot consisting chiefly of slapstick humor and the tragicomic misadventures of the grotesque, hook-nosed, humpback buffoon Punch and his wife Judy. [1875–80]

punch·ball (punch′bôl′), *n.* a form of playground or street baseball in which a rubber ball is batted with the fist. [1930–35; PUNCH[1] + BALL[1]]

punch·board (punch′bôrd′, -bōrd′), *n.* a small board containing holes filled with slips of paper printed with concealed numbers that are punched out by a player in an attempt to win a prize. Also called **pushcard.** [1910–15; PUNCH[1] + BOARD]

punch′ bowl′, a large bowl from which punch, lemonade, etc., is served, usually with a ladle. [1685–95]

punch′ card′, a card having holes punched in specific positions and patterns so as to represent data to be stored or processed mechanically, electrically, or photoelectrically. Also, **punch′card′, punched′ card′.** [1940–45]

punch-drunk (punch′drungk′), *adj.* **1.** (esp. of a boxer) having cerebral concussion caused by repeated blows to the head and consequently exhibiting unsteadiness of gait, hand tremors, slow muscular movement, hesitant speech, and dulled mentality. **2.** *Informal.* befuddled; dazed. [1915–20, *Amer.*]

punched′ tape′, *Computers.* See **paper tape.** [1880–85]

pun·cheon[1] (pun′chən), *n.* **1.** a large cask of varying capacity, but usually 80 gallons (304 l). **2.** the volume of such a cask, used as a measure. [1425–75; ME *ponchoun, punchon* < MF *ponçon,* perh. to be identified with PUNCHEON[2]]

pun·cheon[2] (pun′chən), *n.* **1.** a heavy slab of timber, roughly dressed, for use as a floorboard. **2.** a short, upright framing timber. **3.** (in goldsmith work) **a.** any of various pointed instruments; a punch. **b.** a stamping tool. [1325–75; ME *ponson, punçon, ponchoun* < MF *poinçon* < L *pūnctiōn-* (s. of *pūnctiō*) a pricking, hence, pricking tool, equiv. to *pūnct(us)* (ptp. of *pungere* to prick; cf. POINT) + *-iōn-* -ION]

Pun·chi·nel·lo (pun′chə nel′ō), *n., pl.* **-los, -loes. 1.** a grotesque or absurd chief character in a puppet show of Italian origin: the prototype of Punch. **2.** any similarly grotesque or absurd person or thing. [1660–70; < It (Naples dial.) *polecenella* character in the puppet show, dim. of *polecana* turkey-cock chick < LL *pullicēnus,* deriv. of L *pullus* PULLET]

punch′ing bag′, **1.** an inflated or stuffed bag, usually suspended, punched with the fists as an exercise. **2.** *Informal.* a person serving as an object of abuse; scapegoat: *I told him that I wasn't going to be a punching bag for anyone.* [1895–1900]

punch′ line′, the climactic phrase or sentence in a joke, speech, advertisement, or humorous story that produces the desired effect. [1920–25, *Amer.*]

punch′ list′, *Informal.* a list of unfinished matters that require attention.

punch-out (punch′out′), *n.* **1.** a small section of cardboard or metal surrounded by perforations so that it can be easily forced out. **2.** *Slang.* a fistfight or brawl. [1925–30; n. use of v. phrase *punch out*]

punch′ press′, *Mach.* a power-driven machine used to cut, draw, or otherwise shape material, esp. metal sheets, with dies, under pressure or by heavy blows. [1910–15]

punch′ spoon′, a spoon having a pierced bowl and a barbed end for removing fruit, ice, etc., from punch.

punch-up (punch′up′), *n. Slang.* punch-out (def. 2). [1955–60; n. use of v. phrase *punch (it) up*]

punch·y (pun′chē), *adj.,* **punch·i·er, punch·i·est.** *Informal.* **1.** punch-drunk. **2.** being or appearing vigorously effective; forceful. [1935–40; PUNCH[1] + -Y[1]] —**punch′i·ness,** *n.*

punc·tate (pungk′tāt), *adj.* marked with points or dots; having minute spots or depressions. Also, **punc′tat·ed.** [1750–60; < NL *pūnctātus* dotted, equiv. to L *pūnct(um)* POINT, dot + *-ātus* -ATE[1]]

punc·ta·tim (po͝ongk tä′tim; *Eng.* pungk tā′tim), *adv. Latin.* point for point.

punc·ta·tion (pungk tā′shən), *n.* **1.** punctate condition or marking. **2.** one of the marks or depressions. [1610–20; < ML *pūnctātiōn-,* s. of *pūnctātiō,* equiv. to *pūnctāt(us)* (ptp. of *pūnctāre* to mark with points; see POINT) + *-iōn-* -ION]

punc·ti·form (pungk′tə fôrm′), *adj.* shaped like or of the nature of a point or dot. [1815–25; < L *pūnct(um)* POINT + -I- + -FORM]

punc·til·i·o (pungk til′ē ō′), *n., pl.* **-til·i·os** for 1. **1.** a fine point, particular, or detail, as of conduct, ceremony, or procedure. **2.** strictness or exactness in the observance of formalities or amenities. [1590–1600; alter. of It *puntiglio* < Sp *puntillo,* dim. of *punto* < L *pūnctum* POINT]

punc·til·i·ous (pungk til′ē əs), *adj.* extremely attentive to punctilios; strict or exact in the observance of the formalities or amenities of conduct or actions. [1625–35; PUNCTILI(O) + -OUS] —**punc·til′i·ous·ly,** *adv.* —**punc·til′i·ous·ness,** *n.*
—**Syn.** precise, demanding; careful, conscientious. See **scrupulous.** —**Ant.** careless.

punc·tu·al (pungk′cho͞o əl), *adj.* **1.** strictly observant of an appointed or regular time; not late; prompt. **2.** made, occurring, etc., at the scheduled or proper time: *punctual payment.* **3.** pertaining to or of the nature of a point. **4.** punctilious. [1350–1400; ME < ML *pūnctuālis* of a point, equiv. to L *pūnctu(s)* a point, a pricking (*pung(ere)* to prick + *-tus* suffix of v. action) + *-ālis* -AL[1]; see PUNGENT] —**punc′tu·al·ly,** *adv.* —**punc′tu·al·ness,** *n.*

punc·tu·al·i·ty (pungk′cho͞o al′i tē), *n.* **1.** the quality or state of being punctual. **2.** strict observance in keeping engagements; promptness. [1610–20; PUNCTUAL + -ITY]

punc·tu·ate (pungk′cho͞o āt′), *v.,* **-at·ed, -at·ing.** —*v.t.* **1.** to mark or divide (something written) with punctuation marks in order to make the meaning clear. **2.** to interrupt at intervals: *Cheers punctuated the mayor's speech.* **3.** to give emphasis or force to; emphasize; underline. —*v.i.* **4.** to insert or use marks of punctuation. [1625–35; < ML *pūnctuātus* (ptp. of *pūnctuāre* to point), deriv. of L *pūnctus* a pricking; see PUNCTUAL] —**punc′tu·a′tor,** *n.*

punc′tuated equilib′rium, theory of, *Biol.* a hypothesis holding that the evolution of species proceeds in a characteristic pattern of relative stability for long periods of time interspersed with much shorter periods during which many species become extinct and new species emerge. Also called **punctuationalism.** Cf. **gradualism** (def. 3).

punc·tu·a·tion (pungk′cho͞o ā′shən), *n.* **1.** the practice or system of using certain conventional marks or characters in writing or printing in order to separate elements and make the meaning clear, as in ending a sentence or separating clauses. **2.** the act of punctuating. **3.** punctuation marks. [1530–40; < ML *pūnctuātiōn-* (s. of *pūnctuātiō*) a marking, pointing. See PUNCTUATE, -ION] —**punc′tu·a′tion·al, punc′tu·a′tive,** *adj.*

punc·tu·a·tion·al·ism (pungk′cho͞o ā′shə nl iz′əm), *n. Biol.* See **punctuated equilibrium.** [1975–80; PUNCTUATIONAL + -ISM] —**punc′tu·a′tion·al,** *adj.* —**punc′·tu·a′tion·al·ist, punc′tu·a′tion·ist,** *n.*

punctua′tion mark′, any of a group of conventional marks or characters used in punctuation, as the period, comma, semicolon, question mark, or dash. [1855–60]

punc·tu·late (pungk′cho͞o lāt′, -lit), *adj.* studded with minute points or dots. Also **punc′tu·lat′ed.** [1840–50; < L *pūnctul(um)* (dim. of *pūnctum* POINT; see -ULE) + -ATE[1]] —**punc′tu·la′tion,** *n.*

punc·ture (pungk′chər), *n., v.,* **-tured, -tur·ing.** —*n.* **1.** the act of piercing or perforating, as with a pointed instrument or object. **2.** a hole or mark so made. **3.** *Zool.* a small pointlike depression. —*v.t.* **4.** to pierce or perforate, as with a pointed instrument: *to puncture leather with an awl.* **5.** to make (a hole, perforation, etc.) by piercing or perforating: *He punctured a row of holes in the cardboard.* **6.** to make a puncture in: *A piece of glass punctured the tire.* **7.** to reduce or diminish as if by piercing; damage; wound: *to puncture a person's pride.* **8.** to cause to collapse or disintegrate; spoil; ruin: *to puncture one's dream of success.* —*v.i.* **9.** to become punctured: *These tires do not puncture easily.* [1350–1400; ME < L *pūnctūra* a pricking, equiv. to *pūnct(us)* (ptp. of *pungere* to pierce; see PUNGENT) + *-ūra* -URE] —**punc′tur·a·ble,** *adj.* —**punc′ture·less,** *adj.* —**punc′tur·er,** *n.*
—**Syn. 2.** break, rupture, perforation.

pun·dit (pun′dit), *n.* **1.** a learned person, expert, or authority. **2.** a person who makes comments or judgments, esp. in an authoritative manner; critic or commentator. **3.** pandit. [1665–75; < Hindi *paṇḍit* < Skt *paṇḍita* learned man, (adj.) learned] —**pun·dit′ic,** *adj.* —**pun·dit′i·cal·ly,** *adv.*
—**Syn. 1.** sage, guru, savant.

pun·dit·ry (pun′di trē), *n.* the opinions or methods of pundits. [1925–30; PUNDIT + -RY]

pung (pung), *n. Chiefly Eastern Canada and New Eng.* a sleigh with a boxlike body. [1815–25, *Amer.*; short for *tom-pung,* ult. < the same Algonquian etymon as TOBOGGAN]

pun·gent (pun′jənt), *adj.* **1.** sharply affecting the organs of taste or smell, as if by a penetrating power; biting; acrid. **2.** acutely distressing to the feelings or mind; poignant. **3.** caustic, biting, or sharply expressive: *pungent remarks.* **4.** mentally stimulating or appealing: *pungent wit.* **5.** *Biol.* piercing or sharp-pointed. [1590–1600; < L *pungent-* (s. of *pungēns*), prp. of *pungere* to prick. See POIGNANT, POINT, -ENT] —**pun′gen·cy,** *n.* —**pun′gent·ly,** *adv.*
—**Syn. 1.** hot, peppery, piquant, sharp. **3.** sarcastic, mordant, cutting; acrimonious, bitter. **4.** keen, sharp.
—**Ant. 1.** mild, bland. **3.** soothing. **4.** dull.

Pu·nic (pyo͞o′nik), *adj.* **1.** of or pertaining to the ancient Carthaginians. **2.** treacherous; perfidious: originally applied by the Romans to the Carthaginians. —*n.* **3.** the language of ancient Carthage, a form of late Phoenician. [< L *Pūnicus,* earlier *Poenicus* Carthaginian, equiv. to *Poen(us)* a Phoenician, a Carthaginian (akin to Gk *Phoînix* a Phoenician) + *-icus* -IC]

Pu′nic Wars′, the three wars waged by Rome against Carthage, 264–241, 218–201, and 149–146 B.C., resulting in the destruction of Carthage and the annexation of its territory by Rome.

pun·ish (pun′ish), *v.t.* **1.** to subject to pain, loss, confinement, death, etc., as a penalty for some offense, transgression, or fault: *to punish a criminal.* **2.** to inflict a penalty for (an offense, fault, etc.): *to punish theft.* **3.** to handle severely or roughly, as in a fight. **4.** to put to painful exertion, as a horse in racing. **5.** *Informal.* to make a heavy inroad on; deplete: *to punish a quart of whiskey.* —*v.i.* **6.** to inflict punishment. [1300–50; ME *punischen* < MF *puniss-,* long s. of *punir* < L *pūnīre;* akin to *poena* PENALTY, PAIN] —**pun′ish·er,** *n.*
—**Syn. 1.** chastise, castigate. PUNISH, CORRECT, DISCIPLINE refer to making evident public or private disapproval of violations of law, wrongdoing, or refusal to obey rules or regulations by imposing penalties. To PUNISH is chiefly to inflict penalty or pain as a retribution for misdeeds, with little or no expectation of correction or improvement: *to punish a thief.* To CORRECT is to reprove or inflict punishment for faults, specifically with the idea of bringing about improvement: *to correct a rebellious child.* TO DISCIPLINE is to give a kind of punish-

ment that will educate or will establish useful habits: *to discipline a careless driver.* **1, 2.** penalize. **—Ant. 1, 2.** reward.

pun·ish·a·ble (pun′i shə bəl), *adj.* liable to or deserving punishment. [1375–1425; late ME. See PUNISH, -ABLE] **—pun′ish·a·bil′i·ty,** *n.*

pun·ish·ing (pun′i shing), *adj.* causing or characterized by harsh or injurious treatment; severe; brutal: *The storm was accompanied by punishing winds.* [1425–75; late ME *punyesand;* see PUNISH, -ING[2]]

pun·ish·ment (pun′ish mənt), *n.* **1.** the act of punishing. **2.** the fact of being punished, as for an offense or fault. **3.** a penalty inflicted for an offense, fault, etc. **4.** severe handling or treatment. [1250–1300; ME *punysshement* < AF *punisement,* OF *punissement.* See PUNISH, -MENT]

pu·ni·tion (pyoo͞ nish′ən), *n.* punishment. [1375–1425; late ME *punicioun* < MF *punition* < L *pūnītiōn-,* s. of *pūnītiō* punishment, equiv. to *pūnīt(us)* (ptp. of *pūnīre* to PUNISH) + *-iōn-* -ION]

pu·ni·tive (pyoo͞′ni tiv), *adj.* serving for, concerned with, or inflicting punishment: *punitive laws; punitive action.* Also, **pu·ni·to·ry** (pyoo͞′ni tôr′ē, -tōr′ē). [1615–25; < ML *pūnītīvus* of punishment, equiv. to L *pūnīt(us)* (ptp. of *pūnīre* to PUNISH) + *-īvus* -IVE] **—pu′ni·tive·ly,** *adv.* **—pu′ni·tive·ness,** *n.*

pu′nitive dam′ages, *Law.* damages awarded to a plaintiff in excess of compensatory damages in order to punish the defendant for a reckless or willful act. Also called **exemplary damages.** Cf. **compensatory damages.** [1970–75]

Pun·jab (pun jäb′, pun′jäb), *n.* **1.** a former province in NW British India: now divided between India and Pakistan. **2.** a state in NW India. 15,230,000; 47,456 sq. mi. (122,911 sq. km). *Cap.:* Chandigarh. **3.** a province in NE Pakistan. 37,374,000; 79,284 sq. mi. (205,330 sq. km). *Cap.:* Lahore.

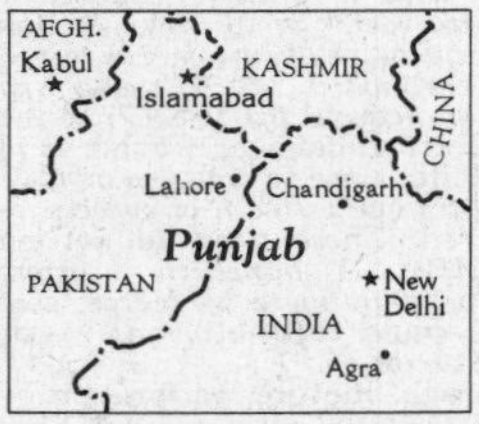

Pun·ja·bi (pun jä′bē), *n., pl.* **-bis** for 1. **1.** a native or inhabitant of the Punjab. **2.** an Indic language of the Punjab. **—***adj.* **3.** of or pertaining to the Punjab, its people, or their language. Also, **Panjabi.** [< Punjabi *Pañjābī* < Pers *panjāb* PUNJAB + *-ī* suffix of appurtenance]

Pun′jab States′, a former group of states in NW India: amalgamated with Punjab state (in India) in 1956.

pun′ji stake′ (po͝on′jē, pun′-), a sharp bamboo stake concealed in high grass at an angle so as to gash the feet and legs of enemy soldiers and often coated with excrement so as to cause an infected wound. Also called **pun′ji stick′.** [1870–75; earlier *punjee, panja,* perh. < Chingpaw, a Tibeto-Burman language of the Kachins of NE Burma and adjacent areas of India and China; the word is first attested in an account of these people]

punk[1] (pungk), *n.* **1.** any prepared substance, usually in stick form, that will smolder and can be used to light fireworks, fuses, etc. **2.** dry, decayed wood that can be used as tinder. **3.** conk[3]. **4.** a spongy substance derived from fungi; amadou; touchwood. [1680–90, *Amer.;* orig. uncert.]

punk[2] (pungk), *n.* **1.** *Slang.* **a.** something or someone worthless or unimportant. **b.** a young ruffian; hoodlum. **c.** an inexperienced youth. **d.** a young male partner of a homosexual. **e.** an apprentice, esp. in the building trades. **f.** *Prison Slang.* a boy. **2.** See **punk rock. 3.** a style or movement characterized by the adoption of aggressively unconventional and often bizarre or shocking clothing, hairstyles, makeup, etc., and the defiance of social norms of behavior, usually associated with punk rock musicians and fans. **4.** a punker. **5.** *Archaic.* a prostitute. **—***adj.* **6.** *Informal.* poor in quality or condition. **7.** of, pertaining to, or characteristic of punk rock: *a punk band.* **8.** pertaining to, characteristic of, or adopting punk styles: *punk youths; punk hairstyles in various colors.* [1590–1600; of obscure orig.; the sense development is appar. "prostitute" > "catamite" > "hoodlum"; the adj. "poor in quality" (1896) is unclearly derived and perh. a distinct word]

pun·kah (pung′kə), *n.* **1.** (esp. in India) a fan, esp. a large, swinging, screenlike fan hung from the ceiling and moved by a servant or by machinery. **—***adj.* **2.** of, pertaining to, used on, or working a punkah: *punkah ropes.* Also, **pun′ka.** [1615–25; < Hindi *paṅkhā*]

punk·er (pung′kər), *n.* a punk rock musician or a devotee of punk rock or punk styles. [PUNK (ROCK) + -ER[1]]

punk·ie (pung′kē), *n.* any of the minute biting gnats of the family Ceratopogonidae. Also called **biting midge, no-see-um.** [1760–70, *Amer.;* < New York D **punkje,* alter. of Munsee Delaware *pónkwəs* (equiv. to Proto-Algonquian **penkw-* dust, ashes + **-ehs-* dim. suffix) + D *-je* dim. suffix]

punk′ rock′, a type of rock-'n'-roll, reaching its peak in the late 1970's and characterized by loud, insistent music and abusive or violent protest lyrics, and whose performers and followers are distinguished by extremes of dress and socially defiant behavior. Also called **punk.** [1970–75] **—punk′ rock′er.**

punk·y[1] (pung′kē), *adj.,* **punk·i·er, punk·i·est. 1.** of, like, or pertaining to spongy punk. **2.** burning very slowly, as a fire. [1870–75, *Amer.;* PUNK[1] + -Y[1]] **—punk′i·ness,** *n.*

punk·y[2] (pung′kē), *adj.,* **punk·i·er, punk·i·est. 1.** *Slang.* of or like punks or hoodlums. **2.** of, pertaining to, or characteristic of punk rock, its performers, or its devotees. [PUNK[2] + -Y[1]] **—punk′i·ness,** *n.*

pun·ner[1] (pun′ər), *n.* a person who puns; punster. [1680–90; PUN + -ER[1]]

pun·ner[2] (pun′ər), *n.* a rammer for compacting earth or fresh concrete. [1605–15; *pun* dial. form of POUND[1] + -ER[1]]

pun·net (pun′it), *n. Brit., Australian.* a small container or basket for strawberries or other fruit. [1815–25; orig. obscure]

pun·ny (pun′ē), *adj.,* **-ni·er, -ni·est.** having, involving, or characteristic of a pun. [1960–65; PUN + -Y[1]] **—pun′ni·ly,** *adv.*

pun·ster (pun′stər), *n.* a person who makes puns frequently. [1690–1700; PUN + -STER]

punt[1] (punt), *n.* **1.** *Football.* a kick in which the ball is dropped and then kicked before it touches the ground. Cf. **drop kick, place kick. 2.** a small, shallow boat having a flat bottom and square ends, usually used for short outings on rivers or lakes and propelled by poling. **—***v.t.* **3.** *Football.* to kick (a dropped ball) before it touches the ground. **4.** to propel (a small boat) by thrusting against the bottom of a lake or stream, esp. with a pole. **5.** to convey in or as if in a punt. **—***v.i.* **6.** to punt a football. **7.** to propel a boat by thrusting a pole against the bottom of a river, stream, or lake. **8.** to travel or have an outing in a punt. **9.** *Informal.* to equivocate or delay: *If they ask you for exact sales figures, you'll have to punt.* [bef. 1000; 1835–45 for def. 1; OE: flat-bottomed boat (not attested in ME) < L *pontō* punt, PONTOON[1]; sense "to kick a dropped ball" perh. via sense "to propel (a boat) by shoving"] **—punt′er,** *n.*

punt[2] (punt), *v.i.* **1.** *Cards.* to lay a stake against the bank, as at faro. **2.** *Slang.* to gamble, esp. to bet on horse races or other sporting events. **—***n.* **3.** *Cards.* a person who lays a stake against the bank. [1705–15; < F *ponter,* deriv. of *ponte* punter, point in faro < Sp *punto* POINT] **—punt′er,** *n.*

punt[3] (po͝ont, punt), *n.* a monetary unit of the Republic of Ireland, equal to 100 pence; Irish pound. [1970–75; < Ir < E POUND[2]]

Punt (po͝ont), *n.* an ancient Egyptian name of an area not absolutely identified but believed to be Somaliland.

Pun·ta A·re·nas (po͞on′tä ä re′näs), a seaport in S Chile, on the Strait of Magellan: the southernmost city in Chile. 64,456. Formerly, **Magallanes.**

Pun·ta·re·nas (po͞on′tä re′näs), *n.* a seaport in W Costa Rica. 30,664.

pun·tat (pun′tat), *n.* a walking catfish, *Clarias fuscus,* introduced in Hawaiian waters. Also called **Chinese catfish.** [orig. undetermined]

pun·til·la (po͞on tē′ə; *Sp.* po͞on tē′lyä, -yä), *n., pl.* **-til·las** (-tē′əz; *Sp.* -tē′lyäs, -yäs). (in bullfighting) a short dagger used for cutting the spinal cord of the bull. [1830–40; < Sp, dim. of *punta* POINT]

pun·til·le·ro (po͞on′tē âr′ō; *Sp.* po͞on′tē lye′rô, -ye′-), *n., pl.* **-til·le·ros** (-tē âr′ōz; *Sp.* -tē lye′rôs, -ye-′). (in bullfighting) a worker, or assistant, who gives the coup de grâce to the fallen bull with a puntilla. [1905–10; < Sp, equiv. to *puntill(a)* PUNTILLA + *-ero* < L *-ārius* -ARY]

Pun·tjak Dja·ja (po͝on′chäk jä′yä). See **Puncak Jaya.**

pun·ty (pun′tē), *n., pl.* **-ties.** an iron rod used in glassmaking for handling the hot glass. Also called **pontil.** [1655–65; var. of PONTIL]

Punx·su·taw·ney (pungk′sə tô′nē), *n.* a town in central Pennsylvania: Groundhog Day celebration. 7479.

pu·ny (pyoo͞′nē), *adj.,* **-ni·er, -ni·est. 1.** of less than normal size and strength; weak. **2.** unimportant; insignificant; petty or minor: *a puny excuse.* **3.** *Obs.* puisne. [1540–50; sp. var. of PUISNE] **—pu′ni·ly,** *adv.* **—pu′ni·ness,** *n.*

pup (pup), *n., v.,* **pupped, pup·ping. —***n.* **1.** a young dog; puppy. **2.** the young of certain other animals, as the rat or fur seal. **3.** a small plant developing as an offshoot from a mature plant. **—***v.i.* **4.** to give birth to pups. [1580–90; apocopated var. of PUPPY]

pu·pa (pyoo͞′pə), *n., pl.* **-pae** (-pē), **-pas.** an insect in the nonfeeding, usually immobile, transformation stage between the larva and the imago. See illus. under **metamorphosis.** [1765–70; < NL, special use of L *pūpa* girl, doll, puppet. See PUPIL[1], PUPPET] **—pu′pal,** *adj.*

pu·pate (pyoo͞′pāt), *v.i.,* **-pat·ed, -pat·ing.** to become a pupa. [1875–80; PUP(A) + -ATE[1]] **—pu·pa′tion,** *n.*

pup·fish (pup′fish′), *n., pl.* (*esp. collectively*) **-fish,** (*esp. referring to two or more kinds or species*) **-fish·es.** any of several tiny, stout killifishes of the genus *Cyprinodon,* inhabiting marshy waters in arid areas of western North America: several species are endangered. [1945–50; PUP + FISH]

pu·pil[1] (pyoo͞′pəl), *n.* **1.** a person, usually young, who is learning under the close supervision of a teacher at school, a private tutor, or the like; student. **2.** *Civil Law.* an orphaned or emancipated minor under the care of a guardian. **3.** *Roman Law.* a person under the age of puberty orphaned or emancipated, and under the care of a guardian. [1350–1400; ME *pupille* < MF < L *pūpillus* (masc.), *pūpilla* (fem.) orphan, ward, diminutives of *pūpus* boy, *pūpa* girl] **—pu′pil·less,** *adj.*

—Syn. 1. apprentice, novice. PUPIL, DISCIPLE, SCHOLAR, STUDENT refer to a person who is studying, usually in a school. A PUPIL is one under the close supervision of a teacher, either because of youth or of specialization in some branch of study: *a grade-school pupil; the pupil of a famous musician.* A DISCIPLE is one who follows the teachings or doctrines of a person whom he or she considers to be a master or authority: *a disciple of Swedenborg.* SCHOLAR, once meaning the same as PUPIL, is today usually applied to one who has acquired wide erudition in some field of learning: *a great Latin scholar.* A STUDENT is a person attending an educational institution or someone who has devoted much attention to a particular problem: *a college student; a student of politics.*

pu·pil[2] (pyoo͞′pəl), *n. Anat.* the expanding and contracting opening in the iris of the eye, through which light passes to the retina. See diag. under **eye.** [1350–1400; ME < L *pūpilla* lit., little doll; for sense cf. Gk *kórē* girl, doll, pupil of the eye, alluding to the tiny reflections visible in the pupils. See PUPA] **—pu′pil·less,** *adj.*

pu·pil·age (pyoo͞′pə lij), *n.* the state or period of being a pupil; tutelage. [1580–90; PUPIL + -AGE]

pu·pil·lar·i·ty (pyoo͞′pə lar′i tē), *n. Civil Law, Scots Law.* the period between birth and puberty, or until attaining majority. Also, **pu′pi·lar′i·ty.** [1575–85; < L *pūpillāri(s)* of an orphan or ward (see PUPIL[1], -AR[1]) + -TY[2]]

pu·pil·lar·y[1] (pyoo͞′pə ler′ē), *adj.* of or pertaining to a pupil or student. [1605–15; < L *pūpill(āris)* (see PUPIL[1], -AR[1]) + -ARY]

pu·pil·lar·y[2] (pyoo͞′pə ler′ē), *adj. Anat.* pertaining to the pupil of the eye. [1785–95; < L *pūpill(a)* PUPIL[2] + -ARY]

Pu·pin (pyoo͞ pēn′, po͞o′pēn), *n.* **Michael Id·vor·sky** (id vôr′skē), 1858–1935, U.S. inventor, physicist, and author, born in Hungary.

pu·pip·a·rous (pyoo͞ pip′ər əs), *adj.* (of an insect) bearing fully developed larvae that are ready to pupate. [1820–30; < NL *pūpiparus.* See PUPA, -I-, -PAROUS]

pup·pet (pup′it), *n.* **1.** an artificial figure representing a human being or an animal, manipulated by the hand, rods, wires, etc., as on a miniature stage. Cf. **hand puppet, marionette. 2.** a person, group, government, etc., whose actions are prompted and controlled by another or others. **3.** a small doll. **4.** *Mach.* poppethead. [1350–1400; earlier *poppet,* ME *popet,* appar. alter. of MLG *poppe* doll < LL *puppa,* L *pūpa* doll; see -ET] **—pup′pet·like′,** *adj.*

—Syn. 2. pawn, figurehead, instrument.

pup·pet·eer (pup′i tēr′), *n.* **1.** a person who manipulates puppets, as in a puppet show. **—***v.i.* **2.** to work as a puppeteer, as by making puppets perform. [1925–30; PUPPET + -EER]

pup·pet·ry (pup′i trē), *n., pl.* **-ries. 1.** the art of making puppets or presenting puppet shows. **2.** the action of puppets. **3.** mummery; mere show. **4.** puppets collectively. [1520–30; see PUPPET, -RY]

pup′pet show′, an entertainment, as a play or musical revue, in which the performers are puppets. Also called **pup′pet play′.** [1640–50]

Pup·pis (pup′is), *n., gen.* **Pup·pis.** *Astron.* the Stern, a southern constellation: one of the subordinate constellations into which Argo is divided. [< L: stern of a ship, poop]

pup·py (pup′ē), *n., pl.* **-pies. 1.** a young dog, esp. one less than a year old. **2.** *Fox Hunting.* a foxhound that has hunted regularly for less than one season. **3.** pup (def. 2). **4.** a presuming, conceited, or empty-headed young man. [1480–90; earlier *popi.* See PUPPET, -Y[2]] **—pup′py·hood′, pup′py·dom,** *n.* **—pup′py·ish,** *adj.* **—pup′py·like′,** *adj.*

pup′py dog′, puppy (def. 1). [1585–95]

pup·py·foot (pup′ē fo͝ot′), *n., pl.* **-feet.** *Cards.* **1.** the ace of clubs. **2.** any card of the club suit. [1905–10, *Amer.;* PUPPY + FOOT; so called from fancied resemblance]

pup′py love′, temporary infatuation of a boy or girl for another person. Also called **calf love.**

pup′ tent′. See **shelter tent.** [1860–65, *Amer.*]

pu·pu (po͞o′po͞o), *n. Polynesian-Hawaiian Cookery.* any hot or cold usually bite-size appetizer, often served in a varied assortment. [< Hawaiian *pūpū*]

pur (pûr), *v.i., v.t., n.* **purred, pur·ring.** purr.

Pu·ra·na (po͝o rä′nə), *n.* any of 18 collections of Hindu legends and religious instructions. [1690–1700; < Skt: of old] **—Pu·ra′nic,** *adj.*

Pur·bach (po͝or′bäk), *n.* a walled plain in the third quadrant of the face of the moon: about 75 mi. (120 km) in diameter.

pur·blind (pûr′blīnd′), *adj.* **1.** nearly or partially blind; dim-sighted. **2.** slow or deficient in understanding, imagination, or vision. **3.** *Obs.* totally blind. [1250–1300; ME *pur blind* completely blind; see PURE (in obs. adv. sense), BLIND] **—pur′blind′ly,** *adv.* **—pur′blind′·ness,** *n.*

—Syn. 1, 2. See **blind.**

Pur·cell (pûr sel′ *for 1;* pûr′səl *for 2*), *n.* **1. Edward Mills** (milz), born 1912, U.S. physicist: Nobel prize 1952. **2. Henry,** 1658?–95, English composer.

Purcell′ Moun′tains, a range in SE British Columbia and NW Montana. Highest peak, Mt. Farnham, 11,340 ft. (3455 m).

Pur·chas (pûr′chəs), *n.* **Samuel,** 1575?–1626, English writer and editor of travel books.

pur·chas·a·ble (pûr′chə sə bəl), *adj.* **1.** capable of being bought. **2.** that may be influenced by bribery; venal. [1605–15; PURCHASE + -ABLE] **—pur′chas·a·bil′·i·ty,** *n.*

pur·chase (pûr′chəs), *v.,* **-chased, -chas·ing,** *n.* **—***v.t.* **1.** to acquire by the payment of money or its equivalent; buy. **2.** to acquire by effort, sacrifice, flattery, etc. **3.** to influence by a bribe. **4.** to be sufficient to buy: *Twenty dollars purchases a subscription.* **5.** *Law.* to acquire

CONCISE ETYMOLOGY KEY: <, descended or borrowed from; >, whence; b., blend of, blended; c., cognate with; cf., compare; deriv., derivative; equiv., equivalent; imit., imitative; obl., oblique; r., replacing; s., stem; sp., spelling, spelled; resp., respelling, respelled; trans., translation; ?, origin unknown; *, unattested; ‡, probably earlier than. See the full key inside the front cover.

(land or other property) by means other than inheritance. **6.** to move, haul, or raise, esp. by applying mechanical power. **7.** to get a leverage on; apply a lever, pulley, or other aid to. **8.** *Obs.* to procure, acquire, or obtain. —*v.i.* **9.** to buy something. —*n.* **10.** acquisition by the payment of money or its equivalent; buying, or a single act of buying. **11.** something that is purchased or bought. **12.** something purchased, with respect to value in relation to price; buy: *At three for a dollar they seemed like a good purchase.* **13.** *Law.* the acquisition of land or other property by means other than inheritance. **14.** acquisition by means of effort, labor, etc.: *the purchase of comfort at the price of freedom.* **15.** a lever, pulley, or other device that provides mechanical advantage or power for moving or raising a heavy object. **16.** an effective hold or position for applying power in moving or raising a heavy object; leverage. **17.** any means of applying or increasing power, influence, etc. **18.** the annual return or rent from land. **19.** a firm grip or grasp, footing, etc., on something. **20.** *Obs.* booty. [bef. 1150; (v.) ME *purchasen* < AF *purchacer* to seek to obtain, procure (OF *pourchacier*), equiv. to *pur-* (< L *prō* PRO[1]) + *chacer* to CHASE[1]; (n.) ME < AF *purchas* (OF *porchas*), deriv. of the v.] —**pur′chas•er,** *n.*
—**Syn. 1.** get, obtain, procure. See **buy. 15.** winch, capstan. —**Ant. 1.** sell.

pur′chase tax′, *Brit.* a sales tax on nonessential and luxury goods. [1935–40]

pur′chasing a′gent, 1. a person who buys materials, supplies, equipment, etc., for a company. **2.** an independent buyer acting as a hired agent. [1920–25]

pur′chasing pow′er, 1. Also called **buying power.** the ability to purchase goods and services. **2.** the value of money in terms of what it can buy at a specified time compared to what it could buy at some period established as a base: *the purchasing power of the dollar.* [1815–25]

pur•dah (pûr′də), *n.* (in India, Pakistan, etc.) **1.** the seclusion of women from the sight of men or strangers, practiced by some Muslims and Hindus. **2.** a screen, curtain, or veil used for this purpose. Also, **pur′da, pardah.** [1790–1800; < Hindi, Urdu *pardah* curtain < Pers]

pure (pyŏŏr), *adj.,* **pur•er, pur•est. 1.** free from anything of a different, inferior, or contaminating kind; free from extraneous matter: *pure gold; pure water.* **2.** unmodified by an admixture; simple or homogeneous. **3.** of unmixed descent or ancestry: *a pure breed of dog.* **4.** free from foreign or inappropriate elements: *pure Attic Greek.* **5.** clear; free from blemishes: *pure skin.* **6.** (of literary style) straightforward; unaffected. **7.** abstract or theoretical (opposed to *applied*): *pure science.* **8.** without any discordant quality; clear and true: *pure tones in music.* **9.** absolute; utter; sheer: *to sing for pure joy.* **10.** being that and nothing else; mere: *a pure accident.* **11.** clean, spotless, or unsullied: *pure hands.* **12.** untainted with evil; innocent: *pure in heart.* **13.** physically chaste; virgin. **14.** ceremonially or ritually clean. **15.** free of or without guilt; guiltless. **16.** independent of sense or experience: *pure knowledge.* **17.** *Biol., Genetics.* **a.** homozygous. **b.** containing only one characteristic for a trait. **18.** *Phonet.* monophthongal. [1250–1300; ME *pur* < OF < L *pūrus* clean, unmixed, plain, pure] —**pure′ness,** *n.*
—**Syn. 1.** unmixed, unadulterated, unalloyed, uncontaminated, untainted, unstained, undefiled, untarnished, immaculate, unpolluted, uncorrupted. See **clean. 12.** modest, virtuous, undefiled.

pure•blood (pyŏŏr′blud′), *n.* **1.** an individual, esp. an animal, whose ancestry consists of a single strain or type unmixed with any other. —*adj.* Also, **pure′blood′ed, pure′-blood′ed. 2.** of or pertaining to a pureblood. **3.** purebred (def. 1). [1770–80; PURE + BLOOD]

pure•bred (*adj.* pyŏŏr′bred′; *n.* pyŏŏr′bred′), *adj.* **1.** of or pertaining to an animal, all of whose ancestors derive over many generations from a recognized breed. —*n.* **2.** a purebred animal, esp. one of registered pedigree. [1865–70; PURE + BRED]

pure′ cul′ture, the growth of only one microorganism in a culture. [1890–95]

pure′ democ′racy, a form of democracy in which the laws and policies are made directly by the citizens rather than by representatives. [1905–10]

pu•rée (pyŏŏ rā′, -rē′, pyŏŏr′ā), *n., v.* **-réed, -rée•ing.** —*n.* **1.** a cooked food, esp. a vegetable or fruit, that has been put through a sieve, blender, or the like. **2.** a soup made with ingredients that have been puréed. —*v.t.* **3.** to make a purée of. Also, **pu•ree′.** [1700–10; < F, n. use of fem. ptp. of *purer* to strain, lit., make pure; see PURE]

Pure′ Food′ and Drug′ Act′, *U.S. Hist.* a law passed in 1906 to remove harmful and misrepresented foods and drugs from the market and regulate the manufacture and sale of drugs and food involved in interstate trade.

pure•heart•ed (pyŏŏr′här′tid), *adj.* (of a person) without malice, treachery, or evil intent; honest; sincere; guileless. [1825–35; PURE + HEARTED]

pure′ imag′inary num′ber, *Math.* a complex number of the form *iy* where *y* is a real number and $i = \sqrt{-1}$.

Pure′ Land′, *Buddhism.* a paradise believed by the followers of a Mahayana sect **(Pure′ Land′ sect′)** to be ruled over by a Buddha **(Amida),** whose hope it is to bring all beings into it. Chinese, **Ching-t'u.** Japanese, **Jodo.** [1930–35]

pure′ line′, *Genetics.* a uniform strain of organisms that is relatively pure genetically because of continued inbreeding and artificial selection. [1905–10]

pure•ly (pyŏŏr′lē), *adv.* **1.** in a pure manner; without admixture. **2.** merely; only; solely: *purely accidental.* **3.** entirely; completely. **4.** innocently, virtuously, or chastely. [1250–1300; ME *purliche.* See PURE, -LY]

pure′ rea′son, *Kantianism.* reason based on a priori principles and providing a unifying ground for the perception of the phenomenal world.

pur•fle (pûr′fəl), *v.,* **-fled, -fling,** *n.* —*v.t.* **1.** to finish with an ornamental border. **2.** to decorate (a shrine or tabernacle) with architectural forms in miniature. —*n.* **3.** Also called **pur′fling.** an ornamental border, as the inlaid border near the outer edge of the table and back of a stringed instrument. [1275–1325; ME *purfilen* < MF *porfiler* to make or adorn a border, equiv. to *por-* PRO[1] + *filer* to spin, deriv. of *fil* thread < L *fīlum.* See PROFILE] —**pur′fler,** *n.*

pur•ga•tion (pûr gā′shən), *n.* the act of purging. [1325–75; ME *purgacioun* (< AF) < L *pūrgātiōn-* (s. of *pūrgātiō*) a cleansing, purging, equiv. to *pūrgāt(us)* (ptp. of *pūrgāre* to make clean or pure, deriv. of *pūrus* PURE) + *-iōn-* -ION]

pur•ga•tive (pûr′gə tiv), *adj.* **1.** purging or cleansing, esp. by causing evacuation of the bowels. —*n.* **2.** a purgative medicine or agent; cathartic. [1350–1400; < LL *pūrgātīvus* (see PURGATION, -IVE); r. ME *purgatyf* < MF < LL, as above] —**pur′ga•tive•ly,** *adv.*

pur•ga•to•ri•al (pûr′gə tôr′ē əl, -tōr′-), *adj.* **1.** removing or purging sin; expiatory: *purgatorial rites.* **2.** of, pertaining to, or like purgatory. [1490–1500; PURGATORY + -AL[1]]

pur•ga•to•ry (pûr′gə tôr′ē, -tōr′ē), *n., pl.* **-ries,** *adj.* —*n.* **1.** (in the belief of Roman Catholics and others) a condition or place in which the souls of those dying penitent are purified from venial sins, or undergo the temporal punishment that, after the guilt of mortal sin has been remitted, still remains to be endured by the sinner. **2.** (*cap., italics*) Italian, ***Pur•ga•to•rio*** (pōōr′gä tô′ryô). the second part of Dante's *Divine Comedy,* in which the repentant sinners are depicted. Cf. **inferno** (def. 3), **paradise** (def. 7). **3.** any condition or place of temporary punishment, suffering, expiation, or the like. —*adj.* **4.** serving to cleanse, purify, or expiate. [1175–1225; (n.) ME *purgatorie* (< AF) < ML *pūrgātōrium,* n. use of neut. of LL *pūrgātōrius* purging, equiv. to *pūrgā(re)* to PURGE + *-tōrius* -TORY[1]; (adj.) ME *purgatorie* < LL *pūrgātōrius*]

purge (pûrj), *v.,* **purged, purg•ing,** *n.* —*v.t.* **1.** to rid of whatever is impure or undesirable; cleanse; purify. **2.** to rid, clear, or free (usually fol. by *of* or *from*): *to purge a political party of disloyal members.* **3.** to clear of imputed guilt or ritual uncleanliness. **4.** to clear away or wipe out legally (an offense, accusation, etc.) by atonement or other suitable action. **5.** to remove by cleansing or purifying (often fol. by *away, off,* or *out*). **6.** to clear or empty (the bowels) by causing evacuation. **7.** to cause evacuation of the bowels of (a person). **8.** to put to death or otherwise eliminate (undesirable or unwanted members) from a political organization, government, nation, etc. **9.** *Metall.* **a.** to drive off (undesirable gases) from a furnace or stove. **b.** to free (a furnace or stove) of undesirable gases. —*v.i.* **10.** to become cleansed or purified. **11.** to undergo or cause purging of the bowels. —*n.* **12.** the act or process of purging. **13.** the removal or elimination of members of a political organization, government, nation, etc., who are considered disloyal or otherwise undesirable. **14.** something that purges, as a purgative medicine or dose. [1250–1300; (v.) ME *purgen* < OF *purg(i)er* < L *pūrgāre* to cleanse; (n.) ME < OF, deriv. of the v.] —**purge′a•ble,** *adj.* —**purg′er,** *n.*
—**Syn. 8.** oust, liquidate, extirpate.

purg′ing nut′. See **physic nut.** [1750–60]

Pu•ri (pŏŏr′ē, pŏŏ rē′), *n.* a seaport in E Orissa, in E India, on the Bay of Bengal: temple of Krishna; Hindu pilgrimage center. 72,712. Cf. **Juggernaut** (def. 2).

pu•ri•fi•ca•tor (pyŏŏr′ə fi kā′tər), *n. Eccles.* **1.** the linen cloth used by the celebrant for wiping the chalice after each communicant has drunk from it. **2.** a sponge wrapped in cloth used by the celebrant for wiping the hands. [1850–55; < L *pūrificā(re)* to PURIFY + *-tor* -TOR]

pu•ri•form (pyŏŏr′ə fôrm′), *adj. Pathol.* resembling pus; purulent. [1790–1800; < L *pūr-* (s. of *pūs*) PUS + -I- + -FORM]

pu•ri•fy (pyŏŏr′ə fī′), *v.,* **-fied, -fy•ing.** —*v.t.* **1.** to make pure; free from anything that debases, pollutes, adulterates, or contaminates: *to purify metals.* **2.** to free from foreign, extraneous, or objectionable elements: *to purify a language.* **3.** to free from guilt or evil. **4.** to clear or purge (usually fol. by *of* or *from*). **5.** to make clean for ceremonial or ritual use. —*v.i.* **6.** to become pure. [1250–1300; ME *purifien* < MF *purifier* < L *pūrificāre.* See PURE, -IFY] —**pu′ri•fi•ca′tion,** *n.* —**pu•rif•i•ca•to•ry** (pyŏŏ rif′i kə tôr′ē, -tōr′ē), *adj.* —**pu′ri•fi′er,** *n.*

Pu•rim (pŏŏr′im; *Seph. Heb.* pōō rēm′; *Ashk. Heb.* pŏŏr′im), *n.* a Jewish festival celebrated on the 14th day of the month of Adar in commemoration of the deliverance of the Jews in Persia from destruction by Haman. [< Heb *pūrīm,* pl. of *pūr* lot]

pu•rine (pyŏŏr′ēn, -in), *n. Chem., Biochem.* **1.** a white, crystalline compound, $C_5H_4N_4$, from which is derived a group of compounds including uric acid, xanthine, and caffeine. **2.** one of several purine derivatives, esp. the bases adenine and guanine, which are fundamental constituents of nucleic acids. [1895–1900; < G *Purin.* See PURE, URIC, -INE[2]]

pur•ism (pyŏŏr′iz əm), *n.* **1.** strict observance of or insistence on purity in language, style, etc. **2.** an instance of this. **3.** (*often cap.*) *Fine Arts.* a style of art developed in France in the early 20th century, characterized by the use of simple geometric forms and images evocative of objects produced by machine. [1795–1805; PURE + -ISM] —**pur′ist,** *n.* —**pu•ris′tic, pu•ris′ti•cal,** *adj.* —**pu•ris′ti•cal•ly,** *adv.*

Pu•ri•tan (pyŏŏr′i tn), *n.* **1.** a member of a group of Protestants that arose in the 16th century within the Church of England, demanding the simplification of doctrine and worship, and greater strictness in religious discipline: during part of the 17th century the Puritans became a powerful political party. **2.** (*l.c.*) a person who is strict in moral or religious matters, often excessively so. —*adj.* **3.** of or pertaining to the Puritans. **4.** (*l.c.*) of, pertaining to, or characteristic of a moral puritan; puritanical. [1540–50; < LL *pūrit(ās)* PURITY + -AN] —**pu′ri•tan•like′,** *adj.* —**pu′ri•tan•ly,** *adv.*

Pu′ritan eth′ic. See **work ethic.** Also called **Pu′ritan work′ eth′ic.** [1970–75]

pu•ri•tan•i•cal (pyŏŏr′i tan′i kəl), *adj.* **1.** very strict in moral or religious matters, often excessively so; rigidly austere. **2.** (*sometimes cap.*) of, pertaining to, or characteristic of Puritans or Puritanism. Also, **pu′ri•tan′ic.** [1600–10; PURITAN + -ICAL] —**pu′ri•tan′i•cal•ly,** *adv.* —**pu′ri•tan′i•cal•ness,** *n.*

Pu•ri•tan•ism (pyŏŏr′i tn iz′əm), *n.* **1.** the principles and practices of the Puritans. **2.** (*sometimes l.c.*) extreme strictness in moral or religious matters, often to excess; rigid austerity. [1565–75; PURITAN + -ISM]

Pu′ritan spoon′, a silver spoon having an ovoid bowl and a straight, flat, completely plain stem. [1955–60]

pu•ri•ty (pyŏŏr′i tē), *n.* **1.** the condition or quality of being pure; freedom from anything that debases, contaminates, pollutes, etc.: *the purity of drinking water.* **2.** freedom from any admixture or modifying addition. **3.** ceremonial or ritual cleanness. **4.** freedom from guilt or evil; innocence. **5.** physical chastity; virginity. **6.** freedom from foreign or inappropriate elements; careful correctness: *purity of expression.* **7.** *Optics.* the chroma, saturation, or degree of freedom from white of a given color. **8.** cleanness or spotlessness, as of garments. [1175–1225; < LL *pūritās* (see PURE, -ITY); r. ME *pur(e)te* < AF < LL, as above]

Pur•kin′je cell′ (pər kin′jē), *Biol.* a large, densely branching neuron in the cerebellar cortex of the brain. [1885–90; see PURKINJE FIBER]

Purkin′je fi′ber, any of the specialized cardiac muscle fibers forming a network in the ventricular walls that conduct electric impulses responsible for the contractions of the ventricles. [named after Jan Evangelista *Purkinje* (Czech *Purkyně*) (1787–1869), Czech physiologist, who discovered the fibers in 1839]

Purkin′je shift′, *Psychol.* the changes in perception of the relative lightness and darkness of different colors as illumination changes from daylight to twilight. [1970–75; see PURKINJE FIBER]

purl[1] (pûrl), *v.t., v.i.* **1.** to knit with a reverse stitch. **2.** to finish with loops or a looped edging. —*n.* **3.** a basic stitch in knitting, the reverse of the knit, formed by pulling a loop of the working yarn back through an existing stitch and then slipping that stitch off the needle. Cf. **knit** (def. 11). **4.** one of a series of small loops along the edge of lace braid. **5.** thread made of twisted gold or silver wire. Also, **pearl.** [1520–30; var. of obs. or dial. *pirl* to twist (threads, etc.) into a cord]

purl[2] (pûrl), *v.i.* **1.** to flow with curling or rippling motion, as a shallow stream does over stones. **2.** to flow with a murmuring sound. **3.** to pass in a manner or with a sound likened to this. —*n.* **4.** the action or sound of purling. **5.** a circle or curl made by the motion of water; ripple; eddy. [1545–55; orig. uncert.; akin to Norw *purla* to bubble up, gush]

pur•lieu (pûr′lōō, pûrl′yōō), *n.* **1. purlieus,** environs or neighborhood. **2.** a place where one may range at large; confines or bounds. **3.** a person's haunt or resort. **4.** an outlying district or region, as of a town or city. **5.** a piece of land on the edge of a forest, originally land that, after having been included in a royal forest, was restored to private ownership, though still subject, in some respects, to the operation of the forest laws. [1475–85; alter. (simulating F *lieu* place) of earlier *parlewe, parley, paraley* purlieu of a forest < AF *purale(e)* a going through, equiv. to *pur* (< L *prō* for, PRO[1], confused with *per* through) + *alee* (see ALLEY)]

pur•lin (pûr′lin), *n.* a longitudinal member in a roof frame, usually for supporting common rafters or the like between the plate and the ridge. Also, **pur′line.** See diags. under **king post, queen post.** [1400–50; late ME *purlyn, purloyne,* akin to AL *perliō;* of uncert. orig.]

pur′lin plate′, *Carpentry.* (in a curb roof) a purlin at the top of a lower slope supporting the ends of the upper rafters at the curb. Also called **curb.**

pur•loin (pər loin′, pûr′loin), *v.t.* **1.** to take dishonestly; steal; filch; pilfer. —*v.i.* **2.** to commit theft; steal. [1400–50; late ME *purloynen* < AF *purloigner* to put off, remove, equiv. to *pur-* (< L *prō-* PRO-[1]) + *-loigner,* deriv. of *loin* at a distance, far off < L *longē*] —**pur•loin′er,** *n.*

pur•part (pûr′pärt), *n. Law.* a purparty. [< ML *purpart-* (s. of *purpars*) < OF *pur* for + L *part-* PART]

pur•par•ty (pûr′pär′tē), *n. Law.* a share of an estate held by coparceners that is apportioned to one upon the division of the estate among them. Also, **pourparty.** [1275–1325; ME *purpartie* < AF, OF, equiv. to *pur, pour* for (see PRO[1]) + *partie* partition, share; see PARTY]

pur•ple (pûr′pəl), *n.,* **-pler, -plest,** *adj., v.,* **-pled, -pling.** —*n.* **1.** any color having components of both red and blue, such as lavender, esp. one deep in tone. **2.** cloth or clothing of this hue, esp. as formerly worn distinctively by persons of imperial, royal, or other high rank. **3.** the rank or office of a cardinal. **4.** the office of a bishop. **5.** imperial, regal, or princely rank or position. **6.** deep red; crimson. **7.** any of several nymphalid butterflies, as *Basilarchia astyanax* **(red-spotted purple),** having blackish wings spotted with red, or *Basilarchia arthemis* **(banded purple** or **white admiral),** having brown wings banded with white. **8. born in** or **to the purple,** of royal or exalted birth: *Those born to the purple are destined to live in the public eye.* —*adj.* **9.** of the color purple. **10.** imperial, regal, or princely. **11.** brilliant or showy. **12.** full of exaggerated literary devices and effects; marked by excessively ornate rhetoric: *a purple passage in a novel.* **13.** profane or shocking, as language. —*v.t., v.i.* **14.** to make or become purple. [bef. 1000; ME *purpel* (n. and adj.), OE *purple* (adj.), var. of *purpure* < L *purpura* kind of shellfish yielding purple dye, the dye, cloth so dyed < Gk *porphýra;* cf. PURPURE, PORPHYRY] —**pur′ple·ness,** *n.*

pur′ple bacte′ria, a group of Gram-negative pink to purplish-brown bacteria, comprising the purple sulfur bacteria and purple nonsulfur bacteria, that occur in anaerobic aquatic environments and carry out a unique form of photosynthesis without oxygen, using the pigment bacteriochlorophyll. [1895–1900]

pur′ple beech′. See **copper beech.** [1865–70]

pur′ple bone′set. See **joe-pye weed** (def. 1).

pur′ple choke′berry. See under **chokeberry** (def. 1).

pur′ple finch′, a North American finch, *Carpodacus purpureus,* having a raspberry-red head, breast, and rump. See illus. under **finch.** [1720–30, *Amer.*]

pur′ple fox′glove, a medicinal plant, *Digitalis purpurea,* of western Europe, having finger-shaped, spotted, purple flowers and leaves from which digitalis is obtained. Also called **fairy glove, fingerflower.**

pur′ple-fringed or′chid (pûr′pəl frinjd′), either of two orchids, *Habenaria fimbriata* or *H. psycodes,* of eastern North America, having a cluster of fragrant purple flowers with a fringed lip. Also called **pur′ple-fringed or′chis.**

pur′ple gal′linule, **1.** a purple, blue, green, and white gallinule, *Porphyrula martinica,* inhabiting warmer areas of the New World, having a bright red, yellow, and blue bill, and lemon-yellow legs and feet. **2.** any of several large, Old World gallinules of the genus *Porphyrio.* [1805–15, *Amer.*]

pur′ple grack′le, the eastern subspecies of the common grackle, *Quiscalus quiscula,* of North America, having an iridescent purple back. [1775–85, *Amer.*]

pur′ple granadil′la. See under **granadilla** (def. 1).

Pur′ple Heart′, *U.S. Armed Forces.* a medal awarded for wounds received in action against an enemy or as a direct result of an act of the enemy. [1930–35, *Amer.*]

pur·ple·heart (pûr′pəl härt′), *n.* the hard, purplish wood of any of several South American trees belonging to the genus *Peltogyne,* of the legume family, used for making furniture. [1790–1800; PURPLE + HEART]

pur′ple her′on, an Old World heron, *Ardea purpurea,* having maroon, buff, and black plumage. [1830–40]

pur′ple loose′strife, an Old World plant, *Lythrum salicaria,* of the loosestrife family, widely naturalized in North America, growing in wet places and having spikes of reddish-purple flowers. [1540–50]

pur′ple mar′tin, a large American swallow, *Progne subis,* the male of which is blue-black. [1735–45, *Amer.*]

pur′ple mite′. See **citrus red mite.**

pur′ple mom·bin′ (mōm bēn′), a tree, *Spondias purpurea,* of tropical America, having clusters of purple or greenish flowers and yellow or dark red fruit that is edible either raw or cooked. Also called **red mombin, Spanish plum.** [see YELLOW MOMBIN]

pur′ple of Cas′sius (kash′əs, kash′ē əs, kä′sē əs), a purple pigment precipitated as a sol by the interaction of gold chloride and a solution of stannic acid and stannous chloride: used chiefly in the manufacture of ruby glass, ceramic glazes, and enamels. [1830–40; named after A. *Cassius,* 17th-century German physician]

pur′ple pas′sion, a variety of the velvet plant, *Gynura aurantiaca,* having trailing stems and leaves densely covered with purple hairs, grown as a houseplant.

pur′ple prose′, writing that calls attention to itself because of its obvious use of certain effects, as exaggerated sentiment or pathos, esp. in an attempt to enlist or manipulate the reader's sympathies.

pur′ple sage′, a plant, *Salvia leucophylla,* of the mint family, native to California, having silvery leaves and purple spikes of flowers.

pur′ple sand′piper, a sandpiper, *Calidris maritima,* of arctic regions of the New and Old World, having in winter a slate-gray back with purplish reflections. [1815–25]

pur′ple shore′ crab′. See under **shore crab.** [1880–85, *Amer.*]

pur′ple tril′lium, birthroot (def. 1). [1930–35]

pur·plish (pûr′plish), *adj.* of or having a somewhat purple hue. Also, **pur′ply.** [1555–65; PURPLE + -ISH[1]] —**pur′plish·ness,** *n.*

pur·port (*v.* pər pôrt′, -pōrt′, pûr′pôrt, -pōrt; *n.* pûr′pôrt, -pōrt), *v.t.* **1.** to present, esp. deliberately, the appearance of being; profess or claim, often falsely: *a document purporting to be official.* **2.** to convey to the mind as the meaning or thing intended; express or imply. —*n.* **3.** the meaning, import, or sense: *the main purport of your letter.* **4.** purpose; intention; object: *the main purport of their visit to France.* [1375–1425; (v.) late ME *purporten* < AF *purporter* to convey, equiv. to *pur-* PRO-[1] + *porter* to carry (< L *portāre*); (n.) late ME < AF, deriv. of the v.] —**pur′port·less,** *adj.*
—**Syn. 2.** mean, intend, signify. **3.** implication, drift, trend, gist. See **meaning.**

pur·port·ed (pər pôr′tid, -pōr′-), *adj.* reputed or claimed; alleged: *We saw no evidence of his purported wealth.* [1890–95; PURPORT + -ED[2]] —**pur·port′ed·ly,** *adv.*

CONCISE ETYMOLOGY KEY: <, descended or borrowed from; >, whence; b., blend of, blended; c., cognate with; cf., compare; deriv., derivative; equiv., equivalent; imit., imitative; obl., oblique; r., replacing; s., stem; sp., spelling, spelled; resp., respelling, respelled; trans., translation; ?, origin unknown; *, unattested; ‡, probably earlier than. See the full key inside the front cover.

pur·pose (pûr′pəs), *n., v.,* **-posed, -pos·ing.** —*n.* **1.** the reason for which something exists or is done, made, used, etc. **2.** an intended or desired result; end; aim; goal. **3.** determination; resoluteness. **4.** the subject in hand; the point at issue. **5.** practical result, effect, or advantage: *to act to good purpose.* **6. on purpose,** by design; intentionally: *How could you do such a thing on purpose?* **7. to the purpose,** relevant; to the point: *Her objections were not to the purpose.* —*v.t.* **8.** to set as an aim, intention, or goal for oneself. **9.** to intend; design. **10.** to resolve (to do something): *He purposed to change his way of life radically.* —*v.i.* **11.** to have a purpose. [1250–1300; (n.) ME *purpos* < OF, deriv. of *purposer,* var. of *proposer* to PROPOSE; (v.) ME *purposen* < AF, OF *purposer*]
—**Syn. 1.** object, point, rationale. See **intention. 9.** mean, contemplate, plan.

pur·pose·ful (pûr′pəs fəl), *adj.* **1.** having a purpose. **2.** determined; resolute. **3.** full of meaning; significant. [1850–55; PURPOSE + -FUL] —**pur′pose·ful·ly,** *adv.* —**pur′pose·ful·ness,** *n.*

pur·pose·less (pûr′pəs lis), *adj.* **1.** having no purpose or apparent meaning. **2.** having no aim or goal; aimless: *to lead a purposeless existence.* [1545–55; PURPOSE + -LESS] —**pur′pose·less·ly,** *adv.* —**pur′pose·less·ness,** *n.*

pur·pose·ly (pûr′pəs lē), *adv.* **1.** intentionally; deliberately: *He tripped me purposely.* **2.** with the particular purpose specified; expressly: *I wore that suit purposely to make a good impression.* [1485–95; PURPOSE + -LY]

pur·pos·ive (pûr′pə siv), *adj.* **1.** having, showing, or acting with a purpose, intention, or design. **2.** adapted to a purpose or end. **3.** serving some purpose. **4.** determined; resolute. **5.** of or characteristic of purpose. [1850–55; PURPOSE + -IVE] —**pur′pos·ive·ly,** *adv.* —**pur′pos·ive·ness,** *n.*

pur·pres·ture (pər pres′chər), *n. Law.* the wrongful enclosure of or intrusion upon lands, waters, or other property rightfully belonging to the public at large. [1150–1200; ME < OF *pourpres(t)ure, porpresure* enclosure, occupied space, equiv. to *pourprise, porprise* (ptp. of *purprendre* to seize upon, encroach upon, enclose, equiv. to *pur- por-* PRO-[1] + *prendre* to take < L *prehendere;* see PREHENSION) + *-ure* -URE]

pur·pu·ra (pûr′pyŏŏr ə), *n. Pathol.* a disease characterized by purple or brownish-red spots on the skin or mucous membranes, caused by the extravasation of blood. [1680–90; < NL, special use of L *purpura.* See PURPLE] —**pur·pu·ric** (pûr pyŏŏr′ik), *adj.*

pur·pure (pûr′pyŏŏr), *Heraldry.* —*n.* **1.** the tincture or color purple. —*adj.* **2.** of the tincture or color purple. [bef. 900; ME, OE < L *purpura* PURPLE]

pur·pu·rin (pûr′pyə rin), *n. Chem.* a reddish, crystalline, anthraquinone dye, $C_{14}H_5O_2(OH)_3$, isomeric with flavopurpurin. [1830–40; < L *purpur(a)* PURPLE + -IN[2]]

purr (pûr), *v.i.* **1.** to utter a low, continuous, murmuring sound expressive of contentment or pleasure, as a cat does. **2.** (of things) to make a sound suggestive of the purring of a cat: *The new motor of the car purred.* —*v.t.* **3.** to express by or as if by purring. —*n.* **4.** the low, vibrating sound made by a cat by the contracting of the laryngeal muscles and the diaphragm as it breathes. **5.** a sound resembling this. **6.** the act of purring. Also, **pur.** [1595–1605; imit.] —**purr′ing·ly,** *adv.*

pur·ree (pŏŏr′ē, pûr′ē), *n.* **1.** See **Indian yellow** (defs. 1, 2a). —*adj.* **2.** having the color Indian yellow. [1850–55; < Hindi *piyūṛī*]

purse (pûrs), *n., v.,* **pursed, purs·ing.** —*n.* **1.** a woman's handbag or pocketbook. **2.** a small bag, pouch, or case for carrying money. **3.** anything resembling a purse in appearance, use, etc. **4.** a sum of money offered as a prize or reward. **5.** a sum of money collected as a present or the like. **6.** money, resources, or wealth. —*v.t.* **7.** to contract into folds or wrinkles; pucker: *to purse one's lips.* **8.** to put into a purse. [bef. 1100; (n.) ME, OE *purs,* b. *pusa* bag (c. ON *posi*) and ML *bursa* bag (<< Gk *býrsa* hide, leather); (v.) ME *pursen* to put in a purse, deriv. of the n.] —**purse′less,** *adj.* —**purse′like′,** *adj.*

purse′ crab′. See **coconut crab.** [1705–15]

purse-proud (pûrs′proud′), *adj.* proud of one's wealth, esp. in an arrogant or showy manner. [1675–85]

purs·er (pûr′sər), *n.* an officer on a ship who handles financial accounts and various documents relating to the ship and who keeps money and valuables for passengers. [1400–50; late ME; see PURSE, -ER[1]]

purse′ seine′, **1.** a large seine, for use generally by two boats, that is drawn around a school of fish and then closed at the bottom by means of a line passing through rings attached along the lower edge of the net. **2.** a technique of fishing that utilizes a purse seine to capture large schools of fish, esp. tuna. [1865–70, *Amer.*]

purse-seine (pûrs′sān′), *v.i.,* **-seined, -sein·ing.** to fish using a purse seine. —**purse′ sein′er.**

purse′ strings′, **1.** the right or power to manage the disposition of money: *in control of the family purse strings.* **2. hold the purse strings,** to have the power to determine how money shall be spent. **3. loosen** or **tighten the purse strings,** to increase or decrease expenditures or the availability of money: *The budget committee is in the process of tightening the purse strings.* [1375–1425; late ME]

purse′-string su′ture (pûrs′string′), *Surg.* a suture for a circular opening, stitched around the edge, that closes it when pulled. [1900–05]

purs·lane (pûrs′lān, -lin), *n.* **1.** a low, trailing plant, *Portulaca oleracea,* having yellow flowers, used as a salad plant and potherb. Cf. **purslane family. 2.** any other plant of the purslane family. [1350–1400; ME *purcelan(e)* < MF *porcelaine* < LL *porcillāgin-* (s. of *porcillāgō*), for L *porcilāca,* var. of *portulāca* PORTULACA]

purs′lane fam′ily, the plant family Portulacaceae, characterized by chiefly herbaceous plants having simple, often fleshy leaves, sometimes showy flowers, and capsular fruit, and including bitterroot, purslane, red maids, rose moss, and spring beauty.

pur·su·ance (pər sōō′əns), *n.* the following or carrying out of some plan, course, injunction, or the like. [1590–1600; PURSUE + -ANCE]

pur·su·ant (pər sōō′ənt), *adj.* **1.** proceeding after; following (usually fol. by *to*): *Pursuant to his studies he took a job in an office.* **2.** pursuing. —*adv.* Also, **pur·su′ant·ly. 3.** according (usually fol. by *to*): *to do something pursuant to an agreement.* **4.** in a manner conformable (usually fol. by *to*): *to act pursuant to the dictates of one's conscience.* [1425–75; late ME, var. of *pursevant* PURSUIVANT]

pur·sue (pər sōō′), *v.,* **-sued, -su·ing.** —*v.t.* **1.** to follow in order to overtake, capture, kill, etc.; chase. **2.** to follow close upon; go with; attend: *Bad luck pursued him.* **3.** to strive to gain; seek to attain or accomplish (an end, object, purpose, etc.). **4.** to proceed in accordance with (a method, plan, etc.). **5.** to carry on or continue (a course of action, a train of thought, an inquiry, studies, etc.). **6.** to continue to annoy, afflict, or trouble. **7.** to practice (an occupation, pastime, etc.). **8.** to continue to discuss (a subject, topic, etc.). **9.** to follow: *They pursued the river to its source. I felt their eyes pursuing me.* **10.** to continue; go on with (one's course, a journey, etc.). —*v.i.* **11.** to follow in pursuit. **12.** to continue. [1250–1300; ME *pursuen* < AF *pursuer* << L *prōsequī* to pursue, follow, continue. See PRO-[1], SUE, PROSECUTE] —**pur·su′a·ble,** *adj.*
—**Syn. 1.** trail, hunt. **2.** dog.

pur·su·er (pər sōō′ər), *n.* **1.** a person or thing that pursues. **2.** *Scots Law, Eccles. Law.* a plaintiff or complainant. [1350–1400; ME; see PURSUE, -ER[1]]

pur·suit (pər sōōt′), *n.* **1.** the act of pursuing: *in pursuit of the fox.* **2.** an effort to secure or attain; quest: *the pursuit of happiness.* **3.** any occupation, pastime, or the like, in which a person is engaged regularly or customarily: *literary pursuits.* [1300–50; ME < AF *purseute* << VL **prōsequita* for L *prōsecūta,* fem. of *prōsecūtus,* ptp. of *prōsequī* to PURSUE; cf. SUIT]
—**Syn. 1.** chase, hunt. **2.** search. **3.** activity, preoccupation, inclination.

pursuit′ plane′, *Mil.* (formerly) an armed airplane designed for speed and maneuverability in fighting enemy aircraft. [1915–20]

pur·sui·vant (pûr′swi vənt), *n.* **1.** a heraldic officer of the lowest class, ranking below a herald. **2.** an official attendant on heralds. **3.** any attendant or follower. [1350–1400; < F *poursuivant* (prp. of *poursuivre* to PURSUE, follow << L *prōsequī*); r. ME *pursevant* < MF *pursivant* < L, as above]

pur·sy[1] (pûr′sē), *adj.,* **-si·er, -si·est. 1.** short-winded, esp. from corpulence or fatness. **2.** corpulent or fat. [1400–50; late ME *purcy,* var. of ME *pursif* < AF *porsif,* var. of OF *polsif,* deriv. (see -IVE) of *polser* to pant, heave. See PUSH] —**pur′si·ly,** *adv.* —**pur′si·ness,** *n.*

purs·y[2] (pûr′sē), *adj.,* **purs·i·er, purs·i·est.** vain about one's wealth; purse-proud. [1545–55; PURSE + -Y[1]]

pur·te·nance (pûr′tn əns), *n.* the liver, heart, and lungs of an animal. [1300–50; ME; aph. var. of APPURTENANCE]

pu·ru·lence (pyŏŏr′ə ləns, pyŏŏr′yə-), *n.* **1.** the condition of containing or forming pus. **2.** pus. Also, **pu′ru·len·cy.** [1590–1600; < LL *pūrulentia.* See PURULENT, -ENCE]

pu·ru·lent (pyŏŏr′ə lənt, pyŏŏr′yə-), *adj.* **1.** full of, containing, forming, or discharging pus; suppurating: *a purulent sore.* **2.** attended with suppuration: *purulent appendicitis.* **3.** of the nature of or like pus: *purulent matter.* [1590–1600; < L *pūrulentus,* equiv. to *pūr-,* s. of *pūs* PUS + *-ulentus* -ULENT] —**pu′ru·lent·ly,** *adv.*

pu·ru·loid (pyŏŏr′ə loid′, pyŏŏr′yə-), *adj. Med.* resembling pus. [1865–70; PURUL(ENT) + -OID]

Pu·rús (*Sp.* pōō rōōs′; *Port.* pōō rōōs′), *n.* a river in NW central South America, flowing NE from E Peru through W Brazil to the Amazon. 2000 mi. (3200 km) long.

pu·ru·sha (pŏŏr′ə shə), *n. Hinduism.* (in Sankhya and Yoga) one's true self, regarded as eternal and unaffected by external happenings. Cf. **prakriti.** [< Skt *puruṣa* lit., man]

pur·vey (pər vā′), *v.t.* to provide, furnish, or supply (esp. food or provisions) usually as a business or service. [1250–1300; ME *purveien* < AF *purveier* < L *prōvidēre* to foresee, provide for. See PROVIDE]

pur·vey·ance (pər vā′əns), *n.* **1.** the act of purveying. **2.** something that is purveyed, as provisions. **3.** *Eng. Law.* a prerogative of the crown, abolished in 1660, allowing provisions, supplies, or services for the sovereign or the royal household to be purchased or acquired at an appraised value. [1225–75; PURVEY + -ANCE; r. ME *purvea(u)nce, purvya(u)nce* < OF *purveance* < L *prōvidentia.* See PROVIDENCE]

pur·vey·or (pər vā′ər), *n.* **1.** a person who purveys, provides, or supplies: *a purveyor of foods; a purveyor of lies.* **2.** *Old Eng. Law.* an officer who provided or acquired provisions for the sovereign under the prerogative of purveyance. [1250–1300; ME *pourveour* < AF; see PURVEY, -OR[2]]

pur·view (pûr′vyōō), *n.* **1.** the range of operation, authority, control, concern, etc. **2.** the range of vision, insight, or understanding. **3.** *Law.* **a.** that which is provided or enacted in a statute, as distinguished from the preamble. **b.** the purpose or scope of a statute. **4.** the full scope or compass of any document, statement, subject, book, etc. [1225–75; ME *purveu* < AF: ptp. of *purveier* to PURVEY]
—**Syn. 1.** scope, responsibility, compass, extent.

pus (pus), *n.* a yellow-white, more or less viscid substance produced by suppuration and found in abscesses, sores, etc., consisting of a liquid plasma in which white blood cells are suspended. [1535–45; < L; akin to Gk *pýon* pus. See PYO-] —**pus′like′,** *adj.*

Pu•san (po͞o′sän′), *n.* a seaport in SE South Korea. 2,454,051.

Pu•sey (pyo͞o′zē), *n.* **1. Edward Bou•ve•rie** (bo͞o′və rē), 1800–82, English clergyman. **2. Nathan Marsh,** born 1907, U.S. educator: president of Harvard University 1953–71.

Pu•sey•ism (pyo͞o′zē iz′əm), *n.* Tractarianism. [1830–40; (E. B.) PUSEY + -ISM] **—Pu′sey•is′ti•cal, Pu′sey•is′tic,** *adj.* **—Pu•sey•ite** (pyo͞o′zē īt′), *n.*

push (po͝osh), *v.t.* **1.** to press upon or against (a thing) with force in order to move it away. **2.** to move (something) in a specified way by exerting force; shove; drive: *to push something aside; to push the door open.* **3.** to effect or accomplish by thrusting obstacles aside: *to push one's way through the crowd.* **4.** to cause to extend or project; thrust. **5.** to press or urge to some action or course: *His mother pushed him to get a job.* **6.** to press (an action, proposal, etc.) with energy and insistence: *to push a bill through Congress.* **7.** to carry (an action or thing) toward a conclusion or extreme: *She pushed the project to completion.* **8.** to press the adoption, use, sale, etc., of: *to push inferior merchandise on customers.* **9.** to press or bear hard upon, as in dealings with someone: *The prosecutor pushed him for an answer.* **10.** to put into difficulties because of the lack of something specified (usually fol. by *for*): *to be pushed for time.* **11.** *Slang.* to peddle (illicit drugs). **12.** *Informal.* to be approaching a specific age, speed, or the like: *The maestro is pushing ninety-two.* **13.** *Photog.* to modify (film processing) to compensate for underexposure.
—*v.i.* **14.** to exert a thrusting force upon something. **15.** to use steady force in moving a thing away; shove. **16.** to make one's way with effort or persistence, as against difficulty or opposition. **17.** to extend or project; thrust: *The point of land pushed far out into the sea.* **18.** to put forth vigorous or persistent efforts. **19.** *Slang.* to sell illicit drugs. **20.** to move on being pushed: *a swinging door that pushes easily.* **21. push around,** to treat contemptuously and unfairly; bully: *She's not the kind of person who can be pushed around.* **22. push off,** *Informal.* to go away; depart: *We stopped at Denver for the night and were ready to push off again the following morning.* **23. push on,** to press forward; continue; proceed: *The pioneers, despite overwhelming obstacles, pushed on across the plains.* **24. push one's luck.** See **luck** (def. 9).
—*n.* **25.** the act of pushing; a shove or thrust. **26.** a contrivance or part to be pushed in order to operate a mechanism. **27.** a vigorous onset or effort. **28.** a determined advance against opposition, obstacles, etc. **29.** a vigorous and determined military attack or campaign: *The big push began in April.* **30.** the pressure of circumstances, activities, etc. **31.** *Informal.* persevering energy; enterprise. **32.** *Informal.* a crowd or company of people. **33.** *Brit.* dismissal from a job; sack. **34.** *Australian Slang.* a gang of hoodlums. **35. when** or **if push comes to shove,** when or if matters are ultimately confronted or resolved; when or if a problem must be faced; in a crucial situation: *If push comes to shove, the government will impose quotas on imports.* [1250–1300; ME *pushen, poshen, posson* (v.) < MF *pousser,* OF *po(u)lser* < L *pulsāre.* See PULSATE]
—Syn. 3. shoulder. **5.** persuade, impel.

push•ball (po͝osh′bôl′), *n.* **1.** a game played with a large, heavy ball, usually about 6 ft. (1.8 m) in diameter, which two sides attempt to push to opposite goals. **2.** the ball used in this game. [1895–1900, *Amer.*; PUSH + BALL[1]]

push-bike (po͝osh′bīk′), *n. Brit.* a standard bicycle, operated by pedals rather than a motor. Also, **push′ bi′•cycle, push cycle.** [1905–10]

push′ broom′, a wide broom with a long handle, pushed by hand and used for sweeping large areas. [1925–30]

push′ but′ton, 1. a device designed to close or open an electric circuit when a button or knob is depressed, and to return to a normal position when it is released. **2.** the button or knob depressed. Also, **push′but′ton.** [1875–80, *Amer.*]

push-but•ton (po͝osh′but′n), *adj.* **1.** operated by or as if by push buttons: *push-button tuning.* **2.** using complex, automated weapons, as long-range missiles, that require only simple initial steps to put them into action: *push-button warfare.* [1875–80, *Amer.*]

push•card (po͝osh′kärd′), *n.* punchboard. [PUSH + CARD[1]]

push•cart (po͝osh′kärt′), *n.* any of various types of wheeled light cart to be pushed by hand, as one used by street vendors. [1890–95; PUSH + CART]

push′ cy′cle, *Brit.* push-bike. [1900–05]

push-down (po͝osh′doun′), *n. Aeron.* a sudden, downward shift by an aircraft in the direction of the flight path. Also called **pushover.** [1935–40; n. use of v. phrase *push down*]

push•er (po͝osh′ər), *n.* **1.** a person or thing that pushes. **2.** *Slang.* a peddler of illegal drugs. **3.** *Aeron.* an airplane that is driven by pusher propellers. **4.** *Naut.* one of the masts abaft the mizzen on a sailing vessel having more than three masts, either the sixth or seventh from forward. Cf. **driver** (def. 10b), **spanker** (def. 1b). **5.** *Railroads.* a helper attached to the rear of a train, usually to provide extra power for climbing a steep grade. [1585–95; PUSH + -ER[1]]

push′er propel′ler, a propeller located on the trailing edge of an aircraft wing. [1950–55]

push•ful (po͝osh′fəl), *adj.* self-assertive and aggressive; pushing. [1895–1900; PUSH + -FUL] **—push′ful•ly,** *adv.* **—push′ful•ness,** *n.*

push-in (po͝osh′in′), *adj.* (of a crime) accomplished by waiting until a victim has unlocked or opened the door before making a forced entry. [1975–80; adj. use of v. phrase *push in*]

push•ing (po͝osh′ing), *adj.* **1.** that pushes. **2.** enterprising; energetic. **3.** tactlessly or officiously aggressive; forward; intrusive. [1520–30; PUSH + -ING[2]] **—push′•ing•ly,** *adv.* **—push′ing•ness,** *n.*
—Syn. 2. ambitious. **3.** offensive.

Push•kin (po͝osh′kin; *Russ.* po͞o′shkyin), *n.* **A•le•xan•der Ser•ge•e•vich** (al′ig zan′dər sûr gā′ə vich, -zän′-; *Russ.* u lyi ksän′dʀ syiʀ gye′yi vyich), 1799–1837, Russian poet, short-story writer, and dramatist.

push•mi•na (push mē′nə), *n.* pashm.

push•out (po͝osh′out′), *n. Informal.* throwaway (def. 5). [n. use of v. phrase *push out*]

push•o•ver (po͝osh′ō′vər), *n.* **1.** *Informal.* anything done easily. **2.** *Informal.* an easily defeated person or team. **3.** *Informal.* a person who is easily persuaded, influenced, or seduced. **4.** *Rocketry.* a displacement in a horizontal direction of the trajectory of a missile or rocket. **5.** *Aeron.* push-down. [1905–10, *Amer.*; n. use of v. phrase *push over*]

push•pin (po͝osh′pin′), *n.* **1.** a short pin having a spool-shaped head of plastic, glass, or metal, used for affixing material to a bulletin board, wall, or the like. **2.** an early children's game. **3.** *Archaic.* child's play; triviality. [1580–90, for an earlier sense; PUSH + PIN]

push′ plate′, a rectangular protective plate of metal, plastic, ceramic, or other material applied vertically to the lock stile of a door. [1905–10]

push-pull (po͝osh′po͝ol′), *n.* **1.** *Radio.* a two-tube symmetrical arrangement in which the grid excitation voltages are opposite in phase. —*adj.* **2.** of or pertaining to electronic devices having components with balanced signals opposite in phase. [1925–30]

push•rod (po͝osh′rod′), *n. Auto.* a rod in an overhead-valve engine that is part of the linkage used to open and close the valves. Also, **push′ rod′.** [1905–10; PUSH + ROD]

push′ shot′, 1. *Basketball.* a shot with one hand from a point relatively distant from the basket, in which a player shoots the ball from shoulder level or above. **2.** *Golf.* a shot, played with an iron, in which a player with the weight forward on the front foot and with the wrists firm strikes the ball a sharp, descending blow in hitting a low ball with backspin. [1905–10]

Push•tu (push′to͞o), *n.* Pashto. Also, **Push•to** (push′tō).

push-up (po͝osh′up′), *n.* **1.** an exercise in which a person, keeping a prone position with the hands palms down under the shoulders, the balls of the feet on the ground, and the back straight, pushes the body up and lets it down by an alternate straightening and bending of the arms. —*adj.* **2.** (of a brassiere) having padding and usually underwires in the lower part of the cups so as to raise the breasts and make them seem fuller. **3.** (of a sleeve) made to be pushed up the arm, away from the wrist or elbow, so as to create a puffed or creased fullness. [1905–10; n. use of v. phrase *push up*]

push•y (po͝osh′ē), *adj.,* **push•i•er, push•i•est.** *Informal.* obnoxiously forward or self-assertive. [1935–40, *Amer.*; PUSH + -Y[1]] **—push′i•ly,** *adv.* **—push′i•ness,** *n.*
—Syn. brazen, brash, cheeky.

pu•sil•la•nim•i•ty (pyo͞o′sə lə nim′i tē), *n.* the state or condition of being pusillanimous; timidity; cowardliness. [1350–1400; ME < LL *pusillanimitās.* See PUSILLANIMOUS, -ITY]

pu•sil•lan•i•mous (pyo͞o′sə lan′ə məs), *adj.* **1.** lacking courage or resolution; cowardly; faint-hearted; timid. **2.** proceeding from or indicating a cowardly spirit. [1580–90; < LL *pusillanimis* petty-spirited, equiv. to L *pusill(us)* very small, petty + *-anim(is)* -spirited, -minded (*anim(us)* spirit + *-is* adj. suffix); see -OUS] **—pu′sil•lan′i•mous•ly,** *adv.*
—Syn. 1. timorous, fearful, frightened.

puss[1] (po͝os), *n.* **1.** a cat. **2.** *Informal.* a girl or woman: often used as a form of affectionate address. **3.** *Brit.* a hare. [1520–30; akin to D *poes,* LG *puus-katte,* dial. Sw *kattepus,* Norw *puse(kat)*] **—puss′like′,** *adj.*

puss[2] (po͝os), *n. Slang.* **1.** face: *She smacked him in the puss.* **2.** mouth: *Shut your puss before I shut it for you.* [1880–85; < Ir *pus* lip, mouth]

puss′ in the cor′ner, a parlor game for children in which one player in the middle of a room tries to occupy any of the positions along the walls that become vacant as other players dash across to exchange places at a signal. Also, **puss′y wants′ a cor′ner.** [1705–15]

puss•y[1] (po͝os′ē), *n., pl.* **puss•ies. 1.** a cat, esp. a kitten. **2.** the game of tipcat. **3.** the tapering piece of wood used in tipcat. [1575–85; PUSS[1] + -Y[2]]

pus•sy[2] (pus′ē), *adj.,* **-si•er, -si•est.** *Med.* puslike. [1840–50; PUS + -Y[1]]

pus•sy[3] (po͝os′ē), *n., pl.* **-sies.** *Slang* (*vulgar*). **1.** the vulva. **2.** sexual intercourse. [1875–80; perh. < D, a dim. of *poes* vulva, akin to LG *pūse* vulva, OE *pusa* bag; see PURSE]

puss•y•cat (po͝os′ē kat′), *n.* **1.** a cat; pussy. **2.** *Informal.* a person or thing not at all threatening: *a pussycat underneath all his gruffness.* [1795–1805; PUSSY[1] + CAT[1]]

puss•y•foot (po͝os′ē fo͝ot′), *v., n., pl.* **-foots.** —*v.i.* **1.** to go or move in a stealthy or cautious manner. **2.** to act cautiously or timidly, as if afraid to commit oneself on a point at issue. —*n.* **3.** a person with a catlike, or soft and stealthy, tread. **4.** *Chiefly Brit.* a teetotaler or prohibitionist. [1890–95, *Amer.*; PUSSY[1] + FOOT]
—Syn. 2. hedge, dodge, sidestep, straddle.

puss•y-toes (po͝os′ē tōz′), *n., pl.* **-toes.** (*used with a singular or plural v.*) any of various woolly composite plants of the genus *Antennaria,* having small white or grayish flower heads. Also called **ladies-tobacco.** [1890–95, *Amer.*]

puss′y wil′low (po͝os′ē), **1.** a small willow, *Salix discolor,* of eastern North America, having silky catkins. **2.** any of various similar willows. [1865–70, *Amer.*]

pussy willow,
Salix discolor

pus•tu•lant (pus′chə lənt), *adj.* **1.** causing the formation of pustules. —*n.* **2.** a medicine or agent causing pustulation. [1870–75; < LL *pūstulant-* (s. of *pūstulāns*), prp. of *pūstulāre* to blister. See PUSTULE, -ANT]

pus•tu•lar (pus′chə lər), *adj.* **1.** of, pertaining to, or of the nature of pustules. **2.** characterized by or covered with pustules. [1730–40; < NL *pūstulāris.* See PUSTULE, -AR[1]]

pus•tu•late (*v.* pus′chə lāt′; *adj.* pus′chə lit, -lāt′), *v.,* **-lat•ed, -lat•ing,** *adj. Pathol.* —*v.t.* **1.** to cause to form pustules. —*v.i.* **2.** to become pustular. —*adj.* **3.** covered with pustules. [1600–10; < LL *pūstulātus,* ptp. of *pūstulāre* to blister. See PUSTULE, -ATE[1]]

pus•tu•la•tion (pus′chə lā′shən), *n.* the formation or breaking out of pustules. [1870–75; < LL *pūstulātiōn-* (s. of *pūstulātiō*) a blistering. See PUSTULATE, -ION]

pus•tule (pus′cho͞ol), *n.* **1.** *Pathol.* a small elevation of the skin containing pus. **2.** any pimplelike or blisterlike swelling or elevation. [1350–1400; ME < L *pūstula, pusula* a pimple, blister; akin to Gk *physaléos* inflated] **—pus′tuled,** *adj.*

pus•tu•lous (pus′chə ləs), *adj.* pustular. [1535–45; PUSTULE + -OUS]

put (po͝ot), *v.,* **put, put•ting,** *adj., n.* —*v.t.* **1.** to move or place (anything) so as to get it into or out of a specific location or position: *to put a book on the shelf.* **2.** to bring into some relation, state, etc.: *to put everything in order.* **3.** to place in the charge or power of a person, institution, etc.: *to put a child in a special school.* **4.** to subject to the endurance or suffering of something: *to put convicted spies to death.* **5.** to set to a duty, task, action, etc.: *I put him to work setting the table.* **6.** to force or drive to some course or action: *to put an army to flight.* **7.** to render or translate, as into another language: *He put the novel into French.* **8.** to provide (words) with music as accompaniment; set: *to put a poem to music.* **9.** to assign or attribute: *You put a political interpretation on everything.* **10.** to set at a particular place, point, amount, etc., in a scale of estimation: *I'd put the distance at five miles.* **11.** to bet or wager: *to put two dollars on a horse.* **12.** to express or state: *To put it mildly, I don't understand.* **13.** to apply, as to a use or purpose: *to put one's knowledge to practical use.* **14.** to set, give, or make: *to put an end to an ancient custom.* **15.** to propose or submit for answer, consideration, deliberation, etc.: *to put a question before a committee.* **16.** to impose, as a burden, charge, or the like: *to put a tax on luxury articles.* **17.** to invest (often fol. by *in* or *into*): *to put one's money in real estate; to put one's savings into securities.* **18.** to lay the blame of (usually fol. by *on, to,* etc.): *He put my failure to lack of experience.* **19.** to throw or cast, esp. with a forward motion of the hand when raised close to the shoulder: *to put the shot.*
—*v.i.* **20.** to go, move, or proceed: *to put to sea.* **21.** *Informal.* to begin to travel: *to put for home.* **22.** to shoot out or grow, or send forth shoots or sprouts. **23. put about, a.** *Naut.* to change direction, as on a course. **b.** to start (a rumor); circulate. **c.** to inconvenience; trouble. **d.** to disturb; worry. **e.** to turn in a different direction. **24. put across, a.** to cause to be understood or received favorably: *She put across her new idea. He puts himself across well.* **b.** to do successfully; accomplish: *to put a project across.* **c.** to be successful in (a form of deception): *It was obviously a lie, but he put it across.* **25. put aside** or **by, a.** to store up; save. **b.** Also, **set aside.** to put out of the way; place to one side: *Put aside your books and come for a walk.* **26. put away, a.** to put in the designated place for storage: *Put away the groceries as soon as you get home.* **b.** to save, esp. for later use: *to put away a few dollars each week.* **c.** to discard: *Put away those childish notions.* **d.** to drink or eat, esp. in a large quantity; finish off: *to put away a hearty supper after jogging.* **e.** to confine in a jail or a mental institution: *He was put away for four years.* **f.** to put to death by humane means: *The dog was so badly injured that the veterinarian had to put it away.* **27. put down, a.** to write down; register; record. **b.** to enter in a list, as of subscribers or contributors: *Put me down for a $10 donation.* **c.** to suppress; check; squelch: *to put down a rebellion.* **d.** to attribute; ascribe: *We put your mistakes down to nervousness.* **e.** to regard or categorize: *He was put down as a chronic complainer.* **f.** *Informal.* to criticize, esp. in a contemptuous manner; disparage; belittle. **g.** *Informal.* to humble, humiliate, or embarrass. **h.** to pay as a deposit. **i.** to store for future use: *to put down a case of wine.* **j.** to dig or sink, as a well. **k.** *Brit.* to put (an animal) to death; put away. **l.** to land an aircraft or in an aircraft: *We put down at Orly after six hours.* **28. put forth, a.** to bring out; bear; grow: *The trees are putting forth new green shoots.* **b.** to propose; present: *No one has put forth a workable solution.* **c.** to bring to public notice; publish: *A new interpretation of the doctrine has been put forth.* **d.** to exert; exercise: *We will have to put forth our best efforts to win.* **e.** to set out; depart: *Dark clouds threatened as we put forth from the shore.* **29. put forward, a.** to propose; advance: *I hesitated to put*

forward my plan. **b.** to nominate, promote, or support, as for a position: *We put him forward for treasurer.* **30. put in, a.** Also, **put into.** *Naut.* to enter a port or harbor, esp. for shelter, repairs, or provisions. **b.** to interpose; intervene. **c.** to spend (time) as indicated. **31. put in for,** to apply for or request (something): *I put in for a transfer to another department.* **32. put it to,** *Slang.* **a.** to overburden with work, blame, etc.: *They really put it to him in officer-training school.* **b.** to take advantage of; cheat: *That used car dealer put it to me good.* **33. put off, a.** to postpone; defer. **b.** to confuse or perturb; disconcert; repel: *We were put off by the book's abusive tone.* **c.** to get rid of by delay or evasion. **d.** to lay aside; take off. **e.** to start out, as on a voyage. **f.** to launch (a boat) from shore or from another vessel: *They began to put off the lifeboats as the fire spread.* **34. put on, a.** to clothe oneself with (an article of clothing). **b.** to assume insincerely or falsely; pretend. **c.** to assume; adopt. **d.** to inflict; impose. **e.** to cause to be performed; produce; stage. **f.** *Informal.* to tease (a person), esp. by pretending the truth of something that is untrue: *You can't be serious—you're putting me on, aren't you?* **g.** to act in a pretentious or ostentatious manner; exaggerate: *All that putting on didn't impress anyone.* **35. put oneself out,** to take pains; go to trouble or expense: *She has certainly put herself out to see that everyone is comfortable.* **36. put out, a.** to extinguish, as a fire. **b.** to confuse; embarrass. **c.** to be vexed or annoyed: *He was put out when I missed our appointment.* **d.** to subject to inconvenience. **e.** *Baseball, Softball, Cricket.* to cause to be removed from an opportunity to reach base or score; retire. **f.** to publish. **g.** to go out to sea. **h.** to manufacture; prepare; produce. **i.** to exert; apply: *They were putting out their best efforts.* **j.** *Slang (vulgar).* (of a woman) to engage in coitus. **37. put over, a.** to succeed in; accomplish: *It will take an exceptional administrator to put over this reorganization.* **b.** to postpone; defer: *Discussion of this point will be put over until new evidence is introduced.* **38. put something over on,** to take advantage of; deceive: *He suspected that his friend had put something over on him, but he had no proof.* **39. put through, a.** to complete successfully; execute: *He was not able to put through his project.* **b.** to bring about; effect: *The proposed revisions have not as yet been put through.* **c.** to make a telephone connection for: *Put me through to Los Angeles.* **d.** to make (a telephone connection): *Put a call through to Hong Kong.* **e.** to cause to undergo or endure: *She's been put through a lot the past year.* **40. put to it,** to be confronted with a problem; have difficulty: *We were put to it to find the missing notebook.* **41. put up, a.** to construct; erect. **b.** to can (vegetables, fruits, etc.); preserve (jam, jelly, etc.). **c.** to set or arrange (the hair). **d.** to provide (money); contribute. **e.** to accommodate; lodge. **f.** to display; show. **g.** to stake (money) to support a wager. **h.** to propose as a candidate; nominate: *Someone is going to put him up for president.* **i.** to offer, esp. for public sale. **j.** *Archaic.* to sheathe one's sword; stop fighting. **42. put upon,** to take unfair advantage of; impose upon: *Some of the employees felt put upon when they were asked to work late.* **43. put up to,** to provoke; prompt; incite: *Someone put him up to calling us.* **44. put up with,** to endure; tolerate; bear: *I couldn't put up with the noise any longer.* —*adj.* **45. stay put,** *Informal.* to remain in the same position; refuse to move: *The baby wouldn't stay put, and kept trying to climb out of the playpen.* —*n.* **46.** a throw or cast, esp. one made with a forward motion of the hand when raised close to the shoulder. **47.** Also called **put option.** *Finance.* an option that gives the right to sell a fixed amount of a particular stock at a predetermined price within a given time, purchased by a person who expects the stock to decline. Cf. **call** (def. 65). [bef. 1000; ME *put(t)en* to push, thrust, put, OE **putian* (as v. noun *putung* an impelling, inciting); akin to *pytan, potian* to push, goad, c. ON *pota* to thrust, poke]
—**Syn. 1.** PUT, PLACE, LAY, SET mean to bring or take an object (or cause it to go) to a certain location or position, there to leave it. PUT is the general word: *to put the dishes on the table; to put one's hair up.* PLACE is a more formal word, suggesting precision of movement or definiteness of location: *He placed his hand on the Bible.* LAY, meaning originally to cause to lie, and SET, meaning originally to cause to sit, are used particularly to stress the position in which an object is put: LAY usually suggests putting an object rather carefully into a horizontal position: *to lay a pattern out on the floor.* SET usually means to place upright: *to set a child on a horse.* **16.** levy, inflict.

pu·ta·men (pyo͞o tā′min), *n., pl.* **-tam·i·na** (-tam′ə nə). **1.** *Bot.* a hard or stony endocarp, as a peach stone. **2.** a shell membrane. [1820–30; < L *putāmen,* equiv. to *putā(re)* to prune, clean + *-men* resultative suffix] —**pu·tam·i·nous** (pyo͞o tam′ə nəs), *adj.*

put-and-take (po͝ot′n tāk′), *n.* any of various games of chance played with a teetotum or other special type of top, in which each player puts in an equal stake before starting to spin the top. [1920–25]

pu·ta·tive (pyo͞o′tə tiv), *adj.* commonly regarded as such; reputed; supposed: *the putative boss of the mob.* [1400–50; late ME < LL *putātīvus* reputed, equiv. to *putāt(us)* (ptp. of *putāre* to think, consider, reckon, orig. to clean, prune) + *-īvus* -IVE] —**pu′ta·tive·ly,** *adv.*

pu′tative mar′riage, *Law.* a marriage contracted in violation of an impediment, but in good faith on the part of one or both of the contracting persons. [1805–15]

put-down (po͝ot′doun′), *n.* **1.** a landing of an aircraft. **2.** *Informal.* **a.** a disparaging, belittling, or snubbing remark. **b.** a remark or act intended to humiliate or embarrass someone. Also, **put′down′.** [1960–65; n. use of v. phrase *put down*]

Put·nam (put′nəm), *n.* **1. Herbert,** 1861–1955, U.S. librarian: headed Library of Congress 1899–1939. **2. Israel,** 1718–90, American Revolutionary general. **3. Rufus,** 1738–1824, American Revolutionary officer: engineer and colonizer in Ohio.

put·off (po͝ot′ôf′, -of′), *n.* **1.** an act or instance of putting off. **2.** a delaying, postponing, or avoiding of something. **3.** an expressed excuse or evasion; demur: *She responded with a polite but firm putoff.* [1540–50; n. use of v. phrase *put off*]

put-on (*n.* po͝ot′on′, -ôn′; *adj.* po͝ot′on′, -ôn′), *n. Informal.* **1.** an act or instance of putting someone on. **2.** a prank or pretense, esp. one perpetrated or assumed in mock seriousness; hoax; spoof. **3.** affected manner or behavior; pretentiousness. —*adj.* **4.** assumed, feigned, pretended, or disguised: *a put-on manner that didn't fool anyone.* [1855–60; adj., n. use of v. phrase *put (someone) on*]

Pu·tong·hua (po͞o′tung′hwä′), *n.* the form of Chinese, based on the Beijing dialect of Mandarin, adopted as the official national language of China. Also, **p'u-t'ung hua.** Also called **Kuo-yü.**

put′ op′tion, *Finance.* put (def. 47).

put-out (po͝ot′out′), *n. Baseball.* an instance of putting out a batter or base runner. [1880–85, *Amer.*; n. use of v. phrase *put out*]

put-put (put′put′, -put′), *n., v.,* **-put·ted, -put·ting.** —*n.* **1.** the sound made by a small internal-combustion engine or imitative of its operation. **2.** *Informal.* a small internal-combustion engine, or something, as a boat or model airplane, equipped with one: *the sound of distant put-puts on the lake.* —*v.i.* **3.** *Informal.* to operate with sounds suggesting a put-put, as a small motor or motor-driven device. Also, **putt-putt.** [1900–05; imit.]

pu·tre·fac·tion (pyo͞o′trə fak′shən), *n.* **1.** the act or process of putrefying; the anaerobic decomposition of organic matter by bacteria and fungi that results in obnoxiously odorous products; rotting. **2.** the state of being putrefied; decay. [1350–1400; ME < LL *putrefactiōn-* (s. of *putrefactiō*) a rotting, equiv. to L *putrefact(us)* (ptp. of *putrefacere* to PUTREFY) + *-iōn-* -ION] —**pu′tre·fac′·tive, pu·tre·fa·cient** (pyo͞o′trə fā′shənt), *adj.*

pu·tre·fy (pyo͞o′trə fī′), *v.,* **-fied, -fy·ing.** —*v.t.* **1.** to render putrid; cause to rot or decay with an offensive odor. —*v.i.* **2.** to become putrid; rot. **3.** to become gangrenous. [1350–1400; ME *putrefien* < MF *putrefier* < VL **putrefīcāre,* for L *putrefacere* to make rotten] —**pu′tre·fi′a·ble,** *adj.* —**pu′tre·fi′er,** *n.*
—**Syn. 2.** decompose, spoil.

pu·tres·cent (pyo͞o tres′ənt), *adj.* **1.** becoming putrid; undergoing putrefaction. **2.** of or pertaining to putrefaction. [1725–35; < L *putrēscent-* (s. of *putrēscēns*), prp. of *putrēscere* to grow rotten] —**pu·tres′cence, pu·tres′cen·cy,** *n.*

pu·tres·ci·ble (pyo͞o tres′ə bəl), *adj.* **1.** liable to become putrid. —*n.* **2.** a putrescible substance. [1790–1800; < L *putrēsc(ere)* to grow rotten + -IBLE] —**pu·tres′ci·bil′i·ty,** *n.*

pu·trid (pyo͞o′trid), *adj.* **1.** in a state of foul decay or decomposition, as animal or vegetable matter; rotten. **2.** of, pertaining to, or attended by putrefaction. **3.** having the odor of decaying flesh. **4.** thoroughly corrupt, depraved, or evil. **5.** of very low quality; rotten. [1375–1425; late ME < L *putridus* rotten, equiv. to *putr(ēre)* to rot + *-idus* -ID[4]] —**pu·trid′i·ty, pu′trid·ness,** *n.* —**pu′trid·ly,** *adv.*
—**Syn. 3.** fetid. **4.** immoral.

pu·tri·lage (pyo͞o′trə lij), *n.* putrid or putrescent matter. [1650–60; < L *putrilāgin-* (s. of *putrilāgō*) putrefaction] —**pu·tri·lag·i·nous** (pyo͞o′trə laj′ə nəs), *adj.* —**pu′tri·lag′i·nous·ly,** *adv.*

putsch (po͝och), *n.* a plotted revolt or attempt to overthrow a government, esp. one that depends upon suddenness and speed. [1915–20; < G *Putsch,* orig. Swiss G: lit., violent blow, clash, shock; introduced in sense "coup" in standard G through Swiss popular uprisings of the 1830's, esp. the Zurich revolt of Sept. 1839]

putsch·ist (po͝och′ist), *n.* **1.** a participant in a putsch. —*adj.* **2.** taking part in or concerned with a putsch. [1895–1900; < G *Putsch* PUTSCH + -IST]

putt (put), *Golf.* —*v.t., v.i.* **1.** to strike (the ball) gently so as to make it roll along the green into the hole. —*n.* **2.** an act of putting. **3.** a stroke made in putting. [1735–45; orig. Scots, var. of PUT]

put·tee (pu tē′, po͝o-, put′ē), *n.* **1.** a long strip of cloth wound spirally round the leg from ankle to knee, worn esp. formerly as part of a soldier's uniform. **2.** a gaiter or legging of leather or other material, as worn by soldiers, riders, etc. Also, **putty, puttie.** [1870–75; < Hindi *paṭṭī* bandage; akin to Skt *paṭṭa* strip of cloth, bandage]

put·ter[1] (put′ər), *v.i.* **1.** to busy or occupy oneself in a leisurely, casual, or ineffective manner: *to putter in the garden.* **2.** to move or go in a specified manner with ineffective action or little energy or purpose: *to putter about the house on a rainy day.* **3.** to move or go slowly or aimlessly; loiter. **4. putter away,** to spend or fill in a random, inconsequential, or unproductive way; fritter away; waste: *We puttered the morning away.* —*n.* **5.** puttering or ineffective action; dawdling. Also, *esp. Brit.,* **potter.** [1875–80; var. of POTTER[2]] —**put′ter·er,** *n.* —**put′ter·ing·ly,** *adv.*

putt·er[2] (put′ər), *n. Golf.* **1.** a person who putts. **2.** a club with a relatively short, stiff shaft and a wooden or iron head, used in putting. [1735–45; PUTT + -ER[1]]

put·ter[3] (po͝ot′ər), *n.* **1.** a person or thing that puts. **2.** *Track.* a shot-putter. [1810–20; PUT + -ER[1]]

put·tie (put′ē), *n.* puttee.

put·ti·er (put′ē ər), *n.* a person who putties, as a glazier. [PUTTY[1] (v.) + -ER[1]]

putt′ing green′, *Golf.* green (def. 24). [1840–50]

put·to (po͞o′tō; *It.* po͝ot′tô), *n., pl.* **-ti** (-tē). *Fine Arts.* a representation of a cherubic infant, often shown winged. [1635–45; < It: lit., boy < L *putus*]

putt-putt (put′put′, -put′), *n., v.i.* put-put.

put·ty[1] (put′ē), *n., pl.* **-ties,** *v.,* **-tied, -ty·ing.** —*n.* **1.** a compound of whiting and linseed oil, of a doughlike consistency when fresh, used to secure windowpanes, patch woodwork defects, etc. **2.** any of various other compounds used for similar purposes. **3.** any of various substances for sealing the joints of tubes or pipes, composed of linseed oil with red lead, white lead, iron oxide, etc. **4.** a creamy mixture of lime and water, partially dried and mixed with sand and plaster of Paris to make a finish plaster coat. **5.** See **putty powder. 6.** any person or thing easily molded, influenced, etc.: *We were putty in his hands.* **7.** light brownish- or yellowish-gray. **8. up to putty,** *Australian Slang.* worthless or useless. —*v.t.* **9.** to secure, cover, etc., with putty. [1625–35; < F *potée,* lit., (something) potted. See POT[1], -EE]

put·ty[2] (put′ē), *n., pl.* **-ties.** puttee.

put′ty knife′, a tool for puttying, having a broad flexible blade. [1855–60]

put′ty pow′der, an abrasive consisting chiefly of stannic oxide, used for polishing hard surfaces. Also called **putty, jeweler's putty.** [1825–35]

put·ty·root (put′ē ro͞ot′, -ro͝ot′), *n.* an American orchid, *Aplectrum hyemale,* having a slender naked rootstock that produces a leafless stalk with a loose cluster of yellowish-brown flowers. [1810–20, *Amer.*; PUTTY[1] + ROOT[1]]

Pu·tu·ma·yo (po͞o′to͞o mä′yô), *n.* a river in NW South America, flowing SE from S Colombia into the Amazon in NW Brazil. 900 mi. (1450 km) long. Portuguese, **Içá.**

p'u-t'ung hua (po͞o′tung′hwä′), *n.* Putonghua.

put-up (po͝ot′up′), *adj. Informal.* planned beforehand in a secret or crafty manner: *a put-up job.* [1800–10; adj. use of v. phrase *put up*]

put-up·on (po͝ot′ə pon′, -pôn′), *adj.* imposed upon; ill-used. [1915–20]

putz (puts), *n. Slang.* **1.** fool; jerk. **2.** *Vulgar.* penis. [1900–05; < Yiddish *puts* lit., ornament, finery, prob. n. deriv. of *putsn* to clean, shine; cf. early mod. G *butzen* to decorate (G *putzen* to clean, brighten)]

PUVA, a therapy for psoriasis combining the oral drug psoralen and high-intensity long-wave ultraviolet light. [P(SORALEN) + *UV-A* ultraviolet light of a wavelength between 320 and 400 nanometers]

Pu·vis de Cha·vannes (py vē də shA vAn′), **Pierre Cé·cile** (pyer sā sēl′), 1824–98, French painter.

Puy·al·lup (pyo͞o al′əp), *n.* a city in W Washington, SE of Tacoma. 18,251.

Puy·al·lup (pyo͞o al′əp), *n., pl.* **-lups,** *(esp. collectively)* **-lup.** a member of a Salishan-speaking North American Indian tribe living in the Puget Sound area of Washington.

Puy-de-Dôme (pwē də dōm′), *n.* **1.** a mountain in central France. 4805 ft. (1465 m). **2.** a department in central France. 580,033; 3095 sq. mi. (8015 sq. km). *Cap.:* Clermont-Ferrand.

Pu-yi (po͞o′yē′), *n.* **Henry,** 1906–67, as Hsüan T'ung, last emperor of China 1908–12; as K'ang Tê, puppet emperor of Manchukuo 1934–45. Also, **P'u-i.**

puz·zle (puz′əl), *n., v.,* **-zled, -zling.** —*n.* **1.** a toy, problem, or other contrivance designed to amuse by presenting difficulties to be solved by ingenuity or patient effort. **2.** something puzzling; a puzzling question, matter, or person. **3.** a puzzled or perplexed condition; bewilderment. **4.** a crossword puzzle: *Did you do the puzzle in the newspaper today?* **5.** a jigsaw puzzle. —*v.t.* **6.** to put (someone) at a loss; mystify; confuse; baffle: *Her attitude puzzles me.* **7.** to frustrate or confound, as the understanding; perplex: *The problem puzzled him for weeks.* **8.** to exercise (oneself, one's brain, etc.) over some problem or matter. **9.** *Archaic.* to make intricate or complicated. —*v.i.* **10.** to be perplexed or confused. **11.** to ponder or study over some perplexing problem or matter. **12. puzzle out,** to solve by careful study or effort: *I was unable to puzzle out the message.* [1585–95; orig. uncert.] —**puz′zled·ly,** *adv.* —**puz′zled·ness,** *n.*
—**Syn. 2.** PUZZLE, RIDDLE, ENIGMA refer to something baffling or confusing that is to be solved. A PUZZLE is a question or problem, intricate enough to be perplexing to the mind; it is sometimes a contrivance made purposely perplexing to test one's ingenuity: *a crossword puzzle; The reason for their behavior remains a puzzle.* A RIDDLE is an intentionally obscure statement or question, the meaning of or answer to which is to be arrived at only by guessing: *the famous riddle of the Sphinx.* ENIGMA, originally meaning riddle, now refers to some baffling problem with connotations of mysteriousness: *He will always be an enigma to me.* **6.** confound.

puz′zle box′, *Psychol.* an enclosure, used in experiments in animal learning, from which an animal must escape or in which it must manipulate various devices. [1865–70]

puz·zle·head·ed (puz′əl hed′id), *adj.* **1.** having, deriving from, or characterized by confused thoughts or ideas. **2.** given to or characterized by puzzling over common things. [1775–85; PUZZLE + HEADED] —**puz′·zle·head′ed·ness,** *n.*

puz′zle jug′, a drinking jug of the 17th and 18th centuries, so made as to challenge the drinker to drink without spilling or spraying the contents. [1875–80]

puz·zle·ment (puz′əl mənt), *n.* **1.** the state of being puzzled; perplexity. **2.** something puzzling. [1815–25; PUZZLE + -MENT]

puz·zler (puz′lər), *n.* **1.** a person who puzzles. **2.** a baffling thing or problem. **3.** a person who is occupied or amused by solving puzzles. [1645–55; PUZZLE + -ER[1]]

puz·zling (puz′ling), *adj.* **1.** confusing or baffling: *a puzzling answer.* —*n.* **2.** the skill or pastime of constructing or working crossword or other puzzles. [1590–1600; PUZZLE + -ING[2]] —**puz′zling·ly,** *adv.*

CONCISE ETYMOLOGY KEY: <, descended or borrowed from; >, whence; b., blend of, blended; c., cognate with; cf., compare; deriv., derivative; equiv., equivalent; imit., imitative; obl., oblique; r., replacing; s., stem; sp., spelling, spelled; resp., respelling, respelled; trans., translation; ?, origin unknown; *, unattested; ‡, probably earlier than. See the full key inside the front cover.

puz·zo·la·na (po͞ot′sə lä′nə; *It.* po͞ot′tsô lä′nä), *n.* pozzolana. Also, **puz·zo·lan** (po͞ot′sə lən).

PVA, See **polyvinyl acetate.**

PVC, See **polyvinyl chloride.**

PVP, polyvinylpyrrolidone.

Pvt., Private.

PW, 1. *Auto.* power windows. **2.** prisoner of war. **3.** public works.

PWA, 1. person with AIDS. **2.** Also, **P.W.A.** Public Works Administration.

P wave, a longitudinal earthquake wave that travels through the interior of the earth and is usually the first conspicuous wave to be recorded by a seismograph. Also called **primary wave.** Cf. **L wave, S wave.** [1935–40]

P.W.D., Public Works Department. Also, **PWD**

pwr, power.

pwt, pennyweight. Also, **pwt.**

Pwyll (po͞ol), *n. Welsh Legend.* a prince who stole his wife, Rhiannon, from her suitor, Gwawl, and was the father of Pryderi.

PX, *pl.* **PXs.** *U.S. Army.* See **post exchange.**

P.X., please exchange.

pxt., pinxit.

py-, var. of **pyo-** before a vowel: *pyemia.*

pya (pyä, pē ä′), *n.* an aluminum coin of Burma, the 100th part of a kyat. [1950–55; < Burmese (sp. *prāḥ*)]

py·ae·mi·a (pī ē′mē ə), *n. Pathol.* pyemia. —**py·ae′·mic,** *adj.*

Pya·ti·gorsk (pyä′ti gôrsk′; *Russ.* pyi tyi gôrsk′), *n.* a city in the SW Russian Federation in Europe, in Caucasia. 110,000. Also, **Piatigorsk.**

pycn-, var. of **pycno-** before a vowel: *pycnium.*

pyc·nid·i·um (pik nid′ē əm), *n., pl.* **-nid·i·a** (-nid′ē ə). *Mycol.* (in certain ascomycetes and fungi imperfecti) a globose or flask-shaped fruiting body bearing conidia on conidiophores. [1855–60; < NL < Gk *pykn(ós)* close, thick, dense + *-idion* dim. suffix] —**pyc·nid′i·al,** *adj.*

pyc·ni·o·spore (pik′nē ə spôr′, -spōr′), *n. Mycol.* the spore produced in a pycnium. [PYCNI(UM) + -O- + SPORE]

pyc·ni·um (pik′nē əm), *n., pl.* **-ni·a** (-nē ə). *Mycol.* a flask-shaped or conical sporangium of a rust fungus, which develops below the epidermis of the host and bears pycniospores. [1900–05; < NL; see PYCN-, -IUM] —**pyc′ni·al,** *adj.*

pycno-, a combining form meaning "dense," "close," "thick," used in the formation of compound words: *pycnometer.* Also, *esp. before a vowel,* **pycn-.** [< NL, comb. form repr. Gk *pyknós*]

pyc·nom·e·ter (pik nom′i tər), *n.* a container used for determining the density of a liquid or powder, having a specific volume and often provided with a thermometer to indicate the temperature of the contained substance. [1880–85; PYCNO- + -METER]

pyc·no·style (pik′nə stīl′), *adj. Archit.* having an intercolumniation of 1½ diameters. See illus. under **intercolumniation.** [1555–65; < L *pycnostȳlus* < Gk *pyknóstȳlos,* equiv. to *pyknós* PYCNO- + *-stylos* -STYLE[2]]

Pyd·na (pid′nə), *n.* a town in ancient Macedonia, W of the Gulf of Salonika: decisive Roman victory over the Macedonians 186 B.C.

pye (pī), *n. Eccles.* pie[4]. [1530–40]

pye-dog (pī′dôg′, -dog′), *n.* an ownerless half-wild dog of uncertain breeding, common in the villages and towns of India and other countries in east and south Asia. [1860–65; *pye* said to be < Hindi *pāhī* outsider]

py·e·li·tis (pī′ə lī′tis), *n. Pathol.* inflammation of the pelvis or outlet of the kidney. [1835–45; < NL; see PYELO-, -ITIS] —**py·e·lit·ic** (pī′ə lit′ik), *adj.*

pyelo-, a combining form meaning "pelvis," used in the formation of compound words: *pyelogram.* Also, *esp. before a vowel,* **pyel-.** [< NL, comb. form repr. Gk *pýelos* basin, on the model of the NL use of L *pelvis*]

py·e·lo·gram (pī′ə lə gram′, pī el′ə-), *n.* an x-ray produced by pyelography. Also, **py·e·lo·graph** (pī′ə lə-graf′, -gräf′, pī el′ə-). [1920–25; PYELO- + -GRAM[1]]

py·e·log·ra·phy (pī′ə log′rə fē), *n.* the science or technique of making photographs of the kidneys, renal pelves, and ureters by means of x-rays, after the injection of an opaque solution or of a radiopaque dye. [1905–10; PYELO- + -GRAPHY] —**py·e·lo·graph·ic** (pī′ə lə graf′ik, pī el′ə-), *adj.*

py·e·lo·ne·phri·tis (pī′ə lō nə frī′tis, pī el′ō-), *n. Pathol.* inflammation of the kidney and its pelvis, caused by a bacterial infection. [1865–70; PYELO- + NEPHRITIS] —**py·e·lo·ne·phrit·ic** (pī′ə lō nə frit′ik, pī el′ō-), *adj.*

py·e·lo·ne·phro·sis (pī′ə lō nə frō′sis, pī el′ō-), *n. Pathol.* any disease of the kidney and its pelvis. [PYELO- + NEPHROSIS]

py·e·mi·a (pī ē′mē ə), *n. Pathol.* a diseased state in which pyogenic bacteria are circulating in the blood, characterized by the development of abscesses in various organs. Also, **pyaemia.** [1855–60; < NL; see PY-, -EMIA] —**py·e′mic,** *adj.*

py·gid·i·um (pī jid′ē əm), *n., pl.* **-gid·i·a** (-jid′ē ə). *Zool.* any of various structures or regions at the caudal end of the body in certain invertebrates. [1840–50; < NL < Gk *pȳg(ḗ)* rump + *-idion* dim. suffix] —**py·gid′i·al,** *adj.*

pyg·mae·an (pig mē′ən, pig′mē-), *adj.* pygmy. Also, **pyg·me′an.** [1545–55; < L *pygmae(us)* dwarfish (see PYGMY) + -AN]

Pyg·ma·li·on (pig mā′lē ən, -māl′yən), *n.* **1.** *Class. Myth.* a sculptor and king of Cyprus who carved an ivory statue of a maiden and fell in love with it. It was brought to life, in response to his prayer, by Aphrodite. **2.** (*italics*) a comedy (1912) by George Bernard Shaw.

Pyg·my (pig′mē), *n., pl.* **-mies,** *adj.* —*n.* **1.** *Anthropol.* **a.** a member of a small-statured people native to equatorial Africa. **b.** a Negrito of southeastern Asia, or of the Andaman or Philippine islands. **2.** (*l.c.*) a small or dwarfish person. **3.** (*l.c.*) anything very small of its kind. **4.** (*l.c.*) a person who is of small importance, or who has some quality, attribute, etc., in very small measure. **5.** *Class. Myth.* (in the *Iliad*) one of a race of dwarfs who fought battles with cranes, who preyed on them and destroyed their fields. —*adj.* **6.** (*often l.c.*) of or pertaining to the Pygmies. **7.** (*l.c.*) of very small size, capacity, power, etc. Also, **Pigmy.** [1350–1400; ME *pigmēis,* pl. of *pigmē* < L *Pygmaeus* < Gk *pygmaîos* dwarfish (adj.), Pygmy (n.), equiv. to *pygm(ḗ)* distance from elbow to knuckles + *-aios* adj. suffix] —**pyg′·moid,** *adj.* —**pyg′my·ish,** *adj.* —**pyg′my·ism,** *n.*
—**Syn. 2.** See **dwarf.**

pyg′my chimpanzee′, a small chimpanzee, *Pan paniscus,* primarily of swamp forests in Zaire: a threatened species.

pyg′my glid′er, a gliding marsupial, *Acrobates pygmaeus,* of Australia, growing to about the size of a mouse and having a featherlike tail. Also called **feather-tail glider.**

pyg′my owl′, any of several small, diurnal owls of the genus *Glaucidium,* that feed chiefly on insects. [1855–60, *Amer.*]

pyg′my wea′sel. See **least weasel.**

py·go·style (pī′gə stīl′), *n. Ornith.* the bone at the posterior end of the spinal column in birds, formed by the fusion of several caudal vertebrae. [1870–75; < Gk *pȳgo-* (comb. form repr. *pȳgḗ* rump) + *stȳlos* pillar] —**py′go·styled′,** *adj.* —**py′go·sty′lous,** *adj.*

py·in (pī′in), *n. Biochem.* an albuminous constituent of pus. [1835–45; PY- + -IN[2]] —**py′ic,** *adj.*

py·jam·as (pə jä′məz, -jam′əz), *n.* (*used with plural v.*) *Chiefly Brit.* pajamas.

pyk·nic (pik′nik), *Psychol.* —*adj.* **1.** (of a physical type) having a fat, rounded build or body structure. Cf. **asthenic** (def. 2), **athletic** (def. 5). —*n.* **2.** a person of the pyknic type. [1920–25; < Gk *pykn(ós)* thick + -IC]

Pyl·a·des (pil′ə dēz′), *n. Class. Myth.* a son of Strophius who befriended Orestes, accompanied him in his wanderings, and eventually married Electra, sister of Orestes.

Pyle (pīl), *n.* **1. Ernest** ("*Ernie*"), 1900–45, U.S. war correspondent and journalist. **2. Howard,** 1853–1911, U.S. illustrator and author.

py·lon (pī′lon), *n.* **1.** a marking post or tower for guiding aviators, frequently used in races. **2.** a relatively tall structure at the side of a gate, bridge, or avenue, marking an entrance or approach. **3.** a monumental tower forming the entrance to an ancient Egyptian temple, consisting either of a pair of tall quadrilateral masonry masses with sloping sides and a doorway between them or of one such mass pierced with a doorway. **4.** a steel tower or mast carrying high-tension lines, telephone wires, or other cables and lines. **5.** *Aeron.* a finlike device used to attach engines, auxiliary fuel tanks, bombs, etc., to an aircraft wing or fuselage. [1840–50; < Gk *pylṓn* gateway, gate tower]

pylor′ic steno′sis, *Pathol.* an abnormal narrowing of the valve at the outlet from the stomach, preventing normal passage of food into the small intestine. [1895–1900]

py·lo·ro·plas·ty (pī lôr′ə plas′tē, -lōr′-, pi-), *n.* the surgical alteration of the pylorus, usually a widening to facilitate the passage of food from the stomach to the duodenum. [PYLOR(US) + -O- + -PLASTY]

py·lo·rus (pī lôr′əs, -lōr′-, pi-), *n., pl.* **-lo·ri** (-lôr′ī, -lōr′ī). *Anat.* the opening between the stomach and the duodenum. See diag. under **intestine.** [1605–15; < LL < Gk *pylōrós* lit., gatekeeper] —**py·lor·ic** (pī lôr′ik, -lor′-, pi-), *adj.*

Py·los (pē′lôs; *Eng.* pī′los, -lōs), *n.* Greek name of **Navarino.**

Pym (pim), *n.* **John,** 1584–1643, English statesman.

pymt., payment.

Pyn·chon (pin′chən), *n.* **William,** 1590?–1662, English colonist in America.

pyo-, a combining form meaning "pus," used in the formation of compound words: *pyogenesis.* Also, *esp. before a vowel,* **py-.** [< Gk, comb. form of *pýon;* akin to L *pūs* PUS]

py·o·gen·e·sis (pī′ə jen′ə sis), *n. Pathol.* the generation of pus; the process of the formation of pus. [1840–50; PYO- + -GENESIS]

py·o·gen·ic (pī′ə jen′ik), *adj. Pathol.* **1.** producing or generating pus. **2.** attended with or pertaining to the formation of pus. [1830–40; PYO- + -GENIC]

py·oid (pī′oid), *adj. Pathol.* pertaining to pus; puslike. [1850–55; < Gk *pyoeidḗs.* See PY-, -OID]

py·o·ne·phri·tis (pī′ō nə frī′tis), *n. Pathol.* suppurative inflammation of the kidney. [PYO- + NEPHRITIS]

Pyong·yang (pyung′yäng′, -yang′, pyong′-), *n.* a city in and the capital of North Korea, in the SW part. 1,500,000.

py·oph·thal·mi·a (pī′of thal′mē ə, -op-), *n. Pathol.* suppurative inflammation of the eye. Also, **py·oph·thal·mi·tis** (pī′of thal mī′tis, -op-). [PY- + OPHTHALMIA]

py·or·rhe·a (pī′ə rē′ə), *n.* **1.** *Pathol.* a discharge of pus. **2.** Also called **pyorrhe′a al·ve·o·lar′is** (al vē′ə-lar′is), **Riggs' disease.** *Dentistry.* a chronic form of periodontitis occurring in various degrees of severity, characterized in its severe forms by the formation of pus in the pockets between the roots of the teeth and their surrounding tissues, and frequently accompanied by the loosening and subsequent loss of the teeth. Also, **py′or·rhoe′a.** [1805–15; < NL; see PYO-, -RHEA] —**py′or·rhe′al, py′or·rhe′ic,** *adj.*

py·o·sis (pī ō′sis), *n. Pathol.* the formation of pus; suppuration. [1685–95; < NL < Gk *pýōsis;* see PY-, -OSIS]

py·o·tho·rax (pī′ō thôr′aks, -thōr′-), *n. Pathol.* empyema. [1850–55; PYO- + THORAX]

py·o·u·re·ter (pī′ō yo͝o rē′tər), *n. Pathol.* distention of a ureter with pus. [PYO- + URETER]

pyr-, var. of **pyro-,** used before *h* or a vowel: *pyran.*

pyr·a·lid (pir′ə lid), *n.* **1.** any of numerous slender-bodied moths of the family Pyralidae, having elongated triangular forewings, and in the larval phase including many crop pests. —*adj.* **2.** belonging or pertaining to the family Pyralidae. [1580–90; < NL *Pyralidae,* equiv. to *Pyral(is)* type genus (< L *pyralis* < Gk *pyralís* an insect thought to live in fire; akin to *pŷr* FIRE) + *-idae* -ID[2]]

pyr·a·mid (pir′ə mid), *n.* **1.** *Archit.* **a.** (in ancient Egypt) a quadrilateral masonry mass having smooth, steeply sloping sides meeting at an apex, used as a tomb. **b.** (in ancient Egypt and pre-Columbian Central America) a quadrilateral masonry mass, stepped and sharply sloping, used as a tomb or a platform for a temple. **2.** anything of such form. **3.** a number of persons or things arranged or heaped up in this manner: *a pyramid of acrobats; a pyramid of boxes.* **4.** a system or structure resembling a pyramid, as in hierarchical form. **5.** *Geom.* a solid having a polygonal base, and triangular sides that meet in a point. **6.** *Crystall.* any form the planes of which intersect all three of the axes. **7.** *Anat., Zool.* any of various parts or structures of pyramidal form. **8.** Also called **pyramid scheme.** a scheme that pyramids, as in speculating on the stock exchange or writing a chain letter. **9.** a tree pruned or trained to grow in conical form. **10. pyramids,** (*used with a singular v.*) *Brit.* a form of pocket billiards for two or four players in which 15 colored balls, initially placed in the form of a triangle, are pocketed with one white cue ball. —*v.i.* **11.** to take, or become disposed in, the form of a pyramid. **12.** *Stock Exchange.* (in speculating on margin) to enlarge one's operations in a series of transactions, as on a continued rise or decline in price, by using profits in transactions not yet closed, and consequently not yet in hand, as margin for additional buying or selling in the next transaction. **13.** to increase gradually, as with the completion of each phase: *Our problems are beginning to pyramid.* —*v.t.* **14.** to arrange in the form of a pyramid. **15.** to raise or increase (costs, wages, etc.) by adding amounts gradually. **16.** to cause to increase at a steady and progressive rate: *New overseas markets have pyramided the company's profits.* **17.** *Stock Exchange.* (in speculating on margin) to operate in, or employ in, pyramiding. [1350–1400; < L *pȳramid-* (s. of *pȳramis*) < Gk *pȳramís;* r. ME *pyramis* < L, as above] —**pyr′a·mid·like′,** *adj.*

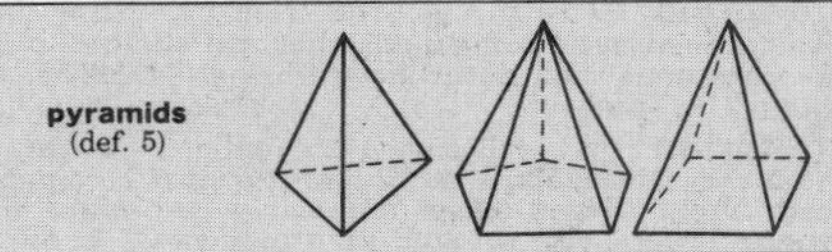

pyramids (def. 5)

py·ram·i·dal (pi ram′i dl), *adj.* **1.** of, pertaining to, or shaped like a pyramid: *the pyramidal form.* **2.** of the nature of a pyramid; pyramidlike. [1565–75; < ML *pȳramidālis;* see PYRAMID, -AL[1]] —**py·ram′i·dal·ly,** *adv.*

pyram′idal tract′, *Anat.* any of four tracts of descending motor fibers that extend in pairs down each side of the spinal column and function in voluntary movement. [1885–90]

pyr′amid bet′, a set of bets on two or more horse races or other sporting events in which the stake and winnings from the first bet automatically become the stake in the next bet, and so on as long as each bet wins. Also called **if-come bet.**

pyr·a·mid·i·cal (pir′ə mid′i kəl), *adj.* pyramidal. Also, **pyr′a·mid′ic.** [1615–25; < Gk *pȳramidik(ós)* of a pyramid (*pȳramid-,* s. of *pȳramís* PYRAMID + *-ikos* -IC) + -AL[1]] —**pyr′a·mid′i·cal·ly,** *adv.*

pyr·a·mid·i·on (pir′ə mid′ē ən, -on′), *n., pl.* **-mid·i·a** (-mid′ē ə). a miniature pyramid, as at the apex of an obelisk. [1830–40; < NL, equiv. to *pȳramid-* PYRAMID + *-ion* dim. suffix < Gk]

pyr′amid let′ter. See **chain letter.**

pyr′amid scheme′, pyramid (def. 8).

Pyr′a·mus and This′be (pir′ə məs), *Class. Myth.* two young lovers of Babylon who held conversations clandestinely, and in defiance of their parents, through a crack in a wall. On believing Thisbe dead, Pyramus killed himself. When Thisbe discovered his body she committed suicide.

py·ran (pī′ran, pī ran′), *n. Chem.* either of two compounds having the formula C_5H_6O, containing one oxygen and five carbon atoms arranged in a six-membered ring. [1900–05; PYR(ONE) + *-an,* var. of -ANE]

py·ra·nose (pī′rə nōs′, -nōz′), *n. Biochem.* any monosaccharide having a pyran ring structure. [1925–30; PYRAN + -OSE[2]]

py·ran·o·side (pī ran′ə sīd′), *n. Biochem.* a glycoside containing a pyran ring structure. [1930–35; PYRANOSE + -IDE]

py·rar·gy·rite (pī rär′jə rīt′), *n.* a blackish mineral, silver antimony sulfide, $AgSbS_3$, showing, when transparent, a deep ruby-red color by transmitted light; ruby silver: an ore of silver. [1840–50; PYR- + Gk *árgyr(on)* silver + -ITE[1]]

CONCISE PRONUNCIATION KEY: act, cāpe, dâre, pärt; set, ēqual; if, īce; ox, ōver, ôrder, oil, bo͝ok, bo͞ot, out; up, ûrge; child; sing; shoe; thin, t͟hat; zh as in *treasure.* ə = *a* as in *alone, e* as in *system, i* as in *easily, o* as in *gallop, u* as in *circus;* ᵊ as in *fire* (fīᵊr), *hour* (ouᵊr). l and n can serve as syllabic consonants, as in *cradle* (krād′l), and *button* (but′n). See the full key inside the front cover.

pyr·a·zin·a·mide (pir′ə zin′ə mīd′, -mid), *n. Pharm.* a substance, $C_5H_5N_3O$, used in the treatment of tuberculosis. [1950–55; *pyrazine* (< G *Pyrazin,* alter. of *Pyridin* PYRIDINE, by insertion of *az-* AZ-) + AMIDE]

pyr·a·zole (pir′ə zōl′, -zôl′), *n. Chem.* **1.** any of the group of heterocyclic compounds containing three carbon atoms, two adjacent nitrogen atoms, and two double bonds in the ring. **2.** the parent compound, $C_3H_4N_2$. [1885–90; PYR- + AZOLE]

py·raz·o·line (pi raz′ə lēn′, -lin, pī-), *n. Chem.* **1.** any of the group of heterocyclic compounds containing three carbon atoms, two adjacent nitrogen atoms, and one double bond in the ring. **2.** the parent compound, $C_3H_6N_2$. [1885–90; PYRAZOLE + -INE[2]]

py·raz·o·lone (pi raz′ə lōn′, pī-), *n. Chem.* **1.** any of the group of heterocyclic compounds containing the pyrazoline ring in which one carbon atom is doubly linked to an oxygen atom not in the ring. **2.** the parent compound, $C_3H_4N_2O$. [1885–90; PYRAZOLE + -ONE]

pyraz′olone dye′, *Chem.* any of the group of dyes, as tartrazine, derived from a pyrazolone: used chiefly to dye silk and wool.

pyre (pīᵊr), *n.* **1.** a pile or heap of wood or other combustible material. **2.** such a pile for burning a dead body, esp. as part of a funeral rite, as in India. [1650–60; < L *pyra* < Gk *pyrá* hearth, funeral pile]

py·rene[1] (pī′rēn, pī rēn′), *n. Bot.* a putamen or stone, esp. when there are several in a single fruit; a nutlet. [1830–40; < NL *pȳrēna* < Gk *pȳrḗn* fruit stone]

py·rene[2] (pī′rēn), *n. Chem.* a polycyclic, aromatic crystalline hydrocarbon, $C_{16}H_{10}$, consisting of four fused benzene rings, found in coal tar and believed to be carcinogenic. [1880–85; PYR- + -ENE]

Pyr·e·nees (pir′ə nēz′), *n.* a mountain range between Spain and France. Highest peak, Pic de Néthou, 11,165 ft. (3400 m). —**Pyr′e·ne′an,** *adj.*

Py·ré·nées-At·lan·tiques (pē rā nā′zat län tēk′), *n.* a department in SW France. 534,748; 2978 sq. mi. (7710 sq. km). *Cap.:* Pau. Formerly, **Basses-Pyrénées.**

Py·ré·nées-O·ri·en·tales (pē rā nā′zô rē än tal′), *n.* a department in S France. 299,506; 1600 sq. mi. (4145 sq. km). *Cap.:* Perpignan.

py·re·no·carp (pī rē′nə kärp′), *n.* **1.** *Mycol.* a perithecium. **2.** *Bot.* a drupe. [1885–90; PYRENE + -O- + -CARP] —**py·re′no·car′pic, py·re′no·car′pous,** *adj.*

py·re·thrin (pī rē′thrin, -reth′rin), *n. Chem.* **1.** Also called **pyrethrin I.** a viscous, water-insoluble liquid, $C_{21}H_{28}O_3$, extracted from pyrethrum flowers, used as an insecticide. **2.** Also called **pyrethrin II.** a like compound, $C_{22}H_{28}O_5$, obtained and used similarly. [1830–40; PYRETHR(UM) + -IN[2]]

py·re·throid (pī rē′throid, -reth′roid), *n. Chem.* any of several synthetic compounds that are similar to but more persistent than natural pyrethrins. [1950–55; PYRETHR(IN) + -OID]

py·re·thrum (pī rē′thrəm, -reth′rəm), *n.* **1.** any of several chrysanthemums, as *Chrysanthemum coccineum,* having finely divided leaves and showy red, pink, lilac, or white flowers, cultivated as an ornamental. **2.** any of several chrysanthemums, as *C. cinerariifolium,* or *C. coccineum,* cultivated as a source of insecticides. **3.** *Pharm.* the dried flower heads of these plants, used chiefly as an insecticide and sometimes in medicine for certain skin disorders. [1555–65; < L: pellitory < Gk *pýrethron,* akin to *pyretós* fever; cf. PELLITORY]

py·ret·ic (pī ret′ik), *adj.* of, pertaining to, affected by, or producing fever. [1685–95; < NL *pyreticus,* equiv. to Gk *pyret(ós)* fever + L *-icus* -IC]

pyr·e·to·ther·a·py (pir′i tō ther′ə pē, pī′ri-), *n. Med.* therapy by raising the body temperature, as by diathermy or by artificially inducing fever. [< Gk *pyretó(s)* fever + THERAPY]

Py·rex (pī′reks), *Trademark.* a brand name for any of a class of heat- and chemical-resistant glassware products of varying composition used for cooking.

py·rex·i·a (pī rek′sē ə), *n. Pathol.* **1.** fever. **2.** feverish condition. [1760–70; < NL < Gk *pýrex(is)* feverishness + *-ia* -IA] —**py·rex′i·al, py·rex′ic,** *adj.*

pyr·he·li·om·e·ter (pīᵊr′hē lē om′i tər, pir′-), *n. Astrophysics.* an instrument for measuring the total intensity of the sun's energy radiation. [1860–65; PYR- + HELIO- + -METER] —**pyr·he·li·o·met·ric** (pīᵊr′hē lē ə me′trik, pir′-), *adj.*

Pyr·i·ben·za·mine (pir′ə ben′zə mēn′, pī′rə-), *Pharm., Trademark.* a brand of tripelennamine.

pyr·i·dine (pir′i dēn′, -din), *n. Chem.* a colorless, flammable, liquid organic base, C_5H_5N, having a disagreeable odor, usually obtained from coal or synthesized from acetaldehyde and ammonia: used chiefly as a solvent and in organic synthesis. [1850–55; PYR- + -ID[3] + -INE[2]] —**pyr·id·ic** (pi rid′ik), *adj.*

Py·rid·i·um (pī rid′ē əm, pi-), *Pharm., Trademark.* a brand of phenazopyridine.

pyr·i·do·stig′mine bro′mide (pir′i dō stig′mēn), *Pharm.* a cholinesterase inhibitor, $C_9H_{13}BrN_2O_2$, used in its bromide form in the treatment of myasthenia gravis. [1960–65; PYRID(INE) + -O- + (PHYSO)STIGMINE]

pyr·i·dox·ine (pir′i dok′sēn, -sin), *n. Biochem.* a derivative of pyridine, $C_8H_{11}NO_3$, occurring in whole-grain cereals, meats, fish, etc., and also made synthetically: required for the prevention of pellagra and the formation of hemoglobin; vitamin B_6. Also, **pyr·i·dox·in** (pir′i dok′sin). [1935–40; PYRID(INE) + OX(YGEN) + -INE[2]]

pyr·i·form (pir′ə fôrm′), *adj.* pear-shaped. [1695–1705; < NL *pyriformis* pear-shaped, equiv. to *pyri-* (for *piri-;* L *pir(um)* PEAR + *-i-* -I-) + *-formis* -FORM]

CONCISE ETYMOLOGY KEY: <, descended or borrowed from; >, whence; b., blend of, blended; c., cognate with; cf., compare; deriv., derivative; equiv., equivalent; imit., imitative; obl., oblique; r., replacing; s., stem; sp., spelling, spelled; resp., respelling, respelled; trans., translation; ?, origin unknown; *, unattested; ‡, probably earlier than. See the full key inside the front cover.

py·ri·meth·a·mine (pī′rə meth′ə mēn′, -min), *n. Pharm.* a potent substance, $C_{12}H_{13}ClN_4$, used against susceptible plasmodia in the prophylactic treatment of malaria and against *Toxoplasma gondi* in the treatment of toxoplasmosis. [1950–55; PYRIM(IDINE) + ETH(YL) + -AMINE]

py·rim·i·dine (pī rim′i dēn′, pi-, pir′ə mi dēn′, -din), *n. Biochem.* **1.** a heterocyclic compound, $C_4H_4N_2$, that is the basis of several important biochemical substances. **2.** one of several pyrimidine derivatives, esp. the bases cytosine, thymine, and uracil, which are fundamental constituents of nucleic acids. [1880–85; b. PYRIDINE and IMIDE]

Pyr·i·phleg·e·thon (pir′ə fleg′ə thon′, -flej′-), *n. Class. Myth.* Phlegethon (def. 1).

py·rite (pī′rīt), *n.* a very common brass-yellow mineral, iron disulfide, FeS_2, with a metallic luster, burned to sulfur dioxide in the manufacture of sulfuric acid: chemically similar to marcasite, but crystallizing in the isometric system. Also, **pyrites.** Also called **iron pyrites.** [1560–70; < L *pyrītēs* < Gk *pyrī́tēs,* n. use of adj.: of fire, so called because it produces sparks when struck. See PYR-, -ITE[1]] —**py·rit·ic** (pī rit′ik, pə-), **py·rit′i·cal, py·ri·tous** (pə rī′təs, pī-), *adj.*

py·ri·tes (pī rī′tēz, pə-, pī′rīts), *n., pl.* **-tes.** *Mineral.* **1.** pyrite. **2.** marcasite. **3.** any of various other metallic sulfides, as of copper or tin. [1545–55; < L *pyrītes* (pl.); see PYRITE]

py·ri·to·he·dron (pī rī′tə hē′drən, pə-, pī′rī-), *n. Crystall.* a crystal form of 12 pentagonal faces. Also called **pentagonal dodecahedron.** See diag. under **dodecahedron.** [1865–70; *pyrito-* (comb. form of PYRITE) + -HEDRON] —**py·ri′to·he′dral,** *adj.*

py·ro (pī′rō), *n., pl.* **-ros.** *Informal.* a pyromaniac. [by shortening; cf. -O]

pyro-, **1.** a combining form meaning "fire," "heat," "high temperature," used in the formation of compound words: *pyrogen; pyrolusite; pyromancy.* **2.** *Chem.* a combining form used in the names of inorganic acids, indicating that the acid's water content is intermediate between that of the corresponding ortho- (more water) and meta- (least water) acids (*pyroantimonic,* $H_4Sb_2O_7$, *pyroarsenic,* $H_4As_2O_7$, and *pyrosulfuric,* $H_2S_2O_7$, *acids*). The combining form is also used in the names of the salts of these acids. If the acid ends in *-ic,* the corresponding salt ends in *-ate* (*pyroboric acid,* $H_2B_4O_7$, and *potassium pyrobate,* $K_2B_4O_7$, or *pyrosulfuric,* $H_2S_2O_7$, and *pyrosulfate,* $N_2S_2O_7$); if the acid ends in *-ous,* the corresponding salt ends in *-ite* (*pyrophosphorous acid,* $H_4P_2O_5$, *potassium pyrophosphite,* $K_4P_2O_5$). Also, **pyr-.** [< Gk *pyro-,* comb. form of *pŷr* FIRE]

py·ro·bi·tu·men (pī′rō bi to͞o′mən, -tyo͞o′-, -bich′o͞o-), *n.* any of the dark, solid hydrocarbons including peat, coal, and bituminous shale. [1900–05; PYRO- + BITUMEN] —**py′ro·bi·tu′mi·nous, py′ro·bi·tu′mi·noid′,** *adj.*

py·ro·bo·rate (pī′rə bôr′āt, -it, -bōr′-), *n.* borax. [PYRO- + BORATE]

py·ro·cat·e·chol (pī′rə kat′i chôl′, -chol′, -kôl′, -kol′), *n. Chem.* catechol. Also, **py·ro·cat·e·chin** (pī′rə kat′ə chin, -kin). [1885–90; PYRO- + CATECHOL]

py·ro·cel·lu·lose (pī′rə sel′yə lōs′), *n.* cordite. [1905–10; PYRO- + (NITRO)CELLULOSE]

py·ro·chem·i·cal (pī′rə kem′i kəl), *adj.* pertaining to or producing chemical change at high temperatures. [PYRO- + CHEMICAL] —**py′ro·chem′i·cal·ly,** *adv.*

py·ro·chlore (pī′rə klôr′, -klōr′), *n.* a mineral, chiefly composed of niobates of the cerium metals, occurring in syenites in the form of brown crystals. [1820–30; < G *Pyrochlor.* See PYRO-, CHLOR-[1]]

py·ro·clas·tic (pī′rə klas′tik), *adj. Geol.* composed chiefly of fragments of volcanic origin, as agglomerate, tuff, and certain other rocks; volcaniclastic. [1885–90; PYRO- + CLASTIC]

py·ro·con·duc·tiv·i·ty (pī′rə kon′duk tiv′i tē), *n. Elect.* conductivity brought about by the application of heat, esp. in solids that are not conductors at normal temperatures. [PYRO- + CONDUCTIVITY]

py·ro·crys·tal·line (pī′rə kris′tl in, -īn′, -ēn′), *adj. Petrog.* crystallized from a molten magma or highly heated solution. [PYRO- + CRYSTALLINE]

py·ro·e·lec·tric (pī′rō i lek′trik), *adj.* **1.** pertaining to, subject to, or manifesting pyroelectricity. —*n.* **2.** a substance manifesting pyroelectricity. [1850–55; back formation from PYROELECTRICITY]

py·ro·e·lec·tric·i·ty (pī′rō i lek tris′i tē, -ē′lek-), *n.* electrification or electrical polarity produced in certain crystals by temperature changes. [1825–35; PYRO- + ELECTRICITY]

py·ro·gal·late (pī′rə gal′āt, -gô′lāt), *n. Chem.* a salt or ether of pyrogallol. [1830–40; PYROGALL(OL) + -ATE[2]]

py·ro·gal·lol (pī′rə gal′ôl, -ol, -gə lôl′, -lol′), *n.* a white, crystalline, water-soluble, poisonous, solid, phenolic compound, $C_6H_3(OH)_3$, obtained by heating gallic acid and water: used chiefly as a developer in photography, as a mordant for wool, in dyeing, and in medicine in the treatment of certain skin conditions. Also called **py′rogal′lic ac′id.** [1875–80; PYRO- + GALL(IC)[2] + -OL[1]] —**py·ro·gal·lic** (pī′rə gal′ik, -gô′lik), *adj.*

py·ro·gen (pī′rə jən, -jen′), *n.* a substance, as a thermostable bacterial toxin, that produces a rise in temperature in a human or animal. [1855–60; PYRO- + -GEN]

py·ro·gen·ic (pī′rə jen′ik), *adj.* **1.** producing or produced by heat or fever. **2.** Also, **py·ro·ge·net·ic** (pī′rō jə net′ik). *Geol.* produced by heat, as the anhydrous minerals of an igneous rock. [1850–55; PYRO- + -GENIC]

py·rog·e·nous (pī roj′ə nəs), *adj. Geol.* pyrogenic (def. 2). [1830–40; PYRO- + -GENOUS]

py·rog·nos·tics (pī′rəg nos′tiks), *n.pl.* those properties of a mineral that it exhibits when heated, alone or with fluxes, in the blowpipe flame, as the fusibility, intumescence, or other phenomena of fusion, flame coloration, etc. [1840–50; PYRO- + GNOST(IC) + -ICS]

py·ro·graph (pī′rə graf′, -gräf′), *n.* **1.** an object ornamented by pyrography. —*v.t., v.i.* **2.** to decorate or work with pyrography. [1890–95; back formation from PYROGRAPHY]

py·rog·ra·phy (pī rog′rə fē), *n., pl.* **-phies** for 2. **1.** the process of burning designs on wood, leather, etc., with a heated tool. **2.** a design made by this process. Also called **py·ro·gra·vure** (pī′rə grə vyo͝or′, -grā′vyər). [1875–80, *Amer.;* PYRO- + -GRAPHY] —**py·rog′ra·pher,** *n.* —**py·ro·graph·ic** (pī′rə graf′ik), *adj.*

py·ro·ki·ne·sis (pī′rō ki nē′sis, -kī-), *n.* (in science fiction) the ability to set objects or people on fire through the concentration of psychic power. [PYRO- + (TELE)KINESIS] —**py·ro·ki·net·ic** (pī′rō ki net′ik, -kī-), *adj.*

py·ro·lig·ne·ous (pī′rə lig′nē əs), *adj.* produced by the distillation of wood. Also, **py′ro·lig′nic.** [1780–90; PYRO- + LIGNEOUS]

pyrolig′neous ac′id, *Chem.* a yellowish, acidic, water-soluble liquid, containing about 10 percent acetic acid, obtained by the destructive distillation of wood: used for smoking meats. Also called **wood vinegar.** [1780–90]

pyrolig′neous al′cohol. See **methyl alcohol.** Also called **pyrolig′neous spir′it.** [1860–65]

py·ro·lize (pī′rə līz′), *v.t.,* **-lized, -liz·ing.** *Chem.* to subject (a substance) to pyrolysis. Also, **py′ro·lyze′;** *esp. Brit.,* **py′ro·lyse′.** [1930–35; back formation from PYROLYSIS; see -IZE] —**py′ro·liz′er,** *n.*

py·ro·lu·site (pī′rə lo͞o′sīt, pī rol′yə sīt′), *n.* a common mineral, manganese dioxide, MnO_2, the principal ore of manganese, used in various manufactures, as a decolorizer of brown or green tints in glass, and as a depolarizer in dry-cell batteries. [1820–30; PYRO- + Gk *loûs(is)* washing + -ITE[1]]

py·rol·y·sis (pī rol′ə sis), *n. Chem.* **1.** the subjection of organic compounds to very high temperatures. **2.** the resulting decomposition. [1885–90; PYRO- + -LYSIS] —**py·ro·lyt·ic** (pī′rə lit′ik), *adj.*

py·ro·mag·net·ic (pī′rō mag net′ik), *adj. Physics.* (formerly) thermomagnetic (def. 1). [1885–90; PYRO- + MAGNETIC]

py·ro·man·cy (pī′rə man′sē), *n.* divination by fire, or by forms appearing in fire. [1325–75; ME *piromancie* < ML *pyromantīa* < Gk *pyromanteía* divination by fire. See PYRO-, -MANCY] —**py′ro·man′cer,** *n.* —**py′ro·man′tic,** *adj.*

py·ro·ma·ni·a (pī′rə mā′nē ə, -mān′yə), *n.* a compulsion to set things on fire. [1835–45; PYRO- + -MANIA] —**py·ro·ma·ni·ac** (pī′rə mā′nē ak′), *n.* —**py·ro·ma·ni·a·cal** (pī′rō mə nī′ə kəl), *adj.*

py·ro·met·al·lur·gy (pī′rə met′l ûr′jē), *n.* the process or technique of refining ores with heat so as to accelerate chemical reactions or to melt the metallic or nonmetallic content. [1905–10; PYRO- + METALLURGY] —**py′ro·met′al·lur′gi·cal,** *adj.*

py·rom·e·ter (pī rom′i tər), *n.* an apparatus for measuring high temperatures that uses the radiation emitted by a hot body as a basis for measurement. [1740–50; PYRO- + -METER] —**py·ro·met·ric** (pī′rə me′trik), **py′ro·met′ri·cal,** *adj.* —**py′ro·met′ri·cal·ly,** *adv.* —**py·rom′e·try,** *n.*

py′romet′ric bead′, (in a kiln) a ball of material that indicates by changing color that a certain temperature has been reached. [1825–35]

py′romet′ric cone′, (in a kiln) a triangular piece of material that indicates by bending or melting that a certain temperature has been reached. [1945–50]

py·ro·mor·phite (pī′rə môr′fīt), *n.* a mineral, lead chlorophosphate, $Pb_5P_3O_{12}Cl$, occurring in crystalline and massive forms, and of a green, yellow, or brown color; green lead ore: a minor ore of lead. [1805–15; < G *Pyromorphit.* See PYRO-, MORPH-, -ITE[1]]

py′ro·mu′cic al′dehyde (pī′rə myo͞o′sik, pī′-), *Chem.* furfural. [1785–95; PYRO- + MUCIC (ACID)]

py·rone (pī′rōn, pī rōn′), *n. Chem.* either of two heterocyclic ketones having the formula $C_5H_4O_2$. [1890–95; PYR- + -ONE]

py·ro·nine (pī′rə nēn′), *n. Histol.* a xanthine dye used for detecting the presence of RNA. [1890–95; < G *Pyronin,* orig. a trademark]

py·rope (pī′rōp), *n.* a mineral, magnesium-aluminum garnet, $Mg_3Al_2Si_3O_{12}$, occurring in crystals of varying shades of red, and frequently used as a gem. [1300–50; ME *pirope* < L *pyrōpus* gold-bronze < Gk *pyrōpós* lit., fire-eyed, equiv. to *pyr-* PYR- + *ōp-* (s. of *ṓps*) EYE + *-os* adj. suffix]

py·ro·pho·bi·a (pī′rə fō′bē ə), *n.* an abnormal fear of fire. [1885–90; PYRO- + -PHOBIA] —**py′ro·pho′bic,** *adj.*

py·ro·phor·ic (pī′rə fôr′ik, -for′-), *adj. Chem.* capable of igniting spontaneously in air. [1830–40; < Gk *pyrophór(os)* fire-bearing (see PYRO-, -PHOROUS) + -IC]

py·ro·phos·phate (pī′rə fos′fāt), *n. Chem.* a salt or ester of pyrophosphoric acid. [1830–40; PYROPHOSPH(ORIC ACID) + -ATE[2]]

py′ro·phos·phor′ic ac′id (pī′rō fos fôr′ik, -for′-, pī′-), *Chem.* a crystalline, water-soluble powder, $H_4P_2O_7$, formed by the union of one molecule of phosphorus pentoxide with two molecules of water. [1865–70; PYRO- + PHOSPHORIC]

py·ro·pho·tom·e·ter (pī′rō fō tom′i tər), *n. Physics.* a form of pyrometer that measures temperature by optical or photometric means. [PYRO- + PHOTOMETER]

py·ro·phyl·lite (pī′rə fil′īt, pī rof′ə līt′), *n. Mineral.* a phyllosilicate, $AlSi_2O_5(OH)$, usually having a white or greenish color, and occurring in either foliated or compact masses, the latter variety being used like soapstone.

[1820–30; < G *Pyrophyllit;* so called because it exfoliates when heated. See PYRO-, -PHYLL, -ITE[1]]

py′ro·ra·ce′mic ac′id (pī′rō rā sē′mik, -sem′ik, -rō rə-, pī′rō-), *Chem.* See **pyruvic acid.** [1830–40; PYRO- + RACEMIC ACID]

py·ro·sis (pī rō′sis), *n. Pathol.* heartburn (def. 1). [1780–90; < NL < Gk *pýrōsis;* see PYR-, -OSIS]

py·ro·stat (pī′rə stat′), *n.* **1.** a thermostat for high temperatures. **2.** a safety device that, when a fire breaks out in its vicinity, automatically causes a mechanism to sound a warning alarm. [PYRO- + -STAT]

py·ro·sul·fate (pī′rə sul′fāt), *n. Chem.* a salt of pyrosulfuric acid. [PYROSULF(URIC ACID) + -ATE[2]]

py·ro·sul·fu·ric (pī′rō sul fyŏŏr′ik), *adj. Chem.* of or derived from pyrosulfuric acid; disulfuric. Also, **py′ro·sul·phu′ric.** [1870–75; PYRO- + SULFURIC]

py′rosulfu′ric ac′id, *Chem.* an oily, hygroscopic, corrosive liquid, $H_2S_2O_7$, that, depending on purity, is colorless or dark brown: used chiefly as a dehydrating agent in the manufacture of explosives and as a sulfating or sulfonating agent in the manufacture of dyes. Also called **fuming sulfuric acid, oleum.** [1870–75]

py·ro·tech·nic (pī′rə tek′nik), *adj.* **1.** of or pertaining to pyrotechnics. **2.** pertaining to, resembling, or suggesting fireworks. Also, **py′ro·tech′ni·cal.** [1695–1705; PYRO- + TECHNIC] **—py′ro·tech′ni·cal·ly,** *adv.*

py·ro·tech·ni·cian (pī′rō tek nish′ən), *n.* **1.** a specialist in the origin of fires, their nature and control, etc. **2.** a fireworks technician or expert; pyrotechnist. **3.** a performer capable of dazzling virtuosity: *a pyrotechnician of the keyboard.* [1720–30; PYRO(TECHNICS) + TECHNICIAN]

py·ro·tech·nics (pī′rə tek′niks), *n.* (*used with a singular or plural v.*) **1.** the art of making fireworks. **2.** the use of fireworks for display, military purposes, etc. **3.** a display of fireworks. **4.** a brilliant or sensational display, as of rhetoric or musicianship. **5.** *Mil.* ammunition containing chemicals for producing smoke or light, as for signaling, illuminating, or screening. Also, **py′ro·tech′ny** (for defs. 1, 2). [1710–20; see PYROTECHNIC, -ICS]

py·ro·tech·nist (pī′rə tek′nist), *n.* a person skilled in pyrotechnics, esp. in the manufacture or use of fireworks. [1785–95; PYROTECHN(ICS) + -IST]

py·ro·tox·in (pī′rə tok′sin), *n.* pyrogen. [PYRO- + TOXIN]

py·ro·trau·mat′ic dermati′tis (pī′rō trə mat′ik, -trô-, -trou-), *Vet. Pathol.* See **hot spot.** [PYRO- + TRAUMATIC]

py·rox·ene (pī rok′sēn, pə-, pī′rok sēn′), *n.* any of a very common group of minerals of many varieties, silicates of magnesium, iron, calcium, and other elements, occurring as important constituents of many kinds of rocks, esp. basic igneous rocks. Cf. **augite, diopside, hypersthene.** [1790–1800; < F; see PYRO-, XENO-; orig. supposed to be a foreign substance when found in igneous rocks] **—py·rox·en·ic** (pī′rok sen′ik), *adj.*

py·rox·e·nite (pī rok′sə nīt′, pə-), *n. Petrol.* any rock composed essentially, or in large part, of pyroxene of any kind. [1860–65; PYROXENE + -ITE[1]]

py·rox·y·lin (pī rok′sə lin, pə-), *n.* a nitrocellulose compound containing fewer nitrate groups than guncotton, used in the manufacture of artificial silk, leather, oilcloth, etc. Also, **py·rox·y·line** (pī rok′sə lin, -lēn′, pə-). [1830–40; PYRO- + XYL- + -IN[2]]

pyr·rhic[1] (pir′ik), *Pros.* **—adj. 1.** consisting of two short or unaccented syllables. **2.** composed of or pertaining to pyrrhics. **—n. 3.** Also called **dibrach.** a pyrrhic foot. [1620–30; < L *pyrrhichius* < Gk *pyrrhíchios* pertaining to the *pyrrhíchē* PYRRHIC[2]]

pyr·rhic[2] (pir′ik), *n.* **1.** an ancient Greek warlike dance in which the motions of actual warfare were imitated. **—adj. 2.** of, pertaining to, or denoting this dance. [1590–1600; < L *pyrrhicha* < Gk *pyrrhíchē* a dance; said to be named after Pyrrhichus, the inventor]

Pyr·rhic (pir′ik), *adj.* of, pertaining to, or resembling Pyrrhus, king of Epirus, or his costly victory. [1880–85; PYRRH(US) + -IC]

Pyr′rhic vic′tory, a victory or goal achieved at too great a cost. Cf. **Cadmean victory.** [1880–85; < Gk *Pyrrikós;* after a remark attributed by Plutarch to PYRRHUS, who declared, after a costly victory over the Romans, that another similar victory would ruin him]

Pyr·rho (pir′ō), *n.* c365–c275 B.C., Greek philosopher.

Pyr·rho·nism (pir′ə niz′əm), *n.* **1.** the Skeptic doctrines of Pyrrho and his followers. **2.** extreme or absolute skepticism. [1660–70; < Gk *Pýrrhōn* PYRRHO + -ISM] **—Pyr′rho·nist,** *n.* **—Pyr′rho·nis′tic,** *adj.*

pyr·rho·tite (pir′ə tīt′), *n.* a common mineral, iron sulfide, approximately FeS but variable because of a partial absence of ferrous ions, occurring in massive and in crystal forms with a bronze color and metallic luster; magnetic pyrites: generally slightly magnetic. [1868; < Gk *pyrrhót(ēs)* redness + -ITE[1]]

pyr·rhu·lox·i·a (pir′ə lok′sē ə), *n.* a cardinallike grosbeak, *Cardinalis (Pyrrhuloxia) sinuatus,* of the southwestern U.S. and Mexico, having a bill superficially resembling that of a parrot. [< NL *Pyrrhu(la)* finch genus (< Gk *pyrrhoúlas* a red bird, deriv. of *pyrrhós* red) + NL *Loxia* crossbill genus, equiv. to Gk *lox(ós)* oblique + *-ia* -IA]

Pyr·rhus (pir′əs), *n.* **1.** c318–272 B.C., king of Epirus c300–272. **2.** *Class. Myth.* Neoptolemus.

pyr·role (pi rōl′, pir′ōl), *n. Chem.* a colorless, toxic, liquid, five-membered ring compound, C_4H_5N, that is a component of chlorophyll, hemin, and many other important naturally occurring substances. [1825–35; irreg. < Gk *pyrr(hós)* red + -OLE] **—pyr·rol·ic** (pi rol′ik, -rō′lik), *adj.*

pyr·rol·i·dine (pi rō′li dēn′, -din, -rol′i-), *n. Chem.* a colorless, water-soluble, unpleasant smelling, poisonous liquid, C_4H_9N, from which proline and certain alkaloids are derived, prepared by reducing pyrrole: used chiefly in organic synthesis. [1880–85; PYRROLE + -ID[3] + -INE[2]]

Pyr·roph·y·ta (pi rof′i tə), *n. Biol.* a phylum in the kingdom Protista comprising the dinoflagellates and cryptomonads. [< NL < Gk *pyrrh(ós)* red + *-o-* -O- + *phytá,* pl. of *phytón* -PHYTE]

pyr·ro·phyte (pir′ə fīt′), *n.* any of various single-celled, biflagellated algae, of the phylum Pyrrophyta, esp. the dinoflagellates. [see PYRROPHYTA]

pyr·u·vate (pī rōō′vāt, pi-), *n. Chem.* an ester or salt of pyruvic acid. [1850–55; PYRUV(IC ACID) + -ATE[2]]

py·ru·vic (pī rōō′vik, pi-), *adj. Chem.* of or derived from pyruvic acid. [1830–40; PYR- + L *ūv(a)* grape + -IC]

pyru′vic ac′id, *Chem., Biochem.* a water-soluble liquid, $C_3H_4O_3$, important in many metabolic and fermentative processes, having an odor resembling that of acetic acid, prepared by the dehydration of tartaric acid: used chiefly in biochemical research. Also called **acetylformic acid, pyroracemic acid.** [1830–40]

pyru′vic al′dehyde, *Chem.* a yellow, liquid compound, $C_3H_4O_2$, containing both an aldehyde and a ketone group, usually obtained in a polymeric form: used chiefly in organic synthesis. Also, **py·ruv·al·de·hyde** (pī′rōō val′də hīd′, pir′ōō-). Also called **methylglyoxal.**

Py·thag·o·ras (pi thag′ər əs), *n.* c582–c500 B.C., Greek philosopher, mathematician, and religious reformer.

Py·thag·o·re·an (pi thag′ə rē′ən), *adj.* **1.** of or pertaining to Pythagoras, to his school, or to his doctrines. **—n. 2.** a follower of Pythagoras. [1540–50; < L *Pȳthagorē(us)* (< Gk *Pȳthagóreios* of Pythagoras) + -AN]

Py·thag·o·re·an·ism (pi thag′ə rē′ə niz′əm), *n.* the doctrines of Pythagoras and his followers, esp. the belief that the universe is the manifestation of various combinations of mathematical ratios. [1720–30; PYTHAGOREAN + -ISM]

Pythag′ore′an scale′, *Music.* the major scale as derived acoustically by Pythagoras from the perfect fifth.

Pythag′ore′an the′orem, *Geom.* the theorem that the square of the hypotenuse of a right triangle is equal to the sum of the squares of the other two sides. [1905–10]

Pyth·i·a (pith′ē ə), *n. Gk. Myth.* the priestess of Apollo at Delphi who delivered the oracles. [< L *Pȳthia* < Gk *Pȳthía,* fem. of *Pȳthiós* PYTHIAN]

Pyth·i·ad (pith′ē ad′), *n.* the four-year period between two celebrations of the Pythian Games. [1835–45; < Gk *Pȳthiad-* (s. of *Pȳthiás*)]

Pyth·i·an (pith′ē ən), *adj.* Also, **Pyth′ic. 1.** of or pertaining to Delphi, in ancient Greece. **2.** of or pertaining to Apollo, with reference to his oracle at Delphi. **—n. 3.** a Pythian priestess. [1590–1600; < L *Pȳthi(us)* (< Gk *Pȳthios* of Delphi and the oracle) + -AN]

Pyth′ian Games′, one of the great national festivals of ancient Greece, held every four years at Delphi in honor of Apollo. [1595–1605]

Pyth·i·as (pith′ē əs), *n.* See **Damon and Pythias.**

py·tho·gen·ic (pī′thə jen′ik, pith′ə-), *adj.* originating from filth or putrescence. Also, **py·thog·e·nous** (pī thoj′ə nəs, pi-). [1860–65; < Gk *pȳ́th(ein)* to rot + -o- + -GENIC] **—py′tho·gen′e·sis,** *n.*

py·thon[1] (pī′thon, -thən), *n.* any of several Old World boa constrictors of the subfamily Pythoninae, often growing to a length of more than 20 ft. (6 m): the Indian python, *Python molurus,* is endangered. [1580–90; < NL; special use of PYTHON]

py·thon[2] (pī′thon, -thən), *n.* **1.** a spirit or demon. **2.** a person who is possessed by a spirit and prophesies by its aid. [1595–1605; < LGk *pȳ́thōn;* relation to PYTHON unclear]

Py·thon (pī′thon, -thən), *n. Class. Myth.* a large dragon who guarded the chasm at Delphi from which prophetic vapors emerged. He was finally killed by Apollo, who established his oracle on the site. [< L *Pȳthōn* < Gk *Pȳ́thōn*]

py·tho·ness (pī′thə nis, pith′ə-), *n.* **1.** a woman believed to be possessed by a soothsaying spirit, as the priestess of Apollo at Delphi. **2.** a woman who practices divination. [1325–75; PYTHON[2] + -ESS; r. ME *phytonesse* < MF]
—Usage. See **-ess.**

py·thon·ic[1] (pī thon′ik, pi-), *adj.* **1.** of or pertaining to pythons. **2.** pythonlike. **3.** gigantic or monstrous. [1855–60; PYTHON[1] + -IC]

py·thon·ic[2] (pī thon′ik, pi-), *adj.* prophetic; oracular. [1650–60; < LL *pythōnicus* < Gk *pythōnikós* prophetic. See PYTHON[2], -IC]

py·u·ri·a (pī yŏŏr′ē ə), *n. Pathol.* the presence of pus in the urine. [1805–15; PY- + URIA]

pyx (piks), *n.* **1.** *Eccles.* **a.** the box or vessel in which the reserved Eucharist or Host is kept. **b.** a watch-shaped container for carrying the Eucharist to the sick. **2.** Also called **pyx′ chest′.** a box or chest at a mint, in which specimen coins are deposited and reserved for trial by weight and assay. Also, **pix.** [1350–1400; ME *pyxe* < L *pyxis* < Gk *pyxís* a box, orig. made of boxwood]

pyx·id·i·um (pik sid′ē əm), *n., pl.* **pyx·id·i·a** (pik sid′ē ə). *Bot.* a seed vessel that opens transversely, the top part acting as a lid, as in the purslane. [1825–35; < NL < Gk *pyxídion* a little box, equiv. to *pyxid-* (s. of *pyxís*) a box + *-ion* dim. n. suffix]

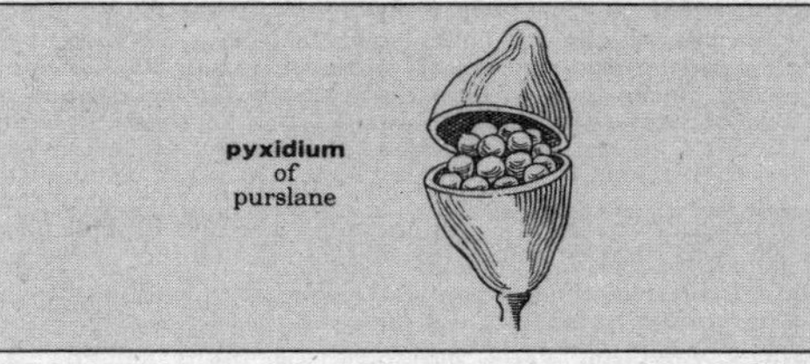

pyxidium of purslane

pyx·ie (pik′sē), *n.* either of two trailing, shrubby, evergreen plants, *Pyxidanthera barbulata* or *P. brevifolia,* of the eastern U.S., having numerous small, starlike blossoms and growing in sandy soil. Also called **flowering moss.** [1880–85; short for NL *Pyxidanthera,* equiv. to L *pyxid-* (s. of *pyxis*) box (see PYX) + NL *-anthera* ANTHER]

pyx·is (pik′sis), *n., pl.* **pyx·i·des** (pik′si dēz′). **1.** *Gk. and Rom. Antiq.* a box of a usually cylindrical shape having a lid with a knob in the center, used for toilet articles. **2.** pyx (def. 1). **3.** *Bot.* a pyxidium. [1350–1400; ME < L < Gk *pyxís* a box]

Pyx·is (pik′sis), *n., gen.* **Pyx·i·dis** (pik′si dis). *Astron.* the Compass, a southern constellation: one of the subordinate constellations into which Argo is now divided. [1680–90; < L < Gk *pyxís* a box, PYX]

Pyx′is Nau′ti·ca (nô′ti kə), *gen.* **Pixidis Nau·ti·cae** (nô′ti kē′). Pyxis.

CONCISE PRONUNCIATION KEY: *act, cāpe, dâre, pärt; set, ēqual; if, īce; ox, ōver, ôrder, oil, bŏŏk, bōōt, out; up, ûrge; child; sing; shoe; thin, that;* zh as in *treasure.* ə = *a* as in *alone, e* as in *system, i* as in *easily, o* as in *gallop, u* as in *circus;* ᵊ as in *fire* (fīᵊr), *hour* (ouᵊr). l and n can serve as syllabic consonants, as in *cradle* (krād′l), and *button* (but′n). See the full key inside the front cover.

DEVELOPMENT OF MAJUSCULE								
NORTH SEMITIC	GREEK		ETR.	LATIN		MODERN		
						GOTHIC	ITALIC	ROMAN
					Q	𝔔	*Q*	Q

DEVELOPMENT OF MINUSCULE					
ROMAN CURSIVE	ROMAN UNCIAL	CAROL. MIN	MODERN		
			GOTHIC	ITALIC	ROMAN
	q	q	q	*q*	q

*The seventeenth letter of the English alphabet developed in its present form from Latin. Its equivalent in Greek was kappa (Κ), which became obsolete except as a numeral, and in North Semitic, it was qoph, which represented a guttural k-like sound. When adopted from the Etruscans, the Latin alphabet contained three symbols for the k-sound (see **C, K**), and the use of Q was limited to representing the sound (k) when it was labialized and followed in spelling by U, a practice maintained today with only rare exceptions. In Old English the Q does not appear, its labialized sound being written CW or, later, KW.*

Q, q (kyo͞o), *n., pl.* **Q's** or **Qs, q's** or **qs. 1.** the 17th letter of the English alphabet, a consonant. **2.** any spoken sound represented by the letter *Q* or *q,* as in *quick, acquit,* or *Iraq.* **3.** something having the shape of a Q. **4.** a written or printed representation of the letter Q or *q.* **5.** a device, as a printer's type, for reproducing the letter *Q* or *q.*

Q, 1. quarterly. **2.** *Chess.* queen.

Q, *Symbol.* **1.** the 17th in order or in a series, or, when *I* is omitted, the 16th. **2.** (*sometimes l.c.*) the medieval Roman numeral for 500. Cf. **Roman numerals. 3.** *Biochem.* glutamine. **4.** *Physics.* heat. **5.** *Thermodynam.* a unit of heat energy, equal to 10^{18} British thermal units (1.055×10^{21} joules). **6.** Also called **Q-factor.** *Electronics.* the ratio of the reactance to the resistance of an electric circuit or component. **7.** *Biblical Criticism.* the symbol for material common to the Gospels of Matthew and Luke that was not derived from the Gospel of Mark.

Q., 1. quarto. **2.** Quebec. **3.** Queen. **4.** question. **5.** (in Guatemala) quetzal; quetzals.

q., 1. farthing. [< L *quadrāns*] **2.** quart; quarts. **3.** query. **4.** question. **5.** quintal. **6.** quire.

Qad·a·rite (kad′ə rīt′), *n. Islam.* a member of the Qadariyah. [< Ar *qadar*(*ī*) Qadarite (*qadar* fate + -*ī* suffix of appurtenance) + -ITE[1]]

Qa·da·ri·yah (kä′də rē′yə), *n. Islam.* (in classical thought) the group who defended free will against the doctrine of predestination. Also, **Qa′da·ri′ya.** [< Ar *qadariyyah,* deriv. of *qadarī* Qadarite (equiv. to *qadar* fate + -*ī* suffix of appurtenance)]

Qa·dha·fi (kə dä′fē), *n.* **Mu·am·mar (Muhammad) al-** or **el-** (mo͞o ä′mär, al, el), born 1942, Libyan army colonel and political leader: chief of state since 1969. Also, **Qad·da′fi, Gaddafi, Kaddafi, Khadafy.**

qa·di (kä′dē, kā′-), *n., pl.* **-dis.** a judge in a Muslim community, whose decisions are based on Islamic religious law. Also, **cadi, kadi.** [< Ar *qāḍī* judge]

Qa·di·a·nis (kä′dē ä′nis), *n.* See under **Ahmadiya.**

Qa·di·ri·yah (kä′də rē′yə), *n. Islam.* a Sufi fraternity founded by ʿAbd al-Qadir al-Jilani (1077–1166) in the 12th century. Also, **Qa′di·ri′ya.** [< Ar *qādiriyyah,* equiv. to *qādir* (deriv. of founder's name) + -*iyyah* abstract n. suffix]

qāf (käf), *n.* the 21st letter of the Arabic alphabet, representing a uvular stop consonant sound. [< Ar]

Qa·har (chä′här′), *n. Pinyin.* a former province of Inner Mongolia in NE China: divided 1952 among adjacent provinces. Also, **Chahar.**

qa·id (kä ēth′, kīth), *n.* caid.

qal·an·dar (kal′ən dər), *n.* (in Islamic countries) one of an order of mendicant dervishes founded in the 14th century. Also, **Calender.** [< Pers]

Q and A (kyo͞o′ ən ā′, ənd), *Informal.* an exchange of questions and answers. Also, **Q&A**

Qa·ra Qum (kar′ə ko͞om′, ko͝om′, kär′ə). See **Kara Kum.**

qa·si·da (kə sē′də), *n., pl.* **-da, -das.** *Pros.* an Arabic poem, usually in monorhyme, that may be satirical, elegiac, threatening, or laudatory. [1810–20; < Ar *qaṣīdah*]

qat (kät), *n.* kat.

Qa·tar (kä′tär, kə tär′), *n.* an independent emirate on the Persian Gulf; under British protection until 1971. 190,000; 8500 sq. mi. (22,000 sq. km). *Cap.:* Doha. Also, **Katar. —Qa·tar′i,** *adj., n.*

CONCISE ETYMOLOGY KEY: <, descended or borrowed from; >, whence; b., blend of, blended; c., cognate with; cf., compare; deriv., derivative; equiv., equivalent; imit., imitative; obl., oblique; r., replacing; s., stem; sp., spelling, spelled; resp., respelling, respelled; trans., translation; ?, origin unknown; *, unattested; ‡, probably earlier than. See the full key inside the front cover.

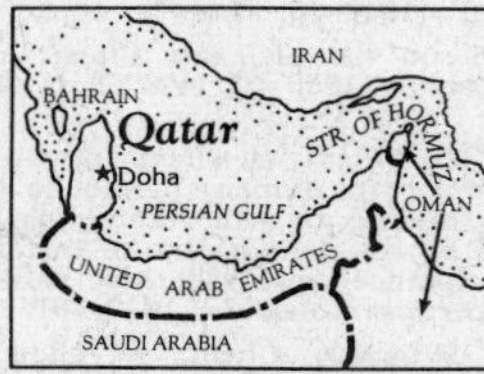

Qaz·vin (kaz vēn′), *n.* a city in NW Iran, NW of Teheran: capital of Persia in the 16th century. 107,000. Also, **Kazvin.**

QB, *Chess.* queen's bishop.

Q.B., Queen's Bench.

q.b., *Football.* quarterback.

Q-boat (kyo͞o′bōt′), *n.* Q-ship.

QBP, *Chess.* queen's bishop's pawn.

Q.C., 1. See **quality control. 2.** Quartermaster Corps. **3.** Queen's Counsel. Also, **QC**

QCD, *Physics.* See **quantum chromodynamics.**

Q-Celt·ic (kyo͞o′sel′tik, -kel′-), *n., adj.* Goidelic. [1940–45]

Q clearance, (in the Nuclear Regulatory Commission) the highest level of security clearance, permitting access to secret information, documents, etc., relating to nuclear research.

q.d., (in prescriptions) every day. [< L *quāque diē*]

q.e., which is. [< L *quod est*]

QED, *Physics.* See **quantum electrodynamics.**

Q.E.D., which was to be shown or demonstrated (used esp. in mathematical proofs). [1810–20; < L *quod erat dēmōnstrandum*]

Q.E.F., which was to be done. [< L *quod erat faciendum*]

Q.F., quick-firing.

Q-fac·tor (kyo͞o′fak′tər), *n.* Q (def. 6). [1960–65]

Q fever, *Pathol.* an acute, influenzalike disease caused by the rickettsia *Coxiella burnetti.* [1935–40; abbrev. of *query*]

Q gauge. See **O gauge** (def. 2).

q.h., (in prescriptions) each hour; every hour. [< L *quāque hōrā*]

Qi (chœ), *n. Pinyin.* Ch'i.

Qi·a·na (kē ä′nə), *Trademark.* a brand of lightweight, lustrous, silklike, synthetic fiber chemically classed as nylon.

Qian·long (chyän′lông′), *n. Pinyin.* See **Ch'ien Lung.**

qib·la (kib′lə), *n. Islam.* the point toward which Muslims turn to pray, esp. the Ka'ba, or House of God, at Mecca. Also, **qib′lah, kibla, kiblah.** [< Ar *qiblah*]

q.i.d., (in prescriptions) four times a day. [< L *quater in diē*]

Qi·lian Shan (chē′lyän′ shän′), *Pinyin.* a mountain range in W China, bordered between Qinghai and Gansu provinces. Also, **Chilien Shan.** Formerly, **Nan Shan.**

Qin (chin), *n. Pinyin.* Ch'in.

Qing (ching), *n. Pinyin.* Ch'ing.

Qing·dao (ching′dou′), *n. Pinyin.* Tsingtao.

Qing Hai (ching′ hī′), *Pinyin.* a lake in W central China, in NE Qinghai province. 2300 sq. mi. (5950 sq. km). Also, **Ch'ing Hai, Tsing Hai.** Also called **Koko Nor.**

Qing·hai (ching′hī′), *n. Pinyin.* a province in W central China. 2,140,000; 269,187 sq. mi. (697,194 sq. km). *Cap.:* Xining. Also, **Ch'inghai, Tsinghai.** Formerly, **Koko Nor.**

Qing·yuan (ching′ywän′), *n. Pinyin.* former name of **Baoding.** Also, **Tsingyuan.**

Qin·huang·dao (chin′hwäng′dou′), *n. Pinyin.* a seaport in NE Hebei province, in NE China, on the Bohai. 186,800. Also, **Chinhuangtao, Chinwangtao.**

Qin Shi Huang Di (chin′ shœ′ hwäng′ dē′), *Pinyin.* Ch'in Shih Huang Ti.

qin·tar (kin tär′), *n.* a money of account of Albania, the 100th part of a lek. Also, **qin·dar** (kin där′). [1925–30; < Albanian]

Qiong·shan (chyông′shän′), *n. Pinyin.* a port on N Hainan island, in S China: chief city of the island. 376,294. Also, **Ch'iungshan, Kiungshan.** Formerly, **Qiongzhou.**

Qiong·zhou (chyông′jō′), *n. Pinyin.* former name of **Qiongshan.** Also, **Chiungchou, Kiungchow.**

Qiong′zhou′ Strait′. See **Hainan Strait.**

Qi·qi·har (chē′chē′här′), *n. Pinyin.* a city in W Heilongjiang province, in NE China. 760,000. Also, **Chichihaerh, Chichihar, Tsitsihaerh, Tsitsihar.**

qirsh (kûrsh), *n., pl.* **qu·rush** (ko͞o ro͞osh′). **1.** a cupronickel coin and monetary unit of Saudi Arabia, the 20th part of a riyal. **2.** a former coin and fractional monetary unit of several Middle Eastern and North African countries. Also, **qursh, gursh, girsh, ghirsh.** [1910–15; < Ar]

Qishm (kish′əm), *n.* an island S of and belonging to Iran, in the Strait of Hormuz. 68 mi. (109 km) long; ab. 510 sq. mi. (1320 sq. km).

Qiu Chu·ji (chyo͞o′ cho͞o′jē′), *Pinyin.* See **Ch'iu Ch'u-chi.**

qiv·i·ut (kē′vē ət, -o͞ot′), *n.* the soft, dense, light-brown woolly undercoat of the musk ox, used in making fabrics. [1955–60; < Inuit]

qi·yas (kē yäs′), *n. Islam.* judgment of an act or belief by application of established principles governing some analogous act or belief. Also, **kiyas.** [< Ar *qiyās* analogy]

Qi·zil Qum (ki zil′ ko͞om′, ko͝om′). See **Kyzyl Kum.**

QKt, *Chess.* queen's knight.

QKtP, *Chess.* queen's knight's pawn.

ql., quintal.

q.l., (in prescriptions) as much as is desired. [< L *quantum libet*]

qlty., quality.

QM, 1. Also, **Q.M.** Quartermaster. **2.** *Physics.* See **quantum mechanics.**

QMC, Quartermaster Corps. Also, **Q.M.C.**

QMG, Quartermaster-General. Also, **Q.M.G., Q.M.Gen.**

QN, *Chess.* queen's knight.

QNP, *Chess.* queen's knight's pawn.

Qom (ko͝om), *n.* a city in NW Iran, SW of Teheran, on the Qom river. 170,000. Also, **Qum.**

qoph (kôf), *n.* koph.

QP, *Chess.* queen's pawn.

q.p., (in prescriptions) as much as you please. Also, **q. pl.** [< L *quantum placet*]

Qq., quartos.

qq., questions.

qq. hor., (in prescriptions) every hour. [< L *quāque hōrā*]

qq. v., (in formal writing) which (words, things, etc.) see. Cf. **q.v.** [< L *quae vidē*]

QR, *Chess.* queen's rook.

qr., *pl.* **qrs.** **1.** farthing. [< L *quadrāns,* pl. *quadrantēs*] **2.** quarter. **3.** quire.

Q-ra·tio (kyōō′rā′shō, -shē ō′), *n.* the ratio of the total market value of a corporation's physical assets, as existing plants and equipment, to the cost of replacing these assets.

QRP, *Chess.* queen's rook's pawn.

q.s., **1.** (in prescriptions) as much as is sufficient; enough. [< L *quantum sufficit*] **2.** See **quarter section.**

Q-ship (kyōō′ship′), *n.* an armed combat ship disguised as a merchant vessel to attract submarines within attack range. Also called **Q-boat.** [1915–20; *Q* a naval classification]

QSO, *Astron.* quasi-stellar object.

QSS, *Astron.* See **quasi-stellar radio source.**

qt., **1.** quantity. **2.** *pl.* **qt., qts.** quart.

q.t., *Informal.* **1.** quiet. **2. on the q.t.,** stealthily; secretly: *to meet someone on the q.t.* Also, **Q.T.** [1905–10]

Q-Tip (kyōō′tip′), *Trademark.* a brand of cotton-tipped swab used esp. for cleansing a small area or for applying medications or cosmetics.

qtly., quarterly.

qto., quarto.

qtr., **1.** quarter. **2.** quarterly.

qty., quantity.

qu., **1.** quart. **2.** quarter. **3.** quarterly. **4.** queen. **5.** query. **6.** question.

qua (kwā, kwä), *adv.* as; as being; in the character or capacity of: *The work of art qua art can be judged by aesthetic criteria only.* [1640–50; < L *quā* fem. abl. sing. of *quī* WHO]

Quaa·lude (kwā′lōōd), *Pharm., Trademark.* a brand of methaqualone.

quack[1] (kwak), *n.* **1.** the harsh, throaty cry of a duck or any similar sound. —*v.i.* **2.** to utter the cry of a duck or a sound resembling it. [1610–20; imit.; cf. D *kwakken,* G *quacken*]

quack[2] (kwak), *n.* **1.** a fraudulent or ignorant pretender to medical skill. **2.** a person who pretends, professionally or publicly, to skill, knowledge, or qualifications he or she does not possess; a charlatan. —*adj.* **3.** being a quack: *a quack psychologist who complicates everyone's problems.* **4.** presented falsely as having curative powers: *quack medicine.* **5.** of, pertaining to, or befitting a quack or quackery: *quack methods.* —*v.t.* **6.** to treat in the manner of a quack. **7.** to advertise or sell with fraudulent claims. [1620–30; short for QUACKSALVER] **—quack′ish,** *adj.* **—quack′ish·ly,** *adv.* **—quack′ish·ness,** *n.*
—Syn. 2. mountebank, phony.

quack·er·y (kwak′ə rē), *n., pl.* **-er·ies.** **1.** the practice or methods of a quack. **2.** an instance of this. [1700–10; QUACK[2] + -ERY]

quack′ grass′, *Inland North and North Midland U.S.* a couch grass, *Agropyron repens,* a pernicious weed in cultivated fields. [1810–20]

quack·sal·ver (kwak′sal′vər), *n.* **1.** a quack doctor. **2.** a charlatan. [1570–80; < early D (now *kwakzalver*); see QUACK[1], SALVE, -ER[1]]

Qua·co (kwä′kōō), *n.* a male day name for Wednesday. See under **day name.**

quad[1] (kwod), *n. Informal.* a quadrangle, as on a college campus. [1810–20; shortened form]

quad[2] (kwod), *n., v.,* **quad·ded, quad·ding.** *Print.* —*n.* **1.** Also called **quadrat.** a piece of type metal of less height than the lettered types, serving to cause a blank in printed matter, used for spacing. —*v.t.* **2.** to space out (matter) by means of quads. [1875–80; short for QUADRAT]

quad[3] (kwod), *n. Informal.* a quadruplet. [1895–1900; shortened form]

quad[4] (kwod), *Informal.* —*adj.* **1.** quadraphonic. —*n.* **2.** quadraphonic sound, or an electronic system for reproducing it: *The recording sounded best in quad.* [by shortening]

quad[5] (kwod), *adj.* **1.** designating or comprising four persons or things: *rates for quad occupancy; a quad-level house.* —*n.* **2.** *Informal.* quadruple occupancy: *Rates are based on quad.* [shortening of QUADRUPLE or words formed with QUADRI-]

quad[6] (kwod), *n. Informal.* quadriplegic: *a special ward for quads.* [by shortening]

quad., **1.** quadrangle. **2.** quadrant.

Quad′ Cit′ies, the cities of Davenport and Bettendorf, Iowa, together with Rock Island and Moline, Illinois.

quad′ left′, (in computer typesetting) flush left.

quad·plex (kwod′pleks′), *adj.* **1.** fourfold; quadruple. —*n.* **2.** Also called **fourplex.** a building having four dwelling or commercial units. [QUAD[5] + -PLEX]

quadr-, var. of **quadri-** before a vowel: *quadrennial.*

quad·ra (kwod′rə), *n., pl.* **-rae** (-rē). *Archit.* a small molding, as a fillet. [1655–65; < L: fillet, side of a square, quadrant section]

quad·ra·ge·nar·i·an (kwod′rə jə nâr′ē ən), *adj.* **1.** 40 years of age. **2.** between the ages of 40 and 50. —*n.* **3.** a person who is 40 years old or whose age falls between 40 and 50. [1830–40; < L *quadrāgēnāri(us)* consisting of forty (*quadrāgēn(ī)* forty each + *-ārius* -ARY) + -AN]

Quad·ra·ges·i·ma (kwod′rə jes′ə mə), *n.* the first Sunday in Lent. [1350–1400; ME < ML *quadrāgēsima,* short for L *quadrāgēsima diēs* fortieth day]

Quad·ra·ges·i·mal (kwod′rə jes′ə məl), *adj.* **1.** of, pertaining to, or suitable for Lent; Lenten. **2.** (*sometimes l.c.*) lasting 40 days, as the fast of Lent. [1620–30; QUADRAGESIM(A) + -AL[1]]

quad·ran·gle (kwod′rang′gəl), *n.* **1.** a plane figure having four angles and four sides, as a square. **2.** a square or quadrangular space or court that is surrounded by a building or buildings, as on a college campus. **3.** the building or buildings around such a space or court. **4.** the area shown on one of the standard topographic map sheets published by the U.S. Geological Survey: approximately 17 mi. (27 km) north to south and from 11 to 15 mi. (17 to 24 km) east to west. [1400–50; late ME < LL *quadrangulum,* n. use of neut. of L *quadrangulus, quadriangulus* four-cornered. See QUADR-, ANGLE] **—quad′ran′gled,** *adj.*

quad·ran·gu·lar (kwo drang′gyə lər), *adj.* having four angles and four sides; having the shape of a quadrangle. [1585–95; < LL *quadrangulāris,* equiv. to *quadrangul(um)* QUADRANGLE + *-āris* -AR[1]] **—quad·ran′·gu·lar·ly,** *adv.* **—quad·ran′gu·lar·ness,** *n.*

quad·rans (kwod′ranz), *n., pl.* **quad·ran·tes** (kwodran′tēz). a bronze coin of ancient Rome, the fourth part of an as. [< L *quadrāns* lit., fourth part]

quad·rant (kwod′rənt), *n.* **1.** a quarter of a circle; an arc of 90°. **2.** the area included between such an arc and two radii drawn one to each extremity. **3.** something shaped like a quarter of a circle, as a part of a machine. **4.** *Geom., Astron.* one of the four parts into which a plane, as the face of a heavenly body, is divided by two perpendicular lines, numbered counterclockwise from upper right: *the first quadrant of the moon.* **5.** an instrument, usually containing a graduated arc of 90°, used in astronomy, navigation, etc., for measuring altitudes. **6.** *Astrol.* one of the four quarters of the horoscope: determined by the ascendant, nadir, descendant, and midheaven and numbered counterclockwise from the ascendant. **7.** *Furniture.* one of two metal sliding pieces, of quadrant form, used to support the fall front of a desk from above. [1350–1400; ME < L *quadrant-* (s. of *quadrāns*) fourth part] **—quad·ran·tal** (kwo dran′tl), *adj.* **—quad′rant·like′,** *adj.*

quadran′tal correc′tor, *Naut.* either of two soft-iron spheres attached to each side of a binnacle, intended to correct the compass deviation **(quadran′tal devia′·tion)** resulting from magnetism from ferrous metal in a ship. See diag. under **binnacle**[1].

Quad·ran·tids (kwo dran′tidz), *n.* (*used with a plural v.*) *Astron.* a collection of meteors comprising a meteor shower **(Quadran′tid me′teor show′er)** visible around January 31 and having its apparent origin in the constellation Boötes. [1875–80; < NL *Quadrant-* (s. of *Quadrāns,* in *Quadrāns* (*Mūrālis*) (mural) quadrant, obs. constellation name) + -ID[1] + -S[3]]

quad·ra·phon·ic (kwod′rə fon′ik), *adj.* of, noting, or pertaining to the recording and reproduction of sound over four separate transmission or direct reproduction channels instead of the customary two of the stereo system: *a quadraphonic recording.* Also, **four-channel, quadriphonic, quad·ra·son·ic** (kwod′rə son′ik). Cf. **monophonic, stereophonic.** [1965–70; *quadra-,* var. of QUADRI- + *-phonic,* as in STEREOPHONIC]

qua·draph·o·ny (kwo draf′ə nē), *n.* high-fidelity sound reproduction involving signals transmitted through four different channels. Also called **quad·ra·phon·ics** (kwod′rə fon′iks), **quadriphonics, quad·ra·son·ics** (kwod′rə son′iks), **quadrisonics.** [1965–70; *quadra-,* var. of QUADRI- + -PHONY]

quad·ra·ple·gic (kwod′rə plē′jik, -plej′ik), *adj.* quadriplegic.

quad·rat (kwod′rət), *n.* **1.** *Print.* quad[2] (def. 1). **2.** *Ecol.* a square or rectangular plot of land marked off for the study of plants and animals. [1675–85; var. of QUADRATE]

quad·rate (*adj., n.* kwod′rit, -rāt; *v.* kwod′rāt), *adj., n., v.,* **-rat·ed, -rat·ing.** —*adj.* **1.** square or rectangular. **2.** *Zool.* of or pertaining to the quadrate. **3.** *Heraldry.* (of a cross) having an enlarged square at the junction of the limbs: *a cross quadrate.* —*n.* **4.** a square. **5.** something square or rectangular. **6.** *Zool.* one of a pair of bones in the skulls of many lower vertebrates, to which the lower jaw is articulated. —*v.t.* **7.** to cause to conform or harmonize; adapt. —*v.i.* **8.** to agree; conform. [1350–1400; ME *quadrat* (n. and adj.) < L *quadrātus* (ptp. of *quadrāre* to make square)]

quad·rat·ic (kwo drat′ik), *adj.* **1.** square. **2.** *Algebra.* involving the square and no higher power of the unknown quantity; of the second degree. —*n.* **3.** a quadratic polynomial or equation. [1650–60; QUADRATE + -IC] **—quad·rat′i·cal·ly,** *adv.*

quadrat′ic equa′tion, *Math.* an equation containing a single variable of degree 2. Its general form is $ax^2 + bx + c = 0$, where x is the variable and a, b, and c are constants ($a \neq 0$). [1680–90]

quadrat′ic form′, *Math.* a polynomial all of whose terms are of degree 2 in two or more variables, as $5x^2 - 2xy + 3y^2$. [1855–60]

quadrat′ic for′mula, *Math.* the formula for determining the roots of a quadratic equation from its coefficients: $x = (-b \pm \sqrt{b^2 - 4ac})/2a$.

quadrat′ic res′idue, *Math.* a number x that is relatively prime to a given integer y and for which a number z exists whose square gives the same remainder as x when divided by y.

quad·rat·ics (kwo drat′iks), *n.* (*used with a singular v.*) the branch of algebra that deals with quadratic equations. [1675–85; see QUADRATIC, -ICS]

quad·ra·ture (kwod′rə chər, -chŏŏr′), *n.* **1.** the act of squaring. **2.** *Math.* **a.** the act or process of finding a square equal in area to a given surface, esp. a surface bounded by a curve. **b.** the act or process of finding an area or calculating an integral, esp. by numerical methods. **c.** a definite integral. **3.** *Astron.* **a.** the situation of two heavenly bodies when their longitudes differ by 90°. **b.** either of the two points in the orbit of a body, as the moon, midway between the syzygies. **c.** (of the moon) those points or moments at which a half moon is visible. **4.** *Electronics.* the relation between two signals having the same frequency that differ in phase by 90°. [1545–55; < L *quadrātūra,* equiv. to *quadrāt(us)* (ptp. of *quadrāre;* see QUADRATE) + *-ūra* -URE]

quad′rature of the cir′cle, *Math.* the insoluble problem of constructing, by the methods of Euclidean geometry, a square equal in area to a given circle. Also called **squaring the circle.** [1590–1600]

quad·rel (kwod′rəl), *n.* a square stone, brick, or tile. [1680–90; < It *quadrello,* dim. of *quadro* square < L *quadrum;* see -ELLE]

quad·ren·ni·al (kwo dren′ē əl), *adj.* **1.** occurring every four years: *a quadrennial festival.* **2.** of or lasting for four years: *a quadrennial period.* —*n.* **3.** an event occurring every four years, as an anniversary or its celebration. [1640–50; earlier *quadriennial* < L *quadrienni(um)* (see QUADRENNIUM) + -AL[1]] **—quad·ren′ni·al·ly,** *adv.*

quad·ren·ni·um (kwo dren′ē əm), *n., pl.* **quad·ren·ni·ums, quad·ren·ni·a** (kwo dren′ē ə). a period of four years. [1815–25; < NL, alter. of L *quadriennium,* equiv. to *quadri-* QUADRI- + *-enn-,* comb. form of *annus* year (cf. ANNUAL) + *-ium* -IUM]

quadri-, a combining form meaning "four," used in the formation of compound words: *quadrilateral.* Also, **quadru-;** *esp. before a vowel,* **quadr-.** [< L; akin to *quattuor* FOUR]

quad·ri·ad (kwod′rē ad′), *n.* a group of four, esp. a group of four persons with an interest or task in common. [QUADRI- + -AD[1]]

quad·ric (kwod′rik), *Math.* —*adj.* **1.** of the second degree (said esp. of functions with more than two variables). —*n.* **2.** a quadric function. **3.** a surface such as an ellipsoid or paraboloid as defined by a second-degree equation in three real variables. [1855–60; QUADR- + -IC]

quad·ri·cen·ten·ni·al (kwod′rə sen ten′ē əl), *adj.* **1.** of, pertaining to, or marking the completion of a period of four hundred years. —*n.* **2.** a quadricentennial anniversary. **3.** its celebration. [1880–85; QUADRI- + CENTENNIAL]

quad·ri·ceps (kwod′rə seps′), *n., pl.* **-ceps·es** (-sep′siz), **-ceps.** *Anat.* a large muscle in front of the thigh, the action of which extends the leg or bends the hip joint. [1830–40; < NL, equiv. to *quadri-* QUADRI- + *-ceps;* see BICEPS] **—quad·ri·cip·i·tal** (kwod′rə sip′i tl), *adj.*

quad′ric sur′face, a three-dimensional surface whose equation is a quadratic equation. [1880–85]

quad·ri·cy·cle (kwod′rə sī′kəl), *n.* a vehicle similar to the bicycle and tricycle but having four wheels. [1880–85; QUADRI- + CYCLE] **—quad′ri·cy′cler, quad′·ri·cy′clist,** *n.*

quad·ri·en·ni·al (kwod′rē en′ē əl), *adj.* quadrennial. **—quad′ri·en′ni·al·ly,** *adv.*

quad·ri·en·ni·um (kwod′rē en′ē əm), *n., pl.* **-ni·ums, -ni·a** (-nē ə). quadrennium.

quad·ri·fid (kwod′rə fid), *adj.* cleft into four parts or lobes. [1655–65; < L *quadrifidus.* See QUADRI-, -FID]

quad·ri·ga (kwo drē′gə, -drī′-), *n., pl.* **quad·ri·gae** (kwo drē′gī, -drī′jē). *Class. Antiq.* a two-wheeled chariot drawn by four horses harnessed abreast. Cf. **biga, triga.** [1720–30; < L *quadriga,* earlier pl. *quadrigae,* contr. of *quadrijugae* a team of four; cf. QUADRI-, YOKE]

quad·ri·ga·tus (kwod′ri gā′təs), *n., pl.* **-ti** (-tī). a silver coin of ancient Rome, bearing an image of Jupiter in a quadriga on the reverse. [< L, equiv. to *quadrig(a)* QUADRIGA + *-ātus* -ATE[1]]

quad′ right′, (in computer typesetting) flush right.

quad·ri·lat·er·al (kwod′rə lat′ər əl), *adj.* **1.** having four sides. —*n.* **2.** a plane figure having four sides and four angles. **3.** something of this form. **4.** *Geom.* **a.** a figure formed by four straight lines that have six points of intersection. **b.** a polygon with four sides. **5.** the space enclosed between and defended by four fortresses. [1640–50; < L *quadrilater(us)* four-sided + -AL[1]. See QUADRI-, LATERAL] **—quad′ri·lat′er·al·ly,** *adv.* **—quad′ri·lat′er·al·ness,** *n.*

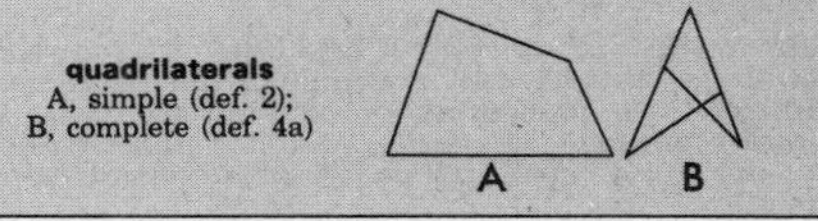

quadrilaterals
A, simple (def. 2);
B, complete (def. 4a)

quad·ri·lin·gual (kwod′rə ling′gwəl *or, Can.,* -ling′gyōō əl), *adj.* using or involving four languages: *a quadrilingual person; a quadrilingual translation of the Bible.* [1960–65; QUADRI- + LINGUAL]

quad·ri·lit·er·al (kwod′rə lit′ər əl), *adj.* **1.** using or consisting of four letters. —*n.* **2.** a quadriliteral word or root. [1765–75; QUADRI- + LITERAL]

quad·rille[1] (kwo dril′, kwə-, kə-), *n.* **1.** a square dance for four couples, consisting of five parts or movements, each complete in itself. **2.** the music for such a dance. [1730–40; < F < Sp *cuadrilla* company, troop, dim. of *cuadra* square < L *quadra*]

quad·rille[2] (kwo dril′, kwə-, kə-), *n.* a card game played by four persons. [1720–30; < F < Sp *cuartillo,* dim. of *cuarto* FOURTH < L *quartus*]

quad·rille[3] (kwo dril′, kwə-, kə-), *adj.* ruled in squares, as graph paper. [1880–85; < F *quadrillé,* ptp. of *quadriller* to rule in squares, deriv. of *quadrille* lozenge < Sp *cuadrilla;* see QUADRILLE[1]]

CONCISE PRONUNCIATION KEY: *act, cāpe, dâre, pärt; set, ēqual; if, īce; ox, ōver, ôrder, oil, bŏŏk, bōōt, out; up, ûrge; child; sing; shoe; thin, that;* zh *as in treasure.* ə = *a* as in *alone, e* as in *system, i* as in *easily, o* as in *gallop, u* as in *circus;* ᵊ as in *fire* (fīᵊr), *hour* (ouᵊr). l and n can serve as syllabic consonants, as in *cradle* (krād′l), and *button* (but′n). See the full key inside the front cover.

quad•ril•lion (kwo dril′yən), *n., pl.* **-lions,** (*as after a numeral*) **-lion,** *adj.* —*n.* **1.** a cardinal number represented in the U.S. by 1 followed by 15 zeros, and in Great Britain by 1 followed by 24 zeros. —*adj.* **2.** amounting to one quadrillion in number. [1665–75; QUADR- + *-illion* (as in *million*)] —**quad•ril′lionth,** *n., adj.*

quad•ri•no•mi•al (kwod′rə nō′mē əl), *Algebra.* —*adj.* **1.** consisting of four terms. —*n.* **2.** a quadrinomial expression. [QUADRI- + (BI)NOMIAL]

quad•ri•par•tite (kwod′rə pär′tīt), *adj.* **1.** divided into or consisting of four parts. **2.** involving four participants: *a quadripartite treaty.* [1400–50; late ME < L *quadripartītus.* See QUADRI-, PARTITE] —**quad′ri•par′•tite•ly,** *adv.*

quad•ri•phon•ic (kwod′rə fon′ik), *adj.* quadraphonic.

quad•ri•phon•ics (kwod′rə fon′iks), *n.* (*used with a singular v.*) quadraphony. Also called **quad•ri•son•ics** (kwod′rə son′iks). [see QUADRAPHONIC, -ICS]

quad•ri•ple•gi•a (kwod′rə plē′jē ə, -jə), *n. Pathol.* paralysis of all four limbs or of the entire body below the neck. Also called **tetraplegia.** [1920–25; QUADRI- + -PLEGIA]

quad•ri•ple•gic (kwod′rə plē′jik, -plej′ik), *n. Pathol.* a person with quadriplegia. [1960–65; QUADRIPLEG(IA) + -IC]

quad•ri•reme (kwod′rə rēm′), *n.* (in classical antiquity) a galley having four banks of oars. [1590–1600; < L *quadrirēmis,* equiv. to *quadri-* QUADRI- + *-rēmis* (deriv. of *rēmus* oar)]

quad•ri•sect (kwod′rə sekt′), *v.t.* to divide (something) into four equal parts. [1800–10; QUADRI- + -SECT] —**quad′ri•sec′tion,** *n.*

quad•ri•syl•la•ble (kwod′rə sil′ə bəl), *n.* a word of four syllables. [1650–60; QUADRI- + SYLLABLE] —**quad•ri•syl•lab•ic** (kwod′rə si lab′ik), **quad′ri•syl•lab′i•cal,** *adj.*

quad•ri•va•lent (kwod′rə vā′lənt, kwo driv′ə-), *adj. Chem.* **1.** having a valence of four; tetravalent. **2.** exhibiting four different valences, as antimony with valences of 5, 4, 3, and −3. [1860–65; QUADRI- + -VALENT] —**quad′ri•va′lence, quad′ri•va′len•cy,** *n.* —**quad′ri•va′lent•ly,** *adv.*

quad•riv•i•al (kwo driv′ē əl), *adj.* **1.** having four ways or roads meeting in a point. **2.** (of ways or roads) leading in four directions. **3.** of or pertaining to the quadrivium. [1375–1425; late ME < ML *quadriviālis,* equiv. to LL *quadrivi(um)* QUADRIVIUM + *-ālis* -AL[1]]

quad•riv•i•um (kwo driv′ē əm), *n., pl.* **quad•riv•i•a** (kwo driv′ē ə). (during the Middle Ages) the more advanced division of the seven liberal arts, comprising arithmetic, geometry, astronomy, and music. Cf. **trivium.** [1795–1805; < LL, special use of L *quadrivium* place where four ways meet; see QUADRI-, VIA, -IUM]

quad•ro•min•i•um (kwod′rə min′ē əm), *n.* a building consisting of four individually owned apartments or living units. [1970–75; QUADR- + (COND)OMINIUM]

quad•roon (kwo dro͞on′), *n.* a person having one-fourth black ancestry; the offspring of a mulatto and a white. [1640–50; alter. of Sp *cuarterón,* deriv. of *cuarto* FOURTH < L *quartus;* see -OON]

quadru-, var. of **quadri-.** [< L: var. of *quadri-* before labial consonants, as in *quadrupēs* QUADRUPED, *quadruplex* QUADRUPLEX]

quad•ru•mane (kwod′ro͝o mān′), *n.* a quadrumanous animal, as a monkey. [1820–30; < NL *quadrumana,* n. use of fem. of *quadrumanus* QUADRUMANOUS]

quad•ru•ma•nous (kwo dro͞o′mə nəs), *adj.* four-handed; having all four feet adapted for use as hands, as monkeys. [1690–1700; < NL *quadrumanus,* equiv. to L *quadru-* QUADRU- + *-manus,* adj. deriv. of *manus* hand (cf. MANUAL)]

quad•rum•vir (kwo drum′vər), *n.* a member of a quadrumvirate. [1780–90; back formation from QUADRUMVIRATE, by analogy with TRIUMVIR]

quad•rum•vi•rate (kwo drum′vər it, -və rāt′), *n.* a governing or managing group, coalition, or the like, of four persons. [1745–55; QUADR- + *-umvirate* (as in TRIUMVIRATE)]

quad•ru•ped (kwod′ro͝o ped′), *adj.* **1.** four-footed. —*n.* **2.** an animal, esp. a mammal, having four feet. [1640–50; < L *quadruped-* (s. of *quadrupēs*), equiv. to *quadru-* QUADRU- + *-ped-* -PED] —**quad•ru•pe•dal** (kwo dro͞o′pi dl, kwod′ro͝o ped′l), *adj.* —**quad′ru•ped′•ism,** *n.*

quad•ru•ple (kwo dro͞o′pəl, -drup′əl, kwod′ro͝o pəl), *adj., n., v.,* **-pled, -pling.** —*adj.* **1.** fourfold; consisting of four parts: *a quadruple alliance.* **2.** four times as great. **3.** *Music.* having four beats to a measure. —*n.* **4.** a number, amount, etc., four times as great as another. **5.** something, as a series of acrobatic somersaults, made up of four clearly defined parts or stages: *the first trapeze artist to perform a quadruple successfully.* —*v.t., v.i.* **6.** to make or become four times as great: *To serve 24 people, quadruple the recipe. My savings quadrupled in 20 years.* [1325–75; ME < L *quadruplus;* cf. QUADRU-, DUPLE] —**quad•ru′ple•ness,** *n.* —**quad•ru′ply,** *adv.*

quadru′ple run′, *Cribbage.* a set of five cards consisting of a three-card run plus two other cards that duplicate different denominations in the run, as 5,5,6,6,7, worth 16 points.

quad•ru•plet (kwo drup′lit, -dro͞o′plit, kwod′ro͝o plit), *n.* **1.** any group or combination of four. **2. quadruplets,** four children or offspring born of one pregnancy. **3.** one of four such children or offspring. **4.** *Music.* a group of four notes of equal value performed in the time normally taken for three. [1780–90; QUADRUPLE + -ET (modeled on *triplet*)]

quadru′ple time′, *Music.* **1.** a measure consisting of four beats or pulses with accent on the first and third. **2.** the rhythm created by use of this measure. [1895–1900]

quad•ru•plex (kwod′ro͝o pleks′, kwo dro͞o′pleks), *adj.* **1.** fourfold; quadruple. **2.** noting or pertaining to a system of telegraphy by which four messages may be transmitted simultaneously over one wire or communications channel. [1870–75; < L; see QUADRU-, -PLEX]

quad•ru•pli•cate (*n., adj.* kwo dro͞o′pli kit; *v.* kwo-dro͞o′pli kāt′), *n., adj., v.,* **-cat•ed, -cat•ing.** —*n.* **1.** one of four copies or identical items, esp. copies of typewritten material. **2. in quadruplicate,** in four identical copies. —*adj.* **3.** consisting of four identical parts. **4.** pertaining to a fourth item or copy of something. —*v.t.* **5.** to produce or copy in quadruplicate. **6.** to make four times as great. [1650–60; < L *quadruplicātus* (ptp. of *quadruplicāre*), equiv. to *quadruplic-* (s. of *quadruplex* QUADRUPLEX) + *-ātus* -ATE[1]] —**quad•ru′pli•ca′tion, quad•ru•pli•ca•ture** (kwo dro͞o′pli kə chər), *n.*

quad•ru•plic•i•ty (kwod′ro͝o plis′i tē), *n.* **1.** the state or fact of being quadruple or fourfold. **2.** *Astrol.* the division of the signs of the zodiac into three groups of four signs each, the cardinal signs, the fixed signs, and the mutable signs, with each sign separated from the next nearest within the group by 90 degrees of the ecliptic. [1580–90; < L *quadruplic-,* s. of *quadruplex* QUADRUPLEX + -ITY, on the model of DUPLICITY, etc.]

quads (kwodz), *n.pl. Informal.* quadriceps muscles. [by shortening]

quae•re (kwēr′ē), *Archaic.* —*v. imperative.* **1.** ask; inquire (used to introduce or suggest a question). —*n.* **2.** a query or question. [1525–35; < L, 2nd person sing. impv. of *quaerere* to seek, ask]

quaes•tor (kwes′tər, kwē′stər), *n. Rom. Hist.* **1.** one of two subordinates of the consuls serving as public prosecutors in certain criminal cases. **2.** (later) one of the public magistrates in charge of the state funds, as treasury officers or those attached to the consuls and provincial governors. Also, **questor.** [1350–1400; ME *questor* < L *quaestor,* equiv. to *quaes-,* base of *quaerere* to seek + *-tor* -TOR] —**quaes•to•ri•al** (kwe stôr′ē əl, -stōr′-, kwē-), *adj.* —**quaes′tor•ship′,** *n.*

quaff (kwof, kwaf, kwôf), *v.i.* **1.** to drink a beverage, esp. an intoxicating one, copiously and with hearty enjoyment. —*v.t.* **2.** to drink (a beverage) copiously and heartily: *We spent the whole evening quaffing ale.* —*n.* **3.** an act or instance of quaffing. **4.** a beverage quaffed. [1515–25; orig. uncert.] —**quaff′er,** *n.*
—**Syn. 1.** swallow, gulp, swig, guzzle.

quag (kwag, kwog), *n.* a quagmire. [1580–90; expressive word, obscurely akin to QUAKE]

quag•ga (kwag′ə, kwog′ə), *n.* an extinct equine mammal, *Equus quagga,* of southern Africa, related to and resembling the zebra, but striped only on the forepart of the body and the head. [1775–85; < Afrik (now sp. *kwagga*) < Khoikhoi, first recorded as *quácha* (1691); said to be imit. of the animal's yelp]

quag•gy (kwag′ē, kwog′ē), *adj.,* **-gi•er, -gi•est. 1.** of the nature of or resembling a quagmire; marshy; boggy. **2.** soft or flabby: *quaggy flesh.* [1600–10; QUAG + -Y[1]] —**quag′gi•ness,** *n.*

quag•mire (kwag′mīər′, kwog′-), *n.* **1.** an area of miry or boggy ground whose surface yields under the tread; a bog. **2.** a situation from which extrication is very difficult: *a quagmire of financial indebtedness.* **3.** anything soft or flabby. [1570–80; QUAG + MIRE] —**quag′mir′y,** *adj.*
—**Syn. 2.** predicament, dilemma, quandary, scrape, jam.

qua•hog (kwô′hôg, -hog, kwō-, kō′-, kwə hôg′, -hog′), *n.* an edible clam, *Venus (Mercenaria) mercenaria,* inhabiting waters along the Atlantic coast, having a relatively thick shell. Also, **qua′haug.** [1745–55, *Amer.;* < Narragansett (E sp.) *poquaûhock*]

quaich (kwākh), *n.* a Scottish drinking cup of the 17th and 18th centuries having a shallow bowl with two or three flat handles. [1665–75; < ScotGael *cuach*]

Quai d'Or•say (ke dôr se′; *Eng.* kā′ dôr sā′, kwā′), **1.** the quay along the south bank of the Seine in Paris, on which are located the Ministry of Foreign Affairs and other French government offices. **2.** the French Ministry of Foreign Affairs.

bobwhite quail,
Colinus virginianus,
length 9 in. (23 cm)

quail[1] (kwāl), *n., pl.* **quails,** (*esp. collectively*) **quail. 1.** a small, migratory, gallinaceous game bird, *Coturnix coturnix,* of the Old World. **2.** any of several other birds of the genus *Coturnix* and allied genera. **3.** any of various New World gallinaceous game birds of the genus *Colinus* and allied genera, esp. the bobwhite. **4.** *Slang.* a woman or girl. [1300–50; ME *quaille* < OF < Gmc; cf. D *kwakkel* quail, MD, MLG *quackele;* akin to QUACK[1]] —**quail′like′,** *adj.*

quail[2] (kwāl), *v.i.* to lose heart or courage in difficulty or danger; shrink with fear. [1400–50; late ME < MD *quelen, queilen*]
—**Syn.** recoil, flinch, blench, cower. See **wince.**

quail-brush (kwāl′brush′), *n.* a salt-tolerant, silvery gray shrub, *Atriplex lentiformis breweri,* of the goosefoot family, native to southern California. [1920–25, *Amer.*]

quail′ clock′, a clock that announces the hours by a sound resembling that of a quail. [1895–1900]

quail′ dove′, any of several tropical American pigeons of the genera *Starnoenas* or *Geotrygon.* [1890–95, *Amer.*]

quaint (kwānt), *adj.,* **-er, -est. 1.** having an old-fashioned attractiveness or charm; oddly picturesque: *a quaint old house.* **2.** strange, peculiar, or unusual in an interesting, pleasing, or amusing way: *a quaint sense of humor.* **3.** skillfully or cleverly made. **4.** *Obs.* wise; skilled. [1175–1225; ME *queinte* < OF, var. of *cointe* clever, pleasing << L *cognitus* known (ptp. of *cognōscere;* see COGNITION)] —**quaint′ly,** *adv.* —**quaint′•ness,** *n.*
—**Syn. 1.** antiquated, archaic. **2.** curious, uncommon.
—**Ant. 2.** ordinary.

quake (kwāk), *v.,* **quaked, quak•ing,** *n.* —*v.i.* **1.** (of persons) to shake or tremble from cold, weakness, fear, anger, or the like: *He spoke boldly even though his legs were quaking.* **2.** (of things) to shake or tremble, as from shock, internal convulsion, or instability: *The earth suddenly began to quake.* —*n.* **3.** an earthquake. **4.** a trembling or tremulous agitation. [bef. 900; ME; OE *cwacian* to shake, tremble] —**quak′ing•ly,** *adv.*
—**Syn. 1.** shudder. See **shiver**[1]. **2.** quiver.

quake•proof (kwāk′pro͞of′), *adj.* **1.** designed or built to withstand the destructive forces of an earthquake. —*v.t.* **2.** to make quakeproof. [1935–40; QUAKE + -PROOF]

Quak•er (kwā′kər), *n.* a popular name for a member of the Religious Society of Friends. [1590–1600; QUAKE + -ER[1]] —**Quak′er•ish, Quak′er•like′,** *adj.*

Quak•er•ess (kwā′kər is), *n.* a woman or girl who is a Quaker. [1715–25; QUAKER + -ESS]
—**Usage.** See **-ess.**

Quak′er gun′, a dummy gun, as on a ship or fort: so called in allusion to the Quakers' opposition to war. [1800–10, *Amer.*]

Quak•er•ism (kwā′kə riz′əm), *n.* the beliefs, principles, and practices of Quakers. [1650–60; QUAKER + -ISM]

Quak•er-la•dies (kwā′kər lā′dēz), *n.* (*used with a plural v.*) bluet (def. 1). [1870–75, *Amer.*]

Quak•er•ly (kwā′kər lē), *adj.* **1.** like a Quaker. —*adv.* **2.** in the manner of the Quakers. [1675–85; QUAKER + -LY]

Quak′er meet′ing, 1. a meeting of Quakers, at which all members, except those moved to speak, remain silent. **2.** *Informal.* a gathering at which there is considerable silence. [1650–60]

quak′ing as′pen. See under **aspen** (def. 1). [1785–95]

quak′ing grass′, any of several grasses of the genus *Briza,* having spikelets with slender, drooping stalks. [1590–1600]

quak•y (kwā′kē), *adj.,* **quak•i•er, quak•i•est.** tending to quake; shaky or tremulous. [1860–65; QUAKE + -Y[1]] —**quak′i•ly,** *adv.* —**quak′i•ness,** *n.*

qua•le (kwä′lē, -lā, kwā′lē), *n., pl.* **-li•a** (-lē ə). *Philos.* **1.** a quality, as bitterness, regarded as an independent object. **2.** a sense-datum or feeling having a distinctive quality. [1665–75; < L *quāle,* neut. sing. of *quālis* of what sort]

qual•i•fi•a•ble (kwol′ə fī′ə bəl), *adj.* capable of being qualified: *qualifiable statements.* [1605–15; QUALIFY + -ABLE]

qual•i•fi•ca•tion (kwol′ə fi kā′shən), *n.* **1.** a quality, accomplishment, etc., that fits a person for some function, office, or the like. **2.** a circumstance or condition required by law or custom for getting, having, or exercising a right, holding an office, or the like. **3.** the act of qualifying; state of being qualified. **4.** modification, limitation, or restriction: *to endorse a plan without qualification.* **5.** an instance of this: *He protected his argument with several qualifications.* [1535–45; < ML *quālificātiōn-* (s. of *quālificātiō*), equiv. to *quālificāt(us)* (ptp. of *quālificāre* to QUALIFY) + *-iōn-* -ION]
—**Syn. 4.** reservation, stipulation, condition.

qual•i•fi•ca•tor (kwol′ə fi kā′tər), *n. Rom. Cath. Ch.* (in an ecclesiastical court) an officer charged with examining cases and preparing them for trial. [1680–90; < ML *quālificātor,* equiv. to *quālificā(re)* to QUALIFY + L *-tor* -TOR]

qual•i•fied (kwol′ə fīd′), *adj.* **1.** having the qualities, accomplishments, etc., that fit a person for some function, office, or the like. **2.** having the qualities, accomplishments, etc., required by law or custom for getting, having, or exercising a right, holding an office, or the like. **3.** modified, limited, or restricted in some way: *a qualified endorsement.* [1550–60; QUALIFY + -ED[2]] —**qual′i•fied′ly,** *adv.* —**qual′i•fied′ness,** *n.*
—**Syn. 1.** able, capable, competent, fitted. —**Ant.** unqualified.

qual•i•fi•er (kwol′ə fī′ər), *n.* **1.** a person or thing that qualifies. **2.** *Gram.* **a.** a word that qualifies the meaning of another, as an adjective or adverb; modifier. **b.** an adverb that modifies adjectives or other adverbs and typically expresses degree or intensity, as *very, somewhat,* or *quite.* [1555–65; QUALIFY + -ER[1]]

qual•i•fy (kwol′ə fī′), *v.,* **-fied, -fy•ing.** —*v.t.* **1.** to provide with proper or necessary skills, knowledge, credentials, etc.; make competent: *to qualify oneself for a job.* **2.** to modify or limit in some way; make less strong or positive: *to qualify an endorsement.* **3.** *Gram.* to modify. **4.** to make less violent, severe, or unpleasant; moderate; mitigate. **5.** to attribute some quality or qualities to; characterize, call, or name: *She cannot qualify his attitude as either rational or irrational.* **6.** to modify or alter the flavor or strength of: *He qualified his coffee with a few drops of brandy.* **7.** *Law.* to certify as legally competent. —*v.i.* **8.** to be fitted or competent

for something. **9.** to get authority, license, power, etc., as by fulfilling required conditions, taking an oath, etc. **10.** *Sports.* to demonstrate the required ability in an initial or preliminary contest: *He qualified in the trials.* **11.** to fire a rifle or pistol on a target range for a score high enough to achieve a rating of marksman, sharpshooter, or expert. **12.** *Mil.* to pass a practical test in gunnery. **13.** *Law.* to perform the actions necessary to acquire legal power or capacity: *By filing a bond and taking an oath he qualified as executor.* [1525–35; < ML *quālificāre,* equiv. to L *quāl(is)* of what sort + *-ificāre* -IFY] —**qual•i•fi•ca•to•ry** (kwol′ə fi kə tôr′ē, -tōr′ē), *adj.* —**qual′i•fy′ing•ly,** *adv.*
—**Syn. 1.** fit, suit, adapt, prepare, equip. **2.** narrow, restrict. See **modify. 4.** meliorate, soften, temper, reduce, diminish. **5.** designate, label.

qual•i•ta•tive (kwol′i tā′tiv), *adj.* pertaining to or concerned with quality or qualities. [1600–10; < LL *quālitātīvus,* equiv. to *quālitāt-* (s. of *quālitās*) QUALITY + *-īvus* -IVE] —**qual′i•ta′tive•ly,** *adv.*

qual′itative anal′ysis, *Chem.* the analysis of a substance in order to ascertain the nature of its chemical constituents. Cf. **quantitative analysis.** [1835–45]

qual•i•ty (kwol′i tē), *n., pl.* **-ties,** *adj.* —*n.* **1.** an essential or distinctive characteristic, property, or attribute: *the chemical qualities of alcohol.* **2.** character or nature, as belonging to or distinguishing a thing: *the quality of a sound.* **3.** character with respect to fineness, or grade of excellence: *food of poor quality; silks of fine quality.* **4.** high grade; superiority; excellence: *wood grain of quality.* **5.** a personality or character trait: *kindness is one of her many good qualities.* **6.** native excellence or superiority. **7.** an accomplishment or attainment. **8.** good or high social position: *a man of quality.* **9.** the superiority or distinction associated with high social position. **10.** *Acoustics.* the texture of a tone, dependent on its overtone content, that distinguishes it from others of the same pitch and loudness. **11.** *Phonet.* the tonal color, or timbre, that characterizes a particular vowel sound. **12.** *Logic.* the character of a proposition as affirmative or negative. **13.** *Thermodynam.* the proportion or percentage of vapor in a mixture of liquid and vapor, as wet steam. **14.** social status or position. **15.** a person of high social position: *He's quality, that one is.* —*adj.* **16.** of or having superior quality: *quality paper.* **17.** producing or providing products or services of high quality or merit: *a quality publisher.* **18.** of or occupying high social status: *a quality family.* **19.** marked by a concentrated expenditure of involvement, concern, or commitment: *Counselors are urging that working parents try to spend more quality time with their children.* [1250–1300; ME *qualite* < OF < L *quālitās,* equiv. to *quāl(is)* of what sort + *-itās* -ITY] —**qual′i•ty•less,** *adj.*
—**Syn. 1.** trait, character, feature. QUALITY, ATTRIBUTE, PROPERTY agree in meaning a particular characteristic (of a person or thing). A QUALITY is a characteristic, innate or acquired, that, in some particular, determines the nature and behavior of a person or thing: *naturalness as a quality; the quality of meat.* An ATTRIBUTE was originally a quality attributed, usually to a person or something personified; more recently it has meant a fundamental or innate characteristic: *an attribute of God; attributes of a logical mind.* PROPERTY applies only to things; it means a characteristic belonging specifically in the constitution of, or found (invariably) in, the behavior of a thing: *physical properties of uranium or of limestone.* **3.** nature, kind, grade, sort, condition.

qual′ity cir′cle, a group of workers performing similar duties who meet periodically to discuss work-related problems, offer suggestions for improved production or product quality, etc. [1975–80]

qual′ity control′, a system for verifying and maintaining a desired level of quality in a product or process by careful planning, use of proper equipment, continued inspection, and corrective action as required. [1930–35]

qual•i•ty-of-life (kwol′i tē əv līf′), *adj.* affecting the quality of urban life: *such quality-of-life crimes as fare-beating and graffiti writing.* [1940–45]

qual′ity pa′perback. See **trade paperback.**

qual′ity point′, *Educ.* See **grade point.**

qual′ity point′ av′erage, *Educ.* See **grade point average.** [1970–75]

qual′ity time′, time devoted exclusively to nurturing a cherished person or activity. [1985–90]

qualm (kwäm, kwôm), *n.* **1.** an uneasy feeling or pang of conscience as to conduct; compunction: *He has no qualms about lying.* **2.** a sudden feeling of apprehensive uneasiness; misgiving: *a sudden qualm about the success of the venture.* **3.** a sudden sensation or onset of faintness or illness, esp. of nausea. [1520–30; orig. uncert.]

qualm•ish (kwä′mish, kwô′-), *adj.* **1.** tending to have, or having, qualms. **2.** nauseous; nauseated. **3.** of the nature of a qualm. **4.** likely to cause qualms. [1540–50; QUALM + -ISH[1]] —**qualm′ish•ly,** *adv.* —**qualm′ish•ness,** *n.*

quam•ash (kwom′ash, kwə mash′), *n.* camass.

Qua•min (kwä′min), *n.* a male day name for Saturday. See under **day name.** Also, **Qua•me** (kwä′mē).

Qua•nah (kwä′nə), *n.* (*Quanah Parker*), 1845?–1911, Comanche leader.

quan•da•ry (kwon′də rē, -drē), *n., pl.* **-ries.** a state of perplexity or uncertainty, esp. as to what to do; dilemma. [1570–80; perh. fancifully < L *quand(ō)* when + *-āre* inf. suffix]
—**Syn.** See **predicament.**

quan•dong (kwon′dong′), *n.* **1.** an Australian tree, *Fusanus acuminatus,* bearing a fruit with an edible, nutlike seed. **2.** the fruit, or the seed or nut. Also, **quan′•dang′, quantong.** [1830–40; < Wiradjuri *guwandhaŋ*]

quan•go (kwang′gō), *n., pl.* **-gos.** a government organization, agency, or other body that operates autonomously. [1975–80; *qu(asi)-a(utonomous) n(ational) g(overnmental) o(rganization)*]

quan•ta (kwon′tə), *n.* pl. of **quantum.**

quan•tal (kwon′tl), *adj. Physics.* of or pertaining to quanta or quantum mechanics. [1915–20; QUANT(UM) + -AL[1]]

quan•tic (kwon′tik), *n. Math.* a rational, integral, homogeneous function of two or more variables. [1850–55; < L *quant(us)* how much + -IC]

Quan•ti•co (kwon′ti kō′), *n.* a U.S. Marine Corps base and development and education command in NE Virginia, NE of Fredericksburg on the Potomac River.

quan•ti•fi•er (kwon′tə fī′ər), *n.* **1.** *Logic.* an expression, as "all" or "some," that indicates the quantity of a proposition. Cf. **existential quantifier, universal quantifier. 2.** a word, esp. a modifier, that indicates the quantity of something. [1875–80; QUANTIFY + -ER[1]]

quan•ti•fy (kwon′tə fī′), *v.t.,* **-fied, -fy•ing. 1.** to determine, indicate, or express the quantity of. **2.** *Logic.* to make explicit the quantity of (a proposition). **3.** to give quantity to (something regarded as having only quality). [1830–40; < ML *quantificāre,* equiv. to L *quant(us)* how much + *-ificāre* -IFY] —**quan′ti•fi′•a•ble,** *adj.* —**quan′ti•fi′a•bly,** *adv.* —**quan′ti•fi•ca′•tion,** *n.*

quan•tile (kwon′tīl, -til), *n. Statistics.* one of the class of values of a variate that divides the total frequency of a sample or population into a given number of equal proportions. Cf. **decile, percentile, quartile, quintile.** [1935–40; QUANT(ITY) + *-ile* n. suffix, on the model of PERCENTILE]

quan•ti•tate (kwon′ti tāt′), *v.t.,* **-tat•ed, -tat•ing.** to determine the quantity of, esp. with precision. [1955–60; QUANTIT(Y) + -ATE[1]] —**quan′ti•ta′tion,** *n.*

quan•ti•ta•tive (kwon′ti tā′tiv), *adj.* **1.** that is or may be estimated by quantity. **2.** of or pertaining to the describing or measuring of quantity. **3.** of or pertaining to a metrical system, as that of classical verse, based on the alternation of long and short, rather than accented and unaccented, syllables. **4.** of or pertaining to the length of a spoken vowel or consonant. [1575–85; < ML *quantitātīvus,* equiv. to L *quantitāt-* (s. of *quantitās*) QUANTITY + *-īvus* -IVE] —**quan′ti•ta′tive•ly, quan′ti•tive•ly,** *adv.* —**quan′ti•ta′tive•ness, quan′ti•tive•ness,** *n.*

quan′titative anal′ysis, *Chem.* the analysis of a substance to determine the amounts and proportions of its chemical constituents. Cf. **qualitative analysis.** [1840–50]

quan′titative genet′ics. See **population genetics.**

quan′titative inher′itance, *Genetics.* the process in which the additive action of numerous genes results in a trait, as height, showing continuous variability. Cf. **polygenic inheritance.** [1925–30]

quan•ti•ty (kwon′ti tē), *n., pl.* **-ties. 1.** a particular or indefinite amount of anything: *a small quantity of milk; the ocean's vast quantity of fish.* **2.** an exact or specified amount or measure: *Mix the ingredients in the quantities called for.* **3.** a considerable or great amount: *to extract ore in quantity.* **4.** *Math.* **a.** the property of magnitude involving comparability with other magnitudes. **b.** something having magnitude, or size, extent, amount, or the like. **c.** magnitude, size, volume, area, or length. **5.** *Music.* the length or duration of a note. **6.** *Logic.* the character of a proposition as singular, universal, particular, or mixed, according to the presence or absence of certain kinds of quantifiers. **7.** that amount, degree, etc., in terms of which another is greater or lesser. **8.** *Pros., Phonet.* the relative duration or length of a sound or a syllable, with respect to the time spent in pronouncing it; length. **9.** *Law.* the nature of an estate as affected by its duration in time. [1250–1300; ME *quantite* < OF < L *quantitās,* equiv. to *quant(us)* how much + *-itās* -ITY]

quan•tize (kwon′tīz), *v.t.,* **-tized, -tiz•ing. 1.** *Math., Physics.* to restrict (a variable quantity) to discrete values rather than to a continuous set of values. **2.** *Physics.* to change the description of (a physical system) from classical to quantum-mechanical, usually resulting in discrete values for observable quantities, as energy or angular momentum. Also, *esp. Brit.,* **quan′tise.** [1920–25; QUANT(UM) + -IZE] —**quan′ti•za′tion,** *n.*

quan•tong (kwon′tong′), *n.* quandong.

Quan•trill (kwon′tril), *n.* **William Clarke,** 1837–65, Confederate guerrilla leader.

quan•tum (kwon′təm), *n., pl.* **-ta** (-tə), *adj.* —*n.* **1.** quantity or amount: *the least quantum of evidence.* **2.** a particular amount. **3.** a share or portion. **4.** a large quantity; bulk. **5.** *Physics.* **a.** the smallest quantity of radiant energy, equal to Planck's constant times the frequency of the associated radiation. **b.** the fundamental unit of a quantized physical magnitude, as angular momentum. —*adj.* **6.** sudden and significant: *a quantum increase in productivity.* [1610–20; n. use of neut. of L *quantus* how much]

quan′tum chem′istry, the application of quantum mechanics to the study of chemical phenomena.

quan′tum chromodynam′ics, *Physics.* a quantum field theory that describes quarks and gluons and their interactions, with the color of the quarks playing a role analogous to that of electric charge. *Abbr.:* QCD Also called **chromodynamics.** Cf. **color** (def. 18). [1975–80]

quan′tum electrodynam′ics, *Physics.* the quantum field theory that deals with the electromagnetic field and its interaction with electrons and positrons. *Abbr.:* QED [1925–30]

quan′tum field′ the′ory, *Physics.* any theory in which fields are treated by the methods of quantum mechanics; each field can then be regarded as consisting of particles of a particular kind, which may be created and annihilated. [1945–50]

quan′tum jump′, 1. *Physics.* an abrupt transition of a system described by quantum mechanics from one of its discrete states to another, as the fall of an electron in an atom to an orbit of lower energy. **2.** any sudden and significant change, advance, or increase. Also called **quan′tum leap′.** [1925–30]

quan′tum mechan′ics, *Physics.* a theory of the mechanics of atoms, molecules, and other physical systems that are subject to the uncertainty principle. *Abbr.:* QM Cf. **nonrelativistic quantum mechanics, relativistic quantum mechanics.** [1920–25] —**quan′tum-me•chan′i•cal,** *adj.*

quan′tum num′ber, *Physics.* **1.** any integer or half of an odd integer that distinguishes one of the discrete states of a quantum-mechanical system. **2.** any number that distinguishes among different members of a family of elementary particles. [1915–20]

quan′tum op′tics, the branch of optics dealing with light as a stream of photons, each possessing a quantum of energy proportional to the frequency of light when it is considered as a wave motion.

quan′tum state′, *Physics.* the condition in which a physical system exists, usually described by a wave function or a set of quantum numbers. [1920–25]

quan′tum statis′tics, *Physics, Chem.* the branch of statistical mechanics that incorporates quantum mechanics. Cf. **Bose-Einstein statistics, Fermi-Dirac statistics, statistical mechanics.** [1930–35]

quan•tum suf•fi•cit (kwän′tŏŏm sōōf′i kit; *Eng.* kwon′təm suf′ə sit), *Latin.* as much as suffices; enough.

quan′tum the′ory, *Physics.* **1.** any theory predating quantum mechanics that encompassed Planck's radiation formula and a scheme for obtaining discrete energy states for atoms, as Bohr theory. **2.** any theory that treats certain phenomena by the methods of quantum mechanics: *a quantum theory of gravitation.* [1910–15]

Quantz (kvänts), *n.* **Jo•hann Jo•a•chim** (yō′hän yō′ä-KHim), 1697–1773, German flutist and composer: teacher of Frederick the Great.

Quan•zhou (chwän′jō′), *n. Pinyin.* a seaport in SE Fujian province, in SE China, on Taiwan Strait. 130,000. Also, **Chuanchow.** Formerly, **Tsinkiang.**

Qua•o (kwä′ō), *n.* a male day name for Thursday. See under **day name.**

Qua•paw (kwô′pô′), *n., pl.* **-paws,** (*esp. collectively*) **paw** for 1. **1.** a member of a North American Indian people formerly of Arkansas, now living mostly in northeastern Oklahoma. **2.** the Siouan language of the Quapaw.

qua•qua•ver•sal (kwā′kwə vûr′səl), *adj.* (of a geological formation) sloping downward from the center in all directions. [1720–30; < L *quāquā vers(us)* lit., wheresoever turned, turned everywhere + -AL[1]] —**qua′qua•ver′sal•ly,** *adv.*

quar., 1. quarter. **2.** quarterly.

quar•an•tine (kwôr′ən tēn′, kwor′-, kwôr′ən tēn′, kwor′-), *n., v.,* **-tined, -tin•ing.** —*n.* **1.** a strict isolation imposed to prevent the spread of disease. **2.** a period, originally 40 days, of detention or isolation imposed upon ships, persons, animals, or plants on arrival at a port or place, when suspected of carrying some infectious or contagious disease. **3.** a system of measures maintained by governmental authority at ports, frontiers, etc., for preventing the spread of disease. **4.** the branch of the governmental service concerned with such measures. **5.** a place or station at which such measures are carried out, as a special port or dock where ships are detained. **6.** the detention or isolation enforced. **7.** the place, esp. a hospital, where people are detained. **8.** a period of 40 days. **9.** social, political, or economic isolation imposed as a punishment, as in ostracizing an individual or enforcing sanctions against a foreign state. —*v.t.* **10.** to put in or subject to quarantine. **11.** to exclude, detain, or isolate for political, social, or hygienic reasons. [1600–10; < It *quarantina,* var. of *quarantena,* orig. Upper It (Venetian): period of forty days, group of forty, deriv. of *quaranta* forty << L *quadrāgintā*] —**quar′an•tin′a•ble,** *adj.* —**quar′an•tin′er,** *n.*

quar′antine an′chorage, an anchorage for ships awaiting a pratique.

quar′antine flag′, *Naut.* a yellow flag, designating the letter Q in the International Code of Signals: flown by itself to signify that a ship has no disease on board and requests a pratique, or flown with another flag to signify that there is disease on board ship. Also called **yellow flag.** [1870–75]

quark (kwôrk, kwärk), *n. Physics.* any of the hypothetical particles with spin ½, baryon number ⅓, and electric charge ⅓ or −⅔ that, together with their antiparticles, are believed to constitute all the elementary particles classed as baryons and mesons; they are distinguished by their flavors, designated as up (u), down (d), strange (s), charm (c), bottom or beauty (b), and top or truth (t), and their colors, red, green, and blue. Cf. **color** (def. 18), **flavor** (def. 5), **quantum chromodynamics, quark model.** [coined in 1963 by U.S. physicist Murray Gell-Mann (b. 1929), who associated it with a word in Joyce's *Finnegans Wake,* read variously as E *quark* croak and G *Quark* curd, (slang) rubbish, tripe]

quark′ mod′el, *Physics.* a scheme that explains the quantum numbers of all the baryons and mesons by assuming that baryons are composed of three quarks and mesons of a quark and an antiquark, with different combinations of quark and antiquark flavors giving different sets of quantum numbers.

quar•ko•ni•um (kwôr kō′nē əm, kwär-), *n. Physics.* a meson composed of a quark and an antiquark of the same flavor. [1975–80; QUARK + -ON[1] + -IUM, on the model of POSITRONIUM and similarly named particles]

Quarles (kwôrlz, kwärlz), *n.* **Francis,** 1592–1644, English poet.

Quar•ne•ro (*It.* kwär ne′RÔ), *n.* **Gulf of,** an arm of the Adriatic Sea, in NW Yugoslavia.

quar·rel[1] (kwôr′əl, kwor′-), *n., v.,* **-reled, -rel·ing** or (*esp. Brit.*) **-relled, -rel·ling.** —*n.* **1.** an angry dispute or altercation; a disagreement marked by a temporary or permanent break in friendly relations. **2.** a cause of dispute, complaint, or hostile feeling: *She has no quarrel with her present salary.* —*v.i.* **3.** to disagree angrily; squabble; wrangle. **4.** to end a friendship as a result of a disagreement. **5.** to make a complaint; find fault. [1300–50; ME *querele* < OF < L *querēla, querella* a complaint, deriv. of *querī* to complain] —**quar′rel·er,** *n.* —**quar′rel·ing·ly,** *adv.*
—**Syn. 1.** argument, contention, controversy, difference, fight. QUARREL, DISSENSION refer to disagreement and conflict. QUARREL applies chiefly to a verbal disagreement between individuals or groups and is used with reference to a large variety of situations, from a slight and petty difference of opinion to a violent altercation: *It was little more than a domestic quarrel. Their quarrel led to the barroom brawl.* DISSENSION usually implies a profound disagreement and bitter conflict. It also applies chiefly to conflict within a group or to members of the same group: *dissension within the union; dissension among the Democrats.* **3.** bicker, argue, brawl, fight.

quar·rel[2] (kwôr′əl, kwor′-), *n.* **1.** a square-headed bolt or arrow, formerly used with a crossbow. **2.** Also, **quarry.** a small, square or diamond-shaped pane of glass, as used in latticed windows. **3.** any of various tools with pyramidal heads. [1175–1225; ME *quarel* < OF < ML *quadrellus,* dim. of L *quadrus* square]

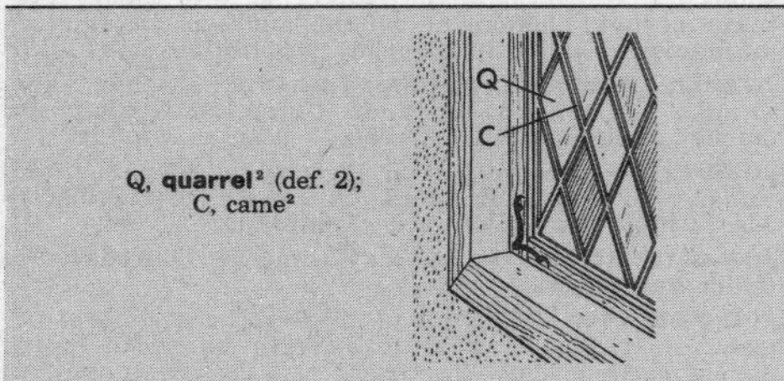

Q, **quarrel**[2] (def. 2); C, came[2]

quar·rel·some (kwôr′əl səm, kwor′-), *adj.* inclined to quarrel; argumentative; contentious. [1590–1600; QUARREL[1] + -SOME[1]] —**quar′rel·some·ly,** *adv.* —**quar′rel·some·ness,** *n.*

quar·ri·er (kwôr′ē ər, kwor′-), *n.* a person who quarries stone. [1325–75; ME *quaryer, quarriour* < OF *quarrier,* equiv. to **quarre* QUARRY[1] + *-ier* -IER[2]]

quar·ry[1] (kwôr′ē, kwor′ē), *n., pl.* **-ries,** *v.,* **-ried, -ry·ing.** —*n.* **1.** an excavation or pit, usually open to the air, from which building stone, slate, or the like, is obtained by cutting, blasting, etc. **2.** an abundant source or supply. —*v.t.* **3.** to obtain (stone) from or as if from a quarry. **4.** to make a quarry in. [1375–1425; ME *quarey* (n.) < ML *quareia,* var. of *quareria* < OF *quarriere* < VL **quadrāria* place where stone is squared, deriv. of L *quadrāre* to square] —**quar′ri·a·ble, quar′ry·a·ble,** *adj.*

quar·ry[2] (kwôr′ē, kwor′ē), *n., pl.* **-ries. 1.** an animal or bird hunted or pursued. **2.** game, esp. game hunted with hounds or hawks. **3.** any object of search, pursuit, or attack. [1275–1325; ME *querre* < OF *cuiree,* deriv. of *cuir* skin, hide < L *corium*]

quar·ry[3] (kwôr′ē, kwor′ē), *n., pl.* **-ries. 1.** a square stone or tile. **2.** quarrel[2] (def. 2). [1545–55; n. use of obs. *quarry* (adj.) square < OF *quarre* < L *quadrātus* QUADRATE]

quar·ry-faced (kwôr′ē fāst′, kwor′-), *adj. Masonry.* rock-faced.

quar·ry·man (kwôr′ē mən, kwor′-), *n., pl.* **-men.** a person who quarries stone; quarrier. [1605–15; QUARRY[1] + -MAN]

quar′ry tile′, a machine-made, unglazed, ceramic floor tile. Also called **promenade tile.** [1935–40]

quart[1] (kwôrt), *n.* **1.** a unit of liquid measure of capacity, equal to one fourth of a gallon, or 57.749 cubic inches (0.946 liter) in the U.S. and 69.355 cubic inches (1.136 liters) in Great Britain. **2.** a unit of dry measure of capacity, equal to one eighth of a peck, or 67.201 cubic inches (1.101 liters). **3.** a container holding, or capable of holding, a quart. [1275–1325; ME < OF *quarte* fourth part, quarter < L *quarta,* n. use of fem. of *quartus* FOURTH (in order)]

quart[2] (kärt), *n.* **1.** *Piquet.* a sequence of four cards of the same suit, as an ace, king, queen, and jack (**quart major**), or king, queen, jack, and ten (**quart minor**). **2.** *Fencing Rare.* quarte. [1685–95; < F *quarte,* n. use of fem. of *quart* < L *quartus;* see QUART[1]]

quart., 1. quarter. **2.** quarterly.

quar·tan (kwôr′tn), *adj.* **1.** (of a fever, ague, etc.) characterized by paroxysms that recur every fourth day, both days of consecutive occurrence being counted. —*n.* **2.** a quartan fever or ague. **3.** quartan malaria. [1250–1300; ME *quartaine* < OF < L (*febris*) *quartāna* quartan (fever), fem. of *quartānus,* equiv. to *quart(us)* FOURTH + *-ānus* -AN]

quarte (kärt; *Fr.* KART), *n., pl.* **quartes** (kärts; *Fr.* KART). *Fencing.* the fourth of eight defensive positions. [1690–1700; < F, fem. of *quart* FOURTH < L *quartus*]

quar·ter (kwôr′tər), *n.* **1.** one of the four equal or equivalent parts into which anything is or may be divided: *a quarter of an apple; a quarter of a book.* **2.** a fourth part, esp. of one (¼). **3.** one fourth of a U.S. or Canadian dollar, equivalent to 25 cents. **4.** a coin of this value. **5.** one fourth of an hour: *He stayed there for an hour and a quarter.* **6.** the moment marking this period: *The clock struck the quarter.* **7.** one fourth of a calendar or fiscal year: *The bank sends out a statement each quarter.* **8.** *Astron.* **a.** a fourth of the moon's period or monthly revolution, being that portion of its period or orbital course between a quadrature and a syzygy. **b.** either quadrature of the moon. Cf. **first quarter, last quarter. 9.** (in schools, colleges, and universities) one of the terms or periods into which instruction is organized, generally 10 to 12 weeks in length. **10.** *Sports.* any of the four periods that make up certain games, as football and basketball. Cf. **half** (def. 3). **11.** one fourth of a pound. **12.** one fourth of a mile; two furlongs. **13.** one fourth of a yard; 9 inches. **14.** a unit of weight: one fourth of a hundredweight. In the U.S. this equals 25 lbs. and in Britain 28 lbs. **15.** *Brit.* a measure of capacity for grain, etc., equal to 8 bushels, or, locally, to approximately this. **16.** the region of any of the four principal points of the compass or divisions of the horizon. **17.** such a point or division. **18.** any point or direction of the compass: *The wind is blowing in that quarter.* **19.** a region, district, or place. **20.** a particular district of a city or town, esp. one generally occupied by a particular group of people: *the Turkish quarter; an artists' quarter.* **21.** Usually, **quarters. a.** housing accommodations, as a place of residence; lodgings. **b.** *Mil.* the buildings, houses, barracks, or rooms occupied by military personnel or their families. **22.** Often, **quarters.** an unspecified part or member of a community, government, etc., that serves as a source of information or authority: *He received secret information from a high quarter.* **23.** mercy or indulgence, esp. as shown in sparing the life and accepting the surrender of a vanquished enemy: *to give quarter; to ask for quarter.* **24.** one of the four parts, each including a leg, of the body or carcass of a quadruped. **25.** *Vet. Med.* the part of a horse's hoof between heel and toe. **26.** *Shoemaking.* the part of a boot or shoe on each side of the foot, from the middle of the back to the vamp. **27.** *Naut.* **a.** the after part of a ship's side, usually from about the aftermost mast to the stern. **b.** the general horizontal direction 45° from the stern of a ship on either side: *Another boat is coming near on the port quarter.* **c.** one of the stations to which crew members are called for battle, emergencies, or drills. **d.** the part of a yard between the slings and the yardarm. **e.** See **quarter point. 28.** *Heraldry.* **a.** any of the four equal areas into which an escutcheon may be divided by a vertical and a horizontal line passing through the center. **b.** any of the variously numbered areas into which an escutcheon may be divided for the marshaling of different arms. **c.** any of the arms marshaled on an escutcheon. **d.** a charge occupying one quarter of an escutcheon, esp. that in dexter chief. Cf. **canton** (def. 3). **29.** each half of a cask, consisting of the portion from the bilge to the top chime and the portion from the bilge to the bottom chime.
—*v.t.* **30.** to divide into four equal or equivalent parts. **31.** to divide into parts fewer or more than four: *Quarter the pie into six pieces.* **32.** to cut the body of (a person) into quarters, esp. in executing for treason or the like. **33.** *Mach.* to make holes in, fix, etc., a quarter of a circle apart. **34.** to furnish with lodging in a particular place. **35.** to impose (soldiers) on persons, towns, etc., to be lodged and fed: *He quartered his men with the farmer.* **36.** to assign to a particular place for service, action, etc., as on a battleship. **37.** to traverse (the ground) from left to right and right to left while advancing, as dogs in search of game. **38.** *Heraldry.* **a.** to divide (an escutcheon) into four or more parts. **b.** to place or bear quarterly (different coats of arms, etc.) on an escutcheon. **c.** to display (a coat of arms) with one's own on an escutcheon.
—*v.i.* **39.** to take up, or be in quarters; lodge: *to quarter in a cheap hotel.* **40.** to range to and fro, as dogs in search of game. **41.** *Naut.* to sail so as to have the wind or sea on the quarter.
—*adj.* **42.** being one of four equal or approximately equal parts into which anything is or may be divided. **43.** being equal to only about one fourth of the full measure. [1250–1300; (n.) ME < AF; OF *quartier* < L *quartārius,* equiv. to *quart(us)* FOURTH + *-ārius* -ARY; (v.) ME *quarteren,* deriv. of the n.] —**quar′ter·er,** *n.*

quar·ter·age (kwôr′tər ij), *n.* **1.** the act of providing troops with living accommodations. **2.** the cost of such accommodations. **3.** a shelter or lodging. **4.** a quarterly payment, charge, or allowance. [1350–1400; ME. See QUARTER, -AGE]

quar·ter·back (kwôr′tər bak′), *n.* **1.** a back in football who usually lines up immediately behind the center and directs the offense of the team. **2.** the position played by this back. **3.** a person who leads or directs a group or activity. —*v.t.* **4.** to direct the offense of (a team). **5.** to lead or direct: *to quarterback a public-relations campaign.* —*v.i.* **6.** to play the position of quarterback. [1875–80, *Amer.*; QUARTER + BACK[1]]

quar′terback sneak′, *Football.* a play in which the quarterback charges into the middle of the line, usually immediately after receiving the ball from the center. [1920–25]

quar′ter bar′, a strut for bracing the central post of a windmill.

quar′ter bend′, a 90° bend, as in a plumbing pipe. [1880–85]

quar′ter bind′ing, a style of bookbinding in which the spine is leather and the sides are cloth or paper. Cf. **full binding, half binding, three-quarter binding.** [1910–15] —**quar·ter-bound** (kwôr′tər bound′), *adj.*

quar′ter blan′ket, a horse blanket, usually placed under a saddle or harness and extending to the horse's tail.

quar·ter-breed (kwôr′tər brēd′), *n. Often Disparaging and Offensive.* a person with one white grandparent, esp. a person of American Indian ancestry. [1820–30]

quar′ter crack′, *Vet. Pathol.* See **sand crack.** [1895–1900]

quar′ter day′, 1. (in England, Ireland, and Wales) one of the four days, Lady Day, Midsummer Day, Michaelmas, or Christmas, regarded as marking off the quarters of the year, on which quarterly payments are due, tenancies begin and end, etc. **2.** (in Scotland) one of the four days, Candlemas, Whitsunday, Lammas, or Martinmas, regarded as marking off the quarters of the year. [1470–80]

quar·ter·deck (kwôr′tər dek′), *n. Naut.* the part of a weather deck that runs aft from the midship area or the mainmast to the stern or poop of a vessel. [1620–30]

A, **quarterdeck;** B, poop deck; C, mizzenmast; D, mainmast

quar′ter dol′lar, quarter (def. 3). [1785–95, *Amer.*]

quar′ter ea′gle, a gold coin of the U.S. (issued 1796–1929), one fourth of an eagle.

quar·tered (kwôr′tərd), *adj.* **1.** divided into quarters. **2.** furnished with quarters or lodging. **3.** (of wood) quartersawed. **4.** *Heraldry.* **a.** (of an escutcheon) divided into four or more parts. **b.** (of a cross) having the central square portion removed. [1475–85; QUARTER + -ED[2]]

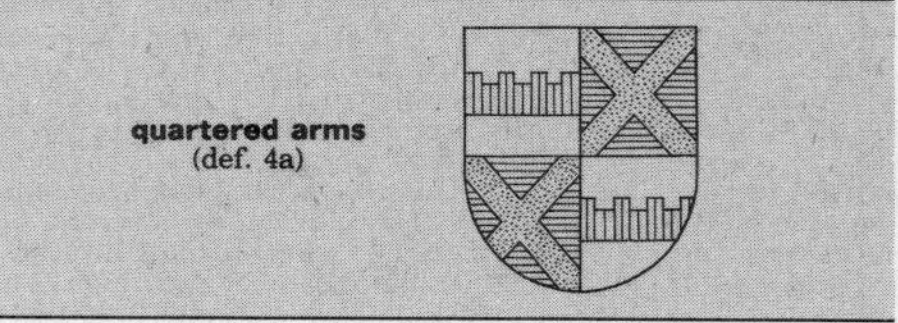
quartered arms (def. 4a)

quar·ter·fi·nal (kwôr′tər fīn′l), *Sports.* —*adj.* **1.** of or pertaining to the contest or round preceding the semifinal one. —*n.* **2.** a quarterfinal contest or round. [1925–30; QUARTER + FINAL]

quar·ter·fi·nal·ist (kwôr′tər fīn′l ist), *n. Sports.* a participant in a quarterfinal contest. [QUARTER + FINALIST]

quar′ter grain′, the grain appearing in quartersawed wood. [1695–1705]

quar′ter hol′low, *Archit.* a deep cove or cavetto. [1890–95]

quar·ter-hoop (kwôr′tər ho͞op′, -ho͝op′), *n.* a hoop, esp. of steel, fastened around a cask between the bilge and the chime. [1880–85]

quar′ter horse′, 1. one of a breed of strong horses developed in the U.S. for short-distance races, usually a quarter of a mile. **2.** a horse of this breed used in herding livestock. [1825–35, *Amer.*]

quar·ter-hour (kwôr′tər ouᵊr′, -ou′ər), *n.* **1.** a period of 15 minutes. **2.** a point 15 minutes after or before the hour. [1880–85]

quar·ter·ing (kwôr′tər ing), *n.* **1.** the act of a person or thing that quarters. **2.** the assignment of quarters or lodgings. **3.** *Heraldry.* **a.** the division of an escutcheon into quarters. **b.** the marshaling of various coats of arms on an escutcheon. **c.** any of the coats of arms so marshaled. —*adj.* **4.** that quarters. **5.** lying at right angles. **6.** *Naut.* (of a wind) blowing on a ship's quarter. [1585–95; QUARTER + -ING[1], -ING[2]]

quar·ter·ly (kwôr′tər lē), *adj., n., pl.* **-lies,** *adv.* —*adj.* **1.** occurring, done, paid, issued, etc., at the end of every quarter of a year: *a quarterly report; quarterly interest.* **2.** pertaining to or consisting of a quarter. —*n.* **3.** a periodical issued every three months. —*adv.* **4.** by quarters; once each quarter of a year: *The bank pays interest quarterly.* **5.** *Heraldry.* **a.** with division into four quarters. **b.** in the four quarters of an escutcheon. [1400–50; late ME; see QUARTER, -LY]

quar·ter·mas·ter (kwôr′tər mas′tər, -mä′stər), *n.* **1.** *Mil.* an officer charged with providing quarters, clothing, fuel, transportation, etc., for a body of troops. **2.** *Navy.* a petty officer having charge of signals, navigating apparatus, etc. [1400–50; late ME *quarter maister.* See QUARTER, MASTER] —**quar′ter·mas′ter·like′,** *adj.* —**quar′ter·mas′ter·ship′,** *n.*

Quar′termaster Corps′, *Mil.* the branch of the U.S. Army responsible for supplying food, clothing, fuel, and equipment and for the operation of commissaries, laundries, etc.

quar′termaster gen′eral, *pl.* **quartermasters general, quartermaster generals.** *Mil.* a general in command of the Quartermaster Corps. [1695–1705]

quar·tern (kwôr′tərn), *n. Chiefly Brit.* a quarter, or a fourth part, esp. of certain weights and measures, as of a pound, ounce, peck, or pint. [1250–1300; ME *quartroun, quartron, quartern* < OF *quarteron,* deriv. of *quart* fourth. See QUART[1]]

quar′ter nel′son, *Wrestling.* a hold in which a wrestler, from a kneeling position beside an opponent, puts one hand on the opponent's head, passes the free arm under the far arm of the opponent, and locks the free arm to the other arm by clasping the wrist. Cf. **nelson.**

quar′ter note′, *Music.* a note equivalent to one fourth of a whole note; a crotchet. See illus. under **note.** [1755–65]

quar·ter-phase (kwôr′tər fāz′), *adj. Elect.* differing in phase by a quarter of a cycle; two-phase.

quar′ter point′, the fourth part of the distance between any two adjacent points of the 32 marked on a compass, being 2° 48′ 45″. Also called **quarter.** [1720–30]

CONCISE ETYMOLOGY KEY: <, descended or borrowed from; >, whence; b., blend of, blended; c., cognate with; cf., compare; deriv., derivative; equiv., equivalent; imit., imitative; obl., oblique; r., replacing; s., stem; sp., spelling, spelled; resp., respelling, respelled; trans., translation; ?, origin unknown; *, unattested; ‡, probably earlier than. See the full key inside the front cover.

quar′ter rest′, *Music.* a rest equal in time value to a quarter note. See illus. under **rest**[1]. [1885–90]

quar′ter round′, a molding, as on an ovolo, whose section is a quarter circle. [1700–10]

quar·ter·saw (kwôr′tər sô′), *v.t.,* **-sawed, -sawed** or **-sawn, -saw·ing.** to saw (lumber) from quarter sections of logs so that the annual rings in any board form at least a 45° angle with the faces of the board. [1905–10; QUARTER + SAW[1]]

quar′ter sec′tion, *Western U.S.* (in surveying and homesteading) a square tract of land, half a mile on each side, thus containing ¼ sq. mi. or 160 acres. *Abbr.:* q.s. [1795–1805, *Amer.*]

quar′ter ses′sions, *Law.* **1.** an English court of general criminal jurisdiction for crimes less than homicide, held quarterly. **2.** (in the U.S.) a court with limited criminal jurisdiction, having local administrative powers in some states. [1570–80]

quar·ter·staff (kwôr′tər staf′, -stäf′), *n., pl.* **-staves** (-stāvz′), **-staffs. 1.** a former English weapon consisting of a stout pole 6 to 8 ft. (1.8 to 2.4 m) long, tipped with iron. **2.** exercise or fighting with this weapon. [1540–50; QUARTER + STAFF[1]]

quar′ter tone′, *Music.* an interval equivalent to half of a semitone. [1770–80]

quar′ter-wave plate′ (kwôr′tər wāv′), *Optics.* a crystal thin enough to cause a phase difference of 90° between the ordinary and extraordinary rays of polarized light, thereby converting circularly polarized light into plane polarized light. Cf. **half-wave plate.** [1880–85]

quar·tet (kwôr tet′), *n.* **1.** any group of four persons or things. **2.** an organized group of four singers or players. **3.** a musical composition for four voices or instruments. Also, *esp. Brit.,* **quar·tette′.** [1765–75; < It *quartetto,* dim. of *quarto* < L *quartus* FOURTH]

quar·tic (kwôr′tik), *Algebra.* —*adj.* **1.** of or pertaining to the fourth degree. —*n.* **2.** Also called **biquadratic.** a quartic polynomial or equation. [1855–60; < L *quart(us)* FOURTH + -IC]

quar·tile (kwôr′tīl, -til), *n.* **1.** *Statistics.* (in a frequency distribution) one of the values of a variable that divides the distribution of the variable into four groups having equal frequencies. Cf. **first quartile, median, third quartile. 2.** *Astrol.* a quartile aspect. —*adj.* **3.** *Astrol.* of or pertaining to the aspect of two heavenly bodies when their longitudes differ by 90°. [1500–10; < ML *quartīlis,* equiv. to L *quart(us)* FOURTH + *-īlis* -ILE]

quart′ ma′jor. See under **quart**[2] (def. 1). [1740–50]

quart′ mi′nor. See under **quart**[2] (def. 1).

quar·to (kwôr′tō), *n., pl.* **-tos,** *adj.* —*n.* **1.** a book size of about 9½ × 12 in. (24 × 30 cm), determined by folding printed sheets twice to form four leaves or eight pages. *Symbol:* 4to, 4° **2.** a book of this size. —*adj.* **3.** bound in quarto. [1580–90; short for NL *in quartō* in fourth (*quartō,* abl. sing. of *quartus* FOURTH)]

quartz (kwôrts), *n.* one of the commonest minerals, silicon dioxide, SiO_2, having many varieties that differ in color, luster, etc., and occurring either in masses (as agate, bloodstone, chalcedony, jasper, etc.) or in crystals (as rock crystal, amethyst, citrine, etc.): the chief constituent of sand and sandstone, and an important constituent of many other rocks. It is piezoelectric and used to control the frequencies of radio transmitters. [1750–60; < G *Quarz*] —**quartz·ose** (kwôrt′sōs), **quartz·ous** (kwôrt′səs), *adj.*

quartz′ glass′, lechatelierite. [1900–05]

quartz·if·er·ous (kwôrt sif′ər əs), *adj.* consisting of or containing quartz: *quartziferous rock.* [1825–35; QUARTZ + -I- + -FEROUS]

quartz·ite (kwôrt′sīt), *n.* a granular metamorphic rock consisting essentially of quartz in interlocking grains. [1840–50; QUARTZ + -ITE[1]] —**quartz·it·ic** (kwôrt sit′ik), *adj.*

quartz′ lamp′, a lamp consisting of an ultraviolet light source, as mercury vapor, contained in a fused-silica bulb that transmits ultraviolet light with little absorption. [1920–25]

quartz′ move′ment, *Horol.* an extremely accurate electronic movement utilizing the natural frequency of vibrations of a quartz crystal to regulate the operation of the timepiece **(quartz′ clock′** or **quartz′ watch′).**

quartz′ plate′, *Electronics.* a carefully cut quartz crystal that is piezoelectrically active. Cf. **crystal** (def. 10).

qua·sar (kwā′zär, -zər, -sär, -sər), *n. Astron.* one of over a thousand known extragalactic objects, starlike in appearance and having spectra with characteristically large redshifts, that are thought to be the most distant and most luminous objects in the universe. Also called **quasi-stellar object.** [1960–65; *quas(i-stell)ar,* in QUASI-STELLAR RADIO SOURCE, the first type of quasar discovered]

quash (kwosh), *v.t.* **1.** to put down or suppress completely; quell; subdue: *to quash a rebellion.* **2.** to make void, annul, or set aside (a law, indictment, decision, etc.). [1300–50; ME *quashen* to smash, break, overcome, suppress < OF *quasser,* in part < L *quassāre* to shake (freq. of *quatere* to shake; cf. CONCUSSION); in part < LL *cassāre* to annul, deriv. of L *cassus* empty, void]
—**Syn. 1.** crush, squash, quench, repress.

Qua·she·ba (kwä shē′bä), *n.* a female day name for Sunday. See under **day name.**

Qua·shee (kwä′shē), *n.* a male day name for Sunday. See under **day name.**

qua·si (kwā′zī, -sī, kwä′sē, -zē), *adj.* resembling; seeming; virtual: *a quasi member.* [independent use of QUASI-]

quasi-, a combining form meaning "resembling," "having some, but not all of the features of," used in the formation of compound words: *quasi-definition; quasi-monopoly; quasi-official; quasi-scientific.* [< L *quasi* as if, as though, equiv. to *qua(m)* as + *sī* if]
—**Note.** The lists at the bottom of this and the following page provide the spelling, syllabification, and stress for words whose meanings may be easily inferred by com-

CONCISE PRONUNCIATION KEY: act, cāpe, dâre, pärt; set, ēqual; *if,* īce; ox, ōver, ôrder, oil, bŏŏk, bōōt, out; up, ûrge; child; sing; shoe; thin, *th*at; zh as in *treasure.* ə = *a* as in *alone, e* as in *system, i* as in *easily, o* as in *gallop, u* as in *circus;* ᵊ as in *fire* (fīᵊr), *hour* (ouᵊr). l and n can serve as syllabic consonants, as in *cradle* (krād′l), and *button* (but′n). See the full key inside the front cover.

qua′si-ab′so·lute′, *adj.;* **-ly,** *adv.*
qua′si-ac′a·dem′ic, *adj.*
qua′si-ac′a·dem′i·cal·ly, *adv.*
qua′si-ac·cept′ed, *adj.*
qua′si-ac′ci·den′tal, *adj.;* **-ly,** *adv.*
qua′si-ac·quaint′ed, *adj.*
qua′si-ac′tive, *adj.;* **-ly,** *adv.*
qua′si-ad′e·quate, *adj.;* **-ly,** *adv.*
qua′si-ad·just′ed, *adj.*
qua′si-ad·mire′, *v.,* **-mired, -mir·ing.**
qua′si-a·dopt′, *v.t.*
qua′si-a·dopt′ed, *adj.*
qua′si-a·dult′, *adj.*
qua′si-ad′van·ta′geous, *adj.;* **-ly,** *adv.*
qua′si-af·fec′tion·ate, *adj.;* **-ly,** *adv.*
qua′si-af·firm′a·tive, *adj.;* **-ly,** *adv.*
qua′si-al′ter·nat′ing, *adj.;* **-ly,** *adv.*
qua′si-al·ter′na·tive, *adj.;* **-ly,** *adv.*
qua′si-am′a·teur′ish, *adj.;* **-ly,** *adv.*
qua′si-A·mer′i·can, *adj.*
qua′si-A·mer′i·can·ized′, *adj.*
qua′si-a′mi·a·ble, *adj.;* **-bly,** *adv.*
qua′si-a·mus′ing, *adj.;* **-ly,** *adv.*
qua′si-an′cient, *adj.;* **-ly,** *adv.*
qua′si-an·gel′ic, *adj.*
qua′si-an·gel′i·cal·ly, *adv.*
qua′si-an·tique′, *adj.*
qua′si-anx′ious, *adj.;* **-ly,** *adv.*
qua′si-a·pol′o·get′ic, *adj.*
qua′si-a·pol′o·get′i·cal·ly, *adv.*
qua′si-ap·peal′ing, *adj.;* **-ly,** *adv.*
qua′si-ap·point′ed, *adj.*
qua′si-ap·pro′pri·ate, *adj.;* **-ly,** *adv.*
qua′si-ar·tis′tic, *adj.*
qua′si-ar·tis′ti·cal·ly, *adv.*
qua′si-a·side′, *adv.*
qua′si-a·sleep′, *adj., adv.*
qua′si-ath·let′ic, *adj.*
qua′si-ath·let′i·cal·ly, *adv.*
qua′si-at·tempt′, *v.*
qua′si-au′di·ble, *adj.;* **-bly,** *adv.*
qua′si-au·then′tic, *adj.*
qua′si-au·then′ti·cal·ly, *adv.*
qua′si-au′thor·ized′, *adj.*
qua′si-au′to·mat′ic, *adj.*
qua′si-au′to·mat′i·cal·ly, *adv.*
qua′si-aw′ful, *adj.;* **-ly,** *adv.*
qua′si-bad′, *adj.*
qua′si-bank′rupt, *adj.*
qua′si-ba′sic, *adj.*
qua′si-ba′si·cal·ly, *adv.*
qua′si-ben′e·fi′cial, *adj.;* **-ly,** *adv.*
qua′si-be·nev′o·lent, *adj.;* **-ly,** *adv.*
qua′si-bi′o·graph′i·cal, *adj.;* **-ly,** *adv.*
qua′si-blind′, *adj.;* **-ly,** *adv.*
qua′si-brave′, *adj.;* **-ly,** *adv.*
qua′si-bril′liant, *adj.;* **-ly,** *adv.*
qua′si-bronze′, *adj.*
qua′si-broth′er·ly, *adj.*
qua′si-calm′, *adj.;* **-ly,** *adv.*
qua′si-can′did, *adj.;* **-ly,** *adv.*
qua′si-ca′pa·ble, *adj.;* **-bly,** *adv.*
qua′si-care′ful, *adj.;* **-ly,** *adv.*
qua′si-char′ac·ter·is′tic, *adj.*
qua′si-char′ac·ter·is′ti·cal·ly, *adv.*
qua′si-char′i·ta·ble, *adj.;* **-bly,** *adv.*
qua′si-cheer′ful, *adj.;* **-ly,** *adv.*
qua′si-civ′il, *adj.;* **-ly,** *adv.*
qua′si-clas′sic, *adj.*
qua′si-clas′si·cal·ly, *adv.*
qua′si-cler′i·cal, *adj.;* **-ly,** *adv.*
qua′si-col·le′giate, *adj.*
qua′si-col·lo′qui·al, *adj.;* **-ly,** *adv.*
qua′si-com′fort·a·ble, *adj.;* **-bly,** *adv.*
qua′si-com′ic, *adj.*
qua′si-com′i·cal, *adj.;* **-ly,** *adv.*
qua′si-com·mand′ing, *adj.;* **-ly,** *adv.*
qua′si-com·mer′cial, *adj.;* **-ly,** *adv.*
qua′si-com·mer′cial·ized′, *adj.*
qua′si-com′mon, *adj.;* **-ly,** *adv.*
qua′si-com·pact′, *adj.;* **-ly,** *adv.*
qua′si-com·pet′i·tive, *adj.;* **-ly,** *adv.*
qua′si-com·plete′, *adj.;* **-ly,** *adv.*
qua′si-com·plex′, *adj.;* **-ly,** *adv.*
qua′si-com·pli′ant, *adj.;* **-ly,** *adv.*
qua′si-com′pli·men′ta·ry, *adj.*
qua′si-com′pre·hen′sive, *adj.;* **-ly,** *adv.*
qua′si-com′pro·mis′ing, *adj.;* **-ly,** *adv.*
qua′si-com·pul′sive, *adj.;* **-ly,** *adv.*
qua′si-com·pul′so·ri·ly, *adv.*
qua′si-com·pul′so·ry, *adj.*
qua′si-con′fi·dent, *adj.;* **-ly,** *adv.*
qua′si-con′fi·den′tial, *adj.;* **-ly,** *adv.*
qua′si-con·fin′ing, *adj.*
qua′si-con·form′ing, *adj.*
qua′si-con·gen′ial, *adj.;* **-ly,** *adv.*
qua′si-con·grat′u·la·to′ry, *adj.*
qua′si-con·nec′tive, *adj.;* **-ly,** *adv.*
qua′si-con′sci·en′tious, *adj.;* **-ly,** *adv.*
qua′si-con′scious, *adj.;* **-ly,** *adv.*
qua′si-con′se·quen′tial, *adj.;* **-ly,** *adv.*
qua′si-con·serv′a·tive, *adj.;* **-ly,** *adv.*
qua′si-con·sid′er·ate, *adj.;* **-ly,** *adv.*
qua′si-con·sist′ent, *adj.;* **-ly,** *adv.*
qua′si-con·sol′i·dat′ed, *adj.*
qua′si-con′stant, *adj.;* **-ly,** *adv.*
qua′si-con′sti·tu′tion·al, *adj.;* **-ly,** *adv.*
qua′si-con·struct′ed, *adj.*
qua′si-con·struc′tive, *adj.;* **-ly,** *adv.*
qua′si-con·sum′ing, *adj.*
qua′si-con·tent′, *adj.*
qua′si-con·tent′ed, *adj.;* **-ly,** *adv.*
qua′si-con·tin′u·al, *adj.;* **-ly,** *adv.*
qua′si-con·tin′u·ous, *adj.;* **-ly,** *adv.*
qua′si-con′trar·i·ly, *adv.*
qua′si-con′trar·y, *adj.*
qua′si-con·trast′ed, *adj.*
qua′si-con·trolled′, *adj.*
qua′si-con·trol′ling, *adj.*
qua′si-con·ven′ient, *adj.;* **-ly,** *adv.*
qua′si-con·ven′tion·al, *adj.;* **-ly,** *adv.*
qua′si-con·vert′ed, *adj.*
qua′si-con·veyed′, *adj.*
qua′si-con·vinced′, *adj.*
qua′si-cor′dial, *adj.;* **-ly,** *adv.*
qua′si-cor·rect′, *adj.;* **-ly,** *adv.*
qua′si-cour′te·ous, *adj.;* **-ly,** *adv.*
qua′si-craft′i·ly, *adv.*
qua′si-craft′y, *adj.*
qua′si-crim′i·nal, *adj.;* **-ly,** *adv.*
qua′si-crit′i·cal, *adj.;* **-ly,** *adv.*
qua′si-cul′ti·vat′ed, *adj.*
qua′si-cun′ning, *adj.;* **-ly,** *adv.*
qua′si-cyn′i·cal, *adj.;* **-ly,** *adv.*
qua′si-dam′aged, *adj.*
qua′si-dan′ger·ous, *adj.;* **-ly,** *adv.*
qua′si-dar′ing, *adj.;* **-ly,** *adv.*
qua′si-deaf′, *adj.;* **-ly,** *adv.*
qua′si-deaf′en·ing, *adj.*
qua′si-dec′o·rat′ed, *adj.*
qua′si-de·feat′ed, *adj.*
qua′si-de·fi′ant, *adj.;* **-ly,** *adv.*
qua′si-def′i·nite, *adj.;* **-ly,** *adv.*
qua′si-de·ject′ed, *adj.;* **-ly,** *adv.*
qua′si-de·lib′er·ate, *adj.;* **-ly,** *adv.*
qua′si-del′i·cate, *adj.;* **-ly,** *adv.*
qua′si-de·light′ed, *adj.;* **-ly,** *adv.*
qua′si-de·mand′ing, *adj.;* **-ly,** *adv.*
qua′si-dem′o·crat′ic, *adj.*
qua′si-dem′o·crat′i·cal·ly, *adv.*
qua′si-de·pend′ent, *adj.;* **-ly,** *adv.*
qua′si-de·pressed′, *adj.*
qua′si-des′o·late, *adj.;* **-ly,** *adv.*
qua′si-des′per·ate, *adj.;* **-ly,** *adv.*
qua′si-de·spond′ent, *adj.;* **-ly,** *adv.*
qua′si-de·ter′mine, *v.,* **-mined, -min·ing.**
qua′si-de·vot′ed, *adj.;* **-ly,** *adv.*
qua′si-dif′fi·cult′, *adj.;* **-ly,** *adv.*
qua′si-dig′ni·fied′, *adj.*
qua′si-dig′ni·fy′ing, *adj.*
qua′si-dip′lo·mat′ic, *adj.*
qua′si-dip′lo·mat′i·cal·ly, *adv.*
qua′si-dis·ad′van·ta′geous, *adj.;* **-ly,** *adv.*
qua′si-dis·as′trous, *adj.;* **-ly,** *adv.*
qua′si-dis·creet′, *adj.;* **-ly,** *adv.*
qua′si-dis·crim′i·nat′ing, *adj.;* **-ly,** *adv.*
qua′si-dis·graced′, *adj.*
qua′si-dis·gust′ed, *adj.;* **-ly,** *adv.*
qua′si-dis′tant, *adj.;* **-ly,** *adv.*
qua′si-dis·tressed′, *adj.*
qua′si-di·verse′, *adj.;* **-ly,** *adv.*
qua′si-di·ver′si·fied′, *adj.*
qua′si-di·vid′ed, *adj.;* **-ly,** *adv.*
qua′si-dou′ble, *adj.;* **-bly,** *adv.*
qua′si-doubt′ful, *adj.;* **-ly,** *adv.*
qua′si-dra·mat′ic, *adj.*
qua′si-dra·mat′i·cal·ly, *adv.*
qua′si-dread′ful, *adj.;* **-ly,** *adv.*
qua′si-dumb′, *adj.;* **-ly,** *adv.*
qua′si-du′pli·cate, *adj.*
qua′si-du′ti·ful, *adj.;* **-ly,** *adv.*
qua′si-ea′ger, *adj.;* **-ly,** *adv.*
qua′si-ec′o·nom′ic, *adj.*
qua′si-ec′o·nom′i·cal, *adj.;* **-ly,** *adv.*
qua′si-ed′u·cat′ed, *adj.*
qua′si-ed′u·ca′tion·al, *adj.;* **-ly,** *adv.*
qua′si-ef·fec′tive, *adj.;* **-ly,** *adv.*
qua′si-ef·fi′cient, *adj.;* **-ly,** *adv.*
qua′si-e·lab′o·rate, *adj.;* **-ly,** *adv.*
qua′si-el′e·men′ta·ry, *adj.*
qua′si-el′i·gi·ble, *adj.;* **-bly,** *adv.*
qua′si-el′o·quent, *adj.;* **-ly,** *adv.*
qua′si-em′i·nent, *adj.;* **-ly,** *adv.*
qua′si-e·mo′tion·al, *adj.;* **-ly,** *adv.*
qua′si-emp′ty, *adj.*
qua′si-end′less, *adj.;* **-ly,** *adv.*
qua′si-en′er·get′ic, *adj.*
qua′si-en′er·get′i·cal·ly, *adv.*
qua′si-en·forced′, *adj.*
qua′si-en·gag′ing, *adj.;* **-ly,** *adv.*
qua′si-Eng′lish, *adj.*
qua′si-en′ter·tain′ing, *adj.*
qua′si-en·thused′, *adj.*
qua′si-en·thu′si·as′tic, *adj.*
qua′si-en·thu′si·as′ti·cal·ly, *adv.*
qua′si-en′vi·ous, *adj.;* **-ly,** *adv.*
qua′si-e·pis′co·pal, *adj.;* **-ly,** *adv.*
qua′si-e′qual, *adj.;* **-ly,** *adv.*
qua′si-eq′ui·ta·ble, *adj.;* **-bly,** *adv.*
qua′si-e·quiv′a·lent, *adj.;* **-ly,** *adv.*
qua′si-e·rot′ic, *adj.*
qua′si-e·rot′i·cal·ly, *adv.*
qua′si-es·sen′tial, *adj.;* **-ly,** *adv.*
qua′si-es·tab′lished, *adj.*
qua′si-e·ter′nal, *adj.;* **-ly,** *adv.*
qua′si-ev′er·last′ing, *adj.;* **-ly,** *adv.*
qua′si-e′vil, *adj.;* **-ly,** *adv.*
qua′si-ex·act′, *adj.;* **-ly,** *adv.*
qua′si-ex·cep′tion·al, *adj.;* **-ly,** *adv.*
qua′si-ex·ces′sive, *adj.;* **-ly,** *adv.*
qua′si-ex·empt′, *adj.*
qua′si-ex′iled, *adj.*
qua′si-ex·ist′ent, *adj.*
qua′si-ex·pect′ant, *adj.;* **-ly,** *adv.*
qua′si-ex·pe′di·ent, *adj.;* **-ly,** *adv.*
qua′si-ex·pen′sive, *adj.;* **-ly,** *adv.*
qua′si-ex·pe′ri·enced, *adj.*
qua′si-ex·per′i·men′tal, *adj.;* **-ly,** *adv.*
qua′si-ex·plic′it, *adj.;* **-ly,** *adv.*
qua′si-ex·posed′, *adj.*
qua′si-ex·pressed′, *adj.*
qua′si-ex·ter′nal, *adj.;* **-ly,** *adv.*
qua′si-ex′tra·ter′ri·to′ri·al, *adj.;* **-ly,** *adv.*
qua′si-ex·treme′, *adj.*
qua′si-fab′ri·cat′ed, *adj.*
qua′si-fair′, *adj.;* **-ly,** *adv.*
qua′si-faith′ful, *adj.;* **-ly,** *adv.*
qua′si-false′, *adj.;* **-ly,** *adv.*
qua′si-fa·mil′iar, *adj.;* **-ly,** *adv.*
qua′si-fa′mous, *adj.;* **-ly,** *adv.*
qua′si-fas′ci·nat′ed, *adj.*
qua′si-fas′ci·nat′ing, *adj.;* **-ly,** *adv.*
qua′si-fash′ion·a·ble, *adj.;* **-bly,** *adv.*
qua′si-fa′tal, *adj.;* **-ly,** *adv.*
qua′si-fa′tal·is′tic, *adj.*
qua′si-fa′tal·is′ti·cal·ly, *adv.*
qua′si-fa′vor·a·ble, *adj.;* **-bly,** *adv.*
qua′si-fed′er·al, *adj.;* **-ly,** *adv.*
qua′si-feu′dal, *adj.;* **-ly,** *adv.*
qua′si-fic·ti′tious, *adj.;* **-ly,** *adv.*
qua′si-fi′nal, *adj.*
qua′si-fi·nan′cial, *adj.;* **-ly,** *adv.*
qua′si-fire′proof′, *adj.*
qua′si-fis′cal, *adj.;* **-ly,** *adv.*
qua′si-fit′, *adj.*
qua′si-fool′ish, *adj.;* **-ly,** *adv.*
qua′si-forced′, *adj.*
qua′si-for′eign, *adj.*
qua′si-for·get′ful, *adj.;* **-ly,** *adv.*
qua′si-for·got′ten, *adj.*
qua′si-for′mal, *adj.;* **-ly,** *adv.*
qua′si-for′mi·da·ble, *adj.;* **-bly,** *adv.*
qua′si-for′tu·nate, *adj.;* **-ly,** *adv.*
qua′si-frank′, *adj.;* **-ly,** *adv.*

bining the meanings of QUASI- and an attached base word, or base word plus a suffix. Appropriate parts of speech are also shown. Words prefixed by QUASI- that have special meanings or uses are entered in their proper alphabetical places in the main vocabulary or as derived forms run on at the end of a main vocabulary entry.

CONCISE ETYMOLOGY KEY: <, descended or borrowed from; >, whence; b., blend of, blended; c., cognate with; cf., compare; deriv., derivative; equiv., equivalent; imit., imitative; obl., oblique; r., replacing; s., stem; sp., spelling, spelled; resp., respelling, respelled; trans., translation; ?, origin unknown; *, unattested; ‡, probably earlier than. See the full key inside the front cover.

qua′si con′tract, *Law.* an obligation imposed by law in the absence of a contract to prevent unjust enrichment. [1720–30]

qua·si·crys·tal (kwā′zī crys′tl, kwā′sī-, kwä′sē-, -zē-), *n.* a form of solid matter whose atoms are arranged like those of a crystal but assume patterns that do not exactly repeat themselves. [1985–90]

qua·si-ju·di·cial (kwā′zī jo͞o dish′əl, kwā′sī-, kwä′sē-, -zē-), *adj.* noting, pertaining to, or exercising powers or functions that resemble those of a court or a judge: *a quasi-judicial agency.* [1830–40]

Qua·si·mo·do (kwä′sə mō′dō, -zə mō′-; *It.* kwä′zē-mô′dô), *n.* **Sal·va·to·re** (säl′vä tô′re), 1901–68, Italian poet: Nobel prize 1959.

Qua·si·mo·do (kwä′sə mō′dō, -zə mō′-), *n.* **1.** See **Low Sunday. 2.** the ugly, humpbacked protagonist of *The Hunchback of Notre Dame,* by Victor Hugo. [1840–50; < LL, from the opening words of the introit antiphon for the Sunday: *Quasi modo genitī infantēs* . . . As just born children . . . (1 Pet. 2:2)]

qua·si·par·ti·cle (kwā′zī pär′ti kəl, kwā′sī-, kwä′sē, -zē-), *n. Physics.* an entity, as an exciton or phonon, that interacts with elementary particles, but does not exist as a free particle. [1955–60; QUASI- + PARTICLE]

qua′si-stel′lar ob′ject (kwā′zī stel′ər, kwā′sī-, kwä′sē-, -zē-), quasar. *Abbr.:* QSO [1960–65]

qua′si-stel′lar ra′dio source′, *Astron.* a quasar having detectable radio emission. *Abbr.:* QSS [1960–65]

qua′si-fra·ter′nal, *adj.;* **-ly,** *adv.*
qua′si-free′, *adj.;* **-ly,** *adv.*
qua′si-French′, *adj.*
qua′si-ful·fill′ing, *adj.*
qua′si-full′, *adj.*
qua′si-ful′ly, *adv.*
qua′si-gal′lant, *adj.;* **-ly,** *adv.*
qua′si-gas′e·ous, *adj.*
qua′si-gay′, *adj.*
qua′si-gen′er·ous, *adj.;* **-ly,** *adv.*
qua′si-gen·teel′, *adj.;* **-ly,** *adv.*
qua′si-gen′tle·man·ly, *adv.*
qua′si-gen′u·ine, *adj.;* **-ly,** *adv.*
qua′si-Ger′man, *adj.*
qua′si-glad′, *adj.;* **-ly,** *adv.*
qua′si-glo′ri·ous, *adj.;* **-ly,** *adv.*
qua′si-good′, *adj.*
qua′si-gra′cious, *adj.;* **-ly,** *adv.*
qua′si-grate′ful, *adj.;* **-ly,** *adv.*
qua′si-grave′, *adj.;* **-ly,** *adv.*
qua′si-great′, *adj.;* **-ly,** *adv.*
qua′si-Gre′cian, *adj.*
qua′si-Greek′, *adj.*
qua′si-guar′an·teed′, *adj.*
qua′si-guilt′i·ly, *adv.*
qua′si-guilt′y, *adj.*
qua′si-ha·bit′u·al, *adj.;* **-ly,** *adv.*
qua′si-hap′py, *adj.*
qua′si-harm′ful, *adj.;* **-ly,** *adv.*
qua′si-health′ful, *adj.;* **-ly,** *adv.*
qua′si-heart′i·ly, *adv.*
qua′si-heart′y, *adj.*
qua′si-help′ful, *adj.;* **-ly,** *adv.*
qua′si-he·red′i·tar′y, *adj.*
qua′si-he·ro′ic, *adj.*
qua′si-he·ro′i·cal·ly, *adv.*
qua′si-his·tor′ic, *adj.*
qua′si-his·tor′i·cal, *adj.;* **-ly,** *adv.*
qua′si-hon′est, *adj.;* **-ly,** *adv.*
qua′si-hon′or·a·ble, *adj.;* **-bly,** *adv.*
qua′si-hu′man, *adj.;* **-ly,** *adv.*
qua′si-hu′man·is′tic, *adj.*
qua′si-hum′ble, *adj.;* **-bly,** *adv.*
qua′si-hu′mor·ous, *adj.;* **-ly,** *adv.*
qua′si-i·de′al, *adj.;* **-ly,** *adv.*
qua′si-i·de′al·is′tic, *adj.*
qua′si-i·de′al·is′ti·cal·ly, *adv.*
qua′si-i·den′ti·cal, *adj.;* **-ly,** *adv.*
qua′si-ig′no·rant, *adj.;* **-ly,** *adv.*
qua′si-im·me′di·ate, *adj.;* **-ly,** *adv.*
qua′si-im·mor′tal, *adj.;* **-ly,** *adv.*
qua′si-im·par′tial, *adj.;* **-ly,** *adv.*
qua′si-im·por′tant, *adj.;* **-ly,** *adv.*
qua′si-im·proved′, *adj.*
qua′si-in·clined′, *adj.*
qua′si-in·clu′sive, *adj.;* **-ly,** *adv.*
qua′si-in·creased′, *adj.*
qua′si-in′de·pend′ent, *adj.;* **-ly,** *adv.*
qua′si-in·dif′fer·ent, *adj.;* **-ly,** *adv.*
qua′si-in·duced′, *adj.*
qua′si-in·dulged′, *adj.*
qua′si-in·dus′tri·al, *adj.;* **-ly,** *adv.*
qua′si-in·ev′i·ta·ble, *adj.;* **-bly,** *adv.*
qua′si-in·fe′ri·or, *adj.*
qua′si-in·ferred′, *adj.*
qua′si-in′fi·nite, *adj.;* **-ly,** *adv.*
qua′si-in′flu·en′tial, *adj.;* **-ly,** *adv.*
qua′si-in·for′mal, *adj.;* **-ly,** *adv.*
qua′si-in·formed′, *adj.*
qua′si-in·her′it·ed, *adj.*
qua′si-in·i′ti·at′ed, *adj.*
qua′si-in′jured, *adj.*
qua′si-in·ju′ri·ous, *adj.;* **-ly,** *adv.*
qua′si-in′no·cent, *adj.;* **-ly,** *adv.*
qua′si-in·nu′mer·a·ble, *adj.;* **-bly,** *adv.*
qua′si-in·sist′ent, *adj.;* **-ly,** *adv.*
qua′si-in·spect′ed, *adj.*
qua′si-in′spi·ra′tion·al, *adj.*
qua′si-in·stalled′, *adj.*
qua′si-in·struct′ed, *adj.*
qua′si-in·sult′ed, *adj.*
qua′si-in′tel·lec′tu·al, *adj.;* **-ly,** *adv.*
qua′si-in·tel′li·gent, *adj.;* **-ly,** *adv.*
qua′si-in·tend′ed, *adj.*
qua′si-in′ter·est·ed, *adj.;* **-ly,** *adv.*
qua′si-in·ter′nal, *adj.;* **-ly,** *adv.*
qua′si-in·ter′nal·ized′, *adj.*
qua′si-in′ter·na′tion·al, *adj.;* **-ly,** *adv.*
qua′si-in′ter·na′tion·al·is′tic, *adj.*
qua′si-in′ter·viewed′, *adj.*
qua′si-in′ti·mate, *adj.;* **-ly,** *adv.*
qua′si-in′ti·mat′ed, *adj.*
qua′si-in·tol′er·a·ble, *adj.;* **-bly,** *adv.*
qua′si-in·tol′er·ant, *adj.;* **-ly,** *adv.*
qua′si-in′tro·duced′, *adj.*
qua′si-in·tu′i·tive, *adj.;* **-ly,** *adv.*
qua′si-in·vad′ed, *adj.*
qua′si-in·ves′ti·gat′ed, *adj.*
qua′si-in·vis′i·ble, *adj.;* **-bly,** *adv.*
qua′si-in·vit′ed, *adj.*
qua′si-ir·reg′u·lar, *adj.;* **-ly,** *adv.*
qua′si-Jac′o·be′an, *adj.*
qua′si-Jap′a·nese′, *adj.*
qua′si-jo·cose′, *adj.;* **-ly,** *adv.*
qua′si-joc′und, *adj.;* **-ly,** *adv.*
qua′si-joint′ly, *adv.*
qua′si-kind′, *adj.;* **-ly,** *adv.*
qua′si-knowl′edge·a·ble, *adj.;* **-bly,** *adv.*
qua′si-la·bo′ri·ous, *adj.;* **-ly,** *adv.*
qua′si-la·ment′ed, *adj.*
qua′si-Lat′in, *adj.*
qua′si-law′ful, *adj.;* **-ly,** *adv.*
qua′si-le′gal, *adj.;* **-ly,** *adv.*
qua′si-leg′end·ar′y, *adj.*
qua′si-leg′is·lat′ed, *adj.*
qua′si-leg′is·la′tive, *adj.;* **-ly,** *adv.*
qua′si-le·git′i·mate, *adj.;* **-ly,** *adv.*
qua′si-lib′er·al, *adj.;* **-ly,** *adv.*
qua′si-lit′er·ar′y, *adj.*
qua′si-liv′ing, *adj.*
qua′si-log′i·cal, *adj.;* **-ly,** *adv.*
qua′si-loy′al, *adj.;* **-ly,** *adv.*
qua′si-lux·u′ri·ous, *adj.;* **-ly,** *adv.*
qua′si-mad′, *adj.;* **-ly,** *adv.*
qua′si-mag′ic, *adj.*
qua′si-mag′i·cal, *adj.;* **-ly,** *adv.*
qua′si-ma·li′cious, *adj.;* **-ly,** *adv.*
qua′si-man′aged, *adj.*
qua′si-man′a·ge′ri·al, *adj.;* **-ly,** *adv.*
qua′si-ma·te′ri·al, *adj.;* **-ly,** *adv.*
qua′si-ma·ter′nal, *adj.;* **-ly,** *adv.*
qua′si-me·chan′i·cal, *adj.;* **-ly,** *adv.*
qua′si-me′di·ae′val, *adj.*
qua′si-med′i·cal, *adj.;* **-ly,** *adv.*
qua′si-me′di·e′val, *adj.*
qua′si-men′tal, *adj.;* **-ly,** *adv.*
qua′si-mer′can·tile′, *adj.*
qua′si-met′a·phys′i·cal, *adj.;* **-ly,** *adv.*
qua′si-me·thod′i·cal, *adj.;* **-ly,** *adv.*
qua′si-might′y, *adj.*
qua′si-mil′i·ta·ris′tic, *adj.*
qua′si-mil′i·ta·ris′ti·cal·ly, *adv.*
qua′si-mil′i·tar′y, *adj.*
qua′si-min′is·te′ri·al, *adj.*
qua′si-mi·rac′u·lous, *adj.;* **-ly,** *adv.*
qua′si-mis′er·a·ble, *adj.;* **-bly,** *adv.*
qua′si-mod′ern, *adj.*
qua′si-mod′est, *adj.;* **-ly,** *adv.*
qua′si-mor′al, *adj.;* **-ly,** *adv.*
qua′si-mor′al·is′tic, *adj.*
qua′si-mor′al·is′ti·cal·ly, *adv.*
qua′si-mu·nic′i·pal, *adj.;* **-ly,** *adv.*
qua′si-mu′si·cal, *adj.;* **-ly,** *adv.*
qua′si-mu′tu·al, *adj.;* **-ly,** *adv.*
qua′si-mys·te′ri·ous, *adj.;* **-ly,** *adv.*
qua′si-myth′i·cal, *adj.;* **-ly,** *adv.*
qua′si-name′less, *adj.*
qua′si-na′tion·al, *adj.;* **-ly,** *adv.*
qua′si-na′tion·al·is′tic, *adj.*
qua′si-na′tive, *adj.*
qua′si-nat′u·ral, *adj.;* **-ly,** *adv.*
qua′si-neb′u·lous, *adj.;* **-ly,** *adv.*
qua′si-nec′es·sar′y, *adj.*
qua′si-neg′a·tive, *adj.;* **-ly,** *adv.*
qua′si-ne·glect′ed, *adj.*
qua′si-neg′li·gent, *adj.*
qua′si-neg′li·gi·ble, *adj.;* **-bly,** *adv.*
qua′si-neu′tral, *adj.;* **-ly,** *adv.*
qua′si-new′, *adj.;* **-ly,** *adv.*
qua′si-nor′mal, *adj.;* **-ly,** *adv.*
qua′si-no·tar′i·al, *adj.*
qua′si-nup′tial, *adj.*
qua′si-o·be′di·ent, *adj.;* **-ly,** *adv.*
qua′si-ob·jec′tive, *adj.;* **-ly,** *adv.*
qua′si-ob′li·gat′ed, *adj.*
qua′si-ob·served′, *adj.*
qua′si-of·fen′sive, *adj.;* **-ly,** *adv.*
qua′si-of·fi′cial, *adj.;* **-ly,** *adv.*
qua′si-op·posed′, *adj.*
qua′si-or′di·nar′y, *adj.*
qua′si-or·gan′ic, *adj.*
qua′si-or·gan′i·cal·ly, *adv.*
qua′si-o′ri·en′tal, *adj.;* **-ly,** *adv.*
qua′si-o·rig′i·nal, *adj.;* **-ly,** *adv.*
qua′si-par′ti·san, *adj.*
qua′si-pas′sive, *adj.;* **-ly,** *adv.*
qua′si-pa·thet′ic, *adj.*
qua′si-pa·thet′i·cal·ly, *adv.*
qua′si-pa′tient, *adj.;* **-ly,** *adv.*
qua′si-pa′tri·ar′chal, *adj.*
qua′si-pa′tri·ot′ic, *adj.*
qua′si-pa′tri·ot′i·cal·ly, *adv.*
qua′si-pa′tron·iz′ing, *adj.;* **-ly,** *adv.*
qua′si-peace′ful, *adj.;* **-ly,** *adv.*
qua′si-per′fect, *adj.;* **-ly,** *adv.*
qua′si-pe′ri·od′ic, *adj.*
qua′si-pe′ri·od′i·cal·ly, *adv.*
qua′si-per′ma·nent, *adj.;* **-ly,** *adv.*
qua′si-per·pet′u·al, *adj.;* **-ly,** *adv.*
qua′si-per′son·a·ble, *adj.;* **-bly,** *adv.*
qua′si-per′son·al, *adj.;* **-ly,** *adv.*
qua′si-pe·rus′a·ble, *adj.*
qua′si-phil′o·soph′i·cal, *adj.;* **-ly,** *adv.*
qua′si-phys′i·cal, *adj.;* **-ly,** *adv.*
qua′si-pi′ous, *adj.;* **-ly,** *adv.*
qua′si-pleas′ur·a·ble, *adj.;* **-bly,** *adv.*
qua′si-pledge′, *v.,* **-pledged, -pledg·ing.**
qua′si-plen′ti·ful, *adj.;* **-ly,** *adv.*
qua′si-po·et′ic, *adj.*
qua′si-po·et′i·cal, *adj.;* **-ly,** *adv.*
qua′si-pol′i·tic, *adj.*
qua′si-po·lit′i·cal, *adj.;* **-ly,** *adv.*
qua′si-poor′, *adj.;* **-ly,** *adv.*
qua′si-pop′u·lar, *adj.;* **-ly,** *adv.*
qua′si-pos′i·tive, *adj.;* **-ly,** *adv.*
qua′si-pow′er·ful, *adj.;* **-ly,** *adv.*
qua′si-prac′ti·cal, *adj.;* **-ly,** *adv.*
qua′si-pre·ced′ent, *adj.*
qua′si-pref′er·en′tial, *adj.;* **-ly,** *adv.*
qua′si-prej′u·diced, *adj.*
qua′si-prep′o·si′tion·al, *adj.;* **-ly,** *adv.*
qua′si-pre·vent′ed, *adj.*
qua′si-pri′vate, *adj.;* **-ly,** *adv.*
qua′si-priv′i·leged, *adj.*
qua′si-prob′a·ble, *adj.;* **-bly,** *adv.*
qua′si-prob′lem·at′ic, *adj.*
qua′si-pro·duc′tive, *adj.;* **-ly,** *adv.*
qua′si-pro·gres′sive, *adj.;* **-ly,** *adv.*
qua′si-prom′ised, *adj.*
qua′si-prompt′, *adj.;* **-ly,** *adv.*
qua′si-pro·phet′ic, *adj.*
qua′si-pro·phet′i·cal, *adj.;* **-ly,** *adv.*
qua′si-pros′e·cut′ed, *adj.*
qua′si-pros′per·ous, *adj.;* **-ly,** *adv.*
qua′si-pro·tect′ed, *adj.*
qua′si-proud′, *adj.;* **-ly,** *adv.*
qua′si-pro·vin′cial, *adj.;* **-ly,** *adv.*
qua′si-pro·voc′a·tive, *adj.;* **-ly,** *adv.*
qua′si-pub′lic, *adj.;* **-ly,** *adv.*
qua′si-pun′ished, *adj.*
qua′si-pu′pil·lar′y, *adj.*
qua′si-pur′chased, *adj.*
qua′si-qual′i·fied′, *adj.*
qua′si-rad′i·cal, *adj.;* **-ly,** *adv.*
qua′si-ra′tion·al, *adj.;* **-ly,** *adv.*
qua′si-re′al·is′tic, *adj.*
qua′si-re′al·is′ti·cal·ly, *adv.*
qua′si-rea′son·a·ble, *adj.;* **-bly,** *adv.*
qua′si-re·bel′lious, *adj.;* **-ly,** *adv.*
qua′si-re′cent, *adj.;* **-ly,** *adv.*
qua′si-rec′og·nized′, *adj.*
qua′si-rec′on·ciled′, *adj.*
qua′si-re·duced′, *adj.*
qua′si-re·fined′, *adj.*
qua′si-re·formed′, *adj.*
qua′si-re·fused′, *adj.*
qua′si-reg′is·tered, *adj.*
qua′si-reg′u·lar, *adj.;* **-ly,** *adv.*
qua′si-reg′u·lat′ed, *adj.*
qua′si-re·ject′ed, *adj.*
qua′si-re·li′a·ble, *adj.;* **-bly,** *adv.*
qua′si-re·lieved′, *adj.*
qua′si-re·li′gious, *adj.;* **-ly,** *adv.*
qua′si-re·mark′a·ble, *adj.;* **-bly,** *adv.*
qua′si-re·newed′, *adj.*
qua′si-re·paired′, *adj.*
qua′si-re·placed′, *adj.*
qua′si-re·port′ed, *adj.*
qua′si-rep′re·sent′ed, *adj.*
qua′si-re·quired′, *adj.*
qua′si-res′cued, *adj.*
qua′si-res′i·den′tial, *adj.;* **-ly,** *adv.*
qua′si-re·sist′ed, *adj.*
qua′si-re·spect′a·ble, *adj.;* **-bly,** *adv.*
qua′si-re·spect′ed, *adj.*
qua′si-re·spect′ful, *adj.;* **-ly,** *adv.*
qua′si-re·spon′si·ble, *adj.;* **-bly,** *adv.*
qua′si-re·spon′sive, *adj.;* **-ly,** *adv.*
qua′si-re·stored′, *adj.*
qua′si-re·tired′, *adj.*
qua′si-rev′o·lu′tion·ized′, *adj.*
qua′si-re·ward′ing, *adj.*
qua′si-ri·dic′u·lous, *adj.;* **-ly,** *adv.*
qua′si-right′eous, *adj.;* **-ly,** *adv.*
qua′si-ro·man′tic, *adj.*
qua′si-ro·man′ti·cal·ly, *adv.*
qua′si-roy′al, *adj.;* **-ly,** *adv.*
qua′si-ru′ral, *adj.;* **-ly,** *adv.*
qua′si-sad′, *adj.;* **-ly,** *adv.*
qua′si-safe′, *adj.;* **-ly,** *adv.*
qua′si-sa·ga′cious, *adj.;* **-ly,** *adv.*
qua′si-saint′ly, *adj.*
qua′si-sanc′tioned, *adj.*
qua′si-san′guine, *adj.;* **-ly,** *adv.*
qua′si-sar·cas′tic, *adj.*
qua′si-sar·cas′ti·cal·ly, *adv.*
qua′si-sa·tir′i·cal, *adj.;* **-ly,** *adv.*
qua′si-sat′is·fied′, *adj.*
qua′si-sav′age, *adj.;* **-ly,** *adv.*
qua′si-schol′ar·ly, *adj.*
qua′si-scho·las′tic, *adj.*
qua′si-scho·las′ti·cal·ly, *adv.*
qua′si-sci′en·tif′ic, *adj.*
qua′si-sci′en·tif′i·cal·ly, *adv.*
qua′si-se′cret, *adj.;* **-ly,** *adv.*
qua′si-se′cre·tive, *adj.;* **-ly,** *adv.*
qua′si-se·cure′, *adj.;* **-ly,** *adv.*
qua′si-sen′ti·men′tal, *adj.;* **-ly,** *adv.*
qua′si-se′ri·ous, *adj.;* **-ly,** *adv.*
qua′si-set′tled, *adj.*
qua′si-sim′i·lar, *adj.;* **-ly,** *adv.*
qua′si-sin·cere′, *adj.;* **-ly,** *adv.*
qua′si-sin′gle, *adj.;* **-gly,** *adv.*
qua′si-skill′ful, *adj.;* **-ly,** *adv.*
qua′si-slan′der·ous, *adj.;* **-ly,** *adv.*
qua′si-so′ber, *adj.;* **-ly,** *adv.*
qua′si-so′cial·is′tic, *adj.*
qua′si-so′cial·is′ti·cal·ly, *adv.*
qua′si-sov′er·eign, *adj.*
qua′si-Span′ish, *adj.*
qua′si-spa′tial, *adj.;* **-ly,** *adv.*
qua′si-spher′i·cal, *adj.;* **-ly,** *adv.*
qua′si-spir′it·ed, *adj.;* **-ly,** *adv.*
qua′si-spir′it·u·al, *adj.;* **-ly,** *adv.*
qua′si-stand′ard·ized′, *adj.*
qua′si-sta′tion·ar′y, *adj.*
qua′si-stren′u·ous, *adj.;* **-ly,** *adv.*
qua′si-stu′di·ous, *adj.;* **-ly,** *adv.*
qua′si-styl′ish, *adj.;* **-ly,** *adv.*
qua′si-sub·jec′tive, *adj.;* **-ly,** *adv.*
qua′si-sub·mis′sive, *adj.;* **-ly,** *adv.*
qua′si-suc·cess′ful, *adj.;* **-ly,** *adv.*
qua′si-suf·fi′cient, *adj.;* **-ly,** *adv.*
qua′si-su′per·fi′cial, *adj.;* **-ly,** *adv.*
qua′si-su·pe′ri·or, *adj.*
qua′si-su′per·vised′, *adj.*
qua′si-sup·port′ed, *adj.*
qua′si-sup·pressed′, *adj.*
qua′si-sym′pa·thet′ic, *adj.*
qua′si-sym′pa·thet′i·cal·ly, *adv.*
qua′si-sys′tem·at′ic, *adj.*
qua′si-sys′tem·at′i·cal·ly, *adv.*
qua′si-sys′tem·a·tized′, *adj.*
qua′si-tan′gent, *adj.*
qua′si-tan′gi·ble, *adj.;* **-bly,** *adv.*
qua′si-tech′ni·cal, *adj.;* **-ly,** *adv.*
qua′si-tem′po·ral, *adj.;* **-ly,** *adv.*
qua′si-ter′ri·to′ri·al, *adj.;* **-ly,** *adv.*
qua′si-the·at′ri·cal, *adj.;* **-ly,** *adv.*
qua′si-thor′ough, *adj.;* **-ly,** *adv.*
qua′si-tol′er·ant, *adj.;* **-ly,** *adv.*
qua′si-to′tal, *adj.;* **-ly,** *adv.*
qua′si-tra·di′tion·al, *adj.;* **-ly,** *adv.*
qua′si-trag′ic, *adj.*
qua′si-trag′i·cal·ly, *adv.*
qua′si-trib′al, *adj.;* **-ly,** *adv.*
qua′si-truth′ful, *adj.;* **-ly,** *adv.*
qua′si-typ′i·cal, *adj.;* **-ly,** *adv.*
qua′si-ty·ran′ni·cal, *adj.;* **-ly,** *adv.*
qua′si-u·nan′i·mous, *adj.;* **-ly,** *adv.*
qua′si-un·con′scious, *adj.;* **-ly,** *adv.*
qua′si-u′ni·fied′, *adj.*
qua′si-u′ni·ver′sal, *adj.;* **-ly,** *adv.*
qua′si-u′ti·lized′, *adj.*
qua′si-val′id, *adj.;* **-ly,** *adv.*
qua′si-val′ued, *adj.*
qua′si-ven′er·a·ble, *adj.;* **-bly,** *adv.*
qua′si-vic·to′ri·ous, *adj.;* **-ly,** *adv.*
qua′si-vi′o·lat′ed, *adj.*
qua′si-vi′o·lent, *adj.;* **-ly,** *adv.*
qua′si-vir′tu·ous, *adj.;* **-ly,** *adv.*
qua′si-vi′tal, *adj.;* **-ly,** *adv.*
qua′si-vo·ca′tion·al, *adj.;* **-ly,** *adv.*
qua′si-war′rant·ed, *adj.*
qua′si-wealth′y, *adj.*
qua′si-whis′pered, *adj.*
qua′si-wick′ed, *adj.;* **-ly,** *adv.*
qua′si-will′ing, *adj.;* **-ly,** *adv.*
qua′si-wrong′, *adj.*
qua′si-young′, *adj.*
qua′si-zeal′ous, *adj.;* **-ly,** *adv.*

quas•qui•cen•ten•ni•al (kwos′kwi sen ten′ē əl), *adj.* **1.** pertaining to or marking a period of 125 years. —*n.* **2.** a 125th anniversary. **3.** a celebration marking such an anniversary. [*quasqui-* one and a quarter (pseudo-L, appar. QUA(DRI-) + (SE)SQUI-) + CENTENIAL]

quass (kväs, kwäs), *n.* kvass.

quas•sia (kwosh′ə, -ē ə), *n.* **1.** a shrub or small tree, *Quassia amara,* of tropical America, having pinnate leaves, showy red flowers, and wood with a bitter taste. Cf. **quassia family. 2.** any of several other trees having bitter-tasting wood. **3.** Also called **bitterwood.** *Chem., Pharm.* a prepared form of the heartwood of any of these trees, used as an insecticide and in medicine as a tonic to dispel intestinal worms. [1755–65; < NL, named after *Quassi,* 18th-century slave in Dutch Guiana who discovered its medicinal properties; see -IA]

quas′sia fam′ily, the plant family Simaroubaceae, characterized by tropical and subtropical trees and shrubs having pinnately compound leaves, clusters of flowers, fruit in the form of a capsule or berry, or fleshy or winged fruit, and a bitter bark used medicinally, and including the ailanthus and quassia.

quat., (in prescriptions) four. [< L *quattuor*]

quat•er (kwat′ər), *adv.* (in prescriptions) four times. [< L]

quat•er•cen•ten•ar•y (kwot′ər sen ten′ə rē, -sen′tn-er′ē; *esp. Brit.* kwot′ər sen tē′nə rē), *adj., n., pl.,* **-ar•ies.** —*n.* **1.** a 400th anniversary. —*adj.* **2.** pertaining to or marking a period of 400 years; quatercentennial. [1880–85; < L *quater* four times + CENTENARY]

quat•er•cen•ten•ni•al (kwot′ər sen ten′ē əl), *adj.* pertaining to or marking a period of 400 years. [1960–65; < L *quater* four times + CENTENNIAL]

quat•er•nar•y (kwot′ər ner′ē, kwə tûr′nə rē), *adj., n., pl.* **-nar•ies.** —*adj.* **1.** consisting of four. **2.** arranged in fours. **3.** (*cap.*) *Geol.* noting or pertaining to the present period of earth history, forming the latter part of the Cenozoic Era, originating about 2 million years ago and including the Recent and Pleistocene Epochs. See table under **geologic time. 4.** (of an alloy) having four principal constituents. —*n.* **5.** a group of four. **6.** the number four. **7.** (*cap.*) *Geol.* the Quaternary Period or System. [1400–50; late ME < L *quaternārius* consisting of four, equiv. to *quatern(ī)* four at a time + *-ārius* -ARY]

quat′ernary ammo′nium com′pound, *Chem.* any of a class of salts derived from ammonium in which the nitrogen atom is attached to four organic groups, as in benzalkonium chloride; the salts are cationic surface-active compounds used as antiseptics and disinfectants. Also called **quat′ernary ammo′nium salt′.** [1815–25]

quat•er•nate (kwot′ər nāt′, kwə tûr′nit), *adj.* having four parts, as the leaves of certain plants. [1745–55; < L *quatern(ī)* four at a time + -ATE[1]]

qua•ter•ni•on (kwə tûr′nē ən), *n.* **1.** a group or set of four persons or things. **2.** *Bookbinding.* four gathered sheets folded in two for binding together. **3.** *Math.* **a.** an expression of the form $a + bi + cj + dk$, where a, b, c, and d are real numbers; $i^2 = j^2 = k^2 = -1$; and $ij = -ji = k$, $jk = -kj = i$, and $ki = -ik = j$. **b.** a quantity or operator expressed as the sum of a real number and three complex numbers, equivalent to the quotient of two vectors. The field of quaternions is not commutative under multiplication. [1350–1400; ME *quaternioun* < LL *quaterniōn-* (s. of *quaterniō*), equiv. to L *quatern(ī)* four at a time + *-iōn-* -ION]

qua•ter•ni•ty (kwə tûr′ni tē), *n., pl.* **-ties.** a group or set of four. [1520–30; < LL *quaternitās,* equiv. to L *quatern(ī)* four each, four at a time + *-itās* -ITY]

Quath•lam•ba (kwät läm′bə), *n.* Drakensberg.

qua•torze (kə tôrz′; *Fr.* KA TÔRZ′), *n., pl.* **-torz•es** (-tôr′ziz; *Fr.* -TÔRZ′). *Piquet.* a set of four cards of the same denomination, aces, kings, queens, jacks, or tens, scoring 14 points. [1695–1705; < F: fourteen < L *quattuordecim,* equiv. to *quattuor* FOUR + *-decim,* comb. form of *decem* TEN]

quat•rain (kwo′trān), *n.* a stanza or poem of four lines, usually with alternate rhymes. [1575–85; < F, equiv. to *quatre* FOUR (< L *quattuor*) + *-ain* < L *-ānus* -AN]

qua•tre (kä′tər; *Fr.* KA′TRᵊ), *n.* the four at cards, dice, or the like. [1540–50; < F]

Qua•tre Bras (kä′trə brä′; *Fr.* KA TRᵊ BRÄ′), a village in central Belgium, near Brussels: battle preliminary to the battle of Waterloo fought here 1815.

quat•re•foil (kat′ər foil′, ka′trə-), *n.* **1.** a leaf composed of four leaflets. **2.** *Archit.* a panellike ornament composed of four lobes, divided by cusps, radiating from a common center. [1375–1425; ME < MF *quatre* four + *-foil* (as in TREFOIL)] —**quat′re•foiled′,** *adj.*

quatrefoils (def. 2)

quat•tro•cen•to (kwä′trō chen′tō; *It.* kwät′trô chen′tô), *n.* (*often cap.*) the 15th century, used in reference to the Italian art and literature of that time. [1870–75; < It, short for *mil quattro cento* 1400, occurring in the names of all the years from 1400 to 1499] —**quat′tro•cen′tist,** *n.*

quat•tu•or•de•cil•lion (kwot′o͞o ôr′di sil′yən, kwot′yo͞o-), *n., pl.* **-lions,** (*as after a numeral*) **-lion,** *adj.* —*n.* **1.** a cardinal number represented in the U.S. by 1 followed by 45 zeros, and in Great Britain by 1 followed by 84 zeros. —*adj.* **2.** amounting to one quattuordecillion in number. [1900–05; < L *quattuordec(im)* fourteen (see QUATORZE) + *-illion* (as in *million*)] —**quat′tu•or′de•cil′lionth,** *adj., n.*

qua•ver (kwā′vər), *v.i.* **1.** to shake tremulously; quiver or tremble: *He stood there quavering with fear.* **2.** to sound, speak, or sing tremulously: *Her voice quavered a moment and then she regained control.* **3.** to perform trills in singing or on a musical instrument. —*v.t.* **4.** to utter, say, or sing with a quavering or tremulous voice. —*n.* **5.** a quavering or tremulous shake, esp. in the voice. **6.** a quavering tone or utterance. **7.** *Music, Chiefly Brit.* an eighth note. See illus. under **note.** [1400–50; late ME *quaveren* (v.), b. QUAKE and WAVER[1]] —**qua′ver•er,** *n.* —**qua′ver•ing•ly,** *adv.* —**qua′ver•y, qua′ver•ous,** *adj.*

quay (kē, kā, kwā), *n.* a landing place, esp. one of solid masonry, constructed along the edge of a body of water; wharf. [1690–1700; sp. var. (after F *quai*) of earlier *kay* (also *key,* whence the mod. pronunciation) < OF *kay, cay;* akin to Sp *cayo* shoal. See KEY[2]] —**quay′like′,** *adj.* —**Syn.** pier, dock, landing, levee.

quay•age (kē′ij, kā′-, kwā′-), *n.* **1.** quays collectively. **2.** space appropriated to quays. **3.** a charge for the use of a quay or quays. [1750–60; < F, equiv. to *quay* QUAY + *-age* -AGE]

Quayle (kwāl), *n.* **James Dan•forth** (dan′fôrth) (*Dan*), born 1947, U.S. politician: senator 1981–89; vice president of the U.S. 1989–93.

qub•ba (ko͝ob′ə), *n.* a small Moslem shrine. [< Ar *qubboh* lit., dome]

′que (kyo͞o), *n. Chiefly California.* barbecue. [by shortening]

Que., Quebec.

quean (kwēn), *n.* **1.** an overly forward, impudent woman; shrew; hussy. **2.** a prostitute. **3.** *Brit. Dial.* a girl or young woman, esp. a robust one. [bef. 1000; ME *quene,* OE *cwene;* c. MD *quene, kone,* OS, OHG *quena,* Goth *qino* < Gmc **kwenōn-;* akin to OE *cwēn* woman, QUEEN] —**quean′ish,** *adj.* —**quean′like′,** *adj.*

quea•sy (kwē′zē), *adj.,* **-si•er, -si•est. 1.** inclined to or feeling nausea, as the stomach, a person, etc.; nauseous; nauseated. **2.** tending to cause nausea; nauseating. **3.** uneasy or uncomfortable, as feelings, the conscience, etc. **4.** squeamish; excessively fastidious. [1425–75; late ME *qweysy, coisi,* of uncert. orig.] —**quea′si•ly,** *adv.* —**quea′si•ness,** *n.* —**Syn. 3.** upset, troubled, anxious, worried.

Que•bec (kwi bek′, ki-), *n.* **1.** a province in E Canada. 6,141,491; 594,860 sq. mi. (1,540,685 sq. km). **2.** a seaport in and the capital of this province, on the St. Lawrence: capital of New France from 1663 to 1759, when it was taken by the English; wartime conferences 1943, 1944. 177,082. **3.** a word used in communications to represent the letter Q. French, **Qué•bec** (kā bek′) (for 1, 2).

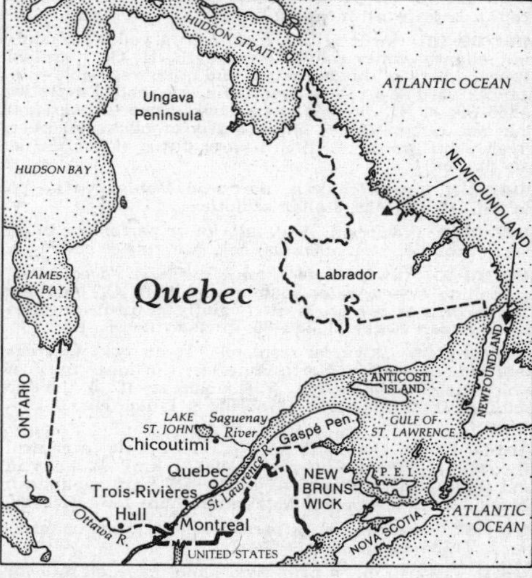

Que•bec•er (kwi bek′ər), *n.* a native or inhabitant of Quebec, esp. one who is from the city of Quebec and whose native language is French. Also, **Que•beck′er, Québecois, Quebecois.** [1830–40; QUEBEC + -ER[1]]

Qué•bec•ois (kā′be kwä′; *Fr.* kā be KWA′), *n., pl.* **-bec•ois** (-be kwä′, -kwäz′; *Fr.* -be KWA′). **1.** Quebecer. **2.** a person, esp. a member of the Parti Québecois, who supports the separation and independence of the province of Quebec from the rest of Canada. Also, **Que′bec•ois′.** [1870–75; < F; see QUEBEC, -ESE]

que•bra•cho (kā brä′chō; *Sp.* ke VRÄ′chô), *n., pl.* **-chos** (-chōz; *Sp.* -chôs). **1.** any of several tropical American trees of the genus *Schinopsis,* having very hard wood, esp. *S. lorentzii,* the wood and bark of which are important in tanning and dyeing. **2.** a tree, *Aspidosperma quebrachoblanco,* of the dogbane family, yielding a medicinal bark. **3.** the wood or bark of any of these trees. [1880–85; < AmerSp, var. of *quiebracha, quiebrahacha* lit., (it) breaks (the) hatchet; see QUEBRADA, HATCHET]

que•bra•da (kā brä′də), *n.* **1.** *Southwestern U.S.* a ravine. **2.** a brook. [1825–35; < Sp, n. use of fem. ptp. of *quebrar* to break << L *crepāre* to clatter, crack, rattle]

Quech•ua (kech′wä, -wə), *n., pl.* **-uas,** (*esp. collectively*) **-ua** for 2. **1.** the language of the Inca civilization, presently spoken by about 7 million people in Peru, Ecuador, Bolivia, Chile, and Argentina. **2.** a member of an Indian people of Peru speaking Quechua. Also, **Kechua, Kechuan, Quechuan, Quichua.**

Quech•uan (kech′wən), *adj., n., pl.* **-uans,** (*esp. collectively*) **-uan.** —*adj.* **1.** of or pertaining to the Quechua language or people. —*n.* **2.** Quechua. [1835–45; QUECHU(A) + -AN]

queen (kwēn), *n.* **1.** a female sovereign or monarch. **2.** the wife or consort of a king. **3.** a woman, or something personified as a woman, that is foremost or preeminent in any respect: *a movie queen; a beauty queen; Athens, the queen of the Aegean.* **4.** *Slang (disparaging and offensive).* **a.** a male homosexual, esp. one who is flamboyantly campy. **b.** See **drag queen. 5.** a playing card bearing a picture of a queen. **6.** *Chess.* the most powerful piece of either color, moved across any number of empty squares in any direction. **7.** *Entomol.* a fertile female ant, bee, termite, or wasp. **8.** a word formerly used in communications to represent the letter Q. —*v.i.* **9.** to reign as queen. **10.** to behave in an imperious or pretentious manner (usually fol. by *it*). **11.** *Chess.* to become promoted to a queen. [bef. 900; ME *quene, quen,* OE *cwēn* woman, queen; c. OS *quān,* ON *kvān,* Goth *qēns* < Gmc **kwēni-;* akin to OIr *ben,* Gk *gynḗ* woman, Russ *zhená,* Skt *jani* wife] —**queen′less,** *adj.* —**queen′like′,** *adj.*

Queen′ Anne′, 1. noting or pertaining to the style of architecture, furnishings, and decoration prevailing in England in the early 18th century, characterized by simplicity and refinement of forms, with increasing attention to French and Italian models. **2.** noting or pertaining to the style of architecture, furnishings, and decoration prevailing in England from c1865 to c1885, imitated in the U.S. from c1875 to c1890, characterized by imitation of English vernacular work of the middle and late 17th century, often with an eclectic mixture of medieval, 18th-century, and Japanese motifs. [1765–75]

Queen′ Anne′s′ lace′, a plant, *Daucus carota,* the wild form of the cultivated carrot, having broad umbels of white flowers. Also called **wild carrot.** [1890–95]

Queen′ Anne′s′ War′, the war (1702–13) in which England and its American colonies opposed France and its Indian allies. It constituted the American phase of the War of the Spanish Succession.

queen′ bee′, 1. a fertile female bee. See illus. under **bee. 2.** a woman who is in a favored or preeminent position. [1600–10]

Queen′ Char′lotte Is′lands, a group of islands in British Columbia off the W coast of Canada. 2222; 3970 sq. mi. (10,280 sq. km).

Queen′ Cit′y, *Canadian Informal.* Toronto.

queen′ clos′er (klō′zer), *Masonry.* **1.** a brick of normal length and thickness but of half normal width, used to complete a course or to space regular bricks. **2.** a brick of half the usual length, for completing a course or for spacing regular bricks. Also called **queen′ clo′sure.** Cf. **king closer.** [1835–45]

queen′ con′sort, the wife of a ruling king. [1755–65]

queen-cup (kwēn′kup′), *n.* a North American plant, *Clintonia uniflora,* of the lily family, having solitary, white flowers and blue berries.

queen•dom (kwēn′dəm), *n.* **1.** the position or status of a queen. **2.** the realm of a queen. [1600–10; QUEEN + -DOM]

queen′ dow′ager, the widow of a king. [1615–25]

Queen′ Eliz′abeth Is′lands, a group of islands, including Ellesmere Island, in the Arctic Ocean, in the N Northwest Territories, N Canada.

queen•fish (kwēn′fish′), *n., pl.* **-fish•es,** (*esp. collectively*) **-fish.** a silvery and bluish drum, *Seriphus politus,* inhabiting shallow waters along the coast of California. [1880–85, *Amer.;* QUEEN + FISH]

queen•hood (kwēn′ho͝od), *n.* the state, dignity, or rank of a queen. [1855–60; QUEEN + -HOOD]

Queen•ie (kwē′nē), *n.* a female given name.

queen•ing (kwē′ning), *n. Chess.* promotion (def. 6). [QUEEN + -ING[1]]

queen•ly (kwēn′lē), *adj.,* **-li•er, -li•est,** *adv.* —*adj.* **1.** belonging or proper to a queen: *queenly propriety.* **2.** befitting, or suggestive of, a queen: *queenly grace.* —*adv.* **3.** in a queenly manner. [1530–40; QUEEN + -LY] —**queen′li•ness,** *n.*

Queen′ Mab′ (mab), *Irish and English Folklore.* a mischievous, tantalizing fairy who governs and produces people's dreams.

Queen′ Maud′ Land′ (môd), a coastal region of Antarctica, S of Africa: Norwegian explorations.

Queen′ Maud′ Range′, a mountain range in Antarctica, in Ross Dependency, S of the Ross Sea.

queen′ moth′er, a queen dowager who is mother of a reigning sovereign. [1570–80]

Queen′ of Heav′en, 1. a designation of the Virgin Mary. **2.** (*l.c.*) an ancient Semitic goddess, variously identified with other ancient goddesses, as Isis and Ashtoreth. **3.** an epithet of Ishtar. [1200–50; ME]

queen′ of the prai′rie, a tall plant, *Filipendula rubra,* of the rose family, having branching clusters of pink flowers, growing in meadows and prairies. Also, **queen′-of-the-prai′rie.** [1850–55, *Amer.*]

queen′ ol′ive, 1. any large, meaty olive suitable for pickling or processing. **2.** such an olive grown esp. in the area of Seville, Spain. [1910–15]

queen′ palm′, a feather palm, *Arecastrum romanzoffianum,* of South America, having leaves from 7 to 12 ft. (2 to 3½ m) in length, and large, hanging clusters of small fruit.

queen′ post′, either of a pair of timbers or posts extending vertically upward from the tie beam of a roof truss or the like, one on each side of the center. [1815–25]

A, **queen post;** B, tie beam; C, strut; D, straining piece; E, purlin; F, common rafter; G, ridgepole

queen′ re′gent, **1.** a queen who reigns in behalf of another. **2.** See **queen regnant.** [1755–65]

queen′ reg′nant, a queen who reigns in her own right. Also, **queen regent.** [1840–50]

Queens (kwēnz), *n.* a borough of E New York City, on Long Island. 1,891,325; 113.1 sq. mi. (295 sq. km).

Queen's′ Bench′. See **King's Bench.**

Queens′ber·ry rules′ (kwēnz′ber′ē, -bə rē). See **Marquis of Queensberry rules.**

queen's′ boun′ty, *Brit.* See **king's bounty.** Also, **Queen's′ boun′ty, Queen's′ Boun′ty.**

Queen's′ Cham′pion. See under **Champion of England.**

Queen's′ Coun′sel. See **King's Counsel.** [1855–60]

queen's′ Eng′lish. See **king's English.** [1585–95]

queen's′ ev′idence. See **king's evidence.**

queen's′ high′way. See **king's highway.** Also, **Queen's′ high′way, Queen's′ High′way.**

queen·ship (kwēn′ship), *n.* the state, office, or dignity of a queen. [1530–40; QUEEN + -SHIP]

queen-size (kwēn′sīz′), *adj.* **1.** (of a bed) larger than a double bed, but smaller than king-size, usually 60 in. (152 cm) wide and 80 in. (203 cm) long. **2.** pertaining to or made for a queen-size bed: *queen-size blankets.* Cf. **full-size, king-size, twin-size. 3.** of a size larger than average: often used as a euphemism: *a store specializing in queen-size clothing.* Also, **queen′-sized′.** [1955–60; by analogy with KING-SIZE]

Queens·land (kwēnz′land′, -lənd), *n.* a state in NE Australia. 2,295,123; 670,500 sq. mi. (1,736,595 sq. km). *Cap.:* Brisbane.

Queens′land nut′, macadamia. [1880–85]

Queen's′ pat′tern, **1.** a pattern of ceramic decoration consisting of bands of swirling radial lines, white on blue alternating with red on white. **2.** an early 19th-century silver pattern having a shell at the stem terminal and an ornament resembling a fleur-de-lis on the stem enclosed by elaborate scrolls. [1760–70]

queen's′-pawn′ o′penings (kwēnz′pôn′), (*used with a singular v.*) a class of chess openings in which the pawn in front of the queen is advanced two squares on the first move.

Queen's′ Proc′tor. See **King's Proctor.**

Queen's′ Remem′brancer. See **King's Remembrancer.**

queen's′ scout′. See **king's scout.** [1950–55]

queen's′ shil′ling. See **king's shilling.** [1875–80]

Queen's′ speech′. See **King's speech.**

Queens·town (kwēnz′toun′), *n.* former name of **Cóbh.**

queen′ sub′stance, a pheromone secreted from the mandibular glands of a queen honeybee and smelled, eaten, and absorbed by the worker bees, having the effect of preventing them from producing or rearing rival queens. [1950–55]

queen's′ ware′, a hard, cream-colored earthenware, perfected c1765 by Wedgwood. Also, **queens′ware′.** [1760–70]

queen′ truss′, a truss having queen posts with no king post. [1860–65]

queer (kwēr), *adj.,* **-er, -est,** *v., n.* —*adj.* **1.** strange or odd from a conventional viewpoint; unusually different; singular: *a queer notion of justice.* **2.** of a questionable nature or character; suspicious; shady: *Something queer about the language of the prospectus kept investors away.* **3.** not feeling physically right or well; giddy, faint, or qualmish: *to feel queer.* **4.** mentally unbalanced or deranged. **5.** *Slang* (*disparaging and offensive*). **a.** homosexual. **b.** effeminate; unmanly. **6.** *Slang.* bad, worthless, or counterfeit. —*v.t.* **7.** to spoil; ruin. **8.** to put (a person) in a hopeless or disadvantageous situation as to success, favor, etc. **9.** to jeopardize. **10. queer the pitch,** *Brit. Informal.* to spoil the chances of success. —*n.* **11.** *Slang* (*disparaging and offensive*). a homosexual, esp. a male homosexual. **12.** *Slang.* counterfeit money. [1500–10; perh. < G *quer* oblique, cross, adverse] —**queer′ly,** *adv.* —**queer′ness,** *n.*
—**Syn. 1.** unconventional, curious, freakish, eccentric, weird. See **strange.** —**Ant. 1.** ordinary.

Queer′ Street′, a condition of financial instability or embarrassment: *Such extravagance will surely put them in Queer Street.* [1830–40]

que·le·a (kwē′lē ə), *n.* any of several African weaverbirds of the genus *Quelea,* esp. *Q. quelea* (**red-billed quelea**), noted for its vast flocks that destroy grain crops. [1925–30; < NL: genus name (1850; earlier as a species name), perh. alter. of ML *qualea* quail]

CONCISE ETYMOLOGY KEY: <, descended or borrowed from; >, whence; b., blend of, blended; c., cognate with; cf., compare; deriv., derivative; equiv., equivalent; imit., imitative; obl., oblique; r., replacing; s., stem; sp., spelling, spelled; resp., respelling, respelled; trans., translation; ?, origin unknown; *, unattested; ‡, probably earlier than. See the full key inside the front cover.

Quel·i·ma·ne (kel′ə mä′nə), *n.* a seaport in E Mozambique. 70,000.

quell (kwel), *v.t.* **1.** to suppress; put an end to; extinguish: *The troops quelled the rebellion quickly.* **2.** to vanquish; subdue. **3.** to quiet or allay (emotions, anxieties, etc.): *The child's mother quelled his fears of the thunder.* [bef. 900; ME *quellen,* OE *cwellan* to kill; akin to ON *kvelja* to torment, G *quälen* to vex; cf. KILL[1]] —**quell′a·ble,** *adj.* —**quell′er,** *n.*
—**Syn. 1, 2.** crush, quash, overpower, overcome, defeat, conquer, quench. **3.** calm, pacify, compose, hush. —**Ant. 1, 2.** foster. **3.** agitate.

Quel·part (kwel′pärt), *n.* former name of **Cheju** (def. 1).

quel·que-chose (kel′kə shōz′), *n.* kickshaw. [< F: something]

Que·moy (ki moi′), *n.* an island off the SE coast of China, in the Taiwan Strait: controlled by Taiwan. 61,305; 50 sq. mi. (130 sq. km). Also called **Chinmen, Jinmen, Kinmen.** Cf. **Matsu.**

quench (kwench), *v.t.* **1.** to slake, satisfy, or allay (thirst, desires, passion, etc.). **2.** to put out or extinguish (fire, flames, etc.). **3.** to cool suddenly by plunging into a liquid, as in tempering steel by immersion in water. **4.** to subdue or destroy; overcome; quell: *to quench an uprising.* **5.** *Electronics.* to terminate (the flow of electrons in a vacuum tube) by application of a voltage. [1150–1200; ME *quenchen,* earlier *cwenken;* cf. OE *-cwencan* in *ācwencan* to quench (cf. A-[3])] —**quench′a·ble,** *adj.* —**quench′a·ble·ness,** *n.* —**quench′er,** *n.*

quench·less (kwench′lis), *adj.* not capable of being quenched; unquenchable. [1550–60; QUENCH + -LESS] —**quench′less·ly,** *adv.* —**quench′less·ness,** *n.*

que·nelle (kə nel′), *n. French Cookery.* a dumpling of finely chopped fish or meat that is poached in water or stock and usually served with a sauce. [1835–45; < F < G *Knödel* dumpling]

Quen·tin (kwen′tn), *n.* a male or female given name: from a Latin word meaning "fifth."

quer·ce·tin (kwûr′si tin), *n. Chem.* a yellow, crystalline, slightly water-soluble powder, $C_{15}H_{10}O_7$, obtained from the bark of the quercitron and other vegetable substances, used as a yellow dye; flavin. Also called **meletin.** [1855–60; < NL *quercēt(um)* an oak grove (L *querc(us)* oak (see QUERCINE) + *-ētum* suffix of places where a given plant grows) + -IN[2]] —**quer·cet·ic** (kwər set′ik, -sē′tik), *adj.*

Quer·cia (kweʀ′chä), *n.* **Ja·co·po Del·la** (yä′kô pô del′lä), 1374?–1438, Italian sculptor.

quer·cine (kwûr′sin, -sīn), *adj.* of or pertaining to an oak. [1650–60; < L *querc(us)* oak (see FIR) + -INE[2]]

quer·ci·tol (kwûr′si tôl′, -tol′), *n. Chem.* a colorless, crystalline, sweet, water-soluble solid, $C_6H_{12}O_5$, obtained from acorns or oak bark: used chiefly in medicine. Also called **acorn sugar.** [1880–85; QUERCET(IN) + -OL[1]]

quer·ci·tron (kwûr′si trən), *n.* **1.** an oak, *Quercus velutina,* of eastern North America, the inner bark of which yields a yellow dye. **2.** the bark itself. **3.** the dye obtained from this bark. [1785–95; < L *quer(cus)* oak + CITRON]

Que·ré·ta·ro (ke ʀe′tä ʀô′), *n.* **1.** a state in central Mexico. 618,000; 4432 sq. mi. (11,480 sq. km). **2.** a city in and the capital of this state, in the SW part: republican forces executed Emperor Maximilian here 1867. 150,226.

que·rist (kwēr′ist), *n.* a person who inquires or questions. [1625–35; QUER(Y) + -IST]

quern (kwûrn), *n.* a primitive, hand-operated mill for grinding grain. [bef. 950; ME; OE *cweorn;* akin to ON *kvern* hand-mill]

quer·sprung (kvâr′shprŏŏng′), *n. Skiing.* a jump turn in which a skier lands at right angles to the pole or poles. [< G: diagonal jump]

quer·u·lous (kwer′ə ləs, kwer′yə-), *adj.* **1.** full of complaints; complaining. **2.** characterized by or uttered in complaint; peevish: *a querulous tone; constant querulous reminders of things to be done.* [1490–1500; < L *querulus,* equiv. to *quer(i)* to complain + *-ulus* -ULOUS] —**quer′u·lous·ly,** *adv.* —**quer′u·lous·ness,** *n.*
—**Syn. 1, 2.** petulant, testy; caviling, carping, discontented. —**Ant. 1.** contented.

que·ry (kwēr′ē), *n., pl.* **-ries,** *v.,* **-ried, -ry·ing.** —*n.* **1.** a question; an inquiry. **2.** mental reservation; doubt. **3.** *Print.* a question mark (?), esp. as added on a manuscript, proof sheet, or the like, indicating doubt as to some point in the text. **4.** an inquiry from a writer to an editor of a magazine, newspaper, etc., regarding the acceptability of or interest in an idea for an article, news story, or the like: usually presented in the form of a letter that outlines or describes the projected piece. —*v.t.* **5.** to ask or inquire about: *No one queried his presence.* **6.** to question as doubtful or obscure: *to query a statement.* **7.** *Print.* to mark (a manuscript, proof sheet, etc.) with a query. **8.** to ask questions of. [1625–35; alter. (cf. -Y[3]) of earlier *quere* < L *quaere* QUAERE] —**que′ry·ing·ly,** *adv.*

ques., question.

que·sa·dil·la (kā′sə dē′ə; *Sp.* ke′sä thē′yä), *n., pl.* **-dil·las** (-dē′əz; *Sp.* -thē′yäs). *Mexican Cookery.* a tortilla folded over a filling of shredded cheese, onions, and chilies and broiled or fried. [1940–45; < MexSp; Sp: pastry or cake made with cheese, equiv. to *quesad(a)* (*ques(o)* cheese (< L *cāseus;* cf. CHEESE[1]) + *-ada* -ADE[1]) + *-illa* dim. suffix]

qué se·rá, se·rá (ke′ se ʀä′ se ʀä′; *Eng.* kā′ sə rä′ sə rä′), *Spanish.* what will be, will be.

Ques·nay (ke ne′), *n.* **Fran·çois** (fʀäɴ swa′), 1694–1774, French economist and physician.

quest (kwest), *n.* **1.** a search or pursuit made in order to find or obtain something: *a quest for uranium mines; a quest for knowledge.* **2.** *Medieval Romance.* an adventurous expedition undertaken by a knight or knights to secure or achieve something: *the quest of the Holy Grail.* **3.** those engaged in such an expedition. **4.** *Brit. Dial.* inquest. **5.** *Obs.* a jury of inquest. —*v.i.* **6.** to search; seek (often fol. by *for* or *after*): *to quest after hidden treasure.* **7.** to go on a quest. **8.** *Hunting.* (of a dog) **a.** to search for game. **b.** to bay or give tongue in pursuit of game. —*v.t.* **9.** to search or seek for; pursue. [1275–1325; (n.) ME *queste* < OF < L *quaesīta,* fem. ptp. of *quaerere* to seek; (v.) ME *questen* < OF *quester,* deriv. of the n.] —**quest′er,** *n.* —**quest′ing·ly,** *adv.*
—**Syn. 1.** hunt, seeking, journey, mission, enterprise.

ques·tion (kwes′chən), *n.* **1.** a sentence in an interrogative form, addressed to someone in order to get information in reply. **2.** a problem for discussion or under discussion; a matter for investigation. **3.** a matter of some uncertainty or difficulty; problem (usually fol. by *of*): *It was simply a question of time.* **4.** a subject of dispute or controversy. **5.** a proposal to be debated or voted on, as in a meeting or a deliberative assembly. **6.** the procedure of putting a proposal to a vote. **7.** *Politics.* a problem of public policy submitted to the voters for an expression of opinion. **8.** *Law.* **a.** a controversy that is submitted to a judicial tribunal or administrative agency for decision. **b.** the interrogation by which information is secured. **c.** *Obs.* judicial examination or trial. **9.** the act of asking or inquiring; interrogation; query. **10.** inquiry into or discussion of some problem or doubtful matter. **11. beg the question.** See **beg** (def. 9). **12. beyond question,** beyond dispute; without doubt: *It was, beyond question, a magnificent performance.* Also, **beyond all question. 13. call in** or **into question, a.** to dispute; challenge. **b.** to cast doubt upon; question: *This report calls into question all previous research on the subject.* **14. in question, a.** under consideration. **b.** in dispute. **15. out of the question,** not to be considered; unthinkable; impossible: *She thought about a trip to Spain but dismissed it as out of the question.* —*v.t.* **16.** to ask (someone) a question; ask questions of; interrogate. **17.** to ask or inquire. **18.** to make a question of; doubt: *He questioned her sincerity.* **19.** to challenge or dispute: *She questioned the judge's authority in the case.* —*v.i.* **20.** to ask a question or questions. [1250–1300; (n.) ME *questio(u)n, questiun* < AF *questiun,* MF *question* < L *quaestiōn-* (s. of *quaestiō*), equiv. to *quaes-,* s. of *quaerere* to ask + *-tiōn-* -TION; (v.) late ME < MF *questioner,* deriv. of the n.] —**ques′tion·er,** *n.*
—**Syn. 1.** inquiry, query, interrogation. **16.** query, examine. **17.** See **inquire.** —**Ant. 1, 16.** answer, reply.

ques·tion·a·ble (kwes′chə nə bəl), *adj.* **1.** of doubtful propriety, honesty, morality, respectability, etc.: *questionable activities; in questionable taste.* **2.** open to question or dispute; doubtful or uncertain: *a statement of questionable accuracy.* **3.** open to question as to being of the nature or value suggested: *a questionable privilege.* [1580–90; QUESTION + -ABLE] —**ques′tion·a·ble·ness, ques′tion·a·bil′i·ty,** *n.* —**ques′tion·a·bly,** *adv.*
—**Syn. 2.** debatable, disputable, controvertible, dubitable, dubious. —**Ant. 1.** certain.

ques·tion·ar·y (kwes′chə ner′ē), *n., pl.* **-ar·ies.** a questionnaire. [1535–45; < ML *quaestiōnārium* or F *questionnaire;* see QUESTION, -ARY]

ques·tion·ing (kwes′chə ning), *adj.* **1.** indicating or implying a question: *a questioning tone in her voice.* **2.** characterized by or indicating intellectual curiosity; inquiring: *an alert and questioning mind.* —*n.* **3.** an inquiry or interrogation. [1795–1805; QUESTION + -ING[2], -ING[1]] —**ques′tion·ing·ly,** *adv.*

ques·tion·less (kwes′chən lis), *adj.* **1.** unquestionable; doubtless: *a questionless fact.* **2.** unquestioning: *questionless faith in God.* —*adv.* **3.** without question; unquestionably. [1375–1425; late ME; see QUESTION, -LESS] —**ques′tion·less·ly,** *adv.*

ques′tion mark′, **1.** Also called **interrogation point, interrogation mark.** a mark indicating a question: usually, as in English, the mark (?) placed after a question. **2.** something unanswered or unknown: *His identity is still a question mark to most of us.* **3.** an anglewing butterfly, *Polygonia interrogationis,* having silver spots shaped like a question mark on the underside of each hind wing. [1865–70]

ques·tion·mas·ter (kwes′chən mas′tər, -mä′stər), *n. Brit.* quizmaster. [1945–50; QUESTION + MASTER]

ques·tion·naire (kwes′chə nâr′), *n.* a list of questions, usually printed, submitted for replies that can be analyzed for usable information: *a questionnaire used in market research.* [1895–1900; < F, equiv. to *question(er)* to QUESTION + *-aire;* see -ARY]

ques′tion of fact′, a question concerning the reality of an alleged event or circumstance in a trial by jury, usually determined by the jury. Cf. **question of law.**

ques′tion of law′, a question concerning a rule or the legal effect or consequence of an event or circumstance, usually determined by a court or judge. Cf. **question of fact.**

ques′tion time′, *Parl. Proc.* a time set aside in a session during which members of a parliament may question a minister or ministers regarding state affairs. [1850–55]

ques•tor (kwes′tər, kwē′stər), *n. Rom. Hist.* quaestor.

quetsch (kwech, kvech), *n.* **1.** *Hort.* a variety of plum. **2.** a dry, white, unaged brandy distilled from quetsch plums in Alsace. [1830–40; < G *Quetsche* plum]

Quet•ta (kwet′ə), *n.* a city in W central Pakistan: the capital of Baluchistan; almost totally destroyed by an earthquake 1935. 285,000.

quet•zal (ket säl′), *n., pl.* **-zals, -za•les** (-sä′läs). **1.** any of several large Central and South American trogons of the genus *Pharomachrus,* having golden-green and scarlet plumage, esp. *P. mocino* **(resplendent quetzal),** the national bird of Guatemala: rare and possibly endangered. **2.** a paper money and monetary unit of Guatemala, equal to 100 centavos. *Abbr.:* Q. Also, **que•zal** (ke-säl′). [1820–30; < AmerSp < Nahuatl *quetzalli* plumage of the quetzal bird]

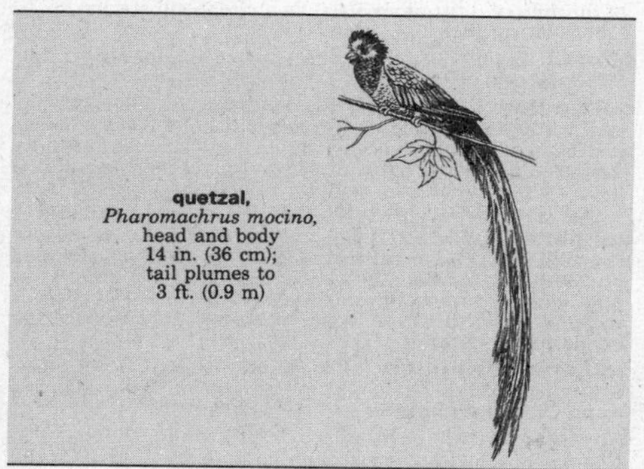

quetzal, *Pharomachrus mocino,* head and body 14 in. (36 cm); tail plumes to 3 ft. (0.9 m)

Quet•zal•co•a•tl (ket säl′kō ät′l), *n.* the feathered serpent god of the Aztec and Toltec cultures. [< Sp *Quetzalcóatl* < Nahuatl *Quetzalcōātl,* equiv. to *quetzal(li)* (see QUETZAL) + *cōātl* snake]

queue (kyōō), *n., v.,* **queued, queu•ing.** —*n.* **1.** a braid of hair worn hanging down behind. **2.** a file or line, esp. of people waiting their turn. **3.** *Computers.* a FIFO-organized sequence of items, as data, messages, jobs, or the like, waiting for action. —*v.i., v.t.* **4.** to form in a line while waiting (often fol. by *up*). **5.** *Computers.* to arrange (data, jobs, messages, etc.) into a queue. [1585–95; < MF < L *cauda, cōda* tail] —**queu′er,** *n.*

queue′ fourché′, *Heraldry.* (of a lion) having a single tail divided in two partway along its length so as to have two complete ends. Cf. **double-tailed.** [< F: lit., forked tail]

queu′ing the′ory, a theory that deals with providing a service on a waiting line, or queue, esp. when the demand for it is irregular and describable by probability distributions, as processing phone calls arriving at a telephone exchange or collecting highway tolls from drivers at tollbooths. [1950–55]

quey (kwā), *n., pl.* **queys.** *Scot. and North Eng.* a heifer. [1325–75; ME *quy* < ON *kvīga*]

Que•zal•te•nan•go (ke säl′te näng′gô), *n.* a city in SW Guatemala: earthquake 1902. 65,733.

Que′zon Cit′y (kā′zon, -sōn), a city on W central Luzon Island, in the Philippines, NE of Manila: former national capital (1948–76). 1,165,865.

Que•zon y Mo•li•na (kā′zon ē mō lē′nə, -sōn; *Sp.* ke′sôn ē mô lē′nä), **Ma•nuel Luis** (mä nwel′ lwēs), 1878–1944, Philippine political leader; 1st president of the Philippine Commonwealth 1933–44.

quib•ble (kwib′əl), *n., v.,* **-bled, -bling.** —*n.* **1.** an instance of the use of ambiguous, prevaricating, or irrelevant language or arguments to evade a point at issue. **2.** the general use of such arguments. **3.** petty or carping criticism; a minor objection. —*v.i.* **4.** to equivocate. **5.** to carp; cavil. [1605–15; perh. deriv. (cf. -LE) of *quib* gibe, appar. akin to QUIP] —**quib′bler,** *n.*
—**Syn. 1.** evasion, equivocation, sophism, shift, ambiguity.

quib•bling (kwib′ling), *adj.* **1.** characterized by or consisting of quibbles; carping; niggling: *quibbling debates.* —*n.* **2.** the act of a person who quibbles. **3.** an instance of quibbling: *a relationship marked by frequent quibblings.* [1650–60; QUIBBLE + -ING[2], -ING[1]] —**quib′•bling•ly,** *adv.*

Quib•dó (kēv thô′), *n.* a city in W Colombia. 46,871.

Qui•be•ron (kēbᵊ RÔN′), *n.* a peninsula in NW France, on the S coast of Brittany: British naval victory over the French 1759. 6 mi. (10 km) long.

quiche (kēsh), *n.* a pielike dish consisting of an unsweetened pastry shell filled with a custard and usually containing cheese and other ingredients, as vegetables, seafood, or ham: *spinach quiche.* [1945–50; < F < G (dial.) *Küche,* dim. of *Küchen* CAKE]

Qui•ché (kē chā′), *n.* a Mayan language of Guatemala.

quiche′ Lorraine′, a quiche containing bits of bacon or ham and often cheese. [1940–45]

Quich•ua (kēch′wä, -wə), *n., pl.* **-uas,** (*esp. collectively*) **-ua.** Quechua.

quick (kwik), *adj.,* **-er, -est,** *n., adv.,* **-er, -est.** —*adj.* **1.** done, proceeding, or occurring with promptness or rapidity, as an action, process, etc.; prompt; immediate: *a quick response.* **2.** that is over or completed within a short interval of time: *a quick shower.* **3.** moving, or able to move, with speed: *a quick fox; a quick train.* **4.** swift or rapid, as motion: *a quick flick of the wrist.* **5.** easily provoked or excited; hasty: *a quick temper.* **6.** keenly responsive; lively; acute: *a quick wit.* **7.** acting with swiftness or rapidity: *a quick worker.* **8.** prompt or swift to do something: *quick to respond.* **9.** prompt to perceive; sensitive: *a quick eye.* **10.** prompt to understand, learn, etc.; of ready intelligence: *a quick student.* **11.** (of a bend or curve) sharp: *a quick bend in the road.* **12.** consisting of living plants: *a quick pot of flowers.* **13.** brisk, as fire, flames, heat, etc. **14.** *Archaic.* **a.** endowed with life. **b.** having a high degree of vigor, energy, or activity. —*n.* **15.** living persons: *the quick and the dead.* **16.** the tender, sensitive flesh of the living body, esp. that under the nails: *nails bitten down to the quick.* **17.** the vital or most important part. **18.** *Chiefly Brit.* **a.** a line of shrubs or plants, esp. of hawthorn, forming a hedge. **b.** a single shrub or plant in such a hedge. **19. cut to the quick,** to injure deeply; hurt the feelings of: *Their callous treatment cut her to the quick.* —*adv.* **20.** quickly. [bef. 900; ME *quik* lively, moving, swift; OE *cwic, cwicu* living; c. OS *quik,* G *queck, keck,* ON *kvikr;* akin to L *vīvus* living (see VITAL), Skt *jīvas* living, Gk *bíos* life (see BIO-), *zōē* animal life (see ZOO-)] —**quick′ness,** *n.*
—**Syn. 1.** fleet, expeditious. QUICK, FAST, SWIFT, RAPID describe speedy tempo. QUICK applies particularly to something practically instantaneous, an action or reaction, perhaps, of very brief duration: *to give a quick look around; to take a quick walk.* FAST and SWIFT refer to actions, movements, etc., that continue for a time, and usually to those that are uninterrupted; when used of communication, transportation, and the like, they suggest a definite goal and a continuous trip. SWIFT, the more formal word, suggests the greater speed: *a fast train; a swift message.* RAPID, less speedy than the others, applies to a rate of movement or action, and usually to a series of actions or movements, related or unrelated: *rapid calculation; a rapid walker.* **5.** abrupt, curt, short, precipitate. **7.** nimble, agile, brisk. **10.** See **sharp.** —**Ant. 1, 10.** slow.
—**Usage.** The difference between the adverbial forms QUICK and QUICKLY is frequently stylistic. QUICK is more often used in short spoken sentences, especially imperative ones: *Come quick! The chimney is on fire.* QUICKLY is the usual form in writing, both in the preverb position (*We quickly realized that attempts to negotiate would be futile*) and following verbs other than imperatives (*She turned quickly and left*). See also **slow, sure.**

quick′-and-dirt′y, *adj.* **1.** *Informal.* slipshod. —*n.* **2.** *Slang.* See **greasy spoon.** [1970–75]

quick′ as′sets, *Accounting.* liquid assets including cash, receivables, and marketable securities. [1890–95]

quick′ bread′, bread, muffins, etc., made with a leavening agent, as baking powder or soda, that permits immediate baking. [1850–55]

quick′-change′ art′ist (kwik′chānj′), a person adept at changing from one thing to another, as an entertainer who changes costumes quickly during a performance. [1885–90]

quick′ draw′, a game or competition in which the winner is the quickest person to draw a handgun from a holster and sometimes to fire it and hit a target.

quick•en (kwik′ən), *v.t.* **1.** to make more rapid; accelerate; hasten: *She quickened her pace.* **2.** to give or restore vigor or activity to; stir up, rouse, or stimulate: *to quicken the imagination.* **3.** to revive; restore life to: *The spring rains quickened the earth.* —*v.i.* **4.** to become more active, sensitive, etc.: *This drug causes the pulse to quicken.* **5.** to become alive; receive life. **6.** (of the mother) to enter that stage of pregnancy in which the fetus gives indications of life. **7.** (of a fetus in the womb) to begin to manifest signs of life. [1250–1300; ME *quikenen.* See QUICK, -EN[1]] —**quick′en•er,** *n.*
—**Syn. 2.** animate, vitalize, enliven. **3.** vivify.

quick′ fire′, a single shot or several shots fired at a rapid rate from small arms at a target, esp. one presented unexpectedly. [1890–95]

quick-fire (kwik′fīᵊr′), *adj.* firing or equipped for firing rapidly, esp. at moving targets. Also, **quick′-fir′•ing.** [1890–95]

quick′ fix′, *Informal.* an expedient, temporary solution, esp. one that merely postpones having to cope with an overall problem. [1965–70]

quick-freeze (kwik′frēz′), *v.t.,* **-froze, -fro•zen, -freez•ing.** to freeze (cooked or uncooked food) rapidly, permitting it to be stored almost indefinitely at freezing temperatures. Also called **flash-freeze, sharp-freeze.** [1925–30]

quick′ grass′, the couch grass, *Agropyron repens.* [1875–80]

quick•hatch (kwik′hach′), *n.* a wolverine. [1675–85; earlier *quiquahatch* < East Cree **kwi·hkwaha·če·w* (c. Cree *kwi·hkwaha·ke·w,* Ojibwa *kwi·nkwaʔa·ke·*); cf. CARCAJOU, KINKAJOU]

quick•ie (kwik′ē), *Informal.* —*n.* **1.** a book, story, movie, etc., usually trivial in quality, requiring only a short time to produce. **2.** a quickly consumed alcoholic drink. **3.** anything taking only a short time, esp. a hurried sexual encounter. —*adj.* **4.** done, made, assembled, etc., quickly or hurriedly: *I'll fix a quickie meal after I get home from the office.* **5.** achieved or acquired with a minimum of formality: *a quickie divorce.* [1925–30; QUICK + -IE]

quick′ie strike′. See **wildcat strike.**

quick′ kick′, *Football.* a punt, usually on second or third down, made from an offensive formation not usually used for kicking, intended to go beyond the opposing safety men in order to prevent a possible runback. [1935–40]

quick•lime (kwik′līm′), *n.* lime[1] (def. 1). [1350–1400; ME *quyk lym,* trans. L *calx vīva;* see QUICK, LIME[1]]

quick•ly (kwik′lē), *adv.* with speed; rapidly; very soon. [bef. 1000; ME *quikly.* See QUICK, -LY]
—**Usage.** See **quick.**

quick′ march′, a march in quick time. [1745–55]

quick•sand (kwik′sand′), *n.* a bed of soft or loose sand saturated with water and having considerable depth, yielding under weight and tending to suck down any object resting on its surface. [1275–1325; ME *qwykkesand.* See QUICK, SAND] —**quick′sand′y,** *adj.*

quick•set (kwik′set′), *n. Chiefly Brit.* **1.** a plant or cutting, esp. of hawthorn, set to grow, as in a hedge. **2.** such plants collectively. **3.** a hedge of such plants. —*adj.* **4.** formed of quickset, or of growing plants. [1400–50; late ME; see QUICK, SET]

quick-set•ting (kwik′set′ing), *adj.* setting quickly, as a cement, paint, or gelatin. [1515–25]

quick•sil•ver (kwik′sil′vər), *n.* **1.** the metallic element mercury. —*v.t.* **2.** to amalgamate (metal) with mercury. [bef. 1000; ME *qwyksilver,* OE *cwicseolfor* (trans. L *argentum vīvum*) lit., living silver] —**quick′•sil′ver•y,** *adj.*

quick•step (kwik′step′), *n.* **1.** (formerly) a lively step used in marching. **2.** music adapted to such a march, or in a brisk march rhythm. **3.** a lively step or combination of steps in ballroom dancing. [1795–1805; QUICK + STEP]

quick′ stud′y, **1.** someone who is able to learn a new job or adjust to a new social environment in a short time. **2.** an actor who can learn lines and become proficient in a role on short notice.

quick-tem•pered (kwik′tem′pərd), *adj.* easily angered. [1820–30]
—**Syn.** quarrelsome, testy, churlish, irascible.

quick′ time′, *Mil.* a rate of marching in which 120 paces, each of 30 in. (76.2 cm), are taken in a minute. [1795–1805]

quick′ trick′, *Bridge.* a card, or group of cards, that will probably win the first or second trick in a suit, regardless of who plays it or at what declaration. [1925–30]

quick•wa•ter (kwik′wô′tər, -wot′ər), *n.* the part of a river or other stream having a strong current. [1855–60; QUICK + WATER]

quick-wit•ted (kwik′wit′id), *adj.* having a nimble, alert mind. [1520–30; QUICK + WIT[1] + -ED[3]] —**quick′-wit′ted•ly,** *adv.* —**quick′-wit′ted•ness,** *n.*
—**Syn.** keen, perceptive, smart, clever, sharp.

quid[1] (kwid), *n.* a portion of something, esp. tobacco, that is to be chewed but not swallowed. [1720–30; dial. var. of CUD]

quid[2] (kwid), *n., pl.* **quid.** *Brit. Informal.* one pound sterling. [1680–90; orig. uncert.]

Quid•de (kvid′ə), **Lud•wig** (lōōt′viкн, lōōd′-), 1858–1941, German historian and pacifist: Nobel peace prize 1927.

quid•di•ty (kwid′i tē), *n., pl.* **-ties.** **1.** the quality that makes a thing what it is; the essential nature of a thing. **2.** a trifling or subtle distinction, as in argument. [1530–40; < ML *quidditās,* equiv. to L *quid* what + *-itās* -ITY]

quid•nunc (kwid′nungk′), *n.* a person who is eager to know the latest news and gossip; a gossip or busybody. [1700–10; < L *quid nunc* what now?]

quid pro quo (kwid′ prō kwō′), *pl.* **quid pro quos, quids pro quo** for 2. **1.** (*italics*) *Latin.* one thing in return for another. **2.** something that is given or taken in return for something else; substitute. [1555–65; L *quid prō quō* lit., something for something; see WHAT, PRO[1]]

qui•es•cent (kwē es′ənt, kwī-), *adj.* being at rest; quiet; still; inactive or motionless: *a quiescent mind.* [1600–10; < L *quiēscent-* (s. of *quiēscēns,* prp. of *quiēscere*), equiv. to *qui-,* base meaning "rest, quiet" + *-ēsc-* inchoative suffix + *-ent-* -ENT] —**qui•es′cent•ly,** *adv.* —**qui•es′cence, qui•es′cen•cy,** *n.*
—**Syn.** dormant, latent.

qui•et[1] (kwī′it), *adj.,* **-er, -est,** *v.* —*adj.* **1.** making no noise or sound, esp. no disturbing sound: *quiet neighbors.* **2.** free, or comparatively free, from noise: *a quiet street.* **3.** silent: *Be quiet!* **4.** restrained in speech, manner, etc.; saying little: *a quiet person.* **5.** free from disturbance or tumult; tranquil; peaceful: *a quiet life.* **6.** being at rest. **7.** refraining or free from activity, esp. busy or vigorous activity: *a quiet Sunday afternoon.* **8.** making no disturbance or trouble; not turbulent; peaceable: *The factions remained quiet for twenty years.* **9.** motionless or moving very gently: *quiet waters.* **10.** free from disturbing thoughts, emotions, etc.; mentally peaceful: *a quiet conscience.* **11.** said, expressed, done, etc., in a restrained or unobtrusive way: *a quiet reproach; a quiet admonition.* **12.** not showy or obtrusive; subdued: *quiet colors.* **13.** not busy or active: *The stock market was quiet last week.* —*v.t.* **14.** to make quiet. **15.** to make tranquil or peaceful; pacify: *to quiet a crying baby.* **16.** to calm mentally, as a person. **17.** to allay (tumult, doubt, fear, etc.). **18.** to silence. —*v.i.* **19.** to become quiet (often fol. by *down*). [1350–1400; (adj.) ME (< MF) < L *quiētus,* ptp. of *quiēscere* (see QUIESCENT); (v.) ME *quieten,* partly deriv. of the adj., partly < LL *quiētāre,* deriv. of *quiētus.* Cf. COY] —**qui′et•er,** *n.* —**qui′et•ly,** *adv.* —**qui′et•ness,** *n.*
—**Syn. 2.** See **still[1].** **5.** calm, serene. **9.** unmoving. **14.** still, hush, silence. **15, 17.** lull, soothe. —**Ant. 2.** noisy. **5.** perturbed. **9.** active.

qui•et[2] (kwī′it), *n.* **1.** freedom from noise, unwanted sound, etc.: *At least there's quiet here.* **2.** freedom from disturbance or tumult; tranquillity; rest; repose: *to live in quiet.* **3.** peace; peaceful condition of affairs. [1300–50; ME *quiet(e)* (< MF *quiete*) < L *quiēt-* (s. of *quiēs*) rest, peace; akin to *quiēscere* (see QUIESCENT)]
—**Syn. 1.** silence. **2.** calm, stillness. —**Ant. 1.** noise. **2.** disturbance.

qui•et•en (kwī′i tn), *Chiefly Brit.* —*v.i.* **1.** to become quiet (often fol. by *down*). —*v.t.* **2.** to make quiet. [1820–30; QUIET[1] + -EN[1]] —**qui′et•en•er,** *n.*

qui•et•ism (kwī′i tiz′əm), *n.* **1.** a form of religious mysticism taught by Molinos, a Spanish priest, in the

CONCISE PRONUNCIATION KEY: *act, cāpe, dâre, pärt; set, ēqual; if, ice; ox, ōver, ôrder, oil, bŏŏk, bōōt, out; up, ûrge; child; sing; shoe; thin, that;* zh as in *treasure.* ə = *a* as in *alone, e* as in *system, i* as in *easily, o* as in *gallop, u* as in *circus;* ᵊ as in *fire* (fīᵊr), *hour* (ouᵊr). l and n can serve as syllabic consonants, as in *cradle* (krād′l), and *button* (but′n). See the full key inside the front cover.

latter part of the 17th century, requiring extinction of the will, withdrawal from worldly interests, and passive meditation on God and divine things; Molinism. **2.** some similar form of religious mysticism. **3.** mental or bodily repose or passivity. [1680–90; < It *quietismo* orig., prayer in a state of quietude. See QUIET², -ISM] —**qui′·et·ist,** *n., adj.* —**qui′et·is′tic,** *adj.*

qui′et sun′, *Astron.* **1.** the sun at the minimum of solar activity, occurring every 11 years. **2.** the unchanging background of solar phenomena. Cf. **active sun, solar cycle.**

qui·e·tude (kwī′i to͞od′, -tyo͞od′), *n.* the state of being quiet; tranquillity; calmness; stillness; quiet. [1590–1600; < LL *quiētūdō,* deriv. of L *quiētus* QUIET²; see -TUDE]

qui·e·tus (kwī ē′təs), *n., pl.* **-tus·es. 1.** a finishing stroke; anything that effectually ends or settles: *Having given a quietus to the argument, she left.* **2.** discharge or release from life. **3.** a period of retirement or inactivity. [1530–40; < ML *quiētus* quit (in *quiētus est* (he) is quit, a formula of acquittance), L: (he) is quiet, at rest (see QUIET¹); cf. QUIT¹ (adj.)]

quiff¹ (kwif), *n., pl.* **quiff, quiffs.** *Slang.* a woman, esp. one who is promiscuous. [1920–25; orig. uncert.]

quiff² (kwif), *n. Brit.* a lock or curl of hair brought forward over the forehead. [1885–90; orig. uncert.]

quill (kwil), *n.* **1.** one of the large feathers of the wing or tail of a bird. **2.** the hard, hollow, basal part of a feather. See illus. under **feather. 3.** a feather, as of a goose, formed into a pen for writing. **4.** one of the hollow spines on a porcupine or hedgehog. **5.** a plectrum of a harpsichord. **6.** a roll of bark, as of cinnamon, formed in drying. **7.** a reed or other hollow stem on which yarn is wound. **8.** a bobbin or spool. **9.** a toothpick. **10.** *Mach.* **a.** a hollow shaft or sleeve through which another independently rotating shaft may pass. **b.** a shaft, joined to and supported by two other shafts or machines, for transmitting motion from one to the other. **c.** a rotating toolholder used in boring or facing internal angles. **11.** a musical pipe, esp. one made from a hollow reed. —*v.t.* **12.** *Textiles.* **a.** to arrange (fabric) in flutes or cylindrical ridges, as along the edge of a garment, hem, etc. **b.** to wind on a quill, as yarn. **13.** to penetrate with, or as if with, a quill or quills. **14.** to extract a quill or quills from: *to quill a duck before cooking it.* [1375–1425; late ME *quil;* cf. LG *quiele,* G *Kiel*] —**quill′-like′,** *adj.*

quil·lai (ki lī′), *n.* soapbark (def. 1). [1865–70; < AmerSp < Araucanian]

quillai′ bark′, soapbark (def. 2).

quill·back (kwil′bak′), *n., pl.* **-backs,** (*esp. collectively*) **-back.** a carpsucker, *Carpiodes cyprinus,* inhabiting waters in the central and eastern U.S., having one ray of the dorsal fin greatly elongated. Also called **quill′back carp′sucker.** [1880–85, *Amer.;* QUILL + BACK¹]

quill′ driv′er, *Facetious.* a person who does a great deal of writing. —**quill′ driv′ing.** [1750–60]

quilled (kwild), *adj.* rolled or incurved into a narrow tubular form. [1720–30; QUILL + -ED³]

quill·er (kwil′ər), *n.* **1.** a machine for quilling yarn. **2.** a person who operates such a machine. [1850–55; QUILL + -ER¹]

Quil·ler-Couch (kwil′ər ko͞och′), *n.* **Sir Arthur Thomas** (*"Q"*), 1863–1944, English novelist and critic.

quil·let (kwil′it), *n. Archaic.* a subtlety or quibble. [1580–90; earlier *quillity,* var. of QUIDDITY] —**quil′let·ed,** *adj.*

quill·fish (kwil′fish′), *n., pl.* **-fish·es,** (*esp. collectively*) **-fish.** a fish, *Ptilichthys goodei,* of the Bering Sea, having an eellike body with long, many-rayed fins. [QUILL + FISH]

quill·ing (kwil′ing), *n.* **1.** the flutes or ridges in quilled material. **2.** quilled fabric, lace, ribbon, etc. **3.** copping. [1630–40; QUILL + -ING¹]

quill·wort (kwil′wûrt′, -wôrt′), *n.* any fernlike, aquatic marsh plant of the genus *Isoëtes,* characterized by clustered, quill-like leaves bearing sporangia in their bases. [1780–90; QUILL + WORT²]

Quil·mes (kēl′mes), *n.* a city in E Argentina, near Buenos Aires. 445,662.

quilt (kwilt), *n.* **1.** a coverlet for a bed, made of two layers of fabric with some soft substance, as wool or down, between them and stitched in patterns or tufted through all thicknesses in order to prevent the filling from shifting. **2.** anything quilted or resembling a quilt. **3.** a bedspread or counterpane, esp. a thick one. **4.** *Obs.* a mattress. —*v.t.* **5.** to stitch together (two pieces of cloth and a soft interlining), usually in an ornamental pattern. **6.** to sew up between pieces of material. **7.** to pad or line with material. —*v.i.* **8.** to make quilts or quilted work. [1250–1300; ME *quilte* < OF *cuilte* < L *culcita* mattress, cushion] —**quilt′er,** *n.*

quilt·ed (kwil′tid), *adj.* **1.** resembling a quilt, as in texture, design, stitching, etc. **2.** padded, filled, or stitched in the manner of a quilt. [1525–35; QUILT + -ED²]

quilt·ing (kwil′ting), *n.* **1.** the act of a person who quilts. **2.** material for making quilts. **3.** a heavily padded wrapping, as for fragile cargo. [1605–15; QUILT + -ING¹]

quilt′ing bee′, a social gathering at which the participants make quilts. [1825–35, *Amer.*]

quim (kwim), *n. Slang* (*vulgar*). vagina; vulva. [1725–35; orig. obscure]

Quim·per (kaɴ pᴇʀ′), *n.* a port in and the capital of Finistère, in NW France: noted for pottery manufacture. 60,510.

quin·a·crine (kwin′ə krēn′), *n. Pharm.* an alkaloid, $C_{23}H_{30}ClN_3O$, similar in its properties to pamaquine, used in the treatment of malaria. [1930–35; QUIN(INE) + ACR(ID) + -INE²]

qui·nar·i·us (kwi nâr′ē əs), *n., pl.* **-nar·i·i** (-nâr′ē ī′). a denomination of ancient Roman coinage, issued in silver or gold at various times and undergoing many changes of value. [1595–1605; < L *quīnārius; see* QUINARY]

qui·na·ry (kwī′nə rē), *adj., n., pl.* **-ries.** —*adj.* **1.** pertaining to or consisting of five. **2.** arranged in fives. **3.** of, pertaining to, or noting a numerical system based on the number 5. —*n.* **4.** a number in a quinary system. [1595–1605; < L *quīnārius,* equiv. to *quīn(ī)* five each + *-ārius* -ARY]

qui·nate (kwī′nāt), *adj. Bot.* arranged in groups of five. [1800–10; < L *quīn(ī)* five each + -ATE¹]

quin·az·o·line (kwi naz′ə lēn′, -lin), *n. Chem.* **1.** a colorless, crystalline, heterocyclic compound, $C_8H_6N_2$. **2.** any derivative of this compound. [1885–90; QUIN(INE) + AZOLE + -INE²]

quince (kwins), *n.* **1.** either of two small trees, *Cydonia oblonga* or *C. sinensis,* of the rose family, bearing hard, fragrant, yellowish fruit used chiefly for making jelly or preserves. **2.** the fruit of such a tree. [1275–1325; ME *quince,* appar. orig. pl. (taken as sing.) of *quyne, coyn* < MF *cooin* < L *cotōneum,* akin to *cydōnium* < Gk (*mêlon*) *Kydṓnion* quince, lit., (apple) of Cydonia]

quin·cen·ten·ar·y (kwin′sen ten′ə rē, kwin sen′tn er′ē; *esp. Brit.* kwin′sen tē′nə rē), *n., pl.* **-ar·ies,** *adj.* —*n.* **1.** a 500th anniversary or its celebration. —*adj.* **2.** pertaining to or marking a period of 500 years; quincentennial. [QUIN(QUE-) + CENTENARY]

quin·cen·ten·ni·al (kwin′sen ten′ē əl), *adj.* pertaining to or marking a period of 500 years. [1880–85; QUIN(QUE-) + CENTENNIAL]

quin·cun·cial (kwin kun′shəl, kwing-), *adj.* **1.** consisting of, arranged, or formed like a quincunx or quincunxes. **2.** *Bot.* noting a five-ranked arrangement of leaves. [1595–1605; < L *quincunciālis,* equiv. to *quīncunci-* (s. of *quīncunx* QUINCUNX) + *-ālis* -AL¹] —**quin·cun′cial·ly,** *adv.*

quin·cunx (kwing′kungks, kwin′-), *n.* **1.** an arrangement of five objects, as trees, in a square or rectangle, one at each corner and one in the middle. **2.** *Bot.* an overlapping arrangement of five petals or leaves, in which two are interior, two are exterior, and one is partly interior and partly exterior. [1640–50; < L: five twelfths (*quinc-,* var. of *quīnque-* QUINQUE- + *uncia* twelfth; see OUNCE¹); orig. a Roman coin worth five twelfths of an as and marked with a quincunx of spots]

Quin·cy (kwin′zē, -sē *for 1, 2;* kwin′sē *for 3, 4*), *n.* **1. Josiah,** 1744–75, American patriot and writer. **2.** a city in E Massachusetts, near Boston. 84,743. **3.** a city in W Illinois, on the Mississippi. 42,352. **4.** a male given name.

quin·dec·a·gon (kwin dek′ə gon′), *n. Geom.* a polygon having 15 angles and 15 sides. [1560–70; < L *quindec(im)* fifteen + *-agon* (extracted from PENTAGON, HEXAGON, etc.)]

quin·de·cen·ni·al (kwin′di sen′ē əl), *adj.* **1.** of or pertaining to a period of 15 years or the 15th occurrence of a series, as an anniversary. —*n.* **2.** a 15th anniversary. [< L *quindec(im)* fifteen + *-ennial* (as in DECENNIAL)]

quin·de·cil·lion (kwin′di sil′yən), *n., pl.* **-lions,** (*as after a numeral*) **-lion,** *adj.* —*n.* **1.** a cardinal number represented in the U.S. by 1 followed by 48 zeros, and in Great Britain by 1 followed by 90 zeros. —*adj.* **2.** amounting to one quindecillion in number. [1900–05; < L *quindec(im)* fifteen + *-illion* (as in *million*)] —**quin′·de·cil′lionth,** *adj., n.*

qui·nel·la (kē nel′ə, kwi-), *n.* **1.** a type of bet, esp. on horse races, in which the bettor, in order to win, must select the first- and second-place finishers without specifying their order of finishing. **2.** a race in which such bets are made. Cf. **exacta.** Also, **qui·nel′a, quiniela.** [1940–45, *Amer.;* < AmerSp *quiniela,* equiv. to Sp *quin(a)* (< F *quine* KENO) + *-iela* n. suffix]

quin·es·trol (kwin es′trôl, -trol), *n. Pharm.* a synthetic estrogen, $C_{25}H_{32}O_2$, used in oral contraceptives. [1965–70; QUIN(IC ACID) + ESTR(OGEN) + -OL¹]

Qui Nhon (kwē nyôn′), a seaport in SE Vietnam, on the South China Sea coast. 213,757.

quin·hy·drone (kwin hī′drōn, kwin′hī′drōn), *n. Chem.* a dark green, crystalline, slightly water-soluble solid, $C_{12}H_{10}O_4$, used in solution, together with a platinum wire, as an electrode (**quinhy′drone elec′trode**). [1855–60; QUIN(INE) + HYDR(OQUIN)ONE]

quin′ic ac′id (kwin′ik), *Chem.* a white, crystalline, water-soluble, solid cyclic compound, $C_7H_{12}O_6$, present in cinchona bark, coffee beans, and the leaves of many plants. Also, **chinic acid.** [1805–15; < Sp *quin(a)* quinine + -IC]

quin·i·dine (kwin′i dēn′, -din), *n. Pharm.* a colorless, crystalline alkaloid, $C_{20}H_{24}N_2O_2$, isomeric with quinine, obtained from the bark of certain species of cinchona trees or shrubs, used chiefly to regulate heart rhythm and to treat malaria. [1830–40; QUIN(INE) + -ID³ + -INE²]

qui·nie·la (kēn yel′ə; *Sp.* kē nye′lä), *n.* quinella.

qui·nine (kwī′nīn, kwin′īn *or, esp. Brit.,* kwi nēn′), *n. Chem., Pharm.* **1.** a white, bitter, slightly water-soluble alkaloid, $C_{20}H_{24}N_2O_2$, having needlelike crystals, obtained from cinchona bark: used in medicine chiefly in the treatment of resistant forms of malaria. **2.** a salt of this alkaloid, esp. the sulfate. [1820–30; < Sp *quin(a)* (< Quechua *kina* bark) + -INE²]

qui′nine wa′ter, carbonated water containing lemon, lime, sweetener, and quinine, often used as a mixer. Also called **tonic, tonic water.** [1950–55]

quin′nat salm′on (kwin′at). See **chinook salmon.** [1820–30; *quinnat* < Lower Chinook *i-kʷanat*]

qui·noa (kēn′wä), *n.* a tall crop plant, *Chenopodium quinoa,* of the goosefoot family, cultivated in Peru and Chile for its small, ivory-colored seed, which is used as a food staple. Also, **quinua.** [1615–25; < Sp < Quechua *kinua, kinoa*]

quin·oid (kwin′oid), *Chem.* —*n.* **1.** a quinonoid substance. —*adj.* **2.** quinonoid. [1905–10; QUIN(ONE) + -OID]

qui·noi·dine (kwi noi′dēn, -din), *n. Pharm.* a brownish-black, resinous substance consisting of a mixture of alkaloids, obtained as a by-product in the manufacture of quinine and formerly used as a cheap substitute for it. [1835–45; QUIN(INE) + -OID + -INE²]

quin·ol (kwin′ôl, -ol), *n. Chem.* hydroquinone. [1880–85; QUIN(INE) + -OL¹]

quin·o·line (kwin′l ēn′, -in), *n. Chem.* a colorless, liquid, water-immiscible, nitrogenous base, C_9H_7N, having a disagreeable odor, occurring in coal tar, and usually prepared by oxidizing a mixture of glycerol and aniline: used as a solvent and reagent and to make dyes. Also called **leucoline.** [1835–45; QUIN(INE) + -OL¹ + -INE²]

qui·none (kwi nōn′, kwin′ōn), *n. Chem.* **1.** a yellow, crystalline, cyclic unsaturated diketone, $C_6H_4O_2$, formed by oxidizing aniline or hydroquinone: used chiefly in photography and in tanning leather. **2.** any of a class of compounds of this type. Also, **chinone.** [1850–55; QUIN(IC ACID) + -ONE]

quinone′ di′i·mine (dī′ə mēn′), *Chem.* a colorless, crystalline solid, $C_6H_6N_2$, the parent of the indamine dyes. Cf. **quinonimine.** [DI-¹ + -IMINE]

qui·non·i·mine (kwi non′ə mēn′, -min, -nō′nə-), *n. Chem.* a colorless, crystalline compound, C_6H_5NO, the parent of the indophenol dyes, derived from quinone. Cf. **quinone diimine.** [QUINONE + -IMINE]

quin·o·noid (kwin′ə noid′, kwi nō′noid), *adj. Chem.* of or resembling quinone. Also, **quinoid, qui·noi·dal** (kwi noid′l). [1875–80; QUINONE + -OID]

quin·ox·a·line (kwi nok′sə lēn′, -lin), *n. Chem.* a colorless, crystalline, water-soluble powder, $C_8H_6N_2$, used chiefly in organic synthesis. Also, **quin·ox·a·lin** (kwi-nok′sə lin). [1880–85; QUIN(INE) + (GLY)OXAL + -INE²]

quinq., (in prescriptions) five. [< L *quīnque;* see QUINQUE-]

quin·qua·ge·nar·i·an (kwing′kwə jə nâr′ē ən, kwin′-), *adj.* **1.** 50 years of age. **2.** between the ages of 50 and 60. —*n.* **3.** a person who is 50 years old or whose age is between 50 and 60. [1560–70; < L *quinquāgēnāri(us)* (see QUINQUAGENARY)]

quin·quag·e·nar·y (kwin kwä′jə ner′ē, kwing-), *n., pl.* **-nar·ies.** a 50th anniversary. [1580–90; < L *quinquāgēnārius* containing fifty, equiv. to *quīnquāgēn(ī)* fifty each + *-ārius* -ARY]

Quin·qua·ges·i·ma (kwing′kwə jes′ə mə, kwin′-), *n.* the Sunday before Lent; Shrove Sunday. [1350–1400; ME < ML, short for L *quīnquāgēsima diēs* fiftieth day] —**Quin′qua·ges′i·mal,** *adj.*

quinque-, a combining form meaning "five," used in the formation of compound words: *quinquevalent.* [< L, comb. form of *quīnque;* see FIVE]

quin·que·fid (kwing′kwə fid, kwin′-), *adj.* cleft into five parts or lobes. [1695–1705; QUINQUE- + -FID]

quin·que·foil (kwing′kwə foil′, kwin′-), *n.* cinquefoil (def. 2). [1610–20; QUINQUE- + *-foil* (as in *trefoil*)]

quin·quen·ni·al (kwin kwen′ē əl, kwing-), *adj.* **1.** of or lasting for five years. **2.** occurring every five years. —*n.* **3.** something that occurs every five years. **4.** a fifth anniversary. **5.** a five-year term in office. **6.** a quinquennium. [1425–75; late ME < L *quīnquenni(s)* of five years + -AL¹] —**quin·quen′ni·al·ly,** *adv.*

quin·quen·ni·um (kwin kwen′ē əm, kwing-), *n., pl.* **-quen·ni·ums, -quen·ni·a** (-kwen′ē ə). a period of five years. Also, **quin·quen·ni·ad** (kwin kwen′ē ad′, kwing-). [1615–25; < L *quinquennium;* see QUINQUE-, BIENNIUM]

quin·que·par·tite (kwing′kwə pär′tīt, kwin′-), *adj.* divided into or consisting of five parts. [1585–95; QUINQUE- + PARTITE]

quin·que·va·lent (kwing′kwə vā′lənt, kwin′-, kwin-kwev′ə lənt, kwing-), *adj. Chem.* **1.** pentavalent. **2.** exhibiting five valences, as phosphorus with valences 5, 4, 3, 1, and −3. [1875–80; QUINQUE- + -VALENT] —**quin·que·va·lence** (kwing′kwə vā′ləns, kwin′-, kwin kwev′ə ləns, kwing-), **quin′que·va′len·cy,** *n.*

quin·sy (kwin′zē), *n. Pathol.* a suppurative inflammation of the tonsils; suppurative tonsillitis; tonsillar abscess. [1300–50; ME *quin(e)sie* < ML *quinancia,* LL *cynanchē* < Gk *kynánchē* sore throat] —**quin′sied,** *adj.*

quint¹ (kwint, kint), *n.* **1.** an organ stop sounding a fifth higher than the corresponding digitals. **2.** *Piquet.* a sequence of five cards of the same suit, as an ace, king, queen, jack, and ten (**quint major**), or a king, queen, jack, ten, and nine (**quint minor**). [1520–30; < F *quinte* (fem. of *quint*) < L *quīnta,* fem. of *quīntus* FIFTH]

quint² (kwint), *n. Informal.* a quintuplet. [1930–35; shortened form]

quint., (in prescriptions) fifth. [< L *quīntus*]

quin·ta (*Sp.* kēn′tä; *Port.* kᴇɴ′tä, -tə), *n., pl.* ***-tas*** (*Sp.* -täs; *Port.* -täs, -təsh). *Spanish, Portuguese.* an inn, esp. one in the countryside.

quin·tain (kwin′tn), *n.* **1.** an object mounted on a post or attached to a movable crossbar mounted on a post, used as a target in the medieval sport of tilting. See illus. on next page. **2.** the sport of tilting at a quintain. [1400–50; late ME *quyntain* object for tilting at < MF *quintaine* or ML *quintāna,* of obscure orig.; the alleged connection with L *quīntāna* "market place in a military camp" is dubious]

CONCISE ETYMOLOGY KEY: <, descended or borrowed from; >, whence; b., blend of, blended; c., cognate with; cf., compare; deriv., derivative; equiv., equivalent; imit., imitative; obl., oblique; r., replacing; s., stem; sp., spelling, spelled; resp., respelling, respelled; trans., translation; ?, origin unknown; *, unattested; ‡, probably earlier than. See the full key inside the front cover.

quintain (def. 1)

quin·tal (kwin′tl), *n.* **1.** a unit of weight equal to 100 kilograms (220.5 avoirdupois pounds). **2.** hundredweight. [1425–75; late ME < ML *quintāle* < Ar *qinṭār* weight of a hundred pounds, prob. << L *centēnārius.* Cf. CENTENARY, KANTAR, KILDERKIN]

quin·tan (kwin′tn), *adj.* **1.** (of a fever, ague, etc.) characterized by paroxysms that recur every fifth day. —*n.* **2.** a quintan fever or ague. [1740–50; < L *quintāna (febris)* quintan (fever); see QUINTAIN]

Quin·ta·na Ro·o (kēn tä′nä RÔ′ô), a sparsely populated state in SE Mexico, on the E Yucatán peninsula. 91,044. *Cap.:* Chetumal. 19,435 sq. mi. (50,335 sq. km).

quin·tant (kwin′tnt), *n. Navig.* a sextant having an arc equal to one fifth of a circle. [1675–85; *quint-* (< L *quintus* FIFTH) + *-ant* (as in *quadrant*)]

quinte (kANt, kant), *n. Fencing.* the fifth of eight defensive positions. [1700–10; < F; see QUINT[1]]

quinte·foil (kwint′foil′), *n.* cinquefoil (def. 2). [*quinte-* five, fifth (< F) + *-foil* (as in *trefoil*)]

quin·ter·ni·on (kwin tûr′nē ən), *n. Bookbinding.* five gathered sheets folded in two for binding together. [1645–55; *quint-* five (< L *quintus* FIFTH) + *-ternion* (extracted from *quaternion*)]

Quin·te·ro (*Sp.* kēn te′RÔ), *n.* See **Álvarez Quintero.**

quin·tes·sence (kwin tes′əns), *n.* **1.** the pure and concentrated essence of a substance. **2.** the most perfect embodiment of something. **3.** (in ancient and medieval philosophy) the fifth essence or element, ether, supposed to be the constituent matter of the heavenly bodies, the others being air, fire, earth, and water. [1400–50; ME < ML *quinta essentia* fifth essence] —**quin·tes·sen·tial** (kwin′tə sen′shəl), *adj.* —**quin′tes·sen′tial·ly,** *adv.*

quin·tet (kwin tet′), *n.* **1.** any set or group of five persons or things. **2.** an organized group of five singers or players. **3.** a musical composition scored for five voices or instruments. Also, **quin·tette′.** [1805–15; < F *quintette* < It *quintetto,* dim. of *quinto* FIFTH < L *quīntus*]

quin·tic (kwin′tik), *Math.* —*adj.* **1.** of the fifth degree. —*n.* **2.** a quantity of the fifth degree. **3.** an equation of the fifth degree. [1850–55; < L *quīnt(us)* FIFTH + -IC]

quin·tile (kwin′til, -tīl), *n.* **1.** *Statistics.* a quantile for the special case of five equal proportions. **2.** *Astrol.* a quintile aspect. —*adj.* **3.** *Astrol.* of or pertaining to the aspect of two heavenly bodies that are one fifth of the zodiac, or 72°, apart. [1600–10; < L *quīnt(us)* FIFTH + -ILE (as in *quartile*)]

Quin·til·ian (kwin til′yən, -ē ən), *n.* (*Marcus Fabius Quintilianus*) A.D. c35–c95, Roman rhetorician.

quin·til·lion (kwin til′yən), *n., pl.* **-lions,** (*as after a numeral*) **-lion,** *adj.* —*n.* **1.** a cardinal number represented in the U.S. by 1 followed by 18 zeros, and in Great Britain by 1 followed by 30 zeros. —*adj.* **2.** amounting to one quintillion in number. [1665–75; < L *quīnt(us)* FIFTH + *-illion* (as in *million*)] —**quin·til′lionth,** *n., adj.*

quint′ ma′jor. See under **quint**[1] (def. 2). [1655–65]

quint′ mi′nor. See under **quint**[1] (def. 2). [1650–60]

quin·tu·ple (kwin to͞o′pəl, -tyo͞o′-, -tup′əl, kwin′to͞o-pəl, -tyo͞o-), *adj., n., v.,* **-pled, -pling.** —*adj.* **1.** fivefold; consisting of five parts. **2.** five times as great or as much. **3.** *Music.* having five beats to a measure. —*n.* **4.** a number, amount, etc., five times as great as another. —*v.t., v.i.* **5.** to make or become five times as great. [1560–70; < MF < NL or ML *quīntuplus,* deriv. of *quīntus* fifth (see QUINT[1]), on the model of *duplus* DUPLE, *quadruplus* QUADRUPLE]

quin·tu·plet (kwin tup′lit, -to͞o′plit, -tyo͞o′-, kwin′-to͞o plit, -tyo͞o-), *n.* **1.** any group or combination of five, esp. of the same kind. **2. quintuplets,** five children or offspring born of one pregnancy. **3.** one of five such children or offspring. **4.** *Music.* a group of five notes of equal value performed in the time normally taken for four. [1870–75; QUINTUPLE + -ET]

quin·tu·plex (kwin′to͝o pleks′, -tyo͝o-, kwin to͞o′pleks, -tyo͞o′-, -tup′leks), *adj.* fivefold; quintuple. [QUINTU(PLE) + -PLEX]

quin·tu·pli·cate (*n., adj.* kwin to͞o′pli kit, -tyo͞o′-; *v.* kwin to͞o′pli kāt′, -tyo͞o′-), *n., adj., v.,* **-cat·ed, -cat·ing.** —*n.* **1.** a group, series, or set of five copies or identical items, esp. copies of typewritten matter. **2. in quintuplicate,** in five identical copies. —*adj.* **3.** noting or consisting of five identical parts; fivefold. **4.** pertaining to a fifth item or copy of something. —*v.t.* **5.** to produce or copy in quintuplicate. **6.** to make five times as great, as by multiplying. [1650–60; QUINTU(PLE) + *-plicate,* after DUPLICATE, TRIPLICATE, etc.] —**quin·tu′pli·ca′tion,** *n.*

qui·nua (kēn′wä), *n.* quinoa.

quip (kwip), *n., v.,* **quipped, quip·ping.** —*n.* **1.** a clever or witty remark or comment. **2.** a sharp, sarcastic remark; a cutting jest. **3.** a quibble. **4.** an odd or fantastic action or thing. —*v.i.* **5.** to utter quips. [1525–35; back formation from *quippy* quip < L *quippe* indeed] —**quip′pish,** *adj.* —**quip′pish·ness,** *n.*
—**Syn. 1.** joke, witticism. **2.** gibe, sally, jape.

quip·ster (kwip′stər), *n.* a person who frequently makes quips. [1875–80; QUIP + -STER]

qui·pu (kē′po͞o, kwip′o͞o), *n.* a device consisting of a cord with knotted strings of various colors attached, used by the ancient Peruvians for recording events, keeping accounts, etc. [1695–1705; < Sp < Quechua *khipu*]

quire[1] (kwīᵊr), *n.* **1.** a set of 24 uniform sheets of paper. **2.** *Bookbinding.* a section of printed leaves in proper sequence after folding; gathering. [1175–1225; ME *quayer* < MF *quaier* < VL **quaternum* set of four sheets, deriv. of L *quaternī* four each]

quire[2] (kwīᵊr), *n., v.i., v.t.,* **quired, quir·ing.** *Archaic.* choir.

Quir·i·nal (kwir′ə nl), *n.* **1.** one of the seven hills on which ancient Rome was built. **2.** the Italian civil authority and government (distinguished from the *Vatican*). —*adj.* **3.** noting or pertaining to the Quirinal. **4.** of or pertaining to Quirinus. [1850–55; < L *Quirīnālis.* See QUIRINUS, -AL[1]]

Qui·ri·nus (kwi rī′nəs, -rē′-), *n.* an ancient Roman god of war, identified with the deified Romulus; a personification of the Roman nation.

Qui·ri·tes (kwi rī′tēz, -rē′-), *n.pl.* the citizens of ancient Rome considered in their civil capacity. [< L *Quirītēs,* pl. of *Quirīs,* associated, perh. by folk etym., with *Cures,* a Sabine town]

quirk (kwûrk), *n.* **1.** a peculiarity of action, behavior, or personality; mannerism: *He is full of strange quirks.* **2.** a shift, subterfuge, or evasion; quibble. **3.** a sudden twist or turn: *He lost his money by a quirk of fate.* **4.** a flourish or showy stroke, as in writing. **5.** *Archit.* **a.** an acute angle or channel, as one dividing two parts of a molding or one dividing a flush bead from the adjoining surfaces. **b.** an area taken from a larger area, as a room or a plot of ground. **c.** an enclosure for this area. **6.** *Obs.* a clever or witty remark; quip. —*adj.* **7.** formed with a quirk or channel, as a molding. [1540–50; orig. uncert.]
—**Syn. 1.** See **eccentricity.**

quirk·y (kwûr′kē), *adj.,* **quirk·i·er, quirk·i·est.** having or full of quirks. [1800–10; QUIRK + -Y[1]] —**quirk′i·ly,** *adv.* —**quirk′i·ness,** *n.*

quirt (kwûrt), *n.* **1.** a riding whip consisting of a short, stout stock and a lash of braided leather. —*v.t.* **2.** to strike with a quirt. [1835–45, *Amer.*; perh. < Sp *cuerda* CORD]

quis cus·to·di·et ip·sos cus·to·des? (kwis ko͞o-stō′dē et′ ip′sōs ko͞o stō′dās; *Eng.* kwis kə stō′dē it ip′sōs kə stō′dēz), *Latin.* who shall keep watch over the guardians?

quis·ling (kwiz′ling), *n.* a person who betrays his or her own country by aiding an invading enemy, often serving later in a puppet government; fifth columnist. [1940; after Vidkun *Quisling* (1887–1945), pro-Nazi Norwegian leader]

quis se·pa·ra·bit? (kwis se′pä RÄ′bit; *Eng.* kwis sep′ə rā′bit), *Latin.* who shall separate (us)?

quit[1] (kwit), *v.,* **quit** or **quit·ted, quit·ting,** *adj.* —*v.t.* **1.** to stop, cease, or discontinue: *She quit what she was doing to help me paint the house.* **2.** to depart from; leave (a place or person): *They quit the city for the seashore every summer.* **3.** to give up or resign; let go; relinquish: *He quit his claim to the throne. She quit her job.* **4.** to release one's hold of (something grasped). **5.** to acquit or conduct (oneself). **6.** to free or rid (oneself): to quit oneself of doubts. **7.** to clear (a debt); repay. —*v.i.* **8.** to cease from doing something; stop. **9.** to give up or resign one's job or position: *He keeps threatening to quit.* **10.** to depart or leave. **11.** to stop trying, struggling, or the like; accept or acknowledge defeat. —*adj.* **12.** released from obligation, penalty, etc.; free, clear, or rid (usually fol. by *of*): *quit of all further responsibilities.* [1175–1225; (adj.) ME *quit(te)* exempt, freed, acquitted of (< OF *quite*) < ML *quittus,* by-form of *quītus* (> > ME *quit(e);* see QUITE), for L *quiētus* QUIET[1]; (v.) ME *quit(t)en* to pay, acquit oneself < OF *quit(t)er* < ML *quittāre, quiētāre* to release, discharge, LL *quiētare* to put to rest, QUIET[1]] —**quit′ta·ble,** *adj.*
—**Syn. 3.** surrender, release. **12.** acquitted, discharged. —**Ant. 1, 8.** start. **2.** enter.

quit[2] (kwit), *n.* any of various small tropical birds. [1845–50; orig. Jamaican E, of uncert. orig.]

quitch (kwich), *n.* See **couch grass.** Also, **quitch′ grass′.** [bef. 900; late ME *quich,* OE *cwice;* c. D *kweek,* Norw *kvike;* akin to QUICK (adj.)]

quit·claim (kwit′klām′), *n. Law.* **1.** a transfer of all one's interest, as in a parcel of real estate, esp. without a warranty of title. —*v.t.* **2.** to quit or give up claim to (a possession, right, etc.). [1275–1325; ME *quitclayme* < AF *quiteclame,* deriv. of *quiteclamer* to declare quit. See QUIT[1] (adj.), CLAIM]

quit′claim deed′, *Law.* a deed that conveys to the grantee only such interests in property as the grantor may have, the grantee assuming responsibility for any claims brought against the property. Cf. **warranty deed.** [1750–60]

quite (kwīt), *adv.* **1.** completely, wholly, or entirely: *quite the reverse; not quite finished.* **2.** actually, really, or truly: *quite a sudden change.* **3.** to a considerable extent or degree: *quite small; quite objectionable.* [1300–50; ME, adv. use of *quit(e),* a var. of *quit(te)* QUIT[1], the meaning of the two forms not being distinct in ME]

Qui·to (kē′tô), *n.* a city in and the capital of Ecuador, in the N part. 599,828; 9348 ft. (2849 m) above sea level.

qui trans·tu·lit sus·ti·net (kwē tRäns′to͞o lit so͞os′-ti net′; *Eng.* kwī trans′to͞o lit sus′tə net′, -tyo͞o lit, kwē), *Latin.* he who transplanted (it) sustains (it): motto of Connecticut.

quit·rent (kwit′rent′), *n.* rent paid by a freeholder or copyholder in lieu of services that might otherwise have been required. [1425–75; late ME; see QUIT[1], RENT[1]]

quits (kwits), *adj.* **1.** on equal terms by repayment or retaliation. **2. call it quits, a.** to end one's activity, esp. temporarily: *At 10 o'clock I decided to call it quits for the day.* **b.** to abandon an effort. **3. cry quits,** to agree to end competition and consider both sides equal: *It became too dark to continue play and they decided to cry quits.* [1470–80; perh. < ML *quittus* QUIT[1]]

quit·tance (kwit′ns), *n.* **1.** recompense or requital. **2.** discharge from a debt or obligation. **3.** a document certifying discharge from debt or obligation, as a receipt. [1175–1225; ME *quitaunce* < OF *quitance,* equiv. to *quit(er)* to QUIT[1] + *-ance* -ANCE]

quit′ted trick′, *Cards.* a trick the cards of which have been collected by the taker and turned face down, further examination being prohibited.

quit·ter (kwit′ər), *n.* a person who quits or gives up easily, esp. in the face of some difficulty, danger, etc. [1605–15; QUIT[1] + -ER[1]]

quit·tor (kwit′ər), *n. Vet. Pathol.* purulent infection of horses and other hoofed animals, characterized by chronic inflammation of the lateral cartilage of the foot and formation of fistulas that open above the coronet, usually resulting in lameness. [1250–1300; ME *quittere* < OF *cuiture* cooking < L *coctūra,* equiv. to *coct(us)* (ptp. of *coquere* to COOK[1]) + *-ūra* -URE]

quiv·er[1] (kwiv′ər), *v.t., v.i.* **1.** to shake with a slight but rapid motion; vibrate tremulously; tremble. —*n.* **2.** the act or state of quivering; a tremble or tremor. [1480–90; orig. uncert.; cf. MD *quiveren* to tremble] —**quiv′er·er,** *n.* —**quiv′er·ing·ly,** *adv.* —**quiv′er·y,** *adj.*
—**Syn. 1.** quake, shudder, shiver. See **shake. 2.** shudder, shiver, shake.

quiv·er[2] (kwiv′ər), *n.* **1.** a case for holding or carrying arrows. **2.** the arrows in such a case. [1250–1300; ME < AF *quiveir,* var. of OF *quivre;* perh. < Gmc; cf. OE *cocer* quiver]

quiv′er leg′, a round, tapered chair leg used in the Louis Quinze style and similar styles.

qui vive (kē vēv′), **1.** (*italics*) *French.* who goes there? **2. on the qui vive,** on the alert; watchful: *Special guards were on the qui vive for trespassers.* [1720–30; < F lit., (long) live who? (i.e., on whose side are you?)]

Qui·xo·te (kē hō′tē, kwik′sət; *Sp.* kē hô′te), *n.* **Don.** See **Don Quixote.**

quix·ot·ic (kwik sot′ik), *adj.* **1.** (*sometimes cap.*) resembling or befitting Don Quixote. **2.** extravagantly chivalrous or romantic; visionary, impractical, or impracticable. **3.** impulsive and often rashly unpredictable. Also, **quix·ot′i·cal.** [1805–15; (DON) QUIXOTE + -IC] —**quix·ot′i·cal·ly,** *adv.*
—**Syn. 2.** fanciful, fantastic, imaginary. —**Ant. 2.** realistic, practical.

quix·o·tism (kwik′sə tiz′əm), *n.* **1.** (*sometimes cap.*) quixotic character or practice. **2.** a quixotic idea or act. [1660–70; (DON) QUIXOTE + -ISM]

quiz (kwiz), *n., pl.* **quiz·zes,** *v.,* **quizzed, quiz·zing.** —*n.* **1.** an informal test or examination of a student or class. **2.** a questioning. **3.** a practical joke; a hoax. **4.** *Chiefly Brit.* an eccentric, often odd-looking person. —*v.t.* **5.** to examine or test (a student or class) informally by questions. **6.** to question closely: *The police quizzed several suspects.* **7.** *Chiefly Brit.* to make fun of; ridicule; mock; chaff. [1775–85 in sense "odd person"; 1840–50 for def. 1; orig. uncert.] —**quiz′za·ble,** *adj.* —**quiz′zer,** *n.*

quiz′ kid′, *Informal.* an unusually intelligent child. [1940–45, *Amer.*]

quiz·mas·ter (kwiz′mas′tər, -mä′stər), *n.* a person who asks questions of contestants in a game, esp. as part of a radio or television program. [1885–90; QUIZ + MASTER]

quiz′ pro′gram, a radio or television program in which contestants compete, often for prizes, by answering questions. Also called **quiz′ show′.** Cf. **game show.** [1940–45]

quiz·zi·cal (kwiz′i kəl), *adj.* **1.** odd, queer, or comical. **2.** questioning or puzzled: *a quizzical expression on her face.* **3.** derisively questioning, ridiculing, or chaffing. [1790–1800; QUIZ + -ICAL] —**quiz′zi·cal′i·ty, quiz′zi·cal·ness,** *n.* —**quiz′zi·cal·ly,** *adv.*

Qum (ko͝om), *n.* Qom.

Qum·ran (ko͝om′rän), *n.* See **Khirbet Qumran.** Also, **Qûm′ran.**

quo (kwō), *v.t. Archaic.* quoth.

quo·ad hoc (kwô′äd hōk′; *Eng.* kwō′ad hok′), *Latin.* as much as this; to this extent.

quo a·ni·mo? (kwō ä′ni mō′; *Eng.* kwō an′ə mō′), *Latin.* with what spirit or intention?

quod (kwod), *n. Chiefly Brit. Slang.* jail. Also, **quad.** [1690–1700; orig. uncert.]

quod e·rat de·mon·stran·dum (kwôd e′Rät dā′-mōn stRän′do͝om; *Eng.* kwod er′ət dem′ən stran′dəm), *Latin.* which was to be shown or demonstrated.

quod e·rat fa·ci·en·dum (kwôd e′Rät fä′kē en′-do͝om; *Eng.* kwod er′ət fā′shē en′dəm), *Latin.* which was to be done.

quod·li·bet (kwod′lə bet′), *n.* **1.** a subtle or elaborate argument or point of debate, usually on a theological or scholastic subject. **2.** *Music.* a humorous composition consisting of two or more independent and harmonically complementary melodies, usually quotations of well-known tunes, played or sung together, usually to different texts, in a polyphonic arrangement. [1350–1400; ME < ML *quodlibetum;* cf. L *quod libet* what pleases, as you please] —**quod′li·bet′ic, quod′li·bet′i·cal,** *adj.* —**quod′li·bet′i·cal·ly,** *adv.*

CONCISE PRONUNCIATION KEY: *act, cāpe, dâre, pärt; set, ēqual; if, īce; ox, ōver, ôrder, oil, bo͝ok, bo͞ot, out; up, ûrge; child; sing; shoe; thin, that;* zh *as in treasure.* ə = *a* as in *alone, e* as in *system, i* as in *easily, o* as in *gallop, u* as in *circus;* ᵊ as in *fire* (fīᵊr), *hour* (ouᵊr). l and n can serve as syllabic consonants, as in *cradle* (krād′l), and *button* (but′n). See the full key inside the front cover.

quod vi•de (kwod vī′dē, vē′dā). See **q.v.** (def. 2). [< L: which see]

quoin (koin, kwoin), *n.* **1.** an external solid angle of a wall or the like. **2.** one of the stones forming it; cornerstone. **3.** any of various bricks of standard shape for forming corners of brick walls or the like. **4.** a wedge-shaped piece of wood, stone, or other material, used for any of various purposes. **5.** *Print.* a wedge of wood or metal for securing type in a chase. —*v.t.* **6.** to provide with quoins, as a corner of a wall. **7.** to secure or raise with a quoin or wedge. Also, **coign, coigne.** [1525–35; var. of COIN]

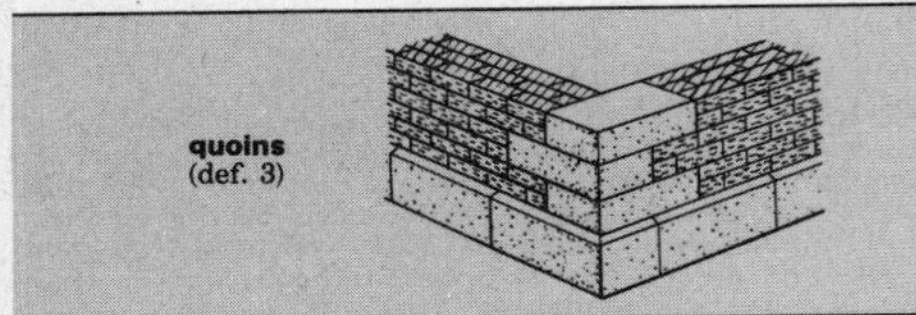
quoins (def. 3)

quoit (kwoit, koit), *n.* **1. quoits,** (*used with a singular v.*) a game in which rings of rope or flattened metal are thrown at an upright peg, the object being to encircle it or come as close to it as possible. **2.** a ring used in the game of quoits. —*v.t.* **3.** to throw as or like a quoit. —*v.i.* **4.** to play quoits. [1350–1400; ME *coyte* < ?] —**quoit′er,** *n.* —**quoit′like′,** *adj.*

quo ju•re? (kwō yo͞o′ʀe; *Eng.* kwō jo͝or′ē), *Latin.* by what right?

quok•ka (kwok′ə), *n.* a small wallaby, *Setonix brachyurus,* inhabiting islands and swampy areas in southwestern Australia. [1860–65; < Nyungar *kwaka*]

quon•dam (kwon′dəm, -dam), *adj.* former; onetime: *his quondam partner.* [1580–90; < L]

Quon′set hut′ (kwon′sit), *Trademark.* a semicylindrical metal shelter having end walls, usually serving as a barracks, storage shed, or the like, developed for the U.S. military forces from the British Nissen hut at Quonset Naval Base in Rhode Island.

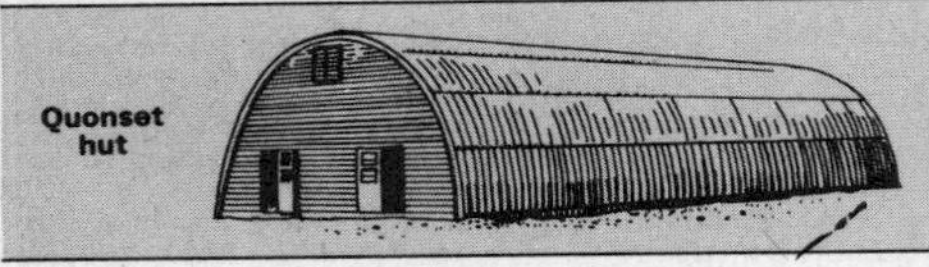
Quonset hut

quor., (in prescriptions) of which. [< L *quōrum*]

quo•rum (kwôr′əm, kwōr′-), *n.* **1.** the number of members of a group or organization required to be present to transact business legally, usually a majority. **2.** a particularly chosen group. [1425–75; < L *quōrum* of whom; from a use of the word in commissions written in Latin specifying a quorum]

quot., quotation.

quo•ta (kwō′tə), *n.* **1.** the share or proportional part of a total that is required from, or is due or belongs to, a particular district, state, person, group, etc. **2.** a proportional part or share of a fixed total amount or quantity. **3.** the number or percentage of persons of a specified kind permitted to enroll in a college, join a club, immigrate to a country, etc. [1660–70; < ML, short for L *quota pars* how great a part?]
—**Syn. 1.** allotment, apportionment, allocation.

quot•a•ble (kwō′tə bəl), *adj.* **1.** able to be quoted or easily quoted, as by reason of effectiveness, succinctness, or the like: *the most quotable book of the season.* **2.** suitable or appropriate for quotation: *His comments were hilarious but unfortunately not quotable.* [1815–25; QUOTE + -ABLE] —**quot′a•bil′i•ty, quot′a•ble•ness,** *n.* —**quot′a•bly,** *adv.*

quo′ta sys′tem, 1. a system, originally determined by legislation in 1921, of limiting by nationality the number of immigrants who may enter the U.S. each year. **2.** a policy of limiting the number of minority group members in a business firm, school, etc. **3.** any hiring or admissions policy requiring that a specified number or percentage of minority group members be hired or admitted. [1920–25]

quo•ta•tion (kwō tā′shən), *n.* **1.** something that is quoted; a passage quoted from a book, speech, etc.: *a speech full of quotations from Lincoln's letters.* **2.** the act or practice of quoting. **3.** *Com.* **a.** the statement of the current or market price of a commodity or security. **b.** the price so stated. [1525–35; 1810–15 for def. 3; < ML *quotātiōn-* (s. of *quotātiō*), equiv. to *quotāt(us)* (ptp. of *quotāre;* see QUOTE) + *-iōn-* -ION]
—**Syn. 1.** extract, citation, selection.

quota′tion mark′, one of the marks used to indicate the beginning and end of a quotation, in English usually shown as " at the beginning and " at the end, or, for a quotation within a quotation, of single marks of this kind, as *"He said, 'I will go.'"* Frequently, esp. in Great Britain, single marks are used instead of double, the latter being then used for a quotation within a quotation. Also, **quote′ mark′.** [1880–85]

quote (kwōt), *v.,* **quot•ed, quot•ing,** *n.* —*v.t.* **1.** to repeat (a passage, phrase, etc.) from a book, speech, or the like, as by way of authority, illustration, etc. **2.** to repeat words from (a book, author, etc.). **3.** to use a brief excerpt from: *The composer quotes Beethoven's Fifth in his latest work.* **4.** to cite, offer, or bring forward as evidence or support. **5.** to enclose (words) within quotation marks. **6.** *Com.* **a.** to state (a price). **b.** to state the current price of. —*v.i.* **7.** to make a quotation or quotations, as from a book or author. **8.** (used by a speaker to indicate the beginning of a quotation.) **9. quote unquote,** so called; so to speak; as it were: *If you're a liberal, quote unquote, they're suspicious of you.* —*n.* **10.** a quotation. **11.** See **quotation mark.** [1350–1400; 1880–85 for def. 10; ME *coten, quoten* (< OF *coter*) < ML *quotāre* to divide into chapters and verses, deriv. of L *quot* how many] —**quot′er,** *n.*

quote•wor•thy (kwōt′wûr′thē), *adj.* quotable. [1865–70; QUOTE + -WORTHY] —**quote′wor′thi•ness,** *n.*

quoth (kwōth), *v. Archaic.* said (used with nouns, and with first- and third-person pronouns, and always placed before the subject): *Quoth the raven, "Nevermore."* Also, **quo.** [1150–1200; preterit of *quethe* (otherwise obs.), ME *quethen,* OE *cwethan* to say. Cf. BEQUEATH]

quoth•a (kwō′thə), *interj. Archaic.* indeed! (used ironically or contemptuously in quoting another). [1510–20; from *quoth a* quoth he]

quotid., (in prescriptions) daily. [< L *quotīdiē*]

quo•tid•i•an (kwō tid′ē ən), *adj.* **1.** daily: *a quotidian report.* **2.** usual or customary; everyday: *quotidian needs.* **3.** ordinary; commonplace: *paintings of no more than quotidian artistry.* **4.** (of a fever, ague, etc.) characterized by paroxysms that recur daily. —*n.* **5.** something recurring daily. **6.** a quotidian fever or ague. [1300–50; < L *quotīdiānus, cottīdiānus* daily, equiv. to *cottīdi(ē)* every day (adv.) (**quot(t)ī* a locative form akin to *quot* however many occur, every + *diē,* abl. of *diēs* day; cf. MERIDIAN) + *-ānus* -AN; r. ME *cotidien* < OF < L, as above] —**quo•tid′i•an•ly,** *adv.* —**quo•tid′i•an•ness,** *n.*

quo•tient (kwō′shənt), *n. Math.* the result of division; the number of times one quantity is contained in another. [1400–50; late ME *quocient, quociens* < L *quotiēns* (adv.) how many times]

quo′tient group′, *Math.* a group, the elements of which are cosets with respect to a normal subgroup of a given group. Also called **factor group.** [1890–95]

quo′tient ring′, *Math.* a ring whose elements are cosets with respect to a given ideal. Also called **difference ring.** [1955–60]

quo′tient space′, *Math.* a topological space whose elements are the equivalence classes of a given topological space with a specified equivalence relation.

quo war•ran•to (kwō wô ran′tō, wo-), *Law.* **1.** (formerly, in England) a writ calling upon a person to show by what authority he or she claims an office, franchise, or liberty. **2.** (in England and the U.S.) a trial, hearing, or other legal proceeding initiated to determine by what authority one has an office, franchise, or liberty. **3.** the pleading initiating such a proceeding. [1250–1300; ME < ML *quō warrantō* by what warrant]

Qu•r'an (ko͝o rän′, -ran′), *n.* Koran.

qursh (kûrsh), *n.* qirsh.

qu•rush (ko͝o ro͞osh′), *n.* pl. of **qirsh.**

Qutb (ko͞o′təb), *n. Islam.* (in Sufism) the highest-ranking saint, the focal point of all spiritual energy. [1895–1900; < Ar *quṭb* lit., axis]

Qu Yuan (cho͞o′ yyän′), *Pinyin.* See **Ch'ü Yüan.**

q.v., 1. (in prescriptions) as much as you wish. [< L *quantum vīs*] **2.** *pl.* **qq.v.** (in formal writing) which see. [< L *quod vidē*]

QWERTY (kwûr′tē, kwer′-), *adj.* of or pertaining to a keyboard having the keys in traditional typewriter arrangement, with the letters *q, w, e, r, t,* and *y* being the first six of the top row of alphabetic characters, starting from the left side. Cf. **Dvorak Keyboard.** See illus. under **keyboard.** [1925–30]

Qy., query. Also, **qy.**

CONCISE ETYMOLOGY KEY: <, descended or borrowed from; >, whence; b., blend of, blended; c., cognate with; cf., compare; deriv., derivative; equiv., equivalent; imit., imitative; obl., oblique; r., replacing; s., stem; sp., spelling, spelled; resp., respelling, respelled; trans., translation; ?, origin unknown; *, unattested; ‡, probably earlier than. See the full key inside the front cover.

DEVELOPMENT OF MAJUSCULE								
NORTH SEMITIC	GREEK			ETR.	LATIN		MODERN	
							GOTHIC	ITALIC	ROMAN
9	4	P	4	R	R	𝕽	*R*	R

DEVELOPMENT OF MINUSCULE					
ROMAN CURSIVE	ROMAN UNCIAL	CAROL. MIN.	MODERN		
			GOTHIC	ITALIC	ROMAN
r	R	r	𝔯	*r*	r

The eighteenth letter of the English alphabet developed from North Semitic. The Greek *rho* (ρ, P) is a later version of the same symbol. Its form in Latin (R) derives from a variant used in a local Greek script, which added the short stroke at the right.

R, r (är), *n., pl.* **R's** or **Rs, r's** or **rs. 1.** the 18th letter of the English alphabet, a consonant. **2.** any spoken sound represented by the letter *R* or *r,* as in *ran, carrot,* or *rhyme.* **3.** something having the shape of R. **4.** a written or printed representation of the letter *R* or *r.* **5.** a device, as a printer's type, for reproducing the letter *R* or *r.* **6.** See **three R's.**

R (är), *v. Informal.* are: *Oysters R in season.*

R, 1. *Chem.* radical. **2.** *Math.* ratio. **3.** regular: a man's suit or coat size. **4.** *Elect.* resistance. **5.** restricted: a rating assigned to a motion picture by the Motion Picture Association of America indicating that children under the age of 17 will not be admitted unless accompanied by an adult. Cf. **G** (def. 7), **PG, PG-13, X.** [abbrev. for RESTRICTED] **6.** *Theat.* stage right. **7.** *Physics.* roentgen. **8.** *Chess.* rook.

R, *Symbol.* **1.** the 18th in order or in a series, or, when *I* is omitted, the 17th. **2.** (*sometimes l.c.*) the medieval Roman numeral for 80. Cf. **Roman numerals. 3.** *Biochem.* arginine. **4.** *Physics.* See **universal gas constant. 5.** registered trademark: written as superscript ® following a name registered with the U.S. Patent and Trademark Office.

r, 1. radius. **2.** *Com.* registered (def. 2). **3.** *Elect.* resistance. **4.** *Physics.* roentgen. **5.** royal. **6.** ruble. **7.** *pl.* **rs,** rupee.

r, *Ecol.* the theoretical intrinsic rate of increase of a population, equivalent to the difference between the birth and death rates divided by the number of individuals in the population. Also called **Malthusian parameter.**

R., 1. rabbi. **2.** Radical. **3.** radius. **4.** railroad. **5.** railway. **6.** (in South Africa) rand; rands. **7.** Réaumur. **8.** Also, **R** (in prescriptions) take. [< L *recipe*] **9.** rector. **10.** redactor. **11.** regina. **12.** Republican. **13.** response. **14.** rex. **15.** river. **16.** road. **17.** royal. **18.** ruble. **19.** rupee. **20.** *Theat.* stage right.

r., 1. rabbi. **2.** railroad. **3.** railway. **4.** range. **5.** rare. **6.** *Com.* received. **7.** recipe. **8.** replacing. **9.** residence. **10.** right. **11.** rises. **12.** river. **13.** road. **14.** rod. **15.** royal. **16.** rubber. **17.** ruble. **18.** *Baseball.* run; runs. **19.** *pl.* **rs.** rupee.

rā (rä), *n.* the 10th letter of the Arabic alphabet. [< Ar]

Ra (rä), *n. Egyptian Religion.* a sun god of Heliopolis, a universal creator worshiped throughout Egypt (typically represented as a hawk-headed man bearing on his head the solar disk and the uraeus). Also, **Re.**

RA, regular army.

Ra, *Symbol, Chem.* radium.

R.A., 1. rear admiral. **2.** *Astron.* right ascension. **3.** royal academician. **4.** Royal Academy.

raab (räb), *n.* See **broccoli rabe.**

Raab (rab), *n.* **Julius,** 1891–1964, Austrian engineer and statesman: chancellor of Austria 1953–61.

R.A.A.F., Royal Australian Air Force.

Ra•am•ses (rā am′sēz), *n.* a city that was built for the Pharaoh by the Israelites and from which the Exodus began. Ex. 1:11. Also, **Rameses.** Cf. **Pithom.**

rab (rab), *n.* a wooden beater for mixing plaster or mortar. [1815–25; < F *rabot*]

ra•bal (rā′bəl), *n. Meteorol.* the measurement and computation of the speed and direction of winds aloft by theodolitic tracking of a radiosonde. Cf. **pibal.** [*ra(diosonde) bal(loon wind data)*]

ra•bat[1] (rab′ē, rə bat′), *n. Eccles.* a sleeveless, backless, vestlike garment extending to the waist, worn by a cleric beneath the clerical collar, esp. in the Roman Catholic and Anglican churches. Also called **rabbi.** [1860–65; < MF; see REBATE[1]]

rab•at[2] (rab′ət), *n.* a piece of unglazed and imperfectly fired pottery, used for polishing hard surfaces. [< F, MF. See REBATE[1]]

Ra•bat (rä bät′, rə-), *n.* a seaport in and the capital of Morocco, in the NW part. 724,100.

ra•ba•to (rə bä′tō, -bā′-), *n., pl.* **-tos. 1.** a wide, stiff collar of the 17th century, worn flat over the shoulders or open in front and standing at the back. **2.** a stiff frame of wire or wood worn in the 17th century as a support for a ruff or stand-up collar. Also, **rebato.** [1585–95; < F (obs.) *rabateau;* cf. RABAT[1]]

Ra•baul (rä boul′, rə-, rä′boul), *n.* a seaport on NE New Britain island, in the Bismarck Archipelago, Papua New Guinea. 21,453.

Rab•bah (rab′ə), *n.* **1.** the ancient Biblical capital of the Ammonite kingdom east of the Jordan River. **2.** a city in Judah, near Jerusalem.

rab•ban (rab′ən, rə bän′; *Seph. Heb., Ashk. Heb.* RÄ-bän′), *n., pl.* **rab•ba•nim** (rə bä′nim, rä′bə nēm′; *Seph. Heb.* RÄ bä nēm′; *Ashk. Heb.* RÄ′bə nim′, RÄ bô′nim). *Judaism.* master; teacher (used as a term of address and title of respect for a person ranking higher than a rabbi). [< Heb *rabbān* < Aram]

Rab•bath Am•mon (rab′əth am′ən), Amman.

rab•bet (rab′it), *n., v.,* **-bet•ed, -bet•ing.** —*n.* **1.** a deep notch formed in or near one edge of a board, framing timber, etc., so that something else can be fitted into it or so that a door or the like can be closed against it. **2.** a broad groove let into the surface of a board or the like; dado. —*v.t.* **3.** to cut a rabbet in (a board or the like). **4.** to join (boards or the like) by means of a rabbet or rabbets. —*v.i.* **5.** to join by a rabbet (usually fol. by *on* or *over*). Also, **rebate.** [1350–1400; ME *rabet* < OF *rabat,* deriv. of *rabattre* to beat back, beat down; see REBATE[1]]

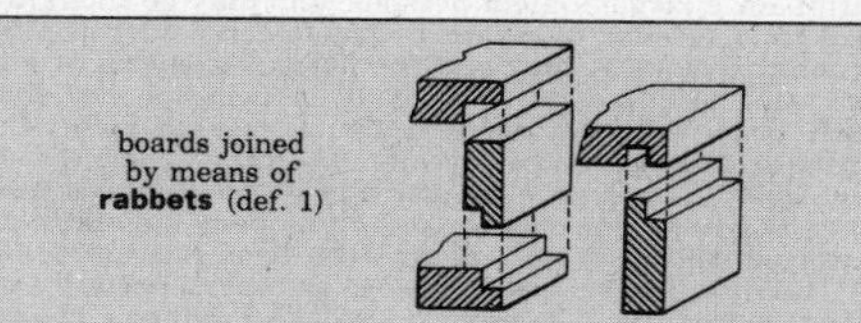

boards joined by means of **rabbets** (def. 1)

rab′bet joint′, *Carpentry.* a joint between rabbeted parts. [1820–30]

rab′bet plane′, *Carpentry.* a plane for cutting rabbets or the like, having a blade set to one side at right angles or diagonally to the direction of motion. [1670–80]

rab•bi[1] (rab′ī), *n., pl.* **-bis. 1.** the chief religious official of a synagogue, trained usually in a theological seminary and duly ordained, who delivers the sermon at a religious service and performs ritualistic, pastoral, educational, and other functions in and related to his or her capacity as a spiritual leader of Judaism and the Jewish community. Cf. **cantor** (def. 2). **2.** a title of respect for a Jewish scholar or teacher. **3.** a Jewish scholar qualified to rule on questions of Jewish law. **4.** any of the Jewish scholars of the 1st to 6th centuries A.D. who contributed to the writing, editing, or compiling of the Talmud. **5.** *Slang.* a personal patron or adviser, as in business. [1250–1300; ME *rabi* (< OF *rab(b)i*) < LL *rabbī* < Gk *rhabbí* < Heb *rabbī* my master (*rabh* master + *-ī* my)]

rab•bi[2] (rab′ē), *n. Eccles.* rabat[1]. [by alter.]

rab•bin (rab′in), *n. Archaic.* rabbi[1]. [1525–35; < MF << Aram *rabbīn* masters (pl. of *rab*)]

rab•bin•ate (rab′ə nit, -nāt′), *n.* **1.** the office or term of office of a rabbi. **2.** a group of rabbis: *the Orthodox rabbinate.* [1695–1705; RABBIN + -ATE[3]]

Rab•bin•ic (rə bin′ik), *n.* the Hebrew language as used by rabbis in post-Biblical times. [1605–15; < ML *rabbīn(us)* of a RABBI[1] + -IC]

rab•bin•i•cal (rə bin′i kəl), *adj.* **1.** of or pertaining to rabbis or their learning, writings, etc. **2.** for the rabbinate: *a rabbinical school.* Also, **rab•bin′ic.** [1615–25; < ML *rabbīn(us)* of a RABBI[1] + -ICAL]

rab•bin•ism (rab′ə niz′əm), *n.* the beliefs, practices, and precepts of the rabbis of the Talmudic period. [1645–55; RABBIN + -ISM]

Rab•bin•ite (rab′ə nīt′), *n. Judaism.* a proponent of the Talmud and the teachings and traditions of the rabbis in the face of rejection by the Karaites. Also, **Rab•bin•ist** (rab′ə nist). Cf. **Karaite.** [1825–35; RABBIN + -ITE[1]] —**rab•bin•it•ic** (rab′ə nit′ik), **rab′bin•is′tic, rab′bin•is′ti•cal,** *adj.*

swamp rabbit, *Sylvilagus aquaticus,* length about 15 in. (38 cm)

rab•bit (rab′it), *n., pl.* **-bits,** (*esp. collectively*) **-bit** for 1–3. **1.** any of several soft-furred, large-eared, rodentlike burrowing mammals of the family Leporidae, allied with the hares and pikas in the order Lagomorpha, having a divided upper lip and long hind legs, usually smaller than the hares and mainly distinguished from them by bearing blind and furless young in nests rather than fully developed young in the open. **2.** any of various small hares. **3.** the fur of a rabbit or hare, often processed to imitate another fur. **4.** See **Welsh rabbit. 5.** a runner in a distance race whose goal is chiefly to set a fast pace, either to exhaust a particular rival so that a teammate can win or to help another entrant break a record; pacesetter. **6.** *Brit. Informal.* a person who is poor at sports, esp. golf, tennis, or cricket. **7. pull a rabbit out of the hat,** to find or obtain a sudden solution to a problem: *Unless somebody pulls a rabbit out of the hat by next week, we'll be bankrupt.* [1375–1425; late ME *rabet(te)* young rabbit, bunny, prob. < ONF; cf. Walloon *robett,* dial. D *robbe*] —**rab′bit•like′, rab′bit•y,** *adj.*

rab′bit ball′, a lively baseball, esp. the ball used in present-day baseball: *The pitchers keep complaining about the rabbit ball.* [1920–25, *Amer.*]

rab•bit•brush (rab′it brush′), *n.* any of several composite shrubs of the genus *Chrysothamnus,* of the western U.S. and Mexico, having whitish, hairy branches and yellow flowers. [1860–65; RABBIT + BRUSH[2]; so called because it provides shelter for jackrabbits]

rab′bit-eared ban′dicoot (rab′it ērd′), any of several bandicoots of the genus *Macrotis,* esp. *M. lagotis,* of the Australian region, having leathery, rabbitlike ears and a long, pointed snout: an endangered species. Also called **bilby, rab′bit ban′dicoot.** [1825–35]

rab′bit ears′, 1. an indoor television antenna consisting of two telescoping, swivel-based aerials. **2.** *Sports Slang.* acute sensitivity to gibes, insults, or sarcasm: *Players with rabbit ears are the favorite targets of bench jockeys.* [1965–70]

rab′bit eye′, a blueberry, *Vaccinium ashei,* of the southeastern U.S., having pink flowers and blackish fruits. Also called **rab′bit-eye blue′berry.**

rab′bit fe′ver, *Pathol., Vet. Pathol.* tularemia. [1920–25]

rab•bit•fish (rab′it fish′), *n., pl.* (*esp. collectively*) **-fish,** (*esp. referring to two or more kinds or species*) **-fish•es.** **1.** a puffer, *Lagocephalus laevigatus.* **2.** a chimaera, *Chimaera monstrosa.* [1820–30; RABBIT + FISH, from the resemblance of its nose to a rabbit's]

rab′bit food′, *Informal.* raw vegetables, esp. those used in salads, as lettuce, carrots, radishes, or celery. [1905–10, for literal sense]

rab′bit-foot clo′ver (rab′it fo͝ot′), a plant, *Trifolium arvense,* having trifoliate leaves with narrow leaflets and fuzzy, cylindrical, grayish-pink flower heads. Also, **rab′bit's-foot clo′ver.** [1810–20, *Amer.*]

rab•bit-kill•er (rab′it kil′ər), *n. Australian.* a rabbit punch. [1920–25]

rab′bit punch′, a short, sharp blow to the nape of the neck or the lower part of the skull. [1910–15]

rab•bit•ry (rab′i trē), *n., pl.* **-ries.** **1.** a collection of rabbits. **2.** a place where rabbits are kept. [1830–40; RABBIT + -RY]

rab′bit's foot′, the foot of a rabbit, esp. the left hind foot carried as a good-luck charm. Also, **rab′bit foot′, rab′bit-foot′.** [1810–20, *Amer.*]

rab′bit's-foot fern′ (rab′its fo͝ot′). See **hare's-foot fern.** [1950–55]

rab′bit war′ren, warren. [1760–70]

rab•ble[1] (rab′əl), *n., v.,* **-bled, -bling.** —*n.* **1.** a disorderly crowd; mob. **2. the rabble,** the lower classes; the common people: *The nobility held the rabble in complete contempt.* —*v.t.* **3.** to beset as a rabble does; mob. [1350–1400; ME *rabel* (n.), of uncert. orig.]

rab•ble[2] (rab′əl), *n., v.,* **-bled, -bling.** *Metall.* —*n.* **1.** a tool or mechanically operated device used for stirring or mixing a charge in a roasting furnace. —*v.t.* **2.** to stir (a charge) in a roasting furnace. [1655–65; < F *râble* fire-shovel, tool, MF *raable* < L *rutābulum* implement for shifting hot coals, equiv. to **rutā(re)* presumed freq. of *ruere* to churn up, disturb + *-bulum* suffix of instrument] —**rab′bler,** *n.*

rab•ble•ment (rab′əl mənt), *n.* a tumult; disturbance. [1535–45; RABBLE[1] + -MENT]

rab•ble-rouse (rab′əl rouz′), *v.i.,* **-roused, -rousing.** to stir up the emotions or prejudices of the public; agitate. [1955–60; back formation from RABBLE-ROUSER]

rab•ble-rous•er (rab′əl rou′zər), *n.* a person who stirs up the passions or prejudices of the public, usually for his or her own interests; demagogue. [1835–45]

rab•ble-rous•ing (rab′əl rou′zing), *adj.* **1.** of, pertaining to, or characteristic of a rabble-rouser. —*n.* **2.** an instance or the practice of stirring up the passions or prejudices of the public. [1795–1805]

Rabe (räb), *n.* **David (William),** born 1940, U.S. playwright.

Rab•e•lais (rab′ə lā′, rab′ə lā′; *Fr.* RA ble′), *n.* **François** (fräN swa′), c1490–1553, French satirist and humorist.

Rab•e•lai•si•an (rab′ə lā′zē ən, -zhən), *adj.* **1.** of, pertaining to, or suggesting François Rabelais, whose work is characterized by broad, coarse humor and keen satire. —*n.* **2.** a person who admires or studies the works of Rabelais. [1855–60; RABELAIS + -IAN]

Ra•bi (rä′bē), *n.* **Isidor Isaac,** 1898–1988, U.S. physicist: Nobel prize 1944.

Ra•bi I (rub′ē), the third month of the Muslim calendar. Also, **Ra•bi•a I** (rə bē′ə). Cf. **Muslim calendar.**

Rabi II, the fourth month of the Muslim calendar. Also, **Rabia II.** Cf. **Muslim calendar.**

rab•id (rab′id), *adj.* **1.** irrationally extreme in opinion or practice: *a rabid isolationist; a rabid baseball fan.* **2.** furious or raging; violently intense: *a rabid hunger.* **3.** affected with or pertaining to rabies; mad. [1605–15; < L *rabidus* raving, furious, mad, equiv. to *rab(ere)* to rave, be mad + *-idus* -ID[4]] —**ra•bid•i•ty** (rə bid′i tē, ra-), **rab′id•ness,** *n.* —**rab′id•ly,** *adv.*
—**Syn. 1.** zealous, fervent, ardent, fanatical, bigoted.

ra•bies (rā′bēz), *n. Pathol.* an infectious disease of dogs, cats, and other animals, transmitted to humans by the bite of an infected animal and usually fatal if prophylactic treatment is not administered: caused by an RNA virus of the rhabdovirus group; hydrophobia. [1655–65; < L *rabiēs* rage, madness, deriv. of *rabere* to be mad, rave] —**rab•ic** (rab′ik, rā′bik), *adj.*

Ra•bin (rä bēn′), *n.* **Yitz•hak** (yits KHäk′), 1922–95, Israeli military and political leader: prime minister 1974–77 and 1992–95: Nobel peace prize 1994.

Ra•bi•no•witz (rə bin′ə vits, -wits; *Russ.* rə byi nô′-vyich), *n.* **Solomon.** See **Aleichem, Sholom.**

ra•bi•ru•bi•a (rä′bə ro͞o′bē ə), *n.* yellowtail (def. 2). [< Caribbean Sp *rabirrubia,* alter. of Sp *rabo* tail (prob. < L *rapum* turnip) + *rubio* blond, fair (< L *rūbeus, robeus* red (of animals))]

Ra•born (rā′bərn), *n.* **William F.,** 1905–90, U.S. admiral and government official: CIA director 1965–66.

rab•ot (rab′ət), *n.* a hardwood block used for rubbing marble before polishing. [< F: plane]

rac•coon (ra ko͞on′), *n., pl.* **-coons,** (*esp. collectively*) **-coon.** **1.** a nocturnal carnivore, *Procyon lotor,* having a masklike black stripe across the eyes, a sharp snout, and a bushy, ringed tail, native to North and Central America and introduced elsewhere for its valuable fur. **2.** the thick, brownish-gray fur of this animal, with gray, black-tipped guard hairs. **3.** any of various related animals of the genus *Procyon,* of Central American islands, some now rare. [1600–10, *Amer.*; < Virginia Algonquian (E sp.) *aroughcun*]

CONCISE ETYMOLOGY KEY: <, descended or borrowed from; >, whence; b., blend of, blended; c., cognate with; cf., compare; deriv., derivative; equiv., equivalent; imit., imitative; obl., oblique; r., replacing; s., stem; sp., spelling, spelled; resp., respelling, respelled; trans., translation; ?, origin unknown; *, unattested; ‡, probably earlier than. See the full key inside the front cover.

raccoon, *Procyon lotor,* head and body 2 ft. (0.6 m); tail 1 ft. (0.3 m)

raccoon′ dog′, a small wild dog of the genus *Nyctereutes,* common in Asia, resembling a raccoon in coat and coloration. [1865–70]

race[1] (rās), *n., v.,* **raced, rac•ing.** —*n.* **1.** a contest of speed, as in running, riding, driving, or sailing. **2. races,** a series of races, usually of horses or dogs, run at a set time over a regular course: *They spent a day at the races.* **3.** any contest or competition, esp. to achieve superiority: *the arms race; the presidential race.* **4.** urgent need, responsibility, effort, etc., as when time is short or a solution is imperative: *the race to find an effective vaccine.* **5.** onward movement; an onward or regular course. **6.** the course of time. **7.** the course of life or a part of life. **8.** *Geol.* **a.** a strong or rapid current of water, as in the sea or a river. **b.** the channel or bed of such a current or of any stream. **9.** an artificial channel leading water to or from a place where its energy is utilized. **10.** the current of water in such a channel. **11.** Also called **raceway.** *Mach.* a channel, groove, or the like, for sliding or rolling a part or parts, as the balls of a ball bearing. **12.** *Textiles.* **a.** the float between adjacent rows of pile. **b.** See **race plate.** —*v.i.* **13.** to engage in a contest of speed; run a race. **14.** to run horses or dogs in races; engage in or practice horse racing or dog racing. **15.** to run, move, or go swiftly. **16.** (of an engine, wheel, etc.) to run with undue or uncontrolled speed when the load is diminished without corresponding diminution of fuel, force, etc. —*v.t.* **17.** to run a race against; try to beat in a contest of speed: *I'll race you to the water.* **18.** to enter (a horse, car, track team, or the like) in a race or races. **19.** to cause to run, move, or go at high speed: *to race a motor.* [1250–1300; (n.) ME *ras(e)* < ON *rās* a running, race (c. OE *rǣs* a running); (v.) ME *rasen,* deriv. of the n. (cf. ON *rasa* to rush headlong)]

race[2] (rās), *n.* **1.** a group of persons related by common descent or heredity. **2.** a population so related. **3.** *Anthropol.* **a.** any of the traditional divisions of humankind, the commonest being the Caucasian, Mongoloid, and Negro, characterized by supposedly distinctive and universal physical characteristics: no longer in technical use. **b.** an arbitrary classification of modern humans, sometimes, esp. formerly, based on any or a combination of various physical characteristics, as skin color, facial form, or eye shape, and now frequently based on such genetic markers as blood groups. **c.** a human population partially isolated reproductively from other populations, whose members share a greater degree of physical and genetic similarity with one another than with other humans. **4.** a group of tribes or peoples forming an ethnic stock: *the Slavic race.* **5.** any people united by common history, language, cultural traits, etc.: *the Dutch race.* **6.** the human race or family; humankind: *Nuclear weapons pose a threat to the race.* **7.** *Zool.* a variety; subspecies. **8.** a natural kind of living creature: *the race of fishes.* **9.** any group, class, or kind: *Journalists are an interesting race.* **10.** the characteristic taste or flavor of wine. —*adj.* **11.** of or pertaining to the races of humankind. [1490–1500; < F < It *razza,* of obscure orig.]
—**Syn. 1.** tribe, clan, family. RACE, PEOPLE, NATION are terms for a large body of persons who may be thought of as a unit because of common characteristics. In the traditional biological and anthropological systems of classification RACE refers to a group of persons who share such genetically transmitted traits as skin color, hair texture, and eye shape or color: *the white race; the yellow race.* In reference to classifying the human species, RACE is now under dispute among modern biologists and anthropologists. Some feel that the term has no biological validity; others use it to specify only a partially isolated reproductive population whose members share a considerable degree of genetic similarity. In certain broader or less technical senses RACE is sometimes used interchangeably with PEOPLE. PEOPLE refers to a body of persons united usually by common interests, ideals, or culture but sometimes also by a common history, language, or ethnic character: *We are one people; the peoples of the world; the Swedish people.* NATION refers to a body of persons living under an organized government or rule, occupying a defined area, and acting as a unit in matters of peace and war: *the English nation.*

race[3] (rās), *n.* a ginger root. [1540–50; < MF *rais* < L *rādic-* (s. of *rādix*) ROOT[1]]

Race (rās), *n.* **Cape,** a cape at the SE extremity of Newfoundland.

race•a•bout (rās′ə bout′), *n.* a small, sloop-rigged racing yacht with a short bowsprit. [1895–1900, *Amer.*; n. use of v. phrase *race about*]

race•car (rās′kär′), *n.* See **racing car.** [RACE[1] + CAR[1]]

race•course (rās′kôrs′, -kōrs′), *n.* **1.** racetrack. **2.** a current of water, as a millrace. [1755–65; RACE[1] + COURSE]

race•horse (rās′hôrs′), *n.* a horse bred or kept for racing, esp. in flat races or steeplechases. [1620–30; RACE[1] + HORSE]

ra•ce•mate (rā sē′māt, rə-), *n. Chem.* **1.** a salt or ester of racemic acid. **2.** a racemic compound. [1825–35; RACEM(IC ACID) + -ATE[2]]

ra•ceme (rā sēm′, rə-), *n. Bot.* **1.** a simple indeterminate inflorescence in which the flowers are borne on short pedicels lying along a common axis, as in the lily of the valley. See illus. under **inflorescence. 2.** a compound inflorescence in which the short pedicels with single flowers of the simple raceme are replaced by racemes. [1775–85; < L *racēmus* cluster of grapes, bunch of berries] —**ra•cemed′,** *adj.*

ra•ce•mic (rā sē′mik, -sem′ik, rə-), *adj. Chem.* noting or pertaining to any of various organic compounds in which racemism occurs. [1830–40; < F *racémique* < L *racēm(us)* RACEME + F *-ique* -IC]

race′mic ac′id, *Chem.* an isomeric modification of tartaric acid that is sometimes found in the juice of grapes in conjunction with the common dextrorotatory form and is optically inactive but can be separated into the two usual isomeric forms, dextrorotatory and levorotatory. [1830–40]

rac•e•mism (ras′ə miz′əm, rā sē′miz əm), *n. Chem.* (of a compound) the state of being optically inactive and separable into two other substances of the same chemical composition as the original substance, one of which is dextrorotatory and the other levorotatory, as racemic acid. [1895–1900; RACEME + -ISM]

rac•e•mi•za•tion (ras′ə mə zā′shən, rā sē′mə-), *n. Chem.* the conversion of an optically active substance into an optically inactive mixture of equal amounts of the dextrorotatory and levorotatory forms. [1890–95; RACEME + -IZATION]

rac•e•mose (ras′ə mōs′), *adj.* **1.** *Bot.* **a.** having the form of a raceme. **b.** arranged in racemes. **2.** *Anat.* (of a gland) resembling a bunch of grapes; having branching ducts that end in acini. [1690–1700; < L *racēmōsus* full of clusters, clustering. See RACEME, -OSE[1]] —**rac′e•mose′ly,** *adv.*

rac•e•mous (ras′ə məs), *adj.* racemose. [1650–60] —**rac′e•mous•ly,** *adv.*

race′ mu′sic, *Older Use.* blues or jazz by and for American blacks, regarded as a distinctive market by the music industry in the 1920's and 1930's. [1925–30, *Amer.*]

race′ norm′ing, the process of statistically adjusting the scores of minority job applicants on job-qualification tests by rating each test-taker's score against the results of others in his or her racial or ethnic group. [1991]

race′ plate′, a metallic, plastic, or wooden strip directly in front of the reed on the lay of a loom, along which the shuttle travels in its passage through the shed. Also, **race′plate′.** Also called **race.**

rac•er (rā′sər), *n.* **1.** a person, animal, or thing that races or takes part in a race, as a racehorse, bicycle, etc. **2.** anything having great speed. **3.** See **racing skate. 4.** a turntable on which a heavy gun is turned. **5.** any of several slender, active snakes of the genera *Coluber* and *Masticophis.* [1640–50; RACE[1] + -ER[1]]

race′ ri′ot, a riot resulting from racial tensions or animosity. [1885–90, *Amer.*]

race•run•ner (rās′run′ər), *n.* a whiptail lizard, *Cnemidophorus sexlineatus,* common in the eastern and central U.S., that runs with great speed. [1640–50; RACE[1] + RUNNER]

race′ su′icide, the extinction of a race or people that tends to result when, through the unwillingness or forbearance of its members to have children, the birthrate falls below the death rate. [1900–05, *Amer.*]

race•track (rās′trak′), *n.* **1.** a plot of ground, usually oval, laid out for horse racing. **2.** the course for any race. [1855–60]

race•track•er (rās′trak′ər), *n.* a person who regularly attends horse races, esp. for the purpose of betting. [1950–55; RACETRACK + -ER[1]]

race-walk (rās′wôk′), *v.i.* to participate in race walking. [1970–75]

race′ walk′ing, the sport of rapid, continuous-foot-contact walking, requiring that the trailing foot not be lifted until the other meets the ground and the knee locks momentarily, and executed in an upright, rhythmic stride with the arms usually held bent and high and pumped close to the body. Also called **walking, the walk, heel-and-toe racing.** —**race′ walk′er.**

race•way (rās′wā′), *n.* **1.** *Chiefly Brit.* a passage or channel for water, as a millrace. **2.** a racetrack on which harness races are held. **3.** *Elect.* a channel for protecting and holding electrical wires and cables, esp. a metal rectangular tube used for such purposes. **4.** *Mach.* race[1] (def. 11). [1820–30; RACE[1] + WAY[1]]

Ra•chel (rā′chəl), *n.* **1.** Jacob's favorite wife, the mother of Joseph and Benjamin. Gen. 29–35. **2.** a female given name: from a Hebrew word meaning "lamb."

ra•chil•la (rə kil′ə), *n., pl.* **-chil•lae** (-kil′ē). *Bot.* a small or secondary rachis, as the axis of a spikelet in a grass inflorescence. [1835–45; < NL, dim. of *rachis* RACHIS]

ra•chis (rā′kis), *n., pl.* **ra•chis•es, rach•i•des** (rak′i-dēz′, rā′ki-). **1.** *Bot.* **a.** the axis of an inflorescence when somewhat elongated, as in a raceme. **b.** (in a pinnately compound leaf or frond) the prolongation of the petiole along which the leaflets are disposed. **c.** any of various axial structures. **2.** *Ornith.* the part of the shaft of a feather bearing the web. See illus. under **feather. 3.** *Anat.* See **spinal column.** Also, **rhachis.** [1775–85; < NL < Gk *rháchis* spine, ridge, backbone] —**ra•chid•i•an** (rə kid′ē ən), **ra•chi•al** (rā′kē əl), **ra•chid′i•al,** *adj.*

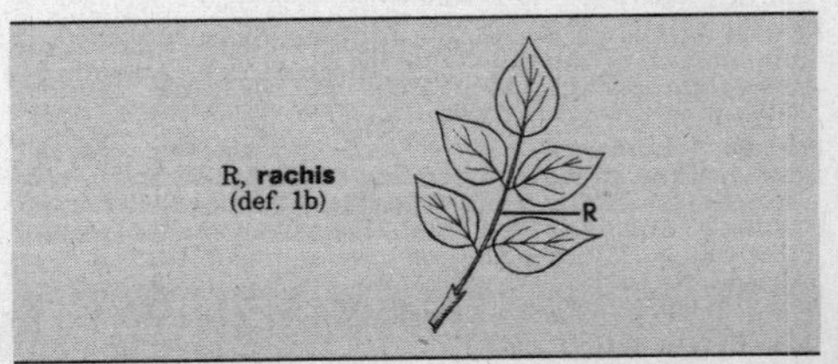

R, **rachis** (def. 1b)

ra•chi•tis (rə kī′tis), *n. Pathol.* rickets. [1720–30; < NL < Gk *rhachîtis* inflammation of the spine. See RACHIS, -ITIS] —**ra•chit•ic** (rə kit′ik), *adj.*

Rach•ma•ni•noff (räkн mä′nə nôf′, -nof′, räk-; *Russ.* RUKH mä′nyi nəf), *n.* **Ser•gei Was•si•lie•vitch** (sûr gā′ və sēl′yə vich; *Russ.* syir gyā′ vu syē′lyi vyich), 1873–1943, Russian pianist and composer. Also, **Rach•ma′ni•nov′.**

ra•cial (rā′shəl), *adj.* **1.** of, pertaining to, or characteristic of one race or the races of humankind. **2.** arising, occurring, or existing because of differences between races or racial attitudes: *racial conflict; racial motivations.* [1860–65; RACE² + -IAL] —**ra′cial•ly,** *adv.*

ra•cial•ism (rā′shə liz′əm), *n.* racism. [1905–10; RACIAL + -ISM] —**ra′cial•ist,** *n., adj.* —**ra′cial•is′tic,** *adj.*

ra′cial mem′ory, *Psychol.* feelings, patterns of thought, and fragments of experience that have been transmitted from generation to generation in all humans and have deeply influenced the mind and behavior.

ra•ci•nage (ras′ə näzh′; *Fr.* RA sē NAZH′), *n.* decorative treatment of leather with colors and acids to produce a branchlike effect. [< F, equiv. to *racine* root (< LL *rādīcīna,* for L *rādīx,* s. *rādīc-* ROOT¹) + *-age* -AGE]

Ra•cine (rə sēn′, ra- *or, Fr.,* RA sēn′ *for 1;* rə sēn′, rā- *for 2*), *n.* **1. Jean Bap•tiste** (zhäN BA tēst′), 1639–99, French dramatist. **2.** a city in SE Wisconsin. 85,725.

rac′ing car′, a car used for racing, as a specially designed and modified car or stock car. [1905–10]

rac′ing flag′, a distinguishing flag flown by a yacht during the period of its participation in a race. [1855–60]

rac′ing form′, a sheet that provides detailed information about horse races, including background data on the horses, jockeys, etc. [1945–50]

rac′ing skate′, a tubular ice skate having a long blade extending beyond the heel and toe. Also called **racer, speed skate.** Cf. **figure skate, hockey skate, tubular skate.**

rac•ism (rā′siz əm), *n.* **1.** a belief or doctrine that inherent differences among the various human races determine cultural or individual achievement, usually involving the idea that one's own race is superior and has the right to rule others. **2.** a policy, system of government, etc., based upon or fostering such a doctrine; discrimination. **3.** hatred or intolerance of another race or other races. [1865–70; < F *racisme.* See RACE², -ISM] —**rac′ist,** *n., adj.*

rack¹ (rak), *n.* **1.** a framework of bars, wires, or pegs on which articles are arranged or deposited: *a clothes rack; a luggage rack.* **2.** a fixture containing several tiered shelves, often affixed to a wall: *a book rack; a spice rack.* **3.** a spreading framework set on a wagon for carrying hay, straw, or the like, in large loads. **4.** *Pool.* **a.** a wooden frame of triangular shape within which the balls are arranged before play. **b.** the balls so arranged: *He took aim at the rack.* **5.** *Mach.* **a.** a bar, with teeth on one of its sides, adapted to engage with the teeth of a pinion (**rack and pinion**) or the like, as for converting circular into rectilinear motion or vice versa. **b.** a bar having a series of notches engaging with a pawl or the like. **6.** a former instrument of torture consisting of a framework on which a victim was tied, often spread-eagled, by the wrists and ankles, to be slowly stretched by spreading the parts of the framework. **7.** a cause or state of intense suffering of body or mind. **8.** torment; anguish. **9.** violent strain. **10.** a pair of antlers. **11.** *Slang.* a bed, cot, or bunk: *I spent all afternoon in the rack.* —*v.t.* **12.** to torture; distress acutely; torment: *His body was racked with pain.* **13.** to strain in mental effort: *to rack one's brains.* **14.** to strain by physical force or violence. **15.** to strain beyond what is normal or usual. **16.** to stretch the body of (a person) in torture by means of a rack. **17.** *Naut.* to seize (two ropes) together side by side. **18. rack out,** *Slang.* to go to bed; go to sleep: *I racked out all afternoon.* **19. rack up, a.** *Pool.* to put (the balls) in a rack. **b.** *Informal.* to tally, accumulate, or amass as an achievement or score: *The corporation racked up the greatest profits in its history.* [1250–1300; ME *rakke, rekke* (n.) < MD *rac, rec, recke;* cf. MLG *reck,* G *Reck*] —**rack′ing•ly,** *adv.*
—**Syn. 7.** torture, pain, agony, tribulation, ordeal. **12.** See **torment.**

R, rack¹ (def. 5a); P, pinion

rack² (rak), *n.* **1.** ruin or destruction; wrack. **2. go to rack and ruin,** to decay, decline, or become destroyed: *His property went to rack and ruin in his absence.* —*v.* **3. rack up,** *Slang.* to wreck, esp. a vehicle. [1590–1600; var. of WRACK¹]

rack³ (rak), *n.* **1.** the fast pace of a horse in which the legs move in lateral pairs but not simultaneously. —*v.i.* **2.** (of horses) to move in a rack. [1570–80; perh. var. of ROCK²]

rack⁴ (rak), *n.* **1.** Also called **cloud rack.** a group of drifting clouds. —*v.i.* **2.** to drive or move, esp. before the wind. Also, **wrack.** [1350–1400; ME *rak, reck(e);* orig. uncert.]

rack⁵ (rak), *v.t.* to draw off (wine, cider, etc.) from the lees. [1425–75; late ME < OF; cf. obs. F *raqué* (of wine) pressed from the dregs of grapes]

rack⁶ (rak), *n.* **1.** the neck portion of mutton, pork, or veal. **2.** the rib section of a foresaddle of lamb, mutton, or sometimes veal. [1560–70; orig. uncert.]

rack′ and pin′ion, *Mach., Auto.* See under **rack¹** (def. 5a).

rack-and-pin•ion (rak′ən pin′yən), *adj.* of or pertaining to a mechanism in which a rack engages a pinion: *rack-and-pinion steering.* See illus. under **rack¹.** [1900–05]

rack•board (rak′bôrd′, -bōrd′), *n.* a board with holes into which organ pipes are fitted. [1850–55; RACK¹ + BOARD]

rack′ car′, *Railroads.* a flatcar containing a frame or frames for carrying various objects, as automobiles, logs, girders, etc. [1870–75]

rack•et¹ (rak′it), *n.* **1.** a loud noise or clamor, esp. of a disturbing or confusing kind; din; uproar: *The traffic made a terrible racket in the street below.* **2.** social excitement, gaiety, or dissipation. **3.** an organized illegal activity, such as bootlegging or the extortion of money from legitimate business people by threat or violence. **4.** a dishonest scheme, trick, business, activity, etc.: *the latest weight-reducing racket.* **5.** Usually, **the rackets.** organized illegal activities: *Some say that the revenue from legalized gambling supports the rackets.* **6.** *Slang.* **a.** an occupation, livelihood, or business. **b.** an easy or profitable source of livelihood. —*v.i.* **7.** to make a racket or noise. **8.** to take part in social gaiety or dissipation. [1555–65; 1890–95 for def. 6; metathetic var. of dial. *rattick;* see RATTLE¹]
—**Syn. 1.** tumult, disturbance, outcry. See **noise.**
—**Ant. 1, 2.** tranquillity.

rack•et² (rak′it), *n.* **1.** a light bat having a netting of catgut or nylon stretched in a more or less oval frame and used for striking the ball in tennis, the shuttlecock in badminton, etc. **2.** the short-handled paddle used to strike the ball in table tennis. **3. rackets,** (*used with a singular v.*) racquet (def. 1). **4.** a snowshoe made in the form of a tennis racket. Also, **racquet** (for defs. 1, 2, 4). [1490–1500; < MF *raquette, rachette,* perh. < Ar *rāḥet,* var. of *rāḥah* palm of the hand] —**rack′et•like′,** *adj.*

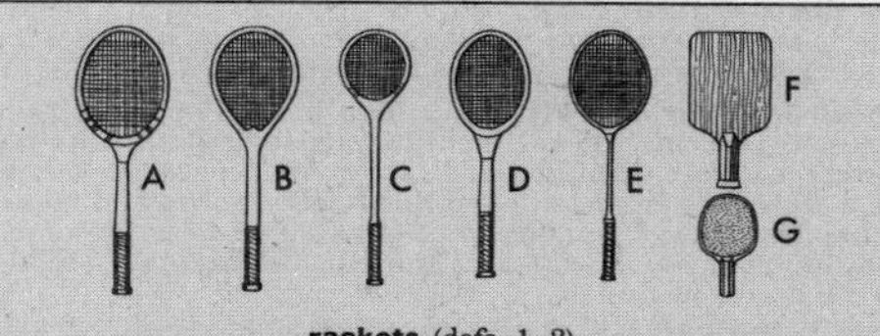

rackets (defs. 1, 2)
A, tennis; B, court tennis; C, squash; D, squash tennis; E, badminton; F, paddle tennis; G, table tennis

rack•et•eer (rak′i tēr′), *n.* **1.** a person engaged in a racket. —*v.i.* **2.** to engage in a racket. [1925–30, *Amer.;* RACKET¹ + -EER]

rack•et•eer•ing (rak′i tēr′ing), *n.* the practice of conducting or engaging in a racket, as extortion or bootlegging. [1925–30, *Amer.;* RACKETEER + -ING¹]

rack•ett (rak′it), *n.* ranket.

rack•et•y (rak′i tē), *adj.* **1.** making or causing a racket; noisy. **2.** fond of excitement or dissipation. [1765–75; RACKET¹ + -Y¹]

Rack•ham (rak′əm), *n.* **Arthur,** 1867–1939, English illustrator and painter.

rack•ing (rak′ing), *n. Masonry.* the stepping back of the ends of courses successively from bottom to top in an unfinished wall to facilitate resumption of work or bonding with an intersecting wall. [1890–95; RACK¹ + -ING¹]

rack•le (rak′əl), *adj. Chiefly Scot.* headstrong; rash. [1250–1300; ME; perh. var. of RATTLE¹; cf. RACKET¹]

rack′ locomo′tive, a locomotive designed for operation on a rack railway. Also called **cog locomotive.**

rack′ rail′, (in an inclined-plane or mountain-climbing railway) a rail between the running rails having cogs or teeth with which cogwheels on the locomotive engage. [1830–40]

rack′ rail′way. See **cog railway.** [1880–85]

rack-rent (rak′rent′), *n.* **1.** Also, **rack′ rent′.** rent equal to or nearly equal to the full annual value of a property. —*v.t.* **2.** to exact the highest possible rent for. **3.** to demand rack-rent from. [1600–10] —**rack′-rent′•er,** *n.*

rack•work (rak′wûrk′), *n.* a mechanism utilizing a rack, as a rack and pinion. [1760–70; RACK¹ + WORK]

ra•clette (rä klet′, ra-), *n. Swiss Cookery.* **1.** a dish made by heating a piece of cheese, as over a hearth, and scraping off the melted part onto a plate: served with boiled potatoes. **2.** the cheese used in making this dish. [1930–35; < F]

ra•con (rā′kon), *n.* See **radar beacon.** [1940–45, *Amer.; ra(dar bea)con*]

rac•on•teur (rak′ən tûr′; *Fr.* RA kôN tœR′), *n., pl.* **-teurs** (-tûrz′; *Fr.* -tœR′). a person who is skilled in relating stories and anecdotes interestingly. [1820–30; < F, equiv. to *racont(er)* to tell (OF *r(e)-* RE- + *aconter* to tell, ACCOUNT) + *-eur* -EUR]

rac•on•teuse (rak′ən tœz′, -to͞oz′, -to͞os′; *Fr.* RA kôN-tœz′), *n., pl.* **-teus•es** (-tœ′ziz, -to͞o′-, -to͞o′siz; *Fr.* -tœz′). a woman who is skilled in relating stories and anecdotes interestingly. [1860–65; < F, fem. of *raconteur* RACONTEUR; see -EUSE]

ra•coon (ra ko͞on′), *n., pl.* **-coons,** (*esp. collectively*) **-coon.** raccoon.

rac•quet (rak′it), *n.* **1. racquets,** (*used with a singular v.*) a game played with rackets and a ball by two or four persons on a four-walled court. **2.** racket² (defs. 1, 2, 4). [var. of RACKET²]

rac•quet•ball (rak′it bôl′), *n.* a game similar to handball, played on a four-walled court but with a short-handled, strung racket and a larger, somewhat softer ball. [1965–70; RACQUET + BALL¹] —**rac′quet•ball′er,** *n.*

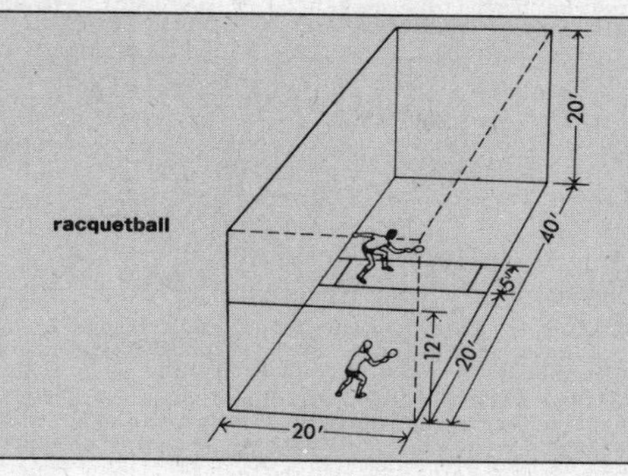

rac•y (rā′sē), *adj.,* **rac•i•er, rac•i•est. 1.** slightly improper or indelicate; suggestive; risqué. **2.** vigorous; lively; spirited. **3.** sprightly; piquant; pungent: *a racy literary style.* **4.** having an agreeably peculiar taste or flavor, as wine, fruit, etc. [1645–55; RACE² + -Y¹] —**rac′i•ly,** *adv.* —**rac′i•ness,** *n.*
—**Syn. 2.** animated. **3.** strong. —**Ant. 2.** slow.

rad¹ (rad), *n. Physics.* a unit of absorbed dose equal to 0.01 Gy. Cf. **dose** (def. 4a). [1915–20; shortened form of RADIATION]

rad² (rad), *n.* **1.** *Informal.* radical. —*adj.* **2.** *Slang.* fine; wonderful. [by shortening of RADICAL]

rad, *Math.* radian; radians.

rad., *Math.* **1.** radical. **2.** radix.

ra•dar (rā′där), *n. Electronics.* a device for determining the presence and location of an object by measuring the time for the echo of a radio wave to return from it and the direction from which it returns. [1940–45, *Amer.; ra(dio) d(etecting) a(nd) r(anging)*]

ra′dar astron′omy, the branch of astronomy that uses radar to map the surfaces of planetary bodies, as the moon and Venus, and to determine periods of rotation. [1955–60]

ra′dar bea′con, a radar device at a fixed location that, on receiving a radar signal, automatically transmits a particular radar signal in reply, identifying itself and enabling navigators of ships and aircraft to determine their distance and direction from it. Also called **racon.** [1940–45]

ra•dar•man (rā′där mən, -man′), *n., pl.* **-men** (-mən, -men′). a person who operates or helps to operate radar equipment. [1940–45; RADAR + MAN¹]

ra′dar pick′et, *Mil.* a ship, vehicle, or aircraft stationed at a distance from a protected force to increase radar detection range. [1950–55]

ra•dar•scope (rā′där skōp′), *n.* the viewing screen of radar equipment. [1945–50; RADAR + -SCOPE]

Rad•cliff (rad′klif), *n.* a city in central Kentucky. 14,519.

Rad•cliffe (rad′klif), *n.* **Ann (Ward),** 1764–1823, English writer of Gothic romances.

rad•dle¹ (rad′l), *v.t.,* **-dled, -dling.** to interweave; wattle. [1665–75; v. use of *raddle* lath < AF *reidele* pole, rail of a cart (OF *redelle;* cf. F *ridelle*)]

rad•dle² (rad′l), *n., v.,* **-dled, -dling.** —*n.* **1.** ruddle. —*v.t.* **2.** ruddle. **3.** to color coarsely.

rad•dle•man (rad′l mən), *n., pl.* **-men.** ruddleman.

ra•deau (rə dō′), *n., pl.* **-deaux** (-dō′, -dōz′). an armed scow, variously rigged, used as a floating battery during the American Revolution. [1750–60; < F: raft < Pr *radel* < VL **ratellus,* dim. of L *ratis* raft]

ra•dec•to•my (rə dek′tə mē), *n., pl.* **-mies.** *Dentistry, Surg.* excision of part or all of the root of a tooth. [RAD(IX) + -ECTOMY]

Ra•dek (rä′dek; *Russ.* Rä′dyik), *n.* **Karl** (kärl), 1885–1939?, Russian writer and politician.

Ra•detz•ky (rä dets′kē), *n.* **Count Jo•seph** (yō′zef), 1766–1858, Austrian field marshal.

Rad•ford (rad′fərd), *n.* **1. Arthur William,** 1896–1973, U.S. admiral: chairman of Joint Chiefs of Staff 1953–57. **2.** a town in SW Virginia. 13,225.

Ra•dha (rä′dä), *n. Hindu Legend.* the milkmaid who became the consort of Krishna.

Ra•dha•krish•nan (rä′də krish′nən), *n.* **Sir Sar•ve•pal•li** (sur′və pul′ē), 1888–1975, president of India 1962–67.

ra•di•al (rā′dē əl), *adj.* **1.** arranged like radii or rays. See diag. on next page. **2.** having spokes, bars, lines, etc., arranged like radii, as a machine. **3.** made in the direction of a radius; going from the center outward or from the circumference inward along a radius: *a radial cut.* **4.** *Zool.* pertaining to structures that radiate from a central point, as the arms of a starfish. **5.** of, like, or pertaining to a radius or a ray. **6.** *Mach.* **a.** having pistons moving inward and outward from a central point or shaft: *a radial engine; a radial pump.* **b.** noting a bearing designed primarily to take thrusts radial to the center of rotation. **7.** *Anat., Entomol.* of, pertaining to, or situated near the radius. **8.** acting along or in the direction of the radius of a circle: *radial motion; radial velocity.* —*n.* **9.** a radial section or construction. **10.** *Auto.* See **radial tire.** [1560–70; < ML *radiālis,* equiv. to L *radi(us)* beam, ray (see RADIUS) + *-ālis* -AL[1]] —**ra′di·al′i·ty,** *n.* —**ra′di·al·ly,** *adv.*

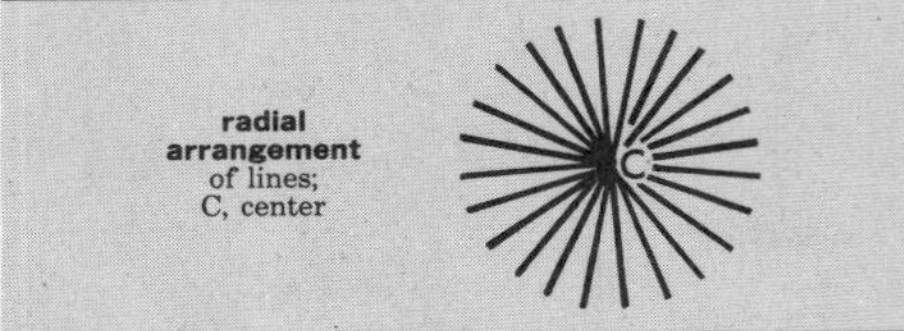

ra′dial en′gine, *Aeron.* an internal-combustion engine having the cylinders arranged in radial opposition, found mainly on older aircraft. [1905–10]

ra′dial keratot′omy, *Ophthalm.* a surgical technique for correcting nearsightedness by making a series of spokelike incisions in the cornea to change its shape and focusing properties. [1975–80; KERATO- + -TOMY]

ra′dial mo′tion, *Astron.* the component of the motion of a star away from or toward the earth along its line of sight, expressed in miles or kilometers per second and determined by the shift in the wavelength of light emitted by the star. Also called **ra′dial veloc′ity.** Cf. **redshift, tangential motion.**

ra′dial saw′, a cantilevered circular saw adjustable at various angles to the length of the work and to the perpendicular.

ra′dial sym′metry, *Biol.* a basic body plan in which the organism can be divided into similar halves by passing a plane at any angle along a central axis, characteristic of sessile and bottom-dwelling animals, as the sea anemone and starfish. Cf. **bilateral symmetry.** [1885–90]

ra′dial tire′, a motor-vehicle tire in which the plies or cords run from one bead to the other at right angles to both beads. See illustration under **tire**[2]. Also called **radial.** [1965–70]

ra′dial triangula′tion, *Photogrammetry.* triangulation based upon lines radiating from the center of each of two overlapping photographs to certain objects appearing on each photograph.

ra·di·an (rā′dē ən), *n. Math.* the measure of a central angle subtending an arc equal in length to the radius: equal to 57.2958°. *Abbr.:* rad [1875–80; RADI(US) + -AN]

ra·di·ance (rā′dē əns), *n.* **1.** radiant brightness or light: *the radiance of the tropical sun.* **2.** warm, cheerful brightness: *the radiance of her expression.* **3.** *Rare.* radiation. Also, **radiancy.** [1595–1605; RADI(ANT) + -ANCE]
—**Syn. 1.** resplendence, splendor, brilliance.

ra·di·an·cy (rā′dē ən sē), *n., pl.* **-cies.** radiance. [1640–50; RADI(ANT) + -ANCY]

ra·di·ant (rā′dē ənt), *adj.* **1.** emitting rays of light; shining; bright: *the radiant sun; radiant colors.* **2.** bright with joy, hope, etc.: *radiant smiles; a radiant future.* **3.** *Physics.* emitted or propagated by radiation. **4.** *Heraldry.* **a.** noting a partition line having a series of flamelike indentations formed by ogees joined in zigzags; rayonny. **b.** (of a charge, as an ordinary) having an edge or edges so formed. —*n.* **5.** a point or object from which rays proceed. **6.** *Astron.* the point in the heavens from which a shower of meteors appears to radiate. **7.** a refractory absorbing and radiating heat from the flames of a gas fireplace or the like. [1400–50; late ME < L *radiant-* (s. of *radiāns,* prp. of *radiāre* to radiate light, shine), equiv. to *radi(us)* beam, ray (see RADIUS) + *-ant-* -ANT] —**ra′di·ant·ly,** *adv.*
—**Syn. 1.** beaming, refulgent, resplendent. See **bright.**
—**Ant. 1.** dim.

ra′diant emit′tance, *Optics.* radiant flux emitted per unit area. Also called **ra′diant ex·cit′ance** (ik sīt′ns).

ra′diant en′ergy, *Physics.* **1.** energy transmitted in wave motion, esp. electromagnetic wave motion. **2.** light[1] (def. 2a). [1910–15]

ra′diant flux′, *Physics.* the time rate of flow of radiant energy. [1915–20]

ra′diant heat′, *Thermodynam.* heat energy transmitted by electromagnetic waves in contrast to heat transmitted by conduction or convection. [1500–10]

ra′diant heat′ing, 1. the means of heating objects or persons by radiation in which the intervening air is not heated. **2.** a system for heating by radiation from a surface, esp. from a surface heated by means of electric resistance, hot water, etc. [1910–15]

Ra·di·a·ta (rā′dē ā′tə, -ä′tə), *n. Biol.* (in some classification systems) a major grouping that includes more or less radially symmetrical animals, as coelenterates (jellyfish, sea anemones, corals), ctenophores (comb jellies), and echinoderms (starfish, sea urchins, sea cucumbers). [1820–30; < NL, n. use of neut. pl. of L *radiātus* RADIATE (adj.)]

ra·di·ate (*v.* rā′dē āt′; *adj.* rā′dē it, -āt′), *v.,* **-at·ed, -at·ing,** *adj.* —*v.i.* **1.** to extend, spread, or move like rays or radii from a center. **2.** to emit rays, as of light or heat; irradiate. **3.** to issue or proceed in rays. **4.** (of persons) to project or glow with cheerfulness, joy, etc.: *She simply radiates with good humor.* —*v.t.* **5.** to emit in rays; disseminate, as from a center. **6.** (of persons) to project (joy, goodwill, etc.). —*adj.* **7.** radiating from a center. **8.** having rays extending from a central point or part: *a coin showing a radiate head.* **9.** radiating symmetrically. [1610–20; < L *radiātus* (ptp. of *radiāre* to radiate light, shine). See RADIANT, -ATE[1]] —**ra′di·a·ble,** *adj.* —**ra′di·a·bil′i·ty, ra′di·a·ble·ness,** *n.* —**ra′di·a·bly, ra′di·ate·ly,** *adv.*

ra·di·a·tion (rā′dē ā′shən), *n.* **1.** *Physics.* **a.** the process in which energy is emitted as particles or waves. **b.** the complete process in which energy is emitted by one body, transmitted through an intervening medium or space, and absorbed by another body. **c.** the energy transferred by these processes. **2.** the act or process of radiating. **3.** something that is radiated. **4.** radial arrangement of parts. [1545–55; < L *radiātiōn-* (s. of *radiātiō*) a glittering, shining. See RADIATE, -ION] —**ra′di·a′tion·al,** *adj.*

radia′tion belt′, *Physics.* See **Van Allen belt.** [1955–60]

radia′tion fog′, fog produced by the nocturnal cooling of the surface boundary layer to a temperature at which its content of water vapor condenses. Also called **ground fog.** [1855–60]

radia′tion poten′tial, *Physics.* the potential in volts that must be applied to an atom or molecule to cause it to emit radiation at one of its characteristic frequencies.

radia′tion pres′sure, *Physics.* the pressure exerted on a surface by electromagnetic radiation or by sound waves. [1900–05]

radia′tion sick′ness, *Pathol.* sickness caused by irradiation with x-rays or other nuclear radiation as a result of therapeutic treatment, accidental exposure, or a nuclear bomb explosion and characterized by nausea, vomiting, headache, cramps, diarrhea, loss of hair and teeth, destruction of white blood cells, and prolonged hemorrhage. [1920–25]

radia′tion ther′apy, radiotherapy.

ra·di·a·tive (rā′dē ā′tiv), *adj.* giving off radiation. Also, **ra·di·a·to·ry** (rā′dē ə tôr′ē, -tōr′ē). [1830–40; RADIAT(ION) + -IVE]

ra′diative cap′ture, *Physics.* the capture of a particle, as a neutron, by a nucleus, inducing the emission of electromagnetic radiation, as a gamma ray. [1930–35]

ra·di·a·tor (rā′dē ā′tər), *n.* **1.** a person or thing that radiates. **2.** any of various heating devices, as a series or coil of pipes through which steam or hot water passes. **3.** a device constructed from thin-walled tubes and metal fins, used for cooling circulating water, as in an automobile engine. **4.** *Radio.* a transmitting antenna. [1830–40; RADIATE + -OR[2]]

ra′diator grille′, a grille in an automobile or the like for air cooling of the liquid in the cooling system. [1955–60]

ra·di·a·tus (rā′dē ā′təs), *adj. Meteorol.* (of a cloud) having bands that appear to converge toward a point on the horizon. [< NL, L: arranged radially, orig., having rays of light; see RADIATE]

rad·i·cal (rad′i kəl), *adj.* **1.** of or going to the root or origin; fundamental: *a radical difference.* **2.** thoroughgoing or extreme, esp. as regards change from accepted or traditional forms: *a radical change in the policy of a company.* **3.** favoring drastic political, economic, or social reforms: *radical ideas; radical and anarchistic ideologues.* **4.** forming a basis or foundation. **5.** existing inherently in a thing or person: *radical defects of character.* **6.** *Math.* **a.** pertaining to or forming a root. **b.** denoting or pertaining to the radical sign. **c.** irrational (def. 5b). **7.** *Gram.* of or pertaining to a root. **8.** *Bot.* of or arising from the root or the base of the stem. —*n.* **9.** a person who holds or follows strong convictions or extreme principles; extremist. **10.** a person who advocates fundamental political, economic, and social reforms by direct and often uncompromising methods. **11.** *Math.* **a.** a quantity expressed as a root of another quantity. **b.** the set of elements of a ring, some power of which is contained in a given ideal. **c.** See **radical sign. 12.** *Chem.* **a.** group (def. 3). **b.** See **free radical. 13.** *Gram.* root (def. 11). **14.** (in Chinese writing) one of 214 ideographic elements used in combination with phonetics to form thousands of different characters. [1350–1400; ME < LL *rādīcālis* having roots, equiv. to L *rādīc-* (s. of *rādīx*) ROOT[1] + *-ālis* -AL[1]] —**rad′i·cal·ness,** *n.*
—**Syn. 1.** basic, essential; original, innate, ingrained. **2.** complete, unqualified, thorough; drastic, excessive, immoderate, violent. RADICAL, EXTREME, FANATICAL denote that which goes beyond moderation or even to excess in opinion, belief, action, etc. RADICAL emphasizes the idea of going to the root of a matter, and this often seems immoderate in its thoroughness or completeness: *radical ideas; radical changes or reforms.* EXTREME applies to excessively biased ideas, intemperate conduct, or repressive legislation: *to use extreme measures.* FANATICAL is applied to a person who has extravagant views, esp. in matters of religion or morality, which render that person incapable of sound judgments; and excessive zeal which leads him or her to take violent action against those who have differing views: *fanatical in persecuting others.* —**Ant. 1, 2.** superficial.

rad′ical ax′is, *Geom.* the line such that tangents drawn from any point of the line to two given circles are equal in length. [1840–50]

rad′ical chic′, the patronage of extremists or left-wing radicals by rich or famous people, as through invitations to social functions or public expressions of support. [coined by Tom Wolfe (b. 1931), American journalist, in an essay of the same title published in 1970] —**rad′i·cal-chic′,** *adj.*

rad′ical empir′icism, 1. (in the philosophy of William James) the doctrine that the only proper subject matter of philosophy is that which can be defined in terms of experience, and that relations are a part of experience. **2.** sensationalism (def. 3b). [1895–1900] —**rad′ical empir′icist.**

rad·i·cal·ism (rad′i kə liz′əm), *n.* **1.** the holding or following of radical or extreme views or principles. **2.** the principles or practices of radicals. [1810–20; RADICAL + -ISM]

rad·i·cal·ize (rad′i kə līz′), *v.,* **-ized, -iz·ing.** —*v.t.* **1.** to make radical or more radical, esp. in politics. —*v.i.* **2.** to become radical or more radical, esp. in politics. Also, *esp. Brit.,* **rad′i·cal·ise′.** [1815–20; RADICAL + -IZE] —**rad′i·cal·i·za′tion,** *n.*

rad′ical left′, the faction representing extreme left-wing political views, often Marxist or Maoist in ideology. Cf. **New Left.** [1965–70]

rad·i·cal·ly (rad′ik lē), *adj.* **1.** with regard to origin or root. **2.** in a complete or basic manner; thoroughly; fundamentally. [1600–10; RADICAL + -LY]

rad′ical right′, the faction representing extreme right-wing political views; ultraconservatives; reactionaries. [1950–55] —**rad′ical right′ism.** —**rad′ical right′ist.**

rad′ical sign′, *Math.* the symbol $\surd$ or $\sqrt{\ }$ indicating extraction of a root of the quantity that follows it, as $\sqrt{25}=5$ or $\sqrt[3]{a^3b^3}=ab$. [1660–70]

rad·i·cand (rad′i kand′, rad′i kand′), *n. Math.* the quantity under a radical sign. [1895–1900; < L *rādīcandum,* neut. gerundive of *rādīcāre,* deriv. of *rādīx* ROOT[1]]

rad·i·cant (rad′i kənt), *adj. Bot.* rooting from the stem, as ivy. [1745–55; < L *rādīcant-* (s. of *rādīcāns,* prp. of *rādīcārī* to grow roots, take root), equiv. to *rādīc-* (s. of *rādīx*) ROOT[1] + *-ant-* -ANT]

ra·dic·chi·o (rä dē′kē ō′, rə-), *n.* a variety of chicory originating in Italy, having a compact head of reddish, white-streaked leaves: leaves and roots may be cooked or used raw in salads. Also, **ra·di′chi·o.** Also called **ra·di·chet·ta** (rä′di ket′ə). [< It]

rad·i·cel (rad′ə sel′), *n. Bot.* a minute root; a rootlet. [1810–20; < NL *rādīcella* small root, rootlet, equiv. to L *rādīc-* (s. of *rādīx*) ROOT[1] + *-ella* -ELLE]

rad·i·ces (rad′ə sēz′, rā′də-), *n.* a pl. of **radix.**

rad·i·cle (rad′i kəl), *n.* **1.** *Bot.* **a.** the lower part of the axis of an embryo; the primary root. See diag. under **plumule. b.** a rudimentary root; radicel or rootlet. **2.** *Chem.* (formerly) radical (def. 12). **3.** *Anat.* a small rootlike part or structure, as the beginning of a nerve or vein. [1665–75; < L *rādīcula* small root, equiv. to *rādīc-* (s. of *rādīx*) ROOT[1] + *-ula* -ULE]

ra·dic·u·lar (rə dik′yə lər), *adj.* **1.** *Bot.* of or pertaining to a radicle or root. **2.** *Anat.* of, pertaining to, or involving a radicle. [1820–30; < L *rādīcul(a)* RADICLE + -AR[1]]

ra·dic·u·li·tis (rə dik′yə lī′tis), *n. Pathol.* inflammation of a spinal nerve root. [1905–10; < NL; see RADICLE, -ITIS]

ra·di·i (rā′dē ī′), *n.* a pl. of **radius.**

Ra·din (rād′n), *n.* **Paul,** 1883–1959, U.S. anthropologist, born in Poland.

ra·di·o (rā′dē ō′), *n., pl.* **-di·os,** *adj., v.,* **-di·oed, -di·o·ing.** —*n.* **1.** wireless telegraphy or telephony: *speeches broadcast by radio.* **2.** an apparatus for receiving or transmitting radio broadcasts. **3.** a message transmitted by radio. —*adj.* **4.** pertaining to, used in, or sent by radio. **5.** pertaining to or employing radiations, as of electrical energy. —*v.t.* **6.** to transmit (a message, music, etc.) by radio. **7.** to send a message to (a person) by radio. —*v.i.* **8.** to transmit a message, music, etc., by radio. [1910–15; shortening of RADIOTELEGRAPH or RADIOTELEGRAPHY]

radio-, a combining form with the meanings "dealing with radiant energy" (*radiometer*), "employing or dealing with radio waves" (*radioacoustics; radiolocation; radiotelephone*), "emitting rays as a result of the breakup of atomic nuclei" (*radioactive; radiocarbon*), "characterized by, employing or dealing with such rays" (*radiography; radiopaque; radiotherapy*). [< F, comb. form repr. L *radius* beam, ray, RADIUS]

ra·di·o·a·cous·tics (rā′dē ō ə ko͞o′stiks), *n.* (*used with a singular v.*) the science and technology of the production, transmission, and reproduction of sounds carried by radio waves. [RADIO- + ACOUSTICS]

ra·di·o·ac·tin·i·um (rā′dē ō ak tin′ē əm), *n. Chem.* the radioactive isotope of thorium having a mass number 227 and a half-life of 18.8 days. *Symbol:* RdAc, Th 227 [1905–10; RADIO- + ACTINIUM]

ra·di·o·ac·ti·vate (rā′dē ō ak′tə vāt′), *v.t.,* **-vat·ed, -vat·ing.** *Physics.* to make (a substance) radioactive. [1900–05; RADIOACTIVE + -ATE[1]]

ra·di·o·ac·tive (rā′dē ō ak′tiv), *adj. Physics, Chem.* of, pertaining to, exhibiting, or caused by radioactivity. [1895–1900; RADIO- + ACTIVE] —**ra′di·o·ac′tive·ly,** *adv.*

ra′dioac′tive dat′ing. See **radiometric dating.**

radioac′tive decay′, *Physics.* decay (def. 8). [1960–65]

ra′dioac′tive fall′out. See under **fallout.**

ra′dioac′tive se′ries, *Physics, Chem.* a succession of elements initiated in the radioactive decay of a parent, as thorium or uranium, each of which decays into the next until a stable element, usually lead, is produced. Also called **decay series.** [1920–25]

ra′dioac′tive waste′, the radioactive by-products from the operation of a nuclear reactor or from the reprocessing of depleted nuclear fuel. Also called **nuclear waste.** [1945–50]

ra·di·o·ac·tiv·i·ty (rā′dē ō ak tiv′i tē), *n. Physics, Chem.* the phenomenon, exhibited by and being a property of certain elements, of spontaneously emitting radiation resulting from changes in the nuclei of atoms of the element. Also called **activity.** [1895–1900; RADIO- + ACTIVITY]

ra′dio astron′omy, the branch of astronomy that utilizes extraterrestrial radiation in radio wavelengths rather than visible light for the study of the universe. [1945–50]

ra·di·o·au·to·graph (rā′dē ō ô′tə graf′, -gräf′), *n.* autoradiograph. [1940–45; RADIO- + AUTOGRAPH]

CONCISE ETYMOLOGY KEY: <, descended or borrowed from; >, whence; b., blend of, blended; c., cognate with; cf., compare; deriv., derivative; equiv., equivalent; imit., imitative; obl., oblique; r., replacing; s., stem; sp., spelling, spelled; resp., respelling, respelled; trans., translation; ?, origin unknown; *, unattested; ‡, probably earlier than. See the full key inside the front cover.

ra·di·o·au·tog·ra·phy (rā′dē ō ô tog′rə fē), *n.* autoradiography. [1940–45; RADIO- + AUTO- + -GRAPHY]

ra′dio bea′con, a radio station that sends a characteristic signal so as to enable ships or airplanes to determine their position or bearing by means of a radio compass. [1915–20]

ra′dio beam′, beam (def. 12). [1920–25]

ra·di·o·bi·ol·o·gy (rā′dē ō bī ol′ə jē), *n.* the branch of biology dealing with the effects of radiation on living matter. [1915–20; RADIO- + BIOLOGY] —**ra·di·o·bi·o·log·i·cal** (rā′dē ō bī′ə loj′i kəl), **ra′di·o·bi′o·log′ic,** *adj.* —**ra′di·o·bi·ol′o·gist,** *n.*

ra·di·o·broad·cast (*n.* rā′dē ō brôd′kast, -käst; *v.* rā′dē ō brôd′kast′, -käst′), *n., v.,* **-cast** or **-cast·ed, -cast·ing.** —*n.* **1.** a broadcast by radio. —*v.t., v.i.* **2.** to broadcast by radio. [1955–60; RADIO- + BROADCAST] —**ra′di·o·broad′cast′er,** *n.*

ra′dio car′, an automobile, esp. a police car or taxi, equipped with a two-way radio for communication. [1920–25]

ra·di·o·car·bon (rā′dē ō kär′bən), *n. Chem.* **1.** Also called **carbon 14.** a radioactive isotope of carbon with mass number 14 and a half-life of about 5730 years: widely used in the dating of organic materials. **2.** any radioactive isotope of carbon. [1935–40; RADIO- + CARBON]

radiocar′bon dat′ing, the determination of the age of objects of organic origin by measurement of the radioactivity of their carbon content. Also called **carbon-14 dating.** Cf. **radiometric dating.** [1950–55]

ra·di·o·cast (rā′dē ō kast′, -käst′), *n., v.,* **-cast** or **-cast·ed, -cast·ing.** —*n.* **1.** a radiobroadcast. —*v.t., v.i.* **2.** to broadcast via radio. [1920–25; RADIO + (BROAD)CAST]

ra·di·o·ce·si·um (rā′dē ō sē′zē əm), *n. Chem.* See **cesium 137.** [1950–55; RADIO- + CESIUM]

ra·di·o·chem·i·cal (rā′dē ō kem′i kəl), *adj. Chem.* pertaining to or involving radiochemistry. [1910–15; RADIO- + CHEMICAL]

ra·di·o·chem·is·try (rā′dē ō kem′ə strē), *n.* the chemical study of radioactive elements, both natural and artificial, and their use in the study of chemical processes. [1900–05; RADIO- + CHEMISTRY] —**ra′di·o·chem′ist,** *n.*

ra·di·o·chro·ma·tog·ra·phy (rā′dē ō krō′mə tog′rə fē), *n. Chem.* chromatography in which radiolabeled substances on the chromatogram are determined quantitatively or qualitatively by measuring their radioactivity. [RADIO- + CHROMATOGRAPHY]

ra′dio com′pass, a radio receiver with a directional antenna for determining the bearing of the receiver from a radio transmitter. [1915–20]

ra·di·o·di·ag·no·sis (rā′dē ō dī′əg nō′sis), *n., pl.* **-ses** (-sēz). *Med.* diagnosis by means of radiography or radioscopy. [1900–05; RADIO- + DIAGNOSIS]

ra′dio direc′tion find′er, a navigational aid establishing a fix by means of the bearings of two known radio stations. *Abbr.:* RDF [1920–25]

ra·di·o·el·e·ment (rā′dē ō el′ə mənt), *n. Chem.* a radioactive element. [1900–05; RADIO- + ELEMENT]

Ra′dio Free′ Eu′rope/Ra′dio Lib′erty, a federally funded private organization that broadcasts news and entertainment to Communist countries, esp. the Soviet Union, Poland, Czechoslovakia, Hungary, Rumania, and Bulgaria: founded 1952.

ra·di·o·fre·quen·cy (rā′dē ō frē′kwən sē), *n., pl.* **-cies. 1.** the frequency of the transmitting waves of a given radio message or broadcast. **2.** a frequency within the range of radio transmission, from about 15,000 to 10^{11} hertz. *Abbr.:* RF, rf Also, **ra′dio fre′quency.** [1910–15; RADIO- + FREQUENCY]

ra′dio gal′axy, a galaxy that emits much more strongly in the radio part of the spectrum than does a typical galaxy. [1955–60]

ra·di·o·gen·ic (rā′dē ō jen′ik), *adj.* **1.** *Physics.* produced by radioactive decay: *radiogenic lead; radiogenic heat.* **2.** having qualities or characteristics that broadcast well; suitable for presentation on the radio. [1925–30; RADIO- + -GENIC]

ra·di·o·gram[1] (rā′dē ō gram′), *n.* a message transmitted by radiotelegraphy. [1900–05; RADIO- + -GRAM[1]]

ra·di·o·gram[2] (rā′dē ō gram′), *n. Brit.* a combination radio and record player. [1905–10; RADIO + GRAM(OPHONE)]

ra·di·o·graph (rā′dē ō graf′, -gräf′), *n.* **1.** Also called **shadowgraph.** a photographic image produced by the action of x-rays or nuclear radiation. —*v.t.* **2.** to make a radiograph of. [1875–80; RADIO- + -GRAPH]

ra·di·og·ra·phy (rā′dē og′rə fē), *n.* the production of radiographs. [1895–1900; RADIO- + -GRAPHY] —**ra′di·og′ra·pher,** *n.* —**ra·di·o·graph·ic** (rā′dē ō graf′ik), **ra′di·o·graph′i·cal,** *adj.* —**ra′di·o·graph′i·cal·ly,** *adv.*

ra′dio hori′zon, the locus of points on the earth's surface where rays from a transmitting antenna are tangent to the surface. The radio horizon for a fixed antenna varies with refraction by the atmosphere of radio waves.

ra·di·o·im·mu·no·as·say (rā′dē ō im′yə nō as′ā, -a sā′, -i myōō′-), *n.* a test procedure that integrates immunologic and radiolabeling techniques to measure minute quantities of a substance, as a protein, hormone, or drug, in a given sample of body fluid or tissue. [1960–65; RADIO- + IMMUNOASSAY]

ra·di·o·im·mu·nol·o·gy (rā′dē ō im′yə nol′ə jē), *n.* the study of biological substances or processes with the aid of antigens or antibodies labeled with a radioactive isotope. [1960–65; RADIO- + IMMUNOLOGY] —**ra·di·o·im·mu·no·log·i·cal** (rā′dē ō im′yə nl oj′i kəl, -i myōō′-), *adj.*

ra′dio interferom′eter, *Astron.* any of several different types of instrumentation designed to observe interference patterns of electromagnetic radiation at radio wavelengths: used in the discovery and measurement of radio sources in the atmosphere.

ra·di·o·i·o·dine (rā′dē ō ī′ə dīn′, -din, -dēn′), *n. Chem.* any of nine radioisotopes of iodine, esp. iodine 131 and iodine 125, used as radioactive tracers in research and clinical diagnosis and treatment. [1935–40; RADIO- + IODINE]

ra·di·o·i·ron (rā′dē ō ī′ərn), *n. Chem.* the radioactive isotope of iron, with atomic weight 59 and a half-life of 46 days: used chiefly as a tracer in biochemistry. [1955–60; RADIO- + IRON]

ra·di·o·i·so·tope (rā′dē ō ī′sə tōp′), *n.* a radioactive isotope, usually artificially produced: used in physical and biological research, therapeutics, etc. [1940–45; RADIO- + ISOTOPE] —**ra·di·o·i·so·top·ic** (rā′dē ō ī′sə top′ik), *adj.*

ra′dio knife′, *Surg.* an electrical instrument for cutting tissue that by searing severed blood vessels seals them and prevents bleeding.

ra·di·o·la·bel (rā′dē ō lā′bəl), *v.t.,* **-beled, -bel·ing** or (*esp. Brit.*) **-belled, -bel·ling.** *Chem.* label (def. 12). [1950–55; RADIO- + LABEL]

ra·di·o·land (rā′dē ō land′), *n.* (*sometimes cap.*) *Often Facetious.* the aggregate of listeners within the reach of a radio station's transmission. [RADIO + -LAND]

ra·di·o·lar·i·an (rā′dē ō lâr′ē ən), *n.* any minute, marine protozoan of the class Radiolaria, or, in some classification schemes, the superclass Actinopoda, having an amebalike body with radiating, filamentous pseudopodia and a usually elaborate outer skeleton. [1875–80; < NL *Radiolari(a)* name of the group (L *radiol(us)* a small beam, equiv. to *radi(us)* RADIUS + *-olus* -OLE[1] + *-aria* -ARIA) + -AN]

ra·di·o·lo·ca·tion (rā′dē ō lō kā′shən), *n.* the method or process of determining the position and velocity of an object by radar. [1940–45; RADIO- + LOCATION]

ra·di·o·lo·ca·tor (rā′dē ō lō′kā tər, -lō kā′tər), *n. Brit.* radar. [1940–45; RADIO- + LOCATOR]

ra·di·o·log·i·cal (rā′dē ə loj′i kəl), *adj.* **1.** of or pertaining to radiology. **2.** involving radioactive materials: *radiological warfare.* Also, **ra′di·o·log′ic.** [1905–10; RADIOLOG(Y) + -ICAL] —**ra′di·o·log′i·cal·ly,** *adv.*

ra′di·ol·o·gy (rā′dē ol′ə jē), *n.* **1.** the science dealing with x-rays or nuclear radiation, esp. for medical uses. **2.** the examination or photographing of organs, bones, etc., with such rays. **3.** the interpretation of medical x-ray photographs. [1895–1900; RADIO- + -LOGY] —**ra′di·ol′o·gist,** *n.*

ra·di·o·lu·cent (rā′dē ō lōō′sənt), *adj.* almost entirely transparent to radiation; almost entirely invisible in x-ray photographs and under fluoroscopy. Cf. **radiopaque, radiotransparent.** [1915–20; RADIO- + LUCENT] —**ra′di·o·lu′cence, ra′di·o·lu′cen·cy,** *n.*

ra·di·o·lu·mi·nes·cence (rā′dē ō lōō′mə nes′əns), *n. Physics.* luminescence induced by nuclear radiation. [1910–15; RADIO- + LUMINESCENCE] —**ra′di·o·lu′mi·nes′cent,** *adj.*

ra·di·ol·y·sis (rā dē ol′ə sis), *n. Chem.* the dissociation of molecules by ionizing radiation. [1945–50; RADIO- + -LYSIS] —**ra·di·o·lyt·ic** (rā′dē ō lit′ik), *adj.*

ra·di·o·man (rā′dē ō man′), *n., pl.* **-men.** a person who operates a radio. [1920–25; RADIO + MAN[1]]

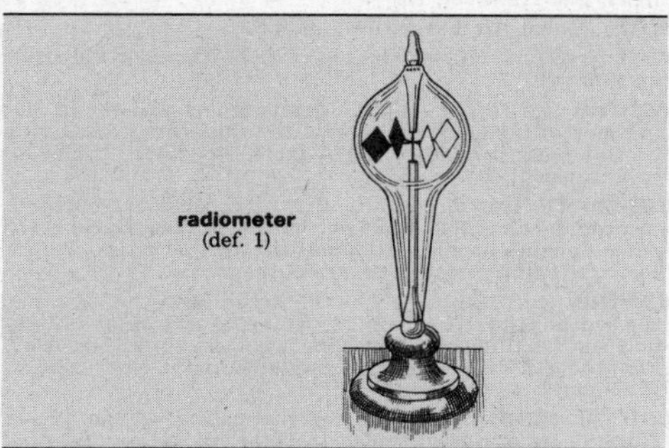

radiometer (def. 1)

ra·di·om·e·ter (rā′dē om′i tər), *n.* **1.** Also called **Crookes radiometer.** an instrument for demonstrating the transformation of radiant energy into mechanical work, consisting of an exhausted glass vessel containing vanes that revolve about an axis when exposed to light. **2.** an instrument for detecting and measuring small amounts of radiant energy. [1870–75; RADIO- + -METER] —**ra·di·o·met·ric** (rā′dē ō me′trik), *adj.* —**ra′di·om′e·try,** *n.*

ra′diomet′ric dat′ing, any method of determining the age of earth materials or objects of organic origin based on measurement of either short-lived radioactive elements or the amount of a long-lived radioactive element plus its decay product. Also called **radioactive dating.** [1965–70]

ra·di·o·mi·crom·e·ter (rā′dē ō mī krom′i tər), *n.* an instrument for measuring small amounts of radiant energy, consisting of a sensitive thermocouple connected to a galvanometer. [1885–90; RADIO- + MICROMETER]

ra·di·o·nu·clide (rā′dē ō nōō′klīd, -nyōō′-), *n. Physics.* a radioactive nuclide. [1945–50; RADIO- + NUCLIDE]

ra·di·o·paque (rā′dē ō pāk′), *adj.* opaque to radiation; visible in x-ray photographs and under fluoroscopy (opposed to *radiotransparent*). Cf. **radiolucent.** [1925–30; RADI(O)- + OPAQUE] —**ra·di·o·pac·i·ty** (rā′dē ō pas′i tē), *n.*

ra·di·o·phare (rā′dē ō fâr′), *n.* a radiotelegraphic station used by vessels to determine their positions; radio beacon. [1910–15; RADIO- + *-phare* < L *pharos* lighthouse < Gk *pháros*]

ra·di·o·phar·ma·ceu·ti·cal (rā′dē ō fär′mə sōō′ti kəl), *n. Pharm.* any of a number of radioactive drugs used diagnostically or therapeutically. [1950–55; RADIO- + PHARMACEUTICAL]

ra·di·o·phone (rā′dē ō fōn′), *n.* **1.** a radiotelephone. **2.** any of various devices for producing sound by the action of radiant energy. —*v.t., v.i.* **3.** to radiotelephone. [1880–85; RADIO- + -PHONE] —**ra·di·o·phon·ic** (rā′dē ō fon′ik), *adj.* —**ra·di·oph·o·ny** (rā′dē of′ə nē), *n.*

ra·di·o·phos·pho·rus (rā′dē ō fos′fər əs), *n. Chem.* See **phosphorus 32.** [1935–40; RADIO- + PHOSPHOROUS]

ra·di·o·pho·to·graph (rā′dē ō fō′tə graf′, -gräf′), *n.* a photograph or other image transmitted by radio. Also called **ra′di·o·pho′to, ra·di·o·pho·to·gram** (rā′dē ō fō′tə gram′). [1920–25; RADIO- + PHOTOGRAPH] —**ra·di·o·pho·tog·ra·phy** (rā′dē ō fə tog′rə fē), *n.*

ra′dio range′ bea′con, a radio transmitter that utilizes two or more directional antennas and transmits signals differing with direction, permitting a flier receiving a signal to determine his or her approximate bearing from the transmitter without a radio compass. [1925–30]

ra·di·os·co·py (rā′dē os′kə pē), *n.* the examination of objects opaque to light by means of another form of radiation, usually x-rays. [1895–1900; RADIO- + -SCOPY] —**ra·di·o·scop·ic** (rā′dē ō skop′ik), **ra′di·o·scop′i·cal,** *adj.*

ra·di·o·sen·si·tive (rā′dē ō sen′si tiv), *adj. Pathol.* (of certain tissues or organisms) sensitive to or destructible by various types of radiant energy, as x-rays, rays from radioactive material, or the like. [1915–20; RADIO- + SENSITIVE] —**ra′di·o·sen′si·tiv′i·ty, ra·di·o·sen·si·bil·i·ty** (rā′dē ō sen′sə bil′i tē), *n.*

ra·di·o·sen·si·tiz·er (rā′dē ō sen′si tī′zər), *n.* a substance, as a drug, that enhances the sensitivity of tissues or cells to radiation therapy. [1950–55; RADIO- + SENSITIZER]

ra′dio shack′, *Informal.* a room or structure, as on a ship, for housing radio equipment. [1945–50]

ra·di·o·so·di·um (rā′dē ō sō′dē əm), *n. Chem.* the radioactive isotope of sodium having an atomic mass of 24 and a half-life of 14.9 hours: used as a tracer in biochemistry. [1930–35; RADIO- + SODIUM]

ra·di·o·sonde (rā′dē ō sond′), *n. Meteorol.* an instrument that is carried aloft by a balloon to send back information on atmospheric temperature, pressure, and humidity by means of a small radio transmitter. Cf. **rawinsonde** [1935–40; RADIO- + SONDE]

ra′dio source′, *Astron.* a cosmic object or phenomenon, as a galaxy, pulsar, quasar, or the remnant of a supernova or of a galactic collision, that emits radio waves. [1945–50]

ra′dio spec′trum, the portion of the electromagnetic spectrum that includes radio waves. [1925–30]

ra′dio star′, *Astron. Now Rare.* a radio source. [1945–50]

ra′dio sta′tion. station (def. 8). [1910–15]

ra·di·o·stron·ti·um (rā′dē ō stron′shē əm, -shəm, -tē əm), *n. Chem.* See **strontium 90.** [1940–45; RADIO- + STRONTIUM]

ra·di·o·sym·met·ri·cal (rā′dē ō si me′tri kəl), *adj.* radially symmetrical. [RADI(AL) + -O- + SYMMETRICAL]

ra′dio tax′i, a taxi in two-way radio communication with a dispatcher, who sends it directly to persons who phone in for a taxi.

ra·di·o·tech·nol·o·gy (rā′dē ō tek nol′ə jē), *n.* **1.** the technical application of any form of radiation to industry. **2.** the technical application of x-rays to industry. **3.** the technology of radio. [RADIO- + TECHNOLOGY]

ra·di·o·tel·e·gram (rā′dē ō tel′ə gram′), *n.* a message transmitted by radiotelegraphy. [1900–05; RADIO- + TELEGRAM]

ra·di·o·tel·e·graph (rā′dē ō tel′ə graf′, -gräf′), *n.* **1.** a telegraph in which messages or signals are sent by means of radio waves rather than through wires or cables. —*v.t., v.i.* **2.** to telegraph by radiotelegraphy. [1905–10; RADIO- + TELEGRAPH] —**ra′di·o·tel′e·graph′ic,** *adj.*

ra·di·o·te·leg·ra·phy (rā′dē ō tə leg′rə fē), *n.* the constructing or operating of radiotelegraphs. [1895–1900; RADIO- + TELEGRAPHY]

ra·di·o·tel·e·phone (rā′dē ō tel′ə fōn′), *n., v.,* **-phoned, -phon·ing.** —*n.* **1.** a telephone in which sound or speech is transmitted by means of radio waves instead of through wires or cables. —*v.t., v.i.* **2.** to telephone by radiotelephony. [1905–10; RADIO- + TELEPHONE] —**ra·di·o·tel·e·phon·ic** (rā′dē ō tel′ə fon′ik), *adj.*

ra·di·o·te·leph·o·ny (rā′dē ō tə lef′ə nē), *n.* the constructing or operating of radiotelephones. [1905–10; RADIO- + TELEPHONY]

ra′dio tel′escope, *Astron.* a system consisting of an antenna, either parabolic or dipolar, used to gather radio waves emitted by celestial sources and bring them to a receiver placed in the focus. [1925–30]

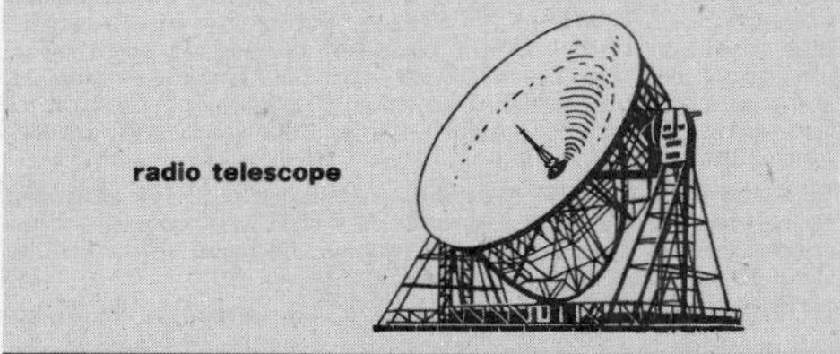

radio telescope

ra·di·o·tel·e·type (rā′dē ō tel′i tīp′), *n.* **1.** Also called **ra·di·o·tel·e·type·writ·er.** (rā′dē ō tel′i tīp′rī′tər, -tel′i tīp rī′-). a teletypewriter equipped for transmitting or receiving messages by radio instead of wire. **2.** the equipment relating to transmission by radioteletypes, taken as a whole. [1935–40; RADIO- + TELETYPE]

ra·di·o·ther·a·py (rā′dē ō ther′ə pē), *n. Med.* treatment of disease by means of x-rays or of radioactive substances. Also called **radiation therapy.** [1900–05; RADIO- + THERAPY] **—ra′di·o·ther′a·pist,** *n.*

ra·di·o·ther·my (rā′dē ō thûr′mē), *n. Med.* therapy that utilizes the heat from a shortwave radio apparatus or diathermy machine. [RADIO- + -THERMY]

ra·di·o·thon (rā′dē ō thon′), *n.* an on-the-air radio campaign, often lasting 24 hours or more, designed to raise money for a radio station, charity, the arts, etc., as from listeners phoning in and pledging specific donations, sometimes in exchange for gifts or premiums. Cf. **telethon.** [1960–65, *Amer.*; RADIO + -THON]

ra·di·o·tho·ri·um (rā′dē ō thôr′ē əm, -thōr′-), *n. Chem.* a disintegration product of thorium. [1920–25; < NL; see RADIO-, THORIUM]

ra·di·o·tox·ic (rā′dē ō tok′sik), *adj. Pathol.* causing radiation sickness. [1945–50; RADIO- + TOXIC]

ra·di·o·trac·er (rā′dē ō trā′sər), *n. Chem.* a radioactive isotope used as a tracer. [1945–50; RADIO- + TRACER]

ra·di·o·trans·par·ent (rā′dē ō trans pâr′ənt, -par′-), *n.* transparent to radiation; invisible in x-ray photographs and under fluoroscopy (opposed to *radiopaque*). Cf. **radiolucent.** [RADIO- + TRANSPARENT] **—ra′di·o·trans·par′en·cy,** *n.*

ra′dio tube′, a vacuum tube used in a radio receiving set.

ra·di·o·vi·sion (rā′dē ō vizh′ən), *n. Now Rare.* television. [1960–65; RADIO- + VISION]

ra′dio wave′, *Elect.* an electromagnetic wave having a wavelength between 1 millimeter and 30,000 meters, or a frequency between 10 kilohertz and 300,000 megahertz. [1915–20]

ra′dio win′dow, *Astron.* the range of wavelengths at which the earth's atmosphere is transparent to radio waves.

rad·ish (rad′ish), *n.* **1.** the crisp, pungent, edible root of the plant, *Raphanus sativus,* of the mustard family, usually eaten raw. **2.** the plant itself. [bef. 1000; late ME *radish(e),* var. (cf. OF *radise,* var. of *radice*) of ME *radich(e),* OE *rǣdic* < L *rādīc-* (s. of *rādīx* ROOT[1]); cf. OHG *rātih,* G *Rettich*] **—rad′ish·like′,** *adj.*

ra·di·um (rā′dē əm), *n.* **1.** *Chem.* a highly radioactive metallic element whose decay yields radon gas and alpha rays. *Symbol:* Ra; *at. wt.:* 226; *at. no.:* 88. **2.** a lustrous rayon or silk fabric constructed in plain weave and used in women's apparel, lining, and drapery. [1895–1900; < NL, equiv. to L *rad(ius)* ray (see RADIUS) + *-ium* -IUM]

radium A, *Chem.* a substance, formed by decay of radon, that gives rise to radium B. [1900–05]

radium B, *Chem.* an isotope of lead, formed by decay of radium A, that gives rise to radium C, which is an isotope of bismuth, from which radium D, radium E, and radium F, or polonium 210, are derived. [1900–05]

ra′dium eman′tion, *Chem.* (formerly) radon.

radium F, *Chem.* an isotope of polonium: polonium 210. [1900–05]

ra′dium sul′fate, *Chem.* a white, crystalline, water-insoluble, poisonous, radioactive solid, $RaSO_4$, used chiefly in radiotherapy. [1970–75]

ra′dium ther′apy, treatment of disease by means of radium. [1900–05]

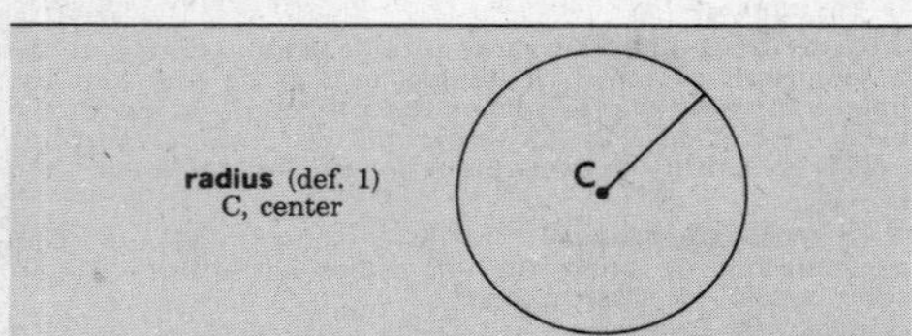

radius (def. 1)
C, center

ra·di·us (rā′dē əs), *n., pl.* **-di·i** (-dē ī′), **-di·us·es. 1.** a straight line extending from the center of a circle or sphere to the circumference or surface: *The radius of a circle is half the diameter.* **2.** the length of such a line. **3.** any radial or radiating part. **4.** a circular area having an extent determined by the length of the radius from a given or specified central point: *every house within a radius of 50 miles.* **5.** a field or range of operation or influence. **6.** extent of possible operation, travel, etc., as under a single supply of fuel: *the flying radius of an airplane.* **7.** *Anat.* the bone of the forearm on the thumb side. Cf. **ulna** (def. 1). See diag. under **skeleton. 8.** *Zool.* a corresponding bone in the forelimb of other vertebrates. **9.** *Mach. Now Rare.* the throw of an eccentric wheel or cam. **10.** a rounded corner or edge on a machined or cast piece of metal. **11.** *Entomol.* one of the principal longitudinal veins in the anterior portion of the wing of an insect. [1590–1600; < L: staff, rod, spoke, beam, orig., RAY[1]]

ra′dius of conver′gence, *Math.* a positive number so related to a given power series that the power series converges for every number whose absolute value is less than this particular number.

ra′dius of cur′vature, *Math.* the absolute value of the reciprocal of the curvature at a point on a curve. Cf. **circle of curvature.** [1745–55]

ra′dius of gyra′tion, *Physics.* the distance from an axis at which the mass of a body may be assumed to be concentrated and at which the moment of inertia will be equal to the moment of inertia of the actual mass about the axis, equal to the square root of the quotient of the moment of inertia and the mass. [1875–80]

ra′dius rod′, (in a feathering paddle wheel) any of the rods, meeting in a hub mounted eccentrically with the paddle-wheel shaft, for feathering the paddles while in the water. See illus. under **paddle wheel.** [1855–60]

ra′dius vec′tor, *pl.* **radii vec·to·res** (vek tôr′ēz, -tōr′-), **radius vectors. 1.** *Math.* the length of the line segment joining a fixed point or origin to a given point. **2.** *Astron.* **a.** the straight line joining two bodies in relative orbital motion, as the line from the sun to a planet at any point in its orbit. **b.** the distance between two such bodies at any point in the orbit. [1745–55]

ra·dix (rā′diks), *n., pl.* **rad·i·ces** (rad′ə sēz′, rā′də-), **ra·dix·es. 1.** *Math.* a number taken as the base of a system of numbers, logarithms, or the like. **2.** *Anat., Bot.* a root; radicle. [1565–75; < L *rādīx* root (cf. RACE[3], RADICAL, RAMUS); akin to Gk *rhíza* root, *rhádix* branch, frond; see ROOT[1]]

rad-lib (rad′lib′), *Informal.* **—n. 1.** *Usually Disparaging.* a liberal, esp. a liberal politician, considered to have radical or extremist tendencies. **—adj. 2.** being or of such a liberal; liberal tending toward radical: *The congressman accused his opponent of holding rad-lib ideas.* Also, **rad′/lib′.** [RAD(ICAL) + LIB(ERAL)]

RAdm, rear admiral. Also, **RADM**

Rad·nor (rad′nər), *n.* **1.** a town in SE Pennsylvania, near Philadelphia. 27,676. **2.** Radnorshire.

Rad·nor·shire (rad′nər shēr′, -shər), *n.* a historic county in Powys, in E Wales. Also called **Radnor.**

Ra·dom (rä′dôm), *n.* a city in E Poland. 175,000.

ra·dome (rā′dōm′), *n.* a dome-shaped device used to house a radar antenna. [1940–45; b. RADAR and DOME]

ra·don (rā′don), *n. Chem.* a chemically inert, radioactive gaseous element produced by the decay of radium: emissions produced by outgassing of rock, brick, etc. are a health hazard. *Symbol:* Rn; *at. no.:* 86; *at. wt.:* 222. [1915–20; RAD(IUM) + -ON[2]]

rad/s, radians per second. Also, **rad/sec**

rad·u·la (raj′o͝o lə), *n., pl.* **-lae** (-lē′). a chitinous band in the mouth of most mollusks, set with numerous, minute, horny teeth and drawn backward and forward over the floor of the mouth in the process of breaking up food. [1745–55; < NL *rādula,* L: scraper, equiv. to *rā-d(ere)* to scrape, rub + *-ula* -ULE] **—rad′u·lar,** *adj.*

rad·waste (rad′wāst′), *n.* See **radioactive waste.** [by shortening]

Rae (rā), *n.* **1.** a male given name, form of **Raymond** or **Ray. 2.** a female given name, form of **Rachel.**

Rae·burn (rā′bərn), *n.* **Sir Henry,** 1756–1823, Scottish painter.

Rae·tic (rē′tik), *n.* **1.** an extinct language of uncertain affinities that was spoken in Rhaetia and written with the Etruscan alphabet. **—adj. 2.** of or pertaining to Raetic. Also, **Rhaetian.** [1930–35; < L *Raeticus, Rhaeticus.* See RHAETIA, -IC]

RAF, Royal Air Force. Also, **R.A.F.**

raff (raf), *n.* riffraff; rabble. [1665–75; extracted from RIFF-RAFF]

raf·fee (ra fē′), *n. Naut.* a triangular sail set in the manner of a square sail above the uppermost yard of a topsail schooner. Also, **raffe** (raf), **raf·fie′.** [1885–90; orig. uncert.]

raf·fer·ty (raf′ər tē), *adj. Brit., Australian.* confused; disorganized. [1925–30; orig. in the phrase *Rafferty('s) rules* no rules at all; perh. identical with Brit. dial. *raffatory, ref(f)atory,* alters. of REFRACTORY]

raf·fi·a (raf′ē ə), *n.* a fiber obtained from the leaves of the raffia palm, used for tying plants and other objects and for making mats, baskets, hats, and the like. Also, **raphia.** [1880–85; earlier *rofia* raffia palm, said to be < Malagasy]

raf′fia palm′, any of various palms of the genus *Raphia,* as *R. farinifera* of tropical Africa, having pinnate leaves that yield a strong, flexible fiber. [1895–1900]

raf·fi·nate (raf′ə nāt′), *n. Chem.* the part of a liquid, esp. an oil, remaining after its more soluble components have been extracted by a solvent. [1925–30; < F *raffin(er)* to refine (*r(e)-* RE- + *affiner* to refine; see AFFINE) + -ATE[1]]

raf·fi·nose (raf′ə nōs′), *n. Biochem.* a colorless, crystalline trisaccharide, $C_{18}H_{32}O_{16}·5H_2O$, with little or no sweetness, occurring in the sugar beet, cottonseed, etc., and breaking down to fructose, glucose, and galactose on hydrolysis. Also called **gossypose, melitose, melitriose.** [1875–80; < F *raffin(er)* to refine (see RAFFINATE) + -OSE[2]]

raff·ish (raf′ish), *adj.* **1.** mildly or sometimes engagingly disreputable or nonconformist; rakish: *a matinee idol whose raffish offstage behavior amused millions.* **2.** gaudily vulgar or cheap; tawdry. [1795–1805; RAFF + -ISH[1]] **—raff′ish·ly,** *adv.* **—raff′ish·ness,** *n.*

raf·fle[1] (raf′əl), *n., v.,* **-fled, -fling.** **—n. 1.** a form of lottery in which a number of persons buy one or more chances to win a prize. **—v.t. 2.** to dispose of by a raffle (often fol. by *off*): *to raffle off a watch.* **—v.i. 3.** to take part in a raffle. [1350–1400; ME *rafle* dice game < MF, deriv. of *rafler* to snatch; cf. RAFF] **—raf′fler,** *n.*

raf·fle[2] (raf′əl), *n.* **1.** rubbish. **2.** *Naut.* a tangle, as of ropes, canvas, etc. [1790–1800; RAFF + -LE]

raf·fles (raf′əlz), *n.* (*often cap.*) a gentlemanly burglar, amateur housebreaker, or the like. [1925–30; after *Raffles,* hero of *The Amateur Cracksman,* by E. W. Hornung (1866–1921), English novelist]

Raf·fles (raf′əlz), *n.* **Sir Thomas Stamford,** 1781–1826, English colonial administrator in the East Indies.

raf·fle·sia (rə flē′zhə, -zhē ə, -zē ə, ra-), *n.* any stemless, leafless, parasitic plant of the genus *Rafflesia,* of the Malay Peninsula and Republic of Indonesia, characterized by apetalous flowers, measuring 3 in.–3 ft. (8 cm–90 cm) in diameter, that exude a putrid odor: now greatly reduced in number. [< NL (1821), after T. S. RAFFLES, who obtained the type specimen]

Ra·fi·nesque (rä′fē nesk′), *n.* **Constantine Samuel,** 1783–1840, U.S. naturalist, born in Turkey.

ra·fraî·chis·soir (RA fre shē swar′), *n. Fr. Furniture.* a table of the 18th century having a cooler for bottles and shelves for plates. [< F: lit., refresher]

Raf·san·ja·ni (räf′sän jä′nē), *n.* **Hojatolislam Ali Akbar Hashemi,** born 1935, president of Iran since 1989.

raft[1] (raft, räft), *n.* **1.** a more or less rigid floating platform made of buoyant material or materials: *an inflatable rubber raft.* **2.** a collection of logs, planks, casks, etc., fastened together for floating on water. **3.** See **life raft. 4.** a slab of reinforced concrete providing a footing on yielding soil, usually for a whole building, so that the weight of the soil that would be displaced by the settlement of the building exceeds the weight of the building itself; mat. **—v.t. 5.** to transport on a raft. **6.** to form (logs or the like) into a raft. **7.** to travel or cross by raft. **8.** (of an ice floe) to transport (embedded organic or rock debris) from the shore out to sea. **—v.i. 9.** to use a raft; go or travel on a raft. **10.** (of an ice floe) to overlap another ice floe. [1250–1300; ME *rafte,* perh. < ON *raptr* RAFTER[1]]

raft[2] (raft, räft), *n. Informal.* a great quantity; a lot: *a raft of trouble.* [1825–35; var. of RAFF large number (ME: abundance)]

raf·ter[1] (raf′tər, räf′-), *n.* **1.** any of a series of timbers or the like, usually having a pronounced slope, for supporting the sheathing and covering of a roof. **—v.t. 2.** *Brit. Dial.* to plow (a field) so that the soil of a furrow is pushed over onto an unplowed adjacent strip. [bef. 900; ME; OE *rǣfter;* c. MLG *rafter,* ON *raptr.* See RAFT[1]]

raft·er[2] (raf′tər, räf′-), *n.* a person who engages in the sport or pastime of rafting. [1800–10; RAFT[1] + -ER[1]]

raft·er[3] (raf′tər, räf′-), *n.* a flock, esp. of turkeys. [RAFT[2] + -ER[1]]

raft′ ice′, ice in cakes or sheets overlapping or piled on top of one another. Also called **raft′ed ice′.**

raft·ing (raf′ting, räf′-), *n.* the sport of traveling on rivers and streams by raft. [1690–1700; RAFT[1] + -ING[1]]

rafts·man (rafts′mən, räfts′-), *n., pl.* **-men.** a person who manages or is employed on a raft. [1770–80; RAFT[1] + -'S[1] + -MAN]

rag[1] (rag), *n.* **1.** a worthless piece of cloth, esp. one that is torn or worn. **2. rags,** ragged or tattered clothing: *The tramp was dressed in rags.* **3.** any article of apparel regarded deprecatingly or self-deprecatingly, esp. a dress: *It's just an old rag I had in the closet.* **4.** a shred, scrap, or fragmentary bit of anything. **5.** *Informal.* **a.** something of very low value or in very poor condition. **b.** a newspaper or magazine regarded with contempt or distaste: *Are you still subscribing to that rag?* **6.** a person of shabby or exhausted appearance. **7.** a large roofing slate that has one edge untrimmed. **8. chew the rag.** See **chew** (def. 9). **9. from rags to riches,** from extreme poverty to great wealth: *He went from rags to riches in only three years.* [1275–1325; ME *ragge* < Scand; cf. Norw, Sw *ragg* coarse hair < ON *rǫgg*]

rag[2] (rag), *v.,* **ragged, rag·ging,** *n. Informal.* **—v.t. 1.** to scold. **2.** to subject to a teasing, esp. in an intense or prolonged way (often fol. by *on*): *Some of the boys were ragging on him about his haircut.* **3.** *Brit.* to torment with jokes; play crude practical jokes on. **—n. 4.** *Brit.* an act of ragging. [1790–1800; orig. uncert.]

rag[3] (rag), *v.t.,* **ragged, rag·ging.** to break up (lumps of ore) for sorting. [1870–75; orig. uncert.]

rag[4] (rag), *n., v.,* **ragged, rag·ging.** **—n. 1.** a musical composition in ragtime: *a piano rag.* **—v.t. 2.** to play (music) in ragtime. [1895–1900; shortened form of RAGTIME]

ra·ga (rä′gə), *n.* one of the melodic formulas of Hindu music having a prescribed melodic shape, rhythm, and ornamentation. [1780–90; < Skt *rāga* color, tone]

rag·a·muf·fin (rag′ə muf′in), *n.* **1.** a ragged, disreputable person; tatterdemalion. **2.** a child in ragged, ill-fitting, dirty clothes. [1350–1400; ME *Ragamoffyn,* name of a demon in the poem *Piers Plowman*]
—Syn. 2. waif, urchin, guttersnipe, street arab.

rag′-and-bone′ man′ (rag′ən bōn′), *Brit.* a peddler who buys and sells used clothes, rags, etc.; junkman. [1850–55]

rag·bag (rag′bag′), *n.* **1.** a bag in which small pieces of cloth are kept for use in mending. **2.** a mixture or conglomeration: *a ragbag of facts, half-truths, and blatant lies.* Also, **rag′-bag′.** [1810–20; RAG[1] + BAG]

rag′ bolt′. See **barb bolt.** [1620–30]

rag′ busi′ness. See **rag trade.**

rag′ doll′, a stuffed doll, esp. of cloth. [1850–55]

rage (rāj), *n., v.,* **raged, rag·ing.** **—n. 1.** angry fury; violent anger. **2.** a fit of violent anger. **3.** fury or violence of wind, waves, fire, disease, etc. **4.** violence of feeling, desire, or appetite: *the rage of thirst.* **5.** a violent desire or passion. **6.** ardor; fervor; enthusiasm: *poetic rage.* **7.** the object of widespread enthusiasm, as for being popular or fashionable: *Raccoon coats were the rage on campus.* **8.** *Archaic.* insanity. **9. all the rage,** widely popular or in style. **—v.i. 10.** to act or speak with fury; show or feel violent anger; fulminate. **11.** to move, rush, dash, or surge furiously. **12.** to proceed, continue, or prevail with great violence: *The battle raged ten days.* **13.** (of feelings, opinions, etc.) to hold sway with unabated violence. [1250–1300; (n.) ME < OF < LL *rabia,* L *rabiēs* madness, rage, deriv. of *rabere* to rage;

CONCISE ETYMOLOGY KEY: <, descended or borrowed from; >, whence; b., blend of, blended; c., cognate with; cf., compare; deriv., derivative; equiv., equivalent; imit., imitative; obl., oblique; r., replacing; s., stem; sp., spelling, spelled; resp., respelling, respelled; trans., translation; ?, origin unknown; *, unattested; ‡, probably earlier than. See the full key inside the front cover.

(v.) *ragen* < OF *ragier*, deriv. of *rage* (n.)] **—rage′ful,** *adj.* **—rag′ing·ly,** *adv.*
—Syn. 1. wrath, frenzy, passion, ire, madness. See **anger. 3.** turbulence. **6.** eagerness, vehemence. **7.** vogue, fad, fashion, craze. **10, 11.** rave, fume, storm. **—Ant. 1.** calm.

rag·fish (rag′fish′), *n., pl. (esp. collectively)* **-fish,** *(esp. referring to two or more kinds or species)* **-fish·es.** a deep-sea fish of the family Icosteidae, inhabiting the North Pacific, having a very flexible body owing to its soft, highly cartilaginous skeleton. [RAG[1] + FISH]

rag·ged (rag′id), *adj.* **1.** clothed in tattered garments: *a ragged old man.* **2.** torn or worn to rags; tattered: *ragged clothing.* **3.** shaggy, as an animal, its coat, etc. **4.** having loose or hanging shreds or fragmentary bits: *a ragged wound.* **5.** full of rough or sharp projections; jagged: *ragged stones.* **6.** in a wild or neglected state: *a ragged garden.* **7.** rough, imperfect, or faulty: *a ragged piece of work.* **8.** harsh, as sound, the voice, etc. **9.** (of a column of type) set or printed with one side unjustified; either flush left with the right side unjustified **(rag′ged right′)** or flush right with the left side unjustified **(rag′·ged left′).** [1250–1300; ME *ragget.* See RAG[1], -ED[3]] **—rag′ged·ly,** *adv.* **—rag′ged·ness,** *n.*
—Syn. 1. shabby, poor. **2.** shredded, rent.

rag′ged edge′, 1. the brink, as of a cliff. **2.** any extreme edge; verge. **3. on the ragged edge,** in a dangerous or precarious position; on the verge or brink of: *on the ragged edge of despair.* [1875–80, *Amer.*]

rag′ged jack′et, *Newfoundland.* a young seal that, having lost parts of its initially white fur, presents a parti-colored or piebald appearance. [1875–80]

rag′ged rob′in, a plant, *Lychnis flos-cuculi,* of the pink family, having pink or white flowers with dissected petals. [1735–45]

rag·ged·y (rag′i dē), *adj.* ragged. [1885–90; RAGGED + -Y[1]]

rag·ging (rag′ing), *n. Metalworking.* (in the rolls of a rolling mill) corrugations affording a grip on a piece being roughed. [RAG[3] + -ING[1]]

rag·gle (rag′əl), *n.* **1.** a groove cut in masonry to receive flashing. **2.** Also called **rag′gle block′.** a manufactured masonry unit, usually of terra cotta, having a groove for receiving flashing. [1880–85; orig. uncert.]

rag·gle-tag·gle (rag′əl tag′əl), *adj.* ragtag. [1900–05; alter. of RAGTAG]

rag′ gourd′, loofah (def. 1).

rag·i (rag′ē), *n.* a cereal grass, *Eleusine coracana,* cultivated in the Old World for its grain. Also, **rag′gee, rag′gy.** [1785–95; said to be < Deccan Hindi *rāgī*]

rag·lan (rag′lən), *n.* a loose overcoat with raglan sleeves. [1860–65; after Lord *Raglan* (1788–1855), British field marshal]

rag′lan sleeve′, a sleeve that begins at the neck and has a long, slanting seam line from the neck to the armhole, giving the garment a relatively undefined shoulder. Cf. **set-in sleeve.** [1925–30]

rag·man (rag′man′, -mən), *n., pl.* **-men** (-men′, -mən). a person who gathers or deals in rags. [1350–1400; RAG[1] + MAN[1]]

rag′man roll′, 1. Usually, **ragman rolls.** a series of documents in which the Scottish nobles acknowledged their allegiance to Edward I of England, 1291–92 and 1296. **2.** *Obs.* a long list or record; register; catalogue. [1350–1400; ME *rageman rolle,* of uncert. orig.]

Rag·nar Lod·brok (räg′när lôth′brōk), *Scand. Legend.* a possibly historical Danish king of the 9th century, the subject of an Old Icelandic saga and of accounts in the Danish history by Saxo Grammaticus: also associated with the story of Sigurd and the Volsungs. Also called **Rag′nar Shag′gy-breech·es** (shag′ē brich′iz). [*Lodbrok* < ON *Lothbrōk,* equiv. to *loth(in)* hairy, shaggy + *brōk* breeches]

Rag·na·rok (räg′nə rok′), *n. Scand. Myth.* the destruction of the gods and of all things in a final battle with the evil powers. Also, **Rag·na·rök** (räg′nə rok′, -rœk′). [1760–70; < ON *Ragnarǫk,* equiv. to *ragna,* gen. of *regin* gods + *rǫk* fate, misread by some as *Ragnarökkr* lit., twilight of the gods; cf. GÖTTERDÄMMERUNG]

ra·gout (ra go͞o′), *n., v.,* **-gouted** (-go͞od′), **-gout·ing** (-go͞o′ing). **—***n.* **1.** *French Cookery.* a highly seasoned stew of meat or fish, with or without vegetables. **—***v.t.* **2.** to make into a ragout. [1650–60; < F *ragoût,* deriv. of *ragoûter* to restore the appetite of, equiv. to *r(e)-* RE- + *á* (< L *ad* to) + *goût* (< L *gustus* taste)]

rag′ pa′per, a high-quality paper made from cotton or linen pulp. [1825–35]

rag·pick·er (rag′pik′ər), *n.* a person who picks up rags and other waste material from the streets, refuse heaps, etc., for a livelihood. [1855–60; RAG[1] + PICKER]

rag′ rug′, a rug, often multicolored, made of rags or strips of fabric stitched together. [1915–20, *Amer.*]

rag·tag (rag′tag′), *adj.* **1.** ragged or shabby; disheveled. **2.** made up of mixed, often diverse, elements: *a ragtag crowd.* [1880–85; RAG[1] + TAG[1]]

rag′tag and bob′tail, the riffraff; rabble: *The ragtag and bobtail of every nation poured into the frontier in search of gold.* Also, **rag′, tag′, and bob′tail; tagrag and bobtail.** [1810–20]

rag·time (rag′tīm′), *n. Music.* **1.** rhythm in which the accompaniment is strict two-four time and the melody, with improvised embellishments, is in steady syncopation. **2.** a style of American music having this rhythm, popular from about 1890 to 1915. [1895–1900; prob. RAG(GED) + TIME] **—rag′time′y,** *adj.*

rag·top (rag′top′), *n. Slang.* **1.** an automobile having a folding canvas top; convertible. **2.** the top itself: *a ragtop that folds flush with the body.* [1950–55; RAG[1] + TOP[1]]

rag′ trade′, *Slang.* the garment, clothing, or fashion industry. Also called **rag business.** [1835–45] **—rag′ trad′er.**

Ra·gu·sa (rä go͞o′zä), *n.* **1.** a province in SE Italy. **2.** a city in and the capital of this province. 59,787. **3.** a city in SE Sicily. 62,472. **4.** Italian name of **Dubrovnik.**

rag·weed (rag′wēd′), *n.* any of the composite plants of the genus *Ambrosia,* the airborne pollen of which is the most prevalent cause of autumnal hay fever, as the common North American species, *A. trifida* **(great ragweed** or **giant ragweed)** and *A. artemisiifolia.* [1650–60; RAG[1] + WEED[1], so called from its ragged appearance]

rag·work (rag′wûrk′), *n.* masonry of thin, undressed rubble. [1830–40; RAG[1] + WORK]

rag·wort (rag′wûrt′, -wôrt′), *n.* any of various composite plants of the genus *Senecio,* as *S. jacobaea,* of the Old World, having yellow flowers and irregularly lobed leaves, or *S. aureus* **(golden ragwort),** of North America, also having yellow flowers. [1325–75; ME; see RAG[1], WORT[2]]

rah (rä), *interj.* (used as an exclamation of encouragement to a player or team.) [1865–70; short for HURRAH]

Ra·hab (rā′hab), *n.* a harlot of Jericho who gave shelter to the two agents sent by Joshua to spy on the city. Josh. 2.

Ra·him·yar Khan (rə hēm′yər KHän′), a city in E Pakistan. 129,000.

Rah·man (rä′män), *n.* **Prince Ab·dul** (äb′do͝ol), 1903–90, Malayan political leader: prime minister of Malaya 1957–63; premier of Malaysia 1963–70.

rah-rah (rä′rä′), *adj. Informal.* marked by or expressive of ardently enthusiastic spirit: *a group of rah-rah undergraduates; a rah-rah attitude.* [1910–15, *Amer.*; redupl. of RAH]

Rah·way (rô′wā), *n.* a city in NE New Jersey. 26,723.

rai (rī), *n.* a style of Algerian popular music played on electric guitar, synthesizer, and percussion instruments. [1985–90; of undetermined orig.]

ra·ia (rä′yə, rī′ə), *n.* rayah.

raid (rād), *n.* **1.** a sudden assault or attack, as upon something to be seized or suppressed: *a police raid on a gambling ring.* **2.** *Mil.* a sudden attack on the enemy, as by air or by a small land force. **3.** a vigorous, large-scale effort to lure away a competitor's employees, members, etc. **4.** *Finance.* a concerted attempt of speculators to force stock prices down. **—***v.t.* **5.** to make a raid on. **6.** to steal from; loot: *a worry that the investment fund is being raided.* **7.** to entice away from another: *Large companies are raiding key personnel from smaller companies.* **8.** to indulge oneself by taking from, esp. in order to eat: *raiding the cookie jar.* **—***v.i.* **9.** to engage in a raid. [1375–1425; ME (north and Scots) *ra(i)de,* OE *rād* expedition, lit., a riding; doublet of ROAD]
—Syn. 1. seizure. **2.** incursion, invasion, inroad.

raid·er (rā′dər), *n.* **1.** a person or thing that raids. **2.** a commando, ranger, or the like, specially trained to participate in military raids. **3.** a light, fast warship, aircraft, etc., used in such a raid. **4.** a person who seizes control of a company, as by secretly buying stock and gathering proxies. **5.** *Informal.* a person who works within an organization for the purpose of gathering evidence of wrongdoing. [1860–65; RAID + -ER[1]]

rail[1] (rāl), *n.* **1.** a bar of wood or metal fixed horizontally for any of various purposes, as for a support, barrier, fence, or railing. **2.** a fence; railing. **3.** one of two fences marking the inside and outside boundaries of a racetrack. **4.** one of a pair of steel bars that provide the running surfaces for the wheels of locomotives and railroad cars. See illus. under **flange. 5.** the railroad as a means of transportation: *to travel by rail.* **6. rails,** stocks or bonds of railroad companies. **7.** *Naut.* a horizontal member capping a bulwark. **8.** *Carpentry, Furniture.* any of various horizontal members framing panels or the like, as in a system of paneling, paneled door, window sash, or chest of drawers. Cf. **stile**[2]. **9.** *Slang.* a line of cocaine crystals or powder for inhaling through the nose. **—***v.t.* **10.** to furnish or enclose with a rail or rails. [1250–1300; ME *raile* < OF *raille* bar, beam < L *rēgula* bar, straight piece of wood, REGULA] **—rail′less,** *adj.* **—rail′like′,** *adj.*

rail[2] (rāl), *v.i.* **1.** to utter bitter complaint or vehement denunciation (often fol. by *at* or *against*): *to rail at fate.* **—***v.t.* **2.** to bring, force, etc., by railing. [1425–75; late ME *railen* < MF *railler* to deride < Pr *ralhar* to chatter < VL **ragulāre,* deriv. of LL *ragere* to bray] **—rail′er,** *n.* **—rail′ing·ly,** *adv.*
—Syn. 1. fulminate, inveigh, castigate, rant, revile.

rail[3] (rāl), *n.* any of numerous birds of the family Rallidae, that have short wings, a narrow body, long toes, and a harsh cry and inhabit grasslands, forests, and marshes in most parts of the world. [1400–50; late ME *rale* < OF *raale* (c. Pr *rascla*), n. deriv. of *raler* < VL **rāsculāre* freq. of L *rādere* (ptp. *rāsus*) to scratch]

Virginia rail, *Rallus limicola,* length 9½ in. (24 cm)

rail·age (rā′lij), *n.* an amount charged for transporting goods by rail. [1890–95; RAIL[1] + -AGE]

rail′ an′chor, a fastening device for attaching the base of a rail to a crosstie.

rail′ bead′, a long, straight, cock bead.

rail·bird (rāl′bûrd′), *n. Informal* **1.** a horse-racing fan who watches races or workouts from the railing along the track. **2.** any kibitzer or self-styled critic or expert. [1890–95, *Amer.*; RAIL[1] + BIRD in sense "frequenter," as in JAILBIRD, YARDBIRD]

rail′ detec′tor car′, *Railroads.* a car equipped with special instruments and used to locate defects in rails.

rail′ fence′, a fence made of rails resting on crossed stakes or across one another at an angle. Also called **Virginia fence.** [1640–50, *Amer.*]

rail·head (rāl′hed′), *n. Railroads.* **1.** the farthest point to which the rails of a railroad have been laid. **2.** the upper part of a rail, used for supporting and guiding the wheels of railroad cars. **3.** a railroad depot at which supplies are unloaded to be distributed or forwarded by truck or other means. [1895–1900; RAIL[1] + HEAD]

rail·ing (rā′ling), *n.* **1.** a fencelike barrier composed of one or more horizontal rails supported by widely spaced uprights; balustrade. **2.** banister. **3.** rails collectively. [1350–1400; RAIL[1] + -ING[1]]

rail·ler·y (rā′lə rē), *n., pl.* **-ler·ies. 1.** good-humored ridicule; banter. **2.** a bantering remark. [1645–55; < F *raillerie,* equiv. to MF *raill(er)* to RAIL[2] + *-erie* -ERY]
—Syn. 1. jesting, joking, badinage, chaff, pleasantry.

rail′ rap′id tran′sit, a system of rail transit within an urban area that has exclusive right of way either below, above, or on the ground and so is capable of relatively high operating speed. *Abbr.:* RRT Cf. **elevated railroad, subway.**

rail·road (rāl′rōd′), *n.* **1.** a permanent road laid with rails, commonly in one or more pairs of continuous lines forming a track or tracks, on which locomotives and cars are run for the transportation of passengers, freight, and mail. **2.** an entire system of such roads together with its rolling stock, buildings, etc.; the entire railway plant, including fixed and movable property. **3.** the company of persons owning or operating such a plant. **4.** *Bowling.* a split. **5. railroads,** stocks or bonds of railroad companies. **—***v.t.* **6.** to transport by means of a railroad. **7.** to supply with railroads. **8.** *Informal.* to push (a law or bill) hastily through a legislature so that there is not time enough for objections to be considered. **9.** *Informal.* to convict (a person) in a hasty manner by means of false charges or insufficient evidence: *The prisoner insisted he had been railroaded.* **—***v.i.* **10.** to work on a railroad. [1750–60; 1875–85 for def. 9; RAIL[1] + ROAD]

rail·road·er (rāl′rō′dər), *n.* a person employed in the operation or management of a railroad. [1855–60, *Amer.*; RAILROAD + -ER[1]]

rail′road flat′, an apartment whose series of narrow rooms forms a more or less straight line. Also called **rail′road apart′ment.** [1925–30]

rail·road·ing (rāl′rō′ding), *n.* **1.** the construction or operation of railroads. **2.** travel by railroad. [1850–55, *Amer.*; RAILROAD + -ING[1]]

rail′road pen′, a pen for drawing two parallel lines.

rail′road worm′, the larva of a fruit fly, *Rhagoletis pomonella,* that burrows through apples, forming tunnels that sometimes appear on the skin as faint depressions or darkened trails: a serious pest of apples in colder regions of North America. Also called **apple maggot.** [1905–10]

rail-split·ter (rāl′split′ər), *n.* **1.** a person or thing that splits logs into rails, esp. for fences. **2.** *(cap.)* nickname of Abraham Lincoln. [1855–60, *Amer.*; RAIL[1] + SPLITTER]

rail·way (rāl′wā′), *n.* **1.** a rail line with lighter-weight equipment and roadbed than a main-line railroad. **2.** a railroad, esp. one operating over relatively short distances. **3.** Also called **trackway.** any line or lines of rails forming a road of flanged-wheel equipment. **4.** *Chiefly Brit.* railroad. [1770–80; RAIL[1] + WAY[1]] **—rail′·wayed′,** *adj.* **—rail′way′less,** *adj.*

rai·ment (rā′mənt), *n.* clothing; apparel; attire. [1350–1400; ME *rayment,* aph. var. of *arrayment.* See ARRAY, -MENT]

Rai·mon·di (rī mōn′dē, -mon′-; *It.* RĪ môn′dē), *n.* **Marc·an·to·nio** (mär′kan tō′nē ō′; *It.* mäR′kän tô′nyô), c1480–c1534, Italian engraver. Also called **Marcantonio.**

rain (rān), *n.* **1.** water that is condensed from the aqueous vapor in the atmosphere and falls to earth in drops more than ¹⁄₅₀ in. (0.5 mm) in diameter. Cf. **drizzle** (def. 6). **2.** a rainfall, rainstorm, or shower: *We had a light rain this afternoon.* **3. rains,** the rainy season; seasonal rainfall, as in India. **4.** weather marked by steady or frequent rainfall: *We had rain most of last summer.* **5.** a heavy and continuous descent or inflicting of anything: *a rain of blows; a rain of vituperation.* **—***v.i.* **6.** (of rain) to fall (usually used impersonally with *it* as subject): *It rained all night.* **7.** to fall like rain: *Tears rained from their eyes.* **8.** to send down rain: *The lightning flashed and the sky rained on us in torrents.* **—***v.t.* **9.** to send down in great quantities, as small pieces or objects: *People on rooftops rained confetti on the parade.* **10.** to offer, bestow, or give in great quantity: *to rain favors upon a person.* **11.** to deal, hurl, fire, etc., repeatedly: *to rain blows on someone's head.* **12. rain cats and dogs,** *Informal.* to rain very heavily or steadily: *We canceled our picnic because it rained cats and dogs.* **13. rain out,** to cause, by raining, the cancellation or postponement of a sports event, performance, or the like: *The doubleheader was rained out yesterday.* [bef. 900; (n.) ME *rein;* OE *regn, rēn,* c. D, G *regen,* ON *regn,* Goth *rign;* (v.) ME *reinen,* OE *regnian*] **—rain′less,** *adj.* **—rain′less·ness,** *n.*
—Syn. 10. lavish, shower, pour.

rain·band (rān′band′), *n.* a dark band in the solar spectrum caused by water vapor in the atmosphere. [1880–85; RAIN + BAND[2]]

rain·bird (rān′bûrd′), *n.* any of several birds, esp. the black-billed cuckoo (*Coccyzus erythropthalmus*) and the yellow-billed cuckoo (*C. americanus*), that are said to

CONCISE PRONUNCIATION KEY: act, cāpe, dâre, pärt; set, ēqual; if, īce; ox, ōver, ôrder, oil, bo͝ok, bo͞ot, out; up, ûrge; child; sing; shoe; thin, *th*at; zh as in *treasure.* ə = *a* as in *alone, e* as in *system, i* as in *easily, o* as in *gallop, u* as in *circus;* ᵊ as in *fire* (fīᵊr), *hour* (ouᵊr). l and n can serve as syllabic consonants, as in *cradle* (krād′l), and *button* (but′n). See the full key inside the front cover.

call frequently before a rainstorm. [1910–15; RAIN + BIRD]

rain•bow (rān′bō′), *n.* **1.** a bow or arc of prismatic colors appearing in the heavens opposite the sun and caused by the refraction and reflection of the sun's rays in drops of rain. Cf. **primary rainbow, secondary rainbow. 2.** a similar bow of colors, esp. one appearing in the spray of a waterfall or fountain. **3.** any brightly multicolored arrangement or display. **4.** a wide variety or range; gamut. **5.** a visionary goal: *He pursued the rainbow of a singing career for years before becoming a success.* **6.** See **rainbow trout.** —*adj.* **7.** made up of diverse races, ethnic groups, etc.: *a rainbow coalition of supporters.* [bef. 1000; ME *reinbowe,* OE *regnboga;* c. ON *regnbogi,* G *Regenbogen.* See RAIN, BOW[2]] —**rain′bow′y, rain′bow•like′,** *adj.*

Rain′bow Bridge′, a natural stone bridge in S Utah: a national monument. 290 ft. (88 m) high; 275-ft. (84-m) span.

rain′bow cac′tus, an erect stiff cactus, *Echinocereus pectinatus rigidissimus,* of Arizona and Mexico, having a cylindrical body, numerous interlocking spines, and pink flowers. [1890–95]

rain•bow-col•lar (rān′bō′kol′ər), *adj. Informal.* **1.** being or of an employee who combines work or experience on the assembly line with more technical or administrative duties; having both blue-collar and white-collar duties or experience. **2.** being, of, or for a factory worker supplanted by automated equipment and retrained for technical or administrative duties.

rain′bow dart′er, a stout darter, *Etheostoma caeruleum,* inhabiting the Great Lakes and Mississippi River drainages, the spawning male of which has the sides marked with oblique blue bars with red interspaces. Also called **soldierfish.** [1880–85, *Amer.*]

rain′bow fish′, guppy. [1885–90, *Amer.*]

rain′bow roof′, a gable roof in the form of a broad Gothic arch, with gently sloping convex surfaces.

rain′bow run′ner, a streamlined, cigar-shaped swift jack, *Elagatis bipinnulata,* of warm seas, having a blue back, light-colored abdomen, and blue-bordered yellow stripes on its sides: a food and game fish. [1935–40]

rain′bow sea′perch, an embiotocid fish, *Hypsurus caryi,* living off the Pacific coast of North America, having red, orange, and blue stripes on the body. Also called **rain′bow perch′.**

rain′bow snake′, a burrowing snake, *Farancia erytrogramma,* of the southeastern U.S., having red and black stripes along the body, a red and yellow underside, and a sharp-tipped tail used in maneuvering prey. [1905–10, *Amer.*]

rain′bow trout′, a trout, *Salmo gairdnerii,* native in the coastal waters and streams from Lower California to Alaska, used as a food and game fish. [1880–85, *Amer.*]

rain′ check′, 1. a ticket for future use given to spectators at an outdoor event, as a baseball game or concert, that has been postponed or interrupted by rain. **2.** an offered or requested postponement of an invitation until a more convenient, usually unspecified time: *Since you can't join us for dinner, we'll give you a rain check.* **3.** a ticket, coupon, or the like, entitling a customer to purchase at a later date and for the same amount a sale item that is temporarily out of stock. Also, **rain′check′.** [1880–85]

rain′ cloud′, a cloud or a mass of clouds that yields rain. [1830–40]

rain•coat (rān′kōt′), *n.* a waterproof or water-repellent coat worn as protection against rain. [1820–30, *Amer.;* RAIN + COAT]

rain′ dance′, (esp. among American Indians) a ritualistic dance performed to bring rain. [1925–30]

rain•drop (rān′drop′), *n.* a drop of rain. [bef. 1000; ME *rein-drop(e);* OE *regndropa;* see RAIN, DROP]

Rai•ney (rā′nē), *n.* **1. Gertrude** (*"Ma"*), 1886–1939, U.S. blues singer. **2. Joseph Hayne** (hān), 1832–87, U.S. politician: first black congressman 1870–79.

rain•fall (rān′fôl′), *n.* **1.** a fall or shower of rain. **2.** the amount of water falling in rain, snow, etc., within a given time and area, usually expressed as a hypothetical depth of coverage: *a rainfall of 70 inches a year.* [1840–50; RAIN + FALL]

rain′ for′est, a tropical forest, usually of tall, densely growing, broad-leaved evergreen trees in an area of high annual rainfall. Also, **rain′for′est.** [1900–05]

rain′ frog′, *Chiefly Southern U.S.* a tree frog, esp. a spring peeper. [1820–30, *Amer.*]

rain′ gauge′, an instrument for measuring rainfall. Also called **pluviometer.** [1760–70]

Rai•nier (rā nēr′, rā-, rā′nēr), *n.* **Mount,** a volcanic peak in W Washington, in the Cascade Range. 14,408 ft. (4392 m).

Rai•nier III (rā nēr′, re-, rə-; *Fr.* ʀe nyā′), *n.* **Rainier Louis Hen•ri Max•ence Ber•trand de Gri•mal•di** (lwē äN ʀē′ mak säNs′ beʀ träN′ də gʀē mal dē′), **Prince of Monaco,** born 1923, reigning prince of Monaco since 1949.

rain•mak•er (rān′mā′kər), *n.* **1.** (among American Indians) a medicine man who by various rituals and incantations seeks to cause rain. **2.** a person who induces rainfall by using various scientific techniques, as the seeding of clouds with silver iodide crystals from an airplane. **3.** *Slang.* an executive or lawyer with exceptional ability to attract clients, use political connections, increase profits, etc.: *The president has several rainmakers among his advisers.* [1765–75, *Amer.;* RAIN + MAKER] —**rain′mak′ing,** *n.*

rain′ or shine′, regardless of the weather or circumstances; in any event: *The concert will be held, rain or shine. He's always a reliable friend, rain or shine.*

rain•out (rān′out′), *n.* **1.** a contest, performance, or the like, that has been rained out. **2.** Also called **washout.** the removal of radioactive particles or other foreign substances from the atmosphere by precipitation. Also, **rain′-out′.** Cf. **fallout.** [1945–50, *Amer.;* n. use of v. phrase *rain out*]

rain•proof (rān′pro͞of′), *adj.* **1.** impervious to rain; keeping out or unaffected by rain: *a rainproof cover; a rainproof coat.* —*v.t.* **2.** to make rainproof. [1825–35; RAIN + -PROOF]

rain′ shad′ow, *Meteorol.* a region in the lee of mountains that receives less rainfall than the region windward of the mountains. [1900–05]

rain′ show′er, a brief rainfall, usually of variable intensity. [bef. 1000; ME; OE]

rain•spout (rān′spout′), *n.* waterspout (def. 1). [1920–25; RAIN + SPOUT]

rain•squall (rān′skwôl′), *n.* squall[1] (def. 1). [1840–50; RAIN + SQUALL[1]]

rain•storm (rān′stôrm′), *n.* a storm with heavy rain. [1810–20; RAIN + STORM]

rain′ tree′, monkeypod. [1875–80]

rain•wash (rān′wosh′, -wôsh′), *n.* material eroded or swept away by rain. [1875–80; RAIN + WASH]

rain•wa•ter (rān′wô′tər, -wot′ər), *n.* water fallen as rain. [bef. 1000; ME *rein water,* OE *regn-wæter;* see RAIN, WATER]

Rain•wa•ter (rān′wô′tər, -wot′ər), *n.* **(Leo) James,** 1917–86, U.S. physicist: Nobel prize 1975.

rain•wear (rān′wâr′), *n.* waterproof or water-repellent clothing. [1950–55; RAIN + WEAR]

rain•y (rā′nē), *adj.,* **rain•i•er, rain•i•est. 1.** characterized by rain: *rainy weather; a rainy region.* **2.** wet with rain: *rainy streets.* **3.** bringing rain: *rainy clouds.* [bef. 1000; ME *reyny,* OE *rēnig.* See RAIN, -Y[1]] —**rain′i•ly,** *adv.* —**rain′i•ness,** *n.*

rain′y day′, a time of need or emergency: *saving money for a rainy day.* [1570–80] —**rain′y-day′,** *adj.*

Rai•pur (rī′po͝or), *n.* a city in SE Madhya Pradesh, in E central India. 174,518.

Rais (res; *Fr.* ʀes), *n.* **Gilles de.** See **Retz, Gilles de Laval, Baron de.**

raise (rāz), *v.,* **raised, rais•ing,** *n.* —*v.t.* **1.** to move to a higher position; lift up; elevate: *to raise one's hand; sleepy birds raising their heads and looking about.* **2.** to set upright: *When the projection screen toppled, he quickly raised it again.* **3.** to cause to rise or stand up; rouse: *The sound of the bugle raised him from his bed.* **4.** to build; erect: *to raise a monument.* **5.** to set up the framework of: *to raise a house.* **6.** to set in motion; activate: *to raise a storm of protest.* **7.** to grow or breed, care for, or promote the growth of: *to raise corn; to raise prizewinning terriers.* **8.** to serve in the capacity of parent to; rear: *to raise children.* **9.** to give rise to; bring up or about: *His comments raised a ripple of applause.* **10.** to put forward; present for public consideration: *He raised the issue of his opponent's eligibility.* **11.** *Law.* to make (an issue at law). **12.** to restore to life: *to raise the dead.* **13.** to stir up: *to raise a rebellion with stirring speeches.* **14.** to give vigor to; animate: *The news raised his spirits.* **15.** to advance in rank or position: *to raise someone to the peerage.* **16.** to assemble or collect: *to raise an army; to raise money for a charity.* **17.** to increase the height or vertical measurement of: *The blocks raise the table three inches.* **18.** to increase in degree, intensity, pitch, or force: *to raise the volume of a radio.* **19.** to utter (a cry, shout, etc.) in a loud voice. **20.** to cause (the voice) to be heard: *to raise one's voice in opposition.* **21.** to cause (dough or bread) to rise by expansion and become light, as by the use of yeast. **22.** to increase in amount: *to raise rents; to raise salaries.* **23.** to increase (the value or price) of a commodity, stock, bond, etc. **24.** *Poker.* **a.** to increase (another player's bet). **b.** to bet at a higher level than (a preceding bettor). **25.** *Bridge.* to increase (the bid for a contract) by repeating one's partner's bid at a higher level. **26.** *Phonet.* to alter the articulation of (a vowel) by bringing the tongue closer to the palate: *The vowel in "pen" is raised to* (i) *in some dialects.* **27.** to increase the amount specified in (a check, money order, or the like) by fraudulent alteration. **28.** *Mil.* to end (a siege) by withdrawing the besieging forces or by compelling the besieging forces to withdraw. **29.** *Naut.* **a.** to cause (something) to rise above the visible horizon by approaching it. **b.** to come in sight of (land, a whale, etc.). **30.** to establish communication with by radio: *The radioman was able to raise shore headquarters after three tries.* **31.** *Mining.* to excavate (an opening) upward from a level below. —*v.i.* **32.** to be able to be lifted or pulled up: *The window raises easily.* **33.** (in cards, poker, etc.) to increase a previous bet or bid: *My cards weren't good enough to let me raise.* **34. raise Cain.** See **Cain** (def. 3). —*n.* **35.** an increase in amount, as of wages: *a raise in pay.* **36.** the amount of such an increase: *His raise was five dollars.* **37.** a raising, lifting, etc.: *a raise in spirits.* **38.** a raised or ascending place; rise. **39.** *Mining.* a shaft excavated upward from below. Cf. **winze[1].** [1150–1200; ME *reisen* (v.) < Scand (cf. ON *reisa*); cf. also Goth *-raisjan* (causative v. formed on Gmc base of OE *risan* to RISE), OE *rǣran* to REAR[2]] —**rais′a•ble, raise′a•ble,** *adj.* —**rais′er,** *n.*

—**Syn. 1, 2.** loft. RAISE, LIFT, HEAVE, HOIST imply bringing something up above its original position. RAISE, the most general word, may mean to bring something to or toward an upright position with one end resting on the ground; or it may be used in the sense of LIFT, moving an object a comparatively short distance upward but breaking completely its physical contact with the place where it had been: *to raise a ladder; to raise* (*lift*) *a package.* HEAVE implies lifting with effort or exertion: *to heave a huge box onto a truck.* HOIST implies lifting slowly and gradually something of considerable weight, usually with mechanical help, such as given by a crane or derrick: *to hoist steel beams to the top of the framework of a building.* **3.** arouse, awaken. **4.** construct, rear. **7.** cultivate. **9.** originate, produce, effect. **13.** excite. **14.** invigorate, inspirit. **15.** elevate, promote, exalt. **17.** heighten, enlarge. **18.** amplify, augment. —**Ant. 1.** lower.

—**Usage.** RAISE and RISE are similar in form and meaning but different in grammatical use. RAISE is the causative of RISE; to RAISE something is to cause it to RISE. RAISE is almost always used transitively. Its forms are regular: *Raise the window. The flag had been raised before we arrived.* RAISE in the intransitive sense "to rise up, arise" is nonstandard: *Dough raises better when the temperature is warm.*

RISE is almost exclusively intransitive in its standard uses. Its forms are irregular: *My husband usually rises before seven. The earliest I have ever risen is eight. The sun rose in a cloudless sky. The dough is rising now.*

Both RAISE and REAR are used in the United States to refer to the upbringing of children. Although RAISE was formerly condemned in this sense ("You raise hogs but you rear children"), it is now standard.

In American English, a person receives a RAISE in salary. In British English it is a RISE.

raised (rāzd), *adj.* **1.** fashioned or made as a surface design in relief. **2.** *Cookery.* made light by the use of yeast or other ferment but not with baking powder, soda, or the like. [1595–1605; RAISE + -ED[2]]

rai•sin (rā′zin), *n.* **1.** a grape of any of various sweet varieties dried in the sun or by artificial means, often used in cookery. **2.** dark purplish blue. [1350–1400; ME *raisin, reisin* < OF < VL **racimus,* for L *racēmus* RACEME] —**rai′sin•y,** *adj.*

rais•ing (rā′zing), *n. Ling.* a rule of transformational grammar that shifts the subject or object of an embedded clause into the subject or object position of the main clause, as in the derivation of *The suspect appears to be innocent* from *It appears that the suspect is innocent.* [RAISE + -ING[1]]

rais′ing plate′. See **wall plate** (def. 1). [1670–80]

rai•son d'é•tat (ʀe zôN dā ta′), *French.* for the good of the country. [lit., reason of state]

rai•son d'ê•tre (rā′zōn de′trə; *Fr.* ʀe zôN de′tʀᵊ), *pl.* **rai•sons d'ê•tre** (rā′zōnz de′trə; *Fr.* ʀe zôN de′tʀᵊ). reason or justification for being or existence: *Art is the artist's raison d'être.* [1865–70; < F]

rai•son•neur (rez′ə nûr′; *Fr.* ʀe zô nœʀ′), *n., pl.* **-neurs** (-nûrz′; *Fr.* -nœʀ′). a character in a play, novel, or the like who voices the central theme, philosophy, or point of view of the work. [1900–05; < F: lit., one who reasons or argues, equiv. to *raisonn(er)* to REASON, argue + *-eur* -EUR]

raj (räj), *n.* (*often cap.*) (in India) rule, esp. the British rule prior to 1947. [1790–1800; < Hindi *rāj* < Pali, Prakrit *rajja* < Skt *rājya* kingdom, rule]

Ra•jab (rə jab′), *n.* the seventh month of the Muslim calendar. Cf. **Muslim calendar.** [1760–70; < Ar]

ra•jah (rä′jə), *n.* **1.** a king or prince in India. **2.** a minor chief or dignitary. **3.** an honorary title conferred on Hindus in India. **4.** a title of rulers, princes, or chiefs in Java, Borneo, etc. Also, **ra′ja.** [1545–55; < Hindi *rājā* < Skt *rājan;* c. L *rēx* king]

ra•jas (ruj′əs), *n. Hinduism.* See under **guna.** [< Skt] —**ra•jas•ic** (rə jas′ik), *adj.*

Ra•ja•sthan (rä′jə stän′), *n.* a state in NW India; formerly Rajputana and a group of small states. 29,590,000; 132,078 sq. mi. (342,056 sq. km). *Cap.:* Jaipur.

Ra•ja•stha•ni (rä′jə stä′nē), *n.* **1.** an Indic language, the vernacular of Rajasthan. —*adj.* **2.** of, pertaining to, or characteristic of Rajasthan, its people, culture, or language.

Raj•kot (räj′kōt), *n.* a city in S Gujarat, in W India. 300,152.

Raj•put (räj′po͝ot), *n.* a member of a Hindu people claiming descent from the ancient Kshatriya, or warrior caste, and noted for their military spirit. [< Hindi, equiv. to Skt *rāj* king (see RAJ) + *putra* son]

Raj•pu•ta•na (räj′po͝o tä′nə), *n.* a former region in NW India, now making up the principal part of Rajasthan.

Raj•ya Sab•ha (räj′yə sub′hä), the upper house of parliament in India.

ra•k'a (ruk′ə), *n. Islam.* a portion of the salat, the prescribed prayers said five times a day, that combines a ritual of bows and prostrations with the recitation of prayers. Also, **ra′k'ah.** [< Ar *rak'ah*]

rake[1] (rāk), *n., v.,* **raked, rak•ing.** —*n.* **1.** an agricultural implement with teeth or tines for gathering cut grass, hay, or the like or for smoothing the surface of the ground. **2.** any of various implements having a similar form, as a croupier's implement for gathering in money on a gaming table. —*v.t.* **3.** to gather, draw, or remove with a rake: *to rake dead leaves from a lawn.* **4.** to clear, smooth, or prepare with a rake: *to rake a garden bed.* **5.** to clear (a fire, embers, etc.) by stirring with a poker or the like. **6.** to gather or collect abundantly (usually fol. by *in*): *He marketed his invention and has been raking in money ever since.* **7.** to bring to light, usually for discreditable reasons (usually fol. by *up*): *to rake up an old scandal.* **8.** to search thoroughly through: *They raked the apartment for the missing jewels.* **9.** to scrape; scratch: *The sword's tip raked his face lightly.* **10.** to scoop out (a masonry joint) to a given depth while the mortar is still green. **11.** to fire guns along the length of (a position, body of troops, ship, etc.). **12.** to sweep with the eyes: *He raked the horizon with his gaze.* —*v.i.* **13.** to use a rake: *The gardener raked along the border of the garden.* **14.** to search, as with a rake: *His gaze raked over the room.* **15.** to scrape; search: *She frantically raked through her belongings.* **16. rake over the coals.** See **coal** (def. 5). [bef. 900; (n.) ME *rak(e),* OE *raca* (masc.), *racu* (fem.); c. G *Rechen,*

ON *reka* shovel; (v.) ME *raken,* partly deriv. of the n., partly < ON *raka* to scrape, rake] **—rak′a·ble, rake′a·ble,** *adj.* **—rak′er,** *n.*
—Syn. 8. comb, scour, ransack.

rake[2] (rāk), *n.* a dissolute or profligate person, esp. a man who is licentious; roué. [1645–55; see RAKEHELL]
—Syn. libertine, profligate, lecher, womanizer.

rake[3] (rāk), *v.,* **raked, rak·ing,** *n.* **—***v.i.* **1.** to incline from the vertical, as a mast, or from the horizontal. **—***v.t.* **2.** to cause (something) to incline from the vertical or the horizontal. **—***n.* **3.** inclination or slope away from the perpendicular or the horizontal. **4.** a board or molding placed along the sloping sides of a frame gable to cover the ends of the siding. **5.** *Aeron.* the angle measured between the tip edge of an aircraft or missile wing or other lifting surface and the plane of symmetry. **6.** *Mach.* the angle between the cutting face of a tool and a plane perpendicular to the surface of the work at the cutting point. [1620–30; orig. uncert.]

rake[4] (rāk), *v.i.,* **raked, rak·ing. 1.** *Hunting.* **a.** (of a hawk) to fly after game. **b.** (of a dog) to hunt with the nose close to the ground instead of in the wind. **2.** *Chiefly Scot.* to go or proceed, esp. with speed. [bef. 1000; ME *raken* to go, hasten, OE *racian*]

raked (rākt), *adj.* inclining from the vertical or from the horizontal: *raked masts; a raked stage.* [1945–50; RAKE[3] + -ED[2]]

rake·hell (rāk′hel′), *n.* **1.** a licentious or dissolute man; rake. **—***adj.* **2.** Also, **rake·hell·y** (rāk′hel′ē). dissolute; profligate. [1540–50; alter. by folk etym. (see RAKE[1], HELL) of ME *rakel* (adj.) rash, rough, coarse, hasty (akin to RAKE[4]); cf. ON *reikall* wandering, unsettled]

rake-off (rāk′ôf′, -of′), *n.* **1.** a share or amount taken or received illicitly, as in connection with a public enterprise. **2.** a share, as of profits. **3.** a discount in the price of a commodity: *a 20 percent rake-off on the car.* [1885–90, *Amer.*; n. use of v. phrase *rake off*]

rak·er[1] (rā′kər), *n.* **1.** a person or thing that rakes. **2.** See **raker tooth.** [1325–75; ME. See RAKE[1], -ER[1]]

rak·er[2] (rā′kər), *n. Building Trades.* an inclined member, as a pile or shore. [1880–85; RAKE[3] + -ER[1]]

rak′er tooth′, a saw tooth for cleaning loose chips from a kerf. Also called **raker, cleaner tooth.**

Rake's′ Prog′ress, The, **1.** a series of paintings and engravings by William Hogarth. **2.** an opera (1951) by Igor Stravinsky.

ra·ki (rä kē′, rə-, rak′ē, rä′kē), *n.* a spirituous liquor distilled from grain, grapes, plums, etc., in southeastern Europe and the Near East. Also, **ra·kee′.** [1665–75; < Turk < Ar *ʿaraqī,* equiv. to *ʿaraq* ARRACK + *-ī* suffix of appurtenance]

rak′ing bond′, a brickwork bond in which concealed courses of diagonally laid bricks are used to bond exposed brickwork to the wall structure. Cf. **herringbone bond.** [1875–80]

rak′ing cor′nice, *Archit.* either of two straight, sloping cornices on a pediment following or suggesting the slopes of a roof.

rak′ing course′, a concealed course of bricks laid diagonally to the wall surface in a raking bond. [1875–80]

rak′ing piece′, 1. a sloping piece of scenery, as on a television or stage set, esp. such a piece used for masking the side of a ramp. **2.** a wedge used for leveling scenery on a sloping stage. [1880–85]

rak·ish[1] (rā′kish), *adj.* like a rake; dissolute: *rakish behavior.* [1700–10; RAKE[2] + -ISH[1]] **—rak′ish·ly,** *adv.* **—rak′ish·ness,** *n.*

rak·ish[2] (rā′kish), *adj.* **1.** smart; jaunty; dashing: *a hat worn at a rakish angle.* **2.** (of a vessel) having an appearance suggesting speed. [1815–25; RAKE[3] + -ISH[1]]
—Syn. 1. sporting, dapper, debonair, breezy.

ra·ku (rä′ko͞o), *n.* a thick-walled, rough, dark lead-glazed Japanese earthenware used in the tea ceremony. [1870–75; < Japn *raku(-yaki)* "pleasure" glaze, originated by Chōjirō of Kyoto, who was given the seal-stamp with the character "pleasure" from Hideyoshi as an artisan-household designation]

rale (ral, räl), *n. Pathol.* an abnormal crackling or rattling sound heard upon auscultation of the chest, caused by disease or congestion of the lungs. [1820–30; < F *râle,* deriv. of *râler* to make a rattling sound in the throat; cf. RAIL[3]]

Ra·leigh (rô′lē, rä′-), *n.* **1. Sir Walter.** Also, **Ra′legh.** 1552?–1618, English explorer and writer, a favorite of Elizabeth I. **2.** a city in and the capital of North Carolina, in the central part. 149,771. **3.** a male given name.

rall., rallentando.

ral·len·tan·do (rä′lən tän′dō; *It.* räl′len tän′dô), *adj.* slackening; becoming slower (used as a musical direction). [1805–15; < It, ger. of *rallentare* to slow down; see LENTO]

ral·li·form (ral′ə fôrm′), *adj. Zool.* raillike in shape, anatomy, etc. [1895–1900; < NL *Rall(us)* name of genus (see RAIL[3]) + -I- + -FORM]

ral·line (ral′īn, -in), *adj.* belonging or pertaining to the family Rallidae, comprising the rails and allied species. [1880–85; < NL *Rall(us)* name of genus (see RAIL[3]) + -INE[1]]

ral·ly[1] (ral′ē), *v.,* **-lied, -ly·ing,** *n., pl.* **-lies. —***v.t.* **1.** to bring into order again; gather and organize or inspire anew: *The general rallied his scattered army.* **2.** to draw or call (persons) together for a common action or effort: *He rallied his friends to help him.* **3.** to concentrate or revive, as one's strength, spirits, etc.: *They rallied their energies for the counterattack.* **—***v.i.* **4.** to come together for common action or effort: *The disunited party rallied in time for the election campaign.* **5.** to come together or into order again: *The captain ordered his small force to rally at the next stream.* **6.** to come to the assistance of a person, party, or cause (often fol. by *to* or *around*): *to rally around a political candidate.* **7.** to recover partially from illness: *He spent a bad night but began to rally by morning.* **8.** to find renewed strength or vigor: *The runner seemed to be rallying for a final sprint.* **9.** *Finance.* **a.** (of securities) to rise sharply in price after a drop. **b.** (of the persons forming a stock market) to begin to trade with increased activity after a slow period. **10.** (in tennis, badminton, etc.) to engage in a rally. **11.** to participate in a long-distance automobile race. **12.** *Baseball.* (of a team) to score one or more runs in one inning. **—***n.* **13.** a recovery from dispersion or disorder, as of troops. **14.** a renewal or recovery of strength, activity, etc. **15.** a partial recovery of strength during illness. **16.** a drawing or coming together of persons, as for common action, as in a mass meeting: *A political rally that brought together hundreds of the faithful.* **17.** a get-together of hobbyists or other like-minded enthusiasts, primarily to meet and socialize. **18.** *Finance.* a sharp rise in price or active trading after a declining market. **19.** (in tennis, badminton, etc.) **a.** an exchange of strokes between players before a point is scored. **b.** the hitting of the ball back and forth prior to the start of a match. **20.** *Boxing.* an exchange of blows. **21.** *Baseball.* the scoring of one or more runs in one inning. **22.** *Theat. Brit.* a quickening of pace for heightening the dramatic effect in a scene. **23.** *Shipbuilding.* a series of blows with battering rams, made in order to drive wedges under a hull to raise it prior to launching. **24.** Also, **rallye.** a long-distance automobile race held over public roads unfamiliar to the drivers, with numerous checkpoints along the route. [1585–95; < F *rallier* (v.), OF, equiv. to *r(e)-* RE- + *allier* to join; see ALLY] **—ral′li·er,** *n.*
—Syn. 2, 4. muster. **3.** reanimate, reinvigorate. **4.** assemble. **5.** reassemble.

ral·ly[2] (ral′ē), *v.t.,* **-lied, -ly·ing.** to ridicule in a good-natured way; banter. [1660–70; < F *railler* to RAIL[2]]
—Syn. chaff, tease, twit.

ral·lye (ral′ē), *n.* rally[1] (def. 24).

ral·ly·ing (ral′ē ing), *n.* the sport of driving in automobile rallies. [1955–60; RALLY + -ING[1]]

ral·ly·ist (ral′ē ist), *n.* a person who participates in automobile rallies. [1960–65; RALLY[1] + -IST]

ral·ly·mas·ter (ral′ē mas′tər, -mä′stər), *n.* an organizer and director of an automobile rally. [1965–70, RALLY[1] + MASTER]

ralph (ralf), *v.i. Slang.* to vomit. [1970–75; appar. of expressive orig.]

Ralph (ralf *or, esp. Brit.,* rāf, räf, rälf), *n.* a male given name: from Old Norse words meaning "counsel" and "wolf."

Ralph′ Rois′ter Dois′ter (roi′stər doi′stər), a play (1553?) by Nicholas Udall: the earliest known English comedy.

ram[1] (ram), *n., v.,* **rammed, ram·ming. —***n.* **1.** a male sheep. **2.** (*cap.*) *Astron., Astrol.* the constellation or sign of Aries. **3.** any of various devices for battering, crushing, driving, or forcing something, esp. a battering ram. **4.** (formerly) a heavy beak or spur projecting from the bow of a warship for penetrating the hull of an enemy's ship. **5.** (formerly) a warship so equipped, esp. one used primarily for ramming enemy vessels. **6.** the heavy weight that strikes the blow in a pile driver or the like. **7.** a piston, as on a hydraulic press. **8.** a reciprocating part of certain machine tools, as the toolholder of a slotter or shaper. **9.** See **hydraulic ram. —***v.t.* **10.** to drive or force by heavy blows. **11.** to strike with great force; dash violently against: *The car went out of control and rammed the truck.* **12.** to cram; stuff: *They rammed the gag in his mouth.* **13.** to push firmly: *to ram a bill through the Senate.* **14.** to force (a charge) into a firearm, as with a ramrod. [bef. 900; ME: male sheep, machine for ramming, OE *ram(m)*; c. D, LG *ram,* G *Ramme;* (v.) ME *rammen,* deriv. of the n.; cf. OHG *rammen*] **—ram′like′,** *adj.*
—Syn. 10. jam, thrust, beat, hammer.

ram[2] (ram), *Australian.* a confidence man's associate who acts as a decoy; confederate; shill. [1940–45; orig. obscure; Brit. criminal argot *ramp* swindle (earlier, as v.: snatch, tear) is a phonetically implausible source]

RAM (ram), *n.* computer memory available to the user for creating, loading, or running programs and for the temporary storage and manipulation of data, in which time of access to each item is independent of the storage sequence. Cf. **ROM.** [*r(andom)-a(ccess) m(emory)*]

RAM, See **reverse annuity mortgage.**

R.A.M., Royal Academy of Music.

Ra·ma (rä′mə), *n.* (in the Ramayana) any of the three avatars of Vishnu: Balarama, Parashurama, or Ramachandra.

-rama, var. of **-orama,** occurring as the final element in compounds when the first element is disyllabic and does not end in *-r,* used so that the entire word maintains the same number of syllables as **panorama:** *Cinerama; telerama.*

Rama IX, (*Phumiphon Aduldet* or *Bhumibol-Adulyadej*) born 1927, king of Thailand since 1950.

Ra·ma·chan·dra (rä′mə chun′drə), *n.* the hero of the Ramayana, and a character in the Mahabharata.

ra·ma·da (rə mä′də), *n.* an open shelter, often having a dome-shaped thatched roof, and installed esp. on beaches and picnic grounds. [1865–70, *Amer.*; < AmerSp: open shelter roofed with branches; earlier Sp *enramada* arbor, bower, n. use of fem. ptp. of *enramar* to intertwine branches equiv. to *en-* IN-[2] + *-ramar,* v. deriv. of *ramo* branch < L *rāmus*]

Ram·a·dan (ram′ə dän′), *n. Islam.* **1.** the ninth month of the Muslim calendar. Cf. **Muslim calendar. 2.** the daily fast that is rigidly enjoined from dawn until sunset during this month. [1590–1600; < Ar *ramaḍān*]

ram·age (ram′ij), *n. Anthropol.* a descent group composed of individuals descended from one ancestor through any combination of male and female links. [1610–20, in sense "the branches of a tree" (1936 in this sense); < F, equiv. to *ram-* (OF *ram, raim*) branch (< L *rāmus*) + *-age* -AGE]

Ra·ma·krish·na (rä′mə krish′nə), *n.* **Sri** (srē, shrē), 1836–86, Hindu religious reformer and mystic.

ra·mal (rā′məl), *adj.* of or pertaining to a ramus. [1855–60; < L *rām(us)* branch (see RAMUS) + -AL[1]]

ra·ma·morph (rä′mə môrf′), *n.* any of a group of extinct Miocene apes of Europe, Asia, and Africa, characterized by large molars and small incisors and typified by the genera *Ramapithecus* and *Sivapithecus.* [appar. RAMA(PITHECUS) + -MORPH]

Ra·man (rä′mən), *n.* **Sir Chan·dra·se·kha·ra Ven·ka·ta** (chun′drə shä′kər ə veng′kə tə), 1888–1970, Indian physicist: Nobel prize 1930.

Ra′man effect′ (rä′mən), *Optics.* the change in wavelength of light scattered while passing through a transparent medium, the collection of new wavelengths **(Ra′man spec′trum)** being characteristic of the scattering medium and differing from the fluorescent spectrum in being much less intense and in being unrelated to an absorption band of the medium. [1925–30; named after Sir C. RAMAN]

Rā·mā·nu·ja (rä mä′no͝o jə), *n.* 1017–1134, Indian leader of the Shri-Vaishnavite sect.

Ra·ma·nu·jan (rä mä′no͝o jən), *n.* **Sri·ni·va·sa** (shrē′ni vä′sə, srē′-), 1887–1920, Indian mathematician.

Ra·ma·pith·e·cus (rä′mə pith′i kəs, -pə thē′kəs), *n.* a genus of extinct Miocene ape known from fossils found in India and Pakistan and formerly thought to be a possible human ancestor. [< NL (1934), equiv. to Skt *Rāma* RAMA + Gk *píthēkos* ape]

ra·mark (rā′märk), *n.* a radar beacon developed by the U.S. Coast Guard as a marine navigational aid. [RA(DAR) + MARK(ER)]

ra·mate (rā′māt), *adj.* having branches; branching out or off. [1895–1900; RAM(US) + -ATE[1]]

Ra·mat Gan (rä′mät gän′), a city in central Israel, near Tel Aviv. 120,300.

Ra·ma·ya·na (rä mä′yə nə), *n.* an epic of India, one of the Puranas attributed to Valmiki and concerned with Ramachandra and his wife Sita.

Ram·a·zan (ram′ə zän′), *n.* (esp. in India) Ramadan.

Ram·bert (räm bâr′) *n.* **Dame Marie** (*Cyvia Rambam; Myriam Rambam*), 1888–1982, English ballet dancer, producer, and director, born in Poland.

ram·bla (räm′blə), *n.* a dry ravine. [1820–30; < Sp < Ar *ramlah*]

ram·ble (ram′bəl), *v.,* **-bled, -bling,** *n.* **—***v.i.* **1.** to wander around in a leisurely, aimless manner: *They rambled through the shops until closing time.* **2.** to take a course with many turns or windings, as a stream or path. **3.** to grow in a random, unsystematic fashion: *The vine rambled over the walls and tree trunks.* **4.** to talk or write in a discursive, aimless way (usually fol. by *on*): *The speaker rambled on with anecdote after anecdote.* **—***v.t.* **5.** to walk aimlessly or idly over or through: *They spent the spring afternoon rambling woodland paths.* **—***n.* **6.** a walk without a definite route, taken merely for pleasure. [1610–20; orig. uncert.]
—Syn. 1. stroll, saunter, amble, stray, straggle. See **roam.**

ram·bler (ram′blər), *n.* **1.** a person, animal, or thing that rambles. **2.** See **ranch house** (def. 2). **3.** any of several climbing roses having clusters of small flowers. [1615–25; RAMBLE + -ER[1]]

ram·bling (ram′bling), *adj.* **1.** aimlessly wandering. **2.** taking an irregular course; straggling: *a rambling brook.* **3.** spread out irregularly in various directions: *a rambling mansion.* **4.** straying from one subject to another; desultory: *a rambling novel.* [1615–25; RAMBLE + -ING[2]] **—ram′bling·ly,** *adv.* **—ram′bling·ness,** *n.*
—Syn. 4. discursive.

Ram·bo (ram′bō), *n., pl.* **-bos.** a fanatically militant or violently aggressive person. [after John *Rambo,* a Vietnam veteran in the motion picture *First Blood* (1982) and its sequels]

Ram·bouil·let (ram′bo͞o lā′; *Fr.* RäN bo͞o ye′), *n.* one of a breed of hardy sheep, developed from the Merino, yielding good mutton and a fine grade of wool. [1905–10; after *Rambouillet,* town and forest in N France, source of the breed]

ram·bunc·tious (ram bungk′shəs), *adj.* **1.** difficult to control or handle; wildly boisterous: *a rambunctious child.* **2.** turbulently active and noisy: *a social gathering that became rambunctious and out of hand.* [1820–30, *Amer.*; orig. uncert.] **—ram·bunc′tious·ly,** *adv.* **—ram·bunc′tious·ness,** *n.*

ram·bu·tan (ram bo͞ot′n), *n.* **1.** the bright-red oval fruit of a Malayan, sapindaceous tree, *Nephelium lappaceum,* covered with soft spines, or hairs, and having a subacid taste. **2.** the tree itself. [1700–10; < Malay, equiv. to *rambut* hair + *-an* nominalizing suffix]

Ra·meau (RA mō′), *n.* **Jean Phi·lippe** (zhäN fē lēp′), 1683–1764, French composer and musical theorist.

Ra·mée (rə mā′), *n.* **Louise de la** (*"Ouida"*), 1839–1908, English novelist.

ram·e·kin (ram′i kin), *n.* **1.** a small, separately cooked portion of a cheese preparation or other food mixture baked in a small dish without a lid. **2.** a small dish in which food can be baked and served. Also, **ram·equin.** [1700–10; < F *ramequin* < dial. D, MD *rammeken*]

ra·men (rä′mən), *n. Japanese Cookery.* a bowl of clear soup containing noodles, vegetables, and often bits of meat. Also called **larmen.** [< Japn *rāmen* < Chin *lāmiàn* lit., pull noodle]

ram·en·ta·ceous (ram′ən tā′shəs), *adj. Bot.* resembling or covered with ramenta. [1810–20; RAMENT(UM) + -ACEOUS]

ra·men·tum (rə men′təm), *n., pl.* **-ta** (-tə). **1.** a scraping, shaving, or particle. **2.** *Bot.* one of the thin, chafflike scales covering the shoots or leaves of certain ferns. [1655–65; < L *rāmentum* a shaving, shred < **rādmentum,* equiv. to *rād(ere)* to scrape + *-mentum* -MENT]

ram·e·quin (ram′i kin), *n.* ramekin.

Ram·e·ses (ram′ə sēz′), *n.* **1.** Ramses (def. 1). **2.** Raamses.

ra·met (rā′mit), *n.* an individual of a clone. [1925–30; < L *rām(us)* branch + -ET]

ra·mi (rā′mī), *n.* pl. of **ramus.**

ram·ie (ram′ē, rā′mē), *n.* **1.** an Asian shrub, *Boehmeria nivea,* of the nettle family, yielding a fiber used esp. in making textiles. **2.** the fiber itself. [1810–20; < Malay *rami* a kind of grass]

ram·i·fi·ca·tion (ram′ə fi kā′shən), *n.* **1.** the act or process of ramifying. **2.** a branch: *ramifications of a nerve.* **3.** a related or derived subject, problem, etc.; outgrowth; consequence; implication: *The new tax law proved to have many ramifications unforeseen by the lawmakers.* **4.** *Bot.* **a.** a structure formed of branches. **b.** a configuration of branching parts. [1670–80; < MF < ML *rāmificāt(us)* (ptp. of *rāmificāre* to RAMIFY) + MF *-ion* -ION]

ram·i·form (ram′ə fôrm′), *adj.* **1.** having the form of a branch; branchlike. **2.** branched. [1815–25; < L *rām(us)* branch (see RAMUS) + -I- + -FORM]

ram·i·fy (ram′ə fī′), *v.t., v.i.,* **-fied, -fy·ing.** to divide or spread out into branches or branchlike parts; extend into subdivisions. [1535–45; < MF *ramifier* < ML *rāmificāre,* equiv. to L *rām(us)* branch (see RAMUS) + *-ificāre* -IFY]

Ra·mil·lies (*Fr.* RA mē yē′), *n.* a village in central Belgium: Marlborough's defeat of the French 1706.

ram·jet (ram′jet′), *n.* a jet engine operated by the injection of fuel into a stream of air compressed by the forward speed of the aircraft. Also called **ram′jet en′gine.** [1940–45; RAM + JET[1]]

rammed′ earth′, a mixture of sand, loam, clay, and other ingredients rammed hard within forms as a building material. Also called **pisé, pisé de terre, pisay.** [1825–35]

ram·mels·berg·ite (ram′əlz bûr′gīt), *n.* a mineral, essentially nickel diarsenide, $NiAs_2$. [< G *Rammelsbergit* (1845), named after Karl Friedrich *Rammelsberg* (1813–99), German chemist; see -ITE[1]]

ram·mer (ram′ər), *n.* a person or thing that rams. [1490–1500; RAM[1] + -ER[1]]

ram·mish (ram′ish), *adj.* **1.** resembling a ram. **2.** having a disagreeable taste or smell; rank. [1350–1400; ME; see RAM[1], -ISH[1]] **—ram′mish·ness,** *n.*

ra·mon (rə mōn′), *n.* any of several tropical American trees belonging to the genus *Brosimum,* of the mulberry family, the leaves of which are used as forage, esp. *B. alicastrum,* which bears the breadnut. Also, **ra·moon** (ra mo͞on′). [1750–60; < Sp *ramón* browse, aug. of *ramo* branch (< L *rāmus;* see RAMUS)]

Ra·mon (rā′mən, rə mōn′), *n.* a male given name, form of **Raymond.**

Ra·mo·na (rə mō′nə), *n.* a female given name.

Ra·món y Ca·jal (rä môn′ ē kä häl′), **San·tia·go** (sän tyä′gô), 1852–1934, Spanish histologist: Nobel prize for medicine 1906.

ra·mose (rā′mōs, rə mōs′), *adj.* **1.** having many branches. **2.** branching. [1680–90; < L *rāmōsus* full of boughs, equiv. to *rām(us)* branch (see RAMUS) + *-ōsus* -OSE[1]] **—ra′mose·ly,** *adv.* **—ra·mos·i·ty** (rə mos′i tē), *n.*

Ra′mos gin′ fizz′ (rā′mōs), a cocktail of gin, egg white, lime and lemon juice, sugar, and cream, shaken with ice and often topped with soda or seltzer. [after Henry C. *Ramos,* U.S. bartender, inventor of the drink]

ra·mous (rā′məs), *adj.* **1.** ramose. **2.** resembling or pertaining to branches. [1555–65; < L *rāmōsus.* See RAMOSE, -OUS]

ramp[1] (ramp), *n.* **1.** a sloping surface connecting two levels; incline. **2.** a short concave slope or bend, as one connecting the higher and lower parts of a staircase railing at a landing. **3.** any extensive sloping walk or passageway. **4.** the act of ramping. **5.** Also called **boarding ramp.** a movable staircase for entering or leaving a cabin door of an airplane. **6.** Also called **parking ramp.** apron (def. 6). —*v.i.* **7.** (of animals) to stand or move with the forelegs or arms raised, as in animosity or excitement. **8.** (of a lion or other large quadruped represented on a coat of arms) to rise or stand on the hind legs. **9.** to rear as if to spring. **10.** to leap or dash with fury (often fol. by *about*). **11.** to act violently; rage; storm: *ramping and raging in a great fury.* —*v.t.* **12.** to provide with a ramp or ramps: *Entrances will be ramped to accommodate those in wheelchairs.* **13. ramp along,** *Naut.* to sail on a tack with all sails filled. [1350–1400; (v.) ME *rampen* < OF *ramper* to creep, crawl, climb; (n.) < F *rampe,* deriv. of *ramper*] **—ramp′ing·ly,** *adv.*

ramp[2] (ramp), *n.* Usually, **ramps.** a wild onion, *Allium tricoccum,* of the amaryllis family, of eastern North America, having flat leaves and rounded clusters of whitish flowers; eaten raw or used as a flavoring in cooked foods. Also called **wild leek.** [1530–40; back formation from *ramps* ramson, var. (with intrusive *p*) of *rams,* earlier *rammys,* orig. the sing. of RAMSON]

ram·page (*n.* ram′pāj; *v.* ram pāj′, ram′pāj), *n., v.,* **-paged, -pag·ing.** —*n.* **1.** violent or excited behavior that is reckless, uncontrolled, or destructive. **2.** a state of violent anger or agitation: *The smallest mistake sends him into a rampage. The river has gone on a rampage and flooded the countryside.* —*v.i.* **3.** to rush, move, or act furiously or violently: *a bull elephant rampaging through the jungle.* [1705–15; RAMP[1] + -AGE] **—ram·pag′er,** *n.*
—Syn. 3. storm, rage, tear.

ram·pa·geous (ram pā′jəs), *adj.* violent; unruly; boisterous. [1815–25; RAMPAGE + -OUS] **—ram·pa′geous·ly,** *adv.* **—ram·pa′geous·ness,** *n.*

ramp·an·cy (ram′pən sē), *n.* a rampant condition or position. [1655–65; RAMP(ANT) + -ANCY]

ramp·ant (ram′pənt), *adj.* **1.** violent in action or spirit; raging; furious: *a rampant leopard.* **2.** growing luxuriantly, as weeds. **3.** in full sway; prevailing or unchecked: *a rampant rumor.* **4.** (of an animal) standing on the hind legs; ramping. **5.** *Heraldry.* (of a beast used as a charge) represented in profile facing the dexter side, with the body upraised and resting on the left hind leg, the tail and other legs elevated, the right foreleg highest, and the head in profile unless otherwise specified: *a lion rampant.* **6.** *Archit.* (of an arch or vault) springing at one side from one level of support and resting at the other on a higher level. See illus. under **arch**[1]. [1350–1400; ME < OF, prp. of *ramper* to RAMP[1]] **—ramp′ant·ly,** *adv.*
—Syn. 3. rife, widespread, unrestrained.

rampant (heraldic lion)

ram·part (ram′pärt, -pərt), *n.* **1.** *Fort.* **a.** a broad elevation or mound of earth raised as a fortification around a place and usually capped with a stone or earth parapet. See diag. under **bastion. b.** such an elevation together with the parapet. **2.** anything serving as a bulwark or defense. —*v.t.* **3.** to furnish with or as if with a rampart. [1575–85; < MF, deriv. of *remparer,* equiv. to *re-* RE- + *emparer* to take possession of < Pr *amparar* << L *ante-* ANTE- + *parāre* to PREPARE]
—Syn. 2. fortification, breastwork, barricade, guard.

ram·pas·ture (ram′pas′chər), *n. Canadian.* **1.** a room in a boarding or lodging house used as a communal dormitory for unmarried men. **2.** a large attic room. [1910–15; RAM[1] + PASTURE]

ram·pike (ram′pīk′), *n. Chiefly Canadian.* a dead tree, esp. the bleached skeleton or splintered trunk of a tree killed by fire, lightning, or wind. Also called **rampick** (ram′pik′), **ram·pole** (ram′pōl′). [1585–95; orig. uncert.]

ram·pi·on (ram′pē ən), *n.* **1.** a European bellflower, *Campanula rapunculus,* having an edible white tuberous root used in Europe for salad. **2.** any related plant of the genus *Phyteuma,* having heads or spikes of blue flowers. [1565–75; prob. alter. of MF *raiponce* < It *raponzo,* deriv. of *rapa* turnip (< L *rāpa;* see RAPE[2])]

ram·rod (ram′rod′), *n., v.,* **-rod·ded, -rod·ding.** —*n.* **1.** a rod for ramming down the charge of a muzzleloading firearm. **2.** a cleaning rod for the barrel of a firearm. **3.** a strict disciplinarian; martinet. —*v.t.* **4.** to exert discipline and authority on. **5.** to strike or injure with or as if with a ramrod. **6.** to accomplish or put into action by force, intimidation, etc.: *to ramrod a bill through Congress.* [1750–60; RAM[1] + ROD]

Ram·say (ram′zē), *n.* **1. Allan,** 1686–1758, Scottish poet. **2. George.** Dalhousie (def. 1). **3. James Andrew Broun.** Dalhousie (def. 2). **4. Sir William,** 1852–1916, English chemist: Nobel prize 1904.

Rams′den eye′piece *Optics.* an eyepiece consisting of two plano-convex crown-glass lenses of equal focal length, placed with the convex sides facing each other and with a separation between the lenses of about two-thirds of the focal length of each. [1840–50; named after Jesse *Ramsden* (1735–1800), English maker of astronomical instruments]

Ram·ses (ram′sēz), *n.* **1.** the name of several kings of ancient Egypt. **2.** Raamses. Ex. 12:37; Num. 33:3–5. Also, **Rameses.**

Ramses I, 1324?–1258 B.C., king of ancient Egypt.

Ramses II, 1292–1225 B.C., king of ancient Egypt.

Ramses III, 1198–1167 B.C., king of ancient Egypt.

Ram·sey (ram′zē), *n.* **1. Arthur Michael,** (Baron Ramsey of Canterbury), born 1904, English clergyman and scholar: archbishop of Canterbury 1961–74. **2.** a town in NE New Jersey. 12,899. **3.** a town in SE Minnesota. 10,093. **4.** a male given name: from a Scandinavian word meaning "wooded island."

Rams·gate (ramz′gāt′; *Brit.* ramz′git), *n.* a seaport in NE Kent, in SE England: resort. 39,482.

ram·shack·le (ram′shak′əl), *adj.* loosely made or held together; rickety; shaky: *a ramshackle house.* [1815–25; cf. earlier *rans(h)ackled,* obscurely akin to RANSACK] **—ram′shack′le·ness,** *n.*
—Syn. tumbledown, dilapidated, derelict, flimsy.

ram's′-head la′dy's-slipper (ramz′hed′), a rare, slender-stemmed orchid, *Cypripedium arietinum,* of northeastern North America, that has crimson-streaked, whitish-lipped flowers with purple sepals and grows in moist soil. [1865–70]

ram·son (ram′zən, -sən), *n.* **1.** a garlic, *Allium ursinum,* having broad leaves. **2.** Usually, **ramsons.** its bulbous root, used as a relish. [bef. 1000; ME *ramsyn* (orig. pl., taken as sing.); OE *hramesan,* pl. of *hramsa* broad-leafed garlic; c. Gk *krómmyon* onion]

ram·stam (ram′stam), *Scot. and North Eng.* —*adj.* **1.** obstinate; headstrong. —*n.* **2.** a stubborn or thoughtless person. [1780–90; perh. rhyming compound based on RAM[1] and STAMP]

ram·til (ram′til), *n.* See **niger seed.** [1855–60; perh. < Bengali]

ram·u·lose (ram′yə lōs′), *adj. Bot., Zool.* having many small branches. Also, **ram·u·lous** (ram′yə ləs). [1745–55; < L *rāmulōsus* full of branching veins, equiv. to *rāmul(us)* little branch, twig (*rām(us)* branch + *-ulus* -ULE) + *-ōsus* -OSE[1]; see RAMUS]

ra·mus (rā′məs), *n., pl.* **-mi** (-mī). *Bot., Zool., Anat.* a branch, as of a plant, vein, bone, etc. [1795–1805; < L *rāmus* branch, twig, bough; akin to *rādix* ROOT[1] (see RADIX)]

ran (ran), *v.* pt. of **run.**

Ran (rän), *n. Scand. Myth.* a sea goddess who drags down ships and drowns sailors: the wife of Aegir.

Ran·ca·gua (RÄNG kä′gwä), *n.* a city in central Chile. 108,010.

ranch (ranch), *n.* **1.** an establishment maintained for raising livestock under range conditions. **2.** *Chiefly Western U.S. and Canada.* a large farm used primarily to raise one kind of crop or animal: *a mink ranch.* **3.** a dude ranch. **4.** the persons employed or living on a ranch. **5.** See **ranch house.** —*v.i.* **6.** to manage or work on a ranch. [1800–10, *Amer.;* < Sp *rancho* RANCHO] **—ranch′less,** *adj.* **—ranch′like′,** *adj.*

ranch·er (ran′chər), *n.* a person who owns or works on a ranch. [1830–40, *Amer.;* RANCH + -ER[1]]

ranch·er·ie (ran′chə rē), *n. Canadian.* **1.** an Indian village or settlement, esp. one located on a reserve. **2.** any one of the large rectangular cedar buildings erected by Pacific Coast Indians for communal living and ceremonial purposes. [1590–1600, *Amer.;* earlier *rancheria* < Sp, deriv. of *rancho;* see RANCHO]

ran·che·ro (ran châr′ō; *Sp.* rän che′rô), *n., pl.* **-che·ros** (-châr′ōz; *Sp.* -che′rôs). (in Spanish America and the southwestern U.S.) a rancher. [1820–30; < Sp, equiv. to *ranch(o)* RANCH + *-ero* < L *-ārius* -ARY]

ranch·ette (ran chet′), *n.* a small-scale ranch, typically of only a few acres. [1955–60, *Amer.;* RANCH + -ETTE]

ranch′ house′, 1. the house of the owner of a ranch, usually of one story and with a low-pitched roof. **2.** Also called **rambler.** any one-story house of the same general form, esp. one built in the suburbs. [1860–65, *Amer.*]

Ran·chi (rän′chē), *n.* a city in S Bihar, in E India. 256,011.

ranch·man (ranch′mən), *n., pl.* **-men.** a rancher. [1855–60, *Amer.;* RANCH + -MAN]

ranch′ mink′, a semiaquatic mink, *Mustela vision,* raised commercially for its fur. [1950–55]

ran·cho (ran′chō, rän′-; *Sp.* rän′chô), *n., pl.* **-chos** (-chōz; *Sp.* -chôs). **1.** a ranch. **2.** a hut or collection of huts for herders, laborers, or travelers. [1800–10, *Amer.;* < AmerSp: small farm, camp (Sp: camp) < OSp *rancharse* to lodge, be billeted < MF *(se) ranger* to be arranged, be installed; see RANGE]

Ran·cho Cor·do·va (ran′chō kôr′də və), a town in central California. 42,881.

Ran′cho Cu·ca·mon′ga (ko͞o′kə mung′gə, -mong′-), a city in SE California. 55,250.

Ran′cho Pal′os Ver′des, a town in SW California. 35,227.

ran·cid (ran′sid), *adj.* **1.** having a rank, unpleasant, stale smell or taste, as through decomposition, esp. of fats or oils: *rancid butter.* **2.** (of an odor or taste) rank, unpleasant, and stale: *a rancid smell.* **3.** offensive or nasty; disagreeable. [1640–50; < L *rancidus* rank, stinking, equiv. to *ranc(ēre)* to be rotten + *-idus* -ID[4]] **—ran′cid·ly,** *adv.* **—ran′cid·ness, ran·cid′i·ty,** *n.*

ran·cor (rang′kər), *n.* bitter, rankling resentment or ill will; hatred; malice. Also, *esp. Brit.,* **ran′cour.** [1175–1225; ME *rancour* < MF < LL *rancōr-* (s. of *rancor*) rancidity, equiv. to L *ranc(ēre)* (see RANCID) + *-ōr-* -OR[1]] **—ran′cored;** *esp. Brit.,* **ran′coured,** *adj.*
—Syn. bitterness, spite, venom, animosity. See **malevolence. —Ant.** benevolence.

ran·cor·ous (rang′kər əs), *adj.* full of or showing rancor. [1580–90; RANCOR + -OUS] **—ran′cor·ous·ly,** *adv.* **—ran′cor·ous·ness,** *n.*

rand[1] (rand), *n.* **1.** (in shoemaking) a strip of leather set in a shoe at the heel before the lifts are attached. **2.** *Brit. Dial.* **a.** a strip or long slice. **b.** a border or margin. —*v.t.* **3.** to provide (footwear) with rands. [bef. 900; ME, OE; c. D, G *rand* border, margin]

rand[2] (rand), *n.* a coin and monetary unit of the Republic of South Africa, equal to 100 cents. *Abbr.:* R. [1960–65; < Afrik, after THE RAND (Witwatersrand), a major gold mining area]

Rand (rand), *n.* **Ayn** (īn), 1905–82, U.S. novelist and essayist, born in Russia.

Rand, The (rand), Witwatersrand.

Ran·dall (ran′dl), *n.* a male given name. Also, **Ran′dal.**

Ran·dalls·town (ran′dlz toun′), *n.* a city in N Maryland, near Baltimore. 25,927.

R&B, rhythm-and-blues. Also, **r&b, R and B**

R&D, research and development. Also, **R and D**

Rand·ers (rä′nərs), *n.* a seaport in E Jutland, in Denmark. 58,409.

R. & I., 1. king and emperor. [< L *Rēx et Imperātor*] **2.** queen and empress. [< L *Rēgina et Imperātrix*]

Ran·dolph (ran′dolf, -dəlf), *n.* **1. A(sa) Philip,** 1889–1979, U.S. labor leader: president of the Brotherhood of Sleeping Car Porters 1925–68. **2. Edmund Jennings** (jen′ings), 1753–1813, U.S. statesman: first U.S. Attorney General 1789–94; Secretary of State 1794–95. **3. John,**

CONCISE ETYMOLOGY KEY: <, descended or borrowed from; >, whence; b., blend of, blended; c., cognate with; cf., compare; deriv., derivative; equiv., equivalent; imit., imitative; obl., oblique; r., replacing; s., stem; sp., spelling, spelled; resp., respelling, respelled; trans., translation; ?, origin unknown; *, unattested; ‡, probably earlier than. See the full key inside the front cover.

1773–1833, U.S. statesman and author. **4.** a town in E Massachusetts, S of Boston. 28,218. **5.** a male given name.

ran•dom (ran′dəm), *adj.* **1.** proceeding, made, or occurring without definite aim, reason, or pattern: *the random selection of numbers.* **2.** *Statistics.* of or characterizing a process of selection in which each item of a set has an equal probability of being chosen. **3.** *Building Trades.* **a.** (of building materials) lacking uniformity of dimensions: *random shingles.* **b.** (of ashlar) laid without continuous courses. **c.** constructed or applied without regularity: *random bond.* —*n.* **4.** *Chiefly Brit.* bank[3] (def. 7b). **5. at random,** without definite aim, purpose, method, or adherence to a prior arrangement; in a haphazard way: *Contestants were chosen at random from the studio audience.* —*adv.* **6.** *Building Trades.* without uniformity: *random-sized slates.* [1275–1325; ME *raundon, random* < OF *randon,* deriv. of *randir* to gallop < Gmc] —**ran′dom•ly,** *adv.* —**ran′dom•ness,** *n.*
—**Syn. 1.** haphazard, chance, fortuitous.

ran′dom ac′cess, 1. the capacity of a videodisc or compact disc player that allows the user to select and replay any portion without starting at the beginning. **2.** availability, as of a service or facility, whenever needed or desired: *an executive's need for random access to legal experts.* [1950–55]

ran•dom-ac•cess (ran′dəm ak′ses), *adj. Computers.* **1.** of or pertaining to a storage medium in which records can be read or written at the same time from or to any main storage address. **2.** See **direct-access.**

ran′dom-access mem′ory, *Computers.* See **RAM.**

ran′dom er′ror, *Statistics.* an error that has a random distribution and can be attributed to chance. Cf. **systematic error.** [1935–40]

ran•dom•ize (ran′də mīz′), *v.t.,* **-ized, -iz•ing.** to order or select in a random manner, as in a sample or experiment, esp. in order to reduce bias and interference caused by irrelevant variables; make random. Also, *esp. Brit.,* **ran′dom•ise′.** [1925–30; RANDOM + -IZE] —**ran′•dom•i•za′tion,** *n.* —**ran′dom•iz′er,** *n.*

ran′dom line′, *Survey.* a trial survey line run from a station toward a predetermined point that cannot be seen from the station.

ran′dom num′ber, *Statistics.* a number chosen by a random sampling, as from a table (**ran′dom num′ber ta′ble**) or generated by a computer. [1925–30]

ran′dom sam′pling, *Statistics.* a method of selecting a sample (**ran′dom sam′ple**) from a statistical population in such a way that every possible sample that could be selected has a predetermined probability of being selected. [1895–1900]

ran′dom var′iable, *Statistics.* a quantity that takes any of a set of values with specified probabilities. Also called **variate.** [1935–40]

ran′dom walk′, 1. *Statistics.* the path taken by a point or quantity that moves in steps, where the direction of each step is determined randomly. **2.** *Physics.* the tendency of particles in random motion to achieve a net displacement or to drift in a particular direction. [1900–05]

R and R, 1. rest and recreation. **2.** rest and recuperation. **3.** rock-'n'-roll. Also, **R&R**

rand•y (ran′dē), *adj.,* **rand•i•er, rand•i•est,** *n., pl.* **rand•ies.** —*adj.* **1.** sexually aroused; lustful; lecherous. **2.** *Chiefly Scot.* rude and aggressive. —*n.* **3.** *Chiefly Scot.* a rude or coarse beggar. [1690–1700; *rand* (obs. var. of RANT) + -Y[1]] —**rand′i•ness,** *n.*

Ran•dy (ran′dē), *n.* **1.** a male given name, form of **Randall** or **Randolph. 2.** a female given name.

ra•nee (rä′nē, rä nē′), *n.* (in India) **1.** the wife of a rajah. **2.** a reigning queen or princess. Also, **rani.** [1690–1700; < Hindi *rānī* < Skt *rājñī* queen (fem. deriv. of *rājan* king)]

rang[1] (rang), *v.* pt. of **ring**[2].

rang[2] (rang), *n. Informal.* a boomerang. [by shortening]

range (rānj), *n., adj., v.,* **ranged, rang•ing.** —*n.* **1.** the extent to which or the limits between which variation is possible: *the range of steel prices; a wide range of styles.* **2.** the extent or scope of the operation or action of something: *within range of vision.* **3.** the distance to which a projectile is or may be sent by a weapon. **4.** the distance of the target from the weapon. **5.** an area equipped with targets for practice in shooting weapons: *a rifle range.* **6.** an area used for flight-testing missiles. **7.** the distance of something to be located from some point of operation, as in sound ranging. **8.** the distance that can be covered by an aircraft, ship, or other vehicle, carrying a normal load without refueling. **9.** *Statistics.* the difference between the largest and smallest values in a statistical distribution. **10.** a continuous course of masonry of the same height from end to end. **11.** *Music.* compass (def. 4). **12.** *Survey.* **a.** the horizontal direction or extension of a survey line established by two or more marked points. **b.** (in U.S. public-land surveys) one of a series of divisions numbered east or west from the principal meridian of the survey and consisting of a row of townships, each six miles square, that are numbered north or south from a base line. **13.** *Navig.* a line established by markers or lights on shore for the location of soundings. **14.** a rank, class, or order: *in the higher ranges of society.* **15.** a row, line, or series, as of persons or things. **16.** an act of ranging or moving around, as over an area or region. **17.** Also called **rangeland.** an area or tract that is or may be ranged over, esp. an open region for the grazing of livestock. **18.** the region over which a population or species is distributed: *the range of the Baltimore oriole.* **19.** *Math.* the set of all values attained by a given function throughout its domain. **20.** a chain of mountains forming a single system: *the Catskill Range.* **21.** a large portable or stationary cooking stove having burners built into the top surface and containing one or more ovens. **22.** *Physics.* the maximum distance that a charged particle, as a proton, can penetrate a given medium and still maintain sufficient kinetic energy to produce ionization in the medium. **23.** *Naut.* **a.** a large cleat for securing various lines, esp. the tacks and sheets of courses. **b.** a length of anchor cable laid on deck. **24. in range,** (of two or more objects observed from a vessel) located one directly behind the other.
—*adj.* **25.** working or grazing on a range: *range horses; range animals like steer and sheep.*
—*v.t.* **26.** to draw up or arrange (persons or things) in rows or lines or in a specific position, company, or group: *The sergeant ranged the troops in columns of six across.* **27.** to place or arrange systematically; set in order; dispose: *The members of the cast were ranged in their proper places on stage.* **28.** to place in a particular class; classify: *They ranged themselves with the liberals.* **29.** to make straight, level, or even, as lines of type. **30.** to pass over or through (an area or region) in all directions, as in exploring or searching: *They ranged the entire countryside.* **31.** to pasture (cattle) on a range. **32.** to direct or train, as a telescope, upon an object. **33.** to obtain the range of (something aimed at or to be located). **34.** *Naut.* to lay out (an anchor cable) so that the anchor may descend smoothly.
—*v.i.* **35.** to vary within certain limits: *prices ranging from $5 to $10.* **36.** to have a certain variety of things somehow related: *emotions ranging from smugness to despair.* **37.** to move around or through a region in all directions, as people or animals. **38.** to rove, roam, or wander: *The talk ranged over a variety of subjects.* **39.** to stretch out or extend in a line, as things: *shabby houses ranged along the road.* **40.** to extend, run, or go in a certain direction: *a boundary ranging from east and west.* **41.** to lie or extend in the same line or plane, as one thing with another or others. **42.** to take up a position in a line or in order. **43.** to extend, be found, or occur over an area or throughout a period, as an animal or plant. **44.** to have a specified range, as a gun, missile, etc. **45.** to find the range, as of something aimed at or to be located. **46.** *Naut.* (of an anchored vessel) to swerve or sheer (often fol. by *about*). [1350–1400; (n.) ME < OF *renge* row, deriv. of *renc* line; see RANK[1]; (v.) ME *rangen* < MF *ranger,* OF *rengier,* deriv. of *renc*]
—**Syn. 1.** sweep, reach. RANGE, COMPASS, LATITUDE, SCOPE refer to extent or breadth. RANGE emphasizes extent and diversity: *the range of one's interests.* COMPASS suggests definite limits: *within the compass of one's mind.* LATITUDE emphasizes the idea of freedom from narrow confines, thus breadth or extent: *granted latitude of action.* SCOPE suggests great freedom but a proper limit: *the scope of one's activities; the scope of one's obligations.* **14.** kind, sort. **15.** tier, file. **26.** align, rank. **27.** array. **37.** See **roam. 39.** lie.

ranged (rānjd), *adj. Building Trades.* coursed. [1520–30; RANGE + -ED[2]]

range′ find′er, any of various instruments for determining the distance from the observer to a particular object, as for sighting a gun or adjusting the focus of a camera. Also, **range′find′er.** [1870–75]

range•land (rānj′land′), *n.* range (def. 17). [1930–35; RANGE + -LAND]

Range′ley Lakes′ (rānj′lē), a group of lakes in W Maine.

range′ line′, (in U.S. public-land surveys) one of two parallel lines running north and south that define the east and west borders of a township. Cf. **township** (def. 2), **township line.** [1810–20, *Amer.*]

range•mas•ter (rānj′mas′tər, -mä′stər), *n.* a person in charge of a firing range. [RANGE + MASTER]

range′ of accommoda′tion, *Ophthalm.* the range of distance over which an object can be accurately focused on the retina by accommodation of the eye.

range′ of stabil′ity, *Naval Archit.* the angle to the perpendicular through which a vessel may be heeled without losing the ability to right itself.

range′ oil′, oil suitable for burning as the fuel of a kitchen stove.

range′ paral′ysis, *Vet. Pathol.* See **Marek's disease.** [1930–35]

range′ pole′, *Survey.* a conspicuously painted pole held upright to show the position of a survey mark.

rang•er (rān′jər), *n.* **1.** See **forest ranger. 2.** one of a body of armed guards who patrol a region. **3.** (*cap.*) a U.S. soldier in World War II specially trained for making surprise raids and attacks in small groups. Cf. **commando** (def. 1). **4.** a soldier specially trained in the techniques of guerrilla warfare, esp. in jungle terrain. **5.** a person who ranges or roves. **6.** (esp. in Texas) a member of the state police. **7.** *Brit.* a keeper of a royal forest or park. **8.** *Building Trades.* wale[1] (def. 5). **9.** (*cap.*) one of a series of instrumented U.S. space probes launched in the 1960's that transmitted closeup pictures of the moon before impacting the lunar surface. [1350–1400; ME; see RANGE, -ER[1]]

range′ ta′ble, one of a number of identical small tables that can be used together to form a single table. [1870–75]

range′ wool′. See **territory wool.**

Ran•goon (rang go͞on′), *n.* former name of **Yangon.**

rang•pur (rung′po͝or, rung po͝or′), *n.* a variety of mandarin orange, bearing a tart fruit. [named after *Rangpur,* region of Bangladesh]

rang•y (rān′jē), *adj.,* **rang•i•er, rang•i•est. 1.** (of animals or people) slender and long-limbed. **2.** given to or fitted for ranging or moving about, as animals. **3.** mountainous. [1865–70; RANGE + -Y[1]] —**rang′i•ness,** *n.*

ra•ni (rä′nē, rä nē′), *n., pl.* **-nis.** ranee.

ran•id (ran′id, rā′nid), —*adj.* **1.** belonging or pertaining to the frog family Ranidae, characterized by smooth, moist skin and semiaquatic habits. —*n.* **2.** frog[1] (def. 2). [1885–90; < NL *Ranidae,* equiv. to *Ran*(*a*) a genus (L *rāna* frog) + *-idae* -ID[2]]

Ra′ni•khet disease′ (rä′ni ket′), *Vet. Pathol.* See **Newcastle disease.** [named after *Ranikhet,* town in northern India]

Ran•jit Singh (run′jit sing′), (*"Lion of the Punjab"*) 1780–1839, Indian maharaja: founder of the Sikh kingdom of Punjab.

rank[1] (rangk), *n.* **1.** a number of persons forming a separate class in a social hierarchy or in any graded body. **2.** a social or official position or standing, as in the armed forces: *the rank of captain.* **3.** high position or station in the social or some similar scale: *a woman of rank.* **4.** a class in any scale of comparison. **5.** relative position or standing: *a writer of the first rank.* **6.** a row, line, or series of things or persons: *orchestra players arranged in ranks.* **7. ranks, a.** the members of an armed service apart from its officers; enlisted personnel. **b.** military enlisted personnel as a group. See table on next page. **8.** Usually, **ranks.** the general body of any party, society, or organization apart from the officers or leaders. **9.** orderly arrangement; array. **10.** a line of persons, esp. soldiers, standing abreast in close-order formation (distinguished from *file*). **11.** *Brit.* a place or station occupied by vehicles available for hire; stand: *a taxi rank.* **12.** *Chess.* one of the horizontal lines of squares on a chessboard. **13.** a set of organ pipes of the same kind and tonal color. **14.** Also called **determinant rank.** *Math.* the order of the nonzero determinant of greatest order that can be selected from a given matrix by the elimination of rows and columns. **15.** *Mining.* the classification of coal according to hardness, from lignite to anthracite. **16. break ranks, a.** to leave an assigned position in a military formation. **b.** to disagree with, defect from, or refuse to support one's colleagues, party, or the like. **17. pull rank (on),** to make use of one's superior rank to gain an advantage over (someone). Also, **pull one's rank (on).** —*v.t.* **18.** to arrange in ranks or in regular formation: *The men were ranked according to height. He ranked the chess pieces on the board.* **19.** to assign to a particular position, station, class, etc.: *She was ranked among the most admired citizens.* **20.** to outrank: *The colonel ranks all other officers in the squadron.* **21.** *Slang.* to insult; criticize.
—*v.i.* **22.** to form a rank or ranks. **23.** to take up or occupy a place in a particular rank, class, etc.: *to rank well ahead of the other students.* **24.** to have rank or standing. **25.** to be the senior in rank: *The colonel ranks at this camp.* **26.** *Slang.* to complain. [1560–70; < F *ranc* (n., obs.), OF *renc, ranc, rang* row, line < Gmc, akin to RING[1]] —**rank′less,** *adj.*
—**Syn. 3.** distinction, eminence, dignity. **6.** range, tier. **9.** alignment. **18.** align, range, array.

rank[2] (rangk), *adj.,* **-er, -est. 1.** growing with excessive luxuriance; vigorous and tall of growth: *tall rank weeds.* **2.** producing an excessive and coarse growth, as land. **3.** having an offensively strong smell or taste: *a rank cigar.* **4.** offensively strong, as a smell or taste. **5.** utter; absolute: *a rank amateur; rank treachery.* **6.** highly offensive; disgusting: *a rank sight of carnage.* **7.** grossly coarse, vulgar, or indecent: *rank language.* **8.** *Slang.* inferior; contemptible. [bef. 1000; ME; OE *ranc* bold, proud; c. ON *rakkr* straight, bold] —**rank′ish,** *adj.* —**rank′ly,** *adv.* —**rank′ness,** *n.*
—**Syn. 1.** abundant, exuberant. **5.** complete, sheer, entire. **6.** repulsive, repellent. See **flagrant. 7.** foul.

Rank (rängk), *n.* **Ot•to** (ôt′ō), 1884–1939, Austrian psychoanalyst.

rank′ and file′, 1. the members of a group or organization apart from its leaders or officers. **2.** rank[1] (def. 7a). [1590–1600] —**rank′-and-file′,** *adj.*

rank-and-fil•er (rangk′ən fī′lər), *n.* a member of the rank and file. [1935–40, *Amer.*; *rank and file* + -ER[1]]

Ran•ke (räng′kə), *n.* **Le•o•pold von** (lā′ô pôlt′ fən), 1795–1886, German historian.

rank•er (rang′kər), *n.* **1.** a person who ranks. **2.** *Brit.* a soldier in the ranks or a commissioned officer promoted from the ranks. [1825–35; RANK[1] + -ER[1]]

ran•ket (rang′kit), *n.* a double-reed wind instrument of the 16th and 17th centuries. Also, **ran′kett, rackett.** Also called **sausage bassoon.** [1875–80; < G *Rankett*]

Ran•kin (rang′kin), *n.* **Jeannette,** 1880–1973, U.S. women's-rights leader and pacifist: first woman elected to Congress; served 1917–19, 1941–43.

Ran•kine (rang′kin), *n.* **1. William John Mac•quorn** (mə kwôrn′), 1820–70, Scottish engineer and physicist. —*adj.* **2.** *Thermodynam.* pertaining to an absolute temperature scale (**Ran′kine scale′**) in which the degree intervals are equal to those of the Fahrenheit scale and in which 0° Rankine equals −459.7° Fahrenheit. Cf. **absolute temperature scale, Kelvin** (defs. 2, 3).

Ran′kine cy′cle, *Thermodynam.* the hypothetical cycle of a steam engine in which all heat transfers take place at constant pressure and in which expansion and compression occur adiabatically. Also called **Clausius cycle.** [1895–1900; named after W. J. M. RANKINE]

rank•ing (rang′king), *adj.* **1.** senior or superior in rank, position, etc.: *a ranking diplomat.* **2.** prominent or highly regarded: *a ranking authority on Soviet affairs.* **3.** occupying a specific rank, position, etc. (often used in combination): *a low-ranking executive.* —*n.* **4.** an act or instance of indicating relative standing. **5.** a list showing such standing. [1860–65; RANK[1] + -ING[2], -ING[1]]

ran•kle (rang′kəl), *v.,* **-kled, -kling.** —*v.i.* **1.** (of unpleasant feelings, experiences, etc.) to continue to cause keen irritation or bitter resentment within the mind; fester; be painful. —*v.t.* **2.** to cause keen irritation or bitter resentment in: *His colleague's harsh criticism rankled him for days.* [1250–1300; ME *ranclen* < MF *rancler,* OF *raoncler,* var. of *draoncler* to fester, deriv. of *draoncle* a sore < LL *dracunculus* small serpent, dim. of L *dracō* serpent; see DRAGON, CARBUNCLE] —**ran′kling•ly,** *adv.*
—**Syn. 1, 2.** irritate, gall, chafe.

COMPARATIVE RANKS IN THE UNITED STATES ARMED FORCES

Army	Navy	Air Force	Marine Corps
General of the Army	Fleet Admiral	General of the Air Force	NA
General	Admiral	General	General
Lieutenant General	Vice Admiral	Lieutenant General	Lieutenant General
Major General	Rear Admiral	Major General	Major General
Brigadier General	Commodore	Brigadier General	Brigadier General
Colonel	Captain	Colonel	Colonel
Lieutenant Colonel	Commander	Lieutenant Colonel	Lieutenant Colonel
Major	Lieutenant Commander	Major	Major
Captain	Lieutenant	Captain	Captain
First Lieutenant	Lieutenant Junior Grade	First Lieutenant	First Lieutenant
Second Lieutenant	Ensign	Second Lieutenant	Second Lieutenant
Chief Warrant Officer (in three grades)	Chief Warrant Officer (in three grades)	NA	Chief Warrant Officer (in three grades)
Warrant Officer	Warrant Officer	NA	Warrant Officer
Sergeant Major of the Army	Master Chief Petty Officer of the Navy	Chief Master Sergeant of the Air Force	Sergeant Major of the Marine Corps
Command Sergeant Major / Sergeant Major	Master Chief Petty Officer	Chief Master Sergeant	Sergeant Major / Master Gunnery Sergeant
First Sergeant / Master Sergeant	Senior Chief Petty Officer	Senior Master Sergeant	First Sergeant / Master Sergeant
Sergeant First Class	Chief Petty Officer	Master Sergeant	Gunnery Sergeant
Staff Sergeant	Petty Officer First Class	Technical Sergeant	Staff Sergeant
Sergeant	Petty Officer Second Class	Staff Sergeant	Sergeant
Corporal / Specialist 4	Petty Officer Third Class	Sergeant / Senior Airman	Corporal
Private First Class	Seaman	Airman First Class	Lance Corporal
Private	Seaman Apprentice	Airman	Private First Class
Private (no insignia)	Seaman Recruit	Airman Basic (no insignia)	Private (no insignia)

NA = not applicable

rank′ scale′, *Ling.* (in systemic linguistics) a hierarchical ordering of grammatical units such that a unit of a given rank normally consists of units of the next lower rank, as, in English, the ordering sentence, clause, group or phrase, word, morpheme.

rank•shift (rangk′shift′), *Ling.* —*v.t.* **1.** (in systemic linguistics) to use a unit as a constituent of another unit of the same or lower rank on the rank scale, as in using the phrase *next door* within the phrase *the boy next door* or the clause *that you met yesterday* within the phrase *the girl that you met yesterday.* —*n.* **2.** the process of rankshifting. [1960–65; RANK[1] + SHIFT]

ran•sack (ran′sak), *v.t.* **1.** to search thoroughly or vigorously through (a house, receptacle, etc.): *They ransacked the house for the missing letter.* **2.** to search through for plunder; pillage: *The enemy ransacked the entire town.* [1200–50; ME *ransaken* < ON *rannsaka* to search, examine (for evidence of crime), equiv. to *rann* house + *saka* search (var. of *soekja* to SEEK)] —**ran′•sack•er,** *n.*

ran•som (ran′səm), *n.* **1.** the redemption of a prisoner, slave, or kidnapped person, of captured goods, etc., for a price. **2.** the sum or price paid or demanded. **3.** a means of deliverance or rescue from punishment for sin, esp. the payment of a redemptive fine. —*v.t.* **4.** to redeem from captivity, bondage, detention, etc., by paying a demanded price. **5.** to release or restore on receipt of a ransom. **6.** to deliver or redeem from punishment for sin. [1150–1200; (n.) ME *ransoun* < OF *rançon* < LL *redēmptiōn-* (s. of *redēmptiō*) REDEMPTION; (v.) ME *ransounen* < OF *rançonner,* deriv. of *rançon*] —**ran′som•er,** *n.*
—**Syn. 1.** deliverance, liberation, release. **4.** See **redeem.**

Ran•som (ran′səm), *n.* **John Crowe** (krō), 1888–1974, U.S. poet, critic, and teacher.

rant (rant), *v.i.* **1.** to speak or declaim extravagantly or violently; talk in a wild or vehement way; rave: *The demagogue ranted for hours.* —*v.t.* **2.** to utter or declaim in a ranting manner. —*n.* **3.** ranting, extravagant, or violent declamation. **4.** a ranting utterance. [1590–1600; < D *ranten* (obs.) to talk foolishly] —**rant′•er,** *n.* —**rant′ing•ly,** *adv.*
—**Syn. 3.** bombast, extravagance.

Ran•toul (ran to͞ol′), *n.* a city in E Illinois. 20,161.

ran•u•la (ran′yə lə), *n. Pathol.* a cystic tumor formed beneath the tongue, caused by obstruction of the sublingual or submaxillary gland or of a mucous gland. [1650–60; < L *rānula* little frog, swelling, equiv. to *rān(a)* frog + *-ula* -ULE] —**ran′u•lar,** *adj.*

ra•nun•cu•la•ceous (rə nung′kyə lā′shəs), *adj.* belonging to the Ranunculaceae, the buttercup family of plants. Cf. **buttercup family.** [1825–35; < NL *Ranunculac(eae)* name of family (*Ranuncul(us)* genus name (L *rānunculus* little frog; *rān(a)* frog + *-unculus* dim. suffix, extracted from n-stem derivatives; see HOMUNCULUS) + *-aceae* -ACEAE) + -OUS]

ra•ob (rā′ob), *n. Meteorol.* a radiosonde or rawinsonde observation. Cf. **rawin.** [*ra(diosonde) ob(servation)*]

Ra•oult's′ law′ (rä o͞olz′), *Physical Chem.* the principle that the fraction by which the vapor pressure of a solvent is lowered by the addition of a nonvolatile, nonelectrolytic solute is equal to the mole fraction of the solute in the solution. [1890–95; named after François *Raoult* (1830–1901), French chemist and physicist]

rap[1] (rap), *v.,* **rapped, rap•ping,** *n.* —*v.t.* **1.** to strike, esp. with a quick, smart, or light blow: *He rapped the door with his cane.* **2.** to utter sharply or vigorously: *to rap out a command.* **3.** (of a spirit summoned by a medium) to communicate (a message) by raps (often fol. by *out*). **4.** *Slang.* to criticize sharply: *Critics could hardly wait to rap the play.* **5.** *Slang.* to arrest, detain, or sentence for a crime. **6.** *Metall.* to jar (a pattern) loose from a sand mold. —*v.i.* **7.** to knock smartly or lightly, esp. so as to make a noise: *to rap on a door.* **8.** *Slang.* to talk or discuss, esp. freely, openly, or volubly; chat. **9.** *Slang.* to talk rhythmically to the beat of rap music. —*n.* **10.** a quick, smart, or light blow: *a rap on the knuckles with a ruler.* **11.** the sound produced by such a blow: *They heard a loud rap at the door.* **12.** *Slang.* blame or punishment, esp. for a crime. **13.** *Slang.* a criminal charge: *a murder rap.* **14.** *Slang.* response, reception, or judgment: *The product has been getting a very bad rap.* **15.** *Slang.* **a.** a talk, conversation, or discussion; chat. **b.** talk designed to impress, convince, etc.; spiel: *a high-pressure sales rap.* **16.** See **rap music. 17. beat the rap,** *Slang.* to succeed in evading the penalty for a crime; be acquitted: *The defendant calmly insisted that he would beat the rap.* **18. take the rap,** *Slang.* to take the blame and punishment for a crime committed by another: *He took the rap for the burglary.* [1300–50; 1960–65 for def. 8; ME *rappen* (v.), *rap(p)e* (n.); akin to Sw *rappa* to beat, drub, G *rappeln* to rattle; senses "to talk," "conversation, talk" perh. of distinct orig., though the hypothesis that it is a shortening of REPARTEE is questionable]

rap[2] (rap), *n.* **1.** the least bit: *I don't care a rap.* **2.** a counterfeit halfpenny formerly passed in Ireland. [1715–25; orig. uncert.]

rap[3] (rap), *v.t.,* **rapped** or **rapt, rap•ping.** *Archaic.* **1.** to carry off; transport. **2.** to transport with rapture. **3.** to seize for oneself; snatch. [1520–30; back formation from RAPT]

ra•pa•cious (rə pā′shəs), *adj.* **1.** given to seizing for plunder or the satisfaction of greed. **2.** inordinately greedy; predatory; extortionate: *a rapacious disposition.* **3.** (of animals) subsisting by the capture of living prey; predacious. [1645–55; < L *rapāci-* (s. of *rapāx* greedy, akin to *rapere* to seize; see RAPE[1]) + -OUS] —**ra•pa′cious•ly,** *adv.* —**ra•pac•i•ty** (rə pas′i tē), **ra•pa′cious•ness,** *n.*
—**Syn. 2.** ravenous, voracious, grasping; preying. See **avaricious.** —**Ant. 2.** generous.

Ra•pal•lo (rä päl′lô), *n.* a seaport in NW Italy, on the Gulf of Genoa: treaties 1920, 1922. 27,042.

Ra•pa Nu•i (rä′pə no͞o′ē). See **Easter Island.**

rape[1] (rāp), *n., v.,* **raped, rap•ing.** —*n.* **1.** the unlawful compelling of a woman through physical force or duress to have sexual intercourse. **2.** any act of sexual intercourse that is forced upon a person. **3.** See **statutory rape. 4.** an act of plunder, violent seizure, or abuse; despoliation; violation: *the rape of the countryside.* **5.** *Archaic.* the act of seizing and carrying off by force. —*v.t.* **6.** to force to have sexual intercourse. **7.** to plunder (a place); despoil. **8.** to seize, take, or carry off by force. —*v.i.* **9.** to commit rape. [1250–1300; (v.) ME *rapen* < AF *raper* < L *rapere* to seize, carry off by force, plunder; (n.) ME < AF *ra(a)p(e),* deriv. of *raper*] —**rap′a•ble, rape′a•ble,** *adj.* —**rap′ist, rap′er,** *n.*

rape[2] (rāp), *n.* a plant, *Brassica napus,* of the mustard family, whose leaves are used for food for hogs, sheep, etc., and whose seeds yield rape oil. [1350–1400; ME (< MF) < L *rāpum* (neut.), *rāpa* (fem.) turnip; c. Gk *rháp̄ys*]

rape[3] (rāp), *n.* the residue of grapes, after the juice has been extracted, used as a filter in making vinegar. [1590–1600; < F *râpe* < Gmc; cf. OHG *raspōn* to scrape]

Rape′ of Lu•crece′, The (lo͞o krēs′, lo͞o′krēs), a narrative poem (1594) by Shakespeare.

Rape′ of the Lock′, The, a mock-epic poem (1712) by Alexander Pope.

rape′ oil′, *Chem.* a brownish-yellow oil obtained by expression from rapeseed and used chiefly as a lubricant, an illuminant, and in the manufacture of rubber substitutes. Also called **rape′seed oil′, colza oil.** [1535–45]

rape•seed (rāp′sēd′), *n.* **1.** the seed of the rape. **2.** the plant itself. [1525–35; RAPE[2] + SEED]

rap′ full′, *Naut.* **1.** (of a sail or sails) filled with wind; clean full. **2.** with all sails full of wind. [1865–70]

rap′ group′, an informal discussion group, often supervised by a trained leader, that meets to discuss shared concerns or interests. [1965–70]

Raph•a•el (raf′ē əl, rā′fē-, rä′fī el′), *n.* **1.** (*Raffaello Santi* or *Sanzio*) 1483–1520, Italian painter. **2.** one of the archangels. **3.** a male given name: from a Hebrew word meaning "healing of the Lord."

Raph•a•el•esque (raf′ē ə lesk′, rā′fē-, rä′fē-), *adj.* of, pertaining to, or characteristic of the style of the painter Raphael. [1830–35; RAPHAEL + -ESQUE]

ra•phe (rā′fē), *n., pl.* **-phae** (-fē). **1.** *Anat.* a seamlike union between two parts or halves of an organ or the like. **2.** *Bot.* **a.** (in certain ovules) a ridge connecting the hilum with the chalaza. **b.** a median line or slot on a cell wall of a diatom. [1745–55; < NL < Gk *rhaphḗ* seam, suture, akin to *rháptein* to sew, stitch together]

ra•phi•a (rā′fē ə, raf′ē ə), *n.* raffia.

raph•i•des (raf′i dēz′), *n.pl. Bot.* acicular crystals, usually composed of calcium oxalate, that occur in bundles in the cells of many plants. [1835–45; < NL < Gk *rhaphídes,* pl. of *rhaphís* needle]

-raphy, var. of **-rraphy.**

rap•id (rap′id), *adj.,* **-er, -est,** *n.* —*adj.* **1.** occurring within a short time; happening speedily: *rapid growth.* **2.** moving or acting with great speed; swift: *a rapid worker.* **3.** characterized by speed: *rapid motion.* —*n.* **4.** Usually, **rapids.** a part of a river where the current runs very swiftly. [1625–35; < L *rapidus* tearing away, seizing, swift. See RAPE[1], -ID[4]] —**rap′id•ly,** *adv.*
—**Syn. 2.** See **quick.**

Rap•i•dan (rap′i dan′), *n.* a river in N Virginia, flowing E from the Blue Ridge Mountains into the Rappahannock River: Civil War battle 1862.

Rap′id Cit′y, a city in SW South Dakota. 46,492.

Rap′id Deploy′ment Force′, a U.S. military organization consisting of one Marine division and four Army divisions, established in 1979 to respond quickly to any distant threat to national interests.

rap′id eye′ move′ment. rapidly shifting, continuous movements of the eyes beneath closed lids during the stage of sleep characterized by dreaming. Also called **REM** [1915–20]

rap′id eye′ move′ment sleep′. See **REM sleep.** [1960–65]

rap′id fire′, *Mil.* a rate of firing small arms that is intermediate between slow fire and quick fire.

rap•id-fire (rap′id fīər′), *adj.* **1.** characterized by, delivered, or occurring in rapid succession: *rapid-fire questions; rapid-fire events.* **2.** *Mil.* discharging in rapid fire: *rapid-fire rifles.* **3.** discharging, operating, etc., at a rate more rapid than normal: *a rapid-fire staple gun.* [1885–90]

ra•pid•i•ty (rə pid′i tē), *n.* a rapid state or quality; quickness; celerity. Also, **rap•id•ness** (rap′id nis). [1610–20; < L *rapiditās.* See RAPID, -ITY]
—**Syn.** swiftness, fleetness. See **speed.**

rap′idly advanc′ing ju′venile periodonti′tis, *Dentistry.* a rare, rapidly progressive and destructive infectious periodontal disease that usually affects the front teeth and first permanent molars of children.

ra•pi•do (rä′pē dō′; *Sp.* Rä′pē t͟hō′; *It.* Rä′pē dô), *n., pl.* **-dos** (-dōz′; *Sp.* -t͟hōs′), *It.* **-di** (-dē). (esp. in Spain, Italy, and Latin America) an express train. [1955–60; < It *rapido,* Sp *rápido* (n. use of adj.). See RAPID]

rap′id tran′sit, a system of public transportation in a metropolitan area, usually a subway or elevated train system. Cf. **mass transit.** [1870–75, *Amer.*] —**rap′•id-tran′sit,** *adj.*

ra•pi•er (rā′pē ər), *n.* **1.** a small sword, esp. of the 18th century, having a narrow blade and used for thrusting. **2.** a longer, heavier sword, esp. of the 16th and 17th centuries, having a double-edged blade and used for slashing and thrusting. [1545–55; < MF *(espee) rapiere* lit., rasping (sword); see RAPE[3]] —**ra′pi•ered,** *adj.*

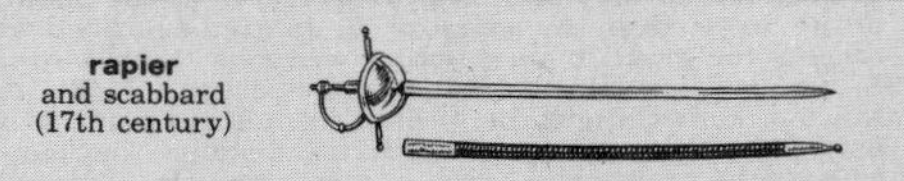
rapier and scabbard (17th century)

rap•ine (rap′in, -īn), *n.* the violent seizure and carrying off of another's property; plunder. [1375–1425; late ME < L *rapīna* robbery, pillage. See RAPE[1], -INE[2]]

ra•pi•ni (ra pē′nē), *n.* the leaves of the turnip, *Brassica rapa,* eaten cooked or raw as greens. Also, **rappini.** [perh. < It, pl. of *rapino* a plant of the genus *Erysimum,* perh. orig. dim. of *rapa* RAPE[2]]

rap′ mu′sic, a style of popular music, developed by disc jockeys and urban blacks in the late 1970's, in which an insistent, recurring beat pattern provides the background and counterpoint for rapid, slangy, and often boastful rhyming patter glibly intoned by a vocalist or vocalists. Also called **rap.**

Rapp (rap; *Ger.* räp), *n.* **George,** 1757–1847, U.S. religious preacher, born in Germany: leader of the Harmonists.

Rap•pa•han•nock (rap′ə han′ək), *n.* a river flowing SE from N Virginia into the Chesapeake Bay: Civil War battle 1863. 185 mi. (300 km) long.

rap•pa•ree (rap′ə rē′), *n.* **1.** an armed Irish freebooter or plunderer, esp. of the 17th century. **2.** any freebooter or robber. [1680–90; < Ir *rapaire*]

rap•pee (ra pē′), *n.* a strong snuff made from dark,

CONCISE ETYMOLOGY KEY: <, descended or borrowed from; >, whence; b., blend of, blended; c., cognate with; cf., compare; deriv., derivative; equiv., equivalent; imit., imitative; obl., oblique; r., replacing; s., stem; sp., spelling, spelled; resp., respelling, respelled; trans., translation; ?, origin unknown; *, unattested; ‡, probably earlier than. See the full key inside the front cover.

rank tobacco leaves. [1730–40; < F *râpé* grated (ptp. of *râper*); see RAPE[3]]

rap•pel (ra pel′, rə-), *n.*, *v.*, **-pelled, -pel•ling.** —*n.* **1.** (in mountaineering) the act or method of moving down a steep incline or past an overhang by means of a double rope secured above and placed around the body, usually under the left thigh and over the right shoulder, and paid out gradually in the descent. —*v.i.* **2.** to descend by means of a rappel. [1930–35; < F: mountaineering term, lit., a recall. See REPEAL]

rap•pen (rä′pən), *n.*, *pl.* **rap•pen.** a bronze coin and monetary unit of Switzerland; centime. [1830–40; < Swiss G; late MHG *rappen* a type of coin first minted in Alsace, lit., raven (a jocular reference to the eagle on the coin), declensional var. of MHG *rappe,* a by-form of *raben,* OHG *hraban;* see RAVEN[1]]

rap′pé pie′ (rap′ē, rä′pē), *Canadian* (*chiefly the Maritime Provinces*). a pie containing grated potatoes and chicken, duck, or rabbit meat. Also, **rap′pie pie′.** [1930–35; < CanF (Acadian) (*tarte*) *râppée* grated (pie); see RAPE[3]]

rap•per (rap′ər), *n.* **1.** a person or thing that raps or knocks. **2.** the knocker of a door. **3.** *Slang.* a person who chats or talks, esp. freely. **4.** a person who performs rap music, esp. professionally. [1605–15; 1970–75, *Amer.* for def. 3; RAP[1] + -ER[1]]

rap•ping (rap′ing), *n.* **1.** the act or sound of a person or thing that raps. **2.** communication by the sound of taps or knocks, as between medium and spirit during a séance. [1350–1400; ME. See RAP[1], -ING[1]]

rap•pi•ni (ra pē′nē), *n.* rapini.

Rapp•ist (rap′ist), *n.* Harmonist. Also, **Rapp•ite** (rap′īt). [1835–45, *Amer.*; after G. RAPP; see -IST]

rap•port (ra pôr′, -pōr′, rə-), *n.* relation; connection, esp. harmonious or sympathetic relation: *a teacher trying to establish close rapport with students.* [1530–40; < F, deriv. of *rapporter* to bring back, report, equiv. to *r(e)-* RE- + *apporter* (OF *aporter* < L *apportāre,* equiv. to *ap-* AP-[1] + *portāre* to carry; see PORT[5])]
—**Syn.** fellowship, camaraderie, understanding.

rap•por•teur (rap′ôr tûr′; *Fr.* RA pôr tœr′), *n.*, *pl.* **-teurs** (-tûrz′; *Fr.* -tœr′). a person responsible for compiling reports and presenting them, as to a governing body. [1490–1500; < F, deriv. of *rapporter.* See RAPPORT, -EUR]

rap•proche•ment (rap′rōsh män′; *Fr.* RA prôsh-män′), *n.* an establishment or reestablishment of harmonious relations: *a rapprochement reached between warring factions.* [1800–10; < F, equiv. to *rapproche(r)* to bring near, bring together (*r(e)-* RE- + *approcher;* see APPROACH) + *-ment* -MENT]
—**Syn.** reconciliation, understanding, accommodation.

rap•scal•lion (rap skal′yən), *n.* a rascal; rogue; scamp. [1690–1700; earlier *rascallion,* based on RASCAL]

rap′ ses′sion, a usually informal or unstructured group discussion, attended esp. by people with shared interests, concerns, or problems. [1965–70]

rap′ sheet′, *Slang.* a record kept by law-enforcement authorities of a person's arrests and convictions. [1955–60; see RAP[1] (def. 12)]

rapt (rapt), *adj.* **1.** deeply engrossed or absorbed: *a rapt listener.* **2.** transported with emotion; enraptured: *rapt with joy.* **3.** showing or proceeding from rapture: *a rapt smile.* **4.** carried off spiritually to another place, sphere of existence, etc. [1350–1400; ME (ptp. of *rapen* to carry off, abduct, rape) < L *raptus* seized, carried off (ptp. of *rapere*), equiv. to *rap-* (see RAPE[1]) + *-tus* ptp. suffix] —**rapt′ly,** *adv.* —**rapt′ness,** *n.*
—**Syn. 2.** ecstatic, spellbound, bewitched.

rap•tor (rap′tər, -tôr), *n.* a raptorial bird. [1600–10; < L *raptor* one who seizes by force, robber, equiv. to *rap(ere)* (see RAPE[1]) + *-tor* -TOR]

rap•to•ri•al (rap tôr′ē əl, -tōr′-), *adj.* **1.** preying upon other animals; predatory. **2.** adapted for seizing prey, as the bill or claws of a bird. **3.** belonging or pertaining to the Raptores, a former order in which the falconiform and strigiform birds were erroneously grouped together. [1815–25; < L *raptōr-* (s. of *raptor* RAPTOR) + -IAL]

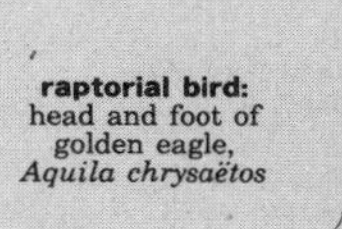

raptorial bird: head and foot of golden eagle, *Aquila chrysaëtos*

rap•ture (rap′chər), *n.*, *v.* **-tured, -tur•ing.** —*n.* **1.** ecstatic joy or delight; joyful ecstasy. **2.** Often, **raptures.** an utterance or expression of ecstatic delight. **3.** the carrying of a person to another place or sphere of existence. **4. the Rapture,** *Theol.* the experience, anticipated by some fundamentalist Christians, of meeting Christ midway in the air upon his return to earth. **5.** *Archaic.* the act of carrying off. —*v.t.* **6.** to enrapture. [1590–1600; RAPT + -URE] —**rap′ture•less,** *adj.*
—**Syn. 1.** bliss, beatitude; transport, exaltation. See **ecstasy.** —**Ant. 1.** misery.

rap•tured (rap′chərd), *adj. Theol.* (esp. of saints) experiencing religious ecstasy as a result of one's faith. [1675–85; RAPTURE + -ED[2]]

rap′ture of the deep′, *Pathol.* See **nitrogen narcosis.** [1950–55; coined by J. Y. Cousteau as a trans. of the F phrase *ivresse des grandes profondeurs*]

rap•tur•ous (rap′chər əs), *adj.* **1.** full of, feeling, or manifesting ecstatic joy or delight. **2.** characterized by, attended with, or expressive of such rapture: *rapturous praise.* [1670–80; RAPTURE + -OUS] —**rap′tur•ous•ly,** *adv.* —**rap′tur•ous•ness,** *n.*

rap•tus (rap′təs), *n.* a state of intense or overwhelming excitement; rapture; ecstasy. [1840–50; < L: a seizing, equiv. to *rap(ere)* to seize, abduct, RAPE[1] + *-tus* suffix of v. action]

ra•ra a•vis (râr′ə ā′vis; *Lat.* RÄ′RÄ Ä′wis), *pl.* **ra•rae a•ves** (râr′ē ā′vēz; *Lat.* RÄ′RĪ Ä′wes). a rare person or thing; rarity. [1600–10; < L *rāra avis* rare bird]

rare[1] (râr), *adj.*, **rar•er, rar•est. 1.** coming or occurring far apart in time; unusual; uncommon: *a rare disease; His visits are rare occasions.* **2.** thinly distributed over an area; few and widely separated: *Lighthouses are rare on that part of the coast.* **3.** having the component parts not closely compacted together; not dense: *rare gases; lightheaded from the rare mountain air.* **4.** unusually great: *a rare display of courage.* **5.** unusually excellent; admirable; fine: *She showed rare tact in inviting them.* [1350–1400; ME < L *rārus* loose, wide apart, thin, infrequent] —**rare′ness,** *n.*
—**Syn. 1.** exceptional, extraordinary, singular. **2.** sparse, infrequent. **5.** choice, incomparable, inimitable. —**Ant. 1.** common. **2.** frequent. **5.** inferior.

rare[2] (râr), *adj.*, **rar•er, rar•est.** (of meat) cooked just slightly: *He likes his steak rare.* [1645–55; var. of earlier *rear,* ME *rere,* OE *hrēr* lightly boiled] —**rare′ness,** *n.*

rare[3] (râr), *v.i.*, **rared, rar•ing.** *Older Use.* rear[2] (def. 6).

rare•bit (râr′bit), *n.* See **Welsh rabbit.** [1715–25]

rare′ book′, a book that is distinguished by its early printing date, its limited issue, the special character of the edition or binding, or its historical interest. [1890–95]

rare′ earth′, *Chem.* the oxide of any of the rare-earth elements contained in various minerals. [1875–80]

rare′-earth′ el′ement (râr′ûrth′), *Chem.* any of a group of closely related metallic elements, comprising the lanthanides, scandium, and yttrium, that are chemically similar by virtue of having the same number of valence electrons. Also called **rare′-earth′ met′al.** [1955–60]

rar′ee show′ (râr′ē), **1.** See **peep show. 2.** a carnival or street show; spectacle. [1695–1705; allegedly imit. of a foreign pron. of *rare show*]

rar•e•fac•tion (râr′ə fak′shən), *n.* **1.** the act or process of rarefying. **2.** the state of being rarefied. [1595–1605; < ML *rārēfactiōn-* (s. of *rārēfactiō*), equiv. to L *rārēfact(us)* (ptp. of *rārēfacere;* see RAREFY) + *-iōn-* -ION] —**rar′e•fac′tion•al,** *adj.* —**rar•e•fac•tive** (râr′ə-fak′tiv), *adj.*

rar•e•fied (râr′ə fīd′), *adj.* **1.** extremely high or elevated; lofty; exalted: *the rarefied atmosphere of a scholarly symposium.* **2.** of, belonging to, or appealing to an exclusive group; select; esoteric: *rarefied tastes.* [1625–35; RAREFY + -ED[2]]

rar•e•fy (râr′ə fī′), *v.*, **-fied, -fy•ing.** —*v.t.* **1.** to make rare or rarer; make less dense: *to rarefy a gas.* **2.** to make more refined, spiritual, or exalted. —*v.i.* **3.** to become rare or less dense; become thinned: *Moisture rarefies when heated.* [1350–1400; ME *rarefien* < MF *rarefier* < L *rārēfacere,* equiv. to *rārē-,* comb. form of *rārus* RARE[1] (for expected *rāri-;* orig. of *-ē-* unclear) + *facere* to make; see -FY] —**rar′e•fi′a•ble,** *adj.* —**rar′e•fi′er,** *n.*

rare•ly (râr′lē), *adv.* **1.** on rare occasions; infrequently; seldom: *I'm rarely late for appointments.* **2.** exceptionally; in an unusual degree. **3.** unusually or remarkably well; excellent. [1515–25; RARE[1] + -LY]

rare•ripe (râr′rīp′), *Bot.* —*adj.* **1.** ripening early. —*n.* **2.** a fruit or vegetable that ripens early. [1715–25, *Amer.; rare,* early var. (obs. except Brit. dial.) of RATHE + RIPE]

rar•ing (râr′ing), *adj. Informal.* very eager or anxious; enthusiastic: *raring to go.* [1905–10; RARE[3] + -ING[2]]

rar•i•ty (râr′i tē), *n.*, *pl.* **-ties. 1.** something rare, unusual, or uncommon: *Snowstorms are a rarity in the South.* **2.** something esteemed or interesting in being rare, uncommon, or curious: *That folio is a rarity that will bring a good price.* **3.** the state or quality of being rare. **4.** rare occurrence; infrequency: *Volcanic eruptions on the island occur with great rarity.* **5.** unusual excellence. **6.** thinness, as of air or a gas. [1550–60; < L *rāritās* thinness, equiv. to *rār(us)* RARE[1] + *-itās* -ITY]

Ra•ro•tong•a (rar′ə tong′gə), *n.* one of the Cook Islands, in the S Pacific, 11,433; 26 sq. mi. (67 sq. km). —**Ra′ro•tong′an,** *adj.*, *n.*

ra•sa (rus′ə), *n.* (in Hindu aesthetics) flavor, sentiment, or emotion: regarded as one of the fundamental qualities of classical music, dance, and poetry. [1790–1800; < Skt *rasa* sap, fluid, essence]

Ras Ad•dar (räs′ a där′). See **Bon, Cape.**

ras•bo•ra (raz bôr′ə, -bōr′ə, raz′bər ə), *n.* any of several minnows of the genus *Rasbora,* inhabiting fresh waters of southeastern Asia and the Malay Archipelago, esp. the silvery *R. heteromorpha,* that has a black triangular marking near the tail and is often kept in aquariums. [1930–35; < NL, of undetermined orig.]

ras•cal (ras′kəl), *n.* **1.** a base, dishonest, or unscrupulous person. **2.** a mischievous person or animal: *That child is a real rascal.* [1300–50; ME *rascaile, raskaille* < OF *rascaille* rabble; perh. akin to RASH[2]] —**ras′cal•like′,** *adj.*
—**Syn. 1.** rapscallion, scamp, villain, miscreant, scapegrace. See **knave.**

ras•cal•i•ty (ra skal′i tē), *n.*, *pl.* **-ties. 1.** rascally or knavish character or conduct. **2.** a rascally act. [1570–80; RASCAL + -ITY]

ras•cal•ly (ras′kə lē), *adj.* being, characteristic of, or befitting a rascal. —*adv.* **1.** in a rascally manner. [1590–1600; RASCAL + -LY]

ras•casse (ra skas′), *n.* any of several scorpionfishes, as *Scorpaena scrofa* or *S. porcus,* of the Mediterranean Sea, used in making bouillabaisse. [1920–25; < F < Pr *rascasso,* deriv. of *rasca* to scrape < VL **rāsicāre;* see RAZE]

rase (rāz), *v.t.*, **rased, ras•ing.** raze. —**ras′er,** *n.*

rash[1] (rash), *adj.* **-er, -est. 1.** acting or tending to act too hastily or without due consideration. **2.** characterized by or showing too great haste or lack of consideration: *rash promises.* [1350–1400; ME; c. D, G *rasch* quick, brisk, ON *rǫskr* brave] —**rash′ly,** *adv.* —**rash′•ness,** *n.*
—**Syn. 1.** hasty, impetuous, reckless, venturous, incautious, precipitate, indiscreet, foolhardy. —**Ant. 1.** cautious.

rash[2] (rash), *n.* **1.** an eruption or efflorescence on the skin. **2.** a multitude of instances of something occurring more or less during the same period of time: *a rash of robberies last month.* [1700–10; < F *rache* (obs.), OF *rasche* skin eruption, deriv. of *raschier* to scratch, ult. < L *rādere* to scratch] —**rash′like′,** *adj.*

rash•er[1] (rash′ər), *n.* **1.** a thin slice of bacon or ham for frying or broiling. **2.** a portion or serving of bacon, usually three or four slices. [1585–95; orig. uncert.]

rash•er[2] (rash′ər), *n.* See **vermilion rockfish.** [1875–80, *Amer.*; perh. < Sp *rascacio;* see RASCASSE]

Ra•shi (rä′shē), *n.* (*Solomon ben Isaac*) 1040–1105, French Hebrew scholar.

Ra•shi•da (rä shē′də, rä′shi dä′), *n.* a female given name: from a Swahili word meaning "righteous."

Rasht (rasht), *n.* a city in NW Iran, about 10 mi. (16 km) S of the Caspian Sea. 175,000. Also, **Resht.**

Rask (rask; *Dan.* räsk), *n.* **Ras•mus Chris•tian** (ras′-məs kris′chən; *Dan.* Räs′mŏŏs krēs′tyän), 1787–1832, Danish philologist.

Ras•kol•nik (rə skôl′nik), *n.*, *pl.* **-niks, -ni•ki** (-ni kē′). a member of any of several sects founded by dissenters from the Russian Orthodox Church who opposed the liturgical reforms of Nikon in the 17th century. Also called **Old Believer, Old Ritualist.** [< Russ *raskól′nik* schismatic, equiv. to *raskól* split, schism (n. deriv. of *raskolót′* to split; *ras-* v. prefix marking dissolution, fracture + *kolot′* to chop) + *-nik* agent suffix]

Ras•mus•sen (Ras′mŏŏ sən), *n.* **Knud Jo•han Vic•tor** (knōōth yō hän′ vēk′tôr), 1879–1933, Danish arctic explorer.

ra•son (Rä′sôn; *Eng.* ras′on), *n.*, *pl.* **ra•sa** (Rä′sä; *Eng.* ras′ə). *Gk. Orth. Ch.* a long, loose, black gown with wide sleeves, worn by the clergy. [1930–35; < MGk *rháson* a woolen cloth]

ras•o•phore (raz′ə fôr′, -fōr′), *n. Gk. Orth. Ch.* a monk authorized to wear the rason. [1885–90; < MGk *rhasophóros.* See RASON, -PHORE]

ra•so•ri•al (rə sôr′ē əl, -sōr′-), *adj.* **1.** given to scratching the ground for food, as chickens; gallinaceous. **2.** pertaining to a bird's foot adapted for scratching. [1830–40; < NL *Rasor(es)* former name of the order, LL *rāsōrēs,* pl. of *rāsor* scratcher (L *rād(ere)* to scrape, scratch + *-tor* -TOR, with *dt* > s; cf. RAZE) + -IAL]

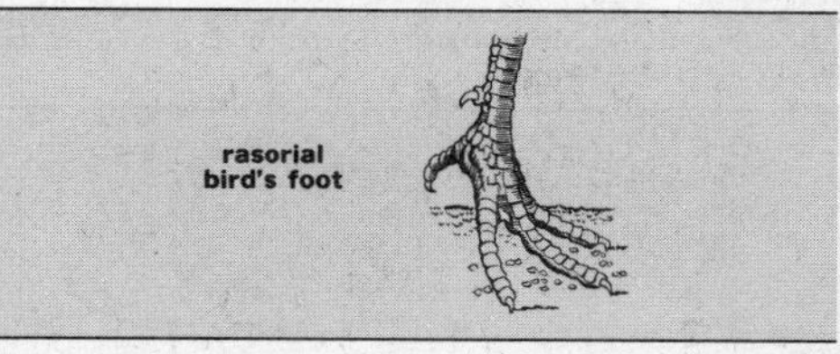

rasorial bird's foot

rasp (rasp, räsp), *v.t.* **1.** to scrape or abrade with a rough instrument. **2.** to scrape or rub roughly: *The glacier rasped the valley floor.* **3.** to grate upon or irritate: *The sound rasped his nerves.* **4.** to utter with a grating sound: *to rasp out an answer.* —*v.i.* **5.** to scrape or grate. **6.** to make a grating sound. —*n.* **7.** an act of rasping. **8.** a rasping sound. **9.** a coarse file, used mainly on wood, having separate conical teeth. **10.** (in an insect) a roughened surface used in stridulation. [1200–50; ME *raspen* < OF *rasper* to scrape, grate < Gmc; see RAPE[3]] —**rasp′ish,** *adj.*

rasp•ber•ry (raz′ber′ē, -bə rē, räz′-), *n.*, *pl.* **-ries. 1.** the fruit of any of several shrubs belonging to the genus *Rubus,* of the rose family, consisting of small and juicy red, black, or pale yellow drupelets forming a detachable cap about a convex receptacle. **2.** any shrub bearing this fruit. **3.** a dark reddish-purple color. **4.** *Informal.* **a.** See **Bronx cheer. b.** any sign or expression of dislike or derision. [1615–25; earlier *rasp(is)* raspberry (< ?) + BERRY; (def. 4) by shortening of *raspberry tart,* rhyming slang for *fart*]

rasp′berry saw′fly, a black sawfly, *Monophadnoides geniculatus,* the larvae of which feed on the leaves of the raspberry and blackberry.

rasp•er (ras′pər, rä′spər), *n.* **1.** a person or thing that rasps. **2.** a machine for scraping sugarcane. [1715–25; RASP + -ER[1]]

rasp•ing (ras′ping, rä′sping), *adj.* **1.** harsh; grating: *a rasping voice.* —*n.* **2.** a minute piece removed by rasping: *raspings of sawed wood.* **3. raspings,** dry bread crumbs. [1650–60; RASP + -ING[2], -ING[1]] —**rasp′ing•ly,** *adv.* —**rasp′ing•ness,** *n.*

Ra•spu•tin (ra spyōō′tin, -tn; *Russ.* RU spōō′tyin), *n.* **1. Gri•go•ri E•fi•mo•vich** (gri gôr′ē i fē′mə vich; *Russ.* gRyi gô′Ryē yi fyē′mə vyich), 1871–1916, Siberian peasant monk who was very influential at the court of Czar Nicholas II and Czarina Alexandra. **2.** any person who exercises great but insidious influence.

rasp•y (ras′pē, rä′spē), *adj.*, **rasp•i•er, rasp•i•est. 1.**

CONCISE PRONUNCIATION KEY: act, cāpe, dâre, pärt; set, ēqual; *if,* īce; ox, ōver, ôrder, oil, bŏŏk, bōōt, out; up, ûrge; child; sing; shoe; thin, *that;* zh as in *treasure.* ə = *a* as in *alone, e* as in *system, i* as in *easily, o* as in *gallop, u* as in *circus;* ᵊ as in *fire* (fīᵊr), *hour* (ouᵊr). l and n can serve as syllabic consonants, as in *cradle* (krād′l), and *button* (but′n). See the full key inside the front cover.

harsh; grating; rasping. **2.** easily annoyed; irritable. [1830–40; RASP + -Y[1]] **—rasp′i•ness,** *n.*

Ras Sham•ra (räs shäm′rə), a locality in W Syria, near the Mediterranean Sea: site of ancient Ugarit; many archaeologically important objects dating to the Bronze Age.

ras•sle (ras′əl), *v.i., v.t.,* **-sled, -sling,** *n. Dial.* wrestle.

Ras•ta (ras′tə, rä′stə), *n.* **1.** Rastafarian (def. 1). **2.** Rastafarianism. *—adj.* **3.** Rastafarian (def. 2). [by shortening]

Ras•ta•far•i (ras′tə fâr′ē, -fär′ē, -fâr′ī, rä′stə-; *in Jamaica often* rä′stä fä rī′), *n.* **1.** Rastafarian (def. 1). **2.** Rastafarianism. *—adj.* **3.** Rastafarian (def. 2).

Ras•ta•far•i•an (ras′tə fâr′ē ən, -fär′-, rä′stə-), *n.* **1.** a follower of Rastafarianism. *—adj.* **2.** of, pertaining to, or characteristic of Rastafarianism or Rastafarians. [< Amharic *ras tāfāri* Prince Tafari, the pre-coronation name of Haile Selassie (*ras* prince, orig., head; *tāfāri* an Amharic personal name, lit., (one to be) feared, respected, prp. from passive s. *fārra* (v.) fear, respect) + -AN]

Ras•ta•far•i•an•ism (ras′tə fâr′ē ə niz′əm, -fär′-, rä′stə-), *n.* a religious cult, originally of Jamaica, that regards Africa as the Promised Land, to which all true believers will someday return, and the late Haile Selassie I, former emperor of Ethiopia, as the messiah. [RASTAFARIAN + -ISM]

ras•ter (ras′tər), *n.* **1.** *Television.* a pattern of scanning lines covering the area upon which the image is projected in the cathode-ray tube of a television set. **2.** *Computers.* a set of horizontal lines composed of individual pixels, used to form an image on a CRT or other screen. [1950–55; < G < L *rāstrum* toothed hoe, rake, deriv. of *rādere* to scratch, scrape]

ras•tle (ras′əl), *v.i., v.t.,* **-tled, -tling,** *n. Dial.* wrestle.

ra•sure (rā′zhər, -shər), *n.* an erasure. [< MF < LL *rāsūra,* equiv. to L *rās(us)* (ptp. of *rādere* to scratch, scrape; cf. RASORIAL, RAZE) + *-ūra* -URE]

rat (rat), *n., interj., v.,* **rat•ted, rat•ting.** *—n.* **1.** any of several long-tailed rodents of the family Muridae, of the genus *Rattus* and related genera, distinguished from the mouse by being larger. **2.** any of various similar or related animals. **3.** *Slang.* a scoundrel. **4.** *Slang.* **a.** a person who abandons or betrays his or her party or associates, esp. in a time of trouble. **b.** an informer. **c.** a scab laborer. **5.** a pad with tapered ends formerly used in women's hair styles to give the appearance of greater thickness. **6. smell a rat,** to suspect or surmise treachery; have suspicion: *After noting several discrepancies in his client's story, the attorney began to smell a rat.* *—interj.* **7. rats,** *Slang.* (an exclamation of disappointment, disgust, or disbelief.) *—v.i.* **8.** *Slang.* **a.** to desert one's party or associates, esp. in a time of trouble. **b.** to turn informer; squeal: *He ratted on the gang, and the police arrested them.* **c.** to work as a scab. **9.** to hunt or catch rats. *—v.t.* **10.** to dress (the hair) with or as if with a rat. [bef. 1000; ME *rat(t)e,* OE *ræt;* c. D *rat,* G *Ratz, Ratte*] **—rat′like′,** *adj.*

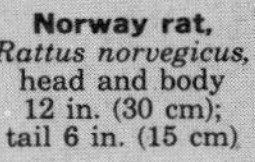

Norway rat, *Rattus norvegicus,* head and body 12 in. (30 cm); tail 6 in. (15 cm)

rat•a•ble (rā′tə bəl), *adj.* **1.** capable of being rated or appraised. **2.** proportional: *ratable distribution of wealth.* Also, **rateable.** [1495–1505; RATE[1] + -ABLE] **—rat′a•bil′i•ty, rat′a•ble•ness,** *n.* **—rat′a•bly,** *adv.*

rat•a•fi•a (rat′ə fē′ə), *n.* a sweet liqueur made from wine or grape juice combined with brandy or other spirits and often flavored with almonds, fruit, or fruit kernels. Also, **rat•a•fee** (rat′ə fē′). [1690–1700; < F]

ratafi′a bis′cuit, *Brit.* a macaroon.

rat•al (rāt′l), *n. Brit.* the amount on which rates or taxes are assessed. [1855–60; RATE[1] + -AL[1]]

ra•tan (ra tan′, rə-), *n.* rattan.

rat•a•plan (rat′ə plan′), *n., v.,* **-planned, -plan•ning.** *—n.* **1.** a sound of or as of the beating of a drum. *—v.i.* **2.** to produce such a sound. [1840–50; < F; imit.]

rat-a-tat (rat′ə tat′), *n.* a sound of knocking or rapping: *a sharp rat-a-tat on the window.* Also, **rat′-a-tat′-tat′.** [1675–85; imit.]

ra•ta•touille (rat′ə to͞o′ē, -twē′; *Fr.* RA TA to͞o′yᵊ), *n.* a vegetable stew of Provence, typically consisting of eggplant, zucchini, onions, green peppers, tomatoes, and garlic, served hot or cold. [1875–80; < F]

rat′bite fe′ver (rat′bīt′), *Pathol.* either of two relapsing febrile diseases, widely distributed geographically, caused by infection with *Streptobacillus moniliformis* or *Spirillum minor* and transmitted by rats. [1905–10; RAT + BITE]

rat•catch•er (rat′kach′ər), *n.* **1.** a person, animal, or thing that catches and exterminates rats, esp. a person whose business it is to rid a property of rats. **2.** *Chiefly Brit.* an informal fox-hunting costume, as a tweed jacket and tan riding breeches. [1585–95; RAT + CATCHER]

ratch (rach), *n.* a ratchet.

rat′ cheese′, *Informal.* inexpensive cheese, esp. domestic cheddar. [1935–40, *Amer.;* presumably so called because it is deemed suitable only for rattraps]

CONCISE ETYMOLOGY KEY: <, descended or borrowed from; >, whence; b., blend of, blended; c., cognate with; cf., compare; deriv., derivative; equiv., equivalent; imit., imitative; obl., oblique; r., replacing; s., stem; sp., spelling, spelled; resp., respelling, respelled; trans., translation; ?, origin unknown; *, unattested; ‡, probably earlier than. See the full key inside the front cover.

ratch•et (rach′it), *n.* **1.** a toothed bar with which a pawl engages. **2.** (not in technical use) a pawl or the like used with a ratchet or ratchet wheel. **3.** a mechanism consisting of such a bar or wheel with the pawl. **4.** See **ratchet wheel. 5.** a steady progression up or down: *the upward ratchet of oil prices.* *—v.t., v.i.* **6.** to move by degrees (often fol. by *up* or *down*): *to ratchet prices up; Interest rates have been ratcheting downward.* [1650–60; alter. of F *rochet;* MF *rocquet* a blunt lance-head < Gmc]

ratch′et effect′, intermittent growth, increase, expansion, or the like: *the ratchet effect of defense expenditures.* [1965–70]

ratch′et jack′, a screw jack rotated by a ratchet mechanism. [1870–75]

ratch′et wheel′, a wheel, with teeth on the edge, into which a pawl drops or catches, as to prevent reversal of motion or convert reciprocating motion into rotatory motion. [1770–80]

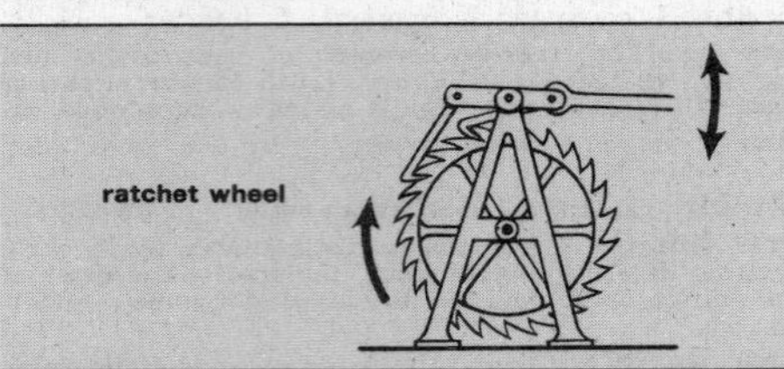

ratchet wheel

rat′ claw′ foot′, *Furniture.* an elongated foot having the form of a thin claw grasping a ball.

rate[1] (rāt), *n., v.,* **rat•ed, rat•ing.** *—n.* **1.** the amount of a charge or payment with reference to some basis of calculation: *a high rate of interest on loans.* **2.** a certain quantity or amount of one thing considered in relation to a unit of another thing and used as a standard or measure: *at the rate of 60 miles an hour.* **3.** a fixed charge per unit of quantity: *a rate of 10 cents a pound.* **4.** price; cost: *to cut rates on all home furnishings.* **5.** degree of speed, progress, etc.: *to work at a rapid rate.* **6.** degree or comparative extent of action or procedure: *the rate of increase in work output.* **7.** relative condition or quality; grade, class, or sort. **8.** assigned position in any of a series of graded classes; rating. **9.** *Insurance.* the premium charge per unit of insurance. **10.** a charge by a common carrier for transportation, sometimes including certain services involved in rendering such transportation. **11.** a wage paid on a specified time basis: *a salary figured on an hourly rate.* **12.** a charge or price established in accordance with a scale or standard: *hotel rates based on length of stay.* **13.** *Horol.* the relative adherence of a timepiece to perfect timekeeping, measured in terms of the amount of time gained or lost within a certain period. **14.** Usually, **rates.** *Brit.* **a.** a tax on property for some local purpose. **b.** any tax assessed and paid to a local government, as any city tax or district tax. **15. at any rate, a.** in any event; in any case. **b.** at least: *It was a mediocre film, but at any rate there was one outstanding individual performance.* *—v.t.* **16.** to estimate the value or worth of; appraise: *to rate a student's class performance.* **17.** to esteem, consider, or account: *He was rated one of the best writers around.* **18.** to fix at a certain rate, as of charge or payment. **19.** to value for purposes of taxation or the like. **20.** to make subject to the payment of a certain rate or tax. **21.** to place in a certain rank, class, etc., as a ship or a sailor; give a specific rating to. **22.** to be considered or treated as worthy of; merit: *an event that doesn't even rate a mention in most histories of the period.* **23.** to arrange for the conveyance of (goods) at a certain rate. *—v.i.* **24.** to have value, standing, etc.: *a performance that didn't rate very high in the competition.* **25.** to have position in a certain class. **26.** to rank very high in estimation: *The new teacher really rates with our class.* [1375–1425; (n.) late ME *rate* monetary value, estimated amount, proportional part < ML *rata* < L (*prō*) *ratā* (*parte*) (according to) an estimated (part), *ratā* abl. sing. of *rata,* fem. of *ratus,* ptp. of *rērī* to judge; (v.) late ME *raten* to estimate the value (of), deriv. of the n.]
—Syn. 5. pace. **16.** rank, classify, measure.

rate[2] (rāt), *v.t., v.i.,* **rat•ed, rat•ing.** to chide vehemently; scold. [1350–1400; ME *(a)raten,* perh. < Scand; cf. Sw, Norw *rata* to reject] **—rat′er,** *n.*

rate•a•ble (rā′tə bəl), *adj.* ratable. **—rate′a•bil′i•ty, rate′a•ble•ness,** *n.* **—rate′a•bly,** *adv.*

rate′ base′, 1. a guaranteed minimum amount or number used to compute advertising rates, as the number of subscribers to a publication. **2.** a basic amount or number used to compute charges to a customer, as the number of monthly phone calls. **3.** the valuation of property upon which tax rates are based.

rate′ card′, a list showing the rates charged by a magazine, newspaper, radio or television station, etc., for various types of advertising. [1900–05, *Amer.*]

rat′ed load′, 1. the load a machine or vehicle is rated to carry. **2.** the power an engine, dynamo, etc., is rated at or designed to produce. [1920–25]

ra•tel (rāt′l, rät′l), *n.* a badgerlike carnivore, *Mellivora capensis,* of Africa and India. Also called **honey badger.** [1770–80; < Afrik < D dial. *ratel,* var. of *raat* honeycomb; perh. orig. a compound with this word, referring to the animal's fondness for honey]

ratel, *Mellivora capensis,* 11 in. (28 cm) high at shoulder; head and body 2 ft. (0.6 m); tail 9 in. (23 cm)

rate′-of-climb′ in′dicator (rāt′əv klīm′), *Aeron.* a flight instrument that indicates the rate of climb or descent of an aircraft. [1945–50]

rate′ of exchange′. See **exchange rate.** [1720–30]

rate•pay•er (rāt′pā′ər), *n.* **1.** a person who pays a regular charge for the use of a public utility, as gas or electricity, usually based on the quantity consumed. **2.** *Brit.* a person who pays rates; a taxpayer of the local government. [1835–45; RATE[1] + PAYER] **—rate′pay′•ing,** *adj., n.*

rat•er (rā′tər), *n.* **1.** a person who makes rates or ratings. **2.** a person or thing that is of a specific rating (usually used in combination): *The show's star is a first-rater.* **3.** *Slang.* any of various small, popular yachts belonging to standard classes. [1605–15; RATE[1] + -ER[1]]

rat•fink (rat′fingk′), *n. Slang.* fink (defs. 3, 4). [1960–65; RAT + FINK]

rat•fish (rat′fish′), *n., pl.* (*esp. collectively*) **-fish,** (*esp. referring to two or more kinds or species*) **-fish•es.** a chimaera, *Hydrolagus colliei,* of the Pacific Ocean from Alaska to Lower California, having a ratlike tail. [1880–85, *Amer.;* RAT + FISH]

rat′ guard′, a disk of sheet metal fitted around a hawser to prevent rats from boarding a vessel moored at a dock.

Rath•bone (rath′bōn), *n.* **Basil,** 1892–1967, English actor, born in South Africa.

rathe (rāth), *adj. Archaic.* growing, blooming, or ripening early in the year or season. Also, **rath** (rath). [bef. 900; ME; OE *hræth, hræd* quick, active; c. D *rad,* ON *hrathr*] **—rathe′ly,** *adv.* **—rathe′ness,** *n.*

Ra•the•nau (rät′n ou′), *n.* **Wal•ther** (väl′tər), 1867–1922, German industrialist, writer, and statesman.

rath•er (*adv.* rath′ər, rä′thər; *interj.* rath′ûr′, rä′-thûr′), *adv.* **1.** in a measure; to a certain extent; somewhat: *rather good.* **2.** in some degree: *I rather thought you would regret it.* **3.** more properly or justly; with better reason: *The contrary is rather to be supposed.* **4.** sooner; more readily or willingly: *to die rather than yield.* **5.** more properly or correctly speaking; more truly: *He is a painter or, rather, a watercolorist.* **6.** on the contrary: *It's not generosity, rather self-interest.* **7. had** or **would rather,** to prefer that or to: *I had much rather we not stay. We would rather go for dinner after the show.* *—interj.* **8.** *Chiefly Brit.* emphatically yes; assuredly; without doubt: *Is the book worth reading? Rather!* [bef. 900; ME; OE *hrathor,* comp. of *hræth* quick, RATHE]

Rath′ke's pouch′ (rät′kəz), *Embryol.* an invagination of stomodeal ectoderm developing into the anterior lobe of the pituitary gland. Also called **Rath′ke's pock′•et.** [1940–45; named after Martin Heinrich *Rathke* (1793–1860), German anatomist]

rat•hole (rat′hōl′), *n.* **1.** a hole made by a rat, as into a room, barn, etc.: *The first chore in the old building is to plug up the ratholes.* **2.** the burrow or shelter of a rat. **3.** any small and uncomfortable room, office, apartment, etc., esp. one that is dirty or disordered: *He lives in a rathole near the docks.* **4. down the rathole,** for a worthless purpose or purposes: *seeing your inheritance disappear down the rathole.* [1805–15; RAT + HOLE]

raths•kel•ler (rät′skel′ər, rat′-, rath′-), *n.* **1.** (in Germany) the cellar of a town hall, often used as a beer hall or restaurant. **2.** a restaurant patterned on the German rathskeller, usually located below street level. [1860–65; < G, equiv. to *Rath* (extracted from *Rathaus* town hall) + -s 's[1] + *Keller* CELLAR]

rat•i•cide (rat′ə sīd′), *n.* a substance or preparation for killing rats. [1840–50; RAT + -I- + -CIDE] **—rat′i•cid′al,** *adj.*

rat•i•fi•ca•tion (rat′ə fi kā′shən), *n.* **1.** the act of ratifying; confirmation; sanction. **2.** the state of being ratified. [1400–50; late ME < ML *ratificātiōn-* (s. of *ratificātiō*), equiv. to *ratificāt(us)* (ptp. of *ratificāre* to RATIFY) + *-iōn-* -ION] **—rat′i•fi•ca′tion•ist,** *n., adj.*

rat•i•fy (rat′ə fī′), *v.t.,* **-fied, -fy•ing. 1.** to confirm by expressing consent, approval, or formal sanction: *to ratify a constitutional amendment.* **2.** to confirm (something done or arranged by an agent or by representatives) by such action. [1325–75; ME *ratifien* < MF *ratifier* < ML *ratificāre,* equiv. to L *rat(us)* calculated (see RATE[1]) + *-ificāre* -IFY] **—rat′i•fi′er,** *n.*
—Syn. 1. corroborate, approve. **2.** validate, establish.
—Ant. 1. veto, disapprove.

rat•i•né (rat′n ā′; *Fr.* RA tē nā′), *n.* a loosely woven fabric made with nubby or knotty yarns. Also, **ra•ti•ne** (rat′n ā′, ra tēn′). Also called **sponge cloth.** [1675–85; < F, ptp. of *ratiner* to make a nap on cloth]

rat•ing[1] (rā′ting), *n.* **1.** classification according to grade or rank. **2.** assigned position in a particular class or grade, or relative standing, as of a ship or a member of the armed forces. **3.** the credit standing of a person or firm. **4.** *Radio, Television.* a percentage indicating the number of listeners to or viewers of a specific program. **5.** a designated operating limit for a machine, apparatus, etc., as of voltage, load, or frequency, based on specified conditions. **6.** an amount fixed as a rate. **7.** *Brit.* apportioning of a tax. **8.** *Chiefly Brit.* one of the enlisted personnel in the British navy. [1525–35; RATE[1] + -ING[1]]

rat•ing[2] (rā′ting), *n.* an angry reprimand or rebuke; scolding. [1570–80; RATE[2] + -ING[1]]

rat′ing badge′, *U.S. Navy.* a badge that indicates the rank and specialty of a petty officer: worn on the upper left sleeve. [1905–10]

rat′ing nut′, *Horol.* a nut that screws onto the lower end of the rod of a clock pendulum for raising or lowering the weight to alter the rate of the clock.

ra•tio (rā′shō, -shē ō′), *n., pl.* **-tios. 1.** the relation between two similar magnitudes with respect to the number of times the first contains the second: *the ratio of 5 to 2, written 5:2 or 5/2.* **2.** proportional relation; rate: *the* ratio between acceptances and rejections. **3.** *Finance.* the relative value of gold and silver in a bimetallic currency system. [1630–40; < L *ratiō* a reckoning, account, calculation, deriv. (see -TION) of the base of *rērī* to judge, think]

ra•ti•oc•i•nate (rash′ē os′ə nāt′, -ō′sə-, rat′ē-), *v.i.*, **-nat•ed, -nat•ing.** to reason; carry on a process of reasoning. [1635–45; < L *ratiōcinātus* ptp. of *ratiōcinārī* to reckon, calculate, conclude, v. deriv. of *ratiō* reason] **—ra′ti•oc′i•na′tor,** *n.*

ra•ti•oc•i•na•tion (rash′ē os′ə nā′shən, -ō′sə-, rat′ē-), *n.* the process of logical reasoning. [1520–30; < L *ratiōcinātiōn-* (s. of *ratiōcinātiō*), equiv. to *ratiōcināt(us)* (see RATIOCINATE) + *-iōn-* -ION] **—ra′ti•oc′i•na′tive,** *adj.*

ra•ti•om•e•ter (rā′shē om′i tər), *n.* (in three-color photography) a device for determining the exposure factors of the filters to be used. [1920–25, for an earlier sense; RATIO + -METER]

ra•tion (rash′ən, rā′shən), *n.* **1.** a fixed allowance of provisions or food, esp. for soldiers or sailors or for civilians during a shortage: *a daily ration of meat and bread.* **2.** an allotted amount: *They finally saved up enough gas rations for the trip.* **3. rations, a.** provisions: *Enough rations were brought along to feed all the marchers.* **b.** *Chiefly South Atlantic States.* food or meals: *The old hotel still has the best rations in town.* **—***v.t.* **4.** to supply, apportion, or distribute as rations (often fol. by *out*): *to ration out food to an army.* **5.** to supply or provide with rations: *to ration an army with food.* **6.** to restrict the consumption of (a commodity, food, etc.): *to ration meat during war.* **7.** to restrict the consumption of (a consumer): *The civilian population was rationed while the war lasted.* [1540–50; < F < L *ratiōn-* (s. of *ratiō*); see REASON]
—Syn. 1, 2. portion, allotment. **1, 3.** See **food. 4.** mete, dole, allot.

ra•tion•al (rash′ə nl, rash′nl), *adj.* **1.** agreeable to reason; reasonable; sensible: *a rational plan for economic development.* **2.** having or exercising reason, sound judgment, or good sense: *a calm and rational negotiator.* **3.** being in or characterized by full possession of one's reason; sane; lucid: *The patient appeared perfectly rational.* **4.** endowed with the faculty of reason: *rational beings.* **5.** of, pertaining to, or constituting reasoning powers: *the rational faculty.* **6.** proceeding or derived from reason or based on reasoning: *a rational explanation.* **7.** *Math.* **a.** capable of being expressed exactly by a ratio of two integers. **b.** (of a function) capable of being expressed exactly by a ratio of two polynomials. **8.** *Class. Pros.* capable of measurement in terms of the metrical unit or mora. **—***n.* **9.** *Math.* See **rational number.** [1350–1400; ME *racional* < L *ratiōnālis*, equiv. to *ratiōn-* (s. of *ratiō*) REASON + *-ālis* -AL[1]] **—ra′tion•al•ly,** *adv.* **—ra′tion•al•ness,** *n.*
—Syn. 2. intelligent, wise, judicious, sagacious, enlightened. **6.** See **reasonable. —Ant. 2.** stupid. **3.** insane.

ra•tion•ale (rash′ə nal′), *n.* **1.** the fundamental reason or reasons serving to account for something. **2.** a statement of reasons. **3.** a reasoned exposition of principles. [1650–60; < L: neut. of *ratiōnālis* RATIONAL]
—Syn. 1. logic, basis, grounds.

ra′tion•al-e•mo′tive ther′apy (rash′ə nl i mō′tiv), *Psychol.* a form of therapy in which a patient is asked to reject irrational attitudes and assumptions in order to deal effectively with stressful situations.

ra′tional form′, *Math.* a quotient of two polynomials with integral coefficients.

ra′tional func′tion, *Math.* a function that can be written as the quotient of two polynomials with integral coefficients. [1880–85]

ra•tion•al•ism (rash′ə nl iz′əm), *n.* **1.** the principle or habit of accepting reason as the supreme authority in matters of opinion, belief, or conduct. **2.** *Philos.* **a.** the doctrine that reason alone is a source of knowledge and is independent of experience. **b.** (in the philosophies of Descartes, Spinoza, etc.) the doctrine that all knowledge is expressible in self-evident propositions or their consequences. **3.** *Theol.* the doctrine that human reason, unaided by divine revelation, is an adequate or the sole guide to all attainable religious truth. **4.** *Archit.* (*often cap.*) **a.** a design movement principally of the mid-19th century that emphasized the development of modern ornament integrated with structure and the decorative use of materials and textures rather than as added adornment. **b.** the doctrines and practices of this movement. Cf. **functionalism** (def. 1). [1790–1800; RATIONAL + -ISM] **—ra′tion•al•ist,** *n.* **—ra′tion•al•is′tic, ra′tion•al•is′ti•cal,** *adj.* **—ra′tion•al•is′ti•cal•ly,** *adv.*

ra•tion•al•i•ty (rash′ə nal′i tē), *n., pl.* **-ties. 1.** the state or quality of being rational. **2.** the possession of reason. **3.** agreeableness to reason; reasonableness. **4.** the exercise of reason. **5.** a reasonable view, practice, etc. [1560–70; < LL *ratiōnālitās* reasonableness. See RATIONAL, -ITY]

ra•tion•al•ize (rash′ə nl īz′, rash′nl īz′), *v.*, **-ized, -iz•ing. —***v.t.* **1.** to ascribe (one's acts, opinions, etc.) to causes that superficially seem reasonable and valid but that actually are unrelated to the true, possibly unconscious and often less creditable or agreeable causes. **2.** to remove unreasonable elements from. **3.** to make rational or conformable to reason. **4.** to treat or explain in a rational or rationalistic manner. **5.** *Math.* to eliminate radicals from (an equation or expression): *to rationalize the denominator of a fraction.* **6.** *Chiefly Brit.* to reorganize and integrate (an industry). **—***v.i.* **7.** to invent plausible explanations for acts, opinions, etc., that are actually based on other causes: *He tried to prove that he was not at fault, but he was obviously rationalizing.* **8.** to employ reason; think in a rational or rationalistic manner. Also, esp. *Brit.,* **ra′tion•al•ise′.** [1810–20; RATIONAL + -IZE] **—ra′tion•al•i•za′tion,** *n.* **—ra′tion•al•iz′er,** *n.*
—Usage. Although RATIONALIZE retains its principal 19th-century senses "to make conformable to reason" and "to treat in a rational manner," 20th-century psychology has given it the now more common meaning "to ascribe (one's acts, opinions, etc.) to causes that seem reasonable but actually are unrelated to the true, possibly unconscious causes." Although the possibility of ambiguity exists, the context will usually make clear which sense is intended.

ra′tional num′ber, *Math.* a number that can be expressed exactly by a ratio of two integers. [1900–05]

ra′tional opera′tion, any of the mathematical operations of addition, subtraction, multiplication, and division. [1900–05]

ra′tio test′, *Math.* the theorem that a given infinite series converges if the absolute value of the ratio of the term succeeding the *n*th term to the *n*th term approaches a limit less than 1 as *n* increases without bound.

Rat•is•bon (rat′is bon′, -iz-), *n.* Regensburg.

rat•ite (rat′īt), *adj.* **1.** having a flat, unkeeled sternum, as an ostrich, cassowary, emu, or moa. **—***n.* **2.** a bird having a ratite breastbone. [1875–80; < L *rat(is)* raft + -ITE[2]]

rat-kan•ga•roo (rat′kang′gə ro͞o′), *n., pl.* **-roos.** any of several rabbit-sized, ratlike Australian kangaroos of the subfamily Potoroinae. [1840–50]

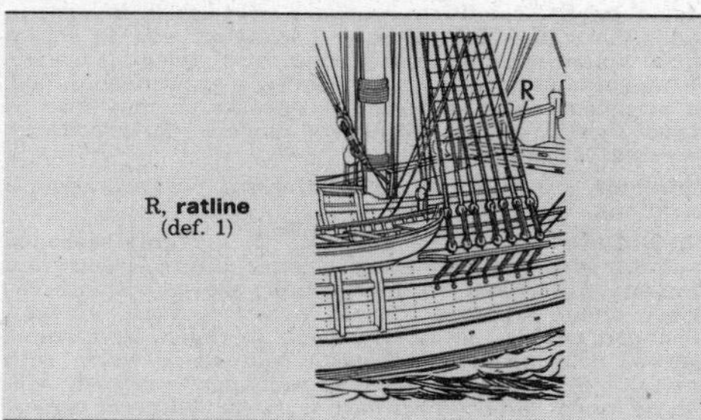

R, ratline
(def. 1)

rat•line (rat′lin), *n. Naut.* **1.** any of the small ropes or lines that traverse the shrouds horizontally and serve as steps for going aloft. **2.** Also, **rat′line stuff′.** three-stranded, right-laid, tarred hemp stuff of from 6 to 24 threads, used for ratlines, lashings, etc. Also, **rat′lin.** [1475–85; earlier *ratling, radelyng* < ?]

RATO (rā′tō), *n. Rocketry.* rocket-assisted takeoff.

ra•toon (ra to͞on′), *n.* **1.** a sprout or shoot from the root of a plant, esp. a sugarcane, after it has been cropped. **—***v.i., v.t.* **2.** to put forth or cause to put forth ratoons. Also, **rattoon.** [1625–35; < Sp *retoño* sprout, deriv. of *retoñar* to sprout again in the fall, equiv. to *re-* RE- + *-(o)toñar*, deriv. of *otoño* AUTUMN] **—ra•toon′er,** *n.*

rat′ race′, *Informal.* any exhausting, unremitting, and usually competitive activity or routine, esp. a pressured urban working life spent trying to get ahead with little time left for leisure, contemplation, etc. [1935–40, *Amer.*]

rats•bane (rats′bān′), *n.* **1.** rat poison. **2.** the trioxide of arsenic. [1515–25; RAT + -'S[1] + BANE]

rat′ snake′, any of several New and Old World colubrid snakes, of the genus *Elaphe*, that feed chiefly on small mammals and birds. Also called **house snake.** [1855–60]

rat's′ nest′. See **mare's nest** (def. 2).

rat-tail (rat′tāl′), *n.* grenadier (def. 4). Also, **rat′tail′.** [1695–1705]

rat′-tail cac′tus, a cactus, *Aporocactus flagelliformis*, of Mexico, having slim, cylindrical stems that are easily trained into strange designs, and crimson flowers. [1895–1900]

rat′tail comb′, a comb for the hair having a narrow, pointed handle used in styling the hair. [1975–80]

rat′-tailed mag′got (rat′tāld′), the aquatic larva of any of several syrphid flies of the genus *Eristalis*, that breathes through a long, thin tube at the posterior end of its body.

rat′-tail file′, a long, narrow file having a circular cross section. [1840–50]

rat•tan (ra tan′, rə-), *n.* **1.** Also called **rattan′ palm′.** any of various climbing palms of the genus *Calamus* or allied genera. **2.** the tough stems of such palms, used for wickerwork, canes, etc. **3.** a stick or switch of this material. Also, **ratan.** [1650–60; by uncert. mediation < Malay *rotan*, alleged to derive from *rout* scrape off, with *-an* nominalizing suffix]

rat•teen (ra tēn′), *n. Obs.* ratiné.

rat•ter (rat′ər), *n.* a person, animal, or thing that catches rats, as a terrier or a cat. [1825–35; RAT + -ER[1]]

rat′ ter′rier, a terrier of any of several breeds developed esp. for catching rats, as the Manchester terrier. [1850–55]

Rat•ti•gan (rat′i gən), *n.* **Terence,** 1911–77, English playwright.

rat•tish (rat′ish), *adj.* **1.** of, pertaining to, characteristic of, or resembling a rat. **2.** infested with rats. [1680–90; RAT + -ISH[1]]

rat•tle[1] (rat′l), *v.*, **-tled, -tling,** *n.* **—***v.i.* **1.** to give out or cause a rapid succession of short, sharp sounds, as in consequence of agitation and repeated concussions: *The windows rattled in their frames.* **2.** to move or go, esp. rapidly, with such sounds: *The car rattled along the highway.* **3.** to talk rapidly; chatter: *He rattled on for an hour about his ailments.* **—***v.t.* **4.** to cause to rattle: *He rattled the doorknob violently.* **5.** to drive, send, bring, etc., esp. rapidly, with rattling sounds: *The wind rattled the metal can across the roadway.* **6.** to utter or perform in a rapid or lively manner: *to rattle off a list of complaints.* **7.** to disconcert or confuse (a person): *A sudden noise rattled the speaker.* **8.** *Hunting.* to stir up (a cover). **—***n.* **9.** a rapid succession of short, sharp sounds, as from the collision of hard bodies. **10.** an instrument contrived to make a rattling sound, esp. a baby's toy filled with small pellets that rattle when shaken. **11.** the series of horny, interlocking elements at the end of the tail of a rattlesnake, with which it produces a rattling sound. **12.** a rattling sound in the throat, as the death rattle. [1250–1300; ME *ratelen* (v.), *ratele* (n.) (c. D *ratelen*, G *rasseln*); imit.]
—Syn. 1. clatter, knock. **7.** discompose. **9.** clatter.

rat•tle[2] (rat′l), *v.t.*, **-tled, -tling.** *Naut.* to furnish with ratlines (usually fol. by *down*). [1720–30; back formation from *ratling* RATLINE (taken as verbal n.)]

rat•tle•brain (rat′l brān′), *n.* a giddy, empty-headed, talkative person. [1700–10; RATTLE[1] + BRAIN]

rat•tle•brained (rat′l brānd′), *adj.* foolish; flighty; scatterbrained. [1710–20; RATTLE + BRAIN + -ED[3]]

rat•tle-bush (rat′l bo͝osh′), *n.* See **blue false indigo.** [1740–50]

rat•tle•head (rat′l hed′), *n.* a rattlebrain. [1635–45; RATTLE[1] + HEAD] **—rat′tle•head′ed,** *adj.*

rat•tle•pate (rat′l pāt′), *n.* a rattlebrain. [1635–45; RATTLE[1] + PATE] **—rat′tle•pat′ed,** *adj.*

rat•tler (rat′lər), *n.* **1.** a rattlesnake. **2.** a person or thing that rattles. **3.** *Informal.* a fast freight train. [1400–50; late ME; see RATTLE[1], -ER[1]]

rat•tle•snake (rat′l snāk′), *n.* any of several New World pit vipers of the genera *Crotalus* and *Sistrurus*, having a rattle composed of a series of horny, interlocking elements at the end of the tail. [1620–30, *Amer.*; RATTLE[1] + SNAKE]

timber rattlesnake,
Crotalus horridus,
length 3½ to 6 ft.
(1 to 1.8 m)

rat′tlesnake fern′, any of several American grape ferns, esp. *Botrychium virginianum*, having clusters of sporangia resembling the rattles of a rattlesnake. [1805–15, *Amer.*]

rat′tlesnake mas′ter, 1. any of various plants of the genus *Eryngium*, esp. *E. yuccifolium*, having spiny leaves and dense, rounded flower heads. **2.** any of several other plants, esp. of the genus *Liatris.* [1800–10, *Amer.*]

rat′tlesnake plan′tain, any of several low, terrestrial orchids, as *Goodyera repens*, of northern temperate regions, having a basal rosette of leaves with white veins and a one-sided spike of white flowers. [1770–80, *Amer.*]

rat′tlesnake root′, 1. any of certain composite plants of the genus *Prenanthes*, whose roots or tubers have been regarded as a remedy for snake bites, as *P. serpentaria* or *P. alba.* **2.** the root or tuber. **3.** the snakeroot, *Polygala senega.* **4.** its root. [1675–85]

rat′tlesnake weed′, 1. a hawkweed, *Hieracium venosum*, of eastern North America, whose leaves and root are thought to possess medicinal properties. **2.** a carrotlike weed, *Daucus pusillus*, of southern and western North America. **3.** any of certain other plants, as an umbelliferous plant, *Eryngium aquaticum.* **4.** See **rattlesnake plantain.** [1750–60, *Amer.*]

rat•tle•trap (rat′l trap′), *n.* a shaky, rattling object, as a rickety vehicle. [1760–70; RATTLE[1] + TRAP[1]]

rat•tling (rat′ling), *adj.* **1.** that rattles: *a rattling door.* **2.** remarkably good, lively, or fast: *a rattling talk; a rattling gallop.* **—***adv.* **3.** very: *a rattling good time.* [1350–1400; ME *ratelinge;* see RATTLE[1], -ING[2]] **—rat′•tling•ly,** *adv.*

rat•tly (rat′lē), *adj.* tending to rattle; making or having a rattling sound. [1880–85; RATTLE[1] + -Y[1]]

rat•ton (rat′n), *n. Dial.* a rat. [1250–1300; ME *ratoun* < OF *raton*, dim. of *rat* RAT]

rat•toon (ra to͞on′), *n., v.i., v.t.* ratoon.

rat•trap (rat′trap′), *n.* **1.** a device for catching rats. **2.** a run-down, filthy, or dilapidated place. **3.** a difficult, involved, or entangling situation. [1425–75; late ME. See RAT, TRAP[1]]

rat•ty (rat′ē), *adj.*, **-ti•er, -ti•est. 1.** full of rats. **2.** of or characteristic of a rat. **3.** wretched; shabby: *a ratty old overcoat.* **4.** *Slang.* irritable or angry; bad-tempered; nasty: *I always feel ratty when I wake up.* [1860–65; RAT + -Y[1]]

Rau (rou), *n.* **San•tha Ra•ma** (san′thə rä′mə), born 1923, Indian writer and astrologer.

rau•cous (rô′kəs), *adj.* **1.** harsh; strident; grating: *raucous voices; raucous laughter.* **2.** rowdy; disorderly: *a raucous party.* [1760–70; < L *raucus* hoarse, harsh, rough; see -OUS] **—rau′cous•ly,** *adv.* **—rau′cous•ness, rau•ci•ty** (rô′si tē), *n.*

CONCISE PRONUNCIATION KEY: *act, cāpe, dâre, pärt; set, ēqual; if, īce; ox, ōver, ôrder, oil, bo͝ok, bo͞ot, out; up, ûrge; child; sing; shoe; thin, that;* zh as in *treasure.* ə = *a* as in *alone, e* as in *system, i* as in *easily, o* as in *gallop, u* as in *circus;* ᵊ as in *fire* (fīᵊr), *hour* (ouᵊr). l and n can serve as syllabic consonants, as in *cradle* (krād′l), and *button* (but′n). See the full key inside the front cover.

—**Syn.** **1.** rough, jarring, raspy. —**Ant.** **1.** soft, mellow, dulcet.

raunch (rônch, ränch), *n. Informal.* **1.** smuttiness or vulgarity; crudeness; obscenity: *porno magazines and other purveyors of raunch.* **2.** slovenliness; grubbiness. **3.** an earthy, raw musical style derived from blues and gospel: *a singer who can go easily from raunch to rock.* [1960–65, *Amer.*; back formation from RAUNCHY]

raun·chy (rôn′chē, rän′-), *adj.* **-chi·er, -chi·est.** *Informal.* **1.** vulgar or smutty; crude; earthy; obscene: *a raunchy joke.* **2.** dirty; slovenly; grubby. **3.** lecherous. [1935–40, *Amer.*; orig. uncert.] —**raun′chi·ly,** *adv.* —**raun′chi·ness,** *n.*

Rau·schen·berg (rou′shən bûrg′), *n.* **Robert,** born 1925, U.S. artist.

Rau·schen·busch (rou′shən bo͝osh′), *n.* **Walter,** 1861–1918, U.S. clergyman and social reformer.

rau·wol·fi·a (rô wo͝ol′fē ə, rou-), *n.* **1.** any tropical tree or shrub of the genus *Rauwolfia,* as *R. serpentina,* of India. **2.** an extract from the roots of the rauwolfia, *R. serpentina,* containing alkaloids the most important of which is reserpine: used in medicine chiefly for the treatment of hypertension and as a sedative. [1745–55; < NL, named after L. *Rauwolf,* 16th-century German botanist; see -IA]

rav·age (rav′ij), *v.,* **-aged, -ag·ing,** *n.* —*v.t.* **1.** to work havoc upon; damage or mar by ravages: *a face ravaged by grief.* —*v.i.* **2.** to work havoc; do ruinous damage. —*n.* **3.** havoc; ruinous damage: *the ravages of war.* **4.** devastating or destructive action. [1605–15; < F, MF, equiv. to *rav(ir)* to RAVISH + *-age* -AGE] —**rav′age·ment,** *n.* —**rav′ag·er,** *n.*

—**Syn.** **1.** ruin, despoil, plunder, pillage, sack. RAVAGE, DEVASTATE, LAY WASTE all refer, in their literal application, to the wholesale destruction of a countryside by an invading army (or something comparable). LAY WASTE has remained the closest to the original meaning of destruction of land: *The invading army laid waste the towns along the coast.* But RAVAGE and DEVASTATE are used in reference to other types of violent destruction and may also have a purely figurative application. RAVAGE is often used of the results of epidemics: *The Black Plague ravaged 14th-century Europe;* and even of the effect of disease or suffering on the human countenance: *a face ravaged by despair.* DEVASTATE, in addition to its concrete meaning (*vast areas devastated by bombs*), may be used figuratively: *a devastating remark.* **4.** ruin, waste, desolation. —**Ant.** **1.** build, repair. **4.** creation.

Ra·va·na (rä′və nə), *n.* (in the Ramayana) the king of Ceylon who abducts Sita, the wife of Ramachandra, and is later defeated by Ramachandra.

rave[1] (rāv), *v.,* **raved, rav·ing,** *n., adj.* —*v.i.* **1.** to talk wildly, as in delirium. **2.** to talk or write with extravagant enthusiasm: *She raved about her trip to Europe.* **3.** (of wind, water, storms, etc.) to make a wild or furious sound; rage. —*v.t.* **4.** to utter as if in madness. —*n.* **5.** an act of raving. **6.** an extravagantly enthusiastic appraisal or review of something. **7.** *Chiefly Brit. Slang.* a boisterous party, esp. a dance. —*adj.* **8.** extravagantly flattering or enthusiastic: *rave reviews of a new play.* [1325–75; 1915–25 for def. 2; ME *raven* (v.), prob. < MF *resver* to wander, be delirious] —**rav′er,** *n.*

rave[2] (rāv), *n.* a vertical sidepiece of a wagon or other vehicle. [1520–30; alter. of dial. *rathe,* ME < ?]

rave′ hook′, *Naut.* a hooklike tool for reaming old oakum out of seams in planking. [1840–50; perh. obs. *rave* to drag, pull, ME *raven* < ?]

rav·el (rav′əl), *v.,* **-eled, -el·ing** or (*esp. Brit.*) **-elled, -el·ling,** *n.* —*v.t.* **1.** to disentangle or unravel the threads or fibers of (a woven or knitted fabric, rope, etc.). **2.** to tangle or entangle. **3.** to involve; confuse; perplex. **4.** to make clear; unravel (often fol. by *out*). —*v.i.* **5.** to become disjoined thread by thread or fiber by fiber; fray. **6.** to become tangled. **7.** to become confused or perplexed. **8.** (of a road surface) to lose aggregate. —*n.* **9.** a tangle or complication. [1575–85; < D *rafelen*] —**rav′el·er;** *esp. Brit.,* **rav′el·ler,** *n.* —**rav′el·ly,** *adj.*

Ra·vel (rə vel′; *Fr.* RA vel′), *n.* **Mau·rice Jo·seph** (mō rēs′ zhō zef′), 1875–1937, French composer.

rave·lin (rav′lin), *n. Fort.* a V-shaped outwork outside the main ditch and covering the works between two bastions. [1580–90; < MF, earlier *revelin* < It *rivellino,* dim. of *riva* bank, rim]

rav·el·ing (rav′ə ling), *n.* something raveled out, as a thread drawn or separated from a knitted or woven fabric. Also, *esp. Brit.,* **rav′el·ling.** [1650–60; RAVEL + -ING[1]]

rav·el·ment (rav′əl mənt), *n.* entanglement; confusion. [1825–35; RAVEL + -MENT]

ra·ven[1] (rā′vən), *n.* **1.** any of several large, corvine birds having lustrous, black plumage and a loud, harsh call, esp. *Corvus corax,* of the New and Old Worlds. **2.** the divine culture hero and trickster of the North Pacific Coast Indians. **3.** (*cap.*) *Astron.* the constellation Corvus. —*adj.* **4.** lustrous black: *raven locks of hair.* [bef. 900; ME; OE *hrǣfn;* c. G *Rabe,* ON *hrafn*] —**ra′ven·like′,** *adj.*

raven[1], *Corvus corax,* length 26 in. (66 cm)

CONCISE ETYMOLOGY KEY: <, descended or borrowed from; >, whence; b., blend of, blended; c., cognate with; cf., compare; deriv., derivative; equiv., equivalent; imit., imitative; obl., oblique; r., replacing; s., stem; sp., spelling, spelled; resp., respelling, respelled; trans., translation; ?, origin unknown; *, unattested; ‡, probably earlier than. See the full key inside the front cover.

rav·en[2] (rav′ən), *v.i.* **1.** to seek plunder or prey. **2.** to eat or feed voraciously or greedily: *to raven like an animal.* **3.** to have a ravenous appetite. —*v.t.* **4.** to seize as spoil or prey. **5.** to devour voraciously. —*n.* **6.** rapine; robbery. **7.** plunder or prey. Also, **ravin.** [1485–95; earlier *ravine* < MF *raviner,* ult. < L *rapīna* RAPINE]

Raven, The, a lyric poem (1845) by Edgar Allan Poe.

rav·en·ing (rav′ə ning), *adj.* **1.** rapacious; voracious. —*n.* **2.** rapacity. [1520–30; RAVEN[2] + -ING[2], -ING[1]] —**rav′en·ing·ly,** *adv.*

—**Syn.** **1.** See **ravenous.**

Ra·ven·na (rə ven′ə; *for 1 also It.* rä ven′nä), *n.* **1.** a city in NE Italy: the capital of Italy in the period of the Byzantine Empire; tomb of Dante. 138,352. **2.** a city in NE Ohio. 11,987.

rav·en·ous (rav′ə nəs), *adj.* **1.** extremely hungry; famished; voracious: *feeling ravenous after a hard day's work.* **2.** extremely rapacious: *a ravenous jungle beast.* **3.** intensely eager for gratification or satisfaction. [1350–1400; ME < OF *ravineus,* equiv. to *ravin(er)* to RAVEN[2] + *-eus* -OUS] —**rav′en·ous·ly,** *adv.* —**rav′en·ous·ness,** *n.*

—**Syn.** **1.** greedy, starved, devouring. RAVENOUS, RAVENING, VORACIOUS suggest a greediness for food and usually intense hunger. RAVENOUS implies extreme hunger, or a famished condition: *ravenous wild beasts.* RAVENING adds the idea of fierceness and savagery, esp. as shown in a violent manner of acquiring food: *ravening wolves.* VORACIOUS implies craving or eating a great deal of food: *a voracious child; a voracious appetite.* It may also be used figuratively: *a voracious reader.* **2.** predatory. —**Ant.** **1.** sated.

rave-up (rāv′up′), *n. Brit. Informal.* a party, esp. a wild one. [1965–70]

ra·vi·gote (*Fr.* RA vē gôt′), *n.* **1.** a highly seasoned velouté with white wine and vinegar, butter, cream, and mushrooms cooked in liquor, usually served hot with variety meats and poultry. **2.** a sauce of oil, vinegar, chopped capers, parsley, chervil, tarragon, and onion, served cold with vegetables or seafood or warm with meat. [1820–30; < F, deriv. of *ravigoter* to refresh; MF, equiv. to *ra-* (alter. of *re-* RE-) + *vigoter* (alter. of *vigorer* to be vigorous; see VIGOR)]

rav·in (rav′in), *v.i., v.t., n.* raven[2].

ra·vine (rə vēn′), *n.* a narrow steep-sided valley commonly eroded by running water. [1400–50; late ME < MF: torrent, OF: a violent rushing; see RAVEN[2]] —**ra·vine′y,** *adj.*

ra·vined (rə vēnd′), *adj.* marked or furrowed with ravines. [1850–55; RAVINE + -ED[3]]

rav·ing (rā′ving), *adj.* **1.** talking wildly; delirious; frenzied: *a raving maniac.* **2.** *Informal.* extraordinary or remarkable: *a raving beauty.* —*adv.* **3.** furiously or wildly: *a remark that made me raving mad.* —*n.* **4.** Usually, **ravings. a.** irrational, incoherent talk: *Putting him in a straitjacket did not stop his ravings.* **b.** wildly extravagant or outrageous talk; bombast. [1400–50; late ME; see RAVE, -ING[2], -ING[1]] —**rav′ing·ly,** *adv.*

ra·vi·o·li (rav′ē ō′lē, rä′vē-; *It.* rä vyô′lē), *n.* (*used with a singular or plural v.*) small cases of pasta, often square, stuffed with a filling, usually of meat or cheese, and often served with a tomato sauce. [1835–45; < It, pl. of dial. *raviolo* little turnip, dim. of *rava* < L *rāpa;* see RAPE[2]]

rav·ish (rav′ish), *v.t.* **1.** to fill with strong emotion, esp. joy. **2.** to seize and carry off by force. **3.** to carry off (a woman) by force. **4.** to rape (a woman). [1250–1300; ME *ravishen* < MF *raviss-,* long s. of *ravir* to seize << L *rapere;* see RAPE[1]] —**rav′ished·ly,** *adv.* —**rav′ish·er,** *n.*

—**Syn.** **1.** enrapture, transport, enthrall, delight, captivate.

rav·ish·ing (rav′i shing), *adj.* extremely beautiful or attractive; enchanting; entrancing. [1300–50; ME; see RAVISH, -ING[2]] —**rav′ish·ing·ly,** *adv.*

rav·ish·ment (rav′ish mənt), *n.* **1.** rapture or ecstasy. **2.** violent removal. **3.** the forcible abduction of a woman. **4.** rape[1] (def. 1). [1470–80; < MF *ravissement,* equiv. to *raviss-* (see RAVISH) + *-ment* -MENT]

raw (rô), *adj.,* **-er, -est,** *n.* —*adj.* **1.** uncooked, as articles of food: *a raw carrot.* **2.** not having undergone processes of preparing, dressing, finishing, refining, or manufacture: *raw cotton.* **3.** unnaturally or painfully exposed, as flesh, by removal of the skin or natural integument. **4.** painfully open, as a sore or wound. **5.** crude in quality or character; not tempered or refined by art or taste: *raw humor.* **6.** ignorant, inexperienced, or untrained: *a raw recruit.* **7.** brutally or grossly frank: *a raw portrayal of human passions.* **8.** brutally harsh or unfair: *a raw deal; receiving raw treatment from his friends.* **9.** disagreeably damp and chilly, as the weather or air: *a raw, foggy day at the beach.* **10.** not diluted, as alcoholic spirits: *raw whiskey.* **11.** unprocessed or unevaluated: *raw data.* —*n.* **12.** a sore or irritated place, as on the flesh. **13.** unrefined sugar, oil, etc. **14. in the raw, a.** in the natural, uncultivated, or unrefined state: *nature in the raw.* **b.** *Informal.* in the nude; naked: *sunbathing in the raw.* [bef. 1000; ME; OE *hrēaw, hrǣw;* c. D *rauw,* G *roh;* akin to L *crūdus* raw (see CRUDE), *cruor* blood, Gk *kréas* raw flesh] —**raw′ish,** *adj.* —**raw′ish·ness,** *n.* —**raw′ly,** *adv.* —**raw′ness,** *n.*

—**Syn.** **2.** unprepared, rough, makeshift. RAW, CRUDE, RUDE refer to something not in a finished or highly refined state. RAW applies particularly to material not yet changed by a process, by manufacture, or by preparation for consumption: *raw cotton; raw leather.* CRUDE refers to that which still needs refining: *crude petroleum.* RUDE refers to what is still in a condition of rough simplicity or in a makeshift or roughly made form: *rude agricultural implements; the rude bridge that arched the flood.* **6.** undisciplined, green, unskilled, unpracticed. **9.** cold, wet. **10.** straight, neat. —**Ant.** **1.** cooked.

Ra·wal·pin·di (rä′wəl pin′dē), *n.* a city in N Pakistan: former provisional capital. 806,000.

raw·boned (rô′bōnd′), *adj.* having little flesh, esp. on a large-boned frame; gaunt. [1585–95; RAW + BONED]

raw′ fi′bers, textile fibers, as cotton or wool, or textile filaments, as silk or nylon, that have received no manipulation or treatment.

raw·hide (rô′hīd′), *n., v.,* **-hid·ed, -hid·ing.** —*n.* **1.** untanned skin of cattle or other animals. **2.** a rope or whip made of rawhide. —*v.t.* **3.** to whip with a rawhide. [1650–60; RAW + HIDE[2]]

ra·win (rā′win), *n.* a method of observation of upper-air winds conducted by means of a weather balloon tracked by radar or a radio direction finder. Cf. **raob, rawinsonde.** [1945–50; *ra(dio)* + *win(ds-aloft)*]

ra·win·sonde (rā′win sond′), *n.* a method of upper-atmosphere meteorological observation conducted by means of a radiosonde tracked by radar. Cf. **raob, rawin.** [1945–50; *ra(dar)* + *win(d)* + *(radio)sonde*]

Raw·lings (rô′lingz), *n.* **Marjorie Kin·nan** (ki nan′), 1896–1953, U.S. novelist and journalist.

Raw·lins (rô′linz), *n.* a town in S Wyoming. 11,547.

Raw·lin·son (rô′lin sən), *n.* **1. George,** 1812–1902, English historian. **2.** his brother, **Sir Henry Cres·wicke** (krez′ik), 1810–95, English archaeologist, diplomat, and soldier.

raw′ mate′rial, material before being processed or manufactured into a final form. [1790–1800]

raw′-pack meth′od (rô′pak′). See **cold pack** (def. 2).

raw′ score′, the original score, as of a test, before it is statistically adjusted. [1925–30]

raw′ sien′na. See under **sienna** (def. 1). [1885–90]

raw′ silk′, reeled silk that has not had the sericin removed. [1300–50; ME]

raw′ um′ber. See under **umber** (def. 1). [1890–95]

rax (raks), *Scot. and North Eng.* —*v.i.* **1.** to stretch oneself, as after sleeping. **2.** to extend the hand. —*v.t.* **3.** to elongate; stretch. [bef. 1000; ME (north) *raxen,* OE *raxan;* akin to OE *reccean* to stretch, G *recken*]

ray[1] (rā), *n.* **1.** a narrow beam of light. **2.** a gleam or slight manifestation: *a ray of hope.* **3.** a raylike line or stretch of something. **4.** light or radiance. **5.** a line of sight. **6.** *Physics, Optics.* **a.** any of the lines or streams in which light appears to radiate from a luminous body. **b.** the straight line normal to the wave front in the propagation of radiant energy. **c.** a stream of material particles all moving in the same straight line. **7.** *Math.* **a.** one of a system of straight lines emanating from a point. **b.** Also called **half-line.** the part of a straight line considered as originating at a point on the line and as extending in one direction from that point. **8.** any of a system of parts radially arranged. **9.** *Zool.* **a.** one of the branches or arms of a starfish or other radiate animal. **b.** one of the bony or cartilaginous rods in the fin of a fish. **10.** *Bot.* **a.** See **ray flower. b.** one of the branches of an umbel. **c.** See **vascular ray. d.** (in certain composite plants) the marginal part of the flower head. **11.** *Astron.* one of many long, bright streaks radiating from some of the large lunar craters. **12.** a prominent upright projection from the circlet of a crown or coronet, having a pointed or ornamented termination. **13. get** or **grab some rays,** *Slang.* to relax in the sun, esp. to sunbathe. —*v.i.* **14.** to emit rays. **15.** to issue in rays. —*v.t.* **16.** to send forth in rays. **17.** to throw rays upon; irradiate. **18.** to subject to the action of rays, as in radiotherapy. **19.** *Informal.* to make a radiograph of; x-ray. **20.** to furnish with rays or radiating lines. [1300–50; ME *raie, raye* < OF *rai* < L *radius* RADIUS] —**ray′like′,** *adj.*

—**Syn.** **1.** See **gleam.**

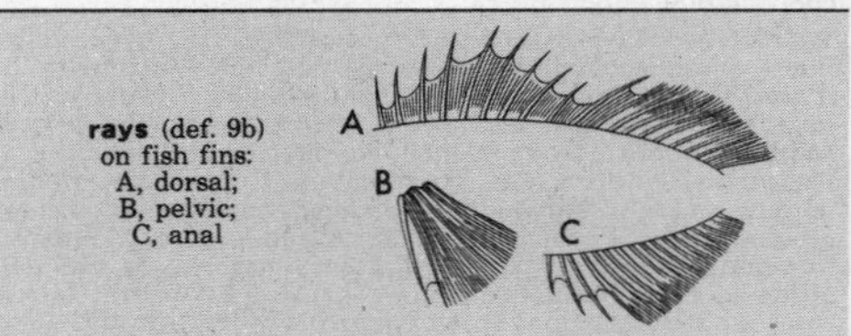

rays (def. 9b) on fish fins: A, dorsal; B, pelvic; C, anal

ray[2] (rā), *n.* any of numerous elasmobranch fishes, adapted for life on the sea bottom, having a flattened body and greatly enlarged pectoral fins with the gills on the undersides. [1275–1325; ME *raye* (< OF *rai*) < L *raia*]

Ray (rā *for 1, 2, 4, 5;* rī *for 3*), *n.* **1. John,** 1627?–1705, English naturalist. **2. Man** (man), 1890–1976, U.S. painter and photographer. **3. Sat·ya·jit** (sut′yə jit), 1921–92, Indian film director. **4.** a male given name, form of **Raymond. 5.** Also, **Raye.** a female given name, form of **Rachel.**

ra·yah (rä′yə, rī′ə), *n.* a Christian subject of an Ottoman ruler. Also, **ra′ya.** [1805–15; < Turk *reaya* < Ar *ra'īyah* subject, lit., flock; cf. RYOT]

Ray·burn (rā′bûrn), *n.* **Sam,** 1882–1961, U.S. lawyer and political leader: Speaker of the House 1940–47, 1949–53, 1955–61.

rayed (rād), *adj.* **1.** having or represented as having emanating rays; radiate: *The saint was painted with a rayed, beatific face.* **2.** having zoological or botanical rays (often used in combination): *a five-rayed fin.* [1740–50; RAY[1] + -ED[3]]

ray′ flow′er, *Bot.* one of the marginal florets surrounding the disk of tubular florets in the flower heads of certain composite plants, as the daisy. Also called **ray′ flo′ret.** [1850–55]

ray′ gun′, 1. a gun that can fire bursts of usually destructive or lethal rays: *a science fiction novel whose hero has a ray gun made of gold.* **2.** a child's futuristic toy gun that emits sparks, whirring noises, etc. [1930–35]

Ray·leigh (rā′lē), *n.* **John William Strutt** (strut), **3rd Baron,** 1842–1919, English physicist: Nobel prize 1904.

Ray′leigh disk′, *Acoustics, Mech.* a small circular disk, usually of mica, that is suspended from a fiber and tends to be deflected at right angles to a stream of air, indicating by its deflection the intensity of a sound wave. [1910–15; named after J. W. S. RAYLEIGH]

Ray′leigh scat′tering, *Optics.* the scattering of light by particles that are very small in relation to the wavelength of the light, and in which the intensity of the scattered light varies inversely with the fourth power of the wavelength. Cf. **Mie scattering.** [1935–40; named after J. W. S. RAYLEIGH]

Ray′leigh wave′, *Mech., Geol.* a wave along the surface of a solid, elastic body, esp. along the surface of the earth. [1915–20; named after J. W. S. RAYLEIGH]

ray·less (rā′lis), *adj.* **1.** lacking rays or raylike parts. **2.** unlit, dark, or gloomy: *a rayless cave.* [1755–45; RAY[1] + -LESS] **—ray′less·ness,** *n.*

Ray·mond (rā′mənd), *n.* **1. Henry Jar·vis** (jär′vis), 1820–69, U.S. publicist: founder of *The New York Times.* **2.** a male given name: from Germanic words meaning "counsel" and "protection."

Ray·naud's′ disease′ (rā nōz′), *Pathol.* a vascular disorder of unknown cause, characterized by recurrent episodes of blanching and numbness of the fingers and toes and sometimes the tip of the nose and ears, usually triggered by stress or exposure to cold. [1880–85; named after Maurice *Raynaud* (1834–81), French physician who described it]

ray·on (rā′on), *n.* **1.** a regenerated, semisynthetic textile filament made from cellulose, cotton linters, or wood chips by treating these with caustic soda and carbon disulfide and passing the resultant solution, viscose, through spinnerets. **2.** fabric made of this filament. *—adj.* **3.** made of rayon. [1920–25; appar. based on RAY[1]]

ray·on·ny (rā′ə nē), *adj. Heraldry.* radiant (def. 4). [< F *rayonné* (ptp. of *rayonner* to radiate, beam), equiv. to *rayon* (see RAYON) + *-é* -ATE[1]]

Ray·side-Bal·four (rā′sīd′bal′fŏŏr, -fər), *n.* a town in S Ontario, in S Canada. 15,017.

Ray·town (rā′toun′), *n.* a city in W Missouri, near Kansas City. 31,759.

ra·za (rä′sä), *n.* ***la.*** *(sometimes caps.) Mexican Spanish.* See ***la raza.***

raze (rāz), *v.t.,* **razed, raz·ing. 1.** to tear down; demolish; level to the ground: *to raze a row of old buildings.* **2.** to shave or scrape off. Also, **rase.** [1540–50; ME *rasen* < MF *raser* < *VL *rāsāre* to scrape, freq. of L *rādere* to scrape] **—raz′er,** *n.*
—Syn. 1. See **destroy.**

ra·zee (rā zē′), *n., v.,* **-zeed, -zee·ing.** *—n.* **1.** a ship, esp. a warship, reduced in height by the removal of the upper deck. *—v.t.* **2.** to cut down (a wooden ship) by removing the upper deck. [1785–95; < F (*vaisseau*) *rasé* razed (ship), ptp. of *raser* to RAZE]

ra·zor (rā′zər), *n.* **1.** a sharp-edged instrument used esp. for shaving the face or trimming the hair. **2.** an electrically powered instrument used for the same purpose. *—v.t.* **3.** to shave, cut, or remove with or as if with a razor. **4. on the razor's edge,** in a difficult or precarious position. [1250–1300; ME *rasour* < OF *rasor,* equiv. to *ras(er)* to RAZE + *-or* -OR[2]] **—ra′zor·less,** *adj.*

ra·zor·back (rā′zər bak′), *n.* **1.** a finback or rorqual. **2.** a wild or semiwild hog with a ridgelike back, common in the southern U.S. **3.** a sharp narrow ridge or range of hills. *—adj.* **4.** Also, **ra′zor-backed′, ra′zor-backed′.** having a sharp ridge along the back. [1815–25; RAZOR + BACK[1]]

ra′zor-billed auk′ (rā′zər bild′), a black and white auk, *Alca torda,* of the American and European coasts of the northern North Atlantic, having a compressed black bill encircled by a white band. Also called **ra′zor·bill′.** See illus. under **auk.** [1815–25]

ra′zor clam′, any bivalve mollusk of the family Solenidae, esp. of the genus *Ensis,* having a long, rectangular, slightly curved shell. Also called **jackknife clam.** [1880–85, *Amer.*]

ra·zor·fish (rā′zər fish′), *n., pl. (esp. collectively)* **-fish,** *(esp. referring to two or more kinds or species)* **-fish·es.** any of several wrasses of the genus *Hemipteronatus* having a compressed, sharp-edged head, as *H. novacula* **(pearly razorfish),** of the West Indies and the Mediterranean Sea. [1595–1605; RAZOR + FISH]

ra′zor wire′. See **concertina wire.** Also called **ra′zor rib′bon.**

razz (raz), *Slang.* *—v.t.* **1.** to deride; make fun of; tease. *—n.* **2.** raspberry (def. 4). [1910–15, *Amer.*; short for RASPBERRY]

razz·ber·ry (raz′ber′ē, -bə rē, räz′-), *n., pl.* **-ries.** raspberry (def. 4).

raz·zi·a (raz′ē ə), *n.* a plundering raid. [1835–45; < F < Ar (Algerian) *ghāzya* military raid, var. of Ar *ghazwah*]

raz·zle-daz·zle (raz′əl daz′əl), *n. Informal.* **1.** showiness, brilliance, or virtuosity in technique or effect, often without concomitant substance or worth; flashy theatricality: *The razzle-dazzle of the essay's metaphors cannot disguise its shallowness of thought.* **2.** *Chiefly Football.* deceptive action typically consisting of a series of complex maneuvers, as a double reverse or hand-off, usually executed in a flashy manner: *a team relying more on power and speed than razzle-dazzle.* **3.** confusion, commotion, or riotous gaiety. *—adj.* **4.** impressively opulent or decorative, esp. in a new way; showy; flashy; eye-catching: *a shopping center lined with razzle-dazzle boutiques.* **5.** energetic, dynamic, or innovative: *razzle-dazzle technology; a razzle-dazzle sales pitch.* [1890–95; rhyming compound based on DAZZLE]

razz·ma·tazz (raz′mə taz′), *n. Informal.* razzle-dazzle (def. 1). [1895–1900, *Amer.*; by alter.]

Rb, *Symbol, Chem.* rubidium.

RBC, red blood cell.

R.B.I., *Baseball.* run batted in; runs batted in. Also, **RBI, rbi, r.b.i.**

R.C., 1. Red Cross. **2.** Reserve Corps. **3.** Roman Catholic. Also, **RC**

R.C.A.F., Royal Canadian Air Force. Also, **RCAF**

R.C.Ch., Roman Catholic Church.

rcd., received.

R.C.M.P., Royal Canadian Mounted Police. Also, **RCMP**

R.C.N., Royal Canadian Navy. Also, **RCN**

r-col·or (är′kul′ər), *n. Phonet.* the auditory quality of an *r*-sound given to a vowel, resulting from retroflex articulation or bunching of the tongue. Also, **r′-col′or·ing.** Also called **r-quality.** **—r′-col′ored,** *adj.*

R.C.P., Royal College of Physicians.

rcpt., receipt.

R.C.S., Royal College of Surgeons.

Rct, 1. receipt. **2.** *Mil.* recruit. Also, **rct**

rcvr, receiver.

Rd, *Symbol, Chem.* (formerly) radium.

rd, rod; rods.

Rd., Road.

rd., 1. rendered. **2.** road. **3.** rod; rods. **4.** round.

R/D, *Banking.* refer to drawer.

R.D., 1. registered dietitian. **2.** Rural Delivery.

RDA, 1. (not in technical use) recommended daily allowance. Cf. **U.S. RDA. 2.** See **recommended dietary allowance.** Also, **R.D.A.**

RdAc, *Symbol, Chem.* radioactinium.

RD&D, research, development, and demonstration.

RD&E, research, development, and engineering.

RDB, *Mil.* Research and Development Board.

RDD, *Marketing.* random digit dialing.

RDF, See **radio direction finder.**

r-drop·ping (är′drop′ing), *adj. Phonet.* (of certain pronunciations of English) characterized by the absence of the sound (r) in postvocalic position in the same syllable, as often encountered in speech identified with the southern and eastern United States and with most of England; r-less. [‡1960–65]

RDS, *Pathol.* See **respiratory distress syndrome.**

RDT&E, research, development, testing, and engineering.

RDX, a white, crystalline, water-insoluble, powerful high explosive, $C_3H_6N_6O_6$, used chiefly in bombs and shells. Also called **cyclonite, cyclotrimethylenetrinitramine.** [1940–45; *R(esearch) D(epartment) (E)x(plosive),* referring to such a department in Woolwich, England]

re[1] (rā), *n. Music.* **1.** the syllable used for the second tone of a diatonic scale. **2.** (in the fixed system of solmization) the tone D. Cf. **sol-fa** (def. 1). [1400–50; late ME; see GAMUT]

re[2] (rē, rā), *prep. Chiefly Law and Com.* in the case of; with reference to; in re. [1700–10; < L *rē* (in the) matter, affair, thing (abl. of *rēs*)]

're (ər), contraction of *are: They're leaving.*
—Usage. See **contraction.**

Re (rā), *n. Egyptian Religion.* Ra.

Re, *Symbol, Chem.* rhenium.

re-, a prefix, occurring originally in loanwords from Latin, used with the meaning "again" or "again and again" to indicate repetition, or with the meaning "back" or "backward" to indicate withdrawal or backward motion: *regenerate; refurbish; retype; retrace; revert.* Also, **red-.** [ME < L *re-, red-*]
—Note. The lists at the bottom of this and following pages provide the spelling, syllabification, and stress for words whose meanings may be easily inferred by combining the meanings of RE- and an attached base word, or base word plus a suffix. Appropriate parts of speech are also shown. Words prefixed by RE- that have special meanings or uses are entered in their proper alphabetical places in the main vocabulary or as derived forms run on at the end of a main vocabulary entry.

Re., rupee. Also, **re.**

R/E, real estate. Also, **RE**

R.E., 1. real estate. **2.** Reformed Episcopal. **3.** Right Excellent.

r.e., *Football.* right end.

REA, Rural Electrification Administration. Also, **R.E.A.**

re·ab·sorp·tion (rē′ab sôrp′shən, -zôrp′-), *n.* resorption (def. 2).

reach (rēch), *v.t.* **1.** to get to or get as far as in moving, going, traveling, etc.: *The boat reached the shore.* **2.** to come to or arrive at in some course of progress, action, etc.: *Your letter never reached me.* **3.** to succeed in touching or seizing with an outstretched hand, a pole, etc.: *to reach a book on a high shelf.* **4.** to stretch or hold out; extend: *reaching out a hand in greeting.* **5.** to stretch or extend so as to touch or meet: *The bookcase reaches the ceiling.* **6.** to establish communication with: *I called but couldn't reach you.* **7.** to amount to, as in the sum or total: *The cost will reach millions.* **8.** to penetrate to: *distant stars the eye cannot reach.* **9.** to succeed in striking or hitting, as with a weapon or missile: *The artillery fire reached the shore.* **10.** to succeed in making contact with, influencing, impressing, interesting, convincing, etc.: *a program that reached a large teenage audience.* *—v.i.* **11.** to make a stretch, as with the hand or arm. **12.** to become outstretched, as the hand or arm. **13.** to make a movement or effort as if to touch or seize something: *to reach for a weapon.* **14.** to extend in operation or effect: *power that reaches throughout the land.* **15.** to stretch in space; extend in direction, length, distance, etc.: *a coat reaching to the knee; a tower reaching to the skies.* **16.** to extend or continue in time. **17.** to get or come to a specified place, person, condition, etc. (often fol. by *to*). **18.** to amount (often fol. by *to*): *sums reaching to a considerable total.* **19.** to penetrate: *Fields of flowers extended as far as the eye could reach.* **20.** to assert or agree without certainty or sufficient evidence; infer hastily: *I'd be reaching if I said I had the answer to your question.* **21.** *Naut.* **a.** to sail on a reach. **b.** to sail with the wind forward of the beam but so as not to require sailing close-hauled. *—n.* **22.** an act or instance of reaching: *to make a reach for a gun.* **23.** the extent or distance of reaching: *within reach of his voice.* **24.** range of effective action, power, or capacity. **25.** a continuous stretch or extent of something: *a reach of woodland.* **26.** Also called **pound.** a level portion of a canal, between locks. **27.** *Naut.* a point of sailing in which the wind is within a few points of the beam, either forward of the beam **(close reach),** directly abeam **(beam reach),** or abaft the beam **(broad reach). 28.** the pole connecting the rear axle of a wagon to the transverse bar or bolster over the front axle supporting the wagon bed. **29.** a straight portion of a river between two bends. [bef. 900; (v.) ME *rechen,* OE *rǣcan* (c. G *reichen,* D *reiken*); (n.) deriv. of the v.] **—reach′a·ble,** *adj.* **—reach′a·bil′i·ty,** *n.* **—reach′er,** *n.*
—Syn. 1. attain. **24.** area, sphere, scope.

reach′ing jib′, *Naut.* genoa. [1920–25]

reach-me-down (rēch′mē doun′), *n., adj. Brit.* hand-me-down. [1860–65]

reach′ rod′, a rod for operating a remote piece of machinery, as a valve. [1905–10]

re-act (rē akt′), *v.t.* to act or perform again. [1650–60; RE- + ACT]

re·act (rē akt′), *v.i.* **1.** to act in response to an agent or influence: *How did the audience react to the speech?* **2.** to act reciprocally upon each other, as two things. **3.** to act in a reverse direction or manner, esp. so as to return to a prior condition. **4.** to act in opposition, as against some force. **5.** to respond to a stimulus in a particular manner: *reacting to a shock by jumping; to react to the word "coward" with anger.* **6.** to undergo a chemical reaction. [1635–45; RE- + ACT, prob. modeled on ML *reagere*]

re·ac·tance (rē ak′təns), *n.* **1.** *Elect.* the opposition of inductance and capacitance to alternating current, expressed in ohms: equal to the product of the sine of the angular phase difference between current and voltage and the ratio of the effective voltage to the effective current. *Symbol:* X Cf. **capacitive reactance, inductive reactance. 2.** *Acoustics.* See **acoustic reactance.** [1890–95; REACT + -ANCE]

re·ac·tant (rē ak′tənt), *n.* **1.** a person or thing that reacts. **2.** Also called **interactant.** *Chem.* any substance that undergoes a chemical change in a given reaction. [1925–30; REACT + -ANT]

re·ac·tion (rē ak′shən), *n.* **1.** a reverse movement or tendency; an action in a reverse direction or manner. **2.** movement in the direction of political conservatism or extreme rightism. **3.** action in response to some influence, event, etc.: *the nation's reaction to the President's speech.* **4.** *Physiol.* action in response to a stimulus, as of the system or of a nerve, muscle, etc. **5.** *Med.* **a.** the action caused by the resistance to another action. **b.** a return to the opposite physical condition, as after shock, exhaustion, or chill. **6.** *Bacteriol., Immunol.* the specific cellular response to foreign matter, as in testing for allergies. **7.** *Chem.* the reciprocal action of chemical agents upon each other; chemical change. **8.** Also called **nuclear reaction.** *Physics.* a process in which a nucleus that is bombarded by a photon, particle, or other nucleus, emits a nucleon, alpha particle, or the like, without a significant change in its atomic weight. **9.** *Mech.* the instantaneous response of a system to an applied force, manifested as the exertion of a force equal in magnitude but opposite in direction to the applied force. **10.** *Com.* a decline in the market after an advance in prices. [1635–45; RE- + ACTION, modeled on *react*] **—re·ac′tion·al,** *adj.* **—re·ac′tion·al·ly,** *adv.*

re·ac·tion·ar·y (rē ak′shə ner′ē), *adj., n., pl.* **-ar·ies.** *—adj.* **1.** of, pertaining to, marked by, or favoring reac-

CONCISE PRONUNCIATION KEY: *act, cāpe, dâre, pärt; set, ēqual; if, īce; ox, ōver, ôrder, oil, bŏŏk, bōōt, out; up, ûrge; child; sing; shoe; thin, that;* zh as in *treasure.* ə = *a* as in *alone, e* as in *system, i* as in *easily, o* as in *gallop, u* as in *circus;* ° as in *fire* (fī°r), *hour* (ou°r). l and n can serve as syllabic consonants, as in *cradle* (krād′l), and *button* (but′n). See the full key inside the front cover.

re′a·ban′don, *v.t.*
re′a·bridge′, *v.t.,* **-bridged, -bridg·ing.**
re′ab·sorb′, *v.t.*
re′ac·cede′, *v.i.,* **-ced·ed, -ced·ing.**
re′ac·cel′er·ate′, *v.,* **-at·ed, -at·ing.**
re′ac·cel′er·a′tion, *n.*
re·ac′cent, *v.t.*
re′ac·cen′tu·ate′, *v.t.,* **-at·ed, -at·ing.**
re′ac·cept′, *v.t.*
re′ac·cept′ance, *n.*
re′ac·ces′sion, *n.*
re′ac·claim′, *v.t.*
re′ac·cla·ma′tion, *n.*
re′ac′cli·mate′, *v.,* **-mat·ed, -mat·ing.**
re′ac·cli′ma·ti·za′tion, *n.*
re′ac·cli′ma·tize′, *v.,* **-tized, -tiz·ing.**
re′ac·com′mo·date′, *v.,* **-dat·ed, -dat·ing.**
re′ac·com′pa·ny, *v.t.,* **-nied, -ny·ing.**
re′ac·cred′it, *v.t.*
re′ac·cred′i·ta′tion, *n.*
re′ac·cu′mu·late′, *v.,* **-lat·ed, -lat·ing.**
re′ac·cu′mu·la′tion, *n.*
re′ac·cu·sa′tion, *n.*
re′ac·cuse′, *v.t.,* **-cused, -cus·ing.**
re′ac·cus′tom, *v.t.*
re′a·cid′i·fi·ca′tion, *n.*
re′a·cid′i·fy′, *v.,* **-fied, -fy·ing.**
re′ac·knowl′edge, *v.t.,* **-edged, -edg·ing.**
re′ac·knowl′edg·ment, *n.*
re′ac·quaint′, *v.t.*

tion, esp. extreme conservatism or rightism in politics; opposing political or social change. —*n.* **2.** a reactionary person. Also, **re•ac′tion•ist.** [1830–40; REACTION + -ARY; cf. F *réactionnaire*] —**re•ac′tion•ism, re•ac′tion•ar′y•ism, re•ac•tion•ar•ism** (rē ak′shə nə riz′əm), *n.*
—**Syn. 1, 2.** ultraconservative. —**Ant. 1, 2.** radical.

reac′tion en′gine, *Aeron., Rocketry.* an engine that produces power as a reaction to the momentum given to gases ejected from it, as a rocket or jet engine. Also called **reac′tion mo′tor.** [1865–70]

reac′tion forma′tion, *Psychoanal.* a behavioral tendency developed in direct opposition to a repressed impulse. [1905–10]

reac′tion time′, *Psychol.* the interval between stimulation and response. [1875–80]

reac′tion tur′bine, a turbine driven by the reactive force of a fluid passing through the rotor blades. Cf. **impulse turbine.** [1880–85]

re•ac•ti•vate (rē ak′tə vāt′), *v.,* **-vat•ed, -vat•ing.** —*v.t.* **1.** to render active again; revive. —*v.i.* **2.** to be active again. [1900–05; RE- + ACTIVATE] —**re•ac′ti•va′•tion,** *n.*

re•ac•tive (rē ak′tiv), *adj.* **1.** tending to react. **2.** pertaining to or characterized by reaction. **3.** *Elect.* pertaining to or characterized by reactance. [1705–15; REACT + -IVE] —**re•ac′tive•ly,** *adv.* —**re•ac′tive•ness,** *n.*

reac′tive compo′nent, *Elect.* the component in an alternating-current circuit that does not contribute power because it is 90° out of phase with the voltage or current. Also called **wattless component.** [1910–15]

reac′tive depres′sion, depression occurring in response to some situational stress, as loss of one's job. Cf. **endogenous depression.** [1920–25]

reac′tive schizophre′nia, *Psychiatry.* a type of schizophrenia of rapid onset and brief duration that occurs in response to environmental factors. [1960–65]

re•ac•tiv•i•ty (rē′ak tiv′i tē), *n.* **1.** the quality or condition of being reactive. **2.** *Chem.* the relative capacity of an atom, molecule, or radical to undergo a chemical reaction with another atom, molecule, or compound. **3.** *Physics.* a measure of the deviation from the condition at which a nuclear reactor is critical. **4.** *Immunol.* the ability of an antigen to combine with an antibody. [1885–90; REACTIVE + -ITY]

re•ac•tor (rē ak′tər), *n.* **1.** a person or thing that reacts or undergoes reaction. **2.** *Elect.* a device whose primary purpose is to introduce reactance into a circuit. **3.** *Immunol., Vet. Med.* a patient or animal that reacts positively towards a foreign material. **4.** Also called **atomic pile, chain reactor, chain-reacting pile, nuclear reactor, pile.** *Physics.* an apparatus in which a nuclear-fission chain reaction can be initiated, sustained, and controlled, for generating heat or producing useful radiation. **5.** *Chem.* (esp. in industry) a large container, as a vat, for processes in which the substances involved undergo a chemical reaction. [1885–90; 1940–45 for def. 4; REACT + -OR[2]]

read[1] (rēd), *v.,* **read** (red), **read•ing** (rē′ding), *n.* —*v.t.* **1.** to look at carefully so as to understand the meaning of (something written, printed, etc.): *to read a book; to read music.* **2.** to utter aloud or render in speech (something written, printed, etc.): *reading a story to his children; The actor read his lines in a booming voice.* **3.** to have such knowledge of (a language) as to be able to understand things written in it: *to be able to read French.* **4.** to apprehend the meaning of (signs, characters, etc.) otherwise than with the eyes, as by means of the fingers: *to read Braille.* **5.** to apprehend or interpret the meaning of (gestures, movements, signals, or the like): *to read a semaphore; to read sign language.* **6.** to make out the significance of by scrutiny or observation: *to read the cloudy sky as the threat of a storm; a fisherman skilled in reading a stream for potential pools.* **7.** to anticipate, expect, or calculate by observation: *At the line of scrimmage, the quarterback read a blitz and called an audible.* **8.** to foresee, foretell, or predict: *to read a person's fortune in tea leaves.* **9.** to make out the character, motivations, desires, etc., of (a person or persons), as by the interpretation of outward signs. **10.** to interpret or attribute a meaning to (a written text), a musical composition, etc.): *How do you read this clause in the contract?* **11.** to infer (something not expressed or directly indicated) from what is read, considered, or observed: *He read an underlying sarcasm into her letter. In your silence I read agreement to my plan.* **12.** to adopt or give as a reading in a particular passage: *For "one thousand" another version reads "ten thousand."* **13.** to substitute or replace (a particular word or phrase) in a written text, usually to correct an error: *Read "cavalry" for "calvary."* **14.** to check (printers' proofs, copy, etc.) for errors; proofread. **15.** to register or indicate, as a thermometer, clock, etc. **16.** *Computers.* to obtain (data, programs, or control information) from an external storage medium or some other source and place in memory. **17.** *Brit.* to study (a subject), as at a university: *to read law.* **18.** to read the work of (an author): *She is reading Kafka.* **19.** to learn by or as if by reading: *to read a person's thoughts.* **20.** to hear and understand (a transmitted radio message or the person transmitting it); receive: *I read you loud and clear.* **21.** to bring, put, etc., by reading: *to read oneself to sleep.* **22.** to give one (a lecture or lesson) by way of admonition or rebuke. **23.** to discover or explain the meaning of (a riddle, dream, etc.).
—*v.i.* **24.** to read or peruse written or printed matter. **25.** to utter aloud or render in speech written or printed words that one is perusing: *to read to a person.* **26.** to give a public reading or recital. **27.** to inspect and apprehend the meaning of written or other signs or characters. **28.** to occupy oneself seriously with reading or study. **29.** to obtain knowledge or learn of something by reading. **30.** to admit of being read, esp. properly or well. **31.** to have a certain wording. **32.** to admit of being interpreted: *a rule that reads in two different ways.* **33.** to register or indicate particular information, as the status or condition of something: *Her blood pressure is reading a little low today.* **34.** to have an effect or make an impression; show forth: *Those battle photographs read with great impact.* **35.** *Computers.* to read data, programs, or control information. **36. read between the lines.** See **line**[1] (def. 69). **37. read for,** (of an actor) to audition for (a role, a play, etc.). **38. read in,** *Computers.* to place (data, programs, or control information) in memory. **39. read lips,** to study the lip movements of a speaker who cannot be heard so as to determine the words being uttered. **40. read out, a.** to read aloud, as for someone's attention. **b.** *Computers.* to retrieve (information) from a computer. **41. read out of,** to oust from membership in (a political party or other group) by a public announcement of dismissal: *He was read out of the association because of alleged subversive activities.* **42. read the green.** *Golf.* See **green** (def. 30). **43. read the riot act.** See **Riot Act** (def. 2). **44. read up on,** to learn about by reading; gather information on; research by reading: *You'd better read up on World War I before taking the history test.*
—*n.* **45.** an act or instance of reading: *Give the agreement a careful read before you sign it.* **46.** something that is read: *Her new novel is a wonderful read.* [bef. 900; ME *reden,* OE *rǣdan* to counsel, read; c. D *raden,* G *raten,* ON *rātha;* akin to Skt *rādhnoti* (he) achieves]
—**Syn. 1.** peruse, scan, note, study.

read[2] (red), *adj.* having knowledge gained by reading (usually used in combination): *a well-read person.* [1580–90; ptp. of READ[1]]

Read (rēd), *n.* **1. George,** 1733–98, American political leader: served in the Continental Congress 1774–77. **2. Sir Herbert,** 1893–1968, English critic and poet. **3.** a male given name: from an Old English word meaning "red."

read•a•bil•i•ty (rē′də bil′i tē), *n.* **1.** Also, **read′a•ble•ness.** the state or quality of being readable. **2.** *Typography.* the property of type that affects the ease with which printed matter can be read for a sustained period. Cf. **legibility** (def. 2). [1835–45; READABLE + -ITY]

read•a•ble (rē′də bəl), *adj.* **1.** easy or interesting to read. **2.** capable of being read; legible: *readable handwriting.* **3.** pertaining to letter mail with addresses and zip codes capable of being read by optical scanning devices. [1560–70; READ[1] + -ABLE] —**read′a•bly,** *adv.*

Reade (rēd), *n.* **Charles,** 1814–84, English novelist.

read•er (rē′dər), *n.* **1.** a person who reads. **2.** a schoolbook for instruction and practice in reading: *a second-grade reader.* **3.** a book of collected or assorted writings, esp. when related in theme, authorship, or instructive purpose; anthology: *a Hemingway reader; a sci-fi reader.* **4.** a person employed to read and evaluate manuscripts offered for publication. **5.** a proofreader. **6.** a person who reads or recites before an audience; elocutionist. **7.** a person authorized to read the lessons, Bible, etc., in a church service. **8.** a lecturer or instructor, esp. in some British universities: *to be appointed reader in English history.* **9.** an assistant to a professor, who grades examinations, papers, etc. **10.** *Computers.* a device that reads data, programs, or control information from an external storage medium for transmission to main storage. Cf. **card reader, optical character reader. 11.** a machine or device that projects or enlarges a microform image on a screen or other surface for reading. **12.** a playing card marked on its back so that the suit or denomination of the card can be identified. **13.** *Library Science.* the user of a library; library patron. [bef. 1000; ME *reder(e), redar(e),* OE *rǣdere.* See READ[1], -ER[1]]

read•er•ship (rē′dər ship′), *n.* **1.** the people who read or are thought to read a particular book, newspaper, magazine, etc.: *The periodical has a dwindling readership.* **2.** the duty, status, or profession of a reader. **3.** (esp. in British universities) the position of instructor or lecturer. **4.** the state or quality of being a reader: *appealing to a higher level of readership.* [1710–20; READER + -SHIP]

read•i•ly (red′l ē), *adv.* **1.** promptly; quickly; easily: *The information is readily available.* **2.** in a ready manner; willingly: *He readily agreed to help us.* [1275–1325; ME *redily.* See READY, -LY]
—**Syn. 2.** freely, graciously, ungrudgingly.

read•i•ness (red′ē nis), *n.* **1.** the condition of being ready. **2.** ready movement; promptness; quickness. **3.** ready action; ease; facility. **4.** willingness; inclination; cheerful consent: *a readiness to help others.* **5.** a developmental stage at which a child has the capacity to receive instruction at a given level of difficulty or to engage in a particular activity. [1350–1400; ME *redyness(e).* See READY, -NESS]

read•ing (rē′ding), *n.* **1.** the action or practice of a person who reads. **2.** *Speech.* the oral interpretation of written language. **3.** the interpretation given in the performance of a dramatic part, musical composition, etc.: *an interesting reading of Beethoven's 5th Symphony.* **4.** the extent to which a person has read; literary knowledge: *a man of wide reading.* **5.** matter read or for reading: *a novel that makes good reading.* **6.** the form or version of a given passage in a particular text: *the various readings of a line in Shakespeare.* **7.** an instance or occasion in which a text or other matter is read or performed, usually without elaborate preparation and often as a means of testing its merits: *The playwright wants to have a reading of the play for prospective producers.* **8.** an interpretation given to anything: *What is your reading of the situation?* **9.** the indication of a graduated instrument: *The reading is 101.2°F.* —*adj.* **10.** pertaining to or used for reading: *reading glasses.* **11.** given to reading: *the reading public.* [bef. 900; ME *redyng* (ger.), OE *rǣdinge.* See READ, -ING[1], -ING[2]]

Read•ing (red′ing), *n.* **1. Rufus Daniel Isaacs, 1st Marquis of,** 1860–1935, Lord Chief Justice of England 1913–21; viceroy of India 1921–26. **2.** a city in Berkshire, in S England. 132,900. **3.** a city in SE Pennsylvania. 78,686. **4.** a town in E Massachusetts, near Boston. 22,678. **5.** a city in SW Ohio. 12,879.

read′ing chair′, a chair of the 18th century having an adjustable reading stand attached to the back and a crest rail extending forward on both sides to form armrests, designed to be sat on facing the back. [1795–1805]

read′ing desk′, 1. a desk for use in reading, esp. by a person standing. **2.** a lectern in a church. [1695–1705]

read′ing no′tice, a short advertisement placed at the bottom of a column, as on the front page of a newspaper, and often set in the same print as other matter. [1905–10, *Amer.*]

read′ing room′, a room set aside for reading, as in a library or club. [1750–60]

re•ad•just (rē′ə just′), *v.t.* to adjust again or anew; rearrange. [1735–45; RE- + ADJUST] —**re′ad•just′a•ble,** *adj.* —**re′ad•just′er,** *n.*

re•ad•just•ment (rē′ə just′mənt), *n.* **1.** an act of readjusting or the state of being readjusted. **2.** *Finance.* a rearrangement in the financial structure of a corporation, usually less drastic than a reorganization. [1765–75; READJUST + -MENT]

read-on•ly (rēd′ōn′lē), *adj. Computers.* of or pertaining to files or memory that can be read but cannot normally be changed.

read′-only mem′ory, *Computers.* See **ROM.** [1965–70]

read•out (rēd′out′), *n.* **1.** *Computers.* the output of information from a computer in readable form. Cf. **printout. 2.** the information displayed on a graduated instrument. Also, **read′-out′.** [1645–55, for an earlier sense; in. use of v. phrase *read out*]

read-through (rēd′thrōō′), *n.* **1.** reading (def. 1). **2.** reading (def. 7). [1960–65; n. use of v. phrase *read through*] Also, **read′through′.**

read′/write′ head′ (rēd′rīt′), *Computers.* an electromagnetic device, as in a disk or tape drive, that reads data from or writes data on a magnetic disk or tape. Also called **head.**

read•y (red′ē), *adj.,* **read•i•er, read•i•est,** *v.,* **read•ied, read•y•ing,** *n., interj.* —*adj.* **1.** completely prepared or in fit condition for immediate action or use: *troops ready for battle; Dinner is ready.* **2.** duly equipped, completed, adjusted, or arranged, as for an occasion or purpose: *The mechanic called to say that the car is ready.* **3.** willing: *ready to forgive.* **4.** prompt or quick in perceiving, comprehending, speaking, writing, etc. **5.** proceeding from or showing such quickness: *a ready reply.* **6.** prompt or quick in action, performance, manifestation, etc.: *a keen mind and ready wit.* **7.** inclined; disposed; apt: *too ready to criticize others.* **8.** in such a condition as to be imminent; likely at any moment: *a tree ready to fall.* **9.** immediately available for use: *a ready source of cash.* **10.** pertaining to prompt payment. **11.** present or convenient: *to lie ready to one's hand.* **12. get ready!** (in calling the start of a race) be prepared to start: *Get ready! Get set! Go!* **13. make ready, a.** to bring to a state of readiness or completion; prepare. **b.** *Print.* to ready a press for printing. —*v.t.* **14.** to make ready; prepare. **15. ready up,** *Brit. and Australian Slang.* to swindle. —*n.* **16.** the state or condition of being ready. **17.** *Informal.* ready money; cash. **18. at the ready,** in a condition of readiness, available for immediate use: *shoppers with their umbrellas at the ready; soldiers keeping their weapons at the ready.* —*interj.* **19.** (used in calling the start of a race to indicate that racers should be prepared to start): *Ready! Set! Go!* [1150–1200; ME *redy,* early ME *rǣdig,* equiv. to OE *rǣde* prompt + *-ig* -Y[1]]
—**Syn. 1.** fit, set. **3.** agreeable, glad, happy. **4.** alert, acute, sharp, keen, adroit, facile, clever, skillful, nimble, adaptable. —**Ant. 1.** unfit. **3.** unwilling.
—**Usage.** See **already.**

read•y-made (red′ē mād′), *adj.* **1.** made in advance for sale to any purchaser, rather than to order: *a ready-made coat.* **2.** made for immediate use. **3.** unoriginal; conventional. —*n.* **4.** readymade. **5.** something that is ready-made, as a garment or a piece of furniture or equipment. [1400–50; late ME]

read•y•made (red′ē mād′), *n.* an everyday manufactured object, as a bottle rack, a snow shovel, a urinal, or a comb, that may by the creative act of selection and designation by an artist attain status as a work of art: associated almost exclusively with the aesthetic activities of Marcel Duchamp during the period 1915 to 1917.

CONCISE ETYMOLOGY KEY: <, descended or borrowed from; >, whence; b., blend of, blended; c., cognate with; cf., compare; deriv., derivative; equiv., equivalent; imit., imitative; obl., oblique; r., replacing; s., stem; sp., spelling, spelled; resp., respelling, respelled; trans., translation; ?, origin unknown; *, unattested; ‡, probably earlier than. See the full key inside the front cover.

re′ac•quaint′ance, *n.*
re′ac•quire′, *v.t.,* **-quired, -quir•ing.**
re′ac•qui•si′tion, *n.*
re′a•dapt′, *v.t.*
re′a•dapt′a•bil′i•ty, *n.*
re′a•dapt′a•ble, *adj.*
re′ad•ap•ta′tion, *n.*
re′a•dap′tive, *adj.;* **-ly,** *adv.;* **-ness,** *n.*
re•add′, *v.t.*
re′ad•di′tion, *n.*
re′ad•dress′, *v.t.,* **-dressed** or **-drest, -dress•ing.**
re′ad•journ′, *v.*
re′ad•journ′ment, *n.*
re′ad•ju′di•cate′, *v.,* **-cat•ed, -cat•ing.**
re′ad•ju′di•ca′tion, *n.*
re′ad•mis′sion, *n.*
re′ad•mit′, *v.,* **-mit•ted, -mit•ting.**
re′ad•mit′tance, *n.*
re′a•dopt′, *v.t.*
re′a•dop′tion, *n.*
re′a•dorn′, *v.t.*
re′a•dorn′ing, *adj.*
re′a•dorn′ment, *n.*
re•ad′ver•tise′, *v.,* **-tised, -tis•ing.**
re′ad•ver•tise′ment, *n.*
re′ad•vise′, *v.,* **-vised, -vis•ing.**
re•ad′vo•cate′, *v.t.,* **-cat•ed, -cat•ing.**
re′ad•vo•ca′tion, *n.*
re′af•fect′, *v.t.*
re′af•fil′i•ate′, *v.,* **-at•ed, -at•ing.**
re′af•fil′i•a′tion, *n.*
re′af•firm′, *v.t.*
re′af•fir•ma′tion, *n.*
re′af•fix′, *v.t.*
re′af•front′, *n., v.t.*

Also, **ready-made.** [< F < E; term introduced by Duchamp in 1915]

read•y-mix (red′ē miks′, -miks′), *n.* **1.** a commercial preparation in which the principal ingredients have already been mixed for easy use: *a novice cook's reliance on ready-mixes.* —*adj.* **2.** Also, **read′y-mixed′.** being a ready-mix; consisting of ingredients that are already mixed: *ready-mix pancakes.* [1945–50]

read′y mon′ey, money that is in hand or may be obtained quickly or easily; cash. [1870–75]

read′y reck′oner, reckoner (def. 2). [1750–60]

read′y room′, a room in which members of an air-crew await their orders for takeoff. [1940–45, *Amer.*]

read•y-to-wear (red′ē tə wâr′), *n.* **1.** clothing made in standard sizes; ready-made clothing. —*adj.* **2.** pertaining to or dealing in such clothing: *the ready-to-wear business; a ready-to-wear shop.* Cf. **made-to-measure, made-to-order.** [1890–95, *Amer.*]

read•y-wit•ted (red′ē wit′id), *adj.* having a quick wit or intelligence. [1575–85] —**read′y-wit′ted•ly,** *adv.* —**read′y-wit′ted•ness,** *n.*

Rea•gan (rā′gən), *n.* **Ronald (Wilson),** born 1911, 40th president of the U.S. 1981–89.

Rea•gan•om•ics (rā′gə nom′iks), *n.* the economic policies put forth by the administration of President Ronald Reagan, esp. as emphasizing supply-side theory. [1980–85; b. REAGAN and ECONOMICS] —**Rea′gan•om′•ic,** *adj.*

re•a•gent (rē ā′jənt), *n. Chem.* a substance that, because of the reactions it causes, is used in analysis and synthesis. [1790–1800; RE(ACT) + AGENT; cf. ACT]

re•a•gin (rē ā′jin, -gin), *n. Immunol.* **1.** Also called **Wassermann antibody.** an antibody formed in response to syphilis and reactive with cardiolipin in various blood tests for the disease. **2.** an antibody found in certain human allergies, as hay fever and asthma. [1910–15; < G *Reagin,* equiv. to *reag(ieren)* to react + *-in* -IN[2]]

re•al[1] (rē′əl, rēl), *adj.* **1.** true; not merely ostensible, nominal, or apparent: *the real reason for an act.* **2.** existing or occurring as fact; actual rather than imaginary, ideal, or fictitious: *a story taken from real life.* **3.** being an actual thing; having objective existence; not imaginary: *The events you will see in the film are real and not just made up.* **4.** being actually such; not merely so-called: *a real victory.* **5.** genuine; not counterfeit, artificial, or imitation; authentic: *a real antique; a real diamond; real silk.* **6.** unfeigned or sincere: *real sympathy; a real friend.* **7.** *Informal.* absolute; complete; utter: *She's a real brain.* **8.** *Philos.* **a.** existent or pertaining to the existent as opposed to the nonexistent. **b.** actual as opposed to possible or potential. **c.** independent of experience as opposed to phenomenal or apparent. **9.** (of money, income, or the like) measured in purchasing power rather than in nominal value: *Inflation has driven income down in real terms, though nominal income appears to be higher.* **10.** *Optics.* (of an image) formed by the actual convergence of rays, as the image produced in a camera (opposed to *virtual*). **11.** *Math.* **a.** of, pertaining to, or having the value of a real number. **b.** using real numbers: *real analysis; real vector space.* —*adv.* **12.** *Informal.* very or extremely: *You did a real nice job painting the house.* —*n.* **13.** See **real number. 14. for real,** *Informal.* **a.** in reality; actually: *You mean she dyed her hair green for real?* **b.** real; actual: *The company's plans to relocate are for real.* **c.** genuine; sincere: *I don't believe his friendly attitude is for real.* **15. the real, a.** something that actually exists, as a particular quantity. **b.** reality in general. [1400–50; late ME < LL *reālis,* equiv. to L *re-,* var. s. of *rēs* thing + *-ālis* -AL[1]] —**re′al•ness,** *n.*

—**Syn. 1–5.** REAL, ACTUAL, TRUE in general use describe objects, persons, experiences, etc., that are what they are said or purport to be. That which is described as REAL is genuine as opposed to counterfeit, false, or merely supposed: *a real emerald; real leather binding; My real ambition is to be a dentist.* ACTUAL usually stresses contrast with another state of affairs that has been proposed or suggested: *The actual cost is much less; to conceal one's actual motive.* TRUE implies a perfect correspondence with actuality and is in direct contrast to that which is false or inaccurate: *a true account of the events; not bravado but true courage.* See also **authentic.**

—**Usage.** The intensifying adverb REAL, meaning "very," is informal and limited to speech or to written representations of speech: *He drives a real beat-up old car.* The adjective REAL meaning "true, actual, genuine, etc.," is standard in all types of speech and writing: *Their real reasons for objecting became clear in the discussion.* The informal adjective sense "absolute, complete" is also limited to speech or representations of speech: *These interruptions are a real bother.*

re•al[2] (rā äl′; *Sp.* re äl′), *n., pl.* **re•als** (rā älz′), *Sp.* **re•a•les** (re ä′les). a former silver coin of Spain and Spanish America, the eighth part of a peso. [1605–15; < Sp: royal < L *rēgālis* REGAL]

re•al[3] (rā äl′; *Port.* re äl′), *n.* sing. of **reis.**

re′al ax′is (rē′əl, rēl), *Math.* the horizontal axis in an Argand diagram.

re′al estate′ (rē′əl, rēl), **1.** property, esp. in land: *three acres of real estate.* **2.** See **real property.** [1705–15] —**re′al-es•tate′,** *adj.*

re′al-estate invest′ment trust′, an unincorporated trust created for the purpose of investing in real property or to extend credit to those engaged in construction. *Abbr.:* REIT

re•al•gar (rē al′gər, -gär), *n.* arsenic disulfide, As_2S_2, found in nature as an orange-red mineral and also produced artificially: used in pyrotechnics. Also called **red orpiment.** [1350–1400; ME < ML *realger* << Ar *rahj al-ghār* powder of the mine or cave]

re•a•li•a (rē ā′lē ə, -al′ē ə, rā ä′lē ə), *n.pl.* **1.** *Educ.* objects, as coins, tools, etc., used by a teacher to illustrate everyday living. **2.** *Philos.* things that are real. [1945–50; < LL *reālia* real (things), neut. pl. of *reālis;* see REAL[1]]

re′al in′come (rē′əl, rēl), the amount of goods and services that money income will buy. [1925–30]

re•al•ism (rē′ə liz′əm), *n.* **1.** interest in or concern for the actual or real, as distinguished from the abstract, speculative, etc. **2.** the tendency to view or represent things as they really are. **3.** *Fine Arts.* **a.** treatment of forms, colors, space, etc., in such a manner as to emphasize their correspondence to actuality or to ordinary visual experience. Cf. **idealism** (def. 4), **naturalism** (def. 2). **b.** (*usually cap.*) a style of painting and sculpture developed about the mid-19th century in which figures and scenes are depicted as they are experienced or might be experienced in everyday life. **4.** *Literature.* **a.** a manner of treating subject matter that presents a careful description of everyday life, usually of the lower and middle classes. **b.** a theory of writing in which the ordinary, familiar, or mundane aspects of life are represented in a straightforward or matter-of-fact manner that is presumed to reflect life as it actually is. Cf. **naturalism** (def. 1b). **5.** *Philos.* **a.** the doctrine that universals have a real objective existence. Cf. **conceptualism, nominalism. b.** the doctrine that objects of sense perception have an existence independent of the act of perception. Cf. **idealism** (def. 5a). [1810–20; REAL[1] + -ISM; cf. F *réalisme*]

re•al•ist (rē′ə list), *n.* **1.** a person who tends to view or represent things as they really are. **2.** an artist or a writer whose work is characterized by realism. **3.** *Philos.* an adherent of realism. —*adj.* **4.** of or pertaining to realism or to a person who embodies its principles or practices: *the realist approach to social ills; realist paintings.* [1595–1605; REAL[1] + -IST; cf. F *réaliste*]

re•al•is•tic (rē′ə lis′tik), *adj.* **1.** interested in, concerned with, or based on what is real or practical: *a realistic estimate of costs; a realistic planner.* **2.** pertaining to, characterized by, or given to the representation in literature or art of things as they really are: *a realistic novel.* **3.** resembling or simulating real life: *a duck hunter skilled at making realistic decoys.* **4.** *Philos.* of or pertaining to realists or realism. [1855–60; REALIST + -IC] —**re′al•is′ti•cal•ly,** *adv.*

—**Syn. 1.** pragmatic, common-sense, hard-headed, sensible.

re•al•i•ty (rē al′i tē), *n., pl.* **-ties** for 3, 5–7. **1.** the state or quality of being real. **2.** resemblance to what is real. **3.** a real thing or fact. **4.** real things, facts, or events taken as a whole; state of affairs: *the reality of the business world; vacationing to escape reality.* **5.** *Philos.* **a.** something that exists independently of ideas concerning it. **b.** something that exists independently of all other things and from which all other things derive. **6.** something that is real. **7.** something that constitutes a real or actual thing, as distinguished from something that is merely apparent. **8. in reality,** in fact or truth; actually: *brave in appearance, but in reality a coward.* [1540–50; < ML *reālitās.* See REAL[1], -ITY]

real′ity prin′ciple, *Psychoanal.* the motivating force or mechanism by which the child, who has previously sought immediate gratification of all wishes, realizes that gratification must sometimes be deferred or forgone. [1920–25]

real′ity test′ing, *Psychiatry.* the objective evaluation of situations, defective in certain psychoses, that enable one to distinguish between the external and the internal worlds and between the self and the nonself. [1920–25]

re•al•i•za•tion (rē′ə lə zā′shən), *n.* **1.** the making or being made real of something imagined, planned, etc. **2.** the result of such a process: *The new church was the realization of a ten-year dream.* **3.** the act of realizing or the state of being realized. **4.** an instance or result of realizing. **5.** *Music.* **a.** the act of realizing a figured bass. **b.** a printed score of a realized figured bass. [1605–15; < F *réalisation,* MF, equiv. to *realis(er)* to REALIZE + *-ation* -ATION]

re•al•ize (rē′ə līz′), *v.,* **-ized, -iz•ing.** —*v.t.* **1.** to grasp or understand clearly. **2.** to make real; give reality to (a hope, fear, plan, etc.). **3.** to bring vividly to the mind. **4.** to convert into cash or money: *to realize securities.* **5.** to obtain as a profit or income for oneself by trade, labor, or investment. **6.** to bring as proceeds, as from a sale: *The goods realized $1000.* **7.** *Music.* to sight-read on a keyboard instrument or write out in notation the full harmony and ornamentation indicated by (a figured bass). **8.** *Ling.* to serve as an instance, representation, or embodiment of (an abstract linguistic element or category): *In "Jack tripped," the subject is realized by "Jack," the predicate by "tripped," and the past tense by "-ed."* —*v.i.* **9.** to convert property or goods into cash or money. Also, *esp. Brit.,* **re′al•ise′.** [1605–15; < F *réaliser,* MF, equiv. to *real* REAL[1] + *-iser* -IZE] —**re′al•iz′•a•ble,** *adj.* —**re′al•iz′a•bil′i•ty, re′al•iz′a•ble•ness,** *n.* —**re′al•iz′a•bly,** *adv.* —**re′al•iz′er,** *n.*

—**Syn. 1.** conceive, comprehend. **2.** accomplish, effect. **3.** See **imagine.** —**Ant. 1.** misunderstand.

re•al-life (rē′əl līf′, rēl′-), *adj.* existing or happening in reality: *real-life drama.* [1830–40]

re′al line′ (rē′əl, rēl), *Math.* **1.** See **number line. 2.** the real axis in the complex plane.

re•al•ly (rē′ə lī′), *v.t., v.i.,* **-lied, -ly•ing.** to ally again or anew. [1425–75; late ME *realy* < MF *real(l)ier;* see RALLY[1]]

re•al•ly (rē′ə lē, rē′lē), *adv.* **1.** in reality; actually: *to see things as they really are.* **2.** genuinely or truly: *a really honest man.* **3.** indeed: *Really, this is too much.* —*interj.* **4.** (used to express surprise, exasperation, etc.) [1400–50; late ME; see REAL[1], -LY]

realm (relm), *n.* **1.** a royal domain; kingdom: *the realm of England.* **2.** the region, sphere, or domain within which anything occurs, prevails, or dominates: *the realm of dreams.* **3.** the special province or field of something or someone: *the realm of physics; facts within the realm of political scientists.* [1250–1300; ME *realme, reaume* < OF *reialme,* deriv. of *reial* < L *rēgālis* REGAL]

—**Syn. 1.** See **kingdom.**

re′al num′ber (rē′əl, rēl), *Math.* a rational number or the limit of a sequence of rational numbers, as opposed to a complex number. Also called **real.** [1905–10]

re′al part′ (rē′əl, rēl), *Math.* the number *a* in the complex number *a* + *bi.* Cf. **imaginary part.** [1960–65]

re•al•po•li•tik (rā äl′pō′li tēk′, rē-), *n.* political realism or practical politics, esp. policy based on power rather than on ideals. Also, **Re•al′po′li•tik′.** [1910–15; < G, equiv. to real REAL[1] + *Politik* politics, policy; see POLITIC] —**re•al•po•li•tik•er,** (rā äl′pō lē′ti kər, rē-), *n.*

re′al pres′ence (rē′əl, rēl), *Theol.* the doctrine that the substance of the body and blood of Christ are present in the Eucharist. [1550–60]

re′al prop′erty (rē′əl, rēl), *Law.* an estate or property consisting of lands and of all appurtenances to lands, as buildings, crops, or mineral rights (distinguished from *personal property*). [1760–70]

re′al stor′age, (rē′əl, rēl), *Computers.* (in a virtual storage system) the portion of addressable memory that consists of main storage. Also called **re′al mem′ory.**

re′al time′ (rē′əl, rēl), **1.** *Computers.* the actual time elapsed in the performance of a computation by a computer, the result of the computation being required for the continuation of a physical process. **2.** the actual time during which a process takes place or an event occurs. **3. in real time,** *Informal.* at once; instantaneously. [1950–55]

re•al-time (rē′əl tīm′, rēl′-), *adj. Computers.* of or pertaining to applications in which the computer must respond as rapidly as required by the user or necessitated by the process being controlled.

Re•al•tor (rē′əl tər, -tôr′, rēl′-), *Trademark.* a person who works in the real-estate business and is a member of the National Association of Real Estate Boards, or one of its constituent boards, and abides by its Code of Ethics.

re•al•ty (rē′əl tē, rēl′-), *n.* real property or real estate. [1400–50; late ME *realte.* See REAL[1], -TY[2]]

re′al var′iable (rē′əl, rēl), *Math.* a variable to which only real numbers are assigned as values.

re′al wag′es (rē′əl, rēl), wages estimated not in money but in purchasing power. Cf. **nominal wages.** [1880–85]

real′ world′ (rē′əl, rēl), the realm of practical or actual experience, as opposed to the abstract, theoretical, or idealized sphere of the classroom, laboratory, etc.: *recent college graduates looking for jobs in the real world of rising unemployment.* [1960–65] —**real′-world′,** *adj.*

ream[1] (rēm), *n.* **1.** a standard quantity of paper, consisting of 20 quires or 500 sheets (formerly 480 sheets), or 516 sheets **(printer's ream** or **perfect ream). 2.** Usually, **reams.** a large quantity: *He has written reams of poetry.* [1350–1400; ME *rem(e)* < MF *reime, rame* < Sp *rezma* < Ar *rizmah* bale]

ream[2] (rēm), *v.t.* **1.** to enlarge to desired size (a previously bored hole) by means of a reamer. **2.** to clear with a reamer; remove or press out by reaming. **3.** to extract the juice from: *to ream an orange.* **4.** *Slang.* **a.** to scold or reprimand severely (usually fol. by *out*). **b.** to cheat; defraud. [1805–15; orig. uncert.]

ream•er (rē′mər), *n.* **1.** any of various rotary tools, with helical or straight flutes, for finishing or enlarging holes drilled in metal. **2.** any bladelike pick or rod used for scraping, shaping, or enlarging a hole: *a pipe reamer.* **3.** a kitchen utensil for extracting and collecting juice from fruits, having a deep saucerlike base and in the center a grooved cone on which the fruit half is pressed down by hand. **4.** *Dentistry.* a drill with a spiral blade, for enlarging root canals. [1815–25; REAM[2] + -ER[1]]

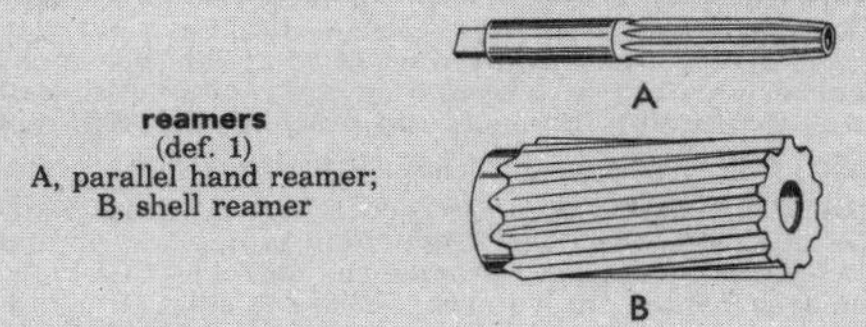

reamers (def. 1) A, parallel hand reamer; B, shell reamer

CONCISE PRONUNCIATION KEY: *act, cāpe, dâre, pärt; set, ēqual; if, īce; ox, ōver, ôrder, oil, bo͝ok, bo͞ot, out; up, ûrge; child; sing; shoe; thin, that;* zh as in *treasure.* ə = *a* as in *alone, e* as in *system, i* as in *easily, o* as in *gallop, u* as in *circus;* ᵊ as in *fire* (fīᵊr), *hour* (ouᵊr). l and n can serve as syllabic consonants, as in *cradle* (krād′l), and *button* (but′n). See the full key inside the front cover.

re•ag′gra•vate′, *v.t.,* **-vat•ed, -vat•ing.**
re•ag′gre•gate′, *v.,* **-gat•ed, -gat•ing.**
re′ag•gre•ga′tion, *n.*
re•ag′i•tate′, *v.,* **-tat•ed, -tat•ing.**
re′ag•i•ta′tion, *n.*
re•al′ien•ate′, *v.t.,* **-at•ed, -at•ing.**
re′al•ien•a′tion, *n.*
re′a•lign′, *v.*
re′a•lign′ment, *n.*
re′al•le•ga′tion, *n.*
re′al•lege′, *v.t.,* **-leged, -leg•ing.**
re′al•li′ance, *n.*
re•al′lo•cate′, *v.t.,* **-cat•ed, -cat•ing.**
re′al•lo•ca′tion, *n.*
re′al•lot′, *v.t.,* **-lot•ted, -lot•ting.**
re′al•lot′ment, *n.*
re•al′ter, *v.*
re•al′ter•a•ble, *adj.;* **-ble•ness,** *n.;* **-bly,** *adv.*
re′al•ter•a′tion, *n.*
re′a•mal′ga•mate′, *v.,* **-at•ed, -at•ing.**
re′a•mal′ga•ma′tion, *n.*
re′a•mass′, *v.t.*
re′a•mass′ment, *n.*
re′a•mend′, *v.*
re′a•mend′ment, *n.*
re′a•nal′y•sis, *n., pl.* **-ses.**
re•an′a•lyz′a•ble, *adj.*
re•an′a•lyze′, *v.t.,* **-lyzed, -lyz•ing.**
re•an′chor, *v.*
re′an•nex′, *v.t.*
re′an•nex•a′tion, *n.*
re•an′no•tate′, *v.,* **-tat•ed, -tat•ing.**

re•an•i•mate (rē an′ə māt′), *v.t.*, **-mat•ed, -mat•ing.** **1.** to restore to life; resuscitate. **2.** to give fresh vigor, spirit, or courage to. **3.** to stimulate to renewed activity. [1605–15; RE- + ANIMATE] —**re•an′i•ma′tion,** *n.*

reap (rēp), *v.t.* **1.** to cut (wheat, rye, etc.) with a sickle or other implement or a machine, as in harvest. **2.** to gather or take (a crop, harvest, etc.). **3.** to get as a return, recompense, or result: *to reap large profits.* —*v.i.* **4.** to reap a crop, harvest, etc. [bef. 900; ME *repen,* OE *repan, riopan;* c. MLG *repen* to ripple (flax); akin to RIPE] —**reap′a•ble,** *adj.*
—**Syn. 3.** gather, earn, realize, gain, win.

reap•er (rē′pər), *n.* **1.** a machine for cutting standing grain; reaping machine. **2.** a person who reaps. **3.** See **Grim Reaper.** [bef. 1000; ME *reper,* OE *ripere.* See REAP, -ER[1]]

reap′ing machine′, any of various machines for reaping grain, often fitted with a device for automatically throwing out bundles of the cut grain. [1805–15]

re•ap•por•tion (rē′ə pôr′shən, -pōr′-), *v.t.* to apportion or distribute anew. [1965–70; RE- + APPORTION]

re•ap•por•tion•ment (rē′ə pôr′shən mənt, -pōr′-), *n.* **1.** the act of redistributing or changing the apportionment of something. **2.** the redistribution of representation in a legislative body. [1930–35; REAPPORTION + -MENT]

rear[1] (rēr), *n.* **1.** the back of something, as distinguished from the front: *The porch is at the rear of the house.* **2.** the space or position behind something: *The bus driver asked the passengers to move to the rear.* **3.** the buttocks; rump. **4.** the hindmost portion of an army, fleet, etc. **5. bring up the rear,** to be at the end; follow behind: *The army retreated, and the fleeing civilian population brought up the rear.* —*adj.* **6.** pertaining to or situated at the rear of something: *the rear door of a bus.* [1590–1600; aph. var. of ARREAR]
—**Syn. 6.** See **back**[1].

rear[2] (rēr), *v.t.* **1.** to take care of and support up to maturity: *to rear a child.* **2.** to breed and raise (livestock). **3.** to raise by building; erect. **4.** to raise to an upright position: *to rear a ladder.* **5.** to lift or hold up; elevate; raise. —*v.i.* **6.** to rise on the hind legs, as a horse or other animal. **7.** (of a person) to start up in angry excitement, hot resentment, or the like (usually fol. by *up*). **8.** to rise high or tower aloft: *The skyscraper rears high over the neighboring buildings.* [bef. 900; ME *reren,* OE *rǣran* to RAISE; c. Goth *-raisjan,* ON *reisa*]
—**Syn. 1.** nurture, raise. **3.** construct. **5.** loft.
—**Usage. 1.** See **raise.**

Rear Adm., Rear Admiral.

rear′ ad′miral, *U.S. Navy, Coast Guard.* a commissioned officer next in rank below a vice-admiral. [1580–90]

rear′ deck′, *Auto.* deck (def. 12).

rear′ ech′elon, (in a military operation) the troops, officers, etc., removed from the combat zone and responsible for administration, matériel, etc. Cf. **forward echelon.** [1930–35]

rear′ end′, 1. the hindmost part of something. **2.** *Informal.* the buttocks; behind. Also called **tail end.** [1865–70]

rear-end (rēr′end′), *v.t.* **1.** to drive a vehicle or other conveyance so as to strike the back end of (another vehicle): *My car was rear-ended by another driver on the highway.* **2.** (of a moving vehicle or other conveyance) to strike the back end of (another vehicle or object): *A freight train rear-ended the commuter train this morning.* [1975–80]

rear-end•er (rēr′en′dər), *n.* an accident in which a vehicle or other conveyance has run into the rear of another. [1930–35; REAR END + -ER[1]]

rear′ guard′, a part of an army or military force detached from the main body to bring up and guard the rear from surprise attack, esp. in a retreat. [1475–85; < AF *reregard,* OF *rereguarde*]

rear•guard (rēr′gärd′), *adj.* **1.** of or pertaining to a rear guard. **2.** designed to oppose or prevent in a defensive way: *a rearguard strategy.* Also, **rear′-guard′.** [1895–1900; attributive use of REAR GUARD]

re•arm (rē ärm′), *v.t.* **1.** to arm again. **2.** to furnish with new or better weapons: *As soon as the new rifle was in production, the troops were rearmed.* —*v.i.* **3.** to become armed again. [1870–75; RE- + ARM[2]] —**re•ar•ma•ment** (rē är′mə mənt), *n.*

rear•most (rēr′mōst′), *adj.* farthest in the rear; last. [1710–20; REAR[1] + -MOST]

rear′ projec′tion, *Motion Pictures.* the projection of filmed action or stills on a translucent screen in front of which actors are lit and filmed: used to simulate an outdoor or location background in the studio. Also called **back projection, background projection.** [1955–60]

rear′ sight′, the sight nearest the breech of a firearm.

rear′view mir′ror (rēr′vyōō′), a mirror mounted on the side, windshield, or instrument panel of an automobile or other vehicle to provide the driver with a view of the area behind the vehicle. [1925–30; REAR[1] + VIEW]

CONCISE ETYMOLOGY KEY: <, descended or borrowed from; >, whence; b., blend of, blended; c., cognate with; cf., compare; deriv., derivative; equiv., equivalent; imit., imitative; obl., oblique; r., replacing; s., stem; sp., spelling, spelled; resp., respelling, respelled; trans., translation; ?, origin unknown; *, unattested; ‡, probably earlier than. See the full key inside the front cover.

rear•ward (rēr′wərd *for 1–4;* rēr′wôrd *for 5*), *adv.* **1.** Also, **rear′wards.** toward or in the rear. —*adj.*, **2.** located in, near, or toward the rear. **3.** directed toward the rear. —*n.* **4.** a position at the rear: *in the rearward of fashion.* **5.** the rear division of a military unit. [1300–50; ME *rerewarde* < AF. See REAR[1], -WARD] —**rear′ward•ness,** *n.*

Re•a Sil•vi•a (rē′ə sil′vē ə), *Rom. Legend.* See **Rhea Silvia.**

rea•son (rē′zən), *n.* **1.** a basis or cause, as for some belief, action, fact, event, etc.: *the reason for declaring war.* **2.** a statement presented in justification or explanation of a belief or action. **3.** the mental powers concerned with forming conclusions, judgments, or inferences. **4.** sound judgment; good sense. **5.** normal or sound powers of mind; sanity. **6.** *Logic.* a premise of an argument. **7.** *Philos.* **a.** the faculty or power of acquiring intellectual knowledge, either by direct understanding of first principles or by argument. **b.** the power of intelligent and dispassionate thought, or of conduct influenced by such thought. **c.** *Kantianism.* the faculty by which the ideas of pure reason are created. **8. bring (someone) to reason,** to induce a change of opinion in (someone) through presentation of arguments; convince: *The mother tried to bring her rebellious daughter to reason.* **9. by reason of,** on account of; because of: *He was consulted about the problem by reason of his long experience.* **10. in** or **within reason,** in accord with reason; justifiable; proper: *She tried to keep her demands in reason.* **11. stand to reason,** to be clear, obvious, or logical: *With such an upbringing it stands to reason that the child will be spoiled.* **12. with reason,** with justification; properly: *The government is concerned about the latest crisis, and with reason.* —*v.i.* **13.** to think or argue in a logical manner. **14.** to form conclusions, judgments, or inferences from facts or premises. **15.** to urge reasons which should determine belief or action. —*v.t.* **16.** to think through logically, as a problem (often fol. by *out*). **17.** to conclude or infer. **18.** to convince, persuade, etc., by reasoning. **19.** to support with reasons. [1175–1225; ME *resoun, reisun* (n.) < OF *reisun, reson* < L *ratiōn-* (s. of *ratiō*) RATIO] —**rea′son•er,** *n.*
—**Syn. 1.** purpose, end, aim, object, objective. REASON, CAUSE, MOTIVE are terms for a circumstance (or circumstances) which brings about or explains certain results. A REASON is an explanation of a situation or circumstance which made certain results seem possible or appropriate: *The reason for the robbery was the victim's display of his money.* The CAUSE is the way in which the circumstances produce the effect, that is, make a specific action seem necessary or desirable: *The cause was the robber's extreme need of money.* A MOTIVE is the hope, desire, or other force which starts the action (or an action) in an attempt to produce specific results: *The motive was to get money to buy food for his family.* **2.** excuse, rationalization. **3.** understanding, intellect, mind, intelligence. **15.** persuade.
—**Usage.** The construction REASON IS BECAUSE is criticized in a number of usage guides: *The reason for the long delays was because the costs greatly exceeded the original estimates.* One objection to this construction is based on its redundancy: the word BECAUSE (literally, *by cause*) contains within it the meaning of REASON; thus saying the REASON IS BECAUSE is like saying "The cause is by cause," which would never be said. A second objection is based on the claim that BECAUSE can introduce only adverbial clauses and that REASON IS requires completion by a noun clause. Critics would substitute *that* for BECAUSE in the offending construction: *The reason for the long delays in completing the project was that the costs. . . .* Although the objections described here are frequently raised, REASON IS BECAUSE is still common in almost all levels of speech and occurs often in edited writing as well.
A similar charge of redundancy is made against THE REASON WHY, which is also a well-established idiom: *The reason why the bill failed to pass was the defection of three key senators.*

rea•son•a•ble (rē′zə nə bəl, rēz′nə-), *adj.* **1.** agreeable to reason or sound judgment; logical: *a reasonable choice for chairman.* **2.** not exceeding the limit prescribed by reason; not excessive: *reasonable terms.* **3.** moderate, esp. in price; not expensive: *The coat was reasonable but not cheap.* **4.** endowed with reason. **5.** capable of rational behavior, decision, etc. [1250–1300; ME *resonable* < MF *raisonnable* < L *ratiōnābilis.* See REASON, -ABLE] —**rea′son•a•ble•ness, rea′son•a•bil′i•ty,** *n.* —**rea′son•a•bly,** *adv.*
—**Syn. 1.** intelligent, judicious, wise, equitable. REASONABLE, RATIONAL refer to the faculty of reasoning. RATIONAL can refer to the reasoning faculty itself or to something derived from that faculty: *rational powers; a rational analysis.* It can also mean sane or sensible: *She was no longer rational; a rational plan.* REASONABLE most often means sensible: *A reasonable supposition is one which appeals to our common sense.* **2.** equitable, fair, just. See **moderate.**

rea•soned (rē′zənd), *adj.* **1.** based on reason: *a carefully reasoned decision.* **2.** containing reasons: *a long, reasoned reply.* [1675–85; REASON + -ED[2]] —**rea′soned•ly,** *adv.*

rea•son•ing (rē′zə ning, rēz′ning), *n.* **1.** the act or process of a person who reasons. **2.** the process of forming conclusions, judgments, or inferences from facts or premises. **3.** the reasons, arguments, proofs, etc., resulting from this process. [1325–75; ME *resoninge.* See REASON, -ING[2]] —**rea′son•ing•ly,** *adv.*

rea•son•less (rē′zən lis), *adj.* **1.** not having any reason or sense: *an utterly reasonless display of anger.* **2.** not having a natural capacity for reason. [1350–1400; ME *resonles.* See REASON, -LESS] —**rea′son•less•ly,** *adv.* —**rea′son•less•ness,** *n.*

re•as•sure (rē′ə shŏŏr′, -shûr′), *v.t.*, **-sured, -sur•ing.** **1.** to restore to assurance or confidence: *His praise reassured me.* **2.** to assure again. **3.** to reinsure. [1590–1600; RE- + ASSURE] —**re′as•sur′ance,** *n.* —**re•as•sur•ed•ly** (rē′ə shŏŏr′id lē, -shûr′-), *adv.* —**re′as•sure′•ment,** *n.* —**re′as•sur′er,** *n.* —**re′as•sur′ing•ly,** *adv.*
—**Syn. 1.** encourage, hearten, comfort, inspirit.

re•a•ta (rē ä′tə, -at′ə), *n.* riata.

Réaum., Réaumur (temperature).

Ré•au•mur (rā′ə myŏŏr′; *Fr.* rā ō myr′), *n.* **1. René Antoine Fer•chault de** (rə nā′ än twan′ fer shō′ də), 1683–1757, French physicist and inventor. —*adj.* **2.** Also, **Re′au•mur′.** noting or pertaining to a temperature scale **(Ré′aumur scale′)** in which 0° represents the ice point and 80° represents the steam point. See illus. under **thermometer.**

reave[1] (rēv), *v.t.*, **reaved** or **reft, reav•ing.** *Archaic.* to take away by or as by force; plunder; rob. [bef. 900; ME *reven,* OE *rēafian;* c. G *rauben,* D *roven* to ROB]

reave[2] (rēv), *v.t., v.i.*, **reaved** or **reft, reav•ing.** *Archaic.* to rend; break; tear. [1175–1225; ME; appar. special use of REAVE[1] (by assoc. with RIVE)]

reb (reb), *n. Informal.* a Confederate soldier. [shortened form of REBEL]

Reb (reb), *n. Yiddish.* Mister (used as a title of respect). [lit., rabbi]

re•bab (ri bäb′), *n.* a Near Eastern fiddle having one to three strings and played with a bow. [1730–40; < Ar *rabāb;* see REBEC]

re•bar (rē′bär′), *n. Building Trades Informal.* a steel bar or rod used to reinforce concrete. Also, **re′-bar′.** [1960–65, *Amer.; re*(*inforcing*) *bar*]

re•bar•ba•tive (rē bär′bə tiv), *adj.* causing annoyance, irritation, or aversion; repellent. [1890–95; < F, fem. of *rébarbatif,* deriv. of *rébarber* to be unattractive, equiv. to *ré-* RE- + *barbe* beard (< L *barba*) + *-atif* -ATIVE]

re•bate[1] (*n.* rē′bāt; *v.* rē′bāt, ri bāt′), *n., v.,* **-bat•ed, -bat•ing.** —*n.* **1.** a return of part of the original payment for some service or merchandise; partial refund. —*v.t.* **2.** to allow as a discount. **3.** to deduct (a certain amount), as from a total. **4.** to return (part of an original payment): *He rebated five dollars to me.* **5.** to provide a rebate for (merchandise) after purchase: *The manufacturer is rebating this air conditioner.* **6.** to blunt (an edged or pointed weapon). **7.** to cover the edge or point of (an edged or pointed weapon) in order to make it incapable of cutting or piercing. —*v.i.* **8.** to allow rebates, esp. as the policy or practice of a company, store, etc. [1400–50; late ME *rebaten* (v.) < OF *rabatre* to beat, put down, equiv. to *re-* RE- + (*a*)*batre;* see ABATE] —**re′bat•a•ble, re′bate•a•ble,** *adj.* —**re′bat•er,** *n.*

re•bate[2] (rē′bāt, rab′it), *n., v.,* **-bat•ed, -bat•ing.** rabbet.

re•bat•ed (ri bā′tid), *adj. Heraldry.* cut off or abridged in some way, as a cross potent formed as a swastika. [1580–90; REBATE[1] + -ED[2]]

re•bate•ment (ri bāt′mənt), *n. Heraldry.* abatement (def. 5). [1555–65; REBATE[1] + -MENT]

re•ba•to (rə bä′tō, -bā′-), *n., pl.* **-tos.** rabato.

reb•be (reb′ə), *n. Yiddish.* **1.** a teacher in a Jewish school. **2.** (*often cap.*) a title of respect for the leader of a Hasidic group.

reb•betz•in (reb′i tsin), *n. Yiddish.* the wife of a rabbi. Also, ***reb′bitz•in.***

re•bec (rē′bek), *n.* a Renaissance fiddle having a pear-shaped body tapering into a neck that ends in a sickle-shaped or scroll-shaped pegbox. Also, **re′beck.** [1745–55; < MF; r. ME *ribibe* < OF *rebebe* << Ar *rabāb* REBAB]

rebec

Re•bec•ca (ri bek′ə), *n.* **1.** a female given name: from a Hebrew word meaning "binding." **2.** *Douay Bible.* Rebekah.

Re•bek•ah (ri bek′ə), *n.* the sister of Laban, wife of Isaac, and mother of Esau and Jacob. Gen. 24–27.

reb•el (*n., adj.* reb′əl; *v.* ri bel′), *n., adj., v.,* **-belled, -bel•ling.** —*n.* **1.** a person who refuses allegiance to, resists, or rises in arms against the government or ruler of his or her country. **2.** a person who resists any authority, control, or tradition. —*adj.* **3.** rebellious; defiant. **4.** of or pertaining to rebels. —*v.i.* **5.** to reject, resist, or rise in arms against one's government or ruler. **6.** to resist or rise against some authority, control, or tradition.

re′an•no•ta′tion, *n.*
re′an•nounce′, *v.t.,* **-nounced, -nounc•ing.**
re′an•nounce′ment, *n.*
re′a•noint′, *v.t.*
re′a•noint′ment, *n.*
re′an•tag′o•nize′, *v.t.,* **-nized, -niz•ing.**
re′a•pol′o•gize′, *v.t.,* **-gized, -giz•ing.**
re′a•pol′o•gy, *n., pl.* **-gies.**
re′ap•peal′, *v.*
re′ap•pear′, *v.i.*
re′ap•pear′ance, *n.*
re′ap•plaud′, *v.*
re′ap•pli′ance, *n.*
re′ap•pli•ca′tion, *n.*
re′ap•ply′, *v.,* **-plied, -ply•ing.**
re′ap•point′, *v.t.*
re′ap•point′ment, *n.*
re′ap•prais′al, *n.*
re′ap•praise′, *v.t.,* **-praised, -prais•ing.**
re′ap•pre•hend′, *v.*
re′ap•pre•hen′sion, *n.*
re′ap•proach′, *v.*
re′ap•proach′a•ble, *adj.*
re′ap•pro′pri•ate′, *v.t.,* **-at•ed, -at•ing.**
re′ap•pro′pri•a′tion, *n.*
re′ap•prov′al, *n.*
re′ap•prove′, *v.,* **-proved, -prov•ing.**
re•ar′bi•trate′, *v.,* **-trat•ed, -trat•ing.**
re′ar•bi•tra′tion, *n.*
re•ar′gue, *v.,* **-gued, -gu•ing.**
re•ar′gu•ment, *n.*

7. to show or feel utter repugnance: *His very soul rebelled at spanking the child.* [1250–1300; (adj.) ME < OF *rebelle* < L *rebellis* renewing a war, equiv. to *re-* RE- + *bell(um)* war + *-is* adj. suffix; (v.) ME *rebellen* (< OF *rebeller*) < L *rebellāre*; (n.) ME *rebel*, deriv. of the adj.] —**reb′el·like′**, *adj.*
—**Syn. 1.** insurrectionist, mutineer, traitor. **1, 3.** insurgent. **3.** mutinous. **5.** revolt, mutiny.

reb·el·dom (reb′əl dəm), *n.* **1.** a region or territory controlled by rebels. **2.** rebels collectively. **3.** rebellious conduct. [1855–60; REBEL + -DOM]

re·bel·lion (ri bel′yən), *n.* **1.** open, organized, and armed resistance to one's government or ruler. **2.** resistance to or defiance of any authority, control, or tradition. **3.** the act of rebelling. [1300–50; ME *rebelliou*n < OF < L *rebelliōn-* (s. of *rebelliō*), equiv. to *rebell(āre)* to REBEL + *-iōn-* -ION]
—**Syn. 1.** mutiny, sedition. **2.** insubordination, disobedience.

re·bel·lious (ri bel′yəs), *adj.* **1.** defying or resisting some established authority, government, or tradition; insubordinate; inclined to rebel. **2.** pertaining to or characteristic of rebels or rebellion. **3.** (of things) resisting treatment; refractory. [1400–50; late ME < ML *rebelliōsus*, equiv. to L *rebelli(ō)* REBELLION + *-ōsus* -OUS] —**re·bel′lious·ly**, *adv.* —**re·bel′lious·ness**, *n.*
—**Syn. 1.** defiant, insurgent, mutinous, seditious, rebel, refractory, disobedient, contumacious.

reb′el yell′, a long, shrill battle cry used by Confederate troops in the U.S. Civil War.

re·bid (*v.* rē bid′; *n.* rē′bid′), *v.*, **-bid, -bid·ding,** *n.* —*v.t.* **1.** *Bridge.* to make a second bid in (a suit that one bid previously): *He opened a spade and then rebid spades on the three level.* **2.** to submit again for bids, as a work contract or project: *The state rebid the proposed road because the original bids were too high.* —*v.i.* **3.** *Bridge.* to make a second bid: *He had enough points to open the bidding but not enough to rebid after his partner's pass.* —*n.* **4.** *Bridge.* a second bid: *a rebid to keep the auction open.* [1920–25; RE- + BID[1]]

re·bid·da·ble (rē bid′ə bəl), *adj. Bridge.* (of a suit) able to be bid twice, owing to length or strength, without support from one's partner. [1940–45; REBID + -ABLE]

re·birth (rē bûrth′, rē′bûrth′), *n.* **1.** a new or second birth: *the rebirth of the soul.* **2.** a renewed existence, activity, or growth; renaissance or revival: *the rebirth of conservatism.* [1830–40; RE- + BIRTH]

reb·o·ant (reb′ō ənt), *adj.* resounding or reverberating loudly. [1820–30; < L *reboant-* (s. of *reboāns*, prp. of *reboāre* to resound), equiv. to *re-* RE- + *bo(āre)* to cry aloud (c. Gk *boân*) + *-ant-* -ANT]

re·bop (rē′bop′), *n.* bop[1]. [imit.; cf. BEBOP]

re·born (rē bôrn′), *adj.* having undergone rebirth. [1590–1600; RE- + BORN]

re·bo·so (ri bō′sō), *n., pl.* **-sos.** rebozo. Also, **re·bo·sa** (ri bō′sə).

re·bo·te (ri bō′tē), *n.* **1.** the rear wall of a cancha or jai alai court. Cf. **frontis. 2.** a shot in which the ball is played as it comes off this wall. [< Sp: a rebound, equiv. to *re-* RE- + *bote* a blow, bounce, akin to *botar* to hurl, throw]

re·bound (*v.* ri bound′, rē′bound′; *n.* rē′bound′, ribound′), *v.i.* **1.** to bound or spring back from force of impact. **2.** to recover, as from ill health or discouragement. **3.** *Basketball.* to gain hold of rebounds: *a forward who rebounds well off the offensive board.* —*v.t.* **4.** to cause to bound back; cast back. **5.** *Basketball.* to gain hold of (a rebound): *The guard rebounded the ball in backcourt.* —*n.* **6.** the act of rebounding; recoil. **7.** *Basketball.* **a.** a ball that bounces off the backboard or the rim of the basket. **b.** an instance of gaining hold of such a ball. **8.** *Ice Hockey.* a puck that bounces off the gear or person of a goalkeeper attempting to make a save. **9. on the rebound, a.** after bouncing off the ground, a wall, etc.: *He hit the ball on the rebound.* **b.** after being rejected by another: *She didn't really love him; she married him on the rebound.* [1300–50; ME (v.) < MF *rebondir*, equiv. to OF *re-* RE- + *bondir* to BOUND[2]]

re·bound·er (rē′boun′dər), *n. Basketball.* a player who excels in gaining hold of rebounds. [1945–50; REBOUND + -ER[1]]

re·bo·zo (ri bō′sō, -zō; *Sp.* rE bô′thô, -sô), *n., pl.* **-zos** (-sōz, -zōz; *Sp.* -thôs, -sôs). a long woven scarf, often of fine material, worn over the head and shoulders by Spanish and Mexican women. Also, **reboso, rebosa, ribozo, ribozo.** [1800–10; < Sp: scarf, shawl, equiv. to *re-* RE- + *bozo* muzzle]

re·broad·cast (rē brôd′kast′, -käst′), *v.*, **-cast** or **-cast·ed, -cast·ing,** *n.* —*v.t.* **1.** to broadcast again from the same station. **2.** to relay (a radio or television program, speech, etc., received from another station). —*n.* **3.** a program that is rebroadcast. [1920–25; RE- + BROADCAST]

re·buff (*n.* ri buf′, rē′buf; *v.* ri buf′), *n.* **1.** a blunt or abrupt rejection, as of a person making advances. **2.** a peremptory refusal of a request, offer, etc.; snub. **3.** a check to action or progress. —*v.t.* **4.** to give a rebuff to; check; repel; refuse; drive away. [1580–90; < MF *rebuffer* < It *ribuffare* to disturb, reprimand, deriv. of *ribuffo* (n.), equiv. to *ri-* RE- + *buffo* puff; see BUFFOON] —**re·buff′a·ble**, *adj.* —**re·buff′a·bly**, *adv.*
—**Syn. 4.** snub, slight, reject, spurn.

re·build (rē bild′), *v.*, **-built** or (*Archaic*) **-build·ed; -build·ing.** —*v.t.* **1.** to repair, esp. to dismantle and reassemble with new parts: *to rebuild an old car.* **2.** to replace, restrengthen, or reinforce: *to rebuild an army.* **3.** to revise, reshape, or reorganize: *to rebuild a shattered career.* —*v.i.* **4.** to build again or afresh: *With the insurance money we can rebuild.* [1605–15; RE- + BUILD] —**re·build′a·ble**, *adj.* —**re·build′a·bil′i·ty**, *n.* —**re·build′er**, *n.*

re·buke (ri byōōk′), *v.*, **-buked, -buk·ing,** *n.* —*v.t.* **1.** to express sharp, stern disapproval of; reprove; reprimand. —*n.* **2.** sharp, stern disapproval; reproof; reprimand. [1275–1325; ME *rebuken* (v.) < AF *rebuker* (OF *rebuchier*) to beat back, equiv. to *re-* RE- + *bucher* to beat, strike < Gmc] —**re·buk′a·ble**, *adj.* —**re·buk′er**, *n.* —**re·buk′ing·ly**, *adv.*
—**Syn. 1.** censure, upbraid, chide, admonish. See **reproach. 2.** reproach, remonstration, censure.

re·bus (rē′bəs), *n., pl.* **-bus·es. 1.** a representation of a word or phrase by pictures, symbols, etc., that suggest that word or phrase or its syllables: *Two gates and a head is a rebus for Gateshead.* **2.** a piece of writing containing many such representations. [1595–1605; < L *rēbus* by things (abl. pl. of *rēs*), in phrase *nōn verbis sed rēbus* not by words but by things]

re·bus sic stan·ti·bus (rē′bəs sik stan′tə bəs), *Internat. Law.* (of the duration of the binding force treaty) for as long as the relevant facts and circumstances remain basically the same. [1840–50; < L *rēbus sīc stantibus* with things remaining thus]

re·but (ri but′), *v.*, **-but·ted, -but·ting.** —*v.t.* **1.** to refute by evidence or argument. **2.** to oppose by contrary proof. —*v.i.* **3.** to provide some evidence or argument that refutes or opposes. [1250–1300; ME *reb(o)uten* < OF *rebouter*, equiv. to *re-* RE- + *bouter* to BUTT[3]] —**re·but′ta·ble**, *adj.*
—**Syn. 1.** disprove, confute.

re·but·tal (ri but′l), *n.* an act of rebutting, as in a debate. [1820–30; REBUT + -AL[2]]
—**Syn.** rejoinder, refutation, denial, confutation.

re·but·ter[1] (ri but′ər), *n.* a person who rebuts. [1785–95; REBUT + -ER[1]]

re·but·ter[2] (ri but′ər), *n. Law.* a defendant's answer to a plaintiff's surrejoinder. [1530–40; < AF *rebuter* rebuttal, n. use of inf.: to REBUT; see -ER[3]]

rec (rek), *n. Informal.* recreation. [1925–30; by shortening]

rec., 1. receipt. **2.** (in prescriptions) fresh. [< L *recēns*] **3.** recipe. **4.** record. **5.** recorder. **6.** recording.

re·cal·ci·trant (ri kal′si trənt), *adj.* **1.** resisting authority or control; not obedient or compliant; refractory. **2.** hard to deal with, manage, or operate. —*n.* **3.** a recalcitrant person. [1835–45; < L *recalcitrant-* (s. of *recalcitrāns*, prp. of *recalcitrāre* to kick back), equiv. to *re-* RE- + *calcitr(āre)* to strike with the heels, kick (deriv. of *calx* heel) + *-ant-* -ANT] —**re·cal′ci·trance, re·cal′ci·tran·cy**, *n.*
—**Syn. 1.** resistant, rebellious, opposed. See **unruly.**

re·cal·ci·trate (ri kal′si trāt′), *v.i.*, **-trat·ed, -trat·ing.** to resist or oppose; show strong objection or repugnance. [1615–25; < L *recalcitrātus*, ptp. of *recalcitrāre*; see RECALCITRANT, -ATE[1]] —**re·cal′ci·tra′tion**, *n.*

re·cal·cu·late (rē kal′kyə lāt′), *v.t.*, **-lat·ed, -lat·ing.** to calculate again, esp. for the purpose of finding an error or confirming a previous computation. [1615–25; RE- + CALCULATE] —**re′cal·cu·la′tion**, *n.*

re·ca·les·cence (rē′kə les′əns), *n. Metall.* a brightening exhibited by cooling iron as latent heat of transformation is liberated. [1870–75; *recal(esce)* to become hot again (< L *recalēscere*, equiv. to *re-* RE- + *cal(ēre)* to be hot (cf. CALORIE) + *-ēsc-* inchoative suffix + *-ere* inf. ending) + -ESCENCE] —**re′ca·les′cent**, *adj.*

re·call (*v.* ri kôl′; *n.* ri kôl′, rē′kôl *for 7–9, 12, 13;* rē′kôl *for 10, 11*), *v.t.* **1.** to bring back from memory; recollect; remember: *Can you recall what she said?* **2.** to call back; summon to return: *The army recalled many veterans.* **3.** to bring (one's thoughts, attention, etc.) back to matters previously considered: *He recalled his mind from pleasant daydreams to the dull task at hand.* **4.** *Internat. Law.* to summon back and withdraw the office from (a diplomat). **5.** to revoke or withdraw: *to recall a promise.* **6.** to revive. —*n.* **7.** an act of recalling. **8.** recollection; remembrance. **9.** the act or possibility of revoking something. **10.** the removal or the right of removal of a public official from office by a vote of the people taken upon petition of a specified number of the qualified electors. **11.** Also called **callback.** a summons by a manufacturer or other agency for the return of goods or a product already shipped to market or sold to consumers but discovered to be defective, contaminated, unsafe, or the like. **12.** a signal made by a vessel to recall one of its boats. **13.** a signal displayed to direct a racing yacht to sail across the starting line again. [1575–85; RE- + CALL] —**re·call′a·ble**, *adj.*
—**Syn. 1.** See **remember. 5.** rescind, retract, recant, repeal; annul. **7.** memory. **9.** revocation, retraction, repeal, withdrawal, recantation; nullification. —**Ant. 1.** forget.

Re·ca·mier (rā′kə myā′), *n.* a backless day bed of the Directoire and Empire periods, having raised ends of equal height. [1920–25; after Madame RÉCAMIER]

Ré·ca·mier (rā kA myā′), *n.* **Madame** (*Jeanne Françoise Julie Adélaïde Bernard*), 1777–1849, French social leader in the literary and political circles of Paris.

re·can·al·i·za·tion (rē kan′l ə zā′shən, rē′kə nal′-), *n. Surg.* the reopening of a previously occluded passageway within a blood vessel. [1950–55; RE- + CANALIZE + -ATION]

re·cant (ri kant′), *v.t.* **1.** to withdraw or disavow (a statement, opinion, etc.), esp. formally; retract. —*v.i.* **2.** to withdraw or disavow a statement, opinion, etc., esp. formally. [1525–35; < L *recantāre* to sing back, sing again, equiv. to *re-* RE- + *cantāre*, freq. of *canere* to sing; cf. CHANT] —**re·can·ta·tion** (rē′kan tā′shən), *n.* —**re·cant′er**, *n.* —**re·cant′ing·ly**, *adv.*
—**Syn. 1.** revoke, recall, rescind, deny.

re·cap[1] (*v.* rē′kap′, rē kap′; *n.* rē′kap′), *v.*, **-capped, -cap·ping,** *n.* —*v.t.* **1.** to recondition (a worn automobile tire) by cementing on a strip of prepared rubber and vulcanizing by subjecting to heat and pressure in a mold. —*n.* **2.** a recapped tire. [1935–40; RE- + CAP[1]] —**re·cap′pa·ble**, *adj.*

re·cap[2] (rē′kap′), *n., v.*, **-capped, -cap·ping.** —*n.* **1.** a recapitulation. —*v.t., v.i.* **2.** to recapitulate. [1945–50; by shortening]

re·cap·i·tal·i·za·tion (rē kap′i tl ə zā′shən), *n.* a revision of a corporation's capital structure by an exchange of securities. [1925–30; RE- + CAPITALIZATION]

re·cap·i·tal·ize (rē kap′i tl īz′), *v.t.*, **-ized, -iz·ing.** to renew or change the capital of. Also, *esp. Brit.*, **re·cap′i·tal·ise′.** [1940–45; RE- + CAPITALIZE]

re·ca·pit·u·late (rē′kə pich′ə lāt′), *v.*, **-lated, -lat·ing.** —*v.t.* **1.** to review by a brief summary, as at the end of a speech or discussion; summarize. **2.** *Biol.* (of an organism) to repeat (ancestral evolutionary stages) in its development. **3.** *Music.* to restate (the exposition) in a sonata-form movement. —*v.i.* **4.** to sum up statements or matters. [1560–70; < LL *recapitulātus* (ptp. of *recapitulāre*), equiv. to *re-* RE- + *capitulātus*; see CAPITULATE]
—**Syn. 1.** See **repeat.**

re·ca·pit·u·la·tion (rē′kə pich′ə lā′shən), *n.* **1.** the act of recapitulating or the state of being recapitulated. **2.** a brief review or summary, as of a speech. **3.** *Biol.* the theory that the stages an organism passes through during its embryonic development repeat the evolutionary stages of structural change in its ancestral lineage. **4.** *Music.* the modified restatement of the exposition following the development section in a sonata-form movement. [1350–1400; ME *recapitulaciou*n < LL *recapitulātiōn-* (s. of *recapitulātiō*), equiv. to *recapitulāt(us)* (see RECAPITULATE) + *-iōn-* -ION] —**re′ca·pit′u·la′tive, re·ca·pit·u·la·to·ry** (rē′kə pich′ə lə tôr′ē, -tōr′ē), *adj.*

re·cap·tion (rē kap′shən), *n. Law.* the taking back without violence of one's property or a member of one's family or household unlawfully in the possession or custody of another. [1600–10; RE- + CAPTION]

re·cap·ture (rē kap′chər), *v.*, **-tured, -tur·ing,** *n.* —*v.t.* **1.** to capture again; recover by capture; retake. **2.** (of a government) to take by recapture. **3.** to recollect or reexperience (something past). —*n.* **4.** the recovery or retaking by capture. **5.** the taking by the government of a fixed part of all earnings in excess of a certain percentage of property value, as in the case of a railroad. **6.** *Internat. Law.* the lawful reacquisition of a former possession. **7.** the state or fact of being recaptured. [1745–55; RE- + CAPTURE] —**re·cap′tur·a·ble**, *adj.*

re·car·bu·rize (rē kär′bə rīz′, -byə-), *v.t.*, **-rized, -riz·ing.** *Metall.* to add carbon to (steel), as in an open-hearth furnace, as by adding pig iron. Also, *esp. Brit.*, **re·car′bu·rise′.** [1925–30; RE- + CARBURIZE] —**re·car′·bu·ri·za′tion**, *n.* —**re·car′bu·riz′er**, *n.*

re·cast (*v.* rē kast′, -käst′; *n.* rē′kast′, -käst′), *v.*, **-cast, -cast·ing,** *n.* —*v.t.* **1.** to cast again or anew. **2.** to form, fashion, or arrange again. **3.** to remodel or reconstruct (a literary work, document, sentence, etc.). **4.** to supply (a theater or opera work) with a new cast. —*n.* **5.** a recasting. **6.** a new form produced by recasting. [1890–95; RE- + CAST] —**re·cast′er**, *n.*

rec·ce (rek′ē), *n.* (esp. in British military use) reconnaissance: *a pilot who spent three months on recce.* Also, **rec·co** (rek′ō), **rec·cy** (rek′ē). [1940–45; by shortening and alter.]

recd., received. Also, **rec'd.**

re·cede[1] (ri sēd′), *v.i.*, **-ced·ed, -ced·ing. 1.** to go or move away; retreat; go to or toward a more distant point; withdraw. **2.** to become more distant. **3.** (of a color, form, etc., on a flat surface) to move away or be perceived as moving away from an observer, esp. as giving the illusion of space. Cf. **advance** (def. 15). **4.** to slope backward: *a chin that recedes.* **5.** to draw back or withdraw from a conclusion, viewpoint, undertaking, promise, etc. [1470–80; < L *recēdere* to go, fall back, equiv. to *re-* RE- + *cēdere* to withdraw, go; see CEDE]
—**Syn. 5.** retire, retreat.

re·cede[2] (rē sēd′), *v.t.*, **-ced·ed, -ced·ing.** to cede back; yield or grant to a former possessor. [1765–75; RE- + CEDE]

re·ceipt (ri sēt′), *n.* **1.** a written acknowledgment of having received a specified amount of money, goods, etc. **2. receipts,** the amount or quantity received. **3.** the act of receiving or the state of being received. **4.** something that is received. **5.** a recipe. —*v.t.* **6.** to acknowledge in writing the payment of (a bill). **7.** to give a receipt for (money, goods, etc.). —*v.i.* **8.** to give a receipt, as for money or goods. [1350–1400; ME *receite* < AF (OF *recoite*) < L *recepta*, fem. ptp. of *recipere* to RECEIVE]

CONCISE PRONUNCIATION KEY: act, cāpe, dâre, pärt; set, ēqual; *if*, īce; ox, ōver, ôrder, oil, bŏŏk, bōōt, out; up, ûrge; child; sing; shoe; thin, *th*at; zh as in *treasure*. ə = *a* as in *alone*, *e* as in *system*, *i* as in *easily*, *o* as in *gallop*, *u* as in *circus*; ᵊ as in *fire* (fīᵊr), *hour* (ouᵊr). l and n can serve as syllabic consonants, as in *cradle* (krād′l), and *button* (but′n). See the full key inside the front cover.

re′a·rise′, *v.i.*, **-rose, -ris·en, -ris·ing.**
re′a·rous′al, *n.*
re′a·rouse′, *v.*, **-roused, -rous·ing.**
re′ar·range′, *v.*, **-ranged, -rang·ing.**
re′ar·range′a·ble, *adj.*
re′ar·range′ment, *n.*
re′ar·rest′, *v.t., n.*
re′ar·tic′u·late′, *v.*, **-lat·ed, -lat·ing.**
re′ar·tic′u·la′tion, *n.*
re′as·cend′, *v.*
re′as·cent′, *n.*
re′as·sem′blage, *n.*
re′as·sem′ble, *v.*, **-bled, -bling.**
re′as·sem′bly, *n., pl.* **-blies.**
re′as·sent′, *v.i.*
re′as·sert′, *v.t.*
re′as·ser′tion, *n.*
re′as·sess′, *v.t.*
re′as·sess′ment, *n.*
re′as·sign′, *v.t.*
re′as·sig·na′tion, *n.*
re′as·sign′ment, *n.*
re′as·sim′i·late′, *v.*, **-lat·ed, -lat·ing.**
re′as·sim′i·la′tion, *n.*
re′as·sist′, *v.t.*
re′as·sist′ance, *n.*
re′as·so′ci·ate′, *v.*, **-at·ed, -at·ing.**
re′as·so′ci·a′tion, *n.*
re′as·sort′, *v.*
re′as·sort′ment, *n.*
re′as·sume′, *v.t.*, **-sumed, -sum·ing.**
re′as·sump′tion, *n.*
re′at·tach′, *v.*
re′at·tach′a·ble, *adj.*
re′at·tach′ment, *n.*

re·ceipt·or (ri sē′tər), *n.* **1.** a person who receipts. **2.** *Law.* a person to whom attached property is delivered for safekeeping in return for a bond to produce it when the litigation ends. [1805–15, *Amer.*; RECEIPT + -OR[2]]

re·ceiv·a·ble (ri sē′və bəl), *adj.* **1.** fit for acceptance; acceptable. **2.** awaiting receipt of payment: *accounts receivable.* **3.** capable of being received. —*n.* **4. receivables,** business assets in the form of obligations due from others. [1350–1400; RECEIVE + -ABLE; r. ME *rescevable* < AF *receivable* (OF *recevable*)] —**re·ceiv′a·bil′i·ty, re·ceiv′a·ble·ness,** *n.*

re·ceive (ri sēv′), *v.,* **-ceived, -ceiv·ing.** —*v.t.* **1.** to take into one's possession (something offered or delivered): *to receive many gifts.* **2.** to have (something) bestowed, conferred, etc.: *to receive an honorary degree.* **3.** to have delivered or brought to one: *to receive a letter.* **4.** to get or be informed of: *to receive instructions; to receive news.* **5.** to be burdened with; sustain: *to receive a heavy load.* **6.** to hold, bear, or contain: *The nut receives a bolt and a washer. The plaster receives the impression of the mold.* **7.** to take into the mind; apprehend mentally: *to receive an idea.* **8.** to accept from another by hearing or listening: *A priest received his confession.* **9.** to meet with; experience: *to receive attention.* **10.** to suffer the injury of: *He received a terrific blow on the forehead.* **11.** to be at home to (visitors): *They received their neighbors on Sunday.* **12.** to greet or welcome (guests, visitors, etc.) upon arriving: *They received us at the front door.* **13.** to admit (a person) to a place: *The butler received him and asked him to wait in the drawing room.* **14.** to admit into an organization, membership, etc.: *to receive someone into the group.* **15.** to accept as authoritative, valid, true, or approved: *a principle universally received.* **16.** to react to in the manner specified: *to receive a proposal with contempt; She received the job offer with joy.* —*v.i.* **17.** to receive something. **18.** to receive visitors or guests. **19.** *Radio.* to convert incoming electromagnetic waves into the original signal. **20.** to receive the Eucharist: *He receives every Sunday.* [1250–1300; ME *receven* < ONF *receivre* < L *recipere,* equiv. to *re-* RE- + *-cipere,* comb. form of *capere* to take]
—**Syn. 11.** admit, entertain, welcome. —**Ant. 1.** give.

re·ceived (ri sēvd′), *adj.* generally or traditionally accepted; conventional; standard: *a received moral idea.* [1400–50; late ME; see RECEIVE, -ED[2]]

Received′ Pronuncia′tion, the pronunciation of British English considered to have the widest geographical distribution and the fewest regional peculiarities, originally the pronunciation of educated speakers in southern England and traditionally that used in the public schools and at Oxford and Cambridge universities, adopted by many speakers elsewhere in England and widely used in broadcasting. *Abbr.:* RP [1865–70]

Received′ Stand′ard, the form of educated English spoken originally in southern England and having Received Pronunciation as a chief distinguishing feature. Also called **Received′ Stand′ard Eng′lish.** [1910–15]

re·ceiv·er (ri sē′vər), *n.* **1.** a person or thing that receives. **2.** a device or apparatus that receives electrical signals, waves, or the like, and renders them perceptible to the senses, as the part of a telephone held to the ear, a radio receiving set, or a television receiving set. **3.** *Law.* a person appointed by a court to manage the affairs of a bankrupt business or person or to care for property in litigation. **4.** *Com.* a person appointed to receive money due. **5.** a person who knowingly receives stolen goods for an illegal purpose; a dealer in stolen merchandise. **6.** a device or apparatus for receiving or holding something; receptacle; container. **7.** (in a firearm) the basic metal unit housing the action and to which the barrel and other components are attached. **8.** *Chem.* a vessel for collecting and containing a distillate. See illus. under **alembic. 9.** *Football.* a player on the offensive team who catches, is eligible to catch, or is noted for the ability to catch a forward pass: *Jones was the receiver of the first pass thrown. He sent all his receivers downfield.* **10.** *Baseball.* the catcher. [1300–50; 1875–80 for def. 2; RECEIVE + -ER[1]; r. ME *recevour* < AF *receivour, recevour* (OF *recevere*)]

receiv′er gen′eral, *pl.* **receivers general.** a public official in charge of the government's treasury. [1400–50; late ME]

re·ceiv·er·ship (ri sē′vər ship′), *n. Law.* **1.** the condition of being in the hands of a receiver. **2.** the position or function of being a receiver in charge of administering the property of others. [1475–85; RECEIVER + -SHIP]

receiv′ing blan′ket, a small blanket, usually of cotton, for wrapping an infant, esp. following a bath. [1925–30]

receiv′ing end′, the position in which one is subject to some kind of action or effect, esp. an unpleasant one (usually used in the phrase *at* or *on the receiving end*): *The corporation is on the receiving end of many complaints about its advertising.* [1930–35]

receiv′ing line′, a row formed by the hosts, guests of honor, or the like, for receiving guests formally at a ball, reception, etc. [1930–35, *Amer.*]

receiv′ing set′, *Radio.* a radio receiver. [1915–20]

CONCISE ETYMOLOGY KEY: <, descended or borrowed from; >, whence; b., blend of, blended; c., cognate with; cf., compare; deriv., derivative; equiv., equivalent; imit., imitative; obl., oblique; r., replacing; s., stem; sp., spelling, spelled; resp., respelling, respelled; trans., translation; ?, origin unknown; *, unattested; ‡, probably earlier than. See the full key inside the front cover.

re·cen·sion (ri sen′shən), *n.* **1.** an editorial revision of a literary work, esp. on the basis of critical examination of the text and the sources used. **2.** a version of a text resulting from such revision. [1630–40; < L *recēnsiōn-* (s. of *recēnsiō*) a reviewing, equiv. to *recēns(ēre)* (*re-* RE- + *cēnsēre* to estimate, assess) + *-iōn-* -ION] —**re·cen′sion·ist,** *n.*

re·cent (rē′sənt), *adj.* **1.** of late occurrence, appearance, or origin; lately happening, done, made, etc.: *recent events; a recent trip.* **2.** not long past: *in recent years.* **3.** of or belonging to a time not long past. **4.** (*cap.*) *Geol.* noting or pertaining to the present epoch, originating at the end of the glacial period, about 10,000 years ago, and forming the latter half of the Quaternary Period; Holocene. See table under **geologic time.** —*n.* **5.** Also called **Holocene.** (*cap.*) *Geol.* the Recent Epoch or Series. [1525–35; < L *recent-* (s. of *recēns*) fresh, new] —**re′·cen·cy, re′cent·ness,** *n.* —**re′cent·ly,** *adv.*
—**Syn. 1.** fresh, new. See **modern.** —**Ant. 1.** early, old.

re·cept (rē′sept), *n.* an idea formed by the repetition of similar percepts, as successive percepts of the same object. [1885–90; n. use of L *receptum,* neut. ptp. of *recipere* to RECEIVE] —**re·cep·tu·al** (ri sep′cho͞o əl), *adj.* —**re·cep′tu·al·ly,** *adv.*

re·cep·ta·cle (ri sep′tə kəl), *n.* **1.** a container, device, etc., that receives or holds something: *a receptacle for trash.* **2.** *Bot.* the modified or expanded portion of the stem or axis that bears the organs of a single flower or the florets of a flower head. **3.** *Elect.* a contact device installed at an outlet for the connection of a portable lamp, appliance, or other electric device by means of a plug and flexible cord. [1375–1425; ME (< OF) < L *receptāculum* reservoir, equiv. to *receptā(re)* to take again, receive back (freq. of *recipere* to RECEIVE) + *-culum* -CLE[2]]

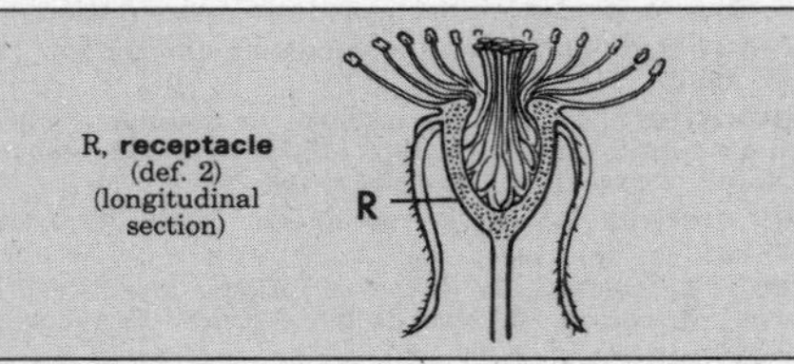

R, **receptacle** (def. 2) (longitudinal section)

re·cep·ti·ble (ri sep′tə bəl), *adj.* adapted to or suitable for reception. [1565–75; < LL *receptibilis* that may be acquired again, equiv. to L *recept(us)* (ptp. of *recipere* to RECEIVE) + *-ibilis* -IBLE] —**re·cep′ti·bil′i·ty,** *n.*

re·cep·tion (ri sep′shən), *n.* **1.** the act of receiving or the state of being received. **2.** a manner of being received: *The book met with a favorable reception.* **3.** a function or occasion when persons are formally received: *a wedding reception.* **4.** the quality or fidelity attained in receiving radio or television broadcasts under given circumstances. [1350–1400; ME *recepcion* < L *receptiōn-* (s. of *receptiō*), equiv. to *recept(us)* (ptp. of *recipere* to RECEIVE) + *-iōn-* -ION]
—**Syn. 2.** response, reaction, treatment.

recep′tion desk′, **1.** a desk at which a receptionist works, as in an office. **2.** a counter, as at a hotel, at which guests are registered. Also called **front desk.** [1935–40]

re·cep·tion·ism (ri sep′shə niz′əm), *n. Theol.* the doctrine that in the communion service the communicant receives the body and blood of Christ but that the bread and wine are not transubstantiated. [1895–1900; RECEPTION + -ISM]

re·cep·tion·ist (ri sep′shə nist), *n.* **1.** a person employed to receive and assist callers, clients, etc., as in an office. **2.** *Theol.* a person who advocates receptionism. [1865–70; RECEPTION + -IST]

recep′tion room′, a room for receiving visitors, clients, patients, etc. [1820–30]

re·cep·tive (ri sep′tiv), *adj.* **1.** having the quality of receiving, taking in, or admitting. **2.** able or quick to receive knowledge, ideas, etc.: *a receptive mind.* **3.** willing or inclined to receive suggestions, offers, etc., with favor: *a receptive listener.* **4.** of or pertaining to reception or receptors: *a receptive end organ.* **5.** (in language learning) of or pertaining to the language skills of listening and reading (opposed to *productive*). [1540–50; < ML *receptīvus.* See RECEPTION, -IVE] —**re·cep′tive·ly,** *adv.* —**re·cep·tiv·i·ty** (rē′sep tiv′i tē), **re·cep′tive·ness,** *n.*
—**Syn. 3.** amenable, hospitable, responsive, open.

re·cep·tor (ri sep′tər), *n.* **1.** *Physiol.* an end organ or a group of end organs of sensory or afferent neurons, specialized to be sensitive to stimulating agents, as touch or heat. **2.** *Cell Biol.* any of various specific protein molecules in surface membranes of cells and organelles to which complementary molecules, as hormones, neurotransmitters, antigens, or antibodies, may become bound. **3.** the panlike base of a stall shower. [1400–50; late ME *receptour* < OF < L *receptor.* See RECEPTION, -TOR]

re·cess (ri ses′, rē′ses), *n.* **1.** temporary withdrawal or cessation from the usual work or activity. **2.** a period of such withdrawal. **3.** a receding part or space, as a bay or alcove in a room. **4.** an indentation in a line or extent of coast, hills, forest, etc. **5. recesses,** a secluded or inner area or part: *in the recesses of the palace.* —*v.t.* **6.** to place or set in a recess. **7.** to set or form as or like a recess; make a recess or recesses in: *to recess a wall.* **8.** to suspend or defer for a recess: *to recess the Senate.* —*v.i.* **9.** to take a recess. [1510–20; < L *recessus* a withdrawal, receding part, equiv. to *recēd(ere)* to RECEDE[1] + *-tus* suffix of v. action, with *dt* > *ss*]
—**Syn. 1.** respite, rest, break, vacation.

re·ces·sion[1] (ri sesh′ən), *n.* **1.** the act of receding or withdrawing. **2.** a receding part of a wall, building, etc. **3.** a withdrawing procession, as at the end of a religious service. **4.** *Econ.* a period of an economic contraction, sometimes limited in scope or duration. Cf. **depression** (def. 7). [1640–50; < L *recessiōn-* (s. of *recessiō*). See RECESS, -ION]

re·ces·sion[2] (rē sesh′ən), *n.* a return of ownership to a former possessor. [1885–90; RE- + CESSION]

re·ces·sion·al (ri sesh′ə nl), *adj.* **1.** of or pertaining to a recession of the clergy and choir after the service. **2.** of or pertaining to a recess, as of a legislative body. —*n.* **3.** a hymn or other piece of music played at the end of a service while the congregation is filing out. [1865–70; RECESSION[1] + -AL[1]]

reces′sional moraine′, *Geol.* a moraine marking a temporary halt in the general retreat of a glacier. Cf. **terminal moraine.** [1905–10]

re·ces·sion·ar·y (ri sesh′ə ner′ē), *adj.* of, pertaining to, or causing recession, esp. economic recession: *recessionary market pressures.* [1955–60; RECESSION + -ARY]

re·ces·sion·proof (ri sesh′ən pro͞of′), *adj.* not susceptible to an economic recession: *a recessionproof economy; He wants a long-term contract to make his job recessionproof.* [1975–80; RECESSION[1] + -PROOF]

re·ces·sive (ri ses′iv), *adj.* **1.** tending to go, move, or slant back; receding. **2.** *Genetics.* of or pertaining to a recessive. **3.** *Phonet.* (of an accent) showing a tendency to recede from the end toward the beginning of a word. —*n. Genetics.* **4.** that one of a pair of alternative alleles whose effect is masked by the activity of the second when both are present in the same cell or organism. **5.** the trait or character determined by such an allele. Cf. **dominant** (def. 6). [1665–75; < L *recess(us)* (see RECESS) + -IVE] —**re·ces′sive·ly,** *adv.* —**re·ces′sive·ness,** *n.*

re·charge (*v.* rē chärj′; *n.* rē chärj′, rē′chärj′), *v.,* **-charged, -charg·ing,** *n.* —*v.t.* **1.** to charge again with electricity. **2.** *Informal.* to refresh or restore; revitalize. —*v.i.* **3.** to make a new charge, esp. to attack again. **4.** *Informal.* to revive or restore energy, stamina, enthusiasm, etc. —*n.* **5.** an act or instance of recharging. **6.** *Geol.* the processes by which ground water is absorbed into the zone of saturation. Cf. **water table.** [1400–50; late ME: to reload (a vessel). See RE-, CHARGE] —**re·charg′er,** *n.*

re·charge·a·ble (rē chär′jə bəl), *adj.* **1.** (of a storage battery) capable of being charged repeatedly. Cf. **cordless** (def. 2). —*n.* **2.** a rechargeable battery. [1945–50; RE- + CHARGEABLE] —**re·charge′a·bil′i·ty,** *n.*

ré·chauf·fé (*Fr.* rā shō fā′), *n., pl.* **-fés** (*Fr.* -fā′). **1.** a warmed-up dish of food. **2.** anything old or stale brought into service again. [1795–1805; < F, ptp. of *réchauffer* (*r(e)-* RE- + *échauffer* to warm; see CHAFE)]

re·cher·ché (rə shâr′shā, rə shâr shā′; *Fr.* rə sher-shā′), *adj.* **1.** sought out with care. **2.** very rare, exotic, or choice; arcane; obscure. **3.** of studied refinement or elegance; precious; affected; pretentious. [1715–25; < F, ptp. of *rechercher* to search for carefully; see RESEARCH]

re·cid·i·vate (ri sid′ə vāt′, rē-), *v.i.* **-vat·ed, -vat·ing.** to engage in recidivism; relapse. [1520–30; < ML *recidivātus* ptp. of *recidivāre* to relapse. See RECIDIVISM, -ATE[1]]

re·cid·i·vism (ri sid′ə viz′əm), *n.* **1.** repeated or habitual relapse, as into crime. **2.** *Psychiatry.* the chronic tendency toward repetition of criminal or antisocial behavior patterns. [1885–90; < L *recidīv(us)* relapsing (*recid(ere)* to fall back (*re-* RE- + *-cidere,* comb. form of *cadere* to fall) + *-īvus* -IVE) + -ISM] —**re·cid′i·vist,** *n., adj.* —**re·cid′i·vis′tic, re·cid′i·vous,** *adj.*

Re·ci·fe (rə sē′fə), *n.* a seaport in and the capital of Pernambuco province, in NE Brazil. 1,249,821. Formerly, **Pernambuco.**

recip., **1.** reciprocal. **2.** reciprocity.

rec·i·pe (res′ə pē), *n.* **1.** a set of instructions for making or preparing something, esp. a food dish: *a recipe for a cake.* **2.** a medical prescription. **3.** a method to attain a desired end: *a recipe for success.* [1350–1400; ME < L: take, impv. sing. of *recipere* to RECEIVE]

re·cip·i·ence (ri sip′ē əns), *n.* **1.** the act of receiving; reception. **2.** the state or quality of being receptive; receptiveness. Also, **re·cip′i·en·cy.** [1880–85; RECIPI(ENT) + -ENCE]

re·cip·i·ent (ri sip′ē ənt), *n.* **1.** a person or thing that receives; receiver: *the recipient of a prize.* —*adj.* **2.** receiving or capable of receiving. [1550–60; < L *recipient-* (s. of *recipiēns*), prp. of *recipere* to RECEIVE; see -ENT]

re·cip·ro·cal (ri sip′rə kəl), *adj.* **1.** given or felt by each toward the other; mutual: *reciprocal respect.* **2.** given, performed, felt, etc., in return: *reciprocal aid.* **3.** corresponding; matching; complementary; equivalent: *reciprocal privileges at other health clubs.* **4.** *Gram.* (of a pronoun or verb) expressing mutual relationship or action: *"Each other" and "one another" are reciprocal pronouns.* **5.** inversely related or proportional; opposite. **6.** *Math.* noting expressions, relations, etc., involving reciprocals: *a reciprocal function.* **7.** *Navig.* bearing in a direction 180° to a given direction; back. —*n.* **8.** something that is reciprocal to something else; equivalent; counterpart; complement. **9.** Also called **multiplication**

re′at·tack′, *v.*
re′at·tain′, *v.t.*
re′at·tain′ment, *n.*
re′at·tempt′, *v.t.*
re′at·test′, *v.t.*
re′at·tire′, *v.t.,* **-tired, -tir·ing.**
re′at·tract′, *v.t.*
re′at·trac′tion, *n.*
re′at·trib′ute, *v.t.,* **-ut·ed, -ut·ing.**
re′at·tri·bu′tion, *n.*
re·au′dit, *n., v.*
re′au·di′tion, *n.*
re′au·then′ti·cate′, *v.t.,* **-cat·ed, -cat·ing.**
re′au·then′ti·ca′tion, *n.*
re′au·thor·i·za′tion, *n.*
re·au′thor·ize′, *v.t.,* **-ized, -iz·ing.**
re′a·vow′, *v.t.*
re′a·vow′al, *n.*
re′a·wake′, *v.,* **-woke** or **-waked, -wak·ing.**
re′a·wak′en, *v.*
re′a·wak′en·ing, *n.*
re·bait′, *v.t.*
re·bake′, *v.t.,* **-baked, -bak·ing.**
re·bal′ance, *v.,* **-anced, -anc·ing.**
re·bale′, *v.t.,* **-baled, -bal·ing.**
re·bal′lot, *n., v.i.*
re·band′age, *v.t.,* **-aged, -ag·ing.**
re·bank′, *v.*
re·bap′tism, *n.*
re·bap′tize, *v.,* **-tized, -tiz·ing.**
re·bathe′, *v.,* **-bathed, -bath·ing.**
re·bend′, *v.t.,* **-bent, -bend·ing.**
re·bend′a·ble, *adj.*
re·bill′, *v.t.*
re·bind′, *v.,* **-bound, -bind·ing.**
re·bleach′, *v.*

inverse. *Math.* the ratio of unity to a given quantity or expression; that by which the given quantity or expression is multiplied to produce unity: *The reciprocal of x is 1/x.* [1560–70; < L *reciproc(us)* returning, reciprocal + -AL[1]] **—re·cip′ro·cal′i·ty, re·cip′ro·cal·ness,** *n.* **—re·cip′ro·cal·ly,** *adv.*
—Syn. 1. See **mutual.**

recip′rocal exchange′, an unincorporated association formed so that its members can participate in reciprocal insurance.

recip′rocal inhibi′tion, *Psychiatry.* the theory that the pairing of an anxiety-provoking stimulus with anxiety-reducing reactions will weaken the association between the stimulus and the anxiety. [1905–10]

recip′rocal insur′ance, insurance in which members of a reciprocal exchange, acting through an attorney-in-fact, insure themselves and each other.

recip′rocal lev′eling, *Survey.* leveling between two widely separated points in which observations are made in both directions to eliminate the effects of atmospheric refraction and the curvature of the earth.

recip′rocal ohm′, *Elect.* siemens.

recip′rocal transloca′tion, *Genetics.* an exchange of segments between two nonhomologous chromosomes. [1940–45]

re·cip·ro·cate (ri sip′rə kāt′), *v.,* **-cat·ed, -cat·ing.** —*v.t.* **1.** to give, feel, etc., in return. **2.** to give and receive reciprocally; interchange: *to reciprocate favors.* **3.** to cause to move alternately backward and forward. —*v.i.* **4.** to make a return, as for something given. **5.** to make interchange. **6.** to be correspondent. **7.** to move alternately backward and forward. [1605–15; < L *reciprocātus* ptp. of *reciprocāre* to move back and forth. See RECIPROCAL, -ATE[1]] **—re·cip′ro·ca′tive, re·cip·ro·ca·to·ry** (ri sip′rə kə tôr′ē, -tōr′ē), *adj.* **—re·cip′ro·ca′·tor,** *n.*
—Syn. 1. return, respond, retaliate.

recip′rocating en′gine, any engine employing the rectilinear motion of one or more pistons in cylinders. Also called **displacement engine, piston engine.** [1815–25]

re·cip·ro·ca·tion (ri sip′rə kā′shən), *n.* **1.** an act or instance of reciprocating. **2.** a returning, usually for something given. **3.** a mutual giving and receiving. **4.** the state of being reciprocal or corresponding. [1520–30; < L *reciprocātiōn-* (s. of *reciprocātiō*). See RECIPROCATE, -ION]

rec·i·proc·i·ty (res′ə pros′i tē), *n.* **1.** a reciprocal state or relation. **2.** reciprocation; mutual exchange. **3.** the relation or policy in commercial dealings between countries by which corresponding advantages or privileges are granted by each country to the citizens of the other. [1760–70; < L *reciproc(us)* (see RECIPROCAL) + -ITY]

re·ci·sion (ri sizh′ən), *n.* an act of canceling or voiding; cancellation. [1605–15; < L *recisiōn-* (s. of *recisiō*) a pruning, reduction, equiv. to *recīs(us),* ptp. of *recīdere* to cut back (*re-* RE- + *-cīd(ere),* comb. form of *caedere* to cut + *-tus* ptp. suffix, with *dt* > *s*) + *-iōn-* -ION]

recit., *Music.* recitative.

re·cit·al (ri sīt′l), *n.* **1.** a musical entertainment given usually by a single performer or by a performer and one or more accompanists. **2.** a similar entertainment in a field other than music: *a dance recital.* **3.** a program or concert by dance or music students to demonstrate their achievements or progress. **4.** an act or instance of reciting. **5.** a formal or public delivery of something memorized. **6.** a detailed statement. **7.** an account, narrative, or description: *He gave a recital of the things he'd been doing since we'd last seen him.* [1505–15; RECITE + -AL[2]] **—re·cit′al·ist,** *n.*
—Syn. 7. See **narrative.**

rec·i·ta·tif (res′i tə tēf′), *n.* recitative[2].

rec·i·ta·tion (res′i tā′shən), *n.* **1.** an act of reciting. **2.** a reciting or repeating of something from memory, esp. formally or publicly. **3.** oral response by a pupil or pupils to a teacher on a prepared lesson. **4.** a period of classroom instruction. **5.** an elocutionary delivery of a piece of poetry or prose, without the text, before an audience. **6.** a piece so delivered or for such delivery. [1475–85; < L *recitātiōn-* (s. of *recitātiō*), equiv. to *recitāt(us)* (ptp. of *recitāre* to RECITE) + *-iōn-* -ION]

rec·i·ta·tive[1] (res′i tā′tiv, ri sī′tə-), *adj.* pertaining to or of the nature of recital. [1855–60; RECITE + -ATIVE]

rec·i·ta·tive[2] (res′i tə tēv′), *Music.* —*adj.* **1.** of the nature of or resembling recitation or declamation. —*n.* **2.** a style of vocal music intermediate between speaking and singing. **3.** a passage, part, or piece in this style. [1635–45; < It *recitativo.* See RECITE, -IVE]

rec·i·ta·ti·vo (res′i tə tē′vō; *It.* re′chē tä tē′vô), *n., pl.* **-vi** (*Eng., It.* -vē), **-vos.** *Music.* recitative[2]. [1610–20; < It]

re·cite (ri sīt′), *v.,* **-cit·ed, -cit·ing.** —*v.t.* **1.** to repeat the words of, as from memory, esp. in a formal manner: *to recite a lesson.* **2.** to repeat (a piece of poetry or prose) before an audience, as for entertainment. **3.** to give an account of: *to recite one's adventures.* **4.** to enumerate. —*v.i.* **5.** to recite a lesson or part of a lesson for a teacher. **6.** to recite or repeat something from memory. [1400–50; late ME *reciten* < L *recitāre* to read aloud, equiv. to *re-* RE- + *citāre* to summon, CITE[1]] **—re·cit′a·ble,** *adj.* **—re·cit′er,** *n.*
—Syn. 3. narrate, describe. See **relate. 4.** count, number, detail.

reck (rek), *v.i.* **1.** to have care, concern, or regard (often fol. by *of, with,* or a clause). **2.** to take heed. **3.** *Archaic.* to be of concern or importance; matter: *It recks not.* —*v.t.* **4.** *Archaic.* to have regard for; mind; heed. [bef. 900; ME *rekken,* OE *reccan;* akin to ON *roekja* to have care, G *(ge)ruhen* to deign]

reck·less (rek′lis), *adj.* **1.** utterly unconcerned about the consequences of some action; without caution; careless (usually fol. by *of*): *to be reckless of danger.* **2.** characterized by or proceeding from such carelessness: *reckless extravagance.* [bef. 900; ME *rekles,* OE *recceléas* careless (c. G *ruchlos*); see RECK, -LESS] **—reck′less·ly,** *adv.* **—reck′less·ness,** *n.*
—Syn. 1. rash, heedless, incautious, negligent, imprudent. **—Ant. 1.** careful.

Reck·ling·hau·sen (rek′ling hou′zən), *n.* a city in North Rhine-Westphalia, in NW Germany. 122,000.

reck·on (rek′ən), *v.t.* **1.** to count, compute, or calculate, as in number or amount. **2.** to esteem or consider; regard as: *to be reckoned an authority in the field.* **3.** *Chiefly Midland and Southern U.S.* to think or suppose. —*v.i.* **4.** to count; make a computation or calculation. **5.** to settle accounts, as with a person (often fol. by *up*). **6.** to count, depend, or rely, as in expectation (often fol. by *on*). **7.** *Chiefly Midland and Southern U.S.* to think or suppose. **8. reckon with, a.** to include in consideration or planning; anticipate: *He hadn't reckoned with so many obstacles.* **b.** to deal with: *I have to reckon with many problems every day.* [bef. 1000; ME *rekenen,* OE *gerecenian* (attested once) to report, pay; c. G *rechnen* to compute] **—reck′on·a·ble,** *adj.*
—Syn. 1. enumerate. **2.** account, deem, estimate, judge.

reck·on·er (rek′ə nər), *n.* **1.** a person who reckons. **2.** Also called **ready reckoner.** a collection of mathematical and other tables for ready calculation. [1175–1225; ME; see RECKON, -ER[1]]

reck·on·ing (rek′ə ning), *n.* **1.** count; computation; calculation. **2.** the settlement of accounts, as between two companies. **3.** a statement of an amount due; bill. **4.** an accounting, as for things received or done. **5.** an appraisal or judgment. **6.** *Navig.* See **dead reckoning. 7.** See **day of reckoning.** [1250–1300; ME; see RECKON, -ING[1]]
—Syn. 4. judgment, retribution.

re·claim (rē klām′), *v.t.* **1.** to claim or demand the return or restoration of, as a right, possession, etc. **2.** to claim again. Also, **reclaim.** [1400–50; late ME. See RE-, CLAIM]

re·claim (ri klām′), *v.t.* **1.** to bring (uncultivated areas or wasteland) into a condition for cultivation or other use. **2.** to recover (substances) in a pure or usable form from refuse, discarded articles, etc. **3.** to bring back to a preferable manner of living, sound principles, ideas, etc. **4.** to tame. **5.** re-claim. —*v.i.* **6.** to protest; object. —*n.* **7.** reclamation: *beyond reclaim.* [1250–1300; (v.) ME *recla(i)men* < OF *reclamer* (tonic s. *reclaim-*) < L *reclāmāre* to cry out against, equiv. to *re-* RE- + *clāmāre* to CLAIM; (n.) ME *reclaim(e)* < OF *reclaim, reclam,* deriv. of *reclamer*] **—re·claim′a·ble,** *adj.* **—re·claim′·er,** *n.*
—Syn. 2. regain, restore. See **recover.**

re·claim·ant (ri klā′mənt), *n.* a person who makes appeals to reclaim. [1740–50; RECLAIM + -ANT]

rec·la·ma·tion (rek′lə mā′shən), *n.* **1.** the reclaiming of desert, marshy, or submerged areas or other wasteland for cultivation or other use. **2.** the act or process of reclaiming. **3.** the state of being reclaimed. **4.** the process or industry of deriving usable materials from waste, by-products, etc. [1525–35, in sense "a protest"; < MF < L *reclāmātiōn-* (s. of *reclāmātiō*) crying out against, equiv. to *reclāmāt(us)* (ptp. of *reclāmāre;* see RECLAIM) + *-iōn-* -ION]

ré·clame (*Fr.* rā klām′), *n.* **1.** publicity; self-advertisement; notoriety. **2.** hunger for publicity; talent for getting attention. [1865–70; < F, deriv. of *réclamer;* see RECLAIM]

re·clas·si·fy (rē klas′ə fī′), *v.t.,* **-fied, -fy·ing. 1.** to classify anew. **2.** to change the security classification of (information, a document, etc.). [1915–20; RE- + CLASSIFY] **—re·clas′si·fi·ca′tion,** *n.*

re·clear·ance (rē klēr′əns), *n.* the revalidation of a person's security clearance, usually done periodically for those handling top-secret material. [RE- + CLEARANCE]

rec·li·nate (rek′lə nāt′, -nit), *adj.* bending or curved downward. [1745–55; < L *reclīnātus* (ptp. of *reclīnāre* to RECLINE); see -ATE[1]]

re·cline (ri klīn′), *v.,* **-clined, -clin·ing.** —*v.i.* **1.** to lean or lie back; rest in a recumbent position. —*v.t.* **2.** to cause to lean back on something; place in a recumbent position. [1375–1425; late ME *reclinen* < L *reclīnāre,* equiv. to *re-* RE- + *clīnāre* to LEAN[1]] **—re·clin′a·ble,** *adj.* **—rec·li·na·tion** (rek′lə nā′shən), *n.*

re·clin·er (ri klī′nər), *n.* **1.** a person or thing that reclines. **2.** Also called **reclin′ing chair′.** an easy chair with a back and footrest adjustable up or down to the comfort of the user. [1660–70; RECLINE + -ER[1]]

re·clos·a·ble (rē klō′zə bəl), *adj.* capable of being closed again easily or tightly after opening: *a reclosable box of crackers.* Also, **re·close′a·ble.** [1960–65; RE- + CLOSE + -ABLE]

rec·luse (*n.* rek′lo͞os, ri klo͞os′; *adj.* ri klo͞os′, rek′lo͞os), *n.* **1.** a person who lives in seclusion or apart from society, often for religious meditation. **2.** Also, **incluse.** a religious voluntary immured in a cave, hut, or the like, or one remaining within a cell for life. —*adj.* **re·cluse.** Also, **re·clu′sive. 3.** shut off or apart from the world; living in seclusion, often for religious reasons. **4.** characterized by seclusion; solitary. [1175–1225; ME < OF *reclus* < LL *reclūsus,* ptp. of *reclūdere* to shut up, equiv. to *re-* RE- + *-clūd-,* comb. form of *claudere* to CLOSE + *-tus* ptp. suffix, with *dt* > *s*]

re·clu·sion (ri klo͞o′zhən), *n.* **1.** the condition or life of a recluse. **2.** an act of shutting or the state of being shut up in seclusion. [1350–1400; ME < LL *reclūsiōn-* (s. of *reclūsiō*) a shutting off, equiv. to L *reclūs(us)* RECLUSE + *-iōn-* -ION]

rec·og·ni·tion (rek′əg nish′ən), *n.* **1.** an act of recognizing or the state of being recognized. **2.** the identification of something as having been previously seen, heard, known, etc. **3.** the perception of something as existing or true; realization. **4.** the acknowledgment of something as valid or as entitled to consideration: *the recognition of a claim.* **5.** the acknowledgment of achievement, service, merit, etc. **6.** the expression of this in the form of some token of appreciation: *This promotion constitutes our recognition of her exceptional ability.* **7.** formal acknowledgment conveying approval or sanction. **8.** acknowledgment of right to be heard or given attention: *The chairman refused recognition to any delegate until order could be restored.* **9.** *Internat. Law.* an official act by which one state acknowledges the existence of another state or government, or of belligerency or insurgency. **10.** the automated conversion of information, as words or images, into a form that can be processed by a machine, esp. a computer or computerized device. Cf. **optical character recognition, pattern recognition. 11.** *Biochem.* the responsiveness of one substance to another based on the reciprocal fit of a portion of their molecular shapes. [1425–75; late ME *recognicion* (< OF) < L *recognitiōn-* (s. of *recognitiō*), equiv. to *recognit(us)* (ptp. of *recognōscere;* see RECOGNIZE) + *-iōn-* -ION] **—rec′og·ni′tion·al,** *adj.* **—re·cog·ni·tive** (ri kog′ni tiv), **re·cog·ni·to·ry** (ri kog′ni tôr′ē, -tōr′ē), *adj.*
—Syn. 5. notice, acceptance.

re·cog·ni·zance (ri kog′nə zəns, -kon′ə-), *n.* **1.** *Law.* **a.** a bond or obligation of record entered into before a court of record or a magistrate, binding a person to do a particular act. **b.** the sum pledged as surety on such a bond. **2.** *Archaic.* recognition. **3.** *Archaic.* a token; badge. [1350–1400; ME *reconissaunce, recognisance* < OF *reconuissance.* See RECOGNIZE, -ANCE]

rec·og·nize (rek′əg nīz′), *v.t.,* **-nized, -niz·ing. 1.** to identify as something or someone previously seen, known, etc.: *He had changed so much that one could scarcely recognize him.* **2.** to identify from knowledge of appearance or characteristics: *I recognized him from the description. They recognized him as a fraud.* **3.** to perceive as existing or true; realize: *to be the first to recognize a fact.* **4.** to acknowledge as the person entitled to speak at a particular time: *The Speaker recognized the Congressman from Maine.* **5.** to acknowledge formally as entitled to treatment as a political unit: *The United States promptly recognized Israel.* **6.** to acknowledge or accept formally a specified factual or legal situation: *to recognize a successful revolutionary regime as the de facto government of the country.* **7.** to acknowledge or treat as valid: *to recognize a claim.* **8.** to acknowledge acquaintance with, as by a greeting, handshake, etc. **9.** to show appreciation of (achievement, service, merit, etc.), as by some reward, public honor, or the like. **10.** *Law.* to acknowledge (an illegitimate child) as one's own. **11.** *Biochem., Immunol.* to bind with, cleave, or otherwise react to (another substance) as a result of fitting its molecular shape or a portion of its shape. Also, *esp. Brit.,* **rec′og·nise′.** [1425–75; RECOGN(ITION) + -IZE; r. late ME *racunnysen, recognisen* < OF *reconuiss-,* s. of *reconuistre* < L *recognōscere,* equiv. to *re-* RE- + *cognōscere* to KNOW[1]; see COGNITION] **—rec·og·niz·a·ble** (rek′əg nī′zə bəl, rek′əg nī′-), *adj.* **—rec′og·niz′a·bil′i·ty,** *n.* **—rec′og·niz′a·bly,** *adv.* **—rec′og·niz′er,** *n.*
—Syn. 3. acknowledge, appreciate, understand, grant, concede.

re·cog·ni·zee (ri kog′nə zē′, -kon′ə-), *n. Law.* the person to whom an obligation is owed in a recognizance. [1585–95; RECOGNIZE + -EE]

re·cog·ni·zor (ri kog′nə zôr′, -kon′ə-), *n. Law.* a person who enters into a recognizance. [1525–35; RECOGNIZE + -OR[2]]

re-coil (rē koil′), *v.t., v.i.* to coil again. [1860–65; RE- + COIL[1]]

re·coil (*v.* ri koil′; *n.* rē′koil′, ri koil′), *v.i.* **1.** to draw back; start or shrink back, as in alarm, horror, or disgust. **2.** to spring or fly back, as in consequence of force of impact or the force of the discharge, as a firearm. **3.** to spring or come back; react (usually fol. by *on* or *upon*): *Plots frequently recoil upon the plotters.* **4.** *Physics.* (of an atom, a nucleus, or a particle) to undergo a change in momentum as a result either of a collision with an atom, a nucleus, or a particle or of the emission of a particle. —*n.* **5.** an act of recoiling. **6.** the distance through which a weapon moves backward after discharging. [1175–1225; ME *recoilen, reculen* (v.) < OF *reculer,* equiv. to *re-* RE- + *-culer,* v. deriv. of *cul* rump, buttocks; see CULET] **—re·coil′ing·ly,** *adv.*
—Syn. 1. withdraw, quail, flinch, falter. See **wince. 2.** rebound.

CONCISE PRONUNCIATION KEY: act, cāpe, dâre, pärt; set, ēqual; *if,* īce; ox, ōver, ôrder, oil, bo͝ok, bo͞ot, out; up, ûrge; child; sing; shoe; thin, *th*at; zh as in *treasure.* ə = *a* as in *alone, e* as in *system, i* as in *easily, o* as in *gallop, u* as in *circus;* ᵊ as in *fire* (fīᵊr), *hour* (ouᵊr). l and n can serve as syllabic consonants, as in *cradle* (krād′l), and *button* (but′n). See the full key inside the front cover.

re·blend′, *v.,* **-blend·ed** or **-blent, -blend·ing.**
re·blis′ter, *v.*
re·block′, *v.t.*
re·bloom′, *v.i.*
re·bloom′er, *n.*
re·blos′som, *v.i.*
re·blown′, *adj.*
re·board′, *v.t.*
re·boil′, *v.*
re·bolt′, *v.*
re·book′, *v.*
re·bore′, *v.,* **-bored, -bor·ing.**
re·bot′tle, *v.t.,* **-tled, -tling.**
re·brace′, *v.t.,* **-braced, -brac·ing.**
re·brand′, *v.t.*
re·break′, *v.,* **-broke, -bro·ken, -break·ing.**
re·break′age, *n.*
re·breed′, *v.,* **-bred, -breed·ing.**
re·brew′, *v.*
re·bright′en, *v.*
re·broad′en, *v.*
re·brush′, *v.t.*
re·buck′le, *v.,* **-led, -ling.**
re·budg′et, *v.t.,* **-et·ed, -et·ing.**
re·bur′i·al, *n.*
re·bur′y, *v.t.,* **-bur·ied, -bur·y·ing.**
re·but′ton, *v.t.*
re·buy′, *v.,* **-bought, -buy·ing.**
re·ca′ble, *v.,* **-bled, -bling.**
re·cage′, *v.t.,* **-caged, -cag·ing.**
re·cal′i·brate′, *v.t.,* **-brat·ed, -brat·ing.**
re·calk′, *v.t.*
re′cam·paign′, *v.*
re·can′cel, *v.t.,* **-celed, -cel·ing** or (*esp. Brit.*) **-celled, -cel·ling.**

re′coil escape′ment, *Horol.* See **anchor escapement.** [1840–50]

re·coil·less (ri koil′lis, rē′koil′-), *adj.* having little or no recoil: *a recoilless rifle.* [1945–50; RECOIL + -LESS]

re·coil-op·er·at·ed (rē′koil′op′ə rā′tid), *adj.* employing the recoil force of an explosive projectile to prepare the firing mechanism for the next shot. [1940–45]

re·col·lect (rē′kə lekt′), *v.t.* **1.** to collect, gather, or assemble again (something scattered). **2.** to rally (one's faculties, powers, spirits, etc.); recover or compose (oneself). [1605–15]

rec·ol·lect (rek′ə lekt′), *v.t.* **1.** to recall to mind; recover knowledge of by memory; remember. **2.** to absorb (oneself) in spiritual meditation, esp. during prayer. —*v.i.* **3.** to have a recollection; remember. [1550–60; < ML *recollēctus,* ptp. of *recolligere* to remember, recollect (L: to gather up again); see RE-, COLLECT[1]] —**rec′ol·lec′tive,** *adj.* —**rec′ol·lec′tive·ly,** *adv.* —**rec′ol·lec′tive·ness,** *n.*
—**Syn. 1.** See **remember.** —**Ant. 1.** forget.

rec·ol·lect·ed (rek′ə lek′tid), *adj.* **1.** calm; composed. **2.** remembered; recalled. **3.** characterized by or given to contemplation. [1620–30; RECOLLECT, RE-COLLECT + -ED[2]] —**rec′ol·lect′ed·ly,** *adv.* —**rec′ol·lect′ed·ness,** *n.*

re-col·lec·tion (rē′kə lek′shən), *n.* the act of re-collecting or the state of being re-collected. [1590–1600; RE- + COLLECTION]

rec·ol·lec·tion (rek′ə lek′shən), *n.* **1.** the act or power of recollecting, or recalling to mind; remembrance. **2.** something that is recollected: *recollections of one's childhood.* [1635–45; < F *récollection* or ML *recollēctiōn-* (s. of *recollēctiō*), equiv. to *recollēct(us)* (see RECOLLECT) + *-iōn-* -ION]
—**Syn. 1.** recall. **1, 2.** memory. **2.** memoir.

ré·colte (rā kôlt′), *n., pl.* ***-coltes*** (-kôlt′). *French.* **1.** a harvest; crop. **2.** (in winemaking) vintage.

re·com·bi·nant (rē kom′bə nənt), *Genetics.* —*adj.* **1.** of or resulting from new combinations of genetic material: *recombinant cells.* —*n.* **2.** a cell or organism whose genetic complement results from recombination. **3.** the genetic material produced when segments of DNA from different sources are joined to produce recombinant DNA. [1940–45; RE- + COMBINE + -ANT]

recombinant DNA, *Genetics.* DNA in which one or more segments or genes have been inserted, either naturally or by laboratory manipulation, from a different molecule or from another part of the same molecule, resulting in a new genetic combination. [1970–75]

recombinant DNA technology, *Genetics.* any of various techniques for separating and recombining segments of DNA or genes, often employing a restriction enzyme to cut a gene from a donor organism and inserting it into a plasmid or viral DNA for transplantation into a host organism, where the gene causes the production of a desired substance either for harvesting or for the benefit of the host organism itself. Also called **gene splicing.** [1970–75]

re·com·bi·na·tion (rē′kom bə nā′shən), *Genetics.* the formation of new combinations of genes, either naturally, by crossing over or independent assortment, or in the laboratory by direct manipulation of genetic material. [1820–30, for general sense; 1900–05 for current sense; RE- + COMBINATION]

rec·om·mend (rek′ə mend′), *v.t.* **1.** to present as worthy of confidence, acceptance, use, etc.; commend; mention favorably: *to recommend an applicant for a job; to recommend a book.* **2.** to represent or urge as advisable or expedient: *to recommend caution.* **3.** to advise, as an alternative; suggest (a choice, course of action, etc.) as appropriate, beneficial, or the like: *He recommended the blue-plate special. The doctor recommended special exercises for her.* **4.** to make desirable or attractive: *a plan that has very little to recommend it.* —*v.i.* **5.** to make a recommendation. —*n.* **6.** *Informal.* a recommendation. [1350–1400; ME *recommenden* < ML *recommendāre,* equiv. to L *re-* RE- + *commendāre* to COMMEND] —**rec′om·mend′a·ble,** *adj.* —**rec′om·mend′er,** *n.*
—**Syn. 1.** approve, condone. **3.** counsel. —**Ant. 1.** condemn.

rec·om·men·da·tion (rek′ə men dā′shən, -mən-), *n.* **1.** an act of recommending. **2.** a letter or the like recommending a person or thing. **3.** representation in favor of a person or thing. **4.** anything that serves to recommend a person or thing, or induce acceptance or favor. [1400–50; late ME *recommendacion* < ML *recommendātiōn-* (s. of *recommendātiō*), equiv. to *recommendāt(us)* (ptp. of *recommendāre* to RECOMMEND; see -ATE[1]) + *-iōn-* -ION]
—**Syn. 1.** See **advice.**

rec·om·mend·a·to·ry (rek′ə men′də tôr′ē, -tōr′ē), *adj.* **1.** serving to recommend; recommending. **2.** serving as or being a recommendation. [1605–15; < ML *recommendāt(us)* (see RECOMMENDATION) + -ORY[1]]

recommend′ed di′etary allow′ance, *Nutrition.* the amount of an essential nutrient, as a vitamin or mineral, that has been established by the Food and Nutrition Board of the National Academy of Sciences as adequate to meet the average daily nutritional needs of most healthy persons according to age group and sex. *Abbr.:* RDA Cf. **U.S. RDA**

re·com·mit (rē′kə mit′), *v.t.,* **-mit·ted, -mit·ting. 1.** to commit again. **2.** to refer again to a committee. [1615–25; RE + COMMIT] —**re′com·mit′ment, re′com·mit′tal,** *n.*

rec·om·pense (rek′əm pens′), *v.,* **-pensed, -pens·ing,** *n.* —*v.t.* **1.** to repay; remunerate; reward, as for service, aid, etc. **2.** to pay or give compensation for; make restitution or requital for (damage, injury, or the like). —*v.i.* **3.** to make compensation for something; repay someone: *no attempt to recompense for our trouble.* —*n.* **4.** compensation, as for an injury, wrong, etc.: *to make recompense for the loss one's carelessness has caused.* **5.** a repayment or requital, as for favors, gifts, etc. **6.** a remuneration or reward, as for services, aid, or the like. [1375–1425; (v.) late ME < MF *recompenser* < LL *recompēnsāre,* equiv. to L *re-* RE- + *compēnsāre* (see COMPENSATE); (n.) late ME < MF, deriv. of *recompenser*] —**rec′om·pen′sa·ble,** *adj.* —**rec′om·pens′er,** *n.*
—**Syn. 1.** reimburse, recoup. **4.** payment, amends, indemnification, satisfaction. **4–6.** See **reward.**

re·com·pose (rē′kəm pōz′), *v.t.,* **-posed, -pos·ing. 1.** to compose again; reconstitute; rearrange. **2.** to restore to composure or calmness. [1605–15; RE- + COMPOSE] —**re·com·po·si·tion** (rē′kom pə zish′ən), *n.*

re′com·pres′sion cham′ber (rē′kəm presh′ən). See **hyperbaric chamber.** [1950–55; RE- + COMPRESSION]

re·con (ri kon′), *n., v.,* **-conned, -con·ning.** *Informal.* —*n.* **1.** reconnaissance. —*v.t., v.i.* **2.** reconnoiter. [1915–20, *Amer.*; by shortening]

re·con·cen·tra·tion (rē′kon sən trā′shən), *n.* **1.** the act of concentrating again. **2.** the state of being concentrated again. [1895–1900; RE- + CONCENTRATION]

rec·on·cil·a·ble (rek′ən sī′lə bəl, rek′ən sī′lə bəl), *adj.* capable of being reconciled. [1605–15; RECONCILE + -ABLE] —**rec′on·cil′a·bil′i·ty, rec′on·cil′a·ble·ness,** *n.* —**rec′on·cil′a·bly,** *adv.*

rec·on·cile (rek′ən sīl′), *v.,* **-ciled, -cil·ing.** —*v.t.* **1.** to cause (a person) to accept or be resigned to something not desired: *He was reconciled to his fate.* **2.** to win over to friendliness; cause to become amicable: *to reconcile hostile persons.* **3.** to compose or settle (a quarrel, dispute, etc.). **4.** to bring into agreement or harmony; make compatible or consistent: *to reconcile differing statements; to reconcile accounts.* **5.** to reconsecrate (a desecrated church, cemetery, etc.). **6.** to restore (an excommunicate or penitent) to communion in a church. —*v.i.* **7.** to become reconciled. [1300–50; ME *reconcilen* < L *reconciliāre* to make good again, repair. See RE-, CONCILIATE] —**rec′on·cile′ment,** *n.* —**rec′on·cil′er,** *n.* —**rec′on·cil′ing·ly,** *adv.*
—**Syn. 2.** pacify, propitiate, placate. **4.** harmonize. —**Ant. 3.** anger.

rec·on·cil·i·ate (rek′ən sil′ē āt′), *v.t., v.i.,* **-at·ed, -at·ing.** reconcile. [1715–25; back formation from RECONCILIATION]

rec·on·cil·i·a·tion (rek′ən sil′ē ā′shən), *n.* **1.** an act of reconciling or the state of being reconciled. **2.** the process of making consistent or compatible. [1300–50; ME *reconsiliacion* < L *reconciliātiōn-* (s. of *reconciliātiō*), equiv. to *reconciliāt(us)* (see RECONCILE, -ATE[1]) + *-iōn-* -ION]

rec·on·cil·i·a·to·ry (rek′ən sil′ē ə tôr′ē, -tōr′ē), *adj.* tending to reconcile. [1580–90; < L *reconciliāt(us)* (see RECONCILE, -ATE[1]) + -ORY[1]]

rec·on·dite (rek′ən dīt′, ri kon′dīt), *adj.* **1.** dealing with very profound, difficult, or abstruse subject matter: *a recondite treatise.* **2.** beyond ordinary knowledge or understanding; esoteric: *recondite principles.* **3.** little known; obscure: *a recondite fact.* [1640–50; earlier *recondit* < L *reconditus* recondite, hidden (orig. ptp. of *recondere* to hide), equiv. to *re-* RE- + *cond(ere)* to bring together (*con-* CON- + *-dere* to put) + *-itus* -ITE[2]] —**rec′on·dite′ly,** *adv.* —**rec′on·dite′ness,** *n.*
—**Syn. 2.** deep. **3.** mysterious, occult, secret. —**Ant. 2.** exoteric. **3.** well-known.

re·con·di·tion (rē′kən dish′ən), *v.t.* to restore to a good or satisfactory condition; repair; make over. [1915–20; RE- + CONDITION]

re·con·fig·ure (rē′kən fig′yər), *v.t.,* **-ured, -ur·ing.** to change the shape or formation of; remodel; restructure. [1965–70; RE- + *configure,* by back formation from CONFIGURATION] —**re′con·fig′u·ra′tion,** *n.*

re·con·nais·sance (ri kon′ə səns, -zəns), *n.* **1.** the act of reconnoitering. **2.** *Mil.* a search made for useful military information in the field, esp. by examining the ground. **3.** *Survey., Civ. Engin.* a general examination or survey of a region, usually followed by a detailed survey. **4.** *Geol.* an examination or survey of the general geological characteristics of a region. Also, **re·con′nois·sance.** [1800–10; < F; MF *reconoissance* RECOGNIZANCE]

recon′naissance car′, a specially equipped and armed car used for making military reconnaissance.

recon′naissance sat′ellite, a military satellite designed to carry out photographic surveillance, gather electronic intelligence, detect nuclear explosions, or provide early warning of strategic-missile launchings.

re·con·noi·ter (rē′kə noi′tər, rek′ə-), *v.t.* **1.** to inspect, observe, or survey (the enemy, the enemy's strength or position, a region, etc.) in order to gain information for military purposes. **2.** to examine or survey (a region, area, etc.) for engineering, geological, or other purposes. —*v.i.* **3.** to make a reconnaissance. [1700–10; < F *reconnoître* (now obs.) to explore, MF *reconoistre.* See RECOGNIZE] —**re′con·noi′ter·er,** *n.*

re·con·noi·tre (rē′kə noi′tər, rek′ə-), *v.t., v.i.,* **-tred, -tring.** *Chiefly Brit.* reconnoiter. —**re′con·noi′trer,** *n.*

re·con·sid·er (rē′kən sid′ər), *v.t.* **1.** to consider again, esp. with a view to change of decision or action: *to reconsider a refusal.* **2.** *Parl. Proc.* to take up for consideration a second time, as a motion or a vote, as with the view of reversing or modifying action taken. —*v.i.* **3.** to reconsider a matter. [1565–75; RE- + CONSIDER] —**re′con·sid′er·a′tion,** *n.*
—**Syn. 1.** rethink, review, reexamine, reevaluate.

re·con·sign·ment (rē′kən sīn′mənt), *n.* **1.** a consigning again. **2.** *Com.* a change in the route, point of delivery, or consignee as stated in the original bill of lading. [1850–55; RE- + CONSIGNMENT]

re·con·sti·tute (rē kon′sti to͞ot′, -tyo͞ot′), *v.,* **-tut·ed, -tut·ing.** —*v.t.* **1.** to constitute again; reconstruct; recompose. **2.** to return (a dehydrated or concentrated food) to the liquid state by adding water: *to reconstitute a bouillon cube with hot water.* —*v.i.* **3.** to undergo reconstitution; become reconstituted. [1805–15; RE- + CONSTITUTE] —**re·con·sti·tu·ent** (rē′kən stich′o͞o ənt), *adj., n.* —**re′con·sti·tut′a·ble, re′con·sti·tut′i·ble,** *adj.* —**re·con′sti·tu′tive,** *adj.* —**re·con′sti·tu′tion,** *n.*

re·con·sti·tut·ed (rē kon′sti to͞o′tid, -tyo͞o′-), *adj.* constituted again, esp. of a liquid product made by adding water to dry solids from which the water has been evaporated: *reconstituted orange juice.* [1840–50; RECONSTITUTE + -ED[2]]

re·con·struct (rē′kən strukt′), *v.t.* **1.** to construct again; rebuild; make over. **2.** to re-create in the mind from given or available information: *to reconstruct the events of the murder.* **3.** *Historical Ling.* to arrive at (hypothetical earlier forms of words, phonemic systems, etc.) by comparison of data from a later language or group of related languages. [1760–70; RE- + CONSTRUCT] —**re′con·struct′i·ble,** *adj.* —**re′con·struc′tor, re′con·struct′er,** *n.*

re·con·struc·tion (rē′kən struk′shən), *n.* **1.** an act of reconstructing. **2.** (*cap.*) *U.S. Hist.* **a.** the process by which the states that had seceded were reorganized as part of the Union after the Civil War. **b.** the period during which this took place, 1865–77. [1785–95; RE- + CONSTRUCTION] —**re′con·struc′tion·al, re′con·struc′tion·ar′y,** *adj.*

Reconstruc′tion Acts′, *U.S. Hist.* the acts of Congress during the period from 1865 to 1877 providing for the reorganization of the former Confederate states and setting forth the process by which they were to be restored to representation in Congress, esp. the acts passed in 1867 and 1868.

Re·con·struc·tion·ism (rē′kən struk′shə niz′əm), *n.* a 20th-century movement among U.S. Jews, founded by Rabbi Mordecai M. Kaplan, advocating that Judaism, being a culture and way of life as well as a religion, is in sum a religious civilization requiring constant adaptation to contemporary conditions so that Jews can identify more readily and meaningfully with the Jewish community. [1940–45; RECONSTRUCTION + -ISM]

Re·con·struc·tion·ist (rē′kən struk′shə nist), *n.* **1.** an advocate or supporter of Reconstruction or Reconstructionism. —*adj.* **2.** of or pertaining to Reconstruction or Reconstructionism. [1860–65, *Amer.*; RECONSTRUCTION + -IST]

re·con·struc·tive (rē′kən struk′tiv), *adj.* tending to reconstruct. [1860–65; RE- + CONSTRUCTIVE] —**re′con·struc′tive·ly,** *adv.* —**re′con·struc′tive·ness,** *n.*

recon′struc′tive sur′gery, the restoration of appearance and function following injury or disease, or the correction of congenital defects, using the techniques of plastic surgery.

re·con·ven·tion (rē′kən ven′shən), *n. Civil Law.* an action brought by the defendant in pending litigation against the plaintiff: the defendant's claim must be connected in some way with the subject matter of the plaintiff's action. [1400–50; late ME *reconvencioun* (< MF *reconvencion*) < ML *reconventiō;* see RE-, CONVENTION]

re·con·vert (rē′kən vûrt′), *v.t.* **1.** to convert again. **2.** to change back to a previous form, opinion, character, or function. [1605–15; RE- + CONVERT[1]] —**re′con·ver′sion,** *n.* —**re′con·vert′er,** *n.*

re·con·vey (rē′kən vā′), *v.t.* **1.** to convey again. **2.** to convey back to a previous position or place. [1500–10; RE- + CONVEY] —**re′con·vey′ance,** *n.*

re·cord (*v.* ri kôrd′; *n., adj.* rek′ərd), *v.t.* **1.** to set down in writing or the like, as for the purpose of preserving evidence. **2.** to cause to be set down or registered: *to record one's vote.* **3.** to state or indicate: *He recorded his protest, but it was disregarded.* **4.** to serve to relate or to tell of: *The document records that the battle took place six years earlier.* **5.** to set down or register in some permanent form, as on a seismograph. **6.** to set down, register, or fix by characteristic marks, incisions, magnetism, etc., for the purpose of reproduction by a phonograph or magnetic reproducer. **7.** to make a recording of: *The orchestra recorded the 6th Symphony.* —*v.i.* **8.** to record something; make a record. —*n.* **rec·ord 9.** an act of recording. **10.** the state of being recorded, as in writing. **11.** an account in writing or the like preserving the memory or knowledge of facts or events. **12.** information or knowledge preserved in writing or the like. **13.** a report, list, or aggregate of actions or achievements: *He made a good record in college. The ship has a fine sailing record.* **14.** a legally

CONCISE ETYMOLOGY KEY: <, descended or borrowed from; >, whence; b., blend of, blended; c., cognate with; cf., compare; deriv., derivative; equiv., equivalent; imit., imitative; obl., oblique; r., replacing; s., stem; sp., spelling, spelled; resp., respelling, respelled; trans., translation; ?, origin unknown; *, unattested; ‡, probably earlier than. See the full key inside the front cover.

re′can·cel·la′tion, *n.*
re·cane′, *v.t.,* **-caned, -can·ing.**
re·car′pet, *v.t.*
re·car′ry, *v.t.,* **-ried, -ry·ing.**
re·carve′, *v.,* **-carved, -carv·ing.**
re·cat′a·log′, *v.t.*
re·cat′a·logue′, *v.t.,* **-logued, -logu·ing.**
re·cat′e·go·rize′, *v.t.,* **-rized, -riz·ing.**
re·cau′tion, *v.t.*
re·cel′e·brate′, *v.,* **-brat·ed, -brat·ing.**
re′cel·e·bra′tion, *n.*
re′ce·ment′, *v.*
re·cen′sor, *v.t.*
re′cen·tral·i·za′tion, *n.*
re·cen′tral·ize′, *v.,* **-ized, -iz·ing.**
re·cen′tri·fuge′, *v.t.,* **-fuged, -fug·ing.**
re′cer·ti·fi·ca′tion, *n.*
re·cer′ti·fy′, *v.t.,* **-fied, -fy·ing.**
re·chal′lenge, *v.t.,* **-lenged, -leng·ing.**
re·chan′nel, *v.t.,* **-neled, -nel·ing** or (*esp. Brit.*) **-nelled, -nel·ling.**
re·char′ac·ter·i·za′tion, *n.*
re·char′ac·ter·ize′, *v.t.,* **-ized, -iz·ing.**
re·chart′, *v.t.*
re·char′ter, *v.t., n.*
re·check′, *v.*
re′check′, *n.*
re·choose′, *v.,* **-chose, -cho·sen, -choos·ing.**
re·cho′re·o·graph′, *v.t.*
re·chris′ten, *v.t.*

documented history of criminal activity: *They discovered that the suspect had a record.* **15.** something or someone serving as a remembrance; memorial: *Keep this souvenir as a record of your visit.* **16.** the tracing, marking, or the like, made by a recording instrument. **17.** something on which sound or images have been recorded for subsequent reproduction, as a grooved disk that is played on a phonograph or an optical disk for recording sound **(audiodisk)** or images **(videodisk).** Cf. **compact disk. 18.** the highest or best rate, amount, etc., ever attained, esp. in sports: *to hold the record for home runs; to break the record in the high jump.* **19.** *Sports.* the standing of a team or individual with respect to contests won, lost, and tied. **20.** an official writing intended to be preserved. **21.** *Computers.* a group of related fields, or a single field, treated as a unit and comprising part of a file or data set, for purposes of input, processing, output, or storage by a computer. **22.** *Law.* **a.** the commitment to writing, as authentic evidence, of something having legal importance, esp. as evidence of the proceedings or verdict of a court. **b.** evidence preserved in this manner. **c.** an authentic or official written report of proceedings of a court of justice. **23. go on record,** to issue a public statement of one's opinion or stand: *He went on record as advocating immediate integration.* **24. off the record, a.** not intended for publication; unofficial; confidential: *The President's comment was strictly off the record.* **b.** not registered or reported as a business transaction; off the books. **25. on record, a.** existing as a matter of public knowledge; known. **b.** existing in a publication, document, file, etc.: *There was no birth certificate on record.* —*adj.* **rec·ord 26.** making or affording a record. **27.** surpassing or superior to all others: *a record year for automobile sales.* [1175–1225; 1875–80 for def. 17; (v.) ME *recorden* < OF *recorder* < L *recordārī* to remember, recollect (*re-* RE- + *cord-* (s. of *cors*) HEART + *-ārī* inf. ending); (n.) ME *record(e)* < OF, deriv. of *recorder;* cf. ML *recordum*] —**re·cord′a·ble,** *adj.* —**rec′ord·less,** *adj.*
—**Syn. 1.** register, enroll, enter, note. **11.** chronicle, history, journal; note, memorandum.

rec·or·da·tion (rek′ər dā′shən, rē′kôr-), *n.* the act or process of recording: *the recordation of documents pertaining to copyright ownership.* [1400–50; late ME *recordacioun* orig., the faculty of recollection < OF *recordacion* < L *recordātiōn-* (s. of *recordātiō*), equiv. to *recordāt(us)* (ptp. of *recordārī;* see RECORD) + *-iōn-* -ION]

rec′ord chang′er, a device that automatically places each of a stack of records in succession onto the turntable of a phonograph. [1930–35]

re·cord·er (ri kôr′dər), *n.* **1.** a person who records, esp. as an official duty. **2.** *Eng. Law.* **a.** a judge in a city or borough court. **b.** (formerly) the legal adviser of a city or borough, with responsibility for keeping a record of legal actions and local customs. **3.** a recording or registering apparatus or device. **4.** a device for recording sound, images, or data by electrical, magnetic, or optical means. **5.** an end-blown flute having a fipple mouthpiece, eight finger holes, and a soft, mellow tone. [1275–1325; ME *recorder* wind instrument (see RECORD, -ER[1]), *recordour* legal official (< AF *recordour,* OF *recordeor*)]

recorder (def. 5)

rec·ord·hold·er (rek′ərd hōl′dər), *n.* a person or thing recognized for the accomplishment of a feat to a better or greater degree than any other. Also, **rec′·ord-hold′er.** [1930–35; RECORD + HOLDER]

re·cord·ing (ri kôr′ding), *n.* **1.** the act or practice of a person or thing that records. **2.** sound recorded on a disk or tape. **3.** a disk or tape on which something is recorded. [1300–50; ME (ger.); see RECORD, -ING[1]]

record′ing head′, the part of a tape recorder that records a sound source by converting the electrical analog of the sound, as from a microphone, into a magnetic signal for storage on magnetic tape. Also, **rec′ord head′.** [1930–35]

record′ing sec′retary, *Parl. Proc.* an officer charged with keeping the minutes of meetings and responsible for the records.

re·cord·ist (ri kôr′dist), *n.* **1.** Also called **sound recordist.** *Motion Pictures.* the person in charge of sound recording on a film set. Cf. **mixer. 2.** Also called **record′ing engineer′.** a similar specialist in charge of recording an album, taping a television show, etc.: *a video recordist.* [1925–30; RECORD + -IST]

rec·ord·keep·ing (rek′ərd kē′ping), *n.* the maintenance of a history of one's activities, as financial dealings, by entering data in ledgers or journals, putting documents in files, etc. [1960–65; RECORD + KEEP + -ING[1]]

rec′ord play′er, phonograph. [1930–35]

re-count (*v.* rē kount′; *n.* rē′kount′, rē kount′), *v.t.* **1.** to count again. —*n.* **2.** a second or additional count, as of votes in an election. [1755–65; RE- + COUNT[1]]

re·count (ri kount′), *v.t.* **1.** to relate or narrate; tell in detail; give the facts or particulars of. **2.** to narrate in order. **3.** to tell one by one; enumerate. [1425–75; late ME *recounten* < MF *reconter,* equiv. to *re-* RE- + *conter* to tell, COUNT[1]]
—**Syn. 1.** describe. See **relate.**

re·count·al (rē koun′tl), *n.* an act of recounting. [1860–65; RECOUNT + -AL[2]]

re·coup (ri ko͞op′), *v.t.* **1.** to get back the equivalent of: *to recoup one's losses by a lucky investment.* **2.** to regain or recover. **3.** to reimburse or indemnify; pay back: *to recoup a person for expenses.* **4.** *Law.* to withhold (a portion of something due), having some rightful claim to do so. —*v.i.* **5.** to get back an equivalent, as of something lost. **6.** *Law.* to plead in defense a claim arising out of the same subject matter as the plaintiff's claim. —*n.* **7.** an act of recouping. [1400–50; late ME < MF *recouper* to cut back, cut again, equiv. to *re-* RE- + *couper* to cut; see COUP[1]] —**re·coup′a·ble,** *adj.* —**re·coup′ment,** *n.*
—**Syn. 1.** recover, restore, retrieve, balance. **3.** recompense, remunerate.

re·course (rē′kôrs, -kōrs, ri kôrs′, -kōrs′), *n.* **1.** access or resort to a person or thing for help or protection: *to have recourse to the courts for justice.* **2.** a person or thing resorted to for help or protection. **3.** the right to collect from a maker or endorser of a negotiable instrument. The endorser may add the words "without recourse" on the instrument, thereby transferring the instrument without assuming any liability. [1350–1400; ME *recours* < OF < LL *recursus,* L: return, retreat, n. use of ptp. of *recurrere* to run back; see RECUR]

re-cov·er (rē kuv′ər), *v.t.* to cover again or anew. [1375–1425; late ME *recoveren;* see RE-, COVER]

re·cov·er (ri kuv′ər), *v.t.* **1.** to get back or regain (something lost or taken away): *to recover a stolen watch.* **2.** to make up for or make good (loss, damage, etc., to oneself). **3.** to regain the strength, composure, balance, or the like, of (oneself). **4.** *Law.* **a.** to obtain by judgment in a court of law, or by legal proceedings: *to recover damages for a wrong.* **b.** to acquire title to through judicial process: *to recover land.* **5.** to reclaim from a bad state, practice, etc. **6.** to regain (a substance) in usable form, as from refuse material or from a waste product or by-product of manufacture; reclaim. **7.** *Mil.* to return (a weapon) to a previously held position in the manual of arms. **8.** *Football.* to gain or regain possession of (a fumble): *They recovered the ball on their own 20-yard line.* —*v.i.* **9.** to regain health after being sick, wounded, or the like (often fol. by *from*): *to recover from an illness.* **10.** to regain a former and better state or condition: *The city soon recovered from the effects of the earthquake.* **11.** to regain one's strength, composure, balance, etc. **12.** *Law.* to obtain a favorable judgment in a suit for something. **13.** *Football.* to gain or regain possession of a fumble: *The Giants recovered in the end zone for a touchdown.* **14.** to make a recovery in fencing or rowing. [1300–50; ME *recoveren* < MF *recoverer* < L *recuperāre* to regain, RECUPERATE] —**re·cov′·er·er,** *n.*
—**Syn. 1.** RECOVER, RECLAIM, RETRIEVE are to regain literally or figuratively something or someone. To RECOVER is to obtain again what one has lost possession of: *to recover a stolen jewel.* To RECLAIM is to bring back from error or wrongdoing, or from a rude or undeveloped state: *to reclaim desert land by irrigation.* To RETRIEVE is to bring back or restore, esp. something to its former, prosperous state: *to retrieve one's fortune.* **9.** heal, mend, recuperate; rally.

re·cov·er·a·ble (ri kuv′ər ə bəl), *adj.* able to recover or be recovered: *a patient now believed to be recoverable; recoverable losses on his investments.* [1425–75; late ME; see RECOVER, -ABLE] —**re·cov′er·a·ble·ness,** *n.*

re·cov·er·y (ri kuv′ə rē), *n., pl.* **-er·ies. 1.** an act of recovering. **2.** the regaining of or possibility of regaining something lost or taken away. **3.** restoration or return to health from sickness. **4.** restoration or return to any former and better state or condition. **5.** time required for recovering. **6.** something that is gained in recovering. **7.** an improvement in the economy marking the end of a recession or decline. **8.** the regaining of substances in usable form, as from refuse material or waste products. **9.** *Law.* the obtaining of right to something by verdict or judgment of a court of law. **10.** *Football.* an act or instance of recovering a fumble. **11.** *Fencing.* the movement to the position of guard after a lunge. **12.** *Rowing.* a return to a former position for making the next stroke. [1350–1400; ME < AF *recoverie.* See RECOVER, -Y[3]]

recov′ery room′, a room near the operating or delivery room of a hospital, equipped with specific apparatus and staffed by specially trained personnel for emergencies, used for the recovery from anesthesia of a postoperative or obstetrical patient before being brought to a hospital room or ward. [1915–20]

recpt, receipt.

rec·re·ant (rek′rē ənt), *adj.* **1.** cowardly or craven. **2.** unfaithful, disloyal, or traitorous. —*n.* **3.** a coward. **4.** an apostate, traitor, or renegade. [1300–50; ME < OF, adj. and n. use of prp. of *recreire* to yield in a contest, equiv. to *re-* RE- + *creire* < L *crēdere* to believe] —**rec′re·ance, rec′re·an·cy,** *n.* —**rec′re·ant·ly,** *adv.*
—**Syn. 1.** dastardly, pusillanimous, base, faint-hearted, yellow. **2.** faithless, untrue, apostate. **3.** dastard. —**Ant. 1.** brave. **2.** loyal. **3.** hero.

re-cre·ate (rē′krē āt′), *v.t.,* **-at·ed, -at·ing.** to create anew. [1580–90; RE- + CREATE] —**re′-cre·at′a·ble,** *adj.* —**re′-cre·a′tive,** *adj.* —**re′-cre·a′tor,** *n.*
—**Syn.** reproduce, remake.

rec·re·ate (rek′rē āt′), *v.,* **-at·ed, -at·ing.** —*v.t.* **1.** to refresh by means of relaxation and enjoyment, as restore physically or mentally. —*v.i.* **2.** to take recreation. [1425–75; late ME *recreaten* < L *recreātus* (ptp. of *recreāre* to create again, revive), equiv. to *re-* RE- + *creātus;* see CREATE] —**rec′re·a′tive,** *adj.* —**rec′re·a′tive·ly,** *adv.* —**rec′re·a′tive·ness,** *n.* —**rec′re·a′tor,** *n.*

re-cre·a·tion (rē′krē ā′shən), *n.* **1.** the act of creating anew. **2.** something created anew. [1515–25; RE- + CREATION]

rec·re·a·tion (rek′rē ā′shən), *n.* **1.** refreshment by means of some pastime, agreeable exercise, or the like. **2.** a pastime, diversion, exercise, or other resource affording relaxation and enjoyment. [1350–1400; ME *recreacioun* (< MF *recreation*) < L *recreātiōn-* (s. of *recreātiō*) restoration, recovery, equiv. to *recreāt(us)* (see RECREATE) + *-iōn-* -ION] —**rec′re·a′tion·al, rec·re·a·to·ry** (rek′rē ə tôr′ē, -tōr′ē), *adj.*

rec·re·a·tion·al·ist (rek′rē ā′shə nl ist), *n.* recreationist. [RECREATIONAL + -IST]

recrea′tional ve′hicle, a van or utility vehicle used for recreational purposes, as camping, and often equipped with living facilities. *Abbr.:* RV [1970–75]

rec·re·a·tion·ist (rek′rē ā′shə nist), *n.* **1.** a person who advocates that national parks, seashores, lakes, etc., be preserved in their natural state for recreation, farming, or scientific study. **2.** a person who frequently enjoys outdoor recreation, as camping and hiking. [1900–05; RECREATION + -IST]

recrea′tion room′, (in a home or public building) a room for informal entertaining, as for dancing, games, cards, etc. [1850–55]

rec·re·ment (rek′rə mənt), *n.* **1.** *Physiol.* a secretion, as saliva, that is reabsorbed by the body. **2.** refuse separated from anything; dross. [1590–1600; < MF < L *recrēmentum* dross, refuse, equiv. to *re-* RE- + *crē-,* var. s. of *cernere* to sift, DISCERN + *-mentum* -MENT] —**rec′re·men′tal,** *adj.*

re·crim·i·nate (ri krim′ə nāt′), *v.,* **-nat·ed, -nat·ing.** —*v.i.* **1.** to bring a countercharge against an accuser. —*v.t.* **2.** to accuse in return. [1595–1605; < ML *recrimināTus* (ptp. of *recrimināRī* to accuse in turn), equiv. to *re-* RE- + *crīmin-,* s. of *crīmen* accusation, blame (see CRIME) + *-ātus* -ATE[1]] —**re·crim′i·na′tion,** *n.* —**re·crim′i·na′tive, re·crim·i·na·to·ry** (ri krim′ə nə tôr′ē, -tōr′ē), *adj.* —**re·crim′i·na′tor,** *n.*

rec′ room′ (rek), *Informal.* a recreation room. [1960–65; by shortening]

re·cru·desce (rē′kro͞o des′), *v.i.,* **-desced, -desc·ing.** to break out afresh, as a sore, a disease, or anything else that has been quiescent. [1880–85; < L *recrūdēscere* to become raw again, equiv. to *re-* RE- + *crūdēscere* to grow harsh, worse (*crūd(us)* bloody (see CRUDE) + *-ēscere* inchoative suffix)]
—**Syn.** erupt, revive.

re·cru·des·cence (rē′kro͞o des′əns), *n.* breaking out afresh or into renewed activity; revival or reappearance in active existence. Also, **re′cru·des′cen·cy.** [1715–25; < L *recrūdēsc(ere)* to RECRUDESCE + -ENCE] —**re′cru·des′cent,** *adj.*

re·cruit (ri kro͞ot′), *n.* **1.** a newly enlisted or drafted member of the armed forces. **2.** a new member of a group, organization, or the like. **3.** a fresh supply of something. —*v.t.* **4.** to enlist (a person) for service in one of the armed forces. **5.** to raise (a force) by enlistment. **6.** to strengthen or supply (an armed force) with new members. **7.** to furnish or replenish with a fresh supply; renew. **8.** to renew or restore (the health, strength, etc.). **9.** to attempt to acquire the services of (a person) for an employer: *She recruits executives for all the top companies.* **10.** to attempt to enroll or enlist (a member, affiliate, student, or the like): *a campaign to recruit new club members.* **11.** to seek to enroll (an athlete) at a school or college, often with an offer of an athletic scholarship. —*v.i.* **12.** to enlist persons for service in one of the armed forces. **13.** to engage in finding and attracting employees, new members, students, athletes, etc. **14.** to recover health, strength, etc. **15.** to gain new supplies of anything lost or wasted. [1635–45; < F, s. of *recruter,* deriv. of *recrue* new growth, n. use of fem. ptp. of *recroître* (*re-* RE- + *croître* < L *crēscere* to grow; cf. CRESCENT)] —**re·cruit′a·ble,** *adj.* —**re·cruit′er,** *n.*

re·cruit·ment (ri kro͞ot′mənt), *n.* **1.** the act or process of recruiting. **2.** *Physiol.* an increase in the response to a stimulus owing to the activation of additional receptors, resulting from the continuous application of the stimulus with the same intensity. [1815–25; RECRUIT + -MENT]

re·crys·tal·lize (rē kris′tl īz′), *v.,* **-lized, -liz·ing.** —*v.i.* **1.** to become crystallized again. **2.** *Metall.* (of a metal) to acquire a new granular structure with new crystals because of plastic deformation, as when hot-worked. —*v.t.* **3.** to crystallize again. Also, *esp. Brit.,* **re·crys′tal·lise′.** [1790–1800; RE- + CRYSTALLIZE] —**re·crys′tal·li·za′tion,** *n.*

Rec. Sec., Recording Secretary. Also, **rec. sec.**

CONCISE PRONUNCIATION KEY: act, cāpe, dâre, pärt; set, ēqual; *if,* ice; ox, ōver, ôrder, oil, bo͝ok, bo͞ot, out; up, ûrge; child; sing; shoe; thin, *th*at; zh as in *treasure.* ə = *a* as in *alone, e* as in *system, i* as in *easily, o* as in *gallop, u* as in *circus;* ᵊ as in *fire* (fīᵊr), *hour* (ouᵊr). l and n can serve as syllabic consonants, as in *cradle* (krād′l), and *button* (but′n). See the full key inside the front cover.

re·chro′ma·to·graph′, *v.t.*
re·cir′cle, *v.,* **-cled, -cling.**
re·cir′cu·late′, *v.,* **-lat·ed, -lat·ing.**
re′cir·cu·la′tion, *n.*
re·clasp′, *v.t.*
re·class′, *v.t.*
re·clean′, *v.t.*
re·cleanse′, *v.t.,* **-cleansed, -cleans·ing.**
re·climb′, *v.t.,* **-climbed, -climb·ing.**
re·clothe′, *v.t.,* **-clothed** or **-clad, -cloth·ing.**
re′co·ag′u·late′, *v.,* **-lat·ed, -lat·ing.**
re′co·ag′u·la′tion, *n.*
re·coat′, *v.t.*
re·coat′, *n.*
re·cock′, *v.*
re·code′, *v.t.,* **-cod·ed, -cod·ing.**
re·cod′i·fi·ca′tion, *n.*
re·cod′i·fy′, *v.t.,* **-fied, -fy·ing.**
re·coin′, *v.t.*
re·coin′age, *n.*
re′col·o·ni·za′tion, *n.*
re·col′o·nize′, *v.t.,* **-nized, -niz·ing.**
re·col′or, *v.t.*
re·col′or·a′tion, *n.*
re·comb′, *v.*
re′com·bine′, *v.,* **-bined, -bin·ing.**
re′com·bin′er, *n.*
re′com·mence′, *v.,* **-menced, -menc·ing.**
re′com·mence′ment, *n.*
re′com·mis′sion, *n., v.t.*
re′com·pare′, *v.t.,* **-pared, -par·ing.**
re′com·par′i·son, *n.*

rect-, var. of **recti-** before a vowel: *rectangle.*

rect., **1.** receipt. **2.** rectangle. **3.** rectangular. **4.** (in prescriptions) rectified. [< L *rēctificātus*] **5.** rector. **6.** rectory.

rec•ta (rek′tə), *n.* a pl. of **rectum.**

rec•tal (rek′tl), *adj.* of, pertaining to, or for the rectum. [1870–75; RECT(UM) + -AL[1]] —**rec′tal•ly,** *adv.*

rec•tan•gle (rek′tang′gəl), *n.* a parallelogram having four right angles. [1565–75; < ML *rēctangulum,* LL *rēctiangulum* right-angled triangle (n. use of neut. of *rēctiangulus* having a right angle), equiv. to *rēcti-* RECTI- + *angulum* ANGLE[1]]

rec•tan•gu•lar (rek tang′gyə lər), *adj.* **1.** shaped like a rectangle. **2.** having the base or section in the form of a rectangle: *a rectangular pyramid.* **3.** having one or more right angles. **4.** forming a right angle. [1615–25; < ML *rēctangul(um)* RECTANGLE + -AR[1]] —**rec•tan•gu•lar•i•ty** (rek tang′gyə lar′i tē), **rec•tan′gu•lar•ness,** *n.* —**rec•tan′gu•lar•ly,** *adv.*

rectan′gular coor′dinates, *Math.* a coordinate system in which the axes meet at right angles. Also called **rectan′gular coor′dinate sys′tem.** [1860–65]

rectan′gular hyper′bola, *Geom.* a hyperbola with transverse and conjugate axes equal to each other. Also called **equiangular hyperbola, equilateral hyperbola.** [1880–85]

rec•ti (rek′tī), *n.* pl. of **rectus.**

recti-, a combining form meaning "right," "straight," used in the formation of compound words: *rectilinear.* Also, *esp. before a vowel,* **rect-.** [< L *rēcti-,* comb. form of *rēctus* RIGHT]

rec•ti•fi•a•ble (rek′tə fī′ə bəl), *adj.* **1.** able to be rectified. **2.** *Math.* of or pertaining to a curve or arc that has finite length. [1640–50; RECTIFY + -ABLE]

rec•ti•fi•ca•tion (rek′tə fi kā′shən), *n.* **1.** the act of rectifying, or the fact of being rectified. **2.** *Astrol.* the method by which the known times of major events in one's life are used to determine an unknown time of birth. [1425–75; late ME; < MF < LL *rēctificātiōn-,* s. of *rēctificātiō.* See RECTIFY, -FICATION]

rec•ti•fi•er (rek′tə fī′ər), *n.* **1.** a person or thing that rectifies. **2.** *Elect.* an apparatus in which current flows more readily in one direction than the other, for changing an alternating current into a direct current. **3.** the apparatus that in distillation separates the most volatile material by condensing it; condenser. [1605–15; RECTIFY + -ER[1]]

rec•ti•fy (rek′tə fī′), *v.t.,* **-fied, -fy•ing.** **1.** to make, put, or set right; remedy; correct: *He sent them a check to rectify his account.* **2.** to put right by adjustment or calculation, as an instrument or a course at sea. **3.** *Chem.* to purify (esp. a spirit or liquor) by repeated distillation. **4.** *Elect.* to change (an alternating current) into a direct current. **5.** to determine the length of (a curve). **6.** *Astron., Geog.* to adjust (a globe) for the solution of any proposed problem. [1350–1400; ME *rectifien* < MF *rectifier* < ML *rēctificāre,* equiv. to L *rēct(us)* RIGHT + *-ificāre* -IFY]
—**Syn. 1.** mend, emend, amend. **2.** adjust, regulate, straighten. —**Ant. 1.** worsen, muddle.

rec•ti•lin•e•ar (rek′tl in′ē ər), *adj.* **1.** forming a straight line. **2.** formed by straight lines. **3.** characterized by straight lines. **4.** moving in a straight line. Also, **rec′ti•lin′e•al.** [1650–60; < LL *rēctiline(us)* (*rēcti-* RECTI- + *līne(a)* LINE[1] + *-us* adj. suffix) + -AR[1]] —**rec′ti•lin′e•ar•ly,** *adv.*

rec•ti•ros•tral (rek′tə ros′trəl), *adj.* (of a bird) having a straight bill. [RECTI- + ROSTRAL]

rec•ti•tude (rek′ti to͞od′, -tyo͞od′), *n.* **1.** rightness of principle or conduct; moral virtue: *the rectitude of her motives.* **2.** correctness: *rectitude of judgment.* **3.** straightness. [1400–50; late ME < MF < LL *rēctitūdin-* (s. of *rēctitūdō*) straightness, equiv. to L *rēct(us)* RIGHT + *-tūdin-* -TUDE]
—**Syn. 1.** integrity, probity, principle.

rec•ti•tu•di•nous (rek′ti to͞od′n əs, -tyo͞od′-), *adj.* **1.** characterized by or given to rectitude. **2.** virtuously self-righteous; pious. [1895–1900; < LL *rēctitūdin-* (s. of *rēctitūdō* RECTITUDE) + -OUS] —**rec′ti•tu′di•nous•ly,** *adv.*

rec•to (rek′tō), *n., pl.* **-tos.** *Print.* a right-hand page of an open book or manuscript; the front of a leaf (opposed to *verso*). [1815–25; < LL *rēctō* (*foliō*) on the right-hand (leaf or page), abl. of L *rēctus* right]

rec•to•cele (rek′tə sēl′), *n.* a hernia of the rectum into the vagina. [1855–60; RECT(UM) + -O- + -CELE[1]]

rec•tor (rek′tər), *n.* **1.** a member of the clergy in charge of a parish in the Protestant Episcopal Church. **2.** *Rom. Cath. Ch.* an ecclesiastic in charge of a college, religious house, or congregation. **3.** *Anglican Ch.* a member of the clergy who has the charge of a parish with full possession of all its rights, tithes, etc. **4.** the head of certain universities, colleges, and schools. [1350–1400; ME *rectour* < L *rēctor* helmsman, ruler, leader, equiv. to *reg(ere)* to rule + *-tor* -TOR] —**rec•to•ri•al** (rek tôr′ē əl, -tōr′-), *adj.*

rec•tor•ate (rek′tər it), *n.* the office, dignity, or term of a rector. Also, **rec′tor•ship′.** [1715–25; < ML *rēctōrātus* office of rector, equiv. to L *rēctōr-* (s. of *rēctor*) RECTOR + *-ātus* -ATE[3]]

rec•to•ry (rek′tə rē), *n., pl.* **-ries.** **1.** a rector's house; parsonage. **2.** *Brit.* a benefice held by a rector. [1530–40; < ML *rēctōria,* equiv. to L *rēctōr-* (s. of *rēctor*) RECTOR + *-ia* -Y[3]]

rec•trix (rek′triks), *n., pl.* **rec•tri•ces** (rek trī′sēz, rek′trə sēz′). *Ornith.* one of the tail feathers of a bird controlling direction during flight. [1605–15; < L *rēctrīx,* fem. of *rēctor* RECTOR] —**rec•tri•cial** (rek trish′əl), *adj.*

rec•tum (rek′təm), *n., pl.* **-tums, -ta** (-tə). *Anat.* the comparatively straight, terminal section of the intestine, ending in the anus. See diag. under **intestine.** [1535–45; < NL *rēctum* (*intestīnum*) the straight (intestine)]

rec•tus (rek′təs), *n., pl.* **-ti** (-tī). *Anat.* any of several straight muscles, as of the abdomen, thigh, eye, etc. [1695–1705; < NL *rēctus* (*musculus*) straight (muscle)]

re•cum•bent (ri kum′bənt), *adj.* **1.** lying down; reclining; leaning. **2.** inactive; idle. **3.** *Zool., Bot.* noting a part that leans or reposes upon its surface of origin. —*n.* **4.** a recumbent person, animal, plant, etc. [1765–75; < L *recumbent-* (s. of *recumbēns*), prp. of *recumbere* to lie back, equiv. to *re-* RE- + *cumb-,* akin to *cubāre* to lie down + *-ent-* -ENT] —**re•cum′ben•cy, re•cum′bence,** *n.* —**re•cum′bent•ly,** *adv.*
—**Syn. 1.** prone, supine; prostrate; inclined.

re•cu•per•ate (ri ko͞o′pə rāt′, -kyo͞o′-) *v.* **-at•ed, -at•ing.** —*v.i.* **1.** to recover from sickness or exhaustion; regain health or strength. **2.** to recover from financial loss. —*v.t.* **3.** to restore to health, vigor, etc. [1535–45; < L *recuperātus* (ptp. of *recuperāre,* var. of *reciperāre* to recover), equiv. to *re-* RE- + *-ciper-,* comb. form of **caper-* (obscure deriv. of *capere* to take) + *-ātus* -ATE[1]] —**re•cu′per•a′tion,** *n.*
—**Syn. 1.** heal, mend.

re•cu•per•a•tive (ri ko͞o′pər ə tiv, -pə rā′tiv, -kyo͞o′-), *adj.* **1.** that recuperates. **2.** having the power of recuperating. **3.** pertaining to recuperation: *recuperative powers.* Also, **re•cu•per•a•to•ry** (ri ko͞o′pər ə tôr′ē, -tōr′ē, -kyo͞o′-). [1640–50; < LL *recuperātīvus* that can be regained, equiv. to *recuperāt(us)* (see RECUPERATE) + *-īvus* -IVE] —**re•cu′per•a′tive•ness,** *n.*

recu′perative fur′nace, a furnace having its incoming air heated by exhaust gases, the passage of air and gases through the furnace being always in the same direction. Cf. **regenerative furnace.**

re•cu•per•a•tor (ri ko͞o′pə rā′tər, -kyo͞o′-), *n.* **1.** a person or thing that recuperates. **2.** (in a recuperative furnace) a system of thin-walled ducts through which incoming air and exhausted gases pass separately so that the air is heated by the gases. [1700–10; < L *recuperātor* regainer, equiv. to *recuperā(re)* to recover (see RECUPERATE) + *-tor* -TOR]

re•cur (ri kûr′), *v.i.,* **-curred, -cur•ring.** **1.** to occur again, as an event, experience, etc. **2.** to return to the mind: *The idea kept recurring.* **3.** to come up again for consideration, as a question. **4.** to have recourse. [1610–20; earlier: to recede < L *recurrere* to run back, equiv. to *re-* RE- + *currere* to run]

re•cur•rence (ri kûr′əns, -kur′-), *n.* **1.** an act or instance of recurring. **2.** return to a previous condition, habit, subject, etc. **3.** recourse. [1640–50; RECUR + -ENCE]

re•cur•rent (ri kûr′ənt, -kur′-), *adj.* **1.** that recurs; occurring or appearing again, esp. repeatedly or periodically. **2.** *Anat.* turned back so as to run in a reverse direction, as a nerve, artery, branch, etc. [1590–1600; < L *recurrent-* (s. of *recurrēns*), prp. of *recurrere* to run back, equiv. to *recurr(ere)* (see RECUR) + *-ent-* -ENT] —**re•cur′rent•ly,** *adv.*
—**Syn. 1.** repeated; persistent, intermittent.

recur′rent fe′ver, *Pathol.* See **relapsing fever.**

re•cur•ring (ri kûr′ing, -kur′-), *adj.* occurring or appearing again. [RECUR + -ING[2]] —**re•cur′ring•ly,** *adv.*

recur′ring dec′imal, *Math.* See **repeating decimal.** [1795–1805]

re•cur•sion (ri kûr′zhən), *n. Math., Computers.* the process of defining a function or calculating a number by the repeated application of an algorithm. [1925–30; < LL *recursiōn-* (s. of *recursiō*) a running back, equiv. to *recurs(us)* (see RECOURSE) + *-iōn-* -ION]

recur′sion for′mula, *Math.* a formula for determining the next term of a sequence from one or more of the preceding terms. Also called **recur′rence for′mula.** [1925–30]

re•cur•sive (ri kûr′siv), *adj.* **1.** pertaining to or using a rule or procedure that can be applied repeatedly. **2.** *Math., Computers.* pertaining to or using the mathematical process of recursion: *a recursive function; a recursive procedure.* [1935–40; RECURS(ION) + -IVE] —**re•cur′sive•ly,** *adv.* —**re•cur′sive•ness,** *n.*

recur′sive defini′tion, *Logic.* a definition consisting of a set of rules such that by repeated application of the rules the meaning of the definiendum is uniquely determined in terms of ideas that are already familiar. [1935–40]

re•cur•vate (ri kûr′vit, -vāt), *adj.* bent back or backward; recurved. [1590–1600; < L *recurvātus* (ptp. of *recurvāre*) to bend backwards, equiv. to *re-* RE- + *curv(us)* CURVE + *-ātus* -ATE[1]]

re•curve (ri kûrv′), *v.t., v.i.,* **-curved, -curv•ing.** to curve or bend back or backward. [1590–1600; < L *recurvāre,* equiv. to *re-* RE- + *curvāre* to CURVE]

re•curved (rē kûrvd′), *adj.* curved upward, as the bill of a bird. [1590–1600; see RECURVE, -ED[2]]

re•cus•al (ri kyo͞o′zəl), *n. Law.* the disqualification of a judge for a particular lawsuit or proceeding, esp. due to some possible conflict of interest or prejudice. [1955–60; RECUSE + -AL[2]]

rec•u•san•cy (rek′yə zən sē, ri kyo͞o′-), *n.* **1.** the state of being recusant. **2.** obstinate refusal or opposition. [1555–65; RECUS(ANT) + -ANCY]

rec•u•sant (rek′yə zənt, ri kyo͞o′zənt), *adj.* **1.** refusing to submit, comply, etc. **2.** obstinate in refusal. **3.** *Eng. Hist.* refusing to attend services of the Church of England. —*n.* **4.** a person who is recusant. **5.** *Eng. Hist.* a person, esp. a Roman Catholic, who refused to attend the services of the Church of England. [1545–55; < L *recūsant-* (s. of *recūsāns*), prp. of *recūsāre* to demur, object, equiv. to *re-* RE- + *-cūsāre,* v. deriv. of *causa* CAUSE; see -ANT]

re•cuse (ri kyo͞oz′), *v.,* **-cused, -cus•ing.** —*v.t.* **1.** to reject or challenge (a judge or juror) as disqualified to act, esp. because of interest or bias. —*v.i.* **2.** to withdraw from a position of judging so as to avoid any semblance of partiality or bias. [1350–1400; ME *recusen* < MF *recuser* < L *recūsāre;* see RECUSANT] —**re•cu•sa•tion** (rek′yo͝o zā′shən), *n.*

re•cy•cle (rē sī′kəl), *v.,* **-cled, -cling,** *n.* —*v.t.* **1.** to treat or process (used or waste materials) so as to make suitable for reuse: *recycling paper to save trees.* **2.** to alter or adapt for new use without changing the essential form or nature of: *The old factory is being recycled as a theater.* **3.** to use again in the original form or with minimal alteration: *The governor recycled some speeches from his early days.* **4.** to cause to pass through a cycle again: *to recycle laundry through a washing machine.* —*v.i.* **5.** to pass through a cycle again; repeat a process from the beginning. **6.** to undergo reuse or renewal; be subject to or suitable for further use, activity, etc.: *The industry will recycle and become profitable once more.* —*n.* **7.** the act or process of recycling. [1925–30; RE- + CYCLE] —**re•cy′cla•ble,** *adj.* —**re•cy′cla•bil′i•ty,** *n.* —**re•cy′cler, re•cy′clist,** *n.*

red[1] (red), *n. adj.,* **red•der, red•dest.** —*n.* **1.** any of various colors resembling the color of blood; the primary color at one extreme end of the visible spectrum, an effect of light with a wavelength between 610 and 780 nm. **2.** something red. **3.** (*often cap.*) a radical leftist in politics, esp. a communist. **4.** *Informal.* See **red light** (def. 1). **5.** *Informal.* red wine: *a glass of red.* **6.** Also called **red devil, red bird.** *Slang.* a capsule of the drug secobarbital, usually red in color. **7. in the red,** operating at a loss or being in debt (opposed to *in the black*): *The newspaper strike put many businesses in the red.* **8. paint the town red.** See **paint** (def. 16). **9. see red,** *Informal.* to become very angry; become enraged: *Snobs make her see red.* —*adj.* **10.** of the color red. **11.** having distinctive areas or markings of red: *a red robin.* **12.** of or indicating a state of financial loss or indebtedness: *the red column in the ledger.* **13.** radically left politically. **14.** (*often cap.*) communist. **15.** of, pertaining to, or characteristic of North American Indian peoples: no longer in technical use. [bef. 900; ME *red,* OE *rēad;* c. G *rot,* D *rood,* ON *raudhr,* L *rūfus, ruber,* Gk *erythrós;* see RUBELLA, RUFESCENT, ERYTHRO-] —**red′ly,** *adv.*

red[2] (red), *v.t.,* **red, red•ding.** redd[1].

Red (red), *n.* a male or female given name.

red-, var. of **re-** before a vowel or *h* in some words: *redintegrate.*

-red, a native English suffix, denoting condition, formerly used in the formation of nouns: *hatred; kindred.* [ME *-rede,* OE *-rǣden*]

re•dact (ri dakt′), *v.t.* **1.** to put into suitable literary form; revise; edit. **2.** to draw up or frame (a statement, proclamation, etc.). [1350–1400; ME < L *redāctus* (ptp. of *redigere* to lead back), equiv. to *red-* RED- + *āctus,* ptp. of *agere* to lead; see ACT] —**re•dac′tion,** *n.* —**re•dac′tion•al,** *adj.* —**re•dac′tor,** *n.*

red′ ad′miral. See under **admiral** (def. 6). [1830–40]

red′ al′der, 1. a tree, *Alnus oregona* (or *A. rubra*), of western North America, having smooth, mottled light gray bark and oval serrate leaves. **2.** the hard, red wood of this tree, used for making furniture. [1905–10] —**red′-al′der,** *adj.*

red′ alert′, 1. (in military or civilian defense) the most urgent form of alert, signaling that an enemy attack is believed to be imminent. **2.** the signal or alarm sounded for this alert. Cf. **blue alert, white alert, yellow alert. 3.** a signal or warning that a critical situation is developing or has occurred. **4.** the period during which a state of crisis or danger is declared to exist. [1960–65]

red′ al′gae, marine algae of the phylum Rhodophyta, in which the chlorophyll is masked by a red or purplish pigment. [1850–55]

re•dan (ri dan′), *n. Fort.* a V-shaped work, usually projecting from a fortified line. [1680–90; < F, var. of *redent* a double notching or jagging, equiv. to *re-* RE- + *dent* TOOTH < L *dent-* (s. of *dēns*)]

CONCISE ETYMOLOGY KEY: <, descended or borrowed from; >, whence; b., blend of, blended; c., cognate with; cf., compare; deriv., derivative; equiv., equivalent; imit., imitative; obl., oblique; r., replacing; s., stem; sp., spelling, spelled; resp., respelling, respelled; trans., translation; ?, origin unknown; *, unattested; ‡, probably earlier than. See the full key inside the front cover.

re′com′pen•sate′, *v.t.,* **-sat•ed, -sat•ing.**
re′com•pen′sa•to′ry, *adj.*
re′com•pi•la′tion, *n.*
re′com•pile′, *v.t.,* **-piled, -pil•ing.**
re•com′pli•cate′, *v.t.,* **-cat•ed, -cat•ing.**
re′com•pli•ca′tion, *n.*
re′com•pound′, *v.*
re′com•pu•ta′tion, *n.*
re′com•pute′, *v.t.,* **-put•ed, -put•ing.**
re′con•ceal′, *v.t.*
re′con•ceal′ment, *n.*
re′con•ceive′, *v.,* **-ceived, -ceiv•ing.**
re′con′cen•trate′, *v.,* **-trat•ed, -trat•ing.**
re′con•cep′tion, *n.*
re′con•cep′tu•al•i•za′tion, *n.*
re′con•cep′tu•al•ize′, *v.t.,* **-ized, -iz•ing.**
re′con•demn′, *v.t.*
re′con•dem•na′tion, *n.*
re′con•den•sa′tion, *n.*
re′con•dense′, *v.,* **-densed, -dens•ing.**
re′con•duct′, *v.t.*
re′con•fer′, *v.,* **-ferred, -fer•ring.**
re′con•fine′, *v.t.,* **-fined, -fin•ing.**
re′con•firm′, *v.t.*
re′con•fir•ma′tion, *n.*
re•con′fis•cate′, *v.t.,* **-cat•ed, -cat•ing.**
re′con•form′, *v.*
re′con•front′, *v.t.*
re′con•fron•ta′tion, *n.*
re′con•fuse′, *v.t.,* **-fused, -fus•ing.**

Red′ and the Black′, The, (French, *Le Rouge et le Noir*), a novel (1832) by Stendhal.

Red′ An′gus, one of a subpopulation of Aberdeen Angus beef cattle having a reddish coat.

red′ ant′, any of various reddish ants, esp. the Pharaoh ant. [1660–70]

re·dar·gue (ri där′gyo͞o), *v.t.*, **-gued, -gu·ing.** *Archaic.* to prove wrong or invalid; disprove; refute. [1350–1400; ME *redarguen* to rebuke (< OF *redargüer*) < L *redarguere*, equiv. to *red-* RED- + *arguere* to ARGUE] **—red′·ar·gu′tion,** *n.*

Red′ Ar′my, the Soviet army.

red′-back spi′der (red′bak′), a venomous spider, *Latrodectus hasselti*, of Australia and New Zealand, related to the black widow spider and having a bright red stripe on the back. [1940–45]

Red′ Badge′ of Cour′age, The, a novel (1895) by Stephen Crane.

red·bait (red′bāt′), *v.i.* to denounce or deprecate as a political radical, esp. to accuse of being communist. [1935–40; back formation from *redbaiter, redbaiting.* See RED[1], BAIT] **—red′bait′er,** *n.*

Red′ Bank′, a borough in E central New Jersey. 12,031.

Red·bank White·oak (red′bank′ hwīt′ōk′, wīt′-), a city in S Tennessee. 13,297.

red′ bay′, an evergreen tree, *Persea borbonia*, of the eastern coast of the U.S., having faintly bluish-green leaves and blue or blue-black, red-stalked fruit, grown as an ornamental. Also called **bull bay.** [1720–30, *Amer.*]

red′-bel·lied tur′tle (red′bel′ēd), any of several freshwater turtles of the genus *Pseudemys*, of the eastern and southern U.S., having red markings on the lower shell.

red′bel·ly dace′ (red′bel′ē), *Ichthyol.* any of the small, brightly colored North American freshwater cyprinids, esp. *Phoxinus oreas* **(northern redbelly dace)** and *P. erythrogaster* **(southern redbelly dace).** [1945–50, *Amer.*; RED[1] + BELLY]

red′-billed que′lea (red′bild′). See under **quelea.** [1955–60]

red′ birch′. See **river birch.** [1775–85, *Amer.*]

red′ bird′, red[1] (def. 6). [1965–70]

red·bird (red′bûrd′), *n.* **1.** the cardinal, *Cardinalis cardinalis.* **2.** any of various other birds having red plumage, as the scarlet tanager. [1660–70; RED[1] + BIRD]

red′ blood′ cell′, *Physiol.* one of the cells of the blood, which in mammals are enucleate disks concave on both sides, contain hemoglobin, and carry oxygen to the cells and tissues and carbon dioxide back to the respiratory organs. Also called **erythrocyte, red cell, red′ blood′ cor′puscle.** *Abbr.:* RBC [1905–10]

red-blood·ed (red′blud′id), *adj.* vigorous; virile. [1795–1805] **—red′-blood′ed·ness,** *n.*
—Syn. robust, sturdy, lusty, hearty.

red·bone (red′bōn′), *n.* an American hound having a red coat, used in hunting raccoons, bears, cougars, and wildcats. Also, **red′ bone′.** [1915–20, *Amer.*; RED[1] + BONE]

Red′ Branch′, *Irish Legend.* the warriors of Conchobar, alienated from him after his treachery to Deirdre and Naoise.

red′ brass′, an alloy of from 77 to 86 percent copper with the balance zinc; Mannheim gold. [1830–40]

red·breast (red′brest′), *n.* **1.** the European robin, *Erithacus rubecula.* **2.** the North American robin, *Turdus migratorius.* **3.** any of various other birds, as a dowitcher or knot. **4.** a freshwater sunfish, *Lepomis auritus*, of the eastern U.S. [1375–1425; late ME; see RED[1], BREAST]

red·brick (red′brik′), *adj. Brit. Informal.* (*sometimes cap.*) of, pertaining to, or associated with a redbrick university. Also, **red′-brick′.** [1705–15; RED[1] + BRICK]

red′brick univer′sity, (*sometimes caps.*) *Brit. Informal.* **1.** any new or little-known university, esp. one built since World War II to educate students in industrial regions, emphasizing technical subjects rather than the classics, and often partially supported by government funds. **2.** any university lacking the prestige of Oxford and Cambridge. [1940–45]

Red·bridge (red′brij′), *n.* a borough of Greater London, England. 231,400.

Red′ Brigades′, an extreme leftist terrorist organization in Italy. [trans. of It *Brigate rosse*]

red·bud (red′bud′), *n.* **1.** an American tree, *Cercis canadensis*, of the legume family, resembling the Eurasian Judas tree and having small, budlike, pink flowers: the state tree of Oklahoma. **2.** any of various related trees. [1695–1705; RED[1] + BUD[1]]

red·bug (red′bug′), *n. Chiefly South Atlantic States.* chigger (def. 1). [1795–1805; RED[1] + BUG[1]]

red′ cab′bage, a variety of the edible cabbage, *Brassica oleracea*, having deep reddish-purple leaves. [1605–15]

red·cap (red′kap′), *n.* **1.** a baggage porter at a railroad station. **2.** *Brit. Informal.* a member of the military police. [1530–40; RED[1] + CAP[1]]

red′ car′pet, 1. a red strip of carpet placed on the ground for high-ranking dignitaries to walk on when entering or leaving a building, vehicle, or the like. **2.** a display of courtesy or deference, as that shown to persons of high station: *The visiting princess was treated to the red carpet in Rome.* [1930–35] **—red′-car′pet,** *adj.*

red′ ce′dar, 1. Also called **eastern red cedar, savin.** an American, coniferous tree, *Juniperus virginiana*, yielding a fragrant, reddish wood used for making lead pencils, etc. **2.** the western red cedar, *Thuja plicata.* **3.** the wood of these trees. [1675–85, *Amer.*]

red′ cell′, a red blood cell. [1880–85]

red′ cent′, *Informal.* a cent, as representative of triviality: *His promise isn't worth a red cent.* [1830–40, *Amer.*]

Red′ Cham′ber, *Canadian Informal.* the Canadian Senate chamber.

Red′ Chi′na, *Informal.* See **China, People's Republic of.**

red′ choke′berry. See under **chokeberry** (def. 1).

red′ clay′, *Geol.* a brown to red, widely distributed deep-sea deposit consisting chiefly of microscopic particles and tinted red by iron oxides and manganese. [1350–1400; ME] **—red′-clay′,** *adj.*

red′ clo′ver, a clover, *Trifolium pratense*, having red flowers, grown for forage: the state flower of Vermont. [bef. 900; OE (not recorded in ME)]

red′ clus′ter pep′per, a tropical, woody plant, *Capsicum annuum fasciculatum*, having erect, very pungent, red fruit in small clusters.

red·coat (red′kōt′), *n.* (esp. during the American Revolution) a British soldier. [1510–20; RED[1] + COAT]

red′ cor′al, any of several alcyonarian corals of the genus *Corallium*, as *C. nobile*, of the Mediterranean Sea, having a red or pink skeleton, used for jewelry. Also called **precious coral.** [1275–1325; ME]

red′ cor′puscle, a red blood cell. [1840–50]

red′ count′, a count of the red cells in a person's blood. Cf. **blood count.**

Red′ Cres′cent, an organization functioning as the Red Cross in Muslim countries.

Red′ Cross′, 1. an international philanthropic organization **(Red′ Cross′ Soci′ety),** formed in consequence of the Geneva Convention of 1864, to care for the sick and wounded in war, secure neutrality of nurses, hospitals, etc., and help relieve suffering caused by pestilence, floods, fires, and other calamities. **2.** a branch of this organization: *the American Red Cross.* **3.** the English national emblem of St. George's cross. **4.** See **Geneva cross.** Also, **red′ cross′** (for defs. 3, 4).

red′ cur′rant, 1. any of various currant shrubs of the genus *Ribes*, bearing an edible, red fruit. **2.** the fruit itself. [1620–30]

redd[1] (red), *v.t.*, **redd** or **redd·ed, redd·ing.** *Northern and Midland U.S.* **1.** to put in order; tidy: *to redd a room for company.* **2.** to clear: *to redd the way.* Also, **red.** [bef. 900; appar. conflation of 2 words: ME (Scots) *reden* to clear, clean up (a space, land), OE *gerǣdan* to put in order (c. MD, MLG *rêden, reiden*; akin to READY); and ME (Scots) *redden* to rid, free, clear, OE *hreddan* to save, deliver, rescue (c. OFris *hredda*, G *retten*)]

redd[2] (red), *n.* the spawning area or nest of trout or salmon. [1640–50; orig. uncert.]

red′ deer′, 1. a deer, *Cervus elaphus*, of Europe and Asia, having a reddish-brown summer coat. See illus. under **stag. 2.** the white-tailed deer, *Odocoileus virginianus*, in its summer coat. [1425–75; late ME]

Red′ Deer′, a city in S central Alberta, in W Canada. 46,393.

Red′ Deli′cious. a deep-red type of Delicious apple.

red·den (red′n), *v.t.* **1.** to make or cause to become red. —*v.i.* **2.** to become red. **3.** to blush; flush. [1605–15; RED[1] + -EN[1]]

Red′ Des′ert. See **Nefud Desert.**

red′ dev′il, *Slang.* red[1] (def. 6). [1965–70]

Red·ding (red′ing), *n.* a city in N California. 41,995.

red·dish (red′ish), *adj.* somewhat red; tending to red; tinged with red. [1350–1400; ME *redische.* See RED[1], -ISH[1]] **—red′dish·ness,** *n.*

red·dle (red′l), *n., v.t.*, **-dled, -dling.** ruddle.

red·dle·man (red′l mən), *n., pl.* **-men.** ruddleman.

red′ dog′, *Cards.* a gambling game played by two to ten persons with a pack of 52 cards, in which players bet in turn that their hands contain a card of the same suit as the top card of the stock and of higher rank. Also called **high-card pool.** [1925–30]

red-dog (red′dôg′, -dog′), *v.*, **-dogged, -dog·ging.** *Football.* (esp. of linebackers) —*v.t.* **1.** to charge directly for (the passer) as soon as the ball is snapped. —*v.i.* **2.** to red-dog the passer. [1950–55] **—red′-dog′·ger,** *n.*

red′ dog′wood, 1. a Eurasian dogwood, *Cornus sanguinea*, having greenish-white flowers and dark-red branches. **2.** a variety of flowering dogwood, *Cornus florida rubra*, having red or pink bracts. [1950–55]

red′ drum′, *Ichthyol.* a large, edible drum, *Sciaenops ocellatus*, living in waters off the Atlantic coast of the U.S. Also called **channel bass.** [1700–10, *Amer.*]

red′ dust′er, a red ensign having the Union Jack as a canton, flown by most British merchant ships. [1880–85]

red′ dwarf′, *Astron.* any of the faint reddish stars having diameters about half that of the sun and low surface temperatures, about 2000–3000 K; a main sequence star of spectral type M. [1915–20]

rede (rēd), *v.*, **red·ed, red·ing,** *n. Chiefly Brit. Dial.* —*v.t.* **1.** to counsel; advise. **2.** to explain. —*n.* **3.** counsel; advice. **4.** a plan; scheme. **5.** a tale; story. [bef. 900; (v.) ME *reden*, OE *rǣdan*; (n.) ME; OE *rǣd*, c. OFris *rēd*, OS *rād*, ON *rāth*; see READ[1], READY]

red′ear sun′fish (red′ēr′), a freshwater sunfish, *Lepomis microlophos*, of the lower Mississippi valley and southeastern states, having the gill cover margined with scarlet. Also called **red′ear shell′cracker.** [1945–50; RED[1] + EAR[1]]

re·deem (ri dēm′), *v.t.* **1.** to buy or pay off; clear by payment: *to redeem a mortgage.* **2.** to buy back, as after a tax sale or a mortgage foreclosure. **3.** to recover (something pledged or mortgaged) by payment or other satisfaction: *to redeem a pawned watch.* **4.** to exchange (bonds, trading stamps, etc.) for money or goods. **5.** to convert (paper money) into specie. **6.** to discharge or fulfill (a pledge, promise, etc.). **7.** to make up for; make amends for; offset (some fault, shortcoming, etc.): *His bravery redeemed his youthful idleness.* **8.** to obtain the release or restoration of, as from captivity, by paying a ransom. **9.** *Theol.* to deliver from sin and its consequences by means of a sacrifice offered for the sinner. [1375–1425; late ME *redemen* < MF *redimer* < L *redimere*, equiv. to *red-* RED- + *-imere*, comb. form of *emere* to purchase (cf. EMPTOR, RANSOM)]
—Syn. 1-3. repurchase. REDEEM, RANSOM both mean to buy back. REDEEM is wider in its application than RANSOM, and means to buy back, regain possession of, or exchange for money, goods, etc.: *to redeem one's property.* To RANSOM is to redeem a person from captivity by paying a stipulated price, or to redeem from sin by sacrifice: *to ransom a kidnapped child.* **8, 9.** free, liberate, rescue, save. **—Ant. 1.** abandon.

re·deem·a·ble (ri dē′mə bəl), *adj.* **1.** capable of being redeemed. **2.** that will be redeemed: *bonds redeemable in 10 years.* Also, **re·demp·ti·ble** (ri demp′tə bəl). [1605–15; REDEEM + -ABLE] **—re·deem′a·bil′i·ty, re·deem′a·ble·ness,** *n.* **—re·deem′a·bly,** *adv.*

re·deem·er (ri dē′mər), *n.* **1.** a person who redeems. **2.** (*cap.*) Jesus Christ. [1400–50; late ME; see REDEEM, -ER[1]]

re·deem·ing (ri dē′ming), *adj.* offsetting or counterbalancing some fault, defect, or the like: *a redeeming quality.* [1745–55; REDEEM + -ING[2]]

red′ eft′. See under **eft[1]** (def. 1).

re·de·liv·er (rē′di liv′ər), *v.t.* **1.** to deliver again. **2.** to deliver back; return. [1485–95; RE- + DELIVER] **—re′de·liv′er·er,** *n.*

re·de·mand (rē′di mand′, -mänd′), *v.t.* **1.** to demand again. **2.** to demand back; demand the return of. [1565–75; RE- + DEMAND] **—re′de·mand′a·ble,** *adj.*

re·demp·tion (ri demp′shən), *n.* **1.** an act of redeeming or the state of being redeemed. **2.** deliverance; rescue. **3.** *Theol.* deliverance from sin; salvation. **4.** atonement for guilt. **5.** repurchase, as of something sold. **6.** paying off, as of a mortgage, bond, or note. **7.** recovery by payment, as of something pledged. **8.** conversion of paper money into specie. [1300–50; ME *redempcioun* (< MF *redemption*) < LL *redēmptiōn-* (s. of *redēmptiō*), equiv. to L *redēmpt(us)* (ptp. of *redimere* to REDEEM) + *-iōn-* -ION] **—re·demp′tion·al,** *adj.* **—re·demp′tion·less,** *adj.*

redemp′tion cen′ter, a commercial establishment at which trading stamps of a specific brand may be exchanged for merchandise.

re·demp·tion·er (ri demp′shə nər), *n. Amer. Hist.* an emigrant from Europe to America who obtained passage by becoming an indentured servant for a specified period of time. [1765–75; REDEMPTION + -ER[1]]

re·demp·tive (ri demp′tiv), *adj.* **1.** serving to redeem. **2.** of, pertaining to, or centering on redemption or salvation: *redemptive religions.* [1640–50; REDEMPT(ION) + -IVE] **—re·demp′tive·ly,** *adv.*

Re·demp·tor·ist (ri demp′tər ist), *n. Rom. Cath. Ch.* a member of the "Congregation of the Most Holy Redeemer," founded by St. Alphonsus Liguori in 1732. [1825–35; < F *rédemptoriste* < LL *redēmptor* (L *redēm-*, var. s. of *redimere* to REDEEM + *-tor* -TOR; cf. EMPTOR) + F *-iste* -IST]

re·demp·to·ry (ri demp′tə rē), *adj.* **1.** of or pertaining to redemption; redemptive. **2.** redeeming; saving: *a redemptory act.* [1590–1600; REDEMPT(ION) + -ORY[1]]

re·de·ploy (rē′di ploi′), *Mil.* —*v.t.* **1.** to transfer (a unit, a person, supplies, etc.) from one theater of operations to another. **2.** to move or allocate to a different position, use, function, or the like; reassign. —*v.i.* **3.** to execute a redeployment. [1940–45; RE- + DEPLOY] **—re′de·ploy′ment,** *n.*

re·de·vel·op (rē′di vel′əp), *v.t.* **1.** to develop (something) again. **2.** *Photog.* to submit (a film or the like) to a second development, as to intensify or tone it. —*v.i.* **3.** to develop again. [1880–85; RE- + DEVELOP] **—re′de·vel′op·er,** *n.*

re·de·vel·op·ment (rē′di vel′əp mənt), *n.* **1.** the act

CONCISE PRONUNCIATION KEY: *act, cāpe, dâre, pärt; set, ēqual; if, īce; ox, ōver, ôrder, oil, bo͝ok, bo͞ot, out; up, ûrge; child; sing; shoe; thin, that;* zh as in *treasure.* ə = *a* as in *alone, e* as in *system, i* as in *easily, o* as in *gallop, u* as in *circus;* ᵊ as in *fire* (fīᵊr), *hour* (ouᵊr). l and n can serve as syllabic consonants, as in *cradle* (krād′l), and *button* (but′n). See the full key inside the front cover.

re′con·fu′sion, *n.*
re′con·nect′, *v.t.*
re′con·nec′tion, *n.*
re·con′quer, *v.t.*
re·con′quest, *n.*
re·con′se·crate′, *v.t.*, **-crat·ed, -crat·ing.**
re′con·se·cra′tion, *n.*
re′con·sent′, *v.i.*
re′con·sign′, *v.t.*
re′con·sole′, *v.t.*, **-soled, -sol·ing.**
re′con·sol′i·date′, *v.*, **-dat·ed, -dat·ing.**
re′con·sol′i·da′tion, *n.*
re′con·sult′, *v.*
re′con·sul·ta′tion, *n.*
re′con′tact, *n., v.*
re′con·tam′i·nate′, *v.t.*, **-nat·ed, -nat·ing.**
re′con·tam′i·na′tion, *n.*
re′con′tem·plate′, *v.*, **-plat·ed, -plat·ing.**
re′con·tem·pla′tion, *n.*
re′con·tend′, *v.i.*
re′con·test′, *v.t.*
re·con′tour, *v.t.*
re′con·tract′, *v.t.*
re′con·trac′tion, *n.*
re′con·vene′, *v.*, **-vened, -ven·ing.**
re′con·verge′, *v.i.*, **-verged, -verg·ing.**
re′con·ver′gence, *n.*
re′con·vict′, *v.t.*
re′con·vic′tion, *n.*
re′con·vince′, *v.t.*, **-vinced, -vinc·ing.**
re·cook′, *v.*
re·cool′, *v.*
re·cop′y, *v.t.*, **-cop·ied, -cop·y·ing.**

or process of redeveloping. **2.** an often publicly financed rebuilding of an urban residential or commercial section in decline. [1870–75; RE- + DEVELOPMENT]

redevel′opment com′pany, a private corporation or a public agency that stimulates the improvement of land, as through a building project subject to certain designs and controls, by financing, selling, or leasing such real estate to interested buyers or lessees.

red-eye (red′ī′), *n.* **1.** the condition of having bloodshot eyes, as from eyestrain or lack of sleep. **2.** Also, **red′ eye′, redeye.** *Informal.* a commercial airline flight between two distant points that departs late at night and arrives early in the morning. **3.** redeye (def. 3). —*adj.* **4.** Also, **redeye.** *Informal.* of or indicating a long-distance flight that leaves late at night: *the red-eye special from New York to Los Angeles.* [1965–70, for def. 2]

red•eye (red′ī′), *n., pl.* **-eyes,** (*esp. collectively*) **-eye** for 1, 2; *adj.* —*n.* **1.** any of several fishes having red eyes, as the rock bass. **2.** See **red-eyed vireo. 3.** Also, **red-eye, red′ eye′.** *Slang.* cheap, strong whiskey. **4.** red-eye (def. 2). **5.** (*cap.*) *Mil.* a shoulder-launched U.S. Army surface-to-air missile capable of destroying low-flying aircraft. —*adj.* **6.** red-eye. [1665–75; 1920–25, for def. 3; RED[1] + EYE]

red′-eyed vir′eo (red′īd′), an American vireo, *Vireo olivaceus,* having olive-green and white plumage and red irises. Also called **redeye, preacher bird.** See illus. under **vireo.** [1830–40, *Amer.*]

red′-eye gra′vy, *Southern Cookery.* a gravy made from the pan juices of fried country ham, thickened with flour and sometimes containing coffee for color and flavor. [1945–50]

red-faced (red′fāst′), *adj.* **1.** having a red face. **2.** blushing or flushed with embarrassment, anger, resentment, or the like. [1570–80] —**red-fac•ed•ly** (red′fā′-sid lē, -fāst′lē), *adv.*

red′ feed′, small red marine crustaceans of various species that are a major source of food for many commercially important fishes.

red′ fes′cue, a grass, *Festuca rubra,* of the meadows of the North Temperate Zone, having green, reddish, or bluish-green flower clusters. [1895–1900]

Red•field (red′fēld′), *n.* **Robert,** 1897–1958, American anthropologist.

red-fig•ure (red′fig′yər), *adj.* pertaining to or designating a style of vase painting developed in Greece in the latter part of the 6th and the 5th centuries B.C., characterized chiefly by figurative representations in red against a black-slip background, details painted in the design, and the introduction of three-dimensional illusion in the rendering of form and space. Also, **red′-fig′•ured.** Cf. **black-figure.** [1890–95]

red•fin (red′fin′), *n.* any of various small freshwater minnows with red fins, esp. a shiner, *Notropis umbratilis,* of streams in central North America. [1785–95; RED[1] + FIN]

red′fin pick′erel. See under **pickerel** (def. 1).

red′ fir′, **1.** any of several firs, as *Abies magnifica,* of the western U.S., having a reddish bark. **2.** the light, soft wood of these trees. **3.** See **Douglas fir.** [1835–45]

red′ fire′, any of various combustible preparations, as one containing strontium nitrate, that burn with a vivid red light: used chiefly in pyrotechnic displays and in signaling. [1810–20]

red•fish (red′fish′), *n., pl.* (*esp. collectively*) **-fish,** (*esp. referring to two or more kinds or species*) **-fish•es. 1.** Also called **ocean perch, rosefish.** a North Atlantic rockfish, *Sebastes marinus,* used for food. **2.** See **red drum. 3.** sheephead. [1400–50; late ME *rede fische;* see RED[1], FISH]

red′ flag′, **1.** the symbol or banner of a left-wing revolutionary party. **2.** a danger signal. **3.** something that provokes an angry or hostile reaction: *The talk about raising taxes was a red flag to many voters.* **4.** Also called **powder flag.** *Naut.* a red burgee, designating in the International Code of Signals the letter "B," flown by itself to show that a vessel is carrying, loading, or discharging explosives or highly inflammable material. **5.** (*caps.*) a war game the U.S. Air Force holds several times each year at Nellis Air Force Base, Nevada, to train personnel in air combat. [1770–80]

red-flag (red′flag′), *v.,* **-flagged, -flag•ging,** *adj.* —*v.t.* **1.** to mark or draw attention to for a particular purpose: *The department has red-flagged the most urgent repair work to be done.* **2.** to provoke the attention of; alert; arouse: *The animal's refusal to eat red-flagged the keeper that something was wrong.* —*adj.* **3.** of or pertaining to a red flag. **4.** intended or serving to emphasize, warn, incite, or provoke. [1880–85]

red′ flash′, a red coloration of the lower portion of the sun, occasionally seen as the sun rises above or sinks to the horizon.

red′ flour′ bee′tle, a reddish-brown flour beetle, *Tribolium castaneum,* that feeds on stored grain, dried fruit, etc.

red′ fox′, a fox, *Vulpes vulpes,* usually having orangish-red to reddish-brown fur. See illus. under **fox.** [1630–40, *Amer.*]

red′ gi′ant, *Astron.* a star in an intermediate stage of evolution, characterized by a large volume, low surface temperature, and reddish hue. [1915–20]

red′ goat′fish, a goatfish, *Mullus auratus.*

Red•grave (red′grāv), *n.* **Sir Michael (Scud•a•more)** (skud′ə môr′, -mōr′, skōō′də-), 1908–85, English actor.

red′ grouse′, a grouse, *Lagopus lagopus scoticus,* of the British Isles, a subspecies of willow ptarmigan lacking white winter plumage. [1770–80]

Red′ Guard′, a member of a Chinese Communist youth movement in the late 1960's, committed to the militant support of Mao Zedong. [1965–70; trans. of Chin *hóng wèibīng*]

red′ gum′, **1.** any of several trees of the genus *Eucalyptus,* esp. *E. camaldulensis,* having smooth, gray bark. **2.** the hard, reddish wood of this tree, used for making railroad ties, fence posts, etc. **3.** See **sweet gum** (defs. 1, 2). [1780–90]

red′ gum′, *Pathol.* strophulus. [1830–40, *Amer.*]

red-hand•ed (red′han′did), *adj., adv.* in the very act of a crime, wrongdoing, etc., or in possession of self-incriminating evidence: *They caught him red-handed dipping into the till.* [1810–20] —**red′-hand′ed•ly,** *adv.* —**red′hand′ed•ness,** *n.*

red′ hat′, **1.** the broad-brimmed official hat of a Roman Catholic cardinal, symbolic of the office or rank of a cardinal. **2.** a cardinal. Also called **scarlet hat.** [1590–1600]

Red′ Hats′, the original sect of Tibetan Buddhist monks, whose doctrines were much influenced by the earlier Bön religion. Cf. **Yellow Hats.**

red•head (red′hed′), *n.* **1.** a person having red hair. **2.** an American diving duck, *Aythya americana,* the male of which has a bright chestnut-red head. [1655–65; RED[1] + HEAD]

red-head•ed (red′hed′id *for 1;* red′hed′id *for 2*), *adj.* **1.** having red hair, as a person. **2.** having a red head, as an animal, esp. a bird. Also, **red′head′ed.** [1555–65]

red′-headed wood′pecker, a black and white North American woodpecker, *Melanerpes erythrocephalus,* having a red head and neck. [1720–30, *Amer.*]

red′ heart′, a treelike Californian shrub, *Ceanothus spinosus,* of the buckthorn family, having pale blue or white flowers. [1825–35]

red′ heat′, **1.** the temperature of a red-hot body. **2.** the condition of being red-hot. [1680–90]

red′ her′ring, **1.** a smoked herring. **2.** something intended to divert attention from the real problem or matter at hand; a misleading clue. **3.** Also called **red′-her′•ring prospec′tus.** *Finance.* a tentative prospectus circulated by the underwriters of a new issue of stocks or bonds that is pending approval by the U.S. Securities and Exchange Commission: so called because the front cover of such a prospectus must carry a special notice printed in red. **4.** any similar tentative financial prospectus, as one concerning a pending or proposed sale of cooperative or condominium apartments. [1375–1425; late ME]

red•hi•bi•tion (red′i bish′ən, red′hi-), *n. Civil Law.* the nullification of a sale because of a defect in the article sold of such nature as to make it totally or virtually unusable or as to have prevented the purchase if known to the buyer. [1650–60; < L *redhibitiōn-* (s. of *redhibitiō*), equiv. to *redhibit(us),* ptp. of *redhibēre* to return (an item bought), take back (an item sold) (*red-* RED- + *-hib(ēre),* comb. form of *habēre* to have + *-itus* -ITE[2]) + *-iōn-* -ION] —**red•hib•i•to•ry** (red hib′i tôr′ē, -tōr′ē), *adj.*

red′ hind′ (hīnd), a grouper, *Epinephelus guttatus,* of Florida, the West Indies, etc., valued as a food fish.

red•horse (red′hôrs′), *n.* any of several suckers of the genus *Moxostoma,* found in the fresh waters of North America, often having reddish fins. Also called **red′•horse suck′er.** [1790–1800, *Amer.;* RED[1] + HORSE]

red-hot (*adj.* red′hot′; *n.* red′hot′), *adj.* **1.** red with heat; very hot. **2.** creating much excitement, demand, or discussion: *The new toy robot is a red-hot item this Christmas.* **3.** violent; furious: *red-hot anger.* **4.** characterized by intense excitement, enthusiasm, or passion. **5.** very fresh or new; most recent: *red-hot tips on the stock market.* —*n.* **6.** a person who has great fervor or intensity, as for a goal or cause. **7.** *Informal.* a hot dog. **8.** a small cinnamon-flavored candy. [1325–75; ME]

red′-hot pok′er, tritoma. [1885–90; so called from the fiery red blossoms at the end of the flower spike]

Re•di (Re′dē), *n.* **Fran•ces•co** (frän ches′kô), 1626?–98, Italian biologist.

re•di•a (rē′dē ə), *n., pl.* **-di•ae** (-dē ē′). *Zool.* a cylindrical larval stage of some trematodes, produced by a sporocyst and giving rise to daughter rediae or to cercariae. [1875–80; < NL, after F. REDI; see -A[2]]

re•di•al (*v.* rē dī′əl, -dīl′; *n.* rē′dī′əl, -dīl′), *Telecommunications.* —*v.t.* **1.** Also, **re•di′al.** to dial again. —*n.* **2.** See **automatic redial.** [1960–65; RE- + DIAL]

Red′ In′dian, *Sometimes Offensive.* Indian (def. 1). [1825–35]

red•in•gote (red′ing gōt′), *n.* **1.** a dress or lightweight coat, usually belted, open along the entire front to reveal a dress or petticoat worn underneath it. **2.** a coatdress with a contrasting gore in front. **3.** a long, double-breasted overcoat worn by men in the 18th century. [1825–35; < F < E *riding coat*]

red′ ink′, **1.** a financial deficit; business loss. **2.** the condition of showing a business loss. [1925–30, *Amer.*]

red•in•te•grate (red in′ti grāt′, ri din′-), *v.t.,* **-grat•ed, -grat•ing.** to make whole again; restore to a perfect state; renew; reestablish. [1400–50; late ME *redintegraten* < L *redintegrātus* (ptp. of *redintegrāre* to make whole again), equiv. to *red-* RED- + *integr-* (s. of *integer*) whole, entire + *-ātus* -ATE[1] (see INTEGRATE)] —**red•in′•te•gra′tive,** *adj.*

red•in•te•gra•tion (red in′ti grā′shən, ri din′), *n.* **1.** the act or process of redintegrating. **2.** *Psychol.* reintegration (def. 3b). [1425–75; < L *redintegrātiōn-* (s. of *redintegrātiō*), equiv. to *redintegrāt(us)* (see REDINTEGRATE) + *-iōn-* -ION]

re•di•rect (rē′di rekt′, -dī-), *v.t.* **1.** to direct again. **2.** to change the direction or focus of: *He redirected the children's energies toward building a sand castle instead of throwing sand at each other.* —*adj.* **3.** *Law.* pertaining to the examination of a witness by the party calling him or her, after cross-examination. [1835–45; RE- + DIRECT] —**re′di•rec′tion,** *n.*

re•dis•count (rē dis′kount), *v.t.* **1.** to discount again. —*n.* **2.** an act of rediscounting. **3.** Usually, **rediscounts.** commercial paper discounted a second time. [1865–70; RE- + DISCOUNT]

redis′count rate′, the rate charged by the Federal Reserve Bank to member banks for rediscounting commercial paper.

re•dis•trib•ute (rē′di strib′yōōt), *v.t.,* **-ut•ed, -ut•ing. 1.** to distribute again or anew: *The corporation will redistribute its share of the profits to its stockholders.* **2.** to alter the distribution of; apportion differently: *Let's redistribute the work more fairly.* [1605–15; RE- + DISTRIBUTE]

re•dis•tri•bu•tion (rē′dis trə byōō′shən), *n.* **1.** a distribution performed again or anew. **2.** *Econ.* the theory, policy, or practice of lessening or reducing inequalities in income through such measures as progressive income taxation and antipoverty programs. [1830–40; RE- + DISTRIBUTION] —**re′dis•tri•bu′tion•al, re•dis•trib•u•to•ry** (rē′di strib′yə tôr′ē, -tōr′ē), *adj.*

re•dis•tri•bu•tion•ist (rē′dis tri byōō′shə nist), *n. Econ.* a person who believes in, advocates, or supports income redistribution. [1975–80; REDISTRIBUTION + -IST]

re•dis•trib•u•tive (rē′di strib′yə tiv), *adj. Econ.* favoring, supporting, or practicing income redistribution: *the redistributive effects of public spending.* [1880–85; REDISTRIBUTE + -IVE]

re•dis•trict (rē dis′trikt), *v.t.* to divide anew into districts, as for administrative or electoral purposes. [1840–50, *Amer.;* RE- + DISTRICT]

red•i•vi•vus (red′ə vī′vəs, -vē′-), *adj.* living again; revived. [1645–55; < L *redivīvus* renewed, renovated]

Red′ Jack′et, (*Sagoyewatha*), c1756–1830, Seneca leader.

red′ jun′gle fowl′. See under **jungle fowl.**

red′ ko′whai (kō′wī), parrot's-bill. [*kowhai* < Maori *kōwhai, kōhai;* cf. PARROT'S-BILL]

red′ la′bel, the phrase warning against fire hazards required by the Interstate Commerce Commission to be shown on the containers and shipping documents of inflammable materials while in transit.

Red•lands (red′ləndz), *n.* a city in SW California, near Los Angeles. 43,619.

red′ lark′spur, a plant, *Delphinium nudicaule,* of the buttercup family, native to the western coast of the U.S., having orange-red or sometimes yellow flowers.

red′ lead′ (led), *n.* an orange to red, heavy, earthy, water-insoluble, poisonous powder, Pb_3O_4, obtained by heating litharge in the presence of air: used chiefly as a paint pigment, in the manufacture of glass and glazes, and in storage batteries. Also called **minium.** Cf. **litharge.** [1400–50; late ME]

red′-lead put′ty (red′led′), a compound for caulking pipe joints, made of red lead, white lead, and boiled linseed oil.

Red•leg (red′leg′), *n. U.S. Hist.* a member of a secret organization, formed in Kansas in 1862, that engaged in guerrilla activities during the Civil War. [so called from the red leggings worn by the members]

red′leg•ged grass′hopper (red′leg′id, -legd′), a migratory grasshopper, *Melanoplus femur-rubrum,* of the southwestern and midwestern U.S., having reddish skin on the underside of the hind legs: an agricultural pest. [1865–70, *Amer.*]

red-let•ter (red′let′ər), *adj.* **1.** marked by red letters, as festival days in the church calendar. **2.** memorable; especially important or happy: *a red-letter day in his life.* [1400–50; late ME]

red′ light′, **1.** a red lamp, used as a traffic signal to mean "stop." **2.** an order or directive to halt an action, project, etc.: *There's a red light on all unnecessary expenses.* **3.** a children's running game in which players must stop when "Red light!" is called. **4.** a signal of danger; warning. [1840–50]

red-light (red′līt′), *v.t.,* **-light•ed, -light•ing.** *Informal.* to stop or deter by means of or as if with a red light. [1895–1900]

CONCISE ETYMOLOGY KEY: <, descended or borrowed from; >, whence; b., blend of, blended; c., cognate with; cf., compare; deriv., derivative; equiv., equivalent; imit., imitative; obl., oblique; r., replacing; s., stem; sp., spelling, spelled; resp., respelling, respelled; trans., translation; ?, origin unknown; *, unattested; ‡, probably earlier than. See the full key inside the front cover.

re•cork′, *v.t.*
re′cor•o•na′tion, *n.*
re′cor•rect′, *v.t.*
re•cost′, *v.t.,* **-cost, -cost•ing.**
re•cos•tume′, *v.t.,* **-tumed, -tum•ing.**
re•coun′sel, *v.t.,* **-seled, -sel•ing** or (*esp. Brit.*) **-selled, -sel•ling.**
re•crate′, *v.t.,* **-crat•ed, -crat•ing.**
re′crim•i•nal•i•za′tion, *n.*
re•crim′i•nal•ize′, *v.t.,* **-ized, -iz•ing.**
re•crit′i•cize′, *v.t.,* **-cized, -ciz•ing.**
re•cross′, *v.*
re•crown′, *v.t.*
re•cul′ti•vate′, *v.t.,* **-vat•ed, -vat•ing.**
re′cul•ti•va′tion, *n.*
re•cut′, *v.,* **-cut, -cut•ting.**
re•dam′age, *v.t.,* **-aged, -ag•ing.**
re•dare′, *v.t.,* **-dared, -dar•ing.**
re•darn′, *v.t.*
re•date′, *v.,* **-dat•ed, -dat•ing.**
re•deal′, *n., v.,* **-dealt, -deal•ing.**
re′de•bate′, *n., v.,* **-bat•ed, -bat•ing.**
re•deb′it, *v.t.*
re′de•cay′, *v.*
re′de•ceive′, *v.t.,* **-ceived, -ceiv•ing.**
re′de•cide′, *v.,* **-cid•ed, -cid•ing.**
re′de•ci′sion, *n.*
re•dec•la•ra′tion, *n.*
re′de•clare′, *v.t.,* **-clared, -clar•ing.**
re′de•cline′, *v.,* **-clined, -clin•ing,** *n.*

red•wing (red′wing′), *n.* **1.** a European thrush, *Turdus iliacus,* having chestnut-red flank and axillary feathers. **2.** See **red-winged blackbird.** [1650–60; RED[1] + WING]

red′-winged black′bird (red′wingd′), a North American blackbird, *Agelaius phoeniceus,* the male of which is black with scarlet patches, usually bordered with buff or yellow, on the bend of the wing. [1770–80]

red′ wolf′, a small, reddish-gray American wolf, *Canis rufus,* similar to the coyote: once abundant in the southeastern U.S., it is now near extinction in the wild. [1940–45]

red•wood[1] (red′wo͝od′), *n.* **1.** a coniferous tree, *Sequoia sempervirens,* of California, noted for its great height, sometimes reaching to more than 350 ft. (107 m): the state tree of California. **2.** its valuable brownish-red timber. **3.** a red-colored wood. **4.** any of various trees yielding a reddish wood. **5.** any tree whose wood produces a red dyestuff. [1610–20; RED[1] + WOOD[1]]

red•wood[2] (red′wo͝od′), *adj. Scot.* **1.** raving mad; insane. **2.** distracted with anger; furious. Also, **red′wud′.** [1550–60; RED[1] + WOOD[2]]

Red′wood Cit′y, a city in W California. 54,965.

Red′wood Na′tional Park′, a national park in N California: redwood forest with some of the world's tallest trees. 172 sq. mi. (445 sq. km).

red′ worm′, *North Central, South Midland, and Southern U.S.* an earthworm. Also, **red′worm′.** [1400–50; late ME]
—**Regional Variation.** See **earthworm.**

ree[1] (rē), *n.* reeve[3].

ree[2] (rē, rā), *v.t.,* **reed, ree•ing.** *Brit. Dial.* to sift (grain, peas, beans, etc.). [1350–1400; ME < ?]

Ree (rē), *n.* Arikara.

re•ech•o (rē ek′ō), *v.,* **-ech•oed, -ech•o•ing,** *n., pl.* **-ech•oes.** —*v.i.* **1.** to echo back, as a sound. **2.** to give back an echo; resound. —*v.t.* **3.** to echo back. **4.** to repeat like an echo. —*n.* **5.** a repeated echo. Also, **re-ech′o.** [1580–90; RE- + ECHO]

reech•y (rē′chē), *adj.,* **reech•i•er, reech•i•est.** *Archaic.* **1.** smoky or sooty. **2.** squalid or filthy. [1425–75; late ME, equiv. to *reech* (dial. var. of REEK) + -Y[1]]

reed (rēd), *n.* **1.** the straight stalk of any of various tall grasses, esp. of the genera *Phragmites* and *Arundo,* growing in marshy places. **2.** any of the plants themselves. **3.** such stalks or plants collectively. **4.** anything made from such a stalk or from something similar, as an arrow. **5.** *Music.* **a.** a pastoral or rustic musical pipe made from a reed or from the hollow stalk of some other plant. **b.** a small, flexible piece of cane or metal that, attached to the mouth of any of various wind instruments, is set into vibration by a stream of air and, in turn, sets into vibration the air column enclosed in the tube of the instrument. **c.** See **reed instrument. 6.** *Textiles.* the series of parallel strips of wires in a loom that force the weft up to the web and separate the threads of the warp. **7.** an ancient unit of length, equal to 6 cubits. Ezek. 40:5. **8. a broken reed,** a person or thing too frail or weak to be relied on for support: *Under stress he showed himself to be a broken reed.* —*v.t.* **9.** to decorate with reed. **10.** to thatch with or as if with reed. **11.** to make vertical grooves on (the edge of a coin, medal, etc.). [bef. 900; ME; OE *hrēod;* c. G, D *riet*] —**reed′like′,** *adj.*

Reed (rēd), *n.* **1. Sir Carol,** 1906–76, British film director. **2. Ishmael (Scott),** born 1938, U.S. novelist and poet. **3. John,** 1887–1920, U.S. journalist and poet. **4. Stanley For•man** (fôr′mən), 1884–1980, U.S. jurist: associate justice of the U.S. Supreme Court 1938–57. **5. Thomas Brackett,** 1839–1902, U.S. politician: Speaker of the House 1889–91, 1895–99. **6. Walter C.,** 1851–1902, U.S. army surgeon who proved that a type of mosquito transmits the yellow fever virus. **7.** a male given name, form of **Read.**

reed•bird (rēd′bûrd′), *n. Southern U.S.* bobolink. [1640–50; REED + BIRD]

reed•buck (rēd′buk′), *n., pl.* **-bucks,** (*esp. collectively*) **-buck.** any of several yellowish African antelopes of the genus *Redunca,* living near lakes and rivers, the male of which has short, forward-curving horns. [1825–35; trans. of Afrik *rietbok*]

reed′ bun′ting, an Old World bunting, *Emberiza schoeniclus,* inhabiting marshy areas. [1775–85]

reed′ canar′y grass′. See under **canary grass.** [1750–60]

reed•ing (rē′ding), *n. Archit.* **1.** a set of moldings, as on a column, resembling small convex fluting. **2.** ornamentation consisting of such moldings. **3.** a number of narrow, vertical grooves on the edge of a coin, medal, etc. [1805–15; REED + -ING[1]]

reed′ in′strument, *Music.* a wind instrument with a single or double reed, as a saxophone or an oboe. Also called **reed.**

Reed•ley (rēd′lē), *n.* a town in central California. 11,071.

reed•ling (rēd′ling), *n. Brit. Dial.* the bearded tit. [1820–30; REED + -LING[1]]

reed′ mace′, cattail. [1540–50]

reed•man (rēd′man′), *n., pl.* **-men.** a musician who plays a reed instrument. [1870–75; REED + MAN[1]]

reed′ or′gan, a musical keyboard instrument, as the harmonium or American organ, having small metal reeds through which air is forced to produce the sound. [1850–55, *Amer.*]

reed′ pipe′, an organ pipe having a reed that is vibrated by air to produce the sound. [1250–1300; ME]

reed′ stop′, a set of reed pipes in a pipe organ. [1720–30]

re•ed•u•cate (rē ej′o͝o kāt′), *v.t.,* **-cat•ed, -cat•ing. 1.** to educate again, as for new purposes. **2.** to educate for resumption of normal activities, as a disabled person. **3.** to rehabilitate or reform through education, training, political indoctrination, etc. Also, **re-ed′u•cate′.** [1800–10; RE- + EDUCATE] —**re•ed′u•ca′tion,** *n.* —**re•ed′u•ca′tive,** *adj.*

reed′ war′bler, a small Old World warbler, *Acrocephalus scirpaceus,* inhabiting marshy places. [1795–1805]

reed•y (rē′dē), *adj.,* **reed•i•er, reed•i•est. 1.** full of reeds: *a reedy marsh.* **2.** consisting or made of a reed or reeds: *a reedy pipe.* **3.** like a reed or reeds: *reedy grass.* **4.** having a sound like that of a reed instrument. [1350–1400; ME; see REED, -Y[1]] —**reed′i•ness,** *n.*

reef[1] (rēf), *n.* **1.** a ridge of rocks or sand, often of coral debris, at or near the surface of the water. **2.** *Mining.* a lode or vein. [1575–85; earlier *riff(e)* < D *rif*]

reef[2] (rēf), *Naut.* —*n.* **1.** a part of a sail that is rolled and tied down to reduce the area exposed to the wind. —*v.t.* **2.** to shorten (sail) by tying in one or more reefs. **3.** to reduce the length of (a topmast, a bowsprit, etc.), as by lowering, sliding inboard, or the like. **4.** to pull (old oakum) out of seams, as with a rave hook (often fol. by *out*). [1350–1400; ME *refe* (n.) < D *reef*]

reef•er[1] (rē′fər), *n.* **1.** *Naut.* a person who reefs. **2.** a short, close-fitting coat or jacket of thick cloth, similar to a pea jacket. **3.** a woman's tailored, fitted, single- or double-breasted coat of durable material with a collar. [1820–30; REEF[2] + -ER[1]]

reef•er[2] (rē′fər), *n. Slang.* a marijuana cigarette. [1930–35; prob. < MexSp *grifa;* see GRIEFO]

ree•fer[3] (rē′fər), *n. Informal.* **1.** a refrigerator, esp. one large enough to be walked into. **2.** a refrigerator car, ship, truck, etc. [1910–15; alter. and shortening of REFRIGERATOR]

reef•fish (rēf′fish′), *n., pl.* (*esp. collectively*) **-fish,** (*esp. referring to two or more kinds or species*) **-fish•es.** any of several damselfishes, as *Chromis insolatus,* that live among reefs. [REEF[1] + FISH]

reef′ knot′, *Naut.* a square knot used in reefing sails. Also called **flat knot.** [1835–45]

reef′ white′tip shark′. See **whitetip shark** (def. 1).

reek (rēk), *n.* **1.** a strong, unpleasant smell. **2.** vapor or steam. —*v.i.* **3.** to smell strongly and unpleasantly. **4.** to be strongly pervaded with something unpleasant or offensive. **5.** to give off steam, smoke, etc. **6.** to be wet with sweat, blood, etc. —*v.t.* **7.** to give off; emit; exude. **8.** to expose to or treat with smoke. [bef. 900; (n.) ME *rek(e),* OE *rēc* smoke; c. G *rauch,* D *rook,* ON *reykr;* (v.) ME *reken* to smoke, steam, OE *rēocan*] —**reek′er,** *n.* —**reek′ing•ly,** *adv.* —**reek′y,** *adj.*
—**Syn. 5.** steam, smoke, fume.

reel[1] (rēl), *n.* **1.** a cylinder, frame, or other device that turns on an axis and is used to wind up or pay out something. **2.** a rotatory device attached to a fishing rod at the butt, for winding up or letting out the line. **3.** *Photog.* **a.** a spool on which film, esp. motion-picture film, is wound. **b.** a roll of motion-picture film. **c.** a holder for roll film in a developing tank. **4.** a quantity of something wound on a reel. **5.** *Chiefly Brit.* a spool of sewing thread; a roller or bobbin of sewing thread. **6. off the reel, a.** without pause; continuously. **b.** without delay or hesitation; immediately. Also, **right off the reel.** —*v.t.* **7.** to wind on a reel, as thread, yarn, etc. **8.** to unwind (silk filaments) from a cocoon. **9.** to pull or draw by winding a line on a reel: *to reel a fish in.* **10. reel off,** to say, write, or produce quickly and easily: *The old sailor reeled off one story after another.* [bef. 1050; (n.) ME *rele,* OE *hrēol;* c. ON *hræll* weaver's rod; (v.) ME *relen,* deriv. of *rele*] —**reel′a•ble,** *adj.*

reel[2] (rēl), *v.i.* **1.** to sway or rock under a blow, shock, etc.: *The boxer reeled and fell.* **2.** to waver or fall back: *The troops reeled and then ran.* **3.** to sway about in standing or walking, as from dizziness, intoxication, etc.; stagger. **4.** to turn round and round; whirl. **5.** to have a sensation of whirling: *His brain reeled.* —*v.t.* **6.** to cause to reel. —*n.* **7.** an act of reeling; a reeling or staggering movement. [1300–50; ME *relen,* appar. deriv. of *rele* REEL[1]]
—**Syn. 3.** See **stagger.**

reel[3] (rēl), *n.* **1.** a lively Scottish dance. **2.** See **Virginia reel. 3.** music for either of these dances. [1575–85; special use of REEL[2]]

reel′ and bead′. See **bead and reel.**

reeled′ silk′, a long strand made of silk reeled from a number of cocoons and not twisted or thrown. Cf. **spun silk** (def. 1). [1825–35]

reel•er (rē′lər), *n.* **1.** a person or thing that reels. **2.** a machine for burnishing the exterior and interior of seamless tubing. [1590–1600; REEL[1] + -ER[1]]

reel-to-reel (rēl′tə rēl′), *adj.* of or pertaining to an audio sound-equipment system or motion-picture camera or projector through which the tape or film must be threaded onto a take-up reel. [1960–65]

reel′-to-reel tape′. See **open-reel tape.** [1975–80]

re•en•force (rē′ən fôrs′, -fōrs′), *v.t.,* **-forced, -forc•ing,** *n.* reinforce. Also, **re′-en•force′.**

re•en•gine (rē en′jən), *v.t.,* **-gined, -gin•ing.** to equip with a new engine or engines, as an aircraft. Also, **re-en′gine.** [1885–90; RE- + ENGINE]

re•en•gi•neer (rē′en jə nēr′), *v.t.* to engineer anew: *to reengineer a motor to make it more efficient.* Also, **re′-en•gi•neer′.** [1940–45; RE- + ENGINEER]

re•en•list (rē′ən list′), *v.i., v.t.* to enlist again. Also, **re′-en•list′.** [1820–30; RE- + ENLIST]

re•en•list•ment (rē′ən list′mənt), *n.* **1.** an act of reenlisting. **2.** a person who reenlists: *We've gained 3000 reenlistments this month.* **3.** the period of service following a reenlistment: *His reenlistment is three years.* Also, **re′-en•list′ment.** [1840–50; RE- + ENLISTMENT]

re•en•ter (rē en′tər), *v.t.* **1.** to enter again: *The guests reentered the reception room after dinner.* **2.** to participate in once more; resume: *to reenter politics after a long absence; mothers reentering the work force after their children are grown.* **3.** to record again, as in a list or account. —*v.i.* **4.** to enter again: *The butler exits and reenters at stage left.* Also, **re-en′ter.** [1400–50; late ME; see RE-, ENTER]

reen′tering an′gle, *Geom.* an interior angle of a polygon that is greater than 180°. Also called **reen′trant an′gle.** See diag. under **salient.** [1690–1700]

reen′tering pol′ygon, a polygon having one or more reentering angles.

re•en•trant (rē en′trənt), *adj.* **1.** reentering or pointing inward: *a reentrant angle.* —*n.* **2.** a reentering angle or part. **3.** a person or thing that reenters or returns: *Reentrants to the engineering program must take the introductory course again.* **4.** *Physical Geog.* a prominent indentation in a coastline. Cf. **salient** (def. 6). Also, **re-en′trant.** [1775–85; RE- + ENTRANT]

re•en•try (rē en′trē), *n., pl.* **-tries. 1.** an act of reentering. **2.** the return from outer space into the earth's atmosphere of an earth-orbiting satellite, spacecraft, rocket, or the like. **3.** *Law.* the retaking of possession under a right reserved in a prior conveyance. **4.** Also called **reen′try card′.** *Bridge, Whist.* a card that will win a trick enabling one to regain the lead previously lost, esp. the lead from a particular hand. Also, **re-en′•try, re•en•trance, re-en•trance** (rē en′trəns). [1425–75; late ME; see RE-, ENTRY]

reen′try ve′hicle, the section of a spacecraft or ballistic missile designed to return to earth.

reest[1] (rēst), *v.t. Scot. and North Eng.* to cure, smoke, or dry (meat or fish). [1500–10; perh. < Scand; cf. Dan, Norw *riste* to roast]

reest[2] (rēst), *v.i. Scot. and North Eng.* (of a horse) to stop or refuse to go; balk. Also, **reist.** [1780–90; dial. var. of REST[1]]

reeve[1] (rēv), *n.* **1.** an administrative officer of a town or district. **2.** *Brit.* an overseer or superintendent of workers, tenants, or an estate. **3.** *Brit.* (formerly) a person of high rank representing the crown. **4.** *Canadian.* the presiding officer of a village or town council. [bef. 900; ME *(i)reve,* OE *gerēfa* high official, lit., head of a *rōf* array, number (of soldiers); cf. SHERIFF]

reeve[2] (rēv), *v.t.,* **rove** or **reeved, reev•ing.** *Naut.* **1.** to pass (a rope or the like) through a hole, ring, or the like. **2.** to fasten by placing through or around something. **3.** to pass a rope through (the swallow of a block). [1620–30; < D *reven* to reef; see REEF[2]]

reeve[3] (rēv), *n.* the female of the ruff, *Philomachus pugnax.* Also called **ree.** [1625–35; orig. uncert.]

re•ex•am (rē′ig zam′), *n. Informal.* reexamination. Also, **re′-ex•am′.** [by shortening]

re•ex•am•ine (rē′ig zam′in), *v.t.,* **-ined, -in•ing. 1.** to examine again. **2.** *Law.* to examine (a witness) again after having questioned him or her previously. Also, **re′-ex•am′ine.** [1585–95; RE- + EXAMINE] —**re′ex•am′in•a•ble,** *adj.* —**re′ex•am′i•na′tion,** *n.* —**re′ex•am′in•er,** *n.*

re•ex•port (*v.* rē′ik spôrt′, -spōrt′, rē ek′spôrt, -spōrt; *n.* rē ek′spôrt, -spōrt), *v.t.* **1.** to export again, as imported goods. —*n.* **2.** the act of reexporting. **3.** a commodity that is reexported. Also, **re′-ex•port′.** [1680–90; RE- + EXPORT] —**re′ex•por•ta′tion,** *n.* —**re′ex•port′•er,** *n.*

ref (ref), *n., v.t., v.i.,* **reffed, ref•fing.** *Sports Slang.* referee. [1895–1900; by shortening]

ref., 1. referee. **2.** reference. **3.** referred. **4.** refining. **5.** reformation. **6.** reformed. **7.** refund. **8.** refunding.

re•face (rē fās′), *v.t.,* **-faced, -fac•ing. 1.** to renew, restore, or repair the face or surface of (buildings, stone, etc.). **2.** to provide with a new facing, as a garment. [1850–55; RE- + FACE]

Ref. Ch., Reformed Church.

re•fect (ri fekt′), *v.t. Archaic.* to refresh, esp. with food or drink. [1425–75; late ME; < L *refectus,* ptp. of *reficere* to make again, renew, equiv. to *re-* RE- + *-fec-,* comb. form of *facere* to make, DO[1] + *-tus* ptp. suffix]

re•fec•tion (ri fek′shən), *n.* **1.** refreshment, esp. with food or drink. **2.** a portion of food or drink; repast.

CONCISE PRONUNCIATION KEY: *act, cāpe, dâre, pärt; set, ēqual; if, īce; ox, ōver, ôrder, oil, bo͝ok, bo͞ot, out; up, ûrge; child; sing; shoe; thin, that;* zh as in *treasure.* ə = *a* as in *alone, e* as in *system, i* as in *easily, o* as in *gallop, u* as in *circus;* ə as in *fire* (fīər), *hour* (ouər). l and n can serve as syllabic consonants, as in *cradle* (krād′l), and *button* (but′n). See the full key inside the front cover.

re′dis•pose′, *v.t.,* **-posed, -pos•ing.**
re′dis•po•si′tion, *n.*
re′dis•pute′, *v.,* **-put•ed, -put•ing.**
re′dis•sect′, *v.t.*
re′dis•sec′tion, *n.*
re′dis•sol′u•ble, *adj.;* **-ble•ness,** *n.;* **-bly,** *adv.*
re′dis•so•lu′tion, *n.*
re′dis•solve′, *v.,* **-solved, -solv•ing.**
re′dis•till′, *v.t.*
re′dis•till′a•ble, *adj.;* **-ness,** *n.*
re′dis•til•la′tion, *n.*
re′dis•tin′guish, *v.*
re′di•vert′, *v.t.*
re′di•vide′, *v.,* **-vid•ed, -vid•ing.**
re′di•vi′sion, *n.*
re′di•vorce′, *n., v.,* **-vorced, -vorc•ing.**
re•dock′, *v.*
re•dock′et, *v.t.,* **-et•ed, -et•ing.**
re•doc′u•ment′, *v.t.*
re•dom′i•nate′, *v.,* **-nat•ed, -nat•ing.**
re•don′, *v.t.,* **-donned, -don•ning.**
re•draft′, *v.t.*
re•draw′, *v.* **-drew, -drawn, -draw•ing,** *n.*
re•draw′er, *n.*
re•dream′, *v.,* **-dreamed** or **-dreamt, -dream•ing.**
re•drill′, *v.*
re•drive′, *v.,* **-drove, -driv•en, -driv•ing.**
re•droop′, *v.i.*
re•drug′, *v.t.,* **-drugged, -drug•ging.**

[1300–50; ME *refeccioun* < L *refectiōn-* (s. of *refectiō*) restoration, equiv. to *refect(us)* (see REFECT) + *-iōn-* -ION] —**re·fec′tive,** *adj.* —**re·fec·to·ri·al** (rē′fek tôr′ē əl, -tōr′-), *adj.*

re·fec·to·ry (ri fek′tə rē), *n., pl.* **-ries.** a dining hall in a religious house, a college, or other institution. [1475–85; < LL *refectōrium,* equiv. to L *refec-,* comb. form of *reficere* to renew (see REFECT) + *-tōrium* -TORY[2]]

refec′tory ta′ble, **1.** a long, narrow table having a single stretcher between trestlelike supports. **2.** a narrow dining table having extensible ends. [1920–25]

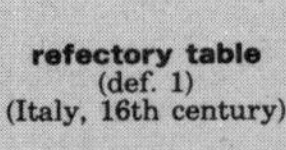
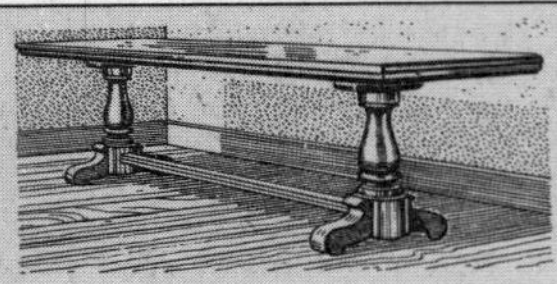

refectory table (def. 1) (Italy, 16th century)

re·fel (ri fel′), *v.t.,* **-felled, -fel·ling.** *Obs.* to refute or disprove. [1520–30; < L *refellere,* equiv. to *re-* RE- + *-fellere* (comb. form of *fallere* to deceive)]

re·fer (ri fûr′), *v.,* **-ferred, -fer·ring.** —*v.t.* **1.** to direct for information or anything required: *He referred me to books on astrology.* **2.** to direct the attention or thoughts of: *The asterisk refers the reader to a footnote.* **3.** to hand over or submit for information, consideration, decision, etc.: *to refer the argument to arbitration.* **4.** to assign to a class, period, etc.; regard as belonging or related. **5.** to have relation; relate; apply. —*v.i.* **6.** to direct attention, as a reference mark does. **7.** to have recourse or resort; turn, as for aid or information: *to refer to one's notes.* **8.** to make reference or allusion: *The author referred to his teachers twice in his article.* [1325–75; ME *referren* < L *referre* to bring back, equiv. to *re-* RE- + *ferre* to bring, BEAR[1]] —**ref·er·a·ble, re·fer·ra·ble, re·fer·ri·ble** (ref′ər ə bəl, ri fûr′-), *adj.* —**re·fer′rer,** *n.*
—**Syn. 4.** attribute, ascribe, impute. **5.** pertain, belong. **8.** advert, allude.

ref·er·ee (ref′ə rē′), *n., v.,* **-eed, -ee·ing.** —*n.* **1.** one to whom something is referred, esp. for decision or settlement; arbitrator. **2.** (in certain games and sports) a judge having functions fixed by the rules of the game or sport; umpire. **3.** an authority who evaluates scientific, technical, or scholarly papers, grant proposals, or the like for the publication or funding institution to which they have been submitted. **4.** *Law.* a person selected by a court to take testimony in a case and return it to the court with recommendations as to the decision. —*v.t.* **5.** to preside over as referee; act as referee in. —*v.i.* **6.** to act as referee. [1605–15; REFER + -EE]
—**Syn. 1.** arbiter. See **judge.**

ref·er·ence (ref′ər əns, ref′rəns), *n., v.,* **-enced, -enc·ing.** —*n.* **1.** an act or instance of referring. **2.** a mention; allusion. **3.** something for which a name or designation stands; denotation. **4.** a direction in a book or writing to some other book, passage, etc. **5.** a book, passage, etc., to which one is directed. **6.** See **reference mark** (def. 2). **7.** material contained in a footnote or bibliography, or referred to by a reference mark. **8.** use or recourse for purposes of information: *a library for public reference.* **9.** a person to whom one refers for testimony as to one's character, abilities, etc. **10.** a statement, usually written, as to a person's character, abilities, etc. **11.** relation, regard, or respect: *all persons, without reference to age.* —*v.t.* **12.** to furnish (a book, dissertation, etc.) with references: *Each new volume is thoroughly referenced.* **13.** to arrange (notes, data, etc.) for easy reference: *Statistical data is referenced in the glossary.* **14.** to refer to: *to reference a file.* [1580–90; REFER + -ENCE]
—**Syn. 4.** note, citation. **10.** endorsement. **11.** consideration, concern.

ref′erence book′, **1.** a book containing useful facts or specially organized information, as an encyclopedia, dictionary, atlas, yearbook, etc. **2.** Also called **pass, passbook.** *South African.* a domestic identity document carried by black citizens. [1885–90]

ref′erence elec′trode, *Physical Chem.* an electrode of known oxidation potential used in determining the electromotive force of a galvanic cell. [1925–30]

ref′erence frame′, *Physics.* See **frame of reference** (def. 2). [1920–25]

ref′erence group′, *Sociol.* a group with which an individual identifies and whose values the individual accepts as guiding principles. [1940–45]

ref′erence mark′, **1.** *Survey.* a permanent mark set at a specific distance in a specific direction from a survey station so as to permit accurate reestablishment of the station. **2.** any of various written or printed symbols, as an asterisk (*), dagger (†), or superscript number, used to indicate the presence of further information in a footnote, bibliography, or other text. [1855–60]

ref·er·en·dum (ref′ə ren′dəm), *n., pl.* **-dums, -da** (-də). **1.** the principle or practice of referring measures proposed or passed by a legislative body to the vote of the electorate for approval or rejection. Cf. **initiative** (def. 4a). **2.** a vote on a measure thus referred. [1840–50; < L: thing to be referred (neut. ger. of *referre* to bring back; see REFER)]

ref·er·ent (ref′ər ənt), *n.* **1.** the object or event to which a term or symbol refers. **2.** *Logic.* the first term in a proposition to which succeeding terms relate. [1835–45; < L *referent-* (s. of *referēns*), prp. of *referre.* See REFER, -ENT]

ref·er·en·tial (ref′ə ren′shəl), *adj.* **1.** having reference: *referential to something.* **2.** containing a reference. **3.** used for reference. [1650–60; REFERENT + -IAL] —**ref′er·en′tial·ly,** *adv.*

re·fer·ral (ri fûr′əl), *n.* **1.** an act of referring; the state of being referred. **2.** an instance of referring. **3.** a person recommended to someone or for something. [1930–35; REFER + -AL[2]]

referred′ pain′, *Pathol.* pain felt in an area remote from the site of origin. Also called **synalgia.** [1895–1900]

ref·fo (ref′ō), *n., pl.* **-fos.** *Australian Informal.* an immigrant, esp. one who has been in Australia only a short time. [1940–45; REF(UGEE) + -O]

re·fill (*v.* rē fil′; *n.* rē′fil′), *v.t., v.i.* **1.** to fill again. —*n.* **2.** a material, supply, or the like, to replace something that has been used up: *a refill for a prescription.* [1680–90; RE- + FILL] —**re·fill′a·ble,** *adj., n.*

re·fi·nance (rē′fi nans′, rē fī′nans), *v.t.,* **-nanced, -nanc·ing.** **1.** to finance again. **2.** to satisfy (a debt) by making another loan on new terms: *to refinance a mortgage.* **3.** to change the financing of, as by selling stock or obtaining additional credit. [1905–10; RE- + FINANCE]

re·fine (ri fīn′), *v.,* **-fined, -fin·ing.** —*v.t.* **1.** to bring to a fine or a pure state; free from impurities: *to refine metal, sugar, or petroleum.* **2.** to purify from what is coarse, vulgar, or debasing; make elegant or cultured. **3.** to bring to a finer state or form by purifying. **4.** to make more fine, subtle, or precise: *to refine one's writing style.* —*v.i.* **5.** to become pure. **6.** to become more fine, elegant, or polished. **7.** to make fine distinctions in thought or language. **8. refine on** or **upon,** to improve by inserting finer distinctions, superior elements, etc.: *to refine on one's previous work.* [1575–85; RE- + FINE[1]] —**re·fin′a·ble,** *adj.* —**re·fin′er,** *n.*

re·fined (ri fīnd′), *adj.* **1.** having or showing well-bred feeling, taste, etc.: *refined people.* **2.** freed or free from coarseness, vulgarity, etc.: *refined taste.* **3.** freed from impurities: *refined sugar.* **4.** very subtle, precise, or exact: *refined distinctions.* [1565–75; REFINE + -ED[2]] —**re·fin·ed·ly** (ri fī′nid lē, -fīnd′-), *adv.* —**re·fin′ed·ness,** *n.*
—**Syn. 1.** cultivated, polished, polite, courteous, civilized, courtly, genteel, elegant. **3.** clarified, distilled, purified. —**Ant. 1.** rude, coarse, crude.

re·fine·ment (ri fīn′mənt), *n.* **1.** fineness or elegance of feeling, taste, manners, language, etc. **2.** an instance of refined feeling, manners, etc. **3.** the act or process of refining. **4.** the quality or state of being refined. **5.** a subtle point or distinction. **6.** subtle reasoning. **7.** an improved, higher, or extreme form of something: *a refinement of the old system.* **8.** *Math.* a set whose elements include the elements of a given set. [1605–15; REFINE + -MENT]

re·fin·er·y (ri fī′nə rē), *n., pl.* **-er·ies.** an establishment for refining something, as metal, sugar, or petroleum. [1720–30; REFINE + -ERY]

re·fin·ish (rē fin′ish), *v.t.* to give a new surface to (wood, furniture, etc.). [1930–35; RE- + FINISH] —**re·fin′ish·er,** *n.*

re·fit (rē fit′), *v.,* **-fit·ted, -fit·ting,** *n.* —*v.t.* **1.** to fit, prepare, or equip again. —*v.i.* **2.** to renew supplies or equipment. **3.** to get refitted. —*n.* **4.** an act of refitting. [1660–70; RE- + FIT[1]]

refl., **1.** reflection. **2.** reflective. **3.** reflex. **4.** reflexive.

re·flag (rē flag′), *v.t.,* **-flagged, -flag·ging.** to register (a foreign ship) so that it flies the flag of the registering nation and thereby comes under the latter's protection. [1985–90]

re·flate (ri flāt′), *v.,* **-flat·ed, -flat·ing.** —*v.i.* **1.** to increase again the amount of money and credit in circulation. —*v.t.* **2.** to increase (money and credit) again. [1930–35; back formation from REFLATION]

re·fla·tion (ri flā′shən), *n.* restoration of economic activity, consumer prices, etc., to higher levels by manipulating monetary policy. [1930–35; RE- + (IN)FLATION] —**re·fla·tion·ar·y** (ri flā′shə ner′ē), *adj.*

re·flect (ri flekt′), *v.t.* **1.** to cast back (light, heat, sound, etc.) from a surface: *The mirror reflected the light onto the wall.* **2.** to give back or show an image of; mirror. **3.** (of an act or its result) to serve to cast or bring (credit, discredit, etc.) on its performer. **4.** to reproduce; show: *followers reflecting the views of the leader.* **5.** to throw or cast back; cause to return or rebound: *Her bitterness reflects gloom on all her family.* —*v.i.* **6.** to be turned or cast back, as light. **7.** to cast back light, heat, etc. **8.** to be reflected or mirrored. **9.** to give back or show an image. **10.** to think, ponder, or meditate: *to reflect on one's faults.* **11.** to serve or tend to bring reproach or discredit by association: *His crimes reflected on the community.* **12.** to serve to give a particular aspect or impression: *The test reflects well on your abilities.* [1350–1400; ME *reflecten* < L *reflectere* to bend back, equiv. to *re-* RE- + *flectere* to bend] —**re·flect′ed·ly,** *adv.* —**re·flect′ed·ness,** *n.* —**re·flect′i·bil′i·ty,** *n.* —**re·flect′i·ble,** *adj.* —**re·flect′ing·ly,** *adv.*
—**Syn. 4.** manifest. **6.** rebound. **10.** ruminate, deliberate, muse, consider, cogitate, contemplate. See **study[1].**

re·flect·ance (ri flek′təns), *n. Physics, Optics.* the ratio of the intensity of reflected radiation to that of the radiation incident on a surface. Cf. **albedo.** [1925–30; REFLECT + -ANCE]

reflect′ed plan′, a plan, as of a room, taken as seen from above but having the outlines of some upper surface, as a vault or compartmented ceiling, projected downward upon it so that a part that would appear at the right when seen from below appears on the plan at the left.

reflect′ing tel′escope. See under **telescope** (def. 1). Also called **reflector.** [1695–1705]

re·flec·tion (ri flek′shən), *n.* **1.** the act of reflecting or the state of being reflected. **2.** an image; representation; counterpart. **3.** a fixing of the thoughts on something; careful consideration. **4.** a thought occurring in consideration or meditation. **5.** an unfavorable remark or observation. **6.** the casting of some imputation or reproach. **7.** *Physics, Optics.* **a.** the return of light, heat, sound, etc., after striking a surface. **b.** something so reflected, as heat or esp. light. **8.** *Math.* **a.** (in a plane) the replacement of each point on one side of a line by the point symmetrically placed on the other side of the line. **b.** (in space) the replacement of each point on one side of a plane by the symmetric point on the other side of the plane. **9.** *Anat.* the bending or folding back of a part upon itself. Also, *esp. Brit.,* **reflexion.** [1350–1400; ME < LL *reflexiōn-* (s. of *reflexiō*) a bending back, equiv. to L *reflex(us)* (see REFLEX) + *-iōn-* -ION] —**re·flec′tion·al,** *adj.* —**re·flec′tion·less,** *adj.*
—**Syn. 3.** meditation, rumination, deliberation, cogitation, study, thinking. **5.** imputation, aspersion, reproach, criticism.

reflec′tion neb′ula, *Astron.* a cloud of interstellar gas and dust that reflects the light of neighboring stars. [1935–40]

reflec′tion plane′, *Crystall.* a plane through a crystal that divides the crystal into two halves that are mirror images of each other. Also called **symmetry plane.** Cf. **symmetry element.** [1970–75]

re·flec·tive (ri flek′tiv), *adj.* **1.** that reflects; reflecting. **2.** of or pertaining to reflection. **3.** cast by reflection. **4.** given to, marked by, or concerned with meditation or deliberation: *a reflective person.* [1620–30; REFLECT + -IVE] —**re·flec′tive·ly,** *adv.* —**re·flec′tive·ness, re·flec·tiv·i·ty** (rē′flek tiv′i tē), *n.*
—**Syn. 4.** contemplative, thoughtful. See **pensive.**

re·flec·tom·e·ter (rē′flek tom′i tər, ri-), *n. Optics.* a device for measuring reflectance. [1890–95; REFLECT + -O- + -METER]

re·flec·tor (ri flek′tər), *n.* **1.** a person or thing that reflects. **2.** a body, surface, or device that reflects light, heat, sound, or the like. **3.** See **reflecting telescope. 4.** a substance, as graphite or heavy water, used to prevent the escape of neutrons from the core of a nuclear reactor. [1655–65; REFLECT + -OR[2]]

re·flec·tor·ize (ri flek′tə rīz′), *v.t.,* **-ized, -iz·ing.** to treat something so that it reflects light: *to reflectorize license plates.* Also, *esp. Brit.,* **re·flec′tor·ise′.** [1940–45, *Amer.;* REFLECTOR + -IZE] —**re·flec′tor·i·za′tion,** *n.*

re·flet (rə flā′), *n.* an effect of brilliance or luster due to the reflection of light on a surface, esp. of pottery; iridescence. [1860–65; < F, earlier *reflès* < It *riflesso* reflection; see REFLEX]

re·flex (*adj., n.* rē′fleks; *v.* ri fleks′), *adj.* **1.** *Physiol.* noting or pertaining to an involuntary response to a stimulus, the nerve impulse from a receptor being transmitted inward to a nerve center that in turn transmits it outward to an effector. **2.** occurring in reaction; responsive. **3.** cast back; reflected, as light, color, etc. **4.** bent or turned back. **5.** designating a radio apparatus in which the same circuit or part performs two functions. —*n.* **6.** *Physiol.* **a.** Also called **re′flex act′.** movement caused by a reflex response. **b.** Also called **re′flex ac′tion.** the entire physiological process activating such movement. **7.** any automatic, unthinking, often habitual behavior or response. **8.** the reflection or image of an object, as exhibited by a mirror or the like. **9.** a reproduction, as if in a mirror. **10.** a copy; adaptation. **11.** reflected light, color, etc. **12.** *Historical Ling.* an element in a language, as a sound, that has developed from a corresponding element in an earlier form of the language: *The (ō) in "stone" is a reflex of Old English ā.* **13.** a reflex radio receiver. **14.** a reflex camera. —*v.t.* **15.** to subject to a reflex process. **16.** to bend, turn, or fold back. **17.** to arrange in a reflex system. [1500–10; < L *reflexus* bent back, ptp. of *reflectere* to REFLECT] —**re′flex·ly,** *adv.* —**re′flex·ness,** *n.*

re′flex an′gle, *Geom.* an angle greater than 180° and less than 360°. [1895–1900]

re′flex arc′, *Physiol.* the nerve pathways followed by an impulse during a reflex. [1880–85]

re′flex cam′era, a camera in which the image appears on a ground-glass viewer **(focusing screen)** after being reflected by a mirror or after passing through a prism or semitransparent glass; in one type **(single-lens reflex camera),** light passes through the same lens to both the ground glass and the film, while in another type **(twin-lens reflex camera),** light passes through one lens **(viewing lens)** to the ground glass and through a second lens **(taking lens)** to the film, the lenses being mechanically coupled for focusing. See illus. on next page. [1925–30]

CONCISE ETYMOLOGY KEY: <, descended or borrowed from; >, whence; b., blend of, blended; c., cognate with; cf., compare; deriv., derivative; equiv., equivalent; imit., imitative; obl., oblique; r., replacing; s., stem; sp., spelling, spelled; resp., respelling, respelled; trans., translation; ?, origin unknown; *, unattested; ‡, probably earlier than. See the full key inside the front cover.

re·dry′, *v.,* **-dried, -dry·ing.**
re·dub′, *v.t.,* **-dubbed, -dub·bing.**
re·dust′, *v.t.*
re·dye′, *v.t.,* **-dyed, -dy·ing.**
re·earn′, *v.t.*
re·ed′i·fy′, *v.t.,* **-fied, -fy·ing.**
re·ed′it, *v.t.*
re′e·ject′, *v.t.*
re′e·lect′, *v.t.*
re′e·lec′ta·bil′i·ty, *n.*
re′e·lec′ta·ble, *adj.*
re′e·lec′tion, *n., adj.*
re′e·lec′tri·fi·ca′tion, *n.*
re′e·lec′tri·fy′, *v.t.,* **-fied, -fy·ing.**
re·el′e·vate′, *v.t.,* **-vat·ed, -vat·ing.**
re′el·e·va′tion, *n.*
re′el·i·gi·bil′i·ty, *n.*
re·el′i·gi·ble, *adj.;* **-bly,** *adv.*
re·em′a·nate′, *v.i.,* **-nat·ed, -nat·ing.**
re′em·bar·ca′tion, *n.*
re′em·bark′, *v.*
re′em·bar·ka′tion, *n.*
re′em·bel′lish, *v.t.*
re′em·bod′y, *v.t.,* **-bod·ied, -bod·y·ing.**
re′em·brace′, *v.t.,* **-braced, -brac·ing.**
re′e·merge′, *v.i.,* **-merged, -merg·ing.**
re′e·mer′gence, *n.*
re′e·mer′gent, *adj.*
re′e·mer′sion, *n.*
re·em′i·grate′, *v.i.,* **-grat·ed, -grat·ing.**
re′em·i·gra′tion, *n.*

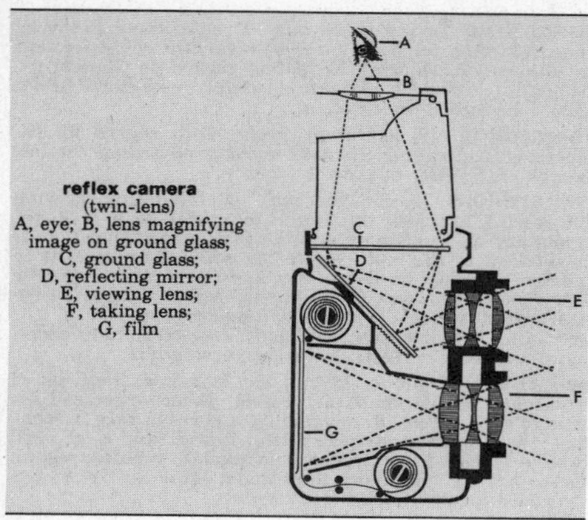

reflex camera
(twin-lens)
A, eye; B, lens magnifying image on ground glass; C, ground glass; D, reflecting mirror; E, viewing lens; F, taking lens; G, film

re•flexed (ri flekst′, rē′flekst), *adj.* bent backward or downward, as a leaf. [1350–1400; ME: reflected; see RE-FLEX, -ED²]

re•flex•ion (ri flek′shən), *n. Chiefly Brit.* reflection.

re•flex•ive (ri flek′siv), *adj.* **1.** *Gram.* **a.** (of a verb) taking a subject and object with identical referents, as *shave* in *I shave myself.* **b.** (of a pronoun) used as an object to refer to the subject of a verb, as *myself* in *I shave myself.* **2.** reflex; responsive. **3.** able to reflect; reflective. **4.** *Math.* **a.** noting a relation in which each element is in relation to itself, as the relation "less than or equal to." Cf. **antireflexive. b.** (of a vector space) having the property that the dual space of the dual space of the given vector space equals the given vector space. —*n.* **5.** *Gram.* a reflexive verb or pronoun. [1580–90; < ML *reflexīvus* turned back, reflected. See REFLEX, -IVE] **—re•flex′ive•ly,** *adv.* **—re•flex′ive•ness, re•flex•iv•i•ty** (rē′flek siv′i tē), *n.*

re•flex•i•vize (ri flek′sə vīz′), *v.t.* to make (a verb or pronoun) reflexive. Also, *esp. Brit.,* **re•flex′i•vise′.** [1960–65; REFLEXIVE + -IZE] **—re•flex′i•vi•za′tion,** *n.*

re•flex•ol•o•gy (rē′flek sol′ə jē), *n.* **1.** a system of massaging specific areas of the foot or sometimes the hand in order to promote healing, relieve stress, etc., in other parts of the body. **2.** *Med.* the study of reflex movements and processes. [1920–25; REFLEX + -O- + -LOGY] **—re′flex•ol′o•gist,** *n.*

ref•lu•ent (ref′lo͞o ənt, rə flo͞o′-), *adj.* flowing back; ebbing, as the waters of a tide. [1690–1700; < L *refluent-* (s. of *refluēns*), prp. of *refluere* to flow back. See RE-, FLUENT] **—ref′lu•ence,** *n.*

re•flux (rē′fluks′), *n.* a flowing back; ebb. [1400–50; late ME < ML *refluxus.* See RE-, FLUX]

re•for•est (rē fôr′ist, -for′-), *v.t.* to replant trees on (land denuded by cutting or fire). [1880–85; RE- + FOREST] **—re′for•est•a′tion,** *n.*

re•form (rē fôrm′), *v.t., v.i.* to form again. [1300–50; ME; orig. identical with REFORM] **re′-for•ma′tion,** *n.* **—re•form′er,** *n.*

re•form (ri fôrm′), *n.* **1.** the improvement or amendment of what is wrong, corrupt, unsatisfactory, etc.: *social reform; spelling reform.* **2.** an instance of this. **3.** the amendment of conduct, belief, etc. —*v.t.* **4.** to change to a better state, form, etc.; improve by alteration, substitution, abolition, etc. **5.** to cause (a person) to abandon wrong or evil ways of life or conduct. **6.** to put an end to (abuses, disorders, etc.). **7.** *Chem.* to subject to the process of reforming, as in refining petroleum. —*v.i.* **8.** to abandon evil conduct or error: *The drunkard promised to reform.* —*adj.* **9.** (*cap.*) of, pertaining to, or characteristic of Reform Jews or Reform Judaism: *a Reform rabbi.* [1300–50; (v.) ME *reformen* < MF *reformer,* OF < L *refōrmāre* (see RE-, FORM); (n.) partly deriv. of the v., partly < F *réforme*] **—re•form′a•ble,** *adj.* **—re•form′a•bil′i•ty, re•form′a•ble•ness,** *n.* **—re•form′a•tive,** *adj.* **—re•form′a•tive•ly,** *adv.* **—re•form′a•tive•ness,** *n.* **—re•form′ing•ly,** *adv.*
—Syn. 1. correction, reformation, betterment, amelioration. **4.** better, rectify, correct, amend, emend, ameliorate, repair, restore. **—Ant. 1.** deterioration.

re•for•mate (ri fôr′māt, -mit), *n. Chem.* the product of the reforming process. [1945–50; REFORM + -ATE¹]

ref•or•ma•tion (ref′ər mā′shən), *n.* **1.** the act of reforming; state of being reformed. **2.** (*cap.*) the religious movement in the 16th century that had for its object the reform of the Roman Catholic Church, and that led to the establishment of the Protestant churches. [1375–1425; late ME *reformacion* < L *refōrmātiōn-* (s. of *refōrmātiō*), equiv. to *refōrmāt(us)* (ptp. of *refōrmāre* to REFORM) + *-iōn-* -ION] **—ref′or•ma′tion•al,** *adj.*
—Syn. 1. improvement, betterment, correction, reform.

re•form•a•to•ry (ri fôr′mə tôr′ē, -tōr′ē), *adj., n., pl.* **-ries.** —*adj.* **1.** serving or designed to reform: *reformatory lectures; reformatory punishments.* —*n.* **2.** Also called **reform school.** a penal institution for reforming young offenders, esp. minors. [1580–90; < L *refōrmāt(us)* (see REFORMATION) + -ORY¹, -ORY²]

Reform′ Bill′, *Eng. Hist.* any of the bills passed by Parliament (1832, 1867, 1884) providing for an increase in the number of voters in elections for the House of Commons, esp. the bill of 1832 by which many rotten boroughs were disfranchised. Also called **Reform′ Act′.**

re•formed (ri fôrmd′), *adj.* **1.** amended by removal of faults, abuses, etc. **2.** improved in conduct, morals, etc. **3.** (*cap.*) noting or pertaining to Protestant churches, esp. Calvinist as distinguished from Lutheran. [1555–65; REFORM + -ED²] **—re•form•ed•ly** (ri fôr′mid lē), *adv.*

Reformed′ Church′ in Amer′ica, a Protestant denomination having a Calvinist theology and originally called the Dutch Reformed Church.

reformed′ spell′ing, a revised orthography intended to simplify the spelling of English words, esp. to eliminate unpronounced letters, as by substituting *thru* for *through, tho* for *though, slo* for *slow,* etc. [1895–1900]

re•form•er (ri fôr′mər), *n.* **1.** a person devoted to bringing about reform, as in politics or society. **2.** (*cap.*) any of the leaders of the Reformation. [1520–30; REFORM + -ER¹]

Reform′ flask′, an English salt-glazed stoneware flask of the early 19th century formed as an effigy of one of the figures connected with the Reform Bill of 1832.

re•form•ing (ri fôr′ming), *n. Chem.* the process of cracking low-octane petroleum fractions in order to increase the octane number. [1920–25; REFORM + -ING¹]

re•form•ist (ri fôr′mist), *n.* **1.** a person who advocates or practices reform; reformer. **2.** a member of any reformed denomination. —*adj.* **3.** Also, **re•form•is′tic.** of or belonging to a movement for reform. [1580–90; REFORM + -IST] **—re•form′ism,** *n.*

Reform′ Jew′, a Jew who adheres to a system of religious worship adapted from Orthodox Judaism to meet the demands of contemporary life, frequently simplifying or rejecting traditional religious law and custom. Cf. **Conservative Jew, Orthodox Jew.** [1865–70]

Reform′ Ju′daism, Judaism as observed by Reform Jews. [1900–05]

reform′ school′, reformatory (def. 2). [1855–60, *Amer.*]

re•for•mu•late (rē fôr′myə lāt′), *v.t.,* **-lat•ed, -lat•ing. 1.** to formulate again. **2.** to formulate in a different way; alter or revise: *to reformulate our plans.* [1880–85; RE- + FORMULATE] **—re′for•mu•la′tion,** *n.*

Ref. Pres., Reformed Presbyterian.

re•fract (ri frakt′), *v.t.* **1.** to subject to refraction. **2.** to determine the refractive condition of (an eye). [1605–15; < L *refrāctus,* ptp. of *refringere* to break, force back, equiv. to *re-* RE- + *frac-* (var. s. of *frangere* to BREAK) + *-tus* ptp. suffix] **—re•fract′a•ble,** *adj.* **—re•fract′ed•ly,** *adv.* **—re•fract′ed•ness,** *n.*

re•frac•tile (ri frak′tl, -tīl), *adj.* refractive (def. 2). [1840–50; REFRACT + -ILE]

refract′ing tel′escope. See under **telescope** (def. 1). Also called **refractor.** [1755–65]

re•frac•tion (ri frak′shən), *n.* **1.** *Physics.* the change of direction of a ray of light, sound, heat, or the like, in passing obliquely from one medium into another in which its wave velocity is different. **2.** *Ophthalm.* **a.** the ability of the eye to refract light that enters it so as to form an image on the retina. **b.** the determining of the refractive condition of the eye. **3.** *Astron.* **a.** Also called **astronomical refraction.** the amount, in angular measure, by which the altitude of a celestial body is increased by the refraction of its light in the earth's atmosphere, being zero at the zenith and a maximum at the horizon. **b.** the observed altered location, as seen from the earth, of another planet or the like due to diffraction by the atmosphere. [1570–80; < LL *refrāctiōn-* (s. of *refrāctiō*). See REFRACT, -ION] **—re•frac′tion•al,** *adj.*

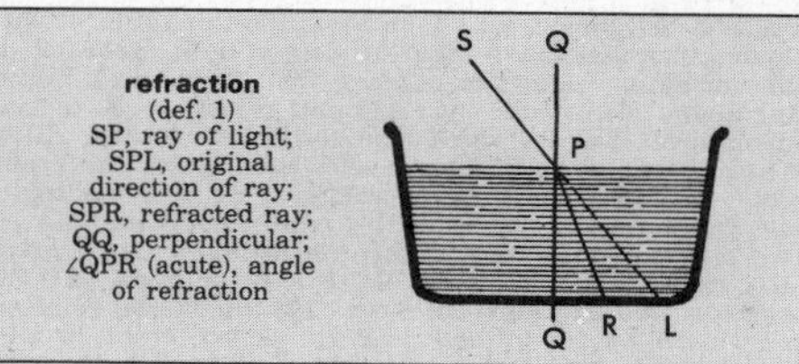

refraction
(def. 1)
SP, ray of light; SPL, original direction of ray; SPR, refracted ray; QQ, perpendicular; ∠QPR (acute), angle of refraction

re•frac•tive (ri frak′tiv), *adj.* **1.** of or pertaining to refraction. **2.** Also, **refractile.** having power to refract. [1665–75; < LL *refrāctīvus* (of pronouns) reflexive. See REFRACT, -IVE] **—re•frac′tive•ly,** *adv.* **—re•frac′tive•ness,** *n.*

refrac′tive in′dex, *Optics.* See **index of refraction.** [1830–40]

re•frac•tiv•i•ty (rē′frak tiv′i tē), *n.* the power to refract. Also called **refringence.** [REFRACTIVE + -ITY]

re•frac•tom•e•ter (rē′frak tom′i tər), *n. Optics.* an instrument for determining the refractive index of a substance. [1875–80; REFRACT + -O- + -METER] **—re•frac•to•met•ric** (ri frak′tə me′trik), *adj.* **—re′frac•tom′e•try,** *n.*

re•frac•tor (ri frak′tər), *n.* **1.** a person or thing that refracts. **2.** See **refracting telescope.** [1630–40; REFRACT + -OR²]

re•frac•to•ry (ri frak′tə rē), *adj., n., pl.* **-ries.** —*adj.* **1.** hard or impossible to manage; stubbornly disobedient: *a refractory child.* **2.** resisting ordinary methods of treatment. **3.** difficult to fuse, reduce, or work, as an ore or metal. —*n.* **4.** a material having the ability to retain its physical shape and chemical identity when subjected to high temperatures. **5. refractories,** bricks of various shapes used in lining furnaces. [1600–10; var. of *refractary* (by analogy with adjectives in -ORY¹) < L *refrāctārius* stubborn, obstinate, equiv. to *refrāct(us)* (see REFRACT) + *-ārius* -ARY] **—re•frac′to•ri•ly,** *adv.* **—re•frac′to•ri•ness,** *n.*
—Syn. 1. obstinate, perverse, mulish, headstrong, intractable, disobedient, recalcitrant, ungovernable. See **unruly. —Ant. 1.** obedient, tractable.

refrac′tory pe′riod, *Physiol.* a short period after a nerve or muscle cell fires during which the cell cannot respond to additional stimulation. [1875–80]

re•frain¹ (ri frān′), *v.i.* **1.** to abstain from an impulse to say or do something (often fol. by *from*): *I refrained from telling him what I thought.* —*v.t.* **2.** *Archaic.* to curb. [1300–50; ME *refreinen* < OF *refrener* < L *refrēnāre* to bridle, equiv. to *re-* RE- + *frēn(um)* bridle + *-āre* inf. suffix] **—re•frain′er,** *n.* **—re•frain′ment,** *n.*
—Syn. 1. forbear, desist.

re•frain² (ri frān′), *n.* **1.** a phrase or verse recurring at intervals in a song or poem, esp. at the end of each stanza; chorus. **2.** *Music.* **a.** a musical setting for the refrain of a poem. **b.** any melody. **c.** the principal, recurrent section of a rondo. [1325–75; ME *refreyne* < OF *refrain,* deriv. of *refraindre* to break sequence < VL **refrangere,* for L *refringere* to REFRACT]

re•fran•gi•ble (ri fran′jə bəl), *adj.* capable of being refracted, as rays of light. [1665–75; RE- + FRANGIBLE] **—re•fran′gi•ble•ness, re•fran′gi•bil′i•ty,** *n.*

re•fres•co (Re fres′kô), *n., pl.* **-cos** (-kôs). *Spanish.* a refreshment, as a soft drink.

re•fresh (ri fresh′), *v.t.* **1.** to provide new vigor and energy by rest, food, etc. (often used reflexively). **2.** to stimulate (the memory). **3.** to make fresh again; reinvigorate or cheer (a person, the mind, spirits, etc.). **4.** to freshen in appearance, color, etc., as by a restorative. **5.** *Computers.* **a.** to display (an image) repeatedly, as on a CRT, in order to prevent fading. **b.** to read and write (the contents of dynamic storage) at intervals in order to avoid loss of data. —*v.i.* **6.** to take refreshment, esp. food or drink. **7.** to become fresh or vigorous again; revive. [1325–75; ME *refreschen* < MF *refreschir,* OF. See RE-, FRESH] **—re•fresh′ful,** *adj.* **—re•fresh′ful•ly,** *adv.*
—Syn. 1. revive. **3.** freshen, enliven, reanimate. **4.** restore, repair, renovate, renew, retouch. **—Ant. 3.** dispirit, discourage.

re•fresh•en (ri fresh′ən), *v.t., v.i.* to make or become fresh again; refresh. [1775–85; RE- + FRESHEN]

re•fresh•er (ri fresh′ər), *n.* **1.** a person or thing that refreshes. **2.** *Brit.* a partial or interim fee paid to a lawyer during a prolonged case. **3.** See **refresher course.** [1375–1425; late ME *refressher.* See REFRESH, -ER¹]

refresh′er course′, a study course serving as a review of previous education. [1910–15]

re•fresh•ing (ri fresh′ing), *adj.* **1.** having the power to restore freshness, vitality, energy, etc.: *a refreshing nap.* **2.** pleasingly fresh or different: *a refreshing lack of pretense.* [1570–80; REFRESH + -ING²] **—re•fresh′ing•ly,** *adv.* **—re•fresh′ing•ness,** *n.*

re•fresh•ment (ri fresh′mənt), *n.* **1.** something that refreshes, esp. food or drink. **2. refreshments,** articles or portions of food or drink, esp. for a light meal. **3.** the act of refreshing or the state of being refreshed. [1350–1400; ME *refresshement* < MF *refreschement.* See REFRESH, -MENT]
—Syn. 3. invigoration, rejuvenation, renewal.

re′fried beans′, *Mexican Cookery.* dried beans, cooked and mashed and then fried in lard, sometimes with onions and other seasonings. Also called **frijoles refritos.** [1955–60; RE- + FRIED]

refrig., **1.** refrigeration. **2.** refrigerator.

re•frig•er•ant (ri frij′ər ənt), *adj.* **1.** refrigerating; cooling. **2.** reducing bodily heat or fever. —*n.* **3.** a refrigerant agent, as a drug. **4.** a liquid capable of vaporizing at a low temperature, as ammonia, used in mechanical refrigeration. **5.** a cooling substance, as ice or solid carbon dioxide, used in a refrigerator. [1590–1600; < L *refrīgerant-* (s. of *refrīgerāns*), prp. of *refrīgerāre.* See REFRIGERATE, -ANT]

re•frig•er•ate (ri frij′ə rāt′), *v.t.,* **-at•ed, -at•ing.** to make or keep cold or cool, as for preservation. [1525–35; < L *refrīgerātus,* ptp. of *refrīgerāre* to make cool, equiv. to *re-* RE- + *frīgerāre* to make cool, deriv. of *frīgus* cold; see -ATE¹] **—re•frig′er•a′tive, re•frig•er•a•to•ry** (ri frij′ər ə tôr′ē, -tōr′ē), *adj.*

re•frig•er•a•tion (ri frij′ə rā′shən), *n.* **1.** the act or process of refrigerating. **2.** the state of being refrigerated. [1425–75; late ME *refrigeracion* < L *refrīgerātiōn-* (s. of *refrīgerātiō*). See REFRIGERATE, -ION]

re•frig•er•a•tor (ri frij′ə rā′tər), *n.* **1.** a box, room, or cabinet in which food, drink, etc., are kept cool by means of ice or mechanical refrigeration. **2.** the part of a distilling apparatus that cools the volatile material, causing

CONCISE PRONUNCIATION KEY: *act, cāpe, dâre, pärt; set, ēqual; if, īce; ox, ōver, ôrder, oil, bo͝ok, bo͞ot, out; up, ûrge; child; sing; shoe; thin, that;* zh as in *treasure.* ə = *a* as in *alone, e* as in *system, i* as in *easily, o* as in *gallop, u* as in *circus;* ᵊ as in *fire* (fīᵊr), *hour* (ouᵊr). l and n can serve as syllabic consonants, as in *cradle* (krād′l), and *button* (but′n). See the full key inside the front cover.

re′e•mis′sion, *n.*
re′e•mit′, *v.t.,* **-mit•ted, -mit•ting.**
re•em′pha•sis, *n., pl.* **-ses.**
re•em′pha•size′, *v.t.,* **-sized, -siz•ing.**
re′em•ploy′, *v.t.*
re′em•ploy′ment, *n.*
re′en•act′, *v.t.*
re′en•act′ment, *n.*
re′en•close′, *v.t.,* **-closed, -clos•ing.**
re′en•coun′ter, *v., n.*
re′en•cour′age, *v.t.,* **-aged, -ag•ing.**
re′en•cour′age•ment, *n.*
re′en•dorse′, *v.t.,* **-dorsed, -dors•ing.**
re′en•dorse′ment, *n.*
re′en•dow′, *v.t.*
re′en•dow′ment, *n.*
re•en′er•gize′, *v.t.,* **-gized, -giz•ing.**
re′en•gage′, *v.,* **-gaged, -gag•ing.**
re′en•gage′ment, *n.*
re′en•grave′, *v.t.,* **-graved, -grav•ing.**
re′en•gross′, *v.t.*
re′en•join′, *v.t.*
re′en•joy′, *v.t.*
re′en•joy′ment, *n.*
re′en•large′, *v.,* **-larged, -larg•ing.**
re′en•large′ment, *n.*
re′en•light′en, *v.t.*
re′en•light′en•ment, *n.*
re′en•roll′, *v.*
re′en•roll′ment, *n.*
re′en•slave′, *v.t.,* **-slaved, -slav•ing.**

it to condense; condenser; rectifier. [1605–15; REFRIGERATE + -OR[2]]

refrig′erator car′, a freight car having either an ice chest or machinery for chilling perishables and sometimes having a heating unit to keep perishables from freezing. [1865–70, *Amer.*]

re·frig·er·a·tor-freez·er (ri frij′ə rā′tər frē′zər), *n.* a large appliance housing one compartment for refrigerating food and another for freezing. [1960–65]

re·frin·gence (ri frin′jəns), *n.* refractivity. [REFRING(ENT) + -ENCE]

re·frin·gent (ri frin′jənt), *adj.* refracting; refractive. [1770–80; < L *refringent-* (s. of *refringēns*), prp. of *refringere* to break up. See REFRACT, -ENT]

Ref. Sp., reformed spelling.

reft (reft), *v.* a pt. and pp. of **reave.**

re·fu·el (rē fyo͞o′əl), *v.,* **-eled, -el·ing** or (*esp. Brit.*) **-elled, -el·ling.** —*v.t.* **1.** to supply again with fuel: *to refuel an airplane.* —*v.i.* **2.** to take on a fresh supply of fuel: *The plane refueled at Paris and flew on.* [1805–15; RE- + FUEL] —**re·fu′el·a·ble,** *adj.*

ref·uge (ref′yo͞oj), *n., v.,* **-uged, -ug·ing.** —*n.* **1.** shelter or protection from danger, trouble, etc.: *to take refuge from a storm.* **2.** a place of shelter, protection, or safety. **3.** anything to which one has recourse for aid, relief, or escape. —*v.t.* **4.** *Archaic.* to afford refuge to. —*v.i.* **5.** *Archaic.* to take refuge. [1350–1400; ME < MF < L *refugium,* equiv. to *refug(ere)* to turn and flee, run away (*re-* RE- + *fugere* to flee; see FUGITIVE) + *-ium* -IUM]
—**Syn. 1.** security, safety. **2.** asylum, retreat, sanctuary, haven, stronghold.

ref·u·gee (ref′yo͝o jē′, ref′yo͝o jē′), *n.* **1.** a person who flees for refuge or safety, esp. to a foreign country, as in time of political upheaval, war, etc. **2.** See **political refugee.** [1675–85; < F *réfugié,* ptp. of *réfugier* to take refuge. See REFUGE, -EE] —**ref′u·gee′ism,** *n.*

re·fu·gi·um (ri fyo͞o′jē əm), *n., pl.* **-gi·a** (-jē ə). an area where special environmental circumstances have enabled a species or a community of species to survive after extinction in surrounding areas. [1940–45; < L; see REFUGE]

re·ful·gent (ri ful′jənt), *adj.* shining brightly; radiant; gleaming: *Crystal chandeliers and gilded walls made the opera house a refulgent setting for the ball.* [1500–10; < L *refulgent-* (s. of *refulgēns,* prp. of *refulgēre* to radiate light). See RE-, FULGENT] —**re·ful′gence, re·ful′gen·cy, re·ful′gent·ness,** *n.* —**re·ful′gent·ly,** *adv.*

re·fund[1] (*v.* ri fund′, rē′fund; *n.* rē′fund), *v.t.* **1.** to give back or restore (esp. money); repay. **2.** to make repayment to; reimburse. —*v.i.* **3.** to make repayment. —*n.* **4.** an act or instance of refunding. **5.** an amount refunded. [1350–1400; ME *refunden* (v.) < L *refundere* to pour back, equiv. to *re-* RE- + *fundere* to pour; see FOUND[3]] —**re·fund′a·ble,** *adj.* —**re·fund′a·bil′i·ty,** *n.* —**re·fund′er,** *n.* —**re·fund′ment,** *n.*

re·fund[2] (rē fund′), *v.t.* **1.** to fund anew. **2.** *Finance.* **a.** to meet (a matured debt structure) by new borrowing, esp. through issuance of bonds. **b.** to replace (an old issue) with a new one. [1855–60; RE- + FUND]

re′fund annu′ity, *Insurance.* an annuity providing for a lump-sum payment or installment payments to the beneficiary for the amount remaining of the purchase price at the death of the annuitant.

re·fur·bish (rē fûr′bish), *v.t.* to furbish again; renovate; brighten: *to refurbish the lobby.* [1605–15; RE- + FURBISH] —**re·fur′bish·ment,** *n.*
—**Syn.** refurnish, redecorate.

re·fus·al (ri fyo͞o′zəl), *n.* **1.** an act or instance of refusing. **2.** priority in refusing or taking something; option. **3.** complete resistance of a driven pile to further driving. [1425–75; late ME *refusell.* See REFUSE[1], -AL[2]]

re·fuse[1] (ri fyo͞oz′), *v.,* **-fused, -fus·ing.** —*v.t.* **1.** to decline to accept (something offered): *to refuse an award.* **2.** to decline to give; deny (a request, demand, etc.): *to refuse permission.* **3.** to express a determination not to (do something): *to refuse to discuss the question.* **4.** to decline to submit to. **5.** (of a horse) to decline to leap over (a barrier). **6.** to decline to accept (a suitor) in marriage. **7.** *Mil.* to bend or curve back (the flank units of a military force) so that they face generally to the flank rather than the front. **8.** *Obs.* to renounce. —*v.i.* **9.** to decline acceptance, consent, or compliance. [1300–50; ME *refusen* < MF *refuser,* OF << L *refūsus,* ptp. of *refundere* to pour back; see REFUND[1]] —**re·fus′a·ble,** *adj.* —**re·fus′er,** *n.*
—**Syn. 1.** rebuff. REFUSE, DECLINE, REJECT, SPURN all imply nonacceptance of something. To DECLINE is milder and more courteous than to REFUSE, which is direct and often emphatic in expressing determination not to accept what is offered or proposed: *to refuse a bribe; to decline an invitation.* To REJECT is even more positive and definite than REFUSE: *to reject a suitor.* To SPURN is to reject with scorn: *to spurn a bribe.* —**Ant. 1.** accept, welcome.

ref·use[2] (ref′yo͞os), *n.* **1.** something that is discarded as worthless or useless; rubbish; trash; garbage. —*adj.* **2.** rejected as worthless; discarded: *refuse matter.* [1325–75; ME < MF; OF *refus* denial, rejection, deriv. of *refuser* to REFUSE[1]]

CONCISE ETYMOLOGY KEY: <, descended or borrowed from; >, whence; b., blend of, blended; c., cognate with; cf., compare; deriv., derivative; equiv., equivalent; imit., imitative; obl., oblique; r., replacing; s., stem; sp., spelling, spelled; resp., respelling, respelled; trans., translation; ?, origin unknown; *, unattested; ‡, probably earlier than. See the full key inside the front cover.

re·fuse·nik (ri fyo͞oz′nik), *n. Informal.* a Soviet citizen, usually Jewish, who has been denied permission to emigrate from the Soviet Union. Also, **re·fus′nik.** [1970–75; REFUSE + -NIK, perh. trans. of Russ *otkáznik* (unless the Russ word is itself a trans. of *refusenik*)]

ref·u·ta·tion (ref′yo͝o tā′shən), *n.* an act of refuting a statement, charge, etc.; disproof. Also, **re·fut·al** (ri fyo͞ot′l). [1540–50; < L *refūtātiōn-* (s. of *refūtātiō*), equiv. to *refūtāt(us)* (ptp. of *refūtāre* to REFUTE; see -ATE[1]) + *-iōn-* -ION]

re·fut·a·tive (ri fyo͞o′tə tiv), *adj.* tending to refute; pertaining to refutation: *refutative evidence.* Also, **re·fut′a·to′ry.** [1645–55; REFUTAT(ION) + -IVE]

re·fute (ri fyo͞ot′), *v.t.,* **-fut·ed, -fut·ing. 1.** to prove to be false or erroneous, as an opinion or charge. **2.** to prove (a person) to be in error. [1505–15; < L *refūtāre* to check, suppress, refute, rebut, equiv. to *re-* RE- + *-fūtāre* presumably, "to beat" (attested only with the prefixes *con-* and *re-;* cf. CONFUTE)] —**re·fut·a·ble** (ri fyo͞o′tə bəl, ref′yə tə-), *adj.* —**re·fut′a·bil′i·ty,** *n.* —**re·fut′a·bly,** *adv.* —**re·fut′er,** *n.*
—**Syn. 1.** disprove, rebut. **1, 2.** confute.

reg (reg), *n.* Usually, **regs.** *Informal.* regulations. [by shortening]

Reg (rej), *n.* a male given name, form of **Reginald.**

Reg., **1.** regiment. **2.** queen. [< L *rēgīna*]

reg., **1.** regent. **2.** regiment. **3.** region. **4.** register. **5.** registered. **6.** registrar. **7.** registry. **8.** regular. **9.** regularly. **10.** regulation. **11.** regulator.

re·gain (rē gān′), *v.t.* **1.** to get again; recover: *to regain one's health.* **2.** to succeed in reaching again; get back to: *to regain the shore.* —*n.* **3.** (in a moisture-free fabric) the percentage of the weight that represents the amount of moisture the material is expected to absorb under normal conditions. [1540–50; RE- + GAIN] —**re·gain′a·ble,** *adj.* —**re·gain′er,** *n.*

re·gal[1] (rē′gəl), *adj.* **1.** of or pertaining to a king; royal: *the regal power.* **2.** befitting or resembling a king. **3.** stately; splendid. [1300–50; ME < L *rēgālis* ROYAL] —**re′gal·ly,** *adv.* —**re′gal·ness,** *n.*
—**Syn. 2.** See **kingly.** —**Ant. 3.** base.

re·gal[2] (rē′gəl), *n.* a portable reed organ of the 16th and 17th centuries. [1540–50; < MF *regale* < ?]

re·gale (ri gāl′), *v.,* **-galed, -gal·ing,** *n.* —*v.t.* **1.** to entertain lavishly or agreeably; delight. **2.** to entertain with choice food or drink. —*v.i.* **3.** to feast. —*n.* **4.** a sumptuous feast. **5.** a choice article of food or drink. **6.** refreshment. [1650–60; < F *régaler,* deriv. of *régal(e),* OF *rigale,* deriv. of *gale* festivity (with prefix of *rigoler* to amuse oneself), deriv. of *galer* to make merry; see GALLANT] —**re·gale′ment,** *n.* —**re·gal′er,** *n.*

re·ga·li·a (ri gā′lē ə, -gāl′yə), *n. pl.* **1.** the ensigns or emblems of royalty, as the crown or scepter. **2.** the decorations, insignia, or ceremonial clothes of any office or order. **3.** rich, fancy, or dressy clothing; finery: *guests wearing formal party regalia.* **4.** royal rights or privileges. [1530–40; < ML *rēgālia* things pertaining to a king, n. use of neut. pl. of L *rēgālis* REGAL[1]]

re·gal·i·ty (ri gal′i tē), *n., pl.* **-ties. 1.** royalty, sovereignty, or kingship. **2.** a right or privilege pertaining to a sovereign. **3.** a kingdom. **4.** (in Scotland) **a.** territorial jurisdiction of a royal nature formerly conferred by the sovereign. **b.** a territory subject to such jurisdiction. [1375–1425; late ME *regalite* < MF < ML *rēgālitās.* See REGAL[1], -ITY]

re′gal moth′, a large moth, *Citheronia regalis,* having yellow spots on gray to olive forewings and on orange-red hind wings. [1850–55]

Re·gan (rē′gən), *n.* (in Shakespeare's *King Lear*) the younger of Lear's two faithless daughters. Cf. **Cordelia** (def. 1), **Goneril.**

re·gard (ri gärd′), *v.t.* **1.** to look upon or think of with a particular feeling: *to regard a person with favor.* **2.** to have or show respect or concern for. **3.** to think highly of; esteem. **4.** to take into account; consider. **5.** to look at; observe: *She regarded him with amusement.* **6.** to relate to; concern: *The news does not regard the explosion.* **7.** to see, look at, or conceive of in a particular way; judge (usually fol. by *as*): *I regard every assignment as a challenge. They regarded his behavior as childish.* —*v.i.* **8.** to pay attention. **9.** to look or gaze. **10. as regards.** See **as**[1] (def. 25). —*n.* **11.** reference; relation: *to err with regard to facts.* **12.** an aspect, point, or particular: *quite satisfactory in this regard.* **13.** thought; attention; concern. **14.** look; gaze. **15.** respect, esteem, or deference: *a high regard for scholarship.* **16.** kindly feeling; liking. **17. regards,** sentiments of esteem or affection: *Give them my regards.* **18. with** or **in regard to,** referring to; concerning: *With regard to the new contract, we have some questions.* [1350–1400; (n.) ME < MF, n. deriv. of *regarder* to look at (cf. REWARD); (v.) late ME < MF *regarder.* See RE-, GUARD]
—**Usage.** Although sometimes considered poor substitutes for *about* or *concerning,* the phrases AS REGARDS, IN REGARD TO, and WITH REGARD TO are standard and occur in all varieties of spoken and written English, especially in business writing: *As regards your letter of January 19 . . . .* IN REGARDS TO, and WITH REGARDS TO are widely rejected as errors.
—**Syn. 3.** respect, honor, revere, value. **5.** notice, note, see, remark, mark.

re·gard·ant (ri gär′dnt), *adj. Heraldry.* (of a beast) looking backward: *a stag regardant.* Also, **reguardant.** [1275–1325; ME < MF, prp. of *regarder* to REGARD]

re·gard·ful (ri gärd′fəl), *adj.* **1.** observant; attentive; heedful (often fol. by *of*): *a man regardful of the feelings of others.* **2.** showing or feeling regard or esteem; respectful. [1580–90; REGARD + -FUL] —**re·gard′ful·ly,** *adv.* —**re·gard′ful·ness,** *n.*

re·gard·ing (ri gär′ding), *prep.* with regard to; respecting; concerning: *He said nothing regarding the lost watch.* [1785–95; REGARD + -ING[2]]

re·gard·less (ri gärd′lis), *adj.* **1.** having or showing no regard; heedless; unmindful (often fol. by *of*). **2. regardless of,** in spite of; without regard for: *They'll do it regardless of the cost.* —*adv.* **3.** without concern as to advice, warning, hardship, etc.; anyway: *I must make the decision regardless.* [1585–95; REGARD + -LESS] —**re·gard′less·ly,** *adv.* —**re·gard′less·ness,** *n.*
—**Syn. 1.** inattentive, negligent, neglectful, indifferent, unconcerned. —**Ant. 1.** attentive, mindful.

re·gat·ta (ri gat′ə, -gä′tə), *n.* **1.** a boat race, as of rowboats, yachts, or other vessels. **2.** an organized series of such races. **3.** (originally) a gondola race in Venice. **4.** a strong, striped cotton fabric that is of twill weave. [1645–55; < Upper It (Venetian) *regatta, regata,* perh. << VL **recaptāre* to contend, equiv. to **re-* RE- + **captāre* to try to seize; see CATCH]

regd., registered.

re·ge·late (rē′jə lāt′, rē′jə lāt′), *v.i.,* **-lat·ed, -lat·ing.** to freeze by regelation. [1855–60; back formation from REGELATION]

re·ge·la·tion (rē′jə lā′shən), *n. Physics.* a phenomenon in which the freezing point of water is lowered by the application of pressure; the melting and refreezing of ice, at constant temperature, caused by varying the pressure. [1855–60; RE- + GELATION]

Ré·gence (rē′jəns; *Fr.* RA ZHÄNS′), *adj.* (*often l.c.*) noting or pertaining to the style of French furnishings and decoration of c1700–20, in which a transition occurs from the Baroque style of Louis XIV to the Rococo of Louis XV. [< F, MF < ML *regentia* REGENCY]

re·gen·cy (rē′jən sē), *n., pl.* **-cies,** *adj.* —*n.* **1.** the office, jurisdiction, or control of a regent or body of regents exercising the ruling power during the minority, absence, or disability of a sovereign. **2.** a body of regents. **3.** a government consisting of regents. **4.** a territory under the control of a regent or regents. **5.** the term of office of a regent. **6.** (*cap.*) *Brit. Hist.* the period (1811–20) during which George, Prince of Wales, later George IV, was regent. **7.** (*cap.*) *Fr. Hist.* the period of the minority of Louis XV. **8.** the office or function of a regent or ruler. —*adj.* **9.** of or pertaining to a regency. **10.** *Hist.* of or pertaining to the Regencies in England or France. **11.** (*often cap.*) of or pertaining to the style of architecture, furnishings, and decoration of the British Regency, somewhat similar to the French Directoire and Empire styles and characterized by close imitation of ancient Greek forms as well as by less frequent and looser adaptations of ancient Roman, Gothic, Chinese, and ancient Egyptian forms. [1400–50; late ME < ML *rēgentia.* See REGENT, -ENCY]

re·gen·er·a·cy (ri jen′ər ə sē), *n.* a regenerate state. [1620–30; REGENER(ATE) + -ACY]

re·gen·er·ate (*v.* ri jen′ə rāt′; *adj.* ri jen′ər it), *v.,* **-at·ed, -at·ing,** *adj.* —*v.t.* **1.** to effect a complete moral reform in. **2.** to re-create, reconstitute, or make over, esp. in a better form or condition. **3.** to revive or produce anew; bring into existence again. **4.** *Biol.* to renew or restore (a lost, removed, or injured part). **5.** *Physics.* to restore (a substance) to a favorable state or physical condition. **6.** *Electronics.* to magnify the amplification of, by relaying part of the output circuit power into the input circuit. **7.** *Theol.* to cause to be born again spiritually. —*v.i.* **8.** to come into existence or be formed again. **9.** to reform; become regenerate. **10.** to produce a regenerative effect. **11.** to undergo regeneration. —*adj.* **12.** reconstituted or made over in a better form. **13.** reformed. **14.** *Theol.* born again spiritually. [1425–75; late ME (adj.) < L *regenerātus,* ptp. of *regenerāre* to bring forth again, equiv. to *re-* RE- + *generātus;* see GENERATE] —**re·gen′er·a·ble,** *adj.* —**re·gen′er·ate·ness,** *n.*
—**Syn. 1.** reform, redeem, uplift.

re·gen·er·a·tion (ri jen′ə rā′shən), *n.* **1.** act of regenerating; state of being regenerated. **2.** *Electronics.* a feedback process in which energy from the output of an amplifier is fed back to the grid circuit to reinforce the input. **3.** *Biol.* the restoration or new growth by an organism of organs, tissues, etc., that have been lost, removed, or injured. **4.** *Theol.* spiritual rebirth; religious revival. [1300–50; ME *regeneracion* < LL *regenerātiōn-* (s. of *regenerātiō*). See REGENERATE, -ION]

re·gen·er·a·tive (ri jen′ər ə tiv, -ə rā′tiv), *adj.* **1.** of, pertaining to, or characterized by regeneration. **2.** tending to regenerate. [1350–1400; ME < ML *regenerātīvus.* See REGENERATE, -IVE] —**re·gen′er·a·tive·ly,** *adv.*

regen′erative cool′ing, **1.** *Physics.* a method of cooling a gas, utilizing the rapid expansion of a compressed portion of the gas, before it becomes liquid, to cool the remainder. **2.** *Rocketry.* the cooling of a reaction engine by circulating around it the liquid propellant prior to its use in the combustion chamber of the engine, the heat energy absorbed by the propellant contributing to the total thrust of the exhaust. [1945–50]

regen′erative fur′nace, a furnace in which the incoming air is heated by regenerators. Cf. **recuperative furnace.** [1860–65]

re·gen·er·a·tor (ri jen′ə rā′tər), *n.* **1.** a person or

re′en·slave′ment, *n.*
re′en·throne′, *v.t.,* **-throned, -thron·ing.**
re′en·throne′ment, *n.*
re′en·trance′, *v.t.,* **-tranced, -tranc·ing.**
re′en·trench′, *v.*
re′en·trench′ment, *n.*
re′e·nu′mer·ate′, *v.t.,* **-at·ed, -at·ing.**
re′e·nu′mer·a′tion, *n.*
re′e·nun′ci·ate′, *v.,* **-at·ed, -at·ing.**
re′e·nun′ci·a′tion, *n.*
re′e·quip′, *v.t.,* **-quipped, -quip·ping.**
re′e·quip′ment, *n.*
re′e·rect′, *v.t.*
re′e·rec′tion, *n.*
re′e·rupt′, *v.i.*
re′e·rup′tion, *n.*
re·es′ca·late′, *v.,* **-lat·ed, -lat·ing.**
re′es·ca·la′tion, *n.*
re′es·tab′lish, *v.t.*
re′es·tab′lish·ment, *n.*
re·es′ti·mate′, *v.t.,* **-mat·ed, -mat·ing.**
re·es′ti·mate, *n.*
re′es·ti·ma′tion, *n.*
re′e·vac′u·ate′, *v.,* **-at·ed, -at·ing.**
re′e·vac′u·a′tion, *n.*
re′e·val′u·ate′, *v.t.,* **-at·ed, -at·ing.**
re′e·val′u·a′tion, *n.*
re′e·va′sion, *n.*
re′e·vict′, *v.t.*
re·ev′i·dence, *v.t.,* **-denced, -denc·ing.**

thing that regenerates. **2.** (in a regenerative furnace) a chamber filled with checkerwork that is repeatedly heated by exhaust gases in order to heat air that is passed through it. [1730–40; REGENERATE + -OR[2]]

Re·gens·burg (rā′gəns bo͝ork′), *n.* a city in central Bavaria, in SE Germany, on the Danube: battle 1809. 131,000. Also called **Ratisbon.**

re·gent (rē′jənt), *n.* **1.** a person who exercises the ruling power in a kingdom during the minority, absence, or disability of the sovereign. **2.** a ruler or governor. **3.** a member of the governing board of a state university or a state educational system. **4.** a university officer who exercises general supervision over the conduct and welfare of the students. **5.** (in certain Catholic universities) a member of the religious order who is associated in the administration of a school or college with a layperson who is its dean or director. —*adj.* **6.** acting as regent of a country; exercising ruling authority in behalf of a sovereign during his or her minority, absence, or disability (usually used postpositively): *a prince regent.* [1350–1400; ME < L *regent-* (s. of *regēns*), prp. of *regere* to rule] —**re′gent·al,** *adj.* —**re′gent·ship′,** *n.*

re′gent bow′erbird, a bowerbird, *Sericulus chrysocephalus,* the males of which have deep black plumage with brilliant golden head, neck, and wing patches and build elaborate bowers. Also called **re′gent bird′.**

Re·ger (rā′gər), *n.* **Max** (mäks), 1873–1916, German composer and pianist.

reg·gae (reg′ā), *n.* a style of Jamaican popular music blending blues, calypso, and rock-'n'-roll, characterized by a strongly syncopated rhythm and lyrics of social protest. [< Jamaican E, resp. of *reggay* (introduced in the song "Do the Reggay" (1968) by Frederick "Toots" Hibbert), a dance name based on *rege,* *strege a dowdy or raggedy fellow; cf. *rege-rege* ragged clothing, quarrel, row]

Reg·gio Ca·la·bria (red′jô kä lä′brya), a seaport in S Italy, on the Strait of Messina: almost totally destroyed by an earthquake 1908. 178,094. Also, **Reg·gio di Ca·la·bria** (red′jô dē′ kä lä′brya).

Reg·gio E·mi·lia (red′jô e mē′lyä), a city in N Italy. 129,725. Also, **Reg·gio nel·l'E·mi·lia** (red′jô nel′le mē′lyä).

Reg·gy (rej′ē), *n.* a male given name, form of **Reginald.** Also, **Reg′gie.**

reg·i·cide (rej′ə sīd′), *n.* **1.** the killing of a king. **2.** a person who kills a king or is responsible for his death, esp. one of the judges who condemned Charles I of England to death. [1540–50; < L *rēg-,* s. of *rēx* king + -I- + -CIDE] —**reg′i·cid′al,** *adj.*

re·gime (rə zhēm′, rā-, *or, sometimes,* -jēm′), *n.* **1.** a mode or system of rule or government: *a dictatorial regime.* **2.** a ruling or prevailing system. **3.** a government in power. **4.** the period during which a particular government or ruling system is in power. **5.** *Med.* regimen (def. 1). Also, **ré·gime′.** [1770–80; < F *régime* < L *regimen* REGIMEN]

reg·i·men (rej′ə mən, -men′, rezh′-), *n.* **1.** *Med.* a regulated course, as of diet, exercise, or manner of living, intended to preserve or restore health or to attain some result. **2.** regime (defs. 1, 2). **3.** *Gram.* government (def. 9). [1350–1400; ME < L: rule, government, guidance, equiv. to *reg(ere)* to rule + *-i-* -I- + *-men,* n. suffix of result]

reg·i·ment (*n.* rej′ə mənt; *v.* rej′ə ment′), *n.* **1.** *Mil.* a unit of ground forces, consisting of two or more battalions or battle groups, a headquarters unit, and certain supporting units. **2.** *Obs.* government. —*v.t.* **3.** to manage or treat in a rigid, uniform manner; subject to strict discipline. **4.** to form into a regiment or regiments. **5.** to assign to a regiment or group. **6.** to form into an organized group, usually for the purpose of rigid or complete control. [1350–1400; ME < MF < LL *regimentum,* equiv. to L *reg(ere)* to rule + *-i-* -I- + *-mentum* -MENT]

reg·i·men·tal (rej′ə men′tl), *adj.* **1.** of or pertaining to a regiment. —*n.* **2. regimentals,** the uniform of a regiment. [1695–1705; REGIMENT + -AL[1]] —**reg′i·men′tal·ly,** *adv.*

reg·i·men·ta·tion (rej′ə men tā′shən, -mən-), *n.* **1.** the act of regimenting or the state of being regimented. **2.** the strict discipline and enforced uniformity characteristic of military groups or totalitarian systems. [1875–85; REGIMENT + -ATION]

Re·gin (rā′gin), *n.* (in the *Volsunga Saga*) a smith, the brother of Fafnir, who raises Sigurd and encourages him to kill Fafnir in the hope of gaining the gold he guards.

re·gi·na (ri jī′nə, -jē′-), *n.* **1.** queen. **2.** (*usually cap.*) the official title of a queen: *Elizabeth Regina.* [1425–75; late ME < L *rēgīna*] —**re·gi′nal,** *adj.*

Re·gi·na (ri jī′nə *for 1;* rə jē′nə, -jī′- *for 2*), *n.* **1.** a city in and the capital of Saskatchewan, in the S part, in S Canada. 149,593. **2.** a female given name: from a Latin word meaning "queen."

Reg·i·nald (rej′ə nəld), *n.* a male given name: from an Old English word meaning "counsel and rule."

Re·gi·o·mon·ta·nus (rē′jē ō mon tā′nəs, -tä′-, rej′ē-; *Ger.* Rā′gē ō mōn tä′no͝os), *n.* See **Müller, Johann.**

re·gion (rē′jən), *n.* **1.** an extensive, continuous part of a surface, space, or body: *a region of the earth.* **2.** Usually, **regions.** the vast or indefinite entirety of a space or area, or something compared to one: *the regions of the firmament; the regions of the mind.* **3.** a part of the earth's surface (land or sea) of considerable and usually indefinite extent: *a tropical region.* **4.** a district without respect to boundaries or extent: *a charming region in Connecticut.* **5.** a part or division of the universe, as the heavens: *a galactic region.* **6.** a large indefinite area or range of something specified; sphere: *a region of authority.* **7.** an area of interest, activity, pursuit, etc.; field: *studies in the region of logic.* **8.** an administrative division of a city or territory. **9.** *Zoogeog.* a major faunal area of the earth's surface, sometimes one regarded as a division of a larger area. **10.** *Anat.* a place in or a division of the body or a part of the body: *the abdominal region.* **11.** *Math.* **a.** Also called **domain.** an open connected set. **b.** the union of such a set and some or all of its boundary points. [1300–50; ME < AF *regiun* < L *regiōn-* (s. of *regiō*) direction, line, boundary, equiv. to *reg(ere)* to rule + *-iōn-* -ION]
—**Syn. 1.** area, section, portion. **4.** locale, site, tract, quarter.

re·gion·al (rē′jə nl), *adj.* **1.** of or pertaining to a region of considerable extent; not merely local: *a regional meeting of the Boy Scouts.* **2.** of or pertaining to a particular region, district, area, or part, as of a country; sectional; local: *regional differences in pronunciation.* **3.** *Anat.* of, pertaining to, or localized in a particular area or part of the body. **4.** having, exhibiting, or characterized by regionalism: *He writes regional novels.* —*n.* **5.** Often, **regionals.** a regional competition or tournament: *The basketball team won the regionals.* **6.** a regional company, branch, stock exchange, etc.: *Regionals are getting stiff competition from the national firms.* [1645–55; < L *regiōnālis.* See REGION, -AL[1]] —**re′gion·al·ly,** *adv.*

re′gional enter′i′tis, *Pathol.* See **Crohn's disease.** Also called **re′gional ilei′tis.**

re·gion·al·ism (rē′jə nl iz′əm), *n.* **1.** *Govt.* the principle or system of dividing a city, state, etc., into separate administrative regions. **2.** advocacy of such a principle or system. **3.** a speech form, expression, custom, or other feature peculiar to or characteristic of a particular area. **4.** devotion to the interests of one's own region. **5.** *Literature.* the theory or practice of emphasizing the regional characteristics of locale or setting, as by stressing local speech. **6.** (*often cap.*) a style of American painting developed chiefly 1930–40 in which subject matter was derived principally from rural areas. [1880–85; REGIONAL + -ISM] —**re′gion·al·ist,** *n., adj.* —**re′gion·al·is′tic,** *adj.*

re·gion·al·ize (rē′jə nl īz′), *v.t., v.i.,* **-ized, -iz·ing.** to separate into or arrange by regions. Also, *esp. Brit.,* **re′gion·al·ise′.** [1920–25; REGIONAL + -IZE] —**re′gion·al·i·za′tion,** *n.*

Re·gis (rē′jis), *n.* a male given name.

ré·gis·seur (rā′zhə sûr′; *Fr.* Rā zhē sœr′), *n., pl.* **-seurs** (-sœr′). someone responsible for the staging of a theatrical work, esp. of a ballet; director. [< F: manager, agent, steward, equiv. to *régiss-,* long s. of *régir* to govern, manage (MF << L *regere;* see REGENT) + *-eur* -EUR]

reg·is·ter (rej′ə stər), *n.* **1.** a book in which records of acts, events, names, etc., are kept. **2.** a list or record of such acts, events, etc. **3.** an entry in such a book, record, or list. **4.** an official document issued to a merchant ship as evidence of its nationality. **5.** registration or registry. **6.** a mechanical device by which certain data are automatically recorded. **7.** See **cash register. 8.** *Music.* **a.** the compass or range of a voice or an instrument. **b.** a part of this range produced in the same way and having the same quality: *the head register; the upper register of the clarinet.* **c.** (in an organ) a stop. **9.** a device for controlling the flow of warmed air or the like through an opening, as from a duct to an interior, composed of a number of narrow, parallel blades, usually behind a grating, that may be adjusted so as to overlap and close the opening. **10.** *Photog.* proper relationship between two plane surfaces in photography, as corresponding plates in photoengraving. **11.** *Print.* **a.** a precise adjustment or correspondence, as of lines, columns, etc., esp. on the two sides of a leaf. **b.** correct relation or exact superimposition, as of colors in color printing. **12.** a bookmark, esp. a ribbon attached to the spine of a book. **13.** *Ling.* a variety of language typically used in a specific type of communicative setting: *an informal register; the register of scientific discourse.* **14.** *Computers.* a high-speed storage location in the CPU, used to store a related string of bits, as a word or phrase. —*v.t.* **15.** to enter or cause to be entered formally in a register. **16.** to cause (mail) to be recorded upon delivery to a post office for safeguarding against loss, theft, damage, etc., during transmission. **17.** to enroll (a student, voter, etc.) in a school or course of study, on the voting rolls, etc. **18.** to indicate by a record, as instruments do: *The thermometer registered 102 degrees today.* **19.** to indicate or show, as on a scale. **20.** *Print.* to adjust so as to secure exact correspondence; cause to be in register. **21.** *Mil.* to adjust (fire) on a known point. **22.** to show (surprise, joy, anger, etc.), as by facial expression or by actions. **23.** to document (a merchant ship engaged in foreign trade) by issuing a certificate of registry. —*v.i.* **24.** to enter one's name or cause it to be entered in a register; enroll: *to register at a motel.* **25.** to apply for and obtain inclusion of one's name on the list of voters. **26.** to enroll in a school or course of study: *I've registered for three English classes.* **27.** *Print.* to be in register. **28.** to show: *A broad smile registered on his face.* **29.** to have some effect; make some impression: *My plea didn't register on him at all.* [1350–1400; ME *registre* < MF, OF < ML *registrum, regestrum,* alter. of LL *regesta* catalog, list, n. use of neut. pl. of L *regestus,* ptp. of *regerere* to carry back, pile up, collect, equiv. to *re-* RE- + *ges-,* s. of *gerere* to bear + *-tus* ptp. suffix; (v.) ME *registren* (< MF *registrer*) < ML *registrāre,* deriv. of *registrum*] —**reg′is·ter·er,** *n.* —**reg·is·tra·bil·i·ty** (rej′ə strə bil′i tē), *n.* —**reg′is·tra·ble, reg′is·ter·a·ble,** *adj.*
—**Syn. 1.** record, ledger, archive. **2.** roll, roster, catalogue, chronicle, schedule, annals. **15.** enroll, list, record, catalogue, chronicle. **22.** demonstrate, evince.

reg·is·tered (rej′ə stərd), *adj.* **1.** recorded, as in a register or book; enrolled. **2.** *Com.* officially listing the owner's name with the issuing corporation and suitably inscribing the certificate, as with bonds to evidence title. *Abbr.:* r **3.** officially or legally certified by a government officer or board: *a registered patent.* **4.** denoting cattle, horses, dogs, etc., having pedigrees verified and filed by authorized associations of breeders. [1665–75; REGISTER + -ED[2]]

reg′istered bond′, a bond recorded in the name of the owner. Cf. **bearer bond.** [1860–65, *Amer.*]

reg′istered dieti′tian, a person who has fulfilled all the educational and examination requirements of the American Dietetic Association for recognition as a qualified nutrition specialist.

reg′istered mail′, prepaid first-class mail that has been recorded at a post office prior to delivery for safeguarding against loss, theft, or damage during transmission. [1850–55]

reg′istered nurse′, a graduate nurse who has passed a state board examination and been registered and licensed to practice nursing. *Abbr.:* R.N. [1895–1900]

reg′istered represent′ative, *Stock Exchange.* an employee of a member firm of a stock exchange, authorized to execute orders for the clients of the firm.

reg′ister of wills′, (in some states of the U.S.) the official charged with the probate of wills or with the keeping of the records of the probate court. [1945–50; *register,* appar. var. of earlier *registrer;* see REGISTRAR]

reg′ister ton′. See under **ton**[1] (def. 6). [1905–10]

reg′ister ton′nage, *Naut.* the volume of a vessel, esp. the net tonnage as measured officially and registered for purposes of taxation. [1855–60]

reg·is·trant (rej′ə strənt), *n.* a person who registers or is registered. [1885–90, *Amer.;* < ML *registrant-* (s. of *registrāns*) prp. of *registrāre.* See REGISTER, -ANT]

reg·is·trar (rej′ə strär′, rej′ə strär′), *n.* **1.** a person who keeps a record; an official recorder. **2.** an agent of a bank, trust company, or other corporation who is responsible for certifying and registering issues of securities. **3.** an official at a school or college who maintains students' personal and academic records, issues reports of grades, mails out official publications, etc. [1350–1400; alter. (see -AR[2]) of earlier *registrary* < ML *registrārius* (see REGISTER, -ARY); r. earlier *registrer,* ME *registrer* < AF (OF *registreur*) < ML *registrātor,* equiv. to *registrā(re)* to REGISTER + *-tor* -TOR] —**reg′is·trar·ship′,** *n.*

reg·is·trate (rej′ə strāt′), *v.i.,* **-trat·ed, -trat·ing.** to select and combine pipe organ stops. [1475–85; < ML *registrātus* (ptp. of *registrāre*). See REGISTER, -ATE[1]]

reg·is·tra·tion (rej′ə strā′shən), *n.* **1.** the act of registering. **2.** an instance of this. **3.** an entry in a register. **4.** the group or number registered. **5.** an official act of registering one's name in the list of qualified voters. **6.** a certificate attesting to the fact that someone or something has been registered: *a boat registration.* **7.** *Music.* **a.** the act or technique of registrating. **b.** the selection of stops made by an organist for a particular piece. [1560–70; < MF < ML *registrātiōn-* (s. of *registrātiō*). See REGISTRATE, -ION] —**reg′is·tra′tion·al,** *adj.*

reg·is·try (rej′ə strē), *n., pl.* **-tries. 1.** the act of registering; registration. **2.** a place where a register is kept; an office of registration. **3.** register (defs. 1, 2). **4.** the state of being registered. **5.** the nationality of a merchant ship as shown on its register. [1475–85; REGIST(ER) + -RY]

reg′istry of′fice, *Brit.* a government office and depository in which records and civil registers are kept and civil marriages performed. [1720–30]

re·gi·us (rē′jē əs, -jəs), *adj.* **1.** of or belonging to a king. **2.** (of a professor in a British university) holding a chair founded by or dependent on the sovereign. [< L *rēgius* worthy of or belonging to a king, royal, equiv. to *rēg-* (s. of *rēx*) king + *-ius* adj. suffix]

re·gle (rē′gəl), *n.* a groove or channel for guiding a sliding door. [1895–1900; < F *règle* straightedge, RULE (< L *regula*)]

reg·let (reg′lit), *n.* **1.** *Archit.* **a.** a groove for guiding or holding a panel, window sash, etc. **b.** a narrow, flat molding; fillet. **2.** *Print.* **a.** a thin strip, usually of wood, less than type-high, used to produce a blank in or about a page of type. **b.** such strips collectively. [1570–80; < F, dim. of *règle* REGLE; see -ET]

reg·ma (reg′mə), *n., pl.* **-ma·ta** (-mə tə). *Bot.* a dry fruit consisting of three or more carpels that separate from the axis at maturity. [1830–40; < NL < Gk

CONCISE PRONUNCIATION KEY: act, cāpe, dâre, pärt; set, ēqual; *if,* īce; ox, ōver, ôrder, oil, bo͝ok, bo͞ot, out; up, ûrge; child; sing; shoe; thin, *th*at; zh as in *treasure.* ə = *a* as in *alone, e* as in *system, i* as in *easily, o* as in *gallop, u* as in *circus;* ᵊ as in *fire* (fīᵊr), *hour* (ouᵊr). l and n can serve as syllabic consonants, as in *cradle* (krād′l), and *button* (but′n). See the full key inside the front cover.

re′ex′ca·vate′, *v.t.,* **-vat·ed, -vat·ing.**
re′ex·ca·va′tion, *n.*
re·ex·change′, *v.,* **-changed, -chang·ing.**
re·ex′e·cute′, *v.t.,* **-cut·ed, -cut·ing.**
re′ex·e·cu′tion, *n.*
re·ex′er·cise′, *v.,* **-cised, -cis·ing.**
re′ex·hib′it, *v.t.*
re′ex·hi·bi′tion, *n.*
re′ex·pand′, *v.*
re′ex·pan′sion, *n.*
re′ex·pel′, *v.t.,* **-pelled, -pel·ling.**
re′ex·pe′ri·ence, *v.,* **-enced, -enc·ing.**
re′ex·per′i·ment, *v.i., n.*
re′ex·plain′, *v.t.*
re′ex·pla·na′tion, *n.*
re·ex′pli·cate′, *v.t.,* **-cat·ed, -cat·ing.**
re′ex·pli·ca′tion, *n.*
re′ex·plo·ra′tion, *n.*
re′ex·plore′, *v.,* **-plored, -plor·ing.**
re′ex·pose′, *v.t.,* **-posed, -pos·ing.**
re′ex·po·si′tion, *n.*
re′ex·po′sure, *n.*
re′ex·press′, *v.t.*
re′ex·pres′sion, *n.*
re′ex·pul′sion, *n.*
re′fa·mil′iar·i·za′tion, *n.*
re′fa·mil′iar·ize′, *v.t.,* **-ized, -iz·ing.**
re·fash′ion, *v.t.*
re·fas′ten, *v.t.*
re′fed·er·al·i·za′tion, *n.*

rhēgma fracture, break, equiv. to *rhēg(nýnai)* to break, shatter + *-ma* n. suffix of result]

reg·nal (reg′nl), *adj.* of or pertaining to a sovereign, sovereignty, or reign: *the second regnal year of Louis XIV.* [1605–15; < ML *rēgnālis,* equiv. to L *rēgn(um)* rule, kingdom + *-ālis* -AL[1]; see REIGN]

reg·nant (reg′nənt), *adj.* **1.** reigning; ruling (usually used following the noun it modifies): *a queen regnant.* **2.** exercising authority, rule, or influence. **3.** prevalent; widespread. [1590–1600; < L *rēgnant-* (s. of *rēgnāns*), prp. of *rēgnāre* to rule; see REIGN, -ANT] —**reg′nan·cy,** *n.*

reg·nat po·pu·lus (reg′nät pô′pŏŏ lŏŏs′; *Eng.* reg′nat pop′yə ləs), *Latin.* let the people rule: motto of Arkansas.

reg·o·lith (reg′ə lith), *n.* See **mantle rock.** [1895–1900; < Gk *rhêgo(s)* rug, blanket + -LITH]

re·gorge (ri gôrj′), *v.* **-gorged, -gorg·ing.** —*v.t.* **1.** to disgorge; cast up again. —*v.i.* **2.** to rush back again; gush: *The waters regorged.* [1595–1605; < F *regorger,* MF. See RE-, GORGE]

regr., registrar.

re·grate[1] (ri grāt′), *v.t.,* **-grat·ed, -grat·ing.** **1.** to buy up (grain, provisions, etc.) in order to sell again at a profit in or near the same market. **2.** to sell again (commodities so bought); retail. [1400–50; late ME *regraten* < OF *regrater,* perh. equiv. to *re-* RE- + *grater* to scrape (see GRATE[2])] —**re·grat′er,** *n.*

re·grate[2] (ri grāt′), *v.t.,* **-grat·ed, -grat·ing.** to dress or tool (existing stonework) anew. [1720–30; < F *regratter,* equiv. to *re-* RE- + *gratter* to GRATE[2]]

re·greet (rē grēt′), *v.t., v.i.* **1.** to greet in return or again. —*n.* **2. regreets,** *Obs.* greetings. [1580–90; RE- + GREET[1]]

re·gress (*v.* ri gres′; *n.* rē′gres), *v.i.* **1.** to move backward; go back. **2.** to revert to an earlier or less advanced state or form. —*n.* **3.** the act of going back; return. **4.** the right to go back. **5.** backward movement or course; retrogression. [1325–75; ME *regresse* (n.) < L *regressus* a returning, going back, equiv. to *re-* RE- + *-gred-,* comb. form of *gradī* to step, walk, go + *-tus* suffix of v. action, with *dt* > *ss*] —**re·gres′sor,** *n.*
—**Syn. 1.** revert, retreat, backslide, lapse, ebb.

re·gres·sion (ri gresh′ən), *n.* **1.** the act of going back to a previous place or state; return or reversion. **2.** retrogradation; retrogression. **3.** *Biol.* reversion to an earlier or less advanced state or form or to a common or general type. **4.** *Psychoanal.* the reversion to a chronologically earlier or less adapted pattern of behavior and feeling. **5.** a subsidence of a disease or its manifestations: *a regression of symptoms.* —*adj.* **6.** of, pertaining to, or determined by regression analysis: *regression curve; regression equation.* [1510–20; < L *regressiōn-* (s. of *regressiō*). See REGRESS, -ION]

regres′sion anal′ysis, *Statistics.* a procedure for determining a relationship between a dependent variable, as predicted success in college, and an independent variable, as a score on a scholastic aptitude test, for a given population. The relationship is expressed as an equation for a line **(regres′sion line′)** or curve **(regres′sion curve′)** in which any coefficient **(regre′ssion coeffi′cient)** of the independent variable in the equation has been determined from a sample population. [1945–50]

re·gres·sive (ri gres′iv), *adj.* **1.** regressing or tending to regress; retrogressive. **2.** *Biol.* of, pertaining to, or effecting regression. **3.** (of tax) decreasing proportionately with an increase in the tax base. **4.** *Logic.* obtained from or characterized by backward reasoning. [1625–35; REGRESS + -IVE] —**re·gres′sive·ly,** *adv.* —**re·gres′sive·ness, re·gres·siv·i·ty** (rē′gre siv′i tē), *n.*

regres′sive assimila′tion, *Phonet.* assimilation in which a following sound has an effect on a preceding one, as in pronouncing *have* in *have to* as (haf), influenced by the voiceless (t) in *to.* Also called **anticipatory assimilation.** Cf. **progressive assimilation.** [1885–90]

re·gret (ri gret′), *v.,* **-gret·ted, -gret·ting,** *n.* —*v.t.* **1.** to feel sorrow or remorse for (an act, fault, disappointment, etc.): *He no sooner spoke than he regretted it.* **2.** to think of with a sense of loss: *to regret one's vanished youth.* —*n.* **3.** a sense of loss, disappointment, dissatisfaction, etc. **4.** a feeling of sorrow or remorse for a fault, act, loss, disappointment, etc. **5. regrets,** a polite, usually formal refusal of an invitation: *I sent her my regrets.* **6.** a note expressing regret at one's inability to accept an invitation: *I have had four acceptances and one regret.* [1300–50; ME *regretten* (v.) < MF *regreter,* OF, equiv. to *re-* RE- + *-greter,* perh. < Gmc (cf. GREET[2])] —**re·gret′ter,** *n.* —**re·gret′ting·ly,** *adv.*
—**Syn. 1.** deplore, lament, bewail, bemoan, mourn, sorrow, grieve. REGRET, PENITENCE, REMORSE imply a sense of sorrow about events in the past, usually wrongs committed or errors made. REGRET is distress of mind, sorrow for what has been done or failed to be done: *to have no regrets.* PENITENCE implies a sense of sin or misdoing, a feeling of contrition and determination not to sin again: *a humble sense of penitence.* REMORSE implies pangs, qualms of conscience, a sense of guilt, regret, and repentance for sins committed, wrongs done, or duty not performed: *a deep sense of remorse.* —**Ant. 1.** rejoice. **4.** joy.

re·gret·ful (ri gret′fəl), *adj.* full of regret; sorrowful because of what is lost, gone, or done. [1640–50; REGRET + -FUL] —**re·gret′ful·ly,** *adv.* —**re·gret′ful·ness,** *n.*

re·gret·ta·ble (ri gret′ə bəl), *adj.* causing or deserving regret; unfortunate; deplorable. Also, **re·gret′a·ble.** [1595–1605; < MF *regret(t)able;* see REGRET, -ABLE] —**re·gret′ta·ble·ness,** *n.* —**re·gret′ta·bly,** *adv.*

re·group (rē grōōp′), *v.t.* **1.** to form into a new or restructured group or grouping. —*v.i.* **2.** to become reorganized in order to make a fresh start: *If the plan doesn't work, we'll have to regroup and try something else.* **3.** *Mil.* to become organized in a new tactical formation. [1880–85; RE- + GROUP] —**re·group′ment,** *n.*

regt., 1. regent. **2.** regiment.

re·guard·ant (ri gär′dnt), *adj. Heraldry.* regardant.

reg·u·la (reg′yə lə), *n., pl.* **-lae** (-lē′). (in a Doric entablature) a fillet, continuing a triglyph beneath the taenia, from which guttae are suspended. Also called **guttae band.** [1555–65; < L *rēgula* ruler, pattern (akin to *rēx* king, *regere* to rule; see -ULE)]

reg·u·la·ble (reg′yə lə bəl), *adj.* that can be regulated; controllable. [1650–60; REGUL(ATE) + -ABLE]

reg·u·lant (reg′yə lənt), *n.* a substance, as a chemical, used to control or regulate: *herbicides and fungicides as regulants for plant growth.* [REGUL(ATE) + -ANT]

reg·u·lar (reg′yə lər), *adj.* **1.** usual; normal; customary: *to put something in its regular place.* **2.** evenly or uniformly arranged; symmetrical: *regular teeth.* **3.** characterized by fixed principle, uniform procedure, etc.: *regular income.* **4.** recurring at fixed times; periodic: *regular bus departures; regular meals.* **5.** rhythmical: *regular breathing.* **6.** occurring with normal frequency, as menses or bowel movements. **7.** having regular menses or bowel movements. **8.** adhering to a rule or procedure; methodical: *regular habits; to be regular in one's diet.* **9.** observing fixed times or habits; habitual: *a regular customer.* **10.** orderly; well-ordered: *a regular life.* **11.** conforming to some accepted rule, discipline, etc. **12.** carried out in accordance with an accepted principle or rule; formally correct: *a regular session of the court.* **13.** qualified to engage in an occupation or profession; legitimate; proper: *I suspected the man wasn't a regular doctor.* **14.** *Informal.* **a.** real or genuine; down-to-earth; decent: *a regular guy.* **b.** absolute; thoroughgoing: *a regular rascal.* **15.** (of a flower) having the members of each of its floral circles or whorls alike in form and size. **16.** *Gram.* conforming to the most prevalent pattern of formation, inflection, construction, etc. **17.** *Math.* **a.** governed by one law throughout. **b.** (of a polygon) having all sides and angles equal. **c.** (of a polyhedron) having all faces congruent regular polygons, and all solid angles congruent. **d.** (of a topological space) having the property that, corresponding to each point and a closed set not containing the point, there are two disjoint open sets, one containing the point, the other containing the closed set. **e.** (of a function of a complex variable) analytic (def. 5a). **18.** *Mil.* noting or belonging to the permanently organized, or standing, army of a state. **19.** *Internat. Law.* noting soldiers recognized as legitimate combatants in warfare. **20.** *Eccles.* subject to a religious rule, or belonging to a religious or monastic order (opposed to *secular*): *regular clergy.* **21.** *U.S. Politics.* of, pertaining to, or selected by the recognized agents of a political party: *the regular ticket.* **22.** (of coffee) containing an average amount of milk or cream. —*n.* **23.** a long-standing or habitual customer or client: *The restaurant can always find tables for its regulars.* **24.** *Eccles.* a member of a duly constituted religious order under a rule. **25.** *Mil.* a professional soldier. **26.** *U.S. Politics.* a party member who faithfully stands by his or her party. **27.** a size of garment designed for men of average build. **28.** a garment, as a suit or overcoat, in this size. **29.** an athlete who plays in most of the games, usually from the start. [1350–1400; ME *reguler* (adj.) < MF < LL *rēgulāris.* See REGULA, -AR[1]] —**reg·u·lar·i·ty** (reg′yə lar′i tē), **reg′u·lar·ness,** *n.*
—**Syn. 2.** even, formal, orderly, uniform. **4.** habitual, established, fixed. **8.** systematic.

Reg′ular Ar′my, the permanent army maintained in peace as well as in war; the standing army: one of the major components of the Army of the United States. [1840–50]

reg′ular bev′el, the bevel of a bolt or lock on a door opening into the building, room, etc., to which the doorway leads (opposed to *reverse bevel*).

reg′ular check′ing account′, a checking account for which the monthly fee is usually based on the average balance maintained and the number of transactions recorded. Cf. **special checking account.**

reg·u·lar·ize (reg′yə lə rīz′), *v.t.,* **-ized, -iz·ing.** to make regular. Also, *esp. Brit.,* **reg′u·lar·ise′.** [1615–25; REGULAR + -IZE] —**reg′u·lar·i·za′tion,** *n.* —**reg′u·lar·iz′er,** *n.*

reg′ular lay′, *Ropemaking.* a right-handed lay, as of a plain-laid rope.

reg·u·lar·ly (reg′yə lər lē), *adv.* **1.** at regular times or intervals. **2.** according to plan, custom, etc. **3.** usually; ordinarily: *The dress is regularly $45 but is now on sale for $30.* [1520–30; REGULAR + -LY]

reg′ular ode′, *Pros.* See **Pindaric ode.**

reg′ular ter′tiaries. See under **tertiary** (def. 5).

reg′ular year′. See under **Jewish calendar.** [1895–1900]

reg·u·late (reg′yə lāt′), *v.t.,* **-lat·ed, -lat·ing. 1.** to control or direct by a rule, principle, method, etc.: *to regulate household expenses.* **2.** to adjust to some standard or requirement, as amount, degree, etc.: *to regulate the temperature.* **3.** to adjust so as to ensure accuracy of operation: *to regulate a watch.* **4.** to put in good order: *to regulate the digestion.* [1620–30; < LL *rēgulātus* (ptp. of *rēgulāre*). See REGULA, -ATE[1]] —**reg·u·la·tive** (reg′yə lā′tiv, -yə lə tiv), **reg·u·la·to·ry** (reg′yə lə tôr′ē, -tōr′ē), *adj.* —**reg′u·la′tive·ly,** *adv.*
—**Syn. 1.** rule, govern, manage, order, adjust, arrange, dispose, conduct. **2.** set. **4.** systematize.

reg·u·la·tion (reg′yə lā′shən), *n.* **1.** a law, rule, or other order prescribed by authority, esp. to regulate conduct. **2.** the act of regulating or the state of being regulated. **3.** *Mach.* the percentage difference in some quantity related to the operation of an apparatus or machine, as the voltage output of a transformer or the speed of a motor, between the value of the quantity at no-load operation and its value at full-load operation. **4.** *Electronics.* the difference between maximum and minimum voltage drops between the anode and the cathode of a gas tube for a specified range of values of the anode current. **5.** *Sports.* the normal, prescribed duration of a game according to the sport's regulations, exclusive of any extra innings, overtime period, etc.: *The Knicks tied the score in the final seconds of regulation, sending the game into overtime.* —*adj.* **6.** prescribed by or conforming to regulation: *regulation army equipment.* **7.** usual; normal; customary: *the regulation decorations for a Halloween party.* [1665–75; REGULATE + -ION]
—**Syn. 2.** direction, management, control, disposition, adjustment.

Regulation T, (in the U.S.) a federal law governing the amount of credit that may be advanced by brokers and dealers to customers for the purchase of securities on margin.

Regulation U, (in the U.S.) a federal law governing the amount of credit that may be advanced by a bank for the purchase of listed securities.

reg·u·la·tor (reg′yə lā′tər), *n.* **1.** a person or thing that regulates. **2.** *Horol.* **a.** an adjustable device in a clock or a watch for making it go faster or slower. **b.** a master clock, usually of great accuracy, against which other clocks are checked. **3.** *Mach.* **a.** a governor mechanism for regulating the flow of fuel, steam, etc., to an engine in order to maintain constant speed under varying load or resistance. **b.** a valve for regulating the pressure of flowing gas or liquid to maintain a predetermined pressure. **c.** any of various mechanisms for maintaining a temperature, a level of liquid in a tank, etc. **4.** *Elect.* a device for maintaining a designated characteristic, as voltage or current, at a predetermined value, or for varying it according to a predetermined plan. **5.** a device on scuba equipment for regulating the rate at which compressed air is fed through a breathing tube in proportion to the depth of water. **6.** a device for maintaining a constant gas pressure. **7.** (*cap.*) *Amer. Hist.* **a.** a member of any of several bands or committees in North Carolina (1767–71), formed to resist certain abuses, as extortion by officials. **b.** (in newly settled areas) a member of any band or committee organized to preserve order before the establishment of regular legal authority. [1645–55; REGULATE + -OR[2]]

reg′ulator pin′, either of two pins on the regulators of certain timepieces, one on each side of the hairspring, that can be moved to adjust the rate of the timepiece.

reg′ulatory gene′, *Genetics.* any gene that exercises control over the expression of another gene or genes. Also, **reg′ulator gene′.** [1960–65]

reg·u·line (reg′yə lin, -līn′), *adj. Metall.* of, pertaining to, or of the nature of, a regulus. [1660–70; REGUL(US) + -INE[1]]

reg·u·lus (reg′yə ləs), *n., pl.* **-lus·es, -li** (-lī′). **1.** (*cap.*) *Astron.* a first magnitude star in the constellation Leo. **2.** *Metall.* **a.** the metallic mass that forms beneath the slag at the bottom of the crucible or furnace in smelting ores. **b.** an impure intermediate product obtained in smelting ores. [1550–60; < L *rēgulus* lit., little king (dim. of *rēx*); in early chemistry, antimony, so called because it readily combines with gold (the king of metals); see -ULE]

Reg·u·lus (reg′yə ləs), *n.* **Marcus A·til·i·us** (ə til′ē əs), died 250? B.C., Roman general.

re·gur·gi·tate (ri gûr′ji tāt′), *v.,* **-tat·ed, -tat·ing.** —*v.i.* **1.** to surge or rush back, as liquids, gases, undigested food, etc. —*v.t.* **2.** to cause to surge or rush back; vomit. **3.** to give back or repeat, esp. something not fully understood or assimilated: *to regurgitate the teacher's lectures on the exam.* [1645–55; < ML *regurgitātus* (ptp. of *regurgitāre*), equiv. to *re-* RE- + *gurgit-,* s. of *gurges* whirlpool, flood, stream + *-ātus* -ATE[1]] —**re·gur·gi·tant** (ri gûr′ji tənt), *n.*

re·gur·gi·ta·tion (ri gûr′ji tā′shən), *n.* **1.** the act of regurgitating. **2.** voluntary or involuntary return of partly digested food from the stomach to the mouth. **3.** *Pathol.* the reflux of blood through defective heart valves. [1595–1605; < ML *regurgitātiōn-* (s. of *regurgitātiō*). See REGURGITATE, -ION]

re·hab (rē′hab′), *n., adj., v.,* **-habbed, -hab·bing.** *Informal.* —*n.* **1.** rehabilitation. **2.** a rehabilitated building. —*adj.* **3.** of or pertaining to rehabilitation: *funds for new rehab projects.* —*v.t.* **4.** to rehabilitate. [by shortening] —**re′hab′ber,** *n.*

re·ha·bil·i·tant (rē′hə bil′i tənt, rē′ə-), *n.* a person

CONCISE ETYMOLOGY KEY: <, descended or borrowed from; >, whence; b., blend of, blended; c., cognate with; cf., compare; deriv., derivative; equiv., equivalent; imit., imitative; obl., oblique; r., replacing; s., stem; sp., spelling, spelled; resp., respelling, respelled; trans., translation; ?, origin unknown; *, unattested; ‡, probably earlier than. See the full key inside the front cover.

re·fed′er·al·ize′, *v.,* **-ized, -iz·ing.**
re·fed′er·ate′, *v.,* **-at·ed, -at·ing.**
re′fed·er·a′tion, *n.*
re·feed′, *v.,* **-fed, -feed·ing.**
re·feel′, *v.,* **-felt, -feel·ing.**
re·fence′, *v.t.,* **-fenced, -fenc·ing.**
re·fer′ti·liz′a·ble, *adj.*
re′fer·ti·li·za′tion, *n.*
re·fer′ti·lize′, *v.t.,* **-lized, -liz·ing.**
re·fight′, *v.,* **-fought, -fight·ing.**
re·fig′ure, *v.t.,* **-ured, -ur·ing.**
re·file′, *v.,* **-filed, -fil·ing.**
re·film′, *v.t.*
re·fil′ter, *v.t.*
re·find′, *v.t.,* **-found, -find·ing.**
re·fin′ger, *v.*
re·fire′, *v.,* **-fired, -fir·ing.**
re·fix′, *v.t.,* **-fixed, -fix·ing.**
re·float′, *v.*
re′flo·res′cence, *n.*
re·flow′, *n., v.*
re·flow′er, *v.*
re·fly′, *v.,* **-flew, -flown, -fly·ing.**
re·fly′a·ble, *adj.*
re·fo′cus, *v.,* **-cused, -cus·ing** or (*esp. Brit.*) **-cussed, -cus·sing.**
re·fold′, *v.*
re·fore′cast′, *v.t.,* **-cast** or **-cast·ed, -cast·ing.**
re·for′feit, *v.t.*
re·for′fei·ture, *n.*
re·forge′, *v.t.,* **-forged, -forg·ing.**
re·forge′a·ble, *adj.*

who is undergoing rehabilitation, esp. for a physical disability. [1960–65; REHABILIT(ATE) + -ANT]

re•ha•bil•i•tate (rē′hə bil′i tāt′, rē′ə-), *v.*, **-tat•ed, -tat•ing.** —*v.t.* **1.** to restore to a condition of good health, ability to work, or the like. **2.** to restore to good condition, operation, or management, as a bankrupt business. **3.** to reestablish the good reputation of (a person, one's character or name, etc.). **4.** to restore formally to former capacity, standing, rank, rights, or privileges. —*v.i.* **5.** to undergo rehabilitation. [1570–80; < ML *rehabilitātus,* ptp. of *rehabilitāre* to restore. See RE-, HABILITATE] —**re′ha•bil′i•ta′tion,** *n.* —**re′ha•bil′i•ta′•tive,** *adj.* —**re′ha•bil′i•ta′tor,** *n.*
—**Syn. 2.** salvage, restore, recondition, reconstruct, refurbish.

re•hash (*v.* rē hash′; *n.* rē′hash′), *v.t.* **1.** to work up (old material) in a new form. —*n.* **2.** the act of rehashing. **3.** something rehashed. [1815–25; RE- + HASH]

re•hear•ing (rē hēr′ing), *n. Law.* a second presentation of the evidence and arguments of a case before the court of original presentation. [1680–90; RE- + HEARING]

re•hears•al (ri hûr′səl), *n.* **1.** a session of exercise, drill, or practice, usually private, in preparation for a public performance, ceremony, etc.: *a play rehearsal; a wedding rehearsal.* **2.** the act of rehearsing. **3.** a repeating or relating: *a rehearsal of grievances.* [1350–1400; ME *rehersaille.* See REHEARSE, -AL²]

re•hearse (ri hûrs′), *v.,* **-hearsed, -hears•ing.** —*v.t.* **1.** to practice (a musical composition, a play, a speech, etc.) in private prior to a public presentation. **2.** to drill or train (an actor, musician, etc.) by rehearsal, as for some performance or part. **3.** to relate the facts or particulars of; recount. —*v.i.* **4.** to rehearse a play, part, etc.; participate in a rehearsal. [1300–50; ME *rehersen, rehercen* < MF *rehercier* to repeat, equiv. to *re-* RE- + *hercier* to strike, harrow (deriv. of *herce, herse* a harrow); see HEARSE] —**re•hears′a•ble,** *adj.* —**re•hears′•er,** *n.*
—**Syn. 3.** delineate, describe, portray; narrate, recapitulate. See **relate.**

re•heat•ing (rē hē′ting), *n.* **1.** heating again. **2.** *Aeron.* a process in certain turbojet engines in which gases are expanded by turbines after combustion, burned again in a second chamber, expanded again by additional turbines, and released through the exhaust nozzle. [1720–30; RE- + HEATING]

Rehn•quist (ren′kwist), *n.* **William H(ubbs)** (hubz), born 1924, U.S. jurist: associate justice of the U.S. Supreme Court 1972–86; Chief Justice since 1986.

Re•ho•bo•am (rē′ə bō′əm), *n.* **1.** the successor of Solomon and the first king of Judah, reigned 922?–915? B.C. I Kings 11:43. **2.** (*often l.c.*) a large wine bottle, used esp. for champagne, equivalent to 6 regular bottles or 4.8 liters (5 quarts).

Re•ho′both Beach′ (rə hō′bəth, -bōth), a town in SE Delaware: beach resort. 1754.

re•house (rē houz′), *v.t.,* **-housed, -hous•ing. 1.** to house again. **2.** to provide with new or different housing: *civic programs to rehouse people living in condemned buildings.* [1810–20; RE- + HOUSE]

Re•ho•vot (rə hō′vōt), *n.* a town in central Israel, SE of Tel Aviv. 66,200. Also, **Re•ho′voth, Re•ho•both** (rə hō′bōt).

re•hy•drate (rē hī′drāt), *v.t.,* **-drat•ed, -drat•ing.** to restore moisture or fluid to (something dehydrated). [1920–25; RE- + HYDRATE, on the model of DEHYDRATE] —**re′hy•dra′tion,** *n.*

Reich (rīk; *Ger.* RĪKH), *n.* **1.** (with reference to Germany) empire; realm; nation. **2.** the German state, esp. during the Nazi period. Cf. **First Reich, Second Reich, Third Reich.** [1920–25; < G: kingdom]

Reich (RĪKH), *n.* **Wil•helm** (vil′helm), 1897–1957, Austrian psychoanalyst in the U.S.

Rei•chen•berg (RĪ′KHən berk′), *n.* German name of **Liberec.**

Reichs•bank (rīks′bangk′; *Ger.* RĪKHS′bängk′), *n.* the former German national bank. [< G; see REICH, 's¹, BANK²]

Reichs•füh•rer (RĪKHS′fy′RəR), *n. German.* the title of the chief of the Schutzstaffel. [lit., Reich leader]

reichs•mark (rīks′märk′; *Ger.* RĪKHS′märk′), *n., pl.* **-marks, -mark.** the monetary unit of Germany from November, 1924, until 1948. Cf. **Deutsche mark, mark²** (def. 1), **ostmark.** [1870–75; < G: Reich mark]

reichs•pfen•nig (rīks′fen′ig; *Ger.* RĪKHS′pfen′iKH), *n., pl.* **-pfen•nigs, -pfen•ni•ge** (*Ger.* -pfen′i gə). a former bronze coin of Germany, the 100th part of a reichsmark. [< G: Reich penny]

Reichs•rat (RĪKHS′rät′), *n.* **1.** *Ger. Hist.* the upper house of the parliament during the period of the Second Reich and the Weimar Republic. **2.** *Hist.* the legislature or parliament in the Austrian division of Austria-Hungary. Also, **Reichs′rath′.** [1855–60; < G: Reich council]

Reichs•tag (rīks′täg′; *Ger.* RĪKHS′täk′), *n. Ger. Hist.* the lower house of the parliament during the period of the Second Reich and the Weimar Republic. [< G: Reich diet]

Reich•stein (rīk′stīn′; *Ger.* RĪKH′shtīn′), *n.* **Ta•de•us** (tä dā′o͞os), born 1897, Swiss chemist, born in Poland: Nobel prize for medicine 1950.

reichs•tha•ler (rīks′tä′lər; *Ger.* RĪKHS′tä′ləR), *n., pl.* **-ler, -lers.** a silver thaler of Germany, originally issued in 1566; rix-dollar. [< G *Reichstaler* (archaic sp. *Reichsthaler*) Reich thaler]

Reichs•wehr (rīks′vâr; *Ger.* RĪKHS′vār′), *n.* the 100,000-man army Germany was permitted to maintain under the Versailles Treaty after World War I: the limit was secretly exceeded. [< G, equiv. to *Reich* realm, empire (see REICH) + *-s* gen. ending + *Wehr* defense, weapon]

Reid (rēd), *n.* **1. Sir George Huston,** 1845–1918, Australian statesman, born in Scotland: prime minister 1904–05. **2. Thomas,** 1710–96, Scottish philosopher. **3. White•law** (hwīt′lô′, wīt′-), 1837–1912, U.S. diplomat and journalist. **4.** a male given name, form of **Read.**

Reids•ville (rēdz′vil), *n.* a city in N North Carolina. 12,492.

reif (rēf), *n. Scot. Obs.* **1.** plunder; booty; loot. **2.** robbery; piracy. **3.** the act of seizing booty. [bef. 950; ME (north) *ref,* OE *rēaf;* akin to REAVE¹, BEREAVE]

re•i•fy (rē′ə fī′, rā′-), *v.t.,* **-fied, -fy•ing.** to convert into or regard as a concrete thing: *to reify a concept.* [1850–55; < L *rē(s)* thing + -IFY] —**re′i•fi•ca′tion,** *n.*

reign (rān), *n.* **1.** the period during which a sovereign occupies the throne. **2.** royal rule or authority; sovereignty. **3.** dominating power or influence: *the reign of law.* —*v.i.* **4.** to possess or exercise sovereign power or authority. **5.** to hold the position and name of sovereign without exercising the ruling power. **6.** to have control, rule, or influence of any kind. **7.** to predominate; be prevalent. [1225–75; (n.) ME *reine, regne* < OF *reigne* < L *rēgnum* realm, reign, deriv. of *rēg-* (s. of *rēx*) king; (v.) ME *reinen, regnen* < OF *reignier* < L *rēgnāre,* deriv. of *rēgnum*]
—**Syn. 2.** dominion, suzerainty. **4.** rule, govern, prevail. —**Ant. 4.** obey.

Reign′ of Ter′ror, 1. a period of the French Revolution, from about March, 1793, to July, 1794, during which many persons were ruthlessly executed by the ruling faction. **2.** (*l.c.*) any period or situation of ruthless administration or oppression.

Reik (rīk; *Ger.* RĪK), *n.* **The•o•dor** (thē′ə dôr′, -dōr′; *Ger.* tā′ô dôR′), 1888–1969, U.S. psychologist and author, born in Austria.

re•im•burse (rē′im bûrs′), *v.t.,* **-bursed, -burs•ing. 1.** to make repayment to for expense or loss incurred: *The insurance company reimbursed him for his losses in the fire.* **2.** to pay back; refund; repay. [1605–15; RE- + obs. *imburse* to put into a purse, pay < ML *imbursāre,* equiv. to L *im-* IM-¹ + ML *-bursāre,* deriv. of *bursa* PURSE, bag] —**re′im•burs′a•ble,** *adj.* —**re′im•burse′ment,** *n.* —**re′im•burs′er,** *n.*
—**Syn. 1.** recompense, remunerate, indemnify, redress, recoup.

re•im•plant (rē′im plant′, -plänt′), *v.t. Surg.* to restore (a tooth, organ, limb, or other structure) to its original site. [1915–20; RE- + IMPLANT]

re•im•plan•ta•tion (rē′im plan tā′shən), *n.* the surgical restoration of a tooth, organ, limb, or other structure to its original site. [1670–80; RE- + IMPLANTATION]

re•im•port (rē′im pôrt′, -pōrt′), *v.t.* to import back into the country of exportation. [1735–45; RE- + IMPORT] —**re′im•por•ta′tion,** *n.*

re•im•pres•sion (rē′im presh′ən), *n.* **1.** a second or repeated impression. **2.** a reprinting or a reprint. [1610–20; RE- + IMPRESSION]

Reims (rēmz; *Fr.* RANS), *n.* a city in NE France: cathedral; unconditional surrender of Germany May 7, 1945. 183,610. Also, **Rheims.**

rein (rān), *n.* **1.** Often, **reins.** a leather strap, fastened to each end of the bit of a bridle, by which the rider or driver controls a horse or other animal by pulling so as to exert pressure on the bit. See illus. under **harness. 2.** any of certain other straps or thongs forming part of a harness, as a checkrein. **3.** any means of curbing, controlling, or directing; check; restraint. **4. reins,** the controlling or directing power: *the reins of government.* **5. draw rein,** to curtail one's speed or progress; halt: *The rider saw the snake and drew rein sharply.* **6. give rein to,** to give complete freedom to; indulge freely: *to give rein to one's imagination.* Also, **give free rein to, give full rein to.** —*v.t.* **7.** to check or guide (a horse or other animal) by exerting pressure on a bridle bit by means of the reins. **8.** to curb; restrain; control. —*v.i.* **9.** to obey the reins: *a horse that reins well.* **10.** to rein a horse or other animal. [1300–50; (n.) ME *rene, reine, raine* < OF *re(s)ne* < VL **retina,* n. deriv. of L *retinēre* to hold back, RETAIN; (v.) ME *rainen, reinen,* deriv. of the n.] —**rein′•less,** *adj.*
—**Syn. 8.** check, bridle, limit.

re•in•car•nate (*v.* rē′in kär′nāt; *adj.* rē′in kär′nit, -nāt), *v.,* **-nat•ed, -nat•ing,** *adj.* —*v.t.* **1.** to give another body to; incarnate again. —*adj.* **2.** incarnate anew. [1855–60; RE- + INCARNATE]

re•in•car•na•tion (rē′in kär nā′shən), *n.* **1.** the belief that the soul, upon death of the body, comes back to earth in another body or form. **2.** rebirth of the soul in a new body. **3.** a new incarnation or embodiment, as of a person. [1855–60; RE- + INCARNATION] —**re′in•car•na′tion•ist,** *n.*

rein•deer (rān′dēr′), *n., pl.* **-deer,** (*occasionally*) **-deers.** any of several large deer of the genus *Rangifer,* of northern and arctic regions of Europe, Asia, and North America, both male and female of which have antlers. [1350–1400; ME *raynder(e)* < ON *hreindȳri,* equiv. to *hreinn* reindeer + *dȳr* animal (c. DEER)]

European reindeer, *Rangifer tarandus,* 4½ ft. (1.4 m) high at shoulder; length 5½ ft. (1.7 m)

Rein′deer Lake′, a lake in central Canada, in NE Saskatchewan and NW Manitoba. 2444 sq. mi. (6330 sq. km).

rein′deer moss′, any of several lichens of the genus *Cladonia,* esp. the gray, many-branched *C. rangiferina,* of arctic and subarctic regions, eaten by reindeer and caribou. [1745–55]

re•in•dus•tri•al•i•za•tion (rē′in dus′trē ə li zā′shən), *n.* the revitalization of an industry or industrial society through government aid and tax incentives, modernization of factories and machinery, etc. [RE- + INDUSTRIALIZATION]

re•in•dus•tri•al•ize (rē′in dus′trē ə līz′), *v.,* **-ized, -iz•ing.** —*v.t.* **1.** to subject to reindustrialization. —*v.i.* **2.** to undergo reindustrialization. Also, *esp. Brit.,* **re′in•dus′tri•al•ise′.** [RE- + INDUSTRIALIZE] —**re′in•dus′tri•al•iz′er,** *n.*

Rei•neck•e (RĪ′ni kə), *n.* **Carl Hein•rich Car•sten** (kärl′ hīn′RIKH kär′stən), 1824–1910, German pianist, conductor, composer, and teacher.

Rei•ner (rī′nər), *n.* **Fritz,** 1888–1963, Hungarian conductor in the U.S.

re•in•force (rē′in fôrs′, -fōrs′), *v.,* **-forced, -forc•ing,** *n.* —*v.t.* **1.** to strengthen with some added piece, support, or material: *to reinforce a wall.* **2.** to strengthen (a military force) with additional personnel, ships, or aircraft: *to reinforce a garrison.* **3.** to strengthen; make more forcible or effective: *to reinforce efforts.* **4.** to augment; increase: *to reinforce a supply.* **5.** *Psychol.* to strengthen the probability of (a response to a given stimulus) by giving or withholding a reward. —*n.* **6.** something that reinforces. **7.** a metal band on the rear part of the bore of a gun, where the explosion occurs. Also, **reenforce, re-enforce.** [1590–1600; RE- + *inforce,* alter. of ENFORCE] —**re′in•forc′er,** *n.*

re′inforced con′crete, concrete containing steel bars, strands, mesh, etc., to absorb tensile and shearing stresses. [1900–05]

re•in•force•ment (rē′in fôrs′mənt, -fōrs′-), *n.* **1.** the act of reinforcing. **2.** the state of being reinforced. **3.** something that reinforces or strengthens. **4.** Often, **reinforcements.** an additional supply of personnel, ships, aircraft, etc., for a military force. **5.** a system of steel bars, strands, wires, or mesh for absorbing the tensile and shearing stresses in concrete work. **6.** *Psychol.* **a.** a procedure, as a reward or punishment, that alters a response to a stimulus. **b.** the act of reinforcing a response. [1600–10; REINFORCE + -MENT]

reinforce′ment ther′apy, *Psychol.* a behavior modification technique in which appropriate behavior is strengthened through systematic reinforcement.

Rein•hardt (rīn′härt; *Ger.* RĪN′härt), *n.* **Max** (maks; *Ger.* mäks), (*Max Goldmann*), 1873–1943, German theatrical director, producer, and actor; born in Austria.

Rein•hold (rīn′hōld), *n.* a male given name.

reins (rānz), *n.pl.* **1.** the kidneys. **2.** the region of the kidneys, or the lower part of the back. **3.** (esp. in Biblical use) the seat of the feelings or affections, formerly identified with the kidneys. [bef. 1000; ME *reines, reenes* < OF *reins;* cf. OE (once) *rēnys;* both < L *rēnēs* kidneys, loins (pl.); cf. RENAL]

reins•man (rānz′mən), *n., pl.* **-men.** a person who rides or drives horses, esp. a skillful one, as a jockey or harness driver. [1850–55; REIN + -s³ + -MAN]

re•in•state (rē′in stāt′), *v.t.,* **-stat•ed, -stat•ing.** to put back or establish again, as in a former position or state: *to reinstate the ousted chairman.* [1620–30; RE- + INSTATE] —**re′in•state′ment, re′in•sta′tion,** *n.* —**re′•in•sta′tor,** *n.*

re•in•sur•ance (rē′in sho͝or′əns, -shûr′-), *n.* the process or business of reinsuring. [1745–55; RE- + INSURANCE]

re•in•sure (rē′in sho͝or′, -shûr′), *v.t.,* **-sured, -sur•ing. 1.** to insure again. **2.** *Insurance.* to insure under a contract by which a first insurer is relieved of part or all of the risk, which devolves upon another insurer. [1745–55; RE- + INSURE] —**re′in•sur′er,** *n.*

CONCISE PRONUNCIATION KEY: *act, cāpe, dâre, pärt; set, ēqual; if, īce; ox, ōver, ôrder, oil, bo͝ok, bo͞ot, out; up, ûrge; child; sing; shoe; thin, that;* zh as in *treasure.* ə = *a* as in *alone, e* as in *system, i* as in *easily, o* as in *gallop, u* as in *circus;* ᵊ as in *fire* (fīᵊr), *hour* (ouᵊr). l and n can serve as syllabic consonants, as in *cradle* (krād′l), and *button* (but′n). See the full key inside the front cover.

re•for′mat, *v.,* **-mat•ted, -mat•ting.**
re′for•ti•fi•ca′tion, *n.*
re•for′ti•fy′, *v.t.,* **-fied, -fy•ing.**
re•for′ward, *v.t.*
re•found′, *v.t.*
re•frac′tur•a•ble, *adj.*
re•frac′ture, *v.,* **-tured, -tur•ing.**
re•frame′, *v.t.,* **-framed, -fram•ing.**
re•freez′a•ble, *adj.*
re•freeze′, *v.,* **-froze, -fro•zen, -freez•ing.**
re•frus′trate, *v.t.,* **-trat•ed, -trat•ing.**
re•fry′, *v.,* **-fried, -fry•ing.**
re•func′tion, *v.i.*
re•fur′nish, *v.t.*
re′gal•va•ni•za′tion, *n.*
re•gal′va•nize′, *v.t.,* **-nized, -niz•ing.**
re•gam′ble, *v.,* **-bled, -bling.**
re•gar′ment, *v.t.*
re•gar′nish, *v.t.*
re•gar′ri•son, *v.t.*
re•gath′er, *v.*
re•gauge′, *v.t.,* **-gauged, -gaug•ing.**
re•gear′, *v.*
re•gel′, *v.i.,* **-gelled, -gel•ling.**
re•ger′mi•nate′, *v.,* **-nat•ed, -nat•ing.**
re′ger•mi•na′tion, *n.*
re•ger′mi•na′tive, *adj.;* **-ly,** *adv.*
re•gild′, *v.t.,* **-gild•ed** or **-gilt, -gild•ing.**
re•gird′, *v.t.,* **-gird•ed,** or **-girt, -gird•ing.**
re•give′, *v.* **-gave, -giv•en, -giv•ing.**

re•in•te•gra•tion (rē in′tə grā′shən, rē′in-), *n.* **1.** restoration to a unified state. **2.** *Psychiatry.* the process of returning the mind to an integrated state after it has been deranged by psychosis. **3.** *Psychol.* **a.** the process of recalling an entire memory from a partial cue, as remembering a speech upon hearing the first few words. **b.** the tendency to repeat the response to a complex stimulus on later experiencing any part of that stimulus. [1595–1605; RE- + INTEGRATION]

re•in•vent (rē′in vent′), *v.t.* to invent again or anew, esp. without knowing that the invention already exists. [1685–90; RE- + INVENT] —**re′in•ven′tion,** *n.*

reis (rās; *Port.* Rās), *n.pl., sing.* **re•al** (rā äl′; *Port.* Re-äl′). a former money of account of Portugal and Brazil. Cf. **milreis.** [1545–55; < Pg, pl. of *real* REAL[2]]

re•is•sue (rē ish′o͞o *or, esp. Brit.,* -is′yo͞o), *n., v.,* **-sued, -su•ing.** —*n.* **1.** something that is issued again, as a book or a motion picture. **2.** an official reprinting of a postage stamp after the original printing has been stopped. —*v.t.* **3.** to issue again. —*v.i.* **4.** to come forth or flow out again. [1610–20; RE- + ISSUE] —**re•is′su•a•ble,** *adj.*

reist (Rēst), *v.i. Scot. and North Eng.* reest[2].

Reis•ters•town (rī′stərz toun′), *n.* a city in N Maryland. 19,385.

REIT (rēt), *n.* real-estate investment trust.

re•it•er•ant (rē it′ər ənt), *adj.* reiterating or repeating, esp. to an intensified degree: *reiterant chatter.* [1600–10; < L *reiterant-* (s. of *reiterāns*), prp. of *reiterāre.* See REITERATE, -ANT]

re•it•er•ate (rē it′ə rāt′), *v.t.,* **-at•ed, -at•ing.** to say or do again or repeatedly; repeat, often excessively. [1520–30; < L *reiterātus,* ptp. of *reiterāre* to repeat, equiv. to *re-* RE- + *iterāre* to repeat, deriv. of *iterum* again; see -ATE[1]] —**re•it′er•a•ble,** *adj.* —**re•it′er•a′tion,** *n.* —**re•it•er•a•tive** (rē it′ə rā′tiv, -ər ə tiv), *adj.*
—**Syn.** See **repeat.**

Rei′ter's syn′drome (rī′tərz), *Pathol.* a disease of unknown cause, occurring primarily in adult males, marked by urethritis, conjunctivitis, and arthritis. Also called **Rei′ter's disease′.** [after Hans Conrad Julius *Reiter* (1881–1969), German bacteriologist, who described it in 1916]

reive (rēv), *v.t., v.i.,* **reived, reiv•ing.** *Chiefly Scot.* to rob; plunder. [1860–65; var. of REAVE[1]] —**reiv′er,** *n.*

Ré•jane (Rā zhan′), *n.* (*Gabrielle-Charlotte Réju*), 1856–1920, French actress.

re•ject (*v.* ri jekt′; *n.* rē′jekt), *v.t.* **1.** to refuse to have, take, recognize, etc.: *to reject a job offer.* **2.** to refuse to grant (a request, demand, etc.). **3.** to refuse to accept (someone or something); rebuff: *The other children rejected him. The publisher rejected the author's latest novel.* **4.** to discard as useless or unsatisfactory: *The mind rejects painful memories.* **5.** to cast out or eject; vomit. **6.** to cast out or off. **7.** *Med.* (of a human or other animal) to have an immunological reaction against (a transplanted organ or grafted tissue): *reject the graft.* —*n.* **8.** something rejected, as an imperfect article. [1485–95; (v.) < L *rējectus,* ptp. of *rējicere* to throw back, equiv. to *re-* RE- + *jec-,* comb. form of *jacere* to throw + *-tus* ptp. suffix] —**re•ject′a•ble,** *adj.* —**re•ject′er,** *n.* —**re•jec′tive,** *adj.*
—**Syn. 1.** See **refuse[1]. 1, 2.** deny. **3.** repel, renounce. **4.** eliminate, jettison. **8.** second.

re•jec•ta•men•ta (ri jek′tə men′tə), *n.pl.* things or matter rejected as useless or worthless. [1810–20; < NL *rējectāmenta* things thrown back (pl. of *rējectāmentum*), equiv. to L *rējectā(re)* (freq. of *rējicere* to REJECT) + *-mentum* -MENT]

re•ject•ee (ri jek tē′, -jek′tē, rē′jek tē′), *n.* a person who is or has been rejected, esp. for military service. [1940–45, *Amer.*; REJECT + -EE]

re•jec•tion (ri jek′shən), *n.* **1.** the act or process of rejecting. **2.** the state of being rejected. **3.** something that is rejected. [1545–55; < L *rējectiōn-* (s. of *rējectiō*) a throwing back, equiv. to *rēject(us)* (see REJECT) + *-iōn-* -ION]
—**Syn. 1, 2.** refusal, spurning, dismissal, elimination.

re•jec•tion•ist (ri jek′shə nist), *n.* **1.** an Arab leader or country that opposes accommodation or compromise in negotiations with Israel. **2.** any person or group that refuses to compromise in a dispute. —*adj.* **3.** of or pertaining to rejectionists. [1975–80; REJECTION + -IST] —**re•jec′tion•ism,** *n.*

rejec′tion re′gion, *Statistics.* the set of values of a test statistic for which the null hypothesis is rejected. Cf. **acceptance region.**

rejec′tion slip′, a notification of rejection, attached by a publisher to a manuscript before returning the work to its author. [1905–10]

rejec′tive art′. See **minimal art.** Also, **Rejec′tive Art′.** [1965–70]

re•jig•ger (rē jig′ər), *v.t. Informal.* to rearrange in a new or different way, esp. by the use of techniques not always considered ethical. [1940–45; RE- + JIGGER[1]]

re•joice (ri jois′), *v.,* **-joiced, -joic•ing.** —*v.i.* **1.** to be glad; take delight (often fol. by *in*): *to rejoice in another's happiness.* —*v.t.* **2.** to make joyful; gladden: *a song to rejoice the heart.* [1275–1325; ME *rejoicen* < OF *rejouiss-,* long s. of *rejouir,* equiv. to *re-* RE- + *jouir* to *rejoice;* see JOY] —**re•joice′ful,** *adj.* —**re•joic′er,** *n.*
—**Syn. 1.** revel, exult, glory.

re•joic•ing (ri joi′sing), *n.* **1.** the act of a person who rejoices. **2.** the feeling or the expression of joy. **3.** Often, **rejoicings.** an occasion for expressing joy. [1325–75; ME; see REJOICE, -ING[1]] —**re•joic′ing•ly,** *adv.*
—**Syn. 1.** celebration, merrymaking.

re•join[1] (rē join′), *v.t.* **1.** to come again into the company of: *to rejoin a party after a brief absence.* **2.** to join together again; reunite. —*v.i.* **3.** to become joined together again. [1535–45; RE- + JOIN]

re•join[2] (ri join′), *v.t.* **1.** to say in answer; reply, esp. to counterreply. —*v.i.* **2.** to answer; reply, esp. to counterreply. **3.** *Law.* to answer a plaintiff's replication. [1425–75; late ME *rejoinen* < AF *rejoyner,* var. of MF *rejoindre,* equiv. to *re-* RE- + *joindre* to JOIN]
—**Syn. 2.** respond, retort.

re•join•der (ri join′dər), *n.* **1.** an answer to a reply; response. **2.** *Law.* a defendant's answer to a plaintiff's replication. [1475–85; < MF *rejoindre* (n. use of inf.); see REJOIN[2]]
—**Syn. 1.** reply, riposte. See **answer.**

re•ju•ve•nate (ri jo͞o′və nāt′), *v.,* **-nat•ed, -nat•ing.** —*v.t.* **1.** to make young again; restore to youthful vigor, appearance, etc.: *That vacation has certainly rejuvenated him.* **2.** to restore to a former state; make fresh or new again: *to rejuvenate an old sofa.* **3.** *Physical Geog.* **a.** to renew the activity, erosive power, etc., of (a stream) by uplift or by removal of a barrier in the stream bed. **b.** to impress again the characters of youthful topography on (a region) by the action of rejuvenated streams. —*v.i.* **4.** to undergo rejuvenation; revive. [1800–10; RE- + L *juven(is)* YOUNG + -ATE[1]] —**re•ju′ve•na′tion,** *n.* —**re•ju′ve•na′tive,** *adj.* —**re•ju′ve•na′tor,** *n.*

re•ju•ve•nes•cent (ri jo͞o′və nes′ənt), *adj.* **1.** becoming young again. **2.** making young again; rejuvenating. [1755–65; < ML *rejuvenēsc(ere)* to become young again (L *re-* RE- + *juven(is)* YOUNG + *-ēsc-* inceptive suffix + *-ere* inf. suffix) + -ENT] —**re•ju′ve•nes′cence,** *n.*

re•ju•ve•nize (ri jo͞o′və nīz′), *v.t.,* **-nized, -niz•ing.** to rejuvenate. Also, *esp. Brit.,* **re•ju′ve•nise′.** [1810–20; RE- + L *juven(is)* YOUNG + -IZE]

re•key (rē kē′), *v.t.,* **-keyed, -key•ing. 1.** to fit with different pins and a different key. **2.** *Computers.* to keyboard (data) again. [RE- + KEY[1]]

-rel, a noun suffix having a diminutive or pejorative force: *wastrel.* Also, **-erel.** [ME < OF *-erel, -erelle*]

rel., 1. relating. **2.** relative. **3.** relatively. **4.** released. **5.** religion. **6.** religious.

re•la•dle (rē lād′l), *v.t.,* **-dled, -dling.** *Metall.* to mix (molten alloy steel) by pouring from ladle to ladle. [RE- + LADLE]

re•laid (rē lād′), *v.* pt. and pp. of **re-lay.**

re•lapse (*v.* ri laps′; *n.* ri laps′, rē′laps), *v.,* **-lapsed, -laps•ing,** *n.* —*v.i.* **1.** to fall or slip back into a former state, practice, etc.: *to relapse into silence.* **2.** to fall back into illness after convalescence or apparent recovery. **3.** to fall back into vice, wrongdoing, or error; backslide: *to relapse into heresy.* —*n.* **4.** an act or instance of relapsing. **5.** a return of a disease or illness after partial recovery from it. [1400–50; (v.) late ME < L *relāpsus,* ptp. of *relābī* to slide back, revert (*re-* RE- + *lāb-* v. stem + *-sus* for *-tus* ptp. suffix); (n.) late ME < ML *relāpsus,* equiv. to L *relāb(ī)* + *-sus* for *-tus* suffix of v. action] —**re•laps′a•ble,** *adj.* —**re•laps′er,** *n.*
—**Syn. 3.** regress, revert, lapse.

relaps′ing fe′ver, *Pathol.* one of a group of fevers characterized by relapses, occurring in many tropical countries, and caused by several species of spirochetes transmitted by several species of lice and ticks. Also called **recurrent fever.** [1840–50]

re•late (ri lāt′), *v.,* **-lat•ed, -lat•ing.** —*v.t.* **1.** to tell; give an account of (an event, circumstance, etc.). **2.** to bring into or establish association, connection, or relation: *to relate events to probable causes.* —*v.i.* **3.** to have reference (often fol. by *to*). **4.** to have some relation (often fol. by *to*). **5.** to establish a social or sympathetic relationship with a person or thing: *two sisters unable to relate to each other.* [1480–90; < L *relātus,* suppletive ptp. of *referre* to carry back (see REFER)] —**re•lat′a•bil′i•ty,** *n.* —**re•lat′a•ble,** *adj.* —**re•lat′er,** *n.*
—**Syn. 1.** narrate, delineate, detail, repeat. RELATE, RECITE, RECOUNT, REHEARSE mean to tell, report, or describe in some detail an occurrence or circumstance. To RELATE is to give an account of happenings, events, circumstances, etc.: *to relate one's adventures.* To RECITE may mean to give details consecutively, but more often applies to the repetition from memory of something learned with verbal exactness: *to recite a poem.* To RECOUNT is usually to set forth consecutively the details of an occurrence, argument, experience, etc., to give an account in detail: *to recount an unpleasant experience.* REHEARSE implies some formality and exactness in telling, sometimes with repeated performance as for practice before final delivery: *to rehearse one's side of a story.*

re•lat•ed (ri lā′tid), *adj.* **1.** associated; connected. **2.** allied by nature, origin, kinship, marriage, etc. **3.** narrated. **4.** *Music.* (of tones) belonging to a melodic or harmonic series, so as to be susceptible of close connection. [1595–1605; RELATE + -ED[2]] —**re•lat′ed•ness,** *n.*
—**Syn. 1.** relevant, affiliated. **2.** linked, united.

re•la•tion (ri lā′shən), *n.* **1.** an existing connection; a significant association between or among things: *the relation between cause and effect.* **2. relations, a.** the various connections between peoples, countries, etc.: *foreign relations.* **b.** the various connections in which persons are brought together: *business and social relations.* **c.** sexual intercourse. **3.** the mode or kind of connection between one person and another, between an individual and God, etc. **4.** connection between persons by blood or marriage. **5.** a person who is related by blood or marriage; relative: *his wife's relations.* **6.** the act of relating, narrating, or telling; narration. **7.** *Law.* a principle whereby effect is given to an act done at one time as if it had been done at a previous time. **8.** *Math.* **a.** a property that associates two quantities in a definite order, as equality or inequality. **b.** a single- or multiple-valued function. **9. in** or **with relation to,** with reference to; concerning: *It's best to plan with relation to anticipated changes.* [1350–1400; ME *relacion* < L *relātiōn-* (s. of *relātiō*). See RELATE, -ION] —**re•la′tion•less,** *adj.*
—**Syn. 1.** relationship; tie, link. **2a, b.** association. **4.** relationship, kinship. **6.** recitation, recital, description. —**Ant. 1.** independence.

re•la•tion•al (ri lā′shə nl), *adj.* **1.** of or pertaining to relations. **2.** indicating or specifying some relation. **3.** *Gram.* serving to indicate relations between various elements in a sentence, as prepositions, conjunctions, etc. Cf. **notional** (def. 6). [1655–65; RELATION + -AL[1]]

rela′tional da′tabase, an electronic database comprising multiple files of related information, usu. stored in tables of rows (records) and columns (fields) and allowing a link to be established between separate files that have a matching field, as a column of invoice numbers, so that the two files can be queried simultaneously by the user. [1970–75]

re•la•tion•ship (ri lā′shən ship′), *n.* **1.** a connection, association, or involvement. **2.** connection between persons by blood or marriage. **3.** an emotional or other connection between people: *the relationship between teachers and students.* **4.** a sexual involvement; affair. [1735–45; RELATION + -SHIP]
—**Syn. 1.** dependence, alliance, kinship. **2.** affinity, consanguinity. RELATIONSHIP, KINSHIP refer to connection with others by blood or by marriage. RELATIONSHIP can be applied to connection either by birth or by marriage: *relationship to a ruling family.* KINSHIP generally denotes common descent and implies a more intimate connection than relationship: *the ties and obligations of kinship.*

rel•a•tive (rel′ə tiv), *n.* **1.** a person who is connected with another or others by blood or marriage. **2.** something having, or standing in, some relation to something else. **3.** something dependent upon external conditions for its specific nature, size, etc. (opposed to *absolute*). **4.** *Gram.* a relative pronoun, adjective, or adverb. —*adj.* **5.** considered in relation to something else; comparative: *the relative merits of democracy and monarchy.* **6.** existing or having its specific nature only by relation to something else; not absolute or independent: *Happiness is relative.* **7.** having relation or connection. **8.** having reference or regard; relevant; pertinent (usually fol. by *to*): *to determine the facts relative to an accident.* **9.** correspondent; proportionate: *Value is relative to demand.* **10.** (of a term, name, etc.) depending for significance upon something else: *"Better" is a relative term.* **11.** *Gram.* **a.** noting or pertaining to a word that introduces a subordinate clause of which it is, or is a part of, the subject or predicate and that refers to an expressed or implied element of the principal clause (the antecedent), as the relative pronoun *who* in *He's the man who saw you* or the relative adverb *where* in *This is the house where she was born.* **b.** noting or pertaining to a relative clause. [1350–1400; ME *relatif* (n.) (< MF) < LL *relātīvus* (adj.); see RELATE, -IVE]
—**Usage. 11.** See **who.**

rel′ative ap′erture, *Optics.* the ratio of the diameter of a lens, esp. a camera lens, to the focal length; the reciprocal of the f number or focal ratio of the lens.

rel′ative bear′ing, *Navig.* the bearing of an object, relative to the heading of a vessel or aircraft.

rel′ative clause′, a subordinate clause introduced by a relative pronoun, adjective, or adverb, either expressed or deleted, esp. such a clause modifying an antecedent, as *who saw you* in *He's the man who saw you* or *(that) I wrote* in *Here's the letter (that) I wrote.* Cf. **definite relative clause, indefinite relative clause.**

rel′ative com′plement, *Math.* the set of elements contained in a given set that are not elements of another specified set. Also called **difference.**

rel′ative den′sity, *Physics.* See **specific gravity.** [1875–80]

rel′ative depriva′tion, *Sociol.* the perception of an unfair disparity between one's situation and that of others. [1945–50]

rel′ative disper′sion, *Optics.* See **Abbe number.**

rel′ative fre′quency, *Statistics.* the ratio of the number of times an event occurs to the number of occasions on which it might occur in the same period.

rel′ative humid′ity, the amount of water vapor in the air, expressed as a percentage of the maximum amount that the air could hold at the given temperature; the ratio of the actual water vapor pressure to the saturation vapor pressure. *Abbr.:* RH, rh Also called **humidity.** Cf. **absolute humidity, dew point, mixing ratio, specific humidity.** [1810–20]

rel′ative imped′iment, *Law.* a fact or circum-

CONCISE ETYMOLOGY KEY: <, descended or borrowed from; >, whence; b., blend of, blended; c., cognate with; cf., compare; deriv., derivative; equiv., equivalent; imit., imitative; obl., oblique; r., replacing; s., stem; sp., spelling, spelled; resp., respelling, respelled; trans., translation; ?, origin unknown; *, unattested; ‡, probably earlier than. See the full key inside the front cover.

re•glaze′, *v.t.,* **-glazed, -glaz•ing.**
re′glo•ri•fi•ca′tion, *n.*
re•glo′ri•fy′, *v.t.,* **-fied, -fy•ing.**
re•glue′, *v.t.,* **-glued, -glu•ing.**
re•gov′ern, *v.t.*
re•gov′ern•ment, *n.*
re•grab′, *v.t.,* **-grabbed, -grab•bing.**
re•gra′date, *v.,* **-dat•ed, -dat•ing.**
re′gra•da′tion, *n.*
re•grade′, *v.t.,* **-grad•ed, -grad•ing.**
re•graft′, *v.*
re•grant′, *v.t., n.*
re•graph′, *v.t.*
re•grasp′, *v.t.*
re•grease′, *v.t.,* **-greased, -greas•ing.**
re•grind′, *v.,* **-ground, -grind•ing.**
re•grip′, *v.,* **-gripped** or **-gript, -grip•ping.**
re•groom′, *v.t.*
re•groove′, *v.t.,* **-grooved, -groov•ing.**
re•grow′, *v.,* **-grew, -grown, -grow•ing.**
re•growth′, *n.*
re′guar•an•tee′, *n., v.t.,* **-teed, -tee•ing.**
re•guar′an•ty′, *n., pl.* **-ties.**
re•guide′, *v.t.,* **-guid•ed, -guid•ing.**
re•ham′mer, *v.t.*
re•han′dle, *v.t.,* **-dled, -dling.**
re•hang′, *v.t.,* **-hung** or **-hanged, -hang•ing.**
re•hard′en, *v.*

stance that disqualifies from lawful marriage persons who are closely related.

rel′ative in′dex of refrac′tion, *Optics.* See under **index of refraction.**

rel·a·tive·ly (rel′ə tiv lē), *adv.* **1.** in a relative manner: *a relatively small difference.* **2.** *Archaic.* **a.** with reference (usually fol. by *to*). **b.** in proportion (usually fol. by *to*). [1555–65; RELATIVE + -LY]

rel′atively prime′ num′bers, *Math.* two numbers whose greatest common divisor is 1.

rel′ative ma′jor, *Music.* the major key whose tonic is the third degree of a given minor key. [1840–50]

rel′ative max′imum, *Math.* maximum (def. 4a).

rel′ative min′imum, *Math.* minimum (def. 5a).

rel′ative mi′nor, *Music.* the minor key whose tonic is the sixth degree of a given major key. [1810–20]

rel·a·tive·ness (rel′ə tiv nis), *n.* the state or fact of being relative. [1665–75; RELATIVE + -NESS]

rel′ative permittiv′ity, *Elect.* permittivity.

rel′ative pitch′, *Music.* **1.** the pitch of a tone as determined by its relationship to other tones in a scale. **2.** the ability to identify or sing a tone by mentally determining the distance of its pitch from that of a tone already sounded. Cf. **absolute pitch.** [1925–30]

rel′ative pro′noun, one of the pronouns *who, whom, which, what,* their compounds with *-ever* or *-soever,* or *that* used as the subordinating word to introduce a subordinate clause, esp. such a pronoun referring to an antecedent. Cf. **definite relative pronoun, indefinite relative pronoun.** [1520–30]
—Usage. See **who.**

rel′ative sun′spot num′ber, *Astron.* See **Wolf number.**

rel′ative topol′ogy, *Math.* a topology of a subset of a topological space, obtained by intersecting the subset with every open set in the topology of the space. Also called **induced topology, subspace topology.**

rel′ative wind′ (wind), the velocity or direction of airflow with respect to the body it surrounds, esp. an airfoil. [1915–20]

rel·a·tiv·ism (rel′ə tə viz′əm), *n. Philos.* any theory holding that criteria of judgment are relative, varying with individuals and their environments. [1860–65; RELATIVE + -ISM]

rel·a·tiv·ist (rel′ə tə vist), *n.* an adherent or advocate of relativism or of the principle of relativity. [1860–65; RELATIVE + -IST]

rel·a·tiv·is·tic (rel′ə tə vis′tik), *adj.* **1.** of or pertaining to relativity or relativism. **2.** *Physics.* **a.** subject to the special or the general theory of relativity. **b.** (of a velocity) having a magnitude that is a significant fraction of the speed of light. **c.** (of a particle) having a relativistic velocity: *radiation from relativistic electrons.* [1885–90; RELATIVIST + -IC] **—rel′a·tiv·is′ti·cal·ly,** *adv.*

rel′ativis′tic mass′, *Physics.* the mass of a body in motion relative to the observer: it is equal to the rest mass multiplied by a factor that is greater than 1 and that increases as the magnitude of the velocity increases.

rel′ativis′tic quan′tum mechan′ics, *Physics.* quantum mechanics based on a wave equation satisfying the mathematical requirements of the special theory of relativity and applying to particles of any velocity. [1935–40]

rel·a·tiv·i·ty (rel′ə tiv′i tē), *n.* **1.** the state or fact of being relative. **2.** *Physics.* a theory, formulated essentially by Albert Einstein, that all motion must be defined relative to a frame of reference and that space and time are relative, rather than absolute concepts: it consists of two principal parts. The theory dealing with uniform motion (**special theory of relativity** or **special relativity**) is based on the two postulates that physical laws have the same mathematical form when expressed in any inertial system, and the velocity of light is independent of the motion of its source and will have the same value when measured by observers moving with constant velocity with respect to each other. Derivable from these postulates are the conclusions that there can be no motion at a speed greater than that of light in a vacuum, mass increases as velocity increases, mass and energy are equivalent, and time is dependent on the relative motion of an observer measuring the time. The theory dealing with gravity (**general theory of relativity** or **general relativity**) is based on the postulate that the local effects of a gravitational field and of acceleration of an inertial system are identical. **3.** dependence of a mental state or process upon the nature of the human mind: *relativity of values; relativity of knowledge.* [1825–35; RELATIVE + -ITY]

rel·a·tiv·ize (rel′ə tə vīz′), *v.t.,* **-ized, -iz·ing.** to regard as or make relative. Also, *esp. Brit.,* **rel′a·tiv·ise′.** [1930–35; RELATIVE + -IZE] **—rel′a·tiv·i·za′tion,** *n.*

re·la·tor (ri lā′tər), *n.* **1.** a person who relates or tells; narrator. **2.** *Law.* **a.** a private person on whose suggestion or complaint certain writs, as a quo warranto, are issued and whose position is analogous to that of a plaintiff. **b.** a party in interest who is allowed to institute a proceeding in the name of a public official when the right to sue rests exclusively in that official. [1585–95; < L *relātor* a proposer, mover. See RELATE, -TOR]

re·lax (ri laks′), *v.t.* **1.** to make less tense, rigid, or firm; make lax: *to relax the muscles.* **2.** to diminish the force of. **3.** to slacken or abate, as effort, attention, etc. **4.** to make less strict or severe, as rules, discipline, etc.: *to relax the requirements for a license.* **5.** to release or bring relief from the effects of tension, anxiety, etc.: *A short swim always relaxes me.* **—*v.i.*** **6.** to become less tense, rigid, or firm. **7.** to become less strict or severe; grow milder. **8.** to reduce or stop work, effort, application, etc., esp. for the sake of rest or recreation. **9.** to release oneself from inhibition, worry, tension, etc. [1350–1400; ME *relaxen* < L *relaxāre* to stretch out again, loosen, equiv. to *re-* RE- + *laxāre* to loosen, deriv. of *laxus* slack, LAX] **—re·lax′a·tive, re·lax·a·tory** (ri lak′sə tôr′ē, -tōr′ē), *adj.* **—re·lax′er,** *n.*
—Syn. 1, 6. loosen, slacken. **2.** mitigate, weaken, lessen, reduce. **4.** ease. **6.** unbend. **7.** relent, soften. **—Ant. 1, 6.** tighten, tense.

re·lax·ant (ri lak′sənt), *adj.* **1.** of, pertaining to, or causing a relaxation. **—*n.*** **2.** *Pharm.* a drug that relaxes, esp. one that lessens strain in muscle. [1765–75; < L *relaxant-* (s. of *relaxāns*), prp. of *relaxāre.* See RELAX, -ANT]

re·lax·a·tion (rē′lak sā′shən), *n.* **1.** abatement or relief from bodily or mental work, effort, application, etc. **2.** an activity or recreation that provides such relief; diversion; entertainment. **3.** a loosening or slackening. **4.** diminution or remission of strictness or severity. **5.** *Math.* a numerical procedure for solving systems of equations by successive approximations of the variables. **6.** *Physics.* **a.** the return of a system undergoing dissipation to an initial state of equilibrium after being displaced from it. **b.** the approach to steady-state operation of a system that has undergone dissipation and a change in state or has been subjected to an abrupt periodic disturbance. [1375–1425; late ME < L *relaxātiōn-* (s. of *relaxātiō*), equiv. to *relaxāt(us)* (ptp. of *relaxāre* to RELAX; see -ATE[1]) + *-iōn-* -ION]
—Syn. 2. fun, amusement, pleasure.

relaxa′tion time′, *Physics.* the time that it takes for an exponentially decaying quantity, as radioactive particles or transient electrical currents, to decrease to 36.8 percent of its initial value. [1970–75]

re·laxed (ri lakst′), *adj.* **1.** being free of or relieved from tension or anxiety: *in a relaxed mood.* **2.** not strict; easy; informal: *the relaxed rules of the club.* [1630–40; RELAX + -ED[2]] **—re·lax·ed·ly** (ri lak′sid lē, -lakst′lē), *adv.* **—re·lax′ed·ness,** *n.*

re·lax·in (ri lak′sin), *n. Biochem., Pharm.* a polypeptide hormone produced by the corpus luteum during pregnancy that causes the pelvic ligaments and cervix to relax during pregnancy and delivery. [1925–30; RELAX + -IN[2]]

re-lay (rē lā′), *v.t.,* **-laid, -lay·ing.** to lay again. Also, **relay.** [1580–90; RE- + LAY[1]]

re·lay[1] (*n.* rē′lā; *v.* rē′lā, ri lā′), *n., v.,* **-layed, -lay·ing.** **—*n.*** **1.** a series of persons relieving one another or taking turns; shift. **2.** a fresh set of dogs or horses posted in readiness for use in a hunt, on a journey, etc. **3.** *Sports.* **a.** See **relay race. b.** a length or leg in a relay race. **4.** *Mach.* an automatic control device in which the settings of valves, switches, etc., are regulated by a powered element, as a motor, solenoid, or pneumatic mechanism actuated by a smaller, sensitive element. **5.** *Elect.* a device, usually consisting of an electromagnet and an armature, by which a change of current or voltage in one circuit is used to make or break a connection in another circuit or to affect the operation of other devices in the same or another circuit. **6.** (*cap.*) *U.S. Aerospace.* one of an early series of experimental low-altitude, active communications satellites. **—*v.t.*** **7.** to carry forward by or as if by relays: *to relay a message.* **8.** to provide with or replace by fresh relays. **9.** *Elect.* to retransmit (a signal, message, etc.) by or as if by means of a telegraphic relay. **—*v.i.*** **10.** *Elect.* to retransmit a signal or message electronically. [1375–1425; (v.) late ME *relaien* to unleash fresh hounds in a hunt < MF *relaier,* OF: to leave behind, RELEASE, equiv. to *re-* RE- + *laier* to leave, dial. var. of *laissier* < L *laxāre* (see RELAX); (n.) late ME *relai* set of fresh hounds < MF, deriv. of *relaier*]

re·lay[2] (rē lā′), *v.t.,* **-laid, -lay·ing.** re-lay.

re′lay race′, *Sports.* a race between two or more teams of contestants, each contestant being relieved by a teammate after running part of the distance. Cf. **medley relay.** [1895–1900]

re-lease (rē lēs′), *v.,* **-leased, -leas·ing,** *n.* **—*v.t.*** **1.** to lease again. **2.** *Law.* to make over (land, property, etc.), as to another. **—*n.*** **3.** a contract for re-leasing land or property. **4.** the land or property re-leased. [1820–30; RE- + LEASE]

re·lease (ri lēs′), *v.,* **-leased, -leas·ing,** *n.* **—*v.t.*** **1.** to free from confinement, bondage, obligation, pain, etc.; let go: *to release a prisoner; to release someone from a debt.* **2.** to free from anything that restrains, fastens, etc.: *to release a catapult.* **3.** to allow to be known, issued, done, or exhibited: *to release an article for publication.* **4.** *Law.* to give up, relinquish, or surrender (a right, claim, etc.). **—*n.*** **5.** a freeing or releasing from confinement, obligation, pain, emotional strain, etc. **6.** liberation from anything that restrains or fastens. **7.** some device or agency for effecting such liberation. **8.** a grant of permission, as to publish, use, or sell something. **9.** the releasing of something for publication, performance, use, exhibition, or sale. **10.** the film, book, record, etc., that is released. **11.** See **press release. 12.** *Law.* **a.** the surrender of a right or the like to another. **b.** a document embodying such a surrender. **13.** *Obs. Law.* a remission, as of a debt, tax, or tribute. **14.** *Mach.* **a.** a control mechanism for starting or stopping a machine, esp. by removing some restrictive apparatus. **b.** the opening of an exhaust port or valve at or near the working stroke of an engine so that the working fluid can be exhausted on the return stroke. **c.** the point in the stroke of an engine at which the exhaust port or valve is opened. **15.** (in jazz or popular music) a bridge. [1250–1300; (v.) ME *reles(s)en* < OF *relesser, relaissier* < L *relaxāre* to loosen (see RELAX); (n.) ME *reles(e)* < OF *reles, relais,* deriv. of *relesser, relaisser*] **—re·leas′a·bil′i·ty,** *n.* **—re·leas′a·ble, re·leas′i·ble,** *adj.*
—Syn. 1. loose, deliver. RELEASE, FREE, DISMISS, DISCHARGE, LIBERATE, EMANCIPATE may all mean to set at liberty, let loose, or let go. RELEASE and FREE, when applied to persons, suggest a helpful action. Both may be used (not always interchangeably) of delivering a person from confinement or obligation: *to free or release prisoners.* FREE (less often, RELEASE) is also used for delivering a person from pain, sorrow, etc.: *to free from fear.* DISMISS, meaning to send away, usually has the meaning of forcing to go unwillingly (*to dismiss a servant*), but may refer to giving permission to go: *The teacher dismissed the class early.* DISCHARGE, meaning originally to relieve of a burden (*to discharge a gun*), has come to refer to that which is sent away, and is often a close synonym to DISMISS; it is used in the meaning permit to go in connection with courts and the armed forces: *The court discharged a man accused of robbery.* LIBERATE and EMANCIPATE, more formal synonyms for RELEASE and FREE, also suggest action intended to be helpful. LIBERATE suggests particularly the release from unjust punishment, oppression, and the like, and often means to set free through forcible action or military campaign: *They liberated the prisoners, the occupied territories, etc.* EMANCIPATE also suggests a release of some size and consequence, but one that is less overt, a more formal or legal freedom; and it sometimes connotes an inner liberation: *Lincoln emancipated the slaves. John emancipated himself.* **2.** loose, extricate, disengage. **3.** announce, publish. **5.** liberation, deliverance, emancipation. **—Ant. 1.** bind. **2.** fasten.

release′ cop′y, *Journalism.* **1.** an article, notice, announcement, or the like, issued in advance for publication or broadcast, bearing a release date. **2.** the contents of such an advance.

release′ date′, *Journalism.* **1.** the time, as the day, part of the day, and sometimes the hour, on or at which release copy may be published or broadcast. **2.** the printed notation of this time on a press release or other advance. [1905–10]

released′ time′, *Educ.* **1.** time or a period allotted to a teacher apart from normal duties for a special activity, as personal research. **2.** a designated period for public-school students to receive religious instruction outside of the public school. Also, **release′ time′.** [1940–45]

release′ print′, *Motion Pictures.* print (def. 33). [1935–40]

re·leas·er (ri lē′sər), *n.* **1.** a person or thing that releases. **2.** *Ethology.* a key stimulus, as a sound, odor, moving shape, or patch of color, that elicits a predictable behavioral response in an animal. [1425–75; late ME. See RELEASE, -ER[1]]

release′ ther′apy, *Psychiatry.* psychotherapy in which the patient finds emotional release in the expression of hostilities and emotional conflicts. [1945–50]

releas′ing fac′tor, *Biochem.* a substance usually of hypothalamic origin that triggers the release of a particular hormone from an endocrine gland. [1950–55]

releas′ing mech′anism, *Ethology.* a hypothetical control complex in the central nervous system of animals that triggers the appropriate behavioral response to a releaser.

rel·e·gate (rel′i gāt′), *v.t.,* **-gat·ed, -gat·ing.** **1.** to send or consign to an inferior position, place, or condition: *He has been relegated to a post at the fringes of the diplomatic service.* **2.** to consign or commit (a matter, task, etc.), as to a person: *He relegates the less pleasant tasks to his assistant.* **3.** to assign or refer (something) to a particular class or kind. **4.** to send into exile; banish. [1375–1425; late ME < L *relēgātus,* ptp. of *relēgāre* to send away, dispatch. See RE-, LEGATE] **—rel·e·ga·ble** (rel′i gə bəl), *adj.* **—rel′e·ga′tion,** *n.*
—Syn. 2. delegate, entrust.

re·lent (ri lent′), *v.i.* **1.** to soften in feeling, temper, or determination; become more mild, compassionate, or forgiving. **2.** to become less severe; slacken: *The winds relented.* **—*v.t.*** **3.** *Obs.* to cause to soften in feeling, temper, or determination. **4.** *Obs.* to cause to slacken; abate. **5.** *Obs.* to abandon; relinquish. [1350–1400; ME < ML **relentāre,* equiv. to L *re-* RE- + *lentāre* to bend, deriv. of *lentus* flexible, viscous, slow] **—re·lent′ing·ly,** *adv.*
—Syn. 1. bend, yield.

re·lent·less (ri lent′lis), *adj.* that does not relent; unyieldingly severe, strict, or harsh; unrelenting: *a relentless enemy.* [1585–95; RELENT + -LESS] **—re·lent′less·ly,** *adv.* **—re·lent′less·ness,** *n.*
—Syn. rigid, unbending, obdurate, adamant, unyielding. See **inflexible. —Ant.** merciful.

CONCISE PRONUNCIATION KEY: *act, cāpe, dâre, pärt; set, ēqual; if, īce; ox, ōver, ôrder, oil, bo͝ok, bo͞ot, out; up, ûrge; child; sing; shoe; thin,* t͟h*at;* zh *as in treasure.* ə = *a* as in *alone, e* as in *system, i* as in *easily, o* as in *gallop, u* as in *circus;* ᵊ as in *fire* (fīᵊr), *hour* (ouᵊr). l and n can serve as syllabic consonants, as in *cradle* (krād′l), and *button* (but′n). See the full key inside the front cover.

re·har′mo·nize′, *v.t.,* **-nized, -niz·ing.**
re·har′ness, *v.t.*
re·har′vest, *v.*
re·haul′, *v.*
re·hear′, *v.,* **-heard, -hear·ing.**
re·heat′, *v.*
re·heat′a·ble, *adj.*
re·heat′er, *n.*
re·heel′, *v.t.*
re·hem′, *v.t.,* **-hemmed, -hem·ming.**
re·hide′, *v.,* **-hid, -hid·den** or **-hid, -hid·ing.**
re·hinge′, *v.t.,* **-hinged, -hing·ing.**
re·hire′, *v.,* **-hired, -hir·ing,** *n.*
re·hitch′, *v.t.*
re·hone′, *v.t.,* **-honed, -hon·ing.**
re·hon′or, *v.t.*
re′hos·pi·tal·i·za′tion, *n.*
re·hos′pi·tal·ize′, *v.t.,* **-ized, -iz·ing.**
re′hu·man·i·za′tion, *n.*
re·hu′man·ize′, *v.,* **-ized, -iz·ing.**
re′hu·mil′i·ate′, *v.t.,* **-at·ed, -at·ing.**
re′hu·mil′i·a′tion, *n.*
re·hyp′no·tize′, *v.t.,* **-tized, -tiz·ing.**
re′hy·poth′e·cate′, *v.t.,* **-cat·ed, -cat·ing.**
re·ice′, *v.,* **-iced, -ic·ing.**
re′i·den′ti·fi·ca′tion, *n.*
re′i·den′ti·fy′, *v.t.,* **-fied, -fy·ing.**
re′ig·nite′, *v.t.,* **-nit·ed, -nit·ing.**
re′ig·ni′tion, *n.*
re′il·lu′mi·nate′, *v.,* **-nat·ed, -nat·ing.**

rel·e·vant (rel′ə vənt), *adj.* bearing upon or connected with the matter in hand; pertinent: *a relevant remark.* [1550–60; < ML *relevant-* (s. of *relevāns*), special use of L, prp. of *relevāre* to raise, lift up. See RELIEVE, -ANT] —**rel′e·vance, rel′e·van·cy,** *n.* —**rel′e·vant·ly,** *adv.*
—**Syn.** applicable, germane, apposite, appropriate, suitable, fitting. See **apt.**
—**Pronunciation.** See **irrelevant.**

re·le·vé (rel′ə vā′; *Fr.* Rəl^ə vā′), *n. Ballet.* a rising up onto full point or half point from the flat of the feet. [1925–30; < F: lit., raised, ptp. of *relever;* see RELIEVE]

re·lex·i·fy (rē lek′sə fī′), *v.t.,* **-fied, -fy·ing.** *Ling.* to replace the vocabulary of (a language, esp. a pidgin) with words drawn from another language, without changing the grammatical structure. [1960–65; RE- + LEXI(CON) + -FY] —**re·lex′i·fi·ca′tion,** *n.*

re·li·a·ble (ri lī′ə bəl), *adj.* that may be relied on; dependable in achievement, accuracy, honesty, etc.: *reliable information.* [1560–70; RELY + -ABLE] —**re·li′a·bil′i·ty, re·li′a·ble·ness,** *n.* —**re·li′a·bly,** *adv.*
—**Syn.** trusty, authentic, consistent. RELIABLE, INFALLIBLE, TRUSTWORTHY apply to persons, objects, ideas, or information that can be depended upon with confident certainty. RELIABLE suggests consistent dependability of judgment, character, performance, or result: *a reliable formula, judge, car, meteorologist.* INFALLIBLE suggests the complete absence of error, breakdown, or poor performance: *an infallible test, system, marksman.* TRUSTWORTHY emphasizes the steady and honest dependability which encourages one's confidence, belief, or trust: *trustworthy and accurate reports.* —**Ant.** undependable, questionable, deceitful.

re·li·ance (ri lī′əns), *n.* **1.** confident or trustful dependence. **2.** confidence. **3.** something or someone relied on. [1600–10; RELY + -ANCE]
—**Syn. 1.** confidence, trust, faith, assurance.

re·li·ant (ri lī′ənt), *adj.* **1.** having or showing dependence: *reliant on money from home.* **2.** confident; trustful. [1855–60; RELY + -ANT] —**re·li′ant·ly,** *adv.*

rel·ic (rel′ik), *n.* **1.** a surviving memorial of something past. **2.** an object having interest by reason of its age or its association with the past: *a museum of historic relics.* **3.** a surviving trace of something: *a custom that is a relic of paganism.* **4. relics, a.** remaining parts or fragments. **b.** the remains of a deceased person. **5.** something kept in remembrance; souvenir; memento. **6.** *Eccles.* (esp. in the Roman Catholic and Greek churches) the body, a part of the body, or some personal memorial of a saint, martyr, or other sacred person, preserved as worthy of veneration. **7.** a once widespread linguistic form that survives in a limited area but is otherwise obsolete. [1175–1225; ME < OF *relique* < L *reliquiae* (pl.) (> OE *reliquias*), equiv. to *reliqu(us)* remaining + *-iae* pl. n. suffix] —**rel′ic·like′,** *adj.*

rel′ic ar′ea, *Ling.* (in dialect geography) an area isolated from the influences of any focal area and preserving older linguistic forms that have been lost in other regions. Cf. **focal area, transition area.** [1950–55]

rel·ict (rel′ikt), *n.* **1.** *Ecol.* a species or community living in an environment that has changed from that which is typical for it. **2.** a remnant or survivor. **3.** a widow. [1525–35; < ML *relicta* widow, n. use of fem. of L *relictus,* ptp. of *relinquere* to RELINQUISH]

re·lief[1] (ri lēf′), *n.* **1.** alleviation, ease, or deliverance through the removal of pain, distress, oppression, etc. **2.** a means or thing that relieves pain, distress, anxiety, etc. **3.** money, food, or other help given to those in poverty or need. **4.** something affording a pleasing change, as from monotony. **5.** release from a post of duty, as by the arrival of a substitute or replacement. **6.** the person or persons acting as replacement. **7.** the rescue of a besieged town, fort, etc., from an attacking force. **8.** the freeing of a closed space, as a tank or boiler, from more than a desirable amount of pressure or vacuum. **9.** *Feudal Law.* a fine or composition which the heir of a feudal tenant paid to the lord for the privilege of succeeding to the estate. **10.** *Literature.* **a.** a distinct or abrupt change in mood, scene, action, etc., resulting in a reduction of intensity, as in a play or novel. **b.** See **comic relief. 11. on relief,** receiving financial assistance from a municipal, state, or federal government because of poverty or need. [1300–50; ME *relef* < OF *relief,* deriv. of *relever* to raise; see RELIEVE] —**re·lief′less,** *adj.*
—**Syn. 1.** mitigation, assuagement, comfort. **3.** succor, aid, redress, remedy. —**Ant. 1.** intensification.

re·lief[2] (ri lēf′), *n.* **1.** prominence, distinctness, or vividness due to contrast. **2.** the projection of a figure or part from the ground or plane on which it is formed, as in sculpture or similar work. **3.** a piece or work in such projection. **4.** an apparent projection of parts in a painting, drawing, etc., giving the appearance of the third dimension. **5.** *Physical Geog.* the differences in elevation and slope between the higher and lower parts of the land surface of a given area. **6.** Also called **relief′ print′ing.** *Print.* any printing process, as letterpress or flexography, in which the printing ink is transferred to paper or another printed surface from areas that are higher than the rest of the block. [1600–10; < F *relief* and It *rilievo;* see RELIEF[1]]

CONCISE ETYMOLOGY KEY: <, descended or borrowed from; >, whence; b., blend of, blended; c., cognate with; cf., compare; deriv., derivative; equiv., equivalent; imit., imitative; obl., oblique; r., replacing; s., stem; sp., spelling, spelled; resp., respelling, respelled; trans., translation; ?, origin unknown; *, unattested; ‡, probably earlier than. See the full key inside the front cover.

relief[2] (defs. 2, 3)
A, bas-relief; B, high relief

re·lief·er (ri lē′fər), *n.* **1.** *Baseball.* See **relief pitcher. 2.** a person who, because of old age, indigence, physical disability, or the like, receives welfare benefits from the state. **3.** a person who temporarily replaces someone else. [1790–1800; RELIEF[1] + -ER[1]]

relief′ map′, a map showing the relief of an area, usually by generalized contour lines. [1875–80]

relief′ pitch′er, *Baseball.* **1.** a pitcher brought into a game to replace another pitcher, often in a critical situation. **2.** a pitcher regularly so used, as opposed to one who regularly starts games. Also called **reliever, reliefer.** [1945–50]

relief′ valve′, a device that, when actuated by static pressure above a predetermined level, opens in proportion to the excess above this level and reduces the pressure to it. Cf. **safety valve** (def. 1).

re·li·er (ri lī′ər), *n.* a person or thing that relies. [1585–95; RELY + -ER[1]]

re·lieve (ri lēv′), *v.,* **-lieved, -liev·ing.** —*v.t.* **1.** to ease or alleviate (pain, distress, anxiety, need, etc.). **2.** to free from anxiety, fear, pain, etc. **3.** to free from need, poverty, etc. **4.** to bring effective aid to (a besieged town, military position, etc.). **5.** to ease (a person) of any burden, wrong, or oppression, as by legal means. **6.** to reduce (a pressure, load, weight, etc., on a device or object under stress): *to relieve the steam pressure; to relieve the stress on the supporting walls.* **7.** to make less tedious, unpleasant, or monotonous; break or vary the sameness of: *curtains to relieve the drabness of the room.* **8.** to bring into relief or prominence; heighten the effect of. **9.** to release (one on duty) by coming as or providing a substitute or replacement. **10.** *Mach.* **a.** to free (a closed space, as a tank, boiler, etc.) of more than a desirable pressure or vacuum. **b.** to reduce (the pressure or vacuum in such a space) to a desirable level. **11.** *Baseball.* to replace (a pitcher). —*v.i.* **12.** *Baseball.* to act as a relief pitcher: *He relieved in 52 games for the Pirates last season.* **13. to relieve oneself,** to urinate or defecate. [1300–50; ME *releven* < MF *relever* to raise < L *relevāre* to reduce the load of, lighten, equiv. to *re-* RE- + *levāre* to raise, deriv. of *levis* light in weight] —**re·liev′a·ble,** *adj.* —**re·liev·ed·ly** (ri lē′vid lē), *adv.*
—**Syn. 1.** mitigate, assuage, allay, lighten, lessen, abate, diminish. See **comfort. 1-4.** aid, help, assist. **3.** support, sustain. **4.** succor. —**Ant. 1.** intensify.

re·liev·er (ri lē′vər), *n.* **1.** a person or thing that relieves. **2.** *Baseball.* See **relief pitcher.** [1475–85; see RELIEVE, -ER[1]]

reliev′ing arch′. See **discharging arch.** [1840–50]

re·lie·vo (ri lē′vō, ril yev′ō), *n., pl.* **-vos.** *Obs.* relief[2] (defs. 2, 3). [1615–25; < It *rilievo* RELIEF[2], deriv. of *rilevare* to raise < L *relevāre;* see RELIEVE]

relig., religion.

re·li·gieuse (Rə lē zhyœz′), *n., pl.* ***-gieuses*** (-zhyœz′). *French.* a woman belonging to a religious order, congregation, etc.

re·li·gieux (Rə lē zhyœ′), *adj., n., pl.* ***-gieux.*** *French.* —*adj.* **1.** religious; devout; pious. —*n.* **2.** a person under monastic vows.

re·li·gion (ri lij′ən), *n.* **1.** a set of beliefs concerning the cause, nature, and purpose of the universe, esp. when considered as the creation of a superhuman agency or agencies, usually involving devotional and ritual observances, and often containing a moral code governing the conduct of human affairs. **2.** a specific fundamental set of beliefs and practices generally agreed upon by a number of persons or sects: *the Christian religion; the Buddhist religion.* **3.** the body of persons adhering to a particular set of beliefs and practices: *a world council of religions.* **4.** the life or state of a monk, nun, etc.: *to enter religion.* **5.** the practice of religious beliefs; ritual observance of faith. **6.** something one believes in and follows devotedly; a point or matter of ethics or conscience: *to make a religion of fighting prejudice.* **7. religions,** *Archaic.* religious rites. **8.** *Archaic.* strict faithfulness; devotion: *a religion to one's vow.* **9. get religion,** *Informal.* **a.** to acquire a deep conviction of the validity of religious beliefs and practices. **b.** to resolve to mend one's errant ways: *The company got religion and stopped making dangerous products.* [1150–1200; ME *religioun* (< OF *religion*) < L *religiōn-* (s. of *religiō*) conscientiousness, piety, equiv. to *relig(āre)* to tie, fasten (*re-* RE- + *ligāre* to bind, tie; cf. LIGAMENT) + *-iōn-* -ION; cf. RELY] —**re·li′gion·less,** *adj.*

re·li·gion·ism (ri lij′ə niz′əm), *n.* **1.** excessive or exaggerated religious zeal. **2.** affected or pretended religious zeal. [1785–95; RELIGION + -ISM] —**re·li′gion·ist,** *n.* —**re·li′gion·is′tic,** *adj.*

re·li·gi·ose (ri lij′ē ōs′, -lij′ē ōs′), *adj.* characterized by religiosity. [1850–55; < L *religiōsus;* see RELIGIOUS]

re·li·gi·os·i·ty (ri lij′ē os′i tē), *n.* **1.** the quality of being religious; piety; devoutness. **2.** affected or excessive devotion to religion. [1350–1400; ME *religiosite* < L *religiōsitās,* equiv. to *religiōs(us)* RELIGIOUS + *-itās* -ITY]

re·li·gious (ri lij′əs), *adj., n., pl.* **-gious.** —*adj.* **1.** of, pertaining to, or concerned with religion: *a religious holiday.* **2.** imbued with or exhibiting religion; pious; devout; godly: *a religious man.* **3.** scrupulously faithful; conscientious: *religious care.* **4.** pertaining to or connected with a monastic or religious order. **5.** appropriate to religion or to sacred rites or observances. —*n.* **6.** a member of a religious order, congregation, etc.; a monk, friar, or nun. **7. the religious,** devout or religious persons: *Each year, thousands of the religious make pilgrimages to the shrine.* [1175–1225; ME (< OF) < L *religiōsus,* equiv. to *religi(ō)* RELIGION + *-ōsus* -OUS] —**re·li′gious·ly,** *adv.* —**re·li′gious·ness,** *n.*
—**Syn. 2.** reverent. RELIGIOUS, DEVOUT, PIOUS indicate a spirit of reverence toward God. RELIGIOUS is a general word, applying to whatever pertains to faith or worship: *a religious ceremony.* DEVOUT indicates a fervent spirit, usually genuine and often independent of outward observances: *a deeply devout though unorthodox church member.* PIOUS implies constant attention to, and extreme conformity with, outward observances. It can also suggest sham or hypocrisy: *a pious hypocrite.* **3.** devoted, unswerving, meticulous. —**Ant. 2.** impious.

reli′gious house′, a convent or monastery.

Reli′gious Soci′ety of Friends′. See **Society of Friends.**

re·lin·quish (ri ling′kwish), *v.t.* **1.** to renounce or surrender (a possession, right, etc.): *to relinquish the throne.* **2.** to give up; put aside or desist from: *to relinquish a plan.* **3.** to let go; release: *to relinquish one's hold.* [1425–75; late ME *relinquissen, relinquisshen* < MF *relinquiss-,* long s. of *relinquir* << L *relinquere* to leave behind, equiv. to *re-* RE- + *linquere* to leave (akin to LEND)] —**re·lin′quish·er,** *n.* —**re·lin′quish·ment,** *n.*
—**Syn. 2.** yield, cede, waive, forego, abdicate, leave, quit, forswear, desert, resign. See **abandon**[1].

rel·i·quar·y (rel′i kwer′ē), *n., pl.* **-quar·ies.** a repository or receptacle for relics. [1650–60; < MF *reliquaire* < ML *reliquiārium,* equiv. to L *reliqui(ae)* remains (see RELIC) + *-ārium* -ARY]

rel·ique (rel′ik; *Fr.* Rə lēk′), *n., pl.* **rel·iques** (rel′iks; *Fr.* Rə lēk′). *Archaic.* relic.

re·liq·ui·ae (ri lik′wē ē′), *n.* (*used with a plural v.*) remains, as those of fossil organisms. [1825–35; < L; see RELIC]

rel·ish (rel′ish), *n.* **1.** liking or enjoyment of the taste of something. **2.** pleasurable appreciation of anything; liking: *He has no relish for obscene jokes.* **3.** *Cookery.* **a.** something savory or appetizing added to a meal, as pickles or olives. **b.** a sweet pickle made of various vegetables, usually chopped or minced. **c.** an appetizer or hors d'oeuvre. **4.** a pleasing or appetizing flavor. **5.** a pleasing or enjoyable quality. **6.** a taste or flavor. **7.** a smack, trace, or touch of something. —*v.t.* **8.** to take pleasure in; like; enjoy: *I don't relish the long drive home.* **9.** to make pleasing to the taste. **10.** to like the taste of. —*v.i.* **11.** to have taste or flavor. **12.** to be agreeable. [1520–30; alter. of ME *reles* aftertaste, scent < OF, var. of *relais* remainder, that left behind; see RELEASE] —**rel′ish·a·ble,** *adj.* —**rel′ish·ing·ly,** *adv.*
—**Syn. 1, 2.** gusto, zest. **2.** inclination, partiality, predilection, preference. **3.** condiment, appetizer. **6.** savor. **8.** appreciate. —**Ant. 1, 2.** distaste, disfavor.

re·live (rē liv′), *v.,* **-lived, -liv·ing.** —*v.t.* **1.** to experience again, as an emotion. **2.** to live (one's life) again. —*v.i.* **3.** to live again. [1540–50; RE- + LIVE[1]] —**re·liv′a·ble,** *adj.*

rel·le·no (rə yā′nō, rəl yā′-; *Sp.* Re ye′nô, Re lye′-), *adj., n., pl.* **-nos** (-nōz; *Sp.* -nôs). *Mexican Cookery.* —*adj.* **1.** stuffed, esp. filled with cheese: *chilis rellenos.* —*n.* **2.** a chili relleno. [< Sp: stuffed, filled]

re·lo·cat·a·ble (rē lō′kā tə bəl, rē′lō kā′-), *adj.* **1.** constructed so as to be movable; portable, prefabricated, or modular: *relocatable classroom units.* **2.** *Computers.* (of a program, code, load module, etc.) capable of being loaded into and executed from different parts of main storage, with appropriate adjustment of address references. —*n.* **3.** a structure that can be relocated. [1870–75; RELOCATE + -ABLE] —**re/lo·cat′a·bil′i·ty,** *n.*

re·lo·cate (rē lō′kāt, rē′lō kāt′), *v.,* **-cat·ed, -cat·ing.** —*v.t.* **1.** to move (a building, company, etc.) to a different location: *plans to relocate the firm to Houston.* —*v.i.* **2.** to change one's residence or place of business; move: *Next year we may relocate to Denver.* [1825–35, *Amer.;* RE- + LOCATE] —**re′lo·ca′tion,** *n.*

rel. pron., relative pronoun.

re·lu·cent (ri lo͞o′sənt), *adj.* shining; bright. [1500–10; < L *relūcent-* (s. of *relūcēns*), prp. of *relūcere.* See RE-, LUCENT]

re·luct (ri lukt′), *v.i.* **1.** to struggle (against something); rebel. **2.** to object; show reluctance. [1520–30; < L *reluctārī,* equiv. to *re-* RE- + *luctārī* to strive, struggle, wrestle]

re·luc·tance (ri luk′təns), *n.* **1.** unwillingness; disinclination: *reluctance to speak in public.* **2.** *Elect.* the resistance to magnetic flux offered by a magnetic circuit, determined by the permeability and arrangement of the

re′il·lu′mi·na′tion, *n.*
re·il′lus·trate′, *v.t.,* **-trat·ed, -trat·ing.**
re′il·lus·tra′tion, *n.*
re·im′age, *v.t.,* **-aged, -ag·ing.**
re′i·mag′ine, *v.t.,* **-ined, -in·ing.**
re′im·merse′, *v.t.,* **-mersed, -mers·ing.**
re·im′ple·ment′, *v.t.*
re′im·ply′, *v.t.,* **-plied, -ply·ing.**
re′im·pose′, *v.,* **-posed, -pos·ing.**
re′im·po·si′tion, *n.*
re′im·preg′nate, *v.t.,* **-nat·ed, -nat·ing.**
re′im·preg·na′tion, *n.*
re′im·press′, *v.t.*
re′im·print′, *v.t.*
re′im·pris′on, *v.t.*
re′im·pris′on·ment, *n.*
re′in·au′gu·rate′, *v.t.,* **-rat·ed, -rat·ing.**
re′in·au′gu·ra′tion, *n.*
re′in·cite′, *v.t.,* **-cit·ed, -cit·ing.**
re′in·cline′, *v.,* **-clined, -clin·ing.**
re′in·clude′, *v.t.,* **-clud·ed, -clud·ing.**
re′in·clu′sion, *n.*
re′in·cor′po·rate′, *v.,* **-rat·ed, -rat·ing.**
re′in·cor′po·rate, *adj.*
re′in·cor′po·ra′tion, *n.*
re′in·crease′, *v.,* **-creased, -creas·ing,** *n.*
re′in·cur′, *v.t.,* **-curred, -cur·ring.**
re·in′dex, *v.t.*
re·in′di·cate′, *v.t.,* **-cat·ed, -cat·ing.**

materials of the circuit. Also, **re•luc′tan•cy.** [1635–45; RELUCT(ANT) + -ANCE]

re•luc•tant (ri luk′tənt), *adj.* **1.** unwilling; disinclined: *a reluctant candidate.* **2.** struggling in opposition. [1655–65; < L *reluctānt-* (s. of *reluctāns*), prp. of *reluctārī.* See RELUCT, -ANT] —**re•luc′tant•ly,** *adv.*
—**Syn. 1.** RELUCTANT, LOATH, AVERSE describe disinclination toward something. RELUCTANT implies some sort of mental struggle, as between disinclination and sense of duty: *reluctant to expel students.* LOATH describes extreme disinclination: *loath to part from a friend.* AVERSE, used with *to* and a noun or a gerund, describes a long-held dislike or unwillingness, though not a particularly strong feeling: *averse to an idea; averse to getting up early.* —**Ant. 1.** willing.

re•luc•tate (ri luk′tāt), *v.i.*, **-tat•ed, -tat•ing.** *Obs.* to show reluctance. [1635–45; < L *reluctātus*, ptp. of *reluctārī.* See RELUCT, -ATE[1]] —**re′luc•ta′tion,** *n.*

rel•uc•tiv•i•ty (rel′ək tiv′i tē), *n. Elect.* the tendency of a magnetic circuit to conduct magnetic flux, equal to the reciprocal of the permeability of the circuit. [1885–90; RELUCT + -IVE + -ITY]

re•lume (ri lo͞om′), *v.t.*, **-lumed, -lum•ing.** to light or illuminate again; relumine. [1595–1605; RE- + (IL)LUME; cf. F *rallumer*, LL *relūmināre.* See RELUMINE]

re•lu•mine (ri lo͞o′min), *v.t.*, **-mined, -min•ing.** to relume. [1775–85; < LL *relūmināre* to restore sight to, equiv. to L *re-* RE- + (*il*)*lūmināre* to ILLUMINE]

re•ly (ri lī′), *v.i.*, **-lied, -ly•ing.** to depend confidently; put trust in (usually fol. by *on* or *upon*): *You can rely on her work.* [1300–50; ME *relien* < MF *relier* < L *religāre* to bind fast, hold firmly. See RE-, LIGAMENT]
—**Syn.** trust, count, bank.

rem (rem), *n. Nucleonics.* the quantity of ionizing radiation whose biological effect is equal to that produced by one roentgen of x-rays. [1945–50; *r*(*oentgen*) *e*(*quivalent in*) *m*(*an*)]

REM (rem), *n.* See **rapid eye movement.** [1955–60]

re•main (ri mān′), *v.i.* **1.** to continue in the same state; continue to be as specified: *to remain at peace.* **2.** to stay behind or in the same place: *to remain at home; I'll remain here when you go to the airport.* **3.** to be left after the removal, loss, destruction, etc., of all else: *The front wall is all that remains of the fort.* **4.** to be left to be done, told, shown, etc.: *Only the dishwashing remains.* **5.** to be reserved or in store. —*n.* **6.** Usually, **remains.** something that remains or is left. **7. remains, a.** miscellaneous, fragmentary, or other writings still unpublished at the time of an author's death. **b.** traces of some quality, condition, etc. **c.** a dead body; corpse. **d.** parts or substances remaining from animal or plant life that occur in the earth's crust or strata: *fossil remains; organic remains.* [1375–1425; late ME *remainen* < AF *remain-*, stressed s. of MF *remanoir* < L *remanēre*, equiv. to *re-* RE- + *manēre* to stay; see MANOR]
—**Syn. 1.** abide, stay. See **continue. 2.** wait, tarry, rest. **3.** endure, abide. —**Ant. 2.** depart.

re•main•der (ri mān′dər), *n.* **1.** something that remains or is left: *the remainder of the day.* **2.** a remaining part. **3.** *Arith.* **a.** the quantity that remains after subtraction. **b.** the portion of the dividend that is not evenly divisible by the divisor. **4.** *Math.* the difference between a function or a number and an approximation to it. **5.** *Law.* a future interest so created as to take effect at the end of another estate, as when property is conveyed to one person for life and then to another. **6. remainders,** *Philately.* the quantities of stamps on hand after they have been demonetized or otherwise voided for postal use. **7.** a copy of a book remaining in the publisher's stock when its sale has practically ceased, frequently sold at a reduced price. —*adj.* **8.** remaining; leftover. —*v.t.* **9.** to dispose of or sell as a remainder. [1350–1400; ME < AF, n. use of MF *remaindre* to REMAIN]
—**Syn. 1.** residuum, remnant, excess, rest, overage. **2.** REMAINDER, BALANCE, RESIDUE, SURPLUS refer to a portion left over. REMAINDER is the general word (*the remainder of one's life*); it may refer in particular to the mathematical process of subtraction: *7 minus 5 leaves a remainder of 2.* BALANCE, originally a bookkeeper's term referring to the amount of money left to one's account (*a bank balance*), is often used as a synonym for REMAINDER: *the balance of the day.* RESIDUE is used particularly to designate what remains as the result of a process; this is usually a chemical process, but the word may also refer to a legal process concerning inheritance: *a residue of ash left from burning leaves.* SURPLUS suggests that what remains is in excess of what was needed: *a surplus of goods.*

re•main•der•man (ri mān′dər mən), *n., pl.* **-men.** *Law.* a person who owns a remainder. [1735–45; REMAINDER + MAN[1]]

re•make (*v.* rē māk′; *n.* rē′māk′), *v.*, **-made, -mak•ing,** *n.* —*v.t.* **1.** to make again or anew. **2.** *Motion Pictures.* to film again, as a picture or screenplay. —*n.* **3.** *Motion Pictures.* a more recent version of an older film. **4.** anything that has been remade, renovated, or rebuilt: *The tailor is offering a special price on remakes.* [1625–35; RE- + MAKE] —**re•mak′er,** *n.*

re•man (rē man′), *v.t.*, **-manned, -man•ning. 1.** to man again; furnish with a fresh supply of personnel. **2.** to restore the manliness or courage of. [1660–70; RE- + MAN[1]]

re•mand (ri mand′, -mänd′), *v.t.* **1.** to send back, remit, or consign again. **2.** *Law.* **a.** to send back (a case) to a lower court from which it was appealed, with instructions as to what further proceedings should be had. **b.** (of a court or magistrate) to send back (a prisoner or accused person) into custody, as to await further proceedings. —*n.* **3.** the act of remanding. **4.** the state of being remanded. **5.** a person remanded. [1400–50; late ME *remaunden* (v.) < OF *remander* < LL *remandāre* to repeat a command, send back word, equiv. to *re-* RE- + *mandāre* to entrust, enjoin; see MANDATE] —**re•mand′•ment,** *n.*

remand′ home′, *Brit.* a detention home for juvenile offenders aged 8–16 years. Cf. **borstal.** [1900–05]

rem•a•nence (rem′ə nəns), *n. Elect.* the magnetic flux that remains in a magnetic circuit after an applied magnetomotive force has been removed. Also called **residual magnetism, retentivity.** [1660–70; REMAN(ENT) + -ENCE]

rem•a•nent (rem′ə nənt), *adj.* remaining; left behind. [1375–1425; late ME < L *remanent-* (s. of *remanēns*), prp. of *remanēre.* See REMAIN, -ENT]

rem′anent mag′netism, *Geol.* magnetization in minerals induced by a former magnetic field and persisting after the field changes. Cf. **paleomagnetism.** [1865–70]

re•man•u•fac•ture (rē′man yə fak′chər), *v.*, **-tured, -tur•ing,** *n.* —*v.t.* **1.** to refurbish (a used product) by renovating and reassembling its components: *to remanufacture a vacuum cleaner.* **2.** to make a new or different product of: *to remanufacture fireplace logs from wood chips.* —*n.* **3.** the act or process of remanufacturing a product. **4.** the product itself. [1790–1800; RE- + MANUFACTURE] —**re′man•u•fac′tur•er,** *n.*

re•mar•gin (rē mär′jin), *v.i.* to provide additional cash or collateral to a broker in order to keep secure stock bought on margin. [1890–95; RE- + MARGIN]

re•mark (ri märk′), *v.t.* **1.** to say casually, as in making a comment: *Someone remarked that tomorrow would be a warm day.* **2.** to note; perceive; observe: *I remarked a slight accent in her speech.* **3.** *Obs.* to mark distinctively. —*v.i.* **4.** to make a remark or observation (usually fol. by *on* or *upon*): *He remarked on her amazing wit and intelligence.* —*n.* **5.** the act of remarking; notice. **6.** comment or mention: *to let a thing pass without remark.* **7.** a casual or brief expression of thought or opinion. **8.** *Fine Arts.* remarque. [1625–35; (v.) < F *remarquer*, MF, equiv. to *re-* RE- + *marquer* to MARK[1]; (n.) < F *remarque*, deriv. of *remarquer*] —**re•mark′er,** *n.*
—**Syn. 2.** heed, regard, notice. **4.** comment. **5.** regard. **7.** REMARK, COMMENT, NOTE, OBSERVATION imply giving special attention, an opinion, or a judgment. A REMARK is usually a casual and passing expression of opinion: *a remark about a play.* A COMMENT expresses judgment or explains a particular point: *a comment on the author's scholarship.* A NOTE is a memorandum or explanation, as in the margin of a page: *a note explaining a passage.* OBSERVATION suggests a comment based on judgment and experience: *an observation on social behavior.* —**Ant. 2.** ignore.

re•mark•a•ble (ri mär′kə bəl), *adj.* **1.** notably or conspicuously unusual; extraordinary: *a remarkable change.* **2.** worthy of notice or attention. [1595–1605; < F *remarquable.* See REMARK, -ABLE] —**re•mark′a•bil′i•ty, re•mark′a•ble•ness,** *n.* —**re•mark′a•bly,** *adv.*
—**Syn. 2.** notable, noteworthy, striking, extraordinary, wonderful, unusual, singular, uncommon. —**Ant. 1, 2.** common, ordinary.

re•marque (ri märk′), *n. Fine Arts.* **1.** a distinguishing mark or peculiarity indicating a particular stage of a plate. **2.** a small sketch engraved in the margin of a plate, and usually removed after a number of early proofs have been printed. **3.** a plate so marked. Also, **remark.** [1880–85; < F; see REMARK]

Re•marque (ri märk′; *Ger.* rə märk′), *n.* **E•rich Ma•ri•a** (er′ik mə rē′ə; *Ger.* ā′rɪκн mä rē′ä), 1898–1970, German novelist in the U.S.

re•mas•ter (rē mas′tər, -mä′stər), *v.t.* to make a new master tape or record from an old master tape, usually to improve the fidelity of an old recording. [1960–65; RE- + MASTER]

re•match (*v.* rē mach′, rē′mach′; *n.* rē′mach′), *v.t.* **1.** to match again; duplicate: *an attempt to rematch a shade of green paint.* **2.** to schedule a second match for or between: *to rematch the winners in each soccer league.* —*n.* **3.** a second match between teams, challengers, etc.; return match. [1855–60; RE- + MATCH[2]]

Rem•brandt (rem′brant, -bränt; *Du.* rem′bränt), *n.* (*Rembrandt Harmenszoon van Rijn* or *van Ryn*) 1606–69, Dutch painter. —**Rem′brandt•esque′, Rem′•brandt•ish,** *adj.*

re•me•di•a•ble (ri mē′dē ə bəl), *adj.* capable of being remedied. [1485–95; (< MF) < L *remediābilis* curable. See REMEDY, -ABLE] —**re•me′di•a•ble•ness,** *n.* —**re•me′di•a•bly,** *adv.*

re•me•di•al (ri mē′dē əl), *adj.* **1.** affording remedy; tending to remedy something. **2.** intended to correct or improve one's skill in a specified field: *remedial math.* [1645–55; < LL *remediālis.* See REMEDY, -AL[1]] —**re•me′di•al•ly,** *adv.*
—**Syn. 2.** corrective.

reme′dial read′ing, instruction in reading aimed at increasing speed and comprehension by correcting poor reading habits. [1925–30]

re•me•di•a•tion (ri mē′dē ā′shən), *n.* the correction of something bad or defective. [1810–20; < L *remediā-t*(*us*), ptp. of *remediāre* to REMEDY + -ION]

rem•e•di•less (rem′i dē lis), *adj.* not admitting of remedy, as disease, trouble, damage, etc.; unremediable. [1400–50; late ME; see REMEDY, -LESS]

rem•e•dy (rem′i dē), *n., pl.* **-dies,** *v.*, **-died, -dy•ing.** —*n.* **1.** something that cures or relieves a disease or bodily disorder; a healing medicine, application, or treatment. **2.** something that corrects or removes an evil of any kind. **3.** *Law.* legal redress; the legal means of enforcing a right or redressing a wrong. **4.** *Coinage.* a certain allowance at the mint for deviation from the standard weight and fineness of coins; tolerance. —*v.t.* **5.** to cure, relieve, or heal. **6.** to restore to the natural or proper condition; put right: *to remedy a matter.* **7.** to counteract or remove: *to remedy an evil.* [1175–1225; (n.) ME *remedie* < AF < L *remedium*, equiv. to *re-* RE- + *med*(*ērī*) to heal, assuage, remedy (cf. MEDICAL) + *-ium* -IUM; (v.) late ME *remedien* (< MF *remedier*) < L *remediāre*, deriv. of *remedium*]
—**Syn. 1.** cure, restorative, specific, medicament, medication. **2.** corrective, antidote. **5.** See **cure. 6.** repair, correct, redress, renew. —**Ant. 5.** worsen.

re•mem•ber (ri mem′bər), *v.t.* **1.** to recall to the mind by an act or effort of memory; think of again: *I'll try to remember the exact date.* **2.** to retain in the memory; keep in mind; remain aware of: *Remember your appointment with the dentist.* **3.** to have (something) come into the mind again: *I just remembered that it's your birthday today.* **4.** to bear (a person) in mind as deserving a gift, reward, or fee: *The company always remembers us at Christmas.* **5.** to give a tip, donation, or gift to: *to remember the needy.* **6.** to mention (a person) to another as sending kindly greetings: *Remember me to your family.* **7.** (of an appliance, computer, etc.) to perform (a programmed activity) at a later time or according to a preset schedule: *The coffeepot remembers to start the coffee at 7* A.M. *every day.* **8.** *Archaic.* to remind. —*v.i.* **9.** to possess or exercise the faculty of memory. **10.** to have recollection (sometimes fol. by *of*): *The old man remembers of his youth.* [1300–50; ME *remembren* < OF *remembrer* < LL *rememorārī*, equiv. to *re-* RE- + L *memor* mindful (see MEMORY) + *-ārī* inf. suffix] —**re•mem′ber•a•ble,** *adj.* —**re•mem′ber•er,** *n.*
—**Syn. 1.** REMEMBER, RECALL, RECOLLECT refer to bringing back before the conscious mind things which exist in the memory. REMEMBER implies that a thing exists in the memory, though not actually present in the thoughts at the moment: *to remember the days of one's childhood.* RECALL implies a voluntary effort, though not a great one: *to recall the words of a song.* RECOLLECT implies an earnest voluntary effort to remember some definite, desired fact or thing: *I cannot recollect the exact circumstances.* —**Ant. 1, 2.** forget.

re•mem•brance (ri mem′brəns), *n.* **1.** a retained mental impression; memory. **2.** the act or fact of remembering. **3.** the power or faculty of remembering. **4.** the length of time over which recollection or memory extends. **5.** the state of being remembered; commemoration: *to hold someone's name in remembrance.* **6.** something that serves to bring to mind or keep in mind some place, person, event, etc.; memento. **7.** a gift given as a token of love or friendship: *I sent her a small remembrance on Mother's Day.* **8. remembrances,** greetings; respects. [1300–50; ME < OF; see REMEMBER, -ANCE]
—**Syn. 1.** recollection, reminiscence. **3.** memory. **6.** keepsake, trophy, souvenir, token, memorial.

Remem′brance Day′, (in Canada) November 11, observed as a legal holiday in memory of those who died in World Wars I and II, similar to Veterans Day in the U.S.

Remem′brance of Things′ Past′, (French, *À la Recherche du Temps Perdu*), a novel (1913–27) by Marcel Proust.

re•mem•branc•er (ri mem′brən sər), *n.* **1.** a person who reminds another of something. **2.** a person engaged to do this. **3.** a reminder; memento; souvenir. **4.** (*usually cap.*) **a.** See **King's Remembrancer. b.** (formerly) any of certain officials of the Court of Exchequer. **5.** an officer of the corporation of the City of London. [1325–75; ME < AF; see REMEMBRANCE, -ER[2]]

re•mex (rē′meks), *n., pl.* **rem•i•ges** (rem′i jēz′). *Ornith.* one of the flight feathers of the wing. [1665–75; < L *rēmex* oarsman, equiv. to *rēm*(*us*) oar + *-eg-* comb. form of *agere* to drive, do (see ACT) + *-s* nom. sing. ending] —**re•mig•i•al** (ri mij′ē əl), *adj.*

rem•i•form (rem′ə fôrm′), *adj.* shaped like an oar. [1855–60; < L *rēm*(*us*) oar + -I- + -FORM]

rem•i•grant (rem′i grənt), *n.* a person or thing that returns. [< L *remigrant-* (s. of *remigrāns*), prp. of *remigrāre.* See RE-, MIGRATE, -ANT]

re•mind (ri mīnd′), *v.t.* to cause (a person) to remember; cause (a person) to think (of someone or something): *Remind me to phone him tomorrow. That woman reminds me of my mother.* [1635–45; RE- + MIND]

re•mind•er (ri mīn′dər), *n.* a person or thing that serves to remind. [1645–55; REMIND + -ER[1]]

re•mind•ful (ri mīnd′fəl), *adj.* **1.** reviving memory of something; reminiscent. **2.** retaining memory of something; mindful. [1800–10; REMIND + -FUL]

Rem•ing•ton (rem′ing tən), *n.* **1. E•liph•a•let** (i lif′ə lit), 1793–1861, U.S. arms manufacturer. **2. Frederic,** 1861–1909, U.S. painter and sculptor.

CONCISE PRONUNCIATION KEY: act, cāpe, dâre, pärt; set, ēqual; *if*, īce; ox, ōver, ôrder, oil, bo͝ok, bo͞ot, out; up, ûrge; child; sing; shoe; thin, *th*at; zh as in *treasure.* ə = a as in *alone*, e as in *system*, i as in *easily*, o as in *gallop*, u as in *circus*; ᵊ as in *fire* (fīᵊr), *hour* (ouᵊr). l and n can serve as syllabic consonants, as in *cradle* (krād′l), and *button* (but′n). See the full key inside the front cover.

re′in•di•ca′tion, *n.*
re′in•dict′, *v.t.*
re′in•dict′ment, *n.*
re′in•doc′tri•nate′, *v.t.*, **-nat•ed, -nat•ing.**
re′in•doc′tri•na′tion, *n.*
re′in•dorse′, *v.t.*, **-dorsed, -dors•ing.**
re′in•dorse′ment, *n.*
re′in•duce′, *v.t.*, **-duced, -duc•ing.**
re′in•duce′ment, *n.*
re′in•duct′, *v.t.*
re′in•duc′tion, *n.*
re′in•dulge′, *v.*, **-dulged, -dulg•ing.**
re′in•dul′gence, *n.*
re′in•fect′, *v.t.*
re′in•fec′tion, *n.*
re′in•fer′, *v.t.*, **-ferred, -fer•ring.**
re′in•fest′, *v.t.*
re′in•fes•ta′tion, *n.*
re′in•fil′trate, *v.*, **-trat•ed, -trat•ing.**
re′in•fil•tra′tion, *n.*
re′in•flame′, *v.*, **-flamed, -flam•ing.**
re′in•flat′a•ble, *adj.*
re′in•flate′, *v.*, **-flat•ed, -flat•ing.**
re′in•fla′tion, *n.*
re•in′flu•ence, *v.t.*, **-enced, -enc•ing.**
re′in•form′, *v.t.*
re′in•fuse′, *v.t.*, **-fused, -fus•ing.**
re′in•fu′sion, *n.*
re′in•gest′, *v.t.*
re′in•hab′it, *v.t.*
re′in•her′it, *v.*

rem·i·nisce (rem′ə nis′), *v.i.*, **-nisced, -nisc·ing.** to recall past experiences, events, etc.; indulge in reminiscence. [1820–30; back formation from REMINISCENCE]
—**Syn.** remember, recollect, muse.

rem·i·nis·cence (rem′ə nis′əns), *n.* **1.** the act or process of recalling past experiences, events, etc. **2.** a mental impression retained and revived. **3.** Often, **reminiscences.** a recollection narrated or told: *reminiscences of an American soldier.* **4.** something that recalls or suggests something else. **5.** (in Platonic philosophy) anamnesis (def. 2). [1580–90; < MF < LL *reminiscentia.* See REMINISCENT, -ENCE]
—**Syn. 1.** recollection. **2.** memory. **3.** anecdote, tale, memoir. **4.** reminder.

rem·i·nis·cent (rem′ə nis′ənt), *adj.* **1.** awakening memories of something similar; suggestive (usually fol. by *of*): *His style of writing is reminiscent of Melville's.* **2.** characterized by or of the nature of reminiscence. **3.** given to reminiscence: *a reminiscent old sailor.* [1755–65; < L *reminiscent-* (s. of *reminiscēns*) remembering, prp. of *reminiscī,* equiv. to *re-* RE- + *-minisc(ī)* (inceptive v., deriv. of the base of *mēns* MIND) + *-ent-* -ENT]
—**rem′i·nis′cent·ly,** *adv.*

rem·i·nis·cen·tial (rem′ə nə sen′shəl), *adj.* of or pertaining to reminiscence; reminiscent. [1640–50; < LL *reminiscenti(a)* REMINISCENCE + -AL[1]] —**rem′i·nis·cen′tial·ly,** *adv.*

rem·i·ped (rem′ə ped′), *Zool.* —*adj.* **1.** having feet adapted for use as oars. —*n.* **2.** a remiped animal. [1820–30; < F *rémipède.* See REMIFORM, -PED]

re·mise (ri mīz′), *v.t.*, **-mised, -mis·ing.** *Law.* to give up a claim to; surrender by deed. [1475–85; < MF, fem. ptp. of *remettre* to put back, deliver < L *remittere* to REMIT]

re·miss (ri mis′), *adj.* **1.** negligent, careless, or slow in performing one's duty, business, etc.: *He's terribly remiss in his work.* **2.** characterized by negligence or carelessness. **3.** lacking force or energy; languid; sluggish. [1375–1425; late ME < L *remissus* (ptp. of *remittere* to send back, slacken, relax); see REMIT] —**re·miss′ly,** *adv.* —**re·miss′ness,** *n.*
—**Syn. 1, 2.** derelict, thoughtless, lax, slack, neglectful. **3.** dilatory, slothful, slow.

re·mis·si·ble (ri mis′ə bəl), *adj.* that may be remitted. [1570–80; < MF < L *remissibilis.* See REMISS, -IBLE] —**re·mis′si·bil′i·ty, re·mis′si·ble·ness,** *n.*

re·mis·sion (ri mish′ən), *n.* **1.** the act of remitting. **2.** pardon; forgiveness, as of sins or offenses. **3.** abatement or diminution, as of diligence, labor, intensity, etc. **4.** the relinquishment of a payment, obligation, etc. **5.** *Med.* **a.** a temporary or permanent decrease or subsidence of manifestations of a disease. **b.** a period during which such a decrease or subsidence occurs: *The patient's leukemia was in remission.* [1175–1225; ME < OF < L *remissiōn-* (s. of *remissiō*). See REMISS, -ION]
—**Syn. 2.** absolution. **3.** lessening, relaxation. **4.** release. —**Ant. 2.** blame, censure. **3.** intensification.

re·mis·sive (ri mis′iv), *adj.* **1.** characterized by remission or decrease. **2.** producing or granting pardon or remission. [1375–1425; late ME: bringing about muscle relaxation < ML *remissīvus.* See REMISS, -IVE] —**re·mis′sive·ly,** *adv.* —**re·mis′sive·ness,** *n.*

re·mit (ri mit′), *v.*, **-mit·ted, -mit·ting,** *n.* —*v.t.* **1.** to transmit or send (money, a check, etc.) to a person or place, usually in payment. **2.** to refrain from inflicting or enforcing, as a punishment, sentence, etc. **3.** to refrain from exacting, as a payment or service. **4.** to pardon or forgive (a sin, offense, etc.). **5.** to slacken; abate; relax: *to remit watchfulness.* **6.** to give back: *to remit an overpayment.* **7.** *Law.* to send back (a case) to an inferior court for further action. **8.** to put back into a previous position or condition. **9.** to put off; postpone; defer. **10.** *Obs.* to set free; release. **11.** *Obs.* to send back to prison or custody. **12.** *Obs.* to give up; surrender. —*v.i.* **13.** to transmit money, a check, etc., as in payment. **14.** to abate for a time or at intervals, as a fever. **15.** to slacken; abate. —*n.* **16.** *Law.* a transfer of the record of an action from one tribunal to another, particularly from an appellate court to the court of original jurisdiction. [1325–75; ME *remitten* < L *remittere* to send back, let go back, concede, allow, equiv. to *re-* RE- + *mittere* to send] —**re·mit′ta·ble,** *adj.*
—**Syn. 1.** forward. **4.** excuse, overlook. **5.** diminish. **6.** return, restore. —**Ant. 1.** retain. **4.** condemn. **5.** increase.

remitt., remittance.

re·mit·tal (ri mit′l), *n.* a remission. [1590–1600; REMIT + -AL[2]]

re·mit·tance (ri mit′ns), *n.* **1.** the sending of money, checks, etc., to a recipient at a distance. **2.** money or its equivalent sent from one place to another. [1695–1705; REMIT + -ANCE]

remit′tance man′, a person who is supported abroad chiefly by remittances from home. [1885–90]

re·mit·tee (ri mi tē′, -mit′ē), *n.* a person or company to which a remittance is made. [1760–70; REMIT + -EE]

re·mit·tent (ri mit′nt), *adj.* **1.** abating for a time or at intervals: *remittent symptoms.* **2.** of, pertaining to, or characterized by a remittent fever. —*n.* **3.** a remittent fever. [1685–95; < L *remittent-* (s. of *remittēns*), prp. of *remittere* to send back. See REMIT, -ENT] —**re·mit′tence, re·mit′ten·cy,** *n.* —**re·mit′tent·ly,** *adv.*

re·mit·ter (ri mit′ər), *n.* **1.** *Law.* **a.** the principle or operation by which a person who enters on an estate by a defective title, and who previously had an earlier and more valid title to it, is adjudged to hold it by the earlier and more valid one. **b.** the act of remitting a case to another court for decision. **2.** restoration, as to a former right or condition. **3.** Also, **re·mit′tor.** a person or company that remits or makes a remittance. [1535–45; REMIT + -ER[3]]

re·mix (*v.* rē miks′; *n.* rē′miks′), *v.*, **-mix, -mix·ing,** *n.* —*v.t.* **1.** to mix again. **2.** to mix and re-record the elements of (a musical recording) in a different way. —*n.* **3.** a remixed recording. [1660–70]

rem·nant (rem′nənt), *n.* **1.** a remaining, usually small part, quantity, number, or the like. **2.** a fragment or scrap. **3.** a small, unsold or unused piece of cloth, lace, etc., as at the end of a bolt. **4.** a trace; vestige: *remnants of former greatness.* —*adj.* **5.** remaining; leftover. [1300–50; ME *remna(u)nt,* contr. of *remenant* < OF, prp. of *remenoir* to REMAIN] —**rem′nant·al,** *adj.*
—**Syn. 1.** remainder, residue, residuum, rest, remains.

re·mod·el (rē mod′l), *v.t.*, **-eled, -el·ing** or (*esp. Brit.*) **-elled, -el·ling.** **1.** to model again. **2.** to reconstruct; make over. [1780–90; RE- + MODEL] —**re·mod′el·er;** *esp. Brit.,* **re·mod′el·ler,** *n.*
—**Syn. 2.** renew, renovate, re-create, repair.

re·mo·lade (rā′mə läd′), *n.* rémoulade.

re·mon·e·tize (rē mon′i tīz′, -mun′-), *v.t.*, **-tized, -tiz·ing.** to restore to use as legal tender: *to remonetize silver.* Also, *esp. Brit.,* **re·mon′e·tise′.** [1875–80, *Amer.*; RE- + MONETIZE] —**re·mon′e·ti·za′tion,** *n.*

re·mon·strance (ri mon′strəns), *n.* **1.** an act or instance of remonstrating. **2.** a protest. [1470–80; < MF, equiv. to *remonstr(er)* (< ML *remōnstrāre* to point out; see REMONSTRATE) + *-ance* -ANCE]

re·mon·strant (ri mon′strənt), *adj.* **1.** remonstrating; expostulatory. —*n.* **2.** a person who remonstrates. **3.** (*cap.*) one of the Dutch Arminians whose doctrinal differences from strict Calvinists were set forth in 1610. [1610–20; < ML *remōnstrant-* (s. of *remōnstrāns,* prp. of *remōnstrāre*). See REMONSTRATE, -ANT] —**re·mon′strant·ly,** *adv.*

re·mon·strate (ri mon′strāt), *v.*, **-strat·ed, -strat·ing.** —*v.t.* **1.** to say or plead in protest, objection, or disapproval. **2.** *Obs.* to show. —*v.i.* **3.** to present reasons in complaint; plead in protest. [1590–1600; < ML *remōnstrātus* (ptp. of *remōnstrāre* to exhibit, demonstrate), equiv. to *re-* RE- + *mōnstrā(re)* to show + *-tus* ptp. suffix; see -ATE[1]] —**re·mon′strat·ing·ly,** *adv.* —**re·mon·stra·tion** (rē′mon strā′shən, rem′ən-), *n.* —**re·mon·stra·tive** (ri mon′strə tiv), *adj.* —**re·mon′stra·tive·ly,** *adv.* —**re·mon·stra·tor** (ri mon′strā tər), *n.*
—**Syn. 3.** argue, object, expostulate.

re·mon·tant (ri mon′tənt), *adj.* **1.** (of certain roses) blooming more than once in a season. —*n.* **2.** a remontant rose. [1880–85; < F, prp. of *remonter* to REMOUNT]

rem·o·ra (rem′ər ə), *n.* **1.** any of several fishes of the family Echeneididae, having on the top of the head a sucking disk by which they can attach themselves to sharks, turtles, ships, and other moving objects. **2.** *Archaic.* an obstacle, hindrance, or obstruction. [1560–70; < L: lit., delay, hindrance, deriv. of *remorārī* to linger, delay, equiv. to *re-* RE- + *morārī* to delay]

remora, *Echeneis naucrates,* length 2 to 3 ft. (0.6 to 0.9 m)

re·morse (ri môrs′), *n.* **1.** deep and painful regret for wrongdoing; compunction. **2.** *Obs.* pity. [1325–75; ME < MF *remors* < ML *remorsus,* equiv. to L *remord(ere)* to bite again, vex, nag (*re-* RE- + *mordere* to bite) + *-tus* suffix of v. action, with *dt* > *s*; see MORDANT]
—**Syn. 1.** contrition. See **regret.**

re·morse·ful (ri môrs′fəl), *adj.* **1.** full of remorse. **2.** characterized by or due to remorse: *a remorseful mood.* [1585–95; REMORSE + -FUL] —**re·morse′ful·ly,** *adv.* —**re·morse′ful·ness,** *n.*
—**Syn. 1, 2.** contrite, regretful, penitent.

re·morse·less (ri môrs′lis), *adj.* without remorse; merciless; relentless. [1585–95; REMORSE + -LESS] —**re·morse′less·ly,** *adv.* —**re·morse′less·ness,** *n.*
—**Syn.** ruthless, unrelenting, implacable, inexorable, cruel.

re·mote (ri mōt′), *adj.*, **-mot·er, -mot·est,** *n.* —*adj.* **1.** far apart; far distant in space; situated at some distance away: *the remote jungles of Brazil.* **2.** out-of-the-way; secluded: *a remote village; a remote mountaintop.* **3.** distant in time: *remote antiquity.* **4.** distant in relationship or connection: *a remote ancestor.* **5.** operating or controlled from a distance, as by remote control: *a remote telephone answering machine.* **6.** far off; abstracted; removed: *principles remote from actions.* **7.** not direct, primary, or proximate; not directly involved or influential: *the remote causes of the war.* **8.** slight or faint; unlikely: *not the remotest idea; a remote chance.* **9.** reserved and distant in manner; aloof; not warmly cordial. —*n.* **10.** *Radio and Television.* a broadcast, usually live, from a location outside a studio. **11.** See **remote control** (def. 2). [1375–1425; late ME < L *remōtus,* ptp. of *removēre* to move back; see REMOVE, MOTION] —**re·mote′ly,** *adv.* —**re·mote′ness,** *n.*
—**Syn. 2.** sequestered, isolated, removed, apart, solitary. **8.** inconsiderable. **9.** withdrawn. —**Ant. 1.** close, near.

remote′ control′, **1.** control of the operation or performance of an apparatus from a distance, as the control of a guided missile by radio signals. **2.** Also called **remote.** a device used to control the operation of an apparatus or machine, as a television set, from a distance. [1900–05] —**re·mote′-con·trol′,** *adj.*

remote′ sens′ing, the science of gathering data on an object or area from a considerable distance, as with radar or infrared photography, to observe the earth or a heavenly body.

re·mo·tion (ri mō′shən), *n.* **1.** the act of removing; removal. **2.** *Obs.* departure. [1350–1400; ME *remosion* < L *remōtiōn-* (s. of *remōtiō*) a putting back, removing. See REMOTE, -ION]

ré·mou·lade (rā′mə läd′; *Fr.* RĀ mōō LAD′), *n.* a cold sauce made with mayonnaise and various condiments and herbs, as chopped pickles, capers, mustard, parsley, chervil, and tarragon. Also, **remolade.** [1835–45; < F, orig. dial. *rémola,* alter. of L *armoracea* horseradish; see -ADE[1]]

re·mount (*v.* rē mount′; *n.* rē′mount′, rē mount′), *v.t., v.i.* **1.** to mount again; reascend. —*n.* **2.** a fresh horse or supply of fresh horses. [1325–75; ME *remounten* < OF *remonter.* See RE-, MOUNT[1]]

re·mov·a·ble (ri mōō′və bəl), *adj.* **1.** that may be removed. **2.** *Math.* **a.** (of a singularity of a function of a complex variable) noting that the function is not analytic at the point but that the function can be redefined so as to be analytic at the point. **b.** (of a discontinuity) noting that the function is discontinuous at the point but that the function can be redefined so as to be continuous at the point. Cf. **essential** (def. 5). [1525–35; REMOVE + -ABLE] —**re·mov′a·bil′i·ty, re·mov′a·ble·ness,** *n.* —**re·mov′a·bly,** *adv.*

re·mov·al (ri mōō′vəl), *n.* **1.** the act of removing. **2.** change of residence, position, etc. **3.** dismissal, as from an office. [1590–1600; REMOVE + -AL[2]]

re·move (ri mōōv′), *v.*, **-moved, -mov·ing,** *n.* —*v.t.* **1.** to move from a place or position; take away or off: *to remove the napkins from the table.* **2.** to take off or shed (an article of clothing): *to remove one's jacket.* **3.** to move or shift to another place or position; transfer: *She removed the painting to another wall.* **4.** to put out; send away: *to remove a tenant.* **5.** to dismiss or force from a position or office; discharge: *They removed him for embezzling.* **6.** to take away, withdraw, or eliminate: *to remove the threat of danger.* **7.** to get rid of; do away with; put an end to: *to remove a stain; to remove the source of disease.* **8.** to kill; assassinate. —*v.i.* **9.** to move from one place to another, esp. to another locality or residence: *We remove to Newport early in July.* **10.** to go away; depart; disappear. —*n.* **11.** the act of removing. **12.** a removal from one place, as of residence, to another. **13.** the distance by which one person, place, or thing is separated from another: *to see something at a remove.* **14.** a mental distance from the reality of something as a result of psychological detachment or lack of experience: *to criticize something at a remove.* **15.** a degree of difference, as that due to descent, transmission, etc.: *a folk survival, at many removes, of a druidic rite.* **16.** a step or degree, as in a graded scale. **17.** *Brit.* a promotion of a pupil to a higher class or division at school. [1250–1300; ME *removen* (v.) < OF *remouvoir* < L *removēre.* See RE-, MOVE]
—**Syn. 1.** dislodge. **3.** displace, transport. **8.** murder.
—**Ant. 1.** leave. **9.** remain.

re·moved (ri mōōvd′), *adj.* **1.** remote; separate; not connected with; distinct from. **2.** distant by a given number of degrees of descent or kinship: *A first cousin once removed is the child of one's first cousin.* [1540–50; REMOVE + -ED[2]] —**re·mov·ed·ly** (ri mōō′vid lē, -mōōvd′-), *adv.* —**re·mov′ed·ness,** *n.*
—**Syn. 1.** withdrawn, abstracted; isolated, solitary, apart.

re·mov·er (ri mōō′vər), *n.* **1.** a person or thing that removes. **2.** *Law.* the transfer of a case from one court to another, as by a writ of error. [1585–95; REMOVE + -ER[1]]

Rem·scheid (rem′shīt), *n.* a city in W Germany, in the Ruhr region. 132,100.

Rem·sen (rem′sən), *n.* **Ira,** 1846–1927, U.S. chemist and educator.

REM′ sleep′, *Physiol.* a recurrent period of sleep, typically totaling about two hours a night, during which most dreaming occurs as the eyes move under closed lids and the skeletal muscles are deeply relaxed. Also called **paradoxical sleep.** Cf. **slow-wave sleep.** [1965–70]

re·mu·da (rə mōō′də; *Sp.* Re mōō′thä), *n., pl.* **-das** (-dəz; *Sp.* -thäs). *Chiefly Southwestern U.S.* a group of saddle horses from which ranch hands choose mounts for the day. [1835–45, *Amer.*; < AmerSp: a change (of horses), Sp: exchange, deriv. of *remudar* to change, replace, equiv. to *re-* RE- + *mudar* to change (< L *mūtāre*)]

re·mu·ner·ate (ri myōō′nə rāt′), *v.t.*, **-at·ed, -at·ing.** **1.** to pay, recompense, or reward for (work, services, etc.). **2.** to yield a recompense for (work, services, etc.). [1515–25; < L *remūnerātus* (ptp. of *remūnerārī* to repay, reward), equiv. to *re-* RE- + *mūner(āre)* to give, bestow (deriv. of *mūner-,* s. of *mūnus* gift, duty) + *-ātus*

CONCISE ETYMOLOGY KEY: <, descended or borrowed from; >, whence; b., blend of, blended; c., cognate with; cf., compare; deriv., derivative; equiv., equivalent; imit., imitative; obl., oblique; r., replacing; s., stem; sp., spelling, spelled; resp., respelling, respelled; trans., translation; ?, origin unknown; *, unattested; ‡, probably earlier than. See the full key inside the front cover.

re′in·i′ti·ate′, *v.t.*, **-at·ed, -at·ing.**
re′in·ject′, *v.t.*
re′in·jec′tion, *n.*
re·in′jure, *v.t.*, **-jured, -jur·ing.**
re·in′ju·ry, *n., pl.* **-ju·ries.**
re·ink′, *v.t.*
re′in·oc′u·late′, *v.*, **-lat·ed, -lat·ing.**
re′in·oc′u·la′tion, *n.*
re′in·quire′, *v.*, **-quired, -quir·ing.**
re′in·quir′y, *n., pl.* **-quir·ies.**
re′in·scribe′, *v.t.*, **-scribed, -scrib·ing.**
re′in·sert′, *v.t.*
re′in·ser′tion, *n.*
re′in·sist′, *v.i.*
re′in·spect′, *v.t.*
re′in·spec′tion, *n.*
re′in·spi·ra′tion, *n.*
re′in·spire′, *v.*, **-spired, -spir·ing.**
re′in·stal′, *v.t.*
re′in·stall′, *v.t.*
re′in·stal·la′tion, *n.*
re′in·stall′ment, *n.*
re′in·stal′ment, *n.*
re·in′sti·tute′, *v.t.*, **-tut·ed, -tut·ing.**
re′in·sti·tu′tion, *n.*
re′in·sti·tu′tion·al·i·za′tion, *n.*
re′in·struct′, *v.t.*
re′in·struc′tion, *n.*
re·in′su·late′, *v.t.*, **-lat·ed, -lat·ing.**
re·in′te·grate′, *v.*, **-grat·ed, -grat·ing.**
re′in·ter′, *v.t.*, **-terred, -ter·ring.**

-ATE[1]] —**re·mu′ner·a·ble,** *adj.* —**re·mu′ner·a·bil′i·ty,** *n.* —**re·mu′ner·a·bly,** *adv.* —**re·mu′ner·a′tor,** *n.*
—**Syn. 1.** reimburse, requite, compensate.

re·mu·ner·a·tion (ri myo͞o′nə rā′shən), *n.* **1.** the act of remunerating. **2.** something that remunerates; reward; pay: *He received little remuneration for his services.* [1470–80; earlier *remuneracion* < L *remūnerātiōn-* (s. of *remūnerātiō*), equiv. to *remūnerāt(us)* (see REMUNERATE) + *-iōn-* -ION]

re·mu·ner·a·tive (ri myo͞o′nər ə tiv, -nə rā′tiv), *adj.* **1.** affording remuneration; profitable: *remunerative work.* **2.** that remunerates. Also, **re·mu′ner·a·to′ry.** [1620–30; REMUNERATE + -IVE] —**re·mu·ner·a·tive·ly** (ri myo͞o′nə rā′tiv lē, -nər ə tiv-), *adv.* —**re·mu′ner·a′·tive·ness,** *n.*

Re·mus (rē′məs), *n.* **1.** *Rom. Legend.* See under **Romulus** (def. 1). **2. Uncle.** See **Uncle Remus.**

Re·na (rē′nə), *n.* a female given name, form of **Marina.**

Ren·ais·sance (ren′ə säns′, -zäns′, -säɴs′, ren′ə-säns′, -zäns′, -säɴs′; *esp. Brit.* ri nā′səns), *n.* Also, **Renascence. 1.** the activity, spirit, or time of the great revival of art, literature, and learning in Europe beginning in the 14th century and extending to the 17th century, marking the transition from the medieval to the modern world. **2.** the forms and treatments in art used during this period. **3.** (*sometimes l.c.*) any similar revival in the world of art and learning. **4.** (*l.c.*) a renewal of life, vigor, interest, etc.; rebirth; revival: *a moral renaissance.* —*adj.* **5.** of, pertaining to, or suggestive of the European Renaissance of the 14th through the 17th centuries: *Renaissance attitudes.* **6.** noting or pertaining to the group of architectural styles existing in Italy in the 15th and 16th centuries as adaptations of ancient Roman architectural details or compositional forms to contemporary uses, characterized at first by the free and inventive use of isolated details, later by the more imitative use of whole orders and compositional arrangements, with great attention to the formulation of compositional rules after the precepts of Vitruvius and the precedents of existing ruins, and at all periods by an emphasis on symmetry, exact mathematical relationships between parts, and a general effect of simplicity and repose. **7.** noting or pertaining to any of the various adaptations of this group of styles in foreign architecture characterized typically by the playful or grotesque use of isolated details in more or less traditional buildings. **8.** noting or pertaining to the furnishings or decorations of the Renaissance, in which motifs of classical derivation frequently appear. [1830–40; < F, MF: rebirth, equiv. to *renaiss-* (s. of *renaistre* to be born again < L *renāscī*; *re-* RE- + *nāscī* to be born) + *-ance* -ANCE]
—**Syn. 4.** resurgence, reawakening.

Renaissance chest
(Florence, 16th century)

Ren′aissance man′, 1. a cultured man of the Renaissance who was knowledgeable, educated, or proficient in a wide range of fields. **2.** (*sometimes l.c.*) a present-day man who has acquired profound knowledge or proficiency in more than one field. [1905–10]

Ren′aissance Reviv′al, a mid-Victorian architectural style adapting the classical forms of 15th- and 16th-century Italian architecture, especially palace architecture, usually characterized by blocklike massing, with refined classicized decorative detail around regularly organized windows.

Ren′aissance wom′an, (*sometimes l.c.*) a woman who has acquired profound knowledge or proficiency in more than one field.

re·nais·sant (ri nā′sənt), *adj.* renascent. [1860–65; < F, prp. of *renaître* to be reborn; see RENAISSANCE, -ANT]

re·nal (rēn′l), *adj.* of or pertaining to the kidneys or the surrounding regions. [1650–60; < LL *rēnālis,* equiv. to L *rēn(ēs)* kidneys (pl.) + *-ālis* -AL[1]]

re′nal cal′culus, *Pathol.* See **kidney stone.**

Re·nan (ri nan′; *Fr.* rə näɴ′), *n.* **Er·nest** (ûr′nist; *Fr.* er nest′), 1823–92, French philologist, historian, and critic.

Ren·ard (ren′ərd), *n.* Reynard. —**Ren·ard·ine** (ren′-ər din, -dēn′), *adj.*

Re·nas·cence (ri nas′əns, -nā′səns), *n.* (*sometimes l.c.*) Renaissance. [1720–30; RENASC(ENT) + -ENCE]

re·nas·cent (ri nas′ənt, -nā′sənt), *adj.* being reborn; springing again into being or vigor: *a renascent interest in Henry James.* [1720–30; < L *renāscent-* (s. of *renāscēns*), prp. of *renāscī.* See RENAISSANCE, -ENT]

Re·na·ta (rə nä′tə; *It.* re nä′tä), *n.* a female given name.

re·na·ture (rē nā′chər), *v.t.,* **-tured, -tur·ing.** to restore (a denatured substance) to its former, natural state. [1925–30; RE- + NATURE; cf. DENATURE]

Re·nault (rə nôlt′; *Fr.* rə nō′), *n.* **Lou·is** (lo͞o′ē; *Fr.* lwē), 1843–1918, French jurist: Nobel peace prize 1907.

ren·con·tre (ren kon′tər; *Fr.* räɴ kôɴ′trᵊ), *n., pl.* **-tres** (-tərz; *Fr.* -trᵊ). rencounter. [< F]

ren·coun·ter (ren koun′tər), *n.* Also, **rencontre. 1.** a hostile meeting; battle. **2.** a contest of any kind. **3.** a casual meeting. —*v.t., v.i.* **4.** to encounter casually. **5.** *Obs.* to meet hostilely. [1495–1505; < MF *rencontrer.* See RE-, ENCOUNTER]

rend (rend), *v.,* **rent, rend·ing.** —*v.t.* **1.** to separate into parts with force or violence: *The storm rent the ship to pieces.* **2.** to tear apart, split, or divide: *a racial problem that is rending the nation.* **3.** to pull or tear violently (often fol. by *away, off, up,* etc.). **4.** to tear (one's garments or hair) in grief, rage, etc. **5.** to disturb (the air) sharply with loud noise. **6.** to harrow or distress (the heart) with painful feelings. —*v.i.* **7.** to split or tear something. **8.** to become torn or split. [bef. 950; ME *renden,* OE *rendan;* c. OFris *renda*] —**rend′i·ble,** *adj.*
—**Syn. 2.** rive, sunder, sever, cleave, chop, fracture, rupture. See **tear**[2].

ren·der[1] (ren′dər), *v.t.* **1.** to cause to be or become; make: *to render someone helpless.* **2.** to do; perform: *to render a service.* **3.** to furnish; provide: *to render aid.* **4.** to exhibit or show (obedience, attention, etc.). **5.** to present for consideration, approval, payment, action, etc., as an account. **6.** to return; to make (a payment in money, kind, or service) as by a tenant to a superior: *knights rendering military service to the lord.* **7.** to pay as due (a tax, tribute, etc.). **8.** to deliver formally or officially; hand down: *to render a verdict.* **9.** to translate into another language: *to render French poems into English.* **10.** to represent; depict, as in painting: *to render a landscape.* **11.** to represent (a perspective view of a projected building) in drawing or painting. **12.** to bring out the meaning of by performance or execution; interpret, as a part in a drama or a piece of music. **13.** to give in return or requital: *to render good for evil.* **14.** to give back; restore (often fol. by *back*). **15.** to give up; surrender. **16.** *Building Trades.* to cover (masonry) with a first coat of plaster. **17.** to melt down; extract the impurities from by melting: *to render fat.* **18.** to process, as for industrial use: *to render livestock carcasses.* —*v.i.* **19.** to provide due reward. **20.** to try out oil from fat, blubber, etc., by melting. —*n.* **21.** *Building Trades.* a first coat of plaster for a masonry surface. [1275–1325; ME *rendren* < MF *rendre* < VL **rendere,* alter. (formed by analogy with *prendere* to take) of L *reddere* to give back, equiv. to *red-* RED- + *-dere,* comb. form of *dare* to give] —**ren′der·a·ble,** *adj.* —**ren′der·er,** *n.*
—**Syn. 3.** give, supply, contribute, afford. **4.** demonstrate. **15.** cede, yield.

rend·er[2] (ren′dər), *n.* a person or thing that rends. [1580–90; REND + -ER[1]]

ren·der·ing (ren′dər ing), *n.* **1.** an act or instance of interpretation, rendition, or depiction, as of a dramatic part or a musical composition: *her rendering of the part of Hedda.* **2.** a translation: *Chapman's rendering of Homer.* **3.** a representation of a building, interior, etc., executed in perspective and usually done for purposes of presentation. **4.** *Building Trades.* render[1] (def. 21). [1400–50; late ME (ger.); see RENDER, -ING[1]]

ren′dering works′, (*used with a singular v.*) a factory or plant that renders and processes livestock carcasses into tallow, hides, fertilizer, etc. Also called **ren′dering plant′.**

ren·dez·vous (rän′də vo͞o′, -dā-; *Fr.* räɴ de vo͞o′), *n., pl.* **-vous** (-vo͞oz′; *Fr.* -vo͞o′), *v.,* **-voused** (-vo͞od′), **-vous·ing** (-vo͞o′ing). —*n.* **1.** an agreement between two or more persons to meet at a certain time and place. **2.** the meeting itself. **3.** a place designated for a meeting or assembling, esp. of troops or ships. **4.** a meeting of two or more spacecraft in outer space. **5.** a favorite or popular gathering place. —*v.t., v.i.* **6.** to assemble at an agreed time and place. [1585–95; < MF, n. use of *rendez-vous* (impv.) present or betake yourselves; see RENDER[1]]

ren·di·tion (ren dish′ən), *n.* **1.** the act of rendering. **2.** a translation. **3.** an interpretation, as of a role or a piece of music. **4.** *Archaic.* surrender. [1595–1605; < MF, alter. of *reddition* (< ME *reddicion*) < LL *redditiōn-* (s. of *redditiō*), equiv. to L *reddit(us)* (ptp. of *reddere;* see RENDER[1]) + *-iōn-* -ION]
—**Syn. 1.** interpretation, version.

Re·née (rə nā′; *Fr.* rə nā′), *n.* a female given name, French form of **Renata.**

ren·e·gade (ren′i gād′), *n.* **1.** a person who deserts a party or cause for another. **2.** an apostate from a religious faith. —*adj.* **3.** of or like a renegade; traitorous. [1575–85; < Sp *renegado* < ML *renegātus* (n. use of ptp. of *renegāre* to desert, RENEGE), equiv. to *re-* RE- + *neg-,* base of *negāre* to deny + *-ātus* -ADE[1]]
—**Syn. 1.** traitor, deserter, betrayer, dissenter.

ren·e·ga·do (ren′i gā′dō, -gä′-), *n., pl.* **-dos.** a renegade. [1590–1600; < Sp]

re·nege (ri nig′, -neg′, -nēg′), *v.,* **-neged, -neg·ing,** *n.* —*v.i.* **1.** *Cards.* to play a card that is not of the suit led when one can follow suit; break a rule of play. **2.** to go back on one's word: *He has reneged on his promise.* —*v.t.* **3.** *Archaic.* to deny; disown; renounce. —*n.* **4.** *Cards.* an act or instance of reneging. [1540–50; earlier *renegue* < ML *renegāre,* equiv. to *re-* RE- + *negāre* to deny (cf. NEGATIVE)] —**re·neg′er,** *n.*

re·ne·go′ti·a·ble-rate mort′gage (rē′ni gō′shē ə-bəl rāt′, -shə bəl-), a type of home mortgage for which monthly payments stay constant for a term, usually of three to five years, and the interest rate is renegotiated at the end of every such term until the loan is paid off. *Abbr.:* RRM Also called **rollover mortgage.**

re·ne·go·ti·ate (rē′ni gō′shē āt′), *v.,* **-at·ed, -at·ing.** —*v.t.* **1.** to negotiate again, as a loan, treaty, etc. **2.** to reexamine (a government contract) with a view to eliminating or modifying those provisions found to represent excessive profits to the contractor. —*v.i.* **3.** to negotiate anew. **4.** to reexamine the costs and profits involved in a government contract for adjustment purposes. [1930–35; RE- + NEGOTIATE] —**re·ne·go·ti·a·ble** (rē′ni gō′shē-ə bəl, -shə bəl), *adj.* —**re′ne·go′ti·a′tion,** *n.*

re·new (ri no͞o′, -nyo͞o′), *v.t.* **1.** to begin or take up again, as an acquaintance, a conversation, etc.; resume. **2.** to make effective for an additional period: *to renew a lease.* **3.** to restore or replenish: *to renew a stock of goods.* **4.** to make, say, or do again. **5.** to revive; reestablish. **6.** to recover (youth, strength, etc.). **7.** to restore to a former state; make new or as if new again. —*v.i.* **8.** to begin again; recommence. **9.** to renew a lease, note, etc. **10.** to be restored to a former state; become new or as if new again. [1325–75; ME *renewen.* See RE-, NEW] —**re·new′a·bly,** *adv.* —**re·new·ed·ly** (ri no͞o′id lē, -nyo͞o′-), *adv.* —**re·new′er,** *n.*
—**Syn. 3.** restock. **7.** re-create, rejuvenate, regenerate, reinstate, mend. RENEW, RENOVATE, REPAIR, RESTORE suggest making something the way it formerly was. To RENEW means to bring back to an original condition of freshness and vigor: *to renew one's enthusiasm.* RENOVATE means to do over or make good any dilapidation of something: *to renovate an old house.* To REPAIR is to put into good or sound condition; to make good any injury, damage, wear and tear, decay, etc.; to mend: *to repair the roof of a house.* To RESTORE is to bring back to its former place or position something which has faded, disappeared, been lost, etc., or to reinstate a person in rank or position: *to restore a king to his throne.*

re·new·a·ble (ri no͞o′, -nyo͞o′), *adj.* **1.** able to be renewed: *a library book that is not renewable.* —*n.* **2.** something that is renewable. [1720–30; RENEW + -ABLE] —**re·new′a·bil′i·ty,** *n.*

renew′able en′ergy, any naturally occurring, theoretically inexhaustible source of energy, as biomass, solar, wind, tidal, wave, and hydroelectric power, that is not derived from fossil or nuclear fuel. Also called **soft energy.** [1970–75]

re·new·al (ri no͞o′əl, -nyo͞o′-), *n.* **1.** the act of renewing. **2.** the state of being renewed. **3.** an instance of this. [1675–85; RENEW + -AL[2]]

Ren·frew (ren′fro͞o), *n.* a historic county in SW Scotland. Also called **Ren·frew·shire** (ren′fro͞o shēr′, -shər).

ren·ga (reng′gə), *n. Pros.* See **linked verse.** [1875–80; < Japn < MChin, equiv. to Chin *lián* link + *gē* song]

Re·ni (ʀe′nē), *n.* **Gui·do** (gwē′dô), 1575–1642, Italian painter.

reni-, a combining form meaning "kidney," used in the formation of compound words: *reniform.* [< L *rēni-,* comb. form of *rēnēs* kidneys]

re·ni·fleur (ren′ə flûr′), *n. Psychiatry.* a person who is sexually aroused or gratified by odors. [< F, equiv. to *renifl(er)* to sniff + *-eur* -EUR]

ren·i·form (ren′ə fôrm′, rē′nə-), *adj.* kidney-shaped: *a reniform leaf; hematite in reniform masses.* [1745–50; < NL *rēniformis.* See RENI-, -FORM]

reniform leaf

re·nin (rē′nin), *n. Biochem.* a proteolytic enzyme secreted by the kidneys that is involved in the release of angiotensin. [1890–95; REN(I)- + -IN[2]]

re·ni·tent (ri nīt′nt, ren′i tənt), *adj.* **1.** resisting pressure; resistant. **2.** persistently opposing; recalcitrant. [1695–1705; < L *renitent-* (s. of *renitēns*), prp. of *renītī* to resist, equiv. to *re-* RE- + *nīt(ī)* to strive, make an effort + *-ent-* -ENT] —**re·ni′ten·cy, re·ni′tence,** *n.*

ren·min·bi (ren′min′bē′), *n.* the currency of the People's Republic of China, the basic unit of which is the yuan. [1955–60; < Chin *rénmínbì,* equiv. to *rénmín* people + *bì* currency]

Rennes (ren), *n.* a city in and the capital of Ille-et-Vilaine, in NW France: former capital of Brittany; scene of trial of Alfred Dreyfus, 1899. 205,733.

ren·net (ren′it), *n.* **1.** the lining membrane of the fourth stomach of a calf or of the stomach of certain other young animals. **2.** the rennin-containing substance from the stomach of the calf. **3.** a preparation or extract of the rennet membrane, used to curdle milk, as in making cheese, junket, etc. [1400–50; late ME; cf. OE *gerennan,* OHG *gerennen* to coagulate; akin to RUN]

Ren·nie (ren′ē), *n.* **John,** 1761–1821, Scottish engineer.

ren·nin (ren′in), *n. Biochem.* a coagulating enzyme oc-

CONCISE PRONUNCIATION KEY: act, cāpe, dâre, pärt; set, ēqual; *if,* īce; ox, ōver, ôrder, oil, bo͝ok, bo͞ot, out; up, ûrge; child; sing; shoe; thin, *th*at; zh as in *treasure.* ə = *a* as in *alone, e* as in *system, i* as in *easily, o* as in *gallop, u* as in *circus;* ᵊ as in *fire* (fīᵊr), *hour* (ouᵊr). l and n can serve as syllabic consonants, as in *cradle* (krād′l), and *button* (but′n). See the full key inside the front cover.

re·in′ter·est, *n., v.t.*
re′in·ter′ment, *n.*
re′in·ter′pret, *v.*
re′in·ter′pre·ta′tion, *n.*
re′in·ter′ro·gate′, *v.,* **-gat·ed, -gat·ing.**
re′in·ter′ro·ga′tion, *n.*
re′in·ter·rupt′, *v.*
re′in·ter·rup′tion, *n.*
re′in·ter·vene′, *v.i.,* **-vened, -ven·ing.**
re′in·ter·ven′tion, *n.*
re·in′ter·view′, *n., v.t.*
re′in·throne′, *v.t.,* **-throned, -thron·ing.**
re′in·trench′, *v.*
re′in·trench′ment, *n.*
re′in·tro·duce′, *v.t.,* **-duced, -duc·ing.**
re′in·tro·duc′tion, *n.*
re′in·vade′, *v.t.,* **-vad·ed, -vad·ing.**
re′in·va′sion, *n.*
re′in·vest′, *v.t.*
re′in·ves′ti·gate′, *v.,* **-gat·ed, -gat·ing.**
re′in·ves′ti·ga′tion, *n.*
re′in·vest′ment, *n.*
re′in·vig′or·ate′, *v.t.,* **-at·ed, -at·ing.**
re′in·vig′or·a′tion, *n.*
re′in·vi·ta′tion, *n.*
re′in·vite′, *v.,* **-vit·ed, -vit·ing.**
re′in·voke′, *v.t.,* **-voked, -vok·ing.**
re′in·volve′, *v.t.,* **-volved, -volv·ing.**
re′in·volve′ment, *n.*
re·ir′ri·gate′, *v.t.,* **-gat·ed, -gat·ing.**

curring in the gastric juice of the calf, forming the active principle of rennet and able to curdle milk. [1895–1900; RENN(ET) + -IN²]

Re·no (rē′nō), *n.* a city in W Nevada. 100,756.

re·nog·ra·phy (rē nog′rə fē), *n. Med.* x-ray examination of the kidney following injection of a radiopaque substance. [1910–15; < L *rēn(ēs)* (see RENAL) + -O- + -GRAPHY] **—re·no·graph·ic** (rē′nə graf′ik), *adj.*

Re·noir (ren′wär, ren wär′; *Fr.* RƏ NWAR′), *n.* **1. Jean** (zhäN), 1894–1979, French film director and writer. **2.** his father, **Pierre Au·guste** (pyer ō gyst′), 1841–1919, French painter.

re·nounce (ri nouns′), *v.*, **-nounced, -nounc·ing,** *n.* —*v.t.* **1.** to give up or put aside voluntarily: *to renounce worldly pleasures.* **2.** to give up by formal declaration: *to renounce a claim.* **3.** to repudiate; disown: *to renounce one's son.* —*v.i.* **4.** *Cards.* **a.** to play a card of a different suit from that led. **b.** to abandon or give up a suit led. **c.** to fail to follow the suit led. —*n.* **5.** *Cards.* an act or instance of renouncing. [1325–75; ME *renouncen* < MF *renoncer* < L *renūntiāre* to bring back word, disclaim, equiv. to *re-* RE- + *nūntiāre* to announce, deriv. of *nūntius* messenger, news] **—re·nounce′a·ble, re·nun·ci·a·ble** (ri nun′sē ə bəl, -shē-), *adj.* **—re·nounce′ment,** *n.* **—re·nounc′er,** *n.*
—Syn. 1. forsake, forgo, forswear, leave, quit. See **abandon¹. 2.** resign, abdicate. **3.** disclaim, reject, disavow, deny. **—Ant. 1.** claim. **3.** accept.

re·no·vas·cu·lar (rē′nō vas′kyə lər), *adj.* of or pertaining to the blood vessels of the kidneys. [1960–65; < L *rēn(ēs)* (see RENAL) + -O- + VASCULAR]

ren·o·vate (ren′ə vāt′), *v.*, **-vat·ed, -vat·ing,** *adj.* —*v.t.* **1.** to restore to good condition; make new or as if new again; repair. **2.** to reinvigorate; refresh; revive. —*adj.* **3.** *Archaic.* renovated. [1400–50; late ME (adj.) < L *renovātus* (ptp. of *renovāre*), equiv. to *re-* RE- + *nov(us)* NEW + *-ātus* -ATE¹] **—ren′o·vat′a·ble,** *adj.* **—ren′o·vat′ing·ly,** *adv.* **—ren′o·va′tion,** *n.* **—ren′o·va′tive,** *adj.* **—ren′o·va′tor,** *n.*
—Syn. 1. See **renew.**

re·nown (ri noun′), *n.* **1.** widespread and high repute; fame. **2.** *Obs.* report or rumor. [1300–50; ME *renoun* < AF; OF *renom,* deriv. of *renomer* to make famous < L *re-* RE- + *nōmināre* to NAME] **—re·nown′less,** *adj.*
—Syn. 1. celebrity, glory, distinction, note, eminence.

re·nowned (ri nound′), *adj.* celebrated; famous. [1325–75; ME; see RENOWN, -ED²] **—re·nown·ed·ly** (ri nou′nid lē, -nound′-), *adv.* **—re·nown′ed·ness,** *n.*
—Syn. famed, distinguished, honored, notable.

rent¹ (rent), *n.* **1.** a payment made periodically by a tenant to a landlord in return for the use of land, a building, an apartment, an office, or other property. **2.** a payment or series of payments made by a lessee to an owner in return for the use of machinery, equipment, etc. **3.** *Econ.* the excess of the produce or return yielded by a given piece of cultivated land over the cost of production; the yield from a piece of land or real estate. **4.** profit or return derived from any differential advantage in production. **5.** *Obs.* revenue or income. **6. for rent,** available to be rented, as a home or store: *an apartment for rent.* —*v.t.* **7.** to grant the possession and enjoyment of (property, machinery, etc.) in return for the payment of rent from the tenant or lessee. (often fol. by *out*). **8.** to take and hold (property, machinery, etc.) in return for the payment of rent to the landlord or owner. —*v.i.* **9.** to be leased or let for rent: *This apartment rents cheaply.* **10.** to lease or let property. **11.** to take possession of and use property by paying rent: *She rents from a friend.* [1125–75; (n.) ME *rente* < OF < VL **rendita,* fem. ptp. of **rendere* (see RENDER¹); (v.) ME *renten* < OF *renter,* deriv. of *rente*] **—rent′a·bil′i·ty,** *n.* **—rent′a·ble,** *adj.*
—Syn. 8. lease, let. See **hire.**

rent² (rent), *n.* **1.** an opening made by rending or tearing; slit; fissure. **2.** a breach of relations or union between individuals or groups; schism. —*v.* **3.** pt. and pp. of **rend.** [1325–75 for v. sense; 1525–35 for def. 1; ME; see REND]
—Syn. 1. tear, split, rift, cleft, rip, rupture, fracture. **2.** division, separation.

rent-a-car (rent′ə kär′), *n.* **1.** a company or service that rents cars, as by the day or week. **2.** a car provided by such a company or service. —*adj.* **3.** Also, *esp. Brit.,* **self-drive.** of or pertaining to such a company or service: *rent-a-car rates.* [1930–35]

rent·al (ren′tl), *n.* **1.** an amount received or paid as rent. **2.** the act of renting. **3.** an apartment, house, car, etc., offered or given for rent. **4.** an income arising from rents received. **5.** a rent-roll. —*adj.* **6.** of or pertaining to rent. **7.** available for rent. **8.** engaged in the business of providing rentals: *a rental agency.* [1325–75; ME < AL *rentāle.* See RENT¹, -AL²]

rent′al collec′tion, a group of books, in a public or other free library, for which a borrower must pay a fee.

rent′al li′brary. See **lending library.** [1925–30, *Amer.*]

rent′ control′, government control over the amount of rent charged, as for housing. [1930–35] **—rent′-con·trolled′,** *adj.*

CONCISE ETYMOLOGY KEY: <, descended or borrowed from; >, whence; b., blend of, blended; c., cognate with; cf., compare; deriv., derivative; equiv., equivalent; imit., imitative; obl., oblique; r., replacing; s., stem; sp., spelling, spelled; resp., respelling, respelled; trans., translation; ?, origin unknown; *, unattested; ‡, probably earlier than. See the full key inside the front cover.

rente (RÄNT), *n., pl.* ***rentes*** (RÄNT). *French.* **1.** revenue or income, or the instrument evidencing a right to such periodic receipts. **2. *rentes.*** Also called ***rentes sur l'é·tat*** (RÄNT SYR lā TA′). perpetual bonds issued by the French government.

rent·er (ren′tər), *n.* a person or organization that holds, or has the use of, property by payment of rent. [1350–1400; ME; see RENT¹, -ER¹]

rent-free (rent′frē′), *adv.* **1.** without payment of rent: *We lived rent-free for six months.* —*adj.* **2.** not subject to rent: *a rent-free apartment.* [1625–35]

ren·tier (RÄN tyā′), *n., pl.* **-tiers** (-tyā′). *French.* a person who has a fixed income, as from lands or bonds.

Ren·ton (ren′tn), *n.* a city in W Washington, near Seattle. 30,612.

rent′ par′ty, (esp. during the Great Depression) a party with music and dancing, given to raise money for the host's rent by collecting a contribution from each guest. [1925–30, *Amer.*]

rent-roll (rent′rōl′), *n.* an account or schedule of rents, the amount due from each tenant, and the total received. Also, **rent′ roll′.** [1525–35]

rent′ seck′ (sek), *pl.* **rents seck.** a right to rent in which the renter does not have the usual power of collection by seizure of the tenant's goods. Also called **dry rent.** [1425–75; late ME < AF *rente seque* lit., dry rent]

rent-sta·bi·lized (rent′stā′bə līzd′), *adj.* (of housing) regulated by law so that rent increases may not exceed a specified amount. **—rent′-sta′bi·li·za′tion,** *n.*

rent′ strike′, a temporary, organized refusal by tenants, as of an apartment building, to pay their rent, as in protest over inadequate services. [1960–65]

rent′ ta′ble, *Eng. Furniture.* a drum table of the 18th century, having six drawers and originally used by landlords to keep rent money and papers pertaining to their estates. [1925–30]

rent table
(18th century)

re·nun·ci·a·tion (ri nun′sē ā′shən, -shē-), *n.* an act or instance of relinquishing, abandoning, repudiating, or sacrificing something, as a right, title, person, or ambition: *the king's renunciation of the throne.* [1350–1400; ME < L *renūnciātiōn-* (s. of *renūnciātiō*) proclamation, equiv. to *renūnciāt(us)* (ptp. of *renūntiāre* to RENOUNCE) + *-iōn-* -ION] **—re·nun′ci·a′tive, re·nun·ci·a·to·ry** (ri nun′sē ə tôr′ē, -tōr′ē, -shē ə-), *adj.*
—Syn. abandonment, repudiation, denial, disavowal, forgoing.

ren·ver·sé (rän′ver sā′; *Fr.* RÄN VER SA′), *adj. Ballet.* performed with the body bent from the waist: *a pirouette renversé.* [1645–55; < F: lit., turned back]

ren·voi (ren voi′), *n.* the expulsion by a government of an alien, esp. a foreign diplomat, from the country. [1895–1900; < F: a return, deriv. of *renvoyer* to send back. See RE-, ENVOY¹]

Ren·wick (ren′wik), *n.* **James,** 1818–95, U.S. architect.

re·o·pen (rē ō′pən), *v.t., v.i.* **1.** to open again. **2.** to start again; resume: *to reopen an argument; to reopen an attack.* [1725–35; RE- + OPEN]

re·o·pen·er (rē ō′pə nər), *n. Informal.* an act or instance of reopening negotiations, as on the provisions of a contract. [REOPEN + -ER¹]

re·or·der (rē ôr′dər), *v.t.* **1.** to put in order again: *to reorder the card file.* **2.** to give a reorder for: *to reorder the books before they're completely sold out.* —*v.i.* **3.** to order goods again. —*n.* **4.** a second or repeated order for the same goods: *to put through a reorder for those lamps.* [1585–95; RE- + ORDER]

re·or·di·na·tion (rē′ôr dn ā′shən), *n.* **1.** a second ordination. **2.** *Rom. Cath. Ch.* the ordination of a priest whose first orders have been held invalid. **3.** *Eccles.* the second ordination of a priest whose first orders were received from another church. **4.** the sacrament elevating a deacon, priest, or bishop to a higher grade or order. [1590–1600; < ML *reōrdinātiōn-* (s. of *reōrdinātiō*). See RE-, ORDINATION]

re·or·gan·i·za·tion (rē′ôr gə nə zā′shən), *n.* **1.** the act or process of reorganizing; state of being reorganized. **2.** *Finance.* a reconstruction of a business corporation, including a marked change in capital structure, often following a failure and receivership or bankruptcy trusteeship. [1805–15; RE- + ORGANIZATION]

re·or·gan·ize (rē ôr′gə nīz′), *v.t., v.i.,* **-ized, -iz·ing.** to organize again. Also, *esp. Brit.,* **re·or′gan·ise′.** [1675–85; RE- + ORGANIZE] **—re·or′gan·iz′er,** *n.*

re·or·i·ent (rē ôr′ē ent′, -ōr′-), *v.t., v.i.* **1.** to orient again or anew. —*adj.* **2.** *Rare.* rising anew. [1930–35; RE- + ORIENT]

re·o·ri·en·ta·tion (rē ôr′ē ən tā′shən, -en-, -ōr′-), *n.* the act or state of reorienting or of being reoriented. [1915–20; RE- + ORIENTATION]

re·o·vi·rus (rē′ō vī′rəs, rē′ō vī′-), *n., pl.* **-rus·es.** any large virus of the family Reoviridae, having double-stranded RNA and a polyhedral capsid, including those causing infantile gastroenteritis. [1955–60; *r(espiratory) e(nteric) o(rphan) virus;* coined by U.S. virologist Albert B. Sabin (b. 1906)]

rep¹ (rep), *n.* a transversely corded fabric of wool, silk, rayon, or cotton. Also, **repp.** [1855–60; < F *reps,* perh. < E *ribs* (see RIB¹)] **—repped,** *adj.*

rep² (rep), *n. Informal.* **1.** a repertory theater or company. **2.** repetition. **3.** a representative, esp. a sales representative. **4.** reputation. [by shortening]

rep³ (rep), *n. Nucleonics.* a unit proposed as a supplement to roentgen for expressing dosage of ionizing radiation: subsequently abandoned. Cf. **rem.** [1945–50; *r(oentgen) e(quivalent) p(hysical)*]

Rep., 1. Representative. **2.** Republic. **3.** Republican.

rep., 1. repair. **2.** repeat. **3.** (in prescriptions) let it be repeated. [< L *repetātur*] **4.** report. **5.** reported. **6.** reporter.

re·pack·age (rē pak′ij), *v.t.,* **-aged, -ag·ing. 1.** to package again or afresh, as in a different style, design, or size: *The soap has been repackaged to be more eye-catching.* **2.** to package for sale under one's own label: *The goods are purchased in bulk and repackaged by the store.* **3.** to remake or alter so as to be more appealing or desirable: *That politician's image needs to be repackaged.* [1945–50; RE- + PACKAGE] **—re·pack′ag·er,** *n.*

re·paint (*v.* rē pānt′; *n.* rē′pānt′, rē pānt′), *v.t.* **1.** to paint again: *to repaint the house.* —*n.* **2.** a part repainted, esp. a part of a picture by a restorer. **3.** the act of repainting. [1690–1700; RE- + PAINT]

re·pair¹ (ri pâr′), *v.t.* **1.** to restore to a good or sound condition after decay or damage; mend: *to repair a motor.* **2.** to restore or renew by any process of making good, strengthening, etc.: *to repair one's health by resting.* **3.** to remedy; make good; make up for: *to repair damage; to repair a deficiency.* **4.** to make amends for; compensate: *to repair a wrong done.* —*n.* **5.** an act, process, or work of repairing: *to order the repair of a building.* **6.** Usually, **repairs. a.** an instance or operation of repairing: *to lay up a boat for repairs.* **b.** a repaired part or an addition made in repairing: *17th-century repairs in brick are conspicuous in parts of the medieval stonework.* **7. repairs,** (in bookkeeping, accounting, etc.) the part of maintenance expense that has been paid out to keep fixed assets in usable condition, as distinguished from amounts used for renewal or replacement. **8.** the good condition resulting from continued maintenance and repairing: *to keep in repair.* **9.** condition with respect to soundness and usability: *a house in good repair.* [1300–50; ME *repairen* < MF *reparer* < L *reparāre,* equiv. to *re-* RE- + *parāre* to PREPARE; see PARE] **—re·pair′a·ble,** *adj.* **—re·pair′a·bil′i·ty, re·pair′a·ble·ness,** *n.*
—Syn. 1. remodel, renovate. **2.** patch, fix, amend. See **renew. 3.** retrieve, recoup. **4.** redress. **—Ant. 1–3.** break, destroy.

re·pair² (ri pâr′), *v.i.* **1.** to betake oneself; go, as to a place: *He repaired in haste to Washington.* **2.** to go frequently or customarily. —*n.* **3.** a resort or haunt. **4.** the act of going or going customarily; resort: *to have repair to the country.* **5.** *Scot. Obs.* a meeting, association, or crowd of people. [1300–50; ME *repairen* < OF *repairier* to return < LL *repatriāre* to return to one's fatherland; see REPATRIATE]

re·pair·er (ri pâr′ər), *n.* **1.** a person or thing that repairs. **2.** *Ceramics.* a person who assembles the modeled parts of a piece and finishes the whole. [1495–1505; REPAIR¹ + -ER¹]

re·pair·man (ri pâr′man′, -mən), *n., pl.* **-men** (-men′, -mən). a person whose occupation is the making of repairs, readjustments, etc. [1870–75; REPAIR¹ + MAN¹]
—Usage. See **-man.**

re·pair·per·son (ri pâr′pûr′sən), *n.* a person whose occupation is the making of repairs, readjustments, etc. [REPAIR(MAN) + -PERSON]
—Usage. See **-person.**

re·pand (ri pand′), *adj.* **1.** *Bot.* having a wavy margin, as a leaf. **2.** slightly wavy. [1750–60; < L *repandus* bent backwards, turned up, equiv. to *re-* RE- + *pandus* bent, curved, deriv. of *pandere* to spread out, extend] **—re·pand′ly,** *adv.*

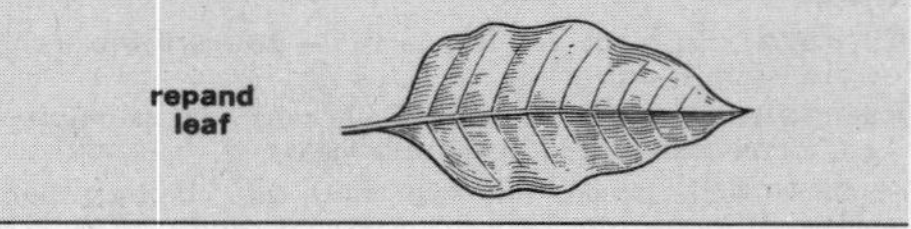
repand
leaf

rep·a·ra·ble (rep′ər ə bəl *or, often,* ri pâr′-), *adj.* capable of being repaired or remedied. [1560–70; < L *reparābilis.* See REPAIR¹, -ABLE] **—rep′a·ra·bly,** *adv.*

rep·a·ra·tion (rep′ə rā′shən), *n.* **1.** the making of amends for wrong or injury done: *reparation for an injustice.* **2.** Usually, **reparations.** compensation in money, material, labor, etc., payable by a defeated country to another country or to an individual for loss suffered during or as a result of war. **3.** restoration to good condition. **4.** repair¹ (def. 7). [1350–1400; ME *reparacion* < MF < LL *reparātiōn-* (s. of *reparātiō*), equiv. to

re′ir·ri·ga′tion, *n.*
re·i′so·late′, *v.t.,* **-lat·ed, -lat·ing.**
re′i·so·la′tion, *n.*
re·i′tem·ize′, *v.t.,* **-ized, -iz·ing.**
re·jail′, *v.t.*
re·jeop′ard·ize′, *v.t.,* **-ized, -iz·ing.**
re·judge′, *v.,* **-judged, -judg·ing.**
re·judg′ment, *n.*
re′jus·ti·fi·ca′tion, *n.*
re·jus′ti·fy′, *v.t.,* **-fied, -fy·ing.**
re·key′board′, *v.*
re·kin′dle, *v.,* **-dled, -dling.**
re·knead′, *v.t.*
re·knit′, *v.,* **-knit·ted** or **-knit, -knit·ting.**
re·knock′, *v.*
re·knot′, *v.,* **-knot·ted, -knot·ting.**
re·la′bel, *v.t.,* **-beled, -bel·ing** or (*esp. Brit.*) **-belled, -bel·ling.**
re·lace′, *v.,* **-laced, -lac·ing.**
re·lac′quer, *v.t.*
re·lance′, *v.t.,* **-lanced, -lanc·ing.**
re·land′, *v.*
re·land′scape′, *v.,* **-scaped, -scap·ing.**
re·latch′, *v.t.*
re·launch′, *v.t.*
re·laun′der, *v.t.*
re·lead′, *v.*
re·learn′, *v.,* **-learned** or **-learnt, -learn·ing.**
re·lend′, *v.t.,* **-lent, -lend·ing.**
re·let′, *v.,* **-let, -let·ting.**
re·let′ter, *v.t.*

L *reparāt(us)* (ptp. of *reparāre* to REPAIR[1]; see -ATE[1]) + -*iōn*- -ION]
—Syn. 1. indemnification, atonement, satisfaction, compensation. See **redress. 3.** renewal, renovation; repair. **—Ant. 3.** destruction.

re·par·a·tive (ri par′ə tiv), *adj.* **1.** tending to repair; repairing; mending. **2.** pertaining to or involving reparation. Also, **re·par·a·to·ry** (ri par′ə tôr′ē, -tōr′ē). [1650–60; < LL *reparātīvus.* See REPARATION, -IVE]

rep·ar·tee (rep′ər tē′, -tā′, -är-), *n.* **1.** a quick, witty reply. **2.** conversation full of such replies. **3.** skill in making such replies. [1635–45; < F *repartie* retort, n. use of fem. ptp. of *repartir,* MF, equiv. to *re-* RE- + *partir* to PART]
—Syn. 2. banter, sparring, fencing.

re·par·ti·tion (rē′pär tish′ən, -pər-), *n.* **1.** distribution; partition. **2.** reassignment; redistribution. *—v.t.* **3.** to divide up. **4.** to partition or subdivide again; reapportion; redistribute. [1545–55; RE- + PARTITION]

re·pass (rē pas′, -päs′), *v.t., v.i.* to pass back or again. [1425–75; late ME *repassen* < MF *repasser,* OF, equiv. to *re-* RE- + *passer* to PASS] **—re·pas·sage** (rē pas′ij), *n.*

re·past (*n.* ri past′, -päst′, rē′past, -päst; *v.* ri past′, -päst′), *n.* **1.** a quantity of food taken or provided for one occasion of eating: *to eat a light repast.* **2.** a meal: *the evening repast.* **3.** the time during which a meal is eaten; mealtime. **4.** *Archaic.* the taking of food, as at a meal. **5.** *Obs.* food. *—v.i.* **6.** to eat or feast (often fol. by *on* or *upon*). [1300–50; ME (n.) < OF, deriv. (cf. *past* < L *pāstus* fodder) of *repaistre* to eat a meal < LL *repāscere* to feed regularly, equiv. to L *re-* RE- + *pāscere* to feed (cf. PASTURE)]

re·pa·tri·ate (*v.* rē pā′trē āt′ *or, esp. Brit.,* -pa′-; *n.* rē pā′trē it *or, esp. Brit.,* -pa′-), *v.t.,* **-at·ed, -at·ing,** *n.* *—v.t.* **1.** to bring or send back (a person, esp. a prisoner of war, a refugee, etc.) to his or her country or land of citizenship. **2.** (of profits or other assets) to send back to one's own country. *—v.i.* **3.** to return to one's own country: *to repatriate after 20 years abroad.* *—n.* **4.** a person who has been repatriated. [1605–15; < LL *repatriātus* (ptp. of *repatriāre* to return to one's fatherland), equiv. to L *re-* RE- + *patri(a)* native country (n. use of fem. of *patrius* paternal, deriv. of *pater* FATHER) + -*ātus* -ATE[1]] **—re·pa·tri·a·ble** (rē pā′trē ə bəl *or, esp. Brit.,* -pa′-), *adj.* **—re·pa′tri·a′tion,** *n.*

re·pay (ri pā′), *v.,* **-paid, -pay·ing.** *—v.t.* **1.** to pay back or refund, as money. **2.** to make return for: *She repaid the compliment with a smile.* **3.** to make return to in any way: *We can never repay you for your help.* **4.** to return: *to repay a visit.* *—v.i.* **5.** to make repayment or return. [1520–30; < MF *repaier.* See RE-, PAY[1]] **—re·pay′a·ble,** *adj.* **—re·pay′a·bil′i·ty,** *n.* **—re·pay′ment,** *n.*
—Syn. 1. reimburse, indemnify. **3.** requite, reward.

re·peal (ri pēl′), *v.t.* **1.** to revoke or withdraw formally or officially: *to repeal a grant.* **2.** to revoke or annul (a law, tax, duty, etc.) by express legislative enactment; abrogate. *—n.* **3.** the act of repealing; revocation; abrogation. [1275–1325; ME *repelen* < AF *repeler,* equiv. to *re-* RE- + *(a)peler* to APPEAL] **—re·peal′a·bil′i·ty, re·peal′a·ble·ness,** *n.* **—re·peal′a·ble,** *adj.* **—re·peal′er,** *n.*
—Syn. 2. nullify, abolish, rescind, invalidate.

re·peat (ri pēt′), *v.t.* **1.** to say or utter again (something already said): *to repeat a word for emphasis.* **2.** to say or utter in reproducing the words, inflections, etc., of another: *to repeat a sentence after the teacher.* **3.** to reproduce (utterances, sounds, etc.) in the manner of an echo, a phonograph, or the like. **4.** to tell (something heard) to another or others. **5.** to do, make, or perform again: *to repeat an action.* **6.** to go through or undergo again: *to repeat an experience.* *—v.i.* **7.** to do or say something again. **8.** to cause a slight regurgitation: *The onions I ate are repeating on me.* **9.** to vote illegally by casting more than one vote in the same election. *—n.* **10.** the act of repeating. **11.** something repeated; repetition. **12.** a duplicate or reproduction of something. **13.** a decorative pattern repeated, usually by printing, on a textile or the like. **14.** *Music.* **a.** a passage to be repeated. **b.** a sign, as a vertical arrangement of dots, calling for the repetition of a passage. **15.** a radio or television program that has been broadcast at least once before. [1325–75; ME *repeten* (v.) < MF *repeter* < L *repetere* to attack again, demand return of, equiv. to *re-* RE- + *petere* to reach towards, seek (cf. PERPETUAL, PETULANT)] **—re·peat′a·ble,** *adj.* **—re·peat′a·bil′i·ty,** *n.*
—Syn. 1. iterate, recite, rehearse. **1, 5.** REPEAT, RECAPITULATE, REITERATE refer to saying a thing more than once. To REPEAT is to do or say something over again: *to repeat a question, an order.* To RECAPITULATE is to restate in brief form, to summarize, often by repeating the principal points in a discourse: *to recapitulate an argument.* To REITERATE is to do or say something over and over again, to repeat insistently: *to reiterate a refusal, a demand.* **3.** echo, reecho.

re·peat·ed (ri pē′tid), *adj.* done, made, or said again and again: *repeated attempts.* [1605–15; REPEAT + -ED[2]] **—re·peat′ed·ly,** *adv.*

re·peat·er (ri pē′tər), *n.* **1.** a person or thing that repeats. **2.** a repeating firearm. **3.** *Horol.* a timepiece, esp. a watch, that may be made to strike the hour or part of the hour. Cf. **clock watch. 4.** *Educ.* a pupil who repeats a course or group of courses that he or she has failed. **5.** a person who votes illegally by casting more than one vote in the same election. **6.** a person who has been convicted and sentenced for one crime, and later for another; recidivist. **7.** *Math.* (no longer in technical use) a repeating decimal. **8.** *Telecommunications.* a device capable of receiving one-way or two-way communications signals and delivering corresponding signals that are either amplified, reshaped, or both. **9.** *Navig.* See **gyro repeater.** [1570–80; REPEAT + -ER[1]]

repeat′ing dec′imal, *Math.* a decimal numeral that, after a certain point, consists of a group of one or more digits repeated ad infinitum, as 2.33333 . . . . or 23.0218181818 . . . . Also called **circulating decimal, periodic decimal, recurring decimal.** [1765–75]

repeat′ing fire′arm, a firearm capable of discharging a number of shots without reloading.

re·pe·chage (rep′ə shäzh′), *n.* (in cycling and rowing) a last-chance qualifying heat in which the runners-up in earlier heats race each other, with the winner advancing to the finals. [1925–30; < F *repêchage* second chance, equiv. to *repêch(er)* to fish up again (*re-* RE + *pêcher* to fish; MF, OF *pescher* < VL **piscāre,* L *piscārī,* deriv. of *piscis* FISH) + *-age* -AGE]

re·pel (ri pel′), *v.,* **-pelled, -pel·ling.** *—v.t.* **1.** to drive or force back (an assailant, invader, etc.). **2.** to thrust back or away. **3.** to resist effectively (an attack, onslaught, etc.). **4.** to keep off or out; fail to mix with: *Water and oil repel each other.* **5.** to resist the absorption or passage of (water or other liquid): *This coat repels rain.* **6.** to refuse to have to do with; resist involvement in: *to repel temptation.* **7.** to refuse to accept or admit; reject: *to repel a suggestion.* **8.** to discourage the advances of (a person): *He repelled me with his harshness.* **9.** to cause distaste or aversion in: *Their untidy appearance repelled us.* **10.** to push back or away by a force, as one body acting upon another (opposed to *attract*): *The north pole of one magnet will repel the north pole of another.* *—v.i.* **11.** to act with a force that drives or keeps away something. **12.** to cause distaste or aversion. [1350–1400; ME *repellen* < L *repellere* to drive back, equiv. to *re-* RE- + *pellere* to drive, push; see REPULSE] **—re·pel′lence, re·pel′len·cy,** *n.* **—re·pel′ler,** *n.* **—re·pel′ling·ly,** *adv.* **—re·pel′ling·ness,** *n.*
—Syn. 1. repulse, parry, ward off. **3.** withstand, oppose, rebuff. **7.** decline, rebuff. **—Ant. 1.** attract.

re·pel·lent (ri pel′ənt), *adj.* **1.** causing distaste or aversion; repulsive. **2.** forcing or driving back. **3.** serving or tending to ward off or drive away. **4.** impervious or resistant to something (often used in combination): *moth-repellant.* *—n.* **5.** something that repels, as a substance that keeps away insects. **6.** a medicine that serves to prevent or reduce swellings, tumors, etc. **7.** any of various durable or nondurable solutions applied to a fabric, garment, surface, etc., to increase its resistance, as to water, moths, mildew, etc. Also, **re·pel′lant.** [1635–45; < L *repellent-* (s. of *repellēns*), prp. of *repellere* to drive back. See REPEL, -ENT] **—re·pel′lent·ly,** *adv.*
—Syn. 1. repugnant, disgusting, distasteful, loathsome.

re·pent[1] (ri pent′), *v.i.* **1.** to feel sorry, self-reproachful, or contrite for past conduct; regret or be conscience-stricken about a past action, attitude, etc. (often fol. by *of*): *He repented after his thoughtless act.* **2.** to feel such sorrow for sin or fault as to be disposed to change one's life for the better; be penitent. *—v.t.* **3.** to remember or regard with self-reproach or contrition: *to repent one's injustice to another.* **4.** to feel sorry for; regret: *to repent an imprudent act.* [1250–1300; ME *repenten* < OF *repentir,* equiv. to *re-* RE- + *pentir* to feel sorrow (< L *paenitēre* to regret, be sorry); see PENITENT] **—re·pent′er,** *n.* **—re·pent′ing·ly,** *adv.*

re·pent[2] (rē′pənt, ri pent′), *adj.* creeping. [1660–70; < L *rēpent-* (s. of *rēpēns*), prp. of *rēpere* to crawl, creep; see -ENT]

re·pent·ance (ri pen′tns, -pen′təns), *n.* **1.** deep sorrow, compunction, or contrition for a past sin, wrongdoing, or the like. **2.** regret for any past action. [1300–50; ME *repentaunce* < OF *repentance.* See REPENT[1], -ANCE]
—Syn. 1. contriteness, penitence, remorse. **2.** sorrow, qualms. **—Ant. 1.** impenitence.

re·pent·ant (ri pen′tnt, -pen′tənt), *adj.* **1.** repenting; penitent; experiencing repentance. **2.** characterized by or showing repentance: *a repentant mood.* [1250–1300; ME *repentaunt* < OF *repentant* (prp. of *repentir*). See REPENT[1], -ANT] **—re·pent′ant·ly,** *adv.*

Re·pen·ti·gny (*Fr.* rə pän tē nyē′), *n.* a town in S Quebec, in E Canada: suburb of Montreal. 34,419.

re·peo·ple (rē pē′pəl), *v.t.,* **-pled, -pling. 1.** to furnish again with people. **2.** to restock with animals. [1475–85; < MF *repeupler,* OF. See RE-, PEOPLE]

re·per·cus·sion (rē′pər kush′ən, rep′ər-), *n.* **1.** an effect or result, often indirect or remote, of some event or action: *The repercussions of the quarrel were widespread.* **2.** the state of being driven back by a resisting body. **3.** a rebounding or recoil of something after impact. **4.** reverberation; echo. **5.** *Music.* (in a fugue) the point after the development of an episode at which the subject and answer appear again. [1375–1425; late ME (< MF) < L *repercussiōn-* (s. of *repercussiō*) a rebounding, equiv. to *repercuss(us)* (ptp. of *repercutere* to strike back) + *-iōn-* -ION. See RE-, PERCUSSION]

re·per·cus·sive (rē′pər kus′iv, rep′ər-), *adj.* **1.** causing repercussion; reverberating. **2.** reflected; reverberated. [1350–1400; ME *repercussif* < OF. See REPERCUSSION, -IVE] **—re′per·cus′sive·ly,** *adv.* **—re′per·cus′sive·ness,** *n.*

re·per·fo·ra·tor (rē pûr′fə rā′tər), *n.* (esp. in teletype transmission) a machine for punching a duplicate perforated paper tape of incoming messages so that they may later be retransmitted: used for automatic typesetting. [1915–20; RE- + PERFORATOR]

rep·er·toire (rep′ər twär′, -twôr′, rep′ə-), *n.* **1.** the list of dramas, operas, parts, pieces, etc., that a company, actor, singer, or the like, is prepared to perform. **2.** the entire stock of works existing in a particular artistic field: *A new play has been added to the theatrical repertoire.* **3.** the entire stock of skills, techniques, or devices used in a particular field or occupation: *a magician's repertoire.* Also, **rép′er·toire′.** [1840–50; < F < LL *repertōrium* catalogue, inventory. See REPERTORY]

rep·er·to·ry (rep′ər tôr′ē, -tōr′ē), *n., pl.* **-ries. 1.** a type of theatrical presentation in which a company presents several works regularly or in alternate sequence in one season. **2.** a theatrical company that presents productions in this manner. **3.** repertoire. **4.** a store or stock of things available. **5.** storehouse. [1545–55; < LL *repertōrium* inventory, equiv. to L *reper(īre)* to discover, find, make up (*re-* RE- + *-perīre,* comb. form of *parere* to bring forth, produce) + *-tōrium* -TORY[2]] **—rep′er·to′ri·al,** *adj.*

rep′ertory cat′alog. See **union catalog.**

rep′ertory the′ater, repertory (def. 2). Also called **rep′ertory com′pany.** [1895–1900]

rep·e·tend (rep′i tend′, rep′i tend′), *n.* **1.** *Math.* the part of a repeating decimal that is repeated, as 1234 in 0.123412341234. . . . **2.** *Music.* a phrase or sound that is repeated. **3.** *Pros.* a word, phrase, line or longer element that is repeated, sometimes with variation, at irregular intervals in a poem. [1705–15; < L *repetendum* that which is to be repeated, neut. ger. of *repetere* to REPEAT]

ré·pé·ti·teur (rā′pā ti tûr′; *Fr.* rā pā tē tœr′), *n., pl.* **-teurs** (-tûrz′; *Fr.* -tœr′). the vocal coach of an opera chorus. [< F: tutor, coach < L *repetīt(us)* (ptp. of *repetere* to REPEAT) + F *-eur* -EUR]

rep·e·ti·tion (rep′i tish′ən), *n.* **1.** the act of repeating; repeated action, performance, production, or presentation. **2.** repeated utterance; reiteration. **3.** something made by or resulting from repeating. **4.** a reproduction, copy, or replica. **5.** *Civil Law.* an action or demand for the recovery of a payment or delivery made by error or upon failure to fulfill a condition. [1375–1425; late ME (< OF *repeticion*) < L *repetītiōn-* (s. of *repetītiō*), equiv. to *repetīt(us)* (ptp. of *repetere* to REPEAT) + *-iōn-* -ION]

rep·e·ti·tious (rep′i tish′əs), *adj.* full of repetition, esp. unnecessary and tedious repetition: *a repetitious account of their vacation trip.* [1665–75; < L *repetīt(us)* (ptp. of *repetere* to REPEAT) + -IOUS] **—rep′e·ti′tious·ly,** *adv.* **—rep′e·ti′tious·ness,** *n.*

re·pet·i·tive (ri pet′i tiv), *adj.* pertaining to or characterized by repetition. [1830–40; < L *repetīt(us)* (ptp. of *repetere* to REPEAT) + -IVE] **—re·pet′i·tive·ly,** *adv.* **—re·pet′i·tive·ness,** *n.*

re·phrase (rē frāz′), *v.t.,* **-phrased, -phras·ing.** to phrase again or differently: *He rephrased the statement to give it less formality.* [1890–95; RE- + PHRASE]

re·pic (ri pēk′), *n. Piquet.* **1.** the scoring of 30 points in the declaration of hands before one's opponent scores a point. **2.** the bonus of 60 points won for so scoring. Cf. **pic**[1]. Also, **re·pique′.** [< F, deriv. of *repiquer* to prick, punch again. See RE-, PIQUE[1]]

re·pine (ri pīn′), *v.i.,* **-pined, -pin·ing.** to be fretfully discontented; fret; complain. [1520–30; RE- + PINE[2]] **—re·pin′er,** *n.*

repl., 1. replace. **2.** replacement.

re·place (ri plās′), *v.t.,* **-placed, -plac·ing. 1.** to assume the former role, position, or function of; substitute for (a person or thing): *Electricity has replaced gas in lighting.* **2.** to provide a substitute or equivalent in the place of: *to replace a broken dish.* **3.** to restore; return; make good: *to replace a sum of money borrowed.* **4.** to restore to a former or the proper place: *to replace the vase on the table.* [1585–95; RE- + PLACE] **—re·place′a·ble,** *adj.* **—re·place′a·bil′i·ty,** *n.* **—re·plac′er,** *n.*
—Syn. 1. succeed. REPLACE, SUPERSEDE, SUPPLANT refer to putting one thing or person in place of another. To REPLACE is to take the place of, to succeed: *Ms. Jones will replace Mr. Smith as president.* SUPERSEDE implies that that which is replacing another is an improvement: *The typewriter has superseded the pen.* SUPPLANT implies that that which takes the other's place has ousted the former holder and usurped the position or function, esp. by art or fraud: *to supplant a former favorite.* **3.** refund, repay.

re·place·ment (ri plās′mənt), *n.* **1.** the act of replacing. **2.** a person or thing that replaces another: *summer replacements for vacationing staff; a replacement for a broken dish.* **3.** *Mil.* a sailor, soldier, or airman assigned to fill a vacancy in a military unit. **4.** Also called **metasomatism.** *Geol.* the process of practically simultaneous removal and deposition by which a new mineral grows in the body of an old one. [1780–90; REPLACE + -MENT]

re·plant (rē plant′, -plänt′), *v.t.* **1.** to plant again. **2.** to cover again with plants, sow with seeds, etc.: *After the drought, we had to replant the south lawn.* **3.** to transfer (a plant) from one soil or container to another. **4.** *Surg.* to reattach, as a severed arm, finger, or toe, esp. with the use of microsurgery to reconnect nerves and blood vessels. [1565–75; RE- + PLANT] **—re·plan·ta·tion** (rē′plan tā′shən), *n.*

re·play (*v.* rē plā′; *n.* rē′plā′), *v.t.* **1.** to play again, as a record or tape. *—n.* **2.** an act or instance of replaying.

CONCISE PRONUNCIATION KEY: *act, cāpe, dâre, pärt; set, ēqual; if, īce; ox, ōver, ôrder, oil, bo͝ok, bo͞ot, out; up, ûrge; child; sing; shoe; thin, that;* zh as in *treasure.* ə = *a* as in *alone, e* as in *system, i* as in *easily, o* as in *gallop, u* as in *circus;* ᵊ as in *fire* (fīᵊr), *hour* (ouᵊr). l and n can serve as syllabic consonants, as in *cradle* (krād′l), and *button* (but′n). See the full key inside the front cover.

re·lev′el, *v.,* **-eled, -el·ing** or (*esp. Brit.*) **-elled, -el·ling.**
re·lev′er, *v.t.*
re·lev′y, *v.t.,* **-lev·ied, -lev·y·ing.**
re·lib′er·ate′, *v.t.,* **-at·ed, -at·ing.**
re·li′cense, *v.t.,* **-censed, -cens·ing.**
re·light′, *v.,* **-light·ed** or **-lit, -light·ing.**
re·lim′it, *v.t.*
re·line′, *v.t.,* **-lined, -lin·ing.**
re·link′, *v.t.*
re·liq′ue·fy′, *v.,* **-fied, -fy·ing.**
re·liq′ui·date′, *v.,* **-dat·ed, -dat·ing.**
re′liq·ui·da′tion, *n.*
re·list′, *v.t.*
re·lis′ten, *v.*
re·lit′i·gate′, *v.t.,* **-gat·ed, -gat·ing.**
re′lit·i·ga′tion, *n.*
re·load′, *n., v.*
re·load′a·bil′i·ty, *n.*
re·load′a·ble, *adj.*
re·loan′, *n., v.t.*
re·lock′, *v.*
re·lose′, *v.t.,* **-lost, -los·ing.**
re·low′er, *v.t.*
re·lu′bri·cate′, *v.t.,* **-cat·ed, -cat·ing.**
re′lu·bri·ca′tion, *n.*
re′mag·net·i·za′tion, *n.*
re·mag′net·ize′, *v.t.,* **-ized, -iz·ing.**
re·mag′ni·fy′, *v.t.,* **-fied, -fy·ing.**
re·mail′, *v.t.*
re·maim′, *v.t.*
re·man′i·fest′, *v.t.*
re′man·i·fes·ta′tion, *n.*

3. a repetition of all or part of a broadcast or of the playing of a phonograph record, videocassette, etc. **4.** See **instant replay. 5.** a rematch. **6.** *Informal.* a repetition, recurrence, or reenactment: *The recession could be a replay of the Great Depression.* [1880–85; RE- + PLAY]

re·plead·er (rē plē′dər), *n. Law.* **1.** a second pleading. **2.** the right or privilege of pleading again. [1600–10; RE- + PLEADER]

re·plen·ish (ri plen′ish), *v.t.* **1.** to make full or complete again, as by supplying what is lacking, used up, etc.: *to replenish one's stock of food.* **2.** to supply (a fire, stove, etc.) with fresh fuel. **3.** to fill again or anew. [1300–50; ME *replenisshen* < MF *repleniss-,* long s. of *replenir* to fill, OF, equiv. to *re-* RE- + *plenir* to fill (deriv. of *plein* < L *plēnus* FULL[1])] **—re·plen′ish·er,** *n.* **—re·plen′ish·ment,** *n.*

re·plete (ri plēt′), *adj.* **1.** abundantly supplied or provided; filled (usually fol. by *with*): *a speech replete with sentimentality.* **2.** stuffed or gorged with food and drink. **3.** complete: *a scholarly survey, replete in its notes and citations.* **—n. 4.** *Entomol.* (among honey ants) a worker with a distensible crop in which honeydew and nectar are stored for the use of the colony. [1350–1400; ME *repleet* < MF *replet* < L *replētus* ptp. of *replēre* to fill up (*re-* RE- + *plē(re)* to fill, akin to *plēnus* FULL[1] + *-tus* ptp. suffix)] **—re·plete′ly,** *adv.* **—re·plete′ness,** *n.* **—re·ple′tive,** *adj.* **—re·ple′tive·ly,** *adv.*
—Syn. 2. sated, satiated, glutted, surfeited.

re·ple·tion (ri plē′shən), *n.* **1.** the condition of being abundantly supplied or filled; fullness. **2.** overfullness resulting from excessive eating or drinking; surfeit. [1350–1400; ME *replecioun* surfeit (< MF) < LL *replētiōn-* (s. of *replētiō*), equiv. to L *replēt(us)* (see REPLETE) + *-iōn-* -ION]

re·plev·in (ri plev′in), *Law.* **—n. 1.** an action for the recovery of goods or chattels wrongfully taken or detained. **2.** the common-law action or writ by which goods are replevied. **—v.t. 3.** to replevy. [1300–50; ME < AF, deriv. of *replevir* to bail out, admit to bail, OF. See RE-, PLEDGE]

re·plev·i·sa·ble (ri plev′ə sə bəl), *adj. Law.* capable of being replevied. Also, **re·plev·i·a·ble** (ri plev′ē ə bəl). [1225–75; < AF, equiv. to *repleviss-* (long s. of *replevir;* see REPLEVIN) + *-able* -ABLE]

re·plev·y (ri plev′ē), *v.,* **-plev·ied, -plev·y·ing,** *n., pl.* **-plev·ies.** *Law.* **—v.t. 1.** to recover possession of by replevin. **—v.i. 2.** to take possession of goods or chattels under a replevin order. **—n. 3.** a seizure in replevin. [1425–75; late ME < MF *replevir;* see REPLEVIN]

rep·li·ca (rep′li kə), *n.* **1.** a copy or reproduction of a work of art produced by the maker of the original or under his or her supervision. **2.** any close or exact copy or reproduction. [1815–25; < It: reply, repetition, deriv. of *replicare* to repeat < LL *replicāre* to REPLY]
—Syn. 2. duplicate, facsimile; imitation.

rep·li·ca·ble (rep′li kə bəl), *adj.* capable of replication: *The scientific experiment must be replicable in all details to be considered valid.* [1950–55; REPLIC(ATE) + -ABLE]

rep·li·car (rep′li kär′), *n.* a custom-made or individually produced automobile whose body is a copy of a vintage or classic automobile. [1975–80; b. REPLICA and CAR[1]]

rep·li·case (rep′li kās′, -kāz′), *n.* See **RNA synthetase.** [1960–65; REPLIC(ATE) + -ASE]

rep·li·cate (*adj., n.* rep′li kit; *v.* rep′li kāt′), *adj., v.,* **-cat·ed, -cat·ing,** *n.* **—adj. 1.** Also, **rep′li·cat′ed.** folded; bent back on itself. **—v.t. 2.** to bend or fold back: *a replicated leaf.* **3.** to repeat, duplicate, or reproduce, esp. for experimental purposes. **—v.i. 4.** to undergo replication. **—n. 5.** something that is replicated, as an experiment or procedure. [1525–35; < LL *replicātus* ptp. of *replicāre* to fold back. See RE-, PLY[2], -ATE[1]]

rep·li·ca·tion (rep′li kā′shən), *n.* **1.** a reply; answer. **2.** a reply to an answer. **3.** *Law.* the reply of the plaintiff or complainant to the defendant's plea or answer. **4.** reverberation; echo. **5.** a copy. **6.** the act or process of replicating, esp. for experimental purposes. **7.** *Genetics.* the process by which double-stranded DNA makes copies of itself, each strand, as it separates, synthesizing a complementary strand. [1325–75; ME *replicacioun* < MF *replication* < L *replicātiōn-* (s. of *replicātiō*) a rolling back, equiv. to *replicāt(us)* (see REPLICATE) + *-iōn-* -ION]

rep·li·ca·tive (rep′li kā′tiv), *adj.* characterized by or capable of replication, esp. of an experiment. [1850–55; REPLICATE + -IVE]

rep·li·con (rep′li kon′), *n. Genetics.* any genetic element that can regulate and effect its own replication from initiation to completion. [< F (1963), shortened form of *réplication;* see -ON[1]]

re·ply (ri plī′), *v.,* **-plied, -ply·ing,** *n., pl.* **-plies. —v.i. 1.** to make answer in words or writing; answer; respond: *to reply to a question.* **2.** to respond by some action, performance, etc.: *to reply to the enemy's fire.* **3.** to return a sound; echo; resound. **4.** *Law.* to answer a defendant's plea. **—v.t. 5.** to return as an answer (usually used in a negative combination or fol. by a clause with *that*): *Not a syllable did he reply. He replied that no one would go.* **—n. 6.** an answer or response in words or writing. **7.** a response made by some action, performance, etc. [1350–1400; ME *replien* (v.) < MF *replier* to fold back, reply < L *replicāre* to unroll, fold back; see REPLICATE] **—re·pli′er,** *n.*
—Syn. 1. rejoin. **6.** rejoinder, riposte. See **answer.**

reply′ card′, a usually postage-paid postcard or coupon that can be mailed back to the sender to place an order, request information, or the like.

re·po[1] (rē′pō), *n., pl.* **-pos.** a repurchase agreement. [1960–65; REP(URCHASE) + -O]

re·po[2] (rē′pō), *n., pl.* **-pos.** *Informal.* repossessed property, esp. a government-financed dwelling repossessed by the government and offered for resale. [by shortening of REPOSSESS; see -O]

ré·pon·dez s'il vous plaît (rā pôn′dā sēl vōō plā′; *Fr.* rā pôn dā sēl vōō ple′). See **RSVP.**

re·port (ri pôrt′, -pōrt′), *n.* **1.** an account or statement describing in detail an event, situation, or the like, usually as the result of observation, inquiry, etc.: *a report on the peace conference; a medical report on the patient.* **2.** a statement or announcement. **3.** a widely circulated statement or item of news; rumor; gossip. **4.** an account of a speech, debate, meeting, etc., esp. as taken down for publication. **5.** a loud noise, as from an explosion: *the report of a distant cannon.* **6.** a statement of a student's grades, level of achievement, or academic standing for or during a prescribed period of time. **7.** *Computers.* output, esp. printed, containing organized information. **8.** a statement of a judicial opinion or decision, or of a case argued and determined in a court of justice. **9. reports,** *Law.* a collection of adjudications. **10.** repute; reputation; fame: *a man of bad report.* **11. on report,** *Mil.* (of personnel) under restriction pending disciplinary action. **—v.t. 12.** to carry and repeat, as an answer or message; repeat, as what one has heard. **13.** to relate, as what has been learned by observation or investigation. **14.** to give or render a formal account or statement of: *to report a deficit.* **15.** to send back (a bill, amendment, etc.) to a legislative body with a formal report outlining findings and recommendations (often fol. by *out*): *The committee reported out the bill.* **16.** to make a charge against (a person), as to a superior: *I intend to report him to the dean for cheating.* **17.** to make known the presence, condition, or whereabouts of: *to report a ship missing.* **18.** to present (oneself) to a person in authority, as in accordance with requirements. **19.** to take down (a speech, lecture, etc.) in writing. **20.** to write an account of (an event, situation, etc.), as for publication in a newspaper. **21.** to relate or tell. **—v.i. 22.** to prepare, make, or submit a report of something observed, investigated, or the like. **23.** to serve or work as a reporter, as for a newspaper. **24.** to make one's condition or whereabouts known, as to a person in authority: *to report sick.* **25.** to present oneself duly, as at a place: *to report to Room 101.* [1325–75; (v.) ME *reporten* < MF *reporter,* OF < L *reportāre* to carry back, equiv. to *re-* RE- + *portāre* to carry (see PORT[5]); (n.) ME < MF, deriv. of *reporter*] **—re·port′a·ble,** *adj.*
—Syn. 1. description, story. **2.** bulletin, dispatch. **5.** shot, detonation. **12, 13.** relay. **16.** accuse. **21.** narrate, rehearse, recount, describe, detail, repeat.

re·port·age (ri pôr′tij, -pōr′-, rep′ôr täzh′, -ər-), *n.* **1.** the act or technique of reporting news. **2.** reported news collectively: *reportage on the war.* **3.** a written account of an act, event, history, etc., based on direct observation or on thorough research and documentation. [1605–15; < F; see REPORT, -AGE]

report′ card′, **1.** a written report containing an evaluation of a pupil's scholarship and behavior, sent periodically to the pupil's parents or guardian, usually on a card containing marks and comments together with a record of attendance. **2.** a history or record of performance or accomplishment as adjudged by others: *The administration has a good report card on farm policy.* [1925–30, *Amer.*]

re·port·ed·ly (ri pôr′tid lē, -pōr′-), *adv.* according to report or rumor: *Reportedly, he is a billionaire.* [1900–05; REPORT + -ED[2] + -LY]

re·port·er (ri pôr′tər, -pōr′-), *n.* **1.** a person who reports. **2.** a person employed to gather and report news, as for a newspaper, wire service, or television station. **3.** a person who prepares official reports, as of legal or legislative proceedings. [1350–1400; ME *reportour* < AF (OF *reporteur*). See REPORT, -ER[1]]

report′ing pay′. See **call-in pay.**

rep·or·to·ri·al (rep′ər tôr′ē əl, -tōr′-, rē′pôr-, -pōr-, -pər-), *adj.* **1.** of or pertaining to a reporter. **2.** of, noting, or characteristic of a report: *His lecture was more reportorial than analytical.* [1855–60, *Amer.*; REPORT(ER) + -ORIAL, by analogy with pairs such as *tutor, tutorial*] **—rep′or·to′ri·al·ly,** *adv.*

re·pos·al (ri pō′zəl), *n.* the act of reposing. [1595–1605; REPOSE[1] + -AL[2]]

re-pose (rē pōz′), *v.t., v.i.,* **-posed, -pos·ing.** to pose again. [RE- + POSE[1]]

re·pose[1] (ri pōz′), *n., v.,* **-posed, -pos·ing. —n. 1.** the state of reposing or being at rest; rest; sleep. **2.** peace; tranquillity; calm. **3.** dignified calmness, as of manner; composure. **4.** absence of movement, animation, etc.: *When in repose, her face recalls the Mona Lisa.* **—v.i. 5.** to lie or be at rest, as from work, activity, etc. **6.** to lie dead: *His body will repose in the chapel for two days.* **7.** to be peacefully calm and quiet: *The sea reposed under the tropical sun.* **8.** to lie or rest on something. **9.** *Archaic.* to depend or rely on a person or thing. **—v.t. 10.** to lay to rest; rest; refresh by rest (often used reflexively). [1425–75; late ME *reposen* (v.) < MF *reposer,* OF < LL *repausāre,* equiv. to L *re-* RE- + LL *pausāre* to rest (deriv. of L *pausa* PAUSE)] **—re·pos·ed·ly** (ri pō′zid lē), *adv.* **—re·pos′ed·ness,** *n.* **—re·pos′er,** *n.*

re·pose[2] (ri pōz′), *v.t.,* **-posed, -pos·ing. 1.** to put (confidence, trust, etc.) in a person or thing. **2.** to put under the authority or at the disposal of a person. **3.** *Archaic.* to deposit. [1375–1425; late ME *reposen* to replace, repr. L *repōnere* to put back; see RE-, POSE]

re·pose·ful (ri pōz′fəl), *adj.* full of or suggesting repose; calm; quiet. [1620–30; REPOSE[1] + -FUL] **—re·pose′ful·ly,** *adv.* **—re·pose′ful·ness,** *n.*
—Syn. restful, tranquil, peaceful, undisturbed.

re·pos·it (ri poz′it), *v.t.* **1.** to put back; replace. **2.** to lay up or store; deposit. [1635–45; < L *repositus* (ptp. of *repōnere* to replace), equiv. to *re-* RE- + *posit(us),* ptp. of *pōnere* to place, put; see POSIT]

re·po·si·tion[1] (rē′pə zish′ən, rep′ə-), *n.* **1.** the act of depositing or storing. **2.** replacement, as of a bone. [1580–90; < LL *repositiōn-* (s. of *repositiō*) a laying up, equiv. to L *reposit(us)* (see REPOSIT) + *-iōn-* -ION]

re·po·si·tion[2] (rē′pə zish′ən), *v.t.* **1.** to put in a new or different position; shift: *to reposition the artwork on the advertising layout.* **2.** to change the image, marketing strategy, etc., of (a product) so as to appeal to a wider or different audience or market: *to reposition a diet drink to appeal to teenagers.* **3.** *Med., Surg.* to place (an organ or bone) in its original position. [1855–60; RE- + POSITION (v.)] **—re′po·si′tion·a·ble,** *adj.*

re·pos·i·to·ri·um (ri poz′i tôr′ē əm, -tōr′-), *n., pl.* **-to·ri·a** (-tôr′ē ə, -tōr′-). a place for the storage of valuables, as in an ancient Roman temple or a church. [< L *repositōrium* REPOSITORY]

re·pos·i·tor·y (ri poz′i tôr′ē, -tōr′ē), *n., pl.* **-tor·ies. 1.** a receptacle or place where things are deposited, stored, or offered for sale: *a repository for discarded clothing.* **2.** an abundant source or supply; storehouse: *a repository of information.* **3.** a burial place; sepulcher. **4.** a person to whom something is entrusted or confided. **5.** *Chiefly Brit.* warehouse. [1475–85; < L *repositōrium* that in which anything is placed; see REPOSIT, -TORY[2]]
—Syn. 1. depot, storehouse, depository.

re·pos·sess (rē′pə zes′), *v.t.* **1.** to possess again; regain possession of, esp. for nonpayment of money due. **2.** to put again in possession of something: *to repossess the Bourbons of their throne.* [1485–95; RE- + POSSESS] **—re′pos·sess′a·ble,** *adj.* **—re·pos·ses·sion** (rē′pə-zesh′ən), *n.* **—re′pos·ses′sor,** *n.*

re·pot (rē pot′), *v.,* **-pot·ted, -pot·ting. —v.t. 1.** to transfer (a plant) to another, esp. larger, pot. **—v.i. 2.** to transfer a plant to another pot. [1835–45; RE- + POT[1]]

re·pous·sage (rə pōō säzh′), *n.* **1.** the art or process of working in repoussé. **2.** the flattening of the hollow areas of an etching or engraving plate by hammering it gently on the reverse side. [< F, equiv. to *repouss(er)* (see REPOUSSÉ) + *-age* -AGE]

re·pous·sé (rə pōō sā′), *adj.* **1.** (of a design) raised in relief by hammering on the reverse side. **2.** ornamented or made in this kind of raised work. **—n. 3.** the art or process of producing repoussé designs. [1850–55; < F, ptp. of *repousser* to push back; see RE-, PUSH]

re·pous·soir (rə pōō swär′), *n. Painting.* a figure or object in the extreme foreground: used as a contrast and to increase the illusion of depth. [1870–75; < F, equiv. to *repouss(er)* to push back (see REPOUSSÉ) + *-oir* -ORY[2]]

repp (rep), *n.* rep[1].

Rep·plier (rep′lēr), *n.* **Agnes,** 1855–1950, U.S. essayist.

repr., **1.** represented. **2.** representing. **3.** reprint. **4.** reprinted.

rep·re·hend (rep′ri hend′), *v.t.* to reprove or find fault with; rebuke; censure; blame. [1300–50; ME *reprehenden* < L *reprehendere* to hold back, restrain, equiv. to *re-* RE- + *prehendere* to seize; see PREHENSION] **—rep′re·hend′a·ble,** *adj.* **—rep′re·hend′er,** *n.*
—Syn. reproach, upbraid, chide, admonish.

rep·re·hen·si·ble (rep′ri hen′sə bəl), *adj.* deserving of reproof, rebuke, or censure; blameworthy. [1350–1400; ME < LL *reprehēnsibilis,* equiv. to L *reprehēns(us)* (ptp. of *reprehendere* to REPREHEND) + *-ibilis* -IBLE] **—rep′re·hen′si·bil′i·ty, rep′re·hen′si·ble·ness,** *n.* **—rep′re·hen′si·bly,** *adv.*
—Syn. culpable. **—Ant.** praiseworthy.

rep·re·hen·sion (rep′ri hen′shən), *n.* the act of reprehending; reproof; censure. [1325–75; ME < L *reprehēnsiōn-* (s. of *reprehēnsiō*), equiv. to *reprehēns(us)* (ptp. of *reprehendere* to REPREHEND) + *-iōn-* -ION] **—rep·re·hen·sive** (rep′ri hen′siv), *adj.* **—rep′re·hen′sive·ly,** *adv.*

re-pre·sent (rē′pri zent′), *v.t.* to present again or anew. [1555–65; RE- + PRESENT[2]]

rep·re·sent (rep′ri zent′), *v.t.* **1.** to serve to express, designate, stand for, or denote, as a word, symbol, or the like does; symbolize: *In this painting the cat represents evil and the bird, good.* **2.** to express or designate by some term, character, symbol, or the like: *to represent musical sounds by notes.* **3.** to stand or act in the place of, as a substitute, proxy, or agent does: *He represents the company in Boston.* **4.** to speak and act for by delegated authority: *to represent one's government in a foreign country.* **5.** to act for or in behalf of (a constituency, state, etc.) by deputy right in exercising a voice in legislation or government: *He represents Chicago's third Congressional district.* **6.** to portray or depict; present the likeness of, as a picture does: *The painting represents*

CONCISE ETYMOLOGY KEY: <, descended or borrowed from; >, whence; b., blend of, blended; c., cognate with; cf., compare; deriv., derivative; equiv., equivalent; imit., imitative; obl., oblique; r., replacing; s., stem; sp., spelling, spelled; resp., respelling, respelled; trans., translation; ?, origin unknown; *, unattested; ‡, probably earlier than. See the full key inside the front cover.

re·map′, *v.t.,* **-mapped, -map·ping.**
re·mar′ket, *v.t.*
re·mar′riage, *n.*
re·mar′ry, *v.,* **-ried, -ry·ing.**
re·mar′shal, *v.t.,* **-shaled, -shal·ing** or (*esp. Brit.*) **-shalled, -shal·ling.**
re·mas′ter·y, *n., pl.* **-ter·ies.**
re·mas′ti·cate′, *v.,* **-cat·ed, -cat·ing.**
re′mas·ti·ca′tion, *n.*
re·mate′, *v.,* **-mat·ed, -mat·ing.**
re′ma·te′ri·al·i·za′tion, *n.*
re′ma·te′ri·al·ize′, *v.,* **-ized, -iz·ing.**
re′ma·tric′u·late′, *v.,* **-lat·ed, -lat·ing.**
re·meas′ure, *v.t.,* **-ured, -ur·ing.**
re·meas′ure·ment, *n.*
re·me′di·ate′, *v.t.,* **-at·ed, -at·ing.**
re·meet′, *v.,* **-met, -meet·ing.**
re·melt′, *v.t.*
re·mem′o·rize′, *v.t.,* **-rized, -riz·ing.**
re·mend′, *v.*
re·men′tion, *v.t.*
re·merge′, *v.,* **-merged, -merg·ing.**
re·mi′grate, *v.i.,* **-grat·ed, -grat·ing.**
re′mi·gra′tion, *n.*
re′mil·i·ta·ri·za′tion, *n.*
re·mil′i·ta·rize′, *v.t.,* **-rized, -riz·ing.**
re·mill′, *v.t.*
re·mill′a·ble, *adj.*
re·mine′, *v.,* **-mined, -min·ing.**
re′min·er·al·i·za′tion, *n.*

him as a man 22 years old. **7.** to present or picture to the mind. **8.** to present in words; set forth; describe; state. **9.** to set forth or describe as having a particular character (usually fol. by *as, to be,* etc.): *The article represented the dictator as a benevolent despot.* **10.** to set forth clearly or earnestly with a view to influencing opinion or action or making protest. **11.** to present, produce, or perform, as on a stage. **12.** to impersonate, as in acting. **13.** to serve as an example or specimen of; exemplify: *a genus represented by two species.* **14.** to be the equivalent of; correspond to: *The llama of the New World represents the camel of the Old World.* —*v.i.* **15.** to protest; make representations against. **16.** *Slang.* to use or display a secret handshake, sign, gesture, etc., for purposes of identification: *The gang members always represent when they see one another.* [1325–75; ME *representen* < MF *representer* < L *repraesentāre* to bring about immediately, make present, equiv. to *re-* RE- + *praesentāre* to PRESENT[2]] —**rep′re·sent′a·ble,** *adj.* —**rep′re·sent′a·bil′i·ty,** *n.*
—**Syn. 1.** exemplify. **6.** delineate. **12.** portray.

rep·re·sen·ta·tion (rep′ri zen tā′shən, -zən-), *n.* **1.** the act of representing. **2.** the state of being represented. **3.** the expression or designation by some term, character, symbol, or the like. **4.** action or speech on behalf of a person, group, business house, state, or the like by an agent, deputy, or representative. **5.** the state or fact of being so represented: *to demand representation on a board of directors.* **6.** *Govt.* the state, fact, or right of being represented by delegates having a voice in legislation or government. **7.** the body or number of representatives, as of a constituency. **8.** *Diplomacy.* **a.** the act of speaking or negotiating on behalf of a state. **b.** an utterance on behalf of a state. **9.** presentation to the mind, as of an idea or image. **10.** a mental image or idea so presented; concept. **11.** the act of portrayal, picturing, or other rendering in visible form. **12.** a picture, figure, statue, etc. **13.** the production or a performance of a play or the like, as on the stage. **14.** Often, **representations.** a description or statement, as of things true or alleged. **15.** a statement of facts, reasons, etc., made in appealing or protesting; a protest or remonstrance. **16.** *Law.* an implication or statement of fact to which legal liability may attach if material: *a representation of authority.* [1375–1425; late ME *representacion* < L *repraesentātiōn-* (s. of *repraesentātiō*), equiv. to *repraesentāt(us)* (ptp. of *repraesentāre* to REPRESENT) + *-iōn-* -ION]

rep·re·sen·ta·tion·al (rep′ri zen tā′shə nl, -zən-), *adj.* **1.** of or pertaining to representation. **2.** representing or depicting an object in a recognizable manner: *representational art.* [1850–55; REPRESENTATION + -AL[1]]

rep·re·sen·ta·tion·al·ism (rep′ri zen tā′shə nl iz′əm, -zən-), *n.* **1.** Also called **represen′tative re′alism.** *Epistemology.* the view that the objects of perception are ideas or sense data that represent external objects, esp. the Lockean doctrine that the perceived idea represents exactly the primary qualities of the external object. **2.** *Fine Arts.* the practice or principle of representing or depicting an object in a recognizable manner, esp. the portrayal of the surface characteristics of an object as they appear to the eye. [1895–1900; REPRESENTATIONAL + -ISM] —**rep′re·sen·ta′tion·al·ist,** *n.* —**rep′re·sen·ta′tion·al·is′tic,** *adj.*

rep·re·sent·a·tive (rep′ri zen′tə tiv), *n.* **1.** a person or thing that represents another or others. **2.** an agent or deputy: *a legal representative.* **3.** a person who represents a constituency or community in a legislative body, esp. a member of the U.S. House of Representatives or a lower house in certain state legislatures. **4.** a typical example or specimen of a group, quality, or kind. —*adj.* **5.** serving to represent; representing. **6.** standing or acting for another or others. **7.** made up of representatives: *a representative assembly.* **8.** of or pertaining to a system of governance by chosen representatives, usually elected from among a large group: *representative government.* **9.** exemplifying a group or kind; typical: *a representative selection of Elizabethan plays.* **10.** corresponding to or replacing some other species or the like, as in a different locality. **11.** of, pertaining to, or characteristic of representationalism. **12.** pertaining to or of the nature of a mental image or representation. [1350–1400; ME (adj.) < ML *repraesentātīvus,* equiv. to *repraesentāt(us)* (see REPRESENTATION) + *-īvus* -IVE] —**rep′re·sent′a·tive·ly,** *adv.* —**rep′re·sent′a·tive·ness,** *n.*
—**Syn. 5.** symbolic, exemplary, typical, characteristic.

re-press (rē′pres′), *v.t., v.i.* to press again or anew. [1870–75; RE- + PRESS[1]]

re·press (ri pres′), *v.t.* **1.** to keep under control, check, or suppress (desires, feelings, actions, tears, etc.). **2.** to keep down or suppress (anything objectionable). **3.** to put down or quell (sedition, disorder, etc.). **4.** to reduce (persons) to subjection. **5.** *Psychoanal.* to reject (painful or disagreeable ideas, memories, feelings, or impulses) from the conscious mind. —*v.i.* **6.** to initiate or undergo repression. [1325–75; ME *repressen* < L *repressus* (ptp. of *reprimere*), equiv. to *re-* RE- + *pressus,* ptp. of *primere* to PRESS[1]] —**re·press′i·ble,** *adj.*
—**Syn. 1.** bridle, control. See **check. 3.** subdue, quash. **4.** crush. —**Ant. 1–4.** foster.

re·pressed (ri prest′), *adj.* subjected to, affected by, or characteristic of psychological repression: *repressed emotional conflicts.* [1900–05; REPRESS + -ED[2]]

re·press·er (ri pres′ər), *n.* a person or thing that represses. Also, **repressor.** [1400–50; late ME; see REPRESS, -ER[1]]

re·pres·sion (ri presh′ən), *n.* **1.** the act of repressing; state of being repressed. **2.** *Psychoanal.* the rejection from consciousness of painful or disagreeable ideas, memories, feelings, or impulses. [1325–75; ME *repressioun* < ML *repressiōn-* (s. of *repressiō*), LL: suppression. See REPRESS, -ION]

re·pres·sive (ri pres′iv), *adj.* tending or serving to repress: *repressive laws.* [1375–1425; late ME < ML *repressīvus* < L *repress(us)* (see REPRESS) + *-īvus* -IVE] —**re·pres′sive·ly,** *adv.* —**re·pres′sive·ness,** *n.*

re·pres·sor (ri pres′ər), *n.* **1.** represser. **2.** *Genetics.* a protein that binds DNA at an operator site and thereby prevents transcription of one or more adjacent genes. [1955–60; < L; see REPRESS, -TOR]

re·priev·al (ri prē′vəl), *n.* reprieve; respite. [1580–90; REPRIEVE + -AL[2]]

re·prieve (ri prēv′), *v.,* **-prieved, -priev·ing,** *n.* —*v.t.* **1.** to delay the impending punishment or sentence of (a condemned person). **2.** to relieve temporarily from any evil. —*n.* **3.** a respite from impending punishment, as from execution of a sentence of death. **4.** a warrant authorizing this. **5.** any respite or temporary relief. [1300–50; perh. conflation of ME *repreven* to REPROVE, appar. taken in literal sense "to test again" (involving postponement), and ME *repried* (ptp.) < OF *repris* (see REPRISE)] —**re·priev′er,** *n.*
—**Syn. 3.** See **pardon. 5.** delay, postponement, stay, deferment.

rep·ri·mand (*n.* rep′rə mand′, -mänd′; *v.* rep′rə mand′, -mänd′, rep′rə mand′, -mänd′), *n.* **1.** a severe reproof or rebuke, esp. a formal one by a person in authority. —*v.t.* **2.** to reprove or rebuke severely, esp. in a formal way. [1630–40; < F *réprimande,* MF *reprimend* < L *reprimenda* that is to be repressed (fem. ger. of *reprimere*), equiv. to *re-* RE- + *prim(ere)* to PRESS[1] + *-enda,* fem. ger. suffix] —**rep′ri·mand′er,** *n.* —**rep′ri·mand′ing·ly,** *adv.*
—**Syn. 1.** condemnation, reprehension. **1, 2.** censure. **2.** condemn, reprehend. REPRIMAND, UPBRAID, ADMONISH, CENSURE all mean to reprove, reproach, or criticize (someone) adversely for behavior deemed reprehensible. REPRIMAND implies a formal rebuke, as by a superior, person in authority, or an official or official body: *reprimanded by the judge and warned of a possible charge of contempt of court.* UPBRAID suggests relatively severe criticism, but of a less formal sort: *The minister upbraided the parishioners for their poor church attendance.* ADMONISH refers to a more gentle warning or expression of disapproval, often including suggestions for improvement: *gently admonished the children to make less noise; admonished the players about promptness at practice sessions.* CENSURE involves harsh, vehement criticism, often from an authoritative source: *censured in the media for her off-the-cuff remarks; voted to censure their fellow senator.*

re·print (*v.* rē print′; *n.* rē′print′), *v.t.* **1.** to print again; print a new impression of. —*n.* **2.** a reproduction in print of matter already printed. **3.** an offprint. **4.** a new impression, without alteration, of a book or other printed work. **5.** *Philately.* an impression from the original plate after the issuance of a stamp has ceased and its use for postage has been voided. [1545–55; RE- + PRINT] —**re·print′er,** *n.*

re·pris·al (ri prī′zəl), *n.* **1.** (in warfare) retaliation against an enemy, for injuries received, by the infliction of equal or greater injuries. **2.** an act or instance of retaliation. **3.** the action or practice of using force, short of war, against another nation, to secure redress of a grievance. **4.** the forcible seizure of property or subjects in retaliation. [1400–50; late ME *reprisail* < OF *reprisaille.* See REPRISE, -AL[2]]
—**Syn. 1.** redress. See **revenge.**

re·prise (ri prīz′ *for 1;* rə prēz′ *for 2, 3*), *n., v.,* **-prised, -pris·ing.** —*n.* **1.** Usually, **reprises.** *Law.* an annual deduction, duty, or payment out of a manor or estate, as an annuity or the like. **2.** *Music.* **a.** a repetition. **b.** a return to the first theme or subject. —*v.t.* **3.** to execute a repetition of; repeat: *They reprised the elaborate dance number in the third act.* [1350–1400; ME < MF: a taking back, OF, n. use of fem. ptp. of *reprendre* to take back < L *reprehendere* to REPREHEND]

re·pris·ti·nate (rē pris′tə nāt′), *v.t.,* **-nat·ed, -nat·ing.** to restore to the first or original state or condition. [1650–60; RE- + PRISTINE + -ATE; cf. ML *repristinātiō*] —**re·pris′ti·na′tion,** *n.*

re·pri·va·tize (rē prī′və tīz′), *v.t.,* **-tized, -tiz·ing.** to restore to private control; remove from governmental jurisdiction. Also, *esp. Brit.,* **re·pri′va·tise′.** [1945–50; RE- + PRIVATE + -IZE]

re·pro (rē′prō), *n., pl.* **-pros. 1.** *Informal.* reproduction (def. 3). **2.** *Print.* See **repro proof.** [1945–50; by shortening]

re·proach (ri prōch′), *v.t.* **1.** to find fault with (a person, group, etc.); blame; censure. **2.** to upbraid. **3.** to be a cause of blame or discredit to. —*n.* **4.** blame or censure conveyed in disapproval: *a term of reproach.* **5.** an expression of upbraiding, censure, or reproof. **6.** disgrace, discredit, or blame incurred: *to bring reproach on one's family.* **7.** a cause or occasion of disgrace or discredit. **8. the Reproaches.** Also called **Improperia.** *Rom. Cath. Ch., Anglican Ch.* a series of antiphons sung in church on Good Friday, consisting of words addressed by Christ to His people, reminding them of His mercies and of their ingratitude. **9.** an object of scorn or contempt. [1375–1425; (n.) late ME *reproche* < OF, deriv. of *reprochier* to reproach < VL **repropiāre* to bring back near, equiv. to L *re-* RE- + LL *-propiāre* (deriv. of L *prope* near; see APPROACH); (v.) late ME *reprochen* < OF *reprochier*] —**re·proach′a·ble,** *adj.* —**re·proach′a·ble·ness,** *n.* —**re·proach′a·bly,** *adv.* —**re·proach′er,** *n.* —**re·proach′ing·ly,** *adv.*
—**Syn. 1.** chide, abuse, reprimand, reprehend, condemn, criticize. REPROACH, REBUKE, SCOLD, REPROVE imply calling one to account for something done or said. REPROACH is censure (often about personal matters, obligations, and the like) given with an attitude of faultfinding and some intention of shaming: *to reproach one for neglect.* REBUKE suggests sharp or stern reproof given usually formally or officially and approaching *reprimand* in severity: *He rebuked him strongly for laxness in his accounts.* SCOLD suggests that censure is given at some length, harshly, and more or less abusively; it implies irritation, which may be with or without justification: *to scold a boy for jaywalking.* A word of related meaning, but suggesting a milder or more kindly censure, often intended to correct the fault in question, is REPROVE: *to reprove one for inattention.* **3.** shame. **4, 5.** reprehension, rebuke, criticism, remonstrance, condemnation, disapproval. **6.** dishonor, shame, disrepute, odium, obloquy, opprobrium, ignominy, infamy, scorn. —**Ant. 1, 4, 5.** praise. **6.** honor.

re·proach·ful (ri prōch′fəl), *adj.* **1.** full of or expressing reproach or censure: *a reproachful look.* **2.** *Obs.* deserving reproach; shameful. [1540–50; REPROACH + -FUL] —**re·proach′ful·ly,** *adv.* —**re·proach′ful·ness,** *n.*

re·proach·less (ri prōch′lis), *adj.* irreproachable. [1820–30; REPROACH + -LESS] —**re·proach′less·ness,** *n.*

rep·ro·bance (rep′rə bəns), *n. Obs.* reprobation. [1595–1605; REPROB(ATE) + -ANCE]

rep·ro·bate (rep′rə bāt′), *n., adj., v.,* **-bat·ed, -bat·ing.** —*n.* **1.** a depraved, unprincipled, or wicked person: *a drunken reprobate.* **2.** a person rejected by God and beyond hope of salvation. —*adj.* **3.** morally depraved; unprincipled; bad. **4.** rejected by God and beyond hope of salvation. —*v.t.* **5.** to disapprove, condemn, or censure. **6.** (of God) to reject (a person), as for sin; exclude from the number of the elect or from salvation. [1400–50; late ME *reprobaten* < L *reprobātus;* ptp. of *reprobāre* to REPROVE] —**rep·ro·ba·cy** (rep′rə bə sē), **rep′ro·bate′·ness,** *n.* —**rep′ro·bat′er,** *n.*
—**Syn. 1.** tramp, scoundrel, wastrel, miscreant, wretch, rascal, cad, rogue. **2.** outcast, pariah. **3.** wicked, sinful, evil, corrupt. **5.** reprehend, blame, rebuke, reprove.

rep·ro·ba·tion (rep′rə bā′shən), *n.* **1.** disapproval, condemnation, or censure. **2.** rejection. **3.** *Theol.* rejection by God, as of persons excluded from the number of the elect or from salvation. [1400–50; late ME *reprobacion* < LL *reprobātiōn-* (s. of *reprobātiō*) rejection, equiv. to *reprobāt(us)* (see REPROBATE) + *-iōn-* -ION] —**rep′ro·ba′tion·ar′y,** *adj.*

rep·ro·ba·tive (rep′rə bā′tiv), *adj.* reprobating; expressing reprobation. [1825–35; REPROBATE + -IVE] —**rep′ro·ba′tive·ly,** *adv.*

re·proc·essed (rē pros′est *or, esp. Brit.,* -prō′sest), *adj.* (of wool) previously spun and woven but not used, as tailors' clippings. [1935–40; RE- + PROCESSED]

re·pro·duce (rē′prə do͞os′, -dyo͞os′), *v.,* **-duced, -duc·ing.** —*v.t.* **1.** to make a copy, representation, duplicate, or close imitation of: *to reproduce a picture.* **2.** to produce again or anew by natural process: *to reproduce a severed branch.* **3.** *Biol.* to produce one or more other individuals of (a given kind of organism) by some process of generation or propagation, sexual or asexual. **4.** to cause or foster the reproduction of (organisms). **5.** to produce, form, make, or bring about again or anew in any manner. **6.** to recall to the mind or have a mental image of (a past incident, scene, etc.), as by the aid of memory or imagination. **7.** to produce again, as a play produced at an earlier time. —*v.i.* **8.** to reproduce its kind, as an organism; propagate; bear offspring. **9.** to turn out in a given manner when copied: *This picture will reproduce well.* [1605–15; RE- + PRODUCE] —**re′pro·duc′er,** *n.* —**re′pro·duc′i·ble,** *adj.* —**re′pro·duc′i·bil′i·ty,** *n.*
—**Syn. 3.** generate, propagate, beget. **5.** repeat. See **imitate.**

reproduce′ head′, *Audio, Television.* See **playback head.**

re·pro·duc·tion (rē′prə duk′shən), *n.* **1.** the act or process of reproducing. **2.** the state of being reproduced. **3.** something made by reproducing an original; copy; duplicate: *a photographic reproduction; a reproduction of a Roman vase.* **4.** *Biol.* the natural process among organisms by which new individuals are generated and the species perpetuated. [1650–60; RE- + PRODUCTION]
—**Syn. 3.** replica, facsimile. **4.** generation, propagation.

reproduc′tion proof′, *Print.* See **repro proof.** [1945–50]

re·pro·duc·tive (rē′prə duk′tiv), *adj.* **1.** serving to reproduce. **2.** concerned with or pertaining to reproduction: *a reproductive process; reproductive organs.* —*n.* **3.** *Entomol.* a sexually mature male or female termite; a member of the reproductive caste. [1745–55; RE- + PRODUCTIVE] —**re′pro·duc′tive·ly,** *adv.* —**re′pro·duc′·tive·ness,** *n.*

reproduc′tive cell′, gamete.

CONCISE PRONUNCIATION KEY: *act, cāpe, dâre, pärt; set, ēqual; if, īce; ox, ōver, ôrder, oil, bo͝ok, bo͞ot, out; up, ûrge; child; sing; shoe; thin, that;* zh as in *treasure.* ə = *a* as in *alone, e* as in *system, i* as in *easily, o* as in *gallop, u* as in *circus;* ˚ as in *fire* (fīˊr), *hour* (ouˊr). l and n can serve as syllabic consonants, as in *cradle* (krād′l), and *button* (but′n). See the full key inside the front cover.

re·min′er·al·ize′, *v.,* **-ized, -iz·ing.**
re·min′er·al·iz′er, *n.*
re·min′gle, *v.,* **-gled, -gling.**
re·mint′, *v.t.*
re·mix′, *v.*
re′mo·bi·li·za′tion, *n.*
re·mo′bi·lize′, *v.,* **-lized, -liz·ing.**
re·mod′ern·i·za′tion, *n.*
re·mod′ern·ize′, *v.,* **-ized, -iz·ing.**
re′mod·i·fi·ca′tion, *n.*
re·mod′i·fy′, *v.,* **-fied, -fy·ing.**
re·mod′u·late′, *v.t.,* **-lat·ed, -lat·ing.**
re·mois′ten, *v.*
re·mold′, *v.*
re·mol′li·fy, *v.t.,* **-fied, -fy·ing.**
re·mort′gage, *v.t.,* **-gaged, -gag·ing.**
re·mo′ti·vate′, *v.t.,* **-vat·ed, -vat·ing.**
re·mo′ti·va′tion, *n.*
re′mul·ti·pli·ca′tion, *n.*
re·mul′ti·ply′, *v.,* **-plied, -ply·ing.**
re·nail′, *v.t.*
re·name′, *v.t.,* **-named, -nam·ing.**
re·na′tion·al·i·za′tion, *n.*
re·na′tion·al·ize′, *v.,* **-ized, -iz·ing.**
re·nav′i·gate′, *v.t.,* **-gat·ed, -gat·ing.**
re′nav·i·ga′tion, *n.*
re′ne·gate′, *v.t.,* **-gat·ed, -gat·ing.**
re′ne·ga′tion, *n.*
re·neu′tral·ize′, *v.,* **-ized, -iz·ing.**

reproduc′tive imagina′tion. See under **imagination** (def. 6).

reproduc′tive isola′tion, the conditions, as physiological or behavioral differences or geographical barriers, that prevent potentially interbreeding populations from cross-fertilization. [1980–85]

re•prog•ra•phy (ri prog′rə fē), *n.* the reproduction and duplication of documents, written materials, drawings, designs, etc., by any process making use of light rays or photographic means, including offset printing, microfilming, photography, office duplicating, and the like. [1960–65; REPRO(DUCTION) + (PHOTO)GRAPHY]

re•proof (ri pro͞of′), *n.* **1.** the act of reproving, censuring, or rebuking. **2.** an expression of censure or rebuke. [1300–50; ME *reprof* < OF *reprove,* deriv. of *reprover* to REPROVE] **—re•proof′less,** *adj.*
—Syn. 1. rebuke, reproach, remonstrance, chiding.

re′pro proof′, *Print.* a proof, usually pulled on glossy paper, of a fidelity suitable for reproduction by photography for making a plate. Also called **repro, reproduction proof.** [1945–50]

re•prov•a•ble (ri pro͞o′və bəl), *adj.* deserving of reproof. [1300–50; ME < MF, equiv. to *reprov(er)* to REPROVE + *-able* -ABLE] **—re•prov′a•ble•ness,** *n.*

re•prov•al (ri pro͞o′vəl), *n.* **1.** the act of reproving. **2.** a reproof. [1840–50; REPROVE + -AL[2]]

re•prove (rē pro͞ov′), *v.t., v.i.,* **-proved, -proved** or **-prov•en, -prov•ing.** to prove again. [1520–30; RE- + PROVE]

re•prove (ri pro͞ov′), *v.,* **-proved, -prov•ing.** **—***v.t.* **1.** to criticize or correct, esp. gently: *to reprove a pupil for making a mistake.* **2.** to disapprove of strongly; censure: *to reprove a bad decision.* **3.** *Obs.* to disprove or refute. **—***v.i.* **4.** to speak in reproof; administer a reproof. [1275–1325; ME *reproven* < OF *reprover* < LL *reprobāre,* equiv. to *re-* RE- + *probāre* to test, PROVE] **—re•prov′er,** *n.* **—re•prov′ing•ly,** *adv.*
—Syn. 1. scold, reprimand, upbraid, chide, reprehend, admonish. See **reproach.** **—Ant. 1.** praise.

rept., report.

rep•tant (rep′tənt), *adj.* repent[2]. [1650–60; < L *rēptant-* (s. of *rēptāns*), prp. of *rēptāre* to creep, equiv. to *rēpt-* (freq. s. of *rēpere* to creep) + *-ant-* -ANT]

rep•tile (rep′til, -tīl), *n.* **1.** any cold-blooded vertebrate of the class Reptilia, comprising the turtles, snakes, lizards, crocodilians, amphisbaenians, tuatara, and various extinct members including the dinosaurs. **2.** (loosely) any of various animals that crawl or creep. **3.** a groveling, mean, or despicable person. **—***adj.* **4.** of or resembling a reptile; creeping or crawling. **5.** groveling, mean, or despicable. [1350–1400; ME *reptil* < LL *rēptile,* n. use of neut. of *rēptilis* creeping, equiv. to L *rēpt(us)* (ptp. of *rēpere* to creep) + *-ilis* -ILE] **—rep′tile•like′,** *adj.* **—rep•ti•loid** (rep′tl oid′), *adj.*

Rep•til•i•a (rep til′ē ə), *n.* the class comprising the reptiles. [1620–30; < NL; see REPTILIAN]

rep•til•i•an (rep til′ē ən, -til′yən), *adj.* **1.** belonging or pertaining to the Reptilia. **2.** groveling, debased, or despicable; contemptible. **3.** mean; treacherous; harmful. **—***n.* **4.** a reptile. [1840–50; < NL *Reptili(a)* reptiles (pl. of *rēptile,* neut. of LL *rēptilis;* see REPTILE) + -AN]

Repub., **1.** Republic. **2.** Republican.

re•pub•lic (ri pub′lik), *n.* **1.** a state in which the supreme power rests in the body of citizens entitled to vote and is exercised by representatives chosen directly or indirectly by them. **2.** any body of persons viewed as a commonwealth. **3.** a state in which the head of government is not a monarch or other hereditary head of state. **4.** (*cap.*) any of the five periods of republican government in France. Cf. **First Republic, Second Republic, Third Republic, Fourth Republic, Fifth Republic.** **5.** (*cap., italics.*) a philosophical dialogue (4th century B.C.) by Plato dealing with the composition and structure of the ideal state. [1595–1605; < F *république,* MF < L *rēs pūblica,* equiv. to *rēs* thing, entity + *pūblica* PUBLIC]

re•pub•li•can (ri pub′li kən), *adj.* **1.** of, pertaining to, or of the nature of a republic. **2.** favoring a republic. **3.** fitting or appropriate for the citizen of a republic: *a very republican notion.* **4.** (*cap.*) of or pertaining to the Republican party. **—***n.* **5.** a person who favors a republican form of government. **6.** (*cap.*) a member of the Republican party. [1685–95; < F *républicain,* MF. See REPUBLIC, -AN]

re•pub•li•can•ism (ri pub′li kə niz′əm), *n.* **1.** republican government. **2.** republican principles or adherence to them. **3.** (*cap.*) the principles or policy of the Republican party. [1680–90; REPUBLICAN + -ISM]

re•pub•li•can•ize (ri pub′li kə nīz′), *v.t.,* **-ized, -iz•ing.** to make republican. Also, *esp. Brit.,* **re•pub′li•can•ise′.** [1790–1800; < F *républicaniser,* equiv. to *républicain* REPUBLICAN + *-iser* -IZE] **—re•pub′li•can•i•za′tion,** *n.* **—re•pub′li•can•iz′er,** *n.*

Repub′lican par′ty, 1. one of the two major political parties in the U.S.: originated 1854–56. **2.** *U.S. Hist.* See **Democratic-Republican party.**

Repub′lican Riv′er, a river flowing E from E Colorado through Nebraska and Kansas into the Kansas River. 422 mi. (680 km) long.

re•pub•li•ca•tion (rē′pub li kā′shən), *n.* **1.** publication anew. **2.** a book or the like published again. [1720–30; RE- + PUBLICATION]

repub′lic of let′ters, 1. the collective body of literary people. **2.** literature. [1695–1705]

Ré•pu•blique Mal•gache (rā py blēk mal gash′), French name of **Malagasy Republic.**

re•pub•lish (rē pub′lish), *v.t.* **1.** to publish again: *to republish a bestseller in a special illustrated edition.* **2.** *Law.* to reexecute (a will). [1615–25; RE- + PUBLISH] **—re•pub′lish•a•ble,** *adj.* **—re•pub′lish•er,** *n.*

re•pu•di•ate (ri pyo͞o′dē āt′), *v.t.,* **-at•ed, -at•ing.** **1.** to reject as having no authority or binding force: *to repudiate a claim.* **2.** to cast off or disown: *to repudiate a son.* **3.** to reject with disapproval or condemnation: *to repudiate a new doctrine.* **4.** to reject with denial: *to repudiate a charge as untrue.* **5.** to refuse to acknowledge and pay (a debt), as a state, municipality, etc. [1535–45; < L *repudiātus* (ptp. of *repudiāre* to reject, refuse), equiv. to *repudi(um)* a casting off, divorce (*re-* RE- + *pud(ere)* to make ashamed, feel shame (see PUDENDUM) + *-ium* -IUM) + *-ātus* -ATE[1]] **—re•pu′di•a•ble,** *adj.* **—re•pu′di•a′tive,** *adj.* **—re•pu′di•a′tor,** *n.*
—Syn. 1. disavow, renounce, discard, disclaim. **3.** condemn, disapprove. **—Ant. 1.** accept. **3.** approve.

re•pu•di•a•tion (ri pyo͞o′dē ā′shən), *n.* **1.** the act of repudiating. **2.** the state of being repudiated. **3.** refusal, as by a state or municipality, to pay a lawful debt. [1535–45; < L *repudiātiōn-* (s. of *repudiātiō*), equiv. to *repudiāt(us)* (see REPUDIATE) + *-iōn-* -ION] **—re•pu•di•a•to•ry** (ri pyo͞o′dē ə tôr′ē, -tōr′ē), *adj.*

re•pugn (ri pyo͞on′), *v.t.* **1.** to oppose or refute. **—***v.i.* **2.** *Archaic.* to resist. [1325–75; ME *repugnen* < MF *repugner* < L *repugnāre* to resist, equiv. to *re-* RE- + *pugnāre* to fight]

re•pug•nance (ri pug′nəns), *n.* **1.** the state of being repugnant. **2.** strong distaste, aversion, or objection; antipathy. **3.** contradictoriness or inconsistency. Also, **re•pug′nan•cy.** [1350–1400; ME < MF < L *repugnantia,* equiv. to *repugn(āre)* to REPUGN + *-antia* -ANCE]
—Syn. 2. hatred, hostility. See **dislike. 3.** contrariety, incompatibility, irreconcilability. **—Ant. 2.** attraction, liking. **3.** compatibility.

re•pug•nant (ri pug′nənt), *adj.* **1.** distasteful, objectionable, or offensive: *a repugnant smell.* **2.** making opposition; averse. **3.** opposed or contrary, as in nature or character. [1350–1400; ME *repugnaunt* < MF < L *repugnant-* (s. of *repugnāns,* prp. of *repugnāre*), equiv. to *repugn(āre)* to REPUGN + *-ant-* -ANT] **—re•pug′nant•ly,** *adv.*
—Syn. 3. antagonistic, adverse, hostile.

re•pulse (ri puls′), *v.,* **-pulsed, -puls•ing,** *n.* **—***v.t.* **1.** to drive back; repel: *to repulse an assailant.* **2.** to repel with denial, discourtesy, or the like; refuse or reject. **3.** to cause feelings of repulsion in: *The scenes of violence in the film may repulse some viewers.* **—***n.* **4.** the act of repelling. **5.** the fact of being repelled, as in hostile encounter. **6.** a refusal or rejection. [1375–1425; late ME < L *repulsus,* ptp. of *repellere* to REPEL] **—re•puls′er,** *n.*
—Syn. 2. rebuff, spurn, shun, snub.

re•pul•sion (ri pul′shən), *n.* **1.** the act of repulsing or the state of being repulsed. **2.** the feeling of being repelled, as by the thought or presence of something; distaste, repugnance, or aversion. **3.** *Physics.* the force that acts between bodies of like electric charge or magnetic polarity, tending to separate them. [1375–1425; late ME < MF < ML *repulsiōn-* (s. of LL *repulsiō*), equiv. to L *repuls(us)* (see REPULSE) + *-iōn-* -ION]

re•pul•sive (ri pul′siv), *adj.* **1.** causing repugnance or aversion: *a repulsive mask.* **2.** capable of causing repulsion; serving to repulse: *to present enough repulsive force to keep the enemy from daring to attack.* **3.** tending to drive away or keep at a distance; cold; forbidding: *arrogant, repulsive airs to frighten the timid.* **4.** *Physics.* of the nature of or characterized by physical repulsion. [1590–1600; REPULSE + -IVE] **—re•pul′sive•ly,** *adv.* **—re•pul′sive•ness,** *n.*
—Syn. 1. loathsome, disgusting, offensive, distasteful.

re•pur•chase (rē pûr′chəs), *v.,* **-chased, -chas•ing,** *n., adj.* **—***v.t.* **1.** to buy again; regain by purchase. **—***n.* **2.** the act of repurchasing. **—***adj.* **3.** of or pertaining to repurchase: *a repurchase contract.* [1585–95; RE- + PURCHASE] **—re•pur′chas•er,** *n.*

repur′chase agree′ment, 1. a contract between a dealer, as a bank, and an investor, whereby the investor purchases securities with the promise that they will be bought back by the dealer on a designated date, for which the investor receives a fixed return. **2.** a contract between a buyer and a seller whereby the seller agrees to repurchase the item sold after a specified length of time or amount of use. *Abbr.:* RP Also called **repo.** [1920–25]

rep•u•ta•ble (rep′yə tə bəl), *adj.* **1.** held in good repute; honorable; respectable; estimable: *a reputable organization.* **2.** considered to be good or acceptable usage; standard: *reputable speech.* [1605–15; REPUTE + -ABLE] **—rep′u•ta•bil′i•ty, rep′u•ta•ble•ness,** *n.* **—rep′u•ta•bly,** *adv.*

rep•u•ta•tion (rep′yə tā′shən), *n.* **1.** the estimation in which a person or thing is held, esp. by the community or the public generally; repute: *a man of good reputation.* **2.** favorable repute; good name: *to ruin one's reputation by misconduct.* **3.** a favorable and publicly recognized name or standing for merit, achievement, reliability, etc.: *to build up a reputation.* **4.** the estimation or name of being, having, having done, etc., something specified: *He has the reputation of being a shrewd businessman.* [1325–75; ME *reputacioun* < L *reputātiōn-* (s. of *reputātiō*) computation, consideration, equiv. to *reputāt(us)* (ptp. of *reputāre;* see REPUTE) + *-iōn-* -ION] **—rep′u•ta′tion•al,** *adj.*
—Syn. 1. regard, name. REPUTATION, CHARACTER are often confused. REPUTATION, however, is the word which refers to the position one occupies or the standing that one has in the opinion of others, in respect to attainments, integrity, and the like: *a fine reputation; a reputation for honesty.* CHARACTER is the combination of moral and other traits which make one the kind of person one actually is (as contrasted with what others think of one): *Honesty is an outstanding trait of his character.* **2.** fame, distinction, renown, esteem, honor, recognition. **3.** See **credit.** **—Ant. 2.** disrepute.

re•pute (ri pyo͞ot′), *n., v.,* **-put•ed, -put•ing.** **—***n.* **1.** estimation in the view of others; reputation: *persons of good repute.* **2.** favorable reputation; good name; public respect. **—***v.t.* **3.** to consider or believe (a person or thing) to be as specified; regard (usually used in the passive): *He was reputed to be a millionaire.* [1400–50; late ME *reputen* (v.) < MF *reputer* < L *reputāre* to compute, consider, equiv. to *re-* RE- + *putāre* to think]
—Syn. 2. distinction, honor. See **credit. 3.** hold, deem, reckon. **—Ant. 2.** dishonor.

re•put•ed (ri pyo͞o′tid), *adj.* reported or supposed to be such: *the reputed author of a book.* [1540–50; REPUTE + -ED[2]]

re•put•ed•ly (ri pyo͞o′tid lē), *adv.* according to reputation or popular belief: *a reputedly honest man.* [1680–90; REPUTED + -LY]

req., 1. require. **2.** required. **3.** requisition.

re•quest (ri kwest′), *n.* **1.** the act of asking for something to be given or done, esp. as a favor or courtesy; solicitation or petition: *At his request, they left.* **2.** an instance of this: *There have been many requests for the product.* **3.** a written statement of petition: *If you need supplies, send in a request.* **4.** something asked for: *to obtain one's request.* **5.** the state of being asked for; demand. **6. by request,** in response or accession to a request: *The orchestra played numbers by request.* **—***v.t.* **7.** to ask for, esp. politely or formally: *He requested permission to speak.* **8.** to ask or beg; bid (usually fol. by a clause or an infinitive): *to request that he leave; to request to be excused.* **9.** to ask or beg (someone) to do something: *He requested me to go.* [1300–50; ME *requeste* (n.) < OF < VL **requaesita* things asked for, n. use of neut. pl. ptp. of **requaerere* to seek, for L *requīrere.* See REQUIRE, QUEST] **—re•quest′er,** *n.*
—Syn. 1. entreaty, supplication, prayer. **7.** petition, supplicate. **8.** See **beg. 9.** entreat, beseech.

Req•ui•em (rek′wē əm, rē′kwē-, rā′-), *n.* **1.** *Rom. Cath. Ch.* **a.** Also called **Req′uiem Mass′.** the Mass celebrated for the repose of the souls of the dead. **b.** a celebration of this Mass. **c.** a plainsong setting for this Mass. **2.** any musical service, hymn, or dirge for the repose of the dead. Also, **req′ui•em.** [1275–1325; ME < L, acc. of *requiēs* rest (the first word of the introit of the mass for the dead)]

req′uiem shark′, any of numerous, chiefly tropical sharks of the family Carcharhinidae, including the tiger shark and soupfin shark. [1895–1900; by folk etym. from F *requin* shark (orig. uncert.; perh. from same source as Pg *requeima, requeime* local name for various serranid fishes)]

re•qui•es•cat (rek′wē es′kät, -kat), *n.* a wish or prayer for the repose of the dead. [1815–25; < L: short for REQUIESCAT IN PACE]

re•qui•es•cat in pa•ce (re′kwē es′kät in pä′che), *Latin.* may he (or she) rest in peace.

re•quire (ri kwīᵊr′), *v.,* **-quired, -quir•ing.** **—***v.t.* **1.** to have need of; need: *He requires medical care.* **2.** to call on authoritatively; order or enjoin to do something: *to require an agent to account for money spent.* **3.** to ask for authoritatively or imperatively; demand. **4.** to impose need or occasion for; make necessary or indispensable: *The work required infinite patience.* **5.** to call for or exact as obligatory; ordain: *The law requires annual income-tax returns.* **6.** to place under an obligation or necessity: *The situation requires me to take immediate action.* **7.** *Chiefly Brit.* to desire; wish to have: *Will you require tea at four o'clock?* **—***v.i.* **8.** to demand; impose obligation: *to do as the law requires.* [1300–50; ME *requiren* < L *requīrere,* equiv. to *re-* RE- + *-quīrere,* comb. form of *quaerere* to seek, search for (cf. QUEST)] **—re•quir′a•ble,** *adj.* **—re•quir′er,** *n.*
—Syn. 1. See **lack. 3.** See **demand. 6.** obligate, necessitate. **—Ant. 3.** forgo.

re•quire•ment (ri kwīᵊr′mənt), *n.* **1.** that which is required; a thing demanded or obligatory: *One of the requirements of the job is accuracy.* **2.** an act or instance of requiring. **3.** a need or necessity: *to meet the requirements of daily life.* [1520–30; REQUIRE + -MENT]
—Syn. 1. REQUIREMENT, REQUISITE refer to that which is necessary. A REQUIREMENT is some quality or performance demanded of a person in accordance with certain fixed regulations: *requirements for admission to college.* A REQUISITE is not imposed from outside; it is a factor which is judged necessary according to the nature of things, or to the circumstances of the case: *Efficiency is a requisite for success in business.* REQUISITE may also refer to a concrete object judged necessary: *the requisites for perfect grooming.* **2.** order, command, injunction, directive, demand, claim.

req•ui•site (rek′wə zit), *adj.* **1.** required or necessary

CONCISE ETYMOLOGY KEY: <, descended or borrowed from; >, whence; b., blend of, blended; c., cognate with; cf., compare; deriv., derivative; equiv., equivalent; imit., imitative; obl., oblique; r., replacing; s., stem; sp., spelling, spelled; resp., respelling, respelled; trans., translation; ?, origin unknown; *, unattested; ‡, probably earlier than. See the full key inside the front cover.

re•nom′i•nate′, *v.t.,* **-nat•ed, -nat•ing.**
re•nom•i•na′tion, *n.*
re′nor•mal•i•za′tion, *n.*
re•nor′mal•ize′, *v.t.,* **-ized, -iz•ing.**
re•no′ta•rize′, *v.t.,* **-rized, -riz•ing.**
re′no•ta′tion, *n.*
re•no′tice, *v.t.,* **-ticed, -tic•ing.**
re′no•ti•fi•ca′tion, *n.*
re•no′ti•fy′, *v.t.,* **-fied, -fy•ing.**
re•nour′ish, *v.t.*
re•nour′ish•ment, *n.*
re•nul′li•fi•ca′tion, *n.*
re•nul′li•fy′, *v.t.,* **-fied, -fy•ing.**
re•num′ber, *v.t.*
re•nu′mer•ate′, *v.t.,* **-at•ed, -at•ing.**
re′ob•ject′, *v.t.*
re•ob′li•gate′, *v.t.,* **-gat•ed, -gat•ing.**
re•ob′li•ga′tion, *n.*
re′o•blige′, *v.t.,* **-bliged, -blig•ing.**
re′ob•ser•va′tion, *n.*
re′ob•serve′, *v.,* **-served, -serv•ing.**
re′ob•tain′, *v.t.*
re′ob•tain′a•ble, *adj.*
re•oc′cu•pa′tion, *n.*
re•oc′cu•py′, *v.t.,* **-pied, -py•ing.**
re′oc•cur′, *v.i.,* **-curred, -cur•ring.**
re′oc•cur′rence, *n.*
re′of•fend′, *v.*
re•of′fer, *v., n.*
re•oil′, *v.*
re•op′er•ate′, *v.t.,* **-at•ed, -at•ing.**
re′op•er•a′tion, *n.*
re′op•pose′, *v.t.,* **-posed, -pos•ing.**

for a particular purpose, position, etc.; indispensable: *the requisite skills of an engineer.* —*n.* **2.** something requisite; a necessary quality, thing, etc. [1425–75; late ME < L *requīsītus* ptp. of *requīrere* to seek; see REQUIRE, -ITE[2]] —**req′ui·site·ly,** *adv.* —**req′ui·site·ness,** *n.*
—**Syn. 1.** needed, needful. See **necessary. 2.** necessity. See **requirement.** —**Ant. 1.** dispensable. **2.** luxury.

req·ui·si·tion (rek′wə zish′ən), *n.* **1.** the act of requiring or demanding. **2.** a demand made. **3.** an authoritative or formal demand for something to be done, given, supplied, etc.: *The general issued a requisition to the townspeople for eight trucks.* **4.** a written request or order for something, as supplies. **5.** the form on which such an order is drawn up. **6.** the state of being required for use or called into service: *to put something in requisition.* **7.** a requirement or essential condition. —*v.t.* **8.** to require or take for use; press into service. **9.** to demand or take, as by authority, for military purposes, public needs, etc.: *to requisition supplies.* [1375–1425; late ME < L *requīsītiōn-* (s. of *requīsītiō*) a searching, equiv. to *requīsīt(us)* REQUISITE + *-iōn-* -ION] —**req′ui·si′tion·ar′y,** *adj.* —**req′ui·si′tion·ist, req′ui·si′tion·er,** *n.*

re·quit·al (ri kwīt′l), *n.* **1.** the act of requiting. **2.** a return or reward for service, kindness, etc. **3.** a retaliation for a wrong, injury, etc. **4.** something given or done as repayment, reward, punishment, etc., in return. [1570–80; REQUITE + -AL[2]]

re·quite (ri kwīt′), *v.t.,* **-quit·ed, -quit·ing. 1.** to make repayment or return for (service, benefits, etc.). **2.** to make retaliation for (a wrong, injury, etc.); avenge. **3.** to make return to (a person, group, etc.) for service, benefits, etc. **4.** to retaliate on (a person, group, etc.) for a wrong, injury, etc. **5.** to give or do in return. [1520–30; RE- + obs. *quite,* var. of QUIT] —**re·quit′a·ble,** *adj.* —**re·quite′ment,** *n.* —**re·quit′er,** *n.*
—**Syn. 1.** repay, reward, recompense, compensate, pay, remunerate, reimburse. **2.** revenge. —**Ant. 2.** forgive.

re·ra·di·a·tion (rē rā′dē ā′shən), *n.* **1.** *Physics.* radiation emitted as a consequence of a previous absorption of radiation. **2.** *Radio.* retransmission of signals, a source of interference, due to frequency oscillations in a radio receiver. [1880–85; RE- + RADIATION]

rere·brace (rēr′brās′), *n. Armor.* a piece of plate armor for the upper arm; an upper cannon. Cf. **vambrace** (def. 1). See diag. under **armor.** [1300–50; ME, equiv. to *rere-* (< MF *rere, riere* behind, backward < L *retrō-* RETRO-) + BRACE]

re·re·cord (rē′ri kôrd′), *v.t.* **1.** to record (something) another time. **2.** to transfer (a recording) from one process to another, as from shellac to long-playing record. [1925–30]

re·re·cord·ing (rē′ri kôr′ding), *n. Motion Pictures.* the preparation of the final sound track of a film or video production, including the mixing of sound effects and dialogue, the recording of additional dialogue, and the addition of music. [1925–30; RE-RECORD + -ING[1]]

rere·dos (rēr′dos, rēr′i-, râr′i-), *n.* **1.** a screen or a decorated part of the wall behind an altar in a church. **2.** the back of a fireplace or of a medieval open hearth. [1325–75; ME, alter. of AF *areredos,* equiv. to MF *arere* behind (see ARREAR) + *dos* back (< L *dorsum*)]

re·re·lease (rē′ri lēs′), *v.,* **-leased, -leas·ing,** *n.* —*v.t.* **1.** to release again: *Some popular films are rereleased every few years.* —*n.* **2.** something, as a film, that has been rereleased. [1945–50; RE- + RELEASE]

rere·mouse (rēr′mous′), *n., pl.* **-mice.** *Archaic.* a bat. [bef. 1100; ME *reremous,* OE *hrēremūs,* equiv. to *hrēre-* (orig. uncert.; perh. akin to *hrēran* to move) + *mūs* MOUSE]

rere·ward (rēr′wərd), *n.* rearward (defs. 2, 3).

re·run (*v.* rē run′; *n.* rē′run′), *v.,* **-ran, -run, -running,** *n.* —*v.t.* **1.** to run again. —*n.* **2.** the act of rerunning. **3.** a showing of a motion picture or television program after its initial run, usually some months or years later. **4.** the motion picture or television program being shown again. **5.** *Informal.* a person or thing that is merely a restatement or imitation of something familiar; rehash: *The plot is just a rerun of every other spy story.* [1795–1805; RE- + RUN]

res (rēz, rās), *n., pl.* **res.** *Chiefly Law.* an object or thing; matter. [1850–55; < L *rēs*]

RES, *Immunol.* See **reticuloendothelial system.**

res., 1. research. **2.** reserve. **3.** residence. **4.** resident; residents. **5.** resigned. **6.** resolution.

Re·sa·ca de la Pal·ma (rä sä′kə dä lä päl′mə, də, rə sak′ə), a locality in S Texas, near Brownsville: battle 1846.

res ad·ju·di·ca·ta (rēz′ ə jo͞o′di kä′tə, rās′), *Law.* See **res judicata.** [1900–05]

re·sail (rē sāl′), *v.i.* to sail back or again. [1580–90; RE- + SAIL]

re·sal·a·ble (rē sā′lə bəl), *adj.* able to be resold; suitable for resale. Also, **re·sale′a·ble.** [1865–70; RESALE + -ABLE]

re·sale (rē′sāl′, rē sāl′), *n.* **1.** the act of selling a second time. **2.** the act of selling something secondhand. —*adj.* **3.** used; secondhand: *a rack of resale clothing.* [1615–25; RE- + SALE]

re·saw (*v.* rē sô′; *n.* rē′sô′), *v.,* **-sawed, -sawed** or **-sawn, -sawing,** *n.* —*v.t.* **1.** to saw again. —*n.* **2.** *Lumbering.* a machine for cutting logs into lumber. [1910–15; RE- + SAW[1]] —**re·saw·yer** (rē sô′yər, -soi′ər), **re·saw′er,** *n.*

re·scale (rē skāl′), *v.t.,* **-scaled, -scal·ing.** to revise the scale of, esp. to make smaller or more modest: *to rescale a budget.* [1940–45; RE- + SCALE[3]]

re·sched·ule (rē skej′o͞ol, -o͞ol, -o͞o əl; *Brit.* rē shed′yo͞ol, -shej′o͞ol), *v.t.,* **-uled, -ul·ing. 1.** to schedule for another or later time: *to reschedule a baseball game because of rain.* **2.** (of a loan) to extend the time for repaying, often granting concessions on interest rates, amount of payments, etc.: *to reschedule debts from developing countries.* [1965–70; RE- + SCHEDULE]

re·scind (ri sind′), *v.t.* **1.** to abrogate; annul; revoke; repeal. **2.** to invalidate (an act, measure, etc.) by a later action or a higher authority. [1630–40; < L *rescindere* to tear off again, cut away, equiv. to *re-* RE- + *scindere* to tear, divide, destroy] —**re·scind′a·ble,** *adj.* —**re·scind′er,** *n.* —**re·scind′ment,** *n.*
—**Syn. 1.** nullify; retract, withdraw. **2.** countermand, repeal, veto.

re·scis·si·ble (ri sis′ə bəl, -siz′-), *adj.* able to be rescinded. [< L *resciss(us)* cut off, repealed (see RESCISSION) + -IBLE]

re·scis·sion (ri sizh′ən), *n.* the act of rescinding. [1605–15; < LL *rescissiōn-* (s. of *rescissiō*) a making void, rescinding, equiv. to *resciss(us)* (ptp. of *rescindere* to RESCIND, equiv. to *re-* RE- + *scid-,* var. s. of *scindere* to cleave, tear in two + *-tus* ptp. suffix, with *dt* > *ss*) + *-iōn-* -ION]

re·scis·so·ry (ri sis′ə rē, -siz′-), *adj.* serving to rescind. [1595–1605; < LL *rescissōrius* pertaining to revoking or rescinding; see RESCISSION, -TORY[1]]

re·script (rē′skript′), *n.* **1.** a written answer, as of a Roman emperor or a pope, to a query or petition in writing. **2.** any edict, decree, or official announcement. **3.** the act of rewriting. **4.** something rewritten. [1520–30; < L *rescrīptum* an imperial rescript (n. use of neut. ptp. of *rescrībere* to write back, reply). See RE-, SCRIPT]

res·cue (res′kyo͞o), *v.,* **-cued, -cu·ing,** *n.* —*v.t.* **1.** to free or deliver from confinement, violence, danger, or evil. **2.** *Law.* to liberate or take by forcible or illegal means from lawful custody. —*n.* **3.** the act of rescuing. [1300–50; (v.) ME *rescuen* < OF *rescourre,* equiv. to *re-* RE- + *escourre* to shake, drive out, remove < L *excutere* (*ex-* EX-[1] + *-cutere,* comb. form of *quatere* to shake); (n.) ME, deriv. of the v.] —**res′cu·a·ble,** *adj.* —**res′cue·less,** *adj.* —**res′cu·er,** *n.*
—**Syn. 1.** liberate, release, save, redeem, ransom, extricate, recover. **3.** liberation, deliverance, release, redemption, recovery.

res′cue grass′, a grass, *Bromus unioloides* (or *B. catharticus*), of tropical America, having clusters of flattened spikelets, grown for forage. [1880–85, *Amer.*; *rescue,* perh. alter. of FESCUE]

res′cue mis′sion, mission (def. 12). [1900–05]

re·search (rē sûrch′), *v.t., v.i.* to search or search for again. [1740–50; RE- + SEARCH]

re·search (ri sûrch′, rē′sûrch), *n.* **1.** diligent and systematic inquiry or investigation into a subject in order to discover or revise facts, theories, applications, etc.: *recent research in medicine.* **2.** a particular instance or piece of research. —*v.i.* **3.** to make researches; investigate carefully. —*v.t.* **4.** to make an extensive investigation into: *to research a matter thoroughly.* [1570–80; (v.) < MF *recercher* to seek, OF, equiv. to *re-* RE- + *cercher* to SEARCH; (n.) < MF *recerche*] —**re·search′a·ble,** *adj.* —**re·search′er, re·search′ist,** *n.*
—**Syn. 1.** scrutiny, study. See **investigation. 4.** study, inquire, examine, scrutinize.

research′ li′brary, a general or specialized library that collects materials for use in intensive research projects. [1960–65]

research′ park′, an industrial park whose facilities are devoted to research and development.

re·seat (rē sēt′), *v.t.* **1.** to provide with a new seat or new seats. **2.** to seat again. [1630–40; RE- + SEAT]

re·seau (rā zō′, rə-), *n., pl.* **-seaux** (-zōz′, -zō′), **-seaus. 1.** a network. **2.** a netted or meshed ground in lace. **3.** *Astron.* a network of fine lines on a glass plate, used in a photographic telescope to produce a corresponding network on photographs of the stars. **4.** *Meteorol.* a system of weather stations under the direction of a single agency or cooperating for common goals. **5.** *Photog.* a screen having minute colored filters, used in some forms of color photography. Also, **ré·seau′.** [1570–80; < F *réseau,* OF *resel,* dim. of *rais* net < VL **rētis* (sing.) or **rētēs* (pl.), for L *rēte*]

re·sect (ri sekt′), *v.t. Surg.* to do a resection on. [1535–45; < L *resectus* ptp. of *resecāre* to cut back, sever at the base, equiv. to *re-* RE- + *sec(āre)* to cut + *-tus* ptp. suffix]

re·sec·tion (ri sek′shən), *n.* **1.** *Survey.* a technique of ascertaining the location of a point by taking bearings from the point on two other points of known location. **2.** *Surg.* the excision of all or part of an organ or tissue. [1605–15; < L *resectiōn-* (s. of *resectiō*) a cutting off, trimming, equiv. to *resect(us)* (see RESECT) + *-iōn-* -ION] —**re·sec′tion·al,** *adj.*

re·se·da (ri sē′də), *n.* **1.** a grayish green. —*adj.* **2.** grayish green, like the flowers of the mignonette. [1745–55 as name of plant genus including mignonette; 1870–75 for current senses; < NL: genus name, L *resēda* (according to Pliny, lit., heal! (impv. of *resēdāre* to heal, assuage), referring to the plant's use in treating tumors)]

re·sem·blance (ri zem′bləns), *n.* **1.** the state or fact of resembling; similarity. **2.** a degree, kind, or point of likeness. **3.** a likeness, appearance, or semblance of something. [1350–1400; ME < AF, equiv. to *resembl(er)* to RESEMBLE + *-ance* -ANCE]
—**Syn. 1.** RESEMBLANCE, SIMILARITY imply that there is a likeness between two or more people or things. RESEMBLANCE indicates primarily a likeness in appearance, either a striking one or one which merely serves as a reminder to the beholder: *The boy has a strong resemblance to his father.* SIMILARITY may imply a surface likeness, but usually suggests also a likeness in other characteristics: *There is a similarity in their tastes and behavior.* **2.** analogy, similitude. **3.** image. —**Ant. 1.** difference.

re·sem·blant (ri zem′blənt), *adj.* **1.** having a resemblance or similarity (sometimes fol. by *to*): *two persons with resemblant features.* **2.** that produces or deals in representations: *sculpture considered as a resemblant art.* [1350–1400; ME < OF, equiv. to *resembl(er)* to RESEMBLE + *-ant* -ANT]

re·sem·ble (ri zem′bəl), *v.t.,* **-bled, -bling. 1.** to be like or similar to. **2.** *Archaic.* to liken or compare. [1300–50; ME *resemblen* < MF *resembler,* OF, equiv. to *re-* RE- + *sembler* to seem, be like < L *similāre,* deriv. of *similis* like; see SIMILAR] —**re·sem′bling·ly,** *adv.*

re·send (rē send′), *v.t.,* **-sent, -send·ing. 1.** to send again. **2.** to send back. [1545–55; RE- + SEND]

re·sent (ri zent′), *v.t.* to feel or show displeasure or indignation at (a person, act, remark, etc.) from a sense of injury or insult. [1595–1605; < F *ressentir* to be angry < OF *resentir,* equiv. to *re-* RE- + *sentir* to feel < L *sentīre;* see SENSE] —**re·sent′ing·ly,** *adv.* —**re·sent′ive,** *adj.*

re·sent·ful (ri zent′fəl), *adj.* full of or marked by resentment. [1645–55; RESENT + -FUL] —**re·sent′ful·ly,** *adv.* —**re·sent′ful·ness,** *n.*

re·sent·ment (ri zent′mənt), *n.* the feeling of displeasure or indignation at some act, remark, person, etc., regarded as causing injury or insult. [1610–20; < F *ressentiment,* MF *resentiment,* equiv. to *resenti(r)* to RESENT + *-ment* -MENT]
—**Syn.** dudgeon, pique, irritation, envy, jealousy.

res·er·pine (res′ər pin, -pēn′, rə sûr′pin, -pēn), *n. Pharm.* an alkaloid, $C_{33}H_{40}N_2O_9$, obtained from the root of the rauwolfia, *Rauwolfia serpentina,* used in the treatment of hypertension. [1950–55; < G *Reserpin,* equiv. to *reserp-* (prob. irreg. < NL *Rauwolfia serpentina* (*Rauwolfia* RAUWOLFIA + LL *serpentīna,* fem. of *serpentīnus* SERPENTINE)) + G *-in* -INE[2]]

res·er·va·tion (rez′ər vā′shən), *n.* **1.** the act of keeping back, withholding, or setting apart. **2.** the act of making an exception or qualification. **3.** an exception or qualification made expressly or tacitly: *to accept something, but with inner reservations.* **4.** a tract of public land set apart for a special purpose, as for the use of an Indian tribe. **5.** an arrangement to secure accommodations at a restaurant or hotel, on a boat or plane, etc. **6.** the record kept or assurance given of such an arrangement: *Sorry, the hotel has no reservation under that name.* [1350–1400; ME *reservacioun* < MF *reservation,* equiv. to *reserv(er)* to RESERVE + *-ation* -ATION]

res·er·va·tion·ist (rez′ər vā′shə nist), *n.* a person who makes or takes reservations, as at an airline office; reservation clerk. [1915–20, *Amer.*; RESERVATION + -IST]

re-serve (rē sûrv′), *v.t., v.i.,* **-served, -serv·ing.** to serve again. [1865–70; RE- + SERVE]

re·serve (ri zûrv′), *v.,* **-served, -serv·ing,** *n., adj.* —*v.t.* **1.** to keep back or save for future use, disposal, treatment, etc. **2.** to retain or secure by express stipulation. **3.** to set apart for a particular use, purpose, service, etc.: *ground reserved for gardening.* **4.** to keep for oneself. **5.** to retain (the original color) of a surface, as on a painted ceramic piece. **6.** to save or set aside (a portion of the Eucharistic elements) to be administered, as to the sick, outside of the Mass or communion service. —*n.* **7.** *Finance.* **a.** cash, or assets readily convertible into cash, held aside, as by a corporation, bank, state or national government, etc., to meet expected or unexpected demands. **b.** uninvested cash held to comply with legal requirements. **8.** something kept or stored for use or need; stock: *a reserve of food.* **9.** a resource not normally called upon but available if needed. **10.** a tract of public land set apart for a special purpose: *a forest reserve.* **11.** an act of reserving; reservation, exception, or qualification: *I will do what you ask, but with one reserve.* **12.** *Mil.* **a.** a fraction of a military force held in readiness to sustain the attack or defense made by the rest of the force. **b.** the part of a country's fighting force not in active service. **c. reserves,** the enrolled but not regular components of the U.S. Army. **13.** formality and self-restraint in manner and relationship; avoidance of familiarity or intimacy with others: *to conduct oneself with reserve.* **14.** reticence or silence. **15. in reserve,** put aside or withheld for a future need; reserved: *money in reserve.* **16. without reserve, a.** without restraint; frankly; freely. **b.** (of articles at auction) without limitation as to the terms of sale, esp. with no stipulated minimum price. —*adj.* **17.** kept in reserve; forming a reserve: *a reserve fund; a reserve supply.* **18.** of or pertaining to the animal awarded second place in livestock shows: *the reserve champion steer.* [1325–75; ME

CONCISE PRONUNCIATION KEY: *act, cāpe, dâre, pärt; set, ēqual; if, īce; ox, ōver, ôrder, oil, bo͝ok, bo͞ot, out; up, ûrge; child; sing; shoe; thin, that;* zh as in *treasure.* ə = *a* as in *alone, e* as in *system, i* as in *easily, o* as in *gallop, u* as in *circus;* ᵊ as in *fire* (fīᵊr), *hour* (ouᵊr). l and n can serve as syllabic consonants, as in *cradle* (krād′l), and *button* (but′n). See the full key inside the front cover.

re′op·press′, *v.t.*
re·or′ches·trate′, *v.,* **-trat·ed, -trat·ing.**
re′or·ches·tra′tion, *n.*
re′or·dain′, *v.t.*
re·o′ri·en·tate′, *v.t.,* **-tat·ed, -tat·ing.**
re·or′na·ment′, *v.t.*
re′out·fit′, *v.t.,* **-fit·ted, -fit·ting.**
re·out′line′, *v.t.,* **-lined, -lin·ing.**
re·ox′i·da′tion, *n.*
re·ox′i·dize′, *v.,* **-dized, -diz·ing.**
re·pac′i·fy′, *v.t.,* **-fied, -fy·ing.**
re·pack′, *v.*
re·pad′, *v.t.,* **-pad·ded, -pad·ding.**
re·pag′i·nate′, *v.t.,* **-nat·ed, -nat·ing.**
re′pag·i·na′tion, *n.*
re·pan′el, *v.t.,* **-eled, -el·ing** or (*esp. Brit.*) **-elled, -el·ling.**
re·pa′per, *v.t.*
re·park′, *v.*
re·paste′, *v.t.,* **-past·ed, -past·ing.**
re·patch′, *v.*
re′pa·trol′, *v.t.,* **-trolled, -trol·ling.**
re·pa′tron·ize′, *v.t.,* **-ized, -iz·ing.**
re·pat′tern, *v.t.*
re·pave′, *v.t.,* **-paved, -pav·ing.**
re·pawn′, *v.t.*
re·ped′dle, *v.t.,* **-dled, -dling.**
re·peg′, *v.,* **-pegged, -peg·ging.**
re·pen′, *v.t.,* **-penned, -pen·ning.**
re·pe′nal·ize′, *v.t.,* **-ized, -iz·ing.**

reserven (v.) < MF *reserver* < L *reservāre* to keep back, retain, equiv. to *re-* RE- + *servāre* to save] —**re·serv′a·ble,** *adj.* —**re·serve′less,** *adj.*
—**Syn. 1.** husband, hold, store. See **keep. 8.** supply. **14.** taciturnity, constraint, coldness. —**Ant. 1.** squander. **13, 14.** warmth.

reserve′ bank′, 1. one of the 12 principal banks of the U.S. Federal Reserve System. **2.** a bank authorized by a government to hold the reserves of other banks.

reserve′ buoy′ancy, *Naut.* the difference between the volume of a hull below the designed waterline and the volume of the hull below the lowest opening incapable of being made watertight. [1900–05]

reserve′ capac′ity, *Auto.* the capacity of a battery, measured in minutes, to keep a vehicle operating if the charging system fails.

reserve′ clause′, *Sports.* the clause in the contract of a professional player in some sports that binds the player to a team for a season beyond the expiration of the contract in the event a new contract has not been made meanwhile or the player has not been sent to another team. [1940–45]

reserve′ cur′rency, any currency, as the U.S. dollar, used as a medium to settle international debts. [1965–70]

re·served (ri zûrvd′), *adj.* **1.** kept or set apart for some particular use or purpose. **2.** kept by special arrangement for some person: *a reserved seat.* **3.** formal or self-restrained in manner and relationship; avoiding familiarity or intimacy with others: *a quiet, reserved man.* **4.** characterized by reserve, as the disposition, manner, etc.: *reserved comments.* **5.** retaining the original color of a surface, esp. when decorating portions of the surface with other colors. [1425–75; late ME; see RESERVE, -ED[2]] —**re·serv·ed·ly** (ri zûr′vid lē), *adv.* —**re·serv′ed·ness,** *n.*
—**Syn. 3, 4.** composed, controlled reticent, constrained, taciturn, withdrawn, distant, cold.

reserved′ pow′er, a political power that a constitution reserves exclusively to the jurisdiction of a particular political authority. [1825–35]

reserve′ of′ficer, a noncareer commissioned officer in a military reserve unit who has served on active duty and who may be recalled to active service during an emergency.

Reserve′ Of′ficers Train′ing Corps′, a body of students at some colleges and universities who are given training toward becoming officers in the armed forces. *Abbr.:* ROTC, R.O.T.C.

reserve′ price′. See **floor price.** [1915–20]

re·serv·ist (ri zûr′vist), *n.* a person who belongs to a reserve military force of a country. [1875–80; RESERVE + -IST]

res·er·voir (rez′ər vwär′, -vwôr′, -vôr′, rez′ə-), *n.* **1.** a natural or artificial place where water is collected and stored for use, esp. water for supplying a community, irrigating land, furnishing power, etc. **2.** a receptacle or chamber for holding a liquid or fluid. **3.** *Geol.* See under **pool**[1] (def. 6). **4.** *Biol.* a cavity or part that holds some fluid or secretion. **5.** a place where anything is collected or accumulated in great amount. **6.** a large or extra supply or stock; reserve: *a reservoir of knowledge.* [1680–90; < F *réservoir,* equiv. to *réserv(er)* to RESERVE + *-oir* -ORY[2]]
—**Syn. 5.** store, pool, fund, stockpile, hoard.

res′ervoir rock′, *Geol.* rock that has sufficient porosity to contain accumulations of oil or gas. [1910–15]

re·set (*v.* rē set′; *n.* rē′set′), *v.,* **-set, -set·ting,** *n.* —*v.t.* **1.** to set again: *to reset an alarm clock.* **2.** to set back the odometer on (an auto or other vehicle) to a lower reading: *a used-car dealer charged with resetting his cars.* —*v.i.* **3.** to become set again: *The alarm bell resets automatically.* —*n.* **4.** the act of resetting. **5.** that which is reset. **6.** a plant which is replanted. **7.** a device used in resetting an instrument or control mechanism. [1645–55; RE- + SET] —**re·set′ta·ble,** *adj.* —**re·set′ter,** *n.*

res ges·tae (rēz′ jes′tē, rās′), **1.** things done; accomplishments; deeds. **2.** *Law.* the acts, circumstances, and statements that are incidental to the principal fact of a litigated matter and are admissible in evidence in view of their relevant association with that fact. [1610–20; < L *rēs gestae*]

resh (räsh), *n.* **1.** the 20th letter of the Hebrew alphabet. **2.** the consonant sound represented by this letter. [1895–1900; < Heb *rēsh,* akin to *rōsh* head]

re·shape (rē shāp′), *v.t.,* **-shaped, -shap·ing.** to shape again or into different form. [1820–30; RE- + SHAPE]

Re·shev·sky (rə shef′skē), *n.* **Samuel,** 1911–92, U.S. chess player, born in Poland.

re·ship (rē ship′), *v.,* **-shipped, -ship·ping.** —*v.t.* **1.** to ship again. **2.** to transfer from one ship to another. —*v.i.* **3.** to go on a ship again. **4.** (of a member of a ship's crew) to sign up for another voyage. [1645–55; RE- + SHIP] —**re·ship′ment,** *n.*

Resht (resht), *n.* Rasht.

CONCISE ETYMOLOGY KEY: <, descended or borrowed from; >, whence; b., blend of, blended; c., cognate with; cf., compare; deriv., derivative; equiv., equivalent; imit., imitative; obl., oblique; r., replacing; s., stem; sp., spelling, spelled; resp., respelling, respelled; trans., translation; ?, origin unknown; *, unattested; ‡, probably earlier than. See the full key inside the front cover.

re·side (*v.* rē sīd′; *n.* rē′sīd′), *v.,* **-sid·ed, -sid·ing,** *n.* —*v.t.* **1.** to replace the siding on (a building). —*v.i.* **2.** to apply new siding, as to a house. —*n.* **3.** a piece or section of siding: *to put backing material on the re-sides.*

re·side (ri zīd′), *v.i.,* **-sid·ed, -sid·ing. 1.** to dwell permanently or for a considerable time: *She resides at 15 Maple Street.* **2.** (of things, qualities, etc.) to abide, lie, or be present habitually; exist or be inherent (usually fol. by *in*). **3.** to rest or be vested, as powers, rights, etc. (usually fol. by *in*). [1425–75; late ME *residen* < MF *resider* < L *residēre,* equiv. to *re-* RE- + *-sidēre,* comb. form of *sedēre* to SIT[1]] —**re·sid′er,** *n.*
—**Syn. 1.** live, abide, sojourn, stay, lodge, remain.

res·i·dence (rez′i dəns), *n.* **1.** the place, esp. the house, in which a person lives or resides; dwelling place; home: *Their residence is in New York City.* **2.** a structure serving as a dwelling or home, esp. one of large proportion and superior quality: *They have a summer residence in Connecticut.* **3.** the act or fact of residing: *during his residence in Spain.* **4.** the act of living or staying in a specified place while performing official duties, carrying on studies or research, awaiting a divorce, etc. **5.** the time during which a person resides in a place: *a residence there of five years.* **6.** the location of the main offices or principal center of business activity of a commercial enterprise, esp. a large corporation, as registered under law. **7.** *Chem.* See **residence time.** [1350–1400; ME < MF < ML *residentia,* equiv. to L *resid(ēre)* to RESIDE + *-entia* -ENCE]
—**Syn. 1.** habitation, domicile. **1, 2.** See **house. 2.** mansion. **5.** stay, abode, sojourn.

res′idence time′, 1. Also called **residence.** *Chem.* the length of time a substance remains in the adsorbed, suspended, or dissolved state. **2.** *Physics.* the length of time radioactive material, as gas or particles, remains in the atmosphere after detonation of a nuclear device.

res·i·den·cy (rez′i dən sē), *n., pl.* **-cies. 1.** residence (def. 3). **2.** the position or tenure of a medical resident. **3.** (formerly) the official residence of a representative of the British governor general at a native Indian court. **4.** (formerly) an administrative division of the Dutch East Indies. [1570–80; RESID(ENT) + -ENCY]

res·i·dent (rez′i dənt), *n.* **1.** a person who resides in a place. **2.** a physician who joins the medical staff of a hospital as a salaried employee for a specified period to gain advanced training usually in a particular field, being in full-time attendance at the hospital and often living on the premises. **3.** a diplomatic representative, inferior in rank to an ambassador, residing at a foreign court. **4.** (formerly) a representative of the British governor general at a native court in India. **5.** (formerly) the governor of a residency in the Dutch East Indies. —*adj.* **6.** residing; dwelling in a place. **7.** living or staying at a place in discharge of duty. **8.** (of qualities) existing; intrinsic. **9.** (of birds) not migratory. **10. a.** encoded and permanently available to a computer user, as a font in a printer's ROM or software on a CD-ROM. **b.** (of a computer program) currently active or standing by in computer memory. [1350–1400; ME < L *resident-* (s. of *residēns*), prp. of *residēre* to RESIDE; see -ENT] —**res′i·dent·ship′,** *n.*

res′ident al′ien, 1. an alien who has legally established residence in the U.S. **2.** an alien who has legally entered the U.S. as an immigrant with the intention of becoming a citizen.

res′ident commis′sioner, a representative from a dependency who is entitled to speak, but not to vote, in the U.S. House of Representatives. [1900–05]

res·i·den·tial (rez′i den′shəl), *adj.* **1.** of or pertaining to residence or to residences: *a residential requirement for a doctorate.* **2.** suited for or characterized by private residences: *a residential neighborhood.* [1645–55; < ML *residenti(a)* RESIDENCE + -AL[1]] —**res·i·den·ti·al·i·ty** (rez′i den′shē al′i tē), *n.* —**res′i·den′tial·ly,** *adv.*

res·i·den·ti·ar·y (rez′i den′shē er′ē, -shə rē), *adj., n., pl.* **-ar·ies.** —*adj.* **1.** residing; resident. **2.** involving or under obligation to be in official residence. —*n.* **3.** a resident. **4.** an ecclesiastic bound to official residence. [1515–25; < ML *residentiārius,* equiv. to *residenti(a)* RESIDENCE + *-ārius* -ARY]

re·sid·ing (rē sī′ding), *n.* material used to replace or augment siding. [see RE-SIDE, SIDING]

re·sid·u·al (ri zij′o͞o əl), *adj.* **1.** pertaining to or constituting a residue or remainder; remaining; leftover. **2.** *Math.* **a.** formed by the subtraction of one quantity from another: *a residual quantity.* **b.** (of a set) having complement of first category. **3.** of or pertaining to the payment of residuals. **4.** *Med.* remaining in an organ or part following normal discharge or expulsion: *residual air.* **5.** *Geol.* remaining after the soluble elements have been dissolved: *residual soil.* —*n.* **6.** a residual quantity; remainder. **7.** Often, **residuals.** something that remains to discomfort or disable a person following an illness, injury, operation, or the like; disability. **8.** *Math.* **a.** the deviation of one of a set of observations or numbers from the mean of the set. **b.** the deviation between an empirical and a theoretical result. **9.** *Navig.* a slight deviation of an adjusted compass on a certain heading. **10.** Usually, **residuals.** additional pay given to a performer for reruns, repeated use of a film, radio or TV commercial, or the like, in which the performer appears. [1550–60; < L *residu(um)* what is left over (n. use of neut. of *residuus* left over, equiv. to *resid(ēre)* to be left over, lit., remain seated (see RESIDE) + *-uus* deverbal adj. suffix) + -AL[1]]
—**Syn. 1.** continuing, lasting, enduring, lingering.

re·sid·u·al·ly (ri zij′o͞o ə lē), *adv.* **1.** in a residual manner. **2.** *Math.* with an element in the directed set such that for every element in the directed set in relation to the given element, the corresponding element of the set is in some given set. [RESIDUAL + -LY]

resid′ual mag′netism, *Elect.* remanence.

resid′ual pow′er, power retained by a governmental authority after certain powers have been delegated to other authorities. [1915–20]

resid′ual stress′, *Metall.* a stress in a metal, on a microscopic scale and resulting from nonuniform thermal changes, plastic deformation, or other causes aside from temporary external forces or applications of heat. [1930–35]

re·sid·u·ar·y (ri zij′o͞o er′ē), *adj.* **1.** entitled to the residue of an estate: *a residuary legatee.* **2.** pertaining to or of the nature of a residue, remainder, or residuum. [1720–30; < L *residu(um)* what is left over (see RESIDUAL) + -ARY]

res·i·due (rez′i do͞o′, -dyo͞o′), *n.* **1.** something that remains after a part is removed, disposed of, or used; remainder; rest; remnant. **2.** *Chem.* **a.** residuum (def. 2). **b.** an atom or group of atoms considered as a group or part of a molecule. **c.** that part remaining as a solid on a filter paper after a liquid passes through in the filtration procedure. **3.** *Law.* the part of a testator's estate that remains after the payment of all debts, charges, special devises, and bequests. **4.** *Math.* **a.** the coefficient of the term with exponent −1 in a Laurent series of a function of a complex variable. **b.** a number related to a given number by a congruence. [1300–50; ME < MF *residu* < L *residuum* what is left over; see RESIDUAL]
—**Syn. 1.** remains, residuum. See **remainder.**

re·sid·u·um (ri zij′o͞o əm), *n., pl.* **-sid·u·a** (-zij′o͞o ə). **1.** the residue, remainder, or rest of something. **2.** Also, **residue.** *Chem.* a quantity or body of matter remaining after evaporation, combustion, distillation, etc. **3.** any residual product. **4.** *Law.* the residue of an estate. [1665–75; < L; see RESIDUAL]

re-sign (rē sīn′), *v.t., v.i.* **1.** to sign again. **2.** to renew or extend a contract. [1795–1805]

re·sign (ri zīn′), *v.i.* **1.** to give up an office or position, often formally (often fol. by *from*): *to resign from the presidency.* **2.** to submit; yield: *to resign before the inevitable.* —*v.t.* **3.** to give up (an office, position, etc.), often formally. **4.** to relinquish (a right, claim, agreement, etc.). **5.** to give or sign over, as to the control or care of another: *She resigned her child to an adoption agency.* **6.** to submit (oneself, one's mind, etc.) without resistance. [1325–75; ME *resignen* < MF *resigner* < L *resignāre* to open, release, cancel, equiv. to *re-* RE- + *signāre* to mark, seal, SIGN]
—**Syn. 1.** withdraw. **3.** abdicate, renounce; quit, leave. **4.** give up, surrender, cede, forgo.

res·ig·na·tion (rez′ig nā′shən), *n.* **1.** the act of resigning. **2.** a formal statement, document, etc., stating that one gives up an office, position, etc. **3.** an accepting, unresisting attitude, state, etc.; submission; acquiescence: *to meet one's fate with resignation.* [1350–1400; ME < MF < ML *resignātiōn-* (s. of *resignātiō*) a canceling, rescinding, equiv. to L *resignāt(us)* (ptp. of *resignāre* to RESIGN; see -ATE[1]) + *-iōn-* -ION]
—**Syn. 1, 2.** abdication. **3.** patience, compliance, forbearance. —**Ant. 3.** recalcitrance.

re·signed (ri zīnd′), *adj.* **1.** submissive or acquiescent. **2.** characterized by or indicative of resignation. [1645–55; RESIGN + -ED[2]] —**re·sign·ed·ly** (ri zī′nid lē), *adv.* —**re·sign′ed·ness,** *n.*

re·sign·ee (ri zī′nē, rē′zī nē′), *n.* a person who has resigned or is about to resign. [1605–15; RESIGN + -EE]

re·sile (ri zīl′), *v.i.,* **-siled, -sil·ing. 1.** to spring back; rebound; resume the original form or position, as an elastic body. **2.** to shrink back; recoil. [1520–30; < MF *resilir* < L *resilīre* to spring back; see RESILIENT] —**re·sile′ment,** *n.*

re·sil·ience (ri zil′yəns, -zil′ē əns), *n.* **1.** the power or ability to return to the original form, position, etc., after being bent, compressed, or stretched; elasticity. **2.** ability to recover readily from illness, depression, adversity, or the like; buoyancy. Also, **re·sil′ien·cy.** [1620–30; < L *resili(ēns),* prp. of *resilīre* to spring back, rebound (see RESILIENT) + -ENCE]

re·sil·ient (ri zil′yənt, -zil′ē ənt), *adj.* **1.** springing back; rebounding. **2.** returning to the original form or position after being bent, compressed, or stretched. **3.** recovering readily from illness, depression, adversity, or the like; buoyant. [1635–45; < L *resilient-* (s. of *resiliēns*), prp. of *resilīre* to spring back, equiv. to *re-* RE- + *-sil-,* comb. form of *salīre* to leap, jump + *-ent-* -ENT); see SALIENT] —**re·sil′ient·ly,** *adv.*
—**Syn. 1.** elastic, flexible, springy.

res·in (rez′in), *n.* **1.** any of a class of nonvolatile, solid or semisolid organic substances, as copal or mastic, that consist of amorphous mixtures of carboxylic acids and are obtained directly from certain plants as exudations or prepared by polymerization of simple molecules: used in medicine and in the making of varnishes and plastics. **2.** a substance of this type obtained from certain pines; rosin. —*v.t.* **3.** to treat or rub with resin. [1350–1400; ME < OF *resine* < L *rēsīna,* prob. < a non-IE language; cf. Gk *rhētínē* pine resin, from a related source] —**res′in·like′,** *adj.*

Res·in (rez′in), *n.* a male given name.

res·in·ate (*v.* rez′ə nāt′; *n.* rez′ə nit, -nāt′), *v.,* **-at·ed,**

re′per·ceive′, *v.t.,* **-ceived, -ceiv·ing.**
re′per·cep′tion, *n.*
re′per·form′, *v.t.*
re′per·form′ance, *n.*
re′pe·rus′al, *n.*
re′pe·ruse′, *v.t.,* **-rused, -rus·ing.**
re′-pe·ti′tion, *v.t.*
re·phase′, *v.t.* **-phased, -phas·ing.**
re·pho′to·graph′, *v.t., n.*
re·pick′, *v.t.*
re·pin′, *v.t.,* **-pinned, -pin·ning.**
re·plan′, *v.t.,* **-planned, -plan·ning.**
re·plane′, *v.t.,* **-planed, -plan·ing.**
re·plas′ter, *v.t.*
re·plate′, *v.t.,* **-plat·ed, -plat·ing.**
re·plead′, *v.,* **-plead·ed** or **-plead** or **-pled, -plead·ing.**
re·pledge′, *v.t.,* **-pledged, -pledg·ing,** *n.*
re·plot′, *v.t.,* **-plot·ted, -plot·ting.**
re·plow′, *v.t.,* **-plowed, -plow·ing.**
re·plumb′, *v.t.*
re·plume′, *v.t.,* **-plumed, -plum·ing.**
re·plunge′, *v.,* **-plunged, -plung·ing;** *n.*
re·po′lar·i·za′tion, *n.*
re·po′lar·ize′, *v.t.,* **-ized, -iz·ing.**
re·pol′ish, *v., n.*
re·poll′, *v.*
re·poll′ing, *n.*
re·pon′der, *v.i.*

-at·ing, *n.* —*v.t.* **1.** to treat with resin, as by impregnation. —*n.* **2.** *Chem.* any of the salts of the acids found in rosin. [1830–40; RESIN + -ATE[1] (def. 1), -ATE[2] (def. 2)]

res′in duct′, *Bot.* a tube or duct in a woody stem or a leaf, esp. in conifers, lined with glandular epithelium that secretes resins. Also called **res′in canal′.** [1880–85]

res·in·if·er·ous (rez′ə nif′ər əs), *adj.* yielding resin. [1665–75; RESIN + -I- + -FEROUS]

res·in·i·fy (re zin′ə fī′), *v.*, **-fied, -fy·ing.** *Chem.* —*v.t.* **1.** to convert into a resin. **2.** to treat with a resin. —*v.i.* **3.** to become a resin. [1810–20; < F *résinifier.* See RESIN, -IFY] —**re·sin′i·fi·ca′tion,** *n.*

res·in·oid (rez′ə noid′), *adj.* **1.** resinlike. —*n.* **2.** a resinoid substance. **3.** a resinous substance synthetically compounded. **4.** a gum resin. [1820–30; RESIN + -OID]

res·in·ous (rez′ə nəs), *adj.* **1.** full of or containing resin. **2.** of the nature of or resembling resin. **3.** pertaining to or characteristic of resin. Also, **res·in·y** (rez′ə nē). [1640–50; < L *rēsinōsus.* See RESIN, -OUS] —**res′in·ous·ly,** *adv.* —**res′in·ous·ness,** *n.*

res ip·sa lo·qui·tur (rēz′ ip′sə lō′kwi tər, lok′wi-, rās′), *Law.* the rule that an injury is due to the defendant's negligence when that which caused it was under his or her control or management and the injury would not have happened had proper management been observed. [1650–60; < L *rēs ipsa loquitur* lit., the thing itself speaks]

re·sist (ri zist′), *v.t.* **1.** to withstand, strive against, or oppose: *to resist infection; to resist temptation.* **2.** to withstand the action or effect of: *to resist spoilage.* **3.** to refrain or abstain from, esp. with difficulty or reluctance: *They couldn't resist the chocolates.* —*v.i.* **4.** to make a stand or make efforts in opposition; act in opposition; offer resistance. —*n.* **5.** a substance that prevents or inhibits some effect from taking place, as a coating on a surface of a metallic printing plate that prevents or inhibits corrosion of the metal by acid. **6.** *Textiles.* a chemically inert substance used in resist printing. [1325–75; ME *resisten* (v.) < L *resistere* to remain standing, equiv. to *re-* RE- + *sistere* to cause to stand, akin to *stāre* to STAND] —**re·sist′er,** *n.* —**re·sist′ing·ly,** *adv.*
—**Syn. 1.** confront, counteract, rebuff. See **oppose.**

re·sist·ance (ri zis′təns), *n.* **1.** the act or power of resisting, opposing, or withstanding. **2.** the opposition offered by one thing, force, etc., to another. **3.** *Elect.* **a.** Also called **ohmic resistance.** a property of a conductor by virtue of which the passage of current is opposed, causing electric energy to be transformed into heat: equal to the voltage across the conductor divided by the current flowing in the conductor: usually measured in ohms. *Abbr.:* R **b.** a conductor or coil offering such opposition; resistor. **4.** *Psychiatry.* opposition to an attempt to bring repressed thoughts or feelings into consciousness. **5.** (*often cap.*) an underground organization composed of groups of private individuals working as an opposition force in a conquered country to overthrow the occupying power, usually by acts of sabotage, guerrilla warfare, etc.: *the resistance during the German occupation in World War II.* **6.** *Stock Exchange.* See **resistance level.** [1300–50; ME < MF. See RESIST, -ANCE]
—**Syn. 1.** opposition, obstinacy, defiance.

resist′ance lev′el, *Stock Exchange.* a point at which the rise in price of a specific stock is arrested due to more substantial selling than buying. Also called **resistance.**

resist′ance thermom′eter, *Metall.* an instrument for measuring the temperature of a metal, utilizing the principle that the electrical resistance of the metal varies with the temperature. [1885–90]

resist′ance train′ing, physical training that utilizes isometric, isotonic, or isokinetic exercise to strengthen or develop the muscles. [1980–85]

resist′ance trans′fer fac′tor. See **R factor.** [1955–60]

resist′ance weld′ing, welding utilizing pressure and heat that is generated in the pieces to be welded by resistance to an electric current. [1910–15]

re·sist·ant (ri zis′tənt), *adj.* **1.** resisting. —*n.* **2.** a person or thing that resists. [1590–1600; < MF *resistant,* prp. of *resister* to RESIST; see -ANT] —**re·sist′ant·ly,** *adv.*

re·sist·ate (ri zis′tāt), *n. Geol.* any of the class of sediments, as sand or sandstone, consisting chiefly of minerals resistant to weathering. [RESIST + -ATE[1]]

Re·sis·ten·cia (Re′sēs ten′syä), *n.* a city in NE Argentina, on the Paraná River. 218,438.

re·sist·i·ble (ri zis′tə bəl), *adj.* that can be resisted. [1635–45; RESIST + -IBLE] —**re·sist′i·bil′i·ty, re·sist′i·ble·ness,** *n.* —**re·sist′i·bly,** *adv.*

re·sis·tive (ri zis′tiv), *adj.* capable of or inclined to resistance; resisting. [1595–1605; RESIST + -IVE] —**re·sis′tive·ly,** *adv.* —**re·sis′tive·ness,** *n.*

re·sis·tiv·i·ty (rē′zis tiv′i tē), *n.* **1.** the power or property of resistance. **2.** Also called **specific resistance.** *Elect.* the resistance between opposite faces of a one-centimeter cube of a given material; ratio of electric intensity to cross-sectional area; reciprocal of conductivity. [1880–85; RESISTIVE + -ITY]

re·sist·less (ri zist′lis), *adj.* **1.** irresistible. **2.** not resisting. [1580–90; RESIST + -LESS] —**re·sist′less·ly,** *adv.* —**re·sist′less·ness,** *n.*

re·sis·tor (ri zis′tər), *n. Elect.* a device designed to introduce resistance into an electric circuit. [1900–05; RESIST + -OR[2]]

resist′ print′ing, a fabric-printing method in which a dye-resistant substance is applied to certain specified areas of the material prior to immersion in a dye bath and subsequently removed so as to permit the original hue to act as a pattern against the colored ground. Cf. **discharge printing.**

res ju·di·ca·ta (rēz′ jo͞o′di kā′tə, rās′), *Law.* a thing adjudicated; a case that has been decided. [1685–95; < L]

re·skin (rē skin′), *v.t.*, **-skinned, -skin·ning.** to replace or repair the exterior surface or coating of: *The space shuttle had to be reskinned before returning to service.* [RE- + SKIN]

res·na·tron (rez′nə tron′), *n. Electronics.* a tetrode with the grid connected to form a drift space for the electrons, formerly used to generate high power at very high frequency. [RES(O)NA(TOR) + -TRON]

Res·nik (rez′nik), *n.* **Regina,** born 1922, U.S. mezzo-soprano.

re·so·cial·i·za·tion (rē sō′shə lə zā′shən), *n.* the process of learning new attitudes and norms required for a new social role. [1960–65; RE- + SOCIALIZE + -ATION]

re·soil (rē soil′), *v.t.* to replace topsoil, esp. that lost by erosion. [1585–95; RE- + SOIL[1]]

res′o·jet en′gine (rez′ō jet′), *Aeron.* a type of pulse-jet engine that burns a continuous flow of fuel but delivers a pulsating thrust due to the resonance of shock waves traveling through it. Also called **resonant-jet engine.** [RESO(NANCE) + JET[1]]

re·sole (rē sōl′), *v.t.*, **-soled, -sol·ing.** to put a new sole on (a shoe, boot, etc.). [1850–55; RE- + SOLE[2]]

re·sol·u·ble[1] (ri zol′yə bəl, rez′əl-), *adj.* capable of being resolved. [1595–1605; < LL *resolūbilis,* equiv. to L *resolū-,* var. s. of *resolvere* to RESOLVE + *-bilis* -BLE] —**re·sol′u·bil′i·ty, re·sol′u·ble·ness,** *n.*

re·sol·u·ble[2] (rē sol′yə bəl), *adj.* able to be redissolved. [1830–40; RE- + SOLUBLE]

res·o·lute (rez′ə lo͞ot′), *adj.* **1.** firmly resolved or determined; set in purpose or opinion. **2.** characterized by firmness and determination, as the temper, spirit, actions, etc. [1375–1425 for earlier sense "dissolved"; 1525–35 for current senses; late ME < L *resolūtus,* ptp. of *resolvere* to RESOLVE] —**res·o·lute·ly** (rez′ə lo͞ot′lē, rez′ə lo͞ot′-), *adv.* —**res′o·lute′ness,** *n.*
—**Syn. 1.** firm, steadfast, fixed. See **earnest[1]. 2.** unwavering, undaunted.

res·o·lu·tion (rez′ə lo͞o′shən), *n.* **1.** a formal expression of opinion or intention made, usually after voting, by a formal organization, a legislature, a club, or other group. Cf. **concurrent resolution, joint resolution. 2.** a resolve or determination: *to make a firm resolution to do something.* **3.** the act of resolving or determining upon an action or course of action, method, procedure, etc. **4.** the mental state or quality of being resolved or resolute; firmness of purpose. **5.** the act or process of resolving or separating into constituent or elementary parts. **6.** the resulting state. **7.** *Optics.* the act, process, or capability of distinguishing between two separate but adjacent objects or sources of light or between two nearly equal wavelengths. Cf. **resolving power. 8.** a solution, accommodation, or settling of a problem, controversy, etc. **9.** *Music.* **a.** the progression of a voice part or of the harmony as a whole from a dissonance to a consonance. **b.** the tone or chord to which a dissonance is resolved. **10.** reduction to a simpler form; conversion. **11.** *Med.* the reduction or disappearance of a swelling or inflammation without suppuration. **12.** the degree of sharpness of a computer-generated image as measured by the number of dots per linear inch in a hard-copy printout or the number of pixels across and down on a display screen. [1350–1400; ME < L *resolūtiōn-* (s. of *resolūtiō*), equiv. to *resolūt(us)* RESOLUTE + *-iōn-* -ION]
—**Syn. 4.** resolve, determination, perseverance.

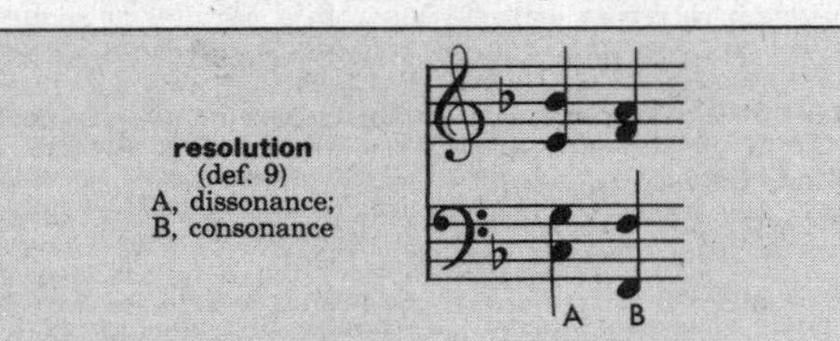

resolution
(def. 9)
A, dissonance;
B, consonance

res·o·lu·tion·er (rez′ə lo͞o′shə nər), *n.* a person joining in or subscribing to a resolution. Also, **res′o·lu′tion·ist.** [1685–95; RESOLUTION + -ER[1]]

re·sol·u·tive (ri zol′yə tiv, rez′ə lo͞o′-), *adj.* **1.** having the ability to dissolve or terminate. **2.** serving to resolve or dispel. [1350–1400; ME *resolutif.* See RESOLUTE, -IVE]

re·solv·a·ble (ri zol′və bəl), *adj.* that can be resolved. [1640–50; RESOLVE + -ABLE] —**re·solv′a·bil′i·ty, re·solv′a·ble·ness,** *n.*

re·solve (ri zolv′), *v.*, **-solved, -solv·ing,** *n.* —*v.t.* **1.** to come to a definite or earnest decision about; determine (to do something): *I have resolved that I shall live to the full.* **2.** to separate into constituent or elementary parts; break up; cause or disintegrate (usually fol. by *into*). **3.** to reduce or convert by, or as by, breaking up or disintegration (usually fol. by *to* or *into*). **4.** to convert or transform by any process (often used reflexively). **5.** to reduce by mental analysis (often fol. by *into*). **6.** to settle, determine, or state formally in a vote or resolution, as of a deliberative assembly. **7.** to deal with (a question, a matter of uncertainty, etc.) conclusively; settle; solve: *to resolve the question before the board.* **8.** to clear away or dispel (doubts, fears, etc.); answer: *to resolve any doubts we may have had.* **9.** *Chem.* to separate (a racemic mixture) into optically active components. **10.** *Music.* to cause (a voice part or the harmony as a whole) to progress from a dissonance to a consonance. **11.** *Optics.* to separate and make visible the individual parts of (an image); distinguish between. **12.** *Med.* to cause (swellings, inflammation, etc.) to disappear without suppuration. —*v.i.* **13.** to come to a determination; make up one's mind; determine (often fol. by *on* or *upon*): *to resolve on a plan of action.* **14.** to break up or disintegrate. **15.** to be reduced or changed by breaking up or otherwise (usually fol. by *to* or *into*). **16.** *Music.* to progress from a dissonance to a consonance. —*n.* **17.** a resolution or determination made, as to follow some course of action. **18.** firmness of purpose or intent; determination. [1325–75; ME *resolven* (v.) < L *resolvere* to unfasten, loosen, release, equiv. to *re-* RE- + *solvere* to loosen; see SOLVE] —**re·solv′er,** *n.*
—**Syn. 1.** confirm. See **decide. 2.** analyze, reduce.

re·solved (ri zolvd′), *adj.* firm in purpose or intent; determined. [1490–1500; RESOLVE + -ED[2]] —**re·solv·ed·ly** (ri zol′vid lē), *adv.* —**re·solv′ed·ness,** *n.*

re·sol·vent (ri zol′vənt), *adj.* **1.** resolving; causing solution; solvent. —*n.* **2.** something resolvent. **3.** *Med.* a remedy that causes resolution of a swelling or inflammation. [1670–80; < L *resolvent-* (s. of *resolvēns*), prp. of *resolvere* to RESOLVE; see -ENT]

resolv′ing pow′er, 1. *Optics.* the ability of an optical device to produce separate images of close objects. **2.** *Photog.* the degree to which a lens or photographic emulsion is able to define the details of an image. [1875–80]

res·o·nance (rez′ə nəns), *n.* **1.** the state or quality of being resonant. **2.** the prolongation of sound by reflection; reverberation. **3.** *Phonet.* **a.** amplification of the range of audibility of any source of speech sounds, esp. of phonation, by various couplings of the cavities of the mouth, nose, sinuses, larynx, pharynx, and upper thorax, and, to some extent, by the skeletal structure of the head and upper chest. **b.** the distribution of amplitudes among interrelated cavities in the head, chest, and throat that are characteristic for a particular speech sound and relatively independent of variations in pitch. **4.** *Physics.* **a.** the state of a system in which an abnormally large vibration is produced in response to an external stimulus, occurring when the frequency of the stimulus is the same, or nearly the same, as the natural vibration frequency of the system. **b.** the vibration produced in such a state. **c.** a hadron with a very short lifetime, of the order of 10^{-23} sec. **5.** *Elect.* that condition of a circuit with respect to a given frequency or the like in which the net reactance is zero and the current flow a maximum. **6.** Also called **mesomerism.** *Chem.* the condition exhibited by a molecule when the actual arrangement of its valence electrons is intermediate between two or more arrangements having nearly the same energy, and the positions of the atomic nuclei are identical. **7.** *Med.* (in percussing for diagnostic purposes) a sound produced when air is present. [1485–95; < MF < L *resonantia* echo, equiv. to *reson(āre)* to RESOUND + *-antia* -ANCE]

res′onance radia′tion, *Physics.* radiation emitted by an atom or molecule, having the same frequency as that of an incident particle, as a photon, and usually involving a transition to the lowest energy level of the atom or molecule. [1900–05]

res·o·nant (rez′ə nənt), *adj.* **1.** resounding or echoing, as sounds: *the resonant thundering of cannons being fired.* **2.** deep and full of resonance: *a resonant voice.* **3.** pertaining to resonance. **4.** producing resonance; causing amplification or sustention of sound. **5.** pertaining to a system in a state of resonance, esp. with respect to sound. —*n.* **6.** *Phonet.* a vowel or a voiced consonant or semivowel that is neither a stop nor an affricate, as, in English, (m, ng, n, l, r, y, w). [1585–95; < L *resonant-* (s. of *resonāns*), prp. of *resonāre* to RESOUND; see -ANT] —**res′o·nant·ly,** *adv.*
—**Syn. 2.** rich, vibrant, sonorant, reverberant.

res′o·nant-jet′ en′gine (rez′ə nənt jet′). See **resojet engine.**

res·o·nate (rez′ə nāt′), *v.*, **-nat·ed, -nat·ing.** —*v.i.* **1.** to resound. **2.** to act as a resonator; exhibit resonance. **3.** *Electronics.* to reinforce oscillations because the natural frequency of the device is the same as the frequency of the source. **4.** to amplify vocal sound by the sympathetic vibration of air in certain cavities and bony structures. —*v.t.* **5.** to cause to resound. [1870–75; < L *resonātus,* ptp. of *resonāre* to RESOUND; see -ATE[1]] —**res′o·na′tion,** *n.*

res·o·na·tor (rez′ə nā′tər), *n.* **1.** anything that resonates. **2.** an appliance for increasing sound by resonance. **3.** an instrument for detecting the presence of a particular frequency by means of resonance. **4.** *Electronics.* **a.**

CONCISE PRONUNCIATION KEY: act, cāpe, dâre, pärt; set, ēqual; *if,* ice; ox, ōver, ôrder, oil, bo͝ok, bo͞ot, out; up, ûrge; child; sing; shoe; thin, *th*at; zh as in *treasure.* ə = *a* as in *alone, e* as in *system, i* as in *easily, o* as in *gallop, u* as in *circus;* ə as in *fire* (fīər), *hour* (ouər). l and n can serve as syllabic consonants, as in *cradle* (krād′l), and *button* (but′n). See the full key inside the front cover.

re′pop·u·lar·i·za′tion, *n.*
re·pop′u·lar·ize′, *v.t.*, **-ized, -iz·ing.**
re·pop′u·late′, *v.t.*, **-lat·ed, -lat·ing.**
re′pop·u·la′tion, *n.*
re·por′tion, *v.t.*
re·post′, *v.t.*
re′post·pone′, *v.t.*, **-poned, -pon·ing.**
re·pos′tu·late′, *v.t.*, **-lat·ed, -lat·ing.**
re·pos′tu·late, *n.*
re′pos·tu·la′tion, *n.*
re·pour′, *v.t.*
re·pow′er, *v.*
re·prac′tice, *v.t.*, **-ticed, -tic·ing.**
re·praise′, *v.t.*, **-praised, -prais·ing.**
re·prem′ise, *v.*, **-ised, -is·ing.**
re′pre·pare′, *v.t.*, **-pared, -par·ing.**
re′pre·scribe′, *v.t.*, **-scribed, -scrib·ing.**
re′pres·su·ri·za′tion, *n.*
re·pres′su·rize′, *v.*, **-rized, -riz·ing.**
re·price′, *v.*, **-priced, -pric·ing.**
re·prime′, *v.t.*, **-primed, -prim·ing.**
re′pri·or′i·ti·za′tion, *n.*
re′pri·or′i·tize′, *v.t.*, **-tized, -tiz·ing.**
re·probe′, *v.*, **-probed, -prob·ing.**
re′pro·ceed′, *v.i.*
re·proc′ess, *v.t.*
re′pro·claim′, *v.t.*

a hollow enclosure **(cavity resonator)** made of conducting material of such dimensions that electromagnetic radiation of a certain frequency will resonate. **b.** any circuit having this frequency characteristic. [1865–70; RESONATE + -OR[2]]

re•sorb (ri sôrb′, -zôrb′), *v.t.* to absorb again, as an exudation. [1630–40; < L *resorbēre,* equiv. to *re-* RE- + *sorbēre* to swallow, suck up] —**re•sorb′ence,** *n.* —**re•sorb′ent,** *adj.* —**re•sorp•tion** (ri sôrp′shən, -zôrp′-), *n.* —**re•sorp•tive** (ri sôrp′tiv, -zôrp′-), *adj.*

res•or•cin•ol (ri zôr′sə nôl′, -nol′, rez ôr′-), *n. Chem., Pharm.* a white, needlelike, water-soluble solid, $C_6H_6O_2$, a benzene derivative originally obtained from certain resins, now usually synthesized: used chiefly in making dyes, as a reagent, in tanning, in the synthesis of certain resins, and in medicine in treating certain skin conditions; meta-dihydroxybenzene. Also, **res•or′cin.** [1880–85; RES(IN) + ORCINOL]

res•or•cin•ol•phthal•e•in (ri zôr′sə nôl thal′ēn, -ē in, -fthal′-, -nol-, rez ôr′-), *n. Chem.* fluorescein. [RESORCINOL + PHTHALEIN]

re•sorp•tion (ri sôrp′shən, -zôrp′-), *n.* **1.** the destruction, disappearance, or dissolution of a tissue or part by biochemical activity, as the loss of bone or of tooth dentin. **2.** Also called **reabsorption.** the selective uptake into the bloodstream of substances previously filtered out of the blood. [1810–20; RE- + (AB)SORPTION; cf. F *résorption*]

re-sort (rē sôrt′), *v.t.* to sort or arrange (cards, papers, etc.) again. [1885–90; RE- + SORT]

re•sort (ri zôrt′), *v.i.* **1.** to have recourse for use, help, or accomplishing something, often as a final available option or resource: *to resort to war.* **2.** to go, esp. frequently or customarily: *a beach to which many people resort.* —*n.* **3.** a place to which people frequently or generally go for relaxation or pleasure, esp. one providing rest and recreation facilities for vacationers: *a popular winter resort.* **4.** habitual or general going, as to a place or person. **5.** use of or appeal to some person or thing for aid, satisfaction, service, etc.; resource: *to have resort to force; a court of last resort.* **6.** a person or thing resorted to for aid, satisfaction, service, etc. [1325–75; (v.) ME *resorten* < OF *resortir,* equiv. to *re-* RE- + *sortir* to go out, leave, escape, perh. ult. < L *sortīrī* to draw lots, though sense development unclear; (n.) ME < OF *ressort,* deriv. of *ressortir*]

re•sort•er (ri zôr′tər), *n.* a person who frequently goes to recreation resorts. [RESORT + -ER[1]]

re-sound (rē sound′), *v.i., v.t.* to sound again. [1895–1900; RE- + SOUND[1]]

re•sound (ri zound′), *v.i.* **1.** to echo or ring with sound, as a place. **2.** to make an echoing sound, or sound loudly, as a metallic object: *A gong resounded.* **3.** to ring or be echoed, as sounds. **4.** to be celebrated or notably important: *His name resounds in the pages of history.* —*v.t.* **5.** to reecho (a sound). **6.** to give forth or utter loudly. **7.** to proclaim loudly (praise, disapproval, etc.). [1350–1400; ME *resounen* < MF *resoner* < L *resonāre,* equiv. to *re-* RE- + *sonāre* to SOUND[1]]

re•sound•ing (ri zoun′ding), *adj.* **1.** making an echoing sound: *a resounding thud.* **2.** uttered loudly: *resounding speech.* **3.** impressively thorough or complete: *a resounding popular success.* [1375–1425; late ME; see RESOUND, -ING[2]] —**re•sound′ing•ly,** *adv.*

re•source (rē′sôrs, -sōrs, -zôrs, -zōrs, ri sôrs′, -sōrs′, -zôrs′, -zōrs′), *n.* **1.** a source of supply, support, or aid, esp. one that can be readily drawn upon when needed. **2. resources,** the collective wealth of a country or its means of producing wealth. **3.** Usually, **resources.** money, or any property that can be converted into money; assets. **4.** Often, **resources.** an available means afforded by the mind or one's personal capabilities: *to have resource against loneliness.* **5.** an action or measure to which one may have recourse in an emergency; expedient. **6.** capability in dealing with a situation or in meeting difficulties: *a woman of resource.* [1640–50; < F *ressource,* OF *ressourse,* n. deriv. of *resourdre* to rise up < L *resurgere,* equiv. to *re-* RE- + *surgere* to rise up, lift; see RESURGE, SOURCE] —**re•source′less,** *adj.* —**re•source′less•ness,** *n.*
—**Syn. 1, 5.** resort. **5.** means, contrivance, shift. **6.** inventiveness, adapability, ingenuity, cleverness.

re•source•ful (ri sôrs′fəl, -sōrs′-, -zôrs′-, -zōrs′-), *adj.* able to deal skillfully and promptly with new situations, difficulties, etc. [1850–55; RESOURCE + -FUL] —**re•source′ful•ly,** *adv.* —**re•source′ful•ness,** *n.*
—**Syn.** talented, able, imaginative, adroit.

resp., 1. respective. **2.** respectively. **3.** respelled; respelling. **4.** respondent.

re•spect (ri spekt′), *n.* **1.** a particular, detail, or point (usually prec. by *in*): *to differ in some respect.* **2.** relation or reference: *inquiries with respect to a route.* **3.** esteem for or a sense of the worth or excellence of a person, a personal quality or ability, or something considered as a manifestation of a personal quality or ability: *I have great respect for her judgment.* **4.** deference to a right, privilege, privileged position, or someone or something considered to have certain rights or privileges; proper acceptance or courtesy; acknowledgment: *respect for a suspect's right to counsel; to show respect for the flag; respect for the elderly.* **5.** the condition of being esteemed or honored: *to be held in respect.* **6. respects,** a formal expression or gesture of greeting, esteem, or friendship: *Give my respects to your parents.* **7.** favor or partiality. **8.** *Archaic.* a consideration. **9. in respect of,** in reference to; in regard to; concerning. **10. in respect that,** *Archaic.* because of; since. **11. pay one's respects, a.** to visit in order to welcome, greet, etc.: *We paid our respects to the new neighbors.* **b.** to express one's sympathy, esp. to survivors following a death: *We paid our respects to the family.* **12. with respect to,** referring to; concerning: *with respect to your latest request.* —*v.t.* **13.** to hold in esteem or honor: *I cannot respect a cheat.* **14.** to show regard or consideration for: *to respect someone's rights.* **15.** to refrain from intruding upon or interfering with: *to respect a person's privacy.* **16.** to relate or have reference to. [1300–50; (n.) ME (< OF) < L *respectus* action of looking back, consideration, regard, equiv. to *respec-,* var. s. of *respicere* to look back (*re-* RE- + *specere* to look) + *-tus* suffix of v. action; (v.) < L *respectus* ptp. of *respicere*]
—**Syn. 1.** regard, feature, matter. **2.** regard, connection. **3.** estimation, reverence, homage, honor. RESPECT, ESTEEM, VENERATION imply recognition of personal qualities by approbation, deference, and more or less affection. RESPECT is commonly the result of admiration and approbation, together with deference: *to feel respect for a great scholar.* ESTEEM is deference combined with admiration and often with affection: *to hold a friend in great esteem.* VENERATION is an almost religious attitude of deep respect, reverence, and love, such as we feel for persons or things of outstanding superiority, endeared by long association: *veneration for one's grandparents, for noble traditions.* **7.** bias, preference. **13.** revere, venerate, consider, admire. **14.** heed.

re•spect•a•bil•i•ty (ri spek′tə bil′i tē), *n., pl.* **-ties** for 3. **1.** the state or quality of being respectable. **2.** respectable social standing, character, or reputation. **3.** a respectable person or persons. **4. respectabilities,** things accepted as respectable. [1775–85; RESPECTABLE + -ITY]

re•spect•a•ble (ri spek′tə bəl), *adj.* **1.** worthy of respect or esteem; estimable; worthy: *a respectable citizen.* **2.** of good social standing, reputation, etc.: *a respectable neighborhood.* **3.** suitable or good enough to be seen or used: *respectable clothes; respectable language.* **4.** of moderate excellence; fairly good; fair: *a respectable performance.* **5.** appreciable in size, number, or amount: *a respectable turnout.* [1580–90; RESPECT + -ABLE] —**re•spect′a•ble•ness,** *n.* —**re•spect′a•bly,** *adv.*
—**Syn. 1.** honorable. **4.** middling, passable.

re•spect•ant (ri spek′tənt), *adj. Heraldry.* aspectant. [1680–90; RESPECT + -ANT]

re•spect•er (ri spek′tər), *n.* someone or something that is influenced by the social standing, importance, power, or any deterrent put forth by persons or things (used chiefly in negative constructions): *Death is no respecter of wealth.* [1605–15; RESPECT + -ER[1]]

re•spect•ful (ri spekt′fəl), *adj.* full of, characterized by, or showing politeness or deference: *a respectful reply.* [1590–1600; RESPECT + -FUL] —**re•spect′ful•ly,** *adv.* —**re•spect′ful•ness,** *n.*
—**Syn.** courteous, polite, decorous, civil, deferential.
—**Ant.** discourteous, disrespectful.

re•spect•ing (ri spek′ting), *prep.* regarding; concerning. [1725–35; RESPECT + -ING[2]]

re•spec•tive (ri spek′tiv), *adj.* pertaining individually or severally to each of a number of persons, things, etc.; particular: *I will now discuss the respective merits of the candidates.* [1515–25; < ML *respectīvus,* equiv. to L *respect(us)* (see RESPECT) + *-īvus* -IVE] —**re•spec′tive•ness,** *n.*
—**Syn.** separate, individual, corresponding. —**Ant.** irrespective.

re•spec•tive•ly (ri spek′tiv lē), *adv.* **1.** in precisely the order given; sequentially. **2.** (of two or more things, with reference to two or more things previously mentioned) referring or applying to in a parallel or sequential way: *Joe and Bob escorted Betty and Alice, respectively.* [1550–60; RESPECTIVE + -LY]

re•spell (rē spel′), *v.t.* to spell again or anew. [1800–10; RE- + SPELL[1]]

Res. Phys., Resident Physician.

Re•spi•ghi (Re spē′gē), *n.* **Ot•to•ri•no** (ôt′tô Rē′nô), 1879–1936, Italian composer.

res•pi•ra•ble (res′pər ə bəl, ri spīər′ə bəl), *adj.* **1.** capable of being respired. **2.** capable of respiring. [1770–80; < LL *respīrābilis.* See RESPIRE, -ABLE] —**res′pi•ra•bil′i•ty, res′pi•ra•ble•ness,** *n.*

res•pi•ra•tion (res′pə rā′shən), *n.* **1.** the act of respiring; inhalation and exhalation of air; breathing. **2.** *Biol.* **a.** the sum total of the physical and chemical processes in an organism by which oxygen is conveyed to tissues and cells, and the oxidation products, carbon dioxide and water, are given off. **b.** an analogous chemical process, as in muscle cells or in anaerobic bacteria, occurring in the absence of oxygen. [1400–50; late ME *respiracioun* < L *respīrātiōn-* (s. of *respīrātiō*) a breathing out, equiv. to *respīrāt(us)* (ptp. of *respīrāre* to RESPIRE) + *-iōn-* -ION] —**res′pi•ra′tion•al,** *adj.*

res•pi•ra•tor (res′pə rā′tər), *n.* **1.** a masklike device, usually of gauze, worn over the mouth, or nose and mouth, to prevent the inhalation of noxious substances or the like. **2.** *Brit.* See **gas mask. 3.** *Med.* an apparatus to produce artificial respiration. [1785–95; < L *respīrāt(us)* (see RESPIRATION) + -OR[2]]

res•pi•ra•to•ry (res′pər ə tôr′ē, -tōr′ē, ri spīər′ə-), *adj.* pertaining to or serving for respiration: *respiratory disease.* [1780–90; < LL *respīrātōrius,* equiv. to L *respīrā(re)* to RESPIRE + *-tōrius* -TORY[1]]

res′piratory chain′, *Biochem.* a series of mitochondrial proteins that transport electrons of hydrogen, released in the Krebs cycle, from acetyl coenzyme A to inhaled oxygen to form H_2O: the energy released in the process is conserved as ATP. Cf. **electron transport.**

res′piratory distress′ syn′drome, *Pathol.* **1.** Also called **hyaline membrane disease.** an acute lung disease of the newborn, occurring primarily in premature babies and babies born to ill mothers, characterized by rapid breathing, flaring of the nostrils, inelastic lungs, edema of the extremities, and in some cases the formation of a hyaline membrane on the lungs caused by a lack of surfactant in the immature lung tissue. **2.** Also called **adult respiratory distress syndrome.** a disorder, caused by an acute illness or injury that affects the lungs either directly or indirectly, resulting in stiffening of the lung tissue, pulmonary edema, and extreme shortness of breath. *Abbr.:* RDS [1965–70]

res′piratory quo′tient, *Physiol.* the ratio of the amount of carbon dioxide released by the lungs to the amount of oxygen taken in during a given period. [1885–90]

res′piratory sys′tem, *Anat.* the system by which oxygen is taken into the body and an exchange of oxygen and carbon dioxide takes place; in mammals the system includes the nasal passages, pharynx, trachea, bronchi, and lungs. [1935–40]

re•spire (ri spīər′), *v.,* **-spired, -spir•ing.** —*v.i.* **1.** to inhale and exhale air for the purpose of maintaining life; breathe. **2.** to breathe freely again, after anxiety, trouble, etc. —*v.t.* **3.** to breathe; inhale and exhale. **4.** to exhale. [1375–1425; late ME *respiren* < L *respīrāre,* equiv. to *re-* RE- + *spīrāre* to breathe; see SPIRIT]

res•pi•rom•e•ter (res′pə rom′i tər), *n.* **1.** an instrument for measuring the extent of respiratory movement. **2.** an instrument for measuring oxygen consumption or carbon dioxide production in an isolated tissue. [1885–90; RESPIRE + -O- + -METER]

res•pi•rom•e•try (res′pə rom′i trē), *n.* the branch of medical science dealing with the measurement and analysis of respiration. [1930–35; RESPIRE + -O- + -METRY]

res•pite (res′pit), *n., v.,* **-pit•ed, -pit•ing.** —*n.* **1.** a delay or cessation for a time, esp. of anything distressing or trying; an interval of relief: *to toil without respite.* **2.** temporary suspension of the execution of a person condemned to death; reprieve. —*v.t.* **3.** to relieve temporarily, esp. from anything distressing or trying; give an interval of relief from. **4.** to grant delay in the carrying out of (a punishment, obligation, etc.). [1200–50; (n.) ME *respit* < OF < L *respectus* (see RESPECT); (v.) ME *respiten* < OF *respitier* < L *respectāre,* freq. of *respicere* to look back; see RESPECT]
—**Syn. 1.** hiatus, rest, recess. **2.** postponement, stay. **3.** alleviate. **4.** postpone, suspend.

re•splend•ence (ri splen′dəns), *n.* a resplendent quality or state; splendor. Also, **re•splend′en•cy.** [1375–1425; late ME < LL *resplendentia.* See RESPLENDENT, -ENCE]

re•splend•ent (ri splen′dənt), *adj.* shining brilliantly; gleaming; splendid: *troops resplendent in white uniforms; resplendent virtues.* [1400–50; late ME < L *resplendent-* (s. of *resplendēns*), prp. of *resplendēre* to shine brightly, equiv. to *re-* RE- + *splend(ēre)* shine (see SPLENDOR) + *-ent-* -ENT] —**re•splend′ent•ly,** *adv.*
—**Syn.** radiant; dazzling, gorgeous, magnificent.

resplend′ent quetzal′. See under **quetzal** (def. 1).

re•spond (ri spond′), *v.i.* **1.** to reply or answer in words: *to respond briefly to a question.* **2.** to make a return by some action as if in answer: *to respond generously to a charity drive.* **3.** to react favorably. **4.** *Physiol.* to exhibit some action or effect as if in answer; react: *Nerves respond to a stimulus.* **5.** to correspond (usually fol. by *to*). **6.** *Bridge.* to make a response. —*v.t.* **7.** to say in answer; reply. —*n.* **8.** *Archit.* a half pier, pilaster, or the like projecting from a wall as a support for a lintel or an arch, the other side of which is supported on a free-standing pier or column. **9.** *Eccles.* **a.** a short anthem chanted at intervals during the reading of a lection. **b.** responsory. **c.** response. [1350–1400; (n.) ME: responsory < OF, deriv. of *respondre* to respond < L *respondēre* to promise in return, reply, answer, equiv. to *re-* RE- + *spondēre* to pledge, promise (see SPONSOR); (v.) < L *respondēre*]
—**Syn. 1.** rejoin. **2.** rise, react, reply.

re•spond•ence (ri spon′dəns), *n.* the act of responding; response: *respondence to a stimulus.* Also, **re•spond′en•cy.** [1580–90; < obs. F; see RESPOND, -ENCE]

re•spond•ent (ri spon′dənt), *n.* **1.** a person who responds or makes reply. **2.** *Law.* a defendant, esp. in appellate and divorce proceedings. —*adj.* **3.** giving a response; answering; responsive. **4.** *Law.* being a respondent. **5.** *Psychol.* of or pertaining to behavior that occurs consistently in response to a particular stimulus. **6.** *Obs.* corresponding. [1520–30; < L *respondent-* (s. of *respondēns*), prp. of *respondēre.* See RESPOND, -ENT]

respond′ent condi′tioning, conditioning (def. 2). [1965–70]

re•spond•er (ri spon′dər), *n.* **1.** a person or thing that

CONCISE ETYMOLOGY KEY: <, descended or borrowed from; >, whence; b., blend of, blended; c., cognate with; cf., compare; deriv., derivative; equiv., equivalent; imit., imitative; obl., oblique; r., replacing; s., stem; sp., spelling, spelled; resp., respelling, respelled; trans., translation; ?, origin unknown; *, unattested; ‡, probably earlier than. See the full key inside the front cover.

re′proc•la•ma′tion, *n.*
re•pro′gram, *v.t.,* **-grammed** or **-gramed, -gram•ming** or **-gram•ing.**
re•pro′gram•ma•ble, *adj.*
re′pro•ject′, *v.*
re•prom′ise, *v.,* **-ised, -is•ing.**
re•prom′ul•gate′, *v.t.,* **-gat•ed, -gat•ing.**
re′prom•ul•ga′tion, *n.*
re•proof′, *v.t.*
re′pro•por′tion, *v.t.*
re′pro•pose′, *v.,* **-posed, -pos•ing.**
re•pros′e•cute′, *v.t.,* **-cut•ed, -cut•ing.**
re•pro′test, *n.*
re′pro•test′, *v.*
re′pro•vi′sion, *v.*
re•prune′, *v.t.,* **-pruned, -prun•ing.**
re•pump′, *v.t.*
re•punc′tu•ate′, *v.t.,* **-at•ed, -at•ing.**
re′punc•tu•a′tion, *n.*
re•pun′ish, *v.*
re•pun′ish•a•ble, *adj.*
re•pun′ish•ment, *n.*
re′pu•ri•fi•ca′tion, *n.*
re•pu′ri•fy′, *v.,* **-fied, -fy•ing.**
re•pur′pose, *v.t.,* **-posed, -pos•ing.**
re′pur•sue′, *v.t.,* **-sued, -su•ing.**
re′qual•i•fi•ca′tion, *n.*
re•qual′i•fy′, *v.,* **-fied, -fy•ing.**
re•ques′tion, *v.t.*
re•quick′en, *v.*
re•quote′, *v.t.,* **-quot•ed, -quot•ing.**
re•rack′, *v.t.*

responds. **2.** *Electronics.* the part of a transponder that transmits the reply. [1875–80; RESPOND + -ER[1]]

Re·spon·sa (ri spon′sə), *n.* the branch of rabbinical literature comprised of authoritative replies in letter form made by noted rabbis or Jewish scholars to questions sent to them concerning Jewish law. [1895–1900; < NL; pl. of RESPONSUM]

re·sponse (ri spons′), *n.* **1.** an answer or reply, as in words or in some action. **2.** *Biol.* any behavior of a living organism that results from an external or internal stimulus. **3.** *Eccles.* **a.** a verse, sentence, phrase, or word said or sung by the choir or congregation in reply to the officiant. Cf. **versicle** (def. 2). **b.** responsory. **4.** *Bridge.* a bid based on an evaluation of one's hand relative to the previous bid of one's partner. [1250–1300; < L *respōnsum,* n. use of neut. ptp. of *respondēre* to RESPOND; r. ME *respounse* < MF *respons* < L, as above] **—re·sponse′less,** *adj.*
—Syn. 1. rejoinder. See **answer.**

response′ generaliza′tion, *Psychol.* generalization (def. 4b).

re·spons·er (ri spon′sər), *n. Electronics.* responsor.

response′ time′, 1. *Psychol.* the time consumed in making a response. **2.** *Computers.* the time that elapses while waiting for a computer to respond to a command. [1955–60]

re·spon·si·bil·i·ty (ri spon′sə bil′i tē), *n., pl.* **-ties. 1.** the state or fact of being responsible. **2.** an instance of being responsible: *The responsibility for this mess is yours!* **3.** a particular burden of obligation upon one who is responsible: *the responsibilities of authority.* **4.** a person or thing for which one is responsible: *A child is a responsibility to its parents.* **5.** reliability or dependability, esp. in meeting debts or payments. **6. on one's own responsibility,** on one's own initiative or authority: *He changed the order on his own responsibility.* [1780–90; RESPONS(IBLE) + -IBILITY]
—Syn. 1. answerability, accountability.

re·spon·si·ble (ri spon′sə bəl), *adj.* **1.** answerable or accountable, as for something within one's power, control, or management (often fol. by *to* or *for*): *He is responsible to the president for his decisions.* **2.** involving accountability or responsibility: *a responsible position.* **3.** chargeable with being the author, cause, or occasion of something (usually fol. by *for*): *Termites were responsible for the damage.* **4.** having a capacity for moral decisions and therefore accountable; capable of rational thought or action: *The defendant is not responsible for his actions.* **5.** able to discharge obligations or pay debts. **6.** reliable or dependable, as in meeting debts, conducting business dealings, etc. **7.** (of a government, member of a government, government agency, or the like) answerable to or serving at the discretion of an elected legislature or the electorate. [1590–1600; < L *respōns(us)* (see RESPONSE) + -IBLE] **—re·spon′si·ble·ness,** *n.* **—re·spon′si·bly,** *adv.*
—Syn. 1. liable. **4.** competent. **5.** solvent. **6.** honest, capable, reliable, trustworthy.

re·spon·sion (ri spon′shən), *n.* **1.** the act of responding or answering. **2. responsions,** the first examination at Oxford University that candidates for the degree of B.A. have to pass. [1425–75; late ME < L *respōnsiōn-* (s. of *respōnsiō*) an answer. See RESPONSE, -ION]

re·spon·sive (ri spon′siv), *adj.* **1.** responding esp. readily and sympathetically to appeals, efforts, influences, etc.: *a responsive government.* **2.** *Physiol.* acting in response, as to some stimulus. **3.** characterized by the use of responses: *responsive worship.* [1375–1425; late ME < LL *respōnsīvus.* See RESPONSE, -IVE] **—re·spon′sive·ly,** *adv.*
—Syn. 1. receptive, understanding, sympathetic.

re·spon·sive·ness (ri spon′siv nis), *n.* **1.** the quality or state of being responsive. **2.** *Mach.* the ability of a machine or system to adjust quickly to suddenly altered external conditions, as of speed, load, or temperature, and to resume stable operation without undue delay. Also, **re·spon·siv·i·ty** (ri spon siv′i tē, rē′spon-). [1840–50; RESPONSIVE + -NESS]

re·spon·sor (ri spon′sər), *n. Electronics.* the portion of an interrogator-responsor that receives and interprets the signals from a transponder. Also, **responser.** [1940–45; RESPONSE + -OR[2]]

re·spon·so·ry (ri spon′sə rē), *n., pl.* **-ries.** *Eccles.* an anthem sung after a lection by a soloist and choir alternately. [1375–1425; late ME < LL *respōnsōrium,* equiv. to L *respond(ēre)* to RESPOND + *-tōrium* -TORY[2], with *dt* > *s*]

re·spon·sum (ri spon′səm), *n., pl.* **-sa** (-sə). the reply of a noted rabbi or Jewish scholar as rendered in the Responsa. [1895–1900; < NL, L *respōnsum* a reply; see RESPONSE]

res pu·bli·ca (räs′ po͞o′bli kä′; *Eng.* rēz′ pub′li kə, räs′), *Latin.* the state; republic; commonwealth. [lit., public matter]

res·sen·ti·ment (*Fr.* Rə sän tē mäN′), *n.* **1.** any cautious, defeatist, or cynical attitude based on the belief that the individual and human institutions exist in a hostile or indifferent universe or society. **2.** an oppressive awareness of the futility of trying to improve one's status in life or in society. [1940–45; < F; see RESENTMENT]

rest[1] (rest), *n.* **1.** the refreshing quiet or repose of sleep: *a good night's rest.* **2.** refreshing ease or inactivity after exertion or labor: *to allow an hour for rest.* **3.** relief or freedom, esp. from anything that wearies, troubles, or disturbs. **4.** a period or interval of inactivity, repose, solitude, or tranquillity: *to go away for a rest.* **5.** mental or spiritual calm; tranquillity. **6.** the repose of death: *eternal rest.* **7.** cessation or absence of motion: *to bring a machine to rest.* **8.** *Music.* **a.** an interval of silence between tones. **b.** a mark or sign indicating it. **9.** *Pros.* a short pause within a line; caesura. **10.** a place that provides shelter or lodging for travelers, as an inn. **11.** any stopping or resting place: *a roadside rest for weary hikers.* **12.** a piece or thing for something to rest on: *a hand rest.* **13.** a supporting device; support. **14.** *Billiards, Pool.* bridge[1] (def. 14). **15. at rest, a.** in a state of repose, as in sleep. **b.** dead. **c.** quiescent; inactive; not in motion: *the inertia of an object at rest.* **d.** free from worry; tranquil: *Nothing could put his mind at rest.* **16. lay to rest, a.** to inter (a dead body); bury: *He was laid to rest last Thursday.* **b.** to allay, suppress, or appease.
—*v.i.* **17.** to refresh oneself, as by sleeping, lying down, or relaxing. **18.** to relieve weariness by cessation of exertion or labor. **19.** to be at ease; have tranquillity or peace. **20.** to repose in death. **21.** to be quiet or still. **22.** to cease from motion, come to rest; stop. **23.** to become or remain inactive. **24.** to stay as is or remain without further action or notice: *to let a matter rest.* **25.** to lie, sit, lean, or be set: *His arm rested on the table.* **26.** *Agric.* to lie fallow or unworked: *to let land rest.* **27.** to be imposed as a burden or responsibility (usually fol. by *on* or *upon*). **28.** to rely (usually fol. by *on* or *upon*). **29.** to be based or founded (usually fol. by *on* or *upon*). **30.** to be found; belong; reside (often fol. by *with*): *The blame rests with them.* **31.** to be present; dwell; linger (usually fol. by *on* or *upon*): *A sunbeam rests upon the altar.* **32.** to be fixed or directed on something, as the eyes, a gaze, etc. **33.** *Law.* to terminate voluntarily the introduction of evidence in a case.
—*v.t.* **34.** to give rest to; refresh with rest: *to rest oneself.* **35.** to lay or place for rest, ease, or support: *to rest one's back against a tree.* **36.** to direct (as the eyes): *to rest one's eyes on someone.* **37.** to base, or let depend, as on some ground of reliance. **38.** to bring to rest; halt; stop. **39.** *Law.* to terminate voluntarily the introduction of evidence on: *to rest one's case.* [bef. 900; (n.) ME, OE; akin to G *Rast;* (v.) ME *resten,* OE *restan;* akin to G *rasten*] **—rest′er,** *n.*
—Syn. 7. stop, halt, standstill.

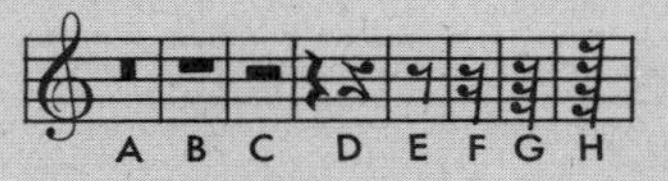

rest[1] (def. 8b)
A, double whole; B, whole; C, half; D, quarter; E, eighth; F, sixteenth; G, thirty-second; H, sixty-fourth

rest[2] (rest), *n.* **1.** the part that is left or remains; remainder: *The rest of the students are in the corridor.* **2.** the others: *All the rest are going.* **3.** *Brit. Banking.* surplus (defs. 1, 2). —*v.i.* **4.** to continue to be; remain as specified: *Rest assured that all is well.* [1375–1425; (v.) late ME *resten* to remain due or unpaid < MF *rester* to remain < L *restāre* to remain standing, equiv. to *re-* RE- + *stāre* to STAND; (n.) late ME < MF *reste,* n. deriv. of *rester*]

rest[3] (rest), *n. Armor.* a support for a lance; lance rest. [1490–1500; aph. var. of ARREST]

re·state (rē stāt′), *v.t.,* **-stat·ed, -stat·ing.** to state again or in a new way. [1705–15; RE- + STATE] **—re·state′ment,** *n.*

res·tau·rant (res′tər ənt, -tə ränt′, -tränt), *n.* an establishment where meals are served to customers. [1820–30, *Amer.;* < F, n. use of prp. of *restaurer* < L *restaurāre* to RESTORE]

res′taurant car′, *Brit.* See **dining car.** [1870–75]

res·tau·ra·teur (res′tər ə tûr′; *Fr.* Res tô Ra tœR′), *n., pl.* **-teurs** (-tûrz′; *Fr.* -tœR′). the owner or manager of a restaurant. [1790–1800; < F; MF: restorer < LL *restaurātor,* equiv. to L *restaurā(re)* to RESTORE + *-tor* -TOR]

rest′ cure′, a treatment for nervous disorders, consisting of a complete rest, usually combined with systematic diet, massage, etc., esp. at a spa or sanitorium. [1885–90]

rest′ en′ergy, *Physics.* the energy equivalent to the mass of a particle at rest in an inertial frame of reference, equal to the rest mass times the square of the speed of light. [1935–40]

rest·ful (rest′fəl), *adj.* **1.** giving or conducive to rest. **2.** being at rest; quiet; tranquil; peaceful. [1300–50; ME; see REST[1], -FUL] **—rest′ful·ly,** *adv.* **—rest′ful·ness,** *n.*
—Syn. 2. calm, serene, undisturbed. **—Ant. 1.** disturbing. **2.** agitated.

rest·har·row (rest′har′ō), *n.* a low, pink-flowered European shrub, *Ononis spinosa,* of the legume family, having tough roots that hinder the plow or harrow. [1540–50; REST[1] + HARROW[1]]

rest′ home′, a residential establishment that provides special care for convalescents and aged or infirm persons. [1920–25]

res′ti·form bod′y (res′tə fôrm′), *Anat.* a cordlike bundle of nerve fibers lying on each side of the medulla oblongata and connecting it with the cerebellum. [1825–35; *restiform* < NL *restiformis,* equiv. to L *resti-,* comb. form of *restis* rope + *-formis* -FORM]

rest·ing (res′ting), *adj.* **1.** that rests; not active. **2.** *Bot.* dormant: applied esp. to spores or seeds that germinate after a period of dormancy. [1350–1400; ME; see REST[1], -ING[2]]

res·ti·tute (res′ti to͞ot′, -tyo͞ot′), *v.,* **-tut·ed, -tut·ing.** —*v.i.* **1.** to make restitution. —*v.t.* **2.** to make restitution for. **3.** to restore to a former state or position. [1350–1400; ME < L *restitūtus,* ptp. of *restituere* to set up again, restore, equiv. to *re-* RE- + *-stitū-,* var. s. of *-stituere* (comb. form of *statuere* to set upright, deriv. of *stāre* to STAND) + *-tus* ptp. suffix]

res·ti·tu·tion (res′ti to͞o′shən, -tyo͞o′-), *n.* **1.** reparation made by giving an equivalent or compensation for loss, damage, or injury caused; indemnification. **2.** the restoration of property or rights previously taken away, conveyed, or surrendered. **3.** restoration to the former or original state or position. **4.** *Physics.* the return to an original physical condition, esp. after elastic deformation. [1350–1400; ME *restitucioun* < OF *restitution, restitucion* < L *restitūtiōn-* (s. of *restitūtiō*) a rebuilding, restoration, equiv. to *restitūt(us)* RESTITUTE + *-iōn-* -ION] **—res′ti·tu′tive, res·ti·tu·to·ry** (res′ti to͞o′tə rē, -tyo͞o′-), *adj.*
—Syn. 1. recompense, amends, compensation, requital, satisfaction, repayment. See **redress.**

res·tive (res′tiv), *adj.* **1.** impatient of control, restraint, or delay, as persons; restless; uneasy. **2.** refractory; stubborn. **3.** refusing to go forward; balky: *a restive horse.* [1375–1425; REST[2] + -IVE; r. late ME *restif* stationary, balking < OF: inert] **—res′tive·ly,** *adv.* **—res′tive·ness,** *n.*
—Syn. 1. nervous, unquiet. **2.** recalcitrant, disobedient, obstinate. **—Ant. 1.** patient, quiet. **2.** obedient, tractable.

rest·less (rest′lis), *adj.* **1.** characterized by or showing inability to remain at rest: *a restless mood.* **2.** unquiet or uneasy, as a person, the mind, or the heart. **3.** never at rest; perpetually agitated or in motion: *the restless sea.* **4.** without rest; without restful sleep: *a restless night.* **5.** unceasingly active; averse to quiet or inaction, as persons: *a restless crowd.* [bef. 1000; ME *restles,* OE *restlēas.* See REST[1], -LESS] **—rest′less·ly,** *adv.* **—rest′less·ness,** *n.*
—Syn. 1, 2, 3. restive, agitated, fretful.

rest′less ca′vy, a wild guinea pig. [1765–75]

rest′ mass′, *Physics.* the mass of a body as measured when the body is at rest relative to an observer, an inherent property of the body. Cf. **relativistic mass.** [1910–15]

re·stock (rē stok′), *v.t., v.i.* to stock again; replenish. [1670–80; RE- + STOCK]

Res·ton (res′tən), *n.* **James (Barrett),** born 1909, U.S. journalist, born in Scotland.

re·stor·al (ri stôr′əl, -stōr′-), *n.* restoration. [1605–15; RESTORE + -AL[2]]

res·to·ra·tion (res′tə rā′shən), *n.* **1.** the act of restoring; renewal, revival, or reestablishment. **2.** the state or fact of being restored. **3.** a return of something to a former, original, normal, or unimpaired condition. **4.** restitution of something taken away or lost. **5.** something that is restored, as by renovating. **6.** a reconstruction or reproduction of an ancient building, extinct animal, or the like, showing it in its original state. **7.** a putting back into a former position, dignity, etc. **8.** *Dentistry.* **a.** the work, process, or result of replacing or restoring teeth or parts of teeth. **b.** something that restores or replaces teeth or parts of teeth, as a filling, crown, or denture. **9. the Restoration, a.** the reestablishment of the monarchy in England with the return of Charles II in 1660. **b.** the period of the reign of Charles II (1660–85), sometimes extended to include the reign of James II (1685–88). —*adj.* **10.** (*cap*) of, pertaining to, or characteristic of the Restoration: *Restoration manners.* [1350–1400; ME < LL *restaurātiōn-* (s. of *restaurātiō*), equiv. to L *restaurāt(us)* (ptp. of *restaurāre* to RESTORE; see -ATE[1]) + *-iōn-* -ION]

Res′tora′tion com′edy, English comedy of the period of the Restoration, stressing manners and social satire.

re·stor·a·tive (ri stôr′ə tiv, -stōr′-), *adj.* **1.** serving to restore; pertaining to restoration. **2.** capable of renewing health or strength. —*n.* **3.** a restorative agent, means, or the like. **4.** a means of restoring a person to consciousness: *Smelling salts serve as a restorative.* [1350–1400; ME *restoratif* (adj. and n.) < MF *restauratif* < L *restaurāt(us)* (ptp. of *restaurāre* to RESTORE) + MF *-if* -IVE]

re·store (ri stôr′, -stōr′), *v.t.,* **-stored, -stor·ing. 1.** to bring back into existence, use, or the like; reestablish: *to restore order.* **2.** to bring back to a former, original, or normal condition, as a building, statue, or painting. **3.** to bring back to a state of health, soundness, or vigor. **4.** to put back to a former place, or to a former position, rank, etc.: *to restore the king to his throne.* **5.** to give back; make return or restitution of (anything taken

CONCISE PRONUNCIATION KEY: act, cāpe, dâre, pärt; set, ēqual; *if,* ice; ox, ōver, ôrder, oil, bo͝ok, bo͞ot, out; up, ûrge; child; sing; shoe; thin, *that;* zh as in *treasure.* ə = *a* as in *alone, e* as in *system, i* as in *easily, o* as in *gallop, u* as in *circus;* ° as in *fire* (fī°r), *hour* (ou°r). l and n can serve as syllabic consonants, as in *cradle* (krād′l), and *button* (but′n). See the full key inside the front cover.

re·ra′di·ate′, *v.,* **-at·ed, -at·ing.**
re·raise′, *v.t.,* **-raised, -rais·ing.**
re·rank′, *v.*
re·rate′, *v.,* **-rat·ed, -rat·ing.**
re·read′, *v.,* **-read, -read·ing.**
re·reel′, *v.*
re·reg′is·ter, *v.*
re′reg·is·tra′tion, *n.*
re·reg′u·late′, *v.t.,* **-lat·ed, -lat·ing.**
re′reg·u·la′tion, *n.*
re′re·mind′, *v.t..*
re·rent′, *v.t.*
re·rent′al, *n.*
re′re·view′, *v.*
re·rise′, *v.,* **-rose, -ris·en, -ris·ing.**
re·roll′, *v.*
re·roof′, *v.t.*
re·root′, *v.*
re·route′, *v.,* **-rout·ed, -rout·ing.**
re·sad′dle, *v.,* **-dled, -dling.**
re·salt′, *v.t.*
re·sa·lute′, *v.,* **-lut·ed, -lut·ing.**
re·sam′ple, *v.t.,* **-pled, -pling.**
re·sanc′tion, *v.t.*
re·school′, *v.t.*
re·score′, *v.,* **-scored, -scor·ing.**
re·screen′, *v.t.*
re·scrub′, *v.,* **-scrubbed, -scrub·bing.**
re·scru′ti·nize′, *v.t.,* **-nized, -niz·ing.**
re·scru′ti·ny, *n., pl.* **-nies.**
re·sculpt′, *v.t.*
re·sculp′ture, *v.t.* **-tured, -tur·ing.**
re·seal′, *v.t.*
re·seal′a·bil′i·ty, *n.*

away or lost). **6.** to reproduce or reconstruct (an ancient building, extinct animal, etc.) in the original state. [1250–1300; ME *restoren* < OF *restorer* < L *restaurāre;* see RE-, STORE] **—re·stor′a·ble,** *adj.* **—re·stor′a·ble·ness,** *n.* **—re·stor′er,** *n.*
—Syn. 2. mend. See **renew. 4.** replace, reinstate. **6.** rebuild.

restor′ing spring′, *Mach.* a spring so located that it returns a displaced part to its normal position.

restr., restaurant.

re-strain (rē strān′), *v.t., v.i.* to strain again. [1870–75; RE- + STRAIN[1]]

re·strain (ri strān′), *v.t.* **1.** to hold back from action; keep in check or under control; repress: *to restrain one's temper.* **2.** to deprive of liberty, as by arrest or the like. **3.** to limit or hamper the activity, growth, or effect of: *to restrain trade with Cuba.* [1350–1400; ME *restreynen* < MF *restreindre* < L *restringere* to bind back, bind fast, equiv. to *re-* RE- + *stringere* to draw together; see STRAIN[1]] **—re·strain′a·ble,** *adj.* **—re·strain′a·bil′i·ty,** *n.* **—re·strain′ing·ly,** *adv.*
—Syn. 1. bridle, suppress, constrain. See **check. 2.** restrict, circumscribe, confine, hinder, hamper. **—Ant. 1.** unbridle. **2.** free, liberate.

re·strained (ri strānd′), *adj.* characterized by restraint: *The actor gave a restrained performance.* [1570–80; RESTRAIN + -ED[2]] **—re·strain′ed·ly,** *adv.*

re·strain·er (ri strā′nər), *n.* **1.** a person or thing that restrains. **2.** *Photog.* a chemical added to a developer to retard its action. [1560–70; RESTRAIN + -ER[1]]

restrain′ing or′der, *Law.* a judicial order to forbid a particular act until a decision is reached on an application for an injunction. [1875–80]

re·straint (ri strānt′), *n.* **1.** a restraining action or influence: *freedom from restraint.* **2.** Sometimes, **restraints.** a means of or device for restraining, as a harness for the body. **3.** the act of restraining, holding back, controlling, or checking. **4.** the state or fact of being restrained; deprivation of liberty; confinement. **5.** constraint or reserve in feelings, behavior, etc. [1350–1400; ME *restreinte* < MF *restrainte,* n. use of fem. ptp. of *restraindre* to RESTRAIN]
—Syn. 4. circumscription, restriction, imprisonment, incarceration. **—Ant. 4.** liberty.

restraint′ of trade′, action tending to interrupt the free flow of goods and services, as by price fixing and other practices that have the effect of reducing competition. [1885–90]

re·strict (ri strikt′), *v.t.* to confine or keep within limits, as of space, action, choice, intensity, or quantity. [1525–35; < L *restrictus* drawn back, tightened, bound, reserved, orig. ptp. of *restringere* to RESTRAIN, equiv. to *re-* RE- + *strictus* STRICT] **re·strict′er, re·stric′tor,** *n.*
—Syn. curb, circumscribe, restrain. **—Ant.** free.

re·strict·ed (ri strik′tid), *adj.* **1.** confined; limited. **2.** (of information, a document, etc.) **a.** bearing the classification *restricted,* usually the lowest level of classified information. **b.** limited to persons authorized to use information, documents, etc., so classified. Cf. **classification** (def. 5). **3.** limited to or admitting only members of a particular group or class: *a restricted neighborhood; a restricted hotel.* [1820–30; RESTRICT + -ED[2]] **—re·strict′·ed·ly,** *adv.* **—re·strict′ed·ness,** *n.*

restrict′ed class′, a class of yachts that, although differing somewhat in design and rigging, are deemed able to race together because of conformity to certain standards.

restrict′ed code′, *Sociolinguistics.* a style of language use associated with informal situations, characterized by linguistic predictability and by its dependence on the external context and on the shared knowledge and experience of the participants for conveying meaning. Cf. **code** (def. 11b), **elaborated code.** [1960–65]

restrict′ed stock′, unregistered stock, as that issued privately as compensation to corporate executives subject to special conditions.

re·stric·tion (ri strik′shən), *n.* **1.** something that restricts; a restrictive condition or regulation; limitation. **2.** the act of restricting. **3.** the state of being restricted. [1375–1425; late ME < LL *restrictiōn-* (s. of *restrictiō*), equiv. to L *restrict(us)* (see RESTRICT) + *-iōn-* -ION]
—Syn. 1. rule, provision, reservation, restraint.

restric′tion en′zyme, *Biochem.* any of a group of enzymes that catalyze the cleavage of DNA molecules at specific sites: used for gene splicing in recombinant DNA technology and for chromosome mapping. [1960–65]

restric′tion frag′ment, a length of DNA cut from the strand by a restriction enzyme.

re·stric·tion·ism (ri strik′shə niz′əm), *n.* a policy, esp. by a national government or legislative body, of enacting restrictions on the amount of imported goods, immigration, etc. [1935–40; RESTRICTION + -ISM] **—re·stric′tion·ist,** *n.*

restric′tion play′, *Checkers.* a limited number of opening moves that are predetermined by their chance selection from an accepted list.

CONCISE ETYMOLOGY KEY: <, descended or borrowed from; >, whence; b., blend of, blended; c., cognate with; cf., compare; deriv., derivative; equiv., equivalent; imit., imitative; obl., oblique; r., replacing; s., stem; sp., spelling, spelled; resp., respelling, respelled; trans., translation; ?, origin unknown; *, unattested; ‡, probably earlier than. See the full key inside the front cover.

restric′tion site′, *Biochem.* the place on a DNA molecule where a restriction enzyme acts.

re·stric·tive (ri strik′tiv), *adj.* **1.** tending or serving to restrict. **2.** of the nature of a restriction. **3.** expressing or implying restriction or limitation of application, as terms, expressions, etc. **4.** *Gram.* limiting the meaning of a modified element: *a restrictive adjective.* [1375–1425; late ME < MF *restrictif* < L *restrict(us)* (see RESTRICT) + MF *-if* -IVE] **—re·stric′tive·ly,** *adv.* **—re·stric′tive·ness,** *n.*

restric′tive clause′, *Gram.* a relative clause that identifies the antecedent and that is usually not set off by commas in English. In *The year that just ended was bad for crops,* the clause *that just ended* is a restrictive clause. Cf. **nonrestrictive clause.** [1900–05]

restric′tive cov′enant, a covenant with a clause that restricts the action of any party to it, esp. an agreement among property owners not to sell to members of particular minority groups. [1880–85]

re·strike (*v.* rē strīk′; *n.* rē′strīk′), *v.,* **-struck, -struck** or **-strick·en, -strik·ing,** *n.* **—***v.t., v.i.* **1.** to strike again. **—***n.* **2.** a coin freshly minted from dies of an earlier issue. **3.** a new print made from an old lithographic stone, metal engraving, woodcut, or the like. [1885–90; RE- + STRIKE]

rest′ room′, rooms or a room having a washbowl, toilet, and other facilities for use by employees, visitors, etc., as in a store, theater, or office. Also, **rest′room′.** [1895–1900, *Amer.*]

re·struc·ture (rē struk′chər), *v.,* **-tured, -tur·ing,** *n.* **—***v.t.* **1.** to change, alter, or restore the structure of: *to restructure a broken nose.* **2.** to effect a fundamental change in (as an organization or system). **3.** to recombine (bits of inexpensive meats), esp. by mechanical means, into simulated steaks, fillets, etc. **—***v.i.* **4.** to restructure something. **—***n.* **5.** the act or an instance of restructuring. [1940–45; RE- + STRUCTURE] **—re·struc′tur·er,** *n.*

rest′ stop′, **1.** a stop made, as during a motor trip, to allow passengers to stretch their legs, use rest rooms, get refreshments, etc. **2.** a rest area, as a roadside parking or picnic area. [1970–75]

re·sult (ri zult′), *v.i.* **1.** to spring, arise, or proceed as a consequence of actions, circumstances, premises, etc.; be the outcome. **2.** to terminate or end in a specified manner or thing. **—***n.* **3.** something that happens as a consequence; outcome. **4.** *Math.* a quantity, expression, etc., obtained by calculation. **5.** Often, **results.** a desirable or beneficial consequence, outcome, or effect: *We had definite results within weeks.* **6. get results,** to obtain a notable or successful result or response; be effective. [1375–1425; late ME *resulten* (v.) < AL *resultāre* to arise as a consequence, L: to spring back, rebound, equiv. to *re-* RE- + *-sultāre,* comb. form of *saltāre* to dance (freq. of *salīre* to leap, spring)]
—Syn. 1. flow, come, issue. See **follow. 2.** resolve, eventuate. **3.** conclusion, issue, end, product, fruit. See **effect. —Ant. 3.** cause.

re·sult·ant (ri zul′tnt), *adj.* **1.** that results; following as a result or consequence. **2.** resulting from the combination of two or more agents: *a resultant force.* **—***n.* **3.** *Math., Physics.* See **vector sum. 4.** *Math.* a determinant the entries of which are the coefficients of each of two polynomials in a specified arrangement and the value of which determines whether the polynomials have a common factor. **5.** something that results. [1400–50; late ME: sum, n. use of L *resultant-* (s. of *resultāns*), prp. of *resultāre.* See RESULT, -ANT]

re·sult·ing·ly (ri zul′ting lē), *adv.* as a result. [1860–65; RESULT + -ING[2] + -LY]

re·sume[1] (ri zōōm′), *v.,* **-sumed, -sum·ing.** **—***v.t.* **1.** to take up or go on with again after interruption; continue: *to resume a journey.* **2.** to take or occupy again: *to resume one's seat.* **3.** to take or assume use or practice of again: *to resume her maiden name.* **4.** to take back: *to resume the title to a property.* **—***v.i.* **5.** to go on or continue after interruption: *The dancing is about to resume.* **6.** to begin again. [1375–1425; late ME *resumen* (< MF *resumer*) < L *resūmere* to take back, take again, equiv. to *re-* RE- + *sūmere* to take (see CONSUME)] **—re·sum′·a·ble,** *adj.* **—re·sum′er,** *n.*

re·su·me[2] (rez′ŏŏ mā′, rez′ŏŏ mā′), *n.* résumé.

ré·su·mé (rez′ŏŏ mā′, rez′ŏŏ mā′), *n.* **1.** a summing up; summary. **2.** a brief written account of personal, educational, and professional qualifications and experience, as that prepared by an applicant for a job. Also, **resume, re′su·mé′.** [1795–1805; < F, n. use of ptp. of *résumer* to RESUME, sum up]

re·sump·tion (ri zump′shən), *n.* **1.** the act of resuming; a reassumption, as of something previously granted. **2.** the act or fact of taking up or going on with again, as of something interrupted. **3.** the act of taking again or recovering something given up or lost. [1400–50; late ME < MF < LL *resūmptiōn-* (s. of *resūmptiō*), equiv. to L *resūmpt(us)* (ptp. of *resūmere* to RESUME) + *-iōn-* -ION]

re·sump·tive (ri zump′tiv), *adj.* **1.** that summarizes: *a resumptive statement.* **2.** that tends to resume or repeat: *a speech so resumptive that its point was lost.* [1850–55; RESUMPT(ION) + -IVE] **—re·sump′tive·ly,** *adv.*

resump′tive pro′noun, *Ling.* a pronoun that appears in a sentence at a position from which something has been copied or moved by a transformational rule, as found in languages such as Irish, Welsh, Hebrew, and Arabic and in some nonstandard varieties of English, as *him* in (nonstandard) *the man that I gave the book to him.*

re·su·pi·nate (ri sōō′pə nāt′, -nit), *adj.* **1.** bent backward. **2.** *Bot.* inverted; appearing as if upside down. [1770–80; < L *resupīnātus* bent backward, turned back (ptp. of *resupīnāre*), equiv. to *re-* RE- + *supīn-* (see SUPINE) + *-ātus* -ATE[1]]

re·su·pi·na·tion (ri sōō′pə nā′shən), *n.* a resupinate condition. [1615–25; < L *resupīnāt(us)* (see RESUPINATE) + -ION]

re·su·pine (rē′sōō pīn′, res′ə-), *adj.* lying on the back; supine. [1620–30; < L *resupīnus* bent back, lying back. See RE-, SUPINE]

re·sur·face (rē sûr′fis), *v.,* **-faced, -fac·ing.** **—***v.t.* **1.** to give a new surface to. **—***v.i.* **2.** to come to the surface again. [1885–90; RE- + SURFACE] **—re·sur′fac·er,** *n.*

re·sur·gam (re sŏŏr′gäm; *Eng.* ri sûr′gam), *Latin.* I shall rise again.

re·surge (ri sûrj′), *v.i.,* **-surged, -surg·ing.** to rise again, as from desuetude or from virtual extinction. [1565–75; < L *resurgere* to rise again, appear again, equiv. to *re-* RE- + *surgere* to lift up, raise, var. of *surrigere* (*sur-* SUR-[2] + *-rigere,* comb. form of *regere* to direct, rule)]

re·sur·gent (ri sûr′jənt), *adj.* rising or tending to rise again; reviving; renascent. [1760–70; < L *resurgent-* (s. of *resurgēns,* prp. of *resurgere*). See RESURGE, -ENT] **—re·sur′gence,** *n.*

res·ur·rect (rez′ə rekt′), *v.t.* **1.** to raise from the dead; bring to life again. **2.** to bring back into use, practice, etc.: *to resurrect an ancient custom.* **—***v.i.* **3.** to rise from the dead. [1765–75; back formation from RESURRECTION] **—res′ur·rec′tor,** *n.*

res·ur·rec·tion (rez′ə rek′shən), *n.* **1.** the act of rising from the dead. **2.** (*cap.*) the rising of Christ after His death and burial. **3.** (*cap.*) the rising of the dead on Judgment Day. **4.** the state of those risen from the dead. **5.** a rising again, as from decay, disuse, etc.; revival. **6.** *Christian Science.* a rising above mortality through the understanding of spiritual life as demonstrated by Jesus Christ. [1250–1300; ME (< OF) < L *resurrēctiōn-* (s. of *resurrēctiō*) the Easter church-festival, equiv. to *resurrēct(us)* (ptp. of *resurgere* to rise again; see RESURGE) + *-iōn-* -ION] **—res′ur·rec′tion·al,** *adj.* **—res′ur·rec′tive,** *adj.*

res·ur·rec·tion·ar·y (rez′ə rek′shə ner′ē), *adj.* **1.** pertaining to or of the nature of resurrection. **2.** pertaining to resurrectionism. [1830–40; RESURRECTION + -ARY]

resurrec′tion fern′, a drought-resistant, evergreen, epiphytic fern, *Polypodium polypodioides,* of subtropical to tropical America, appearing to be a ball of coiled, dead leaves in the dry season but reviving with moisture.

resurrec′tion gate′. See **lich gate.**

res·ur·rec·tion·ism (rez′ə rek′shə niz′əm), *n.* the exhumation and stealing of dead bodies, esp. for dissection. [1855–60; RESURRECTION + -ISM]

res·ur·rec·tion·ist (rez′ə rek′shə nist), *n.* **1.** a person who brings something to life or view again. **2.** a believer in resurrection. **3.** Also called **resurrec′tion man′.** a person who exhumes and steals dead bodies, esp. for dissection; body snatcher. [1770–80; RESURRECTION + -IST]

resurrec′tion plant′, **1.** a desert plant, *Selaginella lepidophylla,* occurring from Texas to South America, having stems that curl inward when dry. **2.** See **Rose of Jericho.** [1865–70, *Amer.*]

re·sur·vey (*v.* rē′sər vā′; *n.* rē sûr′vā, rē′sər vā′), *v., n., pl.* **-veys.** **—***v.t., v.i.* **1.** to survey again. **—***n.* **2.** a new survey. [1590–1600; RE- + SURVEY]

re·sus·ci·tate (ri sus′i tāt′), *v.t.,* **-tat·ed, -tat·ing.** to revive, esp. from apparent death or from unconsciousness. [1525–35; < L *resuscitātus* (ptp. of *resuscitāre* to reawaken), equiv. to *re-* RE- + *sus-* SUS- + *cit(āre)* to move, arouse (see CITE[1]) + *-ātus* ATE[1]] **—re·sus·ci·ta·ble** (ri sus′i tə bəl), *adj.* **—re·sus′ci·ta′tion,** *n.* **—re·sus′ci·ta′tive,** *adj.*

re·sus·ci·ta·tor (ri sus′i tā′tər), *n.* **1.** a person or thing that resuscitates. **2.** *Med.* a device used in the treatment of asphyxiation that, by forcing oxygen or a mixture of oxygen and carbon dioxide into the lungs, initiates respiration. [1840–50; RESUSCITATE + -OR[2]]

Resz·ke (resh′kē; *Pol.* resh′ke), *n.* **1. É·douard de** (*Fr.* ā dwAR′ də), 1853–1917, Polish operatic bass. **2. Jean de** (*Fr.* zhän də), 1850–1925, Polish tenor.

ret (ret), *v.t.,* **ret·ted, ret·ting.** to soak in water or expose to moisture, as flax or hemp, to facilitate the removal of the fiber from the woody tissue by partial rotting. [1400–50; late ME *reten, retten;* c. D *reten* (cf. D *roten,* G *rössen,* Sw *röta*); akin to ROT]

ret., **1.** retain. **2.** retired. **3.** return. **4.** returned.

re·ta·ble (ri tā′bəl, rē′tā′-), *n.* a decorative structure raised above an altar at the back, often forming a frame for a picture, bas-relief, or the like, and sometimes including a shelf or shelves, as for ornaments. [1815–25; < F, equiv. to OF *re(re)* at the back (< L *retrō*) + *table* TABLE; cf. ML *retrōtabulum*]

re·tail (rē′tāl *for 1–4, 6;* ri tāl′ *for 5*), *n.* **1.** the sale of goods to ultimate consumers, usually in small quantities (opposed to *wholesale*). **—***adj.* **2.** pertaining to, connected with, or engaged in sale at retail: *the retail price.* **—***adv.* **3.** in a retail quantity or at a retail price. **—***v.t.* **4.** to sell at retail; sell directly to the consumer. **5.** to

re·seal′a·ble, *adj.*
re·sea′son, *v.*
re′se·cure′, *v.,* **-cured, -cur·ing.**
re·see′, *v.t.,* **-saw, -seen, -see·ing.**
re·seed′, *v.*
re·seek′, *v.t.,* **-sought, -seek·ing.**
re·seg′re·gate′, *v.,* **-gat·ed, -gat·ing.**
re′seg·re·ga′tion, *n.*
re·seize′, *v.t.,* **-seized, -seiz·ing.**
re·sei′zure, *n.*
re′se·lect′, *v.t.*
re′se·lec′tion, *n.*
re·sell′, *v.,* **-sold, -sell·ing.**
re·sell′er, *n.*
re′sen·sa′tion, *n.*
re′sen·si·ti·za′tion, *n.*
re·sen′si·tize′, *v.t.,* **-tized, -tiz·ing.**
re·sen′tence, *n., v.t.,* **-tenced, -tenc·ing.**
re·sep′a·rate′, *v.,* **-rat·ed, -rat·ing.**
re′sep·a·ra′tion, *n.*
re·serv′ice, *v.t.,* **-iced, -ic·ing.**
re·set′tle, *v.,* **-tled, -tling.**
re·set′tle·ment, *n.*
re·sew′, *v.t.,* **-sewed, -sewn** or **sewed, -sew·ing.**
re·shake′, *v.,* **-shook, -shak·en, -shak·ing.**
re·share′, *v.t.,* **-shared, -shar·ing.**
re·sharp′en, *v.*
re·sharp′en·a·ble, *adj.*
re·shave′, *v.,* **-shaved, -shav·ing.**
re·shift′, *v.*
re·shine′, *v.,* **-shone** or **-shined, -shin·ing.**

relate or repeat in detail to others: *to retail scandal.* —*v.i.* **6.** to be sold at retail: *It retails at 50 cents.* [1375–1425; (n.) late ME < AF: a cutting, deriv. of *retailler* to cut, equiv. to *re-* RE- + *tailler* to cut (see TAIL[2]); (v.) ME *retailen* < OF *retailler*] —**re′tail·er,** *n.*

re·tail·ing (rē′tā ling), *n.* the business of selling goods directly to consumers (distinguished from *wholesaling*). [1400–50; late ME; see RETAIL, -ING[1]]

re·tain (ri tān′), *v.t.* **1.** to keep possession of. **2.** to continue to use, practice, etc.: *to retain an old custom.* **3.** to continue to hold or have: *to retain a prisoner in custody; a cloth that retains its color.* **4.** to keep in mind; remember. **5.** to hold in place or position. **6.** to engage, esp. by payment of a preliminary fee: *to retain a lawyer.* [1350–1400; ME *reteinen* < OF *retenir* < L *retinēre* to hold back, hold fast, equiv. to *re-* RE- + *-tinēre*, comb. form of *tenēre* to hold] —**re·tain′a·ble,** *adj.* —**re·tain′a·bil′i·ty, re·tain′a·ble·ness,** *n.* —**re·tain′·ment,** *n.*
—**Syn. 1.** hold, preserve. See **keep.** —**Ant. 1.** loose, lose. **4.** forget.

retained′ earn′ings, the accumulated, undistributed earnings of a corporation. Also called **retained′ in′·come, earned surplus.**

retained′ ob′ject, *Gram.* an object in a passive construction identical with the direct or indirect object in the active construction from which it is derived, as *the picture* in *I was shown the picture,* which is also the direct object in the active construction (*They*) *showed me the picture.* [1930–35]

retained′ ob′ject com′plement, *Gram.* an object complement that is kept in its predicative position following the verb when the verb is transformed into the passive voice, as *genius* in *He was considered a genius* from (*They*) *considered him a genius.*

re·tain·er[1] (ri tā′nər), *n.* **1.** a person or thing that retains. **2.** a servant or attendant who has served a family for many years. **3.** Also called **cage, separator.** *Mach.* a ring separating, and moving with, balls or rollers in a bearing. **4.** *Orthodontics.* **a.** a fixed or removable device worn in the mouth to hold the teeth in their new position during the adaptive period after straightening appliances have been removed. **b.** *Prosthodontics.* a part on a bridge or the like by which the bridge is attached to the natural teeth. [1530–40; RETAIN + -ER[1]] **re·tain′er·ship′,** *n.*

re·tain·er[2] (ri tā′nər), *n.* **1.** the act of retaining in one's service. **2.** the fact of being so retained. **3.** a fee paid to secure services, as of a lawyer. [1425–75; late ME *reteinir*, prob. n. use of MF *retenir* to RETAIN]

re·tain·er·ship (ri tā′nər ship′), *n.* the condition of being a retainer or of having retainers. [1560–70; RETAINER[1] + -SHIP]

retain′ing wall′, a wall for holding in place a mass of earth or the like, as at the edge of a terrace or excavation. Also called **breast wall.** [1830–40]

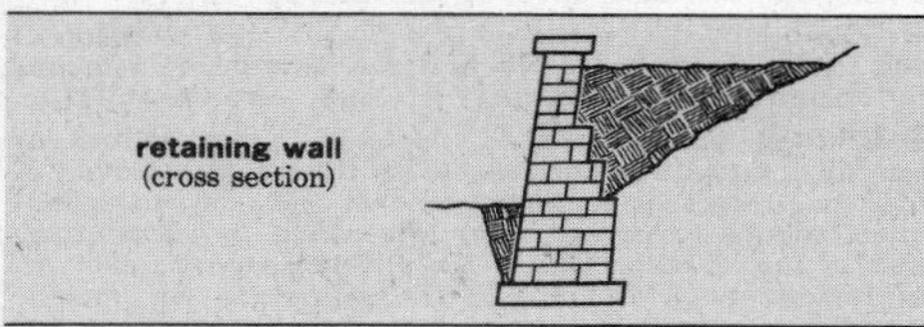

retaining wall (cross section)

re·take (*v.* rē tāk′; *n.* rē′tāk′), *v.*, **-took, -tak·en, -tak·ing,** *n.* —*v.t.* **1.** to take again; take back. **2.** to recapture. **3.** to photograph or film again. —*n.* **4.** the act of photographing or filming again. **5.** a picture, scene, sequence, etc., that is to be or has been photographed or filmed again. [1580–90; RE- + TAKE] —**re·tak′er,** *n.*

re·tal·i·ate (ri tal′ē āt′), *v.*, **-at·ed, -at·ing.** —*v.i.* **1.** to return like for like, esp. evil for evil: *to retaliate for an injury.* —*v.t.* **2.** to requite or make return for (a wrong or injury) with the like. [1605–15; < LL *retāliātus* (ptp. of *retāliāre*), equiv. to *re-* RE- + *tāli(s)* such, of such a nature + *-ātus* -ATE[1]] —**re·tal′i·a′tive, re·tal·i·a·to·ry** (ri tal′ē ə tôr′ē, -tōr′ē), *adj.* —**re·tal′i·a′tor,** *n.*
—**Syn. 1.** counter, repay, reciprocate.

re·tal·i·a·tion (ri tal′ē ā′shən), *n.* the act of retaliating; return of like for like; reprisal. [1575–85; RETALIATE + -ION]

re·tard (ri tärd′, *for 1–3, 5;* rē′tärd *for 4*), *v.t.* **1.** to make slow; delay the development or progress of (an action, process, etc.); hinder. —*v.i.* **2.** to be delayed. —*n.* **3.** a slowing down, diminution, or hindrance, as in a machine. **4.** *Slang* (*disparaging*). **a.** a mentally retarded person. **b.** a person who is stupid, obtuse, or ineffective in some way: *a hopeless social retard.* **5.** *Auto., Mach.* an adjustment made in the setting of the distributor of an internal-combustion engine so that the spark for ignition in each cylinder is generated later in the cycle. Cf. **advance.** [1480–90; < L *retardāre* to delay, protract, equiv. to *re-* RE- + *tardāre* to loiter, be slow, deriv. of *tardus* slow; see TARDY] —**re·tard′ing·ly,** *adv.*
—**Syn. 1.** obstruct, check. —**Ant. 1.** accelerate.

re·tard·ant (ri tär′dnt), *n. Chem.* **1.** any substance capable of reducing the speed of a given reaction. —*adj.* **2.** retarding or tending to retard (usually used in combination): *fire-retardant construction materials.* [1635–45; RETARD + -ANT] —**re·tard′ance, re·tard′an·cy,** *n.*

re·tar·date (ri tär′dāt), *n.* someone who is retarded in some way, as educationally or mentally; retardee. [1955–60; prob. back formation from RETARDATION]

re·tar·da·tion (rē′tär dā′shən), *n.* **1.** the act of retarding or state of being retarded. **2.** something that retards; hindrance. **3.** slowness or limitation in intellectual understanding and awareness, emotional development, academic progress, etc. **4.** *Music.* a form of suspension that is resolved upward. Also, **re·tard·ment** (ri tärd′mənt). [1400–50; late ME *retardacioun* < L *retardātiōn-* (s. of *retardātiō*), equiv. to *retardāt(us)* (see RETARD, -ATE[1]) + *-iōn-* -ION] —**re·tard·a·tive** (ri tär′də tiv), **re·tard·a·to·ry** (ri tär′də tôr′ē, -tōr′ē), *adj.*

re·tard·ed (ri tär′did), *adj.* **1.** characterized by retardation: *a retarded child.* —*n.* **2.** (*used with a plural v.*) mentally retarded persons collectively (usually prec. by *the*): *schools for the retarded.* [1800–10; RETARD + -ED[2]]
—**Syn.** backward, disabled, handicapped.

re·tard·ee (ri tär dē′, -tär′dē), *n.* a retarded person; retardate. [1970–75, *Amer.*; RETARD + -EE]

re·tard·er (ri tär′dər), *n.* **1.** a person or thing that retards. **2.** *Chem.* **a.** any substance added to rubber to delay or prevent vulcanization. **b.** any substance added to delay a process. **3.** *Building Trades.* an admixture of concrete or plaster that retards its set. [1635–45; RETARD + -ER[1]]

re·tar·get (rē tär′git), *v.t.* **1.** to aim toward or calibrate for a different target: *to retarget missiles.* **2.** to change the goal, completion date, recipient, etc., of: *We've retargeted the completion of the job.* [1965–70; RE- + TARGET]

retch (rech), *v.i.* **1.** to make efforts to vomit. —*v.t.* **2.** to vomit. —*n.* **3.** the act or an instance of retching. [1540–50; var. of *reach*, OE *hrǣcan* to clear the throat (not recorded in ME), deriv. of *hrāca* a clearing of the throat; cf. ON *hrǣkja* to hawk, spit]

retd., **1.** retained. **2.** retired. **3.** returned.

re·te (rē′tē), *n., pl.* **re·ti·a** (rē′shē ə, -shə, -tē ə). **1.** a pierced plate on an astrolabe, having projections whose points correspond to the fixed stars. **2.** a network, as of fibers, nerves, or blood vessels. [1350–1400; ME *riet* < L *rēte* net] —**re·ti·al** (rē′shē əl), *adj.*

re·tell·ing (rē tel′ing), *n.* a new, and often updated or retranslated, version of a story. [1635–45; RE- + TELL[1] + -ING[1]]

re·tem (rē′tem), *n.* a shrub, *Retama raetam,* of Syria and Arabia, having white flowers: said to be the juniper of the Old Testament. [< Ar *ratam*]

re·tene (rē′tēn, ret′ēn), *n. Chem.* a crystalline hydrocarbon, $C_{18}H_{18}$, obtained chiefly from the tar of resinous woods and certain fossil resins. [1865–70; < Gk *rhētínē* RESIN + -ENE]

re·ten·tion (ri ten′shən), *n.* **1.** the act of retaining. **2.** the state of being retained. **3.** the power to retain; capacity for retaining. **4.** the act or power of remembering things; memory. [1350–1400; ME *retencion* < L *retentiōn-* (s. of *retentiō*) a keeping back, equiv. to *retent(us)* (ptp. of *retinēre* to RETAIN) + *-iōn-* -ION]

re·ten·tive (ri ten′tiv), *adj.* **1.** tending or serving to retain something. **2.** having power or capacity to retain. **3.** having power or ability to remember; having a good memory. [1325–75; ME *retentif* < MF < ML *retentīvus,* equiv. to L *retent(us)* (see RETENTION) + *-īvus* -IVE] —**re·ten′tive·ly,** *adv.* —**re·ten′tive·ness,** *n.*

re·ten·tiv·i·ty (rē′ten tiv′i tē), *n.* **1.** the power to retain; retentiveness. **2.** *Elect.* remanence. **3.** *Magnetism.* the ability to retain magnetization after the removal of the magnetizing force. [1880–85; RETENTIVE + -ITY]

re·te·pore (rē′tə pôr′, -pōr′), *n.* any bryozoan of the family Reteporidae which forms colonies that have a networklike structure. [< NL *Retepora* name of genus; see RETE, PORE[2]]

re·think (*v.* rē thingk′; *n.* rē′thingk′), *v.*, **-thought, -think·ing,** *n.* —*v.t., v.i.* **1.** to reconsider, esp. profoundly. —*n.* **2.** the act of reconsidering. [1690–1700; RE- + THINK[1]] —**re·think′er,** *n.*

re·ti·ar·i·us (rē′shē âr′ē əs), *n., pl.* **-ar·i·i** (-âr′ē ī′, -âr′ē ē′). *Rom. Hist.* a gladiator equipped with a net for casting over his opponent. [1640–50; < L, equiv. to *rēt-* (s. of *rēte* net) + *-i-* -I- + *-ārius* -ARIUS]

re·ti·ar·y (rē′shē er′ē), *adj.* **1.** using a net or any entangling device. **2.** netlike. **3.** making a net or web, as a spider. [1640–50; < L *rēt-* (s. of *rēte*) net + -I- + -ARY]

ret·i·cent (ret′ə sənt), *adj.* **1.** disposed to be silent or not to speak freely; reserved. **2.** reluctant or restrained. [1825–35; < L *reticent-* (s. of *reticēns*), prp. of *reticēre* to be silent, equiv. to *re-* RE- + *-tic-*, comb. form of *tacēre* to be silent (cf. TACIT) + *-ent-* -ENT] —**ret′i·cence, ret′i·cen·cy,** *n.* —**ret′i·cent·ly,** *adv.*
—**Syn. 1.** taciturn, quiet, uncommunicative. —**Ant. 1.** talkative, voluble.

ret·i·cle (ret′i kəl), *n. Optics.* a network of fine lines, wires, or the like placed in the focus of the eyepiece of an optical instrument. Also, **reticule.** [1650–60; < L *rēticulum* little net, equiv. to *rēt-* (s. of *rēte*) net + *-i-* -I- + *-culum* -CLE[1]]

re·tic·u·lar (ri tik′yə lər), *adj.* **1.** having the form of a net; netlike. **2.** intricate or entangled. **3.** *Anat.* of or pertaining to a reticulum. [1590–1600; < NL *rēticulāris,* equiv. to L *rēticul(um)* RETICLE + *-āris* -AR[1]] —**re·tic′u·lar·ly,** *adv.*

retic′ular forma′tion, a network of neurons in the brainstem involved in consciousness, regulation of breathing, the transmission of sensory stimuli to higher brain centers, and the constantly shifting muscular activity that supports the body against gravity. [1885–90]

re·tic·u·late (*adj.* ri tik′yə lit, -lāt′; *v.* ri tik′yə lāt′), *adj., v.*, **-lat·ed, -lat·ing.** —*adj.* **1.** netted; covered with a network. **2.** netlike. **3.** *Bot.* having the veins or nerves disposed like the threads of a net. —*v.t.* **4.** to form into a network. **5.** to cover or mark with a network. —*v.i.* **6.** to form a network. [1650–60; < L *rēticulātus* net-like, equiv. to *rēticul(um)* RETICLE + *-ātus* -ATE[1]] —**re·tic′u·late·ly,** *adv.*

retic′ulated trac′ery, *Archit.* tracery consisting in large part of a netlike arrangement of repeated geometrical figures. [1840–50]

retic′ulate py′thon, a python, *Python reticulatus,* of southeastern Asia and the East Indies, sometimes growing to a length of 32 ft. (10 m): usually considered to be the largest snake in the world.

re·tic·u·la·tion (ri tik′yə lā′shən), *n.* a reticulated formation, arrangement, or appearance; network. [1665–75; RETICULATE + -ION]

ret·i·cule (ret′i kyōōl′), *n.* **1.** a small purse or bag, originally of network but later of silk, rayon, etc. **2.** *Optics.* reticle. [1720–30; < F *réticule* < L *rēticulum* RETICLE]

re·tic·u·lo·cyte (ri tik′yə lə sīt′), *n. Anat.* a very young red blood cell, sampled as a measure of red blood cell formation; reticulated erythrocyte. [1920–25; RETICUL(UM) + -O- + CYTE]

re·tic·u·lo·en·do·the·li·al (ri tik′yə lō en′dō thē′lē əl), *adj. Cell Biol.* **1.** pertaining to, resembling, or involving cells of the reticuloendothelial system. **2.** of a cell, having both reticular and endothelial characteristics. [1920–25; RETICUL(UM) + -O- + ENDOTHELIAL]

reticuloendothe′lial sys′tem, *Immunol.* the aggregate of the phagocytic cells, including certain cells of the bone marrow, lymphatic system, liver, and spleen, that have reticular and endothelial characteristics and function in the immune system's defense against foreign bodies. *Abbr.:* RES [1920–25]

re·tic·u·lum (ri tik′yə ləm), *n., pl.* **-la** (-lə) for 1–3, *gen.* **-li** (-lī′) for 4. **1.** a network; any reticulated system or structure. **2.** *Anat.* **a.** a network of intercellular fibers in certain tissues. **b.** a network of structures in the endoplasm or nucleus of certain cells. **3.** *Zool.* the second stomach of ruminating animals, between the rumen and the omasum. See diag. under **ruminant.** **4.** (*cap.*) *Astron.* the Net, a southern constellation between Dorado and Hydrus. [1650–60; < L *rēticulum* little net; see RETICLE]

re·ti·form (rē′tə fôrm′, ret′ə-), *adj.* netlike; reticulate. [1685–95; < NL *rētiformis,* equiv. to L *rēt-* (s. of *rēte*) net + *-i-* -I- + *-formis* -FORM]

ret·i·na (ret′n ə, ret′nə), *n., pl.* **ret·i·nas, ret·i·nae** (ret′n ē′). *Anat.* the innermost coat of the posterior part of the eyeball that receives the image produced by the lens, is continuous with the optic nerve, and consists of several layers, one of which contains the rods and cones that are sensitive to light. See diag. under **eye.** [1350–1400; ME *ret(h)ina* < ML *rētina,* perh. equiv. to L *rēt-* (s. of *rēte*) net + *-ina* -INE[1]]

Ret·in-A (ret′n ā′), *Trademark.* a brand of tretinoin, used esp. to reduce wrinkles caused by overexposure to the sun. [1975–80]

ret·i·nac·u·lum (ret′n ak′yə ləm), *n., pl.* **-la** (-lə). **1.** *Anat., Zool.* any of various small structures that hook, clasp, or bind other structures to move them or hold them in place. **2.** *Entomol.* a bristle on the butterfly forewing that clasps to the frenulum of the hindwing. [1815–25; < NL; L *retināculum* tether, rope which holds fast or restrains, equiv. to *retin(ēre)* to hold fast, RETAIN + *-ā-* (from v. stems ending in *-ā-*; cf. GUBERNACULUM) + *-culum* -CULE[2]]

ret·i·nal[1] (ret′n əl), *adj.* of or pertaining to the retina of the eye. [1830–40; RETIN(A) + -AL[1]]

ret·i·nal[2] (ret′n al′, -ôl′), *n. Biochem.* an orange pigment, $C_{20}H_{28}O$, that is the active component of rhodopsin and is liberated upon the absorption of light in the vision cycle; vitamin A aldehyde. Also, **ret·i·nene** (ret′n ēn′). [1940–45; RETIN(A) + -AL[3]]

ret·i·nite (ret′n īt′), *n. Mineral.* any of various fossil resins, esp. one derived from brown coal. [1815–25; < F *rétinite,* equiv. to *rétin-* (comb. form of Gk *rhētínē* RESIN) + *-ite* -ITE[1]]

ret·i·ni·tis (ret′n ī′tis), *n. Ophthalmol.* inflammation of the retina. [1860–65; < NL; see RETINA, -ITIS]

retini′tis pig·men·to′sa (pig′men tō′sə, -mən-), *Ophthalm.* degeneration of the retina manifested by night blindness and gradual loss of peripheral vision, eventually resulting in tunnel vision or total blindness. [1860–65; < NL: pigmentary retinitis. See PIGMENT, -OSE[1]]

ret·ino·blas·to·ma (ret′nō bla stō′mə), *n., pl.* **-mas, -ma·ta** (-mə tə). *Pathol.* an inheritable tumor of the eye. [1920–25; RETIN(A) + -O- + BLASTOMA]

ret·i·noid (ret′n oid′), *n.* **1.** *Biochem.* any of a group of substances related to vitamin A and functioning like vitamin A in the body. —*adj.* **2.** resembling the retina. [1975–80; RETIN(OL) + -OID]

CONCISE PRONUNCIATION KEY: act, cāpe, dâre, pärt; set, ēqual; *if,* īce; ox, ōver, ôrder, oil, bŏŏk, bōōt, out; up, ûrge; child; sing; shoe; thin, *th*at; zh as in *treasure.* ə = *a* as in *alone,* *e* as in *system,* *i* as in *easily,* *o* as in *gallop,* *u* as in *circus;* ᵊ as in *fire* (fīᵊr), *hour* (ouᵊr). l and n can serve as syllabic consonants, as in *cradle* (krād′l), and *button* (but′n). See the full key inside the front cover.

re·shin′gle, *v.t.*, **-gled, -gling.**
re·shoe′, *v.t.*, **-shod, -shoe·ing.**
re·shoot′, *v.*, **-shot, -shoot·ing;** *n.*
re·short′en, *v.*
re·shoul′der, *v.t.*
re·show′, *v.*, **-showed, -shown** or **-showed, show·ing.**
re·show′er, *v.*
re·shuf′fle, *v.* **-fled, -fling,** *n.*
re·shut′, *v.*, **-shut, -shut·ting.**
re·sick′en, *v.*
re·sift′, *v.t.*
re·sight′, *v.t.*
re·sig′nal, *v.* **-naled, -nal·ing** or (*esp. Brit.*) **-nalled, -nal·ling.**
re·sil′ver, *v.t.*
re·sim′mer, *v.*
re·sit′, *v.*, **-sat, -sit·ting.**
re·site′, *v.t.*, **-sit·ed, -sit·ing.**
re·sit′u·ate′, *v.t.*, **-at·ed, -at·ing.**
re·size′, *v.t.*, **-sized, -siz·ing.**
re·sketch′, *v.t.*
re·slan′der, *v.t.*
re·slate′, *v.t.*, **-slat·ed, -slat·ing.**
re·smooth′, *v.t.*
re·soak′, *v.*
re·so′cial·ize′, *v.*, **-ized, -iz·ing.**
re·sod′, *v.t.*, **-sod·ded, -sod·ding.**
re·sof′ten, *v.*
re·sol′der, *v.*
re′so·lic′it, *v.*
re′so·lic′i·ta′tion, *n.*
re′so·lid′i·fi·ca′tion, *n.*
re′so·lid′i·fy′, *v.*, **-fied, fy·ing.**
re·sow′, *v.t.*, **-sowed, -sown** or **-sowed, -sow·ing.**
re·space′, *v.t.*, **-spaced, -spac·ing.**

ret·i·nol (ret′n ôl′, -ol′), *n.* **1.** See **vitamin A. 2.** *Chem.* a yellowish oil, $C_{32}H_{16}$, obtained by the distillation of resin, used as a solvent and as an antiseptic. [1830–40; < Gk *rhētín(ē)* RESIN + -OL[1]]

ret·i·nop·a·thy (ret′n op′ə thē), *n. Ophthalm.* any diseased condition of the retina, esp. one that is noninflammatory. [1930–35; RETIN(A) + -O- + -PATHY]

ret·i·no·scope (ret′n ə skōp′), *n. Ophthalm.* an apparatus that determines the refractive power of the eye by observing the lights and shadows on the pupil when a mirror illumines the retina; skiascope. [RETIN(A) + -O- + -SCOPE]

ret·i·nos·co·py (ret′n os′kə pē, ret′n ə skō′pē), *n. Ophthalm.* an objective method of determining the refractive error of an eye. [1880–85; RETIN(A) + -O- + -SCOPY] —**ret·i·no·scop·ic** (ret′n ə skop′ik), *adj.* —**ret′i·no·scop′i·cal·ly,** *adv.* —**ret′i·nos′co·pist,** *n.*

ret·i·nue (ret′n o͞o′, -yo͞o′), *n.* a body of retainers in attendance upon an important personage; suite. [1325–75; ME *retinue* < MF, n. use of fem. ptp. of *retenir* to RETAIN] —**ret′i·nued′,** *adj.*

re·tin·u·la (ri tin′yə lə), *n., pl.* **-lae** (-lē′). *n. Anat.* a group of elongate neural receptor cells forming part of an arthropod compound eye: each retinula cell leads to a nerve fiber passing to the optic ganglion. [1875–80; < NL; see RETINA, -ULE] —**re·tin′u·lar,** *adj.*

re·tir·ant (ri tīər′ənt), *n.* retiree. [RETIRE + -ANT]

re·tire (ri tīər′), *v.,* **-tired, -tir·ing,** *n.* —*v.i.* **1.** to withdraw, or go away or apart, to a place of privacy, shelter, or seclusion: *He retired to his study.* **2.** to go to bed: *He retired at midnight.* **3.** to withdraw from office, business, or active life, usually because of age: *to retire at the age of sixty.* **4.** to fall back or retreat in an orderly fashion and according to plan, as from battle, an untenable position, danger, etc. **5.** to withdraw or remove oneself: *After announcing the guests, the butler retired.* —*v.t.* **6.** to withdraw from circulation by taking up and paying, as bonds, bills, etc.; redeem. **7.** to withdraw or lead back (troops, ships, etc.), as from battle or danger; retreat. **8.** to remove from active service or the usual field of activity, as an army officer or business executive. **9.** to withdraw (a machine, ship, etc.) permanently from its normal service, usually for scrapping; take out of use. **10.** *Sports.* to put out (a batter, side, etc.). —*n. Literary.* **11.** a place of withdrawal; retreat: *a cool retire from summer's heat.* **12.** retirement or withdrawal, as from worldly matters or the company of others. [1525–35; < MF *retirer* to withdraw, equiv. to *re-* RE- + *tirer* to draw] —**re·tir′er,** *n.*
—**Syn. 5.** leave, withdraw. See **depart.**

re·ti·ré (*Fr.* Rə tē Rā′), *n., pl.* **-ti·rés** (*Fr.* -tē Rā′). *Ballet.* a movement in which the dancer brings one foot to the knee of the supporting leg and then returns it to the fifth position. [< F, ptp. of *retirer* to RETIRE]

re·tired (ri tīərd′), *adj.* **1.** withdrawn from or no longer occupied with one's business or profession: *a retired banker.* **2.** due or given a retired person: *retired pay.* **3.** secluded or sequestered: *a retired little village.* [1580–90; RETIRE + -ED[2]] —**re·tired′ly,** *adv.* —**re·tired′ness,** *n.*
—**Syn. 3.** isolated, removed, solitary.

re·tir·ee (ri tī rē′, -tīər′ē), *n.* a person who has retired from an occupation or profession. [1940–45, *Amer.*; RETIRE + -EE]

re·tire·ment (ri tīər′mənt), *n.* **1.** the act of retiring or the state of being retired. **2.** removal or withdrawal from service, office, or business. **3.** the portion of a person's life during which a person is retired. **4.** a pension or other income on which a retired person lives: *His retirement is barely enough to pay the rent.* **5.** withdrawal into privacy or seclusion. **6.** privacy or seclusion. **7.** a private or secluded place. **8.** *Mil.* orderly withdrawal of a military force, according to plan, without pressure from the enemy. **9.** withdrawal of securities from the market by a corporation, as through payment at maturity, repurchase, or exchange. —*adj.* **10.** noting or pertaining to retirement: *retirement pay.* [1590–1600; < MF; see RETIRE, -MENT]

retire′ment commu′nity, a group of houses in a suburban area or a town designed primarily for retired persons. [1975–80]

retire′ment plan′, **1.** a systematic plan made and kept by an individual for setting aside income for his or her future retirement. **2.** See **pension plan** (def. 1).

re·tir·ing (ri tīər′ing), *adj.* **1.** that retires. **2.** withdrawing from contact with others; reserved; shy. [1540–50; RETIRE + -ING[2]] —**re·tir′ing·ly,** *adv.* —**re·tir′ing·ness,** *n.*
—**Syn. 2.** diffident, bashful, timid.

re·took (rē to͝ok′), *v.* pt. of **retake.**

re·tool (rē to͞ol′), *v.t.* **1.** to replace or rearrange the tools and machinery of (a factory). **2.** to reorganize or rearrange, usually for the purpose of updating: *to retool the industrial organization.* —*v.i.* **3.** to replace or rearrange the tools of a factory. **4.** to replace the stamping machinery of a factory, esp. to make a remodeled product. [1935–40; RE- + TOOL] —**re·tool′a·ble,** *adj.*

CONCISE ETYMOLOGY KEY: <, descended or borrowed from; >, whence; b., blend of, blended; c., cognate with; cf., compare; deriv., derivative; equiv., equivalent; imit., imitative; obl., oblique; r., replacing; s., stem; sp., spelling, spelled; resp., respelling, respelled; trans., translation; ?, origin unknown; *, unattested; ‡, probably earlier than. See the full key inside the front cover.

re·tor·sion (ri tôr′shən), *n. Internat. Law.* retaliation or reprisal by one state identical or similar to an act by an offending state, such as high tariffs or discriminating duties. Also, **retortion.** [1650–60; < ML *retorsiōn-* (s. of *retorsiō,* var. of *retortiō*); see RETORTION]

re·tort[1] (ri tôrt′), *v.t.* **1.** to reply to, usually in a sharp or retaliatory way; reply in kind to. **2.** to return (an accusation, epithet, etc.) upon the person uttering it. **3.** to answer (an argument or the like) by another to the contrary. —*n.* **4.** a severe, incisive, or witty reply, esp. one that counters a first speaker's statement, argument, etc. **5.** the act of retorting. [1590–1600; < L *retortus* (ptp. of *retorquēre* to bend back), equiv. to *re-* RE- + *torqu(ēre)* to twist, bend + *-tus* ptp. suffix, with *-qut-* > *-t-*] —**re·tort′er,** *n.*
—**Syn. 1.** retaliate. **4.** riposte, rejoinder, response. See **answer.**

re·tort[2] (ri tôrt′), *n.* **1.** *Chem.* **a.** a vessel, commonly a glass bulb with a long neck bent downward, used for distilling or decomposing substances by heat. **b.** a refractory chamber, generally cylindrically shaped, within which some substance, as ore or coal, is heated as part of a smelting or manufacturing process. **c.** an airtight, usually cylindrical vessel of fire clay or iron, used in the destructive distillation chiefly of coal and wood in the manufacture of illuminating gas. **2.** a sterilizer for food cans. —*v.t.* **3.** to sterilize food after it is sealed in a container, by steam or other heating methods. **4.** *Chem.* to subject (shale, ore, etc.) to heat and possibly reduced pressure in order to produce fuel oil, metal, etc. [1550–60; < MF *retorte* < ML *retorta,* n. use of fem. of L *retortus;* see RETORT[1]]

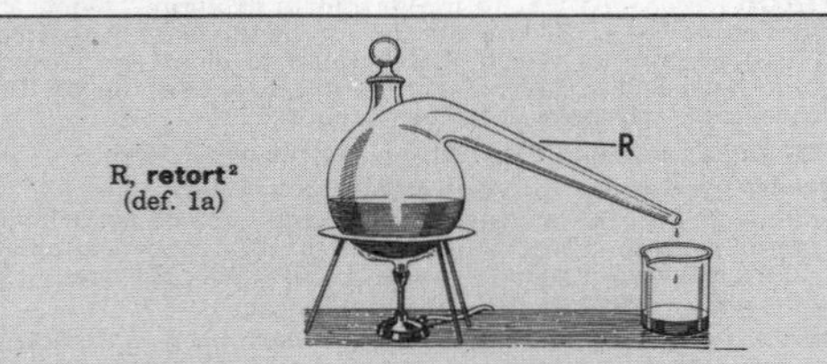

R, **retort**[2] (def. 1a)

re·tor·tion (ri tôr′shən), *n.* **1.** the act of turning or bending back. **2.** retaliation. **3.** *Internat. Law.* retorsion. [1585–95; < ML *retortiōn-* (s. of *retortiō*), equiv. to L *retort(us)* (see RETORT[1]) + *-iōn-* -ION]

re·touch (*v.* rē tuch′; *n.* rē′tuch′, rē tuch′), *v.t.* **1.** to improve with new touches, highlights, or the like; touch up or rework, as a painting or makeup. **2.** *Photog.* to alter (a negative or positive) after development by adding or removing lines, lightening areas, etc., with a pencil, brush, or knife. **3.** to dye, tint, or bleach (a new growth of hair) to match or blend with the color of an earlier and previously dyed growth. —*n.* **4.** an added touch to a picture, painting, paint job, etc., by way of improvement or alteration. **5.** an act or instance of dyeing new growth of hair to blend with previously dyed hair. [1675–85; < MF *retoucher,* equiv. to *re-* RE- + *toucher* to TOUCH] —**re·touch′a·ble,** *adj.* —**re·touch′er,** *n.*

re-trace (rē trās′), *v.t.,* **-traced, -trac·ing.** to trace again, as lines in writing or drawing. Also, **retrace.** [1750–60; RE- + TRACE[1]]

re·trace (ri trās′), *v.t.,* **-traced, -trac·ing. 1.** to trace backward; go back over: *to retrace one's steps.* **2.** to go back over with the memory. **3.** to go over again with the sight or attention. **4.** re-trace. [1690–1700; < F *retracer,* MF *retracier,* equiv. to *re-* RE- + *tracier* to TRACE[1]] —**re·trace′a·ble,** *adj.* —**re·trace′ment,** *n.*

re·tract[1] (ri trakt′), *v.t.* **1.** to draw back or in: *to retract fangs.* —*v.i.* **2.** to draw back within itself or oneself, fold up, or the like, or to be capable of doing this: *The blade retracts.* [1400–50; late ME *retracten* < L *retractus,* ptp. of *retrahere* to draw back, equiv. to *re-* RE- + *tractus* (see TRACT[1])]

re·tract[2] (ri trakt′), *v.t.* **1.** to withdraw (a statement, opinion, etc.) as inaccurate or unjustified, esp. formally or explicitly; take back. **2.** to withdraw or revoke (a decree, promise, etc.). —*v.i.* **3.** to draw or shrink back. **4.** to withdraw a promise, vow, etc. **5.** to make a disavowal of a statement, opinion, etc.; recant. [1535–45; < L *retractāre* to reconsider, withdraw, equiv. to *re-* RE- + *tractāre* to drag, pull, take in hand (freq. of *trahere* to pull)] —**re·tract′a·ble, re·tract′i·ble,** *adj.* —**re·tract′a·bil′i·ty, re·tract′i·bil′i·ty,** *n.* —**re·trac·ta·tion** (rē′trak tā′shən), *n.*
—**Syn. 1, 2.** deny, renounce, recant, abrogate, nullify, annul.

re·trac·tile (ri trak′til), *adj. Zool.* capable of being drawn back or in, as the head of a tortoise; exhibiting the power of retraction. [1770–80; RETRACT[1] + -ILE] —**re·trac·til·i·ty** (rē′trak til′i tē), *n.*

re·trac·tion (ri trak′shən), *n.* **1.** the act of retracting or the state of being retracted. **2.** withdrawal of a promise, statement, opinion, etc.: *His retraction of the libel came too late.* **3.** retractile power. [1350–1400; ME *retraccioun* < L *retractiōn-* (s. of *retractiō*), equiv. to L *retract(us)* (see RETRACT[1]) + *-iōn-* -ION]

re·trac·tive (ri trak′tiv), *adj.* tending or serving to retract. [1350–1400; ME *retractif* < OF; see RETRACT[1], -IVE] —**re·trac′tive·ly,** *adv.* —**re·trac′tive·ness,** *n.*

re·trac·tor (ri trak′tər), *n.* **1.** a person or thing that retracts. **2.** *Anat.* a muscle that retracts an organ or protruded part. **3.** *Surg.* an instrument or appliance for drawing back an impeding part, as the edge of an incision. **4.** a mechanism, device, or the like that regulates retraction: *to adjust the retractor on a seat belt.* [1830–40; RETRACT[1] + -OR[2]]

re·train (rē trān′), *v.t.* **1.** to train again, esp. for a different vocation or different tasks. —*v.i.* **2.** to be retrained. [1930–35; RE- + TRAIN] —**re·train′a·ble,** *adj.*

re·train·ee (rē′trā nē′), *n.* a person who is being retrained. [1940–45; RETRAIN + -EE]

re·tral (rē′trəl, re′-), *adj.* at or toward the back; posterior. [1870–75; RETR(O)- + -AL[1]] —**re′tral·ly,** *adv.*

re-tread (rē tred′), *v.t., v.i.,* **-trod, -trod·den** or **-trod, -tread·ing.** to tread again. [1590–1600; RE- + TREAD]

re·tread (*v.* rē tred′; *n.* rē′tred′), *v.,* **-tread·ed, -tread·ing,** *n.* —*v.t.* **1.** to put a new tread on (a worn pneumatic tire casing) either by recapping or by cutting fresh treads in the smooth surface. **2.** to repeat or do over, esp. without the boldness or inventiveness of the original. —*n.* **3.** a tire that has been retreaded. **4.** *Slang.* a person returned to active work after retirement, dismissal, etc. **5.** a person retrained for a new or more modern job or task. **6.** *Informal.* a repeating, reviving, or reworking of an old or familiar idea, presentation, story, etc., esp. when unimaginative or hackneyed; rehash: *a boring retread of a classic movie.* **7.** *Slang.* a person representing older or previous times, ideas, policies, etc., esp. when they are deemed passé or tiresome. [1885–90; RE- + TREAD]

re-treat (rē trēt′), *v.t., v.i.* to treat again. [1880–85; RE- + TREAT]

re·treat (ri trēt′), *n.* **1.** the forced or strategic withdrawal of an army or an armed force before an enemy, or the withdrawing of a naval force from action. **2.** the act of withdrawing, as into safety or privacy; retirement; seclusion. **3.** a place of refuge, seclusion, or privacy: *The library was his retreat.* **4.** an asylum, as for the insane. **5.** a retirement or a period of retirement for religious exercises and meditation. **6.** *Mil.* **a.** a flag-lowering ceremony held at sunset on a military post. **b.** the bugle call or drumbeat played at this ceremony. **7.** the recession of a surface, as a wall or panel, from another surface beside it. **8. beat a retreat,** to withdraw or retreat, esp. hurriedly or in disgrace. —*v.i.* **9.** to withdraw, retire, or draw back, esp. for shelter or seclusion. **10.** to make a retreat: *The army retreated.* **11.** to slope backward; recede: *a retreating chin.* **12.** to draw or lead back. [1300–50; (n.) ME *retret* < OF, var. of *retrait,* n. use of ptp. of *retraire* to draw back < L *retrahere* (*re-* RE- + *trahere* to draw; see RETRACT[1]); (v.) late ME *retreten* < MF *retraitier* < L *retractāre* to RETRACT[2]] —**re·treat′al,** *adj.* —**re·treat′er,** *n.* —**re·treat′ive,** *adj.*
—**Syn. 2.** departure, withdrawal. **3.** shelter. **9.** leave, pull back. See **depart.** —**Ant. 1, 9, 10.** advance.

re·treat·ant (ri trēt′nt), *n.* a person who takes part in a religious retreat. [1875–80; RETREAT + -ANT]

re·treat·ism (ri trē′tiz əm), *n. Sociol.* the rejection of culturally prescribed goals and the conventional means for attaining them. [RETREAT + -ISM] —**re·treat′ist,** *n.*

re·trench (ri trench′), *v.t.* **1.** to cut down, reduce, or diminish; curtail (expenses). **2.** to cut off or remove. **3.** *Mil.* to protect by a retrenchment. —*v.i.* **4.** to economize; reduce expenses: *They retrenched by eliminating half of the workers.* [1600–10; < F *retrencher* (obs. var. of *retrancher*), MF *retrenchier,* equiv. to *re-* RE- + *trenchier* to TRENCH] —**re·trench′a·ble,** *adj.* —**re·trench′er,** *n.*
—**Syn. 1.** decrease, abridge, cut.

re·trench·ment (ri trench′mənt), *n.* **1.** the act of retrenching; a cutting down or off, as by the reduction of expenses. **2.** *Fort.* an interior work that cuts off a part of a fortification from the rest, and to which a garrison may retreat. [1590–1600; < F *retrenchement.* See RETRENCH, -MENT]

ret·ri·bu·tion (re′trə byo͞o′shən), *n.* **1.** requital according to merits or deserts, esp. for evil. **2.** something given or inflicted in such requital. **3.** *Theol.* the distribution of rewards and punishments in a future life. [1350–1400; ME *retribucioun* < MF < LL *retribūtiōn-* (s. of *retribūtiō*) punishment, reward as result of judgment, equiv. to L *retribūt(us)* (ptp. of *retribuere* to restore, give back; see RE-, TRIBUTE) + *-iōn-* -ION]
—**Syn. 1, 2.** retaliation, repayment, recompense. See **revenge.** —**Ant. 1, 2.** pardon.

re·trib·u·tive (ri trib′yə tiv), *adj.* characterized by or involving retribution: *retributive justice.* Also, **re·trib·u·to·ry** (ri trib′yə tôr′ē, -tōr′ē). [1670–80; obs. *retribute* to make retribution (< L *retribūtus;* see RETRIBUTION) + -IVE] —**re·trib′u·tive·ly,** *adv.*

re·trib·u·tiv·ism (ri trib′yə tə viz′əm), *n.* a policy or theory of criminal justice that advocates the punishment of criminals in retribution for the harm they have inflicted. [1965–70; RETRIBUTIVE + -ISM] —**re·trib′u·tiv·ist,** *adj.*

re·triev·al (ri trē′vəl), *n.* **1.** the act of retrieving. **2.** the chance of recovery or restoration: *lost beyond retrieval.* [1635–45; RETRIEVE + -AL[2]]

re·trieve (ri trēv′), *v.,* **-trieved, -triev·ing,** *n.* —*v.t.* **1.** to recover or regain: *to retrieve the stray ball.* **2.** to bring back to a former and better state; restore: *to retrieve one's fortunes.* **3.** to make amends for: *to retrieve an error.* **4.** to make good; repair: *to retrieve a loss.* **5.** *Hunting.* (of hunting dogs) to fetch (killed or wounded

re·spade′, *v.t.,* **-spad·ed, -spad·ing.**
re·spark′, *v.t.*
re′spec·i·fi·ca′tion, *n.*
re·spec′i·fy′, *v.,* **-fied, -fy·ing.**
re·spice′, *v.t.,* **-spiced, -spic·ing.**
re·spir′it·u·al·ize′, *v.t.,* **-ized, -iz·ing.**
re·splice′, *v.t.,* **-spliced, -splic·ing.**
re·spot′, *v.,* **-spot·ted, -spot·ting.**
re·spray′, *v.*
re·spread′, *v.,* **-spread, -spread·ing.**
re·spring′, *v.,* **-sprang** or, often, **-sprung, -spring·ing.**
re·sprin′kle, *v.,* **-kled, -kling.**
re·sprout′, *v.*
re·squan′der, *v.t.*
re·stab′, *v.,* **-stabbed, -stab·bing.**
re′sta·bi·li·za′tion, *n.*
re·sta′bi·lize′, *v.t.,* **-lized, -liz·ing.**
re·sta′ble, *v.t.,* **-bled, -bling.**
re·stack′, *v.t.*
re·staff′, *v.*
re·stage′, *v.t.,* **-staged, -stag·ing.**
re·stain′, *v.*
re·stamp′, *v.*
re′stand·ard·i·za′tion, *n.*
re·stand′ard·ize′, *v.t.,* **-ized, -iz·ing.**
re·start′, *v., n.*
re·sta′tion, *v.t.*
re′ster·i·li·za′tion, *n.*

game). **6.** to draw back or reel in (a fishing line). **7.** to rescue; save. **8.** (in tennis, squash, handball, etc.) to make an in-bounds return of (a shot requiring running with the hand extended). **9.** *Computers.* to locate and read (data) from storage, as for display on a monitor. —*v.i.* **10.** *Hunting.* to retrieve game. **11.** to retrieve a fishing line. —*n.* **12.** an act of retrieving; recovery. **13.** the possibility of recovery. [1375–1425; late ME *retreven* < MF *retroev-, retreuv-,* tonic s. of *retrouver* to find again, equiv. to *re-* RE- + *trouver* to find; see TROVER] —**re·triev′a·ble,** *adj.* —**re·triev′a·bil′i·ty,** *n.*
—**Syn. 1.** See **recover.**

re·triev·er (ri trē′vər), *n.* **1.** a person or thing that retrieves. **2.** one of any of several breeds of dogs having a coarse, thick, oily coat, trained to retrieve game. **3.** any dog trained to retrieve game. [1480–90; RETRIEVE + -ER[1]]

Labrador retriever, 2 ft. (0.6 m) high at shoulder

ret·ro (re′trō), *adj. Informal.* **1.** retroactive: *retro pay.* **2.** of or designating the style of an earlier time: *retro clothes.* [by shortening]

retro-, a prefix occurring in loanwords from Latin meaning "backward" (*retrogress*); on this model, used in the formation of compound words (*retrorocket*). [< L, repr. *retrō* (adv.), backward, back, behind]

ret·ro·act (re′trō akt′), *v.i.* **1.** to act in opposition; react. **2.** to have reference to or influence on past occurrences. [1785–95; RETRO- + ACT]

ret·ro·ac·tion (re′trō ak′shən), *n.* action that is opposed or contrary to the preceding action. [1560–70; RETRO- + ACTION]

ret·ro·ac·tive (re′trō ak′tiv), *adj.* **1.** operative with respect to past occurrences, as a statute; retrospective: *a retroactive law.* **2.** pertaining to a pay raise effective as of a past date. [1605–15; RETRO- + ACTIVE] —**ret′ro·ac′tive·ly,** *adv.* —**ret′ro·ac·tiv′i·ty,** *n.*

ret·ro·bul·bar (re′trō bul′bər, -bär), *adj. Anat.* situated behind the eyeball. [RETRO- + BULBAR]

ret·ro·cede[1] (re′trə sēd′), *v.i.,* **-ced·ed, -ced·ing.** to go back; recede; retire. [1645–55; < L *retrōcēdere* to go back, retire, equiv. to *retrō-* RETRO- + *cēdere* to go, move; see CEDE] —**ret′ro·ced′ence,** *n.* —**ret·ro·ces·sive** (re′tre ses′iv), *adj.*

ret·ro·cede[2] (re′trə sēd′), *v.t.,* **-ced·ed, -ced·ing. 1.** to cede back: *to retrocede a territory.* **2.** *Insurance.* (of a reinsurance company) to cede (all or part of a reinsured risk) to another reinsurance company. [1810–20; RETRO- + CEDE] —**ret′ro·ced′ence, ret·ro·ces·sion** (re′trə-sesh′ən), *n.*

ret·ro·ces·sion·aire (re′trə sesh′ə nâr′), *n. Insurance.* a reinsurance company that accepts or takes a retrocession. [RETROCESSION + -AIRE]

ret·ro·choir (re′trə kwīər′), *n.* that part of a church behind the choir or the main altar. [1840–50; < ML *retrōchorus.* See RETRO-, CHOIR]

ret·ro·cog·nate (re′trō kog′nāt), *adj. Psychol.* being or pertaining to memory or extrasensory perception of past events. [RETRO- + COGNATE]

ret·ro·di·rec·tive (re′trō di rek′tiv, -dī-), *adj. Optics.* (of a mirror, reflector, etc.) having three reflecting surfaces so oriented that a ray of light is reflected in a direction parallel but opposite to its original direction. [RETRO- + DIRECTIVE]

ret·ro·fire (re′trō fīər′), *v.,* **-fired, -fir·ing.** *Rocketry.* —*v.t.* **1.** to ignite (a retrorocket). —*v.i.* **2.** (of a retrorocket) to become ignited. [1960–65, *Amer.*; RETRO- + FIRE]

ret·ro·fit (*v.* re′trō fit′, re′trō fit′; *n., adj.* re′trō fit′), *v.,* **-fit·ted** or **-fit, -fit·ting,** *n., adj.* —*v.t.* **1.** to modify equipment (in airplanes, automobiles, a factory, etc.) that is already in service using parts developed or made available after the time of original manufacture. **2.** to install, fit, or adapt (a device or system) for use with something older: *to retrofit solar heating to a poorly insulated house.* —*v.i.* **3.** (of new or modified parts, equipment, etc.) to fit into or onto existing equipment. **4.** to replace existing parts, equipment, etc., with updated parts or systems. —*n.* **5.** something that has been retrofitted. **6.** an instance of updating, enlarging, etc., with new or modified equipment: *A retrofit could save thousands of dollars.* —*adj.* **7.** being or characterized by a retrofit: *retrofit units.* [RETRO- + FIT[1]] —**ret′ro·fit′ta·ble,** *adj.*

ret·ro·flex (re′trə fleks′), *adj.* **1.** bent backward; exhibiting retroflexion. **2.** *Phonet.* articulated with the tip of the tongue curled upward and back against or near the juncture of the hard and soft palates; cacuminal; cerebral; coronal. Also, **ret·ro·flexed** (re′trə flekst′). [1910–15; < L *retrōflexus* (ptp. of *retrōflectere* to bend back). See RETRO-, FLEX[1]]

ret·ro·flex·ion (re′trə flek′shən), *n.* **1.** a bending backward. **2.** *Pathol.* a bending backward of the body of the uterus upon the cervix. **3.** *Phonet.* **a.** retroflex articulation. **b.** the acoustic quality resulting from retroflex articulation; r-color. Also, **ret′ro·flec′tion.** [1835–45; < NL *retrōflexiōn-* (s. of *retrōflexiō*), equiv. to L *retrōflex(us)* RETROFLEX + *-iōn-* -ION]

ret′ro·fo·cus lens′ (re′trə fō′kəs), a wide-angle lens, for use on single-lens reflex cameras, of inverted telephoto design, with a back focus greater than the focal length. [1960–65; RETRO- + FOCUS]

ret·ro·gra·da·tion (re′trō grā dā′shən), *n.* **1.** backward movement. **2.** decline or deterioration. [1545–55; < LL *retrōgradātiōn-* (s. of *retrōgradātiō*), prob. equiv. to L *retrōgrad(us)* RETROGRADE + *-ātiō* -ATION, as trans. of Gk *anapodismós*] —**ret·ro·gra·da·to·ry** (re′trə grā′-də tôr′ē, -tōr′ē), *adj.*

ret·ro·grade (re′trə grād′), *adj., v.,* **-grad·ed, -grad·ing.** —*adj.* **1.** moving backward; having a backward motion or direction; retiring or retreating. **2.** inverse or reversed, as order. **3.** *Chiefly Biol.* exhibiting degeneration or deterioration. **4.** *Astron.* **a.** moving in an orbit in the direction opposite to that of the earth in its revolution around the sun. **b.** appearing to move on the celestial sphere in the direction opposite to the natural order of the signs of the zodiac, or from east to west. Cf. **direct** (def. 25). **5.** *Music.* proceeding from the last note to the first: *a melody in retrograde motion.* **6.** *Archaic.* contrary; opposed. —*v.i.* **7.** to move or go backward; retire or retreat. **8.** *Chiefly Biol.* to decline to a worse condition; degenerate. **9.** *Astron.* to have a retrograde motion. —*v.t.* **10.** *Archaic.* to turn back. [1350–1400; ME (adj.) < L *retrōgradus* going back, deriv. of *retrōgradī,* equiv. to *retrō-* RETRO- + *gradī* to step, go; see GRADE] —**ret′ro·grade′ly,** *adv.* —**ret′ro·grad′ing·ly,** *adv.*
—**Syn. 1.** withdrawing, receding. **2.** backward. **7.** withdraw, recede, retrocede.

ret′rograde amne′sia, a memory disorder characterized by an inability to remember events or experiences that occurred before a significant point in time.

ret·ro·gress (re′trə gres′, re′trə gres′), *v.i.* **1.** to go backward into an earlier and usually worse condition: *to retrogress to infantilism.* **2.** to move backward. [1810–20; < L *retrōgressus* ptp. of *retrōgradī* to go back or backward, equiv. to *retrō-* RETRO- + *gred-,* comb. form of *gradī* to step, go (see GRADE) + *-tus* ptp. suffix, with $dt > ss$]
—**Syn. 1.** decline, degenerate, retrograde, withdraw, retreat, revert.

ret·ro·gres·sion (re′trə gresh′ən), *n.* **1.** the act of retrogressing; movement backward. **2.** *Biol.* degeneration; retrograde metamorphosis; passing from a more complex to a simpler structure. [1640–50; < L *retrōgress(us)* (see RETROGRESS) + -ION]

ret·ro·gres·sive (re′trə gres′iv), *adj.* characterized by retrogression; degenerating. [1795–1805; < L *retrōgress(us)* (see RETROGRESS) + -IVE] —**ret′ro·gres′sive·ly,** *adv.*
—**Syn.** backward. —**Ant.** progressive.

ret·ro·len·tal (re′trō len′tl), *adj.* located or occurring behind a lens, as of the eye. [1940–45; RETRO- + L *lent-,* s. of *lēns* (see LENS) + -AL[1]]

retrolen′tal fibropla′sia, *Pathol.* an unusual eye disease occurring in premature infants, usually from being given high concentrations of oxygen, which causes abnormal formation of fibrous tissue behind the lens and often results in blindness. [1940–45]

ret·ro·lin·gual (re′trō ling′gwəl), *adj. Anat.* situated behind or near the base of the tongue. [RETRO- + LINGUAL]

ret·ro·re·flec·tive (re′trō ri flek′tiv), *adj.* of or pertaining to a surface, material, or device (**retroreflector**) that reflects light or other radiation back to its source; reflective. [1850–55; RETRO- + REFLECTIVE] —**ret′ro·re·flec′tion,** *n.*

ret·ro·re·flec·tor (re′trō ri flek′tər), *n.* See under **retroreflective.** [1945–50; RETRO- + REFLECTOR]

ret·ro·rock·et (re′trō rok′it), *n.* a small, auxiliary rocket engine, forming a part of a larger rocket vehicle and having its exhaust nozzle pointed toward the direction of flight, for decelerating the larger rocket, separating one stage from another, etc. Also, **ret′ro-rock′et.** [1945–50; RETRO- + ROCKET]

re·trorse (ri trôrs′, rē′trôrs), *adj.* turned backward. [1815–25; < L *retrōrsus,* contracted form of *retrōversus* bent backward, equiv. to *retrō-* RETRO- + *versus* (ptp. of *vertere* to turn); see RETROVERSION] —**re·trorse′ly,** *adv.*

ret·ro·ser·rate (re′trō ser′it, -āt), *adj. Bot., Zool.* having retrorse teeth or barbs. [1855–60; RETRO- + SERRATE]

ret·ro·ser·ru·late (re′trō ser′yə lit, -lāt′, -ser′ə-), *adj. Bot., Zool.* having tiny retrorse teeth or barbs. [1820–30; RETRO- + SERRULATE]

ret·ro·spect (re′trə spekt′), *n.* **1.** contemplation of the past; a survey of past time, events, etc. **2. in retrospect,** in looking back on past events; upon reflection: *It was, in retrospect, the happiest day of her life.* —*v.i.* **3.** to look back in thought; refer back (often fol. by *to*): *to retrospect to a period in one's youth.* —*v.t.* **4.** to look back upon; contemplate retrospectively. [1595–1605; prob. RETRO- + (PRO)SPECT]

ret·ro·spec·tion (re′trə spek′shən), *n.* **1.** the action, process, or faculty of looking back on things past. **2.** a survey of past events or experiences. [1625–35; RETROSPECT + -ION]

ret·ro·spec·tive (re′trə spek′tiv), *adj.* **1.** directed to the past; contemplative of past situations, events, etc. **2.** looking or directed backward. **3.** retroactive, as a statute. —*n.* **4.** an art exhibit showing an entire phase or representative examples of an artist's lifework. **5.** any exhibition or series of showings or performances, as of musical works or motion pictures, representing the work of an artist or performer over all or a major part of a career: *a retrospective of John Ford's movies.* [1655–65; RETROSPECT + -IVE] —**ret′ro·spec′tive·ly,** *adv.* —**ret′ro·spec′tive·ness,** *n.*

ret·rous·sage (re′trə säzh′; *Fr.* rə trōō sazh′), *n.* the technique or action, in etching or engraving, of drawing up ink from within the incised lines of an inked plate by deftly passing a soft cloth across its surface in order to spread ink to the adjacent areas. [1955–60; < F: a turning up, equiv. to *retrouss(er)* (see RETROUSSÉ) + *-age* -AGE]

re·trous·sé (re′trōō sā′; *Fr.* rə trōō sā′), *adj.* (esp. of the nose) turned up. [1830–40; < F, ptp. of *retrousser,* MF, equiv. to *re-* RE- + *trousser* to turn, tuck up; see TRUSS]

ret·ro·ver·sion (re′trə vûr′zhən, -shən), *n.* **1.** a looking or turning back. **2.** the resulting state or condition. **3.** *Pathol.* a tilting or turning backward of an organ or part: *retroversion of the uterus.* [1580–90; < L *retrōvers(us)* bent backward (*retrō-* RETRO- + *versus* ptp. of *vertere* to turn; see VERSE) + -ION] —**ret·ro·verse** (re′trə-vûrs′, re′trə vûrs′), *adj.* —**ret′ro·vert′ed,** *adj.*

Ret·ro·vir (re′trō vēr′), *Pharm., Trademark.* the international brand name for azidothymidine. Cf. **AZT, zidovudine.**

ret·ro·vi·rus (re′trə vī′rəs, re′trə vī′-), *n., pl.* **-rus·es.** any of a family of single-stranded RNA viruses having a helical envelope and containing an enzyme that allows for a reversal of genetic transcription, from RNA to DNA rather than the usual DNA to RNA, the newly transcribed viral DNA being incorporated into the host cell's DNA strand for the production of new RNA retroviruses: the family includes the AIDS virus and certain oncogene-carrying viruses implicated in various cancers. [1975–80; RETRO- + VIRUS] —**ret′ro·vi′ral,** *adj.*

re·trude (ri trōōd′), *v.t.,* **-trud·ed, -trud·ing.** *Dentistry.* to produce retrusion in. [1640–50; < L *retrūdere* to thrust back, equiv. to *re-* RE- + *trūdere* to thrust]

re·tru·sion (ri trōō′zhən, -shən), *n. Dentistry.* **1.** the act of moving a tooth backward. **2.** a condition characterized by the backward displacement of a tooth or teeth. [1650–60; < L *retrūs(us)* removed, concealed (ptp. of *retrūdere;* see RETRUDE) + -ION] —**re·tru·sive** (ri trōō′-siv), *adj.*

ret·si·na (ret′sə nə, ret sē′nə; *Gk.* re tsē′nä), *n.* a strong, resinated white or red wine of Greece and Cyprus. [1935–40; < ModGk < ML *resina* RESIN]

re·turn (ri tûrn′), *v.i.* **1.** to go or come back, as to a former place, position, or state: *to return from abroad; to return to public office; to return to work.* **2.** to revert to a former owner: *The money I gave him returns to me in the event of his death.* **3.** to revert or recur, as in thought, discourse, etc.: *He returned to his story.* **4.** to make a reply or retort: *She returned with a witty sally.* —*v.t.* **5.** to put, bring, take, give, or send back to the original place, position, etc.: *to return a book to a shelf; to return a child to her mother; to return the switch to off position.* **6.** to send or give back in reciprocation, recompense, or requital: *to return evil for good.* **7.** to reciprocate, repay, or react to (something sent, given, done, etc.) with something similar: *to return the enemy's fire; to return a favor.* **8.** *Law.* **a.** to give to a judge or official (a statement or a writ of actions done). **b.** to render (a verdict, decision, etc.). **9.** to reflect (light, sound, etc.). **10.** to yield (a profit, revenue, etc.), as in return for labor, expenditure, or investment. **11.** to report or announce officially: *to return a list of members.* **12.** to elect, as to a legislative body: *The voters returned him to office by a landslide.* **13.** *Mil.* to put (a weapon) back into its holder. **14.** *Cards.* to respond to (a suit led) by a similar lead: *She returned diamonds.* **15.** to turn back or in the reverse direction, as a served ball in tennis. **16.** *Chiefly Archit.* to cause to turn or proceed in a different direction from the previous line of direction; reverse: *to return a cornice at each end of a façade.* —*n.* **17.** the act or fact of returning as by going or coming back or bringing, sending, or giving back: *We should appreciate your return of the book immediately.* **18.** a recurrence: *the return of the moon each month.* **19.** reciprocation, repayment, or requital: *profits in return for outlay.* **20.** response or reply. **21.** a person or thing that is returned: *returns of mill goods.* **22.** the gain realized on an exchange of goods. **23.** Often, **returns.** a yield or profit, as from labor, land, business, or investment: *He received a quick return on his money.* **24.** Also called **tax return.** a statement, on an officially prescribed form, of income, deductions, exemptions, etc., and taxes due. **25.** Usually, **returns.** an official or unofficial report on a count of votes, candidates elected, etc.: *election returns.* **26.** *Chiefly Brit.* See **return ticket** (def. 2). **27.** *Archit.* **a.** the continuation of a molding, projec-

CONCISE PRONUNCIATION KEY: act, cāpe, dâre, pärt; set, ēqual; if, īce; ox, ōver, ôrder, oil, bŏŏk, bōōt, out; up, ûrge; child; sing; shoe; thin, *th*at; zh as in *treasure.* ə = a as in *alone,* e as in *system,* i as in *easily,* o as in *gallop,* u as in *circus;* ə as in *fire* (fīər), *hour* (ouər). l and n can serve as syllabic consonants, as in *cradle* (krād′l), and *button* (but′n). See the full key inside the front cover.

re·ster′i·lize′, *v.t.,* **-lized, -liz·ing.**
re·stick′, *v.t.*
re·stick′a·ble, *adj.*
re·stim′u·late′, *v.t.,* **-lat·ed, -lat·ing.**
re′stim·u·la′tion, *n.*
re·sting′, *v.,* **-stung, -sting·ing.**
re·stip′u·late′, *v.,* **-lat·ed, -lat·ing.**
re′stip·u·la′tion, *n.*
re·stir′, *v.,* **-stirred, -stir·ring.**
re·stitch′, *v.t.*
re·stow′, *v.t.*
re·straight′en, *v.*
re·strap′, *v.t.,* **-strapped, -strap·ping.**
re·strength′en, *v.*
re·stress′, *v.*
re·string′, *v.,* **-strung, -string·ing.**
re·string′er, *n.*
re·strive′, *v.i.,* **-strove, -striv·en, -striv·ing.**
re·stud′y, *n., pl.* **-stud·ies,** *v.,* **-stud·ied, -stud·y·ing.**
re·stuff′, *v.t.*
re·style′, *v.,* **-styled, -styl·ing.**
re′sub·ject′, *v.t.*
re′sub·jec′tion, *n.*
re·sub′li·mate′, *v.t.,* **-mat·ed, -mat·ing.**
re′sub·li·ma′tion, *n.*
re′sub·merge′, *v.,* **-merged, -merg·ing.**
re′sub·mis′sion, *n.*
re′sub·mit′, *v.,* **-mit·ted, -mit·ting.**
re′sub·scribe′, *v.,* **-scribed, -scrib·ing.**

tion, etc., in a different direction. **b.** a side or part that falls away from the front of any straight or flat member or area. **28.** a tablelike extension attached at a right angle to a desk at typing height, for holding a typewriter, computer, etc. **29.** a key or lever on a typewriter or other business machine that returns the carriage to the extreme right, or the typing element to the extreme left, for the beginning of a new line. **30.** *Computers.* See under **carriage return** (def. 1). **31.** *Sports.* **a.** the act of returning a ball. **b.** the ball that is returned. **32.** *Football.* a runback of a kick, intercepted pass, or fumble recovery. **33.** *Econ.* yield per unit as compared to the cost per unit involved in a specific industrial process. **34.** *Law.* **a.** the bringing or sending back of various documents, such as a writ, summons, or subpoena, with a brief written report usually endorsed upon it, by a sheriff, to the court from which it issued. **b.** a certified document by a great variety of officers, as assessors, collectors, and election officers. **c.** the report or certificate endorsed in such documents. **35.** *Cards.* a lead that responds to a partner's lead. **36.** *Theat.* a flat or drapery parallel to the tormentor for masking the offstage area and often completing the downstage part of a set. **37.** **returns, a.** merchandise shipped back to a supplier from a retailer or distributor as unsold or unsalable. **b.** merchandise returned to a retailer by a consumer.
—*adj.* **38.** of or pertaining to a return or returning: *a return trip.* **39.** sent, given, or done in return: *a return shot.* **40.** done or occurring again: *a return engagement of the opera.* **41.** noting a person or thing that is returned or returning to a place: *return cargo.* **42.** changing in direction; doubling or returning on itself: *a return twist in a road.* **43.** used for returning, recirculating, etc.: *the return road; a return pipe.* **44.** (of a game) played in order to provide the loser of an earlier game with the opportunity to win from the same opponent: *return match.* **45.** adequate, necessary, or provided to enable the return of a mailed package or letter to its sender: *return postage guaranteed; return address; return envelope.* [1275–1325; (v.) ME *retornen* < MF *retorner, returner,* OF (see RE-, TURN); (n.) ME < AF *retorn, return,* deriv. of OF *retorner, returner;* (adj.) deriv. of the n.]
—Syn. 4. rejoin. **5.** replace. **6.** exchange. **10.** pay, repay. **23.** revenue, income.

re·turn·a·ble (ri tûr′nə bəl), *adj.* **1.** that may be returned: *returnable merchandise.* **2.** requiring a return, as a writ to the court from which it is issued. —*n.* **3.** a beverage bottle or can that can be returned when empty for refund of a deposit. [1375–1425; 1960–65 for def. 3; late ME *retournable.* See RETURN, -ABLE] **—re·turn′a·bil′i·ty,** *n.*

return′ bend′, a 180° bend, as in a plumbing pipe.

re·turn-cocked (ri tûrn′kokt′), *adj.* (of a cock bead) situated at an angle or arris.

returned′ man′, *Canadian.* a member of the armed forces discharged in Canada after service overseas. [1910–15]

re·turn·ee (ri tûr nē′, -tûr′nē), *n.* **1.** a person who has returned, as from travels or a long absence. **2.** a person returning from overseas duty in the armed forces. [1940–45, *Amer.;* RETURN + -EE]

re·turn′-flue′ boil′er (ri tûrn′flo͞o′), a fire-tube boiler having flues that collect the combustion gases at the end of the boiler opposite the fire door and pass them through the boiler to an uptake above the fire door. Also called **re·turn′-tu′bu·lar boil′er** (ri tûrn′-to͞o′byə lər, -tyo͞o′-). [1885–90]

return′ing of′ficer, *Brit.* a public official appointed to conduct and preside at an election. [1720–30]

Return′ of the Na′tive, The, a novel (1878) by Thomas Hardy.

return′ on as′sets, *Accounting.* the amount of profit computed by dividing net income before interest and taxes by the cost of assets, usually expressed as a percentage. *Abbr.:* ROA

return′ on eq′uity, *Accounting.* the amount of profit computed by dividing net income before taxes less preferred dividends by the value of stockholders' equity, usually expressed as a percentage. *Abbr.:* ROE

return′ on invest′ment, the amount of profit, before tax and after depreciation, from an investment made, usually expressed as a percentage of the original total cost invested. *Abbr.:* ROI

return′ on net′ as′sets, *Accounting.* the amount of profit computed by dividing net income before interest and taxes by the cost of net assets, usually expressed as a percentage. *Abbr.:* RONA

return′ receipt′, a card bearing the signature of the recipient of registered postal matter, for return to the sender as proof of receipt.

return′ tick′et, 1. a ticket for the return portion of a trip. **2.** *Chiefly Brit.* a round-trip ticket. [1840–50]

re·tuse (ri to͞os′, -tyo͞os′), *adj.* having an obtuse or rounded apex with a shallow notch, as leaves. [1745–55; < L *retūsus* (ptp. of *retundere* to make blunt), equiv. to *re-* RE- + *tud-,* var. s. of *tundere* to beat, strike + *-tus* ptp. suffix, with *dt* > s]

CONCISE ETYMOLOGY KEY: <, descended or borrowed from; >, whence; b., blend of, blended; c., cognate with; cf., compare; deriv., derivative; equiv., equivalent; imit., imitative; obl., oblique; r., replacing; s., stem; sp., spelling, spelled; resp., respelling, respelled; trans., translation; ?, origin unknown; *, unattested; ‡, probably earlier than. See the full key inside the front cover.

Retz (rets; *Fr.* RETS), *n.* **1. Gilles de La·val** (zhēl də LA VAL′), **Baron de,** 1404?–40, French marshal: executed for child murder. **2. Jean Fran·çois Paul de Gon·di** (zhäN fräN swa′ pôl də gôN dē′), **Cardinal de,** 1614–79, French politician and clergyman.

Reu·ben (ro͞o′bən), *n.* **1.** the eldest son of Jacob and Leah. Gen. 29, 30. **2.** one of the 12 tribes of Israel, the tribe traditionally descended from him. **3.** See **Reuben sandwich. 4.** a male given name: from a Hebrew word meaning "behold a son."

Reu·ben·ite (ro͞o′bə nīt′), *n.* a member of the tribe of Reuben. [REUBEN + -ITE[1]]

Reu′ben sand′wich, a grilled sandwich of corned beef, Swiss cheese, and sauerkraut on rye bread. [1965–70, *Amer.;* after Arnold *Reuben* (1883–1970), U.S. restaurateur who created it]

Reuch·lin (ROIKH′lən, ROIKH lēn′), *n.* **Jo·hann** (yō′-hän), 1455–1522, German humanist scholar.

re·un·ion (rē yo͞on′yən), *n.* **1.** the act of uniting again. **2.** the state of being united again. **3.** a gathering of relatives, friends, or associates at regular intervals or after separation: *a family reunion.* [1600–10; RE- + UNION]

Ré·u·nion (rē yo͞on′yən; *Fr.* RĀ Y NYÔN′), *n.* an island in the Indian Ocean, E of Madagascar: an overseas department of France. 476,700; 970 sq. mi. (2512 sq. km). *Cap.:* St. Denis.

re·un·ion·ist (rē yo͞on′yə nist), *n.* a person who advocates the reunion of the Anglican Church with the Roman Catholic Church. [1865–70; REUNION + -IST] **—re·un′ion·ism,** *n.* **—re·un′ion·is′tic,** *adj.*

re·u·nite (rē′yo͞o nīt′), *v.t., v.i.,* **-nit·ed, -nit·ing.** to unite again, as after separation. [1585–95; < ML *reūnīt(us)* (ptp. of *reūnīre*), equiv. to L *re-* RE- + *ūnītus* joined together; see UNITE[1]] **—re′u·nit′a·ble,** *adj.* **—re′u·nit′er,** *n.*

re·up (rē up′), *v.i., v.t.,* **-upped, -up·ping.** *Mil. Informal.* to reenlist. [1905–10, *Amer.*]

re·up·take (rē up′tāk), *n. Physiol.* the process by which the presynaptic terminal of a neuron reabsorbs and recycles the molecules of neurotransmitter it has previously secreted in conveying an impulse to another neuron. [1970–75]

re·used (rē yo͞ozd′), *adj.* noting wool that previously has been spun, woven, and used. [RE- + USED]

Reu·ter (roi′tər), *n.* **Paul Julius, Baron de,** 1816–99, English founder of an international news agency, born in Germany.

Reu·ters (roi′tərz), *n.* a publicly owned international news and information company established in London, 1851.

Reu·ther (ro͞o′thər), *n.* **Walter Philip,** 1907–70, U.S. labor leader: president of the UAW 1946–70; president of the CIO 1952–55.

rev (rev), *n., v.,* **revved, rev·ving.** *Informal.* —*n.* **1.** a revolution (in an engine or the like). —*v.t.* **2.** to accelerate sharply the speed of (an engine or the like) (often fol. by *up*). —*v.i.* **3.** (of an engine) to accelerate; become revved (often fol. by *up*). **4. rev up,** to increase in strength or accelerate sharply: *The economy is beginning to rev up.* [1900–05; short for REVOLUTION]

Rev., 1. Revelation; Revelations. **2.** Reverend.

rev., 1. revenue. **2.** reverse. **3.** review. **4.** reviewed. **5.** revise; revised. **6.** revision. **7.** revolution. **8.** revolving.

Re·val (RĀ′väl), *n.* former German name of **Tallinn.**

re·val·u·ate (rē val′yo͞o āt′), *v.t.,* **-at·ed, -at·ing. 1.** to make a new or revised valuation of; revalue. **2.** to increase the legal exchange value of (a nation's currency) relative to other currencies. [1920–25; prob. back formation from *revaluation;* see RE-, VALUE, -ATE[1]] **—re·val′u·a′tion,** *n.*

re·val·ue (rē val′yo͞o), *v.t.,* **-ued, -u·ing. 1.** to revise or reestimate the value of: *efforts to revalue the dollar.* **2.** to value again. [1605–15; RE- + VALUE]

re·vamp (*v.* rē vamp′; *n.* rē′vamp′), *v.t.* **1.** to renovate, redo, or revise: *We've decided to revamp the entire show.* —*n.* **2.** an act or instance of restructuring, reordering, or revising something; overhaul: *a revamp of the nation's foreign policy.* [1840–50, *Amer.;* RE- + VAMP[1]] **—re·vamp′er,** *n.* **—re·vamp′ment,** *n.*

re·vanche (rə vanch′, -väNsh′), *n.* the policy of a state intent on regaining areas of its original territory that have been lost to other states as a result of war, a treaty signed under duress, etc. [1855–60; < F: REVENGE]

re·vanch·ist (rə van′chist, -väN′shist), *n.* **1.** an advocate or supporter of a political policy of revanche, esp. in order to seek vengeance for a previous military defeat. —*adj.* **2.** of or pertaining to a political policy of revanche. **3.** of or pertaining to revanchists or revanchism. [1925–30; < F *revanchiste;* see REVANCHE, -IST] **—re·vanch′ism,** *n.*

re·vas·cu·lar·i·za·tion (rē vas′kyə lər ə zā′shən), *n.* the restoration of the blood circulation of an organ or area, achieved by unblocking obstructed or disrupted blood vessels or by surgically implanting replacements. [1950–55; REVASCULARIZE + -ATION]

re·vas·cu·lar·ize (rē vas′kyə lə rīz′), *v.t.,* **-ized, -iz·ing.** to surgically improve the blood circulation of (an organ or area of the body). Also, *esp. Brit.,* **re·vas′cu·lar·ise′.** [1965–70; RE- + VASCULAR + -IZE]

re·veal (ri vēl′), *v.t.* **1.** to make known; disclose; divulge: *to reveal a secret.* **2.** to lay open to view; display; exhibit. —*n.* **3.** an act or instance of revealing; revelation; disclosure. **4.** *Archit.* **a.** the part of the jamb of a window or door opening between the outer wall surface and the window or door frame. **b.** the whole jamb of an opening between the outer and inner surfaces of a wall. **5.** the framework or edge of an automobile window. [1325–75; (v.) ME *revelen* < MF *reveler* < L *revēlāre* to unveil (see RE-, VEIL); (in defs. 4 and 5) deriv. of obs. *revale* to lower < OF *revaler* (*re-* RE- + *(a)valer* to lower, v. deriv. of the phrase *à val* down; see VALE)] **—re·veal′a·ble,** *adj.* **—re·veal′a·bil′i·ty, re·veal′a·ble·ness,** *n.* **—re·veal·ed·ly** (ri vē′lid lē, -vēld′-), *adv.* **—re·veal′er,** *n.* **—re·veal′ing·ly,** *adv.* **—re·veal′ing·ness,** *n.* **—re·vel·a·tive** (ri vel′ə tiv, rev′ə lā′-), *adj.*
—Syn. 1, 2. unveil, publish, impart, tell, announce, proclaim. REVEAL, DISCLOSE, DIVULGE share the meaning of making known something previously concealed or secret. To REVEAL is to uncover as if by drawing away a veil: *The fog lifted and revealed the harbor.* To DISCLOSE is to lay open and thereby invite inspection: *to disclose the plans of an organization.* To DIVULGE is to communicate, sometimes to a large number of people, what was at first intended to be private, confidential, or secret: *to divulge the terms of a contract.* **—Ant. 1, 2.** conceal, hide.

revealed′ reli′gion, religion based chiefly on the revelations of God to humans, esp. as described in Scripture. Cf. **natural religion.** [1710–20]

revealed′ theol′ogy, theology based on the doctrine that all religious truth is derived exclusively from the revelations of God to humans. Cf. **natural theology.**

re·veal·ment (ri vēl′mənt), *n.* the act of revealing; revelation. [1575–85; REVEAL + -MENT]

re·veg·e·tate (rē vej′i tāt′), *v.,* **-tat·ed, -tat·ing.** —*v.t.* **1.** to cause vegetation to grow again on: *to revegetate eroded lands.* —*v.i.* **2.** to grow again, as plants. [1760–70; RE- + VEGETATE] **—re·veg′e·ta′tion,** *n.*

rev·eil·le (rev′ə lē; *Brit.* ri val′ē), *n.* **1.** a signal, as of a drum or bugle, sounded early in the morning to awaken military personnel and to alert them for assembly. **2.** a signal to arise. [1635–45; < F *réveillez,* pl. impv. of *réveiller* to awaken, equiv. to *r(e)-* RE- + *éveiller,* OF *esveillier* << L *ēvigilāre* to watch, be vigilant (*ē-* E- + *vigilāre* to watch; see VIGIL)]

rev·el (rev′əl), *v.,* **-eled, -el·ing** or (*esp. Brit.*) **-elled, -el·ling,** *n.* —*v.i.* **1.** to take great pleasure or delight (usually fol. by *in*): *to revel in luxury.* **2.** to make merry; indulge in boisterous festivities. —*n.* **3.** boisterous merrymaking or festivity; revelry. **4.** Often, **revels.** an occasion of merrymaking or noisy festivity with dancing, masking, etc. [1275–1325; (v.) ME *revelen* < OF *reveler* to raise tumult, make merry < L *rebellāre* to REBEL; (n.) ME < OF, deriv. of *reveler*] **—rev′el·er;** *esp. Brit.,* **rev′el·ler,** *n.* **—rev′el·ment,** *n.*
—Syn. 2. celebrate, carouse, roister, caper.

Re·vel (RĀ′vəl; *Russ.* RYE′vyil), *n.* former Russian name of **Tallinn.**

rev·e·la·tion (rev′ə lā′shən), *n.* **1.** the act of revealing or disclosing; disclosure. **2.** something revealed or disclosed, esp. a striking disclosure, as of something not before realized. **3.** *Theol.* **a.** God's disclosure of Himself and His will to His creatures. **b.** an instance of such communication or disclosure. **c.** something thus communicated or disclosed. **d.** something that contains such disclosure, as the Bible. **4.** (*cap.*) Also called **Revelations, The Revelation of St. John the Divine.** the last book in the New Testament; the Apocalypse. *Abbr.:* Rev. [1275–1325; ME *revelacion* (< OF) < LL *revēlātiōn-* (s. of *revēlātiō*), equiv. to L *revēlāt(us)* (ptp. of *revēlāre* to REVEAL) + *-iōn-* -ION] **—rev′e·la′tion·al,** *adj.*
—Syn. 1. divulgation, admission, divulgence, exposure.

rev·e·la·tion·ist (rev′ə lā′shə nist), *n.* a person who believes in divine revelation. [1650–60; REVELATION + -IST]

rev·e·la·tor (rev′ə lā′tər), *n.* a person who makes a revelation. [1795–1805; < LL *revēlātor,* equiv. to L *revēlā(re)* (see REVEAL) + *-tor* -TOR]

re·vel·a·to·ry (ri vel′ə tôr′ē, -tōr′ē, rev′ə lə-), *adj.* **1.** of, pertaining to, or having the characteristics of revelation. **2.** showing or disclosing an emotion, belief, quality, or the like (usually fol. by *of*): *a poem revelatory of the author's deep, personal sorrow.* [1880–85; < L *revēlāt(us)* (see REVELATION) + -ORY[1]]

rev·el·ry (rev′əl rē), *n., pl.* **-ries.** reveling; boisterous festivity: *Their revelry could be heard across the river.* [1400–50; late ME; see REVEL, -RY]
—Syn. merrymaking, celebration, carousal, spree.

Rev·els (rev′əlz), *n.* **Hiram Rhoades** (rōdz), 1822–1901, U.S. clergyman, educator, and politician: first black senator 1870–71.

rev·e·nant (rev′ə nənt), *n.* **1.** a person who returns. **2.** a person who returns as a spirit after death; ghost. [1820–30; < F: ghost, n. use of prp. of *revenir* to return, equiv. to *re-* RE- + *ven(ir)* to come (< L *venīre*) + *-ant* -ANT]

re′sub·scrip′tion, *n.*
re′sub·stan′ti·ate′, *v.t.,* **-at·ed, -at·ing.**
re′sub·stan′ti·a′tion, *n.*
re·suit′, *n., v.t.*
re·sul′fu·rize′, *v.t.,* **-rized, -riz·ing.**
re·sul′phu·rize′, *v.t.,* **-rized, -riz·ing.**
re·sum′mon, *v.t.*
re·sum′mons, *n., pl.* **-mons·es.**
re′sup·ply′, *v.t.,* **-plied, -ply·ing,** *n., pl.* **-plies.**
re′sup·press′, *v.t.*
re′sup·pres′sion, *n.*
re′sus·pend′, *v.*
re′sus·pen′sion, *n.*
re·swear′, *v.,* **-swore, -sworn, -swear·ing.**
re·sweep′, *v.,* **-swept, -sweep·ing.**
re·sweet′en, *v.*
re·swell′, *v.,* **-swelled, -swelled** or **-swol·len, -swell·ing.**
re·sym′bol·ize′, *v.,* **-ized, -iz·ing.**
re·syn′di·cat′ed, *adj.*
re·syn′the·sis, *n., pl.* **-ses.**
re·syn′the·size′, *v.t.,* **-sized, -siz·ing.**
re·syn′the·tize′, *v.t.,* **-tized, -tiz·ing.**
re·sys′tem·a·ti·za′tion, *n.*
re·sys′tem·a·tize′, *v.t.,* **-tized, -tiz·ing.**

re•venge (ri venj′), *v.,* **-venged, -veng•ing,** *n.* —*v.t.* **1.** to exact punishment or expiation for a wrong on behalf of, esp. in a resentful or vindictive spirit: *He revenged his murdered brother.* **2.** to take vengeance for; inflict punishment for; avenge: *He revenged his brother's murder.* —*v.i.* **3.** to take revenge. —*n.* **4.** the act of revenging; retaliation for injuries or wrongs; vengeance. **5.** something done in vengeance. **6.** the desire to revenge; vindictiveness. **7.** an opportunity to retaliate or gain satisfaction. [1350–1400; ME *revengen* (v.) < MF, OF *revenger,* equiv. to *re-* RE- + *venger* to AVENGE < L *vindicāre;* see VINDICATE] —**re•venge′less,** *adj.* —**re•veng′er,** *n.* —**re•veng′ing•ly,** *adv.*
—**Syn. 1.** See **avenge. 4.** requital. REVENGE, REPRISAL, RETRIBUTION, VENGEANCE suggest a punishment, or injury inflicted in return for one received. REVENGE is the carrying out of a bitter desire to injure another for a wrong done to oneself or to those who are felt to be like oneself: *to plot revenge.* REPRISAL, formerly any act of retaliation, is used specifically in warfare for retaliation upon the enemy for its (usually unlawful) actions: *to make a raid in reprisal for one by the enemy.* RETRIBUTION suggests just or deserved punishment, often without personal motives, for some evil done: *a just retribution for wickedness.* VENGEANCE is usually wrathful, vindictive, furious revenge: *implacable vengeance.*

re•venge•ful (ri venj′fəl), *adj.* determined to have revenge; vindictive. [1580–90; REVENGE + -FUL] —**re•venge′ful•ly,** *adv.* —**re•venge′ful•ness,** *n.*
—**Syn.** malevolent, malicious, malignant. See **spiteful.**
—**Ant.** forgiving.

rev•e•nue (rev′ən yo͞o′, -ə no͞o′), *n.* **1.** the income of a government from taxation, excise duties, customs, or other sources, appropriated to the payment of the public expenses. **2.** the government department charged with the collection of such income. **3. revenues,** the collective items or amounts of income of a person, a state, etc. **4.** the return or yield from any kind of property, patent, service, etc.; income. **5.** an amount of money regularly coming in. **6.** a particular item or source of income. [1375–1425; late ME < MF, n. use of fem. ptp. of *revenir* to return < L *revenīre,* equiv. to *re-* RE- + *venīre* to COME] —**rev•e•nu•al** (rev′ən yo͞o′əl, -ə no͞o′-, ri ven′yo͞o-), *adj.* —**rev′e•nued′,** *adj.*

rev′enue a′gent, a government official who is responsible for the collection of revenue. [1860–65, *Amer.*]

rev′enue bond′, a bond issued, as by a municipal utility, to finance a specific project, the income from which will be used for repaying the bond. Cf. **general-obligation bond.** [1855–60]

rev′enue cut′ter, cutter (def. 4). [1780–90]

rev′enue enhance′ment, a new tax or a tax increase. Also called **rev′enue enhanc′er.**

rev•e•nu•er (rev′ən yo͞o′ər, -ə no͞o′-), *n. Informal.* an agent of the U.S. Treasury Department, esp. one whose responsibility is to enforce laws against illegal distilling or bootlegging of alcoholic liquor. [1875–80, *Amer.;* REVENUE + -ER[1]]

rev′enue shar′ing, the system of disbursing part of federal tax revenues to state and local governments for their use. [1970–75] —**rev′e•nue-shar′ing,** *adj.*

rev′enue stamp′, a stamp showing that a governmental tax has been paid. [1860–65]

rev′enue tar′iff, a tariff or duty imposed on imports primarily to produce public revenue. [1810–20, *Amer.*]

re•verb (ri vûrb′), *v.t., v.i.* to reverberate. [1595–1605; irreg. < L *reverberāre* to cause to rebound]

re•ver•ber•ant (ri vûr′bər ənt), *adj.* reverberating; reechoing: *the reverberant booms of cannon.* [1565–75; < L *reverberant-* (s. of *reverberāns*), prp. of *reverberāre,* equiv. to *re-* RE- + *verber(āre)* to beat, lash (deriv. of *verber* whip) + *-ant-* -ANT] —**re•ver′ber•ant•ly,** *adv.*

re•ver•ber•ate (*v.* ri vûr′bə rāt′; *adj.* ri vûr′bər it), *v.,* **-at•ed, -at•ing,** *adj.* —*v.i.* **1.** to reecho or resound: *Her singing reverberated through the house.* **2.** *Physics.* to be reflected many times, as sound waves from the walls of a confined space. **3.** to rebound or recoil. **4.** to be deflected, as flame in a reverberatory furnace. —*v.t.* **5.** to echo back or reecho (sound). **6.** to cast back or reflect (light, heat, etc.). **7.** to subject to reflected heat, as in a reverberatory furnace. —*adj.* **8.** reverberant. [1540–50; < L *reverberātus* (ptp. of *reverberāre* to strike back). See REVERBERANT, -ATE[1]] —**re•ver•ber•a•tive** (ri vûr′bə rā′tiv, -bər ə-), *adj.* —**re•ver′ber•a′tor,** *n.*
—**Syn. 1.** carry, ring, rebound, vibrate.

re•ver•ber•a•tion (ri vûr′bə rā′shən), *n.* **1.** a reechoed sound. **2.** the fact of being reverberated or reflected. **3.** something that is reverberated: *Reverberations from the explosion were felt within a six-mile radius.* **4.** an act or instance of reverberating. **5.** *Physics.* the persistence of a sound after its source has stopped, caused by multiple reflection of the sound within a closed space. **6.** the act or process of subjecting something to reflected heat, as in a reverberatory furnace. [1350–1400; ME *reverberacioun* < ML *reverberātiōn-* (s. of *reverberātiō*). See REVERBERATE, -ION]

reverbera′tion time′, the time it takes for a sound made in a room to diminish by 60 decibels. [1925–30]

re•ver•ber•a•to•ry (ri vûr′bər ə tôr′ē, -tōr′ē), *adj., n., pl.* **-ries.** —*adj.* **1.** characterized or produced by reverberation. **2.** noting a furnace, kiln, or the like in which the fuel is not in direct contact with the ore, metal, etc., to be heated, but furnishes a flame that plays over the material, esp. by being deflected downward from the roof. **3.** deflected, as flame. —*n.* **4.** any device, as a furnace, embodying reverberation. [1595–1605; REVERBERATE + -ORY[1]]

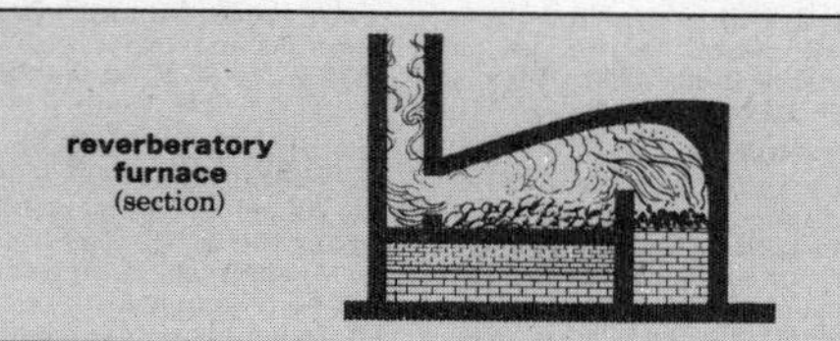

reverberatory furnace
(section)

re•vere[1] (ri vēr′), *v.t.,* **-vered, -ver•ing.** to regard with respect tinged with awe; venerate: *The child revered her mother.* [1655–65; < L *reverērī,* equiv. to *re-* RE- + *verērī* to stand in awe of, fear, feel reverence (akin to WARE[2])] —**re•ver′a•ble,** *adj.* —**re•ver′er,** *n.*
—**Syn.** reverence, honor, adore.

re•vere[2] (ri vēr′), *n.* revers.

Re•vere (ri vēr′), *n.* **1. Paul,** 1735–1818, American silversmith and patriot, famous for his night horseback ride, April 18, 1775, to warn Massachusetts colonists of the coming of British troops. **2.** a city in E Massachusetts, on Massachusetts Bay, near Boston: seaside resort. 42,423.

rev•er•ence (rev′ər əns, rev′rəns), *n., v.,* **-enced, -enc•ing.** —*n.* **1.** a feeling or attitude of deep respect tinged with awe; veneration. **2.** the outward manifestation of this feeling: *to pay reverence.* **3.** a gesture indicative of deep respect; an obeisance, bow, or curtsy. **4.** the state of being revered. **5.** (*cap.*) a title used in addressing or mentioning a member of the clergy (usually prec. by *your* or *his*). —*v.t.* **6.** to regard or treat with reverence; venerate: *One should reverence God and His laws.* [1250–1300; ME < L *reverentia* respect, fear, awe. See REVERE[1], -ENCE] —**rev′er•enc•er,** *n.*
—**Syn. 1.** honor, esteem. **6.** revere, honor, adore.
—**Ant. 1.** contempt.

rev•er•end (rev′ər ənd, rev′rənd), *adj.* **1.** (*cap.*) (used as a title of respect applied or prefixed to the name of a member of the clergy or a religious order): *Reverend Timothy Cranshaw; Reverend Mother.* **2.** worthy to be revered; entitled to reverence. **3.** pertaining to or characteristic of the clergy. —*n.* **4.** *Informal.* a member of the clergy. [1400–50; late ME < L *reverendus* worthy of being revered, ger. of *reverērī* to REVERE[1]] —**rev′er•end•ship′,** *n.*

rev•er•ent (rev′ər ənt, rev′rənt), *adj.* feeling, exhibiting, or characterized by reverence; deeply respectful: *a reverent greeting.* [1350–1400; ME < L *reverent-* (s. of *reverēns*), prp. of *reverērī* to REVERE[1]; see -ENT] —**rev′er•ent•ly,** *adv.* —**rev′er•ent•ness,** *n.*

rev•er•en•tial (rev′ə ren′shəl), *adj.* of the nature of or characterized by reverence; reverent: *reverential awe.* [1545–55; REVERENT + -IAL] —**rev•er•en•ti•al•i•ty** (rev′ə ren′shē al′i tē), **rev′er•en′tial•ness,** *n.* —**rev′er•en′tial•ly,** *adv.*

rev•er•ie (rev′ə rē), *n.* **1.** a state of dreamy meditation or fanciful musing: *lost in reverie.* **2.** a daydream. **3.** a fantastic, visionary, or impractical idea: *reveries that will never come to fruition.* **4.** *Music.* an instrumental composition of a vague and dreamy character. Also, **revery.** [1325–75; ME < OF *reverie,* deriv. of *rever* to speak wildly. See RAVE, -ERY]
—**Syn. 1.** abstraction, brown study.

re•vers (ri vēr′, -vâr′), *n., pl.* **-vers** (-vērz′, -vârz′). **1.** a part of a garment turned back to show the lining or facing, as a lapel. **2.** a trimming simulating such a part. **3.** the facing used. Also, **revere.** [1865–70; < F]

re•ver•sal (ri vûr′səl), *n.* **1.** an act or instance of reversing. **2.** the state of being reversed. **3.** an adverse change of fortune; reverse. **4.** *Law.* the setting aside of a decision of a lower court by a higher court. [1480–90; REVERSE + -AL[2]]

rever′sal film′, *Photog.* film developed by the reversal process. [1930–35]

rever′sal plate′, *Photog.* a plate developed by the reversal process.

rever′sal proc′ess, *Photog.* a process for converting the negative on a film or plate to a positive by bleaching and redeveloping. [1915–20]

re•verse (ri vûrs′), *adj., n., v.,* **-versed, -vers•ing.** —*adj.* **1.** opposite or contrary in position, direction, order, or character: *an impression reverse to what was intended; in reverse sequence.* **2.** with the back or rear part toward the observer: *the reverse side of a fabric.* **3.** pertaining to or producing movement in a mechanism opposite to that made under ordinary running conditions: *a reverse gear; a reverse turbine.* **4.** acting in a manner opposite or contrary to that which is usual, as an appliance or apparatus. **5.** noting or pertaining to an image like that seen in a mirror; backward; reversed. **6.** noting or pertaining to printed matter in which what is normally white, as the page of a book, appears as black, and vice versa. —*n.* **7.** the opposite or contrary of something. **8.** the back or rear of anything. **9.** *Numis.* **a.** the side of a coin, medal, etc., that does not bear the principal design (opposed to *obverse*). **b.** the side of an ancient coin that was struck by the upper die. **10.** an adverse change of fortune; a misfortune, check, or defeat: *to meet with an unexpected reverse.* **11.** *Mach.* **a.** the condition of being reversed: *to throw an engine into reverse.* **b.** a reversing mechanism. **12.** *Football.* a play on offense in which one back running laterally hands the ball to another back who is running in the opposite direction and who then makes either an end run or a cutback. **13.** *Bridge.* See **reverse bid. 14.** *Print.* printed matter in which areas that normally appear as white are printed in black, and vice versa. —*v.t.* **15.** to turn in an opposite position; transpose: *The printer accidently reversed two chapters of the book.* **16.** to turn in the opposite direction; send on the opposite course. **17.** to turn inside out or upside down. **18.** to change the direction of running of (a mechanism). **19.** to cause (a mechanism) to run in a direction opposite to that in which it commonly runs. **20.** to revoke or annul (a decree, judgment, etc.): *to reverse a verdict.* **21.** to alter to the opposite in character or tendency; change completely. **22.** to turn in the opposite order: *to reverse the process of evolution.* **23.** *Print.* to print as a reverse. —*v.i.* **24.** to shift into reverse gear: *The driver drove forward, then reversed.* **25.** (of a mechanism) to be reversed. **26.** to turn or move in the opposite or contrary direction, as in dancing. **27.** *Bridge.* to make a reverse bid. [1275–1325; (n.) ME *revers* < OF < L *reversus,* ptp. of *revertere* to REVERT (see VERSE); (v.) ME *reversen* < OF *reverser* < LL *reversāre,* freq. of *revertere*] —**re•vers•ed•ly** (ri vûr′sid lē, -vûrst′lē), *adv.* —**re•verse′ly,** *adv.* —**re•vers′er,** *n.*
—**Syn. 1.** converse. See **opposite. 7.** converse, counterpart. **10.** mishap, misadventure, affliction. **15, 17.** REVERSE, INVERT agree in meaning to change into a contrary position, order, or relation. To REVERSE is to place or move something so that it is facing in the opposite direction from the one faced previously: *to reverse from right to left; to reverse a decision.* To INVERT is to turn upside down: *to invert a stamp in printing; to invert a bowl over a plate.* **20.** repeal, veto, countermand, rescind, overthrow. —**Ant. 1.** same.

reverse′ an′gle shot′, *Motion Pictures.* See **reverse shot.** [1930–35]

reverse′ annu′ity mort′gage, a type of home mortgage under which an elderly homeowner is allowed a long-term loan in the form of monthly payments against his or her paid-off equity as collateral, repayable when the home is eventually sold. *Abbr.:* RAM Also called **equity conversion, reverse mortgage.**

reverse′ bar′, an angle iron having one leg welded or riveted to a leg of another angle iron to make a member similar to a Z-bar.

reverse′ bev′el, the bevel of a bolt or lock on a door opening outward from the building, room, closet, etc., to which the doorway leads (opposed to *regular bevel*).

reverse′ bid′, *Bridge.* a bid of a higher-ranking suit at the two level or higher by a player whose previous bid was of a lower-ranking suit. [1935–40]

reverse′ commut′er, a commuter who lives in a city and commutes to a job in the suburbs. [1965–70] —**reverse′ commut′ing.**

reverse′ curve′, an S-shaped curve, as on highways and railroad tracks, produced by the joining of two curves that turn in opposite directions.

reversed′ col′lar. See **clerical collar.**

reverse′ dic′tionary, 1. an alphabetical list of words spelled in reversed order, of use esp. to linguists and cryptographers. **2.** a thesauruslike dictionary alphabetizing meanings and concepts under which are listed the related words that are defined or explained. **3.** a dictionary of alphabetized word elements, as prefixes, suffixes, and roots, with lists of the words derived from them.

reverse′ discrimina′tion, the unfair treatment of members of majority groups resulting from preferential policies, as in college admissions or employment, intended to remedy earlier discrimination against minorities. [1965–70]

re•verse-en•gi•neer (ri vûrs′en jə nēr′), *v.t.* to study or analyze (a device, as a microchip for computers) in order to learn details of design, construction, and operation, perhaps to produce a copy or an improved version. —**reverse′ engineer′ing.**

reverse′ Eng′lish, 1. Also called **reverse′ side′.** *Billiards.* a spinning motion imparted to a cue ball in such a manner as to prevent it from moving in a certain direction. Cf. **running English. 2.** words that, because of their misuse or careless syntax, convey an opposite meaning from the one intended or leave their exact meaning in doubt: *"Don't miss it if you can" is reverse English.* [1905–10, *Amer.*]

reverse′ fault′, *Geol.* a fault in which the rock above the fault plane is displaced upward relative to the rock below the fault plane (opposed to *gravity fault*). Cf. **thrust fault.** [1885–90]

reverse′ mort′gage. See **reverse annuity mortgage.**

reverse′ muta′tion, *Genetics.* See **back mutation.**

reverse′ osmo′sis, *Chem.* the process in which pure water is produced by forcing waste or saline water through a semipermeable membrane. [1950–55]

CONCISE PRONUNCIATION KEY: act, cāpe, dâre, pärt; set, ēqual; if, īce; ox, ōver, ôrder, oil, bo͝ok, bo͞ot, out; up, ûrge; child; sing; shoe; thin, that; zh as in *treasure.* ə = *a* as in *alone, e* as in *system, i* as in *easily, o* as in *gallop, u* as in *circus;* ᵊ as in *fire* (fīᵊr), *hour* (ouᵊr). l and n can serve as syllabic consonants, as in *cradle* (krād′l), and *button* (but′n). See the full key inside the front cover.

re•tab′u•late′, *v.t.,* **-lat•ed, -lat•ing.**
re•tack′, *v.t.*
re•tack′le, *v.t.,* **-led, -ling.**
re•tag′, *v.t.,* **-tagged, -tag•ging.**
re•tal′ly, *n., pl.* **-lies,** *v.,* **-lied, -ly•ing.**
re•tan′, *v.t.,* **-tanned, -tan•ning.**
re•tape′, *v.t.,* **-taped, -tap•ing.**
re•tar′, *v.t.,* **-tarred, -tar•ring.**
re•tar′iff, *v.t.*
re•taste′, *v.,* **-tast•ed, -tast•ing.**
re•tax′, *v.t.*
re′tax•a′tion, *n.*
re•teach′, *v.,* **-taught, -teach•ing.**
re•tear′, *v.,* **-tore, -torn, -tear•ing.**
re•tel′e•graph′, *v.*
re•tel′e•phone′, *v.,* **-phoned, -phon•ing.**
re•tel′e•vise′, *v.t.,* **-vised, -vis•ing.**
re•tell′, *v.,* **-told, -tell•ing.**
re•tem′per, *v.t.*
re•test′, *v.t.*
re′test′, *n.*
re•tes′ti•fy′, *v.,* **-fied, -fy•ing.**
re•tes′ti•mo′ny, *n., pl.* **-nies.**
re•tex′ture, *v.t.,* **-tured, -tur•ing.**
re•thank′, *v.t.*
re•thatch′, *v.t.*
re•thaw′, *v.*
re•thick′en, *v.*
re•thread′, *v.*
re•threat′en, *v.*
re•thresh′, *v.*
re•tick′et, *v.t.*
re•tie′, *v.t.,* **-tied, -ty•ing.**
re•tight′en, *v.*

reverse′ plate′, *Print.* a plate for printing a reverse.

reverse′ psychol′ogy, (in nontechnical use) a method of getting another person to do what one wants by pretending not to want it or to want something else or something more.

reverse′ shot′, *Motion Pictures.* a shot that views the action from the opposite side of the previous shot, as during a conversation between two actors, giving the effect of looking from one actor to the other. Also called **reverse angle shot.** [1930–35]

reverse′ snob′, a person overly proud of being one of or sympathetic to the common people, and who denigrates or shuns those of superior ability, education, social standing, etc. **—reverse′ snob′bery, reverse′ snob′bism.**

reverse′ tran•scrip′tase (tran skrip′tās, -tāz), *Biochem.* a retrovirus enzyme that synthesizes DNA from viral RNA, the reverse of the usual DNA-to-RNA replication: used in genetic engineering to clone genes from RNA strands. [1970–75; TRANSCRIPT + -ASE]

reverse′ vid′eo, a mode on the display screen of a computer in which the colors normally used for characters and background are reversed.

re•vers•i•ble (ri vûr′sə bəl), *adj.* **1.** capable of reversing or of being reversed. **2.** capable of reestablishing the original condition after a change by the reverse of the change. **3.** (of a fabric) woven or printed so that either side may be exposed. **4.** that can be worn with either side out: *a reversible jacket.* —*n.* **5.** a garment, esp. a coat, that can be worn with either side exposed. [1640–50; REVERSE + -IBLE] **—re•vers′i•bil′i•ty, re•vers′i•ble•ness,** *n.* **—re•vers′i•bly,** *adv.*

revers′ible reac′tion, *Chem.* a reaction that, depending on ambient conditions, can proceed in either of two directions: the production of the reaction products from the reactants, or the production of the original reactants from the formed reaction products. Cf. **equilibrium** (def. 4).

revers′ing prism′, *Optics.* See **Dove prism.**

re•ver•sion (ri vûr′zhən, -shən), *n.* **1.** the act of turning something the reverse way. **2.** the state of being so turned; reversal. **3.** the act of reverting; return to a former practice, belief, condition, etc. **4.** *Biol.* **a.** reappearance of ancestral characters that have been absent in intervening generations. **b.** return to an earlier or primitive type; atavism. **5.** *Law.* **a.** the returning of an estate to the grantor or the grantor's heirs after the interest granted expires. **b.** an estate which so returns. **c.** the right of succeeding to an estate. **6.** *Archaic.* the remains, esp. of food or drink after a meal. [1350–1400; ME < L *reversiōn-* (s. of *reversiō*) a turning back. See REVERSE, -ION] **—re•ver′sion•al•ly,** *adv.*

re•ver•sion•ar•y (ri vûr′zhə ner′ē, -shə-), *adj.* of, pertaining to, or involving a reversion. Also, **re•ver′sion•al.** [1645–55; REVERSION + -ARY]

rever′sionary annu′ity, *Insurance.* an annuity payable to a beneficiary during the period of time he or she survives the insured.

re•ver•sion•er (ri vûr′zhə nər, -shə-), *n. Law.* a person who possesses a reversion. [1605–15; REVERSION + -ER[1]]

re•ver•sion•ist (ri vur′zhə nist, -shə-), *n.* **1.** a person who advocates reverting to the conditions, customs, ideals, etc., of an earlier era. —*adj.* **2.** of, pertaining to, or characteristic of a reversionist. [REVERSION + -IST] **—re•ver′sion•ism,** *n.*

re•vert (ri vûrt′), *v.i.* —*v.i.* **1.** to return to a former habit, practice, belief, condition, etc.: *They reverted to the ways of their forefathers.* **2.** *Law.* to go back to or return to the former owner or to his or her heirs. **3.** *Biol.* to return to an earlier or primitive type. **4.** to go back in thought or discussion: *He constantly reverted to his childhood.* —*n.* **5.** a person or thing that reverts. **6.** *Law.* a reversion. [1250–1300; ME *reverten* (< OF *revertir*) < L *revertere* to turn back, equiv. to *re-* RE- + *vertere* to turn; see VERSE] **—re•vert′i•ble,** *adj.* **—re•vert′i•bil′i•ty,** *n.* **—re•ver′tive,** *adj.* **—re•ver′tive•ly,** *adv.*
—Syn. 1, 3. retrogress.

re•ver•tant (ri vûr′tnt), *Genetics. n.* **1.** a gene, organism, or strain that has undergone a back mutation. —*adj.* **2.** of or pertaining to a gene, organism, or strain that has undergone a back mutation. [1580–90, for an earlier sense; REVERT + -ANT]

re•vert•er[1] (ri vûr′tər), *n.* a person or thing that reverts. [1885–90; REVERT + -ER[1]]

re•vert•er[2] (ri vûr′tər), *n. Law.* a future interest in property that rests in a grantor. [1485–95; ME < AF, n. use of *reverter* (inf.). See REVERT, -ER[3]]

rev•er•y (rev′ə rē), *n., pl.* **-er•ies.** reverie.

re•vest (rē vest′), *v.t.* **1.** to vest (a person) again, as with ownership or office; reinvest; reinstate. **2.** to vest (powers, office, etc.) again. —*v.i.* **3.** to become vested again in a person; go back again to a former owner. [1555–65; RE- + VEST (v.)]

CONCISE ETYMOLOGY KEY: <, descended or borrowed from; >, whence; b., blend of, blended; c., cognate with; cf., compare; deriv., derivative; equiv., equivalent; imit., imitative; obl., oblique; r., replacing; s., stem; sp., spelling, spelled; resp., respelling, respelled; trans., translation; ?, origin unknown; *, unattested; ‡, probably earlier than. See the full key inside the front cover.

re•vet (ri vet′), *v.t.*, **-vet•ted, -vet•ting.** to face, as an embankment, with masonry or other material. [1805–15; < F *revêtir* lit., to reclothe; cf. REVEST]

re•vet•ment (ri vet′mənt), *n.* **1.** a facing of masonry or the like, esp. for protecting an embankment. **2.** an ornamental facing, as on a common masonry wall, of marble, face brick, tiles, etc. [1765–75; < F *revêtement.* See REVET, -MENT]

re•view (ri vyōō′), *n.* **1.** a critical article or report, as in a periodical, on a book, play, recital, or the like; critique; evaluation. **2.** the process of going over a subject again in study or recitation in order to fix it in the memory or summarize the facts. **3.** an exercise designed or intended for study of this kind. **4.** a general survey of something, esp. in words; a report or account of something. **5.** an inspection or examination by viewing, esp. a formal inspection of any military or naval force, parade, or the like. **6.** a periodical publication containing articles on current events or affairs, books, art, etc.: *a literary review.* **7.** a judicial reexamination, as by a higher court, of the decision or proceedings in a case. **8.** a second or repeated view of something. **9.** a viewing of the past; contemplation or consideration of past events, circumstances, or facts. **10.** *Bridge.* a recapitulation of the bids made by all players. **11.** *Theat.* revue. —*v.t.* **12.** to go over (lessons, studies, work, etc.) in review. **13.** to view, look at, or look over again. **14.** to inspect, esp. formally or officially: *to review the troops.* **15.** to survey mentally; take a survey of: *to review the situation.* **16.** to discuss (a book, play, etc.) in a critical review; write a critical report upon. **17.** to look back upon; view retrospectively. **18.** to present a survey of in speech or writing. **19.** *Law.* to reexamine judicially: *a decision to review the case.* **20.** *Bridge.* to repeat and summarize (all bids made by the players). —*v.i.* **21.** to write reviews; review books, movies, etc., as for a newspaper or periodical: *He reviews for some small-town newspaper.* [1555–65; < MF *revue,* n. use of fem. ptp. of *revoir* to see again << L *revidēre,* equiv. to *re-* RE- + *vidēre* to see; see VIEW] **—re•view′a•ble,** *adj.* **—re•view′a•bil′i•ty,** *n.* **—re•view′less,** *adj.*
—Syn. 1. REVIEW, CRITICISM imply careful examination of something, formulation of a judgment, and statement of the judgment, usually in written form. A REVIEW is a survey over a whole subject or division of it, or esp. an article making a critical reconsideration and summary of something written: *a review of the latest book on Chaucer.* A CRITICISM is a judgment, usually in an article, either favorable or unfavorable or both: *a criticism of a proposed plan.* The words are interchanged when referring to motion pictures or theater, but REVIEW implies a somewhat less formal approach than CRITICISM in referring to literary works: *movie reviews; play reviews; book reviews.* **8.** reconsideration, reexamination.

re•view•al (ri vyōō′əl), *n.* the act of reviewing. [1640–50; REVIEW + -AL[2]]

re•view•er (ri vyōō′ər), *n.* **1.** a person who reviews. **2.** a person who reviews books, plays, etc. [1605–15; REVIEW + -ER[1]]

re•vile (ri vīl′), *v.*, **-viled, -vil•ing.** —*v.t.* **1.** to assail with contemptuous or opprobrious language; address or speak of abusively. —*v.i.* **2.** to speak abusively. [1275–1325; ME *revilen* < MF *reviler.* See RE-, VILE] **—re•vile′ment,** *n.* **—re•vil′er,** *n.* **—re•vil′ing•ly,** *adv.*
—Syn. 1. abuse, vilify, vituperate, berate, disparage.

re•vis•al (ri vī′zəl), *n.* the act of revising; revision. [1605–15; REVISE + -AL[2]]

re•vise (ri vīz′), *v.*, **-vised, -vis•ing,** *n.* —*v.t.* **1.** to amend or alter: *to revise one's opinion.* **2.** to alter something already written or printed, in order to make corrections, improve, or update: *to revise a manuscript.* **3.** *Brit.* to review (previously studied materials) in preparation for an examination. —*n.* **4.** an act of revising. **5.** a revised form of something; revision. **6.** *Print.* a proof sheet taken after alterations have been made, for further examination or correction. [1560–70; < L *revisere* to look back at, revisit, freq. of *revidēre* to see again; see REVIEW] **—re•vis′a•ble, re•vis′i•ble,** *adj.* **—re•vis′a•bil′i•ty,** *n.* **—re•vis′er, re•vi′sor,** *n.*
—Syn. 1. change; emend, correct.

Revised′ Stand′ard Ver′sion, a revision of the Bible, based on the American Standard Version and the King James Version, prepared by American scholars, published in its completed form in 1952. *Abbr.:* RSV

Revised′ Ver′sion of the Bi′ble, a recension of the Authorized Version, prepared by British and American scholars, the Old Testament being published in 1885, and the New Testament in 1881. Also called **Revised′ Ver′sion.**

re•vi•sion (ri vizh′ən), *n.* **1.** the act or work of revising. **2.** a process of revising. **3.** a revised form or version, as of a book. [1605–15; < LL *revisiōn-* (s. of *revisiō*), equiv. to L *revis(us)* (see REVISE) + *-iōn-* -ION] **—re•vi′sion•al, re•vi′sion•ar′y,** *adj.*
—Syn. 1. alteration, correction, emendation.

re•vi•sion•ism (ri vizh′ə niz′əm), *n.* **1.** advocacy or approval of revision. **2.** any departure from Marxist doctrine, theory, or practice, esp. the tendency to favor reform above revolutionary change. **3.** a departure from any authoritative or generally accepted doctrine, theory, practice, etc. [1900–05; REVISION + -ISM]

re•vi•sion•ist (ri vizh′ə nist), *n.* **1.** an advocate of revision, esp. of some political or religious doctrine. **2.** a reviser. **3.** any advocate of doctrines, theories, or practices that depart from established authority or doctrine. —*adj.* **4.** of or pertaining to revisionists or revisionism. **5.** attempting to reevaluate and restate the past based on newly acquired standards. [1860–65; REVISION + -IST]

re•vi•so•ry (ri vī′zə rē), *adj.* pertaining to or for the purpose of revision. [1840–50; REVISE + -ORY[1]]

re•vi•tal•ize (rē vīt′l īz′), *v.t.*, **-ized, -iz•ing. 1.** to give new life to. **2.** to give new vitality or vigor to. Also, *esp. Brit.,* **re•vi′tal•ise′.** [1855–60; RE- + VITALIZE] **—re•vi′tal•i•za′tion,** *n.*

re•viv•al (ri vī′vəl), *n.* **1.** restoration to life, consciousness, vigor, strength, etc. **2.** restoration to use, acceptance, or currency: *the revival of old customs.* **3.** a new production of an old play. **4.** a showing of an old motion picture. **5.** an awakening, in a church or community, of interest in and care for matters relating to personal religion. **6.** an evangelistic service or a series of services for the purpose of effecting a religious awakening: *to hold a revival.* **7.** the act of reviving. **8.** the state of being revived. **9.** *Law.* the reestablishment of legal force and effect. [1645–55; REVIVE + -AL[2]]

re•viv•al•ism (ri vī′və liz′əm), *n.* **1.** the form of religious activity that manifests itself in revivals. **2.** the tendency to revive what belongs to the past. [1805–15; REVIVAL + -ISM]

re•viv•al•ist (ri vī′və list), *n.* **1.** a person, esp. a member of the clergy, who promotes or holds religious revivals. **2.** a person who revives former customs, methods, etc. [1810–20; REVIVAL + -IST] **—re•viv′al•is′tic,** *adj.*

Reviv′al of Learn′ing, the Renaissance in its relation to learning, esp. in literature **(Reviv′al of Lit′erature** or **Reviv′al of Let′ters).** [1775–85]

re•vive (ri vīv′), *v.*, **-vived, -viv•ing.** —*v.t.* **1.** to activate, set in motion, or take up again; renew: *to revive old feuds.* **2.** to restore to life or consciousness: *We revived him with artificial respiration.* **3.** to put on or show (an old play or motion picture) again. **4.** to make operative or valid again. **5.** to bring back into notice, use, or currency: *to revive a subject of discussion.* **6.** to quicken or renew in the mind; bring back: *to revive memories.* **7.** to reanimate or cheer (the spirit, heart, etc., or a person). **8.** *Chem.* to restore or reduce to the natural or uncombined state, as a metal. —*v.i.* **9.** to return to life, consciousness, vigor, strength, or a flourishing condition. **10.** to recover from financial depression. **11.** to be quickened, restored, or renewed, as hope, confidence, suspicions, or memories. **12.** to return to notice, use, or currency, as a subject, practice, or doctrine. **13.** to become operative or valid again. **14.** *Chem.* to recover the natural or uncombined state, as a metal. [1375–1425; late ME *reviven* < L *revīvere* to live again, equiv. to *re-* RE- + *vīvere* to live, be alive; cf. VITAL] **—re•viv′a•ble,** *adj.* **—re•viv′a•bil′i•ty,** *n.* **—re•viv′a•bly,** *adv.* **—re•viv′er,** *n.* **—re•viv′ing•ly,** *adv.*
—Syn. 1, 4. reactivate. **2.** revitalize, reanimate, resuscitate. **6.** rouse, refresh. **—Ant. 2.** kill.

re•viv•i•fy (ri viv′ə fī′), *v.t.*, **-fied, -fy•ing.** to restore to life; give new life to; revive; reanimate. [1665–75; < F *révivifier* < LL *revīvificāre.* See RE-, VIVIFY] **—re•viv•i•fi•ca•tion** (ri viv′ə fi kā′shən), *n.*

rev•i•vis•cence (rev′ə vis′əns), *n.* the act or state of being revived; revival; reanimation. Also, **rev′i•vis′cen•cy.** [1620–30; < L *revīvisc(ere)* to come to life again (*re-* RE- + *vīviscere,* inchoative of *vīvere* to live) + -ENCE] **—rev′i•vis′cent,** *adj.*

re•vi•vor (ri vī′vər), *n. Eng. Law.* the revival of a suit that has been nullified by some circumstance, as the death of one of the parties. [1530–40; REVIVE + -OR[2]]

rev•o•ca•ble (rev′ə kə bəl *or, often,* ri vō′-), *adj.* that may be revoked. Also, **re•vok•a•ble** (ri vō′kə bəl, rev′ə-). [1490–1500; < L *revocābilis.* See REVOKE, -ABLE] **—rev′o•ca•bil′i•ty, rev′o•ca•ble•ness,** *n.* **—rev′o•ca•bly,** *adv.*

rev•o•ca•tion (rev′ə kā′shən), *n.* **1.** the act of revoking; annulment. **2.** *Law.* nullification or withdrawal, esp. of an offer to contract. [1375–1425; late ME *revocacion* < L *revocātiōn-* (s. of *revocātiō*) a calling back, equiv. to *revocāt(us)* (ptp. of *revocāre* to REVOKE) + *-iōn-* -ION] **—rev•o•ca•tive** (rev′ə kā′tiv, ri vok′ə-), **rev•o•ca•to•ry** (rev′ə kə tôr′ē, -tōr′ē), *adj.*

re•voice (rē vois′), *v.t.*, **-voiced, -voic•ing. 1.** to voice again or in return; echo. **2.** to readjust the tone of: *to revoice an organ pipe.* [1600–10; RE- + VOICE]

re•voke (ri vōk′), *v.*, **-voked, -vok•ing,** *n.* —*v.t.* **1.** to take back or withdraw; annul, cancel, or reverse; rescind or repeal: *to revoke a decree.* **2.** to bring or summon back. —*v.i.* **3.** *Cards.* to fail to follow suit when possible and required; renege. —*n.* **4.** *Cards.* an act or instance of revoking. [1300–50; ME *revoken* < L *revocāre* to call again, equiv. to *re-* RE- + *vocāre* to call] **—re•vok′er,** *n.* **—re•vok′ing•ly,** *adv.*
—Syn. 1. retract, recall; nullify, countermand.

re•volt (ri vōlt′), *v.i.* **1.** to break away from or rise against constituted authority, as by open rebellion; rebel: *to revolt against the government.* **2.** to turn away in mental rebellion, disgust, or abhorrence (usually fol. by *from*): *He revolts from eating meat.* **3.** to rebel in feeling (usually fol. by *against*): *to revolt against parental authority.* **4.** to feel horror or aversion (usually fol. by *at*): *to revolt at the sight of blood.* —*v.t.* **5.** to affect with disgust or abhorrence. —*n.* **6.** the act of revolting; an insurrection or rebellion. **7.** an expression or movement of spirited protest or dissent: *a voter revolt at the polls.* [1540–50; (v.) < MF *revolter* < It *rivoltare* to turn around < VL **revolvitāre,* freq. of L *revolvere* to roll back, unroll, REVOLVE; (n.) < F *révolte* < It *rivolta,* deriv. of *rivoltare*] **—re•volt′er,** *n.*
—Syn. 6. uprising, disorder, putsch.

re•tile′, *v.t.,* **-tiled, -til•ing.**
re•till′, *v.t.*
re•time′, *v.t.,* **-timed, -tim•ing.**
re•tin′, *v.t.,* **-tinned, -tin•ning.**
re•tinge′, *v.t.,* **-tinged, -tinge•ing** or **-ting•ing.**
re•tint′, *v.t.*
re•ti′tle, *v.t.,* **-tled, -tling.**
re•toast′, *v.*
re•to′tal, *v.t.,* **-taled, -tal•ing** or (*esp. Brit.*) **-talled, tal•ling,** *n.*
re•track′, *v.*
re•trade′, *v.,* **-trad•ed, -trad•ing,** *n.*
re′tran•scribe′, *v.t.,* **-scribed, -scrib•ing.**
re′tran•scrip′tion, *n.*
re′trans•fer′, *v.t.,* **-ferred, -fer•ring.**
re•trans′fer, *n.*
re′trans•fer′ence, *n.*
re′trans•form′, *v.t.*
re′trans•for•ma′tion, *n.*
re′trans•late′, *v.t.,* **-lat•ed, -lat•ing.**
re′trans•la′tion, *n.*
re′trans•mis′sion, *n.*
re′trans•mit′, *v.t.,* **-mit•ted, -mit•ting.**
re′trans•plant′, *v.t*
re′trans•plan•ta′tion, *n.*
re•trav′erse, *v.,* **-ersed, -ers•ing.**
re•tri′al, *n.*
re•trib′al•i•za′tion, *n.*
re•trib′al•ize′, *v.,* **-ized, -iz•ing.**
re•try′, *v.,* **-tried, -try•ing.**
re•tune′, *v.t.,* **-tuned, -tun•ing.**
re•turf′, *v.t.*
re•twine′, *v.,* **-twined, -twin•ing.**
re•twist′, *v.*

re•volt•ing (ri vōl′ting), *adj.* **1.** disgusting; repulsive: *a revolting sight.* **2.** rebellious. [1585–95; REVOLT + -ING[2]] **—re•volt′ing•ly,** *adv.*

rev•o•lute (rev′ə lo͞ot′), *adj. Biol.* rolled backward or downward; rolled backward at the tip or margin, as a leaf. [1375–1425; late ME < L *revolūtus,* ptp. of *revolvere* to REVOLVE]

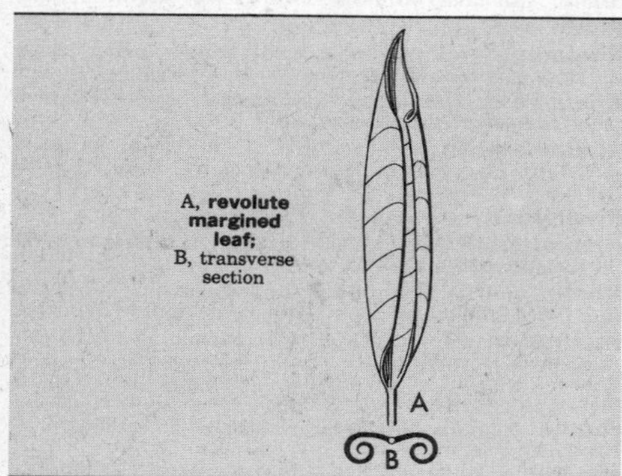

A, **revolute margined leaf;** B, transverse section

rev•o•lu•tion (rev′ə lo͞o′shən), *n.* **1.** an overthrow or repudiation and the thorough replacement of an established government or political system by the people governed. **2.** *Sociol.* a radical and pervasive change in society and the social structure, esp. one made suddenly and often accompanied by violence. Cf. **social evolution. 3.** a sudden, complete or marked change in something: *the present revolution in church architecture.* **4.** a procedure or course, as if in a circuit, back to a starting point. **5.** a single turn of this kind. **6.** *Mech.* **a.** a turning round or rotating, as on an axis. **b.** a moving in a circular or curving course, as about a central point. **c.** a single cycle in such a course. **7.** *Astron.* **a.** (not in technical use) rotation (def. 2). **b.** the orbiting of one heavenly body around another. **c.** a single course of such movement. **8.** a round or cycle of events in time or a recurring period of time. **9.** *Geol.* a time of worldwide orogeny and mountain-building. [1350–1400; ME *revolucion* < LL *revolūtiōn-* (s. of *revolūtiō*), equiv. to *revolūt(us)* (see REVOLUTE) + *-iōn-* -ION]
—Syn. 5. cycle, circuit, round, rotation.

rev•o•lu•tion•ar•y (rev′ə lo͞o′shə ner′ē), *adj., n., pl.* **-ar•ies.** *—adj.* **1.** of, pertaining to, characterized by, or of the nature of a revolution, or a sudden, complete, or marked change: *a revolutionary junta.* **2.** radically new or innovative; outside or beyond established procedure, principles, etc.: *a revolutionary discovery.* **3.** (*cap.*) of or pertaining to the American Revolution or to the period contemporaneous with it in U.S. history: *Revolutionary heroes; Revolutionary weapons.* **4.** revolving. *—n.* **5.** a revolutionist. [1765–75; REVOLUTION + -ARY] **—rev′o•lu′tion•ar′i•ly,** *adv.* **—rev′o•lu′tion•ar′i•ness,** *n.*
—Syn. 2. unprecedented, novel, drastic, unorthodox.

Revolu′tionary cal′endar, the calendar of the French First Republic, adopted in 1793 and abandoned in 1805, consisting of 12 months, each of 30 days, and 5 intercalary days added at the end of the year (6 every fourth year). The months, beginning at the autumnal equinox, are Vendémiaire, Brumaire, Frimaire, Nivôse, Pluviôse, Ventôse, Germinal, Floréal, Prairial, Messidor, Thermidor, and Fructidor.

Revolu′tionary War′. See **American Revolution.** [1790–1800; *Amer.*]

revolu′tion count′er, a device for counting or recording the number of revolutions made by a rotating shaft, as of a motor or engine.

rev•o•lu•tion•ist (rev′ə lo͞o′shə nist), *n,* **1.** a person who advocates or takes part in a revolution. *—adj.* **2.** of, pertaining to, or characteristic of a revolution; revolutionary: *revolutionist ideals.* [1700–10; REVOLUTION + -IST]

rev•o•lu•tion•ize (rev′ə lo͞o′shə nīz′), *v.t.,* **-ized, -iz•ing. 1.** to bring about a revolution in; effect a radical change in: *to revolutionize petroleum refining methods.* **2.** to subject to a political revolution. Also, *esp. Brit.,* **rev′o•lu′tion•ise′.** [1790–1800; REVOLUTION + -IZE] **—rev′o•lu′tion•iz′er,** *n.*

re•volve (ri volv′), *v.,* **-volved, -volv•ing.** *—v.i.* **1.** to move in a circular or curving course or orbit: *The earth revolves around the sun.* **2.** to turn around or rotate, as on an axis: *The wheel revolves slowly.* **3.** to proceed or occur in a round or cycle; come around again in the process of time; recur. **4.** to be revolved in the mind. **5.** to focus or center on. *—v.t.* **6.** to cause to turn around, as on an axis. **7.** to cause to move in a circular or curving course, as about a central point. **8.** to think about; consider. [1350–1400; ME *revolven* < L *revolvere* to roll back, equiv. to *re-* RE- + *volvere* to roll, turn round] **—re•volv′a•ble,** *adj.* **—re•volv′a•bly,** *adv.*
—Syn. 1. orbit, circle. **2.** See **turn. 8.** ponder, study.

re•volv•er (ri vol′vər), *n.* **1.** a handgun having a revolving chambered cylinder for holding a number of cartridges, which may be discharged in succession without reloading. **2.** a person or thing that revolves. [1825–35, *Amer.*; REVOLVE + -ER[1]]

revolver (def. 1)

re•volv•ing (ri vol′ving), *adj.* **1.** that revolves: *a revolving table top.* **2.** *Mach.* noting or pertaining to a radial engine whose cylinders revolve around a stationary crankshaft, as the engine of a helicopter. [1690–1700; REVOLVE + -ING[2]] **—re•volv′ing•ly,** *adv.*

revolv′ing charge′ account′, a charge plan offering revolving credit. [1965–70]

revolv′ing cred′it, credit automatically available up to a predetermined limit while payments are periodically made. Cf. **credit line** (def. 2). [1915–20]

revolv′ing door′, 1. an entrance door for excluding drafts from the interior of a building, usually consisting of four rigid leaves set in the form of a cross and rotating about a central, vertical pivot in the doorway. **2.** *Informal.* **a.** a company, institution, or organization with a high turnover of personnel or members. **b.** a legal, medical, or other system or agency that discharges criminals, patients, etc., in the shortest possible time and without adequate attention or consideration. [1905–10] **—re•volv′ing-door′,** *adj.*

revolv′ing fund′, 1. any loan fund intended to be maintained by the repayment of past loans. **2.** a U.S. government fund, with loans and repayments equalized, used to aid businesses affecting the public interest, as public utilities. [1925–30]

revolv′ing stage′, *Theat.* a circular platform divided into segments enabling multiple theater sets to be put in place in advance and in turn rotated into view of the audience. [1910–15]

Rev. Stat., Revised Statutes.

re•vue (ri vyo͞o′), *n.* **1.** a form of theatrical entertainment in which recent events, popular fads, etc., are parodied. **2.** any entertainment featuring skits, dances, and songs. Also, **review.** [1870–75; < F: REVIEW] **—re•vu′ist,** *n.*

re•vul•sant (ri vul′sənt), *Med. adj., n.* revulsive. [1870–75; < L *revuls(us)* (see REVULSION) + -ANT]

re•vulsed (ri vulst′), *adj.* affected by revulsion. [1930–35; obs. *revulse* (< L *revulsus,* or back formation from REVULSION, etc.) + -ED[2]]

re•vul•sion (ri vul′shən), *n.* **1.** a strong feeling of repugnance, distaste, or dislike: *Cruelty fills me with revulsion.* **2.** a sudden and violent change of feeling or response in sentiment, taste, etc. **3.** the act of drawing something back or away. **4.** the fact of being so drawn. **5.** *Med.* the diminution of morbid action in one part of the body by irritation in another. [1535–45; < L *revulsiōn-* (s. of *revulsiō*) a tearing away, equiv. to *revuls(us)* (ptp. of *revellere* to tear away, equiv. to *re-* RE- + *vellere* to pluck) + *-iōn-* -ION] **—re•vul′sion•ar′y,** *adj.*
—Syn. 1. disgust, repulsion, loathing, aversion.

re•vul•sive (ri vul′siv), *Med. —adj.* **1.** tending to alter the distribution of blood by revulsion. *—n.* **2.** a revulsive agent, esp. one that causes revulsion. Also, **revulsant.** [1610–20; < L *revuls(us)* (see REVULSION) + -IVE] **—re•vul′sive•ly,** *adv.*

Rev. Ver., Revised Version (of the Bible).

re•ward (ri wôrd′), *n.* **1.** a sum of money offered for the detection or capture of a criminal, the recovery of lost or stolen property, etc. **2.** something given or received in return or recompense for service, merit, hardship, etc. *—v.t.* **3.** to recompense or requite (a person or animal) for service, merit, achievement, etc. **4.** to make return for or requite (service, merit, etc.); recompense. [1275–1325; (v.) ME *rewarden* orig., to regard < ONF *rewarder* to look at, var. of OF *reguarder;* (n.) ME: orig., regard < AF, ONF, var. of OF *reguard,* deriv. of *reguarder;* see REGARD] **—re•ward′a•ble,** *adj.* **—re•ward′a•ble•ness,** *n.* **—re•ward′a•bly,** *adv.* **—re•ward′er,** *n.* **—re•ward′less,** *adj.*
—Syn. 2. desert, pay, remuneration; requital; bounty, premium, bonus. REWARD, PRIZE, RECOMPENSE imply something given in return for good. A REWARD is something given or done in return for good (or, more rarely, evil) received; it may refer to something abstract or concrete: *a $50 reward; Virtue is its own reward.* PRIZE refers to something concrete offered as a reward of merit, or to be contested for and given to the winner: *to win a prize for an essay.* A RECOMPENSE is something given or done, whether as reward or punishment, for acts performed, services rendered, etc.; or it may be something given in compensation for loss or injury suffered, etc.: *Renown was his principal recompense for years of hard work.* **3.** compensate, pay, remunerate.

re•ward•ing (ri wôr′ding), *adj.* **1.** affording satisfaction, valuable experience, or the like; worthwhile. **2.** affording financial or material gain; profitable. [1690–1700; REWARD + -ING[2]] **—re•ward′ing•ly,** *adv.*

re•win (rē win′), *v.t.,* **-won, -win•ning.** to win back or again. [1600–10; RE- + WIN[1]]

re•wind (*v.* rē wīnd′; *n.* rē′wīnd′), *v.,* **-wound** or (*Rare*) **-wind•ed; -wind•ing,** *n.* *—v.t., v.i.* **1.** to wind again. **2.** to wind back to or toward the beginning; reverse. *—n.* **3.** an act or instance of rewinding. **4.** a function of a tape recorder or tape deck that causes the tape to wind backward. **5.** a push button or other control for reversing or reeling, as on a tape player. **6.** a camera control or mechanism used to wind film back into a film cassette. [1710–20; RE- + WIND[2]] **—re•wind′er,** *n.*

re•wire (rē wīᵊr′), *v.,* **-wired, -wir•ing.** *—v.t.* **1.** to provide with new wiring: *to rewire a house.* *—v.i.* **2.** to install new wiring. [1900–05; RE- + WIRE] **—re•wir′a•ble,** *adj.*

re•word (rē wûrd′), *v.t.* **1.** to put into other words: *to reword a contract.* **2.** to repeat. [1590–1600; RE- + WORD]

re•work (*v.* rē wûrk′; *n.* rē′wûrk′), *v.,* **-worked** or **-wrought, -work•ing,** *n.* *—v.t.* **1.** to work or form again: *to rework gold.* **2.** to revise or rewrite: *to rework an essay.* **3.** to process again or anew for reuse: *to rework wool.* *—n.* **4.** an act or instance of reworking: *His latest book is merely a rework of his earlier novel.* [1835–45; RE- + WORK]

re′worked wool′ (rē′wûrkt′), used wool which is reprocessed for additional use. [RE- + WORKED]

re•write (*v.* rē rīt′; *n.* rē′rīt′), *v.,* **-wrote, -writ•ten, -writ•ing,** *n.* *—v.t.* **1.** to write in a different form or manner; revise: *to rewrite the entire book.* **2.** to write again. **3.** to write (news submitted by a reporter) for inclusion in a newspaper. *—n.* **4.** the news story rewritten. **5.** something written in a different form or manner; revision. [1560–70; RE- + WRITE] **—re•writ′er,** *n.*

re•write•man (rē′rīt man′), *n., pl.* **-men.** a newspaper employee who writes articles from available information or who reworks the copy written by reporters. [1900–05, *Amer.*; REWRITE + MAN[1]]
—Usage. See **-man.**

re•write•per•son (rē′rīt pûr′sən), *n.* rewriteman. [REWRITE(MAN) + -PERSON]
—Usage. See **-person.**

re′write rule′, *Ling.* a phrase-structure rule in a generative grammar, shown as an instruction to replace or rewrite a single symbol, representing a syntactic structure, on the left with one or more symbols, representing the constituents of the structure, on the right, as in S → NP + VP, where S (sentence) is to be replaced with its constituents NP (noun phrase) and VP (verb phrase). Also, **rewrit′ing rule′.**

rex (reks; *Eng.* reks), *n., pl.* ***re•ges*** (RE′ges; *Eng.* rē′jēz). *Latin.* king.

Rex (reks), *n.* a Belgian fascist party founded in 1935. [after *Christus Rex,* title of a publication put out by its founders] **—Rex′ist,** *n.*

Rex (reks), *n.* a male given name.

rex′ begon′ia, a plant, *Begonia rex,* native to India, having wrinkled, variegated leaves and thick, hairy stems, and cultivated in many varieties.

rex begonia, *Begonia rex*

Rex•burg (reks′bûrg), *n.* a town in E Idaho. 11,559.

Rex•roth (reks′rôth, -roth), *n.* **Kenneth,** 1905–82, U.S. poet, critic, and translator.

Rey (rā) *n.* a city in N Iran, near Teheran. 102,825.

Reye's′ syn′drome (rīz, rāz), *Pathol.* an uncommon, severe disorder occurring primarily in children after a viral illness, as influenza or chickenpox, and associated with aspirin usage, involving swelling of the brain and liver and affecting other organs: symptoms include fever, projectile vomiting, confusion, and, sometimes, respiratory arrest. [after Ralph Douglas Kenneth *Reye* (1912–78), Australian pediatrician, who co-wrote a description of the syndrome in 1963]

Rey•kja•vik (rā′kyə vēk′, -vik), *n.* a seaport in and the capital of Iceland, in the SW part. 84,856.

Rey•mont (rā′mônt), *n.* **Wła•dy•sław Sta•ni•sław** (vwä dē′swäf stä nē′swäf), (*"Ladislas Regmont"*), 1868–1925, Polish novelist: Nobel prize 1924.

Reyn•ard (rā′närd, -nərd, ren′ərd), *n.* a name given to the fox, originally in the medieval beast epic *Reynard the Fox.* Also, **Renard.**

Rey•naud (re nō′), *n.* **Paul** (pôl), 1878–1966, French statesman: premier 1940.

Reyn•old (ren′ld), *n.* a male given name, form of **Reginald.**

Reyn•olds (ren′ldz), *n.* **Sir Joshua,** 1723–92, English painter.

Reyn•olds•burg (ren′ldz bûrg′), *n.* a town in central Ohio. 20,661.

CONCISE PRONUNCIATION KEY: act, cāpe, dâre, pärt; set, ēqual; *if,* īce; ox, ōver, ôrder, oil, bo͝ok, bo͞ot, out; up, ûrge; child; sing; shoe; thin, *th*at; zh as in *treasure.* ə = *a* as in *alone, e* as in *system, i* as in *easily, o* as in *gallop, u* as in *circus;* ᵊ as in *fire* (fīᵊr), *hour* (ouᵊr). l and n can serve as syllabic consonants, as in *cradle* (krād′l), and *button* (but′n). See the full key inside the front cover.

re•type′, *v.t.,* **-typed, -typ•ing.**
re′u•ni•fi•ca′tion, *n.*
re•u′ni•fy′, *v.t.,* **-fied, -fy•ing.**
re′up•hol′ster, *v.t.*
re′up•hol′ster•er, *n.*
re′up•hol′ster•y, *n., pl.* **-ster•ies.**
re′us•a•bil′i•ty, *n.*
re•us′a•ble, *adj.;* **-ness,** *n.*
re•use′, *v.,* **-used, -us•ing,** *n.*
re•use′a•ble, *adj.;* **-ness,** *n.*
re′u•ti•li•za′tion, *n.*
re•u′ti•lize′, *v.t.,* **-lized, -liz•ing.**
re•ut′ter, *v.t.*
re•ut′ter•ance, *n.*
re•va′cate, *v.t.,* **-cat•ed, -cat•ing.**
re•vac′ci•nate′, *v.t.,* **-nat•ed, -nat•ing.**
re′vac•ci•na′tion, *n.*
re•val′i•date′, *v.t.,* **-dat•ed, -dat•ing.**
re′val•i•da′tion, *n.*
re′va•por•i•za′tion, *n.*
re•va′por•ize′, *v.,* **-ized, -iz•ing.**
re•var′nish, *v.t.*
re•vend′, *v.t.*
re•ven′ti•late′, *v.t.,* **-lat•ed, -lat•ing.**
re′ven•ti•la′tion, *n.*
re′ver•i•fi•ca′tion, *n.*
re•ver′i•fy′, *v.t.,* **-fied, -fy•ing.**
re•ve′to, *v.t.,* **-toed, -to•ing.**
re•vi′brate, *v.,* **-brat•ed, -brat•ing.**
re′vi•bra′tion, *n.*
re•vict′ual, *v.,* **-ualed, -ual•ing** or (*esp. Brit.*) **-ualled, -ual•ling.**

Rey·no·sa (rā nô′sä), *n.* a city in N Tamaulipas, in E Mexico, on the Rio Grande. 193,653.

Re·za′i·yeh (ri zī′ə; *Pers.* ʀɪ zä′ē ye), *n.* a city in NW Iran. 155,000. Also, **Rizaiyeh.**

rez-de-chaus·sée (ʀād[ə] shō sā′), *n., pl.* ***rez-de-chaus·sées*** (ʀād[ə] shō sā′). *French.* ground floor.

re·zone (*v.* rē zōn′; *n.* rē zōn′, rē′zōn′), *v.,* **-zoned, -zon·ing,** *n.* —*v.t.* **1.** to reclassify (a property, neighborhood, etc.) as belonging to a different zone or being subject to different zoning restrictions. —*n.* **2.** an act or instance of rezoning. [1950–55; RE- + ZONE]

RF, radiofrequency. Also, **rf**

rf., *Baseball.* right fielder.

R.F., Reserve Force.

r.f., **1.** range finder. **2.** rapid-fire. **3.** reducing flame. **4.** *Baseball.* right field.

R.F.A., Royal Field Artillery.

R factor, a genetic component of some bacteria that provides resistance to antibiotics and can be transferred from one bacterium to another by conjugation. Also called **resistance transfer factor, RTF** [1960–65; *r(esistance) factor*]

r.f.b., *Football.* right fullback. Also, **R.F.B.**

RFC, Reconstruction Finance Corporation.

R.F.D., See **rural free delivery.** Also, **RFD**

RFE, Radio Free Europe. Also, **R.F.E.**

RFI, radio frequency interference.

RFLP (rif′lip′), *n.* restriction fragment length polymorphism: a fragment of DNA, cut by a restriction enzyme, that is different in length for each genetically related group and is used to trace family relationships. Also called **riflip.** [1985–90]

RFQ, *Com.* request for quotation.

r.g., *Football.* right guard.

RGB, *Television.* red-green-blue.

RGNP, real gross national product.

RH, *Meteorol.* See **relative humidity.** Also, **rh**

Rh, *Physiol.* See **Rh factor.**

Rh, *Symbol, Chem.* rhodium.

R.H., Royal Highness.

r.h., right hand.

rhabdo- a combining form meaning "rod," "wand," used in the formation of compound words: *rhabdomyoma.* [comb. form repr. Gk *rhábdos* rod, wand]

rhab·do·coele (rab′də sēl′), *n.* any member of the turbellarian flatworm order Neorhabdocoela, comprising both freshwater and marine species, having a simple saclike digestive system. [1875–80; < NL *Rhabdocoela* order name; see RHABDO-, -COELE]

rhab·dom (rab′dəm, -dom), *n. Anat., Zool.* **1.** any of various rod-shaped structures. **2.** the rod-shaped portion of an arthropod ommatidium. Also, **rhab·dome** (rab′dōm). [1875–80; < LGk *rhábdōma* bundle of rods; see RHABDO-, -OMA] —**rhab·do·mal** (rab dō′məl, rab′də məl), *adj.*

rhab·do·man·cy (rab′də man′sē), *n.* divination by means of a rod or wand, esp. in discovering ores, springs of water, etc. [1640–50; < LGk *rhabdomanteia;* see RHABDO-, -MANCY] —**rhab′do·man′tist,** *n.*

rhab·do·my·o·ma (rab′dō mī ō′mə), *n., pl.* **-mas, -ma·ta** (-mə tə). *Pathol.* a benign tumor made up of striated muscular tissue. Cf. **leiomyoma.** [1875–80; RHABDO- + MYOMA]

rhab·do·my·o·sar·co·ma (rab′dō mī′ō sär kō′mə), *n., pl.* **-mas, -ma·ta** (-mə tə). *Pathol.* a malignant tumor made up of striated muscle tissue. [1895–1900; RHABDO- + MYO- + SARCOMA]

rhab·do·vi·rus (rab′dō vī′rəs), *n., pl.* **-vi·rus·es.** any of various RNA-containing viruses of the family Rhabdoviridae, including the rabies virus. [1965–70; RHABDO- + VIRUS]

rha·chis (rā′kis), *n., pl.* **rha·chis·es, rhach·i·des** (rak′i dēz′, rā′ki-). rachis.

Rhad·a·man·thys (rad′ə man′thəs), *n.* **1.** *Class. Myth.* a son of Zeus and Europa, rewarded for the justice he exemplified on earth by being made, after his death, a judge in the Underworld, where he served with his brothers Minos and Aeacus. **2.** an inflexibly just or severe judge. Also, **Rhad′a·man′thus.** —**Rhad·a·man·thine** (rad′ə man′thin, -thīn), *adj.*

Rhae·ti·a (rē′shē ə, -shə), *n.* an ancient Roman province in central Europe, comprising what is now E Switzerland and a part of the Tyrol: later extended to the Danube.

Rhae·tian (rē′shən, -shē ən), *adj.* **1.** of or pertaining to Rhaetia. **2.** Rhaeto-Romanic. **3.** Raetic. —*n.* **4.** Raetic. **5.** Rhaeto-Romanic. Also, **Rhetian.** [1610–20; RHAETI(A) + -AN]

Rhae′tian Alps′, a chain of the Alps in E Switzerland and W Austria. Highest peak, Mt. Bernina, 13,295 ft. (4052 m).

Rhae·to-Ro·man·ic (rē′tō rō man′ik), *n.* **1.** a Romance language consisting of Friulian, Tyrolese, Ladin, and the Romansh dialects. —*adj.* **2.** of or pertaining to Rhaeto-Romanic. Also, **Rhae′to-Ro·mance′, Rhaetian.** [1865–70; *Rhaeto-* (repr. L *Rhaetus* Rhaetian) + ROMANIC (modeled on G *Rätoromanisch*)]

-rhagia, var. of **-rrhagia.** Also, **-rhage, -rhagy.**

rham·na·ceous (ram nā′shəs), *adj.* belonging to the Rhamnaceae, the buckthorn family of plants. Cf. **buckthorn family.** [< NL *Rhamnace(ae)* family name (*Rhamn(us)* genus name (< Gk *rhámnos* thorn bush) + *-aceae* -ACEAE) + -OUS]

rham·nose (ram′nōs, -nōz), *n. Biochem.* deoxymannose; a deoxy hexose sugar, $C_6H_{12}O_5$, that is an important component of the polysaccharides of plant cell walls. [< G (1887), equiv. to Gk *rhámn(os)* thorn bush + G *-ose* -OSE[2]]

rham·pho·the·ca (ram′fə thē′kə), *n.* the horny covering of a bird's bill. [1865–70; < Gk *rhámpho(s)* beak + THECA]

rhap·sod·ic (rap sod′ik), *adj.* **1.** extravagantly enthusiastic; ecstatic. **2.** pertaining to, characteristic of, or of the nature or form of rhapsody. Also, **rhap·sod′i·cal.** [1775–85; < Gk *rhapsōidikós.* See RHAPSODY, -IC] —**rhap·sod′i·cal·ly,** *adv.*
—**Syn. 1.** elated, transported, overjoyed.

rhap·so·dist (rap′sə dist), *n.* **1.** a person who rhapsodizes. **2.** (in ancient Greece) a person who recited epic poetry, esp. professionally. [1640–50; < Gk *rhapsōid(ós)* rhapsodist (*rhaps-,* var. s. of *rháptein* to stitch, + *-ōid(ē)* ODE + *-os* n. suffix) + -IST] —**rhap′so·dis′tic,** *adj.*

rhap·so·dize (rap′sə dīz′), *v.,* **-dized, -diz·ing.** —*v.i.* **1.** to talk with extravagant enthusiasm. **2.** to speak or write rhapsodies. —*v.t.* **3.** to recite as a rhapsody. Also, *esp. Brit.,* **rhap′so·dise′.** [1600–10; RHAPSOD(Y) + -IZE]

rhap·so·dy (rap′sə dē), *n., pl.* **-dies. 1.** *Music.* an instrumental composition irregular in form and suggestive of improvisation. **2.** an ecstatic expression of feeling or enthusiasm. **3.** an epic poem, or a part of such a poem, suitable for recitation at one time. **4.** a similar piece of modern literature. **5.** an intense or irregular poem or piece of prose. **6.** *Archaic.* a miscellaneous collection. [1535–45; < L *rhapsōdia* < Gk *rhapsōidía* recital of epic poetry, equiv. to *rhapsōid(ós)* RHAPSODIST + *-ia* -Y[3]]

rhat·a·ny (rat′n ē), *n., pl.* **-nies. 1.** either of two South American shrubs belonging to the genus *Krameria,* of the legume family, *K. tiandra* **(knotty rhatany** or **Peruvian rhatany)** or *K. argentea* **(Brazilian rhatany** or **Pará rhatany). 2.** the root of either of these plants, used as an astringent and tonic in medicine and also to color port wine. [1800–10; < NL *rhatania* < AmerSp *rataña*]

rha·thy·mi·a (rə thī′mē ə), *n.* carefree behavior; light-heartedness. [< Gk *rhāithȳmía* easiness of temper, amusement, indifference, equiv. to *rhāíthȳm(os)* easy-going + *-ia* -IA]

r.h.b., *Football.* right halfback. Also, **R.H.B.**

Rh disease, *Pathol.* erythroblastosis (def. 2). [1965–70; see RH FACTOR]

rhe (rē), *n. Physics.* a centimeter-gram-second unit of fluidity, equal to the reciprocal of poise. [1925–30; < Gk *rhéos* flowing substance, stream]

rhe·a (rē′ə), *n.* the ramie plant or fiber. [1850–55; < Assamese *rihā*]

Rhe·a (rē′ə), *n.* **1.** *Class. Myth.* a Titan, the daughter of Uranus and Gaea, the wife and sister of Cronus, and the mother of Zeus, Poseidon, Hera, Hades, Demeter, and Hestia: identified with Cybele and, by the Romans, with Ops. **2.** *Astron.* one of the moons of Saturn. **3.** (*l.c.*) either of two South American, ratite birds, *Rhea americana* or *Pterocnemia pennata,* resembling the African ostrich but smaller and having three toes. **4.** a female given name.

rhea, *Rhea americana,* standing height 4 to 5 ft. (1.2 to 1.5 m); length 4½ ft. (1.4 m)

-rhea, var. of **-rrhea.** Cf. **rheo-.**

Rhe·a Sil·vi·a (rē′ə sil′vē ə), *Rom. Legend.* the mother, by Mars, of Romulus and Remus. Also, **Rea Silvia.**

rhe·bok (rē′bok′), *n., pl.* **-boks,** (*esp. collectively*) **-bok.** a large, deerlike South African antelope, *Pelea capreolus,* with pale-gray, curly fur and straight horns. [1825–35; < Afrik *ribbok,* D *reebok;* c. ROEBUCK, G *Rehbock*]

rhe·da (rē′də), *n., pl.* **-das, -dae** (-dē, -dī). (in ancient Rome) a four-wheeled traveling carriage. [< L *raeda, r(h)ēda* < Gaulish; cf. PALFREY]

Rhee (rē), *n.* **Syng·man** (sing′mən), 1875–1965, president of South Korea 1948–60.

Rheims (rēmz; *Fr.* ʀᴀɴs), *n.* Reims.

Rheims′-Dou′ay Bi′ble (rēmz′dōō′ā). See **Douay Bible.** Also called **Rheims′-Dou′ay Ver′sion.**

Rhein (*Ger.* ʀīn), *n.* the Rhine.

Rhein·gau (rīn′gou), *n.* a small wine-growing region in Hesse, in central Germany, on the Rhine.

Rhein·gold, Das (*Ger.* däs ʀīn′gôlt′). See ***Ring of the Nibelung.*** Also, **Rhinegold.**

Rhein·hes·sen (rīn′hes′ən), *n.* a former Prussian province, now part of Hesse, Germany. Also, **Rhenish Hesse.**

Rhein·land (ʀīn′länt′), *n.* Rhineland.

Rhein·land-Pfalz (ʀīn′länt′pfälts′), *n.* German name of **Rhineland-Palatinate.**

Rhei·ta (rī′tə), *n.* a crater in the fourth quadrant of the face of the moon: about 42 miles (68 km) in diameter.

rhe·mat·ic (ri mat′ik), *adj.* **1.** pertaining to the formation of words. **2.** pertaining to the rheme of a sentence. [1855–60; < Gk *rhēmatikós* belonging to a word, equiv. to *rhēmat-* (s. of *rhêma*) word + *-ikos* -IC]

rheme (rēm), *n. Ling.* comment (def. 6). [1890–95; < Gk *rhêma* saying, word]

rhe·nic (rē′nik), *adj. Chem.* of or containing rhenium. [RHEN(IUM) + -IC]

Rhen·ish (ren′ish), *adj.* **1.** of the river Rhine or the regions bordering on it. —*n.* **2.** *Brit.* See **Rhine wine.** [1325–75; < L *Rhēn(us)* RHINE + -ISH[1]; r. ME *Rhinisch* < OHG]

Rhen′ish Hes′se, Rheinhessen.

rhe·ni·um (rē′nē əm), *n. Chem.* a rare metallic element of the manganese subgroup: used, because of its high melting point, in platinum-rhenium thermocouples. *Symbol:* Re; *at. no.:* 75; *at. wt.:* 186.2. [1920–25; < NL, equiv. to L *Rhēn(us)* RHINE + *-ium* -IUM]

rheo-, a combining form meaning "flow," "current," "stream," used in the formation of compound words: *rheoscope.* Cf. **-rrhea.** [comb. form repr. Gk *rhéos* STREAM, something flowing]

rhe·o·base (rē′ə bās′), *n. Physiol.* the minimum electric current required to excite a given nerve or muscle. [1920–25; RHEO- + BASE[1]]

rhe·ol·o·gy (rē ol′ə jē), *n.* the study of the deformation and flow of matter. [1925–30; RHEO- + -LOGY] —**rhe·o·log·ic** (rē′ə loj′ik), **rhe′o·log′i·cal,** *adj.* —**rhe·ol′o·gist,** *n.*

rhe·om·e·ter (rē om′i tər), *n.* an instrument for measuring the flow of fluids, esp. blood. [1835–45; RHEO- + -METER] —**rhe·o·met·ric** (rē′ə me′trik), *adj.* —**rhe·om′e·try,** *n.*

rhe·o·pex·y (rē′ə pek′sē), *n. Physical Chem.* the property exhibited by certain slow-gelling, thixotropic sols of gelling more rapidly when the containing vessel is shaken gently. [1930–35; RHEO- + *-pexy* < Gk *-pexia,* deriv. of *pêxis* a fixing, solidity; see -Y[3]] —**rhe·o·pec·tic** (rē′ə pek′tik), *adj.*

rhe·o·re·cep·tor (rē′ō ri sep′tər), *n.* a receptor of fishes and aquatic amphibians stimulated by water currents. [1945–50; RHEO- + RECEPTOR]

rhe·o·stat (rē′ə stat′), *n. Elect.* an adjustable resistor so constructed that its resistance may be changed without opening the circuit in which it is connected, thereby controlling the current in the circuit. [1843; RHEO- + -STAT] —**rhe′o·stat′ic,** *adj.*

rhe·o·tax·is (rē′ə tak′sis), *n. Biol.* oriented movement of an organism in response to a current of fluid, esp. water. [1895–1900; RHEO- + -TAXIS] —**rhe·o·tac·tic** (rē′ə tak′tik), *adj.*

rhe·o·tron (rē′ə tron′), *n. Physics.* (formerly) betatron. [RHEO- + -TRON]

rhe·ot·ro·pism (rē o′trə piz′əm), *n.* the effect of a current of water upon the direction of plant growth. [1885–90; RHEO- + -TROPISM] —**rhe·o·trop·ic** (rē′ə-trop′ik, -trō′pik), *adj.*

rhe·sus (rē′səs), *n.* a macaque, *Macaca mulatta,* of India, used in experimental medicine. See illus. under **monkey.** [1830–40; < NL, arbitrary use of L *Rhēsus* name of a Thracian king allied with Troy < Gk *Rhêsos*] —**rhe·sian** (rē′shən), *adj.*

Rhe′sus fac′tor (rē′səs). See **Rh factor.** [1940–45]

rhet., **1.** rhetoric. **2.** rhetorical.

Rhe·tian (rē′shən, -shē ən), *n., adj.* Rhaetian.

rhe·tor (rē′tər, ret′ər), *n.* **1.** a master or teacher of rhetoric. **2.** an orator. [1325–75; < L *rhētor* < Gk *rhḗtōr;* r. ME *rethor* < ML, L, as above]

rhet·o·ric (ret′ər ik), *n.* **1.** (in writing or speech) the undue use of exaggeration or display; bombast. **2.** the art or science of all specialized literary uses of language in prose or verse, including the figures of speech. **3.** the study of the effective use of language. **4.** the ability to use language effectively. **5.** the art of prose in general as opposed to verse. **6.** the art of making persuasive speeches; oratory. **7.** (in classical oratory) the art of influencing the thought and conduct of an audience. **8.** (in older use) a work on rhetoric. [1300–50; < L *rhētorica* < Gk *rhētorikḗ* (*téchnē*) rhetorical (art); r. ME *rethorik* < ML *rēthorica,* L *rhētorica,* as above]

rhe·tor·i·cal (ri tôr′i kəl, -tor′-), *adj.* **1.** used for, be-

CONCISE ETYMOLOGY KEY: <, descended or borrowed from; >, whence; b., blend of, blended; c., cognate with; cf., compare; deriv., derivative; equiv., equivalent; imit., imitative; obl., oblique; r., replacing; s., stem; sp., spelling, spelled; resp., respelling, respelled; trans., translation; ?, origin unknown; *, unattested; ‡, probably earlier than. See the full key inside the front cover.

re·vin′di·cate′, *v.t.,* **-cat·ed, -cat·ing.**
re′vin·di·ca′tion, *n.*
re·vi′o·late′, *v.t.,* **-lat·ed, -lat·ing.**
re′vi·o·la′tion, *n.*
re·vis′it, *v., n.*
re·vis′it·a·ble, *adj.*
re′vis·it·a′tion, *n.*
re′vis·u·al·i·za′tion, *n.*
re·vis′u·al·ize′, *v.,* **-ized, -iz·ing.**
re·vote′, *v.,* **-vot·ed, -vot·ing.**
re′vote′, *n.*
re·voy′age, *n., v.,* **-aged, -ag·ing.**
re·wa′ger, *v., n.*
re·wake′, *v.,* **-waked** or **-woke, -waked** or **-wok·en, -wak·ing.**
re·wak′en, *v.*
re·warm′, *v.*
re·warn′, *v.t.*
re·war′rant, *v.t.*
re·wash′, *v.*
re·wa′ter, *v.*
re·wax′, *v.*
re·weak′en, *v.*
re·wear′, *v.,* **-wore, -worn, -wear·ing.**
re·weave′, *v.,* **-wove, -wo·ven** or **-wove, -weav·ing.**
re·wed′, *v.,* **-wed·ded, -wed·ding.**
re·weigh′, *v.*
re·weld′, *v.*
re·wet′, *v.,* **-wet** or **-wet·ted, -wet·ting.**
re·wid′en, *v.*
re·wound′, *v.t.*
re·wrap′, *v.,* **-wrapped, -wrap·ping.**
re·yoke′, *v.t.,* **-yoked, -yok·ing.**

longing to, or concerned with mere style or effect. **2.** marked by or tending to use bombast. **3.** of, concerned with, or having the nature of rhetoric. [1470–80; < L *rhētoric(us)* (< Gk *rhētorikós*) + -AL[1]] **—rhe·tor′i·cal·ly,** *adv.* **—rhe·tor′i·cal·ness,** *n.*
—Syn. 1. verbal, stylistic, oratorical.

rhetor′ical ques′tion, a question asked solely to produce an effect or to make an assertion and not to elicit a reply, as "What is so rare as a day in June?" [1835–45]

rhetor′ical stress′, stress required by the meaning of a line, as distinguished from that required by the meter. [1720–30]

rhet·o·ri·cian (ret′ə rish′ən), *n.* **1.** an expert in the art of rhetoric. **2.** a person who teaches rhetoric. **3.** a person who writes or speaks in an elaborate or exaggerated style. [1375–1425; late ME *rethoricien* < MF *rethorique* RHETORIC + *-ien* -IAN]

rheum (ro͞om), *n.* **1.** a thin discharge of the mucous membranes, esp. during a cold. **2.** catarrh; cold. [1350–1400; ME *reume* < LL *rheuma* < Gk *rheûma* (*rheu-*, var. s. of *rheîn* to flow, STREAM + *-ma* n. suffix of result)] **—rheum′ic,** *adj.*

rheu·mat·ic (ro͝o mat′ik), *Pathol.* **—adj. 1.** pertaining to or of the nature of rheumatism. **2.** affected with or subject to rheumatism. **—n. 3.** a person affected with rheumatism. [1350–1400; ME *reumatik* < L *rheumaticus* < Gk *rheumatikós*, equiv. to *rheumat-* (s. of *rheûma;* see RHEUM) + *-ikos* -IC] **—rheu·mat′i·cal·ly,** *adv.*

rheumat′ic fe′ver, *Pathol.* a serious disease, associated with streptococcal infections, usually affecting children, characterized by fever, swelling and pain in the joints, sore throat, and cardiac involvement. [1775–85]

rheumat′ic heart′ disease′, *Pathol.* damage to the heart, esp. to the valves, as a result of rheumatic fever, characterized by inflammation of the myocardium or scarring and malfunction of the heart valves.

rheu·ma·tism (ro͞o′mə tiz′əm), *n. Pathol.* **1.** any disorder of the extremities or back, characterized by pain and stiffness. **2.** See **rheumatic fever.** [1595–1605; < L *rheumatismus* catarrh, rheum < Gk *rheumatismós*, equiv. to *rheumat-* (s. of *rheûma;* see RHEUM) + *-ismos* -ISM]

rheu·ma·tism-root (ro͞o′mə tiz′əm ro͞ot′, -ro͝ot′), *n.* See **spotted wintergreen.** [1835–45, *Amer.*]

rheu·ma·toid (ro͞o′mə toid′), *adj.* **1.** resembling rheumatism. **2.** rheumatic. Also, **rheu′ma·toi′dal.** [1855–60; < Gk *rheumat-* (s. of *rheûma;* see RHEUM) + -OID] **—rheu′ma·toi′dal·ly,** *adv.*

rheu′matoid arthri′tis, *Pathol.* a chronic autoimmune disease characterized by inflammation of the joints, frequently accompanied by marked deformities, and ordinarily associated with manifestations of a general, or systemic, affliction. [1855–60]

rheu′matoid fac′tor, *Biochem.* an antibody that is found in the blood of many persons afflicted with rheumatoid arthritis and that reacts against globulins in the blood. [1945–50]

rheu′matoid spondyli′tis, *Pathol.* See **ankylosing spondylitis.**

rheu·ma·tol·o·gist (ro͞o′mə tol′ə jist), *n.* a specialist in rheumatology, esp. a physician who specializes in the treatment of rheumatic diseases, as arthritis, lupus erythematosus, and scleroderma. [1945–50; RHEUMATOL-OG(Y) + -IST]

rheu·ma·tol·o·gy (ro͞o′mə tol′ə jē), *n.* the study and treatment of rheumatic diseases. [1940–45; RHEUMAT(IC) + -O- -LOGY]

rheum·y (ro͞o′mē), *adj.* **rheum·i·er, rheum·i·est.** pertaining to, causing, full of, or affected with rheum. [1585–95; RHEUM + -Y[1]] **—rheum′i·ly,** *adv.* **—rheum′i·ness,** *n.*

rhex·is (rek′sis), *n., pl.* **rhex·es** (rek′sēz). *Pathol.* rupture, as of a blood vessel, organ, or cell. [1375–1425; < NL < Gk *rhêxis* a breaking, cleft, deriv. of *rhēgnýnai* to break, break loose; r. late ME *rixis* (attested once) << Gk, as above]

Rheydt (rīt), *n.* a city in W Germany, adjacent to Mönchen-Gladbach. 96,000 (1963).

Rh fac·tor (är′āch′ fak′tər), *Physiol.* any of a type of specific antigen present on the surface of red blood cells, persons having inherited such antigens being designated Rh+ **(Rh positive)** and persons lacking them, a much smaller group, being designated Rh− **(Rh negative):** blood of Rh− persons is incompatible with Rh+ blood because of antibody reaction, and an Rh− woman who bears an Rh+ baby will have formed antibodies to the fetal blood that, unless removed from her bloodstream by apheresis in a subsequent pregnancy, will be carried across the placenta and destroy red blood cells of the next Rh+ fetus, resulting in erythroblastosis in the newborn. [1940–45; so called because first found in the blood of rhesus monkeys]

Rhi·an·non (rē′an ən), *n. Welsh Legend.* the wife of Pwyll who, accused of having eaten her son, was forced as a penance to carry people on her back until vindicated by her son's return.

rhig·o·lene (rig′ə lēn′), *n. Chem.* a petroleum distillate intermediate between cymogene and gasoline, formerly used to produce local anesthesia by freezing. [1865–70; < Gk *rhîg(os)* frost, cold + -OL[2] + -ENE]

rhin-, var. of **rhino-** before a vowel: *rhinencephalon.*

rhi·nal (rīn′l), *adj.* of or pertaining to the nose; nasal. [1860–65; RHIN- + -AL[1]]

Rhine (rīn), *n.* **1. Joseph Banks,** 1895–1980, U.S. psychologist: pioneer in parapsychology. **2.** German, **Rhein.** French, **Rhin** (RAN). Dutch, **Rijn.** a river flowing from SE Switzerland through Germany and the Netherlands into the North Sea: branches off into the Waal, Lek, and IJssel in its lower course. 820 mi. (1320 km) long.

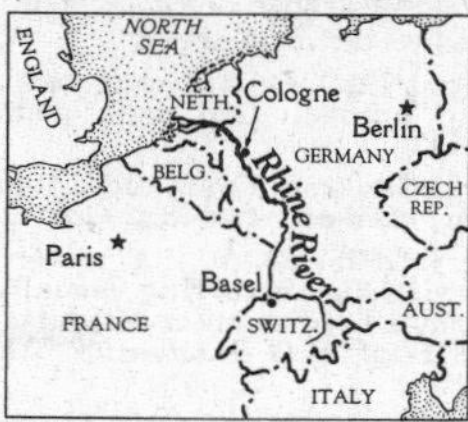

Rhine·gold (rīn′gōld′), *n.* Rheingold.

Rhine′grave breech′es (rīn′grāv′). See **petticoat breeches.** [1930–35; named after the *Rhinegrave* of Salm, who introduced the fashion in Paris about 1650; *Rhinegrave* < MD *rijngraaf,* G *Rheingraf* lit., Rhine count; see RHINE, GRAF]

Rhine·land (rīn′land′, -lənd), *n.* **1.** that part of Germany W of the Rhine. **2.** See **Rhine Province.** German, **Rheinland.**

Rhine·land-Pa·lat·i·nate (rīn′land′pə lat′n āt′, -it, -lənd-), *n.* a state in W Germany: formerly part of Rhine Province. 3,665,800; 7655 sq. mi. (19,825 sq. km). *Cap.:* Mainz. German, **Rheinland-Pfalz.**

rhi·nen·ceph·a·lon (rī′nen sef′ə lon′, -lən), *n., pl.* **-lons, -la** (-lə). *Anat.* the part of the cerebrum containing the olfactory structures. [1840–50; RHIN- + ENCEPHALON] **—rhi·nen·ce·phal·ic** (rī′nen sə fal′ik), **rhi′nen·ceph′a·lous,** *adj.*

Rhine′ Palat′inate. See under **Palatinate** (def. 1).

Rhine′ Prov′ince, a former province in W Germany, mostly W of the Rhine: now divided between Rhineland-Palatinate and North Rhine–Westphalia. Also called **Rhineland.** German, **Rheinland.**

rhine·stone (rīn′stōn′), *n.* an artificial gem of paste, often cut to resemble a diamond. [1885–90; RHINE + STONE (trans. of F *caillou du Rhin*)]

Rhine′ wine′, 1. any of numerous varieties of wine produced in the Rhine valley. **2.** any of a class of white wines, mostly light, still, and dry. [1835–45]

rhi·ni·tis (rī nī′tis), *n. Pathol.* inflammation of the nose or its mucous membrane. [1880–85; RHIN- + -ITIS]

rhi·no[1] (rī′nō), *n., pl.* **-nos,** (*esp. collectively*) **-no.** a rhinoceros. [1880–85; by shortening]

rhi·no[2] (rī′nō), *n. Chiefly Brit. Slang.* money; cash. [1680–90; orig. uncert.]

rhino-, a combining form meaning "nose," used in the formation of compound words: *rhinology.* Also, *esp. before a vowel,* **rhin-.** [< Gk *rhino-,* comb. form of *rhís* (s. *rhīn-*)]

rhi·noc·er·os (rī nos′ər əs), *n., pl.* **-os·es,** (*esp. collectively*) **-os. 1.** any of several large, thick-skinned, perissodactyl mammals of the family Rhinocerotidae, of Africa and India, having one or two upright horns on the snout: all rhinoceroses are endangered. **2.** *Douay Bible.* unicorn (def. 4). [1300–50; ME *rinoceros* < LL *rhinoceros* < Gk *rhīnókerōs,* equiv. to *rhino-* RHINO- + *-kerōs* -horned, adj. deriv. of *kéras* HORN (of an animal)]

Indian rhinoceros, *Rhinoceros unicornis,* 5½ ft. (1.7 m) high at shoulder; horn to 2 ft. (0.6 m); head and body 10 ft. (3 m); tail 2 ft. (0.6 m)

rhinoc′eros bee′tle, any of several scarabaeid beetles, esp. of the genus *Dynastes,* which comprises the largest beetles, characterized by one or more horns on the head and prothorax. Also called **dynastid.** [1675–85]

rhi·nol·o·gy (rī nol′ə jē), *n.* the science dealing with the nose and its diseases. [1830–40; RHINO- + -LOGY] **—rhi·no·log·ic** (rīn′l oj′ik), **rhi′no·log′i·cal,** *adj.* **—rhi·nol′o·gist,** *n.*

rhi·no·phar·yn·gi·tis (rī′nō far′in jī′tis), *n. Pathol.* inflammation of the mucous membranes of the nose and pharynx. [1950–55; RHINO- + PHARYNGITIS]

rhi·no·plas·ty (rī′nə plas′tē), *n., pl.* **-ties.** *Surg.* plastic surgery of the nose. [1835–45; RHINO- + -PLASTY] **—rhi′no·plas′tic,** *adj.*

rhi·nor·rhe·a (rī′nə rē′ə), *n. Pathol.* an excessive discharge of mucus from the nose. Also, **rhi′nor·rhoe′a.** [1865–70; < NL; see RHINO-, -RRHEA]

rhi·no·spo·rid·i·um (rī′nō spô rid′ē əm, -spō-), *n., pl.* **-i·a** (-ē ə). *Mycol.* any fungus of the genus *Rhinosporidium,* members of which produce vascular polyps in the nasal passages. [1900–05; < NL; see RHINO-, SPORE, -IDIUM]

rhi·no·vi·rus (rī′nō vī′rəs, rī′nō vī′-), *n., pl.* **-rus·es.** any of a varied and widespread group of picornaviruses responsible for many respiratory diseases, including the common cold. [1960–65; RHINO- + VIRUS]

-rhiza, var. of **-rrhiza.**

rhizo-, a combining form meaning "root," used in the formation of compound words: *rhizophagous.* Also, *esp. before a vowel,* **rhiz-.** Cf. **-rhiza, -rrhiza.** [< Gk, comb. form of *rhíza* ROOT[1]]

rhi·zo·bi·um (rī zō′bē əm), *n., pl.* **-bi·a** (-bē ə). *Bacteriol.* any of several rod-shaped bacteria of the genus *Rhizobium,* found as symbiotic nitrogen fixers in nodules on the roots of the bean, clover, etc. [< NL (1889), equiv. to *rhizo-* RHIZO- + Gk *bí(os)* life (see BIO-) + L *-um* n. suffix]

rhi·zo·car·pous (rī′zō kär′pəs), *adj. Bot.* having the root perennial but the stem annual, as perennial herbs. Also, **rhi·zo·car·pic** (rī′zō kär′pik). [1825–35; RHIZO- + -CARPOUS]

rhi·zo·ceph·a·lous (rī′zō sef′ə ləs), *adj. Zool.* belonging to the Rhizocephala, a group of degenerate hermaphrodite crustaceans that are parasitic chiefly on crabs. [1890–95; RHIZO- + -CEPHALOUS]

rhi·zoc·to·ni·a (rī′zok tō′nē ə), *n.* any of various soil-inhabiting fungi of the genus *Rhizoctonia,* some species of which are destructive to cultivated plants, causing damping off of seedlings, foliage blight, root and stem cankers, and rot of storage organs. [< NL (1815), equiv. to Gk *rhizo-* RHIZO- + *któn(os)* murder (akin to *kteínein* to kill, slay) + NL *-ia* -IA; so called from its pathogenic activity]

rhi·zo·gen·ic (rī′zō jen′ik), *adj. Bot.* producing roots, as certain cells. Also, **rhi·zog·e·nous** (rī zoj′ə nəs). [1880–85; RHIZO- + -GENIC]

rhi·zoid (rī′zoid), *adj.* **1.** rootlike. **—n. 2.** (in mosses, ferns, etc.) one of the rootlike filaments by which the plant is attached to the substratum. [1855–60; RHIZ- + -OID] **—rhi·zoi′dal,** *adj.*

rhi·zome (rī′zōm), *n. Bot.* a rootlike subterranean stem, commonly horizontal in position, that usually produces roots below and sends up shoots progressively from the upper surface. [1835–45; < NL *rhizoma* < Gk *rhízōma* root, stem, n. of result from *rhizoûn* to fix firmly, take root, deriv. of *rhíza* ROOT[1]] **—rhi·zom·a·tous** (rī zom′ə təs, -zō′mə-), *adj.*

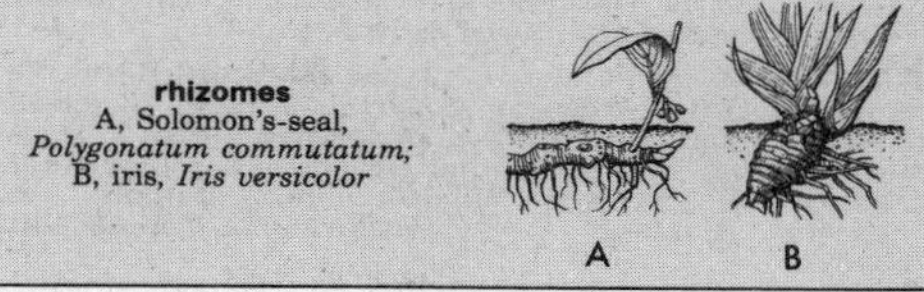

rhizomes
A, Solomon's-seal, *Polygonatum commutatum;* B, iris, *Iris versicolor*

rhi·zo·morph (rī′zə môrf′), *n. Mycol.* a cordlike fusion of hyphae that leads certain fungi across various substrates like a root through soil. [1840–50; RHIZO- + -MORPH]

rhi·zo·mor·phous (rī′zō môr′fəs), *adj. Bot.* rootlike in form. Also, **rhi′zo·mor′phoid.** [1855–60; RHIZO- + -MORPHOUS]

rhi·zoph·a·gous (rī zof′ə gəs), *adj.* feeding on roots. [1825–35; RHIZO- + -PHAGOUS]

rhi·zo·pod (rī′zə pod′), *n.* any of numerous protozoa of the widespread subphylum (or superclass) Rhizopoda, characterized by a pseudopod and comprising most members of the phylum Sarcodina, including the amebas and foraminifers. [1850–55; < NL *Rhizopoda* name of the superclass. See RHIZO-, -POD] **—rhi·zop·o·dan** (rī zop′ə dn), *adj., n.*

rhi·zot·o·my (rī zot′ə mē), *n., pl.* **-mies.** *Surg.* the surgical section or cutting of the spinal nerve roots, usually posterior or sensory roots, to eliminate pain. [1910–15; RHIZO- + -TOMY]

Rh neg·a·tive (är′āch′ neg′ə tiv). See under **Rh factor.** [1955–60]

rho (rō), *n., pl.* **rhos. 1.** the 17th letter of the Greek alphabet (P, ρ). **2.** the consonant sound represented by this letter. [1350–1400; ME < Gk *rhô*]

Rho., Rhodesia. Also, **Rhod.**

rhod-, var. of **rhodo-** before a vowel: *rhodamine.*

Rho·da (rō′də), *n.* a female given name.

rho·da·mine (rō′də mēn′, -min), *n. Chem.* **1.** a red dye obtained by heating an alkyl aminophenol with phthalic anhydride. **2.** any of various related dyes. [1885–90; RHOD- + AMINE]

Rhode′ Is′land (rōd), a state of the NE United States, on the Atlantic coast: a part of New England. 947,154; 1214 sq. mi. (3145 sq. km). *Cap.:* Providence. *Abbr.:* RI (for use with zip code), R.I. **—Rhode′ Is′lander.**

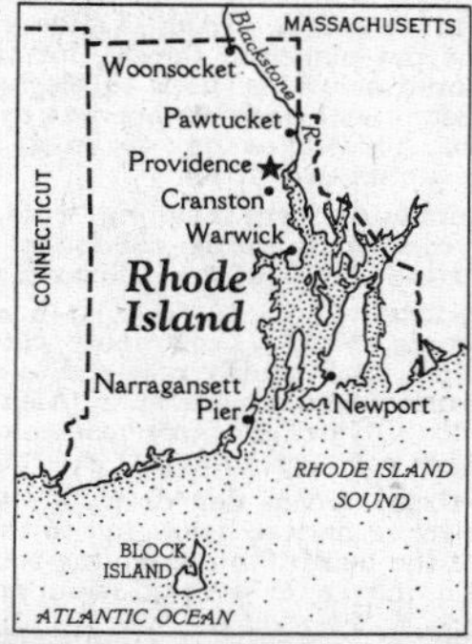

CONCISE PRONUNCIATION KEY: act, cāpe, dâre, pärt; set, ēqual; if, īce; ox, ōver, ôrder, oil, bo͝ok, bo͞ot, out; up, ûrge; child; sing; shoe; thin, *th*at; zh as in *treasure.* ə = *a* as in *alone, e* as in *system, i* as in *easily, o* as in *gallop, u* as in *circus;* ᵊ as in *fire* (fīᵊr), *hour* (ouᵊr). l and n can serve as syllabic consonants, as in *cradle* (krād′l), and *button* (but′n). See the full key inside the front cover.

Rhode′ Is′land bent′, a European pasture grass, *Agrostis tenuis,* naturalized in North America, having red flower clusters. [1780–90, *Amer.*]

Rhode′ Is′land Red′, one of an American breed of chickens having dark reddish-brown feathers and producing brown eggs. [1895–1900]

Rhode′ Is′land White′, one of a dual-purpose American breed of chickens having white feathers and a rose comb. [1920–25, *Amer.*]

Rhodes (rōdz), *n.* **1. Cecil John,** 1853–1902, English colonial capitalist and government administrator in southern Africa. **2. James Ford,** 1848–1927, U.S. historian. **3.** a Greek island in the SE Aegean, off the SW coast of Turkey: the largest of the Dodecanese Islands. 66,606; 542 sq. mi. (1404 sq. km). **4.** a seaport on this island. 32,019. Italian, **Rodi.** Greek, **Rhodos. 5. Colossus of,** a huge bronze statue of Apollo that stood at the entrance to the harbor of Rhodes. Cf. **Seven Wonders of the World.**

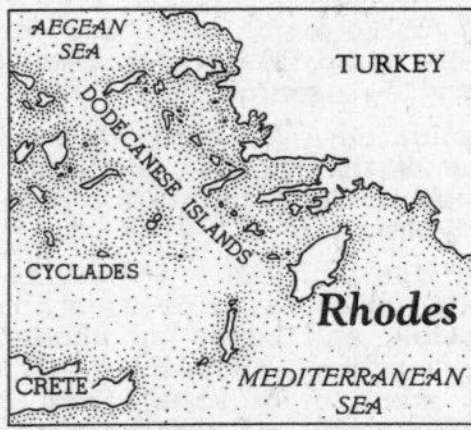

Rhodes′ grass′, a grass, *Chloris gayana,* native to Africa, used as pasturage and fodder in warm climates. [1910–15; named after Cecil J. RHODES]

Rho·de·sia (rō dē′zhə), *n.* **1.** (as **Southern Rhodesia**) a former British colony in S Africa: declared independence 1965; name changed to **Zimbabwe** 1979. **2.** a historical region in S Africa that comprised the British territories of Northern Rhodesia (now Zambia) and Southern Rhodesia (now Zimbabwe). **—Rho·de′sian,** *adj., n.*

Rhode′sia and Nya′saland, Federa′tion of, a former grouping of British territories in S Africa for administrative purposes (1953–63): composed of Southern and Northern Rhodesia and Nyasaland. Also called **Central African Federation.**

Rhode′sian man′, an extinct Pleistocene human whose cranial remains were found at Kabwe, in Zambia: formerly in some classifications *Homo rhodesiensis* but now considered archaic *Homo sapiens.* [1920–25]

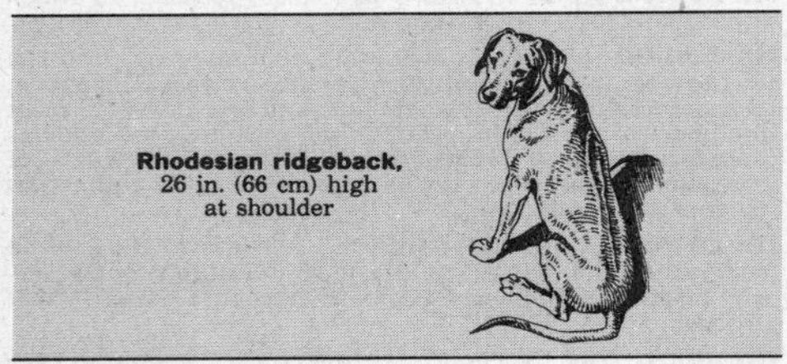
Rhodesian ridgeback, 26 in. (66 cm) high at shoulder

Rhode′sian ridge′back, one of a South African breed of medium-sized muscular hunting dogs having a short, glossy, red or tan coat, with a characteristic ridge of hair along the spine consisting of parallel crowns of hair growing in the opposite direction of the rest of the coat, originally developed for hunting lions but now used primarily as a guard dog. Also called **African lion hound.** [1935–40]

Rhodes′ schol′arship, one of a number of scholarships at Oxford University, established by the will of Cecil Rhodes, for selected students **(Rhodes′ schol′ars)** from the British Commonwealth and the United States. [1900–05]

Rho·di·an (rō′dē ən), *adj.* **1.** of or pertaining to the island Rhodes. **—***n.* **2.** a native or inhabitant of Rhodes. [1585–95; RHOD(ES) + -IAN]

rho·dic (rō′dik), *adj. Chem.* of or containing rhodium, esp. in the tetravalent state. [1835–45; RHOD(IUM) + -IC]

rho·di·um (rō′dē əm), *n. Chem.* a silvery-white metallic element of the platinum family, forming salts that give rose-colored solutions: used to electroplate microscopes and instrument parts to prevent corrosion. *Symbol:* Rh; *at. wt.:* 102.905; *at. no.:* 45; *sp. gr.:* 12.5 at 20°C. [1804; < NL; see RHOD-, -IUM]

rhodo-, a combining form meaning "rose," used in the formation of compound words: *rhodolite.* Also, *esp. before a vowel,* **rhod-.** [< Gk, comb. form of *rhódon* ROSE[1]]

rho·do·chro·site (rō′də krō′sīt), *n.* a mineral, manganese carbonate, $MnCO_3$, commonly containing some iron and calcium, and usually rose-red in color: a minor ore of manganese; manganese spar. Also called **dialogite.** [1830–40; < Gk *rhodóchrōs* rose-colored (*rhódo(n)* RHODO- + *chrṓs* color; cf. CHROMA) + -ITE[1]]

rho·do·den·dron (rō′də den′drən), *n.* any evergreen or deciduous shrub or tree belonging to the genus *Rhododendron,* of the heath family, having rounded clusters of showy, pink, purple, or white flowers and oval or oblong leaves. [1595–1605; < L < Gk *rhodódendron* (*rhódo-* RHODO- + *déndron* tree)]

rho·do·lite (rōd′l īt′), *n.* a rose or reddish-violet garnet, similar to pyrope, used as a gem. [1895–1900; RHODO- + -LITE]

rhod·o·mon·tade (rod′ə mon tād′, -täd′, -mən-, rō′-də-), *n., adj., v.,* **-tad·ed, -tad·ing.** *Obs.* rodomontade.

rho·do·nite (rōd′n īt′), *n.* a mineral, manganese metasilicate, $MnSiO_3$, occurring usually in rose-red masses, sometimes used as an ornamental stone; manganese spar. [1815–25; < G *Rhodonit* < Gk *rhódon* ROSE[1] + G *-it* -ITE[1]]

Rhod·o·pe (rod′ə pē, ro dō′-), *n.* **1.** a mountain range in SW Bulgaria. Highest peak, Mus Allah, 9595 ft. (2925 m). **2.** *Class. Myth.* a maiden skilled in hunting, the companion of Artemis.

rho·dop·sin (rō dop′sin), *n. Biochem.* a bright-red photosensitive pigment found in the rod-shaped cells of the retina of certain fishes and most higher vertebrates: it is broken down by the action of dim light into retinal and opsin. Also called **visual purple.** [1885–90; RHOD- + Gk *óps(is)* sight, vision + -IN[2]]

rho·do·ra (rō dôr′ə, -dōr′ə, rə-), *n.* a low North American shrub, *Rhododendron canadense,* of the heath family, having rose-colored flowers that appear before the leaves. [1780–90; < L *rhodōra* name of a plant]

Rho·dos (RÔ′thôs), *n.* Greek name of **Rhodes.**

-rhoea, var. of **-rrhea.**

Rhoe·cus (rē′kəs), *n.* fl. 6th century B.C., Greek sculptor and architect.

rhomb (rom, romb), *n.* rhombus. [< L *rhombus* RHOMBUS; cf. F *rhombe*]

rhom·ben·ceph·a·lon (rom′ben sef′ə lon′, -lən), *n., pl.* **-lons, -la** (-lə). *Anat.* the hindbrain. [1895–1900; < G; see RHOMB, ENCEPHALON]

rhom·bic (rom′bik), *adj.* **1.** having the form of a rhombus. **2.** having a rhombus as base or cross section. **3.** bounded by rhombuses, as a solid. **4.** *Crystall.* orthorhombic. Also, **rhom′bi·cal.** [1660–70; RHOMB + -IC]

rhom·bo·he·dron (rom′bə hē′drən), *n., pl.* **-drons, -dra** (-drə). a solid bounded by six rhombic planes. [1830–40; < Gk *rhómbo(s)* RHOMBUS + -HEDRON] **—rhom′bo·he′dral,** *adj.*

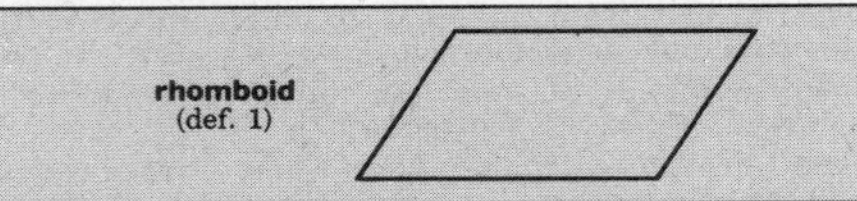
rhomboid (def. 1)

rhom·boid (rom′boid), *n.* **1.** an oblique-angled parallelogram with only the opposite sides equal. **2.** *Anat.* rhomboideus. **—***adj.* **3.** Also, **rhom·boi′dal.** having a form like or similar to that of a rhombus; shaped like a rhomboid. [1560–70; < LL *rhomboīdes* < Gk *rhomboeidḗs* (*schêma*) rhomboid (form, shape). See RHOMBUS, -OID] **—rhom·boi′dal·ly,** *adv.*

rhom·boi·de·us (rom boi′dē əs), *n., pl.* **-de·i** (-dē ī′). *Anat.* either of two back muscles that function to move the scapula. Also called **rhomboid.** [1825–35; < NL (*musculus*) *rhomboideus;* see RHOMBOID, -EUS]

rhom·bus (rom′bəs), *n., pl.* **-bus·es, -bi** (-bī). **1.** an oblique-angled equilateral parallelogram; any equilateral parallelogram except a square. **2.** an equilateral parallelogram, including the square as a special case. **3.** a rhombohedron. [1560–70; < L < Gk *rhómbos* anything that may be spun around, deriv. of *rhémbein* to revolve]

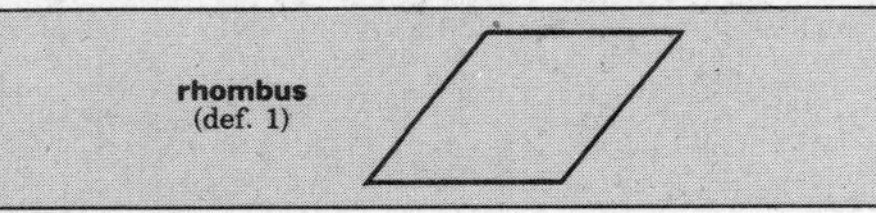
rhombus (def. 1)

rhon·chus (rong′kəs), *n., pl.* **-chi** (-kī). a wheezing or snoring sound heard upon auscultation of the chest, caused by an accumulation of mucus or other material. [1820–30; < L: a snoring, croaking < LGk *rhónchos,* var. of Gk *rhénchos*] **—rhon·chi·al** (rong′kē əl), **rhon·chal** (rong′kəl), *adj.*

Rhon·da (ron′də), *n.* a female given name.

Rhon·dda (ron′də; *Welsh* HRON′thä), *n.* a city in Mid Glamorgan, in S Wales. 86,400.

Rhone (rōn), *n.* **1.** a river flowing from the Alps in S Switzerland through the Lake of Geneva and SE France into the Mediterranean. 504 mi. (810 km) long. **2.** a department in E Central France: wine-growing region. 1,429,647; 1104 sq. mi. (2860 sq. km). *Cap.:* Lyons. French, **Rhône** (RŌN).

Rhone′ wine′, any of numerous varieties of wine produced in the Rhone River valley, between Lyons and the Mediterranean. [1850–55]

rho·pal′id bug′ (rō pal′id, rō′pə lid), any of various hemipterous insects of the family Rhopalidae that feed chiefly on grasses and occasionally on certain trees, as the box elder. Also called **grass bug, scentless plant bug.** [< NL *Rhopalidae* family name, equiv. to Gk *rhopal(on)* club + NL *-idae* -ID[2]]

R horizon, bedrock immediately underlying layers of soil.

rho·ta·cism (rō′tə siz′əm), *n.* **1.** *Historical Ling.* a change of a speech sound, esp. (s), to (r), as in the change from Old Latin *lases* to Latin *lares.* **2.** excessive use of the sound (r), its misarticulation, or the substitution of another sound for it. [1825–35; < Gk *rhô* RHO + (IO)TACISM] **—rho′ta·cis′tic,** *adj.*

rho·ta·cize (rō′tə sīz′), *v.,* **-cized, -ciz·ing.** **—***v.t.* **1.** to change (a sound) to an (r); subject to rhotacism. **2.** to pronounce (a vowel) with r-color. **—***v.i.* **3.** to undergo rhotacism. Also, *esp. Brit.,* **rho′ta·cise′.** [1960–65; RHOTAC(ISM) + -IZE] **—rho′ta·ci·za′tion,** *n.*

rho·tic (rō′tik), *Phonet.* **—***adj.* **1.** of or pertaining to a dialect of English in which the *r* is pronounced at the end of a syllable or before a consonant: *Midwestern American English is rhotic, while Southern British English is not.* **2.** of, pertaining to, or being an *r*-like sound. **—***n.* **3.** a rhotic sound. [*rhot-* (see RHOTACISM) + -IC]

Rh pos·i·tive (är′āch′ poz′i tiv). See under **Rh factor.** [1955–60]

rhu·barb (ro͞o′bärb), *n.* **1.** any of several plants belonging to the genus *Rheum,* of the buckwheat family, as *R. officinale,* having a medicinal rhizome, and *R. rhabarbarum,* having edible leafstalks. **2.** the rhizome of any medicinal species of this plant, forming a combined cathartic and astringent. **3.** the edible, fleshy leafstalks of *R. rhabarbarum,* used in making pies, preserves, etc. **4.** *Slang.* a quarrel or squabble. [1350–1400; ME *rubarb, reubarb* < OF *r(e)ubarbe* < ML *reubarbarum* < Gk *rhéon bárbaron* foreign rhubarb]

rhumb (rum, rumb), *n. Navig.* **1.** See **rhumb line. 2.** a point of the compass. [1570–80; < Sp *rumbo* < L *rhombus* RHOMBUS]

rhum·ba (rum′bə, ro͝om′-, ro͞om′-), *n., pl.* **-bas** (-bəz), *v.i.,* **-baed** (-bəd), **-ba·ing** (-bə ing). rumba.

rhumb′ line′, a curve on the surface of a sphere that cuts all meridians at the same angle. It is the path taken by a vessel or aircraft that maintains a constant compass direction. Also called **loxodrome, rhumb.** [1660–70]

rhumb′ sail′ing, sea navigation along rhumb lines. [1890–95]

rhyme (rīm), *n., v.,* **rhymed, rhym·ing.** **—***n.* **1.** identity in sound of some part, esp. the end, of words or lines of verse. **2.** a word agreeing with another in terminal sound: Find *is a rhyme for* mind *and* womankind. **3.** verse or poetry having correspondence in the terminal sounds of the lines. **4.** a poem or piece of verse having such correspondence. **5.** verse (def. 4). **6. rhyme or reason,** logic, sense, or plan: *There was no rhyme or reason for what they did.* **—***v.t.* **7.** to treat in rhyme, as a subject; turn into rhyme, as something in prose. **8.** to compose (verse or the like) in metrical form with rhymes. **9.** to use (a word) as a rhyme to another word; use (words) as rhymes. **—***v.i.* **10.** to make rhyme or verse; versify. **11.** to use rhyme in writing verse. **12.** to form a rhyme, as one word or line with another: *a word that rhymes with orange.* **13.** to be composed in metrical form with rhymes, as verse: *poetry that rhymes.* Also, **rime.** [1250–1300; ME *rime* < OF, deriv. of *rimer* to rhyme < Gallo-Romance **rimāre* to put in a row << OHG *rīm* series, row; prob. not connected with L *rhythmus* rhythm, although current sp. (from c1600) appar. by assoc. with this word] **—rhym′er,** *n.*

rhyme′ roy′al, *Pros.* a form of verse introduced into English by Chaucer, consisting of seven-line stanzas of iambic pentameter in which there are three rhymes, the first line rhyming with the third, the second with the fourth and fifth, and the sixth with the seventh. [1835–45]

rhyme′ scheme′, the pattern of rhymes used in a poem, usually marked by letters to symbolize correspondences, as rhyme royal, *ababbcc.* [1930–35]

rhyme·ster (rīm′stər), *n.* a writer of inferior verse; poetaster. Also, **rimester.** [1710–20; RHYME + -STER] **—Syn.** versifier.

rhym′ing slang′, **1.** a form of slang in which a rhyming word or phrase is substituted for the word intended, as *Kate and Sidney* for *steak and kidney* or *khaki rocks* for *army socks.* **2.** a further removal from the original word intended by ellipsis of the rhyming part, as *titfer* for *tit for tat* for *hat.* [1855–60]

rhyn·cho·ce·pha·lian (ring′kō sə fāl′yən, -fā′lē ən), *adj.* **1.** belonging or pertaining to the Rhynchocephalia, an order of lizardlike reptiles that are extinct except for the tuatara. **—***n.* **2.** a rhynchocephalian reptile. [1865–70; < NL *Rhynchocephali(a)* name of the order (< Gk *rhýncho(s)* snout + NL *-cephalia;* see CEPHAL-, -IA) + -AN]

rhy·o·lite (rī′ə līt′), *n.* a fine-grained igneous rock rich in silica: the volcanic equivalent of granite. [1865–70; *rhyo-* (irreg. < Gk *rhýax* stream of lava) + -LITE] **—rhy·o·lit·ic** (rī′ə lit′ik), *adj.*

rhythm (rith′əm), *n.* **1.** movement or procedure with uniform or patterned recurrence of a beat, accent, or the like. **2.** *Music.* **a.** the pattern of regular or irregular pulses caused in music by the occurrence of strong and weak melodic and harmonic beats. **b.** a particular form of this: *duple rhythm; triple rhythm.* **3.** measured movement, as in dancing. **4.** *Art, Literature.* a patterned repetition of a motif, formal element, etc., at regular or irregular intervals in the same or a modified form. **5.** the effect produced in a play, film, novel, etc., by the combination or arrangement of formal elements, as length of scenes, speech and description, timing, or recurrent themes, to create movement, tension, and emotional value in the development of the plot. **6.** *Pros.* **a.** metrical or rhythmical form; meter. **b.** a particular kind of metrical form. **c.** metrical movement. **7.** the pattern of recurrent strong and weak accents, vocalization and silence, and the distribution and combination of these elements in speech. **8.** *Physiol.* the regular recurrence of an action or function, as of the beat of the heart, or the menstrual cycle. **9.** procedure marked by the regular recurrence of particular elements, phases, etc.: *the rhythm of the seasons.* **10.** regular recurrence of elements in a system of motion. [1550–60; < L *rhythmus* < Gk *rhythmós;* cf. *rheîn* to flow] **—rhythm′less,** *adj.* **—Syn. 9.** flow, pulse, cadence.

rhythm-and-blues (rith′əm ən blo͞oz′), *n.* a folk-based but urbanized form of black popular music that is marked by strong, repetitious rhythms and simple melodies and was developed, in a commercialized form, into rock-'n'-roll. [1945–50, *Amer.*]

rhythm′ band′, a collection of simple percussion in-

CONCISE ETYMOLOGY KEY: <, descended or borrowed from; >, whence; b., blend of, blended; c., cognate with; cf., compare; deriv., derivative; equiv., equivalent; imit., imitative; obl., oblique; r., replacing; s., stem; sp., spelling, spelled; resp., respelling, respelled; trans., translation; ?, origin unknown; *, unattested; ‡, probably earlier than. See the full key inside the front cover.

struments used esp. with piano accompaniment to teach musical rhythm. [1940–45]

rhyth•mic (riŧħ′mik), *adj.* **1.** cadenced; rhythmical. —*n.* **2.** rhythmics. [1595–1605; < LL *rhythmicus* < Gk *rhythmikós.* See RHYTHM, -IC]

rhyth•mi•cal (riŧħ′mi kəl), *adj.* **1.** periodic, as motion, or a drumbeat. **2.** having a flowing rhythm. **3.** of or pertaining to rhythm: *an excellent rhythmical sense.* [1560–70; RHYTHMIC + -AL[1]] —**rhyth′mi•cal•ly,** *adv.*

rhyth•mic•i•ty (riŧħ mis′i tē), *n.* the state or quality of being rhythmical. [1900–05; RHYTHMIC + -ITY]

rhyth•mics (riŧħ′miks), *n.* (*used with a singular v.*) the science of rhythm and rhythmic forms. Also, **rhythmic.** [1860–65; RHYTHM + -ICS]

rhyth•mist (riŧħ′mist), *n.* **1.** a person versed in or having a fine sense of rhythm. **2.** a person who uses rhythm, esp. in a skilled way: *a film editor who is a good rhythmist.* [1860–65; RHYTHM + -IST]

rhythm′ meth′od, a method of birth control in which the couple abstain from sexual intercourse during the period when ovulation is most likely to occur. Cf. **safe period.** [1935–40]

rhythm′ sec′tion, *Music.* **1.** band instruments, as drums or bass, that supply rhythm rather than harmony or melody. **2.** the group of players in a band who play such instruments. [1925–30]

rhythm′ stick′, a small wooden stick used, esp. by a child, as a simple percussive instrument in learning the rudiments of musical rhythm. [1950–55]

rhyt•i•dec•to•my (rit′i dek′tə mē), *n., pl.* **-mies.** face-lift. [1930–35; < Gk *rhytid-,* s. of *rhytís* wrinkle + -ECTOMY]

rhy•ton (rī′ton), *n., pl.* **-ta** (-tə). an ancient Greek drinking horn, made of pottery or metal, having a base in the form of the head of a woman or animal. [1840–50; < Gk *rhytón,* n. use of neut. of *rhytós* flowing, akin to *rheîn* to flow]

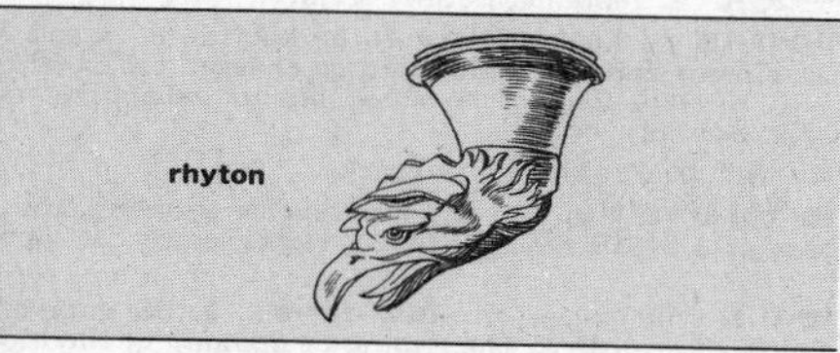
rhyton

RI, Rhode Island (approved esp. for use with zip code).

R.I., **1.** Queen and Empress. [< L *Rēgīna et Imperātrix*] **2.** King and Emperor. [< L *Rēx et Imperātor*] **3.** Rhode Island.

ri•a (rē′ə), *n.* a long, narrow inlet of a river that gradually decreases in depth from mouth to head. [1895–1900; < Sp *ría* river]

ri•al[1] (rē ôl′, -äl′), *n.* a silver or cupronickel coin and monetary unit of Iran, equal to 100 dinars. [1930–35; < Pers < Ar *riyāl* RIYAL]

ri•al[2] (rī′əl), *n.* ryal.

ri•al[3] (rē ôl′, -äl′), *n.* riyal.

rial′ o•ma′ni (ō mä′nē), a paper money, coin, and monetary unit of Oman, equal to 1000 baiza. *Abbr.:* RO. [< Ar *riyāl* RIYAL; *'Umān* Oman + *-ī* suffix of appurtenance]

ri•al•to (rē al′tō), *n., pl.* **-tos.** an exchange or mart. [1590–1660; after the RIALTO in Venice]

Ri•al•to (rē al′tō; *for 1, 2 also It.* Rē äl′tô), *n.* **1.** a commercial center in Venice, Italy, consisting of an island and the surrounding district. **2.** a bridge spanning the Grand Canal in Venice, Italy: constructed of marble in 1590. **3.** a city in SW California, near Los Angeles. 35,615. **4.** the theater district of a city or town, esp. the area around Broadway in New York City.

ri•ant (rī′ənt, rē′-; *Fr.* RYÄN), *adj.* laughing; smiling; cheerful; gay. [1560–70; < F, prp. of *rire* to laugh << L *ridēre;* see -ANT] —**ri′ant•ly,** *adv.*

ri•a•ta (rē ä′tə, -at′ə), *n.* a lariat. Also, **reata.** [1840–50, *Amer.;* < Sp *reata,* deriv. of *reatar* to tie again, equiv. to *re-* RE- + *atar* < L *aptāre* to fit]

rib[1] (rib), *n., v.,* **ribbed, rib•bing.** —*n.* **1.** one of a series of curved bones that are articulated with the vertebrae and occur in pairs, 12 in humans, on each side of the vertebrate body, certain pairs being connected with the sternum and forming the thoracic wall. See diag. under **skeleton.** **2.** a cut of meat, as beef, containing a rib. See diag. under **beef.** **3. ribs,** spareribs (def. 2). **4.** *Archit.* **a.** any of several archlike members of a vault supporting it at the groins, defining its distinct surfaces, or dividing these surfaces into panels: including ogives and tiercerons. **b.** any of several molded members or moldings, including ridge ribs and liernes, on the surface of a vault accenting the ridges or dividing the surface into panels. **5.** something resembling a rib in form, position, or use, as a supporting or strengthening part. **6.** a structural member that supports the shape of something: *an umbrella rib.* **7.** *Naut.* any of the curved framing members in a ship's hull that rise upward and outward from the keel; frame. **8.** a stiffening beam cast as part of a concrete slab. **9.** a primary vein of a leaf. **10.** a vertical ridge in cloth, esp. in knitted fabrics. **11.** a ridge, as in poplin or rep, caused by heavy yarn. **12.** a wife (in humorous allusion to the creation of Eve. Gen. 2:21–22). **13.** *Ceram.* a scraper for smoothing clay being thrown on a potter's wheel. **14.** a metal ridge running along the top of the barrel of a firearm to simplify aligning the sights. **15.** a longitudinal strip of metal joining the barrels of a double-barreled gun. —*v.t.* **16.** to furnish or strengthen with ribs. **17.** to enclose as with ribs. **18.** to mark with riblike ridges or markings. [bef. 900; ME, OE *rib(b);* c. G *Rippe*] —**rib′ber,** *n.* —**rib′less,** *adj.* —**rib′like′,** *adj.*

rib[2] (rib), *v.t.,* **ribbed, rib•bing.** to tease; make fun of. [1925–30, *Amer.;* appar. short for *rib-tickle* (v.)]

R.I.B.A., Royal Institute of British Architects.

rib•ald (rib′əld; *spelling pron.* rī′bəld), *adj.* **1.** vulgar or indecent in speech, language, etc.; coarsely mocking, abusive, or irreverent; scurrilous. —*n.* **2.** a ribald person. [1200–50; ME *ribald, ribaud* (n.) < OF *ribau(l)d,* equiv. to *rib(er)* to be licentious (< OHG *rīben* to copulate, be in heat, lit., rub) + *-au(l)d, -alt* < Frankish **-wald* a suffix in personal names, deriv. of **walden* to rule; cf. parallel development of -ARD] —**rib′ald•ly,** *adv.* —**Syn. 1.** indecent, obscene, gross. —**Ant. 1.** pure.

rib•ald•ry (rib′əl drē; *spelling pron.* rī′bəl drē), *n.* **1.** ribald character, as of language; scurrility. **2.** ribald speech. [1300–50; ME *ribaudrie* < OF. See RIBALD, -RY]

rib•and (rib′ənd), *n.* a decorative ribbon. [1350–1400; ME: RIBBON]

ri•bat (ri bät′), *n. Islam.* a building housing a community of Sufis. [< Ar *ribāṭ* hostelry]

ri•ba•vi•rin (rī′bə vī′rin), *n. Pharm.* a synthetic compound, $C_8H_{12}N_4O_5$, active against several DNA and RNA viruses. [1965–70; prob. by shortening and alter. of *ribofuranosyl,* a component of its chemical name (see RIBOSE, FURAN, -OSE[2], -YL) + VIR(US) + -IN[2]]

rib•band[1] (rib′band′, rib′ənd, -ən), *n.* **1.** Also, **ribbon.** *Shipbuilding.* a strip of wood or metal running fore-and-aft along frames to keep them in the proper position until the shell planking or plating is in place. **2.** *Carpentry.* ribbon (def. 8). [1705–15; RIB[1] + BAND[2]]

rib•band[2] (rib′ənd), *n. Heraldry.* riband.

ribbed-knit (ribd′nit′), *n.* rib-knit (def. 2).

ribbed′ toad′. See **tailed frog.**

ribbed′ vault′, *Archit.* a vault supported by or decorated with diagonal ribs. Also called **rib vault.**

Rib•ben•trop (rib′ən trôp′), *n.* **Jo•a•chim von** (yō′ä-KHIM fən), 1893–1946, German leader in the Nazi party: minister of foreign affairs 1938–45; executed for war crimes.

rib•bing[1] (rib′ing), *n.* **1.** ribs collectively. **2.** an assemblage or arrangement of ribs, as in cloth or a ship. [1555–65; RIB[1] + -ING[1]]

rib•bing[2] (rib′ing), *n.* an act or instance of teasing. [1930–35; RIB[2] + -ING[1]]

rib•bon (rib′ən), *n.* **1.** a woven strip or band of fine material, as silk or rayon, varying in width and finished off at the edges, used for ornament, tying, etc. **2.** material in such strips. **3.** anything resembling or suggesting a ribbon or woven band. **4.** a band of inked material used in a typewriter, adding machine, etc., that supplies ink for printing the figure on the striking typeface onto the paper beneath. **5.** a strip of material, as satin or rayon, being or representing a medal or similar decoration, esp. a military one: *an overseas ribbon.* **6. ribbons, a.** torn or ragged strips; shreds: *clothes torn to ribbons.* **b.** reins for driving. **7.** a long, thin flexible band of metal, as for a spring, a band saw, or a tapeline. **8.** Also, **ribband.** Also called **ledger, ledger board, ribbon strip.** *Carpentry.* a thin horizontal piece let into studding to support the ends of joists. **9.** *Archit.* came[2]. **10.** Also, **ribband.** *Naut.* a distinctive narrow band or stripe painted along the exterior of a hull. **11.** *Shipbuilding.* ribband[1] (def. 1). —*v.t.* **12.** to adorn with ribbon. **13.** to mark with something suggesting ribbon. **14.** to separate into ribbonlike strips. —*v.i.* **15.** to form in ribbonlike strips. Also **riband** (for defs. 8, 10). [1520–30; var. of ME *riban(d)* < OF, var. of *r(e)uban,* perh. < Gmc. See BAND[2]] —**rib′bon•like′, rib′bon•y,** *adj.*

rib′bon cop′y, the original copy of a number of typewritten copies (distinguished from *carbon copy*). [1965–70]

rib′bon devel′opment, housing or commercial buildings built along a stretch of road. [1925–30]

rib•bon•fish (rib′ən fish′), *n., pl.* (*esp. collectively*) **-fish,** (*esp. referring to two or more kinds or species*) **-fish•es. 1.** any of several marine fishes of the families Trachipteridae, Regalicidae, and Lophotidae, having a long, compressed, ribbonlike body. **2.** any of several related fishes, as the oarfish. **3.** any of several unrelated but similar fishes, as the cutlassfish and jackknife-fish. Also called **snakefish.** [1785–95; RIBBON + FISH]

rib′bon light′ning, a repeated lightning discharge in which successive strokes are displaced from each other by wind, resulting in a broadened appearance. [1885–90]

rib′bon mi′crophone, a microphone that utilizes a metal ribbon suspended in a magnetic field. [1930–35]

rib′bon plant′. See **spider plant** (def. 1).

rib′bon snake′, either of two long-tailed garter snakes, *Thamnophis proximus* or *T. sauritus,* of eastern and central North America, having a brownish body and yellow or orange stripes. [1730–40, *Amer.*]

rib′bon strip′, *Carpentry.* ribbon (def. 8).

rib′bon win′dow, a long window made up of a number of individual compartments set together horizontally with little or no division.

rib′bon worm′, any of various slender, unsegmented marine worms of the phylum Nemertea, being able to contract and stretch to an extreme extent. [1850–55]

rib•by[1] (rib′ē), *adj.* **-bi•er, -bi•est.** having prominent ribs: *a ribby fabric.* [1840–50; RIB[1] + -Y[1]]

rib•by[2] (rib′ē), *n., pl.* **-bies.** *Baseball Slang.* a run batted in. [formation based on the abbr. *RBI;* see -Y[2]]

rib′ cage′, *Anat.* the enclosure formed by the ribs and their connecting bones. [1905–10]

Ri•bei•rão Prê•to (rē′bā ROUN′ PRE′tŏŏ), a city in SE Brazil. 190,897.

rib′ eye′, a large beefsteak cut from the outer, or eye, side of the ribs. Also, **rib′-eye′.** Also called **rib′-eye steak′.** [1925–30]

rib•grass (rib′gras′, -gräs′), *n.* See **English plantain.** [1530–40; RIB[1] + GRASS]

rib-knit (rib′nit′), *adj.* **1.** (of a knitted garment or fabric) having a pattern of ribs: *a rib-knit sweater.* —*n.* **2.** Also, **ribbed-knit.** a garment having such a pattern. [1965–70]

ri•bo•fla•vin (rī′bō flā′vin, rī′bō flā′-, -bə-), *n. Biochem.* a vitamin B complex factor appearing as an orange-yellow, crystalline compound, $C_{17}H_{20}N_4O_6$, derived from ribose, essential for growth, found in milk, fresh meat, eggs, leafy vegetables, etc., or made synthetically, and used in enriching flour, in vitamin preparations, and in treating facial lesions. Also, **ri•bo•fla•vine** (rī′bō flā′vin, -vēn). Also called **lactoflavin, vitamin B_2, vitamin G.** [1930–35; RIBO(SE) + FLAVIN]

ri•bo•nu•cle•ase (rī′bō nōō′klē ās′, -āz′, -nyōō′-), *n. Biochem.* any of the class of enzymes that catalyze the hydrolysis of RNA. Also called **RNase, RNAase.** [1940–45; RIBONUCLE(IC ACID) + -ASE]

ri′bo•nu•cle′ic ac′id (rī′bō nōō klē′ik, -klā′-, -nyōō-, rī′-), *Biochem.* See **RNA.** Also, **ri′bose nucle′ic ac′id.** [1930–35; RIBO(SE) + NUCLEIC ACID]

ri•bo•nu•cle•o•pro•tein (rī′bō nōō′klē ō prō′tēn, -tē-in, -nyōō′-), *n. Biochem.* a substance composed of RNA in close association with protein; a nucleoprotein containing RNA. *Abbr.:* RNP [1935–40; RIBO(SE) + NUCLEOPROTEIN]

ri•bo•nu•cle•o•side (rī′bō nōō′klē ə sīd′, -nyōō′-), *n. Biochem.* a ribonucleotide precursor that contains ribose and a purine or pyrimidine base. [1930–35; RIBO(NUCLEIC ACID) + NUCLEOSIDE]

ri•bo•nu•cle•o•tide (rī′bō nōō′klē ə tīd′, -nyōō′-), *n. Biochem.* an ester, composed of a ribonucleoside and phosphoric acid, that is a constituent of ribonucleic acid. [1925–30; RIBO(NUCLEIC ACID) + NUCLEOTIDE]

ri•bose (rī′bōs), *n. Biochem.* a white, crystalline, water-soluble, slightly sweet solid, $C_5H_{10}O_5$, a pentose sugar obtained by the hydrolysis of RNA. [1890–95; < G *Ribose,* earlier *Ribonsäure,* equiv. to *Ribon* (from *Arabinose* ARABINOSE, by arbitrary rearrangement and shortening) + *Säure* acid]

ri•bo•so (ri bō′sō), *n., pl.* **-sos.** rebozo.

ribosomal RNA, *Biochem.* a type of RNA, distinguished by its length and abundance, functioning in protein synthesis as a component of ribosomes. *Abbr.:* rRNA [1960–65; RIBOSOME + -AL[1]]

ri•bo•some (rī′bə sōm′), *n. Cell Biol.* a tiny, somewhat mitten-shaped organelle occurring in great numbers in the cell cytoplasm either freely, in small clusters, or attached to the outer surfaces of endoplasmic reticula, and functioning as the site of protein manufacture. See diag. under **cell.** [1955–60; RIBO(SE) + -SOME[3]] —**ri′bo•so′mal,** *adj.*

ri•bo•zo (ri bō′sō, -zō), *n., pl.* **-zos.** rebozo.

ri•bo•zyme (rī′bə zīm′), *n.* a segment of RNA that can act as a catalyst. [1985–90; RIBO(SOME) + (EN)ZYME] —**ri′bo•zy′mal,** *adj.*

rib′ roast′, a cut of beef taken from the small end of the ribs and containing a large rib eye and two or more ribs. Also called **standing rib roast.** [1885–90]

rib′ steak′. See **club steak.** [1920–25]

rib-tick•ling (rib′tik′ling), *adj.* very amusing; funny or hilarious: *a book of rib-tickling stories.* [1935–40] —**rib′-tick′ler,** *n.*

rib′ vault′. See **ribbed vault.**

rib•wort (rib′wûrt′, -wôrt′), *n.* See **English plantain.** [1325–75; ME. See RIB[1], WORT[2]]

Ri•car′di•an the′ory of rent′ (ri kär′dē ən). See **economic rent.** [after David RICARDO; see -IAN]

Ri•car•do (ri kär′dō), *n.* **David,** 1772–1823, English economist.

Ric•ca′ti equa′tion (ri kä′tē; *It.* Rēk kä′tē), *Math.* a differential equation, $dy/dx + fy^2 + gy + h = 0$, where f, g, and h are functions of x. [named after J. F. *Riccati* (1676–1754), Italian mathematician]

Ric•ci (Rēt′chē), *n.* **Se•bas•tia•no** (se′bäs tyä′nô), 1660?–1734, Italian painter.

Ric•cio (*It.* Rēt′chô), *n.* **Da•vid** (*It.* dä′vēd). See **Rizzio.**

rice (rīs), *n., v.,* **riced, ric•ing.** —*n.* **1.** the starchy seeds or grain of an annual marsh grass, *Oryza sativa,* cultivated in warm climates and used for food. **2.** the grass itself. —*v.t.* **3.** to reduce to a form resembling rice: *to rice potatoes.* [1200–50; ME *ris, rys* < OF < It *riso, risi* (in ML *rīsium*) < MGk *orýzion,* deriv. of Gk *óryza*]

Rice (rīs), *n.* **1. Dan** (*Daniel McLaren*), 1823–1900, U.S. circus clown, circus owner, and Union patriot. **2. Elmer,** 1892–1967, U.S. playwright. **3. Grant•land** (grant′lənd), 1880–1954, U.S. journalist.

rice′ bean′, a southern Asian vine, *Vigna umbellata,* of the legume family, cultivated for its edible seeds.

rice•bird (rīs′bûrd′), *n.* **1.** *Southern U.S.* the bobolink. **2.** See **Java sparrow. 3.** any of several other birds that frequent rice fields. [1695–1705; RICE + BIRD]

rice′ blast′, *Plant Pathol.* a disease of rice caused by the fungus *Pyricularia oryae,* characterized by elliptical leaf spots with reddish-brown margins, brownish lesions and neck rot of the fruiting panicles, and stunting of the plant.

rice′ coal′, anthracite in sizes ranging from under $^5/_{16}$ in. (0.79 cm) to over $^3/_{16}$ in. (0.48 cm).

rice′ pa′per, 1. a thin paper made from the straw of rice. **2.** a Chinese paper consisting of the pith of certain plants cut and pressed into thin sheets. [1815–25]

rice′-pa•per tree′ (rīs′pā′pər), an Asian shrub or small tree, *Tetrapanax papyriferus,* of the ginseng fam-

CONCISE PRONUNCIATION KEY: act, cāpe, dâre, pärt; set, ēqual; if, ice; ox, ōver, ôrder, oil, bŏŏk, bōōt, out; up, ûrge; child; sing; shoe; thin, that; zh as in treasure. ə = a as in alone, e as in system, i as in easily, o as in gallop, u as in circus; ᵊ as in fire (fīᵊr), hour (ouᵊr). l and n can serve as syllabic consonants, as in cradle (krād′l), and button (but′n). See the full key inside the front cover.

ily, the pith of which is used in making rice paper. Also called **rice′-paper plant′.**

ric·er (rī′sər), *n.* an implement for ricing potatoes, squash, etc., by pressing them through small holes. [1895–1900, *Amer.*; RICE + -ER[1]]

rice′ rat′, any rat of the genus *Oryzomys,* having an exceptionally long tail, esp. *O. palustris,* inhabiting rice fields and marshes of the southern U.S., Mexico, and Central America. [1880–85]

ri·cer·car (rē′chər kär′), *n.* **1.** *Music.* a chiefly polyphonic instrumental form of the 16th and 17th centuries closely resembling the vocal motet in structure and style. **2.** a composition, esp. for a keyboard instrument, having this form. Also, **ricercare, ri·cer·ca·ta** (rē′chər kä′tə). [1780–90; apocopated var. of RICERCARE]

ri·cer·ca·re (rē′chər kär′ā; *It.* rē′cher kä′re), *n., pl.* **-ca·ri** (-kär′ē; *It.* -kä′rē). ricercar. [< It, n. use of *ricercare* to seek; see RESEARCH]

rice′ wee′vil, a brown weevil, *Sitophilus oryzae,* that infests stored grains, esp. rice. [1805–15]

ric·ey (rī′sē), *adj.,* **-ey·er, -ey·est.** pertaining to, resembling, or containing rice. [1770–80; RICE + -Y[1]]

rich (rich), *adj.,* **-er, -est,** *n.* **—***adj.* **1.** having wealth or great possessions; abundantly supplied with resources, means, or funds; wealthy: *a rich man; a rich nation.* **2.** abounding in natural resources: *a rich territory.* **3.** having wealth or valuable resources (usually fol. by *in*): *a country rich in traditions.* **4.** abounding (usually fol. by *in* or *with*): *a countryside rich in beauty; a design rich with colors.* **5.** of great value or worth; valuable: *a rich harvest.* **6.** (of food) delectably and perhaps unhealthfully spicy, or sweet and abounding in butter or cream: *a rich gravy; a rich pastry.* **7.** costly, expensively elegant, or fine, as dress or jewels. **8.** sumptuous; elaborately abundant: *a rich feast.* **9.** using valuable materials or characterized by elaborate workmanship, as buildings or furniture. **10.** abounding in desirable elements or qualities: *a man rich in kindness.* **11.** (of wine) strong and finely flavored. **12.** (of color) deep, strong, or vivid: *rich purple.* **13.** full and mellow in tone: *rich sounds; a rich voice.* **14.** strongly fragrant; pungent: *a rich odor.* **15.** producing or yielding abundantly: *a rich soil.* **16.** abundant, plentiful, or ample: *a rich supply.* **17.** *Auto.* (of a mixture in a fuel system) having a relatively high ratio of fuel to air (contrasted with *lean*). **18.** *Informal.* **a.** highly amusing. **b.** ridiculous; absurd. **—***n.* **19.** (*used with a plural v.*) rich persons collectively (usually prec. by *the*): *new tax shelters for the rich.* [bef. 900; ME; OE *rīce* (adj.) << Celtic; c. G *reich* wealthy; akin to L *rēx,* Skt *rājan* king] **—rich′ly,** *adv.* **—rich′ness,** *n.*
—Syn. 1. well-to-do, moneyed. RICH, WEALTHY, AFFLUENT all indicate abundance of possessions. RICH is the general word; it may imply that possessions are newly acquired: *an oilman who became rich overnight.* WEALTHY suggests permanence, stability, and appropriate surroundings: *a wealthy banker.* AFFLUENT usually suggests a generous amount of income, with a high standard of living and some social prestige and privilege: *an affluent family.* **5.** bountiful, copious, luxuriant. **7.** precious, high-priced, dear. **12.** intense, vibrant. **14.** aromatic. **15.** fruitful, productive, prolific, luxuriant. **16.** bountiful, copious, abounding, bounteous. **—Ant. 1–5, 15, 16.** poor.

Rich (rich), *n.* **1. Adrienne,** born 1929, U.S. poet and feminist. **2.** a male given name, form of **Richard.**

Ri·chard (ri shärd′; *Fr.* rē shar′), *n.* **Mau·rice** (mô rēs′; *Fr.* mō rēs′), (*"the Rocket"*), born 1921, Canadian hockey player.

Rich·ard (rich′ərd), *n.* a male given name.

Richard I, (*"Richard the Lion-Hearted," "Richard Coeur de Lion"*) 1157–99, king of England 1189–99.

Richard II, **1.** 1367–1400, king of England 1377–99 (successor to and grandson of Edward III; son of Edward, Prince of Wales). **2.** (*italics*) a drama (1595?) by Shakespeare.

Rich·ard III, **1.** (*Duke of Gloucester*) 1452–85, king of England 1483–85. **2.** (*italics*) a drama (1592–93?) by Shakespeare.

Rich′ard Coeur′ de Li′on (kûr′ də lē′ən; *Fr.* kœr də lē ôɴ′). See **Richard I.**

Rich′ard Roe′ (rō), a fictitious name used in legal proceedings for a male party whose true name is not known, used esp. as the second such name when two male persons are involved whose real names have not been ascertained. Cf. **John Doe.** [1865–70]

Rich·ards (rich′ərdz), *n.* **1. Dickinson Wood·ruff** (wo͝od′ruf), 1895–1973, U.S. physician: Nobel prize 1956. **2. I(vor) A(rmstrong)** (ī′vər, ē′vər), 1893–1979, English literary critic in the U.S. **3. Theodore William,** 1868–1928, U.S. chemist: Nobel prize 1914.

Rich·ard·son (rich′ərd sən), *n.* **1. Henry Handel** (*Henrietta Richardson Robertson*), 1870–1946, Australian novelist. **2. Henry Hob·son** (hob′sən), 1838–86, U.S. architect. **3. Sir Owen Williams,** 1879–1959, English physicist: Nobel prize 1928. **4. Sir Ralph (David),** 1902–83, English actor. **5. Samuel,** 1689–1761, English novelist. **6. Tony,** 1928–91, English motion-picture and theatrical director. **7. Walter Hart,** 1880–1961, U.S. journalist. **8.** a city in NE Texas, near Dallas. 72,496.

Rich′ardson ground′ squir′rel, a ground squirrel, *Citellus richardsoni,* of sagebrush and grassland areas of the northwestern U.S. and adjacent regions in Canada. Also called **flickertail.** [1935–40; named after Sir John Richardson (1787–1865), Scottish naturalist]

Riche·lieu (rish′ə lo͞o′; *Fr.* rēsh° lyœ′), *n.* **1. Armand Jean du Ples·sis** (ar mäɴ′ zhäɴ dy ple sē′), Duc de, 1585–1642, French cardinal and statesman. **2.** a river in SE Canada, in Quebec, flowing N from Lake Champlain to the St. Lawrence. 210 mi. (340 km) long.

rich·en (rich′ən), *v.t., v.i.* to make or become rich or richer. [1875–80; RICH + -EN[1]]

rich·es (rich′iz), *n.pl.* abundant and valuable possessions; wealth. [1175–1225; ME, pl. of ME *riche* wealth, power (OE *rīce* power, rule; c. G *Reich* realm); confused with ME *richesse* wealth < OF, equiv. to *riche* wealthy (< Gmc; see RICH) + *-esse* -ESS]

Ri·chet (ri shā′; *Fr.* rē she′), *n.* **Charles Ro·bert** (sharl rô ber′), 1850–1935, French physician: Nobel prize 1913.

Rich·field (rich′fēld′), *n.* a city in E Minnesota, near Minneapolis. 37,851.

Rich·ie (rich′ē), *n.* a male given name, form of **Richard.**

Ri·chier (rē shyā′), *n.* **Ger·maine** (zher men′), 1904–59, French sculptor.

Rich·land (rich′lənd), *n.* a city in SE Washington, on the Columbia River: residential and administrative quarters for the Hanford Works. 33,578. Cf. **Hanford** (def. 2).

Rich·ler (rich′lər), *n.* **Mordecai,** born 1931, Canadian novelist.

Rich·mond (rich′mənd), *n.* **1.** former name of Staten Island (def. 2). **2.** a port in and the capital of Virginia, in the E part on the James River: capital of the Confederacy 1861–65. 219,214. **3.** Also called **Rich·mond-up·on-Thames** (rich′mənd ə pon′temz′, -pôn′-). a borough of Greater London, England, on the Thames River: site of Kew Gardens. 168,300. **4.** a seaport in W California, on San Francisco Bay. 74,676. **5.** a city in E Indiana. 41,349. **6.** a city in E central Kentucky. 21,705. **7.** a male given name.

Rich′mond Heights′, **1.** a city in E Missouri, near St. Louis. 11,516. **2.** a town in N Ohio. 10,095.

Rich′mond Hill′, a town in SE Ontario, in S Canada, N of Toronto. 37,778.

rich′ rhyme′, *Pros.* See **rime riche.** [1650–60]

Rich·ter (rik′tər; *Ger.* riᴋʜ′tər; *Russ.* ryeᴋʜ′tyir), *n.* **1. Burton,** born 1931, U.S. physicist: Nobel prize 1976. **2. Conrad,** 1890–1968, U.S. novelist. **3. Jean Paul Frie·drich** (zhäɴ poul frē′driᴋʜ), (*"Jean Paul"*), 1763–1825, German author. **4. Svia·to·slav (Te·o·fi·lo·vich)** (svē at′ə släf′ tā′ə fē′lə vich; *Russ.* svyi tu släf′ tyi u fyē′lə vyich), born 1915, Russian pianist.

Rich′ter scale′, a scale, ranging from 1 to 10, for indicating the intensity of an earthquake. [1935–40; after Charles F. *Richter* (1900–85), U.S. seismologist]

Richt·ho·fen (riᴋʜt′hō′fən), *n.* **Baron Man·fred von** (män′frāt fən), (*"Red Baron"* or *"Red Knight"*), 1892–1918, German aviator.

rich·weed (rich′wēd′), *n.* **1.** clearweed. **2.** See **horse balm.** [1755–65, *Amer.*; RICH + WEED[1]]

ri·cin (rī′sin, ris′in), *n. Chem.* a white, poisonous, protein powder from the bean of the castor-oil plant. [1895–1900; < NL *Ricinus* name of genus, L: castor-oil plant]

ric·in·o·le·ic (ris′ə nō lē′ik, -nō′lē ik), *adj. Chem.* of or derived from ricinoleic acid. [1840–50; < L *ricin(us)* castor-oil plant + OLEIC]

ric′inole′ic ac′id, *Chem.* a colorless to yellow, viscous, liquid, water-insoluble, unsaturated hydroxyl acid, $C_{18}H_{34}O_3$, occurring in castor oil in the form of the glyceride: used in soaps and textile finishing. [1840–50]

ric·in·o·le·in (ris′ə nō′lē in), *n. Chem.* the glyceride of ricinoleic acid, the chief constituent of castor oil. [RICINOLE(IC) + -IN[2]]

ric′i·nus oil′ (ris′ə nəs), *Chem.* See **castor oil.** [1685–95; < NL, the genus name; L: lit., tick (parasite), allegedly so called in reference to the appearance of the seeds]

rick[1] (rik), *n.* **1.** Also, **hayrick.** *Chiefly Midland U.S.* a large, usually rectangular stack or pile of hay, straw, corn, or the like, in a field, esp. when thatched or covered by a tarpaulin; an outdoor or makeshift mow. **2.** a stack of cordwood or logs cut to even lengths. **3.** a frame of horizontal bars and vertical supports, as used to hold barrels in a distillery, boxes in a warehouse, etc. **—***v.t.* **4.** to form grain into a stack or pile. **5.** to stack (cordwood) in ricks. [bef. 900; ME *rek(e), reek,* OE *hrēac;* akin to ON *hraukr,* OFris *reak,* MD *rooc, roke*] **—rick′er,** *n.*

rick[2] (rik), *v.t., v.i., n.* wrick.

Rick (rik), *n.* a male given name, form of **Eric** or **Richard.**

Rick·en·back·er (rik′ən bak′ər), *n.* **Edward Vernon** (*"Eddie"*), 1890–1973, U.S. aviator and aviation executive.

rick·ets (rik′its), *n. Pathol.* a disease of childhood, characterized by softening of the bones as a result of inadequate intake of vitamin D and insufficient exposure to sunlight, also associated with impaired calcium and phosphorus metabolism. [1635–45; orig. uncert.]

rick·ett·si·a (ri ket′sē ə), *n., pl.* **-si·ae** (-sē ē′), **-si·as** (-sē əz). **1.** any member of the genus *Rickettsia,* comprising rod-shaped to coccoid microorganisms that resemble bacteria but can be as small as a large virus and reproduce only inside a living cell, parasitic in fleas, ticks, lice, and mites and transmitted by bite to vertebrate hosts, including humans, causing such severe diseases as typhus and Rocky Mountain spotted fever. **2.** any rickettsia or rickettsialike microorganism of the orders Rickettsiales and Chlamydiales. [1915–20; < NL, after Howard T. *Ricketts* (1871–1910), U.S. pathologist; see -IA] **—rick·ett′si·al,** *adj.*

rick·et·y (rik′i tē), *adj.,* **-et·i·er, -et·i·est.** **1.** likely to fall or collapse; shaky: *a rickety chair.* **2.** feeble in the joints; tottering; infirm: *a rickety old man.* **3.** old, dilapidated, or in disrepair. **4.** irregular, as motion or action. **5.** affected with or suffering from rickets. **6.** pertaining to or of the nature of rickets. [1675–85; RICKET(S) + -Y[1]] **—rick′et·i·ness,** *n.*
—Syn. 2. decrepit, frail, withered, unsteady, wobbly.

rick·ey (rik′ē), *n., pl.* **-eys.** a drink made with lime juice, carbonated water, and gin or other liquor. [1890–95, *Amer.*; named after a Colonel *Rickey*]

Rick·ey (rik′ē), *n.* **(Wesley) Branch,** 1881–1965, U.S. baseball executive.

Rick·o·ver (rik′ō vər), *n.* **Hyman George,** 1900–86, U.S. naval officer, born in Poland: helped to develop the nuclear submarine.

rick·rack (rik′rak′), *n.* a narrow, zigzag braid or ribbon used as a trimming on clothing, linens, etc. Also, **ric-rac.** [1880–85, *Amer.*; gradational redupl. of RACK[1]]

rick·shaw (rik′shô, -shä), *n.* jinrikisha. Also, **rick′·sha, rikisha, rikshaw.** [1885–90; by shortening and contr.]

Rick·y (rik′ē), *n.* a male given name, form of **Rick.** Also, **Rick′ie.**

rick·y-tick (rik′ē tik′, -tik′), *Informal.* **—***n.* **1.** the mechanical, repetitive style and beat of ragtime or early swing music. **—***adj.* Also, **rick·y-tick·y** (rik′ē tik′ē, -tik′ē). **2.** of or characteristic of such sound or beat. **3.** corny or outmoded. [1935–40; appar. imit.]

RICO (rē′kō), *n.* Racketeer Influenced and Corrupt Organizations Act: a U.S. law, enacted in 1970, allowing victims of organized crime to sue those responsible for punitive damages.

ric·o·chet (rik′ə shā′, rik′ə shā′ *or, esp. Brit.,* rik′ə shet′), *n., v.,* **-cheted** (-shād′, -shād′), **-chet·ing** (-shā′ing, -shā′ing) or (*esp. Brit.*) **-chet·ted** (-shet′id), **-chet·ting** (-shet′ing). **—***n.* **1.** the motion of an object or a projectile in rebounding or deflecting one or more times from the surface over which it is passing or against which it hits a glancing blow. **—***v.i.* **2.** to move in this way, as a projectile. [1760–70; < F; orig. uncert.]
—Syn. 2. rebound, deflect, glance.

ri·cot·ta (ri kot′ə, -kô′tə; *It.* rē kôt′tä), *n.* a soft Italian cheese that resembles cottage cheese. [1875–80; < It < L *recocta,* fem. of *recoctus,* ptp. of *recoquere* to recook. See RE-, COOK[1]]

ric·rac (rik′rak′), *n.* rickrack.

ric′tal bris′tle, a bristlelike feather growing from the base of a bird's bill. [1815–25; *rictal,* equiv. to RICT(US) + -AL]

ric·tus (rik′təs), *n., pl.* **-tus, -tus·es.** **1.** the gape of the mouth of a bird. **2.** the gaping or opening of the mouth. [1750–60; < L: wide-open mouth, equiv. to *rig-,* var. s. of *ringī* to open the mouth wide + *-tus* suffix of v. action.] **—ric′tal,** *adj.*

rid[1] (rid), *v.t.,* **rid** or **rid·ded, rid·ding.** **1.** to clear, disencumber, or free of something objectionable (usually fol. by *of*): *to rid the house of mice; to rid yourself of a bad habit.* **2.** to relieve or disembarrass (usually fol. by *of*): *to rid the mind of doubt.* **3.** *Archaic.* to deliver or rescue: *to rid him from his enemies.* **4. be rid of,** to be free of or no longer encumbered by: *to be rid of debts.* **5. get rid of,** to eliminate or discard: *It's time we got rid of this trash.* [1150–1200; ME *ridden* (v.), OE *(ge)ryddan* to clear (land); c. ON *rythja* to clear, empty] **—rid′der,** *n.*

rid[2] (rid), *v. Archaic.* a pt. and pp. of **ride.**

rid·a·ble (rī′də bəl), *adj.* **1.** capable of being ridden, as a horse. **2.** capable of being ridden over, through, etc., as a road or a stream. Also, **rideable.** [1895–1900; RIDE + -ABLE] **—rid′a·bil′i·ty,** *n.*

rid·dance (rid′ns), *n.* **1.** the act or fact of clearing away or out, as anything undesirable. **2.** relief or deliverance from something. **3. good riddance,** a welcome relief or deliverance from something: *He's gone, and good riddance!* [1525–35; RID[1] + -ANCE]
—Syn. 1. ouster, clearance, dislodgment.

rid·den (rid′n), *v.* a pp. of **ride.**

-ridden, a combining form meaning "obsessed with," "overwhelmed by" (*torment-ridden*) or "full of," "burdened with" (*debt-ridden*). [special use of RIDDEN]

rid·dle[1] (rid′l), *n., v.,* **-dled, -dling.** **—***n.* **1.** a question or statement so framed as to exercise one's ingenuity in answering it or discovering its meaning; conundrum. **2.** a puzzling question, problem, or matter. **3.** a puzzling thing or person. **4.** any enigmatic or dark saying or speech. **—***v.i.* **5.** to propound riddles; speak enigmatically. [bef. 1000; ME *redel, redels* (n.), OE *rǣdels(e)* counsel, opinion, imagination, riddle (*rǣd(an)* to counsel, REDE + *-els(e)* deverbal n. suffix) with loss of *-s-* in ME through confusion with the pl. form of the n. suffix *-el* -LE (cf. BURIAL); c. G *Rätsel,* D *raadsel*]
—Syn. 1. See **puzzle.**

rid·dle[2] (rid′l), *v.,* **-dled, -dling,** *n.* **—***v.t.* **1.** to pierce with many holes, suggesting those of a sieve: *to riddle the target.* **2.** to fill or affect with (something undesirable, weakening, etc.): *a government riddled with graft.* **3.** to impair or refute completely by persistent verbal attacks: *to riddle a person's reputation.* **4.** to sift through a riddle, as gravel; screen. **—***n.* **5.** a coarse sieve, as one for sifting sand in a foundry. [bef. 1100; (n.) ME *riddil,* OE *hriddel,* var. of *hridder, hrīder;* c. G *Reiter;* akin to L *crībrum* sieve; (v.) ME *ridlen* to sift, deriv. of the n.]

ride (rīd), *v.,* **rode** or (*Archaic*) **rid; rid·den** or (*Archaic*) **rid; rid·ing;** *n.* **—***v.i.* **1.** to sit on and manage a horse or other animal in motion; be carried on the back of an animal. **2.** to be borne along on or in a vehicle or other kind of conveyance. **3.** to move or float on the water: *the surfboarders riding on the crests of the waves.* **4.** to move along in any way; be carried or supported: *He is riding along on his friend's success. Distress is riding among the people.* **5.** to have a specified character for riding purposes: *The car rides smoothly.* **6.** to be conditioned; depend (usually fol. by *on*): *All his hopes are riding on getting that promotion.* **7.** *Informal.* to continue without interruption or interference: *He decided to let the bet ride.* **8.** to be carried on something, as a litter, a

CONCISE ETYMOLOGY KEY: <, descended or borrowed from; >, whence; b., blend of, blended; c., cognate with; cf., compare; deriv., derivative; equiv., equivalent; imit., imitative; obl., oblique; r., replacing; s., stem; sp., spelling, spelled; resp., respelling, respelled; trans., translation; ?, origin unknown; *, unattested; ‡, probably earlier than. See the full key inside the front cover.

person's shoulders, or the like. **9.** to work or move up from the proper place or position (usually fol. by *up*): *Her skirt rode up above her knees.* **10.** to extend or project over something, as the edge of one thing over the edge of another thing. **11.** to turn or rest on something: *the great globe of the world riding on its axis.* **12.** to appear to float in space, as a heavenly body: *A blood-red moon rode in the cloudless sky.* **13.** to lie at anchor, as a ship.
—*v.t.* **14.** to sit on and manage (a horse, bicycle, etc.) so as to be carried along. **15.** to sit or move along on (something); be carried or borne along on: *The ship rode the waves. We ride a bus.* **16.** to ride over, along, or through (a road, boundary, region, etc.); traverse. **17.** to ridicule or harass persistently: *The boys keep riding him about his poor grades.* **18.** to control, dominate, or tyrannize over: *a man ridden by fear; a country that is ridden by a power-mad dictator.* **19.** to cause to ride. **20.** to carry (a person) on something as if on a horse: *He rode the child about on his back.* **21.** to execute by riding: *to ride a race.* **22.** to rest on, esp. by overlapping. **23.** to keep (a vessel) at anchor or moored. **24.** *Jazz.* to play improvisations on (a melody). **25. ride down, a.** to trample or overturn by riding upon or against. **b.** to ride up to; overtake; capture: *The posse rode down the escaping bank robber.* **c.** *Naut.* to bear down upon (a rope of a tackle) with all one's weight. **26. ride for a fall,** to conduct oneself so as to invite misfortune or injury. **27. ride herd on.** See **herd**[1] (def. 5). **28. ride out, a.** to sustain (a gale, storm, etc.) without damage, as while riding at anchor. **b.** to sustain or endure successfully. **29. ride the beam,** *Aeron.* to fly along the course indicated by a radio beam. **30. ride shotgun.** See **shotgun** (def. 3).
—*n.* **31.** a journey or excursion on a horse, camel, etc., or on or in a vehicle. **32.** a means of or arrangement for transportation by motor vehicle: *We'll handle rides to be sure everyone gets home quickly.* **33.** the vehicle used for transportation: *I've got to hang up now—my ride's here.* **34.** a vehicle or device, as a Ferris wheel, roller coaster, or merry-go-round, on which people ride for amusement. **35.** a way, road, etc., made esp. for riding. **36. take for a ride,** *Slang.* **a.** to murder, esp. by abducting the victim for that purpose. **b.** to deceive; trick: *It was obvious to everyone but me that I was being taken for a ride.* [bef. 900; 1915–20 for def. 17; ME *riden* (v.), OE *rīdan;* c. OFris *rida,* G *reiten,* ON *ritha;* akin to OIr *ríad* journey (cf. PALFREY, RHEDA). See ROAD]
—**Syn. 2.** See **drive.**

ride•a•ble (rī′də bəl), *adj.* ridable.

ri•dent (rīd′nt), *adj.* laughing; smiling; cheerful. [1600–10; < L *rīdent-* (s. of *rīdēns,* prp. of *rīdēre* to laugh); see -ENT]

rid•er (rī′dər), *n.* **1.** a person who rides a horse or other animal, a bicycle, etc. **2.** something that rides. **3.** an additional clause, usually unrelated to the main body, attached to a legislative bill in passing it. **4.** an addition or amendment to a document, testament, etc. **5.** any object or device that straddles, is mounted upon, or is attached to something else. **6.** a rail or stake used to brace the corners in a snake fence. **7.** *Shipbuilding.* any of various members following and reinforcing primary framing members, esp. a plate or timber running along the top of a keel. **8.** *Numis.* **a.** a former gold coin of Scotland, first issued by James III in 1475, whose obverse bears an equestrian figure of the king. **b.** any of several gold or silver coins of the Netherlands bearing the figure of a horseman. [bef. 1100; ME *ridere,* OE. See RIDE, -ER[1]] —**rid′er•less,** *adj.*

rid•ered (rī′dərd), *adj.* braced or reinforced with riders, as a snake fence. [1825–35; RIDER + -ED[3]]

rid•er•ship (rī′dər ship′), *n.* the passengers who use a given public transportation system, as buses or trains, or the number of such passengers. [1965–70; RIDER + -SHIP]

ride•shar•ing (rīd′shâr′ing), *adj.* **1.** Also, **ride′•share′.** of or pertaining to sharing rides or transportation, esp. among commuters: *The agency was set up to devise a ridesharing program.* —*n.* **2.** an act or instance of sharing rides or transportation, esp. by commuters: *A statewide campaign to encourage ridesharing would reduce overcrowding on the highways.* [RIDE + SHARE[1] + -ING[1]]

ridge (rij), *n., v.,* **ridged, ridg•ing.** —*n.* **1.** a long, narrow elevation of land; a chain of hills or mountains. **2.** the long and narrow upper edge, angle, or crest of something, as a hill, wave, or vault. **3.** the back of an animal. **4.** any raised, narrow strip, as on cloth. **5.** the horizontal line in which the tops of the rafters of a roof meet. **6.** (on a weather chart) a narrow, elongated area of high pressure. —*v.t.* **7.** to provide with or form into a ridge or ridges. **8.** to mark with or as if with ridges. —*v.i.* **9.** to form ridges. [bef. 900; ME *rigge* (n.), OE *hrycg* spine, crest, ridge; c. D *rug,* G *Rücken,* ON *hryggr*] —**ridge′•like′,** *adj.*

ridge•back (rij′bak′), *n. Informal.* See **Rhodesian ridgeback.** [1935–40; by shortening]

Ridge•crest (rij′krest′), *n.* a town in central California. 15,929.

Ridge•field (rij′fēld′), *n.* **1.** a town in SW Connecticut. 20,120. **2.** a borough in NE New Jersey. 10,294.

Ridge′field Park′, a town in NE New Jersey. 12,738.

ridge•ling (rij′ling), *n. Vet. Med.* any male animal, esp. a colt, with undescended testicles. Also, **ridg′ling.** Also called **ridg•el, ridg•il** (rij′əl). [1545–55; perh. RIDGE + -LING[1], from the belief that the undescended organs were in the animal's back]

ridge•pole (rij′pōl′), *n.* the horizontal timber or member at the top of a roof, to which the upper ends of the rafters are fastened. Also, **ridge′ pole′.** Also called **ridge•piece** (rij′pēs′), **ridge′ board′.** See diag. under **queen post.** [1780–90; RIDGE + POLE[1]] —**ridge′poled′,** *adj.*

Ridge•wood (rij′wo͝od′), *n.* a city in NE New Jersey. 25,208.

Ridg•way (rij′wā′), *n.* **Matthew Bunker,** born 1895, U.S. army general: chief of staff 1953–55.

ridg•y (rij′ē), *adj.,* **ridg•i•er, ridg•i•est.** rising in a ridge or ridges. [1690–1700; RIDGE + -Y[1]]

rid•i•cule (rid′i kyo͞ol′), *n., v.,* **-culed, -cul•ing.** —*n.* **1.** speech or action intended to cause contemptuous laughter at a person or thing; derision. —*v.t.* **2.** to deride; make fun of. [1665–75; < L *rīdiculum* a joke, equiv. to *rīd(ēre)* to laugh + *-i-* -I- + *-culum* -CULE[2]] —**rid′i•cul′er,** *n.*
—**Syn. 1.** mockery, raillery, sarcasm, satire, irony. **2.** banter, chaff, rally, twit, burlesque, satirize, lampoon. RIDICULE, DERIDE, MOCK, TAUNT imply making game of a person, usually in an unkind, jeering way. To RIDICULE is to make fun of, either sportively and good-humoredly, or unkindly with the intention of humiliating: *to ridicule a pretentious person.* To DERIDE is to assail one with scornful laughter: *to deride a statement of belief.* To MOCK is sometimes playfully, sometimes insultingly, to imitate and caricature the appearance or actions of another: *She mocked the seriousness of his expression.* To TAUNT is to call attention to something annoying or humiliating, usually maliciously and exultingly and often in the presence of others: *to taunt a candidate about his defeat in an election.*
—**Ant.** praise.

ri•dic•u•lous (ri dik′yə ləs), *adj.* causing or worthy of ridicule or derision; absurd; preposterous; laughable: *a ridiculous plan.* [1540–50; < LL *rīdiculōsus* laughable, droll, and L *rīdiculus* (adj. deriv. of *rīdiculum* RIDICULE); see -OUS] —**ri•dic′u•lous•ly,** *adv.* —**ri•dic′u•lous•ness, ri•dic•u•los•i•ty** (ri dik′yə los′i tē), *n.*
—**Syn.** nonsensical, ludicrous, funny, droll, comical, farcical. See **absurd.** —**Ant.** sensible.

rid•ing[1] (rī′ding), *n.* **1.** the act of a person or thing that rides. —*adj.* **2.** used in traveling or in riding: *riding clothes.* [bef. 1000; ME (n., adj.); OE *rīdende* (adj.). See RIDE, -ING[1], -ING[2]]

ri•ding[2] (rī′ding), *n.* **1.** any of the three administrative divisions into which Yorkshire, England, is divided, namely, North Riding, East Riding, and West Riding. **2.** any similar administrative division elsewhere. [1250–1300; ME *triding,* OE **thriding* < ON *thridjungr* third part; *t-* (of ME), var. of *th-* (of OE), lost by assimilation to *-t* in *east, west,* which commonly preceded]

rid′ing boot′, a knee-high boot of black or brown leather, without fastenings, forming part of a riding habit. [1850–55]

rid′ing breech′es, calf-length trousers of whipcord or other durable fabric, flaring at the sides of the thighs and fitting snugly at and below the knees, worn with riding boots for horseback riding, hunting, etc. Also called **breeches.** Cf. **jodhpurs.**

rid′ing crop′, crop (def. 7).

rid′ing hab′it, habit (def. 11). [1660–70]

rid′ing light′. See **anchor light.**

rid′ing mas′ter, a person who teaches equitation. [1640–50]

rid′ing sail′, *Naut.* a triangular sail set on the aftermost mast of a vessel, esp. a fishing vessel, to head it into the wind; trysail.

rid′ing school′, a place where equitation is taught. [1670–80]

rid•ley (rid′lē), *n., pl.* **-leys. 1.** Also called **Atlantic ridley, bastard ridley, bastard turtle.** a gray sea turtle, *Lepidochelys kempii,* of the Atlantic and Gulf coasts of North America, about 24 in. (61 cm) long, previously thought to be a hybrid of the loggerhead and green turtles: an endangered species. **2.** Also called **olive ridley, Pacific ridley.** an olive-colored sea turtle, *L. olivacea,* similar to *L. kempii,* inhabiting tropical waters of the Indian, Pacific, and South Atlantic oceans: threatened or endangered throughout its range. [1940–45; of undetermined orig.]

Rid•ley (rid′lē), *n.* **1. Nicholas,** c1500–55, English bishop, reformer, and martyr. **2.** a town in SE Pennsylvania, near Philadelphia. 33,771.

ri•dot•to (ri dot′ō), *n., pl.* **-tos.** a public ball or dance with music and often in masquerade, popular in the 18th century. [1715–25; < It: retreat, resort; see REDOUBT]

rie•beck•ite (rē′be kīt′), *n.* an amphibolic mineral, silicate of sodium and iron, occurring usually in feldspathoid rocks. [1885–90; named after Emil *Riebeck* (d. 1885), German explorer; see -ITE[1]]

Rie•fen•stahl (Rē′fən shtäl′), *n.* **Le•ni** (lā′nē), born 1902, German film director.

Rieg•ger (rē′gər), *n.* **Wal•ling•ford** (wol′ing fərd), 1885–1961, U.S. composer.

Ri•e•ka (rē ek′ə; *Serbo-Croatian.* Rē ye′kä), *n.* Rijeka.

riel (rēl, rē el′), *n.* a paper money and monetary unit of Cambodia, equal to 100 sen.

Ri•el (rē el′), *n.* **Louis,** 1844–85, Canadian revolutionary.

Rie•mann (Rē′män′; *Eng.* rē′män, -mən), *n.* **Ge•org Frie•drich Bern•hard** (gā ôRk′ fRē′dRiKH bern′härt), 1826–66, German mathematician. —**Rie•mann•i•an** (rē-mä′nē ən), *adj.*

Riemann′ian geom′etry, *Geom.* **1.** Also called **elliptic geometry.** the branch of non-Euclidean geometry that replaces the parallel postulate of Euclidean geometry with the postulate that in a plane every pair of distinct lines intersects. Cf. **hyperbolic geometry. 2.** the differential geometry of a metric space that generalizes a Euclidean space. [1915–20]

Rie′mann in′tegral, *Math.* integral (def. 8a). [1910–15; named after G. F. B. RIEMANN]

Rie′mann sphere′, *Math.* a sphere used for a stereographic projection. [named after G. F. B. RIEMANN]

Rie′mann-Stiel′tjes in′tegral (rē′män stēl′chiz, -mən), *Math.* the limit, as the norm of partitions of a given interval approaches zero, of the sum of the product of the first of two functions evaluated at some point in each subinterval multiplied by the difference in functional values of the second function at the endpoints of the subinterval. [named after G. F. B. RIEMANN and T. J. *Stieltjes*]

Rie′mann sur′face, *Math.* a geometric representation of a function of a complex variable in which a multiple-valued function is depicted as a single-valued function on several planes, the planes being connected at some of the points at which the function takes on more than one value. Cf. **branch cut, branch point.** [1890–95; named after G. F. B. RIEMANN]

rien ne va plus (RyaN nə VA plY′), *French.* (in roulette) no further bets.

Ri•en•zi (rē en′zē; *It.* Ryen′dzē), *n.* **Co•la di** (kô′lä dē), (*Nicholas Gabrini*), 1313?–54, Roman orator and tribune. Also, **Ri•en•zo** (rē en′zō; *It.* Ryen′dzō).

Ries•ling (rēz′ling, rēs′-), *n.* **1.** *Hort.* **a.** a variety of grape. **b.** the vine bearing this grape, grown in Europe and California. **2.** a fragrant, white, dry or sweet wine made from this grape. [1825–35; < G]

Ries•man (rēs′mən), *n.* **David,** born 1909, U.S. sociologist.

Riesz′ space′ (rēs), *Math.* a topological space in which sets containing one point are closed. [after Frigyes *Riesz* (1880–1956), Hungarian mathematician]

Rie•ti (rē et′ē; *It.* Rye′tē), *n.* **Vit•to•rio** (vēt tô′Ryô), born 1898, U.S. composer, born in Italy.

Riet•veld (Rēt′felt), *n.* **Ger•rit Tho•mas** (KHer′it tō′-mäs), 1888–1965, Dutch architect.

rif (rif), *v.t.,* **-riffed, -rif•fing.** *Informal.* to discharge (a person) from military or civil service, esp. as part of an economy program. Also, **riff.** [1945–50; special use of RIF]

Rif (rif), *n.* **Er** (er), a mountainous coastal region in N Morocco. Also, **Riff.**

RIF (rif), *n.* **1.** *Mil.* a reduction in the personnel of an armed service or unit. **2.** a reduction in the number of persons employed by a business, government department, etc., esp. for budgetary reasons. [*R(eduction) I(n) F(orce)*]

ri•fa•ci•men•to (ri fä′chi men′tō; *It.* Rē fä′chē men′-tô), *n., pl.* **-ti** (-tē). a recast or adaptation, as of a literary or musical work. [1765–75; < It, deriv. of *rifare* to make over, equiv. to *ri-* RE- + *fare* (<< L *facere* to DO[1]) + *-mento* -MENT]

Ri•fa•'i•ya (rē′fä ē′yə), *n. Islam.* a band of dervishes who achieved ecstasy during prayer by violent body movements and self-inflicted pain: formed in the 12th century; outlawed in 1925.

ri•fam•pin (ri fam′pin), *n. Pharm.* a semisynthetic broad-spectrum antibiotic, $C_{43}H_{58}N_4O_{12}$, used in the treatment of pulmonary tuberculosis, asymptomatic carriers of meningococcal disease, and leprosy. [1965–70; prob. *rifam(yci)n* (orig., *rifomycin,* equiv. to *rifo-* (perh. < It *rifo(rmare)* to REFORM) + -MYCIN) + PI(PERAZINE)]

rife (rīf), *adj.* **1.** of common or frequent occurrence; prevalent; in widespread existence, activity, or use: *Crime is rife in the slum areas of our cities.* **2.** current in speech or report: *Rumors are rife that the government is in financial difficulty.* **3.** abundant, plentiful, or numerous. **4.** abounding (usually fol. by *with*). [bef. 1150; ME; OE *rīfe;* c. MD *rijf* abundant, ON *rīfr*] —**rife′ly,** *adv.* —**rife′ness,** *n.*
—**Syn. 3.** plenteous, multitudinous; teeming, swarming. —**Ant. 3.** scarce.

riff[1] (rif), *Jazz.* —*n.* **1.** a melodic phrase, often constantly repeated, forming an accompaniment or part of an accompaniment for a soloist. —*v.i.* **2.** to perform riffs. [1930–35; perh. alter. and shortening of REFRAIN[2]]

riff[2] (rif), *v.t. Informal.* rif.

Riff (rif), *n., pl.* **Riffs, Riff•i** (rif′ē), (*esp. collectively*) **Riff. 1.** a member of the Berber people living in Er Rif in northern Morocco. **2.** Rif. —**Rif′fi•an,** *adj., n.*

rif•fle (rif′əl), *v.,* **-fled, -fling,** *n.* —*v.t., v.i.* **1.** to turn hastily; flutter and shift: *to riffle a stack of letters; to riffle through a book.* **2.** *Cards.* to shuffle by dividing the deck in two, raising the corners slightly, and allowing them to fall alternately together. **3.** to cause or become a riffle. —*n.* **4.** a rapid, as in a stream. **5.** a ripple, as upon the surface of water. **6.** *Mining.* the lining of transverse bars or slats on the bed of a sluice, arranged so as to catch heavy minerals, as gold or platinum. **7.** a hopper for distributing bulk material. **8.** the act or method of riffling cards. [1630–40; b. RIPPLE[1] and RUFFLE[1]]

rif•fler (rif′lər), *n.* a small curved file. [1790–1800; perh. < G *riffel(n)* to cut grooves into (an object) + -ER[1]; cf. F *rifloir* a kind of file (see RIFLE[2])]

riff•raff (rif′raf′), *n.* **1.** people, or a group of people, regarded as disreputable or worthless: *a pack of riffraff.* **2.** the lowest classes; rabble: *the riffraff of the city.* **3.** trash; rubbish. —*adj.* **4.** worthless, disreputable, or trashy. [1425–75; late ME *rif and raf* every particle, things of small value < OF *rif et raf,* formed on *rifler* to spoil (see RIFLE[2]), *raffler* to ravage, snatch away]

ri•fle[1] (rī′fəl), *n., v.,* **-fled, -fling.** —*n.* **1.** a shoulder firearm with spiral grooves cut in the inner surface of the gun barrel to give the bullet a rotatory motion and thus a more precise trajectory. See illus. on next page. **2.** one of the grooves. **3.** a cannon with such grooves. **4.** (*often cap.*) **rifles,** any of certain military units or bodies equipped with rifles. —*v.t.* **5.** to cut spiral grooves within (a gun barrel, pipe, etc.). **6.** to propel (a ball) at high speed, as by throwing or hitting with a bat. [1745–55; < LG *rifeln* to groove, deriv. of *rive, riefe* groove, flute, furrow; akin to OE *rifelede* wrinkled]

rifle[1] (def. 1)

ri•fle[2] (rī′fəl), *v.t.*, **-fled, -fling.** **1.** to ransack and rob (a place, receptacle, etc.). **2.** to search and rob (a person). **3.** to plunder or strip bare. **4.** to steal or take away. [1325–75; ME *rifel* < OF *rifler* to scratch, strip, plunder] —**ri′fler,** *n.*
—**Syn. 1.** See **rob.**

ri′fle bird′, any of several birds of paradise of Australia, having a long bill, dark plumage, and elaborate courtship displays. Also, **ri′fle•bird′.** [1825–35]

ri′fled slug′, a shotgun projectile with helical grooves on its sides for imparting a spin to it when it is fired through the smooth bore of the shotgun.

ri′fle grenade′, *Mil.* a grenade designed to be fired from a grenade launcher attached to the muzzle of a rifle or carbine. [1910–15]

ri•fle•man (rī′fəl mən), *n., pl.* **-men. 1.** a soldier armed with a rifle. **2.** a person skilled in the use of a rifle. [1765–75, *Amer.*; RIFLE[1] + -MAN] —**ri′fle•man•ship′,** *n.*

ri′fle pit′, a pit or short trench affording shelter to riflemen in firing at an enemy. [1850–55]

ri′fle range′, 1. a firing range for practice with rifles. **2.** the range of, or distance coverable by, a bullet fired from a rifle: *The enemy was within rifle range.* [1840–50]

ri•fle•ry (rī′fəl rē), *n.* the art, practice, or sport of shooting at targets with rifles. [1840–50; RIFLE[1] + -RY]

ri•fle•scope (rī′fəl skōp′), *n.* a telescopic sight mounted on top of a rifle that helps to improve one's aim by magnifying and pinpointing a target. [1960–65, *Amer.*; RIFLE[1] + SCOPE]

ri•fling[1] (rī′fling), *n.* **1.** the act or process of cutting spiral grooves in a gun barrel, pipe, etc. **2.** the system of spiral grooves so cut. [1790–1800; RIFLE[1] + -ING[1]]

ri•fling[2] (rī′fling), *n.* the act or process of ransacking or robbing. [RIFLE[2] + -ING[1]]

rif•lip (rif′lip′), *n.* See **RFLP.**

rift (rift), *n.* **1.** an opening made by splitting, cleaving, etc.; fissure; cleft; chink. **2.** an open space, as in a forest or cloud mass, or a clear interval. **3.** a break in friendly relations: *a rift between two people; a rift between two nations.* **4.** a difference in opinion, belief, or interest that causes such a break in friendly relations. **5.** *Geol.* **a.** a fault. **b.** a graben of regional extent. **6.** the plane or direction along which a log or mass of granite can most easily be split. **7.** wood or a piece of wood that has been split radially from a log. —*v.t., v.i.* **8.** to burst open; split. [1250–1300; ME < ON *ript* breaking of an agreement (cf. Dan, Norw *rift* cleavage), deriv. of *rifa* to tear (c. RIVE)] —**rift′less,** *adj.*
—**Syn. 3.** breach, rupture, estrangement, falling-out.

rift′ saw′, a saw used for cutting wood radially from a log. [1905–10]

rift-sawed (rift′sôd′), *adj.* **1.** (of lumber) sawed radially so that the broader sides of the boards or timbers are approximately perpendicular to the annual rings. **2.** quartersawed. Also, **rift-sawn** (rift′sôn′).

rift′ val′ley, *Geol.* **1.** graben. **2.** a subsea chasm extending along the crest of a mid-ocean ridge, locus of the magma upwellings that accompany seafloor spreading. [1890–95]

Rift′ Val′ley fe′ver (rift), *Pathol.* a highly infectious viral disease of humans and animals, transmitted by mosquitoes and other insects, occurring in Africa and characterized in humans by headache, fever, eye discomfort, and muscle aches, progressing in some cases to encephalitis, blindness, or internal bleeding. [1930–35]

rift′ zone′, *Geol.* a system of related, narrow structural depressions between parallel faults. [1965–70]

rig (rig), *v.*, **rigged, rig•ging,** *n.* —*v.t.* **1.** *Chiefly Naut.* **a.** to put in proper order for working or use. **b.** to fit (a ship, mast, etc.) with the necessary shrouds, stays, etc. **c.** to fit (shrouds, stays, sails, etc.) to the mast, yard, or the like. **2.** to furnish or provide with equipment, clothing, etc.; fit (usually fol. by *out* or *up*). **3.** to assemble, install, or prepare (often fol. by *up*). **4.** to manipulate fraudulently: *to rig prices.* **5. rig down,** *Naut.* to place in an inactive state, stowing all lines, tackles, and other removable parts. **6. rig up,** to equip or set up for use. —*n.* **7.** the arrangement of the masts, spars, sails, etc., on a boat or ship. **8.** apparatus for some purpose; equipment; outfit; gear: *a hi-fi rig; Bring your rod and reel and all the rest of your fishing rig.* **9.** Also called **drill rig.** the equipment used in drilling an oil well. **10.** any combination trucking unit in which vehicles are hooked together, as a tractor-trailer. **11.** any kind of truck. **12.** a carriage, buckboard, sulky, or wagon together with the horse or horses that draw it. **13.** *Informal.* costume or dress, esp. when odd or conspicuous, or when designated for a particular purpose: *He looks quite nifty in a butler's rig.* [1480–90; 1930–35 for def. 4; prob. < Scand; cf. Norw, Sw *rigg* (n.), *rigga* (v.)]

Ri•ga (rē′gə), *n.* **1.** a seaport in and the capital of Latvia, on the Gulf of Riga. 915,000. **2. Gulf of,** an arm of the Baltic between Latvia and Estonia. 90 mi. (145 km) long.

rig•a•doon (rig′ə do͞on′), *n.* **1.** a lively dance, formerly popular, for one couple, characterized by a jumping step and usually in quick duple meter. **2.** a piece of music for this dance or in its rhythm. Also, **rigaudon.** [1685–95; < F *rigaudon,* perh. from name *Rigaud*]

rig•a•ma•role (rig′ə mə rōl′), *n.* rigmarole.

rig•a•to•ni (rig′ə tō′nē), *n.* a tubular pasta in short, ribbed pieces. [1925–30; < It (n. pl.), equiv. to *rigat(o)* furrowed, lined, striped (ptp. of *rigare,* deriv. of *riga* a line < Langobardic **rīga*) + *-oni* pl. aug. suffix]

ri•gau•don (*Fr.* rē gō dôN′), *n., pl.* **-dons** (*Fr.* -dôN′). rigadoon.

Ri•gel (rī′jəl, -gəl), *n. Astron.* a first-magnitude star in the constellation Orion. [1585–95; < Ar *rijl* foot, so called from its position in the left foot of the figure of Orion]

Ri′gel Ken•tau′rus (ken tôr′əs), *Astron.* See **Alpha Centauri.**

rig•ger (rig′ər), *n.* **1.** a person who rigs. **2.** a person whose occupation is the fitting of the rigging of ships. **3.** a person who works with hoisting tackle, cranes, scaffolding, etc. **4.** a protective structure around a construction site. **5.** *Aeron.* **a.** a mechanic skilled in the assembly, adjustment, and alignment of aircraft control surfaces, wings, and the like. **b.** See **parachute rigger.** [1605–15; RIG + -ER[1]]

rig•ging (rig′ing), *n.* **1.** the ropes, chains, etc., employed to support and work the masts, yards, sails, etc., on a ship. **2.** lifting or hauling tackle. **3.** *Informal.* clothing. [1480–90; RIG + -ING[1]]

Riggs′ disease′ (rigz), *Dentistry.* pyorrhea (def. 2). [1875–80; named after John M. *Riggs* (1810–85), American dentist]

right (rīt), *adj.*, **-er, -est,** *n., adv., v.* —*adj.* **1.** in accordance with what is good, proper, or just: *right conduct.* **2.** in conformity with fact, reason, truth, or some standard or principle; correct: *the right solution; the right answer.* **3.** correct in judgment, opinion, or action. **4.** fitting or appropriate; suitable: *to say the right thing at the right time.* **5.** most convenient, desirable, or favorable: *Omaha is the right location for a meatpacking firm.* **6.** of, pertaining to, or located on or near the side of a person or thing that is turned toward the east when the subject is facing north (opposed to *left*). **7.** in a satisfactory state; in good order: *to put things right.* **8.** sound, sane, or normal: *to be in one's right mind; She wasn't right in her head when she made the will.* **9.** in good health or spirits: *I don't feel quite right today.* **10.** principal, front, or upper: *the right side of cloth.* **11.** (*often cap.*) of or pertaining to political conservatives or their beliefs. **12.** socially approved, desirable, or influential: *to go to the right schools and know the right people.* **13.** formed by or with reference to a perpendicular: *a right angle.* **14.** straight: *a right line.* **15.** *Geom.* having an axis perpendicular to the base: *a right cone.* **16.** *Math.* pertaining to an element of a set that has a given property when placed on the right of an element or set of elements of the given set: *a right identity.* **17.** genuine; authentic: *the right owner.* **18. too right,** *Australian Slang.* **a.** (used as an expression of emphatic agreement.) **b.** okay: *"Can we meet tonight?" "Too right."*
—*n.* **19.** a just claim or title, whether legal, prescriptive, or moral: *You have a right to say what you please.* **20.** Sometimes, **rights.** that which is due to anyone by just claim, legal guarantees, moral principles, etc.: *women's rights; Freedom of speech is a right of all Americans.* **21.** adherence or obedience to moral and legal principles and authority. **22.** that which is morally, legally, or ethically proper: *to know right from wrong.* **23.** a moral, ethical, or legal principle considered as an underlying cause of truth, justice, morality, or ethics. **24.** Sometimes, **rights.** the interest or ownership a person, group, or business has in property: *He has a 50-percent right in a silver mine. The author controls the screen rights for the book.* **25.** the property itself or its value. **26.** *Finance.* **a.** the privilege, usually preemptive, that accrues to the owners of the stock of a corporation to subscribe to additional shares of stock or securities convertible into stock at an advantageous price. **b.** Often, **rights.** the privilege of subscribing to a specified amount of a stock or bond issue, or the document certifying this privilege. **27.** that which is in accord with fact, reason, propriety, the correct way of thinking, etc. **28.** the state or quality or an instance of being correct. **29.** the side that is normally opposite to that where the heart is; the direction toward that side: *to turn to the right.* **30.** a right-hand turn: *Make a right at the top of the hill.* **31.** the portion toward the right, as of troops in battle formation: *Our right crumbled.* **32.** (in a pair) the member that is shaped for, used by, or situated on the right side: *Is this shoe a left or a right?* **33.** the right hand: *Jab with your left and punch with your right.* **34. the Right, a.** the complex of individuals or organized groups opposing change in a liberal direction and usually advocating maintenance of the established social, political, or economic order, sometimes by authoritarian means. **b.** the position held by these people: *The Depression led to a movement away from the Right.* Cf. **left**[1] (defs. 6a, b). **c.** See **right wing. 35.** (*usually cap.*) the part of a legislative assembly, esp. in continental Europe, that is situated on the right side of the presiding officer and that is customarily assigned to members of the legislature who hold more conservative or reactionary views than the rest of the members. **36.** the members of such an assembly who sit on the Right. **37.** *Boxing.* a blow delivered by the right hand: *a right to the jaw.* **38.** *Baseball.* See **right field. 39. by rights,** in fairness; justly: *You should by rights have been asked your opinion on the matter.* **40. in one's own right,** by reason of one's own ability, ownership, etc.; in or of oneself, as independent of others: *He is a rich man in his own right.* **41. in the right,** having the support of reason or law; correct: *It pays to be stubborn when one is in the right.* **42. to rights,** into proper condition or order: *to set a room to rights.*
—*adv.* **43.** in a straight or direct line; straight; directly: *right to the bottom; to come right home.* **44.** quite or completely; all the way: *My hat was knocked right off.* **45.** immediately; promptly: *right after dinner.* **46.** exactly; precisely: *right here.* **47.** correctly or accurately: *to guess right.* **48.** uprightly or righteously: *to obey one's conscience and live right.* **49.** properly or fittingly: *to behave right.* **50.** advantageously, favorably, or well: *to turn out right.* **51.** toward the right hand; on or to the right: *to keep right; to turn right.* **52.** *Informal.* very; extremely: *a right fine day.* **53.** very (used in certain titles): *the right reverend.* **54. right and left,** on every side; in all directions: *throwing his clothes right and left; members resigning right and left.* **55. right away** or **off,** without hesitation; immediately: *She made a good impression right off.* **56. right on,** *Slang.* exactly right; precisely.
—*v.t.* **57.** to put in or restore to an upright position: *to right a fallen lamp.* **58.** to put in proper order, condition, or relationship: *to right a crookedly hung picture.* **59.** to bring into conformity with fact; correct: *to right one's point of view.* **60.** to do justice to; avenge: *to be righted in court.* **61.** to redress, as a wrong.
—*v.i.* **62.** to resume an upright or the proper position: *After the storm the saplings righted.* [bef. 900; (n. and adj.) ME; OE *reht, riht;* c. D, G *recht,* ON *rēttr,* Goth *raihts;* akin to L *rēctus,* OIr *recht* law, Gk *orektós* upright; (v.) ME *righten,* OE *rihtan,* c. OFris *riuchta,* G *richten,* ON *rētta;* (adv.) ME; OE *rihte*] —**right′a•ble,** *adj.*
—**Syn. 1.** equitable, fair, honest, lawful. **2.** accurate, true. **4.** fit, seemly. **5.** proper. **10.** obverse. **17.** rightful. **22.** morality, virtue, justice, fairness, integrity, equity, rectitude. **48.** rightfully, lawfully, rightly, justly, fairly, equitably. **49.** appropriately, suitably. —**Ant. 1–5, 10, 22.** wrong.
—**Usage. 52.** RIGHT in the sense of "very, extremely" is neither old-fashioned nor dialectal. It is most common in informal speech and writing: *It's right cold this morning. The editor knew right well where the story had originated.*

right•a•bout (rīt′ə bout′), *n.* **1.** the position assumed by turning about to the right so as to face in the opposite direction. **2.** the act of turning so as to face the opposite direction. —*adv.* **3.** facing or in the opposite direction: *Move that chair rightabout.* Also, **right′-a•bout′.** [1690–1700; RIGHT + ABOUT]

right′ about′ face′, 1. *Mil.* **a.** a command, given to a soldier or soldiers at attention, to turn the body about toward the right so as to face in the opposite direction. **b.** the act of so turning in a prescribed military manner. **2.** rightabout (def. 2). **3.** any complete reversal, as of conduct or opinion. Also, **right′a•bout′-face′, right′-a•bout′-face′.** [1805–15]

right′ an′gle, the angle formed by two radii of a circle that are drawn to the extremities of an arc equal to one quarter of the circle; the angle formed by two perpendicular lines that intersect; an angle of 90°. See diag. under **angle**[1]. [1350–1400; ME] —**right′-an′gled,** *adj.*

right′ ascen′sion, *Astron.* the arc of the celestial equator measured eastward from the vernal equinox to the foot of the great circle passing through the celestial poles and a given point on the celestial sphere, expressed in degrees or hours. [1585–95]

Right′ Bank′, a part of Paris, France, on the N bank of the Seine. Cf. **Left Bank.**

right′ brain′, the cerebral hemisphere on the right side of the corpus callosum, controlling activity on the left side of the body, showing in humans some degree of specialization for spatial and nonverbal concepts. Cf. **left brain.** [1975–80]

right-branch•ing (rīt′bran′ching, -brän′-), *adj. Ling.* (of a grammatical construction) characterized by greater structural complexity in the position following the head, as the phrase *the house of the friend of my brother;* having most of the constituents on the right in a tree diagram (opposed to *left-branching*). [1960–65]

right′ cir′cular cone′, *Geom.* a cone whose surface is generated by lines joining a fixed point to the points of a circle, the fixed point lying on a perpendicular through the center of the circle. Cf. **oblique circular cone.** See illus. under **cone.** [1940–45]

right′ cir′cular cyl′inder, *Geom.* a cylinder generated by the revolution of a rectangle about one of its sides. Cf. **oblique circular cylinder.** [1940–45]

right•eous (rī′chəs), *adj.* **1.** characterized by uprightness or morality: *a righteous observance of the law.* **2.** morally right or justifiable: *righteous indignation.* **3.** acting in an upright, moral way; virtuous: *a righteous and godly person.* **4.** *Slang.* absolutely genuine or wonderful: *some righteous playing by a jazz great.* —*n.* **5. the righteous,** (*used with a plural v.*) righteous persons collectively. [bef. 900; earlier *rightwos, rightwis* (remodeled with -OUS), ME; OE *rihtwīs.* See RIGHT, WISE[2]] —**right′eous•ly,** *adv.*
—**Syn. 3.** good, honest, fair, right. —**Ant. 3.** evil, wicked.

right•eous•ness (rī′chəs nis), *n.* **1.** the quality or state of being righteous. **2.** righteous conduct. **3.** the quality or state of being just or rightful: *They came to realize the righteousness of her position on the matter.* [bef. 900; ME *rightwisnes(se),* OE *rihtwīsnes.* See RIGHTEOUS, -NESS]

right•er (rī′tər), *n.* **1.** a person who rights or redresses: *a righter of wrongs.* **2.** a person who advocates or endorses rights, esp. equal rights, for a particular group: *welfare righters.* [bef. 900; ME *rightar* executioner, OE *rihtere* one who regulates. See RIGHT, -ER[1]]

right′-eyed floun′der (rīt′īd′), any of several flatfishes of the family Pleuronectidae, having both eyes on the right side of the head. Also, **right′eye floun′der.**

right′ face′, *Mil.* **1.** a command, given to a soldier or soldiers at attention, to turn the body 90° toward the right. **2.** the act of so turning in a prescribed military manner.

right′ field′, *Baseball.* **1.** the area of the outfield to

CONCISE ETYMOLOGY KEY: <, descended or borrowed from; >, whence; b., blend of, blended; c., cognate with; cf., compare; deriv., derivative; equiv., equivalent; imit., imitative; obl., oblique; r., replacing; s., stem; sp., spelling, spelled; resp., respelling, respelled; trans., translation; ?, origin unknown; *, unattested; ‡, probably earlier than. See the full key inside the front cover.

the right of center field, as viewed from home plate. **2.** the position of the player covering this area. [1855–60, *Amer.*]

right′ field′er, *Baseball.* the player whose position is right field. [1865–70, *Amer.*]

right•ful (rīt′fəl), *adj.* **1.** having a valid or just claim, as to some property or position; legitimate: *the rightful owner of the farm.* **2.** belonging or held by a valid or just claim: *one's rightful property.* **3.** equitable or just, as actions or a cause. **4.** proper; appropriate; fitting. [bef. 1150; ME; late OE *rihtful;* see RIGHT (n.), -FUL] **—right′ful•ly,** *adv.* **—right′ful•ness,** *n.*

right′ hand′, **1.** the hand that is on the right side, or the side opposite that where the heart is. **2.** the right side, as of a person, esp. this side considered as the side of precedence or courtesy. **3.** a position of honor or special trust. **4.** an extremely efficient or reliable person or, sometimes, tool, esp. a person considered as one's assistant. [bef. 1000; ME; OE]

right-hand (rīt′hand′), *adj.* **1.** on the right. **2.** of, for, or with the right hand. **3.** most reliable, valuable, or useful, as a helper or assistant. **4.** plain-laid. **5.** Also, **right-handed.** *Building Trades.* **a.** (of a door) having the hinges on the right when seen from the exterior of the building, room, closet, etc., to which the doorway leads. **b.** (of a casement sash) having the hinges on the right when seen from inside the window. [adj. use of RIGHT HAND]

right′-hand buoy′, *Navig.* a distinctive buoy marking the side of a channel regarded as the right, or starboard, side.

right-hand•ed (rīt′han′did), *adj.* **1.** having the right hand or arm more serviceable than the left; using the right hand by preference: *a right-handed painter.* **2.** adapted to or performed by the right hand: *a right-handed lever; right-handed penmanship.* **3.** *Mach.* **a.** rotating clockwise. **b.** noting a helical, or spiral, member, as a gear tooth or screw thread, that twists clockwise as it recedes from an observer. **4.** *Building Trades.* right-hand (def. 5). **—***adv.* Also, **right′-hand′ed•ly.** **5.** in a right-handed manner or fashion: *The door opens right-handed.* **6.** with the right hand: *She writes right-handed.* **7.** toward the right hand or in a clockwise direction: *The strands of the rope are laid right-handed.* [1350–1400; ME] **—right′-hand′ed•ness,** *n.*

right-hand•er (rīt′han′dər, -han′-), *n.* **1.** a person who is right-handed, esp. a baseball pitcher who throws with the right hand. **2.** *Informal.* **a.** a slap or punch delivered with the right hand. **b.** a throw or toss, as in basketball, made with the right hand. [1855–60]

right′-hand man′, an indispensable or invaluable assistant; right hand. [1655–65]

right•ism (rī′tiz əm), *n.* (*sometimes cap.*) **1.** conservatism, esp. in politics. **2.** reactionary principles, attitudes, or behavior. [1935–40; RIGHT + -ISM]

right•ist (rī′tist), *adj.* (*sometimes cap.*) **1.** of or pertaining to conservative or reactionary political views; noting or characteristic of the political Right. **—***n.* **2.** a member or supporter of the political Right; conservative or reactionary. [1935–40; RIGHT + -IST]

right-laid (rīt′lād′), *adj.* noting a rope, strand, etc., laid in a right-handed, or clockwise, direction as one looks away along it (opposed to *left-laid*).

right•ly (rīt′lē), *adv.* **1.** in accordance with truth or fact; correctly: *to see rightly; to understand rightly.* **2.** in accordance with morality or equity; uprightly. **3.** properly, fitly, or suitably: *to be rightly dressed.* **4.** *Informal.* with certainty; positively: *I can't rightly say.* [bef. 900; ME; OE *rihtlīce.* See RIGHT, -LY]

right-mind•ed (rīt′mīn′did), *adj.* having correct, honest, or good opinions or principles. [1575–85; RIGHT + MINDED] **—right′-mind′ed•ly,** *adv.* **—right′-mind′•ed•ness,** *n.*

right•ness (rīt′nis), *n.* **1.** correctness or accuracy. **2.** propriety or fitness. **3.** moral integrity. **4.** *Obs.* straightness or directness. [bef. 950; ME; OE *rihtnes.* See RIGHT, -NESS]

right•o (rīt′ō′, rīt′ō′; rī′tō′, -tō′), *interj. Chiefly Brit.* (used to express understanding or assent). [1895–1900; RIGHT + -O]

right′ of asy′lum, **1.** the right of alien fugitives to protection or nonextradition in a country or its embassy. **2.** the right of a nation to extend such protection.

right-of-cen•ter (rīt′əv sen′tər), *adj.* holding conservative views in politics; right-wing. [1955–60]

right′ of search′, *Internat. Law.* the privilege of a nation at war to search neutral ships on the high seas for contraband or other matter, carried in violation of neutrality, that may subject the ship to seizure. [1810–20]

right′ of way′, *pl.* **rights of way, right of ways.** **1.** a common law or statutory right granted to a vehicle, as an airplane or boat, to proceed ahead of another. **2.** a path or route that may lawfully be used. **3.** a right of passage, as over another's land. **4.** the strip of land acquired for use by a railroad for tracks. **5.** land covered by a public road. **6.** land over which a power line passes. **7.** *Fencing.* the right to attack or continue an attack, and thus to be credited with a hit, by virtue of having first extended the sword arm or having parried the opponent's attack. Also, **right′-of-way′.** [1760–70]

right-on (rīt′on′, -ôn′), *adj. Slang.* **1.** exactly right or to the point. **2.** up-to-date; relevant: *a right-on movie that shows conditions as they really are.* [1965–70, *Amer.*]

Right′ Rev′erend, an official form of address for abbots, abbesses, Anglican bishops, and other prelates.

rights (rīts), *Informal.* **—***n.* **1.** (*used with a plural v.*) See **civil rights.** **—***adj.* **2.** civil-rights: *a rights worker.* [1895–1900]

right′ sec′tion, a representation of an object as it would appear if cut by a plane perpendicular to its longest axis. Cf. **cross section.**

right′ stage′. See **stage right.**

right′ stuff′, *Informal.* the necessary or ideal qualities or capabilities, as courage, confidence, dependability, toughness, or daring (usually prec. by *the*). [1925–30]

right-think•ing (rīt′thing′king), *adj.* having acceptably proper or correct convictions, beliefs, etc. [1820–30]

right-to-die (rīt′tə dī′), *adj.* asserting or advocating the right to refuse extraordinary medical measures to prolong one's life when one is terminally ill or irreversibly comatose: *right-to-die laws.* [1975–80]

right-to-know (rīt′tə nō′), *adj.* of or pertaining to laws or policies that make certain government or company data and records available to any individual who has a right or need to know their contents.

right-to-life (rīt′tə līf′), *adj.* pertaining to or advocating laws making abortion, esp. abortion-on-demand, illegal; antiabortion: *right-to-life advocates.* [1970–75] **—right′-to-lif′er,** *n.*

right-to-work (rīt′tə wûrk′), *adj.* of or pertaining to the right of workers to gain or keep employment whether or not they belong to a labor union. [1945–50]

right′-to-work′ law′, a state law making it illegal to refuse employment to a person for the sole reason that he or she is not a union member. [1955–60, *Amer.*]

right′ tri′angle, a triangle having a right angle (contrasted with *oblique triangle*). [1920–25]

right•ward (rīt′wərd), *adv.* **1.** Also, **right′wards.** toward or on the right. **—***adj.* **2.** situated on the right. **3.** directed toward the right. [1805–15; RIGHT + -WARD] **—right′ward•ly,** *adv.*

right′ whale′, any of several large whalebone whales of the genus *Balaena,* of circumpolar seas: the species *B. glacialis* is greatly reduced in numbers. [1715–25; allegedly so called because it was the "right" whale to hunt, alluding to its relative buoyancy when killed, proximity to land, the value of its blubber, etc.]

right′ wing′, **1.** members of a conservative or reactionary political party, or those opposing extensive political reform. **2.** such a political party or a group of such parties. **3.** that part of a political or social organization advocating a conservative or reactionary position: *The union's right wing favored a moderate course of action.* [1930–35] **—right′-wing′,** *adj.* **—right′-wing′er,** *n.*

right•y (rī′tē), *n., pl.* **right•ies,** *adv., adj. Informal.* **—***n.* **1.** a right-handed person; right-hander: *She's a righty.* **—***adv.* **2.** with the right hand; right-handed: *to sketch righty.* **—***adj.* **3.** right-handed: *a righty pitcher.* [1945–50, *Amer.*; RIGHT + -Y[2]]

Ri•gi (rē′gē), *n.* a mountain in central Switzerland, near the Lake of Lucerne. 5906 ft. (1800 m).

rig•id (rij′id), *adj.* **1.** stiff or unyielding; not pliant or flexible; hard: *a rigid strip of metal.* **2.** firmly fixed or set. **3.** inflexible, strict, or severe: *a rigid disciplinarian; rigid rules of social behavior.* **4.** exacting; thorough; rigorous: *a rigid examination.* **5.** so as to meet precise standards; stringent: *lenses ground to rigid specifications.* **6.** *Mech.* of, pertaining to, or noting a body in which the distance between any pair of points remains fixed under all forces; having infinite values for its shear modulus, bulk modulus, and Young's modulus. **7.** *Aeron.* **a.** (of an airship or dirigible) having a form maintained by a stiff, unyielding structure contained within the envelope. **b.** pertaining to a helicopter rotor that is held fixedly at its root. [1530–40; < L *rigidus,* equiv. to *rig(ēre)* to be stiff, stiffen + *-idus* -ID[4]] **—ri•gid′i•ty, rig′id•ness,** *n.* **—rig′id•ly,** *adv.*
—Syn. **1.** unbending, firm, inflexible. **2.** immovable, static. **3.** austere, stern, unyielding. See **strict.** **4, 5.** demanding. **—Ant.** **1.** elastic. **3.** lax.

rig′id frame′, (in iron, steel, and reinforced-concrete construction) a bent having absolutely rigid connections at the knees. **—rig′id-frame′,** *adj.*

ri•gid•i•fy (ri jid′ə fī′), *v.t., v.i.,* **-fied, -fy•ing.** to make or become rigid. [1835–45; RIGID + -IFY]

rig•id•ize (rij′i dīz′), *v.t.,* **-ized, -iz•ing.** to make rigid, as through special processing or the addition of chemicals, plastics, etc.: *rigidized aluminum.* Also, *esp. Brit.,* **rig′id•ise′.** [1945–50; RIGID + -IZE]

rig′id mo′tion, *Math.* any transformation, as a translation or rotation, of a set such that the distance between points is preserved.

Ri•gil Ken•tau•rus (rī′jəl ken tôr′əs, -gəl). *Astron.* See **Alpha Centauri.**

rig•ma•role (rig′mə rōl′), *n.* **1.** an elaborate or complicated procedure: *to go through the rigmarole of a formal dinner.* **2.** confused, incoherent, foolish, or meaningless talk. Also, **rigamarole.** [1730–40; alter. of RAGMAN ROLL]

rig•o•let (rig′ə let′), *n. Southern U.S.* a small stream; rivulet. [1710–20, *Amer.*; < Mississippi Valley F, equiv. to F *rigole* drain, channel + *-et,* -ET]

Rig•o•let•to (rig′ə let′ō; *It.* rē′gô let′tô), *n.* an opera (1851) with music by Giuseppe Verdi.

rig•or (rig′ər), *n.* **1.** strictness, severity, or harshness, as in dealing with people. **2.** the full or extreme severity of laws, rules, etc. **3.** severity of living conditions; hardship; austerity: *the rigor of wartime existence.* **4.** a severe or harsh act, circumstance, etc. **5.** scrupulous or inflexible accuracy or adherence: *the logical rigor of mathematics.* **6.** severity of weather or climate or an instance of this: *the rigors of winter.* **7.** *Pathol.* a sudden coldness, as that preceding certain fevers; chill. **8.** *Physiol.* a state of rigidity in muscle tissues during which they are unable to respond to stimuli due to the coagulation of muscle protein. **9.** *Obs.* stiffness or rigidity. Also, *esp. Brit.,* **rigour.** [1350–1400; ME *rigour* < L *rigor* stiffness, equiv. to *rig(ēre)* to be stiff + *-or* -OR[1]]
—Syn. **1.** inflexibility, stringency. **4.** cruelty.

rig•or•ism (rig′ə riz′əm), *n.* **1.** extreme strictness. **2.** (in Roman Catholic moral philosophy) the theory that in doubtful cases of conscience no course may be followed that is contrary to Catholic law and doctrine. [1695–1705; < F *rigorisme.* See RIGOR, -ISM] **—rig′or•ist,** *n.* **—rig′or•is′tic,** *adj.*

rig•or mor•tis (rig′ər môr′tis, *or, esp. Brit.,* rī′gôr), the stiffening of the body after death. [1830–40; < L: lit., stiffness of death]

rig•or•ous (rig′ər əs), *adj.* **1.** characterized by rigor; rigidly severe or harsh, as people, rules, or discipline: *rigorous laws.* **2.** severely exact or accurate; precise: *rigorous research.* **3.** (of weather or climate) uncomfortably severe or harsh; extremely inclement. **4.** *Logic, Math.* logically valid. [1350–1400; ME < ML *rigōrōsus.* See RIGOR, -OUS] **—rig′or•ous•ly,** *adv.* **—rig′or•ous•ness,** *n.*
—Syn. **1.** stern, austere, hard, inflexible, stiff, unyielding. See **strict.** **2.** demanding, finical. **3.** hard, bitter.
—Ant. **1.** flexible, soft. **2.** inaccurate. **3.** mild.

rig•our (rig′ər), *n. Chiefly Brit.* rigor.

Rigs•dag (rigz′däg′), *n.* the former parliament of Denmark, consisting of an upper house and a lower house: replaced in 1953 by the unicameral Folketing. [< Dan, equiv. to *rigs,* gen. of *rig* kingdom + *dag* diet, assembly. Cf. REICHSTAG]

rigs•da•ler (rigz′dä′lär), *n.* a former silver coin of Denmark, equal to 16 skillings; rix-dollar. [1590–1600; < Dan; see RIX-DOLLAR]

Rig-Ve•da (rig vā′də, -vē′də), *n. Hinduism.* one of the Vedas, a collection of 1028 hymns, dating from not later than the second millennium B.C. Also, **Rig•ve′da.** Cf. **Veda.** [< Skt *ṛgveda*] **—Rig•ve•dic** (rig vā′dik, -vē′-), *adj.*

R.I.I.A., Royal Institute of International Affairs.

Riis (rēs), *n.* **Jacob August,** 1849–1914, U.S. journalist and social reformer, born in Denmark.

Ri•je•ka (rē ek′ə; *Serbo-Croatian.* rē ye′kä), *n.* a seaport in W Croatia, on the Adriatic. 193,044. Also, **Rieka.** Italian, **Fiume.**

rijks•daal•der (rīks′däl′dər), *n.* **1.** a cupronickel or silver coin of the Netherlands, equal to 2½ guilders. **2.** a former silver coin of the Netherlands, equal to 48 stivers; rix-dollar. [1590–1600; < D, equiv. to *rijk* realm, kingdom + connective *-s-* + *daalder* DOLLAR; cf. RIX-DOLLAR]

Rijn (*Du.* rīn), *n.* the Rhine.

rijst•ta•fel (rīs′tä′fəl), *n.* an Indonesian meal consisting of rice served with a large array of small dishes of meat, poultry, seafood, vegetables, and condiments. Also **rijs′ta′fel.** [1885–90; < D, equiv. to *rijst* RICE + *tafel* TABLE]

Rijs•wijk (*Du.* rīs′vīk), *n.* a town in SW Netherlands, near The Hague: Treaty of Ryswick 1697. 52,069.

rik•i•sha (rik′shô, -shä), *n.* jinrikisha. Also, **rik′shaw.**

Riks•dag (riks′däg′), *n.* the parliament of Sweden, consisting of an upper house and a lower house. [< Sw; cf. REICHSTAG]

Riks•mål (riks′môl; *Norw.* rēks′môl′), *n.* Bokmål. Formerly, **Riks′maal.** [< Norw]

rile (rīl), *v.t.,* **riled, ril•ing.** *Chiefly Northern and North Midland U.S.* **1.** to irritate or vex. **2.** to roil (water or the like). [1815–25; var. of ROIL]
—Syn. **1.** irk, annoy, provoke, chafe, nettle.

ri•ley (rī′lē), *adj. Chiefly Northern and North Midland U.S.* **1.** turbid; roily. **2.** angry; vexed. [1795–1805, *Amer.*; RILE + -Y[1]]

Ri•ley (rī′lē), *n.* **1. James Whit•comb** (hwit′kəm, wit′-), 1849–1916, U.S. poet. **2. life of.** See **life of Riley.**

ri•lie•vo (rē lye′vô; *Eng.* ril yev′ō), *n., pl.* **ri•lie•vi** (rē-lye′vē; *Eng.* ril yev′ē). *Italian.* relief[2] (defs. 2, 3).

Ril•ke (ril′kə), *n.* **Rai•ner Ma•ri•a** (rī′nər mä rē′ä), 1875–1926, Austrian poet, born in Prague.

rill[1] (ril), *n.* a small rivulet or brook. [1530–40; < D or LG; cf. Fris *ril*]

rill[2] (ril), *n. Astron.* any of certain long, narrow, straight or sinuous trenches or valleys observed on the surface of the moon. Also, **rille.** [1885–90; < G *Rille;* see RILL[1]]

rill•et (ril′it), *n.* a little rill; streamlet. [1530–40; RILL[1] + -ET]

ril•lettes (ri lets′; *Fr.* rē yet′), *n.* (*used with a singular or plural v.*) *French Cookery.* an appetizer made usually of pork or goose meat that is diced, seasoned, cooked, and then pounded or ground to the consistency of a spread. [1885–90; < F]

rim (rim), *n., v.,* **rimmed, rim•ming.** **—***n.* **1.** the outer edge, border, margin, or brink of something, esp. of a circular object. **2.** any edge, margin, or frame added to or around a central object or area. **3.** the outer circle of a wheel, attached to the hub by spokes. **4.** a circular strip of metal forming the connection between an automobile wheel and tire, either permanently attached to or removable from the wheel. **5.** a drive wheel or flywheel, as on a spinning mule. **6.** *Basketball.* the metal ring from which the net is suspended to form the basket. **7.** *Journalism.* the outer edge of a usually U-shaped copy desk, occupied by the copyreaders. Cf. **slot** (def. 5). **8.** *Metall.* (in an ingot) an outer layer of metal having a composition different from that of the center. **—***v.t.* **9.** to furnish with a rim, border, or margin. **10.** (of a golf ball or putt) to roll around the edge of (a hole) but not go in. **11.** *Basketball.* (of a basketball) to roll around (the rim of the basket) and not go in. **12.** to coat or encrust the rim of (a glass): *Rim each cocktail glass with salt.* [bef. 1150; ME; OE *-rima* (in compounds); c. ON *rimi* raised strip of land, ridge] **—rim′less,** *adj.*

—Syn. 1. lip, verge. RIM, BRIM refer to the boundary of a circular or curved area. A RIM is a line or surface bounding such an area; an edge or border: *the rim of a glass.* BRIM usually means the inside of the rim, at the top of a hollow object (except of a hat), and is used particularly when the object contains something: *The cup was filled to the brim.* **—Ant. 1.** center.

Ri·ma (rē′mə), *n.* a female given name.

Rim·baud (ram bō′; *Fr.* RAN bō′), *n.* **(Jean Ni·co·las) Ar·thur** (zhäN nē kô lä′ AR TYR′), 1854–91, French poet.

rime[1] (rīm), *n., v.,* **rimed, rim·ing.** *—n.* **1.** Also called **rime′ ice′.** an opaque coating of tiny, white, granular ice particles, caused by the rapid freezing of supercooled water droplets on impact with an object. Cf. **frost** (def. 2), **glaze** (def. 17). *—v.t.* **2.** to cover with rime or hoarfrost. [bef. 900; ME *rim,* OE *hrīm;* c. D *rijm,* ON *hrīm*] **—rime′less,** *adj.*

rime[2] (rīm), *n., v.t., v.i.,* **rimed, rim·ing.** rhyme.

rime riche (rēm′ rēsh′), *pl.* **rimes riches** (rēm′ rēsh′). *Pros.* rhyme created by the use of two different words, or groups of words, of which both the stressed syllables and any following syllables are identical, as in *lighted, delighted.* Also called **identical rhyme, perfect rhyme, rich rhyme.** [1900–05; < F: lit., rich rhyme]

rime·ster (rīm′stər), *n.* rhymester.

rime suf·fi·sante (RĒM SY fē zäNt′), *pl.* ***rimes suf·fi·santes*** (RĒM SY fē zäNt′). *French.* See **full rhyme.**

rim·fire (rim′fīər′), *adj.* **1.** (of a cartridge) having the primer in a rim encircling the base. Cf. **center-fire** (def. 1). **2.** (of a firearm) designed for the use of such cartridges. [1865–70, *Amer.*; RIM + FIRE]

Rim·i·ni (rim′ə nē; *It.* RĒ′mē nē), *n.* **1. Francesca da.** See **Francesca da Rimini. 2.** Ancient, **Ariminum.** a seaport in NE Italy, on the Adriatic. 126,025.

rim′ light′ing, backlighting. [1935–40]

rim′ lock′, a lock nailed or screwed to one face of a door, gate, etc., as opposed to one built into its edge. [1835–45]

rim′ man′, copyreader (def. 2). [1930–35]

rimmed (rimd), *adj.* **1.** having a rim: *Do you wear rimmed or rimless glasses?* **2.** having a rim of a specified kind (often used in combination): *Your red-rimmed eyes show that you have been crying.* [1720–30; RIM + -ED[3]]

rimmed′ steel′, a low-carbon steel containing enough iron oxide so that there is continuous generation of carbon monoxide during solidification. [1925–30]

Rim·mer (rim′ər), *n.* **William,** 1816–79, U.S. sculptor and painter, born in England.

ri·mose (rī′mōs, rī mōs′), *adj.* full of crevices, chinks, or cracks. Also, **ri·mous** (rī′məs). [1720–30; < L *rīmōsus* full of cracks, equiv. to *rīm(a)* cleft, crack, chink + *-ōsus* -OSE[1]] **—ri′mose·ly,** *adv.* **—ri·mos·i·ty** (rī mos′i tē), *n.*

Ri·mous·ki (ri mōō′skē), *n.* a city in SE Quebec, in SE Canada, on the St. Lawrence River. 27,897.

rim·ple (rim′pəl), *n., v.,* **-pled, -pling.** *—n.* **1.** a wrinkle. *—v.t., v.i.* **2.** to wrinkle; crumple; crease. [1400–50; late ME; cf. MD, MLG *rimpel;* akin to RUMPLE]

rim·rock (rim′rok′), *n. Geol.* **1.** rock forming the natural boundary of a plateau or other rise. **2.** bedrock forming the natural boundary of a placer or of a gravel deposit. [1855–60, *Amer.*; RIM + ROCK[1]]

Rim·sky-Kor·sa·kov (rim′skē kôr′sə kôf′, -kof′; *Russ.* RYĕm′skyē kôR′sə kəf), *n.* **Ni·co·lai An·dre·e·vich** (nyi kə lī′ un dRye′yi vyich), 1844–1908, Russian composer. Also, **Rim′ski-Kor′sa·kov′, Rim′sky-Kor′·sa·koff′.**

rim·stone (rim′stōn′), *n. Geol.* a calcareous deposit forming a dam at the edge or outlet of an overflowing pool of water, as in a cavern. [1925–30; RIM + STONE]

rim·y (rī′mē), *adj.,* **rim·i·er, rim·i·est.** covered with rime. [bef. 1000; OE *hrīmig* (not recorded in ME). See RIME[1], -Y[1]]

rin (rin), *n., pl.* **rin.** a money of account of Japan, the thousandth part of a yen or the tenth part of a sen. [1870–75; < Japn *ri(n)* < MChin, equiv. to Chin *lí;* cf. LIKIN]

Ri·na (rē′nə), *n.* a female given name.

rin·ceau (*Fr.* RAN sō′), *n., pl.* **-ceaux** (*Fr.* -sō′). an ornamental foliate or floral motif. [1770–80; < F; MF *rainsel* < VL **rāmuscellus,* deriv. of LL *rāmusculus,* dim. of *rāmus* branch (see RAMUS)]

rind[1] (rīnd), *n.* **1.** a thick and firm outer coat or covering, as of certain fruits, cheeses, and meats: *watermelon rind; orange rind; bacon rind.* **2.** the bark of a tree. [bef. 900; ME, OE *rind(e)* tree bark, crust; c. G *Rinde*] **—rind′less,** *adj.* **—rind′y,** *adj.*

rind[2] (rīnd, rind), *n.* a piece of iron running across an upper millstone as a support. Also, **rynd.** Also called **millrind.** [1300–50; ME *rynd;* c. MD *rijn,* MLG *rīn*]

rin·der·pest (rin′dər pest′), *n. Vet. Pathol.* an acute, usually fatal infectious disease of cattle, sheep, etc., caused by a paramyxovirus of the genus *Morbillivirus* and characterized by high fever, diarrhea, and lesions of the skin and mucous membranes. Also called **cattle plague.** [1860–65; < G, equiv. to *Rinder* cattle (pl. of *Rind*) + *Pest* pestilence]

Rine·hart (rīn′härt), *n.* **Mary Roberts,** 1876–1958, U.S. novelist and playwright.

rin·for·zan·do (*It.* RĒN′fôR tsän′dô), *adj., adv.* sforzando. [1795–1805; < It: reinforcing (ger. of *rinforzare,* equiv. to *ri-* RE- + *inforzare* to ENFORCE)]

CONCISE ETYMOLOGY KEY: <, descended or borrowed from; >, whence; b., blend of, blended; c., cognate with; cf., compare; deriv., derivative; equiv., equivalent; imit., imitative; obl., oblique; r., replacing; s., stem; sp., spelling, spelled; resp., respelling, respelled; trans., translation; ?, origin unknown; *, unattested; ‡, probably earlier than. See the full key inside the front cover.

ring[1] (ring), *n., v.,* **ringed, ring·ing.** *—n.* **1.** a typically circular band of metal or other durable material, esp. one of gold or other precious metal, often set with gems, for wearing on the finger as an ornament, a token of betrothal or marriage, etc. **2.** anything having the form of such a band: *a napkin ring; a smoke ring.* **3.** a circular or surrounding line or mark: *dark rings around the eyes.* **4.** a circular course: *to dance in a ring.* **5.** a number of persons or things situated in a circle or in an approximately circular arrangement: *a ring of stones; a ring of hills.* **6.** the outside edge of a circular body, as a wheel; rim. **7.** an enclosed area, often circular, as for a sports contest or exhibition: *a circus ring.* **8.** a bullring. **9.** an enclosure in which boxing and wrestling matches take place, usually consisting of a square, canvas-covered platform with surrounding ropes that are supported at each corner by posts. **10.** the sport of boxing; prizefighting: *the heyday of the ring.* **11.** (formerly in the U.S., now only in Brit.) an area in a racetrack where bookmakers take bets. **12.** a group of persons cooperating for unethical, illicit, or illegal purposes, as to control stock-market prices, manipulate politicians, or elude the law: *a ring of dope smugglers.* **13.** a single turn in a spiral or helix or in a spiral course. **14.** *Geom.* the area or space between two concentric circles. **15.** See **annual ring. 16.** a circle of bark cut from around a tree. **17.** *Chem.* a number of atoms so united that they may be graphically represented in cyclic form. Cf. **chain** (def. 7). **18.** *Archit.* rowlock (def. 1). **19.** a bowlike or circular piece at the top of an anchor, to which the chain or cable is secured. See diag. under **anchor. 20.** Also called **spinning ring.** *Textiles.* (in the ring-spinning frame) a circular track of highly polished steel on which the traveler moves and which imparts twists to the yarn by variations in its vertical movement. **21.** *Auto., Mach.* See **piston ring. 22.** *Math.* a set that is closed under the operations of addition and multiplication and that is an Abelian group with respect to addition and an associative semigroup with respect to multiplication and in which the distributive laws relating the two operations hold. **23. run rings around,** to be obviously superior to; surpass; outdo: *As an artist, she can run rings around her brother.* **24. throw** or **toss one's hat in** or **into the ring.** See **hat** (def. 7).
—v.t. **25.** to surround with a ring; encircle. **26.** to form into a ring. **27.** to insert a ring through the nose of (an animal). **28.** to hem in (animals) by riding or circling about them. **29.** to girdle (def. 11). **30.** (in horseshoes, ringtoss, etc.) to encircle (a stake or peg) with a ring, horseshoe, etc.
—v.i. **31.** to form a ring or rings. **32.** to move in a ring or a constantly curving course: *The road rings around the mountain.* [bef. 900; ME; OE *hring;* c. D, G *ring,* ON *hringr;* akin to RANK[1]] **—ring′less,** *adj.* **—ring′like′,** *adj.*
—Syn. 2. circle, circlet, hoop; annulus. **7.** arena, rink, circle. **12.** bloc, coterie, confederacy, league; gang, mob, syndicate. RING, CLIQUE are terms applied with disapproving connotations to groups of persons. RING suggests a small and intimately related group, combined for selfish and often dishonest purposes: *a gambling ring.* A CLIQUE is a small group that prides itself on its congeniality and exclusiveness: *cliques in a school.*

ring[2] (ring), *v.,* **rang, rung, ring·ing,** *n.* *—v.i.* **1.** to give forth a clear resonant sound, as a bell when struck: *The doorbell rang twice.* **2.** to make a given impression on the mind; appear: *words that rang false; a story that rings true.* **3.** to cause a bell or bells to sound, esp. as a summons: *Just ring if you need anything.* **4.** to sound loudly; be loud or resonant; resound (often fol. by *out*): *His brave words rang out.* **5.** to be filled with sound; reecho with sound, as a place. **6.** (of the ears) to have the sensation of a continued humming sound. **7.** *Chiefly Brit.* to telephone. *—v.t.* **8.** to cause (a bell or device with a bell) to ring; sound by striking: *to ring a bell.* **9.** to produce (sound) by or as if by ringing: *The bell rang a low tone.* **10.** to announce or proclaim, usher in or out, summon, signal, etc., by or as if by the sound of a bell: *to ring someone's praises; The bell rang the hour.* **11.** to test (a coin or other metal object) by the sound it produces when struck against something. **12.** *Chiefly Brit.* to telephone. **13. ring a bell.** See **bell[1]** (def. 10). **14. ring down the curtain, a.** to direct that the curtain of a theater be lowered or closed. **b.** to lower or close the curtain in front of a stage. **15. ring down the curtain on,** to bring to an end: *The accident rang down the curtain on his law career.* **16. ring in, a.** to indicate one's arrival at work by punching in on a time clock. **b.** *Informal.* to introduce artfully or fraudulently: *to ring in an imposter.* **17. ring off, a.** to terminate a telephone conversation. **b.** *Brit. Slang.* to stop talking. **c.** *Brit. Slang.* to go away. **18. ring out, a.** to indicate one's departure from work by punching out on a time clock. **b.** to make a sound or noise; resound: *The church bells rang out.* **19. ring the bell.** See **bell[1]** (def. 11). **20. ring the changes.** See **change** (def. 38). **21. ring up, a.** to register (the amount of a sale) on a cash register. **b.** to accomplish or record: *to ring up a series of successes.* **c.** *Chiefly Brit.* to telephone. **22. ring up the curtain, a.** to direct that the curtain of a theater be raised or opened. **b.** to raise or open the curtain in front of a stage. **23. ring up the curtain on,** to begin; inaugurate; initiate: *The $100-a-plate dinner rang up the curtain on the hospital's fund-raising drive.* *—n.* **24.** a ringing sound, as of a bell or bells: *the ring of sleigh bells.* **25.** a sound or tone likened to the ringing of a bell: *Rings of laughter issued from the school.* **26.** any loud sound; sound continued, repeated, or reverberated: *the ring of iron upon stone.* **27.** a set or peal of bells. **28.** a telephone call: *Give me a ring tomorrow.* **29.** an act or instance of ringing a bell: *No one answered my ring.* **30.** a characteristic sound, as of a coin. **31.** the aspect or impression presented by a statement, an action, etc., taken as revealing a specified inherent quality: *a ring of assurance in her voice; the ring of truth; a false ring.* [bef. 900; ME *ringen,* OE *hringan;* c. ON *hringja,* G *ringen*] **—ring′ing·ly,** *adv.* **—ring′ing·ness,** *n.*
—Syn. 31. sound, tone, quality.

Ring (ring), *n.* a male given name.

ring-a-lie·vi·o (ring′ə lē′vē ō′), *n.* a game played usually between two teams in which the members of one team attempt to find, capture, and imprison the members of the other, who can be freed only by a teammate not yet captured. [1900–05; var. of *ring relievo,* perh. RELIEVE + -O]

ring-a-round-the-ros·ey (ring′ə round′thə rō′zē), *n.* a children's game in which the players sing while going around in a circle and squat when the lyrics "all fall down" are sung. Also, **ring′-a-round′-the-ros′y, ring′-a-round′-a-ros′ey.** [1880–85; prob. ROSE[1] + -EY[2]]

ring·bark (ring′bärk′), *v.t.* girdle (def. 11). [1885–90; RING[1] + BARK[2]]

ring′-billed gull′ (ring′bild′), a North American gull, *Larus delawarensis,* having a black ring around the bill. [1825–35, *Amer.*]

ring′ bind′er, a loose-leaf binder in which the sheets are held in by two or more rings that can be made to snap open. [1925–30]

ring·bolt (ring′bōlt′), *n.* a bolt with a ring fitted in an eye at its head. [1620–30; RING[1] + BOLT[1]]

ring·bone (ring′bōn′), *n. Vet. Pathol.* a morbid bony growth on the pastern bones of a horse, often resulting in lameness. [1515–25; RING[1] + BONE]

ring′ com′pound, *Chem.* a compound whose structural formula contains a closed chain or ring of atoms; a cyclic compound. Cf. **cyclic** (def. 3). [1930–35]

Ring′ Cy′cle. See **Ring of the Nibelung, The.**

ring′ dance′. See **round dance.** [1590–1600]

ring·dove (ring′duv′), *n.* **1.** a small Old World dove, *Streptopelia risoria,* having a black half ring around the nape of the neck. **2.** See **wood pigeon.** Also, **ring′ dove′.** [1530–40; RING[1] + DOVE[1]]

ringed (ringd), *adj.* **1.** having or wearing a ring or rings. **2.** marked or decorated with or as if with a ring or rings. **3.** surrounded by or as if by a ring or rings. **4.** formed of or with rings; ringlike or annular: *a ringed growth.* **5.** *Armor.* noting armor having rings sewn side by side to a flexible backing. [bef. 900; ME; OE *hringed;* see RING[1], -ED[3], -ED[2]]

ringed′ plov′er, any of several cosmopolitan plovers of the genus *Charadrius,* esp. *C. hiaticula,* brownish above and white below with a black band around the breast. [1775–85]

ringed′ snake′. See **ring snake.**

rin·gent (rin′jənt), *adj.* **1.** gaping. **2.** *Bot.* having widely spread lips, as some corollas. [1750–60; < L *ringent-* (s. of *ringēns,* prp. of *ringī* to gape), equiv. to *ring-* open the mouth + *-ent-* -ENT; cf. RICTUS]

ring·er[1] (ring′ər), *n.* **1.** a person or thing that encircles, rings, etc. **2.** a quoit or horseshoe so thrown as to encircle the peg. **3.** the throw itself. **4.** Also, **ring′ers.** Also called **ring taw.** *Marbles.* a game in which players place marbles in a cross marked in the center of a circle, the object being to knock as many marbles as possible outside the circle by using another marble shooter. **5.** *Australian.* a highly skilled sheep shearer. [1815–25; RING[1] + -ER[1]]

ring·er[2] (ring′ər), *n.* **1.** a person or thing that rings or makes a ringing noise: *a ringer of bells; a bell that is a loud ringer.* **2.** See **dead ringer. 3.** *Slang.* **a.** a racehorse, athlete, or the like entered in a competition under false representation as to identity or ability. **b.** a student paid by another to take an exam. **c.** any person or thing that is fraudulent; fake or impostor. **d.** a substitute or addition, as a professional musician hired to strengthen a school orchestra: *We hired three ringers for the commencement concert.* [1375–1425; late ME; see RING[2], -ER[1]]

Ring′er's solu′tion (ring′ərz), *Pharm.* an aqueous solution of the chlorides of sodium, potassium, and calcium in the same concentrations as normal body fluids, used chiefly in the laboratory for sustaining tissue. Cf. **isotonic sodium chloride solution.** [1890–95; named after Sydney *Ringer* (1835–1910), English physician]

ring′ fin′ger, the finger next to the little finger, esp. of the left hand, on which an engagement ring or wedding band is traditionally worn. [bef. 1000; ME, OE]

ring′ frame′. See **ring-spinning frame.**

ring′ gage′, a gage for checking the diameters of circular manufactured objects, consisting of a ring having a hole that is of either the maximum or minimum allowable diameter.

ring′ gal′axy, *Astron.* a galaxy having the shape of an elliptical ring: thought to be the result of a collision of two galaxies.

ring′ gate′, *Metall.* a gate having a widened opening containing a centered disk to prevent molten metal from falling in a direct vertical stream.

ring′ gear′, *Mach.* See **internal gear.**

ring·git (ring′git), *n.* a paper money, cupronickel coin, and monetary unit of Malaysia, equal to 100 sen. Also called **dollar.** [1965–70; < Malay *ringgit* lit., serrated, milled]

ring·hals (ring′hals), *n.* a highly venomous snake, *Hemachatus haemachatus,* of southern Africa, related to the cobras, having one to three light-colored bands across its throat and characterized by its ability to accurately spit its venom up to 7 ft. (2.1 m) away. Also, **rinkhals.** [< Afrik, equiv. to *ring* RING[1] + *hals* neck]

ring·lead·er (ring′lē′dər), *n.* a person who leads others, esp. in opposition to authority, law, etc.: *a ringleader of revolutionary activities.* [1495–1505; RING[1] + LEADER]

ring·let (ring′lit), *n.* **1.** a curled lock of hair. **2.** a small ring or circle. **3.** *Astron.* one of the thin or narrow rings that compose the major rings of Saturn. [1545–55; RING[1] + -LET] **—ring′let·ed,** *adj.*

ring·light (ring′līt′), *n.* a circular electronic flash that surrounds a camera lens, used esp. for even illumination in closeup photography. [RING[1] + LIGHT[1]]

Ring·ling (ring′ling), *n.* **Albert** (1852–1916), and his brothers **Alfred** (1861–1919), **Charles** (1863–1926), **John** (1866–1936), and **Otto** (1858–1911), U.S. circus owners.

ring′ machine′, *Print.* a Linotype used primarily for making corrections.

ring′ man′, **1.** *Print.* an operator of a ring machine. **2.** a person who assists an auctioneer by spotting bids and signaling the information to the auctioneer, often from the ring where livestock is displayed for sale. Also, **ring′man′.** [1475–85]

ring·mas·ter (ring′mas′tər, -mä′stər), *n.* a person in charge of the performances in a circus ring. [1870–75; RING[1] + MASTER]

Ring′ Neb′ula, *Astron.* a planetary nebula in the constellation Lyra that has a ringlike appearance surrounding its central star.

ring·neck (ring′nek′), *n.* a ring-necked animal. [1785–95, *Amer.*; RING[1] + NECK]

ring-necked (ring′nekt′), *adj. Zool.* having a ring of distinctive color around the neck. [1850–55]

ring′-necked duck′, a North American scauplike duck, *Aythya collaris,* having a chestnut ring around the neck. [1825–35, *Amer.*]

ring′-necked pheas′ant, a gallinaceous Asian bird, *Phasianus colchicus,* having a white band around its neck, introduced into Great Britain, North America, and the Hawaiian Islands. See illus. under **pheasant.** [1825–35]

ring′neck snake′, any of several small, nonvenomous North American snakes of the genus *Diadophis,* usually having a conspicuous yellow or orange ring around the neck. Also, **ring′-necked snake′.** Also called **ring snake.** [1825–35]

Ring′ of Fire′, *Geol.* the linear zone of seismic and volcanic activity that coincides in general with the margins of the Pacific Plate.

Ring′ of the Ni′be·lung, The (nē′bə lo͝ong′), Richard Wagner's tetralogy of music dramas: *Das Rheingold* (completed 1869), *Die Walküre* (completed 1870), *Siegfried* (completed 1876), and *Götterdämmerung* (completed 1876): the cycle was first performed at Bayreuth, 1876.

ring-po·rous (ring′pôr′əs, -pōr′-), *adj. Bot.* having annual rings marked by a conspicuous band of large pores in wood formed in spring. Cf. **diffuse-porous.** [1900–05]

ring′ rot′, *Plant Pathol.* a disease of potatoes, characterized by wilted foliage and rotting of the ring of vascular bundles in the tubers, caused by a bacterium, *Corynebacterium sepedonicum.* [1900–05, *Amer.*]

ring·sail (ring′sāl′), *n. Naut.* ringtail (def. 3).

ring′ seiz′ing. See **cuckold's knot.**

ring′ shout′, a group dance of West African origin introduced into parts of the southern U.S. by black revivalists, performed by shuffling counterclockwise in a circle while answering shouts of a preacher with corresponding shouts, and held to be, in its vigorous antiphonal patterns, a source in the development of jazz. [1930–35, *Amer.*]

ring·side (ring′sīd′), *n.* **1.** the area immediately surrounding a ring, esp. the area occupied by the first row of seats on all sides of a boxing or wrestling ring. **2.** any place providing a close view. —*adj.* **3.** in or pertaining to the area immediately surrounding a ring or arena. **4.** close to the point of action; having a close view. [1865–75; RING[1] + SIDE[1]]

ring·sid·er (ring′sī′dər), *n.* a spectator at or near ringside, as of a boxing match or a nightclub performance. [1895–1900; RINGSIDE + -ER[1]]

ring′ snake′, **1.** See **grass snake** (def. 1). **2.** See **ring-neck snake.** Also, **ringed snake.** [1770–80, *Amer.*]

ring′ spin′ning, a process of spinning in which the yarn is twisted and drawn while passing through a small metal device traveling rapidly around a ring in the operation of winding the yarn onto a bobbin. Cf. **mule spinning.** [1880–85]

ring′-spin·ning frame′ (ring′spin′ing), a machine containing the ring, traveler, and bobbin used in spinning yarn. Also called **ring frame, ring′ spin′ner.** [1880–85]

ring′ spot′, *Plant Pathol.* any of various plant diseases caused by a virus or fungus and characterized by concentric rings of discoloration or necrosis on the leaves. [1905–10]

ring·ster (ring′stər), *n.* a member of a ring, esp. a political or price-fixing ring. [1870–75, *Amer.*; RING[1] + -STER]

ring′ stone′, a voussoir appearing on a face of an arch.

ring·straked (ring′strākt′), *adj. Archaic.* ring-streaked. [1605–15; RING[1] + STRAKE (in the obs. sense "stripe of contrasting color") + -ED[3]]

ring-streaked (ring′strēkt′), *adj.* having streaks or bands of color around the body.

ring·tail (ring′tāl′), *n.* **1.** any phalanger of the genus *Pseudocheirus,* having the prehensile tail curled into a ring. **2.** cacomistle. **3.** Also called **ringsail.** *Naut.* a narrow studdingsail set abaft a gaff sail, esp. a spanker, upon spears extending beyond the gaff and boom. —*adj.* **4.** ring-tailed. [1530–40; RING[1] + TAIL[1]]

ring-tailed (ring′tāld′), *adj.* **1.** having the tail ringed with alternating colors, as a raccoon. **2.** having a coiled tail. Also, **ringtail.** [1715–25]

ring′tail mon′key, capuchin (defs. 1, 2).

ring′ taw′, *Marbles.* ringer[1] (def. 4). [1820–30]

ring·toss (ring′tôs′, -tos′), *n.* a game in which rings, often made of rope, are tossed to encircle an upright peg. Also, **ring′-toss′.** [1875–80, *Amer.*; RING[1] + TOSS]

Ring·wood (ring′wo͝od′), *n.* a town in N New Jersey. 12,625.

ring·worm (ring′wûrm′), *n. Pathol.* any of a number of contagious skin diseases caused by certain parasitic fungi and characterized by the formation of ring-shaped eruptive patches. [1375–1425; late ME; see RING[1], WORM]

rink (ringk), *n.* **1.** a smooth expanse of ice for ice-skating, often artificially prepared and inside a building or arena. **2.** a smooth floor, usually of wood, for roller-skating. **3.** a building or enclosure for ice-skating or roller-skating; skating arena. **4.** an area of ice marked off for the game of curling. **5.** a section of a bowling green where a match can be played. **6.** a set of players on one side in a lawn-bowling or curling match. [1325–75; ME (Scots) *renk* area for a battle, joust, or race, appar. < MF *renc* RANK[1]]

rink·hals (ringk′hals), *n.* ringhals.

rink′ rat′, *Canadian.* a youth who spends a great deal of time at a hockey rink, helping with maintenance work, sweeping, etc., often without pay or in return for free admission to the rink. [1940–45]

rink·y-dink (ring′kē dingk′), *Slang.* —*adj.* **1.** inconsequential, amateurish, or of generally inferior quality; small-time: *a rinky-dink college; He plays with some rinky-dink team.* **2.** outmoded or shabby; backward; antiquated: *a rinky-dink airline.* —*n.* **3.** a person or thing that is rinky-dink. [1910–15; rhyming compound (perh. based on alter. and nasalization of RICKETY); cf. RICKY-TICK]

rink·y-tink (ring′kē tingk′), *n., adj.* ricky-tick. [1960–65; perh. b. RICKY-TICK and RINKY-DINK]

rinse (rins), *v.,* **rinsed, rins·ing,** *n.* —*v.t.* **1.** to wash lightly, as by pouring water into or over or by dipping in water: *to rinse a cup.* **2.** to douse or drench in clean water as a final stage in washing. **3.** to remove (soap, dirt, etc.) by such a process (often fol. by *off*). **4.** to use a rinse on (the hair). —*n.* **5.** an act or instance of rinsing. **6.** the water used for rinsing. **7.** any preparation that may be used on the hair after washing, esp. to tint or condition the hair. **8.** an act or instance of using such a preparation on the hair. [1300–50; ME *ryncen* < MF *rincer,* OF *recincier* < VL **recentiāre* to make new, refresh, equiv. to L *recent-* (s. of *recēns*) fresh, RECENT + connective *-i-* + *-āre* inf. suffix] —**rins′a·ble, rinse′a·ble,** *adj.* —**rins′a·bil′i·ty, rinse′a·bil′i·ty,** *n.*

rins·ing (rin′sing), *n.* **1.** an act or instance of rinsing. **2.** Usually, **rinsings.** the liquid with which anything has been rinsed. [1325–75; ME *rinsynge.* See RINSE, -ING[1]]

Rí·o A·zul (rē′ō ə zo͞ol′; *Sp.* rē′ô ä so͞ol′), an archaeological site in the jungles of northern Guatemala, where a 1500-year-old painted Mayan tomb was discovered intact in 1984.

Ri·o·bam·ba (rē′ō bäm′bə; *Sp.* rē′ô väm′bä), *n.* a city in central Ecuador in the Andes, near the Chimborazo volcano. 58,087.

Ri·o Bran·co (rē′o͞o brän′ko͞o), a city in W Brazil. 119,815.

Rí·o Bra·vo (rē′ô vrä′vô), Mexican name of **Rio Grande** (def. 1).

Rí·o Cuar·to (rē′ô kwär′tô), a city in central Argentina. 110,148.

Río da Du·vi·da (*Port.* rē′o͞o dä do͞o′vi dä′), former name of **Roosevelt, Río.**

Ri·o de Ja·nei·ro (rē′ō dā zhə nâr′ō, -nēr′ō, jə-, dē, də; *Port.* rē′o͞o di zhi nā′ro͞o), a seaport in SE Brazil: former capital. 5,184,292. Also called **Ri′o.**

Rí·o de la Pla·ta (*Sp.* rē′ô the lä plä′tä). See **Plata, Río de la.**

Rí·o de O·ro (rē′ô the ô′rô), Western Sahara.

Rí·o Ga·lle·gos (rē′ô gä ye′gôs), a seaport in S Argentina, in S Patagonia. 43,479. Also called **Gallegos.**

Ri·o Grande (rē′ō grand′, gran′dē, grän′dā *for 1;* *Port.* rē′o͞o grän′di *for 2, 3*), **1.** Mexican, **Rio Bravo.** a river flowing from SW Colorado through central New Mexico and along the boundary between Texas and Mexico into the Gulf of Mexico. 1800 mi. (2900 km) long. **2.** a river flowing W from SE Brazil into the Paraná River. 650 mi. (1050 km) long. **3.** Also called **Rio Grande do Sul.** See **São Pedro do Río Grande do Sul.**

Rí·o Gran·de (rē′ō grän′dā, -dē; *Sp.* rē′ô grän′de), **1.** a city in NE Puerto Rico. 12,047. **2.** a river in central Nicaragua, flowing NE to the Caribbean Sea. ab. 200 mi. (320 km) long.

Ri·o Gran·de do Nor·te (rē′o͞o grän′di do͞o nôr′ti), a state in E Brazil. 1,933,131; 20,464 sq. mi. (53,000 sq. km). *Cap.:* Natal.

Ri·o Gran·de do Sul (rē′o͞o grän′di do͞o so͞ol′), **1.** a state in S Brazil. 7,942,047; 107,923 sq. mi. (279,520 sq. km). *Cap.:* Pôrto Alegre. **2.** See **São Pedro de Rio Grande do Sul.**

Ri·o·ja (rē ō′hä; *Sp.* rē ô′hä), *n.* a table wine, esp. a dry red wine, from the Rioja region of northern Spain.

Rí·o Mu·ni (rē′ô mo͞o′nē), the mainland province of Equatorial Guinea on the Guinea coast: formerly the mainland portion of Spanish Guinea. 290,000; 10,040 sq. mi. (26,003 sq. km).

Ri·o Ne·gro (rē′o͞o ne′gro͞o), Portuguese name of **Negro River.**

Rí·o Ne·gro (rē′ō nā′grō; *Sp.* rē′ô ne′grô), Spanish name of **Negro River.**

Ri′on Strait′ (rē′on; *Gk.* rē′ôn), Lepanto (def. 3).

Ri·o·pelle (*Fr.* rē ô pel′), *n.* **Jean Paul** (zhän pôl), born 1923, Canadian painter, in France since 1946.

ri·ot (rī′ət), *n.* **1.** a noisy, violent public disorder caused by a group or crowd of persons, as by a crowd protesting against another group, a government policy, etc., in the streets. **2.** *Law.* a disturbance of the public peace by three or more persons acting together in a disrupting and tumultuous manner in carrying out their private purposes. **3.** violent or wild disorder or confusion. **4.** a brilliant display: *a riot of color.* **5.** something or someone hilariously funny: *You were a riot at the party.* **6.** unrestrained revelry. **7.** an unbridled outbreak, as of emotions, passions, etc. **8.** *Archaic.* loose, wanton living; profligacy. **9. run riot, a.** to act without control or restraint: *The neighbors let their children run riot.* **b.** to grow luxuriantly or abundantly: *Crab grass is running riot in our lawn.* —*v.i.* **10.** to take part in a riot or disorderly public outbreak. **11.** to live in a loose or wanton manner; indulge in unrestrained revelry: *Many of the Roman emperors rioted notoriously.* **12.** *Hunting.* (of a hound or pack) to pursue an animal other than the intended quarry. **13.** to indulge unrestrainedly; run riot. —*v.t.* **14.** to spend (money, time, etc.) in riotous living (usually fol. by *away* or *out*). [1175–1225; (n.) ME: debauchery, revel, violent disturbance < OF *riot(e)* debate, dispute, quarrel, deriv. of *rihoter, riot(t)er* to quarrel; (v.) ME *rioten* < OF *rihoter, riot(t)er*] —**ri′ot·er,** *n.*
—**Syn. 1.** outbreak, brawl, fray, melee. **3.** uproar, tumult, disturbance. **10.** brawl, fight. **11.** carouse.

Ri′ot Act′, **1.** an English statute of 1715 providing that if 12 or more persons assemble unlawfully and riotously, to the disturbance of the public peace, and refuse to disperse upon proclamation they shall be considered guilty of felony. **2. read (someone) the riot act, a.** to reprimand; censure: *The principal read them the riot act for their behavior at the assembly.* **b.** to give (someone) a sharp warning.

ri′ot gun′, a gun, esp. a shotgun with a short barrel, for quelling riots rather than inflicting serious injury. [1925–30]

ri·ot·ous (rī′ə təs), *adj.* **1.** (of an act) characterized by or of the nature of rioting or a disturbance of the peace. **2.** (of a person) inciting or taking part in a riot. **3.** given to or marked by unrestrained revelry; loose; wanton: *riotous living.* **4.** boisterous or uproarious: *riotous laughter.* **5.** hilariously funny. [1300–50; ME; see RIOT, -OUS] —**ri′ot·ous·ly,** *adv.* —**ri′ot·ous·ness,** *n.*

ri′ot squad′, a group of police officers having special training and equipment for quelling riots and other public disturbances. [1945–50]

rip[1] (rip), *v.,* **ripped, rip·ping,** *n.* —*v.t.* **1.** to cut or tear apart in a rough or vigorous manner: *to rip open a seam; to rip up a sheet.* **2.** to cut or tear away in a rough or vigorous manner: *to rip bark from a tree.* **3.** to saw (wood) in the direction of the grain. —*v.i.* **4.** to become torn apart or split open: *Cheap cloth rips easily.* **5.** *Informal.* to move with violence or great speed: *The sports car ripped along in a cloud of dust and exhaust fumes.* **6. let rip,** *Slang.* **a.** to utter a series of oaths; swear. **b.** to speak or write violently, rapidly, or at great length. **c.** to allow to proceed at full speed or without restraint. **7. rip into,** *Informal.* to attack physically or verbally; assail. **8. rip off,** *Slang.* **a.** to steal or pilfer. **b.** to rob or steal from. **c.** to swindle, cheat, or exploit; take advantage of: *phony charity appeals that rip off a gullible public.* **9. rip out,** *Informal.* to utter angrily, as with an oath or exclamation. —*n.* **10.** a rent made by ripping; tear. **11.** *Slang.* a cheat, swindle, or theft; ripoff: *The average consumer doesn't realize that the new tax is a rip.* [1470–80; 1960–65 for def. 8; obscurely akin to Fris *rippe,* dial. D *rippen;* cf. dial. E *ripple* to scratch] —**rip′pa·ble,** *adj.*
—**Syn. 1.** See **tear**[2]. **10.** laceration, cut.

rip[2] (rip), *n.* a stretch of turbulent water at sea or in a river. [1765–75; see RIP[1], RIPPLE[1]]

rip[3] (rip), *n. Informal.* **1.** a dissolute or worthless person. **2.** a worthless or worn-out horse. **3.** something of little or no value. [1770–80; prob. alter. of *rep,* shortened form of REPROBATE]

Rip (rip), *n.* a male given name, form of **Robert.**

R.I.P., **1.** may he or she rest in peace. [< L *requiēscat in pāce*] **2.** may they rest in peace. [< L *requiēscant in pāce*] Also, **RIP**

ri·par·i·an (ri pâr′ē ən, rī-), *adj.* **1.** of, pertaining to, or situated or dwelling on the bank of a river or other body of water: *riparian villas.* —*n.* **2.** *Law.* a person who owns land on the bank of a natural watercourse or body of water. [1840–50; < L *rīpāri(us)* that frequents riverbanks (*rīp(a)* bank of a RIVER + *-ārius* -ARY) + -AN]

ripar′ian right′, *Law.* a right, as fishing or use of water for irrigation or power, enjoyed by a person who owns riparian property. [1885–90]

CONCISE PRONUNCIATION KEY: *act, cāpe, dâre, pärt; set, ēqual; if, ice; ox, ōver, ôrder, oil, bo͝ok, bo͞ot, out; up, ûrge; child; sing; shoe; thin, that;* zh as in *treasure.* ə = *a* as in *alone, e* as in *system, i* as in *easily, o* as in *gallop, u* as in *circus;* ° as in *fire* (fī°r), *hour* (ou°r). l and n can serve as syllabic consonants, as in *cradle* (krād′l), and *button* (but′n). See the full key inside the front cover.

rip′ cord′, **1.** a cord on a parachute that, when pulled, opens the parachute for descent. **2.** a cord fastened in the bag of a passenger balloon or dirigible so that a sharp pull upon it will rip or open the bag and let the gas escape, causing the balloon to descend. [1905–10]

rip′ cur′rent, undertow (def. 1). [1935–40]

ripe (rīp), *adj.,* **rip•er, rip•est.** **1.** having arrived at such a stage of growth or development as to be ready for reaping, gathering, eating, or use, as grain or fruit; completely matured. **2.** resembling such fruit, as in ruddiness and fullness: *ripe, red lips.* **3.** advanced to the point of being in the best condition for use, as cheese or beer. **4.** fully grown or developed, as animals when ready to be killed and used for food. **5.** arrived at the highest or a high point of development or excellence; mature. **6.** of mature judgment or knowledge: *ripe scholars; a ripe mind.* **7.** characterized by full development of body or mind: *of ripe years.* **8.** (of time) advanced: *a ripe old age.* **9.** (of ideas, plans, etc.) ready for action, execution, etc. **10.** (of people) fully prepared or ready to do or undergo something: *He was ripe for a change in jobs.* **11.** fully or sufficiently advanced; ready enough; auspicious: *The time is ripe for a new foreign policy.* **12.** ready for some operation or process: *a ripe abscess.* **13.** *Archaic.* drunk: *reeling ripe.* [bef. 900; ME; OE *ripe;* c. D *rijp,* G *reif;* akin to OE *rīpan* to REAP] —**ripe′ly,** *adv.* —**ripe′ness,** *n.*
—**Syn. 1.** grown, aged. RIPE, MATURE, MELLOW refer to that which is no longer in an incomplete stage of development. RIPE implies completed growth beyond which the processes of decay begin: *a ripe banana.* MATURE means fully grown and developed as used of living organisms: *a mature animal; a mature tree.* MELLOW denotes complete absence of sharpness or asperity, with sweetness and richness such as characterize ripeness or age: *mellow fruit; mellow flavor.*

rip•en (rī′pən), *v.t., v.i.* **1.** to make or become ripe. **2.** to bring or come to maturity, the proper condition, etc.; mature. [1555–65; RIPE + -EN[1]] —**rip′en•er,** *n.*

ripe′ rot′, *Plant Pathol.* a disease of fruit or vegetable storage organs at the ripening stage, caused by any of several fungi or bacteria and characterized by spotting and rapid decay.

ri•pid•o•lite (ri pid′l īt′, rī-), *n.* a mineral of the chlorite group, essentially hydrated magnesium and aluminum silicate with some ferrous iron. [1840–50; < G *Ripidolith* < Gk *rhipid-* (s. of *rhipís*) fan + -o- -o- + G *-lith* -LITE]

ri•pie•no (ri pyā′nō; *It.* rē pye′nô), *n., pl.* **-nos;** *It.* **-ni** (-nē), *adj. Music.* —*n.* **1.** tutti (defs. 3, 4). —*adj.* **2.** tutti (def. 2). [1715–25; < It: full]

Rip•ley (rip′lē), *n.* **George,** 1802–80, U.S. literary critic, author, and social reformer: associated with the founding of Brook Farm.

rip•off (rip′ôf′, -of′), *n. Slang.* **1.** an act or instance of ripping off another or others; a theft, cheat, or swindle. **2.** exploitation, esp. of those who cannot prevent or counter it. **3.** a copy or imitation. **4.** a person who rips off another or others; thief or swindler. Also, **rip′-off′.** [1965–70; n. use of v. phrase *rip off*]

ri•poste (ri pōst′), *n., v.,* **-post•ed, -post•ing.** —*n.* **1.** a quick, sharp return in speech or action; counterstroke: *a brilliant riposte to an insult.* **2.** *Fencing.* a quick thrust given after parrying a lunge. —*v.i.* **3.** to make a riposte. **4.** to reply or retaliate. Also, **ri•post′.** [1700–10; < F, var. of *risposte* prompt answer < It *risposta,* n. use of fem. ptp. of *rispondere* to answer < VL **respondere* for L *respondēre;* see RESPOND]

ripped (ript), *adj. Slang.* **1.** drunk; intoxicated. **2.** under the influence of an illicit drug. [1815–25; RIP[1] + -ED[2]]

rip•per (rip′ər), *n.* **1.** a person or thing that rips. **2.** Also, **rip′per bill′, rip′per act′.** a legislative bill or act for taking powers of appointment to and removal from office away from the usual holders of these powers and conferring them unrestrictedly on a chief executive, as a governor or mayor, or on a board of officials. **3.** a double-ripper. **4.** a killer who dispatches and often mutilates victims with a knife or similar weapon. **5.** *Mining.* a hooklike tool, attached to earth-moving machinery, for tearing away ore, rock, etc. **6.** *Chiefly Brit. Slang.* something especially strong, fine, or good of its kind. [1605–15; RIP[1] + -ER[1]]

rip•ping (rip′ing), *adj. Chiefly Brit. Informal.* excellent; splendid; fine. [1705–15; RIP[1] + -ING[2]] —**rip′ping•ly,** *adv.*

rip′ping bar′. See **pinch bar.**

rip•ple[1] (rip′əl), *v.,* **-pled, -pling,** *n.* —*v.i.* **1.** (of a liquid surface) to form small waves or undulations, as water agitated by a breeze. **2.** to flow with a light rise and fall or ruffling of the surface. **3.** (of a solid surface) to form or have small undulations, ruffles, or folds. **4.** (of sound) to undulate or rise and fall in tone, inflection, or magnitude. —*v.t.* **5.** to form small waves or undulations on; agitate lightly. **6.** to mark as if with ripples; give a wavy form to. —*n.* **7.** a small wave or undulation, as on water. **8.** any similar movement or appearance; a small undulation or wave, as in hair. **9.** a small rapid. **10.** *Geol.* See **ripple mark. 11.** a sound, as of water flowing in ripples: *a ripple of laughter.* [1660–70; orig. uncert.] —**rip′ple•less,** *adj.* —**rip′pling•ly,** *adv.*
—**Syn. 1.** wave, undulate, purl. **5.** ruffle, curl, dimple. **7.** wavelet, ruffling. See **wave.**

rip•ple[2] (rip′əl), *n., v.,* **-pled, -pling.** —*n.* **1.** a toothed or comblike device for removing seeds or capsules from flax, hemp, etc. —*v.t.* **2.** to remove the seeds or capsules from (flax or hemp) with a ripple. [1425–75; late ME *ripel;* c. D *repel,* G *Riffel*]

CONCISE ETYMOLOGY KEY: <, descended or borrowed from; >, whence; b., blend of, blended; c., cognate with; cf., compare; deriv., derivative; equiv., equivalent; imit., imitative; obl., oblique; r., replacing; s., stem; sp., spelling, spelled; resp., respelling, respelled; trans., translation; ?, origin unknown; *, unattested; ‡, probably earlier than. See the full key inside the front cover.

rip′ple effect′, a spreading effect or series of consequences caused by a single action or event. [1965–70]

rip′ple mark′, *Geol.* **1.** one of the wavy lines or ridges produced, esp. on sand, by the action of waves, wind, or the like. **2.** one of such forms preserved in sandstone or siltstone. [1825–35]

rip•pler (rip′lər), *n.* **1.** a person who ripples flax, hemp, etc. **2.** an instrument for rippling; ripple. [1735–45; RIPPLE[2] + -ER[1]]

rip•plet (rip′lit), *n.* a small ripple. [1810–20; RIPPLE[1] + -ET]

rip•ply (rip′lē), *adj.* **1.** characterized by ripples; rippling. **2.** sounding like rippling water. [1765–75; RIPPLE[1] + -Y[1]]

rip•rap (rip′rap′), *n., v.,* **-rapped, -rap•ping.** —*n.* **1.** a quantity of broken stone for foundations, revetments of embankments, etc. **2.** a foundation or wall of stones thrown together irregularly. —*v.t.* **3.** to construct with or strengthen by stones, either loose or fastened with mortar. [1570–80; gradational redupl. of RAP[1]]

rip-roar•ing (rip′rôr′ing, -rōr′-), *adj. Informal.* boisterously wild and exciting; riotous: *Have a rip-roaring good time.* [1825–35, *Amer.;* RIP[1] + ROARING, alter. of *rip-roarious,* modeled on *uproarious*]

rip•saw (rip′sô′), *n., v.,* **-sawed, -sawed** or **-sawn, -saw•ing.** —*n.* **1.** a saw for cutting wood with the grain. —*v.t.* **2.** to saw (wood) in such a manner. [1840–50; RIP[1] + SAW[1]]

rip•snort•er (rip′snôr′tər), *n. Informal.* **1.** something or someone exceedingly strong or violent: *a ripsnorter of a gale.* **2.** something or someone remarkably good or exciting. [1830–40, *Amer.;* RIP[1] + SNORTER]

rip′stop ny′lon (rip′stop′), a nylon fabric woven with a double thread approximately every quarter inch to prevent the expansion of small rips. [1945–50]

rip•tide (rip′tīd′), *n.* a tide that opposes another or other tides, causing a violent disturbance in the sea. [1860–65; RIP[2] + TIDE[1]]
—**Syn.** See **undertow.**

Rip•u•ar•i•an (rip′yo͞o âr′ē ən), *adj.* **1.** designating or pertaining to a group of Franks who lived along the Rhine in the neighborhood of Cologne during the 4th century or the code of laws observed by them. —*n.* **2.** a Ripuarian Frank. [1775–85; < ML *Ripuāri(us)* + -AN]

Rip Van Win•kle (rip′ van wing′kəl), **1.** (in a story by Washington Irving) a ne'er-do-well who sleeps 20 years and upon waking is startled to find how much the world has changed. **2.** (*italics*) the story itself, published in *The Sketch Book* (1819).

RISC (risk), *n.* reduced instruction set computer: a computer whose central processing unit recognizes a relatively small number of instructions, which it can execute very rapidly. Cf. **CISC.**

rise (rīz), *v.,* **rose, ris•en** (riz′ən), **ris•ing,** *n.* —*v.i.* **1.** to get up from a lying, sitting, or kneeling posture; assume an upright position: *She rose and walked over to greet me. With great effort he rose to his knees.* **2.** to get up from bed, esp. to begin the day after a night's sleep: *to rise early.* **3.** to become erect and stiff, as the hair in fright. **4.** to get up after falling or being thrown down. **5.** to become active in opposition or resistance; revolt or rebel. **6.** to be built up, erected, or constructed. **7.** to spring up or grow, as plants: *Weeds rose overnight.* **8.** to become prominent on or project from a surface, as a blister. **9.** to come into existence; appear. **10.** to come into action, as a wind or storm. **11.** to occur: *A quarrel rose between them.* **12.** to originate, issue, or be derived; to have a source. **13.** to move from a lower to a higher position; move upward; ascend: *The bird rose in the air.* **14.** to ascend above the horizon, as a heavenly body. **15.** to extend directly upward; project vertically: *The tower rises to a height of 60 feet. The building rises above the city's other skyscrapers.* **16.** to have an upward slant or curve: *The path rises as it approaches the woods.* **17.** to attain higher rank, status, or importance or a higher economic level: *to rise in the world.* **18.** to advance to a higher level of action, thought, feeling, etc.: *to rise above the commonplace.* **19.** *Angling.* (of fish) to come up toward the surface of the water in pursuit of food or bait. **20.** to prove oneself equal to a demand, emergency, etc. (fol. by *to*): *to rise to the occasion; to rise to one's responsibilities.* **21.** to become animated, cheerful, or heartened, as the spirits. **22.** to become roused or stirred: *to feel one's temper rising.* **23.** to increase in height, as the level of water: *The river rose thirty feet in eight hours.* **24.** to swell or puff up, as dough from the action of yeast. **25.** to increase in amount, as prices. **26.** to increase in price or value, as commodities. **27.** to increase in degree, intensity, or force, as fever, color, etc. **28.** to become louder or of higher pitch, as the voice. **29.** to adjourn or close a session, as a deliberative body or court. **30.** to return from the dead: *Christ rose from the dead and on the third day ascended into heaven.* —*v.t.* **31.** *Nonstandard.* to cause to rise. **32.** *Naut.* to cause (something) to rise above the visible horizon by approaching nearer to it; raise. **33. rise above,** to ignore or be indifferent to, as an insult. —*n.* **34.** an act or instance of rising. **35.** appearance above the horizon, as of the sun or moon. **36.** elevation or increase in rank, fortune, influence, power, etc.: *the rise and fall of ancient Rome.* **37.** an increase in height, as of the level of water. **38.** the amount of such increase. **39.** an increase in amount, as of prices. **40.** an increase in price or value, as of commodities. **41.** *Chiefly Brit.* raise (defs. 33–36). **42.** an increase in degree or intensity, as of temperature. **43.** an increase in loudness or in pitch, as of the voice. **44.** *Archit., Building Trades.* **a.** the measured height of any of various things, as a roof, a flight of steps, a stair step, or the crown of a road. **b.** the measured height of an arch from the springing line to the highest point of the intrados. **45.** the vertical distance through which the floor of an elevator or the like passes. **46.** origin, source, or beginning: *the rise of a stream in a mountain.* **47.** a coming into existence or notice: *the rise of a new talent.* **48.** extension upward. **49.** the amount of such extension. **50.** upward slope, as of ground or a road. **51.** a piece of rising or high ground: *a house built upon a gentle rise.* **52.** the distance between the crotch and the waist of a pair of trousers: *Pants with a high rise are now in style.* **53.** *Angling.* the coming up of a fish toward the surface in pursuit of food or bait. **54. get a rise out of,** *Informal.* **a.** to provoke, as to action or anger. **b.** to evoke the expected or desired response from. **55. give rise to,** to originate; produce; cause: *The Industrial Revolution gave rise to accelerated urbanization.* [bef. 1000; ME *risen* (v.), OE *rīsan;* c. D *rijzen,* OHG *rīsan,* Goth *reisan;* akin to RAISE, REAR[2]]
—**Syn. 12.** arise, proceed. **13.** mount. **17.** succeed, advance. —**Ant. 1.** sink. **4.** fall. **13.** descend. **17.** fail.
—**Usage.** See **raise.**

ris•er (rī′zər), *n.* **1.** a person who rises, esp. from bed: *to be an early riser.* **2.** the vertical face of a stair step. **3.** any of a group of long boards or narrow platforms that can be combined in stepwise fashion. **4.** a vertical pipe, duct, or conduit. **5.** *Metall.* a chamber or enlarged opening at the top of a mold for allowing air to escape or adding extra metal. **6.** *Naut.* **a.** a heavy strake of planking in the vicinity of the garboard strake in a wooden vessel. **b.** rising (def. 10). [1350–1400; ME; see RISE, -ER[1]]

rish•i (rish′ē), *n. Hinduism.* **1.** an inspired sage or poet. **2.** (*cap.*) one of seven of these to whom the Vedas supposedly were revealed. [1760–70; < Skt *ṛṣi*]

ris•i•bil•i•ty (riz′ə bil′i tē), *n., pl.* **-ties. 1.** Often, **risibilities.** the ability or disposition to laugh; humorous awareness of the ridiculous and absurd. **2.** laughter. [1610–20; < LL *rīsibilitās.* See RISIBLE, -ITY]

ris•i•ble (riz′ə bəl), *adj.* **1.** causing or capable of causing laughter; laughable; ludicrous. **2.** having the ability, disposition, or readiness to laugh. **3.** pertaining to or connected with laughing. [1550–60; < LL *rīsibilis* that can laugh, equiv. to L *rīs(us)* (ptp. of *rīdēre* to laugh) + *-ibilis* -IBLE]
—**Syn. 1.** funny, humorous, comical.

ris•ing (rī′zing), *adj.* **1.** advancing, ascending, or mounting: *rising smoke.* **2.** growing or advancing to adult years: *the rising generation.* —*adv. Informal* **3.** somewhat more than: *The crop came to rising 6000 bushels.* **4.** in approach of; almost; well-nigh: *a lad rising sixteen.* —*n.* **5.** the act of a person or thing that rises. **6.** an insurrection; rebellion; revolt. **7.** something that rises; projection or prominence. **8.** a period of leavening of dough preceding baking. **9.** *Chiefly South Midland and Southern U.S.* a morbid swelling, as an abscess or boil. **10.** Also called **riser.** *Naut.* a stringer supporting the thwarts of an open boat. [1150–1200; ME (ger.). See RISE, -ING[2], ING[1]]

ris′ing ac′tion, a related series of incidents in a literary plot that build toward the point of greatest interest. Cf. **falling action.**

ris′ing diph′thong, *Phonet.* a diphthong in which the first of two apparent vocalic elements is of lesser stress or sonority than the second, as the (wä) in *guava* (gwä′və). Cf. **falling diphthong.** [1885–90]

ris′ing hinge′, a gravity hinge causing a door, shutter, etc., to rise slightly when opened. [1800–10]

ris′ing rhythm′, *Pros.* a rhythmic pattern created by a succession of metrical feet each of which is composed of one accented syllable preceded by one or more unaccented ones. [1920–25]

ris′ing sign′, *Astrol.* (in a horoscope) the sign of the zodiac on the eastern horizon at any given moment; ascendant.

risk (risk), *n.* **1.** exposure to the chance of injury or loss; a hazard or dangerous chance: *It's not worth the risk.* **2.** *Insurance.* **a.** the hazard or chance of loss. **b.** the degree of probability of such loss. **c.** the amount that the insurance company may lose. **d.** a person or thing with reference to the hazard involved in insuring him, her, or it. **e.** the type of loss, as life, fire, marine disaster, or earthquake, against which an insurance policy is drawn. **3. at risk, a.** in a dangerous situation or status; in jeopardy: *families at risk in the area of the weakened dam.* **b.** under financial or legal obligation; held responsible: *Are individual investors at risk for the debt part of the real estate venture?* **4. take** or **run a risk,** to expose oneself to the chance of injury or loss; put oneself in danger; hazard; venture. —*v.t.* **5.** to expose to the chance of injury or loss; hazard: *to risk one's life.* **6.** to venture upon; take or run the chance of: *to risk a fall in climbing; to risk a war.* [1655–65; < F *risque* < It *risc(hi)o,* of obscure orig.] —**risk′er,** *n.* —**risk′less,** *adj.*
—**Syn. 1.** venture, peril, jeopardy. **5.** imperil, endanger, jeopardize. **6.** chance.

risk-ben•e•fit (risk′ben′ə fit), *adj.* involving studies, testing, etc., to establish whether the benefits, as of a course of medical treatment, outweigh the risks involved: *to arrive at a risk-benefit ratio.* [1970–75]

risk′ cap′ital. See **venture capital.** [1945–50]

risk′ man′agement, the technique or profession of assessing, minimizing, and preventing accidental loss to a business, as through the use of insurance, safety measures, etc. [1960–65] —**risk′ man′ager.**

risk•tak•er (risk′tā′kər), *n.* a person or corporation inclined to take risks. [1940–45; RISK + TAKER]

risk•y (ris′kē), *adj.,* **risk•i•er, risk•i•est.** attended with or involving risk; hazardous: *a risky undertaking.* [1820–30; RISK + -Y[1]] —**risk′i•ly,** *adv.* —**risk′i•ness,** *n.*
—**Syn.** dangerous, perilous.

Ri•sor•gi•men•to (ri zôr′jə men′tō, -sôr′-; *It.* rē zôr′jē men′tô), *n., pl.* **-tos,** *It.* **-ti** (-tē) for 2. **1.** the period of or the movement for the liberation and unification of Italy 1750–1870. **2.** (*l.c.*) any period or instance of rebirth or renewed activity; resurgence: *The company's risorgimento surprised Wall Street observers.* [< It, equiv. to *risorg(ere)* to rise again (< L *resurgere;* see RESURGE) + *-i-* -I- + *-mento* -MENT]

ri•sot•to (ri sô′tō, -sot′ō; *It.* rē zôt′tô), *n. Italian Cookery.* a dish of rice cooked with broth and flavored with grated cheese and other ingredients. [1850–55; < It, deriv. of *riso* RICE]

ris•qué (ri skā′; *Fr.* rēs kā′), *adj.* daringly close to indelicacy or impropriety; off-color: *a risqué story.* [1865–70; < F, ptp. of *risquer* to RISK]
—Syn. broad, gross, indecent, ribald.

ris•sole (ri sōl′, ris′ōl; *Fr.* rē sôl′), *n., pl.* **ris•soles** (ri-sōlz′, ris′ōlz; *Fr.* rē sôl′). a small pastry, often in turnover form, filled with a mixture containing meat or fish and usually fried in deep fat. [1700–10; < F; MF *roissole, rousole,* perh. < VL **russeola* (fem. adj.) reddish]

ris•so•lé (ris′ə lē, ris′ə lā′; *Fr.* rē sô lā′), *adj.* (of foods) browned in deep fat. [< F, ptp. of *rissoler* to brown, deriv. of *rissole* RISSOLE]

rit., *Music.* ritardando. Also, **ritard.**

rit•a (rit′ə), *n. Hinduism.* the Vedic concept of cosmic and social order. [< Skt *ṛta*]

Ri•ta (rē′tə), *n.* a female given name, form of **Margarita.**

Rit•a•lin (rit′l in), *Pharm., Trademark.* a brand of methylphenidate in its hydrochloride form.

ri•tar•dan•do (rē′tär dän′dō; *It.* rē′tär dän′dô), *adj., adv. Music.* becoming gradually slower. [1805–15; < It, ger. of *ritardare;* see RETARD]

rite (rīt), *n.* **1.** a formal or ceremonial act or procedure prescribed or customary in religious or other solemn use: *rites of baptism; sacrificial rites.* **2.** a particular form or system of religious or other ceremonial practice: *the Roman rite.* **3.** (*often cap.*) one of the historical versions of the Eucharistic service: *the Anglican Rite.* **4.** (*often cap.*) liturgy. **5.** (*sometimes cap.*) *Eastern Ch., Western Ch.* a division or differentiation of churches according to liturgy. **6.** any customary observance or practice: *the rite of afternoon tea.* [1275–1325; ME (< OF *rit(e)*) < L *rītus*] **—rite′less,** *adj.* **—rite′less•ness,** *n.*
—Syn. 1. observance, form, usage. See **ceremony.**

rite de pas•sage (rēt də pä sazh′), *pl.,* ***rites de passage*** (rēt də pä sazh′). *French.* See **rite of passage.**

ri•te•nu•to (rē′tə no͞o′tō; *It.* rē′te no͞o′tô), *adv., adj.* (of a passage in a musical score) immediately slower. [1820–30; < It: lit., held back, ptp. of *ritenere;* see RETAIN]

rite′ of intensifica′tion, *Anthropol.* a ritual or ceremony performed by a community in a time of crisis that affects all members, as a rain dance during a drought. [1945–50]

rite′ of pas′sage, 1. *Anthropol.* a ceremony performed to facilitate or mark a person's change of status upon any of several highly important occasions, as at the onset of puberty or upon entry into marriage or into a clan. **2.** any important act or event that serves to mark a passage from one stage of life to another. [1955–60]

Rite′ of Spring′, The, (French, *Le Sacre du Printemps*), a ballet suite (1913) for orchestra by Igor Stravinsky.

ri•tor•nel•lo (rit′ər nel′ō; *It.* rē′tôr nel′lô), *n., pl.* **-los, -li** (-lē). *Music.* **1.** an orchestral interlude between arias, scenes, or acts in 17th-century opera. **2.** a tutti section in a concerto grosso, aria, etc. [1665–75; < It, dim. of *ritorno* RETURN]

Ritsch•li•an (rich′lē ən), *adj.* **1.** of or pertaining to the theology of Albrecht Ritschl (1822–89), who developed a liberal Christian theology and maintained that religious faith is based on value judgments. —*n.* **2.** a supporter of Ritschlian theology. [1890–95; *Ritschl* + -IAN] **—Ritsch′li•an•ism,** *n.*

rit•ter (rit′ər), *n., pl.* **rit•ter, rit•ters. 1.** a knight. **2.** a member of the lowest order of nobility in Germany or Austria. [1815–25; < G; MHG *riter* RIDER]

Rit•ter (rit′ər), *n.* **1. Joseph Elmer,** 1891–1967, U.S. cardinal. **2. Woodward Maurice** ("**Tex**"), 1907–74, U.S. country-and-western singer, composer, and film actor.

rit•u•al (rich′o͞o əl), *n.* **1.** an established or prescribed procedure for a religious or other rite. **2.** a system or collection of religious or other rites. **3.** observance of set forms in public worship. **4.** a book of rites or ceremonies. **5.** a book containing the offices to be used by priests in administering the sacraments and for visitation of the sick, burial of the dead, etc. **6.** a prescribed or established rite, ceremony, proceeding, or service: *the ritual of the dead.* **7.** prescribed, established, or ceremonial acts or features collectively, as in religious services. **8.** any practice or pattern of behavior regularly performed in a set manner. **9.** a prescribed code of behavior regulating social conduct, as that exemplified by the raising of one's hat or the shaking of hands in greeting. **10.** *Psychiatry.* a specific act, as hand-washing, performed repetitively to a pathological degree, occurring as a common symptom of obsessive-compulsive neurosis. —*adj.* **11.** of the nature of or practiced as a rite or ritual: *a ritual dance.* **12.** of or pertaining to rites or ritual: *ritual laws.* [1560–70; < L *rītuālis,* equiv. to *rītu-,* s. of *rītus* RITE + *-ālis* -AL[1]] **—rit′u•al•ly,** *adv.*
—Syn. 1. See **ceremony. 11.** ceremonial, formal, sacramental.

rit′ual bath′, a mikvah.

rit•u•al•ism (rich′o͞o ə liz′əm), *n.* **1.** adherence to or insistence on ritual. **2.** the study of ritual practices or religious rites. **3.** excessive fondness for ritual. [1835–45; RITUAL + -ISM] **—rit′u•al•is′tic,** *adj.* **—rit′u•al•is′ti•cal•ly,** *adv.*

rit•u•al•ist (rich′o͞o ə list), *n.* **1.** a student of or authority on ritual practices or religious rites. **2.** a person who practices or advocates observance of ritual, as in religious services. **3.** (*cap.*) *Anglican Ch.* **a.** a person who supports High Church principles. **b.** a supporter of the Oxford movement. [1650–60; RITUAL + -IST]

rit•u•al•i•za•tion (rich′o͞o ə lə zā′shən), *n.* **1.** the act of ritualizing. **2.** *Ethology.* the alteration of a behavior pattern, as by a change in intensity, in a way that increases its effectiveness as a signal to other members of the species. [1930–35; RITUALIZE + -ATION]

rit•u•al•ize (rich′o͞o ə līz′), *v.,* **-ized, -iz•ing.** —*v.i.* **1.** to practice ritualism. —*v.t.* **2.** to make into a ritual: *to ritualize the serving of tea.* **3.** to convert (someone) to ritualism; impose ritualism upon. Also, *esp. Brit.,* **rit′u•al•ise′.** [1835–45; RITUAL + -IZE]

rit′ual mur′der, a human sacrifice made to appease a deity. [1945–50]

ritz (rits), *n.* **1.** ostentatious or pretentious display. **2. put on the ritz,** *Informal.* to live in elegance and luxury, esp. to make an ostentatious show of one's wealth: *They put on the ritz to impress their guests.* Also, **put on the Ritz.** —*v.t.* **3.** *Slang.* to treat with condescension; snub: *The star ritzed the reporters and got a bad press.* [1925–30; after the sumptuous hotels founded by César Ritz (d. 1918), Swiss entrepreneur]

Ritz′ combina′tion prin′ciple (rits), *Physics.* the principle that the frequencies of lines in atomic spectra can be represented as differences of a smaller number of terms, all characteristic of the emitting system, interpreted in quantum theory as the emission of exactly one photon in a transition between energy levels. Also called **combination principle.** [after Walther *Ritz* (1878–1909), Swiss physicist, who formulated it]

ritz•y (rit′sē), *adj.,* **ritz•i•er, ritz•i•est.** *Slang.* swanky; elegant; posh: *a ritzy neighborhood; a ritzy hotel.* [1915–20, *Amer.*; see RITZ, -Y[1]] **—ritz′i•ly,** *adv.* **—ritz′i•ness,** *n.*

riv., river.

riv•age (riv′ij, rī′vij), *n. Archaic.* a bank, shore, or coast. [1250–1300; ME < MF, equiv. to *rive* RIVER (< L *rīpa* riverbank) + *-age* -AGE]

ri•val (rī′vəl), *n., adj., v.,* **-valed, -val•ing** or (*esp. Brit.*) **-valled, -val•ling.** —*n.* **1.** a person who is competing for the same object or goal as another, or who tries to equal or outdo another; competitor. **2.** a person or thing that is in a position to dispute another's preeminence or superiority: *a stadium without a rival.* **3.** *Obs.* a companion in duty. —*adj.* **4.** competing or standing in rivalry: *rival suitors; rival businesses.* —*v.t.* **5.** to compete with in rivalry: strive to win from, equal, or outdo. **6.** to prove to be a worthy rival of: *He soon rivaled the others in skill.* **7.** to equal (something) as if in carrying on a rivalry: *The Hudson rivals any European river in beauty.* —*v.i.* **8.** to engage in rivalry; compete. [1570–80; < L *rīvālis* orig., one who uses a stream in common with another, equiv. to *rīv(us)* stream + *-ālis* -AL[1]] **—ri′val•less,** *adj.*
—Syn. 1. contestant, emulator, antagonist. See **opponent. 4.** competitive, opposed. **5.** oppose. **7.** match, emulate. **—Ant. 1.** ally.

ri•val•rous (rī′vəl rəs), *adj.* characterized by rivalry; competitive: *the rivalrous aspect of their friendship.* [1805–15; RIVALR(Y) + -OUS] **—ri′val•rous•ness,** *n.*

ri•val•ry (rī′vəl rē), *n., pl.* **-ries. 1.** the action, position, or relation of a rival or rivals; competition: *rivalry between Yale and Harvard.* **2.** an instance of this. [1590–1600; RIVAL + -RY]
—Syn. 1. opposition, antagonism; jealousy.

Rivals, The, a comedy of manners (1775) by Richard Brinsley Sheridan.

rive (rīv), *v.,* **rived, rived** or **riv•en, riv•ing.** —*v.t.* **1.** to tear or rend apart: *to rive meat from a bone.* **2.** to separate by striking; split; cleave. **3.** to rend, harrow, or distress (the feelings, heart, etc.). **4.** to split (wood) radially from a log. —*v.i.* **5.** to become rent or split apart: *stones that rive easily.* [1225–75; ME *riven* < ON *rīfa* to tear, split. See RIFT]

riv•el (riv′əl), *n. Chiefly Western Canadian.* a very small dumpling made of a batter of butter, egg, flour, and seasoning, cooked in broth. [orig. uncert.]

riv•en (riv′ən), *v.* **1.** a pp. of **rive.** —*adj.* **2.** rent or split apart. **3.** split radially, as a log.

riv•er[1] (riv′ər), *n.* **1.** a natural stream of water of fairly large size flowing in a definite course or channel or series of diverging and converging channels. See table on next page. **2.** a similar stream of something other than water: *a river of lava; a river of ice.* **3.** any abundant stream or copious flow; outpouring: *rivers of tears; rivers of words.* **4.** (*cap.*) *Astron.* the constellation Eridanus. **5.** *Print.* a vertical channel of white space resulting from the alignment in several lines of spaces between words. **6. sell down the river,** to betray; desert; mislead: *to sell one's friends down the river.* **7. up the river,** *Slang.* **a.** to prison: *to be sent up the river for a bank robbery.* **b.** in prison: *Thirty years up the river had made him a stranger to society.* [1250–1300; ME < OF *rivere, riviere* < VL **rīpāria,* n. use of fem. of L *rīpārius* RIPARIAN] **—riv′er•less,** *adj.* **—riv′er•like′,** *adj.*

riv•er[2] (rī′vər), *n.* a person who rives. [1475–85; RIVE + -ER[1]]

Ri•ve•ra (ri vâr′ə; *Sp.* rē ve′rä), *n.* **1. Die•go** (dye′gô), 1886–1957, Mexican painter. **2. Jo•sé Eu•sta•sio** (hô se′ e′o͞os tä′syô), 1889–1928, Colombian poet and novelist. **3. (Jo•sé) Fruc•tuo•so** (hô se′ fro͝ok two′sô), 1790?–1854, Uruguayan revolutionary and political leader: president of Uruguay 1830–34, 1839–42. **4. Mi•guel Pri•mo de** (mē gel′ prē′mô the). See **Primo de Rivera, Miguel. 5.** a city in N Uruguay. 40,000.

riv•er•bank (riv′ər bangk′), *n.* the slopes bordering a river. [1555–65; RIVER[1] + BANK[1]]

riv′erbank grape′, a high-climbing vine, *Vitis riparia,* of eastern North America, having fragrant flowers and nearly black fruit. Also called **frost grape.**

riv′er ba′sin, *Physical Geog.* the area of land drained by a river and its branches. [1875–80]

riv•er•bed (riv′ər bed′), *n.* the channel in which a river flows or formerly flowed. [1825–35; RIVER[1] + BED]

riv′er birch′, a tree, *Betula nigra,* of the eastern U.S., having papery, reddish-brown bark that peels away. Also called **red birch.** [1850–55]

riv′er blind′ness, *Pathol.* onchocerciasis. [1950–55]

riv•er•boat (riv′ər bōt′), *n.* any shallow-draft boat used on rivers. [1555–65; RIVER[1] + BOAT]

riv′er carp′sucker, a carpsucker, *Carpiodes carpio,* found in silty rivers of the central U.S. south to Mexico.

Riv•er•dale (riv′ər dāl′), *n.* a city in NE Illinois. 13,233.

Riv′er Edge′, a borough in NE New Jersey. 11,111.

Riv′er For′est, a city in NE Illinois. 12,392.

Riv′er Grove′, a town in NE Illinois. 10,368.

riv•er•head (riv′ər hed′), *n.* the source or spring of a river. [1675–85; RIVER[1] + HEAD]

riv′er horse′, a hippopotamus. [1595–1605]

riv•er•ine (riv′ə rīn′, -rēn′, -ər in), *adj.* **1.** of or pertaining to a river. **2.** situated or dwelling beside a river. [1855–60; RIVER[1] + -INE[1]]

riv′er ot′ter, a North American otter, *Lutra canadensis,* with brown and silver fur, native to streams and lakes in the U.S. and Canada. [1830–40]

Riv′er Plate′, *Brit.* See **Plata, Río de la.**

Riv′er Rouge′, a city in SE Michigan, near Detroit. 12,912.

Riv•ers (riv′ərz), *n.* **1. Larry** (*Yitzroch Loiza Grossberg*), born 1923, U.S. painter. **2. William Halse** (hôls), 1865–1922, English physiologist and anthropologist.

riv•er•scape (riv′ər skāp′), *n.* a view, painting, etc., of a river and the land surrounding or adjacent to it. [1900–05; RIVER[1] + -SCAPE]

riv•er•side (riv′ər sīd′), *n.* **1.** a bank of a river. —*adj.* **2.** on or near a bank of a river. [1325–75; ME *river-syde.* See RIVER[1], SIDE[1]]

Riv•er•side (riv′ər sīd′), *n.* a city in SW California. 170,876.

Riv•er•view (riv′ər vyo͞o′), *n.* **1.** a town in SE New Brunswick, in SE Canada. 14,907. **2.** a town in SE Michigan. 14,569.

riv•er•ward (riv′ər wərd), *adv.* **1.** Also, **riv′er•wards.** toward a river. —*adj.* **2.** facing a river. [1825–35; RIVER[1] + -WARD]

riv•er•weed (riv′ər wēd′), *n.* any of several chiefly tropical submerged aquatic plants of the genus *Podostemum* and related genera, growing in rapidly moving streams. [1665–75; RIVER[1] + WEED[1]]

riv′er wheat′. See **poulard wheat.**

riv•et (riv′it), *n., v.,* **-et•ed, -et•ing** or (*esp. Brit.*) **-et•ted, -et•ting.** —*n.* **1.** a metal pin for passing through holes in two or more plates or pieces to hold them together, usually made with a head at one end, the other end being hammered into a head after insertion. —*v.t.* **2.** to fasten with a rivet or rivets. **3.** to hammer or spread out the end of (a pin, bolt, etc.) in order to form a head and secure something; clinch. **4.** to fasten or fix firmly. **5.** to hold (the eye, attention, etc.) firmly. [1350–1400; (n.) ME *revette, rivette* < OF *rivet,* deriv. of *river* to attach; (v.) ME *revetten,* deriv. of the n.] **—riv′et•er,** *n.* **—riv′et•less,** *adj.*

riv′et set′, a tool for forming a head on a rivet after driving.

Ri•vi•er•a (riv′ē âr′ə; *for 1 also It.* rē vye′rä), *n.* **1.** a resort area along the Mediterranean coast, extending from Saint Tropez, in SE France, to La Spezia, in NW Italy. See **Côte d'Azur. 2.** (*often l.c.*) any similar coastal resort area: *the Florida riviera.*

Ri•vier′a Beach′ (ri vēr′ə), a town in SE Florida. 26,596.

ri•vière (riv′ē âr′, ri vyâr′; *Fr.* rē vyer′), *n., pl.* **ri•vières** (riv′ē ârz′, ri vyârz′; *Fr.* rē vyer′). a necklace of diamonds or other gems, esp. in more than one string. [1875–80; < F: lit., RIVER]

Ri•vière-du-Loup (*Fr.* rē vyer dy lo͞o′), *n.* a city in SE Quebec, in E Canada, on the St. Lawrence. 13,459.

riv•u•let (riv′yə lit), *n.* a small stream; streamlet; brook. [1580–90; earlier *rivolet* < It *rivoletto,* dim. of *rivolo* < L *rīvulus* small stream]

riv•u•lus (riv′yə ləs), *n., pl.* **-lus.** any of several killifishes of the genus *Rivulus,* native to small streams of tropical America, often kept in aquariums. [< NL, L: RIVULET]

rix-dol•lar (riks′dol′ər), *n.* any of various silver coins, as the Danish rigsdaler, the Dutch rijksdaalder, or the German reichsthaler, of about equal value. [1590–1600; partial trans. of obs. D *rijksdaler* (cf. RIJKSDAALDER); c. G *Reichstaler* REICHSTHALER, Dan *rigsdaler* RIGSDALER]

Ri•yadh (rē yäd′), *n.* a city in and the capital of Saudi Arabia. 450,000.

ri•yal (rē yôl′, -yäl′), *n.* **1.** a bronze coin and monetary unit of Qatar, equal to 100 dirhams. **2.** a silver coin and monetary unit of Saudi Arabia, equal to 100 halala or 20 qurush. **3.** (formerly) a coin and monetary unit of the

CONCISE PRONUNCIATION KEY: act, cāpe, dâre, pärt; set, ēqual; if, īce; ox, ōver, ôrder, oil, bo͝ok, bo͞ot, out; up, ûrge; child; sing; shoe; thin, that; zh as in *treasure.* ə = *a* as in *alone, e* as in *system, i* as in *easily, o* as in *gallop, u* as in *circus;* ᵊ as in *fire* (fīᵊr), *hour* (ouᵊr). l and n can serve as syllabic consonants, as in *cradle* (krād′l), and *button* (but′n). See the full key inside the front cover.

LONGEST RIVERS OF THE WORLD

River	Countries of Transit	Outflow	Approx. Length Miles	Km
Nile	Uganda-Sudan-Egypt	Mediterranean Sea	4160	6695
Missouri-Mississippi	United States	Gulf of Mexico	3990	6420
Amazon	Peru-Brazil	Atlantic Ocean	3900	6280
Chang Jiang (Yangtze)	China	East China Sea	3200	5150
Congo (Zaire)	Zaire-Congo-Angola	Atlantic Ocean	3000	4800
Lena	Russian Federation	Arctic Ocean	2800	4510
Yenisei	Russian Federation	Arctic Ocean	2800	4510
Huang He (Yellow River)	China	Gulf of Bohai	2800	4510
Missouri	United States	Mississippi River	2720	4380
Amur	China-Russian Federation	Sea of Okhotsk	2700	4350
Mekong	China-Burma-Thailand-Laos-Cambodia-Vietnam	South China Sea	2600	4185
Niger	Guinea-Mali-Niger-Nigeria	Gulf of Guinea	2600	4185
Mackenzie	Canada	Beaufort Sea	2525	4065
Ob	Russian Federation	Gulf of Ob	2500	4025
Mississippi	United States	Gulf of Mexico	2470	3975
Volga	Russian Federation	Caspian Sea	2325	3745
Madeira	Brazil	Amazon River	2100	3380
Paraná	Brazil-Paraguay-Argentina	Río de la Plata	2050	3300
Purús	Peru-Brazil	Amazon River	2000	3220
Yukon	Canada-United States	Bering Sea	2000	3220
Indus	Tibet-India-Pakistan	Arabian Sea	1900	3060
Irtysh	China-Kazakhstan-Russian Federation	Ob River	1840	2960
Rio Grande	United States-Mexico	Gulf of Mexico	1800	2900
São Francisco	Brazil	Atlantic Ocean	1800	2900
Japura	Colombia-Brazil	Amazon River	1750	2815
Salween	China-Burma	Bay of Bengal	1750	2815
Danube	Germany-Austria-Slovakia-Hungary-Croatia-Yugoslavia-Rumania-Bulgaria-Ukraine	Black Sea	1725	2775
Euphrates	Turkey-Syria-Iraq	Persian Gulf	1700	2735
Brahmaputra	Tibet-India-Bangladesh	Ganges River	1700	2735
Tocantins	Brazil	Pará River	1700	2735
Zambezi	Angola-Zambia-Zimbabwe-Mozambique	Mozambique Channel	1650	2657
Orinoco	Venezuela-Colombia	Atlantic Ocean	1600	2575
Ganges	India	Bay of Bengal	1550	2495
Aldan	Russian Federation	Lena River	1500	2415
Paraguay	Brazil-Paraguay-Argentina	Paraná River	1500	2415
Arkansas	United States	Mississippi River	1450	2335
Colorado	United States-Mexico	Gulf of California	1450	2335
Amu Darya	Afghanistan-Tadzhikistan-Turkmenistan-Uzbekistan	Aral Sea	1400	2250
Dnieper	Russian Federation-Byelorussia-Ukraine	Black Sea	1400	2250
Negro	Colombia-Brazil	Amazon River	1400	2250
Ural	Russian Federation	Caspian Sea	1400	2250
Orange	Lesotho-South Africa	Atlantic Ocean	1300	2095
Syr Darya	Kirghizia-Uzbekistan-Kazakhstan	Aral Sea	1300	2095
Red	United States	Mississippi River	1300	2095
Xingú	Brazil	Amazon River	1300	2095
Irrawaddy	Burma	Bay of Bengal	1250	2015
Xi Jiang	China	South China Sea	1250	2015
Columbia	Canada-United States	Pacific Ocean	1214	1955
Saskatchewan	Canada	Lake Winnipeg	1205	1940
Kama	Russian Federation	Volga	1200	1930
Don	Russian Federation	Sea of Azov	1200	1930
Juruá	Peru-Brazil	Amazon River	1200	1930
Murray	Australia	Indian Ocean	1200	1930
Salado	Argentina	Paraná River	1200	1930
Ucayali	Peru	Amazon River	1200	1930
Darling	Australia	Murray River	1160	1870
Angara	Russian Federation	Yenisei River	1150	1855
Tigris	Turkey-Syria-Iraq	Euphrates River	1150	1850

Yemen Arab Republic, equal to 100 fils or 40 buqshas. Also, **rial.** [1935–40; < Ar *riyāl* < Sp *real* REAL[2]]

Ri·zai·yeh (ri zī′ə; *Pers.* RI zä′ē ye) *n.* Reza'iyeh.

Ri·zal (RĒ säl′), *n.* **Jo·sé** (hô se′), 1861–96, Philippine patriot, novelist, poet, and physician.

Rizal′ Day′ (ri zäl′, rē säl′), (in the Philippines) December 30: a legal holiday commemorating the death of José Rizal.

Ri·za Shah Pah·la·vi (ri zä′ shä′ pä′lə vē′, shô′), Pahlavi (def. 2).

riz·zar (riz′ər), *Scot.* —*v.t.* **1.** to dry or cure (meat, fish, etc., esp. haddock) in the sun. —*n.* **2.** a haddock dried or cured in the sun. Also, **riz′ar.** [1800–10; prob. < obs. F *ressoré* sun-dried]

Riz·zio (rit′sē ō′, rēt′-; *It.* RĒT′tsyô), *n.* **Da·vid** (dä′-vēd), 1533?–66, Italian musician: private foreign secretary to Mary, Queen of Scots 1564–66. Also, **Riccio.**

RJ, *Mil.* road junction.

R.L.D., retail liquor dealer.

r-less (är′lis), *adj. Phonet.* r-dropping.

RM, reichsmark.

rm., *pl.* **rms. 1.** ream. **2.** room.

r.m., reichsmark.

R.M.A., *Brit.* **1.** Royal Marine Artillery. **2.** Royal Military Academy.

R.M.C., *Brit.* Royal Military College.

rmdr, remainder.

rms, (*often cap.*) See **root mean square.** Also, **r.m.s.**

R.M.S., 1. Railway Mail Service. **2.** *Brit.* Royal Mail Service. **3.** *Brit.* Royal Mail Steamship.

Rn, *Symbol, Chem.* radon.

R.N., 1. See **registered nurse. 2.** *Brit.* Royal Navy.

CONCISE ETYMOLOGY KEY: <, descended or borrowed from; >, whence; b., blend of, blended; c., cognate with; cf., compare; deriv., derivative; equiv., equivalent; imit., imitative; obl., oblique; r., replacing; s., stem; sp., spelling, spelled; resp., respelling, respelled; trans., translation; ?, origin unknown; *, unattested; ‡, probably earlier than. See the full key inside the front cover.

RNA, *Genetics.* ribonucleic acid: any of a class of single-stranded molecules transcribed from DNA in the cell nucleus or in the mitochondrion or chloroplast, containing along the strand a linear sequence of nucleotide bases that is complementary to the DNA strand from which it is transcribed: the composition of the RNA molecule is identical with that of DNA except for the substitution of the sugar ribose for deoxyribose and the substitution of the nucleotide base uracil for thymine. Cf. **messenger RNA, ribosomal RNA, transfer RNA.** [1945–50]

RNA polymerase, *Biochem.* an enzyme that synthesizes the formation of RNA from a DNA template during transcription. Also called **transcriptase.** [1960–65]

R.N.A.S., *Brit.* Royal Naval Air Service.

RNase (är′en′ās, -āz), *n. Biochem.* ribonuclease. Also, **RNAase** (är′en′ā′ās, -āz). [RN(A) + -ASE]

RNA synthetase, *Biochem.* an enzyme that catalyzes the synthesis of RNA in cells infected with RNA viruses, allowing production of copies of the viral RNA. Also called **replicase, RNA replicase.** [1960–65; SYNTHET(IC) + -ASE]

RNA virus, any virus containing RNA; retrovirus. [1960–65]

rnd., round.

rnge, range.

RNP, *Biochem.* ribonucleoprotein.

R.N.R., *Brit.* Royal Naval Reserve.

R.N.W.M.P., *Canadian.* Royal Northwest Mounted Police.

RO., See **rial omani.**

ro., 1. recto. **2.** roan. **3.** rood.

R.O., 1. Receiving Office. **2.** Receiving Officer. **3.** Regimental Order. **4.** *Brit.* Royal Observatory.

ROA, *Accounting.* return on assets.

roach[1] (rōch), *n.* **1.** a cockroach. **2.** *Slang.* the butt of a marijuana cigarette. [1830–40, *Amer.*; 1940–45, *Amer.* for def. 2; short form of COCKROACH]

roach[2] (rōch), *n., pl.* **roach·es,** (*esp. collectively*) **roach. 1.** a European freshwater fish, *Rutilus rutilus,* of the carp family. **2.** any of various similar fishes, as the golden shiner. **3.** a freshwater sunfish of the genus *Lepomis,* found in eastern North America. [1275–1325; ME *roche* < OF < ?]

roach[3] (rōch), *n.* **1.** *Naut.* **a.** the upward curve at the foot of a square sail. **b.** (loosely) a convexity given to any of the edges of a sail; round. **2.** hair combed up from the forehead or temples in a roll or high curve. —*v.t.* **3.** to clip or cut off (the mane of a horse); hog. **4.** to comb (hair) into a roach. [1785–95; orig. uncert.]

roach′ back′, an arched back, as of a dog. [1660–70; special use of ROACH[3]] —**roach′-backed′,** *adj.*

roach′ clip′, *Slang.* a small tweezerlike clip for holding the butt of a marijuana cigarette. [1965–70]

road (rōd), *n.* **1.** a long, narrow stretch with a smoothed or paved surface, made for traveling by motor vehicle, carriage, etc.; street or highway. **2.** a way or course: *the road to peace.* **3.** a railroad. **4.** Often, **roads.** Also called **roadstead.** a partly sheltered area of water near a shore in which vessels may ride at anchor. **5.** any tunnel in a mine used for hauling. **6. burn up the road,** *Slang.* to drive or move very fast. **7. down the road,** in the future: *Economists see higher interest rates down the road.* **8. hit the road,** *Slang.* to begin or resume traveling: *We hit the road before sunrise.* **9. one for the road,** a final alcoholic drink taken just before departing from a party, tavern, etc. **10. on the road, a.** traveling, esp. as a sales representative. **b.** on tour, as a theatrical company: *The musical ends its New York run next week to go on the road.* **c.** started; under way: *Let's get the project on the road.* **11. take to the road,** to begin a journey or tour. Also, **take the road. 12. the road,** the places, usually outside of New York City, at which theatrical companies on tour generally give performances. [bef. 900; ME *rode,* earlier *rade,* OE *rād* a journey on horseback, akin to *rīdan* to RIDE] —**road′·less,** *adj.* —**road′less·ness,** *n.*

road·a·bil·i·ty (rō′də bil′i tē), *n.* the ability of a motor vehicle to maintain a steady, balanced, and comfortable ride, esp. under a variety of road conditions. [1920–25; ROAD + ABILITY] —**road′a·ble,** *adj.*

road′ a′gent, (formerly) a highwayman, esp. along stagecoach routes in the western U.S. [1850–55]

road′ ap′ple, *Slang.* a piece of horse manure on or at the side of a road. [1940–45]

road·bed (rōd′bed′), *n.* **1.** *Railroads.* **a.** the bed or foundation structure for the track of a railroad. **b.** the layer of ballast immediately beneath the ties of a railroad track. **2.** the material of which a road is composed. [1830–40. *Amer.*; ROAD + BED]

road·block (rōd′blok′), *n.* **1.** an obstruction placed across a road, esp. of barricades or police cars, for halting or hindering traffic, as to facilitate the capture of a pursued car or inspection for safety violations. **2.** an obstruction on a road, as a fallen tree or a pile of fallen rocks. **3.** a hastily built barricade, as of barbed wire, erected across a road to hold up the advance of an enemy. **4.** an action, condition, etc., that obstructs progress toward an objective: *Nationalism is a roadblock to European unity.* —*v.t.* **5.** to halt or obstruct with or as if with a roadblock. [1935–40; ROAD + BLOCK]

road′ com′pany, a theatrical group that tours cities and towns, usually performing a single play that is or has been a success in New York City. [1895–1900, *Amer.*]

road·e·o (rō′dē ō′), *n., pl.* **road·e·os.** a competition, usually held annually, for professional truck drivers testing driving skill. [1945–50, *Amer.*; orthographic b. ROAD and RODEO]

road′ gang′, 1. a group of workers employed to repair or build roads. **2.** (in the U.S.) a detail of prisoners set to repairing a road. [1885–90]

road·guard (rōd′gärd′), *n. Mil.* a person assigned to run ahead of a marching formation to stop cross traffic at an intersection. [ROAD + GUARD]

road′ hock′ey, *Canadian.* an imitation of the game of ice hockey played typically by children without ice skates on a public road. [1960–65]

road′ hog′, a driver who obstructs traffic by occupying parts of two lanes. [1890–95] —**road′-hog′gish,** *adj.* —**road′-hog′gism,** *n.*

road·house (rōd′hous′), *n., pl.* **-hous·es** (-hou′ziz). an inn, dance hall, tavern, nightclub, etc., located on a highway, usually beyond city limits. [1855–60; ROAD + HOUSE]

road·ie (rō′dē), *n. Slang.* a member of a crew for a traveling group of musicians or other entertainers, whose work usually includes the setting up of equipment. [1965–70; ROAD (from the idiom *on the road*) + -IE; analogous to GROUPIE]

road′ kill′, the body of an animal killed on a road by a motor vehicle. [1975–80, *Amer.*]

road′ map′, 1. a map designed for motorists, showing the principal cities and towns of a state or area, the chief roads, usually tourist attractions and places of historical interest, and the mileage from one place to another. **2.** any plan or guide: *your road map to financial independence.* [1880–85]

road′ met′al, *Brit.* broken stone, cinders, etc., used for making roads. Also called **metal.** [1810–20]

road′ rac′ing, a competitive event of racing in automobiles, motorcycles, or bicycles over public roads or a twisting course simulating a public road, as opposed to a closed, banked track or a drag strip. [1900–05]

Road·rail·er (rōd′rā′lər), *Trademark.* a combination trailer truck and railroad car with two sets of retractable wheels, one steel, the other rubber, making possible bimodal transportation on rails and highways.

road′ roll′er, 1. a person who rolls roads. **2.** any machine for rolling road materials flat. [1885–90]

road·run·ner (rōd′run′ər), *n.* either of two large terrestrial cuckoos of the genus *Geococcyx* of arid regions of the western U.S., Mexico, and Central America, esp. *G. californianus* **(greater roadrunner).** Also called **chaparral cock.** [1855–60, *Amer.*; ROAD + RUNNER]

roadrunner, *Geococcyx californianus,* length 2 ft. (0.6 m)

road′ show′, **1.** a show, as a play or musical comedy, performed by a touring group of actors. **2.** an important motion picture, usually presented only twice daily on a reserved-seat basis and at increased prices. **3.** any traveling exhibit, as one promoting a company's products or a government program. **4.** *Informal.* any group traveling about the country for a specific purpose, as a political candidate together with his or her entourage. Also, **road′show′** [1905–10, *Amer.*]

road-show (rōd′shō′), *adj., v.,* **-showed, -show·ing.** —*adj.* **1.** of or pertaining to road shows. —*v.t.* **2.** to present as a road show.

road·side (rōd′sīd′), *n.* **1.** the side or border of the road; wayside. —*adj.* **2.** on or near the side of a road. [1705–15; ROAD + SIDE[1]]

road·stead (rōd′sted′), *n. Naut.* road (def. 4). [1325–75; ME *radestede.* See ROAD, STEAD]

road·ster (rōd′stər), *n.* **1.** an early automobile having an open body, a single seat for two or three persons, and a large trunk or a rumble seat. **2.** a horse for riding or driving on the road. [1735–45; ROAD + -STER]

road′ test′, **1.** a check of an automobile's performance in actual operation on the road. **2.** an examination of a person's driving skill, conducted in normal traffic, esp. as a requirement for an automobile driver's license. [1905–10]

road-test (rōd′test′), *v.t.* to test (an automotive vehicle) under normal operating conditions on the road, as by a potential purchaser.

Road′ Town′, a town on SE Tortola, in the NE West Indies: capital of the British Virgin Islands. 3500.

road-train (rōd′trān′), *n.* **1.** a convoy of motor vehicles. **2.** a fleet of motor vehicles traveling together in line. [1955–60]

road·way (rōd′wā′), *n.* **1.** the land over which a road is built; a road together with the land at its edge. **2.** the part of a road over which vehicles travel; road. [1590–1600; ROAD + WAY[1]]

road·work (rōd′wûrk′), *n.* **1.** work, as construction or repairs, done on a road. **2.** a conditioning exercise for an athlete consisting of running considerable distances in areas that are reasonably free of obstructions or traffic, as fields or country roads: performed chiefly by boxers in training for a bout. [1885–90; ROAD + WORK]

road·wor·thy (rōd′wûr′thē), *adj.,* **-thi·er, -thi·est.** in suitable operating condition or meeting accepted standards for safe driving on the road: *a roadworthy automobile.* [1810–20; ROAD + -WORTHY] —**road′wor′thi·ness,** *n.*

roam (rōm), *v.i.* **1.** to walk, go, or travel without a fixed purpose or direction; ramble; wander; rove: *to roam about the world.* —*v.t.* **2.** to wander over or through: *to roam the countryside.* —*n.* **3.** an act or instance of roaming; a ramble. [1300–50; ME *romen* < ?] —**roam′·er,** *n.*
—**Syn. 1.** stray, stroll, prowl. ROAM, RAMBLE, RANGE, ROVE imply wandering about over (usually) a considerable amount of territory. ROAM implies a wandering or traveling over a large area, esp. as prompted by restlessness or curiosity: *to roam through a forest.* RAMBLE implies pleasant, carefree moving about, walking with no specific purpose and for a limited distance: *to ramble through fields near home.* RANGE usually implies wandering over a more or less defined but extensive area in search of something: *Cattle range over the plains.* ROVE sometimes implies wandering with specific incentive or aim, as an animal for prey: *Bandits rove through these mountains.*

roan (rōn), *adj.* **1.** (chiefly of horses) of the color sorrel, chestnut, or bay, sprinkled with gray or white. **2.** prepared from leather of this color. —*n.* **3.** a horse or other animal with a roan coat. **4.** a roan color. **5.** a soft, flexible sheepskin leather, used in bookbinding, often made to imitate morocco. [1520–30; < MF < OSp *roano* < Gmc; cf. Goth *rauths* red]

Ro·a·noke (rō′ə nōk′), *n.* **1.** a city in SW Virginia. 100,427. **2.** a river flowing SE from western Virginia to Albemarle Sound in North Carolina. 380 mi. (610 km) long.

Ro′anoke bells′. See **Virginia cowslip.**

Ro′anoke Is′land, an island off the NE coast of North Carolina, S of Albemarle Sound: site of Raleigh's unsuccessful colonizing attempts 1585, 1587.

Ro′anoke Rap′ids, a city in NE North Carolina. 14,702.

roar (rôr, rōr), *v.i.* **1.** to utter a loud, deep cry or howl, as in excitement, distress, or anger. **2.** to laugh loudly or boisterously: *to roar at a joke.* **3.** to make a loud sound or din, as thunder, cannon, waves, or wind. **4.** to function or move with a loud, deep sound, as a vehicle: *The automobile roared away.* **5.** to make a loud noise in breathing, as a horse. —*v.t.* **6.** to utter or express in a roar: *to roar denials.* **7.** to bring, put, make, etc., by roaring: *to roar oneself hoarse.* —*n.* **8.** a loud, deep cry or howl, as of an animal or a person: *the roar of a lion.* **9.** a loud, confused, constant noise or sound; din; clamor: *the roar of the surf; the roar of lively conversation from the crowded party.* **10.** a loud outburst: *a roar of laughter; a roar of approval from the audience.* [bef. 900; ME *roren* (v.), OE *rārian;* c. OHG *rēren* to bellow] —**roar′·er,** *n.*
—**Syn. 1.** bawl, yell. See **cry. 3.** resound, boom, thunder, peal.

roar·ing (rôr′ing, rōr′-), *n.* **1.** the act of a person, animal, or thing that roars. **2.** a loud, deep cry or sound or a series of such sounds. **3.** *Vet. Pathol.* a disease of horses, caused by respiratory obstruction or vocal cord paralysis, and characterized by loud or rough breathing sounds. —*adj.* **4.** making or causing a roar, as an animal or thunder. **5.** brisk or highly successful, as trade: *He did a roaring business selling watches to tourists.* **6.** characterized by noisy, disorderly behavior; boisterous; riotous: *roaring revelry.* **7.** complete; utter; out-and-out: *a roaring idiot; a roaring success.* —*adv.* **8.** very; extremely: *roaring drunk.* [bef. 1000; ME *roryng* (n., adj.), OE *rarung* (n.). See ROAR, -ING[1], -ING[2]] —**roar′ing·ly,** *adv.*

roar′ing for′ties, either of two areas in the ocean between 40° and 50° N or S latitude, noted for high winds and rough seas. [1875–80]

Roar′ing Twen′ties, the 1920's regarded as a boisterous era of prosperity, fast cars, jazz, speakeasies, and wild youth. [1925–30]

roast (rōst), *v.t.* **1.** to bake (meat or other food) uncovered, esp. in an oven. **2.** to cook (meat or other food) by direct exposure to dry heat, as on a spit. **3.** to brown, dry, or parch by exposure to heat, as coffee beans. **4.** to cook or heat by embedding in hot coals, embers, etc.: *to roast chestnuts.* **5.** to heat excessively: *The summer sun has been roasting the entire countryside.* **6.** *Metall.* to heat (ore or the like) in air in order to oxidize it. **7.** to warm at a hot fire: *She roasted her hands over the fire.* **8.** *Informal.* to ridicule or criticize severely or mercilessly. **9.** to honor with or subject to a roast: *Friends roasted the star at a charity dinner.* —*v.i.* **10.** to roast meat or other food. **11.** to undergo the process of becoming roasted. —*n.* **12.** roasted meat or a piece of roasted meat, as a piece of beef or veal of a quantity and shape for slicing into more than one portion. **13.** a piece of meat for roasting. **14.** something that is roasted. **15.** the act or process of roasting. **16.** *Informal.* severe criticism. **17.** a facetious ceremonial tribute, usually concluding a banquet, in which the guest of honor is both praised and good-naturedly insulted in a succession of speeches by friends and acquaintances. **18.** an outdoor get-together, as a picnic or barbecue, at which food is roasted and eaten: *a weenie roast.* —*adj.* **19.** roasted: *roast beef.* [1250–1300; ME *rosten* (v.) < OF *rostir* < Gmc; cf. D *roosten,* G *rösten*] —**roast′a·ble,** *adj.*

roast·er (rō′stər), *n.* **1.** a contrivance for roasting something, as an oven, a pan for roasting meat, or a machine for roasting coffee beans. **2.** a pig, chicken, or other animal or article of a size convenient and grade suitable for roasting. **3.** a person or thing that roasts. **4.** a guest speaker at a roast. [1400–50; late ME; see ROAST, -ER[1]]

roast·ing (rō′sting), *adj.* **1.** used or suitable to roast. **2.** exceedingly hot; scorching: *a roasting July.* —*n.* **3.** a severely critical notice or review; pan. [1350–1400; ME (ger.); see ROAST, -ING[1], -ING[2]] —**roast′ing·ly,** *adv.*

roast′ing ear′, **1.** an ear of sweet corn suitable for roasting while still in the husk. **2.** *Midland and Southern U.S.* an ear of sweet corn ripe enough to be boiled and eaten on the cob. [1640–50, *Amer.*]

rob (rob), *v.,* **robbed, rob·bing.** —*v.t.* **1.** to take something from (someone) by unlawful force or threat of violence; steal from. **2.** to deprive (someone) of some right or something legally due: *They robbed her of her inheritance.* **3.** to plunder or rifle (a house, shop, etc.). **4.** to deprive of something unjustly or injuriously: *The team was robbed of a home run hitter when the umpire called it a foul ball. The shock robbed him of his speech.* **5.** *Mining.* to remove ore or coal from (a pillar). —*v.i.* **6.** to commit or practice robbery. **7. rob Peter to pay Paul,** to take something from one person or thing to pay one's debt or hypothetical debt to another, as to sacrifice one's health by overworking. [1175–1225; ME *robben* < OF *robber* < Gmc; cf. OHG *roubōn.* See REAVE[1]]
—**Syn. 1.** ROB, RIFLE, SACK refer to seizing possessions that belong to others. ROB is the general word for taking possessions by unlawful force or violence: *to rob a bank, a house, a train.* A term with a more restricted meaning is RIFLE, to make a thorough search for what is valuable or worthwhile, usually within a small space: *to rifle a safe.* On the other hand, SACK is a term for robbery on a huge scale during war; it suggests destruction accompanying pillage, and often includes the indiscriminate massacre of civilians: *to sack a town or district.* **2.** defraud, cheat.

Rob (rob), *n.* a male given name, form of **Robert.**

rob·a·lo (rob′ə lō′, rō′bə-, rō bä′lō), *n., pl.* (*esp. collectively*) **-lo,** (*esp. referring to two or more kinds or species*) **-los.** snook[2] (def. 1). [1885–90; < Pg]

rob·and (rob′ənd), *n. Naut.* a short piece of spun yarn or other material, used to secure a sail to a yard, gaff, or the like. [1755–65; < D *raband,* equiv. to *ra* sailyard + *band* BAND[2]]

Robbe-Gril·let (rôb grē ye′), *n.* **A·lain** (A laN′), born 1922, French writer.

rob·ber (rob′ər), *n.* a person who robs. [1125–75; ME *robbere* < OF *robere.* See ROB, -ER[1]]
—**Syn.** highwayman, bandit, brigand; burglar. See **thief.**

rob′ber bar′on, **1.** *Hist.* a noble who robbed travelers passing through his lands. **2.** a ruthlessly powerful U.S. capitalist or industrialist of the late 19th century considered to have become wealthy by exploiting natural resources, corrupting legislators, or other unethical means. [1875–80]

rob′ber fly′, any of numerous swift-flying, often large, dipterous insects of the family Asilidae that are predaceous on other insects. [1870–75]

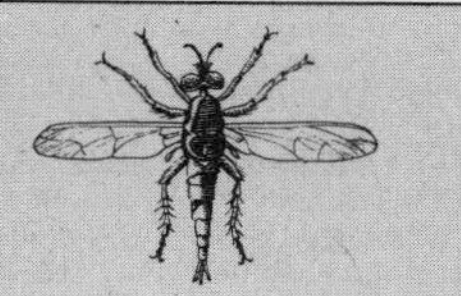
robber fly, *Promachus vertebratus,* length 1 in. (2.5 cm)

rob′ber frog′, any of numerous small frogs of the genera *Eleutherodactylus* and *Hylactophryne,* living chiefly in the American tropics.

rob·ber·y (rob′ə rē), *n., pl.* **-ber·ies.** **1.** the act, the practice, or an instance of robbing. **2.** *Law.* the felonious taking of the property of another from his or her person or in his or her immediate presence, against his or her will, by violence or intimidation. Cf. **theft.** [1150–1200; ME *robberie* < OF. See ROB, -ERY]
—**Syn. 1.** plunder, pillage; theft, burglary.

Rob·bia (rō′bē ə; *It.* rôb′byä), *n.* **An·dre·a del·la** (än drĕ′ä del′lä), 1435–1525, and his uncle, **Lu·ca del·la** (lo͞o′kä del′lä), c1400–82, Italian sculptors.

Rob·bins (rob′inz), *n.* **1. Frederick C(hapman),** born 1916, U.S. physician: Nobel prize 1954. **2. Jerome,** born 1918, U.S. dancer and choreographer.

Rob·bins·dale (rob′inz dāl′), *n.* a city in SE Minnesota, near Minneapolis. 14,422.

robe (rōb), *n., v.,* **robed, rob·ing.** —*n.* **1.** a long, loose or flowing gown or outer garment worn by men or women as ceremonial dress, an official vestment, or garb of office. **2.** any long, loose garment, esp. one for wear while lounging or preparing to dress, as a bathrobe or dressing gown. **3.** a woman's gown or dress, esp. of a more elaborate kind: *a robe for the evening.* **4. robes,** apparel in general; dress; costume. **5.** a piece of fur, cloth, knitted work, etc., used as a blanket, covering, or wrap: *a buffalo robe; a lap robe.* —*v.t.* **6.** to clothe or invest with a robe or robes; dress; array. —*v.i.* **7.** to put on a robe. [1225–75; ME < OF: orig., spoil, booty < Gmc (akin to ROB); cf. OHG *roub* > G *Raub*] —**robe′less,** *adj.* —**rob′er,** *n.*

robe-de-cham·bre (rôb də shäN′brə), *n., pl.* ***robes-de-cham·bre*** (rôb də shäN′brə). *French.* a dressing gown.

Rob·ert (rob′ərt), *n.* **1. Henry Mar·tyn** (mär′tn), 1837–1923, U.S. engineer and authority on parliamentary procedure: author of *Robert's Rules of Order* (1876, revised 1915). **2.** a male given name: from Germanic words meaning "glory" and "bright."

Robert I, **1.** (*"Robert the Devil"*) died 1035, duke of Normandy 1028–35 (father of William I of England). **2.** Also called **Rob′ert the Bruce′, Rob′ert Bruce′.** 1274–1329, king of Scotland 1306–29.

Ro·ber·ta (rə bûr′tə), *n.* a female given name: derived from *Robert.*

Ro·bert Guis·card (*Fr.* RÔ bER gē skAR′). See **Guiscard, Robert.**

Rob·erts (rob′ərts), *n.* **1. Sir Charles George Douglas,** 1860–1943, Canadian poet and novelist. **2. Elizabeth Mad·ox** (mad′əks), 1886–1941, U.S. poet and novelist. **3. Frederick Sleigh** (slā), **Earl** (*"Bobs Bahadur"*), 1832–1914, British field marshal. **4. Glenn** (*"Fireball"*), 1929–64, U.S. racing-car driver. **5. Kenneth (Lewis),** 1885–1957, U.S. novelist and essayist. **6. Oral,** born 1918, U.S. evangelist. **7. Owen Jo·se·phus** (jō sē′fəs), 1875–1955, U.S. jurist: associate justice of the U.S. Supreme Court 1930–45.

Rob·ert·son (rob′ərt sən), *n.* **1. Pat** (*Marion Gordon*), born 1930, U.S. evangelist. **2. William,** 1721–93, Scottish historian. **3. Sir William Robert,** 1860–1933, British field marshal.

Robe·son (rōb′sən), *n.* **Paul,** 1898–1976, U.S. singer and actor.

Robes·pierre (rōbz′pēr, -pē âr′; *Fr.* RÔ bes pyER′), *n.* **Max·i·mil·ien Fran·çois Ma·rie I·si·dore de** (mAK sē mē lyaN′ fRäN swA′ mA Rē′ ē zē dôR′ də), 1758–94, French lawyer and revolutionary leader.

robin, *Turdus migratorius,* length 10 in. (25 cm)

rob·in (rob′in), *n.* **1.** any of several small Old World birds having a red or reddish breast, esp. *Erithacus rubecula,* of Europe. **2.** a large American thrush, *Turdus migratorius,* having a chestnut-red breast and abdomen. **3.** any of several similar thrushes of the New World tropics, not necessarily having reddish underparts, as *T. grayi* **(clay-colored robin),** of Mexico and Central America. Also called **robin redbreast** (for defs. 1, 2). [1540–50; short for ROBIN REDBREAST]

Rob·in (rob′in), *n.* a male or female given name: derived from *Robert.*

Rob′in Good′fel·low (go͝od′fel′ō), Puck (def. 1).

Rob′in Hood′, a legendary English outlaw of the 12th century, hero of many ballads, who robbed the rich to

CONCISE PRONUNCIATION KEY: act, cāpe, dâre, pärt; set, ēqual; if, īce; ox, ōver, ôrder, oil, bo͝ok, bo͞ot, out; up, ûrge; child; sing; shoe; thin, *th*at; zh as in *treasure.* ə = *a* as in *alone, e* as in *system, i* as in *easily, o* as in *gallop, u* as in *circus;* ə as in *fire* (fīər), *hour* (ouər). l and n can serve as syllabic consonants, as in *cradle* (krād′l), and *button* (but′n). See the full key inside the front cover.

give to the poor: a popular model of courage, generosity and justice, as well as of skill in archery, he lived and presided over his band of followers chiefly in Sherwood Forest.

rob′in red′breast, robin (defs. 1, 2). [1400–50; late ME (Scots); *robin,* special use of ROBIN]

rob′in's-egg blue′ (rob′inz eg′), a pale green to a light greenish-blue color. [1880–85]

Rob·in·son (rob′in sən), *n.* **1. Bill** (*"Bojangles"*), 1878–1949, U.S. tap dancer. **2. Board·man** (bôrd′mən, bōrd′-), 1876–1952, U.S. painter and illustrator, born in Nova Scotia. **3. Edward G.** (*Emanuel Goldenberg*), 1893–1973, U.S. actor, born in Rumania. **4. Edwin Arlington,** 1869–1935, U.S. poet. **5. Frederick John, Viscount Gode·rich** (gōd′rich), 1st Earl of Ripon, 1782–1859, British statesman: prime minister 1827–28. **6. Jack Roosevelt** (*Jackie*), 1919–72, U.S. baseball player. **7. James Harvey,** 1863–1936, U.S. historian. **8. Ray** (*Walker Smith*) (*"Sugar Ray"*), born 1921, U.S. boxer. **9. Sir Robert,** 1886–1975, English chemist: Nobel prize 1947. **10.** a male given name.

Rob′inson Cru′soe (kro͞o′sō), **1.** (in a novel by Defoe) a mariner of York who is shipwrecked and lives adventurously for years on a small island. **2.** (*italics*) the novel itself (1719).

Rob′in's plan′tain. See **Poor Robin's plantain.**

ro·ble (rō′blā), *n.* **1.** a Californian white oak, *Quercus lobata,* having a short trunk and large, spreading branches. **2.** any of several other trees, esp. of the oak and beech families. [1860–65; < Sp, Pg << L *rōbur* oak tree]

Ro·bo·am (rō bō′əm), *n. Douay Bible.* Rehoboam.

rob·o·rant (rob′ər ənt), *Med.* —*adj.* **1.** strengthening. —*n.* **2.** a tonic. [1655–65; < L *rōborant-* (s. of *rōborāns*), prp. of *rōborāre* to strengthen, equiv. to *rōbor-* (s. of *rōbur*) oak, hardness + *-ant-* -ANT]

ro·bot (rō′bət, -bot), *n.* **1.** a machine that resembles a human and does mechanical, routine tasks on command. **2.** a person who acts and responds in a mechanical, routine manner, usually subject to another's will; automaton. **3.** any machine or mechanical device that operates automatically with humanlike skill. —*adj.* **4.** operating automatically: *a robot train operating between airline terminals.* [< Czech, coined by Karel Čapek in the play *R.U.R.* (1920) from the base *robot-,* as in *robota* compulsory labor, *robotník* peasant owing such labor] —**ro′·bot·ism,** *n.* —**ro′bot′ic, ro·bot·is·tic** (rō′bə tis′tik, -bo-), *adj.* —**ro′bot·like′,** *adj.*

ro′bot bomb′, a rocket-propelled, gyroscopically steered bomb equipped with wings and control surfaces, usually launched from the ground. Also called **flying bomb.** [1940–45]

ro·bot·i·cist (rō bot′ə sist), *n.* a specialist in robots or robotics. [1940; ROBOTIC + -IST; coined by Isaac Asimov]

ro·bot·ics (rō bot′iks), *n.* (*used with a singular v.*) the use of computer-controlled robots to perform manual tasks, esp. on an assembly line. [1941; ROBOT + -ICS; coined by Isaac Asimov]

ro·bot·ize (rō′bə tīz′, -bot īz′), *v.,* **-ized, -iz·ing** —*v.t.* **1.** to turn (someone) into a robot. **2.** to convert for automated operation or production by robots or robotlike machines: *to robotize an assembly line.* —*v.i.* **3.** to adapt or become adapted to the use of robots or robotics. Also, *esp. Brit.,* **ro′bot·ise′.** [1925–30; ROBOT + -IZE] —**ro′bot·i·za′tion,** *n.*

ro′bot pi′lot, *Aeron.* See **automatic pilot.** [1925–30]

Rob Roy (rob′ roi′), a manhattan made with Scotch whisky. [1865–70; after *Rob Roy,* nickname of Robert Macgregor (1671–1734), Scottish freebooter]

Rob·son (rob′sən), *n.* **Mount,** a mountain in SW Canada, in E British Columbia: highest peak in the Canadian Rockies, 12,972 ft. (3954 m).

Robs·town (robz′toun′), *n.* a city in S Texas. 12,100.

Ro·bus (rō′bəs), *n.* **Hugo,** 1885–1963, U.S. sculptor.

ro·bust (rō bust′, rō′bust), *adj.* **1.** strong and healthy; hardy; vigorous: *a robust young man; a robust faith; a robust mind.* **2.** strongly or stoutly built: *his robust frame.* **3.** suited to or requiring bodily strength or endurance: *robust exercise.* **4.** rough, rude, or boisterous: *robust drinkers and dancers.* **5.** rich and full-bodied: *the robust flavor of freshly brewed coffee.* [1540–50; < L *rōbustus* oaken, hard, strong, equiv. to *rōbus-,* s. of *rōbur* oak, strength + *-tus* adj. suffix] —**ro·bust′ly,** *adv.* —**ro·bust′ness,** *n.*
—**Syn. 1.** powerful, sound. **4.** coarse, rambunctious.
—**Ant. 1.** feeble. **2.** weak.

ro·bus′ta cof′fee (rō bus′tə), **1.** a coffee tree, *Coffea canephora,* native to western tropical Africa and cultivated in warm regions of the Old World. **2.** the seed of this plant. **3.** the coffee made from the seeds. Cf. **arabica coffee.** [1905–10; *robusta* < L *rōbusta,* fem. of *rōbustus* ROBUST]

ro·bus·tious (rō bus′chəs), *adj.* **1.** rough, rude, or boisterous. **2.** robust, strong, or stout. [1540–50; ROBUST + -IOUS] —**ro·bus′tious·ly,** *adv.*

roc (rok), *n. Arabian Myth.* a bird of enormous size and strength. [1570–80; < Ar *rukhkh,* prob. < Pers *rukh;* see ROOK²]

Ro·ca (rō′kə; *Port.* RÔ′kə), *n.* **Cape,** a cape in W Portugal, near Lisbon: the western extremity of continental Europe.

ro·caille (rō kī′; *Fr.* RÔ kä′yᵊ), *n. Fine Arts.* any of the fantastic ornamental, often asymmetrical, combinations characteristic of the Rococo period, consisting of rock, shell, and plant forms combined with artificial forms, esp. C-curves. [1855–60; < F: pebble-work, deriv. of *roc* ROCK¹]

roc·am·bole (rok′əm bōl′), *n.* a European plant, *Allium scorodoprasum,* of the amaryllis family, used like garlic. Also called **giant garlic.** [1690–1700; < F < G *Rockenbolle* lit., distaff bulb (from its shape)]

Ro·cham·beau (rô shäN bō′), *n.* **Jean Bap·tiste Do·na·tien de Vi·meur** (zhäN bA tēst′ dô nA syaN′ də vē mœR′), **Count de,** 1725–1807, French general: marshal of France 1791–1807; commander of the French army in the American Revolution.

Roch·dale (roch′dāl′), *n.* a borough of Greater Manchester, in N England: site of one of the earliest cooperative societies 1844. 211,500.

roche′ al′um (rōch), *Chem.* an alumlike substance derived from alunite. [1400–50; *roche* cliff, rocky height (now obs.), late ME (see ROCK¹); appar. partial trans. of MF *alum en roque, alun de roche*]

Roche′ lim′it (rōsh; *Fr.* RÔsh), *Astron.* the minimum distance below which a moon orbiting a celestial body would be disrupted by tidal forces or below which a moon would not have formed. [1885–90; named after French astronomer Édouard *Roche* (1820–83), who first calculated it]

Ro·chelle (*Fr.* RÔ shel′ *for 1;* rō shel′, rə- *for 2*), *n.* **1. La.** See **La Rochelle. 2.** a female given name: from a French word meaning "small rock."

Rochelle′ pow′ders, (not in technical use). See **Seidlitz powders.** [after LA ROCHELLE]

Rochelle′ salt′, *Chem., Pharm.* a colorless or white, water-soluble solid, $KNaC_4H_4O_6{\cdot}4H_2O$, used in silvering mirrors, in the manufacture of Seidlitz powders and baking powder, and in medicine as a laxative. Also called **potassium sodium tartrate.** [1745–55; after LA ROCHELLE]

roche mou·ton·née (rōsh′ mo͞ot′n ā′; *Fr.* RÔsh mo͞o-tô nā′), *Geol.* a rounded, glacially eroded rock outcrop, usually one of a group, resembling a sheep's back. Also called **sheepback rock.** [1835–45; < F: glaciated rock, lit., fleecy rock]

Roch·es·ter (roch′es tər, -ə stər), *n.* **1. John Wilmot, 2nd Earl of,** 1647–80, English poet and courtier. **2.** a city in W New York, on the Genesee River. 241,741. **3.** a town in SE Minnesota. 57,890. **4.** a city in N Kent, in SE England. 55,460. **5.** a city in SE New Hampshire. 21,560.

roch·et (roch′it), *n.* a vestment of linen or lawn, resembling a surplice, worn esp. by bishops and abbots. [1350–1400; ME < OF: outer garment < Gmc; cf. OE *rocc* outer garment]

Ro·ci·nan·te (*Sp.* RÔ′thē nän′te, -sē-), *n.* Rosinante.

rock¹ (rok), *n.* **1.** a large mass of stone forming a hill, cliff, promontory, or the like. **2.** *Geol.* **a.** mineral matter of variable composition, consolidated or unconsolidated, assembled in masses or considerable quantities in nature, as by the action of heat or water. **b.** a particular kind of such matter: *igneous rock.* **3.** stone in the mass: *buildings that stand upon rock.* **4.** a stone of any size. **5.** something resembling or suggesting a rock. **6.** a firm foundation or support: *The Lord is my rock.* **7.** *Chiefly Brit.* a kind of hard candy, variously flavored. **8.** See **rock candy. 9.** Often, **rocks.** *Slang.* **a.** a piece of money. **b.** a dollar bill. **10.** *Slang.* **a.** a diamond. **b.** any gem. **11.** *Slang.* **a.** crack (def. 41). **b.** a pellet or lump of crack. **12. between a rock and a hard place,** between undesirable alternatives. **13. on the rocks, a.** *Informal.* in or into a state of disaster or ruin: *Their marriage is on the rocks.* **b.** *Informal.* without funds; destitute; bankrupt. **c.** (of a beverage, esp. liquor or a cocktail) with, or containing, ice cubes: *Scotch on the rocks; a vodka martini on the rocks.* **14. get one's rocks off,** *Slang (vulgar).* to have an orgasm. [1300–50; 1905–10 for def. 10; ME *rokk(e)* < OF *ro(c)que, roche* (cf. ROCHE ALUM); cf. Sp, Pr *roca,* It *rocca,* ML *rocha, rocca* (> late OE *-rocc* in *stānrocc* "stone-rock")] —**rock′less,** *adj.* —**rock′like′,** *adj.*

rock² (rok), *v.i.* **1.** to move or sway to and fro or from side to side. **2.** to be moved or swayed powerfully with excitement, emotion, etc. **3.** *Mining.* (of sand or gravel) to be washed in a cradle. **4.** to dance to or play rock music. **5.** (of popular music) to have the driving beat characteristic of rock. —*v.t.* **6.** to move or sway to and fro or from side to side, esp. gently and soothingly. **7.** to lull in security, hope, etc. **8.** to affect deeply; stun; move or sway powerfully, as with emotion: *Everyone in the courtroom was rocked by the verdict.* **9.** to shake or disturb violently: *A thunderous explosion rocked the waterfront.* **10.** *Graphic Arts.* to roughen the surface of (a copperplate) with a rocker preparatory to scraping a mezzotint. **11.** *Mining.* cradle (def. 23). **12. rock the boat,** *Informal.* to disrupt the smooth functioning or routine of something: *Don't rock the boat by demanding special treatment from management.* —*n.* **13.** a rocking movement: *the gentle rock of the boat.* **14.** rock-'n'-roll (def. 1). —*adj.* **15.** rock-'n'-roll (def. 3). [bef. 1100; ME *rocken,* OE *roccian;* c. MD *rocken;* akin to G *rücken;* ON *rykkja* to jerk] —**rock′a·ble,** *adj.* —**rock′ing·ly,** *adv.*
—**Syn. 1.** roll, shake. See **swing**¹.

rock³ (rok), *n.* See **striped bass.** [1690–1700; short for ROCKFISH]

Rock (rok), *n.* a male given name.

rock·a·bil·ly (rok′ə bil′ē), *n.* a style of popular music combining the features of rock-'n'-roll and hillbilly music. [1955–60, *Amer.;* ROCK(-'N'-ROLL) + *-a-* connective + (HILL)BILLY]

rock-and-roll (rok′ən rōl′), *n.* rock-'n'-roll.

rock′ and rye′, a bottled drink made with rye whiskey, rock candy, and fruit. [1875–80]

rock·a·way (rok′ə wā′), *n.* a light, four-wheeled carriage having two or three seats and a fixed top. [1835–45, *Amer.;* appar. named after *Rockaway,* town in N New Jersey]

rockaway

rock′ bar′nacle. See under **barnacle**¹ (def. 1). [1880–85]

rock′ bass′ (bas), **1.** a game fish, *Ambloplites rupestris,* of the sunfish family, inhabiting freshwater streams of the eastern U.S. **2.** See **striped bass.** [1805–15, *Amer.*]

rock′ beau′ty, a gold and black butterflyfish, *Holocanthus tricolor,* ranging from the West Indies to Brazil. [1890–95]

rock′ blen′ny. a prickleback, *Xiphister mucosus,* of the Pacific coast from southern California to Alaska. Also called **rock-eel, rock prickleback.**

rock′ bolt′, *Mining, Civ. Engin.* a steel or fiberglass bolt inserted and anchored in a hole drilled in rock to prevent caving of the roof of a tunnel or subterranean chamber. [1955–60]

rock′ bot′tom, the very lowest level: *He went bankrupt and touched rock bottom.* [1865–70, *Amer.*]

rock-bot·tom (rok′bot′əm), *adj.* at the lowest possible limit or level; extremely low: *rock-bottom prices.* [1880–85]

rock-bound (rok′bound′), *adj.* hemmed in, enclosed, or covered by rocks; rocky: *the rock-bound coast of Maine.* Also, **rock′bound′.** [1830–40]

rock′ can′dy, sugar in large, hard, cohering crystals. [1715–25]

rock′ cod′, rockfish (defs. 1–3). [1625–35]

Rock′ Cor′nish, a small hybrid chicken produced by mating Cornish and White Rock chickens and marketed esp. as a roaster. Also called **Rock′ Cor′nish game′ hen′, Rock′ Cor′nish hen′.** [1955–60]

rock′ crab′, any of several crabs that live along rocky beaches, esp. those of the genus *Cancer,* as *C. irroratus,* of the eastern coast of North America, having the rear legs modified for running. [1830–40, *Amer.*]

rock′ cress′, any of several low growing plants belonging to the genus *Arabis,* of the mustard family, having spikes or one-sided clusters of white, pink, or purple flowers, grown as an ornamental in rock gardens. [1700–10]

rock′ crys′tal, transparent quartz, esp. when colorless. [1660–70]

rock′ dove′, a European pigeon, *Columba livia,* from which most domestic pigeons have been developed. Also called **rock pigeon.** [1645–55]

rock′ dust′, a crushed limestone sprayed on surfaces in mines to make coal dust incombustible in case of a gas explosion. [1930–35]

rock-eel (rok′ēl′), *n.* See **rock blenny.** [1875–80]

Rock·e·fel·ler (rok′ə fel′ər), *n.* **1. John D(a·vi·son)** (dā′və sən), 1839–1937, and his son **John D(avison), Jr.,** 1874–1960, U.S. oil magnates and philanthropists. **2. Nelson A(ldrich),** 1908–79, U.S. political leader: governor of New York 1959–73; vice president of the U.S. 1974–77 (son of John D. Rockefeller, Jr.).

rock′ elm′, **1.** an elm, *Ulmus thomasii,* of eastern North America, having deeply furrowed, grayish-brown bark. **2.** the hard, heavy wood of this tree, used for making furniture and in the manufacture of various types of containers. [1820–30]

rock·er (rok′ər), *n.* **1.** Also called **runner.** one of the curved pieces on which a cradle or a rocking chair rocks. **2.** See **rocking chair. 3.** a rock-'n'-roll song: *She sang a ballad and followed that with two of her well-known rockers.* **4.** any of various devices that operate with a rocking motion. **5.** *Graphic Arts.* a small steel plate with one curved and toothed edge for roughening a copperplate to make a mezzotint. **6.** *Mining.* cradle (def. 13). **7.** an ice skate that has a curved blade. **8.** a performer or fan of rock music. **9. off one's rocker,** *Slang.* insane; crazy: *You're off your rocker if you think I'm going to climb that mountain.* [1400–50; late ME: one who rocks a cradle; see ROCK², -ER¹]

rock′er arm′, *Mach.* a rocking or oscillating arm or lever rotating with a moving shaft or pivoted on a stationary shaft. [1855–60]

rock′er pan′el, body paneling below the passenger compartment of a vehicle. [1920–25]

rock·er·y (rok′ə rē), *n., pl.* **-er·ies.** See **rock garden.** [1835–45; ROCK¹ + -ERY]

rock·et¹ (rok′it), *n.* **1.** any of various simple or complex tubelike devices containing combustibles that on being ignited liberate gases whose action propels the tube through the air: used for pyrotechnic effect, signaling, carrying a lifeline, hurling explosives at an enemy, putting a space vehicle into orbit, etc. **2.** a space capsule or vehicle put into orbit by such devices. **3.** See **rocket engine.** —*v.t.* **4.** to move or transport by means of a rocket. **5.** to attack with rockets. —*v.i.* **6.** to move like a rocket. **7.** (of game birds) to fly straight up rapidly when flushed. [1605–15; < It *rocchetta,* dim. of *rocca* distaff (with reference to its shape) < Goth **rukka*] —**rock′et·like′,** *adj.*

rock·et² (rok′it), *n.* **1.** any of various plants belonging to the genus *Hesperis,* of the mustard family, and related genera. Cf. **dame's rocket. 2.** Also called **rocket salad, roquette.** arugula. **3.** a noxious weed, *Barbarea vulgaris,* of the U.S., having lobed leaves and clusters of small, yellow flowers. [1520–30; < F *roquette* < It *ruchetta* << L *ērūca* kind of herb]

rock′et air′plane, **1.** an airplane propelled wholly or

CONCISE ETYMOLOGY KEY: <, descended or borrowed from; >, whence; b., blend of, blended; c., cognate with; cf., compare; deriv., derivative; equiv., equivalent; imit., imitative; obl., oblique; r., replacing; s., stem; sp., spelling, spelled; resp., respelling, respelled; trans., translation; ?, origin unknown; *, unattested; ‡, probably earlier than. See the full key inside the front cover.

mainly by a rocket engine. **2.** a military airplane armed with rockets. Also called **rock′et plane′.** [1930–35]

rock′et bomb′, **1.** an aerial bomb equipped with a rocket for added velocity after being dropped from an aircraft. **2.** (loosely) any rocket-propelled missile launched from the ground. [1940–45]

rock•e•teer (rok′i tēr′), *n.* **1.** a person who discharges, rides in, or pilots a rocket. **2.** a technician or scientist whose work pertains to rocketry. Also, **rock•et•er** (rok′i tər). [1825–35; ROCKET[1] + -EER]

rock′et en′gine, a reaction engine that produces a thrust due to an exhaust consisting entirely of material, as oxidizer, fuel, and inert matter, that has been carried in the vehicle it propels, none of the propellant being derived from the medium through which the vehicle moves. Also called **rocket, rock′et mo′tor.** [1930–35]

rock′et gun′, any weapon that uses a rocket as a projectile, as a rocket launcher or bazooka. [1880–85]

rock′et launch′er, *Mil.* **1.** a tube attached to a weapon for the launching of rockets. **2.** a vehicle equipped with many such tubes for the simultaneous firing of rockets. [1940–45]

rock•et-pro•pelled (rok′it prə peld′), *adj.* using rocket power as the chief motive force. [1925–30]

rock′et propul′sion, propulsion of an object by thrust developed by a rocket. [1925–30]

rock•et•ry (rok′i trē), *n.* the science of rocket design, development, and flight. [1925–30; ROCKET[1] + -RY]

rock′et sal′ad, rocket[2] (def. 2).

rock′et sci′entist, **1.** a specialist in rocketry. **2.** an exemplar of keen intelligence, esp. mathematical ability.

rock′et ship′, a rocket-propelled aircraft or spacecraft. [1925–30]

rock′et sled′, a sled propelled along a long track by rocket engines, for testing the effects of high rates of acceleration and deceleration. [1950–55]

rock•et•sonde (rok′it sond′), *n. Meteorol.* a telemeter for gathering data on the atmosphere at very high altitudes, carried aloft by rocket and returned to earth by parachute. [1945–50; ROCKET[1] + SONDE]

Rock•eye (rok′ī′), *n.* a 500-pound (225-kg) U.S. cluster bomb, consisting of 247 two-pound (0.9 kg) fragmentation bombs, designed for use against tanks.

rock•face (rok′fās′), *n.* an exposure of rock in a steep slope or cliff. [1850–55; ROCK[1] + FACE]

rock-faced (rok′fāst′), *adj.* **1.** (of a person) having a stiff, expressionless face. **2.** having a rocky surface. **3.** *Masonry.* noting a stone or stonework the visible face of which is dressed with a hammer, with or without a chiseled draft at the edges; quarry-faced. [1940–45]

rock•fall (rok′fôl′), *n.* **1.** an act or instance of the falling of rock, as in a cave-in or an avalanche. **2.** a mass of rocks that have fallen: *to be trapped under a rockfall.* [1920–25; ROCK[1] + FALL]

Rock′ Falls′, a city in NW Illinois. 10,624.

rock′ fence′, *South Midland and Southern U.S.* a wall built of unmortared stones, as one bordering a field. Also called **rock wall.** [1895–1900, *Amer.*]

Rock′ fe′ver, *Pathol.* brucellosis. [1895–1900; so called from the *Rock* of Gibraltar, where it is prevalent]

rock′-fill dam′ (rok′fil′), a dam built mainly of rocks fitted compactly together. [1955–60]

rock•fish (rok′fish′), *n., pl.* (*esp. collectively*) **-fish,** (*esp. referring to two or more kinds or species*) **-fish•es.** **1.** any of various fishes found about rocks. **2.** See **striped bass.** **3.** any of the North Pacific and Atlantic marine fishes of the genus *Sebastes.* **4.** scorpionfish. Also called **rock cod** (for defs. 1–3). [1590–1600; ROCK[1] + FISH]

rock′ flour′. See **glacial meal.** [1880–85]

rock′ flow′er, any shrub of the genus *Crossosoma,* native to the arid regions of the southwestern U.S., having thick, narrow leaves and solitary flowers. [1810–20]

Rock•ford (rok′fərd), *n.* a city in N Illinois. 139,712.

rock′ gar′den, **1.** a garden on rocky ground or among rocks, for the growing of alpine or other plants. **2.** a garden decorated with rocks, usually a wide variety of interestingly shaped, multicolored rocks, esp. quartz. Also called **rockery.** [1830–40]

rock′ gla′cier, a mass of rock resembling a valley glacier that moves down a slope by its own weight or by the action of frost and interstitial ice. [1900–05]

rock′ gun′nel. See under **gunnel**[1].

Rock•hamp•ton (rok hamp′tən, -ham′-), *n.* a city in E Queensland, in E Australia. 56,440.

Rock′ Hill′, a city in N South Carolina. 35,344.

rock′ hind′, a small, orange-spotted grouper, *Epinephelus adscensionis,* inhabiting warm seas from North Carolina to Brazil, esp. in the West Indies, and fished as food. [1865–70]

rock′ hound′, *Informal.* **1.** a geologist. **2.** an amateur collector of rocks, fossils, or minerals. Also, **rock′•hound′.** [1920–25, *Amer.*]

rock′ hound′ing, the activity of searching for and collecting rocks, fossils, or minerals. Also, **rock′hound′•ing.** [1945–50, *Amer.*; ROCK HOUND + -ING[1]]

rock′ hy′rax, an African and Middle Eastern hyrax of the genus *Procavia* that lives in rocky places. [1950–55]

Rock•ies (rok′ēz), *n.* See **Rocky Mountains.**

rock•i•ness[1] (rok′ē nis), *n.* the state or condition of being rocky. [1605–15; ROCKY[1] + -NESS]

rock•i•ness[2] (rok′ē nis), *n.* the state or condition of a person who is shaky or unsteady, as from drinking, fatigue, or illness. [ROCKY[2] + -NESS]

rock′ing chair′, a chair mounted on rockers or springs so as to permit a person to rock back and forth while sitting. Also called **rocker.** [1750–60, *Amer.*]

rock′ing horse′, a toy horse, as of wood, mounted on rockers or springs, on which children may ride; hobbyhorse. [1795–1805]

rock′ing rhythm′, *Pros.* a rhythmic pattern created by a succession of metrical feet each of which consists of one accented syllable between two unaccented ones. [1880–85]

rock′ing shear′, a shear having a curved blade that cuts with a rocking motion.

rock′ing stone′, any fairly large rock so situated on its base that slight forces can cause it to move or sway. Also called **logan stone, loggan stone, logging stone.** [1730–40]

rock′ing valve′, (on a steam engine) a valve mechanism oscillating through an arc to open and close.

Rock′ Is′land, a port in NW Illinois, on the Mississippi: government arsenal. 47,036.

rock′ jas′mine, any of several alpine plants belonging to the genus *Androsace,* of the primrose family, having tufted leaves often in basal rosettes, and umbels of pink, red, purple, or white flowers.

rock′ jock′, *Slang.* a mountaineering enthusiast. [1980–85]

Rock•land (rok′lənd), *n.* a city in SE Massachusetts. 15,695.

Rock•ledge (rok′lij, -lej′), *n.* a city in E central Florida. 11,877.

rock•ling (rok′ling), *n., pl.* **-lings,** (*esp. collectively*) **-ling.** any of several small cods of the genera *Enchalyopus* and *Gaidropsarus,* found in the North Atlantic. [1595–1605; ROCK[1] + -LING[1]]

rock′ lob′ster. See **spiny lobster.** [1880–85]

rock′ ma′ple, *New Eng.* the sugar maple, *Acer saccharum.* [1765–75]

rock′ milk′, a white, powdery surface crust of calcite, formed by efflorescence in limestone caves and fissures. Also called **agaric mineral.** [1795–1805]

Rock•ne (rok′nē), *n.* **Knute (Kenneth)** (no͞ot), 1888–1931, U.S. football coach, born in Norway.

rock-'n'-roll (rok′ən rōl′), *n.* **1.** a style of popular music that derives in part from blues and folk music and is marked by a heavily accented beat and a simple, repetitive phrase structure. —*adj.* **2.** of or pertaining to this music. —*v.i.* **3.** to dance to or play rock-'n'-roll. Also, **rock-and-roll, rock′ 'n' roll′.** [1950–55; contr. of phrase *rock and roll;* see ROCK[2]] —**rock′-'n'-roll′er,** *n.*

Rock′ of Gibral′tar, Gibraltar (def. 2).

rock′ oil′, petroleum. [1660–70; trans. of ML *petroleum*]

rock•oon (rok′o͞on, ro ko͞on′), *n.* a rocket launched from a balloon at a high altitude. [1950–55; ROCK(ET[1]) + (BALL)OON]

rock′ pi′geon. See **rock dove.** [1605–15]

rock′ plant′, a plant found among rocks or in rock gardens. [1605–15]

rock′ prick′leback. See **rock blenny.**

rock′ rab′bit, **1.** See **rock hyrax.** **2.** pika. [1840–50]

rock-ribbed (rok′ribd′), *adj.* **1.** having ribs or ridges of rock: *the rock-ribbed coast of Maine.* **2.** unyielding; confirmed and uncompromising: *a rock-ribbed conservative.* Also, **rock′-rib′.** [1770–80]

rock•rose (rok′rōz′), *n.* **1.** any plant of the genus *Cistus* or some allied genus, as *Helianthemum.* **2.** any related plant. [1620–30; ROCK[1] + ROSE]

rock′rose fam′ily, the plant family Cistaceae, characterized by herbaceous plants and shrubs having simple, usually opposite leaves, solitary or clustered flowers, and capsular fruit, and including the frostweed, pinweed, and rockrose.

rock′ salt′, common salt occurring in extensive, irregular beds in rocklike masses. [1700–10]

rock•shaft (rok′shaft′, -shäft′), *n. Mach.* an oscillating shaft. [1870–75; ROCK[2] + SHAFT]

rock-shel•ter (rok′shel′tər), *n.* a shallow cave or cavelike area, as one formed by an overhanging cliff or standing rocks, occupied by Stone Age peoples, possibly for extended periods. Also, **rock′ shel′ter.** [1860–65]

rock′ spray′, a low, evergreen, Himalayan shrub, *Cotoneaster microphyllus,* of the rose family, having shiny leaves with grayish, hairy undersides, white flowers, and scarlet berries.

Rock′ Springs′, a city in SW Wyoming. 19,458.

rock′ squir′rel, a large, gray ground squirrel, *Spermophilus variegatus,* inhabiting rocky areas of the southwestern U.S. [1850–55]

rock′ stead′y, the style of vocalized Jamaican popular music that succeeded ska and preceded reggae in the 1960's, influenced by American soul music and having a more upbeat tempo with emphasis on electric bass and guitar rather than on horns. [1965–70]

rock′ thrush′, any of several Old World thrushes of the genus *Monticola,* usually having bluish plumage, esp. *M. saxatilis,* of Europe. [1775–85]

rock′ tripe′, any lichen of the genus *Umbilicaria.* Also called **tripe-de-roche.** [1850–55; allegedly so called in reference to the appearance of the thallus]

Rock•ville (rok′vil), *n.* a city in central Maryland. 43,811.

Rock′ville Cen′tre, a city on W Long Island, in SE New York. 25,412.

rock′ wall′. See **rock fence.** [1900–05]

rock′ wal′laby, any wallaby of the genus *Petrogale,* having a banded or striped coat, slender body, and long legs and feet, inhabiting caves and rocky areas in Australia. [1835–45]

rock•weed (rok′wēd′), *n.* a fucoid seaweed growing on rocks exposed at low tide. [1620–30; ROCK[1] + WEED[1]]

Rock•well (rok′wel′, -wəl), *n.* **1. Norman,** 1894–1978, U.S. illustrator. **2.** a male given name.

Rock′well num′ber, *Metall.* a numerical expression of the hardness of a metal as determined by a test **(Rock′well test′)** made by indenting a test piece with a Brale, or with a steel ball of specific diameter, under two successive loads and measuring the resulting permanent indentation. [1930–35, *Amer.*; named after Stanley P. *Rockwell,* 20th-century American metallurgist]

rock′ wool′. See **mineral wool.** [1925–30]

rock•work (rok′wûrk′), *n.* stonework. [1700–10; ROCK[1] + WORK]

rock′ wren′, an American wren, *Salpinctes obsoletus,* inhabiting the foothills, badlands, and mesa country of the western U.S. and Mexico. [1855–60, *Amer.*]

rock•y[1] (rok′ē), *adj.,* **rock•i•er, rock•i•est.** **1.** full of or abounding in rocks. **2.** consisting of rock. **3.** rocklike: *wood with a rocky hardness.* **4.** firm; steadfast: *rocky endurance.* **5.** unfeeling; without sympathy or emotion: *my rocky heart.* [1400–50; late ME; see ROCK[1], -Y[1]]

rock•y[2] (rok′ē), *adj.,* **rock•i•er, rock•i•est.** **1.** inclined or likely to rock; tottering; shaky; unsteady. **2.** difficult or uncertain; full of hazards or obstacles: *a business with a rocky future.* **3.** physically unsteady or weak, as from sickness. [1730–40; ROCK[2] + -Y[1]]

Rock′y Hill′, a town in central Connecticut. 14,559.

Rock′y Mount′, a city in NE North Carolina. 41,283.

Rock′y Moun′tain bee′plant (bē′plant′, -plänt′), a rank-smelling plant, *Cleome serrulata,* of the caper family, native to the western U.S., having showy, dense clusters of pink or white flowers, frequented by bees. Also called **stinking clover.** [1895–1900]

Rock′y Moun′tain big′horn, bighorn. [1910–15, *Amer.*]

Rock′y Moun′tain flow′ering rasp′berry, a shrub, *Rubus deliciosus,* of Colorado, having large white flowers and purple fruit. Also called **boulder raspberry, Rock′y Moun′tain rasp′berry.**

Rock′y Moun′tain goat′, a long-haired, white, antelopelike wild goat, *Oreamnos americanus,* of mountainous regions of western North America, having short, black horns. [1835–45, *Amer.*]

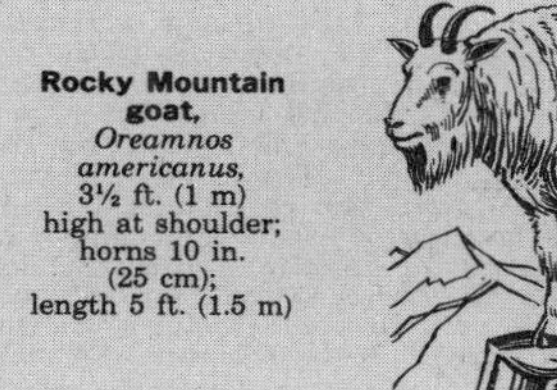

Rocky Mountain goat, *Oreamnos americanus,* 3½ ft. (1 m) high at shoulder; horns 10 in. (25 cm); length 5 ft. (1.5 m)

Rock′y Moun′tain ju′niper, a juniper, *Juniperus scopulorum,* of western North America, that yields a soft, reddish wood used for making fences, pencils, etc., and that is also grown as an ornamental. Also called **Rocky Mountain red cedar.** [1895–1900]

Rock′y Moun′tain lo′cust, a migratory locust, *Melanoplus spretus,* that occurs in North America, esp. the Great Plains, where swarms cause great damage to crops and other vegetation. Also called **Rock′y Moun′tain grass′hopper.** [1875–80, *Amer.*]

Rock′y Moun′tain Na′tional Park′, a national park in N Colorado. 405 sq. mi. (1050 sq. km).

Rock′y Moun′tain oys′ter. See **mountain oyster.** [1885–90]

Rock′y Moun′tain red′ ce′dar. See **Rocky Mountain juniper.**

Rock′y Moun′tains, the chief mountain system in North America, extending from central New Mexico to N Alaska. Highest peak, Mount McKinley, 20,300 ft. (6187 m). Also called **Rockies.**

Rock′y Moun′tain sheep′, bighorn. [1785–95, *Amer.*]

Rock′y Moun′tain spot′ted fe′ver, *Pathol.* an infectious disease characterized by high fever, pains in joints, bones, and muscles, and a cutaneous eruption, caused by *rickettsii* and transmitted by ticks: first reported in the Rocky Mountain area, but now more widely distributed. [1885–90, *Amer.*]

Rock′y Moun′tain States′, those states in the region of the Rocky Mountains, including Colorado, Idaho, Montana, Nevada, Utah, and Wyoming, and sometimes Arizona and New Mexico.

Rock′y Moun′tain white′fish. See **mountain whitefish.** [1880–85, *Amer.*]

Rock′y Riv′er, a city in NE Ohio, near Cleveland. 21,084.

ro•co•co (rə kō′kō, rō′kə kō′), *n.* **1.** a style of architecture and decoration, originating in France about 1720, evolved from Baroque types and distinguished by its elegant refinement in using different materials for a delicate overall effect and by its ornament of shellwork, foliage, etc. **2.** a homophonic musical style of the middle 18th century, marked by a generally superficial elegance and charm and by the use of elaborate ornamentation and stereotyped devices. —*adj.* **3.** (*cap.*) *Fine Arts.* **a.** noting or pertaining to a style of painting developed simultaneously with the rococo in architecture and decoration, characterized chiefly by smallness of scale, delicacy of color, freedom of brushwork, and the selection of playful subjects as thematic material. **b.** designating a corresponding style of sculpture, chiefly characterized by diminutiveness of Baroque forms and playfulness of theme. **4.** of, pertaining to, in the manner of, or suggested by rococo architecture, decoration, or music or the general atmosphere and spirit of the rococo: *rococo charm.* **5.** ornate or florid in speech, literary style, etc. [1830–40; < F, akin to *rocaille* ROCAILLE]

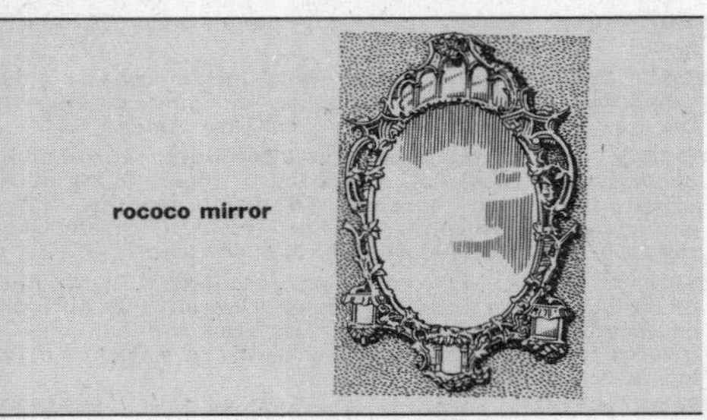
rococo mirror

rod (rod), *n., v.,* **rod·ded, rod·ding.** —*n.* **1.** a stick, wand, staff, or the like, of wood, metal, or other material. **2.** a straight, slender shoot or stem of any woody plant, whether still growing or cut from the plant. **3.** See **fishing rod. 4.** (in plastering or mortaring) a straightedge moved along screeds to even the plaster between them. **5.** a stick used for measuring. **6.** a unit of linear measure, 5½ yards or 16½ feet (5.029 m); linear perch or pole. **7.** a unit of square measure, 30¼ square yards (25.29 sq. m); square perch or pole. **8.** a stick, or a bundle of sticks or switches bound together, used as an instrument of punishment. **9.** punishment or discipline: *Not one to spare the rod, I sent him to bed without dinner.* **10.** a wand, staff, or scepter carried as a symbol of office, authority, power, etc. **11.** authority, sway, or rule, esp. when tyrannical. **12.** See **lightning rod. 13.** a slender bar or tube for draping towels over, suspending a shower curtain, etc. **14.** *Bible.* a branch of a family; tribe. **15.** a pattern, drawn on wood in full size, of one section of a piece of furniture. **16.** *Slang.* **a.** a pistol or revolver. **b.** *Vulgar.* the penis. **17.** *Anat.* one of the rodlike cells in the retina of the eye, sensitive to low intensities of light. Cf. **cone** (def. 5). **18.** *Bacteriol.* a rod-shaped microorganism. **19.** Also called **leveling rod, stadia rod.** *Survey.* a light pole, conspicuously marked with graduations, held upright and read through a surveying instrument in leveling or stadia surveying. **20.** *Metall.* round metal stock for drawing and cutting into slender bars. —*v.t.* **21.** to furnish or equip with a rod or rods, esp. lightning rods. **22.** to even (plaster or mortar) with a rod. **23.** *Metall.* to reinforce (the core of a mold) with metal rods. [bef. 1150; ME *rodd,* late OE; akin to ON *rudda* club] —**rod′less,** *adj.* —**rod′like′,** *adj.*

Rod (rod), *n.* a male given name, form of **Roderick** or **Rodney.**

rod′ bolt′, a long, double-ended bolt. [1825–35]

Rod·chen·ko (rod cheng′kō; *Russ.* RÔT′chyin kə), *n.* **A·le·ksan·dr (Mi·khai·lo·vich)** (al′ig zan′dər, -zän′-, mi kā′lə vich; *Russ.* u lyi ksän′dR myi KHĪ′lə vyich), 1891–1956, Soviet painter, photographer, and designer.

rod·ded (rod′id), *adj.* made of or fitted with rods. [1555–65; ROD + -ED[3]]

rode[1] (rōd), *v.* **1.** a pt. of **ride. 2.** *Nonstandard.* a pp. of **ride.**

rode[2] (rōd), *n.* (in New England and E Canada) a rope by which a boat is anchored. [1625–35; orig. uncert.]

ro·dent (rōd′nt), *adj.* **1.** belonging or pertaining to the gnawing or nibbling mammals of the order Rodentia, including the mice, squirrels, beavers, etc. —*n.* **2.** a rodent mammal. [1825–35; < NL *Rodentia* RODENTIA] —**ro′dent·like′,** *adj.*

Ro·den·tia (rō den′shə, -shē ə, -tē ə), *n.* the order comprising the rodents. [< NL, equiv. to L *rōdent-* (s. of *rōdēns*), prp. of *rōdere* to gnaw (see -ENT) + *-ia* -IA]

ro·den·ti·cide (rō den′tə sīd′), *n.* a substance for killing rodents. [1935–40; RODENT + -I- + -CIDE]

ro′dent ul′cer, *Pathol.* an ulcerating basal cell skin cancer, common on the face. [1850–55]

ro·de·o (rō′dē ō′, rō dā′ō), *n., pl.* **-de·os,** *v.,* **-de·oed, -de·o·ing.** —*n.* **1.** a public exhibition of cowboy skills, as bronco riding and calf roping. **2.** a roundup of cattle. **3.** *Informal.* any contest offering prizes in various events: *a bicycle rodeo for kids under twelve.* **4.** (*cap. italics*) a ballet (1942) choreographed by Agnes de Mille, with musical score by Aaron Copland. —*v.i.* **5.** to participate or compete in a rodeo or rodeos: *He's been rodeoing since he was twelve.* [1825–35; < Sp: cattle ring, deriv. of *rodear* to go round, itself deriv. of *rueda* wheel < L *rota*] —**ro′de·o′er,** *n.*

Rod·er·ick (rod′ə rik, rod′rik), *n.* a male given name: from Germanic words meaning "glory" and "ruler."

Ro·dez (RÔ dez′), *n.* a town in and the capital of Aveyron, in S France. 28,165.

Rodg·er (roj′ər), *n.* a male given name, form of **Roger.**

Rodg·ers (roj′ərz), *n.* **1. James Charles** (*Jimmie*), 1897–1933, U.S. country-and-western singer, guitarist, and composer. **2. Richard,** 1902–79, U.S. composer of popular music. **3. William Henry** (*Bill*), born 1947, U.S. track-and-field athlete.

Ro·di (RÔ′dē), *n.* Italian name of **Rhodes.**

CONCISE ETYMOLOGY KEY: <, descended or borrowed from; >, whence; b., blend of, blended; c., cognate with; cf., compare; deriv., derivative; equiv., equivalent; imit., imitative; obl., oblique; r., replacing; s., stem; sp., spelling, spelled; resp., respelling, respelled; trans., translation; ?, origin unknown; *, unattested; ‡, probably earlier than. See the full key inside the front cover.

Ro·din (rō dan′, -daN′; *Fr.* RÔ daN′), *n.* **(Fran·çois) Au·guste (Re·né)** (fRäN swA′ ō gyst′ Rə nā′), 1840–1917, French sculptor.

rod·man (rod′mən), *n., pl.* **-men. 1.** a person who works with rods, as in making reinforced concrete. **2.** a person who carries the leveling rod in surveying. [1850–55; ROD + -MAN]

rod′ mill′, 1. *Metalworking.* a mill for making metal rods. **2.** a mill for grinding ore or the like by means of steel rods. [1880–85]

Rod·ney (rod′nē), *n.* **1. George Brydg·es** (brij′iz), **Baron,** 1718–92, British admiral. **2.** a male given name: an Old English family name, taken from a placename.

rod·o·mon·tade (rod′ə mon tād′, -täd′, -mən-, rō′-də-), *n., adj., v.,* **-tad·ed, -tad·ing.** —*n.* **1.** vainglorious boasting or bragging; pretentious, blustering talk. —*adj.* **2.** bragging. —*v.i.* **3.** to boast; brag; talk big. [1605–15; < MF < It *Rodomonte,* the boastful king of Algiers in *Orlando Innamorato* and *Orlando Furioso* + MF *-ade* -ADE[1]]

Ro·dzin·ski (rə jin′skē), *n.* **Ar·tur** (är′to͝or), 1894–1958, U.S. orchestra conductor.

roe[1] (rō), *n.* **1.** the mass of eggs, or spawn, within the ovarian membrane of the female fish. **2.** the milt or sperm of the male fish. **3.** the eggs of any of various crustaceans, as the coral of the lobster. [1400–50; late ME *rowe;* c. OHG *rogo*]

roe[2] (rō), *n., pl.* **roes,** (*esp. collectively*) **roe.** See **roe deer.** [bef. 900; ME *roo,* OE *rā, rāha;* c. G *Reh*]

ROE, *Accounting.* return on equity.

Roeb·ling (rō′bling), *n.* **1. John Augustus,** 1806–69, U.S. engineer, born in Germany: pioneer of wire-rope suspension bridges, designer of the Brooklyn Bridge. **2.** his son, **Washington Augustus,** 1837–1926, U.S. engineer: completed Brooklyn Bridge 1883.

roe·buck (rō′buk′), *n., pl.* **-bucks,** (*esp. collectively*) **-buck.** a male roe deer. [1350–1400; ME *robucke.* See ROE[2], BUCK[1]]

roe′ deer′, a small, agile Old World deer, *Capreolus capreolus,* the male of which has three-pointed antlers. Also called **roe.** [bef. 1000; OE *rāhdēor* (not recorded in ME)]

roe deer, *Capreolus capreolus,* 2½ ft. (0.8 m) high at shoulder; antlers 9 in. (23 cm); length 3½ ft. (1 m)

roe·mer (rā′mər; *Ger.* RŒ′məR), *n., pl.* **-mers,** *Ger.* **-mer** (-məR). a German wineglass having a body with a globular top and a cylindrical bottom often decorated with prunts, supported by a conical foot. [1895–1900; < G, orig. a glass for toasting; c. D *roemer;* akin to G *rühmen* to praise]

Roent·gen (rent′gən, -jən, runt′-; *for 1 also Ger.* RŒNT′gən), *n.* **1. Wil·helm Kon·rad** (wil′helm kon′rad; *Ger.* vil′helm kôn′Rät), 1845–1923, German physicist: discoverer of x-rays 1895; Nobel prize 1901. **2.** (*l.c.*) *Physics.* a unit of exposure dose that measures x-rays or gamma rays in terms of the ions or electrons produced in dry air at 0° C and one atmosphere, equal to the amount of radiation producing one electrostatic unit of positive or negative charge per cubic centimeter of air. *Abbr.:* r, R —*adj.* **3.** (*sometimes l.c.*) of or pertaining to Wilhelm Roentgen, the Roentgen unit, or esp. to x-rays. Also, **Röntgen.**

roent·gen·ize (rent′gə nīz′, -jə-, runt′-), *v.t.,* **-ized, -iz·ing.** (formerly) to subject to the action of x-rays. Also, *esp. Brit.,* **roent′gen·ise′.** [1895–1900; ROENTGEN + -IZE] —**roent′gen·i·za′tion,** *n.*

roentgeno-, a combining form of **roentgen:** *roentgenometer.* Also, **röntgeno-.**

roent·gen·o·gram (rent′gə nə gram′, -jə-, runt′-), *n.* a photograph made with x-rays. [1900–05; ROENTGENO- + -GRAM[1]]

roent·gen·o·graph (rent′gə nə graf′, -gräf′, -jə-, runt′-), *n.* (no longer current) roentgenogram. [1905–10; ROENTGENO- + -GRAPH] —**roent·gen·o·graph·ic** (rent′gə nə graf′ik, -jə-, runt′-), *adj.* —**roent′gen·o·graph′i·cal·ly,** *adv.* —**roent·gen·og·ra·phy** (rent′gə-nog′rə fē, -jə-, runt′-), *n.*

roent·gen·ol·o·gy (rent′gə nol′ə jē, -jə-, runt′-), *n.* the branch of medicine dealing with diagnosis and therapy through x-rays. [1910–15; ROENTGENO- + -LOGY] —**roent·gen·o·log·ic** (rent′gə nl oj′ik, -jə-, runt′-), **roent′gen·o·log′i·cal,** *adj.* —**roent′gen·o·log′i·cal·ly,** *adv.* —**roent′gen·ol′o·gist,** *n.*

roent·gen·om·e·ter (rent′gə nom′i tər, -jə-, runt′-), *n.* an instrument for measuring the intensity of x-rays. [ROENTGENO- + -METER] —**roent′gen·om′e·try,** *n.*

roent·gen·o·paque (rent′gə nō pāk′, -jə-, runt′-), *adj.* not permitting the passage of x-rays. [ROENTGEN-(O)- + OPAQUE]

roent·gen·o·par·ent (rent′gə nō pâr′ənt, -par′-, -jə-, runt′-), *adj.* visible by means of x-rays. [ROENTGENO- + (AP)PARENT]

roent·gen·o·scope (rent′gə nə skōp′, -jə-, runt′-), *n.* *Physics.* a fluoroscope. [1920–25; ROENTGENO- + -SCOPE] —**roent·gen·o·scop·ic** (rent′gə nə skop′ik, -jə-, runt′-), *adj.* —**roent·gen·os·co·py** (rent′gə nos′-kə pē, -jə-, runt′-), *n.*

roent·gen·o·ther·a·py (rent′gə nō ther′ə pē, -jə-, runt′-), *n.* treatment of disease by means of x-rays. [1900–05; ROENTGENO- + THERAPY]

Roent′gen ray′, (*sometimes l.c.*) x-ray. [1895–1900]

Roe·rich (rûr′ik; *Russ.* RYÔ′RYIKH), *n.* **Nich·o·las Kon·stan·ti·no·vich** (nik′ə ləs kon′stən tē′nə vich; *Russ.* kən stun tyē′nə vyich), 1874–1947, Russian painter, archaeologist, and author; in the U.S. after 1920.

Roeth·ke (ret′kə), *n.* **Theodore,** 1908–63, U.S. poet and teacher.

R.O.G., receipt of goods. Also, **ROG, r.o.g.**

ro·ga·tion (rō gā′shən), *n.* **1.** Usually, **rogations.** *Eccles.* solemn supplication, esp. as chanted during procession on the three days **(Roga′tion Days′)** before Ascension Day. **2.** *Rom. Hist.* **a.** the proposing by the consuls or tribunes of a law to be passed by the people. **b.** a law so proposed. [1350–1400; ME *rogacio(u)n* < L *rogātiōn-* (s. of *rogātiō*), equiv. to *rogāt(us)* (ptp. of *rogāre* to ask, beg) + *-iōn-* -ION]

rog·a·to·ry (rog′ə tôr′ē, -tōr′ē), *adj.* pertaining to asking or requesting: *a rogatory commission.* [1835–45; < ML *rogātōrius* < L *rogā(re)* (see ROGATION) + *-tōrius* -TORY[1]]

rog·er (roj′ər), *interj.* **1.** *Informal.* all right; O.K. **2.** message received and understood (a response to radio communications). **3.** (*often cap.*) See **Jolly Roger. 4.** (formerly used in communications to represent the letter *R.*) [from the name *Roger;* in def. 2 repr. *r(eceived)*]

Rog·er (roj′ər), *n.* a male given name: from Germanic words meaning "fame" and "spear."

Ro·ger-Du·casse (RÔ zhā′dy KAS′), *n.* **Jean Jules A·ma·ble** (zhäN zhyl A mA′blᵊ), 1873–1954, French composer. Also called **Ducasse.**

Rog·ers (roj′ərz), *n.* **1. Bernard,** 1893–1968, U.S. composer. **2. Bruce,** 1870–1957, U.S. book designer and printer. **3. Carl (Ransom),** 1902–87, U.S. psychologist. **4. Ginger** (*Virginia Katherine McMath*), born 1911, U.S. actress and dancer. **5. James Gamble,** 1867–1947, U.S. architect. **6. Robert,** 1731–95, American pioneer and commander in the British regular army during the French and Indian War. **7. Samuel,** 1763–1855, English poet. **8. Will(iam Penn A·dair)** (ə dâr′), 1879–1935, U.S. actor and humorist. **9. William P(ierce),** born 1913, U.S. lawyer: Attorney General 1957–61; Secretary of State 1969–73. **10.** a city in NW Arkansas. 17,429.

Ro·get (rō zhā′, rō′zhā, rozh′ā), *n.* **Peter Mark,** 1779–1869, English physician and author of a thesaurus.

rogue (rōg), *n., v.,* **rogued, ro·guing,** *adj.* —*n.* **1.** a dishonest, knavish person; scoundrel. **2.** a playfully mischievous person; scamp: *The youngest boys are little rogues.* **3.** a tramp or vagabond. **4.** a rogue elephant or other animal of similar disposition. **5.** *Biol.* a usually inferior organism, esp. a plant, varying markedly from the normal. —*v.i.* **6.** to live or act as a rogue. —*v.t.* **7.** to cheat. **8.** to uproot or destroy (plants, etc., that do not conform to a desired standard). **9.** to perform this operation upon: *to rogue a field.* —*adj.* **10.** (of an animal) having an abnormally savage or unpredictable disposition, as a rogue elephant. **11.** no longer obedient, belonging, or accepted and hence not controllable or answerable; deviating, renegade: *a rogue cop; a rogue union local.* [1555–65; appar. short for obs. *roger* begging vagabond, orig. cant word]
—**Syn. 1.** villain, trickster, swindler, cheat, mountebank, quack. See **knave.**

rogue′ el′ephant, a vicious elephant that has been exiled from the herd. [1855–60]

ro·guer·y (rō′gə rē), *n., pl.* **-guer·ies. 1.** roguish conduct; rascality. **2.** playful mischief. [1590–1600; ROGUE + -ERY]

rogues′ gal′lery, a collection of portraits of criminals and suspects maintained by the police for purposes of identification. [1855–60]

rogue's′ march′, a derisive tune played to accompany a person's expulsion from a regiment, community, etc. [1795–1805]

rogue's′ yarn′, a yarn of distinctive color, material, or twist, laid in a strand or strands of a rope to identify the owner or the maker. Also called **identification thread.** [1760–70]

ro·guish (rō′gish), *adj.* **1.** pertaining to, characteristic of, or acting like a rogue; knavish or rascally. **2.** playfully mischievous: *a roguish smile.* [1565–75; ROGUE + -ISH[1]] —**ro′guish·ly,** *adv.* —**ro′guish·ness,** *n.*

Rohn·ert Park′ (rō′nərt), a city in W California. 22,965.

Roh Tae Woo (nō′ tā′ wo͞o′), born 1932, president of South Korea since 1988.

ROI, return on investment. Also, **R.O.I.**

roil (roil), *v.t.* **1.** to render (water, wine, etc.) turbid by stirring up sediment. **2.** to disturb or disquiet; irritate; vex: *to be roiled by a delay.* —*v.i.* **3.** to move or proceed turbulently. [1580–90; orig. uncert.]
—**Syn. 2.** annoy, fret, ruffle, exasperate, provoke, rile.

roil·y (roi′lē), *adj.,* **roil·i·er, roil·i·est. 1.** turbid; muddy. **2.** turbulent. [1815–25; ROIL + -Y[1]]

roist·er (roi′stər), *v.i.* **1.** to act in a swaggering, boisterous, or uproarious manner. **2.** to revel noisily or without restraint. [1545–55; v. use of *roister* (n.) < MF *ru(i)stre* ruffian, boor, var. of *ru(i)ste* RUSTIC] —**roist′er·er,** *n.* —**roist′er·ous,** *adj.* —**roist′er·ous·ly,** *adv.*

Ro·jas (rō′häs; *Sp.* RÔ′häs), *n.* **Fer·nan·do de** (feR-nän′dô the), c1475–1541?, Spanish writer.

Rok (rok), *n.* a soldier in the army of the Republic of Korea. [*R(epublic) o(f) K(orea)*]

ROK, Republic of Korea.

roke (rōk), *n.* *Metall.* a seam or scratch filled with scale or slag on the surface of an ingot or bar. [1885–90; orig. dial. *roke, rawk* to scratch, flaw]

Ro•land (rō′lənd), *n.* **1.** Italian, **Orlando.** the greatest of the paladins in the Charlemagne cycle of the chansons de geste, renowned for his prowess and the manner of his death in the battle of Roncesvalles (A.D. 778), also for his five days' combat with Oliver in which neither was the victor. **2. a Roland for an Oliver,** retaliation or a retort equal to its provocation; a blow for a blow. **3.** a male given name: from Germanic words meaning "glory" and "land."

role (rōl), *n.* **1.** a part or character played by an actor or actress. **2.** proper or customary function: *the teacher's role in society.* **3.** *Sociol.* the rights, obligations, and expected behavior patterns associated with a particular social status. Also, **rôle.** [1600–10; < F *rôle* ROLL (as of paper) containing the actor's part]
—Syn. 2. capacity, position, responsibility, duty.

role′ con′flict, emotional conflict arising when competing demands are made on an individual in the fulfillment of his or her multiple social roles. [1960–65]

role′ mod′el, a person whose behavior, example, or success is or can be emulated by others, esp. by younger people. [1955–60]

role-play (rōl′plā′), *v.t.* **1.** to assume the attitudes, actions, and discourse of (another), esp. in a make-believe situation in an effort to understand a differing point of view or social interaction: *Management trainees were given a chance to role-play labor negotiators.* **2.** to experiment with or experience (a situation or viewpoint) by playing a role: *trainees role-playing management positions.* —*v.i.* **3.** to engage in role-playing. [1945–50]

role-play•ing (rōl′plā′ing), *n.* **1.** a method of instruction or psychotherapy aimed at changing attitudes and behavior, in which participants act out designated roles relevant to real-life situations. **2.** the modifying of a person's behavior to accord with a desired personal image, as to impress others or conform to a particular environment. [1940–45]

role′-play′ing game′, a game in which participants adopt the roles of imaginary characters in an adventure under the direction of a Game Master.

role′ set′, *Sociol.* the set of roles associated with a single social stratum. [1965–70]

role′ strain′, *Sociol.* the stress or strain experienced by an individual when incompatible behavior, expectations, or obligations are associated with a single social role.

rolf (rolf), *v.i. Slang.* to vomit. [1970–75, *Amer.*; appar. var. of RALPH]

Rolf (rôlf, rolf), *v.t.* to massage using the techniques of Rolfing. [1965–70; after Ida P. *Rolf* (1897–1979), U.S. physiotherapist who invented the techniques] **—Rolf′•er,** *n.*

Rolf (rolf), *n.* **1.** Also called **Rolf′ the Gang′er** (gang′ər). Rollo (def. 1). **2.** a male given name: from Scandinavian words meaning "glory" and "wolf."

Rolfe (rolf), *n.* **John,** 1585–1622, English colonist in Virginia (husband of Pocahontas).

Rolf•ing (rôl′fing, rol′-), *Trademark.* a type of massage therapy involving sometimes intensive manipulation of the fascia of the muscles and internal organs to relieve physical and emotional tension, improve posture, increase vitality, etc.

Rolf′ Kra′ki (krä′kē), *Scand. Legend.* a possibly historical Danish king of the 9th century, the subject of an Old Icelandic saga and in accounts by the Danish historian Saxo Grammaticus: involved in great battles with his stepfather, Adils of Sweden. [< ON *Hrólfr,* equiv. to *hró(thr)* fame + *(ú)lfr* WOLF, c. OE *Hrōthwulf; kraki* wretch (applied ironically)]

roll (rōl), *v.i.* **1.** to move along a surface by revolving or turning over and over, as a ball or a wheel. **2.** to move or be moved on wheels, as a vehicle or its occupants. **3.** to flow or advance in a stream or with an undulating motion, as water, waves, or smoke. **4.** to extend in undulations, as land. **5.** to elapse, pass, or move, as time (often fol. by *on, away,* or *by*). **6.** to move as in a cycle (usually fol. by *round* or *around*): *as soon as summer rolls round again.* **7.** to perform a periodical revolution in an orbit, as a heavenly body. **8.** to emit or have a deep, prolonged sound, as thunder, drums, etc. **9.** to trill, as a bird. **10.** to revolve or turn over, once or repeatedly, as a wheel on an axis or a person or animal lying down. **11.** to turn around in different directions or from side to side and top to bottom, as the eyes in their sockets. **12.** (of a vessel) **a.** to rock from side to side in open water. Cf. **heave** (def. 14b), **pitch**[1] (def. 20). **b.** to sail with a side-to-side rocking motion. **13.** to walk with a swinging or swaying gait. **14.** *Informal.* to begin to move or operate; start; commence: *Let's roll at sunrise.* **15.** *Informal.* to go forward or advance without restrictions or impediments: *The economy is finally beginning to roll.* **16.** to curl up so as to form a tube or cylinder. **17.** to admit of being formed into a tube or cylinder by curling up. **18.** to be spread out after being curled up (usually fol. by *out*). **19.** to spread out as under a roller: *The paint rolls easily.* **20.** *Aviation.* (of an aircraft or rocket) to deviate from a stable flight attitude by rotation about its longitudinal axis.
—*v.t.* **21.** to cause to move along a surface by revolving or turning over and over, as a cask, a ball, or a hoop. **22.** to move along on wheels or rollers; convey in a wheeled vehicle. **23.** to drive, impel, or cause to flow onward with a sweeping or undulating motion: *The wind rolled the waves high on the beach.* **24.** to utter or give forth with a full, flowing, continuous sound: *rolling his orotund phrases.* **25.** to trill: *to roll one's r's.* **26.** to cause to revolve or turn over or over and over: *to roll oneself on one's face.* **27.** to turn around in different directions or from side to side and top to bottom: *He smirked and rolled his eyes.* **28.** to cause to sway or rock from side to side, as a ship. **29.** to wrap (something) around an axis, around upon itself, or into a cylindrical shape, ball, or the like: *to roll string.* **30.** to make by forming a tube or cylinder: *to roll a cigarette.* **31.** to spread out flat (something curled up) (often fol. by *out*): *He rolled the map out on the table.* **32.** to wrap, enfold, or envelop, as in some covering: *to roll a child in a blanket.* **33.** to spread out, level, smooth, compact, or the like, as with a rolling pin, roller, the hands, etc.: *to roll dough; to roll a tennis court.* **34.** to form (metal) in a rolling mill. **35.** to tumble (metal pieces and abrasives) in a box or barrel in such a way that their relative positions remain the same. **36.** to beat (a drum) with rapid, continuous strokes. **37.** (in certain games, as craps) to cast, or throw (dice). **38.** *Print.* to apply (ink) with a roller or series of rollers. **39.** *Slang.* to rob, esp. by going through the pockets of a victim who is either asleep or drunk. **40. roll back,** to reduce (the price of a commodity, wages, etc.) to a former level, usually in response to government action. **41. roll in,** *Informal.* **a.** to luxuriate in; abound in: *rolling in money.* **b.** to go to bed; retire. **c.** to mix and average the cost of (a higher-priced commodity or item) with that of a cheaper one so as to increase the retail price. **d.** to add: *Labor wants to roll in periodic increases with their wage demands.* **e.** to arrive, esp. in large numbers or quantity: *When do my dividends start rolling in?* **42. roll out, a.** to spread out or flatten: *to roll out dough.* **b.** *Informal.* to arise from bed; get up: *It was nearly impossible to roll out on the first day back after vacation.* **c.** *Football.* to execute a rollout. **d.** *Informal.* to introduce; unveil: *a TV advertising campaign to roll out the new car.* **43. roll up, a.** to accumulate; collect: *to roll up a large vote.* **b.** to increase. **c.** to arrive in a conveyance: *He rolled up to the front door in a chauffeur-driven limousine.* **44. roll with the punches.** See **punch**[1] (def. 4).
—*n.* **45.** a document of paper, parchment, or the like, that is or may be rolled up, as for storing; scroll. **46.** a list, register, or catalog, esp. one containing the names of the persons belonging to a company, class, society, etc. **47.** anything rolled up in a ringlike or cylindrical form: *a roll of wire.* **48.** a number of papers or other items rolled up together. **49.** a length of cloth, wallpaper, or the like, rolled up in cylindrical form (often forming a definite measure). **50.** a cylindrical or rounded mass of something: *rolls of fat.* **51.** some article of cylindrical or rounded form, as a molding. **52.** a cylindrical piece upon which something is rolled along to facilitate moving. **53.** a cylinder serving as a core upon which something is rolled up. **54.** a roller with which something is spread out, leveled, crushed, smoothed, compacted, or the like. **55.** *Cookery.* **a.** thin cake spread with jelly or the like and rolled up. **b.** a small cake of bread, originally and still often rolled or doubled on itself before baking. **c.** meat rolled up and cooked. **56.** the act or process or an instance of rolling. **57.** undulation, as of a surface: *the roll of a prairie.* **58.** a sonorous or rhythmical flow of words. **59.** a deep, prolonged sound, as of thunder: *the roll of a breaking wave.* **60.** the trill of certain birds, esp. of the roller canary. **61.** the continuous sound of a drum rapidly beaten. **62.** a rolling motion, as of a ship. **63.** a rolling or swaying gait. **64.** *Aerospace.* **a.** a single, complete rotation of an airplane about the axis of the fuselage with little loss of altitude or change of direction. **b.** (of an aircraft or rocket) the act of rolling. **c.** the angular displacement caused by rolling. **65.** *Informal.* **a.** paper currency carried folded or rolled up: *He took out an impressive roll and paid the check with a $100 bill.* **b.** bankroll; funds: *People were encouraged to shoot their rolls on mining speculation.* **66.** (in various dice games) **a.** a single cast of or turn at casting the dice. **b.** the total number of pips or points made by a single cast; score or point. **67. on a roll, a.** (in a gambling game) having a continuing winning streak. **b.** enjoying continuing good luck or success: *She's been on a roll since taking that course on sales techniques.* **68. roll in the hay,** *Slang.* an instance of sexual intercourse. **69. strike off** or **from the rolls,** to remove from membership or practice, as to disbar. [1175–1225; (n.) (in senses referring to rolled or round objects) ME: scroll, inscribed scroll, register, cylindrical object < OF *ro(u)lle* < L *rotulus, rotula* small wheel, dim. of *rota* wheel (see ROTATE, -ULE); (in senses referring to motion) deriv. of the v.; (v.) ME *rollen* < OF *rol(l)er* < VL **rotulare,* deriv. of L *rotulus, rotula*] **—roll′a•ble,** *adj.*
—Syn. 1. revolve, rotate. **3.** wave, undulate. **4.** undulate. **12.** swing, tilt. **46.** See **list**[1]. **53.** spindle.

Rol•la (rol′ə), *n.* a city in S central Missouri. 13,303.

Rol•land (RÔ län′), *n.* **Ro•main** (RÔ maN′), 1866–1944, French novelist, music critic, and dramatist: Nobel prize 1915.

roll-a•round (rōl′ə round′), *adj.* equipped with wheels or casters so as to be easily movable from one location to another: *a roll-around kitchen counter.* [1970–75; adj. use of v. phrase *roll around*]

rol•la•ti•ni (rō′lə tē′nē), *n.* (*used with a singular or plural v.*) *Italian Cookery.* a dish consisting of thin slices of poultry or meat rolled around a filling, esp. of ham and cheese, and baked in a sauce. [< It]

roll•a•way (rōl′ə wā′), *adj.* **1.** designed to be rolled out of the way or out of sight when not in use: *rollaway bed.* —*n.* **2.** something, as an article of furniture, esp. a bed, that is a rollaway: *a wide selection of cribs and rollaways.* [1935–40; adj. use of v. phrase *roll away*]

roll•back (rōl′bak′), *n.* **1.** an act or instance of rolling back. **2.** a return to a lower level of prices, wages, etc., as by government order. **3.** a pulling back or withdrawal: *a rollback of attack forces.* [1935–40; n. use of v. phrase *roll back*]

roll′ bag′, a small zippered duffel bag for carrying school supplies, sports gear, or the like.

roll′ bar′, a heavy steel transverse bar in the form of an inverted U rising from the framework of an automobile to prevent its occupants from being crushed if the vehicle rolls over. Also, **roll′bar′.** [1950–55]

roll′ book′, a book in which attendance records are kept, as of students or employees.

roll′ cage′, a system of metal bars fitted around the seating area of a vehicle, esp. a racing car, to protect the occupant if the vehicle rolls over. [1965–70]

roll′ call′, 1. the calling of a list of names, as of soldiers or students, for checking attendance. **2.** a military signal for this, as one given by a drum. **3.** a voting process, esp. in the U.S. Congress, in which legislators are called on by name and allowed either to cast their vote or to abstain. [1765–75]

roll′ cloud′, *Meteorol.* **1.** arcus. **2.** See **rotor cloud.**

rolled′ col′lar, a collar that stands up slightly from the point of attachment to the neckline of a garment before folding over to lie flat.

rolled′ glass′, a sheet of glass made by the extrusion of molten glass between two rollers.

rolled′ gold′. See **filled gold.** [1895–1900]

rolled′ oats′, oats that are hulled and steamed, then flattened by rollers. [1885–90, *Amer.*]

rolled′ roast′, meat that has had the bones removed and been rolled and tied for roasting.

roll•er[1] (rō′lər), *n.* **1.** a person or thing that rolls. **2.** a cylinder, wheel, caster, or the like, upon which something is rolled along. **3.** a cylindrical body, revolving on a fixed axis, esp. one to facilitate the movement of something passed over or around it. **4.** a cylindrical object upon which something is rolled up: *the roller of a window shade.* **5.** a hollow, cylindrical object of plastic, stiff net, or the like, upon which hair is rolled up for setting. **6.** a cylindrical body for rolling over something to be spread out, leveled, crushed, smoothed, compacted, impressed, inked, etc. **7.** any of various other revolving cylindrical bodies, as the barrel of a music box. **8.** *Metalworking.* a person in charge of a rolling mill. **9.** a long, swelling wave advancing steadily. **10.** a rolled bandage. [1375–1425; late ME; see ROLL, -ER[1]]
—Syn. 9. breaker, comber.

roll•er[2] (rō′lər), *n. Ornith.* **1.** any of several Old World birds of the family Coraciidae that tumble or roll over in flight, esp. in the breeding season. **2.** tumbler (def. 9). **3.** one of a variety of canaries having a warbling or trilling song. [1655–65; < G *Roller,* deriv. of *rollen* to ROLL]

roll′er bear′ing, *Mach.* a bearing consisting of cylindrical or tapered rollers running between races in two concentric rings, one of which is mounted on a rotating or oscillating part, as a shaft. [1855–60]

roller bearing

Roll•er•blade (rō′lər blād′), *Trademark.* a brand of in-line skates.

roll′er-blind shut′ter (rō′lər blīnd′), *Photog.* See **curtain shutter.**

roll′er chain′, a power chain consisting of parallel pairs of flat links joined by pins covered with rollers, and engaging with the teeth of sprockets. [1895–1900]

roll′er coast′er, 1. a small gravity railroad, esp. in an amusement park, having a train with open cars that moves along a high, sharply winding trestle built with steep inclines that produce sudden, speedy plunges for thrill-seeking passengers. **2.** a car or train of cars for such a railroad. **3.** any phenomenon, period, or experience of persistent or violent ups and downs, as one fluctuating between elation and despair. [1885–90]

roll•er-coast•er (rō′lər kō′stər, rō′li-), *v.i.* **1.** to go up and down like a roller coaster; rise and fall: *a narrow road roller-coastering around the mountain; a light boat roller-coastering over the waves.* **2.** to experience a period of prosperity, happiness, security, or the like, followed by a contrasting period of economic depression, despair, or the like: *The economy was roller-coastering throughout most of the decade.* —*adj.* **3.** of, pertaining to, or characteristic of a roller coaster. **4.** resembling the progress of a ride on a roller coaster in sudden extreme changeableness. [1960–65]

Roll′er Der′by, *Trademark.* a contest between two teams on roller skates, held on a circular, usually banked board track, in which the teams race around the track in each unit of play, working to free a teammate or teammates for the opportunity to score by lapping one or more opponents.

roll′er gate′, (on certain dams) a cylindrical gate that rises and falls by rotating against inclined racks.

roll′er hock′ey, a game similar to ice hockey played on roller skates. [1925–30]

roll′er mill′, any mill that pulverizes, flattens, or otherwise changes material, as grain, by passing it between rolls. [1870–75, *Amer.*]

roll′er skate′, a form of skate with four wheels or rollers instead of a runner, for use on a sidewalk or other surface offering traction. [1860–65, *Amer.*]

roll•er-skate (rō′lər skāt′), *v.i.,* **-skat•ed, -skat•ing.** to glide about by means of roller skates. Also, **roll′er•skate′.** [1870–75; v. use of ROLLER SKATE] **—roll′er skat′er. —roll′er•skat′er,** *n.*

roll′er tow′el, a long towel sewed together at the ends and hung on a roller. [1835–45]

Rolle's′ the′orem (rôlz), *Math.* the theorem that a differentiable function having equal values at the endpoints of an interval has a derivative equal to zero at some point in the interval. [1890–95; named after Michel *Rolle* (d. 1719), French mathematician]

CONCISE PRONUNCIATION KEY: act, cāpe, dâre, pärt; set, ēqual; if, īce; ox, ōver, ôrder, oil, bo͝ok, bo͞ot, out; up, ûrge; child; sing; shoe; thin, *th*at; zh as in *treasure.* ə = *a* as in *alone, e* as in *system, i* as in *easily, o* as in *gallop, u* as in *circus;* ᵊ as in *fire* (fīᵊr), *hour* (ouᵊr). l and n can serve as syllabic consonants, as in *cradle* (krād′l), and *button* (but′n). See the full key inside the front cover.

roll′ film′, *Photog.* a strip of film with space for several exposures, packaged on a spool in roll form so as to permit daylight loading and unloading and ease of handling. [1890–95]

rol•li•che (rol′i chē), *n. Hudson Valley.* roulade (def. 2). [1820–30, *Amer.*; < D *rolletje* little roll]

rol•lick (rol′ik), *v.i.* to move or act in a carefree, frolicsome manner; behave in a free, hearty, gay, or jovial way. [1820–30; b. ROMP and FROLIC] **—rol′lick•er,** *n.*

rol•lick•ing (rol′i king), *adj.* **1.** carefree and joyous: *They had a rollicking good time.* **2.** swaggering; boisterous. [1805–15; ROLLICK + -ING[2]] **—rol′lick•ing•ly,** *adv.* **—rol′lick•ing•ness,** *n.*
—Syn. 1. jolly, hearty, merry, gay, exuberant.

rol•lick•some (rol′ik səm), *adj.* rollicking; frolicsome. [1840–50; ROLLICK + -SOME[1]] **—rol′lick•some•ness,** *n.*

roll•ing (rō′ling), *n.* **1.** the action, motion, or sound of anything that rolls. *—adj.* **2.** moving by revolving or turning over and over. **3.** rising and falling in gentle slopes, as land. **4.** moving in undulating billows, as clouds or waves. **5.** rocking or swaying from side to side. **6.** turning or folding over, as a collar. **7.** producing a deep, continuous sound. [1400–50; late ME (ger.); see ROLL, -ING[1], -ING[2]] **—roll′ing•ly,** *adv.*

roll′ing-el′e•ment bear′ing (rō′ling el′ə mənt), *Mach.* a roller bearing or ball bearing. Also called **antifriction bearing, roll′ing-con′tact bear′ing** (rō′ling kon′takt). Cf. **plain bearing.**

roll′ing hitch′, a hitch on a spar or the like, composed of two round turns and a half hitch so disposed as to jam when a stress is applied parallel to the object on which the hitch is made. [1835–45]

roll′ing kitch′en, a mobile kitchen used for feeding troops outdoors.

Roll′ing Mead′ows, a city in NE Illinois, near Chicago. 20,167.

roll′ing mill′, **1.** a mill where ingots, slabs, sheets, etc., of usually hot metal are passed between rolls to give them a certain thickness or cross-sectional form. **2.** a machine or set of rollers for rolling out or shaping metal. [1780–90, *Amer.*]

roll′ing pa′per, cigarette paper available in small packages to smokers for rolling their own cigarettes. [1975–80, *Amer.*]

roll′ing pin′, a cylinder of wood or other material, usually with a short handle at each end, for rolling out dough. [1490–1500]

roll′ing stock′, the wheeled vehicles of a railroad, including locomotives, freight cars, and passenger cars. Also, **stock.** [1850–55]

Rol•lins (rol′inz), *n.* **Theodore Walter** (*"Sonny"*), born 1929, U.S. jazz saxophonist and composer.

roll′ joint′, (in sheet-metal work) a joint formed by rolling together and flattening the edges of adjoining sheets.

roll•mop (rōl′mop′), *n.* a fillet of herring, rolled, usually around a pickle, marinated in brine, and served as an appetizer. [1910–15; < G *Rollmops,* equiv. to *roll(en)* to ROLL + *Mops* pug (dog)]

Rol•lo (rol′ō), *n.* **1.** Also called **Rolf, Roy, Hrolf, Rolf the Ganger.** A.D. c860–931?, Norse chieftain: 1st duke of Normandy 911?. **2.** a male given name, form of **Rolf.**

rol•lock (rol′ək), *n.* rowlock.

roll-off (rōl′ôf′, -of′), *n.* **1.** *Electronics.* the rate of loss or attenuation of a signal beyond a certain frequency. **2.** *Aeron.* the tendency of an airplane to lower one wing under varying conditions of flight. [n. use of v. phrase *roll off*]

roll-on (rōl′on′, -ôn′), *adj.* **1.** packaged in a tubelike container one end of which is equipped with a rotating ball that dispenses and spreads the liquid content directly. *—n.* **2.** a roll-on preparation: *spray deodorants and roll-ons.* [1945–50; adj., n. use of v. phrase *roll on*]

roll•out (rōl′out′), *n.* **1.** the first public showing of an aircraft. **2.** *Informal.* the introduction or inauguration of a new product or service, as by an advertising campaign, public announcement, or exhibition: *the most lavish rollout in soft-drink history.* **3.** *Football.* an offensive maneuver in which the quarterback, having the option to run or pass, takes the ball from the center, moves back a distance toward his goal line, and then moves forward and toward a sideline. Also, **roll′-out′.** [1955–60; n. use of v. phrase *roll out*]

roll′-o•ver arm′ (rōl′ō′vər), an upholstered chair or sofa arm that curves outward and downward. [1920–25; adj. use of v. phrase *roll over*]

roll′over mort′gage. See **renegotiable-rate mortgage.**

roll′ top′, **1.** a flexible, sliding cover for the working area of a desk, opening by rising upward and back in quadrantal grooves and rolling up beneath the top. **2.** Also called **roll′-top desk′, roll′top desk′.** a desk with such a cover. [1885–90, *Amer.*]

roll-up (rōl′up′), *n.* **1.** Also, **roll′up′.** something, as a carpet or window shade, that can be rolled up when not in use. **2.** *Informal* an increase, as in value or cost. [1745–55; n. use of v. phrase *roll up*]

roll•way (rōl′wā′), *n.* **1.** a place on which things are rolled or moved on rollers. **2.** *Lumbering.* **a.** an incline for rolling or sliding logs into a stream to begin them on their journey from lumber camp to mill. **b.** a pile of logs in or at the side of a river or stream ready to go to the mill. [1850–55, *Amer.*; ROLL + WAY[1]]

CONCISE ETYMOLOGY KEY: <, descended or borrowed from; >, whence; b., blend of, blended; c., cognate with; cf., compare; deriv., derivative; equiv., equivalent; imit., imitative; obl., oblique; r., replacing; s., stem; sp., spelling, spelled; resp., respelling, respelled; trans., translation; ?, origin unknown; *, unattested; ‡, probably earlier than. See the full key inside the front cover.

roll-your-own (rōl′yər ōn′), *n.* a cigarette that one has rolled oneself. [1975–80]

Ro•lo•dex (rō′lə deks′), *Trademark.* a small desktop file containing cards for names, addresses, and phone numbers.

Röl•vaag (rōl′väg), *n.* **O•le Ed•vart** (ō′lə ed′värt), 1876–1931, U.S. novelist and educator, born in Norway.

ro•ly-po•ly (rō′lē pō′lē, -pō′lē), *adj., n., pl.* **-lies.** *—adj.* **1.** short and plumply round, as a person or a young animal. *—n.* **2.** a roly-poly person or thing. **3.** *Chiefly Brit.* a sheet of biscuit dough spread with jam, fruit, or the like, rolled up and steamed or baked. [1595–1605; earlier *rowle powle, rowly-powly* worthless fellow, game involving rolling balls, rhyming compound based on ROLL (v.); for second element cf. POLL[1]]
—Syn. 1. fat, rotund, pudgy. **—Ant. 1.** scrawny.

Rom (rōm), *n.* a Gypsy man or boy. [1835–45; < Romany: a married man; cf. Skt *ḍomba, ḍoma* a low-caste minstrel]

ROM (rom), *n.* computer memory in which program instructions, operating procedures, or other data are permanently stored, generally on electronic chips during manufacture, and that ordinarily cannot be changed by the user. Cf. **PROM, RAM.** [*r(ead)-o(nly) m(emory)*]

Rom., **1.** Roman. **2.** Romance. **3.** Romania. **4.** Romanian. **5.** Romanic. **6.** Romans (New Testament). Also, **Rom** (for defs. 2, 5).

rom., roman (printing type).

Ro•ma (rô′mä), *n.* Rome.

Ro•ma•gna (rō män′yə; *It.* rô mä′nyä), *n.* a former province of the Papal States, in NE Italy. *Cap.:* Ravenna.

Ro•ma•ic (rō mā′ik), *n.* **1.** demotic (def. 5). *—adj.* **2.** of or pertaining to modern Greece, its inhabitants, or their language. [1800–10; < Gk *Rhōmaïkós* Roman, equiv. to *Rhōma(íos)* Roman + *-ikos* -IC]

ro•maine (rō mān′, rə-), *n.* Also called **romaine′ let′tuce, cos, cos lettuce.** a variety of lettuce, *Lactuca sativa longifolia,* having a cylindrical head of long, relatively loose leaves. [1905–10; < F, fem. of *romain* ROMAN]

Ro•mains (rô maɴ′), *n.* **Jules** (zhyl), (*Louis Farigoule*), 1885–1972, French novelist, poet, and dramatist.

ro•ma•ji (rō′mə jē), *n.* (*sometimes cap.*) a system of writing Japanese using the letters of the Latin alphabet. [1885–90; < Japn *roma* Roman + *ji* character]

ro•man (rô mäɴ′), *n., pl.* **-mans** (-mäɴ′). *French.* **1.** a metrical narrative, esp. in medieval French literature. **2.** a novel.

Ro•man (rō′mən), *adj.* **1.** of or pertaining to the ancient or modern city of Rome, or to its inhabitants and their customs and culture: *Roman restaurants.* **2.** of or pertaining to the ancient kingdom, republic, and empire whose capital was the city of Rome. **3.** of a kind or character regarded as typical of the ancient Romans: *Roman virtues.* **4.** (*usually l.c.*) designating or pertaining to the upright style of printing types most commonly used in modern books, periodicals, etc., of which the main text of this dictionary is an example. **5.** of or pertaining to the Roman Catholic Church. **6.** noting, pertaining to, or resembling the architecture of ancient Rome, esp. the public and religious architecture, characterized by the employment of massive brick and concrete construction, with such features as the semicircular arch, the dome, and groin and barrel vaults, by the use in interiors of marble and molded stucco revetments, by the elaboration of the Greek orders as purely decorative motifs for the adornment of façades and interiors, and by an overall effect in which simplicity and grandeur of massing is often combined with much elaboration of detailing. **7.** written in or pertaining to Roman numerals. *—n.* **8.** a native, inhabitant, or citizen of ancient or modern Rome. **9.** the dialect of Italian spoken in Rome. **10.** (*usually l.c.*) roman type or lettering. **11.** *Often Offensive.* a member of the Roman Catholic Church. **12.** *Rare.* the Latin language. **13.** a male given name. [bef. 900; < L *Rōmānus* (see ROME, -AN); r. ME *Romain* < OF < L, as above; r. OE *Roman(e)* < L, as above]

ro•man à clef (rô mä na kle′), *pl.* ***ro•mans à clef*** (rô mäɴ za kle′). *French.* a novel that represents historical events and characters under the guise of fiction.

Ro′man al′phabet. See **Latin alphabet.** [1875–80]

Ro′man arch′, a semicircular arch.

Ro′man brick′, a long, thin face brick, usually yellow-brown and having a length about eight times its thickness.

Ro′man cal′endar, the calendar in use in ancient Rome until 46 B.C., when it was replaced with the Julian calendar. Cf. **Year of Confusion.** [1780–90]

Ro′man can′dle, a firework consisting of a tube that sends out a shower of sparks and a succession of balls of fire. [1825–35]

Ro′man Cath′olic, **1.** of or pertaining to the Roman Catholic Church. **2.** a member of the Roman Catholic Church. Cf. **Catholic.** [1595–1605]

Ro′man Cath′olic Church′, the Christian church of which the pope, or bishop of Rome, is the supreme head. Cf. **Catholic Church.**

Ro′man Cathol′icism, the faith, practice, and system of government of the Roman Catholic Church. [1815–25]

ro•mance[1] (*n., adj.* rō mans′, rō′mans; *v.* rō mans′), *n., v.,* **-manced, -manc•ing,** *adj.* *—n.* **1.** a novel or other prose narrative depicting heroic or marvelous deeds, pageantry, romantic exploits, etc., usually in a historical or imaginary setting. **2.** the colorful world, life, or conditions depicted in such tales. **3.** a medieval narrative, originally one in verse and in some Romance dialect, treating of heroic, fantastic, or supernatural events, often in the form of allegory. **4.** a baseless, made-up story, usually full of exaggeration or fanciful invention. **5.** a romantic spirit, sentiment, emotion, or desire. **6.** romantic character or quality. **7.** a romantic affair or experience; a love affair. **8.** (*cap.*) Also, **Romanic.** Also called **Romance languages.** the group of Italic Indo-European languages descended since A.D. 800 from Latin, as French, Spanish, Italian, Portuguese, Rumanian, Provençal, Catalan, Rhaeto-Romanic, Sardinian, and Ladino. *Abbr.:* Rom. *—v.i.* **9.** to invent or relate romances; indulge in fanciful or extravagant stories or daydreams. **10.** to think or talk romantically. *—v.t.* **11.** *Informal.* **a.** to court or woo romantically; treat with ardor or chivalrousness: *He's currently romancing a very attractive widow.* **b.** to court the favor of or make overtures to; play up to: *They need to romance the local business community if they expect to do business here.* *—adj.* **12.** (*cap.*) Also, **Romanic.** of, pertaining to, or noting Romance: *a Romance language.* [1250–1300; ME *romaunce* Romanic language, composition in such a language < OF, deriv. of *romanz, romans* (adj.) Romanic < VL **Rōmānicē* (adv.) in a Romance language, deriv. of L *Rōmānicus* ROMANIC] **—ro•manc′er,** *n.*
—Syn. 1. story, fiction. **4.** falsehood, fable. **6.** allure, fascination, exoticism.

ro•mance[2] (rō mans′), *n.* **1.** *Music.* a short, simple melody, vocal or instrumental, of tender character. **2.** *Sp. Lit.* a short epic poem, esp. a historical ballad. [1595–1605; < F < Sp: kind of poem, ballad < OF *romanz* ROMANCE[1]]

Ro′mance lan′guages, romance[1] (def. 8). [1770–80]

Ro′man col′lar. See **clerical collar.** [1895–1900]

Ro′man Cu′ria, **1.** the judicial and executive organizations of the papal see comprising the government of the Catholic Church. **2.** the court of the papal see.

Ro′man Em′pire, **1.** the lands and peoples subject to the authority of ancient Rome. **2.** the form of government established in ancient Rome in 27 B.C., comprising the Principate or Early Empire (27 B.C.–A.D. 284) and the Autocracy or Later Empire (A.D. 284–476). **3.** a later empire, as that of Charlemagne or the Byzantine Empire, regarded as a restoration or continuation of the ancient Roman Empire or one of its branches. Cf. **Holy Roman Empire.**

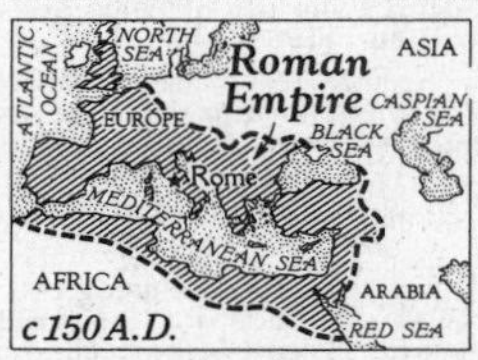

c150 A.D.

Ro•man•esque (rō′mə nesk′), *adj.* **1.** noting or pertaining to the style of architecture prevailing in western or southern Europe from the 9th through the 12th centuries, characterized by heavy masonry construction with narrow openings, features such as the round arch, the groin vault, and the barrel vault, and the introduction or development of the vaulting rib, the vaulting shaft, and central and western towers for churches. **2.** pertaining to or designating the styles of sculpture, painting, or ornamentation of the corresponding period. **3.** (*l.c.*) of or pertaining to fanciful or extravagant literature, as romance or fable; fanciful. *—n.* **4.** the Romanesque style of art or architecture. [1705–15; ROMAN + -ESQUE; cf. F *romanesque* romantic]

ro•man-fleuve (rô mäɴ flœv′), *n., pl.* ***ro•mans-fleuves*** (rô mäɴ flœv′). *French.* saga (def. 3).

Ro′man hol′iday, **1.** a public spectacle or controversy marked by barbarism, vindictiveness, or scandal. **2.** pleasure or advantage gained from the discomfort or suffering of others. [1885–90]

Rom•a•ni (rom′ə nē, rō′mə-), *n.* Romany.

Ro•ma•ni•a (rō mā′nē ə, -mān′yə), *n.* Rumania. **—Ro•ma′ni•an,** *n., adj.*

Ro•mâ•nia (rô mu′nyä; *Eng.* rō mā′nē ə, -mān′yə), *n.* Rumanian name of **Rumania.**

Ro•man•ic (rō man′ik), *adj.* **1.** derived from the Romans. **2.** romance[1] (def. 12). *—n.* **3.** romance[1] (def. 8). [1700–10; < L *Rōmānicus* Roman, equiv. to *Rōmān(us)* ROMAN + *-icus* -IC]

Ro•man•ism (rō′mə niz′əm), *n. Often Disparaging and Offensive.* See **Roman Catholicism.** [1665–75; ROMAN + -ISM]

Ro•man•ist (rō′mə nist), *n.* **1.** *Often Disparaging and Offensive.* a member of the Roman Catholic Church. **2.** one versed in Roman institutions, law, etc. **3.** Also, **Ro•man•i•cist** (rō man′ə sist). a person versed in Romance languages, literature, or linguistics. **4. Romanists,** *Fine Arts.* a group of Flemish and Dutch painters of the 16th century who traveled to Italy and returned to Flanders and Holland with the style and techniques of the High Renaissance and of Mannerism. [1515–25; < NL *Romanista.* See ROMAN, -IST] **—Ro′man•is′tic,** *adj.*

Ro•man•ize (rō′mə nīz′), *v.,* **-ized, -iz•ing.** *—v.t.* **1.** to make Roman Catholic. **2.** (*often l.c.*) to make Roman in character. **3.** (*often l.c.*) to render in the Latin alphabet, esp. a language traditionally written in a different system, as Chinese or Japanese. *—v.i.* **4.** to conform to Roman Catholic doctrine and practices; to become Roman Catholic. **5.** (*often l.c.*) to follow Roman practices. Also, *esp. Brit.,* **Ro′man•ise′.** [1600–10; ROMAN + -IZE] **—Ro′man•i•za′tion,** *n.* **—Ro′man•iz′er,** *n.*

Ro′man law′, the system of jurisprudence elaborated by the ancient Romans, a strong and varied influence on the legal systems of many countries. [1650–60]

Ro′man lit′urgy. See **Latin rite** (def. 1).

Ro′man mile′, a unit of length used by the ancient Romans, equivalent to about 1620 yards (1480 m). [1770–80]

Ro′man nose′, a nose having a prominent upper part or bridge. [1615–25] **—Ro′man-nosed′,** *adj.*

Ro′man nu′merals, the numerals in the ancient Roman system of notation, still used for certain limited purposes, as in some pagination, dates on buildings, etc. The common basic symbols are **I**(=1), **V**(=5), **X**(=10), **L**(=50), **C**(=100), **D**(=500), and **M**(=1000). The Roman numerals for one to nine are: I, II, III, IV, V, VI, VII, VIII, IX. A bar over a letter multiplies it by 1000; thus, $\overline{X}$ equals 10,000. Integers are written according to these two rules: If a letter is immediately followed by one of equal or lesser value, the two values are added; thus, XX equals 20, XV equals 15, VI equals 6. If a letter is immediately followed by one of greater value, the first is subtracted from the second; thus, IV equals 4, XL equals 40, CM equals 900. Examples: XLVII(=47), CXVI(=116), MCXX(=1120), MCMXIV(=1914). Roman numerals may be written in lowercase letters, though they appear more commonly in capitals. [1725–35]

ROMAN NUMERALS

Arabic Numeral	Roman Numeral	Arabic Numeral	Roman Numeral
1	I	29	XXIX
2	II	30	XXX
3	III	31	XXXI
4	IV	32	XXXII
5	V	40	XL
6	VI	41	XLI
7	VII	50	L
8	VIII	60	LX
9	IX	70	LXX
10	X	80	LXXX
11	XI	90	XC
12	XII	100	C
13	XIII	101	CI
14	XIV	102	CII
15	XV	200	CC
16	XVI	300	CCC
17	XVII	400	CD
18	XVIII	500	D
19	XIX	600	DC
20	XX	700	DCC
21	XXI	800	DCCC
22	XXII	900	CM
23	XXIII	1,000	M
24	XXIV	2,000	MM
25	XXV	5,000	$\overline{V}$
26	XXVI	10,000	$\overline{X}$
27	XXVII	100,000	$\overline{C}$
28	XXVIII	1,000,000	$\overline{M}$

Ro•ma•no (rō mä′nō), *n.* (*sometimes l.c.*) a hard, light-colored, sharp, Italian cheese, usually made of ewe's milk. Also called **Roma′no cheese′.** [1905–10; < It: Roman]

Ro•ma•nov (rō′mə nôf′, -nof′, rō mä′nəf; *Russ.* RU-mä′nəf), *n.* **1.** a member of the imperial dynasty of Russia that ruled from 1613 to 1917. **2. Mi•kha•il Feo•do•ro•vich** (myi KHU yēl′ fyô′də rə vyich), 1596–1645, emperor of Russia 1613–45: first ruler of the house of Romanov. Also, **Ro′ma•noff′.**

Ro′man pace′, an ancient Roman unit of measurement, equal to 5 Roman feet or about 58 U.S. inches (147 cm).

Ro′man peace′, the establishment and maintenance of peace by armed force. [trans. of L *pāx Rōmāna*]

Ro′man punch′, *Brit.* a lemon-water ice flavored with rum or other alcoholic beverage. [1820–30]

Ro′man ride′, a method of horseback riding in which a person stands astride a pair of horses.

Ro′man rite′. See **Latin rite** (def. 1).

Ro•mans (rō′mənz), *n.* (*used with a singular v.*) an Epistle of the New Testament, written by Paul to the Christian community in Rome. *Abbr.:* Rom.

Ro•mansh (rō mansh′, -mänsh′), *n.* **1.** a group of three Rhaeto-Romanic dialects spoken in E Switzerland. Cf. **Ladin** (def. 2). —*adj.* **2.** of or pertaining to Romansh.

Ro′man shade′, a window shade that, when raised, is drawn up into a series of concertina folds.

Ro′man strike′, *Horol.* a striking mechanism of c1700, giving the equivalent in tones of Roman numerals, a bell of one pitch striking once for each number I, a bell of another pitch striking once for V, twice for X.

ro•man•tic (rō man′tik), *adj.* **1.** of, pertaining to, or of the nature of romance; characteristic or suggestive of the world of romance: *a romantic adventure.* **2.** fanciful; impractical; unrealistic: *romantic ideas.* **3.** imbued with or dominated by idealism, a desire for adventure, chivalry, etc. **4.** characterized by a preoccupation with love or by the idealizing of love or one's beloved. **5.** displaying or expressing love or strong affection. **6.** ardent; passionate; fervent. **7.** (*usually cap.*) of, pertaining to, or characteristic of a style of literature and art that subordinates form to content, encourages freedom of treatment, emphasizes imagination, emotion, and introspection, and often celebrates nature, the ordinary person, and freedom of the spirit (contrasted with *classical*). **8.** of or pertaining to a musical style characteristic chiefly of the 19th century and marked by the free expression of imagination and emotion, virtuosic display, experimentation with form, and the adventurous development of orchestral and piano music and opera. **9.** imaginary, fictitious, or fabulous. **10.** noting, of, or pertaining to the role of a suitor or lover in a play about love: *the romantic lead.* —*n.* **11.** a romantic person. **12.** a romanticist. **13. romantics,** romantic ideas, ways, etc. [1650–60; < F *romantique,* deriv. of *romant* ROMAUNT; see -IC] —**ro•man′ti•cal•ly,** *adv.* —**ro•man′ti•cal•ness,** *n.*
—**Syn. 2.** extravagant, exaggerated, wild, imaginative, fantastic. **9.** improbable, unreal. —**Ant. 2.** practical, realistic. **9.** probable.

ro•man•ti•cism (rō man′tə siz′əm), *n.* **1.** romantic spirit or tendency. **2.** (*usually cap.*) the Romantic style or movement in literature and art, or adherence to its principles (contrasted with *classicism*). [1795–1805; ROMANTIC + -ISM]

ro•man•ti•cist (rō man′tə sist), *n.* an adherent of romanticism in literature or art (contrasted with *classicist*). [1820–30; ROMANTIC + -IST] —**ro•man′ti•cis′tic,** *adj.*

ro•man•ti•cize (rō man′tə sīz′), *v.,* **-cized, -ciz•ing.** —*v.t.* **1.** to make romantic; invest with a romantic character: *Many people romanticize the role of an editor.* —*v.i.* **2.** to hold romantic notions, ideas, etc. Also, *esp. Brit.,* **ro•man′ti•cise′.** [1810–20; ROMANTIC + -IZE] —**ro•man′ti•ci•za′tion,** *n.*

Roman′tic Move′ment, the late 18th- and early 19th-century movement in France, Germany, England, and America to establish Romanticism in art and literature. [1875–80]

Ro•ma•nus (rō mā′nəs), *n.* died A.D. 897, Italian ecclesiastic: pope 897.

Rom•a•ny (rom′ə nē, rō′mə-), *n., pl.* **-nies,** *adj.* —*n.* **1.** Gypsy (def. 2). **2.** Gypsies collectively. **3.** the Indic language of the Gypsies, its various forms differing greatly because of local influences. —*adj.* **4.** pertaining to Gypsies, their language, or their customs. Also, **Rommany, Romani.**

ro•maunt (rō mänt′, -mônt′), *n. Archaic.* a romantic tale or poem; romance. [1520–30; < AF, var. of OF *romant* ROMANCE[1]]

Rom•berg (rom′bûrg), *n.* **Sig•mund** (sig′mənd), 1887–1951, Hungarian composer of light opera, in the U.S. after 1913.

Rom. Cath., Roman Catholic.

Rom. Cath. Ch., Roman Catholic Church.

Rome (rōm), *n.* **1. Harold (Jacob),** born 1908, U.S. lyricist and composer. **2.** Italian, **Roma.** a city in and the capital of Italy, in the central part, on the Tiber: ancient capital of the Roman Empire; site of Vatican City, seat of authority of the Roman Catholic Church. 2,600,000. **3.** a city in central New York, E of Oneida Lake. 43,826. **4.** a city in NW Georgia. 29,654. **5.** the ancient Italian kingdom, republic, and empire whose capital was the city of Rome. **6.** the Roman Catholic Church. **7.** See **Roman Catholicism.**

Rome′ Beau′ty, a large, red variety of apple, used chiefly for baking.

Ro•me•o (rō′mē ō′), *n.* **1.** the romantic lover of Juliet in Shakespeare's *Romeo and Juliet.* **2.** any man who is preoccupied with or has a reputation for amatory success with women. **3.** a lover: *She found her Romeo at a charity ball.* **4.** (used in communications to represent the letter *R.*) **5.** a male given name.

Ro′meo and Ju′liet, a tragedy (produced between 1591 and 1596) by Shakespeare.

Ro•me•o•ville (rō′mē ō vil′), *n.* a town in NE Illinois. 15,519.

Rome•ward (rōm′wərd), *adv.* to or toward Rome or the Roman Catholic Church. [1300–50; ME; see ROME, -WARD]

Rom•ish (rō′mish), *adj. Often Disparaging and Offensive.* of or pertaining to Rome as the center of the Roman Catholic Church. [1525–35; ROME + -ISH[1]] —**Rom′ish•ly,** *adv.* —**Rom′ish•ness,** *n.*

Rom•ma•ny (rom′ə nē), *n., pl.* **-nies,** *adj.* Romany.

Rom•mel (rom′əl, rum′-; *Ger.* RÔM′əl), *n.* **Er•win** (ûr′-win; *Ger.* ER′vēn), (*"the Desert Fox"*), 1891–1944, German field marshal: commander of the German forces in North Africa in World War II.

Rom•ney (rom′nē, rum′-), *n.* **1. George,** 1734–1802, English painter. **2. George,** born 1907, U.S. businessman and politician: governor of Michigan 1963–69. **3.** former name of **New Romney. 4.** a male given name.

Rom•ney (rom′nē, rum′-), *n.* one of an English breed of hardy sheep, having coarse, long wool. Also called **Rom′ney Marsh′.** [named after a district in southwestern England]

romp (romp), *v.i.* **1.** to play or frolic in a lively or boisterous manner. **2.** to run or go rapidly and without effort, as in racing. **3.** to win easily. —*n.* **4.** a lively or boisterous frolic. **5.** a person who romps. **6.** a quick or effortless pace: *The work was easy, and he went through it in a romp.* **7.** an effortless victory. [1700–10; perh. var. of RAMP[1] (v.); cf. obs. *ramp* rough woman, lit., one who ramps] —**romp′ing•ly,** *adv.*
—**Syn. 1, 4.** gambol.

romp•er (rom′pər), *n.* **1.** a person or thing that romps. **2.** Usually, **rompers.** (*used with a plural v.*) **a.** a loose, one-piece garment combining a shirt or blouse and short, bloomerlike pants, worn by young children. **b.** a similar garment worn by women and girls for sports, leisure activity, etc. [1835–40; ROMP + -ER[1]]

romp′er room′, a playroom for very young children.

romp•ish (rom′pish), *adj.* given to romping; frolicsome. [1700–10; ROMP + -ISH[1]] —**romp′ish•ly,** *adv.* —**romp′ish•ness,** *n.*

Ro•mu•lo (rom′yŏŏ lō′; *Sp.* RÔ′mōō lô′), *n.* **Car•los Pe•na** (kär′lôs pe′nä), 1901–85, Philippine diplomat, journalist, and educator.

Rom•u•lus (rom′yə ləs), *n. Rom. Legend.* **1.** the founder of Rome, in 753 B.C., and its first king: a son of Mars and Rhea Silvia, he and his twin brother **(Remus)** were abandoned as babies, suckled by a she-wolf, and brought up by a shepherd; Remus was finally killed for mocking the fortifications of Rome, which Romulus had just founded. **2.** a town in S Michigan. 24,857.

Ro•mus (rō′məs), *n. Rom. Legend.* a son of either Aeneas or Ascanius: sometimes believed to be the founder of Rome.

RONA, *Accounting.* return on net assets.

Ron•ald (ron′ld), *n.* a male given name: from Scandinavian words meaning "counsel" and "rule."

Ro•nan (rō′nän), *n. Irish Legend.* a king who killed his son, Mael Fothartaigh, after his wife had falsely accused the boy of attempting to seduce her, and who was himself killed by the children of Mael Fothartaigh.

Ron•ces•valles (ron′sə valz′; *Sp.* rôn′thes vä′lyes), *n.* a village in N Spain, in the Pyrenees: defeat of part of Charlemagne's army and the death of Roland A.D. 788. French, **Ronce•vaux** (RÔNS vō′).

ron•co (rong′kō), *n., pl.* **-cos.** any grunt of the genus *Haemulon,* esp. *H. parrai,* the sailor's-choice, of West Indian waters. [1880–85, *Amer.*; < Sp, deriv. of *roncar* to grunt << LGk *rhonchós* a grunt, snore]

rond de jambe (*Fr.* RÔN də zhäNb′), *n., pl.* **ronds de jambe** (*Fr.* RÔN də zhäNb′). *Ballet.* a circular movement of the leg. [1820–30; < F; see ROUND[1], JAMB[1]]

ronde (rond), *n. Print.* a typeface imitative of upright, somewhat angular, handwriting. [1830–40; < F, n. use of fem. of *rond* ROUND[1]]

ron•deau (ron′dō, ron dō′), *n., pl.* **-deaux** (-dōz, -dōz′). **1.** *Pros.* a short poem of fixed form, consisting of 13 or 10 lines on two rhymes and having the opening words or phrase used in two places as an unrhymed refrain. **2.** a 13th-century monophonic song form consisting of two phrases, each repeated several times, and occurring in the 14th and 15th centuries in polyphonic settings. **3.** a 17th-century musical form consisting of a refrain alternating with contrasting couplets, developing in the 18th century into the sonata-rondo form. [1515–25; < MF: little circle; see RONDEL]

ron•del (ron′dl, ron del′), *n.* **1.** *Pros.* a short poem of fixed form, consisting usually of 14 lines on two rhymes, of which four are made up of the initial couplet repeated in the middle and at the end, with the second line of the couplet sometimes being omitted at the end. **2.** *Theat.* roundel (def. 4). [1250–1300; ME < OF *rondel,* dim. of *rond* ROUND[1]]

ron•de•let (ron′dl et′, ron′dl et′), *n.* a short poem of fixed form, consisting of five lines on two rhymes, and having the opening words or word used after the second and fifth lines as an unrhymed refrain. [1565–75; < MF, dim. of *rondel* RONDEL; see -ET]

ron•delle (ron del′), *n.* **1.** a small disk of glass used as an ornament in a stained-glass window. **2.** *Jewelry.* a flat bead, often of rock crystal or onyx, used in a necklace as a spacer between contrasting stones. [1830–40; < F; see RONDEL]

ron•do (ron′dō, ron dō′), *n., pl.* **-dos.** *Music.* a work or movement, often the last movement of a sonata, having one principal subject that is stated at least three times in the same key and to which return is made after the introduction of each subordinate theme. [1790–1800; < It < F *rondeau;* see RONDEL]

Ron•dô•nia (RÔN dô′nyä), *n.* a state in W Brazil. 688,000; 93,815 sq. mi. (242,980 sq. km). *Cap.:* Pôrto Velho. Formerly, **Guaporé.**

ron•dure (ron′jər), *n.* **1.** a circle or sphere. **2.** a graceful curving or roundness. [1590–1600; < F *rondeur,* deriv. of *rond* ROUND[1]]

ron•geur (rôn zhûr′; *Fr.* RÔN ZHŒR′), *n., pl.* **-geurs** (-zhûrz′; *Fr.* -ZHŒR′). *Surg.* a strongly constructed instrument with a sharp-edged, scoop-shaped tip, used for gouging out bone. [1880–85; < F: lit., gnawer]

ron•ion (run′yən), *n. Obs.* ronyon.

Rön•ne (*Dan.* RŒN′ə), *n.* a seaport on W Bornholm island, Denmark, in the S Baltic Sea: stone quarries. 12,440.

Ron′ne Ice′ Shelf′ (rō′nə), an ice barrier in Antarctica, in SW Weddell Sea, bordered by Ellsworth Land on the NW and Berkner Island on the E. [named after Finn *Ronne,* 1899–1980, U.S. explorer]

Ron•nie (ron′ē), *n.* a male or female given name, form of **Ronald** or **Veronica.** Also, **Ron′ni, Ron′ny.**

ron•quil (rong′kil), *n.* any of several percoid fishes of the family Bathymasteridae, ranging along the Pacific coast of North America. [1880–85, *Amer.*; < AmerSp *ronquillo,* dim. of *ronco* RONCO]

Ron•sard (RÔN SAR′), *n.* **Pierre de** (pyeR də), 1524–85, French poet.

Rönt•gen (rent′gən, -jən, runt′-; *Ger.* RŒNT′gən; *Du.* RÔŌNT′KHƏN), *n.* **1. Ju•li•us** (yōō′lē əs), 1855–1932, Dutch pianist, conductor, and composer; born in Germany. **2. Wil•helm Kon•rad** (wil′helm kon′rad; *Ger.* vil′helm kôn′rät). See **Roentgen, Wilhelm Konrad.**

röntgeno-, var. of **roentgeno-:** *röntgenoscope.*

ron•yon (run′yən), *n. Obs.* a mangy creature. Also, **ronion.** [1590–1600; perh. < F *rogne* mange]

'roo (rōō), *n., pl.* **'roos.** *Australian Informal.* kangaroo. [by shortening]

rood (rōōd), *n.* **1.** a crucifix, esp. a large one at the entrance to the choir or chancel of a medieval church, often supported on a rood beam or rood screen. **2.** a cross as used in crucifixion. **3.** a unit of length varying locally from 5½ to 8 yards (5 to 7 m). **4.** a unit of land measure equal to 40 square rods or ¼ acre (0.10117 hectare). **5.** a unit of 1 square rod (25.29 sq. m). **6.** *Archaic.* the cross on which Christ died. [bef. 900; ME; OE *rōd* pole, crucifix; c. G *Rute* rod, twig]

rood′ arch′, **1.** an archway at the center of a rood screen. **2.** the archway between a nave and a chancel. [1840–50]

Roo•de•poort-Ma•rais•burg (rōō′də pōōrt′mä rā′-

CONCISE PRONUNCIATION KEY: *act, cāpe, dâre, pärt; set, ēqual; if, īce; ox, ōver, ôrder, oil, bŏŏk, bōōt, out; up, ûrge; child; sing; shoe; thin, that;* zh as in *treasure.* ə = *a* as in *alone, e* as in *system, i* as in *easily, o* as in *gallop, u* as in *circus;* ᵊ as in *fire* (fīᵊr), *hour* (ouᵊr). l and n can serve as syllabic consonants, as in *cradle* (krād′l), and *button* (but′n). See the full key inside the front cover.

bûrg), *n.* a city in S Transvaal, in the NE Republic of South Africa. 139,810.

rood′ screen′, a screen, often of elaborate design and properly surmounted by a rood, separating the nave from the choir or chancel of a church. [1835–45]

rood′ spire′, a spire over the crossing of a church. Also called **rood′ stee′ple.**

roof (ro͞of, ro͝of), *n., pl.* **roofs,** *v.* —*n.* **1.** the external upper covering of a house or other building. **2.** a frame for supporting this: *an open-timbered roof.* **3.** the highest part or summit: *The Himalayas are the roof of the world.* **4.** something that in form or position resembles the roof of a house, as the top of a car, the upper part of the mouth, etc. **5.** a house. **6.** *Mining.* the rock immediately above a horizontal mineral deposit. **7. go through the roof, a.** to increase beyond all expectations: *Foreign travel may very well go through the roof next year.* **b.** Also, **hit the roof.** *Informal.* to lose one's temper; become extremely angry. **8. raise the roof,** *Informal.* **a.** to create a loud noise: *The applause raised the roof.* **b.** to complain or protest noisily: *He'll raise the roof when he sees that bill.* —*v.t.* **9.** to provide or cover with a roof. [bef. 900; ME (n.); OE *hrōf;* c. D *roef* cover, cabin, ON *hrōf*] —**roof′like′,** *adj.*

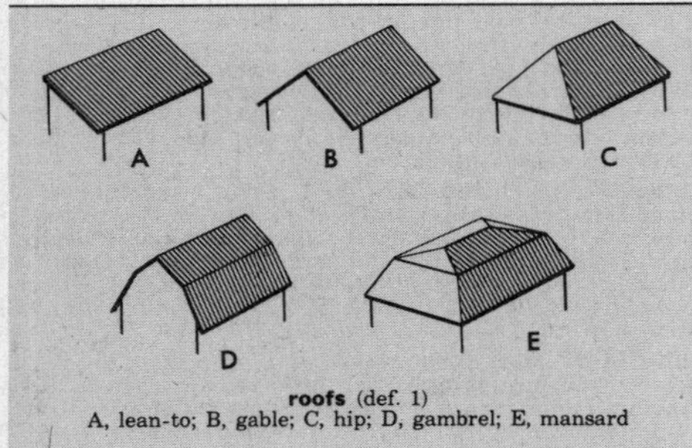

roofs (def. 1)
A, lean-to; B, gable; C, hip; D, gambrel; E, mansard

roof-deck (ro͞of′dek′, ro͝of′-), *n.* a part of a flat roof used for gardening, sunbathing, etc. [1945–50]

roof•er (ro͞o′fər, ro͝of′ər), *n.* a person who makes or repairs roofs. [1840–50; ROOF + -ER[1]]

roof′ gar′den, 1. a garden on the flat roof of a house or other building. **2.** the top or top story of a building, having a garden, restaurant, or the like. [1890–95, *Amer.*]

roof′ guard′. See **snow guard.**

roof•ing (ro͞o′fing, ro͝of′ing), *n.* **1.** the act of covering with a roof. **2.** material for roofs. **3.** a roof. [1400–50; late ME *rovyng.* See ROOF, -ING[1]]

roof′ing nail′, a short nail for nailing asphalt shingles or the like, having a broad head. See illus. under **nail.** [1300–50; ME]

roof′ i′ris, an iris, *Iris tectorum,* of China and Japan, having frilled, violet or white flowers.

roof•less (ro͞of′lis, ro͝of′-), *adj.* **1.** having no roof. **2.** without the shelter of a house: *roofless refugees.* [1600–10; ROOF + -LESS]

roof•line (ro͞of′līn′, ro͝of′-), *n.* the outline of a rooftop. [1855–60; ROOF + LINE[1]]

roof′ prism′, *Optics.* See **Amici prism.**

roof′ rat′, a black rat, *Rattus rattus alexandrinus,* often found on the upper floors of buildings in warm areas. [1810–20]

roof•top (ro͞of′top′, ro͝of′-), *n.* the roof of a building, esp. the outer surface. [1605–15; ROOF + TOP[1]]

roof•tree (ro͞of′trē′, ro͝of′-), *n.* **1.** the ridgepole of a roof. **2.** the roof itself. [1400–50; late ME; see ROOF, TREE]

roo•i•nek (ro͞o′ē nek′), *n. South African.* Briton; Britisher. [1885–90; < Afrik, equiv. to *rooi* red + *nek* neck]

rook[1] (ro͝ok), *n.* **1.** a black, European crow, *Corvus frugilegus,* noted for its gregarious habits. **2.** a sharper at cards or dice; swindler. —*v.t.* **3.** to cheat; fleece; swindle. [bef. 900; ME *rok*(*e*), OE *hrōc;* c. ON *hrōkr,* OHG *hruoh*]

rook[2] (ro͝ok), *n. Chess.* one of two pieces of the same color that may be moved any number of unobstructed squares horizontally or vertically; castle. [1300–50; ME *rok* < OF *roc* < Ar *rukhkh* < Pers *rukh*]

rook•er•y (ro͝ok′ə rē), *n., pl.* **-er•ies. 1.** a breeding place or colony of gregarious birds or animals, as penguins and seals. **2.** a colony of rooks. **3.** a place where rooks congregate to breed. **4.** a crowded tenement house. [1715–25; ROOK[1] + -ERY]

rook•ie (ro͝ok′ē), *n.* **1.** an athlete playing his or her first season as a member of a professional sports team: *The rookie replaced the injured regular at first base.* **2.** a raw recruit, as in the army or on a police force. **3.** a novice; tyro. [1890–95; alter. of RECRUIT; see -Y[2]]

rook•y (ro͝ok′ē), *adj.,* **rook•i•er, rook•i•est.** full of or frequented by rooks. [1595–1605; ROOK[1] + -Y[1]]

room (ro͞om, ro͝om), *n.* **1.** a portion of space within a building or other structure, separated by walls or partitions from other parts: *a dining room.* **2. rooms,** lodgings or quarters, as in a house or building. **3.** the persons present in a room: *The whole room laughed.* **4.** space or extent of space occupied by or available for something: *The desk takes up too much room.* **5.** opportunity or scope for something: *room for improvement; room for doubt.* **6.** status or a station in life considered as a place: *He fought for room at the top.* **7.** capacity: *Her brain had no room for trivia.* **8.** *Mining.* a working area cut between pillars. —*v.i.* **9.** to occupy a room or rooms; lodge. [bef. 900; ME *roum*(*e*), OE *rūm;* c. D *ruim,* G *Raum*]
—**Syn. 5.** provision, margin, allowance.

room′ and board′, lodging and meals. [1950–55]

room-and-pil•lar (ro͞om′ən pil′ər, ro͝om′-), *adj. Mining.* noting a means of extracting coal or other minerals from underground deposits by first cutting out rooms, then robbing the pillars between them; pillar-and-breast. Cf. **longwall.**

room′ clerk′, a clerk at a hotel who assigns rooms to guests, keeps the guest register, sorts the incoming mail, etc. [1915–20]

room′ divid′er, a partition, as a screen or freestanding bookcase, that separates one part of a room from another.

room•er (ro͞o′mər, ro͝om′ər), *n.* a person who lives in a rented room; lodger. [1870–75, *Amer.;* ROOM + -ER[1]]

room•ette (ro͞o met′, ro͝o-), *n.* **1.** a small private compartment in the sleeping car of a train, usually for one person, containing its own washroom facilities and a bed that folds against the wall when not in use. **2.** any small room, esp. one used solely for study or sleeping. **3.** a private room connected to a box at a sports stadium or arena and used for entertaining guests. [1935–40; ROOM + -ETTE]

room′ fa′ther, a male volunteer, often the father of a student, who assists an elementary-school teacher, as by working with students who need extra help.

room•ful (ro͞om′fo͝ol, ro͝om′-), *n., pl.* **-fuls.** an amount or number sufficient to fill a room. [1700–10; ROOM + -FUL]
—**Usage.** See **-ful.**

room•ie (ro͞o′mē, ro͝om′ē), *n. Informal.* roommate. Also, **roomy.** [1915–20, *Amer.;* by shortening and alter.]

room′ing house′, a house with furnished rooms to rent; lodging house. [1890–95, *Amer.*]

room•ing-in (ro͞o′ming in′, ro͝om′ing-), *n.* an arrangement in some hospitals that enables postpartum mothers to keep their babies with them in their rooms rather than in a separate nursery. [1940–45]

room•mate (ro͞om′māt′, ro͝om′-), *n.* a person who is assigned to share or shares a room or apartment with another or others. [1780–90, *Amer.;* ROOM + MATE[1]]

room′ moth′er, a female volunteer, often the mother of a student, who assists an elementary-school teacher, as by working with students who need extra help.

room′ serv′ice, 1. the serving of food, drinks, etc., to a guest in his or her room, as at a hotel. **2.** the department or section, as at a hotel, responsible for rendering this service. [1925–30]

room•y[1] (ro͞o′mē, ro͝om′ē), *adj.,* **room•i•er, room•i•est.** affording ample room; spacious; large. [1615–25; ROOM + -Y[1]] —**room′i•ly,** *adv.* —**room′i•ness,** *n.*
—**Syn.** capacious, generous, ample, extensive.

room•y[2] (ro͞o′mē, ro͝om′ē), *n., pl.* **room•ies.** *Informal.* roomie.

roor•back (ro͝or′bak′), *n.* a false and more or less damaging report circulated for political effect, usually about a candidate seeking an office. Also, **roor′bach.** [1844, *Amer.;* after a fictitious Baron von *Roorback,* in whose travelogue occurred an account of an incident damaging to the character of James K. Polk]

roose (ro͞oz; *Scot. also* RŒZ), *v.t., v.i.,* **roosed, roos•ing,** *n. Chiefly Scot.* praise. [1150–1200; ME *rosen* < ON *hrōsa* to praise]

Roo•se•velt (rō′zə velt′, -vəlt, rōz′velt, -vəlt; *spelling pron.* ro͞o′zə velt′), *n.* **1. (Anna) Eleanor,** 1884–1962, U.S. diplomat, author, and lecturer (wife of Franklin Delano Roosevelt). **2. Franklin Del•a•no** (del′ə nō′), (*"FDR"*), 1882–1945, 32nd president of the U.S. 1933–45. **3. Theodore** (*Teddy, "T.R."*), 1858–1919, 26th president of the U.S. 1901–09: Nobel peace prize 1906. **4. Rio.** Formerly, **Río da Duvida.** a river flowing N from W Brazil to the Madeira River. ab. 400 mi. (645 km) long.

Roo′sevelt Cor′ollary, *U.S. Hist.* a corollary (1904) to the Monroe Doctrine, asserting that the U.S. might intervene in the affairs of an American republic threatened with seizure or intervention by a European country. [after Theodore ROOSEVELT]

Roo′sevelt Dam′, a dam on the Salt River, in central Arizona. 284 ft. (87 m) high; 1080 ft. (329 m) long.

Roo•se•velt•i•an (rō′zə vel′tē ən; *spelling pron.* ro͞o′zə vel′tē ən), *adj.* of, pertaining to, advocating, or following the principles, views, or policies of Franklin Delano Roosevelt or of Theodore Roosevelt. [1905–10, *Amer.,* ROOSEVELT + -IAN]

Roo′sevelt Is′land, 1. Formerly, **Welfare Island, Blackwells Island.** an island in the East River, New York City: residential community. 1½ mi. (2½ km) long. **2.** an island in Antarctica, in the W part of the Ross Ice Shelf: discovered 1934. ab. 90 mi. (145 km) long.

roost (ro͞ost), *n.* **1.** a perch upon which birds or fowls rest at night. **2.** a large cage, house, or place for fowls or birds to roost in. **3.** a place for sitting, resting, or lodging. **4. rule the roost,** to be in charge or control; dominate: *It was only too apparent that his grandfather ruled the roost.* —*v.i.* **5.** to sit or rest on a roost, perch, etc. **6.** to settle or stay, esp. for the night. **7. come home to roost,** (of an action) to revert or react unfavorably to the doer; boomerang: *an evil deed that came home to roost and ruined his life.* [bef. 1100; ME *roost* (n.), OE *hrōst;* c. MD *roest*]

roost•er (ro͞o′stər), *n.* **1.** the male of domestic fowl and certain game birds; cock. **2.** a representation of this bird, used as an emblem of the Democratic party from 1842 to 1874. **3.** *Informal.* a cocky person. [1765–75; ROOST + -ER[1]]

white leghorn rooster (def. 1) (domestic)

roost•er•fish (ro͞o′stər fish′), *n., pl.* **-fish•es,** (*esp. collectively*) **-fish.** a large, edible fish, *Nematistius pectoralis,* inhabiting the warmer waters of the Pacific Ocean, having the first dorsal fin composed of brightly colored filamentous rays. [ROOSTER + FISH]

roost′er tail′, the wake thrown up behind a speeding boat or the dust thrown up behind a speeding vehicle. [1945–50]

root[1] (ro͞ot, ro͝ot), *n.* **1.** a part of the body of a plant that develops, typically, from the radicle and grows downward into the soil, anchoring the plant and absorbing nutriment and moisture. **2.** a similar organ developed from some other part of a plant, as one of those by which ivy clings to its support. **3.** any underground part of a plant, as a rhizome. **4.** something resembling or suggesting the root of a plant in position or function: *roots of wires and cables.* **5.** the embedded or basal portion of a hair, tooth, nail, nerve, etc. **6.** the fundamental or essential part: *the root of a matter.* **7.** the source or origin of a thing: *The love of money is the root of all evil.* **8.** a person or family as the source of offspring or descendants. **9.** an offshoot or scion. **10.** *Math.* **a.** a quantity that, when multiplied by itself a certain number of times, produces a given quantity: *The number 2 is the square root of 4, the cube root of 8, and the fourth root of 16.* **b. rth root,** the quantity raised to the power 1/*r*: *The number 2 is the ⅓ root of 8.* **c.** a value of the argument of a function for which the function takes the value zero. **11.** *Gram.* **a.** a morpheme that underlies an inflectional or derivational paradigm, as *dance,* the root in *danced, dancer,* or *ten-,* the root of Latin *tendere* "to stretch." **b.** such a form reconstructed for a parent language, as **sed-,* the hypothetical proto-Indo-European root meaning "sit." **12. roots, a.** a person's original or true home, environment, and culture: *He's lived in New York for twenty years, but his roots are in France.* **b.** the personal relationships, affinity for a locale, habits, and the like, that make a country, region, city, or town one's true home: *He lived in Tulsa for a few years, but never established any roots there.* **c.** personal identification with a culture, religion, etc., seen as promoting the development of the character or the stability of society as a whole. **13.** *Music.* **a.** the fundamental tone of a compound tone or of a series of harmonies. **b.** the lowest tone of a chord when arranged as a series of thirds; the fundamental. **14.** *Mach.* **a.** (in a screw or other threaded object) the narrow inner surface between threads. Cf. **crest** (def. 18), **flank** (def. 7). **b.** (in a gear) the narrow inner surface between teeth. **15.** *Australian Informal.* an act of sexual intercourse. **16.** *Shipbuilding.* the inner angle of an angle iron. **17. root and branch,** utterly; entirely: *to destroy something root and branch.* **18. take root, a.** to send out roots; begin to grow. **b.** to become fixed or established: *The prejudices of parents usually take root in their children.*
—*v.i.* **19.** to become fixed or established.
—*v.t.* **20.** to fix by or as if by roots: *We were rooted to the spot by surprise.* **21.** to implant or establish deeply: *Good manners were rooted in him like a second nature.* **22.** to pull, tear, or dig up by the roots (often fol. by *up* or *out*). **23.** to extirpate; exterminate; remove completely (often fol. by *up* or *out*): *to root out crime.* [bef. 1150; (n.) ME; late OE *rōt* < ON *rōt;* akin to OE *wyrt* plant, WORT[2], G *Wurzel,* L *rādix* (see RADIX), Gk *rhíza* (see RHIZOME); (v.) ME *roten, rooten,* deriv. of the n.] —**root′like′,** *adj.*
—**Syn. 6.** basis. **7.** beginning, derivation, rise, fountainhead. **8.** parent. **23.** eradicate.

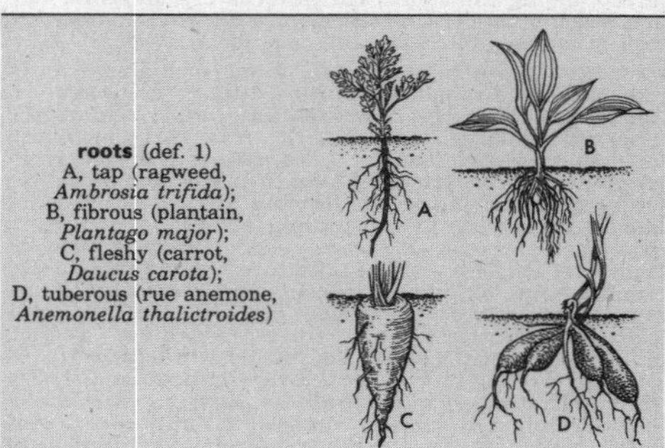

roots (def. 1)
A, tap (ragweed, *Ambrosia trifida*);
B, fibrous (plantain, *Plantago major*);
C, fleshy (carrot, *Daucus carota*);
D, tuberous (rue anemone, *Anemonella thalictroides*)

root[2] (ro͞ot, ro͝ot), *v.i.* **1.** to turn up the soil with the snout, as swine. **2.** to poke, pry, or search, as if to find something: *to root around in a drawer for loose coins.* —*v.t.* **3.** to turn over with the snout (often fol. by *up*). **4.** to unearth; bring to light (often fol. by *up*). [1530–40; var. of obs. *wroot* (OE *wrōtan,* akin to *wrōt* a snout)]

root[3] (ro͞ot *or, sometimes,* ro͝ot), *v.i.* **1.** to encourage a team or contestant by cheering or applauding enthusias-

CONCISE ETYMOLOGY KEY: <, descended or borrowed from; >, whence; b., blend of, blended; c., cognate with; cf., compare; deriv., derivative; equiv., equivalent; imit., imitative; obl., oblique; r., replacing; s., stem; sp., spelling, spelled; resp., respelling, respelled; trans., translation; ?, origin unknown; *, unattested; ‡, probably earlier than. See the full key inside the front cover.

tically. **2.** to lend moral support: *The whole group will be rooting for him.* [1885–90, *Amer.*; perh. var. of ROUT[4]] **—Syn. 1.** cheer, applaud, boost, support.

Root (ro͞ot), *n.* **1. El·i·hu** (el′ə hyo͞o′), 1845–1937, U.S. lawyer and statesman: Nobel peace prize 1912. **2. John Well·born** (wel′bərn), 1851–91, U.S. architect.

root·age (ro͞o′tij, ro͝ot′ij), *n.* **1.** the act of taking root. **2.** a root system or firm fixture by means of roots. [1580–90; ROOT[1] + -AGE]

root·ball (ro͞ot′bôl′, ro͝ot′-), *n.* **1.** a roughly spherical aggregate of roots and soil that is transplanted with a plant, esp. a tree or shrub. **2.** the ball of soil and roots of a plant growing in a pot or other container. [1925–30; ROOT[1] + BALL[1]]

root′ beer′, a carbonated beverage flavored with syrup made from the extracted juices of roots, barks, and herbs that have been fermented with sugar and yeast. [1835–45, *Amer.*]

root′ canal′, *Dentistry.* **1.** Also called **pulp canal.** the root portion of the pulp cavity. **2.** *Informal.* See **root canal therapy** (def. 2). [1890–95]

root′ canal′ ther′apy, 1. endodontics. **2.** a specific treatment for disease of the dental pulp involving removal of the nerve and other tissues from the pulp cavity and their replacement with filling material.

root·cap (ro͞ot′kap′, ro͝ot′-), *n. Bot.* the loose mass of epidermal cells covering the apex of most roots, serving to protect the meristematic cells behind it. [1875–80; ROOT[1] + CAP[1]]

root′ cel′lar, a cellar, partially or wholly underground and usually covered with dirt, where root crops and other vegetables are stored. [1815–25]

root′ climb′er, *Bot.* a plant that clings to a surface and climbs by means of adventitious roots, as the ivy, *Hedera helix.* [1895–1900]

root′ crop′, a crop, as beets, turnips, or sweet potatoes, grown for its large and edible undergound parts. [1825–35]

root′ divi′sion, the act or process of reproducing plants by a division of roots or crowns.

root′ doc′tor, *Chiefly Southern U.S.* See **herb doctor.** [1815–25, *Amer.*]

root·ed (ro͞o′tid, ro͝ot′id), *adj.* **1.** having roots. **2.** firmly implanted (often used in combination): *a deep-rooted belief.* [1350–1400; ME *roted;* see ROOT[1], -ED[2], -ED[3]] **—root′ed·ly,** *adv.* **—root′ed·ness,** *n.*

root·er[1] (ro͞o′tər, ro͝ot′ər), *n.* **1.** a person, animal, or thing that roots, as with the snout. **2.** *South Midland and Southern U.S.* a pig's snout. **3.** See **black buffalo.** [1640–50; ROOT[2] + -ER[1]]

root·er[2] (ro͞o′tər *or, sometimes,* ro͝ot′ər), *n.* **1.** a person who roots for, supports, or encourages a team or contestant. **2.** a loyal and enthusiastic helper, follower, or supporter. [1885–90; ROOT[3] + -ER[1]]

root′er skunk′. See **hog-nosed skunk** (def. 1).

root′ field′, *Math.* See **splitting field.**

root′ graft′, 1. *Hort.* the process of grafting a shoot or stem of one plant onto a section of root of another. **2.** a plant, commonly a young one, that is the result of root grafting. **3.** the natural underground growing together or joining of the roots of nearby plants. [1815–25]

root′ hair′, an elongated tubular extension of an epidermal cell of a root, serving to absorb water and minerals from the soil. [1855–60]

root·i (ro͞o′tē, ro͝ot′ē), *n. Anglo-Indian.* rooty[2].

root′ knot′, *Plant. Pathol.* a disease of plants, characterized by galls or knots on the roots and stunted growth, caused by any of several nematodes of the genus *Meloidogyne.* [1885–90]

root·less (ro͞ot′lis, ro͝ot′-), *adj.* **1.** having no roots. **2.** having no basis of stability; unsteady: *a rootless feeling resulting from economic and social change.* **3.** having no place or position in society; not in accord with the environment: *the homeless, rootless wanderer.* [1325–75; ME *rooteles.* See ROOT[1], -LESS] **—root′less·ness,** *n.*

root·let (ro͞ot′lit, ro͝ot′-), *n. Bot.* **1.** a little root. **2.** a small or fine branch of a root. **3.** one of the adventitious roots by which ivy or the like clings to rocks or other supports. [1785–95; ROOT[1] + -LET]

root′ mean′ square′, *Math.* the square root of the arithmetic mean of the squares of the numbers in a given set of numbers. *Abbr.:* rms [1890–95]

root′ of u′nity, *Math.* a complex number that when raised to some positive integral power results in 1.

root′ posi′tion, *Music.* the position of a triad in which the root is in the bass. [1890–95]

root′ pres′sure, *Bot.* osmotic pressure within the cells of a root system that causes sap to rise through a plant stem to the leaves. [1870–75]

root′ rot′, *Plant Pathol.* **1.** a symptom or phase of many diseases of plants, characterized by discoloration and decay of the roots. **2.** any disease so characterized. [1880–85]

Roots′ blow′er (ro͞ots), a machine for compressing or evacuating air or gas by the rotation of a meshing pair of lobed wheels in a closely fitting case.

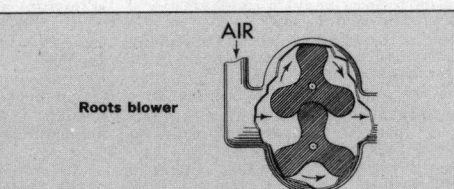

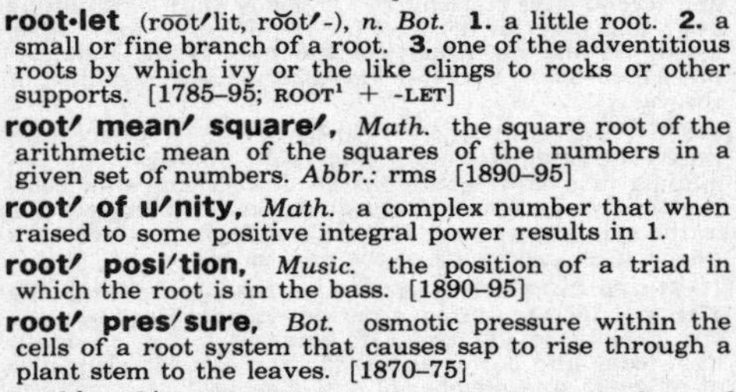

AIR

Roots blower

root·stalk (ro͞ot′stôk′, ro͝ot′-), *n. Bot.* a rhizome. [ROOT[1] + STALK[1]]

root·stock (ro͞ot′stok′, ro͝ot′-), *n.* **1.** *Hort.* a root and its associated growth buds, used as a stock in plant propagation. **2.** *Bot.* a rhizome. [1930–35; ROOT[1] + STOCK]

root′ test′, *Math.* the theorem that a given infinite series converges if the *n*th root of the absolute value of the *n*th term approaches a limit less than 1 as *n* increases without bound.

root·worm (ro͞ot′wûrm′, ro͝ot′-), *n.* **1.** the larva of any of several insects, as the cucumber beetle, that feeds on the roots of plants. **2.** any of several nematodes, esp. of the genus *Heterodera,* that puncture and feed in the roots of plants. [1795–1805; ROOT[1] + WORM]

root·y[1] (ro͞o′tē, ro͝ot′ē), *adj.,* **root·i·er, root·i·est.** abounding in or consisting of roots. [1475–85; ROOT[1] + -Y[1]] **—root′i·ness,** *n.*

root·y[2] (ro͞o′tē, ro͝ot′ē), *n. Anglo-Indian.* bread. Also, **rooti.** [1880–85; < Hindi *roṭī*]

R.O.P., run-of-paper: a designation specifying that the position of a newspaper or magazine advertisement is to be determined by the publisher. Cf. **preferred position.** [1945–50]

rop·a·ble (rō′pə bəl), *adj.* **1.** capable of being roped. **2.** *Australian Informal.* angry. [1870–75; ROPE + -ABLE]

rope (rōp), *n., v.,* **roped, rop·ing.** *—n.* **1.** a strong, thick line or cord, commonly one composed of twisted or braided strands of hemp, flax, or the like, or of wire or other material. **2.** a lasso. **3. ropes, a.** the cords used to enclose a prize ring or other space. **b.** *Informal.* the operations of a business or the details of any undertaking: *The new employee didn't take long to learn the ropes.* **4.** a hangman's noose, halter, or cord. **5.** the sentence or punishment of death by hanging. **6.** a quantity of material or a number of things twisted or strung together in the form of a cord: *a rope of tobacco.* **7.** a stringy, viscid, or glutinous formation in a liquid: *ropes of slime.* **8. at the end of one's rope,** at the end of one's endurance or means; at the limit: *With all her savings gone and bills piling up, she was at the end of her rope.* **9. give someone enough rope,** to allow a person complete freedom to continue his or her misdeeds in hope that retribution will follow. **10. on the ropes, a.** *Boxing.* in a defenseless position, as leaning against the ropes to keep from falling. **b.** *Informal.* in a desperate or hopeless position; close to defeat or failure: *By repeatedly undercutting his prices, his competitors soon had him on the ropes.* *—v.t.* **11.** to tie, bind, or fasten with a rope. **12.** to enclose, partition, or mark off with a rope or ropes (often fol. by *off*). **13.** to catch with a lasso; lasso. **14.** *Naut.* to reinforce (a sail or awning) with a boltrope. *—v.i.* **15.** to be drawn out into a filament of thread; become ropy. **16. rope in,** *Informal.* to lure or entice, esp. by employing deception: *The swindler had roped in a number of gullible persons.* [bef. 900; (n.) ME *rop(e), rap(e),* OE *rāp;* c. D *reep,* G *Reif;* (v.) ME, deriv. of the n.] **—rop′er,** *n.* **—rope′like′,** *adj.*

rope·a·ble (rō′pə bəl), *adj.* ropable.

rope·danc·er (rōp′dan′sər, -dän′-), *n.* a person who walks across or performs acrobatics upon a rope stretched at some height above the floor or ground. [1640–50; ROPE + DANCER] **—rope′dance′,** *n.* **—rope′·danc′ing,** *n.*

rope·mak·ing (rōp′mā′king), *n.* the act, skill, or process of making rope. [1785–95; ROPE + MAKING] **—rope′mak′er,** *n.*

rop·er·y (rō′pə rē), *n., pl.* **-er·ies. 1.** a place where ropes are made. **2.** *Archaic.* knavery; roguery. [1325–75; ME *roperie.* See ROPE, -ERY]

rope′ sock′et, either of a pair of matching fittings fastened to the ends of lengths of wire rope to join them together. [1895–1900]

rope′ stitch′, (in embroidery) a stitch formed from the entwining of stitches. [1875–80]

rope′ tow′. See **ski tow.** [1960–65]

rope·walk (rōp′wôk′), *n.* a long, narrow path or building where ropes are made. [1665–75; ROPE + WALK]

rope·walk·er (rōp′wô′kər), *n.* a ropedancer. [1605–15; ROPE + WALKER]

rope·way (rōp′wā′), *n.* tramway (def. 4). [1885–90; ROPE + WAY]

rope′ yarn′. See under **yarn** (def. 3). [1615–25]

rop·y (rō′pē), *adj.,* **rop·i·er, rop·i·est. 1.** resembling a rope or ropes: *ropy muscles.* **2.** forming viscid or glutinous threads, as a liquid. [1470–80; ROPE + -Y[1]] **—rop′·i·ly,** *adv.* **—rop′i·ness,** *n.*

roque (rōk), *n.* a form of croquet played on a clay or hard-surface court surrounded by a low wall off which the balls may be played. [1895–1900, *Amer.*; back formation from ROQUET]

Roque·fort (rōk′fərt), *Trademark.* a strongly flavored cheese, veined with mold, made of sheep's milk and ripened in caves at Roquefort, a town in S France. Also called **Roque′fort cheese′.** [1830–40]

roq·ue·laure (rok′ə lôr′, -lōr′, rok′ə-; *Fr.* RôKə lôR′), *n., pl.* **-laures** (-lôrz′, -lōrz′; *Fr.* -lôR′). a cloak reaching to the knees, worn by men during the 18th century. [1710–20; named after the Duc de *Roquelaure* (1656–1738), French marshal]

ro·quet (rō kā′), *v.,* **-queted** (-kād′), **-quet·ing** (-kā′-ing), *n. Croquet, Roque.* *—v.t.* **1.** to cause one's ball to strike (another player's ball). **2.** (of a ball) to strike (another player's ball). *—v.i.* **3.** to roquet a ball. *—n.* **4.** an act or instance of roqueting. [1860–65; alter. of CROQUET]

ro·quette (rō ket′), *n.* arugula.

ror·qual (rôr′kwəl), *n.* any of several whales of the genus *Balaenoptera;* finback. [1820–30; < F < Norw *rørkval,* ON *reytharhvalr,* equiv. to *reyth(a)r* rorqual (akin to *rauthr* RED[1]) + *hvalr* WHALE[1]]

Ror′schach test′ (rôr′shäk, rōr′-), *Psychol.* a test for revealing the underlying personality structure of an individual by the use of a standard series of 10 inkblot designs to which the subject responds by telling what image or emotion each design evokes. [1925–30; named after Hermann *Rorschach* (1884–1922), Swiss psychiatrist]

rort (rôrt), *n. Australian.* a rowdy, usually drunken party. [back formation from *rorty* boisterous, rowdy, in earlier Brit. slang: jolly, fine, splendid; of uncert. orig.]

Ro·ry (rôr′ē, rōr′ē), *n.* a male given name.

Ro·sa (*It.* Rô′zä; *Eng.* rō′zə), *n.* **1. Sal·va·tor** (säl′vä-tôR′), 1615–73, Italian painter and poet. **2. Mon·te** (*It.* môn′te; *Eng.* mon′tē), a mountain between Switzerland and Italy, in the Pennine Alps: second highest peak of the Alps. 15,217 ft. (4638 m). **3.** a female given name: derived from *Rose.*

ro·sace (rō zās′, -zäs′), *n.* rosette (def. 3). [1840–50; < F < L *rosāceus* ROSACEOUS]

ro·sa·ce·a (rō zā′shē ə), *n. Pathol.* a chronic form of acne affecting the nose, forehead, and cheeks, characterized by red pustular lesions. Also called **acne rosacea.** [1825–35; < NL (*acnē*) *rosācea* rose-colored (acne), L, fem. of *rosāceus* ROSACEOUS]

ro·sa·ceous (rō zā′shəs), *adj.* **1.** belonging to the plant family Rosaceae. Cf. **rose family. 2.** having a corolla of five broad petals, like that of a rose. **3.** like a rose; roselike: *rosaceous loveliness.* **4.** rose-colored; rosy. [1725–35; < L *rosāceus* made of roses, equiv. to *ros(a)* ROSE[1] + *-āceus* -ACEOUS]

Ro·sa·lie (rō′zə lē, roz′ə-), *n.* a female given name: from a Latin word meaning rose festival.

Ros·a·lind (roz′ə lind, rō′zə-), *n.* a female given name.

Ros·a·mund (roz′ə mənd, rō′zə-), *n.* a female given name: from Germanic words meaning "horse" and "protection." Also, **Ros′a·mond.**

ros·an·i·line (rō zan′l in, -īn′), *n. Chem.* **1.** a red dye, $C_{20}H_{20}N_3Cl$, derived from aniline and orthotoluidine, a constituent of fuchsin. **2.** the base, $C_{20}H_{21}N_3O$, which, with hydrochloric acid, forms this dye. [1860–65; ROSE[1] + ANILINE]

Ros·anne (rō zan′), *n.* a female given name. Also, **Ros·an·na** (rō zan′ə).

ro·sar·i·an (rō zâr′ē ən), *n.* a person who is fond of, develops, or cultivates roses. [1860–65; ROSE[1] + -ARIAN]

Ro·sa·ri·o (rō zär′ē ō′, -sär′-; *Sp.* Rô sä′Ryô), *n.* a port in E Argentina, on the Paraná River. 954,606.

ro·sar·i·um (rō zâr′ē əm), *n., pl.* **-i·ums, -i·a** (-ē ə). a rose garden. [1835–45; < L *rosārium;* see ROSARY]

ro·sa·ry (rō′zə rē), *n., pl.* **-ries. 1.** *Rom. Cath. Ch.* **a.** a series of prayers, usually consisting of 15 decades of aves, each decade being preceded by a paternoster and followed by a Gloria Patri, one of the mysteries or events in the life of Christ or the Virgin Mary being recalled at each decade. **b.** a string of beads used for counting these prayers during their recitation. **c.** a similar string of beads consisting of five decades. **2.** (among other religious bodies) a string of beads similarly used in praying. **3.** a rose garden or a bed of roses. [1350–1400 for earlier sense; 1400–50 for sense "rose garden"; 1540–50 for def. 1; ME *rosarie* < ML *rosārium,* in all current senses, L: rose garden, equiv. to *ros(a)* ROSE[1] + *-ārium* -ARY]

ro′sary pea′. See **Indian licorice.** [1865–70]

ro·sa so·lis (rō′zə sō′lis), *pl.* **ro·sa so·lis·es.** sundew. [1555–65; < NL, alter. (by influence of L *rosa* rose) of L *rōs sōlis* dew of the sun]

Ros·ci·an (rosh′ē ən, rosh′ən), *adj.* of, pertaining to, or involving acting. [1630–40; ROSCI(US) + -AN]

Ros·ci·us (rosh′ē əs, rosh′əs), *n.* **Quin·tus** (kwin′təs), c126–c62 B.C., Roman actor.

ros·coe (ros′kō), *n. Older Slang.* a revolver or pistol. [1910–15, *Amer.*; of uncert. orig.]

Ros·coe (ros′kō), *n.* a male given name: from Germanic words meaning "swift" and "horse."

ros·coe·lite (ros′kō lit′), *n. Mineral.* a brown variety of muscovite in which some aluminum is replaced by vanadium. [1875–80; named after Sir Henry *Roscoe* (1833–1915), English chemist; see -LITE]

Ros·com·mon (ros kom′ən), *n.* a county in Connacht, in the N Republic of Ireland. 54,499; 950 sq. mi. (2460 sq. km). *Co. seat:* Roscommon.

rose[1] (rōz), *n., adj., v.,* **rosed, ros·ing.** *—n.* **1.** any of the wild or cultivated, usually prickly-stemmed, pinnate-leaved, showy-flowered shrubs of the genus *Rosa.* Cf. **rose family. 2.** any of various related or similar plants. **3.** the flower of any such shrub, of a red, pink, white, or yellow color. **4.** the traditional reddish color of this flower, variously a purplish red, pinkish red, or light crimson. **5.** an ornament shaped like or suggesting this flower. **6.** a pink or pinkish-red color in the cheek. **7.** See **rose window. 8.** *Heraldry.* a representation of a wild rose with five petals, usually seeded and barbed in a symmetrical design and used esp. as the cadency mark of a seventh son. **9.** any of various diagrams showing directions radiating from a common center, as a compass card or wind rose. **10.** *Jewelry.* **a.** an obsolete gem style or cut, flat on the bottom and having an upper side with from 12, or fewer, to 32 triangular facets. **b.** a gem with this cut. **11.** a perforated cap or plate, as at the end of a pipe or the spout of a watering pot, to break a flow of water into a spray. **12.** an ornamental plate or socket surrounding the shaft of a doorknob at the face of a door. **13.** *Math.* a plane polar curve consisting of three or more equal loops that meet at the origin. Equation: *r*

= *a*sin*nθ* or *r* = *a*cos*nθ*. **14. come up roses,** *Informal.* to turn out all right; result in success, glory, or profit: *Despite setbacks, things should come up roses in the long run.* —*adj.* **15.** of the color rose. **16.** for, containing, or growing roses: *a rose garden.* **17.** scented like a rose. —*v.t.* **18.** to make rose-colored. **19.** to flush (the face, cheeks, etc.). [bef. 900; ME; OE *rōse* < L *rosa;* akin to Gk *rhódon* (see RHODODENDRON)] —**rose′less,** *adj.* —**rose′like′,** *adj.*

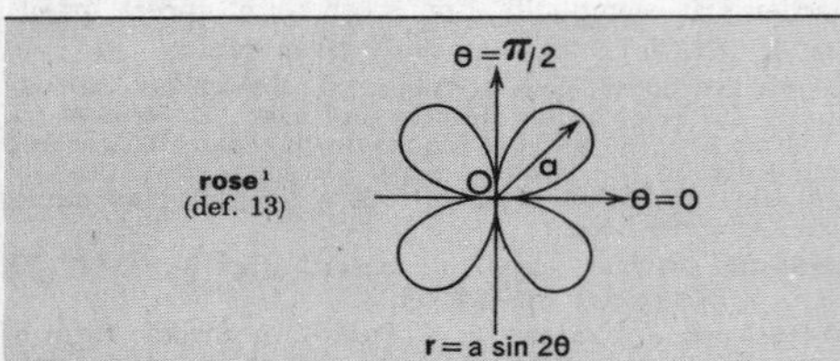

rose[1] (def. 13)

rose[2] (rōz), *v.* **1.** pt. of **rise. 2.** *Nonstandard.* a pp. of **rise.**

Rose (rōz), *n.* **1. Billy,** 1899–1966, U.S. theatrical producer. **2.** a female given name.

ro·sé (rō zā′), *n.* a pink table wine in which the pale color is produced by removing the grape skins from the must before fermentation is completed. [1425–75; < F: lit., pink]

rose′ aca′cia, a small tree, *Robinia hispida,* of the legume family, native to the southeastern U.S., having drooping clusters of large, dark rose-colored flowers. [1810–20]

Rose·an·na (rō zan′ə), *n.* a female given name.

rose′ a′phid, a dark green aphid, *Macrosiphum rosae,* that feeds on roses and related plants.

rose′ ap′ple, 1. any of various tropical trees belonging to the genus *Syzygium,* of the myrtle family, esp. *S. jambos,* of the East Indies, having showy, greenish-white flowers and oval, yellowish fruit. **2.** the fragrant fruit of any of these trees, used in making jellies and confections. [1620–30]

ro·se·ate (rō′zē it, -āt′), *adj.* **1.** tinged with rose; rosy: *a roseate dawn.* **2.** bright or promising: *a roseate future.* **3.** incautiously optimistic: *a roseate forecast for holiday sales.* [1580–90; < L *rose(us)* rose-colored + -ATE[1]] —**ro′se·ate·ly,** *adv.*

ro′seate spoon′bill, a tropical New World spoonbill, *Ajaia ajaja,* having rose-colored plumage and a bare head. See illus. under **spoonbill.** [1775–85, *Amer.*]

Ro·seau (rō zō′), *n.* a seaport on and the capital of Dominica. 10,417.

rose·bay (rōz′bā′), *n.* **1.** any of several rhododendrons, as the great laurel of eastern North America or *Rhododendron macrophyllum,* of the west coast of North America. **2.** *Brit.* the willow herb, *Epilobium angustifolium.* [1540–50; ROSE[1] + BAY[4]]

rose′ bee′tle, 1. See **rose chafer. 2.** See **Fuller rose beetle.** [1775–85]

Rose·ber·y (rōz′bə rē), *n.* **Archibald Philip Primrose** (prim′rōz′), **5th Earl of,** 1847–1929, British statesman and author: prime minister 1894–95.

rose′ box′, a perforated metal box used as a strainer; strum. [1860–65]

rose′-breast·ed gros′beak (rōz′bres′tid), an American grosbeak, *Pheucticus ludovicianus,* the male of which, in nuptial plumage, has a rose-pink triangular breast patch. [1800–10, *Amer.*]

rose·bud (rōz′bud′), *n.* the bud of a rose. [1605–15; ROSE[1] + BUD[1]]

Rose·burg (rōz′bûrg), *n.* a city in W Oregon. 16,644.

rose·bush (rōz′bŏŏsh′), *n.* a shrub that bears roses. [1580–90; ROSE[1] + BUSH[1]]

rose′ cam′pion, a plant, *Lychnis coronaria,* of the pink family, having reddish purple flowers, and leaves covered with whitish down. Also called **dusty miller, mullein pink.** [1520–30]

rose′ chaf′er, a tan scarabaeid beetle, *Macrodactylus subspinosis,* that feeds on the flowers and foliage of roses, grapes, peach trees, etc. Also called **rose beetle.** [1695–1705]

rose′ cold′, *Pathol.* See **rose fever.** [1870–75, *Amer.*]

rose-col·ored (rōz′kul′ərd), *adj.* **1.** of rose color; rosy. **2.** bright; promising; cheerful: *a rose-colored prospect of happiness.* **3.** optimistic; sanguine: *a rose-colored belief that things will turn out well.* [1520–30]

rose′-colored glass′es, a cheerful or optimistic view of things, usually without valid basis: *He saw life through rose-colored glasses.* [1860–65]

rose′ comb′, a low comb with rounded points and a rear-extending spike of some breeds of chickens, as Wyandotte. [1840–50]

Rose·crans (rōz′krans), *n.* **William Starke** (stärk), 1819–98, U.S. general.

Rose·dale (rōz′dāl′), *n.* a city in N Maryland, near Baltimore. 19,956.

rose′ d'An·vers′ (*Fr.* RŌZ DÄN VER′), *Jewelry.* a gem having a rose cut of 12 or fewer facets. [< F: rose of Anvers]

rose′ fam′ily, the plant family Rosaceae, characterized by trees, shrubs, and herbaceous plants having compound or simple leaves with stipules, flowers typically with five sepals and five petals, and fruit in a variety of forms, many of which are fleshy and edible, and including the almond, apple, apricot, blackberry, cherry, cinquefoil, hawthorn, peach, pear, plum, raspberry, rose, spirea, and strawberry.

CONCISE ETYMOLOGY KEY: <, descended or borrowed from; >, whence; b., blend of, blended; c., cognate with; cf., compare; deriv., derivative; equiv., equivalent; imit., imitative; obl., oblique; r., replacing; s., stem; sp., spelling, spelled; resp., respelling, respelled; trans., translation; ?, origin unknown; *, unattested; ‡, probably earlier than. See the full key inside the front cover.

rose′ fe′ver, *Pathol.* a form of hay fever caused by the inhalation of rose pollen, characterized by nasal discharge and lacrimation. Also called **rose cold.** [1850–55, *Amer.*]

rose·fish (rōz′fish′), *n., pl.* (*esp. collectively*) **-fish,** (*esp. referring to two or more kinds or species*) **-fish·es. 1.** redfish (def. 1). **2.** See **blackbelly rosefish.** [1715–25, *Amer.*; ROSE[1] + FISH]

rose′ gera′nium, a geranium, *Pelargonium graveolens,* cultivated for its fragrant, lobed or narrowly divided leaves. [1825–35]

rose′ hip′, hip[2]. [1855–60]

ro·sel·la (rō zel′ə), *n.* any of several large, colorful parakeets of the genus *Platycercus,* of Australia. [1820–30; alter. of *Rosehill,* district in southeast Australia]

ro·selle (rō zel′), *n.* a tropical plant, *Hibiscus sabdariffa,* of the mallow family, grown for its thick, red calyx and bracts, used in making jellies and as a substitute for cranberries. [1855–60; orig. uncert.]

Ro·selle (rō zel′), *n.* **1.** a city in NE New Jersey. 20,641. **2.** a town in NE Illinois. 16,948.

Ros·el·len (rō zel′ən), *n.* a female given name.

Roselle′ Park′, a borough in NE New Jersey. 13,377.

rose′ mad′der, a pigment derived from anthraquinone and hydrated oxide of aluminum, characterized chiefly by its reddish color and permanence: used in painting. Cf. **madder lake** (def. 2). [1885–90]

ro·se·ma·ling (rō′zə mä′ling), *n.* decorative work of Norwegian folk origin consisting of painted or carved floral designs, as on furniture or woodwork. [1940–45; < Norw, equiv. to *rose* ROSE + *maling* painting]

rose′ mal′low, any of several plants of the genus *Hibiscus,* of the mallow family, having rose-colored flowers. [1725–35]

rose′ man′darin. See under **mandarin** (def. 5).

Rose·ma·rie (rōz′mə rē′, rōz′mə rē′), *n.* a female given name.

rose·mar·y (rōz′mâr′ē, -mə rē), *n., pl.* **-mar·ies.** an evergreen shrub, *Rosmarinus officinalis,* of the mint family, native to the Mediterranean region, having leathery, narrow leaves and pale-blue, bell-shaped flowers, used as a seasoning and in perfumery and medicine: a traditional symbol of remembrance. [1400–50; late ME *rose mary* (by folk etym., influenced by ROSE[1] and the name *Mary*) < L *rōs* dew + *marīnus* marine, or *rōs maris* dew of the sea (in E the final -s mistaken for pl. sign)]

Rose·mar·y (rōz′mâr′ē, -mə rē), *n.* a female given name.

Rose·mead (rōz′mēd′), *n.* a city in SW California, near Los Angeles. 42,604.

Rose·mont (rōz′mont), *n.* a town in central California, near Sacramento. 18,888.

rose′ moss′, a portulaca, *Portulaca grandiflora,* widely cultivated for its showy flowers. Also called **moss rose.**

Ro·sen·berg (rō′zən bûrg′), *n.* **1. Julius,** 1918–53, and his wife, **Ethel Green·glass** (grēn′glas′, -gläs′), 1915–53, U.S. citizens executed for passing atomic-bomb secrets to the U.S.S.R. **2.** a town in S Texas. 17,995.

Ro·sen·kav·a·lier, Der (*Ger.* DER RŌ′zən kä vä lēr′), an opera (1911) by Richard Strauss.

rose′ no′ble, a former gold coin of England, first issued by Edward IV, being the existing noble with a figure of a rose added to the types on either side: much imitated on the Continent, esp. in the Netherlands. Also called **ryal.** [1425–75; late ME]

Ro·sen·thal (rō′zən thôl′), *n.* **1. Jean,** 1912–69, U.S. theatrical lighting designer. **2. Emmanuel,** born 1904, French conductor and composer.

Ro·sen·wald (rō′zən wôld′), *n.* **Julius,** 1862–1932, U.S. businessman and philanthropist.

rose′ of Chi′na. See **China rose** (def. 2).

rose′ of Heav′en, a plant, *Lychnis coeli-rosa,* of the pink family, native to the Mediterranean region, having solitary terminal, rose-pink flowers. [1850–55]

rose′ of Jer′icho, an Asian plant, *Anastatica hierochuntica,* of the mustard family, which, after drying and curling up, expands when moistened. Also called **resurrection plant.** [1350–1400; ME]

rose′ of Shar′on, 1. Also called **althea.** a widely cultivated shrub or small tree, *Hibiscus syriacus,* of the mallow family, having showy white, reddish or purplish flowers. **2.** Also called **Aaron's-beard.** a St.-John's-wort, *Hypericum calycinum,* having evergreen foliage and showy yellow flowers. **3.** a plant mentioned in the Bible. Song of Solomon 2:1. [1605–15]

rose′ oil′, a pale yellow, green, or red, volatile, fragrant, sweet-tasting liquid, obtained by steam distillation from fresh roses, esp. damask roses: used in flavoring and perfume. Also called **attar of roses, otto of roses.** [1835–45]

ro·se·o·la (rō zē′ə lə, rō′zē ō′lə), *n. Pathol.* **1.** a kind of rose-colored rash. **2.** rubella. [1810–20; < NL, equiv. to L *rose(us)* rose-colored + *-ola* -OLE[1]] —**ro·se′o·lar,** *adj.*

rose′ pink′, a light pinkish red color. [1725–35] —**rose′-pink′,** *adj.*

rose′ pogo′nia, a North American terrestrial orchid, *Pogonia ophioglossoides,* having a fragrant, usually solitary rose-pink or white flower. Also called **snakemouth, adder's-mouth.**

rose′ quartz′, a rose-red to pink variety of crystalline quartz usually found in massive form and used as a gem or ornamental stone. [1810–20]

rose-slug (rōz′slug′), *n.* the larva of any of several sawflies, esp. *Endelomyia aethiops* or *Cladius isomerus,* that skeletonize the foliage of roses. [1875–80]

ros·et (roz′it), *n. Scot.* resin; rosin. [1495–1505; var. of ME *rosine* ROSIN]

Ro·set·ta (rō zet′ə), *n.* **1.** a town in N Egypt, at a mouth of the Nile. 36,700. **2.** a female given name.

Roset′ta stone′, 1. a stone slab, found in 1799 near Rosetta, bearing parallel inscriptions in Greek, Egyptian hieroglyphic, and demotic characters, making possible the decipherment of ancient Egyptian hieroglyphics. **2.** a clue, breakthrough, or discovery that provides crucial knowledge for the solving of a puzzle or problem.

ro·sette (rō zet′), *n.* **1.** any arrangement, part, object, or formation more or less resembling a rose. **2.** a rose-shaped arrangement of ribbon or other material, used as an ornament or badge. **3.** Also, **rosace.** an architectural ornament resembling a rose or having a generally circular combination of parts. **4.** *Bot.* a circular cluster of leaves or other organs. **5.** a broad ornamental head for a screw or nail. **6.** *Metall.* **a.** any of a number of disks of refined copper formed when cold water is thrown onto the molten metal. **b.** a rounded microconstituent of certain alloys. **7.** *Plant Pathol.* any of several diseases of plants, characterized by the crowding of the foliage into circular clusters owing to a shortening of the internodes of stems or branches, caused by fungi, viruses, or nutritional deficiencies. **8.** one of the compound spots on a leopard. [1780–90; < F: little rose, OF. See ROSE[1], -ETTE]

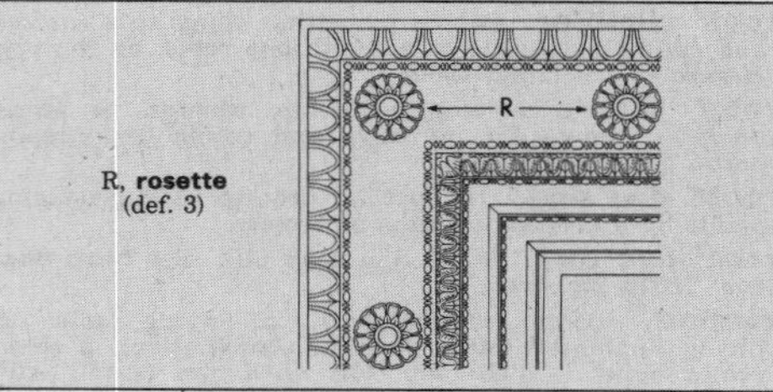

R, **rosette** (def. 3)

Ro·sette (rō zet′), *n.* a female given name.

Rose·ville (rōz′vil), *n.* **1.** a city in SE Michigan, near Detroit. 54,311. **2.** a city in SE Minnesota, near St. Paul. 35,820. **3.** a city in E California. 24,347.

Rose·wall (rōz′wôl′), *n.* **Ken(neth R.),** born 1934, Australian tennis player.

rose′ wa′ter, water tinctured with the essential oil of roses, used as a perfume. [1350–1400; ME]

rose-wa·ter (rōz′wô′tər, -wot′ər), *adj.* **1.** having the aroma or fragrance of rose water. **2.** affectedly delicate, nice, or fine; sentimental: *a Victorian novelist with a genteel, rose-water style.* [1655–65]

rose′ wee′vil. See **Fuller rose beetle.** Also called **rose beetle.**

rose′ win′dow, a circular window decorated with tracery symmetrical about the center. Cf. **wheel window.** [1765–75]

rose·wood (rōz′wŏŏd′), *n.* **1.** any of various reddish cabinet woods, sometimes with a roselike odor, yielded by certain tropical trees, esp. belonging to the genus *Dalbergia,* of the legume family. **2.** a tree yielding such wood. [1650–60; ROSE[1] + WOOD[1]]

rose′wood oil′, a fragrant oil extracted from the wood of a South American tree, *Aniba rosaeodora,* and used in the manufacture of perfumes. [1865–70]

Rosh Ha·sha·nah (rōsh′ hä shô′nə, -shä′-, hə-, rôsh′; *Ashk. Heb.* RŌSH′ hä shô′nə; *Seph. Heb.* RÔSH′ hä shä nä′), a Jewish high holy day that marks the beginning of the Jewish New Year, celebrated on the first and second days of Tishri by Orthodox and Conservative Jews and only on the first day by Reform Jews. Also, **Rosh′ Ha·sha′na, Rosh′ Ha·sho′noh, Rosh′ Ha·sho′no.** [1840–50; < Heb *rōsh hashshānāh* lit., beginning of the year]

Rosh Ho·desh (rōsh′ KHŌ′desh; *Ashk. Heb.* RŌSH KHŌ′desh; *Seph. Heb.* RÔSH KHÔ′desh), *Judaism.* the beginning of a new month in the Jewish calendar, celebrated in a specified manner during the morning service in the synagogue. Also, **Rosh′ Cho′desh.** [< Heb *rōsh ḥōdhesh* lit., beginning of the new moon]

Ro·si·cru·cian (rō′zi kro͞o′shən, roz′i-), *n.* **1.** (in the 17th and 18th centuries) a person who belonged to a secret society laying claim to various forms of occult knowledge and power and professing esoteric principles of religion. **2.** a member of any of several later or modern bodies or societies professing principles derived from or attributed to the earlier Rosicrucians, esp. of an organization **(Rosicru′cian Or′der** or **Ancient Mystic Order Rosae Crucis)** that is active in America. —*adj.* **3.** of, pertaining to, or characteristic of the Rosicrucians. [1615–25; < L *Rosicruc-* (Latinized form of (Christian) *Rosenkreuz,* name of the supposed 15th-century founder of the society, equiv. to *ros(a)* ROSE + *-i-* -I- + *cruc-* (s. of *crux*) CROSS) + -IAN]

Ro·si·cru·cian·ism (rō′zi kro͞o′shə niz′əm, roz′i-), *n.* the practices or principles of Rosicrucians. [1730–40; ROSICRUCIAN + -ISM]

Ro·sie (rō′zē), *n.* a female given name, form of **Rose.**

ros·i·ly (rō′zə lē), *adv.* **1.** with a rosy color. **2.** in a rosy manner; brightly, cheerfully, or optimistically. [1800–10; ROSY + -LY]

ros·in (roz′in), *n.* Also called **colophony. 1.** *Chem.* the yellowish to amber, translucent, hard, brittle, fragmented resin left after distilling the oil of turpentine from the crude oleoresin of the pine: used chiefly in making varnishes, varnish and paint driers, printing inks, and for rubbing on the bows of such string instruments as the violin. **2.** resin. —*v.t.* **3.** to cover or rub with rosin. [1300–50; ME < OF, var. of *resine* RESIN] **—ros′in·y,** *adj.*

Ro·si·na (rō zē′nə; *It.* RÔ zē′nä), *n.* a female given name, Italian form of **Rose.**

Ros·i·nan·te (roz′ə nan′tē, rō′zə nän′tē), *n.* **1.** the old, worn horse of Don Quixote. **2.** (*l.c.*) an old, decrepit horse. Spanish, **Rocinante.**

ros·in·weed (roz′in wēd′), *n.* **1.** any coarse, North American, composite plant of the genus *Silphium,* having a resinous juice and stalkless, paired leaves. **2.** the compass plant, *S. laciniatum.* [1825–35, *Amer.*; ROSIN + WEED[1]]

Ro·si·ta (rō zē′tə; *Sp.* RÔ sē′tä), *n.* a female given name, Spanish form of **Rose.**

ro·so·li·o (rō zō′lē ō′, rə-; *It.* RÔ zô′lyô), *n.* a cordial flavored with rose petals, cloves, cinnamon, or the like, popular in southern Europe. [1810–20; < It, var. of *rosoli* < ML *rōs sōlis* dew of the sun]

ross (rôs, ros), *n.* **1.** the rough exterior of bark. —*v.t.* **2.** to remove the rough exterior of bark from (a log or the like). [1570–80; orig. uncert.]

Ross (rôs, ros), *n.* **1. Betsy Gris·com** (gris′kəm), 1752–1836, maker of the first U.S. flag. **2. Harold Wal·lace,** 1892–1951, U.S. publisher and editor. **3. Sir James Clark,** 1800–62, English navigator: explorer of the Arctic and the Antarctic. **4.** his uncle, **Sir John,** 1777–1856, Scottish naval officer and arctic explorer. **5. John** (*Coowescoowe* or *Kooweskoowe*), 1790–1866, Cherokee leader. **6. Sir Ronald,** 1857–1932, English physician: Nobel prize 1902. **7.** a male given name.

Ross′ and Crom′ar·ty (krom′ər tē, krum′-), a historic county in NW Scotland.

Ross·by (rôs′bē, ros′-), *n.* **Carl-Gu·staf Ar·vid** (kärl′-gōō′stäf är′vid). 1898–1957, U.S. meteorologist, born in Sweden.

Ross′ Depend′ency, a territory in Antarctica, including Ross Island, the coasts along the Ross Sea, and adjacent islands: a dependency of New Zealand. ab. 175,000 sq. mi. (453,250 sq. km).

Ros′sel Cur′rent (rô′səl), a seasonal Pacific Ocean current, a branch of the South Equatorial Current, flowing W and NW past New Guinea. [after Élisabeth-Paul-Édouard, Chevalier de *Rossel* (1765–1829), French naval officer and hydrographer]

Ros·sel·li·ni (rô′sə lē′nē, ros′ə-; *It.* RÔs′sel lē′nē), *n.* **Ro·ber·to** (rə bâr′tō; *It.* RÔ ber′tô), 1906–77, Italian motion-picture director.

ross·er (rô′sər, ros′ər), *n.* **1.** a logger who peels the bark from, and often smooths one side of, a log so that it may be dragged easily. **2.** any of various machines or devices for removing bark from logs and pulpwood. **3.** an attachment on a circular saw for removing ross or bark ahead of the blade. [1870–75, *Amer.*; ROSS + -ER[1]]

Ros·set·ti (rō set′ē, -zet′ē, rə-), *n.* **1. Christina Georgina,** 1830–94, English poet. **2.** her brother, **Dante Gabriel** (*Gabriel Charles Dante Rossetti*), 1828–82, English poet and painter.

Ross′ Ice′ Shelf′, an ice barrier filling the S part of the Ross Sea.

Ros·si·ni (rō sē′nē, rô-; *It.* RÔs sē′nē), *n.* **Gio·ac·chi·no An·to·nio** (jô′äk kē′nô än tô′nyô), 1792–1868, Italian composer.

Ross′ Is′land, an island in the W Ross Sea, off the coast of Victoria Land: part of the Ross Dependency; location of Mt. Erebus.

Ros·si·ya (RU syē′yə), *n.* Russian name of **Russia.**

Ross′ Sea′, an arm of the Antarctic Ocean, S of New Zealand, extending into Antarctica.

Ros·tand (Rôs tän′), *n.* **Ed·mond** (ed môn′), 1868–1918, French dramatist and poet.

ros·tel·late (ros′tl āt′, -it, ro stel′it), *adj.* having a rostellum. [1820–30; < L *rōstell(um)* ROSTELLUM + -ATE[1]]

ros·tel·lum (ro stel′əm), *n., pl.* **ros·tel·la** (ro stel′ə). **1.** *Biol.* any small, beaklike process. **2.** *Bot.* a beaklike modification of the stigma in many orchids. **3.** *Zool.* **a.** a projecting part of the scolex in certain tapeworms. **b.** a part of the mouth in many insects, designed for sucking. [1750–60; < NL; L: little beak, snout, dim. of *rōstrum* snout (see ROSTRUM); for formation, see CASTELLUM]

Ros·ten·kow·ski (ros′tən kou′skē), *n.* **Dan(iel),** born 1928, U.S. politician: congressman since 1959.

ros·ter (ros′tər), *n.* **1.** a list of persons or groups, as of military personnel or units with their turns or periods of duty. **2.** any list, roll, or register: *a roster of famous scientists; a roster of coming events.* [1720–30; < D *rooster* list, roster, lit., gridiron, in reference to the ruled paper used, equiv. to *roost(en)* to ROAST + *-er* -ER[1]] **—Syn. 1, 2.** listing, slate, panel, record.

Ros·tock (ros′tok; *Ger.* RÔs′tôk), *n.* a seaport in N Germany, on the Baltic. 253,990.

Ro·stov (rə stôf′, -stof′; *Russ.* RU stôf′), *n.* a seaport in the SW Russian Federation in Europe, on the Don River, near the Sea of Azov. 1,020,000. Also called **Rostov-on-Don** (rə stôf′on don′, -dôn′, -ŏn-, -stof′-).

Ro·stov·tzeff (rə stôf′tsef, -stof′-), *n.* **Mi·chael I·va·no·vich** (mī′kəl i vä′nə vich), 1870–1952, U.S. historian, born in Russia.

ros·tra (ros′trə), *n.* a pl. of **rostrum.**

ros·tral (ros′trəl), *adj.* of or pertaining to a rostrum. [1700–10; < LL *rōstrālis,* equiv. to L *rōstr(um)* ROSTRUM + *-ālis* -AL[1]] **—ros′tral·ly,** *adv.*

ros′tral col′umn, a memorial column having sculptures representing the rams of ancient ships. [1790–1800]

ros·trate (ros′trāt), *adj.* furnished with a rostrum. Also, **ros′trat·ed.** [1350–1400; < L *rōstrātus* having a beak, curved at the end, equiv. to *rōstr(um)* ROSTRUM + *-ātus* -ATE[1]]

ros·tro·car·i·nate (ros′trō kar′ə nāt′, -nit), *n.* a chipped flint with a beaklike shape found in the late Tertiary sediments of Suffolk, England, once thought to have been worked by humans but now known to have been shaped by natural nonhuman agencies. [1950–55; *rostro-* (comb. form repr. L *rōstrum* ROSTRUM) + CARINATE]

Ros·tro·po·vich (ros′trə pō′vich; *Russ.* RU strə pô′-vyich), *n.* **Msti·slav (Le·o·pol·do·vich)** (mis′tə släv′ lē′ə pōl′də vich; *Russ.* mstyi släf′ lyi ə pôl′də vyich), born 1927, Soviet cellist and conductor, in the U.S. since 1974 (husband of Galina Vishnevskaya).

ros·trum (ros′trəm), *n., pl.* **-tra** (-trə), **-trums. 1.** any platform, stage, or the like, for public speaking. **2.** a pulpit. **3.** a beaklike projection from the prow of a ship, esp. one on an ancient warship for ramming an enemy ship; beak; ram. **4.** *Rom. Antiq.* (in the forum) the raised platform, adorned with the beaks of captured warships, from which orations, pleadings, etc., were delivered. **5.** *Biol.* a beaklike process or extension of some part; rostellum. **6.** *Brit. Theat.* a raised platform or dais, esp. one with hinged sides that can be folded and stored within a relatively small space. [1570–80; < L *rōstrum* snout, bill, beak of a bird, ship's prow (in pl., speaker's platform), equiv. to *rōd(ere)* to gnaw, bite (cf. RODENT) + *-trum* instrumental suffix, with *dt* > *st*] **—Syn. 1.** stand, dais, podium, lectern.

ro·su·late (rō′zə lit, roz′ə-), *adj. Bot.* forming a rosette or rosettes. [1825–35; < LL *rosul(a)* (L *ros(a)* ROSE[1] + *-ula* -ULE) + -ATE[1]]

Ros·well (roz′wel, -wəl), *n.* **1.** a city in SE New Mexico. 39,676. **2.** a town in central Georgia. 23,337.

Ros·wi·tha (*Ger.* Rôs vē′tä), *n.* Hrotsvitha.

ros·y (rō′zē), *adj.,* **ros·i·er, ros·i·est. 1.** pink or pinkish-red; roseate. **2.** (of persons, the cheeks, lips, etc.) having a fresh, healthy redness. **3.** bright or promising: *a rosy future.* **4.** cheerful or optimistic: *rosy anticipations.* **5.** made or consisting of roses: *a rosy bower.* [1325–75; ME; see ROSE[1], -Y[1]] **—ros′i·ness,** *n.* **—Syn. 2.** flushed, blooming, healthy. **—Ant. 2.** pale. **3.** unpromising. **4.** cheerless.

Ro·sy (rō′zē), *n.* a female given name, form of **Rose.**

ros′y finch′, any of several finches of the genus *Leucosticte,* of Asia and western North America, having dark brown plumage with a pinkish wash on the wings and rump. [1795–1805]

ros′y pas′tor. See under **pastor** (def. 3).

Ro·szak (rô′shäk, -shak), *n.* **Theodore,** 1907–81, U.S. sculptor, born in Poland.

rot (rot), *v.,* **rot·ted, rot·ting,** *n., interj.* —*v.i.* **1.** to undergo decomposition; decay. **2.** to deteriorate, disintegrate, fall, or become weak due to decay (often fol. by *away, from, off,* etc.). **3.** to languish, as in confinement. **4.** to become morally corrupt or offensive. —*v.t.* **5.** to cause to rot: *Dampness rots wood.* **6.** to cause moral decay in; cause to become morally corrupt. **7.** to ret (flax, hemp, etc.). —*n.* **8.** the process of rotting. **9.** the state of being rotten; decay; putrefaction: *the rot of an old house.* **10.** rotting or rotten matter: *the rot and waste of a swamp.* **11.** moral or social decay or corruption. **12.** *Pathol.* any disease characterized by decay. **13.** *Plant Pathol.* **a.** any of various forms of decay produced by fungi or bacteria. **b.** any disease so characterized. **14.** *Vet. Pathol.* a bacterial infection of sheep and cattle characterized by decay of the hoofs, caused by *Fusobacterium necrophorum* in cattle and *Bacteroides nodosus* in sheep. **15.** nonsense. —*interj.* **16.** (used to express disagreement, distaste, or disgust.) [bef. 900; (v.) ME *rot(t)en,* OE *rotian,* c. Fris *rotsje,* D *rotten;* (n.) ME, perh. < ON *rot* (perh. partly deriv. of the v.); cf. RET, ROTTEN)] **—Syn. 1.** mold, molder, putrefy, spoil. See **decay. 9.** decomposition, mold. **—Ant. 4, 6.** purify.

ROT, rule of thumb.

rot., 1. rotating. **2.** rotation.

ro·ta[1] (rō′tə), *n.* **1.** *Chiefly Brit.* **a.** a round or rotation of duties; a period of work or duty taken in rotation with others. **b.** an agenda or circuit of sporting events, as a round of golf tournaments, played in different localities throughout the year. **2.** a roster. **3.** Official name, **Sacred Roman Rota.** the ecclesiastical tribunal in Rome, constituting the court of final appeal. [1650–60; < L: wheel]

ro·ta[2] (rō′tə), *n.* rote[2].

Ro·ta (rô′tä), *n.* **Ni·no** (nē′nô), born 1911, Italian composer.

ro·tam·e·ter (rō tam′i tər, rō′tə mē′-), *n.* an instrument for measuring the rate of flow of a liquid, consisting of a tapered vertical tube in which a small float is forced upward until its weight balances the fluid force. [partial trans. of G *Rotamesser* (1911), equiv. to *Rota(tion)* ROTATION + *Messer* measurer, meter]

Ro·tar·i·an (rō târ′ē ən), *n.* **1.** a member of a Rotary Club. —*adj.* **2.** of or pertaining to Rotarians or Rotary Clubs. [1910–15; ROTARY (CLUB) + -AN] **—Ro·tar′i·an·ism,** *n.*

ro·ta·ry (rō′tə rē), *adj., n., pl.* **-ries.** —*adj.* **1.** turning or capable of turning around on an axis, as a wheel. **2.** taking place around an axis, as motion. **3.** having a part or parts that turn on an axis, as a machine. —*n.* **4.** a rotary device or machine. **5.** *Chiefly Northeastern U.S.* See **traffic circle. 6.** Also called **ro′tary convert′er.** *Elect.* See **synchronous converter. 7.** (*cap.*) See **Rotary Club.** [1725–35; < ML *rotārius* (adj.), equiv. to L *rot(a)* wheel + *-ārius* -ARY]

ro′tary beat′er, a culinary utensil or device, as an eggbeater, with one or more sets of rotary blades for beating, whipping, mixing, etc.

Ro′tary Club′, a local club of business and professional men that is a member of a world-wide organization of similar clubs **(Ro′tary Interna′tional)** devoted to serving the community and promoting world peace.

ro′tary di′al, dial (def. 4). **—ro′ta·ry-di′al,** *adj.*

ro′tary en′gine, 1. an engine, as a turbine, in which the impelling fluid produces torque directly rather than by acting upon reciprocating parts. **2.** a revolving radial engine. [1810–20]

ro′tary hoe′, a cultivating implement consisting of a row of wheels each with many fingerlike prongs, pulled over the ground to break up the soil and destroy weeds.

ro′tary plow′, a tined auger mounted on a horizontal power-driven shaft, for pulverizing unplowed soil preparatory to planting. Also called **rotary tiller.** [1885–90]

ro′tary press′, *Print.* a printing press in which the type or plates to be printed are fastened upon a rotating cylinder and are impressed on a continuous roll of moving paper. [1925–30]

ro′tary pump′, a pump for transferring water or other fluids by the rotating action of its component parts, as by the meshing of vanes or screws.

ro′tary shut′ter, a camera shutter consisting of a rotating disk pierced with a slit that passes in front of the lens to expose the film or plate.

ro·ta·ry-till (rō′tə rē til′), *v.t., v.i.* rototill.

ro′tary till′er, 1. rototiller. **2.** rotary plow.

ro′tary valve′, *Mach.* a valve that rotates continuously or through an arc to open and close.

ro′tary wing′, *Aeron.* an airfoil that rotates about an approximately vertical axis, as that supporting a helicopter or autogiro in flight. [1930–35]

ro·tate[1] (rō′tāt *or, esp. Brit.,* rō tāt′), *v.,* **-tat·ed, -tat·ing.** —*v.t.* **1.** to cause to turn around an axis or center point; revolve. **2.** to cause to go through a cycle of changes; cause to pass or follow in a fixed routine of succession: *to rotate farm crops.* **3.** to replace (a person, troops, etc.) by another or others, usually according to a schedule or plan. —*v.i.* **4.** to turn around on or as if on an axis. **5.** to proceed in a fixed routine of succession: *The sentries rotated in keeping watch.* [1800–10; < L *rotātus* (ptp. of *rotāre* to cause to spin, roll, move in a circle), equiv. to *rot(a)* wheel + *-ātus* -ATE[1]] **—ro′tat·a·ble,** *adj.* **—ro′tat·a·bly,** *adv.* **—Syn. 1.** wheel, whirl. See **turn.**

ro·tate[2] (rō′tāt), *adj.* wheel-shaped: applied esp. to a gamopetalous short-tubed corolla with a spreading limb. See illus. under **corolla.** [1775–85; < L *rot(a)* wheel + -ATE[1]]

ro′tating prism′, *Optics.* See **Dove prism.**

ro·ta·tion (rō tā′shən), *n.* **1.** the act of rotating; a turning around as on an axis. **2.** *Astron.* **a.** the movement or path of the earth or a heavenly body turning on its axis. **b.** one complete turn of such a body. **3.** regularly recurring succession, as of officials. **4.** *Agric.* See **crop rotation. 5.** *Math.* **a.** an operation that rotates a geometric figure about a fixed point. **b.** curl (def. 17). **6.** *Pool.* a game in which the balls are played in order by number. **7.** *Baseball.* See **pitching rotation.** [1545–55; < L *rotātiōn-* (s. of *rotātiō*) a rotation, rolling, equiv. to *rotāt(us)* (see ROTATE[1]) + *-iōn-* -ION] **—ro·ta′tion·al,** *adj.*

rota′tional mold′ing, a method for molding hollow plastic objects by placing finely divided particles in a hollow mold that is rotated about two axes, exposing it to heat and then to cold. Also called **rota′tional cast′ing.**

rota′tional quan′tum num′ber, *Physics.* the quantum number that distinguishes the angular momentum states associated with the rotational motion of a molecule. [1935–40]

rota′tion ax′is, *Crystall.* an imaginary line through a crystal about which the crystal may be rotated a specified number of degrees and be brought back to its original position. Also called **axis of symmetry, symmetry axis of rotation.** Cf. **symmetry element.** [1900–05]

ro·ta′tion-in·ver′sion ax′is (rō tā′shən in vûr′-zhən, -shən), *Crystall.* an axis of a crystal such that rotating about the axis and then inverting the crystal brings the crystal back to its original position. Also called **symmetry axis of rotary inversion.** Cf. **symmetry element.**

rota′tion of ax′es (ak′sēz), *Math.* a process of replacing the axes in a Cartesian coordinate system with a new set of axes making a specified angle with and having the same origin as the original axes.

ro·ta·tive (rō′tā tiv), *adj.* **1.** rotating or pertaining to rotation. **2.** producing rotation. **3.** happening in regular succession. [1770–80; < L *rotāt(us)* (see ROTATE[1]) + -IVE] **—ro·ta·tive·ly** (rō′tā tiv lē, -tə-), *adv.*

ro·ta·tor (rō′tā tər *or, esp. Brit.,* rō tā′-), *n., pl.* **ro·ta·tors** for 1, 3, **ro·ta·tor·es** (rō′tə tôr′ēz, -tōr′-) for 2. **1.** a person or thing that rotates. **2.** *Anat.* a muscle serving to rotate a part of the body. **3.** *Naut.* a bladed device streamed to rotate in the water to actuate a patent log. [1670–80; < L *rotātor,* equiv. to *rotā(re)* (see ROTATE[1]) + *-tor* -TOR]

ro′tator cuff′, a bandlike structure encircling and supporting the shoulder joint, formed by four muscles attached to and merging with the joint capsule.

ro·ta·to·ry (rō′tə tôr′ē, -tōr′ē), *adj.* **1.** pertaining to or of the nature of rotation: *rotatory motion.* **2.** rotating, as an object. **3.** passing or following in rotation or succession. **4.** causing rotation, as a muscle. [1745–55; < NL *rotātōrius,* equiv. to L *rotā(re)* (see ROTATE[1]) + *-tōrius* -TORY]

ro·ta·vi·rus (rō′tə vī′rəs), *n., pl.* **-rus·es.** a double-stranded RNA virus of the genus *Rotavirus,* family Reoviridae, that is a major cause of infant diarrhea. [1974; < L *rota* wheel + VIRUS]

R.O.T.C. (är′ō tē sē′, rot′sē). See **Reserve Officers Training Corps.** Also, **ROTC**

rote[1] (rōt), *n.* **1.** routine; a fixed, habitual, or mechanical course of procedure: *the rote of daily living.* **2. by rote,** from memory, without thought of the meaning; in a mechanical way: *to learn a language by rote.* [1275–1325; ME; of obscure orig.]

rote[2] (rōt), *n. Music.* crowd[2]. Also, **rota, rotta, rotte.** [1350–1400; ME < OF < Frankish **hrota* (cf. OHG *hruozza*); akin to CROWD[2]]

rote[3] (rōt), *n.* the sound of waves breaking on the shore. [1600–10; perh. < ON *rauta* roar]

ro·te·none (rōt′n ōn′), *n. Chem., Pharm.* a white, crystalline, water-insoluble, poisonous heterocyclic compound, $C_{23}H_{22}O_6$, obtained from derris root: used chiefly as the active ingredient of certain insecticides and in medicine in the treatment of chiggers and scabies. [1920–25; *roten-* (said to be < Japn) + -ONE]

rot·gut (rot′gut′), *n. Slang.* cheap and inferior liquor. [1590–1600; ROT + GUT]

Roth (rôth, roth), *n.* **Phillip,** born 1933, U.S. novelist and short-story writer.

Roth·er·ham (roth′ər əm), *n.* a city in South Yorkshire, in N England. 248,700.

Roth·er·mere (roth′ər mēr′), *n.* **1st Viscount.** See **Harmsworth, Harold Sidney.**

Rothe·say (roth′sē, -sā), *n.* a town in the Strathclyde region, on Bute island, in SW Scotland: resort; ruins of 11th-century castle. 6524.

Roth·ko (roth′kō), *n.* **Mark,** 1903–70, U.S. painter, born in Russia.

Roth·schild (rôth′chīld, rôths′-, roth-, roths′-; *Ger.* RŌT′shilt), *n.* **1. Lionel Nathan, Baron de** *("Lord Natty"),* 1809–79, English banker: first Jewish member of Parliament (son of Nathan Meyer Rothschild). **2. May·er** (mī′ər, mā′ər; *Ger.* mī′ər) or **Mey·er** (mī′ər; *Ger.* mī′ər) **Am·schel** (am′shəl; *Ger.* äm′shəl) or **An·selm** (an′selm; *Ger.* än′zelm), 1743–1812, German banker: founder of the Rothschild family and international banking firm. **3.** his son, **Nathan Meyer, Baron de,** 1777–1836, English banker, born in Germany.

rô·ti (rō tē′), *n. French.* roast.

ro·ti·fer (rō′tə fər), *n.* any microscopic animal of the phylum (or class) Rotifera, found in fresh and salt waters, having one or more rings of cilia on the anterior end. Also called **wheel animalcule.** [1785–95; < NL; see ROTIFERA] —**ro·tif·er·al** (rō tif′ər əl), **ro·tif′er·ous,** *adj.*

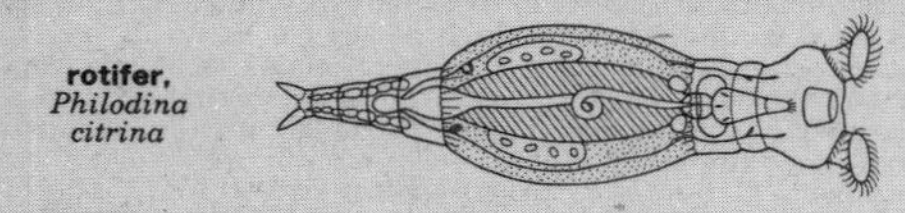

rotifer, *Philodina citrina*

Ro·tif·er·a (rō tif′ər ə), *n.* the phylum or class comprising the rotifers. [1820–30; < NL, equiv. to L *rot(a)* wheel + *-i-* -I- + *-fera,* neut. pl. of *-fer* -FER]

ro·ti·form (rō′tə fôrm′), *adj.* shaped like a wheel. [1850–55; < NL *rotiformis,* equiv. to L *rot(a)* wheel + *-i-* -I- + *-formis* -FORM]

ro·tis·ser·ie (rō tis′ə rē), *n., v.,* **-ied, -i·ing.** —*n.* **1.** a small broiler with a motor-driven spit, for barbecuing fowl, beef, etc. —*v.t.* **2.** to broil on a rotisserie. [1865–70; < F: roasting place]

rot·l (rot′l), *n., pl.* **rotls, ar·tal** (är′täl). **1.** a unit of weight used in Islamic countries, varying widely in value, but of the order of the pound. **2.** a varying unit of dry measure, used in the same areas. [1605–15; < Ar *raṭl* < Gk *lítra* or L *libra* pound]

ro·to (rō′tō), *n., pl.* **ro·tos.** rotogravure. [1930–35; by shortening]

ro·to·gra·vure (rō′tə grə vyŏŏr′, -grā′vyər), *n.* **1.** a photomechanical process by which pictures, typeset matter, etc., are printed from an intaglio copper cylinder. **2.** a print made by this process. **3.** a section of a newspaper consisting of pages printed by the rotogravure process; magazine section. [1910–15; < G *Rotogravur,* orig. in the name of a Berlin printing firm (*Rotogravur Deutsche Tiefdruck Gesellschaft*), allegedly formed from the names of two other firms, *Rotophot* and *Deutshe Photogravur AG;* cf. PHOTOGRAVURE, ROTARY]

ro·tor (rō′tər), *n.* **1.** *Elect.* a rotating member of a machine. Cf. **stator** (def. 1). **2.** *Aeron.* a system of rotating airfoils, as the horizontal ones of a helicopter or of the compressor of a jet engine. **3.** any of a number of tall, cylindrical devices mounted on a special ship **(ro′tor ship′)** and rotated in such a way that the Magnus effect of wind impinging on the cylinders is used to drive and maneuver the vessel. **4.** (in a self-winding watch) a weight eccentrically mounted on an arbor for keeping the mainspring wound. [1873; short for ROTATOR]

ro′tor blade′, *Aeron.* one airfoil of the rotor of a rotary-wing aircraft. [1930–35]

ro′tor cloud′, a cloud within and around which the air is rotating about a horizontal axis, occurring in the lee of a large mountain barrier. Also called **roll cloud.** [1955–60]

ro·tor·craft (rō′tər kraft′, -kräft′), *n.* a rotary-wing aircraft. Also called **ro′tor plane′.** [1950–55; ROTOR + CRAFT]

CONCISE ETYMOLOGY KEY: <, descended or borrowed from; >, whence; b., blend of, blended; c., cognate with; cf., compare; deriv., derivative; equiv., equivalent; imit., imitative; obl., oblique; r., replacing; s., stem; sp., spelling, spelled; resp., respelling, respelled; trans., translation; ?, origin unknown; *, unattested; ‡, probably earlier than. See the full key inside the front cover.

Ro·to·ru·a (rō′tə rōō′ə), *n.* a city on N central North Island, in New Zealand. 46,650.

ro·to·till (rō′tə til′), *v.t.* **1.** to break up (soil) with a rototiller. —*v.i.* **2.** to break up soil with a rototiller. [1935–40; back formation from ROTOTILLER]

ro·to·till·er (rō′tə til′ər), *n.* a motorized device having spinning blades perpendicular to the ground and arranged like spokes, used for tilling soil. Also **ro′to-till′·er, ro′to till′er.** Also called **rotary tiller.** [1920–25; ROT(ARY) + -O- + TILLER[1]]

rot·proof (rot′prōōf′), *adj.* resistant to rotting. [ROT + -PROOF]

rotte (rot), *n. Music.* rote[2]. Also, **rot·ta** (rot′ə).

rot·ten (rot′n), *adj.,* **-er, -est. 1.** decomposing or decaying; putrid; tainted, foul, or bad-smelling. **2.** corrupt or morally offensive. **3.** wretchedly bad, unpleasant, or unsatisfactory; miserable: *a rotten piece of work; a rotten day at the office.* **4.** contemptible; despicable: *a rotten little liar; a rotten trick.* **5.** (of soil, rocks, etc.) soft, yielding, or friable as the result of decomposition. **6.** *Australian Slang.* drunk. [1175–1225; ME *roten* < ON *rotinn,* ptp. of an unrecorded verb meaning "to rot"] —**rot′ten·ly,** *adv.* —**rot′ten·ness,** *n.*
—**Syn. 1.** fetid, rank. **2.** immoral. **4.** disgusting, unwholesome; treacherous. —**Ant. 1.** sound. **2.** moral.

rot′ten bor′ough, 1. (before the Reform Bill of 1832) any English borough that had very few voters yet was represented in Parliament. **2.** an election district that has more representatives in a legislative body than the number of its constituents would normally call for. [1805–15]

rot′ten ice′, *Naut.* ice pitted or honeycombed from melting. [1840–50]

rot·ten·stone (rot′n stōn′), *n.* a friable stone resulting from the decomposition of a siliceous limestone, used as a powder for polishing metals. [1670–80; ROTTEN + STONE]

rot·ter (rot′ər), *n. Chiefly Brit. Slang.* a bad, worthless, or objectionable person. [1890–95; ROT + -ER[1]]

Rot·ter·dam (rot′ər dam′; *for 1 also Du.* RÔT′ƏR-däm′), *n.* **1.** a seaport in SW Netherlands. 558,832. **2.** a town in E New York, on the Mohawk River. 29,451.

Rott·wei·ler (rot′wī lər), *n.* one of a German breed of large, powerful dogs having a short, coarse, black coat with tan to brown markings. [1905–10; < G, after *Rottweil* city in southwest Germany; see -ER[1]]

ro·tund (rō tund′), *adj.* **1.** round in shape; rounded: *rotund fruit.* **2.** plump; fat. **3.** full-toned or sonorous: *rotund speech.* [1695–1705; < L *rotundus* round, circular, deriv. of *rota* wheel; cf. ROUND[1]] —**ro·tund′ly,** *adv.*
—**Syn. 2.** obese, fleshy, corpulent, stout, portly.

ro·tun·da (rō tun′də), *n.* **1.** a round building, esp. one with a dome. **2.** a large and high circular hall or room in a building, esp. one surmounted by a dome. [1680–90; alter. of It *rotonda,* n. use of fem. of *rotondo* < L *rotundus* ROTUND]

rotunda (def. 1)

ro·tun·di·ty (rō tun′di tē), *n., pl.* **-ties. 1.** the condition or quality of roundness or plumpness, as of an object or person. **2.** fullness, as in tone or speech. **3.** a full or rounded tone, phrase, or the like: *oratorical rotundities.* Also, **ro·tund′ness.** [1580–90; < L *rotunditās.* See ROTUND, -ITY]

ro·tu·rier (RÔ TY RYā′; *Eng.* rō tŏŏr′ē ā′, -tyŏŏr′-), *n., pl.* **-tu·riers** (-TY RYā′; *Eng.* -tŏŏr′ē āz′, -tyŏŏr′-). *French.* a person of low rank; plebeian.

Rou·ault (rōō ō′; *Fr.* RWō), *n.* **Georges** (zhôRzh), 1871–1958, French painter.

Rou·baix (Rōō be′), *n.* a city in N France, NE of Lille. 109,797.

rou·ble (rōō′bəl), *n.* ruble.

rou·é (rōō ā′, rōō′ā), *n.* a dissolute and licentious man; rake. [1790–1800; < F, n. use of ptp. of *rouer* to break on the wheel (deriv. of *roue* wheel << L *rota*); name first applied to the profligate companions of the Duc d'Orléans (c1720)]
—**Syn.** profligate, libertine, lecher, cad, bounder, rakehell.

Rou·en (rōō äN′, -än′; *Fr.* RWäN), *n.* **1.** a city in and the capital of Seine-Maritime, in N France, on the Seine: famous cathedral; execution of Joan of Arc 1431. 118,332. **2.** one of a breed of domestic ducks resembling the wild mallard.

Rouen′ li′lac, a shrub, *Syringa chinensis,* of France, having clusters of fragrant, purple flowers. [1880–85]

rou·gail (rōō gī′), *n.* a combination of condiments and spices, as ginger, thyme, pimiento, and tomatoes, used esp. in Creole cookery. [< F < French-based creoles of the Indian Ocean (Mauritius, Réunion, etc.); ulterior orig. undetermined]

rouge (rōōzh), *n., v.,* **rouged, roug·ing.** —*n.* **1.** any of various red cosmetics for coloring the cheeks or lips. **2.** a reddish powder, chiefly ferric oxide, used for polishing metal, glass, etc. **3.** See **Canadian football.** —*v.t.* **4.** to color with rouge. —*v.i.* **5.** to use rouge. [1475–85; < F: red < L *rubeus;* akin to RED[1]]

rouge (Rōōzh), *adj. French.* red; noting the red numbers in roulette. Cf. **noir.**

rouge et noir (rōōzh′ ā nwär′; *Fr.* Rōōzh ā NWAR′), a gambling game using cards, played at a table marked with two red and two black diamond-shaped spots on which the players place their stakes. [1785–95; < F: red and black]

Rou·get de Lisle (Rōō zhe′ də lēl′), **Claude Joseph** (klōd zhô zef′), 1760–1836, French army officer and composer of songs: wrote and composed *Marseillaise.* Also, **Rou·get′ de l'Isle′.**

rough (ruf), *adj.,* **-er, -est,** *n., adv., v.* —*adj.* **1.** having a coarse or uneven surface, as from projections, irregularities, or breaks; not smooth: *rough, red hands; a rough road.* **2.** shaggy or coarse: *a dog with a rough coat.* **3.** (of an uninhabited region or large land area) steep or uneven and covered with high grass, brush, trees, stones, etc.: *to hunt over rough country.* **4.** acting with or characterized by violence: *Boxing is a rough sport.* **5.** characterized by unnecessary violence or infractions of the rules: *It was a rough prize fight.* **6.** violently disturbed or agitated; turbulent, as water or the air: *a rough sea.* **7.** having a violently irregular motion; uncomfortably or dangerously uneven: *The plane had a rough flight in the storm.* **8.** stormy or tempestuous, as wind or weather. **9.** sharp or harsh: *a rough temper.* **10.** unmannerly or rude: *his rough and churlish manner; They exchanged rough words.* **11.** disorderly or riotous: *a rough mob.* **12.** difficult or unpleasant: *to have a rough time of it.* **13.** harsh to the ear; grating or jarring, as sounds. **14.** harsh to the taste; sharp or astringent: *a rough wine.* **15.** coarse, as food. **16.** lacking culture or refinement: *a rough, countrified manner.* **17.** without refinements, luxuries, or ordinary comforts or conveniences: *rough camping.* **18.** requiring exertion or strength rather than intelligence or skill: *rough manual labor.* **19.** not elaborated, perfected, or corrected; unpolished, as language, verse, or style: *a rough draft.* **20.** made or done without any attempt at exactness, completeness, or thoroughness; approximate or tentative: *a rough guess.* **21.** crude, unwrought, nonprocessed, or unprepared: *rough rice.* **22.** *Phonet.* uttered with aspiration; having the sound of *h;* aspirated. —*n.* **23.** something that is rough, esp. rough ground. **24.** *Golf.* any part of the course bordering the fairway on which the grass, weeds, etc., are not trimmed. **25.** the unpleasant or difficult part of anything. **26.** anything in its crude or preliminary form, as a drawing. **27.** *Chiefly Brit.* a rowdy; ruffian. **28. in the rough,** in a rough, crude, or unfinished state: *The country has an exciting potential, but civilization there is still in the rough.* —*adv.* **29.** in a rough manner; roughly. —*v.t.* **30.** to make rough; roughen. **31.** to give a beating to, manhandle, or subject to physical violence (often fol. by *up*): *The mob roughed up the speaker.* **32.** to subject to some rough, preliminary process of working or preparation (often fol. by *down, off,* or *out*): *to rough off boards.* **33.** to sketch roughly or in outline (often fol. by *in* or *out*): *to rough out a diagram; to rough in the conversation of a novel.* **34.** *Sports.* to subject (a player on the opposing team) to unnecessary physical abuse, as in blocking or tackling: *The team was penalized 15 yards for roughing the kicker.* —*v.i.* **35.** to become rough, as a surface. **36.** to behave roughly. **37. rough it,** to live without the customary comforts or conveniences; endure rugged conditions: *We really roughed it on our fishing trip.* [bef. 1000; ME (adj. and n.); OE *rūh* (adj.); c. D *ruig,* G *rauh*] —**rough′ly,** *adv.* —**rough′ness,** *n.*
—**Syn. 1.** irregular, jagged, bumpy, craggy. **2.** hairy, bristly. **13.** noisy, cacophonous, raucous. **16.** impolite, uncivil, unpolished, rude. —**Ant. 1.** smooth, even, regular.

rough·age (ruf′ij), *n.* **1.** rough or coarse material. **2.** any coarse, rough food for livestock. **3.** fiber (def. 9). [1880–85; ROUGH + -AGE]

rough-and-read·y (ruf′ən red′ē), *adj.* **1.** rough, rude, or crude, but good enough for the purpose: *a rough-and-ready estimate of future expenses.* **2.** exhibiting or showing rough vigor rather than refinement or delicacy: *a cowboy—the rough-and-ready type.* [1800–10] —**rough′-and-read′i·ness,** *n.*

rough-and-tum·ble (ruf′ən tum′bəl), *adj.* **1.** characterized by violent, random, disorderly action and struggles: *a rough-and-tumble fight; He led an adventuresome, rough-and-tumble life.* **2.** given to such action. —*n.* **3.** rough and unrestrained competition, fighting, struggling, etc. [1785–95]

rough′ blue′grass, a grass, *Poa trivialis,* native to Eurasia and naturalized in North America, where it is used in mixtures for lawns and pasturage. [1920–25]

rough′ breath′ing, 1. the symbol (ʽ) used in the writing of Greek to indicate aspiration of the initial vowel or of the ρ (rho) over which it is placed. **2.** the aspirated sound indicated by this mark. Cf. **smooth breathing.** [1740–50; trans. of L *spiritus asper*]

rough·cast (ruf′kast′, -käst′), *n., v.,* **-cast, -cast·ing.** —*n.* **1.** Also called **spatter dash.** an exterior wall finish composed of mortar and fine pebbles mixed together and dashed against the wall. Cf. **pebble dash. 2.** a crudely formed pattern or model. —*v.t.* **3.** to cover or coat with roughcast. **4.** to make, shape, or prepare in a rough form: *to roughcast a story.* [1510–20; ROUGH + CAST] —**rough′cast′er,** *n.*

rough′ cut′, *Motion Pictures.* the first assembly of a film following preliminary cutting and editing. Cf. **final cut.** [1935–40]

rough-cut (ruf′kut′), *adj.* cut into small, irregular pieces (contrasted with *fine-cut*): *rough-cut tobacco.* [1965–70]

rough-dry (ruf′drī′), *v.,* **-dried, -dry·ing,** *adj.* —*v.t.* **1.** to dry (laundry) after washing, without smoothing, ironing, etc. —*adj.* **2.** (of laundered clothes, sheets, etc.) dried but not ironed. Also, **rough′dry′.** [1830–40]

rough·en (ruf′ən), *v.t., v.i.* to make or become rough or rougher. [1580–90; ROUGH + -EN[1]] —**rough′en·er,** *n.*

rough′ endoplas′mic retic′ulum. See under **endoplasmic reticulum.**

rough·er (ruf′ər), *n.* a person or thing that roughs or roughs out something, as certain crude cutting tools or a person who performs the first, rough parts of a process. [1880–85; ROUGH + -ER[1]]

rough′ fish′, any fish that is not valued as a sport fish or considered a significant source of food by sport fishers. [1835–45]

rough-hew (ruf′hyo͞o′), *v.t.,* **-hewed, -hewed** or **-hewn, -hew·ing. 1.** to hew (timber, stone, etc.) roughly or without smoothing or finishing. **2.** to shape roughly; give crude form to. Also, **rough′hew′.** [1520–30]

rough·house (*n.* ruf′hous′; *v.* ruf′hous′, -houz′), *n., pl.* **-hous·es** (-hou′ziz), *v.,* **-housed** (-houst′, -houzd′), **-hous·ing** (-hou′sing, -zing). —*n.* **1.** rough, disorderly playing, esp. indoors. —*v.i.* **2.** to engage in rough, disorderly play. —*v.t.* **3.** to handle roughly but with playful intent: *to roughhouse the cat.* [1885–90, *Amer.*; ROUGH + HOUSE]

rough·ing-in (ruf′ing in′), *n. Building Trades.* **1.** the act or process of applying a base coat of plaster to a masonry surface. **2.** the act or process of installing plumbing that will later be concealed. [1815–25]

rough′ing mill′, *Metall.* a rolling mill for converting steel ingots into blooms, billets, or slabs. [1840–50]

rough·ish (ruf′ish), *adj.* rather rough: *a roughish sea.* [1755–65; ROUGH + -ISH[1]]

rough′-leg′ged hawk′ (ruf′leg′id, -legd′), a large hawk, *Buteo lagopus,* of the Northern Hemisphere, that feeds chiefly on small rodents. [1805–15, *Amer.*]

rough′ lem′on, a variety of lemon that has orange-yellow, rough-skinned fruit and is used as a rootstock for the cultivation of other citrus fruits. [1895–1900]

rough·neck (ruf′nek′), *n.* **1.** a rough, coarse person; a tough. **2.** any laborer working on an oil-drilling rig. Cf. **roustabout** (def. 4). —*v.i.* **3.** to work as a roughneck. [1830–40, *Amer.*; ROUGH + NECK]

rough·rid·er (ruf′rī′dər), *n.* **1.** a person who breaks horses to the saddle. **2.** a person accustomed to rough or hard riding. [1725–35; ROUGH + RIDER]

Rough′ Rid′ers, the members of a volunteer regiment of cavalry organized by Theodore Roosevelt and Leonard Wood for service in the Spanish-American War.

rough-sawn (ruf′sôn′), *adj.* (of wood) used as originally cut, without smoothing or sanding: *shingles of rough-sawn cedar.* [1885–90]

rough·shod (ruf′shod′), *adj.* **1.** shod with horseshoes having projecting nails or points. **2. ride roughshod over,** to treat harshly or domineeringly; override; crush: *He rode roughshod over his friends to advance himself in the business world.* [1680–90; ROUGH + SHOD]

rough-spo·ken (ruf′spō′kən), *adj.* coarse or vulgar in speech. [1625–35]

rough′ stuff′, *Informal.* **1.** violence, as physical assault, torture or shooting. **2.** unnecessary violence or infractions of the rules, as in sports. **3.** blatant vulgarity or obscenity. [1885–90]

rough-voiced (ruf′voist′), *adj.* having a harsh or grating voice: *a rough-voiced barker.* [1810–20]

rough′-winged swal′low (ruf′wingd′), **1.** either of two New World swallows of the genus *Stelgidopteryx,* having outer primary feathers with small barblike hooks on the margins. **2.** any of several African swallows of the genus *Psalidoprocne,* having similar feathers. [1830–40, *Amer.*]

roul., *Philately.* roulette.

rou·lade (ro͞o läd′), *n.* **1.** a musical embellishment consisting of a rapid succession of tones sung to a single syllable. **2.** a slice of meat rolled around a filling of minced meat and cooked. [1700–10; < F: a rolling, equiv. to *roul(er)* to roll + *-ade* -ADE[1]]

rou·leau (ro͞o lō′), *n., pl.* **-leaux, -leaus** (-lōz′). **1.** a roll or strip of something, as trimming on a hat brim. **2.** a stack or roll of coins put up in cylindrical form in a paper wrapping. [1685–95; < F; MF *rolel,* dim. of *role* ROLL]

Rou·lers (ro͞o lârs′; *Fr.* RO͞O LER′), *n.* a city in NW Belgium: battles 1914, 1918. 39,826.

engravers' roulettes (def. 2)

rou·lette (ro͞o let′), *n., v.,* **-let·ted, -let·ting.** —*n.* **1.** a game of chance played at a table marked off with numbers from 1 to 36, one or two zeros, and several other sections affording the players a variety of betting opportunities, and having in the center a revolving, dishlike device **(roulette′ wheel′)** into which a small ball is spun to come to rest finally in one of the 37 or 38 compartments, indicating the winning number and its characteristics, as odd or even, red or black, and between 1 and 18 or 19 and 36. **2.** a small wheel, esp. one with sharp teeth, mounted in a handle, for making lines of marks, dots, or perforations: *engravers' roulettes; a roulette for perforating sheets of postage stamps.* **3.** *Philately.* a row of short cuts, in which no paper is removed, made between individual stamps to permit their ready separation. —*v.t.* **4.** to mark, impress, or perforate with a roulette. [1725–35; < F, dim. of *rouelle* wheel. See ROWEL]

Roum., **1.** Roumania. **2.** Roumanian.

Rou·ma·ni·a (ro͞o mā′nē ə, -mān′yə), *n.* Rumania. —**Rou·ma′ni·an,** *adj., n.*

Rou·me·li·a (ro͞o mē′lē ə, -mēl′yə), *n.* Rumelia.

round[1] (round), *adj.,* **-er, -est,** *n., adv., prep., v.* —*adj.* **1.** having a flat, circular surface, as a disk. **2.** ring-shaped, as a hoop. **3.** curved like part of a circle, as an outline. **4.** having a circular cross section, as a cylinder; cylindrical. **5.** spherical or globular, as a ball. **6.** shaped more or less like a part of a sphere; hemispherical. **7.** free from angularity; consisting of full, curved lines or shapes, as handwriting or parts of the body. **8.** executed with or involving circular motion. **9.** full, complete, or entire: *a round dozen.* **10.** noting, formed, or expressed by an integer or whole number with no fraction. **11.** expressed, given, or exact to the nearest multiple or power of ten; in tens, hundreds, thousands, or the like: *in round numbers.* **12.** roughly correct; approximate: *a round guess.* **13.** considerable in amount; ample: *a round sum of money.* **14.** brought to completeness or perfection. **15.** full and sonorous, as sound. **16.** vigorous or brisk: *a round trot.* **17.** straightforward, plain, or candid; outspoken: *a round scolding.* **18.** positive or unqualified: *a round assertion.* —*n.* **19.** any round shape, as a circle, ring or sphere. **20.** a circular, ring-shaped, curved, or spherical object; a rounded form. **21.** something circular in cross section, as a rung of a ladder or chair. **22.** Sometimes, **rounds.** a completed course of time, series of events or operations, etc., ending at a point corresponding to that at the beginning: *We waited through the round of many years.* **23.** any complete course, series, or succession: *The strike was settled after a long round of talks; a round of parties.* **24.** Often, **rounds.** a going around from place to place, as in a habitual or definite circuit: *a doctor's rounds.* **25.** a completed course or spell of activity, commonly one of a series, in some play or sport: *the second round of a tournament.* **26.** a recurring period of time, succession of events, duties, etc.: *the daily round.* **27.** an entire range: *the round of human capabilities.* **28.** a single outburst, as of applause or cheers. **29.** a single discharge of shot by each of a number of guns, rifles, etc. **30.** a single discharge by one firearm. **31.** a charge of ammunition for a single shot. **32.** a single serving, esp. of drink, made more or less simultaneously to everyone present, as at table or at a bar: *The next round is on me.* **33.** See **round dance. 34.** movement in a circle or around an axis. **35.** *Cookery.* **a.** Also, **round of beef.** the portion of the thigh of beef below the rump and above the leg. See diag. under **beef. b.** *Informal.* See **round steak. 36.** a slice, as of bread. **37.** *Archery.* a specified number of arrows shot from a specified distance from the target in accordance with the rules. **38.** one of a series of three-minute periods making up a boxing match: *a 15-round bout.* **39.** *Music.* **a.** a short, rhythmical canon at the unison, in which the several voices enter at equally spaced intervals of time. **b. rounds,** the order followed in ringing a peal of bells in diatonic sequence from the highest to the lowest. **40.** *Golf.* a playing of the complete course. **41.** *Cards.* a division of play in a game, consisting of a turn each for every player to bid, bet, play a card, deal the cards, or be dealt cards. **42. in the round, a.** (of a theater) having a stage completely surrounded by seats for the audience. **b.** in the style of theater-in-the-round: *The play should be done in the round.* **c.** in complete detail; from all aspects: *a character as seen in the round.* **d.** (of sculpture) not attached to a supporting background; freestanding. **43. make the rounds, a.** to go from one place to another, as in making deliveries, paying social visits, or seeking employment. **b.** Also, **go the rounds.** to be reported or told; circulate: *another rumor making the rounds.* —*adv.* **44.** throughout or from the beginning to the end of a recurring period of time: *all year round.* **45.** Also, **'round.** around: *The music goes round and round.* —*prep.* **46.** throughout (a period of time): *a resort visited all round the year.* **47.** around: *It happened round noon.* —*v.t.* **48.** to make round. **49.** to free from angularity; fill out symmetrically; make plump. **50.** to bring to completeness or perfection; finish. **51.** *Jewelry.* to form (a gem) roughly (sometimes fol. by *up*); girdle. **52.** to end (a sentence, paragraph, etc.) with something specified: *He rounded his speech with a particularly apt quotation.* **53.** to encircle or surround. **54.** to make a complete circuit of; pass completely around. **55.** to make a turn or partial circuit around or to the other side of: *to round a corner.* **56.** to cause to move in a circle; turn around. **57.** *Phonet.* **a.** to make the opening at (the lips) relatively round or pursed during an utterance. **b.** to pronounce (a speech sound, esp. a vowel) with rounded lips; labialize. **c.** to contract (the lips) laterally. Cf. **spread** (def. 14), **unround. 58.** *Math.* to replace by the nearest multiple of 10, with 5 being increased to the next highest multiple: 15,837 can be rounded to 15,840; then to 15,800; then to 16,000. —*v.i.* **59.** to become round. **60.** to become free from angularity; become plump. **61.** to develop to completeness or perfection. **62.** to take a circular course; make a circuit, as a guard. **63.** to make a turn or partial circuit around something. **64.** to turn around as on an axis: *to round on one's heels.* **65.** to reduce successively the number of digits to the right of the decimal point of a mixed number by dropping the final digit and adding 1 to the next preceding digit if the dropped digit was 5 or greater, or leaving the preceding digit unchanged if the dropped digit was 4 or less. **66. round off, a.** to complete or perfect; finish. **b.** to express as a round number, usually to the nearest multiple of 10. **67. round out, a.** to complete or perfect: *The new coin rounded out his collection.* **b.** to fill out; become rounder: *She rounded out so nicely that everyone soon forgot she had been so ill.* **68. round to,** *Naut.* to turn a sailing vessel in the direction from which the wind is blowing. **69. round up, a.** to drive or bring (cattle, sheep, etc.) together. **b.** to assemble; gather: *to round up all the suspects in an investigation.* [1250–1300; (adj.) ME *rond, round* < OF, s. of *ront,* earlier *reont* < L *rotundus* round, circular (see ROTUND); (n.) ME, partly deriv. of the adj., partly < OF *rond, ronde* (deriv. of *ront*); (v.) ME, deriv. of the adj.; (adv. and prep.) ME, appar. aph. var. of AROUND] —**round′ness,** *n.*
—**Syn. 9.** whole, unbroken. **20.** cylinder. **22.** cycle, revolution, period. —**Ant. 1.** angular.

round[2] (round), *v.t., v.i. Archaic.* to whisper. [bef. 1000; ME *rounen,* OE *rūnian,* deriv. of *rūn* a secret, RUNE[1]]

round·a·bout (*adj.* round′ə bout′, round′ə bout′; *n.* round′ə bout′), *adj.* **1.** circuitous or indirect, as a road, journey, method, statement or person. **2.** (of clothing) cut circularly at the bottom; having no tails, train, or the like. —*n.* **3.** a short, close-fitting coat or jacket worn by men or boys, esp. in the 19th century. **4.** *Brit.* a merry-go-round. **5.** a circuitous or indirect road, method, etc. **6.** *Chiefly Brit.* See **traffic circle.** [1525–35; ROUND[1] (adv.) + ABOUT]
—**Syn. 1.** meandering, twisting, rambling, tortuous.

round′about chair′. See **corner chair.** [1735–45]

round′ an′gle, perigon. [1930–35]

round′ arch′, an arch formed in a continuous curve, esp. in a semicircle. [1830–40]

round′ bar′row, *Archaeol.* a funerary barrow having a bell, disk, saucer, or pond shape, primarily of the Bronze Age and containing the cremated remains of corpses along with grave artifacts. Cf. **long barrow.** [1865–70]

round′ char′acter, a character in fiction whose personality, background, motives, and other features are fully delineated by the author. Cf. **flat character.** [1925–30]

round′ clam′, quahog. [1835–45, *Amer.*]

round′ dance′, **1.** a dance performed by couples and characterized by circular or revolving movement, as the waltz. **2.** a dance in which the dancers are arranged in or move about in a circle or ring. [1675–85]

round·ed (roun′did), *adj.* **1.** reduced to simple curves; made round. **2.** *Phonet.* pronounced with rounded lips; labialized: *"Boot" has a rounded vowel.* Cf. **spread** (def. 41), **unrounded. 3.** fully developed, perfected, or complete; diversified and well-balanced (sometimes used in combination): *a well-rounded education; a rounded character.* **4.** round[1] (def. 11). [1400–50; late ME; see ROUND[1], -ED[2]] —**round′ed·ly,** *adv.* —**round′ed·ness,** *n.*

roun·del (roun′dl), *n.* **1.** something round or circular. **2.** a small, round pane or window. **3.** a decorative plate, panel, tablet, or the like, round in form. **4.** Also, **rondel.** *Theat.* a round piece of colored gelatin or glass placed over stage lights as a color medium to obtain lighting effects. **5.** *Armor.* **a.** a metal disk that protects the armpit. **b.** a metal disk on a hafted weapon or a dagger to protect the hand. **6.** *Heraldry.* a small circular charge. **7.** *Pros.* **a.** a rondel or rondeau. **b.** a modification of the rondeau, consisting of nine lines with two refrains. **8.** a round dance. [1250–1300; ME *roundele, rundel(le)* < OF *rondel,* deriv. of *rond* ROUND[1] (adj.)]

roun·de·lay (roun′dl ā′), *n.* **1.** a song in which a phrase, line, or the like, is continually repeated. **2.** the music for such a song. **3.** a dance in a circle; round dance. [1565–75; alter. (influenced by LAY[4]) of MF *rondelet,* dim. of *rondel* ROUNDEL]

round·er (roun′dər), *n.* **1.** a person or thing that rounds something. **2.** a person who makes a round. **3.** a habitual drunkard or wastrel. **4.** (*cap.*) *Brit.* a Methodist minister who travels a circuit among congregations. **5. rounders,** (*used with a singular v.*) a game somewhat resembling baseball, played in England. **6.** *Informal.* a boxing match of a specified number of rounds: used in combination: *a 15-rounder.* [1615–25; ROUND[1] + -ER[1]]

round-eye (round′ī′), *n., pl.* **-eyes.** *Disparaging.* a Caucasian, as distinguished from an Oriental, person. [1965–70]

round-faced (round′fāst′), *adj.* having a face that is round. [1670–80]

round′ file′. See **circular file.**

round′ hand′, a style of handwriting in which the letters are round, full, and clearly separated. [1675–85]

Round·head (round′hed′), *n. Eng. Hist.* a member or adherent of the Parliamentarians or Puritan party during the civil wars of the 17th century (so called in derision by the Cavaliers because they wore their hair cut short). [1635–45; ROUND[1] + HEAD]

round·head·ed (round′hed′id), *adj.* **1.** (of a person) possessing a round head; brachycephalic. **2.** rounded or spherical at the head, as a screw. **3.** shaped like a semicircle at the top, as a window. **4.** (*usually cap.*) of or pertaining to the Roundheads. **5.** (*usually cap.*) puritanical (def. 2). [1635–45; ROUND[1] + HEADED] —**round′·head′ed·ness,** *n.*

round′headed ap′ple tree′ bor′er. See **apple tree borer** (def. 2).

round·heels (round′hēlz′), *n.* (*used with a singular v.*) *Slang.* a prostitute. [1940–45; ROUND[1] + HEEL[1]]

round′ her′ring, any of several herringlike fishes of the family Dussumieriidae having a rounded abdomen, living chiefly in tropical marine waters. [1835–45, *Amer.*]

round·house (round′hous′), *n., pl.* **-hous·es** (-hou′ziz). **1.** a building for the servicing and repair of locomotives, built around a turntable in the form of some part of a circle. **2.** *Naut.* a cabin on the after part of a quarterdeck. **3.** *Slang.* a punch in which the arm is typically brought straight out to the side or rear of the body and in which the fist describes an exaggerated circular motion. **4.** Also called **round trip.** *Pinochle.* a meld of one king and queen of each suit. [1580–90; ROUND[1] + HOUSE]

round·ing (roun′ding), *adj.* **1.** round or nearly round. **2.** of, pertaining to, or used for making something round. **3.** turning, curving, or circling around. **4.** pertaining to

CONCISE PRONUNCIATION KEY: act, cāpe, dâre, pärt; set, ēqual; *if,* īce; ox, ōver, ôrder, oil, bo͝ok, bo͞ot, out; up, ûrge; child; sing; shoe; thin, *th*at; zh as in *treasure.* ə = *a* as in *alone, e* as in *system, i* as in *easily, o* as in *gallop, u* as in *circus;* ə as in *fire* (fīər), *hour* (ouər). l and n can serve as syllabic consonants, as in *cradle* (krād′l), and *button* (but′n). See the full key inside the front cover.

the mathematical process of rounding: *a rounding error.* —*n.* **5.** the act or process of making something round. **6.** *Math.* **a.** the process of replacing a number by another number of approximately the same value but having fewer digits: *To the nearest dollar, the rounding of $27.68 yields $28.* **b.** a similar process that specifies one of various rules. Generally, the number is first truncated to one or two digits more than is desired; then the last one or two digits are adjusted in a specified way in order to reflect the magnitude of the original number. In rounding the final digits, 0–4 are simply dropped, 6–9 are dropped after the preceding digit is increased by 1, and 5 is handled in various ways depending on the surrounding digits and the particular convention being followed. Cf. **truncate** (def. 2). [1545–55; ROUND[1] + -ING[2], -ING[1]]

round·ish (roun′dish), *adj.* somewhat round: *a roundish man; roundish furniture.* [1535–45; ROUND[1] + -ISH[1]] —**round′ish·ness,** *n.*

round′ kum′quat, an evergreen, citrus shrub or small tree, *Fortunella japonica,* of Japan, having blunt, broad leaves and globe-shaped, edible fruit. Also called **marumi kumquat.**

Round′ Lake′ Beach′, a town in NE Illinois. 12,921.

round·let (round′lit), *n.* a small circle or circular object. [1350–1400; ME *rondlet* < MF *rondelet;* see ROUNDELAY]

round′ lot′, *Stock Exchange.* **1.** the conventional unit or quantity in which commodities or securities are bought and sold. **2.** (in a transaction) a quantity of 100 shares of a stock that is active or 10 shares of a stock that is inactive. Cf. **odd lot.** [1900–05]

round-lot·ter (round′lot′ər), *n.* a buyer or seller of round lots. Cf. **odd-lotter.** [ROUND LOT + -ER[1]]

round·ly (round′lē), *adv.* **1.** in a round manner. **2.** vigorously or briskly. **3.** outspokenly, severely, or unsparingly. **4.** completely or fully. **5.** in round numbers or in a vague or general way. [1400–50; late ME; see ROUND[1], -LY]

round′ of beef′, round (def. 35).

round-off (round′ôf′, -of′), *Math.* —*adj.* **1.** of or pertaining to the act or process of rounding. —*n.* **2.** an act or instance of rounding off decimal or fractional figures. [1945–50; n. use of v. phrase *round off*]

round′ rob′in, **1.** a sequence or series. **2.** a petition, remonstrance, or the like, having the signatures arranged in circular form so as to disguise the order of signing. **3.** a letter, notice, or the like, circulated from person to person in a group, often with individual comments being added by each. **4.** *Sports.* a tournament in which all of the entrants play each other at least once, failure to win a contest not resulting in elimination. Also, **round′-rob′in.** [1540–50]

Round′ Rock′, a town in central Texas. 11,812.

round-shoul·dered (round′shōl′dərd, -shōl′-), *adj.* having the shoulders bent forward, giving a rounded form to the upper part of the back. [1580–90]

rounds·man (roundz′mən), *n., pl.* **-men.** **1.** a person who makes rounds, as of inspection. **2.** *Brit.* a person who makes deliveries, as of milk or bread. **3.** *Australian.* a journalist covering a specific area of interest: *a political roundsman.* **4.** a police officer who inspects the other officers on duty in a particular district. [1785–95; ROUND[1] + 'S[1] + MAN[1]]

round′ steak′, a steak cut from directly above the hind leg of beef. [1920–25]

round′ ta′ble, **1.** a number of persons gathered together for conference, discussion of some subject, etc., and often seated at a round table. **2.** the discussion, topic of discussion, or the conference itself. **3.** (*cap.*) *Arthurian Romance.* **a.** the table, made round to avoid quarrels as to precedence, about which King Arthur and his knights sat. **b.** King Arthur and his knights. Also, **round′ta′ble** (for defs. 1, 2). [1250–1300; ME]

round-ta·ble (round′tā′bəl), *adj.* noting or pertaining to a conference, discussion, or deliberation in which each participant has equal status, equal time to present views, etc.: *round-table discussions.* [1820–30]

round-the-clock (round′thə klok′), *adj.* around-the-clock.

round′ trip′, **1.** a trip to a given place and back again: *Fares for round trips often have a discount.* **2.** a transportation ticket for such a trip. **3.** *Pinochle.* roundhouse (def. 4). [1850–55, *Amer.*] —**round′-trip′,** *adj.*

round-trip·per (round′trip′ər), *n. Baseball Informal.* a home run. [1970–75; ROUND TRIP + -ER[1]]

round′ turn′, a complete turn of a rope or the like around an object. [1835–45]

round·up (round′up′), *n.* **1.** the driving together of cattle, horses, etc., for inspection, branding, shipping to market, or the like, as in the western U.S. **2.** the people and horses who do this. **3.** the herd so collected. **4.** the gathering together of scattered items or groups of people: *a police roundup of suspects.* **5.** a summary, brief listing, or résumé of related facts, figures, or information: *Sunday's newspaper has a sports roundup giving the final score of every baseball game of the past week.* [1760–70; n. use of v. phrase *round up*]

round′ white′fish, a whitefish, *Prosopium cylindraceum,* found in northern North America and Siberia, having silvery sides and a dark bronze back. Also called **Menominee whitefish.** [1880–85, *Amer.*]

round′ win′dow, a membrane-covered opening in the inner wall of the middle ear that compensates for changes in cochlear pressure. [1900–05]

round·worm (round′wûrm′), *n.* any nematode, esp. *Ascaris lumbricoides,* that infests the intestine of humans and other mammals. [1555–65; ROUND[1] + WORM]

roup[1] (ro͞op), *n. Vet. Pathol.* any catarrhal inflammation of the eyes and nasal passages of poultry. [1800–10; orig. uncert.]

roup[2] (ro͞op), *n.* hoarseness or huskiness. [1575–85; prob. imit.]

roup[3] (roup), *n., v.t. Scot. and North Eng.* auction (defs. 1, 3). [1250–1300; ME *roupen* to cry, shout < ON *raupa* to boast (or *hrōpa* to shout)]

roup·y[1] (ro͞o′pē), *adj.* affected with the disease roup. [1715–25; ROUP[1] + -Y[1]] —**roup′i·ly,** *adv.*

roup·y[2] (ro͞o′pē), *adj.,* **roup·i·er, roup·i·est.** hoarse or husky. [1800–10; ROUP[2] + -Y[1]]

Rous (rous, ro͞os), *n.* **(Francis) Peyton,** 1879–1970, U.S. pathologist: Nobel prize for medicine 1966.

rouse[1] (rouz), *v.,* **roused, rous·ing,** *n.* —*v.t.* **1.** to bring out of a state of sleep, unconsciousness, inactivity, fancied security, apathy, depression, etc.: *He was roused to action by courageous words.* **2.** to stir or incite to strong indignation or anger. **3.** to cause (game) to start from a covert or lair. **4.** *Naut.* to pull by main strength; haul. —*v.i.* **5.** to come out of a state of sleep, unconsciousness, inactivity, apathy, depression, etc. **6.** to start up from a covert or lair, as game. —*n.* **7.** a rousing. **8.** a signal for rousing; reveille. [1480–90 in sense "(of a hawk) to shake the feathers"; 1525–35 for def. 3; orig. uncert.] —**rous·ed·ness** (rou′zid nis), *n.* —**rous′er,** *n.*
—**Syn.** **1.** arouse, stir, excite, animate, stimulate, awaken, kindle, inflame, fire. **1, 2.** See **incite.** **2.** provoke, anger. —**Ant.** **1, 2.** lull, calm, pacify.

rouse[2] (rouz), *n.* **1.** *Archaic.* a carouse. **2.** *Obs.* a bumper of liquor. [1595–1605; perh. var. of CAROUSE (*drink carouse* being wrongly analyzed as *drink a rouse*)]

rous·ing (rou′zing), *adj.* **1.** exciting; stirring: *a rousing song.* **2.** active or vigorous: *a rousing campaign.* **3.** brisk; lively: *a rousing business.* **4.** exceptional; extraordinary: *a rousing lie.* [1635–45; ROUSE[1] + -ING[2]] —**rous′ing·ly,** *adv.*

Rous′ sarco′ma (rous), *Vet. Pathol.* a malignant tumor occurring in the connective tissue of poultry, caused by a transmissible RNA-containing virus. [after F. P. ROUS, who described it in 1910]

Rous·seau (ro͞o sō′; *Fr.* ro͞o sō′), *n.* **1. Hen·ri** (äN rē′), (*"Le Douanier"*), 1844–1910, French painter. **2. Jean Jacques** (zhän zhäk), 1712–78, French philosopher, author, and social reformer; born in Switzerland. **3. (Pierre É·tienne) Thé·o·dore** (pyer ā tyen′ te ô dôr′), 1812–67, French painter.

Rous·seau·ism (ro͞o sō′iz əm), *n.* the doctrines or principles of Jean Jacques Rousseau or his adherents. [1860–65; ROUSSEAU + -ISM] —**Rous·seau′ist, Rous·seau′ite,** *n.* —**Rous′seau·is′tic,** *adj.*

Rous·sel (ro͞o sel′), *n.* **Al·bert (Charles Paul Ma·ri)** (al ber′ sharl pôl ma rē′), 1869–1937, French composer.

roust (roust), *v.t.* to rout, as from a place: *to roust someone out of bed.* [1650–60; perh. alter. of ROUSE[1]]

roust·a·bout (roust′ə bout′), *n.* **1.** a wharf laborer or deck hand, as on the Mississippi River. **2.** an unskilled laborer who lives by odd jobs. **3.** a circus laborer who helps in setting up and taking down the tents and in caring for the animals, equipment, and grounds. **4.** any unskilled laborer working in an oil field. Cf. **roughneck** (def. 2). [1865–70, *Amer.;* ROUST + ABOUT]

roust·er (rou′stər), *n.* roustabout (def. 1). [1880–85, *Amer.;* ROUST + -ER[1]]

rout[1] (rout), *n.* **1.** a defeat attended with disorderly flight; dispersal of a defeated force in complete disorder: *to put an army to rout; to put reason to rout.* **2.** any overwhelming defeat: *a rout of the home team by the state champions.* **3.** a tumultuous or disorderly crowd of persons. **4.** the rabble or mob. **5.** *Law.* a disturbance of the public peace by three or more persons acting together in a manner that suggests an intention to riot although they do not actually carry out the intention. **6.** a large, formal evening party or social gathering. **7.** *Archaic.* a company or band of people. —*v.t.* **8.** to disperse in defeat and disorderly flight: *to rout an army.* **9.** to defeat decisively: *to rout an opponent in conversation.* [1200–50; (n.) ME < AF *rute,* OF *route* a fraction, detachment < L *rupta,* fem. ptp. of *rumpere* to break; (v.) deriv. of the n.]
—**Syn.** **3.** swarm, horde. **9.** overwhelm, overcome, subdue.

rout[2] (rout), *v.i.* **1.** to root: *pigs routing in the garden.* **2.** to poke, search, or rummage. —*v.t.* **3.** to turn over or dig up (something) with the snout. **4.** to find or get by searching, rummaging, etc. (usually fol. by *out*). **5.** to cause to rise from bed (often fol. by *up* or *out*). **6.** to force or drive out. **7.** to hollow out or furrow, as with a scoop, gouge, or machine. [1540–50; alter. of ROOT[2]; cf. MD *ruten* to root out]

rout[3] (rout), *v.i. Archaic.* to snore. [bef. 900; ME *routen,* OE *hrūtan;* c. OHG *hrūzan*]

rout[4] (rout, ro͞ot), *Chiefly Brit. Dial.* —*v.i., v.t.* **1.** to bellow; roar. —*n.* **2.** a bellow. [1250–1300; ME *rowten* < ON *rauta* to bellow; akin to L *rudere*]

route (ro͞ot, rout), *n., v.,* **rout·ed, rout·ing.** —*n.* **1.** a course, way, or road for passage or travel: *What's the shortest route to Boston?* **2.** a customary or regular line of passage or travel: *a ship on the North Atlantic route.* **3.** a specific itinerary, round, or number of stops regularly visited by a person in the performance of his or her work or duty: *a newspaper route; a mail carrier's route.* **4. go the route,** *Informal.* **a.** to see something through to completion: *It was a tough assignment, but he went the route.* **b.** *Baseball.* to pitch the complete game: *The heat and humidity were intolerable, but the pitcher managed to go the route.* —*v.t.* **5.** to fix the route of: *to route a tour.* **6.** to send or forward by a particular route: *to route mail to its proper destination.* [1175–1225; ME: way, course < OF < L *rupta* (*via*) broken (road), fem. ptp. of *rumpere* to break; cf. ROUT[1]]
—**Syn.** **3.** beat, circuit.

route·man (ro͞ot′mən, rout′-), *n., pl.* **-men.** **1.** a person who works in a specified area or covers a specific route, as a mail carrier or truckdriver. **2.** a supervisor who establishes a route for salespersons or the like, maintains office records, and handles customer relations for it. **3.** a person who routes work among a group of employees, as in a plant or shipyard. [1915–20; ROUTE + MAN[1]]

route′ march′, march in which a unit retains its column formation but individuals are allowed to break step.

rout·er[1] (rou′tər), *n.* **1.** any of various tools or machines for routing, hollowing out, or furrowing. **2.** Also called **rout′er plane′.** *Carpentry.* a plane for cutting interior angles, as at the bottom of a groove. See illus. under **plane**[2]. **3.** a machine or tool for cutting into or below a main surface, as of a die or engraving plate. —*v.t.* **4.** to cut with a router. [1840–50; ROUT[2] + -ER[1]]

rout·er[2] (ro͞o′tər, rou′-), *n.* a person or thing that routes. [1900–05; ROUTE + -ER[1]]

rout′er patch′ (rou′tər), a plywood panel patch with parallel sides and rounded ends.

route′ sur′vey, a survey for determining the route, grades, etc., of a railroad, highway, or power line.

routh (ro͞oth, routh), *n. Scot. and North Eng.* abundance; plenty. [1710–20; orig. uncert.]

rou·tine (ro͞o tēn′), *n.* **1.** a customary or regular course of procedure. **2.** commonplace tasks, chores, or duties as must be done regularly or at specified intervals; typical or everyday activity: *the routine of an office.* **3.** regular, unvarying, habitual, unimaginative, or rote procedure. **4.** an unvarying and constantly repeated formula, as of speech or action; convenient or predictable response: *Don't give me that brotherly-love routine!* **5.** *Computers.* **a.** a complete set of coded instructions directing a computer to perform a series of operations. **b.** a series of operations performed by the computer. **6.** an individual act, performance, or part of a performance, as a song or dance, given regularly by an entertainer: *a comic routine; a dance routine.* —*adj.* **7.** of the nature of, proceeding by, or adhering to routine: *routine duties.* **8.** dull or uninteresting; commonplace. [1670–80; < F, deriv. of *route* ROUTE] —**rou·tine′ly,** *adv.* —**rou·tine′ness,** *n.*
—**Syn.** **8.** habitual, ordinary, typical.

rou·ti·neer (ro͞ot′n ēr′), *n.* a person who follows or adheres to routine or a routine. [1870–75; ROUTINE + -EER]

rout·ing (ro͞o′ting, rou′-), *n.* **1.** the scheduling of the route or itinerary of people, freight, etc. **2.** the arranging and scheduling of mail for delivery. **3.** delivery according to scheduled sequence. [1900–05; ROUTE + -ING[1]]

rou·tin·ism (ro͞o tē′niz əm), *n.* adherence to routine. [ROUTINE + -ISM] —**rou·tin·ist** (ro͞o tē′nist), *n.*

rou·tin·ize (ro͞o tē′nīz, ro͞ot′n īz′), *v.t.,* **-ized, -iz·ing.** **1.** to develop into a regular procedure. **2.** to reduce to a customary procedure: *He seems happier now that his life is thoroughly routinized.* Also, *esp. Brit.,* **rou·tin′ise.** [1925–30; ROUTINE + -IZE] —**rou·tin′i·za′tion,** *n.* —**rou·tin′iz·er,** *n.*

roux (ro͞o), *n.* a cooked mixture of butter or other fat and flour used to thicken sauces, soups, etc. [1805–15; < F (*beurre*) *roux* brown (butter) < L *russus* red-brown, red-haired, akin to *ruber* RED]

Rou·yn (ro͞o′in; *Fr.* rwan), *n.* a city in SW Quebec, in E Canada: gold and copper mining. 17,224.

Ro·va·nie·mi (rô′vä nye mē), *n.* a city in N Finland, near the Arctic Circle. 30,800.

rove[1] (rōv), *v.,* **roved, rov·ing,** *n.* —*v.i.* **1.** to wander about without definite destination; move hither and thither at random, esp. over a wide area. —*v.t.* **2.** to wander over or through; traverse: *to rove the woods.* —*n.* **3.** an act or instance of roving. [1490–1500; orig., to shoot at a random target; perh. < Scand; cf. ON *rāfa* to stray; but cf. also OF *raver* to roam]
—**Syn.** **1.** stroll, amble, stray. See **roam.**

rove[2] (rōv), *v.* a pt. and pp. of **reeve**[2].

rove[3] (rōv), *v.,* **roved, rov·ing,** *n.* —*v.t.* **1.** to form (slivers of wool, cotton, etc.) into slightly twisted strands in a preparatory process of spinning. **2.** to draw fibers or the like through an eye or other small opening. **3.** to attenuate, compress, and twist slightly in carding. —*n.* **4.** *Brit.* roving[2]. [1780–90; of obscure orig.]

rove′ bee′tle, any of numerous beetles of the family Staphylinidae, having a slender, elongated body and very short front wings, and capable of running swiftly. Also called **staphylinid.** [1765–75]

rove-o·ver (rōv′ō′vər), *adj. Pros.* (in sprung rhythm) of or pertaining to the completion of a metrical foot, incomplete at the end of one line, with a syllable or syllables from the beginning of the next line.

rov·er[1] (rō′vər), *n.* **1.** a person who roves; wanderer. **2.** *Archery.* **a.** a mark selected at random, as in a competition between two archers wandering over a specified area. **b.** one of a group of fixed marks at a long distance. **c.** an archer who shoots at such a mark. **3.** *Croquet.* a ball that has been driven through all the arches and needs only to strike the last peg to be out of the game. **4.** *Brit.* **a.** (at concerts or the like) a person who has a ticket for standing room only. **b.** a senior boy scout, 18 years of age or older. [1490–1500; ROVE[1] + -ER[1]]

rov·er[2] (rō′vər), *n.* **1.** a pirate. **2.** *Obs.* a pirate ship. [1350–1400; ME < MD or MLG: robber, equiv. to *roven* to rob, REAVE[1] + *-er* -ER[1]]

rov·er[3] (rō′vər), *n.* **1.** a roving or routing machine. **2.** a roving-machine operator. [1735–45; ROVE[3] + -ER[1]]

Ro·ver (rō′vər), *n.* a familiar name for a dog.

Rov′er Boy′, a courageous and principled person who

CONCISE ETYMOLOGY KEY: <, descended or borrowed from; >, whence; b., blend of, blended; c., cognate with; cf., compare; deriv., derivative; equiv., equivalent; imit., imitative; obl., oblique; r., replacing; s., stem; sp., spelling, spelled; resp., respelling, respelled; trans., translation; ?, origin unknown; *, unattested; ‡, probably earlier than. See the full key inside the front cover.

is somewhat naïve and inexperienced. [after the heroes of the *Rover Boys* series, American children's books by Edward Stratemeyer (1862–1930)]

rov•ing[1] (rō′ving), *adj.* **1.** roaming or wandering. **2.** not assigned or restricted to any particular location, area, topic, etc.: *a roving editor.* **3.** not assigned to any particular diplomatic post but having a special mission: *a roving ambassador.* [1590–1600; ROVE[1] + -ING[2]] —**rov′ing•ly,** *adv.* —**rov′ing•ness,** *n.*

rov•ing[2] (rō′ving), *n.* **1.** a soft strand of fiber that has been twisted, attenuated, and freed of foreign matter preparatory to its conversion into yarn. **2.** the final phase of carding, in which this is done. [1785–95; ROVE[3] + -ING[1]]

Ro•vno (Rô′vnə), *n.* a city in NW Ukraine, NE of Lvov. 233,000.

Ro•vu•ma (rŏŏ vōō′mə), *n.* Ruvuma.

row[1] (rō), *n.* **1.** a number of persons or things arranged in a line, esp. a straight line: *a row of apple trees.* **2.** a line of persons or things so arranged: *The petitioners waited in a row.* **3.** a line of adjacent seats facing the same way, as in a theater: *seats in the third row of the balcony.* **4.** a street formed by two continuous lines of buildings. **5.** *Music.* See **tone row. 6.** *Checkers.* one of the horizontal lines of squares on a checkerboard; rank. **7. hard** or **long row to hoe,** a difficult task or set of circumstances to confront: *At 32 and with two children, she found attending medical school a hard row to hoe.* —*v.t.* **8.** to put in a row (often fol. by *up*). [1175–1225; ME *row(e)*; cf. OE *rǣw*]

row[2] (rō), *v.i.* **1.** to propel a vessel by the leverage of an oar or the like. —*v.t.* **2.** to propel (a vessel) by the leverage of an oar or the like. **3.** to convey in a boat that is rowed. **4.** to convey or propel (something) in a manner suggestive of rowing. **5.** to require, use, or be equipped with (a number of oars): *The captain's barge rowed twenty oars.* **6.** to use (oarsmen) for rowing. **7.** to perform or participate in by rowing: *to row a race.* **8.** to row against in a race: *Oxford rows Cambridge.* —*n.* **9.** an act, instance, or period of rowing: *It was a long row to the far bank.* **10.** an excursion in a rowboat: *to go for a row.* [bef. 950; ME *rowen,* OE *rōwan;* c. ON *rōa;* akin to L *rēmus* oar (see REMUS). Cf. RUDDER] —**row′a•ble,** *adj.* —**row′er,** *n.*

row[3] (rou), *n.* **1.** a noisy dispute or quarrel; commotion. **2.** noise or clamor. —*v.i.* **3.** to quarrel noisily. —*v.t.* **4.** *Chiefly Brit.* to upbraid severely; scold. [1740–50; orig. uncert.]
—**Syn. 1.** spat, tiff, scrap, scrape, set-to.

row•an (rō′ən, rou′-), *n.* **1.** the European mountain ash, *Sorbus aucuparia,* having pinnate leaves and clusters of bright red berries. **2.** either of two American mountain ashes, *Sorbus americana* or *S. sambucifolia.* **3.** the berry of any of these trees. [1795–1805; < ON **raun-* in *reynir,* Norw *raun*]

row•boat (rō′bōt′), *n.* a small boat designed for rowing. [1530–40; ROW[2] + BOAT]

row•dy (rou′dē), *n., pl.* **-dies,** *adj.,* **-di•er, -di•est.** —*n.* **1.** a rough, disorderly person. —*adj.* **2.** rough and disorderly: *rowdy behavior at school.* [1810–20, *Amer.;* perh. irreg. from ROW[3]] —**row′di•ly,** *adv.* —**row′di•ness,** *n.*
—**Syn. 2.** boisterous, unruly, obstreperous.

row•dy•ish (rou′dē ish), *adj.* **1.** like or characteristic of a rowdy. **2.** disposed to or characterized by rowdyism. [1835–45, *Amer.;* ROWDY + -ISH[1]] —**row′dy•ish•ly,** *adv.* —**row′dy•ish•ness,** *n.*

row•dy•ism (rou′dē iz′əm), *n.* rough, disorderly behavior. [1835–45, *Amer.;* ROWDY + -ISM]

Rowe (rō), *n.* **Nicholas,** 1674–1718, British poet and dramatist, poet laureate 1715–18.

row•el (rou′əl), *n., v.,* **-eled, -el•ing** or (*esp. Brit.*) **-elled, -el•ling.** —*n.* **1.** a small wheel with radiating points, forming the extremity of a spur. See illus. under **spur**[1]. **2.** *Vet. Med.* a piece of leather or the like inserted beneath the skin of a horse or other animal to promote drainage of an infection. —*v.t.* **3.** to prick or urge with a rowel. **4.** *Vet. Med.* to insert a rowel in. [1350–1400; ME *rowelle* < MF *ruelle,* OF *roel* < LL *rotella,* equiv. to L *rot(a)* wheel + *-ella* -ELLE]

row•en (rou′ən), *n. Chiefly Northern U.S.* the second crop of grass or hay in a season; aftermath. [1300–50; ME *reywayn* < ONF **rewain;* c. F *regain*]

Ro•we•na (rō wē′nə), *n.* a female given name.

row′ house′ (rō), **1.** one of a row of houses having uniform, or nearly uniform, plans and fenestration and usually having a uniform architectural treatment, as in certain housing developments. **2.** a house having at least one side wall in common with a neighboring dwelling. [1935–40]

row′ing boat′ (rō′ing), *Brit.* rowboat. [1810–20]

row′ing machine′ (rō′ing), an exercise machine having a mechanism with two oarlike handles, foot braces, and a sliding seat, allowing the user to go through the motions of rowing in a racing shell. [1870–75, *Amer.*]

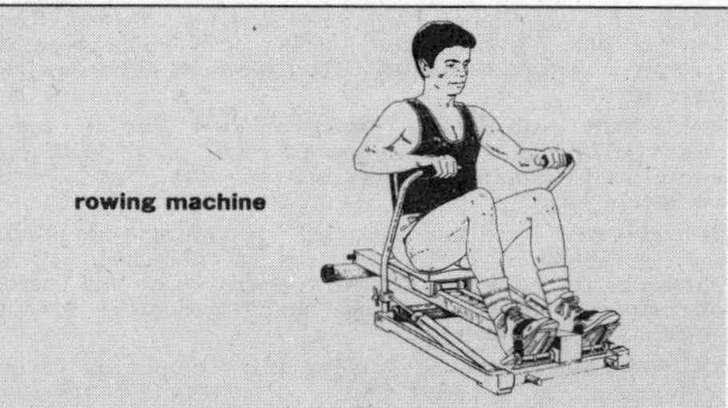
rowing machine

Row′land Heights′ (rō′lənd), a city in SW California, near Los Angeles. 28,252.

Row•land•son (rō′lənd sən), *n.* **Thomas,** 1756–1827, English caricaturist.

row•lock (rō′lok′; *for 3 also Naut.* rol′ək, rul′-), *n.* **1.** *Archit.* one of several concentric rings of masonry forming an arch. **2.** a brick laid on edge, esp. as a header. Cf. **soldier** (def. 7). **3.** *Chiefly Brit.* oarlock. Also, **rollock** (for defs. 1, 2). [1740–50; var. of OARLOCK; see ROW[2]]

row′ vec′tor (rō), *Math.* a collection of numbers, as the components of a vector, written horizontally. Cf. **column vector.** [1925–30]

rox•anne (rok san′), *n. Slang.* crack (def. 41). [orig. uncert.]

Rox•anne (rok san′), *n.* a female given name.

Ro•xas (rō′häs; *Sp.* Rô′häs), *n.* **Ma•nuel** (mä nwel′), 1892–1948, Philippine statesman: 1st president of the Philippines 1946–48.

Rox•burgh (roks′bûr ō, -bur ō *or, esp. Brit.,* -brə), *n.* a historic county in SE Scotland. Also called **Rox•burgh•shire** (roks′bûr ō shēr′, -shər, -bur-, -brə-).

Ro•y (rō′ē), *n.* **Ram•mo•hun** (rä mō′hon), 1774–1833, Indian religious leader: founder of Brahmo Samaj.

Roy (roi), *n.* **1.** a town in N Utah. 19,694. **2.** Rollo (def. 1). **3.** a male given name: from a Scots Gaelic word meaning "red."

roy•al (roi′əl), *adj.* **1.** of or pertaining to a king, queen, or other sovereign: *royal power; a royal palace.* **2.** descended from or related to a king or line of kings: *a royal prince.* **3.** noting or having the rank of a king or queen. **4.** established or chartered by or existing under the patronage of a sovereign: *a royal society.* **5.** (*cap.*) serving or subject to a king, queen, or other sovereign. **6.** proceeding from or performed by a sovereign: *a royal warrant.* **7.** appropriate to or befitting a sovereign; magnificent; stately: *royal splendor.* **8.** (*usually cap.*) *Brit.* in the service of the monarch or of the Commonwealth: *Royal Marines; Royal Air Force.* **9.** fine; excellent: *in royal spirits.* **10.** *Informal.* extreme or persistent; unmitigated: *a royal nuisance; a royal pain.* —*n.* **11.** *Naut.* a sail set on a royal mast. See diag. under **ship. 12.** *Informal.* a royal person; member of the royalty. **13.** Usually, **royals.** *Chiefly Brit.* a member of England's royal family. **14.** a size of printing paper, 20 × 25 in. (51 × 64 cm). **15.** a size of writing paper, 19 × 24 in. (48 × 61 cm). **16.** *Numis.* any of various former coins, as the real or ryal. [1325–75; ME < MF < L *rēgālis* kingly, equiv. to *rēg-* (s. of *rēx*) king + *-ālis* -AL[1]; cf. REGAL] —**roy′al•ly,** *adv.*
—**Syn. 7.** majestic. See **kingly.** —**Ant. 7.** servile.

Roy′al Acad′emy, a society founded in 1768 by George III of England for the establishment of a school of design and the holding of an annual exhibition of the works of living artists.

Roy′al Anne′, a variety of sweet cherry having yellow fruit tinged with red. [1895–1900]

roy′al ant′ler, the third prong from the base of a stag's antler. Also called **tres-tine, trez-tine.** See diag. under **antler.** [1840–50]

roy′al blue′, a deep blue, often with a faint reddish tinge. [1810–20]

Roy′al Cana′dian, in the service of the Canadian federal government and the British monarch: *Royal Canadian Air Force; Royal Canadian Mounted Police.* Also, **roy′al Cana′dian.** [1925–30]

roy′al coach′man, *Angling.* a type of artificial fly, used chiefly for trout and salmon.

roy′al col′ony, 1. a colony ruled or administered by officials appointed by and responsible to the reigning sovereign of the parent state. **2.** *Amer. Hist.* a colony, as New York, administered by a royal governor and council appointed by the British crown, and having a representative assembly elected by the people. Cf. **charter colony.**

roy•ale (roi al′), *n.* custard cut into shapes and used as a garnish in soups. [< F, n. use of fem. of *royal* ROYAL]

roy′al fam′ily, the immediate family of a reigning monarch.

roy′al fern′, a coarse fern, *Osmunda regalis,* having tall, upright fronds. [1770–80]

roy′al fizz′, a beverage consisting of gin, lemon juice, sugar, and an egg.

roy′al flush′, *Poker.* the five highest cards of a suit. [1865–70]

Roy′al Green′wich Observ′atory, the national astronomical observatory of Great Britain, housed in a castle in E Sussex; formerly located at Greenwich. Also called **Greenwich Observatory.**

Roy′al High′ness, 1. (in England) **a.** a title used prior to 1917 and designating a brother, sister, child, grandchild, aunt, or uncle belonging to the male line of the royal family. **b.** a title used since 1917 and designating a child or grandchild of the sovereign. **c.** any person given this title by the Crown. **2.** (in other countries) a person who is a member of a royal family. [1645–55]

roy•al•ist (roi′ə list), *n.* **1.** a supporter or adherent of a king or royal government, esp. in times of rebellion or civil war. **2.** (*cap.*) a Cavalier adherent of Charles I of England. **3.** a loyalist in the American Revolution; Tory. **4.** (*cap.*) an adherent of the house of Bourbon in France. —*adj.* **5.** of or pertaining to royalists: *royalist sympathies.* [1635–45; ROYAL + -IST] —**roy′al•ism,** *n.* —**roy′al•is′tic,** *adj.*

roy′al jel′ly, a viscous substance secreted from the pharyngeal glands of worker honeybees, fed to all larvae during their first few days and afterward only to those larvae selected to be queens. [1850–55]

Roy•all (roi′əl), *n.* **Anne Newport,** 1769–1854, U.S. writer, newspaper publisher, and reformer.

roy′al lil′y, a lily, *Lilium regale,* of western China, having fragrant flowers about six in. (15 cm) wide that are white inside, lilac-colored or purplish outside, and have a yellow base.

roy′al mar′riage, *Cards.* a meld of the king and queen of trumps, as in pinochle. Cf. **marriage** (def. 8).

roy′al mast′, *Naut.* a mast situated immediately above, and generally formed as a single spar with, a topgallant mast. [1785–95]

Roy′al Oak′, a city in SE Michigan, near Detroit. 70,893.

roy′al palm′, any of several tall, showy feather palms of the genus *Roystonea,* as *R. regia,* having a trunk that is swollen in the middle. See illus. under **palm**[2]. [1860–65, *Amer.*]

roy′al poincian′a, a tree, *Delonix regia,* of the legume family, native to Madagascar, having showy clusters of brilliant scarlet flowers and long, flat, woody pods. Also called **flamboyant, flame tree.** [1895–1900]

roy′al pur′ple, a deep bluish purple. [1655–65]

roy′al road′, 1. an auspicious or easy way or means to achieve something: *the royal road to success.* **2.** a highway in ancient Persia, 1677 mi. (2700 km) long, extending from Susa in W Iran to W Asia Minor. Also, **Roy′al Road′.**

Roy′al Soci′ety, The Royal Society of London for the Advancement of Science, a society through which the British government has supported scientific investigation since 1662: awards four annual medals.

roy′al ten′nis. See **court tennis.**

roy•al•ty (roi′əl tē), *n., pl.* **-ties. 1.** royal persons collectively. **2.** royal status, dignity, or power; sovereignty: *to be elevated to royalty.* **3.** a person of royal lineage; member of a royal family. **4. royalties,** *Archaic.* prerogatives, rights, or symbolic emblems of a king, queen, or other sovereign. **5.** a royal domain; kingdom; realm. **6.** character or quality proper to or befitting a sovereign; nobility. **7.** a compensation or portion of the proceeds paid to the owner of a right, as a patent or oil or mineral right, for the use of it. **8.** an agreed portion of the income from a work paid to its author, composer, etc., usually a percentage of the retail price of each copy sold. **9.** a royal right, as over minerals, granted by a sovereign to a person or corporation. **10.** the payment made for such a right. [1350–1400; ME *roialte* < OF. See ROYAL, -TY[2]]

roy′al wa′ter lil′y, a water lily, *Victoria amazonica* (or *V. regia*), of the Amazon River and British Guiana, having floating leaves from three to six ft. (0.9 to 1.8 m) wide, the upturned margins from two to four in. (5 to 10 cm) high, and dull crimson flowers. Also called **water platter.** [1865–70]

roy′al we′, we (def. 5). [1825–35]

Roy′al Worces′ter, *Trademark.* See **Worcester china.**

Royce (rois), *n.* **Josiah,** 1855–1916, U.S. philosopher and educator.

Roy′ Rog′ers, a nonalcoholic cocktail of ginger ale and grenadine, garnished with a maraschino cherry: a child's drink, served esp. to a boy. Cf. **Shirley Temple.**

royst•er (roi′stər), *v.i.* roister.

roze•ner (rōz′nər, rō′zə nər), *n. Australian Informal.* any strong alcoholic beverage. [1930–35; orig. uncert.]

roz•zer (roz′ər), *n. Brit. Slang.* a policeman. [1890–95; orig. uncert.]

RP, 1. See **Received Pronunciation. 2.** See **repurchase agreement. 3.** retinitis pigmentosa.

Rp., (in Indonesia) rupiah; rupiahs.

R.P., 1. Reformed Presbyterian. **2.** Regius Professor.

RPG, role-playing game.

rpm, revolutions per minute. Also, **r.p.m.**

R.P.O., Railway Post Office. Also, **RPO**

RPQ, request for price quotation.

rps, revolutions per second. Also, **r.p.s.**

rpt., 1. repeat. **2.** report.

RPV, remotely piloted vehicle: a military aircraft used esp. for reconnaissance and for confusing enemy radar.

R.Q., respiratory quotient.

r-qual•i•ty (är′kwol′i tē), *n. Phonet.* r-color.

R.R., 1. railroad. **2.** Right Reverend. **3.** rural route.

R-rat•ed (är′rā′tid), *adj.* (of a motion picture) suitable for those under 17 years of age only when accompanied by an adult. [1965–70]

-rrhagia, a combining form with the meanings "rupture," "profuse discharge," "abnormal flow," used in the formation of compound words: *bronchorrhagia.* Also, **-rhagia, -rhage, -rrhage, -rhagy, -rrhagy.** [< Gk *-rrhagia,* comb. form akin to *rhēgnýnai* to break, burst, shatter]

-rrhaphy, a combining form meaning "suture," used in the formation of compound words: *herniorrhaphy.* Also, **-rhaphy.** [< Gk *-rrhaphia;* comb. form akin to *rháptein* to stitch, sew]

-rrhea, a combining form meaning "flow," "discharge," used in the formation of compound words: *gonorrhea.* Also, **-rhea.** Cf. **rheo-.** [< NL *-rrhoea* < Gk *-rrhoia,* comb. form repr. *rhoía* a flow, akin to *rheîn* to flow, STREAM]

-rrhexis, a combining form meaning "rupture," used in the formation of compound words: *enterorrhexis.* [< NL < Gk *rhêxis* a breaking, bursting]

-rrhiza, var. of **rhizo-** as second element of compounds: *mycorrhiza.* Also, **-rhiza.** [< NL < Gk *rhíza* ROOT[1]]

-rrhoea, var. of **-rrhea.**

RR Lyrae star, *Astron.* one of a group of pulsating variable stars found in the halo of the Milky Way, with periods between 1.2 and 30 hours; all have approximately the same luminosity and are therefore used for measuring distances. Also called **cluster variable.** [< NL: RR (variable star designation) of LYRA]

RRM, See **renegotiable-rate mortgage.**

rRNA, *Biochem.* See **ribosomal RNA.**

R.R.R., return receipt requested (used in registered mail). Also, **RRR**

RRT, See **rail rapid transit.**

R.R.T., registered respiratory therapist.

Rs., **1.** reis. **2.** rupees.

R.S., **1.** Recording Secretary. **2.** Reformed Spelling. **3.** Revised Statutes. **4.** Royal Society.

r.s., right side.

RSA, Republic of South Africa.

RSE, Received Standard English.

r* selection,** *Ecol.* selection occurring when a population is far below the carrying capacity of an unstable environment: tends to favor individuals that reproduce early, quickly, and in large numbers so as to make use of ephemeral resources and ensure that at least some offspring survive. Also, ***r*-se•lec•tion** (är′si lek′shən). Cf. ***K* selection.** —r*-se•lect•ed** (är′si lek′tid), *adj.*

RSFSR, See **Russian Soviet Federated Socialist Republic.** Also, **R.S.F.S.R.**

RSV, See **Revised Standard Version.**

RSVP (är′es′vē′pē′), *v.,* **RSVPed** or **RSVP'd, RSVPing** or **RSVP'ing,** *n., pl.* **RSVP's.** —*v.i.* **1.** to reply to an invitation: *Don't forget to RSVP before Thursday.* —*n.* **2.** a reply to an invitation: *He sent a lovely bouquet of flowers with his RSVP.* **3.** (used on an invitation to indicate that the favor of a reply is requested). Also, **R.S.V.P.** [1895–1900; < F *r(épondez) s('il) v(ous) p(laît)* please reply]

RSWC, right side up with care.

RT, radiotelephone.

rt., right.

r.t., *Football.* right tackle.

rte., route.

RTF, resistance transfer factor. See **R factor.**

Rt. Hon., Right Honorable.

Rt. Rev., Right Reverend.

Rts., *Finance.* rights.

rtw, ready-to-wear.

Ru, *Symbol, Chem.* ruthenium.

RU 486, an antigestational drug, in the form of a pill, that prevents a fertilized egg from attaching to the uterine wall by blocking the action of progesterone. [1980; designation given the compound by its French manufacturer, *Roussel UCLAF,* Paris]

ru•a•na (rōō ä′nə), *n.* a poncholike outer garment of heavy wool, worn esp. in the mountains of Colombia. [1940–45; < AmerSp]

Ru•an•da (rōō än′də), *n., pl.* **-das,** (*esp. collectively*) **-da** for 1. **1.** a member of a people living in Rwanda and E Zaire. **2.** Also called **Kinyarwanda.** the Bantu language of the Ruandas, closely related to Rundi, spoken in Zaire and by virtually the entire population of Rwanda.

Ru•an•da-U•run•di (rōō än′də ŏŏ rōōn′dē), *n.* a former territory in central Africa, E of Zaire: formerly part of German East Africa; administered by Belgium as a League of Nations mandate 1923–46 and as a United Nations trust territory 1946–62; now divided into the independent states of Rwanda and Burundi.

rub (rub), *v.,* **rubbed, rub•bing,** *n.* —*v.t.* **1.** to subject the surface of (a thing or person) to pressure and friction, as in cleaning, smoothing, polishing, coating, massaging, or soothing: *to rub a table top with wax polish; to rub the entire back area.* **2.** to move (something) back and forth or with a rotary motion, as against or along another surface: *to rub the cloth over the glass pane.* **3.** to spread or apply (something) with pressure and friction over something else or a person: *to rub lotion on her chapped hands.* **4.** to move (two things) with pressure and friction over or back and forth over each other (often fol. by *together*): *He rubbed his hands together.* **5.** to mark, polish, force, move, etc. (something) by pressure and friction (often fol. by *over, in,* or *into*). **6.** to remove by pressure and friction; erase (often fol. by *off* or *out*). —*v.i.* **7.** to exert pressure and friction on something. **8.** to move with pressure against something. **9.** to admit of being rubbed in a specified manner: *Chalk rubs off easily.* **10.** *Chiefly Brit.* to proceed, continue in a course, or keep going with effort or difficulty (usually fol. by *on, along,* or *through*): *He manages to rub along.* **11. rub down, a.** to smooth off, polish, or apply a coating to: *to rub a chair down with sandpaper.* **b.** to give a massage to. **12. rub it in,** *Informal.* to emphasize or reiterate something unpleasant in order to tease or annoy: *The situation was embarrassing enough without having you rub it in.* **13. rub off on,** to become transferred or communicated to by example or association: *Some of his good luck must have rubbed off on me.* **14. rub out, a.** to obliterate; erase. **b.** *Slang.* to murder: *They rubbed him out before he could get to the police.* **15. rub the wrong way,** to irritate; offend; annoy: *a manner that seemed to rub everyone the wrong way.* **16. rub up,** *Brit. Informal.* to refresh one's memory of (a subject, language, etc.). —*n.* **17.** an act or instance of rubbing: *an alcohol rub.* **18.** something that annoys or irritates one's feelings, as a sharp criticism, a sarcastic remark, or the like: *to resent rubs concerning one's character.* **19.** an annoying experience or circumstance. **20.** an obstacle, impediment, or difficulty: *We'd like to travel, but the rub is that we have no money.* **21.** a rough or abraded area caused by rubbing. [1300–50; 1860–65 for def. 14b; ME *rubben* (v.); c. Fris *rubben,* Dan *rubbe,* Sw *rubba*] —**Syn. 20.** hitch, catch, thing, trouble, pinch.

rub•a•boo (rub′ə bōō′), *n. Canadian.* soup made from pemmican, flour, and water, once common among fur trappers, hunters, etc. [1815–25; orig. uncert.]

rub-a-dub (rub′ə dub′), *n.* the sound of a drum when beaten. [1780–90; imit.]

Ru′bái•yát of O′mar Khayyám′, The (rōō′bī yät′, -bē-), *n.* a free translation (first published in 1859) by Edward FitzGerald of a group of quatrains by the Persian poet Omar Khayyám. [*Rubáiyát* < Pers < Ar, fem. pl. of *rubāʿī* quatrain]

Ru′baiyat stan′za, *Pros.* a quatrain pattern after those in *The Rubáiyát of Omar Khayyám,* of iambic pentameter and rhyming *aaba.*

Rub′ al Kha•li (*Arab.* rōōb′ äl KHä′lē; *Eng.* rōōb′ al kä′lē), a desert in S Arabia, N of Hadhramaut and extending from Yemen to Oman. ab. 250,000 sq. mi. (647,500 sq. km). Also called **Ar Rimal, Dahna, Empty Quarter, Great Sandy Desert.**

Ru′barth's disease′ (rōō′bärts, -bärths), a common, rapidly progressing viral hepatitis of dogs and other carnivores, often confused with canine distemper. Also called **infectious canine hepatitis.** [after Carl Sven *Rubarth* (born 1905), Swedish veterinarian, who described it in 1947]

ru•basse (rōō bas′, -bäs′), *n.* a variety of bright-red rock crystal. [1885–90; < F *rubace,* appar. deriv. of *rubis* RUBY]

ru•ba•to (rōō bä′tō; *It.* rōō bä′tô), *adj., n., pl.* **-tos, -ti** (-tē), *adv. Music.* —*adj.* **1.** having certain notes arbitrarily lengthened while others are correspondingly shortened, or vice versa. —*n.* **2.** a rubato phrase or passage. **3.** a rubato performance. —*adv.* **4.** in a rubato manner. [1880–85; < It (*tempo*) *rubato* stolen (time), ptp. of *rubare* to steal < Gmc; see ROB]

rub•ber[1] (rub′ər), *n.* **1.** Also called **India rubber, natural rubber, gum elastic, caoutchouc.** a highly elastic solid substance, light cream or dark amber in color, polymerized by the drying and coagulation of the latex or milky juice of rubber trees and plants, esp. *Hevea* and *Ficus* species. **2.** a material made by chemically treating and toughening this substance, valued for its elasticity, nonconduction of electricity, shock absorption, and resistance to moisture, used in the manufacture of erasers, electrical insulation, elastic bands, crepe soles, toys, water hoses, tires, and many other products. **3.** any of various similar substances and materials made synthetically. Cf. **synthetic rubber. 4.** See **rubber band. 5.** an eraser of this material, for erasing pencil marks, ink marks, etc. **6.** *Informal.* a rubber tire or a set of rubber tires. **7.** a low overshoe of this material. **8.** an instrument or tool used for rubbing, polishing, scraping, etc. **9.** a person who rubs something, as to smooth or polish it. **10.** cutter (def. 7). **11.** *Brit.* a dishcloth. **12.** a person who gives massages; masseur or masseuse. **13.** swipe (def. 6). **14.** *Baseball.* an oblong piece of white rubber or other material embedded in the mound at the point from which the pitcher delivers the ball. **15.** a coarse file. **16.** *Slang.* a condom. —*v.i.* **17.** *Informal.* to rubberneck. —*adj.* **18.** made of, containing, or coated with rubber: *a rubber bath mat.* **19.** pertaining to or producing rubber: *a rubber plantation.* [1530–40; RUB + -ER[1]] —**rub′ber•less,** *adj.* —**rub′ber•like′,** *adj.*

rub•ber[2] (rub′ər), *n.* (in certain card games, as bridge and whist) **1.** a series or round played until one side reaches a specific score or wins a specific number of hands. **2.** a series consisting of an odd number of games won by the side winning the majority, usually two out of three. **3.** the deciding game in such a series. —*adj.* **4.** Also called **rubber match.** *Sports.* noting a deciding contest between two opponents who have previously won the same number of contests from each other. [1585–95; orig. uncert.]

rub′ber band′, a narrow, circular or oblong band of rubber, used for holding things together, as papers or a box and its lid. [1890–95]

rub′ber-base paint′ (rub′ər bās′). See **latex paint.** [1935–40]

rub′ber bridge′, *Cards.* a form of contract bridge in which deals are not replayed and in which scores are settled after each rubber. Cf. **duplicate bridge.** [1935–40]

rub′ber cement′, a viscous, flammable liquid consisting of unvulcanized rubber dispersed in benzene, gasoline, or the like, used chiefly as an adhesive. [1890–95]

rub′ber check′, a check drawn on an account lacking the funds to pay it; a check that bounces. [1925–30, *Amer.*]

rub′ber-chick′en cir′cuit (rub′ər chik′ən, -in), *Informal.* a monotonous round of dinners, often featuring chicken, that a lecturer or political candidate is obliged to attend. [1955–60]

rub•ber-faced (rub′ər fāst′), *adj.* having mobile facial features: *a rubber-faced comedian.* [1960–65]

rub•ber•ize (rub′ə rīz′), *v.t.,* **-ized, -iz•ing.** to coat or impregnate with rubber or some preparation of it. Also, *esp. Brit.,* **rub′ber•ise′.** [1910–15; RUBBER[1] + -IZE]

rub′ber la′tex, the milky sap of any of several trees of the genus *Hevea,* esp. *H. brasiliensis,* from which natural rubber is derived. [1905–10]

rub′ber•man disease′ (rub′ər man′). See **Ehlers-Danlos syndrome.** [RUBBER[1] + MAN[1]]

rub′ber match′, *Sports.* rubber[2] (def. 4)

rub•ber•neck (rub′ər nek′), *Informal.* —*v.i.* **1.** to look about or stare with great curiosity, as by craning the neck or turning the head. —*v.t.* **2.** to gawk at: *drivers rubbernecking an accident.* —*n.* Also, **rub′ber•neck′er. 3.** a sightseer; tourist. **4.** an extremely curious person. [1895–1900, *Amer.*; RUBBER[1] + NECK]

rub′ber plant′, **1.** a plant, *Ficus elastica,* of the mulberry family, having oblong, leathery leaves, growing native as a tall tree in India, the Malay Archipelago, etc., used as a source of rubber and cultivated in Europe and America as an ornamental house plant. **2.** any plant yielding caoutchouc or India rubber. [1885–90]

rub′ber room′, *Informal.* a room padded with foam rubber for the confinement of a violent mentally ill person. [1975–80]

rub′ber stamp′, **1.** a device with a rubber printing surface that becomes coated with ink by being pressed on an ink-saturated pad, used for imprinting dates, addresses, standard designations or notices, etc., by hand. **2.** a person or government agency that gives approval automatically or routinely. **3.** such approval. [1885–90]

rub•ber-stamp (rub′ər stamp′), *v.t.* **1.** to imprint with a rubber stamp. **2.** to approve automatically: *to rubber-stamp the president's proposals.* —*adj.* **3.** tending to give approval automatically or without due consideration: *a rubber-stamp Congress that passed all the president's bills.* [1915–20; v. use of RUBBER STAMP]

rub′ber tree′, any tree that yields latex from which rubber is produced, esp. *Hevea brasiliensis,* of the spurge family, native to South America, the chief commercial source of rubber. [1840–50]

rub•ber•y (rub′ə rē), *adj.* like rubber; elastic; tough. [1905–10; RUBBER[1] + -Y[1]]

rub•bing (rub′ing), *n.* **1.** an act or action of a person or thing that rubs. **2.** an impression of an incised or sculptured surface made by laying paper over it and rubbing with heelball, graphite, or a similar substance until the image appears. Cf. **brass-rubbing.** [1350–1400; ME; see RUB, -ING[1]]

rub′bing al′cohol, a poisonous solution of about 70 percent isopropyl or denatured ethyl alcohol, used chiefly in massaging. [1925–30]

rub•bish (rub′ish), *n.* **1.** worthless, unwanted material that is rejected or thrown out; debris; litter; trash. **2.** nonsense, as in writing or art: *sentimental rubbish.* [1350–1400; ME *rubbes, rob(b)ous* < ?; cf. RUBBLE] —**Syn. 2.** rot, balderdash, drivel, bosh.

rub•bish•y (rub′i shē), *adj.* **1.** full of rubbish: *a rubbishy cellar.* **2.** suggestive of rubbish; trashy: *a rubbishy book.* [1785–95; RUBBISH + -Y[1]]

rub•ble (rub′əl *or, for 3, 4,* rōō′bəl), *n.* **1.** broken bits and pieces of anything, as that which is demolished: *Bombing reduced the town to rubble.* **2.** any solid substance, as ice, in irregularly broken pieces. **3.** rough fragments of broken stone, formed by geological processes, in quarrying, etc., and sometimes used in masonry. **4.** masonry built of rough fragments of broken stone. [1350–1400; ME *rubel, robil* < ?; cf. RUBBISH]

rub•ble•work (rub′əl wûrk′, rōō′bəl-), *n.* masonry built of rubble or roughly dressed stones. [1815–25; RUBBLE + WORK]

rub•bly (rub′lē), *adj.,* **-bli•er, -bli•est.** made or consisting of rubble. [1725–35; RUBBLE + -Y[1]]

rub•down (rub′doun′), *n.* a massage, esp. after exercise. [1665–75; n. use of v. phrase *rub down*]

rube (rōōb), *n. Informal.* an unsophisticated person from a rural area; hick. [1895–1900; generic use of RUBE; cf. earlier use of REUBEN in same sense]

Rube (rōōb), *n.* a male given name, form of **Reuben.**

ru•be•ba (rōō bā′bə), *n.* a medieval fiddle similar to the rebec. [< ML < Ar *rabāb*; see REBAB, REBEC]

ru•be•fa•cient (rōō′bə fā′shənt), *adj.* **1.** causing redness of the skin, as a medicinal application. —*n.* **2.** *Med.* a rubefacient application, as a mustard plaster. [1795–1805; < L *rubefacient-* (s. of *rubefaciēns,* prp. of *rubefacere* to redden), equiv. to *rube-,* var. s. of *rubēre* to redden, be red + *-facient-* -FACIENT]

ru•be•fac•tion (rōō′bə fak′shən), *n.* **1.** the act or process of making red, esp. with a rubefacient. **2.** redness of the skin caused by a rubefacient. [1650–60; < L *rubefactus* (ptp. of *rubefacere*; see RUBEFACIENT) + -ION]

Rube′ Gold′berg, **1.** having a fantastically complicated, improvised appearance: *a Rube Goldberg arrangement of flasks and test tubes.* **2.** deviously complex and impractical: *a Rube Goldberg scheme for reducing taxes.* Also, **Goldbergian, Rube′ Goldberg′ian.** [1955–60; after *Rube* (*Reuben*) GOLDBERG]

ru•bel•la (rōō bel′ə), *n. Pathol.* a usually mild contagious viral disease characterized by fever, mild upper respiratory congestion, and a fine red rash lasting a few days: if contracted by a woman during early pregnancy, it may cause serious damage to the fetus. Also called **German measles.** [1880–85; < NL, n. use of neut. pl. of L *rubellus* reddish, deriv. of *ruber* RED[1]; for formation see CASTELLUM]

ru•bel•lite (rōō bel′īt, rōō′bə līt′), *n.* a deep-red variety of tourmaline, used as a gem. [1790–1800; < L *rubell(us)* reddish (see RUBELLA) + -ITE[1]]

Ru•ben (rōō′bən), *n.* **1.** *Douay Bible.* Reuben (defs. 1, 2). **2.** a male given name, form of **Reuben.**

Ru•bens (rōō′bənz; *Flem.* RY′bəns), *n.* **Pe•ter Paul** (pē′tər pôl; *Flem.* pā′tər poul), 1577–1640, Flemish painter. —**Ru′ben•esque′, Ru•ben•si•an** (rōō ben′zē ən), *adj.*

ru•be•o•la (rōō bē′ə lə, rōō′bē ō′lə), *n. Pathol.* measles. [1670–80; < NL, n. use of neut. pl. of *rūbeolus,* equiv. to L *rūbe(us), rōbeus* red + *-olus* -OLE[1]] —**ru•be′o•lar,** *adj.*

ru•bes•cent (rōō bes′ənt), *adj.* becoming red; blushing. [1725–35; < L *rubēscent-* (s. of *rubēscēns,* prp. of *rubēscere* to redden), equiv. to *rub(ēre)* to be red (deriv. of *ruber* red; see RUBY) + *-ēsc-* inchoative suffix + *-ent-* -ENT] —**ru•bes′cence,** *n.*

ru•bi•a•ceous (rōō′bē ā′shəs), *adj.* belonging to the Rubiaceae, the madder family of plants. Cf. **madder family.** [1825–35; < NL *Rubiace(ae)* name of family

CONCISE ETYMOLOGY KEY: <, descended or borrowed from; >, whence; b., blend of, blended; c., cognate with; cf., compare; deriv., derivative; equiv., equivalent; imit., imitative; obl., oblique; r., replacing; s., stem; sp., spelling, spelled; resp., respelling, respelled; trans., translation; ?, origin unknown; *, unattested; ‡, probably earlier than. See the full key inside the front cover.

(*Rubi(a)* genus name (L *rubia* madder, akin to *ruber* RED[1]) + *-aceae* -ACEAE) + -OUS]

Ru•bi•con (ro͞o′bi kon′), *n.* **1.** a river in N Italy flowing E into the Adriatic. 15 mi. (24 km) long: in crossing this ancient boundary between Cisalpine Gaul and Italy, to march against Pompey in 49 B.C., Julius Caesar made a major military commitment. **2. cross** or **pass the Rubicon,** to take a decisive, irrevocable step: *Our entry into the war made us cross the Rubicon and abandon isolationism forever.*

ru•bi•cund (ro͞o′bi kund′), *adj.* red or reddish; ruddy: *a rubicund complexion.* [1495–1505; < L *rubicundus,* akin to *ruber* RED[1]] **—ru′bi•cun′di•ty,** *n.*

ru•bid•i•um (ro͞o bid′ē əm), *n. Chem.* a silver-white, metallic, active element resembling potassium, used in photoelectric cells and radio vacuum tubes. *Symbol:* Rb; *at. wt.:* 85.47; *at. no.:* 37; *sp. gr.:* 1.53 at 20°C. [1860–65; < NL, equiv. to L *rubid(us)* red (in allusion to the two red lines in its spectrum) + *-ium* -IUM] **—ru•bid′ic,** *adj.*

ru•bid′i•um-stron′ti•um dat′ing (ro͞o bid′ē əm-stron′shē əm, -shəm, -tē əm), *Geol.* a radiometric dating method whereby the ratio of rubidium isotope to strontium in a mineral is used to calculate the age of the mineral, based on the rate of radioactive decay of rubidium to strontium. [1965–70]

ru•bied (ro͞o′bēd), *adj.* having a color like that of a ruby; deep red. [1600–10; RUBY + -ED[3]]

ru•bi•fy (ro͞o′bə fī′), *v.t.,* **-fied, -fy•ing.** to make red; redden: *a distant fire that rubified the sky.* [1350–1400; ME *rubifien* < OF *rubifier* << L *rubefacere;* see RUBEFACIENT, -IFY]

ru•big•i•nous (ro͞o bij′ə nəs), *adj.* rusty; rust-colored; brownish-red. Also, **ru•big•i•nose** (ro͞o bij′ə nōs′). [1665–75; < L *rōbīginōsus,* equiv. to *rōbīgin-, rūbīgin-,* s. of *rōbīgō, rūbīgō* rust (akin to *ruber* RED[1]) + *-ōsus* -OUS]

Ru′bik's Cube′ (ro͞o′biks), *Trademark.* a puzzle consisting of a cube with colored faces made of 26 smaller colored blocks attached to a spindle in the center, the object being to rotate the blocks until each face of the cube is a single color.

Ru•bin•stein (ro͞o′bin stīn′; *Russ.* RO͞O byin shtyän′; *Pol.* RO͞O′ben stīn′), *n.* **1. An•ton** (an′ton; *Russ.* un-tôn′), 1829–94, Russian pianist and composer. **2. Arthur** or **Ar•tur** (är′tər; *Pol.* äR′to͞oR), 1887–1982, U.S. pianist, born in Poland.

ru•bi•ous (ro͞o′bē əs), *adj.* ruby-colored. [1595–1605; RUBY + -OUS]

ru•ble (ro͞o′bəl), *n.* a silver or copper-alloy coin and monetary unit of Russia, the Soviet Union, and its successor states, equal to 100 kopecks. Also, **rouble.** [1545–55; < Russ *rubl′;* ORuss *rublĭ* lit., stump, plug, deriv. of *rubiti* to chop; prob. orig. denoting a piece cut from a silver bar, or a bar notched for division into smaller pieces]

rub•off (rub′ôf′, -of′), *n.* **1.** an act of rubbing off, as to remove something. **2.** a deep mark, effect, or impact produced esp. through constant close contact. [1935–40; n. use of v. phrase *rub off*]

rub•out (rub′out′), *n. Slang.* a murder or assassination. [1925–30, *Amer.;* n. use of v. phrase *rub out*]

ru•bric (ro͞o′brik), *n.* **1.** a title, heading, or the like, in a manuscript, book, statute, etc., written or printed in red or otherwise distinguished from the rest of the text. **2.** a direction for the conduct of divine service or the administration of the sacraments, inserted in liturgical books. **3.** any established mode of conduct or procedure. **4.** an explanatory comment; gloss. **5.** a class or category **6.** *Archaic.* red ocher. **—***adj.* **7.** written, inscribed in, or marked with or as with red; rubrical. **8.** *Archaic.* red; ruddy. [1325–75; < L *rubrīca* red ocher (deriv. of *ruber* RED); r. ME *rubriche, rubrike* (n.) < OF]

ru•bri•cal (ro͞o′bri kəl), *adj.* **1.** reddish; marked with red. **2.** of, pertaining to, contained in, or prescribed by rubrics, esp. liturgical rubrics. [1635–45; RUBRIC + AL[1]] **—ru′bri•cal•ly,** *adv.*

ru•bri•cate (ro͞o′bri kāt′), *v.t.,* **-cat•ed, -cat•ing.** **1.** to mark or color with red. **2.** to furnish with or regulate by rubrics. [1560–70; < LL *rūbrīcātus* (ptp. of *rūbrīcāre* to color red), equiv. to *rūbrīc(a)* red ocher (see RUBRIC) + *-ātus* -ATE[1]] **—ru′bri•ca′tion,** *n.* **—ru′bri•ca′tor,** *n.*

ru•bri•cat•ed (ro͞o′bri kā′tid), *adj.* (in ancient manuscripts, early printed books, etc.) having titles, catchwords, etc., distinctively colored. [1595–1605; RUBRICATE + -ED[2]]

ru•bri•cian (ro͞o brish′ən), *n.* an expert in or close adherent to liturgical rubrics. [1840–50; RUBRIC + -IAN]

ru′brum lil′y (ro͞o′brəm), either of two cultivated lilies, *Lilium auratum rubrum* or *L. speciosum rubrum,* having showy red flowers.

rub•stone (rub′stōn′), *n.* a stone, esp. a whetstone, used for polishing or sharpening. [1400–50; late ME; see RUB, STONE]

Rub•tsovsk (Ro͞op tsôfsk′), *n.* a city in the SW Russian Federation in Asia. 163,000.

ru•by (ro͞o′bē), *n., pl.* **-bies,** *adj.* **—***n.* **1.** a red variety of corundum, used as a gem. **2.** something made of this stone or one of its imitations, as a bearing in a watch. **3.** a deep-red port wine. **4.** deep red; carmine. **5.** *Brit. Print.* a 5½-point type, nearly corresponding in size to American agate. **—***adj.* **6.** ruby-colored: *ruby lips.* **7.** containing or set or adorned with a ruby or rubies: *a ruby necklace.* [1275–1325; ME *rubi* (n.) < OF < OPr *robi(n)* < ML *rubinus (lapis)* red (stone), deriv. of L *ruber* RED[1]] **—ru′by•like′,** *adj.*

Ru•by (ro͞o′bē), *n.* a female given name.

ru′by-crowned king′let (ro͞o′bē kround′), an olive-gray, American kinglet, *Regulus calendula,* the male of which has an erectile, ruby crest. [1835–45, *Amer.*]

ru′by glass′, **1.** glass having a red color resulting from the addition of gold, copper, or selenium to the batch. **2.** any glass of a dark red color. [1790–1800]

ru′by sil′ver, *Mineral.* **1.** proustite. **2.** pyrargyrite. [1875–80]

ru′by spinel′, *Mineral.* a deep red, transparent variety of spinel, used as a gem. Also called **spinel ruby.**

ru′by-throat•ed hum′mingbird (ro͞o′bē thrō′tid), a small hummingbird, *Archilochus colubris,* the only hummingbird of eastern North America, having metallic-green upper plumage and a bright red throat in the male. [1775–85]

ruche (ro͞osh), *n.* a strip of pleated lace, net, muslin, or other material for trimming or finishing a dress, as at the collar or sleeves. [1820–30; < F: lit., beehive < Gallo-Rom **rūsca* bark, appar. < Gaulish; cf. Welsh *rhisg(l)* bark, rind]

ruch•ing (ro͞o′shing), *n.* **1.** material for making a ruche. **2.** ruches collectively. [1860–65; RUCHE + -ING[1]]

ruck[1] (ruk), *n.* **1.** a large number or quantity; mass. **2.** the great mass of undistinguished or inferior persons or things. [1175–1225; ME *ruke,* perh. < Scand; cf. Norw *ruka* in same senses; akin to RICK[1]]

ruck[2] (ruk), *n.* **1.** a fold or wrinkle; crease. **—***v.t., v.i.* **2.** to make or become creased or wrinkled. [1780–90; < ON *hrukka* a wrinkle]

ruck•sack (ruk′sak′, ro͝ok′-), *n.* a type of knapsack carried by hikers, bicyclists, etc. [1890–95; < G: lit., back sack]

ruck•us (ruk′əs), *n.* **1.** a noisy commotion; fracas; rumpus: *The losers are sure to raise a ruckus.* **2.** a heated controversy: *Newspapers fostered the ruckus by printing the opponents' letters.* [1885–90, *Amer.;* prob. b. RUCTION and RUMPUS]

ruc•tion (ruk′shən), *n.* a disturbance, quarrel, or row. [1815–25; orig. uncert.]

Ru•da Śla•ska (Ro͞o′dä shlôN′skä), a city in S Poland, NW of Katowice. 147,000.

rud•beck•i•a (rud bek′ē ə, ro͞od-), *n.* any composite plant of the genus *Rudbeckia,* having alternate leaves and showy flower heads. [1750–60; < NL; named after Olaus *Rudbeck* (1630–1702), Swedish botanist; see -IA]

rudd (rud), *n.* a European, freshwater fish, *Scardinius erythrophthalmus,* of the carp family. [1600–10; appar. special use of *rud* redness (now dial.), ME *rude,* OE *rudu;* cf. RED[1], RUDDY]

rud•der (rud′ər), *n.* **1.** *Naut.* a vertical blade at the stern of a vessel that can be turned horizontally to change the vessel's direction when in motion. **2.** *Aeron.* a movable control surface attached to a vertical stabilizer, located at the rear of an airplane and used, along with the ailerons, to turn the airplane. **3.** any means of or device for governing, directing, or guiding a course, as a leader or principle: *His ideas provided a rudder for the new company.* [bef. 900; ME *rodder, rother, ruder,* OE *rōther;* c. OFris *rōther,* MD *rōder* (D *roer*), OHG *ruodar* (G *Ruder*); akin to ROW[2]] **—rud′dered,** *adj.* **—rud′der•less,** *adj.* **—rud′der•like′,** *adj.*

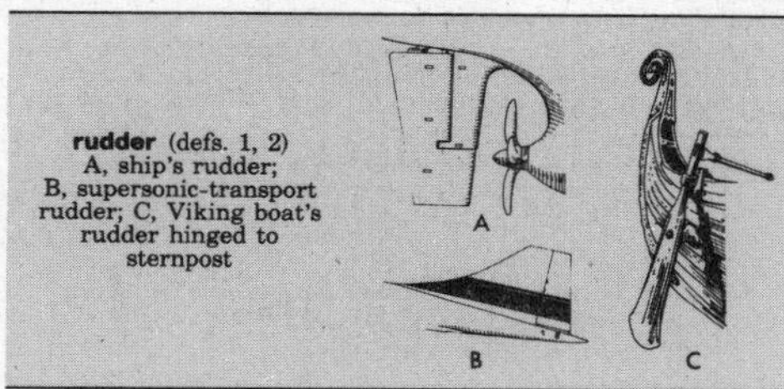

rudder (defs. 1, 2)
A, ship's rudder;
B, supersonic-transport rudder; C, Viking boat's rudder hinged to sternpost

rud•der•fish (rud′ər fish′), *n., pl.* (*esp. collectively*) **-fish,** (*esp. referring to two or more kinds or species*) **-fish•es.** any of various fishes having the habit of following behind ships, as a pilot fish. [1725–35; RUDDER + FISH]

rud•der•head (rud′ər hed′), *n. Naut.* the upper end of a rudderpost, to which a tiller, quadrant, or yoke is attached. [1795–1805; RUDDER + HEAD]

rud•der•post (rud′ər pōst′), *n. Naut.* the vertical member of a stern frame on which the rudder is hung; a sternpost. Also, **rud′der post′.** [1685–95; RUDDER + POST[1]]

rud•der•stock (rud′ər stok′), *n. Naut.* the vertical member at the forward edge of a rudder, hinged at the sternpost and attached to the helm or steering gear. Also, **rud′der stock′.** [1860–65; RUDDER + STOCK]

rud•de•va•tor (rud′ə vā′tər), *n. Aeron.* a control surface functioning both as a rudder and as an elevator. [1960–65; RUDD(ER) + (EL)EVATOR]

rud•dle (rud′l), *n., v.,* **-dled, -dling.** **—***n.* **1.** a red variety of ocher, used for marking sheep, coloring, etc. **—***v.t.* **2.** to mark or color with ruddle. Also, **raddle, reddle.** [1530–40; dial. *rud* (see RUDD) + -LE]

rud•dle•man (rud′l mən), *n., pl.* **-men.** a person who deals in ruddle. Also, **raddleman, reddleman.** [1615–25; RUDDLE + MAN[1]]

rud•dy (rud′ē), *adj.,* **-di•er, -di•est,** *adv.* **—***adj.* **1.** of or having a fresh, healthy red color: *a ruddy complexion.* **2.** red or reddish. **3.** *Brit. Slang.* damned: *a ruddy fool.* **—***adv.* **4.** *Brit. Slang.* damned: *He'd ruddy well better be there.* [bef. 1100; ME *rudi,* OE *rudig.* See RUDD, -Y[1]] **—rud′di•ly,** *adv.* **—rud′di•ness,** *n.*

rud′dy duck′, a stiff-tailed American duck, *Oxyura jamaicensis,* the adult male of which has a brownish-red body, black crown, and white cheeks. [1805–15, *Amer.*]

rud′dy turn′stone, a common shorebird, *Arenaria interpres,* of the New and Old World arctic, wintering south to southern South America and Australia and having striking reddish-brown, black, and white plumage. Also called **turnstone.** [1905–10]

rude (ro͞od), *adj.,* **rud•er, rud•est.** **1.** discourteous or impolite, esp. in a deliberate way: *a rude reply.* **2.** without culture, learning, or refinement: *rude, illiterate peasants.* **3.** rough in manners or behavior; uncouth. **4.** rough, harsh, or ungentle: *rude hands.* **5.** roughly wrought, built, or formed; of a crude construction or kind: *a rude cottage.* **6.** not properly or fully developed; raw: *a rude first stage of development.* **7.** harsh to the ear: *rude sounds.* **8.** without artistic elegance; of a primitive simplicity: *a rude design.* **9.** violent or tempestuous, as the waves. **10.** robust, sturdy, or vigorous: *rude strength.* **11.** approximate or tentative: *a rude first calculation of costs.* [1300–50; ME *rude, ruide* (< OF) < L *rudis*] **—rude′ly,** *adv.* **—rude′ness,** *n.*
—Syn. 1. uncivil, unmannerly, curt, brusque, impertinent, impudent, saucy, pert, fresh. **1, 3.** See **boorish. 2.** unrefined, uncultured, uncivilized, uncouth, coarse, vulgar, rough. **6.** See **raw. 8.** rustic, artless. **9.** stormy, fierce, tumultuous, turbulent.

Rude (RYD), *n.* **Fran•çois** (fräN swa′), 1784–1855, French sculptor.

ru•der•al (ro͞o′dər əl), *Bot.* **—***adj.* **1.** (of a plant) growing in waste places, along roadsides or in rubbish. **—***n.* **2.** a ruderal plant. [1855–60; < NL *rūderālis,* equiv. to L *rūder-* (s. of *rūdus* broken stone, rubble) + *-ālis* -AL[1]]

Rü•des•hei•mer (ro͞o′dəs hī′mər; *Ger.* RY′dəs hī′məR), *n.* any of the Rheingau wines from the vineyards near Rüdesheim, a town on the Rhine River in W Germany. [1790–1800; < G]

ru•di•ment (ro͞o′də mənt), *n.* **1.** Usually, **rudiments. a.** the elements or first principles of a subject: *the rudiments of grammar.* **b.** a mere beginning, first slight appearance, or undeveloped or imperfect form of something: *the rudiments of a plan.* **2.** *Biol.* an organ or part incompletely developed in size or structure, as one in an embryonic stage, one arrested in growth, or one with no functional activity, as a vestige. [1540–50; < L *rudimentum* early training, first experience, initial stage, equiv. to *rudi(s)* unformed, rough (see RUDE) + *-mentum* -MENT (*-ī-* for *-i-* after verbal derivs.)]

ru•di•men•ta•ry (ro͞o′də men′tə rē, -trē), *adj.* **1.** pertaining to rudiments or first principles; elementary: *a rudimentary knowledge of geometry.* **2.** of the nature of a rudiment; undeveloped or vestigial. **3.** primitive. Also, **ru′di•men′tal.** [1830–40; RUDIMENT + -ARY] **—ru•di•men•ta•ri•ly** (ro͞o′də men târ′ə lē, -men′tər ə lē), *adv.* **—ru′di•men′ta•ri•ness,** *n.*
—Syn. 1. fundamental, initial. See **elementary. 2.** embryonic. **—Ant. 1.** advanced. **2.** mature.

Rud•ny (Ro͞od′nē), *n.* a city in N central Kazakhstan, SW of Kustanai. 109,000.

Ru•dolf (ro͞o′dolf), *n.* **1. Max,** born 1902, U.S. orchestra conductor, born in Germany. **2. Lake,** former name of **Turkana** (def. 3). **3.** a male given name, form of **Rolf.**

Ru•dolf I (ro͞o′dolf; *Ger.* Ro͞o′dôlf), 1218–91, king of Germany and emperor of the Holy Roman Empire 1273–91: founder of the Hapsburg dynasty. Also, **Rudolph I.** Also called **Rudolph I of Hapsburg.**

Ru•dolph (ro͞o′dolf), *n.* **1. Paul (Marvin),** born 1918, U.S. architect. **2. Wilma (Glo•de•an)** (glō′dē ən), born 1940, U.S. track and field athlete. **3.** a male given name, form of **Rolf.**

Ru•dra (ro͝od′rə), *n. Vedic Mythology.* father of the storm gods and controller of the powers of nature.

Ru•dy (ro͞o′dē), *n.* a male given name, form of **Rudolf.**

Rud•yard (rud′yərd), *n.* a male given name: from Germanic words meaning "red" and "guarded."

rue[1] (ro͞o), *v.,* **rued, ru•ing,** *n.* **—***v.t.* **1.** to feel sorrow over; repent of; regret bitterly: *to rue the loss of opportunities.* **2.** to wish that (something) had never been done, taken place, etc.: *I rue the day he was born.* **—***v.i.* **3.** to feel sorrow, repentance, or regret. **—***n.* **4.** sorrow; repentance; regret. **5.** pity or compassion. [bef. 900; (v.) ME *ruen, rewen,* OE *hrēowan;* c. D *rouwen,* G *reuen;* (n.) ME *rewe, reowe,* OE *hrēow;* c. D *rouw,* G *Reue;* cf. RUTH] **—ru′er,** *n.*

rue[2] (ro͞o), *n.* any strongly scented plant of the genus *Ruta,* esp. *R. graveolens,* having yellow flowers and leaves formerly used in medicine. Cf. **rue family.** [1350–1400; ME < MF < L *rūta* < Gk *rhytḗ*]

Rue (ro͞o), *n.* **Warren de la.** See **de la Rue, Warren.**

rue′ anem′one, a small, North American plant, *Anemonella thalictroides,* of the buttercup family, having white or pinkish flowers. [1810–20, *Amer.*]

rue′ fam′ily, the plant family Rutaceae, characterized by trees and shrubs having simple or compound aromatic leaves, fragrant flowers, and fruit in a variety of forms, and including the citruses, the gas plant, Hercules'-club, and rue.

rue•ful (ro͞o′fəl), *adj.* **1.** causing sorrow or pity; pitiable; deplorable: *a rueful plight.* **2.** feeling, showing, or expressing sorrow or pity; mournful; doleful: *the rueful look on her face.* [1175–1225; ME *reowful.* See RUE[1], -FUL] **—rue′ful•ly,** *adv.* **—rue′ful•ness,** *n.*

Ru•fen (ro͞o′fən), *Pharm., Trademark.* a brand of ibuprofen.

ru•fes•cent (ro͞o fes′ənt), *adj.* somewhat reddish; tinged with red; rufous. [1810–20; < L *rūfēscent-* (s. of *rūfēscēns,* prp. of *rūfēscere* to redden), equiv. to *rūf(us)* RED[1], tawny + *-ēsc-* inchoative suffix + *-ent-* -ENT] **—ru•fes′cence,** *n.*

ruff[1] (ruf), *n.* **1.** a neckpiece or collar of lace, lawn, or the like, gathered or drawn into deep, full, regular folds, worn in the 16th and 17th centuries. See illus. on next page. **2.** something resembling such a piece in form or position. **3.** a collar, or set of lengthened or specially marked hairs or feathers, on the neck of an animal. **4.** *Ornith.* a species of European and Asian sandpiper, *Philomachus pugnax,* the male of which has a large

CONCISE PRONUNCIATION KEY: act, cāpe, dâre, pärt; set, ēqual; *if,* īce; ox, ōver, ôrder, oil, bo͝ok, bo͞ot, out; up, ûrge; child; sing; shoe; thin, *th*at; zh as in *treasure.* ə = *a* as in *alone, e* as in *system, i* as in *easily, o* as in *gallop, u* as in *circus;* ᵊ as in *fire* (fīᵊr), *hour* (ouᵊr). l and n can serve as syllabic consonants, as in *cradle* (krād′l), and *button* (but′n). See the full key inside the front cover.

erectile ruff of feathers during the breeding season. Cf. **reeve**[3]. **5.** *Alaska and Northern Canada.* a fringe of fur around the edge of a parka hood or along the edges of a jacket. —*v.t.* **6.** tease (def. 3). [1515–25; perh. back formation from RUFFLE[1]] —**ruff′like′,** *adj.*

ruff[1] (def. 1) (16th century)

ruff[2] (ruf), *Cards.* —*n.* **1.** an act or instance of trumping when one cannot follow suit. **2.** an old game of cards, resembling whist. —*v.t., v.i.* **3.** to trump when unable to follow suit. [1580–90; prob. < F *ro(u)ffle;* c. It *ronfa* a card game, prob. < G *Trumpf* TRUMP[1]]

ruff[3] (ruf), *n.* a small European freshwater fish, *Acerina cernua,* of the perch family. [1400–50; ME *ruf, roffe;* perh. special use of ROUGH]

ruffed (ruft), *adj.* displaying or wearing a ruff. [1570–80; RUFF[1] + -ED[2]]

ruffed′ grouse′, a North American grouse, *Bonasa umbellus,* having a tuft of black feathers on each side of the neck. See illus. under **grouse.** [1745–55, *Amer.*]

ruffed′ le′mur, vari. [1830–40]

ruf•fi•an (ruf′ē ən, ruf′yən), *n.* **1.** a tough, lawless person; roughneck; bully. —*adj.* **2.** Also, **ruf′fi•an•ly.** tough; lawless; brutal. [1525–35; < MF < It *ruffiano,* perh. < Langobardic **hruf* scurf + It *-ano* -AN]
—**Syn. 1.** brute, tough, knave, rogue, blackguard.

ruf•fi•an•ism (ruf′ē ə niz′əm, ruf′yə-), *n.* **1.** conduct befitting a ruffian. **2.** ruffian character. [1585–95; RUFFIAN + -ISM]

Ruf•fi′ni's cor′puscle (rōō fē′nēz), *Anat.* an end organ of certain sensory neurons that branches out parallel to the skin and responds to steady pressure. [after Italian anatomist Angelo *Ruffini* (1874–1929), who described them in 1898]

ruf•fle[1] (ruf′əl), *v.,* **-fled, -fling,** *n.* —*v.t.* **1.** to destroy the smoothness or evenness of: *The wind ruffled the sand.* **2.** to erect (the feathers), as a bird in anger. **3.** to disturb, vex, or irritate: *to be ruffled by a perceived slight.* **4.** to turn (the pages of a book) rapidly. **5.** to pass (cards) through the fingers rapidly in shuffling. **6.** to draw up (cloth, lace, etc.) into a ruffle by gathering along one edge. —*v.i.* **7.** to be or become ruffled; undulate; flutter: *Flags ruffle in the wind.* **8.** to be or become vexed or irritated. **9.** to put on airs; swagger. —*n.* **10.** a break in the smoothness or evenness of some surface; undulation. **11.** a strip of cloth, lace, etc., drawn up by gathering along one edge and used as a trimming on a dress, blouse, etc. **12.** some object resembling this, as the ruff of a bird. **13.** disturbance or vexation; annoyance; irritation: *It is impossible to live without some daily ruffles to our composure.* **14.** a disturbed state of mind; perturbation. [1250–1300; ME *ruffelen* (v.); c. LG *ruffelen* to crumple, rumple; cf. ON *hruffa* to scratch] —**ruf′fly,** *adj.* —**ruf′fler,** *n.*
—**Syn. 1.** disarrange, disorder, wrinkle, rumple. **3.** upset, annoy, agitate. **10.** perturbation, flurry, agitation. **11.** frill, ruff. —**Ant. 1.** smooth, arrange, order. **3.** soothe, compose. **13.** tranquillity.

ruf•fle[2] (ruf′əl), *n., v.,* **-fled, -fling.** —*n.* **1.** a low, continuous beating of a drum. —*v.t.* **2.** to beat (a drum) in this manner. [1715–25; archaic *ruff* in same sense (perh. imit.) + -LE]

ruf•fled (ruf′əld), *adj.* (of apparel) having ruffles. [1600–10; RUFFLE[1] + -ED[2]]

Ru•fisque (*Fr.* RY fēsk′), *n.* a city in W Senegal, E of Dakar. 48,101.

ru•fi•yaa (rōō′fē yä′), *n., pl.* **-yaa.** rupee (def. 3).

ru•fous (rōō′fəs), *adj.* reddish; tinged with red; brownish red. [1775–85; < L *rūf(us)* RED[1] + -OUS]

ruf′ter hood′ (ruf′tər), *Falconry.* a temporary, loosely fitted hood used on newly captured hawks. [1565–75; perh. deriv. of RUFF[1]]

Ru•fus (rōō′fəs), *n.* a male given name: from a Latin word meaning "red-headed."

rug (rug), *n.* **1.** a thick fabric for covering part of a floor, often woven of wool and often having an oblong shape with a border design. Cf. **carpet. 2.** the treated skin of an animal, used as a floor covering: *a bear rug.* **3.** *Chiefly Brit.* a piece of thick, warm cloth, used as a coverlet, lap robe, etc. **4.** *Slang.* toupee; hairpiece. **5. cut a rug,** *Older Slang.* to dance, esp. to jitterbug. [1545–55; < ON *rǫgg* wool, long hairs; cf. Norw *rugga* covering of coarse wool, Sw *rugg* coarse hair] —**rug′like′,** *adj.*

ru•ga (rōō′gə), *n., pl.* **-gae** (-jē, -gē). Usually, **rugae.** *Biol., Anat.* a wrinkle, fold, or ridge. [1765–75; < L *rūga*]

rug•a•lach (rug′ə ləKH), *n.pl. Jewish Cookery.* bite-size pastries, often filled with fruit, nuts, raisins, etc. Also, **ro•ge•lach** (rô′gə ləKH, rug′ə-). [< Yiddish *rugelekh, rogelekh,* pl. of *rugele, rogele*]

ru•gate (rōō′gāt, -git), *adj.* wrinkled; rugose. [1840–50; < L *rūgātus,* ptp. of *rūgāre* to become wrinkled. See RUGA, -ATE[1]]

Rug•by (rug′bē), *n.* **1.** a city in E Warwickshire, in central England. 86,400. **2.** a boys' preparatory school located there: founded 1567. **3.** Also, **rugby.** Also called **rugger, Rug′by foot′ball.** a form of football, played between two teams of 15 members each, that differs from soccer in freedom to carry the ball, block with the hands and arms, and tackle, and is characterized chiefly by continuous action and prohibition against the use of substitute players. [‡1835–40 for def. 3]

Rug′by shirt′, a knitted pullover sport shirt usually in bold horizontal stripes and having a white collar and neckline placket, styled after the shirts traditionally worn by the members of Rugby teams. Also, **rug′by shirt′.** Also called **Rug′by jer′sey.**

rug-cut•ter (rug′kut′ər), *n. Older Slang.* a person who jitterbugs. [1935–40, *Amer.*]

rug•ged (rug′id), *adj.* **1.** having a roughly broken, rocky, hilly, or jagged surface: *rugged ground.* **2.** (of a face) wrinkled or furrowed, as by experience or the endurance of hardship. **3.** roughly irregular, heavy, or hard in outline or form; craggy: *Lincoln's rugged features.* **4.** rough, harsh, or stern, as persons or nature. **5.** full of hardship and trouble; severe; hard; trying: *a rugged life.* **6.** tempestuous; stormy: *rugged weather.* **7.** harsh to the ear: *rugged sounds.* **8.** rude, uncultivated, or unrefined. **9.** homely or plain: *rugged fare.* **10.** capable of enduring hardship, wear, etc.; strong and tough: *rugged floor covering; a rugged lumberjack.* [1300–50; ME < Scand; cf. Sw *rugga* to roughen (of cloth); cf. RUG] —**rug′ged•ly,** *adv.* —**rug′ged•ness,** *n.*
—**Syn. 1.** uneven, irregular, craggy. **4.** austere. **6.** turbulent. **7.** grating, cacophonous. **8.** unpolished, crude. —**Ant. 1.** smooth. **4.** mild. **10.** frail.

rug•ged•ize (rug′i dīz′), *v.t.,* **-ized, -iz•ing.** to construct (electronic equipment, cameras, and other delicate instruments) so as to be resistant to shock, vibration, etc. Also, *esp. Brit.,* **rug′ged•ise′.** [1955–60; RUGGED + -IZE]

rug•ger (rug′ər), *n.* Rugby (def. 3). [1890–95; RUG(BY) + -ER[7]]

rug•ging (rug′ing), *n.* a bulky, coarse fabric with a full nap, used as a floor covering. [1855–60; RUG + -ING[1]]

ru•go′sa rose′ (rōō gō′sə), a shrub, *Rosa rugosa,* having densely bristled stems, wrinkled leaves, and fragrant red or white flowers. [1890–95; < NL, L *rūgōsa,* fem. of *rūgōsus* wrinkled; see RUGOSE]

ru•gose (rōō′gōs, rōō gōs′), *adj.* **1.** having wrinkles; wrinkled; ridged. **2.** *Bot.* rough and wrinkled: applied to leaves in which the reticulate venation is very prominent beneath, with corresponding creases on the upper side. [1695–1705; < L *rūgōsus* wrinkled. See RUGA, -OSE[1]] —**ru′gose•ly,** *adv.* —**ru•gos•i•ty** (rōō gos′i tē), *n.*

ru•gu•la (rōō′gə lə), *n.* arugula.

ru•gu•lose (rōō′gyə lōs′), *adj.* finely rugose; having many small wrinkles. [1810–20; < NL *rūgul(a)* (dim. of L *rūga* RUGA) + -OSE[1]]

Ruhm′korff coil′ (rōōm′kôrf), *Elect.* See **induction coil.** [1850–55; named after Heinrich Daniel *Ruhmkorff* (1803–77), German physicist, its inventor]

Ruhr (rŏŏr), *n.* **1.** a river in W Germany, flowing NW and W into the Rhine. 144 mi. (232 km) long. **2.** a mining and industrial region centered in the valley of the Ruhr River.

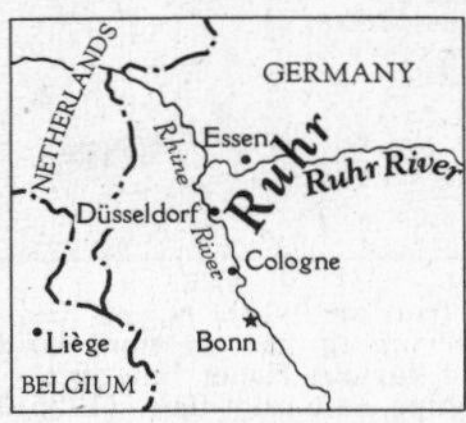

ru•in (rōō′in), *n.* **1. ruins,** the remains of a building, city, etc., that has been destroyed or that is in disrepair or a state of decay: *We visited the ruins of ancient Greece.* **2.** a destroyed or decayed building, town, etc. **3.** a fallen, wrecked, or decayed condition: *The building fell to ruin.* **4.** the downfall, decay, or destruction of anything. **5.** the complete loss of health, means, position, hope, or the like. **6.** something that causes a downfall or destruction; blight: *Alcohol was his ruin.* **7.** the downfall of a person; undoing: *the ruin of Oedipus.* **8.** a person as the wreck of his or her former self; ravaged individual. **9.** the act of causing destruction or a downfall. —*v.t.* **10.** to reduce to ruin; devastate. **11.** to bring (a person, company, etc.) to financial ruin; bankrupt. **12.** to injure (a thing) irretrievably. **13.** to induce (a woman) to surrender her virginity; deflower. —*v.i.* **14.** to fall into ruins; fall to pieces. **15.** to come to ruin. [1325–75; (n.) ME *ruine* < MF < L *ruīna* headlong rush, fall, collapse, equiv. to *ru(ere)* to fall + *-īna* -INE[2]; (v.) (< MF *ruiner*) < ML *ruīnāre,* deriv. of L *ruīna*] —**ru′in•a•ble,** *adj.* —**ru′in•er,** *n.*
—**Syn. 3.** RUIN, DESTRUCTION, HAVOC imply irrevocable and often widespread damage. DESTRUCTION may be on a large or small scale (*destruction of tissue, of enemy vessels*); it emphasizes particularly the act of destroying, while RUIN and HAVOC emphasize the resultant state. RUIN, from the verb meaning to fall to pieces, suggests a state of decay or disintegration (or an object in that state) that is apt to be more the result of the natural processes of time and change than of sudden violent activity from without: *The house has fallen to ruins.* Only in its figurative application is it apt to suggest the result of destruction from without: *the ruin of her hopes.* HAVOC, originally a cry that served as the signal for pillaging, has changed its reference from that of spoliation to devastation, being used particularly of the destruction following in the wake of natural calamities: *the havoc wrought by flood and pestilence.* Today it is used figuratively to refer to the destruction of hopes and plans: *This sudden turn of events played havoc with her carefully laid designs.* **4.** fall, overthrow, defeat, wreck. **10.** demolish, destroy, damage. See **spoil.** —**Ant. 4.** construction, creation.

ru•in•ate (rōō′ə nāt′), *v.,* **-at•ed, -at•ing,** *adj. Chiefly South Midland and Southern U.S.* —*v.t.* **1.** to ruin. —*adj.* **2.** ruined. [1530–40; < ML *ruīnātus,* ptp. of *ruīnāre.* See RUIN, -ATE[1]]

ru•in•a•tion (rōō′ə nā′shən), *n.* **1.** the act or state of ruining or the state of being ruined. **2.** something that ruins. [1655–65; RUINATE + -ION]

ru•in•ous (rōō′ə nəs), *adj.* **1.** bringing or tending to bring ruin; destructive; disastrous: *a ruinous war.* **2.** fallen into ruin; dilapidated: *a ruinous house.* **3.** consisting of ruins: *a ruinous city from antiquity.* [1350–1400; ME *ruynouse* < L *ruīnōsus,* equiv. to *ruīn(a)* RUIN + *-ōsus* -OUS] —**ru′in•ous•ly,** *adv.* —**ru′in•ous•ness,** *n.*
—**Syn. 1.** calamitous, ravaging, devastating, catastrophic.

Ruis•dael (rois′däl, -dāl, rīz′-, rīs′-; *Du.* RŒIS′däl), *n.* **1. Ja•cob van** (yä′kôp vän), 1628?–82, Dutch painter. **2.** his uncle, **Sa•lo•mon van** (sä′lô môn′ vän), 1601?–70, Dutch painter. Also, **Ruysdael.**

Ru•key•ser (rōō′kī zər), *n.* **Muriel,** 1913–80, U.S. poet.

rule (rōōl), *n., v.,* **ruled, rul•ing.** —*n.* **1.** a principle or regulation governing conduct, action, procedure, arrangement, etc.: *the rules of chess.* **2.** the code of regulations observed by a religious order or congregation: *the Franciscan rule.* **3.** the customary or normal circumstance, occurrence, manner, practice, quality, etc.: *the rule rather than the exception.* **4.** control, government, or dominion: *under the rule of a dictator.* **5.** tenure or conduct of reign or office: *during the rule of George III.* **6.** a prescribed mathematical method for performing a calculation or solving a problem. **7.** ruler (def. 2). **8.** (*cap.*) *Astron.* the constellation Norma. **9.** *Print.* a thin, type-high strip of metal, for printing a solid or decorative line or lines. **10.** *Law.* **a.** a formal order or direction made by a court, as for governing the procedure of the court (**general rule**) or for sending the case before a referee (**special rule**). **b.** a legal principle. **c.** a court order in a particular case. **11. rules,** *Penol.* (formerly) **a.** a fixed area in the neighborhood of certain prisons within which certain prisoners were allowed to live. **b.** the freedom of such an area. **12.** *Obs.* behavior. **13. as a rule,** generally; usually: *He arrives at eleven o'clock, as a rule.* —*v.t.* **14.** to control or direct; exercise dominating power, authority, or influence over; govern: *to rule the empire with severity.* **15.** to decide or declare judicially or authoritatively; decree: *The judge ruled that he should be exiled.* **16.** to mark with lines, esp. parallel straight lines, with the aid of a ruler or the like: *to rule paper.* **17.** to mark out or form (a line) by this method: *to rule lines on paper.* **18.** to be superior or preeminent in (a specific field or group); dominate by superiority; hold sway over: *For centuries, England ruled the seas.* —*v.i.* **19.** to exercise dominating power or influence; predominate. **20.** to exercise authority, dominion, or sovereignty. **21.** to make a formal decision or ruling, as on a point at law. **22.** to be prevalent or current: *Higher prices ruled throughout France.* **23. rule out, a.** to prove to be unrelated or not for consideration; eliminate; exclude: *to rule out the possibility of error.* **b.** to make impossible or impracticable: *The rainstorm ruled out the holiday camping.* **24. rule the roost.** See **roost** (def. 4). [1175–1225; (n.) ME *riule, reule* < OF *riule* < L *rēgula* straight stick, pattern (see REGULA); (v.) ME *riwlen, reulen, rewellen* < OF *riuler, rieuler, ruler* < LL *rēgulāre,* deriv. of *rēgula*]
—**Syn. 1.** standard, law, ruling, guide, precept, order. See **principle. 4.** command, domination, mastery, sway, authority, direction. **14.** RULE, ADMINISTER, COMMAND, GOVERN, MANAGE mean to exercise authoritative guidance or direction. RULE implies the exercise of authority as by a sovereign: *to rule a kingdom.* ADMINISTER places emphasis on the planned and orderly procedures used: *to administer the finances of an institution.* COMMAND suggests military authority and the power to exact obedience; to be in command of: *to command a ship.* To GOVERN is authoritatively to guide or direct persons or things, esp. in the affairs of a large administrative unit: *to govern a state.* To MANAGE is to conduct affairs, i.e., to guide them in a unified way toward a definite goal, or to direct or control people, often by tact, address, or artifice: *to manage a business.* **15.** order, judge.

ruled′ sur′face, *Geom.* a surface that can be generated by a straight line, as a cylinder or cone. [1860–65]

rule′ joint′, **1.** (in carpentry and joinery) a joint between two hinged pieces, as between the center and end leaves of a table, consisting of a quarter round and fillet fitting against a cove and fillet. **2.** a pivoted joint between two strips of wood placed end to end, as in a carpenter's folding rule. [1775–85]

rule•less (rōōl′lis), *adj.* being without rule or law. [1400–50; late ME *rewleless;* see RULE, -LESS] —**rule′less•ness,** *n.*

rule′ of elev′en, *Bridge, Whist.* the rule that when a player leads his or her fourth-highest card in any suit its numerical value subtracted from eleven gives the number of higher cards of that suit held by the other players.

rule′ of the road′, *Naut.* any of the regulations concerning the safe handling of vessels under way with respect to one another, imposed by a government on ships in its own waters or upon its own ships on the high seas. [1870–75]

rule′ of three′, *Math.* the method of finding the fourth term in a proportion when three terms are given. [1585–95]

rule′ of thumb′, **1.** a general or approximate principle, procedure, or rule based on experience or practice, as opposed to a specific, scientific calculation or estimate. **2.** a rough, practical method of procedure. [1685–95]

rul•er (rōō′lər), *n.* **1.** a person who rules or governs; sovereign. **2.** Also, **rule.** a strip of wood, metal, or other

CONCISE ETYMOLOGY KEY: <, descended or borrowed from; >, whence; b., blend of, blended; c., cognate with; cf., compare; deriv., derivative; equiv., equivalent; imit., imitative; obl., oblique; r., replacing; s., stem; sp., spelling, spelled; resp., respelling, respelled; trans., translation; ?, origin unknown; *, unattested; ‡, probably earlier than. See the full key inside the front cover.

material having a straight edge and usually marked off in inches or centimeters, used for drawing lines, measuring, etc. **3.** a person or thing that rules paper, wood, etc. **4.** *Astrol.* the planet primarily associated with any sign of the zodiac or any house of the horoscope: *The ruler of Aries is Mars. The ruler of Taurus is Venus.* [1325–75; ME; see RULE, -ER[1]]

rul•er•ship (rōō′lər ship′), *n.* the act or fact of ruling or the state of being ruled. [1640–50; RULER + -SHIP]

rules′ commit′tee, a special committee of a legislature, as of the U.S. House of Representatives, having the authority to establish rules or methods for expediting legislative action, and usually determining the date a bill is presented for consideration. [1915–20]

rules′ of or′der, the rules by which a legislative or deliberative assembly governs its proceedings; parliamentary law.

rul•ing (rōō′ling), *n.* **1.** an authoritative decision, as one by a judge on a debated point of law. **2.** the act of drawing straight lines with a ruler. **3.** ruled lines. **—*adj.* 4.** governing or dominating: *the ruling party.* **5.** controlling; predominating: *the ruling factor in recovery from an illness.* **6.** widespread; prevalent: *ruling values.* [1175–1225; ME (ger.); see RULE, -ING[1], -ING[2]]

rul′ing eld′er, an elder in a Presbyterian church. [1585–95]

rul′ing grade′, *Railroads.* the steepest grade on a given stretch of track, which determines the maximum tonnage that can be hauled in a train having a given horsepower at a stated minimum speed.

rum[1] (rum), *n.* **1.** an alcoholic liquor or spirit distilled from molasses or some other fermented sugar-cane product. **2.** alcoholic drink in general; intoxicating liquor: *He warned against the demon rum.* [1645–55; perh. short for obs. *rumbullion, rumbustion,* of obscure orig.] **—rum′less,** *adj.*

rum[2] (rum), *adj. Chiefly Brit.* **1.** odd, strange, or queer: *a rum fellow.* **2.** problematic; difficult. [1765–75; earlier *rome, room* great, prob. < Romany; see ROM]

rum[3] (rum), *n. Cards.* rummy[1]. [by shortening]

Rum (rōōm), *n.* Arabic name of Rome, once used to designate the Byzantine Empire.

Rum., 1. Rumania. **2.** Also, **Rum** Rumanian.

ru•ma•ki (rə mä′kē), *n.pl. Hawaiian Cookery.* bite-size appetizers, as chicken livers and water chestnuts wrapped in bacon and broiled. [1960–65; of undetermined orig.]

ru•mal (rōō mäl′, rōō′mäl), *n.* a kerchief worn as a headdress by men in India. [1700–10; < Urdu < Pers *rūmāl,* equiv. to *rū* face + *māl* wiping]

Ru•ma•ni•a (rŏŏ mā′nē ə, -mān′yə), *n.* a republic in SE Europe, bordering on the Black Sea: one of the Balkan States. 22,048,305; 91,654 sq. mi. (237,385 sq. km). *Cap.:* Bucharest. Also, **Romania, România, Roumania.**

Ru•ma•ni•an (rŏŏ mā′nē ən, -mān′yən), *adj.* **1.** of or pertaining to Rumania, its inhabitants, or their language. **—*n.* 2.** a native or inhabitant of Rumania. **3.** the language of Rumania, a Romance language. *Abbr.:* Rum., Rum Also, **Romanian, Roumanian.** [1855–60; RUMANI(A) + -AN]

Ruma′nian ten′derloin. See **skirt steak.**

ru•man•ite (rōō′mə nīt′), *n.* a fossil resin similar to amber, used for jewelry. Also called **Ruma′nian am′ber.** [1890–95; named after RUMANIA; see -ITE[1]]

rum•ba (rum′bə, rŏŏm′-, rōōm′-), *n., pl.* **-bas** (-bəz), *v.,* **-baed** (-bəd), **-ba•ing** (-bə ing). **—*n.* 1.** a dance, Cuban in origin and complex in rhythm. **2.** an imitation or adaptation of this dance in the U.S. **3.** music for this dance or in its rhythm. **—*v.i.* 4.** to dance the rumba. Also, **rhumba.** [1920–25; < AmerSp]

rum•ble (rum′bəl), *v.,* **-bled, -bling,** *n.* **—*v.i.* 1.** to make a deep, heavy, somewhat muffled, continuous sound, as thunder. **2.** to move or travel with such a sound: *The train rumbled on.* **3.** *Slang.* to have or take part in a street fight between or among teenage gangs: *Rival gangs rumbled on Saturday afternoon.* **—*v.t.* 4.** to give forth or utter with a rumbling sound: *to rumble a command.* **5.** to cause to make or move with a rumbling sound: *to rumble a wagon over the ground.* **6.** to subject to the action of a rumble or tumbling box, as for the purpose of polishing. **—*n.* 7.** a deep, heavy, somewhat muffled, continuous sound: *the rumble of tanks across a bridge.* **8.** See **rumble seat. 9.** a rear part of a carriage containing seating accommodations, as for servants, or space for baggage. **10.** See **tumbling box. 11.** *Slang.* a street fight between rival teenage gangs. [1325–75; 1940–45 for def. 3; (v.) ME *romblen, rumblen;* cf. D *rommelen,* prob. of imit. orig.; (n.) ME, deriv. of the v.] **—rum′bler,** *n.* **—rum′bling•ly,** *adv.*
—Syn. 1. roar, thunder, roll, boom.

rum′ble seat′, 1. Also called, *Brit.,* **dickey.** a seat recessed into the back of a coupe or roadster, covered by a hinged lid that opens to form the back of the seat when in use. **2.** *Furniture.* See **wagon seat. 3.** *Slang.* the buttocks. [1910–15]

rumble seat (def. 1)

rum′ble strip′, one of a series of rough or slightly raised strips of pavement on a highway, intended to slow down the speed of vehicles, as before a toll booth. [1965–70]

rum•bling (rum′bling), *n.* **1.** Often, **rumblings.** the first signs of dissatisfaction or grievance. **2.** rumble (def. 7). [1350–1400; ME; see RUMBLE, -ING[1]]

rum•bly (rum′blē), *adj.* attended with, making, or causing a rumbling sound. [1870–75; RUMBLE + -Y[1]]

rum•bus•tious (rum bus′chəs), *adj. Chiefly Brit.* rambunctious.

rum-dum (rum′dum′), *Slang.* **—*n.* 1.** a stupid or ignorant person. **2.** drunkard; lush. **—*adj.* 3.** stupid; ignorant. **4.** of, pertaining to, characteristic of, or arising from habitual drunkenness; addled by drink. [1890–95; rhyming compound with RUM[1] and DUMB, perh. influenced in sense by HUMDRUM] Also, **rum′-dumb′, rum′-dumm′.**

Ru•me•li•a (rōō mē′lē ə, -mēl′yə), *n.* **1.** a division of the former Turkish Empire, in the Balkan Peninsula: included Albania, Macedonia, and Thrace. **2. Eastern,** a former autonomous province within this division: later became S Bulgaria. Also, **Roumelia.**

ru•men (rōō′min), *n., pl.* **-mi•na** (-mə nə). the first stomach of ruminating animals, lying next to the reticulum. See diag. under **ruminant.** [1720–30; < L *rūmen* throat, gullet]

Rum•ford (rum′fərd), *n.* **Count.** See **Thompson, Benjamin.**

Ru•mi (*Pers.* rōō′mē), *n.* **Ja•lal ud-din** (*Pers.* jä läl′ ŏŏd dēn′, ŏŏd-, ja-). See **Jalal ud-din Rumi.**

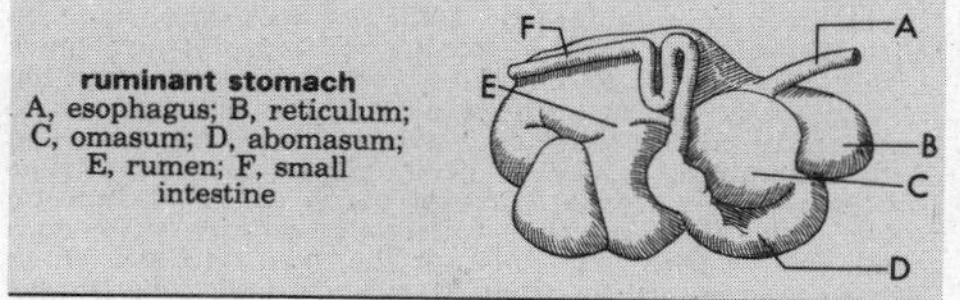

ruminant stomach
A, esophagus; B, reticulum; C, omasum; D, abomasum; E, rumen; F, small intestine

ru•mi•nant (rōō′mə nənt), *n.* **1.** any even-toed, hoofed mammal of the suborder Ruminantia, being comprised of cloven-hoofed, cud-chewing quadrupeds, and including, besides domestic cattle, bison, buffalo, deer, antelopes, giraffes, camels, and chevrotains. **—*adj.* 2.** ruminating; chewing the cud. **3.** contemplative; meditative: *a ruminant scholar.* [1655–65; < L *rūminant-* (s. of *rūmināns,* prp. of *rūminārī, rūmināre* to chew cud, meditate), equiv. to *rūmin-* (s. of *rūmen*) RUMEN + *-ant-* -ANT] **—ru′mi•nant•ly,** *adv.*

ru•mi•nate (rōō′mə nāt′), *v.,* **-nat•ed, -nat•ing.** **—*v.i.* 1.** to chew the cud, as a ruminant. **2.** to meditate or muse; ponder. **—*v.t.* 3.** to chew again or over and over. **4.** to meditate on; ponder. [1525–35; < L *rūminātus* (ptp. of *rūminārī, rūmināre* to ruminate), equiv. to *rūmin-* (s. of *rūmen* RUMEN) + *-ātus* -ATE[1]] **—ru′mi•nat′ing•ly,** *adv.* **—ru′mi•na′tion,** *n.* **—ru′mi•na′tive,** *adj.* **—ru′mi•na′tive•ly,** *adv.* **—ru′mi•na′tor,** *n.*
—Syn. 2. think, reflect.

Rüm•ker (rum′kər), *n.* a crater in the second quadrant of the face of the moon: about 25 miles (40 km) in diameter.

Ruml (rum′əl), *n.* **Beards•ley** (bērdz′lē), 1894–1960, U.S. economist and businessman.

rum•mage (rum′ij), *v.,* **-maged, -mag•ing,** *n.* **—*v.t.* 1.** to search thoroughly or actively through (a place, receptacle, etc.), esp. by moving around, turning over, or looking through contents. **2.** to find, bring, or fetch by searching (often fol. by *out* or *up*). **—*v.i.* 3.** to search actively, as in a place or receptacle or within oneself: *She rummaged in her mind for the forgotten name.* **—*n.* 4.** miscellaneous articles; odds and ends. **5.** a rummaging search. [1520–30; aph. alter. of MF *arrumage,* equiv. to *arrum(er)* to stow goods in the hold of a ship (< ?) + *-age* -AGE] **—rum′mag•er,** *n.*

rum′mage sale′, a sale of miscellaneous articles, old or new, as items contributed to raise money for charity, of unclaimed goods at a wharf or warehouse, or of odds and ends of merchandise at a shop. [1855–60]

rum•mer (rum′ər), *n.* a large drinking glass or cup. [1645–55; < D *roemer* large wine glass, esp. for Rhine wine, perh. deriv. of *roemen* to praise (as in drinking a toast)]

rum•my[1] (rum′ē), *n.* any of various card games for two, three, or four players, each usually being dealt seven, nine, or ten cards, in which the object is to match cards into sets and sequences. Also called **rum.** [1905–10, *Amer.;* perh. special use of RUMMY[3]]

rum•my[2] (rum′ē), *n., pl.* **-mies,** *adj.* **—*n.* 1.** *Slang.* a drunkard. **—*adj.* 2.** of or like rum. [1850–55; RUM[1] + -Y[1]]

rum•my[3] (rum′ē), *adj.,* **-mi•er, -mi•est.** *Chiefly Brit. Slang.* odd; peculiar. [1820–30; RUM[2] + -Y[1]]

ru•mor (rōō′mər), *n.* **1.** a story or statement in general circulation without confirmation or certainty as to facts: *a rumor of war.* **2.** gossip; hearsay: *Don't listen to rumor.* **3.** *Archaic.* a continuous, confused noise; clamor; din. **—*v.t.* 4.** to circulate, report, or assert by a rumor: *It is rumored that the king is dead.* Also, *esp. Brit.,* **ru′mour.** [1325–75; ME *rumour* < MF < L *rūmor;* akin to Skt *rāuti, rāvati* (he) cries]
—Syn. 1. report.

ru•mor•mon•ger (rōō′mər mung′gər, -mong′-), *n.* a person given to spreading rumors, often maliciously. [1930–35; RUMOR + MONGER]

rump (rump), *n.* **1.** the hind part of the body of an animal, as the hindquarters of a quadruped or sacral region of a bird. **2.** a cut of beef from this part of the animal, behind the loin and above the round. See diag. under **beef. 3.** the buttocks. **4.** the last part, esp. that which is unimportant or inferior: *a rump of territory.* **5.** the remnant of a legislature, council, etc., after a majority of the members have resigned or been expelled. **6. the Rump,** *Eng. Hist.* See **Rump Parliament. —*adj.* 7.** constituting a subsidiary or small group or the remnant of a once larger organization: *Our local Shakespeare Club will hold a rump meeting at the Elizabethan Drama Teachers' convention.* [1375–1425; late ME *rumpe* < Scand; cf. Dan, Norw, Sw *rumpe* rump, tail; c. G *Rumpf* body, trunk] **—rump′less,** *adj.*

Rum•pel•stilts•kin (rum′pəl stilt′skin), *n.* a dwarf in a German folktale who spins flax into gold for a young woman to meet the demands of the prince she has married, on the condition that she give him her first child or else guess his name: she guesses his name and he vanishes or destroys himself in a rage.

rumpf (rŏŏmpf), *n. Physical Chem.* kernel (def. 7). [< G; see RUMP]

rum•ple (rum′pəl), *v.,* **-pled, -pling,** *n.* **—*v.t.* 1.** to crumple or crush into wrinkles: *to rumple a sheet of paper.* **2.** to ruffle; tousle (sometimes fol. by *up*): *The wind rumpled her hair.* **—*v.i.* 3.** to become wrinkled or crumpled: *Tissue rumples easily.* **—*n.* 4.** a wrinkle or irregular fold; crease. [1595–1605; < D *rompelen* (v.), *rompel* (n.)]
—Syn. 1. wrinkle, crease, muss.

rum•ply (rum′plē), *adj.,* **-pli•er, -pli•est.** rumpled or tending to rumple: *This suit always looks rumply.* [1825–35; RUMPLE + -Y[1]]

Rump′ Par′liament, *Eng. Hist.* the remnant of the Long Parliament established by the expulsion of the Presbyterian members in 1648, dismissed by force in 1653, and restored briefly in 1659–60.

rum•pus (rum′pəs), *n., pl.* **-pus•es. 1.** a noisy or violent disturbance; commotion; uproar: *There was a terrible rumpus going on upstairs.* **2.** a heated controversy: *a rumpus over the school-bond issue.* [1755–65; orig. uncert.]

rum′pus room′, a recreation room, esp. one for children, as in a house. [1935–40, *Amer.*]

rum•run•ner (rum′run′ər), *n.* a person or ship engaged in smuggling liquor. [1920, *Amer.;* RUM[1] + RUNNER] **—rum′run′ning,** *n., adj.*

Rum•sey (rum′zē), *n.* **James,** 1743–92, U.S. engineer and inventor.

run (run), *v.,* **ran, run, run•ning,** *n., adj.* **—*v.i.* 1.** to go quickly by moving the legs more rapidly than at a walk and in such a manner that for an instant in each step all or both feet are off the ground. **2.** to move with haste; act quickly: *Run upstairs and get the iodine.* **3.** to depart quickly; take to flight; flee or escape: *to run from danger.* **4.** to have recourse for aid, support, comfort, etc.: *He shouldn't run to his parents with every little problem.* **5.** to make a quick trip or informal visit for a short stay at a place: *to run up to New York; I will run over to see you after dinner.* **6.** to go around, rove, or ramble without restraint (often fol. by *about*): *to run about in the park.* **7.** to move, roll, or progress from momentum or from being hurled, kicked, or otherwise propelled: *The wheel ran over the curb and into the street.* **8.** *Sports.* **a.** to take part in a race or contest. **b.** to finish in a race or contest in a certain numerical position: *The horse ran second.* **9.** to be or campaign as a candidate for election. **10.** to migrate, as fish: *to run in huge shoals.* **11.** to migrate upstream or inshore from deep water to spawn. **12.** to move under continuing power or force, as of the wind, a motor, etc.: *The car ran along the highway.* **13.** (of a ship, automobile, etc.) to be sailed or driven from a safe, proper, or given route: *The ship ran aground.* **14.** to ply between places, as a vessel or conveyance: *This bus runs between New Haven and Hartford.* **15.** to move, glide, turn, rotate, or pass easily, freely, or smoothly: *A rope runs in a pulley.* **16.** to creep, trail, or climb, as growing vines: *The ivy ran up the side of the house.* **17.** to come undone or to unravel, as stitches or a fabric: *these stockings run easily.* **18.** to flow, as a liquid: *Let the water run before you drink it.* **19.** to flow along, esp. strongly, as a stream or the sea: *The rapids ran over the rocks.* **20.** to empty or transfer contents: *The river ran into the sea.* **21.** to appear, occur, or exist within a certain limited range; include a specific range of variations (usually fol. by *from*): *Your work runs from fair to bad.* **22.** to melt and flow or drip: *Wax ran down the burning candle.* **23.** *Golf.* (of a golf ball) to bounce or roll along the ground just after landing from a stroke: *The ball struck the green and ran seven feet past the hole.* **24.** to spread on being applied to a surface, as a liquid: *Fresh paint ran over the window molding onto the pane.* **25.** to spread over a material when exposed to moisture: *The dyes in this fabric are*

CONCISE PRONUNCIATION KEY: act, cāpe, dâre, pärt; set, ēqual; if, īce; ox, ōver, ôrder, oil, bŏŏk, bōōt, out; up, ûrge; child; sing; shoe; thin, *th*at; zh as in *treasure.* ə = *a* as in *alone, e* as in *system, i* as in *easily, o* as in *gallop, u* as in *circus;* ᵊ as in *fire* (fīᵊr), *hour* (ouᵊr). l and n can serve as syllabic consonants, as in *cradle* (krād′l), and *button* (but′n). See the full key inside the front cover.

guaranteed not to run in washing. **26.** to undergo a spreading of colors: *materials that run when washed.* **27.** to flow forth as a discharge: *Tears ran from her eyes.* **28.** to discharge or give passage to a liquid or fluid: *Her eyes ran with tears.* **29.** to operate or function: *How does your new watch run? Cars run on gasoline.* **30.** to be in operation: *the noise of a dishwasher running.* **31.** to continue in operation: *The furnace runs most of the day.* **32.** to elapse; pass or go by, as time: *Time is running out, and we must hurry.* **33.** to pass into or meet with a certain state or condition: *to run into debt; to run into trouble.* **34.** to get or become: *The well ran dry.* **35.** to amount; total: *The bill ran to $100.* **36.** to be stated or worded in a certain manner: *The minutes of the last meeting run as follows.* **37.** *Com.* **a.** to accumulate, follow, or become payable in due course, as interest on a debt: *Your interest runs from January 1st to December 31st.* **b.** to make many withdrawals in rapid succession, as from a bank. **38.** *Law.* **a.** to have legal force or effect, as a writ. **b.** to continue to operate. **c.** to go along with: *The easement runs with the land.* **39.** to proceed, continue, or go: *The story runs for eight pages.* **40.** to extend in a given direction: *This road runs north to Litchfield.* **41.** to extend for a certain length: *The unpaved section runs for eight miles.* **42.** to extend over a given surface: *Shelves ran from floor to ceiling.* **43.** to be printed, as on a printing press: *Two thousand copies ran before the typo was caught.* **44.** to appear in print or be published as a story, photograph, etc., in a newspaper, magazine, or the like: *The account ran in all the papers. The political cartoon always runs on the editorial page.* **45.** to be performed on a stage or be played continually, as a play: *The play ran for two years.* **46.** to occur or take place continuously, as a movie: *The picture runs for two hours.* **47.** to pass quickly: *A thought ran through his mind. Her eyes ran over the room.* **48.** to be disseminated, circulated, or spread rapidly: *The news of his promotion ran all over town.* **49.** to continue or return persistently; recur: *The old tune ran through his mind all day.* **50.** to have or tend to have or produce a specified character, quality, form, etc.: *This novel runs to long descriptions. Her sister is fat too, but the family runs to being overweight.* **51.** to be or continue to be of a certain or average size, number, etc.: *Potatoes are running large this year.* **52.** *Naut.* to sail before the wind. —*v.t.* **53.** to move or run along (a surface, way, path, etc.): *Every morning he ran the dirt path around the reservoir to keep in condition. She ran her fingers over the keyboard.* **54.** to traverse (a distance) in running: *He ran the mile in just over four minutes.* **55.** to perform, compete in, or accomplish by or as by running: *to run a race; to run an errand.* **56.** to go about freely on or in or without supervision: *permitting children to run the streets.* **57.** to ride or cause to gallop: *to run a horse across a field.* **58.** to enter in a race: *He ran his best filly in the Florida Derby.* **59.** to bring into a certain state by running: *He ran himself out of breath trying to keep pace.* **60.** to trace, track, pursue or hunt, as game: *to run deer on foot.* **61.** to drive (an animal) or cause to go by pursuing: *to run a fox to cover; to run the stallion into the barn.* **62.** to leave, flee, or escape from: *He ran town before the robbery was discovered.* **63.** to cause to ply between places, as a vessel or conveyance: *to run a ferry between New York and New Jersey.* **64.** to convey or transport, as in a vessel or vehicle: *I'll run you home in my car.* **65.** to cause to pass quickly: *He ran his eyes over the letter. She ran a comb through her hair.* **66.** to get past or through: *to run a blockade.* **67.** (of drivers or cyclists) to disregard (a red or amber traffic light) and continue ahead without stopping. **68.** to smuggle (contraband goods): *to run guns across the border.* **69.** to work, operate, or drive: *Can you run a tractor?* **70.** to publish, print, or make copies of, as on a printing press (sometimes fol. by *off*): *Run off 3000 of these posters. The newspapers ran the story on page one.* **71.** to process, refine, manufacture, or subject to an analysis or treatment: *The doctor wanted to run a blood test. The factory ran 50,000 gallons of paint a day.* **72.** to keep operating or going, as a machine: *They ran the presses 24 hours a day.* **73.** to keep (a motor) idling for an indefinite period: *On cold days he would run the car motor to prevent stalling.* **74.** to allow (a ship, automobile, etc.) to depart from a safe, proper, or given route, as by negligence or error: *He ran the ship aground. She ran the car up on the curb.* **75.** to sponsor, support, or nominate (a person) as a candidate for election. **76.** to manage or conduct: *to run a business; to run one's own life.* **77.** *Computers.* to process (the instructions in a program) by computer. **78.** (in some games, as billiards) to continue or complete a series of successful strokes, shots, or the like. **79.** *Cards.* to lead a series of (one's assured tricks or winners in a given suit): *He ran the heart suit before leading spades.* **80.** to expose oneself to or be exposed to (a chance, risk, etc.): *Through his habitual lateness he ran the danger of being fired.* **81.** to cause (a liquid) to flow: *to run the water for a bath.* **82.** to fill (a tub or bath) with water: *She ran a hot tub for him.* **83.** to give forth or flow with (a liquid); pour forth or discharge: *The well ran 500 barrels of oil daily.* **84.** to charge (an item or items) as on a charge account or to accumulate (bills) to be paid all at one time: *He ran a large monthly tab at the club.* **85.** to cause to move easily, freely, or smoothly: *to run a rope in a pulley.* **86.** *Golf.* to cause (a golf ball) to move forward along the ground after landing from a stroke: *He ran his ball seven feet past the hole.* **87.** to sew or use a running stitch: *to run a seam.* **88.** to cause stitches in (a garment or fabric) to unravel or come undone: *to run a stocking on a protruding nail.* **89.** to bring, lead, or force into a certain state or condition: *He ran his troops into an ambush. They ran themselves into debt.* **90.** to drive, force, or thrust: *to run a nail into a board; to run one's head against a wall; to run one's hand into one's pocket.* **91.** to graze; pasture: *They run sixty head of cattle on their ranch.* **92.** to extend (something) in a particular direction or to a given point or place: *to run a partition across a room; to run a telephone cable from Boston to Buffalo.* **93.** *Carpentry.* to make (millwork) from boards. **94.** to cause to fuse and flow, as metal for casting in a mold. **95.** to draw, trace, or mark out, as a line: *to run a line over a surface; to run a line through a word.* **96.** to cost (an amount or approximate amount): *This watch runs $30.* **97.** to cost (a person) an amount or approximate amount: *The car repair will run you a couple of hundred at least.* **98. run across,** to meet or find accidentally: *She ran across an old friend at the party. He ran across her name in the phone book.* **99. run afoul of, a.** *Naut.* to collide with so as to cause damage and entanglement. **b.** to incur or become subject to the wrath or ill will of: *to run afoul of the law; He argued with his father and has run afoul of him ever since.* **100. run after, a.** to follow; chase: *The dog ran after the burglar.* **b.** to pursue or court the affections of, esp. in an aggressive manner: *He ran after her until she agreed to marry him.* **c.** to attempt to become friendly with or part of the society of: *He runs after the country-club set.* **101. run along,** to leave; go on one's way: *I have to run along now, but I'll see you tonight. Run along—can't you see I'm busy?* **102. run around, a.** (often fol. by *with*) to socialize; consort with: *She runs around with the strangest people.* **b.** to be unfaithful to one's spouse or lover: *It was common knowledge that he was running around.* **103. run away, a.** to flee or escape; leave a place of confinement or control with the intention of never returning: *He ran away from home three times.* **b.** *Naut.* to haul on a line by walking or running steadily. **104. run away with, a.** to go away with, esp. to elope with: *She ran away with a sailor.* **b.** to abscond with; steal: *to run away with some valuable jewelry.* **c.** to surpass others in; be outstanding in: *to run away with academic honors.* **d.** to overwhelm; get the better of: *Sometimes his enthusiasm runs away with him.* **105. run down, a.** to strike and fell or overturn, esp. to drive a vehicle into (someone): *to run down an innocent pedestrian.* **b.** to pursue until captured; chase: *The detective swore that he would run down the criminal.* **c.** to peruse; review: *His eyes ran down the front row and stopped suddenly.* **d.** to cease operation; stop: *My watch has run down.* **e.** to speak disparagingly of; criticize severely: *The students were always running down their math teacher.* **f.** to search out; trace; find: *to run down information.* **g.** *Baseball.* to tag out (a base runner) between bases. **h.** *Naut.* to collide with and sink (another vessel). **i.** *Naut.* to sail closely parallel to (a coast). **106. run for it,** to hurry away or flee, esp. to evade something: *You had better run for it before anyone else arrives.* **107. run in, a.** to visit casually: *If I'm in the neighborhood, I may run in for a few minutes.* **b.** to include in a text, as something to be inserted. **c.** *Slang.* to arrest; take to jail: *They ran him in for burglary.* **d.** *Print.* to add (matter) to text without indenting. **e.** to break in (new machinery). **108. run in place, a.** to go through the motions of running without leaving one's original place. **b.** to exist or work without noticeable change, progress, or improvement. **109. run into, a.** to crash into; collide with: *She was so sleepy that she ran into a lamppost.* **b.** to meet accidentally: *You never know whom you'll run into at a big party.* **c.** to amount to; total: *losses that ran into millions of dollars.* **d.** to succeed; follow: *One year ran into the next, and still there was no change.* **e.** to experience; encounter: *The project ran into difficulty.* **110. run in with,** *Naut.* to sail close to (a coast, vessel, etc.). **111. run off, a.** to leave quickly; depart. **b.** to create or perform rapidly or easily: *to run off a new song.* **c.** to determine the winner of (a contest, race, etc.) by a runoff. **d.** to drive away; expel: *to run someone off one's property.* **e.** to print or otherwise duplicate: *Please run off 500 copies.* **112. run off with, a.** to abscond with (something); steal or borrow; take: *He ran off with the money. Who ran off with the pencil sharpener?* **b.** to elope: *I hear she ran off with the Smith boy.* **113. run on, a.** to continue without interruption: *The account that he gave ran on at some length.* **b.** *Print.* to add (matter) to text without indenting. **c.** to add something, as at the end of a text: *to run on an adverb to a dictionary entry.* **114. run out, a.** to terminate; expire: *My subscription ran out last month. Time ran out before we could score another touchdown.* **b.** to become used up: *His money soon ran out.* **c.** to drive out; expel: *They want to run him out of the country.* **115. run out of,** to exhaust a quantity or supply of: *She couldn't bake a cake because she had run out of sugar.* **116. run out of gas,** *Informal.* **a.** to exhaust or lose one's energy, enthusiasm, etc.: *After the first game of tennis. I ran out of gas and had to rest.* **b.** to falter for lack of impetus, ideas, capital, etc.: *The economic recovery seems to be running out of gas.* **117. run out on,** to withdraw one's support from; abandon: *No one could accuse him of running out on his friends.* **118. run over, a.** to hit and knock down, esp. with a vehicle: *She cried inconsolably when her cat was run over by a car.* **b.** to go beyond; exceed: *His speech ran over the time limit.* **c.** to repeat; review: *We'll run over that song again.* **d.** to overflow, as a vessel. **119. run scared,** to be thrown into a state of fear or uncertainty because of a perceived threat; be apprehensive about survival or the future: *Many businesses are running scared because of increasing competition.* **120. run through, a.** to pierce or stab, as with a sword: *to run someone through.* **b.** to consume or use up recklessly; squander: *to run through a fortune.* **c.** to practice, review, or rehearse quickly or informally: *to run through a scene.* **121. run up, a.** to sew rapidly: *She ran up some curtains.* **b.** to amass; incur: *running up huge debts.* **c.** to cause to increase; raise: *to run up costs unnecessarily.* **d.** to build, esp. hurriedly: *They are tearing down old tenement blocks and running up skyscrapers.* **122. run with,** *Informal.* **a.** to proceed or go ahead with: *If the stockholders like the idea, we'll run with it.* **b.** to carry out with enthusiasm or speed.
—*n.* **123.** an act or instance, or a period of running: *a five-minute run before breakfast.* **124.** a hurrying to or from some point, as on an errand: *a run to reach the store before it closes.* **125.** a fleeing, esp. in great haste; flight: *a run from the police who were hot on his trail.* **126.** a running pace: *The boys set out at a run.* **127.** an act or instance or a period of moving rapidly, as in a boat or automobile: *a run to shore before the storm.* **128.** distance covered, as by racing, running, or during a trip: *a three-mile run.* **129.** an act or instance or a period of traveling or moving between two places; trip: *a truck on its daily run from farm to market; a nonstop run from Louisville to Memphis.* **130.** *Computers.* a single instance of carrying out the sequence of instructions in a program. **131.** *Golf.* the distance that a golf ball moves along the ground after landing from a stroke: *He got a seven-foot run with his chip shot.* **132.** a quick trip for a short stay at a place: *to take a run up to New York.* **133.** *Mil.* **a.** See **bomb run. b.** any portion of a military flight during which the aircraft flies directly toward the target in order to begin its attack: *a strafing run.* **134.** *Aeron.* **a.** the rapid movement, under its own power, of an aircraft on a runway, water, or another surface. **b.** a routine flight from one place to another: *the evening run from New York to London.* **135.** beat (def. 52b). **136.** an interval or period during which something, as a machine, operates or continues operating: *They kept each press in the plant on a 14-hour run.* **137.** the amount of anything produced in such a period: *a daily run of 400,000 gallons of paint.* **138.** pressrun. **139.** a line or place in knitted work where a series of stitches have slipped out or come undone: *a run in a stocking.* **140.** onward movement, development, progress, course, etc.: *the run of our business from a small store to a large chain.* **141.** the direction of something or of its component elements: *the run of the grain of wood.* **142.** the particular course, order, or tendency of something: *the normal run of events.* **143.** freedom to move around in, pass through, or use something: *to allow one's guests the run of the house.* **144.** any rapid or easy course of progress: *a run from trainee to supervisor.* **145.** a continuous series of performances, as of a play: *a long run on Broadway.* **146.** an uninterrupted course of some state or condition; a spell: *a run of good luck; a run of good weather.* **147.** a continuous extent of something, as a vein of ore. **148.** an uninterrupted series or sequence of things, events, etc.: *a run of 30 scoreless innings.* **149.** a sequence of cards in a given suit: *a heart run.* **150.** *Cribbage.* a sequence of three or more cards in consecutive denominations without regard to suits. **151.** any extensive continued demand, sale, or the like: *a run on umbrellas on a rainy day.* **152.** a series of sudden and urgent demands for payment, as on a bank. **153.** a period of being in demand or favor with the public: *Her last book had a briefer run than her first.* **154.** a period during which liquid flows: *They kept each oil well on an eight-hour run.* **155.** the amount that flows during such a period: *a run of 500 barrels a day.* **156.** a small stream; brook; rivulet. **157.** a flow or rush, as of water: *The snow melting on the mountains caused a run of water into the valley.* **158.** a kind or class, as of goods: *a superior run of blouses.* **159.** the typical, ordinary, or average kind: *The run of 19th-century novels tends to be of a sociological nature.* **160.** an inclined course, as on a slope, designed or used for a specific purpose: *a bobsled run; a run for training beginning skiers.* **161.** a fairly large enclosure within which domestic animals may move about freely; runway: *a chicken run.* **162.** *Australian.* a large sheep ranch or area of grazing land. **163.** the beaten track or usual trail used by deer or other wild animals; runway. **164.** a trough or pipe for water or the like. **165.** the movement of a number of fish upstream or inshore from deep water. **166.** large numbers of fish in motion, esp. inshore from deep water or up a river for spawning: *a run of salmon.* **167.** a number of animals moving together. **168.** *Music.* a rapid succession of tones; roulade. **169.** *Building Trades.* **a.** the horizontal distance between the face of a wall and the ridge of a roof. **b.** the distance between the first and last risers of a flight of steps or staircase. **c.** the horizontal distance between successive risers on a flight of steps or a staircase. **170.** *Baseball.* the score unit made by safely running around all the bases and reaching home plate. **171.** a series of successful shots, strokes, or the like, in a game. **172.** *Naut.* the immersed portion of a hull abaft the middle body (opposed to *entrance*). **173. the runs,** (*used with a singular or plural v.*) *Informal.* diarrhea. **174. a run for one's money, a.** close or keen competition: *The out-of-town team gave us a run for our money.* **b.** enjoyment or profit in return for one's expense: *This may not be the best tool kit, but it will give you a run for your money.* **175. in the long run,** in the course of long experience; in the end: *Retribution will come, in the long run.* **176. in the short run,** as an immediate or temporary outcome: *Recession may be averted in the short run if policy changes are made now.* **177. on the run, a.** moving quickly; hurrying about: *He's so busy, he's always on the run.* **b.** while running or in a hurry: *I usually eat breakfast on the run.* **c.** escaping or hiding from the police: *He was on the run for two years.*
—*adj.* **178.** melted or liquefied: *run butter.* **179.** poured in a melted state; run into and cast in a mold: *run bronze.* [bef. 900; (v.) ME *rinnen, rennen*, partly < ON *rinna, renna*, partly continuing OE *rinnan*; c. G *rinnen*; form *run* orig. ptp., later extended to present tense; (n. and adj.) deriv. of the v.] **—run′na·ble,** *adj.* **—run′na·bil′i·ty,** *n.*

run·a·bout (run′ə bout′), *n.* **1.** a small, light automobile or other vehicle, usually with an open top; roadster. **2.** a small pleasure motorboat. **3.** a person who roves around from place to place or group to group. [1540–50; n. use of v. phrase *run about*]

run·a·gate (run′ə gāt′), *n.* **1.** a fugitive or runaway. **2.** a vagabond or wanderer. [1520–30; RUN (v.) + obs. *agate* away; sense influenced by obs. *renegate* (ME *renegat* < ML *renegātus* RENEGADE)]

run·a·round (run′ə round′), *n.* **1.** indecisive or evasive treatment, esp. in response to a request: *Ask for a raise and he'll give you the runaround.* **2.** *Print.* an arrangement of type in which several lines are set in narrower measure than the others in a column to accommodate an illustration, initial, or the like. [1870–75, *Amer.*; n. use of v. phrase *run around*]
—Syn. 1. dodge, evasion, slip.

run·a·way (run′ə wā′), *n.* **1.** a person who runs away; fugitive; deserter. **2.** a horse or team that has broken

CONCISE ETYMOLOGY KEY: <, descended or borrowed from; >, whence; b., blend of, blended; c., cognate with; cf., compare; deriv., derivative; equiv., equivalent; imit., imitative; obl., oblique; r., replacing; s., stem; sp., spelling, spelled; resp., respelling, respelled; trans., translation; ?, origin unknown; *, unattested; ‡, probably earlier than. See the full key inside the front cover.

away from control. **3.** the act of running away. **4.** a decisive or easy victory. **5.** a young person, esp. a teenager, who has run away from home. —*adj.* **6.** having run away; escaped; fugitive. **7.** (of a horse or other animal) having escaped from the control of the rider or driver. **8.** pertaining to or accomplished by running away or eloping: *a runaway marriage.* **9.** easily won, as a contest: *a runaway victory at the polls.* **10.** unchecked; rampant: *runaway prices.* **11.** *Informal.* deserting or revolting against one's group, duties, expected conduct, or the like, esp. to establish or join a rival group, change one's life drastically, etc.: *The runaway delegates nominated their own candidate.* [1505–15; n., adj. use of v. phrase *run away*]
—**Syn. 9.** absolute, complete, perfect.

run′away star′, *Astron.* a star with an unusually high proper motion, believed to result from its ejection from a nearby binary system when its companion star underwent a supernova explosion. [1965–70]

run•back (run′bak′), *n.* **1.** *Football.* **a.** a run made by a player toward the goal line of the opponents after receiving a kick, intercepting a pass, or recovering an opponent's fumble. **b.** the distance covered in making such a run. **2.** *Tennis.* the space on a tennis court between the base line and the backstop. [1905–10; n. use of v. phrase *run back*]

run′ bat′ted in′, *Baseball.* a runner advanced to home for a score by a particular player at bat, as when he or she gets a hit or a walk with the bases loaded: a category important in individual offensive statistics. *Abbr.:* R.B.I.

run′ci•ble spoon′ (run′sə bəl), a forklike utensil with two broad prongs and one sharp, curved prong, as used for serving hors d'oeuvres. [*runcible,* term coined in 1871 by Edward Lear]

Run•cie (run′sē), *n.* **Robert Alexander Kennedy,** born 1921, English clergyman: archbishop of Canterbury 1980–91.

run•ci•nate (run′sə nit, -nāt′), *adj.* (of a leaf) pinnately incised, with the lobes or teeth curved backward. [1770–80; < L *runcinātus* (ptp. of *runcināre* to plane), equiv. to *runcin(a)* carpenter's plane + *-ātus* -ATE[1]]

Run•di (rōōn′dē), *n., pl.* **-dis,** (*esp. collectively*) **-di** for 1. **1.** a member of a people constituting virtually the entire population of Burundi. **2.** Also called **Kirundi.** the Bantu language of the Rundi people, closely related to Ruanda.

run•dle (run′dl), *n.* **1.** a rung of a ladder. **2.** a wheel or similar rotating object. [1275–1325; ME; var. of ROUNDEL]

rund•let (rund′lit), *n.* **1.** an old British measure of capacity, about 15 imperial gallons (68 liters). **2.** a small cask. [1350–1400; ME *rondelet;* see ROUNDLET]

run-down (run′doun′), *adj.* **1.** fatigued; weary; exhausted. **2.** in a state of poor health: *He was in a run-down condition from months of overwork.* **3.** in neglected condition; fallen into disrepair: *a run-down house.* **4.** (of a spring-operated device) not running because it is unwound. [1675–85; adj. use of v. phrase *run down*]
—**Syn. 3.** seedy, tacky, shabby, deteriorated.

run•down (run′doun′), *n.* **1.** a quick review or summary of main points of information, usually oral: *This brief rundown of past events will bring you up to date.* **2.** *Baseball.* a play in which a base runner is caught between bases by two or more players of the opposing team who toss the ball back and forth in an effort to tag the runner out. **3.** *Com.* runoff (def. 4). [1905–10, *Amer.*; n. use of v. phrase *run down*]

Rund•stedt (rōōnt′stet, rōōnd′-; *Ger.* RŌŌNT′shtet), *n.* **Karl Ru•dolf Gerd von** (kärl RŌŌ′dôlf gerd fən), 1875–1953, German field marshal.

rune[1] (rōōn), *n.* **1.** any of the characters of certain ancient alphabets, as of a script used for writing the Germanic languages, esp. of Scandinavia and Britain, from c200 to c1200, or a script used for inscriptions in a Turkic language of the 6th to 8th centuries from the area near the Orkhon River in Mongolia. **2.** something written or inscribed in such characters. **3.** an aphorism, poem, or saying with mystical meaning or for use in casting a spell. [1675–85; < ON *rūn* a secret, writing, runic character; c. OE *rūn* (ME *rune,* obs. E *roun*). See ROUND[2]] —**rune′like′,** *adj.*

rune[2] (rōōn), *n. Literary.* a poem, song, or verse. [1865–70; < Finnish *runo* poem, canto < Scand. See RUNE[1]]

runed (rōōnd), *adj.* having runes inscribed: *a runed ornament.* [1885–90; RUNE[1] + -ED[3]]

rune•smith (rōōn′smith′), *n.* a student, writer, transcriber, or decipherer of runes. [1865–70; RUNE[1] + SMITH]

rune-stone (rōōn′stōn′), *n.* a stone bearing one or more runic inscriptions. [1850–55]

run-flat (run′flat′), *adj.* (of an automobile tire) constructed so as not to deflate completely after a puncture so that a motorist can still drive the vehicle for some distance. [1945–50]

rung[1] (rung), *v.* pt. and pp. of **ring**[2].

rung[2] (rung), *n.* **1.** one of the crosspieces, usually rounded, forming the steps of a ladder. **2.** a rounded or shaped piece fixed horizontally, for strengthening purposes, as between the legs of a chair. **3.** a spoke of a wheel. **4.** a stout stick, rod, or bar, esp. one of rounded section, forming a piece in something framed or constructed. **5.** a stage in a scale, level in a hierarchy, etc.; degree: *He rose a few rungs in the company.* [bef. 1000; ME; OE *hrung;* c. Goth *hrunga* rod, G *Runge*] —**rung′less,** *adj.*

Rung′e-Kut′ta meth′od (rŏŏng′ə kōōt′ä), *Math.* a numerical method, involving successive approximations, used to solve differential equations. [1925–30; named after Carl D. T. *Runge* (1856–1927) and W. *Kutta* (1867–1944), German mathematicians]

ru•nic (rōō′nik), *adj.* **1.** consisting of or set down in runes: *runic inscriptions.* **2.** having some secret or mysterious meaning: *runic rhyme.* **3.** (of ornamental knots, figures, etc.) of an interlaced form seen on ancient monuments, metalwork, etc., of the northern European peoples. **4.** of the ancient Scandinavian class or type, as literature or poetry. [1655–65; RUNE[1] + -IC]

run-in (run′in′), *n.* **1.** a quarrel; argument. **2.** *Print.* matter that is added to a text, esp. without indenting for a new paragraph. —*adj.* **3.** *Print.* added to a text without indenting. [1900–05; n., adj. use of v. phrase *run in*]

Run•jeet Singh (run′jit sing′). See **Ranjit Singh.**

run•less (run′lis), *adj. Baseball.* without having scored a run; without runs: *a runless inning.* [1920–25; RUN + -LESS]

run•nel (run′l), *n.* **1.** a small stream; brook; rivulet. **2.** a small channel, as for water. Also, **run•let** (run′lit). [1570–80; RUN (n.) + *-el* dim. suffix]

run•ner (run′ər), *n.* **1.** a person, animal, or thing that runs, esp. as a racer. **2.** a messenger. **3.** a messenger of a bank or brokerage house. **4.** *Baseball.* See **base runner.** **5.** *Football.* the ball-carrier. **6.** a person whose business it is to solicit patronage or trade. **7.** a person acting as collector, agent, or the like, for a bank, broker, etc. **8.** something in or on which something else runs or moves. **9.** either of the long, bladelike strips of metal or wood on which a sled or sleigh slides. **10.** the blade of an ice skate. **11.** the rotating system of blades driven by the fluid passing through a reaction turbine. **12.** the rotating member of a pair of millstones. Cf. **bed stone.** **13.** a roller on which something moves along. **14.** *Furniture.* **a.** a sliding piece, as a loper. **b.** rocker (def. 1). **15.** an operator or manager, as of a machine. **16.** a long, narrow rug, suitable for a hall or passageway. **17.** a long, narrow strip of line, embroidery, lace, or the like, placed across a table. **18.** *Bot.* **a.** a slender stolon that runs along the surface of the ground and sends out roots and leaves at the nodes, as in the strawberry. **b.** a plant that spreads by such stems. **19.** *Metall.* any of the channels through which molten metal flows. **20.** a smuggler. **21.** a vessel engaged in smuggling. **22.** a person who takes, transmits, and often pays off bets for a bookmaker or a numbers pool. **23.** *Ichthyol.* a jurel, *Caranx crysos,* inhabiting waters from Cape Cod to Brazil. **24.** *Building Trades.* a horizontal longitudinal timber resting upon the uprights of a staging and supporting the footing pieces. **25.** *Theat.* a piece of carpet or matting placed in the wings for deadening offstage sounds. **26.** a tackle or part of a tackle consisting of a line rove through a single block and fixed at one end. See diag. under **tackle.** [1250–1300; ME; see RUN, -ER[1]]

run′ner bean′, *Brit.* See **string bean** (defs. 1, 2). [1780–90]

run′ner foot′, *Furniture.* a foot having the form of a bar connecting the corresponding front and rear legs of a piece. Also called **bar foot.**

run′ner's high′, a state of euphoria experienced during prolonged running or other forms of aerobic, sustained exercise, attributed to an increase of endorphins in the blood.

run′ner's knee′, chondromalacia.

run•ner-up (run′ər up′), *n., pl.* **run•ners-up.** **1.** the competitor, player, or team finishing in second place, as in a race, contest, or tournament. **2. runners-up,** the competitors who do not win a contest but who place ahead of the majority of the contestants and share in prizes or honors, as those who place second, third, and fourth, or in the top ten. [1835–45]

run•ning (run′ing), *n.* **1.** the act of a person, animal, or thing that runs. **2.** managing or directing: *the running of a business.* **3.** an act or instance of racing: *the 113th running of the Kentucky Derby.* **4.** the condition of a track or surface to be run or raced on; footing: *Our track team had muddy running today.* **5.** the amount, quality, or type of a liquid flow. **6. in the running, a.** participating or entered as a competitor. **b.** under consideration as a candidate or possible choice: *Who is still in the running for the directorship?* **c.** among the winners or those making a good showing. **7. out of the running, a.** not competing in a contest or race. **b.** not among the winners or runners-up in a contest or race: *to finish out of the running.* —*adj.* **8.** galloping, racing, moving, or passing rapidly. **9.** (of a horse) **a.** going or proceeding rapidly at the gait of a gallop. **b.** taught to proceed at a gallop. **10.** creeping or climbing, as plants: *a running vine.* **11.** moving or proceeding easily or smoothly. **12.** moving when pulled or hauled, as a rope. **13.** slipping or sliding easily, as a knot or a noose. **14.** operating or functioning, as a machine. **15.** (of measurement) linear; straight-line. **16.** cursive, as handwriting. **17.** flowing, as a stream. **18.** liquid or fluid. **19.** present; current: *the running month.* **20.** prevalent, as a condition or state: *running prices.* **21.** going or carried on continuously; sustained: *a running commentary.* **22.** extending or repeated continuously: *a running pattern.* **23.** performed with or during a run: *a running leap.* **24.** discharging pus or other matter: *a running sore.* **25.** *Naut.* noting any of various objects or assemblages of objects that may be moved in ordinary use: *running bowsprit; running gaff.* **26.** *Naut., Mach.* **a.** noting any block of a tackle that moves. **b.** noting the part of the fall of a tackle that moves through the blocks (opposed to *standing*). —*adv.* **27.** in succession; consecutively: *He slept badly for three nights running.* [1150–1200; ME; see RUN, -ING[1], -ING[2]]

run′ning back′, *Football.* an offensive back, as a halfback or fullback, whose principal role is advancing the ball by running with it on plays from scrimmage.

run′ning board′, a small ledge, step, or footboard, formerly beneath the doors of an automobile, to assist passengers entering or leaving the car. [1810–20, in sense "platform from which a large pole boat is poled," *Amer.*]

run′ning bond′, a brickwork bond having successive courses of overlapping stretchers. Also called **stretcher bond.**

run′ning broad′ jump′. See **long jump.**

run′ning dog′, *Disparaging.* **1.** (esp. in Chinese Communist propaganda) **a.** a person or institution subservient to counter-revolutionary interests. **b.** a manipulable, servile follower; lackey: *to be reviled as a running dog of the colonialists.* **2.** *Archit.* See **Vitruvian scroll.** [1925–30; in political sense, trans. of Chin *zǒugǒu*]

run′ning Eng′lish, *Billiards.* the giving of English or spin to the cue ball to enable it to bounce in the direction of a certain angle. Cf. **reverse English** (def. 1).

run′ning fix′, *Navig.* a fix made from a moving vessel or aircraft from observations made at different times, the course and distance run between the observations being considered. [1915–20]

run′ning gaff′, *Naut.* the hoisting gaff.

run′ning gear′, the working components of a motor-driven or steam-driven vehicle other than those used to develop or transmit power, as wheels, axles or springs, as distinguished from the body. [1655–65, *Amer.*]

run′ning hand′, script or calligraphy characterized by uniformly slanted letters that are written quickly and connected by long, continuous strokes of the pen. [1640–50]

run′ning head′, *Print.* a descriptive word, phrase, title, or the like, usually repeated at the top of each page of a book, periodical, etc. Also called **running title.** [1830–40]

run′ning joke′, **1.** a joke or humorous allusion used recurrently in a play, film, television skit, etc., for a cumulative comic effect. **2.** a subject, reference, remark, etc., that is a continual source of humor. Also called **run′ning gag′.**

run′ning knot′, a knot made around and so as to slide along a part of the same rope, thus forming a noose (**run′ning noose′**) that tightens as the rope is pulled. [1640–50]

run′ning light′, any of various lights required to be displayed by a vessel or aircraft operating between sunset and sunrise. [1880–85]

run′ning mar′tingale, martingale (def. 2).

run′ning mate′, **1.** a candidate for an office linked with another and more important office, as for the vice-presidency. **2.** a horse entered in a race in which another, more important, horse from the same stable, or belonging to the same owner, is run. **3.** a close companion. [1865–70, *Amer.*]

run′ning myr′tle, the periwinkle, *Vinca minor.*

run′ning pine′, a ground pine, *Lycopodium clavatum.*

run′ning rhythm′, *Pros.* the usual English verse rhythm created by a succession of metrical feet each of which consists of a stressed syllable and one or two unstressed ones. Also called **common rhythm.** Cf. **sprung rhythm.** [1880–85]

run′ning rig′ging, *Naut.* **1.** rigging for handling sails, yards, etc. (contrasted with *standing rigging*). **2.** rigging for handling cargo. [1660–70]

run′ning room′, **1.** the space between a racer and the nearby competitors in a running race, esp. enough to run and maneuver as desired. **2.** the space or leeway permitting ample freedom and flexibility to operate, maneuver, or perform without impairment. [‡1980–85]

run′ning start′, **1.** *Sports.* a start, as in the hop, step, and jump or the running broad jump, in which a contestant begins moving before reaching the starting or take-off point. **2.** an initial advantage in undertaking something; a head start: *His background gave him a running start in business.* [1925–30]

run′ning stitch′, a sewing stitch made by passing the needle in and out repeatedly with short, even stitches. [1840–50]

run′ning sto′ry, *Journalism.* **1.** a story continued in subsequent issues of a newspaper or magazine; serial. **2.** a story sent to the compositor in takes.

run′ning text′, the body of text in a newspaper, magazine, or the like, as distinguished from the heads, illustrations, etc.

run′ning time′, *Motion Pictures.* the length or duration, usually expressed in minutes, of a feature film: *The running time of the average film is 90–100 minutes.* [1950–55]

run′ning ti′tle, *Print.* See **running head.** [1660–70]

run•ny (run′ē), *adj.,* **-ni•er, -ni•est.** **1.** tending to run or drip: *a runny paste.* **2.** (of the nose) discharging mucus. [1810–20; RUN + -Y[1]]

Run•ny•mede (run′i mēd′), *n.* a meadow on the S bank of the Thames, W of London, England: reputed site of the granting of the Magna Charta by King John, 1215.

run•off (run′ôf′, -of′), *n.* **1.** something that drains or flows off, as rain that flows off from the land in streams. **2.** a final contest held to determine a victor after earlier contests have eliminated the weaker contestants. **3.** a deciding final contest held after one in which there has been no decisive victor, as between two contestants who have tied for first place. **4.** Also called **rundown.** a continual or prolonged reduction, esp. in quantity or supply: *a runoff in bank deposits; a sharp runoff in business inventories.* **5.** *Stock Exchange.* the final prices appearing on the ticker after the closing bell is rung for the trading day. [1850–55, *Amer.*; n. use of v. phrase *run off;* (def. 2, 3) see -OFF]

run′off pri′mary, (esp. in the southern U.S.) a second primary between the two leading candidates of the first primary to provide nomination by majority rather than by plurality. [1920–25, *Amer.*]

run-of-pa•per (run′əv pā′pər), *adj.* See **R.O.P.** [1950–55]

run-of-the-mill (run′əv *th*ə mil′), *adj.* merely average; commonplace; mediocre: *just a plain, run-of-the-mill house; a run-of-the-mill performance.* [1925–30] **—Syn.** ordinary, routine, everyday.

run-of-the-mine (run′əv *th*ə mīn′), *adj.* **1.** of or pertaining to ore or coal that is crude, ungraded, etc. **2.** common or ordinary; run-of-the-mill: *a boring, run-of-the-mine performance.* Also, **run-of-mine** (run′əv mīn′). [1905–10]

run-on (run′on′, -ôn′), *adj.* **1.** of or designating something that is added or run on: *a run-on entry in a dictionary.* **2.** *Pros.* (of a line of verse) having a thought that carries over to the next line, esp. without a syntactical break. **—*n.*** **3.** run-on matter. **4.** *Auto.* after-run. [1900–05; adj., n. use of v. phrase *run on*]

run′-on sen′tence, a written sequence of two or more main clauses that are not separated by a period or semicolon or joined by a conjunction. Also called **fused sentence.** Cf. **comma fault.** [1910–15]

run-out (run′out′), *n. Manège.* the act of evading a jump or jumping outside of the limiting markers. [1865–70; n. use of v. phrase *run out*]

run•out (run′out′), *n.* **1.** *Mach.* **a.** the gradual termination of a groove on the body of an object not ending there, as the upper termination of a flute in a twist drill. **b.** Also called **back clearance.** a space in a depressed area of an object into which a machine tool or grinding wheel may safely enter at the end of a pass or operation. **2.** the merging of a curved surface into another surface. **3.** an act or instance of running away so as to evade, abandon, or avoid something. **4.** a person who runs away so as to avoid payment or duty. **5.** an act or instance of expiring or becoming depleted: *the runout of a union contract; a runout in office supplies.* **6.** uneven wear on the outer edges of a tire or on the rim of a wheel. [1925–30; n. use of v. phrase *run out*]

run•o•ver (run′ō′vər), *n. Print.* the amount of type matter for a given article, story, etc., that is carried over to another page, column, or line. [1930–35; n. use of v. phrase *run over*]

run•proof (run′proof′), *adj.* made to resist unraveling, runs, or running, as stockings or dyes. [RUN + -PROOF]

runt (runt), *n.* **1.** an animal that is small or stunted as compared with others of its kind. **2.** the smallest or weakest of a litter, esp. of pigs or puppies. **3.** a person who is small and contemptible: *That runt causes most of the trouble at the meetings.* **4.** *Brit. Dial.* **a.** an old or decayed tree stump. **b.** an old cow or ox. **c.** an ugly old woman; hag. [1495–1505; perh. < D *rund* bull, cow, ox; akin to G *Rind* cattle] **—runt′ish,** *adj.* **—runt′ish•ly,** *adv.* **—runt′ish•ness,** *n.*

run-through (run′thrōō′), *n.* **1.** the performing of a sequence of designated actions, esp. as a trial prior to actual performance; rehearsal; practice. **2.** a quick outline or review: *a run-through of his medical history.* **—*adj.*** **3.** (of a freight train) made up of cars for a single destination, usually routed so as to avoid congested areas and stopping only for a change of crew. [1920–25; n. use of v. phrase *run through*]

runt•y (run′tē), *adj.,* **runt•i•er, runt•i•est.** stunted; dwarfish: *The runty puppy seems the most playful of the litter.* [1800–10; RUNT + -Y[1]] **—runt′i•ness,** *n.*

run•up (run′up′), *n.* **1.** the testing of an airplane engine by accelerating the motor. **2.** an advance in prices, as in the stock market. **3.** *Sports.* **a.** the running up to the jump line by a broad jumper. **b.** the running up of the ball in soccer or polo toward the goal. **c.** the running up of a golf ball toward the putting green. [1825–35; n. use of v. phrase *run up*]

run•way (run′wā′), *n.* **1.** a way along which something runs. **2.** a paved or cleared strip on which planes land and take off. **3.** a similar strip on which cars, trucks, or the like may park, load, or enter the stream of traffic. **4.** the beaten track or habitual path of deer or other wild animals. **5.** a fairly large enclosure in which domestic animals may range about: *a runway for dogs.* **6.** the bed of a stream. **7.** *Bowling.* approach (def. 16b). **8.** a narrow platform or ramp extending from a stage into the orchestra pit or into an aisle, as in a theater. [1825–35, *Amer.*; RUN + WAY[1]]

Run•yon (run′yən), *n.* **(Alfred) Da•mon** (dā′mən), 1884–1946, U.S. journalist and short-story writer.

ru•pee (rōō pē′, rōō′pē), *n.* **1.** a cupronickel coin and monetary unit of India, Nepal, and Pakistan, equal to 100 paise. *Abbr.:* R., Re. **2.** a cupronickel coin and monetary unit of Mauritius, the Seychelles, and Sri Lanka, equal to 100 cents. **3.** Also called **rufiyaa.** a coin and monetary unit of the Maldives, equal to 100 laris. **4.** a former monetary unit of Bhutan, equal to 100 naye paise. [1605–15; < Hindi *rupayā*]

Ru•pert (rōō′pərt; *for 1 also Ger.* RŌŌ′pert), *n.* **1. Prince,** 1619–82, German Royalist general and admiral in the English Civil War (nephew of Charles I of England). **2.** a male given name: derived from *Robert.*

Ru•pes Al•tai (rōō′pēz al′tī). a mountain range in the fourth quadrant of the face of the moon: about 315 miles (507 km) long. [< NL: Altai crags]

ru•pes•trine (rōō pes′trin), *adj. Biol.* living or growing on or among rocks. Also, **rupicolous.** [1885–90; < L *rūpēs* steep cliff, crag + *-trine,* extracted from LACUSTRINE]

ru•pi•ah (rōō pē′ə), *n., pl.* **-ah, -ahs.** an aluminum coin, paper money, and monetary unit of Indonesia, equal to 100 sen. *Abbr.:* Rp. [1945–50; see RUPEE]

ru•pic•o•lous (rōō pik′ə ləs), *adj.* rupestrine. [1855–60; < L *rūp(ēs)* crag + -I- + -COLOUS]

rup•ture (rup′chər), *n., v.,* **-tured, -tur•ing.** **—*n.*** **1.** the act of breaking or bursting: *The flood led to the rupture of the dam.* **2.** the state of being broken or burst: *a rupture in the earth's surface.* **3.** a breach of harmonious, friendly, or peaceful relations. **4.** *Pathol.* hernia, esp. abdominal hernia. **—*v.t.*** **5.** to break or burst: *He ruptured a blood vessel.* **6.** to cause a breach of: *to rupture friendly relations.* **7.** *Pathol.* to affect with hernia. **—*v.i.*** **8.** to suffer a break or rupture. [1475–85; < L *ruptūra* (n.), equiv. to *rupt(us)* (ptp. of *rumpere* to break) + *-ūra* -URE] **—rup′tur•a•ble,** *adj.*
—Syn. 2. fracture, break, split, burst. **5.** fracture, split, disrupt. **—Ant. 2.** seam, union. **5.** unite.

rup′tured disk′. See **herniated disk.**

rup′tured duck′, *Slang.* the symbol of an eagle with wings spread appearing in the honorable discharge emblem of the U.S. armed forces. [1925–30, *Amer.*]

ru•ral (rŏŏr′əl), *adj.* **1.** of, pertaining to, or characteristic of the country, country life, or country people; rustic: *rural tranquillity.* **2.** living in the country: *the rural population.* **3.** of or pertaining to agriculture: *rural economy.* **—*n.*** **4.** a person who lives in a rural area. [1375–1425; late ME < MF < L *rūrālis,* equiv. to *rūr-* (s. of *rūs*) the country, rural land (akin to ROOM) + *-ālis* -AL[1]] **—ru′ral•ism,** *n.* **—ru′ral•ist, ru′ral•ite′,** *n.* **—ru′ral•ly,** *adv.* **—ru′ral•ness,** *n.*
—Syn. 1. unsophisticated, rough. RURAL and RUSTIC are terms that refer to the country. RURAL is the official term: *rural education.* It may be used subjectively, and usually in a favorable sense: *the charm of rural life.* RUSTIC, however, may have either favorable or unfavorable connotations. In a derogatory sense, it means provincial, boorish, or crude; in a favorable sense, it may suggest ruggedness or a homelike rural charm: *rustic simplicity.* **—Ant. 1.** urban.

ru′ral dean′, a cleric ranking just below an archdeacon, in charge of an archdeaconry. [1400–50; late ME]

ru′ral deliv′ery serv′ice, mail delivery operated primarily to deliver and collect mail in rural communities with no other convenient postal facilities. Formerly, **rural free delivery.**

Ru′ral Diony′sia. See **Lesser Dionysia.**

ru′ral free′ deliv′ery, former name for **rural delivery service.** *Abbr.:* R.F.D. [1890–95, *Amer.*]

ru•ral•i•ty (rŏŏ ral′i tē), *n., pl.* **-ties. 1.** rural character. **2.** a rural characteristic, matter, or scene. [1720–30; RURAL + -ITY]

ru•ral•ize (rŏŏr′ə līz′), *v.,* **-ized, -iz•ing.** **—*v.t.*** **1.** to make rural. **—*v.i.*** **2.** to spend time in the country; rusticate. Also, *esp. Brit.,* **ru′ral•ise′.** [1795–1805; RURAL + -IZE] **—ru′ral•i•za′tion,** *n.*

ru′ral municipal′ity, any lightly settled area in Canada lacking a local elected government and administered directly by a provincial government. [1860–65]

ru′ral route′, a mail delivery route in a rural area. [1895–1900]

ru′ral sociol′ogy, the sociological study of life in rural areas and the effects of ruralization.

Ru•rik (rŏŏr′ik), *n.* died A.D. 879, Scandinavian prince: founder of the Russian monarchy. Russian, **Ryurik.**

Ru•ri•ta•ni•a (rŏŏr′i tā′nē ə, rŏŏr′i tā′-), *n.* **1.** a mythical, romantic kingdom conceived as the setting for a fairy tale, costume drama, comic operetta, or the like. **2.** *Facetious.* any small, little-known country or region considered remote, backward, or exotic. [after the fictional Central European kingdom in the novel *The Prisoner of Zenda* (1894) by A. Hope] **—Ru′ri•ta′ni•an,** *adj., n.*

Rus., **1.** Russia. **2.** Russian.

ruse (rōōz), *n.* a trick, stratagem, or artifice. [1375–1425; late ME (n. use of obs. *rusen* to detour) < MF, deriv. of *ruser* to retreat. See RUSH[1]]
—Syn. See **trick.**

Ru•se (rōō′sā), *n.* a city in N Bulgaria, on the Danube. 160,351.

rush[1] (rush), *v.i.* **1.** to move, act, or progress with speed, impetuosity, or violence. **2.** to dash, esp. to dash forward for an attack or onslaught. **3.** to appear, go, pass, etc., rapidly or suddenly: *The blood rushed to his face.* **4.** *Football.* to carry the ball on a running play or plays. **—*v.t.*** **5.** to perform, accomplish, or finish with speed, impetuosity, or violence: *They rushed the work to make the deadline.* **6.** to carry or convey with haste: *to rush an injured person to the hospital.* **7.** to cause to move, act, or progress quickly; hurry: *He rushed his roommate to get to the party on time.* **8.** to send, push, force, impel, etc., with unusual speed or haste: *to rush a bill through Congress.* **9.** to attack suddenly and violently; charge. **10.** to overcome or capture (a person, place, etc.). **11.** *Informal.* to heap attentions on; court intensively; woo: *to rush an attractive newcomer.* **12.** to entertain (a prospective fraternity or sorority member) before making bids for membership. **13.** *Football.* **a.** to carry (the ball) forward across the line of scrimmage. **b.** to carry the ball (a distance) forward from the line of scrimmage: *The home team rushed 145 yards.* **c.** (of a defensive team member) to attempt to force a way quickly into the backfield in pursuit of (the back in possession of the ball). **—*n.*** **14.** the act of rushing; a rapid, impetuous, or violent onward movement. **15.** a hostile attack. **16.** an eager rushing of numbers of persons to some region that is being occupied or exploited, esp. because of a new mine: *the gold rush to California.* **17.** a sudden appearance or access: *a rush of tears.* **18.** hurried activity; busy haste: *the rush of city life.* **19.** a hurried state, as from pressure of affairs: *to be in a rush.* **20.** press of work, business, traffic, etc., requiring extraordinary effort or haste. **21.** *Football.* **a.** an attempt to carry or instance of carrying the ball across the line of scrimmage. **b.** an act or instance of rushing the offensive back in possession of the ball. **22.** a scrimmage held as a form of sport between classes or bodies of students in colleges. **23. rushes,** *Motion Pictures.* daily (def. 4). **24.** *Informal.* a series of lavish attentions paid a woman by a suitor: *He gave her a big rush.* **25.** the rushing by a fraternity or sorority. **26.** Also called **flash.** *Slang.* the initial, intensely pleasurable or exhilarated feeling experienced upon taking a narcotic or stimulant drug. **—*adj.*** **27.** requiring or done in haste: *a rush order; rush work.* **28.** characterized by excessive business, a press of work or traffic, etc.: *The cafeteria's rush period was from noon to two in the afternoon.* **29.** characterized by the rushing of potential new members by a sorority or fraternity: *rush week on the university campus.* [1325–75; (v.) ME *ruschen* < AF *russher, russer,* OF *re(h)usser, re(h)user, ruser* < LL *recūsāre,* to push back, L: to refuse. See RECUSE, RUSE; (n.) ME *rus(s)che,* deriv. of the v.] **—rush′ing•ly,** *adv.*
—Syn. 1. hasten, run. RUSH, HURRY, DASH, SPEED imply swiftness of movement. RUSH implies haste and sometimes violence in motion through some distance: *to rush to the store.* HURRY suggests a sense of strain or agitation, a breathless rushing to get to a definite place by a certain time: *to hurry to an appointment.* DASH implies impetuosity or spirited, swift movement for a short distance: *to dash to the neighbor's.* SPEED means to go fast, usually by means of some type of transportation, and with some smoothness of motion: *to speed to a nearby city.* **—Ant. 18.** sloth, lethargy.

rush[2] (rush), *n.* **1.** any grasslike plant of the genus *Juncus,* having pithy or hollow stems, found in wet or marshy places. Cf. **rush family. 2.** any plant of the rush family. **3.** any of various similar plants. **4.** a stem of such a plant, used for making chair bottoms, mats, baskets, etc. **5.** something of little or no value; trifle: *not worth a rush.* [bef. 900; ME *rusch, risch,* OE *rysc, risc;* c. D, obs. G *Rusch*] **—rush′like′,** *adj.*

Rush (rush), *n.* **1. Benjamin,** 1745–1813, U.S. physician and political leader: author of medical treatises. **2.** his son, **Richard,** 1780–1859, U.S. lawyer, politician, and diplomat.

rush′ can′dle, a candle made from a dried, partly peeled rush that has been dipped in grease. Also called **rush′ light′.** [1585–95]

rush•ee (ru shē′), *n.* a college student who is rushed by a fraternity or sorority. [1915–20, *Amer.*; RUSH[1] + -EE]

rush•er (rush′ər), *n.* **1.** a person or thing that rushes. **2.** *Football.* a player whose assignment is to rush or whose special skill is rushing. [1645–55; 1875–80 for def. 2; RUSH[1] + -ER[1]]

rush′ fam′ily, the plant family Juncaceae, characterized by herbaceous plants having narrow, grasslike leaves, small and greenish flowers, and capsular fruit with three compartments, comprising the true rushes.

rush′ hour′, a time of day in which large numbers of people are in transit, as going to or returning from work, and that is characterized by particularly heavy traffic. [1895–1900] **—rush′-hour′,** *adj.*

rush•ing (rush′ing), *n.* a sequence of social events sponsored by a fraternity or sorority for prospective members prior to bidding and pledging. [1900–05, *Amer.*; RUSH[1] + -ING[1]]

Rush•more (rush′môr, -mōr), *n.* **Mount,** a peak in the Black Hills of South Dakota that is a memorial **(Mount Rushmore National Memorial)** having 60-ft. (18-m) busts of Washington, Jefferson, Lincoln, and Theodore Roosevelt, carved into its face between 1927 and 1941, from a design by and under the direction of Gutzon Borglum. 5600 ft. (1707 m).

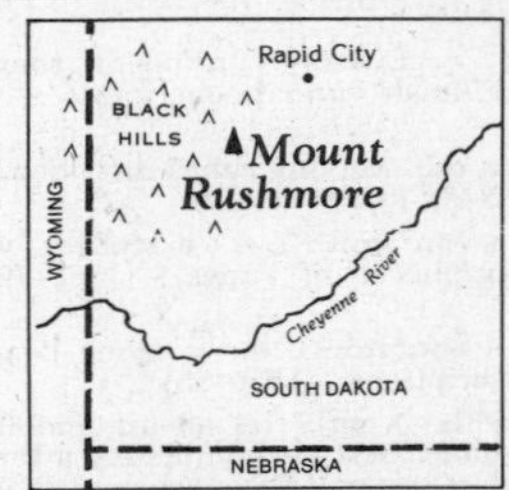

rush•work (rush′wûrk′), *n.* **1.** the handicraft of making objects woven of rushes. **2.** an object so made. [1930–35; RUSH[2] + WORK]

rush•y (rush′ē), *adj.,* **rush•i•er, rush•i•est. 1.** abounding with rushes or their stems. **2.** covered or strewn with rushes. **3.** consisting or made of rushes. **4.** rushlike. [1350–1400; ME; see RUSH[2], -Y[1]] **—rush′i•ness,** *n.*

CONCISE ETYMOLOGY KEY: <, descended or borrowed from; >, whence; b., blend of, blended; c., cognate with; cf., compare; deriv., derivative; equiv., equivalent; imit., imitative; obl., oblique; r., replacing; s., stem; sp., spelling, spelled; resp., respelling, respelled; trans., translation; ?, origin unknown; *, unattested; ‡, probably earlier than. See the full key inside the front cover.

ru′sine ant′ler (ro͞o′sin, -sin), an antler resembling that of the sambar. [1880–85; < NL *Rus(a)* name of the subgenus of sambars (< Malay; cf. BABIRUSA) + -INE[1]]

rusk (rusk), *n.* **1.** a slice of sweet raised bread dried and baked again in the oven; zwieback. **2.** light, soft, sweetened biscuit. [1585–95; alter. Sp or Pg *rosca* twist of bread, lit., screw]

Rusk (rusk), *n.* **(David) Dean,** 1909–94, U.S. statesman: Secretary of State 1961–69.

Rus·ka (rus′kə; *Ger.* ro͝os′kä), *n.* **Ernst (Au·gust Frie·drich)** (ernst ou′go͝ost frē′drikh), 1906–88, German physicist and electrical engineer: developed electron microscope; Nobel prize 1986.

Rus·kin (rus′kin), *n.* **John,** 1819–1900, English author, art critic, and social reformer. **—Rus·kin′i·an, Rus·kin′e·an,** *adj.*

Russ (rus), *n., pl.* **Russ, Russ·es,** *adj.* **—***n.* **1.** a Russian. **2.** *Archaic.* the Russian language. **—***adj.* **3.** Russian. [< F *russe*, G *Russe* or D *rus*, all ult. < ORuss *Rusĭ* the common East Slavic name for the East Slavic-speaking lands and peoples before c1500]

Russ (ro͝os), *n.* Niemen.

Russ., **1.** Russia. **2.** Russian. Also, **Russ**

Rus·sell (rus′əl), *n.* **1. Bertrand (Arthur William), 3rd Earl,** 1872–1970, English philosopher, mathematician, and author: Nobel prize for literature 1950. **2. Charles Edward,** 1860–1941, U.S. journalist, sociologist, biographer, and political leader. **3. Charles Taze** (tāz), (*"Pastor Russell"*), 1852–1916, U.S. religious leader and publisher: founder of Jehovah's Witnesses. **4. Elizabeth Mary, Countess** (*Mary Annette Beauchamp*) (*"Elizabeth"*), 1866–1941, Australian novelist. **5. George William** (*"Æ"*), 1867–1935, Irish poet and painter. **6. Henry Norris,** 1877–1957, U.S. astronomer. **7. John Russell, 1st Earl** (*Lord John Russell*), 1792–1878, British statesman: prime minister 1846–52, 1865–66. **8. Lillian** (*Helen Louise Leonard*), 1861–1922, U.S. singer and actress. **9. William Fel·ton** (fel′tn), (*Bill*), born 1934, U.S. basketball player and coach. **10.** a male given name.

Rus·sell·ite (rus′ə līt′), *n. Offensive.* a member of the Jehovah's Witnesses. [1875–80, *Amer.*; after C. T. RUSSELL; see -ITE[1]]

Rus′sell's par′adox, *Math.* a paradox of set theory in which an object is defined in terms of a class of objects that contains the object being defined, resulting in a logical contradiction. [1920–25; first proposed by Bertrand RUSSELL]

Rus′sell's vi′per, a large venomous snake, *Vipera russelli*, common in India and southeastern Asia, having three rows of large, black-edged brown spots on a light-brown body. [1905–10; named in honor of Patrick *Russell* (1727–1805), Scottish physician and naturalist]

Rus·sell·ville (rus′əl vil′), *n.* a city in central Arkansas. 14,000.

rus·set (rus′it), *n.* **1.** yellowish brown, light brown, or reddish brown. **2.** a coarse reddish-brown or brownish homespun cloth formerly used for clothing. **3.** any of various apples that have a rough brownish skin and ripen in the autumn. **4.** a brownish, roughened area on fruit, resulting from diseases, insects, or spraying. **5.** finished leather that is not yet polished or colored. **—***adj.* **6.** yellowish-brown, light-brown, or reddish-brown. **7.** made of russet. [1225–75; ME < OF *rousset*, dim. of *rous* reddish brown, red (of hair); see ROUX] **—rus′set·ish, rus′set·y,** *adj.* **—rus′set·like′,** *adj.*

Rus·sia (rush′ə), *n.* **1.** Also called **Russian Empire.** Russian, **Rossiya.** a former empire in E Europe and N and W Asia: overthrown by the Russian Revolution 1917. *Cap.:* St. Petersburg (1703–1917). **2.** See **Union of Soviet Socialist Republics. 3.** See **Russian Federation.**

Rus′sia leath′er, a fine, smooth leather produced by careful tanning and dyeing, esp. in dark red: originally prepared in Russia. Also called **rus′sia.** [1650–60]

Rus·sian (rush′ən), *adj.* **1.** of or pertaining to Russia, its people, or their language. **—***n.* **2.** a native or inhabitant of Russia or the Russian Federation. **3.** a member of a Slavic people, the dominant ethnic group in the Russian Federation, whose historical homeland lies along the upper Volga and Oka rivers and adjacent areas. **4.** the Slavic language of this people, written in the Cyrillic alphabet: the official language of Russia or the Russian Federation. *Abbr.:* Russ, Russ. **5.** *Informal.* See **Russian dressing.** [1530–40; < ML *Russiānus.* See RUSS, RUSSIA, -AN]

Rus′sian Church′. See **Russian Orthodox Church.**

Rus′sian dan′delion, kok-saghyz.

Rus′sian dress′ing, a sharp mayonnaise dressing containing chopped pickles, chili sauce or ketchup, pimientos, etc. [1920–25]

Rus′sian Em′pire, Russia (def. 1).

Rus′sian Federa′tion, a republic extending from E Europe to N and W Asia. 147,386,000; 6,593,000 sq. mi. (17,076,000 sq. km). *Cap.:* Moscow. Also called **Russia, Russian Repub′lic.** Formerly (1918–91), **Russian Soviet Federated Socialist Republic.**

Rus·sian·ize (rush′ə nīz′), *v.t.,* **-ized, -iz·ing. 1.** to make Russian; impart Russian characteristics to. **2.** to subordinate and force to adhere to Russian culture, ideology, etc. **3.** (*sometimes l.c.*) to treat (leather) by a process similar to that used on Russia leather or by any process that will produce such leather. Also, *esp. Brit.,* **Rus′sian·ise′.** [1825–35; RUSSIAN + -IZE] **—Rus′sian·i·za′tion,** *n.*

Rus′sian ol′ive, oleaster. [1935–40, *Amer.*]

Rus′sian Or′thodox Church′, the autocephalous Eastern Church in Russia: the branch of the Orthodox Church that constituted the established church in Russia until 1917. Also called **Russian Church.**

Rus′sian Revolu′tion, 1. Also called **February Revolution.** the uprising in Russia in March, 1917 (February Old Style), in which the Czarist government collapsed and a provisional government was established. **2.** Also called **October Revolution.** the overthrow of this provisional government by a coup d'état on November 7, 1917 (October 25 Old Style), establishing the Soviet government.

Rus′sian roulette′, a game of high risk in which each player in turn, using a revolver containing one bullet, spins the cylinder of the revolver, points the muzzle at the head, and pulls the trigger. [1935–40]

Rus′sian So′viet Fed′erated So′cialist Repub′lic, former name (1918–91) of the **Russian Federation.** *Abbr.:* RSFSR, R.S.F.S.R.

Rus′sian this′tle, a saltwort, *Salsola kali tenuifolia*, that has narrow, spinelike leaves, a troublesome weed in the central and western U.S. Also called **Rus′sian tum′bleweed.** [1890–95, *Amer.*]

Rus′sian Tur′kestan. See under **Turkestan.**

Rus′sian wolf′hound, borzoi. [1870–75]

Rus′sian Zone′, a zone in Germany controlled by the Soviet Union since 1945. Cf. **East Germany.**

Rus·si·fy (rus′ə fī′), *v.t.,* **-fied, -fy·ing.** Russianize (defs. 1, 2). [1860–65; RUSS(IAN) + -IFY; cf. F *russifier*] **—Rus′si·fi·ca′tion,** *n.*

Russ·ki (rus′kē, ro͝os′-, ro͞o′skē), *n., pl.* **-kies, -kis.** *Slang* (*disparaging and offensive*). a Russian. Also **Russ′kie, Russky.** [1855–60; < Russ *rússkiĭ* (n. and adj.) Russian]

Russ·ky (rus′kē, ro͝os′-, ro͞o′skē), *n., pl.* **-kies, -kis.** *Slang* (*disparaging and offensive*). Russki.

Russo-, a combining form of **Russia** or **Russian:** *Russophobe.*

Rus′so-Jap′an·ese War′ (rus′ō jap′ə nēz′, -nēs′), the war (1904–1905) between Russia and Japan.

Rus·so·phile (rus′ə fīl′), *n.* a person who is friendly to, admires, or prefers Russia or Russian customs, institutions, etc. [1890–95; RUSSO- + -PHILE] **—Rus·so·phil·i·a** (rus′ə fil′ē ə), *n.*

Rus·so·phobe (rus′ə fōb′), *n.* a person who hates or fears Russia or the Russians. [1880–85; RUSSO- + -PHOBE] **—Rus′so·pho′bi·a,** *n.*

Russ·wurm (rus′wûrm), *n.* **John Brown,** 1799–1851, Jamaican-born journalist in the U.S. and (after 1829) journalist and statesman in Liberia.

rust (rust), *n.* **1.** Also called **iron rust.** the red or orange coating that forms on the surface of iron when exposed to air and moisture, consisting chiefly of ferric hydroxide and ferric oxide formed by oxidation. **2.** any film or coating on metal caused by oxidation. **3.** a stain resembling this coating. **4.** any growth, habit, influence, or agency tending to injure, deteriorate, or impair the mind, character, abilities, usefulness, etc. **5.** *Plant Pathol.* **a.** any of several diseases of plants, characterized by reddish, brownish, or black pustules on the leaves, stems, etc., caused by fungi of the order Uredinales. **b.** Also called **rust′ fun′gus.** a fungus causing this disease. **c.** any of several other diseases of unknown cause, characterized by reddish-brown spots or discolorations on the affected parts. **6.** reddish yellow, reddish brown, or yellowish red. **—***v.i.* **7.** to become or grow rusty, as iron. **8.** to contract rust. **9.** to deteriorate or become impaired, as through inaction or disuse. **10.** to become rust-colored. **—***v.t.* **11.** to affect with rust. **12.** to impair as if with rust. **13.** to make rust-colored. **14. rust out,** (of metal pipes, machinery, etc.) to decay and become unusable through the action of rust. **15. rust through,** to develop holes, breaks, or the like, because of rust. **16. rust together,** to join two metal pieces, as iron pipes, by causing the joint to rust. **—***adj.* **17.** having the color rust. [bef. 900; (n.) ME; OE *rūst*; c. G *Rost*; (v.) ME *rusten*, deriv. of the n.; akin to RED] **—Syn. 2.** corrosion. **9.** decay, decline.

Ru·sta·vi (ro͞o stä′vē; *Russ.* ro͞o stä′vyi), *n.* a city in the SE Georgian Republic, SE of Tbilisi. 129,000.

rust′ belt′, (*sometimes caps.*) the heavily industrial area of the northeastern U.S. containing the older industries and factories. [1980–85]

rust·buck·et (rust′buk′it), *n. Slang.* an old, rundown freighter, esp. one whose hull is covered with rust. [1940–45; RUST + BUCKET]

rust-col·ored (rust′kul′ərd), *adj.* of the color rust. [1685–95]

rus·tic (rus′tik), *adj.* **1.** of, pertaining to, or living in the country, as distinguished from towns or cities; rural. **2.** simple, artless, or unsophisticated. **3.** uncouth, rude, or boorish. **4.** made of roughly dressed limbs or roots of trees, as garden seats. **5.** (of stonework) having the surfaces rough or irregular and the joints sunken or beveled. **—***n.* **6.** a country person. **7.** an unsophisticated country person. [1400–50; late ME < L *rūsticus*, equiv. to *rūs* the country (see RURAL) + *-ticus* adj. suffix] **—rus′ti·cal,** *adj.* **—rus′ti·cal·ly, rus′tic·ly,** *adv.* **—rus′ti·cal·ness, rus′tic·ness,** *n.* **—Syn. 1.** See **rural. —Ant. 1.** urban.

rus·ti·cate (rus′ti kāt′), *v.,* **-cat·ed, -cat·ing. —***v.i.* **1.** to go to the country. **2.** to stay or sojourn in the country. **—***v.t.* **3.** to send to or domicile in the country. **4.** to make rustic, as persons or manners. **5.** to finish (a wall surface) so as to produce or suggest rustication. **6.** *Brit.* to suspend (a student) from a university as punishment. [1650–60; < L *rūsticātus* (ptp. of *rūsticārī* to live in the country), equiv. to *rūstic(us)* RUSTIC + *-ātus* -ATE[1]] **—rus′ti·ca′tor,** *n.*

rus·ti·ca·tion (rus′ti kā′shən), *n.* **1.** Also called **rus′tic work′.** *Archit.* any of various forms of ashlar so dressed and tooled that the visible faces are raised above or otherwise contrasted with the horizontal and usually the vertical joints. **2.** the act of a person or thing that rusticates. [1615–25; < L *rūsticātiōn-* (s. of *rūsticātiō*). See RUSTICATE, -ION]

rus·tic·i·ty (ru stis′i tē), *n., pl.* **-ties. 1.** the state or quality of being rustic. **2.** rural character or life. [1525–35; < MF *rusticite* < L *rūstic(us)* RUSTIC + MF *-ite* -ITY]

rus′tic joint′, *Masonry.* a joint between stones recessed from the faces between sunken drafts or bevels.

Rus·tin (rus′tin), *n.* **Bay·ard** (bā′ərd), born 1910, U.S. civil rights leader.

rust′ joint′, (in plumbing and metalwork) a watertight joint made between two pieces by rusting them together.

rus·tle (rus′əl), *v.,* **-tled, -tling,** *n.* **—***v.i.* **1.** to make a succession of slight, soft sounds, as of parts rubbing gently one on another, as leaves, silks, or papers. **2.** to cause such sounds by moving or stirring something. **3.** to move, proceed, or work energetically: *Rustle around and see what you can find.* **—***v.t.* **4.** to move or stir so as to cause a rustling sound: *The wind rustled the leaves.* **5.** to move, bring, or get by energetic action: *I'll go rustle some supper.* **6.** to steal (livestock, esp. cattle). **7. rustle up,** *Informal.* to find, gather, or assemble by effort or search: *to rustle up some wood for a fire.* **—***n.* **8.** the sound made by anything that rustles: *the rustle of leaves.* [1350–1400; ME *rustlen* (v.); cf. Fris *russelje*, D *ridselen*; of imit. orig.] **—rus′tling·ly,** *adv.*

rus·tler (rus′lər), *n.* **1.** a cattle thief. **2.** a person or thing that rustles. **3.** *Informal.* an active, energetic person. [1810–20; RUSTLE + -ER[1]]

rust·less (rust′lis), *adj.* **1.** free from rust. **2.** rustproof. [1835–45; RUST + -LESS]

rust′ mite′, any of various mites that cause brown or reddish patches on leaves and fruit. [1880–85]

Rus·ton (rus′tən), *n.* a city in N Louisiana. 20,585.

rust·out (rust′out′), *n.* **1.** rust-through. **2.** an area or spot, as on the body of a car, that has rusted through: *scratches, dents, and rustouts.* [n. use of v. phrase *rust out*]

rust·proof (rust′pro͞of′), *adj.* **1.** not subject to rusting. **—***v.t.* **2.** to coat with a substance that prevents rusting. [1685–95; RUST + -PROOF]

rust·proof·ing (rust′pro͞o′fing), *n.* **1.** the process of making metal rustproof. **2.** Also called **rust′proof′er.** a substance used in this process. [1915–20; RUSTPROOF + -ING[1]]

rust-through (rust′thro͞o′), *n.* an act or instance of rusting: *The body of the car is protected against rust-through.* Also, **rustout.** [n. use of v. phrase *rust through*]

rust·y[1] (rus′tē), *adj.,* **rust·i·er, rust·i·est. 1.** covered with or affected by rust. **2.** consisting of or produced by rust. **3.** of or tending toward the color rust; rust-colored. **4.** faded or shabby; impaired by time or wear, as clothes or drapery. **5.** impaired through disuse or neglect: *My Latin is rusty.* **6.** having lost agility or alertness; out of practice: *I am a bit rusty at tennis.* **7.** (of a sound) grating or harsh. [bef. 900; ME *rusti*, OE *rūstig*; see RUST, -Y[1]] **—rust′i·ly,** *adv.* **—rust′i·ness,** *n.*

rust·y[2] (rus′tē), *adj.,* **rust·i·er, rust·i·est. 1.** restive; stubborn: *a rusty horse.* **2.** *Chiefly Dial.* ill-tempered; cross. [1555–65; appar. special use of RUSTY[1]; but cf. obs. *resty* RESTIVE]

Rus·ty (rus′tē), *n.* a male or female given name.

rust′y black′bird, a North American blackbird, *Euphagus carolinus*, the male of which has plumage that is uniformly bluish-black in the spring and rusty-edged in the fall. Also called **rust′y grack′le.** [1850–55, *Amer.*]

rut[1] (rut), *n., v.,* **rut·ted, rut·ting. —***n.* **1.** a furrow or track in the ground, esp. one made by the passage of a vehicle or vehicles. **2.** any furrow, groove, etc. **3.** a fixed or established procedure or course of life, usually dull or unpromising: *to fall into a rut.* **—***v.t.* **4.** to make a rut or ruts in; furrow. [1570–80; perh. var. of ROUTE]

rut[2] (rut), *n., v.,* **rut·ted, rut·ting. —***n.* **1.** the periodically recurring sexual excitement of the deer, goat, sheep, etc. **—***v.i.* **2.** to be in the condition of rut. [1375–1425; late ME *rutte* < MF *rut, ruit* < LL *rugītus* a roaring, equiv. to L *rugī(re)* to roar + *-tus* suffix of v. action]

ru·ta·ba·ga (ro͞o′tə bā′gə, ro͞o′tə bä′-), *n.* **1.** a brassicaceous plant, *Brassica napobrassica*, having a yellow- or white-fleshed, edible tuber. **2.** the edible tuber, a variety of turnip. Also called **Swedish turnip.** [1790–1800, *Amer.*; < Sw (dial.) *rotabagge*]

ru·ta·ceous (ro͞o tā′shəs), *adj. Bot.* **1.** of or like rue. **2.** belonging to the Rutaceae, the rue family of plants. Cf. **rue family.** [1820–30; < NL *Rutace(ae)* name of the family (*Rut(a)* the type genus (L *rūta* RUE[2]) + *-aceae* ACEAE) + -OUS]

ruth (ro͞oth), *n.* **1.** pity or compassion. **2.** sorrow or grief. **3.** self-reproach; contrition; remorse. [1125–75; ME *ruthe, reuthe.* See RUE[1], -TH[1]] **—Syn. 1.** mercy, sympathy. **—Ant. 1.** cruelty.

Ruth (ro͞oth), *n.* **1.** a Moabite woman who married Boaz and became an ancestor of David: the daughter-in-law of Naomi. **2.** a book of the Bible bearing her name. **3.** a female given name.

Ruth (ro͞oth), *n.* **George Herman** (*"Babe"*), 1895–1948, U.S. baseball player.

Ru·the·ni·a (ro͞o thē′nē ə, -thēn′yə), *n.* a former province in E Czechoslovakia. Cf. **Carpatho-Ukraine.**

Ru·the·ni·an (ro͞o thē′nē ən, -thēn′yən), *adj.* **1.** of or pertaining to the Little Russians, esp. a division of them dwelling in Galicia, Ruthenia, and neighboring regions. **—***n.* **2.** one of the Ruthenian people. **3.** the dialect of Ukrainian spoken in Ruthenia. **4.** a member of a former Orthodox religious group that entered into communion with the Roman Catholic Church in 1596 and became the "Uniate Church of the Little Russians." [1840–50; RUTHENI(A) + -AN]

ru·then·ic (ro͞o then′ik, -thē′nik), *adj. Chem.* containing ruthenium in a higher valence state than the corresponding ruthenious compound. [1840–50; RUTHEN(IUM) + -IC]

ru·the·ni·ous (ro͞o thē′nē əs, -thēn′yəs), *adj. Chem.*

CONCISE PRONUNCIATION KEY: act, cāpe, dâre, pärt; set, ēqual; *if*, īce; ox, ōver, ôrder, oil, bo͝ok, bo͞ot, out; up, ûrge; child; sing; shoe; thin, *th*at; zh as in *treasure*. ə = *a* as in *alone*, *e* as in *system*, *i* as in *easily*, *o* as in *gallop*, *u* as in *circus*; ᵊ as in *fire* (fīᵊr), *hour* (ouᵊr). l and n can serve as syllabic consonants, as in *cradle* (krād′l), and *button* (but′n). See the full key inside the front cover.

containing bivalent ruthenium. [1865–70; RUTHENI(UM) + -OUS]

ru•the•ni•um (ro͞o thē′nē əm, -thēn′yəm), *n. Chem.* a steel-gray, rare metallic element, belonging to the platinum group of metals. *Symbol:* Ru; *at. wt.:* 101.07; *at. no.:* 44; *sp. gr.:* 12.2 at 20°C. [1840–50; < NL, named after RUTHENIA (from the fact that it was first found in ore from the region); see -IUM]

Ruth•er•ford (ruth′ər fərd, ruth′-), *n.* **1. Daniel,** 1749–1819, Scottish physician and chemist: discoverer of nitrogen. **2. Ernest** (*1st Baron Rutherford of Nelson*), 1871–1937, English physicist, born in New Zealand: Nobel prize for chemistry 1908. **3. John Sherman** (*Johnny*), born 1938, U.S. racing-car driver. **4. Joseph Franklin,** 1869–1942, U.S. leader of Jehovah's Witnesses. **5. Dame Margaret,** 1892–1972, British actress. **6.** a city in NE New Jersey. 19,068.

ruth•er•for•di•um (ruth′ər fôr′dē əm, -fōr′-), *n. Chem.* unnilquadium. [1969; named in honor of E. RUTHERFORD; see -IUM]

Ruth′erford scat′tering, *Physics.* the scattering of an alpha particle through a large angle with respect to the original direction of motion of the particle, caused by an atom **(Ruth′erford at′om)** with most of the mass and all of the positive electric charge concentrated at a center or nucleus. Also called **alpha-particle scattering, Ruth′erford al′pha-particle scat′tering.** [1925–30; named after E. RUTHERFORD]

ruth•ful (ro͞oth′fəl), *adj.* **1.** compassionate or sorrowful. **2.** causing or apt to cause sorrow or pity. **3.** feeling remorse or self-reproach. [1175–1225; ME; see RUTH, -FUL] **—ruth′ful•ly,** *adv.* **—ruth′ful•ness,** *n.*

ruth•less (ro͞oth′lis), *adj.* without pity or compassion; cruel; merciless: *a ruthless tyrant.* [1300–50; ME; see RUTH, -LESS] **—ruth′less•ly,** *adv.* **—ruth′less•ness,** *n.* **—Syn.** unrelenting, adamant, relentless. See **cruel.**

ru•ti•lant (ro͞ot′l ənt), *adj.* glowing or glittering with ruddy or golden light. [1490–1500; < L *rutilant-* (s. of *rutilāns,* prp. of *rutilāre* to glow red), equiv. to *rutil(us)* red, reddish + *-ant-* -ANT]

ru•ti•lat•ed (ro͞ot′l ā′tid), *adj. Mineral.* containing fine, embedded needles of rutile. [1885–90; < L *rutilā-t(us)* (ptp. of *rutilāre;* see RUTILANT, -ATE[1]) + -ED[2]]

ru•tile (ro͞o′tēl, -tīl), *n.* a common mineral, titanium dioxide, TiO_2, usually reddish-brown in color with a brilliant metallic or adamantine luster, occurring in crystals: used to coat welding rods. [1795–1805; < F < G *Rutil* < L *rutilus* RED[1]]

ru•tin (ro͞ot′n), *n. Pharm.* a bright yellow or greenish-yellow substance, $C_{27}H_{30}O_{16}$, obtained chiefly from buckwheat, and used in the treatment of capillary fragility. [< G *Rutin* (1842) < NL *Rut(a)* rue, a source of the substance (see RUTACEOUS) + G *-in* -IN[2]]

Rut•land (rut′lənd), *n.* **1.** a city in W Vermont. 18,436. **2.** Rutlandshire.

Rut•land•shire (rut′lənd shēr′, -shər), *n.* a former county, now part of Leicestershire, in central England. Also called **Rutland.**

Rut•ledge (rut′lij), *n.* **1. Ann,** 1816–35, fiancée of Abraham Lincoln. **2. Edward,** 1749–1800, U.S. lawyer and statesman. **3.** his brother, **John,** 1739–1800, U.S. jurist and statesman: associate justice of the U.S. Supreme Court 1789–91. **4. Wiley Blount** (blunt), 1894–1949, U.S. jurist: associate justice of the U.S. Supreme Court 1943–49.

rut•ter (rut′ər), *n.* portolano. [1490–1500; var. of *ruttier* < MF *routier,* equiv. to *route* ROUTE + *-ier* -IER[2]]

rut•tish (rut′ish), *adj.* salacious; lustful. [1595–1605; RUT[2] + -ISH[1]] **—rut′tish•ly,** *adv.* **—rut′tish•ness,** *n.*

rut•ty (rut′ē), *adj.,* **-ti•er, -ti•est.** full of or abounding in ruts, as a road. [1590–1600; RUT[1] + -Y[1]] **—rut′ti•ly,** *adv.* **—rut′ti•ness,** *n.*

CONCISE ETYMOLOGY KEY: <, descended or borrowed from; >, whence; b., blend of, blended; c., cognate with; cf., compare; deriv., derivative; equiv., equivalent; imit., imitative; obl., oblique; r., replacing; s., stem; sp., spelling, spelled; resp., respelling, respelled; trans., translation; ?, origin unknown; *, unattested; ‡, probably earlier than. See the full key inside the front cover.

ruvo kale See **broccoli rabe.** [< NL *ruvo* a specific epithet (in some systems) of the genus *Brassica;* of undetermined orig.]

Ru•vu•ma (ro͝o vo͞o′mə), *n.* a river in SE Africa, flowing E along the Tanzania-Mozambique border to the Indian Ocean. ab. 450 mi. (725 km) long. Also, **Rovuma.**

Ru•wen•zo•ri (ro͞o′wən zôr′ē, -zōr′ē), *n.* a mountain group in central Africa between Lake Albert and Lake Edward: sometimes identified with Ptolemy's "Mountains of the Moon." Highest peak, Mt. Ngaliema (Stanley), with two summits: Mt. Margherita, 16,795 ft. (5119 m), and Mt. Alexandra, 16,726 ft. (5098 m).

Ruys•dael (rois′däl, -dāl, rīz′-, rīs′-; *Du.* RŒIS′däl), *n.* Ruisdael.

Ruy•ter (roi′tər; *Du.* RŒI′təR), *n.* **Mi•chel A•dri•aans•soon de** (*Du.* mi′KHəl ä′dRē än′so͞on də), 1607–76, Dutch admiral.

Ru•žič•ka (*Serbo-Croatian* RO͞O′zhēch kä; *Eng.* ro͞o′-zich kə, ro͞o zich′-), *n.* **Le•o•pold** (lā′ō pôlt′), 1887–1976, Swiss chemist, born in Yugoslavia: Nobel prize 1939.

RV, 1. recreational vehicle. **2.** Revised Version (of the Bible).

R-val•ue (är′val′yo͞o), *n.* a measure of the resistance of an insulating or building material to heat flow, expressed as R-11, R-20, and so on; the higher the number, the greater the resistance to heat flow. Cf. **U-value.** [1945–50; *R,* symbol for *resistance*]

R.V.S.V.P., the favor of a prompt reply is requested. Also, **RVSVP, r.v.s.v.p., rvsvp.** [< F *r(épondez) v(ite) s('il) v(ous) p(laît)* please reply quickly]

R/W, right of way.

R.W., 1. Right Worshipful. **2.** Right Worthy.

Rwan•da (ro͞o än′də), *n.* a republic in central Africa, E of Zaire: formerly comprising the northern part of the Belgian trust territory of Ruanda-Urundi; became independent 1962. 4,500,000; 10,169 sq. mi. (26,338 sq. km). *Cap.:* Kigali. **—Rwan′dan,** *adj., n.*

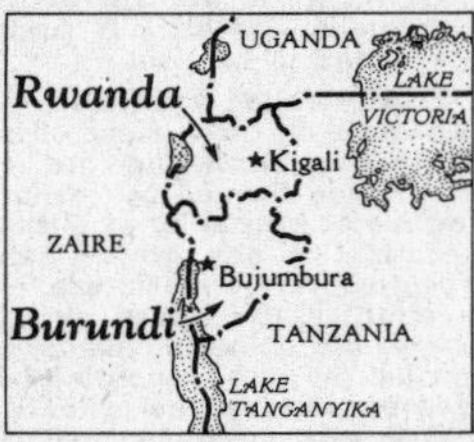

Rwan•dese (ro͞o än′dēz, -dēs), *adj., n., pl.* **-dese.** Rwandan. [RWAND(A) + -ESE]

Rwy., Railway.

Rx, 1. prescription. **2.** (in prescriptions) take. **3.** tens of rupees.

-ry, var. of **-ery:** *heraldry; husbandry; dentistry; tenantry; jewelry.* [ME *-rie* < OF; short form of -ERY]

Ry., Railway.

ry•a (rē′ə, rī′ə), *n.* **1.** a handwoven Scandinavian rug with a thick pile and usually a strong, colorful design. **2.** the weave used for this, comprising warp, weft, and hand-tied knots. [1940–45; after *Rya,* city in Sweden, where originally produced]

ry•al (rī′əl), *n.* **1.** See **rose noble. 2.** a former gold coin of Scotland, equal to 60 shillings. **3.** a former silver coin of Scotland, equal to 30 shillings. Also, **rial.** [1350–1400; ME (Scots): ROYAL]

Ry•an (rī′ən), *n.* a male given name.

Rya•zan (rē′ə zän′, -zan′; *Russ.* Ryi zän′), *n.* a city in the W Russian Federation in Europe, SE of Moscow. 515,000.

Ry•binsk (rib′insk; *Russ.* RI′byinsk), *n.* **1.** a city in the W Russian Federation in Europe, NNE of Moscow, on the Volga near the Rybinsk Reservoir. 254,000. Formerly, **Andropov** (1984–90), **Shcherbakov** (1946–57). **2.** Also called **Ry′binsk Res′ervoir.** a reservoir in the N central Russian Federation in Europe, on the upper Volga River. 1768 sq. mi. (4579 sq. km).

ryd•berg (rid′bûrg), *n. Physics.* a unit of energy used in atomic physics, equal to 13.606 electron-volts. *Abbr.:* ry [named for Johannes Robert *Rydberg* (1854–1919), Swedish physicist]

Ry•der (rī′dər), *n.* **Albert Pink•ham** (ping′kəm), 1847–1917, U.S. painter.

rye[1] (rī), *n.* **1.** a widely cultivated cereal grass, *Secale cereale,* having one-nerved glumes and two- or three-flowered spikelets. **2.** the seeds or grain of this plant, used for making flour and whiskey, and as a livestock feed. **3.** See **rye bread. 4.** a straight whiskey distilled from a mash containing 51 percent or more rye grain. **5.** *Northeastern U.S. and Canada.* a blended whiskey. *—adj.* **6.** made with rye grain or flour: *rye rolls.* Also called **rye whiskey** (for defs. 4, 5). [bef. 900; ME; OE *ryge;* c. ON *rūgr;* akin to D *rogge,* G *Roggen*]

rye[2] (rī), *n.* a male Gypsy. [1850–55; < Romany *rai*]

Rye (rī), *n.* a city in SE New York, on Long Island Sound. 15,083.

rye′ bread′, bread that is made either entirely or partly from rye flour, often with caraway seeds. [1570–80]

rye•grass (rī′gras′, -gräs′), *n.* any of several European grasses of the genus *Lolium,* as *L. perenne* **(perennial ryegrass),** grown for forage in the U.S. [1740–50; RYE[1] + GRASS]

Rye•land (rī′lənd), *n.* one of an English breed of white-faced sheep, yielding wool of high quality. [1795–1805; named after *Ryelands,* a district in Herefordshire, England]

rye′ whis′key, rye[1] (defs. 4, 5). [1775–85, *Amer.*]

Ryle (rīl), *n.* **Sir Martin,** 1918–84, British astronomer: Nobel prize for physics 1974.

rynd (rīnd, rind), *n.* rind[2].

Ryo•jun•ko (RYô′jo͞on kô′), *n.* former Japanese name of **Lüshun.** Also called **Ryo•jun** (RYô′jo͞on′).

ryo•kan (rē′ō kän′; *Japn.* RYô′kän′), *n., pl.* **-kan, -kans.** a traditional Japanese inn or small hotel whose floors are covered with tatami. [1960–65; < Japn]

ry•ot (rī′ət), *n.* (in India) **1.** a peasant. **2.** a person who holds land as a cultivator of the soil. [1615–25; < Hindi *raiyat* < Pers < Ar *ra'iyah* subjects, lit., flock]

Ry•sa•nek (Rē′zä nek′), *n.* **Le•o•nie** (le′ô nē′), born 1926, Austrian soprano.

Ryu•kyu (*Japn.* RYo͞o′kyo͞o; *Eng.* rē o͞o′kyo͞o), *n.* a chain of Japanese islands in the W Pacific between Japan and Taiwan. 1,235,000; 1205 sq. mi. (3120 sq. km).

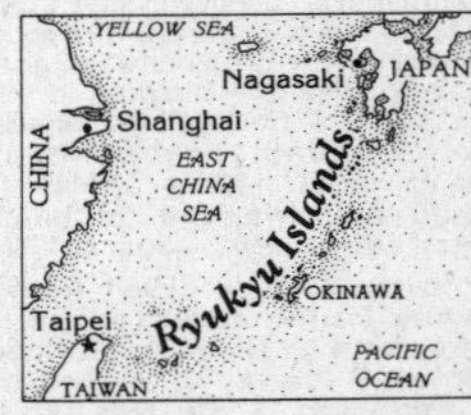

Ryu•kyu•an (rē o͞o′kyo͞o ən, ryo͞o′-), *n.* **1.** a native or inhabitant of Ryukyu. **2.** the group of dialects spoken in the Ryukyu Islands, related to Japanese. *—adj.* **3.** of, pertaining to, or characteristic of Ryukyu.

Ry•un (rī′ən), *n.* **James Ronald** (*Jim*), born 1947, U.S. track-and-field athlete.

Ryu•rik (*Russ.* RYo͞o′Ryik), *n.* Rurik.

DEVELOPMENT OF MAJUSCULE								
NORTH SEMITIC	GREEK		ETR.	LATIN		MODERN		
						GOTHIC	ITALIC	ROMAN
W	ϟ	Σ	ϟ	ϟ	S	𝔖	*S*	S

S

DEVELOPMENT OF MINUSCULE					
ROMAN CURSIVE	ROMAN UNCIAL	CAROL. MIN.	MODERN		
			GOTHIC	ITALIC	ROMAN
ʃ	S	s	𝔰	*s*	s

The nineteenth letter of the English alphabet developed from North Semitic, where its form was similar to that of the modern W. Descending through Greek *sigma* (ς), which itself exhibited some variety of use (ς, σ), it acquired its present form in Latin.

S, s (es), *n., pl.* **S's** or **Ss, s's** or **ss. 1.** the 19th letter of the English alphabet, a consonant. **2.** any spoken sound represented by the letter *S* or *s*, as in *saw, sense*, or *goose*. **3.** something having the shape of an S. **4.** a written or printed representation of the letter *S* or *s*. **5.** a device, as a printer's type, for reproducing the letter *S* or *s*.

S, 1. satisfactory. **2.** Saxon. **3.** sentence. **4.** short. **5.** *Elect.* siemens. **6.** signature. **7.** single. **8.** small. **9.** soft. **10.** *Music.* soprano. **11.** South. **12.** Southern. **13.** state (highway). **14.** *Gram.* subject.

S, *Symbol.* **1.** the 19th in order or in a series, or, when *I* is omitted, the 18th. **2.** (*sometimes l.c.*) the medieval Roman numeral for 7 or 70. Cf. **Roman numerals. 3.** second. **4.** *Biochem.* serine. **5.** *Thermodynam.* entropy. **6.** *Physics.* strangeness. **7.** sulfur.

s, 1. satisfactory. **2.** signature. **3.** small. **4.** soft. **5.** south.

s, *Symbol.* second.

's[1], an ending used in writing to represent the possessive morpheme after most singular nouns, some plural nouns, esp. those not ending in a letter or combination of letters representing an *s* or *z* sound, noun phrases, and noun substitutes, as in *man's, women's, baby's, James's, witness's,* (or *witness'*), *king of England's,* or *anyone's.* [ME -*es,* OE]

's[2], **1.** contraction of *is: She's here.* **2.** contraction of *does: What's he do for a living now?* **3.** contraction of *has: He's just gone.*
—Usage. See **contraction.**

's[3], *Archaic.* a contraction of *God's,* as in *'swounds; 'sdeath; 'sblood.*

's[4], a contraction of *us,* as in *Let's go.*
—Usage. See **contraction.**

's[5], a contraction of *as,* as in *so's to get there on time.*

-s[1], a native English suffix used in the formation of adverbs: *always; betimes; needs; unawares.* Cf. **-ways.** [ME -*es,* OE; ult. identical with 's[1]]

-s[2], an ending marking the third person sing. indicative active of verbs: *walks.* [ME (north) -(*e*)*s,* OE (north); orig. ending of 2nd pers. sing., as in L and Gk; r. ME, OE -*eth* -ETH[1]]

-s[3], an ending marking nouns as plural (*boys; wolves*), occurring also on nouns that have no singular (*dregs; entrails; pants; scissors*), or on nouns that have a singular with a different meaning (*clothes; glasses; manners; thanks*). The pluralizing value of **-s**[3] is weakened or lost in a number of nouns that now often take singular agreement, as the names of games (*billiards; checkers; tiddlywinks*) and of diseases (*measles; mumps; pox; rickets*); the latter use has been extended to create informal names for a variety of involuntary conditions, physical or mental (*collywobbles; d.t.'s; giggles; hots; willies*). A parallel set of formations, where **-s**[3] has no plural value, are adjectives denoting socially unacceptable or inconvenient states (*bananas; bonkers; crackers; nuts; preggers; starkers*); cf. **-ers.** Also, **-es.** [ME -(*e*)*s,* OE -*as,* pl. nom. and acc. ending of some masculine nouns]

-s[4], a suffix of hypocoristic nouns, generally proper names or forms used only in address: *Babs; Fats; Suzykins; Sweetums; Toodles.* [prob. from the metonymic use of nouns formed with -s[3], as *boots* or *Goldilocks*]

S., 1. Sabbath. **2.** Saint. **3.** Saturday. **4.** Saxon. **5.** (in Austria) schilling; schillings. **6.** School. **7.** Sea. **8.** Senate. **9.** September. **10.** shilling; shillings. **11.** (in prescriptions) **a.** mark; write; label. [< L *signā*] **b.** let it be written. [< L *signētur*] **12.** Signor. **13.** Small. **14.** Socialist. **15.** Society. **16.** Fellow. [< L *socius*] **17.** sol[3] (def. 1). **18.** South. **19.** Southern. **20.** (in Ecuador) sucre; sucres. **21.** Sunday.

s., 1. saint. **2.** school. **3.** second. **4.** section. **5.** see. **6.** series. **7.** shilling; shillings. **8.** sign. **9.** signed. **10.** silver. **11.** singular. **12.** sire. **13.** small. **14.** society. **15.** son. **16.** south. **17.** southern. **18.** steamer. **19.** stem. **20.** stem of. **21.** substantive.

Sa, *Symbol, Chem.* (formerly) samarium.

S/A, *Banking.* survivorship agreement.

S.A., 1. Salvation Army. **2.** seaman apprentice. **3.** South Africa. **4.** South America. **5.** South Australia. **6.** (used in French and Spanish as an abbreviation for *corporation.*) [< F *société anonyme* or Sp *sociedad anónima*]

s.a., 1. semiannual. **2.** sex appeal. **3.** without year or date. [< L *sine annō*] **4.** subject to approval.

S.A.A., Speech Association of America.

Saa•di (sä dē′), *n.* (*Muslih ud-Din*) 1184?–1291?, Persian poet. Also, **Sadi.**

Saar (zär, sär), *n.* **1.** Also called **Saar′ Ba′sin.** a coal-producing region in W Germany, in the Saar River valley: governed by the League of Nations 1919–35; returned to Germany 1935 as a result of a plebiscite; under French economic control following World War II until 1956. **2.** French, **Sarre.** a river in W Europe, flowing N from the Vosges Mountains in NE France to the Moselle River in W Germany. 150 mi. (240 km) long. **3.** Saarland.

Saar•brück•en (zär brŏŏk′ən, sär-; *Ger.* zäʀ brʏk′ən), *n.* a city in W Germany: the capital of Saarland. 187,400.

Saa•re•maa (sär′ə mä′), *n.* an island in the Baltic, at the mouth of the Gulf of Riga, belonging to Estonia. 1048 sq. mi. (2714 sq. km). Also, **Sa′re•ma.** German, **Oesel, Ösel.**

Saa•ri•nen (sär′ə nən, sar′-; *Finn.* sä′ʀi nen′), *n.* **1. Ee•ro** (âr′ō), 1910–61, U.S. architect, born in Finland. **2. (Got•tlieb) E•li•el** (got′lēb el′ē əl, ē′lē-; *Finn.* gôt′lēb e′lē el′), 1873–1950, U.S. architect, born in Finland (father of Eero Saarinen).

Saar•land (zär′land′, sär′-; *Ger.* zär′länt′), *n.* a state in W Germany, in the Saar River valley. 1,054,142; 991 sq. mi. (2569 sq. km). *Cap.:* Saarbrücken. **—Saar′land′•er,** *n.*

Sa•a•ve•dra La•mas (sä′ä ve′thrä lä′mäs), **Car•los** (kär′lôs), 1878?–1959, Argentine statesman and diplomat: Nobel peace prize 1936.

Sab., Sabbath.

Sa•ba (sä′bə *for 1;* sā′bə *for 2*), *n.* **1.** an island in the Netherlands Antilles, in the N Leeward Islands. 1011; 5 sq. mi. (13 sq. km). **2.** Biblical name, **Sheba.** an ancient kingdom in southwestern Arabia noted for its extensive trade, esp. in spices and gems.

Sa•ba•dell (sä′bə del′; *Sp.* sä′vä thel′), *n.* a city in NE Spain, N of Barcelona. 159,408.

sab•a•dil•la (sab′ə dil′ə), *n.* **1.** a Mexican plant, *Schoenocaulon officinale,* of the lily family, having long, grasslike leaves. **2.** the bitter seeds of this plant, formerly used medicinally and as a source of veratrine. [1805–15; < Sp *cebadilla* Indian caustic barley, dim. of *cebada* barley (fem.) << L *cibātus* (masc.) fodder, nutriment, equiv. to *cibā(re)* to feed + -*tus* suffix of v. action]

Sa•bae•an (sə bē′ən), *adj., n.* Sabean.

Sa•bah (sä′bä), *n.* a state in Malaysia, on the N tip of Borneo: formerly a British crown colony. 655,622; 29,347 sq. mi. (76,008 sq. km). *Cap.:* Kota Kinabalu. Formerly, **North Borneo, British North Borneo.**

sa•ba•lo (sab′ə lō′), *n., pl.* **-los.** the tarpon. [1885–90; < Sp *sábalo* shad < ?]

Sab•a•oth (sab′ē oth′, -ôth′, sab′ā-, sə bā′ôth), *n.* (*used with a plural v.*) armies; hosts. Rom. 9:29; James 5:4. [1275–1325; < Heb *ṣəbhā'ōth,* pl. of *ṣābhā* army]

Sa•ba•ta (sä bä′tä), *n.* **Vic•tor de** (vēk tôʀ′ də), 1892–1967, Italian composer and conductor.

Sa•ba•tier (sa ba tyā′), *n.* **Paul** (pôl), 1854–1941, French chemist: Nobel prize 1912.

Sab•a•ti•ni (sab′ə tē′nē, sä′bə-), *n.* **Raf•a•el** (raf′ē əl), 1875–1950, English novelist and short-story writer, born in Italy.

sab•a•ton (sab′ə ton′), *n. Armor.* a foot defense of mail or of a number of lames with solid toe and heel pieces. See illus. under **armor.** [1300–50; ME < OPr, equiv. to *sabat(a)* shoe + -*on* aug. suffix. See SABOT]

Sa•bat•tier′ effect′ (sä′bə tyā′, sab′ə-), *Photog.* the alteration of the image tones of a photographic print by briefly reexposing the negative after it has been partially developed. [1925–30; *Sabattier,* erroneous for Armand *Sabatier* (1834–1910), French physician and scientist, who developed the effect]

sa•ba•yon (*Fr.* sa ba yôɴ′), *n.* zabaglione. [< F < It *zabaione;* see ZABAGLIONE]

Sab•bat (sab′ət), *n.* (*sometimes l.c.*) *Demonology.* (in the 14th–16th centuries) a secret rendezvous of witches and sorcerers for worshiping the Devil, characterized by orgiastic rites, dances, feasting, etc. Also, **Sabbath.** Also called **witches' Sabbath.** [1645–55; < F: special use of *sabbat* SABBATH]

Sab•ba•tar•i•an (sab′ə târ′ē ən), *n.* **1.** a person who observes Saturday as the Sabbath. **2.** a person who adheres to or favors a strict observance of Sunday. **—*adj.*** **3.** of or pertaining to the Sabbath and its observance. [1605–15; < LL *sabbatāri(us)* (*sabbat(um)* SABBATH + -*ārius* -ARY) + -AN] **—Sab′ba•tar′i•an•ism,** *n.*

Sab•bath (sab′əth), *n.* **1.** the seventh day of the week, Saturday, as the day of rest and religious observance among Jews and some Christians. Ex. 20:8–11. **2.** the first day of the week, Sunday, similarly observed by most Christians in commemoration of the Resurrection of Christ. **3.** any special day of prayer or rest resembling the Sabbath: *Friday is the Muslim Sabbath.* **4.** (*sometimes l.c.*) a period of rest. **5.** (*sometimes l.c.*) *Demonology.* Sabbat. [bef. 900; ME, var. of *sabbat,* OE < L *sabbatum* < Gk *sábbaton* < Heb *shabbāth* rest] **—Sab′bath•less,** *adj.* **—Sab′bath•like′,** *adj.*
—Syn. 2. See **Sunday.**

Sab′bath school′, 1. See **Sunday school. 2.** (among Seventh-Day Adventists) such a school held on Saturday, their holy day. [1810–20]

Sab•bat•i•cal (sə bat′i kəl), *adj.* **1.** of or pertaining or appropriate to the Sabbath. **2.** (*l.c.*) of or pertaining to a sabbatical year. **3.** (*l.c.*) bringing a period of rest. **—*n.*** **4.** (*l.c.*) See **sabbatical year. 5.** (*l.c.*) any extended period of leave from one's customary work, esp. for rest, to acquire new skills, etc. Also, **Sab•bat′ic.** [1605–15; < Gk *sabbatikós* (*sábbat(on)* SABBATH + -*ikos* -IC) + -AL[1]] **—Sab•bat′i•cal•ly,** *adv.* **—Sab•bat′i•cal•ness,** *n.*

sabbat′ical year′, 1. Also called **sabbat′ical leave′.** (in a school, college, university, etc.) a year, usually every seventh, of release from normal teaching du-

CONCISE PRONUNCIATION KEY: *act, cāpe, dâre, pärt; set, ēqual; if, ice; ox, ōver, ôrder, oil, bŏŏk, bōōt, out; up, ûrge; child; sing; shoe; thin, that;* zh as in *treasure.* ə = *a* as in *alone, e* as in *system, i* as in *easily, o* as in *gallop, u* as in *circus;* ᵊ as in *fire* (fīᵊr), *hour* (ouᵊr). l and n can serve as syllabic consonants, as in *cradle* (krād′l), and *button* (but′n). See the full key inside the front cover.

ties granted to a professor, as for study or travel. **2.** *Chiefly Biblical.* a yearlong period to be observed by Jews once every seven years, during which the fields were to be left untilled and all agricultural labors were to be suspended. Lev. 25. Cf. **jubilee** (def. 6). [1625–35]

Sab·ba·tize (sab′ə tīz′), *v.*, **-tized, -tiz·ing.** *(often l.c.)* —*v.i.* **1.** to keep the Sabbath. —*v.t.* **2.** to keep as the Sabbath. Also, *esp. Brit.,* **Sab′ba·tise′.** [1350–1400; ME *sabbatisen* < LL *sabbatizāre* < Gk *sabbatízein*, equiv. to *sábbat(on)* SABBATH + *-izein* -IZE] —**Sab′ba·ti·za′·tion,** *n.*

Sa·be·an (sə bē′ən), *adj.* **1.** of or pertaining to Saba. —*n.* **2.** an inhabitant of Saba. Also, **Sabaean.** [1580–90; < L *sabae(us)* (< Gk *sabaîos* of Saba or Sheba) + -AN]

Sa·bel·li·an (sə bel′ē ən), *n.* a member of a group of early Italian peoples including the Samnites and Sabines. [1595–1605; < L *Sabell(us)* a member of any of the Oscan-speaking Italic ethnic groups + -IAN]

sa·ber (sā′bər), *n.* **1.** a heavy, one-edged sword, usually slightly curved, used esp. by cavalry. **2.** a soldier armed with such a sword. **3.** *Fencing.* **a.** a sword having two cutting edges and a blunt point. **b.** the art or sport of fencing with the saber, with the target being limited to the head, trunk, and arms, and hits being made with the front edge and the upper part of the back edge of the sword and by thrusts. —*v.t.* **4.** to strike, wound, or kill with a saber. Also, *esp. Brit.,* **sabre.** [1670–80; < F *sabre, sable* < G *Sabel* (now *Säbel*), earlier *sewel, schebel* < Pol *szabla;* cf. Czech *šavle*, Serbo-Croatian *sȁblja*, Russ *sáblya* sword, saber, perh. all ult. < Hungarian *szablya*, though derivation and transmission uncert.] —**sa′ber·like′,** *adj.*

sa·ber·met·rics (sā′bər me′triks), *n.* *(used with a sing. v.)* the computerized measurement of baseball statistics. Also, **SABR·met·rics.** [1980–85; *S(ociety for) A(merican) B(aseball) R(esearch)* + -METRICS] —**sa′·ber·me·tri′cian** (-mi trish′ən), *n.*

sa·ber-rat·tling (sā′bər rat′ling), *n.* a show or threat of military power, esp. as used by a nation to impose its policies on other countries. [1920–25; see SABER, RATTLE[1], -ING[1]]

sa′ber saw′, a portable electric jigsaw. [1950–55]

sa·ber-toothed (sā′bər tōōtht′), *adj.* having long, saberlike upper canine teeth, sometimes extending below the margin of the lower jaw. [1840–50]

sa′ber-toothed ti′ger, any of several extinct members of the cat family Felidae from the Oligocene to Pleistocene Epochs, having greatly elongated, saberlike upper canine teeth. Also called **sa·ber·tooth** (sā′bər-tōōth′). [1840–50]

saber-toothed tiger, *Smilodon californicus,* length 6 ft. (1.8 m); teeth to 8 in. (20 cm)

sa·bin (sā′bin), *n.* *Physics.* a unit of sound absorption, equal to one square foot (929 square centimeters) of a perfectly absorptive surface. [1930–35; named after W. C. SABINE]

Sa·bin (sā′bin), *n.* **Albert Bruce,** 1906–93, U.S. physician, born in Poland: developed Sabin vaccine.

Sa·bi·na (sə bē′nə, -bī′-), *n.* a female given name: from a Latin word meaning "a Sabine woman."

Sa·bine (sā′bīn), *adj.* **1.** of or belonging to an ancient people of central Italy who lived chiefly in the Apennines northeast of Rome and were subjugated by the Romans about 290 B.C. —*n.* **2.** one of the Sabine people. **3.** the Italic language of the Sabines. [1350–1400; ME < L *Sabīnus*]

Sa·bine (sā′bin, -bin *for 1;* sə bēn′ *for 2*), *n.* **1. Wallace Clement (Ware),** 1868–1919, U.S. physicist: pioneered research in acoustics. **2.** a river flowing SE and S from NE Texas, forming the boundary between Texas and Louisiana and then through Sabine Lake to the Gulf of Mexico. ab. 500 mi. (800 km) long.

Sa·bine′ Lake′ (sə bēn′), a shallow lake on the boundary between Texas and Louisiana, formed by a widening of the Sabine River. ab. 17 mi. (27 km) long; 7 mi. (11 km) wide.

Sa·bin·i·a·nus (sə bin′ē ā′nəs), *n.* died A.D. 606, pope 604–606.

Sa′bin vaccine′, an orally administered vaccine of live viruses for immunization against poliomyelitis. [named after A. B. SABIN]

Sa·bir (sə bēr′), *n.* See **lingua franca** (def. 2).

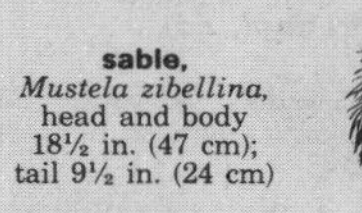

sable, *Mustela zibellina,* head and body 18½ in. (47 cm); tail 9½ in. (24 cm)

sa·ble (sā′bəl), *n., pl.* **-bles,** *(esp. collectively for 1, 2)* **-ble,** *adj.* —*n.* **1.** an Old World weasellike mammal, *Mustela zibellina,* of cold regions in Eurasia and the North Pacific islands, valued for its dark brown fur. **2.** a marten, esp. *Mustela americana.* **3.** the fur of the sable. **4.** the color black, often being one of the heraldic colors. **5. sables,** mourning garments. —*adj.* **6.** of the heraldic color sable. **7.** made of the fur or hair of the sable. **8.** very dark; black. [1275–1325; ME < OF < MLG *sabel* (cf. late OHG *zobel*) < Slavic or Baltic; cf. Russ *sóbol′*, Lith *sàbalas;* ulterior orig. obscure]

CONCISE ETYMOLOGY KEY: <, descended or borrowed from; >, whence; b., blend of, blended; c., cognate with; cf., compare; deriv., derivative; equiv., equivalent; imit., imitative; obl., oblique; r., replacing; s., stem; sp., spelling, spelled; resp., respelling, respelled; trans., translation; ?, origin unknown; *, unattested; ‡, probably earlier than. See the full key inside the front cover.

Sa·ble (sā′bəl), *n.* **Cape, 1.** a cape on a small island at the SW tip of Nova Scotia, Canada: lighthouse. **2.** a cape at the S tip of Florida.

sa′ble an′telope, a large antelope, *Hippotragus niger,* of Africa, with long, saberlike horns and, in the male, a black coat: an endangered species.

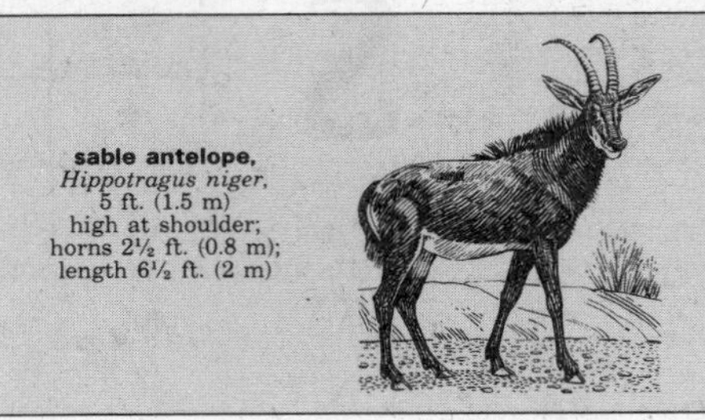

sable antelope, *Hippotragus niger,* 5 ft. (1.5 m) high at shoulder; horns 2½ ft. (0.8 m); length 6½ ft. (2 m)

sa·ble·fish (sā′bəl fish′), *n., pl.* *(esp. collectively)* **-fish,** *(esp. referring to two or more kinds or species)* **-fish·es.** a large, blackish food fish, *Anoplopoma fimbria,* inhabiting waters of the North Pacific. Also called **blackcod.** [1800–10; SABLE + FISH]

sa·bo·ra (sə bôr′ə, -bōr′ə), *n., pl.* **sa·bo·ra·im** (sä′bô-rä′im, -bō-). *(often cap.) Judaism.* one of a group of Jewish scholars, active in the rabbinical academies of Babylonia during the 6th century A.D., whose editing of the work of the Babylonian amoraim constituted the final stage in the preparation of the Babylonian Gemara. Cf. **amora, tanna.** [< Aram *sābhōrā* scholar, thinker, deriv. of *səbhār* to think]

sab·ot (sab′ō; *Fr.* SA bō′), *n., pl.* **sab·ots** (sab′ōz; *Fr.* SA bō′). **1.** a shoe made of a single block of wood hollowed out, worn esp. by farmers and workers in the Netherlands, France, Belgium, etc. **2.** a shoe with a thick wooden sole and sides and a top of coarse leather. **3.** *Mil.* **a.** a wooden or metal disk formerly attached to a projectile in a muzzleloading cannon. **b.** a soft metal ring at the base of a projectile that makes the projectile conform to the rifling grooves of a gun. [1600–10; < F, OF *çabot*, b. *savate* old shoe (of uncert. orig.; akin to OPr *sabata*, It *ciabatta*, Sp *zapato*) and *bot* BOOT] —**sa·boted** (sa bōd′, sab′ōd), *adj.*

sab·o·tage (sab′ə täzh′, sab′ə täzh′), *n., v.,* **-taged, -tag·ing.** —*n.* **1.** any underhand interference with production, work, etc., in a plant, factory, etc., as by enemy agents during wartime or by employees during a trade dispute. **2.** any undermining of a cause. —*v.t.* **3.** to injure or attack by sabotage. [1865–70; < F, equiv. to *sabot(er)* to botch, orig., to strike, shake up, harry, deriv. of *sabot* SABOT + *-age* -AGE]

sab·o·teur (sab′ə tûr′), *n.* a person who commits or practices sabotage. [1920–25; < F, equiv. to *sabot(er)* to botch (see SABOTAGE) + *-eur* -EUR]

sa·bra (sä′brə, -brä), *n.* *(sometimes cap.)* a person born in Israel. [1940–45; < colloquial ModHeb *sabre* lit., prickly pear < Ar *ṣabrah*]

sa·bre (sā′bər), *n., v.t.,* **-bred, -bring.** *Chiefly Brit.* saber.

Sa·bri·na (sə brē′nə, -brī′-), *n.* a female given name: from the Latin word for the river Severn.

sab·u·lous (sab′yə ləs), *adj.* sandy; gritty. [1625–35; < L *sabul(um)* sand + -OUS] —**sab·u·los·i·ty** (sab′yə-los′i tē), *n.*

sac (sak), *n.* a baglike structure in an animal, plant, or fungus. [1735–45; < L *saccus* SACK[1]] —**sac′like′,** *adj.*

Sac (sak, sôk), *n., pl.* **Sacs,** *(esp. collectively)* **Sac.** Sauk.

SAC (sak), *n.* Strategic Air Command. Also, **S.A.C.**

Sac·a·ja·we·a (sak′ə jə wē′ə), *n.* *("Bird Woman")*, 1787?–1812?, Shoshone guide and interpreter: accompanied Lewis and Clark expedition 1804–05. Also, **Sac·a·ga·we·a** (sak′ə gə wē′ə, -jə-), **Sakajawea.**

sac-a-lait (sak′ə lā′, sak′ə lā′), *n.* the white crappie. See under **crappie.** [1880–85, *Amer.*; < LaF < Choctaw *sakli* trout (taken as *sac* SACK[1] + *à* for + *lait* milk)]

sac·cade (sa käd′, sə-), *n.* **1.** the act of checking a horse quickly with a single strong pull of the reins. **2.** *Ophthalm.* the series of small, jerky movements of the eyes when changing focus from one point to another. [1720–30; < F *saccade* jerk, jolt, orig., movement of a horseman who abruptly pulls the reins, equiv. to MF *saqu(er)* to pull violently (N dial. var. of OF *sachier*, ult. deriv. of *sac* SACK[1], hence presumably with sense "withdraw from a sack") + *-ade* -ADE[1]]

sac·cad·ic (sa kä′dik, sə-), *adj.* characterized by discontinuous or sporadic movement; jerky. [1915–20; SACCADE + -IC]

sac·cate (sak′it, -āt), *adj.* having a sac or the form of a sac. [1820–30; < NL *saccātus*, equiv. to *sacc(us)* SACK[1] + *-ātus* -ATE[1]]

sacchar-, a combining form meaning "sugar," used in the formation of technical terms: *saccharoid.* Also, *esp. before a consonant,* **saccharo-.** [comb. form repr. ML *saccharum* Gk *sákkharon*, ult. < an Indo-Aryan source akin to Prakrit *sakkarā* < Skt *śarkarā*; cf. SUGAR]

sac·cha·rate (sak′ə rāt′), *n.* *Chem.* **1.** a salt of saccharic acid. **2.** a compound formed by interaction of sucrose with a metallic oxide, usually lime, and useful in the purification of sugar. [1805–15; SACCHAR(IC ACID) + -ATE[2]]

sac·char·ic (sə kar′ik), *adj.* *Chem.* **1.** of or derived from saccharin or a saccharine substance. **2.** of or derived from saccharic acid. [1790–1800; SACCHAR- + -IC]

sacchar′ic ac′id, *Chem.* a white, needlelike, crystalline, water-soluble solid or syrup, $C_6H_{10}O_8$, usually made by the oxidation of cane sugar, glucose, or starch by nitric acid. Also called **glucaric acid.** [1790–1800]

sac·cha·ride (sak′ə rīd′, -ər id), *n.* *Chem.* **1.** an organic compound containing a sugar or sugars. **2.** a simple sugar; monosaccharide. **3.** an ester of sucrose. [1855–60; SACCHAR- + -IDE]

sac·cha·rif·er·ous (sak′ə rif′ər əs), *adj.* *Chem.* containing or yielding sugar. [1750–60; SACCHAR- + -I- + -FEROUS]

sac·char·i·fy (sə kar′ə fī′, sak′ər ə fī′), *v.t.,* **-fied, -fy·ing.** to convert (starch) into sugar. [1830–40; SACCHAR- + -IFY] —**sac·char·i·fi·ca·tion** (sə kar′ə fi kā′-shən), *n.* —**sac·char′i·fi′er,** *n.*

sac·cha·rim·e·ter (sak′ə rim′i tər), *n.* an optical instrument for determining the strength of sugar solutions by measuring the rotation of the plane of polarized light they produce. [1870–75; SACCHAR- + -I- + -METER]

sac·cha·rim·e·try (sak′ə rim′i trē), *n.* *Biochem.* the process of measuring the amount of sugar in a sample, as with a saccharimeter or by polarimetry. [1850–55; SACCHAR- + -I- + -METRY]

sac·cha·rin (sak′ər in), *n.* *Chem.* a white, crystalline, slightly water-soluble powder, $C_7H_5NO_3S$, produced synthetically, which in dilute solution is 500 times as sweet as sugar: its soluble sodium salt is used as a noncaloric sugar substitute. Also called **benzosulfimide, gluside.** [1875–80; SACCHAR- + -IN[2]]

sac·cha·rine (sak′ər in, -ə rēn′, -ə rīn′), *adj.* **1.** of the nature of or resembling that of sugar: *a powdery substance with a saccharine taste.* **2.** containing or yielding sugar. **3.** very sweet to the taste; sugary: *a saccharine dessert.* **4.** cloyingly agreeable or ingratiating: *a saccharine personality.* **5.** exaggeratedly sweet or sentimental: *a saccharine smile.* [1665–75; SACCHAR- + -INE[1]] —**sac′cha·rine·ly,** *adv.* —**sac·cha·rin·i·ty** (sak′ə rin′-i tē), *n.*

sac·cha·rize (sak′ə rīz′), *v.t.,* **-rized, -riz·ing.** **1.** to convert into sugar; saccharify. **2.** to convert (the starches in grain) to fermentable sugars during mashing. Also, *esp. Brit.,* **sac′cha·rise′.** [1755–65; SACCHAR- + -IZE] —**sac′cha·ri·za′tion,** *n.*

saccharo-, var. of **sacchar-** before a consonant: *saccharometer.*

sac·cha·ro·far·i·na·ceous (sak′ə rō far′ə nā′shəs), *adj.* pertaining to or consisting of sugar and meal. [1895–1900; SACCHARO- + FARINACEOUS]

sac·cha·roid (sak′ə roid′), *adj.* *Geol.* (of rock) having a granular texture like that of loaf sugar. Also, **sac′cha·roi′dal.** [1825–35; SACCHAR- + -OID]

sac′cha·ro·lac′tic ac′id (sak′ə rō lak′tik, sak′-), *Chem.* See **mucic acid.** [SACCHARO- + LACTIC ACID]

sac·cha·ro·lyt·ic (sak′ə rō lit′ik), *adj.* *Chem.* of or causing the hydrolysis of sugars. [1905–10; SACCHARO- + -LYTIC]

sac·cha·rom·e·ter (sak′ə rom′i tər), *n.* *Chem.* an instrument for measuring the amount of sugar in a solution, as by determining the specific gravity of the solution. [1775–85; SACCHARO- + -METER] —**sac·cha·ro·met·ric** (sak′ə rō me′trik), **sac′cha·ro·met′ri·cal,** *adj.* —**sac′cha·rom′e·try,** *n.*

sac·cha·rose (sak′ə rōs′), *n.* *Chem.* sucrose. [1875–80; SACCHAR- + -OSE[2]]

Sac·cid·a·nan·da (such′chid′ä nun′də), *n.* Sat-cit-ananda.

Sac·co (sak′ō; *It.* säk′kô), *n.* **Ni·co·la** (nē kô′lä), 1891–1927, Italian anarchist, in the U.S. after 1908: together with Bartolomeo Vanzetti, found guilty of robbery and murder 1921; executed 1927.

sac·cu·lar (sak′yə lər), *adj.* having the form of a sac. [1860–65; SACCUL(US) + -AR[1]]

sac·cu·late (sak′yə lāt′, -lit), *adj.* formed into or having a sac or saclike dilation. Also, **sac′cu·lat′ed.** [1865–70; SACCUL(US) + -ATE[1]] —**sac′cu·la′tion,** *n.*

sac·cule (sak′yōōl), *n.* **1.** *Anat.* the smaller of two sacs in the membranous labyrinth of the internal ear. Cf. **utricle** (def. 3). **2.** a little sac. [1830–40; < L *sacculus* SACCULUS]

sac·cu·lus (sak′yə ləs), *n., pl.* **-li** (-lī′). a saccule. [1615–25; < L, equiv. to *sacc(us)* SACK[1] + *-ulus* -ULE]

sa·cel·lum (sə kel′əm, -sel′-), *n., pl.* **-cel·la** (-kel′ə, -sel′ə). **1.** a small chapel, as a monument within a church. **2.** (in ancient Rome) a shrine open to the sky. [1800–10; < L: shrine, deriv. of *sacer* holy, SACRED; for formation see CASTELLUM]

sac·er·do·tal (sas′ər dōt′l), *adj.* of priests; priestly. [1350–1400; ME < L *sacerdōtālis*, equiv. to *sacerdōt-* (s. of *sacerdōs*) priest + *-ālis* -AL[1]] —**sac′er·do′tal·ly,** *adv.*

sac·er·do·tal·ism (sas′ər dōt′l iz′əm), *n.* **1.** the system, spirit, or methods of the priesthood. **2.** *Usually Disparaging.* priestcraft. [1840–50; SACERDOTAL + -ISM] —**sac′er·do′tal·ist,** *n.*

sac′ fun′gus, ascomycete. [1925–30; so called because its spores are formed in a sac]

sa·chem (sā′chəm), *n.* **1.** (among some North American Indians) **a.** the chief of a tribe. **b.** the chief of a confederation. **2.** a member of the governing body of the League of the Iroquois. **3.** one of the high officials in the Tammany Society. **4.** *Slang.* a political party leader. [1615–25, *Amer.*; < southeastern New England Algonquian (cf. Narragansett (E sp.) *sâchim, saunchum*, Massachusett *sontim*) < Proto-Algonquian **sa·kima·wa;* cf. SAGAMORE] —**sa′chem·dom,** *n.* —**sa·chem·ic** (sā-chem′ik, sā′chə mik), *adj.* —**sa′chem·ship′,** *n.*

Sa·cher-Ma·soch (zä′KHər mä′zōKH), **Le·o·pold von** (lā′ō pōlt′ fən), 1836–95, Austrian novelist.

Sa·cher torte (sä′kər tôrt′; *Ger.* zä′KHər tôR′tə), *pl.*

Sa•cher tortes, *Ger.* **Sa•cher tor•ten** (zä′KHər tôr′tn). a chocolate cake covered with apricot jam and chocolate icing, usually served with whipped cream. [1905–10; after the *Sacher* Hotel, in Vienna, Austria]

sa•chet (sa shā′ *or, esp. Brit.,* sash′ā), *n.* **1.** a small bag, case, or pad containing perfuming powder or the like, placed among handkerchiefs, lingerie, etc., to impart a pleasant scent. **2.** Also, **sachet′ pow′der.** the powder contained in such a case. [1475–85; < MF, equiv. to *sach-* (comb. form of *sac* SACK[1]) + *-et* -ET]

Sachs (zäks), *n.* **1. Hans** (häns), 1494–1576, German Meistersinger: author of stories, songs, and dramatic works. **2. Nelly (Leonie),** 1891–1970, German poet and playwright, in Sweden after 1940: Nobel prize 1966.

Sach•sen (zäk′sən), *n.* German name of **Saxony.**

Sach•sen-An•halt (zäk′sən än′hält), *n.* German name of **Saxony-Anhalt.**

sack[1] (sak), *n.* **1.** a large bag of strong, coarsely woven material, as for grain, potatoes, or coal. **2.** the amount a sack holds. **3.** a bag. **4.** *Slang.* dismissal or discharge, as from a job: *to get the sack.* **5.** *Slang.* bed: *in the sack.* **6.** Also, **sacque. a.** a loose-fitting dress, as a gown with a Watteau back, esp. one fashionable in the late 17th century and much of the 18th century. **b.** a loose-fitting coat, jacket, or cape. **7.** *Baseball.* a base. **8.** *South Midland U.S.* the udder of a cow. **9. hit the sack,** *Slang.* to go to bed: *He never hits the sack before midnight.* **10. hold the sack.** See **bag** (def. 18). —*v.t.* **11.** to put into a sack or sacks. **12.** *Football.* to tackle (the quarterback) behind the line of scrimmage before the quarterback is able to throw a pass. **13.** *Slang.* to dismiss or discharge, as from a job. **14. sack out,** *Slang.* to go to bed; fall asleep. [bef. 1000; 1940–45 for def. 5; ME *sak* (n.), *sakken* (v.), OE *sacc* (n.) < L *saccus* bag, sackcloth < Gk *sákkos* < Sem; cf. Heb *śaq*] —**sack′like′,** *adj.*
—**Regional Variation.** See **bag.**

sack[2] (sak), *v.t.* **1.** to pillage or loot after capture; plunder: *to sack a city.* —*n.* **2.** the plundering of a captured place; pillage: *the sack of Troy.* [1540–50; < MF phrase *mettre à sac* to put to pillage; *sac,* in this sense < It *sacco* looting, loot, shortened form of *saccomano* < MHG *sakman* pillager (conformed to *sacco* SACK[1])]
—**Syn. 1.** spoil, despoil. See **rob. 2.** looting; ruin.

sack[3] (sak), *n.* a strong light-colored wine formerly imported from Spain and the Canary Islands. [1525–35; < F (*vin*) *sec* dry (wine) < L *siccus* dry; cf. SEC[1]]

sack•but (sak′but′), *n.* **1.** a medieval form of the trombone. **2.** *Bible.* an ancient stringed musical instrument. Dan. 3. [1495–1505; < MF *saquebute,* earlier *saqueboute, saquebot(t)e* orig., a kind of hooked lance, appar. with *saque* (it) pulls (see SACCADE); identity of 2d element uncert.]

sack•cloth (sak′klôth′, -kloth′), *n.* **1.** sacking. **2.** coarse cloth worn as a sign of mourning or penitence. **3. in sackcloth and ashes,** in a state of repentance or sorrow; contrite: *She would be in sackcloth and ashes for days over every trifling error she made.* [1350–1400; ME; see SACK[1], CLOTH] —**sack′clothed′,** *adj.*

sack′ coat′, a short coat or jacket with a straight back and no seam at the waist. [1840–50] —**sack′-coat′ed,** *adj.*

sack′ dress′, a loose, unbelted dress that hangs straight from the shoulder to the hemline. [1955–60]

sack•er[1] (sak′ər), *n.* **1.** bagger (def. 1). **2.** *Baseball.* a baseman: *a slick-fielding third sacker.* [1900–05; SACK[1] + -ER[1]]

sack•er[2] (sak′ər), *n.* a person who sacks; plunderer; pillager. [1580–90; SACK[2] + -ER[1]]

sack•ful (sak′fo͝ol), *n., pl.* **-fuls.** the amount a sack will hold. [1475–85; SACK[1] + -FUL]
—**Usage.** See **-ful.**

sack•ing (sak′ing), *n.* stout, coarse woven material of hemp, jute, or the like, chiefly for sacks. Also called **sackcloth.** [1580–90; SACK[1] + -ING[1]]

sack′ race′, a race in which each contestant jumps ahead while his or her legs are confined in a sack. [1880–85] —**sack′ rac′er.** —**sack′ rac′ing.**

sack′ suit′, a man's suit that has a loose-fitting jacket. [1890–95, *Amer.*]

sack′ time′, *Slang.* time spent sleeping. [1940–45, *Amer.*]

Sack•ville (sak′vil), *n.* **Thomas, 1st Earl of Dorset,** 1536–1608, English statesman and poet.

Sack•ville-West (sak′vil west′), *n.* **Dame Victoria Mary** ("*Vita*"), 1892–1962, English poet and novelist (wife of Harold Nicolson).

Sa•co (sô′kō), *n.* a city in SW Maine. 12,921.

sacque (sak), *n.* sack[1] (def. 6).

sa•cral[1] (sā′krəl, sak′rəl), *adj.* of or pertaining to sacred rites or observances. [1880–85; < L *sacr(um)* sacred thing + -AL[1]]

sa•cral[2] (sā′krəl, sak′rəl), *adj.* of or pertaining to the sacrum. [1760–70; < NL *sacrālis;* see SACRUM, -AL[1]]

sa•cral•ize (sā′krə līz′, sak′rə-), *v.t.,* **-ized, -iz•ing.** to make sacred; imbue with sacred character, esp. through ritualized devotion: *a society that sacralized science.* Also, *esp. Brit.,* **sa′cral•ise′.** [1930–35; SACRAL[1] + -IZE] —**sa′cral•i•za′tion,** *n.*

sa′cral nerve′, *Anat.* any of the nerves arising in five pairs from the spinal cord in the sacrum. [1820–30]

sa′cral plex′us, a nerve network originating from the nerves of the sacral spine and innervating large areas of the lower trunk and legs, esp. via the sciatic nerves.

sac•ra•ment (sak′rə mənt), *n.* **1.** *Eccles.* a visible sign of an inward grace, esp. one of the solemn Christian rites considered to have been instituted by Jesus Christ to symbolize or confer grace: the sacraments of the Protestant churches are baptism and the Lord's Supper; the sacraments of the Roman Catholic and Greek Orthodox churches are baptism, confirmation, the Eucharist, matrimony, penance, holy orders, and extreme unction. **2.** (*often cap.*) Also called **Holy Sacrament.** the Eucharist or Lord's Supper. **3.** the consecrated elements of the Eucharist, esp. the bread. **4.** something regarded as possessing a sacred character or mysterious significance. **5.** a sign, token, or symbol. **6.** an oath; solemn pledge. [1150–1200; ME < ML *sacrāmentum* obligation, oath, LL: mystery, rite, equiv. to L *sacrā(re)* to devote + *-mentum* -MENT]

sac•ra•men•tal (sak′rə men′tl), *adj.* **1.** of, pertaining to, or of the nature of a sacrament, esp. the sacrament of the Eucharist. **2.** powerfully binding: *a sacramental obligation.* —*n.* **3.** *Rom. Cath. Ch.* an action, as the sign of the cross, a ceremony resembling a sacrament, or a sacred object, regarded as being instituted by the church rather than by Christ and serving as a means of receiving sanctifying grace. [1350–1400; ME < LL *sacrāmentālis.* See SACRAMENT, -AL[1]] —**sac′ra•men′tal•ly,** *adv.* —**sac′ra•men′tal•ness, sac′ra•men•tal′i•ty,** *n.*

sac•ra•men•tal•ism (sak′rə men′tl iz′əm), *n.* **1.** a belief in or emphasis on the importance and efficacy of the sacraments for achieving salvation and conferring grace. **2.** emphasis on the importance of sacramental objects and ritual actions. [1860–65; SACRAMENTAL + -ISM] —**sac′ra•men′tal•ist,** *n.*

sac′ramen′tal wine′, wine for use in a Eucharistic service. Also called **altar wine.**

Sac•ra•men•tar•i•an (sak′rə men târ′ē ən), *n.* **1.** a person who maintains that the Eucharistic elements have only symbolic significance and are not corporeal manifestations of Christ. **2.** (*l.c.*) a sacramentalist. —*adj.* **3.** of or pertaining to the Sacramentarians. **4.** (*l.c.*) of or pertaining to the sacraments. [1530–40; SACRAMENT + -ARIAN] —**Sac′ra•men•tar′i•an•ism,** *n.*

Sac•ra•men•to (sak′rə men′tō), *n.* **1.** a port in and the capital of California, in the central part, on the Sacramento River. 275,741. **2.** a river flowing S from N California to San Francisco Bay. 382 mi. (615 km) long.

Sac′ramen′to Moun′tains, a mountain range in S New Mexico and SW Texas: highest peak, Sierra Blanco, 12,003 ft. (3660 m).

Sac′ramen′to stur′geon. See **white sturgeon.**

sa•crar•i•um (sə krâr′ē əm), *n., pl.* **-crar•i•a** (-krâr′ē ə). **1.** *Rom. Cath. Ch.* a piscina. **2.** *Eccles.* the sanctuary or chancel. **3.** *Rom. Hist.* a shrine or sanctuary. [1700–10; < L, equiv. to *sacr-,* s. of *sacer* holy + *-ārium* -ARY] —**sa•crar′i•al,** *adj.*

Sa•cra Ro•ma•na Ro•ta (sä′krə rō mä′nə rō′tə), *Rom. Cath. Ch.* the official name of the Rota.

sa•cred (sā′krid), *adj.* **1.** devoted or dedicated to a deity or to some religious purpose; consecrated. **2.** entitled to veneration or religious respect by association with divinity or divine things; holy. **3.** pertaining to or connected with religion (opposed to *secular* or *profane*): *sacred music; sacred books.* **4.** reverently dedicated to some person, purpose, or object: *a morning hour sacred to study.* **5.** regarded with reverence: *the sacred memory of a dead hero.* **6.** secured against violation, infringement, etc., as by reverence or sense of right: *sacred rights.* **7.** properly immune from violence, interference, etc., as a person or office. [1275–1325; ME, orig. ptp. of *sacren* to consecrate < L *sacrāre* to devote, deriv. of *sacer* holy; see -ED[2]] —**sa′cred•ly,** *adv.* —**sa′cred•ness,** *n.*
—**Syn. 2.** venerable, divine. See **holy. 4.** consecrated. **5.** revered. **6.** sacrosanct. **7.** inviolate, inviolable.
—**Ant. 2.** blasphemous.

sa′cred baboon′. See **hamadryas baboon.** [1890–95]

sa′cred bamboo′, nandina. [1865–70]

Sa′cred Col′lege of Car′dinals, the official name of the **College of Cardinals.**

sa′cred cow′, an individual, organization, institution, etc., considered to be exempt from criticism or questioning. [1905–10; in reference to the traditional inviolability of the cow among Hindus]

Sa′cred Heart′, *Rom. Cath. Ch.* the physical heart of Jesus, to which special devotion is offered as a symbol of His love and redemptive sacrifice. [1755–65]

sa′cred i′bis, an African ibis, *Threskiornis aethiopica,* having a black, naked head and neck and white and black plumage, venerated by the ancient Egyptians. See illus. under **ibis.** [1830–40]

sa′cred lo′tus. See **Indian lotus.** [1865–70]

sa′cred mon′ster, a celebrity whose eccentricities or indiscretions are easily forgiven by admirers. [1980–85; trans. of F *monstre sacré*]

Sa′cred Nine′, *Class. Myth.* the Muses.

sa′cred or′der, *Rom. Cath. Ch.* See **major order.** [1720–30]

Sa′cred Ro′man Ro′ta, rota[1] (def. 3).

sa′cred thread′, *Hinduism.* a cord worn by Hindus of the three upper castes as a sign of being twice-born or initiated into the Vedas.

Sa′cred Writ′, Scripture.

sac•ri•fice (sak′rə fīs′), *n., v.,* **-ficed, -fic•ing.** —*n.* **1.** the offering of animal, plant, or human life or of some material possession to a deity, as in propitiation or homage. **2.** the person, animal, or thing so offered. **3.** the surrender or destruction of something prized or desirable for the sake of something considered as having a higher or more pressing claim. **4.** the thing so surrendered or devoted. **5.** a loss incurred in selling something below its value. **6.** Also called **sac′rifice bunt′, sac′rifice hit′.** *Baseball.* a bunt made when there are fewer than two players out, not resulting in a double play, that advances the base runner nearest home without an error being committed if there is an attempt to put the runner out, and that results in either the batter's being put out at first base, reaching first on an error made in the attempt for the put-out, or being safe because of an attempt to put out another runner. —*v.t.* **7.** to make a sacrifice or offering of. **8.** to surrender or give up, or permit injury or disadvantage to, for the sake of something else. **9.** to dispose of (goods, property, etc.) regardless of profit. **10.** *Baseball.* to cause the advance of (a base runner) by a sacrifice. —*v.i.* **11.** *Baseball.* to make a sacrifice: *He sacrificed with two on and none out.* **12.** to offer or make a sacrifice. [1225–75; (n.) ME < OF < L *sacrificium,* equiv. to *sacri-* (comb. form of *sacer* holy) + *-fic-,* comb. form of *facere* to make, DO[1] + *-ium* -IUM; (v.) ME *sacrifisen,* deriv. of the n.] —**sac′ri•fice′a•ble,** *adj.* —**sac′ri•fic′er,** *n.*
—**Syn. 8.** relinquish, forgo, renounce.

sac′rifice fly′, *Baseball.* a fly ball when there are fewer than two players out that enables a base runner, usually at third base, to score after the ball is caught. [1965–70]

sac•ri•fi•cial (sak′rə fish′əl), *adj.* pertaining to or concerned with sacrifice. [1600–10; < L *sacrifici(um)* SACRIFICE + -AL[1]] —**sac′ri•fi′cial•ly,** *adv.*

sac′rifi′cial an′ode, *Chem.* an anode that is attached to a metal object subject to electrolysis and is decomposed instead of the object. [1975–80]

sac•ri•lege (sac′rə lij), *n.* **1.** the violation or profanation of anything sacred or held sacred. **2.** an instance of this. **3.** the stealing of anything consecrated to the service of God. [1275–1325; ME < OF < L *sacrilegium,* equiv. to *sacri-* (comb. form of *sacrum* holy place) + *leg(ere)* to steal, lit., gather + *-ium* -IUM]

sac•ri•le•gious (sak′rə lij′əs, -lē′jəs), *adj.* **1.** pertaining to or involving sacrilege: *sacrilegious practices.* **2.** guilty of sacrilege: *a sacrilegious person.* [1400–50; late ME *sacrilegiose;* see SACRILEGE, -OUS] —**sac′ri•le′gious•ly,** *adv.* —**sac′ri•le′gious•ness,** *n.*
—**Pronunciation.** The almost universal pronunciation of SACRILEGIOUS as (sak′rə lij′əs) is the result of folk etymology—modifying the pronunciation of an unfamiliar word so that it conforms to a more familiar one—in this case *religious.* Etymologically, SACRILEGIOUS has no direct relationship to *religious.* The historical pronunciation (sak′rə lē′jəs) occurs in American English, though not in British English, and criticism of the newer pronunciation has almost disappeared.

sac•ris•tan (sak′ri stən), *n.* **1.** Also called **sacrist** (sak′rist, sā′krist). an official in charge of the sacred vessels, vestments, etc., of a church or a religious house. **2.** a sexton. [1325–75; ME < ML *sacristānus,* equiv. to *sacrist(a)* custodian of sacred objects + *-ānus* -AN]

sac•ris•ty (sak′ri stē), *n., pl.* **-ties.** an apartment in or a building connected with a church or a religious house, in which the sacred vessels, vestments, etc., are kept. [1400–50; late ME < ML *sacristia* vestry, equiv. to *sacrist(a)* (see SACRISTAN) + *-ia* -Y[3]]

sacro-, a combining form representing **sacrum** in compound words: *sacroiliac.*

sac•ro•il•i•ac (sak′rō il′ē ak′, sā′krō-), *Anat.* —*n.* **1.** the joint where the sacrum and ilium meet. —*adj.* **2.** of, pertaining to, or affecting this joint. [1825–35; SACRO- + ILIAC]

sac•ro•sanct (sak′rō sangkt′), *adj.* **1.** extremely sacred or inviolable: *a sacrosanct chamber in the temple.* **2.** not to be entered or trespassed upon: *She considered her home office sacrosanct.* **3.** above or beyond criticism, change, or interference: *a manuscript deemed sacrosanct.* [1595–1605; < L *sacrō sānctus* made holy by sacred rite. See SACRED, SAINT] —**sac′ro•sanc′ti•ty, sac′ro•sanct′ness,** *n.*

sac•rum (sak′rəm, sā′krəm), *n., pl.* **sac•ra** (sak′rə, sā′krə). *Anat.* a bone resulting from the fusion of two or more vertebrae between the lumbar and the coccygeal regions, in humans being composed usually of five fused vertebrae and forming the posterior wall of the pelvis. See diag. under **pelvis.** [1745–55; < LL (*os*) *sacrum* holy (bone), trans. of Gk *hieròn ostéon*]

sad (sad), *adj.,* **sad•der, sad•dest. 1.** affected by unhappiness or grief; sorrowful or mournful: *to feel sad because a close friend has moved away.* **2.** expressive of or characterized by sorrow: *sad looks; a sad song.* **3.** causing sorrow: *a sad disappointment; sad news.* **4.** (of color) somber, dark, or dull; drab. **5.** deplorably bad; sorry: *a sad attempt.* **6.** *Obs.* firm or steadfast. [bef. 1000; ME; OE *sæd* grave, heavy, weary, orig. sated, full; c. G *satt,* Goth *saths* full, satisfied; akin to L *satis* enough, *satur* sated, Gk *hádēn* enough. See SATIATE, SATURATE] —**sad′ly,** *adv.* —**sad′ness,** *n.*
—**Syn. 1.** unhappy, despondent, disconsolate, discouraged, gloomy, downcast, downhearted, depressed, dejected, melancholy. —**Ant. 1.** happy.

sād (säd), *n.* the 14th letter of the Arabic alphabet. [< Ar]

SAD, seasonal affective disorder.

sa•da•qat (sä′dä kät), *n. Islam.* zakat. [< Ar *ṣadaqah*]

Sa•dat (sə dät′, -dat′), *n.* **An•war el-** (än′wär el), 1918–81, Egyptian political leader: president 1970–81; Nobel peace prize 1978.

sad•den (sad′n), *v.t., v.i.* to make or become sad. [1590–1600; SAD + -EN[1]] —**sad′den•ing•ly,** *adv.*

Sad•dhar•ma-Pun•da•ri•ka (sud dur′mə po͝on dur′ē kə), *n. Buddhism.* a Mahayana sutra, forming with its references to Amida and the Bodhisattvas the basis for the doctrine that there is something of Buddha in everyone, so that salvation is universally available: a central text of Mahayana Buddhism. Also called **Lotus of the Good Law, Lotus of the True Law, Lotus Sutra.**

sad•dle (sad′l), *n., v.,* **-dled, -dling.** —*n.* **1.** a seat for a rider on the back of a horse or other animal. See illus. on next page. **2.** a similar seat on a bicycle, tractor, etc. **3.** a part of a harness laid across the back of an animal and girded under the belly, to which the terrets and check-

CONCISE PRONUNCIATION KEY: *act, cāpe, dâre, pärt; set, ēqual; if, īce; ox, ōver, ôrder, oil, bo͝ok, bo͞ot, out; up, ûrge; child; sing; shoe; thin, that;* zh as in *treasure.* ə = *a* as in *alone, e* as in *system, i* as in *easily, o* as in *gallop, u* as in *circus;* ə as in *fire* (fīər), *hour* (ouər). l and n can serve as syllabic consonants, as in *cradle* (krād′l), and *button* (but′n). See the full key inside the front cover.

hook are attached. See illus. under **harness.** **4.** something resembling a saddle in shape, position, or function. **5.** the part of the back of an animal where a saddle is placed. **6. a.** (of mutton, venison, lamb, etc.) a cut comprising both loins. **b.** this cut, trimmed and prepared for roasting. **7.** (of poultry) the posterior part of the back. **8.** a ridge connecting two higher elevations. **9.** the covering of a roof ridge. **10.** bolster (def. 7). **11.** a raised piece of flooring between the jambs of a doorway. **12.** an inverted bracket bearing on the axle of a railroad car wheel as a support for the car body. **13.** *Ordn.* the support for the trunnion on some gun carriages. **14.** *Mach.* a sliding part for spanning a space or other parts to support something else, as the cross slide and toolholder of a lathe. **15.** a strip of leather, often of a contrasting color, sewn on the vamp or instep of a shoe and extending to each side of the shank. **16.** See **saddle shoe.** **17.** *Ceram.* a bar of refractory clay, triangular in section, for supporting one side of an object being fired. **18.** (in a suspension bridge) a member at the top of a tower for supporting a cable. **19. in the saddle, a.** in a position to direct or command; in control. **b.** at work; on the job. —*v.t.* **20.** to put a saddle on: *to saddle a horse.* **21.** to load or charge, as with a burden: *He has saddled himself with a houseful of impecunious relatives.* **22.** to impose as a burden or responsibility. —*v.i.* **23.** to put a saddle on a horse (often fol. by *up*). **24.** to mount into the saddle (often fol. by *up*). [bef. 900; (n.) ME *sadel,* OE *sadol;* c. G *Sattel,* ON *sǫthull;* (v.) ME *sad(e)len,* OE *sadolian,* deriv. of the n.; akin to SIT[1]] **—sad′dle·less,** *adj.* **—sad′dle·like′,** *adj.*

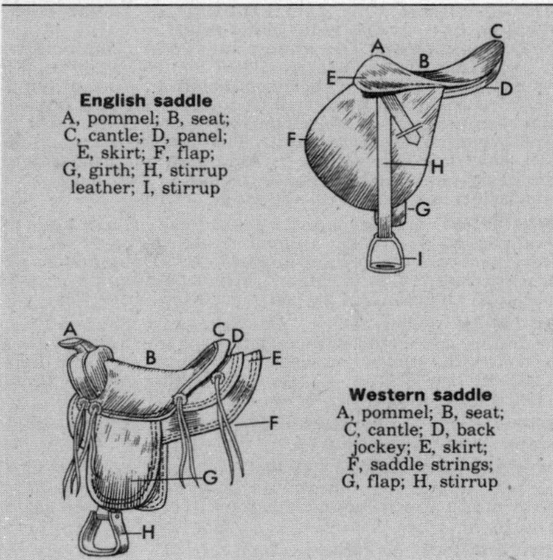

English saddle
A, pommel; B, seat; C, cantle; D, panel; E, skirt; F, flap; G, girth; H, stirrup leather; I, stirrup

Western saddle
A, pommel; B, seat; C, cantle; D, back jockey; E, skirt; F, saddle strings; G, flap; H, stirrup

sad·dle·back (sad′l bak′), *n.* any of various animals having markings on the back that resemble a saddle, as a male harp seal. [1535–45; SADDLE + BACK[1]]

sad·dle-backed (sad′l bakt′), *adj.* **1.** having the back or upper surface curved like a saddle. **2.** having a saddlelike marking on the back, as certain birds. [1535–45]

sad·dle·bag (sad′l bag′), *n.* **1.** a large bag or pouch, usually one of a pair, hung from a saddle, laid over the back of a horse behind the saddle, or mounted over the rear wheel of a bicycle or motorcycle. **2.** Often, **saddlebags.** excess fat around the hips and buttocks. [1765–75; SADDLE + BAG]

sad′dle blan′ket, a saddle-shaped pad, as of felt or sheepskin, placed beneath the saddle to prevent it from irritating the horse's skin. [1730–40, *Amer.*]

sad′dle block′ anesthe′sia, a form of spinal anesthesia that produces loss of sensation in the buttocks, perineum, and inner thighs. [1945–50; so called because the nerve block caused by the anesthesia affects areas that would be numbed by contact with a saddle]

sad·dle·bow (sad′l bō′), *n.* the arched front part of a saddle or saddletree. [bef. 900; ME, OE. See SADDLE, BOW[2]]

sad·dle·cloth (sad′l klôth′, -kloth′), *n., pl.* **-cloths** (-klôthz′, -klothz′, -klôths′, -kloths′). **1.** *Horse Racing.* a cloth placed over the saddle of a racehorse bearing the horse's number. **2.** See **saddle blanket.** [1475–85; SADDLE + CLOTH]

sad′dle horn′, horn (def. 19). [1855–60]

sad′dle horse′, **1.** a horse bred, trained, or used for riding. **2.** See **American saddle horse.** [1655–65]

sad′dle joint′, *Masonry.* (on a sill, coping, or the like) a vertical joint raised above the level of the washes on each side. [1870–75]

sad′dle leath′er, **1.** hide, as from a cow or bull, that undergoes vegetable tanning and is used for saddlery. **2.** leather that simulates the vegetable-tanned product and is used for a variety of goods, as handbags and jackets. [1825–35]

sad′dle ox′ford. See **saddle shoe.** [1945–50]

sad′dle point′, *Math.* a point at which a function of two variables has partial derivatives equal to zero but at which the function has neither a maximum nor a minimum value. [1920–25]

sad·dler (sad′lər), *n.* a person who makes, repairs, or sells saddlery. [1250–1300; ME *sadelere.* See SADDLE, -ER[1]]

sad·dler·y (sad′lə rē), *n., pl.* **-dler·ies.** **1.** saddles, harnesses, and other equipment for horses. **2.** the work, business, or shop of a saddler. [1400–50; late ME *sadelerie.* See SADDLER, -Y[3]]

sad′dle seat′, a chair seat having a double slope downward from a central ridge highest at the front. [1890–95]

sad′dle shoe′, an oxford with a saddle of contrasting color. Also called **saddle oxford, saddle.** [1940–45]

sad′dle soap′, a soap, usually consisting chiefly of Castile, used for cleaning and preserving saddles and other leather articles. [1885–90]

sad′dle sore′, **1.** an irritation or sore on a horse caused by the rubbing of a poorly adjusted saddle. **2.** an irritation or sore on a rider caused by a saddle. [1945–50]

sad·dle·sore (sad′l sôr′, -sōr′), *adj.* **1.** feeling sore or stiff from horseback riding. **2.** irritated or having sores produced by a saddle. [1905–10; SADDLE + SORE]

sad′dle stitch′, **1.** *Sewing.* **a.** an overcasting stitch, esp. one made with a strip of leather or a thick leatherlike cord. **b.** a spaced running stitch in contrasting or heavy thread, used mainly for decoration, usually along an edge. **2.** *Bookbinding.* a binding stitch made by inserting a staple through the center of folded sheets from the back and clinching in the fold. [1930–35]

sad·dle-stitch (sad′l stich′), *v.t.* to sew, bind, or decorate with a saddle stitch. [1930–35] **—sad′dle-stitch′·ing,** *n.*

sad·dle·tree (sad′l trē′), *n.* the frame of a saddle. [1375–1425; late ME *sadeltre.* See SADDLE, TREE]

Sad·du·cee (saj′ə sē′, sad′yə-), *n. Judaism.* a member of a Palestinian sect, consisting mainly of priests and aristocrats, that flourished from the 1st century B.C. to the 1st century A.D. and differed from the Pharisees chiefly in its literal interpretation of the Bible, rejection of oral laws and traditions, and denial of an afterlife and the coming of the Messiah. [bef. 1000; ME *sadducees* (pl.), OE *saddūcēas* < LL *saddūcaei* < Gk *saddoukaîoi* < Heb *ṣədhūqī* adherent of Zadok] **—Sad′du·ce′an,** *adj.* **—Sad′du·cee′ism,** *n.*

Sade (säd, sad; *Fr.* sad), *n.* **Do·na·tien Al·phonse Fran·çois** (dô na syaN′ al fôNs′ fräN swa′), **Comte de** (*Marquis de Sade*), 1740–1814, French soldier and novelist, notorious for his paraphilia.

sad-faced (sad′fāst′), *adj.* having a face characterized by or expressing sorrow. [1580–90]

sa·dha·ka (sä′də kə), *n. Hinduism.* a student of the Tantras. [< Skt *sādhaka;* see SADHU]

sa·dhe (sä′dē, -də, tsä′dē), *n.* **1.** the 18th letter of the Hebrew alphabet. **2.** the consonant sound represented by this letter. Also, **sadi, tsadi.** [1895–1900; < Heb *ṣādhē*]

sa·dhi·ka (sä′di kə), *n. Hinduism.* a female student of the Tantras. [< Skt *sādhikā,* fem. of *sādhaka* SADHAKA]

sa·dhu (sä′do͞o), *n. Hinduism.* an ascetic holy man, esp. a monk. [1835–45; < Skt *sādhu* good, a holy man]

sa·di (sä′dē, tsä′-), *n.* sadhe.

Sa·di (sä dē′), *n.* Saadi.

Sa·die (sā′dē), *n.* **1.** a female given name, form of **Sara** or **Sarah.** **2.** See **Sadie Hawkins.**

Sa′die Haw′kins, **1.** Also called **Sadie, Sa′dies.** a party, dance, or other social event, esp. one held annually among high school or college students, to which each girl escorts the boy of her choice, or invites him to escort her. **2.** a day **(Sa′die Haw′kins Day′)** or night, often in November, when such an event or events are held. [1939, *Amer.;* after the race held on Sadie Hawkins Day (in the cartoon strip *Li'l Abner* by Al Capp), in which single women pursued bachelors]

sad·i·ron (sad′ī′ərn), *n. Northern, North Midland, and Western U.S. Older Use.* a flatiron that is pointed at both ends and has a detachable handle. [1825–35; SAD (in obs. sense "heavy, solid") + IRON]

sa·dism (sā′diz əm, sad′iz-), *n.* **1.** *Psychiatry.* sexual gratification gained through causing pain or degradation to others. Cf. **masochism.** **2.** any enjoyment in being cruel. **3.** extreme cruelty. [1885–90; < F *sadisme;* see SADE, -ISM] **—sa′dist,** *n., adj.* **—sa·dis·tic** (sə dis′tik, sā-, sa-), *adj.* **—sa·dis′ti·cal·ly,** *adv.*

Sa·doc (sā′dok), *n. Douay Bible.* Zadok (def. 1).

sa·do·mas·o·chism (sā′dō mas′ə kiz′əm, -maz′-, sad′ō-), *n.* **1.** interaction, esp. sexual activity, in which one person enjoys inflicting physical or mental suffering on another person, who derives pleasure from experiencing pain. **2.** gratification, esp. sexual, gained through inflicting or receiving pain; sadism and masochism combined. *Abbr.:* S-M, S and M [1930–35; *sad-* (see SADISM) + -O- + MASOCHISM] **—sa′do·mas′o·chist,** *n., adj.* **—sa′do·mas′o·chis′tic,** *adj.*

Sa·do·vá (sä′dô vä′), *n.* a village in NE Bohemia, in the N Czech Republic: Prussian victory over Austrians 1866. German, **Sa·do·wa** (zä dō′vä).

sad′ sack′, *Slang.* a pathetically inept person, esp. a soldier, who continually blunders in spite of good intentions. [after the cartoon character created in 1942 by U.S. cartoonist George Baker (1915–75)] **—sad′-sack′,** *adj.*

sad′ tree′. See **night jasmine** (def. 1). [1865–70; trans. of NL *arbor tristis*]

S.A.E., **1.** self-addressed envelope. **2.** Society of Automotive Engineers. **3.** stamped addressed envelope. Also, **SAE; s.a.e.** (for defs. 1, 3).

Sae·hrim·nir (sâ rim′nir, sâr′im′-), *n. Scand. Myth.* a boar that is roasted and served up every night in Valhalla and grows whole by morning.

Sa′fa and Mar′wa (sä′fə), *Islam.* two hills that must be climbed as a part of the hajj, the pilgrimage to Mecca.

Sa·far (sə fär′), *n.* the second month of the Muslim calendar. Cf. **Muslim calendar.** [< Ar *Ṣafar*]

sa·fa·ri (sə fär′ē), *n., pl.* **-ris,** *v.* **-ried, -ri·ing.** —*n.* **1.** a journey or expedition, for hunting, exploration, or investigation, esp. in eastern Africa. **2.** the hunters, guides, vehicles, equipment, etc., forming such an expedition. **3.** any long or adventurous journey or expedition. —*v.i.* **4.** to go on a safari. [1885–90; < Swahili < Ar *safar* journey]

safa′ri jack′et. See **bush jacket.** [1950–55]

safa′ri park′, a parklike zoo in which wild animals are allowed to roam free in an environment designed to resemble their natural habitat and are observed by visitors riding through the park in cars or buses; animal park. [1970–75]

safa′ri shirt′, a shirt resembling a bush jacket. [1965–70]

safa′ri suit′, a suit consisting of a bush jacket and matching trousers. [1965–70]

Sa·fa·vid (sä fä′wēd), *n.* a member of a dynasty that ruled in Persia from c1500 to 1736. Also, **Sa·fa·wid** (sä-fä′wēd). [1910–15; < Ar *ṣafawī,* adj. deriv. of *Ṣafī al-Dīn Isḥāq,* ancestor of royal house + -ID[1]]

safe (sāf), *adj.,* **saf·er, saf·est,** *n.* —*adj.* **1.** secure from liability to harm, injury, danger, or risk: *a safe place.* **2.** free from hurt, injury, danger, or risk: *to arrive safe and sound.* **3.** involving little or no risk of mishap, error, etc.: *a safe estimate.* **4.** dependable or trustworthy: *a safe guide.* **5.** careful to avoid danger or controversy: *a safe player; a safe play.* **6.** denied the chance to do harm; in secure custody: *a criminal safe in jail.* **7.** *Baseball.* **a.** reaching base without being put out: *safe on the throw to first base.* **b.** making it possible to reach a base: *a safe slide.* —*n.* **8.** a steel or iron box or repository for money, jewels, papers, etc. **9.** any receptacle or structure for the storage or preservation of articles: *a meat safe.* **10.** (in plumbing) **a.** a pan for catching leakage. **b.** template (def. 7). **11.** *Slang.* a condom. [1250–1300; (adj.) ME *sauf, saf* < AF *saf,* OF *sauf* < L *salvus* intact, whole; (n.) late ME *save,* orig. deriv. of SAVE[1], assimilated to the adj.; cf. SALVATION] **—safe′ly,** *adv.* **—safe′ness,** *n.*
—Syn. **1.** protected, sound, guarded. SAFE, SECURE may both imply that something can be regarded as free from danger. These words are frequently interchangeable. SAFE, however, is applied rather to a person or thing that is out of or has passed beyond the reach of danger: *The ship is safe in port.* SECURE is applied to that about which there is no need to fear or worry: *to feel secure about the future; The foundation of the house does not seem very secure.* **4.** sure, reliable. **5.** wary, careful. **8.** strongbox, coffer, chest, safe-deposit box.

safe-con·duct (sāf′kon′dukt), *n.* **1.** a document authorizing safe passage through a region, esp. in time of war. **2.** this privilege. **3.** the act of conducting in safety. [1250–1300; ME *sauf condut* < MF *sauf-conduit*]

safe·crack·er (sāf′krak′ər), *n.* a person who breaks open safes to rob them. [1930–35, *Amer.;* SAFE + CRACKER] **—safe′crack′ing,** *n.*

safe-de·pos·it (sāf′di poz′it), *adj.* providing safe-keeping for valuables: *a safe-deposit vault.* Also, **safety-deposit.** [1775–85, *Amer.*]

safe′-deposit box′, a lockable metal box or drawer, esp. in a bank vault, used for safely storing valuable papers, jewelry, etc. Also, **safety-deposit box.** [1880–85, *Amer.*]

safe·guard (sāf′gärd′), *n.* **1.** something that serves as a protection or defense or that ensures safety. **2.** a permit for safe passage. **3.** a guard or convoy. **4.** a mechanical device for ensuring safety. —*v.t.* **5.** to guard; protect; secure. [1325–75; ME *savegarde* (n.) safe conduct < MF *salvegarde, sauvegarde.* See SAFE, GUARD]
—Syn. **5.** defend, shield.

safe′ har′bor, **1.** a harbor considered safe for a ship, as in wartime or during a storm at sea. **2.** any place or situation that offers refuge or protection.

safe′ house′, a dwelling or building whose conventional appearance makes it a safe or inconspicuous place for hiding, taking refuge, or carrying on clandestine activities. [1960–65]

safe·keep·ing (sāf′kē′ping), *n.* the act of keeping safe or the state of being kept safe; protection; care; custody. [1400–50; late ME *safe kepyng.* See SAFE, KEEPING]

safe·light (sāf′līt′), *n. Photog.* a darkroom light with a filter that transmits only those rays of the spectrum to which films, printing paper, etc., are not sensitive. [1900–05; SAFE + LIGHT[1]]

safe′ pe′riod, an interval of the menstrual cycle when fertilization is considered to be least likely, usually a number of days prior and subsequent to the onset of menstruation. [1915–20]

safe′ sex′, sexual activities in which precautions have been taken, as by the use of a condom, to minimize the chances of spreading or contracting a sexually transmitted disease.

safe·ty (sāf′tē), *n., pl.* **-ties.** **1.** the state of being safe; freedom from the occurrence or risk of injury, danger, or loss. **2.** the quality of averting or not causing injury, danger, or loss. **3.** a contrivance or device to prevent injury or avert danger. **4.** Also called **lock, safety catch, safety lock.** a locking or cutoff device that prevents a gun from being fired accidentally. **5.** the action of keeping safe. **6.** *Football.* **a.** an act or play in which a player on the offensive team is tackled in his own end zone or downs the ball there, or in which the ball goes out of bounds on a fumble, having last been in bounds in or over the end zone and having last been in the possession of an offensive player. Cf. **touchback.** **b.** an award of two points to the opposing team on this play. **c.** Also called **safety man.** a player on defense who lines up farthest behind the line of scrimmage. **7.** *Baseball.* a base hit, esp. a one-base hit. **8.** *Slang.* a condom. **9.** *Obs.* close confinement or custody. [1250–1300; ME *sauvete* < MF. See SAFE, -TY[2]]

safe′ty belt′, 1. See **seat belt.** 2. a belt or strap worn as a safety precaution by a person working at a great height: *The safety belt worn by a window washer is usually secured to each side of the window frame.* 3. See **life belt.** [1855–60]

safe′ty car′, *Naut.* See **life car.** [1830–40]

safe′ty catch′, 1. a device used in mechanisms, as for elevators, to prevent falling in the event of mechanical failure. 2. safety (def. 4). [1875–80]

safe′ty cur′tain, a sheet of asbestos or other fireproof material that can be lowered just inside the proscenium arch in case of fire, sealing off the backstage area from the auditorium. Also called **fire curtain.** [1905–10]

safe·ty-de·pos·it (sāf′tē di poz′it), *adj.* safe-deposit. [1890–95]

safe′ty-deposit box′. See **safe-deposit box.** [1925–30]

safe′ty fac′tor. See **factor of safety.**

safe′ty film′, *Photog.* a film having a nonflammable base of triacetate cellulose. [1925–30]

safe′ty fuze′, a long tube attached to a detonator or percussion cap and filled with a powder that burns slowly when ignited. [1830–40]

safe′ty glass′, a pane made by joining two plates or panes of glass with a layer of usually transparent plastic or artificial resin between them that retains the fragments if the glass is broken. [1920–25]

safe′ty hook′, a hook that can be transformed into an eye by locking a hinged piece in place. [1870–75]

safe′ty is′land, an area provided for the safety of pedestrians from vehicular traffic, as between lanes on a busy street or highway. [1930–35]

Safe′ty Is′lands, a group of three islands in the Caribbean, off the coast of French Guiana, belonging to France. French, **Îles du Salut.**

safe′ty lamp′, a miner's lamp in which the flame is protected by wire gauze to prevent the immediate ignition of explosive gases. [1810–20]

safe′ty lin′tel, an auxiliary lintel concealed behind a visible lintel, arch, etc. [1840–50]

safe′ty lock′, 1. a lock designed to prevent picking. 2. safety (def. 4). [1875–80]

safe′ty man′, *Football.* safety (def. 6c). Also, **safe′·ty·man′.** [1930–35]

safe′ty match′, a match designed to ignite only when rubbed on a specially prepared surface. [1860–65]

safe′ty net′, 1. a large net rigged between a person, as a trapeze performer, and the ground as protection in a fall. 2. something that provides a margin of protection or security: *the safety net of federal credit for financial institutions.* [1945–50] **—safe′ty-net′,** *adj.*

safe′ty pin′, a pin bent back on itself to form a spring, with a guard to cover the point. [1855–60]

safe·ty-pin (sāf′tē pin′), *v.t.*, **-pinned, -pin·ning.** to secure or affix with a safety pin: *to safety-pin a child's mittens to his coat sleeve.* [1915–20]

safe′ty ra′zor, a razor with a guard to prevent the blade from cutting the skin. [1875–80, *Amer.*]

safe′ty squeeze′. See **squeeze play** (def. 1b). Also called **safe′ty squeeze′ play′.**

safe′ty valve′, 1. a device that, when actuated by a gas or vapor pressure above a predetermined level, opens and allows the gas or vapor to escape until its pressure is reduced to a pressure equal to or below that of the predetermined level. Cf. **relief valve.** 2. a harmless outlet for emotion, tension, etc. [1805–15]

saf·fi·an (saf′ē ən), *n.* a leather made of goatskin or sheepskin, usually dyed in bright colors. [1585–95; < Russ *saf′yán* < Turkic (cf. Turk *sahtiyan*) < Pers *sekhtiyān,* akin to *sekht* hard, firm]

saf·flow·er (saf′lou′ər), *n.* 1. a thistlelike composite plant, *Carthamus tinctorius,* native to the Old World, having finely toothed leaves and large, orange-red flower heads. 2. its dried florets, used medicinally or as a red dyestuff. [1575–85; < D *saffloer* < MF *safleur,* alter. (assimilated to *safran* SAFFRON and *fleur* FLOWER) of It *asfori* < Ar *aṣfar* yellow]

saf′flower oil′, an oil expressed or extracted from safflower seeds, used in cooking, as a salad oil, and as a vehicle for medicines, paints, varnishes, etc. [1855–60]

saf·fron (saf′rən), *n.* 1. Also called **vegetable gold.** a crocus, *Crocus sativus,* having showy purple flowers. 2. an orange-colored condiment consisting of its dried stigmas, used to color and flavor foods. 3. Also, **saf′fron yel′low.** yellow-orange. [1150–1200; ME *saffran, saffron* OF *safran* < ML *saffrānum* < Ar *za′farān*]

Sa·fi (saf′ē), *n.* a seaport in W central Morocco, on the Atlantic Ocean coast. 129,100. Also, **Saf′fi.**

Sa·fid Rud (sa fēd′ rōōd′), a river flowing from NW Iran into the Caspian Sea. 450 mi. (725 km) long.

S. Afr., 1. South Africa. 2. South African.

saf·ra·nine (saf′rə nēn′, -nin), *n. Chem.* 1. any of a class of chiefly red organic dyes, phenazine derivatives, used for dyeing wool, silk, etc. 2. Also called **phenosafranine.** a purplish-red, water-soluble dye, $C_{18}H_{14}N_4$, used for textiles and as a stain in microscopy. Also, **saf·ra·nin** (saf′rə nin). [1865–70; < F or G *safran* SAFFRON + *-ine* -INE[2]]

S. Afr. D., South African Dutch. Also, **SAfrD**

saf·role (saf′rōl), *n. Chem.* a colorless or faintly yellow liquid, $C_{10}H_{10}O_2$, obtained from sassafras oil or the like: used chiefly in perfumery, for flavoring, and in the manufacture of soaps. Also, **saf·rol** (saf′rôl, -rōl). [1865–70; (SAS)SAFR(AS) + -OLE]

sag (sag), *v.*, **sagged, sag·ging,** *n.* —*v.i.* 1. to sink or bend downward by weight or pressure, esp. in the middle: *The roof sags.* 2. to hang down unevenly; droop: *Her skirt was sagging.* 3. to droop; hang loosely: *His shoulders sagged.* 4. to yield through weakness, lack of effort, or the like: *Our spirits began to sag.* 5. to decline, as in price: *The stock market sagged today.* 6. *Naut.* **a.** (of a hull) to droop at the center or have excessive sheer because of structural weakness. Cf. **hog** (def. 16). **b.** to be driven to leeward; to make too much leeway. —*v.t.* 7. to cause to sag. —*n.* 8. an act or instance of sagging. 9. the degree of sagging. 10. a place where anything sags; depression. 11. a moderate decline in prices. 12. *Naut.* **a.** deflection downward of a hull amidships, due to structural weakness. **b.** leeway (def. 3). [1375–1425; late ME *saggen* (v.), prob. < Scand; cf. Norw *sagga* to move slowly (akin to LG *sacken* to sink, Norw, Dan *sakke,* Sw *sacka,* Icel *sakka* to slow up, fall behind)]
—Syn. 4. weaken, flag, tire, weary.

SAG (sag), *n.* See **Screen Actors Guild.**

sa·ga (sä′gə), *n.* 1. a medieval Icelandic or Norse prose narrative of achievements and events in the history of a personage, family, etc. 2. any narrative or legend of heroic exploits. 3. Also called **sa′ga nov′el.** a form of the novel in which the members or generations of a family or social group are chronicled in a long and leisurely narrative. [1700–10; < ON; c. SAW[3]]
—Syn. 2. epic, tale, history.

sa·ga·cious (sə gā′shəs), *adj.* 1. having or showing acute mental discernment and keen practical sense; shrewd: *a sagacious lawyer.* 2. *Obs.* keen of scent. [1600–10; SAGACI(TY) + -OUS] **—sa·ga′cious·ly,** *adv.* **—sa·ga′cious·ness,** *n.*
—Syn. 1. wise, sage, discerning, clever, intelligent, judicious, acute, sharp, keen, perspicacious. **—Ant.** 1. unwise.

sa·gac·i·ty (sə gas′i tē), *n.* acuteness of mental discernment and soundness of judgment. [1540–50; < L *sagācitās* wisdom, equiv. to *sagāci-* (s. of *sagāx*) wise (akin to SEEK) + *-tās* -TY[2]]

Sa·ga·mi·ha·ra (sä gä′mē hä′RA) *n.* a city on E central Honshu, in Japan, SW of Tokyo. 439,257.

sag·a·more (sag′ə môr′, -mōr′), *n.* (among the American Indians of New England) a chief or leader. [1605–15, *Amer.*; < Eastern Abenaki *sàkəma* < Proto-Algonquian **sa·kima·wa;* cf. SACHEM]

Sa·gan (sā′gən *for 1;* SA gäN′ *for 2*), *n.* 1. **Carl (Edward),** born 1934, U.S. astronomer and writer. 2. **Fran·çoise** (fräN swaz′), (*Françoise Quoirez*), born 1935, French novelist.

sage[1] (sāj), *n., adj.*, **sag·er, sag·est.** —*n.* 1. a profoundly wise person; a person famed for wisdom. 2. someone venerated for the possession of wisdom, judgment, and experience. —*adj.* 3. wise, judicious, or prudent: *sage advice.* [1250–1300; ME (n. and adj.) < OF < LL *sapidus* wise, tasteful (L: tasty), equiv. to *sap(ere)* to know, be wise, orig. to taste (see SAPIENT) + *-idus* -ID[4]] **—sage′ly,** *adv.* **—sage′ness,** *n.*
—Syn. 1. philosopher. 3. sagacious. **—Ant.** 1. fool.

sage[2] (sāj), *n.* 1. any plant or shrub belonging to the genus *Salvia,* of the mint family. 2. an herb, *Salvia officinalis,* whose grayish-green leaves are used in medicine and for seasoning in cookery. 3. the leaves themselves. 4. sagebrush. [1275–1325; ME *sa(u)ge* < MF *sau(l)ge* < L *salvia,* deriv. of *salvus* SAFE (so named from its supposed healing powers)]

Sage (sāj), *n.* **Russell,** 1816–1906, U.S. financier.

sage·brush (sāj′brush′), *n.* any of several sagelike, bushy composite plants of the genus *Artemisia,* esp. *A. tridentata,* having silvery, wedge-shaped leaves, with three teeth at the tip, common on the dry plains of the western U.S. [1825–35, *Amer.*; SAGE[2] + BRUSH[2]]

sage′ cock′, the male sage grouse. [1830–40, *Amer.*]

sage′ green′, grayish to yellowish green. [1800–10] **—sage′-green′,** *adj.*

sage′ grouse′, a large grouse, *Centrocercus urophasianus,* of the sagebrush regions of western North America, having plumage of gray, buff, and black. [1870–75]

sage′ hen′, the sage grouse, esp. the female. [1835–45, *Amer.*]

sag·e·nite (saj′ə nīt′), *n.* a variety of rutile occurring as needlelike crystals embedded in quartz. Cf. **Venus hairstone.** [1795–1805; < F *sagénite* < Gk *sagḗn(ē)* net (cf. SEINE) + F *-ite* -ITE[1]]

sage′ spar′row, a small gray finch, *Amphispiza belli,* of dry, brushy areas of western North America. [1880–85, *Amer.*]

sage′ thrash′er, a grayish-brown thrasher, *Oreoscoptes montanus,* of sagebrush regions of the western U.S. [1880–85]

sag·ger (sag′ər), *n.* 1. a box or case made of refractory baked clay in which the finer ceramic wares are enclosed and protected while baking. 2. a hard unlayered clay underlying many coal beds. —*v.t.* 3. to place in or on a sagger. Also, **sag′gar, seggar.** [1680–90; perh. var. of SAFEGUARD]

sag·gy (sag′ē), *adj.*, **-gi·er, -gi·est.** sagging or tending to sag: *a saggy roof.* [1850–55; SAG + -Y[1]] **—sag′gi·ness,** *n.*

Sag′ Har′bor, a resort town on E Long Island in SE New York. 2683.

Sag·i·naw (sag′ə nô′), *n.* a port in E Michigan, on the Saginaw River. 77,508.

Sag′inaw Bay′, *n.* an arm of Lake Huron, off the E coast of Michigan. 60 mi. (97 km) long.

Sa·git·ta (sə jit′ə), *n., gen.* **-git·tae** (-jit′ē). *Astron.* the Arrow, a northern constellation between Aquila and Cygnus. [1695–1705; < L: arrow]

sag·it·tal (saj′i tl), *adj.* 1. *Anat.* **a.** of or pertaining to the suture between the parietal bones at the roof of the skull or to a venous canal within the skull and parallel to this suture. **b.** (in direction or location) from front to back in the median plane or in a plane parallel to the median. 2. pertaining to or resembling an arrow or arrowhead. [1535–45; < NL *sagittālis.* See SAGITTA, -AL[1]] **—sag′it·tal·ly,** *adv.*

Sag·it·ta·ri·an (saj′i târ′ē ən), *n. Astrol.* a person born under Sagittarius, the ninth sign of the zodiac; a Sagittarius. [1910–15; SAGITTARI(US) + -AN]

Sag·it·tar·i·us (saj′i târ′ē əs), *n., gen.* **-tar·i·i** (-târ′ē ī′) for 1. 1. *Astron.* the Archer, a zodiacal constellation between Scorpius and Capricorn. 2. *Astrol.* **a.** the ninth sign of the zodiac: the mutable fire sign. See illus. under **zodiac. b.** a person born under this sign, usually between November 22nd and December 21st; a Sagittarian. [1350–1400; ME < L *sagittārius* archer, equiv. to *sagitt(a)* arrow + *-ārius* -ARY]

sag·it·tar·y (saj′i ter′ē), *n., pl.* **-tar·ies.** a centaur with a bow, as Chiron. [1425–75; late ME < L: see SAGITTARIUS]

sag·it·tate (saj′i tāt′), *adj.* shaped like an arrowhead. Also, **sa·git·ti·form** (sə jit′ə fôrm′, saj′i tə-). [1750–60; < NL *sagittātus.* See SAGITTA, -ATE[1]]

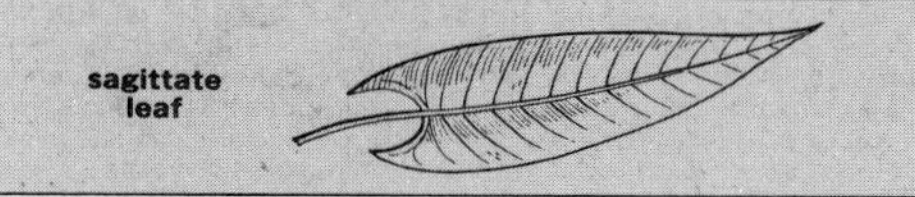
sagittate leaf

sa·go (sā′gō), *n.* a starchy foodstuff derived from the soft interior of the trunk of various palms and cycads, used in making puddings. [1545–55; earlier *sagu* < Malay]

sa′go palm′, 1. any of several tropical Old World palms, as of the genera *Metroxylon* and *Caryota,* that yield sago. 2. a cycad, *Cycas revoluta,* of Japan, having a crown of glossy, fernlike leaves, grown as an ornamental. [1760–70]

sag′ rod′, (in a roof) a rod for preventing the sagging of an open-web steel joist that is used as a purlin with its depth at right angles to a roof slope.

Sa·guache (sə wach′), *n.* Sawatch.

sa·gua·ro (sə gwär′ō, -wär′ō), *n., pl.* **-ros.** a tall, horizontally branched cactus, *Carnegiea* (or *Cereus*) *gigantea,* of Arizona and neighboring regions, yielding a useful wood and bearing an edible fruit: still locally common, though some populations have been reduced. See illus. under **cactus.** [1855–60, *Amer.*; < MexSp *saguaro, sahuaro,* said to be < Opata (now extinct Uto-Aztecan language of Sonora)]

Sag·ue·nay (sag′ə nā′), *n.* a river in SE Canada, in Quebec, flowing SE from Lake St. John to the St. Lawrence. 125 mi. (200 km) long.

Sa·gui·a el Ham·ra (sä′gē ə el ham′rə; *Sp.* sä′gyä el äm′RÄ), the N part of Western Sahara.

Sa·gun·to (sə gōōn′tō; *Sp.* sä gōōn′tô), *n.* a city in E Spain, N of Valencia: besieged by Hannibal 219–218 B.C. 47,026. Ancient, **Sa·gun·tum** (sə gun′təm).

sag′ wag′on, a support vehicle accompanying a bicycle touring group that carries spare parts, luggage, etc., and sometimes also transports bicycles and cyclists. [1960–65]

Sa·hap·tin (sä hap′tən), *n., pl.* **-tins,** (*esp. collectively*) **-tin** for 1, *adj.* —*n.* 1. a member of an American Indian people of Oregon, Washington, and Idaho. 2. a language used by several American Indian tribes, including the Nez Percés, of the Columbia River basin. —*adj.* 3. of or pertaining to the Sahaptins or to their languages. Also, **Shahaptian.** [< Southern Interior Salish *sʿaptnx* Nez Percé, Sahaptin]

Sa·har·a (sə har′ə, -hâr′ə, -här′ə), *n.* 1. a desert in N Africa, extending from the Atlantic to the Nile valley. ab. 3,500,000 sq. mi. (9,065,000 sq. km). 2. any arid waste. **—Sa·har′an, Sa·har′i·an,** *adj.*

Sa·ha·ran·pur (sə här′ən pŏŏr′), *n.* a city in NW Uttar Pradesh, in N India. 225,698.

Sa·hel (sə häl′, -hēl′), *n.* the arid area on the S flank of the Sahara desert that stretches across six countries from Senegal to Chad. **—Sa·hel′i·an,** *adj., n.*

sa·hib (sä′ib, -ēb), *n.* 1. (in India) sir; master: a term of respect used, esp. during the colonial period, when addressing or referring to a European. 2. (*cap.*) sing. of **Ashab.** [1690–1700; < Urdu < Ar *ṣāḥib* master, lit., friend]

saice (sīs), *n.* syce.

said[1] (sed), *v.* 1. pt. and pp. of **say.** —*adj.* 2. *Chiefly Law.* named or mentioned before; aforesaid; aforementioned: *said witness; said sum.*

sa·id[2] (sä′id), *n. Islam.* sayyid.

Sa·i·da (sä′ē dä′), *n.* a seaport in SW Lebanon: the site of ancient Sidon. 24,740.

sai·ga (sī′gə), *n.* a goatlike antelope, *Saiga tatarica,* of western Asia and eastern Russia, having a greatly enlarged muzzle. [1795–1805; (< NL) < Russ *saĭgá(k)* < Turkic; cf. Chagatai *sayğak*]

saiga, *Saiga tatarica,* 2½ ft. (0.8 m) high at shoulder; horns 9 in. (23 cm); length 4½ ft. (1.4 m)

CONCISE PRONUNCIATION KEY: *act, cāpe, dâre, pärt; set, ēqual; if, īce; ox, ōver, ôrder, oil, bŏŏk, bōōt, out; up, ûrge; child; sing; shoe; thin, that;* zh *as in treasure.* ə = *a* as in *alone, e* as in *system, i* as in *easily, o* as in *gallop, u* as in *circus;* ° as in *fire* (fī°r), *hour* (ou°r). l and n can serve as syllabic consonants, as in *cradle* (krād′l), and *button* (but′n). See the full key inside the front cover.

Sai·gon (sī gon′), *n.* former name of **Ho Chi Minh City:** capital of former South Vietnam 1954–76.

Sai′gon cin′namon. See under **cinnamon** (def. 1).

sail (sāl), *n.* **1.** an area of canvas or other fabric extended to the wind in such a way as to transmit the force of the wind to an assemblage of spars and rigging mounted firmly on a hull, raft, iceboat, etc., so as to drive it along. **2.** some similar piece or apparatus, as the part of an arm that catches the wind on a windmill. **3.** a voyage or excursion, esp. in a sailing vessel: *They went for a sail around the island.* **4.** a sailing vessel or ship. **5.** sailing vessels collectively: *The fleet numbered 30 sail.* **6.** sails for a vessel or vessels collectively. **7.** (*cap.*) *Astron.* the constellation Vela. **8. in sail,** with the sails set. **9. make sail,** *Naut.* **a.** to set the sail or sails of a boat or increase the amount of sail already set. **b.** to set out on a voyage: *Make sail for the Leeward Islands.* **10. set sail,** to start a sea voyage: *We set sail at midnight for Nantucket.* **11. trim one's sails,** *Informal.* to cut expenses; economize: *We're going to have to trim our sails if we stay in business.* **12. under sail,** with sails set; in motion; sailing: *It was good to be under sail in the brisk wind and under the warm sun.* —*v.i.* **13.** to move along or travel over water: *steamships sailing to Lisbon.* **14.** to manage a sailboat, esp. for sport. **15.** to begin a journey by water: *We are sailing at dawn.* **16.** to move along in a manner suggestive of a sailing vessel: *caravans sailing along.* **17.** to move along in a stately, effortless way: *to sail into a room.* —*v.t.* **18.** to sail upon, over, or through: *to sail the seven seas.* **19.** to navigate (a vessel). **20. sail in** or **into,** *Informal.* **a.** to go vigorously into action; begin to act; attack. **b.** to attack verbally: *He would sail into his staff when work was going badly.* [bef. 900; (n.) ME *sail(e), seille,* OE *segl;* c. G *Segel,* ON *segl;* (v.) ME *seillen, saylen,* OE *siglan, seglian;* c. D *zeilen,* ON *sigla*] —**sail′a·ble,** *adj.* —**sail′less,** *adj.*

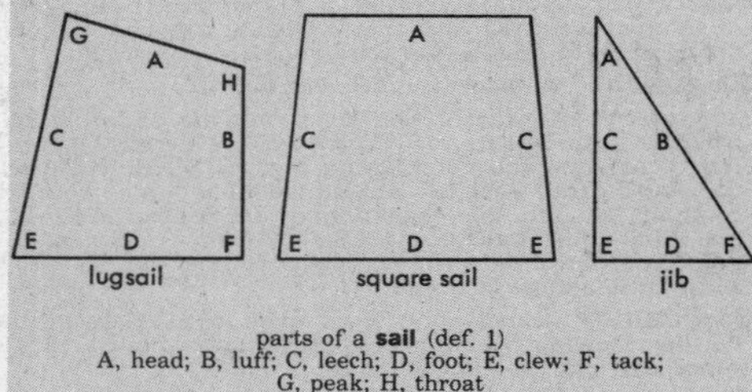

parts of a **sail** (def. 1)
A, head; B, luff; C, leech; D, foot; E, clew; F, tack; G, peak; H, throat

sail·board (sāl′bôrd′, -bōrd′), *n.* **1.** a long board, usually of Plexiglas, used for windsurfing, having a mount for a sail, a daggerboard, and a small skeg. **2.** a small, flat, single-masted sailboat, usually having no cockpit. [1960–65, *Amer.*; SAIL + BOARD]

sail·board·ing (sāl′bôr′ding, -bōr′-), *n.* windsurfing. [1975–80; SAILBOARD + -ING[1]] —**sail′board′er,** *n.*

sail·boat (sāl′bōt′), *n.* a boat having sails as its principal means of propulsion. [1790–1800; SAIL + BOAT] —**sail′boat′er,** *n.* —**sail′boat′ing,** *n.*

sail·cloth (sāl′klôth′, -kloth′), *n.* **1.** any of various fabrics, as of cotton, nylon, or Dacron, for boat sails or tents. **2.** a lightweight canvas or canvaslike fabric used esp. for clothing and curtains. [1175–1225; ME *saylclath;* see SAIL, CLOTH]

sail·er (sā′lər), *n.* **1.** a vessel propelled by a sail or sails. **2.** a vessel with reference to its powers or manner of sailing: *The schooner was judged a good sailer.* [1350–1400; ME; see SAIL, -ER[1]]

Sai·ler (sī′lər; *Ger.* zī′lər), *n.* **An·ton** (än′tōn), (*"Toni"*), born 1935, Austrian skier.

sail·fish (sāl′fish′), *n., pl.* (*esp. collectively*) **-fish,** (*esp. referring to two or more kinds or species*) **-fish·es. 1.** a large tropical and subtropical marine fish, *Istiophorus platypterus,* of the family Istiophoridae, distinguished by a long, high dorsal fin, long pelvic fins, and a double keel on each side of the tail. **2.** any of several related fishes having a high dorsal fin. [1585–95; SAIL + FISH]

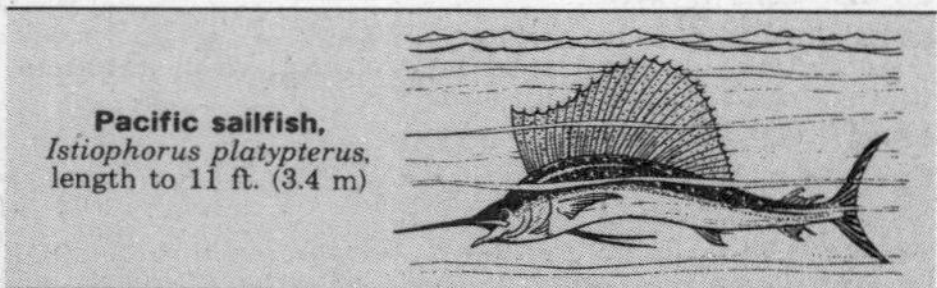
Pacific sailfish,
Istiophorus platypterus,
length to 11 ft. (3.4 m)

sail·ing (sā′ling), *n.* **1.** the activity of a person or thing that sails. **2.** the departure of a ship from port: *The cruise line offers sailings every other day.* **3.** *Navig.* any of various methods for determining courses and distances by means of charts or with reference to longitudes and latitudes, rhumb lines, great circles, etc. [bef. 900; ME *seiling,* OE *seglung.* See SAIL, -ING[1]]

sail′ing boat′, *Brit.* sailboat. [1715–25]

sail′ing length′, a measurement of a yacht, comprising its length on the water line as well as certain measurements taken from the overhangs at bow and stern.

sail′ing ship′, a large ship equipped with sails. [1880–85]

CONCISE ETYMOLOGY KEY: <, descended or borrowed from; >, whence; b., blend of, blended; c., cognate with; cf., compare; deriv., derivative; equiv., equivalent; imit., imitative; obl., oblique; r., replacing; s., stem; sp., spelling, spelled; resp., respelling, respelled; trans., translation; ?, origin unknown; *, unattested; ‡, probably earlier than. See the full key inside the front cover.

sail·mak·er (sāl′mā′kər), *n.* **1.** a person who makes or repairs sails. **2.** a former rank of warrant officer in the U.S. Navy. [1590–1600; SAIL + MAKER]

sail′maker's palm′, palm[1] (def. 4).

sail·or (sā′lər), *n.* **1.** a person whose occupation is sailing or navigation; mariner. **2.** a seaman below the rank of officer. **3.** a naval enlistee. **4.** a person adept at sailing, esp. with reference to freedom from seasickness: *He was such a bad sailor that he always traveled to Europe by plane.* **5.** a flat-brimmed straw hat with a low, flat crown. [1540–50; earlier *sailer;* see SAIL, -OR[2]] —**sail′or·like′,** *adj.* —**sail′or·ly,** *adj.*
—**Syn. 1.** seafarer. SAILOR, MARINER, SALT, SEAMAN, TAR are terms for a person who leads a seafaring life. A SAILOR or SEAMAN is one whose occupation is on board a ship at sea, esp. a member of a ship's crew below the rank of petty officer: *a sailor before the mast; an able-bodied seaman.* MARINER is a term now found only in certain technical expressions: *master mariner* (captain in merchant service); *mariner's compass* (ordinary compass as used on ships); formerly used much as "sailor" or "seafaring man," now the word seems elevated or quaint: *Rime of the Ancient Mariner.* SALT and TAR are informal terms for old and experienced sailors: *an old salt; a jolly tar.* —**Ant. 1.** landlubber.

sail·or·ing (sā′lər ing), *n.* the occupation or duties of a sailor. [1860–65; SAILOR + -ING[1]]

sail′or's breast′plate. See **prolonge knot.**

sail·or's-choice (sā′lərz chois′), *n., pl.* **-choice.** any of several fishes living in waters along the Atlantic coast of the U.S., esp. a pinfish, *Lagodon rhomboides,* ranging from Massachusetts to Texas, and a grunt, *Haemulon parrai,* ranging from Florida to Brazil. [1840–50, *Amer.*]

sail·o·ver (sāl′ō′vər), *n.* a repetition of an indecisive or interrupted run of a racing yacht.

sail′ plan′, *Naval Archit.* a side elevation of a sailing vessel showing all sails and spars and some or all of the standing rigging, as if set directly fore-and-aft so that the true proportions are visible: sometimes combined with the rigging plan of the vessel. [1950–55]

sail·plane (sāl′plān′), *n., v.,* **-planed, -plan·ing.** —*n.* **1.** a very light glider that can be lifted by an upward current of air. —*v.i.* **2.** to soar in a sailplane. [1920–25; SAIL + PLANE[1]] —**sail′plan′er,** *n.*

sail·yard (sāl′yärd′), *n.* a yard for a sail. [bef. 900; ME *seylyarde,* OE *seglgyrd.* See SAIL, YARD[1]]

Sai·maa (sī′mä), *n.* **Lake,** a lake in SE Finland. ab. 500 sq. mi. (1295 sq. km).

sain (sān), *v.t. Archaic.* **1.** to make the sign of the cross on, as for protection against evil influences. **2.** to bless. [bef. 900; ME; OE *segnian* (c. G *segnen* to bless) < LL *signāre* to sign with the cross]

sain·foin (sān′foin), *n.* a Eurasian plant, *Onobrychis viciifolia,* of the legume family, having pinnate leaves and clusters of pink flowers, used for forage. [1620–30; < F, equiv. to MF *sain* (< L *sānus* healthy) + *foin* (< L *fēnum, faenum* hay)]

saint (sānt), *n.* **1.** any of certain persons of exceptional holiness of life, formally recognized as such by the Christian Church, esp. by canonization. **2.** a person of great holiness, virtue, or benevolence. **3.** a founder, sponsor, or patron, as of a movement or organization. **4.** (in certain religious groups) a designation applied by the members to themselves. —*v.t.* **5.** to enroll formally among the saints recognized by the Church. **6.** to give the name of saint to; reckon as a saint. [bef. 1000; ME (n. and v.) < OF (n.) < L *sānctus* sacred, adj. use of ptp. of *sancīre* to consecrate, equiv. to *sanc-* (akin to *sacer* SACRED) + *-tus* ptp. suffix; r. OE *sanct* < L, as above] —**saint′less,** *adj.*

Saint. For entries beginning with this word, see also **St., Ste.**

Saint′ Ag′nes's Eve′ (ag′ni siz), the night of January 20, superstitiously regarded as a time when a young woman who performs certain rites is likely to dream of her future husband.

Saint′ An′drew's Cross′, an X-shaped cross. See illus. under **cross.**

Saint′ An′thony's Cross′, a T-shaped cross. See illus. under **cross.**

Saint′ An′thony's fire′, *Pathol.* (formerly) any of certain skin conditions that are of an inflammatory or gangrenous nature, as erysipelas, hospital gangrene, or ergotism. [1570–80]

Saint′ Barthol′omew's Day′ Mas′sacre, *Fr. Hist.* a massacre of over 3000 Huguenots, instigated by Catherine de Médicis and begun in Paris on St. Bartholomew's Day, August 24, 1572.

Saint′ Bernard′. See **St. Bernard** (def. 3).

Saint′ Bon′iface, a city in SE Manitoba, in S central Canada: suburb of Winnipeg. 46,714.

Sainte-Beuve (sanᴛ bœv′), *n.* **Charles Au·gus·tin** (shᴀʀl ō gʏ stᴀɴ′), 1804–69, French literary critic.

saint·ed (sān′tid), *adj.* **1.** enrolled among the saints. **2.** being a saint in heaven. **3.** sacred or hallowed. **4.** like a saint; saintly. [1590–1600; SAINT + -ED[2]]

Saint′ El′mo's fire′ (el′mōz). See **St. Elmo's fire.**

Saint-Ex·u·pé·ry (saɴ teg zʏ pā ʀē′), *n.* **An·toine de** (äɴ twaɴ′ də), 1900–45, French author and aviator.

saint·foin (sānt′foin), *n.* sainfoin.

Saint-Gau·dens (sānt gôd′nz), *n.* **Augustus,** 1848–1907, U.S. sculptor, born in Ireland.

Saint′ George′'s Cross′, the Greek cross as used in the flag of Great Britain.

Saint′ George′'s Day′, April 23, celebrated in parts of the British Commonwealth in honor of the patron saint of Britain and esp. in New Zealand as a bank holiday.

saint·hood (sānt′ho͝od), *n.* **1.** the character or status of a saint. **2.** saints collectively. Also **saint·dom** (sānt′dəm). [1540–50; SAINT + -HOOD]

Saint′ Joan′, a play (1923) by G. B. Shaw.

Saint′ John′, a seaport in S New Brunswick, in SE Canada, on the Bay of Fundy. 82,976.

Saint-Just (saɴ zhʏst′), *n.* **Louis An·toine Lé·on de** (lwē äɴ twaɴ′ lā ôɴ′ də), 1767–94, French revolutionist.

Saint-Lou·is (*Fr.* saɴ lwē′), *n.* a seaport in and the former capital of Senegal, at the mouth of the Senegal River. 81,204.

saint·ly (sānt′lē), *adj.,* **-li·er, -li·est.** pertaining to, like, or befitting a saint: *saintly lives.* [1650–60; SAINT + -LY] —**saint′li·ness,** *n.*

Saint′ Mar′tin's sum′mer, mild, warm weather similar to Indian summer, occurring in November. [1585–95; from the occurence of such weather around the feast of St. Martin, celebrated on November 11]

Saint′ Pat′rick's Day′, March 17, observed by the Irish in honor of St. Patrick, the patron saint of Ireland.

Saint-Saëns (saɴ säɴs′, -säɴ′), *n.* **Charles Ca·mille** (shᴀʀl kᴀ mē′yᵊ), 1835–1921, French composer and pianist.

Saints·bur·y (sānts′bə rē), *n.* **George Edward Bate·man** (bāt′mən), 1845–1933, English literary critic and historian.

saint's′ day′, a day of celebration commemorating a particular saint. [1400–50; late ME]

saint·ship (sānt′ship), *n.* the qualities or status of a saint. [1600–10; SAINT + -SHIP]

Saint-Si·mon (saɴ sē môɴ′), *n.* **1. Comte de,** 1760–1825, French philosopher and social scientist. **2. Louis de Rou·vroy** (lwē də ʀo͞o vʀwᴀ′), 1675–1755, French soldier, diplomat, and author.

Saint-Tro·pez (san′trə pā′; *Fr.* saɴ tʀô pā′), *n.* a town in SE France, on the French Riviera: beach resort. 4523.

Saint′ Val′entine's Day′. See **Valentine Day.**

Saint′ Vi′tus's dance′ (vī′tə siz). See **St. Vitus's dance.** Also, **Saint′ Vi′tus' dance′.**

Sai·on·ji (sī′ôn jē′), *n.* **Kim·mo·chi** (kēm′mô chē′), 1849–1940, Japanese statesman.

Sai·pan (sī pan′), *n.* an island in and the capital of the North Mariana Islands in the N Pacific, about 1350 mi. (2173 km) S of Japan: taken by U.S. forces June–July 1944. 14,000; 71 sq. mi. (184 sq. km).

Sa·ïs (sā′is), *n.* an ancient city in N Egypt, on the Nile delta: an ancient capital of Lower Egypt.

Sa·ite (sā′īt), *n.* **1.** a native or citizen of Saïs. —*adj.* **2.** Also, **Sa·it·ic** (sā it′ik). of or pertaining to Saïs or its inhabitants. **3.** of or pertaining to the period 663–525 B.C., when the Pharaohs ruled at Saïs. [1670–80; < L *Saïtēs* < Gk *Saïtēs.* See SAÏS, -ITE[1]]

saith (seth, sā′əth), *v. Archaic.* third pers. sing. pres. of **say.**

saithe (sāth, sāth), *n., pl.* **saithe.** *Ichthyol.* pollock. [1625–35; Scots dial. < Scand; cf. ON *seithr,* Icel *seith*]

Sai·va (sī′və), *n. Hinduism.* Shaiva. [< Skt *śaiva*] —**Sai′vite,** *n.*

Sa·kai (sä′kī′), *n.* a seaport on S Honshu, in S Japan, near Osaka. 810,120.

Sa·kai (sä′kī), *n., pl.* **-kais,** (*esp. collectively*) **-kai.** a member of a tribal people of Malaya.

Sak·a·ja·we·a (sak′ə jə wē′ə), *n.* Sacajawea.

sake[1] (sāk), *n.* **1.** cause, account, interest, or benefit: *for the sake of all students.* **2.** purpose or end: *for the sake of appearances.* [bef. 900; ME; OE *sacu* lawsuit, cause; c. G *Sache* thing, ON *sǫk* lawsuit; akin to SEEK]
—**Syn. 1.** regard, consideration, respect. **2.** reason.

sa·ke[2] (sä′kē), *n.* a Japanese fermented, mildly alcoholic beverage made from rice. Also, **sa′ké, saki.** [1680–90; < Japn *sake(y),* earlier **sakai*]

Sa·kel (zä′kəl), *n.* **Manfred (Joshua),** 1906–57, U.S. psychiatrist, born in Austria.

sa·ker[1] (sā′kər), *n.* an Old World falcon, *Falco cherrug,* used in falconry. Also called **sa′ker fal′con.** [1350–1400; ME *sagre, sacre* < MF *sacre* << Ar *ṣaqr*]

sa·ker[2] (sā′kər), *n.* a light field gun that is smaller than a demiculverin and fires a shot weighing 6 lb. (4.5 kg) or less. [1515–25; special use of SAKER[1]]

Sa·kha·lin (sak′ə lēn′; *Russ.* sə ᴋʜᴜ lyēn′), *n.* an island of the Russian Federation in the Sea of Okhotsk, N of Japan: formerly (1905–45) divided between the Soviet Union and Japan. 685,000; 29,100 sq. mi. (75,369 sq. km). Japanese, **Karafuto.**

Sa·kha·rov (sä′kə rôf′, -rof′, sak′ə-; *Russ.* sä′ᴋʜə ʀəf), *n.* **An·drei (Dmi·tri·e·vich)** (än′drā di mē′trē ə vich; *Russ.* un dʀyā′ dmyē′tʀyi yi vyich), born 1921,

Russian nuclear physicist and human-rights advocate: Nobel peace prize 1975.

sa·ki[1] (sak′ē, sä′kē), *n.* any of several monkeys of the genus *Pithecia,* of tropical South America, having a golden-brown to black, thick, shaggy coat and a long, bushy, nonprehensile tail. [1765–75; < F < Tupi *sagui*]

sa·ki[2] (sä′kē), *n.* sake[2].

Sa·ki (sä′kē), *n.* pen name of H. H. Munro.

Sak·ka·ra (sə kär′ə), *n.* Saqqara.

sak·kos (*Gk.* sä′kôs; *Eng.* sak′os), *n., pl.* **sak·koi** (*Gk.* sä′kē; *Eng.* sak′oi). *Eastern Ch.* an embroidered vestment worn by a bishop and corresponding to the dalmatic. [< Gk, special use of *sákkos* SACK[1]]

Sak·ta (shäk′tə), *n. Hinduism.* Shakta.

Sak·ti (shuk′tē), *n. Hinduism.* Shakti.

Sak·tism (shuk′tiz əm), *n. Hinduism.* Shaktism.

Sa·kun·ta·la (sə ko͝on′tə lä, shə-), *n.* a Sanskrit drama written in the 6th century or earlier by Kalidasa. Also, ***Shakuntala.***

Sa·kya·mu·ni (sä′kyə mo͝o′nē), *n.* one of the names of Buddha. Also, **Shakyamuni.** [< Skt *Śākyamuni*]

sal (sal), *n. Chiefly Pharm.* salt. [< L *sāl;* see SALT[1]]

Sal (sal), *n.* a male given name, form of **Salvatore.**

sa·la (sä′lə), *n.* a large hall, living room, or reception room. [1605–15; < AmerSp, Sp: living room, hall < OPr < Gmc, or directly < Gmc; see SALON]

sa·laam (sə läm′), *n.* **1.** a salutation meaning "peace," used esp. in Islamic countries. **2.** a very low bow or obeisance, esp. with the palm of the right hand placed on the forehead. —*v.i., v.t.* **3.** to salute with a salaam. [1605–15; < Ar *salām* peace] —**sa·laam′like′,** *adj.*

sal·a·ble (sā′lə bəl), *adj.* subject to or suitable for sale; readily sold: *The books were sent back by the store in salable condition.* Also, **saleable.** [1520–30; SALE + -ABLE] —**sal′a·bil′i·ty,** *n.* —**sal′a·bly,** *adv.*

sa·la·cious (sə lā′shəs), *adj.* **1.** lustful or lecherous. **2.** (of writings, pictures, etc.) obscene; grossly indecent. [1635–45; < L *salāci-* (s. of *salāx*) lustful (deriv. of *salīre* to jump, move spasmodically, spurt; see SALIENT, SALTATION) + -OUS] —**sa·la′cious·ly,** *adv.* —**sa·la′cious·ness, sa·lac·i·ty** (sə las′i tē), *n.*
—**Syn. 1.** lewd, wanton, lascivious, libidinous. **2.** pornographic. —**Ant. 1.** modest.

sal·ad (sal′əd), *n.* **1.** a usually cold dish consisting of vegetables, as lettuce, tomatoes, and cucumbers, covered with a dressing and sometimes containing seafood, meat, or eggs. **2.** any of various dishes consisting of foods, as meat, seafood, eggs, pasta, or fruit, prepared singly or combined, usually cut up, mixed with a dressing, and served cold: *chicken salad.* **3.** any herb or green vegetable, as lettuce, used for salads or eaten raw. **4.** *South Midland and Southern U.S.* greens. **5.** any mixture or assortment: *The usual salad of writers, artists, and musicians attended the party.* [1350–1400; ME *salad(e)* < MF *salade* < OPr *salada* < VL **salāta,* fem. ptp. of **salāre* to salt, equiv. to *sal-,* s. of *sāl* SALT[1] + *-āta* -ATE[1]]

sal′ad bar′, an assortment of salad ingredients, condiments, and dressings displayed on a serving table or counter, as at a restaurant, so that one can choose and combine ingredients freely. [1970–75]

sal′ad bas′ket, a basket in which washed salad greens are swung or spun to remove excess water. [1905–10]

sal′ad bowl′, 1. a large bowl in which a salad, esp. a tossed salad, is served. **2.** a small bowl for individual servings of salad. [1765–75]

sal′ad bur′net, a plant, *Poterium sanguisorba,* of the rose family, native to Eurasia, having rounded heads of small, greenish flowers in short spikes and edible leaves. [1850–55]

sal′ad days′, a period of youthful inexperience: *a man who never lost the immature attitudes of his salad days.* [1600–10]

sal′ad dress′ing, a sauce for a salad, usually with a base of oil and vinegar or of mayonnaise. [1830–40]

sa·lade (sə läd′, sal′əd), *n. Armor.* sallet.

sal′ad fork′, a small, broad fork, usually one of a set, for eating salad or dessert. [1915–20]

sal′ad green′, a leafy green vegetable, as lettuce, watercress, or escarole, served raw as or in a salad.

Sal·a·din (sal′ə din), *n.* (*Salāh-ed-Din Yūsuf ibn Ayyūb*) 1137–93, sultan of Egypt and Syria 1175–93: opponent of Crusaders.

Sa·la·do (sə lä′dō; *Sp.* sä lä′thô), *n.* **Ri·o** (rē′ō; *Sp.* rē′ô), a river in N Argentina, flowing SE to the Paraná River. ab. 1200 mi. (1930 km) long.

sal′ad oil′, an oil used in salad dressing, esp. olive oil or a vegetable oil, as from sesame, corn, or safflower. [1550–60]

sal′ad plate′, 1. a small plate used chiefly for serving an individual portion of salad. **2.** a selection of salad ingredients served cold, often on a bed of lettuce. [1880–85]

sa·lah (sə lä′), *n. Islam.* salat. [< Ar *ṣalāh*]

sa·lal (sə lal′, sa-), *n.* an evergreen shrub, *Gaultheria shallon,* of the heath family, native to the western coast of North America, having leathery, oblong leaves and clusters of pink or white flowers and purplish-black fruit. [1815–25, *Amer.;* < Chinook Jargon *sallal* < Lower Chinook *sálal*]

Sal·a·man·ca (sal′ə mang′kə; *Sp.* sä′lä mäng′kä), *n.* a city in W Spain: university; Wellington's defeat of the French, 1812. 125,220.

sal·a·man·der (sal′ə man′dər), *n.* **1.** any tailed amphibian of the order Caudata, having a soft, moist, scaleless skin, typically aquatic as a larva and semiterrestrial as an adult: several species are endangered. **2.** a mythical being, esp. a lizard or other reptile, thought to be able to live in fire. **3.** any of various portable stoves or burners. **4.** *Metall.* a mass of iron that accumulates at the bottom of a blast furnace as a result of the escape of molten metal through the hearth. **5.** a metal plate or disk with a handle, heated and held over pastry, etc., to brown or glaze it. **6.** an oven usually heated from the top and bottom by gas, for cooking, browning, and glazing food. [1300–50; ME *salamandre* < L *salamandra* < Gk *salamándrā*] —**sal′a·man′der-like′,** *adj.* —**sal·a·man·drine** (sal′ə man′drin), *adj.* —**sal′a·man′droid,** *adj.*
—**Syn. 2.** See **sylph.**

tiger salamander, *Ambystoma tigrinum,* length 8 in. (20 cm)

Sa·lam·bri·a (sə lam′brē ə, sä′läm brē′ə), *n.* a river in N Greece, in Thessaly, flowing E to the Gulf of Salonika. 125 mi. (200 km) long. Ancient, **Peneus.** Modern Greek, **Peneios.**

sa·la·mi (sə lä′mē), *n.* a kind of sausage, originally Italian, often flavored with garlic. [1850–55; < It, pl. of *salame* < VL **salāmen,* equiv. to **salā(re)* to salt + L *-men* n. suffix; see SAL]

Sal·a·mis (sal′ə mis; *Gk.* sä′lä mēs′), *n.* **1.** an island off the SE coast of Greece, W of Athens, in the Gulf of Aegina: Greeks defeated Persians in a naval battle 480 B.C. 20,000; 39 sq. mi. (101 sq. km). **2.** an ancient city on Cyprus, in the E Mediterranean: the apostle Paul made his first missionary journey to Salamis. Acts 13:5. —**Sal·a·min·i·an** (sal′ə min′ē ən), *adj.*

sal′ ammo′niac, *Chem.* See **ammonium chloride.** [1300–50; ME]

Sa·lam′-Wein′berg the′ory (sä läm′win′bərg), *Physics.* the electroweak theory. Also called **Weinberg-Salam theory.**

sa·lar·i·at (sə lâr′ē ət), *n.* the class of workers in an economy who receive salaries. [1915–20; < F: b. L *salārium* SALARY (F *salaire*) and F *prolétariat* PROLETARIAT]

sal·a·ried (sal′ə rēd), *adj.* **1.** receiving a salary: *a salaried employee.* **2.** having a salary attached: *a salaried job.* [1590–1600; SALARY + -ED[3]]

sal·a·ry (sal′ə rē), *n., pl.* **-ries.** a fixed compensation periodically paid to a person for regular work or services. [1350–1400; ME *salarie* < AF < L *salārium* salt money. See SAL, -ARY] —**sal′a·ry·less,** *adj.*
—**Syn.** See **pay.**

sa·lat (sə lät′), *n. Islam.* prayers, said five times a day: the second of the Pillars of Islam. Also, **salah.** Cf. **rak'a.** [< Ar *ṣalāh, ṣalāt* prayer]

Sa·la·vat (sə lu vät′), *n.* a city in the SW RSFSR, in the W central Soviet Union in Asia, S of Ufa. 137,000.

Sa·la·zar (sal′ə zär′, säl′-; *Port.* sə lä zär′), *n.* **An·to·nio de O·li·vei·ra** (än tô′nyô̂ də ô′lē vā′rə), 1889–1970, premier of Portugal 1933–68.

sal·bu·ta·mol (sal byo͞o′tə môl′, -mol′), *n. Pharm.* the international generic name for albuterol. [1965–70; SAL(ICYLIC ACID) + BUT(YL) + AM(INO) + -OL[1]]

Sal·chow (sal′kou), *n. Ice Skating.* a jump in which the skater leaps from the back inside edge of one skate, making one full rotation of the body in the air, and lands on the back outside edge of the other skate. [1920–25; after Ulrich *Salchow* (1877–1949), Swedish figure skater, who first performed it]

sale (sāl), *n.* **1.** the act of selling. **2.** a quantity sold. **3.** opportunity to sell; demand: *slow sale.* **4.** a special disposal of goods, as at reduced prices. **5.** transfer of property for money or credit. **6.** an auction. **7. for sale,** offered to be sold; made available to purchasers. **8. on sale,** able to be bought at reduced prices. [bef. 1050; ME; late OE *sala;* c. ON, OHG *sala.* Cf. SELL[1]]

sale·a·ble (sā′lə bəl), *adj.* salable.

sale′ and lease′back, leaseback. Also called **sale′-lease′back′.**

Sa·lem (sā′ləm), *n.* **1.** a seaport in NE Massachusetts: founded 1626; execution of persons accused of being witches 1692; home of Nathaniel Hawthorne. 38,220. **2.** a city in and the capital of Oregon, in the NW part, on the Willamette River. 89,233. **3.** a town in SE New Hampshire. 24,124. **4.** a town in SW Virginia, near Roanoke. 23,958. **5.** a city in E Ohio. 12,869. **6.** a city in central Tamil Nadu, in S India. 308,303. **7.** an ancient city of Canaan, later identified with Jerusalem. Gen. 14:18; Psalms 76:2.

Sa′lem sec′retary, *U.S. Furniture.* a tall cabinet having a recessed upper part fitted with drawers and shelves and a lower part with doors and a section falling or pulling out to serve as a writing surface. Also called **Sa′lem desk′.** [after SALEM, Mass.]

sal·ep (sal′ep), *n.* a starchy, demulcent drug or foodstuff consisting of the dried tubers of certain orchids. [1730–40; < Turk *salep* < dial. Ar *saḥlab,* perh. shortened var. of Ar *khusā al-tha'lab* fox's testicles; cf. SALOOP]

sal·e·ra·tus (sal′ə rā′təs), *n.* sodium bicarbonate used in cookery; baking soda. [1830–40, *Amer.;* var. of L *sal aerātus.* See SAL, AERATE]

Sa·ler·no (sə lâr′nō, -lûr′-; *It.* sä ler′nô), *n.* a seaport in SW Italy: taken by U.S. forces September 1943. 161,598.

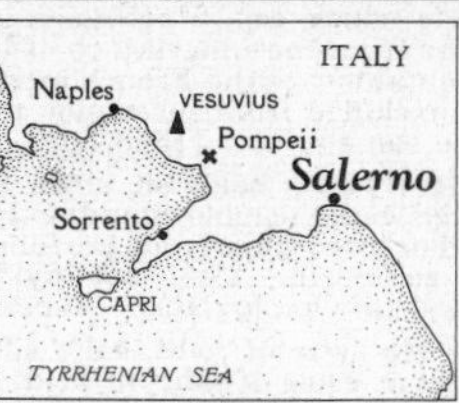

sale·room (sāl′ro͞om′, -ro͝om′), *n. Chiefly Brit.* salesroom (def. 2).

sales (sālz), *n.* **1.** pl. of **sale.** —*adj.* **2.** of, pertaining to, or engaged in sales: *sales records for the month of January; a sales department.*

sales′ check′. See **sales slip.** [1925–30]

sales·clerk (sālz′klûrk′), *n.* a person who sells goods in a store. [1930–35; SALES + CLERK]

sales′ fi′nance com′pany, a finance company that purchases, at a discount, installment contracts from dealers or that finances retail sales.

sales·girl (sālz′gûrl′), *n.* a woman who sells goods, esp. in a store; saleswoman. [1885–90, *Amer.;* SALES + GIRL]

Sa·le·sian (sə lē′zhən, -shən), *Rom. Cath. Ch.* —*n.* **1.** a member of the Society of St. Francis de Sales, a congregation founded in Turin in 1845 and engaged chiefly in missionary and educational work. —*adj.* **2.** of or pertaining to St. Francis de Sales or the Salesians. [St. FRANCIS of Sales + -IAN]

sales·la·dy (sālz′lā′dē), *n., pl.* **-dies.** a saleswoman. [1855–60, *Amer.;* SALES + LADY]

sales·man (sālz′mən), *n., pl.* **-men.** a man who sells goods, services, etc. [1515–25; SALES + -MAN]
—**Usage.** See **-man.**

sales·man·ship (sālz′mən ship′), *n.* **1.** the technique of selling a product: *They used a promotional gimmick that was the last word in salesmanship.* **2.** adeptness at creating interest in new ideas, products, methods, etc.: *The only ingredient lacking in the system was salesmanship.* [1875–80; SALESMAN + -SHIP; cf. -MANSHIP]

sales·peo·ple (sālz′pē′pəl), *n.pl.* people engaged in selling. [1875–80, *Amer.;* SALES + PEOPLE]

sales·per·son (sālz′pûr′sən), *n.* a person who sells goods, services, etc. [1915–20; SALES + PERSON]
—**Usage.** See **-person.**

sales′ promo′tion, the methods or techniques for creating public acceptance of or interest in a product, usually in addition to standard merchandising techniques, as advertising or personal selling, and generally consisting of the offer of free samples, gifts made to a purchaser, or the like. [1915–20]

sales′ reg′ister. See **cash register.**

sales′ rep′, *Informal.* See **sales representative.** [1965–70]

sales′ represent′ative, 1. a person or organization designated by a company to solicit business on its behalf in a specified territory or foreign country: *I suggest you contact our Chicago sales representative.* **2.** See **traveling salesman.** [1945–50]

sales′ resist′ance, the ability or inclination to refuse to buy a product, service, etc., offered. [1920–25]

sales·room (sālz′ro͞om′, -ro͝om′), *n.* **1.** a room in which goods are sold or displayed. **2.** Also, *esp. Brit.,* **saleroom.** an auction room. [1830–40, *Amer.;* SALES + ROOM]

sales′ slip′, a receipt or other slip of paper issued by a store or other vendor showing where a purchase was made and also the amount, date, department, etc. Also called **sales check, sales′ receipt′.** [1925–30]

sales′ talk′, 1. a line of reasoning or argument intended to persuade someone to buy, accept, or do something. **2.** any persuasive argument. [1925–30]

sales′ tax′, a tax on receipts from sales, usually added to the selling price by the seller. [1920–25]

sales·wom·an (sālz′wo͝om′ən), *n., pl.* **-wom·en.** a woman who sells goods, services, etc. [1695–1705; SALES + WOMAN]
—**Usage.** See **-woman.**

Sal·ford (sôl′fərd, sô′-, sal′-), *n.* a city in Greater Manchester, in N England. 266,500.

Sa·li·an (sā′lē ən, sāl′yən), *adj.* **1.** of, pertaining to, or designating a Frankish people who lived in the region of the Rhine near the North Sea. —*n.* **2.** a Salian Frank. [1605–15; < LL *Sali(ī)* (pl.) tribal name + -AN]

Sal·ic (sal′ik, sā′lik), *adj.* of or pertaining to the Salian Franks. Also, **Salique.** [1540–50; < ML *Salicus,* equiv. to LL *Sal(ii)* (pl.) tribal name + *-icus* -IC]

sal·i·ca·ceous (sal′i kā′shəs), *adj.* belonging to the Salicaceae, the willow family of plants. Cf. **willow family.** [1840–50; < NL *Salicace(ae)* (*Salic-,* s. of *Salix* the type genus (L: willow) + *-aceae* -ACEAE) + -OUS]

sal·i·cin (sal′ə sin), *n. Pharm.* a colorless, crystalline, water-soluble glucoside, $C_{13}H_{18}O_7$, obtained from the bark of the American aspen: used in medicine chiefly as an antipyretic and analgesic. Also called **sal′i·cyl al′·cohol glu′coside** (sal′ə sil). [1820–30; < F *salicine* < L *salic-* (s. of *salix*) willow + F *-ine* -INE[2]]

Sal′ic law′, 1. a code of laws of the Salian Franks and

CONCISE PRONUNCIATION KEY: act, cāpe, dâre, pärt; set, ēqual; if, īce; ox, ōver, ôrder, oil, bo͝ok, bo͞ot, out; up, ûrge; child; sing; shoe; thin, *th*at; zh as in *treasure.* ə = *a* as in *alone, e* as in *system, i* as in *easily, o* as in *gallop, u* as in *circus;* ə as in *fire* (fīər), *hour* (ouər). l and n can serve as syllabic consonants, as in *cradle* (krād′l), and *button* (but′n). See the full key inside the front cover.

other Germanic tribes, esp. a provision in this code excluding females from the inheritance of land. **2.** the alleged fundamental law of the French monarchy by which females were excluded from succession to the crown. **3.** any law to the same effect. [1540–50]

sal•i•cyl•al•de•hyde (sal′ə sil al′də hīd′), *n. Chem.* an oily, slightly water-soluble liquid, $C_7H_6O_2$, having an almondlike odor: used chiefly in perfumery and in the synthesis of coumarin. Also, **sal′icyl′ic al′dehyde.** [1865–70; *salicyl* (see SALICYLIC) + ALDEHYDE]

sa•lic•y•late (sə lis′ə lāt′, -lit, sal′ə sil′āt, sal′ə sil′-), *n. Chem.* a salt or ester of salicylic acid. [1835–45; SALICYL(IC ACID) + -ATE[2]]

sal•i•cyl•ic (sal′ə sil′ik), *adj. Chem.* of or derived from salicylic acid. [1830–40; < F *salicyl* the diatomic radical of salicylic acid (< L *salic-,* s. of *salix* willow + F *-yl* -YL; it was orig. derived from salicin) + -IC]

sal′icyl′ic ac′id, *Chem., Pharm.* a white, crystalline, very slightly water-soluble powder, $C_7H_6O_3$, prepared from salicin or phenol: used as a food preservative, in the manufacture of aspirin, and in medicine chiefly in the form of a salicylate as a remedy for rheumatic and gouty conditions. [1830–40]

sa•li•ence (sā′lē əns, sāl′yəns), *n.* **1.** the state or condition of being salient. **2.** a salient or projecting object, part, or feature. [1830–40; see SALIENT, -ENCE]

sa•li•en•cy (sā′lē ən sē, sāl′yən-), *n., pl.* **-cies.** salience. [1655–65; see SALIENT, -ENCY]

sa•li•ent (sā′lē ənt, sāl′yənt), *adj.* **1.** prominent or conspicuous: *salient traits.* **2.** projecting or pointing outward: *a salient angle.* **3.** leaping or jumping: *a salient animal.* **4.** *Heraldry.* (of a beast) represented as leaping: *a lion salient.* —*n.* **5.** a salient angle or part, as the central outward-projecting angle of a bastion or an outward projection in a battle line. **6.** *Physical Geog.* a landform that extends out beyond its surroundings, as a spur projecting from the side of a mountain. Cf. **reentrant** (def. 4). [1555–65; < L *salient-* (s. of *saliēns,* prp. of *salīre* to spring, jump), equiv. to *sali-* verb s. + *-ent-* -ENT] —**sa′li•ent•ly,** *adv.*
—**Syn. 1.** important; striking, remarkable. —**Ant. 1.** inconspicuous, unimportant.

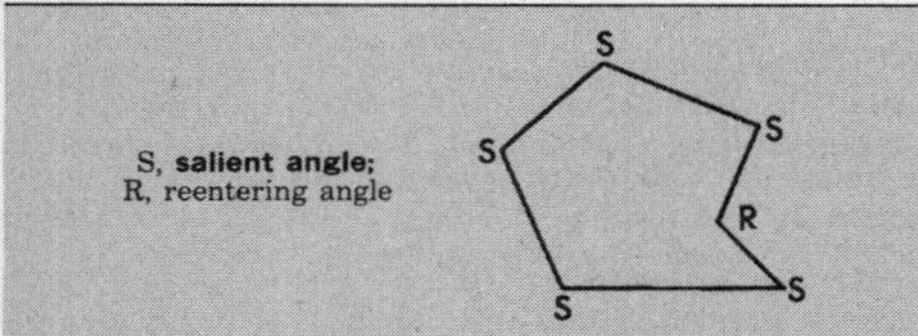

S, **salient angle;**
R, reentering angle

sa•li•en•tian (sā′lē en′shən), *adj.* **1.** belonging or pertaining to the superorder Salientia, comprising the frogs and toads (order Anura) and extinct species. —*n.* **2.** a salientian amphibian. [1945–50; < NL *Salienti(a)* (L: neut. pl. of *saliēns;* see SALIENT) + -AN]

Sa•lie•ri (səl yâr′ē, sal-; *It.* sä lye′rē), *n.* **An•to•nio** (an tō′nē ō; *It.* än tô′nyô), 1750–1825, Italian composer and conductor.

sa•lif•er•ous (sə lif′ər əs), *adj.* containing or producing salt: *saliferous strata.* [1820–30; SAL + -I- + -FEROUS]

sal•i•fy (sal′ə fī′), *v.t.,* **-fied, -fy•ing. 1.** to form into a salt, as by chemical combination. **2.** to mix or combine with a salt. [1780–90; SAL + -IFY] —**sal′i•fi′a•ble,** *adj.* —**sal•i•fi•ca•tion** (sal′ə fi kā′shən), *n.*

Sal•i•i (sal′ē ī′), *n.* (*used with a plural v.*) (in ancient Rome) a college of priests of Mars and Quirinus who guarded the ancilia and led the festivities in their honor. Cf. **ancile.**

sal•im•e•ter (sa lim′i tər), *n. Chem.* salinometer. [1865–70; SAL + -I- + -METER]

sa•li•na (sə lī′nə), *n.* **1.** a saline marsh, spring, or the like. **2.** a saltworks. [1690–1700; < Sp << L *salīnae* saltworks]

Sa•li•na (sə lī′nə), *n.* a city in central Kansas. 41,843.

Sa•li•nas (sə lē′nəs), *n.* a city in W California. 80,479.

sa•line (sā′lēn, -līn), *adj.* **1.** of, containing, or resembling common table salt; salty or saltlike: *a saline solution.* **2.** of or pertaining to a chemical salt, esp. of sodium, potassium, magnesium, etc., as used as a cathartic. **3.** of or pertaining to a method of abortion involving injection of hypertonic saline solution into the amniotic cavity during the second trimester. —*n.* **4.** a sterile solution of sodium chloride used to dilute medications or for intravenous therapy. **5.** salty water; a salty solution. [1400–50; ME: composed of salt < L *salīnus* salty, equiv. to *sal* SAL + *-īnus* -INE[1]] —**sa•lin•i•ty** (sə lin′i tē), *n.*

Sal•in•ger (sal′in jər), *n.* **J(erome) D(avid),** born 1919, U.S. novelist and short-story writer.

sal•i•ni•za•tion (sal′ə nə zā′shən), *n.* the process by which a nonsaline soil becomes saline, as by the irrigation of land with brackish water. [1925–30; SALINIZE + -ATION]

sal•i•nize (sal′ə nīz′, sā′lə-), *v.t.,* **-nized, -niz•ing.** to treat with salt or render saline. Also, *esp. Brit.,* **sal′i•nise′.** [SALINE + -IZE]

sal•i•nom•e•ter (sal′ə nom′i tər), *n. Chem.* an instrument for measuring the amount of salt in a solution. Also, **salimeter, salometer.** [1835–45; SALINE + -O- + -METER] —**sal′i•nom′e•try,** *n.* **sal•i•no•met•ric** (sal′ə nə me′trik), *adj.*

CONCISE ETYMOLOGY KEY: <, descended or borrowed from; >, whence; b., blend of, blended; c., cognate with; cf., compare; deriv., derivative; equiv., equivalent; imit., imitative; obl., oblique; r., replacing; s., stem; sp., spelling, spelled; resp., respelling, respelled; trans., translation; ?, origin unknown; *, unattested; ‡, probably earlier than. See the full key inside the front cover.

Sa•lique (sə lēk′, sal′ik, sā′lik), *adj.* Salic.

Salis•bur•y (sôlz′ber′ē, -bə rē, -brē *or, esp. for 4, 5,* salz′-), *n.* **1. Robert Arthur Tal•bot Gas•coyne Cecil** (tôl′bət gas′koin, tal′-), **3rd Marquis of,** 1830–1903, British statesman: prime minister 1885–86, 1886–92, 1895–1902. **2.** former name of **Harare. 3.** a city in Wiltshire, in S England: cathedral. 104,700. **4.** a city in central North Carolina. 22,677. **5.** a city in E Maryland. 16,429.

Salis′bury Plain′, a plateau in S England, N of Salisbury: the site of Stonehenge.

Salis′bury steak′, ground beef, sometimes mixed with other foods, shaped like a hamburger patty and broiled or fried, often garnished or served with a sauce. [1895–1900, *Amer.;* named after J. H. *Salisbury* (1823–1905), U.S. dietitian, who promoted the eating of such steaks]

Sa•lish (sā′lish), *n.* a member of any of various North American Indian peoples speaking a Salishan language. [< Southern Interior Salish *sé*ʔ*liš* Flatheads]

Sa•lish•an (sā′lish ən, sal′ish-), *n.* **1.** a family of American Indian languages including Coeur d'Alêne, Kalispel, and other languages of British Columbia and the northwestern U.S. —*adj.* **2.** of, pertaining to, or characteristic of this language family or its speakers. [1885–90; SALISH + -AN]

sa•li•va (sə lī′və), *n.* a viscid, watery fluid, secreted into the mouth by the salivary glands, that functions in the tasting, chewing, and swallowing of food, moistens the mouth, and starts the digestion of starches. [1670–80; < L *salīva*] —**sal•i•var•y** (sal′ə ver′ē), *adj.*

sal′ivary am′ylase, ptyalin.

sal′ivary gland′, *Anat.* any of several glands, as the submaxillary glands, that secrete saliva. [1700–10]

sal•i•vate (sal′ə vāt′), *v.,* **-vat•ed, -vat•ing.** —*v.i.* **1.** to produce saliva. —*v.t.* **2.** to produce an excessive secretion of saliva in, as by mercurial poisoning. [1650–60; < L *salīvātus* (ptp. of *salīvāre* to cause to salivate); see SALIVA, -ATE[1]]

sal•i•va•tion (sal′ə vā′shən), *n.* **1.** the act or process of salivating. **2.** an abnormally abundant flow of saliva; ptyalism. **3.** mercurial poisoning. [1590–1600; < L *salīvātiōn-* (s. of *salīvātiō*), equiv. to *salīvāt(us)* (see SALIVATE) + *-iōn-* -ION]

sal•i•va•tor (sal′ə vā′tər), *n. Med.* any agent that causes salivation. [1825–35; SALIVATE + -OR[2]]

Salk (sôk, sôlk), *n.* **Jonas E(dward),** 1914–95, U.S. bacteriologist: developed Salk vaccine.

Salk′ vaccine′, a vaccine that contains three types of inactivated poliomyelitis viruses and induces immunity against the disease. [1950–55; named after J. E. SALK]

salle à man•ger (SAL A mäN zhā′), *pl.* ***salles à manger*** (SAL A mäN zhā′). *French.* a dining room.

sal•len•ders (sal′ən dərz), *n.* (*used with a singular v.*) *Vet. Pathol.* an eruption on the hind leg of a horse, on the inside of a hock. Cf. **malanders.** [1515–25; orig. uncert.]

sal•let (sal′it), *n. Armor.* a light medieval helmet, usually with a vision slit or a movable visor. Also, **salade.** [1400–50; late ME, var. of *salade* < MF < Sp *celada* (or It *celata*) < L *caelāta* (*cassis*) engraved (helmet), fem. of *caelātus* (ptp. of *caelāre* to engrave); see -ATE[1]]

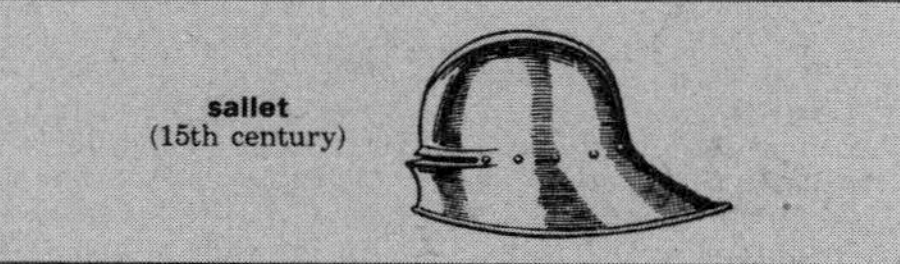
sallet
(15th century)

Sal′lie Mae′. See **Student Loan Marketing Association.**

sal•low[1] (sal′ō), *adj.,* **-er, -est,** *v.* —*adj.* **1.** of a sickly, yellowish color: *sallow cheeks; a sallow complexion.* —*v.t.* **2.** to make sallow. [bef. 1000; ME *sal(o)we,* OE *salo;* c. ON *sǫlr* yellow; cf. F *sale* dirty (< Gmc)] —**sal′low•ish,** *adj.* —**sal′low•ness,** *n.*
—**Syn. 1.** bilious, jaundiced.

sal•low[2] (sal′ō), *n. Brit.* any of several shrubby Old World willows, esp. *Salix atrocinerea* or the pussy willow, *S. caprea.* [bef. 900; ME; OE *sealh;* c. OHG *salaha,* L *salix*]

sal•low•y (sal′ō ē), *adj.* full of sallows: *a sallowy glade.* [1830–40; SALLOW[2] + -Y[1]]

Sal•lust (sal′əst), *n.* (*Caius Sallustius Crispus*) 86–34 B.C., Roman historian.

sal•ly (sal′ē), *n., pl.* **-lies,** *v.,* **-lied, -ly•ing.** —*n.* **1.** a sortie of troops from a besieged place upon an enemy. **2.** a sudden rushing forth or activity. **3.** an excursion or trip, usually off the main course. **4.** an outburst or flight of passion, fancy, etc.: *a sally of anger.* **5.** a clever, witty, or fanciful remark. **6.** *Carpentry.* a projection, as of the end of a rafter beyond the notch by which the rafter is fitted over the wall plate. —*v.i.* **7.** to make a sally, as a body of troops from a besieged place. **8.** to set out on a side trip or excursion. **9.** to set out briskly or energetically. **10.** (of things) to issue forth. [1535–45; < MF *saillie* attack, n. use of fem. ptp. of *saillir* to rush forward < L *salīre* to leap] —**sal′li•er,** *n.*
—**Syn. 5.** quip, witticism.

Sal•ly (sal′ē), *n.* a female given name, form of **Sarah.** Also, **Sal′lie.**

sal′ly lunn′ (lun), a slightly sweetened teacake served hot with butter. Also, **Sal′ly Lunn′.** [1770–80; after a woman who sold them in Bath, England, at the end of the 18th century]

sal′ly port′, (in a fort or the like) **1.** a gateway permitting the passage of a large number of troops at a time. **2.** a postern. [1640–50]

sal•ma•gun•di (sal′mə gun′dē), *n.* **1.** a mixed dish consisting usually of cubed poultry or fish, chopped meat, anchovies, eggs, onions, oil, etc., often served as a salad. **2.** any mixture or miscellany. [1665–75; < MF *salmingondin* (later *salmigondis*), compound based on *salemine* salted food (see SALAMI) and *condir* to season (see CONDIMENT)]

Sal•ma•naz•ar (sal′mə naz′ər), *n.* a wine bottle holding from 10 to 12 quarts (9.5 to 11.4 l). [1930–35; var. of *Shalmaneser,* name of biblical king (2 Kings 18:9)]

sal•mi (sal′mē), *n.* a ragout of partially cooked game, as pheasant or woodcock, stewed in wine and butter. Also, **salmis.** [1750–60; < F, short for *salmigondis* SALAMAGUNDI]

sal•mis (sal′mē; *Fr.* SAL mē′), *n., pl.* **-mis** (-mē; *Fr.* -mē′). salmi.

salm•on (sam′ən), *n., pl.* **-ons,** (*esp. collectively*) **-on** for 1–3, *adj.* —*n.* **1.** a marine and freshwater food fish, *Salmo salar,* of the family Salmonidae, having pink flesh, inhabiting waters off the North Atlantic coasts of Europe and North America near the mouths of large rivers, which it enters to spawn. **2.** See **landlocked salmon. 3.** any of several salmonoid food fishes of the genus *Oncorhynchus,* inhabiting the North Pacific. **4.** a light yellowish-pink. —*adj.* **5.** of the color salmon. [1200–50; ME *salmoun, samoun* < AF (OF *saumon*) < L *salmōn-,* s. of *salmō*] —**salm′on•like′,** *adj.*

chinook salmon,
Oncorhynchus tshawytscha,
length to 4 ft. (1.2 m)

salm•on•ber•ry (sam′ən ber′ē), *n., pl.* **-ries. 1.** the salmon-colored, edible fruit of a raspberry, *Rubus spectabilis,* of the Pacific coast of North America. **2.** the plant itself. [1835–45, *Amer.;* SALMON + BERRY]

salm′on brick′, a soft, imperfectly fired brick having a reddish-orange color.

sal•mo•nel•la (sal′mə nel′ə), *n., pl.* **-nel•lae** (-nel′ē). *Bacteriol.* any of several rod-shaped, facultatively anaerobic bacteria of the genus *Salmonella,* as *S. typhosa,* that may enter the digestive tract of humans and other mammals in contaminated food and cause abdominal pains and violent diarrhea. [< NL (1900), after Daniel E. *Salmon* (1850–1914), U.S. pathologist; see -ELLA]

sal•mo•nel•lo•sis (sal′mə nl ō′sis), *n. Pathol.* food poisoning caused by consumption of food contaminated with bacteria of the genus *Salmonella,* characterized by the sudden onset of abdominal pain, vomiting, diarrhea, and fever. [1910–15; SALMONELL(A) + -OSIS]

sal•mo•nid (sal′mə nid), *adj.* **1.** belonging or pertaining to the family Salmonidae, including the salmons, trouts, chars, and whitefishes. —*n.* **2.** a salmonid fish. [1865–70; < NL *Salmonidae* name of the family. See SALMON, -ID[2]]

sal•mo•noid (sal′mə noid′), *adj.* **1.** resembling a salmon. **2.** belonging or pertaining to the suborder Salmonoidea, to which the salmon family belongs. —*n.* **3.** a salmonoid fish. [1835–45; < NL *Salmonoidea* name of the suborder. See SALMON, -OID]

salm′on pink′, salmon (defs. 4, 5). [1880–85]

Salm′on Riv′er Moun′tains, a range in central Idaho. Highest peak, 10,340 ft. (3150 m).

salm′on trout′, 1. a European trout, *Salmo trutta.* **2.** the lake trout, *Salvelinus namaycush.* **3.** the steelhead. **4.** any large trout. [1350–1400; ME]

salm′on wheel′, a trap for catching salmon, consisting of a revolving wheel with attached nets set in a river so that it is turned by the current to capture the passing fish. Also called **fish wheel.** [1895–1900]

sal•ol (sal′ôl, -ol), *n. Pharm.* a white, crystalline, aromatic powder, $C_{13}H_{10}O_3$, produced by the interaction of salicylic acid and phenol, used as a preservative, a light absorber in suntan preparations, and in medicine chiefly as an antipyretic and as an antiseptic. Also called **phenyl salicylate.** [1885–90; formerly a trademark]

Sa•lo•me (sə lō′mē *for 1, 3;* sal′ə mā′ *for 2*), *n.* **1.** Also, **Sa•lo•mé.** the daughter of Herodias, who is said to have danced for Herod Antipas and so pleased him that he granted her mother's request for the head of John the Baptist. Matt. 14:6–11 (not mentioned by name here). **2.** (*italics*) a one-act opera (1905) by Richard Strauss based on a drama by Oscar Wilde. **3.** a female given name: from a Hebrew word meaning "peace."

sa•lom•e•ter (sə lom′i tər), *n. Chem.* salinometer.

Sal•o•mon (sal′ə mən), *n.* **Haym** (hīm), 1740?–85, American financier and patriot, born in Poland.

sa•lon (sə lon′; *Fr.* SA lôN′), *n., pl.* **-lons** (-lonz′; *Fr.* -lôN′). **1.** a drawing room or reception room in a large house. **2.** an assembly of guests in such a room, esp. an assembly, common during the 17th and 18th centuries, consisting of the leaders in society, art, politics, etc. **3.** a hall or place used for the exhibition of works of art. **4.** a shop, business, or department of a store offering a specific product or service, esp. one catering to a fashionable clientele: *a dress salon; a hair salon.* **5.** (*cap.*) (in France) **a. the Salon,** an annual exhibition of works of art by living artists, originally held at the Salon d'Apollon: it became, during the 19th century, the focal point of artistic controversy and was identified with academicism and official hostility to progress in art. **b.** a national exhibition of works of art by living artists: *Salon des Refusés; Salon des Indépendants.* [1705–15; < F < It *salone,* equiv. to *sal(a)* hall (< Gmc; cf. OE *sæl,* OS *seli,* G *Saal,* ON *salr*) + *-one* aug. suffix]

Sa•lon•i•ka (sə lon′i kə, sal′ə nē′kə), *n.* **1.** Also, **Sa•lon•i•ca** (sə lon′i kə, sal′ə nē′kə), **Sa•lo•ni•ki** (*Gk.* sä′lô-nē′kē). Official name, **Thessalonike.** Ancient, **Therma.** a seaport in south-central Macedonia, in NE Greece, on the Gulf of Salonika. 339,496. **2. Gulf of,** an arm of the Aegean, in NE Greece. 70 mi. (113 km) long.

salon′ mu′sic, music of a simple, agreeable, frequently sentimental character, played usually by a small orchestra. [1910–15]

sa·loon (sə lo͞on′), *n.* **1.** a place for the sale and consumption of alcoholic drinks. **2.** a room or place for general use for a specific purpose: *a dining saloon on a ship.* **3.** a large cabin for the common use of passengers on a passenger vessel. **4.** *Brit.* **a.** (in a tavern or pub) a section of a bar or barroom separated from the public bar and often having more comfortable furnishings and a quieter atmosphere. **b.** See **saloon car. 5.** a drawing room or reception room. [1720–30; var. of SALON]

saloon′ car′, *Brit.* **1.** Also, **saloon′ car′riage.** a railway sleeping, dining, or parlor car similar to a U.S. Pullman. **2.** sedan (def. 1). [1885–90]

saloon′ keep′er, a person who owns or operates a saloon. [1840–50]

sa·loop (sə lo͞op′), *n.* a hot drink prepared originally from salep but later from sassafras, together with milk and sugar. [1705–15; var. of SALEP]

Sal·op (sal′əp), *n.* a county in W England. 354,800; 1348 sq. mi. (3490 sq. km). **—Sa·lo·pi·an** (sə lō′pē ən), *adj., n.*

sal·pa (sal′pə), *n., pl.* **-pas, -pae** (-pē). any free-swimming, oceanic tunicate of the genus *Salpa,* having a transparent, more or less fusiform body. Also, **salp** (salp). [1510–20; < NL, special use of L *salpa* < Gk *sálpē* kind of fish] **—sal·pi·form** (sal′pə fôrm′), *adj.*

sal·pin·gec·to·my (sal′pin jek′tə mē), *n., pl.* **-mies.** *Surg.* excision of the Fallopian tube. [1885–90; SALPING- + -ECTOMY]

sal·pin·gi·tis (sal′pin jī′tis), *n. Pathol.* inflammation of a salpinx. [1860–65; SALPING- + -ITIS] **—sal·pin·git·ic** (sal′pin jit′ik), *adj.*

salpingo-, a combining form representing **salpinx** in compound words: *salpingotomy.* Also, *esp. before a vowel,* **salping-.** [< NL < Gk *salping-* (s. of *sálpinx*) trumpet + *-o-* -O-]

sal·pin·gos·to·my (sal′ping gos′tə mē), *n., pl.* **-mies.** *Surg.* the formation of an artificial opening into a Fallopian tube. Also, **sal·pin·go·sto·mat·o·my** (sal ping′gō-stə mat′ə mē). [1890–95; SALPINGO- + -STOMY]

sal·pin·got·o·my (sal′ping got′ə mē), *n., pl.* **-mies.** *Surg.* incision of a Fallopian tube. [1895–1900; SALPINGO- + -TOMY]

sal·pinx (sal′pingks), *n., pl.* **sal·pin·ges** (sal pin′jēz). *Anat.* a trumpet-shaped tube, as a Fallopian or Eustachian tube. [1835–45; < Gk: trumpet] **—sal·pin·gi·an** (sal pin′jē ən), *adj.*

sal·sa (säl′sə; *Sp.* säl′sä), *n.* **1.** a lively, vigorous type of contemporary Latin American popular music, blending predominantly Cuban rhythms with elements of jazz, rock, and soul music. **2.** a ballroom dance of Puerto Rican origin, performed to this music, similar to the mambo, but faster with the accent on the first beat instead of the second beat of each measure. **3.** *Mexican Cookery.* a sauce, esp. a hot sauce containing chilies. *—v.i.* **4.** to dance the salsa. [1970–75; < AmerSp, Sp: lit., sauce; prob. so called orig. because of its mixture of styles]

sal·si·fy (sal′sə fē), *n., pl.* **-fies.** a purple-flowered, composite plant, *Tragopogon porrifolius,* whose root has an oyster-like flavor and is used as a culinary vegetable. Also called **oyster plant, vegetable oyster.** [1690–1700; < F *salsifis,* var. of *sassefy, sassef(r)ique* < It *sassef(r)ica* < ?]

sal′ so′da. See **sodium carbonate** (def. 2). [1425–75; late ME]

salt[1] (sôlt), *n.* **1.** a crystalline compound, sodium chloride, NaCl, occurring as a mineral, a constituent of seawater, etc., and used for seasoning food, as a preservative, etc. **2.** table salt mixed with a particular herb or seasoning for which it is named: *garlic salt; celery salt.* **3.** *Chem.* any of a class of compounds formed by the replacement of one or more hydrogen atoms of an acid with elements or groups, which are composed of anions and cations, and which usually ionize in solution; a product formed by the neutralization of an acid by a base. **4. salts,** any of various salts used as purgatives, as Epsom salts. **5.** an element that gives liveliness, piquancy, or pungency: *Anecdotes are the salt of his narrative.* **6.** wit; pungency. **7.** a small, usually open dish, as of silver or glass, used on the table for holding salt. **8.** *Informal.* a sailor, esp. an old or experienced one. **9. with a grain of salt,** with reserve or allowance; with an attitude of skepticism: *Diplomats took the reports of an impending crisis with a grain of salt.* **10. worth one's salt,** deserving of one's wages or salary: *We couldn't find an assistant worth her salt.* *—v.t.* **11.** to season with salt. **12.** to cure, preserve, or treat with salt. **13.** to furnish with salt: *to salt cattle.* **14.** to treat with common salt or with any chemical salt. **15.** to spread salt, esp. rock salt, on so as to melt snow or ice: *The highway department salted the roads after the storm.* **16.** to introduce rich ore or other valuable matter fraudulently into (a mine, the ground, a mineral sample, etc.) to create a false impression of value. **17. salt away, a.** Also, **salt down.** to preserve by adding quantities of salt to, as meat. **b.** *Informal.* to keep in reserve; store away; save: *to salt away most of one's earnings.* **18. salt out,** to separate (a dissolved substance) from a solution by the addition of a salt, esp. common salt. *—adj.* **19.** containing salt; having the taste of salt: *salt water.* **20.** cured or preserved with salt: *salt cod.* **21.** inundated by or growing in salt water: *salt marsh.* **22.** producing the one of the four basic taste sensations that is not sweet, sour, or bitter. **23.** pungent or sharp: *salt speech.* [bef. 900; (n. and adj.) ME; OE *sealt;* c. G *Salz,* ON, Goth *salt;* akin to L *sāl,* Gk *háls* (see HALO-); (v.) ME *salten,* OE *s(e)altan;* cf. OHG *salzan,* ON *salta,* D *zouten;* see SALARY] **—salt′like′,** *adj.*
—Syn. 5. flavor, savor. **8.** See **sailor.**

salt[2] (sôlt), *adj. Obs.* lustful; lecherous. [1535–45; aph. var. of *assaut,* ME *a sawt* < MF *a saut* on the jump; *saut* < L *saltus* a jump, equiv. to *sal(ire)* to jump + *-tus* suffix of v. action]

SALT (sôlt), *n.* See **Strategic Arms Limitations Treaty.**

SALT I. See under **Strategic Arms Limitations Treaty.**

SALT II. See under **Strategic Arms Limitations Treaty.**

sal·ta (sal′tə, sôl′-), *n.* a game for two, resembling Chinese checkers, played on a board with 100 squares. [1900–05; < G *Salta* < L *saltā,* 2d sing. impv. of *saltāre* to leap; see SALTANT]

Sal·ta (säl′tä), *n.* a city in NW Argentina. 260,323.

sal·tan·do (säl tän′dō), *Music.* *—adj.* **1.** (of a performance with a stringed instrument) playing each note staccato by bouncing the bow on the strings. *—adv.* **2.** in a saltando manner. Also, **sal·ta·to** (säl tä′tō). [< It, ger. of *saltare* to jump < L *saltāre* to dance, leap; see SALTANT]

salt-and-pep·per (sôlt′n pep′ər), *adj.* pepper-and-salt.

sal·tant (sal′tnt), *adj.* dancing; leaping; jumping. [1595–1605; < L *saltant-* (s. of *saltāns,* prp. of *saltāre* to jump about, dance, freq. of *salīre* to jump), equiv. to *sal-* jump + *-t-* freq. suffix + *-ant-* -ANT]

sal·ta·rel·lo (sal′tə rel′ō, sôl′-; *It.* säl′tä REl′lô), *n., pl.* **-los,** *It.* **-li** (-lē). **1.** a lively Italian dance for one person or a couple. **2.** the music for it. [1590–1600; < It, deriv. of *saltare* to dance; see SALTANT]

sal·ta·tion (sal tā′shən), *n.* **1.** a dancing, hopping, or leaping movement. **2.** an abrupt movement or transition. **3.** *Geol.* intermittent, leaping movement of particles of sand or gravel, as from the force of wind or running water. **4.** *Biol.* **a.** a sudden discontinuity in a line of descent. **b.** a mutation. [1640–50; < L *saltātiōn-* (s. of *saltātiō*) a dancing, equiv. to *saltāt(us)* (ptp. of *saltāre;* see SALTANT) + *-iōn-* -ION] **—sal·ta′tion·al,** *adj.*

sal·ta·tion·ism (sal tā′shə niz′əm), *n. Biol.* any of several theories holding that the evolution of species proceeds in major steps by the abrupt transformation of an ancestral species into a descendant species of a different type, rather than by the gradual accumulation of small changes. [1970–75; SALTATION + -ISM] **—sal·ta′·tion·ist,** *n.*

sal·ta·to·ri·al (sal′tə tôr′ē əl, -tōr′-), *adj.* **1.** pertaining to saltation. **2.** *Zool.* characterized by or adapted for leaping. [1780–90; SALTATORY + -AL[1]]

sal·ta·to·ry (sal′tə tôr′ē, -tōr′ē), *adj.* **1.** pertaining to or adapted for saltation. **2.** proceeding by abrupt movements. [1615–25; < L *saltātōrius,* equiv. to *saltā(re)* to dance + *-tōrius* -TORY[1]]

salt-box (sôlt′boks′), *n.* **1.** a box in which salt is kept. **2.** a type of house found esp. in New England, generally two full stories high in front and one story high in back, the roof having about the same pitch in both directions so that the ridge is well toward the front of the house. Also, **salt′box′.** [1605–15]

salt·bush (sôlt′bo͝osh′), *n.* any of various plants or shrubs of the genus *Atriplex,* having mostly alternate leaves and clusters of inconspicuous flowers, often growing in saline or alkaline soil. [1860–65; SALT[1] + BUSH[1], so called because they thrive in saline or alkaline soils]

salt′ cake′, *Chem.* an impure form of sodium sulfate, esp. as obtained by the interaction of sulfuric acid and common salt in the synthesis of hydrochloric acid: used chiefly in the manufacture of glass, ceramic glazes, soaps, and sodium salts. [1695–1705]

salt′ ce′dar, a shrub or small tree, *Tamarix gallica,* of the Mediterranean region, having bluish foliage and white or pinkish flowers. Also called **French tamarisk.** [1880–85]

salt·cel·lar (sôlt′sel′ər), *n.* a shaker or dish for salt. [1400–50; SALT[1] + CELLAR, for earlier *saler* saltcellar, late ME < OF *saliere* < L *salāria,* n. use of fem. of *salārius* (adj.) pertaining to salt, equiv. to *sal* SALT[1] + *-ārius* -ARY]

salt′ chuck′, *Canadian Informal.* **1.** the ocean. **2.** any body of salt water. [1855–60]

salt′ dome′, *Geol.* a domelike rock structure that is formed beneath the earth's surface by the upward movement of a mass of salt, may reach thousands of feet in vertical extent, and is more or less circular in plan: often associated with oil and gas pools. Cf. **diapir.** [1905–10]

salt·ed (sôl′tid), *adj.* seasoned, cured, or otherwise treated with salt. [1300–50; ME; see SALT[1], -ED[3]]

Sal·ten (sôl′tn; *Ger.* zäl′tən), *n.* **Fe·lix** (fē′liks; *Ger.* fā′liks), (*Siegmund Salzman*), 1869–1945, Austrian novelist, in Switzerland after 1938.

salt·er (sôl′tər), *n.* **1.** a person who makes or sells salt. **2.** a person who salts meat, fish, etc. [bef. 1000; ME; OE *sealtere* saltmaker. See SALT[1], -ER[1]]

salt·ern (sôl′tərn), *n.* **1.** a saltworks. **2.** a plot of land laid out in pools for the evaporation of seawater to produce salt. [bef. 900; OE *sealtærn* saltworks (not recorded in ME), equiv. to *sealt* SALT[1] + *ærn* building, house]

salt′ flat′, an extensive level tract coated with salt deposits left by evaporation of rising ground water or a temporary body of surface water. Cf. **alkali flat.** [1870–75]

salt′ gland′, a gland, located in the head of seabirds and various marine mammals and reptiles, that secretes into the nasal passages the excess salt imbibed or ingested. [1945–50]

salt′ glaze′, a ceramic glaze on stoneware produced by the chemical reaction that occurs when salt is thrown into a kiln during firing. [1850–55] **—salt′ glaz′ing.**

salt·glaze (sôlt′glāz′), *adj. Ceram.* having a salt glaze. Also, **salt′-glazed′, salt′glazed′.** [1860–65; SALT[1] + GLAZE]

salt′ grass′, any of several grasses, as *Distichlis spicata,* that grow in salt marshes or meadows or in alkali soil. [1695–1705]

salt′ hay′, hay made up of salt grass, often used as fodder or as a mulch. [1640–50, *Amer.*]

salt′ horse′, *Naut. Slang.* salted beef; salt junk. [1830–40]

salt·ie (sôl′tē), *n. Canadian Slang.* an ocean-going sailor. [1960–65; SALT[1] + -IE]

salt·i·er[1] (sôl′tē ər), *adj.* comparative of **salty.**

sal·tier[2] (sal′tēr, -tī°r), *n.* saltire.

sal·ti·grade (sal′ti grād′, sôl′-), *adj.* **1.** moving by leaping. **2.** belonging or pertaining to the family Salticidae, comprising the jumping spiders. [1830–40; < L *salt(āre)* to jump (see SALTANT) + -I- + -GRADE]

Sal·ti·llo (säl tē′yō), *n.* a city in and the capital of Coahuila, in northern Mexico. 233,600.

sal·tim·boc·ca (säl′tim bō′kə; *It.* säl′tēm bôk′kä), *n. Italian Cookery.* veal and ham wrapped together and sautéed in butter, often seasoned with sage. [1935–40; < It, contr. of *salta in bocca* (it) jumps into (one's) mouth]

sal·tine (sôl tēn′), *n.* a crisp, salted cracker. [1905–10, *Amer.;* SALT[1] + -INE[2]]

salt′ing out′, *Chem.* the addition of salt to a mixture to precipitate proteins, soaps, and other simple organic compounds. [1885–90]

sal·tire (sal′tīr, -tī°r, sôl′-), *n. Heraldry.* **1.** an ordinary in the form of a cross with arms running diagonally from the dexter chief to the sinister base and from the sinister chief to the dexter base; St. Andrew's cross. **2. in saltire,** (of charges) arranged in the form of a saltire. **3. per saltire,** diagonally in both directions: *party per saltire.* Also, **saltier.** [1350–1400; ME *sawtire* < MF *sautoir* crossed jumping bar < ML *saltātōrium* something pertaining to jumping; see SALTANT, -TORY[2]]

sal·tire·wise (sal′tīr wīz′, -tī°r, sôl′-), *adv. Heraldry.* in the direction or manner of a saltire. Also, **sal·tire·ways** (sal′tīr wāz′, -tī°r-, sôl′-). [1715–25; SALTIRE + -WISE]

salt·ish (sôl′tish), *adj.* somewhat salty. [1470–80; SALT[1] + -ISH[1]] **—salt′ish·ly,** *adv.* **—salt′ish·ness,** *n.*

salt′ junk′, *Naut. Slang.* salted beef or pork. [1785–95]

salt′ lake′, a body of water having no outlet to the sea and containing in solution a high concentration of salts, esp. sodium chloride. [1755–65]

Salt′ Lake′ Cit′y, a city in and the capital of Utah, in the N part, near the Great Salt Lake. 163,033.

salt·less (sôlt′lis), *adj.* **1.** lacking salt. **2.** lacking vitality; dull; insipid: *a saltless person.* [1350–1400; ME; see SALT[1], -LESS]

salt′ lick′, **1.** a place to which animals go to lick naturally occurring salt deposits. **2.** a block of salt or salt preparation provided, as in a pasture, for cattle, horses, etc. [1735–45, *Amer.*]

salt′ marsh′, a marshy tract that is wet with salt water or flooded by the sea. [bef. 1000; ME *saltmerche,* OE *sealtne mersc*]

salt′ mine′, **1.** a mine from which salt is excavated. **2.** Usually, **salt mines.** a place of habitual confinement and drudgery: *After two weeks of vacation it will be back to the salt mines for the staff.* [1675–85]

salt·ness (sôlt′nis), *n.* the state or quality of being salt or salty. [bef. 900; ME *saltnesse;* OE *sealtnes.* See SALT[1], -NESS]

Sal·to (säl′tô), *n.* a city in NW Uruguay, on the Uruguay River. 80,000.

salt′ of phos′phorus. See **sodium ammonium phosphate.**

salt′ of sor′rel, *Chem.* See **potassium binoxalate.**

salt′ of the earth′, an individual or group considered as representative of the best or noblest elements of society. [1350–1400; ME; after Matthew 5:13]

Sal′ton Sea′ (sôl′tən, -tn), a shallow saline lake in S California, in the Imperial Valley, formed by the diversion of water from the Colorado River into a salt-covered depression (**Sal′ton Sink′**). 236 ft. (72 m) below sea level.

salt′ pan′, an undrained natural depression, as a crater or tectonic basin, in which the evaporation of water leaves a deposit of salt. [1485–95]

salt·pe·ter (sôlt′pē′tər), *n.* **1.** the form of potassium nitrate, KNO_3, that occurs naturally, used in the manufacture of fireworks, fluxes, gunpowder, etc.; niter. **2.** See **Chile saltpeter.** Also, **salt′pe′tre.** [1275–1325; earlier *salt peter;* r. ME *sal peter, salpetre* < ML *salpetrē,* for L *sal petrae* salt of rock, so called because it commonly encrusts stones]

salt′ pit′, a pit where salt is obtained. [1350–1400; ME]

salt′ pork′, pork cured with salt, esp. the fat pork taken from the back, sides, and belly. [1715–25]

salt′-ris·ing bread′ (sôlt′rī′zing), a kind of bread leavened with a fermented mixture of salted milk, cornmeal, flour, sugar, and soda. [1825–35, *Amer.*]

Salt′ Riv′er, a river flowing W from E Arizona to the

CONCISE PRONUNCIATION KEY: act, cāpe, dâre, pärt; set, ēqual; if, īce; ox, ōver, ôrder, oil, bo͝ok, bo͞ot, out; up, ûrge; child; sing; shoe; thin, *th*at; zh as in *treasure.* ə = *a* as in *alone, e* as in *system, i* as in *easily, o* as in *gallop, u* as in *circus;* ° as in *fire* (fī°r), *hour* (ou°r). l and n can serve as syllabic consonants, as in *cradle* (krād′l), and *button* (but′n). See the full key inside the front cover.

Gila River near Phoenix: Roosevelt Dam. 200 mi. (322 km) long.

salt′ shake′, *South Midland U.S.* a salt shaker.

salt′ shak′er, a container for salt with a perforated top to allow the salt to be shaken out. Also, **salt′shak′·er.** [1890–95, *Amer.*]

salt′ spoon′, a small spoon with which to take salt at the table. [1810–20]

salt′ stick′, a crusty bread roll sprinkled with salt crystals, made in the shape of a cylinder.

salt′ tree′. See **athel tree.** [1815–25]

sal·tus (sal′təs, sôl′-), *n., pl.* **-tus·es.** *Math.* oscillation (def. 5b). [1655–65; < NL, L: a leap. See SALT²]

salt′ wa′ter, **1.** water containing a large amount of salt. **2.** seawater. [bef. 1000; ME; OE]

salt·wa·ter (sôlt′wô′tər, -wot′ər), *adj.* **1.** of or pertaining to salt water. **2.** inhabiting salt water: *a saltwater fish.* [1520–30; SALT¹ + WATER]

salt′water taf′fy, a taffy sometimes made with seawater but more generally made with salted fresh water. [1890–95, *Amer.*]

salt′ well′, a well from which brine is obtained. [bef. 950; ME; OE]

salt·works (sôlt′wûrks′), *n., pl.* **-works.** (*often used with a plural v.*) a building or plant where salt is made. [1555–65; SALT¹ + WORKS]

salt·wort (sôlt′wûrt′, -wôrt′), *n.* any of various plants of sea beaches, salt marshes, and alkaline regions, esp. belonging to the genus *Salsola,* of the goosefoot family, as *S. kali,* a bushy plant having prickly leaves, or belonging to the genus *Salicornia.* [1560–70; trans. of D *zoutkruid,* equiv. to *zout* salt + *kruid* herb. See SALT¹, WORT¹]

salt·y (sôl′tē), *adj.,* **salt·i·er, salt·i·est. 1.** tasting of or containing salt; saline. **2.** piquant; sharp; witty. **3.** racy or coarse: *salty humor.* **4.** of the sea, sailing, or life at sea. [1400–50; late ME; see SALT¹, -Y¹] —**salt′i·ly,** *adv.* —**salt′i·ness,** *n.*

salt′y dog′, a cocktail of gin or vodka and grapefruit juice, traditionally served in a salt-rimmed glass.

sa·lu·bri·ous (sə lo͞o′brē əs), *adj.* favorable to or promoting health; healthful: *salubrious air.* [1540–50; < L *salūbr(is)* promoting health (akin to *salūs* health) + -IOUS] —**sa·lu′bri·ous·ly,** *adv.* —**sa·lu′bri·ous·ness, sa·lu·bri·ty** (sə lo͞o′bri tē), *n.*

sa·lud (sä lo͞oth′), *interj. Spanish.* (used after a person has sneezed or as a toast.) [lit., health]

sa·lu·gi (sə lo͞o′jē), *n.* **1.** a gamelike prank in which a youth grabs something belonging to another and throws it to a third, preventing the owner from retrieving it as it is tossed back and forth. —*interj.* **2.** (used to signal the beginning of this prank.) [orig. uncert.]

Sa·lu·ki (sə lo͞o′kē), *n.* (*sometimes l.c.*) one of a breed of black and tan, white, gold, or tricolor dogs resembling the greyhound and having fringes of long hair on the ears, legs, and thighs, raised originally in Egypt and southwestern Asia. Also called **gazelle hound.** [1800–10; < Ar *salūqī* lit., of *Salūq* city in Arabia]

Saluki, 2 ft. (0.6 m) high at shoulder

sal·u·ret·ic (sal′yə ret′ik), *Med.* —*adj.* **1.** of or pertaining to a substance that promotes renal excretion of sodium and chloride ions. —*n.* **2.** any such substance, as furosemide. [1955–60; SAL + URETIC] —**sal′u·ret′i·cal·ly,** *adv.*

Sa·lus (sā′ləs), *n.* the ancient Roman goddess of health and prosperity: identified with the Greek goddess Hygeia. [< L *salūs* health]

sa·lus po·pu·li su·pre·ma lex es·to (sä′lo͝os pô′po͝o lē′ so͞o prā′mä leks es′tō; *Eng.* sā′ləs pop′yə lī′ so͞o prē′mə leks es′tō), *Latin.* let the welfare of the people be the supreme law: a motto of Missouri.

sal·u·tar·y (sal′yə ter′ē), *adj.* **1.** favorable to or promoting health; healthful. **2.** promoting or conducive to some beneficial purpose; wholesome. [1480–90; < L *salūt(āris)* (*salūt-* (s. of *salūs*) health + *-āris* -AR¹) + -ARY] —**sal·u·tar·i·ly** (sal′yə ter′ə lē, sal′yə târ′-), *adv.* —**sal′u·tar′i·ness,** *n.*
—**Syn. 1.** salubrious. See **healthy.**

sal·u·ta·tion (sal′yə tā′shən), *n.* **1.** the act of saluting. **2.** something uttered, written, or done by way of saluting. **3.** a word or phrase serving as the prefatory greeting in a letter or speech, as *Dear Sir* in a letter or *Ladies and Gentlemen* in a speech. [1350–1400; ME < L *salūtātiōn-* (s. of *salūtātiō*) greeting, equiv. to *salūtāt(us)* (ptp. of *salūtāre* to greet; see SALUTE, -ATE¹) + *-iōn-* -ION] —**sal′u·ta′tion·al,** *adj.* —**sal′u·ta′tion·less,** *adj.*

sa·lu·ta·to·ri·an (sə lo͞o′tə tôr′ē ən, -tōr′-), *n.* (in some U.S. schools and colleges) the student ranking second highest in the graduating class, who delivers the salutatory. [1840–50, *Amer.*; SALUTATORY + -AN]

CONCISE ETYMOLOGY KEY: <, descended or borrowed from; >, whence; b., blend of, blended; c., cognate with; cf., compare; deriv., derivative; equiv., equivalent; imit., imitative; obl., oblique; r., replacing; s., stem; sp., spelling, spelled; resp., respelling, respelled; trans., translation; ?, origin unknown; *, unattested; ‡, probably earlier than. See the full key inside the front cover.

sa·lu·ta·to·ri·um (sə lo͞o′tə tôr′ē əm, -tōr′-), *n., pl.* **-to·ri·a** (-tôr′ē ə, -tōr′-). a porch or room in a monastery or church serving as a meeting or almsgiving place for monks or priests and the laity. [1650–60; < ML *salūtātōrium,* n. use of neut. of *salūtātōrius* SALUTATORY]

sa·lu·ta·to·ry (sə lo͞o′tə tôr′ē, -tōr′ē), *adj., n., pl.* **-ries.** —*adj.* **1.** pertaining to or of the nature of a salutation. —*n.* **2.** a welcoming address, esp. one given at the beginning of commencement exercises in some U.S. high schools and colleges by the salutatorian. [1635–45; < ML *salūtātōrius,* equiv. to L *salūtā(re)* to SALUTE + *-tōrius* -TORY¹] —**sa·lu′ta·to′ri·ly,** *adv.*

sa·lute (sə lo͞ot′), *v.* **-lut·ed, -lut·ing,** *n.* —*v.t.* **1.** *Mil.* to pay respect to or honor by some formal act, as by raising the right hand to the side of the headgear, presenting arms, firing cannon, dipping colors, etc. **2.** to address with expressions of goodwill, respect, etc.; greet. **3.** to make a bow or other gesture to, as in greeting, farewell, or respect. **4.** to express respect or praise for; honor; commend. —*v.i.* **5.** *Mil.* to give a salute. **6.** to perform a salutation. —*n.* **7.** *Mil.* **a.** the special act of respect paid in saluting. **b.** the position of the hand or rifle in saluting: *at the salute.* **8.** an act of saluting; salutation. **9.** a gold coin, bearing the image of the Virgin Mary receiving Gabriel's salutation, issued by Charles VI of France and by Henry V and Henry VI of England. [1350–1400; (v.) ME *saluten* < L *salūtāre* to greet (lit., to hail), deriv. of *salūt-* (s. of *salūs*) health; r. *salue* < F *saluer* < L, as above; (n.) ME, partly < OF *salut* (deriv. of *saluer*), partly deriv. of the v.] —**sa·lut′er,** *n.*
—**Syn. 4.** applaud, cheer, praise.

sa·lu·te (sä lo͞o′te), *interj. Italian.* (used after a person has sneezed or as a toast.) [lit., health]

sal·u·tif·er·ous (sal′yə tif′ər əs), *adj.* salutary. [1530–40; < L *salūtifer* health-bearing (see SALUTE, -I-, -FER) + -OUS]

Salv., Salvador.

salv·a·ble (sal′və bəl), *adj.* fit for or capable of being saved or salvaged. [1660–70; < LL *salv(āre)* to save + -ABLE] —**sal′va·bil′i·ty, sal′va·ble·ness,** *n.* —**sal′va·bly,** *adv.*

Sal·va·dor (sal′və dôr′; *for 1, 3 also Sp.* säl′vä thôr′; *for 2 also Port.* säl′və dôr′), *n.* **1.** See **El Salvador. 2.** Formerly, **Bahia, São Salvador.** a seaport in E Brazil. 1,525,831. **3.** a male given name. —**Sal′va·do′ran, Sal′va·do′ri·an,** *adj., n.*

sal·vage (sal′vij), *n., v.,* **-vaged, -vag·ing.** —*n.* **1.** the act of saving a ship or its cargo from perils of the seas. **2.** the property so saved. **3.** compensation given to those who voluntarily save a ship or its cargo. **4.** the act of saving anything from fire, danger, etc. **5.** the property saved from danger. **6.** the value or proceeds upon sale of goods recovered from a fire. —*v.t.* **7.** to save from shipwreck, fire, etc. [1635–45; < OF; see SAVE¹, -AGE] —**sal′vage·a·ble,** *adj.* —**sal′vage·a·bil′i·ty,** *n.* —**sal′vag·er,** *n.*

sal′vage archaeol′ogy, the collection of archaeological data and materials from a site in danger of imminent destruction, as from new construction or flooding. [1965–70]

Sal·var·san (sal′vər san′), *Pharm., Trademark.* a brand of arsphenamine.

sal·va·tion (sal vā′shən), *n.* **1.** the act of saving or protecting from harm, risk, loss, destruction, etc. **2.** the state of being saved or protected from harm, risk, etc. **3.** a source, cause, or means of being saved or protected from harm, risk, etc. **4.** *Theol.* deliverance from the power and penalty of sin; redemption. [1175–1225; ME *salvatio(u)n* < LL *salvātiōn-* (s. of *salvātiō*), equiv. to *salvāt(us)* (ptp. of *salvāre* to SAVE¹; see -ATE¹) + *-iōn* -ION; r. ME *sa(u)vaciun, sauvacion* < OF *sauvacion* < LL, as above] —**sal·va′tion·al,** *adj.*

Salva′tion Ar′my, **1.** an international Christian organization founded in England in 1865 by William Booth, organized along quasi-military lines and devoted chiefly to evangelism and to providing social services, esp. to the poor. **2.** a retail store operated by the Salvation Army selling donated clothing, furniture, books, etc., at low prices: *This sofa was a bargain at the Salvation Army.*

Sal·va·tion·ist (sal vā′shə nist), *n.* **1.** a member of the Salvation Army. **2.** (*l.c.*) a person who preaches salvation, deliverance from sin, etc., and the means of obtaining it; evangelist. [1880–85; SALVATION + -IST] —**sal·va′tion·ism,** *n.*

Sal·va·tore (sal′və tôr′, -tōr′; *It.* säl′vä tô′re), *n.* a male given name.

salve¹ (sav, säv), *n., v.,* **salved, salv·ing.** —*n.* **1.** a medicinal ointment for healing or relieving wounds and sores. **2.** anything that soothes, mollifies, or relieves. —*v.t.* **3.** to soothe with or as if with salve; assuage: *to salve one's conscience.* [bef. 900; (n.) ME; OE *sealf;* c. G *Salbe* salve, Skt *sarpis* melted butter; (v.) ME *salven,* OE *sealfian*]
—**Syn. 3.** ease, alleviate, mollify.

salve² (salv), *v.i., v.t.,* **salved, salv·ing.** to save from loss or destruction; to salvage. [1700–10; back formation from SALVAGE]

sal·ve³ (sal′vē; *Lat.* säl′wā), *interj.* hail! [1400–50; late ME < L *salvē!* lit., be in good health!; cf. SALUTE]

Sal·ve·mi·ni (säl ve′mē nē), *n.* **Ga·e·ta·no** (gä′e tä′-nô), 1873–1957, Italian historian in the U.S.

sal·ver (sal′vər), *n.* a tray, esp. one used for serving food or beverages. [1655–65; < Sp *salv(a)* kind of tray (orig. protective foretasting, deriv. of *salvar* to save < L *salvāre*) + -ER¹]

Sal·ve Re·gi·na (säl′vā ri jē′nə), *Rom. Cath. Ch.* a prayer in the form of a hymn to the Virgin Mary.

sal·vi·a (sal′vē ə), *n.* any plant of the genus *Salvia,* comprising the sages, having opposite leaves and whorled flowers. [1835–45; < NL, L: sage]

sal·vif·ic (sal vif′ik), *adj.* of or pertaining to redemptive power. [1585–95; < ML *salvificus,* equiv. to L *salv(us)* SAFE + *-i-* -I- + *-ficus* -FIC]

sal·vo¹ (sal′vō), *n., pl.* **-vos, -voes. 1.** a simultaneous or successive discharge of artillery, bombs, etc. **2.** a round of fire given as a salute. **3.** a round of cheers or applause. [1585–95; earlier *salva* < It << L *salvē* SALVE³]

sal·vo² (sal′vō), *n., pl.* **-vos.** *Archaic.* **1.** an excuse or quibbling evasion. **2.** something to save a person's reputation or soothe a person's feelings. [1635–45; < L *salvō,* abl. of *salvus* safe, found in legal phrases]

sal vo·la·ti·le (sal′ vō lat′l ē′), an aromatic alcoholic solution of ammonium carbonate, the chief ingredient in smelling salts. [1645–55; < NL: volatile salt]

sal·vor (sal′vər), *n.* a person who salvages or helps to salvage a ship, cargo, etc. [1670–80; SALV(AGE) + -OR²]

Sal·ween (sal′wēn), *n.* a river in SE Asia, flowing S from SW China through E Burma (Myanmar) to the Bay of Bengal. 1750 mi. (2815 km) long.

Sal·yut (säl′yo͞ot′), *n.* one of a series of Soviet earth-orbiting space stations, first launched in 1971. [< Russ *Salyút* lit., SALUTE < F]

Salz·burg (sôlz′bûrg; *Ger.* zälts′bo͝ork), *n.* a city in W Austria: the birthplace of Mozart. 138,213.

Salz·git·ter (zälts′git′ər), *n.* a city in Lower Saxony, in central Germany, SE of Hanover. 119,181. Formerly, **Watenstedt-Salzgitter.**

Sam (sam), *n.* **1.** a male given name, form of **Samuel. 2.** a female given name, form of **Samantha.**

SAM (sam), *n.* **1.** surface-to-air missile. **2.** Space Available Mail: a special air service for sending parcels weighing up to 15 lbs. (6.8 kg) to overseas members of the armed forces: only the regular parcel post rate to the U.S. port of shipment is charged. Cf. **PAL.**

SAM, See **shared-appreciation mortgage.**

Sam., *Bible.* Samuel.

S. Am., 1. South America. **2.** South American.

sa·ma‘ (sə mä′), *n. Islam.* the Sufi practice of gathering to listen to religious poetry that is sung, often accompanied by ecstatic dance or other ritual. [< Ar *samā‘* lit., hearing]

sa·ma·dhi (sə mä′dē), *n. Hinduism, Buddhism.* the highest stage in meditation, in which a person experiences oneness with the universe. [1820–30; < Skt *samādhi*]

Sa·main (sä′win), *n.* Samhain.

sa·maj (sə mäj′), *n.* a Hindu religious society or movement. [1870–75; < Hindi *samāj* meeting]

Sa·man (sä′män), *n.* a Persian noble who lived in the 8th century A.D., progenitor of the Samanid dynasty.

Sa·ma′na Cay′ (sə mä′nə), a small, uninhabited island in the central Bahamas: now believed to be first land in the New World seen by Christopher Columbus 1492. 9 mi. (14 km) long.

Sa·ma·nid (sə mä′nid, sam′ə nid), *n.* a member of the rulers of Persia in the 9th and 10th centuries.

Sa·man·tha (sə man′thə), *n.* a female given name: from an Aramaic word meaning "listener."

Sa·mar (sä′mär), *n.* an island in the E central Philippines. 1,200,592; 5309 sq. mi (13,750 sq. km).

sam·a·ra (sam′ər ə, sə mâr′ə), *n. Bot.* an indehiscent, usually one-seeded, winged fruit, as of the elm or maple. [1570–80; < NL; L *samara, samera* elm seed]

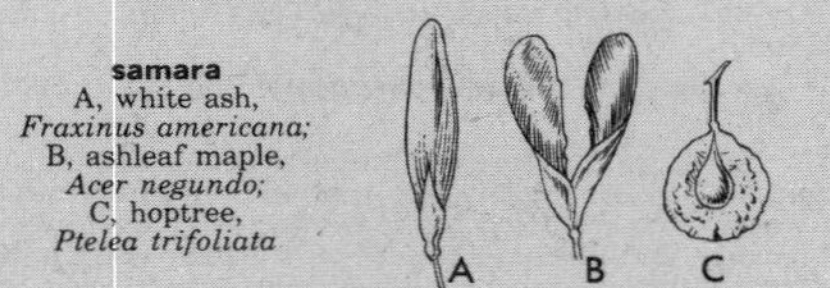

samara A, white ash, *Fraxinus americana;* B, ashleaf maple, *Acer negundo;* C, hoptree, *Ptelea trifoliata*

Sa·ma·ra (sə mär′ə; *Russ.* su mä′rə), *n.* a port in the SE Russian Federation in Europe, on the Volga. 1,257,000. Formerly (1935–91), **Kuibyshev.**

Sa·ma·rang (sə mär′äng), *n.* Semarang.

Sa·mar·i·a (sə mâr′ē ə), *n.* **1.** a district in ancient Palestine: later part of the Roman province of Syria; taken by Jordan 1948; occupied by Israel 1967. **2.** the northern kingdom of the ancient Hebrews; Israel. **3.** the ancient capital of this kingdom.

sam·a·ri·form (sam′ər ə fôrm′), *adj. Bot.* having the form of a samara. [1890–95; SAMAR(A) + -I- + -FORM]

Sam·a·rin·da (sam′ə rin′də), *n.* a city on E Borneo, in Indonesia. 137,521.

Sa·mar·i·tan (sə mar′i tn), *n.* **1.** an inhabitant of Samaria. **2.** See **good Samaritan. 3.** (*often l.c.*) one who is compassionate and helpful to a person in distress. **4.** any of the dialects of Aramaic spoken by the Samaritans in ancient Israel and until recently still spoken in Nablus. —*adj.* **5.** pertaining to Samaria or to Samaritans. [bef. 1000; ME, OE < LL *samarītānus* < Gk *samarī́t(ēs)* dweller in SAMARIA + *-ānus* -AN] —**Sa·mar′i·tan·ism,** *n.*

sa·mar·i·um (sə mâr′ē əm), *n. Chem.* a rare-earth metallic element discovered in samarskite. *Symbol:* Sm; *at. wt.:* 150.35; *at. no.:* 62; *sp. gr.:* 7.49. [1875–80; < NL; see SAMARSKITE, -IUM]

Sam·ar·kand (sam′ər kand′; *Russ.* sə mur känt′), *n.* a city in SE Uzbekistan: taken by Alexander the Great 329 B.C.; Tamerlane's capital in the 14th century. 476,000. Also, **Sam′ar·cand′.** Ancient, **Maracanda.** See map on next page.

Sa•mar•ra (sə mär′ə), *n.* a town in central Iraq, on the Tigris: seat of the early Abassid caliphs.

sa•mar•skite (sə mär′skīt), *n.* a velvet-black mineral, a complex columbate-tantalate of uranium, cerium, etc., occurring in masses: a minor source of uranium, thorium, and rare-earth oxides. [< G *Samarskit* (1847), after Russian mining engineer V.E. *Samarskiĭ*-Bykhovets (1803–70); see -ITE¹]

Sa•ma-Ve•da (sä′mə vā′də, -vē′də), *n. Hinduism.* one of the Samhitas, a collection of mantras and tunes used in connection with the Rig-Veda. Cf. **Veda.**

sam•ba (sam′bə, säm′-), *n., pl.* **-bas,** *v.,* **-baed, -ba•ing.** —*n.* **1.** a rhythmic, Brazilian ballroom dance of African origin. —*v.i.* **2.** to dance the samba. [1880–85; < Pg *samba,* alleged to be of African orig.]

sam•bal (säm′bäl), *n.* a condiment or side dish of Indonesia, Malaysia, and southern India, made with any of various ingredients, as vegetables, fish, or coconut, usually seasoned with chili peppers and spices and served with rice and curries. [< Malay < Tamil *campāl* kind of relish, condiment, akin to *campāram* ingredients for curry, Telugu *sambhāram* preparation of spices for seasoning, Marathi *sā̆bhar* seasoning for dal, all ult. reflecting Prakrit *sambhārei* (he) garnishes, Skt *sambhārayati* (he) causes to be brought together, deriv. with *sam-* SYN- and *bhṛ-* to BEAR¹]

sam•bar (sam′bər, säm′-), *n.* a deer, *Cervus unicolor,* of India, Sri Lanka, southeastern Asia, the East Indies, and the Philippines, having three-pointed antlers. Also, **sam′bur, sam′bhar, sam′bhur.** [1690–1700; < Hindi < Skt *śambara*]

sam•bo (sam′bō), *n., pl.* **-bos.** *Disparaging and Offensive.* **1.** a black person. **2.** a Latin American of black and Indian or mulatto ancestry. Also, **zambo.** [1690–1700, *Amer.*; < AmerSp *zambo* black person, mulatto, perh. special use of Sp *zambo* bowlegged, said to be < L *scambus* < Gk *skambós* crooked]

Sam•bre (*Fr.* säɴ′brᵊ), *n.* a river in W Europe, flowing NE through N France and S Belgium into the Meuse at Namur: battle 1918. 120 mi. (193 km) long.

Sam′ Browne′ belt′ (sam′ broun′), a sword belt having a supporting strap over the right shoulder, formerly worn by officers in the U.S. Army, now sometimes worn as part of the uniform by police officers, guards, and army officers in other nations. [1910–15; named after its inventor, British general *Samuel Browne* (1824–1901)]

sam•bu•ca¹ (sam byo͞o′kə), *n.* **1.** Also, **sam•buke** (sam′byo͞ok). an ancient stringed musical instrument used in Greece and the Near East. **2.** a medieval hurdy-gurdy. [1350–1400; ME *sambuke* < L *sambūca* < Gk *sambýkē* perh. < Sem; cf. Aram *sabbəkhā*]

sam•bu•ca² (sam bo͞o′kə; *It.* säm bo͞o′kä), *n.* a licorice-flavored Italian liqueur made from elderberries. [1970–75; < It, fem. deriv. of *sambuco* elder < L *sa(m)būcus*]

same (sām), *adj.* **1.** identical with what is about to be or has just been mentioned: *This street is the same one we were on yesterday.* **2.** being one or identical though having different names, aspects, etc.: *These are the same rules though differently worded.* **3.** agreeing in kind, amount, etc.; corresponding: *two boxes of the same dimensions.* **4.** unchanged in character, condition, etc.: *It's the same town after all these years.* —*pron.* **5.** the same person or thing. **6.** the same kind or category of thing: *You're having steak? I'll have the same, but very rare.* **7.** the very person, thing, or set just mentioned: *Sighted sub sank same.* **8. all the same, a.** notwithstanding; nevertheless: *You don't have to go but we wish you would, all the same.* **b.** of no difference; immaterial: *It's all the same to me whether our team loses or wins.* **9. just the same, a.** in the same manner. **b.** nevertheless: *It was a success, but it could easily have failed, just the same.* **10. the same,** in the same manner; in an identical or similar way: *I see the same through your glasses as I do through mine.* [1150–1200; ME; OE *same* (adv.); c. ON *samr,* Gk *homós,* Skt *samá*]
—**Syn. 1–3.** corresponding, interchangeable, equal. SAME, SIMILAR agree in indicating a correspondence between two or more things. SAME means alike in kind, degree, quality; that is, identical (with): *to eat the same food every day.* SIMILAR means like, resembling, having certain qualities in common, somewhat the same as, of nearly the same kind as: *similar in appearance; Don't treat them as if they were the same when they are only similar.* —**Ant. 1.** different. **3.** unlike.

sa•mekh (sä′meкн), *n.* **1.** the 15th letter of the Hebrew alphabet. **2.** the consonant sound represented by this letter. Also, **sa′mech.** [< Heb *sāmekh,* akin to *sāmakh* he supported]

same•ness (sām′nis), *n.* **1.** the state or quality of being the same; identity; uniformity. **2.** lack of variety; monotony. [1575–85; SAME + -NESS]

S. Amer., 1. South America. **2.** South American.

Sa•mhain (sä′win), *n.* a festival of the ancient Celts, held around November 1 to celebrate the beginning of winter. Also, **Samain, sa•mh'in** (sä′win). [1885–90; < Ir; OIr *samain*]

Sam′ Hill′, *Slang.* hell (used esp. in WH-questions as a mild oath expressing exasperation and usually prec. by *in* or *the*): *Who in Sam Hill are you?* [1830–40, *Amer.*; *Sam* (orig. *salmon,* var. of *Sal(o)mon* an oath) + *hill,* euphemism for HELL]

Sam•hi•ta (sum′hi tä′), *n. Hinduism.* Veda (def. 2). [< Skt: *saṃhitā*]

Sa•mi (sä′mē), *n.* Lapp.

Sa•mi•an (sā′mē ən), *adj.* **1.** of or pertaining to the Greek island of Samos. —*n.* **2.** a native or inhabitant of Samos. [1570–80; < L *Sami(us)* (< Gk *Sámios* of SAMOS) + -AN]

Sa′mian ware′, a red-glazed terracotta pottery produced in Gaul and the Moselle Valley A.D. 100–300 and copied from Arretine ware. Also called **terra sigillata.** [1835–45; after classical references to a type of pottery produced at Samos, perh. an imitation of the red-glazed ware produced in Gaul and Italy]

sam•i•sen (sam′ə sen′), *n.* a guitarlike Japanese musical instrument having an extremely long neck and three strings, played with a plectrum. [1610–20; < Japn < MChin, equiv. to Chin *sānxiа* three-string banjo]

sam•ite (sam′īt, sā′mīt), *n.* a heavy silk fabric, sometimes interwoven with gold, worn in the Middle Ages. [1300–50; ME *samit* < OF < ML *examitium, samitium* < Gk *hexámiton,* neut. of *hexámitos* having six threads. See HEXA-, MITOSIS]

sam•iz•dat (sä′miz dät′; *Russ.* sə myiz dät′), *n.* **1.** a clandestine publishing system within the Soviet Union, by which forbidden or unpublishable literature is reproduced and circulated privately. **2.** a work or periodical circulated by this system. [1965–70; < Russ *samizdát,* equiv. to *sam(o)-* self- + *izdát(el'stvo)* publishing agency; coined as a jocular allusion to the compound names of official Soviet publishing organs, e.g., *Gosizdát* for *Gosudárstvennoe izdátel'stvo* State Publishing House]

Sam•khya (säng′kyə), *n. Hinduism.* Sankhya.

Saml., Samuel.

sam•let (sam′lit), *n.* a young salmon. [1645–55; SA(L)M(ON) + -LET]

Sam•mar•ti•ni (säm′mär tē′nē), *n.* **Gio•van•ni Bat•ti•sta** (jô vän′nē bät tē′stä), 1698–1775, Italian composer and organist.

Sam•my (sam′ē), *n., pl.* **-mies. 1.** a male given name, form of **Samuel. 2.** a female given name, form of **Samantha.** Also, **Sam′mie.**

Sam•ni•um (sam′nē əm), *n.* an ancient country in central Italy. —**Sam•nite** (sam′nīt), *adj., n.*

Sam•o (sam′ō), *n.* died A.D. 658, first ruler of the Slavs 623–658.

Sa•mo•a (sə mō′ə), *n.* a group of islands in the S Pacific, the islands W of 170° W longitude constituting an independent state and the rest belonging to the U.S. Formerly, **Navigators Islands.** Cf. **American Samoa, Western Samoa.**

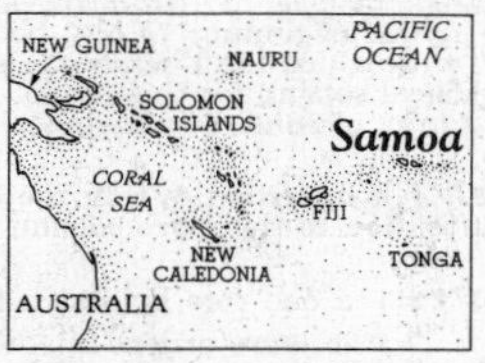

Sa•mo•an (sə mō′ən), *adj.* **1.** pertaining to Samoa or its Polynesian people. —*n.* **2.** a native or inhabitant of Samoa. **3.** the Polynesian language of Samoa. [1840–50; SAMO(A) + -AN]

Sa•mos (sā′mos, sam′ōs; *Gk.* sä′môs), *n.* a Greek island in the E Aegean. 41,709; 194 sq. mi. (502 sq. km).

SAMOS (sam′ōs), *n.* one of a series of U.S. reconnaissance satellites. [*s(atellite) a(nti)m(issile) o(bservation) s(ystem)*]

Sam•o•set (sam′ə set′), *n.* died 1653?, North American Indian leader: aided Pilgrims during early years in New England.

Sam•o•thrace (sam′ə thrās′), *n.* a Greek island in the NE Aegean. 3012. Greek, **Sa•mo•thra•ke** (sä′mô thrä′kē). —**Sam•o•thra•cian** (sam′ə thrā′shən), *adj., n.*

sam•o•var (sam′ə vär′, sam′ə vär′), *n.* a metal urn, used esp. by Russians for heating water for making tea. [1820–30; < Russ *samovár,* equiv. to *samo-* self (see SAME) + *-var,* n. deriv. of *varít'* to cook, boil]

Sam•o•yed (sam′ə yed′, sə moi′id), *n.* **1.** a member of a Uralic people dwelling in W Siberia and the far NE parts of European Russia. **2.** Also, **Samoyedic.** a subfamily of Uralic languages spoken by the Samoyed people. **3.** (*sometimes l.c.*) one of a Russian breed of medium-sized dogs that have long, dense, white or cream hair and are used by the Samoyed people for herding reindeer and pulling sleds. [1580–90; < Russ *samoyéd*]

Sam•o•yed•ic (sam′ə yed′ik), *adj.* **1.** of or pertaining to the Samoyed people or languages. —*n.* **2.** Samoyed (def. 2). [1805–15; SAMOYED + -IC]

samp (samp), *n. Northeastern U.S.* **1.** coarsely ground corn. **2.** a porridge made of it. [1635–45, *Amer.*; < Narragansett (E sp.) *nasàump* cornmeal mush (c. Munsee Delaware *nsà·pa·n* < Proto-Eastern Algonquian **nəhsa·pa·n*)]

sam•pa•gui•ta (sam′pə gē′tə), *n.* (in the Philippines) an Arabian jasmine. [< PhilippineSp < Tagalog *sampag(a)* Arabian jasmine + Sp *-ita* dim. suffix]

sam•pan (sam′pan), *n.* any of various small boats of the Far East, as one propelled by a single scull and provided with a roofing of mats. [1610–20; < Chin *sānbǎn* three-plank (boat), or < cognate dial. forms]

sampan

sam•phire (sam′fīᵊr), *n.* **1.** a European succulent plant, *Crithmum maritimum,* of the parsley family, having compound leaves and small, whitish flowers, growing in clefts of rock near the sea. **2.** glasswort. [1535–45; earlier *sampiere* < MF (*herbe de*) *Saint Pierre* (herb of) Saint Peter]

sam•ple (sam′pəl, säm′-), *n., adj., v.,* **-pled, -pling.** —*n.* **1.** a small part of anything or one of a number, intended to show the quality, style, or nature of the whole; specimen. **2.** *Statistics.* a subset of a population: *to study a sample of the total population.* **3.** a sound of short duration, as a musical tone or a drumbeat, digitally stored in a synthesizer for playback. —*adj.* **4.** serving as a specimen: *a sample piece of cloth.* —*v.t.* **5.** to take a sample or samples of; test or judge by a sample. [1250–1300; ME < OF *essample.* See EXAMPLE]
—**Syn. 1.** See **example.**

sam′ple point′, *Math.* a possible result of an experiment, represented as a point. Cf. **sample space.**

sam•pler (sam′plər, säm′-), *n.* **1.** a person who samples. **2.** a piece of cloth embroidered with various stitches, serving to show a beginner's skill in needlework. **3.** a collection of samples, selections, etc.: *a sampler of French poetry.* **4.** an electronic device that digitally encodes and stores samples of sound. [1250–1300; ME *samplere* < OF *essamplere, exemplaire* < L *exemplārium* EXEMPLAR]

sam′ple room′, a room, as in a hotel suite, in which merchandise is displayed for sale to the trade. [1860–65, *Amer.*]

sam′ple space′, *Math.* the collection of all possible results of an experiment, represented as points. Cf. **sample point.** [1950–55]

sam•pling (sam′pling, säm′-), *n.* **1.** the act or process of selecting a sample for testing, analyzing, etc. **2.** the sample so selected. [1630–40; SAMPLE + -ING¹]

Sam•po (säm′pô), *n. Finnish Legend.* a magical object or substance that was stolen by Ilmarinen, Vainamoinen, and Lemminkainen from Louhi because of its powers.

Samp•son (samp′sən), *n.* **1. William Thomas,** 1840–1902, U.S. admiral. **2.** a male given name.

sam•sa•ra (səm sär′ə), *n.* **1.** *Buddhism.* the process of coming into existence as a differentiated, mortal creature. Cf. **nirvana** (def. 1). **2.** *Hinduism.* the endless series of births, deaths, and rebirths to which all beings are subject. Cf. **nirvana** (def. 2). [1885–90; < Skt *saṃsāra* lit., running together]

sam•shu (sam′sho͞o, -syo͞o), *n.* a Chinese liqueur distilled from millet or rice. [1690–1700; < dial. Chin (Guangdong) *sàam-siu,* akin to Chin *sān shāo* three boilings, brewings]

Sam•son (sam′sən), *n.* **1.** a judge of Israel famous for his great strength. Judges 13–16. **2.** any man of extraordinary physical strength. **3.** a male given name: from a Hebrew word meaning "like the sun." —**Sam•so•ni•an** (sam sō′nē ən), *adj.*

sam′son post′, (*sometimes cap.*) *Naut.* **1.** a strong bitt or post at the bow or stern of a vessel. **2.** a king post for supporting cargo-handling booms on the deck of a ship. [1570–80; perh. named in allusion to the pillars that Samson dislodged]

Sam•sun (säm so͞on′), *n.* a city in N Turkey, in Asia. 169,060.

Sam•u•el (sam′yo͞o əl), *n.* **1.** a judge and prophet of Israel. I Sam. 1–3; 8–15. **2.** either of two books of the Bible bearing his name. *Abbr.:* I Sam., II Sam. **3.** a male given name: from a Hebrew word meaning "name of God."

Sam•u•el•son (sam′yo͞o əl sən, -yəl-), *n.* **Paul A(nthony),** born 1915, U.S. economist: Nobel prize 1970.

sam•u•rai (sam′o͝o rī′), *n., pl.* **-rai.** *Japanese Hist.* **1.** a member of the hereditary warrior class in feudal Japan. **2.** a retainer of a daimyo. [1720–30; < Japn, earlier *samurafi* to serve, equiv. to *sa-* prefix + *morafi* watchfully wait (frequentative of *mor-* to guard)]

San (sän), *n.* a river in central Europe, flowing from the Carpathian Mountains in W Ukraine through SE Poland into the Vistula: battles 1914–15. ab. 280 mi. (450 km) long.

San (sän), *n., pl.* **Sans** (*esp. collectively*) **San** for 1. **1.** a member of a nomadic, racially distinct, short-statured people of southern Africa. **2.** any of more than a dozen related Khoisan languages spoken by the San. Also called **Bushman.**

-san, a suffix used in Japanese as a term of respect after names or titles: *Suzuki-san.* [< Japn, contr. of *-sama* suffix denoting direction, appearance, respect]

Sa•n'a (sä nä′), *n.* a city in and the capital of the Republic of Yemen, in SW Arabia. 150,000. Also, **Sa•naa′.**

San′ An•dre′as fault′ (san′ an drā′əs), *Geol.* an active strike-slip fault in W United States, extending

CONCISE PRONUNCIATION KEY: act, cāpe, dâre, pärt; set, ēqual; *if,* ice; ox, ōver, ôrder, oil, bo͝ok, bo͞ot, out; up, ûrge; child; sing; shoe; thin, *that;* zh as in *treasure.* ə = *a* as in *alone, e* as in *system, i* as in *easily, o* as in *gallop, u* as in *circus;* ᵊ as in *fire* (fīᵊr), *hour* (ouᵊr). l and n can serve as syllabic consonants, as in *cradle* (krād′l), and *button* (but′n). See the full key inside the front cover.

from San Francisco to S California and forming the onland portion of the western margin of the North American Plate. [after *San Andreas* Lake, located in the rift, in San Mateo County]

San An·ge·lo (san an′jə lō′), a city in W Texas. 73,240.

San An·sel·mo (san′ an sel′mō), a city in W California. 11,927.

San An·to·ni·o (san′ an tō′nē ō′), a city in S Texas: site of the Alamo. 785,410. —**San′ An·to′ni·an.**

san·a·tive (san′ə tiv), *adj.* having the power to heal; curative. [1400–50; < ML *sānātīvus* (see SANATORY, -IVE); r. late ME *sanatif* < MF < ML, as above]

san·a·to·ri·um (san′ə tôr′ē əm, -tōr′-), *n., pl.* **-to·ri·ums, -to·ri·a** (-tôr′ē ə, -tōr′ē ə). **1.** a hospital for the treatment of chronic diseases, as tuberculosis or various nervous or mental disorders. **2.** sanitarium. [1830–40; < NL, equiv. to L *sanā(re)* to heal + *-tōrium* -TORY[2]]

san·a·to·ry (san′ə tôr′ē, -tōr′ē), *adj.* favorable for health; curative; healing. [1825–35; < LL *sānātōrius* healthful, equiv. to L *sānā(re)* to heal (deriv. of *sānus* SANE) + *-tōrius* -TORY[1]]

san·be·ni·to (san′bə nē′tō), *n., pl.* **-tos.** (under the Spanish Inquisition) **1.** an ornamented garment worn by a condemned heretic at an auto-da-fé. **2.** a penitential garment worn by a confessed heretic, of yellow for the penitent, of black for the impenitent. [1550–60; < Sp, named after *San Benito* Saint Benedict, from its resemblance to the scapular believed to have been introduced by him]

San Be·ni·to (san′ bə nē′tō), a city in S Texas. 17,988.

San Ber·nar·di·no (san′ bûr′nər dē′nō, -bûr′nə-), **1.** a city in S California. 118,057. **2. Mount,** a mountain in S California, a peak of the San Bernardino Mountains. 10,630 ft. (3240 m). **3.** a mountain pass in the Alps, in SE Switzerland. 6766 ft. (2060 m) high.

San′ Bernardi′no Moun′tains, a mountain range in S California. Highest peak, San Gorgonio, 11,485 ft. (3500 m).

San Ber·nar·do (san′ bər när′dō; *Sp.* sän′ beʀ näʀ′thô), a city in central Chile, S of Santiago. 58,798.

San Blas (sän bläs′), **1. Gulf of,** a gulf of the Caribbean on the N coast of Panama. **2. Isthmus of,** the narrowest part of the Isthmus of Panama. 31 mi. (50 km) wide. **3.** the Cuna Indian people who inhabit the islands in the Gulf of San Blas.

San·born (san′bôrn, -bərn), *n.* a male given name.

San Bru·no (san brōō′nō), a city in W California, S of San Francisco. 35,417.

San Bue·na·ven·tu·ra (san bwā′nə ven tŏŏr′ə), a city in SW California. 74,474.

San Car·los (san kär′ləs), a city in W California, S of San Francisco. 24,710.

San·cerre (säɴ seʀ′), *n.* a dry white wine from the Loire valley region of France. [after *Sancerre,* a town in the region (Cher dept.)]

San·cho Pan·za (san′chō pan′zə; *Sp.* sän′chô pän′thä), the credulous and amusing squire of Don Quixote.

San Cle·men·te (san′ klə men′tē), a town in S California. 27,325.

San Cris·tó·bal (säng′ kʀē stô′väl), a city in SW Venezuela. 151,717.

sanc·ti·fied (sangk′tə fīd′), *adj.* **1.** made holy; consecrated: *sanctified wine.* **2.** sanctimonious: *a sickening, sanctified smile.* [1475–85; SANCTIFY + -ED[2]] —**sanc·ti·fi·ed·ly** (sangk′tə fī′id lē), *adv.*

sanc·ti·fy (sangk′tə fī′), *v.t.,* **-fied, -fy·ing. 1.** to make holy; set apart as sacred; consecrate. **2.** to purify or free from sin: *Sanctify your hearts.* **3.** to impart religious sanction to; render legitimate or binding: *to sanctify a vow.* **4.** to entitle to reverence or respect. **5.** to make productive of or conducive to spiritual blessing. [1350–1400; < LL *sānctificāre* (see SANCTUS, -IFY); r. ME *seintefien* < OF *saintifier* < L, as above] —**sanc′ti·fi′a·ble,** *adj.* —**sanc′ti·fi′a·ble·ness,** *n.* —**sanc′ti·fi′a·bly,** *adv.* —**sanc′ti·fi·ca′tion,** *n.* —**sanc′ti·fi′er,** *n.* —**sanc′ti·fy′ing·ly,** *adv.*
—**Syn. 1.** bless, hallow, anoint, enshrine, exalt.

sanc·ti·mo·ni·ous (sangk′tə mō′nē əs), *adj.* **1.** making a hypocritical show of religious devotion, piety, righteousness, etc.: *They resented his sanctimonious comments on immorality in America.* **2.** *Obs.* holy; sacred. [1595–1605; SANCTIMONY + -OUS] —**sanc′ti·mo′ni·ous·ly,** *adv.* —**sanc′ti·mo′ni·ous·ness,** *n.*

sanc·ti·mo·ny (sangk′tə mō′nē), *n.* **1.** pretended, affected, or hypocritical religious devotion, righteousness, etc. **2.** *Obs.* sanctity; sacredness. [1530–40; < L *sānctimōnia* holiness. See SANCTUS, -MONY]

sanc·tion (sangk′shən), *n.* **1.** authoritative permission or approval, as for an action. **2.** something that serves to support an action, condition, etc. **3.** something that gives binding force, as to an oath, rule of conduct, etc. **4.** *Law.* **a.** a provision of a law enacting a penalty for disobedience or a reward for obedience. **b.** the penalty or reward. **5.** *Internat. Law.* action by one or more states toward another state calculated to force it to comply with legal obligations. —*v.t.* **6.** to authorize, approve, or allow: *an expression now sanctioned by educated usage.* **7.** to ratify or confirm: *to sanction a law.* **8.** to impose a sanction on; penalize, esp. by way of discipline. [1555–65; < L *sānctiōn-* (s. of *sānctiō*), equiv. to *sānct(us)* (ptp. of *sancīre* to prescribe by law) + *-iōn-* -ION] —**sanc′tion·a·ble,** *adj.* —**sanc′tion·a′tive,** *adj.* —**sanc′tion·er,** *n.* —**sanc′tion·less,** *adj.*
—**Syn. 6.** permit. —**Ant. 1.** disapproval. **6.** disapprove.

sanc·ti·tude (sangk′ti tōōd′, -tyōōd′), *n.* holiness; saintliness; sanctity. [1400–50; late ME *sanctitud* < L *sānctitūdō,* equiv. to *sāncti-,* comb. form of *sānctus* (see SANCTUS + *-tūdō* -TUDE]

sanc·ti·ty (sangk′ti tē), *n., pl.* **-ties. 1.** holiness, saintliness, or godliness. **2.** sacred or hallowed character: *the inviolable sanctity of the temple.* **3.** a sacred thing. [1350–1400; < L *sānctitās* holiness, equiv. to *sānct-* (see SANCTUS) + *-itās* -ITY; r. ME *sauntite* < AF < L, as above]

sanc·tu·ar·y (sangk′chōō er′ē), *n., pl.* **-ar·ies. 1.** a sacred or holy place. **2.** *Judaism.* **a.** the Biblical tabernacle or the Temple in Jerusalem. **b.** the holy of holies of these places of worship. **3.** an especially holy place in a temple or church. **4.** the part of a church around the altar; the chancel. **5.** a church or other sacred place where fugitives were formerly entitled to immunity from arrest. **6.** immunity afforded by refuge in such a place. **7.** any place of refuge; asylum. **8.** a tract of land where birds and wildlife, esp. those hunted for sport, can breed and take refuge in safety from hunters. [1300–50; ME < LL *sānctuārium,* equiv. to *sānctu-* (r. L *sānct-*), comb. form of *sanctus* (see SANCTUS) + *-ārium* -ARY] —**sanc′tu·ar′ied,** *adj.*
—**Syn. 1.** church, temple, altar, shrine, sanctum, adytum. **8.** preserve.

sanc·tum (sangk′təm), *n., pl.* **-tums, -ta** (-tə). **1.** a sacred or holy place. **2.** an inviolably private place or retreat. [1570–80; n. use of neut. of L *sānctus;* see SANCTUS]

sanc′tum sanc·to′rum (sangk tôr′əm, -tōr′-), **1.** the holy of holies of the Biblical tabernacle and the Temple in Jerusalem. **2.** sanctum (def. 2). [1350–1400; ME < L *sānctum sānctōrum,* trans. of Heb *qōdhesh haqqodhāshīm* holy of holies]

Sanc·tus (sangk′təs), *n.* **1.** (*italics*) Also called **Tersanctus.** the hymn beginning "Holy, holy, holy, Lord God of hosts," with which the Eucharistic preface culminates. **2.** a musical setting for this hymn. [< L *sānctus* holy, hallowed (ptp. of *sancīre* to hallow), the first word of the hymn]

Sanc′tus bell′, a bell rung during the celebration of Mass to call attention to the more solemn parts. [1470–80]

sanc′tus tur′ret, a bell cote holding a Sanctus bell.

sand (sand), *n.* **1.** the more or less fine debris of rocks, consisting of small, loose grains, often of quartz. **2.** Usually, **sands.** a tract or region composed principally of sand. **3.** the sand or a grain of sand in an hourglass. **4. sands,** moments of time or of one's life: *At this stage of his career the sands are running out.* **5.** a light reddish- or brownish-yellow color. **6.** *Informal.* courage; pluck. **7.** sleeper (def. 10). —*v.t.* **8.** to smooth or polish with sand, sandpaper, or some other abrasive: *to sand the ends of a board.* **9.** to sprinkle with or as if with sand: *to sand an icy road.* **10.** to fill up with sand, as a harbor. **11.** to add sand to: *The mischievous child sanded the sugar.* [bef. 900; ME (n.), OE; c. G *Sand,* ON *sandr*] —**sand′a·ble,** *adj.* —**sand′less,** *adj.* —**sand′like′,** *adj.*

Sand (sand; *Fr.* säɴd), *n.* **George** (jôrj; *Fr.* zhôʀzh) (*Lucile Aurore Dupin Dudevant*), 1804–76, French novelist.

sand., sandwich.

San·dage (san′dij), *n.* **Allan R(ex),** born 1926, U.S. astronomer: codiscoverer of the first quasar 1961.

San·da·kan (sän dä′kän, san dä′kən), *n.* a city in NE Sabah, in E Malaysia. 28,806.

san·dal[1] (san′dl), *n., v.,* **-daled, -dal·ing** or (*esp. Brit.*) **-dalled, -dal·ling.** —*n.* **1.** a shoe consisting of a sole of leather or other material fastened to the foot by thongs or straps. **2.** any of various low shoes or slippers. **3.** a light, low, rubber overshoe covering only the front part of a woman's high-heeled shoe. **4.** a band or strap that fastens a low shoe or slipper on the foot by passing over the instep or around the ankle. —*v.t.* **5.** to furnish with sandals. [1350–1400; < F *sandale;* r. ME *sandalie* < L *sandalium* < Gk *sandálion,* equiv. to *sándal(on)* sandal + *-ion* dim. suffix]

san·dal[2] (san′dl), *n.* sandalwood. [1350–1400; ME *sandell* < ML *sandalum* < LGk *sántalon,* dissimilated var. of *sándanon* << Skt *candana*]

san·dal·foot (san′dl fŏŏt′), *adj.* (of women's hosiery) having no darker or thicker reinforced areas at the toe or heel, so as to be suitable for wear with sandal-type shoes. [SANDAL[1] + FOOT]

san·dal·wood (san′dl wŏŏd′), *n.* **1.** the fragrant heartwood of any of certain Asian trees of the genus *Santalum,* used for ornamental carving and burned as incense. **2.** any of these trees, esp. *S. album* **(white sandalwood),** an evergreen of India, having ovate leaves and yellowish flowers that turn red. **3.** any of various related or similar trees or their woods, esp. an East Indian tree, *Pterocarpus santalinus* **(red sandalwood),** of the legume family, or its heavy dark-red wood that yields a dye. [1505–15; SANDAL[2] + WOOD[1]]

San′dalwood Is′land, Sumba.

san·da·rac (san′də rak′), *n.* **1.** a coniferous tree, *Tetraclinis articulata* (*Callitrus quadrivalvis*), native to northwestern Africa, yielding a resin and a fragrant, hard, dark-colored wood much used in building. **2.** the brittle, usually pale-yellow, faintly aromatic resin exuding from the bark of this tree: used chiefly as incense and in making varnish. [1350–1400; ME *sandaracha* < L *sandaraca* < Gk *sandarákē* realgar, beebread]

sand·bag (sand′bag′), *n., v.,* **-bagged, -bag·ging.** —*n.* **1.** a bag filled with sand, used in fortification, as ballast, etc. **2.** such a bag used as a weapon. —*v.t.* **3.** to furnish with sandbags. **4.** to hit or stun with a sandbag. **5.** *Informal.* **a.** to set upon violently; attack from or as if from ambush. **b.** to coerce or intimidate, as by threats: *The election committee was sandbagged into nominating the officers for a second term.* **c.** to thwart or cause to fail or be rejected, esp. surreptitiously or without warning: *He sandbagged our proposal by snide remarks to the boss.* **6.** *Poker.* to deceive (one or more opponents) into remaining in the pot by refraining from betting on a strong hand, then raising the bet in a later round. —*v.i.* **7.** *Poker.* to sandbag one or more opponents. [1580–90; SAND + BAG] —**sand′bag′ger,** *n.*

sand·bank (sand′bangk′), *n.* a large mass of sand, as on a shoal or hillside. [1580–90; SAND + BANK[1]]

sand′ bar′, a bar of sand formed in a river or sea by the action of tides or currents. [1760–70]

sand·blast (sand′blast′, -bläst′), *n.* **1.** a blast of air or steam laden with sand, used to clean, grind, cut, or decorate hard surfaces, as of glass, stone, or metal. **2.** the apparatus used to apply such a blast. —*v.t., v.i.* **3.** to clean, smooth, etc., with a sandblast. [1870–75; SAND + BLAST] —**sand′blast′er,** *n.*

sand-blind (sand′blīnd′), *adj.* partially blind; dimsighted. [1350–1400; ME; alter. (assimilated to SAND) of OE **samblind* half-blind, equiv. to *sam-* half- (akin to SEMI-) + *blind* BLIND] —**sand′blind′ness,** *n.*

sand′ blue′stem, a grass, *Andropogon hallii,* native to the Great Plains, used as a cover crop for sand dunes. [1945–50]

sand·box (sand′boks′), *n.* a box or receptacle for holding sand, esp. one large enough for children to play in. [1565–75; SAND + BOX[1]]

sand′box tree′, a tropical American tree, *Hura crepitans,* of the spurge family, bearing a furrowed, roundish fruit about the size of an orange that when ripe and dry bursts with a sharp report and scatters the seeds. [1740–50]

sand·bug (sand′bug′), *n.* See **mole crab.** [1850–55, *Amer.;* SAND + BUG[1]]

sand·bur (sand′bûr′), *n.* **1.** any of various grasses of the genus *Cenchrus,* having spikelets enclosed in prickly burs. **2.** any of several bur-bearing weeds growing in sandy places, as *Franseria acanthicarpa* or *Solanum rostratum,* of the western U.S. Also, **sand′burr′.** [1820–30, *Amer.;* SAND + BUR[1]]

Sand·burg (sand′bûrg, san′-), *n.* **Carl,** 1878–1967, U.S. poet and biographer.

sand-cast (sand′kast′, -käst′), *v.t.,* **-cast, -cast·ing.** to produce (a casting) by pouring molten metal into sand molds. [1945–50] —**sand′ cast′ing.**

sand·cas·tle (sand′kas′əl, -kä′səl), *n.* **1.** a small castlelike structure made of wet sand, as by children at a beach. **2.** a plan or idea with little substance. [1850–55; SAND + CASTLE]

sand′ chair′, a low folding beach chair with a frame, usually of tubular metal, that slants outward below the seat, forming a base designed to be rested in the sand.

sand′ cher′ry, 1. any of several low, North American cherries that grow on dry or sandy soil, esp. *Prunus pumila,* of the Great Lakes region. **2.** the fruit of any of these shrubs. Also called **dwarf cherry.** [1945–50]

sand′ crab′, any of several crabs that live on sandy beaches, as the ghost crab or mole crab. [1835–45]

sand′ crack′, *Vet. Pathol.* a crack or fissure in the hoof of a horse, extending from the coronet downward toward the sole, caused by a dryness of horn. Also called **quarter crack.** [1745–55]

sand′ crick′et. See **Jerusalem cricket.** [1880–85; *Amer.*]

sand·cul·ture (sand′kul′chər), *n.* the hydroponic cultivation of plants in sand. [1915–20; SAND + CULTURE]

sand′ dab′, any of several flatfishes used for food, esp. of the genus *Citharichthys,* inhabiting waters along the Pacific coast of North America. [1830–40]

sand′ dol′lar, any of various flat, disklike sea urchins, as *Mellita testudinata* or *Echinarachnius parma,* that live on sandy bottoms off the coasts of the U.S. [1880–85, *Amer.*]

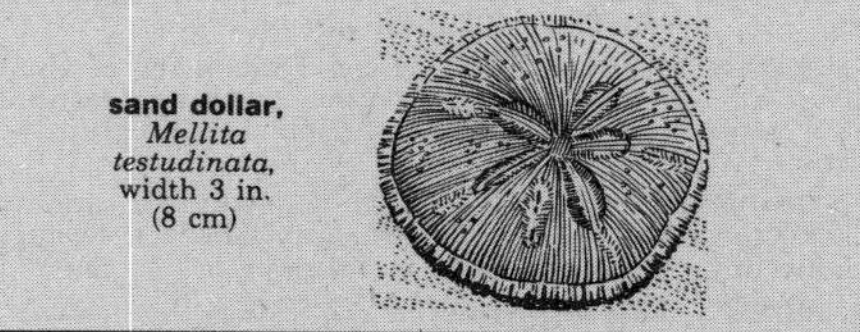
sand dollar, *Mellita testudinata,* width 3 in. (8 cm)

San·de (san′dē), *n.* **Earl,** 1898–1968, U.S. jockey and racehorse trainer.

sand′ eel′, 1. See **sand lance. 2.** *New Zealand.* sandfish (def. 2). [1275–1325; ME *sandel;* see SAND, EEL]

CONCISE ETYMOLOGY KEY: <, descended or borrowed from; >, whence; b., blend of, blended; c., cognate with; cf., compare; deriv., derivative; equiv., equivalent; imit., imitative; obl., oblique; r., replacing; s., stem; sp., spelling, spelled; resp., respelling, respelled; trans., translation; ?, origin unknown; *, unattested; ‡, probably earlier than. See the full key inside the front cover.

san·dek (sän′dek), *n. Yiddish.* the man who holds the child during the Jewish rite of circumcision.

sand·er (san′dər), *n.* a person or thing that sands or sandpapers. [1620–30; SAND + -ER[1]]

San·der (san′dər), *n.* a male given name, form of **Alexander.**

sand·er·ling (san′dər ling), *n.* a common, small sandpiper, *Calidris alba,* inhabiting sandy beaches. [1595–1605; SAND + *-erling,* repr. OE *yrthling* kind of bird (perh. a plover), lit., plowman (cf. obs. E *earthling* plowman), equiv. to *yrth* plowing, tilling (deriv. of *erian* to plow, EAR[3]; for *-th,* cf. BIRTH) + *-ling* -LING[1]]

S.&F., *Insurance.* stock and fixtures.

sand·fish (sand′fish′), *n., pl.* (*esp. collectively*) **-fish,** (*esp. referring to two or more kinds or species*) **-fish·es. 1.** either of two scaleless fishes of the family Trichodontidae, of the North Pacific, that live in sand or mud. **2.** Also called **beaked salmon.** a fish, *Gonorhynchus gonorhynchus,* inhabiting the sandy areas of the western Pacific and Indian oceans, having an angular snout with which it burrows into the sand. **3.** See **belted sandfish.** [1895–1900; SAND + FISH]

sand′ flea′, 1. See **beach flea. 2.** chigoe. [1790–1800]

sand-float·ed (sand′flō′tid), *adj. Building Trades.* noting an exterior wall finish composed of mortar rubbed with sand and floated when it has partly set.

sand·fly (sand′flī′), *n., pl.* **-flies. 1.** any of several small, bloodsucking, dipterous insects of the family Psychodidae that are vectors of several diseases of humans. **2.** any of several other small, bloodsucking, dipterous insects, as one of the family Heleidae or Simuliidae. [1675–85; SAND + FLY[2]]

sand′fly fe′ver, *Pathol.* a usually mild viral disease occurring in hot, dry areas, characterized by fever, eye pain, and sometimes a rash, transmitted by sandflies of the genus *Phlebotomus.* Also called **phlebotomus fever.** [1910–15]

sand·glass (sand′glas′, -gläs′), *n.* an hourglass. [1550–60; SAND + GLASS]

sand-grop·er (sand′grō′pər), *n. Australian Slang.* a native of the arid region of Western Australia. [1895–1900]

sand′ grouse′, any of several birds of the family Pteroclididae inhabiting sandy areas of the Old World, resembling both pigeons and shorebirds and having precocial young. Also, **sand′grouse′.** [1775–85]

S and H, shipping and handling (charges). Also, **S&H**

san·dhi (sun′dē), *n., pl.* **-dhis.** *Ling.* morphophonemic alternation, esp. as determined by phonetic environment, as in *dontcha* for *don't you.* [1800–10; < Skt *saṃdhi* joining, juncture]

sand′hill crane′ (sand′hil′), a North American crane, *Grus canadensis,* having bluish-gray plumage and a red forehead. [1795–1805, *Amer.*; *sandhill,* late ME *sond hille,* OE *sondhyll.* See SAND, HILL]

sand·hog (sand′hog′, -hôg′), *n.* **1.** a laborer who digs or works in sand. **2.** a person who works, usually in a caisson, in digging underwater tunnels. Also, **sand′ hog′.** [1900–05, *Amer.*; SAND + HOG]

sand′ hop′per. See **beach flea.** [1780–90]

Sand·hurst (sand′hûrst), *n.* a village in S England, near Reading, W of London: military college. 6445.

sandh·ya (sund′yä), *n. Hinduism.* a ritual of worship and meditation performed three times a day by Hindus of the higher castes. [1865–70; < Skt *sandhyā*]

San·die (san′dē), *n.* **1.** a male given name, form of **Sandro. 2.** a female given name, form of **Sandra, Saundra,** or **Sondra.**

San Di·e·go (san′ dē ā′gō), a seaport in SW California: naval and marine base. 875,504.

San Di·mas (san dē′məs), a city in SW California. 24,014.

San·di·nis·ta (san′də nē′stə; *Sp.* sän′dē nēs′tä), *n., pl.* **-nis·tas** (-nē′stəz; *Sp.* -nēs′täs). a member of the Nicaraguan revolutionary movement that took control of Nicaragua in 1979. [1925–30, in sense "supporter of Sandino"; < AmerSp; see SANDINO, -IST]

San·di·no (san dē′nō; *Sp.* sän dē′nô), *n.* **Au·gus·to (Cé·sar)** (ou go͞os′tô se′sär), 1893–1934, Nicaraguan revolutionary leader.

san·di·ver (san′də vər), *n.* a whitish, saline scum formed on the surface of molten glass. Also called **glass gall.** [1300–50; ME *saundyver* < MF *suin de verre* grease of glass. See SWEAT, VITRI-]

sand′ jack′, *Shipbuilding.* any of a number of containers of sand driven beneath a hull about to be launched as a temporary support and then drained of sand so as to let the hull down onto the launching cradle.

S&L, *Banking.* See **savings and loan association.** Also, **S and L**

sand′ lance′, any slender marine fish of the family Ammodytidae that burrows into the sand. Also, **sand′ launce′.** [1770–80]

sand′ lil′y, a small, stemless lily, *Leucocrinum montanum,* of the western U.S., having white, fragrant flowers. [1905–10, *Amer.*]

sand′-lime brick′ (sand′līm′), a hard brick composed of silica sand and a lime of high calcium content, molded under high pressure and baked. [1905–10]

sand′ liz′ard, 1. a common lizard, *Lacerta agilis,* of Europe and central Asia. **2.** any of several lizards, as the fringe-toed lizard, that live in sandy areas. [1850–55]

sand·lot (sand′lot′), *n.* **1.** a vacant lot used by youngsters for games or sports. —*adj.* **2.** Also, **sand′-lot′.** of, pertaining to, or played in such a lot: *sandlot baseball.* [1880–85, *Amer.*; SAND + LOT]

sand·lot·ter (sand′lot′ər), *n.* a youngster who plays baseball in a sandlot. [1885–90, *Amer.*; SANDLOT + -ER[1]]

sand′ love′grass. See under **lovegrass.**

S and M, sadomasochism; sadism and masochism. Also, **S&M, s&m** [1965–70]

S.&M., *Insurance.* stock and machinery.

sand·man (sand′man′), *n., pl.* **-men.** the man who, in fairy tales or folklore, puts sand in the eyes of children to make them sleepy. [1860–65; SAND + MAN[1]]

sand′ mar′tin, *Brit.* the bank swallow. [1660–70]

sand′ myr′tle, an evergreen shrub, *Leiophyllum buxifolium,* of the heath family, native to the eastern U.S., having simple, leathery leaves and clusters of white or pink flowers. [1805–15, *Amer.*]

San Do·min·go (san′ də ming′gō; *Sp.* sän′ dô mēng′gô). See **Santo Domingo** (defs. 2, 3).

San·dor (san′dər), *n.* a male given name.

Sán·dor (shän′dôr, shan′-), *n.* **Gyor·gy** (jôr′jē), born 1912, U.S. pianist, born in Hungary.

sand′ paint′ing, 1. the ceremonial practice among Navaho and Pueblo Indians of creating symbolic designs on a flat surface with varicolored sand. **2.** the designs so made. [1895–1900, *Amer.*]

sand·pa·per (sand′pā′pər), *n.* **1.** strong paper coated with a layer of sand or other abrasive, used for smoothing or polishing. —*v.t.* **2.** to smooth or polish with or as if with sandpaper. [1815–25; SAND + PAPER]

sand·pa·per·y (sand′pā′pə rē), *adj.* of or suggesting the grating sound of sandpaper rubbing against wood or the rough texture of sandpaper. [SANDPAPER + -Y[1]]

sand′ pear′. See **Japanese pear.** [1875–80]

sand′ perch′. squirrelfish (def. 2). [1875–80]

sand′ pike′, sauger.

sand′ pile′, *Building Trades.* a base for a footing in soft soil, made by compacting sand in a cavity left by a wooden pile. [1900–05]

sand·pi·per (sand′pī′pər), *n.* any of numerous shore-inhabiting birds of the family Scolopacidae, related to the plovers, typically having a slender bill and a piping call. [1665–75; SAND + PIPER]

spotted sandpiper, *Actitis macularia,* length 7 in. (18 cm)

sand·pit (sand′pit′), *n.* a deep pit in sandy soil from which sand is excavated. [1520–30; SAND + PIT[1]]

sand′ pup′py. See **naked mole rat.**

San·dra (san′drə, sän′-), *n.* a female given name, form of **Alexandra.**

sand′ rat′, 1. gerbil. **2.** See **naked mole rat. 3.** any of various desert rodents. [1775–85]

San·dro (san′drō; *It.* sän′drô), *n.* a male given name.

San·dro·cot·tus (san′drō kot′əs), *n.* Greek name of **Chandragupta.** Also, **San′dra·kot′tos.**

sand·roll·er (sand′rō′lər), *n.* a North American freshwater fish, *Percopsis transmontana,* related to the trout-perch but having a deeper, more compressed body. [1900–05; SAND + ROLLER[1]]

San·dron (san′drən), *n.* a male given name, form of **Sandro.**

s. & s.c., (of paper) sized and supercalendered.

sand′ shark′. See **sand tiger.** [1880–85]

sand′ shoe′, *Brit.* a light tennis shoe; sneaker. [1850–55]

sand-sprayed (sand′sprād′), *adj. Building Trades.* noting an exterior wall finish composed of mortar to which is added a mixture of sand and cement in equal parts while the mortar is still wet.

Sand′ Springs′, a town in NE Oklahoma. 13,246.

sand′ star′gazer, a fish of the family Dactyloscopidae, esp. *Dactyloscopus tridigitatus,* of Atlantic waters from Bermuda to Brazil, having tiny, tubular eyes on top of the head, and capable of emitting electric discharges.

sand·stone (sand′stōn′), *n.* a common sedimentary rock consisting of sand, usually quartz, cemented together by various substances, as silica, calcium carbonate, iron oxide, or clay. [1660–70; SAND + STONE]

sand·storm (sand′stôrm′), *n.* a windstorm, esp. in a desert, that blows along great clouds of sand (distinguished from *dust storm*). [1765–75; SAND + STORM]

sand-struck (sand′struk′), *adj.* (of bricks) made with a mold lined with sand to permit freeing.

sand′ ta′ble, 1. a table with raised edges holding sand for children to play with. **2.** *Mil.* a table holding a scale model of a tract of land, including trees, streams, buildings, etc., made of hardened sand, used for training in gunnery or tactics. [1805–15]

sand′ ti′ger, any of several sharks of the family Odontaspididae, esp. *Odontaspis taurus,* inhabiting shallow waters on both sides of the Atlantic Ocean, having sharp, jagged teeth and sometimes dangerous to humans. [1880–85]

sand′ trap′, (on a golf course) a shallow pit partly filled with sand, usually located near a green, and designed to serve as a hazard. [1875–80]

San·dus·ky (sən dus′kē, san-), *n.* a port in N Ohio, on Lake Erie. 31,360.

sand′ verbe′na, any of several low, mostly trailing plants of the genus *Abronia,* of the western U.S., having showy, verbenalike flowers. [1895–1900, *Amer.*]

sand′ vi′per, 1. See **hognose snake. 2.** See **horned viper.** [1660–70]

sand′ wasp′, any of certain sphecid wasps of the subfamily Bembicinae that nest in the ground and are common along the seashore. [1895–1900]

sand·wich (sand′wich, san′-), *n.* **1.** two or more slices of bread or the like with a layer of meat, fish, cheese, etc., between each pair. **2.** See **open sandwich. 3.** something resembling or suggesting a sandwich, as something in horizontal layers: *a plywood sandwich.* —*v.t.* **4.** to put into a sandwich. **5.** to insert between two other things: *to sandwich an appointment between two board meetings.* [1755–65; named after the fourth Earl of *Sandwich* (1718–92)]

Sand·wich (sand′wich, san′-), *n.* a town in E Kent, in SE England: one of the Cinque Ports. 4467.

sand′wich bat′ten, *Theat.* See **double batten.**

sand′wich beam′. See **flitch beam.** Also called **sand′wich gird′er.** [1885–90]

sand′wich board′, two connected posters or signboards that hang in front of and behind a person and usually bear some advertisement, notice, exhortation, or the like. [1895–1900]

sand′wich coin′, a coin having a layer of one metal between outside layers of another, as a quarter with a layer of copper between layers of silver. [1960–65]

sand′wich genera′tion, the generation of people still raising their children while having to care for their aging parents. [1985–90]

Sand′wich glass′, any glassware manufactured at Sandwich, Mass., from 1825 to c1890. [1930–35, *Amer.*]

Sand′wich Is′lands, former name of **Hawaiian Islands.**

sand′wich man′, a person with advertising boards hung from the shoulders. [1860–65]

sand′wich pan′el, a structural panel consisting of a core of one material enclosed between two sheets of a different material. [1945–50]

sand·worm (sand′wûrm′), *n.* **1.** any of several marine worms that live in sand. **2.** clamworm. [1770–80; SAND + WORM]

sand·wort (sand′wûrt′, -wôrt′), *n.* any plant belonging to the genus *Arenaria,* of the pink family, having narrow leaves and clusters of white flowers, many of which grow in sandy soil. [1590–1600; SAND + WORT[2]]

sand·y (san′dē), *adj.,* **sand·i·er, sand·i·est. 1.** of the nature of or consisting of sand. **2.** containing or covered with sand. **3.** of a yellowish-red color: *sandy hair.* **4.** having hair of a sandy color. **5.** shifting or unstable, like sand. [bef. 1000; ME; OE *sandig.* See SAND, -Y[1]] —**sand′i·ness,** *n.*

San·dy (san′dē), *n.* **1.** a male given name. **2.** a female given name, form of **Sandra, Saundra, Sondra.**

sand′ yacht′. See **land yacht.** [1910–15]

sand′y blight′, *Australian.* trachoma. [1865–70; so called in allusion to the irritation caused by such a disorder]

Sand′y Cit′y, a town in central Utah. 51,022.

Sand′y Hook′, a peninsula in E New Jersey, at the entrance to lower New York Bay. 6 mi. (10 km) long.

sane (sān), *adj.,* **san·er, san·est. 1.** free from mental derangement; having a sound, healthy mind: *a sane person.* **2.** having or showing reason, sound judgment, or good sense: *sane advice.* **3.** sound; healthy. [1620–30; < L *sānus* healthy] —**sane′ly,** *adv.* —**sane′ness,** *n.* —**Syn. 2.** reasonable, sensible, judicious, level-headed.

SANE (sān), *n.* a private nationwide organization in the U.S., established in 1957, that opposes nuclear testing and advocates international peace. [official shortening of its by-name *Committee for a Sane Nuclear Policy*]

San Fe·li·pe (sän′ fe lē′pe), a city in NE Venezuela, on the Orinoco River. 42,905.

San Fer·nan·do (sän′ fer nän′dô *for 1;* san′ fər nan′dō *for 2*), **1.** a city in E Argentina, near Buenos Aires. 88,432. **2.** a city in SW California, near Los Angeles. 17,731.

San·ford (san′fərd), *n.* **1. Mount,** a mountain in SE Alaska. 16,208 ft. (4,940 m). **2.** a city in E Florida. 23,176. **3.** a town in SW Maine. 18,020. **4.** a city in central North Carolina. 14,773. **5.** a male given name.

San·for·ized (san′fə rīzd′), *Trademark.* (of a fabric) treated to resist shrinking.

San Fran·cis·co (san′ frən sis′kō, fran-), a seaport in W California, on San Francisco Bay: earthquake and fire 1906; United Nations Conference 1945. 678,974. —**San′ Fran·cis′can.**

San′ Francis′co Bay′, a bay in W California: the harbor of San Francisco; connected with the Pacific by the Golden Gate strait. 50 mi. (80 km) long; 3–12 mi. (5–19 km) wide.

San Fran·cis·co de Ma·co·rís (san′ frən sis′kō dā mak′ə rēs′, fran-; *Sp.* sän′ fRän sēs′kô the mä′kô-rēs′), a city in the N Dominican Republic. 58,174.

San′ Francis′co Peaks′, a mountain mass in N Arizona: highest point in the state, Humphrey's Peak, 12,611 ft. (3845 m). Also called **San′ Francis′co Mountain.**

sang (sang), *v.* pt. of **sing.**

San Ga·bri·el (san gā′brē əl), a city in SW California, near Los Angeles. 30,072.

CONCISE PRONUNCIATION KEY: *act, cāpe, dâre, pärt; set, ēqual; if, īce; ox, ōver, ôrder, oil, bo͝ok, bo͞ot, out; up, ûrge; child; sing; shoe; thin, that;* zh as in *treasure.* ə = *a* as in *alone, e* as in *system, i* as in *easily, o* as in *gallop, u* as in *circus;* ə as in *fire* (fīər), *hour* (ouər). l and n can serve as syllabic consonants, as in *cradle* (krād′l), and *button* (but′n). See the full key inside the front cover.

San·gal·lo (säng gäl′lô), *n.* **1. An·to·nio Pic·co·ni da** (än tô′nyô pēk kô′nē dä), (*Antonio Cordiani*), 1484?–1546, Italian architect and engineer. **2.** his uncle **Giu·lia·no da** (jo͞o lyä′nô dä), (*Giuliano Giamberti*), 1445–1516, Italian architect, sculptor, and engineer.

San·ga·mon (sang′gə mən), *n. Geol.* the third interglacial stage of the Pleistocene Epoch in North America, after the Illinoian glacial stage and before the Wisconsin. [1930–35; after *Sangamon* County, Ill.]

san·ga·ree (sang′gə rē′), *n.* sangria.

San Gen·na·ro (sän′ jen nä′rô; *Eng.* san′ jə nâr′ō, -när′ō), Italian name of **Januarius.**

Sang·er (sang′ər), *n.* **1. Frederick,** born 1918, English biochemist: Nobel prize for chemistry 1958. **2. Margaret Hig·gins** (hig′inz), 1883–1966, U.S. nurse and author: leader of birth-control movement. **3.** a town in central California. 12,558.

San Ger·mán (sän′ hεr män′), a city in SW Puerto Rico. 13,054.

sang-froid (*Fr.* säɴ fʀwa′), *n.* coolness of mind; calmness; composure: *They committed the robbery with complete sang-froid.* [1740–50; < F: lit., cold blood]
—Syn. self-possession, poise, equanimity, self-control, nerve, courage, steadiness.

San·gha (sung′gə), *n.* a community of Buddhist monks. [1855–60; < Skt *saṅgha*]

San·gli (säng′glē), *n.* a city in S Maharashtra, in SW India, on the Krishna River. 115,138.

sang·li·er (sang′lē ər), *n.* a closely woven fabric made of mohair or worsted, constructed in plain weave, and finished to simulate the coat of a boar. [1350–1400; < MF << LL *singulāris* (*porcus*) solitary (pig or boar); r. ME *singlere* < OF *sengler* < L, as above]

San·go (säng′gō), *n.* a Niger-Congo language of the Adamawa-Eastern branch, used as a lingua franca in the Central African Republic.

San·graal (sang grāl′), *n.* Grail. Also, **San·gre·al** (sang′grē əl). [1400–50; late ME *sangrayle, seynt Graal,* < OF *Saint Graal*]

San·gre de Cris·to (sang′grē də kris′tō; *Sp.* säng′gre the krēs′tô), a mountain range in S Colorado and N New Mexico: a part of the Rocky Mountains. Highest peak, Blanca Peak, 14,390 ft. (4385 m).

san·grí·a (sang grē′ə; *Sp.* säng grē′ä), *n.* an iced drink, typically made with red wine, sugar, fruit juice, soda water, and spices, and containing fruit slices. Also, **san·gri′a.** [1960–65; < Sp: drink of a bloodlike color, equiv. to *sangr(e)* blood (see SANGUINE) + *-ía* n. suffix]

sangui-, a combining form meaning "blood," used in the formation of technical terms: *sanguiferous.* [comb. form of L *sanguis,* s. *sanguin-* blood]

san·guic·o·lous (sang gwik′ə ləs), *adj.* living in the blood, as a parasite. [1890–95; SANGUI- + -COLOUS]

san·guif·er·ous (sang gwif′ər əs), *adj.* conveying blood, as a blood vessel. [1675–85; SANGUI- + -FEROUS]

san·gui·fi·ca·tion (sang′gwə fi kā′shən), *n.* hematopoiesis. [1570–80; < NL *sanguificātiōn-* (s. of *sanguificātiō*). See SANGUI-, -FICATION]

san·gui·nar·i·a (sang′gwə nâr′ē ə), *n.* **1.** the bloodroot, *Sanguinaria canadensis.* **2.** its medicinal rhizome. [1800–10; < NL (*herba*) *sanguināria* bloody (herb), fem. of *sanguinārius* SANGUINARY]

san·gui·nar·y (sang′gwə ner′ē), *adj.* **1.** full of or characterized by bloodshed; bloody: *a sanguinary struggle.* **2.** ready or eager to shed blood; bloodthirsty. **3.** composed of or marked with blood. [1540–50; < L *sanguinārius* bloody. See SANGUINE, -ARY] **—san′gui·nar′i·ly,** *adv.* **—san′gui·nar′i·ness,** *n.*
—Syn. 2. murderous, cruel, savage. **—Ant. 2.** kind.

san·guine (sang′gwin), *adj.* **1.** cheerfully optimistic, hopeful, or confident: *a sanguine disposition; sanguine expectations.* **2.** reddish; ruddy: *a sanguine complexion.* **3.** (in old physiology) having blood as the predominating humor and consequently being ruddy-faced, cheerful, etc. **4.** bloody; sanguinary. **5.** blood-red; red. **6.** *Heraldry.* a reddish-purple tincture. **—*n.* 7.** a red iron-oxide crayon used in making drawings. [1275–1325; ME *sanguyne* a blood-red cloth < OF *sanguin* < L *sanguineus* bloody, equiv. to *sanguin-,* s. of *sanguis* blood + *-eus* -EOUS] **—san′guine·ly,** *adv.* **—san·guin′i·ty, san′guine·ness,** *n.*
—Syn. 1. enthusiastic, buoyant, animated, lively, spirited. **—Ant. 1.** morose.

san·guin·e·ous (sang gwin′ē əs), *adj.* **1.** of, pertaining to, or containing blood. **2.** of the color of blood. **3.** involving much bloodshed. **4.** sanguine; confident. [1510–20; < L *sanguineus* bloody. See SANGUINE] **—san·guin′e·ous·ness,** *n.*

san·guin·o·lent (sang gwin′l ənt), *adj.* **1.** of or pertaining to blood. **2.** containing or tinged with blood; bloody. [1400–50; < L *sanguinolentus,* equiv. to *sanguin-* s. of *sanguis* blood + *-olentus* earlier form of *-ulentus* -ULENT] **—san·guin′o·len·cy,** *n.*

san·guiv·or·ous (sang gwiv′ər əs), *adj.* feeding on blood, as a bat or insect. [1835–45; SANGUI- + -VOROUS]

San·hed·rin (san hed′rin, -hē′drin, sän-, san′i drin), *n. Jewish Hist.* **1.** Also called **Great Sanhedrin.** the highest council of the ancient Jews, consisting of 71 members, and exercising authority from about the 2nd century B.C. **2.** Also called **Lesser Sanhedrin.** a lower tribunal of this period, consisting of 23 members. Also, **San·he·drim** (san′hi drim, san′i-). [1580–90; < late Heb *Sanhedhrīn* < Gk *synédrion,* equiv. to *syn-* SYN- + *hédr(a)* seat (cf. CATHEDRAL) + *-ion* n. suffix]

San′ibel Is′land, (san′ə bəl, -bel′), an island in the Gulf of Mexico off the SW coast of Florida. 16 sq. mi. (41.5 sq. km).

san·i·cle (san′i kəl), *n.* any plant belonging to the genus *Sanicula,* of the parsley family, as *S. marilandica,* of America, used in medicine. [1400–50; late ME < MF < ML *sānicula,* perh. deriv. of L *sānus;* see SANE]

san·i·dine (san′i dēn′, -din), *n. Mineral.* a glassy, often transparent variety of orthoclase in which sodium may replace as much as 50 percent of the potassium: forms phenocrysts in some igneous rocks. [1805–15; < G *Sanidin,* equiv. to Gk *sanid-* (s. of *sanís* plank) + G *-in* -INE[2]] **—san·i·din·ic** (san′i din′ik), *adj.*

sa·ni·es (sā′nē ēz′), *n. Pathol.* a thin, often greenish, serous fluid that is discharged from ulcers, wounds, etc. [1555–65; < L *saniēs*]

San Il·de·fon·so (sän ēl′de fôn′sô), a town in central Spain, near Segovia: termed the "Spanish Versailles" for its 18th-century palace (**La Granja**); treaty 1800. 4164.

sa·ni·ous (sā′nē əs), *adj. Pathol.* characterized by the discharge of sanies. [1555–65; SANI(ES) + -OUS]

sanit., **1.** sanitary. **2.** sanitation.

san·i·tar·i·an (san′i târ′ē ən), *adj.* **1.** sanitary; clean and wholesome. **—*n.* 2.** a specialist in public sanitation and health. [1855–60; SANITARY + -AN]

san·i·tar·i·um (san′i târ′ē əm), *n., pl.* **-tar·i·ums, -tar·i·a** (-târ′ē ə). an institution for the preservation or recovery of health, esp. for convalescence; health resort. Also, **sanatorium.** [1850–55; < L *sānit(ās)* health (see SANITY) + *-ārium* -ARY]

san·i·tar·y (san′i ter′ē), *adj.* **1.** of or pertaining to health or the conditions affecting health, esp. with reference to cleanliness, precautions against disease, etc. **2.** favorable to health; free from dirt, bacteria, etc.: *a sanitary washroom.* **3.** providing healthy cleanliness: *a sanitary wrapper on all sandwiches.* [1835–45; < L *sānit(ās)* health (see SANITY) + -ARY] **—san′i·tar′i·ly,** *adv.* **—san′i·tar′i·ness,** *n.*
—Syn. 1, 2. clean, germ-free, unpolluted, antiseptic. SANITARY, HYGIENIC agree in being concerned with health. SANITARY refers more especially to conditions affecting health or measures for guarding against infection or disease: *to insure sanitary conditions in preparing food.* HYGIENIC is applied to whatever concerns the care of the body and the promotion of health: *to live in hygienic surroundings with plenty of fresh air.* **2.** healthy, salutary. **—Ant. 1, 2.** unclean, unwholesome; unhealthy, polluted, septic.

san′itary belt′, a narrow belt, usually of elastic, for holding a sanitary napkin in place. [1905–10]

san′itary code′. See under **code** (def. 3). Also called **health code.**

san′itary cor′don. See **cordon sanitaire.**

san′itary engineer′ing, a branch of civil engineering dealing with matters affecting public health, as water supply or sewage disposal. [1865–70] **—san′itary engineer′.**

san′itary land′fill, landfill. [1965–70]

san′itary nap′kin, a pad of absorbent material, as cotton, worn by women during menstruation to absorb the uterine flow. Also called **san′itary pad′.** [1915–20, *Amer.*]

san′itary tow′el, *Brit.* See **sanitary napkin.** [1880–85]

san′itary ware′, plumbing fixtures, as sinks or toilet bowls, made of ceramic material or enameled metal. [1870–75]

san·i·tate (san′i tāt′), *v.t.,* **-tat·ed, -tat·ing.** to make sanitary; equip with sanitary appliances: *to sanitate a new town.* [1880–85; back formation from SANITATION]

san·i·ta·tion (san′i tā′shən), *n.* **1.** the development and application of sanitary measures for the sake of cleanliness, protecting health, etc. **2.** the disposal of sewage and solid waste. [1840–50; SANIT(ARY) + -ATION]

san·i·ta·tion·man (san′i tā′shən man′), *n., pl.* **-men.** a sanitation worker. [1935–40, *Amer.;* SANITATION + MAN[1]]
—Usage. See **-man.**

sanita′tion work′er, a person employed to collect, haul away, and dispose of garbage.

san·i·tize (san′i tīz′), *v.t.,* **-tized, -tiz·ing. 1.** to free from dirt, germs, etc., as by cleaning or sterilizing. **2.** to make less offensive by eliminating anything unwholesome, objectionable, incriminating, etc.: *to sanitize a document before releasing it to the press.* Also, *esp. Brit.,* **san′i·tise′.** [1830–40; SANIT(ARY) + -IZE] **—san′i·ti·za′tion,** *n.*

san·i·tiz·er (san′i tī′zər), *n.* a substance or preparation for killing germs, designed for use esp. on food-processing equipment. [1945–50; SANITIZE + -ER[1]]

san·i·ty (san′i tē), *n.* **1.** the state of being sane; soundness of mind. **2.** soundness of judgment. [1400–50; late ME *sanite* < L *sānitās.* See SANE, -ITY]
—Syn. 2. reason, rationality, sensibleness, reasonableness.

San Ja·cin·to (san′ jə sin′tō), a river in E Texas, flowing SE to Galveston Bay: Texans defeated Mexicans near the mouth of this river 1836.

San′ Jacin′to Day′, a legal holiday observed in Texas on April 21.

san·jak (sän′jak′), *n.* (in Turkey) one of the administrative districts into which a vilayet is divided. [1530–40; < Turk *sancak* district (lit., flag, standard)]

San Joa·quin (san′ wo kēn′), a river in California, flowing NW from the Sierra Nevada Mountains to the Sacramento River. 350 mi. (560 km) long.

San′ Joaquin′ Val′ley fe′ver, *Pathol.* coccidioidomycosis. [after the area in which it was first reported]

San Jo·se (san′ hō zā′), a city in W California. 636,550.

San Jo·sé (sän′ hô se′), a city in and the capital of Costa Rica, in the central part. 228,302.

San′ Jo·se′ scale′ (san′ hō zā′), a scale insect, *Aspidiotus perniciosus,* that is highly destructive to fruit trees and shrubs throughout the U.S. Cf. **armored scale.** [1885–90, *Amer.;* named after SAN JOSE, California, where first found]

San Juan (san′ wän′, hwän′; *Sp.* sän hwän′), **1.** a seaport in and the capital of Puerto Rico, in the N part. 424,600. **2.** a city in W Argentina. 290,479. **3.** a river in S Nicaragua, flowing E from Lake Nicaragua along the Nicaragua-Costa Rica border to the Caribbean Sea. ab. 110 mi. (175 km) long.

San′ Juan′ Cap·is·tra′no (kap′i strä′nō), a city in SW California: site of old Spanish mission; known for annual return of swallows, said to occur on March 19. 18,959.

San Juan de la Cruz (*Sp.* sän hwän′ de lä kʀo͞oth′, -kʀo͞os′). See **John of the Cross.**

San′ Juan′ Hill′, a hill in SE Cuba, near Santiago de Cuba: captured by U.S. forces in battle during the Spanish-American War in 1898.

San′ Juan′ Is′lands, a group of islands between NW Washington and SE Vancouver Island, Canada: a part of Washington.

San′ Juan′ Moun′tains, a mountain range in SW Colorado and N New Mexico: a part of the Rocky Mountains. Highest peak, Uncompahgre Peak, 14,306 ft. (4360 m).

sank (sangk), *v.* a pt. of **sink.**

San·ka·ra (sung′kər ə), *n.* Shankara.

San·khya (säng′kyə), *n.* one of the six leading systems of Hindu philosophy, stressing the reality and duality of spirit and matter. Also, **Samkhya.** [1780–90; < Skt *sāṅkhya*]

Sankt Gal·len (zängkt′ gä′lən), German name of **St. Gallen.**

Sankt Mo·ritz (zängkt mō′ʀits), German name of **St. Moritz.**

San Le·an·dro (san′ lē an′drō), a city in W California. 63,952.

San Lo·ren·zo (san′ lə ren′zō), a town in W California, near San Francisco Bay. 20,545.

San Lu·is O·bis·po (san lo͞o′is ə bis′pō), a city in W California. 34,252.

San Lu·is Po·to·sí (sän′ lo͞o ēs′ pô′tô sē′), **1.** a state in central Mexico. 1,527,000; 24,415 sq. mi. (63,235 sq. km). **2.** the capital of this state. 303,000.

San Man·uel (san′ man wel′), a town in S Arizona. 13,481.

San Mar·cos (san mär′kəs), **1.** a city in S central Texas. 23,420. **2.** a city in SW California. 17,479.

San Ma·ri·no (san′ mə rē′nō; *for 1, 2 also It.* sän′ mä ʀē′nô), **1.** a small republic in E Italy: the oldest independent country in Europe. 22,206; 38 sq. mi. (98 sq. km). *Cap.:* San Marino. **2.** a town in and the capital of this republic. 4189. **3.** a city in SW California. 13,307. **—San′ Mar·i·nese′** (mar′ə nēz′, -nēs′).

San Mar·tín (san′ mär tēn′; *Sp.* sän′ mäʀ tēn′), **Jo·sé de** (hô se′ the), 1778–1850, South American general and statesman, born in Argentina: leader in winning independence for Argentina, Peru, and Chile; protector of Peru 1821–22.

San Ma·te·o (san′ mə tā′ō), a city in W California. 77,561.

San·mi·che·li (sän′mē ke′lē), *n.* **Mi·che·le** (mē ke′le), 1484–1559, Italian architect and military engineer.

San Mi·guel (sän′ mē gel′), a city in E El Salvador. 131,977.

san·nup (san′up), *n.* a married American Indian man, esp. a younger one; husband. [1620–30, *Amer.;* < Massachusett (E sp.) *sanomp* (c. Eastern Abenaki *sénape* man, male person)]

sann·ya·si (sun yä′sē), *n. Hinduism.* a wandering beggar and ascetic. [1605–15; < Hindi: one who casts away]

San Pa·blo (san pä′blō, pab′lō), **1.** a city in the Philippines, on S Luzon. 131,655. **2.** a city in W California, near San Pablo Bay. 19,750.

San Pa′blo Bay′, the N part of San Francisco Bay, in W California.

San Pe·dro Su·la (sän pe′thʀô so͞o′lä), a city in NW Honduras. 133,730.

San Quen′tin quail′ (san kwen′tn), *Slang.* jailbait. [1975–80, *Amer.*]

San Ra·fael (san′ rə fel′; *for 1 also Sp.* sän ʀä′fä el′), **1.** a city in W Argentina. 70,477. **2.** a city in W California, N of San Francisco. 44,700.

San Ra·mon (san′ rə mōn′), a town in W California. 22,356.

San Re·mo (san rē′mō, rā′-; *It.* sän ʀe′mô), a seaport in NW Italy, on the Riviera: resort. 64,302.

sans (sanz; *Fr.* säɴ), *prep.* without. [1275–1325; ME < OF *sans*, earlier *sens, seinz* a conflation of L *sine* without, and *absentiā* in the absence of, abl. of *absentia* ABSENCE]

Sans., Sanskrit.

San Sal·va·dor (san sal′və dôr′; *Sp.* sän säl′vä-t͟hôʀ′), *n.* **1.** Also called **Watling Island.** an island in the E central Bahamas: long held to be the first land in the New World sighted by Christopher Columbus 1492. 776; 60 sq. mi. (155 sq. km). Cf. **Samana Cay. 2.** a city in and the capital of El Salvador. 368,313.

sans-cu·lotte (sanz′kyŏŏ lot′, -kŏŏ-; *Fr.* säɴ ky lôt′), *n., pl.* **sans-cu·lottes** (sanz′kyŏŏ lots′, -kŏŏ-; *Fr.* säɴ-ky lôt′). **1.** (in the French Revolution) a revolutionary of the poorer class: originally a term of contempt applied by the aristocrats but later adopted as a popular name by the revolutionaries. **2.** any extreme republican or revolutionary. [1780–90; < F: lit., without knee breeches] **—sans′-cu·lot′tic** (sanz′kyŏŏ lot′ik, -kŏŏ-), *adj.* **—sans′-cu·lot′tism,** *n.* **—sans′-cu·lot′tist,** *n.*

sans doute (säɴ do͞ot′), *French.* without doubt; certainly.

San Se·bas·tián (san′ sə bas′chən; *Sp.* sän′ se väs-tyän′), **1.** a seaport in N Spain: resort. 165,829. **2.** a city in NW Puerto Rico. 10,619. **3.** a tropical American plant, *Cattleya skinneri,* having cylindrical leaves and yellow-throated, rose-purple flowers.

San·sei (sän′sā, san sā′), *n.* a grandchild of Japanese immigrants to the U.S. or Canada. Also, **san′sei′.** Cf. **Issei, Kibei, Nisei.** [1940–45; < Japn: third generation, earlier *san-sei* < MChin, equiv to Chin *sān* three + *shēng* birth]

san·se·vi·e·ri·a (san′sə vē ēr′ē ə, -sə vēr′ē ə), *n.* any plant belonging to the genus *Sansevieria,* of the agave family, grown as a houseplant for its stiff, sword-shaped leaves and white or yellow flowers. [1795–1805; < NL; named after *San Seviero,* principality of Raimondo di Sangro (1710–71), learned Neapolitan; see -IA]

sans gêne (säɴ zhen′), *French.* without constraint or embarrassment; free and easy.

Sansk., Sanskrit.

San·skrit (san′skrit), *n.* **1.** an Indo-European, Indic language, in use since c1200 B.C. as the religious and classical literary language of India. *Abbr.:* Skt —*adj.* **2.** Also, **San·skrit′ic, San·scrit′ic.** of or pertaining to Sanskrit. Also, **San′scrit.** [1610–20; < Skt *saṃskṛta* adorned, perfected] **—San′skrit·ist, San′scrit·ist,** *n.*

San·som (san′səm), *n.* a male given name, form of **Samson.**

San·so·vi·no (san′sō vē′nō; *It.* sän′sô vē′nô), *n.* **1. An·dre·a** (än dre′ä), (*Andrea Contucci*), 1460–1529, Italian sculptor and architect. **2.** his pupil **Ja·co·po** (yä′kô-pô), (*Jacopo Tatti*), 1486–1570, Italian sculptor and architect.

sans peur et sans re·proche (säɴ pœʀ ā säɴ ʀə prôsh), *French.* without fear and without reproach: said originally of the French knight, the Seigneur de Bayard.

sans′ ser′if (sanz), *Print.* a style of monotonal type without serifs. [1820–30] **—sans-ser·if** (sanz′ser′if), *adj.*

sans sou·ci (säɴ so͞o sē′), *French.* carefree.

San Ste·fa·no (sän ste′fä nô′), the former name of Yesilkoy, a town in Turkey, near Istanbul: treaty between Russia and Turkey 1878.

San·ta (san′tə; *for 2 also Sp.* sän′tä), *n.* **1.** See **Santa Claus. 2.** a river in W central Peru, flowing NW into the Pacific Ocean. ab. 200 mi. (322 km) long.

San·ta An·a (san′tə an′ə *or, for 2, 4, Sp.* sän′tä ä′nä), **1.** a city in SW California. 203,713. **2.** a city in NW El Salvador. 174,546. **3.** *Meteorol.* a weather condition in which strong, hot, dust-bearing winds descend to the southern Pacific coast from inland desert regions. **4.** See **Santa Anna.**

San·ta An·na (sän′tä ä′nä; *Eng.* san′tə an′ə), **An·to·nio Ló·pez de** (än tô′nyô lô′pes t͟he), 1795?–1876, Mexican general and revolutionist: dictator 1844–45; president 1833–35, 1853–55. Also, **Santa Ana.**

San·ta Bar·ba·ra (san′tə bär′bər ə, -brə), a city on the SW coast of California: Spanish mission. 74,542.

San′ta Bar′bara Is′lands, a group of islands off the SW coast of California.

San·ta Cat·a·li·na (san′tə kat′l ē′nə), an island off the SW coast of California: resort. 132 sq. mi. (342 sq. km). Also called **Catalina, Catalina Island.**

San·ta Cat·a·ri·na (san′tə kat′ə rē′nə; *Port.* säɴ′tə kä′tə ʀē′nə), a state in S Brazil. 3,687,659; 36,856 sq. mi. (95,455 sq. km). *Cap.:* Florianópolis.

San·ta Cla·ra (san′tə klar′ə; *for 1 also Sp.* sän′tä klä′ʀä), **1.** a city in central Cuba. 189,092. **2.** a city in central California, S of San Francisco. 87,746.

San·ta Claus (san′tə klôz′), a benevolent figure of legend, associated with Saint Nicholas, supposed to bring gifts to children on Christmas Eve. Also, **Santa Klaus.** [1765–75, *Amer.*; < D *Sinterklaas,* equiv. to *sint* SAINT + *heer* (MYN)HEER + *Klaas,* short for *Niklaas* NICHOLAS]

San·ta Co·lo·ma de Gra·ma·net (sän′tä kô lô′mä t͟he grä′mä net′), a city in NE Spain. 106,711.

San·ta Cruz (san′tə kro͞oz′; *for 3 also Sp.* sän′tä kʀo͞os′), **1.** a city on the coast of California. 41,483. **2.** an island in NW Santa Barbara Islands. **3.** a city in central Bolivia. 149,230. **4.** See **St. Croix** (def. 1).

San′ta Cruz′ de Te·ne·rife′ (san′tə kro͞oz′ də ten′ə rif′, -rēf′, -rē′fā; *Sp.* sän′tä kʀo͞oth′ t͟he te′ne-ʀē′fe, kʀo͞os′), a seaport on NE Tenerife island. 151,361.

San′ta Cruz′ Is′lands, a group of islands in the SW Pacific Ocean, part of the Solomon Islands. 380 sq. mi. (984 sq. km).

San′ta Cruz′ wa′ter lil′y, a South American aquatic plant, *Victoria cruziana,* of the water lily family, having floating leaves from 2–5 ft. (0.6–1.5 m) and deep pink or red flowers. Also called **water platter.**

San·ta Fe (san′tə fā′), **1.** a city in and the capital of New Mexico, in the N part: founded c1605. 48,899. **2.** a steam locomotive having a two-wheeled front truck, ten driving wheels, and a two-wheeled rear truck. See table under **Whyte classification. —San′ta Fe′an.**

San·ta Fé (san′tə fā′; *Sp.* sän′tä fe′), a city in E Argentina. 287,240.

San′ta Fe′ Springs′, a city in SW California, near Los Angeles: oil wells. 14,559.

San′ta Fe′ Trail′, an important trade route going between Independence, Missouri, and Santa Fe, New Mexico, used from about 1821 to 1880.

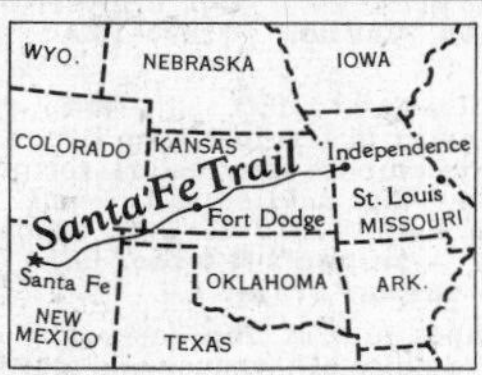

San·ta Ger·tru·dis (san′tə gər tro͞o′dis), one of an American breed of beef cattle, developed from Shorthorn and Brahman stock for endurance to torrid temperatures. [1940–45, *Amer.*; named after a ranch in Texas]

San·ta Is·a·bel (san′tə iz′ə bel′; *Sp.* sän′tä ē′sä-bel′), former name of **Malabo.**

San·ta Klaus (san′tə klôz′). See **Santa Claus.**

san·tal (san′tl), *n.* sandalwood. [see SANDAL[2]]

San·tal (sun täl′), *n., pl.* **-tals,** (*esp. collectively*) **-tal.** a member of a tribal people who live mainly in the state of Bihar in northeastern India.

San·ta·li (sun tä′lē), *n.* the Munda language spoken by the Santal.

San·ta Ma·ri·a (san′tə mə rē′ə; *for 1, 2 also Sp.* sän′-tä mä ʀē′ä; *for 3 also Port.* säɴ′tə mä ʀē′ä), **1.** (*italics*) the flagship used by Columbus when he made his first voyage of discovery to America in 1492. **2.** an active volcano in W Guatemala. 12,300 ft. (3750 m). **3.** a city in S Brazil. 120,667. **4.** a city in W California. 39,685. **5.** calaba.

San·ta Mar·ta (san′tə mär′tə; *Sp.* sän′tä mär′tä), **1.** a seaport in NW Colombia. 102,484. **2.** a cactus, *Heliocereus speciosus,* of Mexico and Central America, having scarlet flowers 6–7 in. (15–17 cm) long.

San·ta Mau·ra (sän′tä mou′ʀä), Italian name of **Levkas.**

San·ta Mon·i·ca (san′tə mon′i kə), a city in SW California, near Los Angeles, on Santa Monica Bay: resort. 88,314.

san·tan·a (san tan′ə), *n. Informal.* See **Santa Ana** (def. 3). [by contr.]

San·ta·na (san tan′ə, -tä′nə; *Sp.* sän tä′nä), *n.* **Pe·dro** (pā′drō; *Sp.* pe′t͟hʀô), 1801–64, Dominican revolutionary and political leader: president 1844–48, 1853–56, 1858–61.

San·tan·der (sän′tän deʀ′), *n.* **1. Fran·cis·co de Pau·la** (frän sēs′kô t͟he pou′lä), 1792–1840, South American soldier and statesman: president of New Granada 1832–37. **2.** a seaport in N Spain: Altamira prehistoric cave drawings nearby. 149,704.

San·ta Pau·la (san′tə pô′lə), a city in SW California. 20,552.

San·ta·rém (san′tə rem′; *Port.* säɴ′tä ʀäɴ′), *n.* a city in N Brazil, on the Amazon River. 111,706.

San·ta Ro·sa (san′tə rō′zə; *for 2 also Sp.* sän′tä ʀô′-sä), **1.** a city in W California, N of San Francisco. 83,205. **2.** a city in central Argentina. 51,689.

San·ta Ro·sa de Co·pán (sän′tä ʀô′sä t͟he kô-pän′), a town in W Honduras: site of extensive Mayan ruins. 18,000. Also called **Copán.**

San·ta Tec·la (san′tə tek′lə; *Sp.* sän′tä te′klä), a city in SW El Salvador, just SW of San Salvador. 38,000. Also called **Nueva San Salvador.**

San·ta·ya·na (san′tē an′ə; -ä′nə; *Sp.* sän′tä yä′nä), *n.* **George,** 1863–1952, Spanish philosopher and writer in the U.S.; in Europe after 1912.

San·tee (san tē′), *n.* **1.** a city in SW California. 47,080. **2.** a river flowing SE from central South Carolina to the Atlantic. 143 mi. (230 km) long. **3.** a branch of the Dakota Indians, comprising the Mdewakanton, Sisseton, Wahpekute, and Wahpeton. **4.** the dialect of Dakota spoken by the Santee. Also called **Dakota** (for defs. 3, 4).

San·te·ri·a (san′tə rē′ə), *n.* (*sometimes l.c.*) a religion merging the worship of Yoruba deities with veneration of Roman Catholic saints: practiced in Cuba and spread to other parts of the Caribbean and to the U.S. by Cuban emigrés. Also, **San′te·rí′a.** [1980–85; < AmerSp, = *santer*(*o*) person practicing Santería (Sp *sant*(*o*)) SAINT + *-ero* < L *-ārius* -ARY) +*ia* -IA]

San·ti·a·go (san′tē ä′gō; *Sp.* sän′tyä′gô), *n.* **1.** a city in and the capital of Chile, in the central part. 1,759,087. **2.** Also called **Santia′go de Com·pos·te′la** (də kom′pə-stel′ə; *Sp.* t͟he kôm′pôs te′lä). a city in NW Spain: pilgrimage center; cathedral. 70,893. **3.** a city in SW Panama. 14,595.

Santia′go de Cu′ba (də kyo͞o′bə; *Sp.* t͟he ko͞o′vä), a seaport in SE Cuba: naval battle 1898. 277,600.

San·tia·go del Es·te·ro (sän tyä′gô t͟hel es te′ʀô), a city in N Argentina. 148,357.

San·tia·go de los Ca·ba·lle·ros (sän tyä′gô t͟he lôs kä′vä ye′ʀôs), a city in the N central Dominican Republic. 155,000.

san·tims (sän′timz), *n., pl.* **-ti·mi** (-tə mē). a former coin of Latvia, the 100th part of a lat. [< Latvian < F *centime* CENTIME]

san·tir (sän′tēr), *n.* a Persian musical instrument resembling a dulcimer. [1850–55; < Ar *ṣanṭir* < Gk *psaltḗrion* PSALTERY]

san·to (san′tō, sän′-; *Sp.* sän′tô), *n., pl.* **-tos** (-tōz; *Sp.* -tôs). a carved wooden figure of a saint, as from Puerto Rico, Mexico, or the southwestern U.S. [1630–40, for an earlier sense; < AmerSp, Sp: lit., SAINT < L *sānctus*]

San·to An·dré (säɴ′to͞o äɴ dʀe′), a city in E Brazil, near São Paulo. 415,025.

San·to Do·min·go (san′tō də ming′gō; *Sp.* sän′tô t͟hô meng′gô), **1.** Formerly, **Ciudad Trujillo.** a city in and the capital of the Dominican Republic, on the S coast: first European settlement in America 1496. 980,000. **2.** a former name of **Dominican Republic. 3.** a former name of **Hispaniola.** Also, **San Domingo** (for defs. 2, 3).

san·ton·i·ca (san ton′i kə), *n.* the dried flower heads of any of several species of wormwood, belonging to the genus *Artemisia,* used as a vermifuge. [1650–60; < NL < L (*herba*) *santonica* (herb) of the *Santonī* a Gaulish tribe of Aquitania]

san·to·nin (san′tə nin), *n. Chem.* a crystalline compound, $C_{15}H_{18}O_3$, the active principle of santonica. [1830–40; SANTON(ICA) + -IN[2]]

San·to·rin (san′tə rēn′), *n.* Thera. Also, **San·to·ri·ni** (san′tə rē′nē; *Gr.* sän′dô rē′nē).

San·tos (san′təs; *Port.* säɴ′to͞os), *n.* a seaport in S Brazil: world's largest coffee-exporting port. 341,317.

San·tos-Du·mont (san′təs do͞o mont′, -dyo͞o-; *Port.* säɴ′to͞oz do͞o môɴt′), *n.* **Al·ber·to** (äl beʀ′to͞o), 1873–1932, Brazilian aeronaut in France: designer and builder of dirigibles and airships.

San·to To·mé de Gua·ya·na (sän′tô tô me′ t͟he gwä yä′nä), a city in NE Venezuela, on the Orinoco River. 143,540. Also called **Ciudad Guayana.**

Sa·nu·si (sə no͞o′sē), *n., pl.* **-sis,** (*esp. collectively*) **-si.** a member of an Islamic brotherhood established among the Bedouins of North Africa. [named after Muhammad ibn Ali al-*Sanūsī* (d. 1859), Algerian founder of the sect]

São Ber·nar·do do Cam·po (souɴ′ beʀ när′do͞o do͞o käɴ′po͞o), a city in SE Brazil, SE of São Paulo. 267,038.

São Ca·e·ta·no do Sul (souɴ′ kī tä′nŏŏ do͞o so͞ol′), a city in SE Brazil, SE of São Paulo. 150,171.

São Fran·cis·co (souɴ′ fʀäɴ sēs′ko͞o), a river flowing NE and E through E Brazil into the Atlantic. 1800 mi. (2900 km) long.

São Gon·ça·lo (souɴ′ go͞oɴ sä′lo͞o), a city in SE Brazil, NE of Rio de Janeiro. 161,392.

São Jo·ão de Me·ri·ti (souɴ′ zho͞o ouɴ′ di mi ʀi-tē′), a city in SE Brazil, NW of Rio de Janeiro. 163,934.

São Jo·sé do Ri·o Prê·to (souɴ′ zho͞o ze′ do͞o ʀē′o͞o pʀe′to͞o), a city in SE Brazil, NW of São Paulo. 108,319.

São Jo·sé dos Cam·pos (souɴ′ zho͞o ze′ do͞os käɴ′po͞os), a city in SE Brazil, NE of São Paulo. 130,118.

São Luís (souɴ′ lwēs′), a seaport on an island off the NE coast of Brazil: capital of Maranhão. 330,311.

São Mi·guel (souɴ′ mē gel′), the largest island of the Azores. 150,000. 288 sq. mi. (746 sq. km).

Sa·o·na (sou′nə; *Sp.* sä ô′nä), *n.* an island in the Caribbean Sea, S of the SE Dominican Republic coast. ab. 13 mi. (21 km) long.

Saône (sōn), *n.* a river flowing S from NE France to the Rhone. 270 mi. (435 km) long.

Saône-et-Loire (sōn′ā lwaʀ′), *n.* a department in E France. 569,810; 3331 sq. mi. (8625 sq. km). *Cap.:* Mâcon.

São Pau·lo (souɴ′ pou′lo͞o; *Eng.* sou′ pou′lō), **1.** a state in S Brazil. 30,942,600; 95,714 sq. mi. (247,898 sq. km). **2.** a city in and the capital of this state. 7,032,547.

São′ Pau′lo de Lu·an′da (də lo͞o äɴ′də), Luanda.

São Pe·dro do Rí·o Gran·de do Sul (souɴ pe′dʀo͞o do͞o ʀē′o͞o gʀäɴ′di do͞o so͞ol′), a seaport in SE Rio Grande do Sul, in SE Brazil. 117,500. Also called **Rio Grande, Rio Grande do Sul.**

Saor·stát Éir·eann (sâr′stät âr′ən; *Irish.* sāʀ′stot ā′ʀyən), Irish name of **Irish Free State.**

CONCISE PRONUNCIATION KEY: *act, cāpe, dâre, pärt; set, ēqual; if, īce; ox, ōver, ôrder, oil, bŏŏk, bo͞ot, out; up, ûrge; child; sing; shoe; thin, that;* zh as in *treasure.* ə = *a* as in *alone, e* as in *system, i* as in *easily, o* as in *gallop, u* as in *circus;* ᵊ as in *fire* (fīᵊr), *hour* (ouᵊr). l and n can serve as syllabic consonants, as in *cradle* (krād′l), and *button* (but′n). See the full key inside the front cover.

São Sal•va•dor (souɴ′ säl′vä dôʀ′), a former name of **Salvador** (def. 2).

Sao•shyant (sou′shyənt), *n. Zoroastrianism.* the World Savior who will come at the end of time.

São Tia•go (souɴ′ tyä′go͞o), the largest of the Cape Verde Islands, S of Cape Verde. ab. 383 sq. mi. (992 sq. km).

São To•mé (souɴ′ to͞o me′; *Eng.* sou′ tə mā′), **1.** an island in the Gulf of Guinea, off the W coast of Gabon, just N of the equator: the larger component of the Democratic Republic of São Tomé and Príncipe. 73,000; 318 sq. mi. (824 sq. km). **2.** a city on this island: capital of the republic. 5714. **3. Pi•co de** (pē′ko͞o də), the highest mountain on this island, 6640 ft. (2024 m). Also, **Sao′ To•me′, São′ Tho•mé′.** —**São′ To•me′an.**

São′ Tomé′ and Prín′cipe, Democratic Republic of, a republic in W Africa, comprising the islands of São Tomé and Príncipe, in the Gulf of Guinea, N of the equator: a former overseas province of Portugal; gained independence in 1975. 80,000; 372 sq. mi. (964 sq. km). *Cap.:* São Tomé. Also, **Sao′ Tome′ and Prin′cipe.**

São Vi•cen•te (souɴ′ vi seɴ′ti), an island city in SE Brazil. 116,075.

sap[1] (sap), *n., v.,* **sapped, sap•ping.** —*n.* **1.** the juice or vital circulating fluid of a plant, esp. of a woody plant. **2.** any vital body fluid. **3.** energy; vitality. **4.** sapwood. **5.** *Slang.* a fool; dupe. **6.** *Metall.* soft metal at the core of a bar of blister steel. —*v.t.* **7.** to drain the sap from. [bef. 900; ME; OE *sæp;* c. D *sap;* akin to G *Saft* juice, ON *safi;* in def. 5 a shortening of SAPHEAD]

sap[2] (sap), *n., v.,* **sapped, sap•ping.** —*n.* **1.** *Fort.* a deep, narrow trench constructed so as to form an approach to a besieged place or an enemy's position. —*v.t.* **2.** *Fort.* **a.** to approach (a besieged place or an enemy position) by means of deep, narrow trenches protected by gabions or parapets. **b.** to dig such trenches in (ground). **3.** to undermine; weaken or destroy insidiously. —*v.i.* **4.** *Fort.* to dig a sap. [1585–95; < F *sape* (n.), deriv. of *saper* to dig a trench < It *zappare,* a military term, based on *zappa* hoe (cf. dial. It *zappo* he-goat < ?)]
—**Syn. 3.** impair, enfeeble, deplete, exhaust, enervate.

sap•a•jou (sap′ə jo͞o′), *n.* a capuchin monkey. [1690–1700; < F]

sa•pan•wood (sə pan′wo͝od′), *n.* sappanwood.

sap′ bush′, *Chiefly Hudson Valley.* sugarbush (def. 2). [1880–85, *Amer.*]

sa•pe•le (sə pē′lē), *n.* **1.** Also called **aboudikro.** the mahoganylike wood of any of several African trees of the genus *Entandrophragma,* used for making furniture. **2.** a tree, esp. *Entandrophragma cylindricum,* of the mahogany family, yielding this wood. Also called **sape′le mahog′any.** [1900–05; after *Sapele,* a port on the Benin River in S Nigeria]

sap′ green′, a green pigment obtained from the juice of buckthorn berries, used chiefly in dyes for wood, paper, and textiles. [1570–80]

sap•head (sap′hed′), *n. Slang.* a simpleton; fool. [1790–1800; SAP[1] + HEAD]

sap•head•ed (sap′hed′id), *adj. Slang.* silly; foolish. [1655–65; SAPHEAD + -ED[3]] —**sap′head′ed•ness,** *n.*

sa•phe•na (sə fē′nə), *n.* See **saphenous vein.** [1350–1400; ME < ML < Ar *ṣāfin*]

sa•phe•nous (sə fē′nəs), *adj.* **1.** of, pertaining to, or situated near the saphenous vein. —*n.* **2.** See **saphenous vein.** [1830–40; SAPHEN(A) + -OUS]

saphe′nous vein′, *Anat.* either of two large veins near the surface of the foot, leg, and thigh, one on the inner side and the other on the outer and posterior sides. [1830–40]

sap•id (sap′id), *adj.* **1.** having taste or flavor. **2.** agreeable to the taste; palatable. **3.** agreeable, as to the mind; to one's liking. [1625–35; < L *sapidus* tasty; cf. SAGE] —**sa•pid′i•ty, sap′id•ness,** *n.*

sa•pi•ens (sā′pē ənz), *adj.* of, pertaining to, or resembling modern humans (*Homo sapiens*). [1935–40; < NL]

sa•pi•ent (sā′pē ənt), *adj.* having or showing great wisdom or sound judgment. [1425–75; late ME *sapyent* < L *sapient-* (s. of *sapiēns,* prp. of *sapere* to be wise, lit., to taste, have taste), equiv. to *sapi-* verb s. + *-ent-* -ENT] —**sa′pi•ence, sa′pi•en•cy,** *n.* —**sa′pi•ent•ly,** *adv.*

sa•pi•en•tial (sā′pē en′shəl), *adj.* containing, exhibiting, or affording wisdom; characterized by wisdom. [1475–85; < LL *sapientiālis,* equiv. to *sapienti(a)* wisdom (see SAPIENT, -IA) + *-ālis* -AL[1]] —**sa′pi•en′tial•ly,** *adv.*

sap•in•da•ceous (sap′in dā′shəs), *adj.* belonging to the Sapindaceae, the soapberry family of plants. Cf. **soapberry family.** [1835–45; < NL *Sapindac(ae)* name of the family (*Sapind(us)* the type genus (L *sāp(ō)* SOAP + *Indus* Indian) + *-aceae* -ACEAE) + -OUS]

Sa•pir (sə pēr′), *n.* **Edward,** 1884–1939, U.S. anthropologist and linguist, born in Germany.

Sa•pir′-Whorf′ hypoth′esis (sə pēr′hwôrf′, -hwôrf′, -wôrf′, -wôrf′), a theory developed by Edward Sapir and Benjamin Lee Whorf that states that the structure of a language determines or greatly influences the modes of thought and behavior characteristic of the culture in which it is spoken. Also called **Whorfian hypothesis.** [1950–55]

sap•less (sap′lis), *adj.* **1.** without sap; withered; dry: *sapless plants.* **2.** lacking vitality or spirit; insipid. [1585–95; SAP[1] + -LESS] —**sap′less•ness,** *n.*

sap•ling (sap′ling), *n.* **1.** a young tree. **2.** a young person. [1375–1425; late ME; see SAP[1], -LING[1]]

sap•o•dil•la (sap′ə dil′ə), *n.* **1.** a large evergreen tree, *Manilkara zapota,* of tropical America, bearing an edible fruit and yielding chicle. Cf. **sapodilla family. 2.** Also called **sap′odil′la plum′.** the fruit itself. Also called **sapota.** [1690–1700; < Sp *zapotillo,* equiv. to *zapot(e)* SAPOTA + *-illo* dim. suffix]

sapodil′la fam′ily, the plant family Sapotaceae, characterized by chiefly tropical trees and shrubs having milky juice, simple leaves, small flowers, and fruit in the form of a berry, and including the buckthorn (genus *Bumelia*), sapodilla, star apple, and trees that are the source of gutta-percha and balata.

sap•o•na•ceous (sap′ə nā′shəs), *adj.* resembling soap; soapy. [1700–10; < NL *sāpōnāceus,* equiv. to L *sāpōn-* (s. of *sāpō*) SOAP + *-āceus* -ACEOUS] —**sap′o•na′ceous•ness,** *n.*

saponifica′tion num′ber, *Chem.* the number of milligrams of potassium hydroxide required to saponify one gram of a given ester, esp. a glyceride. Also called **saponifica′tion val′ue.** [1895–1900; SAPONI(FY) + -FICATION]

sa•pon•i•fy (sə pon′ə fī′), *v.,* **-fied, -fy•ing.** *Chem.* —*v.t.* **1.** to convert (a fat) into soap by treating with an alkali. **2.** to decompose (any ester), forming the corresponding alcohol and acid or salt. —*v.i.* **3.** to become converted into soap. [1815–25; < L *sāpōn-* (s. of *sāpō*) SOAP + -IFY] —**sa•pon′i•fi′a•ble,** *adj.* —**sa•pon′i•fi•ca′tion,** *n.* —**sa•pon′i•fi′er,** *n.*

sap•o•nin (sap′ə nin), *n. Biochem.* any of a group of amorphous glycosides of terpenes and steroids, occurring in many plants, characterized by an ability to form emulsions and to foam in aqueous solutions, and used as detergents. [1825–35; < F *saponine* < L *sāpōn-* (s. of *sāpō*) SOAP + F *-ine* -IN[2]]

sap•o•nite (sap′ə nīt′), *n.* a clay mineral, hydrous magnesium aluminum silicate, belonging to the montmorillonite group: found as a soft filling in rock cavities. [1840–50; < Sw *saponit* < L *sāpōn-* (s. of *sāpō*) SOAP + Sw *-it* -ITE[1]]

sa•por (sā′pər, -pôr), *n.* the quality in a substance that affects the sense of taste; savor; flavor. Also, *Brit.,* **sa′pour.** [1470–80; < L; see SAVOR]

sap′ or′chard, *Chiefly New Eng.* sugarbush (def. 2). [1860–65, *Amer.*]

sap•o•rif•ic (sap′ə rif′ik), *adj.* producing or imparting flavor or taste. [1695–1705; < NL *sapōrificus,* equiv. to L *sapōr-,* s. of *sapor* SAVOR + *-i-* -I- + *-ficus* -FIC]

sap•o•rous (sap′ər əs), *adj.* full of flavor or taste; flavorful. [1660–70; < LL *sapōrōsus,* equiv. to L *sapor* SAVOR + *-ōsus* -OUS] —**sap•o•ros•i•ty** (sap′ə ros′i tē), *n.*

sa•po•ta (sə pō′tə), *n.* **1.** sapote. **2.** sapodilla. [1550–60; < NL < MexSp *zapote* sapodilla < Nahuatl *tzapotl*]

sap•o•ta•ceous (sap′ə tā′shəs), *adj.* belonging to the Sapotaceae, the sapodilla family of plants. Cf. **sapodilla family.** [1835–45; < NL *Sapotace(ae)* name of the family (see SAPOTA, -ACEAE) + -OUS]

sa•po•te (sə pō′tē, -tā), *n.* **1.** Also called **marmalade tree.** a tree, *Pouteria sapota,* of the sapodilla family, native to Mexico and Central America, having large leaves and sweet, edible fruit. **2.** the fruit of this tree. Also, **sapota.** Also called **mammee, marmalade plum.** [1550–60; < AmerSp; see SAPOTA]

sap•pan•wood (sə pan′wo͝od′), *n.* **1.** a dyewood yielding a red color, produced by a small, East Indian tree, *Caesalpinia sappan,* of the legume family. **2.** the tree itself. Also, **sapanwood.** [*sappan-* < Malay *səpang, sapang* (sp. *sepang*) the name of the tree + WOOD[1]]

sap•per (sap′ər), *n.* a soldier employed in the construction of fortifications, trenches, or tunnels that approach or undermine enemy positions. [1620–30; SAP[2] + -ER[1]]

Sap•phic (saf′ik), *adj.* **1.** pertaining to Sappho or to certain meters or a form of strophe or stanza used by or named after her. **2.** Lesbian (def. 2). —*n.* **3.** a Sapphic verse. [1495–1505; < L *sapphicus* < Gk *sapphikós,* equiv. to *Sapph(ṓ)* SAPPHO + *-ikos* -IC]

Sap′phic ode′, *Pros.* See **Horatian ode.** [1870–75]

Sap•phi•ra (sə fī′rə), *n.* **1.** a woman who, with her husband, Ananias, was struck dead for lying. Acts 5. **2.** Also, **Sap•phire** (saf′īᵊr). a female given name.

sap•phire (saf′īᵊr), *n.* **1.** any gem variety of corundum other than the ruby, esp. one of the blue varieties. **2.** a gem of this kind. **3.** the color of this gem, a deep blue. —*adj.* **4.** resembling sapphire; deep blue: *a sapphire sky.* [1225–75; < L *sapphīrus* < Gk *sáppheiros,* prob. < Sem (cf. Heb *sappīr;* ulterior orig. obscure); r. ME *safir* < OF < L, as above]

sap•phir•ine (saf′ər in, -ə rēn′, -ə rīn′), *adj.* **1.** consisting of sapphire; like sapphire, esp. in color. —*n.* **2.** a pale-blue or greenish, usually granular mineral, a silicate of magnesium and aluminum. **3.** a blue variety of spinel. [1375–1425; late ME *saphyryn* (< OF) << Gk *sappheírinos* like lapis lazuli (see SAPPHIRE, -INE[1]); (def. 2) < G *Saphirin* << Gk, as above]

sap•phism (saf′iz əm), *n.* lesbianism. [1885–90; SAPPH(O) + -ISM] —**sap′phist,** *n.*

Sap•pho (saf′ō), *n.* c620–c565 B.C., Greek poet, born in Lesbos.

Sap•po•ro (sə pôr′ō, -pōr′ō; *Japn.* sä′pô ʀô′), *n.* a city on W Hokkaido, in N Japan. 1,401,758.

sap•py (sap′ē), *adj.,* **-pi•er, -pi•est. 1.** abounding in sap, as a plant. **2.** full of vitality and energy. **3.** *Slang.* silly or foolish. [bef. 1100; ME *sapy,* OE *sæpig;* see SAP[1], -Y[1]] —**sap′pi•ness,** *n.*

sa•pre•mi•a (sə prē′mē ə), *n. Pathol.* blood poisoning caused by the toxins produced by bacterial putrefaction, as in gangrene. [1885–90; SAPR- + -EMIA] —**sa•pre′mic,** *adj.*

sapro-, a combining form meaning "rotten," used in the formation of compound words: *saprogenic.* Also, *esp. before a vowel,* **sapr-.** [< Gk, comb. form of *saprós*]

sap•robe (sap′rōb), *n. Biol.* saprophyte. [1932; SAPRO- + (MICRO)BE] —**sa•pro•bic** (sə prō′bik, -prob′ik), *adj.* —**sa•pro′bi•cal•ly,** *adv.*

sap•ro•gen (sap′rə jən, -jen′), *n. Biol.* a plant or animal that can produce decay. [SAPRO- + -GEN]

sap•ro•gen•ic (sap′rō jen′ik), *adj.* **1.** producing putrefaction or decay, as certain bacteria. **2.** formed by putrefaction. Also, **sa•prog•e•nous** (sə proj′ə nəs). [1875–80; SAPRO- + -GENIC]

sap•ro•lite (sap′rə līt′), *n. Petrog.* soft, disintegrated, usually more or less decomposed rock remaining in its original place. [1890–95; SAPRO- + -LITE] —**sap•ro•lit•ic** (sap′rə lit′ik), *adj.*

sap•ro•pel (sap′rə pel′), *n.* mud consisting chiefly of decomposed organic matter formed at the bottom of a stagnant sea or lake. [1905–10; SAPRO- + *-pel* < Gk *pēlós* mud] —**sap′ro•pel′ic,** *adj.*

sa•proph•a•gous (sa prof′ə gəs), *adj. Biol.* (of an organism) feeding on dead or decaying animal matter. [1810–20; SAPRO- + -PHAGOUS]

sap•ro•phyte (sap′rə fīt′), *n.* any organism that lives on dead organic matter, as certain fungi and bacteria. Also called **saprobe.** [1870–75; SAPRO- + -PHYTE] —**sap•ro•phyt•ic** (sap′rə fit′ik), *adj.* —**sap′ro•phyt′i•cal•ly,** *adv.*

sap•sa•go (sap sā′gō, sap′sə gō′), *n.* a strong, hard, usually green cheese of Swiss origin, made with sour skim milk and sweet clover. [1840–50, *Amer.;* alter. of G *Schabziger, Schabzieger,* equiv. to *schab(en)* to grate + *Zi(e)ger* a kind of cheese]

sap•suck•er (sap′suk′ər), *n.* any of several American woodpeckers of the genus *Sphyrapicus* that drill holes in maple, apple, hemlock, etc., drinking the sap and eating the insects that gather there. Cf. **yellow-bellied sapsucker.** [1795–1805, *Amer.;* SAP[1] + SUCKER]

Sa•pul•pa (sə pul′pə), *n.* a city in E central Oklahoma. 15,853.

sap•wood (sap′wo͝od′), *n. Bot.* the softer part of the wood between the inner bark and the heartwood. Also called **alburnum.** [1785–95; SAP[1] + WOOD[1]]

Saq•qa•ra (sə kär′ə), *n.* a village in S Egypt, S of Cairo: site of the necropolis of ancient Memphis; step pyramids; mastabas. 12,700. Also, **Sakkara.**

Sar., Sardinia.

S.A.R., Sons of the American Revolution.

Sa•ra (sär′ə), *n., pl.* **-ras,** (*esp. collectively*) **-ra.** a member of a people of the Central African Republic.

Sar•a (sâr′ə), *n.* **1.** *Douay Bible.* Sarah. **2.** a female given name, form of **Sarah.**

sar•a•band (sar′ə band′), *n.* **1.** a slow, stately Spanish dance, esp. of the 17th and 18th centuries, in triple meter. **2.** a piece of music for or using the rhythm of this dance, usually forming one of the movements in the classical suite and following the courante. Also, **sar′abande′.** [1610–20; < F *sarabande* < Sp *zarabanda,* perh. < Ar *sarband* a kind of dance < Pers]

Sar•a•cen (sar′ə sən), *n.* **1.** *Hist.* a member of any of the nomadic tribes on the Syrian borders of the Roman Empire. **2.** (in later use) an Arab. **3.** a Muslim, esp. in the period of the Crusades. —*adj.* **4.** Also, **Sar•a•cen•ic** (sar′ə sen′ik), **Sar′a•cen′i•cal.** of or pertaining to the Saracens. [bef. 900; ME, OE < ML *Saracēnus* < LGk *Sarakēnós*] —**Sar′a•cen•ism,** *n.*

Sa•ra•gat (sä′ʀä gät′), *n.* **Giu•sep•pe** (jo͞o zep′pe), born 1898, Italian statesman: president 1964–71.

Sar•a•gos•sa (sar′ə gos′ə), *n.* a city in NE Spain, on the Ebro River. 479,845. Spanish, **Zaragoza.**

Sar•ah (sâr′ə), *n.* **1.** the wife of Abraham and mother of Isaac. Gen. 17:15–22. **2.** a female given name. [<< Heb *śārāh* princess]

Sa•rai (sâr′ī, -ā ī′), *n.* an earlier name of Sarah. Gen. 17:15.

Sa•ra•je•vo (sar′ə yā′vō; *Serbo-Croatian.* sä′ʀä ye-vô), *n.* a city in and the capital of Bosnia and Herzegovina, in the central part: assassination of the Austrian Archduke Francis Ferdinand here June 28, 1914, was the final event that precipitated World War I. 448,519. Also, **Serajevo.**

Sar•a•mac•can (sar′ə mak′ən), *n.* an English-based creole spoken in the interior of Suriname. [1955–60; *Saramacc(a)* a river in Surinam (on the upper reaches of which the language is spoken) + -AN]

sa•ran (sə ran′), *n.* a thermoplastic copolymer of vinylidene chloride and usually small amounts of vinyl chloride or acrylonitrile: used as a fiber, for packaging, and for making acid-resistant pipe. [1935–40, *Amer.;* formerly trademark]

Sar′a•nac Lakes′ (sar′ə nak′), a group of three lakes in NE New York, in the Adirondack Mountains: includes the Upper Saranac, the Middle Saranac, and the Lower Saranac.

sa•ran•gi (sär′əng gē), *n.* (in India) a violinlike instrument used to accompany classical dancing. [1850–55; < Skt *sāraṅgī*]

Sa•ransk (su ränsk′), *n.* the capital of the Mordovian Autonomous Republic in the Russian Federation in Europe. 312,000.

CONCISE ETYMOLOGY KEY: <, descended or borrowed from; >, whence; b., blend of, blended; c., cognate with; cf., compare; deriv., derivative; equiv., equivalent; imit., imitative; obl., oblique; r., replacing; s., stem; sp., spelling, spelled; resp., respelling, respelled; trans., translation; ?, origin unknown; *, unattested; ‡, probably earlier than. See the full key inside the front cover.

sa•ra•pe (sə rä′pē; *Sp.* sä RÄ′pe), *n., pl.* **-pes** (-pēz; *Sp.* -pes). serape.

Sa•ra•pis (sə rā′pis), *n.* Serapis (def. 1).

Sa•ra•pul (su RÄ′po͝ol), *n.* a city in the W central RSFSR, in the W central Soviet Union in Asia, S of Izhevsk, on the Kama River. 107,000.

Sar•a•so•ta (sar′ə sō′tə), *n.* a city in W Florida. 48,868.

Sa•ras•va•ti (sə rus′və tē, sur′əs və-), *n.* the Hindu goddess of learning and the arts.

Sar•a•to•ga (sar′ə tō′gə), *n.* **1.** a city in W California. 29,261. **2.** former name of **Schuylerville.**

Sar′ato′ga chip′. See **potato chip.** Also called **Sarato′ga pota′to.** [1870–75, *Amer.*]

Sar′ato′ga Springs′, a city in E New York: health resort; horse races. 23,906.

Sar′ato′ga trunk′, a type of large traveling trunk used mainly by women during the 19th century. [1855–60, *Amer.*; named after SARATOGA SPRINGS]

Sa•ra•tov (su RÄ′təf), *n.* a city in the SW Russian Federation in Europe, on the Volga. 905,000.

Sa•ra•wak (sə rä′wäk, -wä), *n.* a state in the federation of Malaysia, on NW Borneo: formerly a British crown colony (1946–63) and British protectorate (1888–1946). 977,013; ab. 50,000 sq. mi. (129,500 sq. km). *Cap.:* Kuching.

Sar•a•zen (sar′ə zən), *n.* **Gene** (*Eugene Saraceni*), born 1902, U.S. golfer.

sarc-, var. of **sarco-,** esp. before a vowel: *sarcoma.*

-sarc, a combining form meaning "one having flesh or tissue" of the kind specified by the initial element: *ectosarc.* [< Gk *-sarkos,* deriv. of *sárx* flesh]

sar•casm (sär′kaz əm), *n.* **1.** harsh or bitter derision or irony. **2.** a sharply ironical taunt; sneering or cutting remark: *a review full of sarcasms.* [1570–80; < LL *sarcasmus* < Gk *sarkasmós,* deriv. of *sarkázein* to rend (flesh), sneer; see SARCO-]
—**Syn. 1.** sardonicism, bitterness, ridicule. See **irony**[1]. **2.** jeer.

sar•cas•tic (sär kas′tik), *adj.* **1.** of, pertaining to, or characterized by sarcasm: *a sarcastic reply.* **2.** using or given to the use of sarcasm: *to be sarcastic about ambition.* Also, **sar•cas′ti•cal.** [1685–95; SARC(ASM) + -ASTIC] —**sar•cas′ti•cal•ly,** *adv.* —**sar•cas′tic•ness, sar•cas′ti•cal•ness,** *n.*
—**Syn. 2.** biting, cutting, mordant, bitter, derisive, ironic, sardonic. See **cynical.**

sarcas′tic fringe′head. See under **fringehead.**

sarce•net (särs′nit), *n.* a fine, soft fabric, often of silk, made in plain or twill weave and used esp. for linings. Also, **sarsenet, sarsnet.** [1425–75; late ME *sarsenet* < AF *sarzinet,* prob. equiv. to *sarzin-* SARACEN + *-et* -ET]

sar•ci•na (sär′sə nə), *n., pl.* **-nas, -nae** (-nē′). *Bacteriol.* any of several spherical, saprophytic bacteria of the genus *Sarcina,* having a cuboidal cell arrangement. [1835–45; < NL, L: bundle]

sarco-, a combining form meaning "flesh," used in the formation of compound words: *sarcocarp.* Also, *esp. before a vowel,* **sarc-.** [< Gk *sark-* (s. of *sárx*) + -O-]

sar•co•ad•e•no•ma (sär′kō ad′n ō′mə), *n., pl.* **-mas, -ma•ta** (-mə tə). *Pathol.* adenosarcoma. [SARCO- + ADENOMA]

sar•co•car•ci•no•ma (sär′kō kär′sə nō′mə), *n., pl.* **-mas, -ma•ta** (-mə tə). *Pathol.* carcinosarcoma. [SARCO- + CARCINOMA]

sar•co•carp (sär′kō kärp′), *n. Bot.* **1.** the fleshy mesocarp of certain fruits, as the peach. **2.** any fruit of fleshy consistency. [1810–20; SARCO- + -CARP]

sar•code (sär′kōd), *n.* protoplasm, esp. the semifluid content of a protozoan. [1850–55; < F, alter. of Gk *sarkōdēs* fleshy]

sar•co•din•i•an (sär′kə din′ē ən), *adj.* **1.** belonging or pertaining to the protist phylum Sarcodina, comprising protozoa that move and capture food by forming pseudopodia. —*n.* **2.** Also called **sar•co•dine** (sär′kə dīn′, -dēn′). a sarcodinian protozoan. [< NL *Sarcodin(a)* name of the class (Gk *sarkōd(ēs)* fleshy + NL *-ina* neut. pl. suffix) + -IAN]

sar•coid (sär′koid), *Pathol.* —*n.* **1.** a growth resembling a sarcoma. **2.** a lesion of sarcoidosis. **3.** sarcoidosis. —*adj.* **4.** resembling flesh; fleshy. **5.** resembling a sarcoma. [1835–45; SARC- + -OID]

sar•coid•o•sis (sär′koi dō′sis), *n. Pathol.* a disease of unknown cause, characterized by granulomatous tubercles of the skin, lymph nodes, lungs, eyes, and other structures. [1935–40; < NL; see SARCOID, -OSIS]

sar•co•lem•ma (sär′kə lem′ə), *n. Anat.* the membranous sheath of a muscle fiber. [1830–40; SARCO- + LEMMA[2]] —**sar′co•lem′mic, sar′co•lem′mous,** *adj.*

sar•col•o•gy (sär kol′ə jē), *n. Archaic.* the branch of anatomy dealing with the soft or fleshy body parts. [1720–30; SARCO- + -LOGY] —**sar•co•log•i•cal** (sär′kə-loj′i kəl), **sar′co•log′ic,** *adj.*

sar•co•ma (sär kō′mə), *n., pl.* **-mas, -ma•ta** (-mə tə). *Pathol.* any of various malignant tumors composed of neoplastic cells resembling embryonic connective tissue. [1650–60; < NL < Gk *sárkōma* fleshy growth. See SARC-, -OMA] —**sar•co′ma•toid′, sar•co•ma•tous** (sär kō′mə-təs, -kom′ə-), *adj.*

sar•co•ma•to•sis (sär kō′mə tō′sis), *n. Pathol.* **1.** the condition in which a sarcoma has become disseminated throughout the body. **2.** a condition marked by the production of an overwhelming number of sarcomas throughout the body. [1885–90; *sarcomat-* (comb. form of SARCOMA) + -OSIS]

sar•co•mere (sär′kə mēr′), *n. Biol.* any of the segments of myofibril in striated muscle fibers. [1890–95; SARCO- + -MERE]

sar•coph•a•gous (sär kof′ə gəs), *adj.* carnivorous. Also, **sar•co•phag•ic** (sär′kə faj′ik, -fā′jik). [1880–85; < L *sarcophagus* < Gk *sarkophágos* flesh-eating, equiv. to *sarko-* SARCO- + *-phagos* -PHAGOUS]

sar•coph•a•gus (sär kof′ə gəs), *n., pl.* **-gi** (-jī′), **-gus•es. 1.** a stone coffin, esp. one bearing sculpture, inscriptions, etc., often displayed as a monument. **2.** *Gk. Antiq.* a kind of stone thought to consume the flesh of corpses, used for coffins. [1595–1605; < L < Gk *sarkophágos,* n. use of the adj.; see SARCOPHAGOUS]

sar•co•phile (sär′kə fīl′), *n.* a flesh-eating animal, esp. the Tasmanian devil. [SARCO- + -PHILE]

sar•co•plasm (sär′kə plaz′əm), *n. Biol.* the cytoplasm of a striated muscle fiber. [1895–1900; SARCO- + -PLASM]

sar•co•plas′mic retic′ulum (sär′kə plaz′mik), *Cell Biol.* a system of membrane-bound tubules that surrounds muscle fibrils, releasing calcium ions during contraction and absorbing them during relaxation. [1950–55; SARCO- + PLASM(A) + -IC]

sar•cop′tic mange′ (sär kop′tik), *Vet. Pathol.* mange caused by burrowing mites of the genus *Sarcoptes.* [1885–90; < NL *Sarcopt(es)* genus name (irreg. < Gk *sar(k)-* SARC- + *kópt(ein)* to peck, gnaw, strike + NL *-es* n. ending (L *-ēs*)) + -IC]

sar•co•sine (sär′kə sēn′, -sin), *n. Chem.* a crystalline compound, $C_3H_7NO_2$, with a sweet taste, soluble in water, slightly soluble in alcohol: used in the manufacture of toothpaste, cosmetics, and pharmaceuticals. [< G *Sarkosin* (1847), appar. irregular deriv. from Gk *sárx,* s. *sark-* flesh, and G *-in* -INE[2]]

sar•co•some (sär′kə sōm′), *n. Cell Biol.* a mitochondrion occurring in a muscle fiber. [1895–1900; SARCO- + -SOME[3]]

sar•cous (sär′kəs), *adj.* consisting of or pertaining to flesh or skeletal muscle. [1830–40; SARC- + -OUS]

sard (särd), *n.* a reddish-brown chalcedony, used as a gem. Also, **sardius, sardine.** [1350–1400; ME < L *sarda* < Gk *sárdios* SARDIUS]

sar•da•na (sär dä′nə; *Sp.* säR ᴛʜä′nä), *n., pl.* **-nas** (-nəz; *Sp.* -näs). **1.** a dance of the region of Catalonia, Spain, in which the dancers form a moving circle. **2.** the music for this dance. [1920–25; < Sp < Catalan]

Sar•da•na•pa•lian (sär′dn ə pāl′yən, -pā′lē ən), *adj.* excessively luxurious or sensual. [1865–70; *Sardanapal(us)* a legendary Assyrian king proverbial for his decadence (< L < Gk *Sardanápal(l)os,* perh. ult. < Akkadian *Aššur-ban-apli* Ashurbanipal) + -IAN]

sar•dar (sər där′), *n.* sirdar.

sar•dine[1] (sär dēn′), *n., pl.* (*esp. collectively*) **-dine,** (*esp. referring to two or more kinds or species*) **-dines. 1.** the pilchard, *Sardina pilchardus,* often preserved in oil and used for food. **2.** any of various similar, closely related fishes of the herring family Clupeidae. [1400–50; late ME *sardeine* < MF *sardine* < L *sardīna,* deriv. of *sarda* sardine, n. use of fem. of *Sardus* Sardinian]

sar•dine[2] (sär′dīn, -dn), *n.* sard. [1300–50; ME (< LL *sardīnus*) < Gk *sárdinos* SARDIUS]

Sar•din•i•a (sär din′ē ə, -din′yə), *n.* **1.** a large island in the Mediterranean, W of Italy: with small nearby islands it comprises a department of Italy. 1,571,499; 9301 sq. mi. (24,090 sq. km). **2.** a former kingdom 1720–1860, including this island and Savoy, Piedmont, and Genoa (after 1815) in NW Italy: ruled by the House of Savoy. *Cap.:* Turin. Italian, **Sar•de•gna** (säR de′nyä).

Sar•din•i•an (sär din′ē ən, -din′yən), *adj.* **1.** of or pertaining to Sardinia, its inhabitants, or their language. —*n.* **2.** a native or inhabitant of Sardinia. **3.** a Romance language spoken on Sardinia. [1590–1600; SARDINI(A) + -AN]

Sar•dis (sär′dis), *n.* an ancient city in W Asia Minor: the capital of ancient Lydia. Also, **Sar•des** (sär′dēz). Also called **Tarne.** —**Sar•di•an** (sär′dē ən), *n., adj.*

sar•di•us (sär′dē əs), *n.* **1.** sard. **2.** the precious stone, thought to have been a ruby, in the breastplate of the Jewish high priest. Ex. 28:17. [1350–1400; ME < L < Gk *sárdios* (stone) of SARDIS]

sar•don•ic (sär don′ik), *adj.* characterized by bitter or scornful derision; mocking; cynical; sneering: *a sardonic grin.* [1630–40; alter. of earlier *sardonian* (influenced by F *sardonique*) < L *sardoni(us)* (< Gk *sardónios* of Sardinia) + -AN; alluding to a Sardinian plant which when eaten was supposed to produce convulsive laughter ending in death] —**sar•don′i•cal•ly,** *adv.* —**sar•don′i•cism,** *n.*
—**Syn.** biting, mordant, contemptuous.

sar•don•yx (sär don′iks, sär′dn-), *n.* a chalcedony that is used for cameos and has sard and chalcedony of another color, usually white, arranged in straight parallel bands. [1300–50; ME < L < Gk *sardónyx;* see SARD, ONYX]

Sar•dou (säR do͞o′), *n.* **Vic•to•rien** (vēk tô RYEN′), 1831–1908, French dramatist.

sa•ree (sär′ē), *n.* sari.

Sa•re′ra Bay′ (sə rer′ə), a large bay on the NW coast of New Guinea, in Irian Jaya, in Indonesia. Formerly, **Geelvink Bay.**

Sarg (särg), *n.* **Tony** (*Anthony Frederic Sarg*), 1882–1942, U.S. illustrator and marionette maker, born in Guatemala.

sar•gas•so (sär gas′ō), *n., pl.* **-sos.** a gulfweed. [1590–1600; < Pg, perh. special use of *sargaço* rockrose < L *salicastrum,* equiv. to *salic-* (s. of *salix*) willow + *-astrum,* neut. of *-aster* -ASTER[1]]

Sargas′so Sea′, a relatively calm area of water in the N Atlantic, NE of the West Indies.

sar•gas•sum (sär gas′əm), *n.* any seaweed of the genus *Sargassum,* widely distributed in the warmer waters of the globe, as *S. bacciferum,* the common gulfweed. [1900–05; < NL; see SARGASSO]

sar•gas•sum•fish (sär gas′əm fish′), *n., pl.* **-fish•es,** (*esp. collectively*) **-fish.** an olive-brown and black frogfish, *Histrio histrio,* inhabiting tropical Atlantic and western Pacific seas among floating sargassum weed. Also called **mousefish.** [1900–05; SARGASSUM + FISH]

sarge (särj), *n. Informal.* sergeant. [by shortening and resp.]

Sar•gent (sär′jənt), *n.* **1. Sir (Harold) Malcolm (Watts),** 1895–1967, English conductor. **2. John Singer,** 1856–1925, U.S. painter.

sar•go (sär′gō), *n., pl.* **-gos.** *Ichthyol.* a silvery grunt, *Anisotremus davidsonii,* inhabiting waters off the coasts of California and Mexico, having blackish markings and yellowish fins. [1875–80; < Sp < L *sargus* a sea fish < Gk *sárgos*]

Sar•go•dha (sər gō′də), *n.* a city in NE Pakistan. 201,407.

Sar•gon (sär′gon), fl. c2300 B.C., Mesopotamian ruler: founder of Akkadian kingdom.

Sargon II, died 705 B.C., king of Assyria 722–705.

sa•ri (sär′ē), *n., pl.* **-ris.** a garment worn by Hindu women, consisting of a long piece of cotton or silk wrapped around the body with one end draped over the head or over one shoulder. Also, **saree.** [1570–80; < Hindi *sāṛī* < Skt *śāṭī*]

sari

Sa•rit Tha•na•rat (sä RĒT′ tä nä RÄT′), 1908–63, Thai statesman: premier 1952–63.

sark (särk), *n. Scot. and North Eng.* any long, shirtlike garment worn next to the skin, as a chemise, nightshirt, or the like. [bef. 900; ME; OE *serc;* c. ON *serkr* (cf. BERSERK)] —**sark′less,** *adj.*

Sark (särk), *n.* one of the Channel Islands, E of Guernsey. 584; 2 sq. mi. (5 sq. km).

sar•ky (sär′kē), *adj. Brit. Slang.* sarcastic. [by shortening and alter.]

Sar•ma•ti•a (sär mā′shē ə, -shə), *n.* the ancient name of a region in E Europe, between the Vistula and the Volga. —**Sar•ma′ti•an,** *adj., n.*

sar•men•tose (sär men′tōs), *adj. Bot.* having runners. Also, **sar•men•tous** (sär men′təs), **sar•men•ta•ceous** (sär′mən tā′shəs). [1750–60; < L *sarmentōsus,* equiv. to *sarment(um)* twig + *-ōsus* -OSE[1]]

sar•men•tum (sär men′təm), *n., pl.* **-ta** (-tə). *Bot.* a slender running stem; runner. Also, **sar′ment.** [< L: twig]

Sar•mien•to (säR myen′tô), *n.* **Do•min•go Faus•ti•no** (dô mēng′gô fous tē′nô), 1811–88, Argentine writer, educator, and political leader: president 1868–74.

Sar•nath (sär′nät), *n.* an ancient Buddhist pilgrimage center in N India, near Benares: Buddha's first sermon preached here; many ancient Buddhist monuments.

Sar•nen (*Ger.* zäR′nən), *n.* a town in and the capital of Obwalden, in central Switzerland, E of Bern. 7000.

Sar•ni•a (sär′nē ə), *n.* a port in SE Ontario, in S Canada, on the S shore of Lake Huron, on the St. Clair River, across from Port Huron, Michigan. 50,892.

Sar•noff (sär′nôf, -nof), *n.* **David,** 1891–1971, U.S. businessman and broadcasting executive, born in Russia.

sa•rod (sə rōd′), *n.* a lute of northern India, played with a bow. [1860–65; < Hindi < Pers]

sa•rong (sə rông′, -rong′), *n.* **1.** a loose-fitting skirtlike garment formed by wrapping a strip of cloth around the lower part of the body, worn by both men and women in the Malay Archipelago and certain islands of the Pacific Ocean. **2.** a cloth for such garments. [1825–35; < Malay *sarung, sarong*]

Sa·ron′ic Gulf′ (sə ron′ik), an inlet of the Aegean, on the SE coast of Greece, between Attica and the Peloponnesus. 50 mi. (80 km) long; 30 mi. (48 km) wide. Also called **Gulf of Aegina.**

sa·ros (sâr′os), *n. Astron.* the period of 223 synodic months, equaling 6585.32 days or 18 years, 11.32 days (or 10.32 days if 5 leap years occur in the interval), after which eclipses repeat but are shifted 120° west. [1605–15; < Gk *sáros* << Akkadian *shār*] —**sa·ron·ic** (sə ron′ik), *adj.*

Sa·ros (sär′ōs, -ôs), *n.* **Gulf of,** an inlet of the Aegean, N of the Gallipoli Peninsula. 37 mi. (60 km) long; 22 mi. (35 km) wide.

Sa·rouk (sə ro͞ok′), *n.* a tightly woven Oriental rug with soft colors and, usually, a center design. Also, **Saruk.** [1895–1900; named after *Sarouk,* village in western Iran]

Sa·roy·an (sə roi′ən), *n.* **William,** 1908–81, U.S. dramatist, short-story writer, and novelist.

Sar·pe·don (sär pēd′n, -pē′don), *n. Class. Myth.* a Lycian prince, son of Zeus, killed by Patroclus in the Trojan War.

sar·plar (sär′plär, -plər), *n.* **1.** a coarse cloth bagging. **2.** *Obs.* **a.** a bale of wool weighing 2240 lb. (1016 kg) or 80 tods. **b.** the weight of such a bale. Also, **sar·pler** (sär′plər), **sar·pli·er** (sär′plē ər). [1325–75; ME *sarplar* bale of wool < AF (OF *sarpillere*)]

Sar·raute (sᴀ rōt′), *n.* **Na·tha·lie** (nᴀ tᴀ lē′), born 1902, French novelist.

sar·ra·zin (sar′ə zin), *n.* buckwheat (defs. 1–3). [1680–90; < F (*blé*) *sarrasin* SARACEN (wheat)]

Sarre (sᴀʀ), *n.* French name of **Saar.**

sar·ru·so·phone (sə ro͞o′zə fōn′, -rus′ə-), *n.* a metal double-reed wind instrument with a conical bore, related to the oboe and used esp. in military bands. [1870–75; named after *Sarrus* (19th-century French bandmaster); see -O-, -PHONE] —**sar·ru′so·phon′ist,** *n.*

sar·sa·pa·ril·la (sas′pə ril′ə, sär′sə pə-, sär′spə-), *n.* **1.** any of various climbing or trailing tropical American plants belonging to the genus *Smilax,* of the lily family, having alternate leaves, umbels of flowers, and a root that has been used in the treatment of psoriasis. **2.** the root. **3.** an extract or other preparation made of this root. **4.** a soft drink flavored with an extract of this root, as root beer. [1570–80; < Sp *zarzaparrilla,* equiv. to *zarza* bush + *parrilla* (*parr(a)* vine + *-illa* dim. suffix)]

sar·sen (sär′sən), *n.* any of numerous large sandstone blocks or fragments found in south-central England, probably remnants of eroded Tertiary beds. Also called **Druid stone, graywether.** [1635–45; syncopated var. of SARACEN, short for *Saracen boulder* Druid stone]

sarse·net (särs′nit), *n.* sarcenet. Also, **sars′net.**

Sarthe (sᴀʀt), *n.* a department in NW France. 490,385; 2411 sq. mi. (6245 sq. km). *Cap.:* Le Mans.

Sar·to (sär′tō; *It.* säʀ′tô), *n.* **An·dre·a del** (än drā′ə del; *It.* än dʀe′ä del). See **Andrea del Sarto.**

sar·to·ri·al (sär tôr′ē əl, -tōr′-), *adj.* **1.** of or pertaining to tailors or their trade: *sartorial workmanship.* **2.** of or pertaining to clothing or style or manner of dress: *sartorial splendor.* **3.** *Anat.* pertaining to the sartorius. [1815–25; < LL *sartor* tailor + -IAL] —**sar·to′ri·al·ly,** *adv.*

sar·to·ri·us (sär tôr′ē əs, -tōr′-), *n., pl.* **-to·ri·i** (-tôr′ē ī′, -tōr′-). *Anat.* a long, flat, narrow muscle extending obliquely from the front of the hip to the inner side of the tibia, assisting in bending the hip or knee joint and in rotating the thigh outward: the longest muscle in humans. [1695–1705; < NL *sartōrius,* adj. deriv. of LL *sartor* tailor; see -TORY[1]]

Sar·tor Re·sar·tus (sär′tər ri sär′təs), a satirical work (1833–34) by Carlyle.

Sar·tre (sär′trə, särt; *Fr.* sᴀʀ′tʀᵊ), *n.* **Jean-Paul** (zhäɴ pôl′), 1905–80, French philosopher, novelist, and dramatist: declined 1964 Nobel prize for literature.

Sa·ruk (sə ro͞ok′), *n.* Sarouk.

Sar′um use′ (sâr′əm), the liturgy or modified form of the Roman rite used in Salisbury before the Reformation and revived in part by some English churches. [1560–70; after *Sarum* (now *Old Sarum*), a medieval ecclesiastical center, the original site of the cathedral and town of Salisbury]

sa′rus crane′ (sär′əs), a large, gray crane, *Grus antigone,* of Asia, having a naked, red head. [1830–40; < Hindi *sāras* < Skt *sārasa* pertaining to lakes]

SASE, self-addressed stamped envelope. Also, **sase, S.A.S.E., s.a.s.e.**

Sa·se·bo (sä′se bô′), *n.* a seaport on NW Kyushu, in SW Japan. 251,188.

Sa·se·no (sä′sə nô′), *n.* an island off the W coast of Albania, at the entrance to Valona Bay: belongs to Albania. 2 sq. mi. (5 sq. km).

sash[1] (sash), *n.* **1.** a long band or scarf worn over one shoulder or around the waist, as by military officers as a part of the uniform or by women and children for ornament. —*v.t.* **2.** to furnish or adorn with a sash: *a dress sashed at the waist.* [1585–95; dissimilated var. of *shash* (turban of) muslin < Ar *shāsh*] —**sash′less,** *adj.*

sash[2] (sash), *n.* **1.** a fixed or movable framework, as in a window or door, in which panes of glass are set. **2.** such frameworks collectively. —*v.t.* **3.** to furnish with sashes or with windows having sashes. [1675–85; back formation from *sashes* (pl.), dissimilated var. of *shashes* CHASSIS]

CONCISE ETYMOLOGY KEY: <, descended or borrowed from; >, whence; b., blend of, blended; c., cognate with; cf., compare; deriv., derivative; equiv., equivalent; imit., imitative; obl., oblique; r., replacing; s., stem; sp., spelling, spelled; resp., respelling, respelled; trans., translation; ?, origin unknown; *, unattested; ‡, probably earlier than. See the full key inside the front cover.

Sa·sha (sä′shə), *n.* **1.** a female given name, form of **Sandra** or **Alexandra. 2.** a male give name, form of **Alexander.**

sa·shay (sa shā′), *v.i. Informal.* **1.** to glide, move, or proceed easily or nonchalantly: *She just sashayed in as if she owned the place.* **2.** to chassé in dancing. [1830–40, *Amer.*; metathetic var. of CHASSÉ]

sash′ bar′, *Chiefly Brit.* muntin (def. 1). [1830–40]

sash′ chain′, a chain for connecting a vertically sliding window sash with a counterweight.

sash′ cord′, a cord for connecting a vertically sliding window sash with a counterweight. Also called **sash′ line′.** [1770–80]

sa·shi·mi (sä shē′mē; *Japn.* sä′shē mē′), *n. Japanese Cookery.* raw fish cut into very thin slices. Cf. **sushi.** [1875–80; < Japn *sashi* stabbing + *mi(y)* body (< **mui*)]

sash′ rib′bon, a strip of steel or aluminum alloy for connecting a vertically sliding window sash with a counterweight. [1860–65]

sash′ weight′, a counterweight to a vertically sliding window sash. [1730–40]

sa·sin (sā′sin), *n.* See **black buck.** [1825–35; of undetermined orig.]

Sask., Saskatchewan.

Sas·katch·e·wan (sa skach′ə won′, -wən), *n.* **1.** a province in W Canada. 907,650; 251,700 sq. mi. (651,900 sq. km). *Cap.:* Regina. **2.** a river in SW Canada, flowing E to Lake Winnipeg: formed by the junction of the North Saskatchewan and South Saskatchewan rivers. 1205 mi. (1940 km) long.

sas·ka·toon (sas′kə to͞on′), *n. Canadian.* **1.** any of several shad bushes, esp. the serviceberry, *Amelanchier canadensis.* **2.** the berry of these bushes. [1790–1800; < Cree *misa·skwato·min* saskatoon berry, deriv. of *misa·skwat* saskatoon bush (lit., that which is solid wood), with *-min* berry]

Sas·ka·toon (sas′kə to͞on′), *n.* a city in S Saskatchewan, in SW Canada. 133,750.

Sas·quatch (sas′kwoch, -kwach), *n.* See **Big Foot.** [1925–30; < Mainland Halkomelem *sésq̓ec*]

sass[1] (sas), *n. Chiefly New Eng., Midland, and Southern U.S.* **1.** stewed fruit; fruit sauce. **2.** fresh vegetables. [1765–75; var. of SAUCE]

sass[2] (sas), *Informal.* —*n.* **1.** impudent or disrespectful back talk: *Both parents refuse to take any sass from their kids.* —*v.t.* **2.** to answer back in an impudent manner: *Don't sass your mother.* [1855–60, *Amer.*; back formation from SASSY[1]]

sas·sa·by (sas′ə bē), *n., pl.* **-bies.** a large, blackish-red South African antelope, *Damaliscus lunatus,* having curved horns. [1810–20; said to be < Tswana]

sas·sa·fras (sas′ə fras′), *n.* **1.** an American tree, *Sassafras albidum,* of the laurel family, having egg-shaped leaves and long clusters of greenish-yellow flowers. **2.** the aromatic bark of its root, used medicinally and esp. for flavoring beverages, confectionery, etc. [1570–80; < Sp *sasafrás*]

sas′safras oil′, a yellowish or reddish-yellow, aromatic volatile oil distilled from sassafras root, used in flavoring, perfumery, and medicine. [1790–1800]

sas′safras tea′, a tea made from the aromatic dried bark of the root of the sassafras tree, often used medicinally as a stimulant, diaphoretic, and diuretic. [1775–85]

Sas·sa·nid (sə sä′nid, -san′id), *n., pl.* **-sa·nids, -sa·ni·dae** (-sä′ni dē′, -san′i-), *adj.* —*n.* **1.** a member of a dynasty that ruled in Persia A.D. 226–651. —*adj.* **2.** of or pertaining to the Sassanids or their dynasty. Also, **Sas·sa·ni·an** (sə sā′nē ən), **Sas·sa·nide** (sas′ə nid). [1770–80; *Sassan* grandfather of first king of dynasty + -ID[1]]

Sas·sa·ri (*It.* säs′sä ʀē), *n.* a city in NW Sardinia. 114,561.

Sas·se·nach (sas′ə nᴇᴋʜ, -nak), *n.* an English inhabitant of the British Isles: used, often disparagingly, by the Gaelic inhabitants. [1765–75; < ScotGael *Sasunnach,* Ir *Sasanach* English, English person, Protestant, MIr *Saxanach,* deriv. of *Saxain, Sagsuin, Sachsain* the Saxons, England << LL *Saxonēs;* see SAXON]

Sas·set·ta (säs set′tä), *n.* **Ste·fa·no di Gio·van·ni** (ste′fä nô dē jô vän′nē), 1392?–1450, Italian painter.

Sas·soon (sa so͞on′), *n.* **Sieg·fried (Lo·raine)** (sēg′frēd lô rān′, lō-), 1886–1967, English poet and novelist.

sass·wood (sas′wo͝od′), *n.* a tropical African tree, *Erythrophleum suavolens,* of the legume family, having a poisonous bark and hard, durable wood. Also called **sassy bark, sas·sy·wood** (sas′ē wo͝od′). [1895–1900; SASS(Y)[2] + WOOD[1]]

sas·sy[1] (sas′ē), *adj.,* **-si·er, -si·est.** *Informal.* saucy.

sas·sy[2] (sas′ē), *n.* See **sassy bark.** [1855–60; of uncert. orig.]

sas′sy bark′, 1. sasswood. **2.** the bark of the sasswood, used as a poison in certain tribal ordeals. [1855–60]

sas·tru·ga (sas′trə gə, sä′strə-, sa stro͞o′-, sä-), *n., pl.* **-gi** (-gē). Usually, **sastrugi.** ridges of snow formed on a snowfield by the action of the wind. Also, **zastruga.** [1830–40; < G < dial. Russ. *zastrúga,* n. deriv. of *zastrugát′, zastrogát′* to plane, shave down (wood), equiv. to *za-* perfective v. prefix + *strugát′, strogát′* to plane, smooth (wood)]

sat[1] (sat), *v.* a pt. and pp. of **sit.**

sat[2] (sut), *n. Hinduism.* **1.** (in Vedic mythology) the realm of existence, populated by people and gods. Cf. **Asat. 2.** reality. Cf. **Sat-cit-ananda.** [< Skt: lit., being]

SAT, *Trademark.* Scholastic Aptitude Test.

Sat., 1. Saturday. **2.** Saturn.

sat., 1. saturate. **2.** saturated.

Sa·tan (sāt′n), *n.* the chief evil spirit; the great adversary of humanity; the devil. [bef. 900; ME, OE < LL < Gk *Satân, Satán* < Heb *sāṭān* adversary]

sa·tang (sä tang′), *n., pl.* **-tang.** a monetary unit and former coin of Thailand, the 100th part of a baht. [1910–15; < Thai *sataaŋ* (sp. *sataṅg*) ult. < Pali *sata-* HUNDRED + *aṅga* portion, division]

sa·tan·ic (sə tan′ik, sā-), *adj.* **1.** of Satan. **2.** characteristic of or befitting Satan; extremely wicked; devillike; diabolical. Also, **sa·tan′i·cal.** [1660–70; < MGk *satanikós.* See SATAN, -IC] —**sa·tan′i·cal·ly,** *adv.* —**sa·tan′i·cal·ness,** *n.*
—**Syn. 2.** evil, devilish, hellish, fiendish, infernal.

Sa·tan·ism (sāt′n iz′əm), *n.* **1.** the worship of Satan or the powers of evil. **2.** a travesty of Christian rites in which Satan is worshiped. **3.** diabolical or satanic disposition, behavior, or activity. [1555–65; SATAN + -ISM] —**Sa′tan·ist,** *n.*

SATB, *Music.* soprano, alto, tenor, bass.

satch·el (sach′əl), *n.* a small bag, sometimes with a shoulder strap. [1300–50; ME *sachel* < OF < L *saccellus,* double dim. of *saccus* SACK[1]; see -ELLE] —**satch′·eled,** *adj.*

Sat-cit-a·nan·da (sut′chit′ä nun′də), *n. Hinduism.* reality, seen through the discovery of Brahman as *sat* or ultimate being, *cit* or pure consciousness, and *ananda* or perfect bliss. Also, **Saccidananda, Sat′-chit′-a·nan′da.**

Sat·com (sat′kom′), *n.* one of a series of privately financed geosynchronous communications satellites that provide television, voice, and data transmissions to the U.S. [1965–70; *sat(ellite) com(munications)*]

sate[1] (sāt), *v.t.,* **sat·ed, sat·ing. 1.** to satisfy (any appetite or desire) fully. **2.** to fill to excess; surfeit; glut. [1595–1605; var. of obs. *sade* to satiate, OE *sadian* (akin to SAD), perh. influenced by SATIATE]
—**Syn. 1.** satiate, fill. **2.** gorge, stuff.

sate[2] (sat, sāt), *v. Archaic.* pt. and pp. of **sit.**

sa·te[3] (sä tā′), *n.* a Southeast Asian, esp. Indonesian and Malaysian, dish of marinated, bite-size pieces of meat, skewered, barbecued, and usually served with a peanut-flavored dipping sauce. Also, **sa·tay′, sa·té′.** [1930–35; < Malay *satay, sate*]

sa·teen (sa tēn′), *n.* a strong cotton fabric constructed in satin weave and having a lustrous face. [1875–80; var. of SATIN, by assoc. with *velveteen*]

sat·el·lite (sat′l īt′), *n.* **1.** *Astron.* a natural body that revolves around a planet; a moon. **2.** a country under the domination or influence of another. **3.** something, as a branch office or an off-campus facility of a university, that depends on, accompanies, or serves something else. **4.** an attendant or follower of another person, often subservient or obsequious in manner. **5.** a device designed to be launched into orbit around the earth, another planet, the sun, etc. —*adj.* **6.** of, pertaining to, or constituting a satellite: *the nation's new satellite program.* **7.** subordinate to another authority, outside power, or the like: *satellite nations.* [1540–50; 1955–60 for def. 2; < L *satellit-* (s. of *satelles*) attendant, member of bodyguard or retinue] —**sat′el·lit′ed,** *adj.*
—**Syn. 4.** follower, supporter, companion, associate; lackey, parasite, sycophant, toady, flunky.

sat′ellite chro′mosome, *Genetics.* See **B chromosome.**

sat′ellite cit′y. See **new town.** Also called **sat′ellite town′.** [1910–15]

sat′ellite dish′, dish (def. 8).

sat·el·loid (sat′l oid′), *n. Aerospace.* a low-altitude satellite using engines with small thrust to maintain its orbit. [1950–55; SATELL(ITE) + -OID]

sa·tem (sä′təm), *adj.* belonging to or consisting of those branches of the Indo-European family in which alveolar or palatal fricatives, as the sounds (s) or (sh), developed in ancient times from Proto-Indo-European palatal stops: the satem branches are Indo-Iranian, Armenian, Slavic, Baltic, and Albanian. Cf. **centum[2].** [1900–05; < Avestan *satəm* hundred (c. L *centum;* see CENTUM[2]), exemplifying in *s-* the outcome of Indo-European palatal stops characteristic of the group]

sa•ti (su tē′, sut′ē), *n.* **1.** a Hindu practice whereby a widow immolates herself on the funeral pyre of her husband: now abolished by law. **2.** a Hindu widow who so immolates herself. Also, **sa•tī′, suttee.** [1780–90; < Skt *satī* good woman, woman devoted to her husband]

Sa•ti (su tē′, sut′ē), *n. Hindu Mythology.* the wife of Rudra, who immolated herself following a quarrel between her father and her husband. Also, **Sa•tī′.**

sa•tia•ble (sā′shə bəl, -shē ə-), *adj.* capable of being satiated. [1560–70; SATI(ATE) + -ABLE] —**sa′tia•bil′i•ty, sa′tia•ble•ness,** *n.* —**sa′tia•bly,** *adv.*

sa•ti•ate (*v.* sā′shē āt′; *adj.* sā′shē it, -āt′), *v.,* **-at•ed, -at•ing,** *adj.* —*v.t.* **1.** to supply with anything to excess, so as to disgust or weary; surfeit. **2.** to satisfy to the full; sate. —*adj.* **3.** satiated. [1400–50; late ME (adj.) < L *satiātus* (ptp. of *satiāre* to satisfy), equiv. to *sati-* enough (akin to SAD) + *-ātus* -ATE[1]] —**sa′ti•a′tion,** *n.*
—**Syn. 1.** glut, stuff, gorge.

sa•ti•at•ed (sā′shē ā′tid), *adj.* satisfied, as one's appetite or desire, to the point of boredom. [1685–95; SATIATE + -ED[2]]

Sat•i•con (sat′i kon′), *Television, Trademark.* a camera tube similar to the vidicon in construction and operation but using a combination of the semiconductors selenium, arsenic, and tellurium (rather than antimony sulfide) as its photoconductive surface.

Sa•tie (sä tē′), *n.* **E•rik Al•fred Les•lie** (e rēk′ al fred′ les lē′), 1866–1925, French composer.

sa•ti•e•ty (sə tī′i tē), *n.* the state of being satiated; surfeit. [1525–35; < L *satietās;* r. earlier *sacietie* < MF *sacieté* < L]

sat•in (sat′n), *n.* **1.** a fabric in a warp-effect or filling-effect satin weave, as acetate, rayon, nylon, or silk, often having a glossy face and a soft, slippery texture. **2.** See **satin weave. 3.** a dress or other garment of satin: *She wore her green satin.* —*adj.* **4.** of or like satin; smooth; glossy. **5.** made of or covered or decorated with satin: *a satin pillow.* [1325–75; ME *satyn(e)* < MF *satin,* prob. < Ar (*aṭlas*) *zaytūnī* (satin) of *Zaitun* a city in China where the cloth was made, prob. Tsinkiang] —**sat′in•like′,** *adj.*

sat•i•net (sat′n et′), *n.* **1.** a satin-weave fabric made with cotton warp and wool filling, fulled and finished to resemble wool. **2.** a thin, light satin. Also, **sat′i•nette′.** [1695–1705; < F; see SATIN, -ET]

sat•in•flow•er (sat′n flou′ər), *n.* a Californian plant, *Clarkia amoena,* of the evening primrose family, having cup-shaped pink or purplish flowers blotched with red. [1590–1600]

sat′in glass′, an American art glassware having colored glass set into indentations in a thickness of opaque glass, the whole covered with clear glass and etched slightly with acid. Also called **mother-of-pearl glass.**

sat•in•pod (sat′n pod′), *n.* either of two European plants belonging to the genus *Lunaria,* of the mustard family, *L. annua* or *L. rediviva,* cultivated for their shiny flowers and large, round, flat, satiny pods. [SATIN + POD[1]]

Sat′in Slip′per, The, (French, *Le Soulier de Satin*), a play (1925–28) by Paul Claudel.

sat′in spar′, *Mineral.* a fibrous variety of gypsum having a silky luster, used as a gem. [1795–1805]

sat′in stitch′, a long, straight embroidery stitch worked closely parallel in rows to form a pattern that resembles satin. [1675–85]

sat′in weave′, one of the basic weave structures in which the filling threads are interlaced with the warp at widely separated intervals, producing the effect of an unbroken surface. Also called **satin.** Cf. **plain weave, twill weave.** [1895–1900]

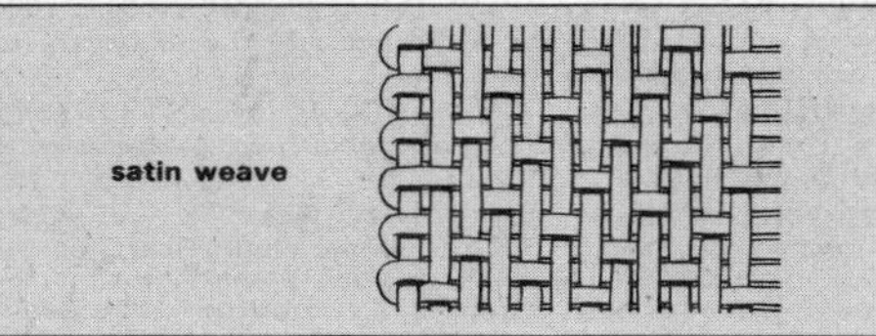

sat•in•wood (sat′n wŏŏd′), *n.* **1.** the satiny wood of an East Indian tree, *Chloroxylon swietenia,* of the rue family, used esp. for making furniture. **2.** the tree itself. [1785–95; SATIN + WOOD[1]]

sat•in•y (sat′n ē), *adj.* satinlike; smooth; glossy. [1780–90; SATIN + -Y[1]]

sat•ire (sat′īər), *n.* **1.** the use of irony, sarcasm, ridicule, or the like, in exposing, denouncing, or deriding vice, folly, etc. **2.** a literary composition, in verse or prose, in which human folly and vice are held up to scorn, derision, or ridicule. **3.** a literary genre comprising such compositions. [1500–10; < L *satira,* var. of *satura* medley, perh. fem. deriv. of *satur* sated (see SATURATE)]
—**Syn. 1.** See **irony[1]. 2, 3.** burlesque, caricature, parody, travesty. SATIRE, LAMPOON refer to literary forms in which vices or follies are ridiculed. SATIRE, the general term, often emphasizes the weakness more than the weak person, and usually implies moral judgment and corrective purpose: *Swift's satire of human pettiness and bestiality.* LAMPOON refers to a form of satire, often political or personal, characterized by the malice or virulence of its attack: *lampoons of the leading political figures.*

sa•tir•i•cal (sə tir′i kəl), *adj.* **1.** of, pertaining to, containing, or characterized by satire: *satirical novels.* **2.** indulging in or given to satire: *a satirical poet.* Also, **sa•tir′ic.** [1520–30; < LL *satiric(us)* (*satir(a)* SATIRE + *-icus* -IC) + -AL[1]] —**sa•tir′i•cal•ly,** *adv.* —**sa•tir′i•cal•ness,** *n.*
—**Syn. 1.** sardonic, ironical, taunting, cutting, mordant, biting, acid. See **cynical.**

sat•i•rist (sat′ər ist), *n.* **1.** a writer of satires. **2.** one who indulges in satire. [1580–90; SATIRE + -IST]

sat•i•rize (sat′ə rīz′), *v.t.,* **-rized, -riz•ing.** to attack or ridicule with satire. Also, *esp. Brit.,* **sat′i•rise′.** [1595–1605; SATIRE + -IZE] —**sat′i•riz′a•ble,** *adj.* —**sat′i•ri•za′tion,** *n.* —**sat′i•riz′er,** *n.*

sat•is•fac•tion (sat′is fak′shən), *n.* **1.** an act of satisfying; fulfillment; gratification. **2.** the state of being satisfied; contentment. **3.** the cause or means of being satisfied. **4.** confident acceptance of something as satisfactory, dependable, true, etc. **5.** reparation or compensation, as for a wrong or injury. **6.** the opportunity to redress or right a wrong, as by a duel. **7.** payment or discharge, as of a debt or obligation. **8.** *Eccles.* **a.** an act of doing penance or making reparation for venial sin. **b.** the penance or reparation made. [1250–1300; < L *satisfactiōn-* (s. of *satisfactiō*) a doing enough, equiv. to *satisfact(us)* (ptp. of *satisfacere,* equiv. to *satis* enough + *facere* to make, DO[1]) + *-iōn-* -ION; r. ME *satisfaccioun* < AF < L, as above] —**sat′is•fac′tion•al,** *adj.* —**sat′is•fac′tion•less,** *adj.*
—**Syn. 2.** enjoyment, pleasure, comfort. **5.** amends, expiation, atonement, indemnity, indemnification, requital, recompense. **7.** repayment, remuneration.
—**Ant. 2.** displeasure, discontent.

sat•is•fac•to•ry (sat′is fak′tə rē, -fak′trē), *adj.* **1.** giving or affording satisfaction; fulfilling all demands or requirements: *a satisfactory solution.* **2.** *Theol.* atoning or expiating. [1520–30; < ML *satisfactōrius,* equiv. to L *satisfac(ere)* to do enough + *-tōrius* -TORY[1]] —**sat′is•fac′to•ri•ly,** *adv.* —**sat′is•fac′to•ri•ness,** *n.*
—**Syn. 1.** competent, adequate, suitable, passable.

sat•is•fied (sat′is fīd′), *adj.* **1.** content: *a satisfied look.* **2.** completely paid, as a bill. **3.** convinced, as in an argument: *Their opponents were finally satisfied.* [1565–75; SATISFY + -ED[2]]

sat•is•fy (sat′is fī′), *v.,* **-fied, -fy•ing.** —*v.t.* **1.** to fulfill the desires, expectations, needs, or demands of (a person, the mind, etc.); give full contentment to: *The hearty meal satisfied him.* **2.** to put an end to (a desire, want, need, etc.) by sufficient or ample provision: *The hearty meal satisfied his hunger.* **3.** to give assurance to; convince: *to satisfy oneself by investigation.* **4.** to answer sufficiently, as an objection. **5.** to solve or dispel, as a doubt. **6.** to discharge fully (a debt, obligation, etc.). **7.** to make reparation to or for: *to satisfy an offended person; to satisfy a wrong.* **8.** to pay (a creditor). **9.** *Math.* **a.** to fulfill the requirements or conditions of: *to satisfy a theorem.* **b.** (of a value of an unknown) to change (an equation) into an identity when substituted for the unknown: *x = 2 satisfies 3x = 6.* —*v.i.* **10.** to give satisfaction. [1400–50; late ME *satisfien* < MF *satisfier* < VL **satisficāre* (for L *satisfacere* to do enough; see SATISFACTION); see -FY] —**sat′is•fi′a•ble,** *adj.* —**sat′is•fi′er,** *n.* —**sat′is•fy′ing•ly,** *adv.* —**sat′is•fy′ing•ness,** *n.*
—**Syn. 1.** gratify, appease, pacify, please. SATISFY, CONTENT refer to meeting one's desires or wishes. To SATISFY is to meet to the full one's wants, expectations, etc.: *to satisfy a desire to travel.* To CONTENT is to give enough to keep one from being disposed to find fault or complain: *to content oneself with a moderate meal.* **3.** persuade.

Sa•to (sä′tō; *Japn.* sä′tô), *n.* **Ei•sa•ku** (ā sä′kōō; *Japn.* ā′sä kōō′), 1901–75, Japanese political leader: prime minister 1964–72; Nobel peace prize 1974.

sa•to•ri (sə tôr′ē, -tōr′ē), *n. Zen.* sudden enlightenment. [1720–30; < Japn: n. deriv. of v. "to awaken" (*sato-* aware + *-r-* formative affix)]

sa•trap (sā′trap, sa′-), *n.* **1.** a governor of a province under the ancient Persian monarchy. **2.** a subordinate ruler, often a despotic one. [1350–1400; ME < L *satrapa* < Gk *satrápēs* < OPers *khshathra-pāvan-* country-protector]

sa•trap•y (sā′trə pē, sa′-), *n., pl.* **-trap•ies.** the province or jurisdiction of a satrap. [1595–1605; < L *satrapia* < Gk *satrapeía,* equiv. to *satrape-,* s. of *satrápēs* SATRAP + *-ia* -Y[3]]

Sat•su•ma (sat sōō′mə, sat′sə mə; *Japn.* sä′tsōō mä′), *n.* a former province on S Kyushu, in SW Japan: famous for its porcelain ware.

Satsu′ma ware′, a Japanese pottery from Kyushu, first produced in the early 17th century and after 1800 having a crackle glaze and overglaze polychrome enameling and gilding. Also, **sat•su′ma.** [1870–75; named after SATSUMA, Japan]

satt•va (sut′və), *n. Hinduism.* See under **guna.** [< Skt]

satt•vic (sut′vik, sat′-), *adj. Hinduism.* characterized by sattva: having a serene, harmonious, balanced mind or attitude. [SATTV(A) + -IC]

Sa•tu-Ma•re (sä′tōō mä′re), *n.* a city in NW Rumania. 108,152.

sat•u•ra•ble (sach′ər ə bəl), *adj.* capable of being saturated. [1560–70; < L *saturābilis,* equiv. to *saturā(re)* to SATURATE + *-bilis* -BLE] —**sat′u•ra•bil′i•ty,** *n.*

sat•u•rant (sach′ər ənt), *n.* **1.** something that causes saturation. —*adj.* **2.** that saturates; saturating. [1745–55; < L *saturant-* (s. of *saturāns,* prp. of *saturāre* to SATURATE), equiv. to *satur-* full, well-fed (akin to SAD) + *-ant-* -ANT]

sat•u•rate (*v.* sach′ə rāt′; *adj., n.* sach′ər it, -ə rāt′), *v.,* **-rat•ed, -rat•ing,** *adj., n.* —*v.t.* **1.** to cause (a substance) to unite with the greatest possible amount of another substance, through solution, chemical combination, or the like. **2.** to charge to the utmost, as with magnetism. **3.** to soak, impregnate, or imbue thoroughly or completely: *to saturate a sponge with water; a town saturated with charm.* **4.** to destroy (a target) completely with bombs and missiles. **5.** to send so many planes over (a target area) that the defensive electronic tracking equipment becomes ineffective. **6.** to furnish (a market) with goods to its full purchasing capacity. —*v.i.* **7.** to become saturated. —*adj.* **8.** saturated. —*n.* **9.** a saturated fat or fatty acid. [1530–40; < L *saturātus* (ptp. of *saturāre* to fill), equiv. to *satur-* full, well-fed (see SAD) + *-ātus* -ATE[1]]
—**Syn. 3.** See **wet.**

sat•u•rat•ed (sach′ə rā′tid), *adj.* **1.** soaked, impregnated, or imbued thoroughly; charged thoroughly or completely; brought to a state of saturation. **2.** (of colors) of maximum chroma or purity; of the highest intensity of hue; free from admixture of white. **3.** *Chem.* **a.** (of a solution) containing the maximum amount of solute capable of being dissolved under given conditions. **b.** (of an organic compound) containing no double or triple bonds; having each single bond attached to an atom or group. **c.** (of an inorganic compound) having no free valence electrons. [1660–70; SATURATE + -ED[2]]

sat′urated fat′, *Nutrition.* a type of single-bond animal or vegetable fat, as that found in butter, meat, egg yolks, and coconut or palm oil, that in humans tends to increase cholesterol levels in the blood. Cf. **saturated** (def. 3). [1970–75]

sat′urated liq′uid, *Thermodynam.* a liquid whose temperature and pressure are such that any decrease in pressure without change in temperature causes it to boil. Cf. **saturated vapor.**

sat′urated va′por, *Thermodynam.* a vapor whose temperature and pressure are such that any compression of its volume at constant temperature causes it to condense to liquid at a rate sufficient to maintain a constant pressure. Cf. **saturated liquid.**

sat•u•rat•er (sach′ə rā′tər), *n.* a person or thing that saturates. Also, **saturator.**

sat•u•ra•tion (sach′ə rā′shən), *n.* **1.** the act or process of saturating. **2.** the state of being saturated. **3.** *Meteorol.* a condition in the atmosphere corresponding to 100 percent relative humidity. **4.** the degree of chroma or purity of a color; the degree of freedom from admixture with white. **5.** *Magnetism.* the state of maximum magnetization of a ferromagnetic material. [1545–55; < LL *saturātiōn-* (s. of *saturātiō*) a filling, equiv. to *saturāt(us)* (see SATURATE) + *-iōn-* -ION]

satura′tion bomb′ing, intense area bombing intended to destroy everything in the target area. [1940–45]

satura′tion div′ing, a method of prolonged diving, using an underwater habitat to allow divers to remain in the high-pressure environment of the ocean depths long enough for their body tissues to become saturated with the inert components of the pressurized gas mixture that they breathe: when this condition is reached, the amount of time required for decompression remains the same, whether the dive lasts a day, a week, or a month. [1965–70] —**satura′tion dive′.**

satura′tion lev′el. See **carrying capacity.**

satura′tion point′, 1. the point at which a substance will receive no more of another substance in solution, chemical combination, etc. **2.** a point at which some capacity is at its fullest; limit: *After a while she reached the saturation point and could absorb nothing more from the lectures.* [1855–60]

sat•u•ra•tor (sach′ə rā′tər), *n.* **1.** saturater. **2.** *Chem.* a device for saturating an inert gas with the vapor of a volatile liquid by slowly bubbling the gas through it. [1880–85; SATURATE + -OR[2]]

Sat•ur•day (sat′ər dā′, -dē), *n.* the seventh day of the week, following Friday. [bef. 900; ME *Saturdai;* OE *Sæternesdæg,* partial trans. of L *Sāturnī diēs* Saturn's day; c. D *zaterdag,* LG *saterdag*]

Sat′ur•day-night spe′cial (sat′ər dā nīt′, -dē-), *Informal.* a cheap, small-caliber handgun that is easily obtainable and concealable. [1965–70]

Sat•ur•days (sat′ər dāz′, -dēz), *adv.* on Saturdays: *Saturdays we go to the movies.* [SATURDAY + -S[1]]

Sat•urn (sat′ərn), *n.* **1.** an ancient Roman god of agriculture, the consort of Ops, believed to have ruled the earth during an age of happiness and virtue, identified with the Greek god Cronus. **2.** *Astron.* the planet sixth in order from the sun, having an equatorial diameter of 74,600 mi. (120,000 km), a mean distance from the sun of 886.7 million mi. (1427 million km), a period of revolution of 29.46 years, and 21 known moons. It is the second largest planet in the solar system, encompassed by a series of thin, flat rings composed of small particles of ice. See table under **planet. 3.** *Alchemy.* the metal lead. **4.** a U.S. space-vehicle booster developing from 2 million to 9 million lb. (900,000 to 4 million kg) of thrust for launching satellites, probes, and spaceships.

Sat•ur•na•li•a (sat′ər nā′lē ə, -nāl′yə), *n., pl.* **-li•a, -li•as. 1.** (*sometimes used with a plural v.*) the festival of Saturn, celebrated in December in ancient Rome as a time of unrestrained merrymaking. **2.** (*l.c.*) unrestrained revelry; orgy. [1585–95; < L *Sāturnālia,* equiv. to *Sāturn(us)* SATURN + *-ālia,* neut. pl. of *-ālis* -AL[1]] —**Sat′ur•na′li•an,** *adj.*

Sa•tur•ni•an (sə tûr′nē ən), *adj.* **1.** of or pertaining to the planet Saturn. **2.** of or pertaining to the god Saturn, whose reign is referred to as the "golden age." **3.** prosperous, happy, or peaceful: *Saturnian days.* [1550–60; < L *Sāturni(us)* of Saturn + -AN]

sa•tur•ni•id (sə tûr′nē id), *n.* **1.** any of several large, brightly colored moths of the family Saturniidae, comprising the giant silkworm moths. —*adj.* **2.** belonging

CONCISE PRONUNCIATION KEY: *act, cāpe, dâre, pärt; set, ēqual; if, īce; ox, ōver, ôrder, oil, bŏŏk, bōōt, out; up, ûrge; child; sing; shoe; thin, that;* zh as in *treasure.* ə = *a* as in *alone, e* as in *system, i* as in *easily, o* as in *gallop, u* as in *circus;* ᵊ as in *fire* (fīᵊr), *hour* (ouᵊr). l and n can serve as syllabic consonants, as in *cradle* (krād′l), and *button* (but′n). See the full key inside the front cover.

or pertaining to the family Saturniidae. [1890–95; < NL *Saturniidae* name of the family. See SATURNIAN, -ID²]

sat·ur·nine (sat′ər nīn′), *adj.* **1.** sluggish in temperament; gloomy; taciturn. **2.** suffering from lead poisoning, as a person. **3.** due to absorption of lead, as bodily disorders. [1400–50; late ME < ML *sāturnīnus* (see SATURN, -INE¹)] —**sat′ur·nine′ly,** *adv.* —**sat′ur·nine′ness, sat·ur·nin·i·ty** (sat′ər nin′i tē), *n.*

sat·ur·nism (sat′ər niz′əm), *n. Pathol.* See **lead poisoning** (def. 1b). [1850–55; < ML *Sāturn(us)* lead + -ISM; in alchemy the planet was thought to have leadlike properties]

Sat·ya·gra·ha (sut′yə gru′hə, sət yä′grə-), *n.* (*sometimes l.c.*) (in India) the policy of passive resistance inaugurated by Mohandas Gandhi in 1919 as a method of gaining political and social reforms. [1915–20; < Hindi, equiv. to Skt *satya* truth + *āgraha* strong attachment, persistence]

sat·ya·lo·ka (sut′yə lō′kə), *n. Hindu Myth.* the highest heaven, where Brahma and Sarasvati live with Brahmins. [< Skt: world of truth, equiv. to *satya* true, truth + *loka* world]

Sat·ya Yu·ga (sut′yə yŏŏg′ə), *Hinduism.* the first and best of the four Yugas. Also called **Krita Yuga.**

sa·tyr (sā′tər, sat′ər), *n.* **1.** *Class. Myth.* one of a class of woodland deities, attendant on Bacchus, represented as part human, part horse, and sometimes part goat and noted for riotousness and lasciviousness. **2.** a lascivious man; lecher. **3.** a man who has satyriasis. **4.** Also, **sa·tyr·id** (sā′tər id, sat′ər-, sə tī′rid). Also called **sa′tyr but′terfly.** any of several butterflies of the family Satyridae, having gray or brown wings marked with eyespots. [1325–75; ME < L *satyrus* < Gk *sátyros*] —**sa·tyr·ic** (sə tir′ik), **sa·tyr′i·cal,** *adj.* —**sa′tyr·like′,** *adj.*

sa·ty·ri·a·sis (sā′tə rī′ə sis, sat′ə-), *n.* See **Don Juanism.** [1620–30; < NL < Gk *satyríāsis.* See SATYR, -IASIS]

Sa·tyr·i·con (sa tir′i kon′), *n.* a satirical novel, interspersed with verse, written in the 1st century A.D. by Petronius, extant in fragments.

sa·tyr·o·ma·ni·ac (sā′tə rō mā′nē ak′, sat′ə-), *n.* a lascivious man; lecher. [1885–90; < Gk *sátyro(s)* SATYR + MANIAC]

sa′tyr play′, a burlesque or ribald drama having a chorus of satyrs, usually written by a poet to follow the poet's trilogy of tragedies presented at the Dionysian festival in ancient Greece.

Sau (sou), *n.* German name of **Sava.**

sauce (sôs), *n., v.,* **sauced, sauc·ing.** —*n.* **1.** any preparation, usually liquid or semiliquid, eaten as a gravy or as a relish accompanying food. **2.** stewed fruit, often puréed and served as an accompaniment to meat, dessert, or other food: *cranberry sauce.* **3.** something that adds piquance or zest. **4.** *Informal.* impertinence; sauciness. **5.** *Slang.* hard liquor (usually prec. by *the*): *He's on the sauce again.* **6.** *Archaic.* garden vegetables eaten with meat. —*v.t.* **7.** to dress or prepare with sauce; season: *meat well sauced.* **8.** to make a sauce of: *Tomatoes must be sauced while ripe.* **9.** to give piquance or zest to. **10.** to make agreeable or less harsh. **11.** *Informal.* to speak impertinently or saucily to. [1300–50; ME < MF < LL *salsa,* n. use of fem. of L *salsus* salted, ptp. of *sallere* to salt, deriv. of *sāl* SALT] —**sauce′less,** *adj.*

sauce a·mé·ri·caine (sō SA mā rē ken′), *French Cookery.* américaine.

sauce Bercy (sōs ber sē′), *French.* Bercy.

sauce·boat (sôs′bōt′), *n.* a low, boat-shaped container for serving sauce or gravy, typically having a handle at one end and a long, wide lip at the other end. [1740–50; SAUCE + BOAT]

sauce·box (sôs′boks′), *n. Informal* (*older use*). a saucy person. [1580–90; SAUCE + BOX¹]

sauced (sôst), *adj. Slang.* intoxicated; drunk. [prob. b. SOUSED and SAUCE (in sense "liquor")]

sauce es·pag·nole (sôs′ es′pən yōl′, -pan-; *Fr.* sō ses pA nyôl′). See **brown sauce.** [< F: Spanish sauce]

sauce·pan (sôs′pan′), *n.* a metal container of moderate depth, usually having a long handle and sometimes a cover, for stewing, boiling, etc. [1680–90; SAUCE + PAN¹]

sauce·pot (sôs′pot′), *n.* a cooking pot having a handle on each side and a close-fitting lid, used esp. for stewing and simmering. [SAUCE + POT¹]

sau·cer (sô′sər), *n.* **1.** a small, round, shallow dish to hold a cup. **2.** something resembling a saucer, as in shape. [1300–50; ME < OF *saussier.* See SAUCE, -ER²]

sau′cer dome′, *Archit.* a dome having the form of a segment of a sphere, with the center well below the springing line; a shallow dome, as in Roman or Byzantine architecture. [1890–95]

sauce su·prême (sôs′ sə prēm′, -prām′, sŏŏ-; *Fr.* sōs sY prem′), suprême (def. 1).

sauch (soukh, sôkh, säkh), *n. Scot. and North Eng.* saugh.

sau·cier (sôs yā′; *Fr.* sō sye′), *n., pl.* **sau·ciers** (sôs-yāz′; *Fr.* sō sye′). *French Cookery.* a chef or cook who specializes in making sauces. [1960–65; < F; see SAUCE, -IER²]

sau·cy (sô′sē), *adj.,* **-ci·er, -ci·est.** **1.** impertinent; insolent: *a saucy remark; a saucy child.* **2.** pert; boldly smart: *a saucy little hat for Easter.* [1500–10; SAUCE + -Y¹] —**sau′ci·ly,** *adv.* —**sau′ci·ness,** *n.*
—**Syn. 1.** rude, impudent, fresh, brazen. **2.** jaunty.

Sa·ud (sä ŏŏd′), *n.* **1.** (*Saud ibn Abdul-Aziz*), 1901?–69, king of Saudi Arabia 1953–64 (son of ibn-Saud and brother of Faisal). **2. Ab·dul-A·ziz ibn-** (äb dŏŏl′-ä zēz′ ib′ən). See **ibn-Saud, Abdul-Aziz.**

Sau·di (sou′dē, sô′-, sä ōō′-), *n., pl.* **-dis,** *adj.* —*n.* **1.** a native or inhabitant of Saudi Arabia. —*adj.* **2.** of, pertaining to, or characteristic of Saudis or Saudi Arabia. [1930–35; < Ar *Sa'ūdī,* equiv. to *Sa'ūd* personal name of the founder of the present dynasty + *-ī* suffix of appurtenance]

Sau′di Ara′bia, a kingdom in N and central Arabia, including Hejaz, Nejd, and dependencies. 7,800,000; ab. 600,000 sq. mi. (1,554,000 sq. km). *Cap.:* Riyadh. Cf. **Mecca.**

sau·er·bra·ten (sou°r′brät′n, sou′ər-; *Ger.* zou′ər-brät′n), *n.* a pot roast of beef, marinated before cooking in a mixture of vinegar, sugar, and seasonings. [1885–90, *Amer.*; < G, equiv. to *sauer* SOUR + *Braten* roast]

sau·er·kraut (sou°r′krout′, sou′ər-), *n.* cabbage cut fine, salted, and allowed to ferment until sour. [1610–20; < G, equiv. to *sauer* SOUR + *Kraut* greens]

sau·ger (sô′gər), *n.* a freshwater, North American pikeperch, *Stizostedion canadense.* Also called **sand pike.** [1880–85, *Amer.*; orig. uncert.]

saugh (soukh, sôkh, säkh), *n. Scot. and North Eng.* sallow². Also, **sauch.** [bef. 1000; ME (north); OE (Anglian) *salh* (var. of West Saxon *sealh* SALLOW²)]

Sau·gus (sô′gəs), *n.* a town in E Massachusetts, near Boston. 24,746.

Sauk (sôk), *n., pl.* **Sauks,** (*esp. collectively*) **Sauk. 1.** a member of a North American Indian people formerly of Wisconsin and Iowa, now living mostly in Oklahoma. **2.** the dialect of the Fox language spoken by the Sauk. Also, **Sac.**

Sauk′ Cen′tre, a town in central Minnesota: model for town in Sinclair Lewis's novel *Main Street.* 3709.

Sauk′ Vil′lage, a town in NE Illinois. 10,906.

Saul (sôl), *n.* **1.** the first king of Israel. I Sam. 9. **2.** Also called **Saul′ of Tar′sus.** the original name of the apostle Paul. Acts 9:1–30; 22:3. **3.** a male given name: from a Hebrew word meaning "asked for."

sault (sōō), *n.* a waterfall or rapid. [1590–1600; < F; OF *saut* < L *saltus* a leap. See SALT²]

Saul·teaux (sō′tō), *n., pl.* **-teaux** (-tōz; *esp. collectively* -tō) for 1. **1.** a member of an American Indian people of Ontario, Manitoba, and Saskatchewan, a division of the Ojibwa. **2.** the Algonquian language of the Saulteaux, a dialect of Ojibwa.

Sault Ste. Ma·rie (sōō′ sānt′ mə rē′), **1.** the rapids of the St. Marys River, between NE Michigan and Ontario, Canada. **2.** a city in S Ontario, in S Canada, near these rapids. 81,048. **3.** a city opposite it, in NE Michigan. 14,448. Also, **Sault′ Sainte′ Marie′.**

Sault Ste. Marie Canals, two ship canals, one in Canada and the other in Michigan, N and S of Sault Ste. Marie rapids and connecting Lakes Superior and Huron. 1½ mi. (2.4 km) long. Also, **Sault′ Sainte′ Marie′ Canals′, Soo Canals.**

sau·na (sô′nə, sou′-), *n., v.,* **-naed, -na·ing.** —*n.* **1.** a bath that uses dry heat to induce perspiration, and in which steam is produced by pouring water on heated stones. **2.** a bathhouse or room, usually of wood, equipped for such a bath. —*v.i.* **3.** to take a sauna: *to sauna after exercising.* [1880–85; < Finnish]

saun·cy (son′sē, sôn′sē), *adj.,* **-ci·er, -ci·est.** *Scot. and North Eng., Irish Eng.* sonsy.

Saun·dra (sôn′drə, sän′-), *n.* a female given name.

saun·ter (sôn′tər, sän′-), *v.i.* **1.** to walk with a leisurely gait; stroll: *sauntering through the woods.* —*n.* **2.** a leisurely walk or ramble; stroll. **3.** a leisurely gait. [1660–70; of uncert. orig.] —**saun′ter·er,** *n.*
—**Syn. 1–3.** amble, ramble, meander.

-saur, a combining form used in the names of extinct reptiles, esp. archosaurs, usually Anglicized forms of Latin taxonomic names: *dinosaur; pterosaur.* [< Gk *saûros* lizard]

Sau·rash·tra (sou räsh′trə), *n.* a former state in W India, comprising most of Kathiawar peninsula: now part of Gujarat state. 21,062 sq. mi. (54,550 sq. km).

sau·rel (sôr′əl), *n.* any of several elongated marine fishes of the genus *Trachurus,* having bony plates along each side. [1880–85; < F, equiv. to *saur-* (< LL *saurus* jack mackerel < Gk *saûros* sea fish) + *-el* n. suffix]

sau·ri·an (sôr′ē ən), *adj.* **1.** belonging or pertaining to the *Sauria,* a group of reptiles originally including the lizards, crocodiles, and several extinct forms but now technically restricted to the lizards. **2.** resembling a lizard. —*n.* **3.** a saurian animal, as a dinosaur or lizard. [1800–10; < NL *Sauri(a)* an order of reptiles + -AN; see -SAUR]

saur·is·chi·an (sô ris′kē ən), *n.* **1.** any herbivorous or carnivorous dinosaur of the order Saurischia, having a three-pronged pelvis resembling that of a crocodile. Cf. **ornithischian.** —*adj.* **2.** belonging or pertaining to the Saurischia. [1885–90; < NL *Saurischi(a)* name of the order (*Saur(ia)* (see -SAUR) + L *-ischi(um)* ISCHIUM + *-a* -A¹) + -AN]

sau·ro·pod (sôr′ə pod′), *n.* **1.** any herbivorous dinosaur of the suborder Sauropoda, from the Jurassic and Cretaceous periods, having a small head, long neck and tail, and five-toed limbs: the largest known land animal. —*adj.* **2.** belonging or pertaining to the sauropods. [1890–95; < NL *Sauropoda* suborder name < Gk *saûro(s)* lizard + *-poda* -PODA; cf. -POD]

-saurus, Latinized var. of **-saur:** *brontosaurus.*

sau·ry (sôr′ē), *n., pl.* **-ries. 1.** a sharp-snouted fish, *Scomberesox saurus,* inhabiting temperate regions of the Atlantic Ocean. **2.** any of various related fishes. [1765–75; < NL *saur(us)* + -Y². See SAUREL]

sau·sage (sô′sij *or, esp. Brit.,* sos′ij), *n.* **1.** minced pork, beef, or other meats, often combined, together with various added ingredients and seasonings, usually stuffed into a prepared intestine or other casing and often made in links. **2.** *Aeron.* a sausage-shaped observation balloon, formerly used in warfare. [1400–50; late ME *sausige* < dial. OF *sausiche* < LL *salsīcia,* neut. pl. of *salsīcius* seasoned with salt, deriv. of L *salsus* salted. See SAUCE, -ITIOUS] —**sau′sage·like′,** *adj.*

sau′sage curl′, a lock of hair formed into a curl resembling a sausage in shape. [1820–30]

sau′sage turn′ing, *Furniture.* turning of members to resemble a continuous row of sausages flattened at the ends.

Sau·sa·li·to (sô′sə lē′tō), *n.* a town in W California on San Fransisco Bay: resort; formerly artist's colony. 7090.

Saus·sure (*Fr.* sō sYR′), *n.* **Fer·di·nand de** (*Fr.* ferdē nän′ də), 1857–1913, Swiss linguist.

Saus·sur·e·an (sō sŏŏr′ē ən, -syŏŏr′-), *adj.* pertaining to or characteristic of the theories of Ferdinand de Saussure, esp. the view that a language consists of a network of interrelated elements in contrast. [SAUSSURE + -EAN]

saus·su·rite (sô′sə rīt′), *n.* a mineral aggregate of albite, zoisite, and other calcium aluminum silicates, formed by alteration of plagioclase feldspars in igneous rocks. [1805–15; named after H. B. de *Saussure* (1740–99), Swiss geologist and physicist; see -ITE¹] —**saus·su·rit·ic** (sô′sə rit′ik), *adj.*

saut de basque (*Fr.* sō də bask′), *pl.* **sauts de basque** (*Fr.* sō də bask′), *Ballet.* a jump in which the dancer turns in the air while keeping the foot of one leg drawn up to the knee of the other. [1945–50; < F: lit., Basque jump]

sau·té (sō tā′, sô-), *adj., v.,* **-téed** (-tād′), **-té·ing** (-tā′-ing), *n.* —*adj.* **1.** cooked or browned in a pan containing a small quantity of butter, oil, or other fat. —*v.t.* **2.** to cook in a small amount of fat; pan-fry. —*n.* **3.** a dish of sautéed food. [1805–15; < F, ptp. of *sauter* to jump (causative: to toss) < L *saltāre,* freq. of *salīre* to jump]

Sau·terne (sō tûrn′, sô-), *n.* (*sometimes l.c.*) a semi-sweet white wine of California, commonly sold as a jug wine. [see SAUTERNES]

Sau·ternes (sō tûrn′, sô-; *Fr.* sō tern′), *n.* **1.** a rich, sweet white table wine of France. **2.** the district near Bordeaux producing this wine.

sau·til·lé (*Fr.* sō tē yā′), *adj., adv. Music.* saltando. [< F, ptp. of *sautiller* to jump about, freq. of *sauter* to jump. See SAUTÉ]

sau·toir (sō twär′, sô-; *Fr.* sō twar′), *n., pl.* **-toirs** (-twärz′; *Fr.* -twar′). **1.** a ribbon, chain, scarf, or the like, tied around the neck in such a manner that the ends cross over each other. **2.** a chain to which a pendant is attached, worn around the neck. [1935–40; < F; see SALTIRE]

Sau·vi·gnon (sō′vin yōn′; *Fr.* sō vē nyōn′), *n.* a small blue-black grape grown primarily in the Médoc region of Bordeaux, in SW France, and highly prized in winemaking. [see CABERNET SAUVIGNON]

Sau·vi·gnon Blanc (sō′vin yōn′ blängk′; *Fr.* sō vē-nyōn blän′), **1.** a white grape grown primarily in France and California. **2.** a white table wine made from this grape. [1940–45; < F: white Sauvignon]

Sa·va (sä′vä), *n.* a river flowing E from W Slovenia, through Croatia to the Danube at Belgrade, Yugoslavia. 450 mi. (725 km) long. Also, **Save.** German, **Sau.**

sav·age (sav′ij), *adj., n., v.,* **-aged, -ag·ing.** —*adj.* **1.** fierce, ferocious, or cruel; untamed: *savage beasts.* **2.** uncivilized; barbarous: *savage tribes.* **3.** enraged or furiously angry, as a person. **4.** unpolished; rude: *savage manners.* **5.** wild or rugged, as country or scenery: *savage wilderness.* **6.** *Archaic.* uncultivated; growing wild. —*n.* **7.** an uncivilized human being. **8.** a fierce, brutal, or cruel person. **9.** a rude, boorish person. **10.** a member of a preliterate society. —*v.t.* **11.** to assault and maul by biting, rending, goring, etc.; tear at or mutilate: *numerous sheep savaged by dogs.* **12.** to attack or criticize thoroughly or remorselessly; excoriate: *a play savaged by the critics.* [1250–1300; ME *savage, sauvage*

CONCISE ETYMOLOGY KEY: <, descended or borrowed from; >, whence; b., blend of, blended; c., cognate with; cf., compare; deriv., derivative; equiv., equivalent; imit., imitative; obl., oblique; r., replacing; s., stem; sp., spelling, spelled; resp., respelling, respelled; trans., translation; ?, origin unknown; *, unattested; ‡, probably earlier than. See the full key inside the front cover.

(adj.) < MF *sauvage, salvage* < ML *salvāticus,* for L *silvāticus,* equiv. to *silv(a)* woods + *-āticus* adj. suffix] **—sav′age·ly,** *adv.* **—sav′age·ness,** *n.*
—Syn. 1. wild, feral, fell; bloodthirsty. See **cruel. 2.** wild. **3.** infuriated. **5.** rough, uncultivated. **9.** churl, oaf. **—Ant. 1.** mild. **2, 4.** cultured. **5.** cultivated.

Sav·age (sav′ij), *n.* **1. Michael Joseph,** 1872–1940, New Zealand statesman and labor leader: prime minister 1935–40. **2. Richard,** 1697?–1743, English poet.

Sav′age Is′land, Niue.

sav·age·ry (sav′ij rē), *n., pl.* **-ries. 1.** an uncivilized or barbaric state or condition; barbarity. **2.** savage action, nature, disposition, or behavior. [1585–95; SAVAGE + -RY]

Sav′age's Sta′tion, a locality in E Virginia, near Richmond: Civil War battle in 1862.

sav·ag·ism (sav′ə jiz′əm), *n.* barbarism; savagery. [1790–1800; SAVAGE + -ISM]

Sa·vai·i (sä vī′ē), *n.* an island in Western Samoa: largest of the Samoa group. 40,572; 703 sq. mi. (1821 sq. km).

sa·van·na (sə van′ə), *n.* **1.** a plain characterized by coarse grasses and scattered tree growth, esp. on the margins of the tropics where the rainfall is seasonal, as in eastern Africa. **2.** grassland region with scattered trees, grading into either open plain or woodland, usually in subtropical or tropical regions. Also, **sa·van′nah.** [1545–55; earlier *zavana* < Sp (now *sabana*) < Taino *zabana*]

Sa·van·nah (sə van′ə), *n.* **1.** a seaport in E Georgia, near the mouth of the Savannah River. 141,634. **2.** a river flowing SE from E Georgia along most of the boundary between Georgia and South Carolina and into the Atlantic. 314 mi. (505 km) long.

Savan′nah spar′row, a North American sparrow, *Passerculus sandwichensis,* having brown and white plumage with a yellow stripe over each eye. [1805–15, *Amer.*]

Sa·van·na·khet (sä wän nä ket′), *n.* a city in S central Laos. 50,690.

savan′na mon′key, any of several common, closely allied long-tailed monkeys of African savannas ranging from Senegal to South Africa, including the green monkey, grivet, tantalus, and vervet, which are sometimes considered subspecies and classified together as *Cercopithecus aethiops.*

sa·vant (sa vänt′, sav′ənt; *Fr.* SA VÄN′), *n., pl.* **savants** (sa vänts′, sav′ənts; *Fr.* SA VÄN′). a person of profound or extensive learning; learned scholar. [1710–20; < F: man of learning, scholar, old prp. of *savoir* to know << L *sapere* to be wise; see SAPIENT]

sav·a·rin (sav′ə rin), *n.* a spongelike cake leavened with yeast, baked in a ring mold, and often soaked with a rum syrup. [1875–80; < F, named after Anthelme Brillat-*Savarin* (d. 1826), French politician and gourmet]

sa·vate (sə vat′), *n.* a sport resembling boxing but permitting blows to be delivered with the feet as well as the hands. [1860–65; < F: lit., old shoe. See SABOT]

save[1] (sāv), *v.,* **saved, sav·ing,** *n.* **—***v.t.* **1.** to rescue from danger or possible harm, injury, or loss: *to save someone from drowning.* **2.** to keep safe, intact, or unhurt; safeguard; preserve: *God save the king.* **3.** to keep from being lost: *to save the game.* **4.** to avoid the spending, consumption, or waste of: *to save fuel.* **5.** to keep, as for reuse: *to save leftovers for tomorrow's dinner.* **6.** to set aside, reserve, or lay by: *to save money.* **7.** to treat carefully in order to reduce wear, fatigue, etc.: *to save one's eyes by reading under proper light.* **8.** to prevent the occurrence, use, or necessity of; obviate: *to come early in order to save waiting.* **9.** *Theol.* to deliver from the power and consequences of sin. **10.** *Computers.* to copy (a file) from RAM onto a disk or other storage medium. **11.** *Sports.* to stop (a ball or puck) from entering one's goal. **—***v.i.* **12.** to lay up money as the result of economy or thrift. **13.** to be economical in expenditure. **14.** to preserve something from harm, injury, loss, etc. **15.** to admit of being kept without spoiling, as food. **—***n.* **16.** an act or instance of saving, esp. in sports. **17.** *Baseball.* a statistical credit given a relief pitcher for preserving a team's victory by holding its lead in a game. [1175–1225; ME *sa(u)ven* < OF *sauver* < LL *salvāre* to save; see SAFE] **—sav′a·ble, save′a·ble,** *adj.* **—sav′a·ble·ness, save′a·ble·ness,** *n.* **—sav′er,** *n.*
—Syn. 1. salvage. **6.** store up, husband. **12.** economize, hoard.

save[2] (sāv), *prep.* **1.** except; but: *All the guests had left save one.* **—***conj.* **2.** except; but (usually fol. by *that*): *He would have gone, save that he had no means.* [1250–1300; ME; var. of SAFE]
—Syn. 1. See **except**[1].

Save (sä′və), *n.* Sava.

save-all (sāv′ôl′), *n.* **1.** a means, contrivance, or receptacle for preventing loss or waste. **2.** *Older Use.* overalls. **3.** *Naut.* **a.** a net secured between a pier and a ship, beneath cargo being transferred from one to the other. **b.** a sail for utilizing wind spilled from the regular sails of a vessel: used in very light winds. [1635–45; n. use of v. phrase *save all*]

sav·e·loy (sav′ə loi′), *n. Chiefly Brit.* a highly seasoned, dried sausage. [1830–40; prob. < F *cervelas,* MF *cervelat* < It *cervellato* Milanese sausage, orig. containing pig's brains, equiv. to *cervell(o)* brain (see CEREBELLUM) + *-ato* -ATE[1]]

sav·in (sav′in), *n.* **1.** a juniper, *Juniperus sabina,* of Europe and Asia. **2.** the drug derived from the dried tops of this plant, formerly used in treating amenorrhea. **3.** See **red cedar** (def. 1). Also, **sav′ine.** [bef. 1000; ME; OE *safine, savene* << L *(herba) Sabina* Sabine (herb)]

sav·ing (sā′ving), *adj.* **1.** tending or serving to save; rescuing; preserving. **2.** compensating; redeeming: *a saving sense of humor.* **3.** thrifty; economical: *a saving housekeeper.* **4.** making a reservation: *a saving clause.* **—***n.* **5.** a reduction or lessening of expenditure or outlay: *a saving of 10 percent.* **6.** something that is saved. **7. savings,** sums of money saved by economy and laid away. **8.** *Law.* a reservation or exception. **—***prep.* **9.** except: *Nothing remains saving these ruins.* **10.** with all due respect to or for: *saving your presence.* **—***conj.* **11.** except; save. [1250–1300; ME; see SAVE[1], -ING[2], -ING[1]] **—sav′ing·ly,** *adv.*
—Syn. 2. restoring, redemptory, qualifying.

sav′ing grace′, a quality that makes up for other generally negative characteristics; redeeming feature. [1590–1600]

sav′ings account′, a bank account on which interest is paid, traditionally one for which a bankbook is used to record deposits, withdrawals, and interest payments. Cf. **checking account.** [1910–15]

sav′ings and loan′ associa′tion, a cooperative savings institution, chartered and regulated by a state or the federal government, that receives deposits in exchange for shares of ownership and invests its funds chiefly in loans secured by first mortgages on homes. Also called **building and loan association, cooperative bank;** *Brit.,* **building society.**

sav′ings bank′, a bank that receives savings accounts only and pays interest to its depositors. [1810–20]

sav′ings bond′, a U.S. government bond with principal amounts up to $10,000. [1945–50]

sav′ings certif′icate, a certificate of deposit for a specific sum of money in a savings account, esp. a deposit for a fixed term at a specified interest rate. [1915–20]

sav·ior (sāv′yər), *n.* **1.** a person who saves, rescues, or delivers: *the savior of the country.* **2.** *(cap.)* a title of God, esp. of Christ. **3.** *(cap.) Class. Myth.* an epithet of Artemis. Also, **sav′iour.** [1250–1300; ME *saveour, sauveur* < OF *sauvēour* < LL *salvātor,* equiv. to L *salvā(re)* to SAVE[1] + *-tor* -TOR] **—sav′ior·hood′, sav′ior·ship′,** *n.*
—Usage. See **-or**[1].

Sa·voie (SA VWA′), *n.* **1.** a department in E France. 305,118; 2389 sq. mi. (6185 sq. km). *Cap.:* Chambéry. **2.** French name of **Savoy.**

sa·voir-faire (sav′wär fâr′; *Fr.* SA VWAR FER′), *n.* knowledge of just what to do in any situation; tact. [1805–15; < F: lit., knowing how to do]
—Syn. adaptability, adroitness, diplomacy, discernment, skill, ability.

sa·voir-vi·vre (sav′wär vē′vrə, -vēv′; *Fr.* SA VWAR-VĒ′VR[ə]), *n.* knowledge of the world and the ways or usages of polite society. [1745–55; < F: lit., knowing how to live]

Sa·vo·na (sä vô′nä), *n.* a city in N Italy on the Mediterranean. 79,393.

Sav·o·na·ro·la (sav′ə nə rō′lə; *It.* sä′vô nä RÔ′lä), *n.* **Gi·ro·la·mo** (ji rol′ə mō′; *It.* jē RÔ′lä mô), 1452–98, Italian monk, reformer, and martyr.

Savonaro′la chair′, *Italian Furniture.* a chair of the Renaissance having a number of transverse pairs of curved legs, crossing beneath the seat and rising to support the arms and back. Cf. **Dante chair.** [1915–20; after G. SAVONAROLA]

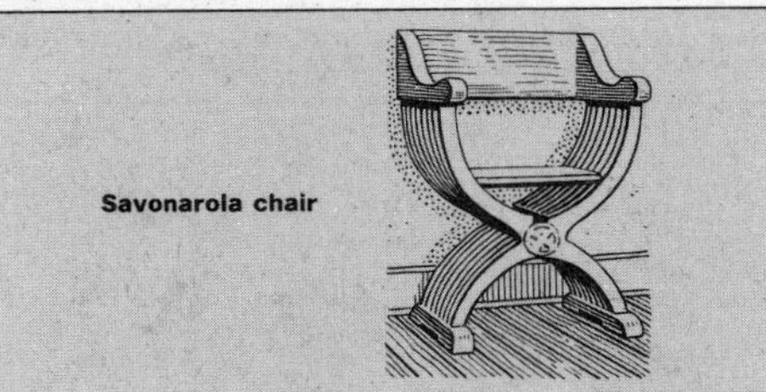
Savonarola chair

sa·vor (sā′vər), *n.* **1.** the quality in a substance that affects the sense of taste or of smell. **2.** a particular taste or smell. **3.** distinctive quality or property. **4.** power to excite or interest. **5.** *Archaic.* repute. **—***v.i.* **6.** to have savor, taste, or odor. **7.** to exhibit the peculiar characteristics; smack (often fol. by *of*): *His business practices savor of greed.* **—***v.t.* **8.** to give a savor to; season; flavor. **9.** to perceive by taste or smell, esp. with relish: *to savor the garden's odors.* **10.** to give oneself to the enjoyment of: *to savor the best in life.* Also, *esp. Brit.,* **sa′vour.** [1175–1225; (n.) ME *sav(o)ur* < OF *savour* < L *sapōrem,* acc. of *sapor* taste, deriv. of *sapere* to taste (cf. SAPIENT); (v.) ME *sav(o)uren* < OF *savourer* < LL *sapōrāre,* deriv. of *sapor*] **—sa′vor·er,** *n.* **—sa′vor·ing·ly,** *adv.* **—sa′vor·less,** *adj.* **—sa′vor·ous,** *adj.*
—Syn. 1. relish, smack; odor, scent, fragrance. See **taste.**
—Usage. See **-or**[1].

sa·vor·y[1] (sā′və rē), *adj.,* **-vor·i·er, -vor·i·est,** *n., pl.* **-vor·ies.** **—***adj.* **1.** pleasant or agreeable in taste or smell: *a savory aroma.* **2.** piquant: *a savory jelly.* **3.** pleasing, attractive, or agreeable. **—***n.* **4.** *Brit.* an aromatic, often spicy course or dish served either as an appetizer or as a dessert, as pickled fish or brandied fruit. Also, *esp. Brit.,* **savoury.** [1175–1225; ME *savori* (see SAVOR, -Y[1]); r. ME *savure* < OF *savoure,* ptp. of *savourer* to savor] **—sa′vor·i·ly,** *adv.* **—sa′vor·i·ness,** *n.*
—Syn. 1, 2. See **palatable.**

sa·vor·y[2] (sā′və rē), *n., pl.* **-vor·ies.** any of several aromatic herbs belonging to the genus *Satureja,* of the mint family, esp. *S. hortensis* **(summer savory)** or *S. montana* **(winter savory),** having narrow leaves used in cookery. [1350–1400; ME *saverey,* perh. for OE *sætherie* < L *saturēia* (whence also OE *saturege,* ME *satureie*)]

sa·vour·y (sā′və rē), *adj.,* **-vour·i·er, -vour·i·est,** *n., pl.* **-vour·ies.** *Chiefly Brit.* savory[1].

Sa·voy (sə voi′), *n.* **1.** a member of the royal house of Italy that ruled from 1861 to 1946. **2.** French, **Savoie.** a region in SE France, adjacent to the Swiss-Italian border: formerly a duchy; later a part of the kingdom of Sardinia; ceded to France, 1860.

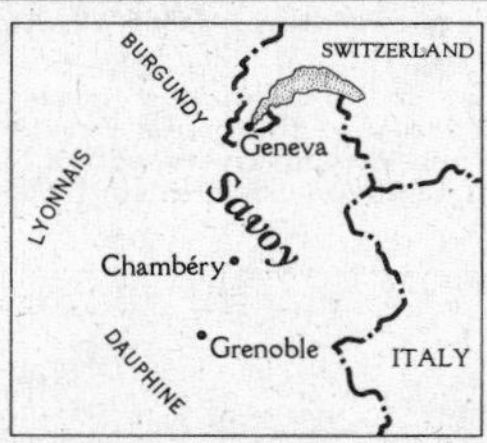

Savoy′ Alps′, a mountain range in SE France: a part of the Alps. Highest peak, Mont Blanc, 15,781 ft. (4810 m).

Sa·voy·ard (sə voi′ərd, sav′oi ärd′; *Fr.* SA VWA YAR′), *n., pl.* **Sa·voy·ards** (sə voi′ərdz, sav′oi ärdz′; *Fr.* SA-VWA YAR′), *adj.* **—***n.* **1.** a native or inhabitant of Savoy. **2.** a person enthusiastic about or connected with Gilbert and Sullivan operas: so called from the Savoy Theater in London, where the operas were first presented. **—***adj.* **3.** of or pertaining to Savoy, its people, or their dialect. [1690–1700; < F; see SAVOY, -ARD]

Savoy′ cab′bage, a variety of cabbage having a compact head of crinkled, blistered leaves. [1700–10]

sav·vy (sav′ē), *v.,* **-vied, -vy·ing,** *n., adj.,* **-vi·er, -vi·est.** *Informal.* **—***v.t., v.i.* **1.** to know; understand. **—***n.* **2.** Also, **sav′vi·ness.** practical understanding; shrewdness or intelligence; common sense: *a candidate who seemed to have no political savvy.* **—***adj.* **3.** shrewdly informed; experienced and well-informed; canny. [1775–85; < Sp *sabe,* pres. 3rd sing. of *saber* to know < L *sapere* to be wise; see SAPIENT]

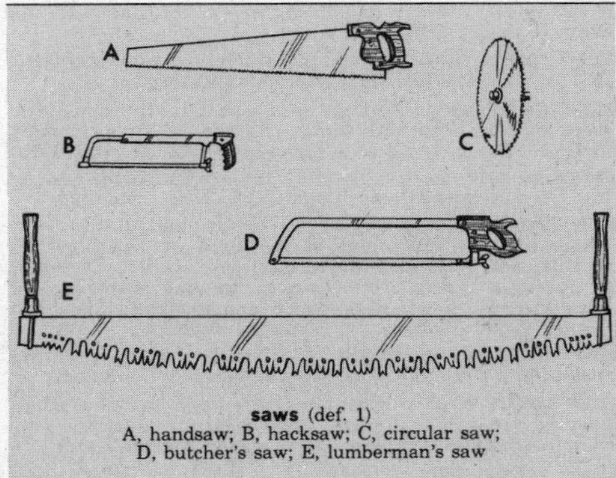

saws (def. 1)
A, handsaw; B, hacksaw; C, circular saw; D, butcher's saw; E, lumberman's saw

saw[1] (sô), *n., v.,* **sawed, sawed** or **sawn, saw·ing.** **—***n.* **1.** a tool or device for cutting, typically a thin blade of metal with a series of sharp teeth. **2.** any similar tool or device, as a rotating disk, in which a sharp continuous edge replaces the teeth. **—***v.t.* **3.** to cut or divide with a saw. **4.** to form by cutting with a saw. **5.** to make cutting motions as if using a saw: *to saw the air with one's hands.* **6.** to work (something) from side to side like a saw. **—***v.i.* **7.** to use a saw. **8.** to cut with or as if with a saw. **9.** to cut as a saw does. **10. saw wood,** *Informal.* to snore loudly while sleeping. [bef. 1000; (n.) ME *sawe,* OE *saga,* **sagu;* c. D *zaag,* ON *sǫg;* akin to G *Säge* saw, L *secāre* to cut (see SECTION), OE *seax* knife, SAX[2]; (v.) ME *sawen,* deriv. of the n.] **—saw′er,** *n.* **—saw′like′,** *adj.*

saw[2] (sô), *v.* pt. of **see**[1].

saw[3] (sô), *n.* a sentensious saying; maxim; proverb: *He could muster an old saw for every occasion.* [bef. 950; ME; OE *sagu;* c. G *Sage,* ON *saga* SAGA; akin to SAY[1]]

Sa·watch (sə wäch′), *n.* a mountain range in central Colorado: part of the Rocky Mountains. Highest peak, Mount Elbert, 14,431 ft. (4400 m). Also, **Saguache.**

saw·bones (sô′bōnz′), *n., pl.* **-bones, -bones·es.** *(used with a singular v.) Slang.* a surgeon or physician. [1830–40; SAW[1] + BONE + -S[3]]

saw·buck[1] (sô′buk′), *n.* a sawhorse. [1860–65, *Amer.;* cf. D *zaagbok*]

saw·buck[2] (sô′buk′), *n. Slang.* a ten-dollar bill. [1840–50, *Amer.;* so called from the resemblance of the Roman numeral X to the crossbars of a SAWBUCK[1]]

saw′buck ta′ble, a table that has X-shaped legs.

saw·dust (sô′dust′), *n.* small particles of wood produced in sawing. [1520–30; SAW[1] + DUST]

saw′dust trail′, **1.** the road to conversion or rehabilitation, as for a sinner or criminal. **2.** Also called **saw′·dust cir′cuit.** the itinerary of revival meetings. [1910–15, *Amer.;* so called from the sawdust-covered aisles in the temporary constructions put up for revival meetings]

saw·dust·y (sô′dus′tē), *adj.* **1.** filled with or suggesting sawdust. **2.** without profound meaning or interest; tiresome. [1860–65; SAWDUST + -Y[1]]

sawed-off (sôd′ôf′, -of′), *adj.* **1.** sawed off at the end, as a shotgun or broomstick. **2.** *Slang.* smallish; of less than average size or stature. [1865–70, *Amer.*]

saw·fish (sô′fish′), *n., pl.* (*esp. collectively*) **-fish,** (*esp. referring to two or more kinds or species*) **-fish·es.** a large, elongated ray of the genus *Pristis,* living along tropical coasts and lowland rivers, with a bladelike snout bearing strong teeth on each side. [1655–65; SAW[1] + FISH]

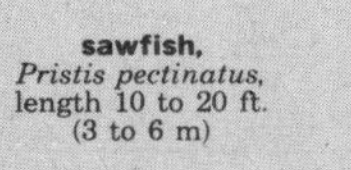

sawfish, *Pristis pectinatus,* length 10 to 20 ft. (3 to 6 m)

saw·fly (sô′flī′), *n., pl.* **-flies.** any of numerous hymenopterous insects of the family Tenthredinidae, the female of which has a sawlike ovipositor for inserting the eggs in the tissues of a host plant. [1765–75; SAW[1] + FLY[2]]

saw·horse (sô′hôrs′), *n.* a movable frame or trestle for supporting wood being sawed. [1770–80; SAW[1] + HORSE]

saw′ log′, a log large enough to saw into boards. [1750–60, *Amer.*]

sawm (sôm), *n.* fasting, esp. during the month of Ramadan; the fourth of the Pillars of Islam.

saw·mill (sô′mil′), *n.* a place or building in which timber is sawed into planks, boards, etc., by machinery. [1545–55; SAW[1] + MILL[1]]

sawn (sôn), *v.* a pp. of **saw**[1].

saw′ palmet′to, 1. a shrublike palmetto, *Serenoa repens,* of the palm family, native to the southern U.S., having green or blue leafstalks set with spiny teeth. **2.** a tall palm, *Acoelorraphe wrightii,* of Florida and the West Indies. [1790–1800, *Amer.*]

saw′ pit′, a place for pit sawing. Also, **saw′pit′.** [1375–1425; late ME *sawpytt.* See SAW[1], PIT[1]]

saw′ set′, an instrument used to bend out slightly the point of each alternate tooth of a saw so that the kerf made by the saw will be wider than its blade. [1840–50]

saw·tim·ber (sô′tim′bər), *n.* trees suitable for sawing into planks, boards, etc. [1930–35; SAW[1] + TIMBER]

saw·tooth (sô′to͞oth′), *n., pl.* **-teeth** (-tēth′), *adj.* —*n.* **1.** one of the cutting teeth of a saw. **2.** any of the small parallel roof structures forming a sawtooth roof. —*adj.* **3.** having a zigzag profile, similar to that of the cutting edge of a saw; sawtoothed; serrate: *a sawtooth mountain range.* [1595–1605; SAW[1] + TOOTH]

saw-toothed (sô′to͞otht′), *adj.* **1.** having pointing resembling the edge of a saw. **2.** serrate. [1580–90]

saw′tooth roof′, a roof composed of a series of small parallel roofs of triangular cross section, usually asymmetrical with the shorter slope glazed. [1895–1900]

saw′-whet owl′ (sô′hwet′, -wet′), a very small North American owl, *Aegolius acadicus,* having streaked, brown plumage and lacking ear tufts. [1825–35, *Amer.*; allegedly so called because its cry was likened to the noise of a saw being whetted]

saw·yer (sô′yər, soi′ər), *n.* **1.** a person who saws wood, esp. as an occupation. **2.** Also called **saw′yer bee′tle.** any of several long-horned beetles, esp. one of the genus *Monochamus,* the larvae of which bore in the wood of coniferous trees. [1300–50; ME *sawier,* equiv. to *sawe* SAW[1] + *-ier* -IER[1]]

sax[1] (saks), *n. Informal.* saxophone. [by shortening]

sax[2] (saks), *n.* a short, single-edged sword of ancient Scandinavia. [bef. 900; ME *sexe,* OE *seax, sæx;* c. ON *sax* (Sw, Dan *sax* scissors). See SAW[1]]

Sax., 1. Saxon. **2.** Saxony.

sax·a·tile (sak′sə til), *adj.* living or growing on or among rocks. [1645–55; < L *saxātilis* frequenting rocks, equiv. to *sax(um)* rock + *-āt-* formative suffix + *-ilis* -ILE]

Saxe (saks), *n.* **1. Comte Her·mann Mau·rice de** (er man′ mô rēs′ də), 1696–1750, French military leader: marshal of France 1744. **2.** French name of **Saxony.**

Saxe-Al·ten·burg (saks′äl′tn bûrg′), *n.* a former duchy in Thuringia in central Germany.

Saxe-Co·burg-Go·tha (saks′kō′bûrg gō′thə), *n.* **1.** a member of the present British royal family, from the establishment of the house in 1901 until 1917 when the family name was changed to Windsor. **2. Albert Francis Charles Augustus Emanuel, Prince of.** See **Albert, Prince. 3.** a former duchy in central Germany.

Saxe-Mei·ning·en (saks′mī′ning ən), *n.* a former duchy in Thuringia in central Germany.

Saxe-Wei·mar-Ei·sen·ach (saks′vī′mär ī′zən äkh′), *n.* a former grand duchy in Thuringia in central Germany.

sax·horn (saks′hôrn′), *n.* any of a family of brass instruments close to the cornets and tubas. [1835–45; named after A. *Sax* (1814–94), a Belgian who invented such instruments]

CONCISE ETYMOLOGY KEY: <, descended or borrowed from; >, whence; b., blend of, blended; c., cognate with; cf., compare; deriv., derivative; equiv., equivalent; imit., imitative; obl., oblique; r., replacing; s., stem; sp., spelling, spelled; resp., respelling, respelled; trans., translation; ?, origin unknown; *, unattested; ‡, probably earlier than. See the full key inside the front cover.

saxhorn

sax·ic·o·line (sak sik′ə lin, -līn′), *adj. Bot., Zool.* living or growing among rocks. Also, **sax·ic·o·lous** (sak sik′ə ləs). [1895–1900; < NL *saxicol(a)* (L *saxi-,* comb. form of *saxum* rock + *-cola* dweller; see -COLOUS) + -INE[1]]

sax·i·fra·ga·ceous (sak′sə frə gā′shəs), *adj.* belonging to the plant family Saxifragaceae. Cf. **saxifrage family.** [1835–45; SAXIFRAGE + -ACEOUS]

sax·i·frage (sak′sə frij), *n.* any plant of the genus *Saxifraga,* certain species of which grow wild in the clefts of rocks, other species of which are cultivated for their flowers. Cf. **saxifrage family.** [1400–50; late ME < L *saxifraga* (*herba*) stone-breaking (herb), equiv. to *saxi-,* comb. form of *saxum* stone + *-fraga,* fem. of *-fragus* breaking; see FRAGILE]

sax′ifrage fam′ily, the plant family Saxifragaceae, characterized by herbaceous plants, shrubs, and small trees having alternate or opposite leaves, clustered or solitary flowers, and fruit in the form of a berry or capsule, and including the astilbe, currant, deutzia, gooseberry, hydrangea, mock orange, piggy-back plant, saxifrage, and strawberry geranium.

sax·i·tox·in (sak′si tok′sin), *n.* a powerful neurotoxin, $C_{10}H_{17}N_7O_4$, produced by the dinoflagellate *Gonyaulax catenella,* the causative agent of red tide. [1960–65; < NL *Saxi(domus),* a clam genus infected by the dinoflagellates (equiv. to L *sax(um)* stone + *-i-* -I- + *domus* house) + TOXIN]

Sax·o Gram·mat·i·cus (sak′sō grə mat′i kəs), c1150–1206?, Danish historian and poet.

Sax·on (sak′sən), *n.* **1.** a member of a Germanic people in ancient times dwelling near the mouth of the Elbe, a portion of whom invaded and occupied parts of Britain in the 5th and 6th centuries. **2.** the Old English dialects of the regions settled by the Saxons. **3.** a native or inhabitant of Saxony in modern Germany. **4.** an English person; Britisher. **5.** an Anglo-Saxon. **6.** (not in scholarly use) the Old English language. **7.** a member of the royal house of Germany that ruled from 919 to 1024. —*adj.* **8.** of or pertaining to the early Saxons or their language. **9.** of or pertaining to Saxony in modern Germany. **10.** English (defs. 1, 2). [1250–1300; ME, prob. < LL *Saxō, Saxonēs* (pl.) < Gmc; r. OE *Seaxan* (pl.)]

Sax·on·ism (sak′sə niz′əm), *n.* an English word or idiom of Anglo-Saxon rather than foreign origin. Also called **Anglo-Saxonism.** [1765–75; SAXON + -ISM]

sax·o·ny (sak′sə nē), *n.* **1.** a fine, three-ply woolen yarn. **2.** a soft-finish, compact fabric, originally of high-grade merino wool from Saxony, for topcoats and overcoats. **3.** a pile carpet woven in the manner of a Wilton but with yarns of lesser quality. [1825–35]

Sax·o·ny (sak′sə nē), *n.* **1.** a state in E central Germany. 4,900,000; 6561 sq. mi. (16,990 sq. km). *Cap:* Dresden. **2.** a former state of the Weimar Republic in E central Germany. 5788 sq. mi. (14,990 sq. km). *Cap:* Dresden. **3.** a medieval division of N Germany with varying boundaries: extended at its height from the Rhine to E of the Elbe. German, **Sachsen;** French, **Saxe.** —**Sax·o·ni·an** (sak sō′nē ən), *n., adj.* —**Sax·on·ic** (sak son′ik), *adj.*

Sax·ony-An·halt (sak′sə nē än′hält), *n.* a state in central Germany. 3,000,000; 9515 sq. mi. (24,644 sq. km). *Cap.:* Magdeburg. Germany, **Sachsen-Anhalt.**

sax·o·phone (sak′sə fōn′), *n.* a musical wind instrument consisting of a conical, usually brass tube with keys or valves and a mouthpiece with one reed. [1850–55; *Sax* (see SAXHORN) + -O- + -PHONE] —**sax·o·phon·ic** (sak′sə fon′ik), *adj.* —**sax′o·phon′ist,** *n.*

saxophone

sax·tu·ba (saks′to͞o′bə, -tyo͞o′-), *n.* a large bass saxhorn. [1860–65; *Sax* (see SAXHORN) + TUBA]

say[1] (sā), *v.,* **said, say·ing,** *adv., n., interj.* —*v.t.* **1.** to utter or pronounce; speak: *What did you say? I said "Hello!"* **2.** to express in words; state; declare; word: *Say it clearly and simply. It's hard to know how to say this tactfully.* **3.** to state as an opinion or judgment: *I say her plan is the better one.* **4.** to be certain, precise, or assured about; determine: *It is hard to say what is wrong.* **5.** to recite or repeat: *to say one's prayers.* **6.** to report or allege; maintain: *People say he will resign.* **7.** to express (a message, viewpoint, etc.), as through a literary or other artistic medium: *a writer with something to say.* **8.** to indicate or show: *What does your watch say?* **9.** to assume as a hypothesis or estimate: *Let's say, for the sake of argument, that it's true.* —*v.i.* **10.** to speak; declare; express an opinion. **11. that is to say,** that is what is meant; in other words: *I believe his account of the story, that is to say, I have no reason to doubt it.* —*adv.* **12.** approximately; about: *It's, say, 14 feet long.* **13.** for example: *If you serve, say tuna fish and potato chips, it will cost much less.* —*n.* **14.** what a person says or has to say. **15.** the right or opportunity to speak, decide, or exercise influence: *to have one's say in choosing the candidate.* **16.** a turn to say something: *It is now my say.* —*interj.* **17.** (used to express surprise, get attention, etc.) [bef. 900; ME *seyen, seggen,* OE *secgan;* c. D *zeggen,* G *sagen,* ON *segja;* akin to SAW[3]] —**say′er,** *n.*

say[2] (sā), *v.t., n. Brit. Dial.* assay. [1350–1400; ME *sayen,* aph. var. of *assayen* to ASSAY]

say[3] (sā), *n.* a thin silk or woolen fabric similar to serge, much used in the 16th century. [1250–1300; ME < OF *saie* < L *saga,* pl. of *sagum* woolen cloak, said to be < Gaulish]

Say (sā), *n.* **1. Jean Bap·tiste** (zhän ba tēst′), 1767–1832, French economist. Cf. **Say's law. 2. Thomas,** 1787–1834, U.S. entomologist.

say·a·ble (sā′ə bəl), *adj.* **1.** of the sort that can be said or spoken; utterable: *He felt a great deal that was not sayable.* **2.** capable of being said or stated clearly, effectively, etc.: *The speech is as sayable today as when Demosthenes first composed it.* [1855–60; SAY[1] + -ABLE]

Sa·yan′ Moun′tains (sä yän′), a mountain range in the S Russian Federation in central Asia. Highest peak, Munku Sardik, 11,447 ft. (3490 m).

Sa·yão (sä you′, -yä′o͞o; *Port.* sä youn′), *n.* **Bi·dú** (bē′do͞o; *Port.* bi do͞o′), (*Balduina de Oliveira Sayão*), born 1906?, Brazilian soprano.

Say·ers (sā′ərz, sârz), *n.* **Dorothy L(eigh),** 1893–1957, English novelist, essayist, and dramatist.

say·est (sā′ist), *v. Archaic.* 2nd pers. sing. of **say**[1]. **Also, sayst** (sāst).

say·ing (sā′ing), *n.* **1.** something said, esp. a proverb or apothegm. **2. go without saying,** to be completely self-evident; be understood: *It goes without saying that you are welcome to visit us at any time.* [1250–1300; ME (ger.); see SAY[1], -ING[1]]
—**Syn. 1.** maxim, adage, saw, aphorism.

sa·yo·na·ra (sī′ə när′ə; *Japn.* sä′yô nä′rä), *interj., n.* farewell; good-bye. [1870–75; < Japn *sayō-nara,* equiv. to *sayō* thus (*sa* that + *yō,* earlier *yaū* < MChin, equiv. to Chin *yàng* appearance) + *nara* if it be (*ni* essive particle + *ara* subjunctive s. of existential v.)]

Sayre·ville (sâr′vil), *n.* a city in central New Jersey. 29,969.

says (sez), *v.* 3rd pers. sing. pres. ind. of **say.**

Say's′ law′ (sāz), the principle, propounded by Jean Baptiste Say, that the supply of goods is always matched by the demand for them. [1930–35]

say-so (sā′sō′), *n., pl.* **say-sos. 1.** one's personal statement or assertion. **2.** final authority; directing influence. **3.** an authoritative statement. [1630–40; orig., one's mere word on a matter, as opposed to proof]

Say·ville (sā′vil), *n.* a town on the S shore of Long Island, in SE New York. 12,013.

say·yid (sä′yid, sā′id), *n.* **1.** (in Islamic countries) a supposed descendant of Muhammad through his grandson Hussein, the second son of his daughter Fatima. **2.** a title of respect, esp. for royal personages. Also, **said, say′ed, say′id.** [1780–90; < Ar: lord]

Saz·e·rac (saz′ə rak′), *Trademark.* a cocktail made with rye or bourbon, bitters, Pernod, and sugar, stirred or shaken with ice, strained and served with a twist of lemon rind.

Sb, *Symbol, Chem.* antimony. [< LL *stibium*]

sb., substantive.

S.B., 1. Bachelor of Science. [< L *Scientiae Baccalaureus*] **2.** South Britain (England and Wales).

s.b., *Baseball.* stolen base; stolen bases.

SBA, See **Small Business Administration.** Also, **S.B.A.**

SbE, See **south by east.**

SBIC, Small Business Investment Company.

SBLI, Savings Bank Life Insurance.

'sblood (zblud), *interj. Obs.* (used as an oath.) [1590–1600; euphemistic shortening of *God's blood;* see 's[3]]

SBN, Standard Book Number.

SbW, See **south by west.**

SC, South Carolina (approved esp. for use with zip code).

Sc, *Symbol, Chem.* scandium.

Sc., 1. Scotch. **2.** Scotland. **3.** Scots. **4.** Scottish.

sc., 1. scale. **2.** scene. **3.** science. **4.** scientific. **5.** namely. [< L *scīlicet,* contr. of *scīre licet* it is permitted to know] **6.** screw. **7.** scruple. **8.** sculpsit.

S.C., 1. Sanitary Corps. **2.** Security Council (of the U.N.). **3.** Signal Corps. **4.** South Carolina. **5.** Staff Corps. **6.** Supreme Court.

s.c., 1. *Print.* small capitals. **2.** supercalendered.

scab (skab), *n., v.,* **scabbed, scab·bing.** —*n.* **1.** the incrustation that forms over a sore or wound during healing. **2.** *Vet. Pathol.* a mangy disease in animals, esp. sheep; scabies. Cf. **itch** (def. 10). **3.** *Plant Pathol.* **a.** a disease of plants characterized by crustlike lesions on the affected parts and caused by a fungus or bacterium. **b.** one of these crustlike lesions. **4.** a worker who refuses to join a labor union or to participate in a union strike, who takes a striking worker's place on the job, or the like. **5.** *Slang.* a rascal or scoundrel. **6.** *Metall.* **a.** a projection or roughness on an ingot or casting from a defective mold. **b.** a surface defect on an iron or steel piece resulting from the rolling in of scale. **7.** *Carpentry.* a short, flat piece of wood used for various purposes, as binding two timbers butted together or strengthening a timber at a weak spot. —*v.i.* **8.** to become covered with a scab. **9.** to act or work as a scab. [1200–50; 1800–10 for def. 4; ME < ON *skabb* scab, itch; cf. SHABBY, SHAVE] —**scab′like′,** *adj.*

scab·bard (skab′ərd), *n.* **1.** a sheath for a sword or the like. See illus. under **scimitar.** —*v.t.* **2.** to put into a scabbard; sheathe. [1250–1300; ME *scalburde, scauberge* (cf. AF *escauberz, escauberge,* ML *escauberca*) << dissimilated var. of OHG **skārberga* sword-protection. See SHEAR, HARBOR] —**scab′bard·less,** *adj.*

scab·bed (skab′id, skabd), *adj.* **1.** covered with or affected by scabs. **2.** *Obs.* mean or petty. [1250–1300; ME; see SCAB, -ED[3]] —**scab′bed·ness,** *n.*

scab·ble (skab′əl), *v.t.,* **-bled, -bling.** to shape or dress (stone) roughly. [1610–20; var. of *scapple* < MF *escapeler* to dress (timber)]

scab·by (skab′ē), *adj.,* **-bi·er, -bi·est.** **1.** covered with scabs; having many scabs. **2.** consisting of scabs. **3.** (of an animal or plant) having scab. **4.** *Informal.* mean or contemptible: *a scabby trick.* [1520–30; SCAB + -Y[1]] —**scab′bi·ly,** *adv.* —**scab′bi·ness,** *n.*

scab·i·cide (skab′ə sīd′), *adj.* **1.** Also, **scab′i·ci′dal.** destructive to the organisms causing scabies. —*n.* **2.** a scabicide agent. [SCABI(ES) + -CIDE]

sca·bies (skā′bēz, -bē ēz′), *n.* (*used with a singular v.*) *Pathol., Vet. Pathol.* a contagious skin disease occurring esp. in sheep and cattle and also in humans, caused by the itch mite, *Sarcoptes scabiei,* which burrows under the skin. Cf. **itch** (def. 10), **mange.** [1350–1400; ME < L *scabiēs* roughness, the itch, deriv. of *scabere* to scratch, scrape; c. SHAVE] —**sca·bi·et·ic** (skā′bē et′ik), *adj.*

sca·bi·ous[1] (skā′bē əs), *adj.* **1.** covered with or consisting of scabs; scabby. **2.** pertaining to or of the nature of scabies. [1595–1605; SCABI(ES) + -OUS]

sca·bi·ous[2] (skā′bē əs), *n.* **1.** Also called **pincushion flower.** any of various plants belonging to the genus *Scabiosa,* of the teasel family, having opposite leaves and often showy flower heads in a variety of colors. **2.** any of various similar or related plants. [1350–1400; ME *scabiose* < ML *scabiōsa* (*herba*) scabies-curing (herb); see SCABIES, -OUS]

scab·land (skab′land′), *n. Physical Geog.* rough, barren, volcanic topography with thin soils and little vegetation. [1920–25, *Amer.*; SCAB + LAND]

scab·rous (skab′rəs), *adj.* **1.** having a rough surface because of minute points or projections. **2.** indecent or scandalous; risqué; obscene: *scabrous books.* **3.** full of difficulties. [1575–85; < L *scab(e)r* rough + -OUS] —**scab′rous·ly,** *adv.* —**scab′rous·ness,** *n.*
—**Syn. 2.** lewd, wanton, improper.

scad[1] (skad), *n., pl.* (*esp. collectively*) **scad,** (*esp. referring to two or more kinds or species*) **scads. 1.** any carangid fish of the genus *Decapterus,* inhabiting tropical and subtropical shore waters. **2.** any of several related carangid fishes, as of the genera *Trachurus* or *Selar.* [1595–1605; orig. uncert.]

scad[2] (skad), *n.* Usually, **scads. 1.** *Informal.* a great number or quantity: *scads of money.* **2.** *Archaic.* a piece of money; dollar. [1855–60, *Amer.*; of obscure orig.; cf. Brit. dial *scal(d)* a great quantity]

Scae·vo·la (sē′və lə, sev′ə-), *n.* **Ga·ius** (gā′əs) (or **Ca·ius**) (kā′əs) **Mu·ci·us** (myo͞o′shē əs, -shəs), fl. 6th century B.C., Roman hero.

Sca′fell Pike′ (skô′fel′), a mountain in NW England, in Cumberland: highest peak in England. 3210 ft. (978 m).

scaf·fold (skaf′əld, -ōld), *n.* **1.** a temporary structure for holding workers and materials during the erection, repair, or decoration of a building. **2.** an elevated platform on which a criminal is executed, usually by hanging. **3.** a raised platform or stage for exhibiting spectacles, seating spectators, etc. **4.** any raised framework. **5.** a suspended platform that is used by painters, window washers, and others for working on a tall structure, as a skyscraper. **6.** *Metall.* any piling or fusion of materials in a blast furnace, obstructing the flow of gases and preventing the uniform descent of the charge. **7.** a system of raised frameworks; scaffolding. —*v.t.* **8.** to furnish with a scaffold or scaffolding. **9.** to support by or place on a scaffold. [1300–50; ME *scaffot, skaffaut, scaffalde* < OF *escadafaut;* akin to CATAFALQUE]

scaf·fold·ing (skaf′əl ding, -ōl-), *n.* **1.** a scaffold or system of scaffolds. **2.** materials for scaffolds. [1300–50; ME *skaf(f)aldyng;* see SCAFFOLD, -ING[1]]

scaf′fold nail′, a nail used in building temporary structures, having a stop on its shank to prevent its being driven in all the way and to leave the head free for pulling. Also called **form nail.**

scag (skag), *n. Slang.* heroin. Also, **skag.** [1965–70; of obscure orig.; cf. earlier *scag* cigarette butt]

scagl·io·la (skal yō′lə), *n.* plasterwork imitating marble, granite, or the like. [1575–85; < It, equiv. to *scagli(a)* a chip (< Goth *skalja* tile; c. SHELL) + *-ola* dim. suffix] —**scagl·io′list,** *n.*

scal·a·ble (skā′lə bəl), *adj.* capable of being scaled: *the scalable slope of a mountain.* [1570–80; SCALE[3] + -ABLE] —**scal′a·ble·ness,** *n.* —**scal′a·bly,** *adv.*

sca·la cor·do·na·ta (*It.* skä′lä kôʀ′dô nä′tä), *pl.* **sca·le cor·do·na·te** (*It.* skä′le kôʀ′dô nä′te). a ramp having the form of broad, slightly inclined steps. [< It; see SCALE[3], CORDON, -ATE[1]]

sca·lade (skə lād′), *n. Archaic.* escalade. [1585–95; var. of ESCALADE]

scal·age (skā′lij), *n.* **1.** an assessed percentage deduction, as in weight or price, granted in dealings with goods that are likely to shrink, leak, or otherwise vary in the amount or weight originally stated. **2.** the amount of lumber estimated to be contained in a log being scaled. [1850–55, *Amer.*; SCALE[3] + -AGE]

sca·lar (skā′lər), *adj.* **1.** representable by position on a scale or line; having only magnitude: *a scalar variable.* **2.** of, pertaining to, or utilizing a scalar. **3.** ladderlike in arrangement or organization; graduated: *a scalar structure for promoting personnel.* —*n.* **4.** *Math., Physics.* a quantity possessing only magnitude. Cf. **vector** (def. 1a). [1650–60; < L *scālāris* of a ladder. See SCALE[3], -AR[1]]

sca·lar·e (skə lâr′ē, -lär′ē), *n.* any of three deep-bodied, cichlid fishes, *Pterophyllum scalare, P. altum,* and *P. eimekei,* inhabiting northern South American rivers, often kept in aquariums. [1925–30; < NL; L *scālāre,* neut. of *scālāris* SCALAR; from its ladderlike markings]

sca′lar field′, *Math., Physics.* a region with a number assigned at each point. Cf. **vector field.** [1930–35]

sca·lar·i·form (skə lar′ə fôrm′), *adj. Biol.* ladderlike. [1830–40; < NL *scālāriformis.* See SCALAR, -FORM]

sca′lar prod′uct, *Math.* See **inner product** (def. 1). [1875–80]

sca′lar tri′ple prod′uct, *Math.* the volume of the parallelepiped defined by three given vectors, *u, v,* and *w,* usually represented as *u·v′*(*v×w*), [*uvw*], or (*uvw*), where × denotes a cross product and • denotes an inner product. Also, **triple scalar product.** [1900–05]

sca·la·tion (skā lā′shən), *n.* **1.** an arrangement of scales, as on a fish. **2.** ichthyosis. [SCALE[1] + -ATION]

scal·a·wag (skal′ə wag′), *n.* **1.** a scamp; rascal. **2.** *U.S. Hist.* a native white Southerner who collaborated with the occupying forces during Reconstruction, often for personal gain. Also, **scallywag;** *esp. Brit.,* **scallawag.** [1840–50, *Amer.*; orig. uncert.] —**scal′a·wag′ger·y,** *n.* —**scal′a·wag′gy,** *adj.*

scald[1] (skôld), *v.t.* **1.** to burn or affect painfully with or as if with hot liquid or steam. **2.** to subject to the action of boiling or hot liquid. **3.** to heat to a temperature just short of the boiling point: *to scald milk.* **4.** to parboil or blanch (fruit, vegetables, etc.). —*v.i.* **5.** to be or become scalded. —*n.* **6.** a burn caused by the action of hot liquid or steam. **7.** any similar condition, esp. as the result of too much heat or sunlight. **8.** *Plant Pathol.* **a.** a blanching of the epidermis and adjacent tissues, which turn pale or dark brown, caused by extreme heat or sun exposure. **b.** a condition resembling scald caused by improper conditions of growth or storage, as in apples, or by fungi, as in cranberries. [1175–1225; ME *scalden* (v.) < dial. OF *escalder* < LL *excaldāre* to wash in hot water. See EX-, CALDARIUM]

scald[2] (skôld, skäld), *n.* skald.

scald[3] (skôld), *adj. Archaic.* **1.** Also, **scalled.** scabby; scurvy. —*n.* **2.** a scab. [1490–1500; SCALL + -ED[3]]

scale[1] (skāl), *n., v.,* **scaled, scal·ing.** —*n.* **1.** *Zool.* **a.** one of the thin, flat, horny plates forming the covering of certain animals, as snakes, lizards, and pangolins. **b.** one of the hard, bony or dentinal plates, either flat or denticulate, forming the covering of certain other animals, as fishes. **2.** any thin, platelike piece, lamina, or flake that peels off from a surface, as from the skin. **3.** *Bot.* **a.** Also called **bud scale.** a rudimentary body, usually a specialized leaf and often covered with hair, wax, or resin, enclosing an immature leaf bud. **b.** a thin, scarious or membranous part of a plant, as a bract of a catkin. **4.** See **scale insect. 5.** a coating or incrustation, as on the inside of a boiler, formed by the precipitation of salts from the water. **6.** Often, **scales.** *Metall.* **a.** an oxide, esp. an iron oxide, occurring in a scaly form on the surface of metal brought to a high temperature. **b.** Also called **mill scale.** such scale formed on iron or steel during hot-rolling. **7. scales, a.** a cause of blindness or ignorance, as regarding the true nature of a person, situation, etc.: *You're infatuated with her now, but the scales will soon fall from your eyes.* **b.** *Bible.* an unspecified affliction that caused Paul to become temporarily blind. Acts 9:18. —*v.t.* **8.** to remove the scales or scale from: *to scale a fish.* **9.** to remove in scales or thin layers. **10.** to cover with an incrustation or scale. **11.** to skip, as a stone over water. **12.** *Dentistry.* to remove (calculus) from the teeth with instruments. —*v.i.* **13.** to come off in scales. **14.** to shed scales. **15.** to become coated with scale, as the inside of a boiler. [1250–1300; (n.) ME < MF *escale* < WGmc **skāla;* akin to SCALE[2]; (v.) late ME *scalen* to remove scales from, deriv. of the n.] —**scale′less,** *adj.* —**scale′like′,** *adj.*

scale[2] (skāl), *n., v.,* **scaled, scal·ing.** —*n.* **1.** Often, **scales.** a balance or any of various other instruments or devices for weighing: *We gave the parents a baby scale. The butcher placed the meat on the scales.* **2.** Also called **scalepan.** either of the pans or dishes of a balance. **3. Scales,** *Astron., Astrol.* the constellation or sign of Libra; Balance. **4. tip the scale** or **scales, a.** to weigh: *He tips the scales at 190 lbs.* **b.** to turn the trend of favor, control, etc.: *The present crisis should tip the scales for our candidate.* **5. turn the scale** or **scales,** to decide in favor of one side or faction; determine the outcome: *It would take a miracle to turn the scales for us now.* —*v.t.* **6.** to weigh in or as if in scales. **7.** to have a weight of. [1175–1225; ME < ON *skālar* (pl.), c. OE *scealu* scale (of a balance)]

scale[3] (skāl), *n., v.,* **scaled, scal·ing.** —*n.* **1.** a succession or progression of steps or degrees; graduated series: *the scale of taxation; the social scale.* **2.** a series of marks laid down at determinate distances, as along a line, for purposes of measurement or computation: *the scale of a thermometer.* **3.** a graduated line, as on a map, representing proportionate size. **4.** a table of graduated rates, as of prices or wages: *These unions use different scales.* **5.** a wage that conforms to such rates: *How much is scale?* **6.** Also called **union scale.** a wage fixed by contract that is the minimum permitted to be paid to or accepted by a particular category of employed persons: *All actors and musicians for the performance, including the stars, are working for scale.* **7.** an instrument with graduated spaces, as for measuring. **8.** the proportion that a representation of an object bears to the object itself: *a model on a scale of one inch to one foot.* **9.** the ratio of distances or sometimes of areas on a map to the corresponding values on the earth. **10.** a certain relative or proportionate size or extent: *They built a residence on a yet more magnificent scale.* **11.** a standard of measurement or estimation; point of reference by which to gauge or rate: *We have no scale by which to judge his achievements.* **12.** *Music.* a succession of tones ascending or descending according to fixed intervals, esp. such a series beginning on a particular note: *the major scale of C.* **13.** *Educ., Psychol.* a graded series of tests or tasks for measuring intelligence, achievement, adjustment, etc. **14.** *Arith.* a system of numerical notation: *the decimal scale.* **15.** anything by which one may ascend. **16.** *Obs.* **a.** a ladder. **b.** a flight of stairs. —*v.t.* **17.** to climb by or as if by a ladder; climb up or over. **18.** to make according to scale. **19.** to adjust in amount according to a fixed scale or proportion (often fol. by *down* or *up*): *to scale down wages.* **20.** to measure by or as if by a scale. **21.** *Lumbering.* **a.** to measure (logs). **b.** to estimate the amount of (standing timber). **22.** *Australian Informal.* to ride on (public transportation) without paying the fare. —*v.i.* **23.** to climb; ascend; mount. **24.** to progress in a graduated series. [1350–1400; (n.) ME < L *scālae* ladder, stairs; (v.) ME < OF *escaler* or ML *scālāre,* both << L *scāla, scālae*]
—**Syn. 17.** See **climb.**

scale·board (skāl′bôrd′, -bōrd′, skab′ərd), *n.* **1.** a very thin board, as for the back of a picture. **2.** *Print.* a thin strip of wood used in justifying. **3.** a thin sheet of wood used as veneer. [1705–15; SCALE[1] + BOARD]

scaled (skāld), *adj. Armor.* noting armor having imbricated metal plates sewn to a flexible backing. [1350–1400; ME *scalid.* See SCALE[1], -ED[3]]

scale·down (skāl′doun′), *n.* a reduction in size, quantity, or activity according to a fixed scale or proportion: *a scaledown of military expenditures.* Also called **scale·back** (skāl′bak′). [1930–35; n. use of v. phrase *scale down*]

scale′ in′sect, any of numerous small, plant-sucking homopterous insects of the superfamily Coccoidea, the males of which are winged and the females wingless, often covered by a waxy secretion resembling scales. [1830–40]

scale′ leaf′, a scalelike leaf, as a bud scale or certain bracts. [1880–85]

scale′ moss′, any thalloid liverwort. [1840–50]

sca·lene (skā lēn′), *adj.* **1.** *Geom.* **a.** (of a cone or the like) having the axis inclined to the base. **b.** (of a triangle) having three unequal sides. **2.** *Anat.* of or pertaining to a scalenus muscle. [1635–45; < LL *scalēnus* < Gk *skalēnós* unequal]

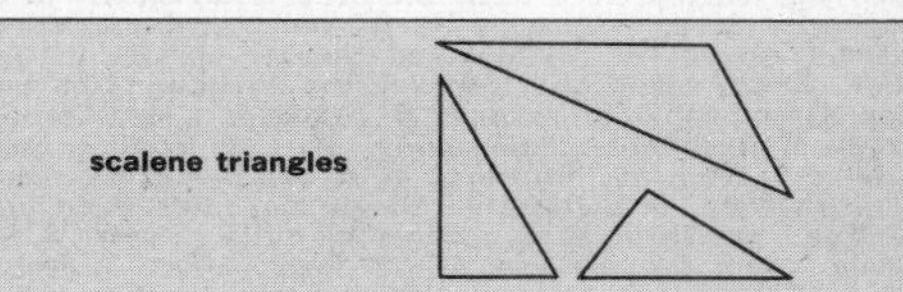
scalene triangles

sca·le·no·he·dron (skā lē′nə hē′drən), *n., pl.* **-drons, -dra** (-drə). *Crystall.* a hemihedral crystal form of 8 or 12 faces, each face being a scalene triangle. [1850–55; < Gk *skalēnó(s)* unequal + -HEDRON] —**sca·le′no·he′dral,** *adj.*

sca·le·nus (skā lē′nəs), *n., pl.* **-ni** (-nī). *Anat.* any of three muscles on each side of the neck, the action of which raises the first and second ribs in respiration and assists in bending the neck to one side. [1695–1705; < NL, LL. See SCALENE]

scale·pan (skāl′pan′), *n.* scale[2] (def. 2). [1820–30; SCALE[2] + PAN[1]]

scal·er (skā′lər), *n.* **1.** a person or thing that scales. **2.** Also called **counter, scal′ing cir′cuit.** *Electronics.* an electronic circuit devised to give a single pulse as output after a certain number of input pulses. [1605–15; SCALE[1], SCALE[3] + -ER[1]]

scale·up (skāl′up′), *n.* an increase in size, quantity, or activity according to a fixed scale or proportion: *a scaleup of an engineering design; a scaleup program of energy conservation.* [1940–45; n. use of v. phrase *scale up*]

Sca·li·a (skə lē′ə), *n.* **An·to·nin** (an′tə nin), born 1936, U.S. jurist: associate justice of the U.S. Supreme Court since 1986.

Scal·i·ger (skal′i jər), *n.* **1. Joseph Jus·tus** (jus′təs), 1540–1609, French scholar and critic. **2.** his father, **Julius Caesar,** 1484–1558, Italian scholar, philosopher, and critic in France.

scal·ing (skā′ling), *n. Dentistry.* the removal of calculus and other deposits on the teeth by means of instruments. [SCALE[1] + -ING[1]]

scal′ing lad′der, a ladder for climbing high walls. [1350–1400; ME]

scall (skôl), *n.* dandruff. [1250–1300; ME < ON *skalli* bald head. Cf. SKULL]

CONCISE PRONUNCIATION KEY: *act, cāpe, dâre, pärt; set, ēqual; if, īce; ox, ōver, ôrder, oil, bo͝ok, bo͞ot, out; up, ûrge; child; sing; shoe; thin, that;* zh as in *treasure.* ə = *a* as in *alone, e* as in *system, i* as in *easily, o* as in *gallop, u* as in *circus;* ᵊ as in *fire* (fīᵊr), *hour* (ouᵊr). l and n can serve as syllabic consonants, as in *cradle* (krād′l), and *button* (but′n). See the full key inside the front cover.

scal·la·wag (skal′ə wag′), *n. Chiefly Brit.* scalawag.

scalled (skôld), *adj.* scald[3] (def. 1).

scal·lion (skal′yən), *n.* **1.** any onion that does not form a large bulb; green onion. **2.** a shallot. **3.** a leek. [1300–50; late ME *scalyon(e)* < OF **escaloigne* < VL **escalonia,* var. of L *Ascalōnia (caepa)* onion of Ascalon, a seaport of Palestine; r. ME *scalone, scaloun* < AF *scaloun* < VL, as above]

scal·lop (skol′əp, skal′-), *n.* **1.** any of the bivalve mollusks of the genus *Argopecten (Pecten)* and related genera that swim by rapidly clapping the fluted shell valves together. **2.** the adductor muscle of certain species of such mollusks, used as food. **3.** one of the shells of such a mollusk, usually having radial ribs and a wavy outer edge. **4.** a scallop shell or a dish in which food, esp. seafood, is baked and served. **5.** *Cookery.* a thin slice of meat, usually further flattened by pounding with a mallet or other implement. **6.** any of a series of curved projections cut along the edge, as of a fabric. —*v.t.* **7.** to finish (an edge) with scallops. **8.** *Cookery.* to escallop. —*v.i.* **9.** to dredge for scallops. Also, **scollop.** [1350–1400; ME *scalop,* aph. var. of *escal(l)op* ESCALLOP; sense "thin slice of meat" prob. by assoc. with F *escalope* ESCALOPE]

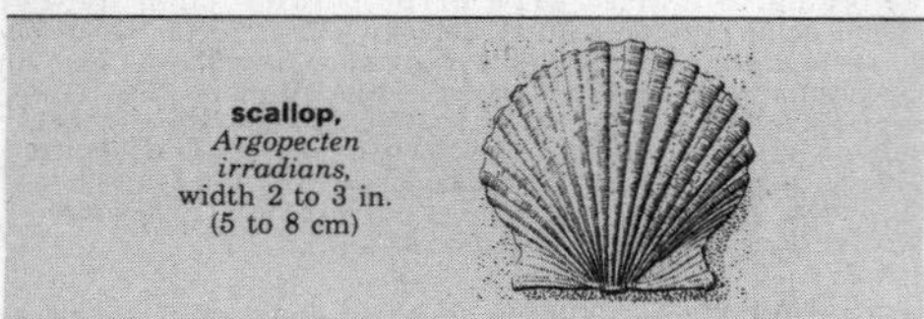
scallop, *Argopecten irradians,* width 2 to 3 in. (5 to 8 cm)

scal·lop·er (skol′ə pər, skal′-), *n.* a person or thing that scallops. [1880–85; SCALLOP + -ER[1]]

scal·lop·ing (skol′ə ping, skal′-), *n.* **1.** the act or occupation of collecting scallops. **2.** a pattern or contour in the form of scallops, as along the edge of a garment. **3.** the act of finishing an edge with scallops. [1790–1800; SCALLOP + -ING[1]]

scal′lop squash′. See **pattypan squash.**

scal·ly·wag (skal′ē wag′), *n.* scalawag.

scal·o·gram (skā′lə gram′), *n. Psychol.* an attitude scale in which a positive answer to an item implies agreement with items appearing lower on the scale. [1940–45; SCALE[3] + -O- + -GRAM[1]]

sca·lop·pi·ne (skä′lə pē′nē, skal′ə-), *n. Italian Cookery.* scallops, esp. of veal, flattened by pounding and usually dredged in flour or breadcrumbs and sautéed quickly: *scaloppine alla Marsala.* Also, **scal′lo·pi′ni.** [1945–50; < It *scaloppine,* pl. of *scaloppina,* equiv. to *scalopp(a)* thin slice (of veal, poultry, etc.) (< F *escalope* ESCALOPE) + *-ina* dim. suffix]

scalp (skalp), *n.* **1.** the integument of the upper part of the head, usually including the associated subcutaneous structures. **2.** a part of this integument with the accompanying hair, severed from the head of an enemy as a sign of victory, as by some North American Indians and others during the colonial and frontier periods in the U.S. **3.** any token of victory. **4.** the integument on the top of the head of an animal. **5.** *Informal.* a small profit made in quick buying and selling. —*v.t.* **6.** to cut or tear the scalp from. **7.** *Informal.* **a.** to resell (tickets, merchandise, etc.) at higher than the official rates. **b.** to buy and sell (stocks) so as to make small quick profits. **8.** to plane down the surfaces of (an ingot, billet, or slab). —*v.i.* **9.** *Informal.* to scalp tickets, stocks, or the like. [1250–1300; ME (north) (n.), perh. < ON *skālpr* sheath (hence, metaphorically a covering)] —**scalp′er,** *n.* —**scalp′less,** *adj.*

scal·pel (skal′pəl), *n.* a small, light, usually straight knife used in surgical and anatomical operations and dissections. [1735–45; < L *scalpellum,* dim. of *scalprum* tool for scraping or paring (deriv. of *scalpere* to scratch); for formation see CASTELLUM] —**scal·pel·lic** (skal pel′ik), *adj.*

scalp′ lock′, a long lock or tuft of hair left on the shorn scalp by some North American Indian men. [1815–25, *Amer.*]

scal·pri·form (skal′prə fôrm′), *adj.* chisel-shaped, as the incisors of certain rodents. [1820–30; < L *scalpri-* (comb. form of *scalprum;* see SCALPEL) + -FORM]

scal·y (skā′lē), *adj.,* **scal·i·er, scal·i·est. 1.** covered with or abounding in scales or scale. **2.** characterized by or consisting of scales; scalelike. **3.** peeling or flaking off in scales. **4.** *Slang.* shabby; despicable. [1520–30; SCALE[1] + -Y[1]] —**scal′i·ness,** *n.*

scal′y ant′eater, pangolin. [1830–40]

scam (skam), *n., v.,* **scammed, scam·ming.** —*n.* **1.** a confidence game or other fraudulent scheme, esp. for making a quick profit; swindle. —*v.t.* **2.** to cheat or defraud with a scam. [1960–65; orig. carnival argot; of obscure orig.] —**scam′mer,** *n.*

Sca·man·der (skə man′dər), *n.* ancient name of the river **Menderes.** Also, **Skamandros.**

sca·mil·lus (skə mil′əs), *n. Archit.* **1.** a slight bevel at an arris of a stone, as in the necking of a Greek Doric column. **2.** a plain stone beneath the plinth of a column. [< L, dim. of *scamnum* stool, bench]

scam·mo·ny (skam′ə nē), *n., pl.* **-nies.** a twining, Asian convolvulus, *Convolvulus scammonia.* [bef. 1000; ME *scamonie,* OE < L *scamōnia* < Gk *skamōnía*] —**scam·mo·ni·ate** (skə mō′nē it), *adj.*

scamp (skamp), *n.* **1.** an unscrupulous and often mischievous person; rascal; rogue; scalawag. **2.** a playful, mischievous, or naughty young person; upstart. **3.** a grouper, *Mycteroperca phenax,* of Florida: so called from its habit of stealing bait. —*v.t.* **4.** to do or perform in a hasty or careless manner: *to scamp work.* [1775–85; obs. *scamp* to travel about idly or for mischief, perh. < obs. D *schampen* to be gone < OF *escamper* to DECAMP] —**scamp′er,** *n.* —**scamp′ing·ly,** *adv.* —**scamp′ish,** *adj.* —**scamp′ish·ly,** *adv.* —**scamp′ish·ness,** *n.*

scamp·er (skam′pər), *v.i.* **1.** to run or go hastily or quickly. **2.** to run playfully about, as a child. —*n.* **3.** a scampering; a quick run. [1680–90; obs. *scamp* to go (see SCAMP) + -ER[6]]

scam·pi (skam′pē, skäm′-), *n., pl.* **-pi.** *Italian Cookery.* **1.** a large shrimp or prawn. **2.** a dish of shrimp or prawns grilled or sautéed in oil or butter and garlic. [1920–25; < It, pl. of *scampo*]

scan (skan), *v.,* **scanned, scan·ning,** *n.* —*v.t.* **1.** to examine the particulars or points of minutely; scrutinize. **2.** to glance at or over or read hastily: *to scan a page.* **3.** to peer out at or observe repeatedly or sweepingly, as a large expanse; survey. **4.** to analyze (verse) as to its prosodic or metrical structure; read or recite (verse) so as to indicate or test the metrical form. **5.** to read (data) for use by a computer or computerized device, esp. using an optical scanner. **6.** *Television.* to traverse (a surface) with a beam of light or electrons in order to reproduce or transmit a picture. **7.** *Radar.* to traverse (a region) with a beam from a radar transmitter. **8.** *Med., Biol.* to examine (a body, organ, tissue, or other biologically active material) with a scanner. —*v.i.* **9.** to examine the meter of verse. **10.** (of verse) to conform to the rules of meter. **11.** *Television.* to scan a surface or the like. —*n.* **12.** an act or instance of scanning; close examination. **13.** a visual examination by means of a television camera, as for the purpose of making visible or relaying pictures from a remote place: *a satellite scan of the dark side of the moon; video scans of property listings available to customers.* **14.** a particular image or frame in such video observation or a photograph made from it. **15.** *Med., Biol.* **a.** examination of the body or an organ or part, or a biologically active material, by means of a technique such as computed axial tomography, nuclear magnetic resonance, ultrasonography, or scintigraphy. **b.** the image or display so obtained. [1350–1400; ME *scannen,* var. of **scanden* < LL *scandere* to scan verse, L: to climb (see ASCEND)] —**scan′na·ble,** *adj.*
—**Syn. 1.** study, investigate, inspect, search. **2.** skim.

Scan., Scandinavia.

Scand, Scandinavian (def. 3).

Scand., **1.** Scandinavia. **2.** Scandinavian.

scan·dal (skan′dl), *n., v.,* **-daled, -dal·ing** or (*esp. Brit.*) **-dalled, -dal·ling.** —*n.* **1.** a disgraceful or discreditable action, circumstance, etc. **2.** an offense caused by a fault or misdeed. **3.** damage to reputation; public disgrace. **4.** defamatory talk; malicious gossip. **5.** a person whose conduct brings disgrace or offense. —*v.t.* **6.** *Brit. Dial.* to defame (someone) by spreading scandal. **7.** *Obs.* to disgrace. [1175–1225; < LL *scandalum* < LGk *skándalon* snare, cause of moral stumbling; r. ME *scandle* < OF (north) *escandle* < LL, as above]
—**Syn. 3.** discredit, dishonor, shame, disrepute, opprobrium, ignominy. **4.** slander, calumny, aspersion, obloquy. See **gossip.** —**Ant. 4.** honor, praise.

scan·dal·ize (skan′dl īz′), *v.t.,* **-ized, -iz·ing. 1.** to shock or horrify by something considered immoral or improper. **2.** *Naut.* to spill the wind from or reduce the exposed area of (a sail) in an unusual manner. Also, *esp. Brit.,* **scan′dal·ise′.** [1480–90; < LL *scandalizāre* < LGk *skandalízein.* See SCANDAL, -IZE] —**scan′dal·i·za′tion,** *n.* —**scan′dal·iz′er,** *n.*

scan·dal·mon·ger (skan′dl mung′gər, -mong′-), *n.* a person who spreads scandal or gossip. [1715–25; SCANDAL + MONGER]

scan·dal·ous (skan′dl əs), *adj.* **1.** disgraceful; shameful or shocking; improper: *scandalous behavior in public.* **2.** defamatory or libelous, as a speech or writing. **3.** attracted to or preoccupied with scandal, as a person: *a scandalous, vicious gossip.* [1585–95; < ML *scandalōsus.* See SCANDAL, -OUS] —**scan′dal·ous·ly,** *adv.* —**scan′dal·ous·ness,** *n.*

scan′dal sheet′, a newspaper or magazine that emphasizes scandal or gossip. [1900–05]

scan·dent (skan′dənt), *adj.* climbing, as a plant. [1675–85; < L *scandent-* (s. of *scandēns,* prp. of *scandere* to climb); see SCAN, -ENT]

Scan·der·beg (skan′dər beg′), *n.* (*George Castriota*) 1403?–68, Albanian chief and revolutionary leader. Turkish, **Iskander Bey.**

scan·di·a (skan′dē ə), *n. Chem.* See **scandium oxide.** [< NL; see SCANDIUM, -IA]

Scan·di·a (skan′dē ə), *n.* ancient name of the S Scandinavian Peninsula.

Scan·di·an (skan′dē ən), *adj.* **1.** of or pertaining to Scandia. —*n.* **2.** a Scandinavian. [1660–70; SCANDI(A) + -AN]

scan·dic (skan′dik), *adj. Chem.* of or pertaining to scandium: *scandic oxide.* [SCAND(IUM) + -IC]

Scan·di·na·vi·a (skan′də nā′vē ə), *n.* **1.** Norway, Sweden, Denmark, and sometimes Finland, Iceland, and the Faeroe Islands. **2.** Also called **Scandina′vian Penin′sula.** the peninsula consisting of Norway and Sweden.

Scan·di·na·vi·an (skan′də nā′vē ən), *adj.* **1.** of or pertaining to Scandinavia, its inhabitants, or their languages. —*n.* **2.** a native or inhabitant of Scandinavia. **3.** the group of languages composed of Danish, Icelandic, Norwegian, Old Norse, Swedish, and the language of the Faeroe Islands; North Germanic. *Abbr.:* Scand [1775–85; SCANDINAVI(A) + -AN]

Scandina′vian lox′. See under **lox**[1].

scan·di·um (skan′dē əm), *n. Chem.* a rare, trivalent, metallic element obtained from thortveitite. *Symbol:* Sc; *at. wt.:* 44.956; *at. no.:* 21; *sp. gr.:* 3.0. [1875–80; < NL; see SCANDIA, -IUM]

scan′dium ox′ide, *Chem.* a white infusible powder, Sc_2O_3, soluble in acids. Also called **scandia.**

scan·ner (skan′ər), *n.* **1.** a person or thing that scans. **2.** optical scanner. See under **optical scanning. 3.** *Photog.* any device for exposing an image on film, a sensitized plate, etc., by tracing light along a series of many closely spaced parallel lines. **4.** (in aerial photography) a device for estimating the ratio of aircraft speed to aircraft altitude. **5.** a photoelectric device for scanning a picture to determine automatically the density of the hue or value in each area for transmission by wire or radio or for preparation of color process printing plates. **6.** a computer-aided electronic system using photoelectric cells to separate copy, as color illustrations, into its primary colors, correct color copy, and produce a set of color separations ready for proofing or printing. **7.** *Radio.* a radio receiver, used esp. by police, firefighters, and the press, that continuously tunes to preselected frequencies, broadcasting any signal that it detects. **8.** *Med., Biol.* a device for examining a body, organ, tissue, or other biologically active material. Cf. **CAT scanner, MRI scanner, PET scanner, sonogram.** [1550–60; SCAN + -ER[1]]

scan′ning disk′, *Television.* (in mechanical scanning) a disk with a line of holes spiraling in from its edge, rotated in front of a surface so as to expose a small segment as each hole passes before it for transmitting or reproducing a picture. [1925–30]

scan′ning elec′tron mi′croscope, a device in which the specimen is examined point by point directly in a moving electron beam, and electrons reflected by the specimen are used to form a magnified, three-dimensional image on a television screen. *Abbr.:* SEM [1950–55]

scan′ning line′, (in a cathode-ray or television tube) a single horizontal trace made by the electron beam in one traversal of the fluorescent screen. Cf. **frame** (def. 9). [1925–30]

scan′ning tun′neling mi′croscope, a device that uses a moving needle and the tunnel effect to generate a maplike image of the atomic surface structure of matter, thereby achieving even greater magnification than the scanning electron microscope.

scan·sion (skan′shən), *n. Pros.* the metrical analysis of verse. The usual marks for scansion are ˘ for a short or unaccented syllable, ¯ or ′ for a long or accented syllable, ˆ for a rest, | for a foot division, and ‖ for a caesura or pause. [1645–55; < LL *scānsiōn-* (s. of *scānsiō*), L: a climbing, equiv. to *scāns(us)* (ptp. of *scandere* to climb) + *-iōn-* -ION]

scan·so·ri·al (skan sôr′ē əl, -sōr′-), *adj. Zool.* **1.** capable of or adapted for climbing, as the feet of certain birds, lizards, etc. **2.** habitually climbing, as a woodpecker. [1800–10; < L *scānsōri(us)* for climbing (*scand(ere)* to climb (see SCAN) + *-tōrius* -TORY[1], with *dt* > *s*) + -AL[1]]

scant (skant), *adj.,* **-er, -est,** *v., adv.* —*adj.* **1.** barely sufficient in amount or quantity; not abundant; almost inadequate: *to do scant justice.* **2.** limited; meager; not large: *a scant amount.* **3.** barely amounting to as much as indicated: *a scant two hours; a scant cupful.* **4.** having an inadequate or limited supply (usually fol. by *of*): *scant of breath.* —*v.t.* **5.** to make scant; diminish. **6.** to stint the supply of; withhold. **7.** to treat slightly or inadequately. —*adv.* **8.** *Scot. and North Eng. Dial.* scarcely; barely; hardly. [1325–75; ME (adj.) < ON *skamt,* neut. of *skammr* short] —**scant′ly,** *adv.* —**scant′ness,** *n.*
—**Syn. 2.** scanty, small, restricted. **4.** short, lacking, wanting, deficient. **5.** lessen, reduce, decrease, curtail. **6.** limit, restrict, skimp, scrimp. **7.** slight, neglect.

scant·ling (skant′ling), *n.* **1.** a timber of relatively slight width and thickness, as a stud or rafter in a house frame. **2.** such timbers collectively. **3.** the width and thickness of a timber. **4.** the dimensions of a building stone. **5.** *Naut.* **a.** a dressed timber or rolled metal member used as a framing member in a vessel. **b.** the dimension, in cross section, of a framing member. **6.** a small quantity or amount. [1520–30; SCANT + -LING[1]; r. ME *scantilon* < OF *escantillon* gauge]

scant·y (skan′tē), *adj.,* **scant·i·er, scant·i·est,** *n., pl.* **scant·ies.** —*adj.* **1.** scant in amount, quantity, etc.; barely sufficient. **2.** meager; not adequate. **3.** lacking amplitude in extent or compass. —*n.* **4. scanties,** very brief underpants, esp. for women. [1650–60; SCANT + -Y[1]; (def. 4) b. *scanty* and PANTIES] —**scant′i·ly,** *adv.* —**scant′i·ness,** *n.*
—**Syn. 1, 2.** SCANTY, MEAGER, SPARSE refer to insufficiency or deficiency in quantity, number, etc. SCANTY denotes smallness or insufficiency of quantity, number, supply, etc.: *a scanty supply of food.* MEAGER indicates that something is poor, stinted, or inadequate: *meager fare; a meager income.* SPARSE applies particularly to that which grows thinly or is thinly strewn or sown, often over a wide area: *sparse vegetation; a sparse population.* —**Ant. 1, 2.** plentiful, ample.

Sca′pa Flow′ (skä′pə, skap′ə), an area of water off the N coast of Scotland, in the Orkney Islands: British naval base; German warships scuttled 1919.

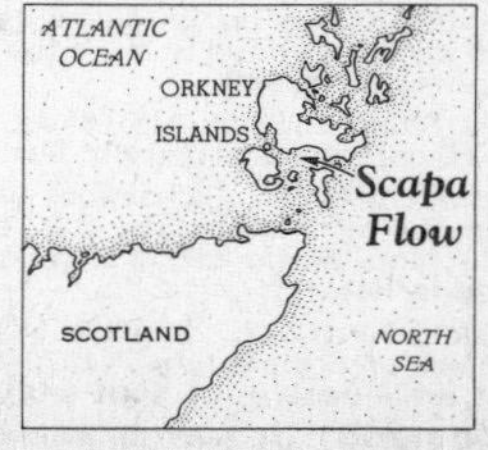

CONCISE ETYMOLOGY KEY: <, descended or borrowed from; >, whence; b., blend of, blended; c., cognate with; cf., compare; deriv., derivative; equiv., equivalent; imit., imitative; obl., oblique; r., replacing; s., stem; sp., spelling, spelled; resp., respelling, respelled; trans., translation; ?, origin unknown; *, unattested; ‡, probably earlier than. See the full key inside the front cover.

scape[1] (skāp), *n.* **1.** *Bot.* a leafless peduncle rising from the ground. **2.** *Zool.* a stemlike part, as the shaft of a feather. **3.** *Archit.* the shaft of a column. **4.** *Entomol.* the stemlike basal segment of the antenna of certain insects. [1595–1605; < L *scāpus* stalk < Doric Gk *skâpos,* akin to Attic *skêptron* staff, SCEPTER]

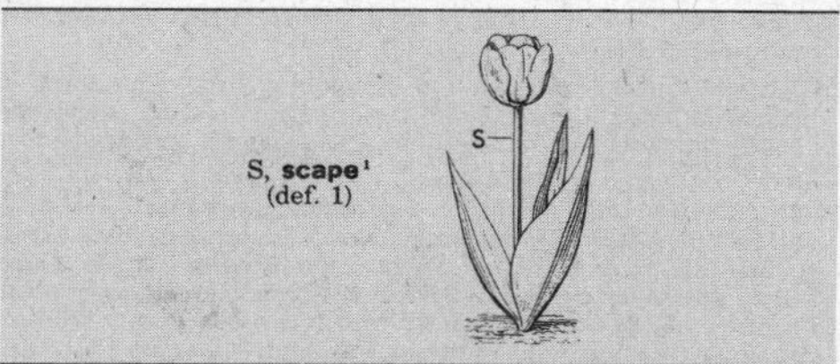

S, **scape**[1] (def. 1)

scape[2] (skāp), *n., v.t., v.i.,* **scaped, scap•ing.** *Archaic.* escape. Also, **'scape.**

-scape, a combining form extracted from **landscape,** denoting "an extensive view, scenery," or "a picture or representation" of such a view, as specified by the initial element: *cityscape; moonscape; seascape.*

scape•goat (skāp′gōt′), *n.* **1.** a person or group made to bear the blame for others or to suffer in their place. **2.** *Chiefly Biblical.* a goat let loose in the wilderness on Yom Kippur after the high priest symbolically laid the sins of the people on its head. Lev. 16:8, 10, 26. —*v.t.* **3.** to make a scapegoat of: *Strike leaders tried to scapegoat foreign competitors.* [1520–30; SCAPE[2] + GOAT]

scape•goat•ism (skāp′gō tiz′əm), *n.* the act or practice of assigning blame or failure to another, as to deflect attention or responsibility away from oneself. Also called **scape′goat′ing.** [SCAPEGOAT + -ISM]

scape•grace (skāp′grās′), *n.* a complete rogue or rascal; a habitually unscrupulous person; scamp. [1800–10; SCAPE[2] + GRACE]

scape′ wheel′, *Horol.* See **escape wheel.** [1815–25]

scapho-, a combining form meaning "boat," used in the formation of compound words: *scaphocephaly.* Also, *esp. before a vowel,* **scaph-.** [comb. form repr. Gk *skáphē* boat]

scaph•o•ceph•a•ly (skaf′ə sef′ə lē), *n. Pathol.* premature closure of the sagittal suture resulting in a deformed skull having an elongated, keellike shape. Also, **scaph′o•ceph′a•lism.** Also called **cymbocephaly.** [1900–05; SCAPHO- + -CEPHALY] —**scaph•o•ce•phal•ic** (skaf′ō sə fal′ik), **scaph′o•ceph′a•lous,** *adj.*

scaph•oid (skaf′oid), *adj.* **1.** boat-shaped; navicular. —*n.* **2.** *Anat.* a navicular. [1735–45; < NL *scaphoīdēs* < Gk *skaphoeidēs* like a boat. See SCAPH-, -OID]

scaph•o•pod (skaf′ə pod′), *n.* **1.** any mollusk of the class Scaphopoda, comprising the tooth shells. —*adj.* **2.** Also, **sca•phop•o•dous** (skə fop′ə dəs). belonging or pertaining to the Scaphopoda. [1910–15; < NL *Scaphopoda.* See SCAPHO-, -POD]

scap•o•lite (skap′ə līt′), *n.* **1.** any of a group of minerals of variable composition, essentially silicates of aluminum, calcium, and sodium, occurring as massive aggregates or tetragonal crystals. **2.** the member of the scapolite group intermediate in composition between meionite and marialite; wernerite. [1795–1805; < G *Skapolith.* See SCAPE, -O-, -LITE]

sca•pose (skā′pōs), *adj.* **1.** having scapes; consisting of a scape. **2.** resembling a scape. [1900–05; SCAPE[1] + -OSE[1]]

s. caps., *Print.* small capitals.

scapul-, var. of **scapulo-** before a vowel: *scapulalgia.*

scap•u•la (skap′yə lə), *n., pl.* **-las, -lae** (-lē′). **1.** *Anat.* either of two flat, triangular bones, each forming the back part of a shoulder in humans; shoulder blade. See diags. under **shoulder, skeleton. 2.** *Zool.* a dorsal bone of the pectoral girdle. [1570–80; < L: shoulder]

scap•u•lar[1] (skap′yə lər), *adj.* of or pertaining to the shoulders or the scapula or scapulae. [1680–90; < NL *scapulāris.* See SCAPULA, -AR[1]]

scap•u•lar[2] (skap′yə lər), *n.* **1.** *Eccles.* a loose, sleeveless monastic garment, hanging from the shoulders. **2.** two small pieces of woolen cloth, joined by strings passing over the shoulders, worn under the ordinary clothing as a badge of affiliation with a religious order, a token of devotion, etc. **3.** *Anat., Zool.* scapula. **4.** *Ornith.* one of the scapular feathers. See illus. under **bird.** [1475–85; < ML *scapulāre,* n. use of neut. of *scapulāris* (adj.). See SCAPULAR[1]]

scap•u•lar•y (skap′yə ler′ē), *adj., n., pl.* **-lar•ies.** —*adj.* **1.** scapular[1]. —*n.* **2.** *Surg.* a shoulder dressing that keeps the shoulder or another bandage in place. [1175–1225; ME *scapelori, scapelry* < ML *scapulōrium, scapulārium,* assimilated to -ARY. See SCAPULA, -ARY]

scap•u•li•man•cy (skap′yə lə man′sē), *n.* divination of the future by observation of the cracking of a mammal's scapula that has been heated by a fire or hot instrument. Also, **scap′u•lo•man′cy.** Cf. **oracle bone.** [1870–75; SCAPUL(A) + -I- + -MANCY]

scapulo-, a combining form representing **scapula** in compound words: *scapulohumeral.* Also, *esp. before a vowel,* **scapul-.**

scap•u•lo•hum•er•al (skap′yə lō hyōō′mər əl *or, often,* -yōō′-), *adj. Anat.* of, pertaining to, or involving the scapula and humerus. [1830–40; SCAPULO- + HUMERAL]

scar[1] (skär), *n., v.,* **scarred, scar•ring.** —*n.* **1.** a mark left by a healed wound, sore, or burn. **2.** a lasting aftereffect of trouble, esp. a lasting psychological injury resulting from suffering or trauma. **3.** any blemish remaining as a trace of or resulting from injury or use. **4.** *Bot.* a mark indicating a former point of attachment, as where a leaf has fallen from a stem. —*v.t.* **5.** to mark with a scar. —*v.i.* **6.** to form a scar in healing. [1350–1400; ME; aph. var. of ESCHAR] —**scar′less,** *adj.*

scar[2] (skär), *n. Brit.* **1.** a precipitous, rocky place; cliff. **2.** a low or submerged rock in the sea. [1300–50; ME *skerre* < ON *sker* SKERRY]

scar•ab (skar′əb), *n.* **1.** any scarabaeid beetle, esp. *Scarabaeus sacer,* regarded as sacred by the ancient Egyptians. **2.** a representation or image of a beetle, much used among the ancient Egyptians as a symbol, seal, amulet, or the like. **3.** a gem cut to resemble a beetle. Also, **scarabaeus** (for defs. 2, 3). [1570–80; short for SCARABAEUS]

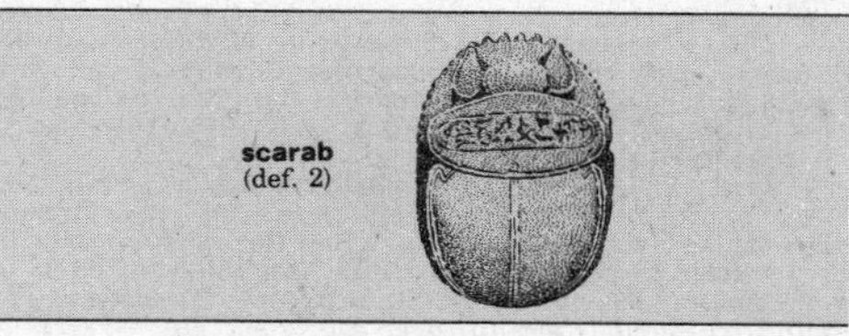
scarab (def. 2)

scar•a•bae•id (skar′ə bē′id), *adj.* **1.** belonging or pertaining to the Scarabaeidae, a family of lamellicorn beetles, including the scarabs, dung beetles, June bugs, and cockchafers. —*n.* **2.** any scarabaeid beetle. Also, **scar′•a•bae′an.** [1835–45; < NL *scarabaeidae.* See SCARABAEUS, -ID[2]]

scar•a•bae•oid (skar′ə bē′oid), *adj.* Also, **scar•a•boid** (skar′ə boid′). **1.** resembling a scarab. —*n.* **2.** an imitation or counterfeit scarab. [1885–90; SCARABAE(US) + -OID]

scar•a•bae•us (skar′ə bē′əs), *n., pl.* **-bae•us•es, -bae•i** (-bē′ī). scarab (defs. 2, 3). [1400–50; late ME < L; cf. Gk *kárabos* kind of beetle]

Scar•a•mouch (skar′ə mouch′, -mōōsh′), *n.* **1.** a stock character in commedia dell'arte and farce who is a cowardly braggart, easily beaten and frightened. **2.** (*l.c.*) a rascal or scamp. Also, **Scar′a•mouche′.** [1655–65; < F *Scaramouche* < It *Scaramuccia,* proper use of *scaramuccia* skirmish (applied in jest); of Gmc orig.]

Scar•bor•ough (skär′bûr′ō, -bur′ō, -bər ə), *n.* **1.** a seaport in North Yorkshire, in NE England. 97,900. **2.** a city in SW Maine. 11,347.

Scar′borough lil′y, a plant, *Vallota speciosa,* of the amaryllis family, native to southern Africa, having clusters of funnel-shaped, scarlet flowers. [1880–85; after SCARBOROUGH, England]

scarce (skârs), *adj.,* **scarc•er, scarc•est,** *adv.* —*adj.* **1.** insufficient to satisfy the need or demand; not abundant: *Meat and butter were scarce during the war.* **2.** seldom met with; rare: *a scarce book.* **3. make oneself scarce,** *Informal.* **a.** to depart, esp. suddenly. **b.** to stay away; avoid. —*adv.* **4.** scarcely. [1250–1300; ME *scars* < ONF (*e*)*scars* < VL **excarpsus* plucked out, for L *excerptus;* see EXCERPT] —**scarce′ness,** *n.*
—**Syn. 1.** deficient. **2.** uncommon, infrequent.
—**Ant. 1.** abundant.

scarce•ly (skârs′lē), *adv.* **1.** barely; hardly; not quite: *The light is so dim we can scarcely see.* **2.** definitely not: *This is scarcely the time to raise such questions.* **3.** probably not: *You could scarcely have chosen better.* [1250–1300; ME; see SCARCE, -LY]
—**Syn. 1.** See **hardly.**
—**Usage. 1.** See **hardly.**

scarce•ment (skârs′mənt), *n.* a footing or ledge formed by a setoff in a wall. [1495–1505; obs. *scarce* to lessen (v. deriv. of SCARCE) + -MENT]

scar•ci•ty (skâr′si tē), *n., pl.* **-ties. 1.** insufficiency or shortness of supply; dearth. **2.** rarity; infrequency. [1300–50; ME *scarsete(e)* < ONF *escarsete.* See SCARCE, -ITY]
—**Syn. 1.** shortage, want, lack, paucity.

scare (skâr), *v.,* **scared, scar•ing,** *n.* —*v.t.* **1.** to fill, esp. suddenly, with fear or terror; frighten; alarm. —*v.i.* **2.** to become frightened: *That horse scares easily.* **3. scare up,** *Informal.* to obtain with effort; find or gather: *to scare up money.* —*n.* **4.** a sudden fright or alarm, esp. with little or no reason. **5.** a time or condition of alarm or worry: *For three months there was a war scare.* [1150–1200; (v.) ME *skerren* < ON *skirra* to frighten, deriv. of *skjarr* timid, shy; (n.) late ME *skere,* deriv. of the v.] —**scar′er,** *n.* —**scar′ing•ly,** *adv.*
—**Syn. 1.** startle, intimidate. See **frighten.**

scare•crow (skâr′krō′), *n.* **1.** an object, usually a figure of a person in old clothes, set up to frighten crows or other birds away from crops. **2.** anything frightening but not really dangerous. **3.** a person in ragged clothes. **4.** an extremely thin person. [1545–55; SCARE + CROW[1]] —**scare′crow′ish, scare′crow′y,** *adj.*

scared•y-cat (skâr′dē kat′), *n. Informal.* fraidy-cat. [1930–35; SCARED + -Y[2]]

scare•head (skâr′hed′), *n.* a headline in exceptionally large type. Cf. **screamer** (def. 4). [1885–90; SCARE + HEAD]

scare•mon•ger (skâr′mung′gər, -mong′-), *n.* a person who creates or spreads alarming news. [1885–90; SCARE + MONGER] —**scare′mon′ger•ing,** *n.*

scarf[1] (skärf), *n., pl.* **scarfs, scarves** (skärvz), *v.* —*n.* **1.** a long, broad strip of wool, silk, lace, or other material worn about the neck, shoulders, or head, for ornament or protection against cold, drafts, etc.; muffler. **2.** a necktie or cravat with hanging ends. **3.** a long cover or ornamental cloth for a bureau, table, etc. —*v.t.* **4.** to cover or wrap with or as if with a scarf. **5.** to use in the manner of a scarf. [1545–55; perh. special use of SCARF[2]] —**scarf′less,** *adj.* —**scarf′like′,** adj.

scarf[2] (skärf), *n., pl.* **scarfs,** *v.* —*n.* **1.** a tapered or otherwise-formed end on each of the pieces to be assembled with a scarf joint. **2.** *Whaling.* a strip of skin along the body of the whale. —*v.t.* **3.** to assemble with a scarf joint. **4.** to form a scarf on (the end of a timber). **5.** *Steelmaking.* to burn away the surface defects of (newly rolled steel). **6.** *Whaling.* to make a groove in and remove (the blubber and skin). Also, **scarph** (for defs. 1, 3, 4). [1490–1500; < ON *skarfr* (deriv. of *skera* to cut) end cut from a beam (hence perh. a piece of cloth cut off, i.e., SCARF[1]); cf. Sw *skarv* patch] —**scarf′er,** *n.*

scarf[3] (skärf), *v.t., v.i. Slang.* to eat, esp. voraciously (often fol. by *down* or *up*): *to scarf down junk food.* [1955–60, *Amer.*; var. of SCOFF[2], with *r* inserted prob. through r-dialect speakers' mistaking the underlying vowel as an r-less *ar*]

scar-faced (skär′fāst′), *adj.* with a face marked by a scar or scars.

scarf′ cloud′, pileus (def. 3).

scarf′ joint′, 1. a joint in which two timbers or other structural members are fitted together with long end laps of various forms and held in place with bolts, straps, keys, fishplates, etc., to resist tension or compression. **2.** (in welding) a butt joint between two pieces beveled on their meeting surfaces. [1785–95]

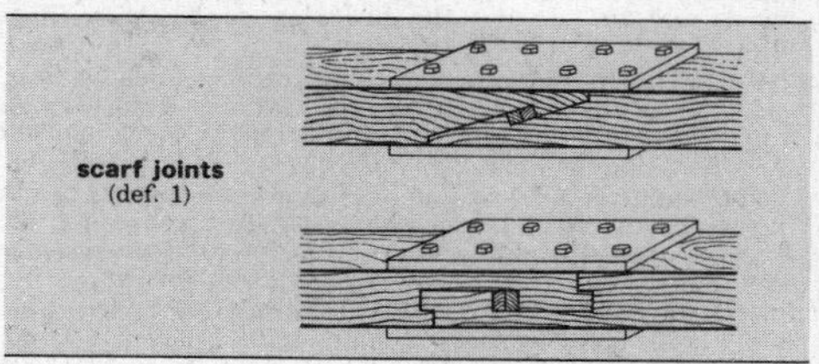
scarf joints (def. 1)

scarf•pin (skärf′pin′), *n.* tiepin. [1855–60; SCARF[1] + PIN]

scarf•skin (skärf′skin′), *n.* the outermost layer of the skin; epidermis. [1605–15; SCARF[1] + SKIN]

scar•i•fi•ca•tion (skar′ə fi kā′shən), *n.* **1.** an act or instance of scarifying. **2.** the result of scarifying; a scratch or scratches. [1350–1400; ME *scarificacioun* < LL *scarificātiōn-* (s. of *scarificātiō*). See SCARIFY, -ATION]

scar•i•fi•ca•tor (skar′ə fi kā′tər), *n.* **1.** a person who scarifies. **2.** a surgical instrument for scarifying. [1605–15; < NL (coined by Ambroise Paré); see SCARIFY, -ATOR]

scar•i•fy (skar′ə fī′), *v.t.,* **-fied, -fy•ing. 1.** to make scratches or superficial incisions in (the skin, a wound, etc.), as in vaccination. **2.** to lacerate by severe criticism. **3.** to loosen (the soil) with a type of cultivator. **4.** to hasten the sprouting of (hard-covered seeds) by making incisions in the seed coats. **5.** to break up (a road surface). [1400–50; late ME *scarifie* < MF *scarifier* < LL *scarīficāre,* alter. of L *scarīfāre, scarīphāre* to make scratches < Gk *skarīphâsthai* to sketch, deriv. of *skárīphos* stylus; see -IFY] —**scar′i•fi′er,** *n.*

scar•i•ous (skâr′ē əs), *adj. Bot.* thin, dry, and membranous, as certain bracts; chaffy. [1800–10; alter. of *scariose* < NL *scariōsus* < ?; see -OUS]

scar•la•ti•na (skär′lə tē′nə), *n. Pathol.* **1.** See **scarlet fever. 2.** a mild form of scarlet fever. [1795–1805; < NL (*febris*) *scarlatina* scarlet fever, deriv. of ML *scarlata* scarlet (cloth); see SCARLET, -INE[1]] —**scar′la•ti′nal, scar•la•ti•nous** (skär′lə tē′nəs, skär lat′n əs), *adj.*

scar•la•ti•noid (skär′lə tē′noid, skär lat′n oid′), *adj. Pathol.* resembling scarlatina or its eruptions. [1885–90; SCARLATIN(A) + -OID]

Scar•lat•ti (skär lä′tē; *It.* skär lät′tē), *n.* **1. A•les•san•dro** (ä′lə sän′drō; *It.* ä′les sän′drô), 1659–1725, Italian composer. **2.** his son **Do•me•ni•co** (də men′i kō′; *It.* dô me′nē kô′), 1685–1757, Italian harpsichordist, organist, and composer.

scar•let (skär′lit), *n.* **1.** a bright-red color inclining toward orange. **2.** cloth or clothing of this color. —*adj.* **3.** of the color scarlet. **4.** flagrantly offensive: *Their sins were scarlet.* [1200–50; ME < OF *escarlate* < ML *scarlata, scarletum,* perh. < Ar *saqirlāṭ, siqillāṭ* < MGk *sigillátos* < L *sigillātus* decorated with patterns in relief; see SIGILLATE]

scar′let clem′atis, a slightly woody vine, *Clematis texensis,* of Texas, having bluish-green leaves, plumed fruit, and solitary, urn-shaped, scarlet-to-pink flowers.

scar′let cup′, a small, fleshy, saucer-shaped fungus, *Sarcoscypha coccinea,* of the family Sarcoscyphaceae, marked by a scarlet inner surface and white exterior, seen on fallen branches in the spring.

scar′let egg′plant, a hairy, prickly plant, *Solanum integrifolium,* of the nightshade family, native to Africa, grown for its furrowed, nearly round, scarlet or yellow ornamental fruit. Also called **tomato eggplant.**

scar′let fe′ver, *Pathol.* a contagious febrile disease caused by streptococci and characterized by a scarlet eruption. [1670–80]

scar′let fire′thorn, a Eurasian evergreen, thorny shrub, *Pyracantha coccinea,* of the rose family, having white, hairy flower clusters and bright red berries.

scar′let gil′i•a (jil′ē ə), skyrocket. [1840–50, *Amer.*; *gilia* < NL, a genus name, after Felipe *Gil,* 18th century Spanish botanist; see -IA]

scar′let hat′. See **red hat.**

scar′let let′ter, a scarlet letter "A," formerly worn by one convicted of adultery. [1840–50, *Amer.*]

Scar′let Let′ter, The, a novel (1850) by Nathaniel Hawthorne.

CONCISE PRONUNCIATION KEY: *act, cāpe, dâre, pärt; set, ēqual; if, īce; ox, ōver, ôrder, oil, bŏŏk, bōōt, out; up, ûrge; child; sing; shoe; thin, that;* zh *as in treasure.* ə = *a as in alone, e as in system, i as in easily, o as in gallop, u as in circus;* ᵊ *as in fire* (fīᵊr), *hour* (ouᵊr). l and n can serve as syllabic consonants, as in *cradle* (krād′l), and *button* (but′n). See the full key inside the front cover.

scar′let light′ning, 1. See **scarlet lychnis.** 2. See **red valerian.**

scar′let lobel′ia. See **cardinal flower.**

scar′let lych′nis, a plant, *Lychnis chalcedonica,* of the pink family, having scarlet or sometimes white flowers, the arrangement and shape of the petals resembling a Maltese cross. Also called **Maltese cross, Jerusalem cross, scarlet lightning.**

scar′let mon′key flow′er. See under **monkey flower.**

scar′let pim′pernel. See under **pimpernel.** [1850–55]

scar′let run′ner, a twining, South American bean plant, *Phaseolus coccineus,* having clusters of scarlet flowers. [1780–90]

scar′let sage′, a tender shrub, *Salvia splendens,* of Brazil, having ovate leaves and bell-shaped scarlet flowers. [1905–10]

scar′let tan′ager, an American tanager, *Piranga olivacea,* the male of which is bright red with black wings and tail during the breeding season. See illus. under **tanager.** [1800–10, *Amer.*]

scar′let wom′an, 1. a sexually promiscuous woman, esp. a prostitute or a woman who commits adultery. 2. a symbol of pagan Rome or, opprobriously, of the church of Rome. Rev. 17:1–6. [1810–20]

scarp (skärp), *n.* 1. a line of cliffs formed by the faulting or fracturing of the earth's crust; an escarpment. 2. *Fort.* an escarp. —*v.t.* 3. to form or cut into a steep slope. [1580–90; < It *scarpa* a slope. See ESCARP]

scarp·er (skär′pər), *v.i. Brit.* to flee or depart suddenly, esp. without having paid one's bills. [1840–50; orig. argot, prob. < Polari << It *scappare* to flee (see ESCAPE)]

scarph (skärf), *n., v.t. Shipbuilding.* scarf² (defs. 1, 3, 4).

Scar·ron (ska rôn′), *n.* **Paul** (pôl), 1610–60, French novelist, dramatist, and poet.

scar·ry¹ (skär′ē), *adj.,* **-ri·er, -ri·est.** marked with the scars of wounds. [1645–55; SCAR¹ + -Y¹]

scar·ry² (skär′ē), *adj.* full of precipitous, rocky places. [1350–1400; ME; see SCAR², -Y¹]

Scars·dale (skärz′dāl′), *n.* a town in SE New York, N of New York City. 17,650.

scart (skärt), *v.t., v.i. Scot.* to scratch, scrape, mark, or scar. [1325–75; ME (Scots), metathetic var. of *scrat* to SCRATCH]

scar′ tis′sue, connective tissue that has contracted and become dense and fibrous. Also called **cicatricial tissue.** [1870–75]

scarves (skärvz), *n.* a pl. of **scarf¹.**

scar·y (skâr′ē), *adj.,* **scar·i·er, scar·i·est.** 1. causing fright or alarm. 2. easily frightened; timid. [1575–85; SCARE + -Y¹]

scat¹ (skat), *v.i.,* **scat·ted, scat·ting.** *Informal.* to go off hastily (often used in the imperative). [1865–70, *Amer.*; of uncert. orig.]

scat² (skat), *v.,* **scat·ted, scat·ting,** *n. Jazz.* —*v.i.* 1. to sing by making full or partial use of the technique of scat singing. —*n.* 2. See **scat singing.** [1925–30; of uncert. orig.]

scat³ (skat), *n.* the excrement of an animal. [1925–30; orig. uncert.; cf. Brit. dial. (SW) *scat* to scatter, fling down, bespatter; Gk *skat-* (s. of *skôr* dung; see SCATO-) is unlikely source, given popular character of the word and unmotivated derivation pattern]

scat⁴ (skat), *n. Slang.* heroin. [1945–50; of uncert. orig.; cf. earlier *scat* (slang) whiskey]

scat⁵ (skat), *n.* (in the Shetland and Orkney Islands) a crown tax, as for use of common lands. Also, **scatt.** [1300–50; ME < ON *skattr* tax, treasure]

scat-, var. of **scato-** before a vowel.

scat·back (skat′bak′), *n. Football.* a fast and agile running back, often small in stature, skilled at eluding tacklers. [1945–50; *Amer.*; SCAT¹ + BACK¹]

scathe (skāth), *v.,* **scathed, scath·ing,** *n.* —*v.t.* 1. to attack with severe criticism. 2. to hurt, harm, or injure, as by scorching. —*n.* 3. hurt, harm, or injury. [bef. 1000; (n.) ME *scath(e), scade, schath(e)* < ON *skathi* damage, harm, c. OE *sc(e)atha* malefactor, injury (with which the ME forms with *sch-* might be identified); (v.) ME *scath(e), skath(e)* < ON *skatha,* c. OE *sceathian*] —**scathe′less,** *adj.* —**scathe′less·ly,** *adv.*

scath·ing (skā′thing), *adj.* 1. bitterly severe, as a remark: *a scathing review of the play.* 2. harmful, injurious, or searing. [1785–95; SCATHE + -ING²] —**scath′·ing·ly,** *adv.*

scato-, a combining form meaning "excrement," used in the formation of compound words: *scatology.* Also, *esp. before a vowel,* **scat-.** [< Gk *skato-,* comb. form of *skôr* dung; akin to OE *scearn,* ON *skarn* dung]

sca·tol·o·gy (skə tol′ə jē), *n.* 1. the study of or preoccupation with excrement or obscenity. 2. obscenity, esp. words or humor referring to excrement. 3. the study of fossil excrement. Also called **coprology.** [1875–80; SCATO- + -LOGY] —**scat·o·log·i·cal** (skat′l oj′i kəl), **scat′o·log′ic,** *adj.*

sca·to·ma (skə tō′mə), *n., pl.* **-mas, -ma·ta** (-mə tə). *Med.* a tumorlike mass of feces in the colon or rectum. [SCAT- + -OMA]

sca·tos·co·py (skə tos′kə pē), *n. Med.* examination of the feces for diagnostic purposes. [SCATO- + -SCOPY]

*CONCISE ETYMOLOGY KEY: <, descended or borrowed from; >, whence; b., blend of, blended; c., cognate with; cf., compare; deriv., derivative; equiv., equivalent; imit., imitative; obl., oblique; r., replacing; s., stem; sp., spelling, spelled; resp., respelling, respelled; trans., translation; ?, origin unknown; *, unattested; ‡, probably earlier than. See the full key inside the front cover.*

scat′ sing′ing, *Jazz.* singing in which the singer substitutes improvised nonsense syllables for the words of a song, and tries to sound and phrase like a musical instrument. [1925–30]

scatt (skat), *n.* scat⁵.

scat·ter (skat′ər), *v.t.* 1. to throw loosely about; distribute at irregular intervals: *to scatter seeds.* 2. to separate and drive off in various directions; disperse: *to scatter a crowd.* 3. *Physics.* **a.** to refract or diffract (light or other electromagnetic radiation) irregularly so as to diffuse in many directions. **b.** (of a medium) to diffuse or deflect (light or other wave phenomena) by collisions between the wave and particles of the medium. —*v.i.* 4. to separate and disperse; go in different directions. —*n.* 5. the act of scattering. 6. something that is scattered. [1125–75; ME *scatere;* cf. D *schateren* to burst out laughing] —**scat′ter·a·ble,** *adj.* —**scat′ter·er,** *n.* —**scat′ter·ing·ly,** *adv.*

—**Syn.** 1. broadcast. See **sprinkle.** 2. SCATTER, DISPEL, DISPERSE, DISSIPATE imply separating and driving something away so that its original form disappears. To SCATTER is to separate something tangible into parts at random, and drive these in different directions: *The wind scattered leaves all over the lawn.* To DISPEL is to drive away or scatter usually intangible things so that they vanish or cease to exist: *Photographs of the race dispelled all doubts as to which horse won.* To DISPERSE is usually to cause a compact or organized tangible body to separate or scatter in different directions, to be reassembled if desired: *Tear gas dispersed the mob.* To DISSIPATE is usually to scatter by dissolving or reducing to small atoms or parts that cannot be brought together again: *He dissipated his money and his energy in useless activities.*

scat·ter·a·tion (skat′ə rā′shən), *n.* 1. the act of scattering. 2. the state of being scattered. 3. something scattered. [1770–80; SCATTER + -ATION]

scat·ter·brain (skat′ər brān′), *n.* a person incapable of serious, connected thought. Also, **scat′ter·brains′.** [1780–90; SCATTER + BRAIN] —**scat′ter·brained′,** *adj.*

scat′ter di′agram, *Statistics.* a graphic representation of bivariate data as a set of points in the plane that have Cartesian coordinates equal to corresponding values of the two variates. Also called **scat·ter·gram** (skat′ər gram′), **scat·ter·graph** (skat′ər graf′, -gräf′), **scat·ter·plot** (skat′ər plot′). [1920–25]

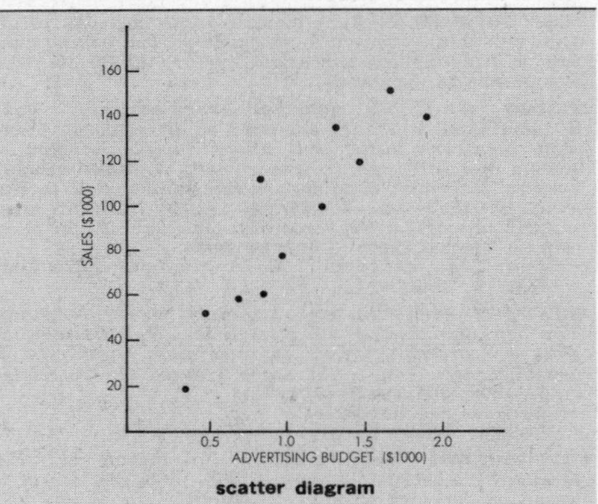

scatter diagram

scat·tered (skat′ərd), *adj.* 1. distributed or occurring at widely spaced and usually irregular intervals: *scattered villages; scattered showers.* 2. dispersed; disorganized: *scattered forces.* 3. distracted or disorganized: *scattered thoughts.* 4. *Meteorol.* (of clouds) covering up to one-half of the sky. Cf. **broken** (def. 5). [SCATTER + -ED²] —**scat′tered·ly,** *adv.* —**scat′tered·ness,** *n.*

scat·ter·good (skat′ər go͝od′), *n.* a spendthrift. [1570–80; SCATTER + GOOD]

scat·ter·ing (skat′ər ing), *adj.* 1. distributed or occurring here and there at irregular intervals; scattered. 2. straggling, as an assemblage of parts. 3. (of votes) cast in small numbers for various candidates. 4. distributing, dispersing, or separating. —*n.* 5. a small, scattered number or quantity. 6. *Physics.* the process in which a wave or beam of particles is diffused or deflected by collisions with particles of the medium that it traverses. Cf. **elastic scattering, Rayleigh scattering.** [1300–50; ME; see SCATTER, -ING², -ING¹]

scat′ter pin′, a woman's small ornamental pin, usually worn with other similar pins on a dress, suit jacket, etc. [1955–60]

scat′ter rug′, a small rug, placed on the floor in front of a chair, under a table, etc. Also called **throw rug.** [1930–35]

scat′ter shot′, shot prepared for a weapon having a rifled bore or barrel. [1960–65]

scat·ter·shot (skat′ər shot′), *adj.* delivered over a wide area and at random; generalized and indiscriminate: *a scattershot attack on the proposed program.* [1960–65; adj. use of SCATTER SHOT]

scat′ter·site hous′ing (skat′ər sit′), public housing, esp. for low-income families, built throughout an urban area rather than being concentrated in a single neighborhood. Also, **scat′ter-site hous′ing.** [1970–75, *Amer.*; SCATTER + SITE]

scat·ty (skat′ē), *adj.,* **-ti·er, -ti·est.** *Brit. Informal.* scatterbrained. [1910–15; appar. SCATT(ERBRAIN) + -Y¹]

sca·tu·ri·ent (skə to͝or′ē ənt, -tyo͝or′-), *adj.* 1. gushing; overflowing. 2. overly demonstrative; effusive. [1675–85; < L *scatūr(r)ient-,* s. of *scatūr(r)iēns,* prp. of *scatūr(r)ire* to gush out, bubble up; see -ENT] —**sca·tu′ri·ence,** *n.*

scaup (skôp), *n.* any of several diving ducks of the genus *Aythya,* esp. *A. marila* **(greater scaup),** of the Northern Hemisphere, having a bluish-gray bill. Also called **scaup′ duck′.** [1665–75; by ellipsis from *scaup duck,* prob. with Scots, N dial. *scaup, scalp* mussel bed (of uncert. orig.)]

scau·per (skô′pər), *n.* a graver with a flattened or hollowed blade, used in engraving. Also, **scorper.** [1815–25; var. of *scalper* < L *scalprum* scraper. See SCALPEL]

scav·enge (skav′inj), *v.,* **-enged, -eng·ing.** —*v.t.* 1. to take or gather (something usable) from discarded material. 2. to cleanse of filth, as a street. 3. to expel burnt gases from (the cylinder of an internal-combustion engine). 4. *Metall.* to purify (molten metal) by introducing a substance that will combine chemically with impurities. —*v.i.* 5. to act as a scavenger. 6. (of an engine or cylinder) to become scavenged of burnt gases. 7. to search, esp. for food. [1635–45; back formation from SCAVENGER]

scav·en·ger (skav′in jər), *n.* 1. an animal or other organism that feeds on dead organic matter. 2. a person who searches through and collects items from discarded material. 3. a street cleaner. 4. *Chem.* a chemical that consumes or renders inactive the impurities in a mixture. [1520–30; earlier *scavager* < AF *scawageour,* equiv. to *(e)scawage* inspection *(escaw(er)* to inspect < MD *schauwen* to look at (c. SHOW) + *-age* -AGE) + *-eour* -OR²]

scav′enger hunt′, a game in which individuals or teams are sent out to accumulate, without purchasing, a series of common, outlandish, or humorous objects, the winner being the person or team returning first with all the items. [1935–40, *Amer.*]

scav′enger's daugh′ter, an instrument of torture that doubled over and squeezed the body so strongly and violently that blood was brought forth from the ears and nose: invented in 16th-century England. [1555–65; *scavenger,* alter. of the name of its inventor, Leonard *Skevington,* Lieutenant of the Tower of London under Henry VIII]

Sc.B., See **Bachelor of Science.** [< L *Scientiae Baccalaureus*]

Sc.B.C., Bachelor of Science in Chemistry.

Sc.B.E., Bachelor of Science in Engineering.

Sc.D., Doctor of Science. [< L *Scientiae Doctor*]

Sc.D.Hyg., Doctor of Science in Hygiene.

Sc.D.Med., Doctor of Medical Science.

sceat (shat), *n.* a silver Anglo-Saxon coin of the 7th and 8th centuries, sometimes including an amount of gold. Also, **sceat·ta** (shat′ə). [learned borrowing (18th century) of OE *sceat, sceǣt;* c. OS *skat,* OHG *scaz* (G *Schatz*) treasure, tribute. See SCAT⁵]

scelp (skelp), *n., v.t. Scot. and North Eng.* skelp¹.

sce·na (shā′nə), *n.* an extended operatic vocal solo, usually including an aria and a recitative. [1810–20; < It: lit., SCENE]

sce·nar·i·o (si nâr′ē ō′, -när′-), *n., pl.* **-nar·i·os.** 1. an outline of the plot of a dramatic work, giving particulars as to the scenes, characters, situations, etc. 2. the outline or the manuscript of a motion picture or television program, giving the action in the order in which it takes place, the description of scenes and characters, etc. 3. an imagined or projected sequence of events, esp. any of several detailed plans or possibilities: *One scenario calls for doubling profits by increasing our advertising, the other by reducing costs.* [1875–80; < It < L *scēnārium.* See SCENE, -ARY]

—**Syn.** 3. scheme, plan, concept, sketch.

sce·nar·ist (si nâr′ist, -när′-), *n.* a writer of motion-picture or television scenarios. [1915–20; SCENAR(IO) + -IST]

scend (send), *Naut.* —*v.i.* (of a vessel) 1. to heave in a swell. 2. to lurch forward from the motion of a heavy sea. —*n.* 3. the heaving motion of a vessel. 4. the forward impulse imparted by the motion of a sea against a vessel. Also, **send.** [1615–25; cf. SEND²; perh. aph. var. of ASCEND, DESCEND]

scene (sēn), *n.* 1. the place where some action or event occurs: *He returned to the scene of the murder.* 2. any view or picture. 3. an incident or situation in real life. 4. an embarrassing outbreak or display of anger, strong feeling, or bad manners: *Please don't make a scene in such a public place.* 5. a division of a play or of an act of a play, usually representing what passes between certain of the actors in one place. 6. a unit of action or a segment of a story in a play, motion picture, or television show. 7. the place in which the action of a play or part of a play is supposed to occur. 8. scenery (def. 2). 9. *Literature.* **a.** an episode, situation, or the like, as in a narrative. **b.** the setting or locale of a story. 10. the stage, esp. of an ancient Greek or Roman theater. 11. an area or sphere of activity, current interest, etc.: *the rock music scene; the fashion scene.* 12. **behind the scenes,** in secret or in private. 13. **make the scene,** *Slang.* to appear in a particular place or engage in a particular activity: *Let's make the scene downtown tonight. She was never one to make the drug scene.* [1530–40; < L *scēna* background (of the stage) < Gk *skēnḗ* booth (where actors dressed)]

—**Syn.** 1. arena, stage, location; center, focus. 2. See **view.** 3. episode. 4. demonstration, spectacle, show.

scene′ dock′, dock¹ (def. 7). [1880–85]

scene′ mas′ter, *Theat.* (on a switchboard) a master switch that controls several lighting circuits.

scen·er·y (sē′nə rē), *n., pl.* **-er·ies.** 1. the general appearance of a place; the aggregate of features that give character to a landscape. 2. hangings, draperies, structures, etc., used on a stage to represent a locale or furnish decorative background. **3. chew the scenery,** to act melodramatically; overact. [1740–50; SCENE + -ERY] **—Syn. 1.** terrain, view, surroundings.

scene-steal•er (sēn′stē′lər), *n.* a performer in a play, motion picture, etc., who by charm, talent, or artifice, draws most of the audience's attention, often away from the leading performers. [1945–50]

sce•nic (sē′nik, sen′ik), *adj.* Also, **sce′ni•cal. 1.** of or pertaining to natural scenery. **2.** having pleasing or beautiful scenery. **3.** of or pertaining to the stage or to stage scenery. **4.** representing a scene, action, or the like. **—*n.* 5.** a photograph, graphic representation, etc., depicting natural scenery. **6.** a scenic tour: *to arrange scenics in advance.* [1615–25; < L *scēnicus* < Gk *skēnikós* theatrical. See SCENE, -IC] **—sce′ni•cal•ly,** *adv.*

sce′nic rail′way, a railroad that carries its passengers on a brief tour of an amusement park, resort, etc. [1890–95]

sce•nog•ra•phy (sē nog′rə fē), *n.* **1.** the art of representing objects in accordance with the rules of perspective. **2.** scene painting (used esp. with reference to ancient Greece). [1635–45; < Gk *skēnographía.* See SCENE, -O-, -GRAPHY] **—sce•nog′raph•er,** *n.* **—sce•no•graph•ic** (sē′nə graf′ik, sen′ə-), **sce′no•graph′i•cal,** *adj.* **—sce′no•graph′i•cal•ly,** *adv.*

scent (sent), *n.* **1.** a distinctive odor, esp. when agreeable: *the scent of roses.* **2.** an odor left in passing, by means of which an animal or person may be traced. **3.** a track or trail as or as if indicated by such an odor: *The dogs lost the scent and the prisoner escaped.* **4.** perfume. **5.** the sense of smell: *a remarkably keen scent.* **6.** small pieces of paper dropped by the hares in the game of hare and hounds. **—*v.t.* 7.** to perceive or recognize by or as if by the sense of smell: *to scent trouble.* **8.** to fill with an odor; perfume. **—*v.i.* 9.** to hunt by the sense of smell, as a hound. [1325–75; (v.) earlier *sent,* ME *senten* < MF *sentir* to smell < L *sentīre* to feel; (n.) ME, deriv. of the v. Cf. SENSE] **—scent′less,** *adj.* **—scent′less•ness,** *n.* **—Syn. 1.** See **odor. 7.** smell, sniff.

scent′ gland′, any of various specialized skin glands, occurring in many kinds of animals, that emit an odor commonly functioning as a social or sexual signal or a defensive weapon. [1675–85]

scent′less plant′ bug′. See **rhopalid bug.**

scent′ mark′, *Animal Behav.* a distinctive odor that an animal deposits on the ground or other surface, as by urinating, which functions as an identifying signal to other animals of the species.

scent-mark (sent′märk′), *Animal Behav.* **—*v.i.* 1.** to deposit a scent mark; mark. **—*v.t.* 2.** to deposit a scent mark on; mark.

scep•ter (sep′tər), *n.* **1.** a rod or wand borne in the hand as an emblem of regal or imperial power. **2.** royal or imperial power or authority; sovereignty. **—*v.t.* 3.** to give a scepter to; invest with authority. Also, *esp. Brit.,* **sceptre.** [1250–1300; ME *(s)ceptre* < OF < L *scēptrum* < Gk *skêptron* staff; akin to SHAFT] **—scep′ter•less,** *adj.* **—scep•tral** (sep′trəl), *adj.*

S. scepter (def. 1)

scep•tic (skep′tik), *n., adj.* skeptic.

scep•ti•cal (skep′ti kəl), *adj.* skeptical.

scep•ti•cism (skep′tə siz′əm), *n.* skepticism.

scep•tre (sep′tər), *n., v.t.,* **-tred, -tring.** *Chiefly Brit.* scepter.

scf, standard cubic foot.

scfh, standard cubic feet per hour

scfm, standard cubic feet per minute.

Sch., (in Austria) schilling; schillings.

sch., 1. school. **2.** schooner.

Schacht (shäkht), *n.* **(Horace Greeley) Hjal•mar** (yäl′mär), 1877–1970, German financier: acting minister of national economy 1934–37.

scha•den•freu•de (shäd′n froi′də), *n.* satisfaction or pleasure felt at someone else's misfortune. [1890–95; < G, equiv. to *Schaden* harm + *Freude* joy]

Schaer•beek (*Flemish.* skhär′bāk), *n.* a city in central Belgium, near Brussels. 118,950.

Schaerf (sherf), *n.* **A•dolf** (ä′dôlf), 1890–1965, Austrian statesman: president 1957–65.

Scha′fer meth′od (shā′fər). See **prone pressure method.** Also, **Scha′fer's Meth′od.** [named after Sir Edward A. Sharpey-*Schafer* (1850–1935), English physiologist]

Schaff•hau•sen (shäf′hou′zən), *n.* **1.** a canton in N Switzerland. 70,700; 100 sq. mi. (259 sq. km). **2.** a city in and the capital of this canton, on the Rhine. 34,000.

schafs•kopf (shafs′kôpf′), *n. Cards.* sheepshead (def. 4). [< G: sheepshead]

Schal•ly (shal′ē), *n.* **Andrew Victor,** born 1926, U.S. physiologist, born in Poland: Nobel prize 1977.

schap•pe (shä′pə), *v.,* **schapped** (shäpt), **schap•ping,** *n.* **—*v.t.* 1.** to remove sericin from (silk waste) by fermentation. **—*n.* 2.** See **schappe silk.** [1880–85; < Swiss G: raw silk leavings; cf. F *échappement* leakage]

schap′pe silk′, a yarn or fabric of or similar to spun silk. Also called **schappe, chappe.**

Scharn•horst (shärn′hôrst), *n.* **Ger•hard Jo•hann Da•vid von** (gâr′härt yō′hän dä′vēt fən), 1755–1813, Prussian general.

Schar•wen•ka (shär veng′kä), *n.* **1. (Lud•wig) Phi•lipp** (lo͝ot′vikh fē′lip), 1847–1917, German composer. **2.** his brother, **(Franz) Xa•ver** (fränts ksä′vər, ksä vär′), 1850–1924, German pianist and composer.

schat•chen (*Yiddish, Ashk. Heb., Eng.* shät′khən; *Seph. Heb.* shät khän′), *n., pl.* **schat•cha•nim** (*Yiddish, Ashk. Heb.* shät khô′nim; *Seph. Heb.* shät khä nēm′), *Eng.* **schat•chens.** *Yiddish and Hebrew.* shadkhan.

schat•zi (shät′sē), *n. Slang.* sweetheart; darling. [1955–60; < G *Schatzi* (orig. dial., esp. Swiss G), equiv. to *Schatz* treasure (MHG *scha(t)z,* OHG *scaz* property, piece of money; see SCEAT) + *-i* dim. suffix (MHG *-īn;* see -EN[5])]

Schau•dinn (shou′din), *n.* **Fritz** (frits), 1871–1906, German zoologist.

Schaum•burg (shôm′bûrg), *n.* a city in NE Illinois. 52,319.

Schaum•burg-Lip•pe (shoum′bo͝ork lip′ə), *n.* a former state in NW Germany.

schav (shäv, shchäv), *n. Jewish or Eastern European Cookery.* a cold soup of sorrel to which chopped egg, sour cream, lemon juice, and chopped scallions are sometimes added. [< Yiddish *shtshav* sorrel, soup made with sorrel < Pol *szczaw,* akin to Czech *št′avel,* Serbo-Croatian *štȁvelj,* Russ *shchavél′* sorrel]

Schech•ter (shek′tər), *n.* **Solomon,** 1847–1915, U.S. Hebraist, born in Rumania.

sched., schedule.

sched•ule (skej′o͞ol, -o͞ol, -o͞o əl; *Brit.* shed′yo͞ol, shej′o͞ol), *n., v.,* **-uled, -ul•ing. —*n.* 1.** a plan of procedure, usually written, for a proposed objective, esp. with reference to the sequence of and time allotted for each item or operation necessary to its completion: *The schedule allows three weeks for this stage.* **2.** a series of things to be done or of events to occur at or during a particular time or period: *He always has a full schedule.* **3.** a timetable. **4.** a written or printed statement of details, often in classified or tabular form, esp. one forming an appendix or explanatory addition to another document. **5.** *Obs.* a written paper. **—*v.t.* 6.** to make a schedule of or enter in a schedule. **7.** to plan for a certain date: *to schedule publication for June.* [1350–1400; < LL *schedula,* equiv. to L *sched(a)* leaf of paper + *-ula* -ULE; r. ME *cedule, sedule* < MF < LL, as above] **—sched′u•lar,** *adj.* **—sched′ul•er,** *n.* **—Syn. 4.** table, register. See **list**[1]. **6.** register, list, enroll, tabulate.

Schee•le (shā′lə), *n.* **Karl Wil•helm** (kärl vil′helm), 1742–86, Swedish chemist.

Schee′le's green′, copper arsenite used as a pigment, esp. in paints. [1810–20; named after K.W. SCHEELE]

scheel•ite (shā′līt, shē′-), *n. Mineral.* calcium tungstate, $CaWO_4$, usually occurring in tetragonal crystals: an important ore of tungsten. [1830–40; < G *Scheelit,* named after K. W. SCHEELE, who first isolated tungstic acid; see -ITE[1]]

schef•fler•a (shef′lər ə, shef lēr′ə), *n.* **1.** any of various tropical trees or shrubs belonging to the genus *Schefflera,* of the ginseng family, having glossy, palmately compound leaves and often cultivated as a houseplant. **2.** a similar, related plant, *Brassaia actinophylla.* [< NL (1776), after J. C. *Scheffler,* 18th century German botanist; see -A[2]]

Sche•her•a•za•de (shə her′ə zä′də, -zäd′, -hēr′-), *n.* **1.** (in *The Arabian Nights' Entertainments*) the wife of the sultan of India, who relates such interesting tales nightly that the sultan spares her life. **2.** (*italics*) a symphonic suite (1888) by Nikolai Rimski-Korsakov.

Scheldt (skelt), *n.* a river in W Europe, flowing from N France through W Belgium and SW Netherlands into the North Sea. 270 mi. (435 km) long. Flemish, **Schel•de** (skhel′də). French, **Escaut.**

Schel•ling (shel′ing), *n.* **Frie•drich Wil•helm Jo•seph von** (frē′drikh vil′helm yō′zef fən), 1775–1854, German philosopher. **—Schel′ling•ism, Schel•ling•i•an•ism** (she ling′ē ə niz′əm), *n.*

sche•ma (skē′mə), *n., pl.* **sche•ma•ta** (skē′mə tə *or, sometimes,* skē mä′tə, ski-), **sche•mas. 1.** a diagram, plan, or scheme. **2.** an underlying organizational pattern or structure; conceptual framework. **3.** (in Kantian epistemology) a concept, similar to a universal but limited to phenomenal knowledge, by which an object of knowledge or an idea of pure reason may be apprehended. [1790–1800; < Gk *schêma* form]

sche•mat•ic (skē mat′ik, ski-), *adj.* **1.** pertaining to or of the nature of a schema, diagram, or scheme; diagrammatic. **—*n.* 2.** a diagram, plan, or drawing: *Read the schematic before attempting any repairs.* [1695–1705; < NL *schēmaticus* < Gk *schēmatikós.* See SCHEME, -IC] **—sche•mat′i•cal•ly,** *adv.*

sche•ma•tism (skē′mə tiz′əm), *n.* **1.** the particular form or disposition of a thing. **2.** a schematic arrangement. [1610–20; < Gk *schēmatismós.* See SCHEMATIZE, -ISM]

sche•ma•tize (skē′mə tīz′), *v.t.,* **-tized, -tiz•ing.** to reduce to or arrange according to a scheme. Also, *esp. Brit.,* **sche′ma•tise′.** [1640–50; < Gk *schēmatízein* to form. See SCHEME, -IZE] **—sche′ma•ti•za′tion,** *n.* **—sche′ma•tiz′er,** *n.*

scheme (skēm), *n., v.,* **schemed, schem•ing. —*n.* 1.** a plan, design, or program of action to be followed; project. **2.** an underhand plot; intrigue. **3.** a visionary or impractical project. **4.** a body or system of related doctrines, theories, etc.: *a scheme of philosophy.* **5.** any system of correlated things, parts, etc., or the manner of its arrangement. **6.** a plan, program, or policy officially adopted and followed, as by a government or business: *The company's pension scheme is very successful.* **7.** an analytical or tabular statement. **8.** a diagram, map, or the like. **9.** an astrological diagram of the heavens. **—*v.t.* 10.** to devise as a scheme; plan; plot; contrive. **—*v.i.* 11.** to lay schemes; devise plans; plot. [1545–55; < ML *schēma* (s. *schēmat-*) < Gk *schêma* form, figure] **—scheme′less,** *adj.* **—schem′er,** *n.* **—Syn. 1, 6.** See **plan. 2.** stratagem, cabal, conspiracy. **5.** pattern, schema. **10.** See **plot**[1].

schem•ing (skē′ming), *adj.* given to making plans, esp. sly and underhand ones; crafty. [1830–40; SCHEME + -ING[2]] **—schem′ing•ly,** *adv.* **—Syn.** artful, calculating, cunning.

Sche•nec•ta•dy (skə nek′tə dē), *n.* a city in E New York, on the Mohawk River. 67,972.

Scher•er•ville (shēr′ər vil′), *n.* a town in NW Indiana. 13,209.

scherm (skerm, skûrm), *n.* (in South Africa) a hut, screen, or shelter constructed from branches and canvas, scraped animal hides, or the like. [1860–65; < Afrik *skerm* screen, shelter < D *scherm* screen, (earlier) shelter]

scher•zan•do (skert sän′dō, -san′-), *adj.* (a musical direction) playful; sportive. [1805–15; < It, ger. of *scherzare* to joke; see SCHERZO]

scher•zo (skert′sō), *n., pl.* **scher•zos, scher•zi** (skert′sē). *Music.* a movement or passage of light or playful character, esp. as the second or third movement of a sonata or a symphony. [1850–55; < It: joke, deriv. of *scherzare* to joke, of Langobardic orig.]

Sche•ven•ing•en (skhā′vən ing′ən), *n.* a town in the W Netherlands, near The Hague: seaside resort.

Schia•pa•rel•li (skyä′pə rel′ē *or, esp. for 1,* skap′ə-rel′ē, shap′-; *It.* skyä′pä rel′lē), *n.* **1. El•sa** (el′sä), 1890–1973, French fashion designer, born in Italy. **2. Gio•van•ni Vir•gin•io** (jô vän′nē vēr jē′nyô), 1835–1910, Italian astronomer.

Schick (shik), *n.* **Bé•la** (bā′lə; *Hung.* bā′lo), 1877–1967, U.S. pediatrician, born in Hungary.

Schick′ test′, *Med.* a diphtheria immunity test in which diphtheria toxoid is injected intracutaneously, nonimmunity being indicated by an inflammation at the injection site. [1915–20; named after B. SCHICK]

Schie•dam (skhē däm′), *n.* a city in SW Netherlands. 71,280.

schiff•li (shif′lē), *n.* **1.** a large, loomlike machine for embroidering textiles and working patterns in lace. **2.** the delicate work produced by such a machine, used on clothing, as lingerie and millinery, on furniture coverings, etc. [< SwissG: lit., little ship]

Schiff′ rea′gent (shif), *Chem.* a solution of rosaniline and sulfurous acid in water, used to test for the presence of aldehydes. Also, **Schiff's′ rea′gent.** [1895–1900; named after Hugo *Schiff,* 1834–1915, German chemist]

schil•ler (shil′ər), *n.* a bronzelike luster, sometimes with iridescence, occurring on certain minerals. [1795–1805; < G: play of colors, glitter]

Schil•ler (shil′ər), *n.* **1. Ferdinand Can•ning Scott** (kan′ing), 1864–1937, English philosopher in the U.S. **2. Jo•hann Chris•toph Frie•drich von** (yō′hän kris′tôf frē′drikh fən), 1759–1805, German poet, dramatist, and historian. **3.** *Astron.* an elliptical walled plain in the third quadrant of the face of the moon: about 112 miles (180 km) in length and 60 miles (100 km) in width.

schil•ler•ize (shil′ə rīz′), *v.t.,* **-ized, -iz•ing.** to give a schiller to (a crystal) by developing microscopic inclusions along certain planes. Also, *esp. Brit.,* **schil′ler•ise′.** [1880–85; SCHILLER + -IZE] **—schil′ler•i•za′tion,** *n.*

Schil′ler Park′, a town in NE Illinois. 11,458.

schil•ling (shil′ing), *n.* **1.** a copper and aluminum coin and monetary unit of Austria, equal to 100 groschen. *Abbr.:* S., Sch. **2.** any of various former minor coins of Germany. [1745–55; < G; c. SHILLING]

Schi•pa (skē′pä), *n.* **Ti•to** (tē′tô), 1890–1965, Italian operatic tenor.

schip•per•ke (skip′ər kē, -kə), *n.* one of a Belgian breed of small dogs having erect ears and a thick, black coat, originally used as a watchdog on boats in the Netherlands and Belgium. [1885–90; < dial. D: little boatman, equiv. to *schipper* SKIPPER[1] + *-ke* -KIN]

Schip•pers (ship′ərz), *n.* **Thomas,** 1930–77, U.S. orchestra conductor.

Schir•mer (shûr′mər), *n.* **Gus•tav** (go͝os′täf), 1829–93, born in Germany, and his sons **Rudolph Edward,** 1859–1919, and **Gustave,** 1864–1907, U.S. music publishers.

Schir•ra (shi rä′), *n.* **Walter Mar•ty, Jr.** (mär′tē), born 1923, U.S. astronaut.

schism (siz′əm, skiz′-), *n.* **1.** division or disunion, esp. into mutually opposed parties. **2.** the parties so formed. **3.** *Eccles.* **a.** a formal division within, or separation from, a church or religious body over some doctrinal difference. **b.** the state of a sect or body formed by such division. **c.** the offense of causing or seeking to cause such a division. [1350–1400; < LL (Vulgate) *sc(h)isma* (s. *sc(h)ismat-*) < Gk, deriv. of *schízein* to split, with *-ma* (s. *-mat-*) n. suffix of result; r. ME *(s)cisme, sisme* < MF < LL, as above] **—schism′less,** *adj.*

schis•mat•ic (siz mat′ik, skiz-), *adj.* **1.** Also, **schis•mat′i•cal.** of, pertaining to, or of the nature of schism; guilty of schism. **—*n.* 2.** a person who promotes schism or is an adherent of a schismatic body. [1350–1400; < LL *schismaticus* < Gk *schismatikós* (see SCHISM, -IC); r.

CONCISE PRONUNCIATION KEY: act, cāpe, dâre, pärt; set, ēqual; *if,* ice; ox, ōver, ôrder, oil, bo͝ok, bo͞ot, out; up, ûrge; child; sing; shoe; thin, *th*at; zh as in *treasure.* ə = *a* as in *alone, e* as in *system, i* as in *easily, o* as in *gallop, u* as in *circus;* ᵊ as in *fire* (fīᵊr), *hour* (ouᵊr). l and n can serve as syllabic consonants, as in *cradle* (krād′l), and *button* (but′n). See the full key inside the front cover.

ME *scismatik* < MF *scismatique* < LL, as above] —**schis·mat′i·cal·ly,** *adv.* —**schis·mat′i·cal·ness,** *n.*

schis·ma·tist (siz′mə tist, skiz′-), *n.* schismatic (def. 2). [1745–55; < LL *schismat-* (see SCHISM) + -IST]

schis·ma·tize (siz′mə tīz′, skiz′-), *v.*, **-tized, -tiz·ing.** —*v.i.* **1.** to take part in a schism. —*v.t.* **2.** to cause schism in. Also, *esp. Brit.*, **schis′ma·tise′.** [1595–1605; < LL *schismat-* (see SCHISM) + -IZE]

schist (shist), *n.* any of a class of crystalline metamorphic rocks whose constituent mineral grains have a more or less parallel or foliated arrangement. [1775–85; < NL *schistus,* L (*lapis*) *schistos* < Gk *schistós* divided, curdled, divisible, deriv. of *schízein* to split, with *-tos* adj. suffix]

schis·tose (shis′tōs), *adj.* of, resembling, or in the form of schist. Also, **schis·tous** (shis′təs). [1785–95; SCHIST + -OSE[1]] —**schis·tos·i·ty** (shi stos′i tē), *n.*

schis·to·sis (shi stō′sis), *n. Pathol.* fibrosis of the lungs caused by inhaling dust from slate. [SCHIST + -OSIS]

schis·to·some (shis′tə sōm′), *n.* **1.** Also called **bilharzia.** any elongated trematode of the genus *Schistosoma,* parasitic in the blood vessels of humans and other mammals; a blood fluke. —*adj.* **2.** Also, **schis′to·so′mal.** pertaining to or caused by schistosomes. [1900–05; < NL *Schistosoma,* equiv. to *schist(us)* (see SCHIST) + *-o-* -O- + *-soma* (neut. pl.) -SOME[3]]

schis·to·so·mi·a·sis (shis′tə sō mī′ə sis), *n. Pathol.* an infection caused by parasitic flukes of the genus *Schistosoma,* occurring commonly in eastern Asia and in tropical regions and transmitted to humans through feces-contaminated fresh water or snails: symptoms commonly include pain, anemia, and malfunction of the infected organ. Also called **bilharziasis, snail fever.** [1905–10; SCHISTOSOME + -IASIS]

schit·zo (skit′sō), *n., pl.* **-zos,** *adj. Informal.* schizo (defs. 1, 2).

schiz (skits), *n., adj. Informal.* schizo (defs. 1, 2). Also, **schitz.** [1950–55; by shortening]

schi·zan·thus (ski zan′thəs), *n.* any of several plants of the genus *Schizanthus,* native to Chile, having numerous variously colored flowers resembling small orchids. Also called **butterfly flower.** [< NL (1794) < Gk *schiz-* SCHIZ- + *ánthos* flower; cf. ANTHO-]

schiz·o (skit′sō), *n., pl.* **schiz·os,** *adj. Informal.* —*n.* **1.** a schizophrenic or schizoid person. —*adj.* **2.** schizophrenic or schizoid. **3.** crazy; wildly eccentric; lunatic. Also, **schitzo, schitz, schiz** (for defs. 1, 2). [1940–45; by shortening; cf. -O]

schizo-, a combining form meaning "split," used in the formation of compound words: *schizogenetic.* Also, *esp. before a vowel,* **schiz-.** [< Gk, comb. form repr. *schízein* to part, split]

schiz′o·af·fec′tive disor′der (skit′sō ə fek′tiv, skit′sō-), a psychotic disorder in which symptoms of schizophrenia and affective disorder occur simultaneously. [1930–35; SCHIZO(PHRENIC) + AFFECTIVE]

schiz·o·carp (skiz′ə kärp′, skit′sə-), *n. Bot.* a dry, dehiscent fruit that at maturity splits into two or more one-seeded carpels. [1865–70; SCHIZO- + -CARP] —**schiz′o·car′pous, schiz′o·car′pic,** *adj.*

schi·zog·a·my (ski zog′ə mē, skit sog′-), *n. Biol.* reproduction characterized by division of the organism into sexual and asexual parts, as in certain polychaetes. [SCHIZO- + -GAMY]

schiz·o·gen·e·sis (skiz′ə jen′ə sis, skit′sə-), *n. Biol.* reproduction by fission. [1890–95; SCHIZO- + -GENESIS]

schiz·o·ge·net·ic (skiz′ō jə net′ik, skit′sō-), *adj. Biol.* reproducing or formed by fission. Also, **schiz·o·gen·ic** (skiz′ə jen′ik, skit′sə-), **schizogenous.** [1880–85; SCHIZO- + GENETIC] —**schiz′o·ge·net′i·cal·ly,** *adv.*

schi·zog·e·nous (ski zoj′ə nəs, skit soj′-), *adj. Biol.* **1.** schizogenetic. **2.** schizogonous. [1880–85; SCHIZO- + -GENOUS] —**schi·zog′e·nous·ly,** *adv.*

schi·zog·o·nous (ski zog′ə nəs, skit sog′-), *adj. Biol.* pertaining to or reproducing by schizogony. Also, **schiz·o·gon·ic** (skiz′ə gon′ik, skit′sə-), **schizogenous.** [SCHIZO- + -GONOUS]

schi·zog·o·ny (ski zog′ə nē, skit sog′-), *n. Biol.* (in the asexual reproduction of certain sporozoans) the multiple fission of a trophozoite or schizont into merozoites. [1885–90; SCHIZO- + -GONY]

schiz·oid (skit′soid), *adj.* **1.** *Psychol.* of or pertaining to a personality disorder marked by dissociation, passivity, withdrawal, inability to form warm social relationships, and indifference to praise or criticism. **2.** *Informal.* of or pertaining to schizophrenia or to multiple personality. —*n.* **3.** a schizoid person. [1920–25; SCHIZ- + -OID]

schiz·o·my·cete (skiz′ō mī′sēt, -mī sēt′, skit′sō-), *n.* any of numerous microorganisms of the subkingdom (or phylum) Schizophyta, kingdom Monera, comprising the bacteria. [1875–80; < NL; see SCHIZO-, -MYCETE] —**schiz′o·my·ce′tic, schiz′o·my·ce′tous,** *adj.*

schiz·o·my·co·sis (skiz′ō mī kō′sis, skit′sō-), *n. Pathol.* any disease due to schizomycetes. [SCHIZO- + MYCOSIS]

schiz·ont (skiz′ont, skit′sont), *n. Biol.* (in the asexual reproduction of certain sporozoans) a cell developed from a trophozoite, which undergoes multiple fission to form merozoites. [1895–1900; SCHIZ- + *-ont* being; see ONTO-]

schiz·o·phre·ni·a (skit′sə frē′nē ə, -frēn′yə), *n.* **1.** *Psychiatry.* Also called **dementia praecox.** a severe mental disorder characterized by some, but not necessarily all, of the following features: emotional blunting, intellectual deterioration, social isolation, disorganized speech and behavior, delusions, and hallucinations. **2.** a state characterized by the coexistence of contradictory or incompatible elements. [1910–15; SCHIZO- + -PHRENIA] —**schiz·o·phren·ic** (skit′sə fren′ik), *adj., n.*

schiz·o·phre·no·gen·ic (skit′sə frē′nə jen′ik, -fren′-), *adj.* causative of schizophrenia. [1945–50; SCHIZOPHREN(IA) + -O- + -GENIC]

schiz·o·phy·ceous (skiz′ə fī′shəs, -fish′əs, skit′sə-), *adj.* belonging to the Schizophyceae, a group of unicellular bluish-green algae, occurring in both salt and fresh water and often causing pollution of drinking water. [< NL *Schizophyce(ae)* (see SCHIZO-, PHYCO-, -EAE) + -OUS]

schiz·o·phyte (skiz′ə fīt′, skit′sə-), *n.* any of the Schizophyta, a group of organisms comprising the schizomycetes and the schizophyceous algae, characterized by a simple structure and reproduction by simple fission or spores. [1875–80; SCHIZO- + -PHYTE] —**schiz·o·phyt·ic** (skiz′ə fit′ik, skit′sə-), *adj.*

schiz·o·pod (skiz′ə pod′, skit′sə-), *n.* **1.** any crustacean of the former order or division Schizopoda, now divided into the orders Mysidacea, comprising the opossum shrimps, and Euphausiacea, comprising krill. —*adj.* **2.** Also, **schi·zop·o·dous** (ski zop′ə dəs, skit sop′-). belonging or pertaining to the Schizopoda. [1835–45; < NL *Schizopoda;* see SCHIZO-, -POD]

schiz·o·typ′al personal′ity (skit′sə tī′pəl), a personality disorder characterized by a group of symptoms similar to but less severe than schizophrenia, as odd behavior, peculiar thinking, and social isolation. [1960–65; SCHIZO(PHRENIA) + -TYPE + -AL[1]]

schiz·y (skit′sē), *adj.,* **schiz·i·er, schiz·i·est.** *Informal.* schizoid or schizophrenic. Also, **schiz′zy.** [1925–30; SCHIZ(OPHRENIA) + -Y[1]; cf. SCHIZ, SCHIZO]

schlag (shläg), *n. Viennese Cookery.* whipped cream, used esp. as a topping for cake, coffee, etc. [< Austrian G *Schlag,* short for *Schlagobers* whipped cream, equiv. to G *Schlag* blow (n. corresponding to *schlagen* to strike, hit; see SLAY) + Austrian G *Obers* (cf. G *ober* UPPER)]

Schle·gel (shlā′gəl), *n.* **1. Au·gust Wil·helm von** (ou′go͝ost vil′helm fən), 1767–1845, German poet, critic, and translator. **2.** his brother, **Frie·drich von** (frē′drɪKH fən), 1772–1829, German critic, philosopher, and poet.

Schlei·cher (shlī′kər; *Ger.* shlī′KHəR), *n.* **August,** 1821–68, German linguist.

Schlei·den (shlīd′n), *n.* **Mat·thi·as Ja·kob** (mä tē′äs yä′kôp), 1804–81, German botanist.

Schlei·er·ma·cher (shlī′əR mä′KHəR), *n.* **Frie·drich Ernst Da·ni·el** (frē′drɪKH ernst dä′nē el′), 1768–1834, German theologian and philosopher.

schle·miel (shlə mēl′), *n. Slang.* an awkward and unlucky person for whom things never turn out right. Also, **schle·mihl′, shlemiel.** [1890–95; < Yiddish *shlemil* < Heb *shəlumī'ēl* Shelumiel, a Biblical and Talmudic figure]

schlep (shlep), *v.,* **schlepped, schlep·ping,** *n. Slang.* —*v.t.* **1.** to carry; lug: *to schlep an umbrella on a sunny day.* —*v.i.* **2.** to move slowly, awkwardly, or tediously: *We schlepped from store to store all day.* —*n.* **3.** Also, **schlep′per.** someone or something that is tedious, slow, or awkward; drag. Also, **schlepp, shlep, shlepp.** [1920–25; < Yiddish *shlepn* to pull, drag, (intrans.) trudge < MHG dial. *sleppen* < MLG, MD *slēpen;* c. MHG, OHG *sleifen* (G *schleifen*); akin to SLIP[1], SLIPPERY]

schlep·py (shlep′ē), *adj.,* **-pi·er, -pi·est.** *Slang.* **1.** slovenly, dowdy, or run-down; frumpy: *a schleppy hotel; a schleppy old bathrobe.* **2.** awkward, clumsy, or dull. [SCHLEP + -Y[1]]

Schle·si·en (shlā′zē ən), *n.* German name of **Silesia.**

Schles·in·ger (shles′in jər, shlā′zing ər), *n.* **1. Arthur Mei·er** (mī′ər), 1888–1965, U.S. historian. **2.** his son, **Arthur Meier, Jr.,** born 1917, U.S. historian and writer.

Schles·wig (shles′wig; *Ger.* shläs′vik), *n.* **1.** a seaport in N Germany, on the Baltic. 30,700. **2.** a historic region in S Jutland: a former duchy of Denmark; annexed by Prussia 1864; the N part was returned to Denmark as the result of a plebiscite 1920. Also **Sleswick.** Danish, **Slesvig.**

Schles·wig-Hol·stein (shles′wig hōl′stīn; *Ger.* shläs′vik hôl′shtīn), *n.* **1.** two contiguous duchies of Denmark that were a center of international tension in the 19th century: Prussia annexed Schleswig 1864 and Holstein 1866. **2.** a state of N Germany, including the former duchies of Holstein and Lauenburg and part of Schleswig. 2,564,565; 6073 sq. mi. (15,728 sq. km). *Cap.:* Kiel.

Schley (slī), *n.* **Win·field Scott** (win′fēld′), 1839–1911, U.S. rear admiral.

Schlie·mann (shlē′män′), *n.* **Hein·rich** (hīn′rɪKH), 1822–90, German archaeologist: excavated ancient cities of Troy and Mycenae.

schlie·ren (shlēr′ən), *n.* (*used with a plural v.*) **1.** *Petrog.* streaks or irregularly shaped masses in an igneous rock that differ in texture or composition from the main mass. **2.** *Physics.* the visible streaks in a turbulent, transparent fluid, each streak being a region that has a density and index of refraction differing from that of the greater part of the fluid. [1885–90; < G, pl. of *Schliere* streak]

schlie′ren meth′od, *Physical Chem.* a method for detecting regions of differing densities in a clear fluid by photographing a beam of light passed obliquely through it. [1930–35]

schli·ma·zel (shli mä′zəl), *n. Slang.* an inept, bungling person who suffers from unremitting bad luck. Also, **schli·mazl′, shlimazel, shlimazl.** [1945–50; < Yiddish, equiv. to *shlim* bad (cf. MHG *slimp* wrong) + *mazl* luck < ModHeb *mazzāl*]

schlock (shlok), *Slang.* —*adj.* **1.** Also, **schlocky.** cheap; trashy: *a schlock store.* —*n.* **2.** something of cheap or inferior quality; junk. Also, **shlock.** [1910–15; appar. < Yiddish *shlak* apoplectic stroke, evil, nuisance, wretch (cf. MHG *slac(g)* blow; see SLAY); though development of E sense is unclear]

schlock·meis·ter (shlok′mī′stər), *n. Slang.* a person who deals in or sells inferior or worthless goods; junk dealer. [1960–65, *Amer.;* SCHLOCK + Yiddish *mayster* or G *Meister* master craftsman; MHG *meister,* OHG *meistar* < L *magister;* see MASTER]

schlock·y (shlok′ē), *adj.,* **schlock·i·er, schlock·i·est.** *Slang.* schlock (def. 1). Also, **shlocky.** [SCHLOCK + -Y[1]]

Schloss (shlôs), *n., pl.* ***Schlös·ser*** (shlœ′səR). *German.* a castle or palace.

schlub (shlub), *n.* zhlob.

schlump (shlo͝omp), *Slang.* —*n.* **1.** a dull, colorless person. **2.** a slovenly person; slob. —*v.i.* **3.** to loaf or idle. Also, **shlump.** [1950–55; prob. of expressive orig.]

Schmal·kal·den (shmäl′käl′dn), *n.* a town in SW East Germany: a league to defend Protestantism formed here 1531. 16,806.

schmaltz (shmälts, shmôlts), *n.* **1.** *Informal.* exaggerated sentimentalism, as in music or soap operas. **2.** fat or grease, esp. of a chicken. Also, **schmalz.** [1930–35; < Yiddish *shmalts* or G *Schmaltz;* c. SMELT[1]]

schmaltz·y (shmält′sē, shmôlt′-), *adj.* **schmaltz·i·er, schmaltz·i·est.** *Informal.* of, pertaining to, or characterized by schmaltz. Also, **schmalz′y.** [1930–35; SCHMALTZ + -Y[1]]

schmat·te (shmä′tə), *n. Slang.* **1.** an old ragged garment; tattered article of clothing. **2.** any garment. Also, **shmatte.** [1965–70, *Amer.;* < Yiddish *shmate* rag < Pol *szmata*]

schmear (shmēr), *Slang.* —*n.* **1.** a dab, as of cream cheese, spread on a roll, bagel, or the like. **2.** a number of related things, ideas, etc., resulting in a unified appearance, attitude, plan, or the like (usually used in the phrase *the whole schmear*). **3.** a bribe. —*v.t.* **4.** to spread; smear: *Schmear it on the bread.* **5.** to bribe. [1960–65; appar. < Yiddish *shmirn* to smear, grease; cf. MHG *smirwen* (G *schmieren*); see SMEAR]

Schme·ling (shmel′ing; *Ger.* shmā′ling), *n.* **Max** (maks; *Ger.* mäks) born 1905, German boxer: world heavyweight champion 1930–32.

Schmidt (shmit), *n.* **Hel·mut (Hein·rich Wal·de·mar)** (hel′mo͞ot hīn′rik väl′də mär′; *Ger.* hel′mo͞ot hīn′rɪKH väl′də mäR′), born 1918, West German political leader: chancellor 1974–82.

Schmidt′ tel′escope, a wide-angle reflecting telescope used primarily for astronomical photography, in which spherical aberration and coma are reduced to a minimum by means of a spherical mirror with a corrector plate near its focus. Also called **Schmidt′ reflec′tor.** [1935–40; named after Bernard *Schmidt* (1879–1935), German inventor]

schmier·kase (shmēr′käz′, -kä′zə), *n.* See **cottage cheese.** [1900–05; < G: lit., smear-cheese]

Schmitt (shmit), *n.* **1. Ber·na·dotte Ev·er·ly** (bûr′nə dot′ ev′ər lē), 1886–1969, U.S. historian. **2. Harrison (Ha·gan)** (hā′gən), ("*Jack*"), born 1935, U.S. astronaut, geologist, and politician: U.S. senator 1977–83.

schmo (shmō), *n., pl.* **schmoes.** *Slang.* a foolish, boring, or stupid person; a jerk. Also, **schmoe.** [1945–50, *Amer.;* of obscure orig.]

schmoose (shmo͞oz, shmo͞os), *v.i.,* **schmoosed, schmoos·ing.,** *n.* schmooze. Also, **schmoos.**

schmooze (shmo͞oz), *v.,* **schmoozed, schmooz·ing,** *n. Slang.* —*v.i.* **1.** to chat idly; gossip. —*n.* **2.** idle conversation; chatter. Also, **schmoose, schmoos.** [1895–1900, *Amer.;* < Yiddish, v. use of *schmues* < Heb *shəmū'ōth* reports, gossip] —**schmooz′er,** *n.*

schmuck (shmuk), *n. Slang.* an obnoxious or contemptible person. [1890–95; < Yiddish *shmok* (vulgar) lit., penis (of uncert. orig.)]

Sch.Mus.B., Bachelor of School Music.

schmutz (shmo͝ots), *n. Slang.* dirt; filth; garbage. [1965–70; < Yiddish *shmuts* or G *Schmutz,* MHG *smuz;* cf. SMUDGE, SMUT, ME *bismotered* bespattered, soiled (all presumably expressive vars. of same Gmc base)]

schmutz·y (shmo͝ot′sē), *adj.,* **schmutz·i·er, schmutz·i·est.** *Slang.* dirty; grimy. Also, **schmutz·ig** (shmo͝ot′sik, -sig). [1965–70; SCHMUTZ + -Y[1], as trans. of Yiddish *shmutsik* or G *schmutzig*]

Schna·bel (shnä′bəl), *n.* **Ar·tur** (äR′to͞oR), 1882–1951, Austrian pianist.

schnap·per (shnap′ər, snap′-), *n.* a food fish, *Pagrosomus auratus,* occurring in large numbers off the shores of Australia and New Zealand. [1820–30; var. of SNAPPER; *sch* < G]

schnapps (shnäps, shnaps), *n.* **1.** (in Europe) any strong, dry spirit, as slivovitz, aquavit, or kirsch. **2.** a drink of schnapps. Also, **schnaps.** [1810–20; < G < D or LG *snaps* lit., gulp, mouthful, der. of *snappen* to SNAP]

schnau·zer (shnou′zər; *Ger.* shnou′tsəR), *n.* one of a German breed of sturdy medium-sized dogs having a tight, wiry, pepper-and-salt or pure black coat, bristly

CONCISE ETYMOLOGY KEY: <, descended or borrowed from; >, whence; b., blend of, blended; c., cognate with; cf., compare; deriv., derivative; equiv., equivalent; imit., imitative; obl., oblique; r., replacing; s., stem; sp., spelling, spelled; resp., respelling, respelled; trans., translation; ?, origin unknown; *, unattested; ‡, probably earlier than. See the full key inside the front cover.

eyebrows and beardlike whiskers, and a docked tail, used originally as a ratter and a guard dog and later used in police work. Also called **standard schnauzer.** Cf. **giant schnauzer, miniature schnauzer.** [1920–25; < G, equiv. to *Schnauze* SNOUT + *-er* -ER[1]]

schnauzer, 19 in. (48 cm) high at shoulder

schneck·en (shnek′ən), *n.pl., sing.* **schneck·e** (shnek′ə). sweet, spiral, snail-shaped rolls made from raised dough with chopped nuts, butter, and cinnamon. [< G: lit., snail, OHG *snecko.* See SNAIL]

schnei·der (shnī′dər), (in gin rummy) —*v.t.* **1.** to prevent (an opponent) from scoring a point in a game or match. —*n.* **2.** an act of schneidering or the fact of being schneidered. [1930–35; < G: tailor]

Schnei·der·man (shnī′dər mən), *n.* **Rose,** 1884–1972, U.S. labor leader, born in Poland.

schnit·zel (shnit′səl), *n.* a cutlet, esp. of veal. [1850–55, *Amer.*; < G: a shaving, deriv. of *schnitzeln* to whittle]

Schnitz·ler (shnits′lər; *Ger.* shnits′ləʀ), *n.* **Ar·thur** (är′thər; *Ger.* äʀ′to͝oʀ), 1862–1931, Austrian dramatist and novelist.

schnook (shno͝ok), *n. Slang.* an unimportant or stupid person; dope. [1945–50, *Amer.*; of uncert. orig.]

schnor·kle (shnôr′kəl), *n.* (formerly) snorkel (def. 1). Also, **schnor′kel.**

schnor·rer (shnôr′ər, shnōr′-), *n. Slang.* a person who habitually borrows or lives at the expense of others with no intention of repaying; sponger; moocher; beggar. Also, **shnorrer.** [1890–95; < Yiddish *shnorer* beggar, sponger, equiv. to *shnor(n)* to beg (cf. MHG *snurren* to hum, buzz, whir; sense "beg" from beggars' custom of playing a small pipe or whistle (G *Schnurrpfeife*)) + *-er* -ER[1]]

schnoz (shnoz), *n. Slang.* a nose, esp. one of unusually large size. Also, **schnozz, schnoz·zle** (shnoz′əl), **schnoz·zo·la** (schno zō′lə) [1935–40, *Amer.*; prob. expressive alter. of NOSE, NOZZLE; *schn-* by assoc. with any of several semantically related Yiddish words, e.g. *shnabl* beak, *shnoyts* SNOUT, *shnuk* beak, trunk; for suffix of *schnozzola* see -OLA]

Schoen·heim·er (shōn′hī′mər; *Ger.* shœn′hī′məʀ), *n.* **Ru·dolf** (ro͞o′dolf; *Ger.* ʀo͞o′dôlf), 1898–1941, U.S. biochemist, born in Germany.

Scho·field (skō′fēld′), *n.* **John Mc·Al·lis·ter** (məkal′i stər), 1831–1906, U.S. general.

Scho′field Bar′racks, a town on central Oahu, in central Hawaii. 18,851.

scho·la can·to·rum (skō′lə kan tôr′əm, -tōr′-), *pl.* **scho·lae can·to·rum** (skō′lē kan tôr′əm, -tōr′-). **1.** an ecclesiastical choir or choir school. **2.** a section of a church, cathedral, or the like, for use by the choir. [1775–85; < ML *schola cantōrum* school of singers]

schol·ar (skol′ər), *n.* **1.** a learned or erudite person, esp. one who has profound knowledge of a particular subject. **2.** a student; pupil. **3.** a student who has been awarded a scholarship. [bef. 1000; < LL *scholāris,* equiv. to L *schol(a)* SCHOOL[1] + *-āris* -AR[1]; r. ME *scoler(e),* OE *scolere* < LL, as above] —**schol′ar·less,** *adj.*
—**Syn. 1.** savant. **2.** See **pupil**[1].

schol·arch (skol′ärk), *n.* **1.** the head of a school. **2.** the head of a school of philosophy in ancient Athens. [1860–65; < Gk *scholárchēs.* See SCHOOL[1], -ARCH]

schol·ar·ly (skol′ər lē), *adj.* **1.** of, like, or befitting a scholar: *scholarly habits.* **2.** having the qualities of a scholar: *a scholarly person.* **3.** concerned with academic learning and research. —*adv.* **4.** like a scholar. [1590–1600; SCHOLAR + -LY] —**schol′ar·li·ness,** *n.*

schol·ar·ship (skol′ər ship′), *n.* **1.** learning; knowledge acquired by study; the academic attainments of a scholar. **2.** a sum of money or other aid granted to a student, because of merit, need, etc., to pursue his or her studies. **3.** the position or status of such a student. **4.** a foundation to provide financial assistance to students. [1525–35; SCHOLAR + -SHIP]
—**Syn. 1.** See **learning.**

scho·las·tic (skə las′tik), *adj.* Also, **scho·las′ti·cal. 1.** of or pertaining to schools, scholars, or education: *scholastic attainments.* **2.** of or pertaining to secondary education or schools: *a scholastic meet.* **3.** pedantic. **4.** of or pertaining to the medieval schoolmen. —*n.* **5.** (*sometimes cap.*) a schoolman, a disciple of the schoolmen, or an adherent of scholasticism. **6.** a pedantic person. **7.** *Rom. Cath. Ch.* a student in a scholasticate. [1590–1600; < L *scholasticus* < Gk *scholastikós* studious, learned, deriv. of *scholázein* to be at leisure to study. See SCHOOL[1], -TIC] —**scho·las′ti·cal·ly,** *adv.*

Scholas′tic Ap′titude Test′, *Trademark.* a standardized aptitude test for college admission developed by the College Entrance Examination Board, consisting of questions testing verbal and mathematical skills that are graded on a scale from 200 to 800 points and according to percentile rank. *Abbr.:* SAT

scho·las·ti·cate (skə las′ti kāt′, -kit), *n. Rom. Cath. Ch.* **1.** a course of study for seminarians, taken prior to their theological studies. **2.** a school for this course of study. [1870–75; < NL *scholasticātus.* See SCHOLASTIC, -ATE[3]]

scho·las·ti·cism (skə las′tə siz′əm), *n.* **1.** (*sometimes cap.*) the system of theological and philosophical teaching predominant in the Middle Ages, based chiefly upon the authority of the church fathers and of Aristotle and his commentators. **2.** narrow adherence to traditional teachings, doctrines, or methods. [1750–60; SCHOLASTIC + -ISM]

scho·li·ast (skō′lē ast′), *n.* **1.** an ancient commentator on the classics. **2.** a person who writes scholia. [1575–85; < Gk *scholiastḗs.* See SCHOLIUM, -IST] —**scho′li·as′tic,** *adj.*

scho·li·um (skō′lē əm), *n., pl.* **-li·a** (-lē ə). **1.** Often, **scholia. a.** an explanatory note or comment. **b.** an ancient annotation upon a passage in a Greek or Latin text. **2.** a note added to illustrate or amplify, as in a mathematical work. [1525–35; < ML < Gk *schólion,* equiv. to *schol(ḗ)* SCHOOL[1] + *-ion* dim. suffix]

Schom·burg (shom′bûrg), *n.* **Arthur Alfonso,** 1874–1938, U.S. scholar and collector of books on black literature and history, born in Puerto Rico.

Schön·bein (shœn′bīn), *n.* **Chris·ti·an Frie·drich** (kʀis′tē än′ fʀē′dʀiKH), 1799–1868, Swiss chemist.

Schön·berg (shœn′bûrg; *Ger.* shœn′berk), *n.* **Ar·nold** (är′nəld; *Ger.* äʀ′nôlt), 1874–1951, Austrian composer in the U.S.

Schö·ne Mül·ler·in, Die (*Ger.* dē shœ′nə mʏ′ləʀ in), a song cycle (1823), by Franz Schubert, consisting of 20 songs set to poems by Wilhelm Müller.

Schon·gau·er (shōn′gou ər; *Ger.* shōn′gou əʀ), *n.* **Mar·tin** (mär′tn; *Ger.* mäʀ′tēn), c1430–91, German engraver and painter.

school[1] (sko͞ol), *n.* **1.** an institution where instruction is given, esp. to persons under college age: *The children are at school.* **2.** an institution for instruction in a particular skill or field. **3.** a college or university. **4.** a regular course of meetings of a teacher or teachers and students for instruction; program of instruction: *summer school.* **5.** a session of such a course: *no school today; to be kept after school.* **6.** the activity or process of learning under instruction, esp. at a school for the young: *As a child, I never liked school.* **7.** one's formal education: *They plan to be married when he finishes school.* **8.** a building housing a school. **9.** the body of students, or students and teachers, belonging to an educational institution: *The entire school rose when the principal entered the auditorium.* **10.** a building, room, etc., in a university, set apart for the use of one of the faculties or for some particular purpose: *the school of agriculture.* **11.** a particular faculty or department of a university having the right to recommend candidates for degrees, and usually beginning its program of instruction after the student has completed general education: *medical school.* **12.** any place, situation, etc., tending to teach anything. **13.** the body of pupils or followers of a master, system, method, etc.: *the Platonic school of philosophy.* **14.** *Art.* **a.** a group of artists, as painters, writers, or musicians, whose works reflect a common conceptual, regional, or personal influence: *the modern school; the Florentine school.* **b.** the art and artists of a geographical location considered independently of stylistic similarity: *the French school.* **15.** any group of persons having common attitudes or beliefs. **16.** *Mil., Navy.* parts of close-order drill applying to the individual **(school of the soldier),** the squad **(school of the squad),** or the like. **17.** *Australian and New Zealand Informal.* a group of people gathered together, esp. for gambling or drinking. **18. schools,** *Archaic.* the faculties of a university. **19.** *Obs.* the schoolmen in a medieval university. —*adj.* **20.** of or connected with a school or schools. **21.** *Obs.* of the schoolmen. —*v.t.* **22.** to educate in or as if in a school; teach; train. **23.** *Archaic.* to reprimand. [bef. 900; ME *scole* (n.), OE *scōl* < L *schola* < Gk *scholḗ* leisure employed in learning] —**school′a·ble,** *adj.* —**school′·less,** *adj.* —**school′like′,** *adj.*

school[2] (sko͞ol), *n.* **1.** a large number of fish, porpoises, whales, or the like, feeding or migrating together. —*v.i.* **2.** to form into, or go in, a school, as fish. [1350–1400; ME *schol(e)* < D *school*; c. OE *scolu* troop; see SHOAL[2]]

school′ age′, 1. the age set by law for children to start school attendance. **2.** the period of school attendance required by law. [1735–45] —**school′-age′,** *adj.*

school·bag (sko͞ol′bag′), *n.* a bag used for carrying books, school supplies, etc. [1890–95; SCHOOL[1] + BAG]

school′ board′, a local board or committee in charge of public education. [1820–30]

school·book (sko͞ol′bo͝ok′), *n.* a book for study in schools. [1735–45; SCHOOL[1] + BOOK]

school·boy (sko͞ol′boi′), *n.* a boy attending school. [1580–90; SCHOOL[1] + BOY] —**school′boy′ish,** *adj.*

school′ bus′, a vehicle used to transport students to and from school or used for other related purposes. [1905–10, *Amer.*]

school·child (sko͞ol′chīld′), *n., pl.* **-chil·dren.** a child attending school. [1830–40; SCHOOL[1] + CHILD]

School·craft (sko͞ol′kraft′, -kräft′), *n.* **Henry Rowe** (rō), 1793–1864, U.S. explorer, ethnologist, and author.

school′ day′, 1. any day on which school is conducted. **2.** the daily hours during which school is conducted: *The school day here is from nine to three.* [1580–90]

school′ edi′tion. See **text edition.**

school·er (sko͞o′lər), *n.* a person who attends school, esp. a child (usually used in combination): *a new course for junior-high-schoolers.* [from parasynthetic derivatives with SCHOOL[1] and a preceding attributive; see -ER[1]]

school·fel·low (sko͞ol′fel′ō), *n.* a schoolmate. [1400–50; late ME; see SCHOOL[1], FELLOW]

school′ fig′ure, (in ice skating) any one of a group of sixty-nine different figures, skated in two- or three-circle figure-eight patterns, used to test various skating movements, a skater usually being required to perform six selected ones in competition.

School′ for Scan′dal, The, a comedy of manners (1777) by Richard Brinsley Sheridan.

school·girl (sko͞ol′gûrl′), *n.* a girl attending school. [1770–80; SCHOOL[1] + GIRL] —**school′girl′ish,** *adj.*

school·house (sko͞ol′hous′), *n., pl.* **-hous·es** (-hou′ziz). a building in which a school is conducted. [1400–50; late ME *scolehous.* See SCHOOL[1], HOUSE]

school·ing (sko͞o′ling), *n.* **1.** the process of being taught in a school. **2.** instruction, education, or training, esp. when received in a school. **3.** the act of teaching. **4.** *Archaic.* a reprimand. [1400–50; late ME *scoling.* See SCHOOL[1], -ING[1]]

school·ma'am (sko͞ol′mam′, -mäm′), *n.* schoolmarm. [1825–35, *Amer.*; SCHOOL[1] + MA'AM]

school·man (sko͞ol′mən, -man′), *n., pl.* **-men** (-mən, -men′), **1.** a person versed in scholastic learning or engaged in scholastic pursuits. **2.** (*sometimes cap.*) a master in one of the schools or universities of the Middle Ages; one of the medieval writers who dealt with theology and philosophy. [1530–40; SCHOOL[1] + MAN[1]]

school·marm (sko͞ol′märm′), *n. Older Use.* a female schoolteacher, esp. of the old-time country school type, popularly held to be strict and priggish. Also, **school·ma'am.** [1835–45, *Amer.*; var. of SCHOOLMA'AM] —**school′marm′ish,** *adj.*

school·mas·ter (sko͞ol′mas′tər, -mä′stər), *n.* **1.** a man who presides over or teaches in a school. **2.** anything that teaches or directs: *Life can be a harsh schoolmaster.* **3.** a snapper, *Lutjanus apodus,* a food fish found in Florida, the West Indies, etc. —*v.t., v.i.* **4.** to teach or direct in the capacity of schoolmaster. [1175–1225; ME *scolemaister.* See SCHOOL[1], MASTER] —**school′mas′ter·ship′,** *n.*

school·mate (sko͞ol′māt′), *n.* a companion or associate at school. [1555–65; SCHOOL[1] + MATE[1]]

school·mis·tress (sko͞ol′mis′tris), *n.* a woman who presides over or teaches in a school. [1490–1500; SCHOOL[1] + MISTRESS]
—**Usage.** See **-ess.**

school′ of hard′ knocks′, the experience gained from living, esp. from disappointment and hard work, regarded as a means of education: *The only school he ever attended was the school of hard knocks.* [1910–15]

School′ of Law′, (in Chinese philosophy) a Neo-Confucian school asserting the existence of transcendent universals, which form individual objects from a primal matter otherwise formless. Also called **Ch'eng-Chu school.**

School′ of Mind′, (in Chinese philosophy) a Neo-Confucian school asserting the original unity of all things, to be grasped through the perfect attainment of jen. Also called **Hsin Hsüeh, Lu-Wang school.**

school′ of the sol′dier. See under **school** (def. 16).

school′ of the squad′. See under **school** (def. 16).

school·room (sko͞ol′ro͞om′, -ro͝om′), *n.* a room in which a class is conducted or pupils are taught. [1765–75; SCHOOL[1] + ROOM]

school′ ship′, a vessel used in training students for nautical careers. [1835–45, *Amer.*]

school·teach·er (sko͞ol′tē′chər), *n.* a teacher in a school, esp. in one below the college level. [1840–50; SCHOOL[1] + TEACHER]

school·teach·er·ish (sko͞ol′tē′chər ish), *adj. Disparaging.* showing characteristics thought to be typical of a schoolteacher, as strictness and primness. [1925–30; SCHOOLTEACHER + -ISH[1]]

school·teach·ing (sko͞ol′tē′ching), *n.* the profession of a schoolteacher. [1840–50; SCHOOL[1] + TEACHING]

school′ tie′. See **old school tie.** [1930–35]

school′ without′ walls′, a nontraditional educational program that uses community facilities as learning resources.

school·work (sko͞ol′wûrk′), *n.* the material studied in or for school, comprising homework and work done in class. [1855–60; SCHOOL[1] + WORK]

school·yard (sko͞ol′yärd′), *n.* a playground or sports field near a school. [1865–70; SCHOOL[1] + YARD[2]]

school′ year′, 1. the months of the year during which school is open and attendance at school is required. **2.** See **academic year.** [1855–60]

schoon·er (sko͞o′nər), *n.* **1.** *Naut.* any of various types of sailing vessel having a foremast and mainmast, with or without other masts, and having fore-and-aft sails on all lower masts. Cf. **ketch, topsail schooner, yawl** (def. 2). **2.** a very tall glass, as for beer. **3.** See **prairie schooner.** [1705–15, *Amer.*; perh. *scoon,* var. of dial. *scun* SCUD[1] (cf. dial. Sw *skunna,* OE *scyndan*) + -ER[1]]

fishing schooner

CONCISE PRONUNCIATION KEY: act, cāpe, dâre, pärt; set, ēqual; *if,* ice; ox, ōver, ôrder, oil, bo͝ok, bo͞ot, out; up, ûrge; child; sing; shoe; thin, *th*at; zh as in *treasure.* ə = *a* as in *alone, e* as in *system, i* as in *easily, o* as in *gallop, u* as in *circus;* ᵊ as in *fire* (fīᵊr), *hour* (ouᵊr). l and n can serve as syllabic consonants, as in *cradle* (krād′l), and *button* (but′n). See the full key inside the front cover.

schoon·er-rigged (sko͞o′nər rigd′), *adj.* rigged as a schooner, esp. with gaff sails and staysails only. [1760–70]

Scho·pen·hau·er (shō′pən hou′ər; *Ger.* shō′pən-hou′əʀ), *n.* **Ar·thur** (är′to͝oʀ), 1788–1860, German philosopher. —**Scho·pen·hau·er·i·an** (shō′pən hou°r′ē ən, -hou′ər-, shō′pən hou ėr′ē ən), *adj.*

Scho·pen·hau·er·ism (shō′pən hou′ə riz′əm), *n.* the philosophy of Schopenhauer, who taught that only the cessation of desire can solve the problems arising from the universal impulse of the will to live. [1880–85; SCHOPENHAUER + -ISM]

schorl (shôrl), *n.* *Mineral.* a black tourmaline. Also called **schorl·ite** (shôr′līt). [1755–65; < G *Schörl*]

schot·tische (shot′ish), *n.* **1.** a round dance resembling the polka. **2.** the music for this dance. [1840–50; < G: SCOTTISH (dance))]

Schott′ky de′fect (shot′kē), *Crystall.* an unoccupied position in a crystal lattice caused by the relocation of an atom or ion from the interior to the surface of the crystal. [named after Walter Hans *Schottky* (1886–1976), German physicist, who described it]

Schott′ky noise′, *Electronics.* See **shot effect.** [see SCHOTTKY DEFECT]

schrank (shrangk), *n.* (in Pennsylvania Dutch furniture) a two-door clothes cabinet one side of which has drawers and shelves and the other side an open space for hanging clothes. [< PaG; cf. G *Schrank* cupboard]

Schreck·lich·keit (shʀek′likh kīt′), *n.* *German.* frightfulness; horror.

schrei·ber·site (shrī′bər sīt′, -zīt′), *n.* a mineral, iron-nickel phosphide, $(Fe, Ni)_3P$, found only in meteorites. [1840–50; < G *Schreibersit,* named after Carl von *Schreibers,* Viennese official; see -ITE[1]]

Schrei·ner (shrī′nər), *n.* **Olive** (*"Ralph Iron"*), c1862–1920, English author and feminist.

schrei′ner fin′ish, a lustrous surface imparted to a fabric by schreinerizing. [1900–05; after Ludwig *Schreiner* (fl. 1900), German textile manufacturer]

schrei·ner·ize (shrī′nə rīz′), *v.t.,* **-ized, -iz·ing.** to produce a lustrous finish on (a fabric) by subjecting it to pressure exerted by rollers engraved with many fine lines. Also, **schrei·ner** (shrī′nər); *esp. Brit.,* **schrei′ner·ise′.** [1905–10; see SCHREINER FINISH, -IZE]

Schrief·fer (shrē′fər), *n.* **John Robert,** born 1931, U.S. physicist: Nobel prize 1972.

schrod (skrod), *n.* scrod.

Schrö′der-Bern′stein the′orem (shrō′dər bûrn′stēn, -stīn, shrā′-), *Math.* the theorem of set theory that if two sets are so related that each can be placed in one-to-one correspondence with a subset of the other, then the sets are equivalent. [after Ernst *Schröder* (1841–1902), German logician and mathematician; *Bernstein* is unidentified]

Schrö·ding·er (shrō′ding ər, shrā′-; *Ger.* shʀœ′ding-əʀ), *n.* **Er·win** (eʀ′vin), 1887–1961, German physicist: Nobel prize 1933.

Schrö′dinger equa′tion, *Physics.* the wave equation of nonrelativistic quantum mechanics. Also called **Schrö′dinger wave′ equa′tion.** Cf. **wave equation** (def. 2). [1950–55; after E. SCHRÖDINGER]

schry·a·ri (shrī′ə rī′), *n.* a musical woodwind instrument of the 16th and 17th centuries having a double reed concealed in a cylinder and producing a shrill tone. [1935–40; < MLG *schry(en)* to shriek + L *-ārium* -ARY]

schtick (shtik), *n.* *Slang.* shtick. Also, **schtik.**

schtup (shto͝op), *v.,* **schtupped, schtup·ping.** *Slang (vulgar).* —*v.t.* **1.** to have sexual intercourse with. —*v.i.* **2.** to engage in sexual intercourse. Also, **shtup.** [< Yiddish *shtupn* lit., to push (in), press]

Schu·bert (sho͞o′bərt; *Ger.* sho͞o′beʀt), *n.* **Franz** (fʀänts), 1797–1828, Austrian composer.

schul (sho͞ol, sho͝ol), *n., pl.* ***schuln*** (sho͞oln, sho͝oln), *Yiddish.* shul.

Schul·berg (sho͝ol′bərg), *n.* **Budd** (bud), born 1914, U.S. novelist, short-story writer, and scenarist.

Schultz (sho͝olts), *n.* **Dutch,** nickname of Arthur Flegenheimer.

Schulz (sho͝olts), *n.* **Charles M(onroe),** born 1922, U.S. cartoonist: creator of the comic strip "Peanuts."

Schu·man (sho͞o′mən *or, for 1, Fr.* sho͞o mäN′), *n.* **1. Ro·bert** (rob′ərt; *Fr.* ʀô beʀ′), 1886–1963, French political leader: premier of France 1947–48. **2. William (Howard),** 1910–92, U.S. composer and teacher.

Schu·mann (sho͞o′män), *n.* **Ro·bert** (rob′ərt; *Ger.* ʀō′-beʀt), 1810–56, German composer.

Schu·mann-Heink (sho͞o′män hīngk′), *n.* **Ernestine,** 1861–1936, U.S. contralto, born in Bohemia.

Schu′man Plan′, the plan for establishing the European Coal and Steel Community, proposed by Robert Schuman, French political leader, in 1950.

Schum·pe·ter (sho͝om′pā tər), *n.* **Joseph A·lois** (ə lois′), 1883–1950, U.S. economist, born in Austria.

Schurz (shûrz, shûrts, sho͝orts), *n.* **Carl,** 1829–1906, U.S. general, statesman, and newspaperman; born in Germany.

Schusch·nigg (sho͝osh′nik), *n.* **Kurt von** (kûrt von; *Ger.* ko͝oʀt fən), (1897–1977), Austrian statesman in the U.S.: Chancellor of Austria 1934–38.

schuss (sho͞os, sho͝os), *Skiing.* —*n.* **1.** a straight downhill run at high speed. —*v.i.* **2.** to execute a schuss. —*v.t.* **3.** to schuss over: *to schuss the slopes around Aspen.* [1935–40; < G; c. SHOT[1]] —**schuss′er,** *n.*

schuss·boom·er (sho͝os′bo͞o′mər, sho͞os′-), *n.* *Informal.* a skier who is skilled at schussing. [1950–55, *Amer.*; SCHUSS + BOOMER]

Schütz (shyts), *n.* **Hein·rich** (hīn′ʀikh), 1585–1672, German composer.

Schutz·staf·fel (sho͝ots′shtä′fəl), *n.* *German.* an elite military unit of the Nazi party that served as Hitler's bodyguard and as a special police force. *Abbr.:* SS [lit., defense echelon]

Schuy·ler (skī′lər), *n.* **Philip John,** 1733–1804, American statesman and general in the Revolutionary War.

Schuy·ler·ville (skī′lər vil′), *n.* a village in E New York, on the Hudson: scene of Burgoyne's defeat and surrender in the Battle of Saratoga 1777. 1256. Formerly, **Saratoga.**

Schuyl·kill (sko͞ol′kil, sko͞o′kəl), *n.* a river flowing SE from E Pennsylvania to the Delaware River at Philadelphia. 131 mi. (210 km) long.

schvartz·e (shvär′tsə; *Eng.* shvärt′sə), *n.* *Yiddish* (*often disparaging and offensive*). a black person. Also, ***shvartze.***

schwa (shwä), *n.* *Phonet.* **1.** the mid-central, neutral vowel sound typically occurring in unstressed syllables in English, however spelled, as the sound of *a* in *alone* and *sofa, e* in *system, i* in *easily, o* in *gallop, u* in *circus.* **2.** the phonetic symbol ə, used to represent this sound. Also, **shwa.** [1890–95; < G < Heb *shəwā,* name of a diacritic marking schwa or no vowel]

Schwa·ben (shvä′bən), *n.* German name of **Swabia.**

Schwann (shvän; *Eng.* shwän), *n.* **The·o·dor** (tā′ō-dôʀ′), 1810–82, German zoologist.

Schwann′ cell′, *Biol.* a cell of the peripheral nervous system that wraps around a nerve fiber, jelly-roll fashion, forming the myelin sheath. [1930–35; after T. SCHWANN, who first described it]

Schwär·me·rei (shveʀ′mə ʀī′), *n.* (*sometimes l.c.*) *German.* excessive enthusiasm or sentimentality.

Schwartz (shwôrts), *n.* **Del·more** (del′môr, -mōr), 1913–1966, U.S. poet, short-story writer, and critic.

Schwarz (shwôrts; *Ger.* shvärts), *n.* **Her·mann A·man·dus** (heʀ′män ä män′do͝os), 1843–1921, German mathematician.

Schwarz′ inequal′ity, *Math.* **1.** Also called **Cauchy's inequality.** the theorem that the inner product of two vectors is less than or equal to the product of the magnitudes of the vectors. **2.** Also called **Cauchy-Schwarz inequality.** the theorem that the square of the integral of the product of two functions is less than or equal to the product of the integrals of the square of each function. [1950–55; named after H. A. SCHWARZ]

Schwarz·kopf (shwôrts′kôpf, -kopf, shwärts′-), *n.* **Elisabeth,** born 1915, German soprano, born in Poland.

Schwarz′schild ra′dius (*Ger.* shvärts′shilt′; *Eng.* shwôrts′chīld′, -shild), *Astron.* the radius at which a gravitationally collapsing celestial body becomes a black hole. [1955–60; named after Karl *Schwarzschild* (1873–1916), German astronomer]

Schwarz·wald (shvärts′vält′), *n.* German name of the **Black Forest.**

Schwed′ler's ma′ple (shwed′lərz), a variety of the Norway maple, *Acer platanoides schwedleri,* producing red leaves that subsequently turn green.

Schwein·furt (shvīn′fo͝oʀt), *n.* a city in N Bavaria, in West Germany, on the Main River. 55,600.

Schweit·zer (shwīt′sər, shvīt′-), *n.* **Albert,** 1875–1965, Alsatian writer, missionary, doctor, and musician in Africa: Nobel peace prize 1952.

Schweiz (shvīts), *n.* German name of **Switzerland.**

Schwei·zer·deutsch (shfīt′sər doich′, shfīt′-, shvīt′-), *n.* Schwyzertütsch.

Schwenk·feld·er (shfengk′fel′dər, shvengk′-), *n.* a member of a Protestant group that emigrated in 1734 from Germany and settled in Pennsylvania, where they organized the Schwenkfelder Church. [1780–90, *Amer.*; < G, after Kaspar von *Schwenkfeld* (1490–1561), German mystic; see -ER[1]]

Schwe·rin (shvā ʀēn′), *n.* a city in and the capital of Mecklenburg-Western Pomerania in N Germany. 130,685.

Schwin·ger (shwing′gər), *n.* **Julian Seymour,** 1918–94, U.S. physicist: Nobel prize 1965.

Schwit·ters (shvit′əʀs), *n.* **Kurt** (ko͝oʀt), 1887–1948, German artist.

Schwyz (shvēts), *n.* **1.** a canton in central Switzerland, bordering on the Lake of Lucerne. 92,400; 350 sq. mi. (900 sq. km). **2.** a city in and the capital of this canton, in the W part. 12,100.

Schwyz·er·tütsch (shfēt′sər tʏch′, shvēt′-), *n.* any of the local dialects of German spoken in Switzerland. Also called **Schweizerdeutsch.**

sci., **1.** science. **2.** scientific.

sci·ae·noid (sī ē′noid), *adj.* **1.** belonging or pertaining to the Sciaenidae, a family of carnivorous fishes that produce a loud sound by snapping the muscles attached to their air bladder, comprising the croakers and drums. —*n.* **2.** a sciaenoid fish. Also, **sci·ae·nid** (sī ē′nid). [1830–40; < L *sciaen(a)* kind of fish (< Gk *skiaina*) + -OID]

sci·am·a·chy (sī am′ə kē), *n., pl.* **-chies.** an act or instance of fighting a shadow or an imaginary enemy. Also, **sciomachy.** [1615–25; < Gk *skiamachía,* equiv. to *skiá* shadow + *-machia* -MACHY]

sci·at·ic (sī at′ik), *adj.* *Anat.* **1.** of, pertaining to, situated near, or affecting the ischium or back of the hip. **2.** affecting the hip or the sciatic nerves. —*n.* **3.** a sciatic part, as a nerve, vein, or artery. [1535–45; < ML *sciaticus,* alter. of Gk *ischiadikós* ISCHIADIC] —**sci·at′i·cal·ly,** *adv.*

sci·at·i·ca (sī at′i kə), *n.* *Pathol.* **1.** pain and tenderness at some points of the sciatic nerve, usually caused by a prolapsed intervertebral disk; sciatic neuralgia. **2.** any painful disorder extending from the hip down the back of the thigh and surrounding area. [1400–50; < ML, n. use of fem. of *sciaticus* SCIATIC]

sciat′ic nerve′, *Anat.* either of a pair of nerves, the largest in the body, that originate in the sacral plexus of the lower back and extend down the buttocks to the back of the knees, where they divide into other nerves: the sciatic nerve and its branches innervate large areas of the pelvis, leg, and foot. [1735–45]

SCID, *Pathol.* See **severe combined immune deficiency.**

sci·ence (sī′əns), *n.* **1.** a branch of knowledge or study dealing with a body of facts or truths systematically arranged and showing the operation of general laws: *the mathematical sciences.* **2.** systematic knowledge of the physical or material world gained through observation and experimentation. **3.** any of the branches of natural or physical science. **4.** systematized knowledge in general. **5.** knowledge, as of facts or principles; knowledge gained by systematic study. **6.** a particular branch of knowledge. **7.** skill, esp. reflecting a precise application of facts or principles; proficiency. [1300–50; ME < MF < L *scientia* knowledge, equiv. to *scient-* (s. of *sciēns*), prp. of *scīre* to know + *-ia* -IA]
—**Syn. 7.** art, technique, method, discipline.

sci′ence fic′tion, a form of fiction that draws imaginatively on scientific knowledge and speculation in its plot, setting, theme, etc. [1925–30]

sci·en·ti·a est po·ten·ti·a (skē en′tē ä′ est pō ten′tē ä′; *Eng.* sē en′shē ə est pō ten′shē ə), *Latin.* knowledge is power.

sci·en·tial (sī en′shəl), *adj.* **1.** having knowledge. **2.** of or pertaining to science or knowledge. [1425–75; late ME < ML *scientiālis,* equiv. to *scienti(a)* SCIENCE + *-ālis* -AL[1]]

sci·en·tif·ic (sī′ən tif′ik), *adj.* **1.** of or pertaining to science or the sciences: *scientific studies.* **2.** occupied or concerned with science: *scientific experts.* **3.** regulated by or conforming to the principles of exact science: *scientific procedures.* **4.** systematic or accurate in the manner of an exact science. [1580–90; < ML *scientificus,* equiv. to *scient-* (see SCIENCE) + *-i-* -I- + *-ficus* -FIC] —**sci′en·tif′i·cal·ly,** *adv.*

scientif′ic crea′tionism, *Theol.* the belief that the account of creation in the early chapters of Genesis is scientifically as well as religiously valid and that it can be supported by scientific evidence apart from scriptural authority. [1980–85] —**scientif′ic crea′tionist.**

sci′entif′ic meth′od, a method of research in which a problem is identified, relevant data are gathered, a hypothesis is formulated from these data, and the hypothesis is empirically tested. [1850–55]

scientif′ic nota′tion, a method for expressing a given quantity as a number having significant digits necessary for a specified degree of accuracy, multiplied by 10 to the appropriate power, as 1385.62 written as 1.386×10^3. [1960–65]

sci·en·tism (sī′ən tiz′əm), *n.* **1.** the style, assumptions, techniques, practices, etc., typifying or regarded as typifying scientists. **2.** the belief that the assumptions, methods of research, etc., of the physical and biological sciences are equally appropriate and essential to all other disciplines, including the humanities and the social sciences. **3.** scientific or pseudoscientific language. [1875–80; SCIENT(IST) + -ISM]

sci·en·tist (sī′ən tist), *n.* an expert in science, esp. one of the physical or natural sciences. [1825–35; < L *scient(ia)* SCIENCE + -IST]

sci·en·tis·tic (sī′ən tis′tik), *adj.* **1.** characterized by or having an exaggerated belief in the principles and methods of science. **2.** of, pertaining to, or characterized by scientism. [1875–80; SCIENTIST + -IC] —**sci′en·tis′ti·cal·ly,** *adv.*

sci·en·tize (sī′ən tīz′), *v.t.,* **-tized, -tiz·ing.** to apply or attempt to apply scientific principles to: *to scientize art criticism.* Also, *esp. Brit.,* **sci′en·tise′.** [1885–90; SCIENT(IFIC) + -IZE]

sci-fi (sī′fī′), *Informal.* —*adj.* **1.** of or pertaining to science fiction: *a writer of sci-fi books.* —*n.* **2.** See **science fiction.** [1950–55; by shortening]

scil., scilicet.

scil·i·cet (sil′ə set′), *adv.* to wit; namely. [1350–1400; ME < L *scīlicet,* short for *scīre licet* it is permitted to know]

Scil·la (sil′ə; *It.* shēl′lä), *n.* modern name of **Scylla.**

scil·lism (sil′iz əm), *n.* *Pathol.* poisoning by squill, characterized by vomiting, slow pulse, cardiac arrhythmia, and ventricular fibrillation. [< L *scill(a)* SQUILL + -ISM]

Scil′ly Isles′ (sil′ē), a group of about 140 small islands, SW of Land's End, England. 2020; 6½ sq. mi. (17 sq. km) *Cap.:* Hugh Town. Also, **Scil′ly Is′lands.** —**Scil·lo·ni·an** (si lō′nē ən), *adj., n.*

scim·i·tar (sim′i tər), *n.* a curved, single-edged sword of Oriental origin. Also, **scim′i·ter, simitar.** [1540–50; < It *scimitarra,* ult. < Pers] —**scim′i·tared,** *adj.*

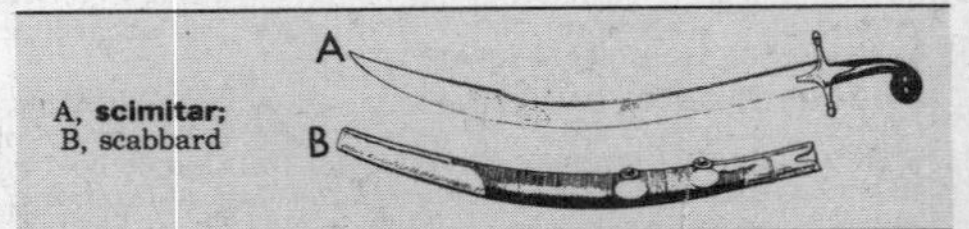

A, scimitar; B, scabbard

CONCISE ETYMOLOGY KEY: <, descended or borrowed from; >, whence; b., blend of, blended; c., cognate with; cf., compare; deriv., derivative; equiv., equivalent; imit., imitative; obl., oblique; r., replacing; s., stem; sp., spelling, spelled; resp., respelling, respelled; trans., translation; ?, origin unknown; *, unattested; ‡, probably earlier than. See the full key inside the front cover.

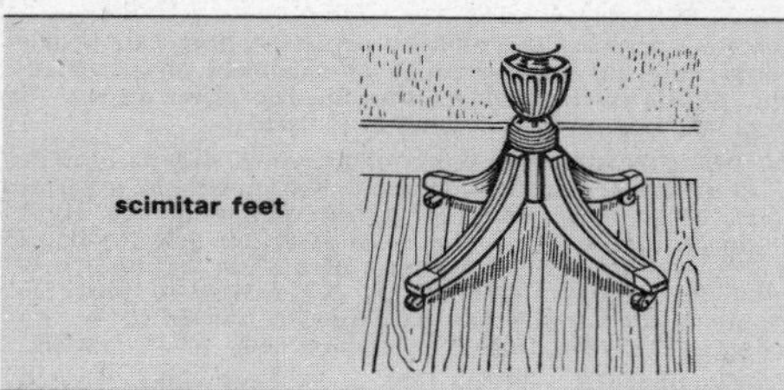
scimitar feet

scim′itar foot′, any short leg or foot, as to a pedestal table, having the form of an arc tangent to the floor plane.

scin•coid (sing′koid), *adj.* **1.** of, pertaining to, or resembling a skink. —*n.* **2.** a scincoid lizard. [1780–90; < L *scinc(us)* SKINK[1] + -OID]

scin•ti•gram (sin′ti gram′), *n.* a paper printout or photographic record indicating the intensity and distribution of radioactivity in tissues after administration of a radioactive tracer. Also called **gammagram.** [1950–55; SCINTI(LLATION) + -GRAM[1]]

scin•tig•ra•phy (sin tig′rə fē), *n.* the process of producing a scintigram. [1955–60; see SCINTIGRAM, -GRAPHY]

scin•til•la (sin til′ə), *n.* a minute particle; spark; trace: *not a scintilla of remorse.* [1685–95; < L: spark]

scin•til•lant (sin′tl ənt), *adj.* scintillating; sparkling. [1600–10; < L *scintillant-* (s. of *scintillāns,* prp. of *scintillāre* to send out sparks; flash). See SCINTILLA, -ANT] —**scin′til•lant•ly,** *adv.*

scin•til•late (sin′tl āt′), *v.,* **-lat•ed, -lat•ing.** —*v.i.* **1.** to emit sparks. **2.** to sparkle; flash: *a mind that scintillates with brilliance.* **3.** to twinkle, as the stars. **4.** *Electronics.* (of a spot of light or image on a radar display) to shift rapidly around a mean position. **5.** *Physics.* **a.** (of the amplitude, phase, or polarization of an electromagnetic wave) to fluctuate in a random manner. **b.** (of an energetic photon or particle) to produce a flash of light in a phosphor by striking it. —*v.t.* **6.** to emit as sparks; flash forth. [1615–25; < L *scintillātus* (ptp. of *scintillāre* to send out sparks, flash). See SCINTILLA, -ATE[1]]

scin•til•lat•ing (sin′tl ā′ting), *adj.* **1.** animated; vivacious; effervescent: *a scintillating personality.* **2.** witty; brilliantly clever: *a scintillating conversationalist; a play full of scintillating dialogue.* [1880–85; SCINTILLATE + -ING[2]] —**scin′til•lat′ing•ly,** *adv.*

scin•til•la•tion (sin′tl ā′shən), *n.* **1.** the act of scintillating; sparkling. **2.** a spark or flash. **3.** *Astron.* the twinkling or tremulous effect of the light of the stars. **4.** *Meteorol.* any small-scale twinkling or shimmering of objects that are viewed through the atmosphere, caused by an interception of the observer's line of view by inhomogeneities in the atmospheric refractive index. **5.** *Physics.* **a.** a flash of light from the ionization of a phosphor struck by an energetic photon or particle. **b.** random fluctuation of the amplitude, phase, or polarization of an electromagnetic wave. **6.** (on a radar display) a slight, rapid shifting of a spot of light or the image of an object about its mean position. [1615–25; < L *scintillātiōn-* (s. of *scintillātiō*). See SCINTILLATE, -ION]

scintilla′tion count′er, a device for detecting and measuring radioactivity, having a crystal scintillator, a photoelectric cell sensitive to the light from scintillations, and an amplifier. Also called **scin•til•lom•e•ter** (sin′tl-om′i tər). [1945–50]

scintilla′tion spectrom′eter, a scintillation counter adapted for measuring the energy distribution of particles emitted in radioactive processes. [1945–50]

scin•til•la•tor (sin′tl ā′tər), *n. Physics.* a phosphor capable of producing scintillations. [1870–75; SCINTILLATE + -OR[2]]

scin•ti•scan•ner (sin′tə skan′ər), *n.* a device that records the distribution and intensity of an internally administered radiopharmaceutical, producing a scintigram. [1950–55; SCINTI(LLATION) + SCANNER] —**scin′ti•scan′•ning,** *n.*

sci•o•lism (sī′ə liz′əm), *n.* superficial knowledge. [1810–20; < LL *sciol(us)* one who knows little (dim. of *scius* knowing; see CONSCIOUS, -OLE[1]) + -ISM] —**sci′o•list,** *n.* —**sci′o•lis′tic,** *adj.*

sci•om•a•chy (sī om′ə kē), *n., pl.* **-chies.** sciamachy.

sci•on (sī′ən), *n.* **1.** a descendant. **2.** Also, **cion.** a shoot or twig, esp. one cut for grafting or planting; a cutting. [1275–1325; ME shoot, twig < OF *cion* < Frankish **ki-* (cf. OE *cīnan,* OS *kīnan,* OHG *chīnan* to sprout, OE *cith,* OS *kith* sprout) + OF *-on* n. suffix] —**Syn. 1.** child, issue, offshoot, progeny.

sci•os•o•phy (sī os′ə fē), *n., pl.* **-phies.** supposed knowledge of natural or supernatural phenomena or forces, usually based on tradition, as astrology or phrenology. [< Gk *skio-* (comb. form of *skiá* shadow) + -SOPHY] —**sci•os′o•phist,** *n.*

Sci•o•to (sī ō′tə, -tō), *n.* a river in central Ohio, flowing S to the Ohio River. 237 mi. (382 km) long.

Scip•i•o (sip′ē ō′, skip′-), *n.* **1. Pub•li•us Cor•ne•li•us Scipio Af•ri•ca•nus Major** (pub′lē əs kôr nēl′yəs, af′ri-kā′nəs, -kan′əs, -kän′-), (*"Scipio the Elder"*), 237–183 B.C., Roman general who defeated Hannibal. **2.** his adopted grandson **Publius Cornelius Scipio Ae•mil•i•a•nus Africanus Minor** (ē mil′ē ā′nəs), (*"Scipio the Younger"*), c185–129 B.C., Roman general: besieger and destroyer of Carthage.

sci•re fa•ci•as (sī′rē fā′shē as′; *Lat.* skē′re fä′kē-äs′), *Law.* **1.** a writ requiring the party against whom it is brought to show cause why a judgment, letters patent, etc., should not be executed, vacated, or annulled. **2.** a judicial proceeding initiated by such a writ. [1400–50; late ME < L *scire faciās* lit., make (him) know]

sci•roc•co (shə rok′ō, sə-), *n., pl.* **-cos.** sirocco.

scir•rhoid (skir′oid, sir′-), *adj. Pathol.* resembling a scirrhus. [1850–55; SCIRRH(US) + -OID]

scir•rhous (skir′əs, sir′-), *adj. Pathol.* **1.** of a hard, fibrous consistency. **2.** of, relating to, or constituting a scirrhus. [1555–65; SCIRRH(US) + -OUS] —**scir•rhos•i•ty** (ski ros′i tē), *n.*

scir•rhus (skir′əs, sir′-), *n., pl.* **scir•rhi** (skir′ī, sir′ī), **scir•rhus•es.** *Pathol.* a firm, densely collagenous cancer. [1595–1605; < NL < L *scirros* < Gk *skírrhos,* var. of *skîros* hard covering, deriv. of *skirós* hard]

scis•sel (sis′əl, siz′-), *n.* the remains of a strip from which coin blanks have been cut; clippings. [1615–25; < F *cisaille,* n. deriv. of *cisailler* to clip. See CHISEL]

scis•sile (sis′il), *adj.* capable of being cut or divided; splitting easily. [1615–25; < L *scissilis,* equiv. to *scis-s(us)* (ptp. of *scindere* to cut) + *-ilis* -ILE]

scis•sion (sizh′ən, sish′-), *n.* **1.** a cutting, dividing, or splitting; division; separation. **2.** *Chem.* cleavage (def. 7). [1400–50; late ME (< MF) < LL *scissiōn-* (s. of *scissiō*) a cutting, equiv. to *sciss(us)* (ptp. of *scindere* to cut) + *-iōn-* -ION]

scis•sor (siz′ər), *v.t.* **1.** to cut or clip out with scissors. **2.** to eliminate or eradicate from a text; expunge: *testimony scissored from the record.* —*v.i.* **3.** to move one's body or legs like the blades of scissors: *a gymnast scissoring over the bar.* —*n.* **4.** scissors. [1605–15; v. use of sing. of SCISSORS]

scis•sor•like (siz′ər līk′), *adj.* like scissors; moving, operating, or crossing in a manner suggesting the blades of scissors. [1865–70; SCISSOR(S) + -LIKE]

scis•sors (siz′ərz), *n.* **1.** (*used with a singular or plural v.*) a cutting instrument for paper, cloth, etc., consisting of two blades, each having a ring-shaped handle, that are so pivoted together that their sharp edges work one against the other (often used with *pair of*). **2.** (*used with a singular v.*) *Gymnastics.* any of several feats in which the legs execute a scissorlike motion. **3.** (*used with a singular v.*) *Wrestling.* a hold secured by clasping the legs around the body or head of the opponent. [1350–1400; ME *cisoures, sisoures* < MF *cisoires* < ML **cīsōria,* pl. of LL *cīsōrium* cutting tool (see CHISEL); current sp. by association with L *scindere* to cut (ptp. *scissus*), ML *scissor* tailor]

scis′sors chair′, a chair, as a Dante or Savonarola chair, having transverse pairs of crossed legs supporting the seat and arms.

scis′sors jack′, a horizontal screw that raises or lowers a hinged, diamond-shaped frame. Also, **scis′sor jack′.**

scissors jack

scis′sors kick′, *Swimming.* a propelling motion of the legs in which they move somewhat like the blades of a pair of scissors, used in the sidestroke. [1970–75]

scis′sors truss′, a roof truss having tension members extending from the foot of each principal rafter to a point on the upper half of its opposite member.

scis•sor•tail (siz′ər tāl′), *n.* **1.** Also called **scis′sor-tailed fly′catcher** (siz′ər tāld′). a flycatcher, *Muscivora forficatus,* of the southern U.S., Mexico, and Central America, having a long, deeply forked tail. **2.** any of various other birds having a long, forked tail. [1830–40; SCISSOR(S) + TAIL[1]]

scis•sure (sizh′ər, sish′-), *n. Archaic.* a longitudinal cleft or opening. [1350–1400; ME (< MF); < L *scissūra,* equiv. to *sciss(us)* (ptp. of *scindere* to cut) + *-ūra* -URE]

sci-tech (sī′tek′), *Informal.* —*adj.* **1.** combining scientific and technical features: *sci-tech culture.* —*n.* **2.** a combination of science and technology: *the amazing world of sci-tech.* [by shortening]

Scit•u•ate (sich′o͞o āt′, -it), *n.* a town in E Massachusetts. 17,317.

sci•u•rine (sī′yo͝o rīn′, -rin), *adj.* of or pertaining to the squirrels and allied rodents of the family Sciuridae. [1835–45; < L *sciūr(us)* SQUIRREL + -INE[1]] —**sci•u•rid** (sī yo͝or′id), *n.*

sci•u•roid (sī yo͝or′oid), *adj.* **1.** sciurine. **2.** *Bot.* resembling a squirrel's tail, as the spikes of certain grasses. [1890–95; < L *sciūr(us)* SQUIRREL + -OID]

sciv•vy (skiv′ē), *n., pl.* **-vies.** skivvy.

sclaff (sklaf), *Golf.* —*v.t.* **1.** to scrape (the ground) with the head of the club just before impact with the ball. —*v.i.* **2.** to sclaff the ground with the club. —*n.* **3.** a sclaffing stroke. [1890–95; special use of Scots *sclaf* to shuffle] —**sclaff′er,** *n.*

SCLC, See **Southern Christian Leadership Conference. Also, S.C.L.C.**

sclent (sklent), *n., v.i. Scot. and North Eng.* sklent.

scler-, var. of **sclero-** before a vowel: *sclerenchyma.*

scle•ra (sklēr′ə), *n. Anat.* a dense, white, fibrous membrane that, with the cornea, forms the external covering of the eyeball. See diag. under **eye.** [1885–90; < NL < Gk *sklērá* (fem.) hard]

scle•ral (sklēr′əl), *adj. Anat.* sclerotic (def. 1). [1865–70; SCLER(A) + -AL[1]]

scle•rec•to•my (skli rek′tə mē), *n., pl.* **-mies.** *Surg.* **1.** excision of part of the sclera. **2.** removal of the adhesions formed in the middle ear during chronic otitis media. [SCLER- + -ECTOMY]

scle•re•ma (skli rē′mə), *n. Pathol.* sclerosis, or hardening, esp. of the skin. [1855–60; SCLER- + (ED)EMA]

scle•ren•chy•ma (skli reng′kə mə), *n. Bot.* supporting or protective tissue composed of thickened, dry, and hardened cells. [1860–65; SCLER- + (PAR)ENCHYMA] —**scle•ren•chym•a•tous** (sklēr′eng kim′ə təs, skler′-), *adj.*

scle•rite (sklēr′īt, skler′-), *n. Zool.* any chitinous, calcareous, or similar hard part, plate, spicule, or the like. [1860–65; SCLER- + -ITE[1]] —**scle•rit•ic** (skli rit′ik), *adj.*

scle•ri•tis (skli rī′tis), *n. Pathol.* inflammation of the sclera. Also, **sclerotitis.** [1860–65; SCLER- + -ITIS]

sclero-, a combining form meaning "hard," used with this meaning, and as a combining form of **sclera,** in the formation of compound words: *sclerometer.* Also, *esp. before a vowel,* **scler-.** [comb. form of Gk *sklērós* hard]

scle•ro•der•ma (sklēr′ə dûr′mə, skler′-), *n. Pathol.* a disease in which connective tissue anywhere in the body becomes hardened and rigid. [1865–70; SCLERO- + -DERMA]

scle•ro•der•ma•tous (sklēr′ə dûr′mə təs, skler′-), *adj.* **1.** *Zool.* covered with a hardened tissue, as scales. **2.** of or pertaining to scleroderma. [1895–1900; SCLERO- + -DERMATOUS]

scle•roid (sklēr′oid, skler′-), *adj. Biol.* hard or indurated. [1855–60; SCLER- + -OID]

scle•ro•ma (skli rō′mə), *n., pl.* **-mas, -ma•ta** (-mə tə). *Pathol.* a tumorlike hardening of tissue. [1675–85; < Gk *sklḗrōma.* See SCLER-, -OMA]

scle•rom•e•ter (skli rom′i tər), *n.* any instrument for determining with precision the degree of hardness of a substance, esp. a mineral, as by measuring the pressure necessary to pierce or scratch it. [1875–80; SCLERO- + -METER] —**scler•o•met•ric** (sklēr′ə me′trik, skler′-), *adj.*

scle•ro•phyll (sklēr′ə fil), *Bot.* —*adj.* **1.** Also, **scle•ro•phyl•lous** (sklēr′ə fil′əs). of, pertaining to, or exhibiting sclerophylly. —*n.* **2.** a plant exhibiting sclerophylly. [1910–15; SCLERO- + -PHYLL]

scle•ro•phyl•ly (sklēr′ə fil′ē), *n. Bot.* the normal development of much sclerenchyma in the leaves of certain plants, as some desert plants, resulting in thickened, hardened foliage that resists loss of moisture. [1900–05; SCLERO- + -PHYLL + -Y[3]]

scle•ro•pro•tein (sklēr′ə prō′tēn, -tē in), *n. Biochem.* protein that is fibrous and insoluble in water, serving a protective or supportive function in the body. Also called **albuminoid.** [1905–10; SCLERO- + PROTEIN]

Scler•o•scope (sklēr′ə skōp′, skler′-), *Trademark.* a brand name for a sclerometer that determines the hardness of a material by measuring the rebound of a standard ball dropped on the material from a fixed height.

scle•rosed (skli rōst′, sklēr′ōzd, skler′-), *adj. Pathol.* hardened or indurated, as by sclerosis. [1875–80; SCLEROS(IS) + -ED[2]]

scle•ro•sis (skli rō′sis), *n., pl.* **-ses** (-sēz). **1.** *Pathol.* a hardening or induration of a tissue or part, or an increase of connective tissue or the like at the expense of more active tissue. **2.** *Bot.* a hardening of a tissue or cell wall by thickening or lignification. [1350–1400; ME < ML < Gk *sklḗrōsis* hardening. See SCLER-, -OSIS] —**scle•ro′sal,** *adj.*

scle•ro•ther•a•py (sklēr′ə ther′ə pē, skler′-), *n. Med.* a treatment for varicose veins in which blood flow is diverted and the veins collapsed by injection of a hardening solution, also used cosmetically in spider veins to eliminate discoloration. [1940–45; SCLERO- + THERAPY]

scle•rot•ic (skli rot′ik), *adj.* **1.** Also, **scleral.** *Anat.* of or pertaining to the sclera. **2.** *Pathol., Bot.* pertaining to or affected with sclerosis. [1535–45; < NL *sclērōticus* of hardening, equiv. to Gk *sklērōt(ēs)* hardness (deriv. of *sklērós* hard; see SCLERO-) + NL *-icus* -IC]

scle•ro•tin (sklēr′ə tin, skler′-), *n. Biochem.* an insoluble protein that serves to stiffen the chitin of the cuticle of arthropods. [1935–40; < Gk *sklērót(ēs)* hardness + -IN[2]]

scle•ro•ti•tis (sklēr′ə tī′tis, skler′-), *n. Pathol.* scleritis. [1815–25; SCLEROT(IC) + -ITIS]

scle•ro•ti•um (skli rō′shē əm), *n., pl.* **-ti•a** (-shē ə). *Mycol.* a vegetative, resting food-storage body in certain higher fungi, composed of a compact mass of hardened mycelia. [1810–20; < NL; see SCLEROTIN, -IUM] —**scle•ro′tial** (skli rō′shəl), *adj.*

scle•ro•ti•za•tion (sklēr′ə tə zā′shən, skler′-), *n.* the state of being sclerotized. [1955–60; SCLEROTIZ(ED) + -ATION]

scle•ro•tized (sklēr′ə tīzd′, skler′-), *adj.* **1.** (esp. of the cuticle of an arthropod) hardened by the presence of substances other than chitin, as by scleroproteins, waxes, or calcium salts. **2.** *Pathol.* sclerosed. [1960–65; SCLEROT(IC) + -IZE + -ED[2]]

scle•ro•tome (sklēr′ə tōm′, skler′-), *n.* **1.** *Embryol.* the part of a mesodermal somite contributing to the development of the vertebrae and ribs. **2.** *Surg.* an instrument for use in performing a sclerotomy. **3.** *Zool.* a fibrous partition separating successive myotomes. [1855–60; SCLERO- + -TOME] —**scle•ro•tom•ic** (sklēr′ə-tom′ik, skler′-), *adj.*

scle•rot•o•my (skli rot′ə mē), *n., pl.* **-mies.** *Surg.* incision into the sclera, as to extract foreign bodies. [1875–80; SCLERO- + -TOMY]

scle•rous (sklēr′əs, skler′-), *adj.* hard; firm; bony. [1835–45; SCLER- + -OUS]

Sc.M., See **Master of Science.** [< L *Scientiae Magister*]

Sc.M.Hyg., Master of Science in Hygiene.

scoff[1] (skôf, skof), *v.i.* **1.** to speak derisively; mock; jeer (often fol. by *at*): *If you can't do any better, don't scoff. Their efforts toward a peaceful settlement are not to be scoffed at.* —*v.t.* **2.** to mock at; deride. —*n.* **3.** an expression of mockery, derision, doubt, or derisive scorn; jeer. **4.** an object of mockery or derision. [1300–50; ME *scof;* orig. uncert., but cf. ON *skopa* to scorn] —**scoff′er,** *n.* —**scoff′ing•ly,** *adv.*
—**Syn. 1.** gibe. SCOFF, JEER, SNEER imply behaving with scornful disapproval toward someone or about something. To SCOFF is to express insolent doubt or derision, openly and emphatically: *to scoff at a new invention.* To JEER suggests expressing disapproval and scorn more loudly, coarsely, and unintelligently than in scoffing: *The crowd jeered when the batter struck out.* To SNEER is to show by facial expression or tone of voice ill-natured contempt or disparagement: *He sneered unpleasantly in referring to his opponent's misfortunes.* —**Ant. 3.** praise.

scoff[2] (skôf, skof), *Slang.* —*v.i., v.t.* **1.** to eat voraciously. —*n.* **2.** food; grub. [1855–60; earlier *scaff;* orig. uncert.]

scoff•law (skôf′lô′, skof′-), *n.* **1.** a person who flouts the law, esp. one who fails to pay fines owed. **2.** a person who flouts rules, conventions, or accepted practices. [1920–25; SCOFF[1] + LAW[1]]

scoin′son arch′ (skoin′sən). See **sconcheon arch.** [1840–50]

scoke (skōk), *n.* pokeweed. [1785–95, *Amer.;* < a New England Algonquian language; cf. Eastern Abenaki *skōkimin* pokeberry (equiv. to Proto-Algonquian **aθkoka* snake + **-i-min* berry); cf. PERSIMMON]

scold (skōld), *v.t.* **1.** to find fault with angrily; chide; reprimand: *The teacher scolded me for being late.* —*v.i.* **2.** to find fault; reprove. **3.** to use abusive language. —*n.* **4.** a person who is constantly scolding, often with loud and abusive speech. **5.** See **common scold.** [1150–1200; (n.) ME, var. of *scald* < ON *skald* poet (as author of insulting poems); see SKALD; (v.) ME *scolden,* deriv. of the n.] —**scold′a•ble,** *adj.* —**scold′er,** *n.* —**scold′ing•ly,** *adv.*
—**Syn. 1.** reprove; censure. See **reproach.** —**Ant. 1.** praise.

scold•ing (skōl′ding), *n.* the action of a person who scolds; a rebuke; reproof: *I got a scolding for being late again.* [1425–75; late ME; see SCOLD, -ING[1]]

scold′ing bri′dle, *Brit. Dial.* branks. Also called **scold's′ bri′dle** (skōldz).

scol•e•cite (skol′ə sīt′, skō′lə-), *n.* a monoclinic white zeolite mineral, a hydrous calcium aluminum silicate, $CaAl_2Si_3O_{10} \cdot 3H_2O$, occurring in masses and in needle-shaped crystals. [1815–25; < Gk *skōlēk-* (s. of *skṓlēx*) SCOLEX + -ITE[1]]

sco•lex (skō′leks), *n., pl.* **sco•le•ces** (skō lē′sēz), **scol•i•ces** (skol′ə sēz′, skō′lə-). *Zool.* the anterior, headlike segment of a tapeworm, having suckers, hooks, or the like, for attachment. [1850–55; < Gk *skṓlēx* worm]

sco•li•on (skō′lē on′), *n., pl.* **-li•a** (-lē ə). a song sung at banquets in ancient Greece. [1595–1605; < Gk *skolión,* n. use of neut. of *skoliós* crooked, bent]

sco•li•o•sis (skō′lē ō′sis, skol′ē-), *n. Pathol.* an abnormal lateral curvature of the spine. Cf. **kyphosis, lordosis.** [1700–10; < Gk *skolíōsis* a bending] —**sco•li•ot•ic** (skō′lē ot′ik), *adj.*

scol•lop (skol′əp), *n., v.t., v.i.* scallop.

scol•o•pen•drid (skol′ə pen′drid), *n.* any myriapod of the order Scolopendrida, including many large, poisonous centipedes. [< NL *Scolopendrida* order name, equiv. to *scolopendr(a)* (< Gk *skolópendra* millipede) + *-ida* -IDA; see -ID[2]] —**scol•o•pen•drine** (skol′ə pen′drin, -drīn), *adj.*

scom•brid (skom′brid), *n.* **1.** any fish of the family Scombridae, comprising the mackerels and tunas. —*adj.* **2.** belonging or pertaining to the family Scombridae. [1835–45; < NL *Scombridae* name of the family < L *scombr-* (s. of *scomber*) mackerel (< Gk *skómbros*) + *-idae* -IDAE; see -ID[2]]

scom•broid (skom′broid), *adj.* **1.** resembling the mackerel. **2.** resembling or related to the mackerel family Scombridae. —*n.* **3.** a mackerel or related scombroid fish. [1835–45; < Gk *skómbr(os)* mackerel + -OID]

sconce[1] (skons), *n.* **1.** a bracket for candles or other lights, placed on a wall, mirror, picture frame, etc. **2.** the hole or socket of a candlestick, for holding the candle. [1350–1400; ME *sconce, sconse* (< OF *esconce*) < ML *scōnsa,* aph. var. of *absconsa,* n. use of fem. ptp. of *abscondere* to conceal; see ABSCOND]

sconce[2] (skons), *n., v.,* **sconced, sconc•ing.** —*n.* **1.** *Fort.* a small detached fort or defense work, as to defend a pass, bridge, etc. **2.** a protective screen or shelter. —*v.t.* **3.** *Fort.* to protect with a sconce. **4.** *Obs.* to protect; shelter. [1565–75; < D *schans* < G *Schanze,* orig. bundle of wood; cf. ENSCONSE]

sconce[3] (skons), *v.,* **sconced, sconc•ing,** *n.* —*v.t.* **1.** (at English universities, esp. formerly) to fine (an undergraduate) for a breach of rules or etiquette. —*n.* **2.** a fine so imposed. [1610–20; orig. uncert.]

sconce[4] (skons), *n.* **1.** the head or skull. **2.** sense or wit. [1560–70; orig. uncert.]

scon•cheon (skon′chən), *n. Archit.* the reveal of a window or doorway from the frame to the inner face of the wall. Also, **scuncheon, esconson.** [1325–75; ME *sconchon, sconcheon* < OF *escoinson* corner, cut angle, deriv. of *coin, cuigne* angle; see COIN]

scon′cheon arch′, an archway that includes the sconcheons of a door or window. Also, **scoinson arch.**

scone (skōn, skon), *n.* **1.** a small, light, biscuitlike quick bread made of oatmeal, wheat flour, barley meal, or the like. **2.** biscuit (def. 1). [1505–15; shortened < earlier D *schoonbrot* fine bread, white bread. See SHEEN, BREAD]

Scone (skōōn, skōn), *n.* **1.** a village in central Scotland: site of coronation of Scottish kings until 1651. **2. Stone of,** a stone, formerly at Scone, Scotland, upon which Scottish kings sat at coronation, now placed beneath the coronation chair in Westminster Abbey.

S. Con. Res., Senate concurrent resolution.

scoop (skōōp), *n.* **1.** a ladle or ladlelike utensil, esp. a small, deep-sided shovel with a short, horizontal handle, for taking up flour, sugar, etc. **2.** a utensil composed of a palm-sized hollow hemisphere attached to a horizontal handle, for dishing out ice cream or other soft foods. **3.** a hemispherical portion of food as dished out by such a utensil: *two scoops of chocolate ice cream.* **4.** the bucket of a dredge, steam shovel, etc. **5.** *Surg.* a spoonlike apparatus for removing substances or foreign objects from the body. **6.** a hollow or hollowed-out place. **7.** the act of ladling, dipping, dredging, etc. **8.** the quantity held in a ladle, dipper, shovel, bucket, etc. **9.** a news item, report, or story first revealed in one paper, magazine, newscast, etc.; beat. **10.** *Informal.* news, information, or details, esp. as obtained from experience or an immediate source: *What's the scoop on working this machine?* **11.** a gathering to oneself or lifting with the arms or hands. **12.** *Informal.* a big haul, as of money. **13.** *Television, Motion Pictures.* a single large floodlight shaped like a flour scoop. —*v.t.* **14.** to take up or out with or as if with a scoop. **15.** to empty with a scoop. **16.** to form a hollow or hollows in. **17.** to form with or as if with a scoop. **18.** to get the better of (other publications, newscasters, etc.) by obtaining and publishing or broadcasting a news item, report, or story first: *They scooped all the other dailies with the story of the election fraud.* **19.** to gather up or to oneself or to put hastily by a sweeping motion of one's arms or hands: *He scooped the money into his pocket.* —*v.i.* **20.** to remove or gather something with or as if with a scoop: *to scoop with a ridiculously small shovel.* [1300–50; (n.) ME *scope* < MD *schōpe;* (v.) ME *scopen,* deriv. of the n.] —**scoop′er,** *n.*

scoop•ful (skōōp′fŏŏl), *n., pl.* **-fuls.** the amount that a scoop can hold. [1715–25; SCOOP + -FUL]
—**Usage.** See **-ful.**

scoop′ neck′, a round, usually low, neckline on a dress, blouse, etc. Also called **scoop′ neck′line.** [1950–55]

scoop′ seat′, *Furniture.* See **dropped seat.**

scoot (skōōt), *Informal.* —*v.i.* **1.** to go swiftly or hastily; dart. —*v.t.* **2.** to send or impel at high speed. —*n.* **3.** a swift, darting movement or course. [1750–60; prob. < ON *skota* to push or *skjōta* to SHOOT[1]]

scoot•er[1] (skōō′tər), *n.* **1.** a child's vehicle that typically has two wheels with a low footboard between them, is steered by a handlebar, and is propelled by pushing one foot against the ground while resting the other on the footboard. **2.** Also called **motor scooter.** a similar but larger and heavier vehicle for adults, having a saddlelike seat mounted on the footboard and being propelled by a motor. **3.** (in the U.S. and Canada) a sailboat equipped with runners for use on ice. **4.** See **Pacific barracuda.** —*v.i.* **5.** to sail or travel in or on a scooter. [1800–10; SCOOT + -ER[1]]

scoot•er[2] (skōō′tər), *n., pl.* **-ers,** (*esp. collectively*) **-er.** scoter.

scop (skop), *n.* an Old English bard or poet. [bef. 900; learned borrowing (19th century) of OE *scop;* c. ON *skop* mocking, OHG *skof* derision]

sco•pa (skō′pə), *n., pl.* **-pae** (-pē), **-pas.** See **pollen brush.** [1795–1805; < L *scōpae* (pl., sing. *scopa* rare) twigs, shoots] —**sco•pate** (skō′pāt), *adj.*

Sco•pas (skō′pəs), *n.* fl. 4th century B.C., Greek sculptor and architect.

scope (skōp), *n., v.,* **scoped, scop•ing.** —*n.* **1.** extent or range of view, outlook, application, operation, effectiveness, etc.: *an investigation of wide scope.* **2.** space for movement or activity; opportunity for operation: *to give one's fancy full scope.* **3.** extent in space; a tract or area. **4.** length: *a scope of cable.* **5.** aim or purpose. **6.** *Ling., Logic.* the range of words or elements of an expression over which a modifier or operator has control: *In "old men and women," "old" may either take "men and women" or just "men" in its scope.* **7.** (used as a short form of *microscope, oscilloscope, periscope, radarscope, riflescope, telescopic sight,* etc.) —*v.t.* **8.** *Slang.* to look at, read, or investigate, as in order to evaluate or appreciate. **9. scope out,** *Slang.* **a.** to look at or over; examine; check out: *a rock musician scoping out the audience before going on stage.* **b.** to master; figure out: *By the time we'd scoped out the problem, it was too late.* [1525–35; < It *scopo* < Gk *skopós* aim, mark to shoot at; akin to *skopeîn* to look at (see -SCOPE)] —**scope′less,** *adj.*
—**Syn. 1.** See **range. 2.** margin, room, liberty.

-scope, a combining form meaning "instrument for viewing," used in the formation of compound words: *telescope.* Cf. **-scopy.** [< NL *-scopium* < Gk *-skopion, -skopeion,* equiv. to *skop(eîn)* to look at (akin to *sképtesthai* to look, view carefully; cf. SKEPTIC) + *-ion, -eion* n. suffix]

Scopes (skōps), *n.* **John Thomas,** 1901–70, U.S. high-school teacher whose teaching of the Darwinian theory of evolution became a cause célèbre **(Scopes′ Tri′al** or **Monkey Trial)** in 1925.

scop•ing (skō′ping), *n.* **1.** *Slang.* the act or practice of eyeing or examining, as in order to evaluate or appreciate. —*adj.* **2.** of or involving an investigation or discussion to determine the effect a proposed policy or project would have on a community or the local environment: *The public is invited to the scoping meeting on the proposed new refinery.* [SCOPE + -ING[1]]

sco•pol•a•mine (skə pol′ə mēn′, -min, skō′pə lam′in), *n. Pharm.* a colorless, syrupy, water-soluble alkaloid, $C_{17}H_{21}NO_4$, obtained from certain plants of the nightshade family, used chiefly as a sedative and mydriatic and to alleviate the symptoms of motion sickness. Also called **hyoscine.** [1890–95; < NL *Scopol(ia japonica)* Japanese belladonna (genus *Scopolia* named after G.A. *Scopoli* (1723–88), Italian naturalist; see -A[2]) + AMINE]

sco•po•phil•i•a (skō′pə fil′ē ə), *n. Psychiatry.* the obtaining of sexual pleasure by looking at nude bodies, erotic photographs, etc. Also, **scop•to•phil•i•a** (skop′tə-fil′ē ə). [1920–25; < NL; see -SCOPE, -O-, -PHILIA] —**sco•po•phil•i•ac** (skō′pə fil′ē ak′), **scop•to•phil•i•ac** (skop′tə fil′ē ak′), *n., adj.* —**sco′po•phil′ic, scop′to•phil′ic,** *adj.*

scops′ owl′ (skops), any of a group of small owls having ear tufts and a whistling call, esp. *Otus scops* **(Old World scops owl)** and *O. sunia* **(Oriental scops owl).** [1815–25; < NL < Gk *skṓps* little horned owl]

scop•u•la (skop′yə lə), *n., pl.* **-las, -lae** (-lē′). *Zool.* a dense tuft of hairs, as on the feet of certain spiders. [1795–1805; < NL *scōpula,* L: a broom twig, equiv. to *scōp(a)* broom + *-ula* -ULE]

scop•u•late (skop′yə lāt′, -lit), *adj. Zool.* broom-shaped; brushlike. [1820–30; SCOPUL(A) + -ATE[1]]

-scopy, a combining form used to form abstract action nouns corresponding to nouns with stems ending in **-scope:** *telescopy.* [< Gk *skopía* watching. See -SCOPE, -Y[3]]

scor•bu•tic (skôr byōō′tik), *adj. Pathol.* pertaining to, of the nature of, or affected with scurvy. Also, **scor•bu′ti•cal.** [1645–55; < NL *scorbūticus,* equiv. to ML *scorbūt(us)* scurvy (<< MLG *scorbûk*) + *-icus* -IC] —**scor•bu′ti•cal•ly,** *adv.*

scorch (skôrch), *v.t.* **1.** to affect the color, taste, etc., of by burning slightly: *The collar of the shirt was yellow where the iron had scorched it.* **2.** to parch or shrivel with heat: *The sun scorched the grass.* **3.** to criticize severely. **4.** *Mach.* burn[1] (def. 23). **5.** to destroy (crops, towns, etc.) by or as if by fire in the path of an invading army's advance. —*v.i.* **6.** to become scorched: *Milk scorches easily.* **7.** *Informal.* to travel or drive at high speed: *The car scorched along the highway.* —*n.* **8.** a superficial burn. [1400–50; late ME *scorchen,* perh. b. *scorcnen* (< Scand; cf. ON *skorpna* to shrivel) and TORCH[1]]
—**Syn. 1.** char, blister. See **burn**[1]. **3.** excoriate, condemn. —**Ant. 3.** laud.

scorched′-earth′ pol′icy (skôrcht′ûrth′), a military practice of devastating the property and agriculture of an area before abandoning it to an advancing enemy. [1935–40; appar. trans. of Chin *jiāotǔ zhèngcè*]

scorch•er (skôr′chər), *n.* **1.** a person or thing that scorches. **2.** *Informal.* a very hot day: *Tomorrow is supposed to be a scorcher.* **3.** something caustic or severe: *a scorcher of a critique.* **4.** *Informal.* a person who drives extremely fast. **5.** *Print.* a device for drying and forming flong into a curve before casting. [1835–45; SCORCH + -ER[1]]

scorch•ing (skôr′ching), *adj.* **1.** burning; very hot. **2.** caustic or scathing: *a scorching denunciation.* [1555–65; SCORCH + -ING[2]] —**scorch′ing•ly,** *adv.*

scor•da•tu•ra (skôr′də tŏŏr′ə; *It.* skôr′dä tōō′rä), *n., pl.* **-tu•re** (-tŏŏr′ā; *It.* -tōō′re), **-tu•ras.** *Music.* the tuning of a stringed instrument in other than the usual way to facilitate the playing of certain compositions. [1875–80; < It, equiv. to *scordat(o),* ptp. of *scordare* to be out of tune (< L *discordāre;* see DISCORD) + *-ura* n. suffix]

score (skôr, skōr), *n., pl.* **scores, score** for 11, *v.,* **scored, scor•ing.** —*n.* **1.** the record of points or strokes made by the competitors in a game or match. **2.** the total points or strokes made by one side, individual, play, game, etc. **3.** an act or instance of making or earning a point or points. **4.** *Educ., Psychol.* the performance of an individual or sometimes of a group on an examination or test, expressed by a number, letter, or other symbol. **5.** a notch, scratch, or incision; a stroke or line. **6.** a notch or mark for keeping an account or record. **7.** a reckoning or account so kept; tally. **8.** any account showing indebtedness. **9.** an amount recorded as due. **10.** a line drawn as a boundary, the starting point of a race, a goal line, etc. **11.** a group or set of 20: *about a score of years ago.* **12. scores,** a great many: *Scores of people were at the dance.* **13.** a reason, ground, or cause: *to complain on the score of low pay.* **14.** *Informal.* **a.** the basic facts, point of progress, etc., regarding a situation: *What's the score on Saturday's picnic?* **b.** a successful move, remark, etc. **15.** *Music.* **a.** a written or printed piece of music with all the vocal and instrumental parts arranged on staves, one under the other. **b.** the music itself. **c.** the music played as background to or part of a movie, play, or television presentation. **16.** *Slang.* **a.** a success in finding a willing sexual partner; sexual conquest. **b.** a purchase or acquisition of illicit drugs, as heroin or cocaine. **c.** a single payoff obtained through graft by a police officer, esp. from a narcotics violator. **d.** a successful robbery; theft. **e.** any success, triumph, happy acquisition, gift, or win. **f.** the victim of a robbery or swindle. **17. pay off** or **settle a score,** to avenge a wrong; retaliate: *In the Old West they paid off a score with bullets.* —*v.t.* **18.** to gain for addition to one's score in a game or match. **19.** to make a score of: *He scored 98 on the test.* **20.** to have as a specified value in points: *Four aces score 100.* **21.** *Educ., Psychol.* to evaluate the responses a person has made on (a test or an examination). **22.** *Music.* **a.** to orchestrate. **b.** to write out in score. **c.** to compose the music for (a movie, play, television show, etc.) **23.** *Cookery.* to cut ridges or lines into (meat, fish, etc.) with shallow slashes, usually in a diamond pattern, before cooking. **24.** to make notches, cuts, marks, or lines in or on. **25.** to record or keep a record of (points, items, etc.), by or as if by notches, marks, etc.; tally; reckon (often fol. by *up*). **26.** to write down as a debt. **27.** to record as a debtor. **28.** to

CONCISE ETYMOLOGY KEY: <, descended or borrowed from; >, whence; b., blend of, blended; c., cognate with; cf., compare; deriv., derivative; equiv., equivalent; imit., imitative; obl., oblique; r., replacing; s., stem; sp., spelling, spelled; resp., respelling, respelled; trans., translation; ?, origin unknown; *, unattested; ‡, probably earlier than. See the full key inside the front cover.

gain, achieve, or win: *The play scored a great success.* **29.** *Slang.* **a.** to obtain (a drug) illicitly. **b.** to steal. **c.** to acquire; be given. **30.** to berate or censure: *The newspapers scored the mayor severely for the announcement.* **31.** to crease (paper or cardboard) so that it can be folded easily and without damage. —*v.i.* **32.** to make a point or points in a game or contest. **33.** to keep score, as of a game. **34.** to achieve an advantage or a success: *The new product scored with the public.* **35.** to make notches, cuts, lines, etc. **36.** to run up a score or debt. **37.** *Slang.* **a.** to succeed in finding a willing sexual partner; have coitus. **b.** to purchase or obtain drugs illicitly. **c.** to elicit and accept a bribe. [bef. 1100; (n.) ME; late OE *scora, score* (pl.; sing. *scoru) group of twenty (appar. orig. notch) < ON *skor* notch; (v.) ME *scoren* to incise, mark with lines, tally debts < ON *skora* to notch, count by tallies; later v. senses deriv. of the n.; akin to SHEAR] —**score′less,** *adj.* —**scor′er,** *n.*

score•board (skôr′bôrd′, skōr′bōrd′), *n.* a large, usually rectangular board in a ballpark, sports arena, or the like, that shows the score of a contest and often other relevant facts and figures, as the count of balls and strikes on a baseball batter. [1820–30; SCORE + BOARD]

score•card (skôr′kärd′, skōr′-), *n.* a card for keeping score of a sports contest and, esp. in team sports, for identifying the players by name, number, and position. [1875–80; SCORE + CARD[1]]

score•keep•er (skôr′kē′pər, skōr′-), *n.* an official of a sports contest who keeps record of the score. [1875–80, *Amer.*; SCORE + KEEPER] —**score′keep′ing,** *n.*

score•pad (skôr′pad′, skōr′-), *n.* a pad whose sheets are printed with headings, vertical or horizontal lines, symbols, or the like, to facilitate the recording of scores in a game, as bowling or bridge. [SCORE + PAD[1]]

sco•ri•a (skôr′ē ə, skōr′-), *n., pl.* **sco•ri•ae** (skôr′ē ē′, skōr′-). **1.** *Metall.* the refuse, dross, or slag left after melting or smelting metal; scum. **2.** *Geol.* a cinderlike basic cellular lava. [1350–1400; ME < L *scōria* < Gk *skōría,* deriv. of *skôr* dung] —**sco•ri•a•ceous** (skôr′ē ā′shəs, skōr′-), *adj.*

sco•ri•fi•ca•tion (skôr′ə fi kā′shən, skōr′-), *n. Metall.* an assaying process whereby gold or silver is separated from ore by fusion with lead. [1745–55; SCORI(A) + -FICATION]

sco•ri•fy (skôr′ə fī′, skōr′-), *v.t.,* **-fied, -fy•ing.** to subject to scorification. [1745–55; SCORI(A) + -FY] —**sco′ri•fi′er,** *n.*

scorn (skôrn), *n.* **1.** open or unqualified contempt; disdain: *His face and attitude showed the scorn he felt.* **2.** an object of derision or contempt. **3.** a derisive or contemptuous action or speech. **4. laugh to scorn,** to ridicule; deride: *Her good advice was laughed to scorn.* —*v.t.* **5.** to treat or regard with contempt or disdain: *They scorned the old beggar.* **6.** to reject, refuse, or ignore with contempt or disdain: *She scorned my help.* —*v.i.* **7.** to mock; jeer. [1150–1200; (n.) ME *scorn, scarn* < OF *escarn* < Gmc (cf. obs. D *schern* mockery, trickery); (v.) ME *skarnen, sc(h)ornen* < OF *escharnir, eschernir* << Gmc] —**scorn′er,** *n.* —**scorn′ing•ly,** *adv.*
—**Syn. 1.** contumely. See **contempt. 5.** disdain, contemn, despise, detest. —**Ant. 3.** praise.

scorn•ful (skôrn′fəl), *adj.* full of scorn; derisive; contemptuous: *He smiled in a scornful way.* [1350–1400; ME; see SCORN, -FUL] —**scorn′ful•ly,** *adv.* —**scorn′ful•ness,** *n.*

scor•pae•nid (skôr pē′nid), *adj.* **1.** belonging or pertaining to the Scorpaenidae, a family of marine fishes with spiny fins, including the rockfishes, scorpionfishes, and lionfishes. —*n.* **2.** a scorpaenid fish. [1880–85; < NL *Scorpaenidae* family name, equiv. to L *scorpaen(a)* (< Gk *skórpaina* kind of fish; akin to *skorpíos* SCORPION) + *-idae* -IDAE; see -ID[2]]

scor•pae•noid (skôr pē′noid), *adj.* **1.** resembling or related to the family Scorpaenidae. —*n.* **2.** a scorpaenoid fish. [1835–45; < L *scorpaen(a)* (see SCORPAENID) + -OID]

scor•per (skôr′pər), *n.* scauper.

Scor•pi•o (skôr′pē ō′), *n.* **1.** *Astron.* Scorpius. **2.** *Astrol.* **a.** the eighth sign of the zodiac: the fixed water sign. See illus. under **zodiac. b.** a person born under this sign, usually between October 23rd and November 21st. [1350–1400; ME < L *Scorpiō* SCORPION]

scor•pi•oid (skôr′pē oid′), *adj.* **1.** resembling a scorpion. **2.** belonging or pertaining to the Scorpionida, the order of arachnids comprising the scorpions. **3.** curved at the end like the tail of a scorpion. [1830–40; < L *scorpi(ō)* SCORPION + -OID]

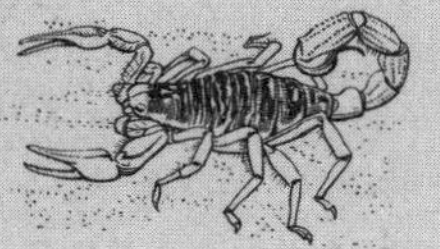

scorpion, *Centruroides sculpturatus,* length ¼ in. (0.6 cm)

scor•pi•on (skôr′pē ən), *n.* **1.** any of numerous arachnids of the order Scorpionida, widely distributed in warmer parts of the world, having a long, narrow, segmented tail that terminates in a venomous sting. **2. the Scorpion,** *Astron.* Scorpius. **3.** any of various harmless lizards, esp. the red- or orange-headed males of certain North American skinks. **4.** *Bible.* a whip or scourge that has spikes attached. I Kings 12:11. [1175–1225; ME < L *scorpiōn-* (s. of *scorpiō*), equiv. to *scorp(ius)* scorpion (< Gk *skorpíos*) + *-iōn-* n. suffix, perh. after *pāpiliō* (s. *pāpiliōn-*) butterfly, or *stelliō* (s. *stelliōn-*) gecko] —**scor•pi•on•ic** (skôr′pē on′ik), *adj.*

scor•pi•on•fish (skôr′pē ən fish′), *n., pl.* (*esp. collectively*) **-fish,** (*esp. referring to two or more kinds or species*) **-fish•es.** any of several tropical and temperate marine scorpaenid fishes, esp. members of the genus *Scorpaena,* many having venomous dorsal spines. Also called **sea scorpion, rockfish.** [1655–65; SCORPION + FISH]

scor•pi•on•fly (skôr′pē ən flī′), *n., pl.* **-flies.** any of several harmless insects of the order Mecoptera, the male of certain species having a reproductive structure that resembles the sting of a scorpion. Also, **scor′pion fly′.** [1660–70; SCORPION + FLY[2]]

scor′pion spi′der. whipscorpion. [1795–1805]

Scor•pi•us (skôr′pē əs), *n., gen.* **-pi•i** (-pē ī′). *Astron.* the Scorpion, a zodiacal constellation between Sagittarius and Libra, containing the bright star Antares. Also, **Scorpio.** [< L < Gk *skorpíos* SCORPION]

scot (skot), *n. Hist.* **1.** a payment or charge. **2.** one's share of a payment or charge. **3.** an assessment or tax. [1200–50; ME < ON *skattr* tax, treasure; c. OE *gescot* payment]

Scot (skot), *n.* **1.** a native or inhabitant of Scotland. **2.** one of an ancient Gaelic people who came from northern Ireland about the 6th century A.D. and settled in the northwestern part of Great Britain, and after whom Scotland was named. [bef. 900; ME; OE *Scottas* (pl.) < LL *Scottī* the Irish]
—**Usage.** See **Scotch.**

Scot, 1. Scots. **2.** Scottish.

Scot., 1. Scotch. **2.** Scotland. **3.** Scottish.

scot′ and lot′, 1. *Brit. Hist.* a municipal tax assessed proportionately upon the members of a community. **2. pay scot and lot,** to pay in full; settle finally. [1275–1325; ME, rhyming phrase; see SCOT, LOT]

scotch[1] (skoch), *v.t.* **1.** to put a definite end to; crush; stamp out; foil: *to scotch a rumor; to scotch a plan.* **2.** to cut, gash, or score. **3.** to injure so as to make harmless. **4.** to block or prop with a wedge or chock. —*n.* **5.** a cut, gash, or score. **6.** a block or wedge put under a wheel, barrel, etc., to prevent slipping. [1375–1425; late ME *scocche* (n. and v.), perh. b. SCORE and NOTCH (>AF *escocher*)]

scotch[2] (skoch), *v.t., n. Masonry.* scutch (defs. 2, 4).

Scotch (skoch), *adj.* **1.** of Scottish origin; resembling or regarded as characteristic of Scotland or the Scottish people (used outside Scotland): *Scotch plaid.* **2.** *Sometimes Offensive.* Scottish (def. 1). **3.** (*usually l.c.*) *Informal.* frugal; provident; thrifty. —*n.* **4.** (*used with a plural v.*) *Sometimes Offensive.* the Scottish people; Scots. **5.** (*often l.c.*) See **Scotch whisky. 6.** *Sometimes Offensive.* Scots (def. 1). [1585–95; syncopated var. of SCOTTISH]
—**Usage.** The natives of Scotland refer to themselves as SCOTS or, in the singular, SCOT, SCOTSMAN, or SCOTSWOMAN. The related adjectives are SCOTTISH or, less commonly, SCOTS. SCOTCH as a noun or adjective is objected to except when used of whisky and in established phrases like *Scotch egg* and *Scotch pine.* In the United States, SCOTCH is often used where the Scots themselves, or some Americans of Scottish descent, would prefer SCOTTISH or SCOTS. The term SCOTCH-IRISH is standard in the United States for the descendants of the Scots of Ulster who immigrated to America beginning in the 18th century.

Scotch′ Black′face, one of a Scottish breed of mountain sheep having a black face and growing long, coarse wool. [1940–45]

Scotch′ broom′, the broom, *Cytisus scoparius.* [1810–20, *Amer.*]

Scotch′ broth′, a thick soup prepared from mutton, vegetables, and barley. [1825–35]

Scotch′ cro′cus, a garden plant, *Crocus biflorus,* of southeastern Europe and Turkey, having purple-striped, yellow-throated flowers. [1880–85]

Scotch′ egg′, *British Cookery.* a hard-boiled egg encased in sausage meat, breaded, and deep-fried. [1800–10]

Scotch′ four′some, *Golf.* foursome (def. 2b).

Scotch′ fur′nace, *Metall.* See **ore hearth.** Also called **Scotch′ hearth′.** [1890–95]

Scotch′ Gael′ic, (not in technical use) See **Scots Gaelic.**

Scotch•gard (skoch′gärd′), *Trademark.* a brand name for a fluorocarbon chemical used for the treatment of upholstery and other fabrics to render them water- and oil-repellent and stain-resistant.

Scotch′ High′land. See **West Highland.**

Scotch-I•rish (skoch′ī′rish), *n.* **1.** (*used with a plural v.*) the descendants of the Lowland Scots who were settled in Ulster in the 17th century. —*adj.* **2.** of or pertaining to the Scotch-Irish. **3.** of mixed Scottish and Irish descent. Also, **Scots-Irish.** [1735–45]
—**Usage.** See **Scotch.**

Scotch•man (skoch′mən), *n., pl.* **-men. 1.** *Sometimes Offensive.* Scotsman. **2.** (*l.c.*) lingcod. [1560–70; SCOTCH + -MAN]
—**Usage.** See **Scotch.**

Scotch′ mist′, 1. a combination of mist or fog and drizzle, occurring frequently in Scotland and parts of England. **2.** a cocktail made by pouring Scotch whisky over finely crushed ice. [1655–65]

Scotch′ pine′, a pine, *Pinus sylvestris,* of Eurasia, having a reddish trunk and twisted, bluish-green needles. [1725–35]

Scotch′ Plains′, a township in NE New Jersey. 20,774.

Scotch′ rose′, a rose, *Rosa spinosissima,* of Eurasia, having pink, white, or yellow flowers. Also called **burnet rose.** [1725–35]

Scotch′ tape′, *Trademark.* a brand name for various transparent or semitransparent adhesive tapes made chiefly of cellulose acetate or cellophane, for sealing, attaching, mending, etc.

Scotch-tape (skoch′tāp′), *v.t.,* **-taped, -tap•ing.** to fasten or mend with Scotch tape. [1950–55; after the trademark]

Scotch′ ter′rier. See **Scottish terrier.** [1800–10]

Scotch′ this′tle, a tall, prickly plant, *Onopordum acanthium,* native to Eurasia, having stems and leaves covered with cottony down and solitary purple flower heads: the national emblem of Scotland. Also called **cotton thistle.**

Scotch′ ver′dict, 1. a verdict of not proven: acceptable in certain cases in Scottish criminal law. **2.** any inconclusive decision or declaration. [1910–15]

Scotch′ whis′ky, whiskey distilled in Scotland, esp. from malted barley in a pot still. [1825–35]

Scotch•wom•an (skoch′wo͝om′ən), *n., pl.* **-wom•en.** *Sometimes Offensive.* Scotswoman. [1810–20; SCOTCH(MAN) + -WOMAN]
—**Usage.** See **Scotch.**

Scotch′ wood′cock, toast spread with anchovy paste and topped with loosely scrambled eggs. [1875–80]

sco•ter (skō′tər), *n., pl.* **-ters,** (*esp. collectively*) **-ter.** any of the large diving ducks of the genus *Melanitta,* inhabiting northern parts of the Northern Hemisphere. Also, **scooter.** [1665–75; orig. uncert.]

scot-free (skot′frē′), *adj.* completely free from harm, restraint, punishment, or obligation: *The driver of the car escaped from the accident scot-free. The judge let the defendant off scot-free.* [1200–50; ME; see SCOT, FREE]

ScotGael, Scots Gaelic.

sco•tia (skō′shə), *n. Archit.* a deep concave molding between two fillets, as in the Attic base. Also called **trochilus.** See illus. under **molding.** [1555–65; < L < Gk *skotía* darkness (from its shadow)]

Sco•tia (skō′shə), *n. Literary.* Scotland. [< L: Scotland. See SCOT, -IA]

Sco•tism (skō′tiz əm), *n. Philos.* the set of doctrines of Duns Scotus. [1635–45; (DUNS) SCOT(US) + -ISM] —**Sco′tist,** *n.* —**Sco•tis′tic, Sco•tis′ti•cal,** *adj.*

Scot•land (skot′lənd), *n.* a division of the United Kingdom in the N part of Great Britain. 5,205,000; 30,412 sq. mi. (78,772 sq. km). *Cap.:* Edinburgh.

Scot′land Yard′, 1. a short street in central London, England: formerly the site of the London police headquarters, which were removed 1890 to a Thames embankment (**New Scotland Yard**). **2.** the metropolitan police of London, esp. the branch engaged in crime detection. [1860–65]

scoto-, a combining form meaning "darkness," used in the formation of compound words: *scotoma.* [< L < Gk *skoto-* comb. form of *skótos* darkness]

Scoto-, a combining form representing **Scots** or **Scottish** in compound words: *Scoto-Irish.* [comb. form of ML *Scōtus* SCOT]

sco•to•ma (skə tō′mə), *n., pl.* **-mas, -ma•ta** (-mə tə). *Pathol.* loss of vision in a part of the visual field; blind spot. [1535–45; < LL < Gk *skótōma* dizziness. See SCOTO-, -OMA] —**sco•tom•a•tous** (skə tom′ə təs), *adj.*

sco•to•pi•a (skə tō′pē ə, skō-), *n. Ophthalm.* vision in dim light (opposed to *photopia*). Cf. **dark adaptation.** [SCOT(O)- + -OPIA] —**sco•top•ic** (skə top′ik, skō-), *adj.*

Scots (skots), *n.* **1.** Also called **Scottish.** the English language as spoken in Scotland. Cf. **Scots Gaelic.** —*adj.* **2.** Scottish (def. 1). [1325–75; syncopated form of *Scottis,* ME, var. (north) of SCOTTISH]
—**Usage.** See **Scotch.**

Scots′ Gael′ic, the Gaelic of the Hebrides and the Highlands of Scotland, also spoken as a second language in Nova Scotia. *Abbr.:* ScotGael Also, **Scottish Gaelic.**

Scots-I•rish (skots′ī′rish), *n., adj.* See **Scotch-Irish.**

Scots•man (skots′mən), *n., pl.* **-men.** a person, esp. a man, who is a native or inhabitant of Scotland; Scot. [1325–75; ME. See SCOTS, -MAN]
—**Usage.** See **Scotch.**

Scots•wom•an (skots′wo͝om′ən), *n., pl.* **-wom•en.** a woman who is a native or inhabitant of Scotland; Scot. [1810–20; SCOTS(MAN) + -WOMAN]
—**Usage.** See **Scotch.**

Scott (skot), *n.* **1. Barbara Ann,** born 1928, Canadian figure skater. **2. Dred** (dred), 1795?–1858, a black slave whose suit for freedom (1857) was denied by the U.S. Supreme Court **(Dred Scott Decision)** on the grounds that a slave was not a citizen and therefore could not sue in a federal court. **3. Duncan Campbell,** 1862–1947, Canadian poet and public official. **4. Sir George Gilbert,** 1811–78, English architect. **5.** his grandson, **Sir Giles Gilbert,** 1880–1960, English architect. **6. Robert Fal•con** (fôl′kən, fal′-, fô′kən), 1868–1912, British naval officer and antarctic explorer. **7. Sir Walter,** 1771–1832, Scottish novelist and poet. **8. Win•field** (win′fēld′), 1786–1866, U.S. general. **9.** a male given name.

Scot•ti (skôt′tē), *n.* **1. An•to•nio** (än tô′nyô), 1866–1936, Italian baritone.

Scot•ti•cism (skot′ə siz′əm), *n.* a word or idiom peculiar to or characteristic of Scots. [1710–20; < ML *scotic(us),* var. of *scōticus* SCOTTISH (*Scōt(us)* SCOT + *-icus* -IC) + -ISM]

Scot•tie (skot′ē), *n.* **1.** See **Scottish terrier. 2.** a male given name, form of **Scott. 3.** a female given name. [1905–10; SCOT + -IE]

Scot•tish (skot′ish), *adj.* **1.** Also, **Scots.** of or pertaining to Scotland, its people, or their language. —*n.* **2.** the people of Scotland. **3.** Scots (def. 1). [bef. 900; ME < LL *Scott(us)* SCOT + -ISH[1]; r. OE *Scyttisc*] —**Scot′tish•ly,** *adv.* —**Scot′tish•ness,** *n.*
—**Usage.** See **Scotch.**

Scot′tish deer′hound, one of a Scottish breed of

CONCISE PRONUNCIATION KEY: act, cāpe, dâre, pärt; set, ēqual; if, īce; ox, ōver, ôrder, oil, bo͝ok, bo͞ot, out; up, ûrge; child; sing; shoe; thin, *th*at; zh as in *treasure.* ə = *a* as in *alone, e* as in *system, i* as in *easily, o* as in *gallop, u* as in *circus;* ᵊ as in *fire* (fīᵊr), *hour* (ouᵊr). l and n can serve as syllabic consonants, as in *cradle* (krād′l), and *button* (but′n). See the full key inside the front cover.

large, tall hunting dogs having a medium-length, wiry, gray or reddish-fawn coat, originally developed for hunting and bringing down deer, and known as the royal dog of Scotland. [1930–35]

Scottish deerhound, 2½ ft. (0.8 m) high at shoulder

Scot′tish Gael′ic. See **Scots Gaelic.**

Scot′tish rite′, one of the two advanced divisions of Masonic membership, leading to the 33rd degree. Cf. **York rite.** [1900–05]

Scot′tish star′, mullet[2].

Scot′tish ter′rier, one of a Scottish breed of small terriers having short legs and a wiry, steel-gray, brindled, black, sandy, or wheaten coat. Also called **Scotch terrier.** [1830–40]

Scottish terrier, 10 in. (25 cm) high at shoulder

Scotts•bluff (skots′bluf′), *n.* a city in W Nebraska, on the North Platte River. 14,156.

Scotts•bor•o (skots′bûr ō, -bur ō), *n.* a town in NE Alabama. 14,758.

Scotts•dale (skots′dāl′), *n.* a city in central Arizona, near Phoenix. 88,364.

Scot•ty (skot′ē), *n., pl.* **-ties. 1.** (*often l.c.*) *Informal.* a Scot; Scotsman or Scotswoman. **2.** See **Scottish terrier. 3.** a male given name, form of **Scott. 4.** a female given name. [SCOT + -Y[2]]

Sco•tus (skō′təs), *n.* **John Duns.** See **Duns Scotus, John.**

scoun•drel (skoun′drəl), *n.* **1.** an unprincipled, dishonorable person; villain. —*adj.* **2.** mean or base in nature; villainous; unprincipled; dishonorable. [1580–90; orig. uncert.]
—**Syn. 1.** scamp, rapscallion, miscreant. See **knave.**

scoun•drel•ly (skoun′drə lē), *adj.* **1.** having the character of a scoundrel; unscrupulous; villainous. **2.** of or like a scoundrel. [1780–90; SCOUNDREL + -LY]

scour[1] (skouᵊr, skou′ər), *v.t.* **1.** to remove dirt, grease, etc., from or to cleanse or polish by hard rubbing, as with a rough or abrasive material: *to scour pots and pans.* **2.** to remove (dirt, grease, etc.) from something by hard rubbing: *to scour grease from pots and pans.* **3.** to clear or dig out (a channel, drain, etc.) as by the force of water, by removing debris, etc. **4.** to purge thoroughly, as an animal. **5.** to clear or rid of what is undesirable: *to scour the nation of spies.* **6.** to remove by or as if by cleansing; get rid of. **7.** to clean or rid of debris, impurities, etc., by or as if by washing, as cotton or wool. **8.** *Metall.* (of the contents of a blast furnace) to rub against and corrode (the refractory lining). —*v.i.* **9.** to rub a surface in order to cleanse or polish it. **10.** to remove dirt, grease, etc. **11.** to become clean and shiny. **12.** to be capable of being cleaned by rubbing: *The roasting pan scours easily.* **13.** (of a plow, cultivator, etc.) to pass through the ground without soil clinging to the blade. **14.** (of a plow, shovel, etc.) to become polished from use. —*n.* **15.** the act of scouring. **16.** the place scoured. **17.** an apparatus or material used in scouring; scourer: *Sand is a good scour.* **18.** the erosive force of moving water, as in a river or sea. **19.** Usually, **scours.** (*used with a singular or plural v.*) *Vet. Pathol.* diarrhea in horses and cattle caused by intestinal infection. [1250–1300; ME *scouren* (v.) < MD *scūren* < OF *escurer* < L *excūrāre* to take care of (ML *escūrāre* to clean), equiv. to *ex-* EX-[1] + *cūrāre* to care for]
—**Syn. 1.** burnish, buff, shine, rub.

scour[2] (skouᵊr, skou′ər), *v.t.* **1.** to range over, as in a search: *They scoured the countryside for the lost child.* **2.** to run or pass quickly over or along. —*v.i.* **3.** to range about, as in search of something. **4.** to move rapidly or energetically. [1250–1300; ME *scouren*; perh. < ON *skūr* SHOWER[1]]
—**Syn. 1.** comb, rake, scan.

scour•er[1] (skouᵊr′ər, skou′ər ər), *n.* **1.** a person who scours or cleanses. **2.** an implement, device, or preparation for scouring. [1425–75; late ME *scourour.* See SCOUR[1], -ER[1]]

scour•er[2] (skouᵊr′ər, skou′ər ər), *n.* **1.** a person who scours or ranges about. **2.** (in the 17th and 18th centuries) a prankster who roamed the streets at night. [1350–1400; ME; see SCOUR[2], -ER[1]]

scourge (skûrj), *n., v.,* **scourged, scourg•ing.** —*n.* **1.** a whip or lash, esp. for the infliction of punishment or torture. **2.** a person or thing that applies or administers punishment or severe criticism. **3.** a cause of affliction or calamity: *Disease and famine are scourges of humanity.* —*v.t.* **4.** to whip with a scourge; lash. **5.** to punish, chastise, or criticize severely. [1175–1225; (n.) ME < AF *escorge,* deriv. of *escorgier* to whip < VL **excorrigiāre,* deriv. of L *corrigia* thong, whip (see EX-[1]); (v.) ME < OF *escorgier*] —**scourg′er,** *n.* —**scourg′ing•ly,** *adv.*
—**Syn. 3.** plague, bane. **5.** correct, castigate.

scour′ing pad′, a small pad, as of steel wool or plastic mesh, used for scouring pots, pans, etc.

scour′ing rush′, any of certain horsetails, esp. *Equisetum hyemale,* used for scouring and polishing. Also called **Dutch rush.** [1810–20]

scour•ings (skouᵊr′ingz, skou′ər-), *n.* (*used with a plural v.*) **1.** dirt or refuse removed by scouring. **2.** refuse removed from grain. [1580–90; see SCOUR[1], -ING[1], -S[3]]

scouse (skous), *n. Brit. Naut.* a baked dish or stew made usually with meat and hardtack. [1830–40; short for LOBSCOUSE]

scout[1] (skout), *n.* **1.** a soldier, warship, airplane, etc., employed in reconnoitering. **2.** a person sent out to obtain information. **3.** *Sports.* **a.** a person who observes and reports on the techniques, players, etc., of opposing teams. **b.** a person sent out by a team to observe and recommend new talent for recruitment. **4.** a talent scout, as in the entertainment field. **5.** an act or instance of reconnoitering, inspecting, observing, etc. **6.** (*sometimes cap.*) a Boy Scout or Girl Scout. **7.** *Informal.* a person: *He's a good scout.* **8.** a man acting as servant to a student at Oxford University. —*v.i.* **9.** to act as a scout; reconnoiter. **10.** to make a search; hunt. **11.** to work as a talent scout. —*v.t.* **12.** to examine, inspect, or observe for the purpose of obtaining information; reconnoiter: *to scout the enemy's defenses.* **13.** to seek; search for (usually fol. by *out* or *up*): *to scout up a date for Friday night.* **14.** to find by seeking, searching, or looking (usually fol. by *out* or *up*): *Scout out a good book for me to read.* [1300–50; (v.) ME *skowten* < OF *escouter, escolter, ascolter* (F *écouter* to listen) < LL *ascultāre,* L *auscultāre* to listen; see AUSCULTATE; (n.) < MF *escoute,* deriv. of *escouter*]

scout[2] (skout), *v.t.* **1.** to treat with scorn; dismiss. **2.** to make fun of; deride; mock. —*v.i.* **3.** to scoff; jeer. [1595–1605; perh. < ON *skūta, skūt* abuse, angry words. See SHOUT]

scout′ car′, a fast, lightly-armored military vehicle equipped with guns and used chiefly for reconnaissance. [1940–45, *Amer.*]

scout•craft (skout′kraft′, -kräft′), *n.* **1.** practice of or skill at scouting. **2.** skill in the program of activities of the Boy Scouts or the Girl Scouts. [1900–05; SCOUT[1] + CRAFT]

scout•er (skou′tər), *n.* **1.** a person who scouts. **2.** (*often cap.*) a Boy Scout who is 18 years of age or over. [1635–45; SCOUT[1] + -ER[1]]

scouth (sko͞oth), *n. Scot.* **1.** abundance; plenty. **2.** opportunity; scope. Also, **skouth.** [1585–95; orig. uncert.]

scout•hood (skout′ho͝od), *n.* **1.** (*sometimes cap.*) the state of being a scout, esp. a Boy Scout or a Girl Scout. **2.** the qualities or spirit of the Boy Scouts or the Girl Scouts. [SCOUT[1] + -HOOD]

scout•ing (skou′ting), *n.* **1.** an act or instance of reconnoitering; reconnaissance. **2.** the activities of a scout or scouts. **3.** (*often cap.*) the program of activities of the Boy Scouts or the Girl Scouts. [1635–45; SCOUT[1] + -ING[1]] —**scout′ing•ly,** *adv.*

scout•mas•ter (skout′mas′tər, -mä′stər), *n.* **1.** the leader or officer in charge of a band of scouts. **2.** the adult leader of a troop of Boy Scouts. [1570–80; SCOUT[1] + MASTER]

scow (skou), *n.* **1.** any of various vessels having a flat-bottomed rectangular hull with sloping ends, built in various sizes with or without means of propulsion, as barges, punts, rowboats, or sailboats. **2.** *Eastern U.S.* a barge carrying bulk material in an open hold. **3.** an old or clumsy boat; hulk; tub. —*v.t.* **4.** to transport by scow. [1660–70, *Amer.*; < D *schouw* ferryboat]

scowl (skoul), *v.i.* **1.** to draw down or contract the brows in a sullen, displeased, or angry manner. **2.** to have a gloomy or threatening look. —*v.t.* **3.** to affect or express with a scowl. —*n.* **4.** a scowling expression, look, or aspect. [1300–50; ME *scoulen* (v.); perh. < Scand; cf. Dan *skule* to scowl, Norw *skule* to look furtively, though these may be < LG *schūlen* to spy] —**scowl′er,** *n.* —**scowl′ful,** *adj.* —**scowl′ing•ly,** *adv.*
—**Syn. 1.** frown, lower, glare. **2.** glower, gloom.

SCR, *Electronics.* silicon-controlled rectifier.

scr., scruple.

scrab•ble (skrab′əl), *v.,* **-bled, -bling,** *n.* —*v.t.* **1.** to scratch or scrape, as with the claws or hands. **2.** to grapple or struggle with or as if with the claws or hands. **3.** to scrawl; scribble. —*v.i.* **4.** to scratch or dig frantically with the hands; claw (often fol. by *at*): *scrabbling at a locked door to escape the flames.* **5.** to jostle or struggle for possession of something; grab or collect something in a disorderly way; scramble. —*n.* **6.** a scratching or scraping, as with the claws or hands. **7.** a scrawled or scribbled writing. **8.** a disorderly struggle for possession of something; scramble: *After the fumble, there was a scrabble for the football.* [1530–40; < D *schrabbelen* to scratch, freq. of *schrabben* to SCRAPE] —**scrab′bler,** *n.*

Scrab•ble (skrab′əl), *Trademark.* a brand name for a game combining anagrams and crosswords in which two to four players use counters of various point values to form words on a playing board.

scrab•bly (skrab′lē), *adj.,* **-bli•er, -bli•est. 1.** insignificantly small or sparse: *scrabbly tufts of grass sprouting from the parched lawn.* **2.** scratchy; raspy. [1940–45; SCRABBLE + -Y[1]]

scrag (skrag), *n., v.,* **scragged, scrag•ging.** —*n.* **1.** a lean or scrawny person or animal. **2.** the lean end of a neck of veal or mutton. **3.** *Slang.* the neck of a human being. —*v.t.* **4.** *Slang.* to wring the neck of; hang; garrote. **5.** *Metall.* to test (spring steel) by bending. [1535–45; obscurely akin to CRAG[2]]

scrag•gly (skrag′lē), *adj.,* **-gli•er, -gli•est. 1.** irregular; uneven; jagged. **2.** shaggy; ragged; unkempt. [1865–70; SCRAG + -LY]

scrag•gy (skrag′ē), *adj.,* **-gi•er, -gi•est. 1.** lean or thin; scrawny. **2.** meager. **3.** irregular; craggy; jagged. [1565–75; SCRAG + -Y[1]] —**scrag′gi•ly,** *adv.* —**scrag′gi•ness,** *n.*

scram[1] (skram), *v.i.,* **scrammed, scram•ming.** *Informal.* to go away; get out (usually used as a command): *I said I was busy, so scram.* [1925–30; prob. shortened form of SCRAMBLE (but cf. G *schramm,* impv. sing. of *schrammen* to depart)]

scram[2] (skram), *Informal.* —*n.* **1.** the rapid shutdown of a nuclear reactor in an emergency. —*v.t.* **2.** to shut down (a nuclear reactor) rapidly in an emergency. [1945–50; perh. identical with SCRAM[1], though sense development is unclear]

scram•a•sax (skram′ə saks′), *n.* a single-edged knife or sword used by the Anglo-Saxons. Also, **scram′a•saxe′.** [1860–65; < LL *scramasaxus* < Gmc; cf. OHG *scrāma* big knife, OE *seax* short sword, SAX[2]]

scram•ble (skram′bəl), *v.,* **-bled, -bling,** *n.* —*v.i.* **1.** to climb or move quickly using one's hands and feet, as down a rough incline. **2.** to compete or struggle with others for possession or gain: *The children scrambled for the coins we tossed.* **3.** to move hastily and with urgency: *She scrambled into her coat and ran out the door.* **4.** *Mil.* (of pilots or aircraft) to take off as quickly as possible to intercept enemy planes. —*v.t.* **5.** to collect or organize (things) in a hurried or disorderly manner (often fol. by *together* or *up*): *He scrambled the papers up from the desk. I scrambled the report together at the last minute.* **6.** to mix together confusedly: *The teacher has hopelessly scrambled our names and faces.* **7.** to cause to move hastily, as if in panic: *He scrambled everyone out of the burning building.* **8.** to cook (eggs) in a pan while stirring, usually after mixing whites and yolks together. **9.** to make (a radio or telephonic message) incomprehensible to interceptors by systematically changing the transmission frequencies. **10.** to mix the elements of (a television signal) so that only subscribers with a decoding box can receive the signal. **11.** *Mil.* to cause (an intercepting aircraft or pilot) to take off in the shortest possible time, in response to an alert. —*n.* **12.** a quick climb or progression over rough, irregular ground. **13.** a struggle for possession or gain: *a scramble for choice seats in the stadium.* **14.** any disorderly or hasty struggle or proceeding. **15.** *Mil.* an emergency takeoff of interceptors performed in the shortest possible time. [1580–90; b. dial. *scamble* to stumble along, and SCRABBLE (in the same sense)]

scram′bled eggs′, 1. eggs cooked in a pan while stirring, usually after the whites and yolks have been mixed together, sometimes with milk. **2.** *Mil. Slang.* military gold braid, esp. that decorating the brim of an officer's hat. [1860–65]

scram•bler (skram′blər), *n.* **1.** a person or thing that scrambles. **2.** an electronic device that mixes and confuses telecommunications signals in order to make them unintelligible through certain circuits. Cf. **unscrambler** (def. 2). [1680–90; SCRAMBLE + -ER[1]]

scram•jet (skram′jet′), *n. Aeron.* a ramjet engine in which the flow through the combustor itself is supersonic. [1965–70; *s*(*upersonic*) *c*(*ombustion*) *ramjet*]

scran•nel (skran′l), *adj. Archaic.* **1.** thin or slight. **2.** squeaky or unmelodious. [1630–40; orig. uncert.]

Scran•ton (skran′tn), *n.* **1. William Warren,** born 1917, U.S. politician. **2.** a city in NE Pennsylvania. 88,117.

scrap[1] (skrap), *n., adj., v.,* **scrapped, scrap•ping.** —*n.* **1.** a small piece or portion; fragment: *a scrap of paper.* **2. scraps, a.** bits or pieces of food, esp. of leftover or discarded food. **b.** the remains of animal fat after the oil has been tried out. **3.** a detached piece of something written or printed: *scraps of poetry.* **4.** an old, discarded, or rejected item or substance for use in reprocessing or as raw material, as old metal that can be melted and reworked. **5.** chips, cuttings, fragments, or other small pieces of raw material removed, cut away, flaked off, etc., in the process of making or manufacturing an item. —*adj.* **6.** consisting of scraps or fragments. **7.** existing in the form of fragments or remnants of use only for reworking, as metal. **8.** discarded or left over. —*v.t.* **9.** to make into scraps or scrap; break up: *to scrap old cars.* **10.** to discard as useless, worthless, or ineffective: *He urged that we scrap the old method of teaching mathematics.* [1350–1400; ME *scrappe* (n.) < ON *skrap,* deriv. of *skrapa* to SCRAPE] —**scrap′ping•ly,** *adv.*

scrap[2] (skrap), *n., v.i.,* **scrapped, scrap•ping.** *Informal.* —*n.* **1.** a fight or quarrel: *She got into a scrap with her in-laws.* —*v.i.* **2.** to engage in a fight or quarrel. [1670–80; var. of SCRAPE]

scrap•book (skrap′bo͝ok′), *n.* an album in which pictures, newspaper clippings, etc., may be pasted or mounted. [1815–25; SCRAP[1] + BOOK]

scrape (skrāp), *v.,* **scraped, scrap•ing,** *n.* —*v.t.* **1.** to deprive of or free from an outer layer, adhering matter, etc., or to smooth by drawing or rubbing something, esp. a sharp or rough instrument, over the surface: *to scrape a table to remove paint and varnish.* **2.** to remove (an outer layer, adhering matter, etc.) in this way: *to scrape the paint and varnish from a table.* **3.** to scratch, injure, or mar the surface of in this way: *to scrape one's arm on a rough wall.* **4.** to produce by scraping: *He scraped his initials on the rock.* **5.** to collect or do by or as if by scraping; do or gather laboriously or with difficulty (usually fol. by *up* or *together*): *They managed to scrape together a football team.* **6.** to rub harshly on or across (something): *Don't scrape the floor with your boots!* **7.** to draw or rub (a thing) roughly across something: *Scrape your shoes on the doormat before you come in.* **8.** to level (an unpaved road) with a grader. —*v.i.* **9.** to scrape something. **10.** to rub against something gratingly. **11.** to produce a grating and unmusical tone from

CONCISE ETYMOLOGY KEY: <, descended or borrowed from; >, whence; b., blend of, blended; c., cognate with; cf., compare; deriv., derivative; equiv., equivalent; imit., imitative; obl., oblique; r., replacing; s., stem; sp., spelling, spelled; resp., respelling, respelled; trans., translation; ?, origin unknown; *, unattested; ‡, probably earlier than. See the full key inside the front cover.

a string instrument. **12.** to draw one's foot back noisily along the ground in making a bow. **13.** to manage or get by with difficulty or with only the barest margin: *I barely scraped through on the test.* **14.** to economize or save by attention to even the slightest amounts: *By careful scraping they managed to survive.* —*n.* **15.** an act or instance of scraping. **16.** a drawing back of the foot noisily along the ground in making a bow. **17.** a harsh, shrill, or scratching sound made by scraping. **18.** a scraped place: *a scrape on one's elbow.* **19.** an embarrassing or distressing situation; predicament: *He is always in some kind of a scrape.* **20.** a difference of opinion, fight, or quarrel; scrap. [bef. 1000; (v.) ME *scrapen* < ON *skrapa*; r. ME *shrapen*, OE *scrapian* to scratch (c. ON *skrapa*); (n.) late ME: scraper, deriv. of the v.] —**scrap′a·ble,** *adj.* —**scrape′age,** *n.*
—**Syn. 14.** scrimp, stint, pinch.

scrap·er (skrā′pər), *n.* **1.** a person or thing that scrapes. **2.** any of various tools or utensils for scraping. [1545–55; SCRAPE + -ER[1]]

scrap·er·board (skrā′pər bôrd′, -bōrd′), *n.* scratchboard. [1890–95; SCRAPER + BOARD]

scrap′ heap′, **1.** a pile of old, discarded material, as metal. **2.** a place for dumping old, useless things. Also, **scrap′heap′.** [1830–40; SCRAP[1] + HEAP]

scrap·ie (skrā′pē, skrap′ē), *n. Vet. Pathol.* an infectious, usually fatal brain disease of sheep, characterized by twitching of the neck and head, grinding of the teeth, and scraping of itching portions of skin against fixed objects with a subsequent loss of wool: caused by an unidentified sticky agent that clings to cell membranes. [1905–10; SCRAPE + -IE]

scrap·ing (skrā′ping), *n.* **1.** the act of a person or thing that scrapes. **2.** the sound of something being scraped. **3.** Usually, **scrapings.** something that is scraped off, up, or together. [1400–50; late ME; see SCRAPE, -ING[1]] —**scrap′ing·ly,** *adv.*

scrap′ i′ron, old iron to be remelted or reworked.

scrap·per[1] (skrap′ər), *n.* a person who removes or does away with scraps. [1640–50; SCRAP[1] + -ER[1]]

scrap·per[2] (skrap′ər), *n. Informal.* a fighter or aggressive competitor, esp. one always ready or eager for a fight, argument, or contest: *the best lightweight scrapper in boxing; a rugged political scrapper.* [1870–75; SCRAP[2] + -ER[1]]

scrap·ple (skrap′əl), *n. Pennsylvania Dutch Cookery.* cornmeal mush mixed with pork scraps, seasoned with onions, spices, herbs, etc., and shaped into loaves and sliced for frying. [1810–20, *Amer.*; SCRAP[1] + -LE]

scrap·py[1] (skrap′ē), *adj.*, **-pi·er, -pi·est.** made up of scraps or of odds and ends; fragmentary; disconnected. [1830–40; SCRAP[1] + -Y[1]] —**scrap′pi·ly,** *adv.* —**scrap′pi·ness,** *n.*

scrap·py[2] (skrap′ē), *adj.*, **-pi·er, -pi·est.** *Informal.* fond of fighting, arguing, or competing. [1890–95, *Amer.*; SCRAP[2] + -Y[1]]

scratch (skrach), *v.t.* **1.** to break, mar, or mark the surface of by rubbing, scraping, or tearing with something sharp or rough: *to scratch one's hand on a nail.* **2.** to dig, scrape, or tear (something) out or off with or as if with the nails, claws, etc.: *to scratch the burs off one's coat.* **3.** to rub or scrape slightly, as with the fingernails, to relieve itching. **4.** to rub or draw along a rough, grating surface: *to scratch a match on the sidewalk.* **5.** to erase, cancel, strike out, or eliminate (a name, something written, etc.) by or as if by drawing a line through it (often fol. by *out*): *Scratch out the third name on the list.* **6.** to withdraw (an entry) from a race or competition. **7.** *U.S. Politics.* **a.** to divide (one's vote) though predominantly supporting one political party or faction. **b.** to strike out or reject a particular name or names on (a party ticket) in voting. **8.** to write or draw by scraping or cutting the lines into a surface: *She scratched her initials on the glass.* **9.** to manipulate (a phonograph record) back and forth under the stylus to produce rhythmic sounds. —*v.i.* **10.** to use the nails, claws, etc., for tearing, digging, etc. **11.** to relieve itching by rubbing or scraping lightly, as with the fingernails. **12.** to make a slight grating noise, as a pen. **13.** to earn a living or to manage in any respect with great difficulty: *We scratched along that year on very little money.* **14.** to withdraw or be withdrawn from a contest or competition. **15.** (in certain card games) to make no score; earn no points. **16.** *Billiards, Pool.* to make a shot that results in a penalty, esp. to pocket the cue ball without hitting the object ball. —*n.* **17.** a slight injury, mar, or mark, usually thin and shallow, caused by scratching: *three scratches on my leg; a noticeable scratch on the table.* **18.** a rough mark made by a pen, pencil, etc.; scrawl. **19.** an act of scratching. **20.** the slight grating sound caused by scratching. **21.** the starting place, starting time, or status of a competitor in a handicap who has no allowance and no penalty. **22.** *Billiards, Pool.* **a.** a shot resulting in a penalty, esp. a pocketing of the cue ball without hitting the object ball. **b.** a fluke or lucky shot. **23.** (in certain card games) a score of zero; nothing. **24.** *Baseball.* See **scratch hit. 25.** See **scratch wig. 26.** *Slang.* money; cash. **27. from scratch, a.** from the very beginning or starting point. **b.** from nothing; without resources: *After the depression he started another business from scratch.* **28. up to scratch,** in conformity with a certain standard; adequate; satisfactory: *The local symphony orchestra has improved this year, but it is still not up to scratch.* —*adj.* **29.** used for hasty writing, notes, etc.: *scratch paper.* **30.** without any allowance, penalty, or handicap, as a competitor or contestant. **31.** *Informal.* done by or dependent on chance: *a scratch shot.* **32.** *Informal.* gathered hastily and indiscriminately: *a scratch crew.* **33.** done or made from scratch: *a scratch cake.* [1425–75; late ME *scracche* (v.), b. ME *scratte* to scratch, and *cracche* to scratch; c. MD *cratsen*] —**scratch′a·ble,** *adj.* —**scratch′a·bly,** *adv.* —**scratch′er,** *n.* —**scratch′less,** *adj.* —**scratch′like′,** *adj.*

Scratch (skrach), *n.* Old Scratch; Satan. [1730–40; alter. of *scrat* hermaphrodite (late ME *scratte*; cf. OE *scritta* (once), which may be an error for **scratta*); c. ON *skratti* devil, goblin, wizard, OHG *skraz* wood-demon]

scratch′ awl′, *Carpentry.* an awllike device for scribing wood. [1890–95]

scratch·board (skrach′bôrd′, -bōrd′), *n.* a cardboard coated with impermeable white clay and covered by a layer of ink that is scratched or scraped in patterns revealing the white surface below. Also called **scratch′card′, scraperboard.** [1925–30; SCRATCH + BOARD]

scratch′ coat′, (in plastering) a rough, deeply scored first coat upon which the brown coat is laid. [1815–25, *Amer.*] —**scratch′-coat′ed,** *adj.*

scratch·es (skrach′iz), *n.* (*used with a singular v.*) *Vet. Pathol.* a disease of horses marked by dry rifts or chaps that appear on the skin near the fetlock, behind the knee, or in front of the hock. [1605–15; see SCRATCH, -S[3]]

scratch′ hard′ness, resistance of a material, as a stone or metal, to scratching by one of several other materials, the known hardnesses of which are assembled into a standard scale, as the Mohs' scale of minerals. [1925–30]

scratch′ hit′, *Baseball.* a batted ball, usually poorly hit, barely enabling the batter to reach base safely: *a scratch hit off the end of the bat.* [1915–20]

scratch′ing post′, a block or post of wood, usually covered with carpeting, on which a cat can use its claws. [1890–95]

scratch′ line′, **1.** a line that marks the start of a race. **2.** *Track and Field.* a line that a competitor is not allowed to step over while performing in certain events, as the triple jump or javelin throw. [1895–1900]

scratch′ pad′, a pad of paper used for jotting down ideas, informal notes, preliminary writing, etc. [1890–95]

scratch′ sheet′, a racing publication giving the betting odds and other information on the horses entered at a racetrack or racetracks during a racing day. [1935–40]

scratch′ test′, a test for a suspected allergy in which the skin is scratched and an allergen applied to the area, redness indicating a positive reaction. [1935–40]

scratch′ wig′, a short wig, esp. one that covers only part of the head. Also called **scratch.** [1765–75]

scratch·y (skrach′ē), *adj.*, **scratch·i·er, scratch·i·est. 1.** causing or liable to cause a slight grating noise: *a scratchy record.* **2.** consisting of or marked by scratches: *a scratchy drawing.* **3.** uneven; haphazard: *He plays a scratchy game.* **4.** causing itching or other minor irritation of the skin: *a scratchy woolen sweater.* **5.** causing or liable to cause a scratch or scratches: *scratchy bushes.* **6.** *Chiefly Brit. Slang.* peevish; spiteful. [1700–10; SCRATCH + -Y[1]] —**scratch′i·ly,** *adv.* —**scratch′i·ness,** *n.*

scrawl (skrôl), *v.t.* **1.** to write or draw in a sprawling, awkward manner: *He scrawled his name hastily across the blackboard.* —*v.i.* **2.** to write awkwardly, carelessly, or illegibly. —*n.* **3.** awkward, careless, or illegible handwriting. **4.** something scrawled, as a letter or a note. [1605–15; perh. to be identified with late ME *scraule* to sprawl, crawl (b. SPRAWL and CRAWL)]

scrawl·er (skrô′lər), *n.* **1.** a person who scrawls. **2.** an agricultural machine for laying out fields in which plants are to be placed in ridged rows. [1725–35; SCRAWL + -ER[1]]

scrawl·y (skrô′lē), *adj.*, **scrawl·i·er, scrawl·i·est.** written or drawn awkwardly or carelessly. [1825–35; SCRAWL + -Y[1]] —**scrawl′i·ness,** *n.*

scrawn·y (skrô′nē), *adj.*, **scrawn·i·er, scrawn·i·est.** excessively thin; lean; scraggy: *a long, scrawny neck.* [1825–35, *Amer.*; var. of dial. *scranny* < Norw *skran* lean + -Y[1]] —**scrawn′i·ly,** *adv.* —**scrawn′i·ness,** *n.*
—**Syn.** gaunt, emaciated. —**Ant.** fleshy, plump.

screak (skrēk), *v.i.* **1.** to screech. **2.** to creak. —*n.* **3.** a screech. **4.** a creak. [1490–1500; < Scand; cf. Norw *skrike*, Dan *skrige*; c. ON *skrækja* to screech; see SCREECH] —**screak′y,** *adj.*

scream (skrēm), *v.i.* **1.** to utter a loud, sharp, piercing cry. **2.** to emit a shrill, piercing sound: *The sirens and whistles screamed.* **3.** to laugh immoderately or uncontrollably: *The comedian had the audience screaming.* **4.** to shout or speak shrilly, esp. with harsh or exaggerated words: *They screamed across the back fence.* **5.** to play or sing in a high, loud, harsh manner. **6.** to be conspicuous or startling: *That red dress really screams.* —*v.t.* **7.** to utter with or as if with a scream or screams. **8.** to make by screaming: *to scream oneself hoarse.* —*n.* **9.** a loud, sharp, piercing cry: *Her scream frightened off the burglar.* **10.** a shrill, piercing sound: *the scream of the tires as the car rounded the curve.* **11.** *Informal.* someone or something that is hilariously funny: *The movie was a scream.* [1150–1200; 1905–10 for def. 11; ME *screamen* (v.), OE **scrǣman*; akin to ON *skraumi* chatterbox, braggart, *skruma* to jabber; *sc-* (for regular *sh-* as in ME *shreame*) from obs. *scritch* to SCREECH]
—**Syn. 1.** SCREAM, SHRIEK, SCREECH apply to crying out in a loud, piercing way. To SCREAM is to utter a loud, piercing cry, esp. of pain, fear, anger, or excitement: *to scream with terror.* The word is used also for a little, barely audible cry given by one who is startled. SHRIEK usually refers to a sharper and briefer cry than SCREAM; when caused by fear or pain, it is often indicative of more terror or distress; SHRIEK is also used for shrill uncontrolled cries: *to shriek with laughter.* SCREECH emphasizes disagreeable shrillness and harshness, often with a connotation of lack of dignity: *to screech approval at a rock concert.* **9.** outcry, shriek, screech, screak.

scream·er (skrē′mər), *n.* **1.** a person or thing that screams. **2.** *Informal.* something or someone causing screams of excitement, laughter, or the like. **3.** *Print. Slang.* an exclamation point. **4.** *Journalism.* **a.** a sensational headline. **b.** banner (def. 7). Cf. **scarehead. 5.** *Baseball Slang.* an extremely hard-hit line drive. **6.** *Ornith.* any of several South American birds of the family Anhimidae, having a harsh, trumpeting call. Cf. **horned screamer.** [1705–15; SCREAM + -ER[1]]

scream·ing (skrē′ming), *adj.* **1.** uttering screams. **2.** boldly striking or startling: *screaming colors; screaming headlines.* **3.** causing hilarious laughter; extremely funny: *a screaming farce.* —*n.* **4.** the act or sound of a person or thing that screams. [1350–1400; ME (ger.); see SCREAM, -ING[2], -ING[1]] —**scream′ing·ly,** *adv.*

scream·ing-mee·mies (skrē′ming mē′mēz), *n.* (*used with a singular or plural v.*) *Informal.* extreme nervousness; hysteria (usually prec. by *the*). [1925–30; redupl. with alter. of SCREAMING; see -Y[2], -S[3]]

scree (skrē), *n.* a steep mass of detritus on the side of a mountain. [1775–85; < ON *skritha* landslide]

screech (skrēch), *v.i.* **1.** to utter or make a harsh, shrill cry or sound: *The child screeched hysterically. The brakes screeched.* —*v.t.* **2.** to utter with a screech: *She screeched her warning.* —*n.* **3.** a harsh, shrill cry or sound: *an owl's screech; the screech of brakes.* [1550–60; var. of obs. *scritch* to scream; akin to SCREAK] —**screech′er,** *n.*
—**Syn. 1.** See **scream.**

screech·ing (skrē′ching), *adj.* **1.** causing or uttering screeches: *screeching bats.* **2.** characteristic of screeches; harshly shrill: *a screeching tone.* —*n.* **3.** the act or sound of a person or thing that screeches. [1610–20; SCREECH + -ING[2], -ING[1]] —**screech′ing·ly,** *adv.*

screech′ owl′, **1.** any of numerous small American owls of the genus *Otus*, having hornlike tufts of feathers, as *O. asio*, of eastern North America. **2.** (not in technical use) any owl having a harsh cry, esp. the barn owl. Also, **screech′-owl′.** [1585–95]

screech owl, *Otus asio,* length 9 in. (23 cm)

screech·y (skrē′chē), *adj.*, **screech·i·er, screech·i·est. 1.** like or suggesting screeching. **2.** producing screeches: *a screechy door.* [1820–30; SCREECH + -Y[1]]

screed (skrēd), *n.* **1.** a long discourse or essay, esp. a diatribe. **2.** an informal letter, account, or other piece of writing. **3.** *Building Trades.* **a.** a strip of plaster or wood applied to a surface to be plastered to serve as a guide for making a true surface. **b.** a wooden strip serving as a guide for making a true level surface on a concrete pavement or the like. **c.** a board or metal strip dragged across a freshly poured concrete slab to give it its proper level. **4.** *Brit. Dial.* a fragment or shred, as of cloth. **5.** *Scot.* **a.** a tear or rip, esp. in cloth. **b.** a drinking bout. —*v.t., v.i.* **6.** *Scot.* to tear, rip, or shred, as cloth. [1275–1325; ME *screde* torn fragment, irreg. (with *sc-* for *sh-*) repr. OE *scrēade* SHRED]

screen (skrēn), *n.* **1.** a movable or fixed device, usually consisting of a covered frame, that provides shelter, serves as a partition, etc. **2.** a permanent, usually ornamental partition, as around the choir of a church or across the hall of a medieval house. **3.** a specially prepared, light-reflecting surface on which motion pictures, slides, etc., may be projected. **4.** motion pictures collectively or the motion-picture industry. **5.** *Electronics, Television.* the external surface of the large end of a cathode-ray tube of a television set, radar receiver, etc., on which an electronically created picture or image is formed. **6.** *Computers.* **a.** Also called **video screen.** the portion of a terminal or monitor upon which information is displayed. **b.** frame (def. 10). **7.** anything that shelters, protects, or conceals: *a screen of secrecy; A screen of fog prevented our seeing the ship.* **8.** a frame holding a mesh of wire, cloth, or plastic, for placing in a window or doorway, around a porch, etc., to admit air but exclude insects. **9.** a sieve, riddle, or other meshlike device used to separate smaller particles or objects from larger ones, as for grain or sand. **10.** a system for screening or grouping people, objects, etc. **11.** *Mil.* a body of troops sent out to protect the movement of an army. **12.** *Navy.* a protective formation of small vessels, as destroyers, around or in front of a larger ship or ships. **13.** *Physics.* a shield designed to prevent interference between various agencies: *electric screen.* **14.** *Electronics.* See **screen grid. 15.** *Photog.* a plate of ground glass or the like on which the image is brought into focus in a camera before being photographed. **16.** *Photoengraving.* a transparent plate containing two sets of fine parallel lines, one crossing the other, used in the halftone process. **17.** *Sports.* **a.** any of various offensive plays in which teammates form a protective formation around the ball carrier, pass receiver, shooter, etc. **b.** any of various defensive plays in which teammates conceal or block an opposing ball carrier, pass receiver, shooter, or the goal, basket, net, etc., itself. —*v.t.* **18.** to shelter, protect, or conceal with or as if with a screen. **19.** to select, reject, consider, or group (people, objects, ideas, etc.) by examining systematically: *Job applicants were screened by the personnel department.* **20.** to provide with a screen or screens to exclude insects: *He screened the porch so they could enjoy sitting out on summer evenings.* **21.** to sift or sort by passing through a screen. **22.** to project (a motion picture, slide, etc.) on a screen. **23.** *Motion Pictures.* **a.** to show (a motion picture), esp. to an invited audience, as of exhibitors and critics. **b.** to photograph with a motion-picture camera; film. **c.** to adapt (a story, play, etc.) for presentation as a motion picture. **24.** to lighten (type or areas of a line engraving) by etching a regular pattern of dots or lines into the printing surface. —*v.i.* **25.** to be projected on a motion-picture screen. [1350–1400; ME *screne* (n.) < AF; OF *escren* (F *écran*) < Frankish **skrank*, c. OHG *scrank* barrier (G *Schrank* cupboard)] —**screen′a·ble,** *adj.*

CONCISE PRONUNCIATION KEY: act, cāpe, dâre, pärt; set, ēqual; if, īce; ox, ōver, ôrder, oil, bo͝ok, bo͞ot, out; up, ûrge; child; sing; shoe; thin, *th*at; zh as in *treasure*. ə = *a* as in *alone*, *e* as in *system*, *i* as in *easily*, *o* as in *gallop*, *u* as in *circus*; ᵊ as in *fire* (fīᵊr), *hour* (ouᵊr). l and n can serve as syllabic consonants, as in *cradle* (krād′l), and *button* (but′n). See the full key inside the front cover.

—**screen′er,** *n.* —**screen′less,** *adj.* —**screen′like′,** *adj.*

—**Syn. 7.** guard, shield. See **cover. 18.** veil, defend, shield, hide, mask.

Screen′ Ac′tors Guild′, a labor union for motion-picture performers, founded in 1933. *Abbr.:* SAG

screen′ grid′, *Electronics.* a grid placed between the anode and the control electrode in a vacuum tube, usually maintained at a fixed positive potential. [1925–30]

screen·ing (skrē′ning), *n.* **1.** the act or work of a person who screens, as in ascertaining the character and competence of applicants, employees, etc. **2.** the showing of a motion picture: *There will be screenings at 6 P.M. and 8 P.M.* **3. screenings,** (*used with a singular or plural v.*) **a.** undesirable material that has been separated from usable material by means of a screen or sieve: *screenings of imperfect grain.* **b.** extremely fine coal. **4.** the meshed material used in screens for windows and doors. [1715–25; SCREEN + -ING[1]]

screen·land (skrēn′land′), *n.* filmdom. [1920–25; SCREEN + -LAND]

screen′ mem′ory, *Psychoanal.* a childhood memory, perhaps recalled falsely, that screens out a more distressing recollection. [1920–25]

screen·o (skrē′nō), *n.* (*sometimes cap.*) (formerly) bingo played in a movie theater. [SCREEN + (BING)O]

screen′ pass′, *Football.* a pass thrown to a receiver who is directly in back of a wall of blockers and who is behind or not far beyond the line of scrimmage. [1950–55]

screen·play (skrēn′plā′), *n.* **1.** a motion-picture or television scenario. **2.** *Older Use.* a motion picture. [1915–20; SCREEN + PLAY]

screen′ test′, a filmed audition to determine the suitability of an individual for appearing or acting in a motion picture. [1920–25]

screen-test (skrēn′test′), *v.t.* **1.** to give a screen test to: *The studio screen-tested 400 children before casting the part.* —*v.i.* **2.** to undergo a screen test: *Dozens of actors have screen-tested for the role.* [1965–70; v. use of n. phrase *screen test*]

screen-wip·er (skrēn′wī′pər), *n. Brit.* See **windshield wiper.** [1925–30]

screen-writ·er (skrēn′rī′tər), *n.* a person who writes screenplays, esp. as an occupation or profession. [1920–25; SCREEN + WRITER]

screev·er (skrē′vər), *n. Chiefly Brit.* an artist who draws pictures on sidewalks, as with colored chalks, earning a living from the donations of spectators and passersby. [1875–80; earlier *screeve* (v.) (< Polari) < It *scrivere* to write (< L *scrībere*) + -ER[1]]

screw (skro͞o), *n.* **1.** a metal fastener having a tapered shank with a helical thread, and topped with a slotted head, driven into wood or the like by rotating, esp. by means of a screwdriver. **2.** a threaded cylindrical pin or rod with a head at one end, engaging a threaded hole and used either as a fastener or as a simple machine for applying power, as in a clamp, jack, etc. Cf. **bolt**[1] (def. 3). **3.** *Brit.* a tapped or threaded hole. **4.** something having a spiral form. **5.** See **screw propeller. 6.** Usually, **screws.** physical or mental coercion: *The terrified debtor soon felt the gangster's screws.* **7.** a single turn of a screw. **8.** a twist, turn, or twisting movement. **9.** *Chiefly Brit.* **a.** a little salt, sugar, tobacco, etc., carried in a twist of paper. **b.** *Slang.* a mean, old, or worn-out horse; a horse from which one can obtain no further service. **c.** *Slang.* a friend or employer from whom one can obtain no more money. **d.** *Slang.* a miser. **10.** *Brit. Informal.* salary; wages. **11.** *Slang.* a prison guard. **12.** *Slang* (*vulgar*). **a.** an act of coitus. **b.** a person viewed as a sexual partner. **13. have a screw loose,** *Slang.* to be eccentric or neurotic; have crazy ideas: *You must have a screw loose to keep so many cats.* **14. put the screws on,** to compel by exerting pressure on; use coercion on; force: *They kept putting the screws on him for more money.* —*v.t.* **15.** to fasten, tighten, force, press, stretch tight, etc., by or as if by means of a screw or device operated by a screw or helical threads. **16.** to operate or adjust by a screw, as a press. **17.** to attach with a screw or screws: *to screw a bracket to a wall.* **18.** to insert, fasten, undo, or work (a screw, bolt, nut, bottle top with a helical thread, etc.) by turning. **19.** to contort as by twisting; distort: *Father screwed his face into a grimace of disgust.* **20.** to cause to become sufficiently strong or intense (usually fol. by *up*): *I screwed up my courage to ask for a raise.* **21.** to coerce or threaten. **22.** to extract or extort. **23.** to force (a seller) to lower a price (often fol. by *down*). **24.** *Slang.* to cheat or take advantage of (someone). **25.** *Slang* (*vulgar*). to have coitus with. —*v.i.* **26.** to turn as or like a screw. **27.** to be adapted for being connected, taken apart, opened, or closed by means of a screw or screws or parts with helical threads (usually fol. by *on, together,* or *off*): *This top screws on easily.* **28.** to turn or move with a twisting or rotating motion. **29.** to practice extortion. **30.** *Slang* (*vulgar*). to have coitus. **31. screw around,** *Slang.* **a.** to waste time in foolish or frivolous activity: *If you'd stop screwing around we could get this job done.* **b.** *Vulgar.* to engage in promiscuous sex. **32. screw off,** *Slang.* **a.** to do nothing; loaf. **b.** to leave; go away. **33. screw up,** *Slang.* **a.** to ruin through bungling or stupidity: *Somehow the engineers screwed up the entire construction project.* **b.** to make a botch of something; blunder. **c.** to make confused, anxious, or neurotic. [1375–1425; late ME *scrwe, screw(e)* (n.); cf. MF *escro(ue)* nut, MD *schrûve,* MHG *schrûbe* screw] —**screw′a·ble,** *adj.* —**screw′er,** *n.* —**screw′less,** *adj.* —**screw′like′,** *adj.*

—**Syn. 22.** wring, wrest, force, exact, squeeze.

CONCISE ETYMOLOGY KEY: <, descended or borrowed from; >, whence; b., blend of, blended; c., cognate with; cf., compare; deriv., derivative; equiv., equivalent; imit., imitative; obl., oblique; r., replacing; s., stem; sp., spelling, spelled; resp., respelling, respelled; trans., translation; ?, origin unknown; *, unattested; ‡, probably earlier than. See the full key inside the front cover.

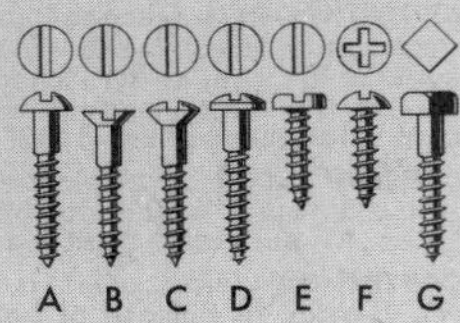

screws (def. 1) and screwheads A, round head; B, flat head; C, oval head; D, fillister head; E, metal screw; F, Phillips head screw; G, lag screw

screw′ an′chor, *Naut.* See **mooring screw.**

screw′ au′ger, an auger having a helical outer surface suggesting a screw thread. [1785–95, *Amer.*]

screw′ ax′is, *Crystall.* a symmetry element of a space group such that a rotation of the lattice about the axis and a translation of the lattice some fraction of the lattice's unit distance brings the lattice back to its original position. [1900–05]

screw·ball (skro͞o′bôl′), *n.* **1.** *Slang.* an eccentric or whimsically eccentric person; a nut. **2.** *Baseball.* a pitched ball that curves toward the side of the plate from which it was thrown. —*adj.* **3.** *Slang.* eccentric or whimsically eccentric: *What a screwball idea!* [1865–70; 1935–40 for def. 2; SCREW + BALL[1]]

screw′ bean′, **1.** a tree, *Prosopis pubescens,* of the legume family, native to the southwestern U.S., bearing twisted pods used as fodder. **2.** the pod itself. Also called **tornillo.** [1865–70, *Amer.*]

screw′ cap′, a cap designed to screw onto the threaded mouth of a bottle, jar, or the like. [1870–75]

screw′ convey′or, a device for moving loose materials, consisting of a shaft with a broad, helically wound blade rotating in a tube or trough. Also called **worm.**

screw·driv·er (skro͞o′drī′vər), *n.* **1.** a hand tool for turning a screw, consisting of a handle attached to a long, narrow shank, usually of metal, which tapers and flattens out to a tip that fits into the slotted head of a screw. **2.** a mixed drink made with vodka and orange juice. [1770–80; SCREW + DRIVER]

screwed (skro͞od), *adj.* **1.** fastened with screws. **2.** having grooves like a screw; threaded. **3.** twisted; awry. **4.** *Slang.* bilked; cheated. **5.** *Chiefly Brit. Slang.* drunk; intoxicated. [1640–50; SCREW + -ED[2]]

screw′ eye′, a screw having a ring-shaped head. [1870–75]

screw′ fly′. See **screwworm fly.** [1880–85]

screw·head (skro͞o′hed′), *n.* the head or top of a screw having a slot for the end of a screwdriver. See diag. under **screw.** [1680–90; SCREW + HEAD]

screw′ hook′, a hook having a shank in the form of a screw. [1680–90]

screw′ jack′, jackscrew. [1710–20]

screw′ log′, *Naut.* See **patent log.**

screw′ moor′ing, *Naut.* See **mooring screw.**

screw′ nail′. See **drive screw.** [1650–60]

screw′ nut′, a nut threaded to receive a screw. [1805–15]

screw-off (skro͞o′ôf′, -of′), *n. Slang.* a loafer; idler. Also, **screw′off′.** [n. use of v. phrase *screw off*]

screw-on (skro͞o′on′, -ôn′), *adj.* **1.** attached, connected, or closed by screwing onto another part of a container or receptacle. **2.** (of an earring) held on the earlobe by a small screwlike post with a disk at the tip. [1925–30; adj. use of v. phrase *screw on*]

screw′ pile′, a pile that is used for the foundations of bridges, lighthouses, etc., and has a screwlike lower end for drilling through and taking firm hold in compacted material. [1830–40] —**screw′ pil′ing.**

screw′ pine′, any tropical Asian tree or shrub of the genus *Pandanus,* having a palmlike or branched stem, long, narrow, rigid, spirally arranged leaves and aerial roots, and bearing an edible fruit. [1830–40]

screw·plate (skro͞o′plāt′), *n.* a metal plate having threaded holes, used for cutting screw threads by hand. Also, **screw′ plate′.** [1650–60; SCREW + PLATE[1]]

screw′ press′, a device for applying pressure by the turning of a threaded shaft. [1680–90]

screw′ propel′ler, a rotary propelling device, as for a ship or airplane, consisting of a number of blades that radiate from a central hub and are so inclined to the plane of rotation as to tend to drive a helical path through the substance in which they rotate. [1830–40] —**screw′-pro·pelled′,** *adj.*

screw′ thread′, **1.** Also called **worm.** the helical ridge of a screw. **2.** a full turn of the helical ridge of a screw. [1805–15]

screw-top (skro͞o′top′), *adj.* **1.** (of a container) having a top that screws on. —*n.* **2.** a top that can be screwed onto a container. **3.** a container having such a top. [1890–95]

screw-up (skro͞o′up′), *n. Slang.* **1.** a mistake or blunder: *The package was delayed through an addressing screwup.* **2.** a habitual blunderer. Also, **screw′-up′.** [1955–60; *Amer.*; n. use of v. phrase *screw up*]

screw·worm (skro͞o′wûrm′), *n.* the larva of any of certain flies of the genus *Callitroga,* which sometimes infests wounds and the nose and navel of domestic animals and humans. [1875–80, *Amer.*; SCREW + WORM]

screw′worm fly′, the adult screwworm. Also called **screw fly.** [1905–10; *Amer.*]

screw·y (skro͞o′ē), *adj.,* **screw·i·er, screw·i·est.** *Slang.* **1.** crazy; nutty: *I think you're screwy, refusing an invitation to the governor's dinner.* **2.** disconcertingly strange: *There's something screwy about his story.* **3.** absurdly peculiar or impractical; ridiculous: *screwy ideas.* [1810–20; SCREW + -Y[1]]

Scria·bin (skrē ä′bin; *Russ.* skryä′byin), *n.* **A·le·ksan·dr Ni·ko·la·e·vich** (al′ig zan′dər nik′ə lī′ə vich, -zän′-; *Russ.* u lyi ksän′dr nyi ku lä′yi vyich), 1872–1915, Russian composer and pianist.

scrib·ble[1] (skrib′əl), *v.,* **-bled, -bling,** *n.* —*v.t.* **1.** to write hastily or carelessly: *to scribble a letter.* **2.** to cover with meaningless writing or marks: *to scribble all over a page.* —*v.i.* **3.** to write or draw in a hasty or careless way. **4.** to make meaningless marks, scrolls, lines, etc., with a pencil, pen, or the like. —*n.* **5.** a note or other writing that has little or no meaning. **6.** a hasty or careless drawing or piece of writing. **7.** handwriting, esp. when illegible. [1425–75; late ME *scribblen* (v.) < ML *scrībillāre* to scribble, deriv. of L *scrībere* to write; see SHRIVE] —**scrib′bling·ly,** *adv.*

scrib·ble[2] (skrib′əl), *v.t.,* **-bled, -bling.** to tear apart (wool fibers) in the first stages of carding. [1675–85; < D *schribbelen* to scratch; c. *schrobbelen* to card wool coarsely, freq. of *schrobben* to SCRUB[1]]

scrib·bler[1] (skrib′lər), *n.* **1.** a writer whose work has little or no value or importance. **2.** a person who scribbles. [1545–55; SCRIBBLE[1] + -ER[1]]

scrib·bler[2] (skrib′lər), *n.* a machine for scribbling wool fibers. [1675–85; SCRIBBLE[2] + -ER[1]]

scrib′bling block′, *Brit.* See **scratch pad.** [1905–10]

scribe[1] (skrīb), *n., v.,* **scribed, scrib·ing.** —*n.* **1.** a person who serves as a professional copyist, esp. one who made copies of manuscripts before the invention of printing. **2.** a public clerk or writer, usually one having official status. **3.** Also called **sopher, sofer.** *Judaism.* one of the group of Palestinian scholars and teachers of Jewish law and tradition, active from the 5th century B.C. to the 1st century A.D., who transcribed, edited, and interpreted the Bible. **4.** a writer or author, esp. a journalist. —*v.i.* **5.** to act as a scribe; write. —*v.t.* **6.** to write down. [1350–1400; ME < L *scrība* clerk, deriv. of *scrībere* to write] —**scrib′al,** *adj.*

scribe[2] (skrīb), *v.,* **scribed, scrib·ing,** *n.* —*v.t.* **1.** to mark or score (wood or the like) with a pointed instrument as a guide to cutting or assembling. —*n.* **2.** scriber. [1670–80; perh. aph. form of INSCRIBE]

Scribe (skrēb), *n.* **Au·gus·tin Eu·gène** (ō gys tan′ œ zhen′), 1791–1861, French dramatist.

scrib·er (skrī′bər), *n.* a tool for scribing wood or the like. Also, **scribe.** [1825–35; SCRIBE[2] + -ER[1]]

scrim (skrim), *n.* **1.** a cotton or linen fabric of open weave used for bunting, curtains, etc. **2.** *Theat.* a piece of such fabric used as a drop, border, or the like, for creating the illusion of a solid wall or backdrop under certain lighting conditions or creating a semitransparent curtain when lit from behind. [1785–95; orig. uncert.]

scrim·mage (skrim′ij), *n., v.,* **-maged, -mag·ing.** —*n.* **1.** a rough or vigorous struggle. **2.** *Football.* **a.** the action that takes place between the teams from the moment the ball is snapped until it is declared dead. Cf. **line of scrimmage. b.** a practice session or informal game, as that played between two units of the same team. —*v.t., v.i.* **3.** to engage in a scrimmage. [1425–75; late ME, var. of *scrimish,* metathetic form of SKIRMISH] —**scrim′mag·er,** *n.*

scrim′mage line′. See **line of scrimmage.** [1875–80]

scrimp (skrimp), *v.i.* **1.** to be sparing or frugal; economize (often fol. by *on*): *They scrimped and saved for everything they have. He spends most of his money on clothes, and scrimps on food.* —*v.t.* **2.** to be sparing or restrictive of or in; limit severely: *to scrimp food.* **3.** to keep on short allowance; provide sparingly for: *to scrimp their elderly parents.* [1710–20; < Scand; cf. Sw *skrympa,* Norw, Dan *skrumpe* (orig. **skrimpa,* strong v.) to shrivel, c. MHG *schrimpfen* to contract; see SHRIMP] —**Syn. 1.** skimp, stint, save, scrape.

scrimp·y (skrim′pē), *adj.,* **scrimp·i·er, scrimp·i·est.** **1.** scanty; meager; barely adequate. **2.** tending to scrimp; frugal; parsimonious. [1850–55; SCRIMP + -Y[1]] —**scrimp′i·ly,** *adv.* —**scrimp′i·ness,** *n.*

scrim·shank (skrim′shangk′), *v.i. Brit. Slang.* to avoid one's obligations or share of work; shirk. [1885–90; orig. uncert.] —**scrim′shank′er,** *n.*

scrim·shaw (skrim′shô′), *n.* **1.** a carved or engraved article, esp. of whale ivory, whalebone, walrus tusks, or the like, made by whalers as a leisure occupation. **2.** such articles or work collectively. **3.** the art or technique of carving or engraving whale ivory, whalebone, walrus tusks, etc. —*v.i.* **4.** to produce scrimshaw. —*v.t.* **5.** to carve or engrave (whale ivory or whalebone) into scrimshaw. [1860–65; of obscure orig.]

scrin·i·um (skrin′ē əm), *n., pl.* **scrin·i·a** (skrin′ē ə). a cylindrical container used in ancient Rome to hold papyrus rolls. [< L *scrīnium;* see SHRINE]

scrip[1] (skrip), *n.* **1.** a receipt, certificate, list, or similar brief piece of writing. **2.** a scrap of paper. **3.** *Finance.* **a.** a certificate representing a fraction of a share of stock. **b.** a certificate to be exchanged for goods, as at a company store. **c.** a certificate indicating the right of the holder to receive payment later in the form of cash, goods, or land. **4.** paper currency in denominations of less than one dollar, formerly issued in the United States. [1610–20; earliest sense "scrap of paper" perh. gradational var. of SCRAP[1]; subsequent sense development shows influence of SCRIPT and SUBSCRIPTION, with def. 3a specifically a shortening of *subscription receipt*] —**scrip′less,** *adj.*

scrip[2] (skrip), *n. Archaic.* a bag or wallet carried by wayfarers. [1250–1300; ME *scrippe* < ML *scrippum* pilgrim's pack < ?]

scrip[3] (skrip), *n. Informal.* a prescription, as for a drug. [1965–70; shortening of PRESCRIPTION]

scrip′ div′idend, a dividend issued in the form of a note entitling the holder to a cash payment at a specified later date. [1880–85]

scrip·o·phile (skrip′ə fīl′), *n.* a person who practices scripophily. Also, **scri·poph·i·list** (skri pof′ə list). [1975–80; SCRIP[1] + -O- + -PHILE]

scri•poph•i•ly (skri pof′ə lē), *n.* the collecting by hobbyists of old stock certificates and bonds that have no intrinsic value other than their aesthetic appeal or relative rarity. [1975–80; SCRIP[1] + -O- + -PHILY]

Scripps (skrips), *n.* **Edward Wyl•lis** (wil′is), 1854–1926, U.S. newspaper publisher.

scrip•sit (skrip′sit; *Eng.* skrip′sit), *v. Latin.* he wrote (it); she wrote (it).

script (skript), *n.* **1.** the letters or characters used in writing by hand; handwriting, esp. cursive writing. **2.** a manuscript or document. **3.** the text of a manuscript or document. **4.** the manuscript or one of various copies of the written text of a play, motion picture, or radio or television broadcast. **5.** any system of writing. **6.** *Print.* a type imitating handwriting. Cf. **cursive.** —*v.t.* **7.** to write a script for. **8.** to plan or devise; make arrangements for: *The week-long festivities were scripted by a team of experts.* [1325–75; ME (n.) < L *scrīptum,* n. use of neut. ptp. of *scrībere* to write; r. ME *scrit* < OF *escrit* < L , as above] —**script′er,** *n.*

Script., **1.** Scriptural. **2.** Scripture.

script′ doc′tor, one who revises or alters a script to improve it.

script′ girl′, a female secretarial assistant to the director of a motion picture. [1925–30]

scrip•to•ri•um (skrip tôr′ē əm, -tōr′-), *n., pl.* **-to•ri•ums, -to•ri•a** (-tôr′ē ə, -tōr′-). a room, as in a monastery, library, or other institution, where manuscripts are stored, read, or copied. [1765–75; < ML *scrīptōrium;* see SCRIPT, -TORY[2]]

script′ read′er, playreader. [1955–60]

scrip•tur•al (skrip′chər əl), *adj.* **1.** (*sometimes cap.*) of, pertaining to, or in accordance with sacred writings, esp. the Scriptures. **2.** rendered in or related to writing. [1635–45; < LL *scrīptūrālis.* See SCRIPTURE, -AL[1]] —**scrip′tur•al•ly,** *adv.* —**scrip′tur•al•ness,** *n.*

Scrip•ture (skrip′chər), *n.* **1.** Often, **Scriptures.** Also called **Holy Scripture, Holy Scriptures.** the sacred writings of the Old or New Testaments or both together. **2.** (*often l.c.*) any writing or book, esp. when of a sacred or religious nature. **3.** (*sometimes l.c.*) a particular passage from the Bible; text. [1250–1300; ME < L *scrīptūra* writing. See SCRIPT, -URE]

script•writ•er (skript′rī′tər), *n.* a person who writes scripts, as for movies, radio, or television. [1910–15; SCRIPT + WRITER] —**script′writ′ing,** *n.*

scrive′ board′ (skrīv, skrēv), *Shipbuilding.* a floorlike construction on which the lines of a vessel can be drawn or scribed at full size. [1865–70; *scrive,* var. of SCRIBE[2]]

scrive•ner (skriv′nər), *n.* **1.** scribe[1] (defs. 1, 2). **2.** a notary. [1325–75; ME *scriveyner,* equiv. to *scrivein* (< OF *escrivein;* see SCRIBE[1], -AN) + *-er* -ER[1]]

scro•bic•u•late (skrō bik′yə lit, -lāt′), *adj. Bot., Zool.* furrowed or pitted. [1800–10; < L *scrobicul(us)* small planting hole (*scrobi(s)* ditch + *-culus* -CULE[1]) + -ATE[1]]

scrod (skrod), *n.* a young Atlantic codfish or haddock, esp. one split for cooking. Also, **schrod.** [1835–45, *Amer.*; orig. uncert.]

scrof•u•la (skrof′yə lə), *n. Pathol.* primary tuberculosis of the lymphatic glands, esp. those of the neck. [1350–1400; ME (pl.) < LL *scrōfulae* (L *scrōf(a)* sow + *-ulae* (pl.) -ULE), from the belief that breeding sows were susceptible]

scrof•u•lous (skrof′yə ləs), *adj.* **1.** pertaining to, resembling, of the nature of, or affected with scrofula. **2.** morally tainted. [1605–15; SCROFUL(A) + -OUS] —**scrof′u•lous•ly,** *adv.* —**scrof′u•lous•ness,** *n.*

scrog (skrog), *n. Scot. and North Eng.* **1.** any naturally short or stunted tree or bush, as a crab apple tree or blackthorn bush. **2.** **scrogs,** underbrush; brushwood. [1350–1400; ME *skrogg;* prob. akin to SCRAG] —**scrog′gy,** *adj.*

scroll (skrōl), *n.* **1.** a roll of parchment, paper, copper, or other material, esp. one with writing on it: *a scroll containing the entire Old Testament.* **2.** something, esp. an ornament, resembling a partly unrolled sheet of paper or having a spiral or coiled form. **3.** a list, roll, roster, or schedule. **4.** (in Japanese and Chinese art) a painting or text on silk or paper that is either displayed on a wall **(hanging scroll)** or held by the viewer **(hand scroll)** and is rolled up when not in use. Cf. **kakemono, makimono.** **5.** the curved head of a violin or other bowed instrument. **6.** a note, message, or other piece of writing. —*v.t.* **7.** to cut into a curved form with a narrow-bladed saw. **8.** *Computers.* to move (text) up, down, or across a display screen, with new text appearing on the screen as old text disappears. —*v.i.* **9.** *Computers.* to move text vertically or horizontally on a display screen in searching for a particular section, line, etc. [1350–1400; ME *scrowle;* b. *scrow,* aph. var. of ESCROW and *rowle* ROLL] —**scroll′-like′,** *adj.*

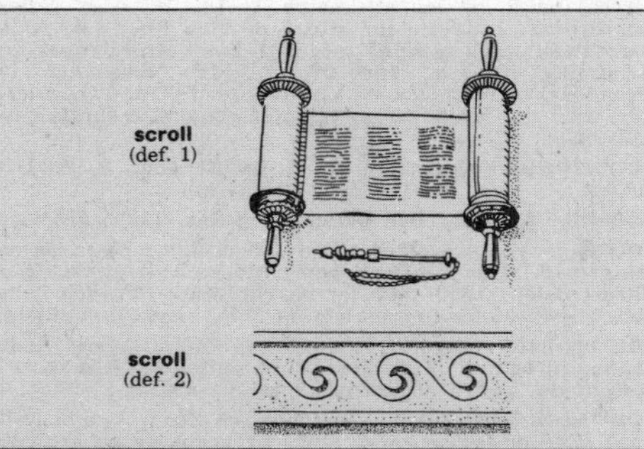

scroll (def. 1)

scroll (def. 2)

scroll′ foot′. See **French foot** (def. 1). [1930–35]

scroll•head (skrōl′hed′), *n. Naut.* billethead. [1865–70; SCROLL + HEAD]

scroll′ saw′, **1.** a narrow saw mounted vertically in a frame and operated with an up-and-down motion, used for cutting curved ornamental designs. **2.** such a saw mounted in a power-driven machine. [1850–55]

scroll•work (skrōl′wûrk′), *n.* **1.** decorative work in which scroll forms figure prominently. **2.** ornamental work cut out with a scroll saw. [1730–40; SCROLL + WORK]

scrooch (skrōōch), *v.i. Chiefly Midland and Southern U.S.* to crouch, squeeze, or huddle (usually fol. by *down, in,* or *up*). Also, **scrootch.** [1835–45; appar. var. of SCROUGE, influenced in meaning by CROUCH]

scrooge (skrōōj), *v.t., v.i.,* **scrooged, scroog•ing.** scrouge.

Scrooge (skrōōj), *n.* **1. Eb•e•ne•zer** (eb′ə nē′zər), a miserly curmudgeon in Dickens' *Christmas Carol.* **2.** (*often l.c.*) any miserly person. [1935–40, for def. 2]

scroop (skrōōp), *v.i.* **1.** to emit a harsh, grating sound: *The gate scrooped as he swung it shut.* —*n.* **2.** a scrooping sound. **3.** ability to make a rustling sound added to silk or rayon fabrics during finishing by treating them with certain acids. [1780–90; b. SCRAPE and WHOOP]

scroph•u•lar•i•a•ceous (skrof′yə lâr′ē ā′shəs), *adj.* belonging to the Scrophulariaceae, the figwort family of plants. Cf. **figwort family.** [1840–50; < NL *scrophulariace(ae)* family name (see SCROFULA, -ARIA, -ACEAE) + -OUS]

scro•tum (skrō′təm), *n., pl.* **-ta** (-tə), **-tums.** *Anat.* the pouch of skin that contains the testes. [1590–1600; < L *scrōtum,* var. of *scrautum* quiver] —**scro′tal,** *adj.*

scrouge (skrouj, skrōōj), *v.t., v.i.,* **scrouged, scroug•ing.** to squeeze; crowd. Also, **scrooge.** [1820–30; b. obs. *scruze* (itself b. SCREW and BRUISE) and GOUGE]

scrounge (skrounj), *v.,* **scrounged, scroung•ing,** *n.* —*v.t.* **1.** to borrow (a small amount or item) with no intention of repaying or returning it: *to scrounge a cigarette.* **2.** to gather together by foraging; seek out: *We'll try to scrounge enough food for supper from the neighbors.* —*v.i.* **3.** to borrow, esp. a small item one is not expected to return or replace. **4. scrounge around,** to search or forage for something, esp. in a haphazard or disorganized fashion; hunt for: *We scrounged around for something to eat.* —*n.* **5.** a habitual borrower; sponger. **6.** an act or instance of scrounging. **7.** a person who exists by foraging. Also, **scroung′er** (for defs. 5, 7). [1905–10; alter. of dial. *scringe* to glean]

scroung•y (skroun′jē), *adj.,* **scroung•i•er, scroung•i•est.** **1.** given to or characterized by scrounging. **2.** shabby or slovenly: *scroungy clothes.* [SCROUNGE + -Y[1]]

Scro•ve′gni Chap′el (skrō vān′yē; *It.* skrô ve′nyē). See **Arena Chapel.**

scrub[1] (skrub), *v.,* **scrubbed, scrub•bing,** *n.* —*v.t.* **1.** to rub hard with a brush, cloth, etc., or against a rough surface in washing. **2.** to subject to friction; rub. **3.** to remove (dirt, grime, etc.) from something by hard rubbing while washing. **4.** *Chem.* to remove (impurities or undesirable components) from a gas by chemical means, as sulfur dioxide from smokestack gas or carbon dioxide from exhaled air in life-support packs. **5.** to cancel or postpone (a space flight or part of a mission): *Ground control scrubbed the spacewalk.* **6.** *Slang.* to do away with; cancel: *Scrub your vacation plans—there's work to do!* —*v.i.* **7.** to cleanse something by hard rubbing. **8.** to cleanse one's hands and arms as a preparation to performing or assisting in surgery (often fol. by *up*). —*n.* **9.** an act or instance of scrubbing. **10.** a canceled or postponed space flight, launching, scheduled part of a space mission, etc. **11.** something, as a cosmetic preparation, used for scrubbing. [1300–50; ME *scrobben* (n.) < MD *schrobben*] —**scrub′ba•ble,** *adj.*

scrub[2] (skrub), *n.* **1.** low trees or shrubs collectively. **2.** a large area covered with low trees and shrubs, as the Australian bush. **3.** a domestic animal of mixed or inferior breeding; mongrel. **4.** a small or insignificant person. **5.** anything undersized or inferior. **6.** *Sports.* a player not belonging to the varsity or regular team; a player who is not first-string. —*adj.* **7.** small, undersized, or stunted. **8.** inferior or insignificant. **9.** abounding in or covered with low trees and shrubs: *They rode through scrub country.* [1350–1400; ME < Scand; cf. dial. Dan *skrub* brushwood; see SHRUB[1]]

scrub•bed (skrub′id), *adj. Archaic.* stunted; scrubby. [1590–1600; SCRUB[2] + -ED[3]]

scrub•ber[1] (skrub′ər), *n.* **1.** a person who scrubs. **2.** a device or process for removing pollutants from smoke or gas produced by burning high-sulfur fuels. **3.** a machine or appliance used in scrubbing: *an automatic floor scrubber.* [1830–40; SCRUB[1] + -ER[1]]

scrub•ber[2] (skrub′ər), *n.* **1.** a mongrel, esp. a mongrel steer. **2.** a thin or stunted steer. **3.** *Australian.* **a.** an inhabitant of the bush. **b.** any domestic animal that has run off into the bush and become wild, esp. a steer. [1855–60; SCRUB[2] + -ER[1]]

scrub•ber[3] (skrub′ər), *n. Brit. Slang.* a prostitute or promiscuous woman. [1955–60; variously explained as sense development of either SCRUBBER[1] or SCRUBBER[2]; cf. earlier *scrub* in same sense]

scrub•bird (skrub′bûrd′), *n.* either of two Australian passerine birds of the genus *Atrichornis,* related to the lyrebirds, having a loud voice and reduced powers of flight: *A. clamosus* is endangered. [1865–70; SCRUB[2] + BIRD]

scrub•board (skrub′bôrd′, -bōrd′), *n.* washboard (defs. 1, 2). [SCRUB[1] + BOARD]

scrub′ brush′, a brush with stiff, short bristles for scrubbing. Also called **scrub′bing brush′.** [1675–85]

scrub•by (skrub′ē), *adj.,* **-bi•er, -bi•est.** **1.** low or stunted, as trees. **2.** consisting of or covered with scrub, stunted trees, etc. **3.** undersized or inferior, as animals. **4.** wretched; shabby. [1745–55; SCRUB[2] + -Y[1]] —**scrub′bi•ly,** *adv.* —**scrub′bi•ness,** *n.*

scrub•down (skrub′doun′), *n.* an act or instance of scrubbing, esp. a thorough washing of a surface or object: *The decks of the ship get a scrubdown every morning.* [n. use of v. phrase *scrub down*]

scrub′ fowl′, megapode. [1940–45]

scrub′ jay′, a crestless jay, *Aphelocoma coerulescens,* of the western and southern U.S. and Mexico, having blue and grayish plumage. [1935–40, *Amer.*]

scrub•land (skrub′land′), *n.* land on which the natural vegetation is chiefly scrub. [1770–80, *Amer.*; SCRUB[2] + -LAND]

scrub′ nurse′, a nurse specially trained to assist surgeons in the operating room and serving as part of the surgically clean medical team handling instruments during an operation. [1925–30]

scrub′ oak′, any of several oaks, as *Quercus ilicifolia* and *Q. prinoides,* characterized by a scrubby manner of growth, usually found in dry, rocky soil. [1760–70, *Amer.*]

scrub′ pine′, any of several pines, as the jack pine, characterized by a scrubby or irregular manner of growth, usually found in dry, sandy soil. [1785–95, *Amer.*]

scrub′ suit′, a loose-fitting, usually two-piece garment, often of green cotton, worn by surgeons and assisting personnel in an operating room.

scrub′ ty′phus, *Pathol.* an infectious disease occurring chiefly in Japan and the East Indies, caused by the organism *Rickettsia tsutsugamushi,* transmitted by mites through biting. Also called **Japanese river fever, tsutsugamushi disease.** [1925–30]

scrub-up (skrub′up′), *n.* the act of washing or bathing thoroughly, esp. the aseptic washing by doctors, nurses, etc., before a surgical operation. [1915–20]

scrub•wom•an (skrub′wŏŏm′ən), *n., pl.* **-wom•en.** a woman hired to clean a place; charwoman. [1870–75; SCRUB[1] + WOMAN]
—**Usage.** See **woman.**

scruff[1] (skruf), *n.* the nape or back of the neck. [1780–90; var. of dial. *scuff, scuft* < D *schoft* horse's withers]

scruff[2] (skruf), *n. Metall.* (in tin-plating) dross formed in the bath. [metathetic var. of SCURF]

scruff•y (skruf′ē), *adj.,* **scruff•i•er, scruff•i•est.** untidy; shabby. [1650–60; SCRUFF[2] + -Y[1]]

scrum (skrum), *n., v.,* **scrummed, scrum•ming.** —*n.* **1.** a Rugby play in which, typically, three members of each team line up opposite one another with a group of two and a group of three players behind them, making an eight-person, three-two-three formation on each side; the ball is then rolled between the opposing front lines, the players of which stand with arms around a teammate's waist, meeting the opponent shoulder to shoulder, and attempt to kick the ball backward to a teammate. **2.** *Brit.* a place or situation of confusion and racket; hubbub. —*v.i.* **3.** to engage in a scrum. Also, **scrummage** (for defs. 1, 3). [1885–90; short for SCRUMMAGE]

scrum•mage (skrum′ij), *n., v.i.,* **-maged, -mag•ing.** scrum (defs. 1, 3). [perh. orig. a dial. var. of SCRIMMAGE] —**scrum′mag•er,** *n.*

scrum•my (skrum′ē), *adj.,* **-mi•er, -mi•est.** *Chiefly Brit. Informal.* scrumptious. [1910–15; SCRUM(PTIOUS) + -Y[1]]

scrump•tious (skrump′shəs), *adj.* very pleasing, esp. to the senses; delectable; splendid: *a scrumptious casserole; a scrumptious satin gown.* [1820–30; perh. alter. of SUMPTUOUS] —**scrump′tious•ly,** *adv.* —**scrump′tious•ness,** *n.*

scrunch (skrunch, skrŏŏnch), *v.t.* **1.** to crunch, crush, or crumple. **2.** to contract; squeeze together: *I had to scrunch my shoulders to get through the door.* —*v.i.* **3.** to squat or hunker (often fol. by *down*). —*n.* **4.** the act or sound of scrunching. [1815–25; perh. expressive var. of CRUNCH]

scru•ple (skrōō′pəl), *n., v.,* **-pled, -pling.** —*n.* **1.** a moral or ethical consideration or standard that acts as a restraining force or inhibits certain actions. **2.** a very small portion or amount. **3.** a unit of weight equal to 20 grains (1.295 grams) or $\frac{1}{3}$ of a dram, apothecaries' weight. **4.** an ancient Roman unit of weight equivalent to $\frac{1}{24}$ of an ounce or $\frac{1}{288}$ of an as or pound. Cf. **as[2]** (def. 2). —*v.i.* **5.** to have scruples. —*v.t.* **6.** to have scruples about; hesitate at. [1350–1400; (< F *scrupule*) < L *scrūpulus* unit of weight, worry, precaution equiv. to *scrūp(us)* rough pebble + *-ulus* -ULE; r. earlier *scriple,* ME < L *scrīpulum* (var. *scriptulum*) small weight, pebble, alter. of *scrūpulus* by assoc. with *scrīptum* writing (see SCRIPT; for sense relation cf. GRAM)] —**scru′ple•less,** *adj.*
—**Syn. 1.** qualm, compunction, restraint. **6.** waver.

scru•pu•lous (skrōō′pyə ləs), *adj.* **1.** having scruples; having or showing a strict regard for what one considers right; principled. **2.** punctiliously or minutely careful, precise, or exact: *a scrupulous performance.* [1400–50; late ME < L *scrūpulōsus.* See SCRUPLE, -OUS] —**scru•pu•los•i•ty** (skrōō′pyə los′i tē), **scru′pu•lous•ness,** *n.* —**scru′pu•lous•ly,** *adv.*
—**Syn. 1.** conscientious, cautious, careful, circumspect. **2.** exacting, rigorous. SCRUPULOUS, PUNCTILIOUS imply abiding exactly by rules. SCRUPULOUS implies conscientious carefulness in attending to details: *scrupulous attention to details.* PUNCTILIOUS suggests strictness, preciseness, and rigidity, esp. in observance of social conventions. —**Ant. 2.** careless.

scru•ta•ble (skrōō′tə bəl), *adj.* capable of being understood by careful study or investigation. [1590–1600; < L *scrūt(ārī)* (see SCRUTINY) + -ABLE] —**scru′ta•bil′i•ty,** *n.*

scru•ta•tor (skrōō tā′tər), *n.* a person who investigates. [1570–80; < L *scrūtātor* searcher, examiner,

CONCISE PRONUNCIATION KEY: act, cāpe, dâre, pärt; set, ēqual; if, īce; ox, ōver, ôrder, oil, bŏŏk, bōōt, out; up, ûrge; child; sing; shoe; thin, *th*at; zh as in *treasure.* ə = *a* as in *alone, e* as in *system, i* as in *easily, o* as in *gallop, u* as in *circus;* ə as in *fire* (fīər), *hour* (ouər). l and n can serve as syllabic consonants, as in *cradle* (krād′l), and *button* (but′n). See the full key inside the front cover.

equiv. to *scrūtā(rī)* to examine (see SCRUTINY) + *-tor* -TOR]

scru·ti·neer (skrōōt′n ēr′), *n. Chiefly Brit. and Canadian.* an official examiner, esp. of votes in an election. [1550–60; SCRUTIN(Y) + -EER]

scru·ti·nize (skrōōt′n īz′), *v.*, **-nized, -niz·ing.** —*v.t.* **1.** to examine in detail with careful or critical attention. —*v.i.* **2.** to conduct a scrutiny. Also, *esp. Brit.,* **scru′ti·nise′.** [1665–75; SCRUTIN(Y) + -IZE] —**scru′ti·ni·za′tion,** *n.* —**scru′ti·niz′er,** *n.* —**scru′ti·niz′ing·ly,** *adv.*

scru·ti·ny (skrōōt′n ē), *n., pl.* **-nies. 1.** a searching examination or investigation; minute inquiry. **2.** surveillance; close and continuous watching or guarding. **3.** a close and searching look. [1400–50; late ME < L *scrūtinium* the action of searching, of scrutinizing, deriv. of *scrūtārī* to search]
—**Syn. 1.** See **examination.**

scru·toire (skrōō twär′), *n.* See **writing desk** (def. 1).

SCS, Soil Conservation Service.

SCSI (skuz′ē), *n.* a standard for computer interface ports featuring faster data transmission and greater flexibility than normal ports. [1985–90; *s(mall) c(omputer) s(ystem) i(nterface)*]

scu·ba (skōō′bə), *n., v.,* **scu·baed, scu·ba·ing.** —*n.* **1.** a portable breathing device for free-swimming divers, consisting of a mouthpiece joined by hoses to one or two tanks of compressed air that are strapped on the back. **2.** See **scuba diving.** —*v.i.* **3.** scuba-dive. [1950–55; *s(elf)-c(ontained) u(nderwater) b(reathing) a(pparatus)*]

scu·ba-dive (skōō′bə dīv′), *v.i.,* **-dived** or **-dove, dived, -div·ing.** to descend and swim underwater using a scuba device. Also, **scu′ba dive′, scuba.** [1960–65]

scu′ba div′ing, the activity or recreation of diving or exploring underwater through use of a scuba device. Also called **scuba.** [1960–65] —**scu′ba div′er.**

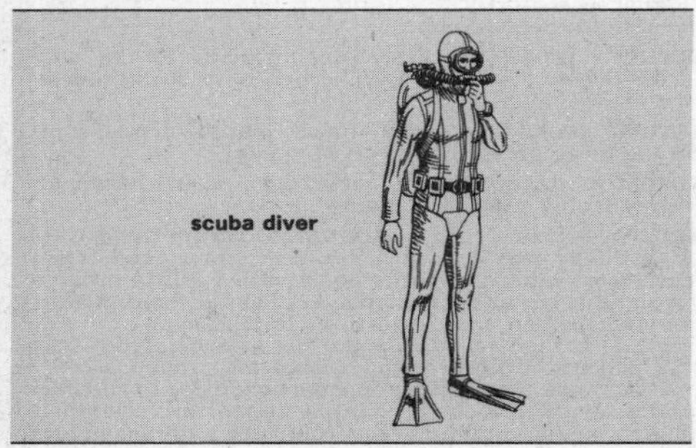

scuba diver

scud[1] (skud), *v.,* **scud·ded, scud·ding,** *n.* —*v.i.* **1.** to run or move quickly or hurriedly. **2.** *Naut.* to run before a gale with little or no sail set. **3.** *Archery.* (of an arrow) to fly too high and wide of the mark. —*n.* **4.** the act of scudding. **5.** clouds, spray, or mist driven by the wind; a driving shower or gust of wind. **6.** low-drifting clouds appearing beneath a cloud from which precipitation is falling. [1525–35; < MLG *schudden* to shake]

scud[2] (skud), *v.,* **scud·ded, scud·ding,** *n.* —*v.t.* **1.** to cleanse (a trimmed and roughly depilated skin or hide) of remaining hairs or dirt. —*n.* **2.** the hairs or dirt removed by scudding. [1635–45; perh. to be identified with obs. *scud* dirt < ?]

Scu·dé·ry (skʏ dā rē′), *n.* **Mag·de·leine de** (mag də-len′ də), 1607–1701, French novelist.

scu·do (skōō′dō), *n., pl.* **-di** (-dē). any of various gold or silver coins, of various Italian states, issued from the late 16th through the early 19th centuries. [1635–45; < It < L *scūtum* shield]

scuff (skuf), *v.t.* **1.** to scrape (something) with one's foot or feet. **2.** to rub or scrape (one's foot or feet) over something. **3.** to mar by scraping or hard use, as shoes or furniture. **4.** *Chiefly Scot.* **a.** to brush against, as in passing. **b.** to brush off; wipe off. —*v.i.* **5.** to walk without raising the feet from the ground; shuffle. **6.** to scrape or rub one's foot back and forth over something. **7.** to be or become marred or scratched by scraping or wear. **8.** (of machine parts, as gear teeth) to creep from pressure and friction so that ridges appear transversely to the direction of wear. —*n.* **9.** the act or sound of scuffing. **10.** a flat-heeled slipper with a full-length sole and an upper part covering only the front of the foot. **11.** a marred or scratched place on an item, as from scraping or wear. [1585–95; < MLG *schūven* to shove]

scuf·fle (skuf′əl), *v.,* **-fled, -fling,** *n.* —*v.i.* **1.** to struggle or fight in a rough, confused manner. **2.** to go or move in hurried confusion. **3.** to move or go with a shuffle; scuff. —*n.* **4.** a rough, confused struggle or fight. **5.** a shuffling: *a scuffle of feet.* **6.** Also called **scuf′fle hoe′.** a spadelike hoe that is pushed instead of pulled. **7.** (in tap dancing) a forward and backward movement of the foot. [1570–80; see SCUFF, -LE] —**scuf′fler,** *n.* —**scuf′fling·ly,** *adv.*
—**Syn. 4.** scrap, tussle, row.

sculch (skulch), *n. Eastern New Eng.* culch (def. 3).

scul·dud·der·y (skul dud′ə rē), *n., pl.* **-der·ies.** *Chiefly Brit.* obscene behavior; lewdness. [1705–15; orig. uncert.]

scul·dug·ger·y (skul dug′ə rē), *n.* skulduggery. Also, **scull·dug′ger·y.**

sculk (skulk), *v.i., n.* skulk.

scull (skul), *n.* **1.** an oar mounted on a fulcrum at the stern of a small boat and moved from side to side to propel the boat forward. **2.** either of a pair of oars rowed by one rower. **3.** a boat propelled by an oar or oars. **4.** a light, narrow racing boat for one, two, or sometimes four rowers, each equipped with a pair of oars. **5.** **sculls,** a race involving such boats. Cf. **double sculls, single sculls.** —*v.t.* **6.** to propel or convey by means of a scull or sculls. —*v.i.* **7.** to propel a boat with a scull or sculls. [1300–50; ME *sculle* < ?] —**scull′er,** *n.*

CONCISE ETYMOLOGY KEY: <, descended or borrowed from; >, whence; b., blend of, blended; c., cognate with; cf., compare; deriv., derivative; equiv., equivalent; imit., imitative; obl., oblique; r., replacing; s., stem; sp., spelling, spelled; resp., respelling, respelled; trans., translation; ?, origin unknown; *, unattested; ‡, probably earlier than. See the full key inside the front cover.

S, **scull** (def. 1)

scul·ler·y (skul′ə rē, skul′rē), *n., pl.* **-ler·ies.** *Chiefly Brit.* **1.** a small room or section of a pantry in which food is cleaned, trimmed, and cut into cooking portions before being sent to the kitchen. **2.** a small room or section of a pantry or kitchen in which cooking utensils are cleaned and stored. [1300–50; ME *squillerye* < MF *escuelerie,* equiv. to *escuele* dish (< L *scutella,* dim. of *scutra* pan) + *-rie* -RY]

Scul·lin (skul′in), *n.* **James Henry,** 1876–1953, Australian statesman: prime minister 1929–31.

scul·lion (skul′yən), *n.* **1.** a kitchen servant who does menial work. **2.** a low or contemptible person. [1475–85; perh. < MF *escouvillon* dishcloth, equiv. to *escouve* broom (< L *scōpa*) + *-illon* dim. suffix]

sculp (skulp), *v.t.* to sculpture; carve or model. [1525–35; < L *sculpere* to carve]

sculp., 1. sculptor. **2.** sculptural. **3.** sculpture. Also, **sculpt.**

scul·pin (skul′pin), *n., pl. (esp. collectively)* **-pin,** *(esp. referring to two or more kinds or species)* **-pins. 1.** any small, freshwater fish of the genus *Cottus,* of the family Cottidae, having a large head with one or more spines on each side; bullhead. **2.** any of numerous marine fishes of the same family. **3.** (in California) a common scorpionfish, *Scorpaena guttata.* [1665–75; orig. uncert.]

sculp·ing (skul′ping), *n. Newfoundland.* the act of cutting the skin and its adhering fat from the body of a seal. [1810–20; *sculp* the skin of a seal with the blubber attached (perh. a convergence of Ir *scealbóg* layer of flesh, slice, *scealp, scealb* slice, fragment, splinter, with E SCALP) + -ING[1]]

sculp·sit (skŏŏlp′sit; *Eng.* skulp′sit), *v. Latin.* he engraved, carved, or sculptured (it); she engraved, carved, or sculptured (it). *Abbr.:* sc.

sculpt (skulpt), *v.t., v.i.* **1.** *Fine Arts.* to carve, model, or make by using the techniques of sculpture. **2.** to form, shape, or manipulate, as in the manner of sculpture: *Her hair was sculpted by a leading hairdresser.* [1860–65; < F *sculpter* < L *sculpt-* (ptp. s. of *sculpere* to carve); or as back formation from SCULPTOR]

sculp·tor (skulp′tər), *n., gen.* **Sculp·to·ris** (skulp tôr′is, -tōr′-) for 2. **1.** a person who practices the art of sculpture. **2.** *(cap.) Astron.* a southern constellation between Phoenix and Cetus. [1625–35; < L, equiv. to *sculp(ere)* to carve + *-tor* -TOR]

Sculp′tor's Tool′, *Astron.* the constellation Caelum. [1850–55]

sculp·tress (skulp′tris), *n.* a woman who practices the art of sculpture. [1655–65; SCULPT(O)R + -ESS]
—**Usage.** See **-ess.**

sculp·ture (skulp′chər), *n., v.,* **-tured, -tur·ing.** —*n.* **1.** the art of carving, modeling, welding, or otherwise producing figurative or abstract works of art in three dimensions, as in relief, intaglio, or in the round. **2.** such works of art collectively. **3.** an individual piece of such work. —*v.t.* **4.** to carve, model, weld, or otherwise produce (a piece of sculpture). **5.** to produce a portrait or image of in this way; represent in sculpture. **6.** *Physical Geog.* to change the form of (the land surface) by erosion. —*v.i.* **7.** to work as a sculptor. [1350–1400; ME (n.) < L *sculptūra,* equiv. to *sculpt(us)* (ptp. of *sculpere* to carve) + *-ūra* -URE] —**sculp′tur·al,** *adj.* —**sculp′tur·al·ly,** *adv.*

sculp·tured (skulp′chərd), *adj.* having a surface or shape molded, marked, carved, indented, etc., by or as if by sculpture: *sculptured leather belts.* [1700–10]

sculp·tur·esque (skulp′chə resk′), *adj.* suggesting sculpture: *the sculpturesque beauty of her face.* [1825–35; SCULPTURE + -ESQUE] —**sculp′tur·esque′ly,** *adv.* —**sculp′tur·esque′ness,** *n.*

scum (skum), *n., v.,* **scummed, scum·ming.** —*n.* **1.** a film or layer of foul or extraneous matter that forms on the surface of a liquid. **2.** refuse or offscourings. **3.** a low, worthless, or evil person. **4.** such persons collectively; riffraff; dregs. **5.** scoria (def. 1). —*v.t.* **6.** to remove the scum from. **7.** to remove as scum. —*v.i.* **8.** to form scum; become covered with scum. [1200–50; ME *scume* < MD *schūme* (D *schuim*) foam; c. G *Schaum* foam] —**scum′less,** *adj.* —**scum′like′,** *adj.*

scum·bag (skum′bag′), *n. Slang (vulgar).* **1.** a condom. **2.** a mean, despicable person. [1965–70; SCUM + BAG]

scum·ble (skum′bəl), *v.,* **-bled, -bling,** *n. Painting.* —*v.t.* **1.** to soften (the color or tone of a painted area) by overlaying parts with opaque or semiopaque color applied thinly and lightly with an almost dry brush. —*n.* **2.** the act or technique of scumbling. **3.** the effect produced by this technique. [1790–1800; perh. equiv. to SCUM (v.) + -LE, with intrusive *b*]

scum·board (skum′bôrd′, -bōrd′), *n.* a board or strip of material partly immersed in flowing water to hold back scum. [1895–1900; SCUM + BOARD]

scum·my (skum′ē), *adj.,* **-mi·er, -mi·est. 1.** consisting of or having scum. **2.** *Informal.* despicable; contemptible: *That was a scummy trick.* [1570–80; SCUM + -Y[1]]

scun·cheon (skun′chən), *n. Archit.* sconcheon.

scun·ner (skun′ər), *n.* **1.** an irrational dislike; loathing: *She took a scunner to him.* —*v.i.* **2.** *Scot. and North Eng.* to feel or show violent disgust, esp. to flinch, blanch, or gag. —*v.t.* **3.** *Scot. and North Eng.* to disgust; nauseate. [1325–75; ME (Scots) *skunner* to shrink back in disgust, equiv. to *skurn* to flinch (akin to SCARE) + *-er* -ER[6], with loss of first *r* by dissimilation]

scup (skup), *n.* a sparid food fish, *Stenotomus chrysops,* found along the Atlantic coast of the U.S., having a compressed body and high back. [1840–50, *Amer.*; short for earlier and dial. *scuppaug, skippaug, skapaug* < Narragansett (E sp.) *mishcuppaûog,* pl. (sing. *mishcùp*)]

scup·per[1] (skup′ər), *n.* **1.** *Naut.* a drain at the edge of a deck exposed to the weather, for allowing accumulated water to drain away into the sea or into the bilges. Cf. **freeing port. 2.** a drain, closed by one or two flaps, for allowing water from the sprinkler system of a factory or the like to run off a floor of the building to the exterior. **3.** any opening in the side of a building, as in a parapet, for draining off rain water. [1475–85; earlier *skoper.* See SCOOP, -ER[1]]

scup·per[2] (skup′ər), *v.t. Brit.* **1.** *Mil.* to overwhelm; surprise and destroy, disable, or massacre. **2.** *Informal.* to prevent from happening or succeeding; ruin; wreck. [1880–85; orig. uncert.]

scup·per·nong (skup′ər nông′, -nong′), *n.* **1.** a silvery amber-green variety of muscadine grape. **2.** the vine bearing this fruit, grown in the southern U.S. [1805–15, *Amer.*; short for *scuppernong grape,* after a river in North Carolina]

scurf (skûrf), *n.* **1.** the scales or small shreds of epidermis that are continually exfoliated from the skin. **2.** any scaly matter or incrustation on a surface. [bef. 1000; ME, OE < ON *skurfa* scurf, crust] —**scurf′like′,** *adj.*

scurf·y (skûr′fē), *adj.,* **scurf·i·er, scurf·i·est.** resembling, producing, or covered with or as if with scurf. [1475–85; SCURF + -Y[1]]

scur·rile (skûr′il, -īl, skur′-), *adj. Archaic.* scurrilous. [1560–70; < L *scurrīlis* jeering, equiv. to *scurr(a)* buffoon + *-īlis* -ILE]

scur·ril·i·ty (skə ril′i tē), *n., pl.* **-ties** for 2. **1.** a scurrilous quality or condition. **2.** a scurrilous remark or attack. [1500–10; < L *scurrīlitās.* See SCURRILE, -ITY]
—**Syn. 2.** vituperation, abuse, vilification, invective.

scur·ril·ous (skûr′ə ləs, skur′-), *adj.* **1.** grossly or obscenely abusive: *a scurrilous attack on the mayor.* **2.** characterized by or using low buffoonery; coarsely jocular or derisive: *a scurrilous jest.* [1570–80; SCURRILE + -OUS] —**scur′ril·ous·ly,** *adv.* —**scur′ril·ous·ness,** *n.*
—**Syn. 1.** vituperative, insulting, offensive. **2.** vulgar.

scur·ry (skûr′ē, skur′ē), *v.,* **-ried, -ry·ing,** *n., pl.* **-ries.** —*v.i.* **1.** to go or move quickly or in haste. —*v.t.* **2.** to send hurrying along. —*n.* **3.** a scurrying rush: *the scurry of little feet on the stairs.* **4.** a short run or race. [1800–10; extracted from HURRY-SCURRY]

S-curve (es′kûrv′), *n.* a curve shaped like an S. [1975–80]

scur·vy (skûr′vē), *n., adj.,* **-vi·er, -vi·est.** —*n.* **1.** *Pathol.* a disease marked by swollen and bleeding gums, livid spots on the skin, prostration, etc., due to a diet lacking in vitamin C. —*adj.* **2.** contemptible; despicable; mean: *a scurvy trick.* [1555–65; SCURF + -Y[1]] —**scur′vi·ly,** *adv.* —**scur′vi·ness,** *n.*

scur′vy grass′, a plant, *Cochlearia officinalis,* of the mustard family, purported to be a remedy for scurvy. [1590–1600]

scut[1] (skut), *n.* a short tail, esp. that of a hare, rabbit, or deer. [1400–50; late ME: hare < ON *skutr* stern]

scut[2] (skut), *n. Slang.* a worthless, contemptible person. [1870–75; orig. uncert.; perh. continuation of Scots and dial. *scout, scoot,* ME *scoute* in same sense; perh. n. use of Scots *scout* to spurt, squirt out, SCOOT]

scu·ta (skyōō′tə), *n.* pl. of **scutum.**

scu·tage (skyōō′tij), *n.* (in the feudal system) a payment exacted by a lord in lieu of military service due to him by the holder of a fee. [1425–75; late ME < ML *scūtāgium.* See SCUTUM, -AGE]

Scu·ta·ri (skōō′tə rē; *for 2 also It.* skōō′tä rē), *n.* **1.** **Lake,** a lake between NW Albania and S Yugoslavia. ab. 135 sq. mi. (350 sq. km). **2.** Italian name of **Shkodër. 3.** former name of **Üsküdar.**

scu·tate (skyōō′tāt), *adj.* **1.** *Bot.* formed like a round buckler. **2.** *Zool.* having scutes, shields, or large scales. [1820–30; < L *scūtātus.* See SCUTUM, -ATE[1]]

scutch (skuch), *v.t.* **1.** to dress (flax) by beating. **2.** to dress (brick or stone); scotch. —*n.* **3.** Also called **scutch′er.** a device for scutching flax fiber. **4.** Also, **scotch.** a small picklike tool with two cutting edges for trimming brick. [1680–90; < MF **escoucher* (F *écoucher*) to beat flax < VL **excuticāre,* for L *excutere* (*ex-* EX-[1] + *-cutere,* comb. form of *quatere* to shatter; cf. QUASH)]

scutch·eon (skuch′ən), *n.* **1.** escutcheon. **2.** *Zool.* a scute.

scutch′ grass′. See **Bermuda grass.** [1675–85]

scute (skyōōt), *n. Zool.* **1.** a dermal bony plate, as on an armadillo, or a large horny plate, as on a turtle. **2.** a large scale. [1350–1400 for earlier sense "French coin, ÉCU"; 1840–50 for current senses; ME < L *scūtum* shield]

scu·tel·late (skyōō tel′it, -āt, skyōōt′l āt′), *adj. Zool.* **1.** having scutes. **2.** formed into a scutellum. Also, **scu′·tel·lat′ed.** [1775–85; SCUTELL(UM) + -ATE[1]]

scu·tel·la·tion (skyōōt′l ā′shən), *n. Zool.* **1.** a scutellate state or formation; a scaly covering, as on a bird's foot. **2.** an arrangement of scutella or scales. [1870–75; SCUTELL(UM) + -ATION]

scu·tel·lum (skyo͞o tel′əm), *n., pl.* **-tel·la** (-tel′ə). **1.** *Bot.* the shieldlike cotyledon of certain monocots. **2.** *Zool.* a small plate, scutum, or other shieldlike part, as on the thorax of insects or the feet of birds. [1750–60; < NL, equiv. to L *scūt(um)* shield (see SCUTE) + *-ellum* dim. suffix]

scu·ti·form (skyo͞o′tə fôrm′), *adj.* shield-shaped. Also, **scu·tel·li·form** (skyo͞o tel′ə fôrm′). [1650–60; < NL *scūtiformis.* See SCUTUM, -I-, -FORM]

scut·ter (skut′ər), *v.i., n. Brit. Dial.* scurry. [1775–85; var. of SCUTTLE[2]]

scut·tle[1] (skut′l), *n.* **1.** a deep bucket for carrying coal. **2.** *Brit. Dial.* a broad, shallow basket. [bef. 1050; ME; OE *scutel* dish, trencher, platter < L *scutella,* dim. of *scutra* shallow pan]

scut·tle[2] (skut′l), *v.,* **-tled, -tling,** *n.* —*v.i.* **1.** to run with quick, hasty steps; scurry. —*n.* **2.** a quick pace. **3.** a short, hurried run. [1400–50; late ME *scottlynge* (ger.), var. of *scuddle,* freq. of SCUD[1]]
—**Syn. 1.** hasten, hurry, scamper, scramble.

scut·tle[3] (skut′l), *n., v.,* **-tled, -tling.** —*n.* **1.** *Naut.* **a.** a small hatch or port in the deck, side, or bottom of a vessel. **b.** a cover for this. **2.** a small hatchlike opening in a roof or ceiling. —*v.t.* **3.** to sink (a vessel) deliberately by opening seacocks or making openings in the bottom. **4.** to abandon, withdraw from, or cause to be abandoned or destroyed (as plans, hopes, rumors, etc.). [1490–1500; perh. << Sp *escotilla* hatchway, equiv. to *escot(e)* a cutting of cloth (< Goth *skaut* seam; akin to SHEET[1]) + *-illa* dim. suffix]

scut·tle·butt (skut′l but′), *n.* **1.** *Naut.* **a.** an open cask of drinking water. **b.** a drinking fountain for use by the crew of a vessel. **2.** *Informal.* rumor or gossip. [1795–1805; 1900–05 for def. 2; SCUTTLE[3] + BUTT[4]]

scu·tum (skyo͞o′təm), *n., pl.* **-ta** (-tə) for 1, 2, *gen.* **Scu·ti** (sko͞o′tī) for 3. **1.** *Zool.* scute (def. 1). **2.** a large, oblong shield used by the heavy legionaries of ancient Rome. **3.** (*cap.*) *Astron.* the Shield, a southern constellation north of Sagittarius and east of Aquila, containing a small, very bright star cloud. [1765–75; < L *scūtum* shield]

scut·work (skut′wûrk′), *n. Informal.* menial, routine work, as that done by an underling: *the scutwork of scrubbing pots and pans.* Also, **scut′ work′.** [1960–65; *scut* (< ?) + WORK]

scuzz (skuz), *Slang.* —*n.* **1.** a dirty, grimy, sordid, or repulsive person or thing. —*adj.* **2.** scuzzy. [1965–70; prob. by back formation from SCUZZY, though relative chronology of coinage uncert.]

scuzz·y (skuz′ē), *adj.,* **scuzz·i·er, scuzz·i·est.** *Slang.* dirty, grimy, sordid, or repulsive; disgusting. Also, **scuzz.** [1965–70; expressive coinage; cf. similar phonetic components of SCUM, FUZZY, LOUSY, SLEAZY]

Scyl·la (sil′ə), *n.* **1.** Modern, **Scilla.** a rock in the Strait of Messina off the S coast of Italy. **2.** *Class. Myth.* a sea nymph who was transformed into a sea monster: later identified with the rock Scylla. Cf. **Charybdis** (def. 2). **3. between Scylla and Charybdis,** between two equally perilous alternatives, neither of which can be passed without encountering and probably falling victim to the other.

scy·phate (sī′fāt), *adj.* cup-shaped. [SCYPH(I)- + -ATE[1]]

scyphi-, a combining form representing **scyphus** in compound words: *scyphiform.* Also, **scyph-, scypho-.**

scy·phi·form (sī′fə fôrm′), *adj. Bot.* shaped like a cup or goblet. [1870–75; SCYPHI- + -FORM]

scy·pho·zo·an (sī′fə zō′ən), *n.* **1.** any coelenterate of the class Scyphozoa, comprising the true marine jellyfishes. —*adj.* **2.** belonging or pertaining to the scyphozoans. [1910–15; < NL *Scyphozo(a)* (see SCYPHI-, -O-, -ZOA) + -AN]

scy·phus (sī′fəs), *n., pl.* **-phi** (-fī). **1.** a cup-shaped part, as of a flower. **2.** skyphos. [1770–80; < L < Gk *skýphos* drinking bowl]

Scy·ros (skī′ros, -rōs; *Gk.* skē′rôs), *n.* Skyros.

scythe (sīth), *n., v.,* **scythed, scyth·ing.** —*n.* **1.** an agricultural implement consisting of a long, curving blade fastened at an angle to a handle, for cutting grass, grain, etc., by hand. —*v.t.* **2.** to cut or mow with a scythe. [bef. 900; ME *sith,* OE *sithe,* earlier *sigdi;* c. ON *sigthr;* spelling *sc* by pseudoetymological assoc. with L *scindere* to cut or with SCISSORS] —**scythe′less,** *adj.* —**scythe′like′,** *adj.*

scythe (def. 1)

Scyth·i·a (sith′ē ə), *n.* the ancient name of a region in SE Europe and Asia, between the Black and Aral seas.

Scyth·i·an (sith′ē ən), *adj.* **1.** pertaining to Scythia, its people, or their language. —*n.* **2.** a native or inhabitant of Scythia. **3.** the Iranian language spoken by the ancient Scythians. [1535–45; SCYTHI(A) + -AN]

Scyth′ian lamb′, a fern, *Cibotium barometz,* of southeastern Asia, having stalks covered with shaggy, brownish hair and large, feathery leaves, formerly believed to be a source of vegetable wool. [1650–60]

SD, 1. sea-damaged. **2.** South Dakota (approved esp. for use with zip code). **3.** *Statistics.* standard deviation. **4.** the intelligence and counterespionage service of the Nazi SS. [< G *Sicherheitsdienst*]

sd., sound.

S/D, 1. school district. **2.** sight draft.

S.D., 1. doctor of science. [< L *Scientiae Doctor*] **2.** sea-damaged. **3.** senior deacon. **4.** South Dakota. **5.** special delivery. **6.** *Statistics.* standard deviation.

s.d., 1. sine die. **2.** *Statistics.* standard deviation.

S.D.A., Seventh Day Adventists.

S. Dak., South Dakota.

'sdeath (zdeth), *interj. Archaic.* (used as a mild oath). [euphemistic shortening of *God's death;* see 's[3]]

SDI, Strategic Defense Initiative: technical name of **Star Wars.**

S. Doc., Senate document.

SDR, special drawing rights. Also, **S.D.R.**

SDS, Students for a Democratic Society: a radical political organization, esp. of college students, active in the U.S. in the 1960's.

SE, 1. southeast. **2.** southeastern. **3.** Standard English. Also, **S.E.**

Se, *Symbol, Chem.* selenium.

se-, a prefix occurring in loanwords from Latin, where it meant "apart": *seduce; select.* [< L *sē(d)* (prep.), *sē-* (prefix) without, apart]

sea (sē), *n.* **1.** the salt waters that cover the greater part of the earth's surface. **2.** a division of these waters, of considerable extent, more or less definitely marked off by land boundaries: *the North Sea.* See table on page 1340. **3.** one of the seven seas; ocean. **4.** a large lake or landlocked body of water. **5.** the degree or amount of turbulence of the ocean or other body of water, as caused by the wind. **6.** the waves. **7.** a large wave: *The heavy seas almost drowned us.* **8.** a widely extended, copious, or overwhelming quantity: *a sea of faces; a sea of troubles.* **9.** the work, travel, and shipboard life of a sailor: *The sea is a hard life but a rewarding one.* **10.** *Astron.* mare[3]. **11. at sea, a.** on the ocean. **b.** perplexed; uncertain: *completely at sea as to how to answer the question.* Also, **asea. 12. follow the sea,** to pursue a nautical career: *Many boys then dreamed of following the sea.* **13. go to sea, a.** to set out on a voyage. **b.** to embark on a nautical career. **14. half seas over,** *Slang.* partly or completely drunk: *They came home at dawn, looking half seas over.* Also, **half-seas over. 15. put to sea,** to embark on a sea voyage: *The expedition is nearly ready to put to sea.* Also, **put out to sea.** —*adj.* **16.** of, pertaining to, or adapted for use at sea. [bef. 900; ME *see,* OE *sǣ;* c. D *zee,* G *See,* ON *sær* sea, Goth *saiws* marsh]
—**Syn. 8.** multitude, host, abundance, mass.

sea′ an′chor, *Naut.* any of various devices, as a drogue, that have great resistance to being pulled through the water and are dropped forward of a vessel at the end of a cable to hold the bow into the wind or sea during a storm. [1760–70]

sea′ anem′one, any sedentary marine animal of the phylum Coelenterata, having a columnar body and one or more circles of tentacles surrounding the mouth. [1735–45]

sea anemone, *Epiactis prolifera,* width 3/4 in. (1.9 cm)

sea′ bag′, a tubular canvas bag closed by a drawstring, used by a sailor for gear. [1920–25]

sea′ bass′ (bas), **1.** any of numerous marine fishes of the family Serranidae. Cf. **black sea bass. 2.** any of numerous related or similar marine food fishes. [1755–65, *Amer*]

sea·beach (sē′bēch′), *n.* a beach lying along a sea or ocean. [1765–75; SEA + BEACH]

sea·bed (sē′bed′), *n.* seafloor. [1830–40; SEA + BED]

Sea·bee (sē′bē′), *n.* **1.** a member of the construction battalions of the U.S. Navy, established in December, 1941, to build landing facilities, airfields, etc., in combat areas. **2.** Also, **See-Bee.** a large, ocean-going, barge-carrying vessel equipped with a heavy-duty elevator situated at the stern to facilitate the loading and unloading of barges. [sp. form of the letters *CB,* for *Construction Battalion*]

sea·bird (sē′bûrd′), *n.* a bird frequenting the sea or coast. Also, **sea′ bird′.** Also called **seafowl.** [1580–90; SEA + BIRD]

sea′ bis′cuit, ship biscuit; hardtack. [1670–80]

sea′ blite′ (blīt), any of several halophytic herbs of the genus *Suaeda,* having fleshy leaves. [1755–60]

sea·board (sē′bôrd′, -bōrd′), *n.* **1.** the line where land and sea meet. **2.** a region bordering a seacoast: *the Eastern seaboard.* —*adj.* **3.** bordering on or adjoining the sea. [1350–1400 for earlier sense "porthole cover"; 1480–90 in phrases *at, on, to seaboard* on the seaward side; 1815–25 for def. 1; ME *seebord.* See SEA, STARBOARD]

sea·boot (sē′bo͞ot′), *n.* a high, waterproof wading boot worn for fishing and sailing. [1850–55; SEA + BOOT[1]]

Sea·borg (sē′bôrg), *n.* **Glenn T(heodor),** born 1912, U.S. chemist: chairman of the Atomic Energy Commission 1961–71; Nobel prize 1951.

sea·born (sē′bôrn′), *adj.* **1.** born in or of the sea, as naiads. **2.** produced in or rising from the sea, as reefs. [1585–95]

sea·borne (sē′bôrn′, -bōrn′), *adj.* **1.** transported by ship over the sea. **2.** carried on or over the sea: *a seaborne fog; seaborne cargoes.* [1815–25; SEA + BORNE]

sea′ bread′, ship biscuit; hardtack. [1830–40]

sea′ bream′, 1. any of numerous marine sparid fishes, as *Pagellus centrodontus,* inhabiting waters off the coasts of Europe. **2.** a porgy, *Archosargus rhomboidalis,* inhabiting the Atlantic Ocean. [1520–30]

sea′ breeze′, a thermally produced wind blowing from a cool ocean surface onto adjoining warm land. Cf. **lake breeze, land breeze.** [1690–1700]

Sea·bur·y (sē′ber′ē, -bə rē), *n.* **1. Samuel,** 1729–96, American clergyman: first bishop of the Protestant Episcopal Church. **2. Samuel,** 1873–1958, U.S. jurist (great-great-grandson of Samuel Seabury).

sea′ but′terfly, any member of the gastropod order Pteropoda, shelled marine mollusks so called for their ability to swim using winglike extensions of the foot. [1880–85]

sea′ cab′bage, a brown alga, *Hedophyllum sessile,* of the North Pacific, characterized by a compact mass of fronds resembling a cabbage. [1725–35]

sea′ calf′. See **harbor seal.** [1350–1400; ME]

sea′ cap′tain, the master of a seagoing vessel. [1605–15]

sea′ change′, 1. a striking change, as in appearance, often for the better. **2.** any major transformation or alteration. **3.** a transformation brought about by the sea. [1600–10]

sea′ chest′, *Naut.* **1.** a fitting in a hull below the water line, for admitting or discharging water. **2.** a chest for the personal belongings of a sailor. [1660–70]

sea·coast (sē′kōst′), *n.* the land immediately adjacent to the sea. [1300–50; ME *see cost.* See SEA, COAST]

sea·cock (sē′kok′), *n. Naut.* a valve in the hull of a vessel for admitting outside water into some part of the hull, as a ballast tank. Also called **sea′ connec′tion.** [1660–70; SEA + COCK[1]]

sea′ cow′, 1. any sirenian, as the manatee or dugong. **2.** *Obs.* the hippopotamus. [1605–15]

sea′ cra′dle, chiton (def. 1).

sea′ cray′fish. See **spiny lobster.** Also, **sea′ craw′·fish.** [1595–1605]

sea′ cu′cumber, any echinoderm of the class Holothuroidea, having a long, leathery body with tentacles around the anterior end. [1595–1605]

sea′ dahl′ia, a garden plant, *Coreopsis maritima,* of the southwestern coast of North America, having long-stalked, solitary, yellow flower heads nearly 3 in. (7.6 cm) wide.

Sea′ Day′ak, Iban (def. 1).

sea′ dev′il, manta (def. 4). [1585–95]

sea′ dog′, 1. a sailor, esp. an old or experienced one. **2.** See **harbor seal. 3.** a dogfish. **4.** a pirate or privateer. [1590–1600]

sea·dog (sē′dôg′, -dog′), *n.* fogbow. [1815–25; SEA + DOG]

sea·drome (sē′drōm′), *n. Aeron.* a floating airdrome serving as an intermediate or emergency landing place for aircraft flying over water. [1920–25; SEA + -DROME]

sea′ duck′, any of various diving ducks, as the scaups, goldeneyes, scoters, and eiders, found principally on seas. [1745–55]

sea′ ea′gle, any of several large eagles of the genus *Haliaetus,* that usually feed on fish. Cf. **gray sea eagle.** [1660–70]

sea′ el′ephant. See **elephant seal.** [1595–1605]

sea′ fan′, any of certain anthozoans, esp. *Gorgonia flabellum,* of the West Indies, in which the colony assumes a fanlike form. [1625–35]

sea·far·er (sē′fâr′ər), *n.* **1.** a sailor. **2.** a traveler on the sea. [1505–15; SEA + FARER]

sea·far·ing (sē′fâr′ing), *adj.* **1.** traveling by sea. **2.** following the sea as a trade, business, or calling. **3.** of, pertaining to, or occurring during a voyage on the sea. —*n.* **4.** the business or calling of a sailor. **5.** traveling by sea. [1150–1200; early ME *safarinde* (adj.); see SEA, FARE, -ING[2], -ING[1]]

sea′ feath′er, any of several anthozoans of the order Gorgonacea, in which the colony assumes a featherlike shape. [1615–25]

sea′ fight′, a fight between ships at sea. [1590–1600]

sea′ fire′, a bioluminescent glow produced by phosphorescent marine organisms. [1805–15]

sea·floor (sē′flôr′, -flōr′), *n.* the solid surface underlying a sea or an ocean. Also called **seabed.** [1850–55; SEA + FLOOR]

sea′ foam′, 1. the foam of the sea. **2.** meerschaum (def. 1). [1250–1300; ME] —**sea′-foam′,** *adj.*

sea·food (sē′fo͞od′), *n.* any fish or shellfish from the sea used for food. [1830–40, *Amer.*]

Sea·ford (sē′fərd), *n.* a city on SW Long Island, in SE New York. 16,117.

sea·fowl (sē′foul′), *n., pl.* **-fowls,** (*esp. collectively*) **-fowl.** seabird. [1300–50; ME *seafoule.* See SEA, FOWL]

sea′ fox′, thresher (def. 2). [1585–95]

CONCISE PRONUNCIATION KEY: *act, cāpe, dâre, pärt; set, ēqual; if, ice; ox, ōver, ôrder, oil, bo͝ok, bo͞ot, out; up, ûrge; child; sing; shoe; thin, that;* zh as in *treasure.* ə = *a* as in *alone, e* as in *system, i* as in *easily, o* as in *gallop, u* as in *circus;* ᵊ as in *fire* (fīᵊr), *hour* (ouᵊr). l and n can serve as syllabic consonants, as in *cradle* (krād′l), and *button* (but′n). See the full key inside the front cover.

sea′ front′, an area, including buildings, along the edge of the sea; waterfront. [1875–80]

sea′ gate′, a navigable channel giving access to the sea. [1860–65]

sea′ gauge′, **1.** an automatic sounding device registering the depth to which it is lowered. **2.** the draft of a vessel. [1745–55]

sea•girt (sē′gûrt′), *n.* surrounded by the sea. [1615–25; SEA + GIRT[1]]

sea•go•ing (sē′gō′ing), *adj.* **1.** designed or fit for going to sea, as a vessel. **2.** going to sea; seafaring. —*n.* **3.** the activity of a person who travels by sea. [1820–30; SEA + GOING]

sea′ goose′berry, a comb jelly, esp. of the genus *Pleurobrachia.*

sea′ grant′ col′lege, a college or university doing research on marine resources under the U.S. National Sea Grant College and Program Act of 1966. [1970–75]

sea′ grape′, **1.** a tropical American tree, *Coccoloba uvifera,* of the buckwheat family, bearing grapelike clusters of edible purple berries. **2.** the fruit itself. **3.** a gulfweed. [1570–80]

sea′ green′, a clear, light, bluish green. [1590–1600] —**sea′-green′,** *adj.*

sea′ gull′, a gull, esp. any of the marine species. [1535–45]

Sea′ Gull′, The, a play (1896) by Anton Chekhov.

sea′ hare′, any gastropod of the order Aplysiacea, comprising large marine sluglike mollusks with a reduced, internal shell. [1585–95]

Sea•hawk (sē′hôk′), *n.* a twin-engine, four-seat U.S. Navy helicopter used for surveillance, targeting, and antisubmarine warfare.

sea′ hibis′cus. See **hau tree.**

sea′ hog′, a porpoise. [1570–80]

sea′ hol′ly, the eryngo, *Eryngium maritimum.* [1540–50]

sea′ hol′lyhock, a rose mallow, *Hibiscus moscheutos.*

sea′ horse′, **1.** any fish of the genus *Hippocampus,* of the pipefish family, having a prehensile tail, an elongated snout, and a head bent at right angles to the body. **2.** a fabled marine animal with the foreparts of a horse and the hind parts of a fish. **3.** a walrus. Also, **sea′•horse′.** [1425–75; late ME *sehors* walrus; cf. G *Seepferd*]

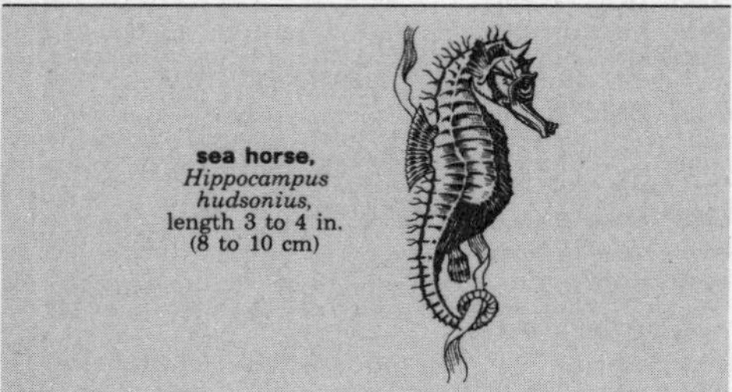

sea horse, *Hippocampus hudsonius,* length 3 to 4 in. (8 to 10 cm)

sea′-is•land cot′ton (sē′ī′lənd), a long-staple cotton, *Gossypium barbadense,* raised originally in the Sea Islands and now grown chiefly in the West Indies. Also, **Sea′ Is′land cot′ton.** [1795–1805, *Amer.*]

Sea′ Is′lands, a group of islands in the Atlantic, along the coasts of South Carolina, Georgia, and N Florida.

sea•jack (sē′jak′), *n.* **1.** the hijacking of a ship, esp. one that occurs while the vessel is under way. —*v.t.* **2.** to hijack (a ship) while at sea. [SEA + (HI)JACK] —**sea′•jack′er,** *n.*

sea′ kale′, a European broad-leaved maritime plant, *Crambe maritima,* of the mustard family, having fleshy, blue basal leaves, used as a pot plant. [1690–1700]

sea•kind•ly (sē′kīnd′lē), *adj. Naut.* (of a vessel) sailing easily in a rough sea. [1875–80; SEA + KINDLY] —**sea′kind′li•ness,** *n.*

sea′ king′, **1.** one of the piratical Scandinavian chiefs who ravaged the coasts of medieval Europe. **2.** (*caps.*) a twin-engine U.S. Navy helicopter for rescue work and antisubmarine warfare. [1575–85; trans. of ON *sǣkonungr;* c. OE *sǣcyning*]

seal[1] (sēl), *n.* **1.** an embossed emblem, figure, symbol, word, letter, etc., used as attestation or evidence of authenticity. **2.** a stamp, medallion, ring, etc., engraved with such a device, for impressing paper, wax, lead, or the like: *The king took the seal from his finger and applied it to the document.* **3.** the impression so obtained: *It was unmistakably the royal seal on the document.* **4.** a mark or symbol attached to a legal document and imparting a formal character to it, originally wax with an impression. **5.** a piece of wax or similar adhesive substance so attached to an envelope, folded document, etc., that it must be broken when the object is opened, insuring that the contents have not been tampered with or altered. **6.** anything that tightly or completely closes or secures a thing, as closures or fastenings for doors and railroad cars, adhesive stamps and tapes used to secure the flap of an envelope, etc. **7.** something that keeps a thing secret: *Her vow was the seal that kept her silent.* **8.** a decorative stamp, esp. as given to contributors to a charitable fund: *a Christmas seal.* **9.** a mark, sign, symbol, or the like, serving as visible evidence of something. **10.** anything that serves as assurance, confirmation, or bond: *She gave the plan her seal of approval.* **11.** *Plumbing.* **a.** a small amount of water held by a trap to exclude foul gases from a sewer or the like. **b.** the depth of the part of the water that actually excludes the gases. **12. set one's seal to,** to give one's approval to; authorize; endorse: *Both families have set their seal to the marriage.* **13. the seals,** *Brit.* the tokens or signs of public office. —*v.t.* **14.** to affix a seal to in authorization, testimony, etc. **15.** to assure, confirm, or bind with or as if with a seal: *They sealed the bargain with a handshake.* **16.** to impress a seal upon as evidence of legal or standard exactness, measure, quality, etc. **17.** to close by any form of fastening that must be broken before access can be gained. **18.** to fasten or close tightly by or as if by a seal: *She was sealing envelopes. My lips are sealed.* **19.** to decide irrevocably: *to seal someone's fate.* **20.** to grant under one's seal or authority, as a pardon. **21.** *Mormon Ch.* to make (a marriage or adoption) forever binding; solemnize. **22.** *Elect.* to bring (a plug and jack or socket) into locked or fully aligned position. **23. seal off, a.** to close hermetically: *to seal off a jar.* **b.** to block (an entrance, area, etc.) completely so as to prevent escape or entrance: *The police sealed off the area after the bomb threat was received.* [1175–1225; (n.) ME *seel, seil(e), seale* mark on a document, token < OF *seel* (F *sceau*) < LL **sigellum,* L *sigillum,* dim. of *signum* SIGN; r. ME *seil,* OE *(in)segel* seal < LL, as above; (v.) *sealen, seilen* < OF *seeler, seieler,* deriv. of *seel*] —**seal′a•ble,** *adj.*

seal[1] (def. 4): Great Seal of the United States

seal[2] (sēl), *n., pl.* **seals,** (*esp. collectively for 1*) **seal,** *v.* —*n.* **1.** any of numerous marine carnivores of the suborder Pinnipedia, including the eared or fur seals, as the sea lion, and the earless or hair seals, as the harbor seal. **2.** the skin of such an animal. **3.** leather made from this skin. **4.** the fur of the fur seal; sealskin. **5.** a fur used as a substitute for sealskin. **6.** a dark, gray brown. —*v.i.* **7.** to hunt, kill, or capture seals. [bef. 900; ME *sele,* OE *seolh;* c. ON *selr*] —**seal′like′,** *adj.*

seal[3] (sēl), *v.t. Falconry.* seel (def. 1).

Sea•lab (sē′lab′), *n.* any of several experimental U.S. Navy underwater habitats for aquanauts. [1965–70; SEA + LAB]

sea′ lad′der, a set of rungs fixed to the side of a vessel, forming a ladder from the weather deck to the water line. [1900–05]

sea′ lam′prey, a parasitic marine lamprey, *Petromyzon marinus,* that spawns in fresh water along both Atlantic coasts and in the Great Lakes, where it is responsible for losses of economically valuable fish. [1875–80]

sea′ lane′, a standard navigational route for ships traversing an ocean or sea. Also called **shipping lane.** [1875–80]

seal•ant (sē′lənt), *n.* **1.** a substance used for sealing, as sealing wax or adhesives. **2.** any of various liquids, paints, chemicals, or soft substances that may be applied to a surface or circulated through a system of pipes or the like, drying to form a hard, watertight coating. **3.** *Dentistry.* any of several transparent synthetic resins applied to the chewing surfaces of molars and premolars in young children and teenagers as a preventive measure against tooth decay in the occlusal pits and fissures. [1940–45; SEAL[1] + -ANT, prob. by analogy with COOLANT]

sea′-launched ballis′tic mis′sile (sē′lôncht′, -läncht′), a ballistic missile designed for launch by a submarine or surface ship. *Abbr.:* SLBM, S.L.B.M.

sea′-launched cruise′ mis′sile, a cruise missile launched by surface ships or submarines against land or sea targets and equipped with nuclear or conventional warheads, with a range of 2210 miles (3556 km). *Abbr.:* SLCM, S.L.C.M.

sea′ lav′ender, **1.** an Old World, maritime plant, *Limonium vulgare,* of the leadwort family, having one-sided spikes of small, lavender-colored flowers. **2.** a similar plant, *Limonium carolinianum,* of the eastern coast of North America. [1590–1600]

sea′ law′yer, *Naut. Slang.* a sailor inclined to question or complain about the orders given. [1805–15]

Seal′ Beach′, a town in S California. 25,975.

seal′ brown′, a rich, dark brown suggestive of dressed and dyed sealskin. [1880–85] —**seal′-brown′,** *adj.*

seal′ dog′, *Newfoundland.* an iron hook used for dragging seal carcasses over the ice.

sea′ leath′er, the skin of sharks, porpoises, dogfishes, etc., prepared and used for the same purposes as ordinary leather.

sealed′-beam′ head′light (sēld′bēm′), a headlight in which the reflector and lens are hermetically sealed together with the filament in a single unit. Also called **sealed′ beam′.**

sealed′ book′, something beyond understanding and therefore unknown. [1810–20]

sealed′ or′ders, written orders or instructions that are not to be looked at until a specified time, esp. orders that are given in sealed form to a commander of a vessel to be opened after the vessel is out of contact with the shore.

sea′ legs′, **1.** the ability to adjust one's balance to the motion of a ship at sea: *He stumbled about the deck for three days before getting his sea legs.* **2.** the ability to remain free of seasickness. **3.** surimi. [1705–15]

seal•er[1] (sē′lər), *n.* **1.** an officer appointed to examine and test weights and measures, and to set a stamp upon such as are true to the standard. **2.** a substance applied to a porous surface as a basecoat for paint, varnish, etc. [1350–1400; ME *seler.* See SEAL[1], -ER[1]]

seal•er[2] (sē′lər), *n.* a person or ship engaged in hunting seals. [1760–70; SEAL[2] + -ER[1]]

seal•er•y (sē′lə rē), *n., pl.* **-er•ies.** **1.** a place where seals are caught. **2.** the occupation of hunting or taking seals. [1890–95; SEAL[2] + -ERY]

sea′ let′tuce, any seaweed of the genus *Ulva,* having large leaflike blades. [1660–70]

sea′ lev′el, the horizontal plane or level corresponding to the surface of the sea at mean level between high and low tide. [1800–10]

sea′-lev•el pres′sure (sē′lev′əl), the atmospheric pressure, at any elevation, reduced by formula to a value approximating the pressure at sea level.

sea•lift (sē′lift′), *n.* **1.** a system for transporting persons or cargo by ship, esp. in an emergency. **2.** the act of transporting such persons or cargo. —*v.t.* **3.** to transport (persons or cargo) by sealift. [1955–60; SEA + (AIR)LIFT]

sea′ lil′y, a stalked, sessile crinoid. See illus. under **crinoid.** [1875–80]

seal′ing wax′, a resinous preparation, soft when heated, used for sealing letters, documents, etc. [1300–50; ME]

sea′ li′on, **1.** any of several large eared seals, as *Eumetopias jubatus* (**Steller's sea lion**), of the northern Pacific, and *Zalophus californicus* (**California sea lion**), of the Pacific coast of North America. **2.** *Heraldry.* a monster having the forepart of a lion, webbed forepaws, and the dorsal fin and tail of a fish. [1595–1605]

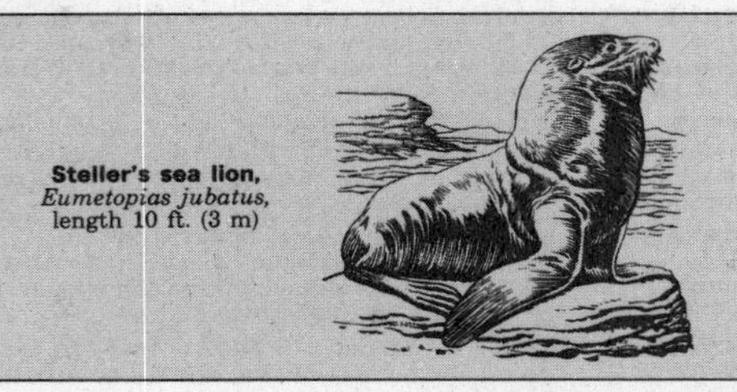

Steller's sea lion, *Eumetopias jubatus,* length 10 ft. (3 m)

seal′ point′, a Siamese cat having a fawn-colored body and dark-brown points. [1935–40]

seal′ ring′, a finger ring bearing an incised design for embossing a wax seal. [1600–10]

seal•skin (sēl′skin′), *n.* **1.** the skin of a seal. **2.** the skin or fur of the fur seal when prepared for making garments or leather items. **3.** a garment or article made of this fur. —*adj.* **4.** made of sealskin: *a sealskin purse.* [1275–1325; ME *seleskin.* See SEAL[2], SKIN]

sea′ lung′wort, a plant, *Mertensia maritima,* of the borage family, growing on northern seacoasts and having leaves with an oysterlike flavor. [1590–1600]

Sea′ly•ham ter′rier (sē′lē ham′, -lē əm), one of a Welsh breed of small terriers having short legs, a docked tail, and a wiry, mostly white coat. [1890–95; named after *Sealyham,* Wales, where it was first bred]

Sealyham terrier, 10½ in. (27 cm) high at shoulder

sea′ lyme′ grass′, a stout grass, *Elymus arenarius,* of Eurasia, used as a binder for shifting sand. Also called **dune grass.** [*lyme,* perh. alter. (based on the genus name) of LIME[1], with reference to its binding properties; cf. BIRDLIME]

seam (sēm), *n.* **1.** the line formed by sewing together pieces of cloth, leather, or the like. **2.** the stitches used to make such a line. **3.** any line formed by abutting edges. **4.** any linear indentation or mark, as a wrinkle or scar. **5.** *Knitting.* a line of stitches formed by purling. **6.** *Geol.* a comparatively thin stratum; a bed, as of coal. —*v.t.* **7.** to join with or as if with stitches; make the seam or seams of. **8.** to furrow; mark with wrinkles, scars, etc. **9.** *Knitting.* to knit with or in a seam. —*v.i.* **10.** to become cracked, fissured, or furrowed. **11.** *Knitting.* to make a line of stitches by purling. [bef. 1000; ME *seme* (n.), OE *sēam;* c. G *Saum* hem; akin to SEW[1], Gk *hymḗn* membrane (see HYMEN)] —**seam′er,** *n.*

sea•maid (sē′mād′), *n.* **1.** a mermaid. **2.** a goddess or nymph of the sea. Also, **sea-maid•en** (sē′mād′n). [1580–90; SEA + MAID]

sea•man (sē′mən), *n., pl.* **-men.** **1.** a person skilled in seamanship. **2.** a person whose trade or occupation is assisting in the handling, sailing, and navigating of a ship during a voyage, esp. one below the rank of officer; sailor. **3.** *Navy.* an enlisted person ranking below petty

CONCISE ETYMOLOGY KEY: <, descended or borrowed from; >, whence; b., blend of, blended; c., cognate with; cf., compare; deriv., derivative; equiv., equivalent; imit., imitative; obl., oblique; r., replacing; s., stem; sp., spelling, spelled; resp., respelling, respelled; trans., translation; ?, origin unknown; *, unattested; ‡, probably earlier than. See the full key inside the front cover.

officer. [bef. 900; ME *seeman,* OE *sǣmann.* See SEA, MAN[1]]
—Syn. See **sailor.**

Sea·man (sē′mən), *n.* **Elizabeth Coch·rane** (kok′rən), original name of Nellie Bly.

sea·man·like (sē′mən līk′), *adj.* like or befitting a seaman; showing good seamanship. Also, **sea·man·ly** (sē′mən lē). [1790–1800; SEAMAN + -LIKE]

sea·man·ship (sē′mən ship′), *n.* knowledge and skill pertaining to the operation, navigation, management, safety, and maintenance of a ship. [1760–70; SEAMAN + -SHIP]

sea·mark (sē′märk′), *n.* a conspicuous object on land, visible from the sea, serving to guide or warn mariners, as a beacon. [1475–85; SEA + MARK[1]]

seam′ bind′ing, a narrow strip of fabric attached to the unfinished edge of a seam or hem to keep it from raveling.

sea′ mile′. See **nautical mile.** [1790–1800]

sea′ milk′wort, a maritime plant, *Glaux maritima,* having small, pinkish-white flowers.

sea′ mist′, a mist over or from the sea.

seam·less (sēm′lis), *adj.* **1.** having no seams: *seamless stockings.* **2.** smoothly continuous or uniform in quality; combined in an inconspicuous way: *a seamless blend of art and entertainment.* [1475–85; SEAM + -LESS] **—seam′less·ly,** *adv.* **—seam′less·ness,** *n.*

sea′ moss′, **1.** *Bot.* any of certain frondlike red algae. **2.** *Zool.* a bryozoan. [1540–50]

sea·moth (sē′môth′, -moth′), *n.* dragonfish (def. 2). [1900–05; SEA + MOTH]

sea·mount (sē′mount′), *n.* a submarine mountain rising several hundred fathoms above the floor of the sea but having its summit well below the surface of the water. [1945–50; SEA + MOUNT[2]]

sea′ mouse′, any of several large, marine annelids of the genus *Aphrodite* and related genera, having a covering of long, fine, hairlike setae. [1510–20]

seam·ster (sēm′stər *or, esp. Brit.,* sem′-), *n.* a person whose occupation is sewing; tailor. [bef. 1000; ME *semster(e),* OE *sǣmestre, sēamystre,* fem. deriv. of *sēamere* tailor; see SEAM, -STER]

seam·stress (sēm′stris *or, esp. Brit.,* sem′-), *n.* a woman whose occupation is sewing. Also, **sempstress.** [1605–15; SEAMST(E)R + -ESS]
—Usage. See **-ess.**

seam·y (sē′mē), *adj.,* **seam·i·er, seam·i·est.** **1.** unpleasant or sordid; low; disagreeable: *the seamy side of life.* **2.** having, showing, or of the nature of a seam. [1595–1605; SEAM + -Y[1]; in transferred senses alluding to the unpresentable appearance of the inside of a garment, i.e., where the seams show] **—seam′i·ness,** *n.*
—Syn. 1. squalid, rough, coarse, nasty.

Sean (shôn), *n.* a male given name, form of **John.**

Sean·ad Éir·eann (shôn′əd â′rən), the upper house of the parliament of the Republic of Ireland. Cf. **Oireachtas** (def. 1). [< Ir: senate of Ireland]

sé·ance (sā′äns), *n.* **1.** a meeting in which a spiritualist attempts to communicate with the spirits of the dead. **2.** a session or sitting, as of a class or organization. [1795–1805; < F: session, equiv. to *sé-,* base of *seoir* to SIT[1] (< L *sedēre*) + *-ance* -ANCE]

sea′ net′tle, any large, stinging jellyfish. [1595–1605]

sea′ oats′, a tall grass, *Uniola paniculata,* of coastal areas of southeastern North America, having as its inflorescence a densely crowded panicle, used to control sand erosion. [1890–95; *Amer.*]

Sea′ of Tranquil′lity, *Astron.* See **Mare Tranquillitatis.**

sea′ on′ion, **1.** Also called **sea squill.** a Mediterranean plant, *Urginea maritima,* of the lily family, yielding medicinal squill. **2.** a squill, *Scilla verna,* of the Isle of Wight, having narrow leaves and clusters of violet flowers. [1350–1400; ME]

sea′ ot′ter, a marine otter, *Enhydra lutris,* of the shores of the northern Pacific, with a very valuable fur: now greatly reduced in number and rare in many areas. [1655–65]

sea otter, *Enhydra lutris,* head and body 4 ft. (1.2 m); tail 1 ft. (0.3 m)

sea′ palm′, a kelp, *Postelsia palmaeformis,* of the Pacific coast of North America, that resembles a miniature palm tree.

sea′ pen′, any of several colonial coelenterates of the genus *Pennatula* and related genera, having the shape of a fleshy feather. [1755–65]

sea·perch (sē′pûrch′), *n., pl.* (*esp. collectively*) **-perch,** (*esp. referring to two or more kinds or species*) **-perch·es.** surfperch. [1595–1605; SEA + PERCH[2]]

sea·piece (sē′pēs′), *n.* seascape (def. 1). [1650–60; SEA + PIECE]

sea′ pink′, thrift (def. 3). [1725–35]

sea·plane (sē′plān′), *n.* an airplane provided with floats for taking off from or landing on water. [1910–15; SEA + PLANE[1]]

sea·poach·er (sē′pō′chər), *n.* poacher[1] (def. 2). [1800–10]

sea′ pop′py. See **horn poppy.** [1555–65]

sea·port (sē′pôrt′, -pōrt′), *n.* **1.** a port or harbor on or accessible to a seacoast and providing accommodation for seagoing vessels. **2.** a town or city at such a place. [1590–1600; SEA + PORT[1]]

sea′ pow′er, **1.** naval strength. **2.** a nation that possesses formidable naval power. [1840–50]

sea′ purse′, the horny egg case of certain rays and sharks. [1800–10]

sea′ puss′ (po͝os), *Oceanog.* a strong nearshore current resulting from the seaward flow of water, esp. through a channel in a bar. [1645–55, *Amer.* in sense "brook;" alter., by folk etym., of earlier *seapoose* < Unquachog (E sp.) *seépus* river < Proto-Algonquian **si·po·wi* (>Fox *si·po·wi*) + dim. suffix]

sea·quake (sē′kwāk′), *n.* an agitation of the sea caused by a submarine eruption or earthquake. [1670–80; SEA + (EARTH)QUAKE]

sear[1] (sēr), *v.t.* **1.** to burn or char the surface of: *She seared the steak to seal in the juices.* **2.** to mark with a branding iron. **3.** to burn or scorch injuriously or painfully: *He seared his hand on a hot steam pipe.* **4.** to make callous or unfeeling; harden: *The hardship of her youth has seared her emotionally.* **5.** to dry up or wither; parch. —*v.i.* **6.** to become dry or withered, as vegetation. —*n.* **7.** a mark or scar made by searing. —*adj.* **8.** sere[1]. [bef. 900; (adj.) ME *sere,* OE *sēar;* c. D *zoor;* (v.) ME *seren,* OE *sēarian,* deriv. of *sēar*]
—Syn. 1. See **burn**[1].

sear[2] (sēr), *n.* a pivoted piece that holds the hammer at full cock or half cock in the firing mechanism of small arms. [1550–60; < MF *serre* a grip, deriv. of *serrer* to lock up, close < VL **serrāre,* for LL *serāre* to bar (a door), deriv. of L *sera* door-bar; VL *-rr-* unexplained]

sea′ ra′ven, a large marine fish of the genus *Hemitripterus,* as *H. americanus,* common on the northern Atlantic coast of America. [1595–1605]

search (sûrch), *v.t.* **1.** to go or look through (a place, area, etc.) carefully in order to find something missing or lost: *They searched the woods for the missing child. I searched the desk for the letter.* **2.** to look at or examine (a person, object, etc.) carefully in order to find something concealed: *He searched the vase for signs of a crack. The police searched the suspect for weapons.* **3.** to explore or examine in order to discover: *They searched the hills for gold.* **4.** to look at, read, or examine (a record, writing, collection, repository, etc.) for information: *to search a property title; He searched the courthouse for a record of the deed to the land.* **5.** to look at or beneath the superficial aspects of to discover a motive, reaction, feeling, basic truth, etc.: *He searched her face for a clue to her true feelings.* **6.** to look into, question, or scrutinize: *She searched her conscience.* **7.** (of natural elements) to pierce or penetrate: *The sunlight searched the room's dark corners.* **8.** to uncover or find by examination or exploration (often fol. by *out*): *to search out all the facts.* **9.** *Mil.* to fire artillery over (an area) with successive changes in gun elevation. **10.** *Computers.* to examine (one or more files, as databases or texts) electronically, to locate specified items. —*v.i.* **11.** to inquire, investigate, examine, or seek; conduct an examination or investigation. **12. search me,** I don't know: *Why has it taken so long to reach a decision? Search me.* —*n.* **13.** an act or instance of searching; careful examination or investigation. **14.** the practice, on the part of naval officers of a belligerent nation, of boarding and examining a suspected neutral vessel at sea in order to ascertain its true nationality and determine if it is carrying contraband: *the right of visit and search.* [1300–50; (v.) ME *serchen, cerchen* (< AF *sercher*) < OF *cerchier* < LL *circāre* to go around, deriv. of L *circus* circle; (n.) ME *serche* < AF *serche,* OF *cerche,* deriv. of *cerchier*] **—search′a·ble,** *adj.* **—search′a·ble·ness,** *n.* **—search′er,** *n.*
—Syn. 1. investigate. **2.** inspect. **13.** inspection, scrutiny.

search·ing (sûr′ching), *adj.* **1.** examining carefully or thoroughly: *a searching inspection.* **2.** acutely observant or penetrating: *a searching glance; a searching mind.* **3.** piercing or sharp: *a searching wind.* [1570–80; SEARCH + -ING[2]] **—search′ing·ly,** *adv.* **—search′ing·ness,** *n.*

search·less (sûrch′lis), *adj.* unsearchable; inscrutable. [1595–1605; SEARCH + -LESS]

search·light (sûrch′līt′), *n.* **1.** a device, usually consisting of a light and reflector, for throwing a beam of light in any direction. **2.** a beam of light so thrown. [1880–85; SEARCH + LIGHT[1]]

search′ par′ty, a group of persons conducting an organized search for someone or something lost or hidden. [1880–85]

search′ war′rant, *Law.* a court order authorizing the examination of a dwelling or other private premises by police officials, as for stolen goods. [1730–40]

Sear·cy (sûr′sē), *n.* a city in central Arkansas. 13,612.

sea′ reach′, a straight course at the mouth of a river, connecting with the sea. [1865–70]

sea′ return′, *Electronics.* radar signals that are reflected by a body of water and hamper target identification.

sea′ risk′, Often, **sea risks.** the hazard of traveling or transporting by sea. [1720–30]

Searle (sûrl), *n.* **Ronald (William Ford·ham)** (fôr′dəm, fōr′-), born 1920, British cartoonist and artist.

sea′ rob′ber, a pirate. [1560–70]

sea′ rob′in, any of various gurnards, esp. certain American species of the genus *Prionotus,* having large pectoral fins used to move across the ocean bottom. [1805–15, *Amer.*]

sea′ room′, unobstructed space at sea in which a vessel can be easily maneuvered or navigated. [1545–55]

sea′ rov′er, **1.** a pirate. **2.** a pirate ship. [1570–80] **—sea′-rov′ing,** *adj., n.*

Sears (sērz), *n.* **Richard Warren,** 1863–1914, U.S. mail-order retailer.

sea′ salt′, table salt produced through the evaporation of seawater. [1595–1605]

sea′ scal′lop, **1.** Also called **giant scallop.** a large scallop, *Pecten magellanicus,* of deep waters off the Atlantic coast of North America. **2.** the abductor muscle of this scallop, eaten as food.

sea·scape (sē′skāp′), *n.* **1.** a sketch, painting, or photograph of the sea. **2.** a view of the sea. [1790–1800; SEA + *-scape,* modeled on LANDSCAPE]

sea′ scor′pion, *Ichthyol.* scorpionfish. [1595–1605]

sea′ scout′, (*often caps.*) a member of a scouting program that provides training in boating and other water activities.

sea′ ser′pent, **1.** an enormous, imaginary, snakelike or dragonlike marine animal. **2.** (*caps.*) *Astron.* the constellation Hydra. [1640–50]

sea·shell (sē′shel′), *n.* the shell of any marine mollusk. Also, **sea′ shell′.** [bef. 900; OE *sǣscill* (not recorded in ME) see SEA, SHELL]

sea·shore (sē′shôr′, -shōr′), *n.* **1.** land along the sea or ocean. **2.** *Law.* the ground between the ordinary high-water and low-water marks. [1520–30; SEA + SHORE[1]]

Sea′shore test′, *Psychol.* a test of musical ability in which items measuring tonal memory, rhythm sense, etc., are presented to the subject by means of recordings. [named after Carl *Seashore* (1866–1949), American psychologist]

sea·sick (sē′sik′), *adj.* afflicted with seasickness. [1560–70; SEA + SICK]

sea·sick·ness (sē′sik′nis), *n.* nausea and dizziness, sometimes accompanied by vomiting, resulting from the rocking or swaying motion of a vessel in which one is traveling at sea. Cf. **motion sickness.** [1615–25; SEA + SICKNESS]

sea·side (sē′sīd′), *n.* **1.** the land along the sea; seacoast. —*adj.* **2.** situated on or pertaining to the seaside. [1175–1225; ME *seeside.* See SEA, SIDE[1]]

Sea·side (sē′sīd′), *n.* a city in W California, on Monterey Bay. 36,567.

sea′side dai′sy. See **beach aster.**

sea′side gold′enrod. See **beach goldenrod.**

sea′side knot′weed. See under **knotweed.**

sea′side spar′row, a species of sparrow, *Ammospiza maritima,* existing in two subspecies, one **(Cape Sable seaside sparrow)** having dark olive-drab plumage with a lighter breast and underbelly, and the other **(dusky seaside sparrow)** having bold black and white markings on the breast and underbelly: the dusky seaside sparrow is almost extinct.

sea′ slug′, a nudibranch. [1770–80]

sea′ smoke′. See **steam fog.**

sea·snail (sē′snāl′), *n., pl.* (*esp. collectively*) **-snail,** (*esp. referring to two or more kinds or species*) **-snails.** **1.** any of several snailfishes of the genus *Liparis,* of the North Atlantic. **2.** any of several marine gastropods having a spirally coiled shell, as a whelk. [bef. 1000; ME *seesnail,* OE *sǣsnægl.* See SEA, SNAIL]

sea′ snake′, any of several venomous marine snakes of the family Hydrophidae, having a finlike tail. [1745–55]

sea·son (sē′zən), *n.* **1.** one of the four periods of the year (spring, summer, autumn, and winter), beginning astronomically at an equinox or solstice, but geographically at different dates in different climates. **2.** a period of the year characterized by particular conditions of weather, temperature, etc.: *the rainy season.* **3.** a period of the year when something is best or available: *the oyster season.* **4.** a period of the year marked by certain conditions, activities, etc.: *baseball season.* **5.** a period of the year immediately before and after a special holiday or occasion: *the Christmas season.* **6.** *Sports.* **a.** a period with reference to the total number of games to be played by a team: *a 162-game season.* **b.** a period with reference to the won-lost record of a team after it has completed its schedule: *a .700 season.* **7.** any period or time: *in the season of my youth.* **8.** a suitable, proper, fitting, or right time: *This is not the season for frivolity.* **9. for a season,** for a time, esp. a short time: *He lived in Paris for a season.* **10. in good season,** in enough time; sufficiently early: *Applicants will be notified of our decision in good season.* **11. in season, a.** in the time or state for use, eating, etc.: *Asparagus is now in season.* **b.** in the period regulated by law, as for hunting and fishing. **c.** at the right time; opportunely. **d.** (of an animal, esp. female) in a state of readiness for mating; in heat. **e.** in good season. **12. in season and out of season,** regardless of time or season; at all times: *Misfortunes plague this family in season and out of season.* **13. out of season,** not in season: *The price is so high because lilacs are out of season now.* —*v.t.* **14.** to heighten or improve the flavor of (food) by adding condiments, spices, herbs, or the like. **15.** to give relish or a certain character to: *conversation seasoned with wit.* **16.** to mature, ripen, or condition by exposure to suitable conditions or treatment: *a writer seasoned by experience.* **17.** to dry or otherwise treat (lumber) so as to harden and render immune to shrinkage, warpage, etc. **18.** to accustom or harden: *troops seasoned by battle.* —*v.i.* **19.** to become seasoned, matured, hardened, or the like. [1250–1300; (n.) ME *sesoun, seson* < OF *se(i)son* < L *satiōn-* (s. of *satiō*) a sowing (VL: sowing time), equiv. to *sa-* (var. s. of *serere* to sow) + *-tiōn-* -TION; (v.) ME *seso(u)nen* < OF *saisonner* to ripen, make palatable by aging, deriv. of

CONCISE PRONUNCIATION KEY: *act, cāpe, dâre, pärt; set, ēqual; if, īce; ox, ōver, ôrder, oil, bo͝ok, bo͞ot, out; up, ûrge; child; sing; shoe; thin, that;* zh as in *treasure.* ə = *a* as in *alone, e* as in *system, i* as in *easily, o* as in *gallop, u* as in *circus;* ᵊ as in *fire* (fīᵊr), *hour* (ouᵊr). l and n can serve as syllabic consonants, as in *cradle* (krād′l), and *button* (but′n). See the full key inside the front cover.

seison] **—sea′soned·ly,** *adv.* **—sea′son·er,** *n.* **—sea′son·less,** *adj.*
—Syn. 19. mature, harden, toughen.

sea·son·a·ble (sē′zə nə bəl), *adj.* **1.** suitable to or characteristic of the season: *seasonable weather.* **2.** timely; opportune: *a seasonable suggestion.* [1350–1400; ME *sesounable.* See SEASON, -ABLE] **—sea′son·a·ble·ness,** *n.* **—sea′son·a·bly,** *adv.*
—Syn. 1. fit, appropriate. **2.** See **opportune.**
—Usage. See **seasonal.**

sea·son·al (sē′zə nl), *adj.* **1.** pertaining to, dependent on, or accompanying the seasons of the year or some particular season; periodical: *seasonal work.* **—***n.* **2.** a seasonal product, employee, etc.: *to hire seasonals.* [1830–40; SEASON + -AL[1]] **—sea′son·al·ly,** *adv.* **—sea′son·al·ness,** *n.*
—Usage. SEASONAL and SEASONABLE are sometimes interchanged, probably because of their obvious connection with SEASON. In edited prose and in formal speech these two adjectives are almost always distinguished. SEASONAL describes phenomena that occur with or depend upon a season or the seasons: *seasonal fluctuations in rainfall; seasonal sales.* SEASONABLE in reference to weather means "suitable to or characteristic of the season": *a seasonable December; seasonable temperatures for July.* SEASONABLE also has the sense "timely, opportune": *a seasonable offer of financial assistance.*

sea′sonal affec′tive disor′der, recurrent winter depression characterized by oversleeping, overeating, and irritability, and relieved by the arrival of spring or by light therapy. *Abbr.:* SAD [1980–85]

sea·son·ing (sē′zə ning), *n.* **1.** salt or an herb, spice, or the like, for heightening or improving the flavor of food. **2.** the process by which a person becomes conditioned or seasoned: *That pitcher had a year of seasoning.* [1505–15; SEASON + -ING[1]] **—sea′son·ing·like′,** *adj.*

Seasons, The, an oratorio (1801) by Franz Joseph Haydn.

sea′son tick′et, a ticket for a specified series or number of events or valid for unlimited use during a specified time, often sold at a reduced rate, for athletic events, concerts, transportation, etc. [1810–20]

sea′ spi′der, any member of the arthropod class Pycnogonida, marine invertebrates with eight long walking legs attached to a small body consisting of a cephalothorax and vestigial abdomen. [1660–70]

sea′ squab′, the blowfish: used esp. on menus as a euphemism.

sea′ squill′. See **sea onion** (def. 1).

sea′ squirt′, any tunicate, esp. a sessile ascidian, so called from its habit of contracting its body and ejecting streams of water when disturbed. [1840–50]

sea′ stack′, a pillarlike mass of rock detached by wave action from a cliff-lined shore and surrounded by water. [1895–1900]

sea′ star′, *n.* starfish. [1560–70]

sea′ stores′, provisions and supplies to be used on a sea voyage. Also called **sea′ stock′.** [1650–60]

sea·strand (sē′strand′), *n.* seashore. [bef. 1000; ME *see stronde;* OE *sǣstrand;* see SEA, STRAND[1]]

sea′ swal′low, 1. any of several terns, esp. *Sterna hirundo.* **2.** *Brit. Dial.* any of several small petrels, esp. the storm petrel, *Hydrobates pelagicus.* [1590–1600]

seat (sēt), *n.* **1.** something designed to support a person in a sitting position, as a chair, bench, or pew; a place on or in which one sits. **2.** the part of a chair, sofa, or the like, on which one sits. **3.** the part of the body on which one sits; the buttocks. **4.** the part of the garment covering it: *the seat of one's pants.* **5.** a manner of or posture used in sitting, as on a horse. **6.** something on which the base of an object rests. **7.** the base itself. **8.** a place in which something belongs, occurs, or is established; site; location. **9.** a place in which administrative power or the like is centered: *the seat of the government.* **10.** a part of the body considered as the place in which an emotion or function is centered: *The heart is the seat of passion.* **11.** the office or authority of a king, bishop, etc.: *the episcopal seat.* **12.** a space in which a spectator or patron may sit; accommodation for sitting, as in a theater or stadium. **13.** right of admittance to such a space, esp. as indicated by a ticket. **14.** a right to sit as a member in a legislative or similar body: *to hold a seat in the senate.* **15.** a right to the privileges of membership in a stock exchange or the like. **16. by the seat of one's pants,** using experience, instinct, or guesswork. **—***v.t.* **17.** to place on a seat or seats; cause to sit down. **18.** to usher to a seat or find a seat for: *to be seated in the front row.* **19.** to have seats for; accommodate with seats: *a theater that seats 1200 people.* **20.** to put a seat on or into (a chair, garment, etc.). **21.** to install in a position or office of authority, in a legislative body, etc. **22.** to fit (a valve) with a seat. **23.** to attach to or place firmly in or on something as a base: *Seat the telescope on the tripod.* **—***v.i.* **24.** (of a cap, valve, etc.) to be closed or in proper position: *Be sure that the cap of the dipstick seats.* [1150–1200; ME *sete* (n.) < ON *sæti*] **—seat′er,** *n.* **—seat′less,** *adj.*
—Syn. 1. throne, stool. **3.** bottom, fundament.

sea′ tan′gle, any of various seaweeds, esp. of the genus *Laminaria.* [1860–65]

seat′ an′gle. See **angle cleat.**

seat′ belt′, a belt or strap in an automobile, airplane, etc., fastened around or sometimes diagonally across the midsection to keep the person safely secured, as during a sudden stop. Also, **seat′belt′.** Also called **safety belt.** Cf. **lap belt.** [1945–50]

CONCISE ETYMOLOGY KEY: <, descended or borrowed from; >, whence; b., blend of, blended; c., cognate with; cf., compare; deriv., derivative; equiv., equivalent; imit., imitative; obl., oblique; r., replacing; s., stem; sp., spelling, spelled; resp., respelling, respelled; trans., translation; ?, origin unknown; *, unattested; ‡, probably earlier than. See the full key inside the front cover.

seat·er (sē′tər), *n.* **1.** a person or thing that seats. **2.** a vehicle that seats a specified number of persons (usually used in combination): *The car is a four-seater.* [1685–95; SEAT + -ER[1]]

seat·ing (sē′ting), *n.* **1.** an act or instance of furnishing with, assigning, or escorting to a seat. **2.** the arrangement of seats in a theater, stadium, etc. **3.** material for seats, esp. upholstery. **—***adj.* **4.** of or pertaining to seats or those who are sitting: *the seating plan of a theater.* [1590–1600; SEAT + -ING[1], -ING[2]]

seat·mate (sēt′māt′), *n.* a person who shares a seat or occupies the seat next to oneself on a bus, plane, etc. [1855–60, *Amer.;* SEAT + MATE[1]]

SEATO (sē′tō), *n.* an organization formed in Manila (1954), comprising Australia, Great Britain, France, New Zealand, Pakistan, the Philippines, Thailand, and the United States, for collective defense against aggression in southeastern Asia and the southwestern Pacific: abolished in 1977. [*S*(*outh*)*e*(*ast*) *A*(*sia*) *T*(*reaty*) *O*(*rganization*)]

seat-of-the-pants (sēt′əv *th*ə pants′), *adj.* **1.** using or based on experience, instinct, or guesswork: *a seat-of-the-pants management style.* **2.** done without the aid of instruments: *The pilot made a seat-of-the-pants landing.* [1940–45]

sea·train (sē′trān′), *n.* a ship for the transportation of loaded railroad cars. [1930–35; SEA + TRAIN]

sea′ tri′als, a series of trial runs to test the performance of a new ship.

sea′ trout′, 1. any of various species of trout inhabiting salt water, as the salmon trout, *Salmo trutta.* **2.** any of several fishes of the genus *Cynoscion.* [1735–45]

Se·at·tle (sē at′l), *n.* **1.** (*Seatlh*), c1790–1866, Suquamish leader: Seattle, Washington, named after him. **2.** a seaport in W Washington, on Puget Sound. 493,846.

sea′ tur′tle, any of several large turtles of the families Cheloniidae and Dermochelyidae, widely distributed in tropical and subtropical seas, having the limbs modified into paddlelike flippers: all sea turtles are either threatened or endangered through most of their range because of ocean pollution. [1670–80]

seat·work (sēt′wûrk′), *n. Educ.* work that can be done by a child at his or her seat in school without supervision. [SEAT + WORK]

sea′ ur′chin, 1. any echinoderm of the class Echinoidea, having a somewhat globular or discoid form, and a shell composed of many calcareous plates covered with projecting spines. **2.** a tall evergreen shrub or small tree, *Hakea laurina,* of Australia, having narrow leaves and dense, globe-shaped clusters of crimson flowers with long yellow stamens. [1585–95]

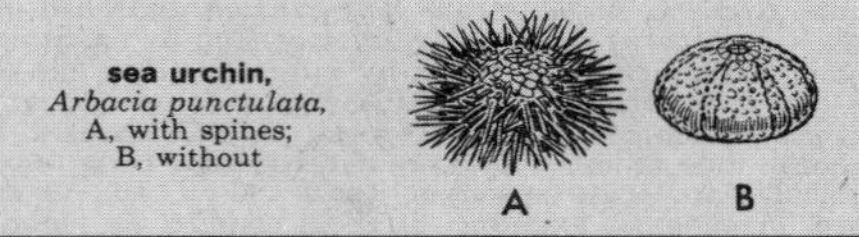

sea urchin, *Arbacia punctulata,* A, with spines; B, without

sea′ wall′, a strong wall or embankment to prevent the encroachments of the sea, serve as a breakwater, etc. [bef. 1000; ME; OE: cliff over the sea] **—sea′-walled′,** *adj.*

sea′ wal′nut, a comb jelly, as of the genus *Mnemiopsis,* shaped like a walnut.

sea·wan (sē′wən), *n.* wampum (def. 1). Also, **sea·want** (sē′wänt′), **sewan.** [1620–30, *Amer.;* < New York D *sewan, zeewan, zeewant,* etc. < Munsee Delaware **sé·wan* unstrung wampum, lit., that which is in a scattered state, deriv of *se·*(*w*)- scatter(ed)]

sea·ward (sē′wərd), *adv.* **1.** Also, **sea′wards.** toward the sea: *a storm moving seaward.* **—***adj.* **2.** facing or tending toward the sea: *a seaward course.* **3.** coming from the sea: *a seaward wind.* **—***n.* **4.** the direction toward the sea or away from the land. [1350–1400; ME; see SEA, -WARD]

sea·ware (sē′wâr′), *n.* seaweed, esp. coarse, large seaweed, used chiefly as a fertilizer. [bef. 1000; OE *sǣwār,* equiv. to *sǣ* SEA + *wār* seaweed (not recorded in ME)]

sea′ wasp′, any of various highly poisonous stinging jellyfishes of the order Cubomedusae, of tropical seas. [1935–40]

sea·wa·ter (sē′wô′tər, -wot′ər), *n.* the salt water in or from the sea. [bef. 1000; ME *see water,* OE *sǣwæter;* see SEA, WATER]

sea·way (sē′wā′), *n.* **1.** a way over the sea. **2.** the open sea. **3.** the progress of a ship through the waves. **4.** a more or less rough sea: *a hard vessel to steer in a seaway.* **5.** a canal, enlarged river, etc., giving access to a landlocked port by oceangoing vessels. [bef. 1000; ME *seewey,* OE *sǣweg.* See SEA, WAY[1]]

sea·weed (sē′wēd′), *n.* **1.** any plant or plants growing in the ocean. **2.** a marine alga. [1570–80; SEA + WEED[1]]

sea′weed mar′quetry, marquetry having the form of symmetrical, foliate scrolls, as on English cabinetwork of the late 17th and early 18th centuries.

sea′ whip′, a gorgonian coral that forms a flexible colony resembling shrubbery on the ocean floor. [1825–35]

sea′ wolf′, 1. any of several large, voracious, marine fishes, as the wolffish or sea bass. **2.** a pirate. [1250–1300; ME]

sea·wor·thy (sē′wûr′*th*ē), *adj.,* **-thi·er, -thi·est.** (of a vessel) **1.** constructed, outfitted, manned, and in all respects fitted for a voyage at sea. **2.** safe for a voyage at sea. [1800–10; SEA + -WORTHY] **—sea′wor′thi·ness,** *n.*

sea′ wrack′, seaweed or a growth of seaweed, esp. of the larger kinds cast up on the shore. [1540–50]

se·ba·ceous (si bā′shəs), *adj. Physiol.* **1.** pertaining to, of the nature of, or resembling tallow or fat; fatty; greasy. **2.** secreting a fatty substance. [1720–30; < NL *sēbāceus.* See SEBUM, -ACEOUS]

seba′ceous gland′, any of the cutaneous glands that secrete oily matter for lubricating hair and skin. See diag. under **hair.** [1720–30]

se·bac·ic (si bas′ik, -bā′sik), *adj. Chem.* of or derived from sebacic acid. [1780–90; SEBAC(EOUS) + -IC]

sebac′ic ac′id, *Chem.* a crystalline, slightly water-soluble, dibasic acid, $C_{10}H_{18}O_4$, usually obtained from castor oil: used chiefly in the manufacture of plasticizers and resins. [1780–90]

Se·bas·tian (si bas′chən), *n.* **1. Saint,** died A.D. 288?, Roman martyr. **2.** a male given name.

Se·bas·to·pol (si bas′tə pōl′), *n.* Sevastopol.

SEbE, See **southeast by east.**

Se·bo·im (si bō′im), *n. Douay Bible.* Zeboim.

seb·or·rhe·a (seb′ə rē′ə), *n. Pathol.* an excessive and abnormal discharge from the sebaceous glands. Also, **seb′or·rhoe′a.** [1875–80; SEB(UM) + -O- + -RRHEA] **—seb′or·rhe′al, seb′or·rhe′ic,** *adj.*

SEbS, See **southeast by south.**

se·bum (sē′bəm), *n. Physiol.* the fatty secretion of the sebaceous glands. [1700–10; < L *sēbum* tallow, grease]

sec[1] (sek), *adj.* (of wines) dry; not sweet. [1885–90; < F; see SACK[3]]

sec[2] (sek), *n. Informal.* second[2] (def. 2). [1955–60; by shortening]

SEC, *U.S. Govt.* Securities and Exchange Commission: a board, consisting of five members, charged with regulating the public offer and sale of securities. Also, **S.E.C.**

sec, 1. secant. **2.** second. **3.** section.

sec^{-1} *Symbol, Trig.* arc secant.

sec., 1. second. **2.** secondary. **3.** secretary. **4.** section. **5.** sector. **6.** according to. [< L *secundum*]

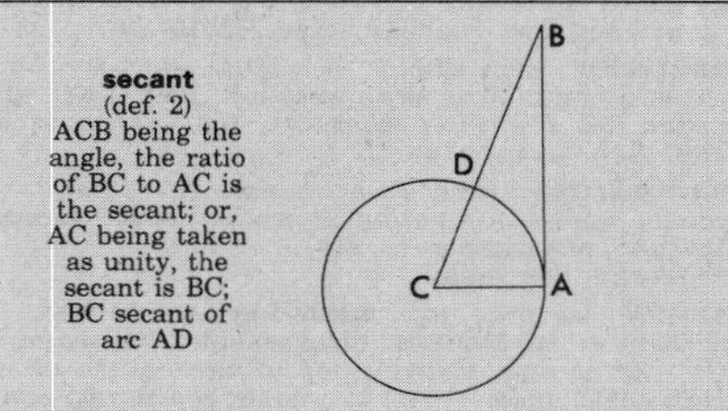

secant (def. 2) ACB being the angle, the ratio of BC to AC is the secant; or, AC being taken as unity, the secant is BC; BC secant of arc AD

se·cant (sē′kant, -kənt), *n.* **1.** *Geom.* an intersecting line, esp. one intersecting a curve at two or more points. **2.** *Trig.* **a.** (in a right triangle) the ratio of the hypotenuse to the side adjacent to a given angle. **b.** (originally) a line from the center of a circle through one extremity of an arc to the tangent from the other extremity. **c.** the ratio of the length of this line to that of the radius of the circle; the reciprocal of the cosine of a given angle or arc. *Abbr.:* sec **—***adj.* **3.** cutting or intersecting, as one line or surface in relation to another. [1585–95; < L *secant-* (s. of *secāns,* prp. of *secāre* to cut), equiv. to *sec-* verb s. (see SAW[1]) + *-ant-* -ANT] **—se′cant·ly,** *adv.*

sec·a·teurs (sek′ə tər, -tûr′), *n.* (*used with a singular or plural v.*) *Chiefly Brit.* scissors or shears, esp. pruning shears. [1880–85; < F < L *sec*(*āre*) to cut (see SECANT) + F *-ateurs* (pl.) < L *-ātor* -ATOR]

Se·cau·cus (si kô′kəs), *n.* a town in NE New Jersey. 13,719.

Sec·chi (sek′ē; *It.* sek′kē), *n.* **Pie·tro An·ge·lo** (pye′trô än′je lô), 1818–78, Italian Jesuit and astronomer.

sec·co (sek′ō; *It.* sek′kô), *n.* **1.** See **fresco secco.** **—***adj.* **2.** (of notes or passages in a musical score) played and released abruptly and without resonance. [1850–55; < It: dry; see SACK[3]]

se·cede (si sēd′), *v.i.,* **-ced·ed, -ced·ing.** to withdraw formally from an alliance, federation, or association, as from a political union, a religious organization, etc. [1695–1705; < L *sēcēdere* to withdraw. See SE-, CEDE] **—se·ced′er,** *n.*

se·cern (si sûrn′), *v.t.* **1.** to discriminate or distinguish in thought. **—***v.i.* **2.** to become secerned. [1620–30; < L *sēcernere,* equiv. to *sē-* SE- + *cernere* to sift (cf. DISCERN)] **—se·cern′ment,** *n.*

se·ces·sion (si sesh′ən), *n.* **1.** an act or instance of seceding. **2.** (*often cap.*) *U.S. Hist.* the withdrawal from the Union of 11 Southern states in the period 1860–61, which brought on the Civil War. **3.** (*usually cap.*) *Fine Arts.* a style of art in Germany and Austria concurrent with and related to Art Nouveau. [1525–35; < L *sēcessiōn-* (s. of *sēcessiō*) withdrawal, equiv. to *sēcess*(*us*) (ptp. of *sēcēdere* to SECEDE; see CESSION) + *-iōn-* -ION] **—se·ces′sion·al,** *adj.*

se·ces·sion·ist (si sesh′ə nist), *n.* **1.** a person who secedes, advocates secession, or claims secession as a constitutional right. **—***adj.* **2.** of or pertaining to secession or secessionists. [1850–55, *Amer.;* SECESSION + -IST] **—se·ces′sion·ism,** *n.*

sech, *Symbol, Math.* hyperbolic secant. [SEC(ANT) + H(YPERBOLIC)]

Seck·el (sek′əl, sik′-), *n.* a small, yellowish-brown variety of pear. [1810–20, *Amer.;* after surname of grower, Pennsylvania orchardist]

sec. leg., according to law. [< L *secundum lēgem*]

se·clude (si klōōd′), *v.t.,* **-clud·ed, -clud·ing. 1.** to place in or withdraw into solitude; remove from social contact and activity, etc. **2.** to isolate; shut off; keep apart: *They secluded the garden from the rest of the property.* [1425–75; late ME < L *sēclūdere,* equiv. to *sē-* SE- + *-clūdere,* comb. form of *claudere* to CLOSE]

se•clud•ed (si klo͞o′did), *adj.* **1.** sheltered or screened from general activity, view, etc.: *a secluded cottage.* **2.** withdrawn from or involving little human or social activity: *a secluded life.* [1595–1605; SECLUDE + -ED[2]] —**se•clud′ed•ly,** *adv.* —**se•clud′ed•ness,** *n.*
—**Syn.** isolated, retired, sequestered, cloistered, private, secret.

se•clu•sion (si klo͞o′zhən), *n.* **1.** an act of secluding. **2.** the state of being secluded; retirement; solitude: *He sought seclusion in his study.* **3.** a secluded place. [1615–25; < ML *sēclūsiōn-* (s. of *sēclūsiō*) < L *sēclūs(us)* (ptp. of *sēclūdere* to SECLUDE) + *-iōn-* -ION]

se•clu•sive (si klo͞o′siv), *adj.* **1.** tending to seclude, esp. oneself. **2.** causing or providing seclusion. [1815–25; *secluse* (< L *sēclūsus* secluded; see SECLUSION) + -IVE] —**se•clu′sive•ly,** *adv.* —**se•clu′sive•ness,** *n.*

sec•o•bar•bi•tal (sek′ō bär′bi tôl′, -tal′), *n. Pharm.* a white, odorless, slightly bitter powder, $C_{12}H_{18}N_2O_3$, used as a sedative and hypnotic. [1950–55; SECO(NAL) + BARBITAL]

Sec•o•nal (sek′ə nôl′, -nal′, -nl), *Pharm., Trademark.* a brand of secobarbital.

sec•ond[1] (sek′ənd), *adj.* **1.** next after the first; being the ordinal number for two. **2.** being the latter of two equal parts. **3.** next after the first in place, time, or value: *the second house from the corner.* **4.** next after the first in rank, grade, degree, status, or importance: *the second person in the company.* **5.** alternate: *I have my hair cut every second week.* **6.** inferior. **7.** *Gram.* noting or pertaining to the second person. **8.** *Music.* being the lower of two parts for the same instrument or voice: *second horn; second alto.* **9.** other or another: *a second Solomon.* **10.** *Auto.* of, pertaining to, or operating at the gear transmission ratio at which drive shaft speed is greater than that of low gear but not so great as that of other gears for a given engine crankshaft speed: *second gear.* —*n.* **11.** a second part. **12.** the second member of a series. **13.** a person who aids or supports another; assistant; backer. **14.** *Boxing.* a person who, between rounds of a prizefight, gives aid, advice, etc., to a boxer. **15.** a person who serves as a representative or attendant of a duelist. **16.** *Auto.* second gear. **17.** a person or thing that is next after the first in place, time, or value. **18.** a person or thing that is next after the first in rank, grade, degree, status, or importance. **19.** Usually, **seconds.** an additional helping of food: *He had seconds on the meat and potatoes.* **20.** (in parliamentary procedure) **a.** a person who expresses formal support of a motion so that it may be discussed or put to a vote. **b.** an act or instance of doing this. **21.** (in certain British universities) a type or grade of college degree granted according to a student's performance on specific written and oral examinations. **22.** *Music.* **a.** a tone on the next degree from a given tone. **b.** the interval between such tones. **c.** the harmonic combination of such tones. **d.** the lower of two parts in a piece of concerted music. **e.** a voice or instrument performing such a part. **f.** an alto. **23.** Usually, **seconds.** goods below the first or highest quality, esp. containing visible flaws. Cf. **first** (def. 19), **third** (def. 12). **24.** *Metall.* a piece of somewhat defective but salable tin plate. **25.** *Baseball.* See **second base.** —*v.t.* **26.** to assist or support. **27.** to further or advance, as aims. **28.** (in parliamentary procedure) to express formal support of (a motion, proposal, etc.), as a necessary preliminary to further discussion or to voting. **29.** to act as second to (a boxer, duelist, etc.). —*adv.* **30.** in the second place, group, etc.; secondly: *The catcher is batting second.* [1250–1300; ME (adj., n. and adv.) < OF (adj.) < L *secundus* following, next, second, equiv. to *sec-* (base of *sequī* to follow) + *-undus* adj. suffix] —**sec′•ond•er,** *n.*
—**Syn. 13.** aide, helper, agent, deputy.

sec•ond[2] (sek′ənd), *n.* **1.** the sixtieth part of a minute of time. **2.** a moment or instant: *It takes only a second to phone.* **3.** the basic unit of time in the International System of Units, equal to the duration of 9,192,631,770 cycles of radiation in a transition, or energy level change, of the cesium atom. *Symbol:* s, S; *Abbr.:* sec **4.** *Geom., Astron.* the sixtieth part of a minute of angular measure, often represented by the sign ″, as in 30″, which is read as 30 seconds. Cf. **angle**[1] (def. 1c). [1350–1400; ME *seconde* < MF < ML *secunda* (*minūta*) second (minute), fem. of *secundus* SECOND[1]]
—**Syn. 2.** jiffy, trice, wink, flash.

se•cond[3] (si kond′), *v.t. Brit.* to transfer (an officer, official, or the like) temporarily to another post. [1795–1805; < F *second,* n. use of the adj. in the phrase *en second,* as in *lieutenant en second* second lieutenant; see SECOND[1]]

Sec′ond Ad′vent. See **Second Coming.** [1730–40]

Sec′ond Ad′ventist, Adventist (def. 1). [1840–50, *Amer.*]

Sec′ond Amend′ment, an amendment to the U.S. Constitution, ratified in 1791 as part of the Bill of Rights, guaranteeing the right to keep and bear arms as necessary to maintain a state militia.

sec•ond•ar•y (sek′ən der′ē), *adj., n., pl.* **-ar•ies.** —*adj.* **1.** next after the first in order, place, time, etc. **2.** belonging or pertaining to a second order, division, stage, period, rank, grade, etc. **3.** derived or derivative; not primary or original: *secondary sources of historical research.* **4.** of minor or lesser importance; subordinate; auxiliary. **5.** of or pertaining to secondary schools. **6.** *Chem.* **a.** involving or obtained by the replacement of two atoms or groups. **b.** noting or containing a carbon atom united to two other carbon atoms in a chain or ring molecule. **7.** *Elect.* noting or pertaining to the current induced by a primary winding or to the winding in which the current is induced in an induction coil, transformer, or the like. **8.** *Geol.* noting or pertaining to a mineral produced from another mineral by decay, alteration, or the like. **9.** *Gram.* **a.** derived. **b.** derived from a word that is itself a derived word: *a secondary derivative.* **c.** having reference to past time; noting or pertaining to a past tense: *the Latin, Greek, or Sanskrit secondary tenses.* Cf. **primary** (def. 13). **10.** *Ornith.* pertaining to any of a set of flight feathers on the second segment of a bird's wing. **11.** *Ling.* of, pertaining to, or characteristic of a secondary accent: *secondary stress.* —*n.* **12.** a person or thing that is secondary. **13.** a subordinate, assistant, deputy, or agent. **14.** *Elect.* a winding in a transformer or the like in which a current is induced by a primary winding. **15.** *Ornith.* a secondary feather. **16.** *Football.* the defensive unit that lines up behind the linemen. **17.** *Ling.* See **secondary accent.** [1350–1400; ME < L *secundārius.* See SECOND[1], -ARY] —**sec•ond•ar•i•ly** (sek′ən der′ə lē, sek′ən dâr′-), *adv.* —**sec′•ond•ar′i•ness,** *n.*
—**Syn. 4.** alternate, subsidiary, backup.

sec′ondary ac′cent, a stress accent weaker than primary accent but stronger than lack of stress. Also called **secondary stress.** [1830–40]

sec′ondary articula′tion, *Phonet.* coarticulation (def. 2).

sec′ondary beam′, *Physics.* a beam of particles of one kind selected from the group of particles produced when a beam of particles from an accelerator (**primary beam**) strikes a target.

sec′ondary boy′cott, a boycott by union members against their employer in order to induce the employer to bring pressure on another company involved in a labor dispute with the union. [1945–50]

sec′ondary cell′, *Elect.* See **storage cell.** [1905–10]

sec′ondary col′or, *Art.* a color, as orange, green, or violet, produced by mixing two primary colors. [1825–35]

sec′ondary con′tact, *Sociol.* communication or relationship between people characterized by impersonal and detached interest on the part of those involved. Cf. **primary contact.**

sec′ondary de′viance, *Sociol.* deviant behavior that results from being publicly labeled as deviant and treated as an outsider. Cf. **primary deviance.**

sec′ondary diag′onal. See under **diagonal** (def. 9).

sec′ondary emis′sion, the emission of electrons (**sec′ondary elec′trons**) from a material that is bombarded with electrons or ions. [1930–35]

sec′ondary gain′, *Psychiatry.* any advantage, as increased attention, disability benefits, or release from unpleasant responsibilities, obtained as a result of having an illness (distinguished from *primary gain*).

sec′ondary group′, *Sociol.* a group of people with whom one's contacts are detached and impersonal. Cf. **primary group.**

sec′ondary inten′tion, *Logic.* See under **intention** (def. 5b).

sec′ondary mar′ket, *Stock Exchange.* the market that exists for an issue after large blocks of shares have been publicly distributed. Also called **aftermarket.**

sec′ondary mem′ory, *Computers.* See **secondary storage.**

sec′ondary met′al, metal derived wholly or in part from scrap. Cf. **primary metal.**

sec′ondary of′fering, *Stock Exchange.* the sale of a large block of outstanding stock off the floor of an exchange, usually by a major stockholder.

sec′ondary phlo′em, phloem derived from the cambium during secondary growth.

sec′ondary proc′ess, *Psychoanal.* the conscious mental activity and logical thinking controlled by the ego and influenced by environmental demands. Cf. **primary process.**

sec′ondary pro′pyl al′cohol, *Chem.* See **isopropyl alcohol.**

sec′ondary qual′ity, *Epistemology.* one of the qualities attributed by the mind to an object perceived, such as color, temperature, or taste. Cf. **primary quality.** [1690–1700]

sec′ondary rain′bow, a faint rainbow formed by light rays that undergo two internal reflections in drops of rain, appearing above the primary rainbow and having its colors in the opposite order. [1785–95]

sec′ondary recov′ery, extraction of oil or natural gas under artificially induced pressure after the natural flow has ceased. Cf. **waterflood.** [1935–40]

sec′ondary road′, a road less important than a main road or highway. [1945–50]

sec′ondary school′, a high school or a school of corresponding grade, ranking between a primary school and a college or university. [1825–35] —**sec′ond•ar′y-school′,** *adj.*

sec′ondary sev′enth chord′, *Music.* a chord formed by superposition of three thirds upon any degree of the scale except the dominant.

sec′ondary sex′ characteris′tic, *Med.* any of a number of manifestations, as development of breasts or beard, muscularity, distribution of fat tissue, and change of pitch in voice, specific to each sex and incipient at puberty but not essential to reproduction. Also called **sec′•ondary sex′ char′acter.** [1925–30]

sec′ondary spermat′ocyte, *Cell Biol.* See under **spermatocyte.**

sec′ondary stor′age, *Computers.* storage, as on disk or tape, supplemental to and slower than main storage, not under the direct control of the CPU and generally contained outside it: *Secondary storage for this system is contained on videodisk.* Also called **auxiliary storage, external storage, secondary memory.**

sec′ondary stress′, **1.** *Engin.* a stress induced by the elastic deformation of a structure under a temporary load. **2.** See **secondary accent.**

sec′ondary syph′ilis, *Pathol.* the second stage of syphilis, characterized by eruptions of the skin and mucous membrane. [1905–10]

sec′ondary tis′sue, *Bot.* tissue derived from cambium.

sec′ondary wave′. See **S wave.**

sec′ondary xy′lem, xylem derived from the cambium during secondary growth.

sec′ond ax′iom of countabil′ity, *Math.* See under **axiom of countability.**

Sec′ond Bal′kan War′. See **Balkan War** (def. 2).

sec′ond banan′a, *Informal.* **1.** a comic who supports the leading comedian, often as a straight man, esp. in burlesque or vaudeville. **2.** any person who plays a secondary role or serves in a subsidiary capacity. Cf. **top banana.** [1950–55]

sec′ond base′, *Baseball.* **1.** the second in order of the bases from home plate. **2.** the position of the player covering the area of the infield between second and first bases. [1835–45, *Amer.*]

sec′ond base′man, *Baseball.* the player whose position is second base. [1855–60, *Amer.*]

sec′ond best′, the next to the best in performance, achievement, craftsmanship, etc. [1400–50; late ME] —**sec′ond-best′,** *adj.*

Sec′ond Birth′, *Theol.* spiritual rebirth. [1505–15]

sec′ond bless′ing, *Rom. Cath. Ch.* an experience of sanctification coming after conversion. [1925–30]

Sec′ond Cham′ber. See under **States-General** (def. 1). [1900–05]

sec′ond child′hood, senility; dotage. [1900–05]

sec′ond class′, **1.** the class of travel accommodations, as on a train, that are less costly and luxurious than first class but are more costly and luxurious than third class. Cf. **cabin class. 2.** (in the U.S. Postal Service) the class of mail consisting of newspapers and periodicals not sealed against postal inspection. **3.** the second of three honors degrees conferred by a British university. [1830–40]

sec•ond-class (sek′ənd klas′, -kläs′), *adj.* **1.** of a secondary class or quality. **2.** second-rate; inferior. —*adv.* **3.** by second-class mail or passenger accommodations: *to travel second-class.* [1830–40]

sec′ond-class cit′izen, **1.** a citizen, esp. a member of a minority group, who is denied the social, political, and economic benefits of citizenship. **2.** a person who is not accorded a fair share of respect, recognition, or consideration: *The boss treats us all like second-class citizens.*

Sec′ond Com′ing, the coming of Christ on Judgment Day. Also called **Advent, Second Advent.** [1635–45]

Sec′ond Command′ment, "Thou shalt not make unto thee any graven image, or any likeness of any thing that is in heaven above, or that is in the earth beneath, or that is in the water under the earth. Thou shalt not bow down thyself to them nor serve them": second of the Ten Commandments. Cf. **Ten Commandments.**

sec′ond con′sonant shift′, the consonant shift by which High German became differentiated from other Germanic languages. Cf. **consonant shift, first consonant shift.** [1935–40]

sec′ond cous′in, a child of a first cousin of one's parent. Cf. **cousin** (def. 1). [1650–60]

sec′ond-de•gree burn′ (sek′ənd di grē′), *Pathol.* See under **burn**[1] (def. 47). [1935–40]

sec′ond-degree mur′der, *Law.* See under **murder** (def. 1). [1945–50, *Amer.*]

sec′ond deriv′ative, *Math.* the derivative of the derivative of a function: *Acceleration is the second derivative of distance with respect to time.* Cf. **first derivative.**

sec′ond divi′sion, *Sports.* the half of a league comprising the teams having the poorest records at a particular time. [1895–1905]

se•conde (si kond′; *Fr.* sə gônd′), *n., pl.* **-condes** (-kondz′; *Fr.* -gônd′). *Fencing.* the second of the eight defensive positions. [1680–90; < F, fem. of *second* SECOND[1]]

Sec′ond Em′pire, the empire established in France (1852–70) by Louis Napoleon: the successor to the Second Republic.

sec′ond estate′, the second of the three estates: the nobles in France; the lords temporal in England. Cf. **estate** (def. 5). [1930–35]

sec′ond fid′dle, **1.** a secondary role: *to play second fiddle to another person.* **2.** a person serving in a subsidiary capacity, esp. to one immediately superior. [1825–35]

sec′ond floor′, **1.** the floor or story above the ground floor. **2.** (in Britain and elsewhere outside the U.S.) the second story completely above ground level. Cf. **first floor.** Also called **second story.** [1815–25]

sec•ond-foot (sek′ənd fo͝ot′), *n.* a unit of measurement of liquid flow, esp. of rivers, equal to one cubic foot per second.

sec•ond-gen•er•a•tion (sek′ənd jen′ə rā′shən), —*adj.* **1.** being the second generation of a family to be born in a particular country: *the oldest son of second-generation Americans.* **2.** being the native-born child of naturalized parents. **3.** being a revised or improved version of a product, system, service, etc.: *Production has been increased with second-generation robots.*

sec′ond growth′, the plant growth that follows the destruction of virgin forest. [1820–30]

CONCISE PRONUNCIATION KEY: *act, cāpe, dâre, pärt; set, ēqual; if, īce; ox, ōver, ôrder, oil, bo͝ok, bo͞ot, out; up, ûrge; child; sing; shoe; thin, that;* zh as in *treasure.* ə = *a* as in *alone, e* as in *system, i* as in *easily, o* as in *gallop, u* as in *circus;* ᵊ as in *fire* (fīᵊr), *hour* (ouᵊr). l and n can serve as syllabic consonants, as in *cradle* (krād′l), and *button* (but′n). See the full key inside the front cover.

sec•ond-guess (sek′ənd ges′), *v.t.* **1.** to use hindsight in criticizing or correcting. **2.** to predict (something) or outguess (someone): *We must try to second-guess what he'll do next.* [1945–50] **—sec′ond-guess′er,** *n.*

sec•ond hand (sek′ənd hand′ *for 1;* sek′ənd hand′ *for 2, 3*), **1.** the hand that indicates the seconds on a clock or watch. **2.** an assistant or helper, as to a worker or foreman. **3. at second hand,** from or through an intermediate source or means; secondhand: *She had the news at second hand.* [1425–75 for def. 3; 1750–60 for def. 1; late ME]

sec•ond•hand (sek′ənd hand′), *adj.* **1.** not directly known or experienced; obtained from others or from books: *Most of our knowledge is secondhand.* **2.** previously used or owned: *secondhand clothes.* **3.** dealing in previously used goods: *a secondhand bookseller.* —*adv.* **4.** after another user or owner: *He bought it secondhand.* **5.** indirectly; at second hand: *He heard the news secondhand.* [1645–55; SECOND[1] + HAND] **—sec′ond-hand′ed•ness,** *n.*

sec′ondhand smoke′, smoke from a cigarette, cigar, or pipe that is involuntarily inhaled, esp. by nonsmokers. [1975–80]

sec′ond home′, **1.** an additional residence, as at the shore or in the country, where one goes on weekends, vacations, and the like. **2.** another residence, as of a close relative or friend, where one spends a great deal of time or feels welcome and at home: *Aunt Sue's house was my second home.* **3.** any place where one spends a great deal of time: *My office is my second home.*

sec′ond inten′tion, *Logic.* See under **intention** (def. 5b).

Sec′ond Interna′tional, an international association formed in 1889 in Paris, uniting socialistic groups or parties of various countries and holding international congresses from time to time: in 1923 it joined with the Vienna International to form the Labor and Socialist International. Cf. **international** (def. 6).

sec′ond lan′guage, **1.** a language learned by a person after his or her native language, esp. as a resident of an area where it is in general use. **2.** a language widely used, esp. in educational and governmental functions in a region where all or most of its speakers are nonnative, as English in India or Nigeria.

sec′ond law′ of mo′tion, *Physics.* See under **law of motion.**

sec′ond law′ of thermodynam′ics. See under **law of thermodynamics** (def. 1).

sec′ond lien′, a lien subordinate to a previous or preferred lien.

sec′ond lieuten′ant, *U.S. Mil.* an Army, Air Force, or Marine officer of the lowest commissioned rank. Cf. **ensign** (def. 4). [1695–1705]

sec•ond•ly (sek′ənd lē), *adv.* in the second place; second. [1325–75; ME; see SECOND[1], -LY]

sec′ond mate′, the officer of a merchant vessel next in command beneath the first mate. Also called **sec′ond of′ficer.**

se•cond•ment (si kond′mənt), *n. Brit.* the transfer of a military officer or corporate executive to another post for temporary duty. [1895–1900; SECOND[3] + -MENT]

sec′ond mes′senger, *Biochem.* any of various intracellular chemical substances, as cyclic AMP, that transmit and amplify the messages delivered by a first messenger to specific receptors on the cell surface. Cf. **first messenger.** [1960–65]

sec′ond mort′gage, a mortgage the lien of which is next in priority to a first mortgage. [1900–05]

sec′ond na′ture, an acquired habit or tendency in one's character that is so deeply ingrained as to appear automatic: *Neatness is second nature to him.* [1655–65]

se•con•do (si kon′dō, -kōn′-; *It.* se kôn′dô), *n., pl.* **-di** (-dē). *Music.* **1.** the second or lower part in a duet, esp. in a piano duet. **2.** the performer playing this part. [1840–50; < It; see SECOND[1]]

sec′ond of arc′, second[2] (def. 4).

sec′ond pa′pers, (before 1952) an official petition for naturalization by a resident alien desiring to become a U.S. citizen, filed two years after his or her first papers and upon having lived in the U.S. for five years. Cf. **citizenship papers.** [1910–15, *Amer.*]

sec′ond per′son, *Gram.* the person used by a speaker in referring to the one or ones being addressed: in English *you* is a second person pronoun. [1665–75]

sec′ond posi′tion, *Ballet.* a position in which the feet are spread apart and are at right angles to the direction of the body, the toes pointing out. See illus. under **first position.**

sec•ond-rate (sek′ənd rāt′), *adj.* **1.** of lesser or minor quality, importance, or the like: *a second-rate poet.* **2.** inferior; mediocre: *a second-rate performance.* [1660–70] **—sec′ond-rate′ness,** *n.* **—sec′ond-rat′er,** *n.*
—Syn. 2. middling, inadequate, undistinguished, pedestrian, commonplace.

Sec′ond Read′er, *Christian Science.* the elected official of a church or society who conducts services and reads from the Scriptures. Cf. **First Reader.** [1890–95]

sec′ond read′ing, the stage in the consideration of a legislative bill that provides an opportunity for debate and amendment. [1640–50]

Sec′ond Reich′, the German Empire 1871–1919. Cf. **Reich.**

Sec′ond Repub′lic, the republic established in France in 1848 and replaced by the Second Empire in 1852.

sec′ond self′, one who associates so closely with a given person as to assume that person's mode of behavior, personality, beliefs, etc. [1580–90]

sec′ond serv′ice, *Ch. of Eng.* the communion service: so called because it follows Morning Prayer. [1645–55]

sec′ond sex′, one sex considered as secondary or subordinate in role to the other, esp. women in a male-dominated society. [1810–20]

sec′ond sheet′, **1.** a sheet of blank stationery, used in a letter as the second and following pages to a sheet having a letterhead. **2.** a sheet of lightweight paper, usually of inferior quality, used behind a carbon to make a duplicate.

sec′ond sight′, the faculty of seeing future events; clairvoyance. [1610–20] **—sec′ond-sight′ed,** *adj.* **—sec′ond-sight′ed•ness,** *n.*

sec′ond sto′ry. See **second floor.**

sec•ond-sto•ry (sek′ənd stôr′ē, -stōr′ē), *adj.* **1.** of or located on the second story or floor. **2.** of or pertaining to a second-story man: *The theft was a second-story job.*

sec′ond-sto′ry man′, a burglar who enters through an upstairs window. [1900–05]

sec′ond string′, **1.** *Sports.* the squad of players available either individually or as a team to replace or relieve those who start a game. **2.** a secondary position, status, or group, as in a level of corporate management. [1635–45 in sense "backup, resort," alluding to a second bowstring; 1860–65, applied to racehorses; 1950–55, to sports teams] **—sec′ond-string′,** *adj.* **—sec′ond-string′er,** *n.*

sec′ond thought′, **1.** Often, **second thoughts.** reservation about a previous action, position, decision, judgment, or the like: *He had second thoughts about his decision.* **2. on second thought,** after reconsideration: *On second thought, I don't think I'll go.* Also, **sec′ond-thought′.** [1625–35]

sec′ond u′nit, *Motion Pictures.* an additional crew on a film production, usually used at a second location for filming crowd scenes, exteriors, and other shots that do not require the principal actors.

Sec′ond Vat′ican Coun′cil, the twenty-first Roman Catholic ecumenical council (1962–65) convened by Pope John XXIII. Its 16 documents redefined the nature of the church, gave bishops greater influence in church affairs, and increased lay participation in liturgy. Also called **Vatican II.**

sec′ond wind′ (wind), **1.** the return of ease in breathing after exhaustion caused by continued physical exertion, as in running. **2.** the energy for a renewed effort to continue an undertaking. [1895–1900]

Sec′ond World′, (*sometimes l.c.*) **1.** the world's industrialized nations other than the U.S. and the U.S.S.R. **2.** the Communist and socialist nations of the world. Cf. **First World, Third World, Fourth World.** [1965–70]

Sec′ond World′ War′. See **World War II.**

se•cos (sē′kōs, -kôs), *n.* sekos.

se•cre•cy (sē′krə sē), *n., pl.* **-cies** for 2, 3. **1.** the state or condition of being secret, hidden, or concealed: *a meeting held in secrecy.* **2.** privacy; retirement; seclusion. **3.** ability to keep a secret. **4.** the habit or characteristic of being secretive; reticence. [1375–1425; obs. *secre* (< MF *secré* SECRET) + -CY; r. late ME *secretee,* equiv. to *secre* + *-tee* -TY[2]]
—Syn. 1. confidentiality, privacy, stealth, covertness.

se•cret (sē′krit), *adj.* **1.** done, made, or conducted without the knowledge of others: *secret negotiations.* **2.** kept from the knowledge of any but the initiated or privileged: *a secret password.* **3.** faithful or cautious in keeping confidential matters confidential; close-mouthed; reticent. **4.** designed or working to escape notice, knowledge, or observation: *a secret drawer; the secret police.* **5.** secluded, sheltered, or withdrawn: *a secret hiding place.* **6.** beyond ordinary human understanding; esoteric. **7.** (of information, a document, etc.) **a.** bearing the classification *secret.* **b.** limited to persons authorized to use information documents, etc., so classified. —*n.* **8.** something that is or is kept secret, hidden, or concealed. **9.** a mystery: *the secrets of nature.* **10.** a reason or explanation not immediately or generally apparent. **11.** a method, formula, plan, etc., known only to the initiated or the few: *the secret of happiness; a trade secret.* **12.** a classification assigned to information, a document, etc., considered less vital to security than top-secret but more vital than confidential, and limiting its use to persons who have been cleared, as by government agencies, as trustworthy to handle such material. Cf. **classification** (def. 5). **13.** (*cap.*) *Liturgy.* a variable prayer in the Roman and other Latin liturgies, said inaudibly by the celebrant after the offertory and immediately before the preface. **14. in secret,** unknown to others; in private; secretly: *a movement organized in secret.* [1350–1400; ME *secrette* < OF *secret* < L *sēcrētus* hidden, orig. ptp. of *sēcernere* to SECERN] **—se′cret•ly,** *adv.* **—se′cret•ness,** *n.*
—Syn. 1. clandestine, hidden, concealed, covert. **1, 2.** private, confidential. **3.** secretive. **6.** occult, obscure, mysterious. **—Ant. 1.** open, manifest.

se′cret a′gent, **1.** an agent of a secret service. **2.** (loosely) a person employed to collect the military secrets of one country and relay them to another, esp. a person living in a foreign country while so working for his or her own nation; spy. [1830–40]

se•cre•ta•gog (si krē′tə gog′, -gôg′), *n. Physiol.* a substance or situation that promotes secretion. Also, **se•cre′ta•gogue′.** [1915–20; SECRETE[1] + -AGOG(UE)]

sec•re•taire (sek′ri târ′), *n. Fr. Furniture.* any writing desk resembling a secretary. [1810–20; < F *secrétaire* SECRETARY]

sec•re•tar•i•al (sek′ri târ′ē əl), *adj.* noting, of, or pertaining to a secretary or a secretary's skills and work: *a secretarial school.* [1795–1805; SECRETARY + -AL[1]]

sec•re•tar•i•at (sek′ri târ′ē ət), *n.* **1.** the officials or office entrusted with administrative duties, maintaining records, and overseeing or performing secretarial duties, esp. for an international organization: *the secretariat of the United Nations.* **2.** a group or department of secretaries. **3.** the place where a secretary transacts business, preserves records, etc. Also, **sec′re•tar′i•ate.** [1805–15; < F *secrétariat* < ML *sēcrētāriātus.* See SECRETARY, -ATE[3]]

sec•re•tar•y (sek′ri ter′ē), *n., pl.* **-tar•ies.** **1.** a person, usually an official, who is in charge of the records, correspondence, minutes of meetings, and related affairs of an organization, company, association, etc.: *the secretary of the Linguistic Society of America.* **2.** a person employed to handle correspondence and do routine work in a business office, usually involving taking dictation, typing, filing, and the like. **3.** See **private secretary.** **4.** (*often cap.*) an officer of state charged with the superintendence and management of a particular department of government, as a member of the president's cabinet in the U.S.: *Secretary of the Treasury.* **5.** Also called **diplomatic secretary.** a diplomatic official of an embassy or legation who ranks below a counselor and is usually assigned as first secretary, second secretary, or third secretary. **6.** a piece of furniture for use as a writing desk. **7.** Also called **sec′retary book′case.** a desk with bookshelves on top of it. [1350–1400; ME *secretarie* one trusted with private or secret matters; confidant < ML *sēcrētārius* < L *sēcrēt(um)* SECRET (n.) + *-ārius* -ARY] **—sec′re•tar′y•ship′,** *n.*

sec′retary bird′, a large, long-legged, raptorial bird, *Sagittarius serpentarius,* of Africa, that feeds on reptiles. [1790–1800; < F *secrétaire,* perh. by folk etym. < Sudanese Ar *ṣaqr al-ṭēr,* equiv. to *ṣaqr* hawk + *al* the + *ṭēr* birds (collective)]

secretary bird,
Sagittarius serpentarius,
height 4 ft. (1.2 m)

sec•re•tar•y-gen•er•al (sek′ri ter′ē jen′ər əl), *n., pl.* **sec•re•tar•ies-gen•er•al.** the head or chief administrative officer of a secretariat. [1695–1705]

sec′retary of state′, **1.** the head and chief administrator of the U.S. Department of State. Cf. **foreign minister.** **2.** *Brit.* any of several ministers in the British government: *A new secretary of state for the Home Department has been appointed.* **3.** (in the U.S.) the appointed or elected official in a state government whose chief function is to distribute statutes, administer elections, keep archives, etc. Also, **Sec′retary of State′.** [1610–20]

se′cret bal′lot, **1.** a vote in which the confidentiality of how one votes is safeguarded. **2.** See **Australian ballot.** [1910–15]

se•crete[1] (si krēt′), *v.t.,* **-cret•ed, -cret•ing.** to discharge, generate, or release by the process of secretion. [1700–10; back formation from SECRETION]

se•crete[2] (si krēt′), *v.t.,* **-cret•ed, -cret•ing.** to place out of sight; hide; conceal: *squirrels secreting nuts in a hollow tree trunk.* [1735–45; alter. of obs. *secret,* v. use of SECRET]
—Syn. cover, shroud, disguise. See **hide**[1].

se•crète (sə kret′), *n. Armor.* a steel skullcap of the 17th century, worn under a soft hat. [< F; see SECRET]

se•cre•tin (si krē′tin), *n. Biochem.* a polypeptide hormone, produced in the small intestine, that activates the pancreas to secrete pancreatic juice. [1900–05; SECRETE[1] + -IN[2]]

se•cre•tion (si krē′shən), *n.* **1.** (in a cell or gland) the act or process of separating, elaborating, and releasing a substance that fulfills some function within the organism or undergoes excretion. **2.** the product of this act or process. [1640–50; < L *sēcrētiōn-* (s. of *sēcrētiō*), equiv. to *sēcrēt(us)* (ptp. of *sēcernere* to SECERN) + *-iōn-* -ION] **—se•cre•tion•ar•y** (si krē′shə ner′ē), *adj.*

se•cre•tive[1] (sē′kri tiv, si krē′-), *adj.* having or showing a disposition to secrecy; reticent: *He seems secretive about his new job.* [1425–75; late ME; back formation from *secretiveness* (itself modeled on F *secrétivité*). See SECRET, -IVE] **—se′cre•tive•ly,** *adv.* **—se′cre•tive•ness,** *n.*
—Syn. secret, close.

se•cre•tive[2] (si krē′tiv), *adj.* secretory. [SECRET(ION) + -IVE]

se•cre•to•ry (si krē′tə rē), *adj., n., pl.* **-ries.** —*adj.* **1.** pertaining to secretion. **2.** performing the process of secretion. —*n.* **3.** a secretory organ, vessel, or the like. [1685–95; SECRET(ION) + -ORY[1]]

se′cret part′ner, a partner whose name as a member of a firm is not revealed to the public. Cf. **silent partner.** [1905–10]

se′cret police′, a police force that functions as the enforcement arm of a government's political policies and whose activities, which often include surveillance, intimidation, and physical violence as a means of suppressing dissent, are usually concealed from the public. Also called **security police.** [1920–25]

se′cret serv′ice, **1.** the branch of governmental service that conducts secret investigations, esp. investigations into the military strength of other nations. **2.**

(*caps.*) the branch of the U.S. Department of the Treasury charged chiefly with the discovery and apprehension of counterfeiters and with providing protection for the president and the president's immediate family. **3.** secret work for a government, esp. espionage. [1730–40] —**se′cret-serv′ice,** *adj.*

se′cret soci′ety, an organization, as a fraternal society, the members of which take secret initiation oaths, share secret passwords and rites, and are bound to assist each other. [1820–30]

secs., **1.** seconds. **2.** sections.

sect (sekt), *n.* **1.** a body of persons adhering to a particular religious faith; a religious denomination. **2.** a group regarded as heretical or as deviating from a generally accepted religious tradition. **3.** (in the sociology of religion) a Christian denomination characterized by insistence on strict qualifications for membership, as distinguished from the more inclusive groups called churches. **4.** any group, party, or faction united by a specific doctrine or under a doctrinal leader. [1300–50; ME *secte* < L *secta* something to follow, pathway, course of conduct, school of thought, prob. n. deriv. of *sectārī* to pursue, accompany, wait upon, freq. of *sequī* to follow]

sect., section.

sec•tar•i•an (sek târ′ē ən), *adj.* **1.** of or pertaining to sectaries or sects. **2.** narrowly confined or devoted to a particular sect. **3.** narrowly confined or limited in interest, purpose, scope, etc. —*n.* **4.** a member of a sect. **5.** a bigoted or narrow-minded adherent of a sect. [1640–50; SECTARY + -AN] —**sec•tar′i•an•ly,** *adv.*

sec•tar•i•an•ism (sek târ′ē ə niz′əm), *n.* sectarian spirit or tendencies; excessive devotion to a particular sect, esp. in religion. [1810–20; SECTARIAN + -ISM]

sec•tar•i•an•ize (sek târ′ē ə nīz′), *v.t.,* **-ized, -iz•ing.** to make sectarian. Also, *esp. Brit.,* **sec•tar′i•an•ise′.** [1835–45; SECTARIAN + -IZE]

sec•ta•ry (sek′tə rē), *n., pl.* **-ries. 1.** a member of a particular sect, esp. an adherent of a religious body regarded as heretical or schismatic. **2.** a Protestant of nonconformist denomination, esp. a minor one. **3.** a person zealously devoted to a particular sect. [1550–60; < ML *sectārius,* equiv. to *sect(a)* SECT + *-ārius* -ARY]

sec•tile (sek′til), *adj.* capable of being cut smoothly with a knife. [1710–20; < L *sectilis* cuttable, equiv. to *sect(us)* (ptp. of *secāre* to cut; see SAW[1]) + *-ilis* -ILE] —**sec•til′i•ty,** *n.*

sec•tion (sek′shən), *n.* **1.** a part that is cut off or separated. **2.** a distinct part or subdivision of anything, as an object, country, community, class, or the like: *the poor section of town; the left section of a drawer.* **3.** a distinct part or subdivision of a writing, as of a newspaper, legal code, chapter, etc.: *the financial section of a daily paper; section 2 of the bylaws.* **4.** one of a number of parts that can be fitted together to make a whole: *sections of a fishing rod.* **5.** (in most of the U.S. west of Ohio) one of the 36 numbered subdivisions, each one square mile (2.59 sq. km or 640 acres), of a township. **6.** an act or instance of cutting; separation by cutting. **7.** *Surg.* **a.** the making of an incision. **b.** an incision. **8.** a thin slice of a tissue, mineral, or the like, as for microscopic examination. **9.** a representation of an object as it would appear if cut by a plane, showing its internal structure. **10.** *Mil.* **a.** a small unit consisting of two or more squads. **b.** Also called **staff section.** any of the subdivisions of a staff. **c.** a small tactical division in naval and air units. **11.** *Railroads.* **a.** a division of a sleeping car containing both an upper and a lower berth. **b.** a length of trackage, roadbed, signal equipment, etc., maintained by one crew. **12.** any of two or more trains, buses, or the like, running on the same route and schedule at the same time, one right behind the other, and considered as one unit, as when a second is necessary to accommodate more passengers than the first can carry: *On holidays the New York to Boston train runs in three sections.* **13.** a segment of a naturally segmented fruit, as of an orange or grapefruit. **14.** a division of an orchestra or band containing all the instruments of one class: *a rhythm section.* **15.** *Bookbinding.* signature (def. 8). **16.** Also called **section mark.** a mark used to indicate a subdivision of a book, chapter, or the like, or as a mark of reference to a footnote. **17.** *Theat.* one of a series of circuits for controlling certain lights, as footlights. **18.** shape (def. 12). —*v.t.* **19.** to cut or divide into sections. **20.** to cut through so as to present a section. **21.** *Surg.* to make an incision. [1550–60; < L *sectiōn-* (s. of *sectiō*) a cutting, equiv. to *sect(us)* (ptp. of *secāre* to cut; see SAW[1]) + *-iōn-* -ION]
—**Syn. 1.** See **part. 8.** specimen, sample, cutting.

sec•tion•al (sek′shə nl), *adj.* **1.** pertaining or limited to a particular section; local or regional: *sectional politics.* **2.** composed of several independent sections: *a sectional sofa.* **3.** of or pertaining to a section: *a sectional view of the machine.* —*n.* **4.** a sofa composed of several independent sections that can be arranged individually or in various combinations. [1800–10, *Amer.;* SECTION + -AL[1]] —**sec′tion•al•ly,** *adv.*

sec•tion•al•ism (sek′shə nl iz′əm), *n.* excessive regard for sectional or local interests; regional or local spirit, prejudice, etc. [1850–55, *Amer.;* SECTIONAL + -ISM] —**sec′tion•al•ist,** *n.*

sec•tion•al•ize (sek′shə nl īz′), *v.t.,* **-ized, -iz•ing. 1.** to render sectional. **2.** to divide into sections, esp. geographical sections. Also, *esp. Brit.,* **sec′tion•al•ise′.** [1850–55; SECTIONAL + -IZE] —**sec′tion•al•i•za′tion,** *n.*

sec′tion boss′, *Railroads.* the boss of a section gang. [1865–70]

sec′tion eight′, **1.** a military discharge for physical or mental unfitness as determined by an Army Regulation in effect from 1922 to 1944. **2.** a soldier receiving such a discharge. [1940–45, *Amer.*]

sec′tion gang′, *Railroads.* a group of workers who take care of a section of railroad track. Cf. **floating gang.** [1885–90, *Amer.*]

sec′tion hand′, *Railroads.* a person who works on a section gang. Also called **tracklayer.** [1870–75]

sec′tion mark′, section (def. 16). [1890–95]

sec•tor (sek′tər), *n.* **1.** *Geom.* a plane figure bounded by two radii and the included arc of a circle. **2.** a mathematical instrument consisting of two flat rulers hinged together at one end and bearing various scales. **3.** *Mach.* a device used in connection with an index plate, consisting of two arms rotating about the center of the plate and set to indicate the angle through which the work is indexed. **4.** *Mil.* a designated defense area, usually in a combat zone, within which a particular military unit operates and for which it is responsible. **5.** *Astron.* an instrument shaped like a sector of a circle, having a variable central angle and sights along the two straight sides, for measuring the angular distance between two celestial bodies. **6.** a distinct part, esp. of society or of a nation's economy: *the housing sector; the educational sector.* **7.** a section or zone, as of a city. **8.** *Computers.* a portion of a larger block of storage, as 1/128 of a track or disk. —*v.t.* **9.** to divide into sectors. [1560–70; < LL: sector, L: cutter, equiv. to *sec(āre)* to cut + *-tor* -TOR] —**sec′tor•al,** *adj.*

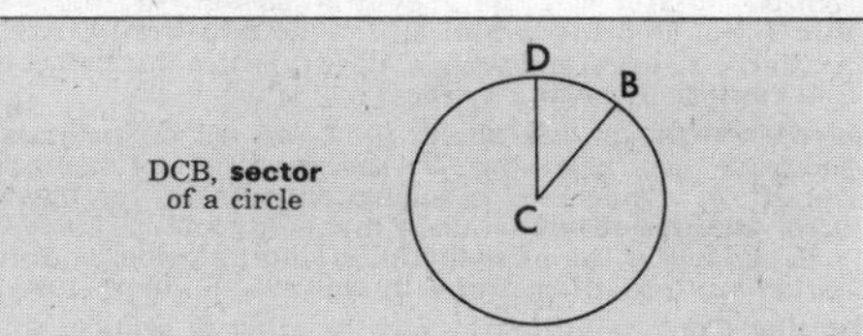

DCB, **sector** of a circle

sec•to•ri•al (sek tôr′ē əl, -tōr′-), *adj.* **1.** of or pertaining to a sector. **2.** *Zool.* (of teeth) adapted for cutting; carnassial. [1795–1805; < NL *sectōri(us)* (see SECTION, -TORY[1]) + -AL[1]]

sec•u•lar (sek′yə lər), *adj.* **1.** of or pertaining to worldly things or to things that are not regarded as religious, spiritual, or sacred; temporal: *secular interests.* **2.** not pertaining to or connected with religion (opposed to *sacred*): *secular music.* **3.** (of education, a school, etc.) concerned with nonreligious subjects. **4.** (of members of the clergy) not belonging to a religious order; not bound by monastic vows (opposed to *regular*). **5.** occurring or celebrated once in an age or century: *the secular games of Rome.* **6.** going on from age to age; continuing through long ages. —*n.* **7.** a layperson. **8.** one of the secular clergy. [1250–1300; < ML *sēculāris,* LL *saeculāris* worldly, temporal (opposed to eternal), L: of an age, equiv. to L *saecul(um)* long period of time + *-āris* -AR[1]; r. ME *seculer* < OF < L, as above] —**sec′u•lar•ly,** *adv.*

sec′ular hu′manism, any set of beliefs that promotes human values without specific allusion to religious doctrines. [1980–85] —**sec′ular hu′manist.**

sec•u•lar•ism (sek′yə lə riz′əm), *n.* **1.** secular spirit or tendency, esp. a system of political or social philosophy that rejects all forms of religious faith and worship. **2.** the view that public education and other matters of civil policy should be conducted without the introduction of a religious element. [1850–55; SECULAR + -ISM] —**sec′u•lar•ist,** *n., adj.* —**sec′u•lar•is′tic,** *adj.*

sec•u•lar•i•ty (sek′yə lar′i tē), *n., pl.* **-ties. 1.** secular views or beliefs; secularism. **2.** the state of being devoted to the affairs of the world; worldliness. **3.** a secular matter. [1350–1400; ME. See SECULAR, -ITY]

sec•u•lar•ize (sek′yə lə rīz′), *v.t.,* **-ized, -iz•ing. 1.** to make secular; separate from religious or spiritual connection or influences; make worldly or unspiritual; imbue with secularism. **2.** to change (clergy) from regular to secular. **3.** to transfer (property) from ecclesiastical to civil possession or use. Also, *esp. Brit.,* **sec′u•lar•ise′.** [1605–15; SECULAR + -IZE] —**sec′u•lar•i•za′tion,** *n.* —**sec′u•lar•iz′er,** *n.*

sec′ular ter′tiaries. See under **tertiary** (def. 5).

sec′ular vic′ar. See **lay vicar.**

se•cund (sē′kund, sek′und), *adj. Bot., Zool.* arranged on one side only; unilateral. [1770–80; < L *secundus* following. See SECOND[1]] —**se′cund•ly,** *adv.*

Se•cun•der•a•bad (sə kun′dər ə bad′), *n.* a city in N Andhra Pradesh, in central India, part of Hyderabad: a former British military cantonment.

sec•un•dine (sek′ən dīn′, -din), *n. Bot.* the inner integument of an ovule. Cf. **primine.** [1350–1400; ME < L *secundinae* (pl.) afterbirth]

se•cun•dus (sə kun′dəs), *adj.* (in prescriptions) second. [1820–30; < L]

se•cure (si kyŏŏr′), *adj.,* **-cur•er, -cur•est,** *v.,* **-cured, -cur•ing.** —*adj.* **1.** free from or not exposed to danger or harm; safe. **2.** dependable; firm; not liable to fail, yield, become displaced, etc., as a support or a fastening: *The building was secure, even in an earthquake.* **3.** affording safety, as a place: *He needed a secure hideout.* **4.** in safe custody or keeping: *Here in the vault the necklace was secure.* **5.** free from care; without anxiety: *emotionally secure.* **6.** firmly established, as a relationship or reputation: *He earned a secure place among the baseball immortals.* **7.** sure; certain; assured: *secure of victory; secure in religious belief.* **8.** safe from penetration or interception by unauthorized persons: *secure radio communications between army units.* **9.** *Archaic.* overconfident. —*v.t.* **10.** to get hold or possession of; procure; obtain: *to secure materials; to secure a high government position.* **11.** to free from danger or harm; make safe: *Sandbags secured the town during the flood.* **12.** to effect; make certain of; ensure: *The novel secured his reputation.* **13.** to make firm or fast, as by attaching: *to secure a rope.* **14.** *Finance.* **a.** to assure payment of (a debt) by pledging property. **b.** to assure (a creditor) of payment by the pledge or mortgaging of property. **15.** to lock or fasten against intruders: *to secure the doors.* **16.** to protect from attack by taking cover, by building fortifications, etc.: *The regiment secured its position.* **17.** to capture (a person or animal): *No one is safe until the murderer is secured.* **18.** to tie up (a person), esp. by binding the person's arms or hands; pinion. **19.** to guarantee the privacy or secrecy of: *to secure diplomatic phone conversations.* —*v.i.* **20.** to be or become safe; have or obtain security. **21.** *Naut.* **a.** to cover openings and make movable objects fast: *The crew was ordered to secure for sea.* **b.** to be excused from duty: *to secure from general quarters.* [1525–35; < L *sēcūrus* carefree, equiv. to *sē-* SE- + *cūr(a)* care (see CURE) + *-us* adj. suffix; cf. SURE] —**se•cur′a•ble,** *adj.* —**se•cure′ly,** *adv.* —**se•cure′ness,** *n.* —**se•cur′er,** *n.*
—**Syn. 1.** protected. See **safe. 2.** stable, fast, fixed. **7.** confident. **10.** gain. See **get. 11.** protect, guard, safeguard. **12.** assure, guarantee. —**Ant. 1.** unsafe.

se•cure•ment (si kyŏŏr′mənt), *n.* **1.** the act of securing. **2.** security or protection. [1615–25; SECURE + -MENT]

Secu′rities and Exchange′ Commis′sion. See **SEC.**

Secu′rities Exchange′ Act′, *U.S. Govt.* a law passed in 1934 establishing the SEC.

se•cu•ri•ty (si kyŏŏr′i tē), *n., pl.* **-ties,** *adj.* —*n.* **1.** freedom from danger, risk, etc.; safety. **2.** freedom from care, anxiety, or doubt; well-founded confidence. **3.** something that secures or makes safe; protection; defense. **4.** freedom from financial cares or from want: *The insurance policy gave the family security.* **5.** precautions taken to guard against crime, attack, sabotage, espionage, etc.: *The senator claimed security was lax and potential enemies know our plans.* **6.** a department or organization responsible for protection or safety: *He called security when he spotted the intruder.* **7.** protection or precautions taken against escape; custody: *The dangerous criminal was placed under maximum security.* **8.** an assurance; guarantee. **9.** *Law.* **a.** something given or deposited as surety for the fulfillment of a promise or an obligation, the payment of a debt, etc. **b.** one who becomes surety for another. **10.** an evidence of debt or of property, as a bond or a certificate of stock. **11.** Usually, **securities.** stocks and bonds. **12.** *Archaic.* overconfidence; cockiness. —*adj.* **13.** of, pertaining to, or serving as security: *The company has instituted stricter security measures.* [1400–50; late ME *securytye, securite(e)* < L *sēcūritās.* See SECURE, -ITY]
—**Syn. 2.** assurance, certainty, positiveness. **3.** safeguard, safety.

secu′rity an′alyst, a person who specializes in evaluating information regarding stocks and bonds. Also, **secu′rities an′alyst.** —**secu′rity anal′ysis, secu′rities anal′ysis.**

secu′rity blan′ket, **1.** a blanket or other familiar item carried esp. by a young child to provide reassurance and a feeling of psychological security. **2.** someone or something that gives a person a sense of protection or a feeling of security: *His wealthy uncle is his security blanket.* [1965–70]

Secu′rity Coun′cil, the division of the United Nations charged with maintaining international peace, composed of five permanent members (U.S., Russian Federation, France, United Kingdom, and the People's Republic of China) and ten temporary members, each serving for two years.

secu′rity guard′, a uniformed guard employed by a bank, airport, office building, etc., to maintain security. [1955–60]

secu′rity police′, **1.** a police force responsible for maintaining order at a specific locale or under specific circumstances, as at an airport or factory. **2.** a police force concerned with detecting and preventing enemy espionage. **3.** See **secret police.** [1915–20]

secu′rity risk′, a person considered by authorities as likely to commit acts that might threaten the security of a country. [1950–55]

secu′rity thread′, a colored thread running through the paper of a piece of paper money, used to deter counterfeiting.

secy, secretary. Also, **sec'y**

SED, shipper's export declaration.

Se•da•li•a (si dā′lē ə, -dāl′yə), *n.* a city in central Missouri. 20,927.

se•dan (si dan′), *n.* **1.** an enclosed automobile body having two or four doors and seating four or more persons on two full-width seats. **2.** See **sedan chair.** [1625–35; of obscure orig.]

Se•dan (si dan′; *Fr.* sə däN′), *n.* a city in NE France, on the Meuse River: defeat and capture of Napoleon III 1870. 25,430.

sedan′ chair′, an enclosed vehicle for one person, borne on poles by two bearers and common during the 17th and 18th centuries. [1740–50]

sedan chair

CONCISE PRONUNCIATION KEY: *act, cāpe, dâre, pärt; set, ēqual; if, ice; ox, ōver, ôrder, oil, bŏŏk, bōōt, out; up, ûrge; child; sing; shoe; thin, that;* zh as in *treasure.* ə = *a* as in *alone, e* as in *system, i* as in *easily, o* as in *gallop, u* as in *circus;* ᵊ as in *fire* (fīᵊr), *hour* (ouᵊr). l and n can serve as syllabic consonants, as in *cradle* (krād′l), and *button* (but′n). See the full key inside the front cover.

Se·da·rim (*Seph. Heb.* se dä RĒM′; *Ashk. Heb.* sə dä′-RIM, sä dä RIM′), *n.* a pl. of **Seder.**

se·date (si dāt′), *adj., v.,* **-dat·ed, -dat·ing.** —*adj.* **1.** calm, quiet, or composed; undisturbed by passion or excitement: *a sedate party; a sedate horse.* —*v.t.* **2.** to put (a person) under sedation. [1640–50; < L *sēdātus* (ptp. of *sēdāre* to allay, quieten); akin to *sedēre* to SIT[1]] —**se·date′ly,** *adv.* —**se·date′ness,** *n.*
—**Syn. 1.** collected, serene, unruffled, unperturbed. See **staid.**

se·da·tion (si dā′shən), *n. Med.* **1.** the calming of mental excitement or abatement of physiological function, esp. by the administration of a drug. **2.** the state so induced. [1535–45; < L *sēdātiōn-* (s. of *sēdātiō*), equiv. to *sēdāt(us)* (see SEDATE) + *-iōn-* -ION]

sed·a·tive (sed′ə tiv), *adj.* **1.** tending to calm or soothe. **2.** allaying irritability or excitement; assuaging pain; lowering functional activity. —*n.* **3.** a sedative drug or agent. [1375–1425; late ME (adj.) (< MF *sédatif*) < ML *sēdātīvus,* equiv. to L *sēdāt(us)* (see SEDATE) + *-īvus* -IVE]

Sed·don (sed′n), *n.* **Richard John,** 1845–1906, New Zealand statesman, born in England: prime minister 1893–1906.

Sed·e·ci·as (sed′i kī′əs), *n. Douay Bible.* Zedekiah.

se de·fen·den·do (sē dē′fen den′dō), *Law.* in self-defense: *homicide committed se defendendo.* [1540–50; < L *sē dēfendendō*]

sed·en·tar·y (sed′n ter′ē), *adj.* **1.** characterized by or requiring a sitting posture: *a sedentary occupation.* **2.** accustomed to sit or rest a great deal or to take little exercise. **3.** *Chiefly Zool.* **a.** abiding in one place; not migratory. **b.** pertaining to animals that move about little or are permanently attached to something, as a barnacle. [1590–1600; < L *sedentārius* sitting, equiv. to *sedent-* (s. of *sedēns,* prp. of *sedēre* to SIT[1]; see -ENT) + *-ārius* -ARY] —**sed·en·tar·i·ly** (sed′n târ′ə lē, sed′n-ter′-), *adj.* —**sed′en·tar′i·ness,** *n.*

Se·der (sā′dər), *n., pl.* **Se·ders,** *Heb.* **Se·da·rim** (*Seph.* se dä RĒM′; *Ashk.* sə dä′RIM, sä dä RIM′). *Judaism.* a ceremonial dinner that commemorates the Exodus from Egypt and includes the reading of the Haggadah and the eating of symbolic foods, generally held on the first night of Passover by Reform Jews and Jews in Israel and on both the first and second nights by Orthodox and Conservative Jews outside of Israel. [1860–65; < Heb *sēdher* lit., order, arrangement]

sedge (sej), *n.* **1.** any rushlike or grasslike plant of the genus *Carex,* growing in wet places. Cf. **sedge family.** **2.** any plant of the sedge family. **3.** siege (def. 5). [bef. 900; ME *segge,* OE *secg;* akin to SAW[1]; presumably so named from its sawlike edges]

sedged (sejd), *adj.* **1.** made of sedge. **2.** abounding or bordered with sedge: *sedged brooks.* [1600–10; SEDGE + -ED[3]]

sedge′ fam′ily, the plant family Cyperaceae, characterized by herbaceous plants, often found in wet areas, having solid stems, narrow, grasslike leaves with closed sheaths, spikes of small flowers set in a scalelike bract, and a dry, flattened, convex fruit, and including the bulrush, chufa, cotton grass, papyrus, and umbrella plant.

Sedge·moor (sej′mŏŏr′), *n.* a plain in SW England, in central Somerset: final defeat of Monmouth 1685.

sedge′ wren′, a small wren, *Cistothorus platensis,* of the Americas, inhabiting wet, sedgy meadows. Also called **marsh wren, short-billed marsh wren.** [1795–1805]

Sedg·wick (sej′wik), *n.* **Ellery,** 1872–1960, U.S. journalist and editor.

sedg·y (sej′ē), *adj.,* **sedg·i·er, sedg·i·est.** **1.** abounding, covered, or bordered with sedge. **2.** of or like sedge. [1275–1325; ME; see SEDGE, -Y[1]]

se·di·le (se dī′lē), *n., pl.* **-dil·i·a** (-dil′ē ə). *Eccles.* one of the seats (usually three) on the south side of the chancel, often recessed, for the use of the officiating clergy. [1785–95; < L *sedīle* sitting-place, equiv. to *sed(ēre)* to SIT[1] + *-īle* neut. n. suffix]

sed·i·ment (*n.* sed′ə mənt; *v.* sed′ə ment′), *n.* **1.** the matter that settles to the bottom of a liquid; lees; dregs. **2.** *Geol.* mineral or organic matter deposited by water, air, or ice. —*v.t.* **3.** to deposit as sediment. —*v.i.* **4.** to form or deposit sediment. [1540–50; < L *sedimentum,* equiv. to *sedi-* (comb. form of *sedēre* to SIT[1], settle) + *-mentum* -MENT] —**sed′i·men′tous,** *adj.*

sed·i·men·ta·ry (sed′ə men′tə rē), *adj.* **1.** of, pertaining to, or of the nature of sediment. **2.** *Geol.* formed by the deposition of sediment, as certain rocks. Also, **sed′i·men′tal.** [1820–30; SEDIMENT + -ARY] —**sed·i·men·tar·i·ly** (sed′ə mən târ′ə lē, sed′ə mən ter′-), *adv.*

sed·i·men·ta·tion (sed′ə mən tā′shən), *n.* the deposition or accumulation of sediment. [1870–75; SEDIMENT + -ATION]

sed·i·men·tol·o·gy (sed′ə mən tol′ə jē), *n. Geol.* the study of sedimentary rocks. [1935–40; SEDIMENT + -O- + -LOGY] —**sed·i·men·to·log·ic** (sed′ə men′tl oj′ik), **sed′i·men′to·log′i·cal,** *adj.* —**sed′i·men·tol′o·gist,** *n.*

sed′iment yeast′. See **bottom yeast.**

se·di·tion (si dish′ən), *n.* **1.** incitement of discontent or rebellion against a government. **2.** any action, esp. in speech or writing, promoting such discontent or rebellion. **3.** *Archaic.* rebellious disorder. [1325–75; < L *sēditiōn-* (s. of *sēditiō*), equiv. to *sēd-* SE- + *-itiōn-* a going (*it(us),* ptp. of *īre* to go + *-iōn-* -ION); r. ME *sedicioun* < AF < L, as above]
—**Syn. 1.** insurrection, mutiny. See **treason.**

CONCISE ETYMOLOGY KEY: <, descended or borrowed from; >, whence; b., blend of, blended; c., cognate with; cf., compare; deriv., derivative; equiv., equivalent; imit., imitative; obl., oblique; r., replacing; s., stem; sp., spelling, spelled; resp., respelling, respelled; trans., translation; ?, origin unknown; *, unattested; ‡, probably earlier than. See the full key inside the front cover.

se·di·tion·ar·y (si dish′ə ner′ē), *adj., n., pl.* **-ar·ies.** —*adj.* **1.** of or pertaining to sedition; seditious. —*n.* **2.** Also, **se·di′tion·ist.** one guilty of sedition. [1600–10; SEDITION + -ARY]

se·di·tious (si dish′əs), *adj.* **1.** of, pertaining to, or of the nature of sedition. **2.** given to or guilty of sedition. [1400–50; late ME *sedicious,* equiv. to *sedici(oun)* SEDITION + *-ous* -OUS; cf. L *sēditiōsus*] —**se·di′tious·ly,** *adv.* —**se·di′tious·ness,** *n.*

Se·drah (*Seph.* sē DRÄ′; *Ashk.* si′DRô; *Eng.* sed′rə), *n., pl.* ***Se·droth, Se·drot, Se·dros*** (*Seph.* sē DRôT′; *Ashk.* si′DRōs), *Eng.* **Sed·rahs.** *Hebrew.* Sidrah.

se·duce (si dōōs′, -dyōōs′), *v.t.,* **-duced, -duc·ing.** **1.** to lead astray, as from duty, rectitude, or the like; corrupt. **2.** to persuade or induce to have sexual intercourse. **3.** to lead or draw away, as from principles, faith, or allegiance: *He was seduced by the prospect of gain.* **4.** to win over; attract; entice: *a market seducing customers with special sales.* [1470–80; < L *sēdūcere* to lead aside, equiv. to *sē-* SE- + *dūcere* to lead; r. earlier *seduise* < MF < L, as above] —**se·duc′er,** *n.* —**se·duc′i·ble, se·duce′a·ble,** *adj.* —**se·duc′ing·ly,** *adv.*
—**Syn. 1.** beguile, inveigle, decoy, allure, lure, deceive. See **tempt.** —**Ant. 1.** repel.

se·duc·tion (si duk′shən), *n.* **1.** an act or instance of seducing, esp. sexually. **2.** the condition of being seduced. **3.** a means of seducing; enticement; temptation. Also, **se·duce·ment** (si dōōs′mənt, -dyōōs′-). [1520–30; < L *sēductiōn-* (s. of *sēductiō*) a leading aside, equiv. to *sēduct(us)* (ptp. of *sēdūcere* to SEDUCE) + *-iōn-* -ION]

se·duc·tive (si duk′tiv), *adj.* tending to seduce; enticing; beguiling; captivating: *a seductive smile.* [1755–65; SEDUCT(ION) + -IVE] —**se·duc′tive·ly,** *adv.* —**se·duc′tive·ness,** *n.*
—**Syn.** tempting, alluring. —**Ant.** repellent.

se·duc·tress (si duk′tris), *n.* a woman who seduces. [1795–1805; obs. *sedut(o)r* (< LL *sēductor;* see SEDUCE, -TOR) + -ESS]
—**Usage.** See **-ess.**

se·du·li·ty (si dōō′li tē, -dyōō′-), *n.* sedulous quality, application, or activity; diligence. [1535–45; < L *sēdulitās,* equiv. to *sēdul(us)* SEDULOUS + *-itās* -ITY]

sed·u·lous (sej′ə ləs), *adj.* **1.** diligent in application or attention; persevering; assiduous. **2.** persistently or carefully maintained: *sedulous flattery.* [1530–40; < L *sēdulus,* adj. deriv. of the phrase *sē dolō* diligently, lit., without guile; r. *sedulious* (see SEDULITY, -OUS)] —**sed′u·lous·ly,** *adv.* —**sed′u·lous·ness,** *n.*
—**Syn. 1.** constant, untiring, tireless.

se·dum (sē′dəm), *n.* any fleshy plant belonging to the genus *Sedum,* of the stonecrop family, usually having small, overlapping leaves and yellow, white, or pink flowers. [1400–50; late ME *cedum* < L *sedum* houseleek]

see[1] (sē), *v.,* **saw, seen, see·ing.** —*v.t.* **1.** to perceive with the eyes; look at. **2.** to view; visit or attend as a spectator: *to see a play.* **3.** to perceive by means of computer vision. **4.** to scan or view, esp. by electronic means: *The satellite can see the entire southern half of the country.* **5.** to perceive (things) mentally; discern; understand: *to see the point of an argument.* **6.** to construct a mental image of; visualize: *He still saw his father as he was 25 years ago.* **7.** to accept or imagine or suppose as acceptable: *I can't see him as president.* **8.** to be cognizant of; recognize: *to see the good in others; to see where the mistake is.* **9.** to foresee: *He could see war ahead.* **10.** to ascertain, learn, or find out: *See who is at the door.* **11.** to have knowledge or experience of: *to see service in the foreign corps.* **12.** to make sure: *See that the work is done.* **13.** to meet and converse with: *Are you seeing her at lunch today?* **14.** to receive as a visitor: *The ambassador finally saw him.* **15.** to visit: *He's gone to see his aunt.* **16.** to court, keep company with, or date frequently: *They've been seeing each other for a long time.* **17.** to provide aid or assistance to; take care of: *He's seeing his brother through college.* **18.** to attend or escort: *to see someone home.* **19.** *Cards.* to match (a bet) or match the bet of (a bettor) by staking an equal sum; call: *I'll see your five and raise you five more.* **20.** to prefer (someone or something) to be as indicated (usually used as a mild oath): *I'll see you in hell before I sell you this house. He'll see the business fail before he admits he's wrong.* **21.** to read or read about: *I saw it in the newspaper.* —*v.i.* **22.** to have the power of sight. **23.** to be capable of perceiving by means of computer vision. **24.** to understand intellectually or spiritually; have insight: *Philosophy teaches us to see.* **25.** to give attention or care: *See, there it goes.* **26.** to find out; make inquiry: *Go and see for yourself.* **27.** to consider; think; deliberate: *Let me see, how does that song go?* **28.** to look about; observe: *They heard the noise and came out to see.* **29. see about, a.** to investigate; inquire about. **b.** to turn one's attention to; take care of: *He said he would see about getting the license plates.* **30. see after,** to attend to; take care of: *Will you please see after my plants while I'm away?* **31. see off,** to take leave of someone setting out on a journey; accompany to the place of departure: *I went to the airport to see them off.* **32. see out,** to remain with (a task, project, etc.) until its completion: *We decided to see it out, even if it meant another year.* **33. see through, a.** to penetrate to the true nature of; comprehend; detect: *He quickly saw through my story.* **b.** to stay with to the end or until completion; persevere: *to see a difficult situation through.* **34. see to,** to take care of; be responsible for: *I'll see to the theater tickets.* [bef. 900; ME *seen,* OE *sēon;* c. D *zien,* G *sehen,* ON *sjá,* Goth *saihwan*] —**see′a·ble,** *adj.* —**see′a·ble·ness,** *n.*
—**Syn. 1.** observe, notice, distinguish, discern, behold, regard. See **watch. 5.** comprehend, penetrate. **10.** determine. **11.** know, undergo. **18.** accompany.

see[2] (sē), *n. Eccles.* the seat, center of authority, office, or jurisdiction of a bishop. [1250–1300; ME *se(e)* < OF *se* (var. of *sie*) < L *sēdes* seat]

See′beck effect′ (sē′bek; *Ger.* zā′bek), *Physics.* See **thermoelectric effect.** [named after Thomas J. Seebeck (1770–1831), German physicist]

See-Bee (sē′bē′), *n.* Seabee (def. 2).

see·catch (sē′kach′), *n., pl.* **-catch·ie** (-kach′ē). the adult male of the fur seal, *Callorhinus alascanus,* of Alaska. [1880–85, *Amer.;* earlier *seecatchie* (collective or pl.) < Russ *sekachí,* pl. of *sekách* mature male fur seal, hog, or wild boar, lit., chopper, cutter (alluding to the tusks of such animals), equiv. to *sek-,* s. of *sech′* to cut, slash + *-ach* n. suffix; cf. HOLLUSCHICK]

seed (sēd), *n., pl.* **seeds,** (*esp. collectively*) **seed,** *v., adj.* —*n.* **1.** the fertilized, matured ovule of a flowering plant, containing an embryo or rudimentary plant. **2.** any propagative part of a plant, including tubers, bulbs, etc., esp. as preserved for growing a new crop. **3.** such parts collectively. **4.** any similar small part or fruit. **5.** *Dial.* pit[2]. **6.** the germ or propagative source of anything: *the seeds of discord.* **7.** offspring; progeny. **8.** birth: *not of mortal seed.* **9.** sperm; semen. **10.** the ovum or ova of certain animals, as the lobster and the silkworm moth. **11.** See **seed oyster. 12.** a small air bubble in a glass piece, caused by defective firing. **13.** *Crystall., Chem.* a small crystal added to a solution to promote crystallization. **14.** *Tennis.* a player who has been seeded in a tournament. **15. go** or **run to seed, a.** (of the flower of a plant) to pass to the stage of yielding seed. **b.** to lose vigor, power, or prosperity; deteriorate: *He has gone to seed in the last few years.* **16. in seed, a.** (of certain plants) in the state of bearing ripened seeds. **b.** (of a field, a lawn, etc.) sown with seed. —*v.t.* **17.** to sow (a field, lawn, etc.) with seed. **18.** to sow or scatter (seed). **19.** to sow or scatter (clouds) with crystals or particles of silver iodide, solid carbon dioxide, etc., to induce precipitation. **20.** to place, introduce, etc., esp. in the hope of increase or profit: *to seed a lake with trout.* **21.** to sprinkle on (a surface, substance, etc.) in the manner of seed: *to seed an icy bridge with chemicals.* **22.** to remove the seeds from (fruit). **23.** *Sports.* **a.** to arrange (the drawings for positions in a tournament) so that ranking players or teams will not meet in the early rounds of play. **b.** to distribute (ranking players or teams) in this manner. **24.** to develop or stimulate (a business, project, etc.), esp. by providing operating capital. —*v.i.* **25.** to sow seed. **26.** to produce or shed seed. —*adj.* **27.** of or producing seed; used for seed: *a seed potato.* **28.** being or providing capital for the initial stages of a new business or other enterprise: *The research project began with seed donations from the investors.* [bef. 900; (n.) ME *sede, side, seed(e),* OE *sǣd, sēd;* c. G *Saat,* ON *sāth,* Goth *-seths;* (v.) ME *seden* to produce seeds, deriv. of the n.; akin to SOW[1]] —**seed′less,** *adj.* —**seed′less·ness,** *n.* —**seed′like′,** *adj.*
—**Syn. 7.** descendants, heirs, posterity, issue, scions.

seed·bed (sēd′bed′), *n.* **1.** land prepared for seeding. **2.** a plot of ground for seedlings. **3.** a place of development; source. [1650–60; SEED + BED]

seed′ bee′tle, any of several beetles of the family Bruchidae that infest the seeds of legumes. Also called **seed weevil.**

seed·cake (sēd′kāk′), *n.* a sweet cake containing aromatic seeds, usually caraway. [1565–75; SEED + CAKE]

seed·case (sēd′kās′), *n.* a seed capsule; pericarp. [1670–80; SEED + CASE[2]]

seed′ coat′, *Bot.* the outer integument of a seed. [1790–1800]

seed′ cor′al, coral fragments used for jewelry. [1875–80]

seed′ corn′, ears or kernels of corn set apart as seed. [1585–95]

seed·eat·er (sēd′ē′tər), *n.* any of numerous small, tropical American finches, esp. of the genus *Sporophila.* [1875–80; SEED + EAT + -ER[1]]

seed·er (sē′dər), *n.* **1.** a person or thing that seeds. **2.** any of various apparatus for sowing seeds in the ground, ranging from simple devices that deposit seed evenly over a plot of land to complex machines that prepare a hole in the earth, insert a seed or seeds at the proper depth, and cover the hole again. **3.** a plant that produces many seeds, esp. one grown mainly to produce seeds for growing other plants. **4.** a device or utensil for removing seeds, as from grapefruit. **5.** a device used to scatter particles of silver iodide, carbon dioxide, etc., in clouds to induce precipitation. [bef. 950; ME *sedere,* OE *sǣdere.* See SEED, -ER[1]]

seed′ fern′, any of various plants of the order Lyginopteridales (or Cycadofilicales), known only as fossils, having fernlike leaves and reproducing by means of seeds. Also called **pteridosperm.** [1925–30]

seed′ leaf′, *Bot.* a cotyledon. [1685–95]

seed·ling (sēd′ling), *n.* **1.** a plant or tree grown from a seed. **2.** a tree not yet 3 ft. (1 m) high. **3.** any young plant, esp. one grown in a nursery for transplanting. [1650–60; SEED + -LING[1]]

seed′ mon′ey, capital for the initial stages of a new business or other enterprise, esp. for the initial operating costs. [1940–45]

seed′ oy′ster, a very young oyster, esp. one used in the cultivating and transplanting of an oyster bed. [1880–85]

seed′ pearl′, a pearl weighing less than ¼ grain. [1545–55]

seed′ plant′, a seed-bearing plant; spermatophyte. [1700–10]

seed·pod (sēd′pod′), *n.* a seed vessel or dehiscent fruit that splits when ripe. [1710–20]

seed′ shrimp′, any of numerous tiny marine and freshwater crustaceans of the subclass Ostracoda, having a shrimplike body enclosed in a hinged bivalve shell. Also called **mussel shrimp, ostracod.**

seeds·man (sēdz′mən), *n., pl.* **-men.** **1.** a sower of seed. **2.** a dealer in seed. Also, **seed·man** (sēd′mən). [1585–95; SEED + -'S[1] + MAN[1]]

seed-snipe (sēd′snīp′), *n.* any of several South American birds of the family Thinocoridae, related to the shorebirds but superficially resembling quail. Also, **seed′snipe′.** [1885–90]

seed•stock (sēd′stok′), *n.* **1.** seed, tubers, or roots selected and kept for planting. **2.** animals, esp. pedigreed livestock, maintained for breeding purposes. **3.** the animals needed to replenish a population, as after hunting or fishing. Also, **seed′ stock′.** [1925–30; SEED + STOCK]

seed′ tick′, the six-legged nymphal form of a tick, somewhat resembling a seed. [1695–1705, *Amer.*]

seed•time (sēd′tīm′), *n.* the season for sowing seed. [bef. 1000; ME; OE *sǣdtīma.* See SEED, TIME]

seed′ ves′sel, *Bot.* a pericarp. [1660–70]

seed′ wee′vil. See **seed beetle.**

seed•y (sē′dē), *adj.,* **seed•i•er, seed•i•est. 1.** abounding in seed. **2.** containing many seeds, as a piece of fruit. **3.** gone to seed; bearing seeds. **4.** poorly kept; run-down; shabby. **5.** shabbily dressed; unkempt: *a seedy old tramp.* **6.** physically run-down; under the weather: *He felt a bit seedy after his operation.* **7.** somewhat disreputable; degraded: *a seedy hotel.* [1565–75; SEED + -Y[1]] **—seed′i•ly,** *adv.* **—seed′i•ness,** *n.*

See•ger (sē′gər), *n.* **1. Alan,** 1888–1916, U.S. poet. **2. Peter** (*Pete*), born 1919, U.S. folk singer and folklorist.

see•ing (sē′ing), *conj.* **1.** in view of the fact that; considering; inasmuch as. *—n.* **2.** the act of a person who sees. **3.** the sense of sight. [1495–1505; SEE[1] + -ING[2]]

See′ing Eye′ dog′, a dog that has been specially trained to lead or guide a blind person in walking about. [named after the *Seeing Eye* organization in Morristown, New Jersey]

see′ing glass′, *Brit. Dial.* a looking glass; mirror. [1555–65]

seek (sēk), *v.,* **sought, seek•ing.** *—v.t.* **1.** to go in search or quest of: *to seek the truth.* **2.** to try to find or discover by searching or questioning: *to seek the solution to a problem.* **3.** to try to obtain: *to seek fame.* **4.** to try or attempt (usually fol. by an infinitive): *to seek to convince a person.* **5.** to go to: *to seek a place to rest.* **6.** to ask for; request: *to seek advice.* **7.** *Archaic.* to search or explore. *—v.i.* **8.** to make inquiry. **9. be sought after,** to be desired or in demand: *Graduates in the physical sciences are most sought after by employers these days.* [bef. 900; ME *seken,* OE *sēcan;* c. G *suchen,* ON *sœkja,* Goth *sōkjan;* akin to L *sāgīre* to perceive by scent (see PRESAGE, SAGACITY); cf. BESEECH]
—Syn. 3. pursue, follow.

seek•er (sē′kər), *n.* **1.** a person or thing that seeks. **2.** *Rocketry.* **a.** a device in a missile that locates a target by sensing some characteristic of the target, as heat emission. **b.** a missile equipped with such a device. [1300–50; ME; see SEEK, -ER[1]]

See•konk (sē′kongk), *n.* a city in SE Massachusetts. 12,269.

seel (sēl), *v.t.* **1.** *Falconry.* to sew shut (the eyes of a falcon) during parts of its training. **2.** *Archaic.* **a.** to close (the eyes). **b.** to blind. [1490–1500; < MF *siller, ciller,* deriv. of *cil* eyelash < L *cilium* eyelid, eyelash; see CILIA]

See•land (sē′lənd), *n.* Zealand.

see•ly (sē′lē), *adj. Archaic.* **1.** insignificant or feeble; poor. **2.** happy; auspicious. **3.** good; pious; blessed. **4.** foolish; simple-minded. [bef. 1000; ME *sely,* OE *gesǣlig* happy, equiv. to *sǣl* happiness + *-ig* -Y[1]; c. D *zalig,* G *selig;* akin to ON *sæll,* Goth *sēls* good, OE *sēl* better; see SILLY] **—see′li•ly,** *adv.*

seem (sēm), *v.i.* **1.** to appear to be, feel, do, etc.: *She seems better this morning.* **2.** to appear to one's own senses, mind, observation, judgment, etc.: *It seems to me that someone is calling.* **3.** to appear to exist: *There seems no need to go now.* **4.** to appear to be true, probable, or evident: *It seems likely to rain.* **5.** to give the outward appearance of being or to pretend to be: *He only seems friendly because he wants you to like him.* [1150–1200; ME *seme* < ON *sœma* to befit, beseem, deriv. of *sœmr* fitting, seemly; akin to *sōmi* honor]
—Syn. 4. SEEM, APPEAR, LOOK refer to an outward aspect that may or may not be contrary to reality. SEEM is applied to something that has an aspect of truth and probability: *It seems warmer today.* APPEAR suggests the giving of an impression that may be superficial or illusory: *The house appears to be deserted.* LOOK more vividly suggests the use of the eye (literally or figuratively) or the aspect as perceived by the eye: *She looked very much frightened.*

seem•er (sē′mər), *n.* a person who constantly pretends. [1595–1605; SEEM + -ER[1]]

seem•ing (sē′ming), *adj.* **1.** apparent; appearing, whether truly or falsely, to be as specified: *a seeming advantage.* *—n.* **2.** appearance, esp. outward or deceptive appearance. [1300–50; ME *semynge;* see SEEM, -ING[2], -ING[1]] **—seem′ing•ly,** *adv.* **—seem′ing•ness,** *n.*
—Syn. 1. ostensible, external, superficial. **2.** semblance, face, pretense.

seem•ly (sēm′lē), *adj.,* **-li•er, -li•est,** *adv.* *—adj.* **1.** fitting or becoming with respect to propriety or good taste; decent; decorous: *Your outburst of rage was hardly seemly.* **2.** suitable or appropriate; fitting: *a seemly gesture.* **3.** of pleasing appearance; handsome. *—adv.* **4.** in a seemly manner; fittingly; becomingly. [1175–1225; ME *semely* < ON *sœmiligr* honorable; deriv. of *sœmr* (see SEEM)] **—seem′li•ness,** *n.*
—Syn. 1, 2. right, proper, appropriate, meet.

seen (sēn), *v.* pp. of **see**[1].

seep (sēp), *v.i.* **1.** to pass, flow, or ooze gradually through a porous substance: *Water seeps through cracks in the wall.* **2.** (of ideas, methods, etc.) to enter or be introduced at a slow pace: *The new ideas finally seeped down to the lower echelons.* **3.** to become diffused; permeate: *Fog seeped through the trees, obliterating everything.* *—v.t.* **4.** to cause to seep; filter: *The vodka is seeped through charcoal to purify it.* *—n.* **5.** moisture that seeps out; seepage. **6.** a small spring, pool, or other place where liquid from the ground has oozed to the surface of the earth. [1780–90; perh. var. of dial. *sipe,* itself perh. continuing OE *sīpian* (c. MLG *sīpen*)]

seep•age (sē′pij), *n.* **1.** the act or process of seeping; leakage. **2.** something that seeps or leaks out. **3.** a quantity that has seeped out. [1815–25; SEEP + -AGE]

seep′age pit′, a pit that is lined with a porous, mortarless masonry wall in which effluent from a septic tank is collected for gradual seepage into the ground, sometimes used as a substitute for a drainfield.

seep•y (sē′pē), *adj.,* **seep•i•er, seep•i•est.** (esp. of ground, a plot of land, or the like) soaked or oozing with water; not drained. [1855–60, *Amer.;* SEEP + -Y[1]]

se•er[1] (sē′ər *for 1;* sēr *for 2–4*), *n.* **1.** a person who sees; observer. **2.** a person who prophesies future events; prophet: *Industry seers predicted higher profits.* **3.** a person endowed with profound moral and spiritual insight or knowledge; a wise person or sage who possesses intuitive powers. **4.** a person who is reputed to have special powers of divination, as a crystal gazer or palmist. [1350–1400; ME; see SEE[1], -ER[1]]
—Syn. 2. oracle, soothsayer, augur.

seer[2] (sēr, sâr), *n.* ser. [1610–20]

seer•ess (sēr′is), *n.* a woman who prophesies future events. [1835–45; SEER[1] + -ESS]
—Usage. See **-ess.**

seer•suck•er (sēr′suk′ər), *n.* a plainwoven cotton, rayon, or linen fabric: traditionally a striped cotton with alternate stripes crinkled in the weaving. [1715–25; < Hindi *sirsakar* < Pers *shīr o shakar* lit., milk and sugar]

see•saw (sē′sô′), *n.* **1.** a recreation in which two children alternately ride up and down while seated at opposite ends of a plank balanced at the middle. **2.** a plank or apparatus for this recreation. **3.** an up-and-down or a back-and-forth movement or procedure. **4.** *Whist.* a crossruff. *—adj.* **5.** moving up and down, back and forth, or alternately ahead and behind: *It was a seesaw game with the lead changing hands many times.* *—v.i.* **6.** to move in a seesaw manner: *The boat seesawed in the heavy sea.* **7.** to ride or play on a seesaw. **8.** to keep changing one's decision, opinion, or attitude; vacillate. *—v.t.* **9.** to cause to move in a seesaw manner. [1630–40 as part of a jingle accompanying a children's game; gradational compound based on SAW[1]]
—Regional Variation. Although SEESAW (def. 2) is the most widely used term in the U.S., TEETERTOTTER is also in wide use in the Northern, North Midland, and Western regions. TILTING BOARD and its variants TILT BOARD and TILTERING BOARD are New Eng. terms, esp. Eastern New Eng., while TINTER and its variant TEENTER are associated with Western New Eng.

seethe (sēth), *v.,* **seethed** or (*Obs.*) **sod; seethed** or (*Obs.*) **sod•den** or **sod; seeth•ing;** *n.* *—v.i.* **1.** to surge or foam as if boiling. **2.** to be in a state of agitation or excitement. **3.** *Archaic* to boil. *—v.t.* **4.** to soak or steep. **5.** to cook by boiling or simmering; boil. *—n.* **6.** the act of seething. **7.** the state of being agitated or excited. [bef. 900; ME; OE *sēothan;* c. G *sieden,* Sw *sjuda*] **—seeth′ing•ly,** *adv.*
—Syn. 2. See **boil**[1].

see-through (sē′thro͞o′), *adj.* **1.** Also, **see-thru** (sē′thro͞o′). transparent: *a see-through blouse.* *—n.* **2.** a degree of or variation in transparency. **3.** a see-through item of clothing. **4.** look-through. [1940–45; adj., n. use of v. phrase *see through*]

Se•fe•ri•a•des (se fe′ʀe ä′thes), *n.* **Gior•gos Sty•lia•nou** (yôr′gôs stē′lyä no͞o′), (*Giorgos Seferis*), 1900–71, Greek poet and diplomat: Nobel prize for literature 1963.

Se•fer To•rah (*Seph.* se′feʀ tô ʀä′; *Ashk.* sā′fər tō′ʀə, toi′ʀə; *Eng.* sā′fər tôr′ə, tôr′ə), *pl.* ***Si•frei To•rah*** (*Seph.* se fʀā′ tô ʀä′; *Ashk.* si′frā tō′ʀə, toi′ʀə), *Eng.* **Sefer Torahs.** *Hebrew.* See ***Sepher Torah.***

Se•gal (sē′gəl), *n.* **George,** born 1924, U.S. sculptor.

se•gar (si gär′), *n.* cigar.

Se•gar (sē′gär), *n.* **El•zie** (**Cris•ler**) (el′zē krīs′lər), 1894–1938, U.S. comic-strip artist: creator of "Popeye."

Se′ger cone′ (zā′gər, sā′-), a pyrometric cone composed of clay and salt. [1890–95; named after Hermann A. Seger (d. 1893), German ceramist]

seg•gar (seg′ər), *n., v.t.* sagger.

Se•ghers (zā′gəʀs), *n.* **An•na** (ä′nä), (*Netty Radvanyi*), born 1900, German novelist.

seg•ment (*n.* seg′mənt; *v.* seg′ment, seg ment′), *n.* **1.** one of the parts into which something naturally separates or is divided; a division, portion, or section: *a segment of an orange.* **2.** *Geom.* **a.** a part cut off from a figure, esp. a circular or spherical one, by a line or plane, as a part of a circular area contained by an arc and its chord or by two parallel lines or planes. **b.** Also called **line segment.** a finite section of a line. **3.** *Zool.* **a.** any of the rings that compose the body of an annelid or arthropod. **b.** any of the discrete parts of the body of an animal, esp. of an arthropod. **4.** an object, as a machine part, having the form of a segment or sector of a circle. **5.** *Computers.* **a.** a portion of a program, often one that can be loaded and executed independently of other portions. **b.** a unit of data in a database. **6.** an arclike support on which the typebars of a typewriter rest when not in use. *—v.t., v.i.* **7.** to separate or divide into segments. [1560–70; < L *segmentum,* equiv. to *sec(āre)* to cut + *-mentum* -MENT] **—seg•men•tar•y** (seg′mən ter′ē), *adj.* **—seg′men•tate′,** *adj.*
—Syn. 1. See **part.**

seg•men•tal (seg men′tl), *adj.* **1.** of, pertaining to, or characterized by segments or segmentation. **2.** *Ling.* noting or pertaining to the discrete elements of sequential speech, as consonants and vowels. [1810–20; SEGMENT + -AL[1]] **—seg•men′tal•ly,** *adv.*

seg•men•tal•ize (seg men′tl īz′), *v.t.,* **-ized, -iz•ing.** to make segmentalized. Also, *esp. Brit.,* **seg•men′tal•ise′.** [SEGMENTAL + -IZE] **—seg•men′tal•i•za′tion,** *n.*

seg•men•tal•ized (seg men′tl īzd′), *adj.* separated into parts, sections, elements, classes, etc.; compartmentalized: *a segmentalized society.* [SEGMENTALIZE + -ED[2]]

seg•men•ta•tion (seg′mən tā′shən), *n.* **1.** division into segments. **2.** *Biol.* **a.** the subdivision of an organism or of an organ into more or less equivalent parts. **b.** cell division. [1850–55; SEGMENT + -ATION]

segmenta′tion cav′ity, *Embryol.* blastocoele. [1885–90]

seg•men•tize (seg′mən tīz′), *v.t.,* **-tized, -tiz•ing.** to segmentalize. Also, *esp. Brit.,* **seg′men•tise′.** [SEGMENT + -IZE]

Se•gni (se′nyē), *n.* **An•to•nio** (än tô′nyô), 1891–1972, Italian teacher, lawyer, and statesman: president 1962–64.

se•gno (sān′yō, sen′yō; *It.* se′nyô), *n., pl.* **se•gni** (sān′yē, sen′yē; *It.* se′nyē). *Music.* **1.** a sign. **2.** a sign or mark at the beginning or end of a section to be repeated. [1905–10; < It < L *signum* a SIGN]

se•go (sē′gō), *n., pl.* **-gos.** See **sego lily.** [1850–55, *Amer.;* < Southern Paiute *siyoʔo*]

se′go lil′y, 1. a plant, *Calochortus nuttallii,* of the lily family, native to the western U.S., having showy, bell-shaped flowers: the state flower of Utah. **2.** its edible root. [1910–15, *Amer.*]

Se•gor (sē′gər), *n. Douay Bible.* Zoar.

Se•go•vi•a (sə gō′vē ə; *Sp.* se gô′vyä), *n.* **1. An•drés** (än dʀes′), 1893–1987, Spanish guitarist. **2.** a city in central Spain: well-preserved Roman aqueduct. 41,880. **3.** Coco.

Se•grè (sə grā′; *It.* se gʀe′), *n.* **E•mil•io** (ə mē′lē ō′, ə mēl′yō; *It.* e mē′lyô), born 1905, U.S. physicist, born in Italy: Nobel prize 1959.

seg•re•ant (seg′rē ənt), *adj. Heraldry.* (of a griffin) rampant. [1540–50; earlier *sergreant;* of uncert. orig.]

seg•re•gate (*v.* seg′ri gāt′; *n.* seg′ri git, -gāt′), *v.,* **-gat•ed, -gat•ing,** *n.* *—v.t.* **1.** to separate or set apart from others or from the main body or group; isolate: *to segregate exceptional children; to segregate hardened criminals.* **2.** to require, often with force, the separation of (a specific racial, religious, or other group) from the general body of society. *—v.i.* **3.** to separate, withdraw, or go apart; separate from the main body and collect in one place; become segregated. **4.** to practice, require, or enforce segregation, esp. racial segregation. **5.** *Genetics.* (of allelic genes) to separate during meiosis. *—n.* **6.** a segregated thing, person, or group. [1400–50 in sense "segregated"; 1535–45 as transit. v.; late ME *segregat* < L *sēgregātus* (ptp. of *sēgregāre* to part from the flock), equiv. to *sē-* SE- + *greg-* (s. of *grex* flock) + *-ātus* -ATE[1]; see GREGARIOUS] **—seg•re•ga•ble** (seg′ri gə bəl), *adj.* **—seg′re•ga′tive,** *adj.*
—Ant. 1. integrate.

seg•re•gat•ed (seg′ri gā′tid), *adj.* **1.** characterized by or practicing racial segregation: *a segregated school system.* **2.** restricted to one group, esp. exclusively on the basis of racial or ethnic membership: *segregated neighborhoods.* **3.** maintaining separate facilities for members of different, esp. racially different, groups: *segregated education.* **4.** discriminating against a group, esp. on the basis of race: *a segregated economy.* **5.** set apart. [1645–55; SEGREGATE + -ED[2]] **—seg′re•gat′ed•ly,** *adv.* **—seg′re•gat′ed•ness,** *n.*

seg•re•ga•tion (seg′ri gā′shən), *n.* **1.** the act or practice of segregating. **2.** the state or condition of being segregated: *the segregation of private clubs.* **3.** something segregated. **4.** *Genetics.* the separation of allelic genes into different gametes during meiosis. Cf. **law of segregation.** [1545–55; < LL *sēgregātiōn-* (s. of *sēgregātiō*), equiv. to *sēgregāt(us)* (see SEGREGATE) + *-iōn-* -ION] **—seg′re•ga′tion•al,** *adj.*

seg•re•ga•tion•ist (seg′ri gā′shə nist), *n.* one who favors, encourages, or practices segregation, esp. racial segregation. [1910–15; SEGREGATION + -IST]

seg•re•ga•tor (seg′ri gā′tər), *n. Med.* an instrument for collecting the urine excreted by one kidney only. [1900–05; SEGREGATE + -OR[2]]

se•gue (sā′gwā, seg′wā), *v.,* **-gued, -gue•ing,** *n.* *—v.i.* **1.** to continue at once with the next musical section or composition (often used as a musical direction). **2.** to perform in the manner of the preceding section (used as a musical direction). **3.** to make a transition from one thing to another smoothly and without interruption: *The conversation segued from travel anecdotes to food.* *—n.* **4.** an uninterrupted transition made between one musical section or composition and another. [1850–55; < It: (there) follows, 3rd pers. sing. pres. ind. of *seguire* << L *sequī* to follow. See SUE]

se•gui•dil•la (sā′gə dēl′yə, -dē′yə, seg′ə-; *Sp.* se′gē-thē′lyä), *n., pl.* **-dil•las** (-dēl′yəz, -dē′yəz; *Sp.* -thē′lyäs). **1.** *Pros.* a stanza of four to seven lines with a distinctive rhythmic pattern. **2.** a Spanish dance in triple meter for two persons. **3.** the music for this dance. [1755–65; < Sp, equiv. to *seguid(a)* sequence (*segui-* (s. of *seguir* << L *sequī* to follow) + *-da* < L *-ta* fem. ptp. suffix) + *-illa* dim. suffix]

Se•guin (si gēn′), *n.* a city in SE Texas. 17,854.

Se•gu•ra (si go͝or′ə; *Sp.* se go͞o′ʀä), *n.* **Fran•cis•co** (fʀän sēs′kô), ("*Pancho*"), born 1921, Ecuadorian tennis player.

Seh′na knot′ (sen′ə), a hand-tied knot, used in rug weaving, in which the ends of yarn looped around a warp thread appear at each of the interstices between adjacent threads and produce a compact and relatively even pile effect. Also, **Senna knot.** Also called **Persian knot.** Cf. **Ghiordes knot.** [var. of *Sinneh,* name of Persian town]

sei (sā), *n.* See **sei whale.**

sei·cen·to (sā chen′tō; *It.* se chen′tô), *n.* (*often cap.*) the 17th century, with reference to the Italian art or literature of that period. [1900–05; < It: short for *mille seicento* lit., a thousand six hundred]

seiche (sāsh), *n.* an occasional and sudden oscillation of the water of a lake, bay, estuary, etc., producing fluctuations in the water level and caused by wind, earthquakes, changes in barometric pressure, etc. [1830–40; < Franco-Provençal]

sei·del (sīd′l, zīd′l), *n.* a large beer mug with a capacity of one liter (1.1 quarts) and often having a hinged lid. [1905–10; < G; MHG *sīdel* < L *situla* bucket]

Seid′litz pow′ders (sed′lits), a mild laxative consisting of tartaric acid, sodium bicarbonate, and Rochelle salt, which are dissolved separately, mixed, and drunk after effervescence. [1805–15; a town in Bohemia]

seif (sāf, sīf), *n.* a long narrow sand dune parallel to the prevailing wind direction. [< Ar *sayf* sword]

Sei·fert (sī′fərt), *n.* **Ja·ro·slav** (yä′rô släf), born 1901, Czech poet: Nobel prize 1984.

sei·gneur (sēn yûr′, sān-; *Fr.* se nyœr′), *n., pl.* **sei·gneurs** (sēn yûrz′, sān-; *Fr.* se nyœr′). (*sometimes cap.*) **1.** a lord, esp. a feudal lord. **2.** (in French Canada) a holder of a seigneury. [1585–95; < F < VL **senior* lord. See SENIOR] **—sei·gneu·ri·al** (sēn yûr′ē əl, sān-), *adj.*

sei·gneur·y (sēn′yə rē, sān′-), *n.* **1.** the domain of a seigneur. **2.** (in French Canada) land originally held by grant from the king of France. [1675–85; < F *seigneurie;* see SEIGNEUR, -Y[3]]

seign·ior (sēn′yər), *n.* (*sometimes cap.*) a lord, esp. a feudal lord; ruler. [1300–50; ME *segnour* < AF; see SEIGNEUR]

seign·ior·age (sēn′yər ij), *n.* **1.** something claimed by a sovereign or superior as a prerogative. **2.** a charge on bullion brought to the mint to be coined. **3.** the difference between the cost of the bullion plus minting expenses and the value as money of the pieces coined, constituting a source of government revenue. Also, **seign′or·age.** [1400–50; late ME *seigneurage* < MF *seignorage, seigneurage;* see SEIGNEUR, -AGE]

seign·ior·y (sēn′yə rē), *n., pl.* **-ior·ies. 1.** the power or authority of a seignior. **2.** *Hist.* a lord's domain. Also, **signory.** [1250–1300; ME *seignorie* < OF; see SEIGNEUR, -Y[3]]

sei·gno·ri·al (sēn yôr′ē əl, -yōr′-), *adj.* of or pertaining to a seignior. Also, **seign·ior·al** (sēn′yər əl), **sei·gnio·ri·al** (sēn yôr′ē əl, -yōr′-), **seign·or·al** (sēn′yər əl). [1810–20; *seignor* (var. of SEIGNIOR) + -IAL]

Sei·le·nos (sī lē′nəs), *n.* Silenus.

seine (sān), *n., v.,* **seined, sein·ing.** **—***n.* **1.** a fishing net that hangs vertically in the water, having floats at the upper edge and sinkers at the lower. **—***v.t.* **2.** to fish for or catch with a seine. **3.** to use a seine in (water). **—***v.i.* **4.** to fish with a seine. [bef. 950; ME *seyne,* OE *segne* < WGmc **sagina* < L *sagēna* < Gk *sagēnē*]

Seine (sān; *Fr.* sen), *n.* **1.** a river in France, flowing NW through Paris to the English Channel. 480 mi. (773 km) long. **2.** a former department in N France.

Seine-et-Marne (sān′ā märn′; *Fr.* sen ā MARN′), *n.* a department in N France. 755,762; 2290 sq. mi. (5930 sq. km). *Cap.:* Melun.

Seine-et-Oise (sen ā WAZ′), *n.* a former department in N France.

Seine-Ma·ri·time (sen mä RĒ tēm′), *n.* a department in NW France. 1,172,743; 2449 sq. mi. (6340 sq. km). *Cap.:* Rouen. Formerly, **Seine-In·fé·rieure** (sen aN fā ryœr′).

sein·er (sā′nər), *n.* **1.** a person who fishes with a seine. **2.** a boat used in fishing with a seine. [1595–1605; SEINE + -ER[1]]

Seine-St-De·nis (sen saN də nē′), *n.* a department in N France. 1,322,127; 91 sq. mi. (236 sq. km). *Cap.:* Bobigny.

Seir·i·os (sir′ē əs), *n. Class. Myth.* Sirius (def. 2).

seise (sēz), *v.t., v.i.* **seised, seis·ing.** *Chiefly Law.* seize. **—seis′a·ble,** *adj.* **—seis′er,** *n.*

sei·sin (sē′zin), *n. Law.* seizin.

seis·ing (sē′zing), *n. Chiefly Law.* seizing.

seism (sī′zəm, -səm), *n.* an earthquake. [1880–85; < Gk *seismós,* equiv. to *seis-,* s. of *seíein* to shake, quake + *-mos* n. suffix; cf. -ISM]

seis·mic (sīz′mik, sīs′-), *adj.* pertaining to, of the nature of, or caused by an earthquake or vibration of the earth, whether due to natural or artificial causes. Also, **seis′mal, seis′mi·cal.** [1855–60; SEISM + -IC] **—seis′mi·cal·ly,** *adv.*

CONCISE ETYMOLOGY KEY: <, descended or borrowed from; >, whence; b., blend of, blended; c., cognate with; cf., compare; deriv., derivative; equiv., equivalent; imit., imitative; obl., oblique; r., replacing; s., stem; sp., spelling, spelled; resp., respelling, respelled; trans., translation; ?, origin unknown; *, unattested; ‡, probably earlier than. See the full key inside the front cover.

seis′mic gap′, the part of an active fault that has experienced little or no seismic activity for a long period, indicating the buildup of stresses that are useful in predicting earthquakes.

seis·mic·i·ty (sīz mis′i tē, sīs-), *n., pl.* **-ties.** the frequency, intensity, and distribution of earthquakes in a given area. [1900–05; SEISMIC + -ITY]

seis′mic sea′ wave′, *Oceanog.* tsunami.

seis·mism (sīz′miz əm, sīs′-), *n.* the natural activity or group of phenomena associated with earthquakes. [1900–05; SEISM + -ISM]

seismo-, a combining form meaning "earthquake," used in the formation of compound words: *seismograph.* [see SEISM, -O-]

seis·mo·gram (sīz′mə gram′, sīs′-), *n.* a record made by a seismograph. [1890–95; SEISMO- + -GRAM[1]]

seis·mo·graph (sīz′mə graf′, -gräf′, sīs′-), *n.* any of various instruments for measuring and recording the vibrations of earthquakes. [1855–60; SEISMO- + -GRAPH] **—seis·mo·graph·ic** (sīz′mə graf′ik, sīs′-), **seis′mo·graph′i·cal,** *adj.*

seis·mog·ra·phy (sīz mog′rə fē, sīs-), *n.* **1.** the scientific measuring and recording of the shock and vibrations of earthquakes. **2.** seismology. [1860–65; SEISMO- + -GRAPHY] **—seis·mog′ra·pher,** *n.*

seismol., 1. seismological. **2.** seismology.

seis·mol·ogy (sīz mol′ə jē, sīs-), *n.* the science or study of earthquakes and their phenomena. Also called **seismography.** [1855–60; SEISMO- + -LOGY] **—seis·mo·log·ic** (sīz′mə loj′ik, sīs′-), **seis′mo·log′i·cal,** *adj.* **—seis′mo·log′i·cal·ly,** *adv.* **—seis·mol′o·gist,** *n.*

seis·mom·e·ter (sīz mom′i tər, sīs-), *n.* a seismograph equipped for measuring the direction, intensity, and duration of earthquakes by measuring the actual movement of the ground. [1835–45; SEISMO- + -METER] **—seis·mo·met·ric** (sīz′mə me′trik, sīs′-), **seis′mo·met′ri·cal,** *adj.* **—seis·mom′et·ry,** *n.*

seis·mo·scope (sīz′mə skōp′, sīs′-), *n.* an instrument for recording the occurrence or time of an earthquake. [1850–55; SEISMO- + -SCOPE] **—seis·mo·scop·ic** (sīz′mə skop′ik, sīs′-), *adj.*

SEIU, Service Employees International Union.

sei′ whale′ (sā), a rorqual, *Balaenoptera borealis,* inhabiting all seas: now greatly reduced in number. [1915–20; < Norw *seihval,* equiv. to *sei* (ON *seithr*) coalfish + *hval* WHALE[1]]

seize (sēz), *v.,* **seized, seiz·ing.** **—***v.t.* **1.** to take hold of suddenly or forcibly; grasp: *to seize a weapon.* **2.** to grasp mentally; understand clearly and completely: *to seize an idea.* **3.** to take possession of by force or at will: *to seize enemy ships.* **4.** to take possession or control of as if by suddenly laying hold: *Panic seized the crowd.* **5.** to take possession of by legal authority; confiscate: *to seize smuggled goods.* **6.** Also, **seise.** *Law.* to put (someone) in seizin or legal possession of property (usually used in passive constructions): *She was seized of vast estates.* **7.** to capture; take into custody. **8.** to take advantage of promptly: *to seize an opportunity.* **9.** *Naut.* to bind or fasten together with a seizing. **—***v.i.* **10.** to grab or take hold suddenly or forcibly (usually fol. by *on* or *upon*): *to seize on a rope.* **11.** to resort to a method, plan, etc., in desperation (usually fol. by *on* or *upon*): *He must seize on a solution, however risky.* **12.** to have moving parts bind and stop moving as a result of excessive pressure, temperature, or friction (usually fol. by *up*): *The engine seized up from cold.* [1250–1300; ME *saisen, seisen* < OF *saisir* < ML *sacīre* to place (in phrase *sacīre ad propriētam* to take as one's own, lay claim to) < Frankish, perh. akin to Goth *satjan* to SET, put, place] **—seiz′a·ble,** *adj.* **—seiz′er;** *Law.* **sei·zor** (sē′zər, -zôr), *n.*
—Syn. 1. clutch, grab. **7.** arrest, apprehend. See **catch. —Ant. 7.** release.

sei·zin (sē′zin), *n. Law.* **1.** (originally) possession of either land or chattel. **2.** the kind of possession or right to possession characteristic of estates of freehold. Also, **seisin.** [1250–1300; ME < OF *saisine,* equiv. to *sais(ir)* to SEIZE + *-ine* -INE[2]]

seiz·ing (sē′zing), *n.* **1.** the act of a person or thing that seizes. **2.** *Naut.* a means of binding or fastening together two objects, as two ropes, by a number of longitudinal and transverse turns of marline, wire, or other small stuff. [1300–50; ME; see SEIZE, -ING[1]]

seizing (def. 2)

sei·zure (sē′zhər), *n.* **1.** the act or an instance of seizing. **2.** the state of being seized. **3.** a taking possession of an item, property, or person legally or by force. **4.** a sudden attack, as of epilepsy or some other disease. [1475–85; SEIZE + -URE]

se·jant (sē′jənt), *adj. Heraldry.* (of an animal) represented in a sitting posture: *a lion sejant.* Also, **se′jeant.** [1490–1500; var. of *seiante* < AF; MF *seant,* equiv. to *se-* (s. of *seoir* < L *sedēre* to SIT[1]) + *-ant* -ANT]

se·jant-e·rect (sē′jənt i rekt′), *adj. Heraldry.* (of an animal) represented as seated upright with forelegs raised: *a lion sejant-erect.* Also, **se′jeant-e·rect′.**

Se·ja·nus (si jā′nəs), *n.* **Lucius Ae·li·us** (ē′lē əs), d. A.D. 31, Roman politician, commander of praetorian guard, and conspirator in the reign of Emperor Tiberius.

Sejm (sām), *n.* the unicameral parliament of Poland. [< Pol: assembly < Slavic **sŭjĭmŭ* equiv. to **sŭ-* with, together + *-jĭmŭ,* n. deriv. of *jĭm-* v. base meaning "take," akin to L *emere* to take, buy (cf. CONSUME, REDEEM)]

Sekh·met (sek′met), *n. Egyptian Myth.* a bloodthirsty goddess, sometimes identified with Hathor, who attempted to destroy humankind. [vocalization of Egyptian *sḫm* powerful (cf. PSCHENT) + *t* fem. marker]

Se·kon·di-Ta·ko·ra·di (sek′ən dē′tä′kə rä′dē), *n.* a seaport in SW Ghana. 161,071.

se·kos (sē′kos), *n.* **1.** (in ancient Greece) **a.** a sanctuary. **b.** the cella of a temple. **2.** any of various other shrines or sanctuaries. Also, **secos.** [1810–20; < Gk *sēkós* enclosed area]

Sekt (zekt), *n. German.* sparkling wine; champagne.

sel (sel), *n., adj., pron. Scot.* self.

sel., 1. select. **2.** selected. **3.** selection; selections.

se·la·chi·an (si lā′kē ən), *adj.* **1.** belonging to the Selachii, a group of fishes comprising the sharks, skates, and rays. **—***n.* **2.** a selachian fish. [1825–35; < NL *Selachi(i)* (pl.) name of the order (< Gk *seláchios* (sing.) resembling a shark, cartilaginous, adj. deriv. of *seláchos* shark, ray) + -AN]

se·la·dang (si lä′däng), *n.* the gaur. [1810–20; < Malay]

se·lah (sē′lə, sel′ə), *n.* an expression occurring frequently in the Psalms, thought to be a liturgical or musical direction, probably a direction by the leader to raise the voice or perhaps an indication of a pause. [1520–30; < Heb *selāh*]

se·lam·lik (si läm′lik), *n.* the portion of a Turkish palace or house reserved for men. [1890–95; < Turk *selamlık*]

Se·lan·gor (sə lang′ər, -ôr, -läng′-), *n.* a state in Malaysia, on the SW Malay Peninsula. 1,467,441; 3160 sq. mi. (8184 sq. km). *Cap.:* Shah Alam.

sel·couth (sel′ko͞oth′), *adj. Archaic.* strange; uncommon. [bef. 900; ME *selcouth,* OE *seldcūth,* equiv. to *seld(an)* SELDOM + *cūth* COUTH[2]] **—sel′couth′ly,** *adv.*

Sel·den (sel′dən), *n.* **1. George Baldwin,** 1846–1922, U.S. inventor of a gasoline-powered car. **2. John,** 1584–1654, English historian, Orientalist, and politician. **3.** a city on N Long Island, in SE New York. 17,259.

sel·dom (sel′dəm), *adv.* **1.** on only a few occasions; rarely; infrequently; not often: *We seldom see our old neighbors anymore.* **—***adj.* **2.** rare; infrequent. [bef. 900; ME; OE *seldum,* var. of *seldan;* c. G *selten,* Goth *silda-*] **—sel′dom·ness,** *n.*

se·lect (si lekt′), *v.t.* **1.** to choose in preference to another or other things; pick out. **—***v.i.* **2.** to make a choice; pick. **—***adj.* **3.** chosen in preference to another or others; selected. **4.** choice; of special value. **5.** careful or fastidious in selecting; discriminating. **6.** carefully or fastidiously chosen; exclusive: *a select group.* [1555–65; < L *sēlēctus* (ptp. of *sēligere* to gather apart), equiv. to *sē-* SE- + *leg(ere)* to gather, choose + *-tus* ptp. suffix] **—se·lec′ta·ble,** *adj.* **—se·lec′ta·bil′i·ty,** *n.* **—se·lect′ly,** *adv.* **—se·lect′ness,** *n.* **—se·lec′tor,** *n.*
—Syn. 1. See **choose. 3.** preferred.

se·lect·ance (si lek′təns), *n.* a measure of the drop in response of a radio receiving set or the like to a given frequency differing from the resonant frequency of the device, expressed as the ratio of the amplitude of the response at the resonant frequency to the amplitude of the response at the given frequency. [SELECT + -ANCE]

select′ commit′tee, a committee, as of a legislative body, that is formed to examine and report on a specific bill or issue. Also called **special committee.** [1780–90, *Amer.*]

se·lect·ee (si lek tē′), *n.* one selected by draft for service in one of the armed forces. [1935–40, *Amer.;* SELECT + -EE]

se·lec·tion (si lek′shən), *n.* **1.** an act or instance of selecting or the state of being selected; choice. **2.** a thing or a number of things selected. **3.** an aggregate of things displayed for choice, purchase, use, etc.; a group from which a choice may be made: *The store had a wide selection of bracelets.* **4.** *Biol.* any natural or artificial process that results in differential reproduction among the members of a population so that the inheritable traits of only certain individuals are passed on, or are passed on in greater proportion, to succeeding generations. Cf. **natural selection, sexual selection, kin selection, artificial selection. 5.** *Ling.* **a.** the choice of one form instead of another in a position where either can occur, as of *ask* instead of *tell* or *with* in the phrase *ask me.* **b.** the choice of one semantic or syntactic class of words in a construction, to the exclusion of others that do not occur there, as the choice of an animate object for the verb *surprise.* [1640–50; < L *sēlēctiōn-* (s. of *sēlēctiō*), equiv. to *sēlēct(us)* (see SELECT) + *-iōn-* -ION] **—se·lec′tion·al,** *adj.*
—Syn. 2. collection, gathering, pick. **—Ant. 1.** rejection.

selec′tion rule′, *Physics.* any of several rules designating allowed transitions between quantum states in terms of the quantum numbers associated with the states.

se·lec·tive (si lek′tiv), *adj.* **1.** having the function or power of selecting; making a selection. **2.** characterized by selection, esp. fastidious selection. **3.** of or pertaining to selection. **4.** *Elect., Radio.* having good selectivity. [1615–25; SELECT + -IVE] **—se·lec′tive·ly,** *adv.* **—se·lec′tive·ness,** *n.*
—Syn. 2. discriminating, particular, discerning.

selec′tive serv′ice, compulsory military service. [1919]

Selec′tive Serv′ice Sys′tem, the U.S. federal agency that facilitates the mobilization of military forces by requiring the registration of males between the ages of 18 and 26 years. *Abbr.:* SSS

selec′tive transmis′sion, *Auto.* a transmission in which the available forward and reverse gears may be engaged in any order, without passing progressively through the different changes of gear.

se·lec·tiv·i·ty (si lek tiv′i tē, sē′lek-), *n.* **1.** the state or quality of being selective. **2.** *Elect.* the property of a circuit, instrument, or the like, by virtue of which it can distinguish oscillations of a particular frequency. **3.** *Radio.* the ability of a receiving set to receive any one of a band of frequencies or waves to the exclusion of others. [1900–05; SELECTIVE + -ITY]

se·lect·man (si lekt′mən), *n., pl.* **-men.** (in most New England states) one of a board of town officers chosen to manage certain public affairs. [1625–35, *Amer.*; SELECT (adj.) + -MAN]

sel·e·nate (sel′ə nāt′), *n. Chem.* a salt or ester of selenic acid. [1810–20; SELEN(IC ACID) + -ATE²]

Se·le·ne (si lē′nē), *n.* **1.** the Greek goddess of the moon. Cf. **Thyone. 2.** Also, **Se·le′na.** a female given name. [< Gk *Selḗnē* the moon]

Sel·en·ga (sel′eng gä′), *n.* a river in N central Asia, flowing E and N through the NW Mongolian People's Republic through the Buryat Autonomous Republic in the SE Russian Federation to Lake Baikal. ab. 700 mi. (1125 km) long.

se·le·nic (si lē′nik, -len′ik), *adj. Chem.* of or containing selenium, esp. in the hexavalent state. [1810–20; SELEN(IUM) + -IC]

sele′nic ac′id, *Chem.* a crystalline, water-soluble, strong, corrosive, dibasic acid, H_2SeO_4, resembling sulfuric acid. [1810–20]

sel·e·nide (sel′ə nīd′, -nid), *n. Chem.* any compound in which bivalent selenium is combined with a positive element, as potassium selenide, K_2Se, or with a group. [1840–50; SELEN(IUM) + -IDE]

sel·e·nif·er·ous (sel′ə nif′ər əs), *adj.* containing or yielding selenium. [1815–25; SELEN(IUM) + -I- + -FEROUS]

se·le·ni·ous (si lē′nē əs), *adj. Chem.* containing tetravalent or bivalent selenium. Also, **selenous.** [1825–35; SELENI(UM) + -OUS]

sele′nious ac′id, *Chem.* a colorless, crystalline, water-soluble, poisonous powder, H_2SeO_3, used chiefly as a reagent. [1825–35]

sel·e·nite (sel′ə nīt′, si lē′nīt), *n.* **1.** *Mineral.* a variety of gypsum, found in transparent crystals and foliated masses. **2.** *Chem.* a salt of selenious acid. [1560–70; < L *selēnītēs* < Gk *selēnī́tēs líthos* moonstone; see SELENE, -ITE¹] **—sel·e·nit·ic** (sel′ə nit′ik), **sel′e·nit′i·cal,** *adj.*

se·le·ni·um (si lē′nē əm), *n. Chem.* a nonmetallic element chemically resembling sulfur and tellurium, occurring in several allotropic forms, as crystalline and amorphous, and having an electrical resistance that varies under the influence of light. *Symbol:* Se; *at. wt.:* 78.96; *at. no.:* 34; *sp. gr.:* (gray) 4.80 at 25°C, (red) 4.50 at 25°C. [< NL (1818) < Gk *selḗn(ē)* moon + NL *-ium* -IUM; named in allusion to its similarity to TELLURIUM]

sele′nium cell′, *Elect.* a photovoltaic cell consisting of a thin strip of selenium placed between two metal electrodes. [1875–80]

sele′nium rec′tifier, a rectifier consisting of laminated plates of metal, usually iron, that have been coated with selenium on one side, with rectification taking place because the flow of electrons from the conductive metal to the selenium occurs more readily than the flow in the opposite direction.

seleno-, a combining form meaning "moon," used in the formation of compound words: *selenography.* [comb. form repr. Gk *selḗnē*]

se·le·no·cen·tric (si lē′nə sen′trik), *adj. Astron.* **1.** having the moon as its center. **2.** of or pertaining to the center of the moon. [1850–55; SELENO- + -CENTRIC, modeled on GEOCENTRIC]

sel·e·nod·e·sy (sel′ə nod′ə sē), *n.* the branch of astronomy that deals with the measurement of the moon's surface and its gravitational field. [1960–65; SELENO- + (GEO)DESY] **—sel′e·nod′e·sist,** *n.*

se·le·no·dont (si lē′nə dont′), *adj.* having molar teeth with crowns formed of crescent-shaped cusps. [1880–85; SELEN(O)- + -ODONT] **—se·le′no·don′ty,** *n.*

sel·e·nog·ra·phy (sel′ə nog′rə fē), *n.* the branch of astronomy that deals with the charting of the moon's surface. [1640–50; SELENO- + -GRAPHY] **—sel′e·nog′ra·pher,** *n.* **—se·le·no·graph·ic** (si lē′nə graf′ik), *adj.*

sel·e·nol·o·gy (sel′ə nol′ə jē), *n.* the branch of astronomy that deals with the nature and origin of the physical features of the moon. [1815–25; SELENO- + -LOGY] **—se·le·no·log·i·cal** (sə lēn′l oj′i kəl), *adj.* **—sel′e·nol′o·gist,** *n.*

se·le·no·tro·pism (si lē′nə trō′piz əm, sel′ə nō-), *n. Biol.* growth in response to moonlight. [1880–85; SELENO- + -TROPISM] **—se·le·no·trop·ic** (sə lē′nə trop′ik, -trō′pik, sel′ə nō-), *adj.*

se·le·nous (sə lē′nəs, sel′ə-), *adj. Chem.* selenious.

Se·ler (zā′lər), *n.* **E·du·ard** (ā′do͞o ärt′), 1859–1922, German archaeologist: first to decipher Mayan calendar and inscriptions.

Se·leu·cia (si lo͞o′shə), *n.* **1.** an ancient city in Iraq, on the Tigris River: capital of the Seleucid empire. **2.** an ancient city in Asia Minor, near the mouth of the Orontes River: the port of Antioch.

Se·leu·cid (si lo͞o′sid), *n., pl.* **-ci·dae** (-si dē′), *adj.* —*n.* **1.** a member of a Macedonian dynasty, 312–64 B.C., that ruled an empire that included much of Asia Minor, Syria, Persia, Bactria, and Babylonia. —*adj.* **2.** of or pertaining to the Seleucids or their dynasty. [1850–55; < NL *Seleucidēs* < Gk *Seleukídēs* offspring of SELEUCUS I; see -ID¹]

Se·leu·ci·dan (si lo͞o′si dn), *adj.* Seleucid. [1795–1805; SELEUCID + -AN]

Se·leu·cus (si lo͞o′kəs), *n.* a crater in the second quadrant of the face of the moon: about 32 miles (51.2 km) in diameter.

Seleucus I, (*Seleucus Nicator*) 358?–281? B.C., Macedonian general under Alexander the Great: founder of the Seleucid dynasty.

self (self), *n., pl.* **selves,** *adj., pron., pl.* **selves,** *v.* —*n.* **1.** a person or thing referred to with respect to complete individuality: *one's own self.* **2.** a person's nature, character, etc.: *his better self.* **3.** personal interest. **4.** *Philos.* **a.** the ego; that which knows, remembers, desires, suffers, etc., as contrasted with that known, remembered, etc. **b.** the uniting principle, as a soul, underlying all subjective experience. —*adj.* **5.** being the same throughout, as a color; uniform. **6.** being of one piece with or the same material as the rest: *drapes with a self lining.* **7.** *Immunol.* the natural constituents of the body, which are normally not subject to attack by components of the immune system (contrasted with *nonself*). **8.** *Obs.* same. —*pron.* **9.** myself, himself, herself, etc.: *to make a check payable to self.* —*v.t., v.i.* **10.** to self-pollinate. [bef. 900; ME; OE *self, selfa;* c. D *zelf,* G *selb-,* ON *sjalfr,* Goth *silba*]

self-, a combining form of **self** and variously used with the meanings "of the self" (*self-analysis*) and "by oneself or itself" (*self-appointed*); and with the meanings "to, with, toward, for, on, in oneself" (*self-complacent*), "inherent in oneself or itself" (*self-explanatory*), "independent" (*self-government*), and "automatic" (*self-operating*). **—Note.** The lists at the bottom of this and following pages provide the spelling, syllabification, and stress for words whose meanings may easily be inferred by combining the meanings of SELF- and an attached base word, or base word plus a suffix. Appropriate parts of speech are also shown. Words prefixed by SELF- that have special meanings or uses are entered in their proper alphabetical places in the main vocabulary or as derived forms run on at the end of a main vocabulary entry.

self-a·ban·don·ment (self′ə ban′dən mənt), *n.* absence or lack of personal restraint. Also, **self′-a·ban′don.** [1810–20]

self-a·base·ment (self′ə bās′mənt, self′-), *n.* humiliation of oneself, esp. as a result of guilt, shame, or the like. [1650–60]

self-ab·ne·ga·tion (self′ab′ni gā′shən), *n.* self-denial or self-sacrifice. [1650–60] **—self′-ab′ne·gat′ing,** *adj.*

self-ab·sorbed (self′ab sôrbd′, -zôrbd′, self′-), *adj.* preoccupied with one's thoughts, interests, etc. [1840–50]

self-ab·sorp·tion (self′ab sôrp′shən, -zôrp′-, self′-), *n.* preoccupation with oneself or one's own affairs. [1860–65]

self-a·buse (self′ə byo͞os′, self′-), *n.* **1.** reproach or blame of oneself. **2.** abuse of one's health. **3.** masturbation. [1595–1605]

self-act·ing (self′ak′ting), *adj.* acting by itself; automatic. [1670–80] **—self′-ac′tion,** *n.*

self-ac·tu·al·i·za·tion (self′ak′cho͞o ə lə zā′shən, self′ak-), *n. Psychol.* the achievement of one's full potential through creativity, independence, spontaneity, and a grasp of the real world. Also called **actualization.** [1935–40]

self-ac·tu·al·ize (self′ak′cho͞o ə līz′, self′-), *v.i.,* **-ized, -iz·ing.** to undergo self-actualization. Also, *esp. Brit.,* **self′-ac′tu·al·ise′.** **—self′-ac′tu·al·iz′er,** *n.*

self-ad·dressed (self′ə drest′), *adj.* addressed for return to the sender. [1840–50]

self-ad·he·sive (self′ad hē′siv), *adj.* having a side or surface coated with an adhesive substance to permit sticking without glue, paste, or the like: *a self-adhesive label; self-adhesive ceramic tiles.*

self-ad·just·ment (self′ə just′mənt, self′-), *n.* **1.** adjustment of oneself or itself, as to the environment. **2.** the process of resolving one's problems or reactions to stress without outside intervention. [1915–20]

self-ad·mit·ted (self′ad mit′id), *adj.* admitting to a specific charge or accusation; self-confessed: *a self-admitted spy.* **—self′-ad·mit′ted·ly,** *adv.*

self-ag·gran·dize·ment (self′ə gran′diz mənt, self′-), *n.* increase of one's own power, wealth, etc., usually aggressively. [1790–1800] **—self-ag·gran·diz·ing** (self′ə-gran′dī zing), *adj.*

self-a·nal·y·sis (self′ə nal′ə sis, self′-), *n.* the application of psychoanalytic techniques and theories to an analysis of one's own personality and behavior, esp. without the aid of a psychiatrist or other trained person. Also called **autoanalysis.** [1860–65] **—self-an·a·lyt·i·cal** (self′an′l it′i kəl, self′-), *adj.*

self-an·a·lyzed (self′an′l īzd′), *adj.* having undergone self-analysis.

self-an·ni·hi·la·tion (self′ə nī′ə lā′shən, self′-), *n.* **1.** self-destruction; suicide. **2.** surrender, abnegation, or immolation of the self in mystic contemplation of or union with God. [1640–50]

self-an·ti·gen (self′an′ti jən, -jen′), *n. Immunol.* autoantigen. Also, **self′ an′tigen.** [1970–75]

self-ap·point·ed (self′ə poin′tid), *adj.* chosen by oneself to act in a certain capacity or to fulfill a certain function, esp. pompously or self-righteously: *a self-appointed guardian of the public's morals.* [1790–1800] **—self′-ap·point′ment,** *n.*

self-as·ser·tion (self′ə sûr′shən, self′-), *n.* insistence on or an expression of one's own importance, wishes, needs, opinions, or the like. [1795–1805] **—self′-as·sert′ing,** *adj.* **—self′-as·sert′ing·ly,** *adv.* **—self′-as·ser′tive,** *adj.* **—self′-as·ser′tive·ly,** *adv.* **—self′-as·ser′tive·ness,** *n.*
—Syn. assertiveness, aggressiveness, belligerence.

self-as·sur·ance (self′ə sho͝or′əns, self′-), *n.* self-confidence. [1585–95]

self-as·sured (self′ə sho͝ord′), *adj.* self-confident. [1705–15] **—self-as·sur·ed·ness** (self′ə sho͝or′id nis), *n.*
—Syn. assured, confident, cocky, positive.

self-bi·as (self′bī′əs), *n. Electronics.* voltage developed on an electrode in a vacuum tube circuit as a result of current flowing through a resistor in a lead to the cathode or to a grid.

self-bind·er (self′bīn′dər), *n. Agric.* binder (def. 5b). [1880–85, *Amer.*]

self-care (self′kâr′), *n.* care of the self without medical or other professional consultation.

CONCISE PRONUNCIATION KEY: act, cāpe, dâre, pärt; set, ēqual; if, īce; ox, ōver, ôrder, oil, bo͝ok, bo͞ot, out; up, ûrge; child; sing; shoe; thin, *th*at; zh as in *treasure.* ə = *a* as in *alone, e* as in *system, i* as in *easily, o* as in *gallop, u* as in *circus;* ᵊ as in *fire* (fīᵊr), *hour* (ouᵊr). l and n can serve as syllabic consonants, as in *cradle* (krād′l), and *button* (but′n). See the full key inside the front cover.

self′-ab·hor′rence, *n.*
self′-a·bom′i·nat′ing, *adj.*
self′-a·bom′i·na′tion, *n.*
self′-ac·cel′er·at′ing, *adj.*
self′-ac·cep′tance, *n.*
self′-ac′cu·sa′tion, *n.*
self′-ac·cu′sa·tive, *adj.*
self′-ac·cu′sa·to′ry, *adj.*
self′-ac·cused′, *adj.*
self′-ac·cus′er, *n.*
self′-ac·cus′ing, *adj.*
self′-ac·knowl′edged, *adj.*
self′-ac·quired′, *adj.*
self′-ac′tu·at′ing, *adj.*
self′-ad·just′ing, *adj.*
self′-ad·min′is·tered, *adj.*
self′-ad·min′is·ter·ing, *adj.*
self′-ad·min′is·tra′tion, *n.*
self′-ad′mi·ra′tion, *n.*
self′-ad·mir′ing, *adj.*
self′-a·dorn′ing, *adj.*
self′-a·dorn′ment, *n.*
self′-ad′u·la′tion, *n.*
self′-ad′u·la·to′ry, *adj.*
self′-ad·vance′ment, *n.*
self′-ad′ver·tise′ment, *n.*
self′-ad′ver·tis′ing, *adj., n.*
self′-af′fir·ma′tion, *n.*
self′-af·flict′ing, *adj.*
self′-af·fright′ed, *adj.*
self′-a·lign′ing, *adj.*
self′-a·lign′ment, *n.*
self′-a·line′ment, *n.*
self′-a·lin′ing, *adj.*
self′-a·mend′ment, *n.*
self′-am′pu·ta′tion, *n.*
self′-a·muse′ment, *n.*
self′-an·nul′ling, *adj.*
self′-an·oint′ed, *adj.*
self′-an·tith′e·sis, *n.*
self′-ap·par′ent, *adj.*
self′-ap·plaud′ing, *adj.*
self′-ap·plause′, *n.*
self′-ap·prais′al, *n.*
self′-ap·pre′ci·at′ing, *adj.*
self′-ap·pre′ci·a′tion, *n.*
self′-ap′pro·ba′tion, *n.*
self′-ap·prov′al, *n.*
self′-ap·proved′, *adj.*
self′-ap·prov′ing, *adj.*
self′-as·sem′bly, *n., pl.* **-blies.**
self′-as·sess′ment, *n.*
self′-as·signed′, *adj.*
self′-as·sumed′, *adj.*
self′-as·sum′ing, *adj.*
self′-as·sump′tion, *n.*
self′-at·tach′ment, *n.*
self′-au·then′ti·cat′ing, *adj.*
self′-au′thor·ized′, *adj.*
self′-au′thor·iz′ing, *adj.*
self′-a·vowed′, *adj.*
self′-a·ware′, *adj.;* **-ness,** *n.*
self′-bal′anced, *adj.*
self′-ban′ished, *adj.*
self′-ban′ish·ment, *n.*
self′-bap′tiz·er, *n.*
self′-be·got′ten, *adj.*
self′-ben′e·fit, *n.*
self′-ben′e·fit·ing, *adj.*
self′-be·tray′al, *n.*
self′-be·tray′ing, *adj.*
self′-bet′ter·ment, *n.*
self′-blame′, *n.*
self′-blind′ed, *adj.*
self′-born′, *adj.*
self′-can′celed, *adj.*
self′-can′celled, *adj.*
self′-car′i·ca·ture, *n.*
self′-cas′ti·gat′ing, *adj.*
self′-cas′ti·ga′tion, *n.*
self′-ca·tal′y·sis, *n.*
self′-cat′a·lyst, *n.*
self′-caused′, *adj.*
self′-cen′sor·ship′, *n.*
self′-chang′ing, *adj.*
self′-char′ac·ter·i·za′tion, *n.*
self′-charg′ing, *adj.*
self′-chas′tise, *v.t.,* **-tised, -tis·ing.**
self′-chas·tise′ment, *n.*
self′-clean′ing, *adj.*
self′-clear′ance, *n.*
self′-clos′ing, *adj.*
self′-cock′er, *n.*
self′-cock′ing, *adj.*
self′-cog·ni′tion, *n.*
self′-cog′ni·zance, *n.*
self′-com·bat′ing, *adj.*
self′-com·bus′tion, *n.*
self′-com′men·da′tion, *n.*
self′-com·mit′ment, *n.*
self′-com·mit′tal, *n.*
self′-com·mit′ting, *adj.*
self′-com·mu′ni·ca′tion, *n.*
self′-com·mun′ing, *adj.*
self′-com·mun′ion, *n.*
self′-com′pre·hend′ing, *adj.*
self′-con·cern′, *n.*
self′-con′dem·na′tion, *n.*
self′-con·dem′na·to′ry, *adj.*
self′-con·demned′, *adj.*
self′-con·demn′ing, *adj.*
self′-con·di′tioned, *adj.*
self′-con·di′tion·ing, *adj.*
self′-con·fine′ment, *n.*
self′-con·fin′ing, *adj.*
self′-con′fir·ma′tion, *n.*
self′-con′flict, *n.*
self′-con′quest, *n.*
self′-con′ser·va′tion, *n.*
self′-con·serv′ing, *adj.*
self′-con·sol′ing, *adj.*
self′-con′sti·tut′ed, *adj.*
self′-con′sti·tut′ing, *adj.*
self′-con·sum′ing, *adj.*
self′-con·sump′tion, *n.*
self′-con·tam′i·nat′ing, *adj.*
self′-con·tam′i·na′tion, *n.*
self′-con·tempt′, *n.*
self′-con·vict′ed, *adj.*
self′-cook′ing, *adj.*
self′-cre·at′ed, *adj.*
self′-cre·at′ing, *adj.*
self′-cre·a′tion, *n.*
self′-cru′el·ty, *n., pl.* **-ties.**
self′-cul′ti·va′tion, *n.*
self′-cure′, *n.*
self′-cut′ting, *adj.*
self′-dam·na′tion, *n.*
self′-damn′ing, *adj.*
self′-de·base′ment, *n.*
self′-ded′i·cat′ed, *adj.*
self′-ded′i·ca′tion, *n.*
self′-de·fined′, *adj.*
self′-de·fin′ing, *adj.*
self′-def′i·ni′tion, *n.*
self′-de·flat′ed, *adj.*
self′-de·fla′tion, *n.*
self′-deg′ra·da′tion, *n.*
self′-de′i·fy′ing, *adj.*
self′-de·jec′tion, *n.*
self′-de·light′, *n.*
self′-de·mag′net·iz′ing, *adj.*
self′-den′i·grat′ing, *adj.*
self′-den·i·gra′tion, *n.*
self′-de·pend′ence, *n.*
self′-de·pend′en·cy, *n.*
self′-de·pend′ent, *adj.;* **-ly,** *adv.*
self′-de·pend′ing, *adj.*
self′-de·praved′, *adj.*
self′-dep′ri·va′tion, *n.*
self′-de·prived′, *adj.*

self-cen•tered (self′sen′tərd), *adj.* **1.** concerned solely or chiefly with one's own interests, welfare, etc.; engrossed in self; selfish; egotistical. **2.** independent, self-sufficient. **3.** centered in oneself or itself. **4.** *Archaic:* fixed; unchanging. Also, *esp. Brit.,* **self′-cen′tred.** [1670–80] —**self′cen′tered•ly,** *adv.* —**self′-cen′tered•ness,** *n.*

self-col•lect•ed (self′kə lek′tid, self′-), *adj.* having or showing self-control; composed; self-possessed. [1705–15] —**self′-col•lect′ed•ness,** *n.*

self-col•ored (self′kul′ərd, self′-), *adj.* **1.** of one color. **2.** of the natural color. Also, *esp. Brit.,* **self′-col′oured.** [1750–60]

self-com•mand (self′kə mand′, -mänd′, self′-), *n.* self-control. [1690–1700]

self-com•pla•cent (self′kəm plā′sənt, self′-), *adj.* pleased with oneself; self-satisfied; smug. [1755–65] —**self′-com•pla′cence, self′-com•pla′cen•cy,** *n.* —**self′-com•pla′cent•ly,** *adv.*

self-com•posed (self′kəm pōzd′, self′-), *adj.* being or appearing to be composed; calm. [1930–35] —**self-com•pos•ed•ly** (self′kəm pō′zid lē, self′-), *adv.* —**self′-com•pos′ed•ness,** *n.*

self-con•ceit (self′kən sēt′, self′-), *n.* an excessively favorable opinion of oneself, one's abilities, etc.; vanity. [1580–90] —**self′-con•ceit′ed,** *adj.* —**self′-con•ceit′ed•ly,** *adv.* —**self′-con•ceit′ed•ness,** *n.*

self-con•cept (self′kon′sept, self′-), *n.* the idea or mental image one has of oneself and one's strengths, weaknesses, status, etc.; self-image. [1920–25]

self-con•fessed (self′kən fest′, self′-), *adj.* openly admitting to being a type of person with a particular quality, habit, character, etc.: *He's a self-confessed gambler.* [1915–20]

self-con•fi•dence (self′kon′fi dəns, self′-), *n.* **1.** realistic confidence in one's own judgment, ability, power, etc. **2.** excessive or inflated confidence in one's own judgment, ability, etc. [1630–40] —**self′-con′fi•dent,** *adj.* —**self′-con′fi•dent•ly,** *adv.*
—**Syn. 1.** assurance, self-possession, self-respect, poise. **2.** conceit, self-esteem.

self-con•grat•u•la•tion (self′kən grach′ə lā′shən, *or, often,* -graj′-, -kəng-, self′-), *n.* the expression or feeling of uncritical satisfaction with oneself or one's own accomplishment, good fortune, etc.; complacency. [1705–15] —**self-con•grat•u•la•to•ry** (self′kən grach′ə lə tôr′ē, -tōr′ē, *or, often,* -graj′-, -kəng-, self′-), *adj.* —**self′-con•grat′u•lat′ing,** *adj.*

self-con•scious (self′kon′shəs, self′-), *adj.* **1.** excessively aware of being observed by others. **2.** conscious of oneself or one's own being. [1670–80] —**self′-con′scious•ly,** *adv.* —**self′-con′scious•ness,** *n.*

self-con•se•cra•tion (self′kon si krā′shən), *n.* the act of setting oneself to a task or vocation without ordination by others or by a religious body.

self-con•se•quence (self′kon′si kwens, self′-), *n.* self-important character or quality; self-importance. [1770–80]

self-con•sist•ent (self′kən sis′tənt, self′-), *n.* consistent with oneself or itself. [1675–85] —**self′-con•sis′ten•cy,** *n.* —**self′-con•sis′tent•ly,** *adv.*

self-con•tained (self′kən tānd′, self′-), *adj.* **1.** containing in oneself or itself all that is necessary; independent. **2.** reserved or uncommunicative. **3.** self-controlled or self-possessed. **4.** (of a machine or mechanism) complete in itself. [1585–95] —**self-con•tain•ed•ly** (self′kən tā′nid lē, self′-), *adv.* —**self′-con•tain′ed•ness,** *n.*

self-con•tain•ment (self′kən tān′mənt, self′-), *n.* the state of being self-contained. [1840–50]

self-con•tem•pla•tion (self′kon′təm plā′shən, self′-), *n.* the act or process of thinking about oneself or one's values, beliefs, behavior, etc.

CONCISE ETYMOLOGY KEY: <, descended or borrowed from; >, whence; b., blend of, blended; c., cognate with; cf., compare; deriv., derivative; equiv., equivalent; imit., imitative; obl., oblique; r., replacing; s., stem; sp., spelling, spelled; resp., respelling, respelled; trans., translation; ?, origin unknown; *, unattested; ‡, probably earlier than. See the full key inside the front cover.

self-con•tent (self′kən tent′, self′-), *n.* **1.** satisfaction with oneself; self-complacency. —*adj.* **2.** content with oneself; self-satisfied. Also, **self′-con•tent′ment.** [1645–55] —**self′-con•tent′ed•ly,** *adv.* —**self′-con•tent′ed•ness,** *n.*

self-con•tra•dic•tion (self′kon′trə dik′shən, self′-), *n.* **1.** an act or instance of contradicting oneself or itself. **2.** a statement containing contradictory elements. [1650–60] —**self′-con′tra•dict′ing,** *adj.* —**self′-con′tra•dic′to•ry,** *adj.*

self-con•trol (self′kən trōl′, self′-), *n.* control or restraint of oneself or one's actions, feelings, etc. [1705–15] —**self′-con•trolled′,** *adj.* —**self′-con•trol′ling,** *adj.*
—**Syn.** self-discipline, self-restraint, willpower, levelheadedness.

self-cor•rect•ing (self′kə rek′ting, self′-), *adj.* automatically adjusting to or correcting mistakes, malfunctions, etc.: *a self-correcting mechanism.* Also, **self′-cor•rec′tive.** [1935–40] —**self′-cor•rec′tion,** *n.*

self-crit•i•cal (self′krit′i kəl, self′-), *adj.* **1.** capable of criticizing oneself objectively. **2.** tending to find fault with one's own actions, motives, etc. —**self′-crit′i•cal•ly,** *adv.*

self-crit•i•cism (self′krit′ə siz′əm, self′-), *n.* the act or fact of being self-critical. [1855–60]

self-deal•ing (self′dē′ling), *n.* financial transaction conducted on a personal, nonbusinesslike basis, as lending or borrowing of corporate money by a director. [1935–40]

self-de•ceived (self′di sēvd′, self′-), *adj.* **1.** holding an erroneous opinion of oneself, one's own effort, or the like. **2.** being mistaken, forming an erroneous judgment, etc., in one's own mind, as from careless or wishful thinking: *If you thought my friendship was love, you were self-deceived.* [1665–75]

self-de•ceiv•ing (self′di sē′ving, self′-), *adj.* **1.** subject to self-deception; tending to deceive or fool oneself: *a self-deceiving person.* **2.** used in deceiving oneself, esp. in justifying a false belief, a morally reprehensible act, or the like: *a self-deceiving argument.* [1605–15]

self-de•cep•tion (self′di sep′shən, self′-), *n.* the act or fact of deceiving oneself. Also called **self-de•ceit** (self′di sēt′, self′-). [1670–80] —**self′-de•cep′tive,** *adj.*

self-de•feat•ing (self′di fē′ting, self′-), *adj.* serving to frustrate, thwart, etc., one's own intention or interests: *His behavior was certainly self-defeating.*

self-de•fense (self′di fens′, self′-), *n.* **1.** the act of defending one's person when physically attacked, as by countering blows or overcoming an assailant: *the art of self-defense.* **2.** a claim or plea that the use of force or injuring or killing another was necessary in defending one's own person from physical attack: *He shot the man who was trying to stab him and pleaded self-defense at the murder trial.* **3.** an act or instance of defending or protecting one's own interests, property, ideas, etc., as by argument or strategy. Also, *esp. Brit.,* **self′-de•fence′.** [1645–55] —**self′-de•fen′sive,** *adj.*

self-de•lu•sion (self′di lo͞o′zhən, self′-), *n.* the act or fact of deluding oneself. [1625–35] —**self-de•lud•ed** (self′di lo͞o′did, self′-), *adj.* —**self′-de•lud′ing,** *adj.*

self-de•ni•al (self′di nī′əl, self′-), *n.* **1.** the sacrifice of one's own desires; unselfishness. **2.** an act or instance of restraining or curbing one's desires: *To reduce, one has to practice self-denial at the dinner table.* [1635–45] —**self′-de•ny′ing,** *adj.* —**self′-de•ny′ing•ly,** *adv.*

self-dep•re•cat•ing (self′dep′ri kā′ting, self′-), *adj.* belittling or undervaluing oneself; excessively modest. Also, **self-dep•re•ca•to•ry** (self′dep′ri kə tôr′ē, -tōr′ē, self′-). —**self′-dep′re•cat′ing•ly,** *adv.* —**self′-dep•re•ca′tion,** *n.*

self-de•pre•ci•at•ing (self′di prē′shē ā′ting, self′-), *adj.* self-deprecating. Also, **self′-de•pre′ci•a′tive.** —**self′-de•pre′ci•a′tion,** *n.*

self-de•struct (self′di strukt′), *v.i.* **1.** to destroy itself or oneself: *The missile is built so that a malfunction will cause it to self-destruct.* **2.** to cause itself or oneself to reach a state of collapse, dysfunction, confusion, or the like: *The committee is so disorganized it will probably self-destruct before it can accomplish anything.* —*adj.* **3.** causing something to self-destruct: *a self-destruct mechanism.* [1965–70, *Amer.*]

self-de•struc•tion (self′di struk′shən, self′-), *n.* **1.** the destruction or ruination of oneself or one's life. **2.** suicide. [1580–90]

self-de•struc•tive (self′di struk′tiv, self′-), *adj.* **1.** harmful, injurious, or destructive to oneself: *His constant arguing with the boss shows he's a self-destructive person.* **2.** reflecting or exhibiting suicidal desires or drives: *Careless driving may be a self-destructive tendency.* [1645–55] —**self′-de•struc′tive•ly,** *adv.*

self-de•ter•mi•na•tion (self′di tûr′mə nā′shən, self′-), *n.* **1.** determination by oneself or itself, without outside influence. **2.** freedom to live as one chooses, or to act or decide without consulting another or others. **3.** the determining by the people of the form their government shall have, without reference to the wishes of any other nation, esp. by people of a territory or former colony. [1670–80; 1915–20 for def. 3] —**self′-de•ter′mined,** *adj.* —**self′-de•ter′min•ing,** *adj.*

self-de•ter•min•ism (self′di tûr′mə niz′əm, self′-), *n. Philos.* a theory that every present state or condition of the self is a result of previous states or conditions of the self.

self-de•vo•tion (self′di vō′shən, self′-), *n.* **1.** intense devotion of oneself to an activity or to a field or profession, as art or science. **2.** devotion of oneself to the care or service of another or others; self-sacrifice: *Her self-devotion to her sick mother prevented her from finishing college.* [1805–15] —**self′-de•vot′ed,** *adj.* —**self′-de•vot′ed•ly,** *adv.* —**self′-de•vot′ed•ness,** *n.*

self-di•ag•no•sis (self′dī′əg nō′sis), *n., pl.* **-ses** (-sēz). **1.** the diagnosis of one's own malady or illness. **2.** the capability of an electronic system to detect and analyze an error or malfunction within itself. —**self′-di′ag•nos′ing,** *adj.* —**self-di•ag•nos•tic** (self′dī′əg nos′tik), *adj.*

self-dis•ci•pline (self′dis′ə plin, self′-), *n.* discipline and training of oneself, usually for improvement: *Acquiring the habit of promptness requires self-discipline.* [1830–40] —**self′-dis′ciplined,** *adj.*

self-dis•trust (self′dis trust′, self′-), *n.* lack of confidence in oneself, in one's abilities, etc. [1780–90] —**self′-dis•trust′ful,** *adj.* —**self′-dis•trust′ing,** *adj.*

self-doubt (self′dout′), *n.* lack of confidence in the reliability of one's own motives, personality, thought, etc. [1840–50] —**self′-doubt′ing,** *adj.*

self-dram•a•tiz•ing (self′dram′ə tī′zing, -drä′mə-, self′-), *adj.* exaggerating one's own qualities, role, situation, etc., for dramatic effect or as an attention-getting device; presenting oneself dramatically. [1935–40] —**self′-dram′a•ti•za′tion,** *n.*

self-drive (self′drīv′), *adj. Chiefly Brit.* of, for, designating, or providing a car that is rented for personal use, without a hired driver. [1950–55]

self-driv•en (self′driv′ən, self′-), *adj.* (of a machine) containing its own power source, as an engine or motor. [1780–90]

self-ed•u•cat•ed (self′ej′o͝o kā′tid, self′-), *adj.* educated by one's own efforts, esp. without formal instruction. [1810–20] —**self′-ed′u•cat′ing,** *adj.* —**self′-ed′u•ca′tion,** *n.*

self-ef•face•ment (self′i fās′mənt, self′-), *n.* the act or fact of keeping oneself in the background, as in humility. [1865–70] —**self′-ef•fac′ing,** *adj.* —**self′-ef•fac′ing•ly,** *adv.* —**self′-ef•fac′ing•ness,** *n.*

self-em•ployed (self′em ploid′, self′-), *adj.* earning one's living directly from one's own profession or business, as a freelance writer or artist, rather than as an employee earning salary or commission from another. [1945–50]

self-em•ploy•ment (self′em ploi′mənt, self′-), *n.* the act or fact of being self-employed. [1735–45]

self-en•er•giz•ing (self′en′ər jī′zing), *adj.* giving rise to energy or power from within itself or oneself; capable of generating energy or power automatically. [1930–35]

self-en•forc•ing (self′en fôr′sing, -fōr′-), *adj.* of or

self′-de•priv′ing, *adj.*
self′-de•rived′, *adj.*
self′-de•scribed′, *adj.*
self′-de•scrip′tion, *n.*
self′-de•scrip′tive, *adj.*
self′-de•ser′tion, *n.*
self′-de•serv′ing, *adj.*
self′-de•sign′, *n.*
self′-de•sign′er, *n.*
self′-de•sire′, *n.*
self′-de•spair′, *n.*
self′-de•stroyed′, *adj.*
self′-de•stroy′er, *n.*
self′-de•stroy′ing, *adj.*
self′-de•tach′ing, *adj.*
self′-de•vel′op•ing, *adj.*
self′-de•vel′op•ment, *n.*
self′-de•vised′, *adj.*
self′-de•vour′ing, *adj.*
self′-di′a•log′, *n.*
self′-di′a•logue′, *n.*
self′-dif′fer•en′ti•at′ing, *adj.*
self′-dif′fer•en′ti•a′tion, *n.*
self′-dif•fu′sion, *n.*
self′-dif•fu′sive, *adj.;* **-ly,** *adv.* **-ness,** *n.*
self′-di•ges′tion, *n.*
self′-di•lat′ed, *adj.*
self′-di•la′tion, *n.*
self′-di•rect′ed, *adj.*
self′-di•rect′ing, *adj.*
self′-di•rec′tion, *n.*
self′-di•rec′tive, *adj.*
self′-di•rec′tor, *n.*
self′-dis′ap•pro•ba′tion, *n.*
self′-dis′ap•prov′al, *n.*
self′-dis•cern′ment, *n.*
self′-dis•closed′, *adj.*
self′-dis•clo′sure, *n.*
self′-dis•col′or•a′tion, *n.*
self′-dis′con•tent′ed, *adj.*
self′-dis•cov′er•y, *n., pl.* **-er•ies.**
self′-dis•crep′ant, *adj.;* **-ly,** *adv.*
self′-dis•crim′i•na′tion, *n.*
self′-dis•dain′, *n.*
self′-dis′en•gag′ing, *adj.*
self′-dis•grace′, *n.*
self′-dis•graced′, *adj.*
self′-dis•grac′ing, *adj.*
self′-dis•gust′, *n.*
self′-dis•like′, *n.*
self′-dis•liked′, *adj.*
self′-dis•par′age•ment, *n.*
self′-dis•par′ag•ing, *adj.*
self′-dis•patch′, *n.*
self′-dis•play′, *n.*
self′-dis•pleased′, *adj.*
self′-dis•pos′al, *n.*
self′-dis•praise′, *n.*
self′-dis•qui′et•ing, *adj.*
self′-dis•sat′is•fac′tion, *n.*
self′-dis•sat′is•fied′, *adj.*
self′-dis•sect′ing, *adj.*
self′-dis•sec′tion, *n.*
self′-dis•serv′ice, *n.*
self′-dis•serv′ing, *adj.*
self′-dis•so′ci•a′tion, *n.*
self′-dis′so•lu′tion, *n.*
self′-dis•solved′, *adj.*
self′-dis•tin′guish•ing, *adj.*
self′-di•vid′ed, *adj.*
self′-di•vi′sion, *n.*
self′-doc′trine, *n.*
self′-dom′i•nance, *n.*
self′-do•min′ion, *n.*
self′-do•na′tion, *n.*
self′-doomed′, *adj.*
self′-draw′ing, *n., adj.*
self′-du′pli•cat′ing, *adj.*
self′-du′pli•ca′tion, *n.*
self′-ease′, *n.*
self′-eas′ing, *adj.*
self′-e•lab′o•rat′ed, *adj.*
self′-e•lab′o•ra′tion, *n.*
self′-e•la′tion, *n.*
self′-e•lect′ed, *adj.*
self′-e•lec′tion, *n.*
self′-e•man′ci•pa′tion, *n.*
self′-e•mas′cu•la′tion, *n.*
self′-e•mit′ted, *adj.*
self′-emp′ti•ness, *n.*
self′-emp′ty•ing, *adj.*
self′-en•am′ored, *adj.*
self′-en•closed′, *adj.*
self′-en•dear′ing, *adj.*
self′-en′er•gy, *n.*
self′-en•grossed′, *adj.*
self′-en•gross′ment, *n.*
self′-en•hance′ment, *n.*
self′-en•joy′ment, *n.*
self′-en•rich′ing, *adj.*
self′-en•rich′ment, *n.*
self′-en′ter•tain′ing, *adj.*
self′-en′ter•tain′ment, *n.*
self′-e•rect′ed, *adj.*
self′-es•cape′, *n.*
self′-es′sence, *n.*
self′-es′ti•mate, *n.*
self′-es′ti•ma′tion, *n.*
self′-es•trange′ment, *n.*
self′-e•val′u•a′tion, *n.*
self′-e•volved′, *adj.*
self′-e•volv′ing, *adj.*
self′-ex•ag′ger•at′ed, *adj.*
self′-ex•ag′ger•a′tion, *n.*
self′-ex′al•ta′tion, *n.*
self′-ex•alt′ed, *adj.*
self′-ex•alt′ing, *adj.*
self′-ex•clu′sion, *n.*
self′-ex′cul•pa′tion, *n.*
self′-ex•cuse′, *n.*
self′-ex•cused′, *adj.*
self′-ex•cus′ing, *adj.*
self′-ex•er′tion, *n.*
self′-ex•hib′it•ed, *adj.*
self′-ex′hi•bi′tion, *n.*
self′-ex•pand′ed, *adj.*
self′-ex•pand′ing, *adj.*
self′-ex•pan′sion, *n.*
self′-ex•pa′tri•a′tion, *n.*
self′-ex′pli•ca′tion, *n.*
self′-ex•ploit′ed, *adj.*
self′-ex•ploit′ing, *adj.*
self′-ex•posed′, *adj.*
self′-ex•pos′ing, *adj.*
self′-ex•po′sure, *n.*
self′-ex•ter′mi•na′tion, *n.*
self′-ex•tinc′tion, *n.*
self′-ex•tin′guish•ing, *adj.*
self′-ex•tolled′, *adj.*
self′-ex′ul•ta′tion, *n.*
self′-ex•ult′ing, *adj.*
self′-fame′, *n.*
self′-farm′ing, *n.*
self′-fear′ing, *adj.*
self′-fe•lic′i•ta′tion, *n.*
self′-fer′men•ta′tion, *n.*
self′-fig′ured, *adj.*
self′-fill′ing, *adj.*
self′-fi•nance′, *v.t.,* **-nanced, -nanc•ing.**
self′-fit′ting, *adj.*
self′-flag′el•la′tion, *n.*
self′-flow′ing, *adj.*
self′-fo′cused, *adj.*
self′-fo′cus•ing, *adj.*
self′-fo′cussed, *adj.*
self′-fo′cus•sing, *adj.*
self′-fold′ing, *adj.*
self′-fond′ness, *n.*
self′-for•bid′den, *adj.*
self′-for•ma′tion, *n.*

having the capability of enforcement within oneself or itself; self-regulating. [1950–55] —**self′-en•force′•ment,** *n.*

self-es•teem (self′i stēm′, self′-), *n.* **1.** a realistic respect for or favorable impression of oneself; self-respect. **2.** an inordinately or exaggeratedly favorable impression of oneself. [1650–60]
—**Syn.** See **pride.** —**Ant.** diffidence.

self-ev•i•dent (self′ev′i dənt, self′-), *adj.* evident in itself without proof or demonstration; axiomatic. [1665–75] —**self′-ev′i•dence,** *n.* —**self′-ev′i•dent•ly,** *adv.*
—**Syn.** obvious, self-explanatory.

self-ex•am•i•na•tion (self′ig zam′ə nā′shən, self′-), *n.* **1.** examination into one's own state, conduct, motives, etc. **2.** *Med.* examination of one's body for signs of illness or disease: *breast self-examination.* [1640–50] —**self′-ex•am′in•ing,** *adj.*

self-ex•cit•ed (self′ik sī′tid), *adj. Elect.* noting a generator with magnets that are excited by the current it produces. [1895–1900] —**self-ex•ci•ta•tion** (self′ek′sī-tā′shən, -si-), *n.* —**self′-ex•cit′er,** *n.*

self-ex•e•cut•ing (self′ek′si kyōō′ting, self′-), *adj.* going into effect immediately without the need of supplementary legislation: *a self-executing treaty.* [1865–70]

self-ex•ile (self′eg′zīl, -ek′sīl, self′-), *n.* **1.** a state of exile imposed by oneself. **2.** a person who lives voluntarily as an exile. [1820–30] —**self′-ex′iled,** *adj.*

self-ex•ist•ent (self′ig zis′tənt, self′-), *adj.* **1.** existing independently of any cause, as God. **2.** having an independent existence. [1695–1705] —**self′-ex•ist′•ence,** *n.*

self-ex•plan•a•to•ry (self′ik splan′ə tôr′ē, -tōr′ē, self′-), *adj.* explaining itself; needing no explanation; obvious. Also, **self-ex•plain•ing** (self′ik splā′ning, self′-). [1895–1900]

self-ex•pres•sion (self′ik spresh′ən, self′-), *n.* the expression or assertion of one's own personality, as in conversation, behavior, poetry, or painting. [1890–95] —**self′-ex•pres′sive,** *adj.*

self-feed (self′fēd′, self′-), *v.t.,* **-fed, -feed•ing.** *Agric.* to provide a supply of food to (animals) so as to allow them to eat as much and as often as they want. Cf. **hand-feed** (def. 1). [1865–70]

self-feed•er (self′fē′dər, self′-), *n.* an apparatus or machine that automatically discharges a supply of some material, esp. one consisting of a hopper and a trough for feeding livestock. [1825–35]

self-fer•tile (self′fûr′tl *or, esp. Brit.,* -tīl, self′-), *adj. Zool.* capable of self-fertilization. [1855–60]

self-fer•ti•li•za•tion (self′fûr′tl ə zā′shən, self′-), *n.* **1.** *Bot.* fertilization of an ovum of a plant by a male gamete from the same flower (opposed to *cross-fertilization*). **2.** *Zool.* fertilization of the ovum of a hermaphroditic animal by a sperm from the same individual, as in some species of tapeworm. [1855–60] —**self′-fer′ti•lized′,** *adj.*

self-flat•ter•y (self′flat′ə rē, self′-), *n.* praise and exaggeration of one's own achievements coupled with a denial or glossing over of one's faults or failings; self-congratulation. [1670–80] —**self′-flat′ter•ing,** *adj.*

self-for•get•ful (self′fər get′fəl, self′-), *adj.* forgetful or not thinking of one's own advantage, interest, etc. [1860–65] —**self′-for•get′ful•ly,** *adv.* —**self′-for•get′ful•ness,** *n.*

self-for•get•ting (self′fər get′ing, self′-), *adj.* self-forgetful. [1840–50] —**self′-for•get′ting•ly,** *adv.*

self-ful•fill•ing (self′fŏŏl fil′ing), *adj.* **1.** characterized by or bringing about self-fulfillment. **2.** happening or brought about as a result of being foretold, expected, or talked about: *a self-fulfilling prophecy.* [1950–55]

self-ful•fill•ment (self′fŏŏl fil′mənt, self′-), *n.* the act or fact of fulfilling one's ambitions, desires, etc., through one's own efforts. Also, *esp. Brit.,* **self′-ful•fil′ment.** [1860–65]

self-gen•er•at•ed (self′jen′ə rā′tid, self′-), *adj.* made without the aid of an external agent; produced spontaneously.

self-gen•er•at•ing (self′jen′ə rā′ting, self′-), *adj.* producing from within itself. Also, **self-gen•er•a•tive** (self′jen′ər ə tiv, -ə rā′tiv, self′-).

self-gen•er•a•tion (self′jen′ə rā′shən), *n.* production or reproduction of something without the aid of an external agent; spontaneous generation.

self-gov•erned (self′guv′ərnd, self′-), *adj.* **1.** governed by itself or having self-government, as a state or community; independent. **2.** self-regulating; self-determining. **3.** exercising self-restraint or self-control. [1700–10] —**self′-gov′ern•ing,** *adj.*
—**Syn. 1.** autonomous. —**Ant. 1.** dependent.

self-gov•ern•ment (self′guv′ərn mənt, -ər mənt, self′-), *n.* **1.** control of the government of a state, community, or other body by its own members; democratic government. **2.** the condition of being self-governed. **3.** self-control. [1725–35]

self-grat•i•fi•ca•tion (self′grat′ə fi kā′shən, self′-), *n.* the act of pleasing or satisfying oneself, esp. the gratifying of one's own impulses, needs, or desires. [1670–80]

self-hard•en•ing (self′här′dn ing, self′-), *adj.* noting or pertaining to any of various steels that harden after heating without quenching or other treatment. [1900–05] —**self′-hard′ened,** *adj.*

self•heal (self′hēl′), *n.* **1.** a plant, *Prunella vulgaris,* of the mint family, having pinnate leaves and tubular violet-blue flowers, formerly believed to have healing properties. **2.** any of various other plants believed to have similar properties. [1350–1400; ME *selfhele.* See SELF, HEAL]

self-help (self′help′, self′-), *n.* **1.** the act of providing for or helping or the ability to provide for or help oneself without assistance from others. **2.** *Law.* the act or right of remedying a wrong, without resorting to legal proceedings. **3.** the acquiring of information or the solving of one's problems, esp. those of a psychological nature, without the direct supervision of professionals or experts, as by independent reading or by joining or forming lay groups that are devoted to one's interests or goals. —*adj.* **4.** of or pertaining to a book, article, home study course, or the like, offering an individual information or counseling intended to be personally beneficial or profitable: *self-help books on overcoming shyness.* [1825–35] —**self′-help′er,** *n.* —**self′-help′ful, self′-help′ing,** *adj.* —**self′-help′ful•ness,** *n.*

self•hood (self′hŏŏd), *n.* **1.** the state of being an individual person; individuality. **2.** one's personality. **3.** selfishness. [1640–50; SELF + -HOOD]

self-hyp•no•sis (self′hip nō′sis, self′-), *n.* autohypnosis. [1900–05] —**self-hyp•not•ic** (self′hip not′ik, self′-), *adj.* —**self-hyp•no•tism** (self′hip′nə tiz′əm), *n.*

self-hyp•no•tized (self′hip′nə tīzd′, self′-), *adj.* hypnotized by oneself. —**self′-hyp′no•ti•za′tion,** *n.*

self-i•den•ti•fi•ca•tion (self′ī den′tə fi kā′shən, -i den′-, self′-), *n.* identification of oneself with some other person or thing. [1950–55]

self-i•den•ti•ty (self′ī den′ti tē, -i den′-, self′-), *n.* the identity or consciousness of identity of a thing with itself. [1865–70]

self-ig•nite (self′ig nīt′, self′-), *v.i.,* **-nit•ed, -nit•ing.** to ignite without spark or flame. [1940–45] —**self-ig•ni•tion** (self′ig nish′ən, self′-), *n.*

self-im•age (self′im′ij), *n.* the idea, conception, or mental image one has of oneself. [1950–55]

self-im•mo•lat•ing (self′im′ə lā′ting, self′-), *adj.* of, pertaining to, or tending toward self-immolation.

self-im•mo•la•tion (self′im′ə lā′shən), *n.* voluntary sacrifice or denial of oneself, as for an ideal or another person. [1810–20]

self-im•por•tant (self′im pôr′tnt, self′-), *adj.* having or showing an exaggerated opinion of one's own importance; pompously conceited or haughty. [1765–75] —**self′-im•por′tance,** *n.* —**self′-im•por′tant•ly,** *adv.*

self-im•posed (self′im pōzd′, self′-), *adj.* imposed on one by oneself: *a self-imposed task.* [1775–85]

self-im•prove•ment (self′im prōōv′mənt, self′-), *n.* improvement of one's mind, character, etc., through one's own efforts. [1735–45] —**self′-im•prov′a•ble,** *adj.* —**self′-im•prov′er,** *n.* —**self′-im•prov′ing,** *adj.*

self-in•clu•sive (self′in klōō′siv, self′-), *adj.* including oneself or itself. [1920–25]

self-in•crim•i•nat•ing (self′in krim′ə nā′ting, self′-), *adj.* serving to incriminate oneself or to expose oneself to prosecution: *self-incriminating testimony.* [1930–35]

self-in•crim•i•na•tion (self′in krim′ə nā′shən, self′-), *n.* the act of incriminating oneself or exposing oneself to prosecution, esp. by giving evidence or testimony. [1920–25]

self-in•duced (self′in dōōst′, -dyōōst′, self′-), *adj.* **1.** induced by oneself or itself. **2.** *Elect.* produced by self-induction. [1885–90]

self-in•duct•ance (self′in duk′təns), *n. Elect.* inductance inducing an electromotive force in the same circuit in which the motivating change of current occurs, equal to the number of flux linkages per unit of current. [1885–90]

self-in•duc•tion (self′in duk′shən), *n. Elect.* the process by which an electromotive force is induced in a circuit by a varying current in that circuit. [1870–75]

self-in•dul•gent (self′in dul′jənt, self′-), *adj.* **1.** indulging one's own desires, passions, whims, etc., esp. without restraint. **2.** characterized by such indulgence. [1785–95] —**self′-in•dul′gence,** *n.* —**self′-in•dul′•gent•ly,** *adv.* —**self′-in•dulg′er,** *n.*

self-in•flict•ed (self′in flik′tid, self′-), *adj.* inflicted by oneself upon oneself: *a self-inflicted wound.* [1775–85] —**self′-in•flic′tion,** *n.*

self-in•i•ti•at•ed (self′i nish′ē ā′tid, self′-), *adj.* initiated or begun by oneself.

self-in•struc•tion•al (self′in struk′shə nəl), *adj. Educ.* pertaining to or constituting learning materials and conditions arranged so that students can proceed to learn on their own with little or no supervision.

self-in•sur•ance (self′in shŏŏr′əns, self′-), *n.* insurance of one's property or interests against possible loss by the establishing of a special fund for the purpose instead of seeking coverage with an underwriter. [1895–1900]

self-in•sure (self′in shŏŏr′, self′-), *v.,* **-sured, -sur•ing.** —*v.t.* **1.** to subject (one's property or interests) to self-insurance. —*v.i.* **2.** to insure with self-insurance. [1930–35]

self-in•sur•er (self′in shŏŏr′ər, self′-), *n.* one insured under self-insurance. [1905–10]

self-in•ter•est (self′in′tər ist, -trist, self′-), *n.* **1.** regard for one's own interest or advantage, esp. with disregard for others. **2.** personal interest or advantage. [1640–50] —**self′-in′ter•est•ed,** *adj.* —**self′-in′ter•est•ed•ness,** *n.*

self•ish (sel′fish), *adj.* **1.** devoted to or caring only for oneself; concerned primarily with one's own interests, benefits, welfare, etc., regardless of others. **2.** characterized by or manifesting concern or care only for oneself: *selfish motives.* [1630–40; SELF + -ISH[1]] —**self′•ish•ly,** *adv.* —**self′ish•ness,** *n.*
—**Syn. 1.** self-interested, self-seeking, egoistic; illiberal, parsimonious, stingy.

self-judg•ment (self′juj′mənt, self′-), *n.* the act or fact of judging oneself. [1650–60]

self-jus•ti•fi•ca•tion (self′jus′tə fi kā′shən, self′-), *n.* the act or fact of justifying oneself, esp. of offering excessive reasons, explanations, excuses, etc., for an act, thought, or the like. [1765–75]

self-jus•ti•fy•ing (self′jus′tə fī′ing, self′-), *adj.* **1.** offering excuses for oneself, esp. in excess of normal demands. **2.** automatically adjusting printed or typed lines to fill a given space, esp. to conform to a rigid margin. [1730–40]

CONCISE PRONUNCIATION KEY: act, cāpe, dâre, pärt; set, ēqual; if, īce; ox, ōver, ôrder, oil, bŏŏk, bōōt, out; up, ûrge; child; sing; shoe; thin, *th*at; zh as in *treasure.* ə = *a* as in *alone, e* as in *system, i* as in *easily, o* as in *gallop, u* as in *circus;* ᵊ as in *fire* (fīᵊr), *hour* (ouᵊr). l and n can serve as syllabic consonants, as in *cradle* (krād′l), and *button* (but′n). See the full key inside the front cover.

self′-formed′, *adj.*
self′-for•sak′en, *adj.*
self′-fric′tion, *n.*
self′-fright′ed, *adj.*
self′-fru•i′tion, *n.*
self′-fur′nished, *adj.*
self′-gain′, *n.*
self′-gaug′ing, *adj.*
self′-giv′en, *adj.*
self′-giv′ing, *adj.*
self′-glazed′, *adj.*
self′-glaz′ing, *adj.*
self′-glo′ri•fi•ca′tion, *n.*
self′-glo′ri•fied′, *adj.*
self′-glo′ri•fy′ing, *adj.*
self′-glo′ry, *n.*
self′-glo′ry•ing, *adj.*
self′-got′ten, *adj.*
self′-guard′, *n.*
self′-guard′ed, *adj.*
self′-guid′ance, *n.*
self′-guid′ed, *adj.*
self′-harm′ing, *adj.*
self′-hate′, *n.*
self′-ha′tred, *n.*
self′-heal′ing, *adj.*
self′-heat′ing, *adj.*
self′-hit′ting, *adj.*
self′-ho′li•ness, *n.*
self′-hom′i•cide′, *n.*
self′-hon′ored, *adj.*
self′-hope′, *n.*
self′-hum′bling, *adj.*
self′-hu•mil′i•at′ing, *adj.*
self′-hu•mil′i•a′tion, *n.*
self′-i•dol′a•ter, *n.*
self′-i•dol′a•try, *n.*
self′-i′dol•ized′, *adj.*
self′-i′dol•iz′ing, *adj.*
self′-ig′no•rance, *n.*
self′-ig′no•rant, *adj.*
self′-il•lu′mined, *adj.*
self′-il•lus′tra•tive, *adj.*
self′-im′i•ta′tion, *n.*
self′-im•mu′ni•ty, *n., pl.* **-ties.**
self′-im•mure′ment, *n.*
self′-im•mur′ing, *adj.*
self′-im•pair′a•ble, *adj.*
self′-im•pair′ing, *adj.*
self′-im•part′ing, *adj.*
self′-im•ped′ance, *n.*
self′-im•preg′nat•ed, *adj.*
self′-im•preg′nat•ing, *adj.*
self′-im′preg•na′tion, *n.*
self′-im•preg′na•tor, *n.*
self′-im•pul′sion, *n.*
self′-in•closed′, *adj.*
self′-in•curred′, *adj.*
self′-in′dig•na′tion, *n.*
self′-in•fat′u•at′ed, *adj.*
self′-in•fla′tion, *n.*
self′-in•i′ti•a•tive, *n.*
self′-in•ju′ri•ous, *adj.*
self′-in′ju•ry, *n., pl.* **-ries.**
self′-in•oc′u•lat′ed, *adj.*
self′-in•oc′u•la′tion, *n.*
self′-in′sig•nif′i•cance, *n.*
self′-in•spect′ed, *adj.*
self′-in•spec′tion, *n.*
self′-in•struct′ed, *adj.*
self′-in•struct′ing, *adj.*
self′-in•struc′tion, *n.*
self′-in•struc′tor, *n.*
self′-in′suf•fi′cien•cy, *n., pl.* **-cies.**
self′-in′te•grat′ing, *adj.*
self′-in′te•gra′tion, *n.*
self′-in•tel′li•gi•ble, *adj.*
self′-in•ten′si•fied′, *adj.*
self′-in•ten′si•fy′ing, *adj.*
self′-in•ter′pre•ta′tion, *n.*
self′-in•ter′pret•ed, *adj.*
self′-in•ter′pret•ing, *adj.*
self′-in•ter′pre•tive, *adj.*
self′-in•ter′ro•ga′tion, *n.*
self′-in′ter•rupt′ing, *adj.*
self′-in′ter•sect′ing, *adj.*
self′-in•ter•view′, *n.*
self′-in•tox′i•ca′tion, *n.*
self′-in′tro•duc′tion, *n.*
self′-in•trud′er, *n.*
self′-in•vent′ed, *adj.*
self′-in•ven′tion, *n.*
self′-in•vit′ed, *adj.*
self′-i′on•i•za′tion, *n.*
self′-i′ro•ny, *n., pl.* **-nies.**
self′-is′sued, *adj.*
self′-is′su•ing, *adj.*
self′-killed′, *adj.*
self′-kill′er, *n.*
self′-kill′ing, *adj.*
self′-kin′dled, *adj.*
self′-kind′ness, *n.*
self′-lac′er•at′ing, *adj.*
self′-lac′er•a′tion, *n.*
self′-lash′ing, *adj., n.*
self′-lau•da′tion, *n.*
self′-laud′a•to′ry, *adj.*
self′-lev′el•er, *n.*
self′-lev′el•ing, *adj.*
self′-lev′el•ler, *n.*
self′-lev′el•ling, *adj.*
self′-lev′ied, *adj.*
self′-lev′i•ta′tion, *n.*
self′-light′ing, *adj.*
self′-lik′ing, *adj., n.*
self′-loath′ing, *adj., n.*
self′-lo′cat•ing, *adj.*
self′-lock′ing, *adj.*
self′-lu′bri•cat′ed, *adj.*
self′-lu′bri•cat′ing, *adj.*
self′-lu′bri•ca′tion, *n.*
self′-lu′mi•nos′i•ty, *n.*
self′-lu′mi•nous, *adj.*
self′-mac′er•a′tion, *n.*
self′-maimed′, *adj.*
self′-main•tained′, *adj.*
self′-main•tain′ing, *adj.*
self′-main′te•nance, *n.*
self′-mak′ing, *adj.*
self′-man′age•ment, *n.*
self′-man′ag•ing, *adj.*
self′-man′i•fest′, *adj.*
self′-man′i•fes•ta′tion, *n.*
self′-mapped′, *adj.*
self′-ma•tured′, *adj.*
self′-meas′ure•ment, *n.*
self′-me′di•at′ing, *adj.*
self′-mer′it, *n.*
self′-mind′ed, *adj.*
self′-mis•trust′, *n.*
self′-mock′er•y, *n.*
self′-mock′ing, *adj.*
self′-mon′i•tor•ing, *adj.*
self′-mo′tion, *n.*
self′-mul′ti•plied′, *adj.*
self′-mul′ti•ply′ing, *adj.*
self′-mur′der, *n.*
self′-mur′dered, *adj.*
self′-mur′der•er, *n.*
self′-mu′ti•lat′ing, *adj.*
self′-mu′ti•la′tion, *n.*
self′-named′, *adj.*
self′-ne•gat′ing, *adj.*
self′-ne•glect′, *n.*
self′-ne•glect′ful, *adj.*
self′-ne•glect′ing, *adj.*
self′-nour′ished, *adj.*
self′-nour′ish•ing, *adj.*
self′-nour′ish•ment, *n.*
self′-ob•jec′ti•fi•ca′tion, *n.*
self′-ob•liv′i•on, *n.*
self′-ob•liv′i•ous, *adj.*
self′-ob′ser•va′tion, *n.*

self-know·ledge (self′nol′ij, self′-), *n.* knowledge or understanding of oneself, one's character, abilities, motives, etc. [1605–15]

self·less (self′lis), *adj.* having little or no concern for oneself, esp. with regard to fame, position, money, etc.; unselfish. [1815–25; SELF + -LESS] —**self′less·ly,** *adv.* —**self′less·ness,** *n.*

self-lim·it·ed (self′lim′i tid, self′-), *adj.* (of a disease) running a definite and limited course. Also, **self-limiting.** [1835–45]

self-lim·it·ing (self′lim′i ting), *adj.* **1.** limiting oneself or itself: *a self-limiting authority.* **2.** (of a disease) self-limited. [1860–65] —**self′-lim′i·ta′tion,** *n.*

self-liq·ui·dat·ing (self′lik′wi dā′ting, self′-), *adj.* **1.** capable of being sold and converted into cash within a short period of time or before the date on which the supplier must be paid. **2.** (of a property, loan, project, investment, etc.) used or operating in such a way as to repay the money needed to acquire it: *He rented half of the house to someone else so that his home loan became self-liquidating.* [1915–20]

self-load·er (self′lō′dər), *n.* semiautomatic (def. 3). [1935–40]

self-load·ing (self′lō′ding, self′-), *adj.* noting or pertaining to an automatic or semiautomatic firearm. [1895–1900]

self-love (self′luv′), *n.* **1.** the instinct by which one's actions are directed to the promotion of one's own welfare or well-being, esp. an excessive regard for one's own advantage. **2.** conceit; vanity. **3.** narcissism (def. 2). [1555–65] —**self′-lov′ing,** *adj.*

self-made (self′mād′), *adj.* **1.** having succeeded in life unaided: *He is a self-made man.* **2.** made by oneself. [1605–15]

self-mail·er (self′mā′lər), *n.* an advertisement, booklet, or the like, that has space for a name, address, and postage and can be mailed without a wrapper or envelope. [1940–45]

self-mas·ter·y (self′mas′tə rē, -mä′stə-, self′-), *n.* self-control. [1855–60]

self-mate (self′māt′), *n. Chess.* a move that will cause a player's king to be mated within a certain number of subsequent moves. Also called **suimate.** [1885–90]

self-med·i·ca·tion (self′med′i kā′shən), *n.* the use of medicine without medical supervision to treat one's own ailment.

self-mor·ti·fi·ca·tion (self′môr′tə fi kā′shən), *n.* the inflicting of pain or privation on oneself: *He was certain that self-mortification was the only road to salvation.* [1815–25] —**self-mor·ti·fied** (self′môr′tə fīd′, self′-), *adj.*

self-mo·ti·va·tion (self′mō′tə vā′shən), *n.* initiative to undertake or continue a task or activity without another's prodding or supervision. —**self′-mo′ti·vat′ed,** *adj.*

self-mov·ing (self′mo͞o′ving, self′-), *adj.* capable of moving without an external agency. [1575–85] —**self′-move′ment,** *n.* —**self′-mov′er,** *n.*

self·ness (self′nis), *n.* selfhood. [1580–90; SELF + -NESS]

self-op·er·at·ing (self′op′ə rā′ting, self′-), *adj.* automatic. Also, **self-op·er·a·tive** (self′op′ər ə tiv, -ə rā′tiv, -op′rə tiv, self′-).

self-o·pin·ion (self′ə pin′yən, self′-), *n.* opinion of oneself, esp. when unduly high. [1570–80]

self-o·pin·ion·at·ed (self′ə pin′yə nā′tid, self′-), *adj.* **1.** conceited; having an inordinately high regard for oneself, one's own opinions, views, etc. **2.** stubborn or obstinate in holding to one's own opinions, views, etc. Also, **self-o·pin·ioned** (self′ə pin′yənd). [1665–75]

self-paced (self′pāst′), *adj.* (of an educational system, course, etc.) done or designed to be accomplished at the student's own speed: *self-paced instruction.* [1970–75]

self-per·pet·u·at·ing (self′pər pech′o͞o ā′ting, self′-), *adj.* **1.** continuing oneself in office, rank, etc., beyond the normal limit. **2.** capable of indefinite continuation. [1815–25] —**self′-per·pet′u·a′tion,** *n.*

self-pit·y (self′pit′ē, self′-), *n.* pity for oneself, esp. a self-indulgent attitude concerning one's own difficulties, hardships, etc.: *We must resist yielding to self-pity and carry on as best we can.* [1615–25] —**self′-pit′y·ing,** *adj.* —**self′-pit′y·ing·ly,** *adv.*

self-pol·li·nate (self′pol′ə nāt′, self′-), *v.i., v.t.* **-nat·ed, -nat·ing.** to undergo or cause to undergo self-pollination. [1885–90]

self-pol·li·na·tion (self′pol′ə nā′shən, self′-), *n. Bot.* the transfer of pollen from the anther to the stigma of the same flower, another flower on the same plant, or the flower of a plant of the same clone. Cf. **cross-pollination.** [1875–80]

self-por·trait (self′pôr′trit, -trāt, -pōr′-, self′-), *n.* a portrait of oneself done by oneself. [1830–40]

self-pos·sessed (self′pə zest′, self′-), *adj.* having or showing control of one's feelings, behavior, etc.; composed; poised. [1830–40] —**self-pos·sess·ed·ly** (self′pə zes′id lē, -zest′lē, self′-), *adv.*
—**Syn.** calm, collected, serene, cool, sedate.

self-pos·ses·sion (self′pə zesh′ən, self′-), *n.* the quality of being self-possessed; control of one's feelings, behavior, etc.; composure; poise. [1735–45]

self-pres·er·va·tion (self′prez′ər vā′shən, self′-), *n.* preservation of oneself from harm or destruction. [1605–15] —**self′-pre·serv′ing,** *adj.*

self-pride (self′prīd′, self′-), *n.* pride in one's abilities, status, possessions, etc.; self-esteem. [1580–90]

self-pro·duced (self′prə do͞ost′, -dyo͞ost′, self′-), *adj.* produced by oneself or itself. —**self-pro·duc·tion** (self′prə duk′shən, self′-), *n.*

self-pro·nounc·ing (self′prə noun′sing), *adj.* having the pronunciation indicated, esp. by diacritical marks added on original spellings rather than by phonetic symbols: *a self-pronouncing dictionary.*

self-pro·pelled (self′prə peld′, self′-), *adj.* **1.** propelled by itself. **2.** (of a vehicle) propelled by its own engine, motor, or the like, rather than drawn or pushed by a horse, locomotive, etc. **3.** (of a gun or a rocket launcher) having a vehicle as a base. Also, **self′-pro·pel′ling.** [1895–1900]

self-pro·pul·sion (self′ prə pul′shən, self′-), *n.* propulsion by a vehicle's own engine, motor, or the like.

self-pro·tec·tion (self′prə tek′shən, self′-), *n.* protection of oneself or itself. [1855–60] —**self′-pro·tect′·ing,** *adj.* —**self′-pro·tec′tive,** *adj.* —**self′-pro·tec′·tive·ness,** *n.*

self-pub·lished (self′pub′lisht), *adj.* **1.** published independently by the author: *self-published books.* **2.** having published one's own work independently: *a self-published author.* [1970–75]

self-ques·tion·ing (self′kwes′chə ning, self′-), *n.* review or scrutiny of one's own motives or behavior. [1860–65]

self-re·al·i·za·tion (self′rē′ə lə zā′shən, self′-), *n.* the fulfillment of one's potential. [1870–75]

self-re·cord·ing (self′ri kôr′ding, self′-), *adj.* recording automatically, as an instrument. [1870–75]

self-ref·er·ence (self′ref′ər əns, -ref′rəns), *n.* **1.** reference made to oneself or one's own experience. **2.** *Logic.* the property of a statement that is a statement about itself, as "This statement is grammatical." —**self-ref·er·en·tial** (self′ref′ə ren′shəl), **self-re·fer·ring** (self′ri fûr′ing), *adj.*

self-re·gard (self′ri gärd′, self′-), *n.* **1.** consideration for oneself or one's own interests. **2.** self-respect. [1585–95] —**self′-re·gard′ing,** *adj.*

self-reg·is·ter·ing (self′rej′ə stər ing, -string, self′-), *adj.* registering automatically, as an instrument; self-recording. [1830–40] —**self′-reg′is·tra′tion,** *n.*

self-reg·u·lat·ed (self′reg′yə lā′tid, self′-), *adj.* governed or controlled from within; self-regulating. [1840–50]

self-reg·u·lat·ing (self′reg′yə lā′ting, self′-), *adj.* **1.** adjusting, ruling, or governing itself without outside interference; operating or functioning without externally imposed controls or regulations: *a self-regulating economy; the self-regulating market.* **2.** functioning automatically: *a self-regulating machine.* [1830–40]

self-reg·u·la·tion (self′reg′yə lā′shən, self′-), *n.* control by oneself or itself, as in an economy, business organization, etc., esp. such control as exercised independently of governmental supervision, laws, or the like. [1685–95]

self-reg·u·la·tive (self′reg′yə lā′tiv, self′-), *adj.* used for or capable of controlling or adjusting oneself or itself: *a self-regulative device.* Also, **self-reg·u·la·to·ry** (self′reg′yə lə tôr′ē, -tōr′ē, self′-). [1865–70]

self-re·li·ance (self′ri lī′əns, self′-), *n.* reliance on oneself or one's own powers, resources, etc. [1825–35]

self-re·li·ant (self′ri lī′ənt, self′-), *adj.* relying on oneself or on one's own powers, resources, etc. [1840–50] —**self′-re·li′ant·ly,** *adv.*
—**Syn.** independent, assured, enterprising, resolute, capable.

self-re·nun·ci·a·tion (self′ri nun′sē ā′shən, self′-), *n.* renunciation of one's own will, interests, etc. [1785–95] —**self-re·nun·ci·a·to·ry** (self′ri nun′sē ə tôr′ē, -tōr′ē, -shē ə-, self′-), *adj.*

self-rep·li·cat·ing (self′rep′li kā′ting, self′-), *adj.* **1.** reproducing itself by its own power or inherent nature: *self-replicating organisms.* **2.** *Genetics.* making an exact copy or copies of itself, as a strand of DNA. [1955–60] —**self′-rep′li·ca′tion,** *n.*

self-re·proach (self′ri prōch′), *n.* blame or censure by one's own conscience. [1770–80] —**self′-re·proach′·ful, self′-re·proach′ing,** *adj.* —**self′-re·proach′ing·ly,** *adv.* —**self′-re·proach′ing·ness,** *n.*

self-re·spect (self′ri spekt′, self′-), *n.* proper esteem or regard for the dignity of one's character. [1605–15] —**self′-re·spect′ful, self′-re·spect′ing,** *adj.*

self-re·straint (self′ri strānt′, self′-), *n.* restraint imposed on one by oneself; self-control. [1765–75] —**self′-re·strained′,** *adj.* —**self′-re·strain′ing,** *adj.*

self-re·veal·ing (self′ri vē′ling, self′-), *adj.* displaying, exhibiting, or disclosing one's most private feelings, thoughts, etc.: *an embarrassingly self-revealing autobiography.* Also, **self-re·vel·a·to·ry** (self′ri vel′ə tôr′ē, -tōr′ē, -rev′ə lə-, self′-), **self-re·vel·a·tive** (self′ri vel′ə tiv, -rev′ə lā′-, self′-). [1830–40]

self-rev·e·la·tion (self′rev′ə lā′shən, self′-), *n.* disclosure of one's private feelings, thoughts, etc., esp. when unintentional. [1850–55]

Sel·fridge (sel′frij), *n.* **Harry Gordon,** 1857?–1947, British retail merchant, born in the U.S.

self-right·eous (self′rī′chəs, self′-), *adj.* confident of one's own righteousness, esp. when smugly moralistic and intolerant of the opinions and behavior of others. [1670–80] —**self′-right′eous·ly,** *adv.* —**self′-right′·eous·ness,** *n.*
—**Syn.** sanctimonious, pharisaical.

self-ris·ing (self′rī′zing), *adj. Cookery.* rising without the addition of leaven: *self-rising pancake flour.* [1860–65, *Amer.*]

self-sac·ri·fice (self′sak′rə fīs′, self′-), *n.* sacrifice of one's interests, desires, etc., as for duty or the good of another. [1795–1805] —**self′-sac′ri·fic′er,** *n.* —**self-sac·ri·fi·cial** (self′sak′rə fish′əl, self′-), *adj.* —**self′-sac′ri·fic′ing,** *adj.* —**self′-sac′ri·fic′ing·ly,** *adv.* —**self′-sac′ri·fic′ing·ness,** *n.*

self·same (self′sām′, -sām′), *adj.* being the very same; identical. [1375–1425; late ME *selve same;* see SELF, SAME; c. Dan *selvsamme,* OHG *selbsama*] —**self′·same′ness,** *n.*
—**Syn.** exact, very, same.

self-sat·is·fac·tion (self′sat′is fak′shən), *n.* a usu-

CONCISE ETYMOLOGY KEY: <, descended or borrowed from; >, whence; b., blend of, blended; c., cognate with; cf., compare; deriv., derivative; equiv., equivalent; imit., imitative; obl., oblique; r., replacing; s., stem; sp., spelling, spelled; resp., respelling, respelled; trans., translation; ?, origin unknown; *, unattested; ‡, probably earlier than. See the full key inside the front cover.

self′-ob·served′, *adj.*
self′-ob·sessed′, *adj.*
self′-ob·ses′sion, *n.*
self′-oc′cu·pa′tion, *n.*
self′-oc′cu·pied′, *adj.*
self′-of·fense′, *n.*
self′-of′fered, *adj.*
self′-oil′ing, *adj.*
self′-o′pened, *adj.*
self′-o′pen·er, *n.*
self′-o′pen·ing, *adj.*
self′-op′er·a′tor, *n.*
self′-op·pres′sion, *n.*
self′-op·pres′sive, *adj.*
self′-op·pres′sor, *n.*
self′-or·dained′, *adj.*
self′-or·dain′er, *n.*
self′-o′ri·ent′ed, *adj.*
self′-o·rig′i·nat′ed, *adj.*
self′-o·rig′i·nat′ing, *adj.*
self′-o·rig′i·na′tion, *n.*
self′-out′law′, *n.*
self′-out′lawed′, *adj.*
self′-own′er·ship′, *n.*
self′-ox′i·da′tion, *n.*
self′-paid′, *adj.*
self′-paint′er, *n.*
self′-pam′pered, *adj.*
self′-pam′per·ing, *adj.*
self′-pan′e·gyr′ic, *adj.*
self′-par′o·dist, *n.*
self′-par′o·dis′tic, *adj.*
self′-par′o·dy, *n., pl.* **-dies.**
self′-pay′ing, *adj.*
self′-peace′, *n.*
self′-pen′e·tra·bil′i·ty, *n.*
self′-pen′e·tra′tion, *n.*
self′-per·ceiv′ing, *adj.*
self′-per·cep′tion, *n.*
self′-per·cep′tive, *adj.*
self′-per·fect′i·bil′i·ty, *n.*
self′-per·fect′ing, *adj.*
self′-per·formed′, *adj.*
self′-per·mis′sion, *n.*
self′-per·plexed′, *adj.*
self′-per·sua′sion, *n.*
self′-pic′tured, *adj.*
self′-pit′i·ful, *adj.;* **-ly,** *adv.;* **-ness,** *n.*
self′-plant′ed, *adj.*
self′-play′er, *n.*
self′-play′ing, *adj.*
self′-pleased′, *adj.*
self′-pleas′er, *n.*
self′-pleas′ing, *adj.*
self′-point′ed, *adj.*
self′-poi′son·er, *n.*
self′-po·lic′ing, *adj.*
self′-pol′i·ti′cian, *n.*
self′-pol·lu′tion, *n.*
self′-posed′, *adj.*
self′-post′ing, *adj.*
self′-post·pone′ment, *n.*
self′-pow′ered, *adj.*
self′-praise′, *n.*
self′-prais′ing, *adj.*
self′-pre·cip′i·ta′tion, *n.*
self′-pref′er·ence, *n.*
self′-pre·oc′cu·pa′tion, *n.*
self′-prep′a·ra′tion, *n.*
self′-pre·pared′, *adj.*
self′-pre·scribed′, *adj.*
self′-pres′en·ta′tion, *n.*
self′-pre·sent′ed, *adj.*
self′-pre·tend′ed, *adj.*
self′-primed′, *adj.*
self′-prim′er, *n.*
self′-prim′ing, *adj.*
self′-priz′ing, *adj.*
self′-pro·claimed′, *adj.*
self′-pro·claim′ing, *adj.*
self′-pro·cured′, *adj.*
self′-pro·cure′ment, *n.*
self′-pro·cur′ing, *adj.*
self′-pro·fessed′, *adj.*
self′-prof′it, *n.*
self′-pro·jec′tion, *n.*
self′-pro·mot′er, *n.*
self′-pro·mot′ing, *adj.*
self′-pro·mo′tion, *n.*
self′-prop′a·gat′ed, *adj.*
self′-prop′a·gat′ing, *adj.*
self′-prop′a·ga′tion, *n.*
self′-prov′ing, *adj.*
self′-pro·vi′sion, *n.*
self′-pun′ished, *adj.*
self′-pun′ish·er, *n.*
self′-pun′ish·ing, *adj.*
self′-pun′ish·ment, *n.*
self′-pu′ni·tive, *adj.*
self′-pu′ri·fy′ing, *adj.*
self′-quo·ta′tion, *n.*
self′-raised′, *adj.*
self′-rais′ing, *adj.*
self′-rat′ing, *adj., n.*
self′-re·act′ing, *adj.*
self′-read′ing, *adj.*
self′-reck′on·ing, *adj., n.*
self′-rec′ol·lec′tion, *n.*
self′-rec′ol·lec′tive, *adj.*
self′-re′con·struc′tion, *n.*
self′-re·crim′i·na′tion, *n.*
self′-rec′ti·fy′ing, *adj.*
self′-re·duc′tion, *n.*
self′-re·du′pli·ca′tion, *n.*
self′-re·fine′ment, *n.*
self′-re·fin′ing, *adj.*
self′-re·flec′tion, *n.*
self′-re·flec′tive, *adj.*
self′-re·form′, *n.*
self′-ref′or·ma′tion, *n.*
self′-re·fut′ed, *adj.*
self′-re·fut′ing, *adj.*
self′-re′in·forc′ing, *adj.*
self′-rel′ish, *n.*
self′-re·new′al, *n.*
self′-re·new′ing, *adj.*
self′-re·nounced′, *adj.*
self′-re·nounce′ment, *n.*
self′-re·nounc′ing, *adj.*
self′-re·pair′ing, *adj.*
self′-re·peat′ing, *adj.*
self′-re·pel′len·cy, *n.*
self′-re·pel′lent, *adj.*
self′-re·pose′, *n.*
self′-rep′re·sen·ta′tion, *n.*
self′-re′pro·duc′ing, *adj.*
self′-re′pro·duc′tion, *n.*
self′-re·proof′, *n.*
self′-re·pul′sive, *adj.*
self′-rep′u·ta′tion, *n.*
self′-re·sent′ment, *n.*
self′-re·signed′, *adj.*
self′-re·source′ful, *adj.;* **-ly,** *adv.;* **-ness,** *n.*
self′-re·splend′ent, *adj.*
self′-re·spon′si·bil′i·ty, *n.*
self′-re·stor′ing, *adj.*
self′-re·strict′ed, *adj.*
self′-re·stric′tion, *n.*
self′-re·tired′, *adj.*
self′-re·vealed′, *adj.*
self′-rev′er·ence, *n.*
self′-rev′er·ent, *adj.*
self′-rid′i·cule′, *n.*
self′-rig′or·ous, *adj.*
self′-roofed′, *adj.*
self′-ru′in, *n.*
self′-ru′ined, *adj.*
self′-rule′, *n.*
self′-safe′ty, *n.*
self′-sanc′ti·fi·ca′tion, *n.*
self′-sat′i·rist, *n.*
self′-scanned′, *adj.*
self′-schooled′, *adj.*

ally smug satisfaction with oneself, one's achievements, etc. [1785–95]

self-sat·is·fied (self′sat′is fīd′, self′-), *adj.* feeling or showing satisfaction with oneself. [1725–35] **—Syn.** complacent, smug, vain, puffed-up.

self-sat·is·fy·ing (self′sat′is fī′ing, self′-), *adj.* effecting satisfaction to oneself. [1665–75]

self-seal·ing (self′sē′ling, self′-), *adj.* capable of sealing itself automatically or without the application of adhesive, glue, or moisture: *a self-sealing automobile tire; self-sealing envelopes.* [1920–25] **—self′-seal′er,** *n.*

self-seek·er (self′sē′kər), *n.* a person who seeks his or her own interest or selfish ends. [1625–35]

self-seek·ing (self′sē′king), *n.* **1.** the seeking of one's own interest or selfish ends. **—***adj.* **2.** given to or characterized by self-seeking; selfish. [1580–90] **—self′-seek′ing·ness,** *n.*

self-se·lec·tion (self′si lek′shən, self′-), *n.* selection made by or for oneself: *goods arranged on shelves for customer self-selection.* **—self′-se·lect′ed,** *adj.*

self-serve (self′sûrv′), *adj.* self-service. [1925–30]

self-serv·ice (self′sûr′vis), *n.* **1.** the serving of oneself in a restaurant, shop, gas station, or other facility, without the aid of a waiter, clerk, attendant, etc. **—***adj.* **2.** noting or pertaining to a cafeteria, grocery, store, etc., designed for the patron or customer to gather food or merchandise from a display or display shelves without the aid of attendants and pay at a cashier's desk upon leaving. **3.** of, for, or pertaining to something designed to be used or enjoyed without the aid of an attendant: *self-service banking; self-service elevators.* [1920–25]

self-serv·ing (self′sûr′ving), *adj.* **1.** preoccupied with one's own interests, often disregarding the truth or the interests, well-being, etc., of others. **2.** serving to further one's own selfish interests. [1900–05]

self-slaugh·ter (self′slô′tər), *n. Law.* suicide. [1595–1605] **—self′-slaugh′tered,** *adj.*

self-slay·er (self′slā′ər), *n. Law.* one who kills oneself. [1680–90] **—self′-slain′,** *adj.*

self-sown (self′sōn′), *adj.* **1.** sown by itself, or without human or animal agency, as of a plant grown from seeds dropped from another plant. **2.** sown by any agency other than humans, as of a plant grown from seeds scattered by birds or the wind. [1600–10]

self-start·er (self′stär′tər), *n.* **1.** starter (def. 3). **2.** *Informal.* a person who begins work or undertakes a project on his or her own initiative, without needing to be told or encouraged to do so. [1890–95] **—self′-start′ing,** *adj.*

self-ster·ile (self′ster′il *or, esp. Brit.,* -il, self′-), *adj. Zool.* incapable of self-fertilization. [1875–80]

self-stick (self′stik′), *adj.* having a surface coated or treated to stick to another surface without the use of glue or moisture; self-adhesive. Also, **self′-stick′ing.** [1945–50]

self-stud·y (self′stud′ē), *n., pl.* **-stud·ies,** *adj.* **—***n.* **1.** the study of something by oneself, as through books, records, etc., without direct supervision or attendance in a class: *She learned to read German by self-study.* **2.** the study of oneself; self-examination. **—***adj.* **3.** designed for or accomplished by self-study: *a self-study course for learning German.* [1675–85]

self-styled (self′stīld′), *adj.* styled, called, or considered by oneself as specified: *a self-styled leader.* [1815–25]

self-suf·fi·cient (self′sə fish′ənt, self′-), *adj.* **1.** able to supply one's own or its own needs without external assistance: *The nation grows enough grain to be self-sufficient.* **2.** having extreme confidence in one's own resources, powers, etc.: *He was self-sufficient, and always reminded you of it.* Also, **self-suf·fic·ing** (self′sə-fī′sing). [1580–90] **—self′-suf·fi′cien·cy,** *n.* **—self′-suf·fi′cient·ly,** *adv.*

self-sup·port (self′sə pôrt′, -pōrt′, self′-), *n.* the supporting or maintaining of oneself or itself without reliance on outside aid. [1760–70] **—self′-sup·port′ed,** *adj.* **—self′-sup·port′ed·ness,** *n.* **—self′-sup·port′·ing,** *adj.* **—self′-sup·port′ing·ly,** *adv.*

self-sur·ren·der (self′sə ren′dər, self′-), *n.* the surrender or yielding up of oneself, one's will, affections, etc., as to another person, an influence, or a cause. [1695–1705]

self-sus·tain·ing (self′sə stā′ning, self′-), *adj.* self-supporting. [1835–45] **—self′-sus·tained′,** *adj.* **—self′-sus·tain′ing·ly,** *adv.* **—self′-sus·tain′ment,** *n.*

self′-tap·ping screw′ (self′tap′ing), a screw designed to tap its corresponding female thread as it is driven. Also called **tapping screw.**

self-taught (self′tôt′), *adj.* **1.** taught to oneself or by oneself to be (as indicated) without the aid of a formal education: *self-taught typing.* **2.** learned by oneself: *a self-taught mastery of the guitar.* [1715–25]

self-test (self′test′), *n.* **1.** a test that can be administered to oneself. **—***v.t.* **2.** to administer a test to (oneself).

self-tor·ment (self′tôr′ment, self′-), *n.* an act or instance of tormenting oneself, as with worry or guilt. [1640–50] **—self′-tor·ment′ed,** *adj.* **—self′-tor·ment′ing,** *adj.* **—self′-tor·ment′ing·ly,** *adv.* **—self′-tor·men′tor,** *n.*

self-to-self (self′tə self′), *adj.* autologous.

self-val·i·dat·ing (self′val′i dā′ting, self′-), *adj.* requiring no external confirmation, sanction, or validation. [1940–45]

self·ward (self′wərd), *adv.* Also, **self′wards. 1.** in the direction of or toward oneself: *a selfward-moving gesture.* **2.** within oneself; inward: *She turned her thoughts selfward.* **—***adj.* **3.** tending toward or directed at oneself. [1885–90; SELF + -WARD] **—self′ward·ness,** *n.*

self-will (self′wil′, self′-), *n.* stubborn or obstinate willfulness, as in pursuing one's own wishes, aims, etc. [bef. 900; ME: one's own will, stubbornness; OE: one's own will; see SELF, WILL[2]] **—self′-willed′,** *adj.* **—self′-willed′ly,** *adv.* **—self′-willed′ness,** *n.*

self-wind·ing (self′wīn′ding), *adj.* (of a timepiece) kept wound or wound periodically by a mechanism, as an electric motor or a system of weighted levers, so that winding by hand is not necessary. [1880–85]

self-worth (self′wûrth′), *n.* the sense of one's own value or worth as a person; self-esteem; self-respect. [1960–65] **—self-wor·thi·ness** (self′wûr′thē nis), *n.*

self-wrong (self′rông′, -rong′), *n.* wrong done to oneself. [1580–90]

Se·li·hoth (*Seph.* sə lē KHôt′, slē-; *Ashk.* sə lē KHōs′, slē′KHəs), *n. Hebrew.* **1.** (*used with a plural v.*) liturgical prayers serving as expressions of repentance and pleas for God's forgiveness, recited by Jews during the period, usually beginning the preceding week, before Rosh Hashanah, during the period between Rosh Hashanah and Yom Kippur, and on fast days. **2.** (*used with a singular v.*) a religious service at which such prayers are recited. Also, ***Se·li·hot′, Se·li·choth′, Se·li·hos′.*** [*səlīḥōth* lit., pardons]

Sel·juk (sel jōōk′), *adj.* **1.** noting or pertaining to any of several Turkish dynasties that ruled over large parts of Asia from the 11th to the 13th centuries. **—***n.* **2.** a member of a Seljuk dynasty or of a tribe ruled by them. Also, **Sel·juk·i·an** (sel jōō′kē ən). [1825–35]

Sel·kirk (sel′kûrk), *n.* **1. Alexander** (originally *Alexander Selcraig*), 1676–1721, Scottish sailor marooned on a Pacific island: supposed prototype of Robinson Crusoe. **2.** Also called **Sel·kirk·shire** (sel′kûrk shēr′, -shər). a historic county in SE Scotland.

Sel′kirk Moun′tains, a mountain range in SW Canada, in SE British Columbia. Highest peak, Mt. Sir Donald, 11,123 ft. (3390 m).

sell[1] (sel), *v.,* **sold, sell·ing,** *n.* **—***v.t.* **1.** to transfer (goods) to or render (services) for another in exchange for money; dispose of to a purchaser for a price: *He sold the car to me for $1000.* **2.** to deal in; keep or offer for sale: *He sells insurance.* **3.** to make a sale or offer for sale to: *He'll sell me the car for $1000.* **4.** to persuade or induce (someone) to buy something: *The salesman sold me on a more expensive model than I wanted.* **5.** to persuade or induce someone to buy (something): *The clerk really sold the shoes to me by flattery.* **6.** to make sales of: *The hot record sold a million copies this month.* **7.** to cause to be accepted, esp. generally or widely: *to sell an idea to the public.* **8.** to cause or persuade to accept; convince: *to sell the voters on a candidate.* **9.** to accept a price for or make a profit of (something not a proper object for such action): *to sell one's soul for political power.* **10.** to force or exact a price for: *The defenders of the fort sold their lives dearly.* **11.** *Informal.* to cheat, betray, or hoax. **—***v.i.* **12.** to engage in selling something. **13.** to be on sale. **14.** to offer something for sale: *I like this house—will they sell?* **15.** to be employed to persuade or induce others to buy, as a salesperson or a clerk in a store: *One sister is a cashier and the other sells.* **16.** to have a specific price; be offered for sale at the price indicated (fol. by *at* or *for*): *Eggs used to sell at sixty cents a dozen. This shirt sells for thirty dollars.* **17.** to be in demand by buyers: *On a rainy day, umbrellas really sell.* **18.** to win acceptance, approval, or adoption: *Here's an idea that'll sell.* **19. sell off,** to sell, esp. at reduced prices, in order to get rid of: *The city is selling off a large number of small lots at public auction.* **20. sell out, a.** to dispose of entirely by selling. **b.** to betray (an associate, one's country, a cause, etc.); turn traitor: *He committed suicide rather than sell out to the enemy.* **21. sell short.** See **short** (def. 33). **22. sell (someone) a bill of goods.** See **bill of goods** (def. 3). **23. sell up,** *Brit.* to sell out: *She was forced to sell up her entire stock of crystal.* **—***n.* **24.** an act or method of selling. **25.** *Stock Exchange.* a security to be sold. **26.** *Informal.* a cheat; hoax. [bef. 900; ME *sellen* (v.), OE *sellan* orig., to give, hence, give up (someone) to an enemy, betray, exchange for money; c. ON *selja,* LG *sellen,* Goth *saljan* to give up, sell, orig., to cause to take; akin to Gk *heleîn* to take] **—sell′a·ble,** *adj.*

—Syn. 1. vend. See **trade. —Ant. 1.** buy.

sell[2] (sel), *n., adj., pron. Scot.* self.

Sel·la (sel′ə), *n. Douay Bible.* Zillah.

sell-back (sel′bak′), *n.* an act or instance of selling something previously purchased.

sell′ date′. See **pull date.**

sell·er (sel′ər), *n.* **1.** a person who sells; salesperson or vender. **2.** an article considered with reference to its sales: *one of the poorest sellers.* [1150–1200; ME; see SELL[1], -ER[1]]

sell′ers′ mar′ket, a market in which goods and services are scarce and prices relatively high. Cf. **buyers' market.**

sell′er's op′tion, (on the New York Stock Exchange) a special transaction that gives the seller the right to make late delivery of a security within a specified period, ranging from 5 to not more than 60 business days for stocks. [1930–35]

sell·ing (sel′ing), *adj.* **1.** of or pertaining to a sale or sales: *the selling price of oranges.* **2.** engaged in selling: *two selling offices in New York.* **3.** readily salable; in strong demand (often used in combination): *This is our fastest-selling model.* [1765–75; SELL[1] + -ING[2]]

sell′ing cli′max, a brief, abrupt decline in stock prices that is succeeded by a rally. [1945–50]

sell′ing floor′. floor (def. 10).

sell·ing-plat·er (sel′ing plā′tər), *n.* a horse that competes in a selling race; an inferior horse. [1885–90]

sell′ing point′, a unique or advantageous feature that appeals to the prospective buyer of a service, product, etc.: *A generous discount is the chief selling point of the book club.* [1920–25]

sell′ing race′, a claiming race at the end of which the winning horse is offered for sale. [1895–1900]

sell-off (sel′ôf′, -of′), *n.* **1.** *Stock Exchange.* a sudden and marked decline in stock or bond prices resulting from widespread selling. **2.** an act or instance of liquidating assets or subsidiaries, as by divestiture. Also, **sell′ing-off′.** [1935–40; n. use of v. phrase *sell off*]

CONCISE PRONUNCIATION KEY: *act, cāpe, dâre, pärt; set, ēqual; if, īce; ox, ōver, ôrder, oil, bŏŏk, bōōt, out; up, ûrge; child; sing; shoe; thin, that;* zh as in *treasure.* ə = *a* as in *alone, e* as in *system, i* as in *easily, o* as in *gallop, u* as in *circus;* ′ as in *fire* (fī′r), *hour* (ou′r). l and n can serve as syllabic consonants, as in *cradle* (krād′l), and *button* (but′n). See the full key inside the front cover.

self′-school′ing, *adj., n.*
self′-scorn′, *n.*
self′-scourg′ing, *adj.*
self′-scru′ti·nized′, *adj.*
self′-scru′ti·niz′ing, *adj.*
self′-scru′ti·ny, *n.*
self′-search′ing, *adj., n.*
self′-se·cu′ri·ty, *n.*
self′-sed′i·men·ta′tion, *n.*
self′-sed′i·ment′ed, *adj.*
self′-sent′, *adj.*
self′-se·ques′tered, *adj.*
self′-set′, *adj.*
self′-shad′owed, *adj.*
self′-shad′ow·ing, *adj.*
self′-shel′ter, *n.*
self′-shel′tered, *adj.*
self′-shine′, *n.*
self′-shin′ing, *adj.*
self′-sig·nif′i·cance, *n.*
self′-sim′i·lar, *adj.*
self′-sink′ing, *adj.*
self′-sold′, *adj.*
self′-so·lic′i·tude′, *n.*
self′-soothed′, *adj.*
self′-sooth′ing, *adj.*
self′-so·phis′ti·ca′tion, *n.*
self′-sought′, *adj.*
self′-sound′ing, *adj.*
self′-sov′er·eign·ty, *n.*
self′-spaced′, *adj.*
self′-spac′ing, *adj.*
self′-speech′, *n.*
self′-spit′ted, *adj.*
self′-sprung′, *adj.*
self′-sta·bil′i·ty, *n.*
self′-sta′bi·lized′, *adj.*
self′-sta′bi·liz′ing, *adj.*
self′-starved′, *adj.*
self′-steered′, *adj.*
self′-steer′ing, *adj.*
self′-ster′i·lized′, *adj.*
self′-stim′u·lat′ed, *adj.*
self′-stim′u·lat′ing, *adj.*
self′-stim′u·la′tion, *n.*
self′-strength′, *n.*
self′-strip′per, *n.*
self′-strong′, *adj.*
self′-stuck′, *adj.*
self′-sub·du′al, *n.*
self′-sub·dued′, *adj.*
self′-sub·jec′tion, *n.*
self′-sub′ju·gat′ing, *adj.*
self′-sub′ju·ga′tion, *n.*
self′-sub·or′di·nat′ing, *adj.*
self′-sub·or′di·na′tion, *n.*
self′-sub·sist′ence, *n.*
self′-sub·sist′ent, *adj.*
self′-sub·sist′ing, *adj.*
self′-sub·ver′sive, *adj.*
self′-sug·ges′tion, *n.*
self′-sup·press′ing, *adj.*
self′-sup·pres′sion, *n.*
self′-sup·pres′sive, *adj.*
self′-sur′vey, *n.*
self′-sur·veyed′, *adj.*
self′-sur·viv′ing, *adj.*
self′-sur·viv′or, *n.*
self′-sus·pend′ed, *adj.*
self′-sus·pi′cion, *n.*
self′-sus·pi′cious, *adj.*
self′-sus′te·nance, *n.*
self′-sus′ten·ta′tion, *n.*
self′-sway′, *n.*
self′-tap′ping, *adj.*
self′-tax·a′tion, *n.*
self′-taxed′, *adj.*
self′-teach′er, *n.*
self′-teach′ing, *adj.*
self′-tempt′ed, *adj.*
self′-ten′der·ness, *n.*
self′-ter′mi·nat′ing, *adj.*
self′-ter′mi·na′tive, *adj.*
self′-test′ing, *adj.*
self′-ther′a·py, *n., pl.* **-pies.**
self′-thin′ning, *adj.*
self′-thought′, *n.*
self′-thread′ing, *adj.*
self′-tight′en·ing, *adj.*
self′-tip′ping, *adj.*
self′-tire′, *v.i.,* **-tired, -tir·ing.**
self′-tol′er·ant, *adj.;* **-ly,** *adv.*
self′-tor′ture, *n.*
self′-tor′tured, *adj.*
self′-tor′tur·ing, *adj.*
self′-trained′, *adj.*
self′-train′ing, *n.*
self′-tran·scend′ence, *n.*
self′-trans′for·ma′tion, *n.*
self′-trans·formed′, *adj.*
self′-treat′ed, *adj.*
self′-treat′ment, *n.*
self′-tri′al, *n.*
self′-trit′u·rat′ing, *adj.*
self′-trou′bled, *adj.*
self′-trou′bling, *adj.*
self′-trust′, *n.*
self′-trust′ing, *adj.*
self′-tu·i′tion, *n.*
self′-un·con′scious, *adj.*
self′-un′der·stand′ing, *n.*
self′-un′der·stood′, *adj.*
self′-un·do′ing, *adj.*
self′-u′ni·form′, *n.*
self′-un′ion, *n.*
self′-u′ni·ty, *n.*
self′-un·load′ing, *adj.*
self′-un·veil′ing, *adj.*
self′-un·wor′thi·ness, *n.*
self′-up·braid′ing, *adj.*
self′-u·surp′, *v.i.*
self′-val′u·a′tion, *n.*
self′-val′ued, *adj.*
self′-val′u·ing, *adj.*
self′-var′i·ance, *n.*
self′-var′i·a′tion, *n.*
self′-var′y·ing, *adj.*
self′-vaunt′ed, *adj.*
self′-vaunt′ing, *adj.*
self′-ven·di′tion, *n.*
self′-ven′ti·lat′ed, *adj.*
self′-vex·a′tion, *n.*
self′-vin′di·cat′ed, *adj.*
self′-vin′di·cat′ing, *adj.*
self′-vin′di·ca′tion, *n.*
self′-vi′o·lence, *n.*
self′-vi′o·lent, *adj.*
self′-viv′i·sec′tor, *n.*
self′-vul′can·iz′ing, *adj.*
self′-want′, *n.*
self′-war′rant·ing, *adj.*
self′-watch′ful·ness, *n.*
self′-wea′ri·ness, *n.*
self′-wea′ry, *adj.*
self′-weight′, *n.*
self′-weight′ed, *adj.*
self′-whip′per, *n.*
self′-whip′ping, *adj.*
self′-whole′, *adj.*
self′-wise′, *adj.*
self′-wit′ness, *n.*
self′-wit′nessed, *adj.*
self′-work′ing, *adj.*
self′-worn′, *adj.*
self′-wor′ship, *n.*
self′-wor′ship·er, *n.*
self′-wor′ship·ing, *adj.*
self′-wor′ship·per, *n.*
self′-wor′ship·ping, *adj.*
self′-wound′ed, *adj.*
self′-wound′ing, *adj.*
self′-writ′ing, *adj.*
self′-writ′ten, *adj.*
self′-wrought′, *adj.*

sell•out (sel′out′), *n.* **1.** an act or instance of selling out. **2.** an entertainment for which all the seats are sold. **3.** *Informal.* a person who betrays a cause, organization, or the like; traitor. **4.** *Informal.* a person who compromises his or her personal values, integrity, talent, or the like, for money or personal advancement. [1855–60, *Amer.*; n. use of v. phrase *sell out*]

Sel•ma (sel′mə), *n.* **1.** a city in central Alabama, on the Alabama River. 26,684. **2.** a town in central California. 10,942. **3.** a female given name.

selt•zer (selt′sər), *n.* **1.** (*sometimes cap.*) a naturally effervescent mineral water containing common salt and small quantities of sodium, calcium, and magnesium carbonates. **2.** tap water that has been commercially filtered, carbonated, and bottled with no addition of minerals or mineral salts. Also called **selt′zer wa′ter.** [1735–45; < G *Selterser* named after *Selters,* a village near Wiesbaden; see -ER[1]]

sel•va (sel′və), *n.* a tropical rain forest, as that in the Amazon basin of South America. [1840–50; < Brazilian Pg; Pg: forest < L *silva*]

sel•vage (sel′vij), *n.* **1.** the edge of woven fabric finished so as to prevent raveling, often in a narrow tape effect, different from the body of the fabric. **2.** any similar strip or part of surplus material, as at the side of wallpaper. **3.** Also called **margin.** *Philately.* the surplus paper or margin around a sheet of stamps. **4.** a plate or surface through which a bolt of a lock passes. Also, **sel′•vedge.** [1425–75; late ME, resp. of SELF + EDGE, modeled on MD *selfegge* (D *zelfegge*)] **—sel′vaged,** *adj.*

selves (selvz), *n.* pl. of **self.**

Sel•ye (zel′ye), *n.* **Hans,** 1907–82, Canadian physician and medical educator, born in Austria.

Selz•nick (selz′nik), *n.* **David O(liver),** 1902–65, U.S. motion-picture producer.

Sem (sem), *n. Douay Bible.* Shem.

SEM, *Optics.* scanning electron microscope.

Sem., **1.** Seminary. **2.** Semitic. Also, **Sem**

sem., semicolon.

se•mai•nier (sə men′yā; *Fr.* sə me nyā′), *n., pl.* **-mai•niers** (-men′yāz; *Fr.* -me nyā′). *Fr. Furniture.* a chest of the 18th century having seven long drawers: originally meant to hold a week's supply of clothing. [< F, equiv. to *semaine* week < LL *septimāna,* n. use of fem. of L *septimānus* of seven (deriv. of *septem* SEVEN; see -AN) + F *-ier* -IER[2]]

se•maise (si mez′), *n.* cymaise.

Se•mang (si mäng′), *n., pl.* **-mangs,** (*esp. collectively*) **-mang.** a member of a Negrito people of the Malay Peninsula.

se•man•teme (si man′tēm), *n. Ling.* one of the minimum elements of lexical meaning in a language. [1920–25; < F *semantème,* equiv. to *sémant(ique)* SEMANTIC + *-ème* -EME]

se•man•tic (si man′tik), *adj.* **1.** of, pertaining to, or arising from the different meanings of words or other symbols: *semantic change; semantic confusion.* **2.** of or pertaining to semantics. Also, **se•man′ti•cal.** [1655–65; < Gk *sēmantikós* having meaning, equiv. to *sēmant(ós)* marked (*sēman-,* base of *sēmaínein* to show, mark + *-tos* verbal adj. suffix; akin to *sêma* sign) + *-ikos* -IC] **—se•man′ti•cal•ly,** *adv.*

seman′tic differen′tial, *Psycholing.* a technique for measuring the connotative meaning of concepts by having an individual rate each concept on a series of graduated scales, each scale defined by a pair of polar adjectives, as *good–bad* or *strong–weak.* [1950–55]

seman′tic field′, *Ling.* an area of human experience or perception, as color, that is delimited and subcategorized by a set of interrelated vocabulary items in a language.

se•man•tics (si man′tiks), *n.* (*used with a singular v.*) **1.** *Ling.* **a.** the study of meaning. **b.** the study of linguistic development by classifying and examining changes in meaning and form. **2.** Also called **significs.** the branch of semiotics dealing with the relations between signs and what they denote. **3.** the meaning, or an interpretation of the meaning, of a word, sign, sentence, etc.: *Let's not argue about semantics.* **4.** See **general semantics.** [1895–1900; see SEMANTIC, -ICS] **—se•man•ti•cist** (si man′tə sist), **se•man•ti•cian** (sē′man tish′ən), *n.*

sem•a•phore (sem′ə fôr′, -fōr′), *n., v.,* **-phored, -phor•ing.** **—n.** **1.** an apparatus for conveying information by means of visual signals, as a light whose position may be changed. **2.** any of various devices for signaling by changing the position of a light, flag, etc. **3.** a system of signaling, esp. one by which a special flag is held in each hand and various positions of the arms indicate specific letters, numbers, etc. **—*v.t., v.i.*** **4.** to signal by semaphore or by some system of flags. [1810–20; < Gk *sêma* sign + -PHORE] **—sem•a•phor•ic** (sem′ə fôr′ik, -for′-), **sem′a•phor′i•cal,** *adj.* **—sem′a•phor′i•cal•ly,** *adv.*

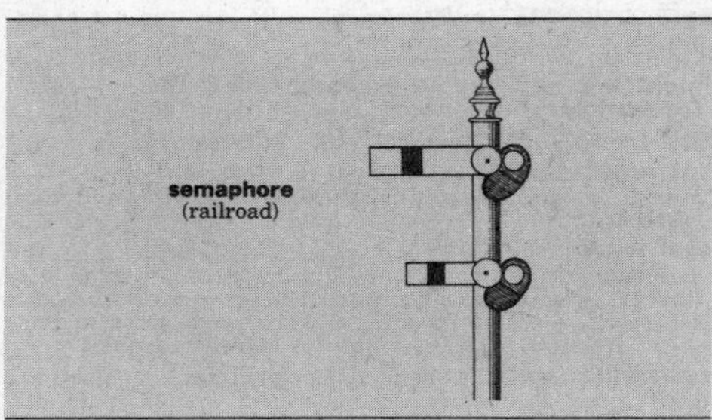

semaphore (railroad)

Se•ma•rang (sə mär′äng), *n.* a seaport on N Java, in S Indonesia. 646,500. Also, **Samarang.**

se•ma•si•ol•o•gy (si mā′sē ol′ə jē, -zē-), *n.* semantics, esp. the study of semantic change. [1875–80; < Gk *sēmasí(a)* signal, mark, meaning + -o- + -LOGY] **—se•ma•si•o•log•i•cal** (si mā′sē ə loj′i kəl, -zē-), *adj.* **—se•ma′si•o•log′i•cal•ly,** *adv.* **—se•ma′si•ol′o•gist,** *n.*

se•mat•ic (si mat′ik), *adj. Biol.* serving as a sign or warning of danger, as the conspicuous colors or markings of certain poisonous animals. [1885–90; < Gk *sēmat-* (s. of *sêma*) sign + -IC]

sem•bla•ble (sem′blə bəl), *n.* **1.** a person or thing that resembles or matches another; counterpart. **2.** *Archaic.* likeness; resemblance. **—*adj. Archaic.*** **3.** like or similar. **4.** seeming or apparent. [1325–75; ME < MF, equiv. to *sembl(er)* to seem + *-able* -ABLE. See SEMBLANCE] **—sem′bla•bly,** *adv.*

sem•blance (sem′bləns), *n.* **1.** outward aspect or appearance. **2.** an assumed or unreal appearance; show. **3.** an electronic device or software program that digitally stores sound for modification and playback through a synthesizer. **4.** a likeness, image, or copy. **5.** a spectral appearance; apparition. [1250–1300; ME < MF, equiv. to *sembl(er)* to seem (see RESEMBLE) + *-ance* -ANCE]
—Syn. **1.** aspect, exterior, mien, air. **2.** seeming.

se•mé (sə mā′), *adj. Heraldry.* covered with many small, identical figures. [1555–65; < F: lit., sown, ptp. of *semer* < L *sēmināre* to sow, equiv. to *sēmin-* (s. of *sēmen*) seed, SEMEN + *-āre* inf. suffix]

se•mei•ol•o•gy (sē′mē ol′ə jē, sem′ē-, sē′mī-), *n.* semiology.

se•mei•ot•ic (sē′mē ot′ik, sem′ē-, sē′mī-), *adj.* semiotic. Also, **se′mei•ot′i•cal.**

se•mei•ot•ics (sē′mē ot′iks, sem′ē-, sē′mī-), *n.* (*used with a singular v.*) semiotics.

Sem•e•le (sem′ə lē′), *n. Class. Myth.* a daughter of Cadmus and mother, by Zeus, of Dionysus. Cf. **Thyone.**

sem•eme (sem′ēm, sē′mēm), *n. Ling.* **1.** the meaning of a morpheme. **2.** a basic unit of meaning or content. [< Gk *sêm(a)* sign + -EME; coined by L. Bloomfield in 1933; cf. SEMANTEME]

se•men (sē′mən), *n.* the viscid, whitish fluid produced in the male reproductive organs, containing spermatozoa. [1350–1400; ME < L *sēmen* seed; akin to *serere* to sow[1]]

Se•më•nov (sim yô′nəf; *Russ.* syi myô′nəf), *n.* **Ni•co•lai N.** (nik′ə lī′; *Russ.* nyi ku lyī′), born 1896, Russian chemist: Nobel prize 1956.

se•mes•ter (si mes′tər), *n.* **1.** (in many educational institutions) a division constituting half of the regular academic year, lasting typically from 15 to 18 weeks. **2.** (in German universities) a session, lasting about six months and including periods of recess. [1820–30; < G < L *sēmē(n)stris* of six months duration < **sex-mēnstris,* equiv. to *sex* SIX + *mēns(is)* month + *-tris* adj. suffix (perh. repr. an earlier **mens(i)-teros*)] **—se•mes′tral, se•mes•tri•al** (si mes′trē əl), *adj.*

semes′ter hour′, *Educ.* a unit of academic credit fulfilled by completing one hour of class instruction each week for one semester. [1945–50, *Amer.*]

sem•i (sem′ē, sem′ī), *n. Informal.* **1.** semitrailer (def. 1). **2.** Often, **semis.** semifinal (def. 3). [by shortening]

semi-, a combining form borrowed from Latin, meaning "half," freely prefixed to English words of any origin, now sometimes with the senses "partially," "incompletely," "somewhat": *semiautomatic; semimonthly.* [ME < L *sēmi-;* c. OE *sōm-, sām-* half (mod. dial. *sam-*), OHG *sāmi-,* Skt *sāmi-,* Gk *hēmi-;* cf. SESQUI-]
—Usage. See **bi-**[1].
—Note. The lists at the bottom of this and following pages provide the spelling, syllabification, and stress for words whose meanings may easily be inferred by combining the meanings of SEMI- and an attached base word, or a base word plus a suffix. Appropriate parts of speech are also shown. Words prefixed by SEMI- that have special meanings or uses are entered in their proper alphabetical places in the main vocabulary or as derived forms run on at the end of a main vocabulary entry.

semi•ab•stract (sem′ē ab′strakt, -ab strakt′, sem′ī-), *adj.* pertaining to or designating a style of painting or sculpture in which the subject remains recognizable although the forms are highly stylized in a manner derived from abstract art. [1940–45] **—sem•i•ab•strac•tion** (sem′ē ab strak′shən, sem′ī-), *n.*

sem•i•am•a•teur (sem′ē am′ə chŏŏr′, -chər, -tər, -am′ə tûr′, sem′ī-), *adj.* **1.** retaining amateur status but receiving prize money or support, as from a sponsor, to cover training expenses. **—n.** **2.** a semiamateur athlete. [1975–80]

sem•i•an•nu•al (sem′ē an′yōō əl, sem′ī-), *adj.* **1.** occurring, done, or published every half year or twice a year; semiyearly. **2.** lasting for half a year: *a semiannual plant.* [1785–95; SEMI- + ANNUAL] **—sem′i•an′•nu•al•ly,** *adv.*
—Usage. See **bi-**[1].

sem•i•a•quat•ic (sem′ē ə kwat′ik, -kwot′-, sem′ī-), *adj. Bot., Zool.* partly aquatic; growing or living in or close to water, or carrying out part of its life cycle in water. [1825–35; SEMI- + AQUATIC]

sem•i•arch (sem′ē ärch′, sem′ī-), *n.* a half arch. [1815–25; SEMI- + ARCH[1]]

sem•i•ar•id (sem′ē ar′id, sem′ī-), *adj.* (of a region, land, etc.) characterized by very little annual rainfall, usually from 10 to 20 in. (25 to 50 cm): *to raise vegetables in semiarid regions.* [1895–1900, *Amer.*; SEMI- + ARID] **—sem•i•a•rid•ity** (sem′ē ə rid′i tē, sem′ī-), *n.*

sem•i•au•to•bi•o•graph•i•cal (sem′ē ô′tə bī′ə graf′i kəl, sem′ī-), *adj.* **1.** pertaining to or being a fictionalized account of an author's own life. **2.** pertaining to or being a work of fiction strongly influenced by events in an author's life. [1935–40; SEMI- + AUTOBIOGRAPHICAL]

sem•i•au•to•mat•ic (sem′ē ô′tə mat′ik, sem′ī-), *adj.* **1.** partly automatic. **2.** (of a firearm) automatically ejecting the cartridge case of a fired shot and loading the next cartridge from the magazine but requiring a squeeze of the trigger to fire each individual shot. **—n.** **3.** a self-loading rifle or other firearm. [1890–95; SEMI- + AUTOMATIC] **—sem′i•au′to•mat′i•cal•ly,** *adv.*

sem•i•au•ton•o•mous (sem′ē ô ton′ə məs, sem′ī-), *adj.* partially self-governing, esp. with reference to internal affairs. [1900–05; SEMI- + AUTONOMOUS]

sem•i•au•ton•o•my (sem′ē ô ton′ə mē, sem′ī-), *n., pl.* **-mies.** **1.** the quality or state of being semiautonomous. **2.** a semiautonomous system of government. [1945–50; SEMI- + AUTONOMY]

sem•i•base•ment (sem′ē bās′mənt, sem′ī-, sem′ē-bās′-, sem′ī-), *n.* a basement partly above ground, as in a house built on a hill. [1870–75; SEMI- + BASEMENT]

sem′i•bi•tu′mi•nous coal′ (sem′ē bi tōō′mə nəs, -tyōō′-, sem′ī-, sem′ē-, sem′ī-), a coal intermediate between bituminous and anthracite coal in hardness, yielding the maximum heat of any ordinary steam coal. [1855–60; SEMI- + BITUMINOUS]

sem•i•breve (sem′ē brēv′, -brev′, sem′ī-), *n. Music Chiefly Brit.* a note half the length of a breve; whole note. See illus. under **note.** [1585–95; SEMI- + BREVE]

CONCISE ETYMOLOGY KEY: <, descended or borrowed from; >, whence; b., blend of, blended; c., cognate with; cf., compare; deriv., derivative; equiv., equivalent; imit., imitative; obl., oblique; r., replacing; s., stem; sp., spelling, spelled; resp., respelling, respelled; trans., translation; ?, origin unknown; *, unattested; ‡, probably earlier than. See the full key inside the front cover.

sem′i•ab•sorb′ent, *adj.*
sem′i•ac′a•dem′ic, *adj.*
sem′i•ac′a•dem′i•cal, *adj.;* **-ly,** *adv.*
sem′i•a•ce′tic, *adj.*
sem′i•ac′id, *adj.*
sem′i•a•cid′ic, *adj.*
sem′i•a•cid′i•fied′, *adj.*
sem′i•a•cid′u•lat′ed, *adj.*
sem′i•ac′ro•bat′ic, *adj.*
sem′i•ac′tive, *adj.;* **-ly,** *adv.;* **-ness,** *n.*
sem′i•ad•he′sive, *adj.;* **-ly,** *adv.;* **-ness,** *n.*
sem′i•ag′ri•cul′tur•al, *adj.*
sem′i•al′co•hol′ic, *adj.*
sem′i•al′le•gor′ic, *adj.*
sem′i•al′le•gor′i•cal, *adj.;* **-ly,** *adv.*
sem′i•a•lu′mi•nous, *adj.*
sem′i•an′aes•thet′ic, *adj.*
sem′i•an′a•lyt′ic, *adj.*
sem′i•an′a•lyt′i•cal, *adj.;* **-ly,** *adv.*
sem′i•an′ar•chism, *n.*
sem′i•an′ar•chist, *n.*
sem′i•an′ar•chis′tic, *adj.*
sem′i•an′a•tom′ic, *adj.*
sem′i•an′a•tom′i•cal, *adj.;* **-ly,** *adv.*
sem′i•an•drog′e•nous, *adj.*
sem′i•an′es•thet′ic, *adj.*
sem′i•an′gle, *n.*
sem′i•an′gu•lar, *adj.*
sem′i•an′i•mal, *n., adj.*
sem′i•an′i•mate, *adj.*
sem′i•an′i•mat′ed, *adj.*
sem′i•an′thro•po•log′ic, *adj.*
sem′i•an′thro•po•log′i•cal, *adj.;* **-ly,** *adv.*
sem′i•ar′chi•tec′tur•al, *adj.;* **-ly,** *adv.*
sem′i•a•rous′al, *n.*
sem′i•ar•tic′u•late, *adj.;* **-ly,** *adv.*
sem′i•bald′, *adj.;* **-ly,** *adv.;* **-ness,** *n.*
sem′i•belt′ed, *adj.*
sem′i•bi′o•graph′ic, *adj.*
sem′i•bi′o•graph′i•cal, *adj;* **-ly,** *adv.*
sem′i•bi′o•log′ic, *adj.*
sem′i•bi′o•log′i•cal, *adj.;* **-ly,** *adv.*
sem′i•blas′phe•mous, *adj.;* **-ly,** *adv.;* **-ness,** *n.*
sem′i•bleached′, *adj.*
sem′i•boiled′, *adj.*
sem′i•bouf•fant′, *adj.*
sem′i•bour•geois′, *adj.*
sem′i•bu′reau•crat′ic, *adj.*
sem′i•bu′reau•crat′i•cal•ly, *adv.*
sem′i•cab′a•lis′tic, *adj.*
sem′i•cab′a•lis′ti•cal, *adj.;* **-ly,** *adv.*
sem′i•cal′cined, *adj.*
sem′i•cap′i•tal•is′tic, *adj.*
sem′i•cap′i•tal•is′ti•cal•ly, *adv.*
sem′i•cap•tiv′i•ty, *n.*
sem′i•car′bon•ate′, *adj.*
sem′i•car′i•ca•tur′al, *adj.*
sem′i•carved′, *adj.*
sem′i•cat′a•lyst, *n.*
sem′i•cat′a•lyt′ic, *adj.*
sem′i•ca•thar′tic, *adj.*
sem′i•cel′lu•lose′, *n.*
sem′i•cel′lu•lous, *adj.*
sem′i•cha•ot′ic, *adj.*
sem′i•cha•ot′i•cal•ly, *adv.*
sem′i•chem′i•cal, *adj.;* **-ly,** *adv.*
sem′i•cler′i•cal, *adj.;* **-ly,** *adv.*
sem′i•clin′i•cal, *adj.;* **-ly,** *adv.*
sem′i•closed′, *adj.*
sem′i•col′loid, *n.*
sem′i•col•loi′dal, *adj.*
sem′i•col•lo′qui•al, *adj.;* **-ly,** *adv.*
sem′i•co•lo′ni•al, *adj.;* **-ly,** *adv.*
sem′i•col′o•ny, *n., pl.* **-nies.**
sem′i•com•bined′, *adj.*
sem′i•com′ic, *adj.*
sem′i•com′i•cal, *adj.;* **-ly,** *adv.*
sem′i•com•mer′cial, *adj.;* **-ly,** *adv.*
sem′i•com•mu′ni•ca′tive, *adj.*
sem′i•con•cealed′, *adj.*
sem′i•con•di′tioned, *adj.*
sem′i•con•fine′ment, *n.*
sem′i•con•form′ist, *n.*
sem′i•con•form′i•ty, *n.*
sem′i•con′i•cal, *adj.;* **-ly,** *adv.*
sem′i•con•serv′a•tive, *adj.;* **-ly,** *adv.*
sem′i•con•tin′u•ous, *adj.;* **-ly,** *adv.*
sem′i•con•ven′tion•al, *adj.;* **-ly,** *adv.*
sem′i•con•ven′tion•al′i•ty, *n., pl.* **-ties.**
sem′i•con•ver′sion, *n.*
sem′i•cor′date, *adj.*
sem′i•cot′ton, *n.*
sem′i•cre′tin, *n.*
sem′i•cul′ti•vat′ed, *adj.*
sem′i•cul′tured, *adj.*
sem′i•cured′, *adj.*
sem′i•cus′tom•ized′, *adj.*
sem′i•cyn′i•cal, *adj.;* **-ly,** *adv.*
sem′i•dan′ger•ous, *adj.;* **-ly,** *adv.;* **-ness,** *n.*
sem′i•deaf′, *adj.;* **-ness,** *n.*
sem′i•dec′a•dent, *adj.;* **-ly,** *adv.*
sem′i•de•cay′, *n.*
sem′i•de•cayed′, *adj.*
sem′i•de•fen′sive, *adj.;* **-ly,** *adv.;* **-ness,** *n.*
sem′i•de•fined′, *adj.*
sem′i•def′i•nite, *adj.;* **-ly,** *adv.;* **-ness,** *n.*
sem′i•de•lir′i•um, *n.*
sem′i•de•ment′ed, *adj.*
sem′i•de•pend′ence, *n.*
sem′i•de•pend′ent, *adj.;* **-ly,** *adv.*
sem′i•de•struc′tion, *n.*
sem′i•de•struc′tive, *adj.*
sem′i•de•ter′min•is′tic, *adj.*
sem′i•di•aph′a•nous, *adj.;* **-ly,** *adv.;* **-ness,** *n.*

sem•i•cen•ten•ar•y (sem′ē sen ten′ə rē, -sen′tn er′ē, sem′ī- *or, esp. Brit.,* -sen tē′nə rē), *adj., n., pl.* **-ar•ies.** semicentennial. [1865–70; SEMI- + CENTENARY]

sem•i•cen•ten•ni•al (sem′ē sen ten′ē əl, sem′ī-), *adj.* **1.** of or pertaining to a fiftieth anniversary. **—n. 2.** a fiftieth anniversary. **3.** the celebration of this anniversary. [1855–60; SEMI- + CENTENNIAL]

sem•i•cir•cle (sem′i sûr′kəl), *n.* **1.** Also called **semi•cir•cum•fer•ence** (sem′ē sər kum′fər əns, -frəns, sem′ī-). half of a circle; the arc from one end of a diameter to the other. **2.** anything having or arranged in the form of a half of a circle. [1520–30; < L *sēmicirculus.* See SEMI-, CIRCLE] **—sem•i•cir•cu•lar** (sem′i sûr′kyə lər), *adj.* **—sem′i•cir′cu•lar•ly,** *adv.* **—sem′i•cir′cu•lar•ness,** *n.*

semicir′cular canal′, *Anat.* any of the three curved tubular canals in the labyrinth of the ear, associated with the sense of equilibrium. See diag. under **ear.** [1740–50]

sem•i•civ•i•lized (sem′ē siv′ə līzd′, sem′ī-), *adj.* half or partly civilized. [1830–40; SEMI- + CIVILIZED] **—sem′i•civ′i•li•za′tion,** *n.*

sem•i•clas•si•cal (sem′ē klas′i kəl, sem′ī-), *adj.* **1.** of or pertaining to music by classical composers that is familiar or appealing to the general public. **2.** of or pertaining to music intermediate in style between classical and popular music. [1900–05; SEMI- + CLASSICAL] **—sem′i•clas′si•cal•ly,** *adv.*

sem•i•co•lon (sem′i kō′lən), *n.* the punctuation mark (;) used to indicate a major division in a sentence where a more distinct separation is felt between clauses or items on a list than is indicated by a comma, as between the two clauses of a compound sentence. [1635–45; SEMI- + COLON[1]]

sem•i•co•ma (sem′ē kō′mə, sem′ī-), *n., pl.* **-mas.** a light coma from which a person can be roused. [1895–1900; SEMI- + COMA] **—sem•i•com•a•tose** (sem′i kom′ə tōs′, -kō′mə-), *adj.*

sem•i•con•duct•ing (sem′ē kən duk′ting, sem′ī-), *adj.* of, pertaining to, or having the characteristics of a semiconductor. Also, **sem′i•con•duc′tive.** [1780–90; SEMI- + CONDUCT + -ING[2]]

sem•i•con•duc•tor (sem′ē kən duk′tər, sem′ī-), *n.* **1.** a substance, as silicon or germanium, with electrical conductivity intermediate between that of an insulator and a conductor: a basic component of various kinds of electronic circuit element **(sem′iconductor device′)** used in communications, control, and detection technology and in computers. **2.** a semiconductor device. [1875–80; SEMI- + CONDUCTOR]

sem•i•con•scious (sem′ē kon′shəs, sem′ī-), *adj.* half-conscious; not fully conscious. [1830–40; SEMI- + CONSCIOUS] **—sem′i•con′scious•ly,** *adv.* **—sem′i•con′scious•ness,** *n.*

sem•i•crys•tal•line (sem′ē kris′tl in, -īn′, sem′ī-), *adj.* partly or imperfectly crystalline. [1810–20; SEMI- + CRYSTALLINE]

sem•i•cyl•in•der (sem′ē sil′in dər, sem′ī-), *n.* half of a cylinder divided lengthwise. [1660–70; SEMI- + CYLINDER] **—sem•i•cy•lin•dri•cal** (sem′ē si lin′dri kəl, sem′ī-), **sem′i•cy•lin′dric,** *adj.*

sem•i•dai•ly (sem′ē dā′lē, sem′ī-), *adj., adv.* twice daily. [1865–70; SEMI- + DAILY]

sem•i•dark•ness (sem′ē därk′nis, sem′ī-), *n.* partial darkness. [1840–50; SEMI- + DARKNESS]

sem•i•de•i•fy (sem′ē dē′ə fī′, sem′ī-), *v.t.,* **-fied, -fy•ing.** to elevate (a person, object, or nature) to the status of a demigod. [1950–55; SEMI- + DEIFY] **—sem′i•de′i•fi•ca′tion,** *n.*

sem•i•des•ert (sem′ē dez′ərt, sem′ī-), *n.* an extremely dry area characterized by sparse vegetation. [1840–50; SEMI- + DESERT[1]]

sem•i•de•tached (sem′ē di tacht′, sem′ī-), *adj.* **1.** partly detached. **2.** of or pertaining to a house joined by a party wall to another house or row of houses. [1855–60; SEMI- + DETACHED] **—sem′i•de•tach′ment,** *n.*

sem•i•di•am•e•ter (sem′ē dī am′i tər, sem′ī-), *n.* half of a diameter; radius. [1545–55; SEMI- + DIAMETER]

sem•i•di•ur•nal (sem′ē dī ûr′nl, sem′ī-), *adj.* **1.** pertaining to, consisting of, or accomplished in half a day. **2.** occurring every 12 hours or twice each day. [1585–95; SEMI- + DIURNAL]

sem•i•di•vine (sem′ē di vīn′, sem′ī-), *adj.* somewhat more than mortal but less than divine. [1590–1600; SEMI- + DIVINE]

sem•i•dome (sem′ē dōm′, sem′ī-), *n.* half a dome, esp. as formed by a vertical section, as over a semicircular apse. [1780–90; SEMI- + DOME] **—sem′i•domed′,** *adj.*

sem•i•do•mes•ti•cat•ed (sem′ē də mes′ti kā′tid, sem′ī-), *adj.* living in a state of partial domestication. [1840–50; SEMI- + DOMESTICATED] **—sem′i•do•mes′ti•ca′tion,** *n.*

sem•i•dom•i•nance (sem′ē dom′ə nəns, sem′ī-), *n. Genetics.* See **incomplete dominance.** [SEMI- + DOMINANCE]

sem•i•dou•ble (sem′ē dub′əl, sem′ī-), *adj. Bot.* having more petals than those of a single flower but fewer than those of a double flower. [1970–75; SEMI- + DOUBLE]

sem•i•dry (sem′ē drī′, sem′ī-), *adj.* partially or nearly dry. [1875–80; SEMI- + DRY]

sem•i•du•ra•bles (sem′ē dŏŏr′ə bəlz, -dyŏŏr′-, sem′ī-), *n.pl.* goods, as clothing or furniture, that are neither perishable nor truly durable. Also called **sem′i•du′ra•ble goods′.** [SEMI- + *durables* (pl. of DURABLE)]

sem•i•el•lipse (sem′ē i lips′, sem′ī-), *n. Geom.* a half ellipse, usually one containing both ends of the major axis. [1725–35; SEMI- + ELLIPSE] **—sem•i•el•lip•tic** (sem′ē i lip′tik, sem′ī-), **sem′i•el•lip′ti•cal,** *adj.*

sem•i•ev•er•green (sem′ē ev′ər grēn′, sem′ī-), *adj. Bot.* retaining green, unwithered leaves for part of the winter or through comparatively mild winters. [1900–05; SEMI- + EVERGREEN]

sem•i•fi•nal (sem′ē fīn′l, sem′ī-), *Sports.* **—adj. 1.** of or pertaining to the round preceding the final one in a tournament from which losers are eliminated. **2.** (in boxing) of or pertaining to the second most important bout on a card, usually immediately preceding the main bout. **—n. 3.** a semifinal contest or round. **4.** (in boxing) the second most important bout on a card. [1880–85; SEMI- + FINAL]

sem•i•fi•nal•ist (sem′ē fīn′l ist, sem′ī-), *n. Sports.* a participant or one qualified to participate in a semifinal. [1920–25; SEMIFINAL + -IST, on the model of FINALIST]

sem•i•fin•ished (sem′ē fin′isht, sem′ī-), *adj.* **1.** partially or almost finished. **2.** (of a manufactured object) being in a form suitable for working easily into a finished product. [1900–05; SEMI- + FINISHED]

sem•i•fit•ted (sem′ē fit′id, sem′ī-), *adj.* designed to fit closely but not snugly: *a semifitted jacket.* [1945–50; SEMI- + FIT[1] + -ED[2]]

sem•i•flex•i•ble (sem′ē flek′sə bəl, sem′ī-), *adj.* moderately or somewhat flexible. [1920–25; SEMI- + FLEXIBLE]

sem•i•float•ing (sem′ē flō′ting, sem′ī-), *adj.* noting or pertaining to a driving axle of an automobile or the like, the inner end of which is carried by the differential gear and the outer end of which is keyed to a wheel supported by the axle housing. [SEMI- + FLOATING]

sem•i•flu•id (sem′ē flōō′id, sem′ī-), *adj.* **1.** imperfectly fluid; having both fluid and solid characteristics; semiliquid. **—n. 2.** a semifluid substance. Also, **semiliquid.** [1725–35; SEMI- + FLUID] **—sem′i•flu•id′i•ty,** *n.*

sem•i•for•mal (sem′ē fôr′məl, sem′ī-), *adj.* partly formal; containing some formal elements: *a semiformal occasion; semiformal attire.* [1930–35; SEMI- + FORMAL]

sem•i•glob•u•lar (sem′ē glob′yə lər, sem′ī-), *adj.* possessing the form of half a globe; hemispheric. [1715–25; SEMI- + GLOBULAR] **—sem′i•glob′u•lar•ly,** *adv.*

sem•i•gloss (sem′ē glos′, -glôs′, sem′ī-), *adj.* **1.** (of paint or a painted surface) having a moderate, satiny luster; having or producing a sheen that is neither flat nor highly glossy. **—n. 2.** a paint that has or produces a moderate, satiny sheen. [1935–40; SEMI- + GLOSS[1]]

sem•i•group (sem′ē grōōp′), *n. Math.* an algebraic system closed under an associative binary operation. [1925–30; SEMI- + GROUP]

semih., (in prescriptions) half an hour. [< L *sēmihōra*]

sem•i•har•dy (sem′ē här′dē, sem′ī-), *adj. Hort.* partially hardy; able to survive moderately low temperatures: *semihardy plants.* [1900–05; SEMI- + HARDY[1]]

sem•i•in•de•pend•ent (sem′ē in′di pen′dənt), *adj.* (of a political entity) having substantial self-government in regard to local matters but subordinate in such external matters as foreign policy; semiautonomous. [1855–60] **—sem′i•in′de•pend′ent•ly,** *adv.*

sem•i•liq•uid (sem′ē lik′wid, sem′ī-), *adj., n.* semifluid. [1675–85; SEMI- + LIQUID] **—sem′i•li•quid′i•ty,** *n.*

sem•i•lit•er•ate (sem′ē lit′ər it, sem′ī-), *adj.* **1.** barely able to read and write. **2.** capable of reading but not writing. **3.** literate but poorly skilled or informed; lacking the proficiency of a literate person. **—n. 4.** a person who is semiliterate. [1925–30; SEMI- + LITERATE] **—sem•i•lit•er•a•cy** (sem′ē lit′ər ə sē, sem′ī-), *n.*

Sé•mil•lon (sā′mē yôN′; *Fr.* sā mē yôN′), *n.* a variety of white grape used in winemaking, esp. in France in the Sauternes district of Bordeaux. [1870–75; < F, earlier *sémilion* < Gascon *semilhoun,* equiv. to OPr *semilh(ar)* to sow, deriv. of *seme* seed (< L *sēmen;* see SEMEN) + Gascon, Pr *-oun* agentive suffix (appar. alluding to the variety's high productivity)]

sem•i•log•a•rith•mic (sem′ē lô′gə rith′mik, -rith′-, -log′ə-, sem′ī-), *adj. Math.* (of graphing) having one scale logarithmic and the other arithmetic or of uniform gradation. Also, **sem′i•log′.** [1915–20; SEMI- + LOGARITHMIC]

sem•i•lu•nar (sem′ē lōō′nər, sem′ī-), *adj.* shaped like a half-moon; crescent. [1590–1600; SEMI- + LUNAR]

sem′ilu′nar bone′, lunate (def. 2). [1825–35]

sem′ilu′nar valve′, *Anat.* either of two valves, one in the aorta and one in the pulmonary artery, consisting of a set of three crescent-shaped flaps of tissue and serving to prevent blood from flowing back into the heart after contraction. Cf. **aortic valve, pulmonary valve.** [1710–20]

sem′i•ma′jor ax′is (sem′ē mā′jər, sem′ī-, sem′ē-, sem′ī-), **1.** *Geom.* one half the major axis of an ellipse. **2.** *Astron.* one half the major axis of the ellipse that one celestial body describes around another, as a planet around the sun or a satellite around a planet, equivalent to the mean distance between the two bodies. [1925–30; SEMI- + MAJOR]

sem•i•matte (sem′ē mat′, sem′ī-), *adj.* midway between matte and glossy, as certain paper or paint. Also, **sem′i•mat′, sem′i•matt′.** [1935–40; SEMI- + MATTE[1]]

sem•i•mi•cro•a•nal•y•sis (sem′ē mī′krō ə nal′ə sis), *n., pl.* **-ses** (-sēz′). *Chem.* any analytical method in which the weight of the sample is between 10 and 100 milligrams. [1950–55; SEMI- + MICROANALYSIS]

sem′i•mi′nor ax′is (sem′ē mī′nər, sem′ī-, sem′ē-, sem′ī-), **1.** *Geom.* one half the minor axis of an ellipse. **2.** *Astron.* one half the minor axis of the ellipse that one celestial body describes around another, as a planet around the sun. [1925–30; SEMI- + MINOR]

sem•i•month•ly (sem′ē munth′lē, sem′ī-), *adj., n., pl.* **-lies,** *adv.* **—adj. 1.** made, occurring, done, or published twice a month. **—n. 2.** something occurring every half month or twice a month. **3.** a semimonthly publication. **—adv. 4.** twice a month: *We went semimonthly to see her.* [1855–60; SEMI- + MONTHLY]
—Usage. See **bi-**[1].

sem•i•nal (sem′ə nl), *adj.* **1.** pertaining to, containing, or consisting of semen. **2.** *Bot.* of or pertaining to seed. **3.** having possibilities of future development. **4.** highly original and influencing the development of future events: *a seminal artist; seminal ideas.* [1350–1400; ME < L *sēminālis,* equiv. to *sēmin-* (s. of *sēmen*) seed, SEMEN + *-ālis* -AL[1]] **—sem′i•nal′i•ty,** *n.* **—sem′i•nal•ly,** *adv.*
—Syn. 4. germinal, primary, formative, innovative.

sem′inal flu′id, the fluid component of semen, excluding the sperm. [1925–30]

sem′inal prin′ciple, *Philos.* a potential, latent within an imperfect object, for attaining full development.

sem′inal ves′icle, *Anat.* either of two small saclike glands, located on each side of the bladder in males, that add nutrient fluid to semen during ejaculation. [1885–90]

CONCISE PRONUNCIATION KEY: *act, cāpe, dâre, pärt; set, ēqual; if, ice; ox, ōver, ôrder, oil, bŏŏk, bōōt, out; up, ûrge; child; sing; shoe; thin, that;* zh *as in treasure.* ə = *a as in alone, e as in system, i as in easily, o as in gallop, u as in circus;* ə *as in fire* (fīər), *hour* (ouər). l and n can serve as syllabic consonants, as in *cradle* (krād′l), and *button* (but′n). See the full key inside the front cover.

sem′i•dic′ta•to′ri•al, *adj.;* **-ly,** *adv.;* **-ness,** *n.*
sem′i•di•gest′ed, *adj.*
sem′i•di•rect′, *adj.;* **-ness,** *n.*
sem′i•dis•a′bled, *adj.*
sem′i•di•vid′ed, *adj.*
sem′i•di•vi′sion, *n.*
sem′i•di•vi′sive, *adj.;* **-ly,** *adv.;* **-ness,** *n.*
sem′i•doc′u•men′ta•ry, *adj., n., pl.* **-ries.**
sem′i•do•mes′tic, *adj.*
sem′i•do•mes′ti•cal•ly, *adv.*
sem′i•dor′mant, *adj.*
sem′i•dra•mat′ic, *adj.*
sem′i•dra•mat′i•cal•ly, *adv.*
sem′i•duc′tile, *adj.*
sem′i•e•las′tic, *adj.*
sem′i•e•las′ti•cal•ly, *adv.*
sem′i•el′e•vat′ed, *adj.*
sem′i•e•mo′tion•al, *adj.;* **-ly,** *adv.*
sem′i•em•pir′i•cal, *adj.;* **-ly,** *adv.*
sem′i•en•clo′sure, *n.*
sem′i•en′tre•pre•neur′i•al, *adj.*
sem′i•ep′ic, *adj., n.*
sem′i•ep′i•cal, *adj.;* **-ly,** *adv.*
sem′i•e•rect′, *adj.;* **-ly,** *adv.;* **-ness,** *n.*
sem′i•ex•clu′sive, *adj.;* **-ly,** *adv.;* **-ness,** *n.*
sem′i•ex•ec′u•tive, *adj.*
sem′i•ex′hi•bi′tion•ist, *n.*
sem′i•ex•pand′ed, *adj.*
sem′i•ex•pan′si•ble, *adj.*
sem′i•ex•per′i•men′tal, *adj.;* **-ly,** *adv.*
sem′i•ex•posed′, *adj.*
sem′i•ex•pos′i•tive, *adj.*
sem′i•ex•pos′i•to′ry, *adj.*
sem′i•ex•po′sure, *n.*
sem′i•ex•pres′sion•is′tic, *adj.*
sem′i•ex•ter′nal, *adj.;* **-ly,** *adv.*
sem′i•ex•ter′nal•ized′, *adj.*
sem′i•fic′tion, *n.*
sem′i•fic′tion•al, *adj.;* **-ly,** *adv.*
sem′i•fic′tion•al•ized′, *adj.*
sem′i•fic•ti′tious, *adj.*
sem′i•fig′ur•a•tive, *adj.;* **-ly,** *adv.;* **-ness,** *n.*
sem′i•fine′, *adj.*
sem′i•fixed′, *adj.*
sem′i•formed′, *adj.*
sem′i•fos′sil•ized′, *adj.*
sem′i•fron•tier′, *n.*
sem′i•func′tion•al, *adj.;* **-ly,** *adv.*
sem′i•func′tion•al•ism, *n.*
sem′i•fur′nished, *adj.*
sem′i•fused′, *adj.*
sem′i•fu′tur•is′tic, *adj.*
sem′i•ge′o•met′ric, *adj.*
sem′i•ge′o•met′ri•cal, *adj.;* **-ly,** *adv.*
sem′i•glaze′, *n.*
sem′i•glazed′, *adj.*
sem′i•god′, *n.*
sem′i•gov′ern•men′tal, *adj.;* **-ly,** *adv.*
sem′i•hard′, *adj.;* **-ness,** *n.*
sem′i•hard′ened, *adj.*
sem′i•her•ba′ceous, *adj.*
sem′i•her′e•tic, *adj., n.*
sem′i•he•ret′i•cal, *adj.*
sem′i•hi′ber•na′tion, *n.*
sem′i•his•tor′ic, *adj.*
sem′i•his•tor′i•cal, *adj.;* **-ly,** *adv.*
sem′i•hos′tile, *adj.;* **-ly,** *adv.*
sem′i•hos•til′i•ty, *n.*
sem′i•hu′man•ism, *n.*
sem′i•hu′man•is′tic, *adj.*
sem′i•hu•man′i•tar′i•an, *adj., n.*
sem′i•hu′man•ized′, *adj.*
sem′i•hy′per•bol′ic, *adj.*
sem′i•hys•ter′i•cal, *adj.;* **-ly,** *adv.*
sem′i•il•lit′er•a•cy, *n.*
sem′i•il•lit′er•ate, *adj.;* **-ly,** *adv.;* **-ness,** *n.*
sem′i•il•lu′mi•nat′ed, *adj.*
sem′i•im•pres′sion•is′tic, *adj.*
sem′i•in′di•rect′, *adj.;* **-ly,** *adv.;* **-ness,** *n.*
sem′i•in•duc′tive, *adj.*
sem′i•in′du•rate, *adj.*
sem′i•in′du•rat′ed, *adj.*
sem′i•in•dus′tri•al, *adj.;* **-ly,** *adv.*
sem′i•in•dus′tri•al•ized′, *adj.*
sem′i•in•hib′it•ed, *adj.*
sem′i•in•sol′u•ble, *adj.*
sem′i•in•stinc′tive, *adj.;* **-ly,** *adv.*
sem′i•in′tel•lec′tu•al, *adj., n.;* **-ly,** *adv.*
sem′i•in′tel•lec′tu•al•ized′, *adj.*
sem′i•in•tel′li•gent, *adj.;* **-ly,** *adv.*
sem′i•in•tel′li•gi•ble, *adj.;* **-bly,** *adv.*
sem′i•in•ter′nal, *adj.;* **-ly,** *adv.*
sem′i•in•ter′nal•ized′, *adj.*
sem′i•in•tox′i•cat′ed, *adj.*
sem′i•in•tox′i•ca′tion, *n.*
sem′i•i•ron′ic, *adj.*
sem′i•i•ron′i•cal, *adj.;* **-ly,** *adv.*
sem′i•i′so•lat′ed, *adj.*
sem′i•joc′u•lar, *adj.;* **-ly,** *adv.*
sem′i•ju•di′cial, *adj.;* **-ly,** *adv.*
sem′i•ju•rid′ic, *adj.*
sem′i•ju•rid′i•cal, *adj.;* **-ly,** *adv.*
sem′i•leg′end•ar′y, *adj.*
sem′i•leg′is•la′tive, *adj.;* **-ly,** *adv.*
sem′i•le′thal, *adj.*
sem′i•lib′er•al, *adj., n.;* **-ly,** *adv.*
sem′i•lib′er•al•ism, *n.*
sem′i•lu′cent, *adj.*
sem′i•lu′mi•nous, *adj.;* **-ly,** *adv.;* **-ness,** *n.*
sem′i•lu′nate, *adj.*
sem′i•lu′nat•ed, *adj.*
sem′i•lus′trous, *adj;* **-ly,** *adv.;* **-ness,** *n.*
sem′i•lux′u•ry, *n., pl.* **-ries.**
sem′i•lyr′ic, *adj.*

sem•i•nar (sem′ə när′), *n.* **1.** a small group of students, as in a university, engaged in advanced study and original research under a member of the faculty and meeting regularly to exchange information and hold discussions. **2.** the gathering place of such a group. **3.** a meeting of such a group. **4.** a course or subject of study for advanced graduate students. **5.** any meeting for exchanging information and holding discussions. [1885–90, *Amer.*; < G < L *sēminārium* SEMINARY]

sem•i•nar•i•an (sem′ə nâr′ē ən), *n.* a student in a theological seminary. Also, **sem•i•na•rist** (sem′ə nər ist). [1575–85; SEMINARY + -AN]

sem•i•nar•y (sem′ə ner′ē), *n., pl.* **-nar•ies. 1.** a special school providing education in theology, religious history, etc., primarily to prepare students for the priesthood, ministry, or rabbinate. **2.** a school, esp. one of higher grade. **3.** a school of secondary or higher level for young women. **4.** seminar (def. 1). **5.** a place of origin and propagation: *a seminary of discontent.* [1400–50; late ME: seed plot, nursery < L *sēminārium,* equiv. to *sēmin-* (s. of *sēmen*) seed, SEMEN + *-ārium* -ARY] **—sem′i•nar′i•al,** *adj.*

sem•i•na•tion (sem′ə nā′shən), *n.* a sowing or impregnating; dissemination. [1525–35; < L *sēminātiōn-* (s. of *sēminātiō*), equiv. to *sēmināt(us)* (ptp. of *sēmināre* to sow, deriv. of *sēmen* seed, SEMEN) + *-iōn-* -ION]

sem•i•nif•er•ous (sem′ə nif′ər əs), *adj.* **1.** *Anat.* conveying or containing semen. **2.** *Bot.* bearing or producing seed. [1685–95; < L *sēmin-* (s. of *sēmen*) seed, SEMEN + -I- + -FEROUS]

seminif′erous tu′bule, *Anat.* any of the coiled tubules of the testis in which spermatozoa are produced. [1855–60]

sem•i•niv•or•ous (sem′ə niv′ər əs), *adj.* feeding on seeds: *seminivorous birds.* [1680–90; < L *sēmin-* (s. of *sēmen*) seed, SEMEN + -I- + -VOROUS]

Sem•i•nole (sem′ə nōl′), *n., pl.* **-noles,** (*esp. collectively*) **-nole,** *adj.* **—n. 1.** a member of any of several groupings of North American Indians comprising emigrants from the Creek Confederacy territories to Florida or their descendants in Florida and Oklahoma, esp. the culturally conservative present-day Florida Indians. **2.** either of the Muskogean languages spoken by the Seminoles, comprising Mikasuki and the Florida or Seminole dialect of Creek. **—*adj.* 3.** of or pertaining to the Seminoles or their languages. [earlier *Seminolie* < Creek *simanó·li* wild, runaway, alter. of earlier and dial. *simaló·ni* < AmerSp *cimarrón;* see MAROON[2]]

Sem′inole Wars′, *U.S. Hist.* **1.** a series of conflicts in 1818–19 between American forces under Andrew Jackson and the Seminole Indians in Spanish-controlled eastern Florida. **2.** a series of conflicts from 1835 to 1842 between U.S. Army forces and the Seminole Indians over the Seminoles' refusal to move from Florida to designated Indian territories.

sem•i•of•fi•cial (sem′ē ə fish′əl, sem′ī-), *adj.* having some degree of official authority. [1800–10; SEMI- + OFFICIAL] **—sem′i•of•fi′cial•ly,** *adv.*

se•mi•ol•o•gy (sē′mē ol′ə jē, sem′ē-, sē′mī-), *n.* the study of signs and symbols; semiotics. Also, **semeiology.** [1885–90; < Gk *sēmeîo(n)* sign + -LOGY] **—se•mi•o•log•ic** (sē′mē ə loj′ik, sem′ē-, se′mī-), **se′mi•o•log′i•cal,** *adj.* **—se′mi•ol′o•gist,** *n.*

sem•i•o•paque (sem′ē ō pāk′, sem′ī-), *adj.* partly or nearly opaque. [1685–95; SEMI- + OPAQUE] **—sem•i•o•pac•i•ty** (sem′ē ō pas′i tē, sem′ī-), *n.*

se•mi•ot•ic (sē′mē ot′ik, sem′ē, sē′mī-), *adj.* Also, **se′mi•ot′i•cal. 1.** of or pertaining to signs. **2.** of or pertaining to semiotics. **3.** *Med.* of or pertaining to symptoms; symptomatic. **—n. 4.** semiotics. [1615–20; (def. 3) < Gk *sēmeiōtikós* significant, equiv. to *sēmeiō-,* verbid s. of *sēmeioûn* to interpret as a sign (deriv. of Gk *sēmeîon* sign) + *-tikos* -TIC; (def. 4) < Gk *sēmeiōtikḗ,* n. use of fem. of *sēmeiōtikós,* adapted by John Locke (on the model of Gk *logikḗ* LOGIC, etc.; see -IC) to mean "the doctrine of signs"; (defs. 1, 2) based on Locke's coinage or a reanalysis of the Gk word]

se•mi•ot•ics (sē′mē ot′iks, sem′ē-, sē′mī-), *n.* (*used with a singular v.*) **1.** the study of signs and symbols as elements of communicative behavior; the analysis of systems of communication, as language, gestures, or clothing. **2.** a general theory of signs and symbolism, usually divided into the branches of pragmatics, semantics, and syntactics. [1875–80; see SEMIOTIC, -ICS] **—se•mi•o•ti•cian** (sē′mē ə tish′ən, sem′ē-, sē′mī-), *n.*

CONCISE ETYMOLOGY KEY: <, descended or borrowed from; >, whence; b., blend of, blended; c., cognate with; cf., compare; deriv., derivative; equiv., equivalent; imit., imitative; obl., oblique; r., replacing; s., stem; sp., spelling, spelled; resp., respelling, respelled; trans., translation; ?, origin unknown; *, unattested; ‡, probably earlier than. See the full key inside the front cover.

sem•i•o•vip•a•rous (sem′ē ō vip′ər əs, sem′ī-), *adj.* bearing young in an incomplete state of development, as a marsupial. [1895–1900; SEMI- + OVIPAROUS]

Se•mi•pa•la•tinsk (sem′i pə lä′tinsk; *Russ.* syi myipu lä′tyinsk), *n.* a city in NE Kazakhstan, on the Irtysh River. 283,000.

sem•i•pal•mate (sem′ē pal′māt, -mit, -päl′-, -pä′māt, sem′ī-), *adj.* partly or imperfectly palmate, as a bird's foot; half-webbed. Also, **sem′i•pal′mat•ed.** [1775–85; SEMI- + PALMATE]

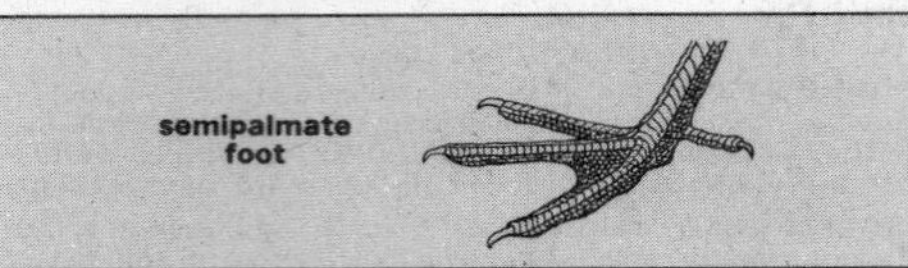

semipal′mated plov′er, a New World plover, *Charadrius semipalmatus,* having a black ring around the chest and semipalmate feet, inhabiting beaches and salt marshes. [1820–30, *Amer.*]

semipal′mated sand′piper, a common North American sandpiper, *Calidris pusillus,* having semipalmate feet. [1800–10, *Amer.*]

sem•i•par•a•sit•ic (sem′ē par′ə sit′ik, sem′ī-), *adj.* **1.** *Biol.* commonly parasitic but also capable of living on dead or decaying animal matter. **2.** *Bot.* partly parasitic and partly photosynthetic. [1875–80; SEMI- + PARASITIC] **—sem•i•par•a•site** (sem′ē par′ə sīt′, sem′ī-), *n.* **—sem•i•par•a•sit•ism** (sem′ē par′ə sī′tiz əm, sem′ī-), *n.*

sem•i•per•ma•nent (sem′ē pûr′mə nənt, sem′ī-), *adj.* not quite permanent. [1885–90; SEMI- + PERMANENT]

sem•i•per•me•a•ble (sem′ē pûr′mē ə bəl, sem′ī-), *adj.* permeable only to certain small molecules: *a semipermeable membrane.* [1895–1900; SEMI- + PERMEABLE] **—sem′i•per′me•a•bil′i•ty,** *n.*

sem•i•plas•tic (sem′ē plas′tik, sem′ī-), *adj.* imperfectly plastic; in a state between rigidity and plasticity. [1850–55; SEMI- + PLASTIC]

sem•i•po•lit•i•cal (sem′ē pə lit′i kəl, sem′ī-), *adj.* of a partially political nature; having some political features. [1855–60; SEMI- + POLITICAL] **—sem•i•pol•i•ti•cian** (sem′ē pol′i tish′ən, sem′ī-), *n.*

sem•i•por•ce•lain (sem′ē pôr′sə lin, -pōr′-, -pôrs′lin, -pōrs′-, sem′ī-), *n.* any of several vitrified ceramic wares lacking the translucency or hardness of true porcelain but otherwise similar to it. [1875–80; SEMI- + PORCELAIN]

sem•i•post•al (sem′ē pōs′tl, sem′ī-), *Philately.* **—n. 1.** a postage stamp sold by a government at a premium above its face value, the excess being used for a nonpostal purpose, as a charity. **—*adj.* 2.** noting or pertaining to such a stamp. [1925–30; SEMI- + POSTAL]

sem•i•pre•cious (sem′ē presh′əs, sem′ī-), *adj.* (of a stone) having commercial value as a gem but not classified as precious, as the amethyst or garnet. [1885–90; SEMI- + PRECIOUS]

sem•i•pri•vate (sem′ē prī′vit, sem′ī-), *adj.* having some degree of privacy but not fully private, as a hospital room with fewer beds than a ward. [1875–80; SEMI- + PRIVATE] **—sem•i•pri•va•cy** (sem′ē prī′və sē, sem′ī-), *n.*

sem•i•pro (*adj.* sem′ē prō′, sem′ī-; *n.* sem′ē prō′, sem′ī-), *adj., n., pl.* **-pros.** *Informal.* semiprofessional. [1910–15; SEMI- + PRO[2]]

sem•i•pro•fes•sion•al (sem′ē prə fesh′ə nl, sem′ī-), *adj.* **1.** actively engaged in some field or sport for pay but on a part-time basis: *semiprofessional baseball players.* **2.** engaged in by paid, part-time people: *semiprofessional football.* **3.** having some features of professional work but requiring less knowledge, skill, and judgment: *a semiprofessional job.* **—n. 4.** a person who is active in some field or sport for pay on a part-time basis. [1895–1900; SEMI- + PROFESSIONAL] **—sem′i•pro•fes′sion•al•ly,** *adv.*

sem•i•pub•lic (sem′ē pub′lik, sem′ī-), *adj.* partly or to some degree public. [1795–1805; SEMI- + PUBLIC]

sem•i•quan•ti•ta•tive (sem′ē kwon′ti tā′tiv, sem′ī-), *adj.* partially quantitative. [1925–30; SEMI- + QUANTITATIVE] **—sem′i•quan′ti•ta′tive•ly,** *adv.*

sem•i•qua•ver (sem′ē kwā′vər), *n. Music Chiefly Brit.* a sixteenth note. See illus. under **note.** Also called **demiquaver.** [1570–80; SEMI- + QUAVER]

sem•i•qui•none (sem′ē kwi nōn′, -kwin′ōn, sem′ī-), *n. Chem.* any of the class of free radicals formed as intermediates in the oxidation of a hydroquinone to a quinone. [SEMI- + QUINONE]

Se•mir•a•mis (si mir′ə mis), *n.* a legendary Assyrian queen, the wife of Ninus and founder of Babylon, noted for her wisdom and beauty.

sem•i•re•li•gious (sem′ē ri lij′əs, sem′ī-), *adj.* having a somewhat religious character. [1860–65; SEMI- + RELIGIOUS]

sem•i•rig•id (sem′ē rij′id, sem′ī-), *adj.* **1.** not fully rigid; partly rigid. **2.** *Aeron.* noting or pertaining to a type of airship whose shape is maintained by means of a rigid keellike structure and by internal gas pressure. [1905–10; SEMI- + RIGID]

sem•i•round (sem′ē round′, sem′ī-), *adj.* having one surface that is round and another that is flat. [SEMI- + ROUND[1]]

se•mis (sā′mis, sē′-), *n.* a copper coin of ancient Rome, the half part of an as. [< L *sēmis,* appar. equiv. to *sēmi-* SEMI- + *as* AS[2]]

sem•i•se•ri•ous (sem′ē sēr′ē əs, sem′ī-), *adj.* having some seriousness; partly serious. [SEMI- + SERIOUS] **—sem′i•se′ri•ous•ly,** *adv.* **—sem′i•se′ri•ous•ness,** *n.*

sem•i•skilled (sem′ē skild′, sem′ī-), *adj.* having or requiring more training and skill than unskilled labor but less than skilled labor. [1915–20; SEMI- + SKILLED]

sem•i•soft (sem′ē sôft′, -soft′, sem′ī-), *adj.* having a somewhat soft consistency or quality. [1900–05; SEMI- + SOFT]

sem•i•sol•id (sem′ē sol′id, sem′ī-), *adj.* **1.** having a somewhat firm consistency; more or less solid. **—n. 2.** a semisolid substance. [1825–35; SEMI- + SOLID]

sem•i•so•phis•ti•cat•ed (sem′ē sə fis′ti kā′tid, sem′ī-), *adj.* somewhat sophisticated. [SEMI- + SOPHISTICATED]

sem•i•spher•ic (sem′ē sfēr′ik, -sfer′-, sem′ī-), *adj.* shaped like half a sphere; hemispheric. Also, **sem′i•spher′i•cal.** [1655–65; SEMI- + SPHERIC] **—sem•i•sphere** (sem′i sfēr′), *n.*

sem•i•star•va•tion (sem′ē stär vā′shən, sem′ī-), *n.* the state of being nearly starved. [1850–55; SEMI- + STARVATION]

sem•i•sub•mers•i•ble (sem′ē səb mûr′sə bəl, sem′ī-), *n.* **1.** Also called **sem′isubmers′ible rig′.** a self-propelled barge that is mounted on partially submerged legs supported by underwater pontoons, rides at anchor, and serves as a work base and living quarters in deep offshore drilling operations. **—*adj.* 2.** of, for, or pertaining to a semisubmersible. [1960–65; SEMI- + SUBMERSIBLE]

sem•i•sub•ter•ra•ne•an (sem′ē sub′tə rā′nē ən, sem′ī-), *adj.* half below the surface of the ground: *the semisubterranean houses of some Indian tribes.* [SEMI- + SUBTERRANEAN]

sem•i•sweet (sem′ē swēt′, sem′ī-), *adj.* somewhat sweet; containing a small amount of sweetening: *a semisweet cookie; semisweet chocolate.* [1950–55; SEMI- + SWEET]

sem•i•syn•thet•ic (sem′ē sin thet′ik, sem′ī-), *adj. Chem.* derived synthetically from one or more substances of natural origin. [1935–40; SEMI- + SYNTHETIC]

Sem•ite (sem′īt *or, esp. Brit.,* sē′mīt), *n.* **1.** a member of any of various ancient and modern peoples originating in southwestern Asia, including the Akkadians, Canaanites, Phoenicians, Hebrews, and Arabs. **2.** a Jew. **3.** a member of any of the peoples descended from Shem, the eldest son of Noah. [1870–75; < NL *sēmīta* < LL *Sēm* (< Gk *Sḗm* < Heb *Shēm* SHEM) + *-ita* -ITE[1]]

sem•i•ter•res•tri•al (sem′ē tə res′trē əl, sem′ī-), *adj. Biol.* living mostly on land but requiring a moist environment or nearby water, esp. as a breeding site: *Most*

sem′i•lyr′i•cal, *adj.;* **-ly,** *adv.*
sem′i•mag′i•cal, *adj.;* **-ly,** *adv.*
sem′i•mag•net′ic, *adj.*
sem′i•mag•net′i•cal, *adj.;* **-ly,** *adv.*
sem′i•ma•li′cious, *adj.;* **-ly,** *adv.;* **-ness,** *n.*
sem′i•ma•lig′nant, *adj.;* **-ly,** *adv.*
sem′i•man′a•ge′ri•al, *adj.;* **-ly,** *adv.*
sem′i•man′ner•is′tic, *adj.*
sem′i•man′u•fac′tured, *adj.*
sem′i•man′u•fac′tur•ing, *n.*
sem′i•ma•rine′, *adj.*
sem′i•ma•te′ri•al•is′tic, *adj.*
sem′i•math′e•mat′i•cal, *adj.;* **-ly,** *adv.*
sem′i•ma•ture′, *adj.;* **-ly,** *adv.;* **-ness,** *n.*
sem′i•ma•tu′ri•ty, *n.*
sem′i•me•chan′i•cal, *adj.*
sem′i•mech′a•nis′tic, *adj.*
sem′i•me•dic′i•nal, *adj.*
sem′i•mem′bra•nous, *adj.*
sem′i•me•tal′lic, *adj.*
sem′i•met′a•phor′ic, *adj.*
sem′i•met′a•phor′i•cal, *adj.;* **-ly,** *adv.*
sem′i•mild′, *adj.;* **-ness,** *n.*
sem′i•min′er•al, *adj.*
sem′i•min′er•al•ized′, *adj.*
sem′i•min′is•te′ri•al, *adj.*
sem′i•mo′bile, *adj.*
sem′i•mod′er•ate, *adj.;* **-ly,** *adv.*
sem′i•moist′, *adj.*
sem′i•mo•nar′chic, *adj.*
sem′i•mo•nar′chi•cal, *adj.;* **-ly,** *adv.*
sem′i•mo•nas′tic, *adj.*
sem′i•mo•nop′o•lis′tic, *adj.*
sem′i•mor′al•is′tic, *adj.*
sem′i•moun′tain•ous, *adj.;* **-ly,** *adv.*
sem′i•mys′tic, *adj.*
sem′i•mys′ti•cal, *adj.;* **-ly,** *adv.;* **-ness,** *n.*
sem′i•myth′ic, *adj.*
sem′i•myth′i•cal, *adj.;* **-ly,** *adv.*
sem′i•na′ked, *adj.*
sem′i•nar•cot′ic, *adj.*
sem′i•nar′ra•tive, *adj.*
sem′i•na′sal, *adj.;* **-ly,** *adv.*
sem′i•na•sal′i•ty, *n.*
sem′i•na′tion•al•ism, *n.*
sem′i•na′tion•al•is′tic, *adj.*
sem′i•na′tion•al•ized′, *adj.*
sem′i•nerv′ous, *adj.;* **-ly,** *adv.;* **-ness,** *n.*
sem′i•neu•rot′ic, *adj.*
sem′i•neu•rot′i•cal•ly, *adv.*
sem′i•neu′tral, *adj.*
sem′i•neu•tral′i•ty, *n.*
sem′i•noc•tur′nal, *adj.*
sem′i•no′mad, *n.*
sem′i•no•mad′ic, *adj.*
sem′i•no•mad′i•cal•ly, *adv.*
sem′i•no′mad•ism, *n.*
sem′i•nor′mal, *adj.;* **-ly,** *adv.;* **-ness,** *n.*
sem′i•nor•mal′i•ty, *n.*
sem′i•nude′, *adj.*
sem′i•nu′di•ty, *n.*
sem′i•ob•jec′tive, *adj.;* **-ly,** *adv.;* **-ness,** *n.*
sem′i•ob•liv′i•ous, *adj.;* **-ly,** *adv.;* **-ness,** *n.*
sem′i•o′pen, *adj.;* **-ly,** *adv.;* **-ness,** *n.*
sem′i•op′ti•mis′tic, *adj.*
sem′i•op′ti•mis′ti•cal•ly, *adv.*
sem′i•or′a•tor′i•cal, *adj.;* **-ly,** *adv.*
sem′i•or•gan′ic, *adj.*
sem′i•or•gan′i•cal•ly, *adv.*
sem′i•o′ri•en′tal, *adj.;* **-ly,** *adv.*
sem′i•or′tho•dox′, *adj.;* **-ly,** *adv.*
sem′i•o′val, *adj.;* **-ly,** *adv.;* **-ness,** *n.*
sem′i•o′vate, *adj.*
sem′i•ox′y•gen•ized′, *adj.*
sem′i•pac′i•fist, *adj., n.*
sem′i•pac′i•fis′tic, *adj.*
sem′i•pa′gan, *n., adj.*
sem′i•pa′gan•ish, *adj.*
sem′i•pa•ral′y•sis, *n., pl.* **-ses.**
sem′i•par′a•lyt′ic, *n., adj.*
sem′i•par′a•lyzed′, *adj.*
sem′i•pa•ro′chi•al, *adj.*
sem′i•pas′sive, *adj.;* **-ly,** *adv.;* **-ness,** *n.*
sem′i•paste′, *n.*
sem′i•pas′to•ral, *adj.;* **-ly,** *adv.*
sem′i•path′o•log′ic, *adj.*
sem′i•path′o•log′i•cal, *adj.;* **-ly,** *adv.*
sem′i•pa′tri•ot, *n.*
sem′i•pa′tri•ot′ic, *adj.*
sem′i•pa′tri•ot′i•cal•ly, *adv.*
sem′i•pat′terned, *adj.*
sem′i•peace′, *n.*
sem′i•peace′ful, *adj.;* **-ly,** *adv.*
sem′i•pe•dan′tic, *adj.*
sem′i•pe•dan′ti•cal, *adj.;* **-ly,** *adv.*
sem′i•pend′ent, *adj.*
sem′i•pen′du•lous, *adj.;* **-ly,** *adv.;* **-ness,** *n.*
sem′i•per•cep′tive, *adj.*
sem′i•per′vi•ous, *adj.;* **-ness,** *n.*
sem′i•pet′ri•fied′, *adj.*
sem′i•phe•nom′e•nal, *adj.;* **-ly,** *adv.*
sem′i•phil′o•soph′ic, *adj.*
sem′i•phil′o•soph′i•cal, *adj.;* **-ly,** *adv.*
sem′i•phos′pho•res′cence, *n.*
sem′i•phos′pho•res′cent, *adj.*
sem′i•phre•net′ic, *adj.*
sem′i•pic•to′ri•al, *adj.;* **-ly,** *adv.*
sem′i•pi′ous, *adj.;* **-ly,** *adv.;* **-ness,** *n.*
sem′i•pneu•mat′ic, *adj.*
sem′i•pneu•mat′i•cal, *adj.;* **-ly,** *adv.*
sem′i•poi′son•ous, *adj.;* **-ly,** *adv.*
sem′i•pop′u•lar, *adj.;* **-ly,** *adv.*
sem′i•pop′u•lar′i•ty, *n.*
sem′i•pop′u•lar•ized′, *adj.*

amphibians are semiterrestrial. [1915–20; SEMI- + TERRESTRIAL]

Se·mit·ic (sə mit′ik), *n.* **1.** a subfamily of Afroasiatic languages that includes Akkadian, Arabic, Aramaic, Ethiopic, Hebrew, and Phoenician. —*adj.* **2.** of or pertaining to the Semites or their languages, esp. of or pertaining to the Jews. [< NL *sēmīticus,* equiv. to *sēmīt(a)* SEMITE + *-icus* -IC]

Se·mit·ics (sə mit′iks), *n.* (*used with a singular v.*) the study of Semitic languages, literature, etc. [1870–75, *Amer.*; see SEMITIC, -ICS]

Sem·i·tism (sem′i tiz′əm *or, esp. Brit.,* sē′mi-), *n.* **1.** Semitic characteristics, esp. the ways, ideas, influence, etc., of the Jewish people. **2.** a word or idiom peculiar to, derived from, or characteristic of a Semitic language, esp. of Hebrew. [1850–55; SEMITE + -ISM]

Sem·i·tist (sem′i tist *or, esp. Brit.,* sē′mi-), *n.* an authority on Semitic languages, literature, etc. [1880–85; SEMITE + -IST]

sem·i·tone (sem′ē tōn′, sem′ī-), *n. Music.* a pitch interval halfway between two whole tones. Also called **half step, half tone.** [1600–10; SEMI- + TONE] —**sem·i·ton·ic** (sem′ē ton′ik, sem′ī-), **sem·i·ton·al** (sem′ē tōn′l, sem′ī-), *adj.* —**sem′i·ton′al·ly,** *adv.*

sem·i·trail·er (sem′i trā′lər), *n.* **1.** Also called **semi.** a detachable trailer for hauling freight, with wheels at the rear end, the forward end being supported by the rear of a truck tractor when attached. Cf. **full trailer. 2.** tractor-trailer. [1915–20; SEMI- + TRAILER]

sem·i·trans·lu·cent (sem′ē trans lo͞o′sənt, -tranz-, sem′ī-), *adj.* imperfectly or almost translucent. [1825–35; SEMI- + TRANSLUCENT]

sem·i·trans·par·ent (sem′ē trans pâr′ənt, -par′-, sem′ī-), *adj.* imperfectly or almost transparent. [1785–95; SEMI- + TRANSPARENT] —**sem′i·trans·par′en·cy, sem′i·trans·par′ent·ness,** *n.* —**sem′i·trans·par′ent·ly,** *adv.*

sem·i·trop·i·cal (sem′ē trop′i kəl, sem′ī-), *adj.* subtropical. Also, **sem′i·trop′ic.** [1855–60; SEMI- + TROPICAL] —**sem′i·trop′ics,** *n.pl.* —**sem′i·trop′i·cal·ly,** *adv.*

sem·i·truck (sem′ē truk′, sem′ī-), *n.* tractor-trailer. Also, **sem′i-truck′.** [1970–75; SEMI(TRAILER) + TRUCK[1]]

sem·i·vit·re·ous (sem′ē vi′trē əs, sem′ī-), *adj.* (of ceramics). partially vitreous. [1775–85; SEMI- + VITREOUS]

sem·i·vow·el (sem′ē vou′əl), *n. Phonet.* a speech sound of vowel quality used as a consonant, as (w) in *wet* or (y) in *yet.* [1520–30; SEMI- + VOWEL; r. *semivocal* < L *sēmivocālis* half vowel]

sem·i·week·ly (sem′ē wēk′lē, sem′ī-), *adj., n., pl.* **-lies,** *adv.* —*adj.* **1.** occurring, done, appearing, or published twice a week: *semiweekly visits.* —*n.* **2.** a semiweekly publication. —*adv.* **3.** twice a week. [1785–95, *Amer.*; SEMI- + WEEKLY]
—**Usage.** See **bi-**[1].

sem·i·year·ly (sem′ē yēr′lē, sem′ī-), *adj.* **1.** semiannual (def. 1). —*adv.* **2.** twice a year; semiannually: *He seeded the lawn semiyearly.* [1925–30; SEMI- + YEARLY]
—**Usage.** See **bi-**[1].

Sem·mel·weis (zem′əl vīs′), *n.* **Ig·naz Phi·lipp** (ig′näts fē′lip), 1818–65, Hungarian obstetrician.

Semmes (semz), *n.* **Raphael,** 1809–77, Confederate admiral in the American Civil War.

sem·o·li·na (sem′ə lē′nə), *n.* a granular, milled product of durum wheat, consisting almost entirely of endosperm particles, used chiefly in the making of pasta. [1790–1800; alter. of It *semolino,* equiv. to *semol(a)* bran (<< L *simila* flour) + *-ino* dim. suffix]

Sem·pach (*Ger.* zem′päKH), *n.* a village in central Switzerland: Austrians defeated by Swiss 1386. 1619.

sem·per fi (sem′pər fī′), *Informal.* See ***semper fidelis.***

sem·per fi·de·lis (sem′peR fi dā′lis; *Eng.* sem′pər fi dā′lis, -dē′-), *Latin.* always faithful: motto of the U.S. Marine Corps.

sem·per i·dem (sem′peR ē′dem; *Eng.* sem′pər ī′dem, id′em), *Latin.* always the same.

sem·per pa·ra·tus (sem′peR pä rä′to͞os; *Eng.* sem′pər pə rā′təs), *Latin.* always ready: motto of the U.S. Coast Guard.

sem·per·vi·vum (sem′pər vī′vəm), *n.* any of various succulent plants belonging to the genus *Sempervivum,* of the stonecrop family, having leaves in dense basal rosettes and a compact, flat-topped cluster of flowers, and including the houseleek, *S. tectorum.* [< NL: genus name, LL *sempervīvum* houseleek, equiv. to L *semper* always + *vīvum,* neut. sing. of *vīvus* alive, in reference to the plant's durable qualities]

sem·pi·ter·nal (sem′pi tûr′nl), *adj. Literary.* everlasting; eternal. [1400–50; late ME < LL *sempiternālis,* equiv. to L *sempitern(us)* everlasting *semp(er)* always + *-i-* -I- + *-ternus* suffix of temporal adjs.; see ETERNE) + *-ālis* -AL[1]] —**sem′pi·ter′nal·ly,** *adv.*

sem·pli·ce (sem′pli chā′; *It.* sem′plē che), *adj., adv.* (used as a musical direction) simple; straightforward. [1885–90; < It: simple; see SIMPLICITY]

sem·pre (sem′prā; *It.* sem′pRe), *adv.* (used in musical directions) throughout. [1885–90; < It: always < L *semper*]

semp·stress (semp′stris, sem′stris), *n.* seamstress.
—**Usage.** See **-ess.**

sen[1] (sen), *n., pl.* **sen.** a money of account of Japan, the 100th part of a yen, now used only in certain quotations, as on foreign exchange. [1795–1805; < Japn < MChin, equiv. to Chin *qián*; cf. CHON]

sen[2] (sen), *n., pl.* **sen.** a money of account of Cambodia, the 100th part of a riel. [< Khmer *sein,* prob. Khmer pron. of the F abbrev. *cent.,* for *centime* CENTIME, on Cambodian coins]

sen[3] (sen), *n., pl.* **sen. 1.** a bronze coin and monetary unit of Brunei, the 100th part of a dollar. **2.** an aluminum coin and monetary unit of Indonesia, the 100th part of a rupiah. **3.** a bronze, cupronickel, or copper-clad coin and monetary unit of Malaysia, the 100th part of a ringgit. Also called **cent.** [1950–55; < Malay < E CENT]

sen., 1. senate. **2.** senator. **3.** senior. Also, **sen**

sen·ar·mon·tite (sen′ər mon′tīt), *n.* a mineral, antimony trioxide, Sb_2O_3, occurring in pearl-colored isometric octahedrons: a dimorph of valentinite. [1850–55; named after Henri de *Sénarmont* (d. 1862), French mineralogist; see -ITE[1]]

sen·a·ry (sen′ə rē), *adj.* of or pertaining to the number six. [1655–65; < L *sēnārius,* equiv. to *sēn(ī)* six each (deriv. of *sex* SIX) + *-ārius* -ARY]

sen·ate (sen′it), *n.* **1.** an assembly or council of citizens having the highest deliberative functions in a government, esp. a legislative assembly of a state or nation. **2.** (*cap.*) the upper house of the legislature of certain countries, as the United States, France, Italy, Canada, Ireland, Republic of South Africa, Australia, and some Latin American countries. **3.** the room or building in which such a group meets. **4.** *Rom. Hist.* the supreme council of state, the membership and functions of which varied at different periods. **5.** a governing, advisory, or disciplinary body, as in certain universities. [1175–1225; ME *senat* < L *senātus* council of elders, equiv. to *sen(ex)* old + *-ātus* -ATE[3]]

sen·a·tor (sen′ə tər), *n.* **1.** a member of a senate. **2.** (*cap.*) (in the U.S.) a title of respect accorded a person who is or has been a member of the Senate. [1175–1225; ME *senatour* < AF < L *senātor,* equiv. to *sen(ātus)* SENATE + *-ātor* -ATOR] —**sen′a·tor·ship′,** *n.*

sen·a·to·ri·al (sen′ə tôr′ē əl, -tōr′-), *adj.* **1.** of, pertaining to, characteristic of, or befitting a senator or senate: *senatorial oratory.* **2.** consisting of senators. [1730–40; < L *senātōri(us)* (see SENATOR, -TORY[1]) + -AL[1]] —**sen′a·to′ri·al·ly,** *adv.*

senato′rial cour′tesy, the practice in the U.S. Senate of confirming only those presidential appointees approved by both senators from the state of the appointee, or by the senior senator of the president's party. [1880–85, *Amer.*]

senato′rial dis′trict, one of a fixed number of districts into which a state of the U.S. is divided, each electing one member to the state senate. Cf. **assembly district, Congressional district.** [1820–30, *Amer.*]

se·na·tus con·sul·tum (se nä′to͞os kôn so͝ol′to͞om; *Eng.* sə nā′təs kən sul′təm), *pl.* ***se·na·tus con·sul·ta*** (se nä′to͞os kôn so͝ol′tä; *Eng.* sə nā′təs kən sul′tə). *Latin.* a decree of the senate of ancient Rome.

send[1] (send), *v.,* **sent, send·ing.** —*v.t.* **1.** to cause, permit, or enable to go: *to send a messenger; They sent their son to college.* **2.** to cause to be conveyed or transmitted to a destination: *to send a letter.* **3.** to order, direct, compel, or force to go: *The president sent troops to Asia.* **4.** to direct, propel, or deliver to a particular point, position, condition, or direction: *to send a punch to the jaw.* **5.** to emit, discharge, or utter (usually fol. by *off, out,* or *through*): *The lion sent a roar through the jungle.* **6.** to cause to occur or befall: *The people beseeched Heaven to send peace to their war-torn village.* **7.** *Elect.* **a.** to transmit (a signal). **b.** to transmit (an electromagnetic wave or the like) in the form of pulses. **8.** *Slang.* to delight or excite: *Frank Sinatra's records used to send her.* —*v.i.* **9.** to dispatch a messenger, agent, message, etc. **10.** *Elect.* to transmit a signal: *The ship's radio sends on a special band of frequencies.* **11. send down,** *Brit.* to expel, esp. from Oxford or Cambridge. **12. send for,** to request the coming or delivery of; summon: *If her temperature goes up, send for the doctor.* **13. send forth, a.** to produce; bear; yield: *plants sending forth new leaves.* **b.** to dispatch out of a country as an export. **c.** to issue, as a publication: *They have sent forth a report to the stockholders.* **d.** to emit or discharge: *The flowers sent forth a sweet odor.* **14. send in,** to cause to be dispatched or delivered to a destination: *Send in your contest entries to this station.* **15. send off,** to cause to depart or to be conveyed from oneself; dispatch; dismiss: *His teacher sent him off to the principal's office.* **16. send out, a.** to distribute; issue. **b.** to send on the way; dispatch: *They sent out their final shipment last week.* **c.** to order delivery: *We sent out for coffee.* **17. send packing,** to dismiss curtly; send away in disgrace: *The cashier was stealing, so we sent him packing.* **18. send round,** to circulate or dispatch widely: *Word was sent round about his illness.* **19. send up, a.** to release or cause to go upward; let out. **b.** *Informal.* to sentence or send to prison: *He was convicted and sent up for life.* **c.** to expose the flaws or foibles of through parody, burlesque, caricature, lampoon, or other forms of satire: *The new movie sends up merchants who commercialize Christmas.* [bef. 900; ME *senden,* OE *sendan*; c. G *senden,* Goth *sandjan* (causative) < Gmc base **sinth-, *santh-* go, whence OE *sīth* journey, *sand* message, messenger] —**send′a·ble,** *adj.*
—**Syn. 2.** transmit, dispatch, forward. **4.** cast, hurl, fling, project. —**Ant. 1.** receive.

send[2] (send), *v.i.,* **sent, send·ing,** *n. Naut.* scend.

Sen·dai (sen′dī′), *n.* a city on NE Honshu, in central Japan. 664,799.

Sendai′ vi′rus, *Pathol., Vet. Pathol.* a paramyxovirus that tends to cause cell fusion: in inactive form, used in biological research to produce cells with multiple nuclei of different genetic constitutions. [1960–65; first described in SENDAI, Japan]

Sen·dak (sen′dak), *n.* **Maurice (Bernard),** born 1928, U.S. author and illustrator of children's books.

sen·dal (sen′dl), *n.* **1.** a silk fabric in use during the Middle Ages. **2.** a piece of this fabric or a garment made of it. Also, **cendal.** [1175–1225; ME *cendal* < OF, prob. through dissimilation < Gk *sindṓn* fine linen, SINDON]

send·ee (sen dē′), *n.* the person to whom something is sent. [1800–10; SEND[1] + -EE]

send·er (sen′dər), *n.* **1.** a person or thing that sends. **2.** a transmitter of electric pulses, as in telegraphy. [1150–1200; ME; SEND[1], -ER[1]]

Sen·de·ro Lu·mi·no·so (sen de′Rô lo͞o′mē nô′sô), *Spanish.* a Maoist guerrilla movement active in Peru since 1980. [lit., Shining Path]

send-off (send′ôf′, -of′), *n.* **1.** a demonstration of good wishes for a person setting out on a trip, career, or other venture: *They gave him a rousing send-off at the pier.* **2.** a start given to a person or thing. [1855–60, *Amer.*; n. use of v. phrase *send off*]

send-up (send′up′), *n.* an entertaining or humorous burlesque or parody; takeoff: *The best skit in the revue was a send-up of TV game shows.* Also, **send′up′.** [1955–60; n. use of v. phrase *send up,* in sense "to parody"; cf. earlier Brit. academic usage "to mock, scoff at"]

se·ne (sā′nā), *n., pl.* **se·ne.** a bronze coin and monetary unit of Western Samoa, the 100th part of a tala. [< Samoan < E CENT]

Sen·e·ca (sen′i kə), *n., pl.* **-cas,** (*esp. collectively*) **-ca**

CONCISE PRONUNCIATION KEY: *act, cāpe, dâre, pärt; set, ēqual; if, īce; ox, ōver, ôrder, oil, bo͝ok, bo͞ot, out; up, ûrge; child; sing; shoe; thin, that;* zh as in *treasure.* ə = *a* as in *alone, e* as in *system, i* as in *easily, o* as in *gallop, u* as in *circus;* ᵊ as in *fire* (fīᵊr), *hour* (ouᵊr). l and n can serve as syllabic consonants, as in *cradle* (krād′l), and *button* (but′n). See the full key inside the front cover.

sem′i·prac′ti·cal, *adj.*
sem′i·pre·served′, *adj.*
sem′i·prim′i·tive, *adj.*
sem′i·proc′essed, *adj.*
sem′i·pro·duc′tive, *adj.;* **-ly,** *adv.;* **-ness,** *n.*
sem′i·pro′duc·tiv′i·ty, *n.*
sem′i·pro·fane′, *adj.;* **-ly,** *adv.;* **-ness,** *n.*
sem′i·pro·fan′i·ty, *n., pl.* **-ties.**
sem′i·pro·gres′sive, *adj., n.;* **-ly,** *adv.;* **-ness,** *n.*
sem′i·prone′, *adj.;* **-ly,** *adv.;* **-ness,** *n.*
sem′i·prop′a·gan′dist, *adj.*
sem′i·pro·tect′ed, *adj.*
sem′i·pro·tec′tive, *adj.;* **-ly,** *adv.*
sem′i·prov′en, *adj.*
sem′i·pro·vin′cial, *adj.;* **-ly,** *adv.*
sem′i·psy′cho·log′ic, *adj.*
sem′i·psy′cho·log′i·cal, *adj.;* **-ly,** *adv.*
sem′i·psy·chot′ic, *adj.*
sem′i·pu′ni·tive, *adj.*
sem′i·pu′ni·to′ry, *adj.*
sem′i·pur′pos·ive, *adj.;* **-ly,** *adv.;* **-ness,** *n.*
sem′i·rad′i·cal, *adj.;* **-ly,** *adv.;* **-ness,** *n.*
sem′i·rare′, *adj.;* **-ly,** *adv.;* **-ness,** *n.*
sem′i·ra′tion·al·ized′, *adj.*
sem′i·raw′, *adj.;* **-ly,** *adv.;* **-ness,** *n.*
sem′i·re·ac′tion·ar′y, *adj., n., pl.* **-ar·ies.**
sem′i·re′al·is′tic, *adj.*
sem′i·re′al·is′ti·cal·ly, *adv.*
sem′i·reb′el, *n.*
sem′i·re·bel′lion, *n.*
sem′i·re·bel′lious, *adj.;* **-ly,** *adv.;* **-ness,** *n.*
sem′i·re·fined′, *adj.*
sem′i·re′flex, *n.*
sem′i·re·flex′ive, *adj.;* **-ly,** *adv.;* **-ness,** *n.*
sem′i·re·lief′, *n.*
sem′i·re·pub′lic, *n.*
sem′i·re·pub′li·can, *adj., n.*
sem′i·res′in·ous, *adj.*
sem′i·res′in·y, *adj.*
sem′i·res′o·lute′, *adj.;* **-ly,** *adv.;* **-ness,** *n.*
sem′i·re·spect′a·bil′i·ty, *n.*
sem′i·re·spect′a·ble, *adj.*
sem′i·re·tired′, *adj.*
sem′i·re·tire′ment, *n.*
sem′i·re·ver′ber·a·to′ry, *adj.*
sem′i·rev′o·lu′tion, *n.*
sem′i·rev′o·lu′tion·ar′y, *adj., n., pl.* **-ar·ies.**
sem′i·rev′o·lu′tion·ist, *n.*
sem′i·rhyth′mic, *adj.*
sem′i·rhyth′mi·cal, *adj.;* **-ly,** *adv.*
sem′i·rig′or·ous, *adj.;* **-ly,** *adv.;* **-ness,** *n.*
sem′i·ro·man′tic, *adj.*
sem′i·ro·man′ti·cal·ly, *adv.*
sem′i·ru′ral, *adj.;* **-ly,** *adv.*
sem′i·ru′ral·ism, *n.*
sem′i-Rus′sian, *adj., n.*
sem′i·sa′cred, *adj.*
sem′i·sa′line, *adj.*
sem′i·sa·tir′ic, *adj.*
sem′i·sa·tir′i·cal, *adj.;* **-ly,** *adv.*
sem′i·sav′age, *adj.*
sem′i·sav′age, *n.*
sem′i·scho·las′tic, *adj.*
sem′i·scho·las′ti·cal·ly, *adv.*
sem′i·se′cre·cy, *n.*
sem′i·se′cret, *adj.;* **-ly,** *adv.*
sem′i·sen′ti·men′tal, *adj.;* **-ly,** *adv.*
sem′i·sen′ti·men′tal·ized′, *adj.*
sem′i·shade′, *n.*
sem′i·slave′, *n.*
sem′i·so′cial·ism, *n.*
sem′i·so′cial·ist, *n.*
sem′i·so′cial·is′tic, *adj.*
sem′i·so′cial·is′ti·cal·ly, *adv.*
sem′i·sol′emn, *adj.;* **-ly,** *adv.;* **-ness,** *n.*
sem′i·so·lem′ni·ty, *n.*
sem′i·som′nam′bu·lis′tic, *adj.*
sem′i·som′no·lence, *n.*
sem′i·som′no·lent, *adj.;* **-ly,** *adv.*
sem′i·spec′u·la′tion, *n.*
sem′i·spec′u·la′tive, *adj.;* **-ly,** *adv.;* **-ness,** *n.*
sem′i·spon·ta′ne·ous, *adj.;* **-ly,** *adv.;* **-ness,** *n.*
sem′i·stiff′, *adj.;* **-ly,** *adv.;* **-ness,** *n.*
sem′i·stim′u·lat′ing, *adj.*
sem′i·strat′i·fied′, *adj.*
sem′i·sub·merged′, *adj.*
sem′i·sub·ur′ban, *adj.*
sem′i·suc·cess′, *adj., n.*
sem′i·suc·cess′ful, *adj.;* **-ly,** *adv.*
sem′i·su′per·nat′u·ral, *adj.;* **-ly,** *adv.;* **-ness,** *n.*
sem′i·tai′lored, *adj.*
sem′i·tex′tur·al, *adj.;* **-ly,** *adv.*
sem′i·the·at′ric, *adj.*
sem′i·the·at′ri·cal, *adj.;* **-ly,** *adv.*
sem′i·the·at′ri·cal·ism, *n.*
sem′i·the′o·log′i·cal, *adj.;* **-ly,** *adv.*
sem′i·tra·di′tion·al, *adj.;* **-ly,** *adv.*
sem′i·trained′, *adj.*
sem′i·truth′ful, *adj.;* **-ly,** *adv.;* **-ness,** *n.*
sem′i·tu′ber·ous, *adj.*
sem′i·un·dressed′, *adj.*
sem′i·ur′ban, *adj.*
sem′i·vol′a·tile, *adj.*
sem′i·vol·can′ic, *adj.*
sem′i·vol·can′i·cal·ly, *adv.*
sem′i·vol′un·tar′y, *adj.*
sem′i·vul′can·ized′, *adj.*
sem′i·war′fare′, *n.*
sem′i·wild′, *adj.;* **-ly,** *adv.;* **-ness,** *n.*

for 1. **1.** a member of the largest tribe of the Iroquois Confederacy of North American Indians, formerly inhabiting western New York and being conspicuous in the wars south and west of Lake Erie. **2.** an Iroquoian language of the Seneca, Onondaga, and Cayuga tribes. [< New York D *Sennecaas,* etc., orig. applied to the Oneida and, more generally, to all the Upper Iroquois (as opposed to the Mohawk), prob. < an unattested Mahican name] **—Sen′e·can,** *adj.*

Sen·e·ca (sen′i kə), *n.* **Lucius An·nae·us** (ə nē′əs), c4 B.C.–A.D. 65, Roman philosopher and writer of tragedies.

Sen′eca Falls′ Conven′tion, *U.S. Hist.* a women's rights convention held at Seneca Falls, New York, in 1848, organized by Elizabeth Cady Stanton and Lucretia Mott. Also called **Sen′eca Falls′ Con′ference.**

Sen′eca Lake′, a lake in W New York: one of the Finger Lakes. 35 mi. (56 km) long.

Sen′eca snake′root. See under **snakeroot** (def. 1). [1755–65, *Amer.*]

se·nec·ti·tude (si nek′ti to͞od′, -tyo͞od′), *n.* the last stage of life; old age. [1790–1800; < L *senect(ūs)* old age (equiv. to *senec-,* extracted as s. from *senex* (gen. *senis*) old man + *-tūs* abstract n. suffix) + -I- + -TUDE, on model of PLENITUDE, RECTITUDE, etc.]

Se·ne·fel·der (zā′nə fel′dər), *n.* **A·lo·ys** (ä′lō ys, ä′lois), 1771–1834, German inventor of lithography.

sen·e·ga (sen′i gə), *n.* **1.** the dried root of a milkwort, *Polygala senega,* of the eastern U.S., used as an expectorant and diuretic. **2.** the plant itself. [1730–40; var. of SENECA, from its use by this tribe]

Sen·e·gal (sen′i gôl′, -gäl′), *n.* **1.** a republic in W Africa: independent member of the French Community; formerly part of French West Africa. 5,400,000; 76,084 sq. mi. (197,057 sq. km). *Cap.:* Dakar. **2.** a river in W Africa, flowing NW from E Mali to the Atlantic at St. Louis. ab. 1000 mi. (1600 km) long. French, **Sé·né·gal** (sā nā gal′).

Sen·e·ga·lese (sen′i gô lēz′, -lēs′, -gə-), *adj., n., pl.* **-lese.** —*adj.* **1.** of or pertaining to the republic of Senegal. —*n.* **2.** a native or inhabitant of Senegal. [1915–20; SENEGAL + -ESE]

Sen·e·gam·bi·a (sen′i gam′bē ə), *n.* **1.** a region in W Africa between the Senegal and Gambia rivers, now mostly in Senegal. **2.** a confederation of Senegal and Gambia, formed in 1982. **—Sen′e·gam′bi·an,** *adj.*

se·nes·cent (si nes′ənt), *adj.* growing old; aging. [1650–60; < L *senēscent-* (s. of *senēscēns*) prp. of *senēscere* to grow old, equiv. to *sen-* old + *-ēscent-* -ESCENT] **—se·nes′cence,** *n.*

sen·e·schal (sen′ə shəl), *n.* an officer having full charge of domestic arrangements, ceremonies, the administration of justice, etc., in the household of a medieval prince or dignitary; steward. [1350–1400; ME < MF < Frankish; cf. ML *seniscalcus* senior servant, c. OHG *senescalh* (*sene-* old, SENIOR + *scalh* servant)]

Sen·ghor (*Fr.* san gôr′), *n.* **Lé·o·pold Sé·dar** (*Fr.* lā ô pôld′ sā där′), born 1906, African poet, teacher, and statesman: president of the Republic of Senegal 1960–80.

se·nhor (sin yôr′, -yōr′; *Port.* si nyôr′), *n., pl.* **se·nhors,** *Port.* **se·nho·res** (si nyô′rish). a Portuguese term of address equivalent to *sir* or *Mr.,* used alone or capitalized and prefixed to the name of a man. *Abbr.:* Sr. [1785–95; < Pg < VL *senior lord; see SENIOR]

se·nho·ra (sin yôr′ə, -yōr′ə; *Port.* si nyô′rə), *n., pl.* **se·nho·ras** (sin yôr′əz, -yōr′əz; *Port.* si nyô′rəsh). a Portuguese term of address equivalent to *Mrs.,* used alone or capitalized and prefixed to the name of a married or older woman. *Abbr.:* Sra. [1795–1805; < Pg, fem. of SENHOR]

se·nho·ri·ta (sēn′yə rē′tə, sän′-; *Port.* se′nyô rē′tə), *n., pl.* **-tas** (-təz; *Port.* -təsh). a Portuguese term of address equivalent to *miss,* used alone or capitalized and prefixed to the name of a girl or unmarried woman. *Abbr.:* Srta. [1870–75; < Pg, dim. of SENHORA]

se·nile (sē′nil, -nil, sen′īl), *adj.* **1.** showing a decline or deterioration of physical strength or mental functioning, esp. short-term memory and alertness, as a result of old age or disease. **2.** of or belonging to old age or aged persons; gerontological; geriatric. **3.** *Physical Geog.* (of topographical features) having been reduced by erosion to a featureless plain that stands everywhere at base level. Cf. **peneplain.** —*n.* **4.** a senile person. [1655–65; < L *senīlis* old, equiv. to *sen(ex)* old man (akin to SENIOR) + *-īlis* -ILE]

se′nile demen′tia, *Pathol.* a syndrome of progressive, irreversible impairment of cognitive function, caused by organic factors and having its onset late in life. [1850–55]

se′nile mac′ular degenera′tion, *Pathol.* a type of macular degeneration that is one of the leading causes of blindness in the elderly and in which tiny blood vessels grow into the macula of the retina, obscuring vision. *Abbr.:* SMD

se·nil·i·ty (si nil′i tē), *n.* the state of being senile, esp. the weakness or mental infirmity of old age. [1770–80; SENILE + -ITY]

sen·ior (sēn′yər), *adj.* **1.** older or elder (usually designating a father whose son is named after him, often written as *Sr.* or *sr.* following the name): *I would like to see the senior Mr. Hansen.* Cf. **junior** (def. 1). **2.** of earlier appointment or admission, as to an office, status, or rank: *a senior partner.* **3.** of higher or the highest rank or standing. **4.** (in American schools, colleges, and universities) of or pertaining to students in their final year or to their class. **5.** (in certain American colleges and universities) of or pertaining to the final two years of education, during which a student specializes in a certain field of study. **6.** of, for, or pertaining to senior citizens: *senior discounts on local bus fares.* **7.** of earlier date; prior to: *His appointment is senior to mine by a year.* **8.** *Finance.* having a claim on payments, assets, dividends, or the like prior to other creditors, mortgages, stockholders, etc. —*n.* **9.** a person who is older than another. **10.** a person of higher rank or standing than another, esp. by virtue of longer service. **11.** (in the U.S.) a student in the final year at a high school, preparatory school, college, or university. **12.** a fellow holding senior rank in a college at an English university. **13.** a senior citizen. **14.** (*cap.*) a member of the Girl Scouts from 14 through 17 years of age. [1350–1400; ME < L, equiv. to *sen(ex)* old, old man + *-ior* comp. adj. suffix]

sen′ior cit′izen, an elderly or aged person, esp. one who is retired or whose principal source of support is a pension or Social Security benefits. [1950–55] **—sen′ior cit′izenship.**

sen′ior high′ school′, a school attended after junior high school and usually consisting of grades 10 through 12. [1910–15]

sen·ior·i·ty (sēn yôr′i tē, -yor′-), *n., pl.* **-ties** for 2. **1.** the state of being senior; priority of birth; superior age. **2.** priority, precedence, or status obtained as the result of a person's length of service, as in a profession, trade, company, or union: *First choice of vacation time will be given to employees with seniority.* [1400–50; late ME < ML *seniōritās,* equiv. to L *senior* SENIOR + *-itās* -ITY]

senior′ity rule′, *U.S. Pol.* the custom in Congress providing for the assignment of a committee chairpersonship to that member of the majority party who has served on the committee the longest.

sen·i·ti (sen′i tē), *n., pl.* **-ti.** a bronze or brass coin and monetary unit of Tonga, the 100th part of a pa'anga. [1965–70; < Tongan < E CENT]

Sen·lac (sen′lak), *n.* a hill in SE England: believed by some historians to have been the site of the Battle of Hastings, 1066.

sen·na (sen′ə), *n.* **1.** any plant, shrub, or tree belonging to the genus *Cassia,* of the legume family, having pinnate leaves and large clusters of flowers. **2.** any of various cathartic drugs consisting of the dried leaflets of certain of these plants, as one drug **(Alexandrian senna)** derived from *C. acutifolia,* or another **(Tinnevelly senna)** derived from *C. angustifolia.* **3.** See **wild senna.** [1535–45; < NL < Ar *sanā*]

Sen·nach·er·ib (sə nak′ər ib), *n.* died 681 B.C., king of Assyria 705–681.

Sen′na knot′. See **Sehna knot.**

Sen·nar (sə när′), *n.* a region in the E Sudan between the White and Blue Nile rivers, S of Khartoum: a former kingdom.

sen·net[1] (sen′it), *n.* any of several small barracudas, as *Sphyraena borealis* **(northern sennet),** ranging along the eastern coast of North and Central America. [1665–75; orig. uncert.]

sen·net[2] (sen′it), *n.* (in Elizabethan drama) a set of notes played on the trumpet or cornet to mark the entrance or exit of a group of actors. [1580–90; var. of SIGNET]

sen·net[3] (sen′it), *n.* sennit.

Sen·nett (sen′it), *n.* **Mack** (*Michael Sinnott*), 1884–1960, U.S. motion-picture director and producer, born in Canada.

sen·night (sen′īt, -it), *n. Archaic.* a week. Also, **se′n′night.** [bef. 1000; ME *sevenyht, seovenihte(e), sennyght,* etc., OE *seofon nihta.* See SEVEN, NIGHT]

sen·nit (sen′it), *n.* **1.** a flat, braided cordage, formed by plaiting strands of rope yarn or other fiber, used as small stuff aboard ships. **2.** braided straw or grass used in making hats. Also, **sennet, sinnet.** [1760–70; orig. uncert.]

se·ñor (sān yôr′, -yōr′, sēn-; *Sp.* se nyôr′), *n., pl.* **se·ñors,** *Sp.* **se·ño·res** (se nyô′res). a Spanish term of address equivalent to *sir* or *Mr.,* used alone or capitalized and prefixed to the name of a man. *Abbr.:* Sr. [1615–25; < Sp < VL *senior. See SENIOR]

se·ño·ra (sān yôr′ə, -yōr′ə, sēn-; *Sp.* se nyô′rä), *n., pl.* **se·ño·ras** (sān yôr′əz, -yōr′-, sēn-; *Sp.* se nyô′räs). a Spanish term of address equivalent to *Mrs.,* used alone or capitalized and prefixed to the name of a married or older woman. *Abbr.:* Sra. [1570–80; < Sp, fem. of SEÑOR]

se·ño·ri·ta (sān′yə rē′tə, sēn′-; *Sp.* se nyô rē′tä), *n., pl.* **-tas** (-təz; *Sp.* -täs). **1.** a Spanish term of address equivalent to *miss,* used alone or capitalized and prefixed to the name of a girl or unmarried woman. *Abbr.:* Srta. **2.** a cigar-shaped wrasse, *Oxyjulis californica,* found off the coast of California, olive brown above shading to creamy white below. [1815–25, *Amer.*; < Sp, dim. of SEÑORA]

sen·sa (sen′sə), *n.* pl. of **sensum.**

sen·sate (sen′sāt), *adj.* perceived by the senses. [1490–1500; < LL *sēnsātus.* See SENSE, -ATE[1]] **—sen′sate·ly,** *adv.*

sen·sa·tion (sen sā′shən), *n.* **1.** the operation or function of the senses; perception or awareness of stimuli through the senses. **2.** a mental condition or physical feeling resulting from stimulation of a sense organ or from internal bodily change, as cold or pain. **3.** *Physiol.* the faculty of perception of stimuli. **4.** a general feeling not directly attributable to any given stimulus, as discomfort, anxiety, or doubt. **5.** a mental feeling, esp. a state of excited feeling. **6.** a state of excited feeling or interest caused among a number of persons or throughout a community, as by some rumor or occurrence. **7.** a cause of such feeling or interest: *The new Brazilian movie was the sensation of the film festival.* [1605–15; < ML *sēnsātiōn-* (s. of *sēnsātiō*), equiv. to LL *sēnsāt(us)* SENSATE + *-iōn-* -ION] **—sen·sa′tion·less,** *adj.*

—Syn. 2, 4. See **sense. 6.** excitement, stimulation, animation; agitation, commotion, perturbation.

sen·sa·tion·al (sen sā′shə nl), *adj.* **1.** producing or designed to produce a startling effect, strong reaction, intense interest, etc., esp. by exaggerated, superficial, or lurid elements: *a sensational novel.* **2.** extraordinarily good; conspicuously excellent: *a sensational quarterback.* **3.** of or pertaining to the senses or sensation. [1830–40; SENSATION + -AL[1]] **—sen·sa′tion·al·ly,** *adv.*

—Syn. 1. exciting, stimulating. **—Ant. 1.** prosaic, dull.

sen·sa·tion·al·ism (sen sā′shə nl iz′əm), *n.* **1.** subject matter, language, or style producing or designed to produce startling or thrilling impressions or to excite and please vulgar taste. **2.** the use of or interest in this subject matter, language, or style: *The cheap tabloids relied on sensationalism to increase their circulation.* **3.** *Philos.* **a.** the doctrine that the good is to be judged only by the gratification of the senses. **b.** the doctrine that all ideas are derived from and are essentially reducible to sensations. **4.** *Psychol.* sensationism. [1840–50; SENSATIONAL + -ISM] **—sen·sa′tion·al·ist,** *n., adj.* **—sen·sa′tion·al·is′tic,** *adj.*

sen·sa·tion·al·ize (sen sā′shə nl īz′), *v.t.,* **-ized, -iz·ing.** to make sensational. Also, *esp. Brit.,* **sen·sa′tion·al·ise′.** [1850–55; SENSATIONAL + -IZE]

sen·sa·tion·ism (sen sā′shə niz′əm), *n. Psychol.* a theory maintaining that experience consists solely of sensations. Also, **sensationalism.** [1860–65; SENSATION + -ISM] **—sen·sa′tion·ist,** *n., adj.* **—sen·sa′tion·is′tic,** *adj.*

sense (sens), *n., v.,* **sensed, sens·ing.** —*n.* **1.** any of the faculties, as sight, hearing, smell, taste, or touch, by which humans and animals perceive stimuli originating from outside or inside the body. **2.** these faculties collectively. **3.** their operation or function; sensation. **4.** a feeling or perception produced through the organs of touch, taste, etc., or resulting from a particular condition of some part of the body: *to have a sense of cold.* **5.** a faculty or function of the mind analogous to sensation: *the moral sense.* **6.** any special capacity for perception, estimation, appreciation, etc.: *a sense of humor.* **7.** Usually, **senses.** clear and sound mental faculties; sanity: *Have you taken leave of your senses?* **8.** a more or less vague perception or impression: *a sense of security.* **9.** a mental discernment, realization, or recognition; acuteness: *a just sense of the worth of a thing.* **10.** the recognition of something as incumbent or fitting: *a sense of duty.* **11.** sound practical intelligence: *He has no sense.* **12.** something that is sensible or reasonable: *to talk sense.* **13.** the meaning or gist of something: *You missed the sense of his statement.* **14.** the value or worth of something; merit: *There's no sense in worrying about the past.* **15.** the meaning of a word or phrase in a specific context, esp. as isolated in a dictionary or glossary; the semantic element in a word or group of words. **16.** an opinion or judgment formed or held, esp. by an assemblage or body of persons: *the sense of a meeting.* **17.** *Genetics.* a DNA sequence that is capable of coding for an amino acid (distinguished from *nonsense*). **18.** *Math.* one of two opposite directions in which a vector may point. **19. come to one's senses,** to regain one's good judgment or realistic point of view; become reasonable. **20. in a sense,** according to one explanation or view; to a certain extent: *In a sense it may have been the only possible solution.* **21. make sense,** to be reasonable or comprehensible: *His attitude doesn't make sense.* —*v.t.* **22.** to perceive (something) by the senses; become aware of. **23.** to grasp the meaning of; understand. **24.** (of certain mechanical devices) to detect physical phenomena, as light, temperature, radioactivity, etc., mechanically, electrically, or photoelectrically. **25.** *Computers.* to read (punched holes, tape, data, etc.) mechanically, electrically, or photoelectrically. [1350–1400; (n.) ME < L *sēnsus* sensation, feeling, understanding, equiv. to *sent(īre)* to feel + *-tus* suffix of v. action, with *tt > s;* (v.) deriv. of the n.]

—Syn. 4. SENSE, SENSATION refer to consciousness of stimulus or of a perception as pleasant or unpleasant. A SENSE is an awareness or recognition of something; the stimulus may be subjective and the entire process may be mental or intellectual: *a sense of failure.* A SENSATION is an impression derived from an objective (external) stimulus through any of the sense organs: *a sensation of heat.* It is also a general, indefinite physical or emotional feeling: *a sensation of weariness.* **5.** awareness, apprehension. **7.** rationality. **9.** estimation, appreciation. **13.** signification, import, denotation, connotation, interpretation. See **meaning. 16.** feeling, sentiment. **22.** discern, appreciate, recognize.

Sense′ and Sensibil′ity, a novel (1811) by Jane Austen.

sense′ da′tum, 1. Also called **sensum.** *Psychol.* the basic unit of an experience resulting from the stimulation of a sense organ; a stimulus or an object of perception or sensation. **2.** *Epistemology.* datum (def. 3). [1920–25]

sense·ful (sens′fəl), *adj.* full of reasonable sense; sound; judicious. [1585–95; SENSE + -FUL]

sen·sei (sen sā′), *n.* a karate or judo instructor. [< Japn: teacher, master, doctor < MChin, equiv. to Chin *xiānsheng* (*xiān* ahead + *shēng* born)]

sense·less (sens′lis), *adj.* **1.** destitute or deprived of sensation; unconscious. **2.** lacking mental perception,

CONCISE ETYMOLOGY KEY: <, descended or borrowed from; >, whence; b., blend of, blended; c., cognate with; cf., compare; deriv., derivative; equiv., equivalent; imit., imitative; obl., oblique; r., replacing; s., stem; sp., spelling, spelled; resp., respelling, respelled; trans., translation; ?, origin unknown; *, unattested; ‡, probably earlier than. See the full key inside the front cover.

appreciation, or comprehension. **3.** stupid or foolish, as persons or actions. **4.** nonsensical or meaningless, as words: *This letter is either cryptic or senseless.* [1550–60; SENSE + -LESS] —**sense′less·ly,** *adv.* —**sense′less·ness,** *n.*
—**Syn. 1.** insensate, insensible. **2.** unperceiving, undiscerning. **3.** silly, idiotic, inane, witless, asinine.
—**Ant. 2.** sensitive. **3.** intelligent.

sense′ or′gan, a specialized bodily structure that receives or is sensitive to internal or external stimuli; receptor. [1850–55]

sense′ percep′tion, perception by the senses rather than by the intellect. [1865–70]

sense′ stress′. See **sentence stress.**

sen·si·bil·i·ty (sen′sə bil′i tē), *n., pl.* **-ties. 1.** capacity for sensation or feeling; responsiveness or susceptibility to sensory stimuli. **2.** mental susceptibility or responsiveness; quickness and acuteness of apprehension or feeling. **3.** keen consciousness or appreciation. **4. sensibilities,** emotional capacities. **5.** Sometimes, **sensibilities.** liability to feel hurt or offended; sensitive feelings. **6.** Often, **sensibilities.** capacity for intellectual and aesthetic distinctions, feelings, tastes, etc.: *a man of refined sensibilities.* **7.** the property, as in plants or instruments, of being readily affected by external influences. [1325–75; ME *sensibilite* < MF < LL *sēnsibilitās.* See SENSIBLE, -ITY]
—**Syn. 1.** SENSIBILITY, SUSCEPTIBILITY, SENSITIVENESS, SENSITIVITY refer to capacity to respond to or be affected by something. SENSIBILITY is, particularly, capacity to respond to aesthetic and emotional stimuli: *the sensibility of the artist.* SUSCEPTIBILITY is the state or quality of being impressionable and responsive, esp. to emotional stimuli; in the plural it has much the same meaning as SENSIBILITY: *a person of keen susceptibilities.* SENSITIVENESS is the state or quality of being sensitive, of having a capacity of sensation and of responding to external stimuli: *sensitiveness to light.* SENSITIVITY is a special capability of being sensitive to physiological, chemical action or a tendency to be easily affected by the adverse reactions of others: *the sensitivity of a nerve; sensitivity to criticism.* **2.** alertness, awareness.

sen·si·ble (sen′sə bəl), *adj.* **1.** having, using, or showing good sense or sound judgment: *a sensible young woman.* **2.** cognizant; keenly aware (usually fol. by *of*): *sensible of his fault.* **3.** significant in quantity, magnitude, etc.; considerable; appreciable: *a sensible reduction in price.* **4.** capable of being perceived by the senses; material: *the sensible universe.* **5.** capable of feeling or perceiving, as organs or parts of the body. **6.** perceptible to the mind. **7.** conscious: *The patient was speechless but still sensible.* **8.** *Archaic.* sensitive. [1325–75; ME < OF < L *sēnsibilis,* equiv. to *sēns(us)* SENSE + *-ibilis* -IBLE] —**sen′si·ble·ness,** *n.* —**sen′si·bly,** *adv.*
—**Syn. 1.** intelligent, sagacious, rational, reasonable. See **practical. 2.** conscious, understanding, observant. **4.** perceptible, discernible, palpable. —**Ant. 1.** stupid.

sen′sible hori′zon, *Astron.* See under **horizon** (def. 2a). [1635–45]

sen·sil·lum (sen sil′əm), *n., pl.* **-la** (-lə). *Zool.* a simple sense organ usually consisting of one or a few cells at the peripheral end of a sensory nerve fiber. [< NL (1895), equiv. to L *sēns-,* ptp. s. of *sentīre* to SENSE + *-illum* dim. suffix]

sen·si·tive (sen′si tiv), *adj.* **1.** endowed with sensation; having perception through the senses. **2.** readily or excessively affected by external agencies or influences. **3.** having acute mental or emotional sensibility; aware of and responsive to the feelings of others. **4.** easily pained, annoyed, etc. **5.** pertaining to or connected with the senses or sensation. **6.** *Physiol.* having a low threshold of sensation or feeling. **7.** responding to stimuli, as leaves that move when touched. **8.** highly responsive to certain agents, as photographic plates, films, or paper. **9.** affected or likely to be affected by a specified stimulus (used in combination): *price-sensitive markets.* **10.** involving work, duties, or information of a highly secret or delicate nature, esp. in government: *a sensitive position in the State Department.* **11.** requiring tact or caution; delicate; touchy: *a sensitive topic.* **12.** constructed to indicate, measure, or be affected by small amounts or changes, as a balance or thermometer. **13.** *Radio.* easily affected by external influences, esp. by radio waves. —*n.* **14.** a person who is sensitive. **15.** a person with psychic powers; medium. [1350–1400; < ML *sēnsitīvus,* irreg. formation on L *sēns-,* ptp. s. of *sentīre* to SENSE (see -IVE); r. ME *sensitif(e)* < MF *sensitif, sensitive* < ML, as above] —**sen′si·tive·ly,** *adv.*

sen′sitive fern′, a common, widely distributed fern, *Onoclea sensibilis,* having large, triangular leaves and beadlike spikes that contain the spores. [1805–15, *Amer.*; so called from the sensitivity of its foliage to frost]

sen·si·tive·ness (sen′si tiv nis), *n.* the state or quality of being sensitive. [1820–30; SENSITIVE + -NESS]
—**Syn.** See **sensibility.**

sen′sitive plant′, 1. Also called **humble plant.** a tropical American plant, *Mimosa pudica,* cultivated in greenhouses, having bipinnate leaves whose leaflets fold together when touched. **2.** any of various other plants that are sensitive to touch. [1650–60]

sen·si·tiv·i·ty (sen′si tiv′i tē), *n., pl.* **-ties** for 2, 3. **1.** the state or quality of being sensitive; sensitiveness. **2.** *Physiol.* **a.** the ability of an organism or part of an organism to react to stimuli; irritability. **b.** degree of susceptibility to stimulation. **3.** *Elect.* **a.** the ability of a radio device to react to incoming signals, expressed as the minimum input signal required to produce a specified output signal with a given noise level. **b.** the input, as voltage, current, or the like, required to produce full deflection in an electric measuring device, expressed as the ratio of the response to the magnitude of the input quantity. [1795–1805; SENSITIVE + -ITY]
—**Syn. 1.** See **sensibility.**

sensitiv′ity group′, a group of persons participating in sensitivity training. Also called **T-group.** [1965–70]

sensitiv′ity train′ing, a form of group therapy designed to develop understanding of oneself and others through free, unstructured discussion. [1950–55]

sen·si·ti·za·tion (sen′si tə zā′shən), *n.* **1.** the state or process of being sensitized. **2.** *Psychol.* the process of becoming susceptible to a given stimulus that previously had no effect or significance. **3.** *Immunol.* **a.** a state or condition in which a previously encountered foreign substance triggers an immune reaction. **b.** an immunologic state or condition that is evidenced by the acquired ability of a cell or individual to detect the presence of a foreign substance upon reexposure to the substance and to react immunologically. [1885–90; SENSITIZE + -ATION]

sen·si·tize (sen′si tīz′), *v.,* **-tized, -tiz·ing.** —*v.t.* **1.** to render sensitive. **2.** *Photog.* to render (a film or the like) sensitive to light or other forms of radiant energy. **3.** *Immunol.* to render sensitive to an antigenic substance. —*v.i.* **4.** to become sensitized. Also, *esp. Brit.,* **sen′si·tise′.** [1855–60; SENSIT(IVE) + -IZE] —**sen′si·tiz′er,** *n.*

sen′sitizing dye′, *Photog.* a dye adsorbed onto the silver halide grains of an emulsion to make the emulsion more sensitive to certain colors.

sen·si·tom·e·ter (sen′si tom′i tər), *n. Photog.* an instrument for testing the sensitivity of various types of film, consisting of an apparatus for exposing successive parts of the film to a light of standard intensity at successively increasing lengths of exposure. [1875–80; SENSIT(IVE) + -O- + -METER] —**sen·si·to·met·ric** (sen′sə tō me′trik), *adj.* —**sen′si·to·met′ri·cal·ly,** *adv.*

sen′sitomet′ric curve′, *Photog.* See **characteristic curve.** [1965–70; SENSITO(METER) + -METRIC]

sen·si·tom·e·try (sen′si tom′i trē), *n.* the science of determining the sensitivity of photographic materials. [1905–10; SENSIT(IVE) + -O- + -METRY]

sen·sor (sen′sôr, -sər), *n.* **1.** a mechanical device sensitive to light, temperature, radiation level, or the like, that transmits a signal to a measuring or control instrument. **2.** a sense organ. [1925–30; SENSE + -OR[2]]

sen·so·ri·mo·tor (sen′sə rē mō′tər), *adj.* **1.** *Psychol.* of or pertaining to motor activity caused by sensory stimuli. Cf. **ideomotor. 2.** *Physiol.* both sensory and motor, as parts of the cerebral cortex. Also, **sen·so·mo·tor** (sen′sə mō′tər). [1850–55; SENSORY + MOTOR]

sen·so·ri·neu·ral (sen′sə rē no͝or′əl, -nyo͝or′-), *adj.* related to or affecting a sensory nerve or a sensory mechanism together with its neural circuitry. [1975–80; SENSORY + NEURAL]

sen·so·ri·um (sen sôr′ē əm, -sōr′-), *n., pl.* **-so·ri·ums, -so·ri·a** (-sôr′ē ə, -sōr′-). **1.** a part of the brain or the brain itself regarded as the seat of sensation. **2.** the sensory apparatus of the body. [1640–50; < LL *sēnsōrium,* equiv. to L *sent(īre)* to feel + *-tōrium* -TORY[2], with *tt* > *s*]

sen·so·ry (sen′sə rē), *adj.* **1.** of or pertaining to the senses or sensation. **2.** *Physiol.* noting a structure for conveying an impulse that results or tends to result in sensation, as a nerve. Also, **sen·so·ri·al** (sen sôr′ē əl, -sōr′-). [1620–30; SENSE + -ORY[1]]

sen′sory cor′tex, the region of the cerebral cortex concerned with receiving and interpreting sensory information from various parts of the body.

sen′sory depriva′tion, *Psychiatry.* the experimental or natural reduction of environmental stimuli, as by physical isolation or loss of eyesight, often leading to cognitive, perceptual, or behavioral changes, as disorientation, delusions, or panic.

sen′sory neu′ron, *Biol.* a nerve cell that conducts impulses from a sense organ to the central nervous system.

sen′sory root′. See under **nerve root.**

sen·su·al (sen′sho͞o əl), *adj.* **1.** pertaining to, inclined to, or preoccupied with the gratification of the senses or appetites; carnal; fleshly. **2.** lacking in moral restraints; lewd or unchaste. **3.** arousing or exciting the senses or appetites. **4.** worldly; materialistic; irreligious. **5.** of or pertaining to the senses or physical sensation; sensory. **6.** pertaining to the philosophical doctrine of sensationalism. [1400–50; late ME < LL *sēnsuālis,* equiv. to *sēnsu-,* s. of *sēnsus* SENSE + *-ālis* -AL[1]] —**sen′su·al·ly,** *adv.*
—**Syn. 1.** SENSUAL, SENSUOUS, VOLUPTUOUS refer to experience through the senses. SENSUAL refers, often unfavorably, to the enjoyments derived from the senses, esp. from the gratification or indulgence of physical appetites: *a sensual delight in eating; sensual excesses.* SENSUOUS refers, favorably or literally, to what is experienced through the senses: *sensuous impressions; sensuous poetry.* VOLUPTUOUS implies the luxurious gratification of sensuous or sensual desires: *voluptuous joys; voluptuous beauty.* See also **carnal. 2.** lascivious.

sen·su·al·ism (sen′sho͞o ə liz′əm), *n.* **1.** subjection to sensual appetites; sensuality. **2.** *Philos.* sensationalism (def. 3). [1795–1805; SENSUAL + -ISM]

sen·su·al·ist (sen′sho͞o ə list), *n.* **1.** a person given to the indulgence of the senses or appetites. **2.** a person who holds the doctrine of sensationalism. [1655–65; SENSUAL + -IST] —**sen′su·al·is′tic,** *adj.*

sen·su·al·i·ty (sen′sho͞o al′i tē), *n., pl.* **-ties. 1.** sensual nature: *the sensuality of Keats's poetry.* **2.** unrestrained indulgence in sensual pleasures. **3.** lewdness; unchastity. Also, **sen′su·al·ness.** [1300–50; ME *sensualite* < OF < LL *sēnsuālitās.* See SENSUAL, -ITY]

sen·su·al·ize (sen′sho͞o ə līz′), *v.t.,* **-ized, -iz·ing.** to render sensual. Also, *esp. Brit.,* **sen′su·al·ise′.** [1605–15; SENSUAL + -IZE] —**sen′su·al·i·za′tion,** *n.*

sen·sum (sen′səm), *n., pl.* **-sa** (-sə). See **sense datum** (def. 1). [1915–20; n. use of L *sēnsum,* neut. of *sēnsus,* ptp. of *sentīre* to feel; see SENSE]

sen·su·ous (sen′sho͞o əs), *adj.* **1.** perceived by or affecting the senses: *the sensuous qualities of music.* **2.** readily affected through the senses: *a sensuous temperament.* **3.** of or pertaining to sensible objects or to the senses. [1630–40; < L *sēnsu(s)* SENSE + -OUS] —**sen′su·ous·ly,** *adv.* —**sen′su·ous·ness, sen·su·os·i·ty** (sen′sho͞o os′i tē), *n.*
—**Syn. 1.** See **sensual. 2.** feeling, sensible. **3.** sentient.

sent[1] (sent), *v.* pt. and pp. of **send.**

sent[2] (sent), *n., pl.* **sent·i** (sen′tē), **sents.** a former coin of Estonia, the 100th part of a kroon: replaced the mark in 1928. [< Estonian *senti* (cf. Finnish *sentti*) < L *centum* hundred; see CENTUM[1]]

sen·te (sen′tē), *n., pl.* **li·sen·te** (li sen′tē). a nickel-brass coin and monetary unit of Lesotho, the 100th part of a loti.

sen·tence (sen′tns), *n., v.,* **-tenced, -tenc·ing.** —*n.* **1.** *Gram.* a grammatical unit of one or more words, bearing minimal syntactic relation to the words that precede or follow it, often preceded and followed in speech by pauses, having one of a small number of characteristic intonation patterns, and typically expressing an independent statement, question, request, command, etc., as *Summer is here.* or *Who is it?* or *Stop!* **2.** *Law.* **a.** an authoritative decision; a judicial judgment or decree, esp. the judicial determination of the punishment to be inflicted on a convicted criminal. **b.** the punishment itself. **3.** *Music.* a period. **4.** *Archaic.* a saying, apothegm, or maxim. **5.** *Obs.* an opinion given on a particular question. —*v.t.* **6.** to pronounce sentence upon; condemn to punishment. [1175–1225; (n.) ME < OF < L *sententia* opinion, decision, equiv. to *sent-* (base of *sentīre* to feel) + *-entia* -ENCE; (v.) ME: to pass judgment, decide judicially < OF *sentencier,* deriv. of *sentence*] —**sen′tenc·er,** *n.*

sen′tence ad′verb, *Gram.* an adverb modifying or commenting upon the content of a sentence as a whole or upon the conditions under which it is uttered, as *frankly* in *Frankly, he can't be trusted.* [1890–95]

sen′tence frag′ment, a phrase or clause written as a sentence but lacking an element, as a subject or verb, that would enable it to function as an independent sentence in normative written English. [1945–50]

sen′tence stress′, the stress pattern or patterns associated with words as arranged in sentences in a particular language. Also called **sense stress, sen′tence ac′·cent.** Cf. **word stress.** [1880–85]

sen·ten·tial (sen ten′shəl), *adj.* pertaining to or of the nature of a sentence. [1425–75; late ME, equiv. to L *sententi(a)* SENTENCE + -AL[1]] —**sen·ten′tial·ly,** *adv.*

senten′tial cal′culus, the branch of symbolic logic dealing with the logical relationships between statements insofar as they can be analyzed into conjunctions, disjunctions, and negations of more elementary statements. Also called **propositional calculus, senten′tial log′ic.** [1935–40]

senten′tial connec′tive, *Logic.* any of several words or their equivalent symbols used in logical formulas to connect propositions, as "or," "not," "and," "if and only if."

senten′tial func′tion, *Logic.* an expression that contains one or more variables and becomes meaningful when suitable constant terms are substituted for them. Also called **propositional function.** [1945–50]

sen·ten·tious (sen ten′shəs), *adj.* **1.** abounding in pithy aphorisms or maxims: *a sententious book.* **2.** given to excessive moralizing; self-righteous. **3.** given to or using pithy sayings or maxims: *a sententious poet.* **4.** of the nature of a maxim; pithy. [1400–50; late ME < L *sententiōsus* meaningful. See SENTENCE, -OUS] —**sen·ten′tious·ly,** *adv.* —**sen·ten′tious·ness, sen·ten·ti·os·i·ty** (sen ten′shē os′i tē), *n.*
—**Syn. 2.** preachy, didactic, sanctimonious, moralistic.

sen·ti (sen′tē), *n., pl.* **senti.** a monetary unit of Tanzania, the 100th part of a shilling; cent.

sen·tience (sen′shəns), *n.* sentient condition or character; capacity for sensation or feeling. Also, **sen′tien·cy.** [1830–40; SENTI(ENT) + -ENCE]

sen·tient (sen′shənt), *adj.* **1.** having the power of perception by the senses; conscious. **2.** characterized by sensation and consciousness. —*n.* **3.** a person or thing that is sentient. **4.** *Archaic.* the conscious mind. [1595–1605; < L *sentient-* (s. of *sentiēns,* prp. of *sentīre* to feel), equiv. to *senti-* v. s. + *-ent-* -ENT] —**sen′tient·ly,** *adv.*

sen·ti·ment (sen′tə mənt), *n.* **1.** an attitude toward something; regard; opinion. **2.** a mental feeling; emotion: *a sentiment of pity.* **3.** refined or tender emotion; manifestation of the higher or more refined feelings. **4.** exhibition or manifestation of feeling or sensibility, or appeal to the tender emotions, in literature, art, or music. **5.** a thought influenced by or proceeding from feeling or emotion. **6.** the thought or feeling intended to be conveyed by words, acts, or gestures as distinguished from the words, acts, or gestures themselves. [1325–75; < ML *sentīmentum,* equiv. to L *sentī(re)* to feel + *-mentum* -MENT; r. ME *sentement* < OF < ML, as above] —**sen′ti·ment·less,** *adj.*
—**Syn. 1.** See **opinion. 2.** See **feeling. 3.** SENTIMENT, SENTIMENTALITY are terms for sensitiveness to emotional feelings. SENTIMENT is a sincere and refined sensibility, a tendency to be influenced by emotion rather than reason or fact: *to appeal to sentiment.* SENTIMENTALITY implies affected, excessive, sometimes mawkish sentiment: *weak sentimentality.*

sen·ti·men·tal (sen′tə men′tl), *adj.* **1.** expressive of or appealing to sentiment, esp. the tender emotions and feelings, as love, pity, or nostalgia: *a sentimental song.* **2.** pertaining to or dependent on sentiment: *We kept the old photograph for purely sentimental reasons.* **3.** weakly emotional; mawkishly susceptible or tender: *the sentimental Victorians.* **4.** characterized by or showing

sentiment or refined feeling. [1740–50; SENTIMENT + -AL¹] **—sen′ti·men′tal·ly,** *adv.*
—Syn. 1. romantic, tender, nostalgic; maudlin, bathetic. **—Ant. 1, 4.** dispassionate.

sen·ti·men·tal·ism (sen′tə men′tl iz′əm), *n.* **1.** sentimental tendency or character; predominance of sentiment over reason. **2.** weak emotionalism; excessive indulgence in sentiment. **3.** a display of sentimentality. [1810–20; SENTIMENTAL + -ISM]

sen·ti·men·tal·ist (sen′tə men′tl ist), *n.* one given to sentiment or sentimentality. [1770–80; SENTIMENTAL + -IST]

sen·ti·men·tal·i·ty (sen′tə men tal′i tē), *n., pl.* **-ties. 1.** the quality or state of being sentimental or excessively sentimental. **2.** an instance of being sentimental. **3.** a sentimental act, gesture, expression, etc. [1760–70; SENTIMENTAL + -ITY]
—Syn. See **sentiment.**

sen·ti·men·tal·ize (sen′tə men′tl īz′), *v.,* **-ized, -iz·ing.** *—v.i.* **1.** to indulge in sentiment. *—v.t.* **2.** to view (someone or something) sentimentally: *He sentimentalized the relationship until all real meaning was lost.* Also, *esp. Brit.,* **sen′ti·men′tal·ise′.** [1790–1800; SENTIMENTAL + -IZE] **—sen′ti·men′tal·i·za′tion,** *n.* **—sen′·ti·men′tal·iz′er,** *n.*

sen·ti·nel (sen′tn l), *n., v.,* **-neled, -nel·ing** or (*esp. Brit.*) **-nelled, -nel·ling.** *—n.* **1.** a person or thing that watches or stands as if watching. **2.** a soldier stationed as a guard to challenge all comers and prevent a surprise attack: *to stand sentinel.* **3.** Also called **tag.** *Computers.* a symbol, mark, or other labeling device indicating the beginning or end of a unit of information. *—v.t.* **4.** to watch over or guard as a sentinel. [1570–80; < MF *sentinelle* < It *sentinella,* deriv. of OIt *sentina* vigilance (L *sent(īre)* to observe) + *-īna* -INE²)] **—sen′ti·nel·like′,** *adj.* **—sen′ti·nel·ship′,** *n.*
—Syn. 1, 2. sentry, guard, watch, lookout.

sen·try (sen′trē), *n., pl.* **-tries. 1.** a soldier stationed at a place to stand guard and prevent the passage of unauthorized persons, watch for fires, etc., esp. a sentinel stationed at a pass, gate, opening in a defense work, or the like. **2.** a member of a guard or watch. [1605–15; short for *sentrinel,* var. of SENTINEL]

sen′try box′, a small structure for sheltering a sentry from bad weather. [1695–1705]

sen′try palm′. See **kentia palm.**

Se·nu·fo (sə nōō′fō), *n., pl.* **-fos,** (*esp. collectively*) **-fo** for 1. **1.** a member of a group of indigenous people of Ivory Coast, Mali, and Burkina Faso, known for their music and art. **2.** any of several dialects spoken by the Senufo, belonging to the Gur branch of the Niger-Congo family.

sen·wood (sen′wŏŏd′), *n.* the light-colored wood of a Japanese tree, *Kalopanax pictus* (or *K. ricinifolium*), used for veneer in the manufacture of plywood. [*sen-* (of undetermined orig.) + WOOD¹]

Se·o de Ur·gel (*Sp.* se′ô the ōōʀ hel′), Urgel.

Se·oul (sōl, sōōl, sā′ŏŏl; *Kor.* syœ′ŏŏl), *n.* a city in and the capital of South Korea, in the W part. 6,889,470.

SEP, simplified employee pension.

Sep., **1.** September. **2.** Septuagint.

sep., **1.** sepal. **2.** separable. **3.** separate. **4.** separated. **5.** separation.

se·pal (sē′pəl), *n. Bot.* one of the individual leaves or parts of the calyx of a flower. [< NL *sepalum* (1790), irreg. coinage based on Gk *sképē* covering and L *petalum* PETAL] **—se′paled, se′palled,** *adj.*

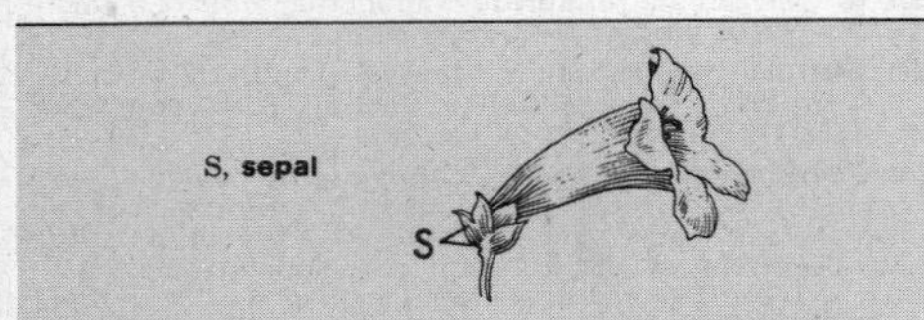

S, sepal

se·pal·oid (sē′pə loid′, sep′ə-), *adj.* resembling a sepal. Also, **sep·al·ine** (sep′ə lin′, -lin, sē′pə-). [1820–30; < NL *sepaloideus.* See SEPAL, -OID]

-sepalous, a combining form meaning "having sepals" of the kind or number specified by the initial element: *polysepalous.* [see SEPAL, -OUS]

sep·a·ra·ble (sep′ər ə bəl, sep′rə-), *adj.* **1.** capable of being separated, parted, or dissociated. **2.** *Math.* **a.** containing a countable dense subset. **b.** (of a differential equation) capable of being written so that coefficients of the differentials of the independent and dependent variables are, respectively, functions of these variables alone. Cf. **separation of variables.** [1350–1400; ME (< MF) < L *sēparābilis,* equiv. to *sēparā(re)* to SEPARATE + *-bilis* -BLE] **—sep′a·ra·bil′i·ty, sep′a·ra·ble·ness,** *n.* **—sep′a·ra·bly,** *adv.*

sep·a·rate (*v.* sep′ə rāt′; *adj., n.* sep′ər it), *v.,* **-rat·ed, -rat·ing,** *adj., n.* *—v.t.* **1.** to keep apart or divide, as by an intervening barrier or space: *to separate two fields by a fence.* **2.** to put, bring, or force apart; part: *to separate two fighting boys.* **3.** to set apart; disconnect; dissociate: *to separate church and state.* **4.** to remove or sever from association, service, etc., esp. legally or formally: *He was separated from the army right after V-E Day.* **5.** to sort, part, divide, or disperse (an assemblage, mass, compound, etc.), as into individual units, components, or elements. **6.** to take by parting or dividing; extract (usually fol. by *from* or *out*): *to separate metal from ore.* **7.** *Math.* to write (the variables of a differential equation) in a form in which the differentials of the independent and dependent variables are, respectively, functions of these variables alone: *We can separate the variables to solve the equation.* Cf. **separation of variables.** *—v.i.* **8.** to part company; withdraw from personal association (often fol. by *from*): *to separate from a church.* **9.** (of a married pair) to stop living together but without getting a divorce. **10.** to draw or come apart; become divided, disconnected, or detached. **11.** to become parted from a mass or compound: *Cream separates from milk.* **12.** to take or go in different directions: *We have to separate at the crossroad.* *—adj.* **13.** detached, disconnected, or disjoined. **14.** unconnected; distinct; unique: *two separate questions.* **15.** being or standing apart; distant or dispersed: *two separate houses; The desert has widely separate oases.* **16.** existing or maintained independently: *separate organizations.* **17.** individual or particular: *each separate item.* **18.** not shared; individual or private: *separate checks; separate rooms.* **19.** (*sometimes cap.*) noting or pertaining to a church or other organization no longer associated with the original or parent organization. *—n.* **20.** Usually, **separates.** women's outer garments that may be worn in combination with a variety of others to make different ensembles, as matching and contrasting blouses, skirts, and sweaters. **21.** offprint (def. 1). **22.** a bibliographical unit, as an article, chapter, or other portion of a larger work, printed from the same type but issued separately, sometimes with additional pages. [1400–50; late ME (n. and adj.) < L *sēparātus* (ptp. of *sēparāre*), equiv. to *sē-* SE- + *par(āre)* to furnish, produce, obtain, PREPARE + *-ātus* -ATE¹] **—sep′a·rate·ly,** *adv.* **—sep′a·rate·ness,** *n.*
—Syn. 1, 2. sever, sunder, split. SEPARATE, DIVIDE imply a putting apart or keeping apart of things from each other. To SEPARATE is to remove from each other things previously associated: *to separate a mother from her children.* To DIVIDE is to split or break up carefully according to measurement, rule, or plan: *to divide a cake into equal parts.* **3.** disjoin, disengage. **13.** unattached, severed, discrete. **15.** secluded, isolated. **16.** independent. **—Ant. 1–3.** unite, connect.

sep′arate but e′qual, pertaining to a racial policy by which blacks may be segregated if granted equal opportunities and facilities, as for education, transportation, or jobs.

sep·a·ra·tion (sep′ə rā′shən), *n.* **1.** an act or instance of separating or the state of being separated. **2.** a place, line, or point of parting. **3.** a gap, hole, rent, or the like. **4.** something that separates or divides. **5.** *Law.* **a.** cessation of conjugal cohabitation, as by mutual consent. **b.** See **judicial separation. 6.** *Aerospace.* the time or act of releasing a burned-out stage of a rocket or missile from the remainder. **7.** *Photog.* See **separation negative.** [1375–1425; late ME < L *sēparātiōn-* (s. of *sēparātiō*), equiv. to *sēparāt(us)* SEPARATE + *-iōn-* -ION]

separa′tion anxi′ety, 1. the normal fear and apprehension expressed by infants when removed from their mothers or approached by strangers. **2.** any similar reaction in later life caused by separation from familiar surroundings or close friends or family.

separa′tion cen′ter, a place at which military personnel are processed for release from active service.

separa′tion en′ergy, *Physics.* See **binding energy** (def. 1).

sep·a·ra·tion·ist (sep′ə rā′shə nist), *n., adj.* separatist. [1880–85; SEPARATION + -IST]

separa′tion lay′er, *Bot.* See **abscission layer.**

separa′tion neg′ative, *Photog.* a black-and-white negative of one of the additive primary colors used to form a color image. Also called **separation.**

separa′tion of pow′ers, the principle or system of vesting in separate branches the executive, legislative, and judicial powers of a government.

separa′tion of var′iables, *Math.* **1.** a grouping of the terms of an ordinary differential equation so that associated with each differential is a factor consisting entirely of functions of the independent variable appearing in the differential. **2.** a process of finding a particular solution of a partial differential equation in the form of a product of factors that each involve only one of the variables.

sep·a·ra·tist (sep′ər ə tist, -ə rā′-), *n.* **1.** a person who separates, withdraws, or secedes, as from an established church. **2.** an advocate of separation, esp. ecclesiastical or political separation. *—adj.* **3.** of, pertaining to, or designating separatism or separatists: *separatist forces; separatist tendencies.* [1600–10; SEPARATE (adj.) + -IST] **—sep′a·ra·tism,** *n.*

sep·a·ra·tive (sep′ər ə tiv, -ə rā′-), *adj.* **1.** tending to separate. **2.** causing separation. [1585–95; < LL *sēparātīvus,* equiv. to L *sēparāt(us)* SEPARATE + *-īvus* -IVE] **—sep′a·ra′tive·ly,** *adv.* **—sep′a·ra′tive·ness,** *n.*

sep·a·ra·tor (sep′ə rā′tər), *n.* **1.** a person or thing that separates. **2.** any of various apparatus for separating one thing from another, as cream from milk, steam from water, or wheat from chaff. **3.** *Elect.* a device that prevents metal contact between plates of opposite charge in a storage battery. **4.** *Mach.* retainer¹ (def. 3). [1600–10; < LL *sēparātor,* equiv. to L *sēparā(re)* to SEPARATE + *-tor* -TOR]

sep·a·ra·to·ry (sep′ər ə tôr′ē, -tōr′ē), *adj.* serving to separate. [1650–60; < NL *sēparātōrius,* equiv. to L *sēparā(re)* to SEPARATE + *-tōrius* -TORY¹]

sep·a·ra·trix (sep′ə rā′triks, sep′ə rā′-), *n., pl.* **sep·a·ra·tri·ces** (sep′ə rā′tri sēz′, -ər ə trī′sēz), **sep·a·ra·trix·es. 1.** something that divides or separates, as the line between light and dark areas on a partially illuminated surface. **2.** virgule. **3.** *Math.* one of several symbols for separating components of a number, as a decimal point or comma. [1650–60; < NL *sēparātrix,* LL; see SEPARATOR, -TRIX]

Seph., Sephardic.

Se·phar·dim (sə fär′dim, -fär dēm′), *n.pl., sing.* **-di** (-dē, -dē′). Jews of Spain and Portugal or their descendants, distinguished from the Ashkenazim and other Jewish communities chiefly by their liturgy, religious customs, and pronunciation of Hebrew: after expulsion from Spain and Portugal in 1492, established communities in North Africa, the Balkans, Western Europe, and elsewhere. [1850–55; < ModHeb *Səphāraddīm,* pl. of *Səphāraddī,* equiv. to < Heb *Səphāradh* (region mentioned in Bible (Obadiah 20) and assumed to be Spain) + *-ī* suffix of appurtenance] **—Se·phar′dic,** *adj.*

Se·phar·vites (sef′är vīts′, si fär′-), *n.pl.* people believed to be of the ancient Babylonian city of Sippar, some of whom later settled in Samaria.

Se·pher To·rah (*Seph.* se′fer tô rä′; *Ashk.* sā′fər tō′rə, toi′rə; *Eng.* sā′fər tôr′ə, tōr′ə), *pl.* ***Si·phrei To·rah*** (*Seph.* sē frā′ tô rä′; *Ashk.* si′frā tō′rə, toi′rə), *Eng.* **Sepher Torahs.** *Hebrew.* a scroll of the Torah, typically of parchment, from which the designated Parashah is chanted or read on the prescribed days. Also, ***Sefer Torah.*** [*sēpher tōrāh* lit., book of law]

Se·phor·a (si fôr′ə, -fōr′ə), *n. Douay Bible.* Zipporah.

se·pi·a (sē′pē ə), *n.* **1.** a brown pigment obtained from the inklike secretion of various cuttlefish and used with brush or pen in drawing. **2.** a drawing made with this pigment. **3.** a dark brown. **4.** *Photog.* a print or photograph made in this color. **5.** any of several cuttlefish of the genus *Sepia,* producing a dark fluid used naturally for defense and, by humans, in ink. *—adj.* **6.** of a brown, grayish brown, or olive brown similar to that of sepia ink. [1560–70; < L *sēpia* cuttlefish, its secretion < Gk *sēpía;* akin to *sēpsis* SEPSIS] **—se′pi·a·like′,** *adj.* **—se·pic** (sē′pik, sep′ik), *adj.*

se·pi·o·lite (sē′pē ə līt′), *n. Mineral.* meerschaum (def. 1). [1850–55; < G *Sepiolit* < Gk *sēpio(n)* cuttlebone, pounce (deriv. of *sēpía* SEPIA) + G *-lit* -LITE]

sepn., separation.

se·poy (sē′poi), *n.* (formerly, in India) a native soldier, usually an infantryman, in the service of Europeans, esp. of the British. [1675–85, in sense "horseman"; 1710–20 for current sense; var. of *sipahi* < Urdu < Pers *sipāhī* horseman, soldier, deriv. of *sipāh* army; cf. SPAHI]

Se′poy Rebel′lion, a revolt of the sepoy troops in British India (1857–59), resulting in the transfer of the administration of India from the East India Company to the crown. Also called **Se′poy Mu′tiny, Indian Mutiny.**

sep·pu·ku (se pōō′kōō), *n.* hara-kiri (def. 1). [1900–05; < Japn, earlier *s(y)et-puku* < MChin, equiv. to Chin *qiè* cut + *fù* belly]

sep·sis (sep′sis), *n. Pathol.* local or generalized invasion of the body by pathogenic microorganisms or their toxins: *dental sepsis; wound sepsis.* [1855–60; < Gk *sêpsis* decay; cf. *sépein* to make rotten]

sept (sept), *n.* **1.** (in Scotland) a branch of a clan. **2.** *Anthropol.* a group believing itself derived from a common ancestor. **3.** *Archaic.* a clan. [1510–20; perh. < L *septum* paddock, enclosure, fold (in figurative use, e.g., *Sept of Christ*)]

sept (set), *n. French.* the number seven.

Sept., **1.** September. **2.** Septuagint.

sep·ta (sep′tə), *n.* pl. of **septum.**

sep·tal (sep′tl), *adj. Biol.* of or pertaining to a septum. [1830–40; SEPT(UM) + -AL¹]

sep·tar·i·um (sep târ′ē əm), *n., pl.* **-tar·i·a** (-târ′ē ə). *Geol.* a concretionary nodule or mass, usually of calcium carbonate or of argillaceous carbonate of iron, traversed within by a network of cracks filled with calcite and other minerals. [1775–85; < NL *sēptārium,* equiv. to L *sēpt(um)* enclosure (see SEPTUM) + *-ārium* -ARIUM] **—sep·tar′i·an,** *adj.* **—sep·tar·i·ate** (sep târ′ē it), *adj.*

sep·tate (sep′tāt), *adj. Biol.* divided by a septum or septa. [1840–50; SEPT(UM) + -ATE¹]

sep·ta·va·lent (sep′tə vā′lənt), *adj. Chem.* septivalent.

sep·tec·to·my (sep tek′tə mē), *n., pl.* **-mies.** *Surg.* excision of part or all of a septum, esp. the nasal septum. [SEPT(UM) + -ECTOMY]

Sep·tem·ber (sep tem′bər), *n.* the ninth month of the year, containing 30 days. *Abbr.:* Sept., Sep. [bef. 1050; ME *Septembre,* OE < L *September* seventh month in the early Roman calendar; for formation see DECEMBER] **—Sep·tem·bral** (sep tem′brəl), *adj.*

Septem′ber Mas′sacre, (in the French Revolution) the massacre of royalists and other inmates of the prisons of Paris, September 2–6, 1792.

Sep·tem·brist (sep tem′brist), *n.* a person who instigated or took part in the September Massacre. [1830–40; SEPTEMBER + -IST, modeled on Pg *setembrista* (with reference to the revolution of September 1836 in Portugal); r. earlier *septembrizer* < F *septembriseur*]

sep·tem·par·tite (sep′tem pär′tīt), *adj.* separated into seven sections. [< L *septem* SEVEN + PARTITE]

sep·tem·vir (sep tem′vər), *n., pl.* **-virs, -vi·ri** (-və rī′). a member of a seven-man ruling body in ancient Rome. [1750–60; sing. of L *septemvirī,* equiv. to *septem* SEVEN + *virī,* pl. of *vir* man]

sep·tem·vi·ral (sep tem′vər əl), *adj.* of or pertaining to septemvirs or a septemvirate. [1635–45; < L *septemvirālis.* See SEPTEMVIR, -AL¹]

sep·tem·vi·rate (sep tem′vər it, -və rāt′), *n.* (in ancient Rome) **1.** the ruling body of septemvirs. **2.** the office or rule of this body. [1630–40; < L *septemvirātus.* See SEPTEMVIR, -ATE³]

sep·te·nar·i·us (sep′tə nâr′ē əs), *n., pl.* **-nar·i·i** (-nâr′ē ī′). *Pros.* a verse consisting of seven feet, usually printed in two lines: used esp. in Latin poems. [1810–20; < L *septēnārius* (see SEPTENARY)]

sep·te·nar·y (sep′tə ner′ē), *adj., n., pl.* **-nar·ies.** *—adj.* **1.** of or pertaining to the number seven or form-

CONCISE ETYMOLOGY KEY: <, descended or borrowed from; >, whence; b., blend of, blended; c., cognate with; cf., compare; deriv., derivative; equiv., equivalent; imit., imitative; obl., oblique; r., replacing; s., stem; sp., spelling, spelled; resp., respelling, respelled; trans., translation; ?, origin unknown; *, unattested; ‡, probably earlier than. See the full key inside the front cover.

ing a group of seven. **2.** septennial. **—***n.* **3.** a group or set of seven. **4.** a period of seven years. **5.** the number seven. **6.** *Pros.* a line of seven feet. [1570–80; < L *septēnārius*, equiv. to *septēn(ī)* seven each (*sept(em)* SEVEN + *-ēnī* distributive suffix) + *-ārius* -ARY]

sep·ten·de·cil·lion (sep′ten di sil′yən), *n., pl.* **-lions,** (*as after a numeral*) **-lion,** *adj.* **—***n.* **1.** a cardinal number represented in the U.S. by 1 followed by 54 zeros, and in Great Britain by 1 followed by 102 zeros. **—***adj.* **2.** amounting to one septendecillion in number. [1935–40; < L *septendec(im)* SEVENTEEN + *-illion*, as in MILLION] **—sep′ten·de·cil′lionth,** *adj., n.*

sep·ten·ni·al (sep ten′ē əl), *adj.* **1.** occurring every seven years. **2.** of or for seven years. **—***n.* **3.** something that occurs every seven years. [1630–40; < LL *septenni(s)* (L *septuennis*) seven years old (*sept(em)* SEVEN + *-enn-*, comb. form of *annus* year + *-is* adj. suffix) + -AL[1]] **—sep·ten′ni·al·ly,** *adv.*

sep·ten·tri·on (sep ten′trē on′, -ən), *n.* *Obs.* the north. [1350–1400; ME *Septemtrio(u)n* < L *septemtriōnēs, septentriōnēs* the seven stars of Ursa Major, the north, equiv. to *septem* SEVEN + *triōnēs* (pl.) plowing oxen] **—sep·ten·tri·o·nal** (sep ten′trē ə nl), *adj.*

sep·tet (sep tet′), *n.* **1.** any group of seven persons or things. **2.** a company of seven singers or musicians. **3.** a musical composition for a septet. Also, *esp. Brit.,* **sep·tette′.** [1830–40; < G; see SEPTI-, -ET]

septi-, a combining form meaning "seven," used in the formation of compound words: *septilateral.*

sep·tic (sep′tik), *adj. Pathol.* **1.** pertaining to or of the nature of sepsis; infected. **2.** putrefactive. [1595–1605; < L *sēpticus* < Gk *sēptikós*, equiv. to *sēpt(ós)* rotted + *-ikos* -IC] **—sep′ti·cal·ly,** *adv.* **—sep·tic·i·ty** (sep tis′i tē), *n.*

sep·ti·ce·mi·a (sep′tə sē′mē ə), *n. Pathol.* the invasion and persistence of pathogenic bacteria in the bloodstream. Also, **sep′ti·cae′mi·a.** [1865–70; < NL; see SEPTIC, -EMIA] **—sep′ti·ce′mic, sep′ti·cae′mic,** *adj.*

sep′tice′mic plague′, *Pathol.* an especially dangerous form of plague in which the infecting organisms invade the bloodstream. Cf. **plague** (def. 2). [SEPTICEM(IA) + -IC]

sep′tic sore′ throat′, *Pathol.* an acute, toxic, streptococcus infection of the throat producing fever, tonsillitis, and other serious effects. [1920–25]

sep′tic tank′, a tank in which solid organic sewage is decomposed and purified by anaerobic bacteria. [1900–05]

sep·ti·lat·er·al (sep′tə lat′ər əl), *adj.* having seven sides. [1650–60; SEPTI- + LATERAL]

Sept-Îles (se tēl′), *n.* French name of **Seven Isles.**

sep·til·lion (sep til′yən), *n., pl.* **-lions,** (*as after a numeral*) **-lion,** *adj.* **—***n.* **1.** a cardinal number represented in the U.S. by 1 followed by 24 zeros, and in Great Britain by 1 followed by 42 zeros. **—***adj.* **2.** amounting to one septillion in number. [1680–90; < F, equiv. to *sept* SEVEN + *-illion*, as in MILLION] **—sep·til′lionth,** *n., adj.*

sep·ti·mal (sep′tə məl), *adj.* of or based on the number seven. [1850–55; < L *septim(us)* seventh (deriv. of *septem* SEVEN) + -AL[1]]

sep·ti·ma·na (sep′tə mā′nə), *n., pl.* **-nae** (-nē). (in prescriptions) a week. [< LL *septimāna*; see SEMAINIER]

sep·time (sep′tēm), *n. Fencing.* the seventh of eight defensive positions. [1885–90; < L *septima (positiō)* seventh (position)]

Sep·ti·mus (sep′tə məs), *n.* a male given name.

sep·ti·syl·la·ble (sep′tə sil′ə bəl), *n.* a word made up of seven syllables. [1825–35; SEPTI- + SYLLABLE] **—sep·ti·syl·lab·ic** (sep′tə si lab′ik), *adj.*

sep·ti·va·lent (sep′tə vā′lənt), *adj. Chem.* having a valence of seven; heptavalent. Also, **septavalent.** [1870–75; SEPTI- + -VALENT]

sep·tu·a·ge·nar·i·an (sep′cho͞o ə jə nâr′ē ən, -to͞o-, -tyo͞o-), *adj.* **1.** of the age of 70 years or between 70 and 80 years old. **—***n.* **2.** a septuagenarian person. [1705–15; < L *septuāgēnāri(us)* (see SEPTUAGENARY) + -AN]

sep·tu·ag·e·nar·y (sep′cho͞o aj′ə ner′ē, -to͞o-, -tyo͞o- *or, esp. Brit.,* -cho͞o ə jē′nə rē), *adj., n., pl.* **-nar·ies.** septuagenarian. [1595–1605; < L *septuāgēnārius*, equiv. to *septuāgēn(ī)* seventy each (distributive of *septuāgintā* seventy) + *-ārius* -ARY]

Sep·tu·a·ges·i·ma (sep′cho͞o ə jes′ə mə, -to͞o-, -tyo͞o-), *n.* the third Sunday before Lent. Also called **Septuages′ima Sun′day.** [1350–1400; < LL *septuāgēsima (diēs)* the seventieth (day), fem. of *septuāgēsimus*, ordinal corresponding to *septuāgintā* seventy; r. ME *septuages(i)me* < OF < LL, as above]

Sep·tu·a·gint (sep′to͞o ə jint′, -tyo͞o-, sep′cho͞o-), *n.* the oldest Greek version of the Old Testament, traditionally said to have been translated by 70 or 72 Jewish scholars at the request of Ptolemy II: most scholars believe that only the Pentateuch was completed in the early part of the 3rd century B.C. and that the remaining books were translated in the next two centuries. [1555–65; < L *septuāgintā* seventy] **—Sep′tu·a·gint′al,** *adj.*

sep·tum (sep′təm), *n., pl.* **-ta** (-tə). *Biol.* a dividing wall, membrane, or the like, in a plant or animal structure; dissepiment. [1710–20; < L *sēptum*, var. of *saeptum* enclosure, n. use of neut. of *saeptus* (ptp. of *saepīre* to fence); akin to *saepēs* hedge, fence]

sep·tu·ple (sep′to͝o pəl, -tyo͝o-, sep to͞o′pəl, -tyo͞o′-, -tup′əl), *adj., v.,* **-pled, -pling.** **—***adj.* **1.** sevenfold; consisting of seven parts. **—***v.t.* **2.** to make seven times as great. [1605–15; < LL *septuplus*, deriv. of L *septem* SEVEN, on the model of *duplus* DUPLE, *quadruplus* QUADRUPLE]

sep·tup·let (sep tup′lit, -to͞o′plit, -tyo͞o′-), *n.* **1.** any group or combination of seven. **2.** one of seven offspring born at one birth. **3. septuplets,** seven offspring born at one birth. **4.** *Music.* a group of seven notes of equal value performed in the same amount of time normally taken to perform four or six. [1890–95; SEPTUPLE + -ET]

sep·tu·pli·cate (*n., adj.* sep to͞o′pli kit, -tyo͞o′-; *v.* sep to͞o′pli kāt′, -tyo͞o′-), *n., adj., v.,* **-cat·ed, -cat·ing.** **—***n.* **1.** a group, series, or set of seven identical copies (usually prec. by *in*). **—***adj.* **2.** having or consisting of seven identical parts; sevenfold. **3.** noting the seventh copy or item. **—***v.t.* **4.** to make seven copies of. **5.** to make seven times as great, as by multiplying. [< ML *septuplicātus* (ptp. of *septuplicāre* to multiply by seven), equiv. to LL *septu(plus)* SEPTUPLE + *-plicātus*, as in *quadruplicātus*; see QUADRUPLICATE]

sep·ul·cher (sep′əl kər), *n.* **1.** a tomb, grave, or burial place. **2.** Also called **Easter sepulcher.** *Eccles.* **a.** a cavity in a mensa for containing relics of martyrs. **b.** a structure or a recess in some old churches in which the Eucharist was ceremonially deposited on Good Friday and taken out at Easter in commemoration of Christ's entombment and Resurrection. **—***v.t.* **3.** to place in a sepulcher; bury. Also, *esp. Brit.,* **sepulchre.** [1150–1200; ME *sepulcre* < OF < L *sepulcrum*, equiv. to *sepul-* (var. stem of *sepelīre* to bury) + *-crum* n. suffix of place] **—Syn. 1.** vault, mausoleum, crypt.

se·pul·chral (sə pul′krəl), *adj.* **1.** of, pertaining to, or serving as a tomb. **2.** of or pertaining to burial. **3.** proper to or suggestive of a tomb; funereal or dismal. **4.** hollow and deep: *sepulchral tones.* [1605–15; < L *sepulcrālis.* See SEPULCHER, -AL[1]] **—se·pul′chral·ly,** *adv.*

sep·ul·chre (sep′əl kər), *n., v.t.,* **-chred, -chring.** *Chiefly Brit.* sepulcher.

sep·ul·ture (sep′əl chər), *n.* **1.** the act of placing in a sepulcher or tomb; burial. **2.** sepulcher; tomb. [1250–1300; ME < OF < L *sepultūra*, equiv. to *sepult(us)* (ptp. of *sepelīre* to bury) + *-ūra* -URE] **—se·pul·tur·al** (sə pul′chər əl), *adj.*

seq., 1. sequel. **2.** the following (one). [< L *sequēns*]

seq. luce, (in prescriptions) the following day. [< L *sequentī lūce*]

seqq., the following (ones). [< L *sequentia*]

se·qua·cious (si kwā′shəs), *adj.* **1.** following with smooth or logical regularity. **2.** *Archaic.* following, imitating, or serving another person, esp. unreasoningly. [1630–40; < L *sequāci-* (s. of *sequāx*) following (akin to *sequī* to follow) + -OUS] **—se·qua′cious·ly,** *adv.* **—se·quac·i·ty** (si kwas′i tē), **se·qua′cious·ness,** *n.*

se·quel (sē′kwəl), *n.* **1.** a literary work, movie, etc., that is complete in itself but continues the narrative of a preceding work. **2.** an event or circumstance following something; subsequent course of affairs. **3.** a result, consequence, or inference. [1375–1425; late ME *sequel(e)* < L *sequēla* what follows, equiv. to *sequ(ī)* to follow + *-ēla* n. suffix] **—Syn. 3.** aftermath, upshot, outgrowth, end.

se·que·la (si kwē′lə), *n., pl.* **-lae** (-lē). *Pathol.* an abnormal condition resulting from a previous disease. [1785–95; < L *sequēla* SEQUEL]

se·quence (sē′kwəns), *n., v.,* **-quenced, -quenc·ing.** **—***n.* **1.** the following of one thing after another; succession. **2.** order of succession: *a list of books in alphabetical sequence.* **3.** a continuous or connected series: *a sonnet sequence.* **4.** something that follows; a subsequent event; result; consequence. **5.** *Music.* a melodic or harmonic pattern repeated three or more times at different pitches with or without modulation. **6.** *Liturgy.* a hymn sometimes sung after the gradual and before the gospel; prose. **7.** *Motion Pictures.* a series of related scenes or shots that make up one episode of a film narrative. **8.** *Cards.* a series of three or more cards following one another in order of value, esp. of the same suit. **9.** *Genetics.* the linear order of monomers in a polymer, as nucleotides in DNA or amino acids in a protein. **10.** *Math.* a set whose elements have an order similar to that of the positive integers; a map from the positive integers to a given set. **—***v.t.* **11.** to place in a sequence. **12.** *Biochem.* to determine the order of (chemical units in a polymer chain), esp. nucleotides in DNA or RNA or amino acids in a protein. [1350–1400; ME < LL *sequentia*, equiv. to *sequ-* (s. of *sequī* to follow) + *-entia* -ENCE] **—Syn. 1.** See **series. 2.** arrangement. **4.** outcome.

se·quenc·er (sē′kwən sər), *n.* **1.** a device for the automatic determination or regulation of a sequence. **2.** *Biochem.* a device that can sequence nucleic acids or protein. **3.** an electronic device or software program that digitally stores sound for modification and playback through a synthesizer. [1970–75; SEQUENCE + -ER[1]]

se·quenc·ing (sē′kwən sing), *n.* the interruption of a career by a woman to bear and care for children until they reach an age that allows her to resume work.

se·quent (sē′kwənt), *adj.* **1.** following; successive. **2.** following logically or naturally; consequent. **3.** characterized by continuous succession; consecutive. **—***n.* **4.** something that follows in order or as a result. [1550–60; < L *sequent-* (s. of *sequēns*, prp. of *sequī* to follow), equiv. to *sequ-* follow + *-ent-* -ENT] **—se′quent·ly,** *adv.*

se·quen·tial (si kwen′shəl), *adj.* **1.** characterized by regular sequence of parts. **2.** following; subsequent; consequent. [1815–25; SEQUENT + -IAL] **—se·quen·ti·al·i·ty** (si kwen′shē al′i tē), *n.* **—se·quen′tial·ly,** *adv.*

se·quen·tial-ac·cess (si kwen′shəl ak′ses), *adj.* *Computers.* **1.** of or pertaining to a storage medium, as magnetic tape, in which records must be accessed by reading or writing from the beginning of the file. **2.** of or pertaining to file processing in which records are organized based on the sequence of keys contained in each record, and in which accessing a record necessitates first accessing all of the preceding records. Cf. **direct-access, random access.** Also, **serial-access.** [1965–70]

sequen′tial anal′ysis, *Statistics.* the analysis of data obtained from a sample the size of which is not fixed in advance, but is selected based on the outcome of the sampling as it proceeds.

sequen′tially compact′ set′, *Math.* a set in which every sequence has a subsequence that converges to a point of the set.

se·ques·ter (si kwes′tər), *v.t.* **1.** to remove or withdraw into solitude or retirement; seclude. **2.** to remove or separate. **3.** *Law.* to remove (property) temporarily from the possession of the owner; seize and hold, as the property and income of a debtor, until legal claims are satisfied. **4.** *Internat. Law.* to requisition, hold, and control (enemy property). [1350–1400; ME *sequestren* < L *sequestrāre* to put in hands of a trustee, deriv. of *sequester* trustee, depositary] **—se·ques′tra·ble,** *adj.* **—Syn. 1, 2.** isolate.

se·ques·trate (si kwes′trāt), *v.t.,* **-trat·ed, -trat·ing.** **1.** *Law.* **a.** to sequester (property). **b.** to confiscate. **2.** to separate; seclude. [1505–15; < L *sequestrātus* (ptp. of *sequestrāre*), equiv. to *sequestr-* (see SEQUESTER) + *-ātus* -ATE[1]] **—se·ques·tra·tor** (sē′kwes trā′tər, si kwes′trā-), *n.*

se·ques·tra·tion (sē′kwes trā′shən, si kwes-), *n.* **1.** removal or separation; banishment or exile. **2.** a withdrawal into seclusion; retirement. **3.** *Law.* **a.** the sequestering of property. **b.** confiscation or seizure. **4.** *Chem.* the combining of metallic ions with a suitable reagent into a stable, soluble complex in order to prevent the ions from combining with a substance with which they would otherwise have formed an insoluble precipitate, from causing interference in a particular reaction, or from acting as undesirable catalysts. [1350–1400; ME < LL *sequestrātiōn-* (s. of *sequestrātiō*), equiv. to *sequestrāt(us)* (ptp. of *sequestrāre* to SEQUESTER) + *-iōn-* -ION]

se·ques·trec·to·my (sē′kwes trek′tə mē), *n., pl.* **-mies.** *Surg.* the removal of dead spicules or portions, esp. of bone. [SEQUESTR(UM) + -ECTOMY]

se·ques·trum (si kwes′trəm), *n., pl.* **-tra** (-trə). *Pathol.* a fragment of bone that has become necrotic as a result of disease or injury and has separated from the normal bone structure. [1825–35; < NL; ML: sequestrated property, deriv. of L *sequester;* see SEQUESTER] **—se·ques′·tral,** *adj.*

se·quin (sē′kwin), *n.* **1.** a small shining disk or spangle used for ornamentation, as on women's clothing and accessories or on theatrical costumes. **2.** a former gold coin of Venice, introduced in 1284; ducat. **3.** a former gold coin of Malta, introduced c1535. **4.** a former gold coin of Turkey, introduced in 1478. Also, **zecchino, zechin** (for defs. 2–4). [1575–85; < F *sequin* < It *zecchino*, equiv. to *zecc(a)* mint (< Ar *sikkah* die, coin) + *-ino* -INE[2]] **—se′quined,** *adj.*

se·quoi·a (si kwoi′ə), *n.* either of two large coniferous trees of California, *Sequoiadendron giganteum* or *Sequoia sempervirens*, both having reddish bark and reaching heights of more than 300 ft. (91 m). [1840–50, *Amer.*; named after SEQUOYA]

Sequoi′a Na′tional Park′, a national park in central California: giant sequoia trees. 604 sq. mi. (1565 sq. km).

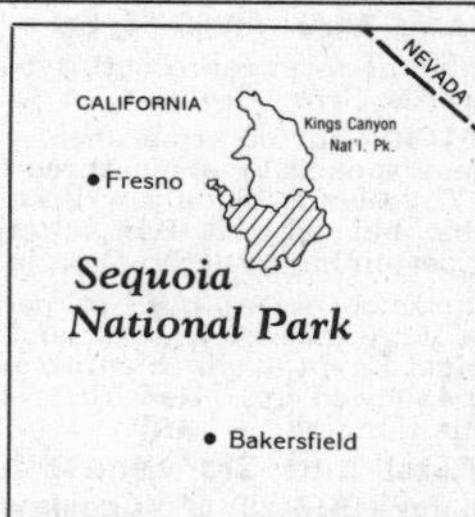

Se·quoy·a (si kwoi′ə), *n.* 1770?–1843, Cherokee Indian scholar: inventor of a syllabary for writing Cherokee. Also, **Se·quoy′ah.**

ser (sēr, sâr), *n.* a unit of weight in India, varying in value but usually 1⁄40 of a maund: the government ser is divided into 80 tolas of 180 English grains and equals nearly 2 pounds 1 ounce avoirdupois (950 grams). Also, **seer.** [1810–20; < Hindi]

ser, 1. serial. **2.** service.

Ser, *Biochem.* serine.

ser-, var. of **sero-** before a vowel: *serous.*

ser., 1. serial. **2.** series. **3.** sermon.

se·ra (sēr′ə), *n.* a pl. of **serum.**

sé·rac (si rak′; *Fr.* sā RAK′), *n., pl.* **-racs** (-raks′; *Fr.* -RAK′). a large irregularity of glacial ice, as a pinnacle found in glacial crevasses and formed by melting or movement of the ice. Also, **se·rac′.** [1855–60; < F *sérac* a white cheese (cf. ML *serācium*), ult. < L *serum* whey]

se·ragl·io (si ral′yō, -räl′-), *n., pl.* **-ragl·ios.** **1.** the part of a Muslim house or palace in which the wives and concubines are secluded; harem. **2.** a Turkish palace, esp. of the sultan. Also called **se·rail** (sə rī′, -ril′, -rāl′). [1575–85; < It *serraglio* < Pers *sarāy* palace; sense development in It perh. influenced by *serrare* to lock up]

se·ra·i (sə rä′ē, sə rī′), *n., pl.* **-ra·is.** (in Eastern countries) a caravansary. [1600–10; < Turk *seray* < Pers *sarāy* abode, palace; see CARAVANSARY]

Se·ra·je·vo (ser′ə yä′vō), *n.* Sarajevo.

ser·al (sēr′əl), *adj. Ecol.* of or pertaining to a sere. [1855–60; SERE[2] + -AL[1]]

Se·rang (se räng′), *n.* Ceram.

CONCISE PRONUNCIATION KEY: act, cāpe, dâre, pärt; set, ēqual; *if,* īce; ox, ōver, ôrder, oil, bo͝ok, bo͞ot, out; up, ûrge; child; sing; shoe; thin, *th*at; zh as in *treasure.* ə = *a* as in *alone, e* as in *system, i* as in *easily, o* as in *gallop, u* as in *circus;* ə as in *fire* (fīər), *hour* (ouər). l and n can serve as syllabic consonants, as in *cradle* (krād′l), and *button* (but′n). See the full key inside the front cover.

se·ra·pe (sə rä′pē), *n.* a blanketlike shawl or wrap, often of brightly colored wool, as worn in Latin America. Also, **sarape.** [1825–35, *Amer.*; < MexSp *sarape*]

Ser·a·pe·um (ser′ə pē′əm), *n., pl.* **-pe·ums, -pe·a** (-pē′ə). a place, as a burial site, building, or group of buildings, dedicated to Serapis. [1835–45; < LL *Serāpēum* < Gk *Serāpeîon*]

ser·aph (ser′əf), *n., pl.* **-aphs, -a·phim** (-ə fim). **1.** one of the celestial beings hovering above God's throne in Isaiah's vision. Isa. 6. **2.** a member of the highest order of angels, often represented as a child's head with wings above, below, and on each side. [1660–70; back formation from SERAPHIM] **—ser′aph·like′,** *adj.*

se·raph·ic (si raf′ik), *adj.* of, like, or befitting a seraph. Also, **se·raph′i·cal.** [1625–35; < ML *seraphicus.* See SERAPHIM, -IC] **—se·raph′i·cal·ly,** *adv.* **—se·raph′i·cal·ness,** *n.*

ser·a·phim (ser′ə fim), *n.* a pl. of **seraph.** [bef. 900; ME; OE *seraphin* < LL (Vulgate) *seraphim* < Heb *śərāphīm*]

Se·ra·pis (si rā′pis), *n.* **1.** Also, **Sarapis.** a Greco-Egyptian deity combining the attributes of Osiris and Apis, identified in Egypt with the Ptolemies: later worshiped throughout the Greek and Roman empires. **2.** (*italics*) the British man-of-war captured by John Paul Jones in 1779.

Serb (sûrb), *n., adj.,* **1.** Serbian. **2.** Serbo-Croatian.

Serb., **1.** Serbia. **2.** Serbian.

Ser·bi·a (sûr′bē ə), *n.* a former kingdom in S Europe: now, with revised boundaries, a constituent republic of Yugoslavia, in the N part; includes the autonomous provinces of Kosovo and Vojvodina. 9,660,000; 34,116 sq. mi. (88,360 sq. km). *Cap.:* Belgrade. Formerly, **Servia.**

Ser·bi·an (sûr′bē ən), *adj.* **1.** of or pertaining to Serbia, its inhabitants, or their language. **—***n.* **2.** a native or inhabitant of Serbia, esp. one of the Slavic peoples inhabiting it. **3.** Serbo-Croatian, esp. as spoken and written in Serbia. Also, **Serb.** [1860–65; SERB + -IAN]

Serbo-, a combining form representing **Serb** or **Serbia** in compound words: *Serbo-Croatian.*

Ser·bo-Cro·a·tian (sûr′bō krō ā′shən, -shē ən), *n.* **1.** a Slavic language spoken by about three-fourths of the population of Yugoslavia, usually written with Cyrillic letters in Serbia but with Roman letters in Croatia. **—***adj.* **2.** of or pertaining to Serbo-Croatian. Also, **Serb.**

Ser·bo·ni·an (sər bō′nē ən), *adj.* of, pertaining to, or designating the large marshy tract of land in the northern part of ancient Egypt in which entire armies are said to have been swallowed up. [1660–70; < Gk *Serbōní(s)* (*límnē*) Serbonian (marsh) + -AN]

Serbs′, Cro′ats, and Slo′venes, Kingdom of the, former name (1918–29) of **Yugoslavia.**

ser·dab (sər dāb′), *n.* a chamber inside a mastaba containing a statue of the deceased. [1835–45; < Ar *sirdāb* underground chamber < Pers *sardāb* cellar for ice, equiv. to *sard* cold + *āb* water]

sere[1] (sēr), *adj.* dry; withered. Also, **sear.** [bef. 900; ME *seer(e),* OE *sēar;* see SEAR[1]]
—Syn. arid, parched, desiccated, wizened.

sere[2] (sēr), *n.* the series of stages in an ecological succession. [1915–20; back formation from SERIES]

se·rein (sə ran′), *n. Meteorol.* fine rain falling after sunset from a sky in which no clouds are visible. [1865–70; < F *serein,* MF *serain* evening, nightfall < VL **serānum,* equiv. to L *sēr(um)* a late hour (neut. of *sērus* late) + *-ānum,* neut. of *-ānus* -AN; cf. obs. E *serene* < MF]

Se·re·na (sə rē′nə), *n.* a female given name.

ser·e·nade (ser′ə nād′), *n., v.,* **-nad·ed, -nad·ing.** **—***n.* **1.** a complimentary performance of vocal or instrumental music in the open air at night, as by a lover under the window of his lady. **2.** a piece of music suitable for such performance. **3.** serenata (def. 2). **—***v.t., v.i.* **4.** to entertain with or perform a serenade. [1640–50; < F *sérénade* < It *serenata;* see SERENATA] **—ser′e·nad′er,** *n.*

ser·e·na·ta (ser′ə nä′tə), *n., pl.* **-tas, -te** (-tā). *Music.* **1.** a form of secular cantata, often of a dramatic or imaginative character. **2.** an instrumental composition in several movements, intermediate between the suite and the symphony. [1715–25; < It *serenata* evening song, equiv. to *seren(o)* SERENE + *-ata* n. suffix, associated with *sera* evening; cf. SOIREE]

Ser·en·dip (ser′ən dip′), *n.* Arabic name of **Sri Lanka.** Also, **Ser·en·dib** (ser′ən dēb′).

ser·en·dip·i·tous (ser′ən dip′i təs), *adj.* **1.** come upon or found by accident; fortuitous: *serendipitous scientific discoveries.* **2.** of, pertaining to, or suggesting serendipity. **3.** good; beneficial; favorable: *serendipitous weather for our vacation.* [1940–45; SERENDIPIT(Y) + -OUS] **—ser′en·dip′i·tous·ly,** *adv.*

ser·en·dip·i·ty (ser′ən dip′i tē), *n.* **1.** an aptitude for making desirable discoveries by accident. **2.** good fortune; luck: *the serendipity of getting the first job she applied for.* [1754; SERENDIP + -ITY; Horace Walpole so named a faculty possessed by the heroes of a fairy tale called *The Three Princes of Serendip*] **—ser′en·dip′it·er, ser′en·dip′i·tist, ser′en·dip′per,** *n.*

serendip′ity ber′ry. See **miracle fruit** (def. 2). [1970–75]

se·rene (sə rēn′), *adj.* **1.** calm, peaceful, or tranquil; unruffled: *a serene landscape; serene old age.* **2.** clear; fair: *serene weather.* **3.** (*usually cap.*) most high or august (used as a royal epithet, usually prec. by *his, your,* etc.): *His Serene Highness.* **—***n.* **4.** serenity; tranquillity. **5.** *Archaic.* a clear or tranquil expanse of sea or sky. [1495–1505; < L *serēnus* (of the sky, weather) clear, unclouded] **—se·rene′ly,** *adv.* **—se·rene′ness,** *n.*
—Syn. 1. undisturbed, imperturbable, unperturbed, composed, collected. See **peaceful. 2.** unclouded.
—Ant. 1. disturbed. **2.** clouded.

Ser·en·get·i (ser′ən get′ē), *n.* a plain in NW Tanzania, including a major wildlife reserve (**Serenget′i Na′tional Park′**).

se·ren·i·ty (sə ren′i tē), *n., pl.* **-ties** for 2. **1.** the state or quality of being serene, calm, or tranquil; sereneness. **2.** (*usually cap.*) a title of honor, respect, or reverence, used in speaking of or to certain members of royalty (usually prec. by *his, your,* etc.). [1400–50; late ME *serenite* < L *serēnitās.* See SERENE, -ITY]
—Syn. 1. composure, calm, peacefulness, peace.
—Ant. 1. agitation.

Se·reth (zā′Rət), *n.* German name of **Siret.**

serf (sûrf), *n.* **1.** a person in a condition of servitude, required to render services to a lord, commonly attached to the lord's land and transferred with it from one owner to another. **2.** a slave. [1475–85; < MF < L *servus* slave] **—serf′dom, serf′hood, serf′age,** *n.*
—Syn. 1. vassal, villein, peasant.

serge[1] (sûrj), *n.* **1.** a twilled worsted or woolen fabric used esp. for clothing. **2.** cotton, rayon, or silk in a twill weave. [1350–1400; < F; r. ME *sarge* < MF < VL **sārica,* for L *sērica* (*lāna*) Chinese (wool), i.e., silk; see SERIC-]

serge[2] (sûrj), *v.t.,* **serged, serg·ing.** to overcast (unfinished seams or edges, as in a fabric or rug), esp. by machine, in order to prevent fraying. [perh. to be identified with SERGE[1], though sense shift is unclear]

Serge (sûrj; *Fr.* serzh), *n.* a male given name.

ser·geant (sär′jənt), *n.* **1.** a noncommissioned army officer of a rank above that of corporal. **2.** *U.S. Air Force.* any noncommissioned officer above the rank of airman first class. **3.** a police officer ranking immediately below a captain or a lieutenant in the U.S. and immediately below an inspector in Britain. **4.** a title of a particular office or function at the court of a monarch (often used in combination): *sergeant of the larder; sergeant-caterer.* **5.** See **sergeant at arms. 6.** Also called **ser′geant at law′.** *Brit.* (formerly) a member of a superior order of barristers. **7.** sergeantfish. **8.** (*cap.*) a surface-to-surface, single-stage, U.S. ballistic missile. **9.** a tenant by military service, below the rank of knight. Also, *esp. Brit.,* **serjeant** (for defs. 1–7, 9). [1150–1200; ME *sergant, serjant, serjaunt* < OF *sergent* < L *servient-* (s. of *serviēns*), prp. of *servīre.* See SERVE, -ENT] **—ser·gean·cy** (sär′jən sē), **ser′geant·ship′,** *n.*

ser′geant at arms′, an executive officer of a legislative or other body, whose duty it is to enforce its commands, preserve order, etc. [1350–1400; ME]

ser′geant first′ class′, *U.S. Army.* a noncommissioned officer ranking next above a staff sergeant and below a first or master sergeant. [1945–50, *Amer.*]

ser·geant·fish (sär′jənt fish′), *n., pl.* (*esp. collectively*) **-fish,** (*esp. referring to two or more kinds or species*) **-fish·es. 1.** the cobia, *Rachycentron canadum.* **2.** any of various other marine fishes with striped fins. [1880–85; SERGEANT + FISH; so called from the striped fins]

ser′geant ma′jor, 1. *U.S. Army, Air Force, and Marine Corps.* a noncommissioned officer serving as chief administrative assistant in a unit headquarters. **2.** *U.S. Marine Corps.* a noncommissioned officer ranking above a first sergeant. **3.** a small damselfish, *Abudefduf saxatilis,* inhabiting warm Atlantic waters, having vertical black stripes on each side. [1565–75]

ser·geant·y (sär′jən tē), *n. Medieval Eng. Law.* serjeanty.

Ser·gi·pe (səR zhē′pə), *n.* a state in NE Brazil. 1,157,176; 8490 sq. mi. (21,990 sq. km). *Cap.:* Aracajú.

Ser·gi·us I (sûr′jē əs), died A.D. 701, Italian ecclesiastic: pope 687–701.

Sergius II, died A.D. 847, pope 844–847.

Sergius III, died A.D. 911, pope 904–911.

Sergius IV, died 1012, pope 1009–12.

Ser·gi·yev Po·sad (sûr′gē əf pə säd′), a city in the NW Russian Federation in Europe, NE of Moscow. 111,000. Formerly (1930–91), **Zagorsk.**

Se·ri (ser′ē, sâr′ē), *n., pl.* **-ris,** (*esp. collectively*) **-ri** for 1. **1.** a member of an American Indian people of western Sonora state, Mexico, on the Gulf of California. **2.** the Hokan language of the Seri.

se·ri·al (sēr′ē əl), *n.* **1.** anything published, broadcast, etc., in short installments at regular intervals, as a novel appearing in successive issues of a magazine. **2.** *Library Science.* a publication in any medium issued in successive parts bearing numerical or chronological designation and intended to be continued indefinitely. **—***adj.* **3.** published in installments or successive parts: *a serial story.* **4.** pertaining to such publication. **5.** of, pertaining to, consisting of, or occurring in a series rather than simultaneously: *Some societies condemn both polygamy and serial marriages.* **6.** effecting or producing a series; sequential: *The police think a serial killer is responsible for five homicides in this city last month.* **7.** *Computers.* **a.** of or pertaining to the apparent or actual performance of data-processing operations one at a time (distinguished from *parallel*). **b.** of or pertaining to the transmission or processing of each part of a whole in sequence, as each bit of a byte or each byte of a computer word (distinguished from *parallel*). **8.** *Music.* of, pertaining to, or composed in serial technique. [1835–45; < NL *seriālis.* See SERIES, -AL[1]] **—se′ri·al·ly,** *adv.*

se·ri·al-ac·cess (sēr′ē əl ak′ses), *adj. Computers.* sequential-access.

se′rial com′ma. See **series comma.**

se·ri·al·ism (sēr′ē ə liz′əm), *n.* See **twelve-tone technique.** [1960–65; SERIAL + -ISM] **—se′ri·al·ist,** *n.*

se·ri·al·ize (sēr′ē ə līz′), *v.t.,* **-ized, -iz·ing. 1.** to publish in serial form. **2.** to broadcast, televise, or film in serial form. Also, *esp. Brit.,* **se′ri·al·ise′.** [1890–95; SERIAL + -IZE] **—se′ri·al·i·za′tion,** *n.*

se′rial monog′amy, a form of monogamy characterized by several successive, short-term marriages over the course of a lifetime. Also called **se′rial mar′riage.** [1970–75]

se′rial num′ber, a number, usually one of a series, assigned for identification: *the serial number of an automobile engine.* [1895–1900]

se′rial rights′, commercial rights to publish an author's work, usually a novel, or to use it on radio or television one chapter or episode at a time. [1875–80]

se′rial technique′. See **twelve-tone technique.**

se·ri·ate (sēr′ē it, -āt′), *adj.* arranged or occurring in one or more series. [1840–50; < L *seri(ēs)* SERIES + -ATE[1]] **—se′ri·ate·ly,** *adv.*

se·ri·a·tim (sēr′ē ā′tim, ser′-), *adv., adj.* in a series; one after another. [1670–80; < ML *seriātim,* equiv. to *seriāt(us)* arranged in order (see SERIES, -ATE[1]) + *-im* adv. suffix]

se·ri·a·tion (sēr′ē ā′shən), *n.* the arrangement of a collection of artifacts into a chronological sequence. [1650–60; < L *seri(ēs)* SERIES + -ATION]

seric-, a combining form meaning "silk," used as a base in English derivatives: *sericin.* [comb. form of ML *sēricum* silk (L *sēricus* Chinese, silken) < Gk *sērikón* silk, neut. of *sērikós* Chinese, silken, equiv. to *sḗr* silkworm + *-ikos* -IC]

ser·i·cate (ser′i kit, -kāt′), *adj.* sericeous; silky. [1615–25; < L *sēricātus* dressed in silk. See SERIC-, -ATE[1]]

se·ri·ceous (si rish′əs), *adj.* **1.** silky. **2.** covered with silky down, as a leaf. [1770–80; < L *sēriceus.* See SERIC-, -EOUS]

ser·i·cin (ser′ə sin), *n.* a gelatinous organic compound that holds the two strands of natural silk together. Also called **silk gum.** [1835–45; SERIC- + -IN[2]]

ser·i·cite (ser′ə sīt′), *n. Mineral.* a fine-grained variety of muscovite produced by the alteration of feldspar. [1850–55; < G *Sericit.* See SERIC-, -ITE[1]] **—ser·i·cit·ic** (ser′i sit′ik), *adj.*

se·ric·te·ry (si rik′tə rē), *n., pl.* **-ries.** a silk gland. [< NL *sērictērium*]

ser·i·cul·ture (ser′i kul′chər), *n.* the raising of silk worms for the production of raw silk. [1850–55; < Gk *sḗr* silkworm + -I- + CULTURE] **—ser′i·cul′tur·al,** *adj.* **—ser′i·cul′tur·ist,** *n.*

ser·i·e·ma (ser′ē ē′mə, -ā′mə), *n.* either of two birds of the family Cariamidae, *Cariama cristata,* of southern Brazil, or *Chunga burmeisteri,* of Argentina, having long legs, an erectile crest, a short, broad bill, and limited ability to fly. Also, **cariama.** [1830–40; < NL < Tupi: crested]

se·ries (sēr′ēz), *n., pl.* **-ries,** *adj.* **—***n.* **1.** a group or a number of related or similar things, events, etc., arranged or occurring in temporal, spatial, or other order or succession; sequence. **2.** a number of games, contests, or sporting events, with the same participants, considered as a unit: *The two baseball clubs played a five-game series.* **3.** a set, as of coins or stamps. **4.** a set of successive volumes or issues of a periodical published in like form with similarity of subject or purpose. **5.** *Radio and Television.* **a.** a daily or weekly program with the same cast and format and a continuing story, as a soap opera, situation comedy, or drama. **b.** a number of related programs having the same theme, cast, or format: *a series of four programs on African wildlife.* **6.** *Math.* **a.** a sequence of terms combined by addition, as $1 + \frac{1}{2} + \frac{1}{4} + \frac{1}{8} + \ldots \frac{1}{2}n$. **b.** See **infinite series. 7.** *Rhet.* a succession of coordinate sentence elements. **8.** *Geol.* a division of stratified rocks that is of next higher rank to a stage and next lower rank to a system, comprising deposits formed during part of a geological epoch. **9.** *Elect.* an end-to-end arrangement of the components, as resistors, in a circuit so that the same current flows through each component. Cf. **parallel** (def. 13). **10.** *Chem.* a group of related chemical elements arranged in order of increasing atomic number: *the lanthanide series.* **—***adj.* **11.** *Elect.* consisting of or having component parts connected in series: *a series circuit; a series generator.* [1605–15; < L *seriēs;* akin to *serere* to connect]
—Syn. 1. SERIES, SEQUENCE, SUCCESSION are terms for an orderly following of things one after another. SERIES is applied to a number of things of the same kind, usually related to each other, arranged or happening in order: *a series of baseball games.* SEQUENCE stresses the continuity in time, thought, cause and effect, etc.: *The scenes came in a definite sequence.* SUCCESSION implies that one thing is followed by another or others in turn, usually though not necessarily with a relation or connection between them: *succession to a throne; a succession of calamities.*

se′ries com′ma, a comma used after the next-to-last item in a series of three or more items when the next-to-last and last items are separated by a conjunction. In the series *A, B, C, or D,* the comma after *C* is the series comma. Also called **serial comma.**

CONCISE ETYMOLOGY KEY: <, descended or borrowed from; >, whence; b., blend of, blended; c., cognate with; cf., compare; deriv., derivative; equiv., equivalent; imit., imitative; obl., oblique; r., replacing; s., stem; sp., spelling, spelled; resp., respelling, respelled; trans., translation; ?, origin unknown; *, unattested; ‡, probably earlier than. See the full key inside the front cover.

se•ries-wound (sēr′ēz wound′), *adj. Elect.* noting a commutator motor in which the field circuit and armature circuit are connected in series. Cf. **shunt-wound.** [1890–95]

ser•if (ser′if), *n. Print.* a smaller line used to finish off a main stroke of a letter, as at the top and bottom of *M.* See diag. under **type.** Also, *esp. Brit.* **ceriph.** [1835–45; perh. < D *schreef* line (in writing), akin to *schrijven* to write]

ser•i•graph (ser′i graf′, -gräf′), *n.* a print made by the silkscreen process. [1885–90; *seri-* (as in SERICULTURE) + -GRAPH] —**se•rig•ra•pher** (si rig′rə fər), *n.* —**se•rig′ra•phy,** *n.*

ser•in (ser′in), *n.* a small finch, *Serinus serinus,* of Europe and northern Africa, closely related to the canary. [1520–30; < MF *sere(i)n;* cf. OPr *serena, sirena* bee-eater (a green bird) < LL *sirēna,* for L *sirēn* SIREN]

ser•ine (ser′ēn, -in, sēr′-), *n. Biochem.* a crystalline amino acid, $HOCH_2CH(NH_2)COOH$, found in many proteins and obtained by the hydrolysis of sericin, the protein constituting silk gum. *Abbr.:* Ser; *Symbol:* S [1875–80; SER(UM) + -INE[2]]

se•rin•ga (sə ring′gə), *n.* any of several Brazilian trees of the genus *Hevea,* yielding rubber. [1730–40; < Pg, var. of SYRINGA]

Se•rin•ga•pa•tam (sə ring′gə pə tam′), *n.* a town in S Karnataka, in S India, former capital of Mysore state: taken by the British 1799.

se•ri•o•com•ic (sēr′ē ō kom′ik), *adj.* partly serious and partly comic: *a seriocomic play.* Also, **se′ri•o•com′i•cal.** [1775–85; SERI(OUS) + -O- + COMIC] —**se′ri•o•com′i•cal•ly,** *adv.*

se•ri•ous (sēr′ē əs), *adj.* **1.** of, showing, or characterized by deep thought. **2.** of grave or somber disposition, character, or manner: *a serious occasion; a serious man.* **3.** being in earnest; sincere; not trifling: *His interest was serious.* **4.** requiring thought, concentration, or application: *serious reading; a serious task.* **5.** weighty or important: *a serious book; Marriage is a serious matter.* **6.** giving cause for apprehension; critical: *The plan has one serious flaw.* **7.** *Med.* (of a patient's condition) having unstable or otherwise abnormal vital signs and other unfavorable indicators, as loss of appetite and poor mobility: patient is acutely ill. —*n.* **8.** that which is of importance, grave, critical, or somber: *You have to learn to separate the serious from the frivolous.* [1400–50; late ME < L *sērius* or LL *sēriōsus;* see -OUS, -OSE[1]] —**se′ri•ous•ness,** *n.*
—**Syn. 2.** sober, sedate, staid. **3.** See **earnest**[1]. **5.** momentous, grave. —**Ant. 3, 5.** trivial.

se•ri•ous•ly (sēr′ē əs lē), *adv.* **1.** in a serious manner: *He shook his head seriously.* **2.** to an alarmingly grave extent: *seriously ill.* **3.** with genuine, earnest intent; sincerely: *Seriously, kids, we have to get home before dark.* [1500–10; SERIOUS + -LY]

se•ri•ous-mind•ed (sēr′ē əs mīn′did), *adj.* characterized by seriousness of intention, purpose, thought, etc.; earnest. [1835–45] —**se′ri•ous-mind′ed•ly,** *adv.* —**se′ri•ous-mind′ed•ness,** *n.*

ser•i•plane (ser′ə plān′), *n.* a test for evaluating the quality of raw silk by inspecting it under controlled conditions for variations in the diameter of the yarn and for imperfections and content. [SERI(C)- + PLANE[1]]

ser•jeant (sär′jənt), *n. Chiefly Brit.* sergeant.

ser•jeant•y (sär′jən tē), *n. Medieval Eng. Law.* a form of land tenure in which a tenant holding of the king rendered him exclusive services in a status below that of a knight. Also, **sergeanty.** Cf. **grand serjeanty, petit serjeanty.** [1300–50; ME *sergeantie, serjantie* < OF *serjantie.* See SERGEANT, -Y[3]]

Ser•kin (sûr′kin; *Ger.* ser′kin), *n.* **1. Ru•dolf** (ro͞o′-dolf; *Ger.* ro͞o′dôlf), 1903–91, U.S. pianist, born in Bohemia. **2. Peter,** born 1947, U.S. pianist (son of Rudolf).

ser•mon (sûr′mən), *n.* **1.** a discourse for the purpose of religious instruction or exhortation, esp. one based on a text of Scripture and delivered by a member of the clergy as part of a religious service. **2.** any serious speech, discourse, or exhortation, esp. on a moral issue. **3.** a long, tedious speech. [1150–1200; ME < ML *sermōn-* (s. of *sermō*) speech from pulpit, L: discourse, equiv. to *ser-* (base of *serere* to link up, organize) + *-mōn-* n. suffix] —**ser′mon•less,** *adj.*
—**Syn. 2, 3.** lecture. **3.** harangue, tirade.

ser•mon•ette (sûr′mə net′), *n.* a brief sermon or homily: *five-minute radio sermonettes.* [1805–15; SERMON + -ETTE]

ser•mon•ic (sər mon′ik), *adj.* of, pertaining to, or resembling a sermon. Also, **ser•mon′i•cal.** [1755–65; SERMON + -IC] —**ser•mon′i•cal•ly,** *adv.*

ser•mon•ize (sûr′mə nīz′), *v.,* **-ized, -iz•ing.** —*v.i.* **1.** to deliver or compose a sermon; preach. —*v.t.* **2.** to give exhortation to; lecture. Also, *esp. Brit.,* **ser′mon•ise′.** [1625–35; SERMON + -IZE] —**ser′mon•iz′er,** *n.*

Ser′mon on the Mount′, a discourse delivered by Jesus to the disciples and others, containing the Beatitudes and important fundamentals of Christian teaching. Matt. 5–7; Luke 6:20–49.

sero-, a combining form representing **serum** in compound words: *serology.* Also, *esp. before a vowel,* **ser-.**

se•ro•di•ag•no•sis (sēr′ō dī′əg nō′sis), *n., pl.* **-ses** (-sēz). *Med.* a diagnosis involving tests on blood serum or other serous fluid of the body. Also called **immunodiagnosis.** [1895–1900; SERO- + DIAGNOSIS] —**se•ro•di•ag•nos•tic** (sēr′ō dī′əg nos′tik), *adj.*

se•rol•o•gy (si rol′ə jē), *n.* the science dealing with the immunological properties and actions of serum. [1905–10; SERO- + -LOGY] —**se•ro•log•ic** (sēr′ə loj′ik), **se′ro•log′i•cal,** *adj.* —**se′ro•log′i•cal•ly,** *adv.* —**se•rol′o•gist,** *n.*

se•ro•neg•a•tive (sēr′ō neg′ə tiv), *adj. Med.* showing no significant level of serum antibodies, or other immunologic marker in the serum, that would indicate previous exposure to the infectious agent being tested. [1930–35; SERO- + NEGATIVE]

se•ro•pos•i•tive (sēr′ō poz′i tiv), *adj. Med.* showing a significant level of serum antibodies, or other immunologic marker in the serum, indicating previous exposure to the infectious agent being tested. [1930–35; SERO- + POSITIVE]

se•ro•re•ac•tion (sēr′ō rē ak′shən), *n. Med., Immunol.* any reaction occurring in serum. [SERO- + REACTION]

se•ro•sa (si rō′sə, -zə), *n., pl.* **-sas, -sae** (-sē, -zē). **1.** *Embryol., Zool.* **a.** the chorion. **b.** a similar membrane in insects and other lower invertebrates. **2.** See **serous membrane.** [1885–90; < NL *serōsa,* fem. of *serōsus,* equiv. to L *ser(um)* SERUM + *-ōsus* -OSE[1]]

se•ro•si•tis (sēr′ō sī′tis, -zī′-), *n. Pathol.* inflammation of a serous membrane. [< NL *serōsitis;* see SEROSA, -ITIS]

se•ro•ther•a•py (sēr′ō ther′ə pē), *n. Med.* therapy by means of injections of a serum obtained esp. from an immune animal. [1890–95; SERO- + THERAPY] —**se′ro•ther′a•pist,** *n.*

se•rot•i•nal (si rot′n l, ser′ə tīn′l), *adj.* pertaining to or occurring in late summer. [1905–10; SEROTINE[1] + -AL[1]]

ser•o•tine[1] (ser′ə tin, -tīn′), *adj.* late in occurring, developing, or flowering. Also, **se•rot•i•nous** (si rot′n əs, ser′ə tī′nəs). [1590–1600; < L *sērōtinus,* equiv. to *sērō* (adv.) late + *-tinus* adj. suffix of time; cf. SEREIN]

ser•o•tine[2] (ser′ə tin, -tīn′), *n.* a small Eurasian brown bat, *Eptesicus serotinus.* [1765–75; < F *sérotine* < L *sērōtina,* fem. of *sērōtinus* SEROTINE[1]]

se•ro•to•ner•gic (ser′ə tn ûr′jik), *adj.* containing or activated by serotonin. [1965–70; SEROTON(IN) + -ERGIC]

ser•o•to•nin (ser′ə tō′nin, sēr′-), *n. Biochem.* a neurotransmitter, derived from tryptophan, that is involved in sleep, depression, memory, and other neurological processes. [1945–50; SERO- + TONE + -IN[2]]

se•ro•type (sēr′ə tīp′, ser′-), *n., v.,* **-typed, -typ•ing.** —*n.* **1.** a group of organisms, microorganisms, or cells distinguished by their shared specific antigens as determined by serologic testing. **2.** the set of antigens that characterizes the group. —*v.t.* **3.** to classify by serotype. [1945–50; SERO- + -TYPE]

se•rous (sēr′əs), *adj.* **1.** resembling serum; of a watery nature. **2.** containing or secreting serum. **3.** of, pertaining to, or characterized by serum. [1585–95; < ML *serōsus;* see SERUM, -OUS] —**se•ros•i•ty** (si ros′i tē), **se′rous•ness,** *n.*

se′rous flu′id, any of various clear, watery fluids in the body.

se′rous mem′brane, *Anat., Zool.* any of various thin membranes, as the peritoneum, that line certain cavities of the body and exude a serous fluid. Also called **serosa.** [1865–70]

Se•rov (sə rôf′, -rof′; *Russ.* syi rôf′), *n.* a city in the RSFSR, in the W Soviet Union in Asia, near the Ural Mountains. 101,000.

ser•ow (ser′ō), *n.* a goat antelope of the genus *Capricornis,* of eastern Asia, related to the goral: the Sumatran serow is endangered. [1840–50; perh. from a source akin to Lepcha *sa-ăr* goat]

Ser•pa•sil (sûr′pə sil), *Pharm., Trademark.* a brand of reserpine.

Ser•pens (sûr′pənz, -penz), *n., gen.* **Ser•pen•tis** (sərpen′tis). *Astron.* the Serpent, a constellation consisting of two separate parts, the head **(Ser′pens Ca′put)** and the tail **(Ser′pens Cau′da),** with Ophiuchus in between. [< L *serpēns* serpent, orig. prp. of *serpere* to creep, crawl; c. Gk *hérpein* (cf. HERPES, HERPETOLOGY)]

ser•pent (sûr′pənt), *n.* **1.** a snake. **2.** a wily, treacherous, or malicious person. **3.** the Devil; Satan. Gen. 3:1–5. **4.** a firework that burns with serpentine motion or flame. **5.** an obsolete wooden wind instrument with a serpentine shape and a deep, coarse tone. Cf. **ophicleide. 6.** *(cap.) Astron.* the constellation Serpens. [1250–1300; ME (< MF) < L *serpent-,* s. of *serpēns;* see SERPENS]

serpent (def. 5)

ser•pen•tar•i•um (sûr′pən târ′ē əm), *n., pl.* **-tar•i•ums, -tar•i•a** (-târ′ē ə). a place where snakes are housed, esp. for exhibition. [SERPENT + -ARIUM]

Ser′pent Bear′er, *Astron.* the constellation Ophiuchus. [1545–55]

ser•pen•ti•form (ser pen′tə fôrm′), *adj.* shaped like a snake. [1770–80; SERPENT + -I- + -FORM]

ser•pen•tine[1] (sûr′pən tēn′, -tīn′), *adj., n., v.,* **-tined, -tin•ing.** —*adj.* **1.** of, characteristic of, or resembling a serpent, as in form or movement. **2.** having a winding course, as a road; sinuous. **3.** shrewd, wily, or cunning. —*n.* **4.** a device on a harquebus lock for holding the match. **5.** a cannon having any of various bore sizes, used from the 15th to the 17th century. **6.** *Skating.* a school figure made by skating two figure eights that share one loop. —*v.i.* **7.** to make or follow a winding course: *The stream serpentines through the valley.* [1350–1400; ME (adj.) < L *serpentīnus* snakelike, equiv. to *serpent-* SERPENT + *-inus* INE[1]]
—**Syn. 2.** twisting, snaking, tortuous.

ser•pen•tine[2] (sûr′pən tēn′, -tīn′), *n.* a common mineral, hydrous magnesium silicate, $H_2Mg_3Si_2O_9$, usually oily green and sometimes spotted, occurring in many varieties: used for architectural and decorative purposes. [1350–1400; ME *serpentyn* < ML *serpentīnum,* n. use. of neut. of *serpentīnus* SERPENTINE[1]]

ser′pentine front′, *Furniture.* a front, as of a chest of drawers, having a horizontal compound curve with a convex section between two concave ones. Cf. **oxbow front.**

serpentine front (18th century)

ser′pentine jade′, *Jewelry.* a green variety of serpentine used as a gem: not a true jade.

ser′pentine stretch′er, *Furniture.* an X-stretcher having curved lines.

ser•pen•tin•ize (sûr′pən tē nīz′), *v.t.,* **-ized, -iz•ing.** *Mineral.* to convert (a mineral or rock) into serpentine. Also, *esp. Brit.,* **ser′pen•tin′ise.** [1785–95; SERPENTINE[2] + -IZE] —**ser′pen•tin′i•za′tion,** *n.*

Ser•pen•tis (sər pen′tis), *n.* gen. of **Serpens.**

ser′pent star′. See **brittle star.** [1850–55]

ser•pi•go (sər pī′gō), *n. Pathol.* (formerly) a creeping or spreading skin disease, as ringworm. [1350–1400; ME < ML *serpīgō,* equiv. to L *serp-* (deriv. of *serpere* to creep) + *-īgō* as in *vertīgō* VERTIGO; cf. HERPES] —**ser•pig•i•nous** (sər pij′ə nəs), *adj.*

Ser•pu•khov (sûr′pə kôf′, -kof′; *Russ.* syer′po͞o-khəf), *n.* a city in the W RSFSR, in the central Soviet Union in Europe, S of Moscow. 140,000.

Ser•ra da Man•ti•quei•ra (se′Rä dä män′ti kā′Rä), a mountain range in SE Brazil, running parallel to the coast. Highest point, 9140 ft. (2785 m).

Ser•ra do Mar (se′Rä do͞o mär′), a mountain range on the SE coast of Brazil. Highest point, 7420 ft. (2262 m).

Ser•ra Ju•ní•pe•ro (seR′Rä ho͞o nē′pe Rō′), **Mi•guel Jo•sé** (mē gel′ hô se′), 1713–84, Spanish Roman Catholic missionary to the Indians in California and Mexico.

ser•ra•nid (sə rä′nid, -rā′-, -ran′id), *n.* **1.** any of numerous percoid fishes of the family Serranidae, living chiefly in warm seas, including the sea basses and groupers. —*adj.* **2.** belonging or pertaining to the family Serranidae. [1895–1900; < NL *Serranidae* family name. See SERRANOID, -ID[2]]

ser•ra•noid (ser′ə noid′), *adj.* **1.** resembling or related to the sea bass family Serranidae. —*n.* **2.** a serranoid fish. [1880–85; < NL *Serran(us)* genus of fishes (L *serr(a)* sawfish + *-ānus* -AN) + -OID]

serrate leaf

ser•rate (*adj.* ser′āt, -it; *v.* ser′āt, sə rāt′), *adj., v.,* **-rat•ed, -rat•ing.** —*adj.* **1.** *Chiefly Biol.* notched on the edge like a saw: *a serrate leaf.* **2.** *Numis.* (of a coin) having a grooved edge. **3.** serrated. —*v.t.* **4.** to make serrate or serrated: *He serrated the knives so they would cut meat easily.* [1590–1600; < L *serrātus,* equiv. to *serr(a)* saw + *-ātus* -ATE[1]]

ser•rat•ed (ser′ā tid, sə rā′-), *adj.* **1.** having a notched edge or sawlike teeth, esp. for cutting; serrate: *the serrated blade of a bread knife.* **2.** serrate. [1695–1705; SERRATE + -ED[2]]

Ser•ra•tia (sə rā′shə, -shē ə, -rä′tē ə), *n. Bacteriol.* a genus of rod-shaped, aerobic bacteria that are saprophytic on decaying plant or animal materials. [< NL, named after Serafino *Serrati,* 19th-century Italian industrialist; see -A[2]]

ser•ra•tion (se rā′shən), *n.* **1.** serrated condition or form. **2.** a serrated edge or formation. **3.** one of the notches or teeth of such an edge or formation. Also, **ser•ra•ture** (ser′ə chər). [1700–10; < NL *serrātiōn-* (s. of *serrātiō*). See SERRATE, -ION]

serre-pa•pier (sâr′pap yā′; *Fr.* seR pA pyā′), *n., pl.* **serre-pa•piers** (sâr pap yāz′; *Fr.* seR pA pyā′). cartonnier. [< F: lit., (it) grips (the) paper; see SEAR[2], PAPER]

ser•ried (ser′ēd), *adj.* pressed together or compacted, as soldiers in rows: serried troops. [1660–70; SERRY + -ED[2]] —**ser′ried•ly,** *adv.* —**ser′ried•ness,** *n.*

ser•ri•form (ser′ə fôrm′), *adj.* resembling the notched edge of a saw; serrated. [1815–25; *serri-* (comb. form of L *serra* saw) + -FORM]

ser•ru•late (ser′yə lit, -lāt′, ser′ə-), *adj.* finely or minutely serrate, as a leaf. Also, **ser′ru•lat′ed.** [1785–95; < NL *serrulātus,* equiv. to L *serrul(a)* small saw (see SERRATE, -ULE[1]) + *-ātus* -ATE[1]]

ser•ru•la•tion (ser′yə lā′shən, ser′ə-), *n.* **1.** serrulate condition or form. **2.** a fine or minute serration. [1815–25; SERRULATE + -ION]

ser•ru•re•rie (se RYRᵊ Rē′), *n. French.* ornamental wrought-iron work. [lit., locksmith's work]

ser•ry (ser′ē), *v.i., v.t.,* **-ried, -ry•ing.** *Archaic.* to crowd closely together. [1575–85; < MF *serré,* ptp. of *serrer* to press tightly together; see SEAR[2]]

Sert (sert), *n.* **Jo•sé Ma•rí•a** (hô se′ mä Rē′ä), 1876–1945, Spanish painter.

Ser•to•ri•us (sər tôr′ē əs, -tōr′-), *n.* **Quin•tus** (kwin′-təs), died 72 B.C., Roman general and statesman.

ser•tu•lar•i•an (sûr′chŏŏ lâr′ē ən), *n. Zool.* a type of hydroid that forms stiff, feathery colonies in which the cups holding the zooids are sessile. [1840–50; < NL *Sertulari(a)* genus name (L *sertul(a),* dim. of *serta* wreath + *-āria* -ARIA) + -AN]

se•rum (sēr′əm), *n., pl.* **se•rums, se•ra** (sēr′ə). **1.** the clear, pale-yellow liquid that separates from the clot in the coagulation of blood; blood serum. **2.** See **immune serum. 3.** any watery animal fluid. **4.** the thin, clear part of the fluid of plants. **5.** milk whey. [1655–65; < L: whey] **—se′rum•al,** *adj.*

se′rum albu′min, **1.** *Biochem.* the principal protein of blood plasma, important in osmotic regulation of the blood and transport of metabolites. **2.** the commercial form of this substance, used in dye preparations, foodstuffs, and in medicine esp. in the treatment of shock. [1875–80]

se′rum hepati′tis. See **hepatitis B.** [1930–35]

se′rum sick′ness, *Pathol.* a generalized allergic reaction to a foreign serum or drug, characterized by fever, skin rash, enlarged lymph nodes, and painful joints. Also called **se′rum disease′.** [1910–15]

serv., service.

ser•val (sûr′vəl), *n., pl.* **-vals,** (*esp. collectively*) **-val.** a long-limbed, nocturnal African cat, *Felis serval,* about the size of a bobcat, having a tawny coat spotted with black: now rare in many former habitats. [1765–75; < NL < Pg (*lobo*) *cerval* lynx, lit., staglike (wolf) < LL *cervālis* deerlike, equiv. to L *cerv(us)* stag + *-ālis* -AL[1]]

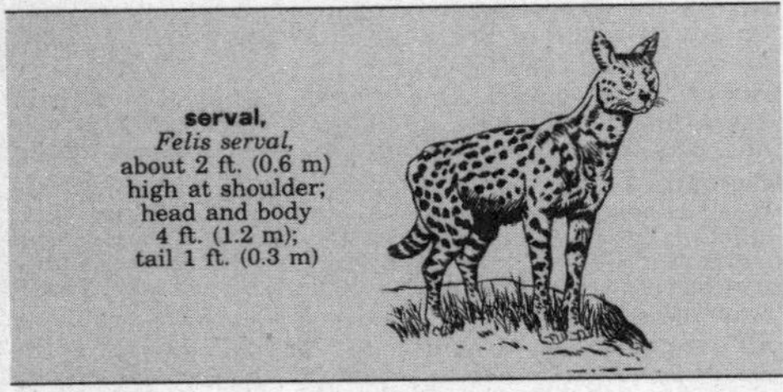

serval, *Felis serval,* about 2 ft. (0.6 m) high at shoulder; head and body 4 ft. (1.2 m); tail 1 ft. (0.3 m)

serv•ant (sûr′vənt), *n.* **1.** a person employed by another, esp. to perform domestic duties. **2.** a person in the service of another. **3.** a person employed by the government: *a public servant.* [1175–1225; ME < OF, n. use of prp. of *servir* to SERVE; see -ANT] **—serv′ant•less,** *adj.* **—serv′ant•like′,** *adj.*

serv′ant church′, *Eccles.* the attitude or practices of a church whose avowed purpose is to serve the world.

serve (sûrv), *v.,* **served, serv•ing,** *n.* **—***v.i.* **1.** to act as a servant. **2.** to wait on table, as a waiter. **3.** to offer or have a meal or refreshments available, as for patrons or guests: *Come early, we're serving at six.* **4.** to offer or distribute a portion or portions of food or a beverage, as a host or hostess: *It was her turn to serve at the faculty tea.* **5.** to render assistance; be of use; help. **6.** to go through a term of service; do duty as a soldier, sailor, senator, juror, etc. **7.** to have definite use: *This cup will serve as a sugar bowl.* **8.** to answer the purpose: *That will serve to explain my actions.* **9.** (in tennis, badminton, handball, etc.) to put the ball or shuttlecock in play with a stroke, swing, or hit. **10.** to be favorable, suitable, or convenient, as weather or time. **11.** *Eccles.* to act as a server. **—***v.t.* **12.** to be in the service of; work for. **13.** to be useful or of service to; help. **14.** to go through (a term of service, imprisonment, etc.). **15.** to render active service to (a sovereign, commander, etc.). **16.** to render obedience or homage to (God, a sovereign, etc.). **17.** to perform the duties of (a position, an office, etc.): *to serve his mayoralty.* **18.** to answer the requirements of; suffice: *This will serve our needs for the moment.* **19.** to contribute to; promote: *to serve a cause.* **20.** to wait upon at table; act as a waiter or waitress to. **21.** to carry and distribute (portions of food or drink) to a patron or a specific table, as a waiter or waitress. **22.** to act as a host or hostess in offering (a person) a portion of food or drink: *May I serve you with some tea and cake?* **23.** to act as a host or hostess in offering or distributing (a portion or portions of food or drink) to another: *They served tea and cake to their guests.* **24.** to provide with a regular or continuous supply of something. **25.** (in tennis, badminton, handball, etc.) to put (the ball or shuttlecock) in play. **26.** to treat in a specified manner: *That served him ill.* **27.** *Law.* **a.** to make legal delivery of (a process or writ). **b.** to present (a person) with a writ. **28.** to gratify (desire, wants, needs, etc.). **29.** (of a male animal) to mate with; service. **30.** to operate or keep in action (a gun, artillery, etc.). **31.** *Naut.* to wrap (a rope) tightly with small stuff, keeping the turns as close together as possible. **32. serve one right,** to treat one as one deserves, esp. to punish justly: *It will serve you right if she never speaks to you again.* **—***n.* **33.** the act, manner, or right of serving, as in tennis. [1125–75; ME *serven* < OF *servir* < L *servīre,* equiv. to *serv(us)* slave (cf. SERF) + *-īre* inf. suffix] **—serv′a•ble, serve′a•ble,** *adj.*

—Syn. 1, 2. attend. **5.** aid, succor.

CONCISE ETYMOLOGY KEY: <, descended or borrowed from; >, whence; b., blend of, blended; c., cognate with; cf., compare; deriv., derivative; equiv., equivalent; imit., imitative; obl., oblique; r., replacing; s., stem; sp., spelling, spelled; resp., respelling, respelled; trans., translation; ?, origin unknown; *, unattested; ‡, probably earlier than. See the full key inside the front cover.

serv•er (sûr′vər), *n.* **1.** a person who serves. **2.** something that serves or is used in serving, as a salver. **3.** a broad fork, spoon, or spatula for dishing out and serving individual portions of food, as vegetables, cake, or pie. **4.** *Eccles.* an attendant on the priest at Mass, who arranges the altar, makes the responses, etc. **5.** (in tennis, badminton, handball, etc.) the player who puts the ball or shuttlecock in play. [1350–1400; ME; see SERVE, -ER[1]]

serv•er•y (sûr′və rē), *n., pl.* **-er•ies.** *Chiefly Brit.* a food counter in a cafeteria or pub. [1940–45; SERVE + -ERY]

Ser•ve•tus (sər vē′təs), *n.* **Michael,** 1511–53, Spanish physician and theologian, accused of heresy and burned at the stake. Spanish, **Mi•guel Ser•ve•to** (mē gel′ ser-ve′tô). **—Ser•ve•tian** (sər vē′shən), *n.* **—Ser•ve′tian•ism,** *n.*

Ser•vi•a (sûr′vē ə), *n.* former name of **Serbia.**

serv•ice[1] (sûr′vis), *n., adj., v.,* **-iced, -ic•ing.** **—***n.* **1.** an act of helpful activity; help; aid: *to do someone a service.* **2.** the supplying or supplier of utilities or commodities, as water, electricity, or gas, required or demanded by the public. **3.** the providing or a provider of accommodation and activities required by the public, as maintenance, repair, etc.: *The manufacturer guarantees service and parts.* **4.** the organized system of apparatus, appliances, employees, etc., for supplying some accommodation required by the public: *a television repair service.* **5.** the supplying or a supplier of public communication and transportation: *telephone service; bus service.* **6.** the performance of duties or the duties performed as or by a waiter or servant; occupation or employment as a waiter or servant. **7.** employment in any duties or work for a person, organization, government, etc. **8.** a department of public employment, an administrative division of a government, or the body of public servants in it: *the diplomatic service.* **9.** the duty or work of public servants. **10.** the serving of a sovereign, state, or government in some official capacity. **11.** *Mil.* **a.** the armed forces: *in the service.* **b.** a branch of the armed forces, as the army or navy: *Which service were you in during the war?* **12.** *Ordn.* the actions required in loading and firing a cannon: *service of the piece.* **13.** Often, **services.** the performance of any duties or work for another; helpful or professional activity: *medical services.* **14.** something made or done by a commercial organization for the public benefit and without regard to direct profit: *Certain books are published at a loss as a public service.* **15.** Also called **divine service.** public religious worship according to prescribed form and order. **16.** a ritual or form prescribed for public worship or for some particular occasion: *the marriage service.* **17.** the serving of God by obedience, piety, etc.: *voluntary service.* **18.** a musical setting of the sung portions of a liturgy. **19.** a set of dishes, utensils, etc., for general table use or for particular use: *a tea service; service for eight.* **20.** See **answering service. 21.** *Law.* the serving of a process or writ upon a person. **22.** *Naut.* tarred spun yarn or other small stuff for covering the exterior of a rope. **23.** (in tennis, badminton, handball, etc.) **a.** the act or manner of putting the ball or shuttlecock into play; serve. **b.** the ball or shuttlecock as put into play. **24.** the mating of a female animal with the male. **25. at someone's service,** ready to be of help or use to someone; at one's disposal: *You will have an English-speaking guide at your service.* **26. be of service,** to be helpful or useful: *If we can be of service, do not hesitate to call.*

—*adj.* **27.** of service; useful. **28.** of, pertaining to, or used by servants, delivery people, etc., or in serving food: *service stairs; the service pieces in a set of dishes.* **29.** supplying aids or services rather than products or goods: *Medicine is one of the service professions.* **30.** supplying maintenance and repair: *He operates a service center for electrical appliances.* **31.** of, for, or pertaining to the armed forces of a country or one of them: *a service academy.* **32.** charged for providing service: *a service fee of 15 percent on the restaurant check.* **33.** providing, authorizing, or guaranteeing service: *a service industry; a service contract.*

—*v.t.* **34.** to make fit for use; repair; restore to condition for service: *to service an automobile.* **35.** to supply with aid, information, or other incidental services. **36.** (of a male animal) to mate with (a female animal). **37.** *Finance.* to pay off (a debt) over a period of time, as by meeting periodic interest payments. [bef. 1100; ME (n.) < OF < L *servitium* servitude, equiv. to *serv(us)* slave + *-itium* -ICE; r. ME *servise,* late OE *serfise* ceremony < OF *servise,* var. of *service*]

serv•ice[2] (sûr′vis), *n.* **1.** a service tree, esp. *Sorbus domestica.* **2.** the shadbush. [1520–30; earlier *serves,* pl. of obs. *serve* service tree; ME; OE *syrfe* < VL **sorbea,* deriv. of L *sorbus* SORB[1]]

Ser•vice (sûr′vis), *n.* **Robert W(illiam),** 1874–1958, Canadian writer, born in England.

serv•ice•a•ble (sûr′və sə bəl), *adj.* **1.** capable of or being of service; useful. **2.** wearing well; durable: *serviceable cloth.* **3.** capable of being used, worn, cleaned, repaired, etc., easily. [1300–50; SERVICE[1] + -ABLE; r. ME *servisable* < MF] **—serv′ice•a•bil′i•ty, serv′ice•a•ble•ness,** *n.* **—serv′ice•a•bly,** *adv.*

—Syn. 1. effective, usable, functional.

serv′ice ace′, ace (def. 3a).

serv•ice•ber•ry (sûr′vis ber′ē), *n., pl.* **-ries.** **1.** the fruit of any service tree. **2.** a North American shrub or small tree, *Amelanchier canadensis,* of the rose family, having serrate, oblong leaves, clusters of white flowers, and a berrylike fruit. **3.** any of various other plants of the genus *Amelanchier.* [1775–85, *Amer.;* SERVICE[2] + BERRY]

serv′ice book′, a book containing the forms of worship used in divine services. [1570–80]

serv′ice break′, *Tennis.* **1.** an instance of a player winning a game against a server. **2.** a game won against an opponent's service. [1950–55]

serv′ice cap′, *Mil.* a saucer-shaped uniform cap with a visor, standard in the U.S. Army and Air Force. [1905–10]

serv′ice cen′ter, an authorized commercial establishment for repairs and replacement parts for appliances or cars. [1960–65]

serv′ice charge′, a fee charged for a service, sometimes in addition to a basic charge. [1915–20]

serv′ice clasp′, clasp (def. 4).

serv′ice club′, **1.** any of several organizations dedicated to the growth and general welfare of its members and the community. **2.** a recreational center for members of the armed forces. [1925–30]

serv′ice court′, the part of the court into which a player must serve in various games, as tennis, badminton, handball, or squash. [1875–80]

serv′ice el′evator, an elevator for the use of servants and delivery people and for carrying large items.

serv′ice en′trance, an entrance for the use of servants, delivery people, or the like.

serv′ice flat′, *Brit.* an apartment with complete hotel services. [1920–25]

serv′ice line′, **1.** *Tennis.* the rear boundary of a service court. **2.** a line running parallel to the front wall in certain court games, as handball or squash, that marks a boundary of the service area. [1870–75]

serv•ice•man (sûr′vis man′, -mən), *n., pl.* **-men** (-men′, -mən). **1.** a member of the armed forces of a country. **2.** a person whose occupation is to maintain or repair equipment: *a television serviceman.* [1920–25; SERVICE[1] + MAN[1]]

—Usage. See **-man.**

serv′ice mark′, a proprietary term, such as Blue Cross and Blue Shield, American Express, or Planned Parenthood, that is registered with the Patent and Trademark Office. *Abbr.:* SM [1945–50]

serv′ice med′al, *Mil.* a medal awarded for performance of specified service, usually in time of war or national emergency. Also called **campaign medal.** [1930–35]

serv′ice mod′ule, (*often caps.*) *U.S. Aerospace.* the section of an Apollo spacecraft containing the principal propulsion system, electrical system, water, and other supplies. [1960–65]

serv•ice•per•son (sûr′vis pûr′sən), *n.* **1.** a person who is a member of the armed forces of a country. **2.** a person who maintains or repairs equipment. [SERVICE(MAN) + -PERSON]

—Usage. See **-person.**

serv′ice pipe′, a pipe connecting a building with a water or gas main.

serv′ice road′, See **frontage road.** [1935–40]

serv′ice sta′tion, **1.** Also called **gas station.** a place equipped for servicing automobiles, as by selling gasoline and oil, making repairs, etc. **2.** a place that provides some service, as the repair of equipment, or where parts and supplies are sold, provided, dispensed, etc. [1915–20]

serv′ice stripe′, *Mil.* a stripe worn on the left sleeve by an enlisted person to indicate a specific period of time served on active duty. [1915–20]

serv′ice tree′, **1.** either of two European trees, *Sorbus domestica,* bearing a small, acid fruit that is edible when overripe, or *S. torminalis* (**wild service tree**), bearing a similar fruit. **2.** serviceberry (defs. 2, 3). [1535–45]

serv′ice u′niform, *Mil.* a uniform for routine duties and service, as distinguished from work, dress, or full-dress uniforms.

serv•ice•wom•an (sûr′vis wŏŏm′ən), *n., pl.* **-wom•en.** **1.** a woman who is a member of the armed forces of a country. **2.** a woman whose occupation is to maintain or repair equipment: *A servicewoman was here to repair the air conditioner.* [1940–45; SERVICE(MAN) + -WOMAN]

—Usage. See **-woman.**

ser′vi•ent ten′ement (sûr′vē ənt), *Law.* land subject to an easement or servitude. Cf. **dominant tenement.** [1675–85; *servient* < L *servient-* (s. of *serviēns,* prp. of *servīre*); see SERVE, -ENT]

ser•vi•ette (sûr′vē et′), *n. Chiefly Brit.* a table napkin. [1480–90; < MF, equiv. to *servi(r)* to SERVE + *-ette* -ETTE; for the formation, cf. OUBLIETTE]

ser•vile (sûr′vil, -vīl), *adj.* **1.** slavishly submissive or obsequious; fawning: *servile flatterers.* **2.** characteristic of, proper to, or customary for slaves; abject: *servile obedience.* **3.** yielding slavishly; truckling (usually fol. by *to*). **4.** extremely imitative, esp. in the arts; lacking in originality. **5.** being in slavery; oppressed. **6.** of, pertaining to, or involving slaves or servants. **7.** of or pertaining to a condition of servitude or property ownership in which a person is held as a slave or as partially enslaved: *medieval rebellions against servile laws.* [1350–1400; ME < L *servīlis,* equiv. to *serv-* (s. of *servire* to be a slave) + *-īlis* -ILE] **—ser′vile•ly,** *adv.* **—ser•vil′i•ty, ser′vile•ness,** *n.*

—Syn. 1, 2. cringing, sycophantic. SERVILE, MENIAL, OBSEQUIOUS, SLAVISH characterize one who behaves like a slave or an inferior. SERVILE suggests cringing, fawning, and abject submission: *servile responses to questions.* MENIAL applies to that which is considered undesirable drudgery: *the most menial tasks.* OBSEQUIOUS implies the ostentatious subordination of oneself to the wishes of another, either from fear or from hope of gain: *an obsequious waiter.* SLAVISH stresses the dependence and laborious toil of one who follows or obeys without question: *slavish attentiveness to orders.* **2.** mean, base, low. **—Ant. 1.** aggressive. **2.** exalted.

serv•ing (sûr′ving), *n.* **1.** the act of a person or thing that serves. **2.** a single portion of food or drink; helping. **3.** *Elect.* a layer of material, as jute yarn or tape, that is applied to the core or the exterior of a lead-covered cable and acts as a protective covering. *—adj.* **4.** for use in distributing food to or at the table: *a serving tray.* [1175–1225; ME; see SERVE, -ING[1]]

Ser•vite (sûr′vit), *n. Rom. Cath. Ch.* a member of an order of mendicant friars, founded in Florence in 1233, engaged in fostering devotion to the Virgin Mary. [1540–50; < ML *Servitēs.* See SERVE, -ITE[1]]

ser•vi•tor (sûr′vi tər), *n.* **1.** a person who is in or at the service of another; attendant. **2.** a glass worker who blocks the gather and does the preliminary blowing of glass for the gaffer. [1300–50; ME *servitour* < AF < LL *servītor,* equiv. to L *servī(re)* to SERVE + *-tor* -TOR]

ser•vi•tude (sûr′vi to͞od′, -tyo͞od′), *n.* **1.** slavery or bondage of any kind: *political or intellectual servitude.* **2.** compulsory service or labor as a punishment for criminals: *penal servitude.* **3.** *Law.* a right possessed by one person to use another's property. [1425–75; late ME < LL *servitūdō,* equiv. to *servi-,* comb. form of *servus* slave + *-tūdō,* -TUDE]
—Syn. 1. serfdom, thralldom. See **slavery. —Ant. 1.** liberty.

Ser•vi•us Tul•li•us (sûr′vē əs tul′ē əs), the legendary sixth king of ancient Rome who built the city walls and whose accession to the throne was prophesied by and secured with the help of Tanaquil, the widow of the previous king: assassinated by his daughter Tullia and her husband Tarquin.

ser•vo (sûr′vō), *adj., n., pl.* **-vos,** *v.,* **-voed, -vo•ing.** *—adj.* **1.** acting as part of a servomechanism: *servo amplifier.* **2.** pertaining to or having to do with servomechanisms: *servo engineer.* **3.** noting the action of certain mechanisms, as brakes, that are set in operation by other mechanisms but which themselves augment the force of that action by the way in which they operate. *—n.* **4.** *Informal.* servomechanism. *—v.t.* **5.** to connect (a mechanism) to another as a servomechanism. [1945–50; independent use of SERVO-, taken as an adj., or shortening of words formed with it]

servo-, a combining form used in the names of devices or operations that employ a servomechanism: *servocontrol.* [extracted from SERVOMOTOR]

ser•vo•con•trol (*n.* sûr′vō kən trōl′; *v.* sûr′vō kən trōl′), *n., v.,* **-trolled, -trol•ling.** *—n.* **1.** control by means of a servomechanism. **2.** a servomechanism used as a control. **3.** Also called **Flettner control, ser′vo tab′.** *Aeron.* a tab that is directly actuated by the control stick and that exerts an aerodynamic force to move a control surface to which it is attached. *—v.t.* **4.** to operate (a mechanism) with such a device. [SERVO- + CONTROL]

ser•vo•mech•an•ism (sûr′vō mek′ə niz′əm, sûr′vō mek′-), *n.* an electronic control system in which a hydraulic, pneumatic, or other type of controlling mechanism is actuated and controlled by a low-energy signal. [1940–45; SERVO- + MECHANISM] **—ser′vo•me•chan′i•cal** (sûr′vō mə kan′i kəl), *adj.* **—ser′vo•me•chan′i•cal•ly,** *adv.*

ser•vo•mo•tor (sûr′vō mō′tər), *n.* a motor or the like forming part of a servomechanism. [1885–90; < F *servomoteur* < L *serv(us)* slave + F *-o-* -O- + *moteur* MOTOR]

ser′vo sys′tem, a system using a servomechanism.

SES, socioeconomic status.

ses•a•me (ses′ə mē), *n.* **1.** a tropical, herbaceous plant, *Sesamum indicum,* whose small oval seeds are edible and yield an oil. **2.** the seeds themselves, used to add flavor to bread, crackers, etc. **3.** See **open sesame.** Also called **benne** (for defs. 1, 2). [1400–50; < Gk *sēsámē* sesame plant << Akkadian *shamashshammū,* derived from *shaman shammī* plant oil; r. *sesam,* late ME *sysane* < L *sēsamum* < Gk *sḗsamon* sesame seed]

ses′ame oil′, a yellow oil expressed from the seeds of the sesame, used in cooking, as a vehicle for medicines, and in the manufacture of margarine, soap, and cosmetics. [1865–70]

ses•a•moid (ses′ə moid′), *adj. Anat.* shaped like a sesame seed, as certain small nodular bones and cartilages. [1690–1700; < L *sēsamoīdes* < Gk *sēsamoeidḗs* like sesame seed. See SESAME, -OID]

Se•so•tho (sə so͞o′to͞o, -sō′tō), *n.* the Bantu language of Lesotho; Sotho.

sesqui-, a combining form meaning "one and a half," used in the formation of compound words: *sesquicentennial.* [< L *sēsqui-* < **sēm(i)sque,* equiv. to *sēmis* half-unit, SEMIS + *-que* and (c. Gk *té,* Skt *ca,* Goth *-uh*)]

ses•qui•car•bon•ate (ses′kwi kär′bə nāt′, -nit), *n. Chem.* a salt intermediate in composition between a carbonate and a bicarbonate or consisting of the two combined. [1815–25; SESQUI- + CARBONATE]

ses•qui•cen•ten•ni•al (ses′kwi sen ten′ē əl), *adj.* **1.** pertaining to or marking the completion of a period of 150 years. *—n.* **2.** a 150th anniversary or its celebration. [1875–80, *Amer.;* SESQUI- + CENTENNIAL] **—ses′qui•cen•ten′ni•al•ly,** *adv.*

ses•qui•ox•ide (ses′kwē ok′sīd, -sid), *n. Chem.* an oxide containing three atoms of oxygen and two of another element, as aluminum oxide, Al_2O_3. [1825–35; SESQUI- + OXIDE]

ses•qui•pe•da•li•an (ses′kwi pi dā′lē ən, -dāl′yən), *adj.* Also, **ses•quip•e•dal** (ses kwip′i dl). **1.** given to using long words. **2.** (of a word) containing many syllables. *—n.* **3.** a sesquipedalian word. [1605–15; < L *sēsquipedālis* measuring a foot and a half (see SESQUI-, PEDAL) + -AN] **—ses•qui•pe•dal•i•ty** (ses′kwi pi dal′i tē), **ses′qui•pe•da′li•an•ism, ses•quip•e•dal•ism** (ses kwip′i dl iz′əm, -kwi pēd′l-), *n.*

ses•qui•plane (ses′kwi plān′), *n. Aeron.* a biplane having one wing with not more than half the surface area of the other wing. [SESQUI- + PLANE[1]]

ses•qui•ter•pene (ses′kwi tûr′pēn), *n. Chem.* See under **terpene.** [1885–90; SESQUI- + TERPENE]

Ses•shu (ses sho͞o′), *n.* 1420?–1506, Japanese Zen Buddhist monk and painter.

ses•sile (ses′il, -il), *adj.* **1.** *Bot.* attached by the base, or without any distinct projecting support, as a leaf issuing directly from the stem. **2.** *Zool.* permanently attached; not freely moving. [1715–25; < L *sessilis* fit for sitting on, low enough to sit on, dwarfish (said of plants), equiv. to *sess(us)* (ptp. of *sedēre* to SIT[1]) + *-ilis* -ILE] **—ses•sil•i•ty** (se sil′i tē), *n.*

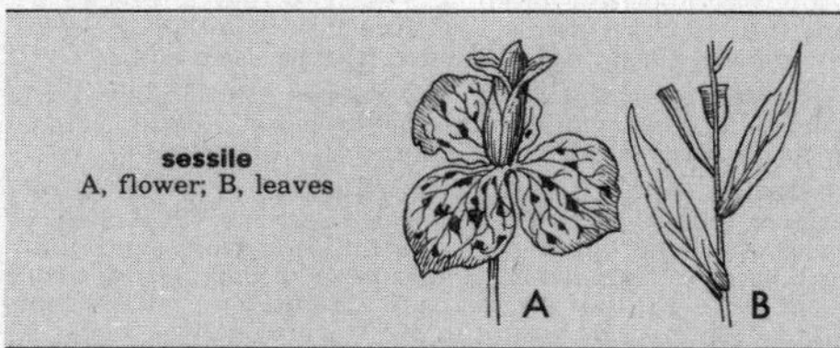

sessile
A, flower; B, leaves

ses•sion (sesh′ən), *n.* **1.** the sitting together of a court, council, legislature, or the like, for conference or the transaction of business: *Congress is now in session.* **2.** a single continuous sitting, or period of sitting, of persons so assembled. **3.** a continuous series of sittings or meetings of a court, legislature, or the like. **4.** the period or term during which such a series is held. **5. sessions,** (in English law) the sittings or a sitting of justices in court, usually to deal with minor offenses, grant licenses, etc. **6.** a single continuous course or period of lessons, study, etc., in the work of a day at school: *two afternoon sessions a week.* **7.** a portion of the year into which instruction is organized at a college or other educational institution. **8.** the governing body of a local Presbyterian church, composed of the pastor who moderates and the elders. **9.** a period of time during which a group of persons meets to pursue a particular activity: *A few of the kids got together for a study session.* [1350–1400; ME < ML *sessiōn-* (s. of *sessiō*) law-court sitting, L: sitting, equiv. to *sess(us)* (ptp. of *sedēre* to SIT[1]) + *-iōn-* -ION] **—ses′sion•al,** *adj.*

ses′sional indem′nity, the remuneration paid to a member of the Canadian parliament. [1895–1900]

ses•sion•man (sesh′ən man′), *n., pl.* **-men.** a professional musician who does studio recording work but is not a member of an established performing group. [1955–60; SESSION + MAN[1]]

Ses•sions (sesh′ənz), *n.* **Roger Huntington,** 1896–1985, U.S. composer.

ses•terce (ses′tûrs), *n.* a silver coin of ancient Rome, the quarter of a denarius, equal to 2½ asses: introduced in the 3rd century B.C. [1590–1600; < L *sēstertius,* equiv. to *sēs-* half-unit (see SESQUI-) + *tertius* THIRD (i.e., 2 units and half a 3rd one equal 2½ asses)]

ses•ter•ti•um (se stûr′shē əm, -shəm), *n., pl.* **-ti•a** (-shē ə, -shə). a money of account of ancient Rome, equal to 1000 sesterces. [1530–40; < L *sēstertium* gen. pl. of *sēstertius* SESTERCE, taken as neut. sing.]

ses•ter•tius (se stûr′shəs, -shē əs), *n., pl.* **-ti•i** (shē ī′). sesterce. [< L *sēstertius;* see SESTERCE]

ses•tet (se stet′, ses′tet), *n.* **1.** *Pros.* the last six lines of a sonnet in the Italian form, considered as a unit. Cf. **octave** (def. 4a). **2.** sextet (def. 2). [1795–1805; < It *sestetto* SEXTET, equiv. to *sest(o)* (< L *sextus* SIXTH) + *-etto* -ET]

ses•ti•na (se stē′nə), *n., pl.* **-nas, -ne** (-nā). *Pros.* a poem of six six-line stanzas and a three-line envoy, originally without rhyme, in which each stanza repeats the end words of the lines of the first stanza, but in different order, the envoy using the six words again, three in the middle of the lines and three at the end. Also called **sextain.** [1580–90; < It, equiv. to *sest(o)* (< L *sextus* SIXTH) + *-ina* -INE[2]]

Ses•tos (ses′tos), *n.* an ancient Thracian town on the Hellespont opposite Abydos: Xerxes crossed the Hellespont here when he began his invasion of Greece.

set (set), *v.,* **set, set•ting,** *n., adj., interj.* *—v.t.* **1.** to put (something or someone) in a particular place: *to set a vase on a table.* **2.** to place in a particular position or posture: *Set the baby on his feet.* **3.** to place in some relation to something or someone: *We set a supervisor over the new workers.* **4.** to put into some condition: *to set a house on fire.* **5.** to put or apply: *to set fire to a house.* **6.** to put in the proper position: *to set a chair back on its feet.* **7.** to put in the proper or desired order or condition for use: *to set a trap.* **8.** to distribute or arrange china, silver, etc., for use on (a table): *to set the table for dinner.* **9.** to place (the hair, esp. when wet) on rollers, in clips, or the like, so that the hair will assume a particular style. **10.** to put (a price or value) upon something: *He set $7500 as the right amount for the car. The teacher sets a high value on neatness.* **11.** to fix the value of at a certain amount or rate; value: *He set the car at $500. She sets neatness at a high value.* **12.** to post, station, or appoint for the purpose of performing some duty: *to set spies on a person.* **13.** to determine or fix definitely: *to set a time limit.* **14.** to resolve or decide upon: *to set a wedding date.* **15.** to cause to pass into a given state or condition: *to set one's mind at rest; to set a prisoner free.* **16.** to direct or settle resolutely or wishfully: *to set one's mind to a task.* **17.** to present as a model; place before others as a standard: *to set a good example.* **18.** to establish for others to follow: *to set a fast pace.* **19.** to prescribe or assign, as a task. **20.** to adjust (a mechanism) so as to control its performance. **21.** to adjust the hands of (a clock or watch) according to a certain standard: *I always set my watch by the clock in the library.* **22.** to adjust (a timer, alarm of a clock, etc.) so as to sound when desired: *He set the alarm for seven o'clock.* **23.** to fix or mount (a gem or the like) in a frame or setting. **24.** to ornament or stud with gems or the like: *a bracelet set with pearls.* **25.** to cause to sit; seat: *to set a child in a highchair.* **26.** to put (a hen) on eggs to hatch them. **27.** to place (eggs) under a hen or in an incubator for hatching. **28.** to place or plant firmly: *to set a flagpole in concrete.* **29.** to put into a fixed, rigid, or settled state, as the face, muscles, etc. **30.** to fix at a given point or calibration: *to set the dial on an oven; to set a micrometer.* **31.** to tighten (often fol. by *up*): *to set nuts well up.* **32.** to cause to take a particular direction: *to set one's course to the south.* **33.** *Surg.* to put (a broken or dislocated bone) back in position. **34.** (of a hunting dog) to indicate the position of (game) by standing stiffly and pointing with the muzzle. **35.** *Music.* **a.** to fit, as words to music. **b.** to arrange for musical performance. **c.** to arrange (music) for certain voices or instruments. **36.** *Theat.* **a.** to arrange the scenery, properties, lights, etc., on (a stage) for an act or scene. **b.** to prepare (a scene) for dramatic performance. **37.** *Naut.* to spread and secure (a sail) so as to catch the wind. **38.** *Print.* **a.** to arrange (type) in the order required for printing. **b.** to put together types corresponding to (copy); compose in type: *to set an article.* **39.** *Baking.* to put aside (a substance to which yeast has been added) in order that it may rise. **40.** to change into curd: *to set milk with rennet.* **41.** to cause (glue, mortar, or the like) to become fixed or hard. **42.** to urge, goad, or encourage to attack: *to set the hounds on a trespasser.* **43.** *Bridge.* to cause (the opposing partnership or their contract) to fall short: *We set them two tricks at four spades. Only perfect defense could set four spades.* **44.** to affix or apply, as by stamping: *The king set his seal to the decree.* **45.** to fix or engage (a fishhook) firmly into the jaws of a fish by pulling hard on the line once the fish has taken the bait. **46.** to sharpen or put a keen edge on (a blade, knife, razor, etc.) by honing or grinding. **47.** to fix the length, width, and shape of (yarn, fabric, etc.). **48.** *Carpentry.* to sink (a nail head) with a nail set. **49.** to bend or form to the proper shape, as a saw tooth or a spring. **50.** to bend the teeth of (a saw) outward from the blade alternately on both sides in order to make a cut wider than the blade itself.
—v.i. **51.** to pass below the horizon; sink: *The sun sets early in winter.* **52.** to decline; wane. **53.** to assume a fixed or rigid state, as the countenance or the muscles. **54.** (of the hair) to be placed temporarily on rollers, in clips, or the like, in order to assume a particular style: *Long hair sets more easily than short hair.* **55.** to become firm, solid, or permanent, as mortar, glue, cement, or a dye, due to drying or physical or chemical change. **56.** to sit on eggs to hatch them, as a hen. **57.** to hang or fit, as clothes. **58.** to begin to move; start (usually fol. by *forth, out, off,* etc.). **59.** (of a flower's ovary) to develop into a fruit. **60.** (of a hunting dog) to indicate the position of game. **61.** to have a certain direction or course, as a wind, current, or the like. **62.** *Naut.* (of a sail) to be spread so as to catch the wind. **63.** *Print.* (of type) to occupy a certain width: *This copy sets to forty picas.* **64.** *Nonstandard.* sit: *Come in and set a spell.* **65. set about, a.** to begin on; start. **b.** to undertake; attempt. **c.** to assault; attack. **66. set against, a.** to cause to be hostile or antagonistic. **b.** to compare or contrast: *The advantages must be set against the disadvantages.* **67. set ahead,** to set to a later setting or time: *Set your clocks ahead one hour.* **68. set apart, a.** to reserve for a particular purpose. **b.** to cause to be noticed; distinguish: *Her bright red hair sets her apart from her sisters.* **69. set aside, a.** to put to one side; reserve: *The clerk set aside the silver brooch for me.* **b.** to dismiss from the mind; reject. **c.** to prevail over; discard; annul: *to set aside a verdict.* **70. set back, a.** to hinder; impede. **b.** to turn the hands of (a watch or clock) to show an earlier time: *When your plane gets to California, set your watch back two hours.* **c.** to reduce to a lower setting: *Set back the thermostat before you go to bed.* **71. set by,** to save or keep for future use. **72. set down, a.** to write or to copy or record in writing or printing. **b.** to consider; estimate: *to set someone down as a fool.* **c.** to attribute; ascribe: *to set a failure down to bad planning.* **d.** to put in a position of rest on a level surface. **e.** to humble or humiliate. **f.** to land an airplane: *We set down in a heavy fog.* **g.** (in horse racing) to suspend (a jockey) from competition because of some offense or infraction of the rules. **73. set forth, a.** to give an account of; state; describe: *He set forth his theory in a scholarly report.* **b.** to begin a journey; start: *Columbus set forth with three small ships.* **74. set forward,** to turn the hands of (a watch or clock) to show a later time: *When your plane lands in New York, set your watch forward two hours.* **75. set in, a.** to begin to prevail; arrive: *Darkness set in.* **b.** (of winds or currents) to blow or flow toward the shore. **76. set off, a.** to cause to become ignited or to explode. **b.** to begin; start. **c.** to intensify or improve by contrast. **d.** to begin a journey or trip; depart. **77. set on, a.** Also, **set upon.** to attack or cause to attack: *to set one's dog on a stranger.* **b.** to instigate; incite: *to set a crew to mutiny.* **78. set one's face against.** See **face** (def. 35). **79. set out, a.** to begin a journey or course: *to set out for home.* **b.** to undertake; attempt: *He set out to prove his point.* **c.** to design; plan: *to set out a pattern.* **d.** to define; describe: *to set out one's arguments.* **e.** to plant: *to set out petunias and pansies.* **f.** to lay out (the plan of a building) in actual size at the site. **g.** to lay out (a building member or the like) in actual size. **80. set store by.** See **store** (def. 9). **81. set to, a.** to make a vigorous effort; apply oneself to work; begin. **b.** to begin to fight; contend. **82. set up, a.** to put upright; raise. **b.** to put into a high or powerful position. **c.** to construct; assemble; erect. **d.** to be assembled or made ready for use: *exercise equipment that sets up in a jiffy.* **e.** to inaugurate; establish. **f.** to enable to begin in business; provide with means. **g.** *Informal.* to make a gift of; treat, as to drinks. **h.** *Informal.* to stimulate;

elate. **i.** to propound; plan; advance. **j.** to bring about; cause. **k.** to become firm or hard, as a glue or cement: *a paint that sets up within five minutes.* **l.** to lead or lure into a dangerous, detrimental, or embarrassing situation, as by deceitful prearrangement or connivance. **m.** to entrap or frame, as an innocent person in a crime or a criminal suspect in a culpable circumstance in order to achieve an arrest. **n.** to arrange the murder or execution of: *His partner set him up with the mob.* **o.** *Bridge.* to establish (a suit): *to set up spades.*

—*n.* **83.** the act or state of setting or the state of being set. **84.** a collection of articles designed for use together: *a set of china; a chess set.* **85.** a collection, each member of which is adapted for a special use in a particular operation: *a set of golf clubs; a set of carving knives.* **86.** a number, group, or combination of things of similar nature, design, or function: *a set of ideas.* **87.** a series of volumes by one author, about one subject, etc. **88.** a number, company, or group of persons associated by common interests, occupations, conventions, or status: *a set of murderous thieves; the smart set.* **89.** the fit, as of an article of clothing: *the set of his coat.* **90.** fixed direction, bent, or inclination: *The set of his mind was obvious.* **91.** bearing or carriage: *the set of one's shoulders.* **92.** the assumption of a fixed, rigid, or hard state, as by mortar or glue. **93.** the arrangement of the hair in a particular style: *How much does the beauty parlor charge for a shampoo and set?* **94.** a plate for holding a tool or die. **95.** an apparatus for receiving radio or television programs; receiver. **96.** *Philately.* a group of stamps that form a complete series. **97.** *Tennis.* a unit of a match, consisting of a group of not fewer than six games with a margin of at least two games between the winner and loser: *He won the match in straight sets of 6–3, 6–4, 6–4.* **98.** a construction representing a place or scene in which the action takes place in a stage, motion-picture, or television production. **99.** *Mach.* **a.** the bending out of the points of alternate teeth of a saw in opposite directions. **b.** a permanent deformation or displacement of an object or part. **c.** a tool for giving a certain form to something, as a saw tooth. **100.** a chisel having a wide blade for dividing bricks. **101.** *Hort.* a young plant, or a slip, tuber, or the like, suitable for planting. **102.** *Dancing.* **a.** the number of couples required to execute a quadrille or the like. **b.** a series of movements or figures that make up a quadrille or the like. **103.** *Music.* **a.** a group of pieces played by a band, as in a night club, and followed by an intermission. **b.** the period during which these pieces are played. **104.** *Bridge.* a failure to take the number of tricks specified by one's contract: *Our being vulnerable made the set even more costly.* **105.** *Naut.* **a.** the direction of a wind, current, etc. **b.** the form or arrangement of the sails, spars, etc., of a vessel. **c.** suit (def. 12). **106.** *Psychol.* a temporary state of an organism characterized by a readiness to respond to certain stimuli in a specific way. **107.** *Mining.* a timber frame bracing or supporting the walls or roof of a shaft or stope. **108.** *Carpentry.* See **nail set. 109.** *Math.* a collection of objects or elements classed together. **110.** *Print.* the width of a body of type. **111.** sett (def. 3).

—*adj.* **112.** fixed or prescribed beforehand: *a set time; set rules.* **113.** specified; fixed: *The hall holds a set number of people.* **114.** deliberately composed; customary: *set phrases.* **115.** fixed; rigid: *a set smile.* **116.** resolved or determined; habitually or stubbornly fixed: *to be set in one's opinions.* **117.** completely prepared; ready: *Is everyone set?* **118. all set,** *Informal.* in readiness; prepared: *They were at the starting line and all set to begin.*

—*interj.* **119.** (in calling the start of a race): *Ready! Set! Go!* Also, **get set!** [bef. 900; (v.) ME *setten,* OE *settan;* c. ON *setja,* G *setzen,* Goth *satjan,* all < Gmc **satjan,* causative of **setjan* to SIT[1]; (n.) (in senses denoting the action of setting or the state of being set) ME *set, set(t)e,* deriv. of the v. and its ptp.; (in senses denoting a group) ME *sette* < OF < L *secta* SECT (in later use influenced by the v. and MLG *gesette* set, suite)]

—**Syn. 1.** position, locate, situate, plant. See **put. 11.** estimate, appraise, evaluate, price, rate. **13.** establish. **55.** solidify, congeal, harden. **88.** clique. See **circle. 90.** attitude. **91.** posture. **112.** predetermined. **116.** stubborn, obstinate.

—**Usage.** The verbs SET and SIT[1] are similar in form and meaning but different in grammatical use. SET is chiefly transitive and takes an object: *Set the dish on the shelf.* Its past tense and past participle are also SET: *Yesterday he set three posts for the fence. The judge has set the date for the trial.* SET also has some standard intransitive uses, as "to pass below the horizon" (*The sun sets late in the northern latitudes during the summer*) and "to become firm, solid, etc." (*This glue sets quickly*). The use of SET for SIT, "to be seated," is nonstandard: *Pull up a chair and set by me.*

SIT is chiefly intransitive and does not take an object: *Let's sit here in the shade.* Its past tense and past participle are SAT: *They sat at the table for nearly two hours. Have they sat down yet?* Transitive uses of SIT include "to cause to sit" (*Pull up a chair and sit yourself down*) and "to provide seating for" (*The waiter sat us near the window*).

Set (set), *n. Egyptian Relig.* the brother and murderer of Osiris, represented as having the form of a donkey or other mammal and regarded as personifying the desert. Also, **Seth.**

se·ta (sē′tə), *n., pl.* **-tae** (-tē). *Biol.* a stiff hair; bristle or bristlelike part. [1785–95; < L *sēta, saeta* bristle] —**se′tal,** *adj.*

se·ta·ceous (si tā′shəs), *adj.* **1.** bristlelike; bristle-shaped. **2.** having bristles. [1655–65; < NL *sētāceus.* See SETA, -ACEOUS] —**se·ta′ceous·ly,** *adv.*

CONCISE ETYMOLOGY KEY: <, descended or borrowed from; >, whence; b., blend of, blended; c., cognate with; cf., compare; deriv., derivative; equiv., equivalent; imit., imitative; obl., oblique; r., replacing; s., stem; sp., spelling, spelled; resp., respelling, respelled; trans., translation; ?, origin unknown; *, unattested; ‡, probably earlier than. See the full key inside the front cover.

se·tar·i·a (si târ′ē ə), *n.* any grass of the genus *Setaria,* having a dense panicle, grown for forage. [< NL; see SETA, -ARIA]

set-a·side (set′ə sīd′), *n.* **1.** something, as land or profits, set aside for a particular purpose. **2.** a tract of federal lands set aside as a wildlife refuge, oil exploration site, etc. **3.** a tract of farmland on which commercial crops or a specific crop will not be grown, as part of a federal plan to decrease production in order to maintain or increase prices. **4.** a specified amount or percentage of an industry's production set aside, esp. for government use: *Ten percent of gasoline production is a set-aside for emergency use by the state.* **5.** a government contract awarded, as to a minority-owned business, without competitive bidding. —*adj.* **6.** pertaining to or constituting a set-aside: *set-aside provisions of the new law.* [1940–45; n., adj. use of v. phrase *set aside*]

set-back (set′bak′), *n.* **1.** *Survey.* the interval by which a chain or tape exceeds the length being measured. **2.** setback (def. 4). [special use of SETBACK]

set·back (set′bak′), *n.* **1.** a check to progress; a reverse or defeat: *The new law was a setback.* **2.** *Archit.* a recession of the upper part of a building from the building line, as to lighten the structure or to permit a desired amount of light and air to reach ground level at the foot of the building. **3.** an act or instance of setting back: *A nightly setback of your home thermostats can save a great deal of fuel.* **4.** Also, **set-back.** a downward temperature adjustment of a thermostat, esp. performed automatically, as by a timer. [1665–75; n. use of v. phrase *set back*]

set′ chis′el, a chisel having a broad edge at the end of a tapered shaft; used to cut the heads off bolts, rivets, etc.

se·ten·ant (sə ten′ənt, set′n än′, sə tə nän′), *n. Philately.* a group of stamps that differ in color, value, or design but are printed together on the same sheet and are collected without separating the stamps. Also, **se ten′ant.** [1910–15; < F: lit., standing, remaining, holding together, equiv. to *se* 3d sing. reflexive pronoun + *tenant* prp. of *tenir* to hold (see TENANT)]

set′ func′tion, *Math.* a function having a collection of sets as domain.

Seth (seth), *n.* **1.** the third son of Adam. Gen. 4:25 **2.** a male given name: from a Hebrew word meaning "substitute."

Seth (sāt), *n. Egyptian Relig.* Set.

SETI, search for extraterrestrial intelligence. [1975–80]

seti-, a combining form meaning "bristle"; used in the formation of compound words: *setiform.* [< L *sēti-, saeti-;* see SETA, -I-]

se·ti·form (sē′tə fôrm′), *adj.* bristle-shaped; setaceous. [1810–20; SETI- + -FORM]

se·tig·er·ous (si tij′ər əs), *adj.* having setae or bristles. Also, **se·tif·er·ous** (si tif′ər əs). [1650–60; < L *sētiger* bristle-bearing + -OUS; see SETI-, -GEROUS]

set-in (set′in′), *adj.* made separately and placed within another unit. [1525–35; adj. use of v. phrase *set in*]

set′-in sleeve′, a sleeve joined to the body of a garment at the shoulder and having a seam at that juncture. Cf. **raglan sleeve.** [1965–70]

se·ti·reme (sē′tə rēm′), *n.* the setose, oarlike leg of an aquatic insect. [1835; SETI- + *-reme* < L *rēmus* oar]

set·off (set′ôf′, -of′), *n.* **1.** something that counterbalances or makes up for something else, as compensation for a loss. **2.** *Accounting.* a counterbalancing debt or claim, esp. one that cancels an amount a debtor owes. **3.** Also called **offset.** *Archit.* **a.** a reduction in the thickness of a wall. **b.** a flat or sloping projection on a wall, buttress, or the like, below a thinner part. **4.** something used to enhance the effect of another thing by contrasting it, as an ornament. **5.** *Print.* offset (def. 7). [1615–25; n. use of v. phrase *set off*]

se·ton (sēt′n), *n. Surg.* a thread or the like inserted beneath the skin to provide drainage or to guide subsequent passage of a tube. [1350–1400; ME < ML *sētōn-* (s. of *sētō*), equiv. to *sēt(a)* SETA + *-ōn-* n. suffix]

Se·ton (sēt′n), *n.* **1. Saint Elizabeth Ann (Bayley)** (*"Mother Seton"*), 1774–1821, U.S. educator, social-welfare reformer, and religious leader: first native-born American to be canonized (1975). **2. Ernest Thompson,** 1860–1946, English writer and illustrator in the U.S.

se·tose (sē′tōs, si tōs′), *adj.* covered with setae or bristles; bristly. [1655–65; < L *sētōsus.* See SETA, -OSE[1]]

set·out (set′out′), *n. Informal.* **1.** preparations, esp. for beginning a journey. **2.** start or outset. **3.** things set or laid out for use or display, as food on a table. **4.** getup or outfit. **5.** an entertaining event. [1800–10; n. use of v. phrase *set out*]

set′ piece′, 1. an arrangement of slow-burning fireworks forming a design or composition when lighted. **2.** *Theat.* a piece of scenery used as part of a stage set, as a profile or three-dimensional construction built to stand independently on the stage floor: *A few set pieces simulating rocks and a fence constituted the scenery for the first act.* **3.** a work of art, literature, music, etc., having a prescribed thematic and formal structure: *the set pieces of Restoration comedy.* **4.** a scene, action, or the like, having a conventional form and functioning as part of the structure of a work of art, literature, etc. **5.** a military operation carried out according to a rigid plan. **6.** (in a novel, narrative poem, or the like) a passage more or less extraneous to the sequence of events, introduced to supply background, color, or the like. [1840–50]

set′ point′, 1. *Tennis.* the point that if won would enable the scorer or his or her side to win the set. **2.** setpoint. [1925–30]

set·point (set′point′), *n.* **1.** the desired value in a closed-loop feedback system, as in regulation of temperature or pressure. **2.** the point at which a thermostat has been set, as for optimum efficiency. **3.** *Physiol.* an internal regulatory system for maintaining a relatively stable physiological condition in the face of changing external circumstances, as body temperature in a varying climate. Cf. **homeostasis. 4.** a hypothetical regulator in the body that maintains a relatively stable body weight. **5.** the weight range thus theoretically maintained. Also, **set point.** [SET + POINT]

set·screw (set′skrōō′), *n.* a screw passing through a threaded hole in a part to tighten the contact of that part with another, as of a collar with the shaft on which it fits. [1850–55; SET + SCREW]

set′ shot′, *Basketball.* a shot with two hands from a point relatively distant from the basket, in which a player stands still and shoots the ball usually from chest level. [1930–35]

sett (set), *n.* **1.** Also called **pitcher.** a small, rectangular paving stone. **2.** Also called **stake.** a hand-held tool that is struck by a hammer to shape or deform a metal object. **3.** Also, **set.** the distinctively colored pattern of crisscrossed lines and stripes against a background in which a Scottish tartan is woven. [1870–75; var. of SET]

Set·tat (se tät′), *n.* a city in W central Morocco. 125,000.

set·te·cen·tesque (set′ā chen tesk′), *adj.* of, pertaining to, or characteristic of the art and literature of 18th-century Italy. [< It *settecentesco,* equiv. to *settecent(o)* seven hundred, the period 1700–99 + *-esco* -ESQUE]

set·tee (se tē′), *n.* a seat for two or more persons, having a back and usually arms, and often upholstered. [1710–20; perh. var. of SETTLE[2]]

set·ter (set′ər), *n.* **1.** a person or thing that sets. **2.** one of any of several breeds of hunting dogs that originally had the habit of crouching when game was scented but that are now trained to stand stiffly and point the muzzle toward the scented game. Cf. **English setter, Gordon setter, Irish setter. 3.** *Volleyball.* a player who lofts the ball high for a teammate near the net to spike. [1375–1425; late ME; see SET, -ER[1]]

set′ the′ory, the branch of mathematics that deals with relations between sets. [1940–45]

set·ting (set′ing), *n.* **1.** the act of a person or thing that sets. **2.** the surroundings or environment of anything: *The garden was a perfect setting for the house.* **3.** the mounting in which a jewel is set. **4.** a group of all the articles, as of china, silver, or glass, required for setting a table or a single place at a table. **5.** the locale or period in which the action of a novel, play, film, etc., takes place: *The setting of this story is Verona in the 15th century.* **6.** Also called **stage setting, stage set.** the scenery and other properties used in a dramatic performance. **7.** *Music.* **a.** a piece of music composed for certain words. **b.** a piece of music composed for a particular medium, or arranged for other than the original medium. [1325–75; ME; see SET, -ING[1]]

—**Syn. 2.** See **environment.**

set′ting-up′ ex′ercises (set′ing up′), any of various exercises, as deep knee bends and push-ups, for improving one's posture, muscle tone, or limberness, or for reducing one's weight. Also called **set-ups.** [1895–1900]

set·tle[1] (set′l), *v.,* **-tled, -tling.** —*v.t.* **1.** to appoint, fix, or resolve definitely and conclusively; agree upon (as time, price, or conditions). **2.** to place in a desired state or in order: *to settle one's affairs.* **3.** to pay, as a bill. **4.** to close (an account) by payment. **5.** to migrate to and organize (an area, territory, etc.); colonize: *The pilgrims settled Plymouth.* **6.** to cause to take up residence: *They settled immigrants in urban areas.* **7.** to furnish (a place) with inhabitants or settlers: *The French settled this colony with army veterans.* **8.** to quiet, calm, or bring to rest (the nerves, stomach, etc.). **9.** to stop from annoying or opposing: *A sharp word will settle that youngster.* **10.** to conclude or resolve: *to settle a dispute.* **11.** to make stable; place in a permanent position or on a permanent basis. **12.** to cause (a liquid) to become clear by depositing dregs. **13.** to cause (dregs, sediment, etc.) to sink or be deposited. **14.** to cause to sink down gradually; make firm or compact. **15.** to dispose of finally; close up: *to settle an estate.* **16.** *Law.* **a.** to secure (property, title, etc.) on or to a person by formal or legal process. **b.** to terminate (legal proceedings) by mutual consent of the parties. —*v.i.* **17.** to decide, arrange, or agree (often fol. by *on* or *upon*): *to settle on a plan of action.* **18.** to arrange matters in dispute; come to an agreement: *to settle with a person.* **19.** to pay a bill; make a financial arrangement (often fol. by *up*). **20.** to take up residence in a new country or place: *Many Frenchmen settled along the Mississippi River following La Salle's explorations.* **21.** to come to rest, as from flight: *A bird settled on a bough.* **22.** to gather, collect, or become fixed in a particular place, direction, etc.: *A cold settled in my head.* **23.** to become calm or composed (often fol. by *down*): *I'll wait until the class settles before starting the lesson.* **24.** to come to rest (often fol. by *down*): *We settled down for the night at an old country inn.* **25.** to sink down gradually; subside. **26.** to become clear by the sinking of suspended particles, as a liquid. **27.** to sink to the bottom, as sediment. **28.** to become firm or compact, as the ground. **29.** (of a female animal) to become pregnant; conceive. **30. settle down, a.** to become established in some routine, esp. upon marrying, after a period of independence or indecision. **b.** to become calm or quiet. **c.** to apply oneself to serious work: *There were so many distractions that we weren't able to settle down to studying.* **31. settle for,** to be satisfied with: *to settle for less.* **32. settle into,** to become established in: *to settle into a new routine.* [bef. 1000; ME *set(t)len,* OE *setlan* (attested once) to place, deriv. of *setl* SETTLE[2]; cf. D *zetelen*] —**set′tle·a·ble,** *adj.* —**set′·tle·a·bil′i·ty,** *n.* —**set′tled·ness,** *n.*

—**Syn. 1.** set, establish. **4.** liquidate. **6.** relocate. **7.** people, colonize. **9.** tranquilize, compose, still, pacify. **11.** stabilize, establish, confirm. **20.** locate, relocate. **25.** decline, fall, abate.

set·tle[2] (set′l), *n.* a long seat or bench, usually wooden, with arms and a high back. See illus. on next page. [bef. 900; ME: seat, sitting place, OE *setl;* c. G *Sessel* armchair, Goth *sitls* seat, L *sella* saddle; akin to SIT[1]]

set•tle•ment (set′l mənt), *n.* **1.** the act or state of settling or the state of being settled. **2.** the act of making stable or putting on a permanent basis. **3.** a state of stability or permanence. **4.** an arrangement or adjustment, as of business affairs or a disagreement. **5.** an agreement signed after labor negotiations between union and management. **6.** the terms reached in this agreement. **7.** the settling of persons in a new country or place. **8.** a colony, esp. in its early stages. **9.** a small community, village, or group of houses in a thinly populated area. **10.** a community formed and populated by members of a particular religious or ideological group: *a Shaker settlement.* **11.** the satisfying of a claim or demand; a coming to terms. **12.** *Law.* **a.** final disposition of an estate or the like. **b.** the settling of property, title, etc., upon a person. **c.** the property so settled. **13.** *Brit.* **a.** legal residence in a specific place. **b.** (of a pauper) the right to claim food and shelter from an official agency or specific town or district. **14.** Also called **set′tlement house′.** *Social Work.* an establishment in an underprivileged area providing social services to local residents. **15.** a subsidence or sinking of all or part of a structure. [1620–30; SETTLE¹ + -MENT]

set′tlement op′tion, *Insurance.* any of the options, other than immediate payment in a lump sum, by which the policyholder or beneficiary may choose to have the benefits of a policy paid.

set′tlement work′er, a person who works with underprivileged people in a settlement house.

set•tler (set′lər, -l ər), *n.* **1.** a person or thing that settles. **2.** a person who settles in a new country or area. [1590–1600; SETTLE¹ + -ER¹]

set•tling (set′ling, -l ing), *n.* **1.** the act of a person or thing that settles. **2.** Usually, **settlings.** sediment. [1400–50; late ME; see SETTLE¹, -ING¹]

set′tling tank′, a tank for holding liquid until particles suspended in it settle. [1905–10]

set•tlor (set′lər, -l ər), *n. Law.* a person who makes a settlement of property. [1810–20; SETTLE¹ + -OR²]

set-to (set′to͞o′), *n., pl.* **-tos.** a usually brief, sharp fight or argument. [1735–45; n. use of v. phrase *set to*]

Se•tú•bal (si to͞o′bäl), *n.* **1. Bay of,** an inlet of the Atlantic, in W Portugal. 20 mi. (32 km) long; 35 mi. (56 km) wide. **2.** a seaport on this bay, near Lisbon. 64,531.

set•u•la (sech′ə lə), *n., pl.* **-lae** (-lē′). *Bot., Zool.* a short, blunt seta. Also, **set•ule** (sech′o͞ol). [1820–30; < NL *sētula;* see SETA, -ULE]

set•u•lose (sech′ə lōs′), *adj. Bot., Zool.* having or covered with setulae. Also, **set•u•lous** (sech′ə ləs). [1855–60; SETUL(A) + -OSE¹]

set-up (set′up′), *n.* **1.** *Survey.* **a.** station (def. 14a). **b.** a surveying instrument precisely positioned for observations from a station. **c.** a gap between the end of a chain or tape being used for a measurement and the point toward which it is laid. **2. set-ups.** See **setting-up exercises.**

set•up (set′up′), *n.* **1.** organization; arrangement. **2.** an act or instance of setting up or getting ready: *The setup of the lights and camera took all morning.* **3.** the carriage of the body; bearing. **4.** a camera position, as for a particular shot. **5.** everything required for an alcoholic drink except the liquor, as a glass, ice, and soda water, as served to patrons who provide their own liquor. **6.** *Informal.* **a.** an undertaking or contest deliberately made easy. **b.** a match or game arranged with an opponent who can be defeated without risk or effort. **c.** an opponent easy to defeat. **7.** *Sports.* **a.** a shot or play that results in a puck, shuttlecock, ball, or balls being so positioned as to provide a player with an easy opportunity for a winning shot. **b.** the position of such a puck, ball, etc. **c.** the puck, ball, etc., itself. **8.** an arrangement of all the tools, parts, apparatus, etc., necessary for any of various specific jobs or purposes. **9.** the equipment or items necessary for a particular activity or period; kit. **10.** a plan or projected course of action. **11.** a prearranged situation or circumstance, usu. created to fool or trap someone; trick; scheme. [1600–10; n. use of v. phrase *set up*]

set′ width′, *Print.* (in automatic typesetting) the width measured by the lowercase alphabet of a particular size and font of type.

Seu•rat (sœ RA′), *n.* **Georges** (zhôrzh), 1859–91, French (pointillist) painter.

Seuss (so͞os), *n.* **Dr.** See **Geisel, Theodor Seuss.**

Se•vas•to•pol (sə vas′tə pōl′, sev′ə stō′pəl; *Russ.* syi-vu stô′pəl), *n.* a fortified seaport in the S Crimea, in S Ukraine: famous for its heroic resistance during sieges of 349 days in 1854–55, and 245 days in 1941–42. 350,000. Also, **Sebastopol.**

sève (sev), *n. French.* the characteristic flavor and body of a wine. [lit., sap]

sev•en (sev′ən), *n.* **1.** a cardinal number, 6 plus 1. **2.** a symbol for this number, as 7 or VII. **3.** a set of this many persons or things. **4.** a playing card with seven pips. **5. sevens,** (*used with a singular v.*) fan-tan (def. 1). —*adj.* **6.** amounting to seven in number. —*v.i.* **7. seven out,** crap² (def. 3a). [bef. 900; ME *seoven(e), seofne, seven,* OE *seofon;* c. G *sieben,* Goth *sibun;* akin to OIr *secht,* Welsh *saith,* L *septem,* Gk *heptá,* Pol *siedem,* Skt *saptá*]

Sev′en against′ Thebes′, **1.** *Class. Myth.* seven heroes, Amphiaraus, Capaneus, Eteoclus, Hippomedon, Parthenopaeus, Polynices, and Tydeus, who led an expedition against Thebes to depose Eteocles in favor of his brother Polynices: the expedition failed, but the Epigoni, the sons of the Seven against Thebes, conquered the city ten years later. **2.** (*italics*) a tragedy (468? B.C.) by Aeschylus.

sev•en•bark (sev′ən bärk′), *n.* See **wild hydrangea.** [1755–65, *Amer.;* SEVEN + BARK²; so called from its many layers]

sev′en-card stud′ (sev′ən kärd′), *Cards.* a variety of poker in which each player is dealt one card face down in each of the first two rounds, one card face up in each of the next four rounds, and one card face down in the last round, each of the last five rounds being followed by a betting interval. Cf. **stud poker** (def. 1).

sev′en dead′ly sins′. See **deadly sins.**

sev•en-e•lev•en (sev′ən i lev′ən), *n.* See **shiner perch.**

Sev•en•er (sev′ə nər), *n. Islam.* Isma'ilian. [SEVEN + -ER¹]

sev•en•fold (sev′ən fōld′), *adj.* **1.** comprising seven parts or members. **2.** seven times as great or as much. —*adv.* **3.** until seven times as many or as great: *multiplied sevenfold.* [bef. 1000; ME; OE *seofonfeald.* See SEVEN, -FOLD]

Sev′en Hills′, a town in N Ohio. 13,650.

Sev′en Hills′ of Rome′, the seven hills (the Aventine, Caelian, Capitoline, Esquiline, Palatine, Quirinal, and Viminal) on and about which the ancient city of Rome was built.

sev•en-inch (sev′ən inch′), *n.* a phonograph record seven inches in diameter, usu. having one popular song on each side. Cf. **twelve-inch.**

Sev′en Isles′, a city in SE Quebec, in E Canada, on the St. Lawrence, near its mouth. 29,262. French, **Sept-Îles.**

sev′en-league boots′ (sev′ən lēg′), fairy-tale boots enabling the wearer to reach seven leagues at a stride. [1805–15; trans. of F *bottes de sept lieues* in the fairy tales of C. Perrault, esp. *Le petit Poucet* (E *Hop-o'-my-Thumb*)]

sev•en•pen•ny (sev′ən pen′ē), *adj.* noting a nail 2¼ in. (6 cm) long. *Symbol:* 7d [1350–1400 for earlier sense "costing seven pence"; ME; see SEVEN, -PENNY]

Sev′en Pines′. See **Fair Oaks** (def. 1).

Sev′en Sag′es, seven wise men of ancient Greece, Bias, Chilon, Cleobulus, Periander, Pittacus, Solon, and Thales, who served their country as rulers, lawgivers, and advisers and who were reputed to have written many popular maxims.

sev′en seas′, the navigable waters of the world. Also, **Sev′en Seas′.** [1870–75]

sev•en-spot (sev′ən spot′), *n Informal.* a playing card the face of which bears seven pips.

sev•en•teen (sev′ən tēn′), *n.* **1.** a cardinal number, 10 plus 7. **2.** a symbol for this number, as 17 or XVII. **3.** a set of this many persons or things. —*adj.* **4.** amounting to 17 in number. **5.** (*cap., italics*) a novel (1916) by Booth Tarkington. [bef. 900; ME *seventene,* OE *seofontēne* (c. D *zeventien,* G *siebzehn*). See SEVEN, -TEEN]

sev•en•teenth (sev′ən tēnth′), *adj.* **1.** next after the sixteenth; being the ordinal number for 17. **2.** being one of 17 equal parts. —*n.* **3.** a seventeenth part, esp. of one (1/17). **4.** the seventeenth member of a series. [bef. 900; SEVENTEEN + -TH²; r. ME *seventethe,* OE *seofontēotha.* (see SEVEN, TITHE)]

Sev′enteenth Amend′ment, an amendment to the U.S. Constitution, ratified in 1913, providing for the election of two U.S. senators from each state by popular vote and for a term of six years.

sev′en•teen′-year lo′cust (sev′ən tēn′yēr′), a cicada, *Magicicada septendecim,* of the eastern U.S., having nymphs that live in the soil, usually emerging in great numbers after 17 years in the North or 13 years in the South. Also called **periodical cicada.** [1810–20]

sev•enth (sev′ənth), *adj.* **1.** next after the sixth; being the ordinal number for seven. **2.** being one of seven equal parts. —*n.* **3.** a seventh part, esp. of one (1/7). **4.** the seventh member of a series. **5.** *Music.* **a.** a tone on the seventh degree from a given tone (counted as the first). **b.** the interval between such tones. **c.** the harmonic combination of such tones. [bef. 950; ME; see SEVEN, -TH²; r. ME *sevethe,* OE *seofotha*]

Sev′enth Amend′ment, an amendment to the U.S. Constitution, ratified in 1791 as part of the Bill of Rights, guaranteeing trial by jury.

Sev′enth Av′enue, **1.** an avenue in the borough of Manhattan, in New York City. **2.** the garment industry of New York City. Cf. **Garment Center.**

sev′enth chord′, *Music.* a chord formed by the superposition of three thirds. [1905–10]

Sev′enth Command′ment, "Thou shalt not commit adultery": seventh of the Ten Commandments. Cf. **Ten Commandments.**

Sev•enth-Day (sev′ənth dā′), *adj.* designating certain Christian denominations that make Saturday their chief day of rest and religious observance: *Seventh-Day Adventists.* Also, **sev′enth-day′.**

sev′enth heav′en, **1.** (esp. in Islam and the cabala) the highest heaven, where God and the most exalted angels dwell. **2.** a state of intense happiness; bliss: *We were in seventh heaven in our new home.* [1810–20]

sev′enth-inn•ing stretch′ (sev′ənth in′ing, -in′-), **1.** *Baseball.* a point in the game when spectators rise from their seats to relax by stretching their legs, usually after six and one-half innings. **2.** any point or period of pause, rest, reconsideration, or the like. [1955–60]

sev•en•ti•eth (sev′ən tē ith), *adj.* **1.** next after the sixty-ninth; being the ordinal number for 70. **2.** being one of 70 equal parts. —*n.* **3.** a seventieth part, esp. of one (1/70). **4.** the seventieth member of a series. [1250–1300; ME *seventithe.* See SEVENTY, -ETH²]

sev•en•ty (sev′ən tē), *n., pl.* **-ties,** *adj.* —*n.* **1.** a cardinal number, 10 times 7. **2.** a symbol for this number, as 70 or LXX. **3.** a set of this many persons or things. **4. seventies,** the numbers, years, degrees, or the like from 70 through 79, as in referring to numbered streets, indicating the years of a lifetime or of a century, or referring to degrees of temperature: *They live in the Seventies. His uncle is in his early seventies.* **5. the Seventy,** the body of scholars who produced the Septuagint. —*adj.* **6.** amounting to 70 in number. [1150–1200; ME; OE *seofontig.* See SEVEN, -TY¹]

sev•en•ty-eight (sev′ən tē āt′), *n.* **1.** a cardinal number, 70 plus 8. **2.** a symbol for this number, as 78 or LXXVIII. **3.** a set of this many persons or things. —*adj.* **4.** amounting to 78 in number.

78 (sev′ən tē āt′), *n., pl.* **78s, 78's.** an early type of shellac-based phonograph record that played at 78 revolutions per minute. [1950–55]

sev•en•ty-eighth (sev′ən tē ātth′, -āth′), *adj.* **1.** next after the seventy-seventh; being the ordinal number for 78. **2.** being one of 78 equal parts. —*n.* **3.** a seventy-eighth part, esp. of one (1/78). **4.** the seventy-eighth member of a series.

sev•en•ty-fifth (sev′ən tē fifth′), *adj.* **1.** next after the seventy-fourth; being the ordinal number for 75. **2.** being one of 75 equal parts. —*n.* **3.** a seventy-fifth part, esp. of one (1/75). **4.** the seventy-fifth member of a series.

sev•en•ty-first (sev′ən tē fûrst′), *adj.* **1.** next after the seventieth; being the ordinal number for 71. **2.** being one of 71 equal parts. —*n.* **3.** a seventy-first part, esp. of one (1/71). **4.** the seventy-first member of a series.

sev•en•ty-five (sev′ən tē fīv′), *n.* **1.** a cardinal number, 70 plus 5. **2.** a symbol for this number, as 75 or LXXV. **3.** a set of this many persons or things. **4.** *Mil.* **a.** a gun with a 75-mm caliber. **b.** the field gun of that caliber used in the French and U.S. armies in World War I. —*adj.* **5.** amounting to 75 in number.

sev•en•ty-four (sev′ən tē fôr′, -fōr′), *n.* **1.** a cardinal number, 70 plus 4. **2.** a symbol for this number, as 74 or LXXIV. **3.** a set of this many persons or things. —*adj.* **4.** amounting to 74 in number.

sev•en•ty-fourth (sev′ən tē fôrth′, -fōrth′), *adj.* **1.** next after the seventy-third; being the ordinal number for 74. **2.** being one of 74 equal parts. —*n.* **3.** a seventy-fourth part, esp. of one (1/74). **4.** the seventy-fourth member of a series.

sev•en•ty-nine (sev′ən tē nīn′), *n.* **1.** a cardinal number, 70 plus 9. **2.** a symbol for this number, as 79 or LXXIX. **3.** a set of this many persons or things. —*adj.* **4.** amounting to 79 in number.

sev•en•ty-ninth (sev′ən tē nīnth′), *adj.* **1.** next after the seventy-eighth; being the ordinal number for 79. **2.** being one of 79 equal parts. —*n.* **3.** a seventy-ninth part, esp. of one (1/79). **4.** the seventy-ninth member of a series.

sev•en•ty-one (sev′ən tē wun′), *n.* **1.** a cardinal number, 70 plus 1. **2.** a symbol for this number, as 71 or LXXI. **3.** a set of this many persons or things. —*adj.* **4.** amounting to 71 in number.

sev•en•ty-sec•ond (sev′ən tē sek′ənd), *adj.* **1.** next after the seventy-first; being the ordinal number for 72. **2.** being one of 72 equal parts. —*n.* **3.** a seventy-second part, esp. of one (1/72). **4.** the seventy-second member of a series.

sev•en•ty-sev•en (sev′ən tē sev′ən), *n.* **1.** a cardinal number, 70 plus 7. **2.** a symbol for this number, as 77 or LXXVII. **3.** a set of this many persons or things. —*adj.* **4.** amounting to 77 in number.

sev•en•ty-sev•enth (sev′ən tē sev′ənth), *adj.* **1.** next after the seventy-sixth; being the ordinal number for 77. **2.** being one of 77 equal parts. —*n.* **3.** a seventy-seventh part, esp. of one (1/77). **4.** the seventy-seventh member of a series.

sev•en•ty-six (sev′ən tē siks′), *n.* **1.** a cardinal number, 70 plus 6. **2.** a symbol for this number, as 76 or LXXVI. **3.** a set of this many persons or things. —*adj.* **4.** amounting to 76 in number.

sev•en•ty-sixth (sev′ən tē siksth′), *adj.* **1.** next after the seventy-fifth; being the ordinal number for 76. **2.** being one of 76 equal parts. —*n.* **3.** a seventy-sixth part, esp. of one (1/76). **4.** the seventy-sixth member of a series.

sev•en•ty-third (sev′ən tē thûrd′), *adj.* **1.** next after the seventy-second; being the ordinal number for 73. **2.** being one of 73 equal parts. —*n.* **3.** a seventy-third part, esp. of one (1/73). **4.** the seventy-third member of a series.

sev•en•ty-three (sev′ən tē thrē′), *n.* **1.** a cardinal number, 70 plus 3. **2.** a symbol for this number, as 73 or LXXIII. **3.** a set of this many persons or things. —*adj.* **4.** amounting to 73 in number.

sev•en•ty-two (sev′ən tē to͞o′), *n.* **1.** a cardinal number, 70 plus 2. **2.** a symbol for this number, as 72 or LXXII. **3.** a set of this many persons or things. —*adj.* **4.** amounting to 72 in number.

sev•en-up (sev′ən up′), *n.* See **all fours** (def. 2). [1820–30]

Sev′en Weeks′ War′. See **Austro-Prussian War.**

Sev′en Won′ders of the World′, the seven most remarkable structures of ancient times: the Egyptian pyramids, the Mausoleum at Halicarnassus, the Temple

CONCISE PRONUNCIATION KEY: act, cāpe, dâre, pärt; set, ēqual; if, īce; ox, ōver, ôrder, oil, bo͝ok, bo͞ot, out; up, ûrge; child; sing; shoe; thin, *that;* zh as in *treasure.* ə = *a* as in *alone, e* as in *system, i* as in *easily, o* as in *gallop, u* as in *circus;* ᵊ as in *fire* (fīᵊr), *hour* (ouᵊr). l and n can serve as syllabic consonants, as in *cradle* (krād′l), and *button* (but′n). See the full key inside the front cover.

of Artemis at Ephesus, the Hanging Gardens of Babylon, the Colossus of Rhodes, the statue of Zeus by Phidias at Olympia, and the Pharos or lighthouse at Alexandria.

sev′en-year itch′ (sev′en yēr′), **1.** scabies. **2.** the temptation to have an affair, held to become a hazard in the seventh year of marriage. [1895–1900, *Amer.*]

Sev′en Years′ War′, the war (1756–63) in which England and Prussia defeated France, Austria, Russia, Sweden, and Saxony.

sev•er (sev′ər), *v.t.* **1.** to separate (a part) from the whole, as by cutting or the like. **2.** to divide into parts, esp. forcibly; cleave. **3.** to break off or dissolve (ties, relations, etc.). **4.** *Law.* to divide into parts; disunite (an estate, titles of a statute, etc.). **5.** to distinguish; discriminate between. —*v.i.* **6.** to become separated from each other; become divided into parts. [1300–50; ME *severen* < MF *sev(e)rer* to SEPARATE]

sev•er•a•ble (sev′ər ə bəl, sev′rə-), *adj.* **1.** capable of being severed. **2.** *Law.* separable or capable of being treated as separate from a whole legal right or obligation: *a severable contract obligation.* [1540–50; SEVER + -ABLE] —**sev′er•a•bil′i•ty,** *n.*

sev•er•al (sev′ər əl, sev′rəl), *adj.* **1.** being more than two but fewer than many in number or kind: *several ways of doing it.* **2.** respective; individual: *They went their several ways.* **3.** separate; different: *several occasions.* **4.** single; particular. **5.** *Law.* binding two or more persons who may be sued separately on a common obligation. —*n.* **6.** several persons or things; a few; some. [1375–1425; late ME < AF < ML *sēparālis,* equiv. to L *sēpar* separate + *-ālis* -AL[1]]

sev•er•al•fold (sev′ər əl fōld′, sev′rəl-), *adj.* **1.** comprising several parts or members. **2.** several times as great or as much: *a severalfold increase.* —*adv.* **3.** in severalfold measure. [1730–40; SEVERAL + -FOLD]

sev•er•al•ly (sev′ər ə lē, sev′rə-), *adv.* **1.** separately; singly. **2.** respectively. [1350–1400; ME; see SEVERAL, -LY]

sev•er•al•ty (sev′ər əl tē, sev′rəl-), *n., pl.* **-ties. 1.** the state of being separate. **2.** *Law.* **a.** (of an estate, esp. land) the condition of being held or owned by separate and individual right. **b.** an estate held or owned by individual right. [1400–50; late ME < AF *severalte.* See SEVERAL, -TY[2]]

sev•er•ance (sev′ər əns, sev′rəns), *n.* **1.** the act of severing or the state of being severed. **2.** a breaking off, as of a friendship. **3.** *Law.* a division into parts, as of liabilities or provisions; removal of a part from the whole. **4.** See **severance pay.** [1375–1425; late ME *severaunce* < AF; see SEVER, -ANCE]

sev′erance pay′, money, exclusive of wages, back pay, etc., paid to an employee who has tenure and who is dismissed because of lack of work or other reasons beyond the employee's control. [1940–45]

sev′erance tax′, a tax levied by a state on the extraction and use of a natural product, as coal, that is sold outside the state or during a certain period. [1925–30]

se•vere (sə vēr′), *adj.,* **-ver•er, -ver•est. 1.** harsh; unnecessarily extreme: *severe criticism; severe laws.* **2.** serious or stern in manner or appearance: *a severe face.* **3.** grave; critical: *a severe illness.* **4.** rigidly restrained in style, taste, manner, etc.; simple, plain, or austere. **5.** causing discomfort or distress by extreme character or conditions, as weather, cold, or heat; unpleasantly violent, as rain or wind, or a blow or shock. **6.** difficult to endure, perform, fulfill, etc.: *a severe test of his powers.* **7.** rigidly exact, accurate, or methodical: *severe standards.* [1540–50; < L *sevērus,* or back formation from SEVERITY] —**se•vere′ly,** *adv.* —**se•vere′ness,** *n.* —**Syn. 2.** strict, hard. See **stern**[1]. **4.** unadorned. **7.** demanding, exacting. —**Ant. 1.** lenient. **2.** gentle.

severe′ combined′ immune′ defi′ciency, *Pathol.* a group of rare congenital disorders in which both cell-mediated and humoral immunity are lacking, causing susceptibility to a wide variety of illnesses and an inability to live in a normal environment. Also, **severe′ combined′ im′munodefi′ciency.** *Abbr.:* SCID

Sev•er•i•nus (sev′ə rī′nəs), *n.* died A.D. 640, pope 640.

se•ver•i•ty (sə ver′i tē), *n., pl.* **-ties. 1.** harshness, sternness, or rigor: *Their lives were marked by severity.* **2.** austere simplicity, as of style, manner, or taste: *The severity of the decor was striking.* **3.** intensity or sharpness, as of cold or pain. **4.** grievousness; hard or trying character or effect: *The severity of his loss was finally becoming apparent.* **5.** rigid exactness or accuracy. **6.** an instance of strict or severe behavior, punishment, etc. [1475–85; < L *sevēritās,* equiv. to *sevēr(us)* SEVERE + *-itās* -ITY]

Sev•ern (sev′ərn), *n.* **1.** a river in Great Britain, flowing from central Wales through W England into the Bristol Channel. 210 mi. (338 km) long. **2.** a city in central Maryland. 20,147.

Se•ver′na Park′ (sə vûr′nə), a city in central Maryland. 21,253.

Se•ve•ro•do•netsk (sev′ər ə də netsk′; *Russ.* syi vyi-RƏ du nyetsk′), *n.* a city in E Ukraine, NE of Donetsk. 113,000.

Se•ve•ro•dvinsk (sev′ər ə dvinsk′; *Russ.* syi vyi RU-dvyĕnsk′), *n.* a city in the N Russian Federation in Europe, on Dvina Gulf, E of Archangel. 239,000. Formerly, **Molotovsk.**

Se•ver•sky (sə ver′skē), *n.* **Alexander Pro•co•fi•eff de** (prə kō′fē ef′ də), 1894–1974, U.S. airplane designer, manufacturer, and writer; born in Russia.

Se•ve•rus (sə vēr′əs), *n.* **Lucius Sep•tim•i•us** (septim′ē əs), A.D. 146–211, Roman emperor 193–211.

CONCISE ETYMOLOGY KEY: <, descended or borrowed from; >, whence; b., blend of, blended; c., cognate with; cf., compare; deriv., derivative; equiv., equivalent; imit., imitative; obl., oblique; r., replacing; s., stem; sp., spelling, spelled; resp., respelling, respelled; trans., translation; ?, origin unknown; *, unattested; ‡, probably earlier than. See the full key inside the front cover.

sev•er•y (sev′ə rē), *n., pl.* **-er•ies.** (in a vaulted structure) one bay between two principal transverse arches. [1350–1400; ME < AF **civorie,* OF *civoire* < L *cibōrium* CIBORIUM]

se•vi•che (sə vē′chā, -chē), *n.* ceviche.

Sé•vi•gné (sā vē nyā′), *n.* **Ma•rie de Ra•bu•tin-Chan•tal** (MA Rē′ də RA BY TAN shäN TAL′), **Marquise de,** 1626–96, French writer, esp. of letters.

Se•ville (sə vil′), *n.* a port in SW Spain, on the Guadalquivir River: site of the Alcazar; cathedral. 560,000. Spanish, **Se•vil•la** (se vē′lyä). —**Se•vil•lian** (sə vil′yən), *adj., n.*

Seville′ or′ange. See under **orange** (def. 2). [1585–95]

Sè•vres (se′VRə; *Eng.* sev′rə, sev), *n.* **1.** a suburb of Paris in N France. 21,296. **2.** Also, **Sè′vres ware′.** the porcelain made in this suburb since 1756.

sew[1] (sō), *v.,* **sewed, sewn** or **sewed, sew•ing.** —*v.t.* **1.** to join or attach by stitches. **2.** to make, repair, etc., (a garment) by such means. **3.** to enclose or secure with stitches: *to sew flour in a bag.* **4.** to close (a hole, wound, etc.) by means of stitches (usually fol. by *up*). —*v.i.* **5.** to work with a needle and thread or with a sewing machine. **6. sew up, a.** *Informal.* to get or have a monopoly of; control exclusively. **b.** *Informal.* to complete or conclude (arrangements, negotiations, etc.) successfully: *to sew up a deal.* **c.** to gain or be assured of: *He tried to sew up as many votes as possible before the convention.* [bef. 900; ME *sewen,* OE *siw(i)an;* c. OHG *siuwan,* Goth *siujan,* L *suere* (see SUTURE); akin to SEAM] —**sew′a•ble,** *adj., n.*

sew[2] (so͞o), *v.,* **sewed, sew•ing,** *n. Naut.* —*v.t.* **1.** to ground (a vessel) at low tide (sometimes fol by *up*). —*v.i.* **2.** (of a vessel) to be grounded at low tide. —*n.* **3.** the amount of additional water necessary to float a grounded vessel. [1505–15; < MF *sewer,* aph. var. of *essewer* < VL **exaquāre,* equiv. to L *ex-* EX-[1] + *aqu(a)* water + *-āre* inf. suffix]

sew•age (so͞o′ij), *n.* the waste matter that passes through sewers. Also, **sewerage.** [1825–35; SEW(ER)[1] (as if the ending was -ER[1]) + -AGE]

Sew•all (so͞o′əl), *n.* **Samuel,** 1652–1730, American jurist, born in England.

se•wan (sē′wən), *n.* seawan.

Sew•ard (so͞o′ərd), *n.* **William Henry,** 1801–72, U.S. statesman: Secretary of State 1861–69.

Sew′ard Penin′sula, a peninsula in W Alaska, on Bering Strait.

Sew′ard's Fol′ly, *U.S. Hist.* the purchase of Alaska in 1867, through the negotiations of Secretary of State W. H. Seward. Cf. **Alaska Purchase.** [so called because Alaska was regarded as worthless land]

se•wel•lel (sə wel′əl), *n.* See **mountain beaver.** [1806, *Amer.;* < Lower Chinook *š-walál* robe of mountain beaver skins, understood as the animal itself]

sew•er[1] (so͞o′ər), *n.* **1.** an artificial conduit, usually underground, for carrying off waste water and refuse, as in a town or city. —*v.t.* **2.** to provide or equip with sewers: *a tax increase necessary to sewer the neighborhood.* [1375–1425; late ME *suer(e)* < dial. OF *se(u)wiere* overflow channel (cf. OF *ess(e)ouer(e)* ditch) < L **exaquāria* drain for carrying water off, equiv. to L *ex-* EX- + *aqu(a)* water + *-āria,* fem. of *-ārius* -ARY; see SEW[2], -ER[2]] —**sew′er•less,** *adj.* —**sew′er•like′,** *adj.*

sew•er[2] (sō′ər), *n.* a person or thing that sews. [1350–1400; ME; see SEW[1], -ER[1]]

sew•er[3] (so͞o′ər), *n.* a former household officer or head servant in charge of the service of the table. [1300–50; ME, aph. < AF *asseour* seater, equiv. to OF *asse(oir)* to seat (< L *assidēre* to attend upon; see ASSIDUOUS) + *-our* -OR[2]]

sew•er•age (so͞o′ər ij), *n.* **1.** the removal of waste water and refuse by means of sewers. **2.** a system of sewers. **3.** sewage. [1825–35; SEWER[1] + -AGE]

sew′er pill′ (so͞o′ər), a ribbed wooden ball for scrapping the walls of a sewer through which it floats.

sew•ing (sō′ing), *n.* **1.** the act or work of one who sews. **2.** something sewn or to be sewn. [1250–1300; ME; see SEW[1], -ING[1]]

sew′ing cir′cle, a group, esp. of women, meeting regularly to sew. [1840–50, *Amer.*]

sew′ing cot′ton, cotton thread used for sewing, embroidery, etc. [1805–15]

sew′ing machine′, any of various foot-operated or electric machines for sewing or making stitches, ranging from machines with a shuttle for a spool of thread and a needle for sewing garments to industrial machines for sewing leather, book pages together, etc. [1840–50, *Amer.*]

sew′ing nee′dle, *Northern U.S.* a dragonfly. —**Regional Variation.** See **dragonfly.**

sew′ing silk′, finely twisted silk thread used for sewing, embroidery, etc. [1470–80]

sew′ing ta′ble, a worktable for holding sewing materials, often supplied with a bag or pouch for needlework. Cf. **bag table.** [1870–75]

sewn (sōn), *v.* a pp. of **sew**[1].

sex (seks), *n.* **1.** either the male or female division of a species, esp. as differentiated with reference to the reproductive functions. **2.** the sum of the structural and functional differences by which the male and female are distinguished, or the phenomena or behavior dependent on these differences. **3.** the instinct or attraction drawing one sex toward another, or its manifestation in life and conduct. **4.** coitus. **5.** genitalia. **6. to have sex,** to engage in sexual intercourse. —*v.t.* **7.** to ascertain the sex of, esp. of newly-hatched chicks. **8. sex up,** *Informal.* **a.** to arouse sexually: *The only intent of that show was to sex up the audience.* **b.** to increase the appeal of; to make more interesting, attractive, or exciting: *We've decided to sex up the movie with some battle scenes.* [1350–1400; ME < L *sexus,* perh. akin to *secāre* to divide (see SECTION)]

sex (seks), *adj. Latin.* six.

sex-, a combining form, occurring in loanwords from Latin, meaning "six" (*sexagenary*); on this model used in the formation of compound words: *sexpartite.* Also, **sexi-.** [< L, comb. form of *sex* SIX]

sex′ abuse′. See **sexual abuse.**

sex′ act′, sexual intercourse; copulation.

sex•a•ge•nar•i•an (sek′sə jə nâr′ē ən), *adj.* **1.** of the age of 60 years or between 60 and 70 years old. —*n.* **2.** a sexagenarian person. [1730–40; < L *sexāgēnāri(us)* SEXAGENARY + -AN]

sex•ag•e•nar•y (sek saj′ə ner′ē), *adj., n., pl.* **-nar•ies.** —*adj.* **1.** of or pertaining to the number 60. **2.** composed of or proceeding by sixties. **3.** sexagenarian. —*n.* **4.** a sexagenarian. [1525–35; < L *sexāgēnārius,* equiv. to *sexāgēn(ī),* distributive of *sexāgintā* sixty + *-ārius* -ARY]

Sex•a•ges•i•ma (sek′sə jes′ə mə, -jā′zə-), *n.* the second Sunday before Lent. Also called **Sexages′ima Sun′day.** [1350–1400; ME < L *sexāgēsima (diēs)* sixtieth (day), fem. of *sexāgēsimus,* ordinal corresponding to *sexāgintā* sixty]

sex•a•ges•i•mal (sek′sə jes′ə məl), *adj.* **1.** pertaining to or based upon the number 60. —*n.* **2.** a fraction whose denominator is 60 or a power of 60. [1675–85; < ML *sexāgēsimālis.* See SEXAGESIMA, -AL[1]]

sex′ appeal′, 1. the ability to excite people sexually. **2.** immediate appeal or obvious potential to interest or excite others, as by appearance, style, or charm: *a house with no sex appeal.* [1920–25]

sex•a•va•lent (sek′sə vā′lənt), *adj. Chem.* hexavalent. Also, **sexivalent.** [1875–80]

sex′ cell′, a spermatozoon or an ovum; gamete. [1885–90]

sex•cen•ten•ar•y (seks′sen ten′ə rē, seks sen′tn er′ē *or, esp. Brit.* -sen tē′nə rē), *adj., n., pl.* **-nar•ies.** —*adj.* **1.** pertaining to 600 or a period of 600 years; marking the completion of 600 years. —*n.* **2.** a 600th anniversary or its celebration. [1770–80; SEX- + CENTENARY]

sex′ change′, the alteration, by surgery and hormone treatments, of a person's morphological sex characteristics to approximate those of the opposite sex. [1975–80]

sex′ chro′matin, *Genetics.* See **Barr body.** [1950–55]

sex′ chro′mosome, *Genetics.* a chromosome, differing in shape or function from other chromosomes, that determines the sex of an individual. [1910–15]

sex•de•cil•lion (seks′di sil′yən), *n., pl.* **-lions,** (*as after a numeral*) **-lion,** *adj.* —*n.* **1.** a cardinal number represented in the U.S. by 1 followed by 51 zeros, and in Great Britain by 1 followed by 96 zeros. —*adj.* **2.** amounting to one sexdecillion in number. [1935–40; SEX- + DECILLION]

sexed (sekst), *adj.* **1.** being of a particular sex or having sexual characteristics. **2.** characterized by sexuality; having sex appeal. [1590–1600; SEX + -ED[3]]

sexed-up (sekst′up′), *adj. Informal.* **1.** sexually aroused. **2.** made sexually attractive or more titillating: *The movie was a sexed-up version of the book.* **3.** made more attractive or interesting, esp. by adding decorative elements: *a sexed-up car.*

sex•e•nar•y (sek′sə ner′ē), *adj.* **1.** senary. **2.** sextuple (def. 1). **3.** (of a numerical system) with a base of six. [1805–15; irreg. < L *sex* SIX + *-enary,* as in SEPTENARY]

sex•en•ni•al (sek sen′ē əl), *adj.* **1.** of or for six years. **2.** occurring every six years. [1640–50; < L *sexenni(s)* six years old (see SIX + *-enn-,* comb. form of *annus* year + *-is* adj. suffix) + -AL[1]] —**sex•en′ni•al•ly,** *adv.*

sex•foil (seks′foil′), *n.* a round ornament consisting of six lobes divided by cusps. [1680–90; SEX- + *-foil,* as in *trefoil*]

sex′ hor′mone, *Biochem.* any of a class of steroid hormones that regulate the growth and function of the reproductive organs or stimulate the development of the secondary sexual characteristics. [1935–40]

sex′ hy′giene, a branch of hygiene concerned with sex and sexual behavior as they relate to individual and community well-being.

sexi-, var. of **sex-:** *sexivalent.*

sex•ism (sek′siz əm), *n.* **1.** attitudes or behavior based on traditional stereotypes of sexual roles. **2.** discrimination or devaluation based on a person's sex, as in restricted job opportunities; esp., such discrimination directed against women. [1965–70; SEX + -ISM, on the model of RACISM]

sex•ist (sek′sist), *adj.* **1.** pertaining to, involving, or fostering sexism: *a sexist remark; sexist advertising.* —*n.* **2.** a person with sexist attitudes or behavior. [1965–70; SEX + -IST, on the model of RACIST]

sex•i•va•lent (sek′sə vā′lənt), *adj. Chem.* hexavalent. Also, **sexavalent.** [1870–75; SEXI- + -VALENT]

sex′ kit′ten, *Informal.* a young woman who is sexy and coquettish. [1955–60]

sex•less (seks′lis), *adj.* **1.** having or seeming to have no sex; neuter. **2.** having or seeming to have no sexual desires. **3.** having no sex appeal; sexually uninteresting. [1590–1600; SEX + -LESS] —**sex′less•ly,** *adv.* —**sex′less•ness,** *n.*

sex-lim•it•ed (seks′lim′i tid), *adj. Genetics.* (of a gene character) expressed in one sex only. [1905–10]

sex-link•age (seks′ling′kij), *n. Genetics.* an association between genes in sex chromosomes such that the characteristics determined by these genes appear more frequently in one sex than in the other. [1910–15]

sex-linked (seks′lingkt′), *adj. Genetics.* **1.** (of a gene) located in a sex chromosome. **2.** (of a character) determined by a gene located in a sex chromosome. [1910–15]

sex′ ob′ject, a person viewed as being of little interest or merit beyond the potential for providing sexual gratification. [1925–30]

sex·ol·o·gy (sek sol′ə jē), *n.* the study of sexual behavior. [1900–05; SEX + -O- + -LOGY] —**sex·o·log·i·cal** (sek′sə loj′i kəl), *adj.* —**sex·ol′o·gist,** *n.*

sex·par·tite (seks pär′tīt), *adj.* **1.** divided into or consisting of six parts. **2.** *Archit.* (of a vault) divided into six compartments by two ogives and three transverse arches, one of which crosses the ogives at the point at which they cross each other. See illus. under **vault**[1]. [1750–60; SEX- + PARTITE]

sex′ play′, erotic caressing, esp. as a prelude to sexual intercourse; foreplay. [1915–20]

sex·ploi·ta·tion (sek′sploi tā′shən), *n. Informal.* the exploitation of sex in films, magazines, etc. [1940–45; b. SEX and EXPLOITATION]

sex·pot (seks′pot′), *n. Informal.* a sexually attractive person. [1955–60, *Amer.*; SEX + POT[1]]

sex′ ra′tio, *Sociol.* the proportional distribution of the sexes in a population aggregate, expressed as the number of males per 100 females. [1905–10]

sex′ shop′, a store that sells products relating to sexual interests or activities. [1970–75]

sex′ sym′bol, a celebrity who is held to possess abundant sex appeal. [1960–65]

sext (sekst), *n. Eccles.* the fourth of the seven canonical hours, or the service for it, originally fixed for the sixth hour of the day taken as noon. [1375–1425; late ME *sexte, syxt* < ML *sexta (hōra)* SIXTH (hour)]

sex·tain (sek′stān), *n. Pros.* **1.** a stanza of six lines. **2.** sestina. [1630–40; b. two obs. F words: *sixain* six-line stanza and *sestine* SESTINA]

sex·tan (sek′stən), *adj.* **1.** (of a fever) characterized by paroxysms that recur every sixth day. —*n.* **2.** a sextan fever. [1650–60; < NL *sextān(a)* *(febris)* sixth day (fever), equiv. to L *sext(us)* SIXTH + *-āna* -AN]

Sex·tans (sek′stənz), *n., gen.* **Sex·tan·tis** (sek stan′tis) for 1. **1.** *Astron.* the Sextant, an equatorial constellation between Hydra and Leo. **2.** (*l.c.*) a bronze coin of ancient Rome, the sixth part of an as, issued during the period of the Republic. [< L *sextāns;* see SEXTANT]

sex·tant (sek′stənt), *n.* **1.** an astronomical instrument used to determine latitude and longitude at sea by measuring angular distances, esp. the altitudes of sun, moon, and stars. **2.** (*cap.*) *Astron.* the constellation Sextans. [1590–1600; < L *sextant-* (s. of *sextāns*) sixth part of a unit. See SEXT, -ANT]

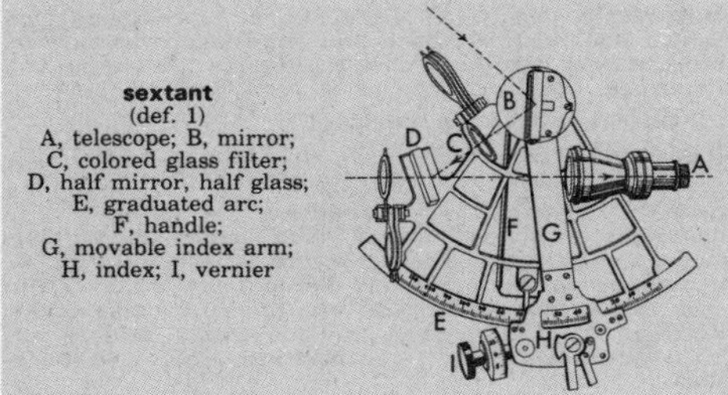

sextant (def. 1)
A, telescope; B, mirror; C, colored glass filter; D, half mirror, half glass; E, graduated arc; F, handle; G, movable index arm; H, index; I, vernier

sex·tern (sek′stərn), *n. Bookbinding.* six gathered sheets folded in two for binding together. [1880–85; < ML *sexternum,* equiv. to L *sex* SIX + *-ternum,* as in VL **quaternum* (see QUIRE[1])]

sex·tet (seks tet′), *n.* **1.** any group or set of six. **2.** Also, **sestet.** *Music.* **a.** a company of six singers or musicians. **b.** a musical composition for a sextet. Also, **sex·tette′.** [1835–45; half-Latinized var. of SESTET; see SEX-]

sex′ ther′apy, *Psychiatry.* treatment of sexual disorders that have psychological causes, as by psychiatric counseling. [1970–75]

sex·tic (sek′stik), *Math.* —*adj.* **1.** of the sixth degree. —*n.* **2.** a quantity of the sixth degree. **3.** an equation of the sixth degree. [1850–55; < L *sext(us)* SIXTH + -IC]

sex·tile (sek′stil, -stīl), *adj.* **1.** *Astron.* noting or pertaining to the aspect or position of two heavenly bodies when 60° distant from each other. —*n.* **2.** *Astron.* a sextile position or aspect. **3.** *Astrol.* a sextile position or aspect, conducive to mental stimulation. **4.** *Statistics.* a quantile for the special case of six equal proportions. [1550–60; < L *sextīlis,* equiv. to *sext(us)* SIXTH + *-īlis* -ILE]

sex·til·lion (seks til′yən), *n., pl.* **-lions,** (*as after a numeral*) **-lion,** *adj.* —*n.* **1.** a cardinal number represented in the U.S. by 1 followed by 21 zeros, and in Great Britain by 1 followed by 36 zeros. —*adj.* **2.** amounting to one sextillion in number. [1680–90; < F < L *sext(us)* SIXTH + *-illion,* as in MILLION] —**sex·til′lionth,** *adj., n.*

sex·to·dec·i·mo (sek′stō des′ə mō′), *n., pl.* **-mos,** *adj. Print.* —*n.* **1.** sixteenmo (def. 1). —*adj.* **2.** sixteenmo (def. 3). [1680–90; < L *sextōdecimō,* abl. sing. of *sextusdecimus* sixteenth]

sex·ton (sek′stən), *n.* **1.** an official who maintains a church building and its contents, rings the bell, etc. **2.** an official who maintains a synagogue and its religious articles, chants the designated portion of the Torah on prescribed days, and assists the cantor in conducting services on festivals. [1275–1325; ME *sexteyn, sekesteyn,* syncopated var. of *segerstane, secristeyn* < AF *segerstaine* SACRISTAN] —**sex′ton·ship′,** *n.*

Sex·ton (sek′stən), *n.* **Anne (Harvey),** 1928–74, U.S. poet.

sex·tu·ple (seks tōō′pəl, -tyōō′-, -tup′əl, seks′tōō pəl, -tyōō-), *adj., v.,* **-pled, -pling.** —*adj.* **1.** consisting of six parts; sexpartite. **2.** six times as great or as many. **3.** *Music.* characterized by six beats or pulses to the measure: *sextuple rhythm.* —*v.t., v.i.* **4.** to make or become six times as great. [1620–30; < L *sext(us)* SIXTH + *-uple,* as in DUPLE, QUADRUPLE]

sex·tu·plet (seks tup′lit, -tōō′plit, -tyōō′-, seks′tōō plit, -tyōō-), *n.* **1.** a group or combination of six things. **2.** one of six offspring born at one birth. **3. sextuplets,** six children or offspring born of one pregnancy. **4.** *Music.* a group of six notes of equal value performed in the same time normally taken to perform four. [1850–55; SEXTUPLE + -ET; cf. TRIPLET]

sex·tu·plex (seks′tōō pleks′, -tyōō-, seks tōō′pleks, -tyōō′-, -tup′leks), *adj.* sixfold; sextuple. [1850–55; SEXTU(PLE) + -PLEX]

sex·tu·pli·cate (*n., adj.* seks tōō′pli kit, -tyōō′-, -tup′li-; *v.* seks tōō′pli kāt′, -tyōō′-, -tup′li-), *n., adj., v.,* **-cat·ed, -cat·ing.** —*n.* **1.** a group, series, or set of six identical copies: *The application is to be submitted in sextuplicate.* —*adj.* **2.** having or consisting of six identical parts; sixfold. **3.** sixth. —*v.t.* **4.** to make six copies of. **5.** to make six times as great. [1650–60; SEXTU(PLE) + *-plicate,* as in DUPLICATE]

sex·u·al (sek′shōō əl *or, esp. Brit.,* seks′yōō-), *adj.* **1.** of, pertaining to, or for sex: *sexual matters; sexual aids.* **2.** occurring between or involving the sexes: *sexual relations.* **3.** having sexual organs or reproducing by processes involving both sexes. [1645–55; < LL *sexuālis,* equiv. to *sexu(s)* SEX + *-ālis* -AL[1]] —**sex′u·al·ly,** *adv.*

sex′ual abuse′, rape, sexual assault, or sexual molestation. Also called **sex abuse.**

sex′ual devia′tion, paraphilia.

sex′ual dimor′phism, the condition in which the males and females in a species are morphologically different, as with many birds. [1885–90] —**sex′ually dimor′phic.**

sex′ual genera′tion, the gametophyte generation in the alternation of generations in plants that produces a zygote from male and female gametes. [1875–80]

sex′ual harass′ment, unwelcome sexual advances made by an employer or superior, esp. when compliance is made a condition of continued employment or advancement. [1975–80]

sex′ual in′tercourse, genital contact, esp. the insertion of the penis into the vagina followed by orgasm; coitus; copulation. [1790–1800]

sex·u·al·i·ty (sek′shōō al′i tē *or, esp. Brit.,* seks′yōō-), *n.* **1.** sexual character; possession of the structural and functional traits of sex. **2.** recognition of or emphasis upon sexual matters. **3.** involvement in sexual activity. **4.** an organism's preparedness for engaging in sexual activity. [1790–1800; SEXUAL + -ITY]

sex·u·al·ize (sek′shōō ə līz′ *or, esp. Brit.,* seks′yōō-), *v.t.,* **-ized, -iz·ing.** to render sexual; endow with sexual characteristics. Also, *esp. Brit.,* **sex′u·al·ise′.** [1830–40; SEXUAL + -IZE] —**sex′u·al·i·za′tion,** *n.*

sex′ually transmit′ted disease′, any disease characteristically transmitted by sexual contact, as gonorrhea, syphilis, genital herpes, and chlamydia. *Abbr.:* STD Also called **venereal disease.**

sex′ual rela′tions, 1. sexual intercourse; coitus. **2.** any sexual activity between individuals. [1945–50]

sex′ual reproduc′tion, *Biol.* reproduction involving the union of gametes. [1880–85]

sex′ual selec′tion, *Biol.* a special type of natural selection in which the sexes acquire distinct forms either because the members of one sex choose mates with particular features or because in the competition for mates among the members of one sex only those with certain traits succeed.

sex′ work′, prostitution. —**sex′ work′er.**

sex·y (sek′sē), *adj.,* **sex·i·er, sex·i·est. 1.** concerned predominantly or excessively with sex; risqué: *a sexy novel.* **2.** sexually interesting or exciting; radiating sexuality: *the sexiest professor on campus.* **3.** excitingly appealing; glamorous: *a sexy new car.* [1920–25; SEX + -Y[1]] —**sex′i·ly,** *adv.* —**sex′i·ness,** *n.*

Sey·chelles (sā shel′, -shelz′), *n.* (*used with a plural v.*) a republic consisting of 115 islands in the Indian Ocean, NE of Madagascar: a member of the Commonwealth of Nations. 67,000; 175 sq. mi. (455 sq. km). *Cap.:* Victoria.

Sey·chel·lois (sā′shel wä′, -shəl-), *n., pl.* **-chel·lois** (-shel wäz′, -wä′, -shəl-), *adj.* —*n.* **1.** a native or inhabitant of Seychelles. —*adj.* **2.** of or noting Seychelles. [< F, equiv. to *Seychell(es)* SEYCHELLES + *-ois* -ESE]

Sey′fert gal′axy (sī′fərt, sē′-), *Astron.* one of a group of spiral galaxies with compact, bright nuclei having characteristically broad emission lines suggestive of very hot gases in violent motion at the center. [1965–70; named after Carl K. Seyfert (1911–60), American astronomer, who first described them]

Sey·han (sā hän′), *n.* **1.** Adana. **2.** a river in S central Turkey, flowing S from the Anatolia plateau to the Mediterranean Sea. 748 mi. (1204 km) long.

Sey·mour (sē′môr, -mōr), *n.* **1. Jane,** c1510–37, third wife of Henry VIII of England and mother of Edward VI. **2.** a city in S Indiana. 15,050. **3.** a town in S Connecticut. 13,434. **4.** a male given name.

SF, 1. science fiction. **2.** sinking fund.

sf, 1. science fiction. **2.** *Music.* sforzando.

s-f, science fiction.

Sfax (sfäks), *n.* a seaport in E Tunisia, in N Africa. 75,000.

Sfc, *Mil.* sergeant first class.

sfer·ics (sfēr′iks, sfer′-), *n.* **1.** (*used with a singular v.*) electronic equipment for determining the position of storms by locating their accompanying atmospherics. **2.** (*used with a plural v.*) the atmospheric discharges located by this device. **3.** Also, **spherics.** (*used with a singular v.*) the study of atmospherics. **4.** spherics[2] (def. 1). [1940–45; shortening and resp. of ATMOSPHERICS]

sfm, surface feet per minute.

Sfor·za (sfôrt′sə; *It.* sfôʀ′tsä), *n.* **1. Count Car·lo** (kär′lô), 1873–1952, Italian statesman: anti-Fascist leader. **2. Fran·ces·co** (frän ches′kô), 1401–66, Italian condottiere and duke of Milan 1450–66. **3.** his father, **Gia·co·muz·zo** (jä′kô mōō′tsô) or **Mu·zio** (mōō′tsyô), 1369–1424, Italian condottiere. **4. Lo·do·vi·co** (lô′dô-vē′kô), (*"the Moor"*), 1451–1508, duke of Milan 1494–1500 (son of Francesco Sforza).

sfor·zan·do (sfôrt sän′dō; *It.* sfôʀ tsän′dô), *adj., adv. Music.* with force; emphatically. Also, **forzando.** [1795–1805; < It, ger. of *sforzare* to show strength < VL **exfortiāre;* see EFFORT]

SFr., (in Switzerland) franc; francs. Also, **Sfr.**

sfu·ma·to (sfōō mä′tō), *n. Fine Arts.* the subtle and minute gradation of tone and color used to blur or veil the contours of a form in painting. [1840–50; < It, ptp. of *sfumare* to gradate tone or color, equiv. to s- < L *ex-* EX-[1] + *fumare* to smoke < L *fūmāre;* see FUME]

sfz, sforzando.

SG, 1. senior grade. **2.** Secretary General. **3.** Solicitor General. **4.** Surgeon General.

sg, *Gram.* singular. Also, **sg.**

s.g., specific gravity.

sga·bel·lo (skä bel′ō; *It.* zgä bel′lô), *n., pl.* **-los,** *It.* **-li** (-lē). *Ital. Furniture.* a side chair of the Renaissance, consisting of a small seat, usually octagonal, often resting on a cubical part and supported either on two carved planks set transversely on edge or on three legs, with a back formed from a carved plank. [1955–60; < It < L *scabellum* footstool, var. of *scabillum,* dim. of *scamnum* stool, bench (< **scabh-nom*)]

S gauge, a model railroad gauge of ⅞ in. (2.2 cm).

sgd., signed.

SGML, Standard Generalized Markup Language: a set of standards, approved by the ISO, enabling a user to create an appropriate markup scheme for tagging the elements of an electronic document, as to facilitate the production of multiple versions in various print and electronic formats.

sgraf·fi·to (skrä fē′tō; *It.* zgräf fē′tô), *n., pl.* **-ti** (-tē). **1.** a technique of ornamentation in which a surface layer of paint, plaster, slip, etc., is incised to reveal a ground of contrasting color. **2.** an object, esp. pottery, decorated by this technique. Cf. **graffito.** [1720–30; < It, ptp. of *sgraffire* to do graffito work; see EX[1], GRAFFITO]

's Gra·ven·ha·ge (sKHRä′vən hä′KHə), Dutch name of The Hague.

Sgt., Sergeant.

Sgt. Maj., Sergeant Major.

sh (sh), *interj.* (used to urge silence.) Also, **shh.** [1840–50]

sh., 1. sheep. **2.** *Bookbinding.* sheet. **3.** shilling; shillings.

SHA, *Navig.* sidereal hour angle.

Shaan·xi (shän′shē′), *n. Pinyin.* a province in N central China. 20,770,000; 75,598 sq. mi. (195,799 sq. km). *Cap.:* Xian. Also, **Shensi.**

Sha·ba (shä′bə), *n.* a province in SE Zaire: important mining area. 3,072,591; 191,878 sq. mi. (496,964 sq. km). *Cap.:* Lubumbashi.

Sha·ban (shə bän′, shä-, shô-), *n.* the eighth month of the Muslim calendar. Cf. **Muslim calendar.** [1760–70; < Ar *sha'bān*]

Shab·bas (shä′bəs), *n. Yiddish.* Sabbath (def. 1). Also, ***Shab′bos, Shab′bes.***

Shab·bas goy (shä′bəs goi′), *Yiddish.* a gentile who performs tasks for Jews in the home or synagogue on the Sabbath or on a holy day that are forbidden Jews on such occasions, as turning on the lights or heat.

Shab·bat (*Seph.* shä bät′), *n. Hebrew.* Sabbath (def. 1).

shab·by (shab′ē), *adj.,* **-bi·er, -bi·est. 1.** impaired by wear, use, etc.; worn: *shabby clothes.* **2.** showing conspicuous signs of wear or neglect: *The rooms on the upper floors of the mansion had a rather shabby appearance, as if they had not been much in use of late.* **3.** wearing worn clothes or having a slovenly or unkempt appearance: *a shabby person.* **4.** run-down, seedy, or dilapidated: *a shabby hotel.* **5.** meanly ungenerous or unfair; contemptible, as persons, actions, etc.: *shabby behavior.* **6.** inferior; not up to par in quality, performance, etc.: *a shabby rendition of the sonata.* [1660–70; *shab* (ME; OE *sceabb* SCAB) + -Y[1]; c. G *schäbig*] —**shab′bi·ly,** *adv.* —**shab′bi·ness,** *n.*

shab·by-gen·teel (shab′ē jen tēl′), *adj.* trying to maintain dignity and self-respect despite shabbiness. [1745–55] —**shab·by-gen·til·i·ty** (shab′ē jen til′i tē), *n.*

Sha·bu·oth (*Seph. Heb.* shä vōō ôt′; *Ashk. Heb.* shə-vōō′ōs, -əs), *n. Judaism.* Shavuoth. Also, **Sha·bu·ot′.**

Sha·cha·rith (*Ashk.* shäKH′ris; *Seph.* shä KHä rēt′), *n. Hebrew.* Shaharith. Also, ***Sha·cha·rit′, Sha′cha·ris.***

Sha·che (shä′chœ′), *n. Pinyin.* a city in W Xinjiang Uygur, in W China, in a large oasis of the Tarim Basin. Also, **Soche.** Also called **Yarkand, Yarkend.**

shack[1] (shak), *n.* **1.** a rough cabin; shanty. **2.** *Informal.* See **radio shack.** —*v.i.* **3. shack up,** *Slang.* **a.** to live together as husband and wife without being legally married. **b.** to have illicit sexual relations. **c.** to live in a shack: *He's shacked up in the mountains.* [1875–80, *Amer.*; cf. earlier *shackly* rickety, prob. akin to RAMSHACKLE (MexSp *jacal* "hut" is a phonetically impossible source)]

CONCISE PRONUNCIATION KEY: act, cāpe, dâre, pärt; set, ēqual; if, īce; ox, ōver, ôrder, oil, bŏŏk, bōōt, out; up, ûrge; child; sing; shoe; thin, *th*at; zh as in *treasure.* ə = *a* as in *alone,* *e* as in *system,* *i* as in *easily,* *o* as in *gallop,* *u* as in *circus;* ᵊ as in *fire* (fīᵊr), *hour* (ouᵊr). l and n can serve as syllabic consonants, as in *cradle* (krād′l), and *button* (but′n). See the full key inside the front cover.

shack² (shak), *v.t. Informal.* to chase and throw back; to retrieve: *to shack a ground ball.* [1825–35, *Amer.*; appar. special use of dial. *shack* to SHAKE]

shack·et (shak′it), *n. Chiefly Rhode Island.* a yellow-jacket or hornet. [orig. uncert.]

shack·le (shak′əl), *n., v.,* **-led, -ling.** —*n.* **1.** a ring or other fastening, as of iron, for securing the wrist, ankle, etc.; fetter. **2.** a hobble or fetter for a horse or other animal. **3.** the U-shaped bar of a padlock, one end of which is pivoted or sliding, the other end of which can be released, as for passing through a staple, and then fastened, as for securing a hasp. **4.** any of various fastening or coupling devices. **5.** Often, **shackles.** anything that serves to prevent freedom of procedure, thought, etc. —*v.t.* **6.** to put a shackle or shackles on; confine or restrain by a shackle or shackles. **7.** to fasten or couple with a shackle. **8.** to restrain in action, thought, etc., as by restrictions; restrict the freedom of. [bef. 1000; (n.) ME *schakle, schakyl(le)*; OE *sceacel* fetter; c. LG *schakel* hobble, ON *skǫkull* wagon pole, (v.) late ME *schaklyn,* deriv. of the n.] —**shack′ler,** *n.*
—**Syn. 1.** chain, manacle, handcuff, gyve, bilboes. **5.** obstacle, obstruction, impediment, encumbrance. **6.** restrict, fetter, chain, handcuff, hobble. **8.** trammel, impede, slow, stultify, dull. —**Ant. 6, 8.** liberate, free.

Shack·le·ton (shak′əl tən), *n.* **Sir Ernest Henry,** 1874–1922, English explorer of the Antarctic.

shack-tap·ping (shak′tap′ing), *n. Canadian Informal.* the making of house-by-house visits to canvass.

shack·up (shak′up′), *n. Slang.* an instance of shacking up: *The census people counted both marriages and shackups.* [1945–50; n. use of v. phrase *shack up*]

shack·y (shak′ē), *adj.,* **shack·i·er, shack·i·est.** rundown; dilapidated: *a shacky old place.* [SHACK + -Y¹]

shad (shad), *n., pl.* (*esp. collectively*) **shad,** (*esp. referring to two or more kinds or species*) **shads. 1.** a deep-bodied herring, *Alosa sapidissima,* of Europe and North America, that migrates up streams to spawn, used for food. **2.** any other fish of the genus *Alosa* or related genera. **3.** any of several unrelated fishes. [bef. 1050; OE *sceadd* (not recorded in ME)]

shad·ber·ry (shad′ber′ē, -bə rē), *n., pl.* **-ries. 1.** the fruit of a shadbush. **2.** the plant itself. [1795–1805, *Amer.*; *shad* (perh. dial. *shad* cool spot, OE *scead* SHADE, shelter) + BERRY]

shad·bush (shad′bo͝osh′), *n.* **1.** the serviceberry, *Amelanchier canadensis.* **2.** any of various other species of *Amelanchier.* Also called **shad·blow** (shad′blō′). [1810–20, *Amer.*; *shad* (see SHADBERRY) + BUSH¹]

shad·chan (*Yiddish, Ashk., Eng.* shät′ᴋʜən; *Seph.* shät ᴋʜän′), *n., pl.* ***shad·cha·nim*** (*Yiddish., Ashk.* shät-ᴋʜô′nim; *Seph.* shät ᴋʜä nēm′), *Eng.* **shad·chans.** *Yiddish and Hebrew.* shadkhan.

Shad·dai (shä dī′), *n. Hebrew.* the Almighty; God. Also, ***Sha·dai′.***

shad·dock (shad′ək), *n.* pomelo. [1690–1700; named after Captain *Shaddock,* 17th-century Englishman who brought the seed to the West Indies from the East Indies]

shade (shād), *n., v.,* **shad·ed, shad·ing.** —*n.* **1.** the comparative darkness caused by the interception or screening of rays of light from an object, place, or area. **2.** a place or an area of comparative darkness, as one sheltered from the sun. **3.** See **window shade. 4.** a lampshade. **5. shades, a.** darkness gathering at the close of day: *Shades of night are falling.* **b.** *Slang.* sunglasses. **c.** a reminder of something: *shades of the Inquisition.* **6.** Usually, **shades.** a secluded or obscure place: *He was living in the shades.* **7.** comparative obscurity. **8.** a specter or ghost. **9.** *Gk. and Rom. Relig.* one of the spirits of the dead inhabiting Hades. **10.** a shadow. **11.** the degree of darkness of a color, determined by the quantity of black or by the lack of illumination. **12.** comparative darkness, as the effect of shadow or dark and light, in pictorial representation; the dark part, or a dark part, of a picture or drawing. **13.** a slight variation or degree: *a shade of difference.* **14.** a little bit; touch, esp. of something that may change the color of or lighten or darken something else: *coffee with a shade of cream.* **15.** anything used for protection against excessive light, heat, etc. **16.** (in architectural shades and shadows) a shadow upon those parts of a solid that are tangent to or turned away from the parallel rays from the theoretical light source. Cf. **shadow** (def. 11). **17. cast** or **put someone in** or **into the shade,** to make another person's efforts seem insignificant by comparison; surpass: *Her playing puts mine in the shade.* **18. the shades,** Hades, as the abode of the spirits of the dead. —*v.t.* **19.** to produce shade in or on. **20.** to obscure, dim, or darken. **21.** to screen or hide from view. **22.** to protect (something) from light, heat, etc., by or as by a screen: *to shade the eyes from a bright light.* **23.** to cover or screen (a candle, light, etc.): *to shade a light to protect the eyes.* **24.** *Fine Arts.* **a.** to introduce degrees of darkness into (a drawing or painting) in order to render light and shadow or give the effect of color. **b.** to render the values of light and dark in (a drawn figure, object, etc.), esp. in order to create the illusion of three-dimensionality. **25.** to change by imperceptible degrees into something else. **26.** to reduce (the price) by way of a concession. —*v.i.* **27.** to pass or change by slight graduations, as one color, quality, or thing into another. **28.** *Agric.* **shade up,** to take shelter (as livestock) from the sun. [bef. 900; 1960–65 for def. 17; (n.) ME *s(c)hade,* OE *sceade* (see SHADOW); c. G *Schatten,* Goth *skadus,* Gk *skótos;* (v.) ME *schaden,* deriv. of the n.] —**shade′less,** *adj.* —**shade′less·ness,** *n.*
—**Syn. 1.** obscurity, gloom, dusk. SHADE, SHADOW imply partial darkness or something less bright than the surroundings. SHADE indicates the lesser brightness and heat of an area where the direct rays of light do not fall: *the shade of a tree.* It differs from SHADOW in that it implies no particular form or definite limit, whereas SHADOW often refers to the form or outline of the object that intercepts the light: *the shadow of a dog.* **8.** apparition, phantom, spirit. **13.** bit. **14.** trace, hint, suggestion. **15.** veil, screen. See **curtain. 20.** cloud, blur, obfuscate. **21.** conceal, shelter. —**Ant. 1.** light, glare.
—**Regional Variation. 3.** See **window shade.**

shade′ cloth′, a covering made of cloth or plastic, esp. one used to control the amount of sunlight to which plants are exposed. Also, **shade′cloth′.**

shad·ed (shā′did), *adj. Print.* noting or pertaining to an ornamented type in which a thin white line appears along one edge of each of the main strokes of a character. [1575–85; SHADE + -ED²] —**shad′ed·ness,** *n.*

shade′ deck′, *Naut.* **1.** a light deck supported by stanchions. **2.** the space below this, open at the sides. [1890–95]

shade-grown (shād′grōn′), *adj. Hort.* grown in the shade, esp. in artificial shade, as under a cloth. [1905–10, *Amer.*]

shade′ tree′, a tree planted or valued for its shade. [1800–10, *Amer.*]

shad·fly (shad′flī′), *n., pl.* **-flies.** mayfly (def. 1). [1830–40, *Amer.*; so called because they hatch at the time of year when shad are running]

shad·ing (shā′ding), *n.* **1.** a slight variation or difference of color, character, etc. **2.** the act of a person or thing that shades. **3.** the representation of the different values of color or light and dark in a painting or drawing. [1605–15; SHADE + -ING¹]

shad·khan (*Yiddish, Ashk., Eng.* shät′ᴋʜən; *Seph.* shät ᴋʜän′), *n., pl.* ***shad·kha·nim*** (*Yiddish, Ashk.* shät-ᴋʜô′nim; *Seph.* shät ᴋʜä nēm′), *Eng.* **shad·khans.** *Yiddish and Hebrew.* a person who arranges Jewish marriages; matchmaker. Also, ***shadchan, schatchen.*** [Yiddish *shatkhn* < Heb *shadhkhān,* deriv. of *shiddēkh* arrange a marriage]

sha·doof (shä do͞of′), *n.* a device used in Egypt and other Eastern countries for raising water, esp. for irrigation, consisting of a long suspended rod with a bucket at one end and a weight at the other. Also, **shaduf.** [1830–40; < Egyptian Ar *shadūf*]

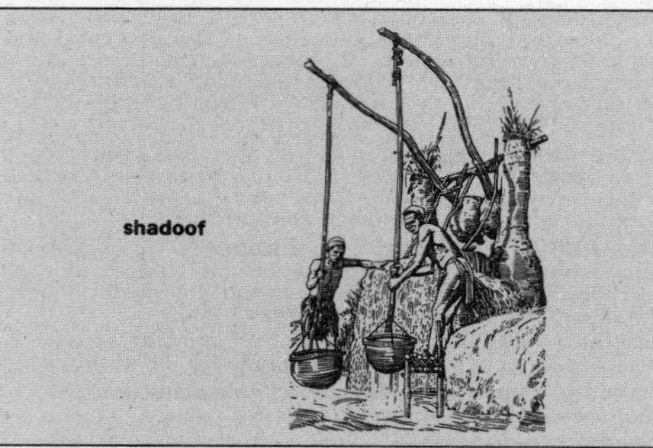
shadoof

shad·ow (shad′ō), *n.* **1.** a dark figure or image cast on the ground or some surface by a body intercepting light. **2.** shade or comparative darkness, as in an area. **3. shadows,** darkness, esp. that coming after sunset. **4.** shelter; protection: *sanctuary in the shadow of the church.* **5.** a slight suggestion; trace: *beyond the shadow of a doubt.* **6.** a specter or ghost: *pursued by shadows.* **7.** a hint or faint, indistinct image or idea; intimation: *shadows of things to come.* **8.** a mere semblance: *the shadow of power.* **9.** a reflected image. **10.** (in painting, drawing, graphics, etc.) **a.** the representation of the absence of light on a form. **b.** the dark part of a picture, esp. as representing the absence of illumination: *Rembrandt's figures often emerge gradually from the shadows.* **11.** (in architectural shades and shadows) a dark figure or image cast by an object or part of an object upon a surface that would otherwise be illuminated by the theoretical light source. Cf. **shade** (def. 16). **12.** a period or instance of gloom, unhappiness, mistrust, doubt, dissension, or the like, as in friendship or one's life: *Their relationship was not without shadows.* **13.** a dominant or pervasive threat, influence, or atmosphere, esp. one causing gloom, fear, doubt, or the like: *They lived under the shadow of war.* **14.** an inseparable companion: *The dog was his shadow.* **15.** a person who follows another in order to keep watch upon that person, as a spy or detective. —*v.t.* **16.** to overspread with shadow; shade. **17.** to cast a gloom over; cloud: *The incident shadowed their meeting.* **18.** to screen or protect from light, heat, etc.; shade. **19.** to follow (a person) about secretly, in order to keep watch over his movements. **20.** to represent faintly, prophetically, etc. (often fol. by *forth*). **21.** *Archaic.* to shelter or protect. **22.** *Archaic.* to shade in painting, drawing, etc. —*adj.* **23.** of or pertaining to a shadow cabinet. **24.** without official authority: *a shadow government.* [bef. 900; (n.) ME *sch(e)adew(e), schadow, shadw(e),* OE *scead(u)we,* obl. case of *sceadu* SHADE; (v.) ME; OE *sceadwian* to protect, cover, OVERSHADOW, deriv. of the n.; cf. OS *skadowan, skadoian,* Goth *-skadwjan*] —**shad′ow·er,** *n.* —**shad′·ow·less,** *adj.* —**shad′ow·like′,** *adj.*
—**Syn. 1.** See **shade.**

shad′ow box′, a shallow, rectangular frame fronted with a glass panel, used to show and at the same time protect items on display, as paintings, coins, or jewelry. Also called **shad′ow box′ frame′.** [1905–10]

shad·ow·box (shad′ō boks′), *v.i.* **1.** to make the motions of attack and defense, as in boxing, as a training or conditioning procedure. **2.** to evade or avoid direct or decisive action. [1915–20; SHADOW + BOX²]

shad′ow cab′inet, (in the British Parliament) a group of prominent members of the opposition who are expected to hold positions in the cabinet when their party assumes power. [1905–10]

shad·owed (shad′ōd), *adj. Print.* noting or pertaining to an ornamented type in which the embellishment is outside the character, esp. one in which a black line at one side and at the top or bottom gives the effect of a cast shadow. [1350–1400 in general sense; ME; see SHADOW, -ED²]

shad·ow·graph (shad′ō graf′, -gräf′), *n.* **1.** a picture produced by throwing a shadow, as of the hands, on a lighted screen, wall, or the like. **2.** See **shadow play. 3.** a radiograph. [1885–90; SHADOW + -GRAPH] —**shad·ow·graph·ic** (shad′ō graf′ik), *adj.* —**shad′ow·graph′·ist,** *n.* —**shad′ow·graph′y,** *n.*

shad·ow·ing (shad′ō ing), *n. Cytol., Histol.* a method of enhancing the visibility of the surface features of a specimen for electron microscopic viewing by spraying it from one side with a coating of metal atoms. [SHADOW + -ING¹]

shad·ow·land (shad′ō land′), *n.* a land or region of shadows, phantoms, unrealities, or uncertainties: *the shadowland of imagination.* [1815–25; SHADOW + -LAND]

shad′ow mask′, *Television.* a perforated metal plate situated behind the faceplate of a color television picture tube and having holes aligned to insure that each of three electron beams strikes only its corresponding red, green, or blue phosphor dot. Also called **aperture mask.** [1950–55]

shad′ow pin′, *Navig.* a vertical pin set in an azimuth instrument or at the center of a compass card, indicating by the direction of its shadow the azimuth of the sun. [1890–95]

shad′ow play′, a show in which shadows of puppets, flat figures, or live actors are projected onto a lighted screen. Also called **shadowgraph, shad′ow pan′·tomime, shad′ow show′, shad′ow the′ater.** [1890–95]

shad′ow roll′, sheepskin that is placed just below the eyes of a pacing horse in order to prevent it from seeing moving shadows cast by its body.

shad·ow·y (shad′ō ē), *adj.,* **-ow·i·er, -ow·i·est. 1.** resembling a shadow in faintness, slightness, etc.: *shadowy outlines.* **2.** unsubstantial, unreal, or illusory: *shadowy preoccupations.* **3.** abounding in shadow; shady: *a shadowy path.* **4.** enveloped in shadow. **5.** casting a shadow. [1325–75; ME *shadewy.* See SHADOW, -Y¹] —**shad′ow·i·ness,** *n.*

Shad·rach (shad′rak, shā′drak), *n.* a companion of Daniel who, with Meshach and Abednego, was thrown into the fiery furnace of Nebuchadnezzar and came out unharmed. Dan. 3:12–30.

sha·duf (shä do͞of′), *n.* shadoof.

Shad·well (shad′wel′, -wəl), *n.* **Thomas,** 1642?–92, English dramatist: poet laureate 1688–92.

shad·y (shā′dē), *adj.,* **shad·i·er, shad·i·est. 1.** abounding in shade; shaded: *shady paths.* **2.** giving shade: *a shady tree.* **3.** shadowy; indistinct; spectral. **4.** of dubious character; rather disreputable: *shady dealings.* **5. on the shady side of,** *Informal.* beyond (the specified age); more than: *on the shady side of 40.* [1570–80; SHADE + -Y¹] —**shad′i·ly,** *adv.* —**shad′i·ness,** *n.*

Shaf·i·'i (shaf′ē ē, shä′fē ē), *n. Islam.* one of the four schools of Islamic law, founded by al-Shafi'i. Cf. **Hanafi, Hanbali, Maliki.** [< Ar *Shāfi'ī,* deriv. of name of founder *al-Shāfi'ī*] —**Shaf′i·'ite′,** *n.*

shaft (shaft, shäft), *n.* **1.** a long pole forming the body of various weapons, as lances, halberds, or arrows. **2.** something directed or barbed as in sharp attack: *shafts of sarcasm.* **3.** a ray or beam: *a shaft of sunlight.* **4.** a long, comparatively straight handle serving as an important or balancing part of an implement or device, as of a hammer, ax, golf club, or other implement. **5.** *Mach.* a rotating or oscillating round, straight bar for transmitting motion and torque, usually supported on bearings and carrying gears, wheels, or the like, as a propeller shaft on a ship, or a drive shaft of an engine. **6.** a flagpole. **7.** *Archit.* **a.** that part of a column or pier between the base and capital. See diag. under **column. b.** any distinct, slender, vertical masonry feature engaged in a wall or pier and usually supporting or feigning to support an arch or vault. **8.** a monument in the form of a column, obelisk, or the like. **9.** either of the parallel bars of wood between which the animal drawing a vehicle is hitched. **10.** any well-like passage or vertical enclosed space, as in a building: *an elevator shaft.* **11.** *Mining.* a vertical or sloping passageway leading to the surface. **12.** *Bot.* the trunk of a tree. **13.** *Zool.* the main stem or midrib of a feather. **14.** Also called **leaf.** *Textiles.* the harness or warp with reference to the pattern of interlacing threads in weave constructions (usually used in combination): *an eight-shaft satin.* **15.** the part of a candelabrum that supports the branches. —*v.t.* **16.** to push or propel with a pole: *to shaft a boat through a tunnel.* **17.** *Informal.* to treat in a harsh, unfair, or treacherous manner. [bef. 1000; ME; OE *sceaft;* c. G *Schaft;* cf. L *scāpus* shaft, Gk *skēptron* SCEPTER] —**shaft′less,** *adj.* —**shaft′like′,** *adj.*

shaft′ al′ley, *Naut.* an enclosure on a ship for housing a propeller shaft and a walk for oilers. Also called **shaft′ tun′nel.**

Shaftes·bur·y (shafts′bə rē, shäfts′-), *n.* **1. Anthony Ashley Cooper, 1st Earl of,** 1621–83, English statesman. **2. Anthony Ashley Cooper, 3rd Earl of,** 1671–1713, English moral philosopher (grandson of Anthony Ashley Cooper, 1st Earl of Shaftesbury). **3. Anthony Ashley Cooper, 7th Earl of,** 1801–85, English philanthropist.

shaft′ grave′, *Archaeol.* a grave consisting of a deep, rectangular pit with vertical sides, roofed over with a stone slab. [1905–10]

CONCISE ETYMOLOGY KEY: <, descended or borrowed from; >, whence; b., blend of, blended; c., cognate with; cf., compare; deriv., derivative; equiv., equivalent; imit., imitative; obl., oblique; r., replacing; s., stem; sp., spelling, spelled; resp., respelling, respelled; trans., translation; ?, origin unknown; *, unattested; ‡, probably earlier than. See the full key inside the front cover.

shaft′ horse′power, the horsepower delivered to the driving shaft of an engine, as measured by a torsion meter. *Abbr.:* shp, SHP [1905–10]

shaft′ house′, a structure housing machinery and other equipment at the top of a mine shaft. [1870–75]

shaft·ing (shaf′ting, shäf′-), *n.* **1.** a number of shafts. **2.** *Mach.* a system of shafts, as the overhead shafts formerly used for driving the machinery of a mill. **3.** steel bar stock used for shafts. **4.** *Archit.* a system of shafts, as those around a pier or in the reveals of an archway. **5.** *Slang.* an instance of unique or unfair treatment: *The owners gave him a real shafting on the deal.* [1815–25; SHAFT + -ING[1]]

shag[1] (shag), *n., v.,* **shagged, shag·ging.** —*n.* **1.** rough, matted hair, wool, or the like. **2.** a mass of this. **3.** a hairdo in which hair is cut in slightly uneven, overlapping layers downward from the crown, sometimes with the hair at the front and back hairlines left longer or wispier than the rest. **4.** a cloth with a nap, as of silk or a heavy or rough woolen fabric. **5.** a rug or carpet with a thick, shaggy pile. **6.** a coarse tobacco cut into fine shreds. —*v.t., v.i.* **7.** to make or become rough or shaggy. [bef. 1050; OE *sceacga* (wooly) hair (not recorded in ME); c. ON *skegg* beard; akin to SHAW] —**shag′like′,** *adj.*

shag[2] (shag), *n.* **1.** a small cormorant, *Phalacrocorax aristotelis,* of European coasts. **2.** any of several small cormorants of the Southern Hemisphere. [1560–70; perh. special use of SHAG[1], applied first to bird's crest]

shag[3] (shag), *v.,* **shagged, shag·ging,** *n.* —*v.i.* **1.** to dance a step with a vigorous hopping on each foot. —*n.* **2.** this dance step. [1350–1400; perh. var. of SHOG]

shag[4] (shag), *v.t.,* **shagged, shag·ging.** **1.** to chase or follow after; pursue. **2.** to go after and bring back; fetch. **3.** *Baseball.* to retrieve and throw back (fly balls) in batting practice. **4.** **shag ass,** *Slang (vulgar).* to depart, esp. hurriedly; get going. [1930–35; orig. uncert.; see SHACK[2]]

shag·a·nap·pi (shag′ə nap′ē, shag′ə nap′ē), *n. Chiefly Canadian.* thongs, straps, or lacings made of rawhide. Cf. **babiche.** [1735–45; < Swampy Cree (dial. of Cree spoken in Manitoba and Ontario) *pi·ša·kana·piy* (cf. Cree *pi·ša·kan* leather, *-a·piy* string)]

shag·bark (shag′bärk′), *n.* **1.** a hickory, *Carya ovata,* having rough, shaggy bark and yielding a valuable wood. **2.** the wood. **3.** the ellipsoidal, slightly angular nut of this tree. Also called **shag′bark hick′ory** (for defs. 1, 2). [1685–95; SHAG(GY) + BARK[2]]

shagged (shagd), *adj. Informal.* weary; exhausted (usually fol. by *out*): *They were completely shagged out from the long trip.* [1930–35; orig. uncert.]

shag·gy (shag′ē), *adj.,* **-gi·er, -gi·est.** **1.** covered with or having long, rough hair. **2.** untidy; unkempt: *a shaggy person.* **3.** rough and matted; forming a bushy mass, as the hair or mane. **4.** having a rough nap, as cloth. **5.** characterized by sloppy planning or execution: *a shaggy production of* Macbeth. [1580–90; SHAG[1] + -Y[1]] —**shag′gi·ly,** *adv.* —**shag′gi·ness,** *n.*

shag′gy-dog′ sto′ry (shag′ē dôg′, -dog′), a funny story, traditionally about a talking dog, that, after an often long and involved narration of unimportant incidents, has an absurd or irrelevant punch line. [1945–50]

shag·gy-mane (shag′ē mān′), *n.* an edible inky-cap mushroom, *Coprinus comatus,* having an elongated, shaggy pileus. Also called, **shag′gy cap′.** [1905–10]

sha·green (shə grēn′), *n.* **1.** an untanned leather with a granular surface, prepared from the hide of a horse, shark, seal, etc. **2.** the rough skin of certain sharks, used as an abrasive. —*adj.* **3.** Also, **sha·greened′.** resembling, covered with, or made of shagreen. [1605–15; < F *chagrin,* var. of *sagrin* < Turk *sağrı* rump, crupper]

shah (shä, shô), *n. (often cap.)* (formerly, in Iran) king; sovereign. [1560–70; < Pers: king] —**shah′dom,** *n.*

sha·ha·da (shä hä′də), *n. Islam.* the Islamic profession of faith, "There is no god but Allah, and Muhammad is his messenger": the first of the Pillars of Islam. Also, **Sha·ha′da, sha·ha′dah.** [< Ar *shahādah* lit., witness]

Shah A·lam (shä′ ä′ləm), a town in and the capital of Selangor state, in W Malaysia. 24,138.

Shah·an·sha (shä′än shä′, shô′än shô′), *n.* the title of the former ruler of Iran. [< Pers: king of kings.]

Sha·hap·ti·an (shä hap′tē ən), *n., pl.* **-ti·ans,** *(esp. collectively)* **-ti·an,** *adj.* Sahaptin.

Sha·ha·rith (*Ashk.* shäKH′ris; *Seph.* shä KHä rēt′), *n. Hebrew.* the religious service celebrated by Jews every morning. Also, ***Sha·ha·rit′, Sha′ha·ris, Shacharith.*** Cf. ***Maariv, Minhah.*** [*Shaḥărīth* lit., morning time]

Shah Ja·han (shä′ jə hän′), 1592?–1666, Mogul emperor in India 1628?–58: built the Taj Mahal. Also, **Shah′ Je·han′.**

Shah·ja·han·pur (shä′jə hän′po͝or′), *n.* a city in central Uttar Pradesh, in N India. 144,058.

Shahn (shän), *n.* **Ben,** 1898–1969, U.S. painter, born in Lithuania.

shaikh (shāk, shīk), *n.* **1.** sheik (def. 1). **2.** Also called **pir.** (in Sufism) the spiritual guide. Also, **shaykh.** [< Ar *shaykh* lit., old man]

Shai·khi (shā kē′, shī-), *n. Islam.* a dissident Shi'ite sect that developed in the 19th century, composed of followers of Ahmad Ahsa'i (c1741–1826). [< Ar *shaykhi,* equiv. to *shaykh* SHAIKH (title of the leader of the sect) + *-ī* suffix of appurtenance]

Shaikh·ism (shā′kiz əm, shī′-), *n. Islam.* the beliefs and practices of the Shaikhi. [SHAIKH(I) + -ISM]

sha·'ir (shä ēr′), *n. Islam.* a person, esp. a poet, endowed with unique perception or insight. [< Ar *shā'ir*]

Shairp (shârp, shärp), *n.* **John Campbell** *("Principal Shairp"),* 1819–85, English critic, poet, and educator.

Shai·tan (shī tän′), *n.* Ash-Shaytān. [< Ar *Shayṭān,* c. Heb *śāṭān* SATAN]

Shai·va (shī′və), *n. Hinduism.* a Bhakti sect devoted to Shiva. Also, **Saiva.** —**Shai′vite,** *n.*

Shak., Shakespeare.

shake (shāk), *v.,* **shook, shak·en, shak·ing,** *n.* —*v.i.* **1.** to move or sway with short, quick, irregular vibratory movements. **2.** to tremble with emotion, cold, etc. **3.** to become dislodged and fall (usually fol. by *off* or *down*): *Sand shakes off easily.* **4.** to move something, or its support or container, briskly to and fro or up and down, as in mixing: *Shake before using.* **5.** to totter; become unsteady. **6.** to clasp another's hand in greeting, agreement, congratulations, etc.: *Let's shake and be friends again.* **7.** *Music.* to execute a trill. —*v.t.* **8.** to move (something or its support or container) to and fro or up and down with short, quick, forcible movements: *to shake a bottle of milk.* **9.** to brandish or flourish: *to shake a stick at someone.* **10.** to grasp (someone or something) firmly in an attempt to move or rouse by, or as by, vigorous movement to and fro: *We shook the tree.* **11.** to dislodge or dispense (something) by short, quick, forcible movements of its support or container: *We shook nuts from the tree.* **12.** to cause to sway, rock, totter, etc.: *to shake the very foundations of society.* **13.** to agitate or disturb profoundly in feeling: *The experience shook him badly.* **14.** to cause to doubt or waver; weaken: *to shake one's self-esteem.* **15.** *Music.* to trill (a note). **16.** to mix (dice) by rolling in the palm of the hand before they are cast. **17.** to get rid of; elude: *They tried to shake their pursuers.* **18.** **shake a leg,** *Informal.* **a.** to hurry up; get a move on. **b.** to dance. **19.** **shake down, a.** to cause to descend by shaking; bring down. **b.** to cause to settle. **c.** to condition; test: *to shake down a ship.* **d.** *Informal.* to extort money from. **e.** *Slang.* to search (someone), esp. to detect concealed weapons. **20.** **shake hands.** See **hand** (def. 64). **21.** **shake off, a.** to rid oneself of; reject. **b.** to get away from; leave behind. **c.** *Baseball, Softball.* (of a pitcher) to indicate rejection of (a sign by the catcher for a certain pitch) by shaking the head or motioning with the glove. **22.** **shake one's head, a.** to indicate disapproval, disagreement, negation, or uncertainty by turning one's head from side to side. **b.** to indicate approval, agreement, or acceptance by nodding one's head up and down. **23.** **shake the dust from one's feet.** See **dust** (def. 18). **24.** **shake up, a.** to shake in order to mix or loosen. **b.** to upset; jar. **c.** to agitate mentally or physically: *The threat of attack has shaken up the entire country.* —*n.* **25.** an act or instance of shaking, rocking, swaying, etc. **26.** tremulous motion. **27.** a tremor. **28.** **shakes,** *(used with a singular v.) Informal.* a state or spell of trembling, as caused by fear, fever, cold, etc. (usually prec. by *the*). **29.** a disturbing blow; shock. **30.** *Informal.* See **milk shake.** **31.** the act or a manner of clasping another's hand in greeting, agreement, etc.: *He has a strong shake.* **32.** *Informal.* chance or fate; deal: *a fair shake.* **33.** a cast of the dice: *He threw an eight on his last shake.* **34.** something resulting from shaking. **35.** an earthquake. **36.** a fissure in the earth. **37.** an internal crack or fissure in timber. **38.** *Music.* trill[1] (def. 9). **39.** an instant: *I'll be with you in a shake.* **40.** *Carpentry.* a shingle or clapboard formed by splitting a short log into a number of tapered radial sections with a hatchet. **41.** *Horol.* (in an escapement) the distance between the nearer corner of one pallet and the nearest tooth of the escape wheel when the other pallet arrests an escape tooth. **42.** *Chiefly South Midland U.S.* shaker (def. 2). **43.** a dance deriving from the twist. **44.** *Slang.* the dried leaves of the marijuana plant. **45.** **no great shakes,** *Informal.* of no particular ability; unimportant; common. **46.** **two shakes** or **two shakes of a lamb's tail,** a very short time; a moment. [bef. 900; (v.) ME *s(c)haken,* OE *sceacan;* c. LG *schacken,* ON *skaka;* (n.) deriv. of the v.] —**shak′a·ble, shake′a·ble,** *adj.*

—**Syn.** **1.** oscillate, waver. SHAKE, QUIVER, TREMBLE, VIBRATE refer to an agitated movement that, in living things, is often involuntary. To SHAKE is to agitate more or less quickly, abruptly, and often unevenly so as to disturb the poise, stability, or equilibrium of a person or thing: *a pole shaking under his weight.* To QUIVER is to exhibit a slight vibratory motion such as that resulting from disturbed or irregular (surface) tension: *The surface of the pool quivered in the breeze.* To TREMBLE (used more often of a person) is to be agitated by intermittent, involuntary movements of the muscles, much like shivering and caused by fear, cold, weakness, great emotion, etc.: *Even stout hearts tremble with dismay.* To VIBRATE is to exhibit a rapid, rhythmical motion: *A violin string vibrates when a bow is drawn across it.* **2.** shudder, shiver. **14.** daunt.

shake·down (shāk′doun′), *n.* **1.** extortion, as by blackmail or threats of violence. **2.** a thorough search: *a shakedown of prison cells to uncover hidden drugs.* **3.** a bed, as of straw or blankets, spread on the floor. **4.** any makeshift bed. **5.** the act or process of shaking down. **6.** Also called **shake′down cruise′, shake′down flight′.** a cruise or flight intended to prepare a new vessel or aircraft for regular service by accustoming the crew to its features and peculiarities, breaking in and adjusting machinery, etc. Also, **shake′-down′.** [1490–1500; n., adj. use of v. phrase *shake down*]

shak′en ba′by syn′drome, a usu. fatal condition of abused infants brought on by violent shaking by the arms or shoulders that causes severe internal bleeding, esp. around the brain and in the eyes. [1985–1990]

shake·out (shāk′out′), *n.* **1.** an elimination or winnowing out of some competing businesses, products, etc., as a result of intense competition in a market of declining sales or rising standards of quality. **2.** a rapid decline in the values of certain securities sold in stock exchanges or the like. [1890–95; n. use of v. phrase *shake out*]

shak·er (shā′kər), *n.* **1.** a person or thing that shakes. **2.** a container with a perforated top from which a seasoning, condiment, sugar, flour, or the like is shaken onto food. **3.** any of various containers for shaking beverages to mix the ingredients: *a cocktail shaker.* **4.** a dredger or caster. **5.** *(cap.)* a member of the Millennial Church, originating in England in the middle of the 18th century and brought to the U.S. in 1774, advocating celibacy, common ownership of property, and a strict and simple way of life: so called from their practice of shaking during religious services. —*adj.* **6.** *(cap.)* noting or pertaining to a style of something produced by Shakers and characterized by simplicity of form, lack of ornamentation, fine craftsmanship, and functionality. [1400–50; late ME; see SHAKE, -ER[1]]

Shak′er Heights′, a city in NE Ohio, near Cleveland. 34,759.

Shak·er·ism (shā′kə riz′əm), *n.* the beliefs and practices of the Shakers. [1800–10, *Amer.;* SHAKER + -ISM]

Shake·speare (shāk′spēr), *n.* **William,** 1564–1616, English poet and dramatist. Also, **Shakspere, Shake′·spear.**

Shake·spear·e·an (shāk spēr′ē ən), *adj.* **1.** of, pertaining to, or suggestive of Shakespeare or his works. —*n.* **2.** a Shakespearean scholar; a specialist in the study of the works of Shakespeare. Also, **Shake·spear′i·an.** [1810–20; SHAKESPEARE + -AN] —**Shake·spear′e·an·ism, Shake·spear′i·an·ism,** *n.*

Shake·spear·e·an·a (shāk spēr′ē an′ə, -ä′nə, -ā′nə), *n.pl.* a collection of historical artifacts, letters, etc., belonging or pertaining to William Shakespeare. [1710–20; SHAKESPEARE + -ANA]

Shakespear′ean son′net, a sonnet form used by Shakespeare and having the rhyme scheme *abab, cdcd, efef, gg.* Also called **English sonnet, Elizabethan sonnet.** [1900–05]

shake-up (shāk′up′), *n.* a thorough change in a business, department, or the like, as by dismissals, demotions, etc. [1900–05; n. use of v. phrase *shake up*]

Shakh·ty (shäKH′tē), a city in the SW Russian Federation in Europe, in the Donets Basin. 210,000.

shak·ing (shā′king), *n.* **1.** the act of a person or thing that shakes. **2.** ague, with or without chill and fever. **3.** **shakings,** *Naut.* waste rope, canvas, etc. [1175–1225; ME; see SHAKE, -ING[1]] —**shak′ing·ly,** *adv.*

shak′ing pal′sy, *Pathol.* parkinsonism. [1605–15]

shak·o (shak′ō, shā′kō), *n., pl.* **shak·os, shak·oes.** a military cap in the form of a cylinder or truncated cone, with a visor and a plume or pompon. [1805–15; < F *schako* < Hungarian *csákó,* short for *csákós (süveg)* peaked (cap), adj. deriv. of *csák* peak < MHG *zacke* peak, point; see TACK[1]]

shako

Shaks., Shakespeare.

Shak·spere (shāk′spēr), *n.* **William.** See **Shakespeare, William.** —**Shak·sper′i·an,** *adj., n.* —**Shak·sper′i·an·ism,** *n.*

Shak·ta (shäk′tə), *n. Hinduism.* a person who worships Shakti as the wife of Shiva. Also, **Sakta.** [< Skt *śākta* pertaining to Shakti]

Shak·ti (shuk′tē), *n. Hinduism.* **1.** the female principle or organ of generative power. **2.** the wife of a deity, esp. of Shiva. Cf. **Divine Mother.** Also, **Sakti.** [< Skt *śakti*]

Shak·tism (shuk′tiz əm, shäk′-), *n. Hinduism.* the worship of Shakti as the wife of Shiva. Also, **Saktism.** [1900–05; SHAKT(I) + -ISM]

Sha·kun·ta·la (shə ko͝on′tə lä′), *n.* Sakuntala.

shak·y (shā′kē), *adj.,* **shak·i·er, shak·i·est.** **1.** tending to shake or tremble. **2.** trembling; tremulous. **3.** liable to break down or give way; insecure; not to be depended upon: *a shaky bridge.* **4.** wavering, as in allegiance: *His loyalty, always shaky, was now nonexistent.* [1695–1705; SHAKE + -Y[1]] —**shak′i·ly,** *adv.* —**shak′i·ness,** *n.*

Sha·kya·mu·ni (shä′kyə mo͝o′nē), *n.* Sakyamuni.

sha·lach ma·noth (*Yiddish, Ashk.* shä′läKH mô′nōs, -nəs, shläKH′; *Seph.* shä läKH′ mä nôt′), *Yiddish and Hebrew.* **1.** the practice of giving gifts to one another or to the needy on Purim. **2.** any such gift, as cake, fruit, or money for charity. Also, ***sha′lach mo′nos.*** [lit., giving out parts]

shale (shāl), *n.* a rock of fissile or laminated structure formed by the consolidation of clay or argillaceous material. [1740–50; orig. uncert.; cf. obs. *shale* to split (said of stone), to shell, deriv. of *shale* shell, husk, OE *scealu* shell, husk; see SCALE[2]] —**shale′like′, shal′ey,** *adj.*

shale′ oil′, petroleum distilled from oil shale. [1855–60]

shall (shal; *unstressed* shəl), *auxiliary v., pres. sing. 1st pers.* **shall,** *2nd* **shall** or *(Archaic)* **shalt,** *3rd* **shall,** *pres. pl.* **shall;** *past sing. 1st pers.* **should,** *2nd* **should** or *(Archaic)* **shouldst** or **should·est,** *3rd* **should,** *past pl.* **should;** *imperative, infinitive, and participles lacking.* **1.** plan to, intend to, or expect to: *I shall go later.* **2.**

CONCISE PRONUNCIATION KEY: act, cāpe, dâre, pärt; set, ēqual; if, īce; ox, ōver, ôrder, oil, bo͝ok, bo͞ot, out; up, ûrge; child; sing; shoe; thin, *that;* zh as in *treasure.* ə = *a* as in *alone, e* as in *system, i* as in *easily, o* as in *gallop, u* as in *circus;* ə as in *fire* (fīər), *hour* (ouər). l and n can serve as syllabic consonants, as in *cradle* (krād′l), and *button* (but′n). See the full key inside the front cover.

will have to, is determined to, or definitely will: *You shall do it. He shall do it.* **3.** (in laws, directives, etc.) must; is or are obliged to: *The meetings of the council shall be public.* **4.** (used interrogatively in questions, often in invitations): *Shall we go?* [bef. 900; ME *shal,* OE *sceal;* c. OS *skal,* OHG *scal,* ON *skal;* cf. G *soll,* D *zal*]

—Usage. The traditional rule of usage guides dates from the 17th century and says that to denote future time SHALL is used in the first person (*I shall leave. We shall go*) and WILL in all other persons (*You will be there, won't you? He will drive us to the airport. They will not be at the meeting*). The rule continues that to express determination, WILL is used in the first person (*We will win the battle*) and SHALL in the other two persons (*You shall not bully us. They shall not pass*). Whether this rule was ever widely observed is doubtful. Today, WILL is used overwhelmingly in all three persons and in all types of speech and writing both for the simple future and to express determination. SHALL has some use in all persons, chiefly in formal writing or speaking, to express determination: *I shall return. We shall overcome.* SHALL also occurs in the language of laws and directives: *All visitors shall observe posted regulations.* Most educated native users of American English do not follow the textbook rule in making a choice between SHALL and WILL. See also **should.**

shal•loon (sha lo͞on′), *n.* a light, twilled woolen fabric used chiefly for linings. [1655–65; < F *chalon,* after *Châlons-sur-Marne,* where made]

shal•lop (shal′əp), *n.* any of various vessels formerly used for sailing or rowing in shallow waters, esp. a two-masted, gaff-rigged vessel of the 17th and 18th centuries. [1570–80; < F *chaloupe* < G *Schaluppe* SLOOP]

shal•lot (shal′ət, shə lot′), *n.* **1.** a plant, *Allium cepa aggregatum* (or *A. ascalonicum*), related to the onion, having a divided bulb used for flavoring in cookery. **2.** the bulb of this plant. [1655–65; aph. var. of earlier *eschalot* < F *échalote,* dim. of MF *eschaloigne* SCALLION]

shal•low (shal′ō), *adj.,* **-er, -est,** *n., adv., v.* **—***adj.* **1.** of little depth; not deep: *shallow water.* **2.** lacking depth; superficial: *a mind that is not narrow but shallow.* **3.** taking in a relatively small amount of air in each inhalation: *shallow breathing.* **4.** *Baseball.* relatively close to home plate: *The shortstop caught the pop fly in shallow left field.* **—***n.* **5.** Usually, **shallows.** (*used with a singular or plural v.*) a shallow part of a body of water; shoal. **—***adv.* **6.** *Baseball.* at a shallow position: *With the pitcher up, the outfielders played shallow.* **—***v.t., v.i.* **7.** to make or become shallow. [1350–1400; ME *schalowe* (adj.); akin to OE *sceald* shallow (see SHOAL¹)] **—shal′low•ly,** *adv.* **—shal′low•ness,** *n.*

Shal•ma•ne•ser III (shal′mə nē′zər), died 824? B.C., Assyrian ruler 859–824?.

sha•lom (shä lôm′; *Eng.* shə lōm′), *interj. Hebrew.* peace (used as a word of greeting or farewell). Also, ***sholom.***

sha•lom a•lei•chem (*Seph.* shä lôm′ ä le KHem′; *Ashk.* shô′ləm ä lā′KHem, ä lā KHem′, shä lōm′), *Hebrew.* peace to you: a conventional Jewish greeting, the reply being *aleichem shalom.*

sha•losh seu•doth (*Ashk.* shä′lōsh so͝o′dōs, -dəs, -ləsh; *Seph.* shä lōsh′ se o͞o dôt′), *Hebrew.* the last of the three prescribed Sabbath meals, taken after *Minhah* and before the evening service. Also, ***sha′losh seu′dot, sha′losh seu′dos.*** [*shālōsh sə'uddōth* lit., three meals]

shalt (shalt), *v. Archaic.* 2nd pers. sing. of **shall.**

shal•war (shul′wär), *n.* (*used with a plural v.*) loose, pajamalike trousers worn by both men and women in India and southeast Asia. Also, **shulwar.** [1880–85; < Hindi < Pers *shalwār*]

sham (sham), *n., adj., v.,* **shammed, sham•ming.** **—***n.* **1.** something that is not what it purports to be; a spurious imitation; fraud or hoax. **2.** a person who shams; shammer. **3.** a cover or the like for giving a thing a different outward appearance: *a pillow sham.* **—***adj.* **4.** pretended; counterfeit; feigned: *sham attacks; a sham Gothic façade.* **5.** designed, made, or used as a sham. **—***v.t.* **6.** to produce an imitation of. **7.** to assume the appearance of; pretend to have: *to sham illness.* **—***v.i.* **8.** to make a false show of something; pretend. [1670–80; orig. uncert.]
—Syn. 1. pretense. **4.** spurious, make-believe, simulated, mock. See **false. 6.** imitate. **7.** feign, fake.
—Ant. 4. genuine.

sha•ma (shä′mə), *n.* a slender long-tailed thrush, *Copsychus malabaricus,* of southern Asia and introduced into Hawaii, having black plumage with a white rump and tail sides and a chestnut belly. [1830–40; said to be < Hindi *sāmā*]

sha•man (shä′mən, shā′-, sham′ən), *n.* (esp. among certain tribal peoples) a person who acts as intermediary between the natural and supernatural worlds, using magic to cure illness, foretell the future, control spiritual forces, etc. [1690–1700; < G *Schamane* < Russ *shamán,* prob. < Evenki *šamān, samān*] **—sha•man•ic** (shə man′ik), *adj.*

sha•man•ism (shä′mə niz′əm, shā′-, sham′ə-), *n.* **1.** the animistic religion of northern Asia, embracing a belief in powerful spirits that can be influenced only by shamans. **2.** any similar religion. [1770–80; SHAMAN + -ISM] **—sha′man•ist,** *n., adj.* **—sha′man•is′tic,** *adj.*

sham•ble¹ (sham′bəl), *n.* **1. shambles,** (*used with a singular or plural v.*) **a.** a slaughterhouse. **b.** any place of carnage. **c.** any scene of destruction: *to turn cities into shambles.* **d.** any scene, place, or thing in disorder: *Her desk is a shambles.* **2.** *Brit. Dial.* a butcher's shop or stall. [bef. 900; ME *shamel,* OE *sc(e)amel* stool, table < LL *scamellum,* L *scamillum,* dim. of L *scamnum* bench; cf. G *Schemel*]

CONCISE ETYMOLOGY KEY: <, descended or borrowed from; >, whence; b., blend of, blended; c., cognate with; cf., compare; deriv., derivative; equiv., equivalent; imit., imitative; obl., oblique; r., replacing; s., stem; sp., spelling, spelled; resp., respelling, respelled; trans., translation; ?, origin unknown; *, unattested; ‡, probably earlier than. See the full key inside the front cover.

sham•ble² (sham′bəl), *v.,* **-bled, -bling,** *n.* **—***v.i.* **1.** to walk or go awkwardly; shuffle. **—***n.* **2.** a shambling gait. [1675–85; perh. short for *shamble-legs* one that walks wide (i.e., as if straddling), reminiscent of the legs of a SHAMBLE¹ (in earlier sense "butcher's table")]

shame (shām), *n., v.,* **shamed, sham•ing.** **—***n.* **1.** the painful feeling arising from the consciousness of something dishonorable, improper, ridiculous, etc., done by oneself or another: *She was overcome with shame.* **2.** susceptibility to this feeling: *to be without shame.* **3.** disgrace; ignominy: *His actions brought shame upon his parents.* **4.** a fact or circumstance bringing disgrace or regret: *The bankruptcy of the business was a shame. It was a shame you couldn't come with us.* **5. for shame!** you should feel ashamed!: *What a thing to say to your mother! For shame!* **6. put to shame, a.** to cause to suffer shame or disgrace. **b.** to outdo; surpass: *She played so well she put all the other tennis players to shame.* **—***v.t.* **7.** to cause to feel shame; make ashamed: *His cowardice shamed him.* **8.** to drive, force, etc., through shame: *He shamed her into going.* **9.** to cover with ignominy or reproach; disgrace. [bef. 900; (n.) ME; OE *sc(e)amu;* c. G *Scham,* ON *skǫmm;* (v.) ME *schamen, shamien* to be ashamed, OE *sc(e)amian,* deriv. of the n.] **—sham′a•ble, shame′a•ble,** *adj.* **—sham′a•bly, shame′a•bly,** *adv.*
—Syn. 1. SHAME, EMBARRASSMENT, MORTIFICATION, HUMILIATION, CHAGRIN designate different kinds or degrees of painful feeling caused by injury to one's pride or self-respect. SHAME is a painful feeling caused by the consciousness or exposure of unworthy or indecent conduct or circumstances: *One feels shame at being caught in a lie.* It is similar to guilt in the nature and origin of the feeling. EMBARRASSMENT usually refers to a feeling less painful than that of SHAME, one associated with less serious situations, often of a social nature: *embarrassment over breaking a teacup at a party.* MORTIFICATION is a more painful feeling, akin to SHAME but also more likely to arise from specifically social circumstances: *his mortification at being singled out for rebuke.* HUMILIATION is mortification at being humbled in the estimation of others: *Being ignored gives one a sense of humiliation.* CHAGRIN is humiliation mingled with vexation or anger: *She felt chagrin at her failure to remember her promise.* **7.** humiliate, mortify, humble, abash, embarrass.
—Ant. 1. pride, self-esteem, self-respect.

shame•faced (shām′fāst′), *adj.* **1.** modest or bashful. **2.** showing shame: *shamefaced apologies.* [1545–55; alter. of SHAMEFAST by folk etym.; see SHAME, FACED] **—shame•fac•ed•ly** (shām′fā′sid lē, shām′fāst′lē), *adv.* **—shame′fac′ed•ness,** *n.*

shame•fast (shām′fast′, -fäst′), *adj. Archaic.* shamefaced. [bef. 900; ME *schamfast* shamefaced, orig., modest, bashful, OE *sc(e)amfæst;* see SHAME, FAST¹] **—shame′fast′ly,** *adv.* **—shame′fast′ness,** *n.*

shame•ful (shām′fəl), *adj.* **1.** causing shame: *shameful behavior.* **2.** disgraceful or scandalous: *shameful treatment.* [bef. 950; ME; OE *scamful.* See SHAME, -FUL] **—shame′ful•ly,** *adv.* **—shame′ful•ness,** *n.*
—Syn. 1. mortifying, humiliating. **2.** dishonorable, ignominious, vile, base, low. **—Ant. 2.** honorable.

shame•less (shām′lis), *adj.* **1.** lacking any sense of shame: immodest; audacious. **2.** insensible to disgrace. **3.** showing no shame. [bef. 900; ME; OE *sceamlēas.* See SHAME, -LESS] **—shame′less•ly,** *adv.* **—shame′less•ness,** *n.*
—Syn. 1. brazen, indecent, impudent, bold, unabashed, unashamed. **2.** hardened, unprincipled, corrupt.
—Ant. 1. modest.

sha•mes (shä′məs), *n., pl.* **sha•mo•sim** (shä mô′sim). shammes.

Sha•mir (shä mēr′), *n.* **Yitz•hak** (yits häk′), born 1915, Israeli political leader: prime minister since 1986.

Sham•mai (shä′mī), fl. 1st century B.C., Hebrew rabbi: founder of Beth Shammai, school of hermeneutics.

sham•mer (sham′ər), *n.* a person who shams. [1670–80; SHAM + -ER¹]

sham•mes (shä′məs), *n., pl.* **sham•mo•sim** (shä mô′sim). **1.** sexton (def. 2). **2.** the candle used to kindle the candles in the Hanukkah menorah. Also, **shames.** [1945–50; < Yiddish *shames* < Heb *shammāsh* server, attendant]

sham•my (sham′ē), *n., pl.* **-mies,** *v.,* **-mied, -my•ing.** chamois (defs. 2–4, 6, 7).

Sha•mo (shä′mô′), *n.* Chinese name of the **Gobi.**

Sha•mo•kin (shə mō′kin), *n.* a borough in E Pennsylvania. 10,357.

sham•oy (sham′ē), *n., pl.* **-oys,** *v.,* **-oyed, -oy•ing.** chamois (defs. 2–4, 6, 7).

sham•poo (sham po͞o′), *v.,* **-pooed, -poo•ing,** *n.* **—***v.t.* **1.** to wash (the head or hair), esp. with a cleaning preparation that does not leave a soap film. **2.** to clean (rugs, upholstery, or the like) with a special preparation. **3.** *Archaic.* to massage. **—***n.* **4.** the act of shampooing. **5.** a preparation used for shampooing, esp. one that does not leave a soap film. [1755–65; earlier *champo* to massage < an inflected form of Hindi *cāmpnā* lit., to press] **—sham•poo′er,** *n.*

sham•rock (sham′rok), *n.* any of several trifoliate plants, as the wood sorrel, *Oxalis acetosella,* or a small, pink-flowered clover, *Trifolium repens minus,* but esp. *Trifolium procumbens,* a small, yellow-flowered clover: the national emblem of Ireland. [1565–75; < Ir *seamróg,* equiv. to *seamair* clover + *-óg* dim. suffix]

shamrock, *Trifolium procumbens*

sham•rock-pea (sham′rok pē′), *n.* a trailing plant, *Parochetus communis,* of the legume family, native to Asia and east Africa, having shamrocklike leaves with a brown crescent at the base and pea-shaped, pink and blue flowers. [1880–85]

sham•shir (sham shēr′), *n.* a curved Persian saber having one edge on the convex side. [1625–35; < Pers *shamshīr.* See SCIMITAR]

sha•mus (shä′məs, shā′-), *n., pl.* **-mus•es.** *Slang.* **1.** a detective. **2.** a police officer. [1925–30; of obscure orig., though popularly derived from either Yiddish *shames* SHAMMES or the Ir male given name *Séamas*]

Shan (shän, shan), *n., pl.* **Shans,** (*esp. collectively*) **Shan.** **1.** a group of Mongoloid tribes in the hills of Burma. **2.** a language spoken in the Shan States and belonging to the Tai group of languages.

Shan•dong (shän′dông′), *n. Pinyin.* **1.** a maritime province in E China. 55,520,000; 59,189 sq. mi. (153,299 sq. km). *Cap.:* Jinan. **2.** a peninsula in the E part of this province, extending into the Yellow Sea. Also, **Shantung.**

shan•dry•dan (shan′drē dan′), *n.* **1.** an old-fashioned hooded chaise. **2.** a rickety, old-fashioned conveyance. [1810–20; orig. uncert.]

shan•dy (shan′dē), *n., pl.* **-dies.** *Chiefly Brit.* **1.** a mixture of beer and lemonade. **2.** shandygaff. [1885–90; short for SHANDYGAFF]

shan•dy•gaff (shan′dē gaf′), *n. Chiefly Brit.* a mixed drink of beer with ginger beer. [1850–55; orig. uncert.]

Shane (shān), *n.* a male given name.

Shang (shäng), *n.* a Chinese dynasty whose dates are usually given as 1766–1122 B.C. and sometimes as 1523–1027 B.C. Also called **Yin.**

shang•hai (shang′hī, shang hī′), *v.t.,* **-haied, -hai•ing.** *Naut.* to enroll or obtain (a sailor) for the crew of a ship by unscrupulous means, as by force or the use of liquor or drugs. [1855–60; after SHANGHAI]

Shang•hai (shang hī′; *Chin.* shäng′hī′), *n.* **1.** *Pinyin, Wade-Giles.* a seaport and municipality in E China, near the mouth of the Chang Jiang. 10,820,000. **2.** a type of long-legged chicken believed to be of Asian origin.

Shang•qiu (shäng′chyʏ′), *n. Pinyin.* a city in E Henan province, in E China. 250,000. Also, **Shang′chiu′, Shang′kiu′.**

Shan•gri-la (shang′grə lä′, shang′grə lä′), *n.* **1.** an imaginary paradise on earth, esp. a remote and exotic utopia. **2.** a faraway haven or hideaway of idyllic beauty and tranquility. [after the fictional Tibetan land of eternal youth in the novel *The Lost Horizon* (1933) by James Hilton]

Shang Ti (shäng′ tē′), the chief of the ancient Chinese gods.

Shan•hai•guan (shän′hī′gwän′), *n. Pinyin.* a city in NE Hebei province, in NE China, on the Gulf of Liaodong: strategically located at the E end of the Great Wall. 50,000. Also, **Shan′hai′kuan′, Shan′hai′kwan′.** Formerly, **Linyu.**

shank (shangk), *n.* **1.** *Anat.* the part of the lower limb in humans between the knee and the ankle; leg. **2.** a corresponding or analogous part in certain animals. See diag. under **horse. 3.** the lower limb in humans, including both the leg and the thigh. **4.** a cut of meat from the top part of the front **(foreshank)** or back **(hind shank)** leg of an animal. See diag. under **beef. 5.** a narrow part of various devices, as a tool or bolt, connecting the end by which the object is held or moved with the end that acts upon another object. **6.** a straight, usually narrow, shaftlike part of various objects connecting two more important or complex parts, as the stem of a pipe. **7.** a knob, small projection, or end of a device for attaching to another object, as a small knob on the back of a solid button, or the end of a drill for gripping in a shaft. **8.** the long, straight part of an anchor connecting the crown and the ring. See diag. under **anchor. 9.** the straight part of a fishhook away from the bent part or prong. See illus. under **fishhook. 10.** *Music.* crook¹ (def. 8). **11.** *Informal.* **a.** the early part of a period of time: *It was just the shank of the evening when the party began.* **b.** the latter part of a period of time: *They didn't get started until the shank of the morning.* **12.** the narrow part of the sole of a shoe, lying beneath the instep. **13.** shankpiece. **14.** *Print.* the body of a type, between the shoulder and the foot. See diag. under **type. 15.** *Golf.* a shot veering sharply to the right after being hit with the base of a club shaft. **16.** the part of a phonograph stylus or needle on which the diamond or sapphire tip is mounted. **17.** *Jewelry.* the part of a ring that surrounds the finger; hoop. **18. shank of the evening,** the main or best part of the evening: *Don't leave yet—it's just the shank of the evening.* **—***v.t.* **19.** *Golf.* to hit (a golf ball) with the base of the shaft of a club just above the club head, causing the ball to go off sharply to the right. **—***v.i.* **20.** *Chiefly Scot.* to travel on foot. Cf. **shanks' mare.** [bef. 900; ME (n.); OE *sc(e)anca;* c. LG *schanke* leg, thigh; akin to G *Schenkel* thigh, *Schinken* ham]

Shan•kar (shän′kär, shäng-), *n.* **Ra•vi** (rä′vē), born 1920?, Indian sitarist.

Shan•ka•ra (shung′kər ə), *n.* A.D. 789?–821?, Hindu Vedantist philosopher and teacher. Also, **Sankara.** Also called **Shan•ka•ra•char•ya** (shung′kər ə chär′yə).

shank•piece (shangk′pēs′), *n.* a piece of metal or fiber for giving form to the shank of a shoe. Also called **shank.** [1880–85; SHANK + PIECE]

shanks′ mare′, **1.** one's own legs, esp. as a means of moving from one place to another: *The only way we can get there is by shanks' mare.* **2. ride shanks' mare,** to go on foot rather than ride; walk: *to ride shanks' mare to the fair.* Also, **shank's′ mare′.** Also called **shanks′ po′ny, shank's′ po′ny.**

Shan•na (shä′nə), *n.* a female given name.

Shan•non (shan′ən), *n.* **1. Claude El•wood** (el′wo͝od′), born 1916, U.S. applied mathematician: early developer of information theory. **2.** a river flowing SW from N Ireland to the Atlantic: the principal river of Ireland. 240 mi. (386 km) long. **3.** international airport in W Ireland, near Limerick. **4.** a female given name.

shan•ny (shan′ē), *n., pl.* **-nies.** a scaleless blenny, *Blennius pholis,* living in waters along the coast of Europe, having an olive-green body marked with dark spots. [1830–40; orig. uncert.]

Shan•si (shän′sē′), *n. Older Spelling.* Shanxi.

Shan′ State′ (shän, shan), a state in E Burma (Myanmar), along the Saiween River. 3,700,000; ab. 56,000 sq. mi. (145,040 sq. km.).

shan't (shant, shänt), contraction of *shall not.* **—Usage.** See **contraction.**

shan•tey (shan′tē), *n., pl.* **-teys.** chantey.

shan•ti (shän′tē), *n. Hinduism.* peace. Also, **shan′tih.** [< Skt *śānti* (nom. sing. *śāntiḥ*)]

Shan•tou (shän′tō′), *n. Pinyin.* a seaport in E Guangdong province, in SE China. 400,000. Also, **Swatow.**

Shan•tung (shan′tung′ *or, for 2,* shan′tung; *for 1, also Chin.* shän′do͝ong′), *n.* **1.** Shandong. **2.** (*often l.c.*) *Textiles.* **a.** a heavy pongee. Cf. **tussah. b.** a fabric imitating this, of rayon or cotton.

shan•ty[1] (shan′tē), *n., pl.* **-ties,** *adj., v.,* **-tied, -ty•ing.** *—n.* **1.** a crudely built hut, cabin, or house. *—adj.* **2.** of, pertaining to, or constituting a shanty or shanties: *a shanty quarter.* **3.** of a low economic or social class, esp. when living in a shanty: *shanty people.* *—v.i.* **4.** to inhabit a shanty. [1810–20; prob. < CanF *chantier* lumber camp, hut; F: yard, depot, gantry, stand for barrels < L *cant(h)ērius* rafter, prop, lit., horse in poor condition, nag < Gk *kanthḗlios* pack ass] **—shan′ty•like′,** *adj.*

shan•ty[2] (shan′tē), *n., pl.* **-ties.** chantey.

shan•ty•town (shan′tē toun′), *n.* **1.** a section, as of a city or town, characterized by shanties and crudely built houses. **2.** a whole town or city that is chiefly made up of shantylike houses. [1880–85; SHANTY[1] + TOWN]

Shan•xi (shän′shē′), *n. Pinyin.* a province in N China. 18,010,000; 60,656 sq. mi. (157,099 sq. km). *Cap.:* Taiyuan. Also, **Shansi.**

Shao•xing (shou′shing′), *n. Pinyin.* a city in NE Zhejiang province, in E China. 225,000. Also, *Older Spelling,* **Shao•hing** (shou′hing′); *Wade-Giles,* **Shao′hsing′.**

Shao•yang (shou′yäng′), *n. Pinyin, Wade-Giles.* a city in central Hunan province, in E China. 275,000. Formerly, **Baoqing.**

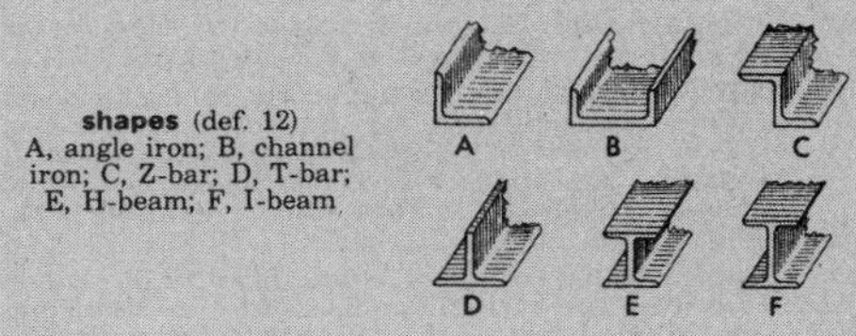

shapes (def. 12) A, angle iron; B, channel iron; C, Z-bar; D, T-bar; E, H-beam; F, I-beam

shape (shāp), *n., v.,* **shaped, shap•ing.** *—n.* **1.** the quality of a distinct object or body in having an external surface or outline of specific form or figure. **2.** this quality as found in some individual object or body form: *This lake has a peculiar shape.* **3.** something seen in outline, as in silhouette. **4.** an imaginary form; phantom. **5.** an assumed appearance; guise: *an angel in the shape of a woman.* **6.** a particular or definite organized form or expression: *He could give no shape to his ideas.* **7.** proper form; orderly arrangement. **8.** condition or state of repair: *The old house was in bad shape.* **9.** the collective conditions forming a way of life or mode of existence: *the shape of the future.* **10.** the figure, physique, or body of a person, esp. of a woman. **11.** something used to give form, as a mold or a pattern. **12.** Also called **section.** *Building Trades, Metalworking.* a flanged metal beam or bar of uniform section, as a channel iron, I-beam, etc. **13.** *Naut.* a ball, cone, drum, etc., used as a day signal, singly or in combinations, to designate a vessel at anchor or engaged in some particular operation. **14. take shape,** to assume a fixed form; become definite: *The house is beginning to take shape.* *—v.t.* **15.** to give definite form, shape, organization, or character to. **16.** to couch or express in words: *to shape a statement.* **17.** to adjust; adapt: *He shaped everything to suit his taste.* **18.** to direct (one's course, future, etc.). **19.** to file the teeth of (a saw) to uniform width after jointing. **20.** *Animal Behav., Psychol.* to teach (a desired behavior) to a human or other animal by successively rewarding the actions that more and more closely approximate that behavior. **21.** *Obs.* to appoint; decree. *—v.i.* **22.** to come to a desired conclusion or take place in a specified way: *If discussions shape properly, the companies will merge.* **23. shape up, a.** to assume a specific form: *The plan is beginning to shape up.* **b.** to evolve or develop, esp. favorably. **c.** to improve one's behavior or performance to meet a required standard. **d.** to get oneself into good physical condition. **e.** (of longshoremen) to get into a line or formation in order to be assigned the day's work. [bef. 900; (n.) ME; OE *gesceapu* (pl.); r. dial. *shap,* ME; OE *gesceap* (sing.); c. ON *skap* state, mood; (v.) ME; OE *sceapen* (ptp.); r. ME *sheppe, shippe,* OE *sceppan, scyppan;* c. G *schaffen,* ON *skepja,* Goth *-skapjan* to make] **—shap′a•ble, shape′a•ble,** *adj.*

—Syn. 1. silhouette, appearance. See **form. 4.** specter, illusion. **7.** order, pattern. **8.** order, situation. **15.** mold, model.

SHAPE (shāp), *n.* Supreme Headquarters Allied Powers, Europe. Also, **Shape.**

shaped (shāpt), *adj.* **1.** of a definite form, shape, or character (often used in combination): *a U-shaped driveway.* **2.** designed to fit a particular form, body, or contour: *a shaped garment.* **3.** *Furniture.* having other than a plane surface. [1530–40; SHAPE + -ED[2]]

shaped′ charge′, *Mil.* a warhead having a concave, hollow end and operating on the Munroe effect.

shape•less (shāp′lis), *adj.* **1.** having no definite or regular shape or form: *a shapeless mass of clay.* **2.** lacking beauty or elegance of form. [1250–1300; SHAPE + -LESS; r. ME *scaples*] **—shape′less•ly,** *adv.* **—shape′less•ness,** *n.*

shape•ly (shāp′lē), *adj.,* **-li•er, -li•est.** having a pleasing shape, esp. with reference to a woman's figure. [1325–75; SHAPE + -LY; r. ME *shaply, schaply;* cf. OE *gesceaplice* (adv.) fitly] **—shape′li•ness,** *n.*

shap•en (shā′pən), *adj.* having a designated shape (usually used in combination): *a sprawling, ill-shapen building.* [1250–1300; ME; OE *-sceapen* (only in compounds); orig. ptp. of SHAPE]

shape′ note′, a musical note in which the degree of the scale is indicated by the shape of the note's head. Also called **buckwheat note.** [1930–35, *Amer.*]

shap•er (shā′pər), *n.* **1.** a person or thing that shapes. **2.** a machine tool for forming flat surfaces, consisting of a frame, usually horizontal, on which the work is held while a cutting tool moves along it with a reciprocating motion. Cf. **planer** (def. 2). **3.** (in woodworking) a stationary power tool driving a vertical spindle to which cutters are locked, used in joinery and for forming decorative edges. [1250–1300; ME; see SHAPE, -ER[1]]

shape-up (shāp′up′), *n.* **1.** an act or instance of shaping up. **2.** a former method of hiring longshoremen in which the applicants appeared daily at the docks and a union hiring boss chose those who would be given work. Also, **shape′up′.** [1940–45; n. use of v. phrase *shape up*]

Sha•pi•ro (shə pēr′ō), *n.* **Karl (Jay),** born 1913, U.S. poet and editor.

shap•ka (shäp′kə), *n.* a round, slightly tapered, brimless fur hat worn esp. in the Soviet Union. [< Russ *shápka* hat, cap, ORuss: headgear for men, c. Serbo-Croatian *šàpka,* prob. < MLG *schapēl* (with Slavic suffix *-ka*) < OF *chapel* (see CHAPEAU); cf. Czech *čapka,* Slovak *čapica,* Pol *czapka,* with *č* perh. directly < OF]

Shap•ley (shap′lē), *n.* **Har•low** (här′lō), 1885–1972, U.S. astronomer.

Sha•ra (shär′ə), *n., pl.* **-ras,** (*esp. collectively*) **-ra.** Sharra.

Sha•ra•ku (shä rä′ko͞o), *n.* **Ta•shu•sai** (tô′sho͞o sī′), fl. 18th century, Japanese printmaker.

shard (shärd), *n.* **1.** a fragment, esp. of broken earthenware. **2.** *Zool.* **a.** a scale. **b.** a shell, as of an egg or snail. **3.** *Entomol.* an elytron of a beetle. Also, **sherd.** [bef. 1000; ME; OE *sceard;* c. LG, D *schaard;* akin to SHEAR]

Shar•da•na (shär dä′nə), *n., pl.* **-na.** a member of an ancient people of the eastern Mediterranean who served as mercenaries in the Egyptian army and may have settled in Sardinia and Sicily.

share[1] (shâr), *n., v.,* **shared, shar•ing.** *—n.* **1.** the full or proper portion or part allotted or belonging to or contributed or owed by an individual or group. **2.** one of the equal fractional parts into which the capital stock of a joint-stock company or a corporation is divided. **3. on** or **upon shares,** on the principle of sharing the profits or losses of an undertaking: *They agreed to work on shares.* *—v.t.* **4.** to divide and distribute in shares; apportion. **5.** to use, participate in, enjoy, receive, etc., jointly. *—v.i.* **6.** to have a share or part; take part (often fol. by *in*). **7.** to divide, apportion, or receive equally. [1325–75; ME (n.) cutting, division; OE *scearu* fork of the body, groin; c. D *schaar,* G *Schar* troop. See SHEAR] **—shar′a•ble, share′a•ble,** *adj.* **—shar′er,** *n.*

—Syn. 1. allotment, allocation; contribution, assessment; quota, lot. **4.** allot, parcel out, deal out, dole, mete. **6.** SHARE, PARTAKE, PARTICIPATE mean to join with others or to receive in common with others. To SHARE is to give or receive a part of something, or to enjoy or assume something in common: *to share in another's experiences.* To PARTAKE is to take for one's own personal use a portion of something: *to partake of food.* To PARTICIPATE is esp. to join with others in some thought, feeling, or, particularly, some action: *to participate in a race, in a conversation.*

share[2] (shâr), *n.* a plowshare. [bef. 900; ME; OE *scear;* c. G *Schar.* See SHEAR]

share′ account′, a savings account in a credit union.

share′ certif′icate, a certificate of deposit issued by a credit union. [1885–90]

share•crop (shâr′krop′), *v.t., v.i.,* **-cropped, -crop•ping.** to farm as a sharecropper. [1865–70, *Amer.;* back formation from SHARECROPPER]

share•crop•per (shâr′krop′ər), *n.* a tenant farmer who pays as rent a share of the crop. [1910–15, *Amer.;* SHARE[1] + CROPPER]

shared′-ap•pre•ci•a′tion mort′gage (shârd′ə prē′shē ā′shən), a type of mortgage that carries a smaller down payment or lower interest rate than usual in return for the lender's sharing in the appreciation of the property at some future date, as at the time of its sale. *Abbr.:* SAM

share′ draft′, **1.** an interest-bearing checking account in a credit union. **2.** a check written against this account.

share•hold•er (shâr′hōl′dər), *n.* a holder or owner of shares, esp. in a company or corporation. Also called **share•own•er** (shâr′ō′nər). [1785–95; SHARE[1] + HOLDER] **—share′hold′ing,** *n.*

Sha•rett (shä ret′), *n.* **Mo•she** (mô she′), (*Moshe Shertok*), 1894–1965, Israeli statesman, born in Russia: prime minister 1953–55. Also, **Sha•ret′.**

share•ware (shâr′wâr′), *n.* computer software distributed without initial charge but for which the user is encouraged to pay a nominal fee to cover support for continued use.

Sha•ri (shär′ē *for 1;* shar′ē *for 2*), *n.* **1.** Also, **Chari.** a river in N central Africa, flowing NW from the Central African Republic into Lake Chad. 1400 mi. (2254 km) long. **2.** a female given name.

sha•ri•'ah (shä rē′ä), *n. Islam.* law, seen as deriving from the Koran, hadith, ijma', and qiyas. Also, **sha•ri′a.** [1875–80; < Ar *sharī'ah*]

sha•rif (shə rēf′), *n.* sherif. [1590–1600]

Sha•rif (shä rēf′), *n.* a male given name: from an Arabic word meaning "exalted."

shark[1] (shärk), *n.* any of a group of elongate elasmobranch, mostly marine fishes, certain species of which are large, voracious, and sometimes dangerous to humans. [1560–70; orig. uncert.] **—shark′like′,** *adj.*

shark[1], *Carcharodon carcharias,* length 30 ft. (9 m)

shark[2] (shärk), *n.* **1.** a person who preys greedily on others, as by cheating or usury. **2.** *Informal.* a person who has unusual ability in a particular field. *—v.t.* **3.** *Archaic.* to obtain by trickery or fraud; steal. *—v.i.* **4.** *Archaic.* to live by shifts and stratagems. [1590–1600; < G dial. *Schork,* var. of *Schurke* rascal]

shark′ repel′lent, any tactic used by a corporation to prevent a takeover by a corporate raider.

shark•skin (shärk′skin′), *n.* **1.** a smooth fabric of acetate or rayon with a dull or chalklike appearance, for apparel. **2.** a fine worsted fabric in twill weave, compact in texture and light to medium in weight, for suits. [1850–55; SHARK[1] + SKIN]

shark•suck•er (shärk′suk′ər), *n.* any of several remoras, as *Echeneis naucrates,* usually found attached to sharks. [1840–50; SHARK[1] + SUCKER]

Shar•leen (shär lēn′), *n.* a female given name.

Sharm al-Sheikh (shärm′ al shāk′; *Arab.* shärm′ el shekh′), a village and military post in E Egypt, on the Sinai Peninsula, guarding the Gulf of Suez.

Shar•on (shar′ən), *n.* **1.** a fertile coastal plain in ancient Palestine: now a coastal region N of Tel Aviv in Israel. **2.** a city in W Pennsylvania. 19,057. **3.** a town in E Massachusetts. 13,601. **4.** Also, **Shar′en.** a female given name: from a Hebrew word meaning "a plain or flat area."

Shar•on•ville (shar′ən vil′), *n.* a town in SW Ohio. 10,108.

sharp (shärp), *adj.,* **-er, -est,** *v., adv., n.* *—adj.* **1.** having a thin cutting edge or a fine point; well-adapted for cutting or piercing: *a sharp knife.* **2.** terminating in an edge or point; not blunt or rounded: *The table had sharp corners.* **3.** involving a sudden or abrupt change in direction or course: *a sharp curve in the road; The car made a sharp turn.* **4.** abrupt, as an ascent: *a sharp drop.* **5.** consisting of angular lines and pointed forms or of thin, long features: *He had a sharp face.* **6.** clearly defined; distinct: *a sharp photographic image.* **7.** distinct or marked, as a contrast: *sharp differences of opinion.* **8.** pungent or biting in taste: *a sharp cheese.* **9.** piercing or shrill in sound: *a sharp cry.* **10.** keenly cold, as weather: *a sharp, biting wind.* **11.** felt acutely; intense; distressing: *sharp pain.* **12.** merciless, caustic, or

CONCISE PRONUNCIATION KEY: act, cāpe, dâre, pärt; set, ēqual; *if,* ice; ox, ōver, ôrder, oil, bo͝ok, bo͞ot, out; up, ûrge; child; sing; shoe; thin, *that;* zh as in *treasure.* ə = *a* as in *alone, e* as in *system, i* as in *easily, o* as in *gallop, u* as in *circus;* ə as in *fire* (fīər), *hour* (ouər). l and n can serve as syllabic consonants, as in *cradle* (krād′l), and *button* (but′n). See the full key inside the front cover.

harsh: *sharp words.* **13.** fierce or violent: *a sharp struggle.* **14.** keen or eager: *sharp desire.* **15.** quick, brisk, or spirited. **16.** alert or vigilant: *They kept a sharp watch for the enemy.* **17.** mentally acute: *a sharp lad.* **18.** extremely sensitive or responsive; keen: *sharp vision; sharp hearing.* **19.** shrewd or astute: *a sharp bargainer.* **20.** shrewd to the point of dishonesty: *sharp practice.* **21.** *Music.* **a.** (of a tone) raised a chromatic half step in pitch: *F sharp.* **b.** above an intended pitch, as a note; too high (opposed to *flat*). **22.** *Informal.* very stylish: *a sharp dresser; a sharp jacket.* **23.** *Radio, Electronics.* of, relating to, or responsive to a very narrow range of frequencies. Cf. **broadband. 24.** *Phonet.* fortis; voiceless. **25.** composed of hard, angular grains, as sand.
—*v.t.* **26.** *Music.* to raise in pitch, esp. by one chromatic half step.
—*v.i.* **27.** to sound above the true pitch.
—*adv.* **28.** keenly or acutely. **29.** abruptly or suddenly: *to pull a horse up sharp.* **30.** punctually: *Meet me at one o'clock sharp.* **31.** vigilantly. **32.** briskly; quickly. **33.** *Music.* above the true pitch: *You're singing a little sharp.*
—*n.* **34.** something sharp. **35.** Usually, **sharps.** a medium-length needle with a rounded eye and a sharp point, used for all-purpose hand sewing. **36.** a sharper. **37.** *Informal.* an expert. **38.** *Music.* **a.** a tone one chromatic half step above a given tone. **b.** (in musical notation) the symbol ♯ indicating this. [bef. 900; (adj.) ME; OE *scearp;* c. G *scharf;* akin to Ir *cearb* a cut (n.), keen (adj.); (adv.) ME; OE *scearpe,* deriv. of the adj.; (n.) ME, deriv. of the adj.; (v.) deriv. of the adj.] —**sharp′ly,** *adv.* —**sharp′ness,** *n.*
—**Syn. 1.** SHARP, KEEN refer to the edge or point of an instrument, tool, and the like. SHARP applies, in general, to a cutting edge or a point capable of piercing: *a sharp knife; a sharp point.* KEEN is usually applied to sharp edges: *a keen sword blade.* **6.** clear. **8.** acrid, bitter, piquant, sour. **10.** piercing, nipping, biting. **11.** severe, excruciating. **12.** unmerciful, cutting, acid, acrimonious, pointed, biting. **16.** attentive. **17.** clever, discriminating, discerning, perspicacious. As applied to mental qualities, SHARP, KEEN, INTELLIGENT, QUICK have varying implications. SHARP suggests an acute, sensitive, alert, penetrating quality: *a sharp mind.* KEEN implies observant, incisive, and vigorous: *a keen intellect.* INTELLIGENT means not only acute, alert, and active, but also able to reason and understand: *an intelligent reader.* QUICK suggests lively and rapid comprehension, prompt response to instruction, and the like: *quick at figures.* **20.** shady, deceitful. —**Ant. 1.** dull.

Sharp (shärp), *n.* **William** (*"Fiona Macleod"*), 1855–?1905, Scottish poet and critic.

sharp•bill (shärp′bil′), *n.* a passerine bird, *Oxyruncus cristatus,* of New World tropical forests, having greenish plumage and a pointed bill, related to the tyrant flycatchers. [SHARP + BILL[2]]

sharp-cut (shärp′kut′), *adj.* **1.** cut so as to have a sharp edge: *a tool with a sharp-cut blade.* **2.** distinctly outlined; clearly defined.

sharp-eared (shärp′ērd′), *adj.* **1.** having pointed ears. **2.** having keen hearing.

sharp-edged (shärp′ejd′), *adj.* **1.** having a fine edge or edges. **2.** acute and caustic: *a sharp-edged wit.* [bef. 1000; OE *scearpecgede* (not recorded in ME); see SHARP, EDGE, -ED[3]]

Shar-Pei (shär′pā′), *n.* one of a Chinese breed of large muscular dogs having a distinctive wrinkly skin covered by a fawn to dark brown smooth coat, originally developed as a guard dog. [< dial. Chin, equiv. to Chin *shā pí* lit., sand fur (cf. Guangdong dial. *sā pèi*); E sp. with *r* perh. r-less speaker's representation of the vowel]

sharp•en (shär′pən), *v.t., v.i.* to make or become sharp or sharper. [1400–50; late ME; see SHARP, -EN[1]] —**sharp′en•er,** *n.*

sharp•er (shär′pər), *n.* **1.** a shrewd swindler. **2.** a professional gambler. Also, **sharpie.** [1560–70; SHARP + -ER[1]]

Sharpe's′ grys′bok. See under **grysbok.** [after British colonial official Sir Alfred *Sharpe* (1853–1935), first European observer of the species, in Nyasaland in 1896]

sharp-eyed (shärp′īd′), *adj.* having keen sight or perception. [1660–70]

sharp′-fo′cus re′alism (shärp′fō′kəs), photorealism. Also, **Sharp′-Focus Re′alism.**

sharp-freeze (shärp′frēz′), *v.t.,* **-froze, -fro•zen, -freez•ing.** quick-freeze. [1940–45]

sharp•ie (shär′pē), *n.* **1.** sharper. **2.** a very alert person. **3.** *Slang.* an ostentatiously stylish person. Also, **sharpy.** [1855–60, *Amer.*; SHARP + -IE]

sharp-nosed (shärp′nōzd′), *adj.* **1.** having a thin, pointed nose. **2.** having a sharp or projecting front: *a sharp-nosed airplane.* **3.** having a keen or sensitive sense of smell. [1555–65] —**sharp-nosed•ly** (shärp′nōz′dlē, -nō′zid-), *adv.* —**sharp′-nosed′ness,** *n.*

Sharps (shärps), *n.* a single-shot, lever-action breechloader rifle patented in the U.S. in 1848 and adopted by the U.S. military in the 1850's. [after Christian *Sharps* (1811–74), U.S. gunsmith, who invented it]

Sharps•burg (shärps′bûrg), *n.* a town in NW Maryland: nearby is the site of the Civil War battle of Antietam 1862. 721.

sharp-set (shärp′set′), *adj.* **1.** eager to satisfy the appetite, esp. for food. **2.** keen or eager. **3.** set to present a sharply angled edge. [1530–40] —**sharp′-set′ness,** *n.*

sharp′-shinned hawk′ (shärp′shind′), a North American hawk, *Accipiter striatus,* having extremely slender legs, a bluish-gray back, and a white, rusty-barred breast. [1805–15, *Amer.*]

sharp•shoot•er (shärp′sho͞o′tər), *n.* **1.** a person skilled in shooting, esp. with a rifle. **2.** *Mil.* **a.** a rating below expert and above marksman, assigned to one who has qualified with a specific score in rifle marksmanship. **b.** a person who has achieved such a rating. **3.** an athlete noted for having accurate aim in a sport, as basketball, hockey, archery, golf, etc. **4.** *Slang.* a person who engages in short-term business dealings with the purpose of making a large, quick profit without regard to scruple. **5.** a spade that has a very narrow blade, used as a garden or nursery tool. [1795–1805; SHARP (i.e., sharp-eyed) + SHOOTER; cf. G *Scharfschütz(e)* expert marksman] —**sharp′shoot′ing,** *n.*

sharp-sight•ed (shärp′sī′tid), *adj.* **1.** having keen sight. **2.** having or showing mental acuteness. [1565–75] —**sharp′-sight′ed•ly,** *adv.* —**sharp′-sight′ed•ness,** *n.*

sharp′-tailed grouse′ (shärp′tāld′), a grouse, *Pedioecetes phasianellus,* of prairies and open forests of western North America, similar in size to the prairie chicken but with a more pointed tail. Also called **sprigtail.** [1775–85, *Amer.*]

sharp′-tailed spar′row, a sparrow, *Ammospiza caudacuta,* inhabiting salt marshes in North America, having narrow, sharply pointed tail feathers. [1825–35, *Amer.*]

sharp′tail mo′la (shärp′tāl′), a fish, *Masturus lanceolatus,* related to the ocean sunfish but having a pointed tail. Also called **headfish.** [SHARP + TAIL[1]]

sharp-tongued (shärp′tungd′), *adj.* characterized by or given to harshness, bitterness, or sarcasm in speech. [1830–40]

sharp-wit•ted (shärp′wit′id), *adj.* having or showing mental acuity; intellectually discerning; acute. [1580–90] —**sharp′-wit′ted•ly,** *adv.* —**sharp′-wit′ted•ness,** *n.*

sharp•y (shär′pē), *n., pl.* **sharp•ies.** sharpie.

Shar•ra (shär′ə), *n., pl.* **-ras,** (*esp. collectively*) **-ra. 1.** a member of a Mongol people inhabiting Outer Mongolia. **2.** the language of the Sharras.

Shar•rie (shar′ē), *n.* a female given name, form of **Sharon.**

Sha•shi (shä′shē), *n.* a river in SE Africa, flowing SE along the Botswana-Zimbabwe border to the Limpopo River. ab. 225 mi. (360 km) long.

shash•lik (shäsh lik′, shäsh′lik), *n.* See **shish kebab.** Also, **shash•lick′, shas•lik′.** [1925–30; < Russ *shashlýk* < Turkic; cf. Turk *şişlik* stewing meat, equiv. to *şiş* skewer (cf. SHISH KEBAB) + *-lik* suffix of appurtenance (*a* in Russ word is unexplained)]

Shas•ta (shas′tə), *n.* **Mount,** a volcanic peak in N California, in the Cascade Range. 14,161 ft. (4315 m).

Shas′ta dai′sy, any of several horticultural varieties of *Chrysanthemum superbum,* having large, white, daisylike flowers. [1890–95, *Amer.*; named after Mt. SHASTA]

shas•tra (shäs′trə), *n.* any of the sacred books of Hinduism. [1620–30; < Skt *śāstra*] —**shas′trik, shas•tra•ik** (shä strä′ik), *adj.*

shas•tra•ca•ra (shäs′trä kä′rə), *n. Hinduism.* an action in accordance with the principles of the shastras. [< Skt]

Shas•tri (shäs′trē), *n.* **Lal Ba•ha•dur** (läl bä hä′do͝or), 1904–66, Indian statesman: prime minister 1964–66.

Shatt-al-A•rab (shat′al ar′əb, shät′-), *n.* a river in SE Iraq, formed by the junction of the Tigris and Euphrates rivers, flowing SE to the Persian Gulf. 123 mi. (198 km) long.

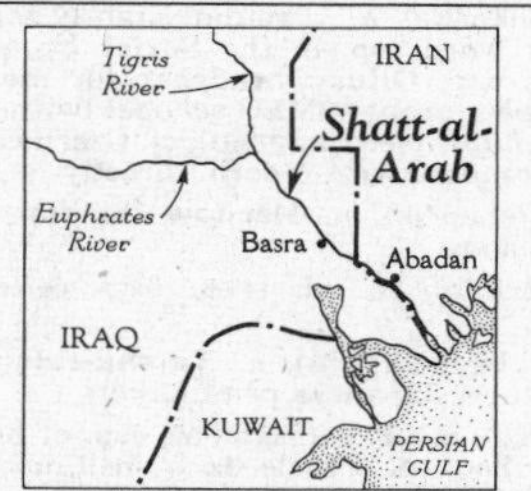

shat•ter (shat′ər), *v.t.* **1.** to break (something) into pieces, as by a blow. **2.** to damage, as by breaking or crushing: *ships shattered by storms.* **3.** to impair or destroy (health, nerves, etc.): *The incident shattered his composure.* **4.** to weaken, destroy, or refute (ideas, opinions, etc.): *He wanted to shatter her illusions.* —*v.i.* **5.** to be broken into fragments or become weak or insubstantial. —*n.* **6.** Usually, **shatters.** fragments made by shattering. [1300–50; ME *schateren* < ?; cf. SCATTER] —**shat′ter•er,** *n.* —**shat′ter•ing•ly,** *adv.*
—**Syn. 1.** shiver, split, crack. See **break.**

shat′ter cone′, *Geol.* a small, radially striated rock structure produced by intense shock, such as generated by meteorite impact. Also called **pressure cone.** [1945–50]

shat•ter•proof (shat′ər pro͞of′), *adj.* designed or made to resist shattering: *shatterproof glass in automobile windows.* [1935–40; SHATTER + -PROOF]

Shaun (shôn), *n.* a male given name, form of **John.**

shave (shāv), *v.,* **shaved, shaved** or (*esp. in combination*) **shav•en, shav•ing,** *n.* —*v.i.* **1.** to remove a growth of beard with a razor. —*v.t.* **2.** to remove hair from (the face, legs, etc.) by cutting it off close to the skin with a razor. **3.** to cut off (hair, esp. the beard) close to the skin with a razor (often fol. by *off* or *away*). **4.** to cut or scrape away the surface of with a sharp-edged tool: *to shave hides in preparing leather.* **5.** to reduce to shavings or thin slices: *to shave wood.* **6.** to cut or trim closely: *to shave a lawn.* **7.** to scrape, graze, or come very near to: *The car just shaved the garage door.* **8.** *Com.* to purchase (a note) at a rate of discount greater than is legal or customary. **9.** to reduce or deduct from: *The store shaved the price of winter suits in the spring.* —*n.* **10.** the act, process, or an instance of shaving or being shaved. **11.** a thin slice; shaving. **12.** any of various tools for shaving, scraping, removing thin slices, etc. [bef. 900; (v.) ME *schaven, schafen,* OE *sc(e)afan;* c. D *schaven* to plane (a plank), abrade (the skin), LG *schaven,* G *schaben,* ON *skafa* to scrape, Goth *skaban* to shear, shave; (n.) ME *schave* tool for shaving, OE *sc(e)afa,* deriv. of the v.] —**shav′a•ble, shave′a•ble,** *adj.*
—**Syn. 7.** brush, glance, touch.

shave•ling (shāv′ling), *n.* **1.** *Often Disparaging.* a head-shaven clergyman. **2.** young fellow; youngster. [1520–30; SHAVE + -LING[1]]

shav•en (shā′vən), *v.* **1.** a pp. of **shave.** —*adj.* **2.** closely trimmed.

shav•er (shā′vər), *n.* **1.** a person or thing that shaves. **2.** an electric razor. **3.** *Informal.* a small boy; youngster. **4.** a fellow. **5.** a person who makes close bargains or is extortionate. [1375–1425; late ME; see SHAVE, -ER[1]; cf. *chip off the old block*]

shave•tail (shāv′tāl′), *n. Slang.* **1.** *U.S. Army.* a second lieutenant. **2.** a young, newly broken mule. [1840–50, *Amer.*; SHAVE + TAIL[1]; orig. in reference to unbroken army mules, whose tails were shaved for identification]

Sha•vi•an (shā′vē ən), *adj.* **1.** of, pertaining to, or characteristic of George Bernard Shaw or his works: *Shavian humor.* —*n.* **2.** a specialist in the study of the works of George Bernard Shaw. [1905–10; *Shav-* (Latinization of SHAW) + -IAN] —**Sha′vi•an•ism,** *n.*

Sha•vi•an•a (shā′vē an′ə, -ä′nə), *n.pl.* collected items pertaining to George Bernard Shaw. [*Shav-* (see SHAVIAN) + -IANA]

shav•ie (shā′vē), *n. Scot.* a trick or prank. [1760–70; SHAVE in obs. sense "swindle" + -IE]

shav•ing (shā′ving), *n.* **1.** Often, **shavings.** a very thin piece or slice, esp. of wood. **2.** the act of a person or thing that shaves. [1325–75; ME; see SHAVE, -ING[1]]

shav′ing brush′, a short, cylindrical brush with long, soft, bristles, used in lathering the face before shaving. [1830–40]

shav′ing cream′, a preparation, as of soap and free fatty acid, that is lathered and applied to the face to soften and condition the beard for shaving. [1825–35]

shav′ing horse′, *Carpentry.* a trestle for supporting and steadying a piece of work being shaved. [1790–1800, *Amer.*]

shav′ing soap′, a special soap for lathering the face to soften and condition the beard for shaving, capable of producing a thick lather due to its high fat content and low alkalinity. [1760–70]

Sha•vu•oth (*Seph. Heb.* shä vo͞o ôt′; *Ashk. Heb.* shəvo͞o′ōs, -əs), *n. Judaism.* a festival, celebrated on the sixth and seventh days of Sivan by Orthodox and Conservative Jews outside Israel but only on the sixth day by Reform Jews and Jews in Israel, that commemorates God's giving of the Ten Commandments to Moses. Also, **Sha•vu•ot′, Sha•vu′os, Shabuoth, Shabuot.** Also called **Feast of Weeks, Pentecost.** [1890–95; < Heb *Shābhū′ōth* lit., weeks]

shaw (shô), *n.* **1.** *Midland U.S.* a small wood or thicket. **2.** *Scot.* the stalks and leaves of potatoes, turnips, and other cultivated root plants. [bef. 900; ME *shawe,* OE *sceaga, scaga;* akin to SHAG[1]]

Shaw (shô), *n.* **1. Artie** (*Arthur Arshawsky*), born 1910, U.S. clarinetist and bandleader. **2. George Bernard,** 1856–1950, Irish dramatist, critic, and novelist: Nobel prize 1925. **3. Henry Wheeler.** See **Billings, Josh. 4. Irwin,** 1913–84, U.S. dramatist and author. **5. Richard Norman,** 1831–1912, English architect, born in Scotland. **6. Thomas Edward.** See **Lawrence, Thomas Edward.**

sha•wab•ti (shə wab′tē), *n.* a figurine placed in an ancient Egyptian tomb to serve as a slave for the soul or as a substitute for the soul in performing forced labor. Also, **ushabti.** [1920–25; < Egyptian *šw′bt(y),* later known as *wšbty* lit., answerer; perh. deriv. of *šw′b* kind of wood]

Sha•win•i•gan (shə win′i gən), *n.* a city in S Quebec, in E Canada. 23,011.

Sha•win•i•gan-Sud (shə win′i gən so͞od′, -syd′), *n.* a town in S Quebec, in E Canada, S of Shawinigan. 11,325.

shawl (shôl), *n.* a square, triangular, or oblong piece of wool or other material worn, esp. by women, about the shoulders, or the head and shoulders, in place of a coat or hat outdoors, and indoors as protection against chill or dampness. [1655–65; < Pers *shāl*] —**shawl′less,** *adj.* —**shawl′like′,** *adj.*

shawl′ col′lar, a rolled collar and lapel in one piece that curves from the back of the neck down to the front closure of a single-breasted or double-breasted garment. [1905–10]

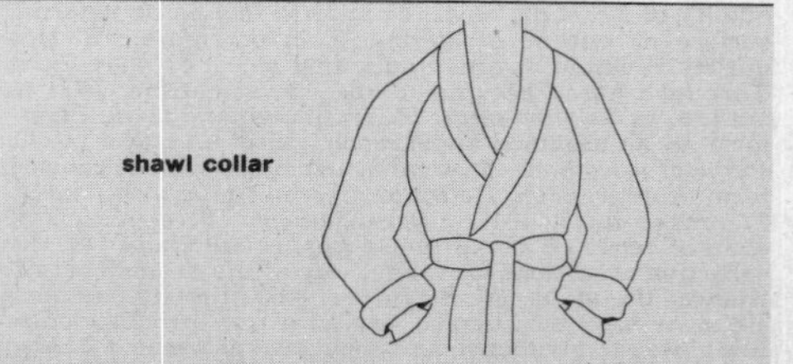
shawl collar

CONCISE ETYMOLOGY KEY: <, descended or borrowed from; >, whence; b., blend of, blended; c., cognate with; cf., compare; deriv., derivative; equiv., equivalent; imit., imitative; obl., oblique; r., replacing; s., stem; sp., spelling, spelled; resp., respelling, respelled; trans., translation; ?, origin unknown; *, unattested; ‡, probably earlier than. See the full key inside the front cover.

shawl′ tongue′, kiltie (def. 3).

shawm (shôm), *n.* an early musical woodwind instrument with a double reed: the forerunner of the modern oboe. [1300–50; ME *schalme* < MF *chaume* < L *calamus* stalk, reed < Gk *kálamos* reed; r. ME *schallemele* < MF *chalemel* (see CHALUMEAU)]

Shawn (shôn), *n.* **1. Ted** (*Edwin M.*), 1891–1972, U.S. dancer and choreographer (husband of Ruth St. Denis). **2.** a male given name, form of **John.**

Shaw·nee (shô nē′), *n., pl.* **-nees,** (*esp. collectively*) **-nee. 1.** a member of an Algonquian-speaking tribe formerly in the east-central U.S., now in Oklahoma. **2.** the Algonquian language of the Shawnee tribe. **3.** a town in E Kansas. 29,653. **4.** a city in central Oklahoma. 26,506. [1720–30, *Amer.*; back formation from earlier *Shawnese, Shawanese* (construed as pl.), reshaping (with -ESE) of earlier *Shawanoes* (pl.) < Munsee Delaware *šá·wano·w* (sing.) < Shawnee *ša·wano·ki* Shawnees, lit., people of the south]

Shaw·wal (shə wäl′), *n.* the tenth month of the Muslim calendar. Cf. **Muslim calendar.** [1760–70; < Ar *shawwāl*]

shay (shā), *n. Chiefly Dial.* a chaise. [1710–20; resp. and back formation from CHAISE (taken as pl.)]

shaykh (shāk, shīk), *n.* shaikh (def. 2).

Shays (shāz), *n.* **Daniel,** 1747–1825, American Revolutionary War soldier: leader of a popular insurrection **(Shays′ Rebel′lion)** in Massachusetts 1786–87.

Shay·tan (shī tän′), *n.* (in Muslim usage) Ash-Shaytān.

Sha·zar (shä zär′, sha-), *n.* **Zal·man** (zäl′män), (*Shneor Zalman Rubashev*), 1889–1974, Israeli statesman, born in Russia: president 1963–73.

Shcha·ran·sky (shə ran′skē; *Russ.* shchu rän′skyē), *n.* **(Na·tan) A·na·to·ly** (nä tän′ an′ə tō′lē; *Russ.* u nu-tô′lyē) born 1948, Soviet mathematician and human-rights activist, in Israel since 1986.

Shcher·ba·kov (sher′bə kôf′, -kof′; *Russ.* shchyir bu-kôf′), *n.* a former name (1946–57) of **Andropov.**

she (shē), *pron., sing. nom.* **she,** *poss.* **her** or **hers,** *obj.* **her;** *pl. nom.* **they,** *poss.* **their** or **theirs,** *obj.* **them;** *n., pl.* **shes.** —*pron.* **1.** the female person or animal being discussed or last mentioned; that female. **2.** the woman: *She who listens learns.* **3.** anything considered, as by personification, to be feminine: *spring, with all the memories she conjures up.* —*n.* **4.** a female person or animal. **5.** an object or device considered as female or feminine. [1125–75; ME, alter. of OE *sēo, sīo, sie,* fem. of *se* THE[1]; r. OE *hēo, hio,* fem. personal pronoun; see HE[1], HER]
—**Usage.** See **he**[1], **me, they.**

s/he (shē′ər hē′, shē′hē′), *pron.* she or he: used as an orthographic device to avoid *he* when the sex of the antecedent is unknown or irrelevant. Cf. **she/he.**
—**Usage.** See **he**[1].

shea (shē, shā), *n.* See **shea tree.** [1799; said to be < Bambara *si* (*shea* is Mungo Park's sp.)]

shea′ but′ter, a solid, greenish, yellowish, or whitish fat derived from the seeds of the shea tree, used for food and in the manufacture of soaps and candles. [1840–50]

sheaf (shēf), *n., pl.* **sheaves,** *v.* —*n.* **1.** one of the bundles in which cereal plants, as wheat, rye, etc., are bound after reaping. **2.** any bundle, cluster, or collection: *a sheaf of papers.* —*v.t.* **3.** to bind (something) into a sheaf or sheaves. [bef. 900; ME *shefe* (n.), OE *scēaf;* c. D *schoof* sheaf, G *Schaub* wisp of straw, ON *skauf* tail of a fox] —**sheaf′like′,** *adj.*

sheal·ing (shē′ling), *n. Scot.* shieling.

shea′ nut′, the seed of the shea tree and the source of shea butter. [1915–20]

shear (shēr), *v.,* **sheared, sheared** or **shorn, shear·ing,** *n.* —*v.t.* **1.** to cut (something). **2.** to remove by or as if by cutting or clipping with a sharp instrument: *to shear wool from sheep.* **3.** to cut or clip the hair, fleece, wool, etc., from: *to shear sheep.* **4.** to strip or deprive (usually fol. by *of*): *to shear someone of power.* **5.** *Chiefly Scot.* to reap with a sickle. **6.** to travel through by or as if by cutting: *Chimney swifts sheared the air.* —*v.i.* **7.** to cut or cut through something with a sharp instrument. **8.** to progress by or as if by cutting: *The cruiser sheared through the water.* **9.** *Mech., Geol.* to become fractured along a plane as a result of forces acting parallel to the plane. **10.** *Chiefly Scot.* to reap crops with a sickle. —*n.* **11.** Usually, **shears.** (*sometimes used with a singular v.*) **a.** scissors of large size (usually used with *pair of*). **b.** any of various other cutting implements or machines having two blades that resemble or suggest those of scissors. **12.** the act or process of shearing or being sheared. **13.** a shearing of sheep (used in stating the age of sheep): *a sheep of one shear.* **14.** the quantity, esp. of wool or fleece, cut off at one shearing. **15.** one blade of a pair of large scissors. **16.** Usually, **shears.** (*usually used with a plural v.*) Also, **sheers.** Also called **shear legs, sheerlegs.** a framework for hoisting heavy weights, consisting of two or more spars with their legs separated, fastened together near the top and steadied by guys, which support a tackle. **17.** a machine for cutting rigid material, as metal in sheet or plate form, by moving the edge of a blade through it. **18.** *Mech., Geol.* the tendency of forces to deform or fracture a member or a rock in a direction parallel to the force, as by sliding one section against another. **19.** *Physics.* the lateral deformation produced in a body by an external force, expressed as the ratio of the lateral displacement between two points lying in parallel planes to the vertical distance between the planes. [bef. 900; (v.) ME *sheren,* OE *sceran,* c. D, G *scheren,* ON *skera;* (n.) (in sense "tool for shearing") ME *sheres* (pl.), continuing OE *scērero, scēar,* two words derived from the same root as the v.] —**shear′er,** *n.* —**shear′less,** *adj.*

sheared (shērd), *adj.* **1.** shaped or completed by or as if by shearing. **2.** trimmed to an even, symmetrical, or uniform length, as fur, shrubbery, etc.: *a sheared muskrat coat.* [1610–20; SHEAR + -ED[2]]

Shear·er (shēr′ər), *n.* **Moira** (*Moira Shearer King*), born 1926, British ballerina.

shear′ legs′, shear (def. 16). Also, **sheerlegs.** [1855–60]

shear·ling (shēr′ling), *n.* **1.** *Chiefly Brit.* a yearling sheep that has been shorn once. **2.** short wool pulled from such a sheep. **3.** the skin from a recently shorn sheep or lamb, tanned with the wool still on it. [1350–1400; ME *scherling.* See SHEAR, -LING[1]]

shear′ mod′ulus, *Physics.* a coefficient of elasticity of a substance, expressing the ratio between the force per unit area **(shear′ing stress′)** that laterally deforms the substance and the shear **(shear′ing strain′)** that is produced by this force. Also called **modulus of rigidity, modulus of torsion, torsion modulus.**

shear′ transforma′tion, *Math.* a map of a coordinate space in which one coordinate is held fixed and the other coordinate or coordinates are shifted. [1880–85]

shear·wa·ter (shēr′wô′tər, -wot′ər), *n.* any of several long-winged petrels of the genus *Puffinus* that appear to shear the water with their wing tips when flying low. [1665–75; SHEAR + WATER]

shear′ zone′, *Geol.* a zone of closely spaced, approximately parallel faults or dispersed displacements. [1910–15]

sheat·fish (shēt′fish′), *n., pl.* **-fish·es,** (*esp. collectively*) **-fish.** a large, freshwater catfish, *Silurus glanis,* inhabiting rivers in central and eastern Europe, sometimes reaching a weight of 400 lb. (181.4 kg). [1580–90; earlier *sheath-fish; sheath* is erroneous trans. of G *Scheide* sheatfish]

sheath (shēth), *n., pl.* **sheaths** (shēthz), *v.* —*n.* **1.** a case or covering for the blade of a sword, dagger, or the like. **2.** any similar close-fitting covering or case. **3.** a condom. **4.** *Biol.* a closely enveloping part or structure, as in an animal or plant. **5.** *Bot.* the leaf base when it forms a vertical coating surrounding the stem. **6.** a close-fitting dress, skirt, or coat, esp. an unbelted dress with a straight drape. **7.** *Elect.* the metal covering of a cable. **8.** *Electronics.* **a.** the metal wall of a wave guide. **b.** a space charge formed by ions near an electrode in a tube containing low-pressure gas. **c.** the region of a space charge in a cathode-ray tube. —*v.t.* **9.** to sheathe. [bef. 950; ME *s(c)heth(e),* OE *scēath;* c. G *Scheide;* see SHED[2]] —**sheath′less,** *adj.* —**sheath′like′, sheath′y,** *adj.*

sheath·bill (shēth′bil′), *n.* either of two white sea birds, *Chionis alba* or *C. minor,* of the colder parts of the Southern Hemisphere: so called from the horny sheath covering the base of the upper bill. [1775–85; SHEATH + BILL[2]]

sheathe (shēth), *v.t.,* **sheathed, sheath·ing. 1.** to put (a sword, dagger, etc.) into a sheath. **2.** to plunge (a sword, dagger, etc.) in something as if in a sheath. **3.** to enclose in or as if in a casing or covering. **4.** to cover or provide with a protective layer or sheathing: *to sheathe a roof with copper.* **5.** to cover (a cable, electrical connector, etc.) with a metal sheath for grounding. [1350–1400; ME *shethen,* deriv. of SHEATH] —**sheath′er,** *n.*

sheath·ing (shē′thing), *n.* **1.** the act of a person who sheathes. **2.** something that sheathes; a covering or outer layer of metal, wood, or other material, as one of metal plates on a ship's bottom, the first covering of boards on a house, etc. **3.** material for forming any such covering. [1490–1500; SHEATHE + -ING[1]]

sheath′ knife′, a knife carried in a sheath. [1830–40]

sheath′ pile′. See **sheet pile.**

shea′ tree′, an African tree, *Butyrospermum parkii,* of the sapodilla family, bearing a round, smooth-skinned fruit that contains one or more seeds yielding shea butter. [1790–1800]

sheave[1] (shēv), *v.t.,* **sheaved, sheav·ing.** to gather, collect, or bind into a sheaf or sheaves. [1570–80; deriv. of SHEAF]

sheave[2] (shiv, shēv), *n.* **1.** a pulley for hoisting or hauling, having a grooved rim for retaining a wire rope. **2.** a wheel with a grooved rim, for transmitting force to a cable or belt. [1300–50; ME *schive;* akin to D *schijf* sheave, G *Scheibe* disk]

sheaves[1] (shēvz), *n.* pl. of **sheaf.**

sheaves[2] (shivz, shēvz), *n.* pl. of **sheave**[2].

She·ba (shē′bə), *n. Bible.* **1. Queen of,** the queen who visited Solomon to test his wisdom. I Kings 10:1–13. **2.** Biblical name of **Saba** (def. 2).

she·bang (shə bang′), *n.* **1.** *Informal.* the structure of something, as of an organization, contrivance, or affair: *The whole shebang fell apart when the chairman quit.* **2.** a primitive dwelling; shack; shanty. [1860–65, *Amer.*; orig. uncert. (perh. alter. of CHAR-À-BANC, though sense shift unclear; SHEBEEN, often cited as the source, is implausible both phonetically and semantically)]

She·bat (shə bät′, shē′bat), *n.* Shevat.

she·been (shə bēn′), *n. Scot., Irish Eng., South African.* a tavern or house where liquor is sold illegally. [1780–90; < Ir *síbín* illicit whiskey, place where such whiskey is sold (ellipsis from *teach síbín* shebeen house), orig., a unit of measure < E CHOPIN[1]]

She·be·li (shi bā′lē), *n.* **We·bi** (wā′bi). See **Webi Shebeli.**

She·boy·gan (shi boi′gən), *n.* a port in E Wisconsin, on Lake Michigan. 48,085.

She·chem (shē′kəm, -kem, shek′əm, -em), *n.* a town of ancient Palestine, near the city of Samaria; occupied by Israel 1967–96; since 1996 under Palestinian self-rule: first capital of the northern kingdom of Israel. Modern name, **Nablus.**

She Chi (shu′ jē′), (in popular Chinese religion) the gods of the earth and the harvest.

She·chi·nah (shə kē′nə, -kī′-; *Seph. Heb.* shə ᴋʜē-nä′; *Ashk. Heb.* shə ᴋʜē′nə), *n. Theol.* Shekhinah.

she·chi·tah (*Seph.* shə ᴋʜē tä′; *Ashk.* shə ᴋʜē′tə), *n. Hebrew.* shehitah.

she′-crab soup′ (shē′krab′), *Southern Atlantic Seaboard Cookery.* a thick, bisquelike soup made with the meat and eggs of the female crab.

shed[1] (shed), *n.* **1.** a slight or rude structure built for shelter, storage, etc. **2.** a large, strongly built structure, often open at the sides or end. [1475–85; var. of SHADE] —**shed′like′,** *adj.*

shed[2] (shed), *v.,* **shed, shed·ding,** *n.* —*v.t.* **1.** to pour forth (water or other liquid), as a fountain. **2.** to emit and let fall, as tears. **3.** to impart or release; give or send forth (light, sound, fragrance, influence, etc.). **4.** to resist being penetrated or affected by: *cloth that sheds water.* **5.** to cast off or let fall (leaves, hair, feathers, skin, shell, etc.) by natural process. **6.** *Textiles.* to separate (the warp) in forming a shed. —*v.i.* **7.** to fall off, as leaves. **8.** to drop out, as hair, seed, grain, etc. **9.** to cast off hair, feathers, skin, or other covering or parts by natural process. **10. shed blood, a.** to cause blood to flow. **b.** to kill by violence; slaughter. —*n.* **11.** *Textiles.* (on a loom) a triangular, transverse opening created between raised and lowered warp threads through which the shuttle passes in depositing the loose pick. [bef. 950; ME *s(c)hed(d)en* (v.), OE *scēadan,* var. of *scēādan;* c. G *scheiden* to divide] —**shed′a·ble, shed′da·ble,** *adj.*
—**Syn. 3.** emit, radiate, effuse, spread. **4.** repel. **9.** molt.

she'd (shēd), **1.** contraction of *she had.* **2.** contraction of *she would.*
—**Usage.** See **contraction.**

shed·der (shed′ər), *n.* **1.** a person or thing that sheds. **2.** a lobster, crab, etc., just before it molts. [1350–1400; ME; see SHED[2], -ER[1]]

she-dev·il (shē′dev′il, -dev′-), *n.* a woman who resembles a devil, as in extreme wickedness, cruelty, or bad temper.

shed′ roof′, a roof having a single slope. Also called **penthouse.** [1730–40]

shed′ room′, *Chiefly Southern U.S.* a storage room. [1815–25, *Amer.*]

shed·row (shed′rō′), *n.* (at a racetrack) a row or double row of horse barns with individual stalls facing a walkway. [SHED[1] + ROW[1]]

shee (shē), *n.* sidh.

shee·fish (shē′fish′), *n., pl.* **-fish·es,** (*esp. collectively*) **-fish.** inconnu (def. 2). [1785–95; *shee* (< a Subarctic Athabaskan language; cf. Eastern Kutchin *ṣyuh*) + FISH]

Shee·lah (shē′lə), *n.* a female given name.

Shee·ler (shē′lər), *n.* **Charles,** 1883–1965, U.S. painter and photographer.

sheen (shēn), *n.* **1.** luster; brightness; radiance. **2.** gleaming attire. —*adj.* **3.** shining. **4.** beautiful. —*v.i.* **5.** *Scot. and North Eng.* to shine. [bef. 900; (adj.) ME *sheene* beautiful, bright, shining, OE *scēne;* c. G *schön;* (v.) ME *s(c)henen,* deriv. of the adj.; (n.) deriv. of the adj.] —**sheen′ful,** *adj.* —**sheen′less,** *adj.* —**sheen′·ly,** *adv.*
—**Syn. 1.** See **polish.**

Sheen (shēn), *n.* **Fulton (John),** 1895–1979, U.S. Roman Catholic clergyman, writer, and teacher.

Shee·na (shē′nə), *n.* a female given name.

shee·ney (shē′nē), *n., pl.* **-neys.** *Slang (disparaging and offensive).* sheeny[2].

sheen·y[1] (shē′nē), *adj.,* **sheen·i·er, sheen·i·est.** shining; lustrous. [1615–25; SHEEN + -Y[1]]

shee·ny[2] (shē′nē), *n., pl.* **-nies.** *Slang (disparaging and offensive).* a Jew. Also, **sheeney, shee′nie.** [1810–20; orig. obscure]

sheep (shēp), *n., pl.* **sheep. 1.** any of numerous ruminant mammals of the genus *Ovis,* of the family Bovidae, closely related to the goats, esp. *O. aries,* bred in a number of domesticated varieties. **2.** leather made from the skin of these animals. **3.** a meek, unimaginative, or easily led person. **4. separate the sheep from the goats,** to separate good people from bad or those intended for a specific end from unqualified people. [bef. 900; ME; OE (north) *scēp;* c. D *schaap,* G *Schaf*] —**sheep′less,** *adj.* —**sheep′like′,** *adj.*

sheep′back rock′ (shēp′bak′), *Geol.* See **roche moutonnée.** [1875–80; SHEEP + BACK[1]]

sheep·ber·ry (shēp′ber′ē, -bə rē), *n., pl.* **-ries. 1.** a North American shrub or small tree, *Viburnum lentago,* of the honeysuckle family, having flat-topped clusters of small white flowers and edible, berrylike black drupes. **2.** the fruit itself. Also called **black haw, nannyberry.** [1805–15, *Amer.*; SHEEP + BERRY]

sheep·cote (shēp′kōt′), *n. Chiefly Brit.* a pen or covered enclosure for sheep. [1375–1425; late ME. See SHEEP, COTE[1]]

sheep-dip (shēp′dip′), *n.* a lotion or wash applied to the fleece or skin of sheep to kill vermin, usually applied by immersing the animals in vats. [1860–65]

sheep•dog (shēp′dôg′, -dog′), *n.* a dog trained to herd and guard sheep. Also, **sheep′ dog′.** [1765–75; SHEEP + DOG]

sheep′ fes′cue, a widely distributed grass, *Festuca ovina*, having densely clustered stems and cultivated for lawns and forage. [1750–60]

sheep•fold (shēp′fōld′), *n. Chiefly Brit.* an enclosure for sheep. [bef. 1000; ME; OE *sceapa falda.* See SHEEP, FOLD[2]]

sheep•head (shēp′hed′), *n., pl.* (*esp. collectively*) **-head,** (*esp. referring to two or more kinds or species*) **-heads.** a large California food fish, *Semicossyphus pulcher*, of the wrasse family. Also called **fathead, redfish.** [1535–45; so called from the resemblance of its teeth to those of a sheep]

sheep•herd•er (shēp′hûr′dər), *n.* shepherd (def. 1). [1870–75, *Amer.*; SHEEP + HERDER] —**sheep′herd′ing,** *n., adj.*

sheep•ish (shē′pish), *adj.* **1.** embarrassed or bashful, as by having done something wrong or foolish. **2.** like sheep, as in meekness, docility, etc. [1150–1200; ME *shepisshe.* See SHEEP, -ISH[1]] —**sheep′ish•ly,** *adv.* —**sheep′ish•ness,** *n.*

sheep′ ked′, sheeptick.

sheep′ lau′rel, a low North American shrub, *Kalmia angustifolia*, of the heath family, having oblong leaves poisonous to grazing animals. Also called **dwarf laurel, lambkill.** [1800–10, *Amer.*]

sheep•man (shēp′mən, -man′), *n., pl.* **-men** (-mən, -men′). **1.** a person engaged in the tending or breeding of sheep, esp. the owner of a sheep ranch. **2.** a shepherd. [1585–95; SHEEP + MAN[1]]

sheep's′ eyes′, shy, amorous, lovesick glances (usually prec. by *make* or *cast*): *making sheep's eyes at the new girl in class.* [1520–30]

sheep•shank (shēp′shangk′), *n.* a kind of knot, hitch, or bend made on a rope to shorten it temporarily. [1635–45; short for *sheepshank knot;* literal sense unclear]

sheeps•head (shēps′hed′), *n., pl.* (*esp. collectively*) **-head,** (*esp. referring to two or more kinds or species*) **-heads** for 1–3. **1.** a deep-bodied, black-banded food fish, *Archosargus probatocephalus*, living along the Atlantic coast of the U.S. **2.** a freshwater drum, *Aplodinotus grunniens*, of eastern North America. **3.** sheephead. **4.** Also called **schafskopf.** *Cards.* an earlier and simpler form of skat. **5.** *Obs.* a foolish or stupid person. [1535–45; SHEEP + 'S[1] + HEAD]

sheep•shear•ing (shēp′shēr′ing), *n.* **1.** an act or instance of shearing sheep. **2.** the time or season of shearing sheep. [1580–90; SHEEP + SHEARING] —**sheep′•shear′er,** *n.*

sheep•skin (shēp′skin′), *n.* **1.** the skin of a sheep, esp. such a skin dressed with the wool on, as for a garment. **2.** leather, parchment, or the like, made from the skin of sheep. **3.** *Informal.* a diploma. —*adj.* **4.** made from the skin of a sheep. **5.** (of a garment) lined with the skin of a sheep dressed with the wool on. [1150–1200; ME *shepskinn.* See SHEEP, SKIN]

sheep′ sor′rel, a slender weed, *Rumex acetosella*, of the buckwheat family, found in poor, dry soils, having arrow-shaped leaves with an acid taste. [1570–80]

sheeps′wool sponge′ (shēps′wo͝ol′). See **wool sponge.** [1880–85]

sheep•tick (shēp′tik′), *n.* a wingless, bloodsucking, dipterous insect, *Melophagus ovinus*, that is parasitic on sheep. Also, **sheep′ tick′.** Also called **ked, sheep ked.** [1375–1425; late ME *scheptyke;* see SHEEP, TICK[2]]

sheeptick, *Melophagus ovinus,* length ¼ in. (0.6 cm)

sheep•walk (shēp′wôk′), *n. Brit.* a tract of land on which sheep are pastured. [1580–90; SHEEP + WALK]

sheer[1] (shēr), *adj.,* **-er, -est,** *adv., n.* —*adj.* **1.** transparently thin; diaphanous, as some fabrics: *sheer stockings.* **2.** unmixed with anything else: *We drilled a hundred feet through sheer rock.* **3.** unqualified; utter: *sheer nonsense.* **4.** extending down or up very steeply; almost completely vertical: *a sheer descent of rock.* **5.** *Brit. Obs.* bright; shining. —*adv.* **6.** clear; completely; quite: *ran sheer into the thick of battle.* **7.** perpendicularly; vertically; down or up very steeply. —*n.* **8.** a thin, diaphanous material, as chiffon or voile. [1175–1225; ME *scere, shere, schere* free, clear, bright, thin; prob. < ON *skǣrr;* change of *sk-* > *s(c)h-* perh. by influence of the related OE *scīr* (E dial. *shire* clear, pure, thin); c. G *schier*, ON *skīr*, Goth *skeirs* clear; see SHINE] —**sheer′ly,** *adv.* —**sheer′ness,** *n.*
—**Syn. 2.** mere, simple, pure, unadulterated. **3.** absolute, downright. **4.** abrupt, precipitous. **6.** totally, entirely. —**Ant. 1.** opaque.

sheer[2] (shēr), *v.i.* **1.** to deviate from a course, as a ship; swerve. —*v.t.* **2.** to cause to sheer. **3.** *Shipbuilding.* to give sheer to (a hull). —*n.* **4.** a deviation or divergence, as of a ship from its course; swerve. **5.** *Shipbuilding.* the fore-and-aft upward curve of the hull of a vessel at the main deck or bulwarks. **6.** *Naut.* the position in which a ship at anchor is placed to keep it clear of the anchor. [1620–30; special use of SHEER[1]; cf. sense development of CLEAR]

CONCISE ETYMOLOGY KEY: <, descended or borrowed from; >, whence; b., blend of, blended; c., cognate with; cf., compare; deriv., derivative; equiv., equivalent; imit., imitative; obl., oblique; r., replacing; s., stem; sp., spelling, spelled; resp., respelling, respelled; trans., translation; ?, origin unknown; *, unattested; ‡, probably earlier than. See the full key inside the front cover.

sheer•legs (shēr′legz′), *n.* (*usually used with a plural v.*) shear (def. 16). [*sheer*, sp. var. of SHEAR + LEG + -S[3]]

Sheer•ness (shēr′nis), *n.* a seaport in N Kent, in SE England on the Isle of Sheppey, at the mouth of the Thames: government dockyards. 31,541.

sheer′ plan′, *Naval Archit.* a diagrammatic fore-and-aft elevation of the hull of a vessel, showing bow and buttock lines, stations, water lines, diagonals, decks, bulwarks, etc. Also called **profile plan.** Cf. **body plan, half-breadth plan.** [1790–1800]

sheers (shērz), *n.* (*usually used with a plural v.*) shear (def. 16).

sheet[1] (shēt), *n.* **1.** a large rectangular piece of cotton, linen, or other material used as an article of bedding, commonly spread in pairs so that one is immediately above and the other immediately below the sleeper. **2.** a broad, relatively thin, surface, layer, or covering. **3.** a relatively thin, usually rectangular form, piece, plate, or slab, as of photographic film, glass, metal, etc. **4.** material, as metal or glass, in the form of broad, relatively thin pieces. **5.** a sail, as on a ship or boat. **6.** a rectangular piece of paper or parchment, esp. one on which to write. **7.** a newspaper or periodical. **8.** *Printing and Bookbinding.* a large, rectangular piece of printing paper, esp. one for printing a complete signature. **9.** *Philately.* the impression from a plate or the like on a single sheet of paper before any division of the paper into individual stamps. **10.** an extent, stretch, or expanse, as of fire or water: *sheets of flame.* **11.** a thin, flat piece of metal or a very shallow pan on which to place food while baking. **12.** *Geol.* a more or less horizontal mass of rock, esp. volcanic rock intruded between strata or poured out over a surface. **13.** *Math.* **a.** one of the separate pieces making up a geometrical surface: *a hyperboloid of two sheets.* **b.** one of the planes or pieces of planes making up a Riemann surface. **14.** *Crystall.* a type of crystal structure, as in mica, in which certain atoms unite strongly in two dimensions to form a layer that is weakly joined to others. —*v.t.* **15.** to furnish with a sheet or sheets. **16.** to wrap in a sheet. **17.** to cover with a sheet or layer of something. [bef. 900; ME *shete*, OE *scēte* (north), *sciete*, deriv. of *scēat* corner, lap, sheet, region; c. D *schoot*, G *Schoss*, ON *skaut*] —**sheet′less,** *adj.* —**sheet′like′,** *adj.*

sheet[2] (shēt), *n.* **1.** *Naut.* **a.** a rope or chain for extending the clews of a square sail along a yard. **b.** a rope for trimming a fore-and-aft sail. **c.** a rope or chain for extending the lee clew of a course. **2. three sheets in** or **to the wind,** *Slang.* intoxicated. —*v.t.* **3.** *Naut.* to trim, extend, or secure by means of a sheet or sheets. [1300–50; ME *shete*, shortening of OE *scēatlīne*, equiv. to *scēat(a)* lower corner of a sail (see SHEET[1]) + *līne* LINE[1], rope; c. LG *schote*]

sheet′ an′chor, 1. *Naut.* a large anchor used only in cases of emergency. **2.** a final reliance or resource, as when in danger. [1485–95]

sheet′ bend′, a knot made between two ropes by forming a bight in one and passing the end of the other through the bight, around it, and under itself. Also called **becket bend, netting knot, weaver's hitch, weaver's knot.** [1835–45]

sheet•case (shēt′kās′), *n.* a covering made of sheet material, esp. one used for a down comforter. Also, **sheet′cas′ing.** [SHEET[1] + (PILLOW)CASE]

sheet′ ero′sion, *Geol.* erosion by sheets of running water, rather than by streams. Also called **sheet′-flood ero′sion** (shēt′flud′). [1915–20]

sheet-fed (shēt′fed′), *adj.* (of a printing press) fed by and designed to print individual flat sheets of paper. Cf. **web-fed.** [1885–90]

sheet′ feed′er, *Computers.* a device that feeds paper into a printer one sheet at a time.

sheet′ film′, *Photog.* a flat piece of film cut to a required size before being loaded into a camera.

sheet′ glass′, glass in sheet form produced by drawing or by the cylinder glass process. [1795–1805]

sheet′ ice′, ice frozen in a relatively thin, smooth, and extensive layer on the surface of a body of water. [1895–1900]

sheet•ing (shē′ting), *n.* **1.** the act of covering with or forming into a sheet or sheets. **2.** wide muslin, chiefly for sheets. **3.** *Engin., Building Trades.* a quantity of sheet piles. [1705–15; SHEET[1] + -ING[1]]

sheet′ light′ning, lightning appearing merely as a general illumination over a broad area, usually because the path of the flash is obscured by clouds. [1820–30]

sheet′ met′al, metal in sheets or thin plates. [1905–10] —**sheet′-metal′,** *adj.*

sheet′ mu′sic, music printed on unbound sheets of paper. [1855–60]

sheet′ pile′, one of a number of piles, usually flat, driven side by side to retain earth, etc., or to prevent seepage into an excavation. Also called **sheath pile.** [1835–45] —**sheet′ pil′ing.**

Sheet•rock (shēt′rok′), *Trademark.* a brand name for a plasterboard of gypsum between paper.

sheet′-web weav′er (shēt′web′), any of numerous spiders of the family Linyphiidae, characterized by a closely woven, sheetlike web.

Shef•field (shef′ēld), *n.* **1.** a city in South Yorkshire, in N England. 559,800. **2.** a city in NW Alabama, on the Tennessee River. 11,903.

Shef′field Lake′, a town in N Ohio. 10,484.

Shef′field plate′, sheet copper with a cladding of silver. [1855–60; named after SHEFFIELD, England]

she•getz (shā′gits), *n., pl.* ***shkotz•im*** (shkôt′sim). *Yiddish* (*often disparaging*). **1.** a boy or man who is not Jewish. **2.** a Jewish boy or man whose attitudes and behavior are felt to resemble those of a gentile. Cf. ***shiksa.***

she/he (shē′ər hē′, shē′hē′), a combined form used to replace a singular nominative pronoun in denoting a person of either sex: *Each employee must sign the register when she/he enters or leaves.* Cf. **s/he.**
—**Usage.** See **he**[1].

she•hi•tah (*Seph.* shə KHĒ tä′; *Ashk.* shə KHĒ′tə), *n. Hebrew.* the slaughtering of animals for food by a duly certified person in the manner prescribed by Jewish law. Also, ***shechitah.*** Cf. ***shohet.***

sheik (shēk, shāk), *n.* **1.** Also, **shaikh, sheikh.** (in Islamic countries) the patriarch of a tribe or family; chief: a term of polite address. **2.** *Slang.* a man held to be masterful and irresistibly charming to women. [1570–80; < Ar *shaykh* old man] —**sheik′like′,** *adj.*

shei•ka (shā′kä), *n.* (in Islamic countries) **1.** the wife of a sheik. **2.** a woman who heads a large family and is revered, esp. as a guardian of religious ways. Also, **shei•kha** (shāk′hä, shā′KHä). [1850–55; < Ar *shaykha*]

sheik•dom (shēk′dəm, shāk′-), *n.* the land or territory under the control of a sheik. Also, **sheikh′dom.** [1835–45; SHEIK + -DOM]

shei•la (shē′lə), *n. Australian Slang.* a girl or young woman. [special use of proper name]

Shei•la (shē′lə), *n.* a female given name, form of **Celia.**

Shei•tan (shī tän′), *n.* Ash-Shaytān.

shei•tel (shāt′l), *n., pl.* ***sheit•len*** (shāt′lən). *Yiddish.* a wig worn by certain Orthodox Jewish married women in keeping with an old rabbinical precept that forbids a woman to leave her hair uncovered in the sight of a man other than her husband.

shek•el (shek′əl), *n.* **1.** Also, **sheqel.** a paper money, cupronickel or silver coin, and monetary unit of Israel equal to 100 agorot: replaced the pound in 1980. **2.** an ancient, orig. Babylonian, unit of weight, of varying value, taken as equal to the fiftieth or the sixtieth part of a mina or to about a quarter to half an ounce. **3.** a coin of this weight, esp. the chief silver coin of the ancient Hebrews. **4. shekels,** *Slang.* money; cash. [1550–60; < Heb *sheqel*]

shekel (def. 3) (Hebrew)
obverse reverse

She•khi•nah (shi kē′nə, -kī′-; *Seph. Heb.* shə KHĒ nä′; *Ashk. Heb.* shə KHĒ′nə), *n. Theol.* the presence of God on earth or a symbol or manifestation of His presence. Also, **She•ki′nah, Shechinah.** [1655–65; < Heb *shěkhīnāh*]

Shel•burne (shel′bûrn), *n.* **William Petty Fitzmaurice, 2nd Earl of, 1st Marquess of Lansdowne.** See **Lansdowne, 1st Marquess of.**

Shel•by (shel′bē), *n.* a city in S North Carolina. 15,310.

Shel•by•ville (shel′bē vil′), *n.* **1.** a city in central Indiana. 14,989. **2.** a city in central Tennessee. 13,530.

Shel•don (shel′dən, -dn), *n.* a male given name.

shel•drake (shel′drāk′), *n., pl.* **-drakes,** (*esp. collectively*) **-drake. 1.** any of several Old World ducks of the genus *Tadorna*, certain species of which have highly variegated plumage. **2.** any of various other ducks, esp. the goosander or merganser. [1275–1325; ME *sheldedrake*, equiv. to *sheld* particolored + *drake* DRAKE[1]]

sheldrake, *Tadorna tadorna,* length 25 in. (64 cm)

shel•duck (shel′duk′), *n., pl.* **-ducks,** (*esp. collectively*) **-duck. 1.** a sheldrake. **2.** a female sheldrake. [1700–10; SHEL(DRAKE) + DUCK[1]]

She•le•pin (shə lep′in; *Russ.* shi lye′pyin), *n.* **A•le•xan•dr Ni•ko•la•ye•vich** (al′ig zan′dər nik′ə lī′ə vich; *Russ.* u lyi ksändr′ nyi ku lä′yi vyich), born 1918, Soviet government official: member of the Politburo 1966–75.

shelf (shelf), *n., pl.* **shelves** (shelvz). **1.** a thin slab of wood, metal, etc., fixed horizontally to a wall or in a frame, for supporting objects. **2.** the contents of this: *a shelf of books.* **3.** a surface or projection resembling this; ledge. **4.** *Physical Geog.* **a.** a sandbank or submerged extent of rock in the sea or river. **b.** the bedrock underlying an alluvial deposit or the like. **c.** See **continental shelf. 5.** *Archery.* the upper part of the bow hand, on which the arrow rests. **6. off the shelf,** readily available from merchandise in stock: *Any of those parts can be purchased off the shelf.* **7. on the shelf,** *Informal.* **a.** put aside temporarily; postponed. **b.** inactive; useless. **c.** without prospects of marriage, as after having broken an engagement. [1350–1400; ME; OE *scylfe;* akin to LG *schelf* shelf, ON *-skjalf* bench] —**shelf′like′,** *adj.*

shelf′ an′gle, an angle iron attached to or suspended from a girder to carry masonry or the ends of a number of joists.

shelf•ful (shelf′fo͝ol), *n., pl.* **-fuls. 1.** an amount adequate to fill a shelf: *They buy canned goods by the shelf-*

ful. **2.** the amount contained on a shelf: *We gave away a shelfful of books.* [1875–80; SHELF + -FUL]
—Usage. See **-ful.**

shelf′ ice′, ice forming part of or broken from an ice shelf. [1910–15]

shelf′ life′, the term or period during which a stored commodity remains effective, useful, or suitable for consumption: *Many medicines have a very short shelf life.* Also called **storage life.** [1925–30]

shelf•list (shelf′list′), *n. Library Science.* a record of the books and other materials in a library arranged in the order in which the materials are stored on shelves. [1905–10; SHELF + LIST[1]]

shelf′ mark′, *Library Science.* a symbol indicating the location of a work on a shelf. [1835–45]

shelf′ pa′per, paper used for covering shelves, esp. those of a cupboard or kitchen cabinet. [1890–95]

shell (shel), *n.* **1.** a hard outer covering of an animal, as the hard case of a mollusk, or either half of the case of a bivalve mollusk. **2.** any of various objects resembling such a covering, as in shape or in being more or less concave or hollow. **3.** the material constituting any of various coverings of this kind. **4.** the hard exterior of an egg. **5.** the usually hard, outer covering of a seed, fruit, etc., as the pod of peas. **6.** a hard, protecting or enclosing case or cover. **7.** an attitude or manner of reserve that usually conceals one's emotions, thoughts, etc.: *One could not penetrate his shell.* **8.** a hollow projectile for a cannon, mortar, etc., filled with an explosive charge designed to explode during flight, upon impact, or after penetration. **9.** a metallic cartridge used in small arms and small artillery pieces. **10.** a metal or paper cartridge, as for use in a shotgun. **11.** a cartridgelike pyrotechnic device that explodes in the air. **12. shells,** *Italian Cookery.* small pieces of pasta having the shape of a shell. **13.** the lower pastry crust of a pie, tart, or the like, baked before the filling is added. **14.** *Computers.* a program providing a menu-driven or graphical user interface designed to simplify use of the operating system, as in loading application programs. **15.** *Physics.* **a.** any of up to seven energy levels on which an electron may exist within an atom, the energies of the electrons on the same level being equal and on different levels being unequal. **b.** a group of nucleons of approximately the same energy. **16.** a light, long, narrow racing boat, for rowing by one or more persons. **17.** the outer part of a finished garment that has a lining, esp. a detachable lining. **18.** a woman's sleeveless blouse or sweater, esp. one meant for wear under a suit jacket. **19.** *Naut.* the plating, planking, or the like, covering the ribs and forming the exterior hull of a vessel. **20.** See **tortoise shell** (def. 1). **21.** a mollusk. **22.** *Engineering.* the curved solid forming a dome or vault. **23.** an arena or stadium covered by a domed or arched roof. **24.** a saucer-shaped arena or stadium. **25.** the framework, external structure, or walls and roof of a building: *After the fire, only the shell of the school was left.* **26.** a small glass for beer. **27.** the metal, pressure-resistant outer casing of a fire-tube boiler. **28.** *Metall.* **a.** a scab on the surface of an ingot. **b.** a length of unfinished tubing. **c.** a pierced forging. **d.** a hollow object made by deep drawing. —*v.t.* **29.** to take out of the shell, pod, etc.; remove the shell of. **30.** to separate (Indian corn, grain, etc.) from the ear, cob, or husk. **31.** to fire shells or explosive projectiles into, upon, or among; bombard. —*v.i.* **32.** to fall or come out of the shell, husk, etc. **33.** to come away or fall off, as a shell or outer coat. **34.** to gather sea shells. **35. shell out,** *Informal.* to hand over (money); contribute; pay. [bef. 900; (n.) ME; OE *scell* (north), *sciell;* c. D *schil* peel, skin, rink, ON *skel* shell, Goth *skalja* tile; (v.) deriv. of the n.; cf. SHALE] **—shell′-less,** *adj.* **—shell′-like′,** *adj.*

shell (def. 16)

she'll (shēl; *unstressed* shil), contraction of *she will.*
—Usage. See **contraction.**

shel•lac (shə lak′), *n., v.,* **-lacked, -lack•ing.** —*n.* **1.** lac that has been purified and formed into thin sheets, used for making varnish. **2.** a varnish **(shellac′ var′•nish)** made by dissolving this material in alcohol or a similar solvent. **3.** a phonograph record made of a breakable material containing shellac, esp. one to be played at 78 r.p.m. —*v.t.* **4.** to coat or treat with shellac. **5.** *Slang.* **a.** to defeat; trounce. **b.** to thrash soundly. Also, **shel•lack′.** [1705–15; SHELL + LAC[1], trans. of F *laque en écailles* lac in thin plates]

shel•lack•ing (shə lak′ing), *n. Slang.* **1.** an utter defeat: *a shellacking their team will remember.* **2.** a sound thrashing: *His father gave him a shellacking for stealing the book.* [1880–85; SHELLAC + -ING[1]]

shell′ back′, an underside of a spoon bowl ornamented with a shell motif.

shell•back (shel′bak′), *n.* **1.** an old sailor. **2.** a person who has crossed the equator by boat. [1880–85; SHELL + BACK[1]]

shell•bark (shel′bärk′), *n.* the shagbark tree. [1750–60; SHELL + BARK[2]]

shell′ bean′, **1.** any of various kinds of bean of which the unripe seeds are removed from the pods before cooking. **2.** the seed itself. [1865–70, *Amer.*]

shell•crack•er (shel′krak′ər), *n.* See **redear sunfish.** [1890–95, *Amer.*; SHELL + CRACKER]

shelled (sheld), *adj.* **1.** having the shell removed: *shelled pecans.* **2.** (esp. of field corn, grain, etc.) removed from the ear or husk. **3.** having or enclosed in a shell. [1570–80; SHELL + -ED[2]]

shell•er (shel′ər), *n.* **1.** a person, device, machine, etc., that shells something, as peas or clams. **2.** a person who collects seashells. [1685–95; SHELL + -ER[1]]

Shel•ley (shel′ē), *n.* **1. Mary Woll•stone•craft (God•win)** (wo͝ol′stən kraft′, -kräft′), 1797–1851, English author (wife of Percy Bysshe Shelley). **2. Percy Bysshe** (bish), 1792–1822, English poet. **3.** a male or female given name.

Shel•ley•an (shel′ē ən), *adj.* **1.** Also, **Shel′li•an.** of, pertaining to, or characteristic of Percy Bysshe Shelley or his works. —*n.* **2.** a student or admirer of the works of Percy Bysshe Shelley. [1840–50; SHELLEY + -AN]

shell•fire (shel′fīᵊr′), *n. Mil.* the firing of explosive shells or projectiles. [1855–60; SHELL + FIRE]

shell•fish (shel′fish′), *n., pl.* (*esp. collectively*) **-fish,** (*esp. referring to two or more kinds or species*) **-fish•es.** an aquatic animal having a shell, as the oyster and other mollusks and the lobster and other crustaceans. [bef. 900; ME; OE *scilfisc.* See SHELL, FISH]

shell•flow•er (shel′flou′ər). *n.* **1.** an eastern Asian plant, *Alpinia zerumbet,* of the ginger family, having pendulous clusters of fragrant white flowers with variegated markings. **2.** See **bells of Ireland. 3.** any of several other plants with flowers or parts thought to resemble shells, as those of the genus *Tigridia.* [1835–45; SHELL + FLOWER]

shell′ game′, **1.** a sleight-of-hand swindling game resembling thimblerig but employing walnut shells or the like instead of thimblelike cups. **2.** any deceit, swindle, fraud, or the like. [1885–90, *Amer.*]

shell′ jack′et, a close-fitting, semiformal jacket, with a short back, worn in the tropics in place of a tuxedo. [1830–40]

shell′ par′akeet, budgerigar.

shell′ pink′, delicate whitish to yellow pink. [1885–90] **—shell′-pink′,** *adj.*

shell•proof (shel′pro͞of′), *adj.* protected against the explosive effect of shells or bombs. [1860–65; SHELL + -PROOF]

shell′ shock′. See **battle fatigue.** [1915–20] **—shell′-shocked′, shell′shocked′,** *adj.*

shell′ star′, *Astron.* a type of star showing bright emission lines superimposed on its normal absorption spectrum, presumably caused by a gaseous shell around the star.

shell′ steak′, *Cookery.* a porterhouse steak with the fillet removed. Also called **New York cut, New York steak.** [1970–75]

shell•work (shel′wûrk′), *n.* decorative work composed of seashells: *an elaborate picture frame decorated with shellwork.* [1605–15; SHELL + WORK]

shell•y (shel′ē), *adj.,* **shell•i•er, shell•i•est. 1.** abounding in shells: *a shelly surf.* **2.** consisting of a shell or shells. **3.** like a shell or shells. [1545–55; SHELL + -Y[1]]

Shel•ly (shel′ē), *n.* a male or female given name.

Shel•ta (shel′tə), *n.* a private language, based in part on Irish, used among Travelers in the British Isles. [1875–80; orig. uncert.]

shel•ter (shel′tər), *n.* **1.** something beneath, behind, or within which a person, animal, or thing is protected from storms, missiles, adverse conditions, etc.; refuge. **2.** the protection or refuge afforded by such a thing: *He took shelter in a nearby barn.* **3.** protection from blame, incrimination, etc. **4.** a dwelling place or home considered as a refuge from the elements: *Everyone's basic needs are food, clothing, and shelter.* **5.** a building serving as a temporary refuge or residence for homeless persons, abandoned animals, etc. **6.** *Finance.* See **tax shelter.** —*v.t.* **7.** to be a shelter for; afford shelter to: *The old barn sheltered him from the rain.* **8.** to provide with a shelter; place under cover. **9.** to protect, as by shelter; take under one's protection: *Parents should not try to shelter their children from normal childhood disappointments.* **10.** *Finance.* to invest (money) in a tax shelter. —*v.i.* **11.** to take shelter; find a refuge: *He sheltered in a barn.* **12.** *Finance.* to invest money in a tax shelter. [1575–85; perh. alter. of obs. *sheltron* testudo, OE *scieldtruma,* equiv. to *sceld* SHIELD + *truma* body of fighting men; see TRIM] **—shel′ter•er,** *n.* **—shel′ter•ing•ly,** *adv.* **—shel′ter•less,** *adj.* **—shel′•ter•less•ness,** *n.*
—Syn. 1. retreat, asylum, sanctuary, shield, haven, harbor. See **cover. 7.** harbor, house. **9.** guard, safeguard, shield, defend.

shel′ter deck′, *Naut.* **1.** a weather deck covering a space not considered fully watertight. **2.** the 'tween deck beneath this. [1910–15]

shel•tered (shel′tərd), *adj.* **1.** protected or shielded from storms, missiles, etc., by a wall, roof, barrier, or the like. **2.** protected from the troubles, annoyances, sordidness, etc., encountered in competitive situations: *a sheltered life.* **3.** (of a business or industry) enjoying noncompetitive conditions, as because of a protective tariff. **4.** of or pertaining to employment or housing, esp. for handicapped persons, in a noncompetitive, supervised environment. [1585–95; SHELTER + -ED[2]]

shel′tered work′shop, a place of employment for handicapped persons where their rights are protected and their needs are met.

shel′tering trust′. See **spendthrift trust.**

shel′ter tent′, a small, two-person, military tent consisting of two halves **(shel′ter halves′)** buttoned or tied together, held up by accessory ropes and poles. Also called **pup tent.** [1860–65, *Amer.*]

Shel•ton (shel′tn), *n.* **1.** a city in SW Connecticut. 31,314. **2.** a male given name.

shel•ty (shel′tē), *n., pl.* **-ties.** *Informal.* **1.** See **Shetland pony. 2.** See **Shetland sheepdog.** Also, **shel′tie.** [1640–50; *shelt* (< ON *hjaltr* native of SHETLAND) + -Y[2]]

shelve[1] (shelv), *v.t.,* **shelved, shelv•ing. 1.** to place (something) on a shelf or shelves. **2.** to put off or aside from consideration: *to shelve the question.* **3.** to remove from active use or service. **4.** to furnish with shelves. [1585–95; v. use of SHELVE(S)] **—shelv′er,** *n.*
—Syn. 2. defer, table, pigeonhole.

shelve[2] (shelv), *v.i.,* **shelved, shelv•ing.** to slope gradually. [1580–90; orig. uncert.; cf. Fris *skelf* not quite level]

shelves (shelvz), *n.* pl. of **shelf.**

shelv•ing (shel′ving), *n.* **1.** material for shelves. **2.** shelves collectively. [1625–35; SHELVE[1] + -ING[1]]

Shem (shem), *n.* the eldest of the three sons of Noah. Gen. 10:21.

She•ma (shə mä′, shmä), *n. Judaism.* a liturgical prayer, prominent in Jewish history and tradition, that is recited daily at the morning and evening services and expresses the Jewish people's ardent faith in and love of God. [< Heb *shəma'* listen!]

She•mi•ni A•tze•reth (shə mē′nē ät ser′es, -min′ē; *Seph. Heb.* shə mē nē′ ä tse′ret; *Ashk. Heb.* shə mē′nē ä tsā′ris), a Jewish festival celebrated on the 22nd day of Tishri, being the 8th day of Sukkoth: marked by a memorial service for the dead and prayers for rain in Israel. Also, **Shemi′ni Atze′ret, Shemi′ni Atze′res.** [1900–05; < Heb *Shəmīnī 'ăṣereth* lit., eighth meeting]

Shem•ite (shem′īt), *n.* a Semite. **—Shem•it•ic** (shə mit′ik), **Shem•it•ish** (shem′ī tish), *adj.*

She•mo•neh Es•reh (*Ashk. Heb.* shə mō′nə es′rā; *Seph. Heb.* shə mō ne′ es rā′), *Judaism.* the *Amidah,* consisting of 19 blessings, recited on days other than the Sabbath and holy days. [*shəmōneh 'eśrēh* eighteen (appar. the number of blessings in earlier times)]

Shen•an•do•ah (shen′ən dō′ə), *n.* **1.** a river flowing NE from N Virginia to the Potomac at Harpers Ferry, West Virginia. ab. 200 mi. (322 km) long. **2.** a valley in N Virginia, between the Blue Ridge and Allegheny mountains: Civil War campaigns 1862–64.

Shen′ando′ah Na′tional Park′, a national park in N Virginia, including part of the Blue Ridge mountain range. 302 sq. mi. (782 sq. km).

she•nan•i•gan (shə nan′i gən), *n. Informal.* **1.** Usually, **shenanigans. a.** mischief; prankishness: *Halloween shenanigans.* **b.** deceit; trickery. **2.** a mischievous or deceitful trick. [1850–55, *Amer.*; of obscure orig.]

Shen Cong•wen (shun′ tsông′wun′), born 1902, Chinese author. Also, *Wade-Giles,* **Shen Ts'ung-wen** (shun′ tso͝ong′wun′).

shend (shend), *v.t.,* **shent, shend•ing.** *Archaic.* **1.** to put to shame. **2.** to reproach or scold. **3.** to destroy or injure; damage. [bef. 900; ME *s(c)henden,* OE *(ge)scendan* (c. D *schenden,* G *schänden*), deriv. of *scand* shame, infamy]

Shen•si (shen′sē′; *Chin.* shun′shē′), *n. Older Spelling.* Shaanxi.

Shen•stone (shen′stən), *n.* **William,** 1714–63, English poet.

Shen•yang (shun′yäng′), *n. Pinyin, Wade-Giles.* a city in and the capital of Liaoning province, in NE China: cultural capital of Manchuria; battle 1905. 3,000,000. Formerly, **Fengtien, Mukden.**

She•ol (shē′ōl), *n.* (in Hebrew theology) **1.** the abode of the dead or of departed spirits. **2.** (*l.c.*) hell. [1590–1600; < Heb *shə'ōl*]

Shep•ard (shep′ərd), *n.* **Alan Bartlett, Jr.,** born 1923, U.S. astronaut: first American in space, May 5, 1961.

shep•herd (shep′ərd), *n.* **1.** a person who herds, tends, and guards sheep. **2.** a person who protects, guides, or watches over a person or group of people. **3.** a member of the clergy. **4. the Shepherd,** Jesus Christ. **5.** See **sheepdog.** —*v.t.* **6.** to tend or guard as a shepherd: *to shepherd the flock.* **7.** to watch over carefully. [bef. 1050; ME *shepherde,* OE *scēphyrde.* See SHEEP, HERD[2]] **—shep′herd•less,** *adj.* **—shep′herd•like′,** *adj.*
—Syn. 2. protector, guardian, defender, keeper.

Shep•herd (shep′ərd), *n.* a male given name.

shep′herd dog′. See **sheepdog.** [1400–50; late ME]

shep•herd•ess (shep′ər dis), *n.* **1.** a girl or woman who herds sheep. **2.** a rural girl. [1350–1400; ME *shepherdesse.* See SHEPHERD, -ESS]
—Usage. See **-ess.**

Shep′herd King′, any of the Hyksos kings.

shep′herd's check′, **1.** a pattern of even checks, used in a variety of fabrics. **2.** a fabric having this pattern. Also called **shep′herd's plaid′.** [1860–65]

shep′herd's pie′, a baked dish of ground or diced meat with a crust of mashed potatoes. [1895–1900]

shep•herd's-purse (shep′ərdz pûrs′), *n.* a European weed, *Capsella bursa-pastoris,* having white flowers and purselike pods, naturalized in North America. [1400–50; late ME]

Shep′pard's correc′tion (shep′ərdz), *Statistics.* a method of correcting the bias in standard deviations and higher moments of distributions that arises from grouping values of the variable. Also called **Shep′pard's adjust′ment.** [named after William F. *Sheppard* (1863–1936), English statistician]

sheq•el (shek′əl), *n.* shekel (def. 1).

sher•ard•ize (sher′ər dīz′), *v.t.,* **-ized, -iz•ing.** *Metall.* to coat (steel) with a thin cladding of zinc by heating in a mixture of sand and powdered zinc. Also, *esp. Brit.,* **sher′ard•ise′.** [1900–05; after *Sherard* Cowper Coles (d. 1936), English inventor; see -IZE]

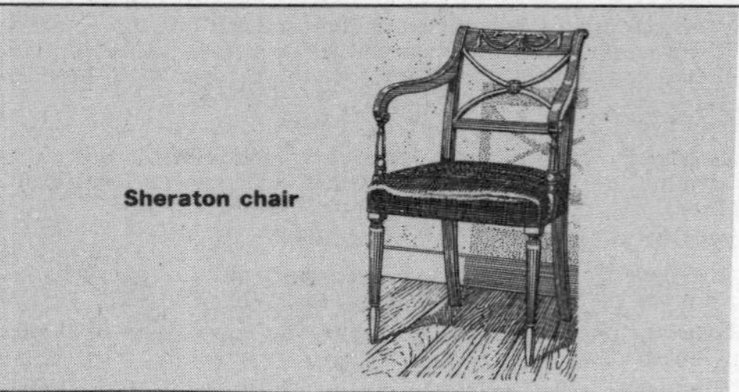
Sheraton chair

Sher·a·ton (sher′ə tn), *n.* **1. Thomas,** 1751–1806, English cabinetmaker and furniture designer. —*adj.* **2.** of the style of furniture designed by Sheraton.

sher·bet (shûr′bit), *n.* **1.** a frozen fruit-flavored mixture, similar to an ice, but with milk, egg white, or gelatin added. **2.** *Brit.* a drink made of sweetened fruit juice diluted with water and ice. **3.** a frozen fruit or vegetable purée, served either between courses to cleanse the palate or as a dessert. [1595–1605; < Turk < Pers *sharbat* < Ar *sharbah* a drink]

Sher·brooke (shûr′brŏŏk), *n.* a city in S Quebec, in SE Canada. 76,804.

sherd (shûrd), *n.* shard.

Sher·i·dan (sher′i dn), *n.* **1. Philip Henry,** 1831–88, Union general in the Civil War. **2. Richard Brins·ley** (brinz′lē), 1751–1816, Irish dramatist and political leader. **3.** a city in N Wyoming. 15,146. **4.** a male given name.

she·rif (she rēf′), *n.* **1.** a governor of Mecca descended from Muhammad. **2.** an Arab chief, prince, or ruler. Also, **sharif, she·reef′.** [1590–1600; < Ar *sharīf* exalted (person)]

sher·iff (sher′if), *n.* **1.** the law-enforcement officer of a county or other civil subdivision of a state. **2.** (formerly) an important civil officer in an English shire. [bef. 1050; ME *sher(r)ef,* OE *scīrgerēfa.* See SHIRE, REEVE[1]] —**sher·iff·dom** (sher′if dəm), *n.*

sher·iff·al·ty (sher′i fəl tē), *n., pl.* **-ties.** shrievalty. [1510–20; alter. of SHRIEVALTY by influence of SHERIFF]

sher·iff·wick (sher′if wik′), *n.* shrievalty. [1425–75; late ME; see SHERIFF, WICK[3]]

sher·lock (shûr′lok), *n. Informal.* **1.** a private detective. **2.** a person remarkably adept at solving mysteries, esp. by using insight and logical deduction: *Who's the sherlock who can tell me where my pen is?* Also, **Sher′·lock.** [after *Sherlock* Holmes, fictitious detective created by Arthur Conan Doyle]

Sher·lock (shûr′lok), *n.* a male given name: from an Old English word meaning "fair-haired."

Sher·lock·ian (shûr lok′ē ən), *adj.* **1.** pertaining to or characteristic of the fictional detective Sherlock Holmes, known for his skill in solving mysteries through deductive reasoning. —*n.* **2.** a devoted fan of or an expert on the adventures of Sherlock Holmes. [see -IAN]

Sher·man (shûr′mən), *n.* **1. Forrest Percival,** 1896–1951, U.S. naval officer. **2. James School·craft** (skōōl′kraft′, -kräft′), 1855–1912, vice president of the U.S. 1909–12. **3. John,** 1823–1900, U.S. statesman (brother of William T.). **4. Roger,** 1721–93, American statesman. **5. Stuart Pratt,** 1881–1926, U.S. critic and educator. **6. William Tecumseh,** 1820–91, Union general in the Civil War. **7.** a city in NE Texas. 30,413. **8.** a male given name. **9.** *U.S. Mil.* a 34-ton medium tank of World War II, with a 75mm gun and a crew of four.

Sher′man Antitrust′ Act′, an act of Congress (1890) prohibiting any contract, conspiracy, or combination of business interests in restraint of foreign or interstate trade. Cf. **Clayton Antitrust Act.** [named after John SHERMAN, who introduced the bill in Congress]

Sher·pa (sher′pə, shûr′-), *n., pl.* **-pas,** (*esp. collectively*) **-pa. 1.** a member of a people of Tibetan stock living in the Nepalese Himalayas, who often serve as porters on mountain-climbing expeditions. **2.** (*sometimes l.c.*) an expert chosen by a chief executive to assist in preparations for a summit meeting.

Sher·riff (sher′if), *n.* **Robert Cedric,** 1896–1975, English playwright and novelist.

Sher·rill (sher′əl), *n.* a male or female given name, form of **Shirley.**

Sher·ring·ton (sher′ing tən), *n.* **Sir Charles Scott,** 1861–1952, English physiologist: Nobel prize for medicine 1932.

sher·ris (sher′is), *n. Archaic.* sherry. [1530–40; < Sp (*vino de*) *Xeres* (wine of) Xeres (now JEREZ)]

sher·ry (sher′ē), *n., pl.* **-ries.** a fortified, amber-colored wine of southern Spain or any of various similar wines made elsewhere. [1590–1600; back formation from SHERRIS, construed as a plural]

Sher·ry (sher′ē), *n.* a female given name, form of **Charlotte.**

sher′ry cob′bler, a cobbler drink made with sherry, sliced fruits, and ice. [1800–10]

's Her·to·gen·bosch (ser′tō KHən bôs′), a city in and the capital of North Brabant, in the S Netherlands. 88,585. French, **Bois-le-Duc.**

Sher·tok (shər tōk′), *n.* **Mo·she** (mō′shə). See **Sharett, Moshe.**

CONCISE ETYMOLOGY KEY: <, descended or borrowed from; >, whence; b., blend of, blended; c., cognate with; cf., compare; deriv., derivative; equiv., equivalent; imit., imitative; obl., oblique; r., replacing; s., stem; sp., spelling, spelled; resp., respelling, respelled; trans., translation; ?, origin unknown; *, unattested; ‡, probably earlier than. See the full key inside the front cover.

Sher·wood (shûr′wŏŏd′), *n.* **1. Robert Em·met** (em′it), 1896–1955, U.S. dramatist. **2.** a town in central Arkansas. 10,586. **3.** a male given name.

Sher′wood For′est, an ancient royal forest in central England, chiefly in Nottinghamshire: the traditional haunt of Robin Hood.

Sher·yl (sher′əl), *n.* a female given name, form of **Shirley.**

she's (shēz), **1.** contraction of *she is.* **2.** contraction of *she has.*
—**Usage.** See **contraction.**

She′ Stoops′ to Con′quer, a comedy (1773) by Oliver Goldsmith.

Shet′land Is′lands (shet′lənd), an island group NE of the Orkney Islands: northernmost part of Great Britain. 18,494; 550 sq. mi. (1425 sq. km). Also called **Shet′·land, Zetland.** —**Shet′land Is′land·er.**

Shet′land po′ny, one of a breed of small but sturdy, rough-coated ponies, raised originally in the Shetland Islands. [1795–1805]

Shetland pony, about 3 ft. (0.9 m) high at shoulder

Shet′land sheep′dog, one of a breed of small sheepdogs resembling a miniature collie, raised originally in the Shetland Islands. [1930–35]

Shet′land wool′, **1.** the fine wool undercoat pulled by hand from Shetland sheep. **2.** thin, loosely twisted wool yarn for knitting or weaving. [1780–90]

sheugh (shōōKH), *Scot. and North Eng.* —*n.* **1.** a furrow, ditch, or trench. —*v.t.* **2.** to plow or dig (a furrow, ditch, etc.). Also, **sheuch** (shōōKH). [1495–1505; N dial. var. of SOUGH[2]]

Shev·ard·na·dze (shev′ərd näd′zə; *Russ.* shi vurd-nä′dzə), *n.* **Ed·uard A.** (ed′wərd; *Russ.* ed wärt′), born 1928, Soviet foreign minister 1985–91; chairman of State Council of his native Georgian Republic since 1992.

She·vat (shə vät′, shvät, shə vôt′), *n.* the fifth month of the Jewish calendar. Also, **Shebat.** Cf. **Jewish calendar.** [1525–35; < Heb *shəbhāṭ*]

shev·e·ret (shev ə ret′, she vret′), *n.* cheveret.

shew (shō), *v.i., v.t.,* **shewed, shewn, shew·ing,** *n. Archaic.* show.

shew·bread (shō′bred′), *n. Judaism.* the 12 loaves of bread placed every Sabbath on a table in the sanctuary of the Biblical tabernacle and the Temple in Jerusalem as an offering by the priests to God. Ex. 25:30; Lev. 24:5–9. Also, **showbread.** [1530; SHEW + BREAD, modeled on G *Schaubrot,* which renders Gk *ártoi enṓpioi,* trans. of Heb *leḥem pānīm*]

she-wolf (shē′wŏŏlf′), *n. pl.* **-wolves. 1.** a female wolf. **2.** a predatory woman.

SHF, See **superhigh frequency.**

shh (sh), *interj.* sh.

Shi·'ah (shē′ə), *n. Islam.* **1.** (*used with a plural v.*) the Shi'ites. **2.** (*used with a singular v.*) Shi'ite. Also, **Shi′·'a.** [1620–30; < Ar *shī'ah* lit., sect]

shi·at·su (shē ät′sōō), *n.* (*sometimes cap.*) a Japanese massage technique that includes the use of acupressure. Also **shi·at′zu.** [< Japn < MChin, equiv. to Chin *chǐ* finger + *yā* pressure]

shi·bah (shiv′ə), *n. Judaism.* shivah.

Shi·bah A·sar Be·tam·muz (*Seph. Heb.* shē vä′ ä sär′ bi tä′mōōz; *Ashk. Heb.* shiv′ə ō′sər bi tä′mōōz, shi vô′ ô sôr′). See **Shivah Asar Betammuz.**

shib·bo·leth (shib′ə lith, -leth′), *n.* **1.** a peculiarity of pronunciation, behavior, mode of dress, etc., that distinguishes a particular class or set of persons. **2.** a slogan; catchword. **3.** a common saying or belief with little current meaning or truth. [< Heb *shibbōleth* lit., freshet, a word used by the Gileadites as a test to detect the fleeing Ephraimites, who could not pronounce the sound *sh* (Judges 12:4–6)]

shi·cer (shī′sər), *n. Australian.* **1.** *Slang.* a swindler. **2.** any unscrupulous person. [1850–55; < G *Scheisser,* equiv. to *scheiss(en)* to SHIT + *-er* -ER[1]]

shick·er (shik′ər), *n. Slang.* **1.** alcoholic liquor. **2.** a drunkard. [1890–95; < Yiddish *shiker* (see SHICKERED) by back formation from SHICKERED]

shick·ered (shik′ərd), *adj. Slang.* intoxicated; drunk. [1910–15; < Yiddish *shiker* (< Heb *shikkōr* drunk, a drunkard) + -ED[2]]

shied (shīd), *v.* pt. and pp. of **shy.**

shiel (shēl), *n. Scot.* shieling. [1250–1300; ME *schele;* cf. ON *skāli* hut, shed; akin to OE *scȳr* hut, OHG *scūr,* ON *skūrr* penthouse]

shield (shēld), *n.* **1.** a broad piece of armor, varying widely in form and size, carried apart from the body, usually on the left arm, as a defense against swords, lances, arrows, etc. **2.** a similar device, often of lightweight plastic, used by riot police to protect themselves from rocks and other thrown objects. **3.** something shaped like a shield, variously round, octagonal, triangular, or somewhat heart-shaped. **4.** a person or thing that protects. **5.** a police officer's, detective's, or sheriff's badge. **6.** *Ordn.* a steel screen attached to a gun to protect its crew, mechanism, etc. **7.** *Mining.* a movable framework for protecting a miner from cave-ins, etc. **8.** *Elect.* a covering, usually made of metal, placed around an electric device or circuit in order to reduce the effects of external electric and magnetic fields. **9.** *Zool.* a protective plate or the like on the body of an animal. **10.** See **dress shield. 11.** *Heraldry.* an escutcheon, esp. one broad at the top and pointed at the bottom, for displaying armorial bearings. **12.** (*cap.*) *Astron.* the constellation Scutum. **13.** *Geol.* a vast area of ancient crustal rocks which, together with a platform, constitutes a craton. **14.** a protective barrier against nuclear radiation, esp. a lead or concrete structure around a reactor.

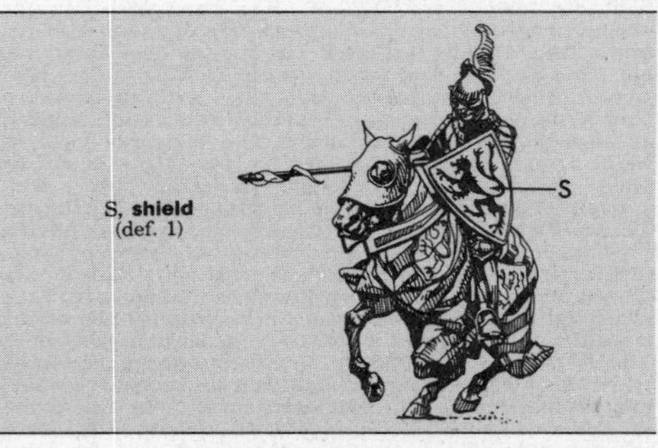

S, **shield** (def. 1)

—*v.t.* **15.** to protect (someone or something) with or as if with a shield. **16.** to serve as a protection for. **17.** to hide or conceal. **18.** *Obs.* to avert; forbid. —*v.i.* **19.** to act or serve as a shield. [bef. 900; (n.) ME *shelde,* OE *sceld;* c. D, G *Schild,* Goth *skildus;* (v.) ME *shelden,* OE *sceldan, scildan,* deriv. of the n.] —**shield′er,** *n.* —**shield′less,** *adj.* —**shield′like′,** *adj.*

shield′ back′, a chair back having a form resembling that of a somewhat heart-shaped medieval shield. Also called **heart back.** [1895–1900]

shield′ bear′er, an attendant who carries the shield or arms of a warrior. [1595–1605]

shield′ fern′, any of numerous ferns of the genera *Dryopteris* and *Polystichum,* having shield-shaped indusia. [1805–15]

shield′ law′, a law protecting journalists from forced disclosure of confidential sources of information. [1970–75]

Shield′ of Da′vid. See **Star of David.**

shield′-tailed snake′ (shēld′tāld′), any of several burrowing snakes of the family Uropeltidae, of the Indian peninsula and Sri Lanka, having a tail that ends in a flat disk. Also called **shield·tail** (shēld′tāl′).

shiel·ing (shē′ling), *n. Scot.* **1.** a pasture or grazing ground. **2.** a shepherd's or herdsman's hut or rough shelter on or near a grazing ground. Also, **shealing, shiel.** [1560–70; SHIEL + -ING[1]]

shi·er[1] (shī′ər), *adj.* a compar. of **shy**[1].

shi·er[2] (shī′ər), *n.* a horse having a tendency to shy. Also, **shyer.** [1820–30; SHY[1] + -ER[1]]

shi·est (shī′ist), *adj.* a superlative of **shy**[1].

shift (shift), *v.t.* **1.** to put (something) aside and replace it by another or others; change or exchange: *to shift friends; to shift ideas.* **2.** to transfer from one place, position, person, etc., to another: *to shift the blame onto someone else.* **3.** *Auto.* to change (gears) from one ratio or arrangement to another. **4.** *Ling.* to change in a systematic way, esp. phonetically. **5. shift gears.** See **gear** (def. 11). —*v.i.* **6.** to move from one place, position, direction, etc., to another. **7.** to manage to get along or succeed by oneself. **8.** to get along by indirect methods; use any expediency, trick, or evasion to get along or succeed: *He shifted through life.* **9.** to change gears in driving an automobile. **10.** *Ling.* to undergo a systematic, esp. phonetic, change. **11.** to press a shift key, as on a typewriter keyboard. **12.** *Archaic.* to change one's clothes. —*n.* **13.** a change or transfer from one place, position, direction, person, etc., to another: *a shift in the wind.* **14.** a person's scheduled period of work, esp. the portion of the day scheduled as a day's work when a shop, service, office, or industry operates continuously during both the day and night: *She prefers the morning shift.* **15.** a group of workers scheduled to work during such a period: *The night shift reported.* **16.** *Baseball.* a notable repositioning by several fielders to the left or the right of their normal playing position, an occasional strategy against batters who usually hit the ball to the same side of the field. **17.** *Auto.* a gearshift. **18.** *Clothing.* **a.** a straight, loose-fitting dress worn with or without a belt. **b.** a woman's chemise or slip. **19.** *Football.* a lateral or backward movement from one position to another, usually by two or more offensive players just before the ball is put into play. **20.** *Mining.* a dislocation of a seam or stratum; fault. **21.** *Music.* a change in the position of the left hand on the fingerboard in playing a stringed instrument. **22.** *Ling.* **a.** a change or system of parallel changes that affects the sound structure of a language, as the series of related changes in the English vowel system from Middle English to Modern English. **b.** a change in the meaning or use of a word. Cf. **functional**

shift. **23.** an expedient; ingenious device. **24.** an evasion, artifice, or trick. **25.** change or substitution. **26.** *Bridge.* See **shift bid. 27.** *Agric.* (in crop rotation) **a.** any of successive crops. **b.** the tract of land used. **28.** an act or instance of using the shift key, as on a typewriter keyboard. [bef. 1000; (v.) ME *shiften* to arrange, OE *sciftan;* c. G *schichten* to arrange in order, ON *skipta* to divide; (n.) ME: contrivance, start, deriv. of the v.] **—shift′ing·ly,** *adv.* **—shift′ing·ness,** *n.*
—Syn. 1. substitute. **23.** contrivance, resource, resort. **24.** wile, ruse, subterfuge, stratagem.

shift·a·ble (shif′tə bəl), *adj.* **1.** able or designed to be shifted, changed, or removed: *shiftable furniture.* **2.** able to be transferred from one owner to another: *shiftable stocks and bonds.* [1735–45; SHIFT + -ABLE]

shift′ bid′, *Bridge.* a bid in a suit different from the suit just bid by one's partner.

shift·er (shif′tər), *n.* **1.** a person or thing that shifts. **2.** *Informal.* See **shift lever.** [1545–55; SHIFT + -ER[1]]

shift′ key′, 1. a typewriter key that determines whether characters are printed in upper or lower case and controls the printing of numbers and symbols. **2.** *Computers.* a key that performs the same functions as on a typewriter keyboard and also controls other functions, depending on the program: *To print a file, depress the shift key and a function key.* [1900–05]

shift·less (shift′lis), *adj.* **1.** lacking in resourcefulness; inefficient; lazy. **2.** lacking in incentive, ambition, or aspiration. [1555–65; SHIFT + -LESS] **—shift′less·ly,** *adv.* **—shift′less·ness,** *n.*
—Syn. 1. slothful, careless, indolent.

shift′ lev′er, *Auto.* the lever mounted on the steering column or floor of a vehicle that enables the driver to shift gears. Also called **gearshift.**

shift′ lock′, a typewriter or computer key that locks the shift key in depressed position. [1905–10]

shift·y (shif′tē), *adj.,* **shift·i·er, shift·i·est. 1.** resourceful; fertile in expedients. **2.** given to or full of evasions; tricky. **3.** suggesting a deceptive or evasive character: *a shifty look.* [1560–70; SHIFT + -Y[1]] **—shift′i·ly,** *adv.* **—shift′i·ness,** *n.*
—Syn. 2. crafty, foxy, slippery.

shi·gel·la (shi gel′ə), *n., pl.* **-gel·lae** (-gel′ē), **-gel·las.** *Bacteriol.* any of several rod-shaped aerobic bacteria of the genus *Shigella,* certain species of which are pathogenic for humans and other warm-blooded animals. [< NL (1918), after Kiyoshi *Shiga* (1870–1957), Japanese scientist; see -ELLA]

shig·el·lo·sis (shig′ə lō′sis), *n. Pathol.* an acute intestinal infection caused by a bacterium of the genus *Shigella,* esp. *S. dysenteriae,* common among children and characterized by fever, abdominal pain, and diarrhea. Also called **bacillary dysentery.** [1945–50; SHIGELL(A) + -OSIS]

Shih Ching (shœ′ jing′). See ***Book of Odes.*** Also, ***Shih′ King′*** (ging), ***Shi′ Jing′.***

Shih Huang Ti (shœ′ hwäng′ tē′), 259–210 B.C., Chinese emperor c247–210 B.C: initiated the building of the Great Wall of China. Also called **Ch'in Shih Huang Ti.** Also, *Pinyin,* **Shi′ Huang′ Di′.**

Shih Tzu (shē′ dzo͞o′), one of a Tibetan breed of toy dogs having a long luxurious coat of any color, formerly bred in imperial China as a pet of the nobility. [1945–50; < Chin (Wade-Giles) *shih*[1]*tzŭ* (*kou*[3]), (pinyin) *shīzi* (*gǒu*) lit., lion (dog)]

shi·i·ta·ke (shē′ē tä′kä), *n., pl.* **-ke.** a large, meaty, black or dark brown mushroom, *Lentinus edodes,* native to eastern Asia and frequently used in Japanese and Chinese cookery. [1875–80; < Japn, equiv. to *shii* oak (earlier *siwi* < *sifi* < **sipi*) + *take* mushroom (perh. *ta* field + *ke*(*y*) hair)]

Shi·'ite (shē′īt), *n. Islam.* a member of one of the two great religious divisions of Islam that regards Ali, the son-in-law of Muhammad, as the legitimate successor of Muhammad, and disregards the three caliphs who succeeded him. Also, **Shi′ite, Shi'a, Shi'ah, Shi·'i** (shē ē′, shē′ē). Cf. **Sunni** (def. 1). [SHI'AH + -ITE[1]] **—Shi·'ism** (shē′iz əm), *n.* **—Shi·'it·ic** (shē it′ik), *adj.*

Shi·jia·zhuang (shœ′jyä′jwäng′), *n. Pinyin.* a city in and the capital of Hebei province, in NE China, SW of Beijing. 1,500,000. Also, *Wade-Giles,* **Shih′chia′·chuang′;** *Older Spelling,* **Shih′kia′chwang′.**

shi·kar (shi kär′), *n., v.,* **-karred, -kar·ring.** (in India) *—n.* **1.** the hunting of game for sport. *—v.t., v.i.* **2.** to hunt. [1600–10; < Urdu < Pers]

shi·ka·ri (shi kär′ē), *n., pl.* **-ris.** (in India) a person who hunts big game, esp. a professional guide or hunter. Also, **shi·ka′ree.** [1815–25; < Urdu < Pers]

Shi·ki·bu (shē′kē bo͞o′), *n.* See **Murasaki Shikibu.**

shi·ki·bu·ton (shē′kē bo͞o′ton), *n.* futon. [< Japn, equiv. to *shiki* spreading + *-buton* comb. form of *futon* FUTON]

Shi·ko·ku (shē′kô ko͞o′), *n.* an island in SW Japan, S of Honshu: the smallest of the main islands of Japan. 5,877,500; 7249 sq. mi. (18,775 sq. km).

shik·sa (shik′sə), *n. Yiddish* (*often disparaging*). **1.** a girl or woman who is not Jewish. **2.** a Jewish girl or woman whose attitudes and behavior are felt to resemble those of a gentile. Also, ***shik′se.*** Cf. ***shegetz.***

Shilh (shilᴋʜ), *n., pl.* **Shluh** (shlo͞o, shlo͞oᴋʜ). **1.** a member of a mountain people of Morocco. **2.** Shilha.

Shil·ha (shil hä′, -ᴋʜä′), *n.* a Berber language, the language of the Shluh. Also, **Shilh.**

shill (shil), *Slang.* *—n.* **1.** a person who poses as a customer in order to decoy others into participating, as at a gambling house, auction, confidence game, etc. **2.** a person who publicizes or praises something or someone for reasons of self-interest, personal profit, or friendship or loyalty. *—v.i.* **3.** to work as a shill: *He shills for a large casino.* *—v.t.* **4.** to advertise or promote (a product) as or in the manner of a huckster; hustle: *He was hired to shill a new TV show.* [1920–25; orig. uncert.]

shil·le·lagh (shə lā′lē, -lə), *n.* (esp. in Ireland) a cudgel, traditionally of blackthorn or oak. Also, **shil·la′·la, shil·la′lah, shil·le′lah.** [1670–80; < Ir *Síol Éiligh* town in Co. Wicklow; the adjoining forest provided wood for the clubs]

shil·ling (shil′ing), *n.* **1.** a cupronickel coin and former monetary unit of the United Kingdom, the 20th part of a pound, equal to 12 pence: retained in circulation equal to 5 new pence after decimalization in 1971. *Abbr.:* s. **2.** a former monetary unit of various other nations, as Australia, Fiji, Ghana, Ireland, Jamaica, New Zealand, and Nigeria, equal to one twentieth of a pound or 12 pence. **3.** the monetary unit of Kenya, Somalia, Tanzania, and Uganda, equal to 100 cents. **4.** any of various coins and moneys of account used in various parts of the U.S. in the 18th and 19th centuries. **5.** See **shilling mark.** [bef. 900; ME; OE *scilling;* c. D *schelling,* G *Schilling,* ON *skillingr,* Goth *skillings*]

shil′ling mark′, a virgule, as used as a divider between shillings and pence: *One reads 2/6 as "two shillings and sixpence" or "two and six."* Also called **shilling.**

Shil·long (shil lông′), *n.* a city in and the capital of Assam state, in NE India: resort. 73,529.

Shil·luk (shi lo͝ok′), *n., pl.* **-luks,** (*esp. collectively*) **-luk** for 1. **1.** a member of a Nilotic people of Sudan. **2.** the Nilotic language of this people.

shil·ly-shal·ly (shil′ē shal′ē), *v.,* **-lied, -ly·ing,** *n., pl.* **-shal·lies,** *adj., adv.* *—v.i.* **1.** to show indecision or hesitation; be irresolute; vacillate. **2.** to waste time; dawdle. *—n.* **3.** irresolution; indecision; vacillation: *It was sheer shilly-shally on his part.* *—adj.* **4.** irresolute; undecided; vacillating. *—adv.* **5.** irresolutely. [1690–1700; orig. repeated question, *shall I? shall I?* later altered on the model of its synonym *dilly-dally*] **—shil′ly-shal′li·er,** *n.*

Shi·loh (shī′lō), *n.* **1.** a national park in SW Tennessee: Civil War battle 1862. **2.** an ancient town in central Palestine, west of the Jordan River.

shil·pit (shil′pit), *adj. Scot.* **1.** (of a person) sickly; puny; feeble. **2.** (of liquor) weak; watery. [1795–1805; orig. uncert.]

shim (shim), *n., v.,* **shimmed, shim·ming.** *—n.* **1.** a thin slip or wedge of metal, wood, etc., for driving into crevices, as between machine parts to compensate for wear, or beneath bedplates, large stones, etc., to level them. *—v.t.* **2.** to fill out or bring to a level by inserting a shim or shims. [1715–25; orig. uncert.]

Shi·ma·za·ki (shē′mä zä′kē), *n.* **Tō·son** (tô′sôn), (*Haruki Shimazaki*), 1872–1943, Japanese author.

shim·mer (shim′ər), *v.i.* **1.** to shine with or reflect a subdued, tremulous light; gleam faintly. **2.** to appear to quiver or vibrate in faint light or while reflecting heat waves. *—n.* **3.** a subdued, tremulous light or gleam. **4.** a quivering or vibrating motion or image as produced by reflecting faint light or heat waves. [bef. 1100; ME *schimeren, s(c)hemeren,* OE *scimrian;* c. D *schemeren,* G *schimmern* to glisten] **—shim′mer·ing·ly,** *adv.*
—Syn. 1. glimmer. See **glisten.**

shim·mer·y (shim′ə rē), *adj.* shimmering; shining softly. [1880–85; SHIMMER + -Y[1]]

shim·my (shim′ē), *n., pl.* **-mies,** *v.,* **-mied, -my·ing.** *—n.* **1.** an American ragtime dance marked by shaking of the hips and shoulders. **2.** excessive wobbling in the front wheels of a motor vehicle. **3.** a chemise. *—v.i.* **4.** to dance the shimmy. **5.** to shake, wobble, or vibrate. [1830–40, for def. 3; 1915–20 for def. 1; back formation and resp. of CHEMISE, construed as a plural]

Shi·mo·no·se·ki (shim′ə nə sā′kē; *Japn.* shē′mô nô·se′kē), *n.* a seaport on SW Honshu, in SW Japan: treaty ending Sino-Japanese War signed 1895. 268,964.

shin[1] (shin), *n., v.,* **shinned, shin·ning.** *—n.* **1.** the front part of the leg from the knee to the ankle. **2.** the lower part of the foreleg in cattle. **3.** the shinbone or tibia, esp. its sharp edge or front portion. **4.** *Chiefly Brit.* a cut of beef similar to the U.S. shank, usually cut into small pieces for stewing. *—v.t., v.i.* **5.** to climb by holding fast with the hands or arms and legs and drawing oneself up. [bef. 1000; ME *shine,* OE *scinu;* c. D *scheen,* G *Schien*(*bein*)]

shin[2] (shēn, shin), *n.* **1.** the 21st letter of the Hebrew alphabet. **2.** the consonant sound represented by this letter. [1895–1900; < Heb *shīn,* akin to *shēn* tooth]

shīn (shēn), *n.* the 13th letter of the Arabic alphabet. [< Ar]

Shin (shin, shēn), *n. Buddhism.* a Japanese offshoot of the Pure Land Sect, requiring only faith in Amida for salvation through his accumulated merit. [1895–1900; < Japn: lit., faith < MChin, equiv. to Chin *zhēn* truth]

Shi·nar (shī′när), *n.* a land mentioned in the Bible, often identified with Sumer.

shin·bone (shin′bōn′), *n.* the tibia. [bef. 1000; ME; OE *scinbān.* See SHIN[1], BONE]

shin·dig (shin′dig′), *n. Informal.* an elaborate or large dance, party, or other celebration. [1855–60, *Amer.;* SHIN[1] + DIG[1]; cf. slang *shinscraper* dance]

shin·dy (shin′dē), *n., pl.* **-dies.** *Informal.* **1.** a row; rumpus. **2.** a shindig. [1810–20; var. of obs. *shinty* row, orig., game resembling field hockey, SHINNY[1]]

shine[1] (shīn), *v.,* **shone** or, esp. for 9, 10, **shined; shin·ing;** *n.* *—v.i.* **1.** to give forth or glow with light; shed or cast light. **2.** to be bright with reflected light; glisten; sparkle. **3.** (of light) to appear brightly or strongly, esp. uncomfortably so: *Wear dark glasses so the sun won't shine in your eyes.* **4.** to be or appear unusually animated or bright, as the eyes or face. **5.** to appear with brightness or clearness, as feelings. **6.** to excel or be conspicuous: *to shine in school.* *—v.t.* **7.** to cause to shine. **8.** to direct the light of (a lamp, mirror, etc.): *Shine the flashlight on the steps so I can see.* **9.** to put a gloss or polish on; polish (as shoes, silverware, etc.). **10. shine up to,** *Informal.* **a.** to attempt to impress (a person), esp. in order to gain benefits for oneself. **b.** to become especially attentive to (one of the opposite sex): *Men shine up to her like moths to a light.* *—n.* **11.** radiance or brightness caused by emitted or reflected light. **12.** luster; polish. **13.** sunshine; fair weather. **14.** a polish or gloss given to shoes. **15.** an act or instance of polishing shoes. **16.** *Informal.* a foolish prank; caper. **17.** *Slang* (*disparaging and offensive*). a black person. **18. come rain or shine, a.** regardless of the weather. **b.** no matter what the circumstances may be: *Come rain or shine, he is always on the job.* Also, **rain or shine. 19. take a shine to,** *Informal.* to take a liking or fancy to: *That little girl has really taken a shine to you.* [bef. 900; ME *s(c)hinen* (v.), OE *scīnan;* c. D *schijnen,* G *scheinen,* ON *skína,* Goth *skeinan*]
—Syn. 1. glimmer, shimmer. SHINE, BEAM, GLARE refer to the emitting or reflecting of light. SHINE refers to a steady glowing or reflecting of light: *to shine in the sun.* That which BEAMS gives forth a radiant or bright light: *to beam like a star.* GLARE refers to the shining of a light that is not only bright but so strong as to be unpleasant and dazzling: *to glare like a headlight.* **9.** buff, burnish, brighten. **12.** gloss, gleam, glow, sheen.

shine[2] (shīn), *n. Slang.* moonshine. [1935–40; by shortening]

shin·er (shī′nər), *n.* **1.** a person or thing that shines. **2.** *Slang.* See **black eye** (def. 1). **3.** any of various small American freshwater fishes having glistening scales, esp. a minnow. **4.** any of various silvery, marine fishes, as the menhaden or butterfish. **5.** a defect in silk or synthetic filament or fabric, produced either in the process of winding or as a result of shuttle friction and appearing on fabric as a shiny streak. [1350–1400; 1900–05 for def. 2; ME; see SHINE[1], -ER[1]]

shin′er perch′, a small, silvery perch, *Cymatogaster aggregata,* inhabiting waters along the Pacific coast of North America and bearing live young. Also called **seven-eleven, shin′er sea′perch.**

shin·gle[1] (shing′gəl), *n., v.,* **-gled, -gling.** *—n.* **1.** a thin piece of wood, slate, metal, asbestos, or the like, usually oblong, laid in overlapping rows to cover the roofs and walls of buildings. **2.** a woman's close-cropped haircut. **3.** *Informal.* a small signboard, esp. as hung before a doctor's or lawyer's office. **4. have** or **be a shingle short,** *Australian Slang.* to be mentally disturbed, mad, or eccentric. **5. hang out one's shingle,** *Informal.* to establish a professional practice, esp. in law or medicine; open an office. *—v.t.* **6.** to cover with shingles, as a roof. **7.** to cut (hair) close to the head. [1150–1200; ME *scincle, sc(h)ingle* < ML *scindula* lath, shingle (ME *-g-* appar. by assoc. with another unidentified word), L *scandula* (ML *-i-* perh. by assoc. with Gk *schíza* lath, splinter, or related words)] **—shin′gler,** *n.*

shin·gle[2] (shing′gəl), *n.* **1.** small, waterworn stones or pebbles such as lie in loose sheets or beds on a beach. **2.** a beach, riverbank, or other area covered with such small pebbles or stones. [1530–40; appar. var. of earlier *chingle;* cf. Norw *singel* small stones]

shin·gle[3] (shing′gəl), *v.t.,* **-gled, -gling.** *Metalworking.* to hammer or squeeze (puddled iron) into a bloom or billet, eliminating as much slag as possible; knobble. [1665–75; < F *cingler* to whip, beat < G *zängeln,* deriv. of *Zange* TONGS]

shin′gle oak′, an oak, *Quercus imbricaria,* yielding a wood used for shingles, clapboards, etc. [1805–15, *Amer.*]

shin·gles (shing′gəlz), *n.* (*used with a singular or plural v.*) *Pathol.* a disease caused by the varicella-zoster virus, esp. by reactivated virus in an older person, characterized by skin eruptions and pain along the course of involved sensory nerves. Also called **herpes zoster.** [1350–1400; < ML *cingulum* (L: girdle; cf. CINCTURE) trans. of Gk *zṓnē* ZONE in its medical sense; see -S[3]]

shin·gling (shing′gling), *n. Geol.* a sedimentary structure in which flat pebbles are uniformly tilted in the same direction. Also called **imbrication.** [1695–1705, for literal sense; SHINGLE[1] + -ING[1]]

shin·gly (shing′glē), *adj.* consisting of or covered with shingle. [1765–75; SHINGLE[2] + -Y[1]]

Shin·gon (shin′gon, shēn′-), *n. Buddhism.* a Japanese form of syncretistic Buddhism founded in the 9th century by Kūkai (A.D. 774–835) and stressing the oral transmission of mystic formulas from master to disciple. [1895–1900; < Japn < MChin, equiv. to Chin *zhēnyán* truth(-speaking)]

shin′ guard′, *Sports.* a protective covering, usually of leather or plastic and often padded, for the shins and sometimes the knees, worn chiefly by catchers in baseball and goalkeepers in ice hockey. [1900–05]

shin·ing (shī′ning), *adj.* **1.** radiant; gleaming; bright. **2.** resplendent; brilliant: *shining talents.* **3.** conspicuously fine: *a shining example.* [bef. 900; ME *s(c)hininge, schininde,* OE *scīnende;* see SHINE[1], -ING[2]] **—shin′ing·ly,** *adv.*

CONCISE PRONUNCIATION KEY: act, cāpe, dâre, pärt; set, ēqual; if, īce; ox, ōver, ôrder, oil, bo͝ok, bo͞ot, out; up, ûrge; child; sing; shoe; thin, *th*at; zh as in *treasure.* ə = *a* as in *alone, e* as in *system, i* as in *easily, o* as in *gallop, u* as in *circus;* ᵊ as in *fire* (fīᵊr), *hour* (ouᵊr). l and n can serve as syllabic consonants, as in *cradle* (krād′l), and *button* (but′n). See the full key inside the front cover.

—**Syn.** **1.** glistening, effulgent. See **bright.** **2.** lustrous. **3.** outstanding, distinguished, eminent, prime, splendid.

shin·leaf (shin′lēf′), *n., pl.* **-leaves.** **1.** a North American plant, *Pyrola elliptica,* having leaves used formerly for shinplasters. **2.** any plant of the genus *Pyrola.* [1810–20, *Amer.;* SHIN^{1} + LEAF]

shin·ner·y (shin′ə rē), *n. Southwestern U.S.* a dense growth of small trees, esp. scrub oaks. [1900–05, *Amer.;* < LaF *chênière* CHENIER (perh. directly < a by-form **chênerie*)]

shin·ny^{1} (shin′ē), *n., pl.* **-nies,** *v.,* **-nied, -ny·ing.** —*n.* **1.** a simple variety of hockey, played with a ball, block of wood, or the like, and clubs curved at one end. **2.** the club used. —*v.i.* **3.** to play shinny. **4.** to drive the ball at shinny. [1665–75; var. of *shin ye,* cry used in the game]

shin·ny^{2} (shin′ē), *v.i.,* **-nied, -ny·ing.** to shin: *He shinnied up the tree.* [1850–55, *Amer.;* appar. deriv. of SHIN^{1}; source of *-y* is unclear]

shin·plas·ter (shin′plas′tər, -plä′stər), *n.* **1.** a plaster for the shin or leg. **2.** *Informal.* (formerly) **a.** a piece of paper money of a denomination lower than one dollar. **b.** money of little value, as that issued on insufficient security. [1815–25, *Amer.;* SHIN^{1} + PLASTER]

shin′ splints′, (*used with a plural v.*) *Pathol.* a painful condition of the front lower leg, associated with tendinitis, stress fractures, or muscle strain, often occurring as a result of running or other strenuous athletic activity, esp. on a nonresilient surface. [1940–45]

Shin·to (shin′tō), *n.* **1.** Also, **Shin′to·ism.** the native religion of Japan, primarily a system of nature and ancestor worship. —*adj.* **2.** Also, **Shin′to·is′tic.** of, pertaining to, or characteristic of Shinto. [< Japn *shintō,* earlier *shintau* < MChin, equiv. to Chin *shéndào* way of the gods] —**Shin′to·ist,** *n., adj.*

shin·y (shī′nē), *adj.,* **shin·i·er, shin·i·est.** **1.** bright or glossy in appearance. **2.** filled with light, as by sunshine. **3.** rubbed or worn to a glossy smoothness, as clothes. [1580–90; SHINE^{1} + -Y^{1}] —**shin′i·ly,** *adv.* —**shin′i·ness,** *n.*
—**Syn. 1, 2.** brilliant, shining, glistening, gleaming.

ship (ship), *n., v.,* **shipped, ship·ping.** —*n.* **1.** a vessel, esp. a large oceangoing one propelled by sails or engines. **2.** *Naut.* **a.** a sailing vessel square-rigged on all of three or more masts, having jibs, staysails, and a spanker on the aftermost mast. **b.** *Now Rare.* a bark having more than three masts. Cf. **shipentine. 3.** the crew and, sometimes, the passengers of a vessel: *The captain gave the ship shore leave.* **4.** an airship, airplane, or spacecraft. **5. jump ship, a.** to escape from a ship, esp. one in foreign waters or a foreign port, as to avoid further service as a sailor or to request political asylum. **b.** to withdraw support or membership from a group, organization, cause, etc.; defect or desert: *Some of the more liberal members have jumped ship.* **6. run a tight ship,** to exercise a close, strict control over a ship's crew, a company, organization, or the like. **7. when one's ship comes in** or **home,** when one's fortune is assured: *She'll buy a car as soon as her ship comes in.* —*v.t.* **8.** to put or take on board a ship or other means of transportation; to send or transport by ship, rail, truck, plane, etc. **9.** *Naut.* to take in (water) over the side, as a vessel does when waves break over it. **10.** to bring (an object) into a ship or boat. **11.** to engage (someone) for service on a ship. **12.** to fix in a ship or boat in the proper place for use. **13.** to place (an oar) in proper position for rowing. Cf. **boat** (def. 13). **14.** to send away: *They shipped the kids off to camp for the summer.* —*v.i.* **15.** to go on board or travel by ship; embark. **16.** to engage to serve on a ship. **17. ship out, a.** to leave, esp. for another country or assignment: *He said goodby to his family and shipped out for the West Indies.* **b.** to send away, esp. to another country or assignment. **c.** *Informal.* to quit, resign, or be fired from a job: *Shape up or ship out!* [bef. 900; (n.) ME; OE *scip;* c. D *schip,* G *Schiff,* ON, Goth *skip;* (v.) ME *s(c)hip(p)en,* deriv. of the n.] —**ship′less,** *adj.* —**ship′less·ly,** *adv.*

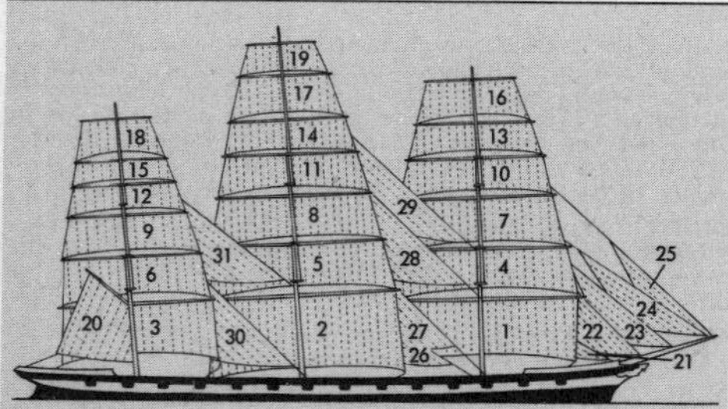

ship (full-rigged)
1, foresail or fore course; 2, mainsail or main course; 3, crossjack or mizzen course; 4, fore lower topsail; 5, main lower topsail; 6, mizzen lower topsail; 7, fore upper topsail; 8, main upper topsail; 9, mizzen upper topsail; 10, fore lower topgallant; 11, main lower topgallant; 12, mizzen lower topgallant; 13, fore upper topgallant; 14, main upper topgallant; 15, mizzen upper topgallant; 16, fore royal; 17, main royal; 18, mizzen royal; 19, skysail; 20, spanker; 21, fore staysail; 22, jib; 23, inner jib; 24, outer jib; 25, flying jib; 26, main staysail; 27, main topmast staysail; 28, main topgallant staysail; 29, main royal staysail; 30, mizzen staysail; 31, mizzen topgallant staysail

CONCISE ETYMOLOGY KEY: <, descended or borrowed from; >, whence; b., blend of, blended; c., cognate with; cf., compare; deriv., derivative; equiv., equivalent; imit., imitative; obl., oblique; r., replacing; s., stem; sp., spelling, spelled; resp., respelling, respelled; trans., translation; ?, origin unknown; *, unattested; ‡, probably earlier than. See the full key inside the front cover.

-ship, a native English suffix of nouns denoting condition, character, office, skill, etc.: *clerkship; friendship; statesmanship.* [ME, OE *-scipe;* akin to SHAPE; c. dial. Fris, dial. D *schip*]

ship′ bis′cuit, hardtack. Also, **ship′ bread′.** [1790–1800]

ship·board (ship′bôrd′, -bōrd′), *n.* **1.** *Archaic.* **a.** the deck or side of a ship. **b.** the situation of being on a ship. **2. on shipboard,** aboard a seagoing vessel. —*adj.* **3.** done, conducted, or designed for use aboard ship, esp. during an ocean voyage: *a shipboard romance; a shipboard telephone.* [1150–1200; late ME *shipbord* (see SHIP, BOARD); r. ME *shipesbord* (see 's^{1})]

ship·boy (ship′boi′), *n.* See **ship's boy.** [1590–1600; SHIP + BOY]

ship·build·er (ship′bil′dər), *n.* **1.** a person whose occupation is the designing or constructing of ships. **2.** a commercial firm for building ships. [1690–1700; SHIP + BUILDER] —**ship′build′ing,** *n.*

ship′ canal′, a canal navigable by ships. [1790–1800, *Amer.*]

ship′ chan′dler, a person who deals in cordage, canvas, and other supplies for ships. [1635–45] —**ship′ chan′dlery.**

ship′ decant′er, a glass decanter with a very wide base.

ship·en·tine (ship′ən tēn′, -tin′), *n. U.S. Naut. Now Rare.* a four-masted bark. [1890–95; SHIP + *-entine* (as in BARKENTINE)]

ship·fit·ter (ship′fit′ər), *n. Shipbuilding.* a person who forms plates, shapes, etc., of ships according to plans, patterns, or molds. [1940–45; SHIP + FITTER]

Ship′ka Pass′ (ship′kä), a mountain pass in central Bulgaria, in the Balkan Mountains. 4375 ft. (1335 m) high.

ship·lap (ship′lap′), *n. Carpentry.* **1.** an overlapping joint, as a rabbet, between two boards joined edge to edge. **2.** boarding joined with such overlapping joints. See illus. under **siding.** [1850–55; SHIP + LAP^{2}]

ship·load (ship′lōd′), *n.* **1.** a full load for a ship. **2.** the cargo or load carried by a ship. [1630–40; SHIP + LOAD]

ship·man (ship′mən), *n., pl.* **-men. 1.** a sailor. **2.** the master of a ship. [bef. 900; ME; OE *scipman;* c. MD *schipman,* G *Schiff(s)mann.* See SHIP, -MAN]

ship·mas·ter (ship′mas′tər, -mä′stər), *n.* a person who commands a ship; master; captain. [1325–75; ME *schipmaster;* c. G *Schiffmeister*]

ship·mate (ship′māt′), *n.* a person who serves with another on the same vessel. [1740–50; SHIP + MATE^{1}]

ship·ment (ship′mənt), *n.* **1.** an act or instance of shipping freight or cargo. **2.** a quantity of freight or cargo shipped at one time. **3.** something that is shipped. [1790–1800; SHIP + -MENT]
—**Syn. 3.** consignment. See **freight.**

ship′ of state′, a nation or its affairs likened to a ship under sail. [1665–75]

ship′ of the line′, a former sailing warship armed powerfully enough to serve in the line of battle, usually having cannons ranged along two or more decks; battleship. [1700–10]

ship′ of war′, warship. [1470–80]

ship·own·er (ship′ō′nər), *n.* a person who owns a ship or ships. [1520–30; SHIP + OWNER]

ship·pa·ble (ship′ə bəl), *adj.* being in a suitable form or condition for shipping. [1475–85; SHIP + -ABLE]

ship·per (ship′ər), *n.* a person who ships goods or makes shipments. [bef. 1100; 1745–55 for current sense; late OE *scipere* sailor (not recorded in ME); see SHIP, -ER^{1}]

ship·ping (ship′ing), *n.* **1.** the act or business of a person or thing that ships. **2.** a number of ships, esp. merchant ships, taken as a whole; tonnage. **3.** *Obs.* a voyage. [1250–1300; ME; see SHIP, -ING^{1}]

ship′ping ar′ticles, *Naut.* See **articles of agreement.** [1830–40]

ship′ping clerk′, a clerk who attends to the packing, unpacking, receiving, sending out, and recording of shipments. [1855–60]

ship′ping fe′ver, *Vet. Pathol.* a respiratory disease of cattle, caused by *Pasteurella haemolytica,* often spread during the shipment of livestock.

ship′ping lane′. See **sea lane.** [1930–35]

ship′ping room′, a place in a business concern where goods are packed and shipped.

ship′ping ton′, See under **ton^{1}** (def. 5).

ship·pon (ship′ən), *n. Brit. Dial.* a cow barn or cattle shed. Also, **ship′pen.** [bef. 900; ME *schepon,* OE *scypen;* c. G *Schuppen;* akin to SHOP]

ship-rigged (ship′rigd′), *adj. Naut.* (of a sailing vessel) rigged as a ship; full-rigged. [1835–45]

ship's′ boy′, a male attendant, as a cabin boy, steward, etc., employed to wait on a ship's passengers or officers. [1545–55]

ship's′ com′pany, company (def. 11). [1635–45]

ship·shape (ship′shāp′), *adj.* **1.** in good order; well-arranged; trim or tidy. —*adv.* **2.** in a shipshape manner. [1635–45; SHIP + SHAPE]

ship·side (ship′sīd′), *n.* the area alongside a ship, as on a pier. [1490–1500; SHIP + SIDE^{1}]

ship's′ iner′tial naviga′tion sys′tem. See **SINS.**

ship's′ pa′pers, necessary papers presented at all legal inspections of a ship, and containing the owner's name, description of cargo, destination, etc. [1655–65]

ship's′ store′, a retail store aboard a navy ship that sells toiletries, cigarettes, etc., to the ship's personnel.

ship's′ stores′, materials, supplies, and equipment for the navigation, maintenance, and operation of a ship. [1790–1800]

ship-to-shore (ship′tə shôr′, -shōr′), *adj.* **1.** operating between a ship and the shore: *a ship-to-shore radio.* —*adv.* **2.** from a ship to the shore: *The message was sent ship-to-shore.* —*n.* **3.** a ship-to-shore radio.

ship·way (ship′wā′), *n.* **1.** the structure that supports a ship being built. **2.** a ship canal. [1825–35; SHIP + WAY^{1}]

ship·worm (ship′wûrm′), *n.* any of various wormlike marine bivalve mollusks that burrow into the timbers of ships, wharves, etc. [1770–80; SHIP + WORM]

ship·wreck (ship′rek′), *n.* **1.** the destruction or loss of a ship, as by sinking. **2.** the remains of a wrecked ship. **3.** destruction or ruin: *the shipwreck of one's hopes.* —*v.t.* **4.** to cause to suffer shipwreck. **5.** to destroy; ruin. —*v.i.* **6.** to suffer shipwreck. [bef. 1100; ME *shipwrech* remains of a shipwreck; see SHIP, WRECK; r. OE *scipwræc* (see WRACK^{1})]

ship·wright (ship′rīt′), *n. Shipbuilding.* a person who builds and launches wooden vessels or does carpentry work in connection with the building and launching of steel or iron vessels. [bef. 1100; ME; OE *scipwyrhta.* See SHIP, WRIGHT]

ship·yard (ship′yärd′), *n.* a yard or enclosure in which ships are built or repaired. [1690–1700; SHIP + YARD^{2}]

shir·a·lee (shir′ə lē), *n. Australian.* swag^{2} (def. 2). [1875–80; orig. uncert.]

Shi·raz (shi räz′), *n.* a city in SW Iran. 373,000.

shire (shīər), *n.* **1.** one of the counties of Great Britain. **2. the Shires,** the counties in the Midlands in which hunting is especially popular. [bef. 900; ME; OE *scīr* office of administration, jurisdiction of such an office, county]

Shire (shīər), *n.* one of an English breed of large, strong draft horses having a usually brown or bay coat with white markings. [1875–80; appar. so called because it was bred in the *shires,* i.e., those counties of west and central England whose names end in *-shire*]

Shi·ré (shē′rā), *n.* a river in SE Africa, flowing S from Lake Malawi to the Zambezi River. 370 mi. (596 km) long.

Shir·er (shīər′ər), *n.* **William Lawrence,** born 1904, U.S. journalist, news broadcaster, and writer.

shirk (shûrk), *v.t.* **1.** to evade (work, duty, responsibility, etc.). —*v.i.* **2.** to evade work, duty, etc. —*n.* **3.** a shirker. [1625–35; obscurely akin to SHARK^{2}]
—**Syn. 1.** shun, avoid, dodge.

shirk·er (shûr′kər), *n.* a person who evades work, duty, responsibility, etc. [1790–1800; SHIRK + -ER^{1}]

Shir·leen (shûr lēn′), *n.* a female given name, form of **Shirley.**

Shir·ley (shûr′lē), *n.* **1. James,** 1596–1666, English dramatist. **2.** a city on the S shore of Long Island, in SE New York. 18,072. **3.** a male or female given name: a family name taken from an Old English placename.

Shir′ley pop′py, a cultivated strain of the corn poppy, having variously colored single or double flowers. [1885–90; after a race of the species selected and named by William Wilks (1843–1923), English horticulturist, of *Shirley* vicarage, Croydon, Surrey]

Shir′ley Tem′ple, a nonalcoholic cocktail of ginger ale and grenadine, garnished with a maraschino cherry: a child's drink, served esp. to a girl. Cf. **Roy Rogers.**

shirr (shûr), *v.t.* **1.** to draw up or gather (cloth or the like) on three or more parallel threads. **2.** to bake (eggs removed from the shell) in a shallow dish or in individual dishes. —*n.* **3.** Also, **shirr′ing.** a shirred arrangement, as of cloth. [1840–50; orig. uncert.]

shirt (shûrt), *n.* **1.** a long- or short-sleeved garment for the upper part of the body, usually lightweight and having a collar and a front opening. **2.** an undergarment of cotton, or other material, for the upper part of the body. **3.** a shirtwaist. **4.** a nightshirt. **5. in one's shirt sleeves,** without a coat: *It was so hot that they worked in their shirt sleeves.* Also, **in one's shirt-sleeves. 6. keep one's shirt on,** *Informal.* to refrain from becoming angry or impatient; remain calm: *Tell him to keep his shirt on until we're ready.* **7. lose one's shirt,** *Informal.* to lose all that one possesses; suffer a severe financial reverse: *He lost his shirt in the stock market.* [bef. 1150; ME *schirte,* OE *scyrte;* c. G *Schürze,* D *schort* apron, ON *skyrta* SKIRT] —**shirt′less,** *adj.*

shirt·band (shûrt′band′), *n.* a band of material sewn into a shirt for stiffening, finishing, or the like, as a neckband to which the collar is sewn or buttoned. [1525–35; SHIRT + BAND^{2}]

shirt-dress (shûrt′dres′), *n.* shirtwaist (def. 2). [1945–50]

shirt′ front′, **1.** the front of a shirt, esp. the part that is exposed when a jacket or vest is worn. **2.** dickey (def. 1). [1830–40]

shirt·ing (shûr′ting), *n.* any shirt fabric, as broadcloth or oxford. [1595–1605; SHIRT + -ING^{1}]

shirt′ jack′et, a shirtlike jacket. Also, **shirt-jac** (shûrt′jak′), **shirt′ jac′.**

shirt·mak·er (shûrt′mā′kər), *n.* a person who makes shirts. [1855–60; SHIRT + MAKER] —**shirt′mak′ing,** *n.*

shirt-sleeve (shûrt′slēv′), *adj.* **1.** not wearing a jacket; informally dressed: *a shirt-sleeve mob.* **2.** warm enough to live or work in without wearing a jacket or coat: *shirt-sleeve weather in November.* **3.** simple, plain, and informal; direct and straightforward in approach, manner, etc.: *shirt-sleeve diplomacy.* Also, **shirt′sleeve′, shirt′-sleeved′, shirt′-sleeves′.** [1560–70]

shirt·tail (shûrt′tāl′), *n.* **1.** the part of a shirt below the waistline. **2.** *Journalism.* a brief item added at the end of a related newspaper story. Cf. **follow-up** (def. 3b). —*adj.* **3.** quite young and immature in behavior. **4.** *Chiefly Midland and Southern U.S.* of distant relation, esp. by marriage: *some shirttail cousins I'd never met.* —*v.t.* **5.** *Informal.* to append or add (an item) to a discussion or writing: *The tariff concessions were shirttailed onto the trade bill.* [1835–45, *Amer.*; SHIRT + TAIL[1]]

shirt·waist (shûrt′wäst′), *n.* **1.** a tailored blouse or shirt worn by women. **2.** Also called **shirt-dress, shirt′waist′ dress′, shirt′waist′er.** a dress with a bodice and a front opening tailored like those of a dress shirt. [1875–80; SHIRT + WAIST]

shirt·y (shûr′tē), *adj.,* **shirt·i·er, shirt·i·est.** *Informal.* bad-tempered; irritable; cranky. [1840–50; SHIRT, in the phrase *get someone's shirt out* to annoy + -Y[1]] —**shirt′·i·ness,** *n.*

shish ke·bab (shish′ kə bob′), a dish consisting of kabobs broiled or roasted on a skewer. Also called **shashlik, shashlick, shaslik.** [1910–15; < Turk *şiş-kebabı,* equiv. to *şiş* spit (cf. SHASHLIK) + *kebap* roast meat (cf. KABOB) + -ı 3d sing. possessive suffix]

shish-ke·bab (shish′kə bob′), *v.,* **-babbed, -bab·bing.** —*v.i.* **1.** to broil or roast food on a skewer. —*v.t.* **2.** to broil or roast (food) on a skewer.

shish·ya (shish′yə), *n. Hinduism.* a pupil of a guru. [< Hindi]

shit (shit), *n., v.,* **shit** or **shat, shit·ting,** *interj. Vulgar.* —*n.* **1.** excrement; feces. **2.** an act of defecating; evacuation. **3. the shits.** diarrhea. **4.** *Slang.* pretense, lies, exaggeration, or nonsense. **5.** *Slang.* something inferior or worthless. **6.** *Slang.* a selfish, mean, or otherwise contemptible person. **7.** *Slang.* narcotic drugs, esp. heroin or marijuana. **8.** *Slang.* possessions, equipment, mementos, etc.; stuff. **9. give a shit,** *Slang.* to care; be concerned. **10. up shit creek,** *Slang.* in a desperate or hopeless situation; in serious trouble. Also, **up shits creek, up shit creek without a paddle.** —*v.i.* **11.** to defecate. —*v.t.* **12.** *Slang.* to exaggerate or lie to. —*interj.* **13.** *Slang.* (used to express disgust, disappointment, frustration, contempt, or the like). **14. no shit,** (used to express amazement, incredulity, or derision). [(v.) var. (with short *i* from ptp. or n.) of earlier *shite,* ME *shiten,* OE *scītan;* cf. MLG, MD *schiten* (D *schijten*), OHG *skizan* (G *scheissen*); (n.) re-formation from the v., or continuation of OE *scite* (in place names)]

shit·faced (shit′fāst′), *adj. Slang* (*vulgar*). very drunk. [1935–40; SHIT + FACE + -ED[3]]

shit·head (shit′hed′), *n. Slang* (*vulgar*). a stupid, inept, unlikable, or contemptible person. [1910–15; SHIT + HEAD]

shit·house (shit′hous′), *n., pl.* **-hous·es** (-hou′ziz). *Slang* (*vulgar*). a privy; outhouse. [1910–15; SHIT + HOUSE]

shit·kick·er (shit′kik′ər), *n. Slang* (*vulgar*). **1.** an unsophisticated farmer, cowboy, or other rural person; country person. **2.** a performer or fan of country-and-western music. **3.** a heavy boot. Also, **shit′-kick′er.** [1965–70; SHIT + KICKER]

shit·list (shit′list′), *n. Slang* (*vulgar*). a list of persons held in extreme disfavor. Also, **shit′ list′.** [1940–45; SHIT + LIST[1]]

shit′ on a shin′gle, *Slang* (*vulgar*). creamed chipped beef or ground beef in a sauce, served on toast.

shit·tah (shit′ə), *n., pl.* **shit·tim** (shit′im), **shit·tahs.** a tree, said to be an acacia, probably *Acacia seyal,* that yielded the shittim wood of the Old Testament. [1605–15; < Heb *shiṭṭāh*]

shit′tim wood′ (shit′im), **1.** the wood, probably acacia, of which the ark of the covenant and various parts of the tabernacle were made. Ex. 25, 26. **2.** the cascara, *Rhamnus purshiana.* **3.** See **false buckthorn.** Also called **shit′tim.** [1580–90; < Heb *shiṭṭīm,* pl. of *shiṭṭāh* (see SHITTAH)]

shit·ty (shit′ē), *adj.,* **-ti·er, -ti·est.** *Slang* (*vulgar*). **1.** inferior or contemptible. **2.** inept or insignificant. **3.** unfortunate or unpleasant. **4.** wretchedly bad; miserable. [1940–45; SHIT + -Y[1]] —**shit′ti·ness,** *n.*

shiv (shiv), *n. Slang.* a knife, esp. a switchblade. [1665–75; perh. alter. of *chiv* blade < Romany]

Shiva

Shi·va (shē′və), *n. Hinduism.* "the Destroyer," the third member of the Trimurti, along with Brahma the Creator and Vishnu the Preserver. Also, **Siva.** [< Skt: lit., the auspicious] —**Shi′va·ism,** *n.* —**Shi′va·ist,** *n.* —**Shi′va·is′tic,** *adj.*

shi·vah (shiv′ə), *n. Judaism.* **1.** the mourning period, following the funeral and lasting traditionally for seven days, observed by Jews for a deceased parent, sibling, child, or spouse. **2. sit shivah,** to observe this period. Also, **shibah.** [< Heb *shibh'āh* lit., seven]

Shi·vah A·sar Be·tam·muz (*Seph. Heb.* shē vä′ ä sär′ bi tä′mo͞oz; *Ashk. Heb.* shiv′ə ô′sər bi tä′mo͝oz, shi vô′ ô sôr′), a Jewish fast day observed on the 17th day of Tammuz in memory of the breach of the walls of Jerusalem by the Romans in A.D. 70. Also, **Shibah Asar Betammuz.** [< Heb *shibh'āh 'āsār bə tammuz* 17th day of Tammuz]

shiv·a·ree (shiv′ə rē′), *n., v.,* **-reed, -ree·ing.** —*n.* **1.** a mock serenade with kettles, pans, horns, and other noisemakers given for a newly married couple; charivari. **2.** *Informal.* an elaborate, noisy celebration. —*v.t.* **3.** to serenade with a shivaree. [1835–45, *Amer.;* alter. of Mississippi Valley F, F *charivari* CHARIVARI]

Shi·va-Shak·ti (shē′və shuk′tē), *n. Hinduism.* the Godhead, of which the masculine, passive, transcendent, eternal principle is Shiva, and the feminine, active, immanent, temporal principle is Shakti, the Divine Mother. Cf. **Tantra.**

shive[1] (shīv), *n.* **1.** a sliver or fragment; splinter. **2.** a thin plug, as of wood or cork, for stopping the bunghole of a cask or the mouth of a bottle. [1175–1225; ME; c. G *Scheibe,* ON *skīfa;* akin to SHEAVE[2]]

shive[2] (shiv, shīv), *n.* **1.** a splinter or fragment of the husk of flax, hemp, etc. **2.** boon[3]. [1475–85; earlier *scyfe;* c. dial. D *schif,* MD *scheve,* G *Schebe;* akin to SHIVER[2]]

Shive·ly (shīv′lē), *n.* a city in N Kentucky, near Louisville. 16,819.

shiv·er[1] (shiv′ər), *v.i.* **1.** to shake or tremble with cold, fear, excitement, etc. **2.** *Naut.* **a.** (of a fore-and-aft sail) to shake when too close to the wind. **b.** (of a sailing vessel) to be headed so close to the wind that the sails shake. —*n.* **3.** a tremulous motion; a tremble or quiver: *The thought sent a shiver down her spine.* **4. shivers,** an attack of shivering or chills (usually preceded by *the*). [1150–1200; ME *chivere* (n.); later *sh-,* appar. for the sake of alliteration in phrase *chiver and shake*] —**shiv′·er·er,** *n.* —**shiv′er·ing·ly,** *adv.*
—**Syn. 1.** SHIVER, QUAKE, SHUDDER refer to a vibratory muscular movement, a trembling, usually involuntary. We SHIVER with cold, or a sensation such as that of cold: *to shiver in thin clothing on a frosty day; to shiver with pleasant anticipation.* We QUAKE esp. with fear: *to quake with fright.* We SHUDDER with horror or abhorrence; the agitation is more powerful and deep-seated than shivering or trembling: *to shudder at pictures of a concentration camp.*

shiv·er[2] (shiv′ər), *v.t., v.i.* **1.** to break or split into fragments. —*n.* **2.** a fragment; splinter. [1150–1200; (n.) ME *schivere* fragment; c. G *Schiefer* schist; (v.) ME *schiveren,* deriv. of the n.]

shiv′ering owl′, *South Atlantic States.* screech owl.

shiv·er·y[1] (shiv′ə rē), *adj.* **1.** inclined to or characterized by shivers, quivers, or tremors. **2.** causing shivering. [1740–50; SHIVER[1] + -Y[1]]

shiv·er·y[2] (shiv′ə rē), *adj.* readily breaking into shivers or fragments; brittle. [1675–85; SHIVER[2] + -Y[1]]

shi·voo (shi vo͞o′), *n., pl.* **-voos.** *Australian.* a boisterous party or celebration. [orig. uncert.]

Shi·zu·o·ka (shē′zo͞o ô′kä), *n.* a city on S Honshu, in central Japan, on Suruga Bay. 458,342.

Shko·dër (shkō′dər; *Albanian.* shkô′dər), *n.* a city in NW Albania, on Lake Scutari: a former capital of Albania. 55,000. Also, **Shko·dra** (shkō′drə; *Albanian.* shkô′drä). Italian, **Scutari.**

shkot·zim (shkô′tsim), *n. Yiddish* (*often disparaging*). pl. of ***shegetz.***

shle·miel (shlə mēl′), *n.* schlemiel.

shlep (shlep), *v.t., v.i.,* **shlepped, shlep·ping,** *n.* schlep. Also, **shlepp.**

shli·ma·zel (shli mä′zəl), *n.* schlimazel. Also, **shli·ma′zl.**

shlock (shlok), *adj., n.* schlock.

shlock·y (shlok′ē), *adj.,* **shlock·i·er, shlock·i·est.** schlock (def. 1).

Shluh (shlo͞o, shlo͝okh), *n.* pl. of **Shilh.**

shlump (shlo͝omp), *n., v.i.* schlump.

S.H.M., See **simple harmonic motion.** Also, **s.h.m.**

shmaltz (shmälts, shmôlts), *n.* schmaltz. Also, **shmalz.**

shmat·te (shmä′tə), *n.* schmatte.

shmear (shmēr), *n., v.t.* schmear.

shmo (shmō), *n., pl.* **shmoes.** schmo.

shmooze (shmo͞oz), *v.,* **shmoozed, shmooz·ing,** *n.* schmooze.

shmuck (shmuk), *n.* schmuck.

shmutz (shmo͝ots), *n.* schmutz.

shnaps (shnäps, shnaps), *n.* schnapps.

shnook (shno͝ok), *n.* schnook.

shnor·rer (shnôr′ər, shnōr′-), *n.* schnorrer.

Sho·a (shō′ä), *n.* a former kingdom in E Africa: now a province of Ethiopia. 5,369,500; 25,290 sq. mi. (65,501 sq. km). *Cap.:* Addis Ababa.

shoad (shōd), *n. Brit. Mining.* float (def. 43). [1595–1605; akin to OE *scādan* to divide, scatter; cf. G *schneiden*]

shoal[1] (shōl), *n.* **1.** a place where a sea, river, or other body of water is shallow. **2.** a sandbank or sand bar in the bed of a body of water, esp. one that is exposed above the surface of the water at low tide. —*adj.* **3.** of little depth, as water; shallow. —*v.i.* **4.** to become shallow or more shallow. —*v.t.* **5.** to cause to become shallow. **6.** *Naut.* to sail so as to lessen the depth of (the water under a vessel). [bef. 900; (adj.) ME (Scots) *shald,* OE *sceald* SHALLOW; (n. and v.) deriv. of the adj.]
—**Syn. 1.** shallow, rapid, riffle. **2.** reef.

shoal[2] (shōl), *n.* **1.** any large number of persons or things. **2.** a school of fish. —*v.i.* **3.** to collect in a shoal; throng. [1570–80; earlier *shole,* prob. < MD, MLG *schōle,* with sound-substitution of *sh-* for LG *skh-;* cf. SCHOOL[2]]

shoal·y (shō′lē), *adj.,* **shoal·i·er, shoal·i·est.** full of shoals or shallows. [1605–15; SHOAL[1] + -Y[1]]

shoat (shōt), *n.* **1.** Also, **shote.** a young, weaned pig. **2.** geep. [1375–1425; late ME *shote;* c. dial. D *schote*]

sho·chet (*Seph.* shô KHet′; *Ashk.* shō′KHāt, shoi′KHit; *Eng.* shō′KHit), *n., pl.* ***shoche·tim*** (shōKH tēm′), *Eng.* **sho·chets.** *Hebrew.* shohet.

shock[1] (shok), *n.* **1.** a sudden and violent blow or impact; collision. **2.** a sudden or violent disturbance or commotion: *the shock of battle.* **3.** a sudden or violent disturbance of the mind, emotions, or sensibilities: *The burglary was a shock to her sense of security. The book provided a shock, nothing more.* **4.** the cause of such a disturbance: *The rebuke came as a shock.* **5.** *Pathol.* a collapse of circulatory function, caused by severe injury, blood loss, or disease, and characterized by pallor, sweating, weak pulse, and very low blood pressure. Cf. **anaphylactic shock, cardiogenic shock, hypovolemic shock. 6.** the physiological effect produced by the passage of an electric current through the body. **7. shocks,** *Informal.* shock absorbers, esp. in the suspension of an automobile. —*v.t.* **8.** to strike or jar with intense surprise, horror, disgust, etc.: *He enjoyed shocking people.* **9.** to strike against violently. **10.** to give an electric shock to. —*v.i.* **11.** to undergo a shock. [1555–65; < MF *choc* armed encounter, n. deriv. of *choquer* to clash (in battle) < Gmc; cf. D *schokken* to shake, jolt, jerk] —**shock′a·ble,** *adj.* —**shock′a·bil′i·ty,** *n.* —**shock′·ed·ness,** *n.* —**shock′like′,** *adj.*
—**Syn. 8.** stagger, astound, stupefy. SHOCK, STARTLE, PARALYZE, STUN suggest a sudden, sharp surprise that affects one somewhat like a blow. SHOCK suggests a strong blow, as it were, to one's nerves, sentiments, sense of decency, etc.: *The onlookers were shocked by the accident.* STARTLE implies the sharp surprise of sudden fright: *to be startled by a loud noise.* PARALYZE implies such a complete shock as to render one temporarily helpless: *paralyzed with fear.* STUN implies such a shock as bewilders or stupefies: *stunned by the realization of an unpleasant truth.*

shock[2] (shok), *n.* **1.** a group of sheaves of grain placed on end and supporting one another in the field. —*v.t.* **2.** to make into shocks. [1275–1325; ME; c. LG *schok* shock of grain, group of sixty, G *Schock* sixty] —**shock′er,** *n.*

shock[3] (shok), *n.* **1.** a thick, bushy mass, as of hair. **2.** Also, **shock′ dog′.** a dog with long, shaggy hair. —*adj.* **3.** shaggy, as hair. [1810–20; special use of SHOCK[2], the hair being compared to a shock of wheat]

shock′ absorb′er, *Mach.* a device for damping sudden and rapid motion, as the recoil of a spring-mounted object from shock. [1905–10]

shock′ cord′. See **bungee cord.**

shock·er (shok′ər), *n.* **1.** a person or thing that shocks. **2.** a sensational novel, play, etc. [1780–90; SHOCK[1] + -ER[1]]

shock′ front′, the forward boundary surface of a shock wave. [1945–50]

shock·head·ed (shok′hed′id), *adj.* having a shock or thick mass of hair on the head. [1810–20; SHOCK[3] + HEAD + -ED[3]]

shock·ing (shok′ing), *adj.* **1.** causing intense surprise, disgust, horror, etc. **2.** very bad: *shocking manners.* [1685–95; SHOCK[1] + -ING[2]] —**shock′ing·ly,** *adv.* —**shock′ing·ness,** *n.*
—**Syn. 1.** staggering, astounding, startling, appalling.

shock′ing pink′, a vivid or intensely bright pink. [1935–40] —**shock′ing-pink′,** *adj.*

Shock·ley (shok′lē), *n.* **William Bradford,** born 1910, U.S. physicist: Nobel prize 1956.

shock·proof (shok′pro͞of′), *adj.* **1.** Also, **shock′-proof′.** (of timepieces, machinery, etc.) protected against damage resulting from anticipated shocks. —*v.t.* **2.** to protect (timepieces, machinery, etc.) against damage resulting from anticipated shocks. [1910–15; SHOCK[1] + -PROOF]

shock-re·sist·ant (shok′ri zis′tənt), *adj.* strong or resilient enough to sustain minor impacts without damage to the internal mechanism: *a shock-resistant watch.*

shock-test (shok′test′), *v.t.* to test (equipment or matériel) for resistance to sudden impact or stress.

shock′ ther′apy, (not in technical use) any of various therapies, as insulin shock therapy or electroconvulsive therapy, that induce convulsions or unconsciousness, used for symptomatic relief in certain mental disorders. Also called **shock′ treat′ment.** [1935–40]

shock′ troops′, *Mil.* troops especially selected, trained, and equipped for engaging in assault. [1915–20]

shock′ wave′, 1. a region of abrupt change of pressure and density moving as a wave front at or above the velocity of sound, caused by an intense explosion or supersonic flow over a body. **2.** a repercussion from a startling event or upheaval; series of aftereffects: *shock waves from the recent collapse of one of the nation's largest banks.* [1945–50]

shock′ wave′ ther′apy, lithotripsy.

shod (shod), *v.* a pt. and pp. of **shoe.**

shod·dy (shod′ē), *adj.,* **-di·er, -di·est,** *n., pl.* **-dies.** —*adj.* **1.** of poor quality or inferior workmanship: *a shoddy bookcase.* **2.** intentionally rude or inconsiderate; shabby: *shoddy behavior.* —*n.* **3.** a fibrous material obtained by shredding unfelted rags or waste. Cf. **mungo. 4.** anything inferior, esp. a handmade item or manufactured product. [1825–35; orig. uncert.] —**shod′di·ly,** *adv.* —**shod′di·ness,** *n.*

shoe (sho͞o), *n., pl.* **shoes,** (*esp. Brit. Dial.*) **shoon;** *v.,* **shod** or **shoed, shod** or **shoed** or **shod·den, shoe·ing.** —*n.* **1.** an external covering for the human foot, usually of leather and consisting of a more or less stiff or heavy sole and a lighter upper part ending a short distance above, at, or below the ankle. **2.** an object or part resembling a shoe in form, position, or use. **3.** a horseshoe or a similar plate for the hoof of some other animal. **4.** a ferrule or the like, as of iron, for protecting the end of a staff, pole, etc. **5.** See **brake shoe. 6.** the outer casing of a pneumatic automobile tire. **7.** a drag or skid for a wheel of a vehicle. **8.** a part having a larger area than the end of an object on which it fits, serving to disperse or apply its weight or thrust. **9.** the sliding contact by which an electric car or locomotive takes its current from the third rail. **10.** *Civ. Engin.* **a.** a member supporting one end of a truss or girder in a bridge. **b.** a hard and sharp foot of a pile or caisson for piercing underlying soil. **11.** a small molding, as a quarter round, closing the angle between a baseboard and a floor. **12.** the outwardly curved portion at the base of a downspout. **13.** a piece of iron or stone, sunk into the ground, against which the leaves of a gateway are shut. **14.** a device on a camera that permits an accessory, as a flashgun, to be attached. **15.** a band of iron on the bottom of the runner of a sleigh. **16.** *Cards.* See **dealing box. 17.** *Furniture.* **a.** a cuplike metal piece for protecting the bottom of a leg. **b.** a fillet beneath an ornamental foot, as a pad or scroll foot. **18.** *Print.* a box into which unusable type is thrown. **19.** a chute conveying grain to be ground into flour. **20.** *Carpentry.* soleplate. **21.** *Naut.* a thickness of planking covering the bottom of the keel of a wooden vessel to protect it against rubbing. **22. drop the other shoe,** to complete an action or enterprise already begun. **23. fill someone's shoes,** to take the place and assume the obligations of another person: *She felt that no stepmother could ever hope to fill her late mother's shoes.* **24. in someone's shoes,** in a position or situation similar to that of another: *I wouldn't like to be in his shoes.* **25. the shoe is on the other foot,** the circumstances are reversed; a change of places has occurred: *Now that we are rich and they are poor the shoe is on the other foot.* **26. where the shoe pinches,** the true cause of the trouble or worry. —*v.t.* **27.** to provide or fit with a shoe or shoes. **28.** to protect or arm at the point, edge, or face with a ferrule, metal plate, or the like. [bef. 900; (n.) ME *scho(o),* OE *sceō(h),* c. G *Schuh,* ON *skōr,* Goth *skōhs;* (v.) ME *schon,* OE *scōg(e)an,* c. MLG *schoi(g)en,* ON *skūa*] —**shoe′less,** *adj.*

shoe·bill (sho͞o′bil′), *n.* a large, African, storklike bird, *Balaeniceps rex,* having a broad, flattened bill shaped somewhat like a shoe. [1870–75; SHOE + BILL[2]]

shoebill, *Balaeniceps rex.* height to 4 ft. (1.2 m)

shoe·black (sho͞o′blak′), *n.* bootblack. [1745–55; SHOE + BLACK]

shoe′ boil′, *Vet. Pathol.* a swelling of the elbow of a horse due to irritation caused by the hoof striking the elbow when lying down. Also called **capped elbow.** [1910–15]

shoe·box (sho͞o′boks′), *n.* **1.** an oblong cardboard box of a standard size used to package a pair of shoes for sale. **2.** any house, building, or other construction likened to a shoebox because of its shape or cramped area. Also, **shoe′ box′.** [1855–60; SHOE + BOX[1]]

shoe·brush (sho͞o′brush′), *n.* a brush used in polishing shoes. [1765–75; SHOE + BRUSH[1]]

shoe·horn (sho͞o′hôrn′), *n.* **1.** a shaped piece of horn, metal, or the like, inserted in the heel of a shoe to make it slip on more easily. —*v.t.* **2.** to force into a limited or tight space: *Can you shoehorn four of us into the back seat of your car?* [1580–90; SHOE + HORN]

shoe·lace (sho͞o′lās′), *n.* a string or lace for fastening a shoe. [1640–50; SHOE + LACE]

shoe·mak·er (sho͞o′mā′kər), *n.* a person who makes or mends shoes. [1350–1400; ME; see SHOE, MAKER] —**shoe′mak′ing,** *n.*

Shoe·mak·er (sho͞o′mā′kər), *n.* **William Lee** (*Willie*), born 1931, U.S. jockey.

shoe·pac (sho͞o′pak′), *n.* a heavy, laced, waterproof boot. Also, **shoe′pack′.** Also called **pac.** [1745–55, *Amer.*; orig., an Indian moccasin with an extra sole, by folk etym. < Delaware Jargon (Sw sp.) *sippack,* (E sp.) *seppock* shoe < Unami Delaware *čipahkə* shoes (sing. *či·p·akw,* c. N Unami (G sp.) *machtschipak*)]

sho·er (sho͞o′ər), *n.* a person who shoes horses or other animals. [bef. 900; OE *scōere* shoemaker (not recorded in ME); see SHOE, -ER[1]]

shoe·shine (sho͞o′shīn′), *n.* **1.** an act or instance of cleaning and polishing a pair of shoes. **2.** the surface of a polished shoe or shoes. [SHOE + SHINE]

CONCISE ETYMOLOGY KEY: <, descended or borrowed from; >, whence; b., blend of, blended; c., cognate with; cf., compare; deriv., derivative; equiv., equivalent; imit., imitative; obl., oblique; r., replacing; s., stem; sp., spelling, spelled; resp., respelling, respelled; trans., translation; ?, origin unknown; *, unattested; ‡, probably earlier than. See the full key inside the front cover.

shoe·string (sho͞o′string′), *n.* **1.** a shoelace. **2.** a very small amount of money. **3. shoestrings.** See **shoestring potatoes.** —*adj.* **4.** consisting of or characterized by a small amount of money: *living on a shoestring budget.* [1610–20; SHOE + STRING]

shoe′string catch′, *Baseball, Football.* a catch of a ball on the fly, made close to the ground while running. [1925–30, *Amer.*]

shoe′string pota′toes, long, sticklike slices of raw potato that are deep-fried until crisp. [1930–35, *Amer.*]

shoe′string root′ rot′, *Plant Pathol.* See **oak root rot.** [1975–80]

shoe′string tack′le, *Football.* a tackle made around the ankles of the ball carrier.

shoe·tree (sho͞o′trē′), *n.* one of a pair of foot-shaped devices, usually of metal or wood, for placing in a shoe to maintain its shape when it is not being worn. [1820–30; SHOE + TREE]

sho·far (shō′fər; *Seph. Heb.* shô fär′; *Ashk. Heb.* shō′fər, shō fär′), *n., pl.* **-fars,** *Heb.* **-froth, -frot, -fros** (*Seph.* -frôt′; *Ashk.* -frōs, -frōs′), *Judaism.* a ram's horn blown as a wind instrument, sounded in Biblical times chiefly to communicate signals in battle and announce certain religious occasions and in modern times chiefly at synagogue services on Rosh Hashanah and Yom Kippur. Also, **shophar.** [1860–65; < Heb *shōphār*]

shofar

shog (shog, shôg), *v.,* **shogged, shog·ging,** *n. Scot. and Brit. Dial.* —*v.t.* **1.** to shake; jolt. —*v.i.* **2.** to jog along. —*n.* **3.** a shake; jolt. [1350–1400; ME *shoggen* (v.); perh. akin to SHOCK[1]]

sho·gi (shō′gē), *n.* the Japanese version of chess. [1880–85; < Japn *shōgi* < MChin, equiv. to Chin *jiàng* commander + *qí* chess]

sho·gun (shō′gən, -gun), *n. Japanese Hist.* the title applied to the chief military commanders from about the 8th century A.D. to the end of the 12th century, then applied to the hereditary officials who governed Japan, with the emperor as nominal ruler, until 1868, when the shogunate was terminated and the ruling power was returned to the emperor. Also, **shō′gun.** [1605–15; < Japn *shōgun,* earlier *shaūgun* < MChin, equiv., to Chin *jiāngjūn* lit., lead the army] —**sho′gun·al,** *adj.*

sho·gun·ate (shō′gə nit, -nāt′), *n.* **1.** the office or rule of a shogun. **2.** a government controlled by shoguns. [1870–75; SHOGUN + -ATE[3]]

sho·het (*Seph.* shô KHet′; *Ashk.* shō′KHăt, shoi′KHit; *Eng.* shō′KHit), *n., pl.* ***shohe·tim*** (shōKH tēm′), *Eng.* **sho·hets.** *Hebrew.* a person certified by a rabbi or Jewish court of law to slaughter animals for food in the manner prescribed by Jewish law. Also, ***shochet.*** Cf. ***shehitah.*** [*shōḥēṭ* lit., one who slaughters]

sho·ji (shō′zhē, -jē), *n., pl.* **-ji, -jis.** a light screen consisting of a framework of wood covered with paper or other translucent material, used originally in Japanese homes as one of a series of sliding panels between the interior and exterior or between two interior spaces. [1875–80; < Japn *shōji,* earlier *shaūji* < MChin, equiv. to Chin *zhàngzi* fence]

Sho·la·pur (shō′lə po͝or′), *n.* a city in S Maharashtra in SW India. 398,122.

Sholes (shōlz), *n.* **Christopher La·tham** (lā′thəm, -thəm), 1819–90, U.S. inventor of the typewriter.

Sho·lo·khov (shô′lə kôf′, -kof′; *Russ.* shô′lə KHəf), *n.* **Mi·kha·il** (mē′hī ēl′; *Russ.* myi KHu yēl′), 1905–84, Russian novelist: Nobel prize 1965.

sho·lom (*Ashk.* shô′ləm, shō′-), *interj. Hebrew.* shalom.

Sho·lom (shô′ləm, shō′-), *n.* a male given name.

Sho′lom A·lei′chem (ä lā′KHəm, ə lā′-). See **Aleichem, Sholom.**

Sho·na (shō′nə), *n., pl.* **-nas,** (*esp. collectively*) **-na** for **1. 1.** Also called **Mashona.** a member of a group of peoples constituting more than two thirds of the population of Zimbabwe. **2.** the Bantu language of the Shona.

shone (shōn; *esp. Brit.* shon), *v.* a pt. and pp. of **shine.**

shoo (sho͞o), *interj., v.,* **shooed, shoo·ing.** —*interj.* **1.** (used to scare or drive away a cat, dog, chickens, birds, etc.) —*v.t.* **2.** to drive away by saying or shouting "shoo." **3.** to request or force (a person) to leave: *I'll have to shoo you out of here now.* —*v.i.* **4.** to call out "shoo." [1475–85; earlier *showe, shough, shooh, ssou* (interjection), imit.; cf. G *schu*]

shoo·fly (sho͞o′flī′), *n., pl.* **-flies.** a child's rocker having a seat supported between two boards cut and painted to resemble animals. [1860–65, *Amer.*; SHOO + FLY[2]]

shoo′-fly pie′ (sho͞o′flī′), an open pie filled with a sweet crumb and molasses mixture and baked. [1925–30; so called in allusion to the attractiveness of the molasses to unwanted flies]

shoo-in (sho͞o′in′), *n. Informal.* a candidate, competitor, etc., regarded as certain to win. [1945–50, *Amer.*; n. use of v. phrase *shoo in*]

shook[1] (sho͝ok), *n.* **1.** a set of staves and headings sufficient for one hogshead, barrel, or the like. **2.** a set of the parts of a box, piece of furniture, or the like, ready to be put together. **3.** a shock of sheaves or the like. [1760–70; short for *shook cask,* var. of *shaken cask* one dismounted for shipment]

shook[2] (sho͝ok), *v.* **1.** pt. of **shake. 2.** *Nonstandard.* a pp. of **shake.** —*adj.* **3.** Also, **shook′ up′.** *Slang.* strongly affected by an event, circumstance, etc.; emotionally unsettled: *She was so shook she couldn't speak.*

shoon (sho͞on), *n. Chiefly Brit. Dial.* pl. of **shoe.**

shoot[1] (sho͞ot), *v.,* **shot, shoot·ing,** *n.* —*v.t.* **1.** to hit, wound, damage, kill, or destroy with a missile discharged from a weapon. **2.** to execute or put to death with a bullet: *to be shot at sunrise.* **3.** to send forth or discharge (a missile) from a weapon: *to shoot a bullet.* **4.** to discharge (a weapon): *to shoot a gun.* **5.** to send forth (words, ideas, etc.) rapidly: *to shoot questions at someone.* **6.** to fling; propel: *The volcano shot lava high into the air.* **7.** to direct suddenly or swiftly: *Shoot the spotlight on the doorway. He shot a smile at his wife.* **8.** to move suddenly; send swiftly along. **9.** to go over (country) in hunting game. **10.** to pass rapidly through, over, down, etc.: *to shoot rapids.* **11.** to emit (a ray or rays, as of light) suddenly, briefly, or intermittently. **12.** to variegate by threads, streaks, etc., of another color. **13.** to cause to extend or project: *He shot out his arm and grabbed the ball.* **14.** to discharge or empty, as down a chute: *Do not shoot rubbish here!* **15.** *Sports.* **a.** to throw, kick, or otherwise propel (a ball, puck, etc.), as at a goal or teammate. **b.** to score (a goal, points, etc.) by propelling the ball, puck, etc. **16.** *Games.* to propel (a marble) from the crook or first knuckle of the forefinger by flicking with the thumb. **17.** (in dice games) **a.** to throw (the dice or a specific number). **b.** to wager or offer to bet (a sum of money): *I'll shoot ten bucks.* **18.** *Photog.* to photograph or film. **19.** to put forth (buds, branches, etc.), as a plant. **20.** to slide (a bolt or the like) into or out of its fastening. **21.** to pull (one's cuffs) abruptly toward one's hands. **22.** *Golf.* to make a final score of (so many strokes): *He shot a 73 on the first 18 holes of the tournament.* **23.** to take the altitude of (a heavenly body): *to shoot the sun.* **24.** to detonate; cause to explode, as a charge of explosives. **25.** *Aeron.* to practice (a maneuver) by repetition: *to shoot landings.* **26.** *Slang.* to inject (an addictive drug) intravenously. —*v.i.* **27.** to send forth missiles from a bow, firearm, or the like. **28.** to be discharged, as a firearm. **29.** to hunt with a gun for sport: *He fishes, but he doesn't shoot.* **30.** to move or pass suddenly or swiftly; spurt: *The car shot ahead and was soon out of sight.* **31.** *Naut.* to acquire momentum and coast into the wind, as a sailboat in a confined area. **32.** to grow forth from the ground, as a stem. **33.** to put forth buds or shoots, as a plant; germinate. **34.** *Photog.* to photograph. **35.** *Motion Pictures.* to film or begin to film a scene or movie. **36.** to extend; jut: *a cape shooting out into the sea.* **37.** *Sports, Games.* **a.** to propel a ball, puck, etc., at a goal, basket, pocket, etc., or in a specific direction: *He shot for the green with a five iron.* **b.** to propel a ball in a specific way: *The center shoots left-handed.* **38.** to be felt by or flow through or permeate the body: *Pain shot through his injured arm. Chills shot up and down her spine.* **39.** to carry by force of discharge or momentum: *The missile left its pad and shot thousands of miles into space.* **40.** *Informal.* to begin, esp. to begin to talk: *I want to hear your complaint, so shoot!* **41. shoot down, a.** to cause to fall by hitting with a shot: *They shot down several ducks.* **b.** *Informal.* to disparage, reject, or expose as false or inadequate; debunk: *to shoot down a popular theory.* **42. shoot for** or **at,** to attempt to obtain or accomplish; strive toward: *He is shooting for a higher production level.* **43. shoot from the hip,** to act or speak without due consideration or deliberation. **44. shoot off one's mouth** or **face,** *Slang.* **a.** to talk indiscreetly, esp. to reveal confidences, make thoughtless remarks, etc. **b.** to exaggerate: *He likes to shoot off his mouth about what a great guy he is.* **45. shoot one's bolt.** See **bolt**[1] (def. 16). **46. shoot one's wad.** See **wad**[1] (def. 7). **47. shoot the breeze.** See **breeze**[1] (def. 5). **48. shoot the bull.** See **bull**[3] (def. 2). **49. shoot the works.** See **work** (def. 18). **50. shoot up, a.** to grow rapidly or suddenly. **b.** *Informal.* to damage or harass by reckless shooting: *cowboys shooting up the town.* **c.** to wound by shooting: *He shot up the lion, but his guide killed it.* **d.** *Slang.* to inject an addictive drug intravenously. —*n.* **51.** the act of shooting with a bow, firearm, etc. **52.** *Chiefly Brit.* a hunting trip or expedition. **53.** a match or contest at shooting. **54.** a growing or sprouting, as of a plant. **55.** a new or young growth that shoots off from some portion of a plant. **56.** the amount of such growth. **57.** a young branch, stem, twig, or the like. **58.** a sprout that is not three feet high. **59.** a chute. **60.** *Rocketry.* the launching of a missile. **61.** *Informal.* a photographic assignment or session, as for a feature film or a television commercial: *The actress is away on a shoot.* **62.** *Rowing.* the interval between strokes. **63.** *Mining.* **a.** a small tunnel branching off from a larger tunnel. **b.** a narrow vein of ore. [bef. 900; ME *shoten* (v.), OE *scēotan;* c. D *schieten,* G *schiessen,* ON *skjōta;* akin to SHOT[1]]
—**Syn. 3, 5.** project, impel, hurl, cast, throw. **17a.** roll. **30.** spring, start, dash, bolt, rush, fly. **36.** project, protrude.

shoot[2] (sho͞ot), *interj.* (used to express irritation or astonishment). [1875–80, *Amer.*; alter. of SHIT, conformed to SHOOT[1]]

shoot-'em-up (sho͞ot′əm up′), *n. Informal.* a motion-picture or television program that emphasizes gunplay, action, and often violence. [1945–50]

shoot·er (sho͞o′tər), *n.* **1.** a person or thing that shoots. **2.** *Games.* a marble used to shoot at other marbles. **3.** a person who sets off explosives in oil-drilling operations. **4.** *Informal.* a photographer, esp. an amateur hobbyist. [1250–1300; ME; see SHOOT[1], -ER[1]]

shoot′ing box′, *Chiefly Brit.* a small house or lodge for use during the shooting season. Also called **shoot′ing lodge′.** [1805–15]

shoot′ing brake′, *Brit.* See **station wagon.** [1910–15; earlier, a light horse-drawn wagonette; cf. *break, brake* bodiless carriage frame, wagonette (< ?)]

shoot′ing gal′lery, 1. a place equipped with targets

and used for practice in shooting. **2.** *Slang.* a place where drug addicts can buy and inject themselves with narcotic drugs. [1830–40]

shoot′ing i′ron, *Informal.* a firearm, esp. a pistol or revolver. [1780–90, *Amer.*]

shoot′ing match′ (sho͞o′ting *for 1;* sho͞ot′n, sho͞o′-ting *for 2*), **1.** a contest in marksmanship. **2.** *Informal.* **a.** a number of persons or things collectively. **b.** everything involved with a particular matter: *He decided to sell the whole shooting match—his house, furniture, and car.* [1740–50]

shoot′ing script′, a motion-picture scenario having the scenes arranged in the order in which they are to be photographed. [1925–30]

shoot′ing star′, **1.** meteor (def. 1b). **2.** Also called **American cowslip, prairie pointer.** any of several North American plants of the genus *Dodecatheon,* esp. *D. meadia,* having pink or white flowers with reflexed petals and stamens forming a pointed beak. [1585–95]

shoot′ing stick′, a device resembling a cane or walking stick, with a spike on one end and a small, folding seat on the other, often used by spectators at outdoor sporting events. [1675–85]

shoot′ing war′, open conflict between hostile nations involving direct military engagements.

shoot·ist (sho͞o′tist), *n.* **1.** a marksman with a pistol or rifle. **2.** a gunfighter, as in the Old West. [1860–65, *Amer.*; SHOOT[1] + -IST]

shoot-off (sho͞ot′ôf′, -of′), *n.* a final or additional contest to decide the winner in a rifle or pistol competition. Also, **shoot′off′.** [see SHOOT, -OFF]

shoot·out (sho͞ot′out′), *n.* **1.** a gunfight that must end in defeat for one side or the other, as between gunfighters in the Old West, criminal groups, or law-enforcement officers and criminals. **2.** *Slang.* any military conflict or skirmish. **3.** *Slang.* a high-scoring or intensely played game or tournament, as of basketball or ice hockey. **4.** *Soccer.* a method of breaking a tie score at the end of overtime in which five players from each team alternate shooting at the opponent's goal, starting from a spot 35 yd. (39 m) from the goal line, in an attempt to kick the ball past the rival goalkeeper in under five seconds. [1945–50; n. use of v. phrase *shoot (it) out* to settle a dispute with firearms]

shoot′ the chutes′. See **chute the chute.** [1920–25]

shoot-up (sho͞ot′up′), *n. Slang.* **1.** an act or instance of injecting an addictive drug intravenously. **2.** shootout (def. 1). [1965–70; n. use of v. phrase *shoot up*]

shop (shop), *n., v.,* **shopped, shop·ping,** *interj.* —*n.* **1.** a retail store, esp. a small one. **2.** a small store or department in a large store selling a specific or select type of goods: *the ski shop at Smith's.* **3.** the workshop of a craftsperson or artisan. **4.** the workshop of a person who works in a manual trade; place for doing specific, skilled manual work: *a carpenter's shop.* **5.** any factory, office, or business: *Our ad agency is a well-run shop.* **6.** *Educ.* **a.** a course of instruction in a trade, as carpentry, printing, etc., consisting chiefly of training in the use of its tools and materials. **b.** a classroom in which such a course is given. **7.** one's trade, profession, or business as a subject of conversation or preoccupation. **8. set up shop,** to go into business; begin business operations: *to set up shop as a taxidermist.* **9. shut up shop, a.** to close a business temporarily, as at the end of the day. **b.** to suspend business operations permanently: *They couldn't make a go of it and had to shut up shop.* **10. talk shop,** to discuss one's trade, profession, or business: *After dinner we all sat around the table and talked shop.* —*v.i.* **11.** to visit shops and stores for purchasing or examining goods. **12.** to seek or examine goods, property, etc., offered for sale: *Retail merchants often stock their stores by shopping in New York.* **13.** to seek a bargain, investment, service, etc. (usually fol. by *for*): *I'm shopping for a safe investment that pays good interest.* —*v.t.* **14.** to seek or examine goods, property, etc., offered for sale in or by: *She's shopping the shoe stores this afternoon.* **15.** *Chiefly Brit. Informal.* **a.** to put into prison; jail. **b.** to behave treacherously toward; inform on; betray. **16.** *Slang.* to try to sell (merchandise or a project) in an attempt to obtain an order or contract. —*interj.* **17.** (used in a store, shop, etc., in calling an employee to wait on a customer.) [1250–1300; ME *shoppe* (n.), OE *sceoppa* booth; akin to *scypen* stall, SHIPPON, G *Schopf* lean-to, *Schuppen* shed]

shop′ assist′ant, *Brit.* a store clerk. [1895–1900]

shop′ chair′man. See **shop steward.**

shop·craft (shop′kraft′, -kräft′), *n.* **1.** any of various skilled trades involving maintenance or repair work, as metalworking or boilermaking, esp. in the railroad industry. **2.** the members of any such trade. [1685–95; SHOP + CRAFT]

shop·ful (shop′fo͝ol), *n., pl.* **-fuls. 1.** the contents of a shop. **2.** a quantity sufficient to fill a shop. [1630–40; SHOP + -FUL]
—**Usage.** See **-ful.**

shop·girl (shop′gûrl′), *n.* a salesgirl; female store clerk. [1760–70; SHOP + GIRL]

sho·phar (shō′fər; *Seph. Heb.* shô fär′; *Ashk. Heb.* shō′fər, shō fär′), *n., pl.* **-phars,** *Heb.* **-phroth, -phrot, -phros** (*Seph.* -frōt′; *Ashk.* -frōs, -frōs′), *Judaism.* shofar.

shop·keep·er (shop′kē′pər), *n.* a retail merchant or tradesman; a person who owns or operates a small store or shop. [1520–30; SHOP + KEEPER] —**shop′keep′ing,** *n.*

shop·lift (shop′lift′), *v.t.* **1.** to steal (merchandise) as a shoplifter. —*v.i.* **2.** to shoplift merchandise. [1810–20; back formation from SHOPLIFTER]

shop·lift·er (shop′lif′tər), *n.* a person who steals goods from the shelves or displays of a retail store while posing as a customer. [1670–80; obs. *shoplift* shoplifter (SHOP + LIFT) + -ER[1]]

shoppe (shop), *n.* shop (used chiefly for quaint effect). [deliberately archaized sp.]

shop·per (shop′ər), *n.* **1.** a person who shops. **2.** See **comparison shopper. 3.** a retail buyer for another person or a business concern. **4.** a locally distributed newspaper of retail advertisements. [1860–65; SHOP + -ER[1]]

shop·ping (shop′ing), *n.* **1.** the act of a person who shops. **2.** the facilities or merchandise available to those who shop: *Chicago has good shopping.* —*adj.* **3.** of, for, or pertaining to examining and buying merchandise: *a shopping trip.* [1755–65; SHOP + -ING[1], -ING[2]]

shop′ping bag′, a strong, usually paper or plastic, bag with handles, used to carry purchases or belongings. [1925–30]

shop′ping-bag la′dy (shop′ing bag′). See **bag lady** (def. 1). [1975–80]

shop′ping cart′, a four-wheeled cart provided by a supermarket or other retail store for a customer's use in collecting purchases. [1925–30]

shop′ping cen′ter, a group of stores within a single architectural plan, supplying most of the basic shopping needs, esp. in suburban areas. [1935–40]

shop′ping list′, **1.** a list made by a shopper of items or goods to be bought. **2.** matters to be discussed, requested, or otherwise attended to: *the president's shopping list at the coming summit conference.* [1965–70]

shop′ping mall′, **1.** mall (def. 1). **2.** a shopping center. [1955–60]

shop′ping pla′za, a complex of stores, banks, movie theaters, etc.; shopping center. Also called **plaza.** [1955–60]

shop′ right′, *Patent Law.* the right of an employer to use an employee's invention without compensating the employee for the use, in cases where the invention was made at the place of and during the hours of employment.

shop′ stew′ard, a unionized employee elected to represent a shop, department, or the like, in dealings with an employer. Also called **committeeman, shop chairman.** [1910–15]

shop·talk (shop′tôk′), *n.* **1.** the specialized vocabulary having to do with work or a field of work: *I don't understand electronics shoptalk.* **2.** talk about one's work or occupation, esp. after the workday is over. [1880–85; SHOP + TALK]

shop·walk·er (shop′wô′kər), *n. Brit.* a floorwalker. [1860–65; SHOP + WALKER]

shop·win·dow (shop′win′dō), *n.* a window used for display of merchandise. [1400–50; late ME; see SHOP, WINDOW]

shop·worn (shop′wôrn′, -wōrn′), *adj.* **1.** worn or marred, as goods handled and exposed in a store. **2.** trite; hackneyed. [1870–75; SHOP + WORN]

shor·an (shôr′an, shōr′-), *n.* a system for aircraft navigation in which two signals sent from an aircraft are received and answered by two fixed transponders, the round-trip times of the signals enabling the navigator to determine the aircraft's position. [1930–35; *sho(rt) ra(nge) n(avigation)*]

shore[1] (shôr, shōr), *n.* **1.** the land along the edge of a sea, lake, broad river, etc. **2.** some particular country: *my native shore.* **3.** land, as opposed to sea or water: *a marine serving on shore.* **4.** *Law.* the space between the ordinary high-water and low-water mark. —*adj.* **5.** of, pertaining to, or located on land, esp. land along the edge of a body of water: *a marine on shore duty.* [1300–50; ME *schore,* OE *scora;* c. MD, MLG *schore;* perh. akin to SHEAR]
—**Syn. 1.** strand, margin. SHORE, BANK, BEACH, COAST refer to an edge of land abutting on an ocean, lake, or other large body of water. SHORE is the general word: *The ship reached shore.* BANK denotes the land along a river or other watercourse, sometimes steep but often not: *The river flows between its banks.* BEACH refers to sandy or pebbly margins along a shore, esp. those made wider at ebb tide: *a private beach for bathers.* COAST applies only to land along an ocean: *the Pacific coast.*

shore[2] (shôr, shōr), *n., v.,* **shored, shor·ing.** —*n.* **1.** a supporting post or beam with auxiliary members, esp. one placed obliquely against the side of a building, a ship in drydock, or the like; prop; strut. —*v.t.* **2.** to support by or as if by a shore or shores; prop (usually fol. by *up*): *to shore up a roof; government subsidies to shore up falling corn prices.* [1300–50; (n.) ME; c. MLG, MD *schore* prop; (v.) *shoren,* deriv. of the n.]
—**Syn. 1.** brace, buttress, stay.

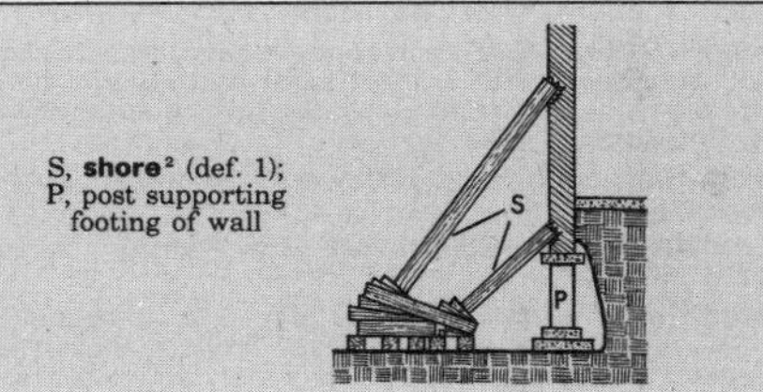

S, **shore[2]** (def. 1); P, post supporting footing of wall

shore[3] (shôr, shōr), *v.t.,* **shored, shor·ing.** *Scot. and North Eng.* **1.** to threaten (someone). **2.** to offer or proffer (something). [1325–75; ME (Scots) *schore* < ?]

Shore (shôr, shōr), *n.* **Jane,** 1445?–1527, mistress of Edward IV of England.

shore·bird (shôr′bûrd′, shōr′-), *n.* a bird that frequents seashores, estuaries, etc., as the snipe, sandpiper, plover, and turnstone; a limicoline bird. [1665–75; SHORE[1] + BIRD]

shore′ bug′, any of various small, predaceous hemipterous insects of the family Saldidae, some of which are burrowers, commonly occurring along grassy shores of ponds, streams, brackish lakes, and seacoasts. [1890–95, *Amer.*]

shore′ crab′, any of numerous crabs that live along the shoreline between the tidemarks, as *Hemigrapsus nudus* **(purple shore crab),** of the Pacific coast of North America. [1840–50]

shore′ din′ner, a meal consisting chiefly of seafood. [1890–95]

shore·front (shôr′frunt′, shōr′-), *n.* **1.** land along a shore. —*adj.* **2.** located on such land: *shorefront cottages.* [1915–20; SHORE[1] + FRONT]

shore′ leave′, *Navy.* **1.** permission to spend time ashore, usually 48 hours or more, granted a member of a ship's company. **2.** the time spent ashore during such leave. [1905–10]

shore·less (shôr′lis, shōr′-), *adj.* **1.** limitless; boundless. **2.** without a shore or beach suitable for landing: *a shoreless island.* [1620–30; SHORE[1] + -LESS]

shore·line (shôr′līn′, shōr′-), *n.* the line where shore and water meet. [1850–55; SHORE[1] + LINE[1]]

shore′ patrol′, (*often caps.*) members of an organization in the U.S. Navy having police duties similar to those performed by military police. *Abbr.:* SP [1940–45]

shore·side (shôr′sīd′, shōr′-), *n.* **1.** land along a shore. —*adj.* **2.** located on such land. [1565–75; SHORE[1] + SIDE[1]]

shore′ ter′race, a terrace or bench produced by wave erosion and biochemical attack along the shore of an ocean or a large lake. [1930–35]

Shore·view (shôr′vyo͞o′, shōr′-), *n.* a town in E Minnesota. 17,300.

shore·ward (shôr′wərd, shōr′-), *adv.* **1.** Also, **shore′·wards.** toward the shore or land. —*adj.* **2.** facing, moving, or tending toward the shore or land: *a shoreward course.* **3.** coming from the shore, as a wind. —*n.* **4.** the direction toward the shore or away from the sea. [1575–85; SHORE[1] + -WARD]

Shore·wood (shôr′wo͝od′, shōr′-), *n.* a city in SE Wisconsin, near Milwaukee. 14,327.

shor·ing (shôr′ing, shōr′-), *n.* **1.** a number or system of shores for steadying or supporting a wall, a ship in drydock, etc. **2.** the act of setting up shores. [1490–1500; SHORE[2] + -ING[1]]

shorn (shôrn, shōrn), *v.* a pp. of **shear.**

short (shôrt), *adj.,* **-er, -est,** *adv., n., v.* —*adj.* **1.** having little length; not long. **2.** having little height; not tall: *a short man.* **3.** extending or reaching only a little way: *a short path.* **4.** brief in duration; not extensive in time: *a short wait.* **5.** brief or concise, as writing. **6.** rudely brief; abrupt; hurting: *short behavior.* **7.** low in amount; scanty: *short rations.* **8.** not reaching a point, mark, target, or the like; not long enough or far enough. **9.** below the standard in extent, quantity, duration, etc.: *short measure.* **10.** having a scanty or insufficient amount of (often fol. by *in* or *on*): *He was short in experience.* **11.** being below a necessary or desired level; lacking: *The office is short due to winter colds and flu.* **12.** *Cookery.* **a.** (of pastry and the like) crisp and flaky; breaking or crumbling readily from being made with a large proportion of butter or other shortening. **b.** (of dough) containing a relatively large amount of shortening. **13.** (of metals) deficient in tenacity; friable; brittle. **14.** (of the head or skull) of less than ordinary length from front to back. **15.** *Stock Exchange.* **a.** not possessing at the time of sale commodities or stocks that one sells. **b.** noting or pertaining to a sale of commodities or stocks that the seller does not possess, depending for profit on a decline in prices. **16.** *Phonet.* **a.** lasting a relatively short time: *"Bit" has a shorter vowel-sound than "bid" or "bead."* **b.** belonging to a class of sounds considered as usually shorter in duration than another class, as the vowel of *but* as compared to that of *bought,* and in many languages serving as a distinctive feature of phonemes, as the *a* in German *Bann* in contrast with the *ah* in *Bahn,* or the *t* in Italian *fato* in contrast with the *tt* in *fatto* (opposed to *long*). **c.** having the sound of the English vowels in *bat, bet, bit, hot, but,* and *put,* historically descended from vowels that were short in duration. **17.** *Pros.* **a.** (of a syllable in quantitative verse) lasting a relatively shorter time than a long syllable. **b.** unstressed. **18.** (of an alcoholic drink) small: *a short drink.* **19.** *Chiefly Brit.* (of whiskey) undiluted; straight. **20.** *Ceram.* (of clay) not plastic enough to be modeled. **21.** *Ropemaking.* hard (def. 39). **22. short and sweet, a.** pleasantly brief. **b.** pertinent: *We're in a hurry, so make it short and sweet.* **23. short for,** being a shorter form of; abbreviated to: *"Phone" is short for "telephone."* **24. short of, a.** less than; inferior to. **b.** inadequately supplied with (money, food, etc.). **c.** without going to the length of; failing of; excluding: *Short of murder, there is nothing he wouldn't have tried to get what he wanted.* **25. make short work of.** See **work** (def. 16). —*adv.* **26.** abruptly or suddenly: *to stop short.* **27.** briefly; curtly. **28.** on the near side of an intended or particular point: *The arrow landed short.* **29.** *Baseball.* **a.** with the hands higher on the handle of the bat than usual: *He held the bat short and flied out.* **b.** in a fielding position closer to home plate than usual. **30. come** or **fall short, a.** to fail to reach a particular standard. **b.** to prove insufficient; be lacking: *Her funds fell short, and she had to wire home for help.* **31. cut short,** to end abruptly; terminate: *Her nap was cut short by a loud noise from outside.* **32. run short,** to be in insufficient supply: *My patience is running short.* **33. sell short, a.** *Stock Exchange.* to sell stocks or the like without having them in one's actual possession at the time of the sale. **b.**

to disparage or underestimate: *Don't sell Tom short; he's really an excellent engineer.* —*n.* **34.** something that is short. **35.** that which is deficient or lacking. **36.** the sum and substance of a matter; gist (usually prec. by *the*). **37. shorts, a.** trousers, knee-length or shorter. **b.** short pants worn by men as an undergarment. **c.** knee breeches, formerly worn by men. **d.** *Finance.* short-term bonds. **e.** *Mining.* crushed ore failing to pass through a given screen, thus being of a larger given size than a specific grade. Cf. **fine** (def. 29a). **f.** remnants, discards, or refuse of various cutting and manufacturing processes. **38.** a size of garment for men who are shorter than average: *He wears a 42 short.* **39.** a garment, as a suit or overcoat, in such a size. **40.** *Mil.* a shot that strikes or bursts short of the target. **41.** *Elect.* See **short circuit. 42.** *Pros.* a short sound or syllable. **43.** *Baseball.* shortstop (def. 1). **44.** *Motion Pictures.* See **short subject. 45.** *Finance.* See **short seller. 46.** a deficiency or the amount of a deficiency. **47.** *Chiefly Brit.* a small drink of straight whiskey; shot. **48. for short,** by way of abbreviation: *Her name is Patricia, and she's called Pat for short.* **49. in short, a.** in summary. **b.** in few words; in brief: *In short, this has been rather a disappointing day.* —*v.t.* **50.** to cause a short circuit in. **51.** to cheat by giving less than is expected or deserved; shortchange. —*v.i.* **52.** to short-circuit. [bef. 900; ME *schort* (adj.), OE *sceort;* c. OHG *scurz* short, ON *skortr* shortness, scarcity] —**short′ness,** *n.*

—**Syn. 4.** SHORT, BRIEF are opposed to *long,* and indicate slight extent or duration. SHORT may imply duration but is also applied to physical distance and certain purely spatial relations: *a short journey.* BRIEF refers esp. to duration of time: *brief intervals.* **5.** terse, succinct, laconic, condensed. **6.** curt, sharp, testy. **7.** poor, deficient, inadequate, wanting, lacking. **12.** crumbly. **14.** brachycephalic. —**Ant. 3, 4.** long.

short′ account′, *Finance.* **1.** the account of a short seller. **2.** See **short interest.** [1900–05]

short·age (shôr′tij), *n.* **1.** a deficiency in quantity: *a shortage of cash.* **2.** the amount of such deficiency. [1865–70; SHORT + -AGE] —**Syn. 1.** lack, want, scarcity.

short′ bal′lot, a ballot containing only candidates for the most important legislative and executive posts, leaving judicial and lesser administrative posts to be filled by appointment. [1910–15]

short′-billed marsh′ wren′ (shôrt′bild′, -bild′). See **sedge wren.** [1870–75]

short·bread (shôrt′bred′), *n.* a butter cookie commonly made in thick, pie-shaped wheels or rolled and cut in fancy shapes. [1795–1805; SHORT + BREAD]

short·cake (shôrt′kāk′), *n.* **1.** a cake made with a relatively large amount of butter or other shortening. **2.** a dessert made of short, sometimes sweetened, biscuit dough baked or split in layers, with a filling or topping of strawberries or other fruit. [1585–95; SHORT + CAKE]

short·change (shôrt′chānj′), *v.t.,* **-changed, -chang·ing. 1.** to give less than the correct change to. **2.** to deal with unfairly or dishonestly, esp. to cheat. [1890–95, *Amer.*] —**short′chang′er,** *n.*

short′ cir′cuit, *Elect.* an abnormal, usually unintentional condition of relatively low resistance between two points of different potential in a circuit, usually resulting in a flow of excess current. [1875–80]

short-cir·cuit (shôrt′sûr′kit), *v.t.* **1.** *Elect.* **a.** to make (an appliance, switch, etc.) inoperable by establishing a short circuit in. **b.** to carry (a current) as a short circuit. **2.** to bypass, impede, hinder, or frustrate: *Bad weather short-circuited my vacation plans.* —*v.i.* **3.** *Elect.* to form a short circuit or become inoperable due to a short circuit. [1870–75]

short·com·ing (shôrt′kum′ing), *n.* a failure, defect, or deficiency in conduct, condition, thought, ability, etc.: *a social shortcoming; a shortcoming of his philosophy.* [1670–80; SHORT + COMING] —**Syn.** fault, flaw, failing, weakness.

short·com·mons (shôrt′kom′ənz), *n.* (*used with a singular v.*) *Southern U.S.* a scanty allowance of food.

short′ con′, *Slang.* any simple confidence game involving a relatively small amount of money.

short′ cov′ering, *Finance.* purchases that close out short sales on stocks or commodities.

short-cut (shôrt′kut′), *v.,* **-cut, -cut·ting.** —*v.t.* **1.** to cause to be shortened by the use of a shortcut. —*v.i.* **2.** to use or take a shortcut. [1560–70] —**short′-cut′ter,** *n.*

short·cut (shôrt′kut′), *n.* **1.** a shorter or quicker way. **2.** a method, procedure, policy, etc., that reduces the time or energy needed to accomplish something. —*adj.* **3.** constituting or providing a shorter or quicker way: *shortcut methods.* [1560–70; SHORT + CUT]

short-day (shôrt′dā′), *adj. Bot.* requiring a short photoperiod. [1915–20]

short′ divi′sion, *Math.* division, esp. by a one-digit divisor, in which the steps of the process are performed mentally and are not written down. [1895–1900]

short′-eared owl′ (shôrt′ērd′), a streaked, buffy brown, cosmopolitan owl, *Asio flammeus,* having very short tufts of feathers on each side of the head. Also called **prairie owl.** [1805–15, *Amer.*]

short·en (shôr′tn), *v.t.* **1.** to make short or shorter. **2.** to reduce, decrease, take in, etc.: *to shorten sail.* **3.** to make (pastry, bread, etc.) short, as with butter or other fat. **4.** *Sports.* choke (def. 8). —*v.i.* **5.** to become short or shorter. **6.** (of odds) to decrease. [1505–15; SHORT + -EN[1]] —**short′en·er,** *n.*

—**Syn. 1.** condense, lessen, limit, restrict. SHORTEN, ABBREVIATE, ABRIDGE, CURTAIL mean to make shorter or briefer. SHORTEN is a general word meaning to make less in extent or duration: *to shorten a dress, a prisoner's sentence.* The other three terms suggest methods of shortening. To ABBREVIATE is to make shorter by omission or contraction: *to abbreviate a word.* To ABRIDGE is to reduce in length or size by condensing, summarizing, and the like: *to abridge a document.* CURTAIL suggests deprivation and lack of completeness because of omitting some part: *to curtail an explanation.* **5.** contract, lessen.

short·en·ing (shôrt′ning, shôr′tn ing), *n.* **1.** butter, lard, or other fat, used to make pastry, bread, etc., short. **2.** *Phonet.* the act, process, or an instance of making or becoming short. **3.** *Ling.* **a.** the act or process of dropping one or more syllables from a word or phrase to form a shorter word with the same meaning, as in forming *piano* from *pianoforte* or *phone* from *telephone.* **b.** See **clipped form.** [1535–45; SHORTEN + -ING[1]]

Shor·ter (shôr′tər), *n.* **Frank,** born 1947, U.S. marathon runner.

Short′er Cat′echism, one of the two catechisms established by the Westminster Assembly in 1647, used chiefly in Presbyterian churches.

short·fall (shôrt′fôl′), *n.* **1.** the quantity or extent by which something falls short; deficiency; shortage. **2.** the act or fact of falling short. [1890–95; SHORT + FALL; from v. phrase *fall short*]

short′ field′, *Baseball.* the area of the infield between third base and second, covered by the shortstop. [1855–60, *Amer.*]

short′fin corvi′na (shôrt′fin′). See under **corvina.**

short′ fuse′, a quick temper: *A person with a short fuse has to be handled diplomatically.* [1965–70]

short′ game′, **1.** the aspect of golf considered in relation to the ability of a player to hit medium or short shots, as chip shots, pitch shots, and putts, with accuracy. Cf. **long game** (def. 1). **2.** a card game in which not all cards in the pack are dealt before play. Cf. **long game** (def. 2). [1850–55, *Amer.*]

short·grass (shôrt′gras′, -gräs′), *n.* any of several range grasses of short stature, as buffalo grass, prevalent in semiarid regions of the Great Plains. [1835–45, *Amer.;* SHORT + GRASS]

short·haired (shôrt′hârd′), *adj.* (of an animal) having short hair lying close to the body. [1615–25; SHORT + HAIR + -ED[3]]

short′ hairs′, *Slang.* pubic hair. [1925–30]

short·hand (shôrt′hand′), *n.* **1.** a method of rapid handwriting using simple strokes, abbreviations, or symbols that designate letters, words, or phrases (distinguished from *longhand*). **2.** a simplified or makeshift manner or system of communication: *We spoke in a kind of pidgin shorthand to overcome the language barrier.* —*adj.* **3.** using or able to use shorthand. **4.** written in shorthand. **5.** of or pertaining to shorthand. [1630–40; SHORT + HAND]

shorthand (def. 1) "This is an example of shorthand" A, Gregg system; B, Pitman system

A

B

short-hand·ed (shôrt′han′did), *adj.* not having the usual or necessary number of workers, helpers, etc. [1615–25] —**short′-hand′ed·ness,** *n.*

short′ haul′. See **haul** (def. 22).

short-haul (shôrt′hôl′), *adj.* of, pertaining to, or engaged in transportation over short distances: *a short-haul trucking firm.* [1925–30]

short·head (shôrt′hed′), *n.* **1.** a brachycephalic person. **2.** a head with a cephalic index of 81 or over. [1890–95; SHORT + HEAD] —**short′head′ed,** *adj.*

Short·horn (shôrt′hôrn′), *n.* one of an English breed of red, white, or roan beef cattle having short horns. Also called **Durham.** [1820–30; SHORT + HORN]

short′-horned grass′hopper (shôrt′hôrnd′), locust (def. 1). [1885–90]

short·ie (shôr′tē), *n., adj.* shorty.

short′ in′terest, *Finance.* the total amount by which a single seller or all sellers are short in a particular stock or commodity or in the market as a whole. Also called **short account, short position.** [1885–90, *Amer.*]

short′ i′ron, *Golf.* a club, as a pitcher, pitching niblick, or niblick, with a short shaft and an iron head the face of which has great slope, for hitting approach shots. Cf. **long iron.** [1930–35]

short·ish (shôr′tish), *adj.* rather short. [1790–1800; SHORT + -ISH[1]]

short-laid (shôrt′lād′), *adj. Ropemaking.* hard-laid. [1785–95]

short′leaf pine′ (shôrt′lēf′), **1.** a pine, *Pinus echinata,* of the southern U.S., having short, flexible leaves. **2.** the hard, brownish-yellow wood of this tree, used in the construction of houses, for making furniture, and for pulp. [1790–1800, *Amer.*]

short′ line′, a bus or rail route covering only a limited distance. [1850–55]

short′ list′, a list of those people or items preferred or most likely to be chosen, as winnowed from a longer list of possibilities. Also, **short′list′.** [1925–30]

short-list (shôrt′list′), *v.t.* to put on a short list.

short-lived (shôrt′līvd′, -livd′), *adj.* living or lasting only a little while. [1580–90] —**short′-lived′ness,** *n.*

short·ly (shôrt′lē), *adv.* **1.** in a short time; soon. **2.** briefly; concisely. **3.** curtly; rudely. [bef. 900; ME *schortly,* OE *scortlīce;* see SHORT, -LY]

short′ or′der, a dish or serving of food that is quickly prepared upon request at a lunch counter. [1890–95]

short-or·der (shôrt′ôr′dər), *adj.* **1.** of, pertaining to, or specializing in short orders: *a short-order cook; short-order diner.* **2.** performed or supplied quickly: *They obtained a short-order divorce decree.* [1900–05]

short′ posi′tion, *Finance.* See **short interest.**

short-range (shôrt′rānj′), *adj.* having a limited extent, as in distance or time: *a short-range shot; a short-range plan.* [1865–70]

short′ rate′, *Insurance.* a charge, proportionately higher than the annual rate, made for insurance issued or continued in force by the insured for less than one year.

short-run (shôrt′run′), *adj.* happening or presented for a short period of time: *a short-run motion picture.* [1935–40]

short′ sale′, an act or instance of selling short. [1865–70]

short′ sell′er, *Finance.* a person, as a speculator, who sells short. —**short′ sell′ing.**

short-sheet (shôrt′shēt′), *v.t.* **1.** to fold and tuck in the top sheet of (a bed) so that it simulates both the top and bottom sheets: when the victim of this joke enters the bed, his or her legs are obstructed by the fold. **2.** to short-sheet the bed of (someone). Cf. **apple-pie bed.**

short′ short′ sto′ry, a very short piece of prose fiction, much more condensed than the average short story.

short′ shrift′, **1.** a brief time for confession or absolution given to a condemned prisoner before his or her execution. **2.** little attention or consideration in dealing with a person or matter: *to give short shrift to an opponent's arguments.* [1585–95]

short·sight·ed (shôrt′sī′tid), *adj.* **1.** unable to see far; nearsighted; myopic. **2.** lacking in foresight: *a shortsighted plan.* [1615–25] —**short′sight′ed·ly,** *adv.* —**short′sight′ed·ness,** *n.* —**Syn. 2.** unthinking, heedless, careless, improvident. —**Ant. 2.** prudent.

short′ splice′, a splice used when an increased thickness of the united rope is not objectionable, made by unlaying the rope ends a certain distance, uniting them so that their strands overlap, then tucking each alternately over and under others several times. Cf. **long splice.** See illus. under **splice.** [1760–70]

short-spo·ken (shôrt′spō′kən), *adj.* speaking in a short, brief, or curt manner. [1860–65]

short·stop (shôrt′stop′), *n.* **1.** *Baseball.* **a.** the position of the player covering the area of the infield between second and third base. **b.** a fielder who covers this position. **2.** Also called **short′stop bath′.** *Photog.* See **stop bath.** [1835–45, *Amer.;* SHORT + STOP]

short′ sto′ry, a piece of prose fiction, usually under 10,000 words. [1885–90] —**short′-sto′ry,** *adj.*

short′ sub′ject, *Motion Pictures.* a short film, as a documentary or travelogue, shown as part of a program with a feature-length film. Also called **short.** [1940–45]

short′ sweet′ening, *Chiefly Southern and Midland U.S.* sugar. Cf. **long sweetening.** [1840–50, *Amer.*]

short′-tailed shear′water (shôrt′tāld′). See under **mutton bird.**

short′-tailed shrew′, a grayish-black shrew, *Blarina brevicauda,* common in eastern North America, that has a tail less than half the length of the body. See illus. under **shrew.**

short-tem·pered (shôrt′tem′pərd), *adj.* having a quick, hasty temper; irascible. [1885–90] —**Syn.** irritable, testy, choleric, waspish.

short-term (shôrt′tûrm′), *adj.* **1.** covering or applying to a relatively short period of time. **2.** maturing over a relatively short period of time: *a short-term loan.* **3.** (of profit, loss, interest, etc.) of or pertaining to a short term, esp. one year or less. [1900–05]

short′-term mem′ory, information retained in the brain and retrievable from it over a brief span of time (contrasted with *long-term memory*). [1965–70]

short′ time′, a period or schedule during which the number of working hours is reduced: *The recession has put most of the manufacturing plants on short time.* —**short′-time′,** *adj.*

short-tim·er (shôrt′tī′mər), *n. Informal.* a person, as a soldier, who has a short period of time left to serve on a tour of duty. [*short time* + -ER[1]]

short′ ti′tle, an abridged listing in a catalog or bibliography, giving only such essential information as the author's name and the book's title, publisher, and date and place of publication. [1865–70]

short′ ton′. See under **ton**[1] (def. 1). Also called **net ton.** [1880–85]

short-waist·ed (shôrt′wā′stid), *adj.* of less than average length between the shoulders and waistline; having a high waistline. Cf. **long-waisted.** [1580–90]

short·wall (shôrt′wôl′), *adj. Mining.* pertaining to a means of extracting coal when the working face is about a third the length of the longwall system and mining is done by a continuous cutter rather than by longwall machinery. [1910–15; SHORT + WALL]

short·wave (shôrt′wāv′), *n., adj., v.,* **-waved, -wav·ing.** —*n.* **1.** *Elect.* a radio wave shorter than that used in AM broadcasting, corresponding to frequencies of over 1600 kilohertz: used for long-distance reception or transmission. **2.** See **shortwave radio. 3.** *Physics.* a wave of electromagnetic radiation equal in length to, or shorter than, the wavelength of visible light. —*adj.* **4.** of, pertaining to, or using shortwaves. —*v.t., v.i.* **5.** to transmit by shortwaves. [1900–05; SHORT + WAVE]

short′wave ra′dio, a radio that transmits or receives shortwaves.

short·weight (shôrt′wāt′), *v.t.* **1.** to give less than

CONCISE ETYMOLOGY KEY: <, descended or borrowed from; >, whence; b., blend of, blended; c., cognate with; cf., compare; deriv., derivative; equiv., equivalent; imit., imitative; obl., oblique; r., replacing; s., stem; sp., spelling, spelled; resp., respelling, respelled; trans., translation; ?, origin unknown; *, unattested; ‡, probably earlier than. See the full key inside the front cover.

the weight charged for: *The firm is accused of short-weighting grain.* —*n.* **2.** the insufficient weight given in this manner. [1925–30; SHORT + WEIGHT]

short-wind·ed (shôrt′win′did), *adj.* **1.** short of breath; liable to difficulty in breathing. **2.** brief or concise; to the point, as in speech or writing. [1400–50; late ME]

short·y (shôr′tē), *n., pl.* **short·ies,** *adj. Informal.* —*n.* **1.** a person of less than average stature. **2.** a garment designed to be of short length. —*adj.* **3.** noting a garment designed to be of short length: *a shorty nightgown.* Also, **shortie.** [1905–10; SHORT + -Y[2]]

Sho·sho·ne (shō shō′nē), *n., pl.* **-nes,** (*esp. collectively*) **-ne** for 2. **1.** a river in NW Wyoming, flowing NE into the Big Horn River. 120 mi. (193 km) long. **2.** a member of any of several Numic-speaking peoples of California, Nevada, Utah, Idaho, and Wyoming. **3.** the language or languages of the Shoshone. Also, **Shoshoni** (for defs. 2, 3). [1805, *Amer.*; < an Eastern Shoshone band name]

Sho·sho·ne·an (shō shō′nē ən, shō′shə nē′ən), *n., pl.* **-ans,** (*esp. collectively*) **-an** for 2, *adj.* —*n.* **1.** (in some, esp. earlier, classifications) a grouping of four branches of the Uto-Aztecan language family including Numic, Hopi, and several languages of southern California. **2.** a member of a group speaking a Shoshonean language. —*adj.* **3.** of or pertaining to the Shoshonean-speaking peoples or their languages. [1890–95; SHOSHONE + -AN]

Shosho′ne Cav′ern, a large cave in NW Wyoming: a national monument.

Shosho′ne Dam′, a dam on the Shoshone River. 328 ft. (100 m) high.

Shosho′ne Falls′, falls of the Snake River, in S Idaho. 210 ft. (64 m) high.

Sho·sho·ni (shō shō′nē), *n., pl.* **-nis,** (*esp. collectively*) **-ni.** Shoshone (defs. 2, 3).

Sho·sta·ko·vich (shos′tə kō′vich; *Russ.* shə stə kô′vyich), *n.* **Di·mi·tri Di·mi·tri·e·vich** (di mē′trē di mē′trē ə vich; *Russ.* dmyē′tryē dmyē′tryi yi vyich), 1906–75, Russian composer.

shot[1] (shot), *n., pl.* **shots** or, for 6, 8, **shot;** *v.,* **shot·ted, shot·ting.** —*n.* **1.** a discharge of a firearm, bow, etc. **2.** the range of or the distance traveled by a missile in its flight. **3.** an aimed discharge of a missile. **4.** an attempt to hit a target with a missile. **5.** an act or instance of shooting a firearm, bow, etc. **6.** a small ball or pellet of lead, a number of which are loaded in a cartridge and used for one charge of a shotgun. **7.** such pellets collectively: *a charge of shot.* **8.** a projectile for discharge from a firearm or cannon. **9.** such projectiles collectively: *shot and shell.* **10.** a person who shoots; marksman: *He was a good shot.* **11.** *Slang.* a blow; punch: *The prizefighter was knocked out by a shot in the chin.* **12.** anything like a shot, esp. in being sudden and forceful. **13.** a heavy metal ball that competitors cast as far as possible in shot-putting contests. **14.** an aimed stroke, throw, or the like, as in certain games, esp. in an attempt to score. **15.** an attempt or try: *He's entitled to a shot at the championship.* **16.** a remark aimed at some person or thing. **17.** a guess at something. **18.** a hypodermic injection, as of a serum, vaccine, narcotic, or anaesthetic. **19.** a small quantity, esp. an ounce, of undiluted liquor. **20.** an amount due, esp. at a tavern. **21.** *Photog.* **a.** a photograph, esp. a snapshot: *Here's a nice shot of my kids.* **b.** the act of making a photograph, esp. a snapshot. **22.** *Motion Pictures, Television.* a unit of action photographed without interruption and constituting a single camera view. **23.** an explosive charge in place for detonation, as in mining or quarrying. **24.** *Metall.* comparatively hard globules of metal in the body of a casting. **25.** *Naut.* a 90-foot (27-m) length of anchor cable or chain. **26.** *Checkers.* a compulsory series of exchanges, especially when it proves favorable to the aggressor. **27.** *Textiles.* **a.** a pick sent through the shed in a single throw of the shuttle. **b.** (in carpet weaving) filling yarn used to bind the pile to the fabric, usually expressed with a preceding number representing the quantity of picks used: *three-shot carpet.* **c.** a defect in a fabric caused by an unusual color or size in the yarn. **28.** a chance with odds for and against; a bet: *a 20 to 1 shot.* **29. by a long shot.** See **long shot** (def. 4). **30. call one's shots,** *Informal.* to indicate beforehand what one intends to do and how one intends to do it. **31. call the shots,** *Informal.* to have the power or authority to make decisions or control policy: *Now that he's chairman of the board, he calls the shots.* **32. have** or **take a shot at,** make an attempt at: *I'll have a shot at solving the problem.* **33. like a shot,** instantly; quickly: *He bolted out of here like a shot.* **34. shot in the arm,** *Informal.* something that results in renewed vigor, confidence, etc.; stimulus: *Her recent promotion has given her a shot in the arm. The new members gave the club a shot in the arm.* **35. shot in the dark,** *Informal.* a wild guess; a random conjecture.
—*v.t.* **36.** to load or supply with shot. **37.** to weight with shot.
—*v.i.* **38.** to manufacture shot, as in a shot tower. [bef. 900; ME; OE *sc(e)ot, (ge)sceot;* c. G *Schoss, Geschoss;* akin to SHOOT] —**shot′less,** *adj.* —**shot′like′,** *adj.*
—**Syn. 15.** chance, go, essay.

shot[2] (shot), *v.* **1.** pt. and pp. of **shoot.** —*adj.* **2.** woven so as to present a play of colors; having a changeable color; variegated, as silk. **3.** spread or streaked with color: *the dawn sky shot with gold.* **4.** in hopelessly bad condition; ruined: *Those sneakers are really shot. His morale is shot.* **5.** *Slang.* intoxicated.

shot′ clock′, a clock used in basketball games to limit to a specific length the time taken between shots. [1980–85]

shote (shōt), *n.* shoat (def. 1).

shot′ effect′, *Electronics.* random fluctuations in the emission of electrons from a hot cathode, causing a hissing or sputtering sound **(shot noise)** in an audio amplifier and causing snow on a television screen. Also called **Schottky noise.** [trans. of G *Schroteffekt* (1918), equiv. to *Schrot* small shot, buckshot + *Effekt* EFFECT]

shot′ glass′, a small, heavy glass for serving a shot of whiskey or liquor.

shot·gun (shot′gun′), *n., adj., v.,* **-gunned, -gun·ning.** —*n.* **1.** a smoothbore gun for firing small shot to kill birds and small quadrupeds, though often used with buckshot to kill larger animals. **2.** *Football.* an offensive formation, designed primarily for passing situations, in which the backfield is spread out with the quarterback positioned a few yards behind the center and the other backs, as potential pass receivers, positioned as slotbacks or flankers. **3. ride shotgun, a.** (formerly) to ride atop a stagecoach as a shotgun-bearing guard. **b.** to protect or keep a watchful eye on something: *riding shotgun over the nation's economy.* —*adj.* **4.** of, pertaining to, used in, or carried out with a shotgun: *a shotgun murder; shotgun pellets.* **5.** covering a wide area in an irregularly effective manner without concern for details or particulars; tending to be all-inclusive, nonselective, and haphazard; indiscriminate in choice and indifferent to specific results: *He favored the shotgun approach in his political attacks.* **6.** seeking a desired result through the use or inclusion of a wide variety of elements. **7.** having all the rooms opening one into the next in a line from front to back: *shotgun apartment; shotgun cottage.* **8.** gained or characterized by coercive methods. —*v.t.* **9.** to fire a shotgun at. [1770–80, *Amer.*; SHOT[1] + GUN[1]]

shot′gun mi′crophone, a directional microphone with a narrow-angle range of sensitivity.

shot′gun wed′ding, 1. a wedding occasioned or precipitated by pregnancy. **2.** *Informal.* a compromise, merger, accord, etc., occasioned by necessity: *The coalition government was obviously a shotgun wedding.* Also, **shot′gun mar′riage.** [1925–30, *Amer.*]

shot′ hole′, a condition in plants in which small, rounded spots drop out of the leaves, appearing as if the leaves were riddled by shot, resulting from infection or injury. [1795–1805]

shot·hole (shot′hōl′), *n.* a hole drilled in rock, coal, ore, etc., to hold explosives used in blasting. [1870–75; SHOT[1] + HOLE]

shot′ met′al, lead hardened with antimony and arsenic, used to manufacture shot for cartridges. Also called **shot′ lead′.** [1870–75]

shot′ noise′, *Electronics.* See under **shot effect.** [1975–80]

shot′ put′, 1. a field event in which a heavy ball or shot is thrown or put for distance. **2.** a single throw or put of the shot. [1895–1900]

shot-put·ter (shot′po͝ot′ər), *n.* a participant in shot put. [1880–85; SHOT PUT + -ER[1]] —**shot′-put′ting,** *n.*

shott (shot), *n.* chott.

shot·ten (shot′n), *adj.* **1.** (of fish, esp. herring) having recently ejected the spawn. **2.** *Obs.* (of a bone) dislocated. [1175–1225; ME, ptp. of SHOOT]

shot·ting (shot′ing), *n.* the act or process of making lead shot in a shot tower. [SHOT[1] + -ING[1]]

shot′ tow′er, a tower from the top of which finely divided streams of molten lead are dropped down a central well, breaking up into spherical drops during their fall to be quenched and hardened in a tank of water at the bottom. [1810–20]

Shot·well (shot′wel′, -wəl), *n.* **James Thomson,** 1874–1965, U.S. diplomat, historian, and educator.

should (sho͝od), *auxiliary v.* **1.** pt. of **shall. 2.** (used to express condition): *Were he to arrive, I should be pleased.* **3.** must; ought (used to indicate duty, propriety, or expediency): *You should not do that.* **4.** would (used to make a statement less direct or blunt): *I should think you would apologize.* [ME *sholde,* OE *sc(e)olde;* see SHALL]
—**Syn. 3.** See **must[1].**
—**Usage.** Rules similar to those for choosing between *shall* and *will* have long been advanced for SHOULD and WOULD, but again the rules have had little effect on usage. In most constructions, WOULD is the auxiliary chosen regardless of the person of the subject: *If our allies would support the move, we would abandon any claim to sovereignty. You would be surprised at the complexity of the directions.*
Because the main function of SHOULD in modern American English is to express duty, necessity, etc. (*You should get your flu shot before winter comes*), its use for other purposes, as to form a subjunctive, can produce ambiguity, at least initially: *I should get my flu shot if I were you.* Furthermore, SHOULD seems an affectation to many Americans when used in certain constructions quite common in British English: *Had I been informed, I should* (American *would*) *have called immediately. I should* (American *would*) *really prefer a different arrangement.* As with *shall* and *will,* most educated native speakers of American English do not follow the textbook rule in making a choice between SHOULD and WOULD. See also **shall.**

shoul·der (shōl′dər), *n.* **1.** the part of each side of the body in humans, at the top of the trunk, extending from each side of the base of the neck to the region where the arm articulates with the trunk. **2.** Usually, **shoulders.** these two parts together with the part of the back joining them. **3.** a corresponding part in animals. See diag. under **horse. 4.** the upper foreleg and adjoining parts of a sheep, goat, etc. **5.** the joint connecting the arm or the foreleg with the trunk. **6.** a shoulderlike part or projection. **7.** *Ornith.* the bend of a bird's wing, between the hand and the forearm, esp. when distinctively colored, as in the red-shouldered hawk, *Buteo lineatus.* **8.** a cut of meat that includes the upper joint of the foreleg. **9.** Often, **shoulders.** *Informal.* capacity for bearing responsibility or blame or sympathizing with other people: *If you want to tell me your troubles, I have broad shoulders.* **10.** a steplike change in the contour of an object, as for opposing or limiting motion along it or for an abutment. **11.** *Carpentry.* **a.** the end surface or surfaces of a piece from which a tenon or tenons project. **b.** an inclined and raised surface, as on a joggle post, for receiving and supporting the foot of a strut or the like. **12.** *Fort.* the angle of a bastion between the face and the flank. **13.** *Print.* the flat surface on a type body extending beyond the base of the letter or character. See diag. under **type. 14.** the part of a garment that covers, or fits over, the shoulder. **15.** (in leather manufacturing) that part of the hide anterior to the butt. **16.** either of the two edges or borders along a road, esp. that portion on which vehicles can be parked in emergencies. Cf. **soft shoulder. 17.** See **shoulder season. 18.** *Furniture.* knee (def. 6). **19. cry on someone's shoulder,** to reveal one's problems to another person in order to obtain sympathy: *Don't cry on my shoulder—this mess is your own fault.* **20. put one's shoulder to the wheel,** to work energetically toward a goal; put forth effort: *If we put our shoulders to the wheel, we'll be able to finish the job soon.* **21. rub shoulders with,** to come into association with; mingle with: *As a social worker in one of the worst slum areas, she rubs shoulders with the poor and the helpless.* **22. shoulder to shoulder,** side by side; with united effort: *The volunteers worked shoulder to shoulder with the natives in harvesting the crops.* **23. straight from the shoulder,** without evasion; directly; candidly: *The lawyer told him straight from the shoulder that his case was weak.* —*v.t.* **24.** to push with or as if with the shoulder, esp. roughly: *to shoulder someone aside.* **25.** to take upon, support, or carry on or as if on the shoulder or shoulders: *He shouldered his knapsack and walked on.* **26.** to assume as a responsibility: *to shoulder the expense.* —*v.i.* **27.** to push with or as if with the shoulder: *to shoulder through a crowd.* **28. shoulder arms,** *Mil.* **a.** to place a rifle muzzle upward on the right or left shoulder, with the buttstock in the corresponding hand. **b.** the command to shoulder arms. [bef. 900; (n.) ME *sholder, s(c)hulder,* OE *sculdor;* c. D *schouder,* G *Schulter;* (v.) ME *shulderen,* deriv. of the n.]
—**Syn. 26.** bear, undertake, carry.

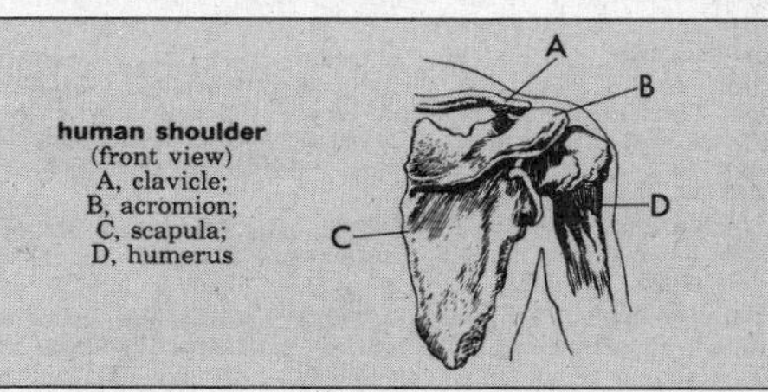

human shoulder (front view) A, clavicle; B, acromion; C, scapula; D, humerus

shoul′der bag′, a handbag with shoulder strap attached. [1940–45]

shoul′der blade′, the scapula. [1250–1300; ME]

shoul′der board′, *U.S. Navy.* one of a pair of narrow, stiff, cloth patches bearing an insignia of rank and worn on the shoulders by a commissioned officer. Also called **shoul′der mark′.** [1940–45]

shoul′der gir′dle. See **pectoral girdle** (def. 2). [1865–70]

shoul′der knot′, 1. a knot of ribbon or lace worn on the shoulder, as by men of fashion in the 17th and 18th centuries, by servants in livery, or by women or children. **2.** one of a pair of detachable ceremonial ornaments consisting of braided cord, worn on the shoulders by a commissioned officer. [1670–80]

shoul′der loop′, a flap on each shoulder of a service uniform on which metallic insignia of rank are worn by commissioned and warrant officers in the Army, Air Force, and Marines. Also called **shoul′der strap′.**

shoul′der patch′, a cloth emblem worn on the upper part of a sleeve of a uniform typically as identification of the organization to which the wearer is assigned. [1940–45]

shoul′der sea′son, a travel season between peak and off-peak seasons, esp. spring and fall, when fares tend to be relatively low. Also called **shoulder.** [1960–65]

shoul′der strap′, 1. a strap worn over the shoulder, as to support a garment. **2.** See **shoulder loop.** [1680–90]

shoul′der weap′on, a firearm that is fired while being held in the hands with the butt of the weapon braced against the shoulder. Also, **shoul′der gun′, shoul′der arm′.**

should·na (sho͝od′nə), *Scot.* contraction of *should not.*

should·n't (sho͝od′nt), contraction of *should not.*
—**Usage.** See **contraction, ought[1].**

shouldst (sho͝odst, sho͝otst), *v. Archaic.* 2nd pers. sing. past of **shall.** Also, **should·est** (sho͝od′ist).

shout (shout), *v.i.* **1.** to call or cry out loudly and vigorously. **2.** to speak or laugh noisily or unrestrainedly. —*v.t.* **3.** to utter or yell (something) loudly. **4.** *Australian.* to treat (another) to a drink, meal, amusement, or the like. —*n.* **5.** a loud call or cry: *He gave a shout for help.* **6.** a sudden loud outburst, as of laughter. **7.** the act of calling or crying out loudly. [1300–50; ME *shoute* (n.), *shouten* (v.); cf. ON *skūta* to scold, chide, *skūti, skūta* a taunt; akin to SHOOT] —**shout′er,** *n.*
—**Syn. 1.** yell, vociferate, exclaim. See **cry.** —**Ant. 1.** whisper.

shout′ing dis′tance. See **hailing distance.** [1950–55]

shout′ing match′, a loud, often abusive quarrel or argument.

shove[1] (shuv), *v.,* **shoved, shov·ing,** *n.* —*v.t.* **1.** to move along by force from behind; push. **2.** to push roughly or rudely; jostle. **3.** *Slang* (*often vulgar*). to go to hell with: *Voters are telling Congress to shove its new* *tax plan.* —*v.i.* **4.** to push. **5. shove** or **stick it,** *Slang (often vulgar).* (used to express contempt or belligerence): *I told them to take the job and shove it.* **6. shove** or **stick it up your** or **one's ass,** *Slang (vulgar).* go to hell: a term of contempt, abuse, disagreement, or the like. **7. shove off, a.** to push a boat from the shore. **b.** *Informal.* to go away; depart: *I think I'll be shoving off now.* —*n.* **8.** an act or instance of shoving. **9. when** or **if push comes to shove.** See **push** (def. 35). [bef. 900; (v.) ME *schouven,* OE *scūfan;* c. D *schuiven,* obs. G *schauben,* ON *skūfa;* akin to Goth *-skiuban;* (n.) ME *scou,* deriv. of the v.] —**shov′er,** *n.*

shove[2] (shōv), *n.* boon[3]. [appar. var. of SHIVE[2]]

shove-ha′·pen·ny (shuv′hā′pə nē, -hāp′nē), *n. Brit.* a shuffleboard game played with coins or brass disks that are pushed by the hand and thumb down a board toward a scoring pit. Also, **shove-half·pen·ny** (shuv′-hā′pə nē, -hāp′nē). [1835–45]

shov·el (shuv′əl), *n., v.,* **-eled, -el·ing** or (*esp. Brit.*) **-elled, -el·ling.** —*n.* **1.** an implement consisting of a broad blade or scoop attached to a long handle, used for taking up, removing, or throwing loose matter, as earth, snow, or coal. **2.** any fairly large contrivance or machine with a broad blade or scoop for taking up or removing loose matter: *a steam shovel.* **3.** a shovelful. **4.** *Informal.* See **shovel hat.** —*v.t.* **5.** to take up and cast or remove with a shovel: *to shovel coal.* **6.** to gather up in large quantity roughly or carelessly with or as if with a shovel: *He shoveled food into his mouth.* **7.** to dig or clear with or as if with a shovel: *to shovel a path through the snow.* —*v.i.* **8.** to work with a shovel. [bef. 900; ME *schovel,* OE *scofl;* c. D *schoffel* hoe; akin to G *Schaufel* shovel]

shov·el·board (shuv′əl bôrd′, -bōrd′), *n.* the game of shuffleboard. [1525–35]

shov·el·er (shuv′ə lər, shuv′lər), *n.* **1.** a person or thing that shovels. **2.** *Ornith.* **a.** a freshwater duck of the Northern Hemisphere, *Anas clypeata,* having a broad, flat bill. **b.** any of several related, similar ducks. Also, *esp. Brit.,* **shov′el·ler.** [1400–50; late ME; see SHOVEL, -ER[1]]

shov·el·ful (shuv′əl fo͝ol′), *n., pl.* **-fuls.** the amount held by a shovel. [1525–35; SHOVEL + -FUL]
—**Usage.** See **-ful.**

shov′el hat′, a hat with a broad brim turned up at the sides and projecting with a shovellike curve in front and behind; worn by some ecclesiastics, chiefly in England. —**shov′el-hat′ted,** *adj.*

shov·el·head (shuv′əl hed′), *n.* bonnethead. [1880–85, *Amer.;* SHOVEL + HEAD]

shov·el·nose (shuv′əl nōz′), *n.* **1.** any of various animals with a shovellike snout or head, as a guitarfish, *Rhinobatos productus,* of California. **2.** See **shovelnose sturgeon.** [1700–10, *Amer.;* SHOVEL + NOSE]

shov′elnose cat′fish. See **flathead catfish.**

shov·el-nosed (shuv′əl nōzd′), *adj.* having the head, snout, or beak broad and flat like the blade of a shovel. [1700–10]

shov′elnose stur′geon, a small sturgeon, *Scaphirhynchus platorhynchus,* of the Mississippi River, having a broad, flat snout. Also called **hackleback.** [1880–85]

show (shō), *v.,* **showed, shown** or **showed, show·ing,** *n.* —*v.t.* **1.** to cause or allow to be seen; exhibit; display. **2.** to present or perform as a public entertainment or spectacle: *to show a movie.* **3.** to indicate; point out: *to show the way.* **4.** to guide, escort, or usher: *He showed me to my room. Show her in.* **5.** to explain or make clear; make known: *He showed what he meant.* **6.** to make known to; inform, instruct, or prove to: *I'll show you what I mean.* **7.** to prove; demonstrate: *His experiment showed the falsity of the theory.* **8.** to indicate, register, or mark: *The thermometer showed 10 below zero.* **9.** to exhibit or offer for sale: *to show a house.* **10.** to allege, as in a legal document; plead, as a reason or cause. **11.** to produce, as facts in an affidavit or at a hearing. **12.** to express or make evident by appearance, behavior, speech, etc.: *to show one's feelings.* **13.** to accord or grant (favor, kindness, etc.): *He showed mercy in his decision.*
—*v.i.* **14.** to be seen; be or become visible: *Does my slip show?* **15.** to be seen in a certain way: *to show to advantage.* **16.** to put on an exhibition or performance; display one's goods or products: *Several dress designers are showing in New York now.* **17.** *Informal.* to be present or keep an appointment; show up: *He said he would be there, but he didn't show.* **18.** to finish third in a horse race, harness race, etc. **19. show off, a.** to display ostentatiously: *The parade was designed to show off all the latest weapons of war.* **b.** to seek to gain attention by displaying prominently one's abilities or accomplishments. **20. show up, a.** to make known, as faults; expose; reveal. **b.** to exhibit in a certain way; appear: *White shows up well against a blue background.* **c.** to come to or arrive at a place: *We waited for two hours, but he didn't show up.* **d.** to make (another) seem inferior; outdo.
—*n.* **21.** a theatrical production, performance, or company. **22.** a radio or television program. **23.** a motion picture. **24.** an exposition for dealers or the public of products by various manufacturers in a particular industry, usually held in an exhibition hall, convention facility, or the like: *the annual boat show.* **25.** any kind of public exhibition or exposition: *a show of Renoirs.* **26.** ostentatious display: *nothing but mere show.* **27.** a display, exhibition, or demonstration: *a true show of freedom.* **28.** an indication; trace: *He frowned on the slightest show of emotion.* **29.** the position of the competitor who comes in third in a horse race, harness race, etc. Cf. **place** (def. 27b), **win**[1] (def. 17). **30.** appearance; impression: *to make a sorry show.* **31.** a sight or spectacle. **32.** an unreal or deceptive appearance: *The actress's tears had the show of grief.* **33.** an act or instance of showing. **34.** a motion-picture theater. **35.** *Informal.* a chance: *to get a fair show.* **36.** *Med.* **a.** the first appearance of blood at the onset of menstruation. **b.** a blood-tinged mucous discharge from the vagina that indicates the onset of labor. **37.** *Chiefly Brit. Informal.* any undertaking, group of persons, event, etc.; affair; thing. **38. make a show of,** to be ostentatious about; affect: *Whenever there are visitors, the bosses make a show of being nice to their employees.* **39. run the show,** to control a business, situation, etc.; be in charge: *My father runs the show in our house.* **40. steal the show, a.** to usurp the credit or get the applause for something: *That woman can act, but the child stole the show. He did all the work, but his partner stole the show.* **b.** to be the most pleasing or spectacular item or person in a group. **41. stop the show,** to win such enthusiastic applause that a theatrical performance is temporarily interrupted. [bef. 900; (v.) ME *showen, s(c)hewen* to look at, show, OE *scēawian* to look at; c. D *schowen,* G *schauen;* (n.) ME *s(c)hew(e),* deriv. of the v.] —**show′a·ble,** *adj.* —**show′less,** *adj.*
—**Syn. 4.** lead, conduct. **5.** interpret, clarify, elucidate; reveal, disclose, divulge. **10.** assert, affirm. **13.** bestow, confer. **25.** spectacle. **26, 27.** SHOW, DISPLAY, OSTENTATION, POMP suggest the presentation of a more or less elaborate, often pretentious, appearance for the public to see. SHOW often indicates an external appearance that may or may not accord with actual facts: *a show of modesty.* DISPLAY applies to an intentionally conspicuous show: *a great display of wealth.* OSTENTATION is vain, ambitious, pretentious, or offensive display: *tasteless and vulgar ostentation.* POMP suggests such a show of dignity and authority as characterizes a ceremony of state: *The coronation was carried out with pomp and ceremonial.* **32.** deception, pretense, simulation, illusion.

Sho·wa (shō′wä), *n.* the designation of the period of the reign of Emperor Hirohito, begun in 1926.

show′ and tell′, **1.** an activity for young children, esp. in school, in which each participant produces an object of unusual interest and tells something about it. **2.** *Facetious.* any informative presentation or demonstration, as to introduce a new product or divulge and explain a special plan. [1950–55] —**show′-and-tell′,** *adj.* —**show′-and-tell′er,** *n.*

show′ bill′, **1.** an advertising poster. **2.** a list of attractions, as for a new theatrical season; roster. Also, **show′bill′.** [1795–1805]

show′ biz′, *Informal.* See **show business.** [1945–50]

show·boat (shō′bōt′), *n.* **1.** a boat, esp. a paddle-wheel steamer, used as a traveling theater. **2.** *Informal.* show-off (def. 1). **3.** a person, esp. an athlete, who performs in an ostentatiously sensational manner calculated to draw attention; show-off. —*v.i.* **4.** to perform or behave in an outrageous or spectacular manner. Also, **show′boat′er** (for defs. 2, 3). [1865–70, *Amer.;* SHOW + BOAT]

show·bread (shō′bred′), *n. Judaism.* shewbread.

show′ busi′ness, the entertainment industry, as theater, motion pictures, television, radio, carnival, and circus. [1925–30]

show′ card′, an advertising placard or card. [1840–50]

show·case (shō′kās′), *n., v.,* **-cased, -cas·ing,** *adj.* —*n.* **1.** a glass case for the display and protection of articles in shops, museums, etc. **2.** an exhibit or display, usually of an ideal or representative model of something. **3.** the setting, place, or vehicle for displaying something on a trial basis: *The club is a showcase for new comics.* —*v.t.* **4.** to exhibit or display. **5.** to present in or as if in an entertainment showcase: *The bar showcases young jazz pianists.* **6.** to show to best advantage: *The part minimizes her acting ability and showcases her singing.* **7.** to present as a special event: *The TV network plans to showcase a new production of the play.* —*adj.* **8.** prominently or proudly regarded or presented: *a showcase city.* [1830–40; SHOW + CASE[2]]

show′ cause′ or′der, *Law.* a court order issued to a party in a lawsuit, directing that party to appear to give reasons why a certain action should not be put into effect by the court.

show·down (shō′doun′), *n.* **1.** the laying down of one's cards, face upward, in a card game, esp. poker. **2.** a conclusive settlement of an issue, difference, etc., in which all resources, power, or the like, are used; decisive confrontation: *An international showdown was inevitable.* [1880–85, *Amer.;* SHOW + DOWN[1]]
—**Syn. 2.** crisis, climax, encounter, clash.

show·er[1] (shou′ər), *n.* **1.** a brief fall of rain or, sometimes, of hail or snow. **2.** Also called **show′er bath′.** a bath in which water is sprayed on the body, usually from an overhead perforated nozzle **(showerhead). 3.** the apparatus for this or the room or stall enclosing it. **4.** a large supply or quantity: *a shower of wealth.* **5.** a party given for a bestowal of presents of a specific kind, esp. such a party for a prospective bride or prospective mother: *a linen shower; a baby shower.* **6.** a fall of many objects, as tears, sparks, or missiles. **7.** *Astron.* See **air shower. 8. showers,** a room or area equipped with several showerheads or stalls for use by a number of people at the same time. **9. send to the showers,** *Baseball.* **a.** to replace (a pitcher) during a game, usually because he or she is ineffective: *The coach sent him to the showers after he walked three batters in a row.* **b.** to cause (a pitcher) to be replaced in a game, as by getting many hits off him or her; knock out of the box: *Two home runs and a line-drive double sent her to the showers.* —*v.t.* **10.** to bestow liberally or lavishly. **11.** to deluge (a person) with gifts, favors, etc.: *She was showered with gifts on her birthday.* **12.** to bathe (oneself) in a shower bath. —*v.i.* **13.** to rain in a shower. **14.** to take a shower bath. [bef. 950; ME *shour* (n.), OE *scūr;* c. G *Schauer,* ON *skūr,* Goth *skūra*] —**show′er·less,** *adj.* —**show′er·like′,** *adj.*
—**Syn. 4.** flood, deluge, torrent, stream.

show·er[2] (shō′ər), *n.* a person or thing that shows. [bef. 900; ME *shewere,* OE *scēawere,* deriv. of *scēawian* to SHOW, see -ER[1]]

show·er·head (shou′ər hed′), *n.* See under **shower**[1] (def. 2). [1965–70; SHOWER[1] + HEAD]

show·er·proof (shou′ər pro͞of′), *adj.* (of clothing, fabric, etc.) treated so as to resist rain; rainproof. [1890–95; SHOWER[1] + -PROOF]

show′er stall′ (shou′ər), an individual compartment or self-contained unit, having a single shower and accommodating one person.

show′er tea′ (shou′ər). See **kitchen tea.**

show·er·y (shou′ə rē), *adj.* **1.** characterized by or abounding with showers: *the showery season in the tropics.* **2.** falling in showers: *showery petals.* **3.** causing or bringing showers: *showery clouds.* **4.** of, pertaining to, or resembling showers: *showery spray from the ocean.* [1585–95; SHOWER[1] + -Y[1]] —**show′er·i·ness,** *n.*

show·folk (shō′fōk′), *n.pl.* persons, esp. performers, whose vocation is in the field of entertainment. [1810–20; SHOW + FOLK]

show′ gera′nium, a geranium, *Pelargonium domesticum,* of southern Africa, having roundish clusters of large white, pink, or red flowers. Also called **fancy geranium, Lady Washington geranium.**

show′ girl′, a woman who appears in the chorus of a show, nightclub act, etc. Also, **show′girl′.** [1920–25]

show′ house′, theater (def. 1). Also, **show′house′.** [1520–30]

show·i·ly (shō′ə lē), *adv.* in a showy manner. [1780–90; SHOWY + -LY]

show·i·ness (shō′ē nis), *n.* the property or characteristic of being showy. [1805–15; SHOWY + -NESS]

show·ing (shō′ing), *n.* **1.** a show, display, or exhibition. **2.** the act of putting something on display. **3.** a performance or record considered for the impression it makes: *She made a bad showing in high school but did better in college.* **4.** a setting forth or presentation, as of facts or conditions. **5.** Also called **show′ piece′.** a rock specimen revealing the presence of a certain mineral. [bef. 950; ME *schewing* (ger.), OE *scēawung;* see SHOW, -ING[1]]

show·man (shō′mən), *n., pl.* **-men. 1.** a person who presents or produces a show, esp. of a theatrical nature. **2.** a person who is gifted in doing or presenting things theatrically or dramatically: *He didn't have much voice but was a great showman.* [1725–35; SHOW + -MAN] —**show′man·ly,** *adv.*

show·man·ship (shō′mən ship′), *n.* the skill or ability of a showman. [1855–60; SHOWMAN + -SHIP]

show-me (shō′mē′), *adj.* demanding proof or evidence before being convinced: *a show-me attitude toward new ideas.* [1905–10, *Amer.*]

Show′ Me′ State′, Missouri (used as a nickname).

shown (shōn), *v.* a pp. of **show.**

show-off (shō′ôf′, -of′), *n.* **1.** a person given to pretentious display. **2.** the act of showing off. [1770–80; n. use of v. phrase *show off*] —**show′-off′ish,** *adj.*
—**Syn. 1.** exhibitionist, braggart.

show′ of hands′, an indication of approval, disapproval, volunteering, etc., on the part of a group of persons, usually made by each assenting person raising his or her hand.

show·piece (shō′pēs′), *n.* **1.** something that is displayed or exhibited. **2.** something exhibited or worthy of exhibiting as a fine example of its kind. [1880–85; SHOW + PIECE]
—**Syn. 1, 2.** masterpiece, prize, gem.

show·place (shō′plās′), *n.* **1.** an estate, mansion, or the like, usually open to the public, renowned for its beauty, excellent design and workmanship, historical interest, etc. **2.** any house, building, office, etc., that is beautifully furnished and is considered of flawless taste: *His home was a showplace.* [1570–80; SHOW + PLACE]

show·room (shō′ro͞om′, -ro͝om′), *n.* a room used for the display of goods or merchandise. [1610–20; SHOW + ROOM]

show-stop·per (shō′stop′ər), *n.* **1.** *Theat.* a performer or performance that wins enthusiastic or prolonged applause. **2.** a spectacularly arresting or appealing person or thing: *This bright plaid suit is a real show-stopper.* Also, **show′stop′per.** [1945–50] —**show′-stop′ping, show′stop′ping,** *adj.*

show-through (shō′thro͞o′), *n.* **1.** the visibility through paper of what is printed on the other side. **2.** a measure of the opacity of a paper. [n. use of v. phrase *show through*]

show·time (shō′tīm′), *n.* the time at which an entertainment is scheduled to begin. [SHOW + TIME]

show′ tri′al, (esp. in a totalitarian state) the public trial of a political offender conducted chiefly for propagandistic purposes, as to suppress further dissent against the government by making an example of the accused. [1945–50]

show′ win′dow, a display window in a store. [1830–40, *Amer.*]

show·y (shō′ē), *adj.,* **show·i·er, show·i·est. 1.** making an imposing display: *showy flowers.* **2.** pompous; ostentatious; gaudy. [1705–15; SHOW + -Y[1]]
—**Syn. 2.** loud. See **gaudy**[1], **grandiose.** —**Ant. 2.** humble.

show′y crab′ ap′ple, a large Japanese bush or tree, *Malus floribunda,* of the rose family, having red fruit and rose-colored flowers that fade to white. [1955–60]

show′y or′chis, a wild orchid, *Orchis spectabilis,* of eastern North America, having a spike of showy flowers, each with purple, pink, or white sepals and petals united into a galea and a white lip. [1855–60, *Amer.*]

shp, See **shaft horsepower.** Also, **SHP, S.H.P., s.hp., s.h.p.**

CONCISE ETYMOLOGY KEY: <, descended or borrowed from; >, whence; b., blend of, blended; c., cognate with; cf., compare; deriv., derivative; equiv., equivalent; imit., imitative; obl., oblique; r., replacing; s., stem; sp., spelling, spelled; resp., respelling, respelled; trans., translation; ?, origin unknown; *, unattested; ‡, probably earlier than. See the full key inside the front cover.

shpt., shipment.

shr., share; shares.

shrad·dha (shrä′də), *n. Hinduism.* one of several funeral rites performed at intervals after a death. [1780–90; < Skt *śrāddha*, deriv. of *śraddhā* faith]

shrank (shrangk), *v.* a pt. of **shrink.**

shrap·nel (shrap′nl), *n.* **1.** *Mil.* **a.** a hollow projectile containing bullets or the like and a bursting charge, designed to explode before reaching the target, and to set free a shower of missiles. **b.** such projectiles collectively. **2.** shell fragments. [1800–10; named after Henry *Shrapnel* (1761–1842), English army officer, its inventor]

shread·head (shred′hed′), *n.* jerkinhead. [1835–45; perh. obs. *shread* SHRED + HEAD]

shred (shred), *n., v.,* **shred·ded** or **shred, shred·ding.** —*n.* **1.** a piece cut or torn off, esp. in a narrow strip. **2.** a bit; scrap: *We haven't got a shred of evidence.* —*v.t.* **3.** to cut or tear into small pieces, esp. small strips; reduce to shreds. —*v.i.* **4.** to be cut up, torn, etc.: *The blouse had shredded.* [bef. 1000; (n.) ME *schrede,* OE *scrēade;* c. ON *skrjōthr* worn-out book, G *Schrot* chips; (v.) ME *schreden,* OE *scrēadian* to pare, trim; akin to SHROUD; cf. SCREED] —**shred′less,** *adj.* —**shred′like′,** *adj.*

shred′ded wheat′, a breakfast cereal made by shredding cooked, dried whole wheat and baking or toasting it in biscuit- or spoon-size pieces. [1895–1900; formerly a trademark]

shred·der (shred′ər), *n.* **1.** a person or thing that shreds. **2.** a machine for destroying secret or private documents by shredding them. **3.** any of various devices used to shred crops, vegetables, wood, metal, etc. [1565–75; SHRED + -ER[1]]

shred·ding (shred′ing), *n.* furring attached to the undersides of rafters. Also, **shread′ing.** [1660–70; orig. uncert.]

Shreve·port (shrēv′pôrt′, -pōrt′), *n.* a city in NW Louisiana, on the Red River. 205,815.

shrew[1] (shro͞o), *n.* a woman of violent temper and speech; termagant. [1200–50; ME; special use of SHREW[2]] —**shrew′like′,** *adj.*
—**Syn.** virago, nag, scold.

shrew[2] (shro͞o), *n.* any of several small, mouselike insectivores of the genus *Sorex* and related genera, having a long, sharp snout. [bef. 900; ME (only in compounds), OE *scrēawa*]

short-tailed shrew, *Blarina brevicauda,* head and body 4 in. (10 cm); tail 1 in. (2.5 cm)

shrewd (shro͞od), *adj.,* **-er, -est.** **1.** astute or sharp in practical matters: *a shrewd politician.* **2.** keen; piercing. **3.** artful. **4.** *Archaic.* malicious. **5.** *Obs.* bad. **6.** *Obs.* shrewish. [1275–1325; ME *shrewed,* in part repr. SHREW[1] + -ED[3] (cf. DOGGED, WICKED); in part prob. ptp. of *shrewen* to curse, v. use of SHREW[1] (see -ED[2])] —**shrewd′ly,** *adv.* —**shrewd′ness,** *n.*
—**Syn. 1.** quick, discerning, perceptive, perspicacious, sagacious, keen; discriminating, intelligent. See **acute.**

shrew·ish (shro͞o′ish), *adj.* having the disposition of a shrew. [1325–75; ME; see SHREW[1], -ISH[1]] —**shrew′ish·ly,** *adv.* —**shrew′ish·ness,** *n.*

shrew′ mole′, **1.** a grayish-black mole, *Neurotrichus gibbsii,* of the western coast of the U.S. and Canada, that grows to a length of about 3 in. (7.6 cm). **2.** any of several Asiatic moles of the genus *Uropsilus.* [1815–25]

shrew·mouse (shro͞o′mous′), *n., pl.* **-mice.** a shrew. [1565–75; SHREW[2] + MOUSE]

Shrews·bur·y (shro͞oz′ber′ē, -bə rē *or, for 1,* shrōz′-), *n.* **1.** a city now part of Shrewsbury and Atcham, in Salop, in W England. 83,900. **2.** a town in central Massachusetts. 22,674.

shriek (shrēk), *n.* **1.** a loud, sharp, shrill cry. **2.** a loud, high sound of laughter. **3.** any loud, shrill sound, as of a whistle. —*v.i.* **4.** to utter a loud, sharp, shrill cry, as birds. **5.** to cry out sharply in a high voice: *to shriek with pain.* **6.** to utter loud, high-pitched sounds in laughing. **7.** (of a musical instrument, a whistle, the wind, etc.) to give forth a loud, shrill sound. —*v.t.* **8.** to utter in a shriek: *to shriek defiance.* [1560–70; earlier *shrick,* N var. of *shritch* (now dial.), ME *schrichen,* back formation from OE *scriccettan;* akin to SHRIKE] —**shriek′er,** *n.* —**shriek′ing·ly,** *adv.* —**shriek′y,** *adj.*
—**Syn. 1, 5.** scream, screech. **5.** See **scream.**

shriev·al (shrē′vəl), *adj.* of, belonging to, or relating to a sheriff. [1670–80; SHRIEVE[1] + -AL[1]]

shriev·al·ty (shrē′vəl tē), *n., pl.* **-ties.** the office, term, or jurisdiction of a sheriff. Also called **sheriffalty.** [1495–1505; SHRIEVE[1] + *-alty,* as in *mayoralty*]

shrieve[1] (shrēv), *n. Archaic.* sheriff.

shrieve[2] (shrēv), *v.t., v.i.,* **shrieved, shriev·ing.** *Archaic.* shrive.

shrift (shrift), *n. Archaic.* **1.** the imposition of penance by a priest on a penitent after confession. **2.** absolution or remission of sins granted after confession and penance. **3.** confession to a priest. [bef. 900; ME; OE *scrift* penance; c. G, D *schrift* writing; see SHRIVE, -TH[1]]

shrike (shrīk), *n.* **1.** any of numerous predaceous oscine birds of the family Laniidae, having a strong, hooked, and toothed bill, feeding on insects and sometimes on small birds and other animals: the members of certain species impale their prey on thorns or suspend it from the branches of trees to tear it apart more easily, and are said to kill more than is necessary for them to eat. **2.** any of several other birds having similar bills, as the vanga shrikes. **3.** (*cap.*) *Mil.* a 10-foot (3-m), 400-pound (180-kg) U.S. air-to-ground missile designed to destroy missile batteries by homing in on their radar emissions. [1535–45; perh. continuing OE *scrīc* thrush; akin to ON *skrīkja* to twitter; see SHRIEK]

shrill (shril), *adj.,* **-er, -est,** *v., n., adv.* —*adj.* **1.** high-pitched and piercing in sound quality: *a shrill cry.* **2.** producing such a sound. **3.** full of or characterized by such a sound: *shrill music.* **4.** betraying some strong emotion or attitude in an exaggerated amount, as antagonism or defensiveness. **5.** marked by great intensity; keen: *the shrill, incandescent light of the exploding bomb.* —*v.t., v.i.* **6.** to cry shrilly. —*n.* **7.** a shrill sound. —*adv.* **8.** in a shrill manner; shrilly. [1300–50; ME *shrille* (adj., v.); akin to OE *scrallettan* to sound loudly; c. G *schrill* (adj.), *schrillen* (v.); cf. ON *skrīll* rabble] —**shrill′ness,** *n.* —**shril′ly,** *adv.*

shrimp (shrimp), *n., pl.* **shrimps,** (*esp. collectively*) **shrimp** for 1, *v., adj.* —*n.* **1.** any of several small, long-tailed, chiefly marine crustaceans of the decapod suborder Natania, certain species of which are used as food. **2.** *Informal.* a diminutive or insignificant person. —*v.i.* **3.** to catch or try to catch shrimps. —*adj.* **4.** (of food) made with or containing shrimp: *shrimp salad.* **5.** of or pertaining to shrimp or their catching, processing, and marketing: *a shrimp boat.* [1300–50; ME *shrimpe* crustacean, puny person; akin to MHG *schrimpfen* to contract, OE *scrimman* to shrink] —**shrimp′like′,** *adj.*

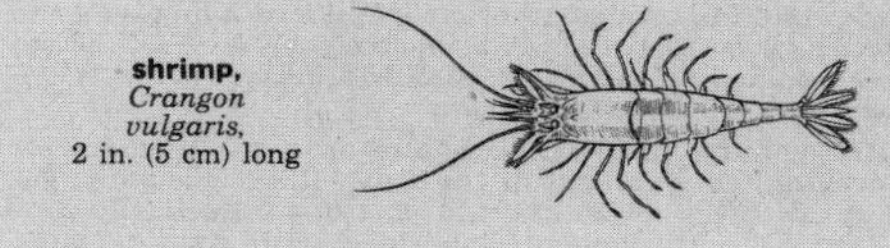

shrimp, *Crangon vulgaris,* 2 in. (5 cm) long

shrimp·er (shrim′pər), *n.* **1.** a shrimp fisherman. **2.** a boat used for shrimping. **3.** *Informal.* a shrimp. [1850–55; SHRIMP + -ER[1]]

shrimp·fish (shrimp′fish′), *n., pl.* (*esp. collectively*) **-fish,** (*esp. referring to two or more kinds or species*) **-fish·es.** any of several fishes of the family Centriscidae, inhabiting shallow waters from eastern Africa to Hawaii, having a compressed body covered with transparent plates. [SHRIMP + FISH]

shrimp′ plant′, a small, sprawling shrub, *Justicia brandegeana* (or *Beloperone guttata*), of the acanthus family, native to Mexico, having small white flowers protruding from a series of overlapping reddish bracts and often cultivated as a houseplant. [1940–45]

shrine (shrīn), *n., v.,* **shrined, shrin·ing.** —*n.* **1.** a building or other shelter, often of a stately or sumptuous character, enclosing the remains or relics of a saint or other holy person and forming an object of religious veneration and pilgrimage. **2.** any place or object hallowed by its history or associations: *a historic shrine.* **3.** any structure or place consecrated or devoted to some saint, holy person, or deity, as an altar, chapel, church, or temple. **4.** a receptacle for sacred relics; a reliquary. —*v.t.* **5.** to enshrine. [bef. 1000; ME *schrine,* OE *scrīn* (c. G *Schrein,* D *schrijn*) < L *scrīnium* case for books and papers] —**shrine′less,** *adj.* —**shrine′like′,** *adj.*

Shrin·er (shrī′nər), *n.* a member of a fraternal order **(Ancient Arabic Order of Nobles of the Mystic Shrine)** that is an auxiliary of the Masonic order and is dedicated to good fellowship, health programs, charitable works, etc. [1885–90, *Amer.*; SHRINE + -ER[1]]

shrink (shringk), *v.,* **shrank** or, often, **shrunk; shrunk** or **shrunk·en; shrink·ing;** *n.* —*v.i.* **1.** to draw back, as in retreat or avoidance: *to shrink from danger; to shrink from contact.* **2.** to contract or lessen in size, as from exposure to conditions of temperature or moisture: *This cloth will not shrink if washed in lukewarm water.* **3.** to become reduced in extent or compass. —*v.t.* **4.** to cause to shrink or contract; reduce. **5.** *Textiles.* to cause (a fabric) to contract during finishing, thus preventing shrinkage, during laundering, of the garments made from it. —*n.* **6.** an act or instance of shrinking. **7.** a shrinking movement. **8.** shrinkage. **9.** Also, **shrinker.** Also called **head shrinker.** *Slang.* a psychotherapist, psychiatrist, or psychoanalyst. [bef. 900; 1955–60 for def. 9; ME *schrinken,* OE *scrincan;* c. MD *schrinken,* Sw *skrynka* to shrink, Norw *skrukka* old shrunken woman] —**shrink′a·ble,** *adj.* —**shrink′ing·ly,** *adv.*
—**Syn. 1.** withdraw, recoil, quail. See **wince. 3.** See **decrease.** —**Ant. 3.** increase.

shrink·age (shring′kij), *n.* **1.** the act or fact of shrinking. **2.** the amount or degree of shrinking. **3.** reduction or depreciation in quantity, value, etc. **4.** contraction of a fabric in finishing or washing. **5.** the difference between the original weight of livestock and that after it has been prepared for marketing. **6.** *Com.* loss of merchandise through breakage, pilferage, shoplifting, etc. [1790–1800; SHRINK + -AGE]

shrink·er (shring′kər), *n.* **1.** a person or thing that shrinks. **2.** a device or chemical substance for shrinking. **3.** *Slang.* shrink (def. 9). [1545–55; SHRINK + -ER[1]]

shrink′ing vi′olet, a shy, modest, or self-effacing person. [1925–30]

shrink-wrap (shringk′rap′), *v.,* **-wrapped, -wrap·ping,** *n.* —*v.t.* **1.** to wrap and seal (a book, a food product, etc.) in a flexible film of plastic that, when exposed to a heating process, shrinks to the contour of the merchandise. —*n.* **2.** the plastic film used to shrink-wrap something. Also, **shrink′wrap′, shrink-pack, shrink·pack** (shringk′pak′). [1965–70]

shrive (shrīv), *v.,* **shrove** or **shrived, shriv·en** or **shrived, shriv·ing.** —*v.t.* **1.** to impose penance on (a sinner). **2.** to grant absolution to (a penitent). **3.** to hear the confession of (a person). —*v.i. Archaic.* **4.** to hear confessions. **5.** to go to or make confession; confess one's sins, as to a priest. [bef. 900; ME *shriven, schrifen,* OE *scrīfan* to prescribe, c. G *schreiben* to write << L *scrībere;* see SCRIBE[1]]

shriv·el (shriv′əl), *v.t., v.i.,* **-eled, -el·ing** or (*esp. Brit.*) **-elled, -el·ling. 1.** to contract and wrinkle, as from great heat, cold, or dryness. **2.** to wither; make or become helpless or useless. [1595–1605; akin to Sw *skroflig* uneven, rough (perh. orig. wrinkled, shrunken), dial. Sw *skryvla* to wrinkle, OE *sceorfan* to roughen; see SCURF]
—**Syn. 1.** shrink. See **wither.**

shriv·en (shriv′ən), *v.* a pp. of **shrive.**

Shri·ver (shrī′vər), *n.* **(Robert) Sar·gent, Jr.** (sär′jənt), born 1915, U.S. businessman and government official: first director of the U.S. Peace Corps, 1961–66.

shroff (shrof), *n.* **1.** (in India) a banker or money-changer. **2.** (in the Far East, esp. China) a native expert employed to test coins and separate the base from the genuine. —*v.t.* **3.** to test (coins) in order to separate the base from the genuine. [1610–20; earlier *sharoffe* < Pg *xarrafo,* prob. < Gujarati *ṣaraf* < Ar *ṣayrāfī* money-changer]

Shrop·shire (shrop′shēr, -shər), *n.* **1.** a former county in W England, now part of Salop. **2.** one of an English breed of dark-faced sheep, yielding good mutton and white wool.

Shrop′shire Lad′, A, a volume of poetry (1896) by A. E. Housman.

shroud (shroud), *n.* **1.** a cloth or sheet in which a corpse is wrapped for burial. **2.** something that covers or conceals like a garment: *a shroud of rain.* **3.** *Naut.* any of a number of taut ropes or wires converging from both sides on the head of a lower or upper mast of the outer end of a bowsprit to steady it against lateral sway: a part of the standing rigging. **4.** Also called **shroud′ line′.** *Aeron.* any of a number of suspension cords of a parachute attaching the load to the canopy. **5.** Also called **shroud′ing.** *Mach.* **a.** (on a nonmetallic gear) an extended metal rim enclosing the ends of the teeth on either side. **b.** (on a water wheel) one of two rings of boards or plates enclosing the buckets at their ends. **6.** *Rocketry.* a cone-shaped shield that protects the payload of a launch vehicle. —*v.t.* **7.** to wrap or clothe for burial; enshroud. **8.** to cover; hide from view. **9.** to veil, as in obscurity or mystery: *They shrouded their past lives in an effort to forget.* **10.** to provide (a water wheel) with a shroud. **11.** *Obs.* to shelter. —*v.i.* **12.** *Archaic.* to take shelter. [bef. 1000; (n.) ME; OE *scrūd;* c. ON *skrūth;* akin to SHRED; (v.) ME *shrouden,* deriv. of the n.; r. ME *shriden,* OE *scrȳdan,* deriv. of *scrūd*] —**shroud′less,** *adj.* —**shroud′like′,** *adj.*
—**Syn. 1.** winding sheet. **8.** conceal, screen.

shroud-laid (shroud′lād′), *adj. Cordage.* noting a fiber rope of four strands laid right-handed with or without a heart. [1790–1800]

Shroud′ of Tu′rin, a linen cloth kept in the Cathedral of Turin, Italy, since the late 1500's that bears a faint life-size human image venerated by some as the imprint of the dead body of Jesus.

shrove (shrōv), *v.* a pt. of **shrive.** [ME *shroof,* OE *scrāf*]

Shrove′ Mon′day, the Monday before Ash Wednesday. [1400–50; late ME *shrovemonday.* See SHROVE, MONDAY]

Shrove′ Sun′day, the Sunday before Ash Wednesday; Quinquagesima. [1425–75; late ME *shrofsunday.* See SHROVE, SUNDAY]

Shrove·tide (shrōv′tīd′), *n.* the three days before Ash Wednesday, once a time of confession and absolution. [1375–1425; late ME *shroftyde.* See SHROVE, TIDE[1]]

Shrove′ Tues′day, the last day of Shrovetide, long observed as a season of merrymaking before Lent. [1490–1500; SHROVE + TUESDAY]

shrub[1] (shrub), *n.* a woody plant smaller than a tree, usually having multiple permanent stems branching from or near the ground. [bef. 1000; ME *shrubbe,* OE *scrybb* brushwood; c. dial. Dan *skrub*] —**shrub′less,** *adj.* —**shrub′like′,** *adj.*

shrub[2] (shrub), *n.* any of various acidulated beverages made from the juice of fruit, sugar, and other ingredients, often including alcohol. [1740–50; < Ar, metathetic var. of *shurb* drink; see SHERBET]

shrub·ber·y (shrub′ə rē), *n., pl.* **-ber·ies. 1.** a planting of shrubs: *He hit the croquet ball into the shrubbery.* **2.** shrubs collectively. [1740–50; SHRUB[1] + -ERY]

shrub·by (shrub′ē), *adj.,* **-bi·er, -bi·est. 1.** consisting of or abounding in shrubs. **2.** resembling a shrub; shrublike. [1530–40; SHRUB[1] + -Y[1]] —**shrub′bi·ness,** *n.*

shrub′by cinque′foil, a small shrub, *Potentilla fruticosa,* of the rose family, native to the Northern temperate region, having pinnate leaves and numerous, showy, bright-yellow flowers. Also called **hardhack.**

shrug (shrug), *v.,* **shrugged, shrug·ging,** *n.* —*v.t.* **1.** to raise and contract (the shoulders), expressing indifference, disdain, etc. —*v.i.* **2.** to raise and contract the shoulders. **3. shrug off, a.** to disregard; minimize: *to shrug off an insult.* **b.** to rid oneself of: *to shrug off the effects of a drug.* —*n.* **4.** the movement of raising and contracting the shoulders. **5.** a short sweater or jacket that ends above or at the waistline. [1350–1400; (v.) ME *schruggen* to shudder, shrug < ?; (n.) late ME *shrugge* a tug, pull, deriv. of the v.]

shrunk (shrungk), *v.* a pp. and pt. of **shrink.**

shrunk·en (shrung′kən), *v.* a pp. of **shrink.**

sht., sheet.

shtetl (shtet′l, shtā′tl), *n., pl.* ***shtet·lach*** (shtet′läKH,

CONCISE PRONUNCIATION KEY: act, cāpe, dâre, pärt; set, ēqual; *if,* īce; ox, ōver, ôrder, oil, bo͝ok, bo͞ot, out; up, ûrge; child; sing; shoe; thin, *th*at; zh as in *treasure.* ə = a as in *alone,* e as in *system,* i as in *easily,* o as in *gallop,* u as in *circus;* ə as in *fire* (fīər), *hour* (ouər). l and n can serve as syllabic consonants, as in *cradle* (krād′l), and *button* (but′n). See the full key inside the front cover.

-ləKH, shtät′-), *Eng.* **shtetls.** *Yiddish.* (formerly) a Jewish village or small-town community in eastern Europe.

shtg., shortage.

shtick (shtik), *n. Slang.* **1.** (esp. in comic acting) a routine or piece of business inserted to gain a laugh or draw attention to oneself. **2.** one's special interest, talent, etc. Also, **shtik.** [1955–60; < Yiddish *shtik* pranks, whims, lit., piece < MHG *stücke,* OHG *stucki* (G *Stück*); cf. STUCCO]

shtup (shtŏŏp), *v.t., v.i.,* **shtupped, shtup•ping.** *Slang.* schtup.

shu (shōō), *n.* the Confucian principle of refraining from actions toward others that would be disagreeable if done to oneself. [< Chin *shù*]

Shu (shōō), *n. Egyptian Religion.* the god of the air, sometimes represented with arms upraised, supporting the vault of heaven. Cf. **Nut.**

Shu•bert (shōō′bərt), *n.* **Lee** (*Levi Shubert*), 1875–1953, and his brothers **Sam S.,** 1876–1905, and **Jacob J.,** 1880–1963, U.S. theatrical managers.

shuck[1] (shuk), *n.* **1.** a husk or pod, as the outer covering of corn, hickory nuts, chestnuts, etc. **2.** Usually, **shucks.** *Informal.* something useless or worthless: *They don't care shucks about the project.* **3.** the shell of an oyster or clam. —*v.t.* **4.** to remove the shucks from: *to shuck corn.* **5.** to remove or discard as or like shucks; peel off: *to shuck one's clothes.* **6.** *Slang.* to get rid of (often fol. by *off*): *a bad habit I couldn't shuck off for years.* —*interj.* **7. shucks,** *Informal.* (used as a mild exclamation of disgust or regret.) [1665–75; orig. uncert.] —**shuck′er,** *n.*

shuck[2] (shuk), *v.t Slang.* to deceive or lie to. [1955–60; orig. uncert.; perh. from exclamation *shucks!* (see SHUCK[1]) taken as a feigned sign of rural ignorance or a sham apology]

shuck•ing (shuk′ing), *n.* husking. [SHUCK[1] + -ING[1]]

shuck′ing and jiv′ing, *Slang.* misleading or deceptive talk or behavior, as to give a false impression. Also, **shuck′ and jive′.** [1965–70; SHUCK[2] + -ING[1]]

shud•der (shud′ər), *v.i.* **1.** to tremble with a sudden convulsive movement, as from horror, fear, or cold. —*n.* **2.** a convulsive movement of the body, as from horror, fear, or cold. [1275–1325; ME *shodderen* (v.) (c. G *schaudern* < LG), freq. of OE *scūdan* to tremble; see -ER[6]]
—**Syn. 1.** quiver. See **shiver**[1].

shud•der•ing (shud′ər ing), *adj.* **1.** trembling or quivering with fear, dread, cold, etc. **2.** Also, **shud′der•y.** characterized by or causing a shudder: *a shuddering plunge of the ship.* [SHUDDER + -ING[2]] —**shud′der•ing•ly,** *adv.*

Shu•dra (shōō′drə), *n.* a Hindu of the lowest caste, that of the workers. Also, **Sudra.** Cf. **Brahman** (def. 1), **Kshatriya, Vaisya.** [< Skt *śūdra*]

shuf•fle (shuf′əl), *v.,* **-fled, -fling,** *n.* —*v.i.* **1.** to walk without lifting the feet or with clumsy steps and a shambling gait. **2.** to scrape the feet over the floor in dancing. **3.** to move clumsily (usually fol. by *into*): *to shuffle into one's clothes.* **4.** to act underhandedly or evasively with respect to a stated situation (often fol. by *in, into,* or *out of*): *to shuffle out of one's responsibilities.* **5.** to intermix so as to change the relative positions of cards in a pack. —*v.t.* **6.** to move (one's feet) along the ground or floor without lifting them. **7.** to perform (a dance) with such movements. **8.** to move (an object or objects) this way and that. **9.** to put, thrust, or bring trickily, evasively, or haphazardly (usually fol. by *in, into, out,* etc.): *to shuffle one's way into favor.* **10.** to mix (cards in a pack) so as to change the relative positions. **11.** to jumble together, mix, or interchange the positions of (objects). **12. shuffle off, a.** to thrust aside; get rid of. **b.** to move away by, or as if by, shuffling: *They shuffled off to school with little enthusiasm.* —*n.* **13.** a scraping movement; dragging gait. **14.** an evasive trick; evasion. **15.** an act or instance of shuffling. **16.** *Cards.* **a.** a shuffling of cards in a pack. **b.** the right or turn to shuffle preparatory to dealing: *You win the shuffle.* **17.** a dance in which the feet are shuffled along the floor. [1525–35; < LG *schuffeln* to walk clumsily or with dragging feet, mix (cards); akin to SHOVEL]
—**Syn. 6.** drag, scrape, scuff.

shuf•fle•board (shuf′əl bôrd′, -bōrd′), *n.* **1.** a game in which standing players shove or push wooden or plastic disks with a long cue toward numbered scoring sections marked on a floor or deck. **2.** the board or marked surface, as on a floor or deck, on which this game is played. [1525–35; alter. of earlier *shove board*]

shuffleboard
(def. 2)

shuf•fler (shuf′lər), *n.* **1.** a person who shuffles. **2.** a person who mixes the cards, as before the deal in a card game. [1605–15; SHUFFLE + -ER[1]]

shuf•fling (shuf′ling), *adj.* **1.** moving in a dragging or clumsy manner. **2.** prevaricating; evasive. [1570–80; SHUFFLE + -ING[2]] —**shuf′fling•ly,** *adv.*

Shu•fu (shōō′fōō′), *n.* former name of **Kashi.**

Shu•ha (shōō′hä), *adj.* of or pertaining to any Shinto sect other than the Kokka.

CONCISE ETYMOLOGY KEY: <, descended or borrowed from; >, whence; b., blend of, blended; c., cognate with; cf., compare; deriv., derivative; equiv., equivalent; imit., imitative; obl., oblique; r., replacing; s., stem; sp., spelling, spelled; resp., respelling, respelled; trans., translation; ?, origin unknown; *, unattested; ‡, probably earlier than. See the full key inside the front cover.

Shu Han (shōō′ hän′), a dynasty that ruled in China A.D. 221–63.

shul (shōōl, shŏŏl), *n., pl.* ***shuln*** (shōōln, shŏŏln), *Yiddish.* a synagogue. Also, ***schul.***

Shu•lam•ite (shōō′lə mīt′), *n.* an epithet meaning "princess," applied to the bride in the Song of Solomon 6:13.

Shul•han A•rukh (*Seph. Heb.* shōōl KHän′ ä RŌŌKH′; *Ashk. Heb.* shŏŏl′KHən ô′RŎŎKH; *Eng.* shŏŏl′kən ô′rək), an authoritative code of Jewish law and custom compiled by the Talmudic scholar Joseph Caro (1488–1575), the original edition published in Vienna in 1565 emphasizing the practices of Sephardic Jews. Also, ***Shulhan′ Aruk′, Shulhan′ Aruch′.*** Cf. ***Mappah.***

Shultz (shŏŏlts), *n.* **George P(ratt),** born 1920, U.S. government official and diplomat: Secretary of State since 1982.

shul•war (shul′wär), *n.* (*used with a plural v.*) shalwar.

shun (shun), *v.t.,* **shunned, shun•ning.** to keep away from (a place, person, object, etc.), from motives of dislike, caution, etc.; take pains to avoid. [bef. 950; ME *shunen,* OE *scunian* to avoid, fear] —**shun′na•ble,** *adj.* —**shun′ner,** *n.*
—**Syn.** evade, eschew. —**Ant.** seek.

Shun (shōōn), *n. Wade-Giles, Pinyin.* See under **Yao.**

shun•pike (shun′pīk′), *n., v.,* **-piked, -pik•ing.** —*n.* **1.** a side road taken instead of a turnpike or expressway to avoid tolls or to travel at a leisurely pace. —*v.i.* **2.** to drive on a shunpike. [1850–55, *Amer.*; SHUN + (TURN)PIKE] —**shun′pik′er,** *n.*

shunt (shunt), *v.t.* **1.** to shove or turn (someone or something) aside or out of the way. **2.** to sidetrack; get rid of. **3.** *Elect.* **a.** to divert (a part of a current) by connecting a circuit element in parallel with another. **b.** to place or furnish with a shunt. **4.** *Railroads.* to shift (rolling stock) from one track to another; switch. **5.** *Surg.* **a.** to divert blood or other fluid by means of a shunt. **b.** the tube itself. **6.** to move or turn aside or out of the way. **7.** (of a locomotive with rolling stock) to move from track to track or from point to point, as in a railroad yard; switch. —*n.* **8.** the act of shunting; shift. **9.** Also called **bypass.** *Elect.* a conducting element bridged across a circuit or a portion of a circuit, establishing a current path auxiliary to the main circuit, as a resistor placed across the terminals of an ammeter for increasing the range of the device. **10.** a railroad switch. **11.** *Surg.* a channel through which blood or other bodily fluid is diverted from its normal path by surgical reconstruction or by a synthetic tube. **12.** *Anat.* an anastomosis. —*adj.* **13.** *Elect.* being, having, or operating by means of a shunt: *a shunt circuit; a shunt generator.* [1175–1225; (v.) ME *schunten, shonten* to shy (said of horses); (n.) ME, deriv. of the v.; akin to SHUN] —**shunt′er,** *n.*

shunt′ing en′gine, *Chiefly Brit.* See **switch engine.**

shun•to (shŏŏn′tō), *n.* the annual sessions of collective bargaining for wage increases sought by Japanese labor unions each spring. [< Japn *shuntō* lit., spring struggle < MChin, equiv. to Chin *chūn* spring + *dòu* struggle]

shunt-wound (shunt′wound′), *adj. Elect.* noting a motor or a generator that has the field circuit connected in parallel with the armature winding. Cf. **series-wound.** [1880–85] —**shunt′ wind′ing.**

shush (shush), *interj.* **1.** hush (used as a command to be quiet or silent). —*v.t.* **2.** to order (someone or something) to be silent; hush. [1920–25; imit.] —**shush′er,** *n.*

Shu•shan (shōō′shan, -shän), *n.* Biblical name of **Susa.**

shut (shut), *v.,* **shut, shut•ting,** *adj., n.* —*v.t.* **1.** to put (a door, cover, etc.) in position to close or obstruct. **2.** to close the doors of (often fol. by *up*): *to shut up a shop for the night.* **3.** to close (something) by bringing together or folding its parts: *Shut your book. Shut the window!* **4.** to confine; enclose: *to shut a bird into a cage.* **5.** to bar; exclude: *They shut him from their circle.* **6.** to cause (a business, factory, store, etc.) to end or suspend operations: *He shut his store, sold his house, and moved away. We're shutting the office for two weeks in June.* **7.** to bolt; bar. —*v.i.* **8.** to become shut or closed; close. **9. shut down, a.** to settle over so as to envelop or darken: *The fog shut down rapidly.* **b.** to close, esp. temporarily, as a factory; cease manufacturing or business operations. **c.** Also, **shut down on** or **upon.** *Informal.* to hinder; check; stop. **10. shut in, a.** to enclose. **b.** to confine, as from illness: *She broke her leg in a fall and has been shut in for several weeks.* **11. shut off, a.** to stop the passage of (water, traffic, electricity, etc.); close off. **b.** to isolate; separate: *an outpost almost completely shut off from civilization.* **12. shut out, a.** to keep from entering; exclude. **b.** to hide from view. **c.** to prevent (an opponent or opposing team) from scoring, as in a game of baseball. **13. shut up, a.** to imprison; confine. **b.** to close entirely. **c.** to stop talking; become silent: *I thought the neighbors would never shut up and let me sleep.* **d.** to stop (someone) from talking; silence. —*adj.* **14.** closed; fastened up: *a shut door.* **15.** *Phonet.* checked. **16. shut of,** *Informal.* free of; rid of: *He wished he were shut of all his debts.* —*n.* **17.** the act or time of shutting or closing. **18.** the line where two pieces of welded metal are united. [bef. 1000; ME *schutten,* OE *scyttan* to bolt (a door); akin to SHOOT]
—**Syn. 1.** See **close. 4.** jail, imprison, cage. **5.** prohibit. —**Ant. 1.** open.

shut•down (shut′doun′), *n.* a shutting down; a closing of a factory or the like for a time. [1855–60, *Amer.*; n. use of v. phrase *shut down*]

Shute (shōōt), *n.* **Nevil** (*Nevil Shute Norway*), 1899–1960, British novelist and aeronautical engineer.

shut-eye (shut′ī′), *n. Informal.* sleep. [1895–1900; SHUT + EYE]

shut-in (shut′in′), *adj.* **1.** confined to one's home, a hospital, etc., as from illness. **2.** *Psychiatry.* disposed to desire solitude; withdrawn; asocial. **3.** (of an oil or gas well) temporarily sealed up. —*n.* **4.** a person confined by infirmity or disease to the house, a hospital, etc. **5.** Also called **shut′-in well′.** an oil or gas well that has been closed down. [1840–50, *Amer.*; adj., n. use of v. phrase *shut in*]

shut•off (shut′ôf′, -of′), *n.* **1.** an object or device that shuts (something) off: *the automatic shutoff on a heater.* **2.** an act or instance of shutting off something, as an opening, a flow, or a service: *a shutoff of electric power due to unpaid bills.* Also, **shut′-off′.** [1865–70; n. use of v. phrase *shut off*]

shut•out (shut′out′), *n.* **1.** an act or instance of shutting out. **2.** the state of being shut out. **3.** *Sports.* **a.** a preventing of the opposite side from scoring, as in baseball. **b.** any game in which one side does not score. [1850–55, *Amer.*; n. use of v. phrase *shut out*]

shut•ter (shut′ər), *n.* **1.** a solid or louvered movable cover for a window. **2.** a movable cover, slide, etc., for an opening. **3.** a person or thing that shuts. **4.** *Photog.* a mechanical device for opening and closing the aperture of a camera lens to expose film or the like. —*v.t.* **5.** to close or provide with shutters: *She shuttered the windows.* **6.** to close (a store or business operations) for the day or permanently. —*v.i.* **7.** to close or close down: *The factory has shuttered temporarily.* [1535–45; SHUT + -ER[1]] —**shut′ter•less,** *adj.*
—**Syn. 1.** See **curtain.**

shut•ter•bug (shut′ər bug′), *n. Informal.* an amateur photographer, esp. one who is greatly devoted to the hobby. [1940–45; SHUTTER + BUG[1]]

shut•ter-pri•or•i•ty (shut′ər prī or′i tē, -ôr′-), *adj. Photog.* of or pertaining to a semiautomatic exposure system in which the photographer presets the shutter speed and the camera selects the aperture. Also, **shut•ter-pre•ferred** (shut′ər pri fûrd′). Cf. **aperture-priority.** [1970–75]

shut′ter release′, *Photog.* a button or similar device used to actuate a camera shutter. [1955–60]

shut′ter speed′, *Photog.* speed (def. 5b). [1885–90]

shut′ting stile′, the stile of a door or shutter that closes against the frame of the opening. Cf. **hanging stile.**

shut•tle (shut′l), *n., v.,* **-tled, -tling.** —*n.* **1.** a device in a loom for passing or shooting the weft thread through the shed from one side of the web to the other, usually consisting of a boat-shaped piece of wood containing a bobbin on which the weft thread is wound. **2.** the sliding container that carries the lower thread in a sewing machine. **3.** a public conveyance, as a train, airplane, or bus, that travels back and forth at regular intervals over a particular route, esp. a short route or one connecting two transportation systems. **4.** shuttlecock (def. 1). **5.** (*often cap.*) See **space shuttle.** —*v.t.* **6.** to cause (someone or something) to move to and fro or back and forth by or as if by a shuttle: *They shuttled me all over the seventh floor.* —*v.i.* **7.** to move to and fro: *constantly shuttling between city and suburb.* [bef. 900; ME *shotil* (n.), OE *scytel* dart, arrow; c. ON *skutill* harpoon; akin to SHUT, SHOOT] —**shut′tle•like′,** *adj.*

shut•tle•cock (shut′l kok′), *n.* **1.** Also called **shuttle.** the object that is struck back and forth in badminton and battledore, consisting of a feathered cork head and a plastic crown. **2.** the game of battledore. —*v.t.* **3.** to send or bandy to and fro like a shuttlecock. —*v.i.* **4.** to move or be bandied to and fro. —*adj.* **5.** of such a state or condition: *a shuttlecock existence.* [1515–25; SHUTTLE + COCK[1]]

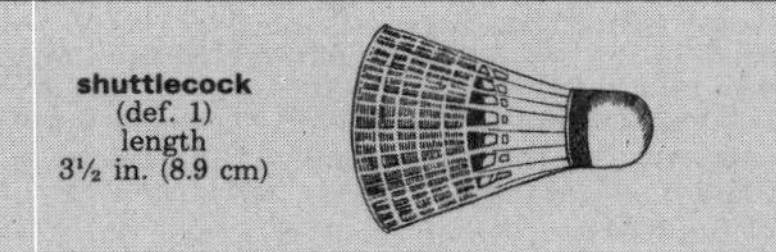
shuttlecock
(def. 1)
length
3½ in. (8.9 cm)

shut′tle diplo′macy, diplomatic negotiations carried out by a mediator who travels back and forth between the negotiating parties. [1970–75]

shvartz•e (shvär′tsə; *Eng.* shvär′tsə), *n. Yiddish* (*often disparaging and offensive*). schvartze. Also, ***shvartz•er*** (shvär′tsər; *Eng.* shvär′tsər).

Shver•nik (shvâr′nik; *Russ.* shvyer′nyik), *n.* **Ni•ko•lai** (nik′ə lī′; *Russ.* nyi ku lī′), 1888–1970, Russian government official: president of the Soviet Union 1946–53.

shwa (shwä), *n.* schwa.

shy[1] (shī), *adj.,* **shy•er** or **shi•er, shy•est** or **shi•est,** *v.,* **shied, shy•ing,** *n., pl.* **shies.** —*adj.* **1.** bashful; retiring. **2.** easily frightened away; timid. **3.** suspicious; distrustful: *I am a bit shy of that sort of person.* **4.** reluctant; wary. **5.** deficient: *shy of funds.* **6.** scant; short of a full amount or number: *still a few dollars shy of our goal; an inch shy of being six feet.* **7.** (in poker) indebted to the pot. **8.** not bearing or breeding freely, as plants or animals. **9. fight shy of,** to keep away from; avoid: *She fought shy of making the final decision.* —*v.i.* **10.** (esp. of a horse) to start back or aside, as in fear. **11.** to draw back; recoil. —*n.* **12.** a sudden start aside, as in fear. [bef. 1000; late ME *schey* (adj.), early ME *scheowe,* OE *scēoh;* c. MHG *schiech;* akin to D *schuw,* G *scheu;* cf. ESCHEW] —**shy′er,** *n.* —**shy′ly,** *adv.* —**shy′ness,** *n.*
—**Syn. 1.** SHY, BASHFUL, DIFFIDENT imply a manner that shows discomfort or lack of confidence in association with others. SHY implies a constitutional shrinking from contact or close association with others, together with a wish to escape notice: *shy and retiring.* BASHFUL suggests timidity about meeting others, and trepidation and awkward behavior when brought into prominence or notice: *a bashful child.* DIFFIDENT emphasizes self-distrust, fear of censure, failure, etc., and a hesitant, tentative manner as a consequence: *a diffident approach to a touchy subject.* **4.** heedful, cautious, chary. **11.** shrink.

—Ant. 1. forward. **2.** trusting. **4.** careless. **11.** advance.

shy² (shī), *v.*, **shied, shy·ing,** *n., pl.* **shies.** *—v.t., v.i.* **1.** to throw with a swift, sudden movement: *to shy a stone.* *—n.* **2.** a quick, sudden throw. **3.** *Informal.* **a.** a gibe or sneer. **b.** a try. [1780–90; orig. uncert.] **—shy′er,** *n.*
—Syn. 1. toss, pitch, fling, cast, flip.

Shy·lock (shī′lok), *n.* **1.** a relentless and revengeful moneylender in Shakespeare's *Merchant of Venice.* **2.** a hard-hearted moneylender. *—v.i.* **3.** (*l.c.*) to lend money at extortionate rates of interest. **—Shy·lock′i·an,** *adj.* **—Shy′lock·y,** *adj.*

shy·ster (shī′stər), *n. Informal.* **1.** a lawyer who uses unprofessional or questionable methods. **2.** a person who gets along by petty, sharp practices. [1835–45, *Amer.*; prob. < G *Scheisser,* equiv. to *scheiss(en)* to SHIT + *-er* -ER¹; final *-ser* conformed to -STER] **—shy′ster·ism,** *n.*

si (sē), *n. Music.* the syllable used for the seventh tone of a scale and sometimes for the tone B. [1720–30; see GAMUT]

SI, See **International System of Units.**

Si, *Symbol, Chem.* silicon.

S.I., 1. Sandwich Islands. **2.** Staten Island.

si·a·bon (sē′ə bən), *n.* a hybrid animal bred from a gibbon and a siamang. [SIA(MANG) + (GIB)BON]

Si·ad Bar·re (sē äd′ bä rā′), **Muhammad,** born 1919, Somali army officer and political leader: president 1969–91.

si·al (sī′al), *n. Geol.* the assemblage of rocks, rich in silica and alumina, that comprise the continental portions of the upper layer of the earth's crust. Cf. **sima¹.** [1920–25; < G, equiv. to *Si(licium)* SILICIUM + *Al(uminium)* ALUMINUM] **—si·al′ic,** *adj.*

si·a·lad·e·ni·tis (sī′ə lad′n ī′tis), *n. Pathol.* inflammation of one or more of the salivary glands. [< Gk *síal(on)* saliva + ADENITIS]

si·al·a·gog·ic (sī′ə lə goj′ik), *Med.* *—adj.* **1.** encouraging salivary flow. *—n.* **2.** sialagogue (def. 2). Also, **si′a·lo·gog′ic.** [1890–95; SIALAGOGUE + -IC]

si·al·a·gogue (sī al′ə gôg′, -gog′), *Med.* *—adj.* **1.** sialagogic (def. 1). *—n.* **2.** a sialagogic agent or medicine. Also, **si·al′o·gogue′.** [1775–85; < NL *sialagōgus* < Gk *síal(on)* saliva + *-agōgós* -AGOGUE]

si·a·lid (sī′ə lid), *n.* **1.** any neuropterous insect of the family Sialidae, comprising the alderflies. *—adj.* **2.** belonging or pertaining to the family Sialidae. [< NL *Sialidae* name of the family, equiv. to *Sialid-,* s. of *Sialis* a genus (Gk *sialís* a kind of bird) + *-idae* -ID²]

Si·al·kot (sē äl′kōt′), *n.* a city in NE Pakistan: military station. 296,000.

Si·am (sī am′, sī′am), *n.* **1.** former name of **Thailand** (def. 1). **2. Gulf of,** Thailand (def. 2).

si·a·mang (sē′ə mang′), *n.* a large, black gibbon, *Hylobates syndactylus,* of Sumatra and the Malay Peninsula, having very long arms and the second and third digits partially united by a web of skin: an endangered species. [1815–25; < Malay]

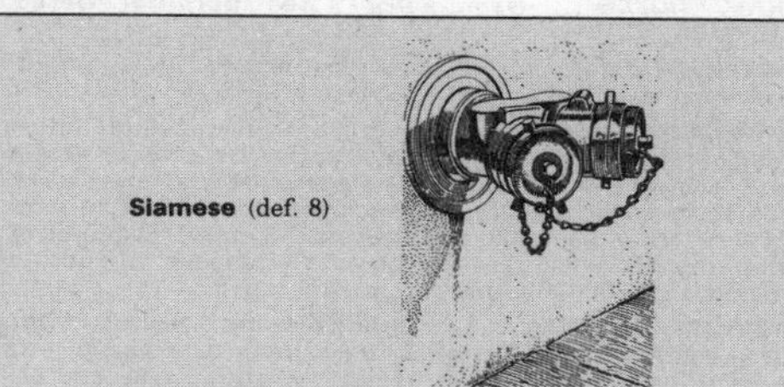
Siamese (def. 8)

Si·a·mese (sī′ə mēz′, -mēs′), *adj., n., pl.* **-mese.** *—adj.* **1.** of or pertaining to Siam, its people, or their language. **2.** Thai (def. 3). **3.** twin; closely connected; similar. **4.** *Informal.* dual; combined; twofold or two-way: *a Siamese sprinkler.* *—n.* **5.** a native of Siam. **6.** Thai (def. 2). **7.** See **Siamese cat. 8.** (*usually l.c.*) a standpipe placed outside a building close to ground level, having two or more openings so that fire engines can pump water to the sprinkler system of the building. [1685–95; SIAM + -ESE]

Si′amese cat′, one of a breed of slender, short-haired cats, raised originally in Siam, having a fawn or grayish body with extremities of a darker shade of the same color. [1905–10]

Siamese cat

Si′amese fight′ing fish′, a labyrinth fish, *Betta splendens,* that has been bred for centuries to develop brilliant coloration, very long fins, and pugnacity. See illus. at **fighting fish.** [1930–35]

Si′amese twins′, 1. congenitally united twins, Chang and Eng (1811–74), born in Siam, who were joined to each other at the chest by a short, tubular, cartilaginous band. **2.** any twins who are born joined together in any manner. [1820–30]

Si·an (sē′än′, shē′-), *n. Older Spelling.* Xian.

Siang·tan (syäng′tän′, shyäng′-), *n. Older Spelling.* Xiangtan.

Šiau·liai (shou lyī′), *n.* a city in N Lithuania, N of Kaunas. 145,000.

sib (sib), *adj.* **1.** related by blood; akin. *—n.* **2.** a kinsman; relative. **3.** one's kin or kindred. **4.** *Anthropol.* a unilateral descent group. [bef. 900; ME *sib(e), sibbe(e),* OE *sib(b)* (orig. adj.); c. ON *sifjar* (pl.) relatives, OFris *sib* (adj.), *sibba* (n.), MD *sibbe* (n. and adj.), G *Sippe* kin; cf. GOSSIP]

Si·be·li·us (si bā′lē əs, -bāl′yəs; *Fin.* si bā′lyŏŏs), *n.* **Jean (Ju·li·us Chris·tian)** (zhän yōō′lyŏŏs kris′tyän), 1865–1957, Finnish composer.

Si·be·ri·a (sī bēr′ē ə), *n.* **1.** Russian, **Sibir′.** an extensive region in the Russian Federation in N Asia, extending from the Ural Mountains to the Pacific. **2.** any undesirable or isolated locale, job, etc., to which one is assigned as punishment, a mark of disfavor, or the like. **—Si·be′ri·an,** *adj., n.*

Sibe′rian crab′ ap′ple, a hardy, round-headed tree, *Malus baccata,* of northern Asia, having white flowers and yellow or red fruit.

Sibe′rian high′, *Meteorol.* the prevailing high pressure system over Asia in winter.

Sibe′rian Husk′y, one of a Siberian breed of medium-size dogs having a thick, soft coat, raised originally as sled dogs. [1930–35]

Sibe′rian lark′spur, a plant, *Delphinium grandiflorum,* of eastern Asia, having blue or whitish flowers and hairy fruit. Also called **bouquet larkspur.**

Sibe′rian mam′moth. See **woolly mammoth.**

Sibe′rian ru′by, a red tourmaline used as a gem: not a true ruby.

Sibe′rian squill′, a bulbous, Eurasian plant, *Scilla siberica,* of the lily family, having nodding, deep blue flowers.

Sibe′rian wall′flower, a North American plant, *Erysimum asperum,* of the mustard family, having orange-yellow flowers. [1920–25]

si·be·rite (sī bēr′īt, sī′bə rīt′), *n.* a violet or violet-red tourmaline, used as a gem. [1795–1805; < F *sibérite,* after *Sibérie* SIBERIA; see -ITE¹]

sib·i·lant (sib′ə lənt), *adj.* **1.** hissing. **2.** *Phonet.* characterized by a hissing sound; noting sounds like those spelled with *s* in *this* (*this*), *rose* (rōz), *pressure* (presh′ər), *pleasure* (plezh′ər), and certain similar uses of *ch, sh, z, zh,* etc. *—n.* **3.** *Phonet.* a sibilant consonant. [1660–70; < L *sībilant-* (s. of *sībilāns*), prp. of *sībilāre* to hiss), equiv. to *sībil(us)* a hissing, whistling (of imit. orig.) + *-ant-* -ANT] **—sib′i·lance, sib′i·lan·cy,** *n.* **—sib′i·lant·ly,** *adv.*

sib·i·late (sib′ə lāt′), *v.,* **-lat·ed, -lat·ing.** *—v.i.* **1.** to hiss. *—v.t.* **2.** to utter or pronounce with a hissing sound. [1650–60; < L *sībilātus* (ptp. of *sībilāre* to hiss); see SIBILANT, -ATE¹] **—sib′i·la′tion,** *n.* **—sib′i·la′tor,** *n.*

Si·bir′ (syi byēʀ′), *n.* Russian name of **Siberia.**

Si·biu (sē byōō′), *n.* a city in central Rumania. 156,854.

sib·ling (sib′ling), *n.* **1.** a brother or sister. **2.** *Anthropol.* a comember of a sib. *—adj.* **3.** of or pertaining to a brother or sister: *sibling rivalry.* [bef. 1000; late ME: relative, OE; see SIB, -LING¹]

sib·ship (sib′ship), *n. Anthropol.* the condition of being a member of a sib. [SIB + -SHIP]

sib·yl (sib′əl), *n.* **1.** any of certain women of antiquity reputed to possess powers of prophecy or divination. **2.** a female prophet or witch. [1250–1300; < Gk *Síbylla* SIBYLLA; r. ME *Sibil* < ML *Sibilla* < Gk, as above]
—Syn. seer, prophetess, oracle, soothsayer.

Sib·yl (sib′əl), *n.* a female given name. Also, **Sib′ylle.**

Si·byl·la (si bil′ə), *n. Class. Myth.* an Asian maiden who gained from her lover Apollo the gift of prophecy and long life.

sib·yl·line (sib′ə lēn′, -līn′, -lin), *adj.* **1.** of, resembling, or characteristic of a sibyl; prophetic; oracular. **2.** mysterious; cryptic. Also, **si·byl·ic, si·byl·lic** (si bil′ik). [1570–80; < L *Sibyllīnus* pertaining to a sibyl. See SIBYL, -INE¹]

sic¹ (sik), *v.t.,* **sicked** or **sicced** (sikt), **sick·ing** or **sic·cing.** **1.** to attack (used esp. in commanding a dog): *Sic 'em!* **2.** to incite to attack (usually fol. by *on*). Also, **sick.** [1835–45; var. of SEEK]

sic² (sik), *adj. Chiefly Scot.* such. [1325–75; ME (north and Scots); see SUCH]

sic (sēk; *Eng.* sik), *adv. Latin.* so; thus: usually written parenthetically to denote that a word, phrase, passage, etc., that may appear strange or incorrect has been written intentionally or has been quoted verbatim: *He signed his name as e. e. cummings* (sic).

SIC, *U.S. Govt.* Standard Industrial Classification: a system used by the federal government to classify business activities for analytical and reporting purposes.

Sic., 1. Sicilian. **2.** Sicily.

Si·ca·ni·an (si kā′nē ən), *adj.* Sicilian. [1640–50; < L *Sicani(us)* (*Sicani(a)* Sicily + *-us* adj. suffix; see -OUS) + -AN]

sic·ca·tive (sik′ə tiv), *adj.* **1.** causing or promoting absorption of moisture; drying. *—n.* **2.** a siccative substance, esp. in paint. [1540–50; < LL *siccātīvus,* equiv. to L *siccāt(us)* (ptp. of *siccāre* to dry up; see SACK³, -ATE¹) + *-īvus* -IVE]

sice (sīs), *n.* syce.

Si·chuan (sich′wän′, sich′ōō än′; *Chin.* sœ′chwän′), *n. Pinyin.* a province in S central China. 67,960,000; 219,691 sq. mi. (569,000 sq. km). *Cap.:* Chengdu. Also, **Szechwan, Szechuan.**

Si·ci·lia (sē chē′lyä *for 1;* si sil′yə, -sil′ē ə *for 2*), *n.* **1.** Italian name of **Sicily. 2.** an ancient name of **Sicily.**

si·cil·i·a·no (si sil′ē ä′nō), *n., pl.* **-nos. 1.** a graceful folk dance of Sicily. **2.** the music for this dance. Also, **si·cil·i·a·na** (si sil′ē ä′nä, -nə). [1715–25; < It: lit., Sicilian]

Sicil′ian Ves′pers, a general massacre of the French in Sicily by the local population, begun at the sound of the vesper bell on Easter Monday, 1282.

Sic·i·lies, Two (sis′ə lēz). See **Two Sicilies.**

Sic·i·ly (sis′ə lē), *n.* an island in the Mediterranean, constituting a region of Italy, and separated from the SW tip of the mainland by the Strait of Messina: largest island in the Mediterranean. 4,909,996; 9924 sq. mi. (25,705 sq. km). *Cap.:* Palermo. Italian, **Sicilia.** Ancient, **Sicilia, Trinacria. —Si·cil·ian** (si sil′yən, -sil′ē ən), *adj., n.*

sick¹ (sik), *adj.,* **-er, -est,** *n.* *—adj.* **1.** afflicted with ill health or disease; ailing. **2.** affected with nausea; inclined to vomit. **3.** deeply affected with some unpleasant feeling, as of sorrow, disgust, or boredom: *sick at heart.* **4.** mentally, morally, or emotionally deranged, corrupt, or unsound: *a sick mind; wild statements that made him seem sick.* **5.** characteristic of a sick mind: *sick fancies.* **6.** dwelling on or obsessed with that which is gruesome, sadistic, ghoulish, or the like; morbid: *a sick comedian; sick jokes.* **7.** of, pertaining to, or for use during sickness: *sick benefits.* **8.** accompanied by or suggestive of sickness; sickly: *a sick pallor.* **9.** disgusted; chagrined. **10.** not in proper condition; impaired. **11.** *Agric.* **a.** failing to sustain adequate harvests of some crop, usually specified: *a wheat-sick soil.* **b.** containing harmful microorganisms: *a sick field.* **12.** *Now Rare.* menstruating. **13. call in sick,** to notify one's place of employment by telephone that one will be absent from work because of being ill. **14. sick and tired,** utterly weary; fed up: *I'm sick and tired of working late.* **15. sick at one's stomach,** *Chiefly Midland and Southern U.S.* nauseated. **16. sick to one's stomach,** *Chiefly Northern, North Midland, and Western U.S.* nauseated. *—n.* **17.** (*used with a plural v.*) sick persons collectively (usually prec. by *the*). [bef. 900; ME *sik, sek,* OE *sēoc;* c. D *ziek,* G *siech,* ON *sjūkr,* Goth *siuks*]
—Syn. 1. infirm, indisposed. See **ill. 2.** nauseous, nauseated. **—Ant. 1.** well, hale, healthy.

sick² (sik), *v.t.* sic¹.

sick′ bay′, a hospital or dispensary, esp. aboard ship. [1805–15]

sick·bed (sik′bed′), *n.* the bed used by a sick person. [1375–1425; late ME; see SICK¹, BED]

sick′ build′ing syn′drome, an illness caused by exposure to pollutants or germs inside an airtight building. [1980–85]

sick′ call′, *Mil.* **1.** a daily formation for those requiring medical attention. **2.** the period during which this formation is held. [1830–40]

sick′ day′, a day for which an employee will be paid while absent because of illness.

sick·en (sik′ən), *v.t., v.i.* to make or become sick. [1150–1200; ME *seknen, sicnen;* c. ON *sjūkna.* See SICK¹, -EN¹]
—Syn. repulse, revolt, disgust, upset.

sick·en·er (sik′ə nər), *n.* something that sickens or disgusts. [1800–10; SICKEN + -ER¹]

sick·en·ing (sik′ə ning), *adj.* causing or capable of causing sickness or loathing: *sickening arrogance.* [1715–25; SICKEN + -ING²] **—sick′en·ing·ly,** *adv.*
—Syn. nauseating, disgusting, loathsome.

sick·er¹ (sik′ər), *adj. compar. of* **sick¹** *with* **sickest** *as superl.*

sick·er² (sik′ər), *Scot. and North Eng.* *—adj.* **1.** safe from danger; secure. **2.** dependable; trustworthy. *—adv.* **3.** certainly; without doubt. Also, **siker.** [bef. 900; ME *siker,* OE *sicor;* c. D *zeker,* G *sicher,* all << L *sēcūrus;* see SECURE]

CONCISE PRONUNCIATION KEY: act, cāpe, dâre, pärt; set, ēqual; *if,* īce; ox, ōver, ôrder, oil, bŏŏk, bōōt, out; up, ûrge; child; sing; shoe; thin, *that;* zh as in *treasure.* ə = *a* as in *alone, e* as in *system, i* as in *easily, o* as in *gallop, u* as in *circus;* ᵊ as in *fire* (fīᵊr), *hour* (ouᵊr). l and n can serve as syllabic consonants, as in *cradle* (krād′l), and *button* (but′n). See the full key inside the front cover.

Sick•ert (sik′ərt), *n.* **Walter Richard,** 1860–1942, English painter.

sick′ head′ache, migraine. [1770–80]

sick•ie (sik′ē), *n. Slang.* **1.** Also, **sicko.** a person who is deranged or perverted. **2.** a morbid or sadistic thing, as a joke. [1965–70; SICK[1] + -IE]

sick•ish (sik′ish), *adj.* **1.** somewhat sick or ill. **2.** somewhat sickening or nauseating. [1575–85; SICK[1] + -ISH[1]] —**sick′ish•ly,** *adv.* —**sick′ish•ness,** *n.*

sick•le (sik′əl), *n.* **1.** an implement for cutting grain, grass, etc., consisting of a curved, hooklike blade mounted in a short handle. **2.** (*cap.*) *Astron.* a group of stars in the constellation Leo, likened to this implement in formation. [bef. 1000; ME *sikel,* OE *sicol;* c. D *zikkel,* G *Sichel,* all << L *secula,* equiv. to *sec(āre)* to cut + *-ula* -ULE]

sickle (def. 1)

sick′ leave′, leave from duty, work, or the like, granted because of illness. [1830–40]

sick′le bar′. See **cutter bar** (def. 1).

sick•le•bill (sik′əl bil′), *n.* any of various birds having a long, curved bill, as the long-billed curlew or curve-billed thrasher. [1870–75, *Amer.;* SICKLE + BILL[2]]

sick′le cell′, *Pathol.* an abnormal red blood cell having an elongated, crescentlike shape due to the presence of an abnormal hemoglobin. [1925–30; so called from the fact that the cells are often sickle-shaped]

sick′le cell′ ane′mia, *Pathol.* a chronic hereditary blood disease, occurring primarily among Africans or persons of African descent, in which abnormal hemoglobin causes red blood cells to become sickle-shaped and nonfunctional, characterized by enlarged spleen, chronic anemia, lethargy, weakness, joint pain, and blood clot formation. Also called **sick•le•mi•a** (sik′ə lē′mē ə, sik-lē′-). [1925–30]

sick′le cell′ trait′, *Pathol.* the usually asymptomatic hereditary condition that occurs when a person inherits from only one parent the abnormal hemoglobin gene characteristic of sickle cell anemia. Also called **sicklemia.** [1925–30]

sick′le feath′er, one of the paired, elongated, sickle-shaped, middle feathers of the tail of the rooster. [1680–90]

sick•le-hocked (sik′əl hokt′), *adj. Vet. Pathol.* noting or pertaining to a condition of horses in which the hock, due to strained tendons and ligaments, is flexed so that the foot is abnormally bowed far under the body. Also called **sick•le-hammed** (sik′əl hamd′). [1600–10]

sick′ list′, 1. a list of persons who are sick. **2. on the sick list,** in poor health; not well; ill. [1785–95]

sick•ly (sik′lē), *adj.,* **-li•er, -li•est,** *adv., v.,* **-lied, -ly•ing.** —*adj.* **1.** not strong; unhealthy; ailing. **2.** of, connected with, or arising from ill health: *a sickly complexion.* **3.** marked by the prevalence of ill health, as a region: *the epidemic left the town sickly.* **4.** causing sickness. **5.** nauseating. **6.** maudlin and insipid; mawkish: *sickly sentimentality.* **7.** faint or feeble, as light or color. —*adv.* **8.** in a sick or sickly manner. —*v.t.* **9.** to cover with a sickly hue. [1300–50; ME *siklich, sekly* (adj.). See SICK[1], -LY] —**sick′li•ness,** *n.*
—**Syn. 1.** frail, weak, puny, sick, feeble, infirm.

sick•ness (sik′nis), *n.* **1.** a particular disease or malady. **2.** the state or an instance of being sick; illness. **3.** nausea; queasiness. [bef. 1000; ME *siknesse, seknesse,* OE *sēocnesse.* See SICK[1], -NESS]

sick•o (sik′ō), *n., pl.* **sick•os.** *Slang.* sickie (def. 1). [SICK[1] + -O]

sick•out (sik′out′), *n.* an organized absence from work by employees on the pretext of sickness, as to avoid the legal problems or antistrike clauses that would be invoked in the case of a formal strike. [1950–55; prob. SICK[1] + (WALK)OUT]

sick′ pay′, wages or other compensation received from an employer during an illness. [1885–90] —**sick′-pay′,** *adj.*

sick•room (sik′ro͞om′, -ro͝om′), *n.* a room in which a sick person is confined. [1740–50; SICK[1] + ROOM]

sic pas•sim (sēk päs′im; *Eng.* sik pas′im), *Latin.* so throughout: used esp. as a footnote to indicate that a word, phrase, or idea recurs throughout the book being cited.

sic sem•per ty•ran•nis (sēk sem′per tʏ rän′nis; *Eng.* sik sem′pər ti ran′is), *Latin.* thus always to tyrants (motto of the State of Virginia).

sic tran•sit glo•ri•a mun•di (sēk trän′sit glō′rē ä′ mo͞on′dē; *Eng.* sik tran′sit glôr′ē ə mun′dī, -dē, glōr′-, -zit), *Latin.* thus passes away the glory of this world.

sic•ut pat•ri•bus, sit De•us no•bis (sē′ko͞ot pä′trē-bo͞os′, sit de′o͞os nō′bis; *Eng.* sik′ət pa′trə bəs, sit dē′əs nō′bis, dā′əs), *Latin.* as with our fathers, may God be with us (motto of Boston).

Si•cy•on (sish′ē on′, sis′-), *n.* an ancient city in S Greece, near Corinth. —**Sic•y•o•ni•an** (sis′ē ō′nē ən), *adj., n.*

Sid (sid), *n.* a male or female given name, form of **Sidney** or **Sydney.**

Si•da•mo (si dä′mō), *n., pl.* **-mos,** (*esp. collectively*) **-mo** for 1. **1.** a member of a people in SW Ethiopia. **2.** the Cushitic language of the Sidamo people.

Sid•dhart•ha (si där′tə, -thə), *n.* **1.** an epithet of Buddha meaning "he who has attained his goal." **2.** (*italics*) a novel (1922) by Hermann Hesse.

sid•dhi (sid′dē), *n.* **1.** *Yoga.* a miraculous power imparted by the late stages of intense meditation. Pali, **iddhi. 2.** *Buddhism.* any occult power acquired through discipline. [< Skt]

Sid•dons (sid′nz), *n.* **Sarah (Kemble),** 1755–1831, English actress.

sid•dur (*Seph.* sē do͞or′; *Ashk.* si′dər, si do͝or′; *Eng.* sid′ər), *n., pl.* ***sid•du•rim*** (*Seph.* sē do͞o rēm′; *Ashk.* si-do͝o′rim), *Eng.* **sid•durs.** *Hebrew.* a Jewish prayer book designed for use chiefly on days other than festivals and holy days; a daily prayer book. Cf. ***mahzor.*** [*siddūr* lit., arrangement]

side[1] (sīd), *n., adj., v.,* **sid•ed, sid•ing.** —*n.* **1.** one of the surfaces forming the outside of or bounding a thing, or one of the lines bounding a geometric figure. **2.** either of the two broad surfaces of a thin, flat object, as a door, a piece of paper, etc. **3.** one of the lateral surfaces of an object, as opposed to the front, back, top, and bottom. **4.** either of the two lateral parts or areas of a thing: *the right side and the left side.* **5.** either lateral half of the body, esp. of the trunk, of a human or animal. **6.** the dressed, lengthwise half of an animal's body, as of beef or pork, used for food. **7.** an aspect or phase, esp. as contrasted with another aspect or phase: *to consider all sides of a problem.* **8.** region, direction, or position with reference to a central line, space, or point: *the east side of a city.* **9.** a slope, as of a hill. **10.** one of two or more contesting teams, groups, parties, etc.: *Our side won the baseball game.* **11.** the position, course, or part of a person or group opposing another: *I am on your side in this issue.* **12.** line of descent through either the father or the mother: *grandparents on one's maternal side.* **13.** the space immediately adjacent to something or someone indicated: *Stand at my side.* **14.** *Informal.* a side dish, as in a restaurant: *I'll have a hamburger and a side of French fries.* **15.** Usually, **sides.** *Theat.* **a.** pages of a script containing only the lines and cues of a specific role to be learned by a performer. **b.** the lines of the role. **16.** *Naut.* the hull portion that is normally out of the water, located between the stem and stern to port or starboard. **17.** *Billiards.* English (def. 8). **18.** *Slang.* a phonograph record. **19.** *Chiefly Brit. Slang.* **a.** affected manner; pretension; assumed haughtiness: *to put on side.* **b.** impudence; gall: *He has a lot of side.* **20. on the side,** *Informal.* **a.** separate from the main issue or point of interest. **b.** in addition to one's regular, or known work, interest, relationships, etc.: *She tried selling cosmetics on the side. He dates another girl on the side.* **c.** as a side dish: *a hamburger with French fries on the side.* **21. on the** (specified) **side,** rather more than less; tending toward (the quality or condition specified): *This cake is a little on the sweet side.* **22. side by side, a.** next to one another; together. **b.** closely associated or related; in proximity: *A divided city in which democracy and communism must live side by side.* **23. take sides,** to give one's support to one person or group in a dispute; be partial to one side: *We were careful not to take sides for fear of getting personally involved.* **24. the far side,** the farther or opposite side: *the far side of the moon.* —*adj.* **25.** being at or on one side: *the side aisles of a theater.* **26.** coming from one side. **27.** directed toward one side: *a side blow.* **28.** subordinate or incidental: *a side issue.* —*v.i.* **29. side with** or **against,** to favor or support or refuse to support one group, opinion, etc., against opposition; take sides, as in a dispute: *He always sides with the underdog.* [bef. 900; ME; OE *side* (n.); c. D *zijde,* G *Seite,* ON *sītha*] —**side′less,** *adj.*
—**Syn. 28.** minor, lesser.

side[2] (sīd), *adj. Scot. and North Eng.* (esp. of a woman's dress or a man's beard) long and loose-flowing. [bef. 900; ME; OE *sīd* ample, large, extending lengthwise; c. ON *sīthr* long, LG *sied* low]

side′ arm′, *Mil.* a weapon, as a pistol or sword, carried at the side or in the belt. [1680–90]

side•arm (sīd′ärm′), *adv.* **1.** with a swinging motion of the arm moving to the side of the body at shoulder level or below and nearly parallel to the ground: *to pitch sidearm.* —*adj.* **2.** thrown or performed sidearm: *a sidearm curve ball; sidearm stroke.* [1925–30; SIDE[1] + ARM[1]]

side′ band′, *Radio.* the band of frequencies at the sides of the carrier frequency of a modulated signal. Also, **side′band′.** [1795–1805]

side•bar (sīd′bär′), *n.* follow-up (def. 3b). [1945–50; SIDE[1] + BAR[1]]

side′ bet′, a bet made, as with another player, in addition to one's principal bet: *a side bet as to which of us would draw the highest card.* [1890–95]

side•board (sīd′bôrd′, -bōrd′), *n.* **1.** a piece of furniture, as in a dining room, often with shelves, drawers, etc., for holding articles of table service. **2.** a board forming a side or a part of a side; sidepiece. **3. sideboards,** *Slang.* See **side whiskers.** [1300–50; ME; see SIDE[1], BOARD]

side•bone (sīd′bōn′), *n. Vet. Pathol.* ossification of the cartilages in the lateral portion of the foot of a horse, resulting in lameness. Also, **side′bones′.** [1810–20; SIDE[1] + BONE]

side•burns (sīd′bûrnz′), *n.pl.* **1.** short whiskers extending from the hairline to below the ears and worn with an unbearded chin. **2.** the projections of the hairline forming a border on the face in front of each ear. [1885–90, *Amer.;* alter. of BURNSIDES]

side•car (sīd′kär′), *n.* **1.** a small car attached on one side to a motorcycle and supported on the other side by a wheel of its own, used for a passenger, parcels, etc. **2.** a cocktail made with brandy, orange liqueur, and lemon juice. [1880–85; SIDE[1] + CAR[1]]

sidecar (def. 1)

side′ card′, *Cards.* **1.** *Poker.* the highest card in a hand that is not part of a scoring combination, as not being one of a pair, three of a kind, etc., and that serves to determine by its denomination the higher ranking of two otherwise equal hands. **2.** a card other than a trump; plain card. [1855–60, *Amer.*]

side′ chain′, *Chem.* an open chain of atoms attached to an atom of a larger chain, or to a ring. Also called **lateral chain.** [1900–05]

side′ chair′, a straight-backed chair without arms. Also, **side•chair** (sīd′châr′). [1920–25]

side•check (sīd′chek′), *n.* a checkrein passing from the bit to the saddle of a harness. See illus. under **harness.** [1890–95, *Amer.;* SIDE[1] + CHECK]

side′ cir′cuit, *Elect.* See under **phantom circuit.**

side′ curl′, earlock. Also, **side•curl** (sīd′kûrl′). [1805–15]

sid•ed (sī′did), *adj.* having a specified number or kind of sides (often used in combination): *five-sided; plastic-sided.* [1425–75; late ME; see SIDE[1], -ED[3]]

side′ dish′, 1. a serving of a portion of food in addition to the principal food, usually on a separate dish. **2.** the small additional dish used for such food. [1715–25]

side-dress (sīd′dres′), *v.t.,* **-dressed, -dress•ing.** to fertilize (growing plants) by mixing fertilizer into the soil along each row. [1965–70]

side′ dress′ing, the fertilizer used to side-dress plants. [1930–35]

side′ drum′. See **snare drum.** [1790–1800]

side′ effect′, 1. any effect of a drug, chemical, or other medicine that is in addition to its intended effect, esp. an effect that is harmful or unpleasant. **2.** any accompanying or consequential and usually detrimental effect: *the side effects of air pollution.* Also, **side′-effect′.** [1880–85]

side-glance (sīd′glans′, -gläns′), *n.* a glance directed to the side; an oblique or sideways look: *a side-glance of displeasure at her interrupter.* [1605–15]

side•head (sīd′hed′), *n. Print.* a heading or subhead run in the margin of a book or magazine. [SIDE[1] + HEAD]

side•hill (sīd′hil′), *n.* a hillside. [1665–75; SIDE[1] + HILL]

side′ horse′, *Gymnastics.* See **pommel horse.** [1930–35]

side•kick (sīd′kik′), *n.* **1.** a close friend. **2.** a confederate or assistant. [1900–05, *Amer.;* SIDE[1] + KICK]

side•light (sīd′līt′), *n.* **1.** an item of incidental information. **2.** either of two lights carried by a vessel under way at night, a red one on the port side and a green on the starboard. **3.** light coming from the side. **4.** a window or other aperture for light in the side of a building, ship, etc. **5.** a window at the side of a door or another window. [1600–10; SIDE[1] + LIGHT[1]]

side•line (sīd′līn′), *n., v.,* **-lined, -lin•ing.** —*n.* **1.** a line at the side of something. **2.** a business or activity pursued in addition to one's primary business; a second occupation. **3.** an additional or auxiliary line of goods: *a grocery store with a sideline of household furnishings.* **4.** *Sports.* **a.** either of the two lines defining the side boundaries of a field or court. **b. sidelines,** the area immediately beyond either sideline, where the substitute players sit. —*v.t.* **5.** to render incapable of participation, esp. in anything involving vigorous, physical action, as a sport: *An injury to his throwing arm sidelined the quarterback for two weeks.* [1685–95, *Amer.;* SIDE[1] + LINE[1]]

side•ling (sīd′ling), *adv.* **1.** sidelong or sideways; obliquely. —*adj.* **2.** having an oblique position; inclined or sloping. [1300–50; ME *sid(e)ling;* see SIDE[1], -LING[2]]

side•lock (sīd′lok′), *n.* earlock. [1840–50; SIDE[1] + LOCK[2]]

side•long (sīd′lông′, -long′), *adj.* **1.** directed to one side: *a sidelong glance.* **2.** inclined or slanting to one side. **3.** indirect; roundabout: *sidelong comments about his appearance.* —*adv.* **4.** toward the side; obliquely. [1515–25; SIDE[1] + LONG[1]]

side•man (sīd′man′, -mən), *n., pl.* **-men** (-men′, -mən). **1.** an instrumentalist in a band or orchestra. **2.** an instrumentalist supporting a soloist or a principal performer. [1560–70; SIDE[1] + MAN[1]]

side′ meat′, *Chiefly Midland and Southern U.S.* salt pork and bacon taken from the sides of a hog. [1870–75, *Amer.*]

side′ mon′ey, (in a poker game) the money or chips in a side pot. [1925–30, *Amer.*]

side-on (sīd′on′, -ôn′), *adj.* **1.** (of two objects) meeting with the sides foremost. —*adv.* **2.** with the side or sides foremost, esp. in a collision: *The other car struck me side-on.* [1905–10]

side•piece (sīd′pēs′), *n.* a piece forming a side or a part of a side, or fixed by the side, of something. [1795–1805; SIDE[1] + PIECE]

side′ pot′, (in poker with table stakes) a second or subsequent pot, separate from the main pot, created

CONCISE ETYMOLOGY KEY: <, descended or borrowed from; >, whence; b., blend of, blended; c., cognate with; cf., compare; deriv., derivative; equiv., equivalent; imit., imitative; obl., oblique; r., replacing; s., stem; sp., spelling, spelled; resp., respelling, respelled; trans., translation; ?, origin unknown; *, unattested; ‡, probably earlier than. See the full key inside the front cover.

when a player's entire table stake has been bet in a main pot or another side pot and other players want to continue betting.

si·de·re·al (sī dēr′ē əl), *adj. Astron.* **1.** determined by or from the stars: *sidereal time.* **2.** of or pertaining to the stars. [1625–35; < L *sīdere(us)* of, belonging to the stars (*sīder-*, s. of *sīdus* star, constellation + *-eus* adj. suffix) + -AL[1]] —**si·de′re·al·ly,** *adv.*

side′real day′, *Astron.* the interval between two successive passages of the vernal equinox over the meridian, being about four minutes shorter than a mean solar day. [1785–95]

side′real hour′ an′gle, *Astron.* the angle, measured westward through 360°, between the hour circle passing through the vernal equinox and the hour circle of a celestial body. Cf. **hour angle.**

side′real month′, *Astron.* See under **month** (def. 5). [1865–70]

side′real time′, *Astron.* time measured by the diurnal motion of stars. A sidereal day is about four minutes shorter than a solar day, with hours, minutes, and seconds all proportionally shorter. [1805–15]

side′real year′, *Astron.* year (def. 4c). [1675–85]

sid·er·ite (sid′ə rīt′), *n.* **1.** Also called **chalybite.** a common mineral, iron carbonate, $FeCO_3$, usually occurring in yellowish to deep-brown cleavable masses: a minor ore of iron. **2.** a meteorite consisting almost entirely of metallic minerals. [1570–80, in sense "loadstone"; 1845–50 for def. 1; SIDER- + -ITE[1]; in obs. sense, var. of *siderites* < L *sidērītēs* < Gk *sidērítēs* loadstone] —**sid·er·it·ic** (sid′ə rit′ik), *adj.*

sidero-[1], a combining form meaning "iron," used in the formation of compound words: *siderolite.* [< Gk *sidēro-,* comb. form of *sídēros* iron]

sidero-[2], a combining form meaning "star," "constellation," used in the formation of compound words: *siderostat.* [< L *sīder-* (s. of *sīdus*) star-group + -o-]

sid·er·o·cyte (sid′ər ə sīt′), *n. Anat.* an erythrocyte that contains iron in forms other than hematin. [SIDERO-[1] + -CYTE]

sid·er·og·ra·phy (sid′ə rog′rə fē), *n.* **1.** the art or technique of engraving on steel. **2.** a method of increasing the number of reproductions obtained from a steel engraving by first rolling a soft-steel cylinder over a hardened steel plate and then rolling the hardened cylinder over a soft-steel plate. [1810–20; SIDERO-[1] + -GRAPHY] —**sid′er·og′ra·pher,** *n.* —**sid·er·o·graph·ic** (sid′ər ə graf′ik), *adj.*

sid·er·o·lite (sid′ər ə līt′), *n.* a meteorite of roughly equal proportions of metallic iron and stony matter. [1860–65; SIDERO-[1] + -LITE]

sid·er·o·phile (sid′ər ə fīl′), *adj.* **1.** (of a cell or tissue) having an affinity for iron. **2.** *Geol.* (of a chemical element in the earth) having an affinity for metallic iron. —*n.* **3.** a siderophile element, tissue, or cell. [SIDERO-[1] + -PHILE]

sid·er·o·scope (sid′ər ə skōp′), *n. Ophthalm.* an apparatus for detecting splinters of iron or steel in the eye. [1820–30; SIDERO-[1] + -SCOPE]

sid·er·o·sis (sid′ə rō′sis), *n. Pathol.* a disease of the lungs caused by inhaling iron or other metallic particles. [1875–80; < Gk *sídēr(os)* iron + -OSIS] —**sid·er·ot·ic** (sid′ə rot′ik), *adj.*

sid·er·o·stat (sid′ər ə stat′), *n.* a telescopic device for reflecting the light of a star in a constant direction, the chief component of which is a plane mirror turned by a clock mechanism to correct for the rotation of the earth. [1875–80; SIDERO-[2] + -STAT] —**sid′er·o·stat′ic,** *adj.*

side·sad·dle (sīd′sad′l), *n.* **1.** a saddle for women on which the rider sits, facing forward, usually with both feet on the left side of the horse. —*adv.* **2.** seated on a sidesaddle: *The girl hunted sidesaddle.* [1485–95; earlier *syd saddyl.* See SIDE[1], SADDLE]

side′saddle flow′er, a pitcher plant, *Sarracenia purpurea.* [1730–40, *Amer.*]

side·show (sīd′shō′), *n.* **1.** a minor show or exhibition in connection with a principal one, as at a circus. **2.** any subordinate event or matter. [1840–50, *Amer.*]

side·slip (sīd′slip′), *v.,* **-slipped, -slip·ping,** *n.* —*v.i.* **1.** to slip to one side. **2.** (of an airplane when banked excessively) to slide sideways in a downward direction, toward the center of the curve described in turning. —*n.* **3.** an act or instance of sideslipping. [1640–50; SIDE[1] + SLIP[1]]

side·spin (sīd′spin′), *n.* a spinning motion imparted to a ball that causes it to rotate in course about its vertical axis. [1925–30; SIDE[1] + SPIN]

side·split·ter (sīd′split′ər), *n.* something that is uproariously funny, as a joke or a situation. [1875–80; from the idiom *to split one's sides (laughing)*; see -ER[1]]

side·split·ting (sīd′split′ing), *adj.* **1.** convulsively uproarious: *sidesplitting laughter.* **2.** producing uproarious laughter; extremely funny: *sidesplitting farce.* [1855–60; SIDE[1] + SPLITTING] —**side′split′ting·ly,** *adv.*

side′ step′, a step to one side, as in dancing, skiing, or boxing. [1840–50]

side·step (sīd′step′), *v.,* **-stepped, -step·ping.** —*v.i.* **1.** to step to one side. **2.** to evade or avoid a decision, problem, or the like. —*v.t.* **3.** to avoid or dodge by stepping aside. **4.** to evade or avoid (a decision, problem, or the like). [1900–05, *Amer.*] —**side′step′per,** *n.*

side′stream smoke′ (sīd′strēm′). See **secondhand smoke.** [1970–75]

side′ street′, a street leading away from a main street; an unimportant street or one carrying but little traffic. Cf. **back street.** [1610–20]

side·stroke (sīd′strōk′), *n., v.,* **-stroked, -strok·ing.** *Swimming.* —*n.* **1.** a stroke in which the body is turned sideways in the water, the hands pull alternately, and the legs perform a scissors kick. —*v.i.* **2.** to swim the sidestroke. [1750–60; SIDE[1] + STROKE[1]]

side′ suit′, *Cards.* See **plain suit.**

side·swipe (sīd′swīp′), *v.,* **-swiped, -swip·ing,** *n.* —*v.t.* **1.** to strike with a sweeping stroke or blow along the side; strike a glancing blow obliquely. —*n.* **2.** such a strike or blow. [1900–05, *Amer.*; SIDE[1] + SWIPE] —**side′swip′er,** *n.*

side′ ta′ble, a table intended to be placed against a wall. [1350–1400; ME]

side·track (sīd′trak′), *v.t., v.i.* **1.** to move from the main track to a siding, as a train. **2.** to move or distract from the main subject or course. —*n.* **3.** any railroad track, other than a siding, auxiliary to the main track. [1825–35, *Amer.*; SIDE[1] + TRACK]

side′ trip′, a brief excursion off the main route of an itinerary, as to visit a particular person or place. [1820–30, *Amer.*] —**side′ trip′per.**

side·walk (sīd′wôk′), *n.* a walk, esp. a paved one, at the side of a street or road. [1660–70; SIDE[1] + WALK]

side′walk art′ist, 1. an artist who draws pictures on the sidewalk, esp. with colored chalk, as a means of soliciting money from passers-by. **2.** an artist working in the streets, who draws portraits of passing individuals who sit for quick sketches executed in charcoal or pastel.

side·walk·ing (sīd′wô′king), *n. Canadian Informal.* the practice of shopkeepers standing on the sidewalk outside their shops to attract customers. [SIDEWALK + -ING[1]]

side′walk sale′, a sale, as at the end of each summer, in which merchants display reduced-price merchandise on the sidewalks in front of their stores.

side′walk superintend′ent, *Informal.* a bystander who watches the building, demolition, repair, or other work being done at a construction site. [1945–50]

side·wall (sīd′wôl′), *n.* **1.** the part of a pneumatic tire between the edge of the tread and the rim of the wheel. **2.** a wall that serves as the side of a structure. **3.** the side part of the upper of a shoe. [1350–1400; ME; see SIDE[1], WALL]

side·ward (sīd′wərd), *adj.* **1.** directed or moving toward one side. —*adv.* **2.** Also, **side′wards.** toward one side. [1400–50; late ME; see SIDE[1], -WARD]

side·way (sīd′wā′), *n.* **1.** a byway. —*adj., adv.* **2.** sideways. [1605–15; SIDE[1] + WAY[1]]

side·ways (sīd′wāz′), *adv.* **1.** with a side foremost. **2.** facing to the side. **3.** toward or from one side. **4.** with a deceitful, scornful, disparaging, or amorous glance. —*adj.* **5.** moving, facing, or directed toward one side. **6.** indirect or evasive. Also, **sideway, side·wise** (sīd′wīz′). [1570–80; SIDE[1] + -WAYS]

side-wheel (sīd′hwēl′, -wēl′), *adj.* having a paddle wheel on each side, as a steamboat. [1855–60] —**side′-wheel′er,** *n.*

side·wheel (sīd′hwēl′, -wēl′), *n. Naut.* either of a pair of paddle wheels on the sides of a vessel. [1825–35; SIDE[1] + WHEEL]

side′ whisk′ers, whiskers worn long and with the chin clean-shaven. [1805–15] —**side′-whisk′ered,** *adj.*

side·wind (sīd′wīnd′), *v.i.,* **-wound** (-wound) or (*Rare*) **-wind·ed, -wind·ing.** to move like a sidewinder. [1925–30; back formation from SIDEWINDER]

side·wind·er (sīd′wīn′dər), *n.* **1.** a severe swinging blow from the side. **2.** a rattlesnake, *Crotalus cerastes,* of southwestern U.S. and northern Mexico, that has a hornlike projection over each eye and that moves in loose sand by raising loops on the body and displacing them sideways. **3.** any Old World snake that moves by sidewinding, as various species of *Bitis* and *Cerastes.* **4.** (*cap.*) an air-to-air, supersonic weapon that intercepts and destroys enemy aircraft using an infrared homing-guidance system. [1830–40; SIDE[1] + WINDER]

sidh (shē), *n., pl.* **sidhe** (shē). *Irish Folklore.* **1.** a mound or hill in which fairies live. **2.** a fairy. **3. sidhe,** the race of fairies. Also, **shee.** [1785–95; < Ir; MIr *síd, sith* fairy mound; cf. BANSHEE]

Si·di-bel-Ab·bès (sē′dē bel ə bes′), *n.* a city in NW Algeria. 91,527.

Si·di If·ni (sē′dē ēf′nē), a seaport in W Morocco: former capital of Ifni. 13,650.

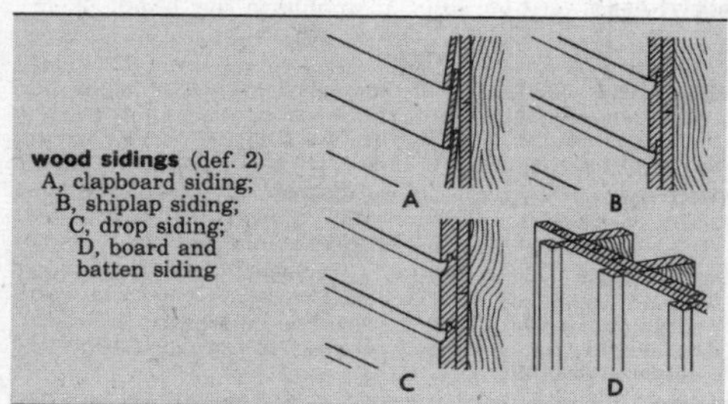

wood sidings (def. 2)
A, clapboard siding;
B, shiplap siding;
C, drop siding;
D, board and batten siding

sid·ing (sī′ding), *n.* **1.** a short railroad track, opening onto a main track at one or both ends, on which one of two meeting trains is switched until the other has passed. **2.** any of several varieties of weatherproof facing for frame buildings, composed of pieces attached separately as shingles, plain or shaped boards, or of various units of sheet metal or various types of composition materials. [1595–1605; SIDE[1] + -ING[1]]

si·dle (sīd′l), *v.,* **-dled, -dling,** *n.* —*v.i.* **1.** to move sideways or obliquely. **2.** to edge along furtively. —*n.* **3.** a sidling movement. [1690–1700; back formation from SIDELING (earlier sp. *sidling* misconstrued as prp. of a verb ending in -LE)] —**si′dling·ly,** *adv.*

Sid·ney (sid′nē), *n.* **1. Sir Philip,** 1554–86, English poet, writer, statesman, and soldier. **2.** a city in N Ohio. 17,657. **3.** a male or female given name: a family name taken from a French placename, *Saint Denis.* Also, **Sydney** (for defs. 1, 3).

Si·don (sīd′n), *n.* a city of ancient Phoenicia: site of modern Saida. —**Si·do·ni·an** (sī dō′nē ən), *adj., n.*

Sid·ra (sid′rä), *n.* **Gulf of,** an inlet of the Mediterranean, on the N coast of Libya.

Si·drah (*Seph.* sē drä′; *Ashk.* si′drô; *Eng.* sid′rə), *n., pl.* ***Si·droth, Si·drot, Si·dros*** (*Seph.* sē drôt′; *Ashk.* si′drôs), *Eng.* **Sid·rahs.** *Hebrew.* a Parashah chanted or read on the Sabbath. Also, ***Sedrah.*** [*sidhrāh* lit., order]

SIDS, See **sudden infant death syndrome.**

siè·cle d'or (sye′klᵊ dôr′), *French.* the period of the reign of Louis XIV of France. [lit., century of gold]

Sieg·bahn (sēg′bän), *n.* **Karl Man·ne Ge·org** (kärl män′nə yā′ôr yᵊ), 1886–1978, Swedish physicist: Nobel prize 1924.

siege (sēj), *n., v.,* **sieged, sieg·ing.** —*n.* **1.** the act or process of surrounding and attacking a fortified place in such a way as to isolate it from help and supplies, for the purpose of lessening the resistance of the defenders and thereby making capture possible. **2.** any prolonged or persistent effort to overcome resistance. **3.** a series of illnesses, troubles, or annoyances besetting a person or group: *a siege of head colds.* **4.** a prolonged period of trouble or annoyance. **5.** Also, **sedge.** *Ornith.* **a.** a flock of herons. **b.** the station of a heron at prey. **6.** the shelf or floor of a glassmaking furnace on which the glass pots are set. **7.** *Obs.* **a.** a seat, esp. one used by a person of distinction, as a throne. **b.** station as to rank or class. **8. lay siege to,** to besiege: *The army laid siege to the city for over a month.* —*v.t.* **9.** to assail or assault; besiege. [1175–1225; (n.) ME *sege* < OF: seat, n. deriv. of *siegier* < VL **sedicāre* to set, deriv. of L *sedēre* to SIT[1]; (v.) ME *segen,* deriv. of the n.] —**siege′a·ble,** *adj.*

—**Syn. 1.** SIEGE, BLOCKADE are terms for prevention of free movement to or from a place during wartime. SIEGE implies surrounding a city and cutting off its communications, and usually includes direct assaults on its defenses. BLOCKADE is applied more often to naval operations that block all commerce, especially to cut off food and other supplies from defenders.

siege′ mental′ity, a state of mind whereby one believes that one is being constantly attacked, oppressed, or isolated. [1965–70]

Siege′ Per′ilous, *Arthurian Romance.* a vacant seat at the Round Table that could be filled only by the predestined finder of the Holy Grail and was fatal to pretenders.

siege′ piece′, a piece of gold or silver stamped as provisional legal tender in a besieged area. Also called **obsidional coin.** [1730–40]

Sieg·fried (sig′frēd, sēg′-; *Ger.* zēk′frēt), *n.* **1.** (in the *Nibelungenlied*) the son of Sigmund and Sieglinde and the husband of Kriemhild. He kills the dragon Fafnir, acquires the treasure of the Nibelungs, wins Brünnhilde for Gunther, and is finally killed by Hagen at the behest of Brünnhilde, whom he had once promised to marry: corresponds to the Sigurd of the *Volsunga Saga.* Cf. **Brünnhilde** (def. 1). **2.** See **Ring of the Nibelung. 3.** a male given name.

Sieg′fried Line′, a zone of fortifications in W Germany facing the Maginot Line, constructed in the years preceding World War II.

Sieg heil (zēk hīl′), *German.* hail to victory: a salute used by the Nazis.

Sieg·lin·de (sig lin′də, sēg-; *Ger.* zēk lin′də), *n.* (in the *Nibelungenlied*) the wife of Sigmund and mother of Siegfried. Cf. **Signy.**

Sieg·mei·ster (sig′mī stər, zig-), *n.* **El·ie** (el′ē), 1909–91, U.S. composer.

sie·mens (sē′mənz), *n.* (*used with a singular v.*) *Elect.* the SI unit of electrical conductance, equal to the reciprocal of the ohm and replacing the equivalent MKS unit **(mho).** *Abbr.:* S [1930–35; named after Sir W. SIEMENS]

Sie·mens (sē′mənz; *Ger.* zē′məns), *n.* **1. (Ernst) Wer·ner von** (ernst′ ver′nər fən), 1816–92, German inventor and electrical engineer. **2.** his brother, **Sir William** (*Karl Wilhelm Siemens*), 1823–83, English inventor, born in Germany.

Si·em Re·ap (sē′əm rē′əp, syem′ ryap′), a city in NW Cambodia, near Angkor. ab. 10,000. Also, ***Si′em·re′ap, Si′em·ré′ap.***

Sie·na (sē en′ə; *It.* sye′nä), *n.* a city in Tuscany, in central Italy, S of Florence: cathedral. 64,745.

Si·en·ese (sē′ə nēz′, -nēs′), *adj., n., pl.* **-ese.** —*adj.* **1.** of or pertaining to Siena or its people. **2.** pertaining to or designating the style of painting developed in Siena during the late 13th and 14th centuries, characterized by a use of Byzantine forms modified by an increased three-dimensional quality, decorative linear rhythms, and harmonious, although sometimes ornamental, color. —*n.* **3.** an inhabitant of Siena. [1750–60; SIEN(A) + -ESE]

Sien·kie·wicz (shen kye′vich; *Eng.* shen kyā′vich), *n.* **Hen·ryk** (hen′rik), 1846–1916, Polish novelist: Nobel prize 1905.

si·en·na (sē en′ə), *n.* **1.** a ferruginous earth used as a yellowish-brown pigment **(raw sienna)** or, after roasting in a furnace, as a reddish-brown pigment **(burnt sienna). 2.** the color of such a pigment. [1750–60; < It (*terra di*) *Sien(n)a* (earth of) SIENA]

Sie·pi (sē ep′ē; *It.* sye′pē), *n.* **Ce·sa·re** (che′zä re), born 1923, Italian basso.

si·er·ra (sē er′ə), *n.* **1.** a chain of hills or mountains, the peaks of which suggest the teeth of a saw. **2.** any of

CONCISE PRONUNCIATION KEY: *act, cāpe, dâre, pärt; set, ēqual; if, ice; ox, ōver, ôrder, oil, bŏŏk, bōōt, out; up, ûrge; child; sing; shoe; thin, that;* zh *as in treasure.* ə = *a as in alone, e as in system, i as in easily, o as in gallop, u as in circus;* ᵊ *as in fire* (fīᵊr), *hour* (ouᵊr). l *and* n *can serve as syllabic consonants, as in cradle* (krād′l), *and button* (but′n). *See the full key inside the front cover.*

several Spanish mackerels of the genus *Scomberomorus,* esp. *S. sierra,* found in western North America. **3.** a word used in communications to represent the letter *S.* [1590–1600; < Sp: lit., saw < L *serra*]

Sier′ra Le·o′ne (lē ō′nē, lē ōn′), an independent republic in W Africa: member of the Commonwealth of Nations; formerly a British colony and protectorate. 3,000,000; 27,925 sq. mi. (72,326 sq. km). *Cap.:* Freetown. —**Sier′ra Le·o′ne·an** (lē ō′nē ən).

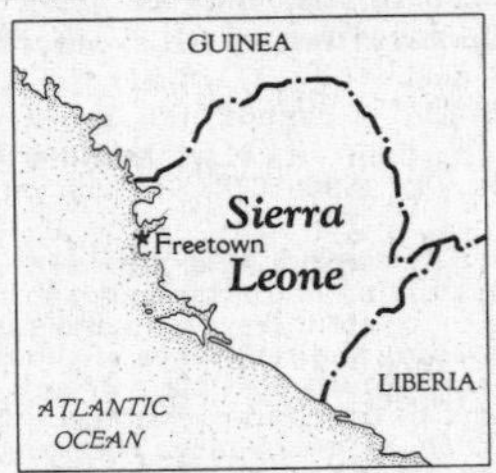

Sier′ra lil′y, a lily, *Lilium parvum,* of the northwestern U.S., having erect, purple-spotted, orange-red flowers with a yellow base.

Si·er·ra Ma·dre (sē er′ə mä′drā; *for 2 also Sp.* syeʀ′rä mä′thre), **1.** a mountain range extending from S Wyoming into N Colorado. **2.** two parallel mountain chains in Mexico, bordering the central plateau on the E and W, and extending SE into N Guatemala. **3.** a town in S California. 10,837.

Si·er·ra Ne·vad·a (sē er′ə nə vad′ə, -vä′də; *for 2 also Sp.* syeʀ′rä ne vä′thä). **1.** a mountain range in E California. Highest peak, Mt. Whitney, 14,495 ft. (4420 m). **2.** a mountain range in S Spain. Highest peak, Mulhacén, 11,420 ft. (3480 m).

Sier′ra Vis′ta, a town in S Arizona. 25,968.

si·es·ta (sē es′tə), *n.* a midday or afternoon rest or nap, esp. as taken in Spain and Latin America. [1645–55; < Sp < L *sexta* (*hōra*) the sixth (hour), midday]

sie′va bean′ (sē′və). See **butter bean.** [1885–90, *Amer.*; perh. alter. of *seewee* or *sewee* bean, prob. after the Sewee, an extinct American Indian tribe of E South Carolina]

sieve (siv), *n., v.,* **sieved, siev·ing.** —*n.* **1.** an instrument with a meshed or perforated bottom, used for separating coarse from fine parts of loose matter, for straining liquids, etc., esp. one with a circular frame and fine meshes or perforations. **2.** a person who cannot keep a secret. —*v.t., v.i.* **3.** to put or force through a sieve; sift. [bef. 900; ME *sive,* OE *sife;* c. D *zeef,* G *Sieb;* akin to SIFT] —**sieve′like′,** *adj.*

sieve′ cell′, *Bot.* an elongated cell whose walls contain perforations **(sieve′ pores′)** that are arranged in circumscribed areas **(sieve′ plates′)** and that afford communication with similar adjacent cells. [1870–75]

sieve′ of Eratos′thenes, *Math.* a method of obtaining prime numbers by sifting out the composite numbers from the set of natural numbers so that only prime numbers remain. [1795–1805]

Sie·vers (zē′fərs), *n.* **E·du·ard** (ā′do͞o ärt), 1850–1932, German philologist.

sie·vert (sē′vərt), *Physics. n.* the SI unit of dose equivalent when the absorbed dose is measured in gray. *Abbr.:* Sv Cf. **gray², rem.** [named in honor of Swedish radiologist Rolf Maximilian *Sievert* (1896–1966)]

sieve′ tube′, *Bot.* **1.** a vertical series of sieve cells in the phloem, specialized for the conduction of food materials. **2.** a single sieve cell. [1870–75]

Sie·yès (sye yes′), *n.* **Em·ma·nu·el Jo·seph** (e mᴀ nyel′ zhô zef′), ("*Abbé Sieyès*"), 1748–1836, French priest and revolutionist.

Sif·nos (sif′nos, -nôs), *n.* Siphnos.

Si·frei To·rah (*Seph.* sē fʀä′ tô ʀä′; *Ashk.* si′frä tō′rə, toi′ʀə), *Hebrew.* a pl. of ***Sefer Torah.***

sift (sift), *v.t.* **1.** to separate and retain the coarse parts of (flour, ashes, etc.) with a sieve. **2.** to scatter or sprinkle through or by means of a sieve: *to sift sugar onto cake.* **3.** to separate by or as if by a sieve. **4.** to examine closely: *The detectives are still sifting the evidence.* **5.** to question closely. —*v.i.* **6.** to sift something. **7.** to pass or fall through or as if through a sieve. [bef. 900; ME *siften,* OE *siftan;* c. D, MLG *siften;* akin to SIEVE] —**Syn. 4.** sort, scrutinize, inspect, search, probe.

sift·er (sif′tər), *n.* **1.** a person or thing that sifts. **2.** a kitchen implement for sifting: *a flour sifter.* [1570–80; SIFT + -ER¹]

sift·ings (sif′tingz), *n.* (*used with a plural v.*) **1.** something sifted: *siftings of flour.* **2.** something that is separated by sifting: *to discard the siftings.* [1590–1600; SIFT + -ING¹ + -S³]

SIG, special-interest group.

Sig., **1.** (in prescriptions) write; mark; label: indicating directions to be written on a package or label for the use of the patient. [< L *signā;* see SIGNA] **2.** let it be written. [< L *signētur*] **3.** signor. **4.** signore; signori.

sig., **1.** signal. **2.** signature. **3.** signor. **4.** signore; signori.

si·gan·id (si gan′id, -gā′nid), *n.* **1.** any fish of the family Siganidae, comprising the rabbitfishes. —*adj.* **2.** belonging or pertaining to the family Siganidae. [< NL *Siganidae,* equiv. to *Sigan(us)* genus name (< Ar *sījān* rabbitfish) + *-idae* -ID²]

Sig·a·to·ka (sig′ə tō′kə), *n. Plant Pathol.* a disease of bananas, characterized by discolored spots on the leaves, caused by a fungus, *Mycosphaerella musicola.* [after *Sigatoka,* river and district on the island of Viti Levu in the Fiji archipelago]

Sig·geir (sig′gâr), *n.* See under **Signy.**

sigh (sī), *v.i.* **1.** to let out one's breath audibly, as from sorrow, weariness, or relief. **2.** to yearn or long; pine. **3.** to make a sound suggesting a sigh: *sighing wind.* —*v.t.* **4.** to express or utter with a sigh. **5.** to lament with sighing. —*n.* **6.** the act or sound of sighing. [1250–1300; (v.) ME *sighen,* back formation from *sihte* sighed, past tense of ME *siken, sichen,* OE *sīcan* to sigh; (n.) ME, deriv. of the v.] —**sigh′er,** *n.*

sigh·ful (sī′fəl), *adj.* mournful; sorrowful: *a sighful ballad.* [1600–10; SIGH + -FUL] —**sigh′ful·ly,** *adv.*

sight (sīt), *n.* **1.** the power or faculty of seeing; perception of objects by use of the eyes; vision. **2.** an act, fact, or instance of seeing. **3.** one's range of vision on some specific occasion: *Land is in sight.* **4.** a view; glimpse. **5.** mental perception or regard; judgment. **6.** something seen or worth seeing; spectacle: *the sights of London.* **7.** *Informal.* something unusual, surprising, shocking, or distressing: *They were a sight after the fight.* **8.** *Com.* **a.** presentation of a bill of exchange: *a draft payable at two months after sight.* **b.** a showing of goods, esp. gems, held periodically for wholesalers. **9.** *Older Use.* a multitude; great deal: *It's a sight better to work than to starve.* **10.** an observation taken with a surveying, navigating, or other instrument to ascertain an exact position or direction. **11.** any of various mechanical or optical viewing devices, as on a firearm or surveying instrument, for aiding the eye in aiming. **12.** *Obs.* skill; insight. **13. at first sight,** at the first glimpse; at once: *It was love at first sight.* **14. at sight, a.** immediately upon seeing, esp. without referring elsewhere for assurance, further information, etc.: *to translate something at sight.* **b.** *Com.* on presentation: *a draft payable at sight.* **15. catch sight of,** to get a glimpse of; espy: *We caught sight of the lake below.* **16. know by sight,** to recognize (a person or thing) seen previously: *I know him by sight, but I know nothing about him.* **17. not by a long sight,** *Informal.* definitely not: *Is that all? Not by a long sight.* **18. on** or **upon sight,** immediately upon seeing: *to shoot him on sight; to recognize someone on sight.* **19. out of sight, a.** beyond one's range of vision. **b.** *Informal.* beyond reason; exceedingly high: *The price is out of sight.* **c.** *Slang.* (often used interjectionally) fantastic; marvelous: *a ceremony so glamorous it was out of sight.* **20. sight for sore eyes,** someone or something whose appearance on the scene is cause for relief or gladness. **21. sight unseen,** without previous examination: *to buy something sight unseen.* —*v.t.* **22.** to see, glimpse, notice, or observe: *to sight a ship to the north.* **23.** to take a sight or observation of (a stake, coastline, etc.), esp. with surveying or navigating instruments. **24.** to direct or aim by a sight or sights, as a firearm. **25.** to provide with sights or adjust the sights of, as a gun. —*v.i.* **26.** to aim or observe through a sight. **27.** to look carefully in a certain direction. [bef. 950; ME (n.); OE *sihth* (more often *gesihth, gesiht*); c. G *Gesicht* face; cf. Y-), deriv. of *sēon* to SEE¹; see -TH¹] —**sight′a·ble,** *adj.* —**sight′er,** *n.*

sight′ draft′, a draft payable upon presentation. [1840–50, *Amer.*]

sight·ed (sī′tid), *adj.* **1.** having functional vision; not blind. **2.** having a particular type of eyesight or perception (used in combination): *sharp-sighted; clear-sighted.* [1545–55; SIGHT + -ED³]

sight′ gag′, a comic effect produced by visual means rather than by spoken lines, as in a play or motion picture. [1945–50]

sight·hole (sīt′hōl′), *n.* a hole, as on a quadrant, through which to see or to sight. [1550–60; SIGHT + HOLE]

sight·hound (sīt′hound′), *n.* gazehound. [SIGHT + HOUND¹]

sight·less (sīt′lis), *adj.* **1.** unable to see; blind. **2.** invisible. [1200–50; ME. See SIGHT, -LESS] —**sight′less·ly,** *adv.* —**sight′less·ness,** *n.*

sight·line (sīt′līn′), *n.* any of the lines of sight between the spectators and the stage or playing area in a theater, stadium, etc.: *Some of the sightlines are blocked by columns.* Also, **sight′ line′.** [1915–20; SIGHT + LINE¹]

sight·ly (sīt′lē), *adj.,* **-li·er, -li·est. 1.** pleasing to the sight; attractive; comely. **2.** affording a fine view. [1525–35; SIGHT + -LY] —**sight′li·ness,** *n.*

sight-read (sīt′rēd′), *v.t., v.i.,* **-read** (-red), **-read·ing.** to read, play, or sing without previous practice, rehearsal, or study of the material to be treated: *to sight-read music; to sight-read another language.* [1900–05] —**sight′-read′er,** *n.*

sight′ rhyme′, *Pros.* agreement in spelling, but not in sound, of the ends of words or of lines of verse, as in *have, grave.* Also called **eye rhyme.** [1935–40]

sight′ screen′, *Cricket.* a white screen set in line with the wicket as an aid to the batsman in seeing the ball when it is bowled.

sight·see (sīt′sē′), *v.i.* **1.** to go about seeing places and things of interest: *In Rome, we only had two days to sightsee.* —*v.t.* **2.** to go about seeing the major sights of: *We had only two days to sightsee Rome.* [1825–35; back formation from *sightseer* or SIGHTSEEING] —**sight′se′·er,** *n.*

sight·see·ing (sīt′sē′ing), *n.* **1.** the act of visiting and seeing places and objects of interest. —*adj.* **2.** seeing, showing, or used for visiting sights: *a sightseeing bus.* [1840–50; SIGHT + SEEING]

sig·il (sij′il), *n.* a seal or signet. [1600–10; < L *sigillum* statuette, figure, stamped figure, dim. of *signum* SIGN; see SEAL¹] —**sig·il·lar·y** (sij′ə ler′ē), *adj.* —**sig′il·is′tic,** *adj.*

sig·il·late (sij′ə lāt′, -lit), *adj.* **1.** (of a ceramic object) having stamped decorations. **2.** *Bot.* having markings that resemble the impressions of a seal. [1425–75; late ME < L *sigillātus.* See SIGIL, -ATE¹] —**sig′il·la′tion,** *n.*

sig·int (sig′int′), *n.* the gathering of military or other intelligence by interception of electronic signals and consisting of comint and elint. Also, **SIGINT** Cf. **humint.** [1965–70; *sig(nal) int(elligence)*]

Sig·is·mund (sij′is mənd, sig′is-; *Ger.* zē′gis mo͝ont′), *n.* 1368–1437, Holy Roman emperor 1411–37.

sig·los (sig′los), *n., pl.* **-loi** (-loi). a silver coin of ancient Persia, the 20th part of a daric. [< Gk *síglos* < Sem; cf. Heb *sheqel* SHEKEL]

sig·ma (sig′mə), *n.* **1.** the 18th letter of the Greek alphabet: Σ, σ, ς. **2.** the consonant sound represented by this letter. [1600–10; < L < Gk *sígma*]

sig′ma par′ticle, *Physics.* an unstable hyperon having positive, negative, or zero electric charge and strangeness −1. *Symbol:* Σ [1960–65]

sig·mate (sig′mit, -māt), *adj.* having the form of the Greek sigma or the letter *S.* [1885–90; SIGM(A) + -ATE¹] —**sig·ma·tion** (sig mā′shən), *n.*

sig·ma·tism (sig′mə tiz′əm), *n.* defective pronunciation of sibilant sounds. [1885–90; < Gk *sigmat-,* s. of *sígma* SIGMA + -ISM]

sig·moid (sig′moid), *adj.* **1.** shaped like the letter *C.* **2.** shaped like the letter *S.* **3.** of, pertaining to, or situated near the sigmoid flexure of the large intestine. Also, **sig·moi′dal.** [1660–70; < Gk *sigmoeidḗs* shaped like a sigma. See SIGMA, -OID] —**sig·moi′dal·ly,** *adv.*

sig′moid flex′ure, **1.** *Zool.* an S-shaped curve in a body part. **2.** Also called **sig′moid co′lon.** an S-shaped curve of the large intestine between the descending colon and the rectum. See diag. under **intestine.** [1780–90]

sig·moid·o·scope (sig moi′də skōp′), *n.* a rigid or flexible endoscope for visual examination of the rectum and sigmoid colon. Also called **proctosigmoidoscope.** [1900–05; SIGMOID (FLEXURE) + -O- + -SCOPE] —**sig·moid·o·scop·ic** (sig moi′də skop′ik), *adj.* —**sig·moid·os·co·pist** (sig′moi dos′kə pist), *n.*

sig·moid·os·co·py (sig′moi dos′kə pē), *n., pl.* **-pies.** an examination by means of a sigmoidoscope. [1895–1900; SIGMOIDOSCOPE + -Y³]

Sig·mund (sig′mənd, sēg′mo͝ond; *Ger.* zēk′mo͝ont), *n.* **1.** (in the *Volsunga Saga*) the son of Volsung and Liod; the father, through his sister, Signy, of Sinfjotli; the husband first of Borghild, then of Hjordis; and the father of Sigurd. **2.** (in the *Nibelungenlied*) the king of the Netherlands and father of Siegfried. **3.** a male given name: from Germanic words meaning "victory" and "protection."

sign (sīn), *n.* **1.** a token; indication. **2.** any object, action, event, pattern, etc., that conveys a meaning. **3.** a conventional or arbitrary mark, figure, or symbol used as an abbreviation for the word or words it represents. **4.** a motion or gesture used to express or convey an idea, command, decision, etc.: *Her nod was a sign that it was time to leave.* **5.** a notice, bearing a name, direction, warning, or advertisement, that is displayed or posted for public view: *a traffic sign; a store sign.* **6.** a trace; vestige: *There wasn't a sign of them.* **7.** an arbitrary or conventional symbol used in musical notation to indicate tonality, tempo, etc. **8.** *Med.* the objective indications of a disease. **9.** any meaningful gestural unit belonging to a sign language. **10.** an omen; portent: *a sign of approaching decadence.* **11.** See **sign of the zodiac. 12.** See **sign language** (def. 1). **13.** Usually, **signs.** traces, as footprints, of a wild animal. **14.** *Math.* **a.** a plus sign or minus sign used as a symbol for indicating addition or subtraction. **b.** a plus sign or minus sign used as a symbol for indicating the positive or negative value of a quantity, as an integer. **c.** See **multiplication sign. d.** See **division sign. e.** a symbol, as $\sqrt{\ }$ or !, used to indicate a radical or factorial operation. —*v.t.* **15.** to affix a signature to: *to sign a letter.* **16.** to write as a signature: *to sign one's name.* **17.** to engage by written agreement: *to sign a new player.* **18.** to mark with a sign, esp. the sign of the cross. **19.** to communicate by means of a sign; signal: *He signed his wish to leave.* **20.** to convey (a message) in a sign language. **21.** *Obs.* to direct or appoint by a sign. —*v.i.* **22.** to write one's signature, as a token of agreement, obligation, receipt, etc.: *to sign for a package.* **23.** to make a sign or signal: *He signed to her to go away.* **24.** to employ a sign language for communication. **25.** to obligate oneself by signature: *He signed with another team for the next season.* **26. sign away** or **over,** to assign or dispose of by affixing one's signature to a document: *She signed over her fortune to the church.* **27. sign in** (or **out**) to record or authorize one's arrival (or departure) by signing a register. **28. sign off, a.** to withdraw, as from some responsibility or connection. **b.** to cease radio or television broadcasting, esp. at the end of the day. **c.** *Informal.* to become silent: *He had exhausted conversation topics and signed off.* **d.** to indicate one's approval explicitly if not formally: *The president is expected to sign off on the new agreement.* **29. sign on, a.** to employ; hire. **b.** to bind oneself to work, as by signing a contract: *He signed on as a pitcher with a major-league team.* **c.** to start radio or television broadcasting, esp. at the beginning of the day. **d.** *Computers.* log¹ (def. 17a). **30. sign up,** to enlist, as in an organization or group; to register or subscribe: *to sign up for the navy; to sign up for class.* [1175–1225; (n.) ME *signe* < OF < L *signum* mark, sign, ensign, signal, image; (v.) ME *signen* to mark with a sign, esp. the sign of the cross < OF *signer* < L *signāre* to mark with a sign, inscribe, affix a seal to, deriv. of *signum*] —**sign′less,** *adj.* —**sign′like′,** *adj.*

—**Syn. 1.** trace, hint, suggestion. **1, 4.** signal. **10.** indication, hint, augury. SIGN, OMEN, PORTENT name that which gives evidence of a future event. SIGN is a general word for whatever gives evidence of an event—past,

CONCISE ETYMOLOGY KEY: <, descended or borrowed from; >, whence; b., blend of, blended; c., cognate with; cf., compare; deriv., derivative; equiv., equivalent; imit., imitative; obl., oblique; r., replacing; s., stem; sp., spelling, spelled; resp., respelling, respelled; trans., translation; ?, origin unknown; *, unattested; ‡, probably earlier than. See the full key inside the front cover.

present, or future: *Dark clouds are a sign of rain or snow.* An OMEN is an augury or warning of things to come; it is used only of the future, in general, as good or bad: *birds of evil omen.* PORTENT, limited, like OMEN, to prophecy of the future, may be used of a specific event, usually a misfortune: *portents of war.*

sig·na (sig′nə), *v.* (used imperatively, in prescriptions) mark; write; label. [< L *signā*, 2nd person sing. pres. impv. active of *signāre;* see SIGN]

sign·a·ble (sī′nə bəl), *adj.* suitable for signing, as in being satisfactory, appropriate, or complete: *a signable legislative bill.* [1795–1805; SIGN + -ABLE]

Si·gnac (sē nyak′), *n.* **Paul** (pôl), 1863–1935, French painter.

sign·age (sī′nij), *n.* graphic designs, as symbols, emblems, or words, used esp. for identification or as a means of giving directions or warning. [SIGN + -AGE]

sig·nal (sig′nl), *n., adj., v.,* **-naled, -nal·ing** or (*esp. Brit.*) **-nalled, -nal·ling.** —*n.* **1.** anything that serves to indicate, warn, direct, command, or the like, as a light, a gesture, an act, etc.: *a traffic signal; a signal to leave.* **2.** anything agreed upon or understood as the occasion for concerted action. **3.** an act, event, or the like that causes or incites some action: *The unjust execution was the signal for revolt.* **4.** a token; indication. **5.** *Electronics.* an electrical quantity or effect, as current, voltage, or electromagnetic waves, that can be varied in such a way as to convey information. **6.** *Cards.* a play that reveals to one's partner a wish that he or she continue or discontinue the suit led. —*adj.* **7.** serving as a signal; used in signaling: *a signal flag.* **8.** unusual; notable; outstanding: *a signal exploit.* —*v.t.* **9.** to make a signal to. **10.** to communicate or make known by a signal. —*v.i.* **11.** to make communication by a signal or signals. [1350–1400; ME (n.) < ML *signāle*, LL, n. use of neut. of *signālis* of a sign. See SIGN, -AL[2], -AL[1]] —**sig′nal·er;** *esp. Brit.* **sig′nal·ler,** *n.*
—**Syn. 1, 4.** sign. **8.** unique, exceptional, remarkable, striking.

sig′nal board′, a board for displaying electrically transmitted signals and indicating their source. Cf. **annunciator.**

sig′nal box′, *Brit.* a railway signal tower. [1820–30]

sig′nal corps′, a branch of the army responsible for military communications, meteorological studies, and related work. [1860–65, *Amer.*]

sig·nal·ize (sig′nl īz′), *v.t.,* **-ized, -iz·ing. 1.** to make notable or conspicuous. **2.** to point out or indicate particularly. **3.** to equip (a particular traffic crossing or an entire transportation route) with traffic signals. Also, *esp. Brit.,* **sig′nal·ise′.** [1645–55; SIGNAL + -IZE] —**sig′nal·i·za′tion,** *n.*

sig·nal·ly (sig′nl ē, -nl lē), *adv.* conspicuously; notably. [1635–45; SIGNAL + -LY]

sig·nal·man (sig′nl mən), *n., pl.* **-men.** a person whose occupation or duty is signaling, as on a railroad or in the army. [1730–40; SIGNAL + -MAN]

sig·nal·ment (sig′nl mənt), *n.* a detailed description, esp. of distinctive features, of a person for identification, usually for police purposes. [1770–80; < F *signalement*, deriv. of *signaler* to signalize. See SIGNAL, -MENT]

sig′nal red′, pimento (def. 3).

sig·na·to·ry (sig′nə tôr′ē, -tōr′ē), *adj., n., pl.* **-ries.** —*adj.* **1.** having signed, or joined in signing, a document: *the signatory powers to a treaty.* —*n.* **2.** a signer, or one of the signers, of a document: *France and Holland were among the signatories of the treaty.* [1640–50, in earlier sense "used in affixing seals"; 1860–65 for def. 2; < L *signātōrius* of, belonging to sealing, equiv. to *signā(re)* to mark, seal (see SIGN) + *-tōrius* -TORY[1]]

sig·na·ture (sig′nə chər, -choor′), *n.* **1.** a person's name, or a mark representing it, as signed personally or by deputy, as in subscribing a letter or other document. **2.** the act of signing a document. **3.** *Music.* a sign or set of signs at the beginning of a staff to indicate the key or the time of a piece. **4.** *Radio.* a song, musical arrangement, sound effect, etc., used as a theme identifying a program. **5.** any unique, distinguishing aspect, feature, or mark. **6.** *Med.* that part of a written prescription that specifies directions for use. **7.** *Biol., Med.* a distinctive characteristic or set of characteristics by which a biological structure or medical condition is recognized. **8.** Also called **section.** *Bookbinding.* a printed sheet folded to page size for binding together, with other such sheets, to form a book, magazine, etc. **9.** *Print.* **a.** a letter or other symbol generally placed by the printer at the foot of the first page of every sheet to guide the binder in folding the sheets and in gathering them in sequence. **b.** a sheet so marked. **10.** *Chem., Physics.* a characteristic trace or sign that indicates the presence of a substance or the occurrence of a physical process or event: *The satellite recorded a spectrum that is the signature of a nuclear explosion.* —*adj.* **11.** serving to identify or distinguish a person, group, etc.: *a signature tune.* [1525–35; < ML *signātūra* a signing, equiv. to L *signāt(us)* ptp. of *signāre* to mark (see SIGN, -ATE[1]) + *-ūra* -URE] —**sig′na·ture·less,** *adj.*

sig′nature loan′, a loan requiring no collateral.

sig′nature tune′. See **theme song** (def. 2). [1930–35]

sign·board (sīn′bôrd′, -bōrd′), *n.* a board bearing a sign. [1625–35; SIGN + BOARD]

signed′ Eng′lish, communication by means of American Sign Language but using English grammar in place of ASL syntax and using invented forms for English grammatical elements, such as *of, to, the,* and *-ing,* where no ASL sign exists. Also, **Sign′ Eng′lish.**

signed′ num′ber, *Math.* a number preceded by a plus sign (+) to indicate a positive quantity or by a minus sign (−) to indicate a negative quantity.

sign·ee (sī nē′, sī′nē), *n.* a person who signs a document, register, etc.; signer; signatory: *a signee of the Declaration of Independence.* [1950–55; SIGN + -EE]

sign·er (sī′nər), *n.* **1.** a person who signs. **2.** a person who writes his or her name, as in token of agreement. **3.** a person who communicates by or interprets into sign language. [1605–15; SIGN + -ER[1]]

sig·net (sig′nit), *n.* **1.** a small seal, as on a finger ring. **2.** a small official seal for legal documents, contracts, etc. **3.** an impression made by or as if by a signet. —*v.t.* **4.** to stamp or mark with a signet. [1300–50; ME < OF (see SIGN, -ET); cf. ML *signētum*]

sig′net ring′, a finger ring containing a small seal, one's initial, or the like. [1675–85]

si·gni·fiant (sē nyē fyän′; *Eng.* sig′nə fī′ənt), *n., pl.* ***-fiants*** (-fyän′; *Eng.* -fī′ənts). *French.* (in linguistics) signifier (def. 2).

sig·nif·i·cance (sig nif′i kəns), *n.* **1.** importance; consequence: *the significance of the new treaty.* **2.** meaning; import: *The familiar place had a new significance for her.* **3.** the quality of being significant or having a meaning: *to give significance to dull chores.* [1400–50; late ME (< MF) < L *significantia* force, meaning, equiv. to *significant-* (see SIGNIFICANT) + *-ia* -IA; see -ANCE]
—**Syn. 1.** moment, weight. See **importance. 2.** See **meaning.** —**Ant. 1.** triviality.

signif′icance lev′el, (in the statistical test of a hypothesis) the maximum probability of a Type I error for all distributions consistent with the null hypothesis. Also called **level of significance.** [1945–50]

sig·nif·i·can·cy (sig nif′i kən sē), *n., pl.* **-cies.** significance. [1585–95; < L *significantia.* See SIGNIFICANCE, -ANCY]

sig·nif·i·cant (sig nif′i kənt), *adj.* **1.** important; of consequence. **2.** having or expressing a meaning; indicative; suggestive: *a significant wink.* **3.** *Statistics.* of or pertaining to observations that are unlikely to occur by chance and that therefore indicate a systematic cause. —*n.* **4.** something significant; a sign. [1570–80; < L *significant-* (s. of *significāns*), prp. of *significāre* to SIGNIFY; see -ANT] —**sig·nif′i·cant·ly,** *adv.*
—**Syn. 1.** consequential, momentous, weighty. **2.** See **expressive.**

signif′icant dig′its, *Math.* all the nonzero digits of a number and the zeros that are included between them or that are final zeros and signify accuracy: *The significant digits of 0.01230 are 1, 2, 3, and the final 0, which signifies accuracy to five places.* Also called **signif′icant fig′ures.** [1920–25]

signif′icant oth′er, **1.** *Sociol.* a person, as a parent or peer, who has great influence on one's behavior and self-esteem. **2.** a spouse or cohabiting lover.

signif′icant sym′bol, *Sociol.* a verbal or nonverbal gesture, as a word or smile, that has acquired a conventionalized meaning.

sig·ni·fi·ca·tion (sig′nə fi kā′shən), *n.* **1.** meaning; import; sense. **2.** the act or fact of signifying; indication. [1250–1300; ME *significacion* (< OF *signification, significaciun*) < L *significātiōn-* (s. of *significātiō*) signal, emphasis, meaning, equiv. to *significāt(us),* ptp. of *significāre* to SIGNIFY (see -ATE[1]) + *-iōn-* -ION]

sig·nif·i·ca·tive (sig nif′i kā′tiv), *adj.* **1.** serving to signify. **2.** significant; suggestive. [1350–1400; ME (< OF *significatif, significative*) < LL *significātīvus* denoting, equiv. to L *significāt(us)* (ptp. of *significāre* to make a sign; see SIGNIFY, -ATE[1]) + *-īvus* -IVE] —**sig·nif′i·ca′tive·ly,** *adv.* —**sig·nif′i·ca′tive·ness,** *n.*

sig·nif·ics (sig nif′iks), *n.* (*used with a singular v.*) semantics (def. 2). [1896; SIGNIF(Y) + -ICS]

si·gni·fié (sē nyē fyā′), *n., pl.* ***-fiés*** (-fyā′), *French.* (in linguistics) the signified.

sig·ni·fied (sig′nə fīd′), *n. Ling.* the thing or concept denoted by a sign. Cf. **signifier.** [1630–40; SIGNIFY + -ED[2]]

sig·ni·fi·er (sig′nə fī′ər), *n.* **1.** a person or thing that signifies. **2.** the configuration of sound elements or other linguistic symbols representing a word or other meaningful unit in a language. Cf. **signified.** [1525–35; SIGNIFY + -ER[1]]

sig·ni·fy (sig′nə fī′), *v.,* **-fied, -fy·ing.** —*v.t.* **1.** to make known by signs, speech, or action. **2.** to be a sign of; mean; portend. —*v.i.* **3.** to be of importance or consequence. [1200–50; ME *signifien* < OF *signifier* < L *significāre* to make a sign, indicate, mention, denote. See SIGN, -IFY] —**sig′ni·fi′a·ble,** *adj.*
—**Syn. 1.** signal, express, indicate. **2.** represent, indicate, denote, betoken, imply.

sig·ni·fy·ing (sig′nə fī′ing), *n.* sounding[1] (def. 4) [1955–60; SIGNIFY + -ING[1]]

sign-in (sīn′in′), *n.* an act, an instance, or a time of signing in. [1945–50; n. use of v. phrase *sign in*]

si·gnior (sēn′yôr, -yōr, sin yôr′, -yōr′), *n.* signor.

sign′ lan′guage, **1.** Also called **sign.** any of several visual-gestural systems of communication, esp. employing manual gestures, as used among deaf people. **2.** any means of communication, as between speakers of different languages, using gestures. [1840–50]

sign′ man′ual, *pl.* **signs manual.** a personal signature, esp. that of a sovereign or official on a public document. [1400–50; late ME]

sign′ of aggrega′tion, *Math.* any of the signs used to indicate grouping in an algebraic expression: vinculum, bar, or raised horizontal line, $\overline{a + b}$; a pair of parentheses, $(a + b)$; a pair of brackets, $[a + b]$; or a pair of braces, $\{a + b\}$. [1940–45]

sign-off (sīn′ôf′, -of′), *n.* **1.** the act or fact of signing off. **2.** personal approval or authorization; endorsement. Also, **sign′off′.** [1925–30; n. use of v. phrase *sign off*]

sign′ of the cross′, a movement of the hand to indicate a cross, as from forehead to breast and left shoulder to right or, in the Eastern Orthodox Church, from right shoulder to left. [1250–1300; ME]

sign′ of the zo′diac, *Astrol.* **1.** one of the twelve constellations along the path of the ecliptic. **2.** (in contemporary Western astrology) one of the twelve divisions of the ecliptic, each consisting of 30 degrees, marked off from the point of the vernal equinox. See illus. at **zodiac.** [1865–70]

sign-on (sīn′on′, -ôn′), *n.* **1.** *Radio and Television.* the opening salutation, station identification, etc., at the beginning of the broadcast day. **2.** an act or instance of signing on. [1880–85; n. use of v. phrase *sign on*]

si·gnor (sēn′yôr, -yōr, sin yôr′, -yōr′; *It.* sē nyôr′), *n., pl.* **-gnors,** *It.* **-gno·ri** (-nyô′rē). a conventional Italian term of address or title of respect for a man, either used separately or prefixed to the name. *Abbr.:* Sig., sig. Also, **signior.** [1570–80; < It; see SIGNORE[1]]

si·gno·ra (sin yôr′ə, -yōr′ə; *It.* sē nyô′rä), *n., pl.* **-ras,** *It.* **-re** (-re). a conventional Italian term of address or title of respect for a married woman, either used separately or prefixed to the name. [1630–40; < It; fem. of *signore* SIGNORE[1]]

si·gno·re[1] (sin yôr′ā, -yōr′ā; *It.* sē nyô′re), *n., pl.* **si·gno·ri** (sin yôr′ē, -yōr′ē; *It.* sē nyô′rē). a conventional Italian title of respect for a man, usually used separately; signor. [1585–95; < It < L *senior;* see SENIOR]

si·gno·re[2] (sin yôr′ā, -yōr′ā; *It.* sē nyô′re), *n.* a pl. of **signora.**

Si·gno·rel·li (sē nyô rel′lē), *n.* **Lu·ca** (lo͞o′kä), c1445–1523, Italian painter.

si·gno·ri·na (sēn′yô rē′nə; *It.* sē′nyô rē′nä), *n., pl.* **-nas,** *It.* **-ne** (-ne). a conventional Italian term of address or title of respect for a girl or unmarried woman, either used separately or prefixed to the name. [1810–20; < It; dim. of *signora* SIGNORA; see -INE[1]]

si·gno·ri·no (sēn′yô rē′nō; *It.* sē′nyô rē′nô), *n., pl.* **-nos,** *It.* **-ni** (-nē). a conventional Italian title of respect for a young man. [1325–75; < It; dim. of *signore* SIGNORE[1]; see -INE[1]]

si·gno·ry (sēn′yə rē), *n., pl.* **-ries.** seigniory.

sign-out (sīn′out′), *n.* an act, instance, or time of signing out. [1945–50; n. use of v. phrase *sign out*]

sign·post (sīn′pōst′), *n.* **1.** a post bearing a sign that gives information or guidance. **2.** any immediately perceptible indication, obvious clue, etc. —*v.t.* **3.** to provide (a place, route, etc.) with signposts. [1610–20; SIGN + POST[1]]

sign-up (sīn′up′), *n.* an act or instance of signing up. Also, **sign′up′.** [1945–50; n. use of v. phrase *sign up*]

Sig·ny (sig′nē, -nY), *n.* (in the *Volsunga Saga*) the daughter of Volsung and mother, by her brother, Sigmund, of Sinfjotli, with whose help she kills her husband **(Siggeir)** to avenge his murder of Volsung. Cf. **Sieglinde.**

Sigr·dri·fa (sig′ər drē′vä), *n.* (in the *Elder Edda*) a Valkyrie who, for disobedience to Odin, sleeps within a circle of fire until awakened by Sigurd. Cf. **Brynhild.**

Si·grid (sē′grid, sig′rid; *Ger.* zē′grit, -grēt; *Nor.* si′gri; *Swed.* sē′grid), *n.* a female given name: from a Scandinavian word meaning "victory."

Sigs·bee (sigz′bē), *n.* **Charles Dwight,** 1845–1923, U.S. naval officer: captain of the *Maine* in 1898.

Sig·urd (sig′ərd; *Ger.* zē′go͝ort), *n.* (in the *Volsunga Saga*) the son of Sigmund and Hjordis and the husband of Gudrun. He kills the dragon Fafnir, acquires the treasure of Andvari, wins Brynhild for Gunnar, and is finally killed at the behest of Brynhild, whom he had once promised to marry: corresponds to Siegfried of the *Nibelungenlied.*

Sig·yn (seg′in, -yn, sē′gin, -gyn), *n. Scand. Myth.* wife of Loki, who held a cup over Loki after his imprisonment in order to spare him the pain of the drops of poison with which he was punished.

Si·ha·nouk (sē′ə no͝ok′), *n.* **Prince Norodom.** See **Norodom Sihanouk.**

Si·irt (sē ûrt′), *n.* a city in SE Turkey, E of Diyarbekir. 110,498.

si·ka (sē′kə), *n.* a small, reddish deer, *Cervus nippon,* native to eastern Asia: most populations are endangered. [1890–95; < Japn, equiv. to *si-* (perh. akin to *sisi* boar, game) + *ka* deer]

Si·kan·dar·a·bad (si kun′drä bäd′), *n.* Secunderabad.

Si·kang (shē′käng′), *n. Older Spelling.* Xikang.

sike (sīk, sik), *n. Scot. and North Eng.* **1.** a small stream. **2.** a gully or ditch, esp. one that fills with water after a heavy rain. Also, **syke.** [1300–50; ME < ON *sik* small stream, ditch, pond, c. OE *sīc* (now *sitch*) rill, MLG *sīk* puddle; akin to OHG *seih* urine, OE *sicerian* to ooze]

sik·er (sik′ər), *adj., adv. Scot. and North Eng.* sicker[2].

Sikes·ton (sīk′stən), *n.* a city in SE Missouri. 17,431.

Sikh (sēk), *n.* **1.** a member of a monotheistic religion, founded in the Punjab c1500 by the guru Nanak, that refuses to recognize the Hindu caste system or the Brahmanical priesthood and forbids magic, idolatry, and pilgrimages. —*adj.* **2.** of or pertaining to the Sikhs or to Sikhism. [1750–60; < Hindi]

si·kha·ra (shik′ər ə, shik′rə), *n.* (in Indian architecture) a convexly tapering tower, capped by an amalaka. Also, **sikra.** [< Skt *śikhara*]

Sikh·ism (sē′kiz əm), *n.* the religion and practices of the Sikhs. [SIKH + -ISM]

Si Kiang (*Chin.* shē′ kyäng′), *Older Spelling.* See **Xi Jiang.**

CONCISE PRONUNCIATION KEY: act, cāpe, dâre, pärt; set, ēqual; if, īce; ox, ōver, ôrder, oil, bo͝ok, bo͞ot, out; up, ûrge; child; sing; shoe; thin, *th*at; zh as in *treasure.* ə = *a* as in *alone,* *e* as in *system,* *i* as in *easily,* *o* as in *gallop,* *u* as in *circus;* ᵊ as in *fire* (fīᵊr), *hour* (ouᵊr). l and n can serve as syllabic consonants, as in *cradle* (krād′l), and *button* (but′n). See the full key inside the front cover.

Sik·kim (sik′im), *n.* a kingdom in NE India, in the Himalayas between Nepal and Bhutan. 315,682; 2818 sq. mi. (7298 sq. km). *Cap.:* Gangtok.

Sik·kim·ese (sik′ə mēz′, -mēs′), *n., pl.* **-ese,** *adj.* —*n.* **1.** a native or inhabitant of Sikkim. —*adj.* **2.** of or pertaining to Sikkim or its people. [SIKKIM + -ESE]

Si·kor·sky (si kôr′skē), *n.* **I·gor** (ē′gôr), 1889–1972, U.S. aeronautical engineer, born in Russia.

si·kra (sik′rə), *n.* sikhara.

si·lage (sī′lij), *n.* fodder preserved through fermentation in a silo; ensilage. [1880–85; shortening of ENSILAGE, influenced by SILO]

sil·ane (sil′ān), *n. Chem.* **1.** Also called **silicon tetrahydride.** a gas with an unpleasant odor, SiH_4, soluble in water: used as a doping agent for semiconductors in the production of solid-state devices. **2.** any of a class of silicon hydrides analogous to the alkanes. [< G *Silan* (1916); see SILICON, -ANE]

Si·las (sī′ləs), *n.* a male given name.

Si·las Mar·ner (sī′ləs mär′nər), a novel (1861) by George Eliot.

Si·las·tic (si las′tik), *Trademark.* a brand name for any of a group of substances containing polymeric silicones, having the properties of rubber but more capable of withstanding extremely high and low temperatures and other causes of deterioration, used in jet-plane engines, medical prosthetic devices, gaskets, electrical insulation, etc.

Sil′bur·y Hill′ (sil′ber′ē, -bə rē), the largest prehistoric artificial mound in Europe, located near Avebury, England, and dating from 2600 B.C.

sild (sild), *n., pl.* **silds,** (*esp. collectively*) **sild.** **1.** (in Scandinavia) any of numerous species of herring. **2.** any immature or small herring, other than a sprat, that is canned and commercially sold as a sardine. [1920–25; < Norw, Dan: herring, ON *síld*]

si·lence (sī′ləns), *n., v.,* **-lenced, -lenc·ing,** *interj.* —*n.* **1.** absence of any sound or noise; stillness. **2.** the state or fact of being silent; muteness. **3.** absence or omission of mention, comment, or expressed concern: *the conspicuous silence of our newspapers on local graft.* **4.** the state of being forgotten; oblivion: *in the news again after years of silence.* **5.** concealment; secrecy. —*v.t.* **6.** to put or bring to silence; still. **7.** to put (doubts, fears, etc.) to rest; quiet. **8.** *Mil.* to still (enemy guns), as by more effective fire. —*interj.* **9.** be silent! *"Silence!" the teacher shouted.* [1175–1225; ME (n.) < OF < L *silentium.* See SILENT, -ENCE]
—**Syn. 6.** hush, quell, muzzle, gag.

si·lenc·er (sī′lən sər), *n.* **1.** a person or thing that silences. **2.** a device for deadening the report of a firearm. **3.** *Chiefly Brit.* the muffler on an internal-combustion engine. [1625–35; SILENCE + -ER[1]]

Si·le·nos (sī lē′nəs), *n.* Silenus.

si·lent (sī′lənt), *adj.* **1.** making no sound; quiet; still: *a silent motor.* **2.** refraining from speech. **3.** speechless; mute. **4.** not inclined to speak; taciturn; reticent. **5.** characterized by absence of speech or sound: *a silent prayer.* **6.** unspoken; tacit: *a silent assent.* **7.** omitting mention of something, as in a narrative: *The records are silent about this crime.* **8.** inactive or quiescent, as a volcano. **9.** not sounded or pronounced: *The "b" in "doubt" is a silent letter.* **10.** *Motion Pictures.* not having spoken dialogue or a soundtrack. **11.** *Med.* producing no symptoms: *silent gallstones.* —*n.* **12.** Usually, **silents.** silent films. [1555–65; < L *silent-* (s. of *silēns*), prp. of *silēre* to be quiet; see -ENT] —**si′lent·ly,** *adv.* —**si′lent·ness,** *n.*
—**Syn. 1.** soundless. See **still**[1]. **8.** dormant. —**Ant. 1.** noisy. **4.** talkative.

si′lent alarm′, **1.** an alarm that alerts security personnel or the police without the knowledge of the intruder or criminal whose presence triggers it: *The silent alarm set off a flashing light at the police station.* **2.** any visual rather than audible alarm.

si′lent auc′tion, an auction at which previously submitted written bids of prospective buyers are opened and compared, with each item being sold to the highest bidder.

si′lent bar′ter. See **dumb barter.** Also, **si′lent trade′.**

si′lent but′ler, a small receptacle having a handle and a hinged lid, used for collecting the contents of ashtrays, crumbs from a dinner table, etc., for disposal. [1935–40]

CONCISE ETYMOLOGY KEY: <, descended or borrowed from; >, whence; b., blend of, blended; c., cognate with; cf., compare; deriv., derivative; equiv., equivalent; imit., imitative; obl., oblique; r., replacing; s., stem; sp., spelling, spelled; resp., respelling, respelled; trans., translation; ?, origin unknown; *, unattested; ‡, probably earlier than. See the full key inside the front cover.

si′lent major′ity, **1.** the U.S. citizens who supported President Nixon's policies but who were not politically vocal, outspoken, or active: considered by him to constitute a majority. **2.** any group of people who are not outspoken and who are considered to constitute a majority. [1870–75]

si′lent part′ner, a partner taking no active part in the conduct of a business. Cf. **secret partner.** [1820–30, *Amer.*]

si′lent serv′ice, (*sometimes caps.*) the submarine service (usually prec. by *the*). [1935–40]

si′lent treat′ment, an act or instance of maintaining silence or aloofness toward another person, esp. as a means of indicating disapproval or rejection. [1945–50]

si′lent vote′, the vote of persons who have not previously expressed or made evident a preference. [1785–95]

Si·le·nus (sī lē′nəs), *n., pl.* **-ni** (-nī) for 2. *Class. Myth.* **1.** a forest spirit, sometimes referred to as the oldest of the satyrs and the foster father, teacher, and companion of Dionysus: often represented as a bearded old man. **2.** (*l.c.*) any of a group of forest spirits similar to satyrs: often represented as a drunken old man with the legs and ears of a horse. Also, **Silenos, Seilenos.**

si·le·sia (si lē′zhə, -shə, sī-), *n.* a lightweight, smoothly finished, twilled fabric of acetate, rayon, or cotton, for garment linings. [1665–70; named after SILESIA]

Si·le·sia (si lē′zhə, -shə, sī-), *n.* a region in central Europe along both banks of the upper Oder River, mainly in SW Poland and the N Czech Republic: formerly divided between Germany (which had the largest portion), Poland, and Czechoslovakia; by provision of the Potsdam agreement 1945, the greater part of German Silesia came under Polish administration; rich deposits of coal, iron, and other minerals. German, **Schlesien.** Polish, **Śląsk.** Czech, **Slezsko.** —**Si·le′sian,** *adj., n.*

si·lex (sī′leks), *n.* flint; silica. [1585–95; < L *silex,* s. *silic-* hard stone, flint, boulder]

silhouette (def. 1)

sil·hou·ette (sil′o͞o et′), *n., v.,* **-et·ted, -et·ting.** —*n.* **1.** a two-dimensional representation of the outline of an object, as a cutout or configurational drawing, uniformly filled in with black, esp. a black-paper, miniature cutout of the outlines of a famous person's face. **2.** the outline or general shape of something: *the slim silhouette of a skyscraper.* **3.** a dark image outlined against a lighter background. —*v.t.* **4.** to show in or as if in a silhouette. **5.** *Print.* to remove the background details from (a halftone cut) so as to produce an outline effect. [1790–1800; < F *à la silhouette,* after Etienne de *Silhouette* (1709–67), French finance minister]

sil·i·ca (sil′i kə), *n.* the dioxide form of silicon, SiO_2, occurring esp. as quartz sand, flint, and agate: used usually in the form of its prepared white powder chiefly in the manufacture of glass, water glass, ceramics, and abrasives. Also called **silicon dioxide.** [1795–1805; < NL, deriv. of L *silex* SILEX]

sil′ica gel′, *Chem.* a highly adsorbent gelatinous form of silica, used chiefly as a dehumidifying and dehydrating agent. [1915–20]

sil′ica glass′, glass made entirely from silica, having a very low rate of thermal expansion. Also called **fused silica.**

sil·i·cate (sil′i kit, -kāt′), *n.* **1.** *Mineral.* any of the largest group of mineral compounds, as quartz, beryl, garnet, feldspar, mica, and various kinds of clay, consisting of SiO_2 or SiO_4 groupings and one or more metallic ions, with some forms containing hydrogen. Silicates constitute well over 90 percent of the rock-forming minerals of the earth's crust. **2.** *Chem.* any salt derived from the silicic acids or from silica. [1805–15; SILIC(A) + -ATE[2]] —**sil·i·ca·tion** (sil′i kā′shən), *n.*

si·li·ceous (sə lish′əs), *adj.* **1.** containing, consisting of, or resembling silica. **2.** growing in soil rich in silica. Also, **si·li·cious** (sə lish′əs). [1650–60; < L *siliceus* of flint or limestone. See SILEX, -EOUS]

si·lic·ic (sə lis′ik), *adj. Chem.* **1.** containing silicon. **2.** of or pertaining to silica or acids derived from it. [1810–20; SILIC(A) + -IC]

silic′ic ac′id, *Chem.* any of certain amorphous gelatinous masses, formed when alkaline silicates are treated with acids, which dissociate readily into silica and water. [1810–20]

sil·i·cide (sil′ə sīd′, -sid), *n. Chem.* a compound of two elements, one of which is silicon. [1865–70; SILIC(ON) + -IDE]

sil·i·cif·er·ous (sil′ə sif′ər əs), *adj.* containing, combined with, or producing silica. [1790–1800; SILIC(A) + -I- + -FEROUS]

silic′ified wood′, wood that has been changed into quartz by a replacement of the cellular structure of the wood by siliceous waters.

si·lic·i·fy (sə lis′ə fī′), *v.t., v.i.,* **-fied, -fy·ing.** to convert or be converted into silica. [1820–30; SILIC(A) + -IFY] —**si·lic′i·fi·ca′tion,** *n.*

si·li·ci·um (sə lish′ē əm, sə lis′-), *n.* (formerly) silicon. [1800–10; < NL; see SILICA, -IUM]

sil·i·cle (sil′i kəl), *n. Bot.* a short silique. [1775–85; < L *silicula* little husk or pod. See SILIQUA, -ULE]

sil·i·con (sil′i kən, -kon′), *n. Chem.* a nonmetallic element, having amorphous and crystalline forms, occurring in a combined state in minerals and rocks and constituting more than one fourth of the earth's crust: used in steelmaking, alloys, etc. *Symbol:* Si; *at. wt.:* 28.086; *at. no.:* 14; *sp. gr.:* 2.4 at 20°C. [1817; SILIC(A) + *-on,* as in *carbon* and *boron*]

sil′icon car′bide, *Chem.* a very hard, insoluble, crystalline compound, SiC, used as an abrasive and as an electrical resistor in objects exposed to high temperatures. [1900–05]

sil′icon diox′ide, *Chem.* silica.

sil·i·cone (sil′i kōn′), *n. Chem.* any of a number of polymers containing alternate silicon and oxygen atoms, as $(\text{–Si–O–Si–O–})_n$, whose properties are determined by the organic groups attached to the silicon atoms, and that are fluid, resinous, rubbery, extremely stable in high temperatures, and water-repellent: used as adhesives, lubricants, and hydraulic oils and in electrical insulation, cosmetics, etc. [1905–10; SILIC(ON) + -ONE]

sil′icone rub′ber, any of the synthetic rubbers made from silicone elastomers. [1940–45]

sil·i·con·ized (sil′i kə nīzd′), *adj.* **1.** (of a material) having silicone added. **2.** *Metall.* (of iron or steel) having silicon added. [1915–20; SILICON + -IZE + -ED[2]]

sil′icon tetrachlo′ride, *Chem.* a colorless, fuming liquid, $SiCl_4$, used chiefly for making smoke screens and various derivatives of silicon. [1865–70]

sil′icon tetrafluor′ide, *Chem.* a colorless, fuming gas, SiF_4, used chiefly in the manufacture of fluosilicic acid.

sil′icon tetrahy′dride, *Chem.* silane (def. 1).

Sil′icon Val′ley, the area in northern California, southwest of San Francisco in the Santa Clara valley region, where many of the high-technology design and manufacturing companies in the semiconductor industry are concentrated. [so called from the silicon wafers employed in semiconductor devices]

sil·i·co·sis (sil′i kō′sis), *n. Pathol.* a disease of the lungs caused by the inhaling of siliceous particles, as by stonecutters. [1890–95; SILIC(A) + -OSIS] —**sil·i·cot·ic** (sil′i kot′ik), *adj.*

si·lic·u·lose (si lik′yə lōs′), *adj. Bot.* **1.** bearing silicles. **2.** having the form or appearance of a silicle. [1725–35; < NL *siliculōsus.* See SILICLE, -OSE[1]]

sil·i·qua (sil′i kwə), *n., pl.* **-quae** (-kwē′). a silver coin of the later Roman Empire, the 24th part of a solidus, first issued by Constantine. [1885–90; < LL; L: pod, carob tree]

si·lique (sə lēk′, sil′ik), *n. Bot.* the long two-valved seed vessel or pod of plants belonging to the mustard family. [1400–50; late ME *selyque, silique* (< MF *silique*) < L *siliqua;* see SILIQUA] —**sil·i·qua·ceous** (sil′i-kwā′shəs), *adj.*

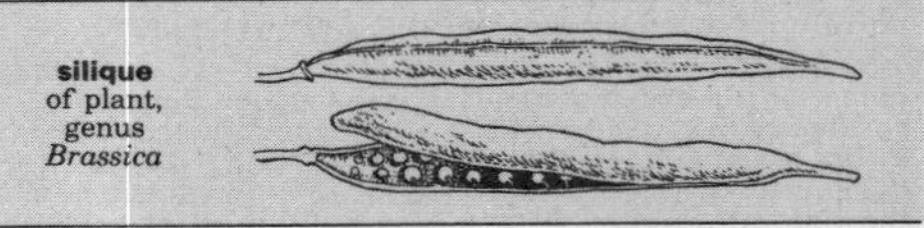
silique of plant, genus *Brassica*

sil·i·quose (sil′i kwōs′), *adj.* **1.** bearing siliques. **2.** resembling a silique or silicle. Also, **sil·i·quous** (sil′ə-kwəs). [1685–95; < NL *siliquōsus.* See SILIQUE, -OSE[1]]

silk (silk), *n.* **1.** the soft, lustrous fiber obtained as a filament from the cocoon of the silkworm. **2.** thread made from this fiber. **3.** cloth made from this fiber. **4.** a garment of this cloth. **5.** a gown of such material worn distinctively by a King's or Queen's Counsel at the English bar. **6. silks,** the blouse and peaked cap, considered together, worn by a jockey or sulky driver in a race. **7.** *Informal.* a parachute, esp. one opened aloft. **8.** any fiber or filamentous matter resembling silk, as a filament produced by certain spiders, the thread of a mollusk, or the like. **9.** the hairlike styles on an ear of corn. **10.** *Brit. Informal.* **a.** a King's or Queen's Counsel. **b.** any barrister of high rank. **11. hit the silk,** *Slang.* to parachute from an aircraft; bail out. **12. take silk,** *Brit.* to become a Queen's or King's Counsel. —*adj.* **13.** made of silk. **14.** resembling silk; silky. **15.** of or pertaining to silk. —*v.i.* **16.** (of corn) to be in the course of developing silk. [bef. 900; ME (n.); OE *sioloc, seol(o)c* (c. ON *silki*), by uncert. transmission < Gk *sērikón* silk, n. use of neut. of *sērikós* silken, lit., Chinese, deriv. of *Sêres* the Chinese (Russ *shëlk,* OPruss *silkas* (gen.) "silk" appear to be < Gmc); cf. SERIC-] —**silk′like′,** *adj.*

silk·a·line (sil′kə lēn′), *n.* a soft, thin cotton fabric with a smooth finish, for curtains, bedspreads, garment linings, etc. Also, **silk′o·line′, silk′o·lene′.** [1895–1900, *Amer.;* SILK + -aline, alter. of *-oline,* as in *crinoline*]

silk′ cot′ton, the silky covering of the seeds of certain tropical trees of the bombax family, used for stuffing cushions, pillows, etc. [1690–1700]

silk′-cot·ton tree′ (silk′kot′n), any of several spiny trees belonging to the genus *Ceiba,* of the bombax family, having palmately compound leaves and seeds surrounded by silk cotton, esp. *C. pentandra,* from which kapok is obtained. [1705–15]

silk·en (silʹkən), *adj.* **1.** made of silk. **2.** like silk in smoothness, softness, glossiness, or delicateness. **3.** clad in silk. **4.** smoothly persuasive or ingratiating; mellifluous: *the senator's silken oratory.* **5.** elegant; luxurious. [bef. 900; ME; OE *seolcen.* See SILK, -EN[2]]

silkʹ glandʹ, any of several glands, as in various insects and spiders, that secrete a viscid protein substance which hardens into silk on contact with air. [1865–70]

silkʹ gumʹ, sericin.

silkʹ hatʹ, a tall, cylindrical, black hat covered with silk plush, worn by men for formal dress. Cf. **beaver**[1] (def. 4), **opera hat, top hat.** [1825–35] **—silkʹ-hatʹted,** *adj.*

silkʹ oakʹ, any of several Australian trees of the genus *Grevillea,* esp. *G. robusta,* having feathery, fernlike leaves and showy orange or yellow flowers, grown as a street tree in Florida and California. Also, **silky oak.** [1865–70]

silkʹ paʹper, paper that contains silk fibers and is sometimes used for printing postage stamps and revenue stamps. Cf. **granite paper.** [1790–1800]

silk·screen (silkʹskrēnʹ), *n.* **1.** Also called **silkʹ·screen procʹess.** a printmaking technique in which a mesh cloth is stretched over a heavy wooden frame and the design, painted on the screen by tusche or affixed by stencil, is printed by having a squeegee force color through the pores of the material in areas not blocked out by a glue sizing. **2.** a print made by this technique. —*v.t.* **3.** to print by silkscreen. —*adj.* **4.** of, made by, or printed with silkscreen. [1940–45; SILK + SCREEN]

silk-stock·ing (silkʹstokʹing), *adj.* **1.** rich or luxurious in dress. **2.** aristocratic or wealthy: *a silk-stocking neighborhood.* —*n.* **3.** a person who dresses richly or luxuriously. **4.** an aristocratic or wealthy person. [1590–1600]

silk-tas·sel (silkʹtasʹəl), *n.* any of several shrubs or small trees of the genus *Garrya,* of the western U.S., having evergreen foliage and flowers in pendulous catkins.

silkʹ treeʹ, a tree, *Albizia julibrissin,* of the legume family, native to Asia, having pinnate leaves and plumelike pink flowers and widely cultivated as an ornamental. Also called **mimosa.** [1850–55]

silk·weed (silkʹwēdʹ), *n.* any milkweed, the pods of which contain a silky down. [1775–85, *Amer.*; SILK + WEED[1]]

silk·worm (silkʹwûrmʹ), *n.* **1.** the larva of the Chinese silkworm moth, *Bombyx mori,* which spins a cocoon of commercially valuable silk. **2.** the larva of any of several moths of the family Saturniidae, which spins a silken cocoon. [bef. 1000; ME *sylkewyrme,* OE *seolcwyrm.* See SILK, WORM]

silkʹworm mothʹ, any of several moths of the families Bombycidae and Saturniidae, the larvae of which are silkworms. [1805–15]

silk·y (silʹkē), *adj.,* **silk·i·er, silk·i·est. 1.** of or like silk; smooth, lustrous, soft, or delicate: *silky skin.* **2.** *Bot.* covered with fine, soft, closely set hairs, as a leaf. [1605–15; SILK + -Y[1]] **—silkʹi·ly,** *adv.* **—silkʹi·ness,** *n.*

silkʹy antʹeater an arboreal, tropical American anteater, *Cyclopes didactylus,* about the size of a rat, having a prehensile tail, glossy, golden fur, and two toes on each forelimb. Also called **two-toed anteater.**

silkʹy corʹnel, a cornel, *Cornus amomum,* of the eastern U.S., having leaves covered with short, silky hairs on the underside and bearing blue berries.

silkʹy flyʹcatcher, any of several passerine birds of the family Ptilogonatidae, of the southwestern U.S. to Panama, related to the waxwings.

silkʹy oakʹ. See **silk oak.** [1885–90]

silkʹy terʹrier, one of an Australian breed of toy dogs having a long, silky, blue coat with tan markings and erect ears, a topknot, and a docked tail. Also called **Sydney silky.** [1955–60]

sill (sil), *n.* **1.** a horizontal timber, block, or the like serving as a foundation of a wall, house, etc. **2.** the horizontal piece or member beneath a window, door, or other opening. See diag. under **double-hung. 3.** *Geol.* a tabular body of intrusive igneous rock, ordinarily between beds of sedimentary rocks or layers of volcanic ejecta. [bef. 900; ME *sille,* OE *syl, sylle;* c. LG *süll,* ON *syll;* akin to G *Schwelle* sill] **—sillʹ-likeʹ,** *adj.*

sil·la·bub (silʹə bubʹ), *n.* syllabub. Also, **silʹli·bubʹ.**

Silʹla Kingʹdom (silʹə), an ancient Korean state that unified Korea; flourished in the 7th–10th centuries A.D.

Sil·lan·pää (silʹlän paʹ), *n.* **Frans Ee·mil** (fräns eʹmil), 1888–1964, Finnish author: Nobel prize 1939.

sill·cock (silʹkokʹ), *n.* hosecock. [SILL + COCK[1]; so called from the fact that it is often attached to a house at about the height of a sill]

sil·ler (silʹər), *n. Scot.* silver.

Sil·le·ry (silʹə rē; *Fr.* sēyᵊ rēʹ), *n.* a city in S Quebec, in E Canada, near Quebec. 12,825.

Sil·li·man (silʹə mən), *n.* **Benjamin,** 1779–1864, U.S. scientist and educator.

sil·li·man·ite (silʹə mə nītʹ), *n.* a mineral, aluminum silicate, Al_2SiO_5, occurring in the form of long, slender, and often fibrous crystals. Also called **fibrolite.** [1825–30; named after B. SILLIMAN; see -ITE[1]]

Sills (silz), *n.* **Beverly** (*Belle Silverman*), born 1929, U.S. coloratura soprano and opera administrator.

sil·ly (silʹē), *adj.,* **-li·er, -li·est,** *n., pl.* **-lies.** —*adj.* **1.** weak-minded or lacking good sense; stupid or foolish: *a silly writer.* **2.** absurd; ridiculous; irrational: *a silly idea.* **3.** stunned; dazed: *He knocked me silly.* **4.** *Cricket.* (of a fielder or the fielder's playing position) extremely close to the batsman's wicket: *silly mid off.* **5.** *Archaic.* rustic; plain; homely. **6.** *Archaic.* weak; helpless. **7.** *Obs.* lowly in rank or state; humble. —*n.* **8.** *Informal.* a silly or foolish person: *Don't be such a silly.* [1375–1425; earlier *sylie, sillie* foolish, feeble-minded, simple, pitiful; late ME *syly,* var. of *sely* SEELY] **—silʹli·ly,** *adv.* **—silʹli·ness,** *n.*

—Syn. 1. witless, senseless, dull-witted, dim-witted. See **foolish. 2.** inane, asinine, nonsensical, preposterous. **—Ant. 1.** sensible.

silʹly bilʹly, a clownish person. [1840–50]

Silʹly Putʹty, *Trademark.* a brand of children's claylike modeling substance that can be shaped, stretched, rolled into a ball and bounced, etc. Cf. **Play-Doh.**

silʹly seaʹson, a time of year, usually in midsummer or during a holiday period, characterized by exaggerated news stories, frivolous entertainments, outlandish publicity stunts, etc.: *The new movie reminds us that the silly season is here.* [1870–75]

sil·ly-sid·er (silʹē sīʹdər), *n. Canadian Slang.* a left-handed person. [*silly side* + -ER[1]]

sil·ly·weed (silʹē wēdʹ), *n. Slang.* marijuana. [SILLY + WEED[1]]

si·lo (sīʹlō), *n., pl.* **-los,** *v.,* **-loed, -lo·ing.** —*n.* **1.** a structure, typically cylindrical, in which fodder or forage is kept. **2.** a pit or underground space for storing grain, green feeds, etc. **3.** *Mil.* an underground installation constructed of concrete and steel, designed to house a ballistic missile and the equipment for firing it. —*v.t.* **4.** to put into or preserve in a silo. [1825–35; < Sp: place for storing grain, hay, etc., orig. subterranean; ulterior orig. uncert.]

Si·lo·am (si lōʹəm, sī-), *n.* a spring and pool near Jerusalem. John 9:7.

Si·lo·ne (si lōʹnē; *It.* sē lôʹne), *n.* **I·gna·zio** (ē nyäʹtsyô), (*Secondo Tranquilli*), 1900–78, Italian author.

si·lox·ane (si lokʹsān), *n. Chem.* any of the class of compounds containing the structural unit R_2SiO, where R is an organic group or hydrogen. [1920–25; SIL(ICON) + OX(YGEN) + -ANE]

silt (silt), *n.* **1.** earthy matter, fine sand, or the like carried by moving or running water and deposited as a sediment. —*v.i.* **2.** to become filled or choked up with silt. —*v.t.* **3.** to fill or choke up with silt. [1400–50; late ME *cylte* gravel, perh. orig. salty deposit; cf. OE *unsylt* unsalted, unseasoned, *sylting* seasoning, *syltan* to salt, season, Norw *sylt* salty swamp, G *Sülze* salt marsh, brine] **—sil·taʹtion,** *n.* **—siltʹy,** *adj.*

silt·stone (siltʹstōnʹ), *n. Petrog.* a very fine-grained sandstone, mainly consolidated silt. [1925–30; SILT + STONE]

Sil·u·res (silʹyə rēzʹ), *n.pl.* a British Celtic tribe resident in southeastern Wales at the time of the Roman conquest of Britain.

Si·lu·ri·an (si lo͝orʹē ən, sī-), *adj.* **1.** of or pertaining to the Silures or their country. **2.** *Geol.* noting or pertaining to a period of the Paleozoic Era, occurring from 425 to 405 million years ago, notable for the advent of air-breathing animals and terrestrial plants. See table under **geologic time.** —*n.* **3.** *Geol.* the Silurian Period or System of rocks. [1700–10; SILUR(ES) + -IAN]

si·lu·rid (si lo͝orʹid, sī-), *n.* **1.** any of numerous Old World freshwater fishes of the family Siluridae, comprising the catfishes. —*adj.* **2.** belonging or pertaining to the family Siluridae. [1890–95; < NL *Siluridae* name of the family, equiv. to *Silur(us)* genus name (L *silūrus* a kind of fish < Gk *sílouros*) + *-idae* -ID[2]]

sil·va (silʹvə), *n.* **1.** the forest trees of a particular area. **2.** a descriptive flora of forest trees. Also, **sylva.** [1840–50; < NL, special use of L *silva* woodland]

Sil·va·dine (silʹvə dēnʹ, -dīnʹ), *Trademark.* a brand name for silver sulfadiazine.

sil·van (silʹvən), *adj., n.* sylvan. **—sil·van·i·ty** (sil vanʹi tē), *n.*

Sil·van·a (sil vanʹə, -väʹnə), *n.* a female given name, form of **Silvia** or **Sylvia.**

Sil·va·nus (sil vāʹnəs), *n., pl.* **-ni** (-nī) for 2. *Rom. Religion.* **1.** the god of forests and uncultivated land, later worshiped under three aspects, as the protector of the house, of the herds, and of the boundaries of the farm. **2.** (*l.c.*) any of a number of forest spirits, identified with fauns. Also, **Sylvanus.** [< L; see SYLVAN]

sil·ver (silʹvər), *n.* **1.** *Chem.* a white, ductile metallic element, used for making mirrors, coins, ornaments, table utensils, photographic chemicals, conductors, etc. *Symbol:* Ag; *at. wt.:* 107.870; *at. no.:* 47; *sp. gr.:* 10.5 at 20°C. **2.** coin made of this metal; specie; money: *a handful of silver.* **3.** this metal as a commodity or considered as a currency standard. **4.** table articles made of or plated with silver, including flatware and hollowware. **5.** any flatware: *The kitchen silver is of stainless steel.* **6.** something resembling this metal in color, luster, etc. **7.** a lustrous grayish white or whitish gray, or the color of the metal: *the silver of the leaves.* **8.** any of the silver halides used for photographic purposes, as silver bromide, silver chloride, or silver iodide. **9.** See **silver medal.** —*adj.* **10.** consisting of, made of, or plated with silver. **11.** of or pertaining to silver. **12.** producing or yielding silver. **13.** resembling silver; silvery: *the silver moon.* **14.** clear and soft: *silver sounds.* **15.** eloquent; persuasive: *a silver tongue.* **16.** urging the use of silver as a currency standard: *silver economists.* **17.** indicating the twenty-fifth event of a series, as a wedding anniversary. See table under **wedding anniversary. 18.** having the color silver: *a silver dress.* —*v.t.* **19.** to coat with silver or some silverlike substance. **20.** to give a silvery color to. —*v.i.* **21.** to become a silvery color. [bef. 900; (n. and adj.) ME *silver(e), selver(e), selfer,* OE *siolfor* (orig. n.); c. G *Silber,* ON *silfr,* Goth *silubr,* akin to Serbo-Croatian *srèbro,* Russ *serebró,* Lith *sidābras;* (v.) late ME *silveren,* deriv. of the n.] **—silʹver·er,** *n.* **—silʹver·ish,** *adj.* **—silʹver·less,** *adj.* **—silʹver·likeʹ,** *adj.* **—silʹver·ness,** *n.*

Sil·ver (silʹvər), *n.* **Ab·ba Hillel** (abʹə), 1893–1963, U.S. rabbi, born in Lithuania.

silʹver ageʹ, 1. *Class. Myth.* the second of the four ages of humankind, inferior to the golden age but superior to the bronze age that followed: characterized by an increase of impiety and of human weakness. **2.** (*usually caps.*) a period in Latin literature, A.D. c14–138, following the Augustan Age: the second phase of classical Latin. Cf. **golden age** (def. 3). [1555–65]

sil·ver·back (silʹvər bakʹ), *n.* an older male gorilla, usually the leader of a troop, whose hairs along the back turn gray with age. [SILVER + BACK[1]]

silʹver bassʹ (bas). See **white bass.** [1880–85, *Amer.*]

silʹver bellʹ, any North American shrub or small tree belonging to the genus *Halesia,* of the storax family, having toothed leaves and drooping white, bell-shaped flowers. Also called **silʹver-bell treeʹ.** [1775–85, *Amer.*]

sil·ver·ber·ry (silʹvər berʹē), *n., pl.* **-ries.** a shrub, *Elaeagnus commutata* (or *E. argentea*), of north-central North America, having silvery leaves and flowers and silvery, drupelike edible fruit. [1855–60; SILVER + BERRY]

silʹver broʹmide, *Chem.* a yellowish, water-insoluble powder, AgBr, which darkens on exposure to light, produced by the reaction of silver nitrate with a bromide: used chiefly in the manufacture of photographic emulsions. [1875–80]

silʹver certifʹicate, a former paper currency first issued in 1878 by the U.S. federal government for circulation, equal to and redeemable for silver to a stated value. [1875–80, *Amer.*]

silʹver chloʹride, *Chem.* a white, granular, water-insoluble powder, AgCl, that darkens on exposure to light, produced by the reaction of silver nitrate with a chloride: used chiefly in the manufacture of photographic emulsions and in the making of antiseptic silver preparations. [1895–1900]

silʹver docʹtor, *Angling.* a type of artificial fly, used chiefly for trout and salmon. [1890–95]

sil·vered (silʹvərd), *adj.* **1.** coated or plated with silver. **2.** coated with a silverlike substance, as quicksilver or tinfoil: *a mirror of silvered glass.* **3.** tinted a silver color, or having silver highlights: *silvered hair.* [1475–85; SILVER + -ED[2]]

sil·ver-eye (silʹvər īʹ), *n., pl.* **-eyes.** white-eye. [1885–90]

silʹver firʹ, a coniferous tree, *Abies alba,* native to Europe, the young branches of which are covered with grayish fuzz. [1700–10]

sil·ver·fish (silʹvər fishʹ), *n., pl.* (*esp. collectively*) **-fish,** (*esp. referring to two or more kinds or species*) **-fish·es. 1.** a white or silvery goldfish, *Carassius auratus.* **2.** any of various other silvery fishes, as the tarpon, silversides, or shiner. **3.** a wingless, silvery-gray thysanuran insect, *Lepisma saccharina,* that feeds on starch, damaging books, wallpaper, etc. [1695–1705; SILVER + FISH]

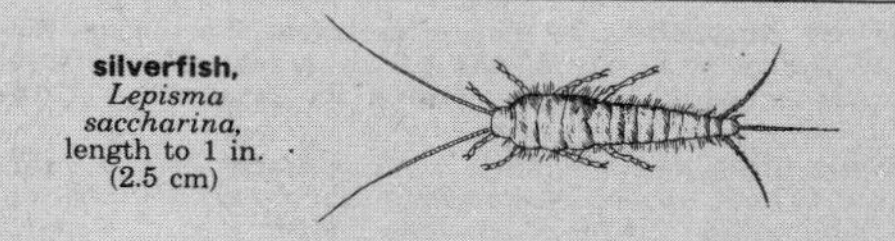
silverfish, *Lepisma saccharina,* length to 1 in. (2.5 cm)

silʹver fizzʹ, an alcoholic drink made with gin, lemon juice, sugar, and egg white.

silʹver fluorʹide, *Chem.* a yellow or brownish, crystalline, water-soluble, hygroscopic solid, AgF, used chiefly as an antiseptic and disinfectant. Also called **tachiol.**

silʹver foilʹ, silver or silver-colored metal in foil form. Also called, *Brit.,* **silver paper.** [1400–50; late ME]

silʹver foxʹ, a red fox in the color phase in which the fur is black with silver-gray ends on the longer hairs. [1760–70]

silʹver frostʹ, glaze (def. 17). [1820–30]

silʹver giltʹ, an ornamental coating of silver, silver leaf, or a silver-colored substance. [1375–1425; late ME]

silʹver grayʹ, a light brownish-gray. [1600–10] **—silʹver-grayʹ,** *adj.*

silʹver hakeʹ, a common hake, *Merluccius bilinearis,* occurring off the Atlantic coast of North America and popular as a food fish. [1880–85, *Amer.*]

silʹver halʹide, *Chem.* a compound in which silver is combined with a halogen, as silver chloride, bromide, or iodide.

sil·ver·ing (silʹvər ing), *n.* **1.** the act or process of coating with silver or a substance resembling silver. **2.** the coating thus applied: *the silvering of the mirror.* [1700–10; SILVER + -ING[1]]

silʹver iʹodate, *Chem.* a white, crystalline, slightly water-soluble powder, $AgIO_3$, used in medicine chiefly as an antiseptic and as an astringent.

silʹver iʹodide, *Chem.* a pale-yellow, water-insoluble solid, AgI, which darkens on exposure to light: used chiefly in medicine, photography, and artificial rainmaking. [1905–10]

Sil·ve·ri·us (sil vērʹē əs), *n.* **Saint,** died A.D. 537, pope 536–37.

sil·ver·ize (silʹvə rīzʹ), *v.t.,* **-ized, -iz·ing.** to cover, plate, or treat with silver. Also, *esp. Brit.,* **silʹver·iseʹ.** [1610–20; SILVER + -IZE] **—silʹver·izʹer,** *n.*

silʹver jenʹny, a silvery mojarra, *Eucinostomus gula,* inhabiting warm waters of the western Atlantic Ocean, along sandy shores.

sil′ver ju′bilee. See under **jubilee** (def. 1).

sil′ver-lace vine′ (sil′vər lās′), a hardy, twining, woody plant, *Polygonum auberti,* of the buckwheat family, native to western China and Tibet, having greenish-white, fragrant flowers in drooping clusters. Also called **Chinese fleece-vine, fleece-vine.**

sil′ver leaf′, silver in the form of very thin foil. [1720–30]

sil′ver lin′ing, a sign of hope in an unfortunate or gloomy situation; a bright prospect: *Every cloud has a silver lining.* [1870–75]

sil′ver·ly (sil′vər lē), *adv.* with a silvery appearance or sound. [1585–95; SILVER + -LY]

sil′ver ma′ple, **1.** a maple, *Acer saccharinum,* having leaves that are light green above and silvery white beneath. **2.** the hard, close-grained wood of this tree, used for making furniture. [1755–65]

sil′ver med′al, a medal, traditionally of silver or silver in color, awarded to a person or team finishing second in a competition, meet, or tournament. Also, **silver.** Cf. **bronze medal, gold medal.** —**sil′ver med′alist.**

sil·vern (sil′vərn), *adj. Archaic.* made of or like silver. [bef. 900; ME *silver(e)n, selvern,* OE *seolfren, seolfern.* See SILVER, -EN[2]]

sil′ver ni′trate, *Chem., Pharm.* a white, crystalline, water-soluble, bitter, corrosive, poisonous powder, $AgNO_3$, produced by the reaction of silver and dilute nitric acid: used chiefly in the manufacture of photographic emulsions and mirrors, as a laboratory reagent, and in medicine as an antiseptic, astringent, and in the routine prophylaxis of ophthalmia neonatorum. [1880–85]

sil′ver pa′per, *Brit.* **1.** See **silver foil.** **2.** tinfoil. [1810–20]

sil′ver perch′, **1.** Also called **mademoiselle.** *Ichthyol.* a drum, *Bairdiella chrysoura,* of southern U.S. waters. **2.** any of various silvery, perchlike fishes, as the white perch. [1810–20, *Amer.*]

sil′ver plate′, **1.** silver tableware. **2.** a coating of silver, esp. one electroplated on base metal. [1520–30]

sil·ver-plate (sil′vər plāt′), *v.t.,* **-plat·ed, -plat·ing.** to coat (base metal) with silver, esp. by electroplating.

sil′ver point′, the melting point of silver, equal to 960.8°C, used as a fixed point on the international temperature scale.

sil·ver·point (sil′vər point′), *n.* **1.** a technique of drawing with a silver stylus on specially prepared paper. **2.** a drawing made by this technique. [1880–85; SILVER + POINT]

sil′ver pop′lar. See **white poplar** (def. 1). [1840–50, *Amer.*]

sil′ver salm′on. See **coho salmon.** [1875–80, *Amer.*]

sil′ver screen′, **1.** motion pictures; the motion-picture industry: *a star of the silver screen.* **2.** a special screen on which motion pictures are projected. [1915–20]

sil·ver·side (sil′vər sīd′), *n.* **1.** *Chiefly Brit.* a rump roast of beef, esp. one taken from the crown of the rump. **2.** silversides. [1810–20; SILVER + SIDE[1]]

sil·ver·sides (sil′vər sīdz′), *n., pl.* **-sides.** any of several small fishes of the family Atherinidae, having a silvery stripe along each side, as *Menidia menidia,* inhabiting the Atlantic coast of the U.S. Also, **silverside.** [1850–55, *Amer.*; SILVER + SIDE[1] + -S[3]]

sil·ver·smith (sil′vər smith′), *n.* a person whose occupation is making and repairing articles of silver. [bef. 1000; ME; OE *seolforsmith.* See SILVER, SMITH] —**sil′·ver·smith′ing,** *n.*

sil′ver spoon′, See **spoon** (def. 7). [1795–1805]

Sil′ver Spring′, a town in central Maryland, near Washington, D.C. 72,893.

sil′ver stand′ard, a monetary standard or system using silver of specified weight and fineness to define the basic unit of currency. [1825–35, *Amer.*]

Sil′ver Star′, *U.S. Army.* a bronze star with a small silver star at the center, awarded to a soldier who has been cited in orders for gallantry in action, when the citation does not warrant the award of a Medal of Honor or the Distinguished Service Cross. Also called **Sil′ver Star′ Med′al.**

Sil′ver State′, Nevada (used as a nickname).

sil·ver·tail (sil′vər tāl′), *n. Australia and New Zealand Informal.* a person of affluence or influence. [1895–1900; SILVER + TAIL[1]]

sil′ver thaw′, glaze (def. 17). [1760–70]

sil·ver·tip (sil′vər tip′), *n.* See **grizzly bear.** [1880–85, *Amer.*; SILVER + TIP[1]]

sil·ver-tongued (sil′vər tungd′), *adj.* persuasive; eloquent: *a silver-tongued orator.* [1585–95]

sil′ver trout′, **1.** a variety of cutthroat trout, *Salmo clarki henshawi,* having silvery coloration, inhabiting Lake Tahoe. **2.** the kokanee.

sil′ver vine′, a vine, *Actinidia polygama,* of eastern Asia, having fragrant, white flowers and yellow, edible fruit and, in the male plant, leaves with silvery-white markings.

sil·ver·ware (sil′vər wâr′), *n.* articles, esp. eating and serving utensils, made of silver, silver-plated metals, stainless steel, etc. [1780–90; SILVER + WARE[1]]

sil′ver wat′tle, a tree, *Acacia dealbata,* of the legume family, native to Australia and Tasmania, having feathery, silver-gray foliage and fragrant yellow flowers. Also called **mimosa.** [1870–75]

CONCISE ETYMOLOGY KEY: <, descended or borrowed from; >, whence; b., blend of, blended; c., cognate with; cf., compare; deriv., derivative; equiv., equivalent; imit., imitative; obl., oblique; r., replacing; s., stem; sp., spelling, spelled; resp., respelling, respelled; trans., translation; ?, origin unknown; *, unattested; ‡, probably earlier than. See the full key inside the front cover.

sil′ver wed′ding, a twenty-fifth wedding anniversary. See table under **wedding anniversary.** [1860–65]

sil·ver·weed (sil′vər wēd′), *n.* **1.** a plant, *Potentilla anserina,* of the rose family, the leaves of which have a silvery pubescence on the underside. **2.** any of several other plants having leaves with a silvery appearance. [1570–80; SILVER + WEED[1]]

sil·ver·work (sil′vər wûrk′), *n.* fine or decorative work executed in silver. [1525–35; SILVER + WORK]

sil·ver·y (sil′və rē), *adj.* **1.** resembling silver; of a lustrous grayish-white color: *the silvery moon.* **2.** having a clear, ringing sound like that of silver: *the silvery peal of bells.* **3.** containing or covered with silver: *silvery deposits.* [1590–1600; SILVER + -Y[1]] —**sil′ver·i·ness,** *n.*

sil′very cinque′foil. See under **cinquefoil** (def. 1).

sil′very spleen′wort, a fern, *Diplazium pycnocarpon,* of eastern North America, having fronds from 20 to 30 in. (50.8 to 76.2 cm) long on yellowish-green stalks.

Sil·ves·ter (sil ves′tər), *n.* a male given name: from a Latin word meaning "of the woodland."

Silvester I. See **Sylvester I.**

Silvester II. See **Sylvester II.**

Sil·vi·a (sil′vē ə), *n.* a female given name: from a Latin word meaning "forest."

sil·vic·o·lous (sil vik′ə ləs), *adj.* living or growing in woodlands. [< L *silvi-* (comb. form repr. *silva* woodland; see SILVA, -I-) + -COLOUS; cf. L *silvicola* in same sense]

sil·vics (sil′viks), *n.* (*used with a singular v.*) the scientific study of trees and their environment. [1945–50; < L *silv(a)* woodland + -ICS]

sil·vi·cul·ture (sil′vi kul′chər), *n.* the cultivation of forest trees; forestry. Also, **sylviculture.** [1875–80; < L *silvi-* (see SILVICOLOUS) + CULTURE] —**sil′vi·cul′tur·al,** *adj.* —**sil′vi·cul′tur·al·ly,** *adv.* —**sil′vi·cul′tur·ist,** *n.*

s'il vous plaît (sēl vo͞o ple′), *French.* if you please; please.

sim., **1.** similar. **2.** simile.

si·ma[1] (sī′mə), *n. Geol.* an assemblage of rocks, rich in silica and magnesium, that constitutes the lower layer of the earth's crust and is found beneath the ocean floors and the sial of continents. [< G (1909), equiv. to L *si(licium)* SILICIUM + *ma(gnesium)* MAGNESIUM] —**si·mat·ic** (sī mat′ik), *adj.*

si·ma[2] (sī′mə), *n. Archit.* the uppermost member of a full classical order, usually a cyma recta, representing a roof gutter; cymatium. [var. of CYMA]

si·mar (si mär′), *n.* **1.** Also, **cymar.** a loose, lightweight jacket or robe for women, fashionable in the 17th and 18th centuries. **2.** zimarra. [1635–45; earlier *simarre* < F < It *zimarra* gown < Sp *zamarra* sheepskin coat, *zamarro* sheepskin < Basque *zamar*]

sim·a·rou·ba (sim′ə ro͞o′bə), *n.* **1.** any tropical American tree belonging to the genus *Simaruba,* of the quassia family, having pinnate leaves, a fleshy fruit, and a root whose bark contains an appetite stimulant. **2.** the bark of this family of trees and shrubs. Also, **sim′a·ru′·ba.** [1745–55; < F < Carib *simaruba*]

sim·a·rou·ba·ceous (sim′ə ro͞o bā′shəs), *adj.* belonging to the Simaroubaceae, the quassia family of plants. Cf. **quassia family.** [1835–45; < NL *Simaroubace(ae)* (see SIMAROUBA, -ACEAE) + -OUS]

si·ma·zine (sī′mə zēn′), *n. Chem.* a colorless crystalline selective herbicide, $C_7H_{12}ClN_5$, used for season-long weed control in corn and other crops. [1955–60; *sim-,* resp. of SYM(METRICAL) + (TRI)AZINE]

Sim·birsk (sim bērsk′; *Russ.* syim byērsk′), *n.* former name of **Ulyanovsk.**

Sim·chath To·rah (sim′khäs tôr′ə, tōr′ə; *Seph. Heb.* sēm khät′ tô rä′; *Ashk. Heb.* sim′khäs tō′rə, toi′rə, -khəs). See **Simhath Torah.** Also, **Sim′chat To′rah.**

Sim·coe (sim′kō), *n.* a town in SE Ontario, in S Canada. 14,326.

Si·me·non (sēm° nôN′), *n.* **Georges (Jo·seph Chris·tian)** (zhôrzh zhō zef′ krēs tyaN′), born 1903, French writer of detective novels, born in Belgium.

Sim·e·on (sim′ē ən), *n.* **1.** a son of Jacob and Leah. Gen. 29:33. **2.** one of the 12 tribes of Israel traditionally descended from him. **3.** a devout man of Jerusalem who praised God for letting him see the infant Jesus. Luke 2:25–35. Cf. **Nunc Dimittis** (def. 1). **4.** a male given name: from a Hebrew word meaning "harkening."

Sim·e·on ben Yo·hai (sim′ē ən ben yō′khī), fl. 2nd century A.D., Palestinian rabbi.

Sim·e·on·ite (sim′ē ə nīt′), *n.* a member of the Israelite tribe of Simeon. [< LL *Simeonītae* (pl.). See SIMEON, -ITE[1]] —**Sim′e·on·ism,** *n.*

Sim′eon Sty·li′tes (stī lī′tēz), **Saint,** A.D. 390?–459, Syrian monk and stylite.

si·meth·i·cone (sī meth′i kōn′), *n. Pharm.* an active ingredient in many antacid preparations that causes small mucus-entrapped air bubbles in the intestines to coalesce into larger bubbles that are more easily passed. [SI(LICA) + METH(YL) + (SIL)ICONE]

Sim·fe·ro·pol (sim′fə rō′pəl; *Russ.* syim fyi rô′pəl), *n.* a city in S Ukraine, on the S Crimean Peninsula. 338,000.

Sim·hath To·rah (sim′khäs tôr′ə, tōr′ə; *Seph. Heb.* sēm khät′ tô rä′; *Ashk. Heb.* sim′khäs tō′rə, toi′rə, -khəs), a Jewish festival, celebrated on the 23rd day of Tishri, being the 9th day of Sukkoth, that marks the completion of the annual cycle of the reading of the Torah in the synagogue and the beginning of the new cycle. Also, **Sim′hat To′rah, Simchath Torah, Simchat Torah.** [< Heb *śimḥath tōrāh* lit., rejoicing of the Law]

sim·i·an (sim′ē ən), *adj.* **1.** of or pertaining to an ape or monkey. **2.** characteristic of apes or monkeys: *long, simian fingers.* —*n.* **3.** an ape or monkey. [1600–10; < L *sīmi(a)* an ape (prob. deriv. of *sīmus* flat-nosed < Gk *simós*) + -AN] —**sim·i·an·i·ty** (sim′ē an′i tē), *n.*

sim′ian shelf′, a shelflike thickening along the inside of the mandible, characteristic of the anthropoid apes.

simian virus 40. See **SV 40.**

sim·i·lar (sim′ə lər), *adj.* **1.** having a likeness or resemblance, esp. in a general way: *two similar houses.* **2.** *Geom.* (of figures) having the same shape; having corresponding sides proportional and corresponding angles equal: *similar triangles.* **3.** *Math.* (of two square matrices) related by means of a similarity transformation. [1605–15; earlier *similary* < F *similaire* or ML *similāris,* equiv. to L *simil(is)* like, similar (akin to *simul* together; cf. SIMPLEX) + *-āris* -AR[1]] —**sim′i·lar·ly,** *adv.*
—**Syn.** **1.** like, resembling. See **same.** —**Ant.** **1.** different.

sim·i·lar·i·ty (sim′ə lar′i tē), *n., pl.* **-ties.** **1.** the state of being similar; likeness; resemblance. **2.** an aspect, trait, or feature like or resembling another or another's: *a similarity of diction.* [1655–65; SIMILAR + -ITY]
—**Syn.** **1.** similitude, correspondence, parallelism. See **resemblance.** —**Ant.** **1.** difference.

similar′ity transforma′tion, *Math.* **1.** Also called **homothetic transformation.** a mapping of a set by which each element in the set is mapped into a positive constant multiple of itself, the same constant being used for all elements. **2.** an operation performed upon a square matrix that leaves invariant its characteristic polynomial, trace, and determinant. The transformation is obtained by multiplying the given matrix on one side by any nonsingular matrix and on the other by the inverse of that nonsingular matrix.

sim·i·le (sim′ə lē), *n.* **1.** a figure of speech in which two unlike things are explicitly compared, as in "she is like a rose." Cf. **metaphor.** **2.** an instance of such a figure of speech or a use of words exemplifying it. [1350–1400; ME < L: image, likeness, comparison, n. use of neut. of *similis* SIMILAR]

si·mil·i·tude (si mil′i to͞od′, -tyo͞od′), *n.* **1.** likeness; resemblance: *a similitude of habits.* **2.** a person or thing that is like or the match or counterpart of another: *This expression is a similitude of the other.* **3.** semblance; image: *a similitude of the truth.* **4.** a likening or comparison in the form of a simile, parable, or allegory: *He spoke by similitudes.* [1325–75; ME < L *similitūdō* likeness, equiv. to *simili(s)* SIMILAR + *-tūdō* -TUDE]

Si·mio·na·to (sē′myô nä′tô), *n.* **Giu·liet·ta** (jo͞o lyet′-tä), born 1910, Italian mezzo-soprano.

sim·i·ous (sim′ē əs), *adj.* pertaining to or characteristic of apes or monkeys; simian. [1795–1805; < L *sīmi(a)* ape (see SIMIAN) + -OUS] —**sim′i·ous·ness,** *n.*

sim·i·tar (sim′i tər), *n.* scimitar.

Si·mi′ Val′ley (si mē′, sē′mē), a city in SW California. 77,500.

Sim·la (sim′lə), *n.* a city in and the capital of Himachal Pradesh, in N India: the summer capital of India. 55,000.

Sim·mel (zim′əl), *n.* **Ge·org** (gā ôrk′), 1858–1918, German sociologist and philosopher.

Sim·men·tal (zim′ən täl′), *n.* one of a large breed of cattle, yellowish-brown to red and white, originally of Switzerland, used for milk and beef and as a draft animal. Also, **Sim′men·thal′, Sim·men·tha·ler** (zim′ən-tä′lər). [1905–10; after *Simmental,* the valley of the river Simme, Bern canton, Switzerland]

sim·mer (sim′ər), *v.i.* **1.** to cook or cook in a liquid at or just below the boiling point. **2.** to make a gentle murmuring sound, as liquids cooking just below the boiling point. **3.** to be in a state of subdued or restrained activity, development, excitement, anger, etc.: *The town simmered with rumors.* —*v.t.* **4.** to keep (liquid) in a state approaching boiling. **5.** to cook in a liquid that is kept at or just below the boiling point. **6. simmer down, a.** to reduce in volume by simmering. **b.** *Slang.* to become calm or quiet, as from a state of anger or turmoil: *We waited for the audience to simmer down.* —*n.* **7.** the state or process of simmering. [1645–55; alter. of earlier *simper* < ?] —**sim′mer·ing·ly,** *adv.*
—**Syn.** **3.** See **boil**[1].

Simms (simz), *n.* **William Gil·more** (gil′môr, -mōr), 1806–70, U.S. author.

sim′nel cake′ (sim′nl), *Chiefly Brit.* any of several kinds of rich fruitcake covered with almond paste. [1830–40; *simnel,* ME *simenel* < OF, ult. < L *simila* or Gk *semidālis* fine flour]

si·mo·le·on (sə mō′lē ən), *n. Slang.* a dollar. [1895–1900, *Amer.*; orig. uncert.]

Si·mon (sī′mən; *Fr.* sē môN′ *for 7*), *n.* **1.** the original name of the apostle Peter. Cf. **Peter.** **2.** Simon the Zealot, one of the twelve apostles. Matt. 10:4. **3. the Canaanite,** one of the twelve apostles. Matt. 10:4; Mark 3:18; Luke 6:15. **4.** a relative, perhaps a brother, of Jesus: sometimes identified with Simon the Canaanite. Matt. 13:55; Mark 6:3. **5.** (*"Simon Magus"*) the Samaritan sorcerer who was converted by the apostle Philip. Acts 8:9–24. **6.** (*"Simon Magus"*) fl. 2nd century A.D.?, founder of a Gnostic sect and reputed prototype of the Faust legend: often identified with the Biblical Simon Magus. **7. Claude** (klōd), born 1913, French novelist: Nobel prize 1985. **8. Herbert Alexander,** born 1916, U.S. social scientist and economist: Nobel prize 1978. **9. Sir John (Allse·brook)** (ôlz′bro͝ok′), 1873–1954, British statesman and lawyer. **10. Neil,** born 1927, U.S. playwright. **11.** a male given name, form of **Simeon.**

Si·mon Boc·ca·ne·gra (sī′mən bō′kə nā′grə, -neg′-rə), an opera (1857) by Giuseppe Verdi. Also, ***Si·mo·ne Boc·ca·ne·gra*** (*It.* sē mō′ne bôk′kä ne′grä).

si·mo·ni·ac (si mō′nē ak′), *n.* a person who practices simony. [1300–50; ME < ML *simoniacus* (n. and adj.). See SIMONY, -AC] —**si·mo·ni·a·cal** (sī′mə nī′ə kəl, sim′ə-), *adj.* —**si′mo·ni′a·cal·ly,** *adv.*

Si·mon·i·des (sī mon′i dēz′), *n.* 556?–468? B.C., Greek poet. Also called **Simon′ides of Ce′os** (sē′os).

si•mon•ize (sī′mə nīz′), *v.t.*, **-ized, -iz•ing.** to shine or polish to a high sheen, esp. with wax: *to simonize an automobile.* Also, *esp. Brit.*, **si′mon•ise′.** [1935–40; after *Simoniz*, a trademark]

Si′mon Le•gree′ (li grē′), **1.** the brutal slave dealer in *Uncle Tom's Cabin.* **2.** any harsh, merciless master: *Our math teacher is a Simon Legree.*

Si′mon Ma′gus, Simon (defs. 5, 6).

Si•mo•nov (sē′mə nôf′, -nof′; *Russ.* syē′mə nəf), *n.* **Kon•stan•tin M.** (kən stun tyēn′), 1915–79, Russian journalist and playwright.

Si′mon Pe′ter, Peter (def. 1).

si•mon-pure (sī′mən pyŏŏr′), *adj.* real; genuine: *a simon-pure accent.* [1710–20; short for *the real Simon Pure,* alluding to the victim of impersonation in Susanna Centlivre's play *A Bold Stroke for a Wife* (1718)]

Si′mon says′, a children's game in which all players must imitate only those movements and commands of a leader that are preceded by the words "Simon says."

Si•mon•son (sī′mən sən), *n.* **Lee,** 1888–1967, U.S. set designer.

si•mo•ny (sī′mə nē, sim′ə-), *n.* **1.** the making of profit out of sacred things. **2.** the sin of buying or selling ecclesiastical preferments, benefices, etc. [1175–1225; ME *simonie* < LL *simōnia;* so called from *Simon Magus,* who tried to purchase apostolic powers; see SIMON (def. 5), -Y[3]] **—si′mon•ist,** *n.*

simp (simp), *n. Informal.* a fool; simpleton. [1905–10; shortening of SIMPLETON]

sim•pa•ti•co (sim pä′ti kō′, -pat′i-), *adj.* congenial or like-minded; likable: *I find our new neighbor simpatico in every respect.* [1860–65; < It: lit., sympathetic, equiv. to *simpat(ia)* SYMPATHY + *-ico* -IC. Cf. Sp *simpático,* F *sympathique,* G *sympatisch*]

sim•per (sim′pər), *v.i.* **1.** to smile in a silly, self-conscious way. *—v.t.* **2.** to say with a simper. *—n.* **3.** a silly, self-conscious smile. [1555–65; akin to MD *zimperlijc,* dial. Dan *simper* affected, Dan *sippe* affected woman, orig. one who sips (see SIP), a way of drinking thought to be affected] **—sim′per•er,** *n.* **—sim′per•ing•ly,** *adv.*
—Syn. 1, 3. smirk, snigger, snicker.

sim•ple (sim′pəl), *adj.*, **-pler, -plest,** *n.* *—adj.* **1.** easy to understand, deal with, use, etc.: *a simple matter; simple tools.* **2.** not elaborate or artificial; plain: *a simple style.* **3.** not ornate or luxurious; unadorned: *a simple gown.* **4.** unaffected; unassuming; modest: *a simple manner.* **5.** not complicated: *a simple design.* **6.** not complex or compound; single. **7.** occurring or considered alone; mere; bare: *the simple truth; a simple fact.* **8.** free of deceit or guile; sincere; unconditional: *a frank, simple answer.* **9.** common or ordinary: *a simple soldier.* **10.** not grand or sophisticated; unpretentious: *a simple way of life.* **11.** humble or lowly: *simple folk.* **12.** inconsequential or rudimentary. **13.** unlearned; ignorant. **14.** lacking mental acuteness or sense: *a simple way of thinking.* **15.** unsophisticated; naive; credulous. **16.** simpleminded. **17.** *Chem.* **a.** composed of only one substance or element: *a simple substance.* **b.** not mixed. **18.** *Bot.* not divided into parts: *a simple leaf; a simple stem.* **19.** *Zool.* not compound: *a simple ascidian.* **20.** *Music.* uncompounded or without overtones; single: *simple tone.* **21.** *Gram.* having only the head without modifying elements included: *The simple subject of "The dappled pony gazed over the fence" is "pony."* Cf. **complete** (def. 5). **22.** (of a verb tense) consisting of a main verb with no auxiliaries, as *takes* (simple present) or *stood* (simple past) (opposed to *compound*). **23.** *Math.* linear (def. 7). **24.** *Optics.* (of a lens) having two optical surfaces only. *—n.* **25.** an ignorant, foolish, or gullible person. **26.** something simple, unmixed, or uncompounded. **27. simples,** *Textiles.* cords for controlling the warp threads in forming the shed on draw-looms. **28.** a person of humble origins; commoner. **29.** an herb or other plant used for medicinal purposes: *country simples.* [1175–1225; (adj.) ME < OF < LL *simplus* simple, L (in *simpla pecunia* simple fee or sum), equiv. to *sim-* one (see SIMPLEX) + *-plus,* as in *duplus* DUPLE, DOUBLE (see -FOLD); c. Gk *háplos* (see HAPLO-); (n.) ME: commoner, deriv. of the adj.] **—sim′ple•ness,** *n.*
—Syn. 1. clear, intelligible, understandable, unmistakable, lucid. **2.** natural, unembellished, neat. **8.** artless, guileless, ingenuous. **10.** See **homely. 12.** trifling, trivial, nonessential, unnecessary. **13.** untutored, stupid.

sim′ple algebra′ic exten′sion, *Math.* a simple extension in which the specified element is a root of an algebraic equation in the given field. Cf. **simple transcendental extension.**

sim′ple arc′, *Math.* a curve that does not cross itself and has no points missing; a curve that can be put into one-to-one correspondence with the closed interval from 0 to 1. Also called **Jordan arc.**

sim′ple carbohy′drate, a carbohydrate, as glucose, that consists of a single monosaccharide unit. Cf. **complex carbohydrate.**

sim′ple chan′cre, *Pathol.* chancroid.

sim′ple closed′ curve′, *Math.* a curve that is closed and that has no loops or points missing; a curve for which there exists a homeomorphism mapping it to a circle. Also called **Jordan curve.** [1965–70]

sim′ple enumera′tion, *Logic, Philos.* a procedure for arriving at empirical generalizations by haphazard accumulation of positive instances.

sim′ple exten′sion, *Math.* an extension field of a given field, obtained by forming all polynomials in a specified element with coefficients contained in the given field.

sim′ple frac′tion, a ratio of two integers. [1585–95]

sim′ple frac′ture, a fracture in which the bone does not pierce the skin. Also called **closed fracture.** [1590–1600]

sim′ple fruit′, a fruit formed from one pistil. [1875–80]

sim′ple group′, *Math.* a group that has no normal subgroup except the group itself and the identity.

sim′ple harmon′ic mo′tion, *Physics.* vibratory motion in a system in which the restoring force is proportional to the displacement from equilibrium. *Abbr.:* S.H.M., s.h.m.

sim•ple-heart•ed (sim′pəl här′tid), *adj.* free of deceit; artless; sincere. [1350–1400; ME *symple herted*]

sim′ple hon′ors, *Auction Bridge.* three honors in the trump suit, or three aces in no-trump, held by a partnership.

sim′ple in′terest, interest payable only on the principal; interest that is not compounded. [1790–1800]

sim′ple in′terval, *Music.* an interval of an octave or less. [1870–75]

sim′ple machine′, *Mech.* machine (def. 3b). [1900–05]

sim′ple major′ity, **1.** less than half of the total votes cast but more than the minimum required to win, as when there are more than two candidates or choices. **2.** less than half the number of voters registered. Cf. **absolute majority.**

sim′ple meas′ure. See **simple time.**

sim′ple mi′croscope, a microscope having a single lens. [1720–30]

sim•ple•mind•ed (sim′pəl mīn′did, -mīn′-), *adj.* **1.** free of deceit or guile; artless or unsophisticated. **2.** lacking in mental acuteness or sense. **3.** mentally deficient. Also, **sim′ple-mind′ed.** [1735–45; SIMPLE + MINDED] **—sim′ple•mind′ed•ly,** *adv.* **—sim′ple•mind′ed•ness,** *n.*
—Syn. 2, 3. stupid, foolish, slow, dull-witted, half-witted.

sim′ple pen′dulum, *Physics.* a hypothetical apparatus consisting of a point mass suspended from a weightless, frictionless thread whose length is constant, the motion of the body about the string being periodic and, if the angle of deviation from the original equilibrium position is small, representing simple harmonic motion (distinguished from *physical pendulum*).

sim′ple pole′, *Math.* a pole of order 1 of a function of a complex variable.

sim′ple pro′tein, *Biochem.* a protein that yields only amino acids and no other major products when hydrolyzed (contrasted with *conjugated protein*). [1920–25]

sim′ple sen′tence, a sentence having only one clause, as *I saw her the day before yesterday.* Cf. **complex sentence, compound-complex sentence, compound sentence.**

Sim′ple Si′mon, a simpleton. [1775–85; after the nursery rhyme character]

sim′ple sug′ar, *Chem.* monosaccharide. [1940–45]

sim′ple syr′up, a thick, sweet liquid, usually prepared from sugar and water and used chiefly as a base for soda fountain flavors. Also called **bar syrup, gomme syrup.**

sim′ple time′, *Music.* rhythm characterized by two or three beats or pulses to a measure. Also called **simple measure.**

sim•ple•ton (sim′pəl tən), *n.* an ignorant, foolish, or silly person. [1640–50; SIMPLE + -TON]
—Syn. dolt, fool, numskull, blockhead, ninny, dope.

sim′ple transcenden′tal exten′sion, *Math.* a simple extension in which the specified element is not a root of any algebraic equation in the given field. Cf. **simple algebraic extension.**

sim′ple vow′, *Rom. Cath. Ch.* a public vow taken by a religious, under which property may be retained and marriage, though held to be illicit, is valid under canon law. Cf. **solemn vow.** [1900–05]

sim•plex (sim′pleks), *adj.*, *n. pl.* **-plex•es, -pli•ces** (-plə sēz′). *—adj.* **1.** simple; consisting of or characterized by a single element. **2.** pertaining to or noting a telecommunications system permitting communication in only one direction at a time. *—n.* **3.** *Math.* a basic geometric element in a Euclidean space, being a line segment in one dimension, a triangle in two dimensions, a tetrahedron in three dimensions, and so on: used in topology and linear programming. **4.** an apartment having all the rooms on one floor. [1585–95; < L: having a single layer, lit., one-fold, equiv. to *sim-,* base meaning "one" (akin to *similis* SIMILAR, Gk *hén* (neut.) one, *homós* same (see HOMO-), E SAME) + *-plex* -PLEX]

sim′plex meth′od, *Math.* a numerical method for solving problems in linear programming.

sim•pli•ci•den•tate (sim′plə si den′tāt), *adj.* belonging or pertaining to the Simplicidentata, formerly regarded as a suborder or division of rodents having only one pair of upper incisor teeth. [< NL *Simplicidentata* group name, equiv. to L *simplici-* (s. of *simplex*) SIMPLEX + *dentāta,* n. use of neut. pl. of *dentatus* DENTATE]

sim•plic•i•ty (sim plis′i tē), *n., pl.* **-ties. 1.** the state, quality, or an instance of being simple. **2.** freedom from complexity, intricacy, or division into parts: *an organism of great simplicity.* **3.** absence of luxury, pretentiousness, ornament, etc.; plainness: *a life of simplicity.* **4.** freedom from deceit or guile; sincerity; artlessness; naturalness: *a simplicity of manner.* **5.** lack of mental acuteness or shrewdness: *Politics is not a field for simplicity about human nature.* [1325–75; ME *simplicite* (< OF *simplicité*) < L *simplicitās* simpleness, equiv. to *simplici-* (s. of *simplex*) SIMPLEX + *-tās* -TY[2]]
—Syn. 4. candor, directness, honesty.

Sim•pli•ci•us (sim plish′ē əs), *n.* **Saint,** died A.D. 483, pope 468–483.

sim•pli•fy (sim′plə fī′), *v.t.*, **-fied, -fy•ing.** to make less complex or complicated; make plainer or easier: *to simplify a problem.* [1645–55; < F *simplifier* < ML *simplificāre* to make simple, equiv. to L *simpli-* (comb. form of *simplus* SIMPLE) + *-ficāre* -FY] **—sim′pli•fi•ca′tion,** *n.* **—sim′pli•fi•ca′tive,** *adj.* **—sim′pli•fi′er, sim′pli•fi•ca′tor,** *n.*

sim•plism (sim′pliz əm), *n.* **1.** exaggerated simplicity, as in concentrating on a single aspect or factor of a problem or situation while disregarding others; oversimplification: *The senator is given to simplism in dealing with international issues.* **2.** an act or instance of oversimplifying: *to offer simplisms instead of analyses.* [1880–85; SIMPLE + -ISM]

sim•plis•tic (sim plis′tik), *adj.* characterized by extreme simplism; oversimplified: *a simplistic notion of good and bad.* [1855–60; SIMPLE + -ISTIC] **—sim•plis′ti•cal•ly,** *adv.*

Sim•plon (sim′plon; *Fr.* saN plôN′), *n.* **1.** a mountain pass in S Switzerland, in the Lepontine Alps: crossed by a carriage road constructed 1800–06 on Napoleon's orders. 6592 ft. (2010 m) high. **2.** a tunnel between Switzerland and Italy, NE of the Simplon Pass: longest tunnel in the world. 12¼ mi. (20 km) long.

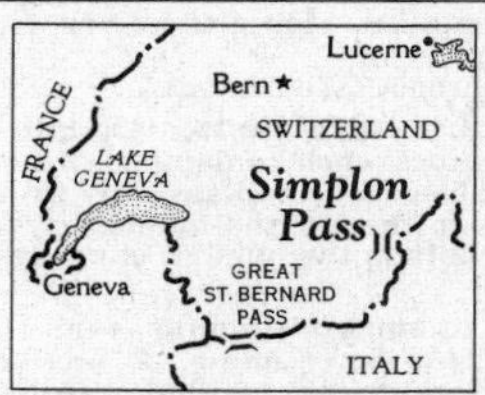

sim•ply (sim′plē), *adv.* **1.** in a simple manner; clearly and easily. **2.** plainly; unaffectedly. **3.** sincerely; artlessly: *to speak simply as a child.* **4.** merely; only: *It is simply a cold.* **5.** unwisely; foolishly: *If you behave simply toward him, you're bound to be betrayed.* **6.** wholly; absolutely: *simply irresistible.* [1250–1300; ME *simpleliche.* See SIMPLE, -LY]

sim•ply-con•nect•ed (sim′plē kə nek′tid), *adj. Math.* **1.** (of a set or domain) having a connected complement. **2.** (of a set or domain) having the property that every simple closed curve in the set can be shrunk to a point without intersecting the boundary of the set. [1930–35]

sim′ply or′dered set′, *Math.* See **totally ordered set.**

Simp•son (simp′sən), *n.* **Wallis Warfield.** See **Windsor, Wallis Warfield, Duchess of.**

Simp′son's rule′, *Math.* a method for approximating the value of a definite integral by approximating, with parabolic arcs, the area under the curve defined by the integrand. [1895–1900; named after Thomas *Simpson* (1710–61), English mathematician]

sim•pu•lum (sim′pyŏŏ ləm), *n., pl.* **-la** (-lə). an ancient dipper having the rim of the bowl at right angles to the handle. [1735–45; < L: ceremonial ladle or pouring vessel]

simp•y (sim′pē), *adj.*, **simp•i•er, simp•i•est.** *Slang.* of or like a simp. [1940–45; SIMP + -Y[1]]

Sims (simz), *n.* **William Sow•den** (soud′n), 1858–1936, U.S. admiral, born in Canada.

Sims•bur•y (simz′ber′ē, -bə rē), *n.* a town in central Connecticut. 21,161.

sim•ul (sim′əl), *adv.* (in prescriptions) together. [< L; cf. SIMILAR, SIMPLEX]

sim•u•la•cre (sim′yə lā′kər), *n. Archaic.* simulacrum. [1325–75; ME < MF < L *simulācrum* SIMULACRUM] **—sim•u•la•cral** (sim′yə lā′krəl), *adj.*

sim•u•la•crum (sim′yə lā′krəm), *n., pl.* **-cra** (-krə). **1.** a slight, unreal, or superficial likeness or semblance. **2.** an effigy, image, or representation: *a simulacrum of Aphrodite.* [1590–1600; < L *simulācrum* likeness, image, equiv. to *simulā(re)* to SIMULATE + *-crum* instrumental suffix]

sim•u•lant (sim′yə lənt), *adj.* **1.** simulating; feigning; imitating. *—n.* **2.** a person or thing that simulates. [1820–30; < L *simulant-* (s. of *simulāns*) imitating (prp. of *simulāre*). See SIMULATE, -ANT]

sim•u•lar (sim′yə lər), *Archaic.* *—n.* **1.** a person or thing that simulates; pretender. *—adj.* **2.** simulated; false; counterfeit. **3.** imitative; simulative. [1520–30; < L *simul(āre)* to SIMULATE + -AR[2], -AR[1]]

sim•u•late (*v.* sim′yə lāt′; *adj.* sim′yə lit, -lāt′), *v.*, **-lat•ed, -lat•ing,** *adj.* *—v.t.* **1.** to create a simulation, likeness, or model of (a situation, system, or the like): *to simulate crisis conditions.* **2.** to make a pretense of; feign: *to simulate knowledge.* **3.** to assume or have the appearance or characteristics of: *He simulated the manners of the rich.* *—adj.* **4.** *Archaic.* simulated. [1400–50; late ME (adj.) < L *simulātus* (ptp. of *simulāre*), equiv. to *simul-* (var. of *simil-,* base of *similis* SIMILAR) + *-ātus* -ATE[1]] **—sim′u•la′tive, sim•u•la•to•ry** (sim′yə lə tôr′ē, -tōr′ē), *adj.* **—sim′u•la′tive•ly,** *adv.*
—Syn. 2. pretend, counterfeit. **3.** affect.

sim•u•la•tion (sim′yə lā′shən), *n.* **1.** imitation or enactment, as of something anticipated or in testing. **2.** the act or process of pretending; feigning. **3.** an assumption or imitation of a particular appearance or form; counterfeit; sham. **4.** *Psychiatry.* a conscious attempt to feign some mental or physical disorder to escape punishment or to gain a desired objective. **5.** the representation of the behavior or characteristics of one system through the use of another system, esp. a computer program designed for the purpose. [1300–50; ME *simulacion* < L *simulātiōn-* (s. of *simulātiō*) a pretense. See SIMULATE, -ION]

sim·u·la·tor (sim′yə lā′tər), *n.* **1.** a person or thing that simulates. **2.** a machine for simulating certain environmental and other conditions for purposes of training or experimentation: *a flight simulator.* [1825–35; < L *simulātor* imitator, counterfeiter. See SIMULATE, -TOR]

si·mul·cast (sī′məl kast′, -käst′, sim′əl-), *n., v.,* **-cast, -cast·ed, -cast·ing.** —*n.* **1.** a program broadcast simultaneously on radio and television, or on more than one channel or station, or in several languages, etc. **2.** a closed-circuit television broadcast of an event, as a horse race, while it is taking place. —*v.t., v.i.* **3.** to broadcast in this manner. [1945–50; SIMUL(TANEOUS) + (BROAD)CAST]

si·mul·ta·ne·ous (sī′məl tā′nē əs, sim′əl-), *adj.* existing, occurring, or operating at the same time; concurrent: *simultaneous movements; simultaneous translation.* [1650–60; < L *simul* together (see SIMILAR) + (INSTAN)TANEOUS] —**si′mul·ta′ne·ous·ly,** *adv.* —**si′·mul·ta′ne·ous·ness, si·mul·ta·ne·i·ty** (sī′məl tə nē′i tē, sim′əl-), *n.*
—**Syn.** synchronous, coincident.

simulta′neous equa′tions, *Algebra.* a set of two or more equations, each containing two or more variables whose values can simultaneously satisfy both or all the equations in the set, the number of variables being equal to or less than the number of equations in the set. [1835–45]

sin[1] (sin), *n., v.,* **sinned, sin·ning.** —*n.* **1.** transgression of divine law: *the sin of Adam.* **2.** any act regarded as such a transgression, esp. a willful or deliberate violation of some religious or moral principle. **3.** any reprehensible action, behavior, etc.; serious fault or offense. —*v.i.* **4.** to commit a sinful act. **5.** to offend against a principle, standard, etc. —*v.t.* **6.** to commit or perform sinfully: *He sinned his crimes without compunction.* **7.** to bring, drive, etc., by sinning: *He sinned his soul to perdition.* [bef. 900; (n.) ME; OE *syn(n)* offense, misdeed; akin to G *Sünde,* ON *synd* sin, L *sōns* guilty; (v.) deriv. of the n., r. ME *sin(i)gen, syn(i)gen,* OE *syngian,* itself deriv. of the n.] —**sin′like′,** *adj.* —**sin′ning·ly,** *adv.*
—**Syn. 1.** trespass, violation. **2.** wrong, wickedness. **4.** transgress, trespass.

sin[2] (sēn), *n.* **1.** the 22nd letter of the Hebrew alphabet. **2.** the consonant sound represented by this letter. [1895–1900; < Heb *sīn*]

sin (sēn), *n.* the 12th letter of the Arabic alphabet. [< Ar]

Sin (sēn), *n.* the Akkadian god of the moon: the counterpart of the Sumerian Nanna.

sin, *Trig.* sine.

sin [1], *Symbol, Trig.* arc sine.

Si·na (sē′nə), *n.* a female given name.

Si·nai (sī′nī, sī′nē ī′), *n.* **1.** Also called **Si′nai Penin′·sula.** a peninsula in NE Egypt, at the N end of the Red Sea between the Gulfs of Suez and Aqaba. 230 mi. (370 km) long. **2. Mount,** the mountain in S Sinai, of uncertain identity, on which Moses received the law. Ex. 19. —**Si·na·it·ic** (sī′nē it′ik), **Si·na·ic** (si nā′ik), *adj.*

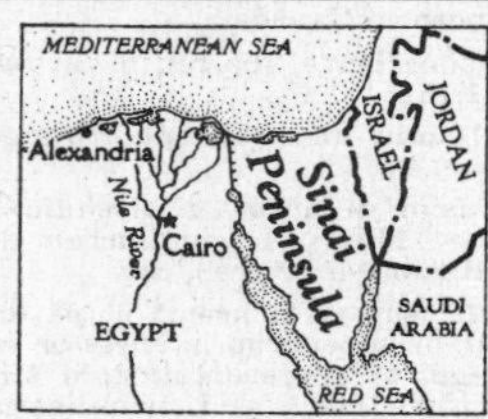

si·nal (sin′l), *adj.* of, pertaining to, or involving a sinus. [SIN(US) + -AL[1]]

sin·al·bin (si nal′bin), *n. Chem.* a white, crystalline, water-soluble glucoside, $C_{30}H_{42}N_2O_{15}S_2$, found in the seeds of the white mustard. [1870–75; < L *sin(āpi)* mustard (< Gk *sināpi*) + *alb(um)* white (see ALB) + -IN[2]]

Si·na·lo·a (sēn′l ō′ə, sin′-; *Sp.* sē′nä lô′ä), *n.* a state in W Mexico, bordering on the Gulf of California. 1,714,000; 22,582 sq. mi. (58,485 sq. km). *Cap.:* Culiacán.

Si·nan (si nän′), *n.* 1489?–1587, Turkish architect, esp. of mosques.

Si·nan·thro·pus (sī nan′thrə pəs, si-, sī′nan thrō′pəs, sin′an-), *n.* the genus to which Peking man was formerly assigned. [< NL (1927), equiv. to *Sin-* SINO- + Gk *ánthrōpos* man]

sin·a·pine (sin′ə pīn′, -pin), *n. Chem.* an alkaloid, $C_{16}H_{25}NO_6$, found in the seeds of the black mustard. [1830–40; < L *sināp(i)* mustard (< Gk *sínāpi*) + -INE[2]]

sin·a·pism (sin′ə piz′əm), *n. Med.* See **mustard plaster.** [1595–1605; < ML *sināpisma* (fem.) < Gk *sinapismós* (masc.) application of mustard, equiv. to *sināp(ízein)* to apply mustard (deriv. of *sínāpi* mustard; see -IZE) + *-ismos* -ISM]

Sin·ar·quist (sin′är kist, -kwist), *n.* a member or advocate of an ultrareactionary, semifascist movement organized in Mexico about 1937. [< AmerSp *sinarquista,* equiv. to Sp *sin* (< L *sine* without) + *(an)arquista* ANARCHIST] —**Sin′ar·quism,** *n.* —**Sin′ar·quis′tic,** *adj.*

CONCISE ETYMOLOGY KEY: <, descended or borrowed from; >, whence; b., blend of, blended; c., cognate with; cf., compare; deriv., derivative; equiv., equivalent; imit., imitative; obl., oblique; r., replacing; s., stem; sp., spelling, spelled; resp., respelling, respelled; trans., translation; ?, origin unknown; *, unattested; ‡, probably earlier than. See the full key inside the front cover.

Si·na·tra (si nä′trə), *n.* **Frank** (*Francis Albert*), born 1915, U.S. singer and actor.

Sin·bad (sin′bad), *n.* See **Sindbad the Sailor.**

since (sins), *adv.* **1.** from then till now (often prec. by *ever*): *He was elected in 1978 and has been president ever since.* **2.** between a particular past time and the present; subsequently: *She at first refused, but has since consented.* **3.** ago; before now: *long since.* —*prep.* **4.** continuously from or counting from: *It has been warm since noon.* **5.** between a past time or event and the present: *There have been many changes since the war.* —*conj.* **6.** in the period following the time when: *He has written once since he left.* **7.** continuously from or counting from the time when: *He has been busy since he came.* **8.** because; inasmuch as: *Since you're already here, you might as well stay.* [1400–50; late ME *syns, sinnes* (adv.) thereupon, afterwards, ME *sithenes* (adv. and conj.) afterwards, from (the specified time), because, equiv. to *sithen* after that, since (OE *siththan,* orig. *sīth thām* after that; see SITH) + *-es* -S[1]]
—**Syn. 8.** See **because.**
—**Usage. 8.** See **as**[1].

sin·cere (sin sēr′), *adj.,* **-cer·er, -cer·est. 1.** free of deceit, hypocrisy, or falseness; earnest: *a sincere apology.* **2.** genuine; real: *a sincere effort to improve; a sincere friend.* **3.** pure; unmixed; unadulterated. **4.** *Obs.* sound; unimpaired. [1525–35; < L *sincērus* pure, clean, untainted] —**sin·cere′ly,** *adv.* —**sin·cere′ness,** *n.*
—**Syn. 1.** frank, candid, honest, open, guileless; unaffected. See **earnest**[1]. —**Ant. 1, 2.** false.

sin·cer·i·ty (sin ser′i tē), *n., pl.* **-ties.** freedom from deceit, hypocrisy, or duplicity; probity in intention or in communicating; earnestness. [1540–50; < L *sincēritās.* See SINCERE, -ITY]
—**Syn.** truth, candor, frankness. See **honor.** —**Ant.** duplicity.

sin·ci·put (sin′sə put′), *n., pl.* **sin·ci·puts, sin·cip·i·ta** (sin sip′i tə). *Anat.* **1.** the forepart of the skull. **2.** the upper part of the skull. [1570–80; < L: lit., half-head < **sēm(i)-caput,* equiv. to *sēmi-* SEMI- + *caput* head] —**sin·cip·i·tal** (sin sip′i tl), *adj.*

Sin·clair (sin klâr′, sing- *or, for 1, 2, 4,* sin′klâr, sing′-), *n.* **1. Harry Ford,** 1876–1956, U.S. oil businessman: a major figure in the Teapot Dome scandal. **2. May,** 1865?–1946, British novelist. **3. Up·ton (Beall)** (up′tən bel), 1878–1968, U.S. novelist, socialist, and reformer. **4.** a male given name: a family name taken from a French placename, *Saint Clair.*

Sind (sind), *n.* a former province of Pakistan, in the lower Indus valley; now part of West Pakistan. 48,136 sq. mi. (125,154 sq. km). *Cap.:* Karachi.

Sind′bad the Sail′or (sind′bad, sin′-), (in *The Arabian Nights' Entertainments*), a wealthy citizen of Baghdad who relates the adventures of his seven wonderful voyages. Also called **Sinbad.**

Sind·hi (sin′dē), *n., pl.* **Sind·his,** (*esp. collectively*) **Sindhi** for 1, *adj.* —*n.* **1.** an inhabitant of Sind. **2.** a modern Indic language of the lower Indus valley. —*adj.* **3.** of or pertaining to Sind or its inhabitants. [1895–1900; < Ar *Sindī,* equiv. to *Sind* SIND (< Hindi *sindhu* sea, ocean; cf. Skt *sindhu* river; cf. HINDI) + *-ī* suffix of appurtenance]

sin·don (sin′dən), *n. Archaic.* cloth of fine linen or silk, used esp. for shrouds. [1400–50; late ME < L *sindōn* < Gk *sindṓn*]

sin·do·nol·o·gy (sin′də nol′ə jē), *n.* the scientific study of the Shroud of Turin. [1965–70; < It *sindon(e)* the shroud in which Christ was interred (< Gk (NT) *sindṓn* winding sheet, Gk: muslin sheet; cf. SINDON) + -O- + -LOGY] —**sin′do·nol′o·gist,** *n.*

sine (sīn), *n.* **1.** *Trig.* **a.** (in a right triangle) the ratio of the side opposite a given acute angle to the hypotenuse. **b.** (of an angle) a trigonometric function equal to the ratio of the ordinate of the end point of the arc to the radius vector of this end point, the origin being at the center of the circle on which the arc lies and the initial point of the arc being on the x-axis. *Abbr.:* sin **2.** *Geom.* (originally) a perpendicular line drawn from one extremity of an arc of a circle to the diameter that passes through its other extremity. **3.** *Math.* (of a real or complex number *x*) the function sin *x* defined by the infinite series $x - (x^3/3!) + (x^5/5!) - + \ldots$, where ! denotes factorial. Cf. **cosine** (def. 2), **factorial** (def. 1). [1585–95; < NL, L *sinus* a curve, fold, pocket, trans. of Ar *jayb* lit., pocket, by folk etym. < Skt *jīyā, jyā* chord of an arc, lit., bowstring]

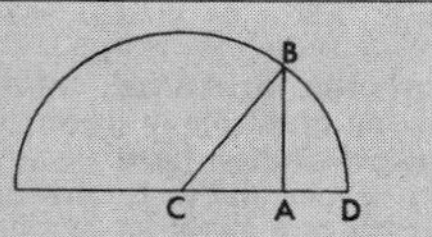

sine (def. 1) ACB being the angle, the ratio of AB to BC is the sine; or BC being taken as unity, the sine is AB

si·ne·cure (sī′ni kyŏŏr′, sin′i-), *n.* **1.** an office or position requiring little or no work, esp. one yielding profitable returns. **2.** an ecclesiastical benefice without cure of souls. [1655–65; < ML (*beneficium*) *sine cūrā* (benefice) without care; see CURE] —**si′ne·cure·ship′,** *n.* —**si′ne·cur·ism,** *n.* —**si′ne·cur′ist,** *n.*

sine′ curve′, *Math.* a curve described by the equation $y = \sin x$, the ordinate being equal to the sine of the abscissa. [1900–05]

si·ne di·e (sī′nē dī′ē, sin′ā dē′ā; *Lat.* si′ne dē′e), without fixing a day for future action or meeting: *The assembly adjourned sine die.* [< L *sine diē* without (a fixed) day]

Si·ne·met (sī′nə met′), *Pharm., Trademark.* a brand name for a tablet preparation used in the symptomatic treatment of parkinsonism.

si·ne pro·le (sī′nē prō′lē, sin′ā), *Law.* without offspring or progeny: *to die sine prole.* [< L]

si·ne qua non (sī′nē kwā non′, kwä, sin′ā; *Lat.* si′ne kwä nōn′), an indispensable condition, element, or factor; something essential: *Her presence was the sine qua non of every social event.* [< LL *sine quā* (*causā*) *nōn* without which (thing) not]

sin·ew (sin′yōō), *n.* **1.** a tendon. **2.** Often, **sinews.** the source of strength, power, or vigor: *the sinews of the nation.* **3.** strength; power; resilience: *a man of great moral sinew.* —*v.t.* **4.** to furnish with sinews; strengthen, as by sinews. [bef. 900; ME; OE *sinu* (nom.), *sinuwe* (gen.); c. D *zenuw,* G *Sehne,* ON *sin;* akin to Skt *snāva* sinew] —**sin′ew·less,** *adj.*

sine′ wave′, *Physics.* a periodic oscillation, as simple harmonic motion, having the same geometric representation as a sine function. [1890–95]

sin·ew·y (sin′yōō ē), *adj.* **1.** having strong sinews: *a sinewy back.* **2.** of or like sinews; tough, firm, braided, or resilient: *a sinewy rope.* **3.** having conspicuous sinews; stringy: *tough, sinewy meat.* **4.** vigorous or forceful, as language, style, etc.: *a sinewy argument.* [1350–1400; ME; see SINEW, -Y[1]] —**sin′ew·i·ness,** *n.*

Sin·fjot·li (sin′fyôt′lē), *n.* (in the *Volsunga Saga*) the son of Signy by her brother Sigmund. [< ON *Sinfjǫtli;* etym. uncert.; cf. OHG *Sintarvizzilo* personal name]

sin·fo·ni·a (sin′fō nē′ə; *It.* sēn′fô nē′ä), *n., pl.* **-ni·as, -ni·e** (-nē′ā; *It.* -nē′e). *Music.* a symphony. [1880–85; < It; see SYMPHONY]

sin·fo·niet·ta (sin′fən yet′ə, -fōn-), *n.* **1.** a short symphony. **2.** a small symphony orchestra, often composed solely of stringed instruments. **3.** a symphony for fewer than the usual number of instruments. [1920–25; < It; dim. of *sinfonia* SINFONIA]

sin·ful (sin′fəl), *adj.* characterized by, guilty of, or full of sin; wicked: *a sinful life.* [bef. 900; ME; OE *synfull.* See SIN[1], -FUL] —**sin′ful·ly,** *adv.* —**sin′ful·ness,** *n.*
—**Syn.** iniquitous, depraved, evil, immoral, corrupt.

sing (sing), *v.,* **sang** or, often, **sung; sung; sing·ing;** *n.* —*v.i.* **1.** to utter words or sounds in succession with musical modulations of the voice; vocalize melodically. **2.** to perform a song or voice composition: *She promised to sing for us.* **3.** to produce melodious sounds, usually high in pitch, as certain birds, insects, etc.: *The nightingale sang in the tree.* **4.** to compose poetry: *Keats sang briefly but gloriously.* **5.** to tell about or praise someone or something in verse or song: *He sang of the warrior's prowess.* **6.** to admit of being sung, as verses: *This lyric sings well.* **7.** to give out a continuous ringing, whistling, murmuring, burbling, or other euphonious sound, as a teakettle or a brook. **8.** to make a short whistling, ringing, or whizzing sound: *The bullet sang past his ear.* **9.** (of an electrical amplifying system) to produce an undesired self-sustained oscillation. **10.** to have the sensation of a ringing or humming sound, as the ears. **11.** *Slang.* to confess or act as an informer; squeal. —*v.t.* **12.** to utter with musical modulations of the voice, as a song. **13.** to escort or accompany with singing. **14.** to proclaim enthusiastically. **15.** to bring, send, put, etc., with or by singing: *She sang the baby to sleep.* **16.** to chant or intone: *to sing mass.* **17.** to tell or praise in verse or song. **18. sing out,** *Informal.* to call in a loud voice; shout: *They lost their way in the cavern and sang out for help.* —*n.* **19.** the act or performance of singing. **20.** a gathering or meeting of persons for the purpose of singing: *a community sing.* **21.** a singing, ringing, or whistling sound, as of a bullet. [bef. 900; ME *singen,* OE *singan;* c. D *zingen,* G *singen,* ON *syngva,* Goth *siggwan*] —**sing′a·ble,** *adj.* —**sing′a·bil′i·ty, sing′a·ble·ness,** *n.* —**sing′ing·ly,** *adv.*

sing., singular.

sing-a·long (sing′ə lông′, -long′), *n.* **1.** an informal or unrehearsed singing of songs by a group of people, usually under the direction of a leader; songfest. **2.** an occasion marked by such singing. Also, **sing′a·long′.** [1955–60; n. use of v. phrase *sing along*]

Si·ngan (*Chin.* sē′ngän′), *n. Older Spelling.* Xian.

Sin·ga·pore (sing′gə pôr′, -pōr′, sing′ə-), *n.* **1.** an island on the Strait of Singapore, off the S tip of the Malay Peninsula. **2.** an independent republic comprising this island and a few adjacent islets: member of the Commonwealth of Nations; formerly a British crown colony (1946–59) and member of the federation of Malaysia (1963–65). 2,300,000; 220 sq. mi. (570 sq. km). *Cap.:* Singapore. **3.** a seaport in and the capital of this republic. 1,400,000. —**Sin′ga·po′re·an,** *n., adj.*

Sin′gapore sling′, a cocktail of gin, cherry brandy, sugar, and water. [1925–30]

singe (sinj), *v.,* **singed, singe·ing,** *n.* —*v.t.* **1.** to burn superficially or slightly; scorch. **2.** to burn the ends, projections, nap, or the like, of (hair, cloth, etc.). **3.** to subject (the carcass of an animal or bird) to flame in order to remove hair, bristles, feathers, etc. —*n.* **4.** a superficial burn. **5.** the act of singeing. [bef. 1000; ME *sengen* (v.), OE *sencgan;* c. D *zengen,* G *sengen;* akin to ON *sangr* singed, burnt] —**singe′ing·ly,** *adv.*
—**Syn. 1.** char. See **burn**[1].

sing·er[1] (sing′ər), *n.* **1.** a person who sings, esp. a trained or professional vocalist. **2.** a poet. **3.** a singing bird. [1300–50; ME; see SING, -ER[1]]

sing·er[2] (sin′jər), *n.* a person or thing that singes. [1870–75; SINGE + -ER[1]]

Sing·er (sing′ər), *n.* **1. Isaac Ba·shev·is** (bä shev′is), 1904–91, U.S. novelist and short-story writer (in Yiddish), born in Poland: Nobel prize 1978. **2. Isaac Mer·rit** (mer′it), 1811–75, U.S. inventor.

Singh., Singhalese.

Sin·gha·lese (sing′gə lēz′, -lēs′), *adj., n., pl.* **-lese.** Sinhalese.

sing·ing·fish (sing′ing fish′), *n., pl.* (*esp. collectively*) **-fish,** (*esp. referring to two or more kinds or species*) **-fish·es.** midshipman (def. 3). [1880–85, *Amer.*; SINGING + FISH; so called because of the humming sound it produces with its air bladder]

sing′ing game′, a children's game in which the players perform certain actions to the words of a song. [1880–85]

sin·gle (sing′gəl), *adj., v.,* **-gled, -gling,** *n.* —*adj.* **1.** only one in number; one only; unique; sole: *a single example.* **2.** of, pertaining to, or suitable for one person only: *a single room.* **3.** solitary or sole; lone: *He was the single survivor.* **4.** unmarried: *a single man.* **5.** pertaining to the unmarried state: *the single life.* **6.** of one against one, as combat or fight. **7.** consisting of only one part, element, or member: *a single lens.* **8.** sincere and undivided: *single devotion.* **9.** separate, particular, or distinct; individual: *Every single one of you must do your best. It's the single most important thing.* **10.** uniform; applicable to all: *a single safety code for all manufacturers.* **11.** (of a bed or bedclothes) twin-size. **12.** (of a flower) having only one set of petals. **13.** *Brit.* of standard strength or body, as ale, beer, etc. Cf. **double** (def. 1). **14.** (of the eye) seeing rightly. —*v.t.* **15.** to pick or choose (one) from others (usually fol. by *out*): *to single out a fact for special mention.* **16.** *Baseball.* **a.** to cause the advance of (a base runner) by a one-base hit. **b.** to cause (a run) to be scored by a one-base hit (often fol. by *in* or *home*). —*v.i.* **17.** *Baseball.* to hit a single. —*n.* **18.** one person or thing; a single one. **19.** an accommodation suitable for one person only, as a hotel room or a table at a restaurant: *to reserve a single.* **20.** a ticket for a single seat at a theater. **21.** *Brit.* **a.** a one-way ticket. **b.** a steam locomotive having one driving wheel on each side. **22.** an unmarried person, esp. one who is relatively young. **23.** *Baseball.* Also called **one-base hit.** a base hit that enables a batter to reach first base safely. **24. singles,** (*used with a singular v.*) a match with one player on each side, as a tennis match. **25.** *Golf.* twosome (def. 4). **26.** *Cricket.* a hit for which one run is scored. **27.** *Informal.* a one-dollar bill. **28.** a phonograph record usually played at 45 r.p.m. and often having one popular song on each side. **29.** the song recorded on one side of a single. **30.** Often, **singles.** *Textiles.* **a.** reeled or spun silk that may or may not be thrown. **b.** a one-ply yarn of any fiber that has been drawn and twisted. [1275–1325; late ME (adj.), ME *sengle* < OF < L *singulus* individual, single, (pl.) one apiece, deriv. of **sem-* one (see SIMPLEX)]
—Syn. 1. distinct, particular. **3.** isolated. **4.** unwed. **15.** select. **18.** individual.

sin·gle-act·ing (sing′gəl ak′ting), *adj.* (of a reciprocating engine, pump, etc.) having pistons accomplishing work only in one direction. Cf. **double-acting** (def. 1). [1815–25]

sin·gle-ac·tion (sing′gəl ak′shən), *adj.* (of a firearm) requiring the cocking of the hammer before firing each shot: *a single-action revolver.* [1850–55]

sin·gle-bar·rel (sing′gəl bar′əl), *n.* a gun having one barrel, esp. a shotgun. [1840–50] **—sin′gle-bar′reled;** *esp. Brit.,* **sin′gle-bar′relled,** *adj.*

sin·gle-blind (sing′gəl blīnd′), *adj.* of or pertaining to an experiment or clinical trial in which the researchers but not the subjects know which subjects are receiving the active medication or treatment and which are not: a technique for eliminating subjective bias, as the placebo effect, from the test results. Cf. **double-blind.** [1960–65]

sin′gle bond′, *Chem.* a chemical linkage consisting of one covalent bond between two atoms of a molecule, represented in chemical formulas by one line or two vertical dots, as C–H or C:H.

sin·gle-breast·ed (sing′gəl bres′tid), *adj.* **1.** (of a coat, jacket, etc.) having a front closure directly in the center with only a narrow overlap secured by a single button or row of buttons. **2.** (of a suit) having a jacket or coat of this type. Cf. **double-breasted.** [1790–1800]

sin′gle bu′oy moor′ing, *Naut.* monobuoy.

sin′gle com′bat, combat between two persons. [1600–10]

sin·gle-cross (sing′gəl krôs′, -kros′), *n. Genetics.* a cross between two inbred lines. [1935–40]

sin′gle cut′, *Jewelry.* a simple form of brilliant cut, having eight facets above and eight facets below the girdle, as well as the table, and usually a culet. Also called **eight cut, Old English cut.** [1825–35]

sin·gle-cut (sing′gəl kut′), *adj.* noting a file having a series of parallel cutting ridges in one direction only. Cf. **double-cut.**

sin·gle-dig·it (sing′gəl dij′it), *adj.* of or denoting a percentage smaller than ten, esp. with reference to rates below that level: *single-digit rates of inflation.*

sin·gle-end·ed (sing′gəl en′did), *adj.* **1.** (of a boiler) fired from one end only. **2.** *Elect.* (of a circuit or transmission line) unbalanced, as when one part of a circuit is grounded.

sin′gle en′try, *Bookkeeping.* **1.** an item noted only once. **2.** a simple accounting system noting only amounts owed by and due to a business. Cf. **double entry.** [1820–30] **—sin′gle-en′try,** *adj.*

sin′gle file′, a line of persons or things arranged one behind the other; Indian file. [1660–70]

sin·gle-foot (sing′gəl fo͝ot′), *n.* **1.** rack[3] (def. 1). —*v.i.* **2.** (of a horse) to go at a rack. [1860–65, *Amer.*]

sin·gle-hand·ed (sing′gəl han′did), *adj.* **1.** accomplished or done by one person alone: *a single-handed victory; single-handed sailing.* **2.** by one's own effort; unaided. —*adv.* **3.** by oneself; alone; without aid: *He built the garage single-handed.* [1700–10] **—sin′gle-hand′ed·ness,** *n.*

sin·gle-hand·ed·ly (sing′gəl han′did lē), *adv.* in a single-handed manner; single-handed. [1880–85]

sin·gle-heart·ed (sing′gəl här′tid), *adj.* sincere and undivided in feeling or spirit; dedicated; not reflecting mixed emotions: *He was single-hearted in his patriotism.* [1570–80] **—sin′gle-heart′ed·ly,** *adv.* **—sin′gle-heart′ed·ness,** *n.*

sin·gle·hood (sing′gəl ho͝od′), *n.* the status of being unmarried. [1830–40; SINGLE + -HOOD]

sin·gle-hung (sing′gəl hung′), *adj.* (of a window) having two sashes, only one of which is movable. [1815–25]

sin·gle-knit (sing′gəl nit′), *n.* **1.** a fabric made on warp knit. **2.** a garment made of single-knit.

sin′gle knot′. See **overhand knot.** [1925–30]

sin′gle-lens re′flex cam′era (sing′gəl lenz′). See under **reflex camera.** *Abbr.:* SLR Also called **sin′gle-lens re′flex.**

sin′gle man′, *Checkers.* an individual checker restricted to forward moves, as contrasted with a king.

sin·gle-mind·ed (sing′gəl mīn′did), *adj.* **1.** having or showing a single aim or purpose: *a single-minded program.* **2.** dedicated; resolute; steadfast: *He was single-minded in his concern for truth.* [1570–80] **—sin′gle-mind′ed·ly,** *adv.* **—sin′gle-mind′ed·ness,** *n.*
—Syn. 2. determined, persevering, inflexible, firm.

sin′gle mod′al, *Transp.* modal (def. 3).

sin′gle-name pa′per (sing′gəl nām′), *Banking.* commercial paper bearing only the signature of the maker.

sin·gle·ness (sing′gəl nis), *n.* the state or quality of being single. [1520–30; SINGLE + -NESS]

sin′gle oc′cupancy, a type of travel accommodation, as at a hotel, for one person in a room. Cf. **double occupancy. —sin′gle-oc′cu·pan·cy,** *adj.*

sin·gle-phase (sing′gəl fāz′), *adj. Elect.* noting or pertaining to a circuit having an alternating current with one phase or with phases differing by 180°. [1895–1900]

sin′gle point′ moor′ing, *Naut.* monobuoy. [1975–80]

sin′gle preci′sion, *Computers.* using one word rather than two or more to represent a number. Cf. **double precision.**

sin′gle pre′mium, a single payment that covers the entire cost of an insurance policy. [1875–80]

sin′gle quotes′, (one pair of single quotation marks, written as (' ') and used esp. for a quotation within another quotation): *He said, "I told you to say 'Open, sesame' when you want to enter the mountain."*

sin′gle rhyme′, a rhyme of monosyllables, as in *heart, part.*

sin′gles bar′, a bar or tavern catering to a clientele composed chiefly of single men and women, esp. those seeking a lover or spouse. Also called **dating bar.** [1965–70]

sin′gle sculls′, a race for sculls each rowed by one oarsman using a pair of oars. Cf. **double sculls.**

sin·gle-sex (sing′gəl seks′), *adj.* designated for, pertaining to, or serving only males or only females: *a single-sex college.* [1935–40]

sin·gle-shot (sing′gəl shot′), *adj.* (of a firearm) requiring loading before each shot; not having or using a cartridge magazine. [1885–90, *Amer.*]

sin·gle-space (sing′gəl spās′), *v.,* **-spaced, -spac·ing.** —*v.t.* **1.** to type (copy) on each line space. —*v.i.* **2.** to type copy leaving no blank spaces between lines. [1935–40]

sin′gle Span′ish bur′ton, a tackle having a runner as well as the fall supporting the load, giving a mechanical advantage of three, neglecting friction. See diag. under **tackle.**

sin′gle stand′ard, 1. a single set of principles or rules applying to everyone, as a single moral code applying to both men and women, esp. in sexual behavior. Cf. **double standard. 2.** monometallism. [1880–85, *Amer.*]

sin·gle·stick (sing′gəl stik′), *n.* **1.** a short, heavy stick. **2.** (formerly) **a.** a wooden stick held in one hand, used instead of a sword in fencing. **b.** fencing with such a stick. [1765–75; SINGLE + STICK[1]]

sin·gle·stick·er (sing′gəl stik′ər), *n. Informal.* a vessel, esp. a sloop or cutter, having one mast. [1885–90; SINGLE + STICK[1] + -ER[1]]

sin·gle-suit·er (sing′gəl so͞o′tər), *n.* one-suiter. [*single suit* + -ER[1]]

sin·glet (sing′glit), *n.* **1.** a sleeveless athletic jersey, esp. a loose-fitting top worn by runners, joggers, etc. **2.** a single unit; an unpaired or separate item. **3.** *Chiefly Brit.* a man's undershirt or jersey. [1740–50; SINGLE + -ET]

sin′gle tape′. See under **magnetic tape.**

sin′gle tax′, *Econ.* a tax, as on land, that constitutes the sole source of public revenue. [1875–80, *Amer.*] **—sin′gle-tax′,** *adj.*

sin′gle tick′et, *Brit.* a one-way ticket.

sin·gle·ton (sing′gəl tən), *n.* **1.** a person or thing occurring singly, esp. an individual set apart from others: *a research program involving twins and singletons.* **2.** *Cards.* a card that is the only one of a suit in a hand. **3.** *Math.* a set consisting of one given element. [1875–80; SINGLE + -TON]

sin·gle-track (sing′gəl trak′), *adj.* **1.** (of a railroad or section of a railroad's route) having but one set of tracks, so that trains going in opposite directions must be scheduled to meet only at points where there are sidings. **2.** having a narrow scope; one-track: *He has a single-track mind.* [1825–35, *Amer.*]

sin·gle·tree (sing′gəl trē′), *n.* whiffletree. [1835–45, *Amer.*; var. of SWINGLETREE]

sin·gle-val·ued (sing′gəl val′yo͞od), *adj. Math.* (of a function) having the property that each element in the domain has corresponding to it exactly one element in the range. Cf. **many-valued.** [1875–80]

sin′gle whip′. See under **whip** (def. 27).

sin′gle wick′et, a rare form of cricket in which only one wicket is used. [1730–40]

sin′gle wing′back forma′tion, *Football.* an offensive formation in which the wingback lines up outside of and about one yard behind an end, the quarterback lines up lateral to the wingback but about midway between the same end and the center, the fullback is three or four yards behind the middle of the line, and the tailback lines up one yard behind the fullback on the other side of the line from the wingback and quarterback. Also called **sin′gle wing′.** Cf. **double wingback formation.** [1905–10, *Amer.*]

sin·gly (sing′glē), *adv.* **1.** apart from others; separately. **2.** one at a time; as single units. **3.** single-handed; alone. [1250–1300; ME *sengley.* See SINGLE, -LY]

Sing Sing (sing′ sing′), **1.** the state prison at Ossining, New York. **2.** former name of **Ossining.**

sing·song (sing′sông′, -song′), *n.* **1.** verse, or a piece of verse, that is monotonously jingly in rhythm and pattern of pitch. **2.** monotonous rhythmical cadence, tone, or sound. **3.** *Brit.* an unrehearsed singing of well-known songs by an audience or other informal, untrained group; a community sing. —*adj.* **4.** monotonous in rhythm and in pitch. [1600–10; SING + SONG]

sing·spiel (sing′spēl′; *Ger.* zing′shpēl′), *n.* a German opera, esp. of the 18th century, using spoken dialogue and resembling ballad opera. [1880–85; < G, equiv. to *sing(en)* to SING + *Spiel* play]

sin·gu·lar (sing′gyə lər), *adj.* **1.** extraordinary; remarkable; exceptional: *a singular success.* **2.** unusual or strange; odd; different: *singular behavior.* **3.** being the only one of its kind; distinctive; unique: *a singular example.* **4.** separate; individual. **5.** *Gram.* noting or pertaining to a member of the category of number found in many languages that indicates that a word form has one referent or denotes one person, place, thing, or instance, as English *boy* and *thing,* which are singular nouns, or *goes,* a singular form of the verb *go.* Cf. **dual** (def. 4), **plural** (def. 4). **6.** *Logic.* **a.** of or pertaining to something individual, specific, or not general. **b.** (of a proposition) containing no quantifiers, as "Socrates was mortal." **7.** *Math.* **a.** of or pertaining to a linear transformation from a vector space to itself that is not one-to-one. **b.** of or pertaining to a matrix having a determinant equal to zero. **8.** *Obs.* private. **9.** *Obs.* single. —*n. Gram.* **10.** the singular number. **11.** a form in the singular. [1300–50; ME < L *singulāris.* See SINGLE, -AR[1]] **—sin′gu·lar·ly,** *adv.* **—sin′gu·lar·ness,** *n.*
—Syn. 1–4. peculiar. **2.** bizarre, queer, curious. **3.** uncommon, rare. **4.** single. **—Ant. 1.** usual.

sin·gu·lar·i·ty (sing′gyə lar′i tē), *n., pl.* **-ties** for 2–4. **1.** the state, fact, or quality of being singular. **2.** a singular, unusual, or unique quality; peculiarity. **3.** *Math.* See **singular point. 4.** *Astron.* (in general relativity) the mathematical representation of a black hole. [1300–50; ME *singularite* < LL *singulāritās.* See SINGULAR, -ITY]

sin·gu·lar·ize (sing′gyə lə rīz′), *v.t.,* **-ized, -iz·ing.** to make singular. Also, *esp. Brit.,* **sin′gu·lar·ise′.** [1580–90; SINGULAR + -IZE] **—sin′gu·lar·i·za′tion,** *n.*

sin′gular point′, *Math.* a point at which a given function of a complex variable has no derivative but of which every neighborhood contains points at which the function has derivatives. Also called **singularity.** [1885–90]

sin·gul·tus (sing gul′təs), *n., pl.* **-tus·es.** *Med.* a hiccup. Also, **sin·gul·ta·tion** (sing′gəl tā′shən). [1745–55; < L: sob, dying breath, hiccup] **—sin·gul′tous,** *adj.*

sinh (sinch), *n. Math.* hyperbolic sine. [SIN(E) + H(YPERBOLIC)]

Sin·hai·lien (*Chin.* shin′hī′lyun′), *n. Older Spelling.* Xinhailian.

Sin·ha·lese (sin′hə lēz′, -lēs′), *adj., n., pl.* **-lese** for 2. —*adj.* **1.** of or pertaining to Sri Lanka, its native people, or their language. —*n.* **2.** a member of the Sinhalese people. **3.** an Indic language that is the language of the majority of the population of Sri Lanka, including Colombo. Also, **Singhalese.**

Sin·i·cism (sin′ə siz′əm), *n.* something characteristic of or peculiar to the Chinese; a Chinese method, custom, or usage. [1890–95; *Sinic* Chinese (< ML *Sinicus* < MGk *Sinikós,* equiv. to LGk *Sîn(ai)* the Chinese + *-ikos* -IC) + -ISM; see SINO-]

Sin·i·cize (sin′ə sīz′), *v.t.,* **-cized, -ciz·ing.** to make Chinese in character or bring under Chinese influence. Also, *esp. Brit.,* **Sin′i·cise′.** [1885–90; *Sinic* (see SINICISM) + -IZE] **—Sin·i·ci·za·tion** (sin′ə sə zā′shən), *n.*

Sin·i·fy (sin′ə fī′), *v.t.,* **-fied, -fy·ing.** to Sinicize. [1895–1900; < LL *Sin(ae)* the Chinese (see SINO-) + -IFY] **—Sin·i·fi·ca·tion** (sin′ə fi kā′shən), *n.*

sin·i·grin (sin′i grin), *n. Chem.* a colorless, crystalline, water-soluble solid, $KC_{10}H_{16}NO_9S_2{\cdot}H_2O$, found chiefly in the seeds of the black mustard, that deters some insect predators. Also called **potassium myronate.** [1875–80;

< NL *Sin(apis n)igr(a)* species yielding black mustard seed (lit., black mustard; see SINAPINE, NEGRO) + -IN[2]

Si·ning (shē′ning′), *n. Older Spelling.* Xining. Also, **Hsining.**

sin·is·ter (sin′ə stər), *adj.* **1.** threatening or portending evil, harm, or trouble; ominous: *a sinister remark.* **2.** bad, evil, base, or wicked; fell: *his sinister purposes.* **3.** unfortunate; disastrous; unfavorable: *a sinister accident.* **4.** of or on the left side; left. **5.** *Heraldry.* noting the side of an escutcheon or achievement of arms that is to the left of the bearer (opposed to *dexter*). [1375–1425; late ME < L: on the left hand or side, hence unfavorable, injurious] —**sin′is·ter·ly,** *adv.* —**sin′is·ter·ness,** *n.*
—**Syn. 1.** inauspicious, portentous. **3.** unlucky.
—**Ant. 1.** benign. **3.** favorable.

sin·is·tral (sin′ə strəl), *adj.* **1.** of, pertaining to, or on the left side; left (opposed to *dextral*). **2.** left-handed. **3.** (of certain gastropod shells) coiling counterclockwise, as seen from the apex. [1425–75; late ME < ML *sinistrālis.* See SINISTER, -AL[1]] —**sin′is·tral·ly,** *adv.*

sin·is·tral·i·ty (sin′ə stral′i tē), *n.* **1.** the state or quality of having the left side or its parts or members different from and, usually, more efficient than the right side or its parts or members; left-handedness. **2.** preference for using the left hand or side. **3.** the state of being sinistral. Cf. **dextrality.** [1850–55; SINISTRAL + -ITY]

sin·is·tra·tion (sin′ə strā′shən), *n.* the quality or state of being left-handed. [1890–95; SINISTR- + -ATION]

sinistro-, a combining form meaning "left, on the left," used in the formation of compound words: *sinistrodextral.* [< L *sinistr-*, s. of *sinister* (see SINISTER) + -O-]

sin·is·troc·u·lar (sin′ə strok′yə lər), *adj. Ophthalm.* favoring the left eye, rather than the right, by habit or for effective vision (opposed to *dextrocular*). [SINISTR(O)- + OCULAR] —**sin′is·troc′u·lar′i·ty,** *n.*

sin·is·tro·dex·tral (sin′ə strō deks′trəl, si nis′trō-), *adj.* moving or extending from the left to the right. [SINISTRO- + DEXTRAL]

sin·is·trorse (sin′ə strôrs′, si nis′trôrs, sin′ə strôrs′), *adj. Bot.* (from a point of view at the center of the spiral) rising spirally in a counterclockwise manner, as a stem (opposed to *dextrorse*). [1855–60; < L *sinistrōrsus* lit., turned leftwards, contr. of **sinistriversus.* See SINISTER, VERSUS] —**sin·is·trorse·ly** (sin′ə strôrs′lē, sin′ə-strôrs′-), *adv.*

sin·is·trous (sin′ə strəs), *adj.* **1.** ill-omened; unlucky; disastrous. **2.** sinistral; left. [1550–60; < L *sinistr-*, s. of *sinister* (see SINISTER) + -OUS] —**sin′is·trous·ly,** *adv.*

Si·nit·ic (si nit′ik), *n.* **1.** a branch of Sino-Tibetan consisting of the various local languages and dialects whose speakers share literary Chinese as their standard language. —*adj.* **2.** of or pertaining to the Chinese, their language, or their culture. [1890–95; < LL *Sīn(ae)* the Chinese (see SINO-) + -ITIC]

sink (singk), *v.,* **sank** or, often, **sunk; sunk** or **sunk·en; sink·ing;** *n.* —*v.i.* **1.** to displace part of the volume of a supporting substance or object and become totally or partially submerged or enveloped; fall or descend into or below the surface or to the bottom (often fol. by *in* or *into*): *The battleship sank within two hours. His foot sank in the mud. Her head sinks into the pillows.* **2.** to fall, drop, or descend gradually to a lower level: *The river sank two feet during the dry spell.* **3.** to settle or fall gradually, as a heavy structure: *The tower is slowly sinking.* **4.** to fall or collapse slowly from weakness, fatigue, distress, etc.: *He gasped and sank to his knees.* **5.** to slope downward; dip: *The field sinks toward the highway.* **6.** to go down toward or below the horizon: *the sun sinks in the west.* **7.** to penetrate, permeate, or seep (usually fol. by *in* or *into*): *Wipe the oil off before it sinks into the wood.* **8.** to become engulfed or absorbed in or gradually to enter a state (usually fol. by *in* or *into*): *to sink into slumber.* **9.** to be or become deeply absorbed or involved in a mood or mental state (usually fol. by *in* or *into*): *sunk in thought. She sank into despair.* **10.** to pass or fall into some lower state, as of fortune, estimation, etc.; degenerate: *to sink into poverty.* **11.** to decline or deteriorate in quality or worth. **12.** to fail in physical strength or health. **13.** to decrease in amount, extent, intensity, etc.: *The temperature sank to 30° at noon.* **14.** to become lower in volume, tone, or pitch: *Her voice sank to a whisper.* **15.** to enter or permeate the mind; become known or understood (usually fol. by *in* or *into*): *He said it four times before the words really sank in.* **16.** to become concave; become hollow, as the cheeks. **17.** to drop or fall gradually into a lower position: *He sank down on the bench.*
—*v.t.* **18.** to cause to become submerged or enveloped; force into or below the surface; cause to plunge in or down: *The submarine sank the battleship. He sank his fist into the pillow.* **19.** to cause to fall, drop, or descend gradually. **20.** to cause to penetrate: *to sink an ax into a tree trunk.* **21.** to lower or depress the level of: *They sank the roadway by five feet.* **22.** to bury, plant, or lay (a pipe, conduit, etc.) into or as if into the ground. **23.** to dig, bore, or excavate (a hole, shaft, well, etc.). **24.** to bring to a worse or lower state or status. **25.** to bring to utter ruin or collapse: *Drinking and gambling sank him completely.* **26.** to reduce in amount, extent, intensity, etc. **27.** to lower in volume, tone, or pitch. **28.** to suppress; ignore; omit. **29.** to invest in the hope of making a profit or gaining some other return: *He sank all his efforts into the business.* **30.** to lose (money) in an unfortunate investment, enterprise, etc. **31.** *Sports.* **a.** to throw, shoot, hit, or propel (a ball) so that it goes through or into the basket, hole, pocket, etc.: *She sank the 10 ball into the side pocket.* **b.** to execute (a stroke or throw) so that the ball goes through or into the basket, hole, pocket, etc.: *to sink a putt; to sink a free throw.* **32. sink one's teeth into, a.** to bite deeply or vigorously. **b.** to do or enter into with great enthusiasm, concentration, conviction, etc.: *to sink my teeth into solving the problem.*
—*n.* **33.** a basin or receptacle, as in a kitchen or laundry, usually connected with a water supply and drainage system, for washing dishes, clothing, etc. **34.** a low-lying, poorly drained area where waters collect and sink into the ground or evaporate. **35.** sinkhole (def. 2). **36.** a place of vice or corruption. **37.** a drain or sewer. **38.** a device or place for disposing of energy within a system, as a power-consuming device in an electrical circuit or a condenser in a steam engine. **39.** any pond or pit for sewage or waste, as a cesspool or a pool for industrial wastes. **40.** any natural process by which contaminants are removed from the atmosphere. [bef. 1000; (v.) ME *sinken,* OE *sincan;* c. D *zinken,* G *sinken,* ON *sǫkkva,* Goth *singkwan;* (n.) late ME: cesspool, deriv. of the v.] —**sink′a·ble,** *adj.* —**sink′like′,** *adj.*

sink·age (sing′kij), *n.* **1.** the act, process, amount, or degree of sinking. **2.** a surface sunk for decorative effect. **3.** *Print.* **a.** the lowering of the first line of body text on a page from its usual position, as at the beginning of a chapter. **b.** the amount of such lowering. [1880–85; SINK + -AGE]

sink·er (sing′kər), *n.* **1.** a person or thing that sinks. **2.** a person employed in sinking, as one who sinks shafts. **3.** a weight, as of lead, for sinking a fishing line or net below the surface of the water. **4.** *Slang.* a doughnut or, sometimes, a biscuit or muffin. **5.** *Baseball.* a pitched ball that curves downward sharply as it reaches the plate. [1520–30; 1920–25 for def. 4; 1925–30 for def. 5; SINK + -ER[1]] —**sink′er·less,** *adj.*

sink·hole (singk′hōl′), *n.* **1.** a hole formed in soluble rock by the action of water, serving to conduct surface water to an underground passage. **2.** Also called **sink.** a depressed area in which waste or drainage collects. [1425–75; late ME; see SINK, HOLE]

Sin·kiang Ui·ghur (*Chin.* shin′jyäng′ wē′gər). See **Xinjiang Uygur.**

sink′ing fund′, a fund to extinguish an indebtedness, usually a bond issue. [1715–25]

sink′ing spell′, a temporary decline, as in health or market values: *Wall Street is over its sinking spell.*

sink·less (singk′lis), *adj.* unsinkable, as a ship. [SINK + -LESS]

sin·less (sin′lis), *adj.* free from or without sin. [bef. 900; ME *sinles,* OE *synlēas.* See SIN[1], -LESS] —**sin′less·ly,** *adv.* —**sin′less·ness,** *n.*

sin·ner (sin′ər), *n.* a person who sins; transgressor. [1275–1325; ME; see SIN[1], -ER[1]]

sin·net (sin′it), *n.* sennit.

Sinn Fein (shin′ fān′), **1.** a political organization in Ireland, founded about 1905, advocating the complete political separation from Great Britain of a unified Ireland. **2.** a member of this organization. [< Ir *sinn féin* we ourselves] —**Sinn′ Fein′er.** —**Sinn′ Fein′ism.**

sin·nin·gi·a (si nin′jē ə), *n.* any of various tropical American plants belonging to the genus *Sinningia,* of the gesneria family, including the gloxinia and other species cultivated as houseplants for their variously colored flowers. [< NL (1825), after Wilhelm *Sinning* (1794–1874), German horticulturist; see -IA]

sino-, a combining form representing **sinus** in compound words: *sinorespiratory.*

Sino-, a combining form meaning "Chinese": *Sino-Tibetan; Sinology.* [< NL, comb. form repr. LL *Sīnae* the Chinese < LGk *Sînai* << Chin *Qin* CH'IN]

si′no·a′tri·al node′ (sī′nō ā′trē əl, si′-), *Anat.* a small mass of tissue in the right atrium functioning as pacemaker of the heart by giving rise to the electric impulses that initiate heart contractions. Also called **sinus node.** [1920–25; SINO- + ATRIAL]

Si′no-Jap′a·nese War′ (sī′nō jap′ə nēz′, -nēs′, -jap′ə nēz′, -nēs′), **1.** the war (1894–95) between China and Japan over the control of Korea that resulted in the nominal independence of Korea and the Chinese cession to Japan of Formosa and the Pescadores. **2.** the war that began in 1937 as a Japanese invasion of China and ended with the World War II defeat of Japan in 1945.

Si·nol·o·gist (si nol′ə jist, si-), *n.* a person who specializes in Sinology. Also, **Si·no·logue** (sīn′l ôg′, -og′, sin′-). [1830–40; *Sinologue* (see SINO-, -LOGUE) + -IST]

Si·nol·o·gy (sī nol′ə jē, si-), *n.* the study of the language, literature, history, customs, etc., of China. [1880–85; SINO- + -LOGY; cf. F, G *sinologie*] —**Si·no·log·i·cal** (sin′l oj′i kəl, sin′-), *adj.*

Si·non (sī′non), *n.* a Greek, posing as a deserter, who persuaded the Trojans to take the Trojan Horse into their city.

Si·no·pe (sə nō′pē), *n. Astron.* a natural satellite of the planet Jupiter.

Si·no·phile (sī′nə fīl′, sin′ə-), *n.* **1.** a person who admires or has a strong liking for China, the Chinese, or their culture. —*adj.* **2.** friendly to or having a strong liking for China or the Chinese. Also, **Si·no·phil** (sī′nə-fil, sin′ə-). [1895–1900; SINO- + -PHILE]

sin·o·pis (sin′ə pəs, si nō′pəs), *n.* a red ocher, used from antiquity to the Middle Ages. Also, **si·no·pi·a** (si-nō′pē ə), **sin·o·per** (sin′ə pər). [< L *Sinōpis* ocher found in Sinope, Greek colony in Paphlagonia; cf. late ME *synopre* << L]

si·no·res·pi·ra·to·ry (sī′nō res′pər ə tôr′ē, -tōr′ē, -ri spī³r′ə-), *adj. Anat.* of, pertaining to, or affecting the paranasal sinuses and the respiratory tract. [SINO- + RESPIRATORY]

Si·no-Ti·bet·an (sī′nō ti bet′n, sin′ō-), *n.* a family of languages including esp. Burmese, Tibetan, and the various local languages and dialects whose speakers share literary Chinese as their standard language. [1915–20; SINO- + TIBETAN]

SINS (sinz), *n.* a gyroscopic device indicating the exact speed and position of a vessel, as indicated by differences in positions over a given period on a given course, as well as the direction of true north. [*s(hip's) i(nertial) n(avigation) s(ystem)*]

sin·se·mil·la (sin′sə mil′ə), *n.* marijuana from seedless female hemp plants that contain very high levels of THC. [1975–80; < AmerSp, equiv. to Sp *sin* without (< L *sine*) + *semilla* seed, appar. continuation of OSp dial. *semilia,* by dissimilation from LL *sēminia,* neut. pl. (taken as fem. sing.) of *sēminium,* deriv. of L *sēmen* seed, SEMEN]

Sin·siang (*Chin.* shin′shyäng′), *n. Older Spelling.* Xinxiang.

sin·syne (sin′sīn), *adv. Scot. and North Eng.* from that time; since then. [1325–75; Scots and N dial. *sin* subsequent to, after (ME, var. of *sithen,* OE *siththan* SITH) + SYNE; r. ME (Scots) *sensyne* (*sen,* var. of *sethen,* var. of *sithen;* see SINCE)]

sin′ tax′, *Informal.* a tax levied on cigarettes, liquor, gambling, or other things considered neither luxuries nor necessities. [1970–75]

sin·ter (sin′tər), *n.* **1.** siliceous or calcareous matter deposited by springs, as that formed around the vent of a geyser. **2.** *Metall.* the product of a sintering operation. —*v.t.* **3.** *Metall.* to bring about agglomeration in (metal particles) by heating. [1770–80; < G: dross; see CINDER]

Sint Maar·ten (sint mär′tn). See **St. Martin.**

sin·u·ate (*adj.* sin′yo͞o it, -āt′, *v.* sin′yo͞o āt′), *adj., v.,* **-at·ed, -at·ing.** —*adj.* Also, **sin′u·at′ed. 1.** bent in and out; winding; sinuous. **2.** *Bot.* having the margin strongly or distinctly wavy, as a leaf. —*v.i.* **3.** to curve or wind in and out; creep in a winding path: *a snake sinuating along the ground.* [1680–90; < L *sinuātus* ptp. of *sinuāre* to bend, curve. See SINUS, -ATE[1]] —**sin′·u·ate·ly,** *adv.*

sin·u·a·tion (sin′yo͞o ā′shən), *n.* a winding; sinuosity. [1645–55; < LL *sinuātiōn-* (s. of *sinuātiō*). See SINUATE, -ION]

Sin·ui·ju (shin′wē′jo͞o′), *n.* a city in W North Korea, on the Yalu River. 165,000.

si·num′bra lamp′ (si num′brə), an unshaded sperm-oil lamp consisting of a translucent glass globe supported on a pedestal: a form of astral lamp. Also, **si·num′bral lamp′.** [1825–35; < L *sin(e)* without + *umbra* shade, shadow]

sin·u·os·i·ty (sin′yo͞o os′i tē), *n., pl.* **-ties. 1.** Often, **sinuosities.** a curve, bend, or turn: *a sinuosity of the road.* **2.** a sinuous form or character. [1590–1600; < ML *sinuōsitās.* See SINUOUS, -ITY]

sin·u·ous (sin′yo͞o əs), *adj.* **1.** having many curves, bends, or turns; winding: *a sinuous path.* **2.** indirect; devious: *sinuous questions.* **3.** characterized by a series of graceful curving motions: *a sinuous dance.* **4.** *Bot.* sinuate, as a leaf. [1570–80; < L *sinuōsus.* See SINUS, -OUS] —**sin′u·ous·ly,** *adv.* —**sin′u·ous·ness,** *n.*
—**Syn. 1.** curving, meandering, twining, twisting, coiled, curved, serpentine. **2.** roundabout. —**Ant. 1.** straight. **2.** direct.

si·nus (sī′nəs), *n., pl.* **-nus·es. 1.** a curve; bend. **2.** a curving part or recess. **3.** *Anat.* **a.** any of various cavities, recesses, or passages, as a hollow in a bone, or a reservoir or channel for venous blood. **b.** one of the hollow cavities in the skull connecting with the nasal cavities. **c.** an expanded area in a canal or tube. **4.** *Pathol.* a narrow passage leading to an abscess or the like. **5.** *Bot.* a small, rounded depression between two projecting lobes, as of a leaf. [1590–1600; < L *sinus* (s. *sinu-*) bent or curved surface, curve, fold] —**si′nus·like′,** *adj.*

Si·nus Ir·i·dum (sē′nəs ir′i dəm, sī′-), (*Bay of Rainbows*) a semicircular dark plain in the second quadrant of the face of the moon.

si·nus·i·tis (sī′nə sī′tis), *n. Pathol.* inflammation of a sinus or the sinuses. [1900–05; < NL; see SINUS, -ITIS]

Si·nus Me·rid·i·a·ni (sē′nəs mə rid′ē ä′nē ē′, sī′nəs mə rid′ē ā′nē ī′), an area on the equator of Mars, appearing as a dark region when viewed telescopically from the earth.

si′nus node′ (sī′nəs), *Anat.* See **sinoatrial node.**

Si·nus of Val·sal·va (sī′nəs əv val sal′və), *Anat.* any of the pouches of the aorta and the pulmonary artery opposite the flaps of the semilunar valves into which blood returning to the heart flows, closing the valves. [see VALSALVA'S MANEUVER]

si·nus·oid (sī′nə soid′), *n. Math.* a curve described by the equation $y = a \sin x$, the ordinate being proportional to the sine of the abscissa. [1815–25; SINUS + -OID]

si·nus·oi·dal (sī′nə soid′l), *adj.* **1.** *Math.* of or pertaining to a sinusoid. **2.** having a magnitude that varies as the sine of an independent variable: *a sinusoidal current.* [1875–80; SINUSOID + -AL[1]] —**si′nus·oi′dal·ly,** *adv.*

sinusoi′dal projec′tion, *Cartog.* an equal-area projection in which parallels are straight lines spaced at regular intervals, the central meridian is a straight line one-half the length of the equator, and the other meridians are curves symmetrical to the central meridian. [1940–45]

Si·nus Sa·bae·us (sē′nəs sa bē′əs, sī′-), an area in the southern hemisphere and near the equator of Mars, appearing dark when viewed telescopically from the earth.

Sion (*Fr.* syôN), *n.* a town in and the capital of Valais, in SW Switzerland. 23,100.

Si·on (sī′ən), *n.* Zion.

CONCISE ETYMOLOGY KEY: <, descended or borrowed from; >, whence; b., blend of, blended; c., cognate with; cf., compare; deriv., derivative; equiv., equivalent; imit., imitative; obl., oblique; r., replacing; s., stem; sp., spelling, spelled; resp., respelling, respelled; trans., translation; ?, origin unknown; *, unattested; ‡, probably earlier than. See the full key inside the front cover.

-sion, a noun suffix appearing in loanwords from Latin: *compulsion.* Cf. **-tion.** [< L, equiv. to *-s(us),* var. of *-tus* ptp. suffix + *-iōn-* -ION]

SIOP (sī′op), *n.* the secret and central U.S. contingency plan for waging a nuclear war with the Soviet Union. [*s(ingle) i(ntegrated) o(perations) p(lan)*]

Siou•an (so͞o′ən), *n.* **1.** an American Indian language family formerly widespread from Saskatchewan to the lower Mississippi, also found in the Virginia and Carolina piedmont, and including Catawba, Crow, Dakota, Hidatsa, Mandan, Osage, and Winnebago. **2.** a member of one of the Siouan-speaking peoples. **—*adj.*** **3.** of or pertaining to the Sioux or the Siouan languages. [1885–90, *Amer.*; SIOUX + -AN]

Sioux (so͞o), *n., pl.* **Sioux** (so͞o, so͞oz). Dakota (defs. 4, 6). [1755–65, *Amer.*; < North American F, shortening of earlier *Nadouessioux* < Ojibwa (Ottawa dial.) *na·towe·s-siw(ak)* pl. (< Proto-Algonquian **na·towe·hsiw-,* deriv. of **na·towe·wa* Iroquoian, prob. lit., speaker of a foreign language) + F *-x* pl. marker]

Sioux′ Cit′y, a port in W Iowa, on the Missouri River. 82,003.

Sioux′ Falls′, a city in SE South Dakota. 81,343.

Sioux′ State′, a nickname of the state of North Dakota.

Sioux′ War′, *U.S. Hist.* any of a series of skirmishes or wars between the Sioux Indians and settlers or the U.S. Army from 1854 to 1890.

sip (sip), *v.,* **sipped, sip•ping,** *n.* **—*v.t.*** **1.** to drink (a liquid) a little at a time; take small tastes of: *He sipped the hot tea noisily.* **2.** to drink from a little at a time: *The bird sipped the flower.* **3.** to take in; absorb: *to sip knowledge at its source.* **—*v.i.*** **4.** to drink by sips. **—*n.*** **5.** an instance of sipping; a small taste of a liquid: *One sip told me that the milk was sour.* **6.** a small quantity taken by sipping: *Take just a sip, not a gulp or a swallow.* [1350–1400; ME *sippen* (v.), akin to LG *sippen* to sip] **—sip′ping•ly,** *adv.*
—Syn. 1. See **drink.**

SIP, supplemental income plan.

sipe (sīp), *v.i.,* **siped, sip•ing.** *Scot. and North Eng.* (of liquid) to drip, ooze, or soak through. [bef. 900; perh. continuing OE *sīpian;* c. D *zijpen,* MLG *sīpen.* See SEEP[1]] **—sip′er,** *n.*

Siph•nos (sif′nos, -nôs), *n.* a Greek island in the SW Aegean Sea, in the Cyclades group: gold and silver mines. 28 sq. mi. (75 sq. km). Also, **Sifnos.**

si•phon (sī′fən), *n.* **1.** a tube or conduit bent into legs of unequal length, for use in drawing a liquid from one container into another on a lower level by placing the shorter leg into the container above and the longer leg into the one below, the liquid being forced up the shorter leg and into the longer one by the pressure of the atmosphere. **2.** See **siphon bottle. 3.** a projecting tubular part of some animals, esp. certain mollusks, through which liquid enters or leaves the body. **—*v.t., v.i.*** **4.** to convey, draw, or pass through or as if through a siphon (sometimes fol. by *off*): *to siphon water; to siphon off profits into a secret bank account.* Also, **syphon.** [1650–60; < L *siphōn-* (s. of *siphō*) < Gk *síphōn, sîphōn* pipe, tube] **—si′phon•al, si•phon•ic** (sī fon′ik), *adj.* **—si′phon•less,** *adj.* **—si′phon•like′,** *adj.*

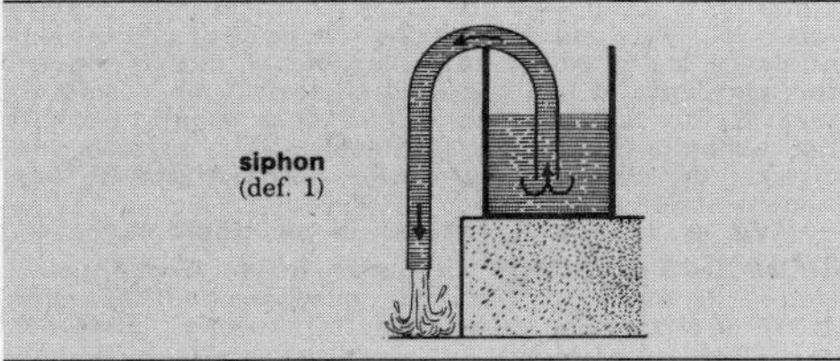
siphon (def. 1)

si•phon•age (sī′fə nij), *n.* the action of a siphon. [1850–55; SIPHON + -AGE]

si•pho•nap•ter•ous (sī′fə nap′tər əs), *adj.* belonging or pertaining to the insect order Siphonaptera, comprising the fleas. [< NL *Siphonapter(a)* (< Gk *siphōn-* SIPHONO- + *a-* A-[6] + *-ptera,* neut. pl. of *-pteros* -PTEROUS) + -OUS]

si′phon bot′tle, a bottle for aerated water, fitted with a bent tube through the neck, the water being forced out, when a valve is opened, by the pressure on its surface of the gas accumulating within the bottle.

siphono-, a combining form meaning "tube," "siphon," used in the formation of compound words: *siphonostele.* [comb. form repr. *síphōn* SIPHON; see -O-]

si•pho•no•phore (sī′fə nə fôr′, -fōr′, sī fon′ə-), *n.* any pelagic hydrozoan of the order Siphonophora, being a floating or swimming colony composed of polyps. [1835–45; < NL *Siphonophora* name of the order < Gk *siphōnophór(os)* tube-carrying (equiv. to *siphōno-* SIPHONO- + *-phóros* -PHORE) + *-a* neut. pl. n. suffix] **—si•pho•noph•o•rous** (sī′fə nof′ər əs), *adj.*

si•phon•o•stele (sī fon′ə stēl′, sī′fə nə stēl′), *n. Bot.* a hollow tube of vascular tissue enclosing a pith and embedded in ground tissue. [1905–10; SIPHONO- + STELE] **—si•pho•no•ste•lic** (sī′fə nə stē′lik), *adj.*

Si•phrei To•rah (*Seph.* sē fʀā′ tô ʀä′; *Ashk.* si′fʀā tō′ʀə, toi′ʀə), *Hebrew.* a pl. of ***Sepher Torah.***

si•phun•cle (sī′fung kəl), *n.* **1.** (in a nautilus) the connecting tube that passes from the end of the body through all of the septa to the innermost chamber. **2.** *Entomol.* an aphid cornicle. [1895–1900; < L *sip(h)unculus* small tube through which water is forced, equiv. to *sīp(h)ōn-,* s. of *sīp(h)ō* SIPHON + *-culus* -CULE[1] (see CARBUNCLE)] **—si•phun′cu•lar, si•phun•cu•late** (sī fung′kyə lit), **si•phun•cu•lat•ed** (sī fung′kyə lā′tid), *adj.*

sip•id (sip′id), *adj.* **1.** having a pleasing taste or flavor. **2.** of agreeably distinctive character. [1615–25; back formation from INSIPID] **—si•pid•i•ty** (si pid′i tē), *n.*

Si•ple (sī′pəl), *n.* **Mount,** a mountain in Antarctica, on the E coast of Marie Byrd Land. 15,000 ft. (4570 m).

Sip•par (si pär′), *n.* an ancient Babylonian city on the Euphrates, in SE Iraq.

sip•per (sip′ər), *n.* **1.** a person who sips. **2.** a paper tube through which to sip; drinking straw. [1605–15; SIP + -ER[1]]

sip•pet (sip′it), *n.* **1.** a small bit; fragment. **2.** a small piece of bread or the like for dipping in liquid food, as in gravy or milk; a small sop. **3.** a crouton. [1520–30; SIP + -ET]

si•pun•cu•lid (sī pung′kyə lid), *n.* **1.** an invertebrate of the phylum Sipuncula, comprising the peanut worms. **—*adj.*** **2.** belonging or pertaining to the sipunculids. [1885–90; orig. a member of the family Sipunculidae < NL, equiv. to *Sipuncul(us)* a genus (L: var. of *sīphunculus;* see SIPHUNCLE) + *-idae* -ID[2]]

si quae•ris pen•in•su•lam a•moe•nam, cir•cum•spi•ce (sē kwī′ʀis pā nin′so͞o läm′ ä moi′näm kēʀ-ko͞om′spi ke′; *Eng.* si kwēr′is pə nin′sə lam′ ə mē′-nam sər kum′spə sē′), *Latin.* if you are seeking a pleasant peninsula, look around you: motto of Michigan.

Si•quei•ros (sē kā′ʀôs), *n.* **Da•vid Al•fa•ro** (dä vēth′ äl fä′ʀô), 1896–1974, Mexican painter.

sir (sûr), *n.* **1.** a respectful or formal term of address used to a man: *No, sir.* **2.** (*cap.*) the distinctive title of a knight or baronet: *Sir Walter Scott.* **3.** (*cap.*) a title of respect for some notable personage of ancient times: *Sir Pandarus of Troy.* **4.** a lord or gentleman: *noble sirs and ladies.* **5.** an ironic or humorous title of respect: *sir critic.* **6.** *Archaic.* a title of respect used before a noun to designate profession, rank, etc.: *sir priest; sir clerk.* [1250–1300; ME; unstressed var. of SIRE]

Si•rach (sī′rak), *n.* **Son of,** Jesus (def. 2).

Si•ra•cu•sa (*It.* sē′ʀä ko͞o′zä), *n.* Syracuse (def. 2).

Si•raj-ud-dau•la (si räj′o͞od dou′lə), *n.* 1728?–57, nawab of Bengal 1756–57. Also, **Surajah Dowlah.**

sir•dar (sər där′), *n.* **1.** (in India, Pakistan, and Afghanistan) a military chief or leader. **2.** (formerly) the British commander of the Egyptian army. Also, **sardar.** [1605–15; < Hindi *sardār* < Pers]

sire (sīᵊr), *n., v.,* **sired, sir•ing.** **—*n.*** **1.** the male parent of a quadruped. **2.** a respectful term of address, now used only to a male sovereign. **3.** *Archaic.* **a.** a father or forefather. **b.** a person of importance or in a position of authority, as a lord. **—*v.t.*** **4.** to beget; procreate as the father. [1175–1225; ME < OF (nom. sing.) < VL **seior,* for L *senior* SENIOR (cf. F *monsieur* orig., my lord, with *sieur* < **seiōr-,* obl. s. of **seior*)] **—sire′less,** *adj.*

sir•ee (sə rē′), *n.* (*sometimes cap.*) sirree.

si•ren (sī′rən), *n.* **1.** *Class. Myth.* one of several sea nymphs, part woman and part bird, who lure mariners to destruction by their seductive singing. **2.** a seductively beautiful or charming woman, esp. one who beguiles men: *a siren of the silver screen.* **3.** an acoustical instrument for producing musical tones, consisting essentially of a disk pierced with holes arranged equidistantly in a circle, rotated over a jet or stream of compressed air, steam, or the like, so that the stream is alternately interrupted and allowed to pass. **4.** an implement of this kind used as a whistle, fog signal, or warning device. **5.** any of several aquatic, eellike salamanders of the family Sirenidae, having permanent external gills, small forelimbs, and no posterior limbs. **—*adj.*** **6.** of or like a siren. **7.** seductive or tempting, esp. dangerously or harmfully: *the siren call of adventure.* **—*v.i.*** **8.** to go with the siren sounding, as a fire engine. **—*v.t.*** **9.** to allure in the manner of a siren. [1300–50; ME *sereyn* < OF *sereine* < LL *Sīrēna,* L *Sīrēn* < Gk *Seirḗn*] **—si′ren•like′,** *adj.*
—Syn. 2. seductress, temptress, vamp.

Si•re•na (sī rē′nə, sə-), *n.* a female given name.

si•re•ni•an (sī rē′nē ən), *n.* an aquatic, herbivorous mammal of the order Sirenia, including the manatee and dugong. [1880–85; < NL *Sireni(a)* (see SIREN, -IA) + -AN]

si•ren•ic (sī ren′ik), *adj.* of or characteristic of a siren; melodious, tempting, or alluring. Also, **si•ren′i•cal.** [1695–1705; SIREN + -IC] **—si•ren′i•cal•ly,** *adv.*

Si•re•num (si rē′nəm), *n.* **Mare.** See **Mare Sirenum.**

Si•ret (si ret′), *n.* a river in SE Europe, flowing SE from the Carpathian Mountains in Ukraine through E Rumania to the Danube. 270 mi. (435 km) long. German, **Sereth.**

Sir′ Ga′wain and the Green′ Knight′, an English alliterative poem of unknown authorship, dating from the 14th century.

si•ri•a•sis (si rī′ə sis), *n. Pathol.* sunstroke. [1595–1605; < L *siriāsis* < Gk *seiriāsis,* equiv. to *seiri(ân)* to be hot, scorching (deriv. of *Seírios* SIRIUS) + *-āsis* -ASIS]

Si•ric•a (sə rik′ə), *n.* **John J(oseph),** born 1904, U.S. jurist: chief judge, district court for District of Columbia 1971–74; tried Watergate cases 1973–74.

Si•ri•ci•us (si rish′ē əs), *n.* **Saint,** died A.D. 399, pope 384–399.

si•ris (sə rēs′), *n.* lebbek (def. 1). [1870–75; < Hindi *siris, siras;* cf. Skt *śiriṣa*]

Sir•i•us (sir′ē əs), *n.* **1.** *Astron.* the Dog Star, the brightest-appearing star in the heavens, located in the constellation Canis Major. **2.** Also, **Seirios.** *Class. Myth.* **a.** the dog of Orion. **b.** Icarius' faithful dog, who was changed into a star. [1325–75; ME < L *Sīrius* < Gk *Seírios*]

sir•loin (sûr′loin), *n.* the portion of the loin of beef in front of the rump. See diag. under **beef.** [1515–25; earlier *surloyn* < OF **surloigne,* var. of *surlonge* (F *surlonge*). See SUR-[1], LOIN]

si•roc•co (sə rok′ō), *n., pl.* **-cos. 1.** a hot, dry, dust-laden wind blowing from northern Africa and affecting parts of southern Europe. **2.** a warm, sultry south or southeast wind accompanied by rain, occurring in the same regions. **3.** any hot, oppressive wind, esp. one in the warm sector of a cyclone. Also, **scirocco.** [1610–20; < It, var. of *scirocco* < Ar *sharq* east]

sir•rah (sir′ə), *n. Archaic.* a term of address used to inferiors or children to express impatience, contempt, etc. [1520–30; extended form of SIR; source of final vowel is unclear]

sir•ree (sə rē′), *n.* (*sometimes cap.*) (used as an intensive with *no* or *yes*): *Will I go there again? No, sirree!* Also, **siree.** [1815–25; prob. a dial. continuation of SIRRAH]

sir-rev•er•ence (sûr′rev′ər əns), *n. Obs.* (used as an expression of apology, as before unseemly or indelicate words.) [1565–75; alter. of *save your reverence*]

Sir Rog′er de Cov′erley, an English country dance performed by two rows of dancers facing each other. [1680–90; earlier *Roger of Coverly,* appar. a fictional name]

sir•up (sir′əp, sûr′-), *n., v.t.* syrup.

sir•up•y (sir′ə pē, sûr′-), *adj.* syrupy.

sir•vente (sər vent′; *Fr.* sēʀ väɴt′), *n., pl.* **-ventes** (-vents′; *Fr.* -väɴt′). a medieval poem or song of heroic or satirical character, as composed by a troubadour. Also, **sir•ventes′.** [1810–20; back formation from Pr *sirventes* lit., pertaining to a servant, i.e., lover (the *-s* being taken as pl. sign). See SERVANT, -ESE]

sis (sis), *n. Informal.* sister. [1825–35, *Amer.*; shortened form; cf. D *zus* for *zuster* SISTER]

-sis, a suffix appearing in loanwords from Greek, where it was used to form from verbs abstract nouns of action, process, state, condition, etc.: *thesis; aphesis.* [< Gk]

si•sal (sī′səl, sis′əl), *n.* **1.** Also called **si′sal hemp′.** a fiber yielded by an agave, *Agave sisalana,* of Yucatán, used for making rope, rugs, etc. **2.** the plant itself. [1835–45; short for *Sisal grass* or *hemp,* named after *Sisal,* port in Yucatán]

sis•co•wet (sis′kə wet′), *n.* a variety of lake trout, *Salvelinus namaycush siscowet,* inhabiting the deeper waters of Lake Superior. [1840–50, *Amer.*; shortening of Ojibwa *pe·mite·wiskawe·t* fish with oily flesh (deriv. of *pimite·w-* oil + *-iskawe·* (of fish) to have flesh (of the specified type), or deriv. of another word with the same final element)]

Sis•er•a (sis′ər ə), *n.* the commander of the Canaanite army of King Jabin: killed by Jael. Judges 4:17–22.

Si•sin•ni•us (si sin′ē əs), *n.* pope A.D. 708.

sis•kin (sis′kin), *n.* any of several small, cardueline finches, esp. *Carduelis spinus,* of Europe. Cf. **pine siskin.** [1555–65; < MD *sijsken,* equiv. to *sijs* (< MLG *czītze* < Slavic; cf. Lusatian *cyž,* Czech *čí̌ž,* Pol *czyż* siskin, ult. of imit. orig.) + *-ken* -KIN]

Sis•ler (sis′lər), *n.* **George Harold,** 1893–1973, U.S. baseball player.

Sis•ley (sis′lē; *Fr.* sēs lā′), *n.* **Al•fred** (al fʀed′), 1839–99, French painter.

Sis•mon•di (sis mon′dē; *Fr.* sēs môɴ dē′), *n.* **Jean Charles Lé•o•nard Si•monde de** (zhäɴ sharl lā ô naʀ′ sē môɴd′ də), 1773–1842, Swiss historian and economist.

Sis•se•ton (sis′i tən, -tn), *n., pl.* **-tons,** (*esp. collectively*) **-ton.** a member of a North American Indian people belonging to the Santee branch of the Dakota.

sis•si•fied (sis′ə fīd′), *adj.* sissy. [1900–05; SISSY + -FY + -ED[2]]

sis•sonne (si son′, -sōn′; *Fr.* sē sôn′), *n., pl.* **-sonnes** (-sonz′, -sōnz′; *Fr.* -sôn′). *Ballet.* a jump in which the dancer lands on one foot, with the other extended to the back, front, or side. [1700–10; named after the Comte de *Sissonne,* 17th-century French noble, said to have invented it]

sis•sy (sis′ē), *n., pl.* **-sies,** *adj.* **—*n.*** **1.** an effeminate boy or man. **2.** a timid or cowardly person. **3.** a little girl. **—*adj.*** **4.** of, pertaining to, or characteristic of a sissy. [1840–50, *Amer.* in sense "sister"; 1885–90, *Amer.* for def. 1; SIS + -Y[2]] **—sis′sy•ish,** *adj.* **—sis′si•ness, sis′sy•ness,** *n.*

sis′sy bar′, a tall, looplike frame fitted to the rear of a bicycle or motorcycle saddle, functioning chiefly as a backrest. [1965–70, *Amer.*]

sis•ter (sis′tər), *n.* **1.** a female offspring having both parents in common with another offspring; female sibling. **2.** Also called **half sister.** a female offspring having only one parent in common with another offspring. **3.** stepsister. **4.** a female friend or protector regarded as a sister. **5.** a thing regarded as feminine and associated as if by kinship with something else: *The ships are sisters.* **6.** a female fellow member, as of a church. **7.** a female member of a religious community that observes the simple vows of poverty, chastity, and obedience. **8.** *Brit.* a nurse in charge of a hospital ward; head nurse. **9.** a fellow black woman. **10.** a woman who supports, promotes, or participates in feminism. **11.** *Informal.* a form of address used to a woman or girl, esp. jocularly or contemptuously: *Listen, sister, you've had enough.* **—*adj.*** **12.** being or considered a sister; related by or as if by sisterhood: *sister ships.* **13.** having a close relationship with another because of shared interests, problems, or the like: *We correspond with school children in our sister city.* **14.** *Biochem.* being one of an identical pair. [bef. 900; ME (n.) < ON *systir;* c. OE *sweoster,* D *zuster,* G *Schwester,* Goth *swistar;* akin to Serbo-Croatian *sèstra,* Lith *sesuō,* L *soror* (< **swesor*), OIr *siur,*

CONCISE PRONUNCIATION KEY: act, cāpe, dâre, pärt; set, ēqual; *if,* ice; ox, ōver, ôrder, oil, bo͝ok, bo͞ot, out; up, ûrge; child; sing; shoe; thin, *that;* zh as in *treasure.* ə = *a* as in *alone, e* as in *system, i* as in *easily, o* as in *gallop, u* as in *circus;* ᵊ as in *fire* (fīᵊr), *hour* (ouᵊr). l and n can serve as syllabic consonants, as in *cradle* (krād′l), and *button* (but′n). See the full key inside the front cover.

Welsh *chwaer,* Skt *svasar* sister, Gk *éor* daughter, niece] **—sis′ter·less,** *adj.* **—sis′ter·like′,** *adj.*

sis·ter·hood (sis′tər ho͝od′), *n.* **1.** the state of being a sister. **2.** a group of sisters, esp. of nuns or of female members of a church. **3.** an organization of women with a common interest, as for social, charitable, business, or political purposes. **4.** congenial relationship or companionship among women; mutual female esteem, concern, support, etc. **5.** Usually, **the sisterhood.** the community or network of women who participate in or support feminism. [1350–1400; ME *sosterhode.* See SISTER, -HOOD]

sis·ter-in-law (sis′tər in lô′), *n., pl.* **sis·ters-in-law. 1.** the sister of one's husband or wife. **2.** the wife of one's brother. **3.** the wife of the brother of one's husband or wife. [1400–50; late ME. See SISTER, IN, LAW[1]]

sis·ter·ly (sis′tər lē), *adj.* **1.** of, like, or befitting a sister: *sisterly affection.* —*adv.* **2.** in the manner of a sister; as a sister. [1560–70; SISTER + -LY] **—sis′ter·li·ness,** *n.*

Sis′ter of Char′ity, *Rom. Cath. Ch.* **1.** a member of one of several congregations of sisters founded in 1634 by St. Vincent de Paul. **2.** any of several other orders of nuns devoted to teaching, care of the sick, etc.

Sis′ter of Lo·ret′to (lə ret′ō), *Rom. Cath. Ch.* a member of a congregation of sisters founded at Loretto, Kentucky, in 1812 and engaged in educational and missionary works.

Sis′ter of Mer′cy, *Rom. Cath. Ch.* a member of a congregation of sisters founded in Dublin in 1827 by Catherine McAuley (1787–1841) and engaged chiefly in works of spiritual and corporal mercy.

Sis·tine (sis′tēn, -tin, -tīn), *adj.* of or pertaining to any pope named Sixtus. Also, **Sixtine.** [1860–65; < It *Sistino,* pertaining to *Sisto* man's name (< L *Sextus* (ML *Sixtus*), special use of *sextus* SIXTH); see -INE[1]]

Sis′tine Chap′el, the chapel of the pope in the Vatican at Rome, built for Pope Sixtus IV and decorated with frescoes by Michelangelo and others.

Sis′tine Madon′na, a Madonna painted by Raphael for the Church of St. Sixtus at Piacenza, Italy.

sis·trum (sis′trəm), *n., pl.* **-trums, -tra** (-trə). an ancient Egyptian percussion instrument consisting of a looped metal frame set in a handle and fitted with loose crossbars that rattle when shaken. [1350–1400; ME < L < Gk *seîstron,* deriv. of *seíein* to shake (cf. SEISMIC)]

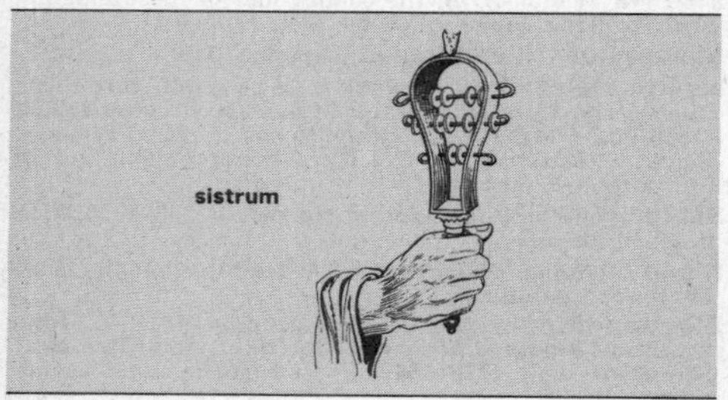
sistrum

Sis·y·phe·an (sis′ə fē′ən), *adj.* **1.** of or pertaining to Sisyphus. **2.** endless and unavailing, as labor or a task. [1625–35; < Gk *Sisýphe(ios)* (*Sísyph(os)* SISYPHUS + *-eios* adj. suffix) + -AN]

Sis·y·phus (sis′ə fəs), *n. Class. Myth.* a son of Aeolus and ruler of Corinth, noted for his trickery: he was punished in Tartarus by being compelled to roll a stone to the top of a slope, the stone always escaping him near the top and rolling down again.

sit[1] (sit), *v.,* **sat** or (*Archaic*) **sate; sat** or (*Archaic*) **sitten; sit·ting.** —*v.i.* **1.** to rest with the body supported by the buttocks or thighs; be seated. **2.** to be located or situated: *The house sits well up on the slope.* **3.** to rest or lie (usually fol. by *on* or *upon*): *An aura of greatness sits easily upon him.* **4.** to place oneself in position for an artist, photographer, etc.; pose: *to sit for a portrait.* **5.** to remain quiet or inactive: *They let the matter sit.* **6.** (of a bird) to perch or roost. **7.** (of a hen) to cover eggs to hatch them; brood. **8.** to fit, rest, or hang, as a garment: *The jacket sits well on your shoulders.* **9.** to occupy a place or have a seat in an official assembly or in an official capacity, as a legislator, judge, or bishop. **10.** to be convened or in session, as an assembly. **11.** to act as a baby-sitter. **12.** (of wind) to blow from the indicated direction: *The wind sits in the west tonight.* **13.** to be accepted or considered in the way indicated: *Something about his looks just didn't sit right with me.* **14.** *Informal.* to be acceptable to the stomach: *Something I ate for breakfast didn't sit too well.* —*v.t.* **15.** to cause to sit; seat (often fol. by *down*): *Sit yourself down. He sat me near him.* **16.** to sit astride or keep one's seat on (a horse or other animal): *She sits her horse gracefully.* **17.** to provide seating accommodations or seating room for; seat: *Our dining-room table only sits six people.* **18.** *Informal.* to serve as baby-sitter for: *A neighbor can sit the children while you go out.* **19. sit down, a.** to take a seat. **b.** to descend to a sitting position; alight. **c.** to take up a position, as to encamp or besiege: *The military forces sat down at the approaches to the city.* **20. sit in, a.** to attend or take part as a visitor or temporary participant: *to sit in at a bridge game; to sit in for the band's regular pianist.* **b.** to take part in a sit-in. **21. sit in on,** to be a spectator, observer, or visitor at: *to sit in on classes.* **22. sit on** or **upon, a.** to inquire into or deliberate over: *A coroner's jury was called to sit on the case.* **b.** *Informal.* to suppress; silence: *They sat on the bad news as long as they could.* **c.** *Informal.* to check or rebuke; squelch: *I'll sit on him if he tries to interrupt me.* **23. sit on one's hands, a.** to fail to applaud. **b.** to fail to take appropriate action. **24. sit out, a.** to stay to the end of: *Though bored, we sat out the play.* **b.** to surpass in endurance: *He sat out his tormentors.* **c.** to keep one's seat during (a dance, competition, etc.); fail to participate in: *We sat out all the Latin-American numbers.* **25. sit tight,** to bide one's time; take no action: *I'm going to sit tight till I hear from you.* **26. sit up, a.** to rise from a supine to a sitting position. **b.** to delay the hour of retiring beyond the usual time. **c.** to sit upright; hold oneself erect. **d.** *Informal.* to become interested or astonished: *We all sat up when the holiday was announced.* [bef. 900; ME *sitten,* OE *sittan;* c. D *zitten,* G *sitzen,* ON *sitja;* akin to Goth *sitan,* L *sedēre,* Gk *hézesthai* (base *hed-*); cf. SET, SEDATE, CATHEDRAL, NEST]
—Syn. 10. meet, assemble, convene, gather.
—Usage. Cf. **set.**

sit[2] (sit), *v.* (in prescriptions) may it be. [< L]

Si·ta (sē′tä), *n.* (in the Ramayana) the wife of Ramachandra, abducted by Ravana and later rescued.

sitar

si·tar (si tär′), *n.* a lute of India with a small, pear-shaped body and a long, broad, fretted neck. [1835–45; < Hindi *sitār*] **—si·tar′ist,** *n.*

sit·a·tun·ga (sit′ə to͝ong′ə), *n.* an antelope, *Tragelaphus spekei,* inhabiting marshy regions of central and eastern Africa. Also, **situtunga.** Also called **marsh buck.** [1880–85; said to be < Lozi, Subiya, or Tonga (Bantu languages of W Zambia)]

sit·com (sit′kom′), *n. Informal.* See **situation comedy.** [1960–65; by shortening]

sit-down (sit′doun′), *adj.* **1.** done or accomplished while sitting down: *sit-down meetings between the two party leaders.* **2.** (of a meal or food) served to or intended for persons seated at a table: *a sit-down dinner.* —*n.* **3.** *Informal.* a period or instance of sitting, as to relax, talk, or the like: *They had a profitable sit-down together.* **4.** See **sit-down strike. 5.** a protest demonstration whereby participants refuse to move from a public place. **6.** *Informal.* a meal, esp. a dinner, served to persons who are seated at a table. [1830–40; adj. and n. use of v. phrase *sit down*]

sit′-down strike′, a strike during which workers occupy their place of employment and refuse to work or allow others to work until the strike is settled. Also called **sit-down, sit-in.** [1930–35, *Amer.*]

site (sīt), *n., v.,* **sit·ed, sit·ing.** —*n.* **1.** the position or location of a town, building, etc., esp. as to its environment: *the site of our summer cabin.* **2.** the area or exact plot of ground on which anything is, has been, or is to be located: *the site of ancient Troy.* —*v.t.* **3.** to place in or provide with a site; locate. **4.** to put in position for operation, as artillery: *to site a cannon.* [1350–1400; ME < L *situs* position, arrangement, site (presumably orig. "leaving, setting down"), equiv. to *si-,* var. s. of *sinere* to leave, allow to be + *-tus* suffix of v. action]
—Syn. 2. position, location, place.

site′ catch′ment anal′ysis, *Archaeol.* the examination by survey, excavation, maps, and graphs of a contained area to evaluate the productivity of the resources customarily exploited by the inhabitants of a settlement, especially a prehistoric one. [1970]

site-spe·cif·ic (sīt′spi sif′ik), *adj.* created, designed, or selected for a specific site: *a site-specific sculpture.*

sith (sith), *adv., conj., prep. Archaic.* since. [bef. 950; ME; OE *siththa,* dial. var. of *siththan,* orig., *sīth thām* after that, subsequently to that, equiv. to *sīth* subsequently (akin to Goth *seithus,* ON *sīth-* late, G *seit* since) + *thām,* dat. of demonstrative pronoun, i.e., "to that" (see THE[1]); cf. ON *sīthan* sith]

sit-in (sit′in′), *n.* **1.** an organized passive protest, esp. against racial segregation, in which the demonstrators occupy seats prohibited to them, as in restaurants and other public places. **2.** any organized protest in which a group of people peacefully occupy and refuse to leave a premises: *Sixty students staged a sit-in outside the dean's office.* **3.** See **sit-down strike.** [1955–60; n. use of v. phrase *sit in* (a place); cf. -IN]

Sit·ka (sit′kə), *n.* a town in SE Alaska, on an island in the Alexander Archipelago: the capital of former Russian America. 7803. **—Sit′kan,** *n.*

Sit′ka spruce′, 1. a spruce, *Picea sitchensis,* of western North America, having long, silvery-white needles, grown as an ornamental. **2.** the soft, pale-brown wood of this tree, used for making furniture and in the construction of houses. [1890–95, *Amer.*]

sito-, a combining form meaning "grain," "food," used in the formation of compound words: *sitomania; sitosterol.* [< Gk *sito-,* comb. form of *sîtos* grain]

si·tol·o·gy (sī tol′ə jē), *n.* the branch of medicine dealing with nutrition and dietetics. [1860–65; SITO- + -LOGY]

si·to·ma·ni·a (sī′tə mā′nē ə, -mān′yə), *n. Pathol.* abnormal craving for food. [1880–85; SITO- + -MANIA]

si·to·pho·bi·a (sī′tə fō′bē ə), *n. Pathol.* abnormal aversion to food. [1880–85; SITO- + -PHOBIA]

si·tos·ter·ol (sī tos′tə rôl′, -rol′), *n. Chem.* any of five steroid alcohols having the formula $C_{22}H_{50}O$, esp. the beta form, obtained from various plant sources: used in organic synthesis. [1915–20; SITO- + STEROL]

Si·tsang (sē′tsäng′), *n. Older Spelling.* Tibet.

sit′ spin′, *Figure Skating.* a spin performed on one skate, in which the skater slowly squats down into a sitting position, with the other leg extended out in front.

sit·ten (sit′n), *v. Archaic.* pp. of **sit**[1].

sit·ter (sit′ər), *n.* **1.** a person who sits. **2.** a brooding hen. **3.** a person who stays with young children while the parents go out; baby-sitter. **4.** a person who provides routine or custodial care temporarily or part-time, as for an elderly person or a pet whose owner is on vacation. **5.** *Slang.* the buttocks; rump. [1300–50; ME; see SIT[1], -ER[1]]

Sit·ter (sit′ər), *n.* **Wil·lem de** (wil′əm də), 1872–1934, Dutch astronomer and mathematician.

sit·ting (sit′ing), *n.* **1.** the act of a person or thing that sits. **2.** a period of remaining seated, as in posing for a portrait or reading a book. **3.** the space on or in which one sits, as in a church. **4.** a brooding, as of a hen upon eggs; incubation. **5.** the number of eggs on which a bird sits during a single hatching; clutch. **6.** a session, as of a court or legislature. **7.** the time or space allotted to the serving of a meal to a group, as aboard a ship. —*adj.* **8.** (of a bird) occupying a nest of eggs for hatching. **9.** of, for, or suited to sitting: *a sitting area in the lobby.* **10.** holding an official position or office; occupying an appointed or elected seat; incumbent: *a sitting pontiff.* **11.** in session or at work; active: *a sitting legislature.* **12. sitting pretty,** in an auspicious position: *He's been sitting pretty since he got that new job.* [1175–1225; ME; see SIT[1], -ING[1], -ING[2]]

Sit′ting Bull′, 1834–90, American Indian warrior: leader of the Hunkpapa; victor at Little Bighorn, 1876.

sit′ting duck′, a helpless or easy target or victim: *a sitting duck for shady financial schemes.* [1940–45]

sit′ting room′, a small living room, often one that forms part of a suite in a hotel, private house, etc. [1765–75]

Sit·twe (sit′wā), *n.* a seaport in W Burma (Myanmar). 107,907. Formerly, **Akyab.**

si·tu (sē′to͞o), *n. Latin.* See **in situ.**

sit·u·ate (*v.* sich′o͞o āt′; *adj.* sich′o͞o it, -āt′), *v.,* **-at·ed, -at·ing,** *adj.* —*v.t.* **1.** to put in or on a particular site or place; locate. —*adj.* **2.** *Archaic.* located; placed; situated. [1515–25; < LL *situātus* situated, equiv. to L *situ-,* s. of *situs* SITE + *-ātus* -ATE[1]]
—Syn. 1. establish, station, set, install.

sit·u·at·ed (sich′o͞o ā′tid), *adj.* **1.** located; placed. **2.** placed in a particular position or condition, esp. with reference to the possession of money: *The inheritance leaves them well situated.* [1550–60; SITUATE + -ED[2]]

sit·u·a·tion (sich′o͞o ā′shən), *n.* **1.** manner of being situated; location or position with reference to environment: *The situation of the house allowed for a beautiful view.* **2.** a place or locality. **3.** condition; case; plight: *He is in a desperate situation.* **4.** the state of affairs; combination of circumstances: *The present international situation is dangerous.* **5.** a position or post of employment; job. **6.** a state of affairs of special or critical significance in the course of a play, novel, etc. **7.** *Sociol.* the aggregate of biological, psychological, and sociocultural factors acting on an individual or group to condition behavioral patterns. [1480–90; < ML *situātiōn-* (s. of *situātiō*). See SITUATE, -ION] **—sit′u·a′tion·al,** *adj.* **—sit′u·a′tion·al·ly,** *adv.*
—Syn. 1. site. **4.** See **state. 5.** See **position.**

sit′ua′tion com′edy, a comedy drama, esp. a television series made up of discrete episodes about the same group of characters, as members of a family. [1945–50]

sit′ua′tion eth′ics, a view of ethics that deprecates general moral principles while emphasizing the source of moral judgments in the distinctive characters of specific situations. [trans. of G *situationsethik* (1950)]

sit·u·a·tion·ism (sich′o͞o ā′shə niz′əm), *n. Psychol.* the theory that behavior is chiefly response to immediate situations. Also, **sit·u·a·tion·al·ism** (sich′o͞o ā′shənl iz′əm). [SITUATION + -ISM] **—sit′u·a′tion·ist,** *n.*

situa′tion room′, a room at a military or political headquarters where the latest information on a military or political situation is channeled. [1965–70]

sit·u·la (sich′ə lə, sit′l ə), *n., pl.* **-u·lae** (-ə lē′, -l ē′). a deep urn, vase, or bucket-shaped vessel, esp. one made in the ancient world. [1895–1900; < L: water vessel, bucket]

sit-up (sit′up′), *n.* an exercise in which a person lies flat on the back, lifts the torso to a sitting position, and then lies flat again without changing the position of the legs: formerly done with the legs straight but now usually done with the knees bent. [1835–45; n. use of v. phrase *sit up*]

sit-up·on (sit′ə pon′, -pôn′), *n.* **1.** a piece of waterproof fabric or other material carried by campers, hikers, etc., and used for sitting on wet surfaces. **2.** *Chiefly Brit. Informal.* the buttocks. [1835–45; n. use of v. phrase *sit upon*]

si·tus (sī′təs, sē′-), *n., pl.* **-tus. 1.** position; situation. **2.** the proper or original position, as of a part or organ. [1695–1705; < L; see SITE]

si′tus in·ver′sus (in vûr′səs), *Med.* a congenital defect in which an organ is on the side opposite from its normal position. [< NL: inverse situs; see INVERSE]

si′tus pick′eting. See **common situs picketing.** [1960–65]

sit·u·tun·ga (sit′ə to͞ong′ə), *n.* sitatunga.

Sit·well (sit′wəl, -wel), *n.* **1. Dame Edith,** 1887–1964, English poet and critic. **2.** her brother, **Sir Osbert,**

1892–1969, English poet and novelist. **3.** her brother, **Sir Sa·chev·er·ell** (sə shev′ər əl), 1897–1988, English poet, novelist, and art critic.

sitz′ bath′ (sits, zits), **1.** a chairlike bathtub in which the thighs and hips are immersed in warm water, usually as part of a therapeutic treatment. **2.** the bath so taken. [1840–50; half adoption, half trans. of G *Sitzbad,* equiv. to *sitz(en)* to SIT[1] + *Bad* BATH[1]]

sitz·krieg (sits′krēg′, zits′-), *n.* slow-moving warfare marked by repeated stalemate. [1935–40; < G, equiv. to *sitz(en)* to SIT[1] + *Krieg* war; modeled on BLITZKRIEG]

sitz·mark (sits′märk′, zits′-), *n. Skiing.* a sunken area in the snow marking a backward fall of a skier. [1935–40; < G, equiv. to *sitz(en)* to SIT[1] + *Mark* MARK[1]]

SI units. See under **International System of Units.**

Si·va (sē′və, shē′və), *n. Hinduism.* Shiva.

Si·van (siv′ən; *Heb.* sē vän′), *n.* the ninth month of the Jewish calendar. Cf. **Jewish calendar.** [< Heb *sīwān*]

Siv·a·pith·e·cus (siv′ə pith′i kəs, -pə thē′kəs), *n.* a genus of extinct Miocene primates of Asia that resemble the modern orang-utan. [< NL, equiv. to *Siva* (< Skt *śiva* SHIVA) + Gk *píthēkos* ape]

Si·vas (sē väs′), *n.* a city in central Turkey. 149,155.

si·wash (sī′wosh, -wôsh), *Pacific Northwest, Northwest Canada, and Alaska.* —*n.* **1.** (*sometimes cap.*) *Disparaging and Offensive.* a North American Indian. —*v.i.* **2.** to camp out without a tent or supplies. [1830–40; < Chinook Jargon < North American F *sauvage* Indian, F: wild, SAVAGE]

Si·wash (sī′wosh, -wôsh), *n.* a conventional designation for any small, provincial college or for such colleges collectively (often prec. by *old*): *students from old Siwash.* [after a fictional college of the same name in *At Good Old Siwash* (1911) and other books by U.S. author George Helgeson Fitch (1877–1915)]

six (siks), *n.* **1.** a cardinal number, five plus one. **2.** a symbol for this number, as 6 or VI. **3.** a set of this many persons or things. **4.** a playing card, die face, or half of a domino face with six pips. **5.** *Cricket.* a hit in which the ball crosses the boundary line of the field without a bounce, counting six runs for the batsman. Cf. **boundary** (def. 3). **6.** an automobile powered by a six-cylinder engine. **7.** a six-cylinder engine. **8. at sixes and sevens, a.** in disorder or confusion. **b.** in disagreement or dispute. —*adj.* **9.** amounting to six in number. [bef. 900; ME *six, sex,* OE *siex, syx, seox, sex;* c. D *zes,* LG *ses,* G *sechs,* ON *sex,* Goth *saihs,* L *sex,* Gk *héx,* Skt *ṣaṣ*]

Six′ Char′acters in Search′ of an Au′thor, a play (1921) by Luigi Pirandello.

Six′-Day War′ (siks′dā′), a war fought in June, 1967, between Israel and the neighboring states of Egypt, Jordan, and Syria, in which Israel captured large tracts of Arab territory.

six·fold (siks′fōld′), *adj.* **1.** having six elements or parts. **2.** six times as great or as much. —*adv.* **3.** in sixfold measure. [bef. 1000; ME *sexfold,* OE *sixfeald.* See SIX, -FOLD]

six-foot·er (siks′fo͝ot′ər), *n.* a person who is roughly six feet tall. [1835–45; SIX + FOOT + -ER[1]]

six-gun (siks′gun′), *n.* a six-shooter. [1910–15]

Six′ Na′tions, the Five Nations of the Iroquois confederacy and the Tuscaroras.

606 (siks′ō′siks′), *n.* arsphenamine. Also, **six′-o′-six′.** [so called because it was the 606th compound prepared in a series of tests conducted ca.1910 by Paul Ehrlich]

six-pack (siks′pak′), *n.* **1.** six bottles or cans of a beverage, as beer or a soft drink, packaged and sold esp. as a unit. **2.** any package of six identical or closely related items, as seedling plants or small batteries, sold as a unit. [1950–55]

six·pence (siks′pəns), *n., pl.* **-pence, -penc·es** for 2. **1.** (*used with a singular or plural v.*) *Brit.* a sum of six pennies. **2.** (*used with a singular v.*) a cupronickel coin of the United Kingdom, the half of a shilling, formerly equal to six pennies: equal to two and one-half new pence after decimalization in 1971. [1350–1400; ME *sexe pans.* See SIX, PENCE]

six·pen·ny (siks′pen′ē, -pə nē), *adj.* **1.** of the amount or value of sixpence; costing sixpence. **2.** of trifling value; cheap; paltry. **3.** noting a nail 2 in. (5 cm) long. *Symbol:* 6d [1400–50; late ME; see SIX, -PENNY]

six-shoot·er (siks′sho͞o′tər, -sho͞o′-), *n.* a revolver from which six shots can be fired without reloading. [1835–45, *Amer.*]

six-spot (siks′spot′), *n.* **1.** a playing card or the upward face of a die bearing six pips. **2.** a domino one half of which bears six pips. [1825–35]

sixte (sikst), *n. Fencing.* the sixth of eight defensive positions. [1880–85; < F < L *sextus* SIXTH]

six·teen (siks′tēn′), *n.* **1.** a cardinal number, ten plus six. **2.** a symbol for this number, as 16 or XVI. **3.** a set of this many persons or things. —*adj.* **4.** amounting to 16 in number. [bef. 900; ME, OE *sixtēne;* c. D *zestien,* G *sechzehn,* ON *sextān.* See SIX, -TEEN]

16-gauge (siks′tēn gāj′), *adj.* **1.** of, pertaining to, or being a size of shotgun shell having a diameter of 0.662 in. (1.68 cm). **2.** of, pertaining to, or being a shotgun using such a shell.

six·teen·mo (siks′tēn′mō), *n., pl.* **-mos,** *adj.* —*n.* **1.** Also called **sextodecimo.** a book size (about 4×6 in.; 10×15 cm) determined by printing on sheets folded to form 16 leaves or 32 pages. **2.** a book of this size. *Symbol:* 16mo, 16° —*adj.* **3.** printed, folded, or bound in sixteenmo; sextodecimo. [1840–50; SIXTEEN + -MO]

six·teen·pen·ny (siks′tēn′pen′ē), *adj.* noting a nail 3½ in. (9 cm) long. *Symbol:* 16d [SIXTEEN + -PENNY]

six·teenth (siks′tēnth′), *adj.* **1.** next after the fifteenth; being the ordinal number for 16. **2.** being one of 16 equal parts. —*n.* **3.** a sixteenth part, esp. of one (1/16). **4.** the sixteenth member of a series. **5.** *Music.* See **sixteenth note.** [bef. 900; ME *sixtenthe* (see SIXTEEN, -TH[2]); r. ME *sixtenthe, sixtethe,* OE *sixtēotha* (see TITHE)]

Six′teenth Amend′ment, an amendment to the U.S. Constitution, ratified in 1913, authorizing Congress to levy a tax on incomes.

six′teenth′ note′, *Music.* a note having one sixteenth of the time value of a whole note; semiquaver. See illus. under **note.** [1860–65]

six′teenth′ rest′, *Music.* a rest equal in time value to a sixteenth note. See illus. under **rest.** [1890–95]

sixth (siksth), *adj.* **1.** next after the fifth; being the ordinal number for six. **2.** being one of six equal parts. —*n.* **3.** a sixth part, esp. of one (1/6). **4.** the sixth member of a series. **5.** *Music.* **a.** a tone on the sixth degree from a given tone (counted as a first). **b.** the interval between such tones. **c.** the harmonic combination of such tones. —*adv.* **6.** in the sixth place; sixthly. [bef. 900; SIX + -TH[2]; r. *sixt,* ME *sixte,* OE *sixta*] —**sixth′ly,** *adv.*

Sixth′ Amend′ment, an amendment to the U.S. Constitution, ratified in 1791 as part of the Bill of Rights, guaranteeing the right to a trial by jury in criminal cases.

sixth′ chord′, *Music.* an inversion of a triad in which the second note (next above the root) is in the bass. [1870–75]

sixth′ col′umn, 1. the persons residing in a country at war who are devoted to aiding the fifth column in its activities, esp. by lowering morale, spreading rumors, etc. **2.** the persons residing in a country at war who are devoted to blocking the efforts of the fifth column.

Sixth′ Command′ment, "Thou shalt not kill": sixth of the Ten Commandments. Cf. **Ten Commandments.**

sixth′ man′ (man), *Basketball.* a team's best substitute.

sixth′ sense′, a power of perception beyond the five senses; intuition: *His sixth sense warned him to be cautious.* [1830–40]

six·ti·eth (siks′tē ith), *adj.* **1.** next after the fifty-ninth; being the ordinal number for 60. **2.** being one of 60 equal parts. —*n.* **3.** a sixtieth part, esp. of one (1/60). **4.** the sixtieth member of a series. [bef. 1000; ME *sixtithe, sixtiaghte,* OE *sixtighetha, sixteoghotha;* see SIXTY, -ETH[2]]

Six·tine (siks′tēn, -tīn), *adj.* Sistine.

Six·tus I (siks′təs), **Saint,** pope A.D. 116?–125?. Also, **Xystus I.**

Sixtus II, Saint, died A.D. 258, pope 257–258. Also, **Xystus II.**

Sixtus III, Saint, pope A.D. 432–440. Also, **Xystus III.**

Sixtus IV, (*Francesco della Rovere*) 1414–84, Italian ecclesiastic: pope 1471–84.

Sixtus V, (*Felice Peretti*) 1521–90, Italian ecclesiastic: pope 1585–90.

six·ty (siks′tē), *n., pl.* **-ties,** *adj.* —*n.* **1.** a cardinal number, ten times six. **2.** a symbol for this number, as 60 or LX. **3.** a set of this many persons or things. **4. sixties,** the numbers, years, degrees, or the like, from 60 through 69, as in referring to numbered streets, indicating the years of a lifetime or of a century, or noting degrees of temperature: *Her grandfather is in his late sixties. The temperature is in the low sixties.* **5. like sixty,** *Informal.* with great speed, ease, energy, or zest: *Everyone was working like sixty to finish up before the holidays.* —*adj.* **6.** amounting to 60 in number. [bef. 900; ME (adj. and n.), OE *sixtig* (adj.); c. D *zestig,* G *sechzig,* ON *sextigir.* See SIX, -TY[1]]

six·ty-eight (sik′stē āt′), *n.* **1.** a cardinal number, 60 plus 8. **2.** a symbol for this number, as 68 or LXVIII. **3.** a set of this many persons or things. —*adj.* **4.** amounting to 68 in number.

six·ty-eighth (siks′tē ātth′, -āth′), *adj.* **1.** next after the sixty-seventh; being the ordinal number for 68. **2.** being one of 68 equal parts. —*n.* **3.** a sixty-eighth part, esp. of one (1/68). **4.** the sixty-eighth member of a series.

six·ty-fifth (siks′tē fifth′), *adj.* **1.** next after the sixty-fourth; being the ordinal number for 65. **2.** being one of 65 equal parts. —*n.* **3.** a sixty-fifth part, esp. of one (1/65). **4.** the sixty-fifth member of a series.

six·ty-first (siks′tē fûrst′), *adj.* **1.** next after the sixtieth; being the ordinal number for 61. **2.** being one of 61 equal parts. —*n.* **3.** a sixty-first part, esp. of one (1/61). **4.** the sixty-first member of a series.

six·ty-five (siks′tē fīv′), *n.* **1.** a cardinal number, 60 plus 5. **2.** a symbol for this number, as 65 or LXV. **3.** a set of this many persons or things. —*adj.* **4.** amounting to 65 in number.

six·ty-four (siks′tē fôr′, -fōr′), *n.* **1.** a cardinal number, 60 plus 4. **2.** a symbol for this number, as 64 or LXIV. **3.** a set of this many persons or things. —*adj.* **4.** amounting to 64 in number.

six′ty-four-dol′lar ques′tion (siks′tē fôr′dol′ər, -fōr′-), the critical or basic question or problem: *Whether the measure will get through Congress this session or not is the sixty-four-dollar question.* Also, **$64 question.** [from the fact that 64 dollars was the largest prize on a popular radio quiz show in the 1940's]

six·ty-four·mo (siks′tē fôr′mō, -fōr′-), *n., pl.* **-mos,** *adj.* —*n.* **1.** a book size (about 2 × 3 inches; 5 × 7 cm) determined by printing on sheets folded to form 64 leaves or 128 pages. **2.** a book of this size. *Symbol:* 64mo, 64° —*adj.* **3.** printed, folded, or bound in sixty-fourmo. [SIXTY-FOUR + -MO]

six·ty-fourth (siks′tē fôrth′, -fōrth′), *adj.* **1.** next after the sixty-third; being the ordinal number for 64. **2.** being one of 64 equal parts. —*n.* **3.** a sixty-fourth part, esp. of one (1/64). **4.** the sixty-fourth member of a series.

six′ty-fourth′ note′, *Music.* a note having one sixty-fourth of the time value of a whole note; hemidemisemiquaver. See illus. under **note.**

six′ty-fourth′ rest′, *Music.* a rest equal in time value to a sixty-fourth note. See illus. under **rest.** [1920–25]

six·ty-nine (siks′tē nīn′), *n.* **1.** a cardinal number, 60 plus 9. **2.** a symbol for this number, as 69 or LXIX. **3.** a set of this many persons or things. **4.** *Slang* (*vulgar*). simultaneous oral-genital sexual activity between two partners. —*adj.* **5.** amounting to 69 in number.

six·ty-ninth (siks′tē nīnth′), *adj.* **1.** next after the sixty-eighth; being the ordinal number for 69. **2.** being one of 69 equal parts. —*n.* **3.** a sixty-ninth part, esp. of one (1/69). **4.** the sixty-ninth member of a series.

six·ty-one (siks′tē wun′), *n.* **1.** a cardinal number, 60 plus 1. **2.** a symbol for this number, as 61 or LXI. **3.** a set of this many persons or things. —*adj.* **4.** amounting to 61 in number.

six·ty·pen·ny (siks′tē pen′ē), *adj.* noting a nail 6 in. (15 cm) long. *Abbr.:* 60d [SIXTY + -PENNY]

six·ty-sec·ond (siks′tē sek′ənd), *adj.* **1.** next after the sixty-first; being the ordinal number for 62. **2.** being one of 62 equal parts. —*n.* **3.** a sixty-second part, esp. of one (1/62). **4.** the sixty-second member of a series.

six·ty-sev·en (siks′tē sev′ən), *n.* **1.** a cardinal number, 60 plus 7. **2.** a symbol for this number, as 67 or LXVII. **3.** a set of this many persons or things. —*adj.* **4.** amounting to 67 in number.

six·ty-sev·enth (siks′tē sev′ənth), *adj.* **1.** next after the sixty-sixth; being the ordinal number for 67. **2.** being one of 67 equal parts. —*n.* **3.** a sixty-seventh part, esp. of one (1/67). **4.** the sixty-seventh member of a series.

six·ty-six (siks′tē siks′), *n.* **1.** a cardinal number, 60 plus 6. **2.** a symbol for this number, as 66 or LXVI. **3.** a set of this many persons or things. **4.** a card game that is played by two players with a 24-card pack made by removing all cards below the nines from a regular 52-card pack, the object being to score 66 points before one's opponent. —*adj.* **5.** amounting to 66 in number.

six·ty-sixth (siks′tē siksth′), *adj.* **1.** next after the sixty-fifth; being the ordinal number for 66. **2.** being one of 66 equal parts. —*n.* **3.** a sixty-sixth part, esp. of one (1/66). **4.** the sixty-sixth member of a series.

six·ty-third (siks′tē thûrd′), *adj.* **1.** next after the sixty-second; being the ordinal number for 63. **2.** being one of 63 equal parts. —*n.* **3.** a sixty-third part, esp. of one (1/63). **4.** the sixty-third member of a series.

six·ty-three (siks′tē thrē′), *n.* **1.** a cardinal number, 60 plus 3. **2.** a symbol for this number, as 63 or LXIII. **3.** a set of this many persons or things. —*adj.* **4.** amounting to 63 in number.

six·ty-two (siks′tē to͞o′), *n.* **1.** a cardinal number, 60 plus 2. **2.** a symbol for this number, as 62 or LXII. **3.** a set of this many persons or things. —*adj.* **4.** amounting to 62 in number.

six-wheel·er (siks′hwē′lər, -wē′-), *n.* **1.** a truck or other vehicle having six wheels. **2.** *CB Slang.* **a.** a small truck. **b.** a passenger car pulling a trailer. [1885–90]

siz·a·ble (sī′zə bəl), *adj.* **1.** of considerable size; fairly large: *He inherited a sizable fortune.* **2.** *Obs.* of convenient or suitable size. Also, **sizeable.** [1605–15; SIZE[1] + -ABLE] —**siz′a·ble·ness,** *n.* —**siz′a·bly,** *adv.*

siz·ar (sī′zər), *n.* (at Cambridge University and at Trinity College, Dublin) an undergraduate who receives maintenance aid from the college. Also, **sizer.** [1580–90; SIZE[1] + -AR[3]] —**siz′ar·ship′,** *n.*

size[1] (sīz), *n., v.,* **sized, siz·ing.** —*n.* **1.** the spatial dimensions, proportions, magnitude, or bulk of anything: *the size of a farm; the size of the fish you caught.* **2.** considerable or great magnitude: *to seek size rather than quality.* **3.** one of a series of graduated measures for articles of manufacture or trade: *children's sizes of shoes.* **4.** extent; amount; range: *a fortune of great size.* **5.** actual condition, circumstance, or state of affairs: *That's about the size of it.* **6.** a number of population or contents: *What size is Springfield, Illinois? The size of that last shipment was only a dozen.* **7.** *Obs.* a fixed standard of quality or quantity, as for food or drink. **8. of a size,** of the same or similar size: *The two poodles are of a size.* **9. try on for size, a.** to put on briefly in order to test the fit of, as a garment or shoes. **b.** to consider, evaluate, do, or use before taking further action: *We'll try the plan on for size to see whether it's practical.* —*v.t.* **10.** to separate or sort according to size. **11.** to make of a certain size. **12.** *Metall.* to press (a sintered compact) to close tolerances. **13.** *Obs.* to regulate or control according to a fixed standard. **14. size up,** *Informal.* **a.** to form an estimate of (a situation, person, etc.); judge: *They sized him up with a look.* **b.** to meet a certain standard: *He doesn't size up to my expectations.* [1250–1300; (n.) ME *syse* orig., control, regulation, limit < OF *sise,* aph. var. of *assise* ASSIZE; (v.) in part repr. late ME *sisen* to regulate (itself partly deriv. of the n., partly aph. var. of *assisen* to fix, ordain, assess < OF *assiser,* deriv. of *assise* ASSIZE), in part deriv. of the n. in later senses]
—**Syn. 1.** SIZE, VOLUME, MASS, BULK are terms referring to the extent or dimensions of that which has magnitude and occupies space. SIZE is the general word: *of great size; small in size.* VOLUME often applies to something that has no fixed shape: *Smoke has volume.* MASS, also, does not suggest shape, but suggests a quantity of matter in a solid body: *a mass of concrete.* BULK suggests weight, and often a recognizable, though perhaps unwieldy, shape: *the huge bulk of an elephant.*

size[2] (sīz), *n., v.,* **sized, siz·ing.** —*n.* **1.** any of various gelatinous or glutinous preparations made from glue, starch, etc., used for filling the pores of cloth, paper, etc., or as an adhesive ground for gold leaf on books. —*v.t.*

2. to coat or treat with size. [1400–50; late ME *sise, syse* (n.); perh. special use of SIZE[1]]

size•a•ble (sī′zə bəl), *adj.* sizable. **—size′a•ble•ness,** *n.* **—size′a•bly,** *adv.*

sized (sīzd), *adj.* having size as specified (often used in combination): *middle-sized.* [1575–85; SIZE[1] + -ED[3]]

siz•er[1] (sī′zər), *n.* **1.** any device for measuring or sorting objects according to size. **2.** a worker who judges or sorts objects according to size. [1670–80; SIZE[1] + -ER[1]]

siz•er[2] (sī′zər), *n.* sizar.

size-up (sīz′up′), *n.* an appraisal or estimation, esp. as the result of sizing up: *asking for a size-up of the new office equipment.* [n. use of v. phrase *size up*]

siz•ing (sī′zing), *n.* **1.** the act or process of applying size or preparing with size. **2.** size, as for glazing paper or strengthening fabric. [1625–35; SIZE[2] + -ING[1]]

siz•y (sī′zē), *adj.*, **siz•i•er, siz•i•est.** *Archaic.* thick; viscous. [1680–90; SIZE[2] + -Y[1]] **—siz′i•ness,** *n.*

siz•zle (siz′əl), *v.*, **-zled, -zling,** *n.* **—***v.i.* **1.** to make a hissing sound, as in frying or burning. **2.** *Informal.* to be very hot: *It's sizzling out.* **3.** *Informal.* to be very angry; harbor deep resentment: *I'm still sizzling over that insult.* **—***v.t.* **4.** to fry or burn with or as if with a hissing sound: *to sizzle steaks on the grill; The sun sizzles the pavement.* **—***n.* **5.** a sizzling sound. [1595–1605; imit.; see -LE] **—siz′zler,** *n.* **—siz′zling•ly,** *adv.*
—Syn. 1. sputter, spatter, crackle, hiss.

S.J., Society of Jesus.

Sjael•land (shel′län), *n.* Zealand.

sjam•bok (sham bok′, -buk′), *n.* **1.** (in southern Africa) a heavy whip, usually of rhinoceros hide. **—***v.t.* **2.** to whip with or as if with such a whip. [1820–30; < Afrik *s(j)ambok* < Malay *cambuk* whip < Hindi *cābuk*]

S.J.D., Doctor of Juridical Science. [< L *Scientiae Jūridicae Doctor*]

S.J. Res., Senate joint resolution.

sk., sack.

ska (skä), *n.* a modern style of vocalized Jamaican popular music, which emerged in the 1950's as a blend of African-Jamaican folk music, calypso, and American rhythm and blues, notable for its shuffling, scratchlike tempo and jazzlike horn riffs on the offbeat. Cf. **reggae, rock steady.** [1960–65; of obscure orig.]

skag (skag), *n. Slang.* scag.

Ska•gen (skä′gən), *n.* See **Skaw, The.**

Skag•er•rak (skag′ə rak′, skä′gə räk′), *n.* an arm of the North Sea, between Denmark and Norway. 150 mi. (240 km) long; 80–90 mi. (130–145 km) wide.

Skag•way (skag′wā′), *n.* a town in SE Alaska, near the famous White and Chilkoot passes to the Klondike gold fields: railway terminus. 768.

skaif (skīf, skāf), *n.* skeif.

skald (skôld, skäld), *n.* one of the ancient Scandinavian poets. Also, **scald.** [1755–65; < ON *skāld* poet] **—skald′ic,** *adj.* **—skald′ship,** *n.*

Skan•da (skun′də), *n.* the Hindu god of war. Cf. **Karttikeya.**

skank (skangk), *v.i. Slang.* to dance rhythmically in a loose-limbed manner. [1980–85; orig. uncert.] **—skank′er,** *n.*

Ska•ra Brae (skar′ə brā′), the site of an excavated Neolithic village on Pomona in the Orkney Islands, dating from c2000 B.C.

skat (skät, skat), *n.* a card game for three players, using a pack of 32 playing cards, sevens through aces, the object being to fulfill any of various contracts, with scoring computed on strategy and on tricks won. [1860–65; < G *skat* < It *scarto,* deriv. of *scartare* to discard, equiv. to *s-* EX-[1] + *-cartare,* deriv. of *carta* CARD[1]]

skate[1] (skāt), *n., v.,* **skat•ed, skat•ing.** **—***n.* **1.** See **ice skate** (def. 1). **2.** See **roller skate. 3.** the blade of an ice skate. **4.** a skid on a lifeboat to facilitate launching from a listing ship. **5. get** or **put one's skates on,** *Brit. Informal.* to make haste. **—***v.i.* **6.** to glide or propel oneself on skates. **7.** to glide or slide smoothly along. **8.** *Slang.* to shirk one's duty; loaf. **9.** (of the tone arm on a record player) to swing toward the spindle while a record is playing. **—***v.t.* **10.** to slide (a flat) across the floor of a stage. **11. skate on thin ice,** to be or place oneself in a risky or delicate situation. [1640–50; orig. pl. *scates* < D *schaats* (sing.) skate, MD *schaetse* stilt (cf. ML *scatia*) < ?] **—skate′a•ble,** *adj.*

skate[2] (skāt), *n., pl.* (*esp. collectively*) **skate,** (*esp. referring to two or more kinds or species*) **skates.** any of several rays of the genus *Raja,* usually having a pointed snout, as *R. binoculata* **(big skate),** inhabiting waters along the Pacific coast of the U.S., growing to a length of 8 ft. (2.4 m). [1300–50; ME *scate* < ON *skati*]

skate[2], *Raja erinacea,* width 1 ft. (0.3 m)

skate[3] (skāt), *n. Slang.* **1.** a person; fellow: *He's a good skate.* **2.** a contemptible person. **3.** an inferior, decrepit horse; nag. [perh. special use of SKATE[2]]

skate•board (skāt′bôrd′, -bōrd′), *n.* **1.** a device for riding upon, usually while standing, consisting of a short, oblong piece of wood, plastic, or aluminum mounted on large roller-skate wheels, used on smooth surfaces and requiring better balance of the rider than the ordinary roller skate does. **—***v.i.* **2.** to ride a skateboard. [1960–65; SKATE[1] + BOARD] **—skate′board′er,** *n.*

skate•board•ing (skāt′bôr′ding, -bōr′-), *n.* the sport of riding a skateboard. Also called **skurfing.** [1960–65; SKATEBOARD + -ING[1]]

skate•mo•bile (skāt′mō bēl′), *n.* a scooterlike vehicle built of boxes, boards, or the like, and mounted on skate wheels. [SKATE[1] + (AUTO)MOBILE]

skat•er (skā′tər), *n.* **1.** a person who skates. **2.** See **water strider.** [1690–1700; SKATE[1] + -ER[1]]

skat•ole (skat′ōl, -ôl), *n.* a white, crystalline, water-soluble solid, C_9H_9N, having a strong, fecal odor: used chiefly as a fixative in the manufacture of perfume. [1875–80; < Gk *skat-* (s. of *skôr*) dung + -OLE[2]]

Skaw (skô), *n.* **The,** a cape at the N tip of Denmark. Also called **Skagen.**

skean (skēn, skē′ən), *n.* a knife or dagger formerly used in Ireland and in the Scottish Highlands. Also, **skene.** [1520–30; < ScotGael *sgian* or Ir *scian*]

skean′ dhu′ (t͟hoo, do͞o), a small knife tucked into or worn against the top of a stocking in the full dress of Highland Scottish males. Also, **skene dhu.** [1810–20; < ScotGael *sgian dhubh* lit., black skean]

Skeat (skēt), *n.* **Walter William,** 1835–1912, English philologist and lexicographer.

sked (sked), *n. Informal.* an airline that maintains a regular schedule of flights. [1925–30, in sense "schedule"; by shortening and resp.]

ske•dad•dle (ski dad′l), *v.,* **-dled, -dling,** *n. Informal.* **—***v.i.* **1.** to run away hurriedly; flee. **—***n.* **2.** a hasty flight. [1860–65, *Amer.*; cf. dial. (Scots, N England) *skedaddle* to spill, scatter, *skiddle* to move away quickly]

ske•dad•dler (ski dad′lər), *n. Informal.* **1.** a person or thing that skedaddles. **2.** *Canadian.* a U.S. citizen who fled to Canada rather than serve in the armed forces during the American Civil War. [1860–65, *Amer.*; SKEDADDLE + -ER[1]]

skee (skē), *n., pl.* **skees, skee,** *v.i., v.t.,* **skeed, skee•ing.** ski.

Skee-Ball (skē′bôl′), *Trademark.* a brand name for a game in which players roll balls up a sloping, table-sized ramp, attempting to score points by making them drop into slots in a target.

skeech (skēkh), *adj., adv. Scot.* skeigh.

skeet[1] (skēt), *n.* a form of trapshooting in which two traps are used and targets are hurled singly or in pairs at varying elevations and speeds so as to simulate the angles of flight taken by game birds. Also called **skeet′ shoot′ing.** [adopted in 1926 as the result of a contest to choose a name for the sport (the winner claimed that the word was "a very old form" of SHOOT[1])]

skeet[2] (skēt), *n. Poker.* a hand consisting of a nine, five, two, and two other cards of denominations below nine but not of the same denomination, being of special value in certain games. Also called **kilter, pelter.** [orig. uncert.]

skeet[3] (skēt), *v.t. Southern U.S. and Brit. Dial.* **1.** to spit (saliva or a mouthful of other liquid) from the mouth, esp. between the teeth. **2.** to splash; spray: *Skeet some cold water on your face to cool off.* [1875–80; cf. Scots *skite,* scoot in same sense, prob. ult. < ON *skýt-,* s. of *skjóta* to shoot, propel dart (see SHOOT[1])]

skee•ter (skē′tər), *n. Informal.* mosquito. [1850–55; by aphesis and resp., with dial. substitution of *-er* for final *-o*]

skeet′er hawk′. See **mosquito hawk.**

skeg (skeg), *n. Naut.* **1.** a projection supporting a rudder at its lower end, located abaft a sternpost or rudderpost. **2.** an extension of the keel of a small craft, designed to improve steering. [1590–1600; < D *scheg* cutwater < Scand; cf. ON *skegg* projection on the stern of a boat]

skeif (skīf, skāf), *n.* a wheel on which diamonds and other gems are ground or polished. Also, **skaif.** [earlier *scaife* < D *schijf* disk, wheel, MD *scīve;* see SHIVE[1]]

skeigh (skēkh), *Scot.* **—***adj.* **1.** (of horses) spirited; inclined to shy. **2.** (of women) proud; disdainful. **—***adv.* **3.** proudly. Also, **skeech, skiech.** [1500–10; earlier *skeich,* late ME *skey,* perh. continuing OE *scēoh* SHY[2], with *sk-* < MD *schu* shy] **—skeigh′ish,** *adj.*

skein (skān), *n.* **1.** a length of yarn or thread wound on a reel or swift preparatory for use in manufacturing. **2.** anything wound in or resembling such a coil: *a skein of hair.* **3.** something suggestive of the twistings of a skein: *an incoherent skein of words.* **4.** a flock of geese, ducks, or the like, in flight. **5.** a succession or series of similar or interrelated things: *a skein of tennis victories.* [1400–50; late ME *skeyne, skayne* < MF *escaigne* < ?]

skel•e•tal (skel′i tl), *adj.* of, pertaining to, or like a skeleton. [1850–55; SKELET(ON) + -AL[1]] **—skel′e•tal•ly,** *adv.*

skel•e•ton (skel′i tn), *n.* **1.** *Anat., Zool.* the bones of a human or an animal considered as a whole, together forming the framework of the body. **2.** any of various structures forming a rigid framework in an invertebrate. **3.** an emaciated person or animal. **4.** a supporting framework, as of a leaf, building, or ship. **5.** an outline, as of a literary work: *the skeleton of the plot.* **6.** something reduced to its essential parts. **7. skeleton at the feast,** a person or thing that casts gloom over a joyful occasion; a note or reminder of sorrow in the midst of joy. **8. skeleton in the closet** or **cupboard, a.** a family scandal that is concealed to avoid public disgrace. **b.** any embarrassing, shameful, or damaging secret. **—***adj.* **9.** of or pertaining to a skeleton. **10.** like or being a mere framework; reduced to the essential or minimal parts or numbers: *a skeleton staff.* [1570–80; < NL < Gk: mummy, n. use of neut. of *skeletós* dried up, verbal of *skéllein* to dry] **—skel′e•ton•less,** *adj.* **—skel′e•ton•like′,** *adj.*

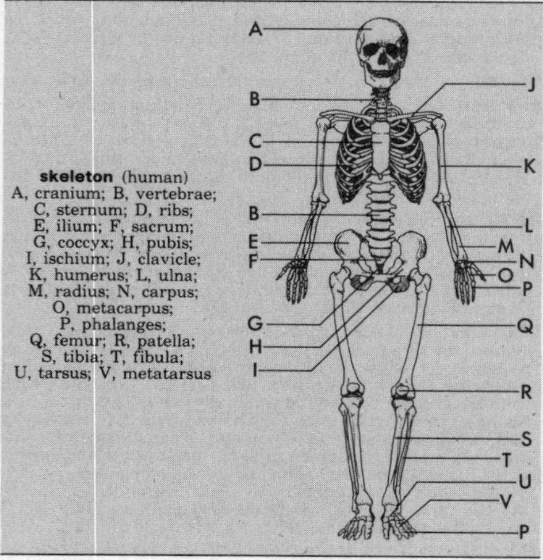

skeleton (human)
A, cranium; B, vertebrae; C, sternum; D, ribs; E, ilium; F, sacrum; G, coccyx; H, pubis; I, ischium; J, clavicle; K, humerus; L, ulna; M, radius; N, carpus; O, metacarpus; P, phalanges; Q, femur; R, patella; S, tibia; T, fibula; U, tarsus; V, metatarsus

skel′eton car′, *Railroads.* a freight car essentially consisting of a central longitudinal girder fastened to the trucks, sometimes supplemented by one or more pairs of cross cantilevers: used for carrying logs or containers. [1935–40]

skel•e•ton•ize (skel′i tn īz′), *v.t.,* **-ized, -iz•ing. 1.** to reduce to a skeleton, outline, or framework. **2.** to reduce in size or number, as a military unit. **3.** to construct in outline. Also, *esp. Brit.,* **skel′e•ton•ise′.** [1635–45; SKELETON + -IZE] **—skel′e•ton•i•za′tion,** *n.* **—skel′e•ton•iz′er,** *n.*

skel′eton key′, a key with nearly the whole substance of the bit filed away so that it may open various locks. Also called **passkey.** [1800–10]

skel′ic in′dex (skel′ik), *Anthropometry.* the ratio of the length of the leg to the length of the torso of a person, multiplied by 100. [< Gk *skél(os)* leg + -IC]

skell (skel), *n. Slang.* **1.** a homeless person who lives on the streets, sleeps in doorways or subways, etc.; derelict. **2.** a slovenly person. [1980–85; perh. shortening of SKELETON]

skel•lum (skel′əm), *n. Chiefly Scot.* a rascal. [1605–15; < D *schelm* rogue, knave < MLG; c. G *Schelm* rogue, OHG *skelmo, scalmo* plague, corpse]

skelp[1] (skelp), *Scot. and North Eng.* **—***n.* **1.** a slap, smack, or blow, esp. one given with the open hand. **2.** the sound of such a slap or smack. **—***v.t.* **3.** to slap, smack, or strike (someone), esp. on the buttocks; spank. **4.** to drive (animals) by slapping or goading them. Also, **scelp.** [1350–1400; ME; prob. imit.]

skelp[2] (skelp), *n.* metal in strip form that is fed into various rolls and welded to form tubing. [1805–15; perh. special use of SKELP[1]]

skel•ter (skel′tər), *v.i.* to scurry. [1850–55; prob. extracted from HELTER-SKELTER]

Skel•ton (skel′tn), *n.* **John,** c1460–1529, English poet.

ske•ne[1] (skē′nē), *n., pl.* **-nai** (-nī). (in the ancient Greek theater) a structure facing the audience and forming the background before which performances were given. [< Gk *skēnḗ;* see SCENE]

skene[2] (skēn), *n.* skean.

skene dhu (skēn′ t͟hoo′, do͞o′). See **skean dhu.**

skep (skep), *n.* **1.** a round farm basket of wicker or wood. **2.** Also, **skepful.** the amount contained in a skep. **3.** a beehive, esp. of straw. [bef. 1100; ME *skeppe,* late OE *sceppe* < ON *skeppa* half-bushel; akin to G *Scheffel*]

skep•ful (skep′fo͝ol), *n., pl.* **-fuls.** skep (def. 2). [1560–70; SKEP + -FUL]
—Usage. See **-ful.**

skep•tic (skep′tik), *n.* **1.** a person who questions the validity or authenticity of something purporting to be factual. **2.** a person who maintains a doubting attitude, as toward values, plans, statements, or the character of others. **3.** a person who doubts the truth of a religion, esp. Christianity, or of important elements of it. **4.** (*cap.*) *Philos.* **a.** a member of a philosophical school of ancient Greece, the earliest group of which consisted of Pyrrho and his followers, who maintained that real knowledge of things is impossible. **b.** any later thinker who doubts or questions the possibility of real knowledge of any kind. **—***adj.* **5.** pertaining to skeptics or skepti-

cism; skeptical. **6.** (*cap.*) pertaining to the Skeptics. Also, **sceptic.** [1565–75; < LL *scepticus* thoughtful, inquiring (in pl. *Sceptici* the Skeptics) < Gk *skeptikós,* equiv. to *sképt(esthai)* to consider, examine (akin to *skopeîn* to look; see -SCOPE) + *-ikos* -IC]
—Syn. 3. doubter. See **atheist.** **—Ant. 3.** believer.

skep·ti·cal (skep′ti kəl), *adj.* **1.** inclined to skepticism; having doubt: *a skeptical young woman.* **2.** showing doubt: *a skeptical smile.* **3.** denying or questioning the tenets of a religion: *a skeptical approach to the nature of miracles.* **4.** (*cap.*) of or pertaining to Skeptics or Skepticism. Also, **sceptical.** [1630–40; SKEPTIC + -AL[1]] **—skep′ti·cal·ly,** *adv.* **—skep′ti·cal·ness,** *n.*
—Syn. 1. skeptic. See **doubtful. 3.** unbelieving.

skep·ti·cism (skep′tə siz′əm), *n.* **1.** skeptical attitude or temper; doubt. **2.** doubt or unbelief with regard to a religion, esp. Christianity. **3.** (*cap.*) the doctrines or opinions of philosophical Skeptics; universal doubt. Also, **scepticism.** [1640–50; < NL *scepticismus,* equiv. to L *sceptic(us)* SKEPTIC + *-ismus* -ISM]
—Syn. 1. questioning, probing, testing. **2.** disbelief, atheism, agnosticism. **—Ant. 2.** faith.

sker·rick (sker′ik), *n. Australian.* a small piece or quantity; a bit: *Not even a skerrick of cake was left.* [1930–35; orig. uncert.]

sker·ry (sker′ē), *n., pl.* **-ries.** *Chiefly Scot.* **1.** a small, rocky island. **2.** a coastline with a series of such islands offshore. [1605–15; Shetland dial. *skerri* a rock in the sea < ON *sker* (gen. pl. *skerja*) rock or reef (in the sea). See SCAR[2]]

sketch (skech), *n.* **1.** a simply or hastily executed drawing or painting, esp. a preliminary one, giving the essential features without the details. **2.** a rough design, plan, or draft, as of a book. **3.** a brief or hasty outline of facts, occurrences, etc.: *a sketch of his life.* **4.** a short, usually descriptive, essay, history, or story. **5.** a short play or slight dramatic performance, as one forming part of a vaudeville program. —*v.t.* **6.** to make a sketch of. **7.** to set forth in a brief or general account: *He sketched his own part in the affair.* **8.** *Metall.* (in a steel mill or the like) to mark (a piece) for cutting. —*v.i.* **9.** to make a sketch or sketches. [1660–70; < D *schets* (n.) << It *schizzo* < L *schedium* extemporaneous poem, n. use of neut. of *schedius* extempore < Gk *schédios*] **—sketch′·er,** *n.* **—sketch′ing·ly,** *adv.* **—sketch′like′,** *adj.*
—Syn. 2. outline. **5.** skit, act, routine. **6.** draw, outline, design, rough out, delineate, represent. See **depict.**

sketch·a·ble (skech′ə bəl), *adj.* suitable for being sketched. [1860–65; SKETCH + -ABLE] **—sketch′a·bil′i·ty,** *n.*

sketch·book (skech′bo͝ok′), *n.* **1.** a book or pad of drawing paper for sketches. **2.** a book of literary sketches. Also, **sketch′ book′.** [1810–20; SKETCH + BOOK]

Sketch′ Book′, The, a collection of essays and stories (1819–20) by Washington Irving.

sketch′ map′, a rough map of the principal features of a locale, as one drawn from memory. [1870–75]

sketch·y (skech′ē), *adj.,* **sketch·i·er, sketch·i·est. 1.** like a sketch; giving only outlines or essentials. **2.** imperfect, incomplete, slight, or superficial: *a sketchy meal.* [1795–1805; SKETCH + -Y[1]] **—sketch′i·ly,** *adv.* **—sketch′i·ness,** *n.*
—Syn. 1. cursory, rough, meager, crude.

ske·te (skē′tē; *Eng.* skēt), *n. Gk. Orth. Ch.* a settlement of monks or ascetics. [1865–70; < Gk *skḗtē,* fem. n. deriv. of *Skḗtis* a desert in Lower Egypt known for its hermits]

skeu·o·morph (skyo͞o′ə môrf′), *n.* an ornament or design on an object copied from a form of the object when made from another material or by other techniques, as an imitation metal rivet mark found on handles of prehistoric pottery. [1889; < Gk *skeû(os)* vessel, implement + -O- + -MORPH (cf. ZOOMORPHIC)] **—skeu′·o·mor′phic,** *adj.*

skew (skyo͞o), *v.i.* **1.** to turn aside or swerve; take an oblique course. **2.** to look obliquely; squint. —*v.t.* **3.** to give an oblique direction to; shape, form, or cut obliquely. **4.** *Slang.* to make conform to a specific concept, attitude, or planned result; slant: *The television show is skewed to the young teenager.* **5.** to distort; depict unfairly. —*adj.* **6.** having an oblique direction or position; slanting. **7.** having a part that deviates from a straight line, right angle, etc.: *skew gearing.* **8.** *Math.* (of a dyad or dyadic) equal to the negative of its conjugate. **9.** (of an arch, bridge, etc.) having the centerline of its opening forming an oblique angle with the direction in which its spanning structure is built. **10.** *Statistics.* (of a distribution) having skewness. —*n.* **11.** an oblique movement, direction, or position. **12.** Also called **skew′ chis′el.** a wood chisel having a cutting edge set obliquely. [1350–1400; (v.) ME *skewen* to slip away, swerve < MD *schuwen* to get out of the way, shun, deriv. of *schu* (D *schuw*) SHY[1]; (adj.) deriv. of the v. (prob. influenced by ASKEW); (n.) deriv. of the v. and adj.]

skew′ arch′, an arch, as at the entrance to a tunnel, having sides, or jambs, that are not at right angles with the face. [1835–45]

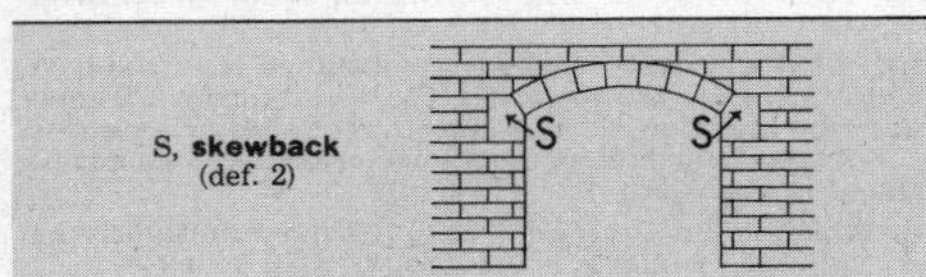

S, **skewback** (def. 2)

skew·back (skyo͞o′bak′), *n. Archit.* **1.** a sloping surface against which the end of an arch rests. **2.** a stone, course of masonry, or the like, presenting such a surface. [1695–1705; SKEW + BACK[1]] **—skew′backed′,** *adj.*

skew·bald (skyo͞o′bôld′), *adj.* **1.** (esp. of horses) having patches of brown and white. —*n.* **2.** a skewbald horse or pony. [1645–55; SKEW + (PIE)BALD]

skew·er (skyo͞o′ər), *n.* **1.** a long pin of wood or metal for inserting through meat or other food to hold or bind it in cooking. **2.** any similar pin for fastening or holding an item in place. —*v.t.* **3.** to fasten with or as if with a skewer. [1670–80; earlier *skiver* < ?]

skew·er·wood (skyo͞o′ər wo͝od′), *n. Brit. Dial.* **1.** the spindle tree, *Euonymus europaeus.* **2.** the red dogwood, *Cornus sanguinea.* [1775–85; SKEWER + WOOD[1]]

skew′ field′, *Math.* a ring in which the equations $ax = b$ and $xa = b$ have solutions for x.

skew·gee (skyo͞o′jē), *adj. Northern U.S.* crooked or slanted; cockeyed. [1840–50; appar. SKEW + GEE[1]]

skew·ing (skyo͞o′ing), *n.* **1.** a process of removing excess gold leaf from a stamped surface. **2. skewings,** the gold leaf so removed. [1850–55; orig. uncert.]

skew′ lines′, *Geom.* any lines in space that do not intersect and are not parallel. [1950–55]

skew·ness (skyo͞o′nis), *n. Statistics.* **1.** asymmetry in a frequency distribution. **2.** a measure of such asymmetry. [1890–95; SKEW + -NESS]

skew-sym·met·ric (skyo͞o′si me′trik), *adj. Math.* noting a square matrix that is equal to the negative of its transpose.

ski (skē), *n., pl.* **skis, ski,** *v.,* **skied, ski·ing.** —*n.* **1.** one of a pair of long, slender runners made of wood, plastic, or metal used in gliding over snow. **2.** See **water ski.** —*v.i.* **3.** to travel on skis, as for sport. —*v.t.* **4.** to use skis on; travel on skis over: *to ski the slopes of Switzerland.* Also, **skee.** [1745–55; < Norw; ON *skíth;* c. OE *scīd* strip of wood, G *Scheit* thin board] **—ski′a·ble,** *adj.*

ski·a·gram (skī′ə gram′), *n.* **1.** a picture made by outlining and shading a subject's shadow. **2.** skiagraph. [1795–1805; < Gk *skiā́* shadow + -GRAM[1]; cf. SKIAGRAPH]

ski·a·graph (skī′ə graf′, -gräf′), *n.* a radiograph. Also, **skiagram.** [1895–1900; back formation from *skiagraphy* the process of making skiagraphs < Gk *skiāgraphía* painting in light and shade, equiv. to *skiā-,* comb. form of *skiā́* shade + *-graphia* -GRAPHY] **—ski·a·graph·ic** (skī′ə graf′ik), **ski′a·graph′i·cal,** *adj.* **—ski·ag·ra·phy** (skī ag′rə fē), *n.*

ski·a·scope (skī′ə skōp′), *n. Ophthalm.* retinoscope. [< Gk *skiā́* a shadow, shade + -SCOPE] **—ski·as·co·py** (skī as′kə pē), *n.*

ski·bob (skē′bob′), *n.* a winter-sport vehicle for riding downhill over snow, often used at mountain resorts, that runs on a fixed ski and has a much shorter, pivoting front ski steered by handlebars, with the rider sitting as on a bicycle and usually wearing miniskis to assist in balancing the vehicle. [1965–70; SKI + BOB(SLED)] **—ski′bob′ber,** *n.* **—ski′bob′bing,** *n.*

ski′ boot′, a heavy, thick-soled, ankle-high shoe for skiing, often having padding and extra supporting straps and laces around the ankle, with grooves at the back of the heel for binding to a ski. [1905–10]

skid (skid), *n., v.,* **skid·ded, skid·ding.** —*n.* **1.** a plank, bar, log, or the like, esp. one of a pair, on which something heavy may be slid or rolled along. **2.** one of a number of such logs or timbers forming a skidway. **3.** a low mobile platform on which goods are placed for ease in handling, moving, etc. Cf. **stillage. 4.** a plank, log, low platform, etc., on or by which a load is supported. **5.** *Naut.* **a.** any of a number of parallel beams or timbers fixed in place as a raised support for boats, spars, etc. **b.** any of a number of timbers on which a heavy object is placed to be shoved along on rollers or slid. **c.** an arrangement of planks serving as a runway for cargo. **d.** an arrangement of planks serving as a fender to protect the side of a vessel during transfer of cargo. **e.** sidewise motion of a vessel; leeway. **6.** a shoe or some other choke or drag for preventing the wheel of a vehicle from rotating, as when descending a hill. **7.** a runner on the under part of some airplanes, enabling the aircraft to slide along the ground when landing. **8.** an unexpected or uncontrollable sliding on a smooth surface by something not rotating, esp. an oblique or wavering veering by a vehicle or its tires: *The bus went into a skid on the icy road.* **9. on the skids,** *Slang.* in the process of decline or deterioration: *His career is on the skids.* **10. put the skids under,** *Informal.* to bring about the downfall of; cause to fail: *Lack of money put the skids under our plans.* **11. the skids,** *Informal.* the downward path to ruin, poverty, or depravity: *After losing his job he began to hit the skids.* —*v.t.* **12.** to place on or slide along a skid. **13.** to check the motion of with a skid: *She skidded her skates to a stop.* **14.** to cause to go into a skid: *to skid the car into a turn.* —*v.i.* **15.** to slide along without rotating, as a wheel to which a brake has been applied. **16.** to slip or slide sideways, as an automobile in turning a corner rapidly. **17.** to slide forward under the force of momentum after forward motion has been braked, as a vehicle. **18.** (of an airplane when not banked sufficiently) to slide sideways, away from the center of the curve described in turning. Cf. **slip[1]** (def. 15). [1600–10; 1925–30 for def. 11; appar. < ON *skíth* (n.), c. OE *scīd* thin slip of wood; see SKI] **—skid′ding·ly,** *adv.*
—Syn. 12, 15. slip. **16.** slither.

Skid·blad·nir (skēd′bläd nir), *n. Scand. Myth.* the huge collapsible ship, made by two dwarfs for Frey, that always had a favoring wind.

skid′ chain′. See **tire chain.**

skid·der (skid′ər), *n.* **1.** a person or thing that skids. **2.** *Mach.* a type of four-wheel tractor equipped with a grapple, used to haul logs or timber, esp. over rough terrain. **3.** *Slang.* **a.** a person who is moving toward or has reached a less desirable status, condition, etc. **b.** a vagrant who lives on the streets or frequents skid row. [1865–70; SKID + -ER[1]]

skid·doo (ski do͞o′), *v.i.,* **-dooed, -doo·ing.** *Informal.* to go away; get out. [1900–05; perh. alter. of SKEDADDLE]

skid·dy (skid′ē), *adj.,* **-di·er, -di·est.** tending to skid or cause skidding: *a skiddy shopping cart; an icy, skiddy driveway.* [1900–05; SKID + -Y[1]]

skid′ fin′, *Aeron.* an upright projection or fin, positioned from leading edge to trailing edge in the center of the upper wing of some early airplanes and used to retard skidding. [1930–35]

skid·proof (skid′pro͞of′), *adj.* preventing or resistant to skidding, as certain road surfaces or vehicle tires. [1930–35; SKID + -PROOF]

skid′ row′ (rō), an area of cheap barrooms and rundown hotels, frequented by alcoholics and vagrants. Also called **Skid′ Road′.** [1930–35, *Amer.;* earlier *skid road* an area of a town frequented by loggers, orig. a skidway]

skid·way (skid′wā′), *n.* **1.** a road or path formed of logs, planks, etc., for sliding objects. **2.** a platform, usually inclined, for piling logs to be sawed or to be loaded onto a vehicle. [1875–80, *Amer.;* SKID + WAY]

skiech (skēKH), *adj., adv. Scot.* skeigh.

skied[1] (skēd), *v.* pt. of **ski.**

skied[2] (skīd), *v.* a pt. of **sky.**

ski·er (skē′ər), *n.* a person who skis. [1890–95; SKI + -ER[1]]

skies (skīz), *n.* **1.** pl. of **sky.** —*v.* **2.** 3rd pers. sing. pres. of **sky.**

ski·ey (skī′ē), *adj.* skyey.

skiff (skif), *n.* any of various types of boats small enough for sailing or rowing by one person. [1565–75; < early It *schifo* < OHG *scif* SHIP] **—skiff′less,** *adj.*

skif·fle[1] (skif′əl), *v.t.,* **-fled, -fling.** knob (def. 7). [perh. akin to SCABBLE]

skif·fle[2] (skif′əl), *n.* **1.** a jazz style of the 1920's deriving from blues, ragtime, and folk music, played by bands made up of both standard and improvised instruments. **2.** a style of popular music developed in England during the 1950's, deriving from hillbilly music and rock-'n'-roll, and played on a heterogeneous group of instruments, as guitar, washboard, ceramic jug, washtub, and kazoo. [1920–25; orig. uncert.]

ski·ing (skē′ing), *n.* the act or sport of gliding on skis. [1890–95; SKI + -ING[1]]

ski·jor·ing (skē jôr′ing, -jōr′-, skē′jôr-, -jōr-), *n.* a sport in which a skier is pulled over snow or ice, generally by a horse. [1905–10, *Amer.;* < Norw *skikjøring,* equiv. to *ski* SKI + *kjøring* driving] **—ski·jor′er,** *n.*

ski′ jump′, 1. a snow-covered chute or slide at the side of a hill or built up on top of the hill, the base of the chute having a horizontal ramp that enables a skier to speed down the chute, take off at the end of the ramp, and land further down the hill. **2.** a jump made by a skier from a ski jump. **3.** to execute or make a ski jump. [1920–25] **—ski′ jump′er.**

ski′ jump′ing, a competitive event, included in the Nordic combined, in which a skier jumps from a ski jump, often traveling 230 to 300 ft. (70 to 90 m) in the air, with scores being based on both the skier's form and the distance of the jump. [1925–30]

Ski·kda (skēk′də), *n.* a seaport in NE Algeria. 60,535. Formerly, **Philippeville.**

skil·fish (skil′fish′), *n., pl.* **-fish·es,** (*esp. collectively*) **-fish.** a sablefish, *Erilepsis zonifer,* of the North Pacific. [< Haida *sqíl* + FISH]

skil·ful (skil′fəl), *adj. Chiefly Brit.* skillful. **—skil′ful·ly,** *adv.* **—skil′ful·ness,** *n.*

ski′ lift′, a conveyance that carries skiers up the side of a slope, consisting typically of a series of chairs suspended from an endless cable driven by motors. [1935–40]

skill[1] (skil), *n.* **1.** the ability, coming from one's knowledge, practice, aptitude, etc., to do something well: *Carpentry was one of his many skills.* **2.** competent excellence in performance; expertness; dexterity: *The dancers performed with skill.* **3.** a craft, trade, or job requiring manual dexterity or special training in which a person has competence and experience: *the skill of cabinetmaking.* **4.** *Obs.* understanding; discernment. **5.** *Obs.* reason; cause. [1125–75; ME < ON *skil* distinction, difference; c. D *geschil* difference, quarrel. See SKILL[2]]
—Syn. 1. proficiency, facility. **2.** deftness, cleverness.
—Ant. 1. inability.

skill[2] (skil), *v.i. Archaic.* **1.** to matter. **2.** to help; avail. [1150–1200; ME *skilien* < ON *skilja* to distinguish, divide, akin to *skil* (see SKILL[1]), OE *scylian* to separate, Goth *skilja* butcher, Lith *skélti* to split]

skilled (skild), *adj.* **1.** having skill; trained or experienced in work that requires skill. **2.** showing, involving, or requiring skill, as certain work. [1545–55; SKILL[1] + -ED[3]]
—Syn. 1. See **skillful.**

skilled′ la′bor, 1. labor that requires special training for its satisfactory performance. **2.** the workers employed in such labor. [1770–80]

skil·less (skil′lis), *adj.* skill-less. **—skil′less·ness,** *n.*

skil·let (skil′it), *n.* **1.** a frying pan. **2.** a cylindrical serving vessel of the late 17th and early 18th centuries, having a hinged lid, a handle, and, sometimes, feet. **3.** *Chiefly Brit.* a long-handled saucepan. [1375–1425; late ME; orig. uncert.]

skill·ful (skil′fəl), *adj.* **1.** having or exercising skill: *a skillful juggler.* **2.** showing or involving skill: *a skillful display of fancy diving.* **3.** *Obs.* reasonable; rational. Also, *esp. Brit.,* **skilful.** [1250–1300; ME; see SKILL[1], -FUL] **—skill′ful·ly,** *adv.* **—skill′ful·ness,** *n.*
—Syn. 1. ready, adroit, deft, adept, apt, clever, ingenious. SKILLFUL, SKILLED, EXPERT refer to readiness and adroitness in an occupation, craft, or art. SKILLFUL suggests esp. adroitness and dexterity: *a skillful watch-*

CONCISE PRONUNCIATION KEY: *act, cāpe, dâre, pärt; set, ēqual; if, īce; ox, ōver, ôrder, oil, bo͝ok, bo͞ot, out; up, ûrge; child; sing; shoe; thin, that;* zh as in *treasure.* ə = *a* as in *alone, e* as in *system, i* as in *easily, o* as in *gallop, u* as in *circus;* ᵊ as in *fire* (fīᵊr), *hour* (ouᵊr). l and n can serve as syllabic consonants, as in *cradle* (krād′l), and *button* (but′n). See the full key inside the front cover.

maker. SKILLED implies having had long experience and thus having acquired a high degree of proficiency: *not an amateur but a skilled worker.* EXPERT means having the highest degree of proficiency; it may mean much the same as SKILLFUL or SKILLED, or both: *expert workmanship.* See also **dexterous.** **—Ant. 1.** awkward, clumsy, amateurish.

skil·ling[1] (skil′ing), *n.* **1.** a former silver coin of Denmark, Sweden, and the Danish West Indies. **2.** any of various former copper coins of Sweden and Norway. [1690–1700; < Dan; c. SHILLING]

skil·ling[2] (skil′ing), *n.* skillion.

skil·lion (skil′yən), *n. Australian.* a lean-to serving as a room or a shed. [1860–65; alter. of *skilling,* orig. dial. (S England), ME *skyling;* sense suggests kinship with dial. *scale* hut, shed (< ON *skāli;* cf. SHIEL), but phonetic development obscure; see -ING[3]]

skill-less (skil′lis), *adj.* **1.** without skill; unskilled or unskillful. **2.** *Archaic.* **a.** without knowledge; ignorant. **b.** (of things) done or made in a clumsy or unskilled manner. Also, **skilless.** [1150–1200; ME; see SKILL[1], -LESS] **—skill′-less·ness,** *n.*

skim (skim), *v.,* **skimmed, skim·ming,** *n.* **—***v.t.* **1.** to take up or remove (floating matter) from the surface of a liquid, as with a spoon or ladle: *to skim the cream from milk.* **2.** to clear (liquid) thus: *to skim milk.* **3.** to move or glide lightly over or along (a surface, as of water): *The sailboat skimmed the lake.* **4.** to throw in a smooth, gliding path over or near a surface, or so as to bounce or ricochet along a surface: *to skim a stone across the lake.* **5.** to read, study, consider, treat, etc., in a superficial or cursory manner. **6.** to cover, as a liquid, with a thin film or layer: *Ice skimmed the lake at night.* **7.** to take the best or most available parts or items from: *Bargain hunters skimmed the flea markets early in the morning.* **8.** to take (the best or most available parts or items) from something: *The real bargains had been skimmed by early shoppers.* **9.** *Metall.* to remove (slag, scum, or dross) from the surface of molten metal. **10.** *Slang.* **a.** to conceal a portion of (winnings, earnings, etc.) in order to avoid paying income taxes, commissions, or the like on the actual total revenue (sometimes fol. by *off*): *The casino skimmed two million a year.* **b.** to take, remove, or appropriate for illegal use: *to skim information from another's credit card.* **—***v.i.* **11.** to pass or glide lightly over or near a surface. **12.** to read, study, consider, etc., something in a superficial or cursory way. **13.** to become covered with a thin film or layer. **14.** *Slang.* to conceal gambling or other profits so as to avoid paying taxes, etc.; practice skimming. **—***n.* **15.** an act or instance of skimming. **16.** something that is skimmed off. **17.** a thin layer or film formed on the surface of something, esp. a liquid, as the coagulated protein material formed on boiled milk. **18.** a thin layer, as of mortar. **19.** *Slang.* the amount taken or concealed by skimming. **20.** See **skim milk. 21.** *Obs.* scum. [1375–1425; late ME *skymen, skemen,* var. of *scumen* to skim; see SCUM] **—Syn. 5.** scan. **12.** glance.

ski′ mask′, a one-piece pullover covering for the head and face, generally of knitted material with holes for the eyes, the mouth, and sometimes the nose, originally worn by skiers and used to protect the face against cold and wind. [1965–70]

skim·ble-scam·ble (skim′bəl skam′bəl; skim′əl skam′əl), *adj.* rambling; confused; nonsensical: *a skimble-scamble explanation.* Also, **skim′ble-skam′ble.** [1590–1600; gradational redupl. of dial. *scamble* to struggle, trample]

skim·mer (skim′ər), *n.* **1.** a person or thing that skims. **2.** a shallow utensil, usually perforated, used in skimming liquids. **3.** any of several gull-like birds of the family Rynchopidae, that skim the water with the elongated lower mandible immersed while in search of food. **4.** a stiff, wide-brimmed hat with a shallow flat crown, usually made of straw. **5.** a woman's A-line dress with side darts that shape it slightly to the body. [1350–1400; SKIM + -ER[1]; r. ME *skemour, skymour,* var. of *schumour* < MF (*e*)*scumoir* ladle for skimming; see SCUM]

skim·mer·ton (skim′ər tən), *n. Chiefly Hudson Valley.* shivaree (def. 1). Also, **skim·mel·ton** (skim′əl tən). [cf., in Britain, *skimmington, skim(m)iting* a similar rural custom intended to ridicule an unfaithful or abusive husband or wife, orig., an effigy of the offending person; of uncert. orig.]

skim·mi·a (skim′ē ə), *n.* any Asian evergreen shrub belonging to the genus *Skimmia,* of the rue family, having simple, alternate leaves, clusters of small, white flowers, and a red, berrylike fruit, grown as an ornamental. [1865–70; < NL]

skim′ milk′, milk from which the cream has been skimmed. Also called **skimmed′ milk′.** [1590–1600]

skim·ming (skim′ing), *n.* **1.** Usually, **skimmings.** something that is removed by skimming. **2. skimmings,** *Metall.* dross. **3.** *Slang.* the practice of concealing gambling or other profits so as to avoid paying taxes, commissions, etc. [1400–50; late ME *skemmyng.* See SKIM, -ING[1]]

ski·mo·bile (skē′mə bēl′), *n.* snowmobile (def. 1). [1940–45; SKI + -MOBILE]

skimp (skimp), *v.i.* **1.** to scrimp. **—***v.t.* **2.** to scrimp. **3.** to scamp. **—***adj.* **4.** skimpy; scanty. [1875–80; orig. uncert.] **—skimp′ing·ly,** *adv.* **—Syn. 1, 2.** stint, pinch.

skimp·y (skim′pē), *adj.,* **skimp·i·er, skimp·i·est. 1.** lacking in size, fullness, etc.; scanty: *a skimpy hem; a skimpy dinner.* **2.** too thrifty; stingy: *a skimpy housekeeper.* [1835–45; SKIMP + -Y[1]] **—skimp′i·ly,** *adv.* **—skimp′i·ness,** *n.*

CONCISE ETYMOLOGY KEY: <, descended or borrowed from; >, whence; b., blend of, blended; c., cognate with; cf., compare; deriv., derivative; equiv., equivalent; imit., imitative; obl., oblique; r., replacing; s., stem; sp., spelling, spelled; resp., respelling, respelled; trans., translation; ?, origin unknown; *, unattested; ‡, probably earlier than. See the full key inside the front cover.

skin (skin), *n., v.,* **skinned, skin·ning,** *adj.* **—***n.* **1.** the external covering or integument of an animal body, esp. when soft and flexible. **2.** such an integument stripped from the body of an animal, esp. a small animal; pelt: *a beaver skin.* **3.** the tanned or treated pelt or hide of an animal, esp. when used in apparel and accessories; leather (usually used in combination): *pigskin; calfskin.* **4.** any integumentary covering, casing, outer coating, or surface layer, as an investing membrane, the rind or peel of fruit, or a film on liquid: *a skin of thin ice; the aluminum skin of an airplane.* **5.** *Jewelry.* **a.** the outermost layer of a pearl. **b.** the outermost layer of a diamond as found: often different in color and refraction from the inner part of the stone. **6.** *Naut.* **a.** the shell or ceiling of a hull. **b.** the outer, exposed part of a furled sail. **7.** *Metall.* an outer layer of a metal piece having characteristics differing from those of the interior. **8.** a container made of animal skin, used for holding liquids, esp. wine. **9.** *Slang.* condom. **10. skins,** *Slang.* drums. **11.** *Slang.* a swindler; cheat. **12.** *Slang.* a skinflint. **13.** *Slang.* a horse. **14.** *Slang.* a dollar bill. **15.** *Rocketry.* the outer surface of a missile or rocket. **16. by the skin of one's teeth,** *Informal.* by an extremely narrow margin; just barely; scarcely: *We made the last train by the skin of our teeth.* **17. get under one's skin,** *Slang.* **a.** to irritate; bother: *His laugh really gets under my skin.* **b.** to affect deeply; impress; penetrate: *That sort of music always gets under my skin.* **18. have a thick skin,** to be insensitive to criticism or rebuffs: *The complaint desk is a job for someone who has a thick skin.* **19. have a thin skin,** to be extremely sensitive to criticism or rebuffs; be easily offended: *Be careful what you say to me, I have a thin skin.* **20. in** or **with a whole skin,** without harm; unscathed; safely: *She escaped from the burning building with a whole skin.* **21. no skin off one's back, nose,** or **teeth,** *Slang.* of no interest or concern or involving no risk to one. **22. save one's skin,** *Informal.* to avoid harm, esp. to escape death: *They betrayed their country to save their skins.* **23. under the skin,** in essence; fundamentally; despite appearances or differences: *sisters under the skin.* **—***v.t.* **24.** to strip or deprive of skin; flay; peel; husk. **25.** to remove or strip off (any covering, outer coating, surface layer, etc.). **26.** to scrape or rub a small piece of skin from (one's hand, leg, etc.), as in falling or sliding against something: *She skinned her knee.* **27.** to urge on, drive, or whip (a draft animal, as a mule or ox). **28.** to climb or jump: *He skinned the rope to the top of the wall.* **29.** to cover with or as if with skin. **30.** *Slang.* to strip of money or belongings; fleece, as in gambling. **31.** *Cards.* to slide cards one at a time off the top of (the pack) in dealing. **32.** *Slang.* to defeat completely: *skinned at the polls.* **33.** *Slang.* to castigate; reprimand: *skinned for his disobedience.* **—***v.i.* **34.** *Slang.* to slip off or depart hurriedly (often followed by *out*). **35. skin alive,** *Informal.* **a.** to reprimand; scold. **b.** to subdue completely, esp. in a cruel or ruthless manner: *The home team was skinned alive this afternoon.* **—***adj.* **36. a.** *Slang.* showing or featuring nude persons, often in a sexually explicit way: *a skin magazine.* **b.** presenting films, stage shows, exhibitions, etc., that feature nude persons, esp. in a sexually explicit way: *a Times Square skin house.* [1150–1200; ME (n.) < ON *skinn;* c. dial. G *Schinde* skin of fruit] **—skin′like′,** *adj.*
—Syn. 2. fur. SKIN, HIDE, PELT are names for the outer covering of animals, including humans. SKIN is the general word: *an abrasion of the skin; the skin of a muskrat.* HIDE applies to the skin of large animals, as cattle, horses, or elephants: *a buffalo hide.* PELT applies to the untanned skin of smaller animals: *a mink pelt.* **4.** hull, shell, husk, crust.

skin′ and bones′, a condition or state of extreme thinness, usually the result of malnutrition; emaciation: *Anorexia had reduced her to skin and bones.* Also, **skin′ and bone′.** [1400–50; late ME]

skin′ care′, the cleansing, massaging, moisturizing, etc., of the skin, esp. the face or hands. Also, **skin′care′.** [1950–55]

skin-deep (skin′dēp′), *adj.* **1.** superficial or slight; not profound or substantial: *Their sincerity is only skin-deep.* **—***adv.* **2.** slightly; superficially: *He went into the subject only skin-deep.* [1605–15]

skin-dive (skin′dīv′), *v.i.,* **-dived** or **-dove** (-dōv′), **-div·ing.** to engage in skin diving. [1950–55] **—skin′ div′er.**

skin′ div′ing, an underwater sport in which the swimmer, equipped with a lightweight mask, foot fins, and either a snorkel or a portable air cylinder and breathing device, can move about quickly and easily underwater, as for exploring or spear fishing. Also called, *esp. Brit.,* **free diving.** [1945–50]

skin′ effect′, *Elect.* the phenomenon in which an alternating current tends to concentrate in the outer layer of a conductor, caused by the self-induction of the conductor and resulting in increased resistance. [1895–1900]

skin′ flick′, *Slang.* a motion picture that features nudity and usually scenes of explicit sexual activity. Also, **skin′flick′.** [1965–70]

skin·flint (skin′flint′), *n.* a mean, niggardly person; miser. [1690–1700; SKIN + FLINT] **—skin′flint′i·ly,** *adv.* **—skin′flint′i·ness,** *n.* **—skin′flint′y,** *adj.*
—Syn. hoarder, pinchpenny, niggard, Scrooge.

skin′ fric′tion drag′, *Aeron.* aerodynamic resistance or drag due to the contact of moving air with the surface of an airplane, a glider, etc.

skin·ful (skin′fo͝ol), *n., pl.* **-fuls. 1.** the amount that a skin container can hold. **2.** *Informal.* a large or satisfying amount of food and drink. **3.** *Informal.* an amount of liquor sufficient to make a person drunk. [1640–50; SKIN + -FUL]
—Usage. See **-ful.**

skin′ game′, 1. a dishonest or unscrupulous business operation, scheme, etc. **2.** any cheating or fraudulent trick. [1865–70, *Amer.*]

skin′ graft′, *Surg.* **1.** skin used for transplanting in skin grafting. **2.** an instance of skin grafting. **3.** the surgical site of a skin graft. [1890–95]

skin′ graft′ing, *Surg.* the transplanting of healthy skin from the patient's or another's body to a wound or burn, to form new skin. Also called **dermatoplasty, dermoplasty.** [1875–80]

skin·head (skin′hed′), *n. Slang.* **1.** a baldheaded man. **2.** a person with closely cropped hair or a shaved head. **3.** a marine recruit; boot. **4.** an antisocial person who affects a hairless head as a symbol of rebellion, racism, or anarchy. [1955–60; SKIN + HEAD]

skink[1] (skingk), *n.* any of numerous lizards of the family Scincidae, common in many regions of the Old and New World, typically having flat, smooth, overlapping scales and comprising terrestrial, arboreal, and fossorial species. [1580–90; < L *scincus* < Gk *skínkos* lizard]

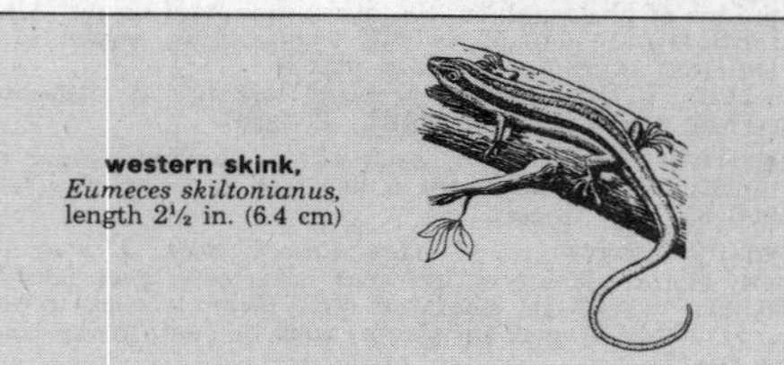
western skink, *Eumeces skiltonianus,* length 2½ in. (6.4 cm)

skink[2] (skingk), *v.t. Scot. Dial.* to serve (a beverage). [1350–1400; ME *skynken* < MD *schenken, schinken;* c. OE *scencan,* G *schenken*]

skink·ing (sking′king), *adj. Scot.* (of liquor, soup, etc.) watery; diluted or thin. [1575–85; SKINK[2] + -ING[2]]

skin·less (skin′lis), *adj.* **1.** deprived of skin: *a skinless carcass.* **2.** (of frankfurters or sausages) having no casing. [1300–50; ME *skinles.* See SKIN, -LESS]

skin·ner (skin′ər), *n.* **1.** a person or thing that skins. **2.** a person who prepares or deals in skins or hides. **3.** a person who drives draft animals, as mules or oxen. **4.** the operator of a piece of heavy equipment used in clearing land or in construction work, as a tractor or bulldozer. **5.** any of a band of irregular cavalry operating in the neutral ground of Westchester County, New York, during the American Revolution and claiming loyalty to both the British and American troops but preying on all persons indiscriminately. Cf. **cowboy** (def. 5). [1350–1400; ME; see SKIN, -ER[1]]

Skin·ner (skin′ər), *n.* **1. B(ur·rhus) F(rederic)** (bûr′-əs), 1904–90, U.S. psychologist and writer. **2. Cornelia Otis,** 1901–79, U.S. actress and author. **3.** her father, **Otis,** 1858–1942, U.S. actor.

Skin′ner box′, *Psychol.* a box used in experiments in animal learning, esp. in operant conditioning, equipped with a mechanism that automatically gives the animal food or other reward or permits escape, as by opening a door. [1940–45; named after B. F. SKINNER]

Skin·ner·i·an (ski nēr′ē ən), *n.* **1.** a psychologist who follows behaviorist theories developed by B. F. Skinner. **—***adj.* **2.** of or pertaining to theories developed by Skinner, esp. concerning operant conditioning. [1955–60; SKINNER + -IAN]

skin·ner·y (skin′ə rē), *n., pl.* **-ner·ies.** a place where skins are prepared, as for the market. [1425–75; late ME; see SKIN, -ERY]

skin·ny (skin′ē), *adj.,* **-ni·er, -ni·est,** *n.* **—***adj.* **1.** very lean or thin; emaciated: *a skinny little kitten.* **2.** of or like skin. **3.** unusually low or reduced; meager; minimal: *skinny profits.* **4.** (of an object) narrow or slender: *a skinny bed.* **—***n.* **5.** *Slang.* **a.** accurate information; data; facts. **b.** news, esp. if confidential; gossip: *Here's the skinny on the latest Hollywood scandal.* [1565–75; SKIN + -Y[1]; def. 5 is unclearly derived and perh. a distinct word] **—skin′ni·ness,** *n.*
—Syn. 1. lank, gaunt, scrawny.

skin·ny-dip (skin′ē dip′), *v.,* **-dipped, -dip·ping,** *n. Informal.* **—***v.i.* **1.** to swim in the nude. **—***n.* **2.** a swim in the nude. [‡1960–65] **—skin′ny-dip′per,** *n.*

Skin′ of Our Teeth′, The, a play (1942) by Thornton Wilder.

skin′ plan′ing, *Surg.* dermabrasion.

skin-pop (skin′pop′), *v.,* **-popped, -pop·ping.** *Slang.* **—***v.t.* **1.** to inject (a drug) under the skin rather than into a vein. **—***v.i.* **2.** to inject a drug under the skin. [1950–55] **—skin′-pop′per,** *n.* **—skin′-pop′ping,** *n., adj.*

skin′ reac′tion, an irritation or inflammation of the skin due to an allergy or infection, brought about by natural means or by a skin test.

skin′ search′. See **strip search.** [1965–70]

skin-search (skin′sûrch′), *v.t.* strip-search.

skint (skint), *adj. Brit. Slang.* having no money; penniless. [1930–35; prob. orig. repr. dial. pron. of *skinned;* see SKIN (v.), -ED[2]]

skin′ test′, a test in which a substance is introduced into the skin, as by application to a purposely abraded area or by injection, for the detection of allergic sensitivity to a specific pollen, protein, etc., or of the presence of a disease. [1925–30]

skin·tight (skin′tīt′), *adj.* fitting almost as tightly as skin: *skintight trousers.* [1880–85; SKIN + TIGHT]

skip[1] (skip), *v.,* **skipped, skip·ping,** *n.* **—***v.i.* **1.** to move in a light, springy manner by bounding forward with alternate hops on each foot. **2.** to pass from one point, thing, subject, etc., to another, disregarding or omitting what intervenes: *He skipped through the book quickly.* **3.** to go away hastily and secretly; flee without notice. **4.** *Educ.* to be advanced two or more classes or grades at once. **5.** to ricochet or bounce along a surface: *The stone skipped over the lake.* **—***v.t.* **6.** to jump lightly over: *The horse skipped the fence.* **7.** to pass over without reading, noting, acting, etc.: *He skipped the bad parts.* **8.** to miss or omit (one of a repeated series of rhythmic actions): *My heart skipped a beat.* **9.** to be absent from; avoid attendance at: *to skip a school class.* **10.** to send (a missile) ricocheting along a surface. **11.** *Informal.* to leave hastily and secretly or to flee from (a place): *They skipped town.* **12. skip out on,** *Informal.* to flee or abandon; desert: *He skipped out on his wife and two children.* —*n.* **13.** a skipping movement; a light jump or bounce. **14.** a gait marked by such jumps. **15.** a passing from one point or thing to another, with disregard of what intervenes: *a quick skip through Europe.* **16.** *Music.* a melodic interval greater than a second. **17.** a natural depression below the surface of a planed board. **18.** *Informal.* a person who has absconded in order to avoid paying debts or meeting other financial responsibilities. [1250–1300; (v.) ME *skippen,* perh. < ON *skopa* to run (cf. Icel *skoppa* to skip); (n.) late ME *skyppe,* deriv. of the v.] —**skip′ping·ly,** *adv.*

—**Syn. 1.** caper, hop. SKIP, BOUND refer to an elastic, springing movement. To SKIP is to give a series of light, quick hops alternating the feet: *to skip about.* BOUND suggests a series of long, rather vigorous leaps; it is also applied to a springing or leaping type of walking or running rapidly and actively: *A dog came bounding up to meet him.* **2.** skim. **13.** leap, spring, caper, hop.

skip[2] (skip), *n., v.,* **skipped, skip·ping.** —*n.* **1.** the captain of a curling or bowling team. **2.** *Informal.* skipper[1]. —*v.t.* **3.** to serve as skip of (a curling or bowling team). **4.** *Informal.* skipper[1]. [1820–30; short for SKIPPER[1]]

skip[3] (skip), *n.* **1.** *Mining.* a metal box for carrying ore, hauled vertically or on an incline. **2.** See **skip car.** [1805–15; alter. of SKEP]

ski′ pants′, pants worn for skiing, having the legs tapered to fit snugly at the ankles and sometimes having a strap going under the arch, often made of a stretch or waterproof fabric.

skip-bomb (skip′bom′), *v.t. Mil.* to attack (a target) by skip bombing. [1940–45]

skip′ bomb′ing, bombing, as by a low-flying plane, carried out so that each bomb, when released, skips along the surface below before striking the target.

skip′ car′, an open car for charging a blast furnace. Also called **skip.**

skip·dent (skip′dent′), *n.* an open-weave effect in fabric, produced by purposely omitting specific warp ends in the drawing-in process. [SKIP[1] + DENT[1]]

skip′ dis′tance, *Radio.* the minimum distance along the earth's surface between the position of a short-wave transmitter and the region where its signal is received after one reflection from the ionosphere. [1925–30]

skip·jack (skip′jak′), *n., pl.* (*esp. collectively*) **-jack,** (*esp. referring to two or more kinds or species*) **-jacks** for 1; **-jacks** for 2, 3. **1.** any of various fishes that leap above the surface of the water, as a tuna, *Euthynnus pelamis,* or the bonito. **2.** *Entomol.* See **click beetle. 3.** *Naut.* an American one-masted sailing vessel. [1545–55; SKIP[1] + JACK[1]]

ski·plane (skē′plān′), *n. Aeron.* an airplane equipped with skis to enable it to land on and take off from snow. [1925–30; SKI + PLANE[1]]

ski′ pole′, a slender pole or stick, usually with a metal point at one end, a loop for the hand at the other, and a disk near the lower end to prevent its sinking into snow, used in skiing to gain momentum, maintain balance, execute certain jumps, etc. [1920–25]

skip·pa·ble (skip′ə bəl), *adj.* able to be skipped, omitted, or passed over without loss; unimportant. [1810–20; SKIP[1] + -ABLE]

skip·per[1] (skip′ər), *n.* **1.** the master or captain of a vessel, esp. of a small trading or fishing vessel. **2.** a captain or leader, as of a team. —*v.t.* **3.** to act as skipper of. [1350–1400; ME < MD *schipper,* equiv. to *schip* SHIP + *-er* -ER[1]]

skip·per[2] (skip′ər), *n.* **1.** a person or thing that skips. **2.** any of various insects that hop or fly with jerky motions. **3.** any of numerous quick-flying, lepidopterous insects of the family Hesperiidae, closely related to the true butterflies. **4.** saury (def. 1). [1200–50; ME: locust. See SKIP[1], -ER[1]]

skip·pet (skip′it), *n.* a small, round box for protecting an official or personal seal, as on a document. [1350–1400; ME *skipet.* See SKIP[3], -ET]

skip′ rope′. See **jump rope.**

skip′ straight′, *Poker.* a hand consisting of five cards following one another by two in order of denomination, as a five, seven, nine, jack, and king, being of special value in certain games. Also called **alternate straight, Dutch straight.** [1885–90, *Amer.*]

skip′ trac′er, an investigator whose job is to locate missing persons, esp. debtors. Also, **skip′-trac′er.** —**skip′ trac′ing.**

skip′ weld′ing, a technique of spacing welds on thin structural members in order to balance and minimize internal stresses due to heat.

ski′ rack′, a rack for holding skis, as one that can be attached to the roof of a car or set up outside a ski lodge.

skirl (skûrl), *v.i.* **1.** to play the bagpipe. **2.** *Scot. and North Eng.* to shriek. —*n.* **3.** the sound of a bagpipe. **4.** *Scot. and North Eng.* any shrill sound. [1350–1400; ME *scirlen, skrillen* (v.), perh. < Scand; cf. Norw *skrella* boom, crash]

skirl·ing (skûr′ling), *n. Scot. and North Eng.* the act of shrieking. [1775–85; SKIRL + -ING[1]]

skir·mish (skûr′mish), *n.* **1.** *Mil.* a fight between small bodies of troops, esp. advanced or outlying detachments of opposing armies. **2.** any brisk conflict or encounter: *She had a skirmish with her landlord about the rent.* —*v.i.* **3.** to engage in a skirmish. [1300–50; (n.) ME *skirmysshe* < OF *eskirmiss-,* long s. of *eskirmir* < Gmc (cf. OHG *skirman*); r. ME *scarmouche* < OF *escaramoucher* (see SCARAMOUCH); (v.) late ME *scarmuchen, scarmusshen* to skirmish, ME *skirmisshen* to brandish a weapon < OF *escar(a)mucher* to skirmish; vowels influenced by OF *eskirmiss-*] —**skir′mish·er,** *n.*

—**Syn. 1.** combat, brush. See **battle**[1].

Skir·nir (skēr′nir), *n. Scand. Myth.* the servant of Frey: symbol of the sun. [< ON *Skirnir,* equiv. to *skír(r)* bright, clear (cf. SHEER[1]) + *-nir* n. suffix]

skirr (skûr), *v.i.* **1.** to go rapidly; fly; scurry. —*v.t.* **2.** to go rapidly over. —*n.* **3.** a grating or whirring sound. [1540–50; var. of SCOUR[2]]

skir·ret (skir′it), *n.* a plant, *Sium sisarum,* of the parsley family, cultivated in Europe for its edible tuberous root. [1300–50; ME *skirwhite* lit., pure white (*skir* < ON *skírr* clear, pure; c. OE *scīr*); alter., by folk etym., of MF *scherwitz,* unexplained var. of OF *carvi* CARAWAY]

skirt (skûrt), *n.* **1.** the part of a gown, dress, slip, or coat that extends downward from the waist. **2.** a one-piece garment extending downward from the waist and not joined between the legs, worn esp. by women and girls. **3.** some part resembling or suggesting the skirt of a garment, as the flared lip of a bell or a protective and ornamental cloth strip covering the legs of furniture. **4.** a small leather flap on each side of a saddle, covering the metal bar from which the stirrup hangs. See diag. under **saddle. 5.** *Building Trades.* **a.** baseboard (def. 1). **b.** apron (def. 13). **6.** Also called **apron.** *Furniture.* **a.** a flat horizontal brace set immediately beneath the seat of a chair, chest of drawers, or the like, to strengthen the legs. **b.** Also called **bed, frieze.** a flat brace or support immediately beneath a tabletop. **7.** Usually, **skirts.** the bordering, marginal, or outlying part of a place, group, etc.; the outskirts. **8.** *Slang* (*disparaging and offensive*). a woman or girl. **9.** *Rocketry.* an outer part of a rocket or missile that provides structural support or houses such systems as avionics or gyroscopes. —*v.t.* **10.** to lie on or along the border of: *The hills skirt the town.* **11.** to border, wrap, or cover with a skirt or something suggesting a skirt in appearance or function. **12.** to pass along or around the border or edge of: *Traffic skirts the town.* **13.** to avoid, go around the edge of, or keep distant from (something that is controversial, risky, etc.): *The senator skirted the issue.* **14.** to remove low-grade wool and foreign matter from (the outer edge of fleece). —*v.i.* **15.** to be or lie on or along the edge of something. **16.** to move along or around the border of something. [1250–1300; ME *skirte* < ON *skyrta* SHIRT] —**skirt′less,** *adj.* —**skirt′like′,** *adj.*

—**Syn. 13.** evade, shun, circle, bypass.

skirt′ chas′er, *Slang.* a womanizer. [1935–40]

skirt·ing (skûr′ting), *n.* **1.** fabric for making skirts. **2.** Often, **skirtings.** low-grade wool and foreign matter removed from the outer edges of fleece. **3.** Also called **skirt′ing board′.** *Brit.* baseboard (def. 1). [1680–90; SKIRT + -ING[1]]

skirt′ steak′, a cut of beef consisting of the diaphragm muscle. Also called **Rumanian tenderloin.** [1905–10]

ski′ run′, a trail, slope, course, or the like, used for skiing. [1920–25]

ski′ suit′, a warm, lightweight outer garment for skiing and other outdoor winter activities, usually consisting of a short, zippered jacket and close-fitting trousers.

skit (skit), *n.* **1.** a short literary piece of a humorous or satirical character. **2.** a short theatrical sketch or act, usually comical. **3.** a gibe or taunt. **4.** *Brit. Dial.* a joke or prank. [1565–75; of obscure orig.]

skite[1] (skit), *n. Scot. and North Eng.* **1.** a quick, oblique blow or stroke; a chopping blow. **2.** a joke or prank. **3.** the butt of a joke or prank. **4.** a person whose opinions are not taken seriously; one held in mild contempt. Also, **skyte.** [1775–85; perh. < Scand; cf. SKEET[3]]

skite[2] (skīt), *v.i.,* **skit·ed, skit·ing.** *Australian.* to boast; brag. [orig. uncert.]

ski′ tour′ing. See **cross-country skiing.** [1930–35] —**ski′ tour′er.**

ski′ tow′, 1. Also called **rope tow.** a type of ski lift in which skiers are hauled up a slope while grasping a looped, endless rope driven by a motor. **2.** a ski lift. [1930–35]

ski′ troops′, a body of soldiers trained to fight on skis. [1935–40]

skit·ter (skit′ər), *v.i.* **1.** to go, run, or glide lightly or rapidly. **2.** to skim along a surface. **3.** *Angling.* to draw a lure or a baited hook over the water with a skipping motion. —*v.t.* **4.** to cause to skitter. [1835–45; *skit,* var. of SKITE[1] + -ER[6]]

skit·ter·y (skit′ə rē), *adj.* skittish. [1900–05; SKITTER + -Y[1]]

skit·tish (skit′ish), *adj.* **1.** apt to start or shy: *a skittish horse.* **2.** restlessly or excessively lively: *a skittish mood.* **3.** fickle; uncertain. **4.** shy; coy. [1375–1425; late ME, perh. deriv. of the Scand source of SKITE[1]; see -ISH[1]] —**skit′tish·ly,** *adv.* —**skit′tish·ness,** *n.*

skit·tle (skit′l), *n. Chiefly Brit.* **1. skittles,** (*used with a singular v.*) ninepins in which a wooden ball or disk is used to knock down the pins. **2.** one of the pins used in this game. [1625–35; perh. < Scand; cf ON *skutill* shuttle, arrow; Dan *skyttel* shuttle]

skive (skīv), *v.t.,* **skived, skiv·ing. 1.** to split or cut, as leather, into layers or slices. **2.** to shave, as hides. **3.** to finish the turning of (a metal object) by feeding a tool against it tangentially. [1815–25; perh. < ON *skīfa* slice]

skiv·er (skī′vər), *n.* **1.** a person or thing that skives. **2.** a thin, soft leather made from sheepskin, used for hat linings and book bindings. [1790–1800; SKIVE + -ER[1]]

skiv·vy[1] (skiv′ē), *n., pl.* **-vies.** *Informal.* **1.** Also called **skiv′vy shirt′.** a man's cotton T-shirt. **2. skivvies,** underwear consisting of cotton T-shirt and shorts. **3.** a thin sweater with a round neck, usually worn over a blouse, turtleneck, or the like. Also, **scivvy.** [1925–30; orig. uncert.]

skiv·vy[2] (skiv′ē), *n., pl.* **-vies,** *v.,* **-vied, -vy·ing.** *Brit. Disparaging.* —*n.* **1.** a female servant, esp. a chambermaid. —*v.i.* **2.** to work as a skivvy. [1910–15; orig. uncert.]

ski·wear (skē′wâr′), *n.* activewear designed to be worn for skiing, as jackets, sweaters, and pants. [1960–65; SKI + WEAR]

sklent (sklent), *Scot. and North Eng.* —*n.* **1.** any slanting surface, as a slope. **2.** a sideways or oblique movement. **3.** a sideways glance. —*v.i.* **4.** to move or lie on a slant. **5.** to deviate from a straight course. **6.** to deviate from the truth; lie. Also, **sclent.** [1505–15; earlier *sklente* (v.), var. of ME *slenten* to SLANT]

skoal (skōl), *interj.* **1.** (used as a toast in drinking someone's health.) —*n.* **2.** a toast. —*v.i.* **3.** to drink a toast. [1590–1600; < Dan *skaal,* Norw, Sw *skål;* cf. ON *skāl* bowl]

Sko·be·lev (skô′bə lef′; *Russ.* skô′byi lyif), *n.* former name of **Fergana.**

Ško·da (skô′də; *Czech.* shkô′dä), *n.* **E·mil von** (e′mil fən), 1839–1900, Czech engineer and manufacturer of artillery.

Sko·kie (skō′kē), *n.* a city in NE Illinois, near Chicago. 60,278.

skoo·kum (skōō′kəm), *adj. Northwest U.S., Canada.* **1.** large; powerful; impressive. **2.** excellent; first-rate. [1825–35, *Amer.;* < Chinook Jargon: strong, powerful < Lower Chehalis (Salishan language of the Washington coast) *skʷəkʷə́m* ghost, spirit, monster (hence, appar. "fearsome" > "powerful" in Chinook Jargon)]

Skop·je (skôp′ye), *n.* a city in and the capital of Macedonia, in the N part. 504,932. Serbo-Croatian, **Skop·lje** (skôp′lye). Turkish, **Üsküb, Üsküp.**

skosh (skōsh), *n. Slang.* a bit; a jot: *We need just a skosh more room.* [< Japn *sukoshi* a little (bit)]

Skou·ras (skŏŏr′əs; *Gk.* skōō′räs), *n.* **Spy·ros (Pa·na·gio·tes)** (spē′ōs pan′ə yō′tis; *Gk.* spē′RÔS pä′nä yô′-tēs), 1893–1971, U.S. film-studio executive, born in Greece.

skouth (skōōth), *n. Scot.* scouth.

skreegh (skrēKH), *v.i., v.t., n. Scot.* screech. Also, **skreigh.**

skrik (skrik), *n. South African.* a sudden fright or panic. [1885–90; < Afrik < D *schrik* fright]

Skry·mir (skrē′mir), *n. Scand. Myth.* See under **Utgard-Loki.**

Skt, Sanskrit. Also, **Skt., Skr., Skrt.**

sku·a (skyōō′ə), *n.* **1.** Also called **bonxie.** any of several large brown gull-like predatory birds of the genus *Catharacta,* related to jaegers, esp. *C. skua* (**great skua**), of colder waters of both northern and southern seas. **2.** *Brit.* jaeger (def. 1). [1670–80; < Faeroese *skū(g)vur;* c. ON *skūfr* tassel, tuft, also skua (in poetry), akin to SHOVE[1]]

skua, *Catharacta skua,* length 22 in. (56 cm)

Skuld (skŏŏld), *n. Scand. Myth.* See under **Norn.** [< ON, prob. lit. future, homonymous with *skuld* debt, bondage in payment of debt, deriv. from root of *skulu* SHALL, must; c. OE *scyld,* OS *sculd,* OHG *scult* (G *Schuld*)]

skul·dug·ger·y (skul dug′ə rē), *n., pl.* **-ger·ies. 1.** dishonorable proceedings; mean dishonesty or trickery: *bribery, graft, and other such skulduggery.* **2.** an instance of dishonest or deceitful behavior; trick. Also, **skullduggery, sculduggery, scullduggery.** [1705–15, *Amer.;* var. of *sculduddery,* orig. Scots: fornication, obscenity < ?]

skulk (skulk), *v.i.* **1.** to lie or keep in hiding, as for some evil reason: *The thief skulked in the shadows.* **2.** to move in a stealthy manner; slink: *The panther skulked through the bush.* **3.** *Brit.* to shirk duty; malinger. —*n.* **4.** a person who skulks. **5.** a pack or group of foxes. **6.** *Rare.* an act or instance of skulking. Also, **sculk.** [1175–1225; ME < Scand (not in ON); cf. Dan, Norw *skulke,* Sw *skolka* play hooky] —**skulk′er,** *n.* —**skulk′ing·ly,** *adv.*

—**Syn. 1.** See **lurk.**

skull (skul), *n.* **1.** the bony framework of the head, enclosing the brain and supporting the face; the skeleton of the head. **2.** the head as the center of knowledge and understanding; mind: *to get literature's great ideas through our skulls.* **3.** *Armor.* the part of a helmet that covers the top of the head. **4. out of one's skull,** *Slang.* crazy; demented. [1175–1225; ME *scolle* < ON *skalli*] —**skull′-less,** *adj.* —**skull′-like′,** *adj.*

human skull (lateral view)
A, frontal bone; B, sphenoid bone; C, eye socket; D, nasal bone; E, zygomatic bone; F, maxilla; G, mandible; H, parietal bone; I, occipital bone; J, temporal bone; K, mastoid process; L, styloid process; M, zygomatic arch

CONCISE PRONUNCIATION KEY: act, cāpe, dâre, pärt; set, ēqual; if, īce; ox, ōver, ôrder, oil, bŏŏk, bōōt, out; up, ûrge; child; sing; shoe; thin, *th*at; zh as in *treasure.* ə = *a* as in *alone, e* as in *system, i* as in *easily, o* as in *gallop, u* as in *circus;* ᵊ as in *fire* (fīᵊr), *hour* (ouᵊr). l and n can serve as syllabic consonants, as in *cradle* (krād′l), and *button* (but′n). See the full key inside the front cover.

skull′ and cross′bones, a representation of a front view of a human skull above two crossed bones, originally used on pirates' flags and now used as a warning sign, as in designating substances as poisons. [1820–30]

skull•cap (skul′kap′), *n.* **1.** a small, brimless close-fitting cap, often made of silk or velvet, worn on the crown of the head, as for religious functions. **2.** the domelike roof of the skull. **3.** *Bot.* any of various plants belonging to the genus *Scutellaria,* of the mint family, having a calyx resembling a helmet. [1675–85; SKULL + CAP[1]]

skull•dug•ger•y (skul dug′ə rē), *n., pl.* **-ger•ies.** skulduggery.

skull′ ses′sion, 1. a meeting for the purpose of discussion, exchange of ideas, solving problems, etc. **2.** a meeting held by an athletic coach, as of football, to instruct team members in new plays or special strategy. Also called **skull′ prac′tice.** [1935–40]

skunk (skungk), *n., pl.* **skunks,** (*esp. collectively*) **skunk,** *v.* —*n.* **1.** a small North American mammal, *Mephitis mephitis,* of the weasel family, having a black coat with a white, V-shaped stripe on the back, and ejecting a fetid odor when alarmed or attacked. **2.** any of several related or similar animals. Cf. **hog-nosed skunk, spotted skunk. 3.** *Informal.* a thoroughly contemptible person. **4.** *U.S. Navy Slang.* an unidentified ship or target. —*v.t.* **5.** *Slang.* to defeat thoroughly in a game, esp. while keeping an opponent from scoring: *The team skunked the favorites in the crucial game.* [1625–35, *Amer.;* < the Massachusett reflex of Proto-Algonquian **šeka·kwa* (deriv. of **šek-* urinate + *-a·kw* fox, foxlike animal]

skunk,
Mephitis mephitis,
head and body
15 in. (38 cm);
tail 8 in. (20 cm)

skunk′ cab′bage, 1. a low, fetid, broad-leaved North American plant, *Symplocarpus foetidus,* of the arum family, having a brownish-purple and green mottled spathe surrounding a stout spadix, growing in moist ground. **2.** a related plant, *Lysichiton americanum,* of western North America, having a cluster of green leaves and a spike of flowers surrounded by a yellow spathe. [1745–55, *Amer.*]

skunk•weed (skungk′wēd′), *n.* any of various plants having an unpleasant odor, as the skunk cabbage. [1730–40; SKUNK + WEED[1]]

Skunk′ Works′, 1. *Trademark.* engineering, technical, consulting, and advisory services for developing aircraft and related equipment at Lockheed Martin Corp. —*n.* **2.** (*usu. l.c.*) Also, **skunk′works′.** *Slang.* an often secret experimental laboratory or facility for producing innovative products, as in computers or aerospace. [1943 for def. 1, 1965–70 for def. 2; after the *Skonk Works,* an illicit distillery in Al Capp's comic strip *Li'l Abner*]

skunk•y (skung′kē), *adj.,* **skunk•i•er, skunk•i•est. 1.** of, pertaining to, or characteristic of a skunk: *a skunky odor.* **2.** having a disagreeable or tainted character: *beer with a skunky taste.* **3.** *Informal.* mean and nasty; contemptible. [1895–1900; SKUNK + -Y[1]] —**skunk′i•ness,** *n.*

skurf•ing (skûr′fing), *n.* skateboarding. [SK(ATEBOARD) + (S)URFING]

skut•te•rud•ite (skut′ə rud′īt), *n.* a mineral, chiefly cobalt and nickel arsenide, $(Co,Ni)As_3$, with some iron, occurring in the form of gray cubic crystals, usually in masses: a source of cobalt and nickel. [1865–70; < G *Skutterudit,* named after *Skutterud* in Norway]

sky (skī), *n., pl.* **skies,** *v.* **skied** or **skyed, sky•ing.** —*n.* Often, **skies** (for defs. 1–4). **1.** the region of the clouds or the upper air; the upper atmosphere of the earth: *airplanes in the sky; cloudy skies.* **2.** the heavens or firmament, appearing as a great arch or vault. **3.** the supernal or celestial heaven: *They looked to the sky for help.* **4.** the climate: *the sunny skies of Italy.* **5.** *Obs.* a cloud. **6. out of a** or **the clear sky,** without advance notice or warning; abruptly: *An old beau phoned her out of a clear sky.* Also, **out of a** or **the clear blue sky. 7. to the skies,** with lavishness or enthusiasm; extravagantly: *to praise someone to the skies.* Also, **to the sky.** —*v.t.* **8.** *Informal.* to raise, throw, or hit aloft or into the air. **9.** *Informal.* to hang (a painting) high on a wall, above the line of vision. **10. sky up,** *Falconry.* (of prey, when flushed) to fly straight upward. [1175–1225; ME < ON *ský* cloud, c. OE *scēo* cloud] —**sky′less,** *adj.* —**sky′like′,** *adj.*

sky′ blue′, the color of the unclouded sky in daytime; azure. [1720–30] —**sky′-blue′,** *adj.*

sky•borne (skī′bôrn′, -bōrn′), *adj.* airborne. [1940–45; SKY + BORNE[1]]

sky•box (skī′boks′), *n.* a private compartment, usu. near the top of a stadium, for viewing a sports contest. [1980–85; SKY + BOX[2]]

sky•bridge (skī′brij′), *n.* **1.** Also called **skywalk.** a bridgelike structure for pedestrians built to link one building with another over a public alley or street. **2.** Also called **flying bridge, walkway.** a similar overhead structure built across an atrium space within a building. [SKY + BRIDGE[1]]

CONCISE ETYMOLOGY KEY: <, descended or borrowed from; >, whence; b., blend of, blended; c., cognate with; cf., compare; deriv., derivative; equiv., equivalent; imit., imitative; obl., oblique; r., replacing; s., stem; sp., spelling, spelled; resp., respelling, respelled; trans., translation; ?, origin unknown; *, unattested; ‡, probably earlier than. See the full key inside the front cover.

sky•cap (skī′kap′), *n.* a porter who carries passenger baggage at an airport or airline terminal. [1940–45; SKY + (RED)CAP]

sky′ cav′alry. See **air cavalry.** Also, **sky′ cav′.**

sky′ com′pass, *Navig.* a device for taking a bearing by means of polarized sunlight when the sun is invisible.

sky′ cov′er, the amount of the sky that is covered by clouds, fog, haze, smoke, or the like, usually expressed in tenths of the total sky. [1955–60]

sky•dive (skī′dīv′), *v.i.,* **-dived** or **-dove; -dived; -div•ing.** to engage in skydiving. [1960–65; SKY + DIVE]

sky•div•ing (skī′dī′ving), *n.* the sport of jumping from an airplane at a moderate or high altitude and free-falling and using one's body to control direction or movements before opening one's parachute. Also, **sky′ div′•ing.** [1955–60; SKY + DIVE + -ING[1]] —**sky′ div′er.**

Skye (skī), *n.* an island in the Hebrides, in NW Scotland: cattle farming. 7372; 670 sq. mi. (1735 sq. km).

Skye′ ter′rier, one of a Scottish breed of small terriers having short legs and a dark or light blue-gray, gray, or fawn coat. [1850–55; after SKYE]

Skye terrier,
9 in. (23 cm)
high at shoulder

sky•ey (skī′ē), *adj.* **1.** of or from the sky. **2.** in the sky; lofty. **3.** skylike; sky blue. [1595–1605; SKY + -EY[1]]

sky-high (skī′hī′), *adv., adj.* very high: *Costs have gone sky-high since the war.* [1810–20]

sky•hook (skī′ho͝ok′), *n.* **1.** a fanciful hook imagined to be suspended in the air. **2.** any of various lifting devices, as one hung from a helicopter, for hoisting heavy loads over a distance. **3.** a high, arching hook shot in basketball. [1910–15; SKY + HOOK[1]]

sky•jack (skī′jak′), *v.t.* to hijack (an airliner), esp. in order to hold the passengers and plane for ransom or for political reasons. [1965–70; SKY + (HI)JACK] —**sky′•jack′er,** *n.*

sky•jack•ing (skī′jak′ing), *n.* an act or instance of hijacking an aircraft. [1965–70; SKYJACK + -ING[1]]

Sky•lab (skī′lab′), *n.* a U.S. earth-orbiting space station that was periodically staffed by three separate crews of astronauts and remained in orbit 1973–79.

sky•lark (skī′lärk′), *n.* **1.** a brown-speckled European lark, *Alauda arvensis,* famed for its melodious song. —*v.i.* **2.** to frolic; sport: *The children were skylarking on the beach.* [1680–90; SKY + LARK[1]] —**sky′lark′er,** *n.*

skylark,
Alauda arvensis,
length 7 in. (18 cm)

sky•light (skī′līt′), *n.* **1.** an opening in a roof or ceiling, fitted with glass, for admitting daylight. **2.** the frame set with glass fitted to such an opening. **3.** *Meteorol.* the diffuse light from the sky, scattered by air molecules, as distinguished from the direct radiation from the sun. [1670–80; SKY + LIGHT[1]]

sky•light•ed (skī′lī′tid), *adj.* having or illuminated by a skylight. Also, **sky•lit** (skī′lit′). [1875–80; SKYLIGHT + -ED[3], or reanalyzed as SKY + LIGHTED (ptp.)]

sky•line (skī′līn′), *n., v.,* **-lined, -lin•ing.** —*n.* Also, **sky′ line′. 1.** the boundary line between earth and sky; the apparent horizon: *A sail appeared against the skyline.* **2.** the outline of something, as the buildings of a city, against the sky. —*v.t.* **3.** to outline (something) against the sky. [1855–60; SKY + LINE[1]]

sky•lounge (skī′lounj′), *n.* a vehicle designed to be lifted by helicopter between an intown passenger terminal and an airport. [1965–70; SKY + LOUNGE]

sky•man (skī′mən), *n., pl.* **-men.** *Informal.* an aviator or paratrooper. [SKY + MAN[1]]

sky′ mar′shal, an armed plainclothes federal marshal riding on an airliner to protect against skyjacking. [1965–70, *Amer.*]

sky•phos (skī′fos), *n., pl.* **-phoi** (-foi). *Gk. and Rom. Antiq.* a cup characterized by a deep bowl, two handles projecting horizontally near the rim, and either a flat base or a foot. Also, **scyphus.** [1855–60; < Gk *skýphos* cup, can]

sky′ pi′lot, *Slang.* a member of the clergy, esp. a chaplain of the armed forces. [1880–85]

sky•rock•et (skī′rok′it), *n.* **1.** a rocket firework that explodes high in the air, usually in a brilliant array of colorful sparks. **2.** Also called **scarlet gilia.** a plant, *Ipomopsis aggregata,* of the phlox family, native to western North America, having finely divided leaves and clusters of red, trumpet-shaped flowers. **3.** an organized group cheer, usually led by a cheerleader, as at a football or basketball game, which begins with a hissing or whistling and ends with a shout. —*v.i.* **4.** to rise or increase rapidly or suddenly, esp. to unexpected or unprecedented levels: *Prices skyrocketed during the war.* —*v.t.* **5.** to cause to rise or increase rapidly and usually suddenly: *Economic changes have skyrocketed prices.* **6.** to thrust with sudden dramatic advancement; catapult: *Talent has skyrocketed him to fame.* [1680–90; SKY + ROCKET[1]]

Sky•ros (skī′ros, -rōs; *Gk.* skē′Rôs), *n.* a Greek island in the W Aegean: the largest island of the Northern Sporades. 3000; 81 sq. mi. (210 sq. km). Also, **Scyros.**

sky•sail (skī′sāl′; *Naut.* skī′səl), *n. Naut.* **1.** (in a square-rigged vessel) a light square sail next above the royal. See diag. under **ship. 2.** a triangular sail set on a stay between the fore and main trucks of a racing schooner. [1820–30; SKY + SAIL]

sky•scape (skī′skāp′), *n.* **1.** a section or portion of the sky, usually extensive and often including part of the horizon, that may be seen from a single viewpoint. **2.** a picture representing this. [1810–20; SKY + -SCAPE]

sky•scrap•er (skī′skrā′pər), *n.* **1.** a relatively tall building of many stories, esp. one for office or commercial use. **2.** *Archit.* a building of exceptional height completely supported by a framework, as of girders, from which the walls are suspended, as opposed to a building supported by load-bearing walls. [1785–95; SKY + SCRAPER]

sky•scrap•ing (skī′skrā′ping), *adj.* of or like a skyscraper; very high: *a skyscraping chimney.* [1830–40; SKY + SCRAPE + -ING[2]; in recent use prob. SKYSCRAP(ER) + -ING[2]]

skyte (skīt), *n. Scot. and North Eng.* skite.

sky′ train′, an airplane towing one or more gliders. Also called **air train.**

sky•troop•er (skī′tro͞o′pər), *n.* a paratrooper. [SKY + (PARA)TROOPER]

sky•troops (skī′tro͞ops′), *n.pl.* paratroops. [SKY + (PARA)TROOPS]

sky•walk (skī′wôk′), *n.* skybridge (def. 1). [1950–55; SKY + WALK]

sky•ward (skī′wərd), *adv.* **1.** Also, **sky′wards.** toward the sky. —*adj.* **2.** directed toward the sky. [1575–85; SKY + -WARD]

sky′ wave′, *Radio.* a radio wave propagated upward from earth, whether reflected by the ionosphere or not. [1925–30]

sky•way (skī′wā′), *n.* **1.** See **air lane. 2.** an elevated highway, esp. one well above ground level and composed of a series of spans. [1915–20; SKY + WAY[1]]

sky•write (skī′rīt′), *v.,* **-wrote, -writ•ten, -writ•ing.** —*v.i.* **1.** to engage in skywriting. —*v.t.* **2.** to produce (a message, advertisement, etc.) by skywriting. [1925–30; SKY + WRITE] —**sky′writ′er,** *n.*

sky•writ•ing (skī′rī′ting), *n.* **1.** the act or technique of writing against the sky with chemically produced smoke released from a maneuvering airplane. **2.** the words, letters, designs, etc., so traced. [1920–25; SKY + WRITING]

SL, See **source language.**

s.l., 1. Also, **sl.** salvage loss. **2.** *Bibliog.* without place (of publication). [< L *sine locō*]

SLA, Special Libraries Association.

slab[1] (slab), *n., v.,* **slabbed, slab•bing.** —*n.* **1.** a broad, flat, somewhat thick piece of stone, wood, or other solid material. **2.** a thick slice of anything: *a slab of bread.* **3.** a semifinished piece of iron or steel so rolled that its breadth is at least twice its thickness. **4.** a rough outside piece cut from a log, as when sawing one into boards. **5.** *Baseball Slang.* rubber (def. 14). **6.** *Building Trades.* a section of concrete pavement or a concrete floor placed directly on the ground or on a base of gravel. —*v.t.* **7.** to make into a slab or slabs. **8.** to cover or lay with slabs. **9.** to cut the slabs or outside pieces from (a log). **10.** to put on in slabs; cover thickly. [1250–1300; ME *sclabbe, slabbe* < ?]

slab[2] (slab), *adj. Scot and North Eng.* thick; viscous. [1595–1605; appar. < Scand; cf. Sw, Norw *slabb* mire, Icel *slabba* to wade in mud]

slab•ber (slab′ər), *v.i., v.t., n.* slobber.

slab•ber•y (slab′ə rē), *adj.* slobbery.

slab′ dash′ing, the act or process of covering an exterior wall with roughcast. Also called **slap dashing.**

slab′ plas′tering, coarse plastering, as between the studs in a half-timbered wall. Also called **slap plastering.**

slab-sid•ed (slab′sī′did), *adj. Informal.* **1.** having the sides long and flat, like slabs. **2.** tall and lank. [1810–20]

slab′ top′, *Furniture.* a top, as to a table, formed from a slab of marble or the like.

slab′ track′, a railroad track in which the rails are attached to and supported by a bed or slab, usually of concrete.

slack[1] (slak), *adj.* **1.** not tight, taut, firm, or tense; loose: *a slack rope.* **2.** negligent; careless; remiss: *slack proofreading.* **3.** slow, sluggish, or indolent: *He is slack in answering letters.* **4.** not active or busy; dull; not brisk: *the slack season in an industry.* **5.** moving very slowly, as the tide, wind, or water. **6.** weak; lax. **7.** *Naut.* easy (def. 15a). —*adv.* **8.** in a slack manner. —*n.* **9.** a slack condition or part. **10.** the part of a rope, sail, or the like, that hangs loose, without strain upon it. **11.** a decrease in activity, as in business or work: *a sudden slack in output.* **12.** a period of decreased activity. **13.** *Geog.* a cessation in a strong flow, as of a current at its turn. **14.** a depression between hills, in a hillside, or in the land surface. **15.** *Pros.* (in sprung rhythm) the unaccented syllable or syllables. **16.** *Brit. Dial.* a morass; marshy ground; a hollow or dell with soft, wet ground at the bottom. **17. take up the slack, a.** to pull in or make taut a loose section of a rope, line, wire, etc.: *Take up the slack before releasing the kite.* **b.** to provide or compensate for something that is missing or incomplete: *New sources of oil will take up the slack resulting from the embargo.* —*v.t.* **18.** to be remiss in respect to (some matter, duty, right, etc.); shirk; leave undone: *He slacked the most important part.* **19.** to make or allow to be-

come less active, vigorous, intense, etc.; relax (efforts, labor, speed, etc.); lessen; moderate (often fol. by *up*). **20.** to make loose, or less tense or taut, as a rope; loosen (often fol. by *off* or *out*). **21.** to slake (lime). —*v.i.* **22.** to be remiss; shirk one's duty or part. **23.** to become less active, vigorous, rapid, etc. (often fol. by *up*): *Business is slacking up.* **24.** to become less tense or taut, as a rope; to ease off. **25.** to become slaked, as lime. [bef. 900; ME *slac* (adj.), OE *sleac, slæc;* c. ON *slakr,* OHG *slach,* L *laxus* LAX] —**slack′ing·ly,** *adv.* —**slack′ly,** *adv.* —**slack′ness,** *n.*
—**Syn. 1.** relaxed. **2.** lazy, weak. **3.** dilatory, tardy, late. **4.** idle, quiet. **11.** slowing, relaxation. **18.** neglect. **19.** reduce, slacken. **22.** malinger.

slack[2] (slak), *n.* the fine screenings of coal. [1400–50; late ME *sleck* < MD *slacke, slecke*]

slack-baked (slak′bākt′), *adj.* **1.** improperly baked. **2.** imperfectly made. [1815–25]

slack·en (slak′ən), *v.t., v.i.* **1.** to make or become less active, vigorous, intense, etc. **2.** to make or become looser or less taut. [1570–80; SLACK[1] + -EN[1]]
—**Syn. 1, 2.** relax, loosen, slack, abate. —**Ant. 2.** tighten, tense.

slack·er (slak′ər), *n.* **1.** a person who evades his or her duty or work; shirker. **2.** a person who evades military service. [1790–1800; SLACK[1] + -ER[1]]
—**Syn. 1.** malingerer, dodger, laggard.

slack-jawed (slak′jôd′), *adj.* having the mouth open, esp. as an indication of astonishment, bewilderment, etc. [*slack jaw* + -ED[3]]

slacks (slaks), *n.* (*used with a plural v.*) trousers for informal wear. [1815–25; SLACK[1] + -S[3]]

slack′ suit′, 1. a man's suit for casual wear consisting of slacks and a matching shirt or loose-fitting jacket. **2.** pantsuit.

slack′ wa′ter, 1. a period when a body of water is between tides. **2.** water that is free of currents. [1760–70]

slag[1] (slag), *n., v.,* **slagged, slag·ging.** —*n.* **1.** Also called **cinder.** the more or less completely fused and vitrified matter separated during the reduction of a metal from its ore. **2.** the scoria from a volcano. **3.** waste left over after the re-sorting of coal. —*v.t.* **4.** to convert into slag. **5.** *Metall.* to remove slag from (a steel bath). —*v.i.* **6.** to form slag; become a slaglike mass. [1545–55; < MLG *slagge;* c. G *Schlacke* dross, slag; see SLACK[2]] —**slag′a·ble,** *adj.* —**slag′a·bil′i·ty,** *n.* —**slag′less,** *adj.* —**slag′less·ness,** *n.*

slag[2] (slag), *n. Brit. Slang.* an abusive woman. [1780–90; orig. an argot word for a worthless person or a thug; perh. identical with SLAG[1]]

slag′ cement′, a cement composed of about 80 percent granulated slag and about 20 percent hydrated lime. [1880–85]

slag·gy (slag′ē), *adj.,* **-gi·er, -gi·est.** of, pertaining to, or like slag. [1680–90; SLAG[1] + -Y[1]]

slain (slān), *v.* pp. of **slay.**

slake (slāk), *v.,* **slaked, slak·ing.** —*v.t.* **1.** to allay (thirst, desire, wrath, etc.) by satisfying. **2.** to cool or refresh: *He slaked his lips with ice.* **3.** to make less active, vigorous, intense, etc.: *His calm manner slaked their enthusiasm.* **4.** to cause disintegration of (lime) by treatment with water. Cf. **slaked lime. 5.** *Obs.* to make loose or less tense; slacken. —*v.i.* **6.** (of lime) to become slaked. **7.** *Archaic.* to become less active, intense, vigorous, etc.; abate. [bef. 1000; ME *slaken* to mitigate, allay, moderate, lessen one's efforts, OE *slacian* to slacken, lessen one's efforts, equiv. to *slæc* SLACK[1] + *-ian* causative v. suffix] —**slak′a·ble, slake′a·ble,** *adj.* —**slake′less,** *adj.*
—**Syn. 1.** satisfy, quench, gratify, relieve.

slaked′ lime′, a soft, white, crystalline, very slightly water-soluble powder, $Ca(OH)_2$, obtained by the action of water on lime: used chiefly in mortars, plasters, and cements. Also called **calcium hydroxide, calcium hydrate, hydrated lime, lime hydrate.** [1605–15]

slak·er (slā′kər), *n.* a person or thing that slakes. [1505–15; SLAKE + -ER[1]]

sla·lom (slä′ləm, -lōm), *n.* **1.** *Skiing.* a downhill race over a winding and zigzag course marked by poles or gates. Cf. **giant slalom. 2.** any winding or zigzag course marked by obstacles or barriers, as one in which automobiles are tested for maneuverability or drivers for reaction time. —*v.i.* **3.** *Skiing.* to ski in or as if in a slalom. **4.** to move in a winding or zigzag fashion; weave. **5.** to follow a course with many twists and turns. —*adj.* **6.** of, for, or designating a zigzag course with obstacles, barriers, or the like: *an excellent slalom skier.* [1920–25; < Norw *slalåm,* equiv. to *sla(d)* sloping + *låm* track]

slam[1] (slam), *v.,* **slammed, slam·ming,** *n.* —*v.t., v.i.* **1.** to shut with force and noise: *to slam the door.* **2.** to dash, strike, knock, thrust, throw, slap down, etc., with violent and noisy impact: *He slammed his books upon the table.* **3.** *Informal.* to criticize harshly; attack verbally: *He slammed my taste mercilessly.* —*n.* **4.** a violent and noisy closing, dashing, or impact. **5.** the noise so made. **6.** Usually, **the slam.** *Slang.* slammer (def. 2). **7.** *Informal.* a harsh criticism; verbal attack. [1650–60; perh < Scand; cf. Icel, Norw, Sw *slamra* to slam]

slam[2] (slam), *n. Cards.* **1.** the winning or bidding of all the tricks or all the tricks but one in a deal. Cf. **grand slam** (def. 1), **little slam. 2.** an old type of card game associated with ruff. [1615–25; perh. special use of SLAM[1]]

slam-bang (slam′bang′), *adv. Informal.* **1.** with noisy violence: *He drove slam-bang through the garage door.* **2.** quickly and carelessly; slapdash. —*adj.* **3.** noisy and violent. **4.** excitingly fast-paced, esp. in a noisy and violent way; action-filled; thrilling: *a slam-bang ending to the movie.* **5.** vigorous and fast but careless; slapdash. **6.** outstanding or powerful; excellent: *a slam-bang keynote address.* —*v.i.* **7.** to act or proceed in a chaotic or disorderly fashion: *The children slam-banged into the furniture.* [1830–40, *Amer.*] —**slam′-bang′er,** *n.*

slam′ dance′, a dance performed to punk rock by groups of people who flail and toss themselves about and slam into one another. [1975–80]

slam′ dunk′, *Basketball.* a particularly forceful, often dramatic dunk shot. [1975–80] —**slam′ dunk′er.**

slam·mer (slam′ər), *n.* **1.** a person or thing that slams. **2.** Usually, **the slammer.** Also called **the slam.** *Slang.* a prison. [1955–60; SLAM[1] + -ER[1]]

slam′ming stile′, doorstop (def. 2).

slan·der (slan′dər), *n.* **1.** defamation; calumny: *rumors full of slander.* **2.** a malicious, false, and defamatory statement or report: *a slander against his good name.* **3.** *Law.* defamation by oral utterance rather than by writing, pictures, etc. —*v.t.* **4.** to utter slander against; defame. —*v.i.* **5.** to utter or circulate slander. [1250–1300; (n.) ME *s(c)laundre* < AF *esclaundre,* OF *esclandre,* alter. of *escandle* < LL *scandalum* cause of offense, snare (see SCANDAL); (v.) ME *s(c)laundren* to cause to lapse morally, bring to disgrace, discredit, defame < OF *esclandrer,* deriv. of *esclandre*] —**slan′der·er,** *n.* —**slan′der·ing·ly,** *adv.* —**slan′der·ous,** *adj.* —**slan′der·ous·ly,** *adv.* —**slan′der·ous·ness,** *n.*
—**Syn. 4.** malign, vilify, revile.

slang[1] (slang), *n.* **1.** very informal usage in vocabulary and idiom that is characteristically more metaphorical, playful, elliptical, vivid, and ephemeral than ordinary language, as *Hit the road.* **2.** (in English and some other languages) speech and writing characterized by the use of vulgar and socially taboo vocabulary and idiomatic expressions. **3.** the jargon of a particular class, profession, etc. **4.** the special vocabulary of thieves, vagabonds, etc.; argot. —*v.i.* **5.** to use slang or abusive language. —*v.t.* **6.** to assail with abusive language. [1750–60; orig. uncert.]
—**Syn. 4.** cant.

slang[2] (slang), *v. Nonstandard.* pt. of **sling**[1].

slan·guage (slang′gwij), *n.* **1.** slang; a vocabulary of slang. **2.** language employing much slang. [1900–05; b. SLANG[1] and LANGUAGE]

slang·y (slang′ē), *adj.,* **slang·i·er, slang·i·est. 1.** of, of the nature of, or containing slang: *a slangy expression.* **2.** using much slang: *slangy speech.* [1840–50; SLANG[1] + -Y[1]] —**slang′i·ly,** *adv.* —**slang′i·ness,** *n.*

slank (slangk), *v. Archaic.* pt. of **slink.**

slant (slant, slänt), *v.i.* **1.** to veer or angle away from a given level or line, esp. from a horizontal; slope. **2.** to have or be influenced by a subjective point of view, bias, personal feeling or inclination, etc. (usually fol. by *toward*). —*v.t.* **3.** to cause to slope. **4.** to distort (information) by rendering it unfaithfully or incompletely, esp. in order to reflect a particular viewpoint: *He slanted the news story to discredit the Administration.* **5.** to write, edit, or publish for the interest or amusement of a specific group of readers: *a story slanted toward young adults.* —*n.* **6.** slanting or oblique direction; slope: *the slant of a roof.* **7.** a slanting line, surface, etc. **8.** virgule. **9.** a mental leaning, bias, or distortion: *His mind shows a curious slant.* **10.** viewpoint; opinion; attitude. **11.** *Informal.* a glance or look. **12.** Also called **angle.** *Journalism.* the particular mood or vein in which something is written, edited, or published: *a column with a humorous slant.* **13.** *Football.* **a.** an offensive play in which the ball-carrier runs toward the line of scrimmage at an angle. **b.** Also called **slant-in.** a pass pattern in which a receiver cuts diagonally across the middle of the field. **14.** Also called **slant-eye** (slant′ī′, slänt′ī′). *Slang (disparaging and offensive).* an Oriental person, esp. a Chinese or Japanese. —*adj.* **15.** sloping; oblique: *a slant roof; a slant approach.* [1485–95; aph. var. of ASLANT] —**slant′ing·ly, slant′ly,** *adv.*
—**Syn. 1.** lean, incline. See **slope. 6.** incline, inclination, pitch, obliquity, obliqueness.

slant′ board′, a tiltable board that allows a person to lie with the feet higher than the head while doing exercises. Also, **slant′board′.**

slant-eyed (slant′īd′, slänt′-), *adj.* (of a person) **1.** having eyes with epicanthic folds. **2.** having eyes that appear to slant. **3.** *Disparaging and Offensive.* being of Far Eastern origin, as a Chinese or Japanese. [1860–65]

slant′ front′, *Furniture.* a flap of a desk, sloping upward and inward to close the desk, and opening forward and downward to a horizontal position as a writing surface: a form of fall front.

slant′ height′, *Geom.* (of a right circular cone) the distance from the vertex to any point on the circumference of the base. [1790–1800]

slant-in (slant′in′), *n. Football.* slant (def. 13b).

slant′ rhyme′, *Pros.* rhyme in which either the vowels or the consonants of stressed syllables are identical, as in *eyes, light; years, yours.* Also called **half rhyme, imperfect rhyme, near rhyme.**

slant-top (slant′top′, slänt′-), *adj.* (esp. of a desk) having a slant front.

slant·wise (slant′wīz′, slänt′-), *adv.* **1.** aslant; obliquely. —*adj.* **2.** slanting; oblique. Also, **slant·ways** (slant′wāz′, slänt′-). [1565–75; SLANT + -WISE]

slap[1] (slap), *n., v.,* **slapped, slap·ping,** *adv.* —*n.* **1.** a sharp blow or smack, esp. with the open hand or with something flat. **2.** a sound made by or as if by such a blow or smack: *the slap of the waves against the dock.* **3.** a sharply worded or sarcastic rebuke or comment. —*v.t.* **4.** to strike sharply, esp. with the open hand or with something flat. **5.** to bring (the hand, something flat, etc.) with a sharp blow against something. **6.** to dash or cast forcibly: *He slapped the package against the wall.* **7.** to put or place promptly and sometimes haphazardly (often fol. by *on*): *The officer slapped a ticket on the car. He slapped mustard on the sandwich.* **8. slap down, a.** to subdue, esp. by a blow or by force; suppress. **b.** to reject, oppose, or criticize sharply: *to slap down dissenting voices.* —*adv.* **9.** *Informal.* directly; straight; smack: *The tug rammed slap into the side of the freighter.* [1625–35; < LG *slapp, slappe;* of expressive orig.] —**slap′per,** *n.*
—**Syn. 1.** See **blow**[1].

slap[2] (slap), *n., v.,* **slapped, slap·ping.** *Scot.* —*n.* **1.** a gap or opening, as in a fence, wall, cloud bank, or line of troops. **2.** a mountain pass. **3.** a wound or gash. —*v.t.* **4.** to make a gap or opening in; breach. [1325–75; ME *slop* < MD or MLG; c. G *Schlupf* hiding place]

slap-bang (slap′bang′), *adv. Brit. Informal.* slambang.

slap·dash (slap′dash′), *adv.* **1.** in a hasty, haphazard manner: *He assembled the motor slapdash.* —*adj.* **2.** hasty and careless; offhand: *a slapdash answer.* [1670–80; SLAP[1] (adv.) + DASH[1]]

slap′ dash′ing. See **slab dashing.** [1810–20]

slap·hap·py (slap′hap′ē), *adj.,* **-pi·er, -pi·est.** *Informal.* **1.** severely befuddled; punch-drunk: *a slaphappy boxer.* **2.** agreeably giddy or foolish: *After a martini he was slaphappy.* **3.** cheerfully irresponsible: *a slaphappy crowd.* [1935–40; SLAP[1] + HAPPY]

slap·jack (slap′jak′), *n.* **1.** a simple card game. **2.** a flapjack or griddlecake. [1790–1800; SLAP[1] + JACK[1]]
—**Regional Variation. 2.** See **pancake.**

slap′ plas′tering. See **slab plastering.**

slap′ shot′, *Ice Hockey.* a very powerful, fast-moving shot of the puck on goal made with a full backswing of the stick and an extended follow-through. [1940–45]

slap·stick (slap′stik′), *n.* **1.** broad comedy characterized by boisterous action, as the throwing of pies in actors' faces, mugging, and obvious farcical situations and jokes. **2.** a stick or lath used by harlequins, clowns, etc., as in pantomime, for striking other performers, esp. a combination of laths that make a loud, clapping noise without hurting the person struck. —*adj.* **3.** using, or marked by the use of, broad farce and horseplay: *a slapstick motion picture.* [1895–1900, *Amer.*; SLAP[1] + STICK[1]]

slap-up (slap′up′), *adj. Brit. Informal.* excellent; first-rate: *a slap-up do.* [1820–30]

slash[1] (slash), *v.t.* **1.** to cut with a violent sweeping stroke or by striking violently and at random, as with a knife or sword. **2.** to lash; whip. **3.** to cut, reduce, or alter: *The editors slashed the story to half its length.* **4.** to make slits in (a garment) to show an underlying fabric. **5.** to criticize, censure, or attack in a savage or cutting manner. —*v.i.* **6.** to lay about one with sharp, sweeping strokes; make one's way by cutting. **7.** to make a sweeping, cutting stroke. —*n.* **8.** a sweeping stroke, as with a knife, sword, or pen. **9.** a cut, wound, or mark made with such a stroke. **10.** a curtailment, reduction, or alteration: *a drastic slash of prices.* **11.** a decorative slit in a garment showing an underlying fabric. **12.** virgule. **13.** (in forest land) **a.** an open area strewn with debris of trees from felling or from wind or fire. **b.** the debris itself. [1350–1400; ME *slaschen* < ?]
—**Syn. 3.** abridge, abbreviate.

slash[2] (slash), *n.* Often, **slashes.** a tract of wet or swampy ground overgrown with bushes or trees. [1645–55, *Amer.*; orig. uncert.]

slash-and-burn (slash′ən bûrn′), *adj.* of a method of agriculture used in the tropics, in which forest vegetation is felled and burned, the land is cropped for a few years, then the forest is allowed to reinvade. [1935–40]

slash·er (slash′ər), *n.* **1.** a person or thing that slashes. **2.** a person who criminally attacks others with a knife, razor, or the like. **3.** a horror film depicting such a criminal and featuring gory special effects. [1550–60; SLASH[1] + -ER[1]]

slash·ing (slash′ing), *n.* **1.** a slash. —*adj.* **2.** sweeping; cutting. **3.** violent; severe: *a slashing wind.* **4.** dashing; impetuous. **5.** vivid; flashing; brilliant. **6.** *Informal.* very large or fine; splendid: *a slashing fortune.* [1590–1600; SLASH[1] + -ING[1], -ING[2]] —**slash′ing·ly,** *adv.*

slash′ pine′, 1. a pine, *Pinus elliotii,* found in slashes and swamps in the southeastern U.S., yielding a hard, durable wood. **2.** the wood of this tree. [1880–85]

slash′ pock′et, a pocket set into a garment, esp. below the waistline, to which easy access is provided by an exterior, vertical or diagonal slit. [1790–1800]

slash-saw (slash′sô′), *v.t.,* **-sawed, -sawed** or **-sawn, -saw·ing.** plain-saw.

Ślask (shlônsk), *n.* Polish name of **Silesia.**

slat[1] (slat), *n., v.,* **slat·ted, slat·ting.** —*n.* **1.** a long thin, narrow strip of wood, metal, etc., used as a support for a bed, as one of the horizontal laths of a Venetian blind, etc. **2.** *Aeron.* a control surface along the leading edge of a wing that can be extended forward to create a gap **(slot)** to improve airflow. **3. slats,** *Slang.* **a.** the ribs. **b.** the buttocks. **c.** (*cap.*) a nickname for a tall, slender man. —*v.t.* **4.** to furnish or make with slats. [1350–1400; ME *sclat, slatt* a slate < MF *esclat* splinter, fragment; see ÉCLAT]

slat[2] (slat), *v.,* **slat·ted, slat·ting,** *n. Chiefly Brit. Dial.* —*v.t.* **1.** to throw or dash with force. —*v.i.* **2.** to flap violently, as sails. —*n.* **3.** a slap; a sharp blow. [1815–25; < ON *sletta* to splash, strike]

S. Lat., south latitude.

slat′ back′, a chair back having two or more horizontal slats between upright posts. [1890–95]

slatch (slach), *n. Naut.* a relatively smooth interval between heavy seas. [1595–1605; obscurely akin to SLACK[1]]

slate[1] (slāt), *n., v.,* **slat·ed, slat·ing.** —*n.* **1.** a fine-grained rock formed by the metamorphosis of clay, shale, etc., that tends to split along parallel cleavage planes, usually at an angle to the planes of stratification. **2.** a thin piece or plate of this rock or a similar material, used esp. for roofing or as a writing surface. **3.** a dull, dark bluish gray. **4.** a list of candidates, officers, etc., to be considered for nomination, appointment, election, or the like. **5. clean slate,** an unsullied record; a record marked by creditable conduct: *to start over with a clean slate.* —*v.t.* **6.** to cover with or as with slate. **7.** to write or set down for nomination or appointment: *the district leader slated for city judge.* **8.** to plan or designate (something) for a particular place and time; schedule: *The premiere was slated for January.* **9.** to censure or criticize harshly or violently; scold. **10.** to punish severely. [1300–50; ME *sclate* < MF *esclate,* fem. of *esclat* piece split off; see SLAT¹]

slate² (slāt), *v.t.,* **slat·ed, slat·ing.** *Brit.* to sic or set a dog on (a person or animal). [1300–50; ME *slayten* < ON **sleita;* c. OE *slǣtan*]

slate′ blue′, a moderate to dark grayish blue. [1790–1800] —**slate′-blue′,** *adj.*

slate′-colored jun′co (slāt′kul′ərd), the eastern subspecies of the dark-eyed junco, *Junco hyemalis,* having grayer plumage than the several western subspecies. [1890–95, *Amer.*]

slat·er (slā′tər), *n.* a person who lays slates, as for roofing. [1375–1425; late ME *sclater.* See SLATE¹, -ER¹]

Sla·ter (slā′tər), *n.* **Samuel,** 1768–1835, U.S. industrialist, born in England.

slath·er (slath′ər), *Informal.* —*v.t.* **1.** to spread or apply thickly: *to slather butter on toast.* **2.** to spread something thickly on (usually fol. by *with*): *to slather toast with butter.* **3.** to spend or use lavishly. —*n.* **4.** Often, **slathers.** a generous amount: *slathers of money.* **5. open slather,** *Australian.* complete freedom. [1810–20, in sense "to slip, slide"; orig. uncert.]

slat·ing (slā′ting), *n.* **1.** the act or work of covering something with slates. **2.** materials for roofing with slates. [1565–75; SLATE¹ + -ING¹]

slat·tern (slat′ərn), *n.* **1.** a slovenly, untidy woman or girl. **2.** a slut; harlot. [1630–40; perh. akin to dial. *slatter* to splash, spill < ?]

slat·tern·ly (slat′ərn lē), *adj.* **1.** slovenly and untidy. **2.** characteristic or suggestive of a slattern. —*adv.* **3.** in the manner of a slattern. [1670–80; SLATTERN + -LY] —**slat′tern·li·ness,** *n.*

slat·ting (slat′ing), *n.* **1.** the act of furnishing with or making from slats. **2.** a number of slats, taken as a whole. [1525–35; SLAT¹ + -ING¹]

slat·y (slā′tē), *adj.,* **slat·i·er, slat·i·est. 1.** consisting of, resembling, or pertaining to slate. **2.** having the color of slate. [1520–30; SLATE¹ + -Y¹] —**slat′i·ness,** *n.*

slaugh·ter (slô′tər), *n.* **1.** the killing or butchering of cattle, sheep, etc., esp. for food. **2.** the brutal or violent killing of a person. **3.** the killing of great numbers of people or animals indiscriminately; carnage: *the slaughter of war.* —*v.t.* **4.** to kill or butcher (animals), esp. for food. **5.** to kill in a brutal or violent manner. **6.** to slay in great numbers; massacre. **7.** *Informal.* to defeat thoroughly; trounce: *They slaughtered our team.* [1250–1300; ME *slaghter, slahter, slauther* (n.) < ON *slātr,* earlier *slāttr, slahtr*] —**slaugh′ter·er,** *n.* —**slaugh′ter·ing·ly,** *adv.*
—**Syn. 2.** murder. **4–6.** SLAUGHTER, BUTCHER, MASSACRE all imply violent and bloody methods of killing. SLAUGHTER and BUTCHER, primarily referring to the killing of animals for food, are used also of the brutal or indiscriminate killing of human beings: *to slaughter cattle; to butcher a hog.* MASSACRE indicates a general slaughtering of helpless or unresisting victims: *to massacre the peasants of a region.*

slaugh·ter·house (slô′tər hous′), *n., pl.* **-hous·es** (-hou′ziz). a building or place where animals are butchered for food; abattoir. [1325–75; ME *slautherhus;* see SLAUGHTER, HOUSE]

slaugh·ter·ous (slô′tər əs), *adj.* murderous; destructive. [1575–85; SLAUGHTER + -OUS] —**slaugh′ter·ous·ly,** *adv.*

Slav (släv, slav), *n.* **1.** one of a group of peoples in eastern, southeastern, and central Europe, including the Russians and Ruthenians **(Eastern Slavs),** the Bulgars, Serbs, Croats, Slavonians, Slovenes, etc. **(Southern Slavs),** and the Poles, Czechs, Moravians, Slovaks, etc. **(Western Slavs).** —*adj.* **2.** of, pertaining to, or characteristic of the Slavs; Slavic. [1350–1400; < ML *Slāvus,* var. of *Sclāvus,* akin to LGk *Sklábos* < a Slavic ethnonym, perh. orig. a name for all Slavic tribes (cf. SLOVAK, SLOVENE, ORuss *Slověnĕ* an East Slavic tribe); r. ME *Sclave* < ML *Sclāvus*]

Slav, Slavic. Also, **Slav.**

slave (slāv), *n., v.,* **slaved, slav·ing.** —*n.* **1.** a person who is the property of and wholly subject to another; a bond servant. **2.** a person entirely under the domination of some influence or person: *a slave to a drug.* **3.** a drudge: *a housekeeping slave.* **4.** a slave ant. **5.** *Photog.* a subsidiary flash lamp actuated through its photoelectric cell when the principal flash lamp is discharged. **6.** *Mach.* a mechanism under control of and repeating the actions of a similar mechanism. Cf. **master** (def. 19). —*v.i.* **7.** to work like a slave; drudge. **8.** to engage in the slave trade; procure, transport, or sell slaves. —*v.t.* **9.** to connect (a machine) to a master as its slave. **10.** *Archaic.* to enslave. [1250–1300; ME *sclave* < ML *sclāvus* (masc.), *sclāva* (fem.) slave, special use of *Sclāvus* Slav, so called because Slavs were commonly enslaved in the early Middle Ages; see SLAV] —**slave′less,** *adj.* —**slave′like′,** *adj.*
—**Syn. 7.** toil, labor, slog, grind.

CONCISE ETYMOLOGY KEY: <, descended or borrowed from; >, whence; b., blend of, blended; c., cognate with; cf., compare; deriv., derivative; equiv., equivalent; imit., imitative; obl., oblique; r., replacing; s., stem; sp., spelling, spelled; resp., respelling, respelled; trans., translation; ?, origin unknown; *, unattested; ‡, probably earlier than. See the full key inside the front cover.

Slave (slāv), *n., pl.* **Slaves,** (*esp. collectively*) **Slave.** a member of a group of Athabaskan-speaking North American Indians living in the upper Mackenzie River valley region of the Northwest Territories and in parts of British Columbia, Alberta, and the Yukon Territory. Also, **Slavey.**

slave′ ant′, an ant taken as a larva or pupa by ants of another species and becoming a working member of the captor colony. [1865–70]

slave′ brace′let, a braceletlike, ornamental circlet or chain worn around the ankle.

Slave′ Coast′, the coast of W equatorial Africa, between the Benin and Volta rivers: a center of slavery traffic 16th–19th centuries.

slave′ driv′er, 1. an overseer of slaves. **2.** a hard taskmaster: *His boss was a slave driver.* [1800–10, *Amer.*]

slave·hold·er (slāv′hōl′dər), *n.* an owner of slaves. [1770–80; SLAVE + HOLDER] —**slave′hold′ing,** *n.*

slave′ la′bor, 1. persons, esp. a large group, performing labor under duress or threats, as prisoners in a concentration camp; a labor force of slaves or slavelike prisoners. **2.** labor done by slaves. **3.** any coerced or poorly remunerated work: *Typing at that salary is slave labor.* [1810–20] —**slave′-la′bor,** *adj.*

slave′ la′bor camp′. See **labor camp** (def. 1). [1935–40]

slave·ling (slāv′ling), *n.* a person in a condition of servility or slavery. [1880–85; SLAVE + -LING¹]

slave′-mak·ing ant′ (slāv′mā′king), an ant of a species that raids the colonies of other ant species, carrying off larvae and pupae to be reared as slaves. [1810–20]

Sla·ven·ska (slä ven′skä), *n.* **Mi·a** (mē′ä), (*Mia Corak*), born 1917, U.S. dancer and choreographer, born in Yugoslavia.

slav·er¹ (slā′vər), *n.* **1.** a dealer in or an owner of slaves. **2.** See **slave ship.** [1815–25; SLAVE + -ER¹]

slav·er² (slav′ər, slā′vər, slä′-), *v.i.* **1.** to let saliva run from the mouth; slobber; drool. **2.** to fawn. —*v.t.* **3.** *Archaic.* to smear with saliva. —*n.* **4.** saliva coming from the mouth. **5.** drivel. [1275–1325; ME *slaver* (n.), *slaveren* (v.), prob. < Scand; cf. Icel *slafra* to slobber]

Slave′ Riv′er, a river in NE Alberta and the Northwest Territories, in Canada: flowing from Lake Athabaska NW to Great Slave Lake. 258 mi. (415 km) long.

slav·er·y (slā′və rē, slāv′rē), *n.* **1.** the condition of a slave; bondage. **2.** the keeping of slaves as a practice or institution. **3.** a state of subjection like that of a slave: *He was kept in slavery by drugs.* **4.** severe toil; drudgery. [1545–55; SLAVE + -ERY]
—**Syn. 1.** thralldom, enthrallment. SLAVERY, BONDAGE, SERVITUDE refer to involuntary subjection to another or others. SLAVERY emphasizes the idea of complete ownership and control by a master: *to be sold into slavery.* BONDAGE indicates a state of subjugation or captivity often involving burdensome and degrading labor: *in bondage to a cruel master.* SERVITUDE is compulsory service, often such as is required by a legal penalty: *penal servitude.* **4.** moil, labor.

slave′ ship′, a ship for transporting slaves from their native homes to places of bondage. [1790–1800]

slave′ state′, 1. any state, nation, etc., where slavery is legal or officially condoned. **2. Slave States,** *U.S. Hist.* the states that permitted slavery between 1820 and 1860: Alabama, Arkansas, Delaware, Florida, Georgia, Kentucky, Louisiana, Maryland, Mississippi, Missouri, North Carolina, South Carolina, Tennessee, Texas, and Virginia. [1800–10, *Amer.*]

slave′ trade′, the business or process of procuring, transporting, and selling slaves, esp. black Africans to the New World prior to the mid-19th century. [1725–35]

slav·ey (slā′vē), *n., pl.* **-eys.** *Brit. Informal.* a female servant, esp. a maid of all work in a boardinghouse. [1800–10; SLAVE + -Y²]

Slav·ey (slā′vē), *n., pl.* **-eys,** (*esp. collectively*) **-ey.** Slave.

Slav·ic (slä′vik, slav′ik), *n.* **1.** a branch of the Indo-European family of languages, usually divided into East Slavic (Russian, Ukrainian, Byelorussian), West Slavic (Polish, Czech, Slovak, Sorbian), and South Slavic (Old Church Slavonic, Macedonian, Bulgarian, Serbo-Croatian, Slovene). Abbr.: Slav —*adj.* **2.** of or pertaining to the Slavs or their languages. Also, **Slavonic.** [1805–15; SLAV + -IC]

Slav·i·cism (slä′və siz′əm, slav′ə-), *n.* Slavism. [SLAVIC + -ISM]

Slav·i·cist (slä′və sist, slav′ə-), *n.* a specialist in the study of the Slavic languages or literatures. Also, **Slavist** (slä′vist, slav′ist). [1940–45; SLAVIC + -IST]

slav·ish (slā′vish), *adj.* **1.** of or befitting a slave: *slavish subjection.* **2.** being or resembling a slave; abjectly submissive: *He was slavish in his obedience.* **3.** base; mean; ignoble: *slavish fears.* **4.** deliberately imitative; lacking originality: *a slavish reproduction.* [1555–65; SLAVE + -ISH¹] —**slav′ish·ly,** *adv.* —**slav′ish·ness,** *n.*
—**Syn. 2.** groveling, sycophantic, fawning, cringing. See **servile.** —**Ant. 2.** independent. **3.** exalted.

Slav·ism (slä′viz əm, slav′iz-), *n.* something that is native to, characteristic of, or associated with the Slavs or Slavic. Also, **Slavicism.** [1875–85; SLAV + -ISM]

Slav·kov (släf′kôf), *n.* Czech name of **Austerlitz.**

Slavo-, a combining form representing **Slav** in compound words: *Slavophile.*

slav·oc·ra·cy (slā vok′rə sē), *n., pl.* **-cies. 1.** the rule or domination of slaveholders: *the slavocracy of the old plantations.* **2.** a dominating body of slaveholders. [1830–40; SLAVE + -O- + -CRACY] —**slav·o·crat** (slā′və-krat′), *n.* —**slav·o·crat·ic** (slā′və krat′ik), *adj.*

Sla·vo·ni·a (slə vō′nē ə), *n.* a historic region in N Croatia.

Sla·vo·ni·an (slə vō′nē ən), *adj.* **1.** of or pertaining to Slavonia or its inhabitants. **2.** Slavic. —*n.* **3.** a native or inhabitant of Slavonia. **4.** a Slav. [1570–80; SLAVONI(A) + -AN]

Sla·von·ic (slə von′ik), *adj.* **1.** Slavonian. **2.** Slavic. [1605–15; < NL *slavonicus,* equiv. to ML *Slavon(ia)* + *-icus* -IC] —**Sla·von′i·cal·ly,** *adv.*

Slav·o·phile (slä′və fīl′, -fil, slav′ə-), *n.* **1.** a person who greatly admires the Slavs and Slavic ways. **2.** one of a group of mid-19th century Russian intellectuals who favored traditional cultural practices over Western innovations, esp. in political and religious life. —*adj.* **3.** admiring or favoring the Slavs and Slavic interests, aims, customs, etc. Also, **Slav·o·phil** (slä′və fil, slav′ə-). [1875–80; SLAVO- + -PHILE; cf. Russ *slavyanofíl*] —**Sla·voph·i·lism** (slə vof′ə liz′əm, slä′və fil iz′əm, slav′ə-), *n.*

Slav·o·phobe (slä′və fōb′, slav′ə-), *n.* a person who fears or hates the Slavs, their influence, or things Slavic. [1885–90; SLAVO- + -PHOBE] —**Slav′o·pho′bi·a,** *n.*

Sla·vyansk (slu vyänsk′), *n.* a city in E central Ukraine, NW of Donetsk. 140,000.

slaw (slô), *n.* coleslaw. [1860–65, *Amer.*; < D *sla,* short for *salade* SALAD]

slay (slā), *v.,* **slew, slain, slay·ing,** *n.* —*v.t.* **1.** to kill by violence. **2.** to destroy; extinguish. **3.** sley. **4.** *Informal.* to impress strongly; overwhelm, esp. by humor: *Your jokes slay me.* **5.** *Obs.* to strike. —*v.i.* **6.** to kill or murder. —*n.* **7.** sley. [bef. 900; ME *sleen, slayn,* OE *slēan;* c. D *slaan,* G *schlagen,* ON *slā,* Goth *slahan* to strike, beat] —**slay′a·ble,** *adj.* —**slay′er,** *n.*
—**Syn. 1.** murder, slaughter, massacre, butcher, assassinate. **2.** annihilate, ruin.

Slay·ton (slāt′n), *n.* **Donald Kent** (*"Deke"*), born 1924, U.S. astronaut.

SLBM, 1. sea-launched ballistic missile. **2.** submarine-launched ballistic missile. Also, **S.L.B.M.**

SLCM, See **sea-launched cruise missile.** Also, **S.L.C.M.**

sld., 1. sailed. **2.** sealed.

SLE, See **systemic lupus erythematosus.**

sleave (slēv), *v.,* **sleaved, sleav·ing,** *n.* —*v.t.* **1.** to divide or separate into filaments, as silk. —*n.* **2.** anything matted or raveled. **3.** a filament of silk obtained by separating a thicker thread. **4.** a silk in the form of such filaments. [1585–95; OE *-slǣfan* (only in the compound *tōslǣfan*), akin to *slīfan* to split; see SLIVER]

sleaze (slēz), *n. Slang.* **1.** a contemptible or vulgar person. **2.** a shabby or slovenly person. **3.** a sleazy quality, character, or atmosphere; shoddiness; vulgarity. **4.** sleazy behavior, content, appearance, or the like. [1950–55; back formation from SLEAZY]

sleaze·bag (slēz′bag′), *n. Slang.* a sleazy person; sleaze. Also, **sleaze′ bag′.** Also called **sleaze·ball** (slēz′bôl′) [SLEAZE + BAG]

slea·zy (slē′zē, slā′zē), *adj.,* **-zi·er, -zi·est. 1.** contemptibly low, mean, or disreputable: *sleazy politics.* **2.** squalid; sordid; filthy; dilapidated: *a sleazy hotel.* **3.** thin or poor in texture, as a fabric; cheap; flimsy: *a sleazy dress; a sleazy excuse.* [1635–45; (def. 3) of obscure orig. (prob. unrelated to SILESIA other than by folk etym.); sense of defs. 1–2 (first attested 1941) perh. represent a distinct word] —**slea′zi·ly,** *adv.* —**slea′zi·ness,** *n.*

sled (sled), *n., v.,* **sled·ded, sled·ding.** —*n.* **1.** a small vehicle consisting of a platform mounted on runners for use in traveling over snow or ice. **2.** a sledge. —*v.i.* **3.** to coast, ride, or be carried on a sled. —*v.t.* **4.** to convey by sled. [1350–1400; ME *sledde* < MD; akin to G *Schlitten* sled, SLEIGH; cf. SLIDE] —**sled′like′,** *adj.*

sled′ cul′tivator, go-devil (def. 5).

sled·der (sled′ər), *n.* **1.** a person who rides on or steers a sled. **2.** a horse or other animal for drawing a sled. [1640–50; SLED + -ER¹]

sled·ding (sled′ing), *n.* **1.** the state of the ground permitting use of a sled: *The mountain roads offer good sledding.* **2.** the going, or kind of travel, for sleds, as determined by ground and weather conditions. **3.** a going, progress, or advance in any field: *The job won't be easy sledding.* **4.** the act of conveying or riding on a sled. [1675–85, *Amer.*; SLED + -ING¹]

sled′ dog′, a dog trained to pull a sled, usually working in a team. [1685–95]

sledge¹ (slej), *n., v.,* **sledged, sledg·ing.** —*n.* **1.** a vehicle of various forms, mounted on runners and often drawn by draft animals, used for traveling or for conveying loads over snow, ice, rough ground, etc. **2.** a sled. **3.** *Brit.* a sleigh. —*v.t., v.i.* **4.** to convey or travel by sledge. —*v.i.* **5.** *Brit.* to sleigh. [1595–1605; < dial. D *sleeds,* deriv. of *slede* SLED; cf. SLEIGH]

sledge² (slej), *n., v.t., v.i.,* **sledged, sledg·ing.** sledgehammer (defs. 1, 2). [bef. 1000; ME *slegge,* OE *slecg;* c. D *slegge,* ON *sleggja;* akin to SLAY]

sledge·ham·mer (slej′ham′ər), *n.* **1.** a large heavy hammer wielded with both hands. —*v.t., v.i.* **2.** to hammer, beat, or strike with or as if with a sledgehammer. —*adj.* **3.** crudely or ruthlessly forceful; lacking all dexterity or grace: *the artist's sledgehammer approach.* [1485–95; SLEDGE² + HAMMER]

sleek¹ (slēk), *adj.,* **-er, -est. 1.** smooth or glossy, as hair, an animal, etc. **2.** well-fed or well-groomed. **3.** trim and graceful; finely contoured; streamlined: *a sleek sports car.* **4.** smooth in manners, speech, etc.; suave. **5.** cleverly or deceitfully skillful; slick: *a sleek confidence man.* [1580–90; var. of SLICK¹] —**sleek′ly,** *adv.* —**sleek′ness,** *n.*
—**Syn. 5.** smooth, suave.

sleek² (slēk), *v.t.* to make sleek; smooth; slick: *to sleek leather.* Also, **sleek′en.** [1400–50; late ME *sleken,* var. of SLICK²] —**sleek′er,** *n.*

sleek·it (slē′kit), *adj. Scot.* sleeky. [ptp. of SLEEK²]

sleek·y (slē′kē), *adj.,* **sleek·i·er, sleek·i·est. 1.** sleek;

smooth. **2.** *Chiefly Scot.* sly; sneaky. Also, *Scot.*, **sleeked** (slēkt), **sleekit.** [1715–25; SLEEK[1] + -Y[1]]

sleep (slēp), *v.*, **slept, sleep·ing,** *n.* —*v.i.* **1.** to take the rest afforded by a suspension of voluntary bodily functions and the natural suspension, complete or partial, of consciousness; cease being awake. **2.** *Bot.* to assume, esp. at night, a state similar to the sleep of animals, marked by closing of petals, leaves, etc. **3.** to be dormant, quiescent, or inactive, as faculties. **4.** to be careless or unalert; allow one's alertness, vigilance, or attentiveness to lie dormant: *While England slept, Germany prepared for war.* **5.** to lie in death: *They are sleeping in their tombs.* —*v.t.* **6.** to take rest in (a specified kind of sleep): *He slept the sleep of the innocent.* **7.** to accommodate for sleeping; have sleeping accommodations for: *This trailer sleeps three people.* **8.** to spend or pass in sleep (usually fol. by *away* or *out*): *to sleep the day away.* **9.** to recover from the effects of (a headache, hangover, etc.) by sleeping (usually fol. by *off* or *away*). **10. sleep around,** *Informal.* to have sexual relations with many partners, esp. in a casual way; be sexually promiscuous. **11. sleep in, a.** (esp. of domestic help) to sleep where one is employed. **b.** to sleep beyond one's usual time of arising. **12. sleep on,** to postpone making a decision about for at least a day: *to sleep on a proposal till the end of the week.* **13. sleep out, a.** (esp. of domestic help) to sleep away from one's place of employment. **b.** *Chiefly Northern U.S.* to sleep away from one's home. **c.** to sleep outdoors. **14. sleep over,** to spend one or more nights in a place other than one's own home: *Two friends will sleep over this weekend.* **15. sleep together,** to be sexual partners; have a sexual relationship. **16. sleep with,** to have sexual relations with. —*n.* **17.** the state of a person, animal, or plant that sleeps. **18.** a period of sleeping: *a brief sleep.* **19.** dormancy or inactivity. **20.** the repose of death. **21.** sleeper (def. 10). **22. put to sleep,** to put (an animal) to death in a humane way: *to put a sick old dog to sleep.* [bef. 900; (n.) ME; OE *slēp* (Anglian), *slǣp, slāp;* c. D *slaap,* G *Schlaf,* Goth *slēps;* (v.) ME *slepen,* OE *slēpan, slǣpan, slāpan,* c. OS *slāpan,* Goth *slēpan*] —**sleep′ful,** *adj.* —**sleep′like′,** *adj.*
—**Syn. 1.** slumber, nap, drowse, doze. **17.** rest, repose. **18.** nap.

sleep′ ap′nea. See under **apnea.** [1975–80]

sleep-a·way (slēp′ə wā′), *adj.* of or pertaining to a place at which one sleeps away from home: *sleep-away camp.* Also, **sleep′a·way′.** [1975–80]

sleep·coat (slēp′kōt′), *n.* a lightweight, knee-length garment for sleep or lounging, styled like a pajama top and having a sash. [SLEEP + COAT]

sleep·er (slē′pər), *n.* **1.** a person or thing that sleeps. **2.** a heavy horizontal timber for distributing loads. **3.** *Building Trades.* **a.** any long wooden, metal, or stone piece lying horizontally as a sill or footing. **b.** any of a number of wooden pieces, laid upon the ground or upon masonry or concrete, to which floorboards are nailed. **4.** a sleeping car. **5.** *Informal.* something or someone that becomes unexpectedly successful or important after a period of being unnoticed, ignored, or considered unpromising or a failure: *The play was the sleeper of the season.* **6.** merchandise that is not quickly sold because its value is not immediately recognized. **7.** Often, **sleepers.** one-piece or two-piece pajamas with feet, esp. for children. **8.** bunting[3]. **9.** a sofa, chair, or other piece of furniture that is designed to open up or unfold into a bed; convertible. **10.** Also called **sleep, sand.** a globule that forms at the inner corner of the eye, esp. during sleep, from the accumulated secretion of the glands of the eyelid. **11.** any of several gobioid fishes of the family Eleotridae, of tropical seas, most species of which have the habit of resting quietly on the bottom. **12.** *Bowling.* a pin that is hidden from view by another pin. **13.** *Chiefly Brit.* a timber or beam laid in a railroad track, serving as a foundation or support for the rails; tie. [1175–1225; ME; see SLEEP, -ER[1]]

sleep′er seat′, a seat, as on an airplane, that can be extended horizontally to permit sleeping.

sleep-in (slēp′in′), *adj.* **1.** live-in (def. 1). —*n.* **2.** a person who sleeps in at a place of employment. [1950–55; adj., n. use of v. phrase *sleep in*]

sleep·ing (slē′ping), *n.* **1.** the condition of being asleep. —*adj.* **2.** asleep. **3.** of, pertaining to, or having accommodations for sleeping: *a sleeping compartment.* **4.** used to sleep in or on: *a sleeping jacket.* **5.** used to induce or aid sleep or while asleep: *sleeping mask.* [1250–1300; ME; see SLEEP, -ING[1], -ING[2]]

sleep′ing bag′, a warmly lined or padded body-length bag, usually waterproof and with a closure, in which one or two persons can sleep, esp. outdoors, as when camping. [1815–25]

Sleep′ing Beau′ty, 1. a beautiful princess, the heroine of a popular fairy tale, awakened from a charmed sleep by the kiss of the prince who is her true love. **2.** (*italics*) the fairy tale itself. **3.** (*italics*) a ballet (1889) by Tchaikovsky.

sleep′ing car′, a railroad car fitted with berths, compartments, bedrooms, or drawing rooms for passengers to sleep in. [1830–40, *Amer.*]

sleep′ing chair′, a chair of the 17th century, having a high back, usually adjustable, with deep wings of the same height. [1665–75]

sleep′ing part′ner, *Brit.* See **silent partner.** [1775–85]

sleep′ing pill′, a pill or capsule containing a drug for inducing sleep. [1940–45]

sleep′ing porch′, a porch enclosed with glass or screening or a room with open sides or a row of windows used for sleeping in the open air. [1880–85]

sleep′ing sick′ness, *Pathol.* **1.** Also called **African sleeping sickness, African trypanosomiasis.** a generally fatal disease, common in parts of Africa, characterized by fever, wasting, and progressive lethargy: caused by a parasitic protozoan, *Trypanosoma gambiense* or *T. rhodesiense,* that is carried by a tsetse fly, *Glossina palpalis.* **2.** Also called **epidemic encephalitis, lethargic encephalitis.** a viral disease affecting the brain, characterized by apathy, sleepiness, extreme muscular weakness, and impairment of vision. Also, *Brit.,* **sleepy sickness.** [1870–75]

sleep′ learn′ing, the act or process of learning during sleep by listening to recordings repeatedly. Also called **hypnopedia.** [1950–55]

sleep·less (slēp′lis), *adj.* **1.** without sleep: *a sleepless night.* **2.** watchful; alert: *sleepless devotion to duty.* **3.** always active: *the sleepless ocean.* [1375–1425; late ME; see SLEEP, -LESS] —**sleep′less·ly,** *adv.* —**sleep′less·ness,** *n.*

sleep-out (slēp′out′), *adj.* **1.** live-out. —*n.* **2.** a person who lives elsewhere than at the place of employment. **3.** an act or instance of sleeping outdoors. [1910–15; adj., n. use of v. phrase *sleep out*]

sleep·o·ver (slēp′ō′vər), *n.* **1.** an instance of sleeping over, as at another person's house. **2.** a person who sleeps over. [1970–75; n. use of v. phrase *sleep over*]

sleep′ shade′, an opaque, masklike covering for the eyes, usually fitted with an elasticized cord that passes around the head, worn to aid sleep by shutting out light.

sleep·shirt (slēp′shûrt′), *n.* a shirtlike garment, usually knee-length or shorter, worn for sleeping. [SLEEP + SHIRT]

sleep′ so′fa, a sofa that can be used as a bed; sofa bed. [1970–75]

sleep′-ter·ror disor′der (slēp′ter′ər). *Psychiatry.* See **night terror.**

sleep′-wake′ cy′cle (slēp′wāk′), *Physiol.* the species-specific biological pattern of alternating sleep and wakefulness, in humans roughly 8 hours of nocturnal sleep and 16 hours of daytime activity.

sleep·walk (slēp′wôk′), *v.i.* **1.** to engage in sleepwalking. —*n.* **2.** an act of sleepwalking; somnambulation. [1920–25; back formation from SLEEPWALKING]

sleep·walk·ing (slēp′wô′king), *n.* **1.** the act or state of walking, eating, or performing other motor acts while asleep, of which one is unaware upon awakening; somnambulism. —*adj.* **2.** of or pertaining to the state of walking while asleep; somnambulistic. [1790–1800; SLEEP + WALKING] —**sleep′walk′er,** *n.*

sleep·wear (slēp′wâr′), *n.* garments, as nightgowns or pajamas, worn for sleeping or at bedtime. [1950–55; SLEEP + WEAR]

sleep·y (slē′pē), *adj.,* **sleep·i·er, sleep·i·est. 1.** ready or inclined to sleep; drowsy. **2.** of or showing drowsiness. **3.** languid; languorous: *a sleepy gesture.* **4.** lethargic; sluggish: *a sleepy brook.* **5.** quiet: *a sleepy village.* **6.** inducing sleep; soporific: *sleepy warmth.* [1175–1225; ME; see SLEEP, -Y[1]] —**sleep′i·ly,** *adv.* —**sleep′i·ness,** *n.*
—**Syn. 1.** tired, somnolent, slumberous.

sleep·y·head (slē′pē hed′), *n.* a sleepy person. [1570–80; SLEEPY + HEAD]

Sleep′y Hol′low chair′, *U.S. Furniture.* an armchair of the mid-19th century, sometimes on rockers, having a single piece forming a high upholstered back and a concave upholstered seat. [1835–45; after *Sleepy Hollow,* New York]

sleep′y sick′ness, *Brit. Pathol.* See **sleeping sickness.**

sleet (slēt), *n.* **1.** precipitation in the form of ice pellets created by the freezing of rain as it falls (distinguished from *hail*). **2.** glaze (def. 17). **3.** *Chiefly Brit.* a mixture of rain and snow. —*v.i.* **4.** to send down sleet. **5.** to fall as or like sleet. [1250–1300; (n.) ME *slete;* akin to LG *slote,* G *Schlossen* hail; (v.) ME *sleten,* deriv. of the n.]

sleet·y (slē′tē), *adj.,* **sleet·i·er, sleet·i·est.** of, pertaining to, or like sleet. [1715–25; SLEET + -Y[1]] —**sleet′i·ness,** *n.*

sleeve (slēv), *n., v.,* **sleeved, sleev·ing.** —*n.* **1.** the part of a garment that covers the arm, varying in form and length but commonly tubular. **2.** an envelope, usually of paper, for protecting a phonograph record. **3.** *Mach.* a tubular piece, as of metal, fitting over a rod or the like. **4. laugh up** or **in one's sleeve,** to be secretly amused or contemptuous; laugh inwardly: *to laugh up one's sleeve at someone's affectations.* **5. have something up one's sleeve,** to have a secret plan, scheme, opinion, or the like: *I could tell by her sly look that she had something up her sleeve.* —*v.t.* **6.** to furnish with sleeves. **7.** *Mach.* to fit with a sleeve; join or fasten by means of a sleeve. [bef. 950; ME *sleve,* OE *slēfe* (Anglian), *sliefe;* akin to D *sloof* apron] —**sleeve′like′,** *adj.*

sleeve·board (slēv′bôrd′, -bōrd′), *n.* a small-scale ironing board for pressing sleeves, esp. a narrow board that fits inside a coat sleeve. Also called **pressboard.** [1820–30; SLEEVE + BOARD]

sleeve′ cou′pling, a cylinder joining the ends of two lengths of shafting or pipe.

sleeve·less (slēv′lis), *adj.* **1.** without sleeves. **2.** amounting to nothing; unprofitable; futile: *a sleeveless errand.* [bef. 950; ME; OE *sliefléas.* See SLEEVE, -LESS] —**sleeve′less·ness,** *n.*

sleeve·let (slēv′lit), *n.* a fitted sleeve or cover worn on the forearm for warmth or to protect a shirt sleeve. [1885–90; SLEEVE + -LET]

sleeve′ link′, *Brit.* See **cuff link.** [1885–90]

sleeve′ valve′, an intake or exhaust valve for an engine, consisting of one or more sleeves reciprocating within a cylinder, so that ports in the cylinder and in the sleeves are opposed at regular intervals to open the valve. [1910–15]

sleigh[1] (slā), *n.* **1.** a light vehicle on runners, usually open and generally horse-drawn, used esp. for transporting persons over snow or ice. **2.** a sled. —*v.i.* **3.** to travel or ride in a sleigh. [1690–1700, *Amer.;* < D *slee,* var. of *slede* SLED; cf. SLIDE] —**sleigh′er,** *n.*

sleigh[2] (slā), *n., v.t.* sley.

sleigh′ bed′, a bed of the Empire period having raised ends terminating in outward scrolls. Also called **boat bed.** [1925–30]

sleigh′ bells′, any of several kinds of small bells attached to a sleigh or to the harness of the animal drawing the sleigh. [1765–75, *Amer.*]

sleight (slīt), *n.* **1.** skill; dexterity. **2.** an artifice; stratagem. **3.** cunning; craft. [1225–75; ME; early ME *slēgth* < ON *slǣgth.* See SLY, -TH[1]]

sleight′ of hand′, 1. skill in feats requiring quick and clever movements of the hands, esp. for entertainment or deception, as jugglery, card or coin magic, etc.; legerdemain. **2.** the performance of such feats. **3.** a feat of legerdemain. **4.** skill in deception. [1350–1400; ME]

Sleip·nir (slāp′nir), *n. Scand. Myth.* the eight-legged horse of Odin. Also, **Sleip·ner** (slāp′nər).

slen·der (slen′dər), *adj.,* **-er, -est. 1.** having a circumference that is small in proportion to the height or length: *a slender post.* **2.** thin or slight; light and graceful: *slender youths.* **3.** small in size, amount, extent, etc.; meager: *a slender income.* **4.** having little value, force, or justification: *slender prospects.* **5.** thin or weak, as sound. [1300–50; ME *slendre, sclendre* < ?] —**slen′der·ly,** *adv.* —**slen′der·ness,** *n.*
—**Syn. 2.** SLENDER, SLIGHT, SLIM imply a tendency toward thinness. As applied to the human body, SLENDER implies a generally attractive and pleasing thinness: *slender hands.* SLIGHT often adds the idea of frailness to that of thinness: *a slight, almost fragile, figure.* SLIM implies a lithe or delicate thinness: *a slim and athletic figure.* **4.** trivial, trifling. **5.** fragile, feeble, fine, delicate, flimsy. —**Ant. 2.** fat, stocky.

slen·der·ize (slen′də rīz′), *v.,* **-ized, -iz·ing.** —*v.t.* **1.** to make slender or more slender. **2.** to cause to appear slender: *dresses that slenderize the figure.* —*v.i.* **3.** to become slender. Also, *esp. Brit.,* **slen′der·ise′.** [1920–25; SLENDER + -IZE] —**slen·der·i·za·tion** (slen′dər ə zā′shən), *n.* —**slen′der·iz′er,** *n.*

slen′der lo′ris, loris (def. 1). [1825–35]

slen′derness ra′tio, *Rocketry.* See **aspect ratio** (def. 4a).

slept (slept), *v.* pt. and pp. of **sleep.**

Sles·vig (sles′vɪκʜ), *n.* Danish name of **Schleswig.**

Sles·wick (sles′wik), *n.* Schleswig.

sleuth (slo͞oth), *n.* **1.** a detective. **2.** a bloodhound. —*v.t., v.i.* **3.** to track or trail, as a detective. [1875–80; short for SLEUTHHOUND] —**sleuth′like′,** *adj.*

sleuth·hound (slo͞oth′hound′), *n.* **1.** a bloodhound. **2.** a detective. [1325–75; ME *sloth* track, trail (< ON *slōth*) + HOUND[1]]

slew[1] (slo͞o), *v.* pt. of **slay.**

slew[2] (slo͞o), *n. Informal.* a large number or quantity: *a whole slew of people.* Also, **slue.** [1830–40, *Amer.;* < Ir *sluagh* crowd, throng, army, host]

slew[3] (slo͞o), *v.t., v.i., n.* slue[1].

slew[4] (slo͞o), *n. U.S., Canadian.* slough[1] (def. 3).

sley (slā), *n., pl.* **sleys,** *v.* —*n.* **1.** the reed of a loom. **2.** the warp count in woven fabrics. **3.** *Brit.* the lay of a loom. —*v.t.* **4.** to draw (warp ends) through the heddle eyes of the harness or through the dents of the reed in accordance with a given plan for weaving a fabric. Also, **slay, sleigh.** [bef. 1050; ME *sleye,* OE *slege* weaver's reed; akin to D *slag,* G *Schlag,* ON *slag,* Goth *slahs* a blow; see SLAY]

Slez·sko (sles′kô), *n.* Czech name of **Silesia.**

SLIC, (Federal) Savings and Loan Insurance Corporation. Also, **S.L.I.C.**

slice (slīs), *n., v.,* **sliced, slic·ing.** —*n.* **1.** a thin, flat piece cut from something: *a slice of bread.* **2.** a part, portion, or share: *a slice of land.* **3.** any of various implements with a thin, broad blade or part, as for turning food in a frying pan, serving fish at the table, or taking up printing ink; spatula. **4.** *Sports.* **a.** the path described by a ball, as in baseball or golf, that curves in a direction corresponding to the side from which it was struck. **b.** a ball describing such a path. **5.** *Tennis.* a stroke executed by hitting down on the ball with an underhand motion and thus creating backspin. —*v.t.* **6.** to cut into slices; divide into parts. **7.** to cut through or cleave with or as if with a knife: *The ship sliced the sea.* **8.** to cut off or remove as a slice or slices (sometimes fol. by *off, away, from,* etc.). **9.** to remove by means of a slice, slice bar, or similar implement. **10.** *Sports.* to hit (a ball) so as to result in a slice. —*v.i.* **11.** to slice something. **12.** to admit of being sliced. **13.** *Sports.* **a.** (of a player) to slice the ball. **b.** (of a ball) to describe a slice in flight. [1300–50; (n.) ME *s(c)lice* < OF *esclice,* n. deriv. of *esclicer* to split up < Frankish **slitjan,* akin to OE *slītan,* ON *slīta,* D *slijten* (see SLIT); (v.) late ME *sklicen* < OF *esclicer*] —**slice′a·ble,** *adj.* —**slic′ing·ly,** *adv.*

slice′ bar′, a long-handled instrument with a blade at the end, for clearing away or breaking up clinkers, coal, etc., in a furnace. [1840–50]

slice-of-life (slīs′əv līf′), *adj.* of, pertaining to, or being a naturalistic, unembellished representation of real life: *a play with slice-of-life dialogue.* [1890–95; attributive use of *slice of life,* trans. of F *tranche de vie,* allegedly coined by dramatist Jean Jullien (1854–1919)]

slic·er (slī′sər), *n.* **1.** a thin-bladed knife or implement used for slicing, esp. food: *a cheese slicer.* **2.** a person or thing that slices. [1520–30; SLICE + -ER[1]]

slick[1] (slik), *adj.,* **-er, -est,** *n., adv.* —*adj.* **1.** smooth and glossy; sleek. **2.** smooth in manners, speech, etc.; suave. **3.** sly; shrewdly adroit: *He's a slick customer, all right.* **4.** ingenious; cleverly devised: *a slick plan to get*

out of work. **5.** slippery, esp. from being covered with or as if with ice, water, or oil. **6.** deftly executed and having surface appeal or sophistication, but shallow or glib in content; polished but superficial; glib: *a writer who has mastered every formula of slick fiction.* **7.** *Slang.* wonderful; remarkable; first-rate. —*n.* **8.** a smooth or slippery place or spot or the substance causing it: *oil slick.* **9.** *Informal.* **a.** a magazine printed on paper having a more or less glossy finish. **b.** such a magazine regarded as possessing qualities, as expensiveness, chic, and sophistication, that hold appeal for a particular readership, as one whose members enjoy or are seeking affluence. **c.** such a magazine regarded as having a sophisticated, deftly executed, but shallow or glib literary content. Cf. **pulp** (def. 6). **10.** any of various paddlelike tools for smoothing a surface. **11.** *Auto.* a wide tire without a tread, used in racing. **12.** *Mil. Slang.* a helicopter. —*adv.* **13.** smoothly; cleverly. [1300–50; ME *slike* (adj.); c. dial. D *sleek* even, smooth; akin to SLICK[2]] —**slick′ly,** *adv.* —**slick′ness,** *n.*
—**Syn. 3.** wily, tricky, foxy, sharp.

slick[2] (slik), *v.t.* **1.** to make sleek or smooth. **2.** to use a slicker on (skins or hides). **3.** *Informal.* to make smart or fine; spruce up (usually fol. by *up*). —*n.* **4.** *Metall.* a small trowel used for smoothing the surface of the mold. **5.** any woodworking chisel having a blade more than 2 in. (5 cm) wide. [bef. 900; ME *slicken* (v.), OE *slician;* akin to ON *slikja* to give a gloss to]

slick•en•side (slik′ən sīd′), *n. Geol.* a rock surface that has become more or less polished and striated by slippage along a fault plane. [1760–70; SLICK[2] + -EN[3] + SIDE[1]]

slick•er[1] (slik′ər), *n.* **1.** a long, loose oilskin raincoat. **2.** any raincoat. **3.** *Informal.* **a.** a swindler; a sly cheat. **b.** See **city slicker.** [1880–85; SLICK[1] + -ER[1]] —**slick′•ered,** *adj.*

slick•er[2] (slik′ər), *n.* a tool, usually of stone or glass, for scraping, smoothing, and working tanning agents into a skin or hide. [1850–55; SLICK[2] + -ER[1]]

slick•rock (slik′rok′), *n.* rock or a rock formation that is smooth and slippery. [SLICK[1] + ROCK[1]]

slick•ster (slik′stər), *n. Slang.* a crafty and opportunistic or deceitful person; hustler; swindler. [1960–65; SLICK[1] + -STER]

slide (slīd), *v.,* **slid** (slid), **slid** or **slid•den** (slid′n), **slid•ing,** *n.* —*v.i.* **1.** to move along in continuous contact with a smooth or slippery surface: *to slide down a snow-covered hill.* **2.** to slip or skid. **3.** to glide or pass smoothly. **4.** to slip easily, quietly, or unobtrusively on or as if on a track, channel, or guide rail (usually fol. by *in, out, away,* etc.). **5.** to pass or fall gradually into a specified state, character, practice, etc. **6.** to decline or decrease: *Interest rates are beginning to slide.* **7.** *Baseball.* (of a base runner) to cast oneself, usually feet first, forward along the ground in the direction of the base being approached, to present less of a target for a baseman attempting to make a tag. —*v.t.* **8.** to cause to slide or coast, as over a surface or with a smooth, gliding motion. **9.** to hand, pass along, or slip (something) easily or quietly (usually fol. by *in, into,* etc.). **10. let slide,** to allow to deteriorate, pursue a natural course, etc., without intervention on one's part: *to let things slide.* —*n.* **11.** an act or instance of sliding. **12.** a smooth surface for sliding on, esp. a type of chute in a playground. **13.** an object intended to slide. **14.** *Geol.* **a.** a landslide or the like. **b.** the mass of matter sliding down. **15.** a single transparency, object, or image for projection in a projector, as a lantern slide. **16.** *Photog.* a small positive color transparency mounted for projection on a screen or magnification through a viewer. **17.** a usually rectangular plate of glass on which objects are placed for microscopic examination. **18.** *Furniture.* a shelf sliding into the body of a piece when not in use. **19.** *Music.* **a.** an embellishment consisting of an upward or downward series of three or more tones, the last of which is the principal tone. **b.** a portamento. **c.** a U-shaped section of the tube of an instrument of the trumpet class, as the trombone, that can be pushed in or out to alter the length of the air column and change the pitch. **20.** a vehicle mounted on runners, for conveying loads, as of grain or wood, esp. over a level surface. **21.** (of a machine or mechanism) **a.** a moving part working on a track, channel, or guide rails. **b.** the surface, track, channel, or guide rails on which the part moves. **22.** any of various chutes used in logging, mining, or materials handling. **23.** a flat or very low-heeled, backless shoe or slipper that can be slipped on and off the foot easily. [bef. 950; ME *sliden* (v.), OE *slīdan;* c. MLG *slīden,* MHG *slīten;* akin to SLED] —**slid′a•ble,** *adj.* —**slid′a•ble•ness,** *n.*
—**Syn. 1.** slither. SLIDE, GLIDE, SLIP suggest movement over a smooth surface. SLIDE suggests a movement of one surface over another in contact with it: *to slide downhill.* GLIDE suggests a continuous, smooth, easy, and (usually) noiseless motion: *a skater gliding over the ice.* To SLIP is to slide in a sudden or accidental way: *to slip on the ice and fall.*

slide-ac•tion (slīd′ak′shən), *adj.* (of a rifle or shotgun) having a lever that when slid back and forth ejects the empty case and cocks and reloads the piece.

slide′ fas′tener, zipper (def. 2). [1935–40]

slide′ guitar′, bottleneck (def. 3). [1965–70]

slide′ knot′, a knot formed by making two half hitches on the standing part of the rope, the second hitch being next to the loop, which can be tightened.

Sli•dell (slī del′), *n.* a town in SE Louisiana. 26,718.

Slide′ Moun′tain, a mountain in SE New York: highest peak of the Catskill Mountains. 4204 ft. (1280 m).

slid•er (slī′dər), *n.* **1.** a person or thing that slides. **2.** *Baseball.* a fast pitch that curves slightly and sharply in front of a batter, away from the side from which it was thrown. **3.** any of several freshwater turtles of the genus *Chrysemys,* of North America, having a smooth shell usually olive brown with various markings above and yellow below: some, esp. *C. scripta,* are raised commercially and the young sold as pets, rarely surviving to adulthood. [1520–30; SLIDE + -ER[1]]

slide′ rule′, a device for performing mathematical calculations, consisting essentially of a ruler having a sliding piece moving along it, both marked with graduated, usually logarithmic, scales: now largely replaced by the electronic calculator. [1655–65 for earlier sense; 1875–80 for current sense]

slide′ trombone′. See under **trombone.**

slide′ valve′, *Mach.* a valve that slides without lifting to open or close an aperture, as the valves of the ports in the cylinders of certain steam engines. [1795–1805]

slide•way (slīd′wā′), *n.* an inclined surface along which something can slide. [1855–60; SLIDE + WAY[1]]

slid•ing (slī′ding), *adj.* **1.** rising or falling, increasing or decreasing, according to a standard or to a set of conditions. **2.** operated, adjusted, or moved by sliding: *a sliding door.* [bef. 900; ME; OE *slīdende.* See SLIDE, -ING[2]] —**slid′ing•ly,** *adv.* —**slid′ing•ness,** *n.*

slid′ing rule′, (formerly) a slide rule. [1655–65]

slid′ing scale′, **1.** a variable scale, esp. of industrial costs, as wages, that may be adapted to changes in demand. **2.** a wage scale varying with the selling price of goods produced, the cost of living, or profits. **3.** a price scale, as of medical fees, in which prices vary according to the ability of individuals to pay. **4.** a tariff scale varying according to changing prices. [1700–10]

slid′ing seat′, a rower's seat that rides on wheels in metal tracks fastened to the boat's frame, allowing the seat to slide back and forth, thereby tapping the rower's leg strength to maximize the stroke. [1870–75]

slid′ing vec′tor, *Mech.* a vector having specified magnitude and lying on a given line. Also called **line vector.**

sli•er (slī′ər), *adj.* a comparative of **sly.**

sli•est (slī′ist), *adj.* a superlative of **sly.**

slight (slīt), *adj.,* **-er, -est,** *v., n.,* —*adj.* **1.** small in amount, degree, etc.: *a slight increase; a slight odor.* **2.** of little importance, influence, etc.; trivial: *a slight cut.* **3.** slender or slim; not heavily built. **4.** frail; flimsy; delicate: *a slight fabric.* **5.** of little substance or strength. —*v.t.* **6.** to treat as of little importance. **7.** to treat (someone) with indifference; ignore, esp. pointedly or contemptuously; snub: *to be slighted by society.* **8.** to do negligently; scamp: *to slight one's studies.* —*n.* **9.** an act or instance of slighting indifference or treatment: *Slights marred his work.* **10.** a pointed and contemptuous discourtesy; affront: *She considered not being invited an unforgivable slight.* [1250–1300; ME (adj.) smooth, sleek, slender; cf. OE *-sliht-* in *earth-slihtes* even with ground; c. G *schlicht,* ON *slēttr,* Goth *slaihts* smooth] —**slight′er,** *n.* —**slight′ly,** *adv.* —**slight′ness,** *n.*
—**Syn. 2.** insignificant, trifling, paltry. **3.** See **slender. 4.** weak, feeble, fragile. **5.** unsubstantial, inconsiderable. **6.** disdain, scorn. SLIGHT, DISREGARD, NEGLECT, OVERLOOK mean to pay no attention or too little attention to someone or something. To SLIGHT is to give only superficial attention to something important: *to slight one's work.* To DISREGARD is to pay no attention to a person or thing: *to disregard the rules;* in some circumstances, to DISREGARD may be admirable: *to disregard a handicap.* To NEGLECT is to shirk paying sufficient attention to a person or thing: *to neglect one's correspondence.* To OVERLOOK is to fail to see someone or something (possibly because of carelessness): *to overlook a bill that is due.* **9.** neglect, disregard, inattention; disdain, scorn. **10.** See **insult.** —**Ant. 1.** considerable.

slight•ing (slī′ting), *adj.* derogatory and disparaging; belittling. [1605–15; SLIGHT + -ING[2]] —**slight′ing•ly,** *adv.*

Sli•go (slī′gō), *n.* **1.** a county in Connaught province, in the NW Republic of Ireland. 55,425; 694 sq. mi. (1795 sq. km). **2.** its county seat: a seaport. 18,609.

sli•ly (slī′lē), *adv.* slyly.

slim (slim), *adj.,* **slim•mer, slim•mest,** *v.,* **slimmed, slim•ming,** *n.* —*adj.* **1.** slender, as in girth or form; slight in build or structure. **2.** poor or inferior: *a slim chance; a slim excuse.* **3.** small or inconsiderable; meager; scanty: *a slim income.* **4.** sized for the thinner than average person. —*v.t.* **5.** to make slim. —*v.i.* **6.** to become slim. **7.** *Chiefly Brit.* to try to become more slender, esp. by dieting. **8. slim down, a.** to lose weight, esp. intentionally. **b.** (of a business) to reduce operating expenses; economize. —*n.* **9.** a garment size meant for a thin person. [1650–60; < D *slim* sly, (earlier) crooked (c. G *schlimm* bad, (earlier) crooked)] —**slim′ly,** *adv.* —**slim′ness,** *n.*
—**Syn. 1.** thin. See **slender. 3.** insignificant, trifling, trivial, paltry. —**Ant. 1.** fat. **3.** considerable; abundant.

slim′ disease′, a form of AIDS common in Africa, marked by emaciation and fever. [1985–90]

slime (slīm), *n., v.,* **slimed, slim•ing.** —*n.* **1.** thin, glutinous mud. **2.** any ropy or viscous liquid matter, esp. of a foul kind. **3.** a viscous secretion of animal or vegetable origin. **4.** *Slang.* a repulsive or despicable person. —*v.t.* **5.** to cover or smear with or as if with slime. **6.** to remove slime from, as fish for canning. [bef. 1000; ME *slyme,* OE *slīm;* c. D *slijm,* G *Schleim,* ON *slīm*]

slime′ bacte′ria. See **gliding bacteria.** [1955–60]

slime′ mold′, **1.** any of various funguslike organisms belonging to the phylum Myxomycota, of the kingdom Protista (or the plant class Myxomycetes), characterized by a noncellular, multinucleate, creeping somatic phase and a propagative phase in which fruiting bodies are produced bearing spores that are covered by cell walls. **2.** any of several similar organisms of the phylum Acrasiomycota (or class Acrasiomycetes), differing from the true slime molds in being cellular and nucleate throughout the life cycle. [1875–80]

slim•line (slim′līn′), *adj.* **1.** slim in appearance. **2.** of, pertaining to, or noting a long, slender shape, design, or item. [SLIM + LINE[1]]

slim•mer (slim′ər), *n. Brit.* a person who is trying to lose weight, esp. by dieting. [SLIM + -ER[1]]

slim•nas•tics (slim nas′tiks), *n.* (*used with a singular or plural v.*) exercises to help someone lose or control weight. [1965–70; b. SLIM and GYMNASTICS]

slim•sy (slim′zē), *adj.* flimsy; frail. Also, **slimp•sy** (slimp′sē). [1835–45, *Amer.;* b. SLIM and FLIMSY]

slim•y (slī′mē), *adj.,* **slim•i•er, slim•i•est. 1.** of or like slime. **2.** abounding in or covered with slime. **3.** offensively foul or vile. [1350–1400; ME; see SLIME, -Y[1]] —**slim′i•ly,** *adv.* —**slim′i•ness,** *n.*

sling[1] (sling), *n., v.,* **slung, sling•ing.** —*n.* **1.** a device for hurling stones or other missiles that consists, typically, of a short strap with a long string at each end and that is operated by placing the missile in the strap, and, holding the ends of the strings in one hand, whirling the instrument around in a circle and releasing one of the strings to discharge the missile. **2.** a slingshot. **3.** a bandage used to suspend or support an injured part of the body, commonly a bandage suspended from the neck to support an injured arm or hand. **4.** a strap, band, or the like, forming a loop by which something is suspended or carried, as a strap attached to a rifle and passed over the shoulder. **5.** sling-back. **6.** an act or instance of slinging. **7.** a rope, chain, net, etc., for hoisting freight or for holding it while being hoisted. **8.** *Naut.* **a.** a chain for supporting a hoisting yard. **b. slings,** the area of a hoisting yard to which such chains are attached; the middle of a hoisting yard. —*v.t.* **9.** to throw, cast, or hurl; fling, as from the hand. **10.** to place in or secure with a sling to raise or lower. **11.** to raise, lower, etc., by such means. **12.** to hang by a sling or place so as to swing loosely: *to sling a rifle over one's shoulder.* **13.** to suspend: *to sling a hammock between two trees.* **14. sling hash,** *Slang.* to work as a waiter or waitress, esp. at a lunch counter or cheap restaurant. [1175–1225; (v.) ME *slyngen* < ON *slyngva* to sling, fling, c. OE *slingan* to wind, twist; (n.) ME, perh. deriv. of the v., though sense "strap, hoist" may be of distinct orig.]
—**Syn. 9.** pitch, toss.

sling[2] (sling), *n.* an iced alcoholic drink, typically containing gin, water, sugar, and lemon or lime juice. [1785–95, *Amer.;* of uncert. orig.]

sling-back (sling′bak′), *n.* **1.** Also called **sling.** a woman's shoe with an open back and a strap or sling encircling the heel of the foot to keep the shoe secure. —*adj.* **2.** having such a strap or sling: *sling-back pumps.*

sling′ chair′, any of several varieties of chairs having a seat and back formed from a single sheet of canvas, leather, or the like, hanging loosely in a frame.

sling•er (sling′ər), *n.* **1.** a person or thing that slings. **2.** *Mach.* flinger (def. 2). [1350–1400; ME; see SLING[1], -ER[1]]

sling′ psychrom′eter, a psychrometer so designed that the wet-bulb thermometer can be ventilated, to expedite evaporation, by whirling in the air.

sling•shot (sling′shot′), *n.* a Y-shaped stick with an elastic strip between the prongs for shooting stones and other small missiles. [1840–50, *Amer.;* SLING[1] + SHOT[1]]

slink (slingk), *v.,* **slunk** or (*Archaic*) **slank; slunk; slink•ing;** *n.; adj.* —*v.i.* **1.** to move or go in a furtive, abject manner, as from fear, cowardice, or shame. **2.** to walk or move in a slow, sinuous, provocative way. —*v.t.* **3.** (esp. of cows) to bring forth (young) prematurely. —*n.* **4.** a prematurely born calf or other animal. —*adj.* **5.** born prematurely: *a slink calf.* [bef. 1150; ME *slynken* (v.), OE *slincan* to creep, crawl; c. LG *slinken,* G *schlinken*] —**slink′ing•ly,** *adv.*
—**Syn. 1.** skulk, sneak; lurk.

slink•y (sling′kē), *adj.,* **slink•i•er, slink•i•est. 1.** characterized by or proceeding with slinking or stealthy movements. **2.** made of soft, often clinging material that follows the figure closely and flows with body movement: *a slinky gown.* [1915–20; SLINK + -Y[1]] —**slink′i•ly,** *adv.* —**slink′i•ness,** *n.*

slip[1] (slip), *v.,* **slipped** or (*Archaic*) **slipt; slipped; slip•ping;** *n.* —*v.i.* **1.** to move, flow, pass, or go smoothly or easily; glide; slide: *Water slips off a smooth surface.* **2.** to slide suddenly or involuntarily; to lose one's foothold, as on a smooth surface: *She slipped on the icy ground.* **3.** to move, slide, or start gradually from a place or position: *His hat had slipped over his eyes.* **4.** to slide out of or become disengaged from a fastening, the grasp, etc.: *The soap slipped from my hand.* **5.** to pass without having been acted upon or used; be lost; get away: *to let an opportunity slip.* **6.** to pass from the mind, memory, or consciousness. **7.** to elapse or pass quickly or imperceptibly (often fol. by *away* or *by*): *The years slipped by.* **8.** to become involved or absorbed easily: *to slip into a new way of life.* **9.** to move or go quietly, cautiously, or unobtrusively: *to slip out of a room.* **10.** to put on or take off a garment easily or quickly: *She slipped on the new sweater.* **11.** to make a mistake or error: *As far as I know, you haven't slipped once.* **12.** to fall below a standard or accustomed level, or to decrease in quantity or quality; decline; deteriorate: *His work slipped last year.* **13.** to be said or revealed inadvertently (usually fol. by *out*): *The words just slipped out.* **14.** to read, study, consider, etc., without attention: *He slipped over the most important part.* **15.** *Aeron.* (of an aircraft when excessively banked) to slide sideways, toward the center of the curve described in turning. Cf. **skid** (def. 18).
—*v.t.* **16.** to cause to move, pass, go, etc., with a smooth, easy, or sliding motion. **17.** to put, place, pass, insert, or withdraw quickly or stealthily: *to slip a letter into a person's hand.* **18.** to put on or take off (a garment) easily or quickly: *He slipped the shirt over his head.* **19.** to let or make (something) slide out of a fastening, the hold, etc.: *I slipped the lock, and the door creaked open.* **20.** to release from a leash, harness, etc., as a hound or a hawk.

21. to get away or free oneself from; escape (a pursuer, restraint, leash, etc.): *The cow slipped its halter.* **22.** to untie or undo (a knot). **23.** *Naut.* to let go entirely, as an anchor cable or an anchor. **24.** to pass from or escape (one's memory, attention, knowledge, etc.). **25.** to put out of joint or position: *I slipped a disk in my back.* **26.** to shed or cast, as a skin. **27.** to ignore, pass over, or omit, as in speaking or writing. **28.** to let pass unheeded; neglect or miss. **29.** *Boxing.* to evade or avoid (a blow) by moving or turning the body quickly: *He slipped a right and countered with a hard left.* **30.** (of animals) to bring forth (offspring) prematurely. **31.** *Brit.* to detach (a railway car) from a moving train as it passes through a station. **32. let slip,** to reveal unintentionally: *to let slip the truth.* **33. slip a cog.** See **cog**[1] (def. 6). **34. slip away, a.** to depart quietly or unobtrusively; steal off. **b.** to recede; slowly vanish: *All those facts I had memorized just slipped away.* **35. slip between the cracks.** See **crack** (def. 52). **36. slip someone's mind,** to be forgotten: *I was supposed to phone, but it slipped my mind.* **37. slip something over on,** to deceive; defraud; trick. Also, **slip one over on. 38. slip up,** to make an error; fail.
—*n.* **39.** an act or instance of slipping. **40.** a sudden losing of one's foothold, as on slippery ground. **41.** a mistake in judgment; blunder. **42.** a mistake or oversight, as in speaking or writing, esp. a small, careless one: *a minor slip in addition; a slip of the tongue.* **43.** an error in conduct; indiscretion. **44.** something easily slipped on or off. **45.** a decline or fall in quantity, quality, extent, etc.: *a slip in prices.* **46.** *Clothing.* **a.** a woman's undergarment, usually having shoulder straps and extending down to the hemline of the outer dress. **b.** an underskirt, as a half-slip or petticoat. **47.** a pillowcase. **48.** an inclined plane, sloping to the water, on which vessels are built or repaired. **49.** *Naut.* the difference between the speed at which a screw propeller or paddle wheel would move if it were working against a solid and the actual speed at which it advances through the water. **50.** a space between two wharves or in a dock for vessels to lie in. **51.** *Elect.* the difference between the synchronous and the operating speeds of a motor. **52.** *Mach.* **a.** the difference between output speed and input or theoretical speed in certain fluid or electromagnetic devices, as couplings or motors. **b.** (in pumps) the difference between the actual volume of water or other liquid delivered by a pump during one complete stroke and the theoretical volume as determined by calculation of the displacement. **53.** unintended movement or play between mechanical parts or the like. **54.** *Cricket.* **a.** the position of a fielder who stands behind and to the offside of the wicketkeeper. **b.** the fielder playing this position. **55.** *Geol.* **a.** the relative displacement of formerly adjacent points on opposite sides of a fault, measured along the fault plane. **b.** a small fault. **56.** Also called **glide.** *Metall.* plastic deformation, by shear, of a metallic crystal. **57. give someone the slip,** to elude a pursuer; escape: *The murderer gave the police the slip.* [1250–1300; (v.) ME *slippen* < MD *slippen*; c. OHG *slipfen*; (n.) late ME *slippe*, deriv. of or akin to the v.; cf. OHG *slipf* a sliding, slipping, error; akin to SLIPPER[2]] —**slip′less,** *adj.* —**slip′ping·ly,** *adv.*
—**Syn. 1, 2.** slither. See **slide. 11.** err, blunder. **42.** error, fault. See **mistake.**

slip[2] (slip), *n., v.,* **slipped, slip·ping.** —*n.* **1.** a small paper form on which information is noted: *a withdrawal slip.* **2.** a piece suitable for propagation cut from a plant; scion or cutting. **3.** any long, narrow piece or strip, as of wood, paper, or land. **4.** a young person, esp. one of slender form: *a mere slip of a girl.* **5.** a long seat or narrow pew in a church. **6.** *Bookbinding.* one of the ends of a band, extending at the sides of a book after sewing. —*v.t.* **7.** to take slips or cuttings from (a plant). **8.** to take (a part), as a slip from a plant. [1400–50; late ME *slippe* < MD *slippe* flap (of a piece of clothing)]

slip[3] (slip), *n.* **1.** *Ceram.* a clay solution of creamy consistency for coating or decorating biscuit. **2.** a glass-bearing liquid fired onto steel as a cladding, as in making enamelware. [bef. 1000; ME *slyppe*, OE *slype* semiliquid mass; cf. SLOP[1], COWSLIP, OXSLIP]

slip[4] (slip), *n. Archit.* slype.

slip′ car′riage, *Brit.* a railway car detached from a moving train as it passes through a station. Also called **slip′ coach′.** [1865–70]

slip·case (slip′kās′), *n.* a box for a book or set of books, open on one side. [1920–25; SLIP[1] + CASE[2]]

slip′ cast′ing, a pottery-making process in which partially liquefied clay is poured into a plaster mold. [1900–05]

slip·cov·er (slip′kuv′ər), *n.* **1.** a cover of cloth or other material, as for an upholstered chair or sofa, made so as to be easily removable. **2.** a book jacket. —*v.t.* **3.** to cover with a slipcover. [1885–90; SLIP[1] + COVER]

slipe (slīp), *n., v.,* **sliped, slip·ing.** *Scot.* —*n.* **1.** a sledge, drag, or sleigh. —*v.t.* **2.** to peel or strip the outer coating from, esp. to peel bark from (a tree or twig). **3.** to slice. [1425–75; late ME *slypen* < ?]

slip′ form′, *Civ. Engin.* a form into which concrete is poured that can be slowly moved and reused in construction, as of a pavement or a building. [1945–50]

slip′ hook′. See **pelican hook.** [1860–65]

slip′ in′dicator. See **bank indicator.**

slip′ joint′, a joint made between an older and a newer masonry wall to form a continuous surface, masonry at the end of the newer wall fitting into a vertical groove cut in the end of the older wall. [1875–80]

slip′-joint pli′ers (slip′joint′), (*sometimes used with a singular v.*) pliers having a sliding joint, permitting the span of the jaws to be adjusted. See illus. under **plier.**

slip·knot (slip′not′), *n.* a knot that slips easily along the cord or line around which it is made. Also, **slip′ knot′.** See illus. under **knot.** [1650–60; SLIP[1] + KNOT[1]]

slip·noose (slip′no͞os′), *n.* a noose formed by means of a slipknot. Also, **slip′ noose′.** [1840–50; SLIP[1] + NOOSE]

slip-on (slip′on′, -ôn′), *adj.* **1.** made without buttons, straps, zippers, etc., so as to be put on easily and quickly: *a slip-on blouse; slip-on shoes.* —*n.* **2.** something made this way, esp. an article of clothing. [1805–15; adj., n. use of v. phrase *slip on*]

slip·o·ver (slip′ō′vər), *n., adj.* pullover. [1915–20; n., adj. use of v. phrase *slip over*]

slip·page (slip′ij), *n.* **1.** an act or instance of slipping. **2.** an amount or extent of slipping. **3.** failure to maintain an expected level, fulfill a goal, meet a deadline, etc.; a falling off. **4.** *Mach.* the amount of work dissipated by slipping of parts, excess play, etc. [1840–50; SLIP[1] + -AGE]

slipped′ disk′. See **herniated disk.** [1940–45]

slip·per[1] (slip′ər), *n.* **1.** any light, low-cut shoe into which the foot may be easily slipped, for casual wear in the home, for dancing, etc. Cf. **bedroom slipper, house slipper.** —*v.t.* **2.** to strike or beat with a slipper. [1470–80; SLIP[1] + -ER[1]] —**slip′per·like′,** *adj.*

slip·per[2] (slip′ər), *adj. Older Use.* slippery. [bef. 1000; ME *sliper*, OE *slipor*; see SLIPPERY]

slip′per chair′, a small bedroom chair with a low seat.

slip·per·ette (slip′ə ret′), *n.* a disposable slipper, often of paper, as for wear during a long airplane or train trip. [SLIPPER[1] + -ETTE]

slip′per foot′, *Furniture.* an elongated pad foot.

slip′per sock′, a sock with a soft leather or vinyl sole sewn onto it, used as indoor footwear.

slip·per·wort (slip′ər wûrt′, -wôrt′), *n.* any of several tropical American plants belonging to the genus *Calceolaria*, of the figwort family, having opposite or whorled leaves and slipper-shaped flowers. [1810–20; SLIPPER[1] + WORT[2]]

slipperwort, *Calceolaria crenatiflora*

slip·per·y (slip′ə rē, slip′rē), *adj.,* **-per·i·er, -per·i·est. 1.** tending or liable to cause slipping or sliding, as ice, oil, a wet surface, etc.: *a slippery road.* **2.** tending to slip from the hold or grasp or from position: *a slippery rope.* **3.** likely to slip away or escape: *slippery prospects.* **4.** not to be depended on; fickle; shifty, tricky, or deceitful. **5.** unstable or insecure, as conditions: *a slippery situation.* [1525–35; alter. of SLIPPER[2]; cf. LG *slipperig*; see -Y[1]] —**slip′per·i·ness,** *n.*

slip′pery dick′, a wrasse, *Halichoeres bivittatus*, inhabiting tropical regions of the Atlantic Ocean. [1875–80]

slip′pery elm′, 1. an elm, *Ulmus rubra*, of eastern North America, having a mucilaginous inner bark. **2.** the bark of this elm, used as a demulcent. [1740–50]

slip′pery slope′, a dangerous and irreversible course: *the slippery slope from narcotics to prison.* [1985–90]

slip·py (slip′ē), *adj.,* **-pi·er, -pi·est. 1.** *Informal.* slippery. **2.** *Chiefly Brit.* quick; alert; sharp. [1540–50; SLIP[1] + -Y[1]] —**slip′pi·ness,** *n.*

slip-rail (slip′rāl′), *n. Australian.* one of a horizontal set of fence rails that can be removed easily to leave a gateway. [1715–25]

slip′ ring′, *Elect.* a metal ring, usually of copper or cast iron, mounted so that current may be conducted through stationary brushes into or out of a rotating member. [1895–1900] —**slip′-ring′,** *adj.*

slip′ seat′, *Furniture.* an upholstered seat having its own frame that fits loosely into the frame of a chair.

slip·sheet (slip′shēt′), *Print.* —*v.t., v.i.* **1.** to insert (blank sheets) between printed sheets as they come off the press to prevent offset. —*n.* **2.** a sheet so inserted. [1905–10; SLIP[1] + SHEET[1]]

slip·shod (slip′shod′), *adj.* **1.** careless, untidy, or slovenly: *slipshod work.* **2.** down-at-heel; seedy; shabby. **3.** *Archaic.* wearing slippers or loose shoes, esp. ones worn at the heel. [1570–80; SLIP[1] + SHOD] —**slip′shod′ness, slip′shod′di·ness,** *n.*
—**Syn. 1.** loose, sloppy, lax, messy.

slip·slop (slip′slop′), *n.* **1.** meaningless or trifling talk or writing. **2.** *Archaic.* sloppy or weak food or drink. [1665–75; gradational compound based on SLOP[1]]

slip·sole (slip′sōl′), *n.* **1.** an insole placed in a shoe for warmth or to adjust the size. **2.** a thin strip of material, as leather, set between the insole and the outsole of a shoe, usually for height. [1905–10; SLIP[1] + SOLE[2]]

slip′ stem′, a spoon handle cut obliquely at the end from top to bottom.

slip·stick (slip′stik′), *n. Informal.* See **slide rule.** [1930–35; SLIP[1] + STICK[1]]

slip′ stitch′, *Sewing.* a loose stitch taken between two layers of fabric, as on a hem, so as to be invisible on the right side or outside surface. [1880–85]

slip-stitch (slip′stich′), *v.t., v.i. Sewing.* to sew with slip stitches. [1895–1900]

slip·stream (slip′strēm′), *n.* Also, **slip′ stream′. 1.** *Aeron.* the airstream pushed back by a revolving aircraft propeller. Cf. **backwash** (def. 2), **wash** (def. 35). **2.** the airstream generating reduced air pressure and forward suction directly behind a rapidly moving vehicle. —*v.i.* **3.** to ride in the slipstream of a fast-moving vehicle. [1910–15; SLIP[1] + STREAM]

slip·stream·ing (slip′strē′ming), *n.* the act of updating a software program without adequately informing the public, as by failing to release it as an official new version. [1985–90]

slipt (slipt), *v. Archaic.* pt. of **slip**[1].

slip′ top′, the end of a slip stem on a spoon.

slip′ trail′ing, *Ceram.* the act of decorating an object with a poured stream of slip. Also called **slip′ trac′ing.**

slip-up (slip′up′), *n.* a mistake, blunder, or oversight. [1850–55; n. use of v. phrase *slip up*]
—**Syn.** error, lapse, bungle.

slip·ware (slip′wâr′), *n.* pottery decorated with slip. [1905–10; SLIP[3] + WARE[1]]

slip·way (slip′wā′), *n. Naut.* **1.** (in a shipyard) the area sloping toward the water, on which the ways are located. **2.** See **marine railway. 3.** a ramp on a factory ship for hauling aboard carcasses of whales for processing. [1830–40; SLIP[1] + WAY[1]]

slit (slit), *v.,* **slit, slit·ting,** *n.* —*v.t.* **1.** to cut apart or open along a line; make a long cut, fissure, or opening in. **2.** to cut or rend into strips; split. —*n.* **3.** a straight, narrow cut, opening, or aperture. [1175–1225; ME *slitte* (n.), *slitten* (v.); c. G *schlitzen* to split, slit; akin to OE *slite* a slit, *geslit* a bite, *slītan* to split; see SLICE] —**slit′·less,** *adj.* —**slit′like′,** *adj.*

slit-drum (slit′drum′), *n.* a hollowed-out log with a long, narrow slit, beaten with a stick or stamped upon to produce a drumming sound, found in many cultures since ancient times. Also, **slit′ drum′.** [1955–60]

slit′ fric′ative, *Phonet.* a fricative, as (f) or (th), in which the tongue is relatively flat, with air channeled over it through a shallow slit. Cf. **groove fricative.**

slith·er (slith′ər), *v.i.* **1.** to slide down or along a surface, esp. unsteadily, from side to side, or with some friction or noise: *The box slithered down the chute.* **2.** to go or walk with a sliding motion: *The snake slithered across the path.* —*v.t.* **3.** to cause to slither or slide. —*n.* **4.** a slithering movement; slide. [1150–1200; ME *slitheren*, var. of *sliddren*, OE *slid(e)rian*, freq. of *slīdan* to SLIDE; see -ER[6]] —**slith′er·y,** *adj.*

slit′ trench′, 1. a narrow trench for one or more persons for protection against enemy fire and fragmentation bombs. **2.** a foxhole. [1940–45]

sliv·er (sliv′ər), *n.* **1.** a small, slender, often sharp piece, as of wood or glass, split, broken, or cut off, usually lengthwise or with the grain; splinter. **2.** any small, narrow piece or portion: *A sliver of sky was visible.* **3.** a strand of loose, untwisted fibers produced in carding. —*v.t.* **4.** to split or cut off (a sliver) or to split or cut into slivers: *to sliver a log into kindling.* **5.** to form (textile fibers) into slivers. —*v.i.* **6.** to split. [1325–75; ME *slivere* (n.), deriv. of *sliven* to split, OE *-slīfan* (in *tōslīfan* to split up)] —**sliv′er·like′,** *adj.*

sliv′er build′ing, a very narrow skyscraper designed in response to restriction of the building site or zoning, frequently containing only a single apartment per floor or comparably limited office space.

sliv·o·vitz (sliv′ə vits, -wits, shliv′-), *n.* a dry, colorless, slightly bitter plum brandy from E Europe. Also, **sliv·o·vic, sliv·o·witz** (sliv′ə vits). [1895–1900; < G *Sliwowitz* < Serbo-Croatian *šljìvovica*, deriv. of *šljìva* plum]

SLMA, See **Student Loan Marketing Association.**

Sloan (slōn), *n.* **1. John,** 1871–1951, U.S. painter. **2.** a male given name.

Sloane (slōn), *n.* **Sir Hans,** 1660–1753, English physician and naturalist.

Sloane′ Rang′er (slōn), a member of a trendy and acquisitive set of largely upper-middle-class young people of London, England. [1970–75, b. *Sloane* Square, London, and *Lone Ranger* hero of radio and television Westerns]

slob (slob), *n.* **1.** a slovenly or boorish person. **2.** *Irish Eng.* mud or ooze, esp. a stretch of mud along a shore. **3.** *Chiefly Canadian.* sludge (def. 5). [1770–80; < Ir *slab(a)* mud, mire]

slob·ber (slob′ər), *v.i.* **1.** to let saliva or liquid run from the mouth; slaver; drivel. **2.** to indulge in mawkish sentimentality: *My family slobbered all over me when I finally got home.* —*v.t.* **3.** to wet or make foul by slobbering: *The baby has slobbered his bib.* **4.** to let (saliva or liquid) run from the mouth: *The baby slobbered milk on his bib.* **5.** to utter with slobbering: *He sobbed and slobbered the bad news.* —*n.* **6.** saliva or liquid dribbling from the mouth; slaver. **7.** mawkishly sentimental speech or actions. Also, **slabber.** [1350–1400; ME (n. and v.), var. of *slabber.* See SLAB[2], -ER[6]] —**slob′ber·er,** *n.*
—**Syn. 1.** drool, dribble, slop.

slob·ber·y (slob′ə rē), *adj.* **1.** characterized by slobbering. **2.** disagreeably wet; sloppy. Also, **slabbery.** [1350–1400; ME; see SLOBBER, -Y[1]]

slob·by (slob′ē), *adj.,* **-bi·er, -bi·est. 1.** pertaining to or characteristic of a slob. **2.** slobbery. [1910–15; SLOB + -Y[1]]

slob′ ice′, *Chiefly Canadian.* sludge (def. 5). [1905–10]

Slo·cum (slō′kəm), *n.* **Joshua,** 1844–c1910, U.S. mariner, author, and lecturer, born in Nova Scotia.

sloe (slō), *n.* **1.** the small, sour, blackish fruit of the blackthorn, *Prunus spinosa*, of the rose family. **2.** the shrub itself. **3.** any of various other plants of the genus *Prunus*, as a shrub or small tree, *P. alleghaniensis*, bearing dark-purple fruit. [bef. 900; ME *slo*, OE *slā(h)*; c. G *Schlehe*, D *slee*]

sloe-eyed (slō′īd′), *adj.* **1.** having very dark eyes; dark-eyed. **2.** having slanted eyes. [1865–70]

sloe′ gin′, a cordial or liqueur made from gin flavored with sloes. [1890–95]

slog (slog), *v.,* **slogged, slog·ging.** *n.* —*v.t.* **1.** to hit hard, as in boxing or cricket; slug. **2.** to drive with blows. —*v.i.* **3.** to deal heavy blows. **4.** to walk or plod heavily. **5.** to toil. —*n.* **6.** a long, tiring walk or march. **7.** long, laborious work. **8.** a heavy blow. [1850–55; var. of SLUG[2]] —**slog′ger,** *n.*

slo·gan (slō′gən), *n.* **1.** a distinctive cry, phrase, or motto of any party, group, manufacturer, or person; catchword or catch phrase. **2.** a war cry or gathering cry, as formerly used among the Scottish clans. [1505–15; < ScotGael *sluagh-ghairm,* equiv. to *sluagh* army, host (cf. SLEW[2]) + *gairm* cry]

slo·gan·eer (slō′gə nēr′), *n.* **1.** a person who creates and uses slogans frequently. —*v.i.* **2.** to create or use slogans, esp. in an effort to change public opinion. [1920–25; SLOGAN + -EER]

slo·gan·ize (slō′gə nīz′), *v.,* **-ized, -iz·ing.** —*v.t.* **1.** to make a slogan of; express as a slogan: *to sloganize one's opinions.* —*v.i.* **2.** to utter slogans; sloganeer. Also, *esp. Brit.,* **slo′gan·ise′.** [1925–30; SLOGAN + -IZE]

sloid (sloid), *n.* sloyd. Also, **slojd.**

sloke (slōk), *n.* **1.** algae or seaweed. **2.** scum or slime, esp. on a body of water. [1425–75; earlier *slawk,* late ME *slauk,* of uncert. orig.]

slo-mo (slō′mō′), *n. Informal.* See **slow motion.**

sloop (slo͞op), *n.* a single-masted, fore-and-aft-rigged sailing vessel, with or without a bowsprit, having a jib-headed or gaff mainsail, the latter sometimes with a gaff topsail, and one or more headsails. Cf. **cutter** (def. 3), **knockabout** (def. 1). [1620–30; < D *sloep;* akin to OE *slūpan* to glide]

sloop′ of war′, (formerly) a sailing or steam naval vessel having cannons on only one deck. [1695–1705]

sloop′ rig′. See **gaff-topsail catfish.** [1890–95]

sloop-rigged (slo͞op′rigd′), *adj.* (of a sailboat) fore-and-aft rigged with a mainsail and a jib. [1760–70]

slop[1] (slop), *v.,* **slopped, slop·ping,** *n.* —*v.t.* **1.** to spill or splash (liquid). **2.** to spill liquid upon. **3.** to feed slop to (pigs or other livestock). —*v.i.* **4.** to spill or splash liquid (sometimes fol. by *about*): *The children happily slopped about in the puddles.* **5.** (of liquid) to spill or splash out of a container (usually fol. by *over*): *The milk slopped over the rim of the glass.* **6.** to walk or go through mud, slush, or water. **7.** *Informal.* to be unduly effusive or sentimental; gush (usually fol. by *over*). **8.** to move in an idle, lazy, casual, or slovenly manner (usually fol. by *around* or *about*): *to spend the weekend slopping around the house.* —*n.* **9.** a quantity of liquid carelessly spilled or splashed about. **10.** badly cooked or unappetizing food or drink. **11.** bran from bolted cornmeal mixed with an equal part of water and used as a feed for swine and other livestock. **12.** any similar, watery feed; swill. **13.** Often, **slops. a.** the dirty water, liquid refuse, etc., of a household or the like. **b.** tasteless or unappetizing soup, stew, or drink. **14.** kitchen refuse; swill. **15.** liquid mud. **16. slops,** *Distilling.* the mash remaining after distilling. [1350–1400; ME *sloppe* (n.), OE *-sloppe* (in *cūsloppe* COWSLIP, lit., cow slime); akin to SLIP[3]]
—**Syn. 2.** splash, slosh, spatter.

slop[2] (slop), *n.* **1. slops, a.** clothing, bedding, etc., supplied to sailors from the ship's stores. **b.** cheap, ready-made clothing in general. **c.** short, baggy trousers, worn by men, esp. sailors, in the 16th and 17th centuries. **2.** a loose-fitting overgarment, as a tunic or smock. [bef. 1000; ME *slop,* OE *-slop* (in *oferslop* overgarment); cf. MD *overslop,* ON *yfirsloppr*]

slop′ ba′sin, *Brit.* a basin or bowl into which the dregs, leaves, and grounds of teacups and coffee cups are emptied at the table. Also called **slop′ bowl′.** [1725–35]

slop′ buck′et. See **slop pail.** [1855–60]

slop′ chest′, **1.** a supply of clothing, boots, tobacco, and other personal goods for sale to the crew of a ship during a voyage. **2.** (formerly) a chest containing this supply. [1830–40]

slope (slōp), *v.,* **sloped, slop·ing,** *n.* —*v.i.* **1.** to have or take an inclined or oblique direction or angle considered with reference to a vertical or horizontal plane; slant. **2.** to move at an inclination or obliquely: *They sloped gradually westward.* —*v.t.* **3.** to direct at a slant or inclination; incline from the horizontal or vertical: *The sun sloped its beams.* **4.** to form with a slope or slant: *to slope an embankment.* **5. slope off,** *Chiefly Brit. Slang.* to make one's way out slowly or furtively. —*n.* **6.** ground that has a natural incline, as the side of a hill. **7.** inclination or slant, esp. downward or upward. **8.** deviation from the horizontal or vertical. **9.** an inclined surface. **10.** Usually, **slopes.** hills, esp. foothills or bluffs: *the slopes of Mt. Kilimanjaro.* **11.** *Math.* **a.** the tangent of the angle between a given straight line and the *x*-axis of a system of Cartesian coordinates. **b.** the derivative of the function whose graph is a given curve evaluated at a designated point. **12.** *Slang (disparaging and offensive).* an Asian, esp. a Vietnamese. [1495–1505; aphetic var. of ASLOPE; akin to SLIP[1]] —**slop′ing·ly,** *adv.* —**slop′ing·ness,** *n.*
—**Syn. 1.** SLOPE, SLANT mean to incline away from a relatively straight surface or line used as a reference. To SLOPE is to incline vertically in an oblique direction: *The ground slopes (upward or downward) sharply here.* To SLANT is to fall to one side, to lie obliquely to some line whether horizontal or perpendicular: *The road slants off to the right.*

slop·er (slō′pər), *n.* **1.** a person or thing that slopes. **2.** *Tailoring.* a basic pattern developed on paper by drafting or in cloth by draping, but with seam allowances omitted, used as a tool to create other patterns. [SLOPE + -ER[1]]

CONCISE ETYMOLOGY KEY: <, descended or borrowed from; >, whence; b., blend of, blended; c., cognate with; cf., compare; deriv., derivative; equiv., equivalent; imit., imitative; obl., oblique; r., replacing; s., stem; sp., spelling, spelled; resp., respelling, respelled; trans., translation; ?, origin unknown; *, unattested; ‡, probably earlier than. See the full key inside the front cover.

slop′ jar′, a large jar or pail for collecting household slop for disposal. [1850–55]

slop-o·ver (slop′ō′vər), *n.* **1.** an act or instance of spilling or slopping over. **2.** an amount spilled; spillover; overflow. [1905–10, *Amer.;* n. use of v. phrase *slop over*]

slop′ pail′, **1.** a pail for conveying slop in feeding livestock, esp. pigs. **2.** a pail into which household slop is collected for disposal. Also called **slop bucket.** [1860–65]

slop·py (slop′ē), *adj.,* **-pi·er, -pi·est.** **1.** muddy, slushy, or very wet: *The field was a sloppy mess after the rain.* **2.** splashed or soiled with liquid. **3.** careless; loose: *sloppy writing.* **4.** untidy; slovenly: *sloppy clothes; a sloppy eater.* **5.** overly emotional; gushy: *sloppy sentimentality.* **6.** (of food or drink) prepared or served in an unappetizing way. **7.** (of clothes) loose-fitting; baggy: *a big, sloppy sweater.* **8.** (of the surface of a racetrack) wet from a recent or continuing heavy rain and containing puddles and mud still too thin and watery to be sticky. [1700–10; SLOP[1] + -Y[1]] —**slop′pi·ly,** *adv.* —**slop′pi·ness,** *n.*
—**Syn. 2, 4.** messy. **3.** slipshod. **4.** slatternly.

Slop′py Joe′, **1.** a sandwich of ground beef cooked in a spicy tomato or barbecue sauce and usually served on a bun. **2.** a baggy, overlarge sweater originally worn by girls and young women in the 1940's. **3.** a man or youth whose appearance is habitually slovenly. Also, **slop′py Joe′, slop′py joe′** (for defs. 1, 2). [1935–40]

Slop′py Joe's′, *Slang.* See **greasy spoon.**

slop·shop (slop′shop′), *n.* a store at which cheap, ready-made clothing may be purchased. [1715–25; SLOP[2] + SHOP]

slop′ sink′, a deep sink for emptying slop pails and the like. [1880–85]

slop·work (slop′wûrk′), *n.* **1.** the manufacture of cheap clothing. **2.** clothing of this kind. **3.** work that is carelessly or poorly done. [1840–50; SLOP[2] + WORK] —**slop′work′er,** *n.*

slosh (slosh), *v.i.* **1.** to splash or move through water, mud, or slush. **2.** (of a liquid) to move about actively within a container. —*v.t.* **3.** to stir or splash (something) around in a fluid: *to slosh the mop in the pail.* **4.** to splash (liquid) clumsily or haphazardly: *She sloshed tea all over her new suit. They sloshed the paint over the wall.* —*n.* **5.** watery mire or partly melted snow; slush. **6.** the lap or splash of liquid: *the slosh of waves against the shore.* **7.** a small quantity of liquid: *a slosh of milk in the pail.* **8.** a watery or weak drink. [1805–15; perh. b. SLOP[1] and SLUSH]

sloshed (slosht), *adj. Slang.* drunk. [1945–50; SLOSH + -ED[2]]

slosh·y (slosh′ē), *adj.,* **slosh·i·er, slosh·i·est.** of or pertaining to slosh; slushy. [1790–1800; SLOSH + -Y[1]] —**slosh′i·ly,** *adv.* —**slosh′i·ness,** *n.*

slot[1] (slot), *n., v.,* **slot·ted, slot·ting.** —*n.* **1.** a narrow, elongated depression, groove, notch, slit, or aperture, esp. a narrow opening for receiving or admitting something, as a coin or a letter. **2.** a place or position, as in a sequence or series: *The program received a new time slot on the broadcasting schedule.* **3.** *Ling.* (esp. in tagmemics) a position having a specific grammatical function within a construction into which any one of a set of morphemes or morpheme sequences can be fit. Cf. **filler** (def. 9). **4.** an assignment or job opening; position: *I applied for the slot in management training.* **5.** *Journalism.* **a.** the interior opening in a copy desk, occupied by the chief copy editor. **b.** the job or position of chief copy editor: *He had the slot at the* Gazette *for 20 years.* Cf. **rim** (def. 7). **6.** an allocated, scheduled time and place for an aircraft to take off or land, as authorized by an airport or air-traffic authority: *40 more slots for the new airline at U.S. airports.* **7.** *Informal.* See **slot machine** (def. 1). **8.** *Aeron.* See under **slat[1]** (def. 2). **9.** *Ornith.* a narrow notch or other similar opening between the tips of the primaries of certain birds, which during flight helps to maintain a smooth flow of air over the wings. **10.** *Ice Hockey.* an unmarked area near the front of an opponent's goal that affords a vantage for an attacking player. —*v.t.* **11.** to provide with a slot or slots; make a slot in. **12.** to place or fit into a slot: *We've slotted his appointment for four o'clock.* —*v.i.* **13.** to fit or be placed in a slot. [1300–50; ME: the hollow of the breastbone < MF *esclot* < ?]

slot[2] (slot), *n.* **1.** the track or trail of a deer or other animal, as shown by the marks of the feet. **2.** a track, trace, or trail of something. [1565–75; < AF, MF *esclot* the hoofprint of a horse, prob. < ON *slōth* track, trail; see SLEUTHHOUND]

slot·back (slot′bak′), *n. Football.* **1.** an offensive back who lines up about one yard behind the gap in the line between a tackle and an end stationed a distance outside of the tackle. **2.** the position played by this back. [1960–65; SLOT[1] + BACK[1]]

slot′ car′, a miniature, electrically-operated toy racing car that runs on a slotted track and is controlled by an operator with a hand-held rheostat. Also called **slot racer.** [1965–70, *Amer.*]

two-toed sloth, *Choloepus hoffmanni,* length 2 ft. (0.6 m)

sloth (slôth *or, esp. for 2,* slōth), *n.* **1.** habitual disinclination to exertion; indolence; laziness. **2.** any of several slow-moving, arboreal, tropical American edentates of the family Bradypodidae, having a long, coarse, grayish-brown coat often of a greenish cast caused by algae, and long, hooklike claws used in gripping tree branches while hanging or moving along in a habitual upside-down position. **3.** a pack or group of bears. [1125–75; ME *slowth* (see SLOW, -TH[1]); r. OE *slǣwth,* deriv. of *slǣw,* var. of *slāw* slow]
—**Syn. 1.** shiftlessness, idleness, slackness.

sloth′ bear′, a coarse-haired, long-snouted bear, *Ursus ursinus,* of India and Indochina: now rare. [1825–35]

sloth bear, *Ursus ursinus,* 2⅔ ft. (0.8 m) high at shoulder; length 5½ ft. (1.7 m)

sloth·ful (slôth′fəl, slōth′-), *adj.* sluggardly; indolent; lazy. [1350–1400; ME; see SLOTH, -FUL] —**sloth′ful·ly,** *adv.* —**sloth′ful·ness,** *n.*
—**Syn.** sluggish; inactive, torpid, slack. See **idle.**

slot′ machine′, **1.** a gambling machine operated by inserting coins into a slot and pulling a handle that activates a set of spinning symbols on wheels, the final alignment of which determines the payoff that is released into a receptacle at the bottom. **2.** any machine operated by inserting coins into a slot, as a vending machine. [1890–95]

slot′ man′, copyeditor (def. 3). Cf. **copyreader.**

slot′ rac′er. See **slot car.** [1965–70]

slot′ rac′ing, the activity of racing slot cars. [1965–70]

slot′ted spoon′, a large spoon whose bowl has several slots or holes for draining liquid from food being ladled. [SLOT[1] + -ED[3]]

slot·ter (slot′ər), *n.* **1.** a person or thing that slots. **2.** a machine tool for shaping vertical surfaces with a cutting tool held in a vertically reciprocating ram. [1880–85; SLOT[1] + -ER[1]]

slouch (slouch), *v.i.* **1.** to sit or stand with an awkward, drooping posture. **2.** to move or walk with loosely drooping body and careless gait. **3.** to have a droop or downward bend, as a hat. —*v.t.* **4.** to cause to droop or bend down, as the shoulders or a hat. —*n.* **5.** a drooping or bending forward of the head and shoulders; an awkward, drooping posture or carriage. **6.** an awkward, clumsy, or slovenly person. **7.** See **slouch hat. 8.** a lazy, inept, or inefficient person. [1505–15; orig. uncert.] —**slouch′er,** *n.* —**slouch′ing·ly,** *adv.*
—**Syn. 8.** laggard, loafer, sluggard.

slouch′ hat′, a soft hat often made of felt and having a supple, usually broad brim. [1830–40]

slouch·y (slou′chē), *adj.,* **slouch·i·er, slouch·i·est.** of or pertaining to a slouch or to a slouching manner, posture, etc. [1685–95; SLOUCH + -Y[1]] —**slouch′i·ly,** *adv.* —**slouch′i·ness,** *n.*

slough[1] (slou *for 1, 2, 4;* slo͞o *for 3*), *n.* **1.** an area of soft, muddy ground; swamp or swamplike region. **2.** a hole full of mire, as in a road. **3.** Also, **slew, slue.** *Northern U.S. and Canadian.* a marshy or reedy pool, pond, inlet, backwater, or the like. **4.** a condition of degradation, despair, or helplessness. [bef. 900; ME; OE *slōh;* c. MLG *slōch,* MHG *sluoche* ditch]

slough[2] (sluf), *n.* **1.** the outer layer of the skin of a snake, which is cast off periodically. **2.** *Pathol.* a mass or layer of dead tissue separated from the surrounding or underlying tissue. **3.** anything that is shed or cast off. **4.** *Cards.* a discard. —*v.i.* **5.** to be or become shed or cast off, as the slough of a snake. **6.** to cast off a slough. **7.** *Pathol.* to separate from the sound flesh, as a slough. **8.** *Cards.* to discard a card or cards. —*v.t.* **9.** to dispose or get rid of; cast (often fol. by *off*): *to slough off a bad habit.* **10.** to shed as or like a slough. **11.** *Cards.* to discard (cards). **12. slough over,** to treat as slight or trivial: *to slough over a friend's mistake.* Also, **sluff.** [1250–1300; ME *slughe, slouh* skin of a snake; c. G *Schlauch* skin, bag] —**slough′i·ness,** *n.* —**slough′y,** *adj.*
—**Syn. 6.** molt.

Slo·vak (slō′väk, -vak), *n.* **1.** one of a Slavic people dwelling in Slovakia. **2.** the language of Slovakia, a Slavic language closely related to Czech. —*adj.* **3.** of or pertaining to the Slovaks or Slovak. [1820–30; < Slovak *slovák,* ult. deriv. of Slavic **slověninŭ* SLAV]

Slo·va·ki·a (slō vä′kē ə, -vak′ē ə), *n.* a republic in central Europe: formerly a part of Czechoslovakia; under German protection 1939–45; independent since 1993. 5,296,768; 18,931 sq. mi. (49,035 sq. km). *Cap.:* Bratislava. Also called **Slo′vak Repub′lic.** Slovak, **Slo·ven·sko** (slô′ven skô). —**Slo·va′ki·an,** *adj., n.*

slov·en (sluv′ən), *n.* **1.** a person who is habitually negligent of neatness or cleanliness in dress, appearance, etc. **2.** a person who works, acts, speaks, etc., in a negligent, slipshod manner. [1400–50; late ME *sloveyn,* perh. < MD *slof* careless (D *slof* careless, *sloven* to toil) + *-inne* fem. n. suffix]

Slo·vene (slō vēn′, slō′vēn), *n.* **1.** one of a Slavic people dwelling in Slovenia. **2.** a South Slavic language spoken in Slovenia. —*adj.* **3.** of or pertaining to the Slovenes or Slovene. Also, **Slo·ve′ni·an.** [1880–85; < G *Slowene* < Slovene *Slovênec* (n.), *slovênski* (adj.), ult. deriv. of Common Slavic **slověninŭ* SLAV]

Slo·ve·ni·a (slō vē′nē ə, -vēn′yə), *n.* a republic in SE Europe: formerly part of Yugoslavia. 1,930,000; 7819 sq. mi. (20,250 sq. km). *Cap.:* Ljubljana.

slov·en·ly (sluv′ən lē), *adj.,* **-li·er, li·est,** *adv.* —*adj.* **1.** untidy or unclean in appearance or habits. **2.** characteristic of a sloven; slipshod: *slovenly work.* —*adv.* **3.** in

an untidy, careless, or slipshod manner. [1505–15; SLOVEN + -LY] —**slov′en·li·ness,** *n.*
—**Syn. 1.** sluttish, slatternly. **2.** careless, loose, disorderly. —**Ant. 1.** neat. **2.** careful.

slow (slō), *adj.*, **-er, -est,** *adv.*, **-er, -est,** *v.* —*adj.* **1.** moving or proceeding with little or less than usual speed or velocity: *a slow train.* **2.** characterized by lack of speed: *a slow pace.* **3.** taking or requiring a comparatively long time for completion: *a slow meal; a slow trip.* **4.** requiring or taking a long time for growing, changing, or occurring; gradual: *a plant of slow growth.* **5.** sluggish in nature, disposition, or function. **6.** dull of perception or understanding; mentally dull: *a slow child.* **7.** not prompt, readily disposed, or in haste (usually fol. by *to* or an infinitive): *slow to anger; slow to take offense.* **8.** burning or heating with little speed or intensity, as a fire or an oven. **9.** slack; not busy: *The market was slow today.* **10.** having some quality that retards speed or causes movement, progress, work, etc., to be accomplished at less than the usual or expected rate of speed: *a slow, careful worker; a slow road.* **11.** running at less than the proper rate of speed or registering less than the proper time, as a clock. **12.** passing heavily or dragging, as time: *It's been a slow afternoon.* **13.** not progressive; behind the times: *a slow town.* **14.** dull, humdrum, uninteresting, or tedious: *What a slow party!* **15.** *Photog.* requiring long exposure, as by having a small lens diameter or low film sensitivity: *a slow lens or film.* **16.** (of the surface of a race track) sticky from a fairly recent rain and in the process of drying out. —*adv.* **17.** in a slow manner; slowly: *Drive slow.* —*v.t.* **18.** to make slow or slower (often fol. by *up* or *down*). **19.** to retard; reduce the advancement or progress of: *His illness slowed him at school.* —*v.i.* **20.** to become slow or slower; slacken in speed (often fol. by *up* or *down*). [bef. 900; ME; OE *slāw* sluggish, dull; c. D *sleeuw;* cf. SLOTH] —**slow′ly,** *adv.* —**slow′ness,** *n.*
—**Syn. 1, 2.** unhurried. SLOW, DELIBERATE, GRADUAL, LEISURELY mean unhurried and not happening rapidly. That which is SLOW acts or moves without haste or rapidity: *a slow procession of cars.* DELIBERATE implies the slowness that marks careful consideration before and while acting: *a deliberate and calculating manner.* GRADUAL suggests the slowness of something that advances one step at a time: *a gradual improvement in service.* That which is LEISURELY moves with the slowness allowed by ample time or the absence of pressure: *an unhurried and leisurely stroll.* **5.** sluggardly, dilatory, indolent, lazy, slothful. **6.** dense. See **dull. 14.** boring. **19.** hinder, impede, obstruct. —**Ant. 1–3.** fast. **19.** advance.
—**Usage.** As an adverb, SLOW has two forms, SLOW and SLOWLY. SLOWLY appeared first in the 15th century; SLOW came into use shortly thereafter. Both are standard today in certain uses.
Originally, SLOW was used both preceding and following the verb it modified. Today, it is used chiefly in imperative constructions with short verbs of motion (*drive, run, turn, walk,* etc.), and it follows the verb: *Drive slow. Don't walk so slow.* This use is more common in speech than in writing, although it occurs widely on traffic and road signs. SLOW also combines with present participles in forming adjectives: *slow-burning; slow-moving.* In this use it is standard in all varieties of speech and writing.
SLOWLY is by far the more common form of the adverb in writing. In both speech and writing it is the usual form in preverb position (*He slowly drove down the street. The couple slowly strolled into the park*) and following verbs that are not imperatives (*He drove slowly down the street. The couple strolled slowly through the park*). See also **quick, sure.**

slow′ burn′, *Informal.* a gradual building up of anger, as opposed to an immediate outburst: *I did a slow burn as the conversation progressed.*

slow·coach (slō′kōch′), *n. Informal.* a slowpoke. Also, **slow′ coach′.** [1830–40; SLOW + COACH]

slow′ cook′er, an electric cooking pot with a tight-fitting lid for cooking meats, casseroles, etc., for several hours at relatively low temperatures, usually around 200° F (93.3° C).

slow·down (slō′doun′), *n.* **1.** a slowing down or delay in progress, action, etc. **2.** a deliberate slowing of pace by workers to win demands from their employers. **3.** *Sports.* a holding or passing tactic by a team to retain possession of the ball, puck, etc., or use up a maximal amount of time, as to safeguard a lead or thwart a high-scoring opponent. [1895–1900; n. use of v. phrase *slow down*]
—**Syn. 1.** slackening, falloff, decline, flagging.

slow′ fire′, a rate of firing small arms that allows time to aim before each shot. —**slow′-fire′,** *adj.*

slow-foot·ed (slō′fo͝ot′id), *adj.* proceeding at a slow pace. [1635–45] —**slow′-foot′ed·ly,** *adv.* —**slow′-foot′ed·ness,** *n.*

slow′ gait′, (of a horse) a slow rack. [1935–40]

slow′ lo′ris, loris (def. 2). [1880–85]

slow′ match′, a slow-burning match or fuse, often consisting of a rope or cord soaked in a solution of saltpeter. [1795–1805]

slow-mo (slō′mō′), *n. Informal.* See **slow motion.** Also, **slo-mo.**

slow′ mo′tion, 1. the process or technique of filming or taping a motion-picture or television sequence at an accelerated rate of speed and then projecting or replaying it at normal speed so that the action appears to be slowed down. **2.** the effect thus created. [1920–25]

slow-mo·tion (slō′mō′shən), *adj.* **1.** of, pertaining to or made in slow motion: *a slow-motion replay.* **2.** moving or proceeding at a strikingly slow rate: *slow-motion progress toward a settlement.* [1925–30]

slow-mov·ing (slō′mo͞o′ving), *adj.* proceeding with or characterized by slow, sluggish, or leisurely movement or activity. [1635–45]

slow′ neu′tron, *Physics.* a neutron with low kinetic energy, esp. one slowed by the moderator in a nuclear reactor. [1930–35] —**slow′-neu′tron,** *adj.*

slow·poke (slō′pōk′), *n. Informal.* a person who makes slow progress. [1915–20; SLOW + POKE[1]]
—**Syn.** laggard, dawdler, dallier, slug.

slow-re·lease (slō′ri lēs′), *adj. Chem., Pharm.* sustained-release. [1925–30]

slow′-scan tel′evision (slō′skan′), a technique or system in which an image is scanned electronically more slowly than is normally done in order to produce images, esp. of still pictures, that can be transmitted economically, as over a telephone line, and displayed on a television screen.

slow′ time′, *Informal.* See **standard time.** Cf. **fast time.** [1895–1900]

slow-twitch (slō′twich′), *adj. Physiol.* of or pertaining to muscle fiber that contracts relatively slowly and is resistant to fatigue (distinguished from fast-twitch). [1975–80]

slow-up (slō′up′), *n.* a delay or retardation in progress or activity; slowdown. [1890–95; n. use of v. phrase *slow up*]

slow′ vi′rus, *Pathol.* a virus that remains dormant in the body for a long time before producing symptoms, as in several neurological diseases, including kuru and Creutzfeldt-Jakob disease. [1950–55]

slow′ wave′, *Physiol.* See **delta wave.**

slow′-wave′ sleep′ (slō′wāv′), *Physiol.* a recurrent period of deep sleep, typically totaling five or six hours a night, distinguished by the presence of slow brain waves and by very little dreaming. Also called **S sleep.** Cf. **REM sleep.** [1965–70]

slow-wit·ted (slō′wit′id), *adj.* mentally slow or dull; slow in comprehension and thinking. [1565–75] —**slow′-wit′ted·ly,** *adv.* —**slow′-wit′ted·ness,** *n.*

slow·worm (slō′wûrm′), *n.* blindworm (def. 2). [bef. 900; SLOW + WORM; r. ME *slowerm, slowurme,* OE *slāwerm, slāwyrm,* equiv. to *slā-* (cf. dial. Sw *slo,* Norw *slō* slowworm) + *wyrm* worm]

sloyd (sloid), *n.* a system of manual training based on experience gained in woodworking, originally developed in Sweden. Also, **sloid, slojd.** [1880–85; < Sw *slöjd* craft, industrial art, woodworking; c. SLEIGHT]

S.L.P., Socialist Labor Party.

SLR, *Photog.* See **single-lens reflex camera.**

slub (slub), *v.,* **slubbed, slub·bing,** *n.* —*v.t.* **1.** to extend (slivers of fiber) and twist slightly in carding. —*n.* **2.** the fibers produced by slubbing. **3.** a slight irregularity in yarn produced either accidentally or purposely by knotting or twisting or by including uneven lengths of fiber in spinning. [1825–35; orig. uncert.]

slub·ber (slub′ər), *v.t.* to perform hastily or carelessly. [1520–30; < LG *slubbern* to do work carelessly] —**slub′·ber·ing·ly,** *adv.*

sludge (sluj), *n.* **1.** mud, mire, or ooze; slush. **2.** a deposit of ooze at the bottom of a body of water. **3.** any of various more or less mudlike deposits or mixtures. **4.** the sediment in a steam boiler or water tank. **5.** broken ice, as on the sea. **6.** a mixture of some finely powdered substance and water. **7.** sediment deposited during the treatment of sewage. **8.** Also called **activated sludge.** *Bacteriol.* sewage sediment that contains a heavy growth of microorganisms, resulting from vigorous aeration. **9.** a fine, mudlike powder produced by a mining drill. [1640–50; var. of dial. *slutch, slitch,* ME *slich* slime, wet mud (cf. its deriv. *slucched* muddy); appar. of expressive orig.]

sludge·worm (sluj′wûrm′), *n.* a small freshwater worm, *Tubifex tubifex,* often inhabiting sewage sludge and the muddy bottoms of lakes, rivers, and pools. [SLUDGE + WORM]

sludg·ing (sluj′ing), *n. Pathol.* intravascular slowing or clumping of red blood cells. [1945–50; SLUDGE + -ING[1]]

sludg·y (sluj′ē), *adj.,* **sludg·i·er, sludg·i·est. 1.** of or pertaining to sludge. **2.** covered, lined with, or containing sludge. [1775–85; SLUDGE + -Y[1]]

slue[1] (slo͞o), *v.,* **slued, slu·ing,** *n.* —*v.t.* **1.** to turn (a mast or other spar) around on its own axis, or without removing it from its place. **2.** to swing around. —*v.i.* **3.** to turn about; swing around. —*n.* **4.** the act of sluing. **5.** a position slued to. Also, **slew.** [1760–70; orig. uncert.]

slue[2] (slo͞o), *n. Informal.* slew[2].

slue[3] (slo͞o), *n.* slough[1] (def. 3).

sluff (sluf), *n., v.t., v.i.* slough[2].

slug[1] (slug), *n., v.,* **slugged, slug·ging.** —*n.* **1.** any of various snaillike terrestrial gastropods having no shell or only a rudimentary one, feeding on plants and a pest of leafy garden crops. **2.** a nudibranch. **3.** a metal disk used as a coin or token, generally counterfeit. **4.** a piece of lead or other metal for firing from a gun. **5.** any heavy piece of crude metal. **6.** *Print.* **a.** a thick strip of type metal less than type-high. **b.** such a strip containing a type-high number or other character for temporary use. **c.** a line of type in one piece, as produced by a Linotype. **7.** *Informal.* a shot of liquor taken neat; belt. **8.** *Slang.* a person who is lazy or slow-moving; sluggard. **9.** a slow-moving animal, vehicle, or the like. **10.** *Journalism.* **a.** Also called **catchline.** a short phrase or title used to indicate the story content of newspaper or magazine copy. **b.** the line of type carrying this information. **11.** *Metalworking.* a small piece of metal ready for processing. **12.** a gold coin of California, privately issued in 1849 and for some time after, worth 50 dollars. **13.** *Physics.* a unit of mass, equivalent to approximately 32.2 lb. (15 kg) and having the property that a force of one pound acting upon a mass of this unit produces an acceleration of one foot per second per second. **14.** an irregular projection or knob on the surface of yarn, usually produced by lint or by defects in weaving. —*v.t.* **15.** *Print.* **a.** to make (corrections) by replacing entire lines of type, esp. as set by a Linotype. **b.** to check the lines of (typeset copy) against copy of the previous typesetting stage to ensure that no line has been omitted, esp. before printing or plating. **16.** *Journalism.* to furnish (copy) with a slug. **17.** to interpolate pieces of metal into (a joint being welded). [1375–1425; late ME *slugge* sluggard < Scand; cf. Norw (dial.) *sluggje* heavy, slow person] —**slug′like′,** *adj.*

slug[1],
Limax maximus,
lenth 4 in.
(10 cm)

slug[2] (slug), *v.,* **slugged, slug·ging,** *n. Informal.* —*v.t.* **1.** to strike heavily; hit hard, esp. with the fist. **2.** to hit or drive (a baseball) very hard or a great distance. —*v.i.* **3.** to hit or be capable of hitting hard. **4.** to trudge, fight, or push onward, as against obstacles or through mud or snow: *The infantry slugged up the hill and dug in.* **5. slug it out, a.** to fight, esp. with fists, until a decisive victory has been achieved. **b.** to succeed or survive by constant and intense struggle. —*n.* **6.** a hard blow or hit, esp. with a fist or baseball bat. [1820–30; orig. in phrase *hit with a slug;* see SLUG[1]]

slug·a·bed (slug′ə bed′), *n.* a lazy person who stays in bed long after the usual time for arising. [1585–95; SLUG[1] + ABED]

slug·fest (slug′fest′), *n. Informal.* **1.** a baseball game in which both teams make many runs and extra-base hits. **2.** a boxing bout in which the boxers exchange powerful blows vigorously and aggressively with little care for defense. **3.** an intense conflict or combat. [1915–20; SLUG[2] + -FEST]

slug·gard (slug′ərd), *n.* **1.** a person who is habitually inactive or lazy. —*adj.* **2.** lazy; sluggardly. [1350–1400; ME *slogarde.* See SLUG[1], -ARD]

slug·gard·ly (slug′ərd lē), *adj.* like or befitting a sluggard; slothful; lazy. [1860–65; SLUGGARD + -LY] —**slug′gard·li·ness,** *n.*

slug·ger (slug′ər), *n.* **1.** a person who strikes hard, esp. a boxer noted for the ability to deliver hard punches. **2.** *Baseball.* a player who frequently gets extra-base hits; a strong hitter. [1875–80, *Amer.;* SLUG[2] + -ER[1]]

slug′ging av′erage, *Baseball.* a measure of the effectiveness of a batter in making base hits, obtained by dividing the total bases reached by hitting by the number of official times at bat and carrying out the result to three decimal places. A batter making 275 total bases in 500 times at bat has a slugging average of .550. Also called **slug′ging percent′age.** Cf. **batting average.** [1965–70]

slug·gish (slug′ish), *adj.* **1.** indisposed to action or exertion; lacking in energy; lazy; indolent: *a sluggish disposition.* **2.** not acting or working with full vigor, as bodily organs: *a sluggish liver.* **3.** slow to act or respond: *a sluggish car engine.* **4.** moving slowly, or having little motion, as a stream. **5.** slow, as motion. **6.** slack, as trade, business, or sales. [1400–50; late ME *sluggissh.* See SLUG[1], -ISH[1]] —**slug′gish·ly,** *adv.* —**slug′·gish·ness,** *n.*
—**Syn. 1.** slow, slothful. See **inactive.** —**Ant. 1.** quick, active.

sluice (slo͞os), *n., v.,* **sluiced, sluic·ing.** —*n.* **1.** an artificial channel for conducting water, often fitted with a gate (**sluice′ gate′**) at the upper end for regulating the flow. **2.** the body of water held back or controlled by a sluice gate. **3.** any contrivance for regulating a flow from or into a receptacle. **4.** a channel, esp. one carrying off surplus water; drain. **5.** a stream of surplus water. **6.** an artificial stream or channel of water for moving solid matter: *a lumbering sluice.* **7.** Also called **sluice′ box′.** *Mining.* a long, sloping trough or the like, with grooves on the bottom, into which water is directed to separate gold from gravel or sand. —*v.t.* **8.** to let out (water) by or as if by opening a sluice. **9.** to drain (a pond, lake, etc.) by or as if by opening a sluice. **10.** to open a sluice upon. **11.** to flush or cleanse with a rush of water: *to sluice the decks of a boat.* **12.** *Mining.* to wash in a sluice. **13.** to send (logs) down a sluiceway. —*v.i.* **14.** to flow or pour through or as if through a sluice. [1300–50; ME *scluse* (n.) < OF *escluse* < LL *exclūsa,* a water barrier, n. use of fem. of L *exclūsus,* ptp. of *exclūdere* to EXCLUDE] —**sluice′like′,** *adj.*

sluice·way (slo͞os′wā′), *n.* **1.** a channel controlled by a sluice gate. **2.** any artificial channel for water. [1770–80, *Amer.;* SLUICE + WAY[1]]

sluit (slo͞ot), *n.* (in South Africa) a deep, dry gulch or channel formed by erosion due to heavy rains. [1860–65; < Afrik *sloot* < D: ditch]

slum (slum), *n., v.,* **slummed, slum·ming.** —*n.* **1.** Often, **slums.** a thickly populated, run-down, squalid part of a city, inhabited by poor people. **2.** any squalid, run-down place to live. —*v.i.* **3.** to visit slums, esp. from curiosity. **4.** to visit or frequent a place, group, or amusement spot considered to be low in social status. [1805–15; cf. earlier argot *slum* room; orig. obscure] —**slum′mer,** *n.*

slum·ber (slum′bər), *v.i.* **1.** to sleep, esp. lightly; doze; drowse. **2.** to be in a state of inactivity, negligence, quiescence, or calm: *Vesuvius is slumbering.* —*v.t.* **3.** to spend or pass (time) in slumbering (often fol. by *away, out,* or *through*): *to slumber the afternoon away.* **4.** to dispel or forget by slumbering (often fol. by *away*): *to slumber cares away.* —*n.* **5.** Sometimes, **slumbers.** sleep, esp. light sleep. **6.** a period of sleep, esp. light sleep. **7.** a state of inactivity, quiescence, etc. [1175–1225; (v.) ME *slumeren,* freq. of *slumen* to doze, deriv. of OE *slūma* sleep (see -ER[6]); cf. G *schlummern;* (n.) ME *slomur, slomber,* deriv. of the v.] —**slum′ber·er,** *n.* —**slum′ber·less,** *adj.*

slum·ber·land (slum′bər land′), *n.* an imaginary land described to children as the place they enter during sleep. [1880–85; SLUMBER + LAND]

slum·ber·ous (slum′bər əs, slum′brəs), *adj.* **1.** sleepy; heavy with drowsiness, as the eyelids. **2.** causing or inducing sleep. **3.** pertaining to, characterized by, or suggestive of slumber. **4.** inactive or sluggish; calm or quiet. Also, **slum′brous.** [1485–95; SLUMBER + -OUS] —**slum′ber·ous·ly,** *adv.* —**slum′ber·ous·ness,** *n.*

slum′ber par′ty, a social gathering typically of teenagers held at the home of one of them for the purpose of sleeping there overnight. Also called **pajama party.** [1920–25]

slum·ber·shade (slum′bər shād′), *n.* See **sleep shade.** [SLUMBER + SHADE]

slum·ber·y (slum′bə rē), *adj. Archaic.* slumberous. [1350–1400; ME *slombry, slomry;* see SLUMBER, -Y[1]]

slum·dwell·er (slum′dwel′ər), *n.* a person who lives in a slum. [1890–95; SLUM + DWELLER]

slum·gul·lion (slum gul′yən, slum′gul′-), *n.* **1.** a stew of meat, vegetables, potatoes, etc. **2.** a beverage made weak or thin, as watery tea, coffee, or the like. **3.** the refuse from processing whale carcasses. **4.** a reddish, muddy deposit in mining sluices. [1840–50, *Amer.;* cf. Scots, Hiberno-E *gullion* quagmire, cesspool]

slum·ism (slum′iz əm), *n.* the prevalence or increase of urban slums and blighted areas. [1965–70; SLUM + -ISM]

slum·lord (slum′lôrd′), *n.* a landlord who owns slum buildings, esp. one who fails to maintain or improve the buildings and charges tenants exorbitant rents. [1950–55; SLUM + LORD]

slum·my (slum′ē), *adj.,* **-mi·er, -mi·est.** of, pertaining to, or characteristic of a slum: *a slummy part of town.* [1855–60; SLUM + -Y[1]] —**slum′mi·ness,** *n.*

slump (slump), *v.i.* **1.** to drop or fall heavily; collapse: *Suddenly she slumped to the floor.* **2.** to assume a slouching, bowed, or bent position or posture: *Stand up straight and don't slump!* **3.** to decrease or fall suddenly and markedly, as prices or the market. **4.** to decline or deteriorate, as health, business, quality, or efficiency. **5.** to sink into a bog, muddy place, etc., or through ice or snow. **6.** to sink heavily, as the spirits. —*n.* **7.** an act or instance of slumping. **8.** a decrease, decline, or deterioration. **9.** a period of decline or deterioration. **10.** any mild recession in the economy as a whole or in a particular industry. **11.** a period during which a person performs slowly, inefficiently, or ineffectively, esp. a period during which an athlete or team fails to play or score as well as usual. **12.** a slouching, bowed, or bent position or posture, esp. of the shoulders. **13.** a landslide or rockslide. **14.** the vertical subsidence of freshly mixed concrete that is a measure of consistency and stiffness. **15.** *New England Cookery.* a dessert made with cooked fruit, esp. apples or berries, topped with a thick layer of biscuit dough or crumbs. [1670–80; orig., to sink into a bog or mud; perh. imit. (cf. PLUMP[2])] —**Syn. 8.** lapse, reverse, setback.

slung (slung), *v.* pt. and pp. of **sling.**

slung′ shot′, a weight, as a stone or a piece of metal, fastened to a short strap, chain, or the like, and used as a weapon. [1835–45, *Amer.*]

slunk (slungk), *v.* a pt. and the pp. of **slink.**

slur
(def. 10b)

slur (slûr), *v.,* **slurred, slur·ring,** *n.* —*v.t.* **1.** to pass over lightly or without due mention or consideration (often fol. by *over*): *The report slurred over her contribution to the enterprise.* **2.** to pronounce (a syllable, word, etc.) indistinctly by combining, reducing, or omitting sounds, as in hurried or careless utterance. **3.** to cast aspersions on; calumniate; disparage; depreciate: *The candidate was viciously slurred by his opponent.* **4.** *Music.* **a.** to sing to a single syllable or play without a break (two or more tones of different pitch). **b.** to mark with a slur. **5.** *Chiefly Brit. Dial.* to smirch, sully, or stain. —*v.i.* **6.** to read, speak, or sing hurriedly and carelessly. —*n.* **7.** a slurred utterance or sound. **8.** a disparaging remark or a slight: *quick to take offense at a slur.* **9.** a blot or stain, as upon reputation: *a slur on his good name.* **10.** *Music.* **a.** the combination of two or more tones of different pitch, sung to a single syllable or played without a break. **b.** a curved mark indicating this. **11.** *Print.* a spot that is blurred or unclear as a result of paper, plate, or blanket slippage. [1595–1605; appar. of multiple orig.; in senses referring to a gliding or smooth transition, cf. LG *slurren* to shuffle, D *sleuren* to trail, drag; in senses referring to a smirch or stain, cf. MD *slore* (D *sloor*) sluttish woman] —**Syn. 1.** slight, disregard, gloss. **3.** slander, asperse. **8.** innuendo, insult, affront. **9.** stigma, disgrace. —**Ant. 8.** compliment.

slurb (slûrb), *n.* a shabby, ill-planned suburban area. [1960–65; SL(UM) + (SUB)URB] —**slurb′an,** *adj.*

CONCISE ETYMOLOGY KEY: <, descended or borrowed from; >, whence; b., blend of, blended; c., cognate with; cf., compare; deriv., derivative; equiv., equivalent; imit., imitative; obl., oblique; r., replacing; s., stem; sp., spelling, spelled; resp., respelling, respelled; trans., translation; ?, origin unknown; *, unattested; ‡, probably earlier than. See the full key inside the front cover.

slurp (slûrp), *v.t.* **1.** to ingest (food or drink) with loud sucking noises: *He slurped his coffee.* —*v.i.* **2.** to make loud sucking noises while eating or drinking: *to slurp when eating soup.* —*n.* **3.** an intake of food or drink with a noisy sucking sound: *He finished his milk in about three slurps.* **4.** any lapping or splashing sound: *the slurp of the waves against the hull.* [1640–50; < D *slurpen* (v.)]

slur·ry (slûr′ē), *n., pl.* **-ries,** *v.,* **-ried, -ry·ing,** *adj.* —*n.* **1.** a thin mixture of an insoluble substance, as cement, clay, or coal, with a liquid, as water or oil. **2.** *Ceram.* a thin slip. —*v.t.* **3.** to prepare a suspension of (a solid in a liquid). —*adj.* **4.** of or pertaining to such a suspension. [1400–50; late ME *slory;* perh. akin to SLUR]

slush (slush), *n.* **1.** partly melted snow. **2.** liquid mud; watery mire. **3.** waste, as fat, grease, or other refuse, from the galley of a ship. **4.** a mixture of grease and other materials for lubricating. **5.** silly, sentimental, or weakly emotional talk or writing: *romantic slush.* **6.** See **slush pile.** —*v.t.* **7.** to splash with slush. **8.** to grease, polish, or cover with slush. **9.** to fill or cover with mortar or cement. **10.** to wash with a large quantity of water, as by dashing it on. [1635–45; appar. c. Norw *slusk* slops, Sw *slask* mud, slops]

slush′ fund′, **1.** a sum of money used for illicit or corrupt political purposes, as for buying influence. **2.** *Naut.* a fund from the sale of slush, refuse fat, etc., spent for any small luxuries. [1855–60]

slush′ pile′, *Informal.* a collection of unsolicited manuscripts submitted to a publisher.

slush·y (slush′ē), *adj.,* **slush·i·er, slush·i·est.** **1.** of or pertaining to slush. **2.** *Informal.* tritely sentimental; mushy. [1785–95; SLUSH + -Y[1]] —**slush′i·ly,** *adv.* —**slush′i·ness,** *n.*

slut (slut), *n.* **1.** a dirty, slovenly woman. **2.** an immoral or dissolute woman; prostitute. [1375–1425; late ME *slutte;* cf. dial. *slut* mud, Norw (dial.) *slutr* sleet, impure liquid]

slut·ty (slut′ē), *adj.,* **-ti·er, -ti·est.** of, resembling, or characteristic of a slut: *slutty behavior.* Also, **slut′tish.** [1350–1400; ME: dirty, slovenly; see SLUT, -Y[1]] —**slut′tish·ly,** *adv.* —**slut′tish·ness,** *n.*

sly (slī), *adj.,* **sly·er** or **sli·er, sly·est** or **sli·est,** *n.* —*adj.* **1.** cunning or wily: *sly as a fox.* **2.** stealthy, insidious, or secret. **3.** playfully artful, mischievous, or roguish: *sly humor.* —*n.* **4. on the sly,** secretly; furtively: *a tryst on the sly.* [1150–1200; ME *sly, sley* < ON *slœgr* sly, cunning] —**sly′ly, sli′ly,** *adv.* —**sly′ness,** *n.* —**Syn. 1.** artful, subtle, foxy, crafty, shrewd, astute. **2.** surreptitious, furtive, underhand, clandestine. —**Ant. 1.** direct, obvious.

sly·boots (slī′bo͞ots′), *n.* (*used with a singular v.*) an engagingly sly or mischievous person. [1690–1700; SLY + *boots* (pl. of BOOT[1]), used metonymically; cf. BOOTS]

sly-grog (slī′grog′), *n. Australian Slang.* bootleg liquor. [1835–45]

slype (slīp), *n. Archit.* a covered passage, esp. one from the transept of a cathedral to the chapter house. Also, **slip.** [1860–65; orig. uncert.; cf. dial. D *slijpe* secret path]

SM, service mark.

Sm, *Symbol, Chem.* samarium.

sm., small.

S-M, **1.** Also, **S and M.** sadomasochism. **2.** sadomasochistic. Also, **s-m, S/M, s/m**

S.M., **1.** Master of Science. [< NL *Scientiae Magister*] **2.** sergeant major. **3.** State Militia.

SMA, Surplus Marketing Administration.

smack[1] (smak), *n.* **1.** a taste or flavor, esp. a slight flavor distinctive or suggestive of something: *The chicken had just a smack of garlic.* **2.** a trace, touch, or suggestion of something. **3.** a taste, mouthful, or small quantity. —*v.i.* **4.** to have a taste, flavor, trace, or suggestion: *Your politeness smacks of condescension.* [bef. 1000; (n.) ME *smacke,* OE *smæc;* c. MLG *smak,* G *Geschmack* taste; (v.) ME *smacken* to perceive by taste, have a (specified) taste, deriv. of the n.; cf. G *schmacken*] —**Syn. 1.** savor. **2.** hint. **4.** taste, suggest.

smack[2] (smak), *v.t.* **1.** to strike sharply, esp. with the open hand or a flat object. **2.** to drive or send with a sharp, resounding blow or stroke: *to smack a ball over a fence.* **3.** to close and open (the lips) smartly so as to produce a sharp sound, often as a sign of relish, as in eating. **4.** to kiss with or as with a loud sound. —*v.i.* **5.** to smack the lips. **6.** to collide, come together, or strike something forcibly. **7.** to make a sharp sound as of striking against something. —*n.* **8.** a sharp, resounding blow, esp. with something flat. **9.** a smacking of the lips, as in relish or anticipation. **10.** a resounding or loud kiss. —*adv. Informal.* **11.** suddenly and violently: *He rode smack up against the side of the house.* **12.** directly; straight: *The street runs smack into the center of town.* [1550–60; imit.; cf. D, LG *smakken,* G (dial.) *schmacken*]

smack[3] (smak), *n.* **1.** *Eastern U.S.* a fishing vessel, esp. one having a well for keeping the catch alive. **2.** *Brit.* any of various small, fully decked, fore-and-aft-rigged vessels used for trawling or coastal trading. [1605–15; < D *smak*]

smack[4] (smak), *n. Slang.* heroin. [1960–65; prob. special use of SMACK[1]; cf. earlier slang *schmeck* with same sense (< Yiddish *shmek* sniff, whiff; cf. MHG *smecken* (G *schmecken*) to taste)]

smack-dab (smak′dab′), *adv. Informal.* directly; squarely: *smack-dab in the middle.* [1890–95]

smack·er (smak′ər), *n. Slang.* a dollar. [1915–20, *Amer.;* SMACK[2] + -ER[1]]

smack·er·oo (smak′ə ro͞o′), *n., pl.* **-er·oos.** *Slang.* **1.** a hard slap or swat: *He gave the ball a smackeroo.* **2.** smacker. [SMACK or SMACK(ER) + -EROO]

smack·ing (smak′ing), *adj.* **1.** smart, brisk, or strong, as a breeze. **2.** *Chiefly Brit. Slang.* smashing. [1585–95; SMACK[2] + -ING[2]] —**smack′ing·ly,** *adv.*

small (smôl), *adj.,* **-er, -est,** *adv.,* **-er, -est,** *n.* —*adj.* **1.** of limited size; of comparatively restricted dimensions; not big; little: *a small box.* **2.** slender, thin, or narrow: *a small waist.* **3.** not large as compared with others of the same kind: *a small elephant.* **4.** (of letters) lowercase (def. 1). **5.** not great in amount, degree, extent, duration, value, etc.: *a small salary.* **6.** not great numerically: *a small army.* **7.** of low numerical value; denoted by a low number. **8.** having but little land, capital, power, influence, etc., or carrying on business or some activity on a limited scale: *a small enterprise.* **9.** of minor importance, moment, weight, or consequence: *a small problem.* **10.** humble, modest, or unpretentious: *small circumstances.* **11.** characterized by or indicative of littleness of mind or character; mean-spirited; petty: *a small, miserly man.* **12.** of little strength or force: *a small effort.* **13.** (of sound or the voice) gentle; with little volume. **14.** very young: *when I was a small boy.* **15.** diluted; weak. **16. feel small,** to be ashamed or mortified: *Her unselfishness made me feel small.* —*adv.* **17.** in a small manner: *They talked big but lived small.* **18.** into small pieces: *Slice the cake small.* **19.** in low tones; softly. —*n.* **20.** something that is small: *Do you prefer the small or the large?* **21.** a small or narrow part, as of the back. **22.** those who are small: *Democracy benefits the great and the small.* **23. smalls,** small goods or products. **24. smalls,** *Brit.* **a.** underclothes. **b.** household linen, as napkins, pillowcases, etc. **25. smalls,** *Brit. Informal.* the responsions at Oxford University. **26. smalls,** *Mining.* coal, ore, gangue, etc., in fine particles. [bef. 900; ME *smale* (adj., n., and adv.), OE *smæl;* c. D *smal,* G *schmal*] —**small′ness,** *n.*

—**Syn. 1.** tiny. See **little. 2.** slight. **1, 3, 5.** SMALLER, LESS indicate a diminution, or not so large a size or quantity in some respect. SMALLER, as applied to concrete objects, is used with reference to size: *smaller apples.* LESS is used of material in bulk, with reference to amount, and in cases where attributes such as value and degree are in question: *A nickel is less than a dime* (in value). *A sergeant is less than a lieutenant* (in rank). As an abstraction, amount may be either SMALLER or LESS, though SMALLER is usually used when the idea of size is suggested: *a smaller opportunity.* LESS is used when the idea of quantity is present: *less courage.* **9.** trifling, petty, unimportant, minor, secondary, nugatory, inconsequential, paltry, insignificant. **11.** small-minded, narrow-minded, mean, selfish, narrow. **12.** feeble. —**Ant. 1.** large, big.

small·age (smô′lij), *n.* the celery, *Apium graveolens,* esp. in its wild state. [1250–1300; ME *smalege, smalache,* equiv. to *smale* SMALL + *ache* parsley < OF < L *apium* celery, parsley]

small′ arm′, Usually, **small arms.** a firearm designed to be held in one or both hands while being fired: in the U.S. the term is applied to weapons of a caliber of up to one in. (2.5 cm). [1680–90] —**small′-armed′,** *adj.*

small′ beer′, **1.** weak beer. **2.** *Chiefly Brit. Slang.* matters or persons of little or no importance. [1560–70]

small-bore (smôl′bôr′, -bōr′), *adj.* **1.** of, noting, or relating to a .22-caliber firearm. **2.** insular or parochial in scope, attitude, etc.: *small-bore officials.* [1895–1900]

Small′ Busi′ness Administra′tion, *U.S. Govt.* a federal agency, created in 1953, that grants or guarantees long-term loans to small businesses. *Abbr.:* SBA, S.B.A.

small′ cal′orie, *Thermodynam.* calorie (def. 1a). [1885–90]

small′ cane′. See under **cane** (def. 5).

small′ cap′ital, a capital letter of a particular font, the same height as the x-high letters. Also called **small′ cap′.** [1760–70]

small′ change′, **1.** coins of small denomination. **2.** someone or something insignificant or trifling: *Those people are small change.* [1810–20]

small′ cir′cle, a circle on a sphere, the plane of which does not pass through the center of the sphere. Cf. **great circle** (def. 1). [1870–75]

small′-claims′ court′ (smôl′klāmz′), a special court established to handle small claims or debts, usually without the services of lawyers. Also called **small′-debts′ court′** (smôl′dets′). [1920–25]

small·clothes (smôl′klōz′, -klōthz′), *n.pl.* **1.** *Brit.* small, personal items of clothing, as underwear, handkerchiefs, etc. **2.** knee breeches, esp. the close-fitting ones worn in the 17th, 18th, and early 19th centuries. [1625–35; SMALL + CLOTHES]

small′ craft′ advi′sory, *Meteorol.* **1.** a U.S. National Weather Service advisory of sustained winds, over coastal and inland waters, with speeds of 20–33 knots (23–38 mph, 10–17 m/sec). Regional NWS offices have discretion over the choice of the lower limit. **2.** an advisory of potentially dangerous sea surface conditions, as high swells, that are not directly related to local winds, accompanied by the reason for the advisory. Cf. **advisory** (def. 4).

small′ cran′berry. See under **cranberry** (def. 1).

Smal·lens (smä′linz), *n.* **Alexander,** 1889–1972, U.S. orchestra conductor, born in Russia.

small′er Eu′ropean elm′ bark′ bee′tle. See **elm bark beetle** (def. 1). [1940–45]

small′ fry′, **1.** children: *a treat for the small fry.* **2.** unimportant persons or objects: *Her parties were closed to the small fry.* **3.** small or young fish. [1895–1900] —**small′-fry′,** *adj.*

small′ game′, wild animals and birds hunted for sport, as rabbits or doves, that are smaller than animals, as deer and bears, classified as big game. [1810–20]

small′ hold′ing, *Brit.* a piece of land rented or sold to a farmer by county authorities for purposes of cultivation. [1890–95] —**small′ hold′er.**

small′ hours′, hours after midnight; early morning hours: *We danced into the small hours.* [1830–40]

small′ intes′tine, *Anat.* intestine (def. 2). [1760–70]

small•ish (smôl′ish), *adj.* rather small. [1325–75; ME; see SMALL, -ISH[1]]

small-mind•ed (smôl′mīn′did), *adj.* selfish, petty, or narrow-minded. [1840–50] **—small′-mind′ed•ly,** *adv.* **—small′-mind′ed•ness,** *n.*

small•mouth bass (smôl′mouth′ bas′), a North American freshwater game fish, *Micropterus dolomieu,* yellowish-green above and lighter below, having the lower jaw extending to the eye. Cf. **largemouth bass.** [1880–85, *Amer.*]

small′ pas′tern bone′. See under **pastern** (def. 2).

small′ pota′toes, *Informal.* a person or thing of little significance, importance, or value: *His salary was small potatoes for an executive of his ability.* [1825–35]

small•pox (smôl′poks′), *n. Pathol.* an acute, highly contagious, febrile disease, caused by the variola virus, and characterized by a pustular eruption that often leaves permanent pits or scars: eradicated worldwide by vaccination programs. [1510–20; SMALL + POX]

small′ print′. See **fine print.**

Smalls (smôlz), *n.* **Robert,** 1839–1915, U.S. captain in the Union navy and politician, born a slave in South Carolina: congressman 1875–79, 1882–87.

small′-sav′er certif′icate (smôl′sā′vər), a savings certificate issued in a small denomination. [1975–80]

small-scale (smôl′skāl′), *adj.* **1.** of limited extent; of small scope: *a small-scale enterprise.* **2.** being a relatively small map, model, etc., of the original and, hence, showing relatively little detail. [1850–55]

small′-scale integra′tion, *Electronics.* See **SSI.**

small′ screen′, **1.** the medium of television. **2.** a television set.

small′ slam′, *Bridge.* See **little slam.**

small′ stores′, *Navy.* personal articles of regulation issue sold to sailors by a supply officer and charged to their pay, as extra clothing. [1830–40]

small′ stuff′, *Naut.* small cordage, as marlines, yarns, etc. [1865–70]

small•sword (smôl′sôrd′, -sōrd′), *n.* a light, tapering sword for thrusting, formerly used in fencing or dueling. [1680–90; SMALL + SWORD]

small′ talk′, light conversation; chitchat. [1745–55] **—Syn.** banter, chatter, gossip.

small-talk (smôl′tôk′), *v.i.* to engage in or have a propensity for small talk. [1780–90]

small′ time′, (in vaudeville) a circuit of minor theaters giving three or more shows daily. [1920–25, *Amer.*]

small-time (smôl′tīm′), *adj.* of modest or insignificant size, importance, or influence: *a small-time politician.* [1910–15] **—small′-tim′er,** *n.*

small-town (smôl′toun′), *adj.* **1.** of, pertaining to, or characteristic of a town or village: *a typical, small-town general store.* **2.** provincial or unsophisticated: *small-town manners.* [1880–85] **—small′-town′er,** *n.*

smalt (smôlt), *n.* a coloring agent made of blue glass produced by fusing silica, potassium carbonate, and cobalt oxide, used in powdered form to add color to vitreous materials. [1550–60; < MF < It *smalto* SMALTO]

smalt•ite (smôl′tīt), *n.* a mineral, originally thought to have been a diarsenide of cobalt, $CoAs_2$, but which is actually a skutterudite rich in cobalt. Also, **smalt•ine** (smôl′tin, -tēn). [1865–70; SMALT + -ITE[1]]

smal•to (smäl′tō, smôl′-; *It.* zmäl′tô), *n., pl.* **-tos,** *It.* **-ti** (-tē). **1.** colored glass or similar vitreous material used in mosaic. **2.** a piece of this. [1695–1705; < It < Gmc; see SMELT[1], ENAMEL]

smar•agd (smar′agd), *n. Rare.* emerald. [1225–75; ME *smaragde* < OF *smaragde, esmaragde;* see EMERALD]

sma•rag•dine (smə rag′din), *adj.* **1.** of or pertaining to emeralds. **2.** emerald-green in color. **—***n.* **3.** *Rare.* smaragd. [1350–1400; ME: smaragd < L *smaragdinus* < Gk *smarágdinos,* equiv. to *smáragd(os)* EMERALD + *-inos* -INE[1]]

sma•rag•dite (smə rag′dīt), *n. Mineral.* a green, foliated member of the amphibole group. [1795–1805; < F < Gk *smáragd(os)* SMARAGD + F *-ite* -ITE[1]]

smarm•y (smär′mē), *adj.,* **smarm•i•er, smarm•i•est.** excessively or unctuously flattering, ingratiating, servile, etc.: *the emcee with the smarmy welcome.* [1905–10; *smarm,* var. of dial. *smalm* to smear, make slick (< ?) + -Y[1]] **—smarm′i•ly,** *adv.*

smart (smärt), *v., adj.,* **-er, -est,** *adv., n.* **—***v.i.* **1.** to be a source of sharp, local, and usually superficial pain, as a wound. **2.** to be the cause of a sharp, stinging pain, as an irritating application, a blow, etc. **3.** to feel a sharp, stinging pain, as in a wound. **4.** to suffer keenly from wounded feelings: *She smarted under their criticism.* **5.** to feel shame or remorse or to suffer in punishment or in return for something. **—***v.t.* **6.** to cause a sharp pain to or in. **—***adj.* **7.** quick or prompt in action, as persons. **8.** having or showing quick intelligence or ready mental capability: *a smart student.* **9.** shrewd or sharp, as a person in dealing with others or as in business dealings: *a smart businessman.* **10.** clever, witty, or readily effective, as a speaker, speech, rejoinder, etc. **11.** dashingly or impressively neat or trim in appearance, as persons, dress, etc. **12.** socially elegant; sophisticated or fashionable: *the smart crowd.* **13.** saucy; pert: *smart remarks.* **14.** sharply brisk, vigorous, or active: *to walk with smart steps.* **15.** sharply severe, as a blow, stroke, etc. **16.** sharp or keen: *a smart pain.* **17.** *Informal.* equipped with, using, or containing electronic control devices, as computer systems, microprocessors, or missiles: *a smart phone; a smart copier.* **18.** *Computers.* intelligent (def. 4). **19.** *Older Use.* considerable; fairly large. **—***adv.* **20.** in a smart manner; smartly. **—***n.* **21.** a sharp local pain, usually superficial, as from a wound, blow, or sting. **22.** keen mental suffering, as from wounded feelings, affliction, grievous loss, etc. **23.** **smarts,** *Slang.* intelligence; common sense: *He never had the smarts to use his opportunities.* [bef. 1050; (v.) ME *smerten,* OE *-smeortan* (only in the compound *fyrsmeortende* painful like fire), c. OHG *smerzan* (G *schmerzen*); (adj.) ME *smerte, smart* quick, prompt, sharp, orig., biting, smarting, late OE *smearte,* akin to the v.; (adv. and n.) ME *smerte,* deriv. of the adj.] **—smart′ing•ly,** *adv.* **—smart′ly,** *adv.* **—smart′ness,** *n.*

—Syn. 1. pain, hurt, sting. **7.** lively, nimble, agile, alert, active. **8.** bright, sharp, expert, adroit. **9.** cunning, adept. **11.** spruce; pretentious, showy. **12.** chic. **14.** energetic. **16.** stinging, poignant, penetrating. **—Ant. 8.** stupid.

smart-al•ec (smärt′al′ik), *n.* **1.** See **smart aleck.** **—***adj.* **2.** smart-alecky.

smart′ al′eck (al′ik), **1.** an obnoxiously conceited person. **2.** a wise guy. [1860–65, *Amer.;* generic use of *Aleck,* nickname for *Alexander*] **—smart′-al′eck•y, smart′-al′eck,** *adj.*

smart′ ass′, *Slang (sometimes vulgar).* a wise guy; know-it-all. Also, **smart′-ass′, smart′ass′.** [1905–10]

smart-ass (smärt′as′), *Slang (sometimes vulgar).* **—***adj.* **1.** Also, **smart′-assed′, smart′assed′.** characteristic of a smart ass or wise guy. **—***n.* **2.** See **smart ass.** [1955–60]

smart′ bomb′, *Mil. Slang.* a steerable air-to-surface bomb that is guided to its target by television or a laser beam. [1970–75]

smart•en (smär′tn), *v.t.* **1.** to make more trim or spruce; improve in appearance (usually fol. by *up*): *Try to smarten up your outfit.* **2.** to make brisker, as a pace. **3.** to sharpen the judgment or broaden the experience of; educate (usually fol. by *up*): *Someone has to smarten him up about dealing with people.* **4. smarten up, a.** to groom oneself: *to smarten up before dinner.* **b.** to become aware of one's mistakes, shortcomings, etc., and make efforts to correct them: *If you don't smarten up, you're going to be out of a job.* [1805–15; SMART + -EN[1]]

smart•ish (smär′tish), *adj.* **1.** rather smart; fairly intelligent or quick-witted: *smartish answers on a quiz.* **2.** rather fashionable; fairly chic or exclusive: *a smartish new restaurant.* **3.** fairly impressive or significant: *a smartish number of supporters at the rally.* **4.** rather saucy or pert. [1730–40; SMART + -ISH[1]]

smart′ mon′ey, **1.** money invested or wagered by experienced investors or bettors. **2.** such knowledgeable investors or bettors. **3.** *Law.* punitive or exemplary damages. [1685–95]

smart′ set′, sophisticated, fashionable people as a group: *a shop catering to the smart set.* [1885–90]

smart•weed (smärt′wēd′), *n.* any of several weeds of the genus *Polygonum,* having a smarting, acrid juice. [1780–90; SMART + WEED[1]]

smart•y (smär′tē), *n., pl.* **smart•ies.** a smart aleck. [1860–65, *Amer.;* SMART + -Y[2]]

smart•y-pants (smär′tē pants′), *n.* (*used with a singular v.*) smarty. [1915–20]

smash (smash), *v.t.* **1.** to break to pieces with violence and often with a crashing sound, as by striking, letting fall, or dashing against something; shatter: *He smashed the vase against the wall.* **2.** to defeat, disappoint, or disillusion utterly. **3.** to hit or strike (someone or something) with force. **4.** to overthrow or destroy something considered as harmful: *They smashed the drug racket.* **5.** to ruin financially: *The depression smashed him.* **6.** *Tennis, Badminton, Table Tennis.* to hit (a ball or shuttlecock) overhead or overhand with a hard downward motion, causing the shot to move very swiftly and to strike the ground or table usually at a sharp angle. **—***v.i.* **7.** to break to pieces from a violent blow or collision. **8.** to dash with a shattering or crushing force or with great violence; crash (usually fol. by *against, into, through,* etc.). **9.** to become financially ruined or bankrupt (often fol. by *up*). **10.** to flatten and compress the signatures of a book in a press before binding. **—***n.* **11.** the act or an instance of smashing or shattering. **12.** the sound of such a smash. **13.** a blow, hit, or slap. **14.** a destructive collision, as between automobiles. **15.** a smashed or shattered condition. **16.** a process or state of collapse, ruin, or destruction. **17.** financial failure or ruin. **18.** *Informal.* See **smash hit.** **19.** a drink made of brandy, or other liquor, with sugar, water, mint, and ice. **20.** *Tennis, Badminton, Table Tennis.* **a.** an overhead or overhand stroke in which the ball or shuttlecock is hit with a hard, downward motion causing it to move very swiftly and to strike the ground or table usually at a sharp angle. **b.** a ball hit with such a stroke. **—***adj.* **21.** of, relating to, or constituting a great success: *That composer has written many smash tunes.* [1690–1700; perh. b. SMACK[2] and MASH] **—smash′a•ble,** *adj.*

—Syn. 1. See **break. 5.** bankrupt. **11.** crash.

smashed (smasht), *adj. Slang.* drunk. [1955–60; SMASH + -ED[2]]

smash•er (smash′ər), *n.* **1.** a person or thing that smashes. **2.** a person or thing that is excellent, impressive, extraordinary, or the like: *That new off-Broadway show is a real smasher.* [1785–95; SMASH + -ER[1]]

smash′ hit′, a person or thing that is overwhelmingly successful or popular: *Both the play and the movie based on it were smash hits.*

smash•ing (smash′ing), *adj.* **1.** impressive or wonderful: *a smashing display.* **2.** crushing or devastating: *a smashing defeat.* [1825–35; SMASH + -ING[2]] **—smash′ing•ly,** *adv.*

smash-up (smash′up′), *n.* a complete smash, esp. a wreck of one or more vehicles. [1855–60, *Amer.;* n. use of v. phrase *smash up*]

smat•ter (smat′ər), *v.t.* **1.** to speak (a language, words, etc.) with superficial knowledge or understanding. **2.** to dabble in. **—***n.* **3.** slight or superficial knowledge; smattering. [1300–50; ME; perh. < Scand; cf. Dan, Norw *smadre* to splash, swash, Sw *smattra* to clatter, rattle; cf. MLG *smetern* to chatter]

smat•ter•ing (smat′ər ing), *n.* **1.** a slight, superficial, or introductory knowledge of something: *a smattering of Latin.* **—***adj.* **2.** slight or superficial. [1530–40; SMATTER + -ING[1], -ING[2]] **—smat′ter•ing•ly,** *adv.*

smaze (smāz), *n.* a mixture of haze and smoke. [1950–55; SM(OKE) + (H)AZE[1]]

S.M.B., Bachelor of Sacred Music.

sm. c., small capital; small capitals. Also, **sm. cap.** or **sm. caps**

SMD, senile macular degeneration.

S.M.D., Doctor of Sacred Music.

smear (smēr), *v.t.* **1.** to spread or daub (an oily, greasy, viscous, or wet substance) on or over something: *to smear butter on bread.* **2.** to spread or daub an oily, greasy, viscous, or wet substance on: *to smear bread with butter.* **3.** to stain, spot, or make dirty with something oily, greasy, viscous, or wet. **4.** to sully, vilify, or soil (a reputation, good name, etc.). **5.** to smudge or blur, as by rubbing: *The signature was smeared.* **6.** *Slang.* to defeat decisively; overwhelm: *They smeared the home team.* **—***n.* **7.** an oily, greasy, viscous, or wet substance, esp. a dab of such a substance. **8.** a stain, spot, or mark made by such a substance. **9.** a smudge. **10.** something smeared or to be smeared on a thing, as a glaze for pottery. **11.** a small quantity of something spread thinly on a slide for microscopic examination. **12.** vilification: *a smear by a cheap gossip columnist.* [bef. 900; (v.) ME *smeren, smirien* to rub with fat, anoint, OE *smirian, smerian, smerwan;* c. D *smeren,* G *schmieren,* ON *smyrja, smyrwa;* (n.) in current senses deriv. of the v.; cf. obs. *smear* fat, grease, ointment, ME *smere,* OE *smeoru,* c. D *smear,* G *Schmer,* ON *smjǫr* grease, Gk *smýris* rubbing powder; see EMERY] **—smear′er,** *n.*

smear′ campaign′, a campaign to tarnish the reputation of a public figure, esp. by vilification or innuendo.

smear•case (smēr′kās′), *n. Chiefly North Midland U.S.* any soft cheese suitable for spreading or eating with a spoon, esp. a sour cottage cheese. Also, **smier•case, schmierkase.** [1820–30, *Amer.;* half trans., half adoption of G *Schmierkäse,* equiv. to *schmier(en)* to spread, SMEAR + *Käse* CHEESE] **—Regional Variation.** See **cottage cheese.**

smear-sheet (smēr′shēt′), *n.* a newspaper, magazine, or other periodical specializing in gossip, scandal, malicious innuendo, etc. [1950–55]

smear′ word′, a slanderous, vilifying epithet.

smear•y (smēr′ē), *adj.,* **smear•i•er, smear•i•est. 1.** showing smears; smeared. **2.** tending to smear or soil. [1520–30; SMEAR + -Y[1]] **—smear′i•ness,** *n.*

Smea•ton (smēt′n), *n.* **John,** 1724–92, English engineer.

smec•tic (smek′tik), *adj. Physical Chem.* (of liquid crystals) noting a mesomorphic state in which the arrangement of the molecules is in layers or planes. Cf. **nematic.** [1665–75 for earlier sense "cleansing"; < L *smēcticus* < Gk *smēktikós,* equiv. to *smēkt(ós)* smeared, verbid of *smḗchein* to wash out, clean + *-tikos* -TIC]

smec•tite (smek′tīt′), *n. Mineral.* montmorillonite. [1805–15; < Gk *smēkt(ós)* smeared + -ITE[1]]

Smed•ley (smed′lē), *n.* a male given name.

smeg•ma (smeg′mə), *n.* a thick, cheeselike, sebaceous secretion that collects beneath the foreskin or around the clitoris. [1810–20; < L < Gk *smêgma* unguent, soap]

smell (smel), *v.,* **smelled** or **smelt, smell•ing,** *n.* **—***v.t.* **1.** to perceive the odor or scent of through the nose by means of the olfactory nerves; inhale the odor of: *I smell something burning.* **2.** to test by the sense of smell: *She smelled the meat to see if it was fresh.* **3.** to perceive, detect, or discover by shrewdness or sagacity: *The detective smelled foul play.* **—***v.i.* **4.** to perceive something by its odor or scent. **5.** to search or investigate (fol. by *around* or *about*). **6.** to give off or have an odor or scent: *Do the yellow roses smell?* **7.** to give out an offensive odor; stink. **8.** to have a particular odor (fol. by *of*): *My hands smell of fish.* **9.** to have a trace or suggestion (fol. by *of*). **10.** *Informal.* to be of inferior quality; stink: *The play is good, but the direction smells.* **11.** *Informal.* to have the appearance or a suggestion of guilt or corruption: *They may be honest, but the whole situation smells.* **12. smell a rat.** See **rat** (def. 6). **13. smell out,** to look for or detect as if by smelling; search out: *to smell out enemy spies.* **14. smell up,** to fill with an offensive odor; stink up: *The garbage smelled up the yard.* **—***n.* **15.** the sense of smell; faculty of smelling. **16.** the quality of a thing that is or may be smelled; odor; scent. **17.** a trace or suggestion. **18.** an act or instance of smelling. **19.** a pervading appearance, character, quality, or influence: *the smell of money.* [1125–75; early ME *smell, smull* (n.), *smellen, smullen* (v.) < ?] **—smell′a•ble,** *adj.* **—smell′-less,** *adj.*

—Syn. 16. See **odor.**

smell•er (smel′ər), *n.* **1.** a person who smells. **2.** a person who tests by smelling. **3.** *Informal.* the nose. **4.** a tactile hair or process, as one of the whiskers of a cat; a feeler. [1510–20; SMELL + -ER[1]]

smell′ing bot′tle, a small bottle or vial for holding smelling salts or perfume. [1765–75]

smell′ing salts′, a preparation for smelling, essentially of ammonium carbonate with some agreeable scent, used as a stimulant and restorative. [1830–40]

smell•y (smel′ē), *adj.,* **smell•i•er, smell•i•est.** emitting a strong or unpleasant odor; reeking. [1860–65; SMELL + -Y[1]] **—smell′i•ness,** *n.*

smelt[1] (smelt), *v.t.* **1.** to fuse or melt (ore) in order to separate the metal contained. **2.** to obtain or refine (metal) in this way. [1535–45; prob. < MD or MLG *smelten*; c. G *schmelzen* to MELT[1], smelt]

smelt[2] (smelt), *n., pl.* (*esp. collectively*) **smelt,** (*esp. referring to two or more kinds or species*) **smelts. 1.** any of various small, silvery food fishes of the family Osmeridae, of cold northern waters, as the rainbow smelt, *Osmerus mordax.* **2.** any of several similar but unrelated fishes, esp. certain silversides, of California. [bef. 900; ME, OE; cf. Norw *smelta* whiting]

smelt[3] (smelt), *v.* a pt. and pp. of **smell.**

smelt·er (smel′tər), *n.* **1.** a person or thing that smelts. **2.** a person who owns or works in a place where ores are smelted. **3.** a place where ores are smelted. [1425–75; late ME; see SMELT[1], -ER[1]]

smelt·er·y (smel′tə rē), *n., pl.* **-er·ies.** smelter (def. 3). [1805–15; SMELT[1] + -ERY]

Sme·ta·na (sme′tä nä; *Eng.* smet′n ə), *n.* **Be·dřich** (*Czech.* be′drzhikh), 1824–84, Czech composer.

Smeth·wick (smeth′ik), *n.* a city in West Midlands, in central England, near Birmingham. 163,388.

smew (smyo͞o), *n.* a Eurasian duck, *Mergus albellus,* closely akin to mergansers: the male is white marked with black and gray. [1665–75; orig. uncert.]

smid·gen (smij′ən), *n.* a very small amount: *a smidgen of jam for your toast.* Also, **smid′gin, smid′geon.** [1835–45; orig. uncert.]

smier·case (smēr′kās′), *n.* smearcase.

smi·lax (smī′laks), *n.* **1.** any plant belonging to the genus *Smilax,* of the lily family, growing in tropical and temperate zones, consisting mostly of vines having woody stems. **2.** a delicate, twining plant, *Asparagus asparagoides,* of the lily family, having glossy, bright-green, egg-shaped leaves, cultivated by florists. [1595–1605; < L *smīlax* bindweed < Gk *smîlax* bindweed, yew]

smile (smīl), *v.,* **smiled, smil·ing,** *n.* —*v.i.* **1.** to assume a facial expression indicating pleasure, favor, or amusement, but sometimes derision or scorn, characterized by an upturning of the corners of the mouth. **2.** to regard with favor: *Luck smiled on us that night.* **3.** to have a pleasant or agreeable appearance or aspect, as natural scenes, objects, etc.: *The landscape smiled in the sunlight.* —*v.t.* **4.** to assume or give (a smile, esp. of a given kind): *She smiled a warm and friendly smile.* **5.** to express by a smile: *to smile approval.* **6.** to bring, put, drive, etc., by or as by smiling: *to smile one's tears away.* **7. smile at, a.** to regard with pleasure or amusement, as with a smile. **b.** to regard with mild derision: *to smile at someone's affectations.* —*n.* **8.** the act or an instance of smiling; a smiling expression. **9.** favor or kindly regard: *fortune's smile.* **10.** a pleasant or agreeable appearance. [1250–1300; ME *smyllen* (v.); c. OHG *smīlan,* Dan *smile*] —**smile′less,** *adj.* —**smile′less·ly,** *adv.* —**smile′less·ness,** *n.* —**smil′er,** *n.* —**smil′ing·ly,** *adv.*
—**Syn. 1, 8.** See **laugh.** —**Ant. 1, 8.** frown.

smile′ face′, a drawing of a face consisting of a yellow circle with an upturned curve for a smile and two dots for eyes. Also, **smil′ey face′.**

smi·lo·don (smī′lə don′), *n.* any of several saber-toothed cats of the extinct genus *Smilodon,* that ranged from California through most of South America during the Pleistocene Epoch and had upper canine teeth more than 6 in. (15 cm) long. See illus. under **saber-toothed tiger.** [< NL (1842) < Gk *smíl*(*ē*) knife + *-odōn* -tooth, having teeth (see -ODONT)]

smirch (smûrch), *v.t.* **1.** to discolor or soil; spot or smudge with or as with soot, dust, dirt, etc. **2.** to sully or tarnish (a person, reputation, character, etc.); disgrace; discredit. —*n.* **3.** a dirty mark or smear, as of soot, dust, dirt, etc. **4.** a stain or blot, as on reputation. [1485–95; orig. uncert.] —**smirch′less,** *adj.*
—**Syn. 1.** smear, smut, dirty. **2.** taint, blot. **3.** smudge, smut, smutch. **4.** taint. —**Ant. 1.** clean.

smirk (smûrk), *v.i.* **1.** to smile in an affected, smug, or offensively familiar way. —*n.* **2.** the facial expression of a person who smirks. [bef. 900; ME *smirken* (v.), OE *sme(a)rcian*] —**smirk′er,** *n.* —**smirk′ing·ly,** *adv.*

smitch (smich), *n. Informal.* smidgen. [1830–40; orig. uncert.]

smite (smīt), *v.,* **smote** or (*Obs.*) **smit; smit·ten** or **smit; smit·ing.** —*v.t.* **1.** to strike or hit hard, with or as with the hand, a stick, or other weapon. **2.** to deliver or deal (a blow, hit, etc.) by striking hard. **3.** to strike down, injure, or slay: *His sword had smitten thousands.* **4.** to afflict or attack with deadly or disastrous effect: *smitten by polio.* **5.** to affect mentally or morally with a sudden pang: *His conscience smote him.* **6.** to affect suddenly and strongly with a specified feeling: *They were smitten with terror.* **7.** to impress favorably; charm; enamor: *He was smitten by her charms.* —*v.i.* **8.** to strike; deal a blow. **9. smite hip and thigh.** See **hip**[1] (def. 6). [bef. 900; ME *smiten,* OE *smītan*; c. G *schmeissen* to throw, D *smijten*] —**smit′er,** *n.*
—**Syn. 1.** knock, cuff, buffet, slap.

smith (smith), *n.* **1.** a worker in metal. **2.** a blacksmith. —*v.t.* **3.** to forge on an anvil; form by heating and pounding: *to smith armor.* [bef. 900; (n.) ME, OE; c. G *Schmied,* ON *smithr,* Goth *-smitha*; (v.) ME *smithen,* OE *smithian*; c. ON *smitha,* Goth *gasmithōn*]

Smith (smith), *n.* **1. Adam,** 1723–90, Scottish economist. **2. Alfred E(manuel),** 1873–1944, U.S. political leader. **3. Bessie,** 1894?–1937, U.S. singer. **4. Charles Henry** (*"Bill Arp"*), 1826–1903, U.S. humorist. **5. David,** 1906–65, U.S. sculptor. **6. Edmond Kir·by** (kûr′bē), 1824–93, Confederate general in the Civil War. **7. Francis Hopkinson,** 1838–1915, U.S. novelist, painter, and engineer. **8. George,** 1840–76, English archaeologist and Assyriologist. **9. Ian Douglas** born 1919, Rhodesian political leader: prime minister 1964–79. **10. John,** 1580–1631, English adventurer and colonist in Virginia. **11. Joseph,** 1805–44, U.S. religious leader: founded the Mormon Church. **12. Lo·gan Pear·sall** (lō′gən pēr′sôl), 1865–1946, U.S. essayist in England. **13. Margaret Chase,** 1897–1995, U.S. politician. **14. Oliver,** born 1918, U.S. set designer and theatrical producer. **15. Red** (*Walter Wellesley Smith*), 1905–82, U.S. sports journalist. **16. Sydney,** 1771–1845, English clergyman, writer, and wit. **17. Tony,** 1912–80, U.S. sculptor. **18. William,** 1769–1839, English geologist. **19.** a male given name.

smith·er·eens (smith′ə rēnz′), *n.pl.* small pieces; bits: *broken into smithereens.* Also, **smith·ers** (smith′ərz). [1820–30; dial. *smithers* (< ?) + Hiberno-E *-een* dim. suffix (< Ir *-ín*)]

smith·er·y (smith′ə rē), *n., pl.* **-er·ies.** the work, craft, or workshop of a smith. [1615–25; SMITH + -ERY]

Smith·field (smith′fēld′), *n.* a town in N Rhode Island. 16,886.

Smith′field ham′, *Trademark.* See **Virginia ham.**

Smith·son (smith′sən), *n.* **James,** 1765–1829, English chemist and mineralogist.

Smith·so′ni·an Institu′tion (smith sō′nē ən), an institution in Washington, D.C., founded 1846 with a grant left by James Smithson, for the increase and diffusion of knowledge: U.S. national museum and repository.

smith·son·ite (smith′sə nīt′), *n. Mineral.* a native carbonate of zinc, $ZnCO_3$, that is an important ore of the metal. [1825–35; named after J. SMITHSON (who distinguished it from calamine); see -ITE[1]]

Smith·town (smith′toun′), *n.* a city on N Long Island, in SE New York. 30,906.

smith·y (smith′ē, smith′ē), *n., pl.* **smith·ies. 1.** the workshop of a smith, esp. a blacksmith. **2.** a blacksmith. [1250–1300; ME *smithi* < ON *smithja*; akin to OE *smiththe.* See SMITH]

smit·ten (smit′n), *adj.* **1.** struck, as with a hard blow. **2.** grievously or disastrously stricken or afflicted. **3.** very much in love. —*v.* **4.** a pp. of **smite.** [1200–50; ME; see SMITE, -EN[3]]

Smit·ty (smit′ē), *n.* a male given name, form of **Smith.**

S.M.M., Master of Sacred Music.

smock (smok), *n.* **1.** a loose, lightweight overgarment worn to protect the clothing while working. —*v.t.* **2.** to clothe in a smock. **3.** to draw (a fabric) by needlework into a honeycomb pattern with diamond-shaped recesses. [bef. 1000; ME (n.), OE *smocc*; orig. name for a garment with a hole for the head; cf. ON *smjūga* to put on (a garment) over the head] —**smock′like′,** *adj.*

smock′ frock′, a loose overgarment of linen or cotton, as that worn by European farm laborers. Cf. **blouse** (def. 3). [1790–1800]

smock·ing (smok′ing), *n.* **1.** smocked needlework. **2.** embroidery stitches used to hold gathered cloth in even folds. [1885–90; SMOCK + -ING[1]]

smock′ mill′, a windmill with sails and shaft carried by a cap rotating on an octagonal tower. [1795–1805]

smog (smog, smôg), *n.* **1.** smoke or other atmospheric pollutants combined with fog in an unhealthy or irritating mixture. **2.** See **photochemical smog.** —*v.t.* **3.** to cover or envelop with or as if with smog. [1900–05; SM(OKE) + (F)OG[1]] —**smog′less,** *adj.*

smog·bound (smog′bound′, smôg′-), *adj. Meteorol.* surrounded by smog. [SMOG + -BOUND[1]]

smog·gy (smog′ē, smô′gē), *adj.,* **-gi·er, -gi·est.** full of or characterized by smog. [1925–30; SMOG + -Y[1]]

smok·a·ble (smō′kə bəl), *adj.* **1.** suitable for being smoked. —*n.* **2.** Usually, **smokables.** things for smoking, as cigars or cigarettes. Also, **smoke′a·ble.** [1830–40; SMOKE + -ABLE]

smoke (smōk), *n., v.,* **smoked, smok·ing.** —*n.* **1.** the visible vapor and gases given off by a burning or smoldering substance, esp. the gray, brown, or blackish mixture of gases and suspended carbon particles resulting from the combustion of wood or other organic matter. **2.** something resembling this, as vapor or mist. **3.** something unsubstantial, evanescent, or without result: *Their hopes and dreams proved to be smoke.* **4.** an obscuring condition: *the smoke of controversy.* **5.** an act or spell of smoking something, esp. tobacco: *They had a smoke during the intermission.* **6.** something for smoking, as a cigar or cigarette: *This is the best smoke on the market.* **7.** *Slang.* marijuana. **8.** *Slang.* a homemade drink consisting of denatured alcohol and water. **9.** *Physics, Chem.* a system of solid particles suspended in a gaseous medium. **10.** a bluish or brownish gray color. **11. go up** or **end in smoke,** to terminate without producing a result; be unsuccessful: *All our dreams went up in smoke.* —*v.i.* **12.** to give off or emit smoke, as in burning. **13.** to give out smoke offensively or improperly, as a stove. **14.** to send forth steam or vapor, dust, or the like. **15.** to draw into the mouth and puff out the smoke of tobacco or the like, as from a pipe or cigarette. **16.** *Slang.* to ride or travel with great speed. **17.** *Australian.* **a.** to flee. **b.** to abscond. —*v.t.* **18.** to draw into the mouth and puff out the smoke of: *to smoke tobacco.* **19.** to use (a pipe, cigarette, etc.) in this process. **20.** to expose to smoke. **21.** to fumigate (rooms, furniture, etc.). **22.** to cure (meat, fish, etc.) by exposure to smoke. **23.** to color or darken by smoke. **24. smoke out, a.** to drive from a refuge by means of smoke. **b.** to force into public view or knowledge; reveal: *to smoke out the leaders of the spy ring.* [bef. 1000; (n.) ME; OE *smoca*; (v.) ME *smoken,* OE *smocian*] —**smoke′like′,** *adj.*

smoke′ and mir′rors, (*used with a sing. or pl. v.*) something that distorts or blurs facts, figures, etc., like a magic or conjuring trick; artful deception. [1980–85]

smoke′ bomb′, a bomb that produces a continuous discharge of smoke rather than an explosion, used to mark a target for aerial attack, indicate wind direction, produce a smoke screen, etc. [1915–20]

smoke′ cham′ber, an enlarged area between the throat of a fireplace and the chimney flue.

smoke·chas·er (smōk′chā′sər), *n.* a person who fights forest fires, esp. one with lightweight equipment. [SMOKE + CHASER[1]]

smoke′ detec′tor, an electronic fire alarm that is activated by the presence of smoke. Also called **smoke′ alarm′.** [1925–30]

smoke′ dome′, the smoke chamber covering of a prefabricated metal fireplace unit.

smoke-dry (smōk′drī′), *v.,* **-dried, -dry·ing.** —*v.t.* **1.** to dry or cure (meat or other food) using smoke. —*v.i.* **2.** to become dried by smoke: *to be eaten as soon as it smoke-dries.* [1695–1705]

smoke-eat·er (smōk′ē′tər), *n. Slang.* a firefighter. [1925–30]

smoke′-filled room′ (smōk′fild′, -fīld′), a place, as a hotel room, for conducting secret negotiations, effecting compromises, devising strategy, etc. [1915–20]

smoke·house (smōk′hous′), *n., pl.* **-hous·es** (-hou′ziz). a building or place in which meat, fish, etc., are cured with smoke. [1565–75; SMOKE + HOUSE]

smoke·jack (smōk′jak′), *n.* an apparatus for turning a roasting spit, set in motion by the current of ascending gases in a chimney. [1665–75; SMOKE + JACK[1]]

smoke·jump·er (smōk′jum′pər), *n.* a firefighter who parachutes to forest fires inaccessible to ground crews. [1925–30; SMOKE + JUMPER[1]]

smoke·less (smōk′lis), *adj.* emitting, producing, or having little or no smoke. [1575–80; SMOKE + -LESS] —**smoke′less·ly,** *adv.* —**smoke′less·ness,** *n.*

smoke′less pow′der, any of various substitutes for ordinary gunpowder that give off little or no smoke, esp. one composed wholly or mostly of guncotton. [1885–90]

smoke′less tobac′co, 1. snuff[1] (def. 9). **2.** See **chewing tobacco.**

smoke·out (smōk′out′), *n.* a day during which smokers are encouraged to abstain from smoking as part of a campaign to emphasize the hazards of the practice. [patterned on phrasal verbs with OUT as a perfective particle, as *put out, stamp out,* etc.]

smoke′ pot′, a can of chemicals that produces a great quantity of smoke when ignited.

smoke·proof (smōk′pro͞of′), *adj.* that cannot be penetrated by smoke: *a fireproof and smokeproof compartment.* [1900–05; SMOKE + -PROOF]

smok·er (smō′kər), *n.* **1.** a person or thing that smokes. **2.** *Railroads.* **a.** Also called **smoking car.** a passenger car for those who wish to smoke. **b.** a compartment for those who wish to smoke. **3.** an informal gathering, esp. of men, for entertainment, discussion, or the like. **4.** an enclosed metal box or similar device for smoking meats, poultry, or fish. **5.** See **smoking stand. 6.** *Brit.* smoking-concert. [1590–1600; SMOKE + -ER[1]]

smok′er's tongue′, *Pathol.* leukoplakia in the mouth caused by irritation due to smoking. Also called **smok′er's patch′es.**

smoke′ screen′, 1. a mass of dense smoke produced to conceal an area, vessel, or plane from the enemy. **2.** something intended to disguise, conceal, or deceive; camouflage. [1910–15]

smoke′ shelf′, a ledge at the bottom of a smoke chamber, so made as to deflect or break downdrafts from the chimney. Also called **wind shelf.**

smoke′ shop′, 1. a shop selling tobacco products. **2.** *Slang.* **a.** a place where marijuana or other illicit drugs are sold surreptitiously. **b.** See **head shop.** [1790–1800]

smoke·stack (smōk′stak′), *n.* **1.** Also called **stack.** a pipe for the escape of the smoke or gases of combustion, as on a steamboat, locomotive, or building. —*adj.* **2.** pertaining to, engaged in, or dependent on a basic heavy industry, as steel or automaking: *smokestack companies.* [1855–60; SMOKE + STACK]

smoke′ tree′, 1. Also called **American smoke tree, chittamwood.** a tree, *Cotinus obovatus,* of the cashew family, native to the southeastern U.S., having egg-shaped leaves and large clusters of small white flowers. **2.** Also called **Venetian sumac.** a related shrub, *C. coggygria,* of Eurasia, having elliptical leaves and clusters of hairy, purple flowers. [1840–50]

smok·ey (smō′kē), *n., pl.* **-eys.** (*often cap.*) *Slang.* **1.** an officer or officers of a state highway patrol. **2.** a state police car. Also called **Smok′ey Bear′.** [1970–75, *Amer.*; shortened from *Smokey the Bear,* a cartoon figure used in the U. S. Forest Service's fire prevention campaign, depicted wearing a hat similar to those worn by state police officers]

smok′ing car′, smoker (def. 2a). [1855–60, *Amer.*]

smok·ing-con·cert (smō′king kon′sərt), *n. Brit.* a concert where smoking is allowed. [1885–90]

smok′ing gun′, indisputable proof or evidence of a crime. [1970–75]

smok′ing jack′et, a loose-fitting jacket for men, often of a heavy fabric and trimmed with braid, worn indoors, esp. as a lounging jacket. [1875–80]

smok′ing lamp′, formerly, a lamp aboard ship for lighting pipes, now used figuratively to indicate when smoking is or is not allowed: *The smoking lamp is lit.* [1880–85]

smok′ing room′, a room set apart for smoking, as in a hotel or clubhouse. [1680–90]

smok′ing stand′, an ashtray mounted on a low pedestal, often placed next to an armchair, sofa, etc. Also called **smoker.**

smok·o (smō′kō), *n., pl.* **smok·os.** *Australia and New Zealand Informal.* **1.** a rest period during work. **2.** an

CONCISE ETYMOLOGY KEY: <, descended or borrowed from; >, whence; b., blend of, blended; c., cognate with; cf., compare; deriv., derivative; equiv., equivalent; imit., imitative; obl., oblique; r., replacing; s., stem; sp., spelling, spelled; resp., respelling, respelled; trans., translation; ?, origin unknown; *, unattested; ‡, probably earlier than. See the full key inside the front cover.

informal evening entertainment, esp. for males. Also, **smoke′-oh.** [1895–1900; SMOKE + -O]

smok·y (smō′kē), *adj.,* **smok·i·er, smok·i·est. 1.** emitting smoke, esp. in large amounts. **2.** hazy; darkened or begrimed with smoke. **3.** having the character or appearance of smoke: *smoky colors.* **4.** pertaining to or suggestive of smoke: *a smoky haze.* **5.** of a dull or brownish gray; cloudy. [1275–1325; ME; see SMOKE, -Y[1]] —**smok′i·ly,** *adv.* —**smok′i·ness,** *n.*

Smok′y Hill′, a river flowing E from E Colorado to the Republican River in central Kansas. 540 mi. (870 km) long.

Smok′y Moun′tains. See **Great Smoky Mountains.**

smok′y quartz′, a smoky-yellow to dark brown or black variety of quartz, used as a gem. Also called **cairngorm, Cairngorm stone.** [1830–40]

smok′y to′paz, *Jewelry.* smoky quartz used as a gemstone: not a true topaz. [1790–1800]

smol·der (smōl′dər), *v.i.* **1.** to burn without flame; undergo slow or suppressed combustion. **2.** to exist or continue in a suppressed state or without outward demonstration: *Hatred smoldered beneath a polite surface.* **3.** to display repressed feelings, as of indignation, anger, or the like: *to smolder with rage.* —*n.* **4.** dense smoke resulting from slow or suppressed combustion. **5.** a smoldering fire. Also, **smoulder.** [1275–1325; (n.) ME *smolder* smoky vapor, dissimilated var. of *smorther* SMOTHER; (v.) ME (as prp. *smolderende*), deriv. of the n.]

Smo·lensk (smō lensk′, *Russ.* smu lyensk′), *n.* a city in the W Russian Federation in Europe, on the upper Dnieper, SW of Moscow: Russians defeated by Napoleon 1812. 338,000.

Smol·lett (smol′it), *n.* **Tobias George,** 1721–71, English novelist.

smolt (smōlt), *n.* a young, silvery salmon in the stage of its first migration to the sea. [1425–75; late ME; perh. akin to SMELT[2]]

S.M.O.M., Sovereign and Military Order of Malta.

smooch[1] (smo͞och), *v.t., n.* smutch.

smooch[2] (smo͞och), *Informal.* —*v.i.* **1.** to kiss. **2.** to pet. —*n.* **3.** a kiss; smack. [1580–90; var. of obs. *smouch* to kiss < ?; cf. dial. G *schmutzen* to kiss, smile] —**smooch′er,** *n.*

smoodge (smo͞oj), *v.i.,* **smoodged, smoodg·ing.** *Australian.* to curry favor; seek unwarranted recognition. [1895–1900; perh. alter. of SMOOCH[2]] —**smoodg′er,** *n.*

smooth (smo͞oth), *adj.,* **-er, -est,** *adv., v., n.* —*adj.* **1.** free from projections or unevenness of surface; not rough: *smooth wood; a smooth road.* **2.** generally flat or unruffled, as a calm sea. **3.** free from hairs or a hairy growth: *a smooth cheek.* **4.** of uniform consistency; free from lumps, as a batter, sauce, etc. **5.** free from or proceeding without abrupt curves, bends, etc.: *a smooth ride.* **6.** allowing or having an even, uninterrupted movement or flow: *smooth driving.* **7.** easy and uniform, as motion or the working of a machine. **8.** having projections worn away: *a smooth tire casing.* **9.** free from hindrances or difficulties: *a smooth day at the office.* **10.** noting a metal file having the minimum commercial grade of coarseness for a single-cut file. Cf. **dead-smooth. 11.** undisturbed, tranquil, or equable, as the feelings, temper, etc.; serene: *a smooth disposition.* **12.** elegant, easy, or polished: *smooth manners.* **13.** ingratiatingly polite or suave: *That salesman is a smooth talker.* **14.** free from harshness, sharpness, or bite; bland or mellow, as cheese or wine. **15.** not harsh to the ear, as sound: *the smooth music of a ballroom dance band.* **16.** *Phonet.* without aspiration.
—*adv.* **17.** in a smooth manner; smoothly.
—*v.t.* **18.** to make smooth of surface, as by scraping, planing, or pressing. **19.** to remove (projections, ridges, wrinkles, etc.) in making something smooth (often fol. by *away* or *out*). **20.** to free from difficulties. **21.** to remove (obstacles) from a path (often fol. by *away*). **22.** to make more polished, elegant, or agreeable, as wording or manners. **23.** to tranquilize, calm, or soothe (a person, the feelings, etc.). **24.** *Math.* to simplify (an expression) by substituting approximate or certain known values for the variables. **25. smooth over,** to make seem less severe, disagreeable, or irreconcilable; allay; mitigate: *He smoothed over my disappointment with kind words.*
—*n.* **26.** act of smoothing: *She adjusted the folds with a smooth of her hand.* **27.** something that is smooth; a smooth part or place: *through the rough and the smooth.* [bef. 1050; (adj.) ME *smothe,* late OE *smōth;* cf. ME *smethe,* OE *smēthe* smooth; c. OS *smōthi;* (v.) late ME *smothen,* deriv. of the adj.; r. ME *smethen,* OE *smēth(i)an*] —**smooth′a·ble,** *adj.* —**smooth′er,** *n.* —**smooth′ly,** *adv.* —**smooth′ness,** *n.*
—**Syn. 1.** glossy, polished, even, flat. See **level.**

smooth·bore (smo͞oth′bôr′, -bōr′), *adj.* **1.** (of firearms) having a smooth bore; not rifled. —*n.* **2.** a smoothbore gun. [1790–1800; SMOOTH + BORE[1]]

smooth′ breath′ing, a symbol (′) used in the writing of Greek to indicate that the initial vowel over which it is placed is unaspirated. Cf. **rough breathing.** [1740–50]

smooth′ dog′fish, any of several requiem sharks having no spines in front of the dorsal fin, esp. *Mustelus canis,* ranging along the American coast of the Atlantic Ocean.

smooth·en (smo͞o′thən), *v.t., v.i.* to make or become smooth. [1625–35; SMOOTH + -EN[1]]

smooth′ endoplas′mic retic′ulum. See under **endoplasmic reticulum.**

smooth-faced (smo͞oth′fāst′), *adj.* **1.** beardless; smooth-shaven. **2.** having a smooth or polished surface, as a stone. **3.** deceitfully ingratiating. [1570–80]

smooth·hound (smo͞oth′hound′), *n.* a smooth dogfish, esp. *Mustelus mustelus,* inhabiting waters along the coast of Europe. Also called **smooth′hound shark′.** [1595–1605; SMOOTH + HOUND[1]]

smooth·ie (smo͞o′thē), *n. Informal.* a person who has a winningly polished manner: *He's such a smoothie he could charm the stripes off a tiger.* Also, **smoothy.** [1920–25; SMOOTH + -IE]

smooth′ mus′cle, *Anat.* involuntary muscle tissue in the walls of viscera and blood vessels, consisting of nonstriated, spindle-shaped cells. [1885–90]

smooth-shav·en (smo͞oth′shā′vən), *adj.* having the beard and mustache shaved off; clean-shaven. [1625–35]

smooth-spo·ken (smo͞oth′spō′kən), *adj.* speaking or spoken easily and softly. [1815–25]

smooth′ su′mac, a shrub or small tree, *Rhus glabra,* of the cashew family, native to North America, having pinnate leaves and green flowers in a dense terminal cluster. [1805–15, *Amer.*]

smooth-talk (smo͞oth′tôk′), *v.t.* to persuade by flattery, cajolery, coaxing, or the like: *We smooth-talked the company into a huge donation.*

smooth-tongued (smo͞oth′tungd′), *adj.* fluent or convincing in speech; glib. [1585–95]

smooth·y (smo͞o′thē), *n., pl.* **smooth·ies.** smoothie.

smor·gas·bord (smôr′gəs bôrd′, -bōrd′ *or, often,* shmôr′-), *n.* **1.** a buffet meal of various hot and cold hors d'oeuvres, salads, casserole dishes, meats, cheeses, etc. **2.** an extensive array or variety: *The company has a smorgasbord of employee benefits.* Also, **smör·gås·bord** (*Swed.* smœr′gôs bo͞ord′). [1915–20; < Sw *smörgåsbord,* equiv. to *smörgås* sandwich + *bord* table]

smor·zan·do (smôrt sän′dō; *It.* zmôr tsän′dô), *adj. Music.* fading away; dying out (a musical direction). [1790–1800; < It, ger. of *smorzare* to extinguish]

smote (smōt), *v.* a pt. of **smite.**

smoth·er (smuth′ər), *v.t.* **1.** to stifle or suffocate, as by smoke or other means of preventing free breathing. **2.** to extinguish or deaden (fire, coals, etc.) by covering so as to exclude air. **3.** to cover closely or thickly; envelop: *to smother a steak with mushrooms.* **4.** to suppress or repress: *to smother feelings.* **5.** *Cookery.* to steam (food) slowly in a heavy, tightly closed vessel with a minimum of liquid: *smothered chicken and onions.* —*v.i.* **6.** to become stifled or suffocated; be prevented from breathing. **7.** to be stifled; be suppressed or concealed. —*n.* **8.** dense, stifling smoke. **9.** a smoking or smoldering state, as of burning matter. **10.** dust, fog, spray, etc., in a dense or enveloping cloud. **11.** an overspreading profusion of anything: *a smother of papers.* [1125–75; (n.) ME *smorther* dense smoke; akin to OE *smorian* to suffocate; (v.) ME *smo(r)theren,* deriv. of the n.] —**smoth′er·a·ble,** *adj.*

smoth′ered mate′, *Chess.* checkmate delivered by a knight when the king's mobility is restricted by his own pieces. [1815–25]

smoth·er·y (smuth′ə rē), *adj.* stifling; close: *a smothery atmosphere.* [1595–1605; SMOTHER + -Y[1]]

smoul·der (smōl′dər), *v.i., n.* smolder.

Smrit·i (smrit′ē), *n. Hinduism.* writings containing traditions concerning law, rituals, teachings of the sages, the epics, and the Puranas. [< Skt *smṛti*]

SMS, Synchronous Meteorological Satellite.

SMSA, Standard Metropolitan Statistical Area.

smudge (smuj), *n., v.,* **smudged, smudg·ing.** —*n.* **1.** a dirty mark or smear. **2.** a smeary state. **3.** a stifling smoke. **4.** a smoky fire, esp. one made for driving away mosquitoes or safeguarding fruit trees from frost. —*v.t.* **5.** to mark with dirty streaks or smears. **6.** to fill with smudge, as to drive away insects or protect fruit trees from frost. —*v.i.* **7.** to form a smudge on something. **8.** to become smudged: *White shoes smudge easily.* **9.** to smolder or smoke; emit smoke, as a smudge pot. [1400–50; late ME *smogen* (v.) < ?] —**smudg′ed·ly,** *adv.* —**smudge′less,** *adj.*

smudge′ pot′, a container for burning oil or other fuels to produce smudge, as for protecting fruit trees from frost. [1880–85]

smudg·y (smuj′ē), *adj.,* **smudg·i·er, smudg·i·est. 1.** marked with smudges; smeared; smeary. **2.** emitting a stifling smoke; smoky. **3.** *Brit. Dial.* humid; sweltering; sultry. [1840–50; SMUDGE + -Y[1]] —**smudg′i·ly,** *adv.* —**smudg′i·ness,** *n.*

smug (smug), *adj.,* **smug·ger, smug·gest. 1.** contentedly confident of one's ability, superiority, or correctness; complacent. **2.** trim; spruce; smooth; sleek. [1545–55; perh. < MD *smuc* neat, pretty, nice] —**smug′ly,** *adv.* —**smug′ness,** *n.*

smug·gle (smug′əl), *v.,* **-gled, -gling.** —*v.t.* **1.** to import or export (goods) secretly, in violation of the law, esp. without payment of legal duty. **2.** to bring, take, put, etc., surreptitiously: *She smuggled the gun into the jail inside a cake.* —*v.i.* **3.** to import, export, or convey goods surreptitiously or in violation of the law. [1680–90; < LG *smuggeln;* c. G *schmuggeln*] —**smug′gler,** *n.*

smush (smush, smo͝osh), *v.t. Informal.* to mash or push, esp. to push down or in; compress: *to smush a pie in someone's face.* [1910–15; prob. b. SMASH and MUSH[1]]

smut (smut), *n., v.,* **smut·ted, smut·ting.** —*n.* **1.** a particle of soot; sooty matter. **2.** a black or dirty mark; smudge. **3.** indecent language or publications; obscenity. **4.** *Plant Pathol.* **a.** a disease of plants, esp. cereal grasses, characterized by the conversion of affected parts into black, powdery masses of spores, caused by fungi of the order Ustilaginales. **b.** a fungus causing this disease. —*v.t.* **5.** to soil or smudge. —*v.i.* **6.** to become affected with smut, as a plant. [1580–90; akin to earlier *smit* (OE *smitte*), by assoc. with SMUDGE, SMUTCH]

smutch (smuch), *v.t.* **1.** to smudge or soil. —*n.* **2.** a smudge or stain. **3.** dirt, grime, or smut. Also, **smooch.** [1520–30; perh. < MHG *smutzen* to smear; cf. G *Schmutz* SMUT] —**smutch′less,** *adj.*

smutch·y (smuch′ē), *adj.,* **smutch·i·er, smutch·i·est.** of or pertaining to smutch; dirty; grimy; soiled; smudged. [1570–80; SMUTCH + -Y[1]]

Smuts (*Du.* smœts; *Eng.* smuts), *n.* **Jan Chris·ti·aan** (*Du.* yän kris′tē än′), 1870–1950, South African statesman and general: prime minister 1919–24, 1939–48.

smut·ty (smut′ē), *adj.,* **-ti·er, -ti·est. 1.** soiled with smut; grimy. **2.** indecent or obscene, as talk or writing: *a smutty novel.* **3.** given to indecent or obscene talk, writing, etc., as a person. **4.** (of plants) affected with smut. [1590–1600; SMUT + -Y[1]] —**smut′ti·ly,** *adv.* —**smut′ti·ness,** *n.*

Smyr·na (smûr′nə), *n.* **1.** former name of **Izmir. 2. Gulf of,** former name of the Gulf of Izmir. **3.** a city in NW Georgia: suburb of Atlanta. 20,312. **4.** *Class. Myth.* Myrrha.

Smyr′na fig′, a variety of the common fig, *Ficus carica,* that requires caprification in order to produce fruit.

Smyr·ne·an (smûr′nē ən), *adj.* of or pertaining to Smyrna, Turkey. [1590–1600; < L *Smyrnae(us)* of SMYRNA + -AN]

Smyth (smith), *n.* **1st Baron.** See **Baden-Powell, Robert Stephenson Smyth.**

Smyth′ sew′ing (smith, smīth), *Bookbinding.* a method of sewing together folded, gathered, and collated signatures with a single thread sewn through the folds of individual signatures. Also, **Smythe′ sew′ing.** [after David M. *Smyth* (1833–1907), Irish-born U.S. inventor, who designed a machine performing this kind of sewing] —**Smyth′-sewn′,** *adj.*

SN, Secretary of the Navy.

Sn, *Symbol, Chem.* tin. [< L *stannum*]

snack (snak), *n.* **1.** a small portion of food or drink or a light meal, esp. one eaten between regular meals. **2.** a share or portion. **3.** *Australian Slang.* something easily done. **4. go snack** or **snacks,** to share (profits or returns). —*v.i.* **5.** to have a snack or light meal, esp. between regular meals: *They snacked on tea and cake.* [1300–50; (n.) ME: a snap or bite, deriv. of *snacken* to snap, bite; cf. MD *snack* a snap; (v.) deriv. of the n.]

snack′ bar′, a lunchroom or restaurant where light meals are sold. [1890–95]

snack′ ta′ble, a small portable folding table used for an individual serving. Also called **TV table.**

snaf·fle[1] (snaf′əl), *n., v.,* **-fled, -fling.** —*n.* **1.** Also called **snaf′fle bit′,** a bit, usually jointed in the middle and without a curb, with a large ring at each end to which a rein and cheek strap are attached. —*v.t.* **2.** to put a snaffle on (a horse). **3.** to control with or as with a snaffle. [1525–35; orig. uncert.; cf. OFris *snavel* mouth, D *snavel,* G *Schnabel* beak, bill]

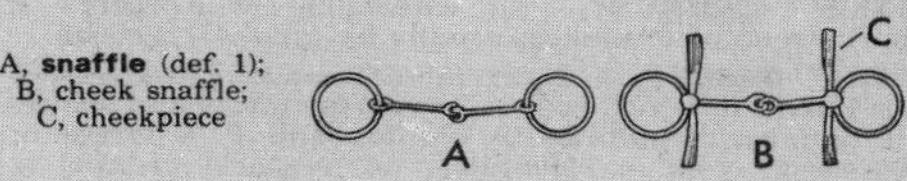

A, **snaffle** (def. 1); B, cheek snaffle; C, cheekpiece

snaf·fle[2] (snaf′əl), *v.t.,* **-fled, -fling.** *Brit. Informal.* to appropriate for one's own use, esp. by devious means; purloin; filch. [1715–25; orig. uncert.]

sna·fu (sna fo͞o′, snaf′o͞o), *n., adj., v.,* **-fued, -fu·ing.** —*n.* **1.** a badly confused or ridiculously muddled situation. —*adj.* **2.** in disorder; out of control; chaotic. —*v.t.* **3.** to throw into disorder; muddle. [1940–45; *s(ituation) n(ormal): a(ll) f(ucked) u(p);* sometimes euphemistically construed as *f(ouled) (u)p*]

snag (snag), *n., v.,* **snagged, snag·ging.** —*n.* **1.** a tree or part of a tree held fast in the bottom of a river, lake, etc., and forming an impediment or danger to navigation. **2.** a short, projecting stump, as of a branch broken or cut off. **3.** any sharp or rough projection. **4.** a jagged hole, tear, pull, or run in a fabric, as caused by catching on a sharp projection. **5.** any obstacle or impediment. **6.** a stump of a tooth or a projecting tooth; snaggletooth. —*v.t.* **7.** to run or catch up on a snag. **8.** to damage by so doing. **9.** to obstruct or impede, as a snag does: *He snagged all my efforts.* **10.** to grab; seize: *to snag the last piece of pie.* —*v.i.* **11.** to become entangled with some obstacle or hindrance. **12.** to become tangled: *This line snags every time I cast.* **13.** (of a boat) to strike a snag. **14.** to form a snag. [1570–80; < ON *snagi* point, projection] —**snag′like′,** *adj.*

snag·gle·tooth (snag′əl to͞oth′), *n., pl.* **-teeth.** a tooth growing out beyond or apart from others. [1815–25; appar. SNAG + -LE + TOOTH] —**snag·gle-toothed** (snag′əl to͞otht′, -to͞othd′), *adj.*

snag·gy (snag′ē), *adj.,* **-gi·er, -gi·est. 1.** having snags or sharp projections, as a tree. **2.** abounding in snags or obstructions, as a river. **3.** snaglike; projecting sharply or roughly. [1575–85; SNAG + -Y[1]]

snail (snāl), *n.* **1.** any mollusk of the class Gastropoda, having a spirally coiled shell and a ventral muscular foot on which it slowly glides about. **2.** a slow or lazy person; sluggard. **3.** a cam having the form of a spiral. **4.** *Midwestern and Western U.S.* a sweet roll in spiral form, esp. a cinnamon roll or piece of Danish pastry. [bef. 900; ME *snail, snayl(e),* OE *snegel;* c. LG *snagel,* G (dial.) *Schnegel*] —**snail′like′,** *adj.*

snail, *Liguus fasciatus,* shell length to 3 in. (8 cm)

CONCISE PRONUNCIATION KEY: act, cāpe, dâre, pärt; set, ēqual; if, īce; ox, ōver, ôrder, oil, bo͝ok, bo͞ot, out; up, ûrge; child; sing; shoe; thin, that; zh as in *treasure.* ə = *a* as in *alone, e* as in *system, i* as in *easily, o* as in *gallop, u* as in *circus;* ᵊ as in *fire* (fīᵊr), *hour* (ouᵊr). l and n can serve as syllabic consonants, as in *cradle* (krād′l), and *button* (but′n). See the full key inside the front cover.

snail′ dart′er, a tan, striped, snail-eating perch, *Percina tanasi,* 3 in. (7.5 cm) long, occurring only in the Tennessee River: a threatened species. [1970–75]

snail′ fe′ver, schistosomiasis. [1945–50; so called because the parasites that cause the disease are carried by snails]

snail•fish (snāl′fish′), *n., pl.* (*esp. collectively*) **-fish,** (*esp. referring to two or more kinds or species*) **-fish•es.** any of several elongate, smooth-skinned fishes of the family Liparididae, inhabiting cold seas, having the ventral fins modified to form a sucking disk. [1830–40; SNAIL + FISH]

snail•flow•er (snāl′flou′ər), *n.* a tropical vine, *Vigna caracalla,* of the legume family, having fragrant, yellowish or purplish flowers, a segment of which is shaped like a snail's shell. Also called **corkscrew flower.** [1680–90; SNAIL + FLOWER]

snail-paced (snāl′pāst′), *adj.* slow of pace or motion, like a snail; sluggish. [1585–95]

snail's′ pace′, an extremely slow rate: *The work progresses at a snail's pace.* [1400–50; late ME]

snake (snāk), *n., v.,* **snaked, snak•ing.** —*n.* **1.** any of numerous limbless, scaly, elongate reptiles of the suborder Serpentes, comprising venomous and nonvenomous species inhabiting tropical and temperate areas. **2.** a treacherous person; an insidious enemy. Cf. **snake in the grass. 3.** *Building Trades.* **a.** Also called **auger, plumber's snake.** (in plumbing) a device for dislodging obstructions in curved pipes, having a head fed into the pipe at the end of a flexible metal band. **b.** Also called **wirepuller.** a length of resilient steel wire, for threading through an electrical conduit so that wire can be pulled through after it. —*v.i.* **4.** to move, twist, or wind: *The road snakes among the mountains.* —*v.t.* **5.** to wind or make (one's course, way, etc.) in the manner of a snake: *to snake one's way through a crowd.* **6.** to drag or haul, esp. by a chain or rope, as a log. [bef. 1000; ME (n.); OE *snaca;* c. MLG *snake,* ON *snākr*] —**snake′like′,** *adj.*

snake•bird (snāk′bûrd′), *n.* anhinga. [1785–95, *Amer.;* SNAKE + BIRD]

snake•bite (snāk′bīt′), *n.* **1.** the bite of a snake, esp. of one that is venomous. **2.** the resulting painful, toxic condition. [1830–40; SNAKE + BITE]

snake′bite rem′edy, *Facetious.* hard liquor.

snake•blen•ny (snāk′blen′ē), *n., pl.* (*esp. collectively*) **-ny,** (*esp. referring to two or more kinds or species*) **-nies.** any of several pricklebacks of the genus *Lumpenus.* [1910–15; SNAKE + BLENNY]

snake′ charm′er, an entertainer who seems to charm venomous snakes, usually by music. [1830–40]

snake′ dance′, 1. a ceremonial dance of the American Indian in which snakes or representations of snakes are handled or imitated by the dancers. **2.** a parade or procession, esp. in celebration of a sports victory, in which the participants weave in single file in a serpentine course. [1765–75, *Amer.*]

snake-dance (snāk′dans′, -däns′), *v.i.,* **-danced, -danc•ing.** to perform a snake dance. [1880–85]

snake′ doc′tor, 1. *South Midland and Southern U.S.* a dragonfly. **2.** a hellgrammite. [1790–1800] —**Regional Variation. 1.** See **dragonfly.**

snake′ eyes′, *Craps.* a cast of two; two aces. [1930–35]

snake′ feed′er, *Midland U.S.* a dragonfly. [1860–65, *Amer.*] —**Regional Variation.** See **dragonfly.**

snake′ fence′, a fence, zigzag in plan, made of rails resting across one another at an angle. Also called **Virginia fence, Virginia rail fence, worm fence.** [1795–1805, *Amer.*]

snake•fish (snāk′fish′), *n., pl.* **-fish•es,** (*esp. collectively*) **-fish. 1.** lizardfish. **2.** ribbonfish. [1790–1800; SNAKE + FISH]

snake•fly (snāk′flī′), *n., pl.* **-flies.** any neuropterous insect of the family Raphidiidae, of western North America, having an elongated prothorax resembling a neck. [1660–70; SNAKE + FLY[2]]

snake′ foot′, *Furniture.* an elongated foot or short leg, as to a pedestal table, having the form of an ogee tangent to the floor surface.

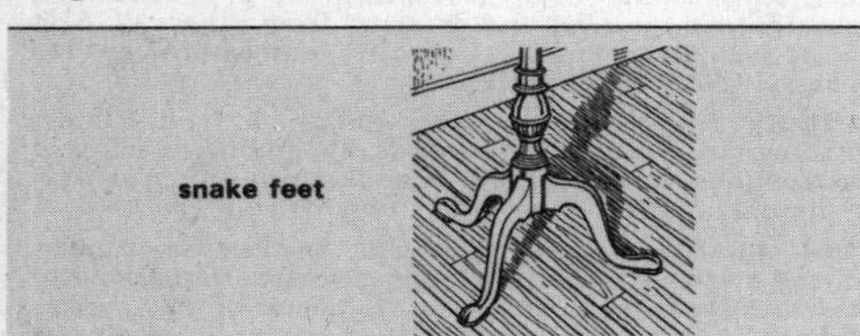
snake feet

snake•head (snāk′hed′), *n.* **1.** a turtlehead plant. **2.** any elongate fish of the family Channidae (or Ophicephalidae), having a large head with a deeply cleft mouth and able to breathe atmospheric oxygen. [1775–85, *Amer.;* SNAKE + HEAD]

snake-hipped (snāk′hipt′), *adj.* having thin, sinuous hips.

snake′ in the grass′, 1. a treacherous person, esp. one who feigns friendship. **2.** a concealed danger. [1690–1700]

snake′ lil′y, a Californian plant, *Dichelostemma volubile,* of the amaryllis family, having a twining stem and an umbel of rose-red or pink flowers. [1825–35, *Amer.*]

snake′ mack′erel, an elongate, deep-sea fish, *Gempylus serpens,* inhabiting tropical and temperate seas, having jutting jaws and strong teeth.

snake•mouth (snāk′mouth′), *n., pl.* **-mouths** (-mouthz′). See **rose pogonia.** [1810–20, *Amer.;* SNAKE + MOUTH; so called because of the resemblance of the flower to a snake's open mouth]

snake′ oil′, 1. any of various liquid concoctions of questionable medical value sold as an all-purpose curative, esp. by traveling hucksters. **2.** *Slang.* deceptive talk or actions; hooey; bunkum: *The governor promised to lower taxes, but it was the same old snake oil.* [1925–30, *Amer.*] —**snake′-oil′,** *adj.*

snake′ palm′, devil's-tongue.

snake′ pit′, *Informal.* **1.** a mental hospital marked by squalor and inhumane or indifferent care for the patients. **2.** an intensely chaotic or disagreeable place or situation. Also, **snake′pit′.** [1945–50]

snake′ plant′, a widely grown houseplant, *Sansevieria trifasciata,* having stiffly erect, mottled, lance-shaped leaves. [1880–85]

Snake′ Riv′er, a river flowing from NW Wyoming through S Idaho into the Columbia River in SE Washington: Shoshone Falls. 1038 mi. (1670 km) long.

snake•root (snāk′ro͞ot′, -ro͝ot′), *n.* **1.** any of various plants whose roots have been regarded as a remedy for snakebites, as the herb *Aristolochia serpentaria* (**Virginia snakeroot**), having a medicinal rhizome and rootlets, and the white-flowered *Polygala senega* (**Seneca snakeroot**), having a medicinal root. **2.** the root or rhizome of such a plant. **3.** the North American bugbane. **4.** a white eupatorium, *Eupatorium rugosum.* **5.** a plant, *Rauwolfia serpentina* (or *Rauvolfia serpentina*), whose roots are the source of reserpine and other drugs. [1625–35; SNAKE + ROOT[1]]

snake's-head (snāks′hed′), *n.* See **checkered lily.** [1730–40]

snake•skin (snāk′skin′), *n.* **1.** the skin of a snake. **2.** leather made from the skin of a snake. [1815–25; SNAKE + SKIN]

snake•stone (snāk′stōn′), *n.* **1.** a piece of porous material popularly supposed to neutralize the toxic effect of a snakebite. **2.** See **ayr stone.** [1655–65; SNAKE + STONE]

snake•weed (snāk′wēd′), *n.* bistort (def. 1). [1590–1600; SNAKE + WEED[1]]

snake•wood (snāk′wo͝od′), *n.* **1.** the heavy, dark-red wood of a South American tree, *Piratinera guianensis,* used for decorative veneers, musical instrument bows, etc. **2.** the tree that is the source of this wood. Also called **letterwood.** [1590–1600; SNAKE + WOOD[1]]

snak•y (snā′kē), *adj.,* **snak•i•er, snak•i•est. 1.** of or pertaining to snakes. **2.** abounding in snakes, as a place. **3.** snakelike; twisting, winding, or sinuous. **4.** venomous; treacherous or insidious: *a snaky remark.* **5.** consisting of, entwined with, or bearing a representation of snakes or serpents, as a ring. **6.** *Australian Informal.* irritable, angry, or spiteful. [1560–70; SNAKE + -Y[1]] —**snak′i•ly,** *adv.* —**snak′i•ness,** *n.*

snap (snap), *v.,* **snapped, snap•ping,** *n., adj., adv.* —*v.i.* **1.** to make a sudden, sharp, distinct sound; crack, as a whip; crackle. **2.** to click, as a mechanism or the jaws or teeth coming together. **3.** to move, strike, shut, catch, etc., with a sharp sound, as a door, lid, or lock. **4.** to break suddenly, esp. with a sharp, cracking sound, as something slender and brittle: *The branch snapped.* **5.** to act or move with quick or abrupt motions of the body: *to snap to attention.* **6.** *Photog.* to take a photograph, esp. without formal posing of the subject. **7.** to make a quick or sudden bite or grab (often fol. by *at*). **8.** to utter a quick, sharp sentence or speech, esp. a command, reproof, retort, etc. (often fol. by *at*). **9.** to be radiant; sparkle; flash, as the eyes. —*v.t.* **10.** to seize with or take, buy, or obtain as with a quick bite or grab (fol. by *up* or *off*): *The bargains were snapped up.* **11.** to secure, judge, vote, etc., hastily: *They snapped the bill through Congress.* **12.** to cause to make a sudden, sharp sound: *to snap one's fingers.* **13.** to crack (a whip). **14.** to bring, strike, shut, open, operate, etc., with a sharp sound or movement: *to snap a lid down.* **15.** to address or interrupt (a person) quickly and sharply. **16.** to say or utter (words, a command, a retort, etc.) in a quick, sharp manner: *to snap complaints.* **17.** to break suddenly, esp. with a cracking sound: *to snap a stick in half.* **18.** *Photog.* to take a photograph of, esp. quickly. **19.** *Building Trades.* to transfer (a line) to a surface by means of a chalk line. **20.** *Football.* to put (the ball) into play by tossing it back to the quarterback or other member of the offensive backfield, esp. from between the legs when bent over double and facing the line of scrimmage; center. **21.** *Hunting.* to fire (a shot) quickly, esp. without raising the gun to aim from the eye. **22. snap one's fingers at.** See **finger** (def. 16). **23. snap out of,** to free oneself from; recover from: *It took him a long time to snap out of his grief.* **24. snap someone's head off.** See **bite** (def. 20). **25. snap to, a.** to come to attention: *The troops snapped to when the colonel walked in.* **b.** to shape up: *If you don't snap to and study, you'll flunk the course.* —*n.* **26.** a quick, sudden action or movement, as the flick of a whip or the breaking of a twig. **27.** a short, sharp sound, as that caused by breaking a twig or closing a latch. **28.** a catch or fastener that closes by pressure and clicks together. **29.** *Informal.* briskness, vigor, or energy: *That song has a lot of snap.* **30.** a quick, sharp speech or manner of speaking: *He uttered his commands with a snap.* **31.** a quick or sudden bite or grab, as at something: *The fish ate with little snaps.* **32.** something obtained by or as by biting or grabbing: *a snap of food.* **33.** a brittle cookie. **34.** a short spell or period, as of cold weather: *an unexpected cold snap.* **35.** *Photog.* a snapshot. **36.** *Informal.* an easy, profitable, or agreeable position, piece of work, or the like: *This job is a snap.* **37.** *Football.* the act or an instance of snapping the ball. **38.** a snap bean. **39.** *Informal.* a snapdragon. **40.** *Brit.* a packed lunch, as that carried by a worker or traveler. **41. not give** or **care a snap of one's fingers for,** to regard with indifference; treat lightly. Also, **not give** or **care a snap.** —*adj.* **42.** fastening or closing with a click or snap, as a device fitted with a spring catch: *a snap lock.* **43.** made, done, taken, etc., suddenly or offhand: *a snap judgment.* **44.** easy or simple. —*adv.* **45.** in a brisk, sudden manner. [1485–95; < D or LG *snappen* to bite, seize] —**snap′less,** *adj.* —**snap′•pa•ble,** *adj.* —**snap′ping•ly,** *adv.*

snap•back (snap′bak′), *n.* **1.** a sudden rebound or recovery. **2.** *Football.* snap (def. 37). [1885–90, *Amer.;* n. use of v. phrase *snap back*]

snap′ bean′, a crisp bean pod, as a green bean or a wax bean, that is easily broken into pieces for cooking. [1760–70, *Amer.*]

snap′ brim′, 1. a hat brim that can be turned up or down. **2.** Also called **snap′-brim hat′.** a man's fedora, usually of felt and often worn with the brim turned up in back and down in front. [1905–10] —**snap′-brim′, snap′-brimmed′,** *adj.*

snap′ course′, an academic course that can be passed with a minimum of effort. Also called **gut course.** [1895–1900]

snap•drag•on (snap′drag′ən), *n.* **1.** any plant belonging to the genus *Antirrhinum,* of the figwort family, esp. *A. majus,* cultivated for its spikes of showy flowers, each having a corolla supposed to resemble the mouth of a dragon. **2.** flapdragon. [1565–75; SNAP + DRAGON]

snap′ fas′tener, a two-pieced fastening device with a projection that fits into a hole, used esp. to hold clothing, pillows, etc., together. Also, *esp. Brit.,* **press stud.** [1925–30]

snap•haunce (snap′hans, -häns), *n.* an early flintlock mechanism for igniting a charge of gunpowder in a gun. [1580–90; < D *snaphaan* (or G *Schnapphahn*) orig., highwayman, equiv. to *snap*(*pen*) to snatch, SNAP + *haan* rooster (D *haan,* G *Hahn,* parallel to COCK[1], mean both "rooster" and "hammer of a firearm"); source of final *s* unclear]

snap-in (snap′in′), *adj.* designed to be attached or held by snapping into position by snaps.

snap′ link′, a link with a latchlike opening through which another link or catch can be fitted. [1870–75]

snap-off (snap′ôf′, of′), *adj.* removed or opened by snapping: *a snap-off lid.* [adj. use of v. phrase *snap off*]

snap-on (snap′on′, -ôn′), *adj.* attached or fitting into place by means of a snap or with a pressing motion: *snap-on bottle tops.* [1920–25; adj. use of v. phrase *snap on*]

snap′ pea′, a variety of the common pea having rounded, crisp, edible pods eaten raw or cooked. Also called **sugar snap pea.**

snap•per (snap′ər), *n., pl.* (*esp. collectively*) **-per,** (*esp. referring to two or more kinds or species*) **-pers** for 1, 2; **-pers** for 3, 4, 5. **1.** any of several large marine food fishes of the family Lutjanidae. **2.** any of various other fishes, as the bluefish, *Pomatomus saltatrix.* **3.** See **snapping turtle. 4.** *Informal.* a person in charge of a group of workers. **5.** a tuft or knot of cotton, horsehair, hemp, etc., at the tip of a whip's lash; cracker; popper. [1525–35; SNAP + -ER[1]]

snap•per•back (snap′ər bak′), *n. Football* (*older use*). the center on the offensive team. [1885–90, *Amer.;* SNAPPER + BACK[1]]

snap′ping bee′tle. See **click beetle.** [1865–70]

snap′ping shrimp′, any common shrimp of the family Alphaeidae, distinguished by the snapping sound made by its enlarged claw. Also called **pistol shrimp.** [1940–45]

snap′ping tur′tle, either of two large, edible, freshwater turtles of the family Chelydridae, of North and Central America, having a large head and powerful hooked jaws, esp. the common snapping turtle, *Chelydra serpentina.* Cf. **alligator snapping turtle.** [1775–85, *Amer.*]

snapping turtle, *Chelydra serpentina,* length of carapace to 1 ft. (0.3 m); tail to 11 in. (28 cm)

snap•pish (snap′ish), *adj.* **1.** apt to snap or bite, as a dog. **2.** disposed to speak or reply in an impatient or irritable manner. **3.** impatiently or irritably sharp; curt: *a snappish reply.* [1535–45; SNAP + -ISH[1]] —**snap′pish•ly,** *adv.* —**snap′pish•ness,** *n.*

snap•py (snap′ē), *adj.,* **-pi•er, -pi•est. 1.** apt to snap or bite; snappish, as a dog. **2.** impatient or irritable, as a person or a reply. **3.** snapping or crackling in sound, as a fire. **4.** quick or sudden in action or performance. **5.** *Informal.* crisp, smart, lively, brisk, etc.: *Only snappy people get ahead in this world.* **6. make it snappy,** *Slang.* to speed up; hurry. [1740–50; SNAP + -Y[1]] —**snap′pi•ly,** *adv.* —**snap′pi•ness,** *n.*

snap′ ring′, *Mach.* any of various kinds of metal rings that must be forced open to be used and snap back into place to make a snug fit. [1900–05]

snap′ roll′, *Aeron.* a maneuver in which an airplane makes a rapid and complete revolution about its longitudinal axis while maintaining approximately level flight. [1930–35]

snap-roll (snap′rōl′), *Aeron.* —*v.t.* **1.** to put (an airplane) through the maneuver of a snap roll. —*v.i.* **2.** to execute a snap roll.

snap•shoot (snap′sho͞ot′), *v.t.,* **-shot, -shoot•ing.** to

CONCISE ETYMOLOGY KEY: <, descended or borrowed from; >, whence; b., blend of, blended; c., cognate with; cf., compare; deriv., derivative; equiv., equivalent; imit., imitative; obl., oblique; r., replacing; s., stem; sp., spelling, spelled; resp., respelling, respelled; trans., translation; ?, origin unknown; *, unattested; ‡, probably earlier than. See the full key inside the front cover.

take a snapshot of (a subject). [back formation from SNAPSHOT]

snap·shoot·er (snap′sho͞o′tər), *n.* an amateur photographer, esp. one who takes snapshots with a simple camera. [1885–90; SNAP(SHOT) + SHOOTER]

snap·shot (snap′shot′), *n., v.,* **-shot** or **-shot·ted, -shot·ting.** —*n.* **1.** an informal photograph, esp. one taken quickly by a hand-held camera. **2.** *Hunting.* a quick shot taken without deliberate aim. **3.** *Informal.* a brief appraisal, summary, or profile. —*v.t., v.i.* **4.** to photograph informally and quickly. [1800–10 for def. 2; 1860–65 for def. 1; SNAP + SHOT[1]]

snap′ the whip′. See **crack the whip** (def. 2).

snare[1] (snâr), *n., v.,* **snared, snar·ing.** —*n.* **1.** a device, often consisting of a noose, for capturing small game. **2.** anything serving to entrap or entangle unawares; trap. **3.** *Surg.* a wire noose for removing tumors or the like by the roots or at the base. —*v.t.* **4.** to catch with a snare; entangle. **5.** to catch or involve by trickery or wile: *to snare her into going.* [bef. 1100; ME (n. and v.); c. ON *snara,* MLG *snare,* OHG *snar(a)ha*] —**snare′less,** *adj.* —**snar′er,** *n.* —**snar′ing·ly,** *adv.*
—**Syn. 1.** See **trap**[1]. **2.** net, seine.

snare[2] (snâr), *n.* one of the strings of gut or of tightly spiraled metal stretched across the skin of a snare drum. [1680–90; < MLG *snare* or MD *snaer* string; r. OE *snēr* string of a musical instrument]

snare′ drum′, a small double-headed drum, carried at the side or placed on a stationary stand, having snares across the lower head to produce a rattling or reverberating effect. Also called **side drum.** [1870–75]

snare drum

snark (snärk), *n.* a mysterious, imaginary animal. [1876; coined by Lewis Carroll in his poem *The Hunting of the Snark*]

snark·y (snär′kē), *adj.,* **snark·i·er, snark·i·est.** *Chiefly Brit. Slang.* testy or irritable. [1910–15; dial. *snark* to nag, find fault with (appar. identical with *snark, snork* to snort, snore, prob. < D, LG *snorken* to snore) + -Y[1]]

snarl[1] (snärl), *v.i.* **1.** to growl angrily or viciously, esp. with teeth bared, as a dog. **2.** to speak in a surly or threatening manner. —*v.t.* **3.** to say by snarling: *to snarl a threat.* —*n.* **4.** the act of snarling. **5.** a snarling sound or utterance. [1580–90; earlier *snarle,* equiv. to obs. *snar* to snarl (c. D, LG *snarren,* G *schnarren*) + -LE] —**snarl′er,** *n.* —**snarl′ing·ly,** *adv.*

snarl[2] (snärl), *n.* **1.** a tangle, as of thread or hair. **2.** a complicated or confused condition or matter: *a traffic snarl.* **3.** a knot in wood. —*v.t.* **4.** to bring into a tangled condition, as thread or hair. **5.** to render complicated or confused: *The questions snarled him up.* **6.** to raise or emboss, as parts of a thin metal vessel, by hammering on a tool **(snarl′ing i′ron)** held against the inner surface of the vessel. —*v.i.* **7.** to become tangled; get into a tangle. [1350–1400; ME *snarle;* see SNARE[1], -LE]

snarl·y[1] (snär′lē), *adj.,* **snarl·i·er, snarl·i·est.** apt to snarl; easily irritated. [1790–1800; SNARL[1] + -Y[1]]

snarl·y[2] (snär′lē), *adj.,* **snarl·i·er, snarl·i·est.** full of knotty snarls; tangled. [1640–50; SNARL[2] + -Y[1]]

snash (snash, snäsh), *Scot.* —*n.* **1.** insolence; impertinence. —*v.i.* **2.** to use abusive language; speak disrespectfully. [1780–90; orig. uncert.]

snatch (snach), *v.i.* **1.** to make a sudden effort to seize something, as with the hand; grab (usually fol. by *at*). —*v.t.* **2.** to seize by a sudden or hasty grasp: *He snatched the old lady's purse and ran.* **3.** to take, get, pull, etc., suddenly or hastily. **4.** to rescue or save by prompt action: *He snatched the baby from the fire.* **5.** *Slang.* to kidnap. —*n.* **6.** an act or an instance of snatching. **7.** a sudden motion to seize something; grab: *He made a snatch as if to stop her.* **8.** a bit, scrap, or fragment of something: *snatches of conversation.* **9.** a brief spell of effort, activity, or any experience: *to work in snatches.* **10.** *Naut.* a sheave or projecting member serving as a fairlead. **11.** a brief period of time. **12.** *Slang.* an act of kidnapping. **13.** *Slang (vulgar).* vulva; vagina. **14.** *Weightlifting.* a lift in which the barbell is brought in a single motion from the floor to an arms-extended position overhead. Cf. **clean and jerk.** [1175–1225; ME *snacche* (n.), *snacchen* (v.) < ?; c. MD *snacken*] —**snatch′a·ble,** *adj.* —**snatch′er,** *n.* —**snatch′ing·ly,** *adv.*

snatch′ block′, *n. Naut.* a fairlead having the form of a block that can be opened to receive the bight of a rope at any point along its length. [1615–25]

snatch·y (snach′ē), *adj.,* **snatch·i·er, snatch·i·est.** consisting of, occurring in, or characterized by snatches; spasmodic; irregular. [1860–65; SNATCH + -Y[1]] —**snatch′i·ly,** *adv.*

snath (snath), *n.* the shaft or handle of a scythe. Also, **snathe** (snāth). [1565–75; unexplained var. of *snead* (ME *snede,* OE *snǣd*)]

snaz·zy (snaz′ē), *adj.,* **-zi·er, -zi·est.** extremely attractive or stylish; flashy; fancy: *a snazzy dresser.* [1930–35; orig. uncert.] —**snaz′zi·ness,** *n.*

SNCC (snik), *n.* a U.S. civil-rights organization formed by students and active esp. during the 1960's, whose aim was to achieve political and economic equality for blacks through local and regional action groups. [orig., *S(tudent) N(onviolent) C(oordinating) C(ommittee)*]

Snead (snēd), *n.* **Samuel Jackson** (*"Slamming Sammy"*), born 1912, U.S. golfer.

sneak (snēk), *v.,* **sneaked** or **snuck, sneak·ing,** *n.* —*v.i.* **1.** to go in a stealthy or furtive manner; slink; skulk. **2.** to act in a furtive or underhand way. **3.** *Brit. Informal.* to tattle; inform. —*v.t.* **4.** to move, put, pass, etc., in a stealthy or furtive manner: *He sneaked the gun into his pocket.* **5.** to do, take, or enjoy hurriedly or surreptitiously: *to sneak a cigarette.* —*n.* **6.** a sneaking, underhand, or contemptible person. **7.** *Informal.* a stealthy or furtive departure. **8.** *Brit. Informal.* tattletale; informer. **9.** **sneaker** (def. 1). **10.** *Informal.* a sneak preview. **11.** *Cards.* the lead of a singleton in a suit other than the trump suit. [1590–1600; var. of ME *sniken,* OE *snīcan* to creep; c. ON *snīkja* to hanker after]
—**Syn. 1.** steal. See **lurk.**
—**Usage.** First recorded in writing toward the end of the 19th century in the United States, SNUCK has become in recent decades a standard variant past tense and past participle of the verb SNEAK: *Bored by the lecture, he snuck out the side door.* SNUCK occurs frequently in fiction and in journalistic writing as well as on radio and television: *In the darkness the sloop had snuck around the headland, out of firing range.* It is not so common in highly formal or belletristic writing, where SNEAKED is more likely to occur. SNUCK is the only spoken past tense and past participle for many younger and middle-aged persons of all educational levels in the U. S. and Canada. SNUCK has occasionally been considered nonstandard, but it is so widely used by professional writers and educated speakers that it can no longer be so regarded.

sneak·er (snē′kər), *n.* **1.** a high or low shoe, usually of fabric such as canvas, with a rubber or synthetic sole. **2.** one who sneaks; a sneak. [1590–1600; SNEAK + -ER[1]]

sneak·ing (snē′king), *adj.* **1.** acting in a furtive or underhand way. **2.** deceitfully underhand, as actions; contemptible. **3.** secret; not generally avowed, as a feeling, notion, suspicion, etc. [1575–85; SNEAK + -ING[2]] —**sneak′ing·ly,** *adv.* —**sneak′ing·ness,** *n.*

sneak′ pre′view, a preview of a motion picture, often shown in addition to an announced film, in order to observe the reaction of the audience. [1935–40]

sneak′ thief′, a burglar who sneaks into houses through open doors, windows, etc. [1855–60, *Amer.*]

sneak·y (snē′kē), *adj.,* **sneak·i·er, sneak·i·est.** like or suggestive of a sneak; furtive; deceitful. [1825–35; SNEAK + -Y[1]] —**sneak′i·ly,** *adv.* —**sneak′i·ness,** *n.*

sneak′y pete′, *Slang.* a homemade or inferior liquor or wine.

sneck[1] (snek), *n. Scot. and North Eng.* a door latch or its lever. [1275–1325; ME *snek(k);* cf. SNATCH]

sneck[2] (snek), *Masonry.* —*n.* **1.** a small stone, as a spall, inserted into the spaces between larger pieces of rubble in a wall. —*v.t.* **2.** to fill (spaces between larger stones) with snecks. [1275–1325; ME; orig. uncert.] —**sneck′er,** *n.*

sneer (snēr), *v.i.* **1.** to smile, laugh, or contort the face in a manner that shows scorn or contempt: *They sneered at his pretensions.* **2.** to speak or write in a manner expressive of derision or scorn. —*v.t.* **3.** to utter or say in a sneering manner. —*n.* **4.** a look or expression of derision, scorn, or contempt. **5.** a derisive or scornful utterance, esp. one that is covert or insinuative. **6.** an act of sneering. [1545–55; orig., to snort; cf. Fris (N dial.) *sneere* scornful remark, SNARL[1]] —**sneer′er,** *n.* —**sneer′ful,** *adj.* —**sneer′ing·ly,** *adv.* —**sneer′less,** *adj.*
—**Syn. 2.** gibe. See **scoff. 5.** scoff, gibe, jeer.

sneesh (snēsh), *n. Scot. and North Eng.* snuff[1] (def. 9). [1675–85; perh. < Scand; cf. Dan *snus* snuff]

sneeze (snēz), *v.,* **sneezed, sneez·ing,** *n.* —*v.i.* **1.** to emit air or breath suddenly, forcibly, and audibly through the nose and mouth by involuntary, spasmodic action. **2. sneeze at,** *Informal.* to treat with contempt; scorn: *$50,000 is nothing to sneeze at.* —*n.* **3.** an act or sound of sneezing. [1485–95; earlier *snese;* r. ME *fnese,* OE *fnēosan;* c. D *fniezen,* ON *fnȳsa*] —**sneeze′less,** *adj.* —**sneez′er,** *n.* —**sneez′y,** *adj.*

sneeze·guard (snēz′gärd′), *n.* a plastic or glass shield overhanging a salad bar, buffet, or the like to protect the food from contamination. [1980–85]

sneeze·weed (snēz′wēd′), *n.* any of several coarse composite plants of the genus *Helenium,* the flowers of which resemble sunflowers and cause sneezing. [1830–40; SNEEZE + WEED[1]]

sneeze·wort (snēz′wûrt′, -wôrt′), *n.* a composite plant, *Achillea ptarmica,* of Europe, the powdered leaves of which cause sneezing. [1590–1600; SNEEZE + WORT[2]]

Snef·ru (snef′ro͞o), *n.* fl. c2920 B.C., Egyptian ruler of the 4th dynasty.

snell[1] (snel), *n.* a short piece of nylon, gut, or the like, by which a fishhook is attached to a line. [1840–50, *Amer.;* orig. uncert.]

snell[2] (snel), *adj. Chiefly Scot.* **1.** active; lively: *a snell lad.* **2.** witty: *a snell remark.* **3.** severe: *snell weather.* [bef. 900; ME, OE; c. OHG *snel* (G *schnell*) quick, ON *snjallr* excellent]

Snell (snel), *n.* **Peter (George),** born 1938, New Zealand track-and-field athlete.

Snell's′ law′ (snelz), *Optics.* the law that, for a ray incident on the interface of two media, the sine of the angle of incidence times the index of refraction of the first medium is equal to the sine of the angle of refraction times the index of refraction of the second medium. [named after Willebrod *Snell* van Royen (d. 1626), Dutch mathematician]

SNG, synthetic natural gas. See under **synthetic fuel.**

snick (snik), *v.t.* **1.** to cut, snip, or nick. **2.** to strike sharply: *He snicked the ball with his cue.* **3.** to snap or click (a gun, trigger, etc.). —*v.i.* **4.** to click. —*n.* **5.** a small cut; nick. **6.** a click. **7.** *Cricket.* **a.** a glancing blow given to the ball. **b.** the ball so hit. [1550–60; orig. uncert.; cf. Scots *sneck* to cut (off), ON *snikka* to whittle]

snick·er (snik′ər), *v.i.* **1.** to laugh in a half-suppressed, indecorous or disrespectful manner. —*v.t.* **2.** to utter with a snicker. —*n.* **3.** a snickering laugh. Also, **snigger.** [1685–95; of expressive orig.] —**snick′er·ing·ly,** *adv.*

snick·er·snee (snik′ər snē′), *n.* a knife, esp. one used as a weapon. [1690–1700; var. (by alliterative assimilation) of earlier *stick or snee* to thrust or cut < D *steken* to STICK[2] + *snij(d)en* to cut]

snide (snīd), *adj.,* **snid·er, snid·est.** derogatory in a nasty, insinuating manner: *snide remarks about his boss.* [1860–65; orig. uncert.] —**snide′ness,** *n.*

sniff (snif), *v.i.* **1.** to draw air through the nose in short, audible inhalations. **2.** to clear the nose by so doing; sniffle. **3.** to smell by short inhalations. **4.** to show disdain, contempt, etc., by or as by sniffing. —*v.t.* **5.** to perceive by or as by smelling: *to sniff a scandal.* **6.** to inhale through the nose: *to sniff the air.* —*n.* **7.** an act of sniffing; a single, short, audible inhalation. **8.** the sound made by such an act. **9.** a scent or odor perceived: *a sniff of perfume.* [1300–50; ME; back formation from SNIVEL] —**sniff′ing·ly,** *adv.*

sniff·er (snif′ər), *n.* **1.** a person or thing that sniffs. **2.** a device or mechanism for detecting something. [1860–65; SNIFF + -ER[1]]

sniff·ish (snif′ish), *adj.* haughtily disdainful; contemptuous: *a sniffish dowager.* [1920–25; SNIFF + -ISH[1]]

snif·fle (snif′əl), *v.,* **-fled, -fling,** *n.* —*v.i.* **1.** to sniff repeatedly, as from a head cold or in repressing tears: *She sniffled woefully.* —*n.* **2.** an act or sound of sniffling. **3. sniffles,** a condition, as a cold, marked by sniffling (usually prec. by *the*): *This draft is giving me the sniffles.* [1625–35; SNIFF + -LE] —**snif′fler,** *n.*

snif·fy (snif′ē), *adj.,* **-fi·er, -fi·est.** *Informal.* inclined to sniff, as in scorn; disdainful; supercilious: *He was very sniffy about breaches of etiquette.* [1865–70; SNIFF + -Y[1]] —**sniff′i·ly,** *adv.* —**sniff′i·ness,** *n.*

snif·ter (snif′tər), *n.* **1.** Also called **inhaler.** a pear-shaped glass, narrowing at the top to intensify the aroma of brandy, liqueur, etc. **2.** *Informal.* a very small drink of liquor. [1840–50; deriv. of *snifter* to sniff, snivel, ME *snyfter;* imit.]

snift′ing valve′, a valve for releasing small quantities of steam, compressed air, or condensate, as from the cylinder of a steam engine. [1870–75]

snig·ger (snig′ər), *v.i., v.t., n.* snicker. —**snig′ger·er,** *n.* —**snig′ger·ing·ly,** *adv.*

snig·gle (snig′əl), *v.,* **-gled, -gling.** —*v.i.* **1.** to fish for eels by thrusting a baited hook into their lurking places. —*v.t.* **2.** to catch by sniggling. [1645–55; *snig* eel (late ME *snigge*) + -LE] —**snig·gler** (snig′lər), *n.*

snig·let (snig′lit), *n.* any word coined for something that has no specific name. [1980–85; said to be der. of obs. *sniggle* to snicker, with -LET]

snip (snip), *v.,* **snipped, snip·ping,** *n.* —*v.t.* **1.** to cut with a small, quick stroke, or a succession of such strokes, with scissors or the like. **2.** to remove or cut off (something) by or as by cutting in this manner: *to snip a rose.* —*v.i.* **3.** to cut with small, quick strokes. —*n.* **4.** the act of snipping, as with scissors. **5.** a small cut made by snipping. **6.** a small piece snipped off. **7.** a small piece, bit, or amount of anything: *a snip of food.* **8.** *Informal.* a small or insignificant person. **9.** *Informal.* a presumptuous or impertinent person. **10. snips,** small, strong hand shears used by sheet metal workers. **11.** *Brit. Informal.* a bargain. [1550–60; orig. uncert.; cf. D, LG *snippen* to snip, catch, clip]

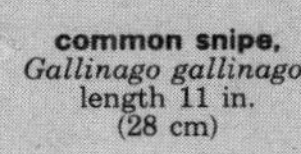

common snipe, *Gallinago gallinago,* length 11 in. (28 cm)

snipe (snīp), *n., pl.* **snipes,** (*esp. collectively*) **snipe** for 1, 2; *v.* **sniped, snip·ing.** —*n.* **1.** any of several long-billed game birds of the genera *Gallinago* (*Capella*) and *Limnocryptes,* inhabiting marshy areas, as *G. gallinago* **(common snipe),** of Eurasia and North America, having barred and striped white, brown, and black plumage. **2.** any of several other long-billed birds, as some sandpipers. **3.** a shot, usually from a hidden position. —*v.i.* **4.** to shoot or hunt snipe. **5.** to shoot at individuals as opportunity offers from a concealed or distant position: *The enemy was sniping from the roofs.* **6.** to attack a person or a person's work with petulant or snide criticism, esp. anonymously or from a safe distance. [1275–1325; ME *snype* (n.) < ON *-snīpa* (in *mȳrisnīpa* moor snipe); c. Norw *snipa,* Icel *snīpa;* cf. Dan *sneppe,* G *Schnepfe*] —**snipe′like′,** *adj.* —**snip′er,** *n.*

snipe·fish (snīp′fish′), *n., pl.* (*esp. collectively*) **-fish,** (*esp. referring to two or more kinds or species*) **-fish·es.** any of several fishes of the family Macrorhamphosidae, of tropical and temperate seas, having a long, tubular snout and a compressed body. Also called **bellows fish.** [1660–70; SNIPE + FISH]

snip·er·scope (snī′pər skōp′), *n.* a snooperscope designed for attaching to a rifle or carbine. [1915–20; SNIPER + -SCOPE]

CONCISE PRONUNCIATION KEY: *act, cāpe, dâre, pärt; set, ēqual; if, īce; ox, ōver, ôrder, oil, bo͝ok, bo͞ot, out; up, ûrge; child; sing; shoe; thin, that;* zh as in *treasure.* ə = *a* as in *alone, e* as in *system, i* as in *easily, o* as in *gallop, u* as in *circus;* ᵊ as in *fire* (fīᵊr), *hour* (ouᵊr). l and n can serve as syllabic consonants, as in *cradle* (krād′l), and *button* (but′n). See the full key inside the front cover.

snip·pet (snip′it), *n.* **1.** a small piece snipped off; a small bit, scrap, or fragment: *an anthology of snippets.* **2.** *Informal.* a small or insignificant person. [1655–65; SNIP + -ET]

snip·py (snip′ē), *adj.,* **-pi·er, -pi·est.** **1.** sharp or curt, esp. in a supercilious or haughty way; impertinent. **2.** scrappy or fragmentary. Also, **snip·pe·ty** (snip′i tē). [1720–30; SNIP + -Y[1]] **—snip′pi·ly,** *adv.* **—snip′pi·ness, snip′pet·i·ness,** *n.*

snit (snit), *n.* an agitated or irritated state. [1935–40; orig. uncert.]

snitch[1] (snich), *v.t. Informal.* to snatch or steal; pilfer. [1900–05; perh. var. of SNATCH]

snitch[2] (snich), *Informal.* —*v.i.* **1.** to turn informer; tattle. —*n.* **2.** Also called **snitch′er.** an informer. [1775–85; orig. uncert.]

snitch·y (snich′ē), *adj.,* **snitch·i·er, snitch·i·est.** *Brit., Australian.* cross; ill-tempered. [SNITCH[2] + -Y[1]]

sniv·el (sniv′əl), *v.,* **-eled, -el·ing** or (*esp. Brit.*) **-elled, -el·ling,** *n.* —*v.i.* **1.** to weep or cry with sniffling. **2.** to affect a tearful state; whine. **3.** to run at the nose; have a runny nose: *She sniveled from the cold.* **4.** to draw up mucus audibly through the nose: *Stop sniveling and use your handkerchief.* —*v.t.* **5.** to utter with sniveling or sniffling. —*n.* **6.** weak, whining, or pretended weeping. **7.** a light sniffle, as in weeping. **8.** a hypocritical show of feeling: *a sentimental snivel.* **9.** mucus running from the nose. **10. snivels,** a sniveling condition; a slight cold; sniffles (usually prec. by *the*). [1275–1325; ME *snyvele;* cf. OE *snyflung* (ger.), deriv. of *snofl* mucus; c. LG *snüfeln*] **—sniv′el·er;** *esp. Brit.,* **sniv′el·ler,** *n.*

sniv·el·y (sniv′ə lē), *adj.* characterized by or given to sniveling. Also, *esp. Brit.,* **sniv′el·ly.** [1570–80; SNIVEL + -Y[1]]

snob (snob), *n.* **1.** a person who imitates, cultivates, or slavishly admires social superiors and is condescending or overbearing to others. **2.** a person who believes himself or herself an expert or connoisseur in a given field and is condescending toward or disdainful of those who hold other opinions or have different tastes regarding this field: *a musical snob.* [1775–85; orig. uncert; first used as a nickname for a cobbler or cobbler's apprentice, hence a townsman, someone of low class or lacking good breeding, commoner, hence someone who imitates persons of higher rank]

snob·ber·y (snob′ə rē), *n., pl.* **-ber·ies.** snobbish character, conduct, trait, or act. [1825–35; SNOB + -ERY]

snob·bish (snob′ish), *adj.* **1.** of, pertaining to, or characteristic of a snob: *snobbish ideas about rank.* **2.** having the character of a snob. [1830–40; SNOB + -ISH[1]] **—snob′bish·ly,** *adv.* **—snob′bish·ness,** *n.*

snob·by (snob′ē), *adj.,* **-bi·er, -bi·est.** condescending, patronizing, or socially exclusive; snobbish. [1840–50; SNOB + -Y[1]] **—snob′bi·ly,** *adv.* **—snob′bi·ness, snob′bism,** *n.*

Sno-Cat (snō′kat′), *Trademark.* a brand of snowmobile with caterpillar treads.

snock·ered (snok′ərd), *adj. Slang.* drunk; intoxicated. [*snocker-* (perh. expressive alter. of KNOCK) + -ED[2]]

snod (snod), *adj. Scot. and North Eng.* **1.** smooth; sleek. **2.** neat; tidy. [1470–80; perh. < Scand; cf. ON *snothin* bald, *snauthr* bare, bald] **—snod′ly,** *adv.*

snog (snog), *v.i.,* **snogged, snog·ging.** *Brit. Informal.* to kiss and cuddle. [1955–60; orig. uncert.]

snol·ly·gos·ter (snol′ē gos′tər), *n. Slang.* a clever, unscrupulous person. [1855–60; orig. uncert.]

snood (snōōd), *n.* **1.** the distinctive headband formerly worn by young unmarried women in Scotland and northern England. **2.** a headband for the hair. **3.** a netlike hat or part of a hat or fabric that holds or covers the back of a woman's hair. **4.** the pendulous skin over the beak of a turkey. —*v.t.* **5.** to bind or confine (the hair) with a snood. [bef. 900; ME: fillet, ribbon; OE *snōd*]

snook[1] (snōōk, snŏŏk), *n., pl.* (*esp. collectively*) **snook,** (*esp. referring to two or more kinds or species*) **snooks.** **1.** any basslike fish of the genus *Centropomus,* esp. *C. undecimalis,* inhabiting waters off Florida and the West Indies and south to Brazil, valued as food and game. **2.** any of several related marine fishes. [1690–1700; < D *snoek*]

snook[2] (snŏŏk, snōōk), *n.* **1.** a gesture of defiance, disrespect, or derision. **2. cock a snook** or **cock one's snook,** to thumb the nose: *a painter who cocks a snook at traditional techniques.* Also, **cock a snoot.** [1875–80; orig. uncert.]

snook·er (snŏŏk′ər, snōō′kər), *n.* **1.** a variety of pool played with 15 red balls and 6 balls of colors other than red, in which a player must shoot one of the red balls, each with a point value of 1, into a pocket before shooting at one of the other balls, with point values of from 2 to 7. —*v.t.* **2.** *Slang.* to deceive, cheat, or dupe: *to be snookered by a mail order company.* [1885–90; orig. uncert.]

snoop (snōōp), *Informal.* —*v.i.* **1.** to prowl or pry; go about in a sneaking, prying way. —*n.* **2.** an act or instance of snooping. **3.** a person who snoops. **4.** a private detective. [1825–35, *Amer.;* < D *snoepen* to take and eat food on the sly] **—snoop′er,** *n.*

snoop·er·scope (snōō′pər skōp′), *n.* a device that displays on a fluorescent screen reflected infrared radiation, enabling the user to see objects obscured by darkness. [1945–50; SNOOPER + -SCOPE]

snoop·y (snōō′pē), *adj.,* **snoop·i·er, snoop·i·est.** *Informal.* characterized by meddlesome curiosity; prying. [1890–95; SNOOP + -Y[1]] **—snoop′i·ly,** *adv.*

CONCISE ETYMOLOGY KEY: <, descended or borrowed from; >, whence; b., blend of, blended; c., cognate with; cf., compare; deriv., derivative; equiv., equivalent; imit., imitative; obl., oblique; r., replacing; s., stem; sp., spelling, spelled; resp., respelling, respelled; trans., translation; ?, origin unknown; *, unattested; ‡, probably earlier than. See the full key inside the front cover.

snoose (snōōs, snōōz), *n.* finely powdered tobacco; snuff. [1910–15; < Sw *snusa,* Dan, Norw *snuse,* short for Sw, Dan, Norw *snustobak(k)* snuff (sniff) tobacco]

snoot (snōōt), *n.* **1.** *Slang.* the nose. **2.** *Informal.* a snob. —*v.t.* **3.** *Informal.* to behave disdainfully toward; condescend to: *New arrivals in the town were snooted by older residents.* [1860–65; var. of SNOUT]

snoot·ful (snōōt′fōōl), *n., pl.* **-fuls.** *Informal.* a sufficient amount of liquor to cause intoxication. [SNOOT + -FUL]
—Usage. See **-ful.**

snoot·y (snōō′tē), *adj.,* **snoot·i·er, snoot·i·est.** *Informal.* snobbish. [1915–20; SNOOT + -Y[1]] **—snoot′i·ly,** *adv.* **—snoot′i·ness,** *n.*

snooze (snōōz), *v.,* **snoozed, snooz·ing,** *n.* —*v.i.* **1.** to sleep; slumber; doze; nap. —*n.* **2.** a short sleep; nap. [1780–90; orig. uncert.] **—snooz′er,** *n.* **—snooz′y,** *adj.*

Sno·qual′mie Falls′ (snō kwol′mē), falls of the Snoqualmie River, in W Washington. 270 ft. (82 m) high.

snore (snôr, snōr), *v.,* **snored, snor·ing,** *n.* —*v.i.* **1.** to breathe during sleep with hoarse or harsh sounds caused by the vibrating of the soft palate. —*v.t.* **2.** to pass (time) in snoring or sleeping (usually fol. by *away* or *out*): *to snore the day away.* —*n.* **3.** the act, instance, or sound of snoring. [1300–50; ME *snoren* (v.); c. MLG, MD *snorren*] **—snor′er,** *n.*

snor·kel (snôr′kəl), *n.* **1.** Also called, *Brit.,* **snort.** a device permitting a submarine to remain submerged for prolonged periods, consisting of tubes extended above the surface of the water to take in air for the diesel engine and for general ventilation and to discharge exhaust gases and foul air. **2.** a hard rubber or plastic tube through which a swimmer can breathe while moving face down at or just below the surface of the water. —*v.i.* **3.** to engage in snorkeling. [1940–45; < G *Schnorchel* air intake] **—snor′kel·er,** *n.*

snor·kel·ing (snôr′kə ling), *n.* the sport of swimming with a snorkel and face mask. [1945–50; SNORKEL + -ING[1]]

Snor·ri Stur·lu·son (snôʀ′rē stœʀ′lə son; *Eng.* snôr′ē stûr′lə sən), 1179–1241, Icelandic historian and poet.

snort (snôrt), *v.i.* **1.** (of animals) to force the breath violently through the nostrils with a loud, harsh sound: *The spirited horse snorted and shied at the train.* **2.** (of persons) to express contempt, indignation, etc., by a similar sound. **3.** *Slang.* to take a drug by inhaling. —*v.t.* **4.** to utter with a snort. **5.** to expel (air, sound, etc.) by or as by snorting. **6.** *Slang.* to take (a drug) by inhaling: *to snort cocaine.* —*n.* **7.** the act or sound of snorting. **8.** *Slang.* a quick drink of liquor; shot. **9.** *Slang.* **a.** an act or instance of taking a drug by inhalation. **b.** the amount of drug inhaled. **10.** *Brit.* snorkel. [1325–75; ME *snorten* (v.); prob. akin to SNORE] **—snort′ing·ly,** *adv.*

snort·er (snôr′tər), *n.* **1.** a person or thing that snorts. **2.** *Informal.* something extraordinary of its kind: *a real snorter of a storm.* [1595–1605; SNORT + -ER[1]]

snot (snot), *n.* **1.** *Vulgar.* mucus from the nose. **2.** *Informal.* a disrespectful or supercilious person. [1350–1400; ME; cf. MLG, MD *snotte,* OE *gesnot,* Dan *snot*]

snot·nosed (snot′nōzd′), *adj. Informal.* impudent; insolent; snotty. [1940–45; SNOT + NOSE + -ED[3]]

snot-rag (snot′rag′), *n. Vulgar.* a handkerchief. [1885–90]

snot·ty (snot′ē), *adj.,* **-ti·er, -ti·est.** **1.** *Vulgar.* of or pertaining to snot. **2.** *Informal.* snobbish; arrogant; supercilious: *a snotty kid.* [1560–70; SNOT + -Y[1]] **—snot′ti·ly,** *adv.* **—snot′ti·ness,** *n.*

snout (snout), *n.* **1.** the part of an animal's head projecting forward and containing the nose and jaws; muzzle. **2.** *Entomol.* an anterior prolongation of the head bearing the mouth parts, as in snout beetles. **3.** anything that resembles or suggests an animal's snout in shape, function, etc. **4.** a nozzle or spout. **5.** a person's nose, esp. when large or prominent. [1175–1225; ME *snute;* c. D *snuite,* G *Schnauze*] **—snout′ed,** *adj.* **—snout′less,** *adj.* **—snout′like′,** *adj.*

snout′ bee′tle, weevil (def. 1). [1860–65, *Amer.*]

snow (snō), *n.* **1.** *Meteorol.* a precipitation in the form of ice crystals, mainly of intricately branched, hexagonal form and often agglomerated into snowflakes, formed directly from the freezing of the water vapor in the air. Cf. **ice crystals, snow grains, snow pellets.** **2.** these flakes as forming a layer on the ground or other surface. **3.** the fall of these flakes or a storm during which these flakes fall. **4.** something resembling a layer of these flakes in whiteness, softness, or the like: *the snow of fresh linen.* **5.** *Literary.* **a.** white blossoms. **b.** the white color of snow. **6.** *Slang.* cocaine or heroin. **7.** white spots or bands on a television screen caused by a weak signal. Cf. **hash**[1] (def. 5). —*v.i.* **8.** to send down snow; fall as snow. **9.** to descend like snow. —*v.t.* **10.** to let fall as or like snow. **11.** *Slang.* **a.** to make an overwhelming impression on: *The view really snowed them.* **b.** to persuade or deceive: *She was snowed into believing everything.* **12. snow under, a.** to cover with or bury in snow. **b.** to overwhelm with a larger amount of something than can be conveniently dealt with. **c.** to defeat overwhelmingly. [bef. 900; (n.) ME; OE *snāw;* c. D *sneeuw,* G *Schnee,* ON *snǣr,* Goth *snaiws,* L *nix* (gen. *nivis*), Gk *nípha* (acc. *nípha*), OCS *sněgŭ;* (v.) ME *snowen,* deriv. of the n.; r. ME *snewen,* OE *sniwan;* c. OHG *sniwan* (G *schneien*), MLG, MD *snien*] **—snow′less,** *adj.* **—snow′like′,** *adj.*

Snow (snō), *n.* **Sir Charles Percy** (*C. P. Snow*), 1905–80, English novelist and scientist. [1665–75]

snow′ ap′ple, Fameuse. [1765–75]

snow·ball (snō′bôl′), *n.* **1.** a ball of snow pressed or rolled together, as for throwing. **2.** any of several shrubs belonging to the genus *Viburnum,* of the honeysuckle family, having large clusters of white, sterile flowers. **3.** a confection of crushed ice, usually in the shape of a ball, which is flavored with fruit or other syrup and served in a paper cup. **4.** a scoop or ball of ice cream covered with shredded coconut and usually chocolate sauce. —*v.t.* **5.** to throw snowballs at. **6.** to cause to grow or become larger, greater, more intense, etc., at an accelerating rate: *to snowball a small business into a great enterprise.* —*v.i.* **7.** to grow or become larger, greater, more intense, etc., at an accelerating rate. [1350–1400; ME (n.); see SNOW, BALL[1]]

snow′ball bush′. See **guelder rose.** [1930–35]

snow·bank (snō′bangk′), *n.* a mound of snow, as a snowdrift or snow shoveled from a road or sidewalk. [1770–80; SNOW + BANK[1]]

snow′ ban′ner, snow being blown off a mountaintop. [1890–95, *Amer.*]

snow·bell (snō′bel′), *n.* a small tree belonging to the genus *Styrax,* of the storax family, having simple, alternate leaves and showy white bell-shaped flowers. [SNOW + BELL[1]]

snow·belt (snō′belt′), *n.* **1.** a region of annual or heavy snowfall. **2.** (*cap.*) Also, **Snow′ Belt′.** Also called **Frostbelt.** the northern parts of the U.S., esp. the Midwest and the Northeast, that are subject to considerable snowfall. [1870–75; SNOW + BELT]

snow·ber·ry (snō′ber′ē, -bə rē), *n., pl.* **-ries.** **1.** a North American shrub, *Symphoricarpos albus,* of the honeysuckle family, cultivated for its ornamental white berries. **2.** any of certain other white-berried plants. [1750–60, *Amer.;* SNOW + BERRY]

snow·bird (snō′bûrd′), *n.* **1.** junco. **2.** See **snow bunting.** **3.** *Informal.* a person who vacations in or moves to a warmer climate during cold weather. **4.** *Slang.* cokehead. [1665–75; SNOW + BIRD]

snow′ blind′ness, the usually temporary dimming of the sight caused by the glare of reflected sunlight on snow. [1740–50] **—snow-blind** (snō′blīnd′), *adj.*

snow·blink (snō′blingk′), *n.* a white luminosity on the underside of clouds, caused by the reflection of light from a snow surface. Cf. **iceblink.** [1860–65; SNOW + BLINK]

snow′ blow′er, a motor-driven machine on wheels used to remove snow by throwing it into the air and to one side. Also, **snow·blow·er** (snō′blō′ər). Also called **snow thrower.** [1945–50]

snow blower

snow′ board′, a board serving as a snow guard.

snow·board (snō′bôrd′, -bōrd′), *n.* a board for gliding on snow, resembling a wide ski, to which both feet are secured and that one rides in an upright position. [SNOW + BOARD] **—snow′board′er,** *n.* **—snow′board′ing,** *n.*

snow·bound (snō′bound′), *adj.* shut in or immobilized by snow. [1805–15; SNOW + -BOUND[1]]

snow-broth (snō′brôth′, -broth′), *n.* **1.** melted snow. **2.** a mixture of snow and water. **3.** ice-cold liquid. [1590–1600]

snow′ bunt′ing, a bunting, *Plectrophenax nivalis,* of the northern parts of the Northern Hemisphere having white plumage. Also called **snowbird, snowflake.** [1765–75]

snow·bush (snō′bŏŏsh′), *n.* **1.** any of several ornamental shrubs having a profusion of white flowers, as *Ceanothus cordulatus,* of the buckthorn family, native to western North America. **2.** a shrub, *Breynia disticha,* of the spurge family, native to the South Sea Islands, having white, speckled leaves, inconspicuous, greenish flowers, and red fruit. [SNOW + BUSH[1]]

snow·cap (snō′kap′), *n.* a layer of snow forming a cap on or covering the top of something, as a mountain peak or ridge. [1870–75; SNOW + CAP[1]]

snow·capped (snō′kapt′), *adj.* topped with snow: *the snowcapped Alps.* Also, **snow′-capped′.** [1790–1800]

snow·cat (snō′kat′), *n.* snowmobile. [1950–55; SNOW + CAT[2]]

snow-clad (snō′klad′), *adj.* covered with snow. [1800–10]

snow′ cone′, a paper cup with shaved or crushed ice over which flavored syrup has been poured. [1960–65]

snow′ cov′er, **1.** a layer of snow on the ground. **2.** the amount of an area that is covered by snow, usually given as a percentage of the total area. **3.** the depth of snow on the ground.

snow′ crab′, an edible spider crab of the North Pacific, *Chionoecetes opilio,* commercially important as a frozen seafood product.

snow·creep (snow′krēp′), *n.* a continuous, slow, downhill movement of snow. [1905–10; SNOW + CREEP]

snow′ crust′, a relatively hard, upper layer or film of ice or compacted snow on a snow surface. [1815–25]

snow′ crys′tal, a crystal of ice sufficiently heavy to fall from the atmosphere. Cf. **snowflake.** [1865–70]

snow′ day′, a day on which public schools or other institutions are closed due to heavy snow.

Snow·don (snōd′n), *n.* a mountain in NW Wales: highest peak in Wales. 3560 ft. (1085 m).

snow·drift (snō′drift′), *n.* **1.** a mound or bank of snow driven together by the wind. **2.** snow driven before the wind. [1250–1300; ME; see SNOW, DRIFT]

snow·drop (snō′drop′), *n.* any of several early-blooming bulbous plants belonging to the genus *Galanthus,* of the amaryllis family, native to Eurasia, esp. *G. nivalis,* having drooping white flowers with green markings. [1655–65; SNOW + DROP]

snow•fall (snō′fôl′), *n.* **1.** a fall of snow. **2.** the amount of snow at a particular place or in a given time. [1815–25; SNOW + FALL]

snow′ fence′, a barrier erected on the windward side of a road, house, barn, etc., serving as a protection from drifting snow. [1870–75, *Amer.*]

snow•field (snō′fēld′), *n. Geol.* a large and relatively permanent expanse of snow. [1835–45; SNOW + FIELD]

snow•flake (snō′flāk′), *n.* **1.** one of the small, feathery masses or flakes in which snow falls. **2.** *Meteorol.* **a.** an agglomeration of snow crystals falling as a unit. **b.** any snow particle. **3.** any of certain European plants belonging to the genus *Leucojum,* of the amaryllis family, resembling the snowdrop. **4.** See **snow bunting.** [1725–35; SNOW + FLAKE[1]]

snow′ gauge′, an instrument for measuring the depth of snow. [1885–90]

snow′ goose′, a white North American wild goose, previously classified as the species *Chen hyperborea* but now considered the light color phase of the blue goose, *C. caerulescens.* [1765–75, *Amer.*]

snow′ grains′, precipitation consisting of white, opaque ice particles usually less than one millimeter in diameter. [1960–65]

snow′ guard′, any device for preventing snow from sliding off a sloping roof. Also called **roof guard.** [1930–35]

snow′ ice′, opaque ice formed from partly melted snow or ice; frozen slush. [1835–45]

snow-in-sum•mer (snō′in sum′ər), *n.* a mat-forming garden plant, *Cerastium tomentosum,* of the pink family, native to Italy, having white flowers and numerous narrow, white, woolly leaves in large patches, growing in sand. [1885–90]

snow′ job′, *Slang.* an attempt to deceive or persuade by using flattery or exaggeration. [1940–45]

snow′ leop′ard, a long-haired, leopardlike feline, *Panthera (Uncia) uncia,* of mountain ranges of central Asia, having a relatively small head and a thick, creamy-gray coat with rosette spots: an endangered species. Also called **ounce**[2]. [1865–70]

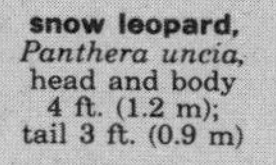

snow leopard, *Panthera uncia,* head and body 4 ft. (1.2 m); tail 3 ft. (0.9 m)

snow′ lil′y. See **glacier lily.** [1905–10]

snow′ line′, **1.** the line, as on mountains, above which there is perpetual snow. **2.** the latitudinal line marking the limit of the fall of snow at sea level. [1825–35]

snow•mak•ing (snō′mā′king), *n.* the creation of artificial snow at ski areas. [1950–55; SNOW + MAKING]

snow•man (snō′man′), *n., pl.* **-men.** a figure of a person made of packed snow. [1820–30; SNOW + MAN[1]]

snow•melt (snō′melt′), *n.* **1.** water from melting snow. **2.** the amount of such water. [1925–30; SNOW + MELT[1]]

snow•mo•bile (snō′mə bēl′), *n., v.* **-biled, -bil•ing.** —*n.* **1.** Also called **skimobile, snowcat.** a motor vehicle with a revolving tread in the rear and steerable skis in the front, for traveling over snow. —*v.i.* **2.** to operate or ride in a snowmobile. [1920–25; SNOW + -MOBILE] —**snow′mo•bil′er,** *n.*

snowmobile (def. 1)

snow′ mold′, *Plant. Pathol.* **1.** a disease of cereals and other grasses, characterized by a dense, cottony growth that covers the affected parts as the snow melts in the spring, caused by any of several fungi of the genera *Calonectria, Fusarium, Pythium,* and *Typhula.* **2.** any fungus causing this disease.

snow-on-the-moun•tain (snō′on thə moun′tn, -ôn-), *n.* a spurge, *Euphorbia marginata,* of the western U.S., having leaves with white margins and white petallike bracts. Also called **ghost-weed.** [1875–80, *Amer.*]

snow•pack (snō′pak′), *n.* the accumulation of winter snowfall, esp. in mountain or upland regions. [1945–50; SNOW + PACK[1]]

snow′ pea′, a variety of the common pea, *Pisum sativum macrocarpon,* having thin, flat, edible pods that are used in cookery. Also called **sugar pea.** [1945–50]

snow′ pear′, a small tree, *Pyrus nivalis,* of eastern Europe and Asia Minor, having showy flowers and nearly globe-shaped fruit. [1855–60]

snow′ pel′lets, precipitation, usually of brief duration, consisting of crisp, white, opaque ice particles, round or conical in shape and about two to five millimeters in diameter. Also called **graupel, soft hail, tapioca snow.** [1940–45]

snow′ plant′, a leafless, parasitic plant, *Sarcodes sanguinea,* of the pine forests of the Sierra Nevada in California, having a stout spike of bright red flowers, a thickly scaled stem, and a corallike mass of roots. [1840–50]

snow•plow (snō′plou′), *n.* **1.** an implement or machine for clearing away snow from highways, railroad tracks, etc. **2.** *Skiing.* a maneuver in which a skier pushes the heels of both skis outward so that they are far apart, as for turning, decreasing speed, or stopping. —*v.t.* **3.** to clear of snow using a snowplow. —*v.i.* **4.** to clear away snow with a snowplow. **5.** *Skiing.* to execute a snowplow. [1785–95, *Amer.*; SNOW + PLOW]

snow′ pud′ding, a pudding, prepared by folding egg whites into a lemon gelatin mixture. [1880–85]

snow′ ring′, *Skiing.* basket (def. 8).

snow•scape (snō′skāp′), *n.* **1.** landscape covered with snow. **2.** a picture of a snowy scene. [1885–90; SNOW + -SCAPE]

snow•shed (snō′shed′), *n.* a structure, as over an extent of railroad track on a mountainside, for protection against snow. [1865–70, *Amer.*; SNOW + SHED[1]]

snow•shoe (snō′sho͞o′), *n., v.,* **-shoed, -shoe•ing.** —*n.* **1.** a contrivance that may be attached to the foot to enable the wearer to walk on deep snow without sinking, esp. a light, racket-shaped frame across which is stretched a network of rawhide. **2.** See **Indian yellow** (def. 1). —*v.i.* **3.** to walk or travel on snowshoes. [1655–65, *Amer.*; SNOW + SHOE] —**snow′sho′er,** *n.*

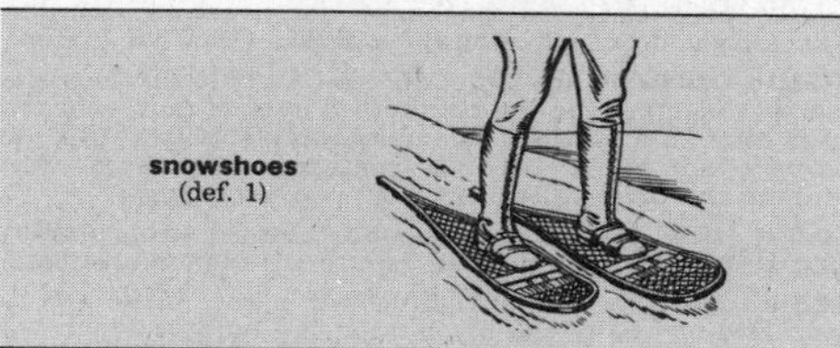

snowshoes (def. 1)

snow′shoe hare′, a large-footed North American hare, *Lepus americanus,* that is white in winter and dark brown in summer. Also called **snow′shoe rab′bit, varying hare.** [1885–90]

snow•slide (snō′slīd′), *n.* an avalanche consisting largely or entirely of snow. Also, *esp. Brit.,* **snow-slip** (snō′slip′). [1835–45, *Amer.*; SNOW + SLIDE]

Snows′ of Kilimanja′ro, The, a short story (1936) by Ernest Hemingway.

snow•storm (snō′stôrm′), *n.* a storm accompanied by a heavy fall of snow. [1765–75, *Amer.*; SNOW + STORM]

snow•suit (snō′so͞ot′), *n.* a child's one- or two-piece outer garment for cold weather, often consisting of heavily lined pants and jacket. [1935–40; SNOW + SUIT]

snow′ throw′er. See **snow blower.** Also, **snow•throw•er** (snō′thrō′ər). [1950–55]

snow′ tire′, an automobile tire with a deep tread or protruding studs to give increased traction on snow or ice. [1940–45]

snow′ train′, a train that takes passengers to and from a winter resort area. [1880–85]

snow-white (snō′hwīt′, -wīt′), *adj.* white as snow. [bef. 1000; ME; OE *snāwhwīt*]

snow•y (snō′ē), *adj.,* **snow•i•er, snow•i•est.** **1.** abounding in or covered with snow: *snowy fields.* **2.** characterized by snow, as the weather: *a snowy day.* **3.** pertaining to, consisting of, or resembling snow. **4.** of the color of snow; snow-white: *snowy skin.* **5.** immaculate; unsullied. [bef. 1000; ME *snawy,* OE *snāwig.* See SNOW, -Y[1]] —**snow′i•ly,** *adv.* —**snow′i•ness,** *n.*

snow′y e′gret, a white egret, *Egretta thula,* of the warmer parts of the Western Hemisphere: formerly hunted in great numbers for its plumes, the species is now protected and has recovered. [1890–95, *Amer.*]

snow′y owl′, a diurnal, arctic and subarctic owl, *Nyctea scandiaca,* having white plumage with dark brown markings. [1775–85]

snub (snub), *v.,* **snubbed, snub•bing,** *n., adj.* —*v.t.* **1.** to treat with disdain or contempt, esp. by ignoring. **2.** to check or reject with a sharp rebuke or remark. **3.** to check or stop suddenly (a rope or cable that is running out). **4.** to check (a boat, an unbroken horse, etc.) by means of a rope or line made fast to a fixed object. **5.** to pull up or stop abruptly in such a manner. —*n.* **6.** an act or instance of snubbing. **7.** an affront, slight, or rebuff. **8.** a sudden check given to a rope or cable running out, a moving boat, or the like. —*adj.* **9.** (of the nose) short and turned up at the tip. **10.** blunt. [1300–50; ME *snubben* < ON *snubba* to scold, reprimand; c. MLG *snūben*] —**snub′ber,** *n* —**snub′bing•ly,** *adv.*
—**Syn. 1.** slight. **2.** stop, reprove, reprimand.

snub•by (snub′ē), *adj.,* **-bi•er, -bi•est.** **1.** somewhat snub, as the nose. **2.** short and thick or wide; stubby; stumpy: *snubby fingers.* **3.** tending to snub people. [1820–30; SNUB + -Y[1]] —**snub′bi•ness,** *n.*

snub-nosed (snub′nōzd′), *adj.* **1.** having a snub nose: *a snub-nosed child.* **2.** having a blunt end: *snub-nosed pliers.* [1715–25]

snuck (snuk), a pp. and pt. of **sneak.**
—**Usage.** See **sneak.**

snuff[1] (snuf), *v.t.* **1.** to draw in through the nose by inhaling. **2.** to perceive by or as by smelling; sniff. **3.** to examine by smelling, as an animal does. —*v.i.* **4.** to draw air into the nostrils by inhaling, as to smell something; snuffle: *After snuffing around, he found the gas leak.* **5.** to draw powdered tobacco into the nostrils; take snuff. **6.** *Obs.* to express disdain, contempt, displeasure, etc., by sniffing (often fol. by *at*). —*n.* **7.** an act of snuffing; an inhalation through the nose; a sniff. **8.** smell, scent, or odor. **9.** a preparation of tobacco, either powdered and taken into the nostrils by inhalation or ground and placed between the cheek and gum. **10.** a pinch of such tobacco. **11. up to snuff,** *Informal.* **a.** *Brit.* not easily imposed upon; shrewd; sharp. **b.** up to a certain standard; satisfactory: *His performance wasn't up to snuff.* [1520–30; < D *snuffen*] —**snuff′ing•ly,** *adv.*

snuff[2] (snuf), *n.* **1.** the charred or partly consumed portion of a candlewick. **2.** a thing of little or no value, esp. if left over. —*v.t.* **3.** to cut off or remove the snuff of (candles, tapers, etc.). **4. snuff out, a.** to extinguish: *to snuff out a candle.* **b.** to suppress; crush: *to snuff out opposition.* **c.** *Informal.* to kill or murder: *Many lives were snuffed out during the epidemic.* [1350–1400; ME *snoffe* < ?]

snuff•box (snuf′boks′), *n.* a box for holding snuff, esp. one small enough to be carried in the pocket. [1680–90; SNUFF[1] + BOX[1]]

snuff•er[1] (snuf′ər), *n.* **1.** a person who snuffs or sniffs. **2.** a person who takes snuff. [1600–10; SNUFF[1] + -ER[1]]

snuff•er[2] (snuf′ər), *n.* **1.** candlesnuffer. **2.** extinguisher (def. 3). **3.** a person who snuffs candles. [1425–75; late ME. See SNUFF[2], -ER[1]]

snuff′ film′, *Slang.* **1.** a pornographic film that shows an actual murder of one of the performers, as at the end of a sadistic act. **2.** See **splatter film.** Also called **snuff′ mov′ie.** [1970–75]

snuf•fle (snuf′əl), *v.,* **-fled, -fling,** *n.* —*v.i.* **1.** to draw air into the nose for the purpose of smelling something; snuff. **2.** to draw the breath or mucus through the nostrils in an audible or noisy manner; sniffle; snivel. **3.** to speak through the nose or with a nasal twang. **4.** to whine; snivel. —*v.t.* **5.** to utter in a snuffling or nasal tone. —*n.* **6.** an act or sound of snuffling. **7. snuffles,** a condition of the nose, as from a cold, causing snuffling (usually prec. by *the*). **8.** a nasal tone of voice. [1575–85; < D *snuffelen* to nose (in something), deriv. of *snuffen* to SNUFF[1] with freq. suffix *-el-*; see -LE] —**snuf′fler,** *n.* —**snuf′fling•ly,** *adv.* —**snuf′fly,** *adj.*

snuff′ stick′, a twig, stick, or brush used to apply snuff on the teeth or gums. Also called **snuff′ brush′.** [1865–70, *Amer.*]

snuff•y (snuf′ē), *adj.,* **snuff•i•er, snuff•i•est.** **1.** resembling snuff. **2.** soiled with snuff. **3.** given to the use of snuff. **4.** having an unpleasant appearance. **5.** having hurt feelings. **6.** easily displeased. [1780–90; SNUFF[1] + -Y[1]] —**snuff′i•ness,** *n.*

snug (snug), *adj.,* **snug•ger, snug•gest,** *v.,* **snugged, snug•ging,** *adv., n.* —*adj.* **1.** warmly comfortable or cozy, as a place, accommodations, etc.: *a snug little house.* **2.** fitting closely, as a garment: *a snug jacket.* **3.** more or less compact or limited in size, and sheltered or warm: *a snug harbor.* **4.** trim, neat, or compactly arranged, as a ship or its parts. **5.** comfortably circumstanced, as persons. **6.** pleasant or agreeable, esp. in a small, exclusive way: *a snug coterie of writers.* **7.** enabling one to live in comfort: *a snug fortune.* **8.** secret; concealed; well-hidden: *a snug hideout.* —*v.i.* **9.** to lie closely or comfortably; nestle. —*v.t.* **10.** to make snug. **11.** *Naut.* to prepare for a storm by taking in sail, lashing deck gear, etc. (usually fol. by *down*). —*adv.* **12.** in a snug manner: *The shirt fit snug around the neck.* —*n.* **13.** *Brit.* a small, secluded room in a tavern, as for private parties. [1575–85; perh. < ON *snøggr* short-haired; c. Sw *snygg* neat] —**snug′ly,** *adv.* —**snug′ness,** *n.*
—**Syn. 4.** tidy, ordered, orderly. **6.** intimate, cozy. **9.** cuddle, snuggle. **10.** settle, arrange. **11.** secure.

snug•ger•y (snug′ə rē), *n., pl.* **-ger•ies.** *Brit.* **1.** a snug place or position. **2.** a comfortable or cozy room. Also, **snug′ger•ie.** [1805–15; SNUG + -ERY]

snug•gies (snug′ēz), *n.* (*used with a plural v.*) *Informal.* warm knitted underwear, esp. long underpants, for women or children. [SNUG + -Y[2] + -S[3]]

snug•gle (snug′əl), *v.,* **-gled, -gling,** *n.* —*v.i.* **1.** to lie or press closely, as for comfort or from affection; nestle; cuddle. —*v.t.* **2.** to draw or press closely against, as for comfort or from affection. —*n.* **3.** the act of snuggling. [1680–90; SNUG + -LE]

Sny•der (snī′dər), *n.* a city in NW central Texas. 12,705.

snye (snī), *n. Canadian* (*chiefly Ontario*). **1.** a backwater. **2.** a side-channel, esp. one that later rejoins the main stream. **3.** a channel joining two rivers. [1810–20; prob. < CanF *chenail, chenal* channel, F *chenal,* b. OF *chanel, chenel* CHANNEL[1] and *canal* CANAL]

so[1] (sō), *adv.* **1.** in the way or manner indicated, described, or implied: *Do it so.* **2.** in that or this manner or fashion; thus: *So it turned out.* **3.** in the aforesaid state or condition: *It is broken and has long been so.* **4.** to the extent or degree indicated or suggested: *Do not walk so fast.* **5.** *Informal.* very or extremely: *I'm so sad.* **6.** very greatly: *My head aches so!* **7.** (used before an adverb or an adverbial clause and fol. by *as*) to such a degree or extent: *so far as I know.* **8.** having the purpose of: *a speech so commemorating the victory.* **9.** for this or that reason; hence; therefore: *She is ill, and so cannot come to the party.* **10.** (used as an affirmative to emphasize or confirm a previous statement) most certainly: *I said I would come, and so I will.* **11.** (used as an emphatic affirmative to contradict a previous statement) indeed; truly; too: *I was so at the party!* **12.** likewise or correspondingly; also; too: *If he is going, then so am I.* **13.** in such manner as to follow or result from: *As he learned, so did he teach.* **14.** in the way that follows; in this way: *The audience was seated, and so the famous speech began.* **15.** in the way that precedes; in that way: *So ended the speech, and the listeners arose and cheered.* **16.** in such way as to end in: *So live your life that old age will bring you no regrets.* **17.** then; subsequently: *and so to bed.* **18. so much as,** even: *He doesn't so much as say hello to me.* **19. so as, a.** with the result

CONCISE PRONUNCIATION KEY: *act, cāpe, dâre, pärt; set, ēqual; if, īce; ox, ōver, ôrder, oil, bo͝ok, bo͞ot, out; up, ûrge; child; sing; shoe; thin, that;* zh as in *treasure.* ə = *a* as in *alone, e* as in *system, i* as in *easily, o* as in *gallop, u* as in *circus;* ° as in *fire* (fī°r), *hour* (ou°r). l and n can serve as syllabic consonants, as in *cradle* (krād′l), and *button* (but′n). See the full key inside the front cover.

or purpose: *to turn up the volume of the radio so as to drown out the noise from the next apartment.* **b.** *Older Use.* provided that: *I like any flower, just so as it's real.* **20. only** or **just so many,** being a limited or small number or amount: *I can eat only so many pieces of fruit.* **21. only** or **just so much,** being a limited amount or quantity; up to a certain point or maximum: *I can eat only so much fruit; just so much that one can do in such a case.* **22. so to speak.** See **speak** (def. 20). **23. so what?** See **what** (def. 17).
—*conj.* **24.** in order that (often fol. by *that*): *Check carefully, so any mistakes will be caught.* **25.** with the result that (often fol. by *that*): *He checked carefully, so that the mistakes were caught.* **26.** on the condition that; if.
—*pron.* **27.** such as has been stated: *to be good and stay so.* **28.** something that is about or near the persons or things in question, as in number or amount: *Of the original twelve, five or so remain.* **29. so much, a.** something, as an amount or cost, that is not specified or determined: *The carpeting is priced at so much per yard.* **b.** all that is or needs to be said or done: *So much for the preliminaries, let's get down to the real issues.*
—*interj.* **30.** (used as an exclamation of surprise, shock, discovery, inquiry, indifference, etc., according to the manner of utterance.)
—*adj.* **31.** true as stated or reported; conforming with reality or the fact: *Say it isn't so.* [bef. 900; ME; OE *swā*; c. D *zoo*, G *so*, Goth *swa*]
—Syn. 9. See **therefore.**
—Usage. 5. The intensive so meaning "very or extremely" (*Everything's so expensive these days*) occurs chiefly in informal speech. In writing and formal speech, intensive so is most often followed by a completing *that* clause: *Everything is so expensive that some families must struggle just to survive.*
24, 25. The conjunction so (often followed by THAT) introduces clauses both of purpose (*We ordered our tickets early so that we could get good seats*) and of result (*The river had frozen during the night so people walked across it all the next day*). In formal speech and writing, SO THAT is somewhat more common than so in clauses of purpose. Otherwise, either SO or SO THAT is standard.
Like AND, BUT[1], and OR, so can occur as a transitional word at the beginning of a sentence: *So all our hard work finally brought results.* See also **as**[1], **and, but**[1].

so[2] (sō), *n. Music.* sol[1].

So., 1. South. **2.** Southern.

S.O., 1. Signal Officer. **2.** Special Order. **3.** Standing Order.

s.o., 1. seller's option. **2.** shipping order.

soak (sōk), *v.i.* **1.** to lie in and become saturated or permeated with water or some other liquid. **2.** to pass, as a liquid, through pores, holes, or the like: *Rain soaked through the roof.* **3.** to be thoroughly wet. **4.** to penetrate or become known to the mind or feelings (fol. by *in*): *The lesson didn't soak in.* **5.** *Informal.* to drink immoderately, esp. alcoholic beverages. —*v.t.* **6.** to place or keep in liquid in order to saturate thoroughly; steep. **7.** to wet thoroughly; saturate or drench. **8.** to permeate thoroughly, as liquid or moisture does. **9.** *Metall.* to heat (a piece) for reworking. **10.** *Informal.* to intoxicate (oneself) by drinking an excess of liquor. **11.** *Slang.* to beat hard; punish severely: *I was soaked for that mistake.* **12.** to extract or remove by or as by soaking (often fol. by *out*): *to soak a stain out of a napkin.* **13.** *Slang.* to overcharge: *The waiter soaked him.* **14. soak up, a.** to absorb or take in or up by absorption: *Blotting paper soaks up ink.* **b.** to absorb with one's mind or senses; take in: *to soak up information.* **c.** *Slang.* to drink to excess: *He can really soak up the booze.* —*n.* **15.** the act or state of soaking or the state of being soaked. **16.** the liquid in which anything is soaked. **17.** *Slang.* a heavy drinker. **18.** *Australian.* any small area of land, as near a spring or at the foot of a hill, that becomes swamplike or holds water after a period of heavy rain. [bef. 1000; ME *soken*, OE *sōcian*; akin to SUCK] **—soak′er,** *n.* **—soak′ing·ly,** *adv.*
—Syn. 2, 4. seep. **7.** See **wet. 8.** infuse, penetrate.

soak·age (sō′kij), *n.* **1.** the act of soaking. **2.** liquid that has seeped out or been absorbed. [1760–70; SOAK + -AGE]

soak·ers (sō′kərz), *n.* (*used with a plural v.*) absorbent, knitted briefs or shorts, often of wool, used as a diaper cover on infants. [SOAKER + -S[3]]

so-and-so (sō′ən sō′), *n., pl.* **so-and-sos. 1.** someone or something not definitely named: *to gossip about so-and-so.* **2.** a bastard; son of a bitch (used as a euphemism): *Tell the old so-and-so to mind his own business.* [1590–1600]

Soane (sōn), *n.* **Sir John,** 1753–1837, English architect.

soap (sōp), *n.* **1.** a substance used for washing and cleansing purposes, usually made by treating a fat with an alkali. **2.** any metallic salt of an acid derived from a fat. **3.** *Slang.* money, esp. as used for bribery in politics. **4.** *Slang.* Also, **soaper.** See **soap opera. 5. no soap,** *Informal.* no go: *He wanted me to vote for him, but I told him no soap.* —*v.t.* **6.** to rub, cover, lather, or treat with soap. [bef. 1000; ME *sope*, OE *sāpe*, c. G *Seife*, D *zeep*, all < WGmc (perh. > > L *sāpō*; cf. SAPONIFY)] **—soap′less,** *adj.* **—soap′like′,** *adj.*

soap·bark (sōp′bärk′), *n.* **1.** a Chilean tree, *Quillaja saponaria*, of the rose family, having evergreen leaves and small, white flowers. **2.** the inner bark of this tree, used as a substitute for soap. [1860–65; SOAP + BARK[2]]

soap·ber·ry (sōp′ber′ē, -bə rē), *n., pl.* **-ries. 1.** the fruit of any tropical or subtropical tree of the genus *Sapindus*, esp. *S. saponaria*, used as a substitute for soap. **2.** the tree itself. [1685–95; SOAP + BERRY]

soap′berry fam′ily, the plant family Sapindaceae, characterized by chiefly tropical trees, shrubs, or herbaceous vines having compound leaves, clustered flowers, and berrylike, fleshy, or capsular fruit, and including the balloon vine, golden rain tree, litchi, and soapberry.

soap·box (sōp′boks′), *n.* **1.** Also, **soap′ box′.** an improvised platform, as one on a street, from which a speaker delivers an informal speech, an appeal, or political harangue. —*adj.* **2.** of, pertaining to, or characteristic of a speaker or speech from a soapbox. [1650–60; SOAP + BOX[1]]

Soap′ Box Der′by, *Trademark.* a race for children driving motorless, wooden vehicles built by the drivers to resemble racing cars.

soap′ bub′ble, 1. a bubble of soapsuds. **2.** something that lacks substance or permanence. [1805–15]

soap′ dish′, a dish designed to hold a bar of soap, esp. as a bathroom or kitchen fixture attached to a sink, lavatory, or bathtub. [1830–40]

soap·er (sō′pər), *n. Slang.* See **soap opera.** [1945–50; SOAP (OPERA) + -ER[1]]

soap·fish (sōp′fish′), *n., pl.* (*esp. collectively*) **-fish,** (*esp. referring to two or more kinds or species*) **-fish·es.** any of several serranid fishes of the genus *Rypticus*, producing a body mucus that gives the skin a soapy quality, as *R. saponaceus*, inhabiting shallow waters of the Atlantic Ocean. [1875–80; SOAP + FISH]

soap′ flakes′, small flakes or chips of soap commercially produced and packaged for washing laundry, dishes, etc. Also called **soap′ chips′.** [1930–35, *Amer.*]

soap′ op′er·a (op′ər ə, op′rə), a radio or television series depicting the interconnected lives of many characters often in a sentimental, melodramatic way. [1935–40, *Amer.*; so called because soap manufacturers were among the original sponsors of such programs]

soap′ pad′, a small pad, usually of steel wool, containing a strong soap and used esp. to scour pots and pans.

soap′ plant′, 1. a Californian plant, *Chlorogalum pomeridianum*, of the lily family, the bulb of which was used by the Indians as a soap. **2.** any of various other plants having parts that can be used as a soap. [1835–45, *Amer.*]

soap′ pow′der, soap produced and packaged in powdered form. [1885–90]

soap·stone (sōp′stōn′), *n.* a massive variety of talc with a soapy or greasy feel, used for hearths, washtubs, tabletops, carved ornaments, etc. Also called **steatite.** [1675–85; SOAP + STONE]

soap·suds (sōp′sudz′), *n.* (*used with a plural v.*) suds made with water and soap. [1605–15; SOAP + SUDS] **—soap′suds′y,** *adj.*

soap·wort (sōp′wûrt′, -wôrt′), *n.* a plant, *Saponaria officinalis*, of the pink family, whose leaves are used for cleansing. Also called **bouncing Bet, bouncing Bess.** [1540–50; SOAP + WORT[2]]

soap·y (sō′pē), *adj.,* **soap·i·er, soap·i·est. 1.** containing or impregnated with soap: *soapy water.* **2.** covered with soap or lather: *soapy dishes.* **3.** of the nature of soap; resembling soap: *a soft, soapy fiber.* **4.** pertaining to or characteristic of soap: *a clean, soapy smell.* **5.** *Informal.* characteristic or reminiscent of a soap opera; melodramatic; corny: *a soapy plot.* [1600–10; SOAP + -Y[1]] **—soap′i·ly,** *adv.* **—soap′i·ness,** *n.*

soar (sôr, sōr), *v.i.* **1.** to fly upward, as a bird. **2.** to fly at a great height, without visible movements of the pinions, as a bird. **3.** to glide along at a height, as an airplane. **4.** to rise or ascend to a height, as a mountain. **5.** to rise or aspire to a higher or more exalted level: *His hopes soared.* —*n.* **6.** an act or instance of soaring. **7.** the height attained in soaring. [1325–75; ME *soren* < MF *essorer* < VL **exaurāre*, equiv. to L *ex-* EX-[1] + *aur(a)* air + *-āre* inf. suffix] **—soar′er,** *n.* **—soar′ing·ly,** *adv.*
—Syn. 1. See **fly**[1]. **4.** tower; mount.

So·a·res (swär′ əsh; *Port.* swä′rəsh), *n.* **Má·rio** (mä′-ryŏŏ), born 1924, Portugese statesman: prime minister 1976–78, 1983–85; president since 1986.

soar·ing (sôr′ing, sōr′-), *n.* the sport of flying a sailplane. [1895–90; SOAR + -ING[1]]

so·a·ve (swä′vā; *It.* sô ä′ve), *n.* a dry, white wine from Verona, Italy. [1940–45; < It < L *suāvis* SWEET]

sob (sob), *v.,* **sobbed, sob·bing,** *n.* —*v.i.* **1.** to weep with a convulsive catching of the breath. **2.** to make a sound resembling this. —*v.t.* **3.** to utter with sobs. **4.** to put, send, etc., by sobbing or with sobs: *to sob oneself to sleep.* —*n.* **5.** the act of sobbing; a convulsive catching of the breath in weeping. **6.** any sound suggesting this. [1150–1200; ME *sobben*, appar. imit.] **—sob′ber,** *n.* **—sob′bing·ly,** *adv.* **—sob′ful,** *adj.*

S.O.B., (*sometimes l.c.*) *Slang.* See **son of a bitch.** Also, **SOB**

so·be·it (sō bē′it), *conj. Archaic.* if it be so that; provided that. [1575–85; SO[1] + BE + IT[1]]

so·ber (sō′bər), *adj.,* **-er, -est,** *v.* —*adj.* **1.** not intoxicated or drunk. **2.** habitually temperate, esp. in the use of liquor. **3.** quiet or sedate in demeanor, as persons. **4.** marked by seriousness, gravity, solemnity, etc., as of demeanor, speech, etc.: *a sober occasion.* **5.** subdued in tone, as color; not gay or showy, as clothes. **6.** free from excess, extravagance, or exaggeration: *sober facts.* **7.** showing self-control: *sober restraint.* **8.** sane or rational: *a sober solution to the problem.* —*v.t., v.i.* **9.** to make or become sober: (often fol. by *up*). [1300–50; ME *sobre* < OF < L *sōbrius*] **—so′ber·ing·ly,** *adv.* **—so′ber·ly,** *adv.* **—so′ber·ness,** *n.*
—Syn. 2. abstinent, abstemious. **4.** serious, quiet, sedate, subdued, staid. See **grave**[2]. **5.** somber, dull. **7.** composed, collected. **8.** reasonable, sound. **—Ant. 4.** gay.

so·ber-head·ed (sō′bər hed′id), *adj.* characterized by clear, logical thinking; not fanciful or capricious.

so·ber·ize (sō′bə rīz′), *v.,* **-ized, -iz·ing.** —*v.t.* **1.** to make sober. —*v.i.* **2.** *Archaic.* to become sober. Also, *esp. Brit.,* **so′ber·ise′.** [1700–10; SOBER + -IZE]

so·ber-mind·ed (sō′bər mīn′did), *adj.* rational; sensible. [1525–35] **—so′ber-mind′ed·ness,** *n.*

so·ber·sid·ed (sō′bər sī′did), *adj.* solemn or grave in disposition, attitude, character, etc.; serious-minded. [1840–50; SOBER + SIDE[1] + -ED[3]]

so·ber·sides (sō′bər sīdz′), *n., pl.* **-sides.** (*used with a singular v.*) *Slang.* a humorless or habitually serious person. [1695–1705; SOBER + SIDE[1] + -S[3]]

So·bhu·za II (sô bo͞o′zə), 1899–1982, king of Swaziland 1921–82.

So·bies·ki (sô byes′kē), *n.* **John.** See **John III** (def. 2).

So·bor (sə bôr′), *n.* (*sometimes l.c.*) *Eastern Ch.* a council, synod, or convention. [< Russ *sobór*, ORuss, OCS *sŭborŭ* council, meeting, equiv. to *sŭ-* together, with + *-borŭ*, n. deriv. of *brati* to take (akin to BEAR[1]); calque of Gk *synagōgḗ* (see SYNAGOGUE)]

So·bran·je (sô brän′yə), *n.* the national assembly of Bulgaria, consisting of a single chamber of elected deputies. [< Bulgarian *sŭbránie* assembly]

so·bri·e·ty (sə brī′i tē, sō-), *n.* **1.** the state or quality of being sober. **2.** temperance or moderation, esp. in the use of alcoholic beverages. **3.** seriousness, gravity, or solemnity: *an event marked by sobriety.* [1375–1425; late ME *sobrietie* (< OF *sobriete*) < L *sōbrietās*, equiv. to *sōbri(us)* SOBER + *-etās*, var. of *-itās* -ITY after vowel stems]

so·bri·quet (sō′brə kā′, -ket′, sō′brə kā′, -ket′; *Fr.* sô brē ke′), *n., pl.* **-quets** (-kāz′, -kets′, -kāz′, -kets′; *Fr.* -ke′). a nickname. Also, **soubriquet.** [1640–50; < F < ?] **—so′bri·quet′i·cal,** *adj.*

sob′ sis′ter, 1. a journalist who writes human-interest stories with sentimental pathos. **2.** a persistently sentimental do-gooder. [1910–15]

sob′ sto′ry, 1. an excessively sentimental human-interest story. **2.** an alibi or excuse, esp. one designed to arouse sympathy: *Instead of a raise, the boss gave us another sob story about her expenses.* [1915–20]

soc (sŏs, sŏsh), *n. Informal.* sociology or a class or course in sociology. [by shortening]

Soc., 1. socialist. **2.** (*often l.c.*) society. **3.** sociology.

so·ca (sō′kä), *n.* a style of Caribbean dance music derived from calypso and American soul music and having a pounding beat. [1975–80; SO(UL) + CA(LYPSO)]

soc·age (sok′ij), *n. Medieval Eng. Law.* a tenure of land held by the tenant in performance of specified services or by payment of rent, and not requiring military service. Also, **soc′cage.** [1275–1325; ME *sokage* < AF *socage*, equiv. to *soc* SOKE + *-age* -AGE]

soc·ag·er (sok′ə jər), *n.* a tenant holding land by socage; sokeman. [1640–50; SOCAGE + -ER[1]]

so-called (sō′kôld′), *adj.* **1.** called or designated thus: *the so-called Southern bloc.* **2.** incorrectly called or styled thus: *so-called intellectuals.* [1650–60]

soc·cer (sok′ər), *n.* a form of football played between two teams of 11 players, in which the ball may be advanced by kicking or by bouncing it off any part of the body but the arms and hands, except in the case of the goalkeepers, who may use their hands to catch, carry, throw, or stop the ball. [1890–95; (*As*)*soc*(*iation football*) + -ER[7]]

So·che (sô′chu′), *n. Wade-Giles.* Shache.

So·chi (sô′chē; *Russ.* sô′chyi), *n.* a seaport in the SW Russian Federation in Europe, on the Black Sea: resort. 317,000.

so·cia·bil·i·ty (sō′shə bil′i tē), *n.* **1.** the act or an instance of being sociable. **2.** the quality, state, disposition, or inclination of being sociable. [1425–75; late ME; see SOCIABLE, -ITY]

so·cia·ble (sō′shə bəl), *adj.* **1.** inclined to associate with or be in the company of others. **2.** friendly or agreeable in company; companionable. **3.** characterized by agreeable companionship: *a sociable evening at the home of friends.* —*n.* **4.** *Chiefly Northern and Midland U.S.* an informal social gathering, esp. of members of a church. [1545–55; < L *sociābilis*, equiv. to *sociā(re)* to unite (deriv. of *socius* partner, comrade) + *-bilis* -BLE] **—so′cia·ble·ness,** *n.* **—so′cia·bly,** *adv.*

so·cial (sō′shəl), *adj.* **1.** pertaining to, devoted to, or characterized by friendly companionship or relations: *a social club.* **2.** seeking or enjoying the companionship of others; friendly; sociable; gregarious. **3.** of, pertaining to, connected with, or suited to polite or fashionable society: *a social event.* **4.** living or disposed to live in companionship with others or in a community, rather than in isolation: *People are social beings.* **5.** of or pertaining to human society, esp. as a body divided into classes according to status: *social rank.* **6.** involved in many social activities: *We're so busy working, we have to be a little less social now.* **7.** of or pertaining to the life, welfare, and relations of human beings in a community: *social problems.* **8.** noting or pertaining to activities designed to remedy or alleviate certain unfavorable conditions of life in a community, esp. among the poor. **9.** pertaining to or advocating socialism. **10.** *Zool.* living habitually together in communities, as bees or ants. Cf. **solitary** (def. 8). **11.** *Bot.* growing in patches or clumps. **12.** *Rare.* occurring or taking place between allies or confederates. —*n.* **13.** a social gathering or party, esp. of or as given by an organized group: *a church social.* [1555–65; < L *sociālis*, equiv. to *soci(us)* partner, comrade + *-ālis* -AL[1]] **—so′cial·ly,** *adv.* **—so′cial·ness,** *n.*

so′cial ac′tion, individual or group behavior that involves interaction with other individuals or groups, esp. organized action toward social reform. [1850–55]

so′cial anthropol′ogy. See **cultural anthropology.** **—so′cial anthropol′ogist.**

so′cial bee′, any of several bees, as the honeybees or bumblebees, that live together in communities. Cf. **solitary bee.**

so′cial class′, *Sociol.* a broad group in society having common economic, cultural, or political status.

so′cial climb′er, a person who attempts to gain admission into a group with a higher social standing. [1920–25] —**so′cial climb′ing.**

so′cial con′tract, **1.** the voluntary agreement among individuals by which, according to any of various theories, as of Hobbes, Locke, or Rousseau, organized society is brought into being and invested with the right to secure mutual protection and welfare or to regulate the relations among its members. **2.** an agreement for mutual benefit between an individual or group and the government or community as a whole. Also, **so′cial com′pact.** [1840–50]

so′cial control′, **1.** *Sociol.* the enforcement of conformity by society upon its members, either by law or by social pressure. **2.** the influence of any element in social life working to maintain the pattern of such life.

So′cial Cred′it, *Econ.* the doctrine that under capitalism there is an inadequate distribution of purchasing power, for which the remedy lies in governmental control of retail prices and the distribution of national dividends to consumers.

so′cial danc′ing, dancing performed by couples or by groups, usually as a form of recreation.

So′cial Dar′winism, *Sociol.* a 19th-century theory, inspired by Darwinism, by which the social order is accounted as the product of natural selection of those persons best suited to existing living conditions and in accord with which a position of laissez-faire is advocated. Also, **so′cial Dar′winism.** [1885–90] —**So′cial Dar′winist, so′cial Dar′winist.**

So′cial Democ′racy, the principles and policies of a Social Democratic party. [1885–90]

So′cial Dem′ocrat, (esp. in Europe) a member of any of certain Social Democratic parties. [1875–80]

So′cial Democrat′ic par′ty, **1.** *Hist.* a political party in Germany advocating a form of social organization based on the economic and political ideology of Karl Marx. **2.** any of several European political parties advocating a gradual transition to socialism or a modified form of socialism by and under democratic processes. **3.** a U.S. political party, organized about 1897, that joined former members of the Socialist Labor party to form the Socialist party.

So′cial Democrat′ic Work′ingmen's par′ty, the name of the Socialist Labor party from 1874 to 1877.

so′cial differentia′tion, *Sociol.* the distinction made between social groups and persons on the basis of biological, physiological, and sociocultural factors, as sex, age, race, nationality, etc.

so′cial disease′, a venereal disease. [1915–20]

so′cial disorganiza′tion, *Sociol.* disruption or breakdown of the structure of social relations and values resulting in the loss of social controls over individual and group behavior, the development of social isolation and conflict, and a sense of estrangement or alienation from the mainstream of one's culture; the condition or state of anomie.

so′cial dis′tance, *Sociol.* the extent to which individuals or groups are removed from or excluded from participating in one another's lives.

so′cial dynam′ics, *Sociol.* the study of social processes, esp. social change. Cf. **social statics.** [1835–45]

so′cial econom′ics, socioeconomics.

so′cial engineer′ing, the application of the findings of social science to the solution of actual social problems. [1895–1900] —**so′cial engineer′.**

so′cial envi′ronment, *Sociol.* the environment developed by humans as contrasted with the natural environment; society as a whole, esp. in its relation to the individual.

so′cial e′vil, **1.** anything detrimental to a society or its citizens, as alcoholism, organized crime, etc. **2.** prostitution. [1855–60]

so′cial evolu′tion, *Sociol.* the gradual development of society and social forms, institutions, etc., usually through a series of peaceful stages. Cf. **revolution** (def. 2).

so′cial gos′pel, *Protestantism.* a movement in America, chiefly in the early part of the 20th century, stressing the social teachings of Jesus and their applicability to public life. [1915–20]

so′cial her′itage, *Sociol.* the entire inherited pattern of cultural activity present in a society.

so′cial insur′ance, any of various forms of insurance in which a government is an insurer, esp. such insurance that provides assistance to disabled or unemployed workers and to aged persons. [1915–20]

so·cial·ism (sō′shə liz′əm), *n.* **1.** a theory or system of social organization that advocates the vesting of the ownership and control of the means of production and distribution, of capital, land, etc., in the community as a whole. **2.** procedure or practice in accordance with this theory. **3.** (in Marxist theory) the stage following capitalism in the transition of a society to communism, characterized by the imperfect implementation of collectivist principles. Cf. **utopian socialism.** [1830–40; SOCIAL + -ISM]

so′cial isola′tion, *Sociol.* a state or process in which persons, groups, or cultures lose or do not have communication or cooperation with one another, often resulting in open conflict.

so·cial·ist (sō′shə list), *n.* **1.** an advocate or supporter of socialism. **2.** (*cap.*) a member of the U.S. Socialist party. —*adj.* **3.** socialistic. [1825–35; SOCIAL + -IST]

so·cial·is·tic (sō′shə lis′tik), *adj.* **1.** of or pertaining to socialists or socialism. **2.** in accordance with socialism. **3.** advocating or supporting socialism. [1840–50; SOCIAL(ISM) + -ISTIC] —**so′cial·is′ti·cal·ly,** *adv.*

So′cialist La′bor par′ty, a U.S. political party, organized in 1874, advocating the peaceful introduction of socialism.

So′cialist par′ty, **1.** a U.S. political party advocating socialism, formed about 1900 chiefly by former members of the Social Democratic party and the Socialist Labor party. **2.** any political party advocating socialism.

so′cialist re′alism, a state-approved artistic or literary style in some socialist countries, as the U.S.S.R., that characteristically celebrates an idealized vision of the life and industriousness of the workers. Also, **So′cialist Re′alism.** [1930–35]

so·cial·ite (sō′shə līt′), *n.* a socially prominent person. [1925–30; SOCIAL + -ITE[1]]

so·ci·al·i·ty (sō′shē al′i tē), *n.* **1.** social nature or tendencies as shown in the assembling of individuals in communities. **2.** the action on the part of individuals of associating together in communities. **3.** the state or quality of being social. [1640–50; < L *sociālitāt-* (s. of *sociālitās*). See SOCIAL, -ITY]

so·cial·i·za·tion (sō′shə lə zā′shən), *n.* **1.** a continuing process whereby an individual acquires a personal identity and learns the norms, values, behavior, and social skills appropriate to his or her social position. **2.** the act or process of making socialistic: *the socialization of industry.* [1885–90; SOCIALIZE + -ATION]

so·cial·ize (sō′shə līz′), *v.,* **-ized, -iz·ing.** —*v.t.* **1.** to make social; make fit for life in companionship with others. **2.** to make socialistic; establish or regulate according to the theories of socialism. **3.** *Educ.* to treat as a group activity: *to socialize spelling quizzes.* —*v.i.* **4.** to associate or mingle sociably with others: *to socialize with one's fellow workers.* Also, *esp. Brit.,* **so′cial·ise′.** [1820–30; SOCIAL + -IZE] —**so′cial·iz′a·ble,** *adj.* —**so′cial·iz′er,** *n.*

so′cialized med′icine, any of various systems to provide the entire population with complete medical care through government subsidization and regularization of medical and health services. [1935–40]

so·cial-mind·ed (sō′shəl mīn′did), *adj.* interested in or concerned with social conditions or the welfare of society. [1925–30] —**so′cial-mind′ed·ly,** *adv.* —**so′cial-mind′ed·ness,** *n.*

so′cial mobil′ity, mobility (def. 2). [1925–30]

so′cial organiza′tion, *Sociol.* the structure of social relations within a group, usually the relations between its subgroups and institutions.

so′cial pathol′ogy, **1.** a social factor, as poverty, old age, or crime, that tends to increase social disorganization and inhibit personal adjustment. **2.** the study of such factors and the social problems they produce.

so′cial proc′ess, *Sociol.* the means by which culture and social organization change or are preserved.

so′cial psychol′ogy, the psychological study of social behavior, esp. of the reciprocal influence of the individual and the group with which the individual interacts. [1905–10]

so′cial re′alism, a style of painting, esp. of the 1930's in the U.S., in which the scenes depicted typically convey a message of social or political protest edged with satire. Also, **So′cial Re′alism.** —**so′cial re′alist.**

So′cial Reg′ister, *Trademark.* the book listing the names, addresses, clubs, etc., of the principal members of fashionable society in a given city or area.

so′cial sci′ence, **1.** the study of society and social behavior. **2.** a science or field of study, as history, economics, etc., dealing with an aspect of society or forms of social activity. [1775–85] —**so′cial sci′entist.**

so′cial sec′retary, a personal secretary employed to make social appointments and handle personal correspondence. [1900–05]

so′cial secu′rity, **1.** (*usually caps.*) a program of old-age, unemployment, health, disability, and survivors insurance maintained by the U.S. federal government through compulsory payments by specific employer and employee groups. **2.** the theory or practice of providing economic security and social welfare for the individual through government programs maintained by moneys from public taxation. [1930–35]

So′cial Secu′rity Act′, *U.S. Govt.* a law passed in 1935 providing old-age retirement insurance, a federal-state program of unemployment compensation, and federal grants for state welfare programs.

So′cial Secu′rity Administra′tion, *U.S. Govt.* a division of the Department of Health and Human Services, created in 1946, that administers federal Social Security programs. *Abbr.:* SSA

so′cial serv′ice, organized welfare efforts carried on under professional auspices by trained personnel. [1850–55] —**so′cial-serv′ice,** *adj.*

so′cial set′tlement, settlement (def. 14).

so′cial stat′ics, *Sociol.* the study of social systems as they exist at a given time. Cf. **social dynamics.** [1850–55]

so′cial struc′ture, structure (def. 9). [1825–35]

so′cial stud′ies, a course of instruction in an elementary or secondary school comprising such subjects as history, geography, civics, etc. [1925–30]

so′cial u′nit, a person or a group of persons, as a family, functioning as a unit in society. [1870–75]

So′cial War′, **1.** *Gk. Hist.* the war between Athens and its confederates, 357–355 B.C. **2.** *Rom. Hist.* the war in Italy between Rome and its allies, 90–88 B.C.

so′cial wasp′, any of several wasps, as the hornets or yellowjackets, that live together in a community. Cf. **solitary wasp.** [1825–35]

so′cial wel′fare, social services provided by a government for its citizens. [1915–20]

so′cial work′, organized work directed toward the betterment of social conditions in the community, as by seeking to improve the condition of the poor, to promote the welfare of children, etc. [1915–20] —**so′cial work′er.**

so·ci·e·tal (sə sī′i tl), *adj.* noting or pertaining to large social groups, or to their activities, customs, etc. [1895–1900; SOCIET(Y) + -AL[1]] —**so·ci′e·tal·ly,** *adv.*

soci′etal devel′opment, *Sociol.* the formation and transformation of social life, customs, institutions, etc.

so·ci·e·ty (sə sī′i tē), *n., pl.* **-ties,** *adj.* —*n.* **1.** an organized group of persons associated together for religious, benevolent, cultural, scientific, political, patriotic, or other purposes. **2.** a body of individuals living as members of a community; community. **3.** the body of human beings generally, associated or viewed as members of a community: *the evolution of human society.* **4.** a highly structured system of human organization for large-scale community living that normally furnishes protection, continuity, security, and a national identity for its members: *American society.* **5.** such a system characterized by its dominant economic class or form: *middle-class society; industrial society.* **6.** those with whom one has companionship. **7.** companionship; company: *to enjoy one's society.* **8.** the social life of wealthy, prominent, or fashionable persons. **9.** the social class that comprises such persons. **10.** the condition of those living in companionship with others, or in a community, rather than in isolation. **11.** *Biol.* a closely integrated group of social organisms of the same species exhibiting division of labor. **12.** *Eccles.* an ecclesiastical society. —*adj.* **13.** of, pertaining to, or characteristic of elegant society: *a society photographer.* [1525–35; < MF *societe* < L *societās,* equiv. to *soci(us)* partner, comrade + *-etās,* var. of *-itās* -ITY] —**so·ci′e·ty·less,** *adj.*
—**Syn.** **1.** association, fellowship, fraternity, brotherhood, company. See **circle.** **7.** fellowship.

Soci′ety Is′lands, a group of islands in the S Pacific: a part of French Polynesia; largest island, Tahiti. (Excluding minor islands) 100,270; 453 sq. mi. (1173 sq. km). *Cap.:* Papeete.

Soci′ety of Friends′, a sect founded by George Fox in England about 1650, opposed to oath-taking and war. Also called **Quakers, Religious Society of Friends.**

Soci′ety of Je′sus. See under **Jesuit** (def. 1).

soci′ety verse′, light, graceful, entertaining poetry considered as appealing to polite society. [trans. of F *vers de société*]

So·cin·i·an (sō sin′ē ən), *n.* **1.** a follower of Faustus and Laelius Socinus who rejected a number of traditional Christian doctrines, as the Trinity, the divinity of Christ, and original sin, and who held that Christ was miraculously begotten and that salvation will be granted to those who adopt Christ's virtues. —*adj.* **2.** of or pertaining to the Socinians or their doctrines. [1635–45; < NL *Sociniānus* of, pertaining to SOCINUS; see -IAN] —**So·cin′i·an·ism,** *n.*

So·ci·nus (sō sī′nəs), *n.* **Faus·tus** (fô′stəs), (*Fausto Sozzini*), 1539–1604, and his uncle, **Lae·li·us** (lē′lē əs), (*Lelio Sozzini*), 1525–62, Italian Protestant theologians and reformers.

socio-, a combining form used, with the meanings "social," "sociological," or "society," in the formation of compound words: *sociometry; socioeconomic.* [comb. form of L *socius* a fellow, companion, comrade; see -o-]

so·ci·o·bi·ol·o·gy (sō′sē ō bī ol′ə jē, sō′shē-), *n.* the study of social behavior in animals with emphasis on the role of behavior in survival and reproduction, engaging branches of ethology, population genetics, and ecology. [1945–50; SOCIO- + BIOLOGY] —**so·ci·o·bi·o·log·i·cal** (sō′sē ō bī′ə loj′i kəl, sō′shē-), *adj.* —**so′ci·o·bi′o·log′i·cal·ly,** *adv.* —**so′ci·o·bi·ol′o·gist,** *n.*

so·ci·o·cen·tric (sō′sē ō sen′trik, sō′shē-), *adj.* **1.** oriented toward or focused on one's own social group. **2.** tending to regard one's own social group as superior to others. **3.** socially oriented. Cf. **egocentric.** [1880–85; SOCIO- + -CENTRIC] —**so·ci·o·cen·tric·i·ty** (sō′sē ō sen-tris′i tē, sō′shē-), *n.* —**so′ci·o·cen′trism,** *n.*

so·ci·oc·ra·cy (sō′sē ok′rə sē, sō′shē-), *n.* a theoretical system of government in which the interests of all members of society are served equally. [1855–60; SOCIO- + -CRACY] —**so·ci·o·crat** (sō′sē ə krat′, sō′shē-), *n.* —**so′ci·o·crat′ic,** *adj.*

so·ci·o·cul·tur·al (sō′sē ō kul′chər əl, sō′shē-), *adj.* of, pertaining to, or signifying the combination or interaction of social and cultural elements. [1925–30; SOCIO- + CULTURAL] —**so′ci·o·cul′tur·al·ly,** *adv.*

so·ci·o·dra·ma (sō′sē ō drä′mə, -dram′ə, sō′shē-), *n.* a method of group psychotherapy in which each patient assumes and dramatizes a variety of roles, usually focusing on problems and conflicts arising in group situations. Cf. **psychodrama.** [1940–45; SOCIO- + DRAMA] —**so·ci·o·dra·mat·ic** (sō′sē ō drə mat′ik, sō′shē-), *adj.*

so·ci·o·ec·o·nom·ic (sō′sē ō ek′ə nom′ik, -ē′kə-, sō′shē-), *adj.* of, pertaining to, or signifying the combination or interaction of social and economic factors: *socioeconomic study; socioeconomic status.* [1880–85; SOCIO- + ECONOMIC] —**so′ci·o·ec′o·nom′i·cal·ly,** *adv.*

so·ci·o·ec·o·nom·ics (sō′sē ō ek′ə nom′iks, -ē′kə-, sō′shē-), *n.* (*used with a singular v.*) the study of the interrelation between economics and social behavior. Also called **social economics.** [SOCIO- + ECONOMICS] —**so·ci·o·e·con·o·mist** (sō′sē ō i kon′ə mist, sō′shē-), *n.*

so·ci·o·ge·net·ic (sō′sē ō jə net′ik, sō′shē-), *adj.* contributing to or affecting the course of social development: *sociogenetic factors leading to war.* [SOCIO- + GENETIC] —**so·ci·o·gen·e·sis** (sō′sē ō jen′ə sis, sō′shē-), *n.*

so·ci·o·gen·ic (sō′sē ō jen′ik, sō′shē-), *adj.* caused or influenced by society or social factors: *sociogenic problems.* [1965–70; SOCIO- + -GENIC]

so·ci·o·gram (sō′sē ə gram′, sō′shē-), *n. Sociol.* a sociometric diagram representing the pattern of relationships between individuals in a group, usually expressed in terms of which persons they prefer to associate with. [1935–40; SOCIO- + -GRAM[1]]

so·ci·og·ra·phy (sō′sē og′rə fē, sō′shē-), *n.* the branch of sociology that uses statistical data to describe social phenomena. [1880–85; SOCIO- + -GRAPHY] —**so·ci·o·graph·ic** (sō′sē ə graf′ik, sō′shē-), *adj.*

sociol., **1.** sociological. **2.** sociology.

so·ci·o·lect (sō′sē ə lekt′, sō′shē-), *n.* a variety of a language used by a particular social group; a social dialect. [1970–75; SOCIO- + (DIA)LECT]

so·ci·o·lin·guis·tics (sō′sē ō ling gwis′tiks, sō′shē-), *n.* (*used with a singular v.*) the study of language as it functions in society; the study of the interaction between linguistic and social variables. [1935–40; SOCIO- + LINGUISTICS] —**so′ci·o·lin′guist,** *n.* —**so′ci·o·lin·guis′tic,** *adj.* —**so′ci·o·lin·guis′ti·cal·ly,** *adv.*

so·ci·o·log·i·cal (sō′sē ə loj′i kəl, sō′shē-), *adj.* **1.** of, pertaining to, or characteristic of sociology and its methodology. **2.** dealing with social questions or problems, esp. focusing on cultural and environmental factors rather than on psychological or personal characteristics: *a sociological approach to art.* **3.** organized into a society; social. Also, **so′ci·o·log′ic.** [1835–45; SOCIOLOG(Y) + -IC + -AL[1]] —**so′ci·o·log′i·cal·ly,** *adv.*

so·ci·ol·o·gism (sō′sē ol′ə jiz′əm, sō′shē-), *n.* an explanation, expression, concept, etc., characteristic of sociology, esp. when lacking reference to other disciplines concerned with human development. [1940–45; SOCIOLOG(Y) + -ISM]

so·ci·ol·o·gis·tic (sō′sē ol′ə jis′tik, sō′shē-), *adj.* making reference only to the concepts of sociology, esp. emphasizing social factors to the exclusion of others. [SOCIOLOGIST + -IC] —**so′ci·ol′o·gis′ti·cal·ly,** *adv.*

so·ci·ol·o·gize (sō′sē ol′ə jīz′, sō′shē-), *v.t., v.i.,* **-gized, -giz·ing.** to explain, study, or interpret in sociological or social terms. Also, *esp. Brit.,* **so′ci·ol′o·gise′.** [1880–85; SOCIOLOG(Y) + -IZE]—**so′ci·ol′o·giz′er,** *n.*

so·ci·ol·o·gy (sō′sē ol′ə jē, sō′shē-), *n.* the science or study of the origin, development, organization, and functioning of human society; the science of the fundamental laws of social relations, institutions, etc. [1835–45; < F *sociologie.* See SOCIO-, -LOGY] —**so′ci·ol′o·gist,** *n.*

so·ci·om·e·try (sō′sē om′i trē, sō′shē-), *n.* the measurement of attitudes of social acceptance or rejection through expressed preferences among members of a social grouping. [1930–35; SOCIO- + -METRY] —**so·ci·o·met·ric** (sō′sē ə me′trik, sō′shē-), *adj.* —**so′ci·om′e·trist,** *n.*

so·ci·o·path (sō′sē ə path′, sō′shē-), *n. Psychiatry.* a person, as a psychopathic personality, whose behavior is antisocial and who lacks a sense of moral responsibility or social conscience. [1940–45; SOCIO- + -PATH] —**so′ci·o·path′ic,** *adj.* —**so·ci·op·a·thy** (sō′sē op′ə thē, sō′shē-), *n.*

so·ci·o·po·lit·i·cal (sō′sē ō pə lit′i kəl, sō′shē-), *adj.* of, pertaining to, or signifying the combination or interaction of social and political factors: *the sociopolitical environment in Japan.* [1880–85; SOCIO- + POLITICAL]

so·ci·o·psy·cho·log·i·cal (sō′sē ō sī′kə loj′i kəl, sō′shē-), *adj.* of, pertaining to, or characterized by interrelated social and psychological factors. [1920–25; SOCIO- + PSYCHOLOGICAL]

so·ci·o·re·li·gious (sō′sē ō ri lij′əs, sō′shē-), *adj.* of, pertaining to, or signifying the combination or interaction of religious and social factors. [1885–90; SOCIO- + RELIGIOUS]

so·ci·o·sex·u·al (sō′sē ō sek′sho͞o əl, sō′shē-), *adj.* of or pertaining to relationships between persons that involve sexuality. [1935–40; SOCIO- + SEXUAL]

so·ci·o·tech·no·log·i·cal (sō′sē ō tek′nə loj′i kəl, sō′shē-), *adj.* of, pertaining to, or signifying the combination or interaction of social and technological factors. [1965–70; SOCIO- + TECHNOLOGICAL]

sock[1] (sok), *n., pl.* **socks** or, for 1, also **sox. 1.** a short stocking usually reaching to the calf or just above the ankle. **2.** a lightweight shoe worn by ancient Greek and Roman comic actors. **3.** comic writing for the theater; comedy or comic drama. Cf. **buskin** (def. 4). **4.** *Furniture.* a raised vertical area of a club or pad foot. **5. knock one's** or **the socks off.** See **knock** (def. 20). [bef. 900; ME *socke,* OE *socc* << L *soccus* slipper] —**sock′less,** *adj.* —**sock′less·ness,** *n.*

sock[2] (sok), *Slang.* —*v.t.* **1.** to strike or hit hard. **2. sock away,** to put into savings or reserve. **3. sock in,** to close or ground because of adverse weather conditions: *The airport was socked in.* —*n.* **4.** a hard blow. **5.** a very successful show, performance, actor, etc.: *The show was a sock.* —*adj.* **6.** extremely successful: *a sock performance.* [1690–1700; orig. uncert.]

sock·dol·a·ger (sok dol′ə jər), *n. Older Slang.* **1.** something unusually large, heavy, etc. **2.** a decisive reply, argument, etc. **3.** a heavy, finishing blow: *His right jab is a real sockdolager.* [1820–30, *Amer.;* SOCK[2] + *-dolager,* of uncert. orig.]

sock·er·oo (sok′ə ro͞o′), *n., pl.* **-oos.** *Slang.* a notable success: *Her performance was a sockeroo.* [1940–45, *Amer.;* SOCK[2] + -EROO]

sock·et (sok′it), *n.* **1.** a hollow part or piece for receiving and holding some part or thing. **2.** *Elect.* **a.** a device intended to hold an electric light bulb mechanically and connect it electrically to circuit wires. **b.** Also called **wall socket.** a socket placed in a wall to receive a plug that makes an electrical connection with supply wiring. **3.** *Anat.* **a.** a hollow in one part that receives another part: *the socket of the eye.* **b.** the concavity of a joint: *the socket of the hip.* —*v.t.* **4.** to place in or fit with a socket. [1300–50; ME *soket* < AF, equiv. to OF *soc* plowshare (< Gaulish **soccos;* cf. Welsh *swch,* OIr *socc*) + *-et* -ET] —**sock′et·less,** *adj.*

sock′et wrench′, a box wrench with a socket that is an extension of the shank. See illus. under **wrench.** [1885–90]

sock′eye salm′on (sok′ī′), an important food fish, *Oncorhynchus nerka,* inhabiting the North Pacific. Also called **blueback salmon, red salmon, sock′eye′.** [1865–70; *sockeye,* alter. (by folk etym.) of Halkomelem (Mainland dial.) *sθəqəy̓*]

sock′ lin′ing, a thin piece of material, as leather, that is laid on top of the insole of a shoe, boot, or other footwear. Also called **sock′ lin′er.**

sock·o (sok′ō), *adj. Slang.* extremely impressive or successful: *a socko performance.* [1935–40; SOCK[2] + -O]

sock′ suspend′er, *Brit.* garter (def. 1). [1915–20]

so·cle (sok′əl, sō′kəl), *n. Archit.* a low, plain part forming a base for a column, pedestal, or the like; plinth. [1695–1705; < F < It *zoccolo* wooden shoe, base of a pedestal < L *socculus* lit., little *soccus;* see SOCK[1], -ULE]

soc·man (sok′mən, sōk′-), *n., pl.* **-men.** sokeman.

So·co·tra (sō kō′trə, sok′ə trə), *n.* an island in the Indian Ocean, S of Arabia: a part of the Republic of Yemen; 1382 sq. mi. (3579 sq. km). Also, **Sokotra.** —**So·co′tran,** *n., adj.*

Soc·ra·tes (sok′rə tēz′), *n.* 469?–399 B.C., Athenian philosopher.

So·crat·ic (sə krat′ik, sō-), *adj.* **1.** of or pertaining to Socrates or his philosophy, followers, etc., or to the Socratic method. —*n.* **2.** a follower of Socrates. **3.** any of the Greek philosophers influenced by Socrates. [1630–40; < L *Sōcraticus* < Gk *Sōkratikós* of, pertaining to SOCRATES; see -IC] —**So·crat′i·cal·ly,** *adv.*

Socrat′ic i′rony, pretended ignorance in discussion. [1870–75]

Socrat′ic meth′od, the use of questions, as employed by Socrates, to develop a latent idea, as in the mind of a pupil, or to elicit admissions, as from an opponent, tending to establish a proposition. [1735–45]

sod[1] (sod), *n., v.,* **sod·ded, sod·ding.** —*n.* **1.** a section cut or torn from the surface of grassland, containing the matted roots of grass. **2.** the surface of the ground, esp. when covered with grass; turf; sward. —*v.t.* **3.** to cover with sods or sod. [1375–1425; late ME < MD or MLG *sode* turf] —**sod′less,** *adj.*

sod[2] (sod), *v. Archaic.* pt. of **seethe.**

sod[3] (sod), *n. Chiefly Brit. Slang.* **1.** sodomite; homosexual. **2.** chap; fellow; guy. **3.** child; kid; brat. Cf. **bugger.** [1875–80; by shortening of SODOMITE]

so·da (sō′də), *n.* **1.** See **sodium hydroxide. 2.** See **sodium monoxide. 3.** See **sodium carbonate** (def. 2). **4.** sodium, as in carbonate of soda. **5.** See **soda water. 6.** a drink made with soda water, flavoring, such as fruit or other syrups, and often ice cream, milk, etc. **7.** soda pop. **8.** (in faro) the card turned up in the dealing box before one begins to play. [1550–60; (< It) < ML < Ar *suwwādah* kind of plant; cf. MF *soulde, soude*] —**so′da·less,** *adj.*

—**Regional Variation. 7.** See **soda pop.**

so′da ash′, *Chem.* See **sodium carbonate** (def. 1). [1830–40]

so′da bis′cuit, 1. a biscuit having soda and sour milk or buttermilk as leavening agents. **2.** See **soda cracker.** [1820–30, *Amer.*]

so′da crack′er, a thin, crisp cracker or wafer prepared from a yeast dough that has been neutralized by baking soda. [1820–30]

so′da foun′tain, 1. a counter, as in a restaurant or drugstore, at which sodas, ice cream, light meals, etc., are served. **2.** a container from which soda water is dispensed, usually through faucets. [1815–25, *Amer.*]

so′da jerk′, *Informal.* a person who prepares and serves sodas and ice cream at a soda fountain. Also, **so′da jerk′er.** [1910–15, *Amer.;* shortened form of *soda jerker*]

so′da lime′, a mixture of sodium hydroxide and calcium hydroxide. [1860–65] —**so′da-lime′,** *adj.*

so′da-lime feld′spar, plagioclase. [1865–70]

so·da·list (sōd′l ist), *n.* a member of a sodality. [1785–95; SODAL(ITY) + -IST]

so·da·lite (sōd′l īt′), *n.* a mineral, sodium aluminum silicate, $Na_4Al_3Si_3O_{12}Cl$, occurring massive and in crystals, usually blue in color and found in certain alkali-rich igneous rocks. [1800–10; SODA + -LITE]

so·dal·i·ty (sō dal′i tē, sə-), *n., pl.* **-ties. 1.** fellowship; comradeship. **2.** an association or society. **3.** *Rom. Cath. Ch.* a lay society for religious and charitable purposes. [1590–1600; < L *sodālitās* companionship, equiv. to *sodāl(is)* companion + *-itās* -ITY]

so·da·mide (sō′də mīd′), *n. Chem.* See **sodium amide.** [1830–40; SOD(IUM) + AMIDE]

so′da ni′ter, a white or transparent mineral, sodium nitrate, $NaNO_3$, used chiefly as a fertilizer and in the manufacture of sulfuric and nitric acids and potassium nitrate. Also called **Chile saltpeter, nitratine.** [1895–1900]

so′da pop′, a carbonated, flavored, and sweetened soft drink. [1905–10]

—**Regional Variation.** The terms SODA POP, SODA, and POP are widely used throughout the U.S., although POP is mainly associated with the Midland U.S. DOPE is used as a synonym in the Southern U.S., esp. in the South Atlantic States, and TONIC is used in eastern New England.

so′da wa′ter, 1. an effervescent beverage consisting of water charged with carbon dioxide. **2.** See **soda pop. 3.** a weak solution of sodium bicarbonate, taken as a stomachic. [1795–1805]

sod·bust·er (sod′bus′tər), *n.* a farmer who works the soil. [1885–90; SOD[1] + BUSTER]

sod·den (sod′n), *adj.* **1.** soaked with liquid or moisture; saturated. **2.** heavy, lumpy, or soggy, as food that is poorly cooked. **3.** having a soaked appearance. **4.** bloated, as the face. **5.** expressionless, dull, or stupid, esp. from drunkenness. **6.** lacking spirit or alertness; inert; torpid; listless. **7.** *Archaic.* boiled. —*v.t., v.i.* **8.** to make or become sodden. **9.** *Obs.* pp. of **seethe.** [1250–1300; ME *soden, sothen,* ptp. of *sethen* to SEETHE] —**sod′den·ly,** *adv.* —**sod′den·ness,** *n.*

sod·dy (sod′ē), *adj.,* **-di·er, -di·est,** *n., pl.* **-dies.** —*adj.* **1.** of or pertaining to sod. **2.** consisting of sod. —*n.* **3.** Also, **sod′die.** *Western U.S.* See **sod house.** [1605–15; SOD[1] + -Y[1], -Y[2]]

Sod·dy (sod′ē), *n.* **Frederick,** 1877–1956, English chemist: Nobel prize 1921.

Sö·der·blom (sœ′dər blo͝om′), *n.* **Nathan,** 1866–1931, Swedish theologian: Nobel peace prize 1930.

sod′ house′, a house built of strips of sod, laid like brickwork, and used esp. by settlers on the Great Plains, when timber was scarce. Also called **soddie, soddy.** [1825–35]

so·dic (sō′dik), *adj.* pertaining to or containing sodium: *sodic soil.* [1855–60; SOD(IUM) + -IC]

sodio-, (in organic chemistry) a combining form representing **sodium** in compound words: *sodio-cupric chloride.*

so·di·um (sō′dē əm), *n.* **1.** *Chem.* a soft, silver-white, metallic element that oxidizes rapidly in moist air, occurring in nature only in the combined state, and used in the synthesis of sodium peroxide, sodium cyanide, and tetraethyllead: a necessary element in the body for the maintenance of normal fluid balance and other physiological functions. *Symbol:* Na; *at. wt.:* 22.9898; *at. no.:* 11; *sp. gr.:* 0.97 at 20°C. **2.** *Med., Pharm.* any salt of sodium, as sodium chloride or sodium bicarbonate, present in or added to foods or beverages as a seasoning or preservative and used in many pharmaceutical products as an antacid, anticoagulant, or other agent. [1800–10; < NL; see SODA, -IUM]

so′dium am′ide, *Chem.* a white, crystalline, water-insoluble, flammable powder, $NaNH_2$, used chiefly in the manufacture of sodium cyanide and in organic synthesis. Also called **sodamide.**

so′dium ammo′nium phos′phate, *Chem.* a colorless, odorless, crystalline, water-soluble solid, $NaNH_4HPO_4 \cdot 4H_2O$, originally obtained from human urine: used as a blowpipe flux in testing metallic oxides. Also called **microcosmic salt, salt of phosphorus.**

so′dium ar′senite, *Chem.* a white or grayish-white, water-soluble, poisonous powder, $NaAsO_2$, used chiefly in arsenical soaps for hides, as an insecticide, and as a weed-killer. Also called **sodium meta-arsenite.**

so′dium ben′zoate, *Chem., Pharm.* a white, crystalline or granular, water-soluble powder, $C_7H_5NaO_2$, used chiefly as a food preservative and antifungal agent, and in diagnostic tests of liver function. Also called **benzoate of soda.** [1895–1900]

so′dium bicar′bonate, *Chem., Pharm.* a white, crystalline, water-soluble solid, in powder or granules, $NaHCO_3$, usually prepared by the reaction of soda ash with carbon dioxide or obtained from the intermediate product of the Solvay process by purification: used chiefly in the manufacture of sodium salts, baking powder, and beverages, as a laboratory reagent, as a fire extinguisher, and in medicine as an antacid. Also called **bicarbonate of soda, baking soda, so′dium ac′id car′bonate.** [1880–85]

so′dium bichro′mate, *Chem.* See **sodium dichromate.**

so′dium bisul′fate, *Chem.* a colorless crystalline compound, $NaHSO_4$, soluble in water: used in dyeing, in the manufacture of cement, paper, soap, and an acid-type cleaner. Also called **sodium hydrogen sulfate.**

so′dium bo′rate, *Chem.* borax[1]. [1895–1900]

so′dium bro′mide, *Chem.* a white, crystalline, hygroscopic, water-soluble solid, NaBr, used chiefly in photography as a developer, and in medicine as a sedative.

so′dium butabar′bital, *Pharm.* See **butabarbital sodium.**

so′dium car′bonate, *Chem.* **1.** Also called **soda ash.** an anhydrous, grayish-white, odorless, water-soluble powder, Na_2CO_3, usually obtained by the Solvay process and containing about 1 percent of impurities consisting of sulfates, chlorides, and bicarbonates of sodium: used in the manufacture of glass, ceramics, soaps, paper, petroleum products, sodium salts, as a cleanser, for bleaching, and in water treatment. **2.** Also called **sal soda, soda, washing soda.** the decahydrated form of this salt, $Na_2CO_3 \cdot 10H_2O$, used similarly. **3.** the monohydrated form of this salt, $Na_2CO_3 \cdot H_2O$, used similarly, esp. in photography. [1865–70]

so′dium chlo′rate, *Chem.* a colorless, water-soluble solid, $NaClO_3$, cool and salty to the taste, used chiefly in the manufacture of explosives and matches, as a textile mordant, and as an oxidizing and bleaching agent. [1880–85]

so′dium chlo′ride, *Chem.* salt[1] (def. 1). [1865–70]

so′dium ci′trate, *Chem.* a white, crystalline or granular, water-soluble, odorless solid, $Na_3C_6H_5O_7 \cdot 2H_2O$, having a cool, saline taste: used in photography, in soft drinks, and in medicine chiefly to prevent the coagulation of blood.

so′dium cy′anide, *Chem.* a white, crystalline, deliquescent, water-soluble, poisonous powder, NaCN, prepared by heating sodium amide with charcoal: used chiefly in casehardening alloys, in the leaching and flotation of ore, and in electroplating. [1880–85]

so′dium cy′clamate, *Chem.* a white, crystalline,

CONCISE ETYMOLOGY KEY: <, descended or borrowed from; >, whence; b., blend of, blended; c., cognate with; cf., compare; deriv., derivative; equiv., equivalent; imit., imitative; obl., oblique; r., replacing; s., stem; sp., spelling, spelled; resp., respelling, respelled; trans., translation; ?, origin unknown; *, unattested; ‡, probably earlier than. See the full key inside the front cover.

water-soluble powder, $NaC_6NH_{12}SO_3$, that has been used as a sweetening agent: banned by the FDA in 1970. Also called **so′dium cy·clo·hex·yl·sul′fa·mate** (sī′klə hek′-səl sul′fə māt′, sik′lə-).

so′dium dichro′mate, *Chem.* a red or orange crystalline, water-soluble solid, $Na_2Cr_2O_7·2H_2O$, used as an oxidizing agent in the manufacture of dyes and inks, as a corrosion inhibitor, a mordant, a laboratory reagent, in the tanning of leather, and in electroplating. Also, **sodium bichromate.** [1900–05]

so′dium eth′ylate, *Chem.* a white, hygroscopic powder, C_2H_5ONa, that is decomposed by water into sodium hydroxide and alcohol: used chiefly in organic synthesis. Also called **caustic alcohol, so′dium eth·ox′ide** (e thok′sīd, -sid).

so′dium fluor′ide, a colorless, crystalline, water-soluble, poisonous solid, NaF, used chiefly in the fluoridation of water, as an insecticide, and as a rodenticide. [1900–05]

so′dium fluor·o·ac′e·tate (flŏŏr′ō as′i tāt′, flôr′ō-, flōr′ō-), *Chem.* a white, amorphous, water-soluble, poisonous powder, $C_2H_2FO_2Na$, used as a rodenticide. Also called **1080.** [1940–45; FLUORO- + ACETATE]

so′dium glu′tamate, *Chem.* See **monosodium glutamate.**

so′dium hex·a·met·a·phos′phate (hek′sə met′ə-fos′fāt). See under **Calgon.** [HEXA- + METAPHOSPHATE]

so′dium hy′drogen sul′fate, *Chem.* See **sodium bisulfate.**

so′dium hydrosul′fite, *Chem.* a white, crystalline, water-soluble powder, $Na_2S_2O_4$, used as a reducing agent, esp. in dyeing, and as a bleach. Also called **hydrosulfite, so′dium di·thi′o·nite** (dī thī′ə nīt′), **sodium hyposulfite.**

so′dium hydrox′ide, *Chem.* a white, deliquescent, water-soluble solid, NaOH, usually in the form of lumps, sticks, chips, or pellets, that upon solution in water generates heat: used chiefly in the manufacture of other chemicals, rayon, film, soap, as a laboratory reagent, and in medicine as a caustic. Also called **caustic soda, soda.** [1880–85]

so′dium hypochlo′rite, *Chem.* a pale-green, crystalline compound, NaOCl, unstable in air, soluble in cold water, decomposes in hot water: used as a bleaching agent for paper and textiles, in water purification, in household use, and as a fungicide. [1880–85]

so′dium hyposul′fite, *Chem.* See **sodium thiosulfate.** [1865–70]

so′dium i′odide, *Chem.* a colorless or white, crystalline, deliquescent, water-soluble solid, NaI, used chiefly in the manufacture of photographic emulsions, in organic synthesis, and as a disinfectant in veterinary medicine.

so′dium lac′tate, *Chem.* a water-soluble, hygroscopic salt, $C_3H_5NaO_3$, used in solution in medicine to treat metabolic acidosis, usually by injection.

so′dium lamp′, *Elect.* See **sodium-vapor lamp.**

so′dium met·a·ar′se·nite (met′ə är′sə nīt′), *Chem.* See **sodium arsenite.**

so′dium met·a·sil′i·cate (met′ə sil′i kit, -kāt′), *Chem.* a white, granular sodium silicate, Na_2SiO_3, soluble in water: used in detergents and in bleaching and cleaning products. [1925–30; META- + SILICATE]

so′dium meth′ylate, *Chem.* a white, free-flowing, flammable powder, CH_3ONa, decomposed by water to sodium hydroxide and methyl alcohol: used chiefly in organic synthesis. Also called **so′dium methox′ide.**

so′dium monox′ide, *Chem.* a white powder, Na_2O, that reacts violently with water to produce sodium hydroxide. Also called **soda, so′dium ox′ide.**

so′dium ni′trate, *Chem.* a crystalline, water-soluble compound, $NaNO_3$, that occurs naturally as soda niter: used in fertilizers, explosives, and glass, and as a color fixative in processed meats.

so′dium ni′trite, 1. *Chem.* a yellowish or white crystalline compound, $NaNO_2$, soluble in water, slightly soluble in alcohol and ether: used in the manufacture of dyes and as a color fixative. **2.** *Nutrition.* this compound added to food as a preservative and for flavor and color, esp. in pork, fish, and beef products: implicated in the formation of suspected carcinogens. Also called **nitrite.** [1900–05]

so′dium pen′tothal, *Pharm.* the sodium salt of thiopental sodium. Also called **sodium thiopental.** [*Pentothal* a trademark]

so′dium perbo′rate, *Chem.* a white, crystalline, water-soluble solid, $NaBO_2·3H_2O$ or $NaBO_3·4H_2O$, used chiefly as a bleaching agent and antiseptic. Also called **perborax.**

so′dium perox′ide, *Chem.* a yellowish-white, hygroscopic, water-soluble powder, Na_2O_2, used chiefly as a bleaching agent and as an oxidizing agent.

so′dium phos′phate, *Chem.* **1.** Also called **monobasic sodium phosphate.** a white, crystalline, slightly hygroscopic, water-soluble powder, NaH_2PO_4, used chiefly in dyeing and in electroplating. **2.** Also called **dibasic sodium phosphate, disodium phosphate.** a water-soluble compound that in its anhydrous form, Na_2HPO_4, occurring as a white, crystalline, hygroscopic powder, is used chiefly in the manufacture of ceramic glazes, enamels, baking powder, and cheeses, and that in its hydrated form, $Na_2HPO_4·xH_2O$, occurring as clear colorless crystals, is used chiefly in the manufacture of dyes, fertilizers, detergents, and pharmaceuticals. **3.** Also called **tribasic sodium phosphate, trisodium phosphate, TSP.** a colorless water-soluble compound, $Na_3PO_4·12H_2O$, occurring as crystals: used chiefly in the manufacture of water-softening agents, detergents, paper, and textiles. [1870–75]

so′dium polysul′fide, *Chem.* a yellow-brown, water-soluble, granular powder, Na_2S_n, used chiefly in the manufacture of sulfur dyes, insecticides, and synthetic rubber.

so′dium pro′pionate, *Chem.* a transparent, crystalline, water-soluble powder, $C_3H_5NaO_2$, used in foodstuffs to prevent mold growth, and in medicine as a fungicide.

so′dium pump′, an energy-consuming mechanism in cell membranes that transports sodium ions across the membrane, in exchange for potassium ions or other substances. [1960–65]

so′dium pyrobo′rate, *Chem.* borax[1]. [PYRO- + BORATE]

so′dium salic′ylate, *Chem.* a white, crystalline compound, $C_7H_5NaO_3$, soluble in water, alcohol, and glycerol: used in medicine as an analgesic, antipyretic, and anti-inflammatory, and as a preservative. [1900–05]

so′dium sil′icate, *Chem.* any of several clear, white, or greenish water-soluble compounds of formulas varying in ratio from $Na_2O·3.75SiO_2$ to $2Na_2O·SiO_2$: used chiefly in dyeing, printing, and fireproofing textiles and in the manufacture of paper products and cement. Also called **liquid glass, water glass.**

so′dium sul′fate, *Chem.* a white, crystalline, water-soluble solid, Na_2SO_4, used chiefly in the manufacture of dyes, soaps, detergents, glass, and ceramic glazes. [1880–85]

so′dium sul′fide, *Chem.* a yellow or brick-red, crystalline, deliquescent, water-soluble solid, Na_2S, used chiefly in the manufacture of dyes, soaps, and rubber, as a depilatory for leather, and in the flotation of powdered lead and copper ores.

so′dium sul′fite, *Chem.* a white, crystalline, water-soluble solid, Na_2SO_3, used chiefly as a food preservative, as a bleaching agent, and as a developer in photography.

so′dium tetrabo′rate, *Chem.* borax[1]. [TETRA- + BORATE]

so′dium thiocy′anate, *Chem., Pharm.* a white powder or colorless, deliquescent crystals, NaSCN, used chiefly in organic synthesis and in medicine in the treatment of hypertension.

so′dium thiopen′tal, *Pharm.* See **sodium pentothal.**

so′dium thiosul′fate, *Chem.* a white, crystalline, water-soluble powder, $Na_2S_2O_3·5H_2O$, used as a bleach and in photography as a fixing agent. Also called **hypo, hyposulfite, sodium hyposulfite.** [1880–85]

so′dium tri·pol·y·phos′phate (trī′pol ē fos′fāt), *Chem.* a white powder, $Na_5P_3O_{10}$, used as a water softener, sequestering agent, and food additive. Also called **so′dium triphos′phate.** [1940–45; TRI- + POLY- + PHOSPHATE]

so′dium-va·por lamp′ (sō′dē əm vā′pər), *Elect.* an electric lamp in which sodium vapor is activated by current passing between two electrodes, producing a yellow, glareless light: used on streets and highways. Also called **sodium lamp.** [1935–40]

Sod·om (sod′əm), *n.* **1.** an ancient city destroyed, with Gomorrah, because of its wickedness. Gen. 18–19. **2.** any very sinful, corrupt, vice-ridden place.

So·do·ma, Il, (ēl sô′dô mä), (*Giovanni Antonio de Bazzi*) (jô vän′nē än tô′nyô de bät′tsē), 1477–1549, Italian painter.

Sod·om·ite (sod′ə mīt′), *n.* **1.** an inhabitant of Sodom. **2.** (*l.c.*) a person who engages in sodomy. [1250–1300; ME < MF < LL *Sodomita* < Gk *Sodomītēs.* See SODOM, -ITE[1]]

sod·om·ize (sod′ə mīz′), *v.t.,* **-ized, -iz·ing.** to subject to sodomy; commit sodomy upon. Also, *esp. Brit.,* **sod′om·ise′.** [1950–55; SODOM(Y) + -IZE] **—sod′om·ist,** *n.*

sod·om·y (sod′ə mē), *n.* **1.** anal or oral copulation with a member of the opposite sex. **2.** copulation with a member of the same sex. **3.** bestiality (def. 4). [1250–1300; ME *sodomie* < OF. See SODOM, -Y[3]] **—sod·o·mit·i·cal** (sod′ə mit′i kəl), **sod′o·mit′ic,** *adj.* **—sod′o·mit′i·cal·ly,** *adv.*

Soe·har·to (sōō här′tō), *n.* Suharto.

Soe·kar·no (sōō kär′nō), *n.* Sukarno.

Soem·ba (sōōm′bä), *n.* Dutch name of **Sumba.**

Soem·ba·wa (sōōm bä′wä), *n.* Dutch name of **Sumbawa.**

Soen′da Is′lands (sōōn′dä). See **Sunda Islands.**

Soe·ra·ba·ja (sōō′rä bä′yä), *n.* Dutch name of **Surabaya.**

so·ev·er (sō ev′ər), *adv.* at all; in any case; of any kind; in any way (used with generalizing force after *who, what, when, where, how, any, all,* etc., sometimes separated by intervening words): *Choose what thing soever you please.* [1510–20; SO[1] + EVER]

SOF, sound on a film.

so·fa (sō′fə), *n.* a long, upholstered couch with a back and two arms or raised ends. [1615–25; < Turk < Ar *ṣuffah* platform used as a seat]

so′fa bed′, a sofa that can be converted into a bed, either by folding out the seat or by lowering the back to be flush with the seat. Also, **so′fa-bed′, so′fa·bed′.** Also called **so·fa-sleep·er, so·fa/sleep·er** (sō′fə slē′-pər). [1810–20]

so·far (sō′fär), *n.* a system for determining a position at sea by exploding a charge under water and measuring the time the shock waves take to reach three widely separated shore stations at known distances from each other. [1945–50; *so(und) f(ixing) a(nd) r(anging)*]

so′fa ta′ble, a table with drawers, having drop leaves at both ends, often placed in front of or behind a sofa. Also called **davenport table.**

so·fer (sō′fər; *Seph. Heb.* sô feʀ′; *Ashk. Heb.* sō′feʀ), *n., pl.* **-fer·im** (-fər im; *Seph. Heb.* -fe ʀēm′; *Ashk. Heb.* -fe ʀim). (*often cap.*) *Judaism.* scribe[1] (def. 3). [< Heb *sōphēr*]

sof·fit (sof′it), *n. Archit.* the underside of an architectural feature, as a beam, arch, ceiling, vault, or cornice. [1605–15; < F *soffite* < It *soffitto* < VL **suffictus,* for L *suffixus;* see SUFFIX]

sof·frit·to (sō frē′tō; *It.* sôf fʀēt′tô), *n.* **1.** Also called **battuto.** *Italian Cookery.* a base for stews and soups, consisting of hot oil, butter, or fat in which a chopped onion or crushed garlic clove has been browned, often with the addition of chopped parsley, celery, and carrot. **2.** sofrito. [< It, ptp. of *soffriggere;* see SUF-, FRY[1]]

So·fi·a (sō′fē ə, sō fē′ə *or, for 2,* sō fī′ə), *n.* **1.** Also **So·fi·ya** (*Bulg.* sô′fē yə). a city in and the capital of Bulgaria, in the W part. 965,728. **2.** a female given name.

so·fri·to (sō frē′tō), *n.* **1.** soffritto. **2.** *Caribbean Cookery.* a sauce of tomatoes, onion, garlic, peppers, coriander, etc.

S. of Sol., Song of Solomon.

soft (sôft, soft), *adj.,* **-er, -est,** *n., adv., interj.* **—*adj.* 1.** yielding readily to touch or pressure; easily penetrated, divided, or changed in shape; not hard or stiff: *a soft pillow.* **2.** relatively deficient in hardness, as metal or wood. **3.** smooth and agreeable to the touch; not rough or coarse: *a soft fabric; soft skin.* **4.** producing agreeable sensations; pleasant or comfortable: *soft slumber.* **5.** low or subdued in sound; gentle and melodious: *soft music; a soft voice.* **6.** not harsh or unpleasant to the eye; not glaring: *soft light; a soft color.* **7.** not hard or sharp: *soft outlines.* **8.** gentle or mild: *soft breezes.* **9.** genial or balmy, as climate or air. **10.** gentle, mild, warm-hearted, or compassionate: *a soft, grandmotherly woman.* **11.** smooth, soothing, or ingratiating: *soft words.* **12.** not harsh or severe, as a penalty or demand. **13.** responsive or sympathetic to the feelings, emotions, needs, etc., of others; tender-hearted. **14.** sentimental or flowery, as language: *soft, meaningless talk.* **15.** not strong or robust; delicate; incapable of great endurance or exertion: *He was too soft for the Marines.* **16.** *Informal.* easy; involving little effort; not difficult, laborious, trying, or severe: *a soft job.* **17.** *Informal.* easily influenced or swayed; easily imposed upon; impressionable. **18.** lenient, permissive, or conciliatory, esp. regarding something that is conceived of as dangerous or threatening: *to be soft on Communism.* **19.** (of water) relatively free from mineral salts that interfere with the action of soap. **20.** (of paper money or a monetary system) not supported by sufficient gold reserves or not easily convertible into a foreign currency. **21.** (of a market, market condition, or prices) declining in value, volume, profitability, etc.; weak: *a soft tourist season.* Cf. **firm**[1] (def. 7). **22.** (of money) plentiful or available at low interest rates or on easy terms: *a soft loan.* **23.** soft-core. **24.** *Metall.* **a.** (of a metal) easily magnetized and demagnetized. **b.** (of solder) fusing readily. **c.** (of a metal or alloy) fully annealed, so as to provide minimum mechanical hardness. **25.** *Photog.* **a.** (of a photographic image) having delicate gradations of tone. **b.** (of a focus) lacking in sharpness. **c.** (of a lens) unable to be focused sharply. **26.** *Phonet.* **a.** (of consonants) lenis, esp. lenis and voiced. **b.** (of *c* and *g*) pronounced as in *cent* and *gem.* **c.** (of consonants in Slavic languages) palatalized. Cf. **hard** (def. 38). **27.** *Mil.* (of a missile-launching base) aboveground and relatively unprotected from enemy attack. **28.** *Aerospace.* (of a landing of a space vehicle) gentle; not harmful to the vehicle or its contents: *a soft landing on the moon.* **29.** *Physics.* (of a beam of particles or electromagnetic radiation) having relatively low energy: *soft x-rays.* Cf. **hard** (def. 40). **30.** (of a delegate, voter, etc.) not committed to any one candidate. **31.** foolish or stupid: *soft in the head.* **32.** (of a detergent) readily biodegradable. **33. be soft on someone,** *Informal.* to be amorously inclined toward a person; have an affection for: *He's been soft on her for years.* **—*n.* 34.** something that is soft or yielding; the soft part. **35.** softness. **—*adv.* 36.** in a soft manner. **—*interj. Archaic.* 37.** be quiet! hush! **38.** not so fast! stop! [bef. 1000; ME *softe* yielding, gentle, mild, OE *sōfte* agreeable; c. G *sanft*] **—soft′ly,** *adv.* **—soft′ness,** *n.*
—Syn. 1. pliable, plastic, malleable. **5.** mellifluous, dulcet, sweet. **10.** tender, sympathetic. **11.** mollifying. **15.** weak, feeble. **17.** compliant, irresolute, submissive.

sof·ta (sôf′tə, sof′-), *n.* a Turkish Muslim theological student. [1605–15; < Turk < Pers *sōkhta* lit., fired (by love of learning)]

soft′ ar′mor, quilted fabric used as armor.

soft·back (sôft′bak′, soft′-), *n., adj.* paperback. [1965–70; SOFT + BACK[1]]

soft·ball (sôft′bôl′, soft′-), *n.* **1.** a form of baseball played on a smaller diamond with a larger and softer ball. **2.** the ball itself. [1925–30; SOFT + BALL[1]]

soft·ball·er (sôft′bô′lər, soft′-), *n.* a person who plays or is an enthusiast of softball. [SOFTBALL + -ER[1]]

soft·bill (sôft′bil′, soft′-), *n.* any of numerous birds, as thrushes or tanagers, having relatively weak bills suited for eating insects, soft-bodied animals, and fruit rather than hard seeds. [1955–60]

soft·board (sôft′bôrd′, -bōrd′, soft′-), *n.* a soft, porous particle board. [SOFT + BOARD]

soft-boiled (sôft′boild′, soft′-), *adj.* (of an egg) boiled in the shell just long enough for the yolk and white to partially solidify, usually three or four minutes. [1900–05]

soft·bound (sôft′bound′, soft′-), *n., adj.* paperback (defs. 1, 2). [1950–55; SOFT + BOUND[1]]

soft′ chan′cre, *Pathol.* chancroid. [1855–60]

soft′ clam′. See **soft-shell clam.** [1850–55, *Amer.*]

CONCISE PRONUNCIATION KEY: *act, cāpe, dâre, pärt; set, ēqual; if, īce; ox, ōver, ôrder, oil, bŏŏk, bōōt, out; up, ûrge; child; sing; shoe; thin, that;* zh as in *treasure.* ə = *a* as in *alone, e* as in *system, i* as in *easily, o* as in *gallop, u* as in *circus;* ə as in *fire* (fīər), *hour* (ouər). l and n can serve as syllabic consonants, as in *cradle* (krād′l), and *button* (but′n). See the full key inside the front cover.

soft′ coal′. See **bituminous coal.** [1780–90]

soft′-coat·ed wheat′en ter′rier (sôft′kō′tid, soft′-), one of an Irish breed of medium-sized sporting terriers having an abundant, soft, medium-length coat, any shade of wheat in color, with its head and face profusely covered with coat. [1945–50]

soft′ cop′y, *Computers.* computer output displayed on the screen of a VDT (opposed to *hard copy*).

soft-core (sôft′kôr′, -kōr′, soft′-), *adj.* of, pertaining to, or containing sexually arousing depictions that are not fully explicit: *soft-core pornography.* Cf. **hard-core** (def. 2). [1965–70]

soft-cov·er (sôft′kuv′ər, soft′-), *n., adj.* paperback (defs. 1, 2). [1950–55]

soft′ drink′, a beverage that is not alcoholic or intoxicating and is usually carbonated, as root beer. [1875–80]

soft′ drug′, a drug, usually illicit, that does not produce significant psychological or physical dependence.

soft·en (sô′fən, sof′ən), *v.t.* **1.** to make soft or softer. —*v.i.* **2.** to become soft or softer. [1325–75; ME; see SOFT, -EN[1]]
—**Syn. 1.** melt; mollify, mitigate, soothe, alleviate, calm, quiet, ease. —**Ant. 1, 2.** harden.

soft·en·er (sô′fə nər, sof′ə-), *n.* **1.** *Chem.* **a.** any admixture to a substance for promoting or increasing its softness, smoothness, or plasticity. **b.** See **water softener. 2.** a person or thing that softens. [1600–10; SOFTEN + -ER[1]]

soft′ en′ergy. See **renewable energy.**

soft′ening of the brain′, *Pathol.* **1.** a softening of the cerebrum, caused by impairment of the blood supply; encephalomalacia. **2.** *Informal.* dementia associated with general paresis. [1825–35]

soft-finned (sôft′find′, soft′-), *adj. Ichthyol.* having fins supported by articulated rays rather than by spines, as a malacopterygian. [1765–75]

soft′ fo′cus, *Photog.* an image, often created by a special lens, that is recognizable but somewhat blurred or diffused. [1915–20] —**soft′-fo′cus,** *adj.*

soft′ goods′, the subclass of nondurable goods as represented esp. by textile products, as clothing, fabrics, and bedding. Also, **soft′goods′.** [1890–95]

soft′ ground′, 1. an etching ground usually mixed with tallow. Cf. **hard ground. 2.** a technique of etching in which a design is drawn on paper placed on a plate covered with a soft ground, resulting in a granular effect resembling pencil, chalk, or crayon.

soft′ hail′. See **snow pellets.** [1890–95]

soft-head·ed (sôft′hed′id, soft′-), *adj.* foolish; stupid. [1660–70] —**soft′head′,** *n.* —**soft′-head′ed·ness,** *n.*

soft-heart·ed (sôft′här′tid, soft′-), *adj.* very sympathetic or responsive; generous in spirit: *a soft-hearted judge.* [1570–80] —**soft′-heart′ed·ly,** *adv.* —**soft′-heart′ed·ness,** *n.*
—**Syn.** tender, kind-hearted.

soft′ hy′phen, a hyphen that is used only in breaking a word at the end of a line of text.

soft·ie (sôf′tē, sof′-), *n.* softy.

soft·ish (sôf′tish, sof′-), *adj.* somewhat or relatively soft. [1580–90; SOFT + -ISH[1]]

soft·key (sôft′kē′, soft′-), *n. Computers.* any key on a keyboard, as a function key, that can be programmed. Also, **soft′ key′.** [SOFT + KEY[1]]

soft-land (sôf′land′, soft′-), *v.t.* **1.** to cause to land slowly and without jarring impact: *to soft-land the module on the planet's surface.* —*v.i.* **2.** to land slowly and without jarring impact: *The craft will soft-land on the moon.* [1955–60] —**soft′-land′er,** *n.*

soft′ land′ing, *Econ.* a slowing down of economic growth at a manageable rate relative to inflation and unemployment. [1960–65]

soft′ lens′, a nonrigid contact lens made of porous plastic, having a high water content that is replenished from eye surface moisture. Also called **hydrophilic.** Cf. **hard lens.**

soft′ line′, a position or policy, as in politics, that is moderate and flexible. [1965–70] —**soft′-line′,** *adj.* —**soft′-lin′er,** *n.*

soft′ pal′ate. See under **palate** (def. 1). [1805–15]

soft′ paste′, any of a variety of artificial porcelains, usually incorporating glass or glass ingredients. French, **pâte tendre.** Cf. **hard paste.**

soft′ ped′al, 1. Also called **una corda pedal.** a pedal, as on a piano, for reducing tonal volume. **2.** *Informal.* something that restrains or dampens: *to put a soft pedal on one's enthusiasm.* [1920–25]

soft-ped·al (sôft′ped′l, soft′-), *v.,* **-aled, -al·ing** or (*esp. Brit.*) **-alled, -al·ling.** —*v.i.* **1.** to use the soft pedal. —*v.t.* **2.** to soften the sound of by using the soft pedal. **3.** *Informal.* to tone or play down; make less strong, as an idea or fact: *The dean soft-pedaled the reports of cheating.* [1915–20; v. use of n. phrase *soft pedal*]

soft′ porn′, soft-core pornography. [1970–75]

soft′ pornog′raphy, soft-core pornography.

soft′ rock′, a comparatively unaggressive, melodic style of rock-'n'-roll in which the arrangement and lyrics are emphasized more than the beat. [1965–70]

soft′-rock geol′ogy (sôft′rok′, soft′-), geology dealing with sedimentary rocks.

soft′ roe′, milt (def. 2). [1790–1800]

soft′ rot′, *Plant Pathol.* a disease of fruits and vegetables, characterized by a soft, watery decay of affected parts, caused by bacteria or fungi. [1900–05]

soft′ scale′, any of numerous homopterous insect pests of the family Coccidae, as leafhoppers, aphids, and whiteflies, that are destructive to crops, shade and fruit trees, and various houseplants. [1890–95]

soft′ sci′ence, any of the specialized fields or disciplines, as psychology, sociology, anthropology, or political science, that interpret human behavior, institutions, society, etc., on the basis of scientific investigations for which it may be difficult to establish strictly measurable criteria. Cf. **hard science.** [1965–70]

soft′ sculp′ture, sculpture principally in vinyl, canvas, or other flexible material reproducing objects of characteristically rigid construction, as an electric fan, a typewriter, a set of drums, or a bathtub, in forms having a malleable texture and a liquescent, somewhat deflated appearance. [1965–70] —**soft′-sculp′ture,** *adj.*

soft′ sell′, a method of advertising or selling that is quietly persuasive, subtle, and indirect (opposed to *hard sell*). [1950–55]

soft-sell (sôft′sel′, soft′-), *v.,* **-sold, -sell·ing,** *adj.* —*v.t.* **1.** to promote (a product, service, etc.) using indirect or gentle persuasion: *an advertising campaign to soft-sell a new perfume.* —*adj.* **2.** (of a sales technique) quietly or indirectly persuasive: *a soft-sell approach to marketing.* [1950–55]

soft-shell (sôft′shel′, soft′-), *adj.* **1.** Also, **soft′-shelled′.** having a soft, flexible, or fragile shell, as a crab that has recently molted. —*n.* **2.** a soft-shell animal, esp. a soft-shell crab. [1795–1805]

soft′-shell clam′, an edible clam, *Mya arenaria,* inhabiting waters along both coasts of North America, having an oval, relatively thin, whitish shell. Also called **long clam, long-neck clam, soft clam, steamer, steamer clam.** [1790–1800, *Amer.*]

soft′-shell crab′, a crab, esp. the blue crab, that has recently molted and therefore has a soft, edible shell. [1835–45]

soft′-shelled tur′tle, any of numerous aquatic turtles of the family Trionychidae, inhabiting North America, Asia, and Africa, having the shell covered with flexible, leathery skin instead of horny plates. [1765–75]

soft-shoe (sôft′shōō′, soft′-), *adj.* of, pertaining to, or characteristic of tap dancing done in soft-soled shoes, without taps. [1915–20]

soft′ shoul′der, the unpaved edge of a road.

soft′ sign′, 1. the Cyrillic letter ( ) as used in Russian to indicate that the preceding consonant is palatalized, or to represent (y) between a palatalized consonant and a vowel. **2.** front jer. See **jer.** [trans. of Russ *myágkiĭ znak*]

soft′ soap′, 1. *Informal.* persuasive talk; flattery: *to use soft soap to get one's way.* **2.** the semifluid soap produced when potassium hydroxide is used in the saponification of a fat or an oil. [1625–35]

soft-soap (sôft′sōp′, soft′-), *v.t.* **1.** *Informal.* to cajole; flatter. **2.** to apply soft soap to. —*v.i.* **3.** to use soft soap in washing. [1820–30]

soft-soap·er (sôft′sō′pər, soft′-), *n. Informal.* a person who flatters or cajoles, esp. for reasons of self-interest or personal advantage: *a soft-soaper specializing in rich, elderly women.* [1850–55; SOFT-SOAP + -ER[1]]

soft′ sol′der, a solder fusible at temperatures below 700°F (370°C), generally an alloy of lead and tin. Cf. **hard solder.** [1835–45]

soft-spo·ken (sôft′spō′kən, soft′-), *adj.* **1.** (of persons) speaking with a soft or gentle voice; mild. **2.** (of words) softly or mildly spoken; persuasive. [1600–10]

soft′ spot′, 1. a weak or vulnerable position, place, condition, etc.: *a soft spot in their fortifications; a soft spot in the economy.* **2.** emotional susceptibility: *a soft spot for dogs and babies.* [1835–45, *Amer.*]

soft′ steel′. See **mild steel.** [1865–70]

soft′ tick′, any of numerous ticks of the family Argasidae, lacking a dorsal shield and having the mouthparts on the underside of the head. Cf. **hard tick.**

soft-top (sôft′top′, soft′-), *n.* **1.** the folding top of a convertible automobile. **2.** an automobile having such a top; convertible. —*adj.* **3.** of or pertaining to such an automobile: *soft-top sales.*

soft′ touch′, *Informal.* **1.** a person who is easily convinced, esp. to give or lend money: *a soft touch for charities.* **2.** a person who is easily influenced, duped, or imposed upon: *a soft touch for anybody with a sob story.* **3.** a person, team, etc., that is easily defeated: *They're a soft touch for any team in the league.* **4.** a task or activity that is easily or quickly done, esp. a job that pays well and requires little work. [1935–40]

soft·ware (sôft′wâr′, soft′-), *n.* **1.** *Computers.* the programs used to direct the operation of a computer, as well as documentation giving instructions on how to use them. Cf. **hardware** (def. 5). **2.** anything that is not hardware but is used with hardware, esp. audiovisual materials, as film, tapes, records, etc.: *a studio fully equipped but lacking software.* **3.** *Television Slang.* prepackaged materials, as movies or reruns, used to fill out the major part of a station's program schedule. [1955–60; SOFT + WARE[1]]

soft′ware plat′form, a major piece of software, as an operating system, an operating environment, or a database, under which various smaller application programs can be designed to run.

soft′ wheat′, a wheat characterized by soft, starchy kernels that yield a flour used in making pastry, breakfast cereals, etc. [1805–15]

soft·wood (sôft′wŏŏd′, soft′-), *n.* **1.** any wood that is relatively soft or easily cut. **2.** a tree yielding such a wood. **3.** *Forestry.* a coniferous tree or its wood. —*adj.* **4.** of, pertaining to, or made of softwood. [1825–35; SOFT + WOOD[1]]

soft·y (sôf′tē, sof′-), *n., pl.* **-ties.** *Informal.* **1.** a person easily stirred to sentiment or tender emotion. **2.** a person who lacks stamina or endurance. **3.** a person who lacks strength of character; a silly or foolish person. Also, **softie.** [1860–65; SOFT + -Y[2]]

Sog·di·an (sog′dē ən), *n.* **1.** a native or inhabitant of Sogdiana. **2.** the extinct Iranian language of Sogdiana. [1770–80; < Gk *Sogdianós.* See SOGDIANA, -IAN]

Sog·di·a·na (sog′dē ā′nə, -an′ə), *n.* a province of the ancient Persian empire between the Oxus and Jaxartes rivers: now in the SW Soviet Union in Asia. *Cap.:* Samarkand.

sog·gy (sog′ē), *adj.,* **-gi·er, -gi·est. 1.** soaked; thoroughly wet; sodden. **2.** damp and heavy, as poorly baked bread. **3.** ponderously dull; boring: *a soggy novel.* [1590–1600; dial. *sog* bog + -Y[1]; cf. Norw (dial.) *soggjast* to get soaked] —**sog′gi·ly,** *adv.* —**sog′gi·ness,** *n.*

So·ho (sō′hō, sō hō′), *n.* **1.** a district in London, England, including Soho Square: a predominantly foreign section since 1685; noted for its restaurants. **2.** SoHo.

So·Ho (sō′hō), *n.* a district in New York City, in lower Manhattan, south of Houston Street, where many of the old warehouses and buildings have been converted into studios, galleries, shops, and restaurants. Also, **Soho.**

So′ho Square′, a formerly fashionable residential district of London, England.

soi-di·sant (swa dē zäɴ′), *adj. French.* **1.** calling oneself thus; self-styled. **2.** so-called or pretended.

soi·gné (swän yā′; *Fr.* swa nyā′), *adj.* **1.** carefully or elegantly done, operated, or designed. **2.** well-groomed. Also, **soi·gnée′.** [1915–20; < F, ptp. of *soigner* to take care of < Gmc (cf. OS *sunnea* care, concern)]

soil[1] (soil), *n.* **1.** the portion of the earth's surface consisting of disintegrated rock and humus. **2.** a particular kind of earth: *sandy soil.* **3.** the ground as producing vegetation or as cultivated for its crops: *fertile soil.* **4.** a country, land, or region: *an act committed on American soil.* **5.** the ground or earth: *tilling the soil.* **6.** any place or condition providing the opportunity for growth or development: *Some believe that poverty provides the soil for crime.* [1300–50; ME *soile* < AF *soyl* < L *solium* seat, confused with *solum* ground] —**soil′less,** *adj.*

soil[2] (soil), *v.t.* **1.** to make unclean, dirty, or filthy, esp. on the surface: *to soil one's clothes.* **2.** to smirch, smudge, or stain: *The ink soiled his hands.* **3.** to sully or tarnish, as with disgrace; defile morally: *to soil one's good name.* —*v.i.* **4.** to become soiled: *White soils easily.* —*n.* **5.** the act or fact of soiling. **6.** the state of being soiled. **7.** a spot, mark, or stain. **8.** dirty or foul matter; sewage. **9.** ordure; manure. [1175–1225; ME *soilen* (v.) < OF *souiller, soillier* to dirty < VL **suculāre,* equiv. to *sū(s)* pig + *-cul(us)* -CLE[1] + *-āre* inf. ending]
—**Syn. 3.** blacken, taint, debase.

soil[3] (soil), *v.t.* to feed (confined cattle, horses, etc.) freshly cut green fodder for roughage. [1595–1605; orig. uncert.]

soil·age[1] (soi′lij), *n.* grass or leafy plants raised as feed for fenced-in livestock. [SOIL[3] + -AGE]

soil·age[2] (soi′lij), *n.* **1.** an act or instance of soiling. **2.** the condition of being soiled. [1585–95; SOIL[2] + -AGE]

soil′ bank′, a plan providing cash payments to farmers who cut production of certain surplus crops in favor of soil-enriching ones. [1950–55] —**soil′-bank′,** *adj.*

soil′ bind′er, a plant that prevents or inhibits erosion by providing a ground cover and forming a dense network of roots that hold the soil. Also, **soil′bind′er.**

soil′ condi′tioner, any of various organic or inorganic materials added to soil to improve its structure.

soil′ conserva′tion, any of various methods to achieve the maximum utilization of the land and preserve its resources through such controls as crop rotation, prevention of soil erosion, etc.

soil′ creep′, *Geol.* creep of soil on even slopes; often accelerated by spring freeze-and-thaw or general periglacial conditions. Cf. **creep** (def. 17a). [1895–1900]

soil′ group′, one of a number of soil classes having the same kinds of horizons in the same sequence and under similar moisture and temperature regimes. [1920–25]

soil′ mechan′ics, the branch of civil engineering that deals with the mechanical behavior of soil and similar materials when they are compressed or sheared or when liquids flow through them.

soil′ pipe′, a pipe carrying wastes from toilets and sometimes from waste pipes. Cf. **waste pipe** (def. 2). [1825–35]

soil′ pro′file, 1. a vertical succession of horizons, commonly lettered A, B, C (beginning at the surface), that have been subjected to soil-forming processes, chiefly leaching and oxidation. **2.** a diagram of a vertical section of soil depicting the horizons. [1920–25]

soil′ rot′, *Plant Pathol.* pox (def. 3).

soil′ sci′ence, pedology[1]. [1935–40] —**soil′ sci′entist.**

soil′ stack′, *Plumbing.* a vertical soil pipe. [1930–35]

soil·ure (soil′yər), *n.* a stain. [1250–1300; ME *soylure* < OF *soilleure,* equiv. to *soill(ier)* (see SOIL[2]) + *-eure* (< L *-ātūra;* see -ATE[1], -URE)]

soi·ree (swä rā′), *n.* an evening party or social gathering, esp. one held for a particular purpose: *a musical soiree.* Also, **soi·rée′.** [1810–20; < F, equiv. to OF *soir* evening (< L *sērō* late (adv.), orig. abl. of *sērus*) + *-ée* < L *-āta,* fem. of *-ātus* -ATE[1]; cf. JOURNEY]

Sois·sons (swa sôɴ′), *n.* a city in N France, on the Aisne River: battles A.D. 486, 1918, 1944. 32,112.

soi·xante-neuf (swä′sänt nûrf′, -nuf′; *Fr.* swa sänt nœf′), *n.* sixty-nine (def. 4). [1915–20; < F]

so·journ (*n.* sō′jûrn; *v.* sō′jûrn, sō jûrn′), *n.* **1.** a temporary stay: *during his sojourn in Paris.* —*v.i.* **2.** to stay for a time in a place; live temporarily: *to sojourn on*

CONCISE ETYMOLOGY KEY: <, descended or borrowed from; >, whence; b., blend of, blended; c., cognate with; cf., compare; deriv., derivative; equiv., equivalent; imit., imitative; obl., oblique; r., replacing; s., stem; sp., spelling, spelled; resp., respelling, respelled; trans., translation; ?, origin unknown; *, unattested; ‡, probably earlier than. See the full key inside the front cover.

the Riviera for two months. [1200–50; (v.) ME *sojurnen* < OF *sojorner* to rest, stay < VL **subdiurnāre,* equiv. to L *sub-* SUB- + *diurn(us)* of a day + *-āre* inf. suffix; (n.) ME *sojurne* < OF *sojorn,* deriv. of the v.; see JOURNEY] **—so′journ•er,** *n.*
—Syn. 2. visit, vacation, rest, stop.

soke (sōk), *n. Early Eng. Law.* **1.** the privilege of holding court, usually connected with the feudal rights of lordship. **2.** a district over which local jurisdiction was exercised. [1250–1300; ME < AL *soca* < OE *sōcn* attack, right of prosecution, jurisdiction (see SOKEN); akin to SAKE[1], SEEK]

soke•man (sōk′mən), *n., pl.* **-men.** a tenant holding land in socage. Also, **socman.** [1250–1300; ME (< AF) < ML *sokemannus* < OE *sōcn* SOKE + *man* MAN[1]]

soke•man•ry (sōk′mən rē), *n., pl.* **-ries. 1.** tenure of land subject to the soke of someone else. **2.** sokemen. [1250–1300; ME < AF *sokemanerie,* equiv. to *sokeman* SOKEMAN + *-erie* -RY]

so•ken (sō′kən), *n.* a district held by socage. [bef. 1000; ME *socne, soken,* OE *sōcn* an attack, visit, resort, soke. See SOKE]

So•ko•to (sō′kō tō′, sō′kō tō′, sə kō′tō), *n.* **1.** a state in NW Nigeria; formerly a sultanate and province; empire in the 19th century. 4,500,000; 57,560 sq. mi. (149,066 sq. km). **2.** a city in and the capital of this state. 104,160.

So•ko•tra (sō kō′trə, sok′ə trə), *n.* Socotra.

sol[1] (sōl), *n. Music.* **1.** the syllable used for the fifth tone of a diatonic scale. **2.** (in the fixed system of solmization) the tone G. Also, **so.** Cf. **sol-fa** (def. 1). [1275–1325; ME < L *solve;* see GAMUT]

sol[2] (sōl, sol), *n.* a former coin and money of account of France, the 20th part of a livre and equal to 12 deniers: originally gold, later silver, finally copper, it was discontinued in 1794. Also, **sou.** Cf. **solidus**[1] (def. 2). [1575–85; < OF *sol* < LL *solidus* SOLIDUS; cf. It *soldo,* Sp *sueldo*]

sol[3] (sōl, sol; *Sp.* sôl), *n., pl.* **sols,** *Sp.* **so•les** (sô′les). **1.** a bronze coin and monetary unit of Peru, equal to 100 centavos. *Abbr.:* S. **2.** Also called **libra.** a former gold coin of Peru. [1880–85; < AmerSp: sun, Sp < L *sōl*]

sol[4] (sôl, sol), *n. Physical Chem.* a fluid colloidal solution. Cf. **aerosol, gel.** [shortened form of HYDROSOL]

Sol (sol), *n.* **1.** an ancient Roman god personifying the sun. **2.** the sun, personified by the Romans as a god. **3.** a male given name, form of **Solomon.**

-sol, a combining form meaning "soil" of the kind specified by the initial element: *spodosol.* [< L *solum* soil]

Sol., 1. Solicitor. **2.** See **Song of Solomon.**

sol., 1. soluble. **2.** solution.

S.O.L., *Slang.* **1.** strictly out (of) luck. **2.** *Vulgar.* shit out (of) luck. Also, **SOL**

so•la (sō′lä), *n.* an Indian shrub, *Aeschynomene aspera,* of the legume family, the pith of which is used for making helmets. Cf. **topee.** [1835–45; < Hindi *solā*]

so•la (sô′lä; *Eng.* sō′lə), *adj. Latin.* (referring to a woman) alone; by oneself (used formerly in stage directions). Cf. ***solus.***

sol•ace (sol′is), *n., v.,* **-aced, -ac•ing.** **—***n.* Also called **sol′ace•ment. 1.** comfort in sorrow, misfortune, or trouble; alleviation of distress or discomfort. **2.** something that gives comfort, consolation, or relief: *The minister's visit was the dying man's only solace.* **—***v.t.* **3.** to comfort, console, or cheer (a person, oneself, the heart, etc.). **4.** to alleviate or relieve (sorrow, distress, etc.). [1250–1300; ME *solas* < OF < L *sōlācium,* equiv. to *sō-l(āri)* to comfort + *-āc-* adj. suffix + *-ium* -IUM] **—sol′ac•er,** *n.*

so•lan (sō′lən), *n.* a gannet. Also called **so′lan goose′.** [1400–50; late ME *soland* < ON *súla* gannet + *ǫnd* duck]

sol•a•na•ceous (sol′ə nā′shəs), *adj.* belonging to the Solanaceae, the nightshade family of plants. Cf. **nightshade family.** [1795–1805; < NL *Solanace(ae)* name of the family (*Solan(um)* a genus (L *solānum* nightshade) + *-aceae* -ACEAE) + -OUS]

so•lan•der (sə lan′dər), *n.* a case for maps, plates, etc., made to resemble a book and having the front cover and fore edge hinged. [1780–90; named after Daniel Charles *Solander* (1736–82), Swedish naturalist who invented it]

so•lar[1] (sō′lər), *adj.* **1.** of or pertaining to the sun: *solar phenomena.* **2.** determined by the sun: *solar hour.* **3.** proceeding from the sun, as light or heat. **4.** utilizing, operated by, or depending on solar energy: *a solar building; a solar stove.* **5.** indicating time by means of or with reference to the sun: *a solar chronometer.* **6.** manufacturing or providing solar power: *the solar industry.* **7.** *Astrol.* subject to the influence of the sun. **—***n.* **8.** *Informal.* See **solar energy.** [1400–50; late ME < L *sōlā-ris,* equiv. to *sōl* SUN + *-āris* -AR[1]]

sol•ar[2] (sol′ər, sō′lər), *n.* a private or upper chamber in a medieval English house. Also, **sollar, soller.** [bef. 900; ME *solar, soler* < AF *soler,* OF *solier* < L *sōlārium* SOLARIUM; cf. OE *solor, soler,* MD *solre* loft < L]

so′lar activ′ity, *Astron.* the sum of all variable and short-lived disturbances on the sun, as sunspots, prominences, and solar flares.

so′lar a′pex, *Astron.* the point on the celestial sphere, near Vega, toward which the solar system is moving relative to the visible stars. [1870–75]

so′lar bat′tery, an array of solar cells, used as a source of electrical power. [1950–55]

so′lar cell′, a photovoltaic cell that converts sunlight directly into electricity.

so′lar char′iot, (in ancient Egypt) a chariot placed in the tomb of a king to transport him to the sun.

so′lar collec′tor, any of numerous devices or systems designed to capture and use solar radiation for heating air or water and for producing steam to generate electricity. Also called **collector.**

so′lar con′stant, the average rate at which radiant energy is received from the sun by the earth, equal to 1.94 small calories per minute per square centimeter of area perpendicular to the sun's rays, measured at a point outside the earth's atmosphere when the earth is at its mean distance from the sun. [1865–70]

so′lar cy′cle, *Astron.* the variation of sunspots, prominences, flares, and other solar activity through an 11-year cycle. Also called **so′lar activ′ity cy′cle.** Cf. **sunspot cycle.**

so′lar day′, 1. *Astron.* the time interval between two successive transits by the sun of the meridian directly opposite that of the observer; the 24-hour interval from one midnight to the following midnight. **2.** *Law.* the period of time from sunrise to sunset. [1755–65]

so′lar eclipse′. See under **eclipse** (def. 1a).

so′lar en′ergy, energy derived from the sun in the form of solar radiation. Also called **solar.**

so′lar flare′, *Astron.* flare (def. 22). [1935–40]

so′lar fur′nace, a furnace using sunlight concentrated by concave mirrors as the direct source of heat.

so•lar-heat (sō′lər hēt′), *v.t.* to heat (a building) by means of solar energy.

so′lar house′, a house designed to absorb and store solar heat. Also called **so′lar home′.**

so•lar•ism (sō′lə riz′əm), *n.* the interpretation of myths by reference to the sun, esp. such interpretation carried to an extreme. [1880–85; SOLAR[1] + -ISM] **—so′lar•ist,** *n.*

so•lar•i•um (sə lâr′ē əm, sō-), *n., pl.* **-lar•i•ums, -lar•i•a** (-lâr′ē ə). a glass-enclosed room, porch, or the like, exposed to the sun's rays, as at a seaside hotel or for convalescents in a hospital. [1815–25; < L *sōlārium* balcony, terrace, equiv. to *sōl* the sun + *-ārium* -ARY]

so•lar•ize (sō′lə rīz′), *v.,* **-ized, -iz•ing.** **—***v.t.* **1.** *Photog.* to reverse (an image) partially, as from negative to positive, by exposure to light during development. **2.** to adapt (a building) to the use of solar energy: *We hope to solarize our house within five years.* **3.** to affect by sunlight. **—***v.i.* **4.** *Photog.* (of material) to become injured by overexposure. Also, *esp. Brit.,* **so′lar•ise′.** [1850–55; SOLAR[1] + -IZE] **—so′lar•i•za′tion,** *n.*

so′lar mass′, the unit, equivalent to the mass of the sun, in which the masses of stars and other celestial objects are given: *a black hole of one million solar masses.*

so′lar month′, month (def. 4).

so′lar pan′el, a bank of solar cells.

so′lar plex′us, 1. Also called **celiac plexus.** *Anat.* a network of nerves situated at the upper part of the abdomen, behind the stomach and in front of the aorta. **2.** a point on the stomach wall, just below the sternum, where a blow will affect this nerve center. [1765–75; so called from the raylike pattern of the nerve fibers]

so′lar pond′, a pool with a bottom layer of salt water and top layer of fresh water, designed to capture solar radiation as a source of energy for generating heat or electricity.

so′lar prom′inence, *Astron.* prominence (def. 3).

so′lar ra′dius, the unit, equivalent to the radius of the sun, in which the radii of stars and other celestial objects are given.

so′lar sail′, *Aerospace.* a design concept for spacecraft propulsion consisting of a very thin, very large sheet of highly polished material that would be driven by the pressure of sunlight. [1955–60]

so′lar ship′, (in ancient Egypt) a boat placed in or near the tomb of a king to transport him to the sun.

so′lar still′, an apparatus that uses solar radiation to distill salt or brackish water to produce drinkable water.

so′lar sys′tem, the sun together with all the planets and other bodies that revolve around it. [1695–1705]

so′lar wind′ an emanation from the sun's corona consisting of a flow of charged particles, mainly electrons and protons, that interacts with the magnetic field of the earth and other planetary bodies. [1955–60]

so′lar year′, year (def. 4b).

sol•ate (sol′āt, sō′lāt), *v.t.,* **-at•ed, -at•ing.** *Chem.* to change from a gel to a sol. [SOL[4] + -ATE[1]] **—sol•a′tion,** *n.*

so•la•ti•um (sō lā′shē əm), *n., pl.* **-ti•a** (-shē ə). **1.** something given in compensation for inconvenience, loss, injury, or the like; recompense. **2.** *Law.* damages awarded to a plaintiff as compensation for personal suffering or grief arising from an injury. [1810–20; < ML *sōlātium,* var. sp. of *sōlācium,* L: SOLACE]

sold (sōld), *v.* pt. and pp. of **sell**[1].

Sol•dan (sol′dən, sōl′-, sōd′n), *n.* **1.** the ruler of an Islamic country. **2.** *Archaic.* a sultan, esp. the sultan of Egypt. [1250–1300; ME < MF < Ar. See SULTAN]

sol•der (sod′ər), *n.* **1.** any of various alloys fused and applied to the joint between metal objects to unite them without heating the objects to the melting point. **2.** anything that joins or unites: *the solder of their common cause.* **—***v.t.* **3.** to join (metal objects) with solder. **4.** to join closely and intimately: *two fates inseparably soldered by misfortune.* **5.** to mend; repair; patch up. **—***v.i.* **6.** to unite things with solder. **7.** to become soldered or united; grow together. [1325–75; (n.) ME *soudour* < OF *soudure, soldure,* deriv. of *solder* to solder < L *solidāre* to make solid, equiv. to *solid(us)* SOLID + *-āre* inf. suffix; (v.) late ME, deriv. of the n.] **—sol′der•a•ble,** *adj.* **—sol′der•er,** *n.* **—sol′der•less,** *adj.*

sol′dering i′ron, an instrument for melting and applying solder. [1680–90]

sol•dier (sōl′jər), *n.* **1.** a person who serves in an army; a person engaged in military service. **2.** an enlisted man or woman, as distinguished from a commissioned officer: *the soldiers' mess and the officers' mess.* **3.** a person of military skill or experience: *George Washington was a great soldier.* **4.** a person who contends or serves in any cause: *a soldier of the Lord.* **5.** Also called **button man.** *Slang.* a low-ranking member of a crime organization or syndicate. **6.** *Entomol.* a member of a caste of sexually underdeveloped female ants or termites specialized, as with powerful jaws, to defend the colony from invaders. **7.** a brick laid vertically with the narrower long face out. Cf. **rowlock** (def. 2). **8.** *Informal.* a person who avoids work or pretends to work; loafer; malingerer. **—***v.i.* **9.** to act or serve as a soldier. **10.** *Informal.* to loaf while pretending to work; malinger: *He was soldiering on the job.* **11. soldier on,** to persist steadfastly in one's work; persevere: *to soldier on until the work is done.* [1250–1300; ME *souldiour* < OF *soudier, so(l)dier,* equiv. to *soulde* pay (< L *solidus;* see SOL[2]) + *-ier* -IER[2]] **—sol′dier•ship′,** *n.*

sol•dier•fish (sōl′jər fish′), *n., pl.* (*esp. collectively*) **-fish,** (*esp. referring to two or more kinds or species*) **-fish•es. 1.** any of several squirrelfishes of the family Holocentridae. **2.** any of various other brightly colored fishes. [1880–85, *Amer.*; so called from its sharp spines and rough scales]

sol′dier fly′, any of several flies of the family Stratiomyidae, characterized by brightly colored abdominal stripes. [1850–55, *Amer.*]

sol•dier•ing (sōl′jər ing), *n.* the activity or career of a person who soldiers. [1690–1700; SOLDIER + -ING[1]]

sol•dier•ly (sōl′jər lē), *adj.* of, like, or befitting a soldier. [1570–80; SOLDIER + -LY] **—sol′dier•li•ness,** *n.*

sol′dier of for′tune, 1. a person who independently seeks pleasure, wealth, etc., through adventurous exploits. **2.** a military adventurer, ready to serve anywhere for pay or for pleasure. [1655–65]

sol′dier's heart′, *Pathol.* See **cardiac neurosis.** [1895–1900]

sol′diers' home′, an institution that provides care and shelter for retired soldiers. [1860–65, *Amer.*]

Sol′dier's Med′al, a medal awarded to any member of the Army of the United States, or of any military organization serving with it, who distinguishes himself or herself by heroism not involving conflict with an enemy.

sol•dier•y (sōl′jə rē), *n., pl.* **-dier•ies** for 2. **1.** soldiers collectively. **2.** a body of soldiers. **3.** military training or skill. [1560–70; SOLDIER + -RY]

sol•do (sol′dō; *It.* sôl′dô), *n., pl.* **-di** (-dē). a former copper coin of Italy, the twentieth part of a lira, equal to five centesimi. [1590–1600; < It < L *solidum;* see SOL[2]]

sold-out (sōld′out′), *adj.* having all tickets sold, as for a performance or engagement. [1905–10]

sole[1] (sōl), *adj.* **1.** being the only one; only: *the sole living relative.* **2.** being the only one of the kind; unique; unsurpassed; matchless: *the sole brilliance of the gem.* **3.** belonging or pertaining to one individual or group to the exclusion of all others; exclusive: *the sole right to the estate.* **4.** functioning automatically or with independent power: *the sole authority.* **5.** *Chiefly Law.* unmarried. **6.** without company or companions; lonely: *the sole splendor of her life.* **7.** *Archaic.* alone. [1350–1400; < L *sōlus* alone; r. ME *soule* alone < OF *sol* < L *sōlus*] **—sole′ness,** *n.*
—Syn. 1. solitary. **2.** individual.

sole[2] (sōl), *n., v.,* **soled, sol•ing.** **—***n.* **1.** the bottom or under surface of the foot. **2.** the corresponding under part of a shoe, boot, or the like, or this part exclusive of the heel. **3.** the bottom, under surface, or lower part of anything. **4.** *Carpentry.* **a.** the underside of a plane. **b.** soleplate. **5.** *Golf.* the part of the head of the club that touches the ground. **—***v.t.* **6.** to furnish with a sole, as a shoe. **7.** *Golf.* to place the sole of (a club) on the ground, as in preparation for a stroke. [1275–1325; ME (n.) < OF < L *solea* sandal, sole, deriv. of *solum* base, bottom] **—sole′less,** *adj.*

sole[3] (sōl), *n., pl.* (*esp. collectively*) **sole,** (*esp. referring to two or more kinds or species*) **soles. 1.** a European flatfish, *Solea solea,* used for food. **2.** any other flatfish of the families Soleidae and Cynoglossidae, having a hooklike snout. [1300–50; ME < MF < OPr < VL **sola* (for L *solea;* see SOLE[2]), so called from its flat shape; cf. Sp *suela,* It *soglia,* Pg *solha*]

sol•e•cism (sol′ə siz′əm, sō′lə-), *n.* **1.** a nonstandard or ungrammatical usage, as *unflammable* and *they was.* **2.** a breach of good manners or etiquette. **3.** any error, impropriety, or inconsistency. [1570–80; < L *soloecismus* < Gk *soloikismós,* equiv. to *sóloik(os)* (*Sólo(i)* a city in Cilicia where a corrupt form of Attic Greek was spoken + *-ikos* -IC) + *-ismos* -ISM] **—sol′e•cist,** *n.* **—sol′e•cis′tic, sol′e•cis′ti•cal,** *adj.* **—sol′e•cis′ti•cal•ly,** *adv.*

sole′ cus′tody, custody, as of a child whose parents are separated, in which one person has sole responsibility. Cf. **joint custody.**

sole•ly (sōl′lē), *adv.* **1.** as the only one or ones: *solely responsible.* **2.** exclusively or only: *plants found solely in the tropics.* **3.** merely: *She wanted solely to get out of the house for a while.* [1485–95; SOLE[1] + -LY]

sol•emn (sol′əm), *adj.* **1.** grave, sober, or mirthless, as a person, the face, speech, tone, or mood: *solemn remarks.* **2.** gravely or somberly impressive; causing serious thoughts or a grave mood: *solemn music.* **3.** serious or earnest: *solemn assurances.* **4.** characterized by dignified or serious formality, as proceedings; of a formal or ceremonious character: *a solemn occasion.* **5.** made in due legal or other express form, as a declaration or agreement: *a solemn oath.* **6.** marked or observed with religious rites; having a religious character: *a solemn holy day.* **7.** uttered, prescribed, or made according to religious forms: *a solemn ban on sacrifice.* [1275–1325; ME *solem(p)ne* (< OF) < LL *sōlennis, sōlempnis,* L

sōlemnis, var. of *sollemnis* consecrated, holy, deriv. of *sollus* whole] —**sol′emn·ly,** *adv.* —**sol′emn·ness,** *n.*
—**Syn. 1.** unsmiling, serious. See **grave**[2]. **2.** august, imposing, stately. **4.** ritual, ceremonial. **6.** devotional, sacred. —**Ant. 1.** humorous. **2.** trivial.

Sol′emn High′ Mass′, a Mass sung with the assistance of a deacon and subdeacon.

so·lem·ni·fy (sə lem′nə fī′), *v.t.,* **-fied, -fy·ing.** to make solemn: *to solemnify an occasion with hymns and prayers.* [1880–85; SOLEMN + -IFY]

so·lem·ni·ty (sə lem′ni tē), *n., pl.* **-ties. 1.** the state or character of being solemn; earnestness; gravity; impressiveness: *the solemnity of a state funeral.* **2.** Often, **solemnities.** a solemn observance, ceremonial proceeding, or special formality: *the solemnities of Easter.* **3.** *Law.* a formality that renders an act or document valid. [1250–1300; ME *solempnete* < OF < L *sollemnitās,* equiv. to *sollemnis* SOLEMN + *-itās* -ITY]

sol·em·nize (sol′əm nīz′), *v.,* **-nized, -niz·ing.** —*v.t.* **1.** to perform the ceremony of (marriage). **2.** to hold or perform (ceremonies, rites, etc.) in due manner. **3.** to observe or commemorate with rites or ceremonies: *to solemnize an occasion with prayer.* **4.** to go through with ceremony or formality. **5.** to render solemn, serious, or grave; dignify. —*v.i.* **6.** to become solemn; conduct oneself with solemnity. Also, *esp. Brit.,* **sol′em·nise′.** [1350–1400; ME *solempnise* < ML *sōlemnizāre,* equiv. to L *sōlemnis* SOLEMN + *-izāre* -IZE] —**sol′em·ni·za′tion,** *n.* —**sol′em·niz′er,** *n.*

Sol′emn League′ and Cov′enant, an agreement (1643) between the parliaments of Scotland and England permitting the promotion of Presbyterianism in Scotland, England, and Ireland. Cf. **National Covenant.**

Sol′emn Mass′. See **High Mass.**

sol′emn vow′, *Rom. Cath. Ch.* a perpetual, irrevocable public vow taken by a religious, in which property may not be owned by the individual, and marriage is held invalid under canon law. Cf. **simple vow.** [1350–1400; ME]

so·le·no·cyte (sə lē′nə sīt′, -len′ə-), *n. Zool.* a type of long, narrow, flagellated cell that functions in excretion of nitrogenous wastes and occurs in a variety of organisms, including certain annelids and mollusks. [1900–05; < Gk *sōlḗn* pipe, channel + -o- + -CYTE] —**so·le·no·cyt·ic** (sə lē′nə sit′ik, -len′ə-), *adj.*

so·le·no·don (sə lē′nə don′, -len′ə-), *n.* either of two insectivores of the genus *Solenodon,* resembling a large shrew and having small eyes, a long and pointy snout, and a scaly tail, including the coarse-haired, reddish-brown to grayish-black *S. paradoxus* of Hispaniola and the finer-haired, usually darker *S. cubanus* of Cuba: *S. paradoxus* is an endangered species; *S. cubanus* is rare and possibly endangered. [1830–40; < NL < Gk *sōlḗn* channel, pipe, syringe + *-odōn* -toothed (see -ODONT)]

solenodon, *Solenodon paradoxus,* head and body 14 in. (36 cm); tail 10 in. (25 cm)

so·le·no·gas·ter (sə lē′nə gas′tər, -len′ə-), *n. Zool.* any of a group of wormlike mollusks, class Solenogastres (formerly Aplacophora), inhabiting deep ocean layers and having fine limy spicules on the covering mantle. Also called **aplacophoran.** [< NL, equiv. to *soleno-* (comb. form of Gk *sōlḗn* pipe, channel; see -o-) + *-gaster* < Gk *gastḗr* paunch, belly]

so·le·noid (sō′lə noid′, sol′ə-), *n.* **1.** *Elect.* an electric conductor wound as a helix with small pitch, or as two or more coaxial helices, so that current through the conductor establishes a magnetic field within the conductor. **2.** Also called **so′lenoid switch′.** a switch controlled by such an arrangement, in which a metal rod moves when the current is turned on: used in automotive starting systems. **3.** *Meteorol.* a space formed by the intersection of isobaric and isosteric surfaces. [1825–35; < F *solénoïde* < Gk *sōlḗn* pipe, channel + F *-oïde* -OID]

so·le·noi·dal (sō′lə noid′l, sol′ə-), *adj.* **1.** of or pertaining to a solenoid. **2.** *Math.* (of a vector or vector function) having divergence equal to zero. [1870–75; SOLENOID + -AL[1]] —**so′le·noi′dal·ly,** *adv.*

So·lent (sō′lənt), *n.* **The,** a channel between the Isle of Wight and the mainland of S England. 2–5 mi. (3.2–8 km) wide.

sole·plate (sōl′plāt′), *n. Carpentry.* a plate upon which studding is erected. Also called **shoe, sole, sole·piece** (sōl′pēs′). [1835–45; SOLE[2] + PLATE[1]]

sole·print (sōl′print′), *n.* a print of the sole of a foot: often used in hospitals for identifying infants. [1930–35; SOLE[2] + PRINT]

So·ler (sō lâr′; *Sp.* sô leʀ′), *n.* **Padre An·to·nio** (än tô′nyô), 1729–83, Spanish organist and composer.

so·le·ra (sō lâr′ə; *Sp.* sô le′ʀä), *n.* **1.** (esp. in Spain) a series of casks, graded according to age, in which sherries and brandies are stored while maturing. **2.** a classification for the sherries or brandies having the greatest maturity in a solera. [< Sp: lit., supporting beam, base (for uprights) < VL **solāria,* equiv. to L *sol(um)* base, ground (> Sp *suelo*) + *-āria* -ARY; cf. *vino de solera* mature wine (presumably from the bottom range of casks) used to fortify younger wine]

CONCISE ETYMOLOGY KEY: <, descended or borrowed from; >, whence; b., blend of, blended; c., cognate with; cf., compare; deriv., derivative; equiv., equivalent; imit., imitative; obl., oblique; r., replacing; s., stem; sp., spelling, spelled; resp., respelling, respelled; trans., translation; ?, origin unknown; *, unattested; ‡, probably earlier than. See the full key inside the front cover.

So·le·ri (sō lâr′ē), *n.* **Pao·lo** (pou′lō), born 1919, U.S. architect, born in Italy.

so·les (*Sp.* sô′les), *n.* a pl. of **sol**[3].

So·lesmes (sô lem′), *n.* a Benedictine monastery in Solesmes, France, known esp. for the work of its monks in editing and performing Gregorian chant.

sole-source (sōl′sôrs′, -sōrs′), *adj.* designating a company contracted, without competition, to be the sole supplier of a product or service, as a firm having an exclusive contract for certain military technology.

sole′ trad′er, *Law.* See **feme-sole trader.**

So·leure (sô lœʀ′), *n.* French name of **Solothurn.**

so·le·us (sō′lē əs), *n., pl.* **-le·i** (-lē ī′), **-le·us·es.** a muscle in the calf of the leg, behind the gastrocnemius muscle, that helps extend the foot forward. [1670–80; < NL, masc. deriv. of L *solea* sandal; see SOLE[2]]

sol-fa (sōl′fä′, sōl′fä′), *n., v.,* **-faed, -fa·ing.** —*n.* **1.** *Music.* the set of syllables, *do, re, mi, fa, sol, la,* and *ti,* sung to the respective tones of the scale. All but *do* and *ti* are attributed to Guido d'Arezzo. **2.** the system of singing tones to these syllables. —*v.i.* **3.** to use the sol-fa syllables in singing, or to sing these syllables. —*v.t.* **4.** to sing to the sol-fa syllables, as a tune. [1560–70; SOL[1] + FA; see GAMUT] —**sol′-fa′ist,** *n.*

sol·fa·ta·ra (sōl′fə tär′ə, sol′-), *n. Geol.* a fumarole that gives off only sulfurous gases. [1770–80; < It (Neapolitan) *solfatara,* deriv. of *solfo* < L *sulfur;* see SULFUR] —**sol′fa·ta′ric,** *adj.*

sol·fège (sol fezh′, -fej′, sōl-), *n. Music.* solfeggio. [< F < It]

sol·feg·gio (sol fej′ō, -fej′ē ō′), *n., pl.* **-feg·gi** (-fej′ē), **-feg·gios.** *Music.* **1.** a vocal exercise in which the sol-fa syllables are used. **2.** the use of the sol-fa syllables to name or represent the tones of a melody or voice part, or the tones of the scale, or of a particular series, as the scale of C; solmization. [1765–75; < It, deriv. of *solfeggiare,* equiv. to *solf(a)* (see SOL-FA) + *-eggiare* v. suffix]

Sol·fe·ri·no (sôl′fe ʀē′nô *for 1;* sol′fə rē′nō *for 2, 3*), *n.* **1.** a village in SE Lombardy, in N Italy: battle 1859. 1811. **2.** (*l.c.*) a dye obtained from rosaniline. **3.** (*l.c.*) vivid purplish pink. [dye so named from its being discovered after the battle of Solferino]

sol·gel (sol′jel′, sōl′-), *adj.* pertaining to alternation between the sol and gel states, as in the pseudopodia of amebas. [1920–25; SOL[4] + GEL]

soli-[1], a combining form meaning "alone," "solitary," used in the formation of compound words: *solifidian.* [< L *sōli-,* comb. form of *sōlus.* See SOLE[1]]

soli-[2], a combining form meaning "sun," used in the formation of compound words: *soliform.* [comb. form repr. L *sōl* SUN; see -I-]

so·lic·it (sə lis′it), *v.t.* **1.** to seek for (something) by entreaty, earnest or respectful request, formal application, etc.: *He solicited aid from the minister.* **2.** to entreat or petition (someone or some agency): *to solicit the committee for funds.* **3.** to seek to influence or incite to action, esp. unlawful or wrong action. **4.** to offer to have sex with in exchange for money. —*v.i.* **5.** to make a petition or request, as for something desired. **6.** to solicit orders or trade, as for a business: *No soliciting allowed in this building.* **7.** to offer to have sex with someone in exchange for money. [1400–50; late ME *soliciten* < MF *solliciter* < L *sollicitāre* to excite, agitate, deriv. of *sollicitus* troubled (*soll(us)* whole + *-i-* -I- + *citus,* ptp. of *ciēre* to arouse)]
—**Syn. 2.** beseech, beg. **3.** excite, arouse, provoke.

so·lic·i·ta·tion (sə lis′i tā′shən), *n.* **1.** the act of soliciting. **2.** entreaty, urging, or importunity; a petition or request. **3.** enticement or allurement. **4.** *Law.* **a.** the crime of asking another to commit or to aid in a crime. **b.** the act of a prostitute soliciting in a public place. [1485–95; < L *sollicitātiōn-* (s. of *sollicitātiō*), equiv. to *sollicitāt(us)* (ptp. of *sollicitāre* to SOLICIT; see -ATE[1]) + *-iōn-* -ION]

so·lic·i·tor (sə lis′i tər), *n.* **1.** a person who solicits. **2.** a person whose business it is to solicit business, trade, etc. **3.** an officer having charge of the legal business of a city, town, etc. **4.** (in England and Wales) a member of that branch of the legal profession whose services consist of advising clients, representing them before the lower courts, and preparing cases for barristers to try in the higher courts. Cf. **barrister** (def. 1). [1375–1425; late ME *solicitour* < AF; MF *soliciteur.* See SOLICIT, -OR[2]] —**so·lic′i·tor·ship′,** *n.*
—**Syn. 4.** lawyer, attorney, counselor.

solic′itor gen′eral, *pl.* **solicitors general. 1.** a law officer who maintains the rights of the state in suits affecting the public interest, next in rank to the attorney general. **2.** the chief legal officer in some states. **3.** (*caps.*) the law officer of the U.S. government next below the Attorney General, having charge of appeals, as to the Supreme Court. [1525–35]

so·lic·i·tous (sə lis′i təs), *adj.* **1.** anxious or concerned (usually fol. by *about, for,* etc., or a clause): *solicitous about a person's health.* **2.** anxiously desirous: *solicitous of the esteem of others.* **3.** eager (usually fol. by an infinitive): *He was always solicitous to please.* **4.** careful or particular: *a solicitous housekeeper.* [1555–65; < L *sollicitus* anxious. See SOLICIT, -OUS] —**so·lic′i·tous·ly,** *adv.* —**so·lic′i·tous·ness,** *n.*
—**Syn. 1.** mindful, regardful, attentive. —**Ant. 1.** unconcerned, careless.

so·lic·i·tude (sə lis′i to͞od′, -tyo͞od′), *n.* **1.** the state of being solicitous; anxiety or concern. **2. solicitudes,** causes of anxiety or care. **3.** an attitude expressing excessive attentiveness: *to show great solicitude about his wife's health.* [1375–1425; late ME < L *sollicitūdō* uneasiness of mind, deriv. of *sollicitus* agitated. See SOLICIT, -TUDE]
—**Syn. 1.** worry, care, unease, disquietude, apprehension.

sol·id (sol′id), *adj.* **1.** having three dimensions (length, breadth, and thickness), as a geometrical body or figure. **2.** of or pertaining to bodies or figures of three dimensions. **3.** having the interior completely filled up, free from cavities, or not hollow: *a solid piece of chocolate.* **4.** without openings or breaks: *a solid wall.* **5.** firm, hard, or compact in substance: *solid ground.* **6.** having relative firmness, coherence of particles, or persistence of form, as matter that is not liquid or gaseous: *solid particles suspended in a liquid.* **7.** pertaining to such matter: *Water in a solid state is ice.* **8.** dense, thick, or heavy in nature or appearance: *solid masses of cloud.* **9.** not flimsy, slight, or light, as buildings, furniture, fabrics, or food; substantial. **10.** of a substantial character; not superficial, trifling, or frivolous: *a solid work of scientific scholarship.* **11.** without separation or division; continuous: *a solid row of buildings.* **12.** whole or entire: *one solid hour.* **13.** forming the whole; consisting entirely of one substance or material: *solid gold.* **14.** uniform in tone or shades, as a color: *a solid blue dress.* **15.** real or genuine: *solid comfort.* **16.** sound or reliable, as reasons or arguments: *solid facts.* **17.** soberminded; fully reliable or sensible: *a solid citizen.* **18.** financially sound or strong: *Our company is solid.* **19.** cubic: *A solid foot contains 1728 solid inches.* **20.** written without a hyphen, as a compound word. **21.** having the lines not separated by leads, or having few open spaces, as type or printing. **22.** thorough, vigorous, great, big, etc. (with emphatic force, often after *good*): *a good solid blow.* **23.** firmly united or consolidated: *a solid combination.* **24.** united or unanimous in opinion, policy, etc. **25.** on a friendly, favorable, or advantageous footing (often prec. by *in*): *He was in solid with her parents.* **26.** *Slang.* excellent, esp. musically. —*n.* **27.** a body or object having three dimensions (length, breadth, and thickness). **28.** a solid substance or body; a substance exhibiting rigidity. [1350–1400; ME < L *solidus*] —**sol′id·ly,** *adv.* —**sol′id·ness,** *n.*
—**Syn. 1.** cubic. **5.** dense. See **firm**[1]. **6.** cohesive, firm. **9.** sound. **11.** unbroken. **18.** solvent. **22.** strong. —**Ant. 1.** flat. **6.** loose. **11, 24.** divided.

sol′id an′gle, *Geom.* an angle formed by three or more planes intersecting in a common point or formed at the vertex of a cone. [1695–1705]

sol·i·dar·i·ty (sol′i dar′i tē), *n., pl.* **-ties. 1.** union or fellowship arising from common responsibilities and interests, as between members of a group or between classes, peoples, etc.: *to promote solidarity among union members.* **2.** community of feelings, purposes, etc. **3.** community of responsibilities and interests. [1840–50; < F *solidarité,* equiv. to *solidaire* SOLIDARY + *-ité* -ITY]
—**Syn. 1.** unity, cooperation, community. **2.** unanimity.

Sol·i·dar·i·ty (sol′i dar′i tē), *n.* a Polish organization of independent trade unions founded in 1980: outlawed by the government of Poland in 1982. Polish, **So·li·dar·ność** (sô lē där′nôshch).

sol·i·da·rize (sol′i də rīz′), *v.i.,* **-rized, -riz·ing.** to unite or come together; become solidified. Also, *esp. Brit.,* **sol′i·da·rise′.** [1885–90; < F *solidariser.* See SOLIDARY, -IZE]

sol·i·dar·y (sol′i der′ē), *adj.* characterized by or involving community of responsibilities and interests. [1810–20; < F *solidaire,* MF; see SOLID, -ARY[1]] —**sol′i·dar′i·ly,** *adv.*

sol′id geom′etry, the geometry of solid figures; geometry of three dimensions. [1725–35]

so·lid·i·fy (sə lid′ə fī′), *v.,* **-fied, -fy·ing.** —*v.t.* **1.** to make solid; make into a hard or compact mass; change from a liquid or gaseous to a solid form. **2.** to unite firmly or consolidate. **3.** to form into crystals; make crystallized. —*v.i.* **4.** to become solid. **5.** to form into crystals; become crystallized. [1790–1800; < F *solidifier.* See SOLID, -IFY] —**so·lid′i·fi′a·bil′i·ty, so·lid′i·fi′a·ble·ness,** *n.* —**so·lid′i·fi′a·ble,** *adj.* —**so·lid′i·fi·ca′tion,** *n.* —**so·lid′i·fi′er,** *n.*

sol′id injec′tion, injection of fuel into an internal-combustion engine without an air blast. Cf. **air injection.**

so·lid·i·ty (sə lid′i tē), *n.* **1.** the state, property, or quality of being solid. **2.** firmness and strength; substantialness: *an argument with little solidity.* **3.** strength of mind, character, finances, etc. **4.** *Obs.* the amount of space occupied by a solid body; volume. [1525–35; < L *soliditās,* equiv. to *solid(us)* SOLID + *-itās* -ITY]

sol·id-look·ing (sol′id lo͝ok′ing), *adj.* reassuringly substantial or stable in appearance: *They're a very solid-looking, intelligent couple.* [1880–85]

sol′id of revolu′tion, a three-dimensional figure formed by revolving a plane area about a given axis. [1810–20]

sol′id propel′lant, a rocket propellant in solid form, usually containing a mixture or combination of fuel and oxidizer. Cf. **liquid propellant.**

sol′id rock′et boost′er, a solid-propellant strap-on rocket used to accelerate a missile or launch vehicle during liftoff. *Abbr.:* SRB

sol′id solu′tion, 1. a solid, homogeneous mixture of substances, as glass or certain alloys. **2.** (in a crystal structure) the more or less complete substitution of one kind of atom, ion, or molecule for another that is chemically different but similar in size and shape; isomorphism.

Sol′id South′, the states of the southern U.S. that traditionally supported the Democratic party after the Civil War.

sol·id-state (sol′id stāt′), *adj. Electronics.* designating or pertaining to electronic devices, as transistors or crystals, that can control current without the use of moving parts, heated filaments, or vacuum gaps. [1965–70]

sol·id·un·gu·late (sol′i dung′gyə lit, -lāt′), *adj. Zool.* **1.** having a single, undivided hoof on each foot, as a horse. —*n.* **2.** Also called **soliped.** a solidungulate animal. [1830–40; < L *solid(us)* SOLID + UNGULATE]

sol·i·dus[1] (sol′i dəs), *n., pl.* **-di** (-dī′). **1.** a gold coin of ancient Rome, introduced by Constantine and continued in the Byzantine Empire; bezant. **2.** (in medieval Europe) a money of account equal to 12 denarii. Cf. **sol²**. **3.** virgule. [1350–1400; ME < LL *solidus* (*nummus*) a solid (coin), a gold (coin)]

sol·i·dus² (sol′i dəs), *n. Physical Chem.* (on a graph of temperature versus composition) the curve connecting the temperatures at which a solid solution is in equilibrium with its vapor and with the liquid solution, and therefore connecting melting temperatures of solid solutions. Cf. **liquidus.** [1900–05; < L: SOLID]

sol·i·fid·i·an (sol′ə fid′ē ən), *n. Theol.* a person who maintains that faith alone, without the performance of good works, is all that is necessary for salvation. [1590–1600; SOLI-¹ + L *fid*(*ēs*) FAITH, belief, trust + -IAN] **—sol′i·fid′i·an·ism,** *n.*

so·li·fluc·tion (sō′lə fluk′shən, sol′ə-), *n. Geol.* creep (def. 17a). [1915–20; < L *sol*(*um*) soil + *-i-* -I- + *fluctiōn-* a flowing (s. of *fluctiō*), equiv. to *fluct*(*us*) (see FLUCTUATE) + *-iōn-* -ION]

so·lif·u·gid (sə lif′yə jid), *n.* See **sun spider.** [var. of SOLPUGID (LL *solifuga,* by folk etym. from L *salpūga*]

so·lil·o·quize (sə lil′ə kwīz′), *v.*, **-quized, -quiz·ing.** *—v.i.* **1.** to utter a soliloquy; talk to oneself. *—v.t.* **2.** to utter in a soliloquy; say to oneself. Also, *esp. Brit.,* **so·lil′o·quise′.** [1750–60; SOLILOQU(Y) + -IZE] **—so·lil·o·quist** (sə lil′ə kwist), **so·lil′o·quiz′er,** *n.* **—so·lil′o·quiz′ing·ly,** *adv.*

so·lil·o·quy (sə lil′ə kwē), *n., pl.* **-quies. 1.** an utterance or discourse by a person who is talking to himself or herself or is disregardful of or oblivious to any hearers present (often used as a device in drama to disclose a character's innermost thoughts): *Hamlet's soliloquy begins with "To be or not to be."* **2.** the act of talking while or as if alone. [1595–1605; < LL *sōliloquium* a talking to oneself, soliloquy, equiv. to *sōli-* SOLI-¹ + *loqu*(*i*) to speak + *-ium* -IUM; see -Y³]

Sol·i·man I (sol′ə mən). See **Suleiman I.**

So·li·me·na (sō′lē me′nä), *n.* **Fran·ces·co** (frän-ches′kô), 1657–1747, Italian painter.

So·li·mões (sô′li moins′), *n.* Brazilian name of the Amazon from its junction with the Río Negro to the border of Peru.

sol·ing (sō′ling), *n.* pitching. [SOLE² + -ING¹]

So·ling·en (zō′ling ən), *n.* a city in W Germany, in the Ruhr region. 159,100.

sol·i·on (sol′ī′ən, -on), *n. Chem., Elect.* a low-frequency amplifying device that operates by controlling the flow of ions in solution: some types, as the micropump, accomplish this by means of electro-osmotic pressure. [1955–60; SOL(UTION) + ION]

sol·i·ped (sol′ə ped′), *n.* solidungulate. [1640–50; < NL *soliped-* (s. of *solipēs*), equiv. to L *soli-* SOLI-¹ + *ped-,* s. of *pēs* foot; see -PED]

sol·ip·sism (sol′ip siz′əm), *n.* **1.** *Philos.* the theory that only the self exists, or can be proved to exist. **2.** extreme preoccupation with and indulgence of one's feelings, desires, etc.; egoistic self-absorption. [1880–85; SOL(I)-¹ + L *ips*(*e*) self + -ISM] **—sol′ip·sis′mal,** *adj.* **—sol′ip·sist,** *n., adj.* **—sol·ip·sis·tic** (sol′ip sis′tik), *adj.*

sol·i·taire (sol′i târ′), *n.* **1.** Also called **patience.** any of various games played by one person with one or more regular 52-card packs, part or all of which are usually dealt out according to a given pattern, the object being to arrange the cards in a predetermined manner. **2.** a game played by one person alone, as a game played with marbles or pegs on a board having hollows or holes. **3.** a precious stone, esp. a diamond, set by itself, as in a ring. **4.** any of several American thrushes of the genus *Myadestes,* having short, broad bills and noted for their beautiful songs. **5.** a large extinct flightless bird of the genus *Pezophaps,* related to the dodo but with a longer neck, smaller bill, and longer legs, that inhabited the Mascarene Islands. [1350–1400; ME < F < L *sōlitārius* SOLITARY]

sol·i·tar·y (sol′i ter′ē), *adj., n., pl.* **-tar·ies.** *—adj.* **1.** alone; without companions; unattended: *a solitary passer-by.* **2.** living alone; avoiding the society of others: *a solitary existence.* **3.** by itself; alone: *one solitary house.* **4.** characterized by the absence of companions: *a solitary journey.* **5.** done without assistance or accompaniment; done in solitude: *solitary chores.* **6.** being the only one: *a solitary exception.* **7.** characterized by solitude, as a place; unfrequented, secluded, or lonely: *a solitary cabin in the woods.* **8.** *Zool.* living habitually alone or in pairs, as certain wasps. Cf. **social** (def. 10). *—n.* **9.** a person who lives alone or in solitude, or avoids the society of others. **10.** a person who lives in solitude from religious motives. **11.** See **solitary confinement.** [1300–50; ME < L *sōlitārius* alone, by itself, solitary, equiv. to *sōlit*(*ās*) solitude (*sōl*(*us*) SOLE¹ + *-itās* -ITY) + *-ārius* -ARY] **—sol′i·tar′i·ly,** *adv.* **—sol′i·tar′i·ness,** *n.*
—Syn. 1. lone. **7.** isolated, retired, sequestered, remote. **9, 10.** hermit, recluse. **10.** eremite.

sol′itary bee′, any of numerous bees, as the leaf-cutting bees, that do not live in a community. Cf. **social bee.** [1820–30]

sol′itary confine′ment, the confinement of a prisoner in a cell or other place in which he or she is completely isolated from others. [1775–85]

sol′itary sand′piper, a North American sandpiper, *Tringa solitaria,* of inland wetlands, having a brownish-gray, white-spotted back and whitish underparts. [1805–15, *Amer.*]

sol′itary vir′eo, a vireo, *Vireo solitarius,* of North and Central America, having the top and sides of the head bluish-gray. Also called **blue-headed vireo.** [1825–35, *Amer.*]

sol′itary wasp′, any of numerous wasps, as the sand wasps or mud wasps, that do not live in a community. Cf. **social wasp.** [1820–30]

sol′itary wave′, *Math., Physics.* a localized disturbance that propagates like a wave but resembles a particle in that it does not disperse, even if it collides with other such waves.

sol·i·ton (sol′i ton′), *Math., Physics.* **1.** a solution of a certain type of partial differential equation that represents a solitary wave. **2.** (loosely) a solitary wave. [1960–65; SOLIT(ARY) + -ON¹]

sol·i·tude (sol′i to͞od′, -tyo͞od′), *n.* **1.** the state of being or living alone; seclusion: *to enjoy one's solitude.* **2.** remoteness from habitations, as of a place; absence of human activity: *the solitude of the mountains.* **3.** a lonely, unfrequented place: *a solitude in the mountains.* [1325–75; ME < MF < L *sōlitūdō.* See SOLI-¹, -TUDE] **—sol·i·tu·di·nous** (sol′i to͞od′n əs, -tyo͞od′-), *adj.*
—Syn. 1. retirement, privacy. SOLITUDE, ISOLATION refer to a state of being or living alone. SOLITUDE emphasizes the quality of being or feeling lonely and deserted: *to live in solitude.* ISOLATION may mean merely a detachment and separation from others: *to be put in isolation with an infectious disease.* **2.** loneliness. **3.** desert, wilderness.

sol·i·tu·di·nar·i·an (sol′i to͞od′n âr′ē ən, -tyo͞od′-), *n.* a person who seeks solitude; recluse. [1685–95; SOLITUDIN(OUS) + -ARIAN]

sol·lar (sol′ər), *n.* solar². Also, **sol′ler.**

sol·lick·er (sol′i kər), *Brit., Australian Informal.* *—n.* **1.** force; momentum. *—adj.* Also **sol′lick·ing. 2.** very large. **3.** remarkable; wonderful. [1915–20; orig. uncert.]

sol·mi·za·tion (sol′mə zā′shən, sōl′-), *n. Music.* the act, process, or system of using certain syllables, esp. the sol-fa syllables, to represent the tones of the scale. [1720–30; < F *solmisation,* equiv. to *solmis*(*er*) (*sol* SOL¹ + *mi* MI + *-iser* -IZE) + *-ation* -ATION]

soln., solution.

so·lo (sō′lō), *n., pl.* **-los, -li** (-lē), *adj., adv., v.* *—n.* **1.** a musical composition or a passage or section in a musical composition written for performance by one singer or instrumentalist, with or without accompaniment: *She sang a solo.* **2.** any performance, as a dance, by one person. **3.** a flight in an airplane during which the pilot is unaccompanied by an instructor or other person: *I'll be ready for my first solo next week.* **4.** a person who works, acts, or performs alone: *He used to sing with a quartet, but now he's a solo.* **5.** a person who performs or accomplishes something without the usual equipment, tools, etc. **6.** *Informal.* an announcement, commercial offering, etc., made to only one person or a selected group of such persons: *Each month the firm sends a solo to its best customers.* **7.** *Cards.* any of certain games in which one person plays alone against others. *—adj.* **8.** *Music.* performing alone: *a part for solo bassoon.* **9.** performed alone; not combined with other parts of equal importance; not concerted. **10.** alone; without a companion or partner: *a solo flight.* *—adv.* **11.** on one's own; alone or unaccompanied: *After six lessons he was flying solo.* *—v.i.* **12.** to perform or do a solo: *to solo on the trumpet.* **13.** to pilot a plane, glider, etc., unaccompanied, esp. for the first time: *After the course the students should be able to solo.* **14.** to perform or accomplish something by oneself. *—v.t.* **15.** to pilot (a plane, glider, etc.) unaccompanied. **16.** to allow (a student pilot) to pilot a plane, glider, etc., alone: *The instructor decided to solo the student.* [1685–95; < It < L *sōlus* alone]

So·lo (sō′lō), *n.* former name of **Surakarta.**

so·lo·ist (sō′lō ist), *n.* a person who performs a solo. [1860–65; SOLO + -IST] **—so′lo·is′tic,** *adj.*

So′lo man′, an early human being of the upper Pleistocene, known from skull fragments found in Java. [after the *Solo* River, central Java, near which the fragments were found]

Sol·o·mon (sol′ə mən), *n.* **1.** fl. 10th century B.C., king of Israel (son of David). **2.** an extraordinarily wise man; a sage. **3.** a male given name.

Sol·o·mon·ic (sol′ə mon′ik), *adj.* **1.** of or pertaining to King Solomon. **2.** wise or reasonable in character: *a Solomonic decision.* Also, **Sol·o·mo·ni·an** (sol′ə mō′nē-ən, -mōn′yən). [1715–25; SOLOMON + -IC]

Sol′omon Is′lands, 1. an archipelago in the W Pacific Ocean, E of New Guinea; important World War II battles; politically divided between Papua New Guinea and the Solomon Islands. **2.** an independent country comprising the larger, SE part of this archipelago: a former British protectorate; gained independence in 1978. 152,000; 11,458 sq. mi. (29,676 sq. km). *Cap.:* Honiara (on Guadalcanal). **—Sol′omon Is′lander.**

Solomon's seal

Sol′omon's seal′, a mystic or talismanic symbol in the form of an interlaced outline of either a five-pointed or six-pointed star. [1535–45]

Sol·o·mon's-seal (sol′ə mənz sēl′), *n.* any of several plants belonging to the genus *Polygonatum,* of the lily family, having a thick rootstock bearing seallike scars, greenish-yellow flowers, and red or blue berries. [1535–45; trans. of ML *sigillum Solomōnis*]

So·lon (sō′lən), *n.* **1.** c638–c558 B.C., Athenian statesman. **2.** (*often l.c.*) a wise lawgiver. **3.** a town in N Ohio. 14,341. **—So·lo·ni·an** (sō lō′nē ən), **So·lon·ic** (sō-lon′ik), *adj.*

so′ long′, *Informal.* good-bye: *I said so long and left.* [1840–50, *Amer.*]

So·lo·thurn (*Ger.* zō′lô to͝orn′), *n.* **1.** a city in NW Switzerland, on the Aar River: capital of canton of Solothurn. 16,200. **2.** a canton in NW Switzerland. 224,800. French, **Soleure.**

so′lo whist′, *Cards.* a variety of whist in which each player can offer to play any of seven specified bids. [1890–95]

sol·pu·gid (sol′pyə jid), *n.* See **sun spider.** [1870–75; < NL *Solpugidae* name of the family, equiv. to *Solpug*(*a*) a genus (L *salpūga* a venomous ant) + *-idae* -ID²]

sol·stice (sol′stis, sōl′-), *n.* **1.** *Astron.* **a.** either of the two times a year when the sun is at its greatest distance from the celestial equator: about June 21, when the sun reaches its northernmost point on the celestial sphere, or about December 22, when it reaches its southernmost point. Cf. **summer solstice, winter solstice. b.** either of the two points in the ecliptic farthest from the equator. **2.** a furthest or culminating point; a turning point. [1200–50; < ME < OF < L *sōlstitium,* equiv. to *sōl* sun + *-stit-,* comb. form of *stat-,* var. s. of *sistere* to make stand (see STAND) + *-ium* -IUM; see -ICE)]

sol·sti·tial (sol stish′əl, sōl-), *adj.* **1.** of or pertaining to a solstice or the solstices: *a solstitial point.* **2.** occurring at or about the time of a solstice. **3.** characteristic of the summer solstice. [1550–60; < L *sōlstitiālis;* see SOLSTICE, -AL¹] **—sol·sti′tial·ly,** *adv.*

Sol·ti (shōl′tē), *n.* **Sir Ge·org** (gā′ôrg, jôrj), born 1912, British orchestra conductor, born in Hungary.

sol·u·bil·i·ty (sol′yə bil′i tē), *n.* the quality or property of being soluble; relative capability of being dissolved. [1670–80; SOLUBLE + -ITY]

solubil′ity prod′uct, *Physical Chem.* the maximum number of undissociated ions, of an electrolyte in a saturated solution, capable at a given temperature of remaining in equilibrium with the undissolved phase of the solution.

sol·u·bi·lize (sol′yə bə līz′), *v.t.,* **-lized, -liz·ing.** *Chem.* to make soluble, or to increase solubility. Also, *esp. Brit.,* **sol′u·bi·lise′.** [1925–30; SOLUBLE + -IZE, with *-i-* inserted as in SOLUBILITY] **—sol′u·bi·li·za′tion,** *n.*

sol·u·ble (sol′yə bəl), *adj.* **1.** capable of being dissolved or liquefied: *a soluble powder.* **2.** capable of being solved or explained: *a soluble problem.* *—n.* **3.** something soluble. [1350–1400; ME < LL *solūbilis,* equiv. to L *solū-,* var. s. of *solvere* to loosen, dissolve + *-bilis* -BLE] **—sol′u·ble·ness,** *n.* **—sol′u·bly,** *adv.*

sol′uble glass′. See **sodium silicate.** [1870–75]

so·lum (sō′ləm), *n., pl.* **-la** (-lə), **-lums.** the upper part of the soil profile, which is influenced by plant roots; the A horizon and the B horizon. [1820–30; < L: base, bottom; see SOLE²]

so·lu·nar (sō lo͞o′nər, so-), *adj.* pertaining to or listing the rising and setting times of the sun and moon, phases of the moon, eclipses, etc.: *The newspaper gives a solunar table each week for hunters and fishermen.* [b. SOLAR¹ and LUNAR]

so·lus (sô′lo͝os; *Eng.* sō′ləs), *adj. Latin.* (referring to a man) alone; by oneself (used formerly in stage directions). Cf. ***sola.***

sol·ute (sol′yo͞ot, sō′lo͞ot), *n.* the substance dissolved in a given solution. [1400–50; late ME < L *solūtus,* ptp. of *solvere* to loosen, dissolve. See SOLVE]

so·lu·tion (sə lo͞o′shən), *n.* **1.** the act of solving a problem, question, etc.: *The situation is approaching solution.* **2.** the state of being solved: *a problem capable of solution.* **3.** a particular instance or method of solving; an explanation or answer: *The solution is as good as any other.* **4.** *Math.* **a.** the process of determining the answer to a problem. **b.** the answer itself. **5.** *Chem.* **a.** the process by which a gas, liquid, or solid is dispersed homogeneously in a gas, liquid, or solid without chemical change. **b.** such a substance, as dissolved sugar or salt in solution. **c.** a homogeneous, molecular mixture of two or more substances. **6.** *Pharm.* Also called **liquor.** a liquid, usually water, in which a medication is dissolved. **7.** *Med.* **a.** the termination of a disease. **b.** a breach or break in anything, esp. one in parts of the body normally continuous, as from fracture or laceration: *solution of continuity.* [1325–75; ME < L *solūtiōn-* (s. of *solūtiō*), equiv. to *solūt*(*us*) (see SOLUTE) + *-iōn-* -ION] **—so·lu′·tion·al,** *adj.*
—Syn. 3. key, resolution.

solu′tion min′ing, removal of a soluble mineral by dissolving it and leaching it out, as in the Frasch process.

sol·u·tiz·er (sol′yə tī′zər), *n. Chem.* any admixture to a substance for promoting or increasing its solubility or that of one or more of its components. [SOLUT(ION) + -IZE + -ER¹]

So·lu·tre·an (sə lo͞o′trē ən), *adj. Archaeol.* of or designating an Upper Paleolithic European culture c18,000–16,000 B.C., characterized by the making of stone projectile points and low-relief stone sculptures. Also, **So·lu′tri·an.** [1885–90; < F *solutréen,* after *Solutré* the type-site, near a village of the same name in France (Saône-et-Loire); see -AN]

solv·a·ble (sol′və bəl), *adj.* **1.** capable of being solved, as a problem. **2.** *Math.* (of a group) having a normal series of subgroups in which successive quotient groups are Abelian. **3.** *Archaic.* soluble (def. 1). [1640–50; SOLVE + -ABLE] **—solv′a·bil′i·ty, solv′a·ble·ness,** *n.*

solv·ate (sol′vāt), *n., v.,* **-at·ed, -at·ing.** *Chem.* *—n.* **1.** a compound formed by the interaction of a solvent and a solute. *—v.t.* **2.** to convert into a solvate. [1900–05; SOLV(ENT) + -ATE¹] **—solv·a′tion,** *n.*

Sol·vay (sol′vā; *Fr.* sôl vā′), *n.* **Er·nest** (ûr′nist; *Fr.* er nest′), 1838–1922, Belgian chemist.

CONCISE PRONUNCIATION KEY: act, cāpe, dâre, pärt; set, ēqual; *if,* ice; ox, ōver, ôrder, oil, bo͝ok, bo͞ot, out; up, ûrge; child; sing; shoe; thin, *th*at; zh as in *treasure.* ə = *a* as in *alone, e* as in *system, i* as in *easily, o* as in *gallop, u* as in *circus;* ᵊ as in *fire* (fīᵊr), *hour* (ouᵊr). l and n can serve as syllabic consonants, as in *cradle* (krād′l), and *button* (but′n). See the full key inside the front cover.

Sol′vay proc′ess, a process for manufacturing sodium carbonate whereby a concentrated solution of sodium chloride is saturated with ammonia, carbon dioxide is passed through it, and the product is calcined. [1885–90; named after E. SOLVAY]

solve (solv), *v.t.,* **solved, solv·ing. 1.** to find the answer or explanation for; clear up; explain: *to solve the mystery of the missing books.* **2.** to work out the answer or solution to (a mathematical problem). [1400–50; late ME *solven* < L *solvere* to loosen, free, release, dissolve] **—solv′er,** *n.*
—Syn. 1. resolve, unravel, untangle, crack.

sol·ven·cy (sol′vən sē), *n.* solvent condition; ability to pay all just debts. [1720–30; SOLV(ENT) + -ENCY]

sol·vent (sol′vənt), *adj.* **1.** able to pay all just debts. **2.** having the power of dissolving; causing solution. **—***n.* **3.** a substance that dissolves another to form a solution: *Water is a solvent for sugar.* **4.** something that solves or explains. [1620–30; < L *solvent-* (s. of *solvēns*), prp. of *solvere* to loosen. See SOLVE, -ENT] **—sol′vent·less,** *adj.* **—sol′vent·ly,** *adv.*

sol·vol·y·sis (sol vol′ə sis), *n. Chem.* a chemical reaction in which the solvent and solute interact; lyolysis. [1920–25; < NL; see SOLVE, -O-, -LYSIS] **—sol·vo·lyt·ic** (sol′və lit′ik), *adj.*

Sol′way Firth′ (sol′wā), an arm of the Irish Sea between SW Scotland and NW England. 38 mi. (61 km) long.

Sol·y·man I (sol′ə mən). See **Suleiman I.**

Sol·zhe·ni·tsyn (sōl′zhə nēt′sin, sôl′-; *Russ.* səl zhi-nyē′tsin), *n.* **Alexander** or **A·le·ksandr (I·sa·ye·vich)** (al′ig zan′dər ē si′ə vich, -zän′-; *Russ.* u lyi ksän′dʀ ē sä′yi vyich), born 1918, Russian novelist: Nobel prize 1970; in the U.S. 1974–94.

so·ma[1] (sō′mə), *n., pl.* **-ma·ta** (-mə tə), **-mas.** *Biol.* the body of an organism as contrasted with its germ cells. [1830–40; < NL < Gk *sôma* body]

so·ma[2] (sō′mə), *n.* haoma (def. 1). [1820–30; < Skt]

So·ma (sō′mə), *Pharm., Trademark.* a brand of carisoprodol.

-soma, a var. of **-some**[3], used esp. in the formation of names of zoological genera: *Schistosoma.* [< NL < Gk *sôma*]

So·ma·li (sō mä′lē, sə-), *n., pl.* **-lis,** (*esp. collectively*) **-li,** *adj.* **—***n.* **1.** a member of a Hamitic population showing an admixture of Arab, black, and other ancestry, and dwelling in Somalia and adjacent regions. **2.** the Cushitic language of the Somali. **—***adj.* **3.** of or pertaining to Somalia, its people, or their language.

So·ma·li·a (sō mä′lē ə, -mäl′yə), *n.* an independent republic on the E coast of Africa, formed from the former British Somaliland and the former Italian Somaliland. 3,400,000; 246,198 sq. mi. (637,653 sq. km). *Cap.:* Mogadishu. Official name, **Soma′li Democrat′ic Repub′lic. —So·ma′li·an,** *adj., n.*

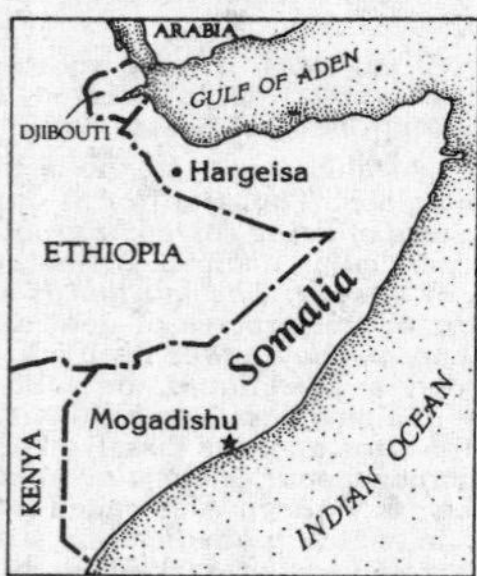

Soma′li Cur′rent, a current of the Indian Ocean, flowing northward along the coast of Somalia in summer and southwestward the rest of the year.

So·ma·li·land (sō mä′lē land′, sə-), *n.* a coastal region in E Africa, including Djibouti, Somalia, and the Ogaden part of Ethiopia.

Soma′liland Protec′torate, official name of the former **British Somaliland.**

somat-, var. of **somato-** before a vowel: *somatist.*

so·mat·ic (sō mat′ik, sə-), *adj.* **1.** of the body; bodily; physical. **2.** *Anat., Zool.* pertaining to the body wall. **3.** *Cell Biol.* pertaining to or affecting the somatic cells, as distinguished from the germ cells. [1765–75; < Gk *sōmatikós* of, pertaining to the body, equiv. to *sōmat-* SOMAT- + *-ikos* -IC] **—so·mat′i·cal·ly,** *adj.*
—Syn. 1. corporal. **—Ant. 1.** psychic.

somat′ic cell′, *Cell Biol.* **1.** one of the cells that take part in the formation of the body, becoming differentiated into the various tissues, organs, etc. **2.** any cell other than a germ cell. [1885–90]

so·mat·i·cize (sə mat′ə sīz′, sō′mə tə-), *v.t.,* **-cized, -ciz·ing.** *v.t. Psychiatry.* to convert (anxiety) into physical symptoms. Also, *esp. Brit.,* **so·mat′i·cise′.** [SOMATIC + -IZE] **—so·mat·i·za·tion** (sə mat′ə zā′shən, sō′mə-tə-), *n.*

somat′ic ther′apy, *Psychiatry.* any of a group of treatments presumed to act on biological factors leading to mental illness.

CONCISE ETYMOLOGY KEY: <, descended or borrowed from; >, whence; b., blend of, blended; c., cognate with; cf., compare; deriv., derivative; equiv., equivalent; imit., imitative; obl., oblique; r., replacing; s., stem; sp., spelling, spelled; resp., respelling, respelled; trans., translation; ?, origin unknown; *, unattested; ‡, probably earlier than. See the full key inside the front cover.

so·ma·tist (sō′mə tist), *n. Psychiatry.* a psychiatrist who considers all mental illnesses to have physical origins. [1670–80, in sense "materialist"; SOMAT- + -IST] **—so′ma·tism,** *n.*

somatiza′tion disor′der, a mental illness, usually beginning before age 20, characterized by multiple physical complaints for which no physical causes can be found and often leading to unnecessary treatment or surgery and to severe disability. Also called **Briquet's syndrome.** [SOMAT- + -IZATION]

somato-, a combining form meaning "body," used in the formation of compound words: *somatotonia.* Also, *esp. before a vowel,* **somat-.** [< Gk *sōmato-,* comb. form equiv. to *sōmat-* (s. of *sôma* body) + *-o-* -O-]

so·mat·o·form (sə mat′ə fôrm′, sō′mə tə-), *adj.* characterized by symptoms suggesting a physical disorder but for which there are no demonstrable organic findings or known physiological mechanisms. [SOMATO- + -FORM]

so·mat·o·gen·ic (sə mat′ə jen′ik, sō′mə tə-), *adj. Biol.* developing from somatic cells. Also, **so·mat·o·ge·net·ic** (sə mat′ə jə net′ik, sō′mə tə-). [1900–05; SOMATO- + -GENIC]

so·ma·tol·o·gy (sō′mə tol′ə jē), *n.* the branch of anthropology that deals with human physical characteristics. [1730–40; SOMATO- + -LOGY] **—so·mat·o·log·ic** (sə mat′l oj′ik, sō′mə tl-), **so′ma·to·log′i·cal,** *adj.* **—so·mat′o·log′i·cal·ly,** *adv.* **—so′ma·tol′o·gist,** *n.*

so·mat·o·me·din (sə mat′ə mēd′n, sō′mə tə-), *n. Biochem.* any of various liver hormones that enhance the activity of a variety of other hormones, as somatotropin. [1970–75; SOMATO- or SOMATO(TROPIN) + *-med-,* as in INTERMEDIARY + -IN[2]]

so·mat·o·plasm (sə mat′ə plaz′əm, sō′mə tə-), *n. Cell Biol.* the cytoplasm of a somatic cell, esp. as distinguished from germ plasm. [SOMATO- + -PLASM] **—so′ma·to·plas′tic,** *adj.*

so·mat·o·pleure (sə mat′ə plŏŏr′, sō′mə tə-), *n. Embryol.* the double layer formed by the association of the upper layer of the lateral plate of mesoderm with the overlying ectoderm, functioning in the formation of the body wall and amnion. Cf. **splanchnopleure.** [1870–75; < NL *somatopleura.* See SOMATO-, PLEURA] **—so·mat′o·pleu′ral, so·mat′o·pleu′ric,** *adj.*

so·mat·o·psy·chic (sə mat′ə sī′kik, sō′mə tə-), *adj.* of or pertaining to the effects of the body on the mind. [1900–05; SOMATO- + PSYCHIC]

so·mat·o·sen·so·ry (sə mat′ə sen′sə rē, sō′mə tə-), *adj.* of or pertaining to sensations that involve parts of the body not associated with the primary sense organs. [1950–55; SOMATO- + SENSORY]

so·mat·o·stat·in (sə mat′ə stat′n, sō′mə tə-), *n. Biochem.* a polypeptide hormone, produced in the brain and pancreas, that inhibits secretion of somatotropin from the hypothalamus and inhibits insulin production by the pancreas. [1973; SOMATO(TROPIN) + *stat-,* extracted from deverbal derivs. of L *stāre* to STAND, stop (cf. STATUS) + -IN[2]]

so·mat·o·tro·pin (sə mat′ə trō′pin, sō′mə tə-), *n. Biochem.* a hormone secreted by the anterior pituitary gland, that stimulates growth in humans. Also called **so·mat′o·troph′ic hor′mone** (sə mat′ə trof′ik, -trō′fik, sō′mə tə-, sə mat′ə-, sō′mə tə-), **human growth hormone.** [1940–45; *somatotrop(hic)* stimulating body growth (see SOMATO-, TROPHIC) + -IN[2]]

so·mat·o·type (sə mat′ə tīp′, sō′mə tə-), *n.* (of humans) physical type; physique. [1935–40; SOMATO- + -TYPE]

som·ber (som′bər), *adj.* **1.** gloomily dark; shadowy; dimly lighted: *a somber passageway.* **2.** dark and dull, as color, or as things in respect to color: *a somber dress.* **3.** gloomy, depressing, or dismal: *a somber mood.* **4.** extremely serious; grave: *a somber expression on his face.* Also, *esp. Brit.,* **som′bre.** [1750–60; < F *sombre,* MF, prob. n. deriv. of **sombrer* to make shady < VL **subumbrāre,* equiv. to L *sub-* SUB- + *umbrāre* to cast a shadow, deriv. of *umbra* shade] **—som′ber·ly,** *adv.* **—som′ber·ness,** *n.*
—Syn. 1. dusky, murky, sunless. **3.** lugubrious, mournful, doleful, melancholy. **—Ant. 1.** bright. **3.** cheerful.

som·bre·ro (som brâr′ō; *Sp.* sôm bʀe′ʀô), *n., pl.* **-bre·ros** (-brâr′ōz; *Sp.* -bʀe′ʀôs). a broad-brimmed hat of straw or felt, usually tall-crowned, worn esp. in Spain, Mexico, and the southwestern U.S. Cf. **cowboy hat, ten-gallon hat.** [1590–1600; < Sp: hat, deriv. of *sombra* shade; see SOMBER] **—som·bre′roed,** *adj.*

sombrero

som·brous (som′brəs), *adj. Archaic.* somber. [1720–30; < F *sombre* SOMBER + -OUS]

some (sum; *unstressed* səm), *adj.* **1.** being an undetermined or unspecified one: *Some person may object.* **2.** (used with plural nouns) certain: *Some days I stay home.* **3.** of a certain unspecified number, amount, degree, etc.: *to some extent.* **4.** unspecified but considerable in number, amount, degree, etc.: *We talked for some time. He was here some weeks.* **5.** *Informal.* of impressive or remarkable quality, consequence, extent, etc.: *That was some storm.* **—***pron.* **6.** certain persons, individuals, instances, etc., not specified: *Some think he is dead.* **7.** an unspecified number, amount, etc., as distinguished from the rest or in addition: *He paid a thousand dollars and then some.* **—***adv.* **8.** (used with numerals and with words expressing degree, extent, etc.) approximately; about: *Some 300 were present.* **9.** *Informal.* to some degree or extent; somewhat: *I like baseball some. She is feeling some better today.* **10.** *Informal.* to a great degree or extent; considerably: *That's going some.* [bef. 900; ME (adj. and pronoun); OE *sum* orig., someone; c. MLG, MHG *sum,* ON *sumr,* Goth *sums*]
—Usage. As pronouns, both SOME and ANY may be used in affirmative or negative questions: *Will you (won't you) have some? Do you (don't you) have any?* But SOME is used in affirmative statements and answers: *You may have some. Yes, I'd like some.* And in negative statements and answers, ANY is the usual choice: *I don't care for any. No, I can't take any.*

-some[1], a native English suffix formerly used in the formation of adjectives: *quarrelsome; burdensome.* [ME; OE *-sum;* akin to Goth *-sama,* G *-sam;* see SAME]

-some[2], a collective suffix used with numerals: *two-some; threesome.* [ME *-sum,* OE *sum;* special use of SOME (pronoun)]

-some[3], a combining form meaning "body," used in the formation of compound words: *chromosome.* Also, **-soma.** [< Gk *sôma* body; see SOMA[1]]

some·bod·y (sum′bod′ē, -bud′ē, -bə dē), *pron., n., pl.* **-bod·ies. —***pron.* **1.** some person. **—***n.* **2.** a person of some note or importance. [1275–1325; ME; see SOME, BODY]

some·day (sum′dā′), *adv.* at an indefinite future time. [bef. 900; ME *sum day,* OE *sum dæg;* see SOME, DAY]
—Usage. The adverb SOMEDAY is written solid: *Perhaps someday we will know the truth.* The two-word form SOME DAY means "a specific but unnamed day": *We will reschedule the meeting for some day when everyone can attend.*

some·deal (sum′dēl′), *adv. Archaic.* somewhat. [bef. 900; ME *somdel,* OE *sume dǣle,* dat. of *sum dǣl* some portion. See SOME, DEAL[1]]

some·how (sum′hou′), *adv.* **1.** in some way not specified, apparent, or known. **2. somehow or other,** in an undetermined way; by any means possible: *She was determined to finish college somehow or other.* [1655–65; SOME + HOW[1]]

some·one (sum′wun′, -wən), *pron.* some person; somebody. [1275–1325; ME; see SOME, ONE]

some·place (sum′plās′), *adv.* somewhere. [1350–1400; ME; see SOME, PLACE]
—Usage. See **anyplace.**

som·er (sum′ər), *n. Obs.* summer[2] (def. 1).

som·er·sault (sum′ər sôlt′), *n.* **1.** an acrobatic movement, either forward or backward, in which the body rolls end over end, making a complete revolution. **2.** such a movement performed in the air as part of a dive, tumbling routine, etc. **3.** a complete overturn or reversal, as of opinion. **—***v.i.* **4.** to perform a somersault. Also, **som·er·set** (sum′ər set′), **summersault, summerset.** [1520–30; < MF *sombresaut,* alter. of *sobresault;* cf. OPr *sobre* over (< L *super*), *saut* a leap (< L *saltus*)]

Som·er·set (sum′ər set′, -sit), *n.* **1.** a city in SE Massachusetts. 18,813. **2.** a town in S Kentucky. 10,649. **3.** Somersetshire.

Som·er·set·shire (sum′ər set shēr′, -shər, -sit-), *n.* a county in SW England. 401,700; 1335 sq. mi. (3455 sq. km). Also called **Somerset.**

Som′ers Point′ (sum′ərz), a town in SE New Jersey. 10,330.

Som·ers·worth (sum′ərz wûrth′), *n.* a town in SE New Hampshire. 10,350.

Som·er·ville (sum′ər vil′), *n.* **1.** a city in E Massachusetts, near Boston. 77,372. **2.** a town in central New Jersey. 11,973.

some·thing (sum′thing′), *pron.* **1.** some thing; a certain undetermined or unspecified thing: *Something is wrong there. Something's happening.* **2.** an additional amount, as of cents or minutes, that is unknown, unspecified, or forgotten: *He charged me ten something for the hat. Our train gets in at two something.* **—***n.* **3.** *Informal.* a person or thing of some value or consequence: *He is really something! This writer has something to say and she says it well.* **—***adv.* **4.** in some degree; to some extent; somewhat. **5.** *Informal.* to a high or extreme degree; quite: *He took on something fierce about my tardiness.* [bef. 1000; ME, OE *sum thing.* See SOME, THING[1]]

some·time (sum′tīm′), *adv.* **1.** at some indefinite or indeterminate point of time: *He will arrive sometime next week.* **2.** at an indefinite future time: *Come to see me sometime.* **3.** *Archaic.* sometimes; on some occasions. **4.** *Archaic.* at one time; formerly. **—***adj.* **5.** having been formerly; former: *The diplomat was a sometime professor of history at Oxford.* **6.** being so only at times or to some extent: *Traveling so much, he could never be more than a sometime husband.* **7.** that cannot be depended upon regarding affections or loyalties: *He was well rid of his sometime girlfriend.* [1250–1300; ME; see SOME, TIME]
—Usage. The adverb SOMETIME is written as one word: *He promised to paint the garage sometime soon.* The two-word form SOME TIME means "an unspecified interval or period of time": *It will take some time for the wounds to heal.*

some·times (sum′tīmz′), *adv.* on some occasions; at times; now and then. [1520–30; SOMETIME + -S[1]]

some·way (sum′wā′), *adv.* in some way; somehow. Also, **some′ way′, some′ways′.** [1400–50; late ME; see SOME, WAY[1]]

some·what (sum′hwut′, -hwot′, -hwət, -wut′, -wot′, -wət), *adv.* **1.** in some measure or degree; to some extent: *not angry, just somewhat disturbed.* **—***n.* **2.** some part, portion, amount, etc. [1150–1200; ME; see SOME, WHAT]

some•when (sum′hwen′, -wen′), *adv. Archaic.* sometime. [1250–1300; ME *sumwhanne;* see SOME, WHEN]

some•where (sum′hwâr′, -wâr′), *adv.* **1.** in or at some place not specified, determined, or known: *They live somewhere in Michigan.* **2.** to some place not specified or known: *They went out somewhere.* **3.** at or to some point in amount, degree, etc. (usually fol. by *about, near,* etc.): *He is somewhere about 60 years old.* **4.** at some point of time (usually fol. by *about, between, in,* etc.): *somewhere about 1930; somewhere between 1930 and 1940; somewhere in the 1930's.* —*n.* **5.** an unspecified or uncertain place. [1150–1200; ME; see SOME, WHERE]
—**Usage.** See **anyplace.**

some•wheres (sum′hwârz′, -wârz′), *adv. Nonstandard.* somewhere. [1805–15; SOMEWHERE + -S[1]]

some•while (sum′hwīl′, -wīl′), *adv. Archaic.* **1.** at some former time. **2.** at one time or another; sometime. **3.** at times; sometimes. **4.** for some time. [1125–75; ME; see SOME, WHILE]

some•whith•er (sum′hwith′ər, -with′-), *adv. Archaic.* to some unspecified place; somewhere. [1350–1400; ME; see SOME, WHITHER]

some•wise (sum′wīz′), *adv. Archaic.* by some means; somehow. [1400–50; late ME; see SOME, WISE[2]]

so•mite (sō′mīt), *n.* **1.** any of the longitudinal series of segments or parts into which the body of certain animals is divided; a metamere. **2.** *Embryol.* one member of a series of paired segments into which the thickened dorsal zone of mesoderm is divided. [1865–70; SOM(A)[1] + -ITE[1]] —**so•mi•tal** (sō′mi tl), **so•mit•ic** (sō mit′ik), *adj.*

Somme (sôm), *n.* **1.** a river in N France, flowing NW to the English Channel: battles, World War I, 1916, 1918; World War II, 1944. 150 mi. (241 km) long. **2.** a department in N France. 538,462; 2424 sq. mi. (6280 sq. km). *Cap.:* Amiens.

som•me•lier (sum′əl yā′; *Fr.* sô mə lyā′), *n., pl.* **som•me•liers** (sum′əl yāz′; *Fr.* sô mə lyā′). a waiter, as in a club or restaurant, who is in charge of wines. [1920–25; < F, MF, dissimilated form of **sommerier,* deriv. of *sommier* one charged with arranging transportation, equiv. to *somme* burden (< LL *sagma* horse load < Gk *ságma* covering, pack saddle) + *-ier* -IER[2]]

Som•mer•feld (zôm′əʀ felt′), *n.* **Ar•nold (Jo•han•nes Wil•helm)** (äʀ′nôlt yō hän′əs vil′helm), 1868–1951, German physicist.

som•nam•bu•late (som nam′byə lāt′, səm-), *v.i.,* **-lat•ed, -lat•ing.** to walk during sleep; sleepwalk. [1825–35; < L *somn(us)* sleep + AMBULATE] —**som•nam′bu•lant,** *adj., n.* —**som•nam′bu•la′tion,** *n.*

som•nam•bu•lism (som nam′byə liz′əm, səm-), *n.* sleepwalking. [1790–1800; < NL *somnambulismus,* equiv. to *somn(us)* sleep + *ambul(āre)* to walk + *-ismus* -ISM] —**som•nam′bu•list,** *n.* —**som•nam′bu•lis′tic,** *adj.*

som•ni•fa•cient (som′nə fā′shənt), *adj.* **1.** causing or inducing sleep. —*n.* **2.** a drug or other agent that induces or tends to induce sleep. [1885–90; < L *somn(us)* sleep + *-i-* -I- + -FACIENT]

som•nif•er•ous (som nif′ər əs, səm-), *adj.* bringing or inducing sleep, as drugs or influences. [1595–1605; < L *somnifer* inducing sleep (*somni-,* comb. form of *somnus* sleep + *-fer* -FER) + -OUS] —**som•nif′er•ous•ly,** *adv.*

som•nif•ic (som nif′ik, səm-), *adj.* causing sleep; soporific; somniferous. [1715–25; < L *somnificus* causing sleep, equiv. to *somni-,* comb. form of *somnus* sleep + *-ficus* -FIC]

som•no•lent (som′nə lənt), *adj.* **1.** sleepy; drowsy. **2.** tending to cause sleep. [1425–75; late ME *sompnolent* < OF < L *somnolentus,* deriv. of *somnus* sleep; see -ULENT] —**som′no•lence, som′no•len•cy,** *n.* —**som′no•lent•ly,** *adv.*
—**Syn. 1.** slumberous. **2.** somniferous, soporific.

Som•nus (som′nəs), *n.* the ancient Roman god of sleep, a son of Night and brother of Death.

So•mo•za (sô mô′sä; *Eng.* sə mō′zə, -mō′sə), *n.* **A•nas•ta•sio** (ä′näs tä′syô), (*Anastasio Somoza García*), 1896–1956, Nicaraguan political leader: president 1937–47, 1950–56 (father of Anastasio and Luis Somoza Debayle).

So•mo•za De•bay•le (sô mô′sä the vi′le; *Eng.* sə mō′zə də bī′lä, -mō′sə), **1. A•nas•ta•sio** (ä′näs tä′syô), 1925–80, Nicaraguan army officer, businessman, and political leader: president 1967–72, 1974–79 (brother of Luis Somoza Debayle). **2. Luis** (lwēs), 1922–67, Nicaraguan political leader: president 1957–63.

son (sun), *n.* **1.** a male child or person in relation to his parents. **2.** a male child or person adopted as a son; a person in the legal position of a son. **3.** any male descendant: *a son of the Aztecs.* **4.** a son-in-law. **5.** a person related as if by ties of sonship. **6.** a male person looked upon as the product or result of particular agencies, forces, influences, etc.: *a true son of the soil.* **7.** a familiar term of address to a man or boy from an older person, an ecclesiastic, etc. **8. the Son,** the second person of the Trinity; Jesus Christ. [bef. 900; ME *sone,* OE *sunu;* c. D *zoon,* G *Sohn,* ON *sunr, sonr,* Goth *sunus,* Lith *sūnùs,* Skt *sūnus;* akin to Gk *huiós*] —**son′less,** *adj.* —**son′like′,** *adj.*

son-, var. of **soni-** before a vowel: *sonance.*

so•nal (sōn′l), *adj.* pertaining to sound; sonic. [1955–60; SON- + -AL[1]]

so•nance (sō′nəns), *n.* **1.** the condition or quality of being sonant. **2.** a sound; a tune. [1590–1600; SON- + -ANCE]
—**Syn. 1.** voice, sound, noise.

so•nant (sō′nənt), *adj.* **1.** sounding; having sound. **2.** *Phonet.* voiced (opposed to *surd*). —*n. Phonet.* **3.** a speech sound that by itself makes a syllable or subordinates to itself the other sounds in the syllable; a syllabic sound (opposed to *consonant*). **4.** a voiced sound (opposed to *surd*). **5.** (in Indo-European) a sonorant. [1840–50; < L *sonant-* (s. of *sonāns*), prp. of *sonāre* to SOUND[1]. See SON-, -ANT] —**so•nan•tal** (sō nan′tl), **so•nan•tic** (sō nan′tik), *adj.*

so•nar (sō′när), *n.* **1.** a method for detecting and locating objects submerged in water by echolocation. **2.** the apparatus used in sonar. Also called, *Brit.,* **asdic.** [1940–45; *so(und) na(vigation) r(anging)*]

so•nar•man (sō′när mən), *n., pl.* **-men.** *U.S. Navy.* a petty officer who operates and maintains sonar. [SONAR + -MAN]

so•na•ta (sə nä′tə), *n. Music.* a composition for one or two instruments, typically in three or four movements in contrasted forms and keys. [1685–95; < It < L *sonāta,* fem. of *sonātus* (ptp. of *sonāre* to SOUND[1]). See SONANT, -ATE[1]]

so•na•ta da ca•me•ra (sə nä′tə də kä′mər ə; *It.* sô nä′tä dä kä′me rä), an instrumental musical form, common in the Baroque period, usually consisting of a series of dances. [1795–1805; < It: lit., sonata of the chamber]

so•na•ta da chie•sa (sə nä′tə də kē ā′zə; *It.* sô nä′tä dä kye′zä), an instrumental musical form, common in the Baroque period, that usually consists of four movements alternating between slow and fast. [1795–1805; < It: lit., sonata of the church]

sona′ta form′, a musical form comprising an exposition, in which the main theme or themes are stated, a development section, a recapitulation of the material in the exposition, and, usually, a coda. [1870–75]

so•na•ta-ron•do (sə nä′tə ron′dō, -ron dō′), *n., pl.* **-dos.** a musical form combining characteristics of both the sonata form and the rondo.

son•a•ti•na (son′ə tē′nə; *It.* sô′nä tē′nä), *n., pl.* **-nas, -ne** (-nā; *It.* -ne). *Music.* a short or simplified sonata. [1715–25; < It, dim. of SONATA]

sonde (sond), *n. Rocketry.* a rocket, balloon, or rockoon used as a probe for observing phenomena in the atmosphere. [1920–25; < F: plumb line; see SOUND[3]]

son•der•class (zon′dər klas′, -kläs′), *n.* a special class of small racing yachts, restricted as to size, sail area, cost, etc. [1910–15, *Amer.;* partial trans. of G *Sonderklasse* special class]

Son•der•kom•man•do (zon′dər kə man′dō; *Ger.* zôn′dəʀ kô män′dô), *n.* (in World War II Nazi concentration camps) a group of prisoners assigned to collect belongings and dispose of the bodies of other prisoners who had died or been killed. Cf. **Kapo.** [< G: special detachment, equiv. to *sonder-* separate, special + *Kommando* detachment, mission, command < It *commando;* see COMMAND, COMMANDO]

Sond•heim (sond′hīm), *n.* **Stephen (Joshua),** born 1930, U.S. composer and lyricist.

Son•dra (son′drə), *n.* a female given name.

sone (sōn), *n.* a unit for measuring the loudness of sound, equal to the loudness of a sound that, in the judgment of a group of listeners, is equal to that of a 1000-cycle-per-second reference sound having an intensity of 40 decibels. [1945–50; < L *sonus* SOUND[1]]

son et lu•mière (sô nā lʏ myeʀ′), *French.* See **sound-and-light show.** [lit., sound and light]

song (sông, song), *n.* **1.** a short metrical composition intended or adapted for singing, esp. one in rhymed stanzas; a lyric; a ballad. **2.** a musical piece adapted for singing or simulating a piece to be sung: *Mendelssohn's "Songs without Words."* **3.** poetical composition; poetry. **4.** the art or act of singing; vocal music. **5.** something that is sung. **6.** an elaborate vocal signal produced by an animal, as the distinctive sounds produced by certain birds, frogs, etc., in a courtship or territorial display. **7. for a song,** at a very low price; as a bargain: *We bought the rug for a song when the estate was auctioned off.* [bef. 900; ME *song, sang,* OE; c. G *Sang,* ON *sǫngr,* Goth *saggws*] —**song′like′,** *adj.*

Song (sông), *n. Pinyin.* **1. Ai•ling** (ī′ling′). See **Soong, Ai-ling. 2. Qing•ling** (ching′ling′). See **Soong, Ching-ling. 3. Mei•ling** (mā′ling′). See **Soong, Mei-ling. 4. Zi•wen** (zœ′wun′). See **Soong, Tse-ven. 5.** Sung.

song′ and dance′, a story or statement, esp. an untrue or misleading one designed to evade the matter at hand: *Every time he's late, he gives me a song and dance about oversleeping.* [1870–75, *Amer.*]

song•bird (sông′bûrd′, song′-), *n.* **1.** a bird that sings. **2.** any passerine bird of the suborder Oscines. **3.** *Slang.* a woman vocalist. [1765–75; SONG + BIRD]

song•book (sông′bo͝ok′, song′-), *n.* a book of songs with words and music. [bef. 1000; OE *sang-bōc* service book (not recorded in ME); see SONG, BOOK]

song′ cy′cle, a group of art songs that are usually all by the same poet and composer and have a unifying subject or idea. [1895–1900]

song•fest (sông′fest, song′-), *n.* **1.** an informal, often spontaneous gathering at which people sing folk songs, popular ballads, etc. **2.** an informal gathering at a studio, concert hall, or the like, in which people participate by singing along with the performers. [1915–20; SONG + -FEST]

song•ful (sông′fəl, song′-), *adj.* abounding in song; melodious. [1350–1400; ME; see SONG, -FUL] —**song′ful•ly,** *adv.* —**song′ful•ness,** *n.*

Son•ghai (song gī′), *n., pl.* **-ghais,** (*esp. collectively*) **-ghai** for 1. **1.** a member of a group of peoples living along the Niger River in the area of Timbuktu and Gao in Mali and in adjacent areas of Niger and Burkina Faso. **2.** a West African empire dominated by the Songhai that flourished in the 15th and 16th centuries. **3.** the Nilo-Saharan language of the Songhai.

Song•hua (sông′hwä′), *n. Pinyin.* a river in NE China, flowing NW and NE through E and central Manchuria into the Amur River on the boundary of Siberia. 800 mi. (1287 km) long. Also, *Wade-Giles,* **Sunghua.** Also called **Song′hua Jiang′** (jyäng), **Sungari.**

Song•jiang (sông′jyäng′), *n. Pinyin.* a former province in NE China, now a part of Inner Mongolia. 79,151 sq. mi. (205,001 sq. km). Also, **Sungchiang, Sungkiang.**

Song•ka (song′kä′), *n.* a river in SE Asia, flowing SE from SW China through Indochina to the Gulf of Tonkin. 500 mi. (800 km) long. Also called **Red River.**

song•less (sông′lis, song′-), *adj.* devoid of song; lacking the power of a song, as a bird. [1795–1805; SONG + -LESS] —**song′less•ly,** *adv.* —**song′less•ness,** *n.*

Song′ of Sol′omon, The, a book of the Bible. Also called, *New American Bible,* **Song′ of Songs′.** *Abbr.:* Sol.

Song′ of the Three′ Chil′dren, a book of the Apocrypha, included as part of the third chapter of Daniel in the Douay Bible.

song•smith (sông′smith′, song′-), *n.* a writer of songs. [1785–95; SONG + SMITH]

song′ spar′row, a small emberizine songbird, *Melospiza melodia,* common in North America. [1800–10, *Amer.*]

song•ster (sông′stər, song′-), *n.* **1.** a person who sings; a singer. **2.** a writer of songs or poems; a poet. **3.** a songbird. [bef. 1000; ME; OE *sangestre* songstress. See SONG, -STER]

song•stress (sông′stris, song′-), *n.* a female singer, esp. one who specializes in popular songs. [1695–1705; SONG + -STRESS]
—**Usage.** See **-ess.**

song′ thrush′, a common, European songbird, *Turdus philomelos.* [1660–70]

song•writ•er (sông′rī′tər, song′-), *n.* a person who writes the words or music, or both, for popular songs. [1815–25; SONG + WRITER]

soni-, a combining form meaning "sound," used in the formation of compound words: *soniferous.* Also, **son-, sono-.** [< L *soni-,* comb. form of *sonus* SOUND[1]]

So•nia (sō′nyə; *Russ.* sô′nyä), *n.* a female given name, Russian form of **Sophia.**

son•ic (son′ik), *adj.* **1.** of or pertaining to sound. **2.** noting or pertaining to a speed equal to that of sound in air at the same height above sea level. [1920–25; < L *son(us)* SOUND[1] + -IC]

son′ic bar′rier. See **sound barrier.** [1945–50]

son′ic boom′, a loud noise caused by the shock wave generated by an aircraft moving at supersonic speed. [1950–55]

son′ic depth′ find′er, a sonar instrument that uses echolocation to measure depths under water. Cf. **Fathometer.** [1925–30]

son′ic mine′. See **acoustic mine.**

son•ics (son′iks), *n.* (*used with a singular v.*) the branch of science that deals with the practical applications of sound. [1955; see SONIC, -ICS]

so•nif•er•ous (sə nif′ər əs, sō-), *adj.* conveying or producing sound. [1705–15; SONI- + -FEROUS]

son-in-law (sun′in lô′), *n., pl.* **sons-in-law.** the husband of one's daughter. [1300–50; ME]

son•net (son′it), *n.* **1.** *Pros.* a poem, properly expressive of a single, complete thought, idea, or sentiment, of 14 lines, usually in iambic pentameter, with rhymes arranged according to one of certain definite schemes, being in the strict or Italian form divided into a major group of 8 lines (the octave) followed by a minor group of 6 lines (the sestet), and in a common English form into 3 quatrains followed by a couplet. —*v.i.* **2.** *Archaic.* to compose sonnets. —*v.t.* **3.** *Older Use.* to celebrate in a sonnet or sonnets. [1550–60; < It *sonnetto* < OPr *sonet,* equiv. to *son* poem (< L *sonus* SOUND[1]) + *-et* -ET] —**son′net•like′,** *adj.*

son•net•eer (son′i tēr′), *n.* **1.** a composer of sonnets. —*v.i.* **2.** to compose sonnets; sonnetize. [1580–90; SONNET + -EER; r. earlier *sonnetier* < It *sonnettiere*]

son•net•ize (son′i tīz′), *v.,* **-ized, -iz•ing.** —*v.i.* **1.** to write sonnets. —*v.t.* **2.** to write sonnets on or to. Also, *esp. Brit.,* **son′net•ise′.** [1790–1800; SONNET + -IZE] —**son′net•i•za′tion,** *n.*

son′net se′quence, a group of sonnets composed by one poet and having a unifying theme or subject. [1880–85]

Son′nets from the Por′tuguese, a sonnet sequence (1850) by Elizabeth Barrett Browning.

son•ny (sun′ē), *n.* **1.** little son (often used as a familiar term of address to a boy). **2.** (used as a term of direct address to express contempt, derision, etc.): *No, sonny, you can't park there!* [1840–50; SON + -Y[2]]

Son•ny (sun′ē), *n.* a male given name.

sono-, var. of **soni-:** *sonometer.*

so•no•bu•oy (son′ə bo͞o′ē, -boi′), *n. Navig.* a buoy that emits a radio signal on receiving an underwater signal from a vessel. [1940–45; SONO- + BUOY]

son′ of a bitch′, *pl.* **sons of bitches.** *Slang (vulgar).* **1.** a contemptible or thoroughly disagreeable person; scoundrel. **2.** a disagreeable matter; a chore. **3.** (used as an exclamation of impatience, irritation, astonishment, etc.) Also, **son′-of-a-bitch′.** [1705–15]

son′-of-a-bitch stew′, (in the Old West) a stew often prepared by chuck-wagon cooks for working cowboys, containing tripe and often also the heart, liver, brains, kidney, etc., of a slaughtered steer. Also called **son′-of-a-gun′ stew′.**

son′ of Ad′am, a man: *He had all the weaknesses to which a son of Adam is heir.*

son′ of a gun′, *pl.* **sons of guns.** *Slang.* **1.** rogue; rascal; scoundrel: *That son of a gun still owes me $20.* **2.** a tiresome or disagreeable matter, chore, etc. **3.** (used as an affectionate greeting, term of address, etc.): *Charlie Humpelmeyer, you old son of a gun, how are you?* **4.** (used as an exclamation of irritation, surprise, dismay, etc.). [1700–10; perh. orig. the illegitimate offspring of a soldier, though later influenced by Brit. argot *gun* thief; cf. GUN MOLL]

Son′ of God′, **1.** Jesus Christ, esp. as the Messiah. **2.** any person responding to God or acknowledging God as Father. Rom. 8:14. [bef. 950; ME; OE]

Son′ of Man′, Jesus Christ, esp. at the Last Judgment. [bef. 900; ME; OE]

son·o·gram (son′ə gram′, sō′nə-), *n. Med.* the visual image produced by reflected sound waves in a diagnostic ultrasound examination. [1955–60; SONO- + GRAM]

son·o·graph (son′ə graf′, -gräf′), *n. Physics.* an instrument that produces a graphic representation of sound. [1955–60; SONO- + -GRAPH]

So·no·ma (sə nō′mə), *n.* a town in W California: center of wine-producing region. 6054.

so·nom·e·ter (sə nom′i tər), *n. Med.* audiometer. [1800–10; SONO- + -METER]

So·no·ra (sə nôr′ə, -nōr′ə; *Sp.* sô nô′rä), *n.* a state in NW Mexico. 1,414,000; 70,484 sq. mi. (182,555 sq. km). *Cap.:* Hermosillo. —**So·no·ran** (sə nôr′ən, -nōr′ən), *adj.*

so·no·rant (sə nôr′ənt, -nōr′-, sō-), *Phonet.* —*n.* **1.** a voiced sound that is less sonorous than a vowel but more sonorous than a stop or fricative and that may occur as either a sonant or a consonant, as (l, r, m, n, y, w). **2.** a speech sound characterized by relatively free air passage through some channel, as a vowel, semivowel, liquid, or nasal. Cf. **obstruent.** —*adj.* **3.** of, pertaining to, or having the properties of a sonorant. [< L *sonōr-* (s. of *sonor*) sound, noise + -ANT; see SONOROUS]

so·nor·i·ty (sə nôr′i tē, -nor′-), *n., pl.* **-ties.** the condition or quality of being resonant or sonorous. [1515–25; < ML *sonōritās* < LL: melodiousness, equiv. to L *sonōr(us)* (see SONOROUS) + *-itās* -ITY]

so·no·rous (sə nôr′əs, -nōr′-, son′ər əs), *adj.* **1.** giving out or capable of giving out a sound, esp. a deep, resonant sound, as a thing or place: *a sonorous cavern.* **2.** loud, deep, or resonant, as a sound. **3.** rich and full in sound, as language or verse. **4.** high-flown; grandiloquent: *a sonorous speech.* [1605–15; < L *sonōrus* noisy, sounding, equiv. to *sonōr-*, s. of *sonor* sound (*son(āre)* to SOUND[1] + *-or* -OR[1]) + *-us* -OUS] —**so·no′rous·ly,** *adv.* —**so·no′rous·ness,** *n.*
—**Syn. 4.** eloquent, florid, grandiose, orotund.

Sons′ and Lov′ers, a novel (1913) by D. H. Lawrence.

son·ship (sun′ship′), *n.* the state, fact, or relation of being a son. [1580–90; SON + -SHIP]

Sons′ of Lib′erty, *Amer. Hist.* **1.** any of several patriotic societies, originally secret, that opposed the Stamp Act and thereafter supported moves for American independence. **2.** (during the Civil War) a secret society of Copperheads.

Son·so·na·te (sôn′sô nä′te), *n.* a city in SW El Salvador. 33,562.

son·sy (son′sē), *adj.,* **-si·er, -si·est.** *Scot. and North Eng., Irish Eng.* **1.** strong and healthy; robust. **2.** agreeable; good-natured. Also, **saucy, son′sie.** [1525–35; *sonse* prosperity, good fortune (ME (Scots) < Scot-Gael *sonas,* MIr *sonus,* deriv. of *sona* prosperous, happy, OIr *son*) + -Y[1]; cf. DONSIE]

Son·ya (sō′nyə; *Russ.* sô′nyä), *n.* a female given name, Russian form of **Sophia.**

Soo (so͞o), *n.* **the,** *Canadian.* Sault Ste. Marie.

Soo′ Canals′. See **Sault Ste. Marie Canals.**

Soo·chow (so͞o′chou′; *Chin.* so͞o′jō′), *n. Older Spelling.* Suzhou.

soo·ey (so͞o′ē), *interj.* (a shout used in calling pigs.) [perh. alter. of SOW[2]]

sook (so͝ok), *n.* **1.** *Australia and New Zealand.* a timid, cowardly person, esp. a young person; crybaby. —*interj.* **2.** *Midland U.S.* (used to summon cows from the pasture). [1890–95; prob. from earlier sense "calf reared by hand," perh. *suck(-calf),* with sp. repr. N England, Scots pron. of SUCK (but earliest cited pron. of *sook* is (so͞ok))]

soon (so͞on), *adv.,* **-er, -est.** **1.** within a short period after this or that time, event, etc.: *We shall know soon after he calls.* **2.** before long; in the near future; at an early date: *Let's leave soon.* **3.** promptly or quickly: *He came as soon as he could.* **4.** readily or willingly: *I would as soon walk as ride.* **5.** early in a period of time; before the time specified is much advanced: *soon at night; soon in the evening.* **6.** *Obs.* immediately; at once; forthwith. **7. would sooner,** to prefer to: *I would sooner not go to their party.* Cf. **rather** (def. 7). **8. sooner or later,** eventually: *Sooner or later his luck will run out.* [bef. 900; ME; OE *sōna;* c. OHG *sān,* Goth *suns*]

soon·er (so͞o′nər), *n.* **1.** a person who settles on government land before it is legally opened to settlers in order to gain the choice of location. **2.** a person who gains an unfair advantage by getting ahead of others. [1885–90, *Amer.*; SOON + -ER[1]]

Soon·er (so͞o′nər), *n.* a native or inhabitant of Oklahoma (the **Sooner State**) (used as a nickname).

Soon′er State′, Oklahoma (used as a nickname).

Soong (so͝ong), *n.* **1. Charles Jones,** 1866–1918, Chinese merchant (father of Ai-ling, Ch'ing-ling, Mei-ling, and Tse-ven Soong). **2. Ai-ling** (ī′ling′), 1888–1973, wife of H. H. Kung. **3. Ching-ling** or **Ch'ing-ling** (ching′-ling′), 1892–1981, widow of Sun Yat-sen. **4. Mei-ling** or **Mayling** (mā′ling′), born 1898, wife of Chiang Kai-shek. **5. Tse-ven** or **Tzu-wen** (tso͞o′wun′), (*T.V.*), 1894–1971, Chinese financier.

soo·ny (so͞o′nē), *adj. Australian.* sentimental; emotional. [*soon,* dial. var. of SWOUND + -Y[1]]

soot (so͝ot, so͞ot), *n.* **1.** a black, carbonaceous substance produced during incomplete combustion of coal, wood, oil, etc., rising in fine particles and adhering to the sides of the chimney or pipe conveying the smoke: also conveyed in the atmosphere to other locations. —*v.t.* **2.** to mark, cover, or treat with soot. [bef. 900; ME; OE *sōt;* c. ON *sōt*] —**soot′less,** *adj.* —**soot′like′,** *adj.*

sooth (so͞oth), *Archaic.* —*n.* **1.** truth, reality, or fact. —*adj.* **2.** soothing, soft, or sweet. **3.** true or real. [bef. 900; ME; OE *sōth;* c. OS *sōth,* ON *sannr,* Goth *sunjis* true, Skt *sat, sant* true, real; akin to IS] —**sooth′ly,** *adv.*

soothe (so͞oth), *v.,* **soothed, sooth·ing.** —*v.t.* **1.** to tranquilize or calm, as a person or the feelings; relieve, comfort, or refresh: *soothing someone's anger; to soothe someone with a hot drink.* **2.** to mitigate, assuage, or allay, as pain, sorrow, or doubt: *to soothe sunburned skin.* —*v.i.* **3.** to exert a soothing influence; bring tranquillity, calm, ease, or comfort. [bef. 950; ME *sothen* to verify, OE *sōthian,* equiv. to *sōth* SOOTH + *-ian* inf. suffix; mod. E sense shift "to verify" > "to support (a person's statement)" > "to encourage" > "to calm"] —**sooth′er,** *n.*
—**Syn. 1.** See **comfort, allay. 2.** alleviate, appease, mollify. —**Ant. 1.** upset, roil.

sooth·fast (so͞oth′fast′, -fäst′), *adj. Archaic.* **1.** based on the truth; true. **2.** truthful; veracious. [bef. 900; ME *sothfast,* OE *sōthfæst.* See SOOTH, FAST[1]] —**sooth′fast′ly,** *adv.* —**sooth′fast′ness,** *n.*

sooth·ing (so͞o′thing), *adj.* **1.** that soothes: *a soothing voice.* **2.** tending to assuage pain: *a soothing cough syrup.* [1590–1600; SOOTHE + -ING[2]] —**sooth′ing·ly,** *adv.* —**sooth′ing·ness,** *n.*

sooth·say (so͞oth′sā′), *v.i.,* **-said, -say·ing.** to foretell events; predict. [1600–10; back formation from SOOTHSAYER]

sooth·say·er (so͞oth′sā′ər), *n.* a person who professes to foretell events. [1300–50; ME *sothseyere, sothseyer.* See SOOTH, SAY[1], -ER[1]]

sooth·say·ing (so͞oth′sā′ing), *n.* **1.** the practice or art of foretelling events. **2.** a prediction or prophecy. [1525–35; SOOTH + SAYING]

soot·y (so͝ot′ē, so͞o′tē), *adj.,* **soot·i·er, soot·i·est.** **1.** covered, blackened, or smirched with soot. **2.** consisting of or resembling soot. **3.** of a black, blackish, or dusky color. [1200–50; ME; see SOOT, -Y[1]] —**soot′i·ly,** *adv.* —**soot′i·ness,** *n.*

soot′y blotch′, *Plant Pathol.* **1.** a disease, esp. of apples and pears, characterized by sootlike spots or blotches on the fruit, caused by a fungus, *Gloeodes pomigena.* **2.** a disease of clover, characterized by black, crusty blotches on the underside of the leaves, caused by a fungus, *Cymadothea trifolii.*

soot′y grouse′. See **blue grouse.** [1880–85]

soot′y mold′, **1.** *Plant Pathol.* a disease of plants, characterized by a black, sooty growth covering the affected parts, caused by any of several fungi. **2.** any fungus causing this disease, as molds of the genera *Capnodium, Phragmocapnias,* and *Scorias.* [1900–05]

soot′y shear′water. See under **mutton bird.**

soot′y tern′, a black and white tern, *Sterna fuscata,* of small tropical islands. Also called **wide-awake.** [1775–85]

sop (sop), *n., v.,* **sopped, sop·ping.** —*n.* **1.** a piece of solid food, as bread, for dipping in liquid food. **2.** anything thoroughly soaked. **3.** something given to pacify or quiet, or as a bribe: *The political boss gave him some cash as a sop.* **4.** a weak-willed or spineless person; milksop. —*v.t.* **5.** to dip or soak in liquid food: *to sop bread in gravy.* **6.** to drench. **7.** to take up (liquid) by absorption (usually fol. by *up*): *He used bread to sop up the gravy.* —*v.i.* **8.** to be or become soaking wet. **9.** (of a liquid) to soak (usually fol. by *in*). [bef. 1000; (n.) ME; OE *sopp;* c. ON *soppa;* (v.) OE *soppian,* deriv. of the n. (not recorded in ME). See SUP[2]]
—**Syn. 3.** tip, gratuity, payoff.

SOP, Standard Operating Procedure; Standing Operating Procedure. Also, **S.O.P.**

sop., soprano.

so·pa (sô′pä), *n. Spanish.* soup.

so·pai·pil·la (sō′pī pē′ə; *Sp.* sô′pī pē′yä), *n., pl.* **-pil·las** (-pē′əz; *Sp.* -pē′yäs). *Mexican Cookery.* a small pastry made of deep-fried yeast dough and usually dipped in honey. [1935–40; < AmerSp, equiv. to Sp *sopaip(a)* fritter or thick pancake soaked in honey (earlier also *xopaipa* < Mozarabic, deriv. of *šúppa, súppa* piece of bread soaked in oil, Sp *sopa* < Gmc; see SOP, SOUP) + *-illa* dim. suffix]

soph (sof), *n.* a sophomore. [by shortening]

So·phar (sō′fər), *n. Douay Bible.* Zophar.

so·pher (sō′fər; *Seph. Heb.* sō fer′; *Ashk. Heb.* sō′fer), *n., pl.* **-pher·im** (-fər im; *Seph. Heb.* -fe rēm′; *Ashk. Heb.* -fe rim), (*often cap.*) *Judaism.* scribe[1] (def. 3). [< Heb *sōphēr*]

So·phi (sō′fē), *n.* (*sometimes l.c.*) Sophy.

So·phi·e (sō′fē), *n.* a female given name. Also, **So·phi·a** (sō fē′ə, -fī′ə, sō′fē ə).

soph·ism (sof′iz əm), *n.* **1.** a specious argument for displaying ingenuity in reasoning or for deceiving someone. **2.** any false argument; fallacy. [1300–50; < L *sophisma* sophistry < Gk *sóphisma* orig., acquired skill, method, deriv. of *sophízesthai* to act the sophist, become wise; r. earlier *sophim,* ME < MF *sophime* < L]

soph·ist (sof′ist), *n.* **1.** (*often cap.*) *Gk. Hist.* **a.** any of a class of professional teachers in ancient Greece who gave instruction in various fields, as in general culture, rhetoric, politics, or disputation. **b.** a person belonging to this class at a later period who, while professing to teach skill in reasoning, concerned himself with ingenuity and specious effectiveness rather than soundness of argument. **2.** a person who reasons adroitly and speciously rather than soundly. **3.** a philosopher. [1535–45; < L *sophista* < Gk *sophistḗs* sage, deriv. of *sophízesthai*]

soph·is·ter (sof′ə stər), *n.* **1.** a specious, unsound, or fallacious reasoner. **2.** *Chiefly Brit.* (esp. formerly) a second or third year student at a university. **3.** *Obs.* an ancient Greek sophist. [1350–1400; ME < MF *sophistre* < L *sophista.* See SOPHIST]

so·phis·tic (sə fis′tik), *adj.* **1.** of the nature of sophistry; fallacious. **2.** characteristic or suggestive of sophistry. **3.** given to the use of sophistry. **4.** of or pertaining to sophists or sophistry. Also, **so·phis′ti·cal.** [1540–50; < L *sophisticus* < Gk *sophistikós,* equiv. to *sophist(ḗs)* (see SOPHIST) + *-ikos* -IC] —**so·phis′ti·cal·ly,** *adv.* —**so·phis′ti·cal·ness,** *n.*

so·phis·ti·cate (*n., adj.* sə fis′ti kit, -kāt′; *v.* sə fis′ti-kāt′), *n., adj., v.,* **-cat·ed, -cat·ing.** —*n.* **1.** a sophisticated person. —*adj.* **2.** sophisticated. —*v.t.* **3.** to make less natural, simple, or ingenuous; make worldly-wise. **4.** to alter; pervert: *to sophisticate a meaning beyond recognition.* —*v.i.* **5.** to use sophistry; quibble. [1350–1400; ME (adj. and v.) < ML *sophisticātus* (ptp. of *sophisticāre* to tamper with, disguise, trick with words), equiv. to L *sophistic(us)* (see SOPHISTIC) + *-ātus* -ATE[1]]

so·phis·ti·cat·ed (sə fis′ti kā′tid), *adj.* **1.** (of a person, ideas, tastes, manners, etc.) altered by education, experience, etc., so as to be worldly-wise; not naive: *a sophisticated young socialite; the sophisticated eye of a journalist.* **2.** pleasing or satisfactory to the tastes of sophisticates: *sophisticated music.* **3.** deceptive; misleading. **4.** complex or intricate, as a system, process, piece of machinery, or the like: *a sophisticated electronic control system.* **5.** of, for, or reflecting educated taste, knowledgeable use, etc.: *Many Americans are drinking more sophisticated wines now.* Also, **sophisticate.** [1595–1605; < ML *sophisticāt(us)* SOPHISTICATE + -ED[2]] —**so·phis′ti·cat′ed·ly,** *adv.*
—**Syn. 1.** worldly, cosmopolitan, experienced, cultivated. —**Ant. 1.** naive.

so·phis·ti·ca·tion (sə fis′ti kā′shən), *n.* **1.** sophisticated character, ideas, tastes, or ways as the result of education, worldly experience, etc.: *the sophistication of the wealthy.* **2.** change from the natural character or simplicity, or the resulting condition. **3.** complexity, as in design or organization. **4.** impairment or debasement, as of purity or genuineness. **5.** the use of sophistry; a sophism, quibble, or fallacious argument. [1350–1400; ME < ML *sophisticātiō* (s. of *sophisticātiō*), equiv. to *sophisticāt(us)* (see SOPHISTICATE) + *-iōn-* -ION]

soph·ist·ry (sof′ə strē), *n., pl.* **-ries.** **1.** a subtle, tricky, superficially plausible, but generally fallacious method of reasoning. **2.** a false argument; sophism. [1300–50; ME *sophistrie* < MF, equiv. to *sophistre* SOPHISTER + *-ie* -Y[3]]

Soph·o·cles (sof′ə klēz′), *n.* 495?–406? B.C., Greek dramatist. —**Soph·o·cle·an** (sof′ə klē′ən), *adj.*

soph·o·more (sof′ə môr′, -mōr′; sof′môr, -mōr), *n.* a student in the second year of high school, college, or a university. [1645–55; earlier *sophumer,* prob. equiv. to *sophum* SOPHISM + -ER[1]]

soph·o·mor·ic (sof′ə môr′ik, -mor′-), *adj.* **1.** of or pertaining to a sophomore or sophomores. **2.** suggestive of or resembling the traditional sophomore; intellectually pretentious, overconfident, conceited, etc., but immature: *sophomoric questions.* Also, **soph′o·mor′i·cal.** [1805–15, *Amer.*; SOPHOMORE + -IC] —**soph′o·mor′i·cal·ly,** *adv.*
—**Syn. 2.** childish, adolescent, juvenile.

Soph·o·ni·as (sof′ə nī′əs), *n. Douay Bible.* Zephaniah.

so·phros·y·ne (sə fros′ə nē), *n.* moderation; discretion; prudence. Cf. **hubris.** [< Gk *sōphrosýnē,* deriv. of *sṓphrōn* prudent]

So·phy (sō′fē, sof′ē), *n., pl.* **-phies.** (*sometimes l.c.*) any of the Safavid rulers of Persia: used as a title. Also, **Sophi.** [1530–40; prob. < Turk *sofi* < Pers *ṣūfī* SUFI, by assoc. with *Safawī* the SAFAVID dynasty]

-sophy, a combining form occurring in loanwords from Greek (*philosophy; theosophy*); on this model used, with the meaning "science of," in the formation of compound words: *anthroposophy.* [< Gk *-sophia,* comb. form of *sophía* skill, wisdom; see -Y[3]]

so·por (sō′pər), *n.* **1.** *Pathol.* a deep, unnatural sleep; lethargy. **2.** Often, **sopors.** *Slang.* methaqualone. [1650–60; 1970–75 for def. 2; < L]

sop·o·rif·er·ous (sop′ə rif′ər əs, sō′pə-), *adj.* bringing sleep; soporific. [1580–90; < L *soporifer* (*sopōr-,* comb. form of *sopor* SOPOR + *-i-* -I- + *-fer* -FER) + -OUS] —**sop′o·rif′er·ous·ly,** *adv.* —**sop′o·rif′er·ous·ness,** *n.*

sop·o·rif·ic (sop′ə rif′ik, sō′pə-), *adj.* **1.** causing or tending to cause sleep. **2.** pertaining to or characterized by sleep or sleepiness; sleepy; drowsy. —*n.* **3.** something that causes sleep, as a medicine or drug. [1655–65; < L *sopor* SOPOR + -I- + -FIC; cf. F *soporifique*] —**sop′o·rif′i·cal·ly,** *adv.*

sop·o·rose (sop′ə rōs′, sō′pə-), *adj.* **1.** sleepy. **2.** *Pathol.* characterized by abnormal slumber. Also, **sop·o·rous** (sop′ər əs, sō′pər-). [1700–10; SOPOR + -OSE[1]]

sop·ping (sop′ing), *adj.* soaked; drenched: *Her clothes were sopping from the rain.* [1525–35; SOP + -ING[2]]

sop·py (sop′ē), *adj.,* **-pi·er, -pi·est.** **1.** soaked, drenched, or very wet, as ground. **2.** rainy, as weather. **3.** *Brit. Slang.* excessively sentimental; mawkish. [1605–15; SOP + -Y[1]] —**sop′pi·ness,** *n.*

so·pra·ni·no (sō′prə nē′nō), *n., pl.* **-nos.** a musical instrument, as a saxophone or recorder, that is a pitch higher than the soprano instrument of its class. [1900–05; < It, equiv. to *sopran(o)* SOPRANO + *-ino* dim. suffix]

CONCISE ETYMOLOGY KEY: <, descended or borrowed from; >, whence; b., blend of, blended; c., cognate with; cf., compare; deriv., derivative; equiv., equivalent; imit., imitative; obl., oblique; r., replacing; s., stem; sp., spelling, spelled; resp., respelling, respelled; trans., translation; ?, origin unknown; *, unattested; ‡, probably earlier than. See the full key inside the front cover.

so•pran•o (sə pran′ō, -prä′nō), *n., pl.* **-pran•os,** *adj. Music.* —*n.* **1.** the uppermost part or voice. **2.** the highest singing voice in women and boys. **3.** a part for such a voice. **4.** a singer with such a voice. —*adj.* **5.** of or pertaining to a soprano; having the compass of a soprano. [1720–30; < It: lit., what is above, high, equiv. to *sopra* (< L *suprā* above) + *-ano* adj. suffix]

sopran′o clef′, *Music.* a sign locating middle C on the bottom line of the staff. See illus. under **C clef.** [1795–1805]

so•ra (sôr′ə, sōr′ə), *n.* a small, short-billed rail, *Porzana carolina,* of marshy areas of North America. Also called **so′ra rail′, Carolina rail.** [1695–1705, *Amer.*; orig. uncert.]

so•ra•li•um (sə rā′lē əm), *n., pl.* **-li•a** (-lē ə). (in a lichen) a group of soredia. [SOR(US) + -AL[1] + -IUM]

So•ra•ta (sô rä′tə), *n.* **Mount,** a mountain in W Bolivia, in the Andes, near Lake Titicaca: two peaks, Ancohuma, 21,490 ft. (6550 m), and Illampu, 21,276 ft. (6485 m).

sorb[1] (sôrb), *n.* **1.** a European tree, *Sorbus domestica.* **2.** Also called **sorb′ ap′ple.** the fruit of this tree. [1520–30; < L *sorbum* serviceberry and *sorbus* service tree] —**sorb′ic,** *adj.*

sorb[2] (sôrb), *v.t. Chem.* to gather on a surface either by absorption, adsorption, or a combination of the two processes. [1905–10; extracted from ABSORB and ADSORB] —**sorb′a•ble,** *adj.* —**sorb′a•bil′i•ty,** *n.*

Sorb (sôrb), *n.* a Wend. [1835–45; < G *Sorbe* << Lusatian *serbje, serbjo*]

sor•bate (sôr′bāt, -bit), *n. Chem.* a sorbed substance. [1925–30; SORB[2] + -ATE[1]]

sor•bent (sôr′bənt), *n. Chem.* a surface that sorbs. [1905–10; SORB[2] + -ENT]

sor•bet (sôr′bit, sôr bā′; *Fr.* sôr be′), *n.* sherbet (defs. 1, 3). [1575–85; < F < It *sorbetto* < Turk *şerbet* cool drink << Ar; see SHERBET]

Sorb•i•an (sôr′bē ən), *adj.* **1.** of or pertaining to the Wends or their language. —*n.* **2.** Also called **Lusatian, Wendish.** a Slavic language spoken by an isolated group in SE East Germany. **3.** a Wend. [1830–40; SORB + -IAN]

sor′bic ac′id (sôr′bik), *Chem.* a white, crystalline compound, $C_6H_8O_2$, slightly soluble in water, soluble in many organic solvents: used as a preservative in pharmaceuticals, cosmetics, and food. [1805–15; SORB[1] + -IC]

sor•bi•tol (sôr′bi tôl′, -tol′), *n. Biochem.* a white, crystalline, sweet, water-soluble powder, $C_6H_8(OH)_6$, occurring in cherries, plums, pears, seaweed, and many berries, obtained by the breakdown of dextrose and used as a sugar substitute for diabetics and in the manufacture of vitamin C, synthetic resins, candy, varnishes, etc.; sorbol. [1890–95; SORB[1] + -ITOL]

sor•bol (sôr′bôl, -bol), *n. Biochem.* sorbitol. [by shortening]

Sor•bon•ist (sôr bon′ist, -bun′-, sôr′bə nist), *n.* a student or graduate of the Sorbonne. [1550–60; < NL *Sorbonista.* See SORBONNE, -IST]

Sor•bonne (sôr bon′, -bun′; *Fr.* sôʀ bôn′), *n.* **1.** the seat of the faculties of arts and letters of the University of Paris. **2.** a theological college founded in Paris in 1253 by Robert de Sorbon, suppressed in 1792, and ceasing to exist about 1850.

sor•bose (sôr′bōs), *n. Biochem.* a ketohexose, $C_6H_{12}O_6$, occurring in mountain ash and obtained industrially from sorbitol by bacterial oxidation: used in the synthesis of vitamin C. [1895–1900; SORB(ITOL) + -OSE[2]]

sor•cer•er (sôr′sər ər), *n.* a person who practices sorcery; black magician; wizard. [1520–30; earlier *sorcer,* ME < MF *sorcier,* perh. < VL **sortiārius* one who casts lots, equiv. to L *sort-* (s. of *sors*) lot, fate + *-i-* -I- + *-ārius* -IER[2]; see -ER[1]]

sor•cer•ess (sôr′sər is), *n.* a woman who practices sorcery; witch. [1350–1400; ME < AF *sorceresse,* equiv. to *sorcer* (see SORCERER) + *-esse* -ESS]
—**Usage.** See **-ess.**

sor•cer•ous (sôr′sər əs), *adj.* **1.** of the nature of or involving sorcery. **2.** using sorcery. [1540–50; SORCER(Y) + -OUS] —**sor′cer•ous•ly,** *adv.*

sor•cer•y (sôr′sə rē), *n., pl.* **-cer•ies.** the art, practices, or spells of a person who is supposed to exercise supernatural powers through the aid of evil spirits; black magic; witchery. [1250–1300; ME *sorcerie* < ML *sorceria.* See SORCERER, -Y[3]]
—**Syn.** enchantment. See **magic.**

sor•did (sôr′did), *adj.* **1.** morally ignoble or base; vile: *sordid methods.* **2.** meanly selfish, self-seeking, or mercenary. **3.** dirty or filthy. **4.** squalid; wretchedly poor and run-down: *sordid housing.* [1590–1600; < L *sordidus,* equiv. to *sord(ēs)* dirt + *-idus* -ID[4]] —**sor′did•ly,** *adv.* —**sor′did•ness,** *n.*
—**Syn. 1.** degraded, depraved. See **mean**[2]. **2.** avaricious, tight, close, stingy. **3.** soiled, unclean, foul.
—**Ant. 1.** honorable. **2.** generous. **3.** clean.

sor•di•no (sôr dē′nō; *It.* sôʀ dē′nô), *n., pl.* **-ni** (-nē). *Music.* mute (def. 10). [1795–1805; < It: a mute, equiv. to *sordo* (< L *surdus* deaf) + *-ino* -INE[1]]

sore (sôr, sōr), *adj.,* **sor•er, sor•est,** *n., adv.* —*adj.* **1.** physically painful or sensitive, as a wound, hurt, or diseased part: *a sore arm.* **2.** suffering bodily pain from wounds, bruises, etc., as a person: *He is sore because of all that exercise.* **3.** suffering mental pain; grieved, distressed, or sorrowful: *to be sore at heart.* **4.** causing great mental pain, distress, or sorrow: *a sore bereavement.* **5.** causing very great suffering, misery, hardship, etc.: *sore need.* **6.** *Informal.* annoyed; irritated; offended; angered: *He was sore because he had to wait.* **7.** causing annoyance or irritation: *a sore subject.* —*n.* **8.** a sore spot or place on the body. **9.** a source or cause of grief, distress, irritation, etc. —*adv.* **10.** *Archaic.* sorely. [bef. 900; ME (adj., n., and adv.); OE *sār;* c. D *zeer,* G *sehr,* ON *sārr*] —**sore′ness,** *n.*
—**Syn. 1.** tender. **3.** aggrieved, hurt, pained, vexed. **4.** grievous, distressing, painful, depressing. **8.** infection, abscess, ulcer, wound.

so•re•di•al (sə rē′dē əl), *adj.* pertaining to or resembling a soredium. [1880–85; SOREDI(UM) + -AL[1]]

so•re•di•um (sə rē′dē əm), *n., pl.* **-di•a** (-dē ə). (in a lichen) a group of algal cells surrounded by hyphal tissue, occurring on the surface of the thallus and functioning in vegetative reproduction. Also called **brood bud, hologonidium.** [1820–30; < NL, dim. of Gk *sōrós* a heap] —**so•re•di•ate** (sə rē′dē it, -āt′), *adj.*

sore•head (sôr′hed′, sōr′-), *n. Informal.* a disgruntled or vindictive person, esp. an unsportsmanlike loser: *Don't be such a sorehead, they won fair and square.* [1840–50; cf. Scots *sorehead* a headache] —**sore′head′•ed•ly,** *adv.* —**sore′head′ed•ness,** *n.*

So•rel (sə rel′; *Fr.* sô ʀel′), *n.* **Georges** (zhôʀzh), **1.** 1847–1922, French engineer and social philosopher. **2.** a city in S Quebec, in E Canada, on the St. Lawrence. 20,347.

sore•ly (sôr′lē, sōr′-), *adv.* **1.** in a painful manner. **2.** extremely; very: *I was sorely tempted to report him.* [bef. 900; ME *sarely, soreli,* OE *sārlīce;* see SORE, -LY]

sore′ mouth′, *Vet. Pathol.* ecthyma.

sore′ shin′, *Plant Pathol.* a disease of plant seedlings, characterized by stem cankers that girdle the stem near the soil line, caused by any of several fungi, esp. *Rhizoctonia solani.* [1850–55, *Amer.*]

sore′ throat′, *Pathol.* a painful or sensitive condition of the throat exaggerated by swallowing or talking, usually caused by bacteria or viruses; laryngitis; pharyngitis; tonsillitis. [1680–90]

sor•gho (sôr′gō), *n., pl.* **-ghos.** sorgo.

sor•ghum (sôr′gəm), *n.* **1.** a cereal grass, *Sorghum bicolor* (or *S. vulgare*), having broad, cornlike leaves and a tall, pithy stem bearing the grain in a dense terminal cluster. **2.** the syrup made from sorgo. [1590–1600; < NL < It *sorgo* (see SORGO)]

sor•go (sôr′gō), *n., pl.* **-gos.** any of several varieties of sorghum grown chiefly for the sweet juice yielded by the stems, used in making sugar and syrup and also for fodder. Also, **sorgho.** Also called **sweet sorghum, sugar sorghum.** [1750–60; < It < VL **syricum (granum)* Syrian (grain), neut. of L *Syricus* (masc.) of SYRIA; see -IC]

so•ri (sôr′ī, sōr′ī), *n.* pl. of **sorus.**

sor•i•cine (sôr′ə sīn′, -sin, sor′ə-), *adj. Zool.* of or resembling the shrews. [1775–85; < L *sōricīnus,* equiv. to *sōric-* (s. of *sōrex*) shrew + *-īnus* -INE[1]]

sor•i•tes (sô rī′tēz, sō-), *n. Logic.* a form of argument having several premises and one conclusion, capable of being resolved into a chain of syllogisms, the conclusion of each of which is a premise of the next. [1545–55; < L *sōrītēs* < Gk *sōreítēs* lit., heaped, piled up, deriv. of *sōrós* a heap] —**so•rit•i•cal** (sô rit′i kəl, sō-), **so•rit′ic,** *adj.*

sor•o•ban (sôr′ə bän′), *n.* a Japanese abacus of Chinese derivation. [< Japn < Chin *suànpan,* equiv. to *suàn* count + *pán* board]

So•ro•ca•ba (sô′ʀŏŏ kä′bä), *n.* a city in SE Brazil, W of São Paulo. 165,990.

So•ro•kin (sə rō′kin, sô-; *Russ.* su ʀô′kyin), *n.* **Pitirim A•le•xan•dro•vitch** (pi ti rēm′ al′ig zan′drə vich, -zän′-; *Russ.* pyi tyi ʀyēm′ u lyi ksän′drə vyich), 1889–1968, U.S. sociologist, born in Russia.

So•rol•la y Bas•ti•da (sô ʀô′lyä ē bäs tē′thä), **Joaquín** (hwä kēn′), 1863–1923, Spanish painter.

so•rop•ti•mist (sə rop′tə mist), *n.* a member of an international association of professional or executive businesswomen **(Sorop′timist Club′),** devoted primarily to welfare work. [1920–25; < L *sor(or)* SISTER + OPTIMIST]

so•ro•ral (sə rôr′əl, -rōr′-), *adj.* of, pertaining to, or characteristic of a sister or sisters; sisterly. [1645–55; < L *soror* SISTER + -AL[1]] —**so•ro′ral•ly,** *adv.*

so•ror•ate (sôr′ə rāt′, sor′-), *n.* subsequent or concurrent marriage with a wife's sister. [1905–10; < L *sorōr-* (s. of *soror*) SISTER + -ATE[3]]

so•ror•i•cide (sə rôr′ə sīd′, -ror′-), *n.* **1.** a person who kills his or her sister. **2.** the act of killing one's own sister. [1650–60; < L *sorōricīda* one who kills his sister, *-cīdium* the act of killing one's sister, equiv. to *sorōr-* (s. of *soror*) SISTER + *-cīda, -cīdium* -CIDE] —**so•ror′i•cid′•al,** *adj.*

so•ror•i•ty (sə rôr′i tē, -ror′-), *n., pl.* **-ties.** a society or club of women or girls, esp. in a college. [1525–35; < ML *sorōritās,* equiv. to L *sorōr-* (s. of *soror*) SISTER + *-itās* -ITY]

soror′ity house′, a house occupied by a college or university sorority. [1910–15]

so•ro•sil•i•cate (sôr′ō sil′i kit, -kāt′, sōr′-), *n. Mineral.* any of the silicates in which each silicate tetrahedron shares one of its four oxygen atoms with a neighboring tetrahedron, the ratio of silicon to oxygen being two to seven. Cf. **cyclosilicate, inosilicate, nesosilicate, tektosilicate.** [< Gk *sōró(s)* heap + SILICATE]

so•ro•sis[1] (sə rō′sis), *n., pl.* **-ses** (-sēz). *Bot.* a fleshy multiple fruit composed of many flowers, seed vessels, and receptacles consolidated, as in the pineapple and mulberry. [1825–35; < NL, equiv. to Gk *sōr(ós)* heap + NL *-ōsis* -OSIS]

so•ro•sis[2] (sə rō′sis), *n., pl.* **-ses** (-sēz), **-sis•es.** a women's society or club. [after the name of a club established in 1868; based on L *soror* SISTER]

sorp•tion (sôrp′shən), *n. Chem.* the state or process of being sorbed. [1905–10; extracted from ABSORPTION, ADSORPTION, etc.] —**sorp′tive,** *adj.*

sor•rel[1] (sôr′əl, sor′-), *n.* **1.** light reddish-brown. **2.** a horse of this color, often with a light-colored mane and tail. —*adj.* **3.** of the color sorrel. [1400–50; late ME < OF *sorel,* equiv. to *sor* brown (< Gmc) + *-el* dim. suffix; see -ELLE]

sor•rel[2] (sôr′əl, sor′-), *n.* **1.** any of various plants belonging to the genus *Rumex,* of the buckwheat family, having edible acid leaves used in salads, sauces, etc. **2.** any of various sour-juiced plants of the genus *Oxalis.* Cf. **wood sorrel. 3.** any of various similar plants. [1350–1400; ME *sorell* < OF *surele,* equiv. to *sur* SOUR (< Gmc; akin to OHG *sūr* sour) + *-el* dim. suffix; see -ELLE]

sor′rel salt′. See **potassium binoxalate.** [1790–1800]

sor′rel tree′, a North American tree, *Oxydendrum arboreum,* of the heath family, having leaves with an acid flavor and drooping clusters of white flowers. Also called **sourwood.** [1680–90, *Amer.*]

Sor•ren•to (sə ren′tō; *It.* sôʀ ʀen′tô), *n.* a seaport in SW Italy, on the Bay of Naples: resort; cathedral; ancient ruins. 15,133. —**Sor•ren•tine** (sôr′ən tēn′, sə ren′tēn), *adj.*

sor•row (sor′ō, sôr′ō), *n.* **1.** distress caused by loss, affliction, disappointment, etc.; grief, sadness, or regret. **2.** a cause or occasion of grief or regret, as an affliction, a misfortune, or trouble: *His first sorrow was the bank failure.* **3.** the expression of grief, sadness, disappointment, or the like: *muffled sorrow.* —*v.i.* **4.** to feel sorrow; grieve. [bef. 900; (n.) ME; OE *sorg;* c. G *Sorge,* D *zorg,* ON *sorg,* Goth *saurga;* (v.) ME *sorwen,* OE *sorgian;* c. OHG *sorgōn*] —**sor′row•er,** *n.* —**sor′row•less,** *adj.*
—**Syn. 1.** SORROW, DISTRESS, GRIEF, MISERY, WOE imply bitter suffering, especially as caused by loss or misfortune. SORROW is the most general term. GRIEF is keen suffering, esp. for a particular reason. DISTRESS implies anxiety, anguish, or acute suffering caused by the pressure of trouble or adversity. MISERY suggests such great and unremitting pain or wretchedness of body or mind as crushes the spirit. WOE is deep or inconsolable grief or misery. **2.** adversity. **4.** mourn, lament.

sor•row•ful (sor′ə fəl, sôr′-), *adj.* **1.** full of or feeling sorrow; grieved; sad. **2.** showing or expressing sorrow; mournful; plaintive: *a sorrowful song.* **3.** involving or causing sorrow; distressing: *a sorrowful event.* [bef. 900; ME *sorowful,* OE *sorgful.* See SORROW, -FUL] —**sor′•row•ful•ly,** *adv.* —**sor′row•ful•ness,** *n.*
—**Syn. 1.** unhappy, grieving. **2.** melancholy. **3.** piteous, heartbreaking.

Sor′rows of Young′ Wer′ther, The, (German, *Die Leiden des Jungen Werther*), a romantic novel (1774) in epistolary form by Goethe.

sor•ry (sor′ē, sôr′ē), *adj.,* **-ri•er, -ri•est. 1.** feeling regret, compunction, sympathy, pity, etc.: *to be sorry to leave one's friends; to be sorry for a remark; to be sorry for someone in trouble.* **2.** regrettable or deplorable; unfortunate; tragic: *a sorry situation; to come to a sorry end.* **3.** sorrowful, grieved, or sad: *Was she sorry when her brother died?* **4.** associated with sorrow; suggestive of grief or suffering; melancholy; dismal. **5.** wretched, poor, useless, or pitiful: *a sorry horse.* **6.** (used interjectionally as a conventional apology or expression of regret): *Sorry, you're misinformed. Did I bump you? Sorry.* [bef. 900; ME; OE *sārig;* c. LG *serig,* OHG *sērag.* See SORE, -Y[1]] —**sor′ri•ly,** *adv.* —**sor′ri•ness,** *n.*
—**Syn. 1.** regretful, sympathetic, pitying. **3.** unhappy, depressed, sorrowing. **4.** grievous, mournful, painful. **5.** abject, contemptible, paltry, worthless, shabby. See **wretched.** —**Ant. 1.** happy.

sort (sôrt), *n.* **1.** a particular kind, species, variety, class, or group, distinguished by a common character or nature: *to develop a new sort of painting; nice people, of course, but not really our sort.* **2.** character, quality, or nature: *young people of a nice sort.* **3.** an example of something that is undistinguished or barely adequate: *He is a sort of poet.* **4.** manner, fashion, or way: *We spoke in this sort for several minutes.* **5.** *Print.* **a.** any of the individual characters making up a font of type. **b.** characters of a particular font that are rarely used. **6.** an instance of sorting. **7. of sorts, a.** of a mediocre or poor kind: *a tennis player of sorts.* **b.** of one sort or another; of an indefinite kind. Also, **of a sort. 8. out of sorts, a.** in low spirits; depressed. **b.** in poor health; indisposed; ill. **c.** in a bad temper; irritable: *to be out of sorts because of the weather.* **d.** *Print.* short of certain characters of a font of type. **9. sort of,** *Informal.* in a way; somewhat; rather: *Their conversation was sort of tiresome.* —*v.t.* **10.** to arrange according to sort, kind, or class; separate into sorts; classify: *to sort socks; to sort eggs by grade.* **11.** to separate or take from other sorts or from others (often fol. by *out*): *to sort the good from the bad; to sort out the children's socks.* **12.** to assign to a particular class, group, or place (often fol. by *with, together,* etc.): *to sort people together indiscriminately.* **13.** *Scot.* to provide with food and shelter. **14.** *Computers.* to place (records) in order, as numerical or alphabetical, based on the contents of one or more keys contained in each record. Cf. **key**[1] (def. 19). —*v.i.* **15.** *Archaic.* to suit; agree; fit. **16.** *Brit. Dial.* to associate, mingle, or be friendly. **17. sort out, a.** evolve; develop; turn out: *We'll just have to wait and see how things sort out.* **b.** to put in order; clarify: *After I sort things out here, I'll be able to concentrate on your problem.* [1200–50; (n.) ME < MF *sorte* < ML *sort-* (s. of *sors*) kind, allotted status or portion, lot, L: orig., voter's lot; (v.) ME *sorten* to allot, arrange, assort (< MF *sortir*) < L *sortīrī* to draw lots, deriv. of *sors;* later senses influenced by the n. and by ASSORT] —**sort′a•ble,** *adj.* —**sort′a•bly,** *adv.* —**sort′•er,** *n.*
—**Syn. 1.** family, order, race, rank, character, nature.
—**Usage.** See **kind**[2].

sort•a (sôr′tə), *adv. Pron. Spelling.* sort of; somewhat: *I'm sorta nervous about asking for a date.*

sort•ed (sôr′tid), *adj. Geol.* **1.** (of sedimentary particles) uniform in size. **2.** (of sedimentary rock) consisting of particles of uniform size. [1945–50; SORT + -ED[2]]

sor•tie (sôr′tē), *n., v.,* **-tied, -tie•ing.** —*n.* **1.** a rapid movement of troops from a besieged place to attack the

CONCISE PRONUNCIATION KEY: *act, cāpe, dâre, pärt; set, ēqual; if, īce; ox, ōver, ôrder, oil, bŏŏk, bōōt, out; up, ûrge; child; sing; shoe; thin, that;* zh as in *treasure.* ə = *a* as in *alone, e* as in *system, i* as in *easily, o* as in *gallop, u* as in *circus;* ᵊ as in *fire* (fīᵊr), *hour* (ouᵊr). l and n can serve as syllabic consonants, as in *cradle* (krād′l), and *button* (but′n). See the full key inside the front cover.

besiegers. **2.** a body of troops involved in such a movement. **3.** the flying of an airplane on a combat mission. —*v.i.* **4.** to go on a sortie; sally forth. [1680–90; < F, n. use of fem. ptp. of *sortir* to go out]

sor·ti·lege (sôr′tl ij), *n.* **1.** the drawing of lots for divination; divination by lot. **2.** sorcery; magic. [1350–1400; ME < ML *sortilegium,* for L *sortilegus,* equiv. to *sort-* (s. of *sors*) lot, chance + *-i-* -I- + *-legus* (deriv. of *legere* to read, count, choose out); see -IUM] —**sor·ti·leg·ic** (sôr′tl ej′ik), **sor·ti·le·gious** (sôr′tl ē′jəs), *adj.*

sort·ing (sôr′ting), *n. Geol.* the process by which sedimentary particles become separated according to some particular characteristic, as size or shape. [SORT + -ING[1]]

sort′ing tracks′, the part of a railroad yard used for the final sorting of cars from a classification yard. Also called **sort′ing yard′.**

sor·ti·tion (sôr tish′ən), *n.* the casting or drawing of lots. [1590–1600; < L *sortītiōn-* (s. of *sortītiō*), equiv. to *sortīt(us)* (ptp. of *sortīrī* to draw lots, deriv. of *sors* lot, portion; see SORT, -ITE[2]) + *-iōn-* -ION]

so·rus (sôr′əs, sōr′-), *n., pl.* **so·ri** (sôr′ī, sōr′ī). **1.** *Bot.* one of the clusters of sporangia on the back of the fronds of ferns. See diag. under **fern.** **2.** *Mycol.* a soruslike spore mass of certain fungi and lichens. [1825–35; < NL < Gk *sōrós* heap]

SOS, 1. the letters represented by the radio telegraphic signal (··· – – – ···) used, esp. by ships in distress, as an internationally recognized call for help. —*n.* **2.** any call for help: *We sent out an SOS for more typists.* —*v.i.* **3.** to send an SOS. [1905–10]

SOS, See **shit on a shingle.**

s.o.s., (in prescriptions) if necessary. [< L *sī opus sit*]

So·se·ki (sô′se kē′), *n.* See **Natsume, Soseki.**

Sos·no·wiec (sôs nô′vyets), *n.* a city in S Poland. 196,000.

so-so (sō′sō′, sō′sō′), *adj.* **1.** Also, **so′so′.** indifferent; neither very good nor very bad. —*adv.* **2.** in an indifferent or passable manner; indifferently; tolerably. Also, **so′ so′.** [1520–30]
—Syn. 1. mediocre, fair, ordinary, average, passable.

sos·te·nu·to (sos′tə nōō′tō, sō′stə-; *It.* sôs′te nōō′tô), *adj., n., pl.* **-tos,** *It.* **-ti** (-tē). *Music.* —*adj.* **1.** sustained or prolonged in the time value of the tones. —*n.* **2.** a movement or passage played in this manner. [1715–25; < It, ptp. of *sostenere;* see SUSTAIN]

sostenu′to ped′al, *Music.* a pedal on a grand piano that raises the dampers, allowing the tone to be sustained for those strings struck at the time the pedal is depressed.

sot (sot), *n.* a drunkard. [bef. 1000; ME: fool, OE *sott* < ML *sottus* < ?]

So·ter (sō′tər), *n.* **Saint,** pope A.D. 166?–175?.

so·te·ri·ol·o·gy (sə tēr′ē ol′ə jē), *n. Theol.* the doctrine of salvation through Jesus Christ. [1760–70; < Gk *sōtēri(a)* salvation, deliverance (*sōtēr-* (s. of *sōtḗr*) deliverer + *-ia* -Y[3]) + -O- + -LOGY] —**so·te·ri·o·log·ic** (sə tēr′ē ə loj′ik), **so·te′ri·o·log′i·cal,** *adj.*

Soth·ern (suth′ərn), *n.* **E(dward) H(ugh),** 1859–1933, U.S. actor, born in England: husband of Julia Marlowe.

So′thic cy′cle, (in the ancient Egyptian calendar) a period of 1460 Sothic years. Also called **So′thic pe′riod.** [1855–60; SOTH(IS) + -IC]

So′thic year′, the fixed year of the ancient Egyptians, determined by the heliacal rising of Sirius, and equivalent to 365 days. [1820–30; SOTH(IS) + -IC]

So·this (sō′this), *n.* the name for the star Sirius, the Dog Star, given by the ancient Egyptians. [< Gk *Sôthis* < Egyptian *spdt*] —**So·thic** (sō′thik, soth′ik), *adj.*

So·tho (sōō′tōō, sō′tō), *n., pl.* **-thos,** (*esp. collectively*) **-tho** for 3. **1.** a group of closely related Bantu languages spoken in Lesotho and South Africa. **2.** any of the Sotho languages, esp. Sesotho. **3.** Also called **Basuto.** a member of any of a cluster of linguistically and culturally related Bantu-speaking peoples of southern Africa, including the Tswana.

so·tie (sō tē′), *n.* a satirical and topical comedy employing actors dressed in traditional fool's costume, popular in France during the late Middle Ages, and often used as a curtain raiser to mystery and morality plays. Also, **sot·tie′.** [1785–95; < F, MF: lit., foolishness, equiv. to *sot* fool + *-ie* -Y[3]]

so·tol (sō′tōl, sō tōl′), *n.* any of several plants belonging to the genus *Dasylirion,* of the agave family, native to the southwestern U.S. and northern Mexico, resembling the yucca. [1880–85, *Amer.;* < MexSp < Nahuatl *zōtōlin*]

sot·ted (sot′id), *adj.* drunken; besotted. [1350–1400; ME, equiv. to *sotten* to be a sot (deriv. of SOT) + -ED[2]]

sot·tish (sot′ish), *adj.* **1.** stupefied with or as if with drink; drunken. **2.** given to excessive drinking. **3.** pertaining to or befitting a sot. [1560–70; SOT + -ISH[1]] —**sot′tish·ly,** *adv.* —**sot′tish·ness,** *n.*

sot·to vo·ce (sot′ō vō′chē; *It.* sôt′tô vô′che), in a low, soft voice so as not to be overheard. [1730–40; < It: lit., under (the) voice]

sou (sōō), *n.* **1.** (formerly) either of two bronze coins of France, equal to 5 centimes and 10 centimes. **2.** sol[2]. [1810–20; < F; OF *sol* SOL[2]]

sou., 1. south. **2.** southern.

sou·a′ri nut′ (sōō är′ē), the large, edible, oily nut of a tall tree, *Caryocar nuciferum,* of tropical South America. Also called **butternut.** [1840–50; < F *saouari* < Galibi *sawarra*]

sou·bise (sōō bēz′), *n.* a brown or white sauce containing strained or puréed onions and served with meat. Also called **soubise′ sauce′.** [1770–80; < F, named after Prince Charles *Soubise* (1715–87), marshal of France]

sou·bre·saut (sōō′brə sō′; *Fr.* sōō brə sō′), *n., pl.* **-sauts** (-sōz′; *Fr.* -sō′). *Ballet.* a jump performed with the legs held together and the body erect but slightly curved to the side. [1840–50; < F; see SOMERSAULT]

sou·brette (sōō bret′), *n.* **1.** a maidservant or lady's maid in a play, opera, or the like, esp. one displaying coquetry, pertness, and a tendency to engage in intrigue. **2.** an actress playing such a role. **3.** any lively or pert young woman. [1745–55; < F: lady's maid < Pr *soubreto,* deriv. of *soubret* affected, ult. deriv. of OPr *sobrar* < L *superāre* to be above] —**sou·bret′tish,** *adj.*

sou·bri·quet (sōō′brə kā′, -ket′, sōō′brə kā′, -ket′), *n.* sobriquet.

sou·car (sou kär′), *n.* a Hindu banker. Also, **sowcar.** [1775–85; < Hindi *sāhūkār* great merchant]

sou·chong (sōō′shong′, -chong′), *n.* a variety of black tea grown in India and Sri Lanka. [1750–60; < Chin dial. (Guangdong) *síu-júng,* akin to Chin *xiǎozhǒng* lit., small sort]

souf·fle (sōō′fəl), *n. Pathol.* a murmuring or blowing sound heard on auscultation. [1875–80; < F; see SOUFFLÉ]

souf·flé (sōō flā′, sōō′flā), *n., adj., v.,* **-fléed, -flé·ing.** —*n.* **1.** a light baked dish made fluffy with beaten egg whites combined with egg yolks, white sauce, and fish, cheese, or other ingredients. **2.** a similar dish made with fruit juices, chocolate, vanilla, etc., and served as dessert. —*adj.* **3.** Also, **souf·fléed′.** puffed up; made light, as by beating and cooking. —*v.t.* **4.** to make (food) puffed up and light, as by beating and cooking, adding stiffly beaten egg whites, etc.: *to soufflé leftover mashed potatoes.* [1805–15; < F, n. use of ptp. of *souffler* to blow, puff < L *sufflāre* to breathe on, blow on]

Souf·flot (sōō flō′), *n.* **Jacques Ger·main** (zhäk zher-maN′), 1713–80, French architect.

Sou·frière (sōō frYeR′), *n.* **1.** Also, **La Soufrière,** a volcano in the West Indies, on St. Vincent island. 4048 ft. (1234 m). **2.** Also, **Grande Soufrière,** a volcano in the West Indies, on Guadeloupe. 4869 ft. (1484 m). **3.** a volcanic peak in the West Indies, on Montserrat island. 3002 ft. (915 m).

sough[1] (sou, suf), *v.i.* **1.** to make a rushing, rustling, or murmuring sound: *the wind soughing in the meadow.* **2.** *Scot. and North Eng.* to speak, esp. to preach, in a whining, singsong voice. —*n.* **3.** a sighing, rustling, or murmuring sound. **4.** *Scot. and North Eng.* **a.** a sigh or deep breath. **b.** a whining, singsong manner of speaking. **c.** a rumor; unconfirmed report. [bef. 900; (v.) ME *swoghen,* OE *swōgan* to make a noise; c. OS *swōgan,* OE *swēgan,* Goth *-swōgjan;* (n.) ME *swow, swo(u)gh,* deriv. of the v.] —**sough′ful·ly,** *adv.* —**sough′less,** *adj.*

sough[2] (suf, sou), *Brit.* —*n.* **1.** drain; drainage ditch, gutter, or sewer. **2.** a swampy or marshy area. —*v.t.* **3.** to drain (land or a mine) by building drainage ditches or the like. Also, *esp. Scot.,* **sugh.** [1250–1300; ME *sogh, sohn* < ?; cf. D (dial.) *zoeg* little ditch]

sought (sôt), *v.* pt. and pp. of **seek.**

sought-af·ter (sôt′af′tər, -äf′-), *adj.* that is in demand; desirable: *a sought-after speaker.* [1880–85]

souk (sōōk, shōōk), *n.* suk.

sou·kous (sōō′kōōs′), *n.* a style of central African popular dance music with electric guitars, Caribbean rhythms, and often several vocalists. [1980–85; said to be < Lingala < F *secouer* to shake]

soul (sōl), *n.* **1.** the principle of life, feeling, thought, and action in humans, regarded as a distinct entity separate from the body, and commonly held to be separable in existence from the body; the spiritual part of humans as distinct from the physical part. **2.** the spiritual part of humans regarded in its moral aspect, or as believed to survive death and be subject to happiness or misery in a life to come: *arguing the immortality of the soul.* **3.** the disembodied spirit of a deceased person. **4.** the emotional part of human nature; the seat of the feelings or sentiments. **5.** a human being; person. **6.** high-mindedness; noble warmth of feeling, spirit or courage, etc. **7.** the animating principle; the essential element or part of something. **8.** the inspirer or moving spirit of some action, movement, etc. **9.** the embodiment of some quality: *He was the very soul of tact.* **10.** (*cap.*) *Christian Science.* God; the divine source of all identity and individuality. **11.** shared ethnic awareness and pride among black people, esp. black Americans. **12.** deeply felt emotion, as conveyed or expressed by a performer or artist. **13.** See **soul music.** —*adj.* **14.** of, characteristic of, or for black Americans or their culture: *soul newspapers.* [bef. 900; ME; OE *sāwl, sāwol;* c. D *ziel,* G *Seele,* ON *sāl,* Goth *saiwala*] —**soul′like′,** *adj.*
—Syn. 1. spirit. **4.** heart. **7.** essence, core, heart.

soul′ broth′er, *Informal.* a black male, esp. a fellow black male. [1955–60]

soul′ cake′, *Brit.* a round, sweet bun or small, oval cake, traditionally made to celebrate All Souls' Day. [1680–90]

soul′ food′, traditional black American cookery, which originated in the rural South, consisting of such foods as chitterlings, pig knuckles, turnip greens, and cornbread. [1960–65, *Amer.*] —**soul′-food′,** *adj.*

soul·ful (sōl′fəl), *adj.* of or expressive of deep feeling or emotion: *soulful eyes.* [1860–65; SOUL + -FUL] —**soul′ful·ly,** *adv.* —**soul′ful·ness,** *n.*

soul′ kiss′, an open-mouthed kiss in which the tongue of one partner is manipulated in the mouth of the other. Also called **deep kiss, French kiss.** [1945–50]

soul-kiss (sōl′kis′), *v.t.* **1.** to give (someone) a soul kiss. —*v.i.* **2.** to be engaged or involved in a soul kiss.

soul·less (sōl′lis), *adj.* **1.** without a soul. **2.** lacking in nobility of soul, as persons; without spirit or courage. [1545–55; SOUL + -LESS] —**soul′less·ly,** *adv.* —**soul′less·ness,** *n.*

soul′ mate′, a person with whom one has a strong affinity. [1815–25]

soul′ mu′sic, a fervent type of popular music developed in the late 1950's by black Americans as a secularized form of gospel music, with rhythm-and-blues influences, and distinctive for its earthy expressiveness, variously plaintive or raucous vocals, and often passionate romanticism or sensuality. Also called **soul.** [1960–65, *Amer.*]

soul-search·ing (sōl′sûr′ching), *n.* the act or process of close and penetrating analysis of oneself, to determine one's true motives and sentiments. [1605–15]

soul′ sis′ter, *Informal.* a black female, esp. a fellow black female. [1965–70]

Soult (sōōlt), *n.* **Ni·co·las Jean de Dieu** (nē kô lä′ zhäN də dyœ), (*Duke of Dalmatia*), 1769–1851, French marshal.

sou mar·qué (sōō′ mär kā′ *or, for 2,* -kē′; *Fr.* sōō maR kā′), *n., pl.* **sous mar·qués** (sōō′ mär kā′ *or, for 2,* -kē′; *Fr.* sōō maR kā′). **1.** a billon coin of France, issued in the 18th century for circulation in the colonies. **2.** something that has little or no value. Also, **sou mar·kee** (sōō′ mär′kē). [1820–30; < F: marked sou]

sound[1] (sound), *n.* **1.** the sensation produced by stimulation of the organs of hearing by vibrations transmitted through the air or other medium. **2.** mechanical vibrations transmitted through an elastic medium, traveling in air at a speed of approximately 1087 ft. (331 m) per second at sea level. **3.** the particular auditory effect produced by a given cause: *the sound of music.* **4.** any auditory effect; any audible vibrational disturbance: *all kinds of sounds.* **5.** a noise, vocal utterance, musical tone, or the like: *the sounds from the next room.* **6.** a distinctive, characteristic, or recognizable musical style, as from a particular performer, orchestra, or type of arrangement: *the big-band sound.* **7.** *Phonet.* **a.** See **speech sound. b.** the audible result of an utterance or portion of an utterance: *the s-sound in "slight."* **8.** the auditory effect of sound waves as transmitted or recorded by a particular system of sound reproduction: *the sound of a stereophonic recording.* **9.** the quality of an event, letter, etc., as it affects a person: *This report has a bad sound.* **10.** the distance within which the noise of something may be heard. **11.** mere noise, without meaning: *all sound and fury.* **12.** *Archaic.* a report or rumor; news; tidings.
—*v.i.* **13.** to make or emit a sound. **14.** to give forth a sound as a call or summons: *The bugle sounded as the troops advanced.* **15.** to be heard, as a sound. **16.** to convey a certain impression when heard or read: *to sound strange.* **17.** to give a specific sound: *to sound loud.* **18.** to give the appearance of being; seem: *The report sounds true.* **19.** *Law.* to have as its basis or foundation (usually fol. by *in*): *His action sounds in contract.*
—*v.t.* **20.** to cause to make or emit a sound: *to sound a bell.* **21.** to give forth (a sound): *The oboe sounded an A.* **22.** to announce, order, or direct by or as by a sound: *His speech sounded a warning to aggressor nations.* **23.** to utter audibly, pronounce, or express: *to sound each letter.* **24.** to examine by percussion or auscultation: *to sound a patient's chest.* **25. sound off,** *Informal.* **a.** to call out one's name, as at military roll call. **b.** to speak freely or frankly, esp. to complain in such a manner. **c.** to exaggerate; boast: *Has he been sounding off about his golf game again?* [1250–1300; (n.) ME *soun* < AF (OF *son*) < L *sonus;* (v.) ME *sounen* < OF *suner* < L *sonāre,* deriv. of *sonus*] —**sound′a·ble,** *adj.*
—Syn. 1. SOUND, NOISE, TONE refer to something heard. SOUND and NOISE are often used interchangeably for anything perceived by means of hearing. SOUND, however, is more general in application, being used for anything within earshot: *the sound of running water.* NOISE, caused by irregular vibrations, is more properly applied to a loud, discordant, or unpleasant sound: *the noise of shouting.* TONE is applied to a musical sound having a certain quality, resonance, and pitch.

sound[2] (sound), *adj.,* **-er, -est,** *adv.* —*adj.* **1.** free from injury, damage, defect, disease, etc.; in good condition; healthy; robust: *a sound heart; a sound mind.* **2.** financially strong, secure, or reliable: *a sound business; sound investments.* **3.** competent, sensible, or valid: *sound judgment.* **4.** having no defect as to truth, justice, wisdom, or reason: *sound advice.* **5.** of substantial or enduring character: *sound moral values.* **6.** following in a systematic pattern without any apparent defect in logic: *sound reasoning.* **7.** uninterrupted and untroubled; deep: *sound sleep.* **8.** vigorous, thorough, or severe: *a sound thrashing.* **9.** free from moral defect or weakness; upright, honest, or good; honorable; loyal. **10.** having no legal defect: *a sound title to property.* **11.** theologically correct or orthodox, as doctrines or a theologian. —*adv.* **12.** deeply; thoroughly: *sound asleep.* [1150–1200; ME *sund,* OE *gesund* (see Y-); c. D *gezond,* G *gesund*] —**sound′ly,** *adv.* —**sound′ness,** *n.*
—Syn. 1. unharmed, whole, hale, unbroken, hardy. **2.** solvent. **4, 6.** valid, rational, logical.

sound[3] (sound), *v.t.* **1.** to measure or try the depth of (water, a deep hole, etc.) by letting down a lead or plummet at the end of a line, or by some equivalent means. **2.** to measure (depth) in such a manner, as at sea. **3.** to examine or test (the bottom, as of the sea or a deep hole) with a lead that brings up adhering bits of matter. **4.** to examine or investigate; seek to fathom or ascertain: *to sound a person's views.* **5.** to seek to elicit the views or sentiments of (a person) by indirect inquiries, suggestive allusions, etc. (often fol. by *out*): *Why not sound him out about working for us?* **6.** *Surg.* to examine, as the urinary bladder, with a sound. —*v.i.* **7.** to use the lead and line or some other device for measuring depth, as at sea. **8.** to go down or touch bottom, as a lead. **9.** to plunge downward or dive, as a whale. **10.** to make investigation; seek information, esp. by indirect inquiries. —*n.* **11.** *Surg.* a long, slender instrument for sounding or exploring body cavities or canals. [1300–50; ME *sounden*

< OF *sonder* to plumb, deriv. of *sonde* sounding line < ?] **—sound′a·ble,** *adj.*

sound[4] (sound), *n.* **1.** a relatively narrow passage of water between larger bodies of water or between the mainland and an island: *Long Island Sound.* **2.** an inlet, arm, or recessed portion of the sea: *Puget Sound.* **3.** the air bladder of a fish. [bef. 900; ME; OE *sund* act of swimming; akin to SWIM]

Sound (sound), *n.* **The,** a strait between SW Sweden and Zealand, connecting the Kattegat and the Baltic. 87 mi. (140 km) long; 3–30 mi. (5–48 km) wide. Swedish and Danish, **Oresund.**

sound·a·like (sound′ə līk′), *n.* a person or thing that sounds like another, esp. a better known or more famous prototype: *a whole spate of Elvis Presley soundalikes.* [1965–70; n. use of v. phrase *sound alike,* on the model of LOOKALIKE]

sound-and-light (sound′ən līt′), *adj.* combining sound effects or music with unusual lighting displays: *a spectacular sound-and-light presentation.* [1960–65]

sound′-and-light′ show′, a nighttime spectacle or performance, at which a building, historic site, etc., is illuminated and the historic significance is imparted to spectators by means of narration, sound effects, and music. [1965–70]

Sound′ and the Fu′ry, The, a novel (1929) by William Faulkner.

sound′ bar′rier, 1. Also called **sonic barrier, transonic barrier.** (not in technical use) a hypothetical barrier to flight beyond the speed of sound, so postulated because aircraft undergo an abruptly increasing drag force induced by compression of the surrounding air when traveling near the speed of sound. **2. break the sound barrier,** to travel faster than the speed of sound. [1950–55]

sound′ bite′, a brief, striking remark or statement excerpted from an audiotape or videotape for insertion in a broadcast news story. [1985–90]

sound′ block′, a small block of wood for rapping with a gavel. Also, **sound′ing block′.**

sound·board (sound′bôrd′, -bōrd′), *n.* See **sounding board.** [1495–1505; SOUND[1] + BOARD]

sound′ bow′ (bō), that part of a bell against which the tongue strikes. [1680–90]

sound·box (sound′boks′), *n.* a chamber in a musical instrument, as the body of a violin, for increasing the sonority of its tone. [1870–75; SOUND[1] + BOX[1]]

sound′ cam′era, a motion-picture camera that is capable of photographing silently at the normal speed of 24 fps and operating in synchronization with separate audio recording equipment. [1900–05]

sound′ effect′, any sound, other than music or speech, artificially reproduced to create an effect in a dramatic presentation, as the sound of a storm or a creaking door. [1925–30]

sound·er[1] (soun′dər), *n.* **1.** a person or thing that makes a sound or noise, or sounds something. **2.** *Telegraphy.* an instrument for receiving telegraphic impulses that emits the sounds from which the message is read. [1585–95; SOUND[1] + -ER[1]]

sound·er[2] (soun′dər), *n.* a person or thing that sounds depth, as of water. [1565–75; SOUND[3] + -ER[1]]

sound′ film′, 1. a film on which sound has been or is to be recorded, as for the soundtrack of a motion picture. **2.** See **sound motion picture.** [1920–25]

sound′ head′, *Motion Pictures.* a mechanism through which film passes in a projector for conversion of the soundtrack into audio-frequency signals that can be amplified and reproduced. Also called **sound′ gate′.** [1930–35]

sound′ hole′, an opening in the soundboard of a musical stringed instrument, as a violin or lute, for increasing the soundboard's capacity for vibration. [1605–15]

sound·ing[1] (soun′ding), *adj.* **1.** emitting or producing a sound or sounds. **2.** resounding or sonorous. **3.** having an imposing sound; high-sounding; pompous. **—*n.*** **4.** a verbal contest or confrontation, as among teenage boys or street-gang members, in which the trading of often elaborate insults and invective takes the place of physical violence. [1275–1325; SOUND[1] + -ING[2]] **—sound′ing·ly,** *adv.* **—sound′ing·ness,** *n.*

sound·ing[2] (soun′ding), *n.* **1.** Often, **soundings.** the act of measuring the depth of an area of water with or as if with a lead and line. **2. soundings, a.** an area of water that can be sounded with an ordinary lead and line, the depth being 100 fathoms (180 m) or less. **b.** the results or measurement obtained by sounding with a lead and line. **3.** *Meteorol.* any vertical penetration of the atmosphere for scientific measurement, esp. a radiosonde observation. **4. off soundings,** *Naut.* in waters beyond the 100-fathom (180-m) depth. **5. on soundings,** *Naut.* in waters less than 100 fathoms (180 m) deep, so that the lead can be used. [1300–50; ME; see SOUND[3], -ING[1]] **—sound′ing·ly,** *adv.* **—sound′ing·ness,** *n.*

sound′ing balloon′, *Meteorol.* a balloon carrying instruments aloft to make atmospheric measurements, esp. a radiosonde balloon. Also called **weather balloon.** [1900–05]

sound′ing board′, 1. a thin, resonant plate of wood forming part of a musical instrument, and so placed as to enhance the power and quality of the tone. **2.** a structure over or behind and above a speaker, orchestra, etc., to reflect the sound toward the audience. **3.** a board used in floors, partitions, etc., for deadening sound. **4.** a person or persons whose reactions serve as a measure of the effectiveness of the methods, ideas, etc., put forth. **5.** a person or group that propagates ideas, opinions, etc. Also called **soundboard.** [1760–70]

sound′ing lead′ (led). See under **sounding line.**

sound′ing line′, a line weighted with a lead or plummet **(sounding lead)** and bearing marks to show the length paid out, used for sounding, as at sea. [1300–50; ME]

sound′ing machine′, *Navig.* any of various machines for taking and recording soundings. [1840–50]

sound′ing rock′et, a rocket equipped with instruments for making meteorological observations in the upper atmosphere. [1940–45]

sound′ law′. See **phonetic law.** [1870–75]

sound·less[1] (sound′lis), *adj.* without sound; silent; quiet. [1595–1605; SOUND[1] + -LESS] **—sound′less·ly,** *adv.* **—sound′less·ness,** *n.*

sound·less[2] (sound′lis), *adj.* unfathomable; very deep. [1580–90; SOUND[3] + -LESS] **—sound′less·ly,** *adv.* **—sound′less·ness,** *n.*

sound′ man′, 1. a technician who produces sound effects. **2.** a technician responsible for the quality of sound that is broadcast or recorded. **3.** *Theat.* a technician responsible for the proper placement of microphones, achieving the desired volume and balance of sound from various sources, and eliminating any distortion caused by amplification. Also, **sound′man′.**

sound′ mo′tion pic′ture, a motion picture with a soundtrack. Also called **sound film.**

sound′ pres′sure, *Physics.* **1.** Also called **excess sound pressure, instantaneous sound pressure.** the difference between the pressure at a point in a medium through which a sound wave is passing and the static pressure of the medium at that point. **2.** See **effective sound pressure.** [1890–95]

sound·proof (sound′pro͞of′), *adj.* **1.** impervious to sound. **—*v.t.*** **2.** to cause to be soundproof. [1875–80; SOUND[1] + -PROOF] **—sound′proof′ing,** *n.*

sound′ rang′ing, a method for determining the distance between a point and the position of a sound source by measuring the time lapse between the origin of the sound and its arrival at the point.

sound′ record′ist, recordist.

sound′ spec′trogram, a graphic representation, produced by a sound spectrograph, of the frequency, intensity, duration, and variation with time of the resonance of a sound or series of sounds.

sound′ spec′trograph, an electronic device for recording a sound spectogram.

sound′ stage′, a large, soundproof studio used for filming motion pictures. [1930–35]

sound′ sym′bolism, *Ling.* a nonarbitrary connection between phonetic features of linguistic items and their meanings, as in the frequent occurrence of close vowels in words denoting smallness, as *petite* and *teeny-weeny.* [1875–80]

sound′ ti′tle, *Law.* See **marketable title.**

sound·track (sound′trak′), *n.* **1.** the narrow band on one or both sides of a motion-picture film on which sound is recorded. **2.** the sound recorded on a motion-picture film; audio portion of a film. **3.** the music or dialogue from a film available on a commercial recording. [1925–30; SOUND[1] + TRACK]

sound′ truck′, a truck carrying a loudspeaker from which speeches, music, etc., are broadcast, as for advertising, campaigning, or the like. [1935–40]

sound′ wave′, *Physics.* a longitudinal wave in an elastic medium, esp. a wave producing an audible sensation. [1865–70]

Sou·ni·on (so͞o′nē ən), *n.* **Cape,** a cape in E central Greece, SE of Athens, at the tip of the Attica peninsula, in W Aegean Sea. Also called **Colonna.**

Sou′nion Head′, the tip of the Attica peninsula, E central Greece: site of ancient temple ruins.

soup (so͞op), *n.* **1.** a liquid food made by boiling or simmering meat, fish, or vegetables with various added ingredients. **2.** *Slang.* a thick fog. **3.** *Slang.* added power, esp. horsepower. **4.** *Slang.* nitroglycerine. **5.** *Photog. Slang.* developing solution. **6. from soup to nuts, a.** from the first through the last course of a meal. **b.** from beginning to end; to a complete, encompassing degree; leaving nothing out. **7. in the soup,** *Informal.* in trouble: *He'll be in the soup when the truth comes out.* **—*v.t.*** **8. soup up,** *Slang.* **a.** to improve the capacity for speed or increase the efficiency of (a motor or engine) by increasing the richness of the fuel mixture or the efficiency of the fuel, or by adjusting the engine. **b.** to give spirit or vivacity to; enliven: *a political rally souped up by the appearance of the candidates.* [1645–55; 1940–45 for def. 8; < F *soupe,* OF *souppe, sope* < Gmc; cf. D *sopen* to dunk. See SOP] **—soup′less,** *adj.* **—soup′like′,** *adj.*
—Syn. 1. broth, stock, potage.

soup-and-fish (so͞op′ən fish′), *n. Informal.* a man's formal evening clothes. [alluding to the early courses of a formal dinner]

soup·bone (so͞op′bōn′), *n.* **1.** a bone used for making soup or broth. **2.** *Baseball Slang.* a pitcher's throwing arm. [1910–15; SOUP + BONE]

soup·çon (so͞op sôN′, so͞op′sôN), *n.* a slight trace, as of a particular taste or flavor. [1760–70; < F: a suspicion, MF *sospeçon* < LL *suspectiōn-* (s. of *suspectiō*), for L *suspīciō* SUSPICION]
—Syn. dash, bit, hint, vestige.

soup du jour (so͞op′ də zho͝or′), the soup featured by a restaurant on a particular day. Also, **soup′ de jour′.** [1940–45; < Fr *soupe du jour* soup of the day]

soup′fin shark′ (so͞op′fin′), a requiem shark, *Galeorhinus zyopterus,* inhabiting the Pacific Ocean, valued for its fins, which are used by the Chinese in the preparation of a soup, and for its liver, which is rich in vitamin A. Also called **soup′fin′.** [1900–05]

Sou·pha·nou·vong (so͞o pä′no͞o vông′), *n.* **Prince,** born 1902, Laotian political leader: president since 1975 (half brother of Prince Souvanna Phouma).

soup′ kitch′en, 1. a place where food, usually soup, is served at little or no charge to the needy. **2.** *Mil. Slang.* (in World War I) a mobile kitchen. [1850–55]

sou·ple (sup′əl), *n.* silk from which only a portion of the sericin has been removed. Also called **sou′ple silk′.** [1885–90; short for F *soie souple* supple silk]

soup·meat (so͞op′mēt′), *n.* beef used for making soup stock. [1835–45; SOUP + MEAT]

soup′ plate′, a deep, concave plate used esp. for serving soup. [1820–30]

soup·spoon (so͞op′spo͞on′), *n.* a large spoon, commonly having a rounded bowl, with which to eat soup. [1695–1705; SOUP + SPOON]

soup-to-nuts (so͞op′tə nuts′), *adj.* **1.** (of a meal) complete or impressive in number of courses. **2.** *Informal.* complete; all-inclusive. [1935–40, *Amer.*]

soup·y (so͞o′pē), *adj.,* **soup·i·er, soup·i·est. 1.** resembling soup in consistency: *soupy oatmeal.* **2.** very thick; dense: *a soupy fog.* **3.** *Informal.* overly sentimental; mawkish: *soupy love scenes.* [1870–75; SOUP + -Y[1]]

sour (souᵊr, sou′ər), *adj.,* **-er, -est,** *n., v.* **—*adj.*** **1.** having an acid taste, resembling that of vinegar, lemon juice, etc.; tart. **2.** rendered acid or affected by fermentation; fermented. **3.** producing the one of the four basic taste sensations that is not bitter, salt, or sweet. **4.** characteristic of something fermented: *a sour smell.* **5.** distasteful or disagreeable; unpleasant. **6.** below standard; poor. **7.** harsh in spirit or temper; austere; morose; peevish. **8.** *Agric.* (of soil) having excessive acidity. **9.** (of gasoline or the like) contaminated by sulfur compounds. **10.** *Music.* off-pitch; badly produced: *a sour note.* **—*n.*** **11.** something that is sour. **12.** any of various cocktails consisting typically of whiskey or gin with lemon or lime juice and sugar and sometimes soda water, often garnished with a slice of orange, a maraschino cherry, or both. **13.** an acid or an acidic substance used in laundering and bleaching to neutralize alkalis and to decompose residual soap or bleach. **—*v.i.*** **14.** to become sour, rancid, mildewed, etc.; spoil: *Milk sours quickly in warm weather. The laundry soured before it was ironed.* **15.** to become unpleasant or strained; worsen; deteriorate: *Relations between the two countries have soured.* **16.** to become bitter, disillusioned, or disinterested: *I guess I soured when I learned he was married. My loyalty soured after his last book.* **17.** *Agric.* (of soil) to develop excessive acidity. **—*v.t.*** **18.** to make sour; cause sourness in: *What do they use to sour the mash?* **19.** to cause spoilage in; rot: *Defective cartons soured the apples.* **20.** to make bitter, disillusioned, or disagreeable: *One misadventure needn't have soured him. That swindle soured a great many potential investors.* [bef. 1000; (adj. and n.) ME *sure, soure,* OE *sūr* (orig. adj.); c. G *sauer,* D *zuur,* ON *sūrr;* (v.) ME *souren,* deriv. of the adj.] **—sour′ish,** *adj.* **—sour′ly,** *adv.* **—sour′ness,** *n.*
—Syn. 5. bitter. **7.** severe, testy, touchy, acrimonious, cross, petulant, crabbed. **—Ant. 1.** sweet.

sour·ball (souᵊr′bôl′, sou′ər-), *n.* **1.** a round piece of hard candy with a tart or acid fruit flavoring. **2.** *Informal.* a chronic grouch. [1895–1900; SOUR + BALL[1]]

sour·ber·ry (souᵊr′ber′ē, sou′ər-), *n., pl.* **-ries.** See **lemonade berry.** [1905–10, *Amer.*; SOUR + BERRY]

source (sôrs, sōrs), *n., v.,* **sourced, sourcing. —*n.*** **1.** any thing or place from which something comes, arises, or is obtained; origin: *Which foods are sources of calcium?* **2.** the beginning or place of origin of a stream or river. **3.** a book, statement, person, etc., supplying information. **4.** the person or business making interest or dividend payments. **5.** a manufacturer or supplier. **6.** *Archaic.* a natural spring or fountain. **—*v.t.*** **7.** to give or trace the source for: *The research paper was not accurately sourced. The statement was sourced to the Secretary of State.* **8.** to find or acquire a source, esp. a supplier, for: *Some of the components are now sourced in Hong Kong.* **—*v.i.*** **9.** to contract a manufacturer or supplier: *Many large companies are now sourcing overseas.* **10.** to seek information about or consider possible options, available personnel, or the like: *a job recruiter who was merely sourcing.* [1300–50; ME *sours* (n.) < OF *sors* (masc.), *sourse, source* (fem.), n. use of ptp. of *sourdre* < L *surgere* to spring up or forth] **—source′ful,** *adj.* **—source′ful·ness,** *n.* **—source′less,** *adj.*
—Syn. 1. supplier, originator. **3.** authority, reference.

source′ book′, 1. an original writing, as a document, record, or diary, that supplies an authoritative basis for future writing, study, evaluation, etc. **2.** a volume containing a small collection of such writings, usually on a specific subject, used in research. Also, **source′book′.** [1895–1900, *Amer.*]

source′ code′, *Computers.* program instructions that must be translated by a compiler, interpreter, or assembler into object code before execution.

source′ lan′guage, 1. the language in which a text appears that is to be translated into another language. Cf. **target language** (def. 1). **2.** a language, usually the learner's native language, that is a source of interference in learning another language. Cf. **target language** (def. 2). [1955–60]

source′ mate′rial, original, authoritative, or basic materials utilized in research, as diaries or manuscripts.

sour′ cher′ry, 1. a cherry, *Prunus cerasus,* characterized by gray bark and the spreading habit of its branches. **2.** the red, tart fruit of this tree, used in making pies and preserves. [1880–85]

sourc·ing (sôr′sing, sōr′-), *n. Econ.* the buying of components of a product from an outside supplier, often one located abroad: *Foreign sourcing in the auto industry has eliminated jobs.* Cf. **outsourcing.** [SOURCE + -ING[1]]

sour′ cream′, cream soured by the lactic acid produced by a ferment. [1815–25, *Amer.*]

sour·dine (so͝or dēn′), *n. Music.* **1.** mute (def. 10). **2.** kit[2]. **3.** an obsolete member of the oboe family. [1670–80; < F: damper, mute < It *sordina* (fem.); see SORDINO]

CONCISE PRONUNCIATION KEY: act, cāpe, dâre, pärt; set, ēqual; if, īce; ox, ōver, ôrder, oil, bo͝ok, bo͞ot, out; up, ûrge; child; sing; shoe; thin, *th*at; zh as in *treasure.* ə = *a* as in *alone, e* as in *system, i* as in *easily, o* as in *gallop, u* as in *circus;* ᵊ as in *fire* (fīᵊr), *hour* (ouᵊr). l and n can serve as syllabic consonants, as in *cradle* (krād′l), and *button* (but′n). See the full key inside the front cover.

sour′ dock′. See under **dock**[4] (def. 1). [1275–1325; ME]

sour•dough (souᵊr′dō′, sou′ər-), *n.* **1.** leaven, esp. fermented dough retained from one baking and used, rather than fresh yeast, to start the next. **2.** a prospector or pioneer, esp. in Alaska or Canada. **3.** any long-time resident, esp. in Alaska or Canada. —*adj.* **4.** leavened with sourdough: *sourdough bread.* [1275–1325; ME; see SOUR, DOUGH]

sour′ gourd′, the acid fruit of any of several African or Australian trees belonging to the genus *Adansonia,* of the bombax family, as the baobab, *A. digitata.* [1630–40]

sour′ grapes′, pretended disdain for something one does not or cannot have: *She said that she and her husband didn't want to join the club anyway, but it was clearly sour grapes.* [1750–60; in allusion to Aesop's fable concerning the fox who, in an effort to save face, dismissed as sour those grapes he could not reach]

sour′ gum′, a tree, *Nyssa sylvatica,* of eastern North America, having elliptic leaves, dark-blue, berrylike fruit, and wood with a variety of commercial uses. Also called **black gum, beetlebung, pepperidge.** Cf. **tupelo.** [1775–85, *Amer.*]

sour′ mash′, a blended grain mash used in the distilling of some whiskeys, consisting of new mash and a portion of mash from a preceding run and yielding a high rate of lactic acid. [1880–85, *Amer.*]

sour′-milk cheese′ (souᵊr′milk′, sou′ər-), *Eastern New Eng.* cottage cheese made from sour milk. —**Regional Variation.** See **cottage cheese.**

sour′ or′ange. See under **orange** (def. 2). [1740–50]

sour•puss (souᵊr′pŏŏs′, sou′ər-), *n. Informal.* a person having a grouchy disposition that is often accompanied by a scowling facial expression. [1935–40; SOUR + PUSS[2]]

sour′ salt′, crystals of citric acid used as a flavoring in foods, carbonated beverages, and pharmaceuticals.

sour•sop (souᵊr′sop′, sou′ər-), *n.* **1.** the large, dark-green, slightly acid, pulpy fruit of a small West Indian tree, *Annona muricata,* of the annona family. **2.** the tree itself. Also called **guanabana.** [1660–70; SOUR + SOP]

sour•wood (souᵊr′wŏŏd′, sou′ər-), *n.* See **sorrel tree.** [1700–10; SOUR + WOOD[1]]

Sou•sa (sōō′zə, -sə), *n.* **John Philip,** 1854–1932, U.S. band conductor and composer.

sou•sa•phone (sōō′zə fōn′, -sə-), *n.* a form of bass tuba, similar to the helicon, used in brass bands. [1920–25; named after J. P. SOUSA; see -PHONE] —**sou′sa•phon′ist,** *n.*

sousaphone

sous-chef (sōō′shef′; *Fr.* sōō shef′), *n., pl.* **chefs** (-shefs′; *Fr.* shef′). the second in command in a kitchen; the person ranking next after the head chef. [< F, equiv. to *sous* under (< L *subtus* (adv.) underneath, below) + *chef* CHEF]

souse[1] (sous), *v.,* **soused, sous•ing,** *n.* —*v.t.* **1.** to plunge into water or other liquid; immerse. **2.** to drench, as with water. **3.** to dash or pour, as water. **4.** to steep in pickling brine; pickle. —*v.i.* **5.** to plunge into water or other liquid. **6.** to be soaked or drenched. **7.** to be steeping or soaking in something. —*n.* **8.** an act of sousing. **9.** something kept or steeped in pickle, esp. the head, ears, and feet of a pig. **10.** a liquid used as a pickle. **11.** *Slang.* a drunkard. [1350–1400; 1915–20 for def. 11; (n.) ME *sows* < MF *souce* pickled < Gmc (akin to SALT[1]); (v.) ME *sousen,* deriv. of the n.] —**Syn. 2.** soak, wet.

souse[2] (sous), *v.,* **soused, sous•ing,** *n. Archaic.* —*v.i.* **1.** to swoop down. —*v.t.* **2.** to swoop or pounce upon. —*n. Falconry.* **3.** a rising while in flight. **4.** a swooping or pouncing. [1480–90; by-form of SOURCE in its earlier literal sense "rising"]

soused (soust), *adj. Slang.* drunk; intoxicated. [1540–50, in sense "pickled"; 1605–15 for current sense; SOUSE[1] + -ED[2]]

sous•lik (sōōs′lik), *n.* suslik.

sous-sous (sōō′sōō′), *n. Ballet.* a small jump beginning and ending in the fifth position, usually performed in series moving forward, backward, or to the side. [< F *sous-sus,* equiv. to (*des*)*sous* (< L *subtus* under) + (*des*)*sus* (< L *sursum* over)]

Sous•telle (sōō stel′), *n.* **Jacques** (zhäk), 1912–90, French anthropologist and government official.

sou•tache (sōō tash′; *Fr.* sōō tash′), *n.* a narrow braid, commonly of mohair, silk, or rayon, used for trimming. [1855–60; < F: braid of a hussar's shako < Hungarian *sujtás* flat braid for trimming]

sou•tane (sōō tän′), *n. Eccles.* a cassock. [1830–40; < F < It *sottana,* fem. of *sottano* placed below, equiv. to *sott(o)* below (< L *subtus*) + *-ano* -AN; form of the F word influenced by *sous* under]

sou•te•nu (sōōt′n ōō′; *Fr.* sōōtᵊ ny′), *adj. Ballet.* performed in a carefully sustained manner. [< F: lit., SUSTAINED]

sou•ter (sōō′tər), *n. Scot. and North Eng.* a person who makes or repairs shoes; cobbler; shoemaker. Also, **soutter.** [bef. 1000; ME *sutor,* OE *sūtere* < L *sūtor,* equiv. to *sū-,* var. s. of *su(ere)* to SEW[1] + *-tor* -TOR]

Sou•ter (sōō′tər), *n.* **David H.,** born 1939, U.S. jurist: associate justice of the U.S. Supreme Court since 1990.

sou•ter•rain (sōō′tə rān′, sōō′tə rān′), *n. Chiefly Archaeol.* a subterranean passage or structure; grotto. [1725–35; < F: lit., underground, calque of L *subterrāneus;* see SOUS-SOUS, TERRAIN]

south (*n., adj., adv.* south; *v.* south, south), *n.* **1.** a cardinal point of the compass lying directly opposite north. *Abbr.:* S **2.** the direction in which this point lies. **3.** (usually cap.) a region or territory situated in this direction. **4. the South,** the general area south of Pennsylvania and the Ohio River and east of the Mississippi, consisting mainly of those states that formed the Confederacy. —*adj.* **5.** lying toward or situated in the south; directed or proceeding toward the south. **6.** coming from the south, as a wind. —*adv.* **7.** to, toward, or in the south. —*v.i.* **8.** to turn or move in a southerly direction. **9.** *Astron.* to cross the meridian. [bef. 900; ME *suth(e), south(e)* (adv., adj., and n.), OE *sūth* (adv. and adj.); c. OHG *sund-*]

South′ Af′rica, Repub′lic of, a country in S Africa; member of the Commonwealth of Nations until 1961. 25,000,000; 472,000 sq. mi. (1,222,480 sq. km). *Capitals:* Pretoria and Cape Town. Formerly, **Union of South Africa.**

South′ Af′rican, 1. of southern Africa. **2.** of the Republic of South Africa. **3.** a native or inhabitant of the Republic of South Africa, esp. one of European descent.

South′ Af′rican Dutch′, the Boers.

South′ Af′rican jade′. See **Transvaal jade.**

South′ Af′rican Repub′lic, former name of **Transvaal.**

South′ Amer′ica, a continent in the S part of the Western Hemisphere. 271,000,000; ab. 6,900,000 sq. mi. (17,871,000 sq. km). See map on next page. —**South′ Amer′ican.**

South′ Amer′ican bull′frog, crapaud.

South′ Amer′ican Plate′, *Geol.* a major tectonic division of the earth's crust, comprising the continent of South America and several ocean basins and bounded on the north by the Caribbean Plate, on the east by the Mid-Atlantic Ridge, on the west by a submarine trench that borders the western coast of the continent, and on the south by the Antarctic Plate.

South•amp•ton (south amp′tən, -hamp′-), *n.* **1. Henry Wri•othes•ley** (rī′əths lē), **3rd Earl of,** 1573–1624, English nobleman, soldier, and patron of writers, including Shakespeare. **2.** a former administrative county in S England: a part of Hampshire. **3.** a town on SE Long Island, in SE New York: resort town. 4000. **4.** a seaport in Hampshire county in S England. 215,400.

Southamp′ton Is′land, an island in N Canada, in the Northwest Territories at the entrance to Hudson Bay. 19,100 sq. mi. (49,470 sq. km).

South′ Ara′bia, 1. Protectorate of, a former protectorate of Great Britain in S Arabia, now part of the Republic of Yemen. **2. Federation of,** a short-lived federation in S Arabia, overlapping the Protectorate of South Arabia, now part of the Republic of Yemen.

South′ A′sia, the countries and land area of Afghanistan, Bangladesh, Bhutan, Sri Lanka, India, the Maldives, Nepal, and Pakistan. —**South′ A′sian.**

South′ Atlan′tic Cur′rent, an eastward-flowing ocean current formed by the merging of the Brazil Current and the southward-flowing current near the Falkland Islands and forming the southern part of the general circulation of the South Atlantic Ocean.

South′ Austral′ia, a state in S Australia. 1,285,033; 380,070 sq. mi. (984,380 sq. km). *Cap.:* Adelaide. —**South′ Austral′ian.**

South′ Bend′, a city in N Indiana. 109,727.

south•bound (south′bound′), *adj.* **1.** traveling southward. **2.** pertaining to southward travel. [1880–85; SOUTH + -BOUND[2]]

South•bridge (south′brij′), *n.* a town in S Massachusetts. 16,665.

South′ Bur′lington, a town in NW Vermont. 10,679.

South•bur•y (south′ber′ē, -bə rē), *n.* a town in S Connecticut. 14,146.

south′ by east′, *Navig., Survey.* a point on the compass 11°15′ east of south. *Abbr.:* SbE

south′ by west′, *Navig., Survey.* a point on the compass 11°15′ west of south. *Abbr.:* SbW

South′ Caroli′na, a state in the SE United States, on the Atlantic coast. 3,119,208; 31,055 sq. mi. (80,430 sq. km). *Cap.:* Columbia. *Abbr.:* SC (for use with zip code), S.C. —**South′ Carolin′ian.**

South′ Cauca′sian, 1. a family of languages including Georgian, Mingrelian, and others that are spoken on the south slopes of the Caucasus and adjacent areas. **2.** of or pertaining to South Caucasian.

South′ Charles′ton, a city in W West Virginia. 15,968.

South′ Chi′na Sea′, a part of the W Pacific, bounded by SE China, Vietnam, the Malay Peninsula, Borneo, and the Philippines. Also called **Nan Hai.**

South′ Dako′ta, a state in the N central United States: a part of the Midwest. 690,178; 77,047 sq. mi. (199,550 sq. km). *Cap.:* Pierre. *Abbr.:* SD (for use with zip code), S. Dak. —**South′ Dako′tan.**

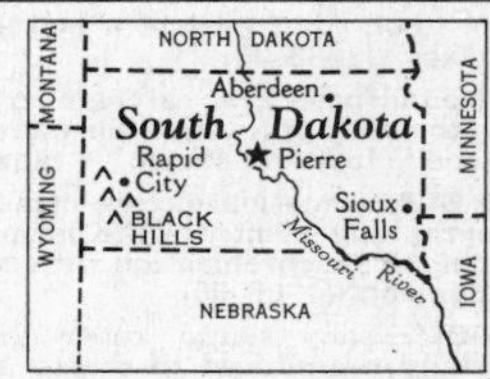

South•down (south′doun′), *n.* one of an English breed of sheep, yielding mutton of high quality. [1780–90; named after SOUTH DOWNS, where the breed was developed]

South′ Downs′, a range of low hills, from Hampshire to East Sussex, in S England.

south•east (south′ēst′; *Naut.* sou′ēst′), *n.* **1.** the point or direction midway between south and east. *Abbr.:* SE **2.** a region in this direction. **3.** (*cap.*) the southeast region of the United States. —*adj.* **4.** lying toward, situated in, or directed toward the southeast. **5.** coming from the southeast, as a wind. —*adv.* **6.** in the direction midway between south and east. [bef. 900; ME *southest,* OE *sūthēast.* See SOUTH, EAST] —**south′east′ern,** *adj.* —**south•east•ern•most** (south′ē′stərn mōst′ *or, esp. Brit.,* -məst), *adj.*

South′east A′sia, the countries and land area of Brunei, Burma, Cambodia, Indonesia, Laos, Malaysia, the Philippines, Singapore, Thailand, and Vietnam. —**South′east A′sian.**

South′east A′sia Trea′ty Organiza′tion. See **SEATO.**

southeast′ by east′, *Navig., Survey.* a point on the compass 11°15′ east of southeast. *Abbr.:* SEbE

southeast′ by south′, *Navig., Survey.* a point on the compass 11°15′ south of southeast. *Abbr.:* SEbS

south•east•er (south′ē′stər; *Naut.* sou′ē′stər), *n.* a wind or storm from the southeast. [1830–40; SOUTHEAST + -ER[1]]

south•east•er•ly (south′ē′stər lē; *Naut.* sou′ē′stər-lē), *adj., adv.* toward or from the southeast. [1700–10; SOUTH + EASTERLY]

south•east•ern•er (south′ē′stər nər), *n.* **1.** a native or inhabitant of the southeast. **2.** (*cap.*) a native or inhabitant of the southeastern U.S. [1915–20; SOUTHEASTERN + -ER[1]]

south•east•ward (south′ēst′wərd; *Naut.* sou′ēst′-wərd), *adv.* **1.** Also, **south′east′wards.** toward the southeast. —*adj.* **2.** facing or tending toward the southeast. **3.** coming from the southeast, as a wind. —*n.* **4.** the southeast. [1520–30; SOUTHEAST + -WARD]

south•east•ward•ly (south′ēst′wərd lē; *Naut.* sou′-ēst′wərd lē), *adj., adv.* toward or from the southeast. [1785–95; SOUTHEASTWARD + -LY]

South′ El Mon′te, a town in SW California. 16,623.

South•end-on-Sea (south′end′on sē′, -ôn-), *n.* a seaport in SE Essex, in SE England, on Thames estuary. 159,400.

South′ Equato′rial Cur′rent, an ocean current, flowing westward, found near the equator in the Atlantic, Pacific, and Indian oceans.

south•er (sou′thər), *n.* a wind or storm from the south. [1860–65; SOUTH + -ER[1]]

south•er•ly (suth′ər lē), *adj., adv., n., pl.* **-lies.** —*adj., adv.* **1.** toward the south: *a southerly course.* **2.** (esp. of

CONCISE ETYMOLOGY KEY: <, descended or borrowed from; >, whence; b., blend of, blended; c., cognate with; cf., compare; deriv., derivative; equiv., equivalent; imit., imitative; obl., oblique; r., replacing; s., stem; sp., spelling, spelled; resp., respelling, respelled; trans., translation; ?, origin unknown; *, unattested; ‡, probably earlier than. See the full key inside the front cover.

a wind) coming from the south: *a gentle southerly breeze.* —*n.* **3.** a wind that blows from the south. [1545–55; SOUTH + *-erly* (see EASTERLY)] —**south′er·li·ness,** *n.*

south·ern (suth′ərn), *adj.* **1.** lying toward, situated in, or directed toward the south. **2.** coming from the south, as a wind. **3.** of or pertaining to the south. **4.** (*cap.*) of or pertaining to the South of the United States. **5.** *Astron.* being or located south of the celestial equator or of the zodiac: *a southern constellation.* —*n.* **6.** (*often cap.*) southerner (def. 2). **7.** (*cap.*) the dialect of English spoken in the eastern parts of Maryland, Virginia, and the Carolinas, in Florida, in the southern parts of Georgia, Alabama, Mississippi, and Louisiana, and in southeastern Texas. [bef. 900; ME; OE *sūtherne.* See SOUTH, -ERN]

South′ern Alps′, a mountain range in New Zealand, on South Island. Highest peak, Mt. Cook, 12,349 ft. (3765 m).

South′ern Bap′tist, a member of the Southern Baptist Convention, founded in Augusta, Georgia, in 1845, that is strictly Calvinistic and active in religious publishing and education.

south′ern blight′, *Plant Pathol.* a disease of peanuts, tomatoes, and other plants, caused by a fungus, *Sclerotium rolfsii,* affecting the roots and resulting in rapid wilting.

South′ern blot′, *Biol., Med.* a procedure for identifying and measuring the amount of a specific DNA sequence or gene in a mixed extract, as in testing for a mutation or a virus: DNA strands from the person or organism under study are cut with restriction enzymes, separated by gel electrophoresis, transferred to special filter paper, and hybridized with a labeled DNA probe. [after Edwin M. *Southern,* originator of the technique]

South′ern Cameroons′. See under **Cameroons** (def. 2).

south′ern cane′. See under **cane** (def. 5).

South′ern Chris′tian Lead′ership Con′ference, a civil-rights organization founded in 1957 by the Rev. Martin Luther King, Jr. *Abbr.:* SCLC, S.C.L.C.

South′ern Coal′sack, *Astron.* Coalsack.

south′ern corn′stalk bor′er, the larva of a grass moth, *Diatraea crambidoides,* occurring in the southeastern U.S. from Maryland to Georgia, that is sometimes a serious pest, esp. of corn.

south′ern crab′ ap′ple, a tree, *Malus angustifolia,* of the eastern U.S., having oblong leaves, fragrant, pink or rose-colored flowers, and small, round, yellow-green fruit. [1900–05, *Amer.*]

South′ern Cross′, **1.** Also called **Cross.** *Astron.* a southern constellation between Centaurus and Musca. Cf. **Northern Cross. 2.** *U.S. Hist.* the battle flag of the Confederate States of America. Cf. **Stars and Bars.** [1690–1700, for def. 1]

South′ern Crown′, *Astron.* the constellation Corona Australis. [1585–95]

south′ern cy′press. See **bald cypress.**

south·ern·er (suth′ər nər), *n.* **1.** a native or inhabitant of the south. **2.** (*cap.*) a native or inhabitant of the southern U.S. [1820–30; SOUTHERN + -ER[1]]

South′ern Fish′, *Astron.* the constellation Piscis Austrinus. [1585–95]

South·ern-fried (suth′ərn frīd′), *adj.* **1.** coated with flour, egg, and bread crumbs and fried in deep fat: *Southern-fried chicken.* **2.** (*often l.c.*) *Slang.* characteristic of or originating in the South: *a vocabulary full of southern-fried expressions.* [1925–30]

South′ern Hem′isphere, the half of the earth between the South Pole and the equator. [1885–90]

south·ern·ism (suth′ər niz′əm), *n.* a pronunciation, expression, or behavioral trait characteristic of the U.S. South. [1860–65, *Amer.*; SOUTHERN + -ISM]

south′ern lights′, *Astron.* See **aurora australis.** [1765–75]

south·ern·ly (suth′ərn lē), *adj.* southerly. [1585–95; SOUTHERN + -LY] —**south′ern·li·ness,** *n.*

south′ern magno′lia. See **evergreen magnolia.**

South′ern Min′, Fukienese.

south·ern·most (suth′ərn mōst′ *or, esp. Brit.,* -məst), *adj.* farthest south. [1715–25; SOUTHERN + -MOST]

South′ern Pai′ute. See under **Paiute** (def. 2).

south′ern red′belly dace′. See under **redbelly dace.**

South′ern Rhode′sia, a former name (until 1964) of **Zimbabwe** (def. 1). —**South′ern Rhode′sian.**

South′ern Slavs′. See under **Slav.**

South′ern Spor′ades. See under **Sporades.**

south′ern stud′fish. See under **studfish.**

south′ern toad′, a common toad, *Bufo terrestris,* of the southeastern U.S., having prominent knoblike crests on its head.

South′ern Tri′angle, *Astron.* the constellation Triangulum Australe. [1870–75]

south·ern·wood (suth′ərn wo͝od′), *n.* a woody-stemmed wormwood, *Artemisia abrotanum,* of southern Europe, having aromatic, finely dissected leaves. Also called **old man.** [bef. 1000; ME *southernwode,* OE *sūtherne wudu.* See SOUTHERN, WOOD[1]]

South′ern Yem′en, a former name of **Yemen** (def. 1).

South′ Eu′clid, a city in NE Ohio, near Cleveland. 25,713.

Sou·they (sou′thē, suth′ē), *n.* **Robert,** 1774–1843, English poet and prose writer: poet laureate 1813–43.

South′ Farm′ingdale, a town on central Long Island, in SE New York. 16,439.

South·field (south′fēld′), *n.* a city in SE Michigan, W of Detroit. 75,568.

South′ Frig′id Zone′, the part of the earth's surface between the Antarctic Circle and the South Pole. See diag. under **zone.**

South·gate (south′gāt′), *n.* a city in SE Michigan, near Detroit. 32,058.

South′ Gate′, a city in SW California, near Los Angeles. 66,784.

South′ Geor′gia, a British island in the S Atlantic, about 800 mi. (1290 km) SE of the Falkland Islands. 22; ab. 1000 sq. mi. (2590 sq. km). —**South′ Geor′gian.**

South′ Glamor′gan, a county in SE Wales. 391,600; 161 sq. mi. (416 sq. km).

South′ Had′ley, a city in W Massachusetts. 16,399.

South′ Hol′land, 1. a province in the SW Netherlands. 3,106,697; 1086 sq. mi. (2810 sq. km). *Cap.:* The Hague. **2.** a city in NE Illinois. 24,977.

South′ Hous′ton, a town in S Texas. 13,293.

South′ Hun′tington, a town in central Long Island, in SE New York. 14,854.

south·ing (sou′thing), *n.* **1.** *Astron.* **a.** the transit of a heavenly body across the celestial meridian. **b.** south declination. **2.** movement or deviation toward the south. **3.** distance due south made by a vessel. [1650–60; SOUTH + -ING[1]]

South·ing·ton (suth′ing tən), *n.* a town in central Connecticut. 36,879.

South′ Is′land, the largest island of New Zealand. 860,990; 58,093 sq. mi. (150,460 sq. km).

South′ Kings′town, a town in S central Rhode Island. 20,414.

South′ Kore′a, a country in E Asia: formed 1948 after the division of the former country of Korea at 38° N. 34,708,542; 36,600 sq. mi. (94,795 sq. km). *Cap.:* Seoul. Cf. **Korea.** Official name, **Republic of Korea.** —**South′ Kore′an.**

South′ Lake′ Ta′hoe, a city in E California. 20,681.

south·land (south′lənd, -land′), *n.* **1.** a southern area. **2.** the southern part of a country. **3. the Southland,** the U.S. South. [bef. 1000; ME *south lond,* OE *sūthland;* see SOUTH, LAND] —**south′land′er,** *n.*

South′ Miam′i, a town in S Florida. 10,884.

South′ Milwau′kee, a city in SE Wisconsin. 21,069.

South′ Modes′to, a town in central California. 12,492.

south·most (south′mōst′ *or, esp. Brit.,* -məst), *adj.* southernmost. [bef. 900; ME *southmest,* OE *sūthmest;* see SOUTH, -MOST]

south′ node′, *Astrol.* (*often caps.*) the descending node of the moon.

South′ Og′den, a town in N Utah. 11,366.

South′ Or′ange, a city in NE New Jersey. 15,864.

South′ Ork′ney Is′lands, a group of islands in the British Antarctic Territory, N of the Antarctic Peninsula: formerly a dependency of the Falkland Islands; claimed by Argentina.

South′ Osse′tian Auton′omous Re′gion, an autonomous region in the Georgian Republic, in the N part. 99,000; 1428 sq. mi. (3900 sq. km). *Cap.:* Tskhinvali.

South′ Pacif′ic Cur′rent, an ocean current that flows E in the South Pacific Ocean parallel to the Antarctic Circumpolar Current.

South′ Pasade′na, a city in SW California, near Los Angeles. 22,681.

south·paw (south′pô′), *Informal.* —*n.* **1.** a person who is left-handed. **2.** *Sports.* **a.** a player who throws with the left hand, esp. a pitcher. **b.** *Boxing.* a boxer who leads with the right hand and stands with the right foot forward, using the left hand for the most powerful blows. —*adj.* **3.** left-handed. [1880–85, *Amer.*; SOUTH + PAW[1]]

South′ Plain′field, a city in N New Jersey. 20,521.

South′ Platte′, a river flowing NE from central Colorado to the Platte River in W Nebraska. 424 mi. (683 km) long.

South′ Pole′, 1. *Geog.* the southern end of the earth's axis, the southernmost point on earth. 2. *Astron.* the point at which the axis of the earth extended cuts the southern half of the celestial sphere; the south celestial pole. 3. (*l.c.*) the pole of a magnet that seeks the earth's south magnetic pole. 4. (*l.c.*) See under **magnetic pole** (def. 1). [1585–95, for def. 1]

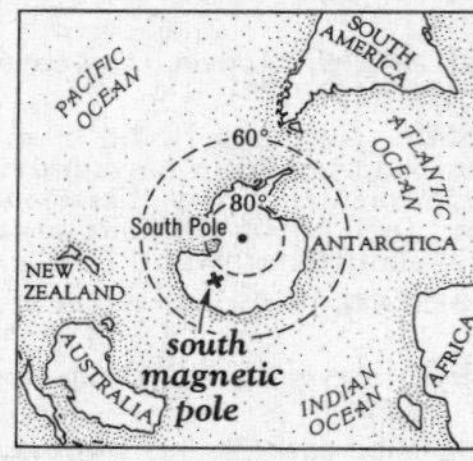

South•port (south′pôrt′, -pōrt′), *n.* a seaport in Merseyside, in W England: resort. 84,348.

South′ Port′land, a city in SW Maine. 22,712.

South′ Riv′er, a borough in central New Jersey. 14,361.

south•ron (suth′rən), *n.* 1. *Southern U.S.* southerner (def. 2). 2. (*usually cap.*) *Scot.* a native or inhabitant of England. [1425–75; late ME; earlier *southren* (var. of SOUTHERN), modeled on *Saxon, Briton,* etc.]

South′ Salt′ Lake′, a town in N Utah. 10,561.

South′ San′ Francis′co, a city in central California. 49,393.

South′ Sea′ Is′lands, the islands in the S Pacific Ocean. Cf. **Oceania.** —**South′ Sea′ Is′lander.**

South′ Seas′, the seas south of the equator.

South′ Shet′land Is′lands, a group of islands in the British Antarctic Territory, N of the Antarctic Peninsula: formerly a dependency of the Falkland Islands; claimed by Argentina and Chile.

South′ Shields′, a seaport in Tyne and Wear, in NE England, at the mouth of the Tyne River. 100,513.

south-south•east (south′south′ēst′; *Naut.* sou′sou′-ēst′), *Navig., Survey.* —*n.* 1. the point on the compass midway between south and southeast. —*adj.* 2. coming from this point: *a south-southeast wind.* 3. directed toward this point: *a south-southeast course.* —*adv.* 4. toward this point: *sailing south-southeast. Abbr.:* SSE

south-south•east•ward (south′south′ēst′wərd; *Naut.* sou′sou′ēst′wərd), *adv., adj.* toward the south-southeast. Also, **south′-south′east′ward•ly.** [1775–85; SOUTH-SOUTHEAST + -WARD]

south-south•west (south′south′west′; *Naut.* sou′-sou′west′), *Navig., Survey.* —*n.* 1. the point on the compass midway between south and southwest. —*adj.* 2. coming from this point: *a south-southwest wind.* 3. directed toward this point: *a south-southwest course.* —*adv.* 4. toward this point: *sailing south-southwest. Abbr.:* SSW

south-south•west•ward (south′south′west′wərd; *Naut.* sou′sou′west′wərd), *adv., adj.* toward the south-southwest. Also, **south′-south′west′ward′ly.** [SOUTH-SOUTHWEST + -WARD]

South St. Paul, a city in SE Minnesota. 21,235.

South′ Subur′ban, a city in SE West Bengal, in E India: a suburb of Calcutta. 227,600. Also called **South′ Sub′urbs City′.**

South′ Tem′perate Zone′, the part of the earth's surface between the tropic of Capricorn and the Antarctic Circle. See diag. under **zone.**

South′ Vietnam′, a former country in SE Asia that comprised Vietnam S of about 17° N latitude; a separate state 1954–75; now part of reunified Vietnam. *Cap.:* Saigon. Cf. **North Vietnam, Vietnam.**

south•ward (south′wərd; *Naut.* suth′ərd), *adj.* 1. moving, bearing, facing, or situated toward the south. 2. coming from the south, as a wind. —*adv.* 3. Also, **south′wards.** toward the south; south. —*n.* 4. the southward part, direction, or point. [bef. 900; ME; OE *sūth weard.* See SOUTH, -WARD]

south•ward•ly (south′wərd lē; *Naut.* suth′ərd lē), *adj., adv.* toward or from the south. [1590–1600; SOUTHWARD + -LY]

South•wark (suth′ərk), *n.* a borough of Greater London, England, S of the Thames. 235,500.

south•west (south′west′; *Naut.* sou′west′), *n.* 1. the point or direction midway between south and west. *Abbr.:* SW 2. a region in this direction. 3. **the Southwest,** the southwest region of the United States. —*adj.* 4. lying toward, situated in, or directed toward the southwest. 5. coming from the southwest, as a wind. —*adv.* 6. in the direction midway between south and west. [bef. 900; ME; OE *sūthwest.* See SOUTH, WEST] —**south′west′ern,** *adj.*

South′-West A′frica (south′west′), a former name of **Namibia.**

southwest′ by south′, *Navig., Survey.* a point on the compass 11°15′ south of southwest. *Abbr.:* SWbS

southwest′ by west′, *Navig., Survey.* a point on the compass 11°15′ west of southwest. *Abbr.:* SWbW

CONCISE ETYMOLOGY KEY: <, descended or borrowed from; >, whence; b., blend of, blended; c., cognate with; cf., compare; deriv., derivative; equiv., equivalent; imit., imitative; obl., oblique; r., replacing; s., stem; sp., spelling, spelled; resp., respelling, respelled; trans., translation; ?, origin unknown; *, unattested; ‡, probably earlier than. See the full key inside the front cover.

south•west•er (south′wes′tər; *Naut.* sou′wes′tər), *n.* 1. a wind, gale, or storm from the southwest. 2. sou'wester (defs. 1, 2). [1825–35; SOUTHWEST + -ER[1]]

south•west•er•ly (south′wes′tər lē; *Naut.* sou′wes′-tər lē), *adj., adv.* toward or from the southwest. [1700–10; SOUTHWEST + *-erly* (see EASTERLY)]

south•west•ern•er (south′wes′tər nər), *n.* 1. a native or inhabitant of the southwest. 2. (*cap.*) a native or inhabitant of the southwestern U.S. [1855–60, *Amer.*; SOUTHWESTERN + -ER[1]]

south•west•ward (south′west′wərd; *Naut.* sou′-west′wərd), *adv.* 1. Also, **south′west′wards.** toward the southwest. —*adj.* 2. facing or tending toward the southwest. 3. coming from the southwest, as a wind. —*n.* 4. the southwest. [1540–50; SOUTHWEST + -WARD]

south•west•ward•ly (south′west′wərd lē; *Naut.* sou′west′wərd lē), *adj., adv.* toward or from the southwest. [1790–1800; SOUTHWESTWARD + -LY]

South′ Whit′tier, a city in SW California, near Los Angeles. 43,815.

South′ Wind′sor, a town in N Connecticut. 17,198.

South′ Yem′en, Yemen (def. 3).

South′ York′shire, a metropolitan county in N England. 1,317,500; 603 sq. mi. (1561 sq. km).

Sou•tine (so͞o tēn′), *n.* **Cha•im** (KHī im′, KHī′im), 1894–1943, Lithuanian painter in France.

sout•er (so͞o′tər), *n. Scot. and North Eng.* souter.

Sou•van•na Phou•ma (so͞o vän′nä po͞o′mä), **Prince,** 1901–84, Laotian statesman: premier 1951–54, 1956–58, 1960, and 1962–75.

sou•ve•nir (so͞o′və nēr′, so͞o′və nēr′), *n.* 1. a usually small and relatively inexpensive article given, kept, or purchased as a reminder of a place visited, an occasion, etc.; memento. 2. a memory. [1765–75; < F, n. use of (*se*) *souvenir* to remember < L *subvenīre* to come to mind, equiv. to *sub-* SUB- + *venīre* to come]
—**Syn.** 1. reminder, keepsake, token.

souvenir′ sheet′, *Philately.* a single stamp or a pair, block, or set of stamps having the same or different designs commemorating a stamp exhibition or other event and having inscriptions in one or all four margins. [1935–40]

souv•la•ki (so͞ov lä′kē), *n. Greek Cookery.* a dish similar to shish kebab made with lamb. Also, **souv•la•kia** (so͞ov lä′kyä). [1945–50; < ModGk *soublάki* small spit, deriv. of *soúbla* spit, skewer << L *sūbula* shoemaker's awl, equiv. to *sū-,* base of *su(ere)* to SEW[1] + *-bula* suffix of instruments]

sou′•west•er (sou′wes′tər), *n.* 1. a waterproof hat, often of oilskin, having the brim very broad behind and slanted, worn esp. by seamen. 2. an oilskin slicker, fastening with buckles, worn esp. by seamen in rough weather. 3. southwester (def. 1). Also called **nor′wester** (for defs. 1, 2). [1830–40; reduced form of SOUTHWESTER]

sou'wester (def. 1)

sov•er•eign (sov′rin, sov′ər in, suv′-), *n.* 1. a monarch; a king, queen, or other supreme ruler. 2. a person who has sovereign power or authority. 3. a group or body of persons or a state having sovereign authority. 4. a gold coin of the United Kingdom, equal to one pound sterling: went out of circulation after 1914. —*adj.* 5. belonging to or characteristic of a sovereign or sovereignty; royal. 6. having supreme rank, power, or authority. 7. supreme; preeminent; indisputable: *a sovereign right.* 8. greatest in degree; utmost or extreme. 9. being above all others in character, importance, excellence, etc. 10. efficacious; potent: *a sovereign remedy.* [1250–1300; ME *soverain* (alter. by influence of REIGN) < OF *soverain* < VL **superānus,* equiv. to L *super-* SUPER- + *-ānus* -AN] —**sov′er•eign•ly,** *adv.*
—**Syn.** 1. emperor, empress, potentate. 3. government. 5. regal, majestic, imperial, princely, monarchical, kingly, queenly. 7. chief, paramount, principal, predominant. 10. effective, effectual.

sov•er•eign•ty (sov′rin tē, suv′-), *n., pl.* **-ties.** 1. the quality or state of being sovereign. 2. the status, dominion, power, or authority of a sovereign; royalty. 3. supreme and independent power or authority in government as possessed or claimed by a state or community. 4. rightful status, independence, or prerogative. 5. a sovereign state, community, or political unit. [1300–50; ME *soverainte* < AF *sovereynete* (OF *soverainete*), equiv. to *soverain* SOVEREIGN + *-ete* -TY[2]]

So•vetsk (sōv yetsk′; *Russ.* su vyetsk′), *n.* a city in the W Russian Federation in Europe, NE of Kaliningrad on the Neman River: formerly in East Prussia; peace treaty (1807) between France, Prussia, and Russia. 40,000. Formerly (until 1945), **Tilsit.**

so•vi•et (sō′vē et′, -it, sō′vē et′), *n.* 1. (in the Soviet Union). a. (before the revolution) any governmental council. b. (after the revolution) a local council, originally elected only by manual workers, with certain powers of local administration. c. (after the revolution) a higher council elected by a local council, being part of a hierarchy of soviets culminating in the Supreme Soviet. 2. any similar council or assembly connected with a socialistic governmental system elsewhere. 3. (*cap.*) Often, **Soviets.** a governing official or person living in the Soviet Union: *The Soviets have denied our charge.* —*adj.* 4. of or pertaining to a soviet. 5. (*cap.*) of the Soviet Union: *a Soviet statesman.* [1915–20; < Russ *sovét* council, counsel, advice, ORuss, OCS *sŭvětŭ,* equiv. to *sŭ-* together, with + *větŭ* counsel; calque of Gk *symboúlion*] —**so•vi•et•dom** (sō′vē et′dəm, -it-, sō′vē et′-), *n.*

So•vi•et•ism (sō′vē i tiz′əm), *n.* 1. (*sometimes l.c.*) a soviet system of government. 2. (*often l.c.*) the practices and principles of a soviet government, esp. as it implies communism. 3. a characteristic, mannerism, phrase, etc., expressive of or identifiable with the ideology of the Soviet Union. [1915–20; SOVIET + -ISM] —**So′vi•et•ist,** *n., adj.*

So•vi•et•ize (sō′vē i tīz′), *v.t.,* **-ized, -iz•ing.** 1. (*sometimes l.c.*) to bring under the influence or domination of the Soviet Union. 2. (*often l.c.*) to impose or institute a system of government similar to that of the Soviet Union. Also, *esp. Brit.,* **So′vi•et•ise′.** [1915–20; SOVIET + -IZE] —**So′vi•et•i•za′tion,** *n.*

So′viet of National′ities. See under **Supreme Soviet.**

So′viet of the Un′ion. See under **Supreme Soviet.**

So•vi•et•ol•o•gy (sō′vē i tol′ə jē), *n.* Kremlinology. [1960–65; SOVIET + -O- + -LOGY] —**So′vi•et•ol′o•gist,** *n.*

So′viet Rus′sia, 1. a conventional name of the Soviet Union. 2. See **Russian Soviet Federated Socialist Republic.**

So′viet Un′ion. See **Union of Soviet Socialist Republics.**

SOV language, *Ling.* a type of language that has basic subject-object-verb order, as Turkish, Japanese, or Tamil. Cf. **OV language, SVO language, VSO language.**

sov•ran (sov′rən, suv′-), *n., adj. Literary.* sovereign. [1625–35; alter. of SOVEREIGN, modeled on It *sovrano*]

Sov. Un., Soviet Union.

sow[1] (sō), *v.,* **sowed, sown** or **sowed, sow•ing.** —*v.t.* 1. to scatter (seed) over land, earth, etc., for growth; plant. 2. to plant seed for: *to sow a crop.* 3. to scatter seed over (land, earth, etc.) for the purpose of growth. 4. to implant, introduce, or promulgate; seek to propagate or extend; disseminate: *to sow distrust or dissension.* 5. to strew or sprinkle with anything. —*v.i.* 6. to sow seed, as for the production of a crop. [bef. 900; ME *sowen,* OE *sāwan;* c. D *zaaien,* G *säen,* ON *sā,* Goth *saian;* akin to SEED, L *sēmen* seed, *serere* to sow] —**sow′a•ble,** *adj.* —**sow′er,** *n.*
—**Syn.** 4. inject, lodge, circulate.

sow[2] (sou), *n.* 1. an adult female swine. 2. the adult female of various other animals, as the bear. 3. *Metall.* a. a large oblong mass of iron that has solidified in the common channel through which the molten metal flows to the smaller channels in which the pigs solidify. b. the common channel itself. c. a basin holding any of certain molten nonferrous metals to be cast. [bef. 900; ME *sowe,* OE *sugu;* c. G *Sau,* ON *sȳr,* L *sūs,* Gk *hŷs,* Tocharian B *suwo;* see SWINE] —**sow′like′,** *adj.*

sow•bel•ly (sou′bel′ē), *n.* fat salt pork taken from the belly of a hog. [1865–70, *Amer.*; SOW[2] + BELLY]

sow•bread (sou′bred′), *n.* any of several species of cyclamen, esp. *Cyclamen hederifolium,* a low-growing Old World plant having mottled leaves and pink or white flowers. [1540–50; SOW[2] + BREAD; so called because the roots are sought after by hogs]

sow′ bug′ (sou), any of several small, terrestrial isopods, esp. of the genus *Oniscus;* wood louse. [1740–50]

sow•car (sou kär′), *n.* soucar.

sow•ens (sō′ənz, so͞o′-), *n.* (*used with a singular v.*) *Scot., Irish Eng.* porridge made from oat bran or husks that have been soaked in water, slightly fermented, and then boiled. [1575–85; < ScotGael *sùghan,* deriv. of *sùgh* sap]

So•we•to (sə wē′tō, -wā′-), *n.* a group of townships in NE South Africa, SW of and administered by Johannesburg: constructed in the 1950's and early 1960's to provide housing and services for black Africans. 550,000; 26 sq. mi. (67 sq. km).

sown (sōn), *v.* a pp. of **sow**[1].

sow′ this′tle (sou), any composite plant belonging to the genus *Sonchus,* esp. *S. oleraceus,* a weed having thistlelike leaves, yellow flowers, and a milky juice. [1200–50; ME *sowethistel,* earlier *sugethistel.* See SOW[2], THISTLE]

sox (soks), *n.* a pl. of **sock**[1].

soy (soi), *n.* 1. See **soy sauce.** 2. the soybean. [1690–1700; perh. via D or NL < Japn *shōyu,* earlier *shaùyu* < MChin, equiv. to Chin *jìngyóu* soybean oil]

soy′a bean′ (soi′ə), *n.* soybean. [*soya* < D *soja* << Japn; see SOY]

soy•bean (soi′bēn′), *n.* 1. a bushy Old World plant, *Glycine max,* of the legume family, grown in the U.S., chiefly for forage and soil improvement. 2. the seed of this plant, used for food, as a livestock feed, and for a variety of other commercial uses. [1795–1805; SOY + BEAN]

soy′bean milk′, a milk substitute made of soy flour and water, used esp. in the making of tofu. Also called **soy′a milk′.**

soy′bean oil′, a pale-yellow oil derived from soybeans by expression or solvent extraction: used as a food and in the manufacture of soap, candles, inks, paints, varnishes, etc. Also called **soy′a oil′.** [1915–20]

soy′ flour′, finely ground soybeans, most commonly used as an additive to other flours, processed meats, cereals, etc. [1895–1900]

So·yin·ka (shô ying′kə), *n.* **Wo·le** (wō′lā), born 1934, Nigerian playwright, novelist, and poet: Nobel prize 1986.

soy′ sauce′, a salty, fermented sauce much used on fish and other dishes in the Orient, prepared from soybeans. Also, **soy′a sauce′.** [1785–95]

So·yuz (sô′yo͞oz; *Russ.* su yo͞oz′), *n.* one of a series of Soviet spacecraft, carrying one, two, or three cosmonauts, who carried out scientific research and developed rendezvous and docking techniques: still used to ferry crews to Soviet space stations. [< Russ *Soyúz* lit., union]

Soz·zi·ni (sôt tsē′nē), *n.* Italian name of **Socinus.**

soz·zled (soz′əld), *adj. Slang.* drunk; inebriated. [1875–80; dial. *sozzle* confused state, sloppy person (earlier *sossle;* akin to SOUSE) + -ED[3]]

SP, 1. Shore Patrol. **2.** Specialist. **3.** Submarine Patrol.

Sp., 1. Spain. **2.** Spaniard. **3.** Also, **Sp** Spanish (def. 3).

sp., 1. special. **2.** species. **3.** specific. **4.** specimen. **5.** spelling. **6.** spirit.

S.P., 1. Shore Patrol. **2.** Socialist party. **3.** Submarine Patrol.

s.p., without issue; childless. [< L *sine prōle*]

spa (spä), *n.* **1.** a mineral spring, or a locality in which such springs exist. **2.** a luxurious resort or resort hotel. **3.** See **health spa. 4.** a hot tub or similar warm-water hydromassage facility, usually for more than one person. **5.** *New Eng.* See **soda fountain.** [1555–65; generalized use of SPA]

Spa (spä), *n.* a resort town in E Belgium, SE of Liège: famous mineral springs. 9391.

Spaak (späk; *Fr.* spak), *n.* **Paul Hen·ri** (pôl hen′rē; *Fr.* pôl äɴ rē′), 1889–1972, Belgian statesman: prime minister of Belgium, 1938–39, 1946–49; first president of the General Assembly of the United Nations 1946–47; secretary-general of NATO 1957–61.

Spaatz (späts), *n.* **Carl,** 1891–1974, U.S. general.

space (spās), *n., v.,* **spaced, spac·ing,** *adj.* —*n.* **1.** the unlimited or incalculably great three-dimensional realm or expanse in which all material objects are located and all events occur. **2.** the portion or extent of this in a given instance; extent or room in three dimensions: *the space occupied by a body.* **3.** extent or area in two dimensions; a particular extent of surface: *to fill out blank spaces in a document.* **4.** *Fine Arts.* **a.** the designed and structured surface of a picture: *In Mondrian's later work he organized space in highly complex rhythms.* **b.** the illusion of depth on a two-dimensional surface. **5.** See **outer space. 6.** See **deep space. 7.** a seat, berth, or room on a train, airplane, etc. **8.** a place available for a particular purpose: *a parking space.* **9.** linear distance; a particular distance: *trees separated by equal spaces.* **10.** *Math.* a system of objects with relations between the objects defined. **11.** extent, or a particular extent, of time: *a space of two hours.* **12.** an interval of time; a while: *After a space he continued his story.* **13.** an area or interval allowed for or taken by advertising, as in a periodical, on the radio, etc. **14.** *Music.* the interval between two adjacent lines of the staff. **15.** an interval or blank area in text: *a space between the letters.* **16.** *Print.* one of the blank pieces of metal, less than type-high, used to separate words, sentences, etc. **17.** *Telegraphy.* an interval during the transmitting of a message when the key is not in contact. **18.** radio or television broadcast time allowed or available for a program, advertisement, etc. **19.** freedom or opportunity to express oneself, resolve a personal difficulty, be alone, etc.; allowance, understanding, or noninterference: *Right now, you can help by giving me some space.* —*v.t.* **20.** to fix the space or spaces of; divide into spaces. **21.** to set some distance apart. **22.** *Print., Writing.* **a.** to separate (words, letters, or lines) by spaces. **b.** to extend by inserting more space or spaces (usually fol. by *out*). —*adj.* **23.** of, pertaining to, or concerned with outer space or deep space: *a space mission.* **24.** designed for or suitable to use in the exploration of outer space or deep space: *space tools; specially packaged space food for astronauts.* [1250–1300; ME (n.) < OF *espace* < L *spatium*] —**spac′er,** *n.*

Space′ Age′, the period in modern history characterized by space exploration, usually considered as beginning October 4, 1957, when the Soviet Union launched the first artificial satellite, Sputnik I, into orbit around the earth. Also, **space′ age′.**

space-age (spās′āj′), *adj.* **1.** pertaining to or characteristic of the Space Age. **2.** using the latest or most advanced technology or design. **3.** modern; up-to-date; forward-looking. [1955–60]

space·band (spās′band′), *Print.* a wedge-shaped piece of metal used in typecasting machines to adjust the space between words and to justify lines of type. [1900–05; SPACE + BAND[2]]

space′ bar′, 1. a horizontal bar on a typewriter keyboard that is depressed in order to resume typing one space to the right. **2.** a horizontal bar on a computer keyboard that is depressed in order to move the cursor one space to the right or, often, to perform some function in a program. [1885–90]

space′ biol′ogy, exobiology. [1955–60]

space·borne (spās′bôrn′, -bōrn′), *adj.* **1.** moving in orbit around the earth: *a spaceborne surveillance system.* **2.** traveling through or operating in space. [1965–70; SPACE + (AIR)BORNE]

space′ cadet′, *Slang.* **1.** a person who appears to be in his or her own world or out of touch with reality. **2.** a person who behaves oddly or seems stupefied or remote because of the influence of drugs; druggie. [1950–55, for sense "spaceman trainee"]

space′ cap′sule, *Aerospace.* capsule (def. 5).

space′ car′rier, *Rocketry.* a vehicle designed to put payloads in orbit about the earth or to boost payloads for extraterrestrial exploration.

space′ charge′, *Elect.* a distribution of an excess of electrons or ions over a three-dimensional region, in contrast to the distribution of an electric charge over the surface of a conductor. [1910–15]

space·craft (spās′kraft′, -kräft′), *n.* a vehicle designed for travel or operation in space beyond the earth's atmosphere or in orbit around the earth. [1955–60; SPACE + CRAFT]

spaced-out (spāst′out′), *adj. Slang.* **1.** dazed or stupefied because of the influence of narcotic drugs. **2.** dreamily or eerily out of touch with reality or seemingly so; spacey. Also, **spaced.** [1965–70, *Amer.*; on the pattern of phrasal verbs with *out* marking perfectivity; *space* appar. by assoc. with "outer space" as, metaphorically, a place outside normal consciousness]

space·flight (spās′flīt′), *n.* the flying of manned or unmanned spacecraft into or in outer space. Also, **space′ flight′.** [1945–50; SPACE + FLIGHT[1]]

space′ group′, *Crystall.* a set of symmetry elements that brings a periodic arrangement of points on a Bravais space lattice to its original position.

space′ heat′ing, the heating of a limited area, as a room, by means of a heater **(space′ heat′er)** within the area. [1930–35] —**space′-heat′ing,** *adj.*

space′ inver′sion, *Physics.* the mathematical operation of reversing the directions of all three space coordinates. *Symbol:* P Also called **parity operation, space reflection.**

Space·lab (spās′lab′), *n.* a manned laboratory in space, developed by the European Space Agency, carried aboard an orbiting space shuttle.

space′ lat′tice, lattice (def. 4). [1905–10]

space′ law′, the projected law that would govern the use of outer space by various nations based on certain treaties. [1950–55]

space·less (spās′lis), *adj.* **1.** having no limits or dimensions in space; limitless; unbounded. **2.** occupying no space. [1600–10; SPACE + -LESS]

space′ man′. See **space writer.** [1890–95]

space·man (spās′man′, -mən), *n., pl.* **-men** (-men′, -mən). **1.** an astronaut. **2.** a visitor to earth from outer space; extraterrestrial. [1935–40; SPACE + MAN[1]] —**Usage.** See **-man.**

space′ mark′, *Print.* a proofreader's symbol used to indicate the need to insert space, as between two typed or printed words that have been run together. *Symbol:* # Cf. **hash mark, number sign, pound sign** (def. 2). [1885–90]

space′ med′icine, the branch of aviation medicine dealing with the effects on humans of flying outside the earth's atmosphere. [1950–55]

space′ op′er·a (op′ər ə, op′rə), a television or radio drama or motion picture that is a science-fiction adventure story. [1945–50]

space′ plat′form. See **space station.** [1955–60]

space·port (spās′pôrt′, -pōrt′), *n.* a site at which spacecraft are tested, launched, sheltered, maintained, etc. [1950–55; SPACE + PORT[1]]

space′ probe′, *Aerospace.* an unmanned spacecraft designed to explore the solar system and transmit data back to earth. Also called **probe.** [1955–60]

space′ rate′, a unit of compensation for written work, based on the amount of space that the submitted material occupies in print, and usually computed in column inches. Cf. **piece rate.** [1905–10]

space′ reflec′tion. See **space inversion.**

space-sav·ing (spās′sā′ving), *adj.* **1.** that saves space. —*n.* **2.** the act or process of saving space.

space′ sci′ence, any of the sciences involved in space travel or the exploration of space, as space medicine. [1975–80] —**space′ sci′entist.**

space·ship (spās′ship′), *n.* spacecraft. [1940–45; SPACE + SHIP]

space·shot (spās′shot′), *n.* a launch of a space vehicle beyond the earth's atmosphere. [1960–65; SPACE + SHOT[1]]

space′ shut′tle, (*often caps.*) any of several U.S. space vehicles consisting of a reusable manned orbiter that touches down on a landing strip after an orbital mission, two reusable solid rocket boosters that drop off after initial ascent, and an expendable external tank containing liquid propellants. [1965–70, *Amer.*]

space′ shut′tle or′biter, (*sometimes caps.*) orbiter (def. 1).

space′ sick′ness, *Pathol.* a complex of symptoms including nausea, lethargy, headache, and sweating, occurring among astronauts under conditions of weightlessness. [1950–55]

space′ stage′, a stage set, often limited to an arrangement of ramps and platforms, in which actors and set pieces are spotlighted against the bare background of a dark or black cyclorama.

space′ sta′tion, an orbiting manned structure that can be used for a variety of purposes, as to assemble or service satellites, refuel spacecraft, etc. Also called **space platform.** [1940–45] —**space′-sta′tion,** *adj.*

space·suit (spās′so͞ot′), *n.* a sealed and pressurized suit designed to allow the wearer to leave a pressurized cabin in outer space or at extremely high altitudes within the atmosphere. Also, **space′ suit′.** [1935–40; SPACE + SUIT]

Space′ Tel′escope, *U.S. Aerospace.* a 7.9-ft. (2.4-m) optical telescope designed for use in orbit around the earth. Also called **Hubble Space Telescope.**

space-time (spās′tīm′), *n.* **1.** Also called **space′-time′ contin′uum.** the four-dimensional continuum, having three spatial coordinates and one temporal coordinate, in which all physical quantities may be located. **2.** the physical reality that exists within this four-dimensional continuum. —*adj.* **3.** of, pertaining to, or noting a system with three spatial coordinates and one temporal coordinate. **4.** noting, pertaining to, or involving both space and time: *a space-time problem.* [1910–15]

space′ trav′el, spaceflight of manned vehicles.

space·walk (spās′wôk′), *n.* **1.** a task or mission performed by an astronaut outside a spacecraft in space. —*v.i.* **2.** to execute such a task or mission. [1960–65, *Amer.*; SPACE + WALK] —**space′walk′er,** *n.*

space·wom·an (spās′wo͝om′ən), *n., pl.* **-wom·en.** a woman astronaut. [1960–65; SPACE(MAN) + -WOMAN] —**Usage.** See **-woman.**

space′ writ′er, a journalist or copywriter paid according to a space rate. Also called **space man.** Cf. **stringer** (def. 6). [1890–95]

spac·ey (spā′sē), *adj.,* **spac·i·er, spac·i·est.** spaced-out (def. 2). Also, **spac′y.** [1965–70, *Amer.*; SPACE + -EY[1]]

spa·cial (spā′shəl), *adj.* spatial. —**spa·ci·al·i·ty** (spā′shē al′i tē), *n.* —**spa′cial·ly,** *adv.*

spac·ing (spā′sing), *n.* **1.** an act of someone or something that spaces. **2.** the fixing or arranging of spaces. [1675–85; SPACE + -ING[1]]

spa·cious (spā′shəs), *adj.* **1.** containing much space, as a house, room, or vehicle; amply large. **2.** occupying much space; vast. **3.** of a great extent or area; broad; large; great: *the spacious prairies.* **4.** broad in scope, range, inclusiveness, etc.: *a spacious approach to a problem.* [1350–1400; ME < L *spatiōsus,* equiv. to *spati(um)* SPACE + *-ōsus* -OUS] —**spa′cious·ly,** *adv.* —**spa′cious·ness,** *n.*
—**Syn. 1.** roomy, capacious. **2.** extensive, huge, tremendous. —**Ant. 1.** small, cramped.

spack·le (spak′əl), *v.,* **-led, -ling. 1.** (*cap.*) *Trademark.* a brand of quick-drying, plasterlike material for patching plasterwork. —*v.t., v.i.* **2.** to patch with Spackle.

spade[1] (spād), *n., v.,* **spad·ed, spad·ing.** —*n.* **1.** a tool for digging, having an iron blade adapted for pressing into the ground with the foot and a long handle commonly with a grip or crosspiece at the top, and with the blade usually narrower and flatter than that of a shovel. **2.** some implement, piece, or part resembling this. **3.** a sharp projection on the bottom of a gun trail, designed to dig into the earth to restrict backward movement of the carriage during recoil. **4. call a spade a spade,** to call something by its real name; be candidly explicit; speak plainly or bluntly: *To call a spade a spade, he's a crook.* **5. in spades,** *Informal.* **a.** in the extreme; positively: *He's a hypocrite, in spades.* **b.** without restraint; outspokenly: *I told him what I thought, in spades.* —*v.t.* **6.** to dig, cut, or remove with a spade (sometimes fol. by *up*): *Let's spade up the garden and plant some flowers.* [bef. 900; ME (n.); OE *spadu;* c. D *spade,* G *Spaten,* ON *spathi* spade, Gk *spáthē* broad, flat piece of wood] —**spade′like′,** *adj.* —**spad′er,** *n.*

spade[2] (spād), *n.* **1.** a black figure shaped like an inverted heart and with a short stem at the cusp opposite the point, used on playing cards. **2.** a card of the suit bearing such figures. **3. spades, a.** (*used with a singular or plural v.*) the suit so marked: *Spades is trump. Spades count double.* **b.** (*used with a plural v.*) *Casino.* the winning of seven spades or more. **4.** *Slang (disparaging and offensive).* a black person. [1590–1600; < It, pl. of *spada* orig., sword < L *spatha* < Gk *spáthē;* see SPADE[1]]

spade·fish (spād′fish′), *n., pl.* (*esp. collectively*) **-fish,** (*esp. referring to two or more kinds or species*) **-fish·es.** a deep-bodied marine fish of the genus *Chaetodipterus,* esp. *C. faber,* of Atlantic coastal waters of North America. [1695–1705; prob. SPADE[2] + FISH, in allusion to its shape]

spade′ foot′, *Furniture.* a square foot, tapering toward its bottom. [1890–95]

spade·foot (spād′fo͝ot′), *n., pl.* **-foots.** See **spadefoot toad.** [1835–45; SPADE[1] + FOOT]

spade′foot toad′, any of several nocturnal toads of the family Pelobatidae, common in the Northern Hemisphere, characterized by a horny, spadelike projection on each hind foot for burrowing under the soil. [1865–70, *Amer.*]

spade·ful (spād′fo͝ol), *n., pl.* **-fuls.** the amount that can be dug out with or carried on a spade. [1635–45; SPADE[1] + -FUL]

spade·work (spād′wûrk′), *n.* preliminary or initial work, such as the gathering of data, on which further activity is to be based. [1770–80; SPADE[1] + WORK]

spa·di·ceous (spā dish′əs), *adj.* **1.** *Bot.* **a.** of the nature of a spadix. **b.** bearing a spadix. **2.** of a bright brown color. [1640–50; < NL *spādiceus,* equiv. to L *spādīc-* (s. of *spādix;* see SPADIX) + *-eus* -EOUS]

spa·dille (spə dil′), *n.* the highest trump in certain card games, as the queen of clubs in omber. [1720–30; < F < Sp *espadilla,* equiv. to *espad(a)* broadsword, spade in cards (< L *spatha;* see SPADE[2]) + *-illa* dim. suffix]

spa·dix (spā′diks), *n., pl.* **spa·di·ces** (spā dī′sēz, spā′-

də sēz′). *Bot.* an inflorescence consisting of a spike with a fleshy or thickened axis, usually enclosed in a spathe. See illus. under **inflorescence.** [1750–60; < L *spādix* a broken palm branch and its fruit < Gk *spádix* a torn-off palm bough, chestnut brown; akin to *spân* to tear off]

spa•do (spā′dō), *n., pl.* **spa•do•nes** (spā dō′nāz, spə-). **1.** *Civil Law.* an impotent person; someone unable to procreate. **2.** a castrated man or animal. [1400–50; late ME < L *spadō* < Gk *spádōn* eunuch; akin to *spân* to tear off]

spae (spā), *v.t.,* **spaed, spae•ing.** *Chiefly Scot.* to prophesy; foretell; predict. [1250–1300; ME *span* < ON *spā*] —**spa′er,** *n.*

spaetz•le (shpet′slə, -səl, -slē), *n.* a dish consisting of lumps or threads made from a batter of flour, milk, eggs, and salt, usually poured through a coarse colander into boiling water, and then either drained and mixed in butter, lightly pan-fried, or added to sauces, stews, etc. [< G (dial.) *Spätzle,* dim. of *Spatz* dumpling, sparrow, MHG, deriv. of *spar* SPARROW]

spa•ghet•ti (spə get′ē), *n.* **1.** a white, starchy pasta of Italian origin that is made in the form of long strings, boiled, and served with any of a variety of meat, tomato, or other sauces. **2.** *Elect.* an insulating tubing of small diameter into which bare wire can be slipped. [1885–90; < It, pl. of *spaghetto,* dim. of *spago* thin rope < LL *spacus* twine, prob. < Gk *sphákos* long-threaded lichen]

spaghet′ti squash′, a variety of a widely cultivated squash, *Cucurbita pepo,* having edible flesh in the form of spaghettilike strands.

spaghet′ti strap′, a thin, often rounded strip of fabric used in women's clothing, as to form a shoulder strap on a bare-shouldered garment. [1970–75]

spaghet′ti west′ern, *Informal.* a low-budget western movie shot in Italy or Spain, usually with Italian actors and an American star. [1965–70]

spa•hi (spä′hē), *n., pl.* **-his. 1.** one of a body of native Algerian cavalry in the French service. **2.** (formerly) a cavalryman in the Turkish army. Also, **spa′hee.** [1555–65; < MF < Turk *sipahi* < Pers *sipāhī.* Cf. SEPOY]

Spain (spān), *n.* a kingdom in SW Europe. Including the Balearic and Canary islands, 36,400,000; 194,988 sq. mi. (505,019 sq. km). *Cap.:* Madrid. Spanish, **España.**

spake (spāk), *v. Archaic.* a pt. of **speak.**

Spa•la•to (spä′lä tô), *n.* Italian name of **Split.**

spal•deen (spôl dēn′), *n. Chiefly New York City.* a smooth, pink rubber ball used in playing catch, stickball, etc. [said to be after *Spalding* a trademark]

Spal•ding (spôl′ding), *n.* **1. Albert,** 1888–1953, U.S. violinist. **2.** a male given name.

spall (spôl), *n.* **1.** a chip or splinter, as of stone or ore. —*v.t.* **2.** to break into smaller pieces, as ore; split or chip. —*v.i.* **3.** to break or split off in chips or bits. [1750–60; orig. uncert.; cf. late ME *spalle* a chip] —**spall′er,** *n.*

Spal•lan•za•ni (spä′lən zä′nē; *It.* späl′län tsä′nē), *n.* **Laz•za•ro** (läd′dzä rô), 1729–99, Italian biologist.

spall•a•tion (spô lā′shən), *n. Physics.* a nuclear reaction in which several nucleons are released from the nucleus of an atom. [1945–50; SPALL + -ATION]

spal•peen (spal pēn′, spal′pēn), *n. Irish Eng.* **1.** a lad or boy. **2.** a rascal; scamp. [1770–80; < Ir *spailpín* seasonal hired laborer, rude person, scamp, equiv. to *spailp* spell, bout, turn + *-ín* n. suffix]

Sp. Am., 1. Spanish America. **2.** Spanish American.

span[1] (span), *n., v.,* **spanned, span•ning.** —*n.* **1.** the distance between the tip of the thumb and the tip of the little finger when the hand is fully extended. **2.** a unit of length corresponding to this distance, commonly taken as 9 in. (23 cm). **3.** a distance, amount, piece, etc., of this length or of some small extent: *a span of lace.* **4.** *Civ. Engin., Archit.* **a.** the distance between two supports of a structure. **b.** the structure so supported. **c.** the distance or space between two supports of a bridge. **5.** the full extent, stretch, or reach of anything: *a long span of memory.* **6.** *Aeron.* the distance between the wing tips of an airplane. **7.** a limited space of time, as the term or period of living: *Our span on earth is short.* **8.** *Math.* the smallest subspace of a vector space that contains a given element or set of elements. —*v.t.* **9.** to measure by the hand with the thumb and little finger extended. **10.** to encircle with the hand or hands, as the waist. **11.** to extend over or across (a section of land, a river, etc.). **12.** to provide with something that extends over: *to span a river with a bridge.* **13.** to extend or reach over (space or time): *a memory that spans 90 years.* **14.** *Math.* to function (in a subspace of a vector space) as a span. **15.** *Archery.* to bend (the bow) in preparation for shooting. [bef. 900; (n.) ME *spanne, sponne, spayn,* OE *span(n), spon(n);* c. G *Spanne,* D *span,* ON *sponn;* (v.) ME *spaynen,* deriv. of the n.]

span[2] (span), *n.* a pair of horses or other animals harnessed and driven together. [1760–70, *Amer.;* < D: team (of oxen, horses)]
—**Syn.** team. See **pair.**

span[3] (span), *v. Archaic.* a pt. of **spin.**

Span., 1. Spaniard. **2.** Spanish.

span•cel (span′səl), *n., v.,* **-celed, -cel•ing** or (*esp. Brit.*) **-celled, -cel•ling.** —*n.* **1.** a noosed rope with which to hobble an animal, esp. a horse or cow. —*v.t.* **2.** to fetter with or as with a spancel. [1600–10; < LG *spansel,* deriv. of *spannen* to stretch; see SPAN[2]]

Span•dau (shpän′dou), *n.* a district of Berlin, in E Germany; site of prison for Nazi war criminals.

span•dex (span′deks), *n. Chem.* a synthetic fiber composed of a long-chain polymer, used chiefly in the manufacture of garments to add elasticity. [1955–60; anagram of *expands*]

span•drel (span′drəl), *n.* **1.** *Archit.* an area between the extradoses of two adjoining arches, or between the extrados of an arch and a perpendicular through the extrados at the springing line. **2.** (in a steel-framed building) a panellike area between the head of a window on one level and the sill of a window immediately above. **3.** *Philately.* the decoration occupying the space at the corner of a stamp between the border and an oval or circular central design. Also, **span′dril.** [1470–80; earlier *spaundrell,* prob. < AF *spaundre,* itself perh. c. OF *espandre* to EXPAND]

S, spandrel (def. 1)

spang (spang), *adv. Informal.* directly, exactly: *The bullet landed spang on target.* [1835–45, *Amer.;* orig. uncert.]

span•gle (spang′gəl), *n., v.,* **-gled, -gling.** —*n.* **1.** a small, thin, often circular piece of glittering metal or other material, used esp. for decorating garments. **2.** any small, bright drop, object, spot, or the like. —*v.t.* **3.** to decorate with spangles. **4.** to sprinkle or stud with small, bright pieces, objects, spots, etc. —*v.i.* **5.** to glitter with or like spangles. [1375–1425; late ME *spangele* (n.), equiv. to *spange* spangle (perh. < MD) + *-le* -LE] —**span′gly,** *adj.*

span′gled glass′, an American art glass having flakes of mica in a layer of clear glass flashed with colored glass.

Spang•lish (spang′glish *or, often,* -lish), *n.* Spanish spoken with a large admixture of English, esp. American, words and expressions. [1965–70; b. SPANISH and ENGLISH]

Span•iard (span′yərd), *n.* a native or inhabitant of Spain. [1350–1400; ME *Spaignarde* < OF *(e)spaignart,* equiv. to *Espaigne* SPAIN + *-art* -ARD]

span•iel (span′yəl), *n.* **1.** one of any of several breeds of small or medium-sized dogs, usually having a long, silky coat and long, drooping ears. **2.** a submissive, fawning, or cringing person. [1350–1400; ME *spaynel* < OF *espaignol* Spanish (dog), deriv. of *Espaigne* SPAIN] —**span′iel•like′,** *adj.*

Span•ish (span′ish), *adj.* **1.** of or pertaining to Spain, its people, or their language. —*n.* **2.** the Spanish people collectively. **3.** a Romance language, the language of Spain, standard also in most of Latin America except Brazil. *Abbr.:* Sp, Sp. [1175–1225; ME; see SPAIN, -ISH[1]]

Span′ish Amer′ica, the Spanish-speaking countries south of the U.S.: Mexico, Central America (with the exception of Belize), South America (with the exceptions of Brazil, French Guiana, Guyana, and Suriname), and most of the West Indies.

Span′ish Amer′ican, 1. a person of Latin-American descent living in the U.S. **2.** a person of Spanish descent living in the U.S. **3.** a native or inhabitant of a Spanish-American country.

Span•ish-A•mer•i•can (span′ish ə mer′i kən), *adj.* **1.** noting or pertaining to the parts of America where Spanish is the prevailing language. **2.** pertaining to Spain and America, sometimes to Spain and the United States: *an example of Spanish-American cooperation.* **3.** of or pertaining to the natives or inhabitants of Spanish America, esp. those of Spanish descent. **4.** of or pertaining to persons of Latin-American descent living in the U.S. **5.** of or pertaining to persons of Spanish descent living in the U.S. [1780–90, *Amer.*]

Span′ish-Amer′ican War′, the war between the U.S. and Spain in 1898.

Span′ish Ar′abic, the Arabic language as used in Spain during the period of Moorish domination and influence, c900–1500. *Abbr.:* SpAr

Span′ish Arma′da, Armada (def. 1).

Span′ish bayonet′, any of certain plants belonging to the genus *Yucca,* of the agave family, having narrow, spine-tipped leaves and a cluster of white flowers. [1835–45, *Amer.;* in allusion to its tropical American origin]

Span′ish blue′bell, a bulbous plant, *Endymion hispanicus,* of the lily family, native to Spain and Portugal, having blue, white, or pink, bell-shaped flowers. Also called **Spanish jacinth.**

Span′ish broom′, a spiny, often leafless shrub, *Genista hispanica,* of the legume family, native to southern Europe, having clustered, golden-yellow flowers and hairy pods. [1555–65]

Span′ish bur′ton, *Naut.* any of several tackles employing a runner in addition to the fall. Cf. **single Spanish burton, double Spanish burton.** [1820–30]

Span′ish but′ton, knapweed.

Span′ish ce′dar, 1. a tropical American tree, *Cedrela odorata,* of the mahogany family. **2.** the hard, fragrant, mahoganylike brown wood of this tree, used for making furniture and esp. cigar boxes. Also called **West Indian cedar.** [1975–80]

Span′ish Civ′il War′, the civil war in Spain 1936–39.

Span′ish dag′ger, a stemless or short-trunked plant, *Yucca gloriosa,* of the agave family, native to the southeastern U.S., having leaves nearly 2½ ft. (75 cm) long, with a stiff, sharp point, and greenish-white or reddish flowers nearly 4 in. (10 cm) wide. [1855–60, *Amer.*]

Spanish fly, *Cantharis vesicatoria,* length ¾ in. (1.9 cm)

Span′ish fly′, 1. Also called **cantharides.** a preparation of powdered blister beetles, esp. the Spanish fly, used medicinally as a counterirritant, diuretic, and aphrodisiac. **2.** Also, **Span′ish•fly′.** Also called **cantharis.** a common European blister beetle, *Cantharis (Lytta) vesicatoria,* that yields this preparation. [1400–50; so called from the fact that the beetles are found in abundance in Spain]

Span′ish foot′, *Furniture.* a carved pyramidal foot having fluted, concave sides usually ending in a scroll at the bottom.

Spanish foot

CONCISE ETYMOLOGY KEY: <, descended or borrowed from; >, whence; b., blend of, blended; c., cognate with; cf., compare; deriv., derivative; equiv., equivalent; imit., imitative; obl., oblique; r., replacing; s., stem; sp., spelling, spelled; resp., respelling, respelled; trans., translation; ?, origin unknown; *, unattested; ‡, probably earlier than. See the full key inside the front cover.

Span′ish Guin′ea, former name of **Equatorial Guinea.**

Span′ish guitar′. See **acoustic guitar.** [1860–65]

Span′ish heel′, a high, curved heel with a straight heel breast, used on women's shoes. Cf. **French heel.**

Span′ish influen′za, *Pathol.* the pandemic respiratory infection that spread throughout the world during 1917–18.

Span′ish Inquisi′tion, the Inquisition in Spain, under state control from 1480 to 1834, marked by the extreme severity and cruelty of its proceedings in the 16th century.

Span′ish i′ris, an iris, *Iris xyphium,* of the Mediterranean region, having blue, white, or yellow flowers with a yellow or orange patch.

Span′ish ja′cinth. See **Spanish bluebell.**

Span′ish jas′mine, a shrub, *Jasminum grandiflorum,* of India, having crimson-tinged, fragrant white flowers, grown as an ornamental and for perfume. Also called **Catalonian jasmine.**

Span′ish lime′, genip (def. 2).

Span′ish mack′erel, 1. an American game fish, *Scomberomorus maculatus,* inhabiting the Atlantic Ocean. **2.** any of various similar scombroid fishes. **3.** (in California) the jack mackerel. [1660–70, *Amer.*]

Span′ish Main′, 1. (formerly) the mainland of America adjacent to the Caribbean Sea, esp. the area between the mouth of the Orinoco River and the Isthmus of Panama. **2.** the Caribbean Sea: the route of the Spanish treasure galleons and a former haunt of pirates.

Span′ish Moroc′co. See under **Morocco** (def. 1).

Span′ish moss′, an epiphytic plant, *Tillandsia usneoides,* of the southern U.S., having narrow, grayish leaves and growing in long festoons that drape the branches of trees. [1815–25, *Amer.*]

Span′ish nee′dles, 1. a composite plant, *Bidens bipinnata,* having achenes with downwardly barbed awns. **2.** the achenes themselves. [1735–45, *Amer.*; in allusion to its tropical American origin]

Span′ish om′elet, an omelet served with a sauce of tomatoes, onions, and green peppers. [1905–10]

Span′ish on′ion, a large-sized, mild, succulent onion, often eaten raw.

Span′ish oys′ter plant′, a composite plant, *Scolymus hispanicus,* of southern Europe, having spiny, thistlelike leaf margins, small yellow flowers, and an edible root. Also called **golden thistle.**

Span′ish papri′ka, 1. a cultivated pepper, *Capsicum annuum,* grown originally in Spain. **2.** a spice or condiment made from the ground-up pod of this plant.

Span′ish plum′. See **purple mombin.**

Span′ish rice′, rice prepared with chopped onions, tomatoes, green peppers, and sometimes diced ham, seasoned with cayenne pepper and mixed with butter. [1925–30]

Span′ish Sahar′a, former name of **Western Sahara.**

Span′ish to′paz, citrine (def. 2).

Span′ish tre′foil, alfalfa. [1835–45, *Amer.*]

spank[1] (spangk), *v.t.* **1.** to strike (a person, usually a child) with the open hand, a slipper, etc., esp. on the buttocks, as in punishment. —*n.* **2.** a blow given in spanking; a smart or resounding slap. [1720–30; imit.]

spank[2] (spangk), *v.i.* to move rapidly, smartly, or briskly. [1800–10; back formation from SPANKING]

spank·er (spang′kər), *n.* **1.** *Naut.* **a.** a fore-and-aft sail on the aftermost lower mast of a sailing vessel having three or more masts. See diag. under **ship. b.** a designation given to the mast abaft a mizzenmast, usually the aftermost mast in any vessel. **2.** *Informal.* a smartly moving person or animal, esp. a fast horse. **3.** *Chiefly New England.* something remarkably fine. —*adj. Naut.* **4.** of or pertaining to a spanker mast or its rigging. [1745–55; akin to SPANKING]

spank·ing (spang′king), *adj.* **1.** moving rapidly and smartly. **2.** quick and vigorous: *a spanking pace.* **3.** blowing briskly: *a spanking breeze.* **4.** *Informal.* unusually fine, great, large, etc.; remarkable; distinctive: *a spanking monogram in gold embroidery.* —*adv.* **5.** *Informal.* extremely, strikingly, or remarkably; very: *three little girls in spanking new dresses.* [1660–70; perh. < Scand; cf. Dan, Norw *spanke,* Sw *spånka* to strut] —**spank′ing·ly,** *adv.*

span′ load′ing, *Aeron.* See under **loading** (def. 4).

span·ner (span′ər), *n.* **1.** a person or thing that spans. **2.** Also called **span′ner wrench′.** a wrench having a curved head with a hook or pin at one end for engaging notches or holes in collars, certain kinds of nuts, etc. Cf. **pin wrench. 3.** *Chiefly Brit.* a wrench, esp. one with fixed jaws. [1630–40; SPAN[1] + -ER[1]]

span-new (span′no͞o′, -nyo͞o′), *adj.* brand-new. [1250–1300; ME *spannewe* < ON *spānnȳr* brand-new, fresh, equiv. to *spānn* chip shavings, shingle + *nȳr* new]

span′ of atten′tion, *Psychol.* See **attention span.**

span·rail (span′rāl′), *n.* a rail connecting two legs of furniture; stretcher. [SPAN[1] + RAIL[1]]

span′ roof′, a roof having two slopes of equal breadth and pitch meeting at a common ridge. [1815–25]

span·worm (span′wûrm′), *n.* measuringworm. [1810–20, *Amer.*; SPAN[1] + WORM]

spar[1] (spär), *n., v.,* **sparred, spar·ring.** —*n.* **1.** *Naut.* a stout pole such as those used for masts, etc.; a mast, yard, boom, gaff, or the like. **2.** *Aeron.* a principal lateral member of the framework of a wing of an airplane. —*v.t.* **3.** to provide or make with spars. [1250–1300; ME *sparre* (n.); c. G *Sparren,* D *spar,* ON *sparri*] —**spar′like′,** *adj.*

spar[2] (spär), *v.,* **sparred, spar·ring,** *n.* —*v.i.* **1.** (of boxers) to make the motions of attack and defense with the arms and fists, esp. as a part of training. **2.** to box, esp. with light blows. **3.** to strike or attack with the feet or spurs, as gamecocks do. **4.** to bandy words; dispute. —*n.* **5.** a motion of sparring. **6.** a boxing match. **7.** a dispute. [1350–1400; ME: orig., thrust (n. and v.); perh. akin to SPUR]

spar[3] (spär), *n.* any of various more or less lustrous crystalline minerals: *fluorspar.* [1575–85; back formation from *sparstone* spar, OE *spærstān* gypsum; cf. MLG *spar*] —**spar′like′,** *adj.*

SPAR (spär), *n.* (during World War II) a woman enlisted in the women's reserve of the U.S. Coast Guard (disbanded in 1946). Also, **Spar.** [1942; < L *S(emper) par(ātus)* "Always ready" the Coast Guard motto]

SpAr, Spanish Arabic.

spar·ag·mos (spə rag′məs), *n.* the tearing to pieces of a live victim, as a bull or a calf, by a band of bacchantes in a Dionysian orgy. [< Gk *sparagmós* lit., tearing]

spa·ras·sis (spə ras′is), *n.* See **cauliflower fungus.** [< NL < Gk *sparássein* to tear + -(s)is -SIS]

spar′ deck′, *Naut.* the upper deck of a vessel, extending from stem to stern. Cf. **main deck.** [1560–70]

spare (spâr), *v.,* **spared, spar·ing,** *adj.,* **spar·er, spar·est,** *n.* —*v.t.* **1.** to refrain from harming or destroying; leave uninjured; forbear to punish, hurt, or destroy: *to spare one's enemy.* **2.** to deal gently or leniently with; show consideration for: *His harsh criticism spared no one.* **3.** to save from strain, discomfort, embarrassment, or the like, or from a particular cause of it: *to spare him the bother; to spare her needless embarrassment.* **4.** to refrain from, forbear, omit, or withhold, as action or speech: *Spare us the gory details.* **5.** to refrain from employing, as some instrument or recourse: *to spare the rod.* **6.** to set aside for a particular purpose: *to spare land for a garden.* **7.** to give or lend, as from a supply, esp. without inconvenience or loss: *Can you spare a cup of sugar? Can you spare me a dollar till payday?* **8.** to dispense with or do without: *We can't spare a single worker during the rush hour.* **9.** to use economically or frugally; refrain from using up or wasting: *A walnut sundae, and don't spare the whipped cream!* **10.** to have remaining as excess or surplus: *We can make the curtains and have a yard to spare.* —*v.i.* **11.** to use economy; be frugal. **12.** to refrain from inflicting injury or punishment; exercise lenience or mercy. **13.** *Obs.* to refrain from action; forbear. —*adj.* **14.** kept in reserve, as for possible use: *a spare part.* **15.** being in excess of present need; free for other use: *spare time.* **16.** frugally restricted or meager, as a manner of living or a diet: *a spare regime.* **17.** lean or thin, as a person. **18.** scanty or scant, as in amount or fullness. **19.** sparing, economical, or temperate, as persons. —*n.* **20.** a spare thing, part, etc., as an extra tire for emergency use. **21.** *Ceram.* an area at the top of a plaster mold for holding excess slip. **22.** *Bowling.* **a.** the knocking down of all the pins with two bowls. **b.** a score so made. Cf. **strike** (def. 78). [bef. 900; (v.) ME *sparen,* OE *sparian;* c. D, G *sparen,* ON *spara;* (n. and adj.) ME; cf. OE *spær* sparing, frugal (c. OHG *spar,* ON *sparr*)] —**spare′a·ble,** *adj.* —**spare′ly,** *adv.* —**spare′ness,** *n.* —**spar′er,** *n.*
—**Syn. 6.** reserve. **14, 15.** extra. **17.** See **thin.**

spare·ribs (spâr′ribz′), *n.* (*used with a plural v.*) **1.** a cut of meat from the rib section, esp. of pork or beef, with some meat adhering to the bones. **2.** a dish of this meat, usually baked, roasted, or barbecued with a pungent sauce. [1590–1600; transposed var. of earlier *ribspare* < MLG *ribbespēr* rib cut; cf. obs. *spare* a cut, slice]

spare′ tire′, 1. a tire used or kept available as an emergency replacement on a vehicle. **2.** *Informal.* excess fat around the waistline. [1920–25]

sparge (spärj), *v.,* **sparged, sparg·ing,** *n.* —*v.t., v.i.* **1.** to scatter or sprinkle. —*n.* **2.** a sprinkling. [1550–60; < L *spargere* to sprinkle, scatter] —**sparg′er,** *n.*

spar·id (spar′id), *n.* **1.** any of numerous fishes of the family Sparidae, chiefly inhabiting tropical and subtropical seas, comprising the porgies, the scups, etc. —*adj.* **2.** belonging or pertaining to the Sparidae. [< NL *Sparidae,* equiv. to *Spar(us)* a genus (L: gilthead < Gk *spáros*) + *-idae* -ID[2]]

Spar·ine (spâr′ēn), *Pharm., Trademark.* a brand of promazine.

spar·ing (spâr′ing), *adj.* **1.** economical (often fol. by *in* or *of*). **2.** lenient or merciful. **3.** scanty; limited. [1325–75; ME; see SPARE, -ING[2]] —**spar′ing·ly,** *adv.* —**spar′ing·ness,** *n.*
—**Syn. 1.** frugal, saving, penurious. **3.** meager, sparse.

spark[1] (spärk), *n.* **1.** an ignited or fiery particle such as is thrown off by burning wood or produced by one hard body striking against another. **2.** Also called **sparkover.** *Elect.* **a.** the light produced by a sudden discontinuous discharge of electricity through air or another dielectric. **b.** the discharge itself. **c.** any electric arc of relatively small energy content. **d.** the electric discharge produced by a spark plug in an internal-combustion engine. **3.** anything that activates or stimulates; inspiration or catalyst. **4.** a small amount or trace of something. **5.** a trace of life or vitality. **6. sparks,** (*used with a singular v.*) *Slang.* a radio operator on a ship or aircraft. **7.** (*usually cap.*) a member of Camp Fire, Inc., who is five years of age. —*v.i.* **8.** to emit or produce sparks. **9.** to issue as or like sparks. **10.** to send forth gleams or flashes. **11.** (of the ignition of an internal-combustion engine) to function correctly in producing sparks. —*v.t.* **12.** to kindle, animate, or stimulate (interest, activity, spirit, etc.): *These bright students have sparked her enthusiasm for teaching. The arrival of the piano player really sparked the party.* [bef. 900; (n.) ME; OE *spearca;* c. MD, MLG *sparke;* (v.) ME *sparken;* c. MD, MLG *sparken*] —**spark′less,** *adj.* —**spark′less·ly,** *adv.* —**spark′like′,** *adj.*
—**Syn. 4.** jot, bit, flicker.

spark[2] (spärk), *n.* **1.** a gay, elegant, or foppish young man. **2.** a beau, lover, or suitor. **3.** a woman of outstanding beauty, charm, or wit. —*v.t.* **4.** *Informal* (*older use*). to woo; court. —*v.i.* **5.** *Informal* (*older use*). to engage in courtship; woo. [1565–75; fig. use of SPARK[1], or < ON *sparkr* quick, lively] —**spark′ish,** *adj.* —**spark′ish·ly,** *adv.* —**spark′ish·ness,** *n.* —**spark′·like′,** *adj.*

Spark (spärk), *n.* **Muriel (Sarah) (Camberg),** born 1918, British novelist and writer, born in Scotland.

spark′ arrest′er, 1. a device, consisting of wire netting or other material, used to stop or deflect sparks thrown from an open fireplace, a smokestack, or the like. **2.** *Elect.* a device to reduce sparking at contacts where a circuit is opened and closed. [1825–35, *Amer.*]

spark′ cham′ber, *Physics.* a device for detecting elementary particles, consisting of a series of charged plates separated by a gas so that the passage of a charged particle causes sparking between adjacent plates. [1960–65]

spark′ coil′, *Elect.* a coil of many turns of insulated wire on an iron core, used for producing sparks. [1895–1900]

spark·er[1] (spär′kər), *n.* **1.** something that produces sparks. **2.** an apparatus used to test insulation on wires. [1860–65; SPARK[1] + -ER[1]]

spark·er[2] (spär′kər), *n.* a lover, swain, or beau. [1825–35, *Amer.*; SPARK[2] + -ER[1]]

spark′ gap′, *Elect.* **1.** a space between two electrodes, across which a discharge of electricity may take place. **2.** the electrodes and the space between, considered as a unit: used in ignition systems. [1885–90]

spark′ gen′erator, an alternating-current power source with a condenser discharging across a spark gap.

spark′ing plug′, *Brit.* See **spark plug** (def. 1). [1900–05]

spark′ing volt′age, *Elect.* the minimum voltage required to produce a spark across a given spark gap.

spark-kil·ler (spärk′kil′ər), *n. Elect.* a device for diminishing sparking, consisting of a capacitor and a resistor connected in series across two points where sparking may occur in a circuit. [SPARK[1] + KILLER]

spar·kle (spär′kəl), *v.,* **-kled, -kling,** *n.* —*v.i.* **1.** to issue in or as if in little sparks, as fire or light: *The candlelight sparkled in the crystal.* **2.** to emit little sparks, as burning matter: *The flames leaped and sparkled.* **3.** to shine or glisten with little gleams of light, as a brilliant gem; glitter; coruscate. **4.** to effervesce, as wine. **5.** to be brilliant, lively, or vivacious. —*v.t.* **6.** to cause to sparkle: *moonlight sparkling the water; pleasure sparkling her eyes.* —*n.* **7.** a little spark or fiery particle. **8.** a sparkling appearance, luster, or play of light: *the sparkle of a diamond.* **9.** brilliance, liveliness, or vivacity. [1150–1200; ME (n. and v.); see SPARK[1], -LE]
—**Syn. 3.** See **glisten. 8.** glitter.

spar·kler (spär′klər), *n.* **1.** a person or thing that sparkles. **2.** a firework that emits little sparks. **3.** a sparkling gem, esp. a diamond. **4.** *Informal.* a bright eye. [1705–15; SPARKLE + -ER[1]]

spark·let (spärk′lit), *n.* **1.** a small spark. **2.** something small that glitters like a spark. [1680–90; SPARK[1] + -LET]

spar′kling wa′ter. See **soda water** (def. 1).

spar′kling wine′, a wine that is naturally carbonated by a second fermentation. [1690–1700]

spark·ly (spär′klē), *adj.,* **-kli·er, -kli·est. 1.** tending to sparkle; animated; lively: *a row of sparkly cheerleaders.* **2.** (of a wine) naturally carbonated; effervescent. [1920–25; SPARKLE + -Y[1]]

spark·o·ver (spärk′ō′vər), *n. Elect.* spark[1] (def. 2). [SPARK[1] + OVER]

spark′ photog′raphy, 1. photography of fast-moving objects, as bullets, by the light of an electric spark. **2.** photography of sparks by their own light.

spark′ plug′, 1. a device designed to fit in each cylinder of a gasoline-powered internal-combustion engine and to produce the electric spark for igniting the mixture of gasoline and air. **2.** *Informal.* a person who leads, inspires, or animates a group. [1900–05]

spark·plug (spärk′plug′), *v.t.,* **-plugged, -plug·ging.** *Informal.* to lead, inspire, or animate something or someone. [v. use of SPARK PLUG]

Sparks (spärks), *n.* **1. Jar·ed** (jâr′id), 1789–1866, U.S. historian and editor. **2.** a city in W Nevada, E of Reno. 40,780.

spark′ spec′trum, *Physics.* a spectrum formed from the light produced by an electric spark, characteristic of the gas or vapor through which the spark passes.

spark′ transmit′ter, *Radio.* a transmitting set that generates electromagnetic waves by the oscillatory discharge from a capacitor through an inductor and a spark gap. [1915–20]

spark·y (spär′kē), *adj.,* **spark·i·er, spark·i·est. 1.** emitting or producing sparks. **2.** animated; lively: *a sparky personality.* [1610–20; SPARK[1] + -Y[1]] —**spark′i·ly,** *adv.*

spar·ling (spär′ling), *n., pl.* **-lings,** (*esp. collectively*) **-ling.** the European smelt, *Osmerus eperlanus.* [1275–1325; ME *sperlynge* < OF *esperlinge* < Gmc; cf. G *Spierling*]

spar·oid (spâr′oid, spar′-), *adj.* **1.** resembling or pertaining to the porgy family, Sparidae. —*n.* **2.** a sparoid fish. [1830–40; < NL *Sparoidēs,* equiv. to *Spar(us)* (see SPARID) + *-oidēs* -OID]

spar′ring part′ner, a boxer who spars with and otherwise serves to train a boxer who is preparing for a bout. Also called **spar′ring mate′.** [1905–10]

spar·row (spar′ō), *n.* **1.** any of numerous American finches of the family Emberizinae. Cf. **chipping sparrow, song sparrow. 2.** any member of the Old World genus *Passer*, formerly thought to be closely related to the weaverbirds but now placed in their own family, Passeridae. **3.** *Brit.* the house sparrow. **4.** any of several other unrelated small birds. Cf. **Java sparrow, hedge sparrow. 5.** (*cap.*) *Mil.* a 12-ft. (4-m), all-weather, radar-guided U.S. air-to-air missile with an 88-lb. (40-kg) high-explosive warhead. [bef. 900; ME *sparowe*, OE *spearwa;* c. Goth *sparwa*, ON *spǫrr*] —**spar′row·less,** *adj.* —**spar′row·like′,** *adj.*

spar·row·grass (spar′ō gras′, -gräs′), *n. Informal.* asparagus. [1650–60; by folk etymology]

spar′row hawk′, 1. a small, short-winged European hawk, *Accipiter nisus*, that preys on smaller birds. **2.** See **American kestrel.** [1400–50; late ME]

spar·ry (spär′ē), *adj.* of or pertaining to mineral spar. [1685–95; SPAR[3] + -Y[1]]

sparse (spärs), *adj.,* **spars·er, spars·est. 1.** thinly scattered or distributed: *a sparse population.* **2.** not thick or dense; thin: *sparse hair.* **3.** scanty; meager. [1715–25; < L *sparsus*, ptp. of *spargere* to scatter, SPARGE] —**sparse′ly,** *adv.* —**sparse′ness, spar·si·ty** (spär′si tē), *n.*
—**Syn. 1–3.** See **scanty.** —**Ant. 1–3.** abundant.

Spar·ta (spär′tə), *n.* an ancient city in S Greece: the capital of Laconia and the chief city of the Peloponnesus, at one time the dominant city of Greece: famous for strict discipline and training of soldiers. Also called **Lacedaemon.**

Spar·ta·cus (spär′tə kəs), *n.* died 71 B.C., Thracian slave, gladiator, and insurrectionist.

Spar·tan (spär′tn), *adj.* Also, **Spar·tan·ic** (spär tan′ik). **1.** of or pertaining to Sparta or its people. **2.** suggestive of the ancient Spartans; sternly disciplined and rigorously simple, frugal, or austere. **3.** brave; undaunted. —*n.* **4.** a native or inhabitant of Sparta. **5.** a person of Spartan characteristics. [1375–1425; late ME < L *Spartānus*, equiv. to *Spart(a)* SPARTA (< Doric Gk *Spártā*) + *-ānus* -AN] —**Spar′tan·ism,** *n.* —**Spar′tan·ly, Spar·tan′i·cal·ly,** *adv.*
—**Syn. 2.** See **austere.**

Spar·tan·burg (spär′tn bûrg′), *n.* a city in NW South Carolina. 43,968.

spar·te·ine (spär′tē ēn′, -in), *n.* a bitter, poisonous, liquid alkaloid obtained from certain species of broom, esp. *Cytisus scoparius*, used in medicine to stimulate the heart and also the uterine muscles in childbirth. [1850–55; irreg. < NL *Sparti(um)* name of a genus of broom (< Gk *spárt(os)* kind of broom + NL *-ium* -IUM) + -INE[1]]

Spar·ti (spär′tī, -tē), *n.* (*used with a plural v.*) *Class. Myth.* a group of fully armed warriors who sprang from the dragon's teeth that Cadmus planted.

Spar·ti·ate (spär′tē āt′, -shē-), *n.* a member of the ruling class of ancient Laconia; a Spartan citizen. Cf. **Helot** (def. 1), **Perioeci.** [1350–1400; ME < L *Spartiātēs* < Doric Gk *Spartiā́tēs*, equiv. to *Spartiā́(s)* of SPARTA + *-tēs* personal n. suffix]

spar′ var′nish, 1. a durable, weather-resistant varnish applied to unpainted wooden areas, esp. on ships. **2.** a varnish made from sulfur, rosin, and linseed oil. [1905–10]

spar·ver (spär′vər), *n.* **1.** a tentlike bed curtain or canopy. **2.** a bed curtain suspended from a flat, circular covering on the ceiling. **3.** a bed having a tentlike curtain or canopy. [1400–50; late ME *sperver* < MF *esprevier* sparrow hawk, canopy bed < Gmc]

spasm (spaz′əm), *n.* **1.** *Pathol.* a sudden, abnormal, involuntary muscular contraction, consisting of a continued muscular contraction **(tonic spasm)** or of a series of alternating muscular contractions and relaxations **(clonic spasm). 2.** any sudden, brief spell of great energy, activity, feeling, etc. [1350–1400; ME *spasme* < L *spasmus* < Gk *spasmós* convulsion, deriv. of *spân* to draw a sword or cord, wrench (off), convulse]
—**Syn. 2.** fit, storm, flash, spurt.

spasm′ band′, an old-time jazz band, flourishing esp. in the late 19th century, the members of which used improvised instruments, as cigar boxes, barrels, kazoos, whistles, and jugs, and often marched in the street while performing. Cf. **jug band.**

spas·mod·ic (spaz mod′ik), *adj.* **1.** pertaining to or of the nature of a spasm; characterized by spasms. **2.** resembling a spasm or spasms; sudden but brief; sporadic: *spasmodic efforts at reform.* **3.** given to or characterized by bursts of excitement. Also, **spas·mod′i·cal.** [1675–85; < ML *spasmodicus* < Gk *spasmṓd(ēs)* spasmodic (deriv. of *spasmós* SPASM; see -ODE[1]) + L *-icus* -IC] —**spas·mod′i·cal·ly,** *adv.*
—**Syn. 2.** occasional, intermittent, periodic, fleeting.

spas·mo·dist (spaz′mə dist), *n.* a person who is spasmodic, esp. in style, as a writer, painter, etc. [1840–50; SPASMOD(IC) + -IST] —**spas′mo·dism,** *n.*

spas·mol·y·sis (spaz mol′ə sis), *n. Med.* the relaxation or relief of muscle spasm. [SPASM + -O- + -LYSIS]

spas·mo·lyt·ic (spaz′mə lit′ik), *Med.* —*adj.* **1.** of or noting spasmolysis. —*n.* **2.** a spasmolytic substance; antispasmodic. Also, **spas·mol·y·sant** (spaz mol′ə zənt). [1930–35; SPASM + -O- + -LYTIC]

spas·mo·phil·i·a (spaz′mə fil′ē ə), *n. Pathol.* a condition in which only moderate mechanical or electrical stimulation produces spasms, convulsions, or tetany. [< NL; see SPASM, -O-, -PHILIA]

spas·mo·phil·ic (spaz′mə fil′ik), *adj.* of or noting spasmophilia. Also, **spas·mo·phile** (spaz′mə fīl′). [SPASM + -O- + -PHILIC]

Spas·sky (spas′kē; *Russ.* spä′skē), *n.* **Bo·ris (Va·si·lye·vich)** (bôr′is və sēl′yə vich, bōr′-, bor′-; *Russ.* bu-ryēs′ vu syē′lyi vyich), born 1937, Russian chess player.

spas·tic (spas′tik), *Pathol.* —*adj.* **1.** pertaining to, of the nature of, or characterized by spasm, esp. tonic spasm. —*n.* **2.** a person exhibiting such spasms. [1745–55; < L *spasticus* afflicted with spasms < Gk *spastikós* of a spasm, equiv. to *spas-*, s. of *spân* to pull off, pluck, convulse + *-tikos* -TIC] —**spas′ti·cal·ly,** *adv.* —**spas·tic·i·ty** (spa stis′i tē), *n.*

spas′tic co′lon, *Pathol.* See **irritable bowel syndrome.**

spas′tic paral′ysis, *Pathol.* a condition in which the muscles affected are marked by tonic spasm and increased tendon reflexes. [1890–95]

spat[1] (spat), *n., v.,* **spat·ted, spat·ting.** —*n.* **1.** a petty quarrel. **2.** a light blow; slap; smack. —*v.i.* **3.** to engage in a petty quarrel or dispute. **4.** to splash or spatter; *rain spatting against the window.* —*v.t.* **5.** to strike lightly; slap. [1795–1805, *Amer.*; perh. imit.]
—**Syn. 1.** tiff, scrap, set-to.

spat[2] (spat), *v.* a pt. and pp. of **spit[1].**

spat[3] (spat), *n.* a short gaiter worn over the instep and usually fastened under the foot with a strap, worn esp. in the late 19th and early 20th centuries. [1795–1805; short for SPATTERDASH]

spat[4] (spat), *n.* **1.** the spawn of an oyster or similar shellfish. **2.** young oysters collectively. **3.** a young oyster. **4.** See **seed oyster.** [1350–1400; ME; orig. uncert.]

spatch·cock (spach′kok′), *n.* **1.** a fowl that has been dressed and split open for grilling. —*v.t.* **2.** to prepare and roast (a fowl) in this manner. **3.** to insert or interpolate, esp. in a forced or incongruous manner: *Additional information has been spatchcocked into the occasional random footnote.* [1775–85; appar. alter. of SPITCHCOCK; popular interpretation as shortening of *dispatch cock* is prob. specious]

spate (spāt), *n.* **1.** a sudden, almost overwhelming, outpouring: *a spate of angry words.* **2.** *Brit.* **a.** a flood or inundation. **b.** a river flooding its banks. **c.** a sudden or heavy rainstorm. [1400–50; late ME (north) < ?]

spa·tha·ceous (spə thā′shəs), *adj. Bot.* **1.** of the nature of or resembling a spathe. **2.** having a spathe. [1750–60; < NL *spathāceus*, equiv. to L *spath(a)* (see SPATHE) + *-āceus* -ACEOUS]

spathe (spāth), *n. Bot.* a bract or pair of bracts, often large and colored, subtending or enclosing a spadix or flower cluster. [1775–85; < L *spatha* < Gk *spáthē* blade, sword, stem; cf. SPADE[2]] —**spathed,** *adj.*

spath·ic (spath′ik), *adj. Mineral.* like spar. [1780–90; < G *Spat* (earlier sp. *Spath*) spar + -IC]

spa·thi·phyl·lum (spā′thə fil′əm, -thə-, spath′ə-), *n.* any of various tropical plants of the genus *Spathiphyllum*, having a white or green spathe and a spike of fragrant flowers and often cultivated as an ornamental. Also called **peace lily, spathe′ flow′er.** [< NL, equiv. to Gk *spáth(ē)* blade, SPATHE + NL *-i-* -I- (irreg. for *-o-*) + Gk *-phyllon*, neut. of *-phyllos* -PHYLLOUS, in reference to the leaflike appearance of the spathes]

spa·those[1] (spā′thōs, spath′ōs), *adj.* spathic. [1770–80; *spath-*, as in SPATHIC + -OSE[1]]

spa·those[2] (spā′thōs, -thōs), *adj.* spathaceous. Also, **spa·thous** (spā′thəs, -thəs). [1830–40; SPATHE + -OSE[1]]

spath·u·late (spath′yə lit, -lāt′), *adj. Chiefly Bot.* spatulate.

spa·tial (spā′shəl), *adj.* **1.** of or pertaining to space. **2.** existing or occurring in space; having extension in space. Also, **spacial.** [1840–50; < L *spati(um)* SPACE + -AL[1]] —**spa·ti·al·i·ty** (spā′shē al′i tē), *n.* —**spa′tial·ly,** *adv.*

spa′tial summa′tion. See under **summation** (def. 5). [1965–70]

spa·ti·og·ra·phy (spā′shē og′rə fē), *n.* the study of the characteristics of space beyond the atmosphere, including the mapping of the movements of celestial bodies and the recording of electrical, magnetic, and gravitational effects, esp. those likely to affect missiles and spacecraft. [< L *spati(um)* SPACE + -O- + -GRAPHY]

spa·ti·o·tem·po·ral (spā′shē ō tem′pər əl), *adj.* **1.** pertaining to space-time. **2.** of or pertaining to both space and time. [1915–20; < L *spati(um)* SPACE + -O- + TEMPORAL[1]] —**spa′ti·o·tem′po·ral·ly,** *adv.*

spat·ter (spat′ər), *v.t.* **1.** to scatter or dash in small particles or drops: *The dog spattered mud on everyone when he shook himself.* **2.** to splash with something in small particles: *to spatter the ground with water.* **3.** to sprinkle or spot with something that soils or stains. —*v.i.* **4.** to send out small particles or drops, as falling water: *rain spattering on a tin roof.* **5.** to strike a surface in or as in a shower, as bullets. —*n.* **6.** the act or the sound of spattering: *the spatter of rain on a roof.* **7.** a splash or spot of something spattered. [1575–85; perh. < D *spatt(en)* to splash + -ER[6]; cf. D *spatterig* lit., spattery] —**spat′ter·ing·ly,** *adv.*

spat′ter cone′, *Geol.* a low, steep-sided volcanic cone built up of droplets or blobs of lava erupted from a fissure or vent. [1900–05]

spat′ter dash′, roughcast (def. 1).

spat·ter·dash (spat′ər dash′), *n.* a long gaiter to protect the trousers or stockings, as from mud while riding. [1680–90; SPATTER + DASH] —**spat′ter·dashed′,** *adj.*

spat·ter·dock (spat′ər dok′), *n.* any of various water lilies of the genus *Nuphar*, having globular yellow flowers and growing in lakes or sluggish streams, esp. *N. advena*, of the eastern U.S. Also called **cow lily.** [1805–15, *Amer.*; SPATTER + DOCK[4]]

spat·u·la (spach′ə lə), *n.* an implement with a broad, flat, usually flexible blade, used for blending foods or removing them from cooking utensils, mixing drugs, spreading plasters and paints, etc. [1515–25; < L: a flat piece, batten, equiv. to *spath(a)* SPATHE + *-ula* -ULE] —**spat′u·lar,** *adj.*

spat·u·late (spach′ə lit, -lāt′), *adj.* **1.** shaped like a spatula; rounded more or less like a spoon. **2.** *Bot.* having a broad, rounded end and a narrow, attenuate base, as a leaf. [1750–60; < NL *spatulātus*. See SPATULA, -ATE[1]]

spätz·le (shpet′slə), *n. German.* spaetzle.

spaul·der (spôl′dər), *n. Armor.* a pauldron, esp. one for protecting only a shoulder. Also called **monnion.** [earlier *spauld* shoulder (ME *spald, spalde* < OF *espalde, espalle* < L *spatula* SPATULA) + -ER[1]]

spav·in (spav′in), *n. Vet. Pathol.* **1.** a disease of the hock joint of horses in which enlargement occurs because of collected fluids **(bog spavin),** bony growth **(bone spavin),** or distention of the veins **(blood spavin). 2.** an excrescence or enlargement so formed. [1400–50; late ME *spaveyne* < OF *(e)spavain, esparvain* swelling < ?]

spav·ined (spav′ind), *adj.* **1.** suffering from or affected with spavin. **2.** being of or marked by a decrepit or broken-down condition: *a spavined old school bus abandoned in a field.* [1400–50; late ME *spaveyned*. See SPAVIN, -ED[3]]

spawn (spôn), *n.* **1.** *Zool.* the mass of eggs deposited by fishes, amphibians, mollusks, crustaceans, etc. **2.** *Mycol.* the mycelium of mushrooms, esp. of the species grown for the market. **3.** a swarming brood; numerous progeny. **4.** (*used with a singular or plural v.*) any person or thing regarded as the offspring of some stock, idea, etc. —*v.i.* **5.** to deposit eggs or sperm directly into the water, as fishes. —*v.t.* **6.** to produce (spawn). **7.** to give birth to; give rise to: *His sudden disappearance spawned many rumors.* **8.** to produce in large number. **9.** to plant with mycelium. [1350–1400; ME *spawnen* (v.), prob. < AF *espaundre* (OF *espandre*) to EXPAND] —**spawn′er,** *n.*
—**Syn. 7.** engender, generate, yield, beget.

spay[1] (spā), *v.t. Vet. Med.* to remove the ovaries of (an animal). [1375–1425; late ME *spayen* < AF *espeier* to cut with a sword (OF *espeer*), deriv. of *espee* sword; see ÉPÉE]

spay[2] (spā), *n.* a three-year-old male red deer. Also called **spay·ad** (spā′əd), **spay·ard** (spā′ərd). [1375–1425; late ME < ?]

spaz (spaz), *n. Slang.* **1.** a grotesquely awkward person. **2.** an eccentric person. Also, **spazz.** [1960–65; shortening and alter. of SPASTIC]

S.P.C.A., Society for the Prevention of Cruelty to Animals.

S.P.C.C., Society for the Prevention of Cruelty to Children.

SPDA, single-premium deferred annuity.

speak (spēk), *v.,* **spoke** or (*Archaic*) **spake; spo·ken** or (*Archaic*) **spoke; speak·ing.** —*v.i.* **1.** to utter words or articulate sounds with the ordinary voice; talk: *He was too ill to speak.* **2.** to communicate vocally; mention: *to speak to a person of various matters.* **3.** to converse: *She spoke with him for an hour.* **4.** to deliver an address, discourse, etc.: *to speak at a meeting.* **5.** to make a statement in written or printed words. **6.** to communicate, signify, or disclose by any means; convey significance. **7.** *Phonet.* to produce sounds or audible sequences of individual or concatenated sounds of a language, esp. through phonation, amplification, and resonance, and through any of a variety of articulatory processes. **8.** (of a computer) to express data or other information audibly by means of an audio response unit. **9.** to emit a sound, as a musical instrument; make a noise or report. **10.** *Chiefly Brit.* (of dogs) to bark when ordered. **11.** *Fox Hunting.* (of a hound or pack) to bay on finding a scent. —*v.t.* **12.** to utter vocally and articulately: *to speak words of praise.* **13.** to express or make known with the voice: *to speak the truth.* **14.** to declare in writing or printing, or by any means of communication. **15.** to make known, indicate, or reveal. **16.** to use, or be able to use, in oral utterance, as a language: *to speak French.* **17.** (of a computer) to express or make known (data, prompts, etc.) by means of an audio response unit. **18.** *Naut.* to communicate with (a passing vessel) at sea, as by voice or signal: *We spoke a whaler on the fourth day at sea.* **19.** *Archaic.* to speak to or with. **20. so to speak,** to use a manner of speaking; figuratively speaking: *We still don't have our heads above water, so to speak.* **21. speak by the book,** to say with great authority or precision: *I can't speak by the book, but I know this is wrong.* **22. speak for, a.** to intercede for or recommend; speak in behalf of. **b.** to express or articulate the views of; represent. **c.** to choose or prefer; have reserved for oneself: *This item is already*

CONCISE ETYMOLOGY KEY: <, descended or borrowed from; >, whence; b., blend of, blended; c., cognate with; cf., compare; deriv., derivative; equiv., equivalent; imit., imitative; obl., oblique; r., replacing; s., stem; sp., spelling, spelled; resp., respelling, respelled; trans., translation; ?, origin unknown; *, unattested; ‡, probably earlier than. See the full key inside the front cover.

spoken for. **23. speak out,** to express one's opinion openly and unreservedly: *He was not afraid to speak out when it was something he believed in strongly.* **24. speak well for,** to be an indication or reflection of (something commendable); testify admirably to: *Her manners speak well for her upbringing.* **25. to speak of,** worth mentioning: *The country has no mineral resources to speak of.* [bef. 900; ME *speken,* OE *specan,* var. of *sprecan;* c. G *sprechen* (OHG *sprehhan;* cf. var. *spehhan*)] **—speak′a·ble,** *adj.* **—speak′a·ble·ness,** *n.* **—speak′a·bly,** *adv.*

—Syn. 1. SPEAK, CONVERSE, TALK mean to make vocal sounds, usually for purposes of communication. To SPEAK often implies conveying information and may apply to anything from an informal remark to a scholarly presentation to a formal address: *to speak sharply; to speak before Congress.* To CONVERSE is to exchange ideas with someone by speaking: *to converse with a friend.* To TALK is a close synonym for TO SPEAK but usually refers to less formal situations: *to talk about the weather; to talk with a friend.* **12.** pronounce, articulate. **13.** say. **15.** disclose.

-speak, a combining form extracted from **newspeak,** used in the formation of compound words, usually derogatory, that denote the style or vocabulary of a discipline, person, era, etc., as specified by the initial element: *adspeak; artspeak; futurespeak.*

speak·eas·y (spēk′ē′zē), *n., pl.* **-eas·ies.** a saloon or nightclub selling alcoholic beverages illegally, esp. during Prohibition. [1885–90, *Amer.;* SPEAK + EASY]

speak·er (spē′kər), *n.* **1.** a person who speaks. **2.** a person who speaks formally before an audience; lecturer; orator. **3.** (*usually cap.*) the presiding officer of the U.S. House of Representatives, the British House of Commons, or other such legislative assembly. **4.** Also called **loudspeaker.** an electroacoustic device, often housed in a cabinet, that is connected as a component in an audio system, its function being to make speech or music audible. **5.** a book of selections for practice in declamation. **6. be** or **not be on speakers,** *Brit.* See **speaking** (defs. 9, 10). [1275–1325; ME; see SPEAK, -ER[1]] **—speak′er·ship′,** *n.*

Speak·er (spē′kər), *n.* **Tris(tram E.),** 1888–1958, U.S. baseball player.

speak·er·phone (spē′kər fōn′), *n.* a telephone or telephone attachment equipped with both loudspeaker and microphone, thus permitting the instrument to be used without being held. [1955–60, *Amer.;* (LOUD)-SPEAKER + (MICRO)PHONE or (TELE)PHONE]

speak·ing (spē′king), *n.* **1.** the act, utterance, or discourse of a person who speaks. **2. speakings,** literary works composed for recitation, as ancient bardic poetry; oral literature. *—adj.* **3.** that speaks. **4.** used in, suited to, or involving speaking or talking: *the speaking voice.* **5.** of or pertaining to declamation. **6.** giving information as if by speech: *a speaking proof of a thing.* **7.** highly expressive: *speaking eyes.* **8.** lifelike: *a speaking likeness.* **9. not on speaking terms,** not or no longer in a relationship of open, willing, or ready communication, as because of resentment or estrangement: *They had a squabble during the holidays, and now they're not on speaking terms.* **10. on speaking terms, a.** in a relationship close enough for or limited to friendly superficialities: *I don't know the hosts well, but we are certainly on speaking terms.* **b.** in a relationship of open, willing, or ready communication: *Now that the debt has been settled, I hope you and your partner are on speaking terms again.* [1200–50; ME; see SPEAK, -ING[1], -ING[2]] **—speak′ing·ly,** *adv.* **—speak′ing·ness,** *n.*

speak′ing in tongues′, a form of glossolalia in which a person experiencing religious ecstasy utters incomprehensible sounds that the speaker believes are a language spoken through him or her by a deity. Also called **gift of tongues.**

speak′ing tube′, a tube for conveying the voice over a somewhat limited distance, as from one part of a building or ship to another. [1825–35]

speak′ing type′, *Numis.* a device on a medal or coin that has a punning reference to a person or thing.

spean (spēn), *v.t. Chiefly Scot.* to wean. [1565–75; var. of dial. *spane,* ME *spanen;* c. LG, D *spenen,* G (dial.) *Spänen*]

spear[1] (spēr), *n.* **1.** a long, stabbing weapon for thrusting or throwing, consisting of a wooden shaft to which a sharp-pointed head, as of iron or steel, is attached. **2.** a soldier or other person armed with such a weapon; spearman: *an army of 40,000 spears.* **3.** a similar weapon or stabbing implement, as one for use in fishing. **4.** the act of spearing. *—adj.* **5.** See **spear side.** *—v.t.* **6.** to pierce with or as with a spear. *—v.i.* **7.** to go or penetrate like a spear: *The plane speared through the clouds.* [bef. 900; ME (n.), OE *spere;* c. D, G *speer*] **—spear′er,** *n.*

spear[2] (spēr), *n.* **1.** a sprout or shoot of a plant, as a blade of grass or an acrospire of grain. *—v.i.* **2.** to sprout; shoot; send up or rise in a spear or spears. [1520–30; var. of SPIRE[1], perh. influenced by SPEAR[1]]

spear′ car′rier, 1. a supernumerary in a theatrical or operatic production, as one of a group of soldiers or a member of a crowd; extra. **2.** any minor member of a group, profession, political party, etc.; subordinate; underling. Also, **spear′-car′ri·er.** [1950–55]

spear·fish (spēr′fish′), *n., pl.* (*esp. collectively*) **-fish,** (*esp. referring to two or more kinds or species*) **-fish·es,** *v.* *—n.* **1.** any of several fishes of the genus *Tetrapturus,* resembling the sailfish but having the first dorsal fin much less developed: inhabiting all seas, but rare. **2.** any of several related fishes. *—v.i.* **3.** to fish underwater using a spearlike implement used manually or propelled mechanically. [1880–85, *Amer.;* SPEAR[1] + FISH]

spear·fish·er·man (spēr′fish′ər mən), *n., pl.* **-men.** a person who engages in spearfishing. [1950–55; SPEAR[1] + FISHERMAN]

spear′ grass′, any of various grasses, as a meadow grass or a bent grass, having lance-shaped leaves or floral spikes. [1540–50]

spear′ gun′, a device for shooting a barbed missile under water, usually by means of gas under pressure, a strong rubber band, or a powerful spring.

spear·head (spēr′hed′), *n.* **1.** the sharp-pointed head that forms the piercing end of a spear. **2.** any person, contingent, or force that leads an attack, undertaking, etc. *—v.t.* **3.** to act as a spearhead for: *She spearheaded the drive for new members.* [1350–1400; ME; see SPEAR[1], HEAD]

—Syn. 3. lead, start, initiate, pioneer.

spear′-head spoon′ (spēr′hed′). See **diamond-point spoon.**

spear·ing (spēr′ing), *n. Ice Hockey.* an illegal check in which a player jabs an opponent with the end of the stick blade or the top end of the stick, resulting in a penalty. [1770–80, for literal sense; SPEAR[1] + -ING[1]]

spear·man (spēr′mən), *n., pl.* **-men.** a person who is armed with or uses a spear. [1250–1300; ME; see SPEAR[1], MAN[1]]

spear·mint (spēr′mint′), *n.* an aromatic herb, *Mentha spicata,* having lance-shaped leaves used for flavoring. [1530–40; SPEAR[1] + MINT[1]]

spear·point (spēr′point′), *n.* **1.** the point at the end of a spearhead. **2.** a spearhead. [1400–50; late ME; see SPEAR[1], POINT]

spear′ side′, the male side, or line of descent, of a family (opposed to *distaff side* or *spindle side*). [1860–65]

spear-throw·er (spēr′thrō′ər), *n. Anthropol.* **1.** a flexible device for launching a spear, usually a short cord wound around the spear so that when thrown the weapon will rotate in the air. **2.** Also called **atlatl.** a rigid device for increasing the speed and distance of a spear when thrown, usually a flat wooden stick with a handhold and a peg or socket to accommodate the butt end of the spear. [1870–75]

spear·wort (spēr′wûrt′, -wôrt′), *n.* any of several buttercups having lance-shaped leaves and small flowers, as *Ranunculus ambigens,* of the eastern U.S., growing in mud. [bef. 1000; ME *sperewort,* OE *sperewyrt.* See SPEAR[1], WORT[2]]

spec (spek), *n, adj., v.,* **spec'd** or **specked** or **specced, spec′·ing** or **speck·ing** or **spec·cing.** *—n.* **1.** Usually, **specs.** specification (def. 2). **2.** speculation. **3. on spec,** made, built, or done with hopes of but no assurance of payment or a sale; without commitment by a client or buyer: *ad illustrations done on spec; luxury homes built on spec and sold before completion.* *—adj.* **4.** built, done, bought, etc., as a speculation: *the construction of spec houses.* *—v.t.* **5.** to provide specifications for: *Their newest truck was spec'd by a computer.* [1785–95, *Amer.;* by shortening] **—spec′er, speck′er,** *n.*

spec., 1. special. **2.** specially. **3.** specifically. **4.** specification.

spe·cial (spesh′əl), *adj.* **1.** of a distinct or particular kind or character: *a special kind of key.* **2.** being a particular one; particular, individual, or certain: *You'd better call the special number.* **3.** pertaining or peculiar to a particular person, thing, instance, etc.; distinctive; unique: *the special features of a plan.* **4.** having a specific or particular function, purpose, etc.: *a special messenger.* **5.** distinguished or different from what is ordinary or usual: *a special occasion; to fix something special.* **6.** extraordinary; exceptional, as in amount or degree; especial: *special importance.* **7.** being such in an exceptional degree; particularly valued: *a special friend.* *—n.* **8.** a special person or thing. **9.** a train used for a particular purpose, occasion, or the like. **10.** a special edition of a newspaper. **11.** *Theat.* a spotlight reserved for a particular area, property, actor, etc.: *Give me the coffin special.* **12.** a temporary, arbitrary reduction in the price of regularly stocked goods, esp. food; a particularly worthwhile offer or price: *The special this week is on sirloin steaks.* **13.** *Television.* a single program not forming part of a regular series. [1175–1225; ME (adj.) < L *speciālis* of a given species, equiv. to *speci(ēs)* SPECIES + *-ālis* -AL[1]; see ESPECIAL] **—spe′cial·ly,** *adv.*

—Syn. 5. singular. SPECIAL, PARTICULAR, SPECIFIC refer to something pointed out for attention and consideration. SPECIAL means given unusual treatment because of being uncommon: *a special sense of a word.* PARTICULAR implies something selected from the others of its kind and set off from them for attention: *a particular variety of orchid.* SPECIFIC implies plain and unambiguous indication of a particular instance, example, etc.: *a specific instance of cowardice.* **—Ant. 1.** general.

—Usage. In American English the adjective SPECIAL is overwhelmingly more common than ESPECIAL in all senses: *He will be of special help if you can't understand the documentation.* The reverse is true of the adverbs; here ESPECIALLY is by far the more common: *He will be of great help, especially if you have trouble understanding the documentation.* Only when the sense "specifically" is intended is SPECIALLY more idiomatic: *The machine was specially designed for use by a left-handed operator.*

spe′cial act′, a legislative act that applies only to specific persons or to a specific area.

spe′cial a′gent, 1. an investigator in a law enforcement agency. **2.** an insurance sales representative. [1830–40, *Amer.*]

spe′cial ar′ea, *Brit.* See **distressed area.**

spe′cial assess′ment, a tax levied by a local government on private property to pay the cost of local public improvements, as sidewalk construction or sewage disposal, that are of general benefit to the property taxed. [1870–75]

Spe′cial Astrophys′ical Observ′atory, an astronomical observatory located on Mount Pastukhov in the Caucasus in the Soviet Union, having a 236-in. (6-m) reflecting telescope, the largest in the world.

spe′cial check′ing account′, a checking account that requires no minimum balance but in which a small charge is made for each check issued or drawn and for monthly maintenance. Cf. **regular checking account.**

spe′cial collec′tion, *Library Science.* a collection of materials segregated from a general library collection according to form, subject, age, condition, rarity, source, or value.

spe′cial commit′tee. See **select committee.**

spe′cial court′-martial, *U.S. Mil.* a court-martial established to try violations of military law less serious than those tried by a general court-martial but more serious than those tried by a summary court-martial.

spe′cial deliv′ery, (in the U.S. Postal Service) delivery of mail outside the regularly scheduled hours, by a special messenger, upon the payment of an extra fee. [1880–85, *Amer.*] **—spe′cial-de·liv′er·y,** *adj.*

spe′cial deliv′ery stamp′, a stamp of special design, having a value indicating an extra fee in addition to the regular postage, and affixed to an item of mail to ensure its special delivery. [1920–25, *Amer.*]

spe′cial div′idend, a dividend paid to stockholders in addition to the regular dividend. Also called **extra dividend.**

spe′cial draw′ing rights′, the reserve asset created through the International Monetary Fund as a supplement to gold and U.S. dollars, for use among the member governments in settling international payments. *Abbr.:* SDR, S.D.R. [1965–70]

spe′cial educa′tion, education that is modified or particularized for those having singular needs or disabilities, as handicapped or maladjusted people, slow learners, or gifted children.

spe′cial effects′, *Motion Pictures, Television.* unusual visual and sound effects beyond the range of normal photography or recording, as simulated fires or earthquakes, explosions, thunder and lightning, miniaturized or enlarged images, or other optical or electronic distortions. [1940–45]

Spe′cial Forc′es, U.S. Army personnel trained to organize, instruct, supply, and supervise indigenous forces engaged in guerrilla warfare and counterinsurgency operations, and to themselves conduct unconventional warfare. Also called **Green Berets.**

spe′cial han′dling, (in the U.S. Postal Service) the handling of third- and fourth-class mail as first-class upon the payment of a fee. [1925–30]

spe′cial in′terest, a body of persons, corporation, or industry that seeks or receives benefits or privileged treatment, esp. through legislation. [1905–10, *Amer.*] **—spe′cial-in′terest,** *adj.*

spe·cial·ism (spesh′ə liz′əm), *n.* devotion or restriction to a particular pursuit, branch of study, etc. [1855–60; SPECIAL + -ISM]

spe·cial·ist (spesh′ə list), *n.* **1.** a person who devotes himself or herself to one subject or to one particular branch of a subject or pursuit. **2.** a medical practitioner who devotes attention to a particular class of diseases, patients, etc. **3.** *U.S. Army.* an enlisted person of one of four grades having technical or administrative duties, the grades corresponding to those of corporal through sergeant first class but not requiring the exercise of command. **4.** *Stock Exchange.* a member of an exchange who executes orders in his or her name or for other stockbrokers in a single stock or a particular group of stocks and thus helps maintain the market in those securities on that exchange. [1855–60; SPECIAL + -IST]

spe·cial·is·tic (spesh′ə lis′tik), *adj.* pertaining to or characteristic of specialists or specialism. [1880–85; SPECIALIST + -IC]

spé·cia·li·té de la mai·son (spe syä lē tā də lᴀ mā-zôɴ′), *French.* the specialty of the house (used in referring to the most important dish served by a restaurant).

spe·ci·al·i·ty (spesh′ē al′i tē), *n., pl.* **-ties.** *Chiefly Brit.* specialty. [1400–50; late ME *specialite* < LL *speciālitās;* see SPECIALTY]

spe·cial·ize (spesh′ə līz′), *v.,* **-ized, -iz·ing.** *—v.i.* **1.** to pursue some special line of study, work, etc.; have a specialty: *The doctor specializes in gastroenterology.* **2.** *Biol.* (of an organism or one of its organs) to be adapted to a special function or environment. *—v.t.* **3.** to render special or specific; invest with a special character, function, etc. **4.** to adapt to special conditions; restrict to specific limits. **5.** to restrict payment of (a negotiable instrument) by endorsing over to a specific payee. **6.** to specify; particularize. Also, *esp. Brit.,* **spe′cial·ise′.** [1605–15; < F *spécialiser.* See SPECIAL, -IZE] **—spe′cial·i·za′tion,** *n.*

spe′cial ju′ry, *Law.* **1.** See **struck jury. 2.** See **blue-ribbon jury.** [1720–30]

spe′cial li′brary, a library maintained by an organization, as a business, association, or government agency, to collect materials and provide information of special relevance to the work of the organization.

spe′cial marine′ warn′ing, *Meteorol.* a National Weather Service warning of high-wind conditions at sea that are expected to last for up to two hours, and generally result from convective storm systems, as thunderstorms or squall lines. Cf. **warning** (def. 3).

Spe′cial Olym′pics, an international program of fitness and athletic competition for children and adults who are mentally and often physically handicapped, founded in 1968 and featuring events and quadrennial games modeled on those of the Olympics as well as regional and national competitions. **—Spe′cial Olym′pian.**

spe·cial-or·der (spesh′əl ôr′dər), *v.t.* **1.** to obtain by specific individual order: *to special-order a dining-room chandelier.* *—v.i.* **2.** to order goods by a special order.

spe′cial or′ders, *Mil.* a set of instructions from a headquarters affecting the activity or status of an individual or group of individuals. Cf. **general order.**

spe′cial part′ner, a partner whose liability for the firm's debts is limited to the amount that partner has invested in the firm. Also called **limited partner.** Cf. **general partner.** [1820–30, *Amer.*]

spe′cial part′nership. See **limited partnership.** [1855–60, *Amer.*]

spe′cial plea′, *Law.* a plea that alleges special or new matter as an answer to the allegations made by the opposite side and not as a denial of them. [1710–20]

spe′cial plead′ing, **1.** *Law.* pleading that alleges special or new matter in avoidance of the allegations made by the opposite side. **2.** pleading or arguing that ignores unfavorable features of a case. [1675–85]

spe′cial pros′ecutor, (formerly) an independent counsel.

spe′cial rule′, *Law.* See under **rule** (def. 10).

spe′cial ses′sion, a session, as of a legislature or council, called to meet in addition to those held regularly. [1840–50, *Amer.*]

spe′cial staff′, *Mil.* all staff officers assigned to headquarters of a division or higher unit who are not members of the general staff or personal staff. Cf. **general staff, personal staff.** [1955–60]

spe′cial term′, *Law.* **1.** the sitting of a court for the trial of a special case. **2.** the sitting of a court at an extraordinary time.

spe′cial the′ory of relativ′ity, *Physics.* See under **relativity** (def. 2). Also called **spe′cial relativ′ity.** [1915–20]

spe·cial·ty (spesh′əl tē), *n., pl.* **-ties,** *adj.* —*n.* **1.** a special or distinctive quality, mark, state, or condition. **2.** a special subject of study, line of work, area of interest, or the like: *His specialty is art criticism.* **3.** an article or service particularly dealt in, rendered, manufactured, etc., or one to which the provider, dealer, or manufacturer claims to devote special care: *The manufacturer's specialty is fine hats.* **4.** an article of unusual or superior design or quality. **5.** a novelty; a new article. **6.** an article with such strong consumer demand that it is at least partially removed from price competition. **7.** a special or particular point, item, matter, characteristic, or peculiarity. **8.** *Law.* **a.** a special agreement, contract, etc., expressed in an instrument under seal. **b.** a negotiable instrument not under seal. —*adj.* **9.** *Theat.* (in vaudeville) **a.** performing or performed in a manner that is unusual or not customary for a type of act, esp. a performance involving dexterity or ingenuity, as a patter song: *specialty actor; specialty act.* **b.** (of a song or dance) isolated from the rest of the show: *specialty number.* Also, *esp. Brit.,* **speciality.** [1300–50; ME *specialte* < MF *especialte* < LL *speciālitās.* See SPECIAL, -ITY]
—**Syn. 3.** trademark, stamp, badge, forte.

spe·ci·a·tion (spē′shē ā′shən, -sē ā′-), *n. Biol.* the formation of new species as a result of geographic, physiological, anatomical, or behavioral factors that prevent previously interbreeding populations from breeding with each other. [1895–1900; SPECI(ES) + -ATION]

spe·cie[1] (spē′shē, -sē), *n.* **1.** coined money; coin. **2. in specie, a.** in the same kind. **b.** (of money) in coin. **c.** in a similar manner; in kind: *Such treachery should be repaid in specie.* **d.** *Law.* in the identical shape, form, etc., as specified. [1545–55; < L *(in) speciē* (in) kind; see SPECIES]

spe·cie[2] (spē′shē, -sē), *n. Nonstandard.* species. [by back formation, construing SPECIES as pl. n.]

spe·cies (spē′shēz, -sēz), *n., pl.* **-cies,** *adj.* —*n.* **1.** a class of individuals having some common characteristics or qualities; distinct sort or kind. **2.** *Biol.* the major subdivision of a genus or subgenus, regarded as the basic category of biological classification, composed of related individuals that resemble one another, are able to breed among themselves, but are not able to breed with members of another species. **3.** *Logic.* **a.** one of the classes of things included with other classes in a genus. **b.** the set of things within one of these classes. **4.** *Eccles.* **a.** the external form or appearance of the bread or the wine in the Eucharist. **b.** either of the Eucharistic elements. **5.** *Obs.* specie; coin. **6. the species,** the human race; mankind: *a study of the species.* —*adj.* **7.** *Hort.* pertaining to a plant that is a representative member of a species, one that is not a hybrid or variety: *a species rose.* [1545–55; < L *speciēs* appearance, form, sort, kind, equiv. to *spec(ere)* to look, regard + *-iēs* abstract n. suffix]

spe·cies·ism (spē′shē ziz′əm, -sē ziz′-), *n.* discrimination in favor of one species, usually the human species, over another, esp. in the exploitation or mistreatment of animals by humans. [1970–75; SPECIES + -ISM] —**spe′cies·ist,** *adj., n.*

spe·cies-spe·cif·ic (spē′shēz spi sif′ik, spē′sēz-), *adj. Ecol.* associated with or limited to one species only.

specif., **1.** specific. **2.** specifically.

spec·i·fi·a·ble (spes′ə fī′ə bəl), *adj.* that can be specified. [1655–65; SPECIFY + -ABLE]

spe·cif·ic (spi sif′ik), *adj.* **1.** having a special application, bearing, or reference; specifying, explicit, or definite: *to state one's specific purpose.* **2.** specified, precise, or particular: *a specific sum of money.* **3.** peculiar or proper to somebody or something, as qualities, characteristics, effects, etc.: *His specific problems got him into trouble.* **4.** of a special or particular kind. **5.** concerned specifically with the item or subject named (used in combination): *The Secretary addressed himself to crop-specific problems.* **6.** *Biol.* of or pertaining to a species: *specific characters.* **7.** *Med.* **a.** (of a disease) produced by a special cause or infection. **b.** (of a remedy) having special effect in the prevention or cure of a certain disease. **8.** *Immunol.* (of an antibody or antigen) having a particular effect on only one antibody or antigen or affecting it in only one way. **9.** *Com.* noting customs or duties levied in fixed amounts per unit, as number, weight, or volume. **10.** *Physics.* **a.** designating a physical constant that, for a particular substance, is expressed as the ratio of the quantity in the substance to the quantity in an equal volume of a standard substance, as water or air. **b.** designating a physical constant that expresses a property or effect as a quantity per unit length, area, volume, or mass. —*n.* **11.** something specific, as a statement, quality, detail, etc. **12.** *Med.* a specific remedy: *There is no specific for the common cold.* [1625–35; < ML *specificus,* equiv. to L *speci(ēs)* SPECIES + *-ficus* -FIC] —**spe·cif′i·cal·ly,** *adv.*
—**Syn. 1.** See **special.** —**Ant. 2.** vague.

CONCISE ETYMOLOGY KEY: <, descended or borrowed from; >, whence; b., blend of, blended; c., cognate with; cf., compare; deriv., derivative; equiv., equivalent; imit., imitative; obl., oblique; r., replacing; s., stem; sp., spelling, spelled; resp., respelling, respelled; trans., translation; ?, origin unknown; *, unattested; ‡, probably earlier than. See the full key inside the front cover.

spec·i·fi·ca·tion (spes′ə fi kā′shən), *n.* **1.** the act of specifying. **2.** Usually, **specifications.** a detailed description or assessment of requirements, dimensions, materials, etc., as of a proposed building, machine, bridge, etc. **3.** a particular item, aspect, calculation, etc., in such a description. **4.** something specified, as in a bill of particulars; a specified particular, item, or article. **5.** an act of making specific. **6.** the state of having a specific character. [1605–15; < ML *specificātiōn-* (s. of *specificātiō*), equiv. to *specificāt(us)* (ptp. of *specificāre* to mention, describe; see SPECIFIC, -ATE[1]) + *-iōn-* -ION]
—**Syn. 4.** requirement, condition, qualification.

specif′ic charge′, *Physics.* the ratio of the charge on a particle to the mass of the particle.

specif′ic conduct′ance, *Elect.* conductivity (def. 2).

specif′ic grav′ity, *Physics.* the ratio of the density of any substance to the density of some other substance taken as standard, water being the standard for liquids and solids, and hydrogen or air being the standard for gases. Also called **relative density.** [1660–70] —**spe·cif′ic-grav′i·ty,** *adj.*

specif′ic heat′, *Physics.* **1.** the number of calories required to raise the temperature of 1 gram of a substance 1°C, or the number of BTU's per pound per degree F. **2.** (originally) the ratio of the thermal capacity of a substance to that of standard material. [1825–35]

specif′ic humid′ity, the ratio of the mass of water vapor in air to the total mass of the mixture of air and water vapor. Cf. **mixing ratio, absolute humidity, dew point, relative humidity.**

specif′ic im′pulse, *Rocketry.* **1.** a measure, usually in seconds, of the efficiency with which a rocket engine utilizes its propellants, equal to the number of pounds of thrust produced per pound of propellant burned per second. **2.** the specific impulse that a given combination of propellants would produce in an ideal rocket engine providing complete combustion, no friction losses, and no lateral expansion of the exhaust. [1945–50]

specif′ic induc′tive capac′ity, *Elect.* permittivity.

spec·i·fic·i·ty (spes′ə fis′i tē), *n.* **1.** the quality or state of being specific. **2.** *Biochem., Pharm.* the selective attachment or influence of one substance on another, as an antibiotic and its target organism or an antibody and its specific antigen. [1875–80; SPECIFIC + -ITY]

specif′ic perfor′mance, *Law.* (esp. in the sale of land) literal compliance with one's contractual promises pursuant to a judicial mandate. [1870–75]

specif′ic resist′ance, *Elect.* resistivity (def. 2).

specif′ic vol′ume, *Physics.* volume per unit mass; the reciprocal of density.

spec·i·fy (spes′ə fī′), *v.,* **-fied, -fy·ing.** —*v.t.* **1.** to mention or name specifically or definitely; state in detail: *He did not specify the amount needed.* **2.** to give a specific character to. **3.** to set forth as a specification. **4.** to name or state as a condition: *He specified that he be given my power of attorney.* —*v.i.* **5.** to make a specific mention or statement. [1250–1300; ME *specyfyen* < OF *specifier* < ML *specificāre.* See SPECIFIC, -FY] —**spec·i·fi·ca·tive** (spes′ə fi kā′tiv), *adj.* —**spec′i·fi·ca′tive·ly,** *adv.* —**spec′i·fi′er,** *n.*
—**Syn. 1.** detail, indicate, enumerate, stipulate.

spec·i·men (spes′ə mən), *n.* **1.** a part or an individual taken as exemplifying a whole mass or number; a typical animal, plant, mineral, part, etc. **2.** (in medicine, microbiology, etc.) a sample of a substance or material for examination or study: *a urine specimen.* **3.** a particular or peculiar kind of person. [1600–10; < L: mark, example, indication, sign, equiv. to *speci-,* s. of *specere* to look, regard + *-men* n. suffix denoting result or means]
—**Syn. 1.** type, model, pattern. See **example.**

spec′imen plant′, *Hort.* a plant grown by itself for ornamental effect, rather than being massed with others in a bed or border.

spe·ci·os·i·ty (spē′shē os′i tē), *n., pl.* **-ties.** the quality or state of being specious. [1425–75; late ME < LL *speciōsitās* good looks, beauty. See SPECIOUS, -ITY]

spe·cious (spē′shəs), *adj.* **1.** apparently good or right though lacking real merit; superficially pleasing or plausible: *specious arguments.* **2.** pleasing to the eye but deceptive. **3.** *Obs.* pleasing to the eye; fair. [1350–1400; ME < L *speciōsus* fair, good-looking, beautiful, equiv. to *speci(ēs)* (see SPECIES) + *-ōsus* -OUS] —**spe′cious·ly,** *adv.* —**spe′cious·ness,** *n.*
—**Syn. 1.** See **plausible. 2.** false, misleading.

spe′cious pres′ent, *Philos.* a short time span in which change and duration are alleged to be directly experienced.

speck (spek), *n.* **1.** a small spot differing in color or substance from that of the surface or material upon which it appears or lies: *Specks of soot on the window sill.* **2.** a very little bit or particle: *We haven't a speck of sugar.* **3.** something appearing small by comparison or by reason of distance: *By then the town was just a speck.* —*v.t.* **4.** to mark with, or as with, a speck or specks. [bef. 900; ME *specke,* OE *specca;* c. D *spikkel*] —**speck·ed·ness** (spek′id nis), *n.* —**speck′less,** *adj.* —**speck′less·ly,** *adv.* —**speck′less·ness,** *n.*

speck·le (spek′əl), *n., v.,* **-led, -ling.** —*n.* **1.** a small speck, spot, or mark, as on skin. **2.** speckled coloring or marking. —*v.t.* **3.** to mark with or as with speckles. [1400–50; late ME; see SPECK, -LE] —**speck′led·ness,** *n.*

speck′led trout′. See **brook trout** (def. 1). [1795–1805, *Amer.*]

speck′le interferom′etry, *Astron.* a photographic technique for clarifying the telescopic images of a star by taking short exposures of the electronic images of the star's speckle pattern and extrapolating properties of the starlight to create a more accurate composite image. [1965–70; INTERFERE + -O- + -METRY]

speck′le pat′tern, *Astron.* the visual appearance of a star as viewed through a large telescope, with irregularities caused by the distorting effect of local turbulence in the earth's atmosphere. [1960–65]

specs (speks), *n.pl. Informal.* **1.** spectacles; eyeglasses. **2.** specifications. [1800–10; by shortening]

SPECT (spekt), *n.* single photon emission computed tomography: a technique for measuring brain function similar to PET. [1985–90]

spec·ta·cle (spek′tə kəl), *n.* **1.** anything presented to the sight or view, esp. something of a striking or impressive kind: *The stars make a fine spectacle tonight.* **2.** a public show or display, esp. on a large scale: *The coronation was a lavish spectacle.* **3. spectacles.** eyeglasses, esp. with pieces passing over or around the ears for holding them in place. **4.** Often, **spectacles. a.** something resembling spectacles in shape or function. **b.** any of various devices suggesting spectacles, as one attached to a semaphore to display lights or different colors by colored glass. **5.** *Obs.* a spyglass. **6. make a spectacle of oneself,** to call attention to one's unseemly behavior; behave foolishly or badly in public: *They tell me I made a spectacle of myself at the party last night.* [1300–50; ME < L *spectāculum* a sight, spectacle, deriv. of *spectāre,* freq. of *specere* to look, regard. See -CLE[2]] —**spec′ta·cle·less,** *adj.* —**spec′ta·cle·like′,** *adj.*
—**Syn. 1.** marvel, wonder, sight, show.

spec·ta·cled (spek′tə kəld), *adj.* **1.** wearing spectacles. **2.** (of an animal) having a marking resembling a pair of spectacles. [1600–10; SPECTACLE + -ED[3]]

spec′tacled co′bra. See **Indian cobra.** [1850–55]

spec·tac·u·lar (spek tak′yə lər), *adj.* **1.** of or like a spectacle; marked by or given to an impressive, large-scale display. **2.** dramatically daring or thrilling: *a spectacular dive from a cliff.* —*n.* **3.** a single television production featuring well-known performers and characterized by elaborate sets, costumes, staging, etc. Cf. **special** (def. 13). **4.** an impressive, large-scale display: *another Hollywood spectacular.* [1675–85; < L *spectācul(um)* (see SPECTACLE) + -AR[1]] —**spec·tac·u·lar·i·ty** (spek tak′yə lar′i tē), **spec·tac′u·lar·ism,** *n.* —**spec·tac′u·lar·ly,** *adv.*
—**Syn. 2.** hair-raising, dramatic, breathtaking.

spec·tate (spek′tāt), *v.i.,* **-tat·ed, -tat·ing.** to participate as a spectator, as at a horse race. [1700–10; back formation from SPECTATOR]

spec·ta·tor (spek′tā tər, spek tā′-), *n.* **1.** a person who looks on or watches; onlooker; observer. **2.** a person who is present at and views a spectacle, display, or the like; member of an audience. **3.** Also called **spec′tator shoe′.** a white shoe with a perforated wing tip and back trim, traditionally of dark brown, dark blue, or black but sometimes of a lighter color. [1580–90; < L *spectātor,* equiv. to *spectā(re),* freq. of *specere* to look, regard + *-tor* -TOR] —**spec·ta·to·ri·al** (spek′tə tôr′ē əl, -tōr′-), *adj.*

Spectator, The, a weekly periodical (1711–12, 1714) issued by Joseph Addison and Richard Steele.

spec′tator pump′, a woman's spectator shoe, closed at the front and back, usually having a medium or medium-high heel.

spec′tator sport′, any sport that can be watched by spectators, as football or basketball, usually for a fee. [1940–45]

spec·ter (spek′tər), *n.* **1.** a visible incorporeal spirit, esp. one of a terrifying nature; ghost; phantom; apparition. **2.** some object or source of terror or dread: *the specter of disease or famine.* Also, *esp. Brit.,* **spectre.** [1595–1605; < L *spectrum;* see SPECTRUM]
—**Syn. 1.** shade. See **ghost.**

spec·ti·no·my·cin (spek′tə nō mī′sin), *n. Pharm.* an antibiotic drug, $C_{14}H_{24}N_2O_7$, produced by the actinomycete *Streptomyces spectabilis,* used in the treatment of susceptible gonorrhea. [1960–65; b. NL *spectabilis* a specific epithet (lit., visible; see SPECTACLE, -ABLE) and ACTINOMYCIN]

spec·tra (spek′trə), *n.* a pl. of **spectrum.**

spec·tral (spek′trəl), *adj.* **1.** of or pertaining to a specter; ghostly; phantom. **2.** resembling or suggesting a specter. **3.** of, pertaining to, or produced by a spectrum or spectra. **4.** resembling or suggesting a spectrum or spectra. [1710–20; < L *spectr(um)* (see SPECTER) + -AL[1]] —**spec·tral′i·ty, spec′tral·ness,** *n.* —**spec′tral·ly,** *adv.*

spec′tral line′, *Optics.* a line in a spectrum due to the absorption or emission of light at a discrete frequency. [1865–70]

spec′tral se′ries, *Physics.* a series of lines in the spectrum of light emitted by excited atoms of an element, each line being related to the others in the series by a simple numerical equation and identified with a particular energy level of an atom of the element.

spec′tral type′, *Astron.* a category for classifying a star, as A star or G star, according to features of its spectrum, as its shape as a function of temperature and wavelength and its absorption spectrum, that indicate the surface temperature of the star and the presence of particular atoms or molecules in its outer layers: principal types are spectral types O, B, A, F, G, K, and M. Also called **spec′tral class′.** [1920–25]

spec′tra yel′low, a vivid yellow color. Also called **Hansa yellow.**

spec·tre (spek′tər), *n. Chiefly Brit.* specter.

spec·trin (spek′trin), *n. Biochem.* a rodlike structural protein of the red blood cell membrane. [1968; SPECT(E)R (cf. GHOST def. 12) + -IN[2]]

spectro-, a combining form representing **spectrum** in compound words: *spectrometer.*

spec·tro·bo·lom·e·ter (spek′trō bō lom′i tər), *n. Physics.* an instrument consisting of a spectroscope and a bolometer, for determining the distribution of radiant energy in a spectrum. [SPECTRO- + BOLOMETER] **—spec·tro·bo·lo·met·ric** (spek′trō bō′lə me′trik), *adj.*

spec·tro·chem·i·cal (spek′trō kem′i kəl), *adj.* of, pertaining to, or utilizing the techniques of spectrochemistry. [SPECTRO- + CHEMICAL]

spec·tro·chem·is·try (spek′trō kem′ə strē), *n.* the branch of chemistry that deals with the chemical analysis of substances by means of the spectra of light they absorb or emit. [SPECTRO- + CHEMISTRY]

spec·tro·col·o·rim·e·try (spek′trō kul′ə rim′i trē), *n.* the quantitative measure of colors by spectrophotometry. [SPECTRO- + COLORIMETRY]

spec·tro·fluo·rim·e·ter (spek′trō flo͝o rim′i tər, -flô-, -flō-), *n. Spectroscopy.* an instrument in which the spectrum of secondarily emitted fluorescent light is used to identify chemical compounds. Also, **spec·tro·fluo·rom·e·ter** (spek′trō flo͝o rom′i tər, -flô-, -flō-). [1955–60; SPECTRO- + FLUORIMETER]

spec·tro·gram (spek′trə gram′), *n.* **1.** a representation or photograph of a spectrum. **2.** See **sound spectrogram.** [1890–95; SPECTRO- + -GRAM[1]]

spec·tro·graph (spek′trə graf′, -gräf′), *n.* **1.** a spectroscope for photographing or producing a representation of a spectrum. **2.** See **sound spectrograph.** [1880–85; SPECTRO- + -GRAPH] **—spec·trog·ra·pher** (spek trog′rə fər), *n.* **—spec·tro·graph·ic** (spek′trə-graf′ik), *adj.* **—spec′tro·graph′i·cal·ly,** *adv.* **—spec·trog′ra·phy,** *n.*

spec·tro·he·li·o·gram (spek′trō hē′lē ə gram′), *n.* a photograph of the sun made with a spectroheliograph. [1905–10; SPECTRO- + HELIOGRAM]

spec·tro·he·li·o·graph (spek′trō hē′lē ə graf′, -gräf′), *n.* an apparatus for making photographs of the sun with a monochromatic light to show the details of the sun's surface and surroundings as they would appear if the sun emitted only that light. [1890–95; SPECTRO- + HELIOGRAPH] **—spec·tro·he·li·o·graph·ic** (spek′trō-hē′lē ə graf′ik), *adj.*

spec·tro·he·li·o·scope (spek′trō hē′lē ə skōp′), *n.* **1.** a spectroheliograph. **2.** a similar instrument, used for visual instead of photographic observations. [1925–30; SPECTRO- + HELIO- + -SCOPE] **—spec·tro·he·li·o·scop·ic** (spek′trō hē′lē ə skop′ik), *adj.*

spec·trol·o·gy (spek trol′ə jē), *n.* the study of ghosts, phantoms, or apparitions. [1810–20; < L *spectr(um)* SPECTER + -O- + -LOGY] **—spec·tro·log·i·cal** (spek′trə-loj′i kəl), *adj.* **—spec′tro·log′i·cal·ly,** *adv.*

spec·trom·e·ter (spek trom′i tər), *n. Optics.* an optical device for measuring wavelengths, deviation of refracted rays, and angles between faces of a prism, esp. an instrument (**prism spectrometer**) consisting of a slit through which light passes, a collimator, a prism that deviates the light, and a telescope through which the deviated light is viewed and examined. [1870–75; SPECTRO- + -METER] **—spec·tro·met·ric** (spek′trə me′trik), *adj.* **—spec·trom′e·try,** *n.*

spec·tro·mi·cro·scope (spek′trō mī′krə skōp′), *n.* a microscope with an attached spectroscope. [SPECTRO- + MICROSCOPE] **—spec·tro·mi·cro·scop·i·cal** (spek′-trō mī′krə skop′i kəl), *adj.*

spec·tro·pho·to·e·lec·tric (spek′trō fō′tō i lek′-trik), *adj. Physics.* pertaining to the relationship between the wavelength of the incident radiation and the number of electrons released by a photoelectric substance. [SPECTRO- + PHOTOELECTRIC]

spec·tro·pho·tom·e·ter (spek′trō fō tom′i tər), *n.* an instrument for making photometric comparisons between parts of spectra. [1880–85; SPECTRO- + PHOTOMETER] **—spec·tro·pho·to·met·ric** (spek′trō fō′tə me′-trik), *adj.* **—spec′tro·pho′to·met′ri·cal·ly,** *adv.* **—spec′tro·pho·tom′e·try,** *n.*

spec·tro·po·lar·im·e·ter (spek′trō pō′lə rim′i tər), *n. Optics.* an instrument for determining the extent to which plane-polarized light of various wavelengths is rotated by certain solutions, consisting of a combination of a spectroscope and a polarimeter. [SPECTRO- + POLARIMETER]

spec·tro·po·lar·i·scope (spek′trō pō lar′ə skōp′), *n. Optics.* an instrument combining the functions of a spectroscope with those of a polariscope. Cf. **spectropolarimeter.** [SPECTRO- + POLARISCOPE]

spec·tro·ra·di·om·e·ter (spek′trō rā′dē om′i tər), *n. Optics.* an instrument for determining the radiant-energy distribution in a spectrum, combining the functions of a spectroscope with those of a radiometer. [SPECTRO- + RADIOMETER] **—spec·tro·ra·di·o·met·ric** (spek′trō rā′dē ə me′trik), *adj.* **—spec′tro·ra′di·om′e·try,** *n.*

spec·tro·scope (spek′trə skōp′), *n. Optics.* an optical device for producing and observing a spectrum of light or radiation from any source, consisting essentially of a slit through which the radiation passes, a collimating lens, and an Amici prism. [1860–65; SPECTRO- + -SCOPE] **—spec·tro·scop·ic** (spek′trə skop′ik), **spec′tro·scop′i·cal,** *adj.* **—spec′tro·scop′i·cal·ly,** *adv.*

spec′troscop′ic bi′nary, *Astron.* a binary star having components that are not sufficiently separated to be resolved by a telescope, known to be a binary only by the variations in wavelength of emitted light that are detected by a spectroscope. Cf. **visual binary.**

spec·tros·co·py (spek tros′kə pē, spek′trə skō′pē), *n.* the science that deals with the use of the spectroscope and with spectrum analysis. [1865–70; SPECTRO- + -SCOPY] **—spec·tros·co·pist** (spek tros′kə pist), *n.*

spec·trum (spek′trəm), *n., pl.* **-tra** (-trə), **-trums. 1.** *Physics.* **a.** an array of entities, as light waves or particles, ordered in accordance with the magnitudes of a common physical property, as wavelength or mass: often the band of colors produced when sunlight is passed through a prism, comprising red, orange, yellow, green, blue, indigo, and violet. **b.** this band or series of colors together with extensions at the ends that are not visible to the eye, but that can be studied by means of photography, heat effects, etc., and that are produced by the dispersion of radiant energy other than ordinary light rays. Cf. **band spectrum, electromagnetic spectrum, mass spectrum. 2.** a broad range of varied but related ideas or objects, the individual features of which tend to overlap so as to form a continuous series or sequence: *the spectrum of political beliefs.* [1605–15; < L: appearance, form, equiv. to *spec(ere)* to look, regard + *-trum* instrumental n. suffix]

spec′trum anal′ysis, 1. the determination of the constitution or condition of bodies and substances by means of the spectra they produce. **2.** the ascertaining of the number and character of the constituents combining to produce a sound spectrogram. [1865–70]

spec·u·lar (spek′yə lər), *adj.* **1.** pertaining to or having the properties of a mirror. **2.** pertaining to a speculum. **3.** *Optics.* (of reflected light) directed, as from a smooth, polished surface (opposed to *diffuse*). [1570–80; < L *speculāris,* equiv. to *specul(um)* a mirror (*spec(ere)* to look, regard + *-ulum* instrumental suffix; see -ULE) + *-āris* -AR[1]] **—spec′u·lar·ly,** *adv.*

spec·u·late (spek′yə lāt′), *v.i.,* **-lat·ed, -lat·ing. 1.** to engage in thought or reflection; meditate (often fol. by *on, upon,* or a clause). **2.** to indulge in conjectural thought. **3.** to engage in any business transaction involving considerable risk or the chance of large gains, esp. to buy and sell commodities, stocks, etc., in the expectation of a quick or very large profit. [1590–1600; < L *speculātus,* ptp. of *speculārī* to watch over, explore, reconnoiter, deriv. of *specula* watch tower, n. deriv. of *specere* to look, regard; see -ATE[1]]
—Syn. 1. think, reflect, cogitate. **2.** conjecture, guess, surmise, suppose, theorize.

spec·u·la·tion (spek′yə lā′shən), *n.* **1.** the contemplation or consideration of some subject: *to engage in speculation on humanity's ultimate destiny.* **2.** a single instance or process of consideration. **3.** a conclusion or opinion reached by such contemplation: *These speculations are impossible to verify.* **4.** conjectural consideration of a matter; conjecture or surmise: *a report based on speculation rather than facts.* **5.** engagement in business transactions involving considerable risk but offering the chance of large gains, esp. trading in commodities, stocks, etc., in the hope of profit from changes in the market price. **6.** a speculative commercial venture or undertaking. [1325–75; ME *speculacioun* < LL *speculātiōn-* (s. of *speculātiō*) exploration, observation. See SPECULATE, -ION]
—Syn. 3. supposition, view, theory, hypothesis.

spec·u·la·tive (spek′yə lā′tiv, -lə tiv), *adj.* **1.** pertaining to, of the nature of, or characterized by speculation, contemplation, conjecture, or abstract reasoning: *a speculative approach.* **2.** theoretical, rather than practical: *speculative conclusions.* **3.** given to speculation, as persons, the mind, etc. **4.** of the nature of or involving commercial or financial speculation: *speculative ventures.* **5.** engaging in or given to such speculation. [1350–1400; ME < LL *speculātīvus.* See SPECULATE, -IVE] **—spec′u·la′tive·ly,** *adv.* **—spec′u·la′tive·ness,** *n.*

spec′ulative philos′ophy, philosophy embodying beliefs insusceptible of proof and attempting to gain insight into the nature of the ultimate by intuitive or a priori means. [1855–60]

spec·u·la·tor (spek′yə lā′tər), *n.* **1.** a person who is engaged in commercial or financial speculation. **2.** a person who makes advance purchases of tickets, as to games or theatrical performances, that are likely to be in demand, for resale later at a higher price. **3.** a person who is devoted to mental speculation. [1545–55; < L *speculātor* explorer, equiv. to *speculā(rī)* to watch over, explore, reconnoiter (see SPECULATE) + *-tor* -TOR]

spec·u·lum (spek′yə ləm), *n., pl.* **-la** (-lə), **-lums. 1.** a mirror or reflector, esp. one of polished metal, as on a reflecting telescope. **2.** See **speculum metal. 3.** *Surg.* an instrument for rendering a part accessible to observation, as by enlarging an orifice. **4.** *Ornith.* a lustrous or specially colored area on the wings of certain birds. [1590–1600; < L: mirror, equiv. to *spec(ere)* to look, behold + *-ulum* instrumental suffix; see -ULE]

spec′ulum met′al, any of several bronze alloys with a high tin content, often containing other materials, as silver, brass, lead, zinc, or arsenic, used for making mirrors and reflectors. Also called **speculum, spec′ulum al′loy.** [1790–1800]

sped (sped), *v.* a pt. and pp. of **speed.**

Sp.Ed., Specialist in Education.

Spee (shpā), *n.* **Ma·xi·mil·i·an von** (mäk′si mē′lē än′ fən), 1861–1941, German admiral.

speech (spēch), *n.* **1.** the faculty or power of speaking; oral communication; ability to express one's thoughts and emotions by speech sounds and gesture: *Losing her speech made her feel isolated from humanity.* **2.** the act of speaking: *He expresses himself better in speech than in writing.* **3.** something that is spoken; an utterance, remark, or declaration: *We waited for some speech that would indicate her true feelings.* **4.** a form of communication in spoken language, made by a speaker before an audience for a given purpose: *a fiery speech.* **5.** any single utterance of an actor in the course of a play, motion picture, etc. **6.** the form of utterance characteristic of a particular people or region; a language or dialect. **7.** manner of speaking, as of a person: *Your slovenly speech is holding back your career.* **8.** a field of study devoted to the theory and practice of oral communication. **9.** *Archaic.* rumor. [bef. 900; ME *speche,* OE *spǣc,* var. of *sprǣc,* deriv. of *sprecan* to SPEAK; c. G *Sprache*]
—Syn. 1. parlance, parley, conversation, communication. SPEECH, LANGUAGE refer to the means of communication used by people. SPEECH is the expression of ideas and thoughts by means of articulate vocal sounds, or the faculty of thus expressing ideas and thoughts. LANGUAGE is a set of conventional signs, not necessarily articulate or even vocal (any set of signs, signals, or symbols that convey meaning, including written words, may be called language): *a spoken language.* Thus, LANGUAGE is the set of conventions, and SPEECH is the action of putting these to use: *He couldn't understand the speech of the natives because it was in a foreign language.* **3.** observation, assertion, asseveration, comment, mention, talk. **4.** talk, discourse. SPEECH, ADDRESS, ORATION, HARANGUE are terms for a communication to an audience. SPEECH is the general word, with no implication of kind or length, or whether planned or not. An ADDRESS is a rather formal, planned speech, appropriate to a particular subject or occasion. An ORATION is a polished, rhetorical address, given usually on a notable occasion, that employs eloquence and studied methods of delivery. A HARANGUE is a violent, informal speech, often addressed to a casually assembled audience, and intended to arouse strong feeling (sometimes to lead to mob action). **6.** tongue, patois.

speech′ act′, *Philos., Ling.* any of the acts that may be performed by a speaker in making an utterance, as stating, asking, requesting, advising, warning, or persuading, considered in terms of the content of the message, the intention of the speaker, and the effect on the listener.

speech′ clin′ic, a place at which specialists in speech therapy reeducate those with a speech handicap.

speech′ commu′nity, *Ling.* **1.** the aggregate of all the people who use a given language or dialect. **2.** a group of people geographically distributed so that there is no break in intelligibility from place to place. [1930–35]

speech′ correc′tion, the reeducation of speech habits that deviate from accepted speech standards.

speech′ form′. See **linguistic form.** [1860–65]

speech·i·fy (spē′chə fī′), *v.i.,* **-fied, -fy·ing.** to make a speech or speeches; harangue. [1715–25; SPEECH + -IFY] **—speech′i·fi·ca′tion,** *n.* **—speech′i·fi′er,** *n.*

speech′ is′land, *Ling.* a speech community that is completely surrounded by another, usually larger, speech community.

speech·less (spēch′lis), *adj.* **1.** temporarily deprived of speech by strong emotion, physical weakness, exhaustion, etc.: *speechless with alarm.* **2.** characterized by absence or loss of speech: *speechless joy.* **3.** lacking the faculty of speech; dumb. **4.** not expressed in speech or words: *speechless compliments.* **5.** refraining from speech. [bef. 1000; ME *specheles,* OE *spǣclēas.* See SPEECH, -LESS] **—speech′less·ly,** *adv.* **—speech′less·ness,** *n.*
—Syn. 1. dumfounded, shocked, mute. See **dumb. 3.** silent, mute. **—Ant. 1–3.** loquacious, voluble, talkative.

speech·mak·er (spēch′mā′kər), *n.* a person who delivers speeches. [1700–10; SPEECH + MAKER] **—speech′mak′ing,** *n.*

speech′ or′gan, any part of the body, as the tongue, velum, diaphragm, or lungs, that participates, actively or passively, voluntarily or involuntarily, in the production of the sounds of speech.

speech′ pathol′ogy, the scientific study and treatment of defects, disorders, and malfunctions of speech and voice, as stuttering, lisping, or lalling, and of language disturbances, as aphasia or delayed language acquisition.

speech·read (spēch′rēd′), *v.t., v.i.,* **-read** (-red′), **-read·ing.** to comprehend by speechreading. Cf. **lip-read.** [SPEECH + READ[1]] **—speech′read′er,** *n.*

speech·read·ing (spēch′rē′ding), *n.* the act or process of determining the intended meaning of a speaker by utilizing all visual clues accompanying speech attempts, as lip movements, facial expressions, and bodily gestures, used esp. by people with impaired hearing. Cf. **lip reading.** [1890–95; SPEECH + READ[1] + -ING[1]]

speech′ recogni′tion, *Computers.* the computerized analysis of spoken words in order to identify the speaker, as in security systems, or to respond to voiced commands: the analysis is performed by finding patterns in the spectrum of the incoming sound and comparing them with stored patterns of elements of sound, as phones, or of complete words. Also called **voice recognition.** Cf. **phone[2].** [1950–55]

speech′ sound′, *Phonet.* **1.** any of the set of distinctive sounds of a given language. Cf. **phoneme. 2.** any audible, elemental, acoustic event occurring in speech: *"Go" contains the speech sound "o."* Cf. **phone[2]. 3.** any of the sounds of the entire phonetic system of a language. Cf. **allophone.** [1865–70]

speech·way (spēch′wā′), *n.* a pattern, style, or feature of spoken language shared by the people of a particular group or area. [SPEECH + WAY[1]]

speech·writ·er (spēch′rī′tər), *n.* a person who writes speeches for others, usually for pay. [1825–35; SPEECH + WRITER]

speed (spēd), *n., v.,* **sped** or **speed·ed, speed·ing.** **—***n.* **1.** rapidity in moving, going, traveling, proceeding,

CONCISE PRONUNCIATION KEY: act, cāpe, dâre, pärt; set, ēqual; *if,* īce; ox, ōver, ôrder, oil, bo͝ok, bo͞ot, out; up, ûrge; child; sing; shoe; thin, *th*at; zh as in *treasure.* ə = *a* as in *alone, e* as in *system, i* as in *easily, o* as in *gallop, u* as in *circus;* ᵊ as in *fire* (fīᵊr), *hour* (ouᵊr). l and n can serve as syllabic consonants, as in *cradle* (krād′l), and *button* (but′n). See the full key inside the front cover.

or performing; swiftness; celerity: *the speed of sound.* **2.** relative rapidity in moving, going, etc.; rate of motion or progress: *full speed ahead.* **3.** full, maximum, or optimum rate of motion: *The car gets to speed in just nine seconds.* **4.** *Auto.* a transmission gear ratio. **5.** *Photog.* **a.** Also called **film speed.** the sensitivity of a film or paper to light, measured by an ASA or DIN index, which assigns low numbers to slow film and higher numbers to faster film. **b.** Also called **shutter speed.** the length of time a shutter is opened to expose film. **c.** the largest opening at which a lens can be used. **6.** *Slang.* a stimulating drug, esp. methamphetamine or amphetamine. **7.** *Informal.* a person or thing that suits one's ability, personality, desires, etc.: *Quiet, easygoing people are more my speed.* **8.** *Archaic.* success or prosperity. **9. at full** or **top speed, a.** at the greatest speed possible. **b.** to the maximum of one's capabilities; with great rapidity: *He worked at full speed.* **10. up to speed, a.** operating at full or optimum speed. **b.** functioning or producing at an expected, acceptable, or competitive level; up to par: *a new firm not yet up to speed.* —*v.t.* **11.** to promote the success of (an affair, undertaking, etc.); further, forward, or expedite. **12.** to direct (the steps, course, way, etc.) with speed. **13.** to increase the rate of speed of (usually fol. by *up*): *to speed up industrial production.* **14.** to bring to a particular speed, as a machine. **15.** to cause to move, go, or proceed with speed. **16.** to expedite the going of: *to speed the parting guest.* **17.** *Archaic.* to cause to succeed or prosper. —*v.i.* **18.** to move, go, pass, or proceed with speed or rapidity. **19.** to drive a vehicle at a rate that exceeds the legally established maximum: *He was arrested for speeding.* **20.** to increase the rate of speed or progress (usually fol. by *up*). **21.** to get on or fare in a specified or particular manner. **22.** *Archaic.* to succeed or prosper. [bef. 900; 1965–70 for def. 6; (n.) ME *spede* good luck, prosperity, rapidity, OE *spēd;* c. D *spoed,* OHG *spōt;* akin to OE *spōwan* to prosper, succeed; (v.) ME *speden* to succeed, prosper, go with speed, OE *spēdan* to succeed, prosper; c. OS *spōdian,* OHG *spuoten*] —**speed′ful,** *adj.* —**speed′ful·ly,** *adv.* —**speed′ful·ness,** *n.* —**speed′ing·ly,** *adv.* —**speed′·ing·ness,** *n.* —**speed′less,** *adj.*
—**Syn. 1, 2.** fleetness, alacrity, dispatch, expedition; hurry. SPEED, VELOCITY, QUICKNESS, RAPIDITY, CELERITY, HASTE refer to swift or energetic movement or operation. SPEED (originally prosperity or success) may apply to human or nonhuman activity and emphasizes the rate in time at which something travels or operates: *the speed of light, of a lens, of an automobile, of thought.* VELOCITY, a more learned or technical term, is sometimes interchangeable with SPEED: *the velocity of light;* it is commonly used to refer to high rates of speed, linear or circular: *velocity of a projectile.* QUICKNESS, a native word, and RAPIDITY, a synonym of Latin origin, suggest speed of movement or operation on a small or subordinate scale; QUICKNESS applies more to people (*quickness of mind, of perception, of bodily movement*), RAPIDITY more to things, often in a technical or mechanical context: *the rapidity of moving parts; a lens of great rapidity.* CELERITY, a somewhat literary synonym of Latin origin, refers usually to human movement or operation and emphasizes expedition, dispatch, or economy in an activity: *the celerity of his response.* HASTE refers to the energetic activity of human beings under stress; it often suggests lack of opportunity for care or thought: *to marry in haste; a report prepared in haste.* **11.** advance, favor. **13.** accelerate. **18.** See **rush**[1]. —**Ant. 1.** slowness.

speed·ball (spēd′bôl′), *n.* **1.** a game similar to soccer with the chief difference that a player catching the ball on the fly can pass it with the hands. **2.** *Slang.* any combination of a stimulant and a depressant taken together, esp. a mixture of heroin and cocaine or heroin and methamphetamine injected into the bloodstream. —*v.i.* **3.** *Slang.* to take a speedball, esp. by injection. [1940–45; SPEED + BALL[1]]

speed·boat (spēd′bōt′), *n.* a motorboat designed for high speeds. [1910–15; SPEED BOAT + -ING[1]]

speed·boat·ing (spēd′bō′ting), *n.* the act or sport of traveling in a speedboat. [1925–30; SPEEDBOAT + -ING[1]]

speed′ bump′, a rounded ridge built crosswise into the pavement of a road or driveway to force vehicles to slow down. [1970–75]

speed′ de′mon, *Informal.* a person who travels or works at high speed.

speed·er (spē′dər), *n.* **1.** a person or thing that speeds. **2.** a driver who exceeds the legal speed limit. **3.** a small self-propelled railroad car powered by a gasoline engine and used by section hands. [1350–1400; ME; see SPEED, -ER[1]]

speed′ freak′ *Slang.* an addict or habitual user of amphetamines, methamphetamines, or similar stimulating drugs. Also, **speed′freak′.** [1965–70]

speed′ gear′, an adjustable gear for driving a machine at various speeds.

speed′ in′dicator, an instrument for counting the number of revolutions of a gasoline engine. Also called **speed′ count′er.** [1855–60]

speed·ing (spē′ding), *n.* the act or practice of exceeding the speed limit: *a $50 fine for speeding.* [1250–1300, for earlier sense "the condition of prospering"; 1905–10 for current sense; ME; see SPEED, -ING[1]]

speed′ light′, *Photog.* an electronic flash lamp. Also called **speed′ flash′, speed′ lamp′.** [1895–1900 for earlier sense]

speed′ lim′it, the maximum speed at which a vehicle is legally permitted to travel, as within a specific area, on a certain road, or under given conditions. [1890–95]

speed′ met′al, a style of heavy-metal music typically played at extremely fast tempos. [1985–90]

CONCISE ETYMOLOGY KEY: <, descended or borrowed from; >, whence; b., blend of, blended; c., cognate with; cf., compare; deriv., derivative; equiv., equivalent; imit., imitative; obl., oblique; r., replacing; s., stem; sp., spelling, spelled; resp., respelling, respelled; trans., translation; ?, origin unknown; *, unattested; ‡, probably earlier than. See the full key inside the front cover.

speed·o (spē′dō), *n., pl.* **speed·os.** *Informal.* speedometer. [1950–55; by shortening; cf. -O]

speed·om·e·ter (spē dom′i tər, spi-), *n.* an instrument on an automobile or other vehicle for indicating the rate of travel in miles or kilometers per hour. [1900–05; SPEED + -O- + -METER]

speed-read (spēd′rēd′), *v.t., v.i.,* **-read** (-red′), **-read·ing.** to read faster than normal, esp. by acquired techniques of skimming and controlled eye movements. Also, **speed′read′.** —**speed′-read′er,** *n.*

speed′ shop′, *Auto. Informal.* a garage that specializes in fitting cars, esp. hot rods, with custom-made mechanical equipment for racing. [1950–55]

speed′ skate′. See **racing skate.** [1890–95]

speed′ skat′ing, ice skating as a form of racing, usually on an oval course and against other competitors or the clock. Also, **speed′skat′ing.** [1880–85] —**speed′ skat′er, speed′skat′er,** *n.*

speed·ster (spēd′stər), *n.* a person who travels at high speed. [1915–20; SPEED + -STER]

speed′ trap′, a section of a road where hidden police, radar, etc., carefully check the speed of motorists and strictly enforce traffic regulations: sometimes characterized by hard-to-see signals, hidden traffic signs, etc. [1920–25]

speed-up (spēd′up′), *n.* **1.** an increasing of speed. **2.** an imposed increase in the rate of production of a worker without a corresponding increase in the rate of pay. [1920–25; n. use of v. phrase *speed up*]

speed·walk (spēd′wôk′), *n.* an endless conveyor belt, moving walk, or the like used to transport standing persons from place to place. [SPEED + WALK]

speed·way (spēd′wā′), *n.* **1.** a road or course for fast driving, motoring, or the like, or on which more than ordinary speed is allowed. **2.** a track on which automobile or motorcycle races are held. [1890–95, *Amer.;* SPEED + WAY[1]]

Speed·way (spēd′wā′), *n.* a town in central Indiana. 12,641.

speed·well (spēd′wel′), *n.* any of several plants, shrubs, or small trees of the genus *Veronica,* of the figwort family, having opposite leaves and small flowers. [1570–80; SPEED + WELL[1]; so called because its petals fade and fall early]

speed·writ·ing (spēd′rī′ting), *n.* a system of shorthand that is based on the sound of words and utilizes letters of the alphabet rather than symbols. [1920–25; SPEED + WRITING; formerly a trademark]

speed·y (spē′dē), *adj.,* **speed·i·er, speed·i·est. 1.** characterized by speed; rapid; swift; fast. **2.** coming, given, or arrived at quickly or soon; prompt; not delayed: *a speedy recovery.* [1325–75; ME *spedy.* See SPEED, -Y[1]] —**speed′i·ly,** *adv.* —**speed′i·ness,** *n.*
—**Syn. 1.** quick. **2.** expeditious.

speel (spēl), *v.t., v.i. Scot. and North Eng.* to climb; ascend; mount. Also, **speil.** [1505–15; orig. uncert.]

speer (spēr), *v.i., v.t. Chiefly Scot.* to ask; inquire. Also, **speir, spier.** [bef. 900; ME *speren, spiren,* OE *spyrian* to make tracks, trace, ask about; c. G *spüren,* ON *spyrja* to ask; akin to SPOOR]

Speer (spēr; *Ger.* shpār), *n.* **Al·bert** (al′bərt; *Ger.* äl′-bert), 1905–81, German Nazi leader: appointed by Hitler as official Nazi architect.

speiss (spīs), *n. Metall.* a product obtained in smelting certain ores, consisting of one or more metallic arsenides, as of iron or nickel. [1790–1800; < G *Speise* lit., food]

spe·lae·an (spi lē′ən), *adj.* of, pertaining to, or inhabiting a cave or caves. Also, **spe·le′an.** [1830–40; < NL *spēlae(us)* (adj. deriv. of L *spēlaeum* cave < Gk *spélaion*) + -AN]

spe·le·ol·o·gy (spē′lē ol′ə jē), *n.* the exploration and study of caves. Also, **spe′lae·ol′o·gy.** [1890–95; < L *spēlae(um)* (see SPELAEAN) + -O- + -LOGY] —**spe·le·o·log·i·cal** (spē′lē ə loj′i kəl), *adj.* —**spe′le·ol′o·gist** *n.*

spell[1] (spel), *v.,* **spelled** or **spelt, spell·ing.** —*v.t.* **1.** to name, write, or otherwise give the letters, in order, of (a word, syllable, etc.): *Did I spell your name right?* **2.** (of letters) to form (a word, syllable, etc.): *The letters spelled a rather rude word.* **3.** to read letter by letter or with difficulty (often fol. by *out*): *She painfully spelled out the message.* **4.** to discern or find, as if by reading or study (often fol. by *out*). **5.** to signify; amount to: *This delay spells disaster for us.* —*v.i.* **6.** to name, write, or give the letters of words, syllables, etc.: *He spells poorly.* **7.** to express words by letters, esp. correctly. **8. spell down,** to outspell others in a spelling match. **9. spell out, a.** to explain something explicitly, so that the meaning is unmistakable. **b.** to write out in full or enumerate the letters of which a word is composed: *The title "Ph.D." is seldom spelled out.* [1250–1300; ME *spellen* < OF *espeller* < Gmc; cf. OE *spellian* to talk, announce (deriv. of *spell* SPELL[2]), OHG *-spellōn,* ON *spjalla,* Goth *spillōn*] —**spell′a·ble,** *adj.*
—**Syn. 5.** foretell, portend, mean, promise.

spell[2] (spel), *n.* **1.** a word, phrase, or form of words supposed to have magic power; charm; incantation: *The wizard cast a spell.* **2.** a state or period of enchantment: *She was under a spell.* **3.** any dominating or irresistible influence; fascination: *the spell of fine music.* [bef. 900; ME *spell,* OE: discourse; c. OHG *spel,* ON *spjall,* Goth *spill* tale; see SPELL[1], GOSPEL] —**spell′ful,** *adj.* —**spell′-like′,** *adj.*

spell[3] (spel), *n.* **1.** a continuous course or period of work or other activity: *to take a spell at the wheel.* **2.** a turn of work so taken. **3.** a turn, bout, fit, or period of anything experienced or occurring: *a spell of coughing.* **4.** an indefinite interval or space of time: *Come visit us for a spell.* **5.** a period of weather of a specified kind: *a hot spell.* **6.** *Australian.* a rest period. **7.** *Archaic.* a person or set of persons taking a turn of work to relieve another. —*v.t.* **8.** to take the place of for a time; relieve: *Let me spell you at the wheel.* **9.** *Australian.* to declare or give a rest period to. —*v.i.* **10.** *Australian.* to have or take a rest period. [1585–95; (v.) alter. of earlier *spele* to stand instead of, relieve, spare, ME *spelen,* OE *spelian;* akin to OE *spala, gespelia* a substitute; (n.) akin to the v. (perh. continuing OE *gespelia*)]
—**Syn. 4.** while, bit, piece.

spell·bind (spel′bīnd′), *v.t.,* **-bound, -bind·ing.** to hold or bind by or as if by a spell; enchant; entrance; fascinate. [1800–10; SPELL[2] + BIND, deduced from SPELLBOUND] —**spell′bind′ing·ly,** *adv.*

spell·bind·er (spel′bīn′dər), *n.* a person or thing that spellbinds, esp. a powerful speaker who can captivate an audience. [1885–90, *Amer.;* SPELLBIND + -ER[1]]

spell·bound (spel′bound′), *adj.* bound by or as if by a spell; enchanted, entranced, or fascinated: *a spellbound audience.* [1790–1800; SPELL[2] + -BOUND[1]]

spell′ check′er, a computer program for checking the spelling of words in an electronic document. Also, **spell′ing check′er.** [1980–85]

spell·down (spel′doun′), *n.* a spelling competition that begins with all the contestants standing and that ends when all but one, the winner, have been required to sit down due to a specified number of misspellings. [1940–45, *Amer.;* from phrase *spell down* to outspell others in a spelling match]

spell·er (spel′ər), *n.* **1.** a person who spells words. **2.** Also called **spell′ing book′.** an elementary textbook or manual to teach spelling. [1400–50; late ME; see SPELL[1], -ER[1]]

spell·er-di·vid·er (spel′ər di vī′dər), *n.* a reference book that lists words in alphabetical order to show spelling and syllabification.

spell·ing (spel′ing), *n.* **1.** the manner in which words are spelled; orthography. **2.** a group of letters representing a word. **3.** the act of a speller. [1400–50; late ME (ger.); see SPELL[1], -ING[1]]

spell′ing bee′, a spelling competition won by the individual or team spelling the greatest number of words correctly; spelldown. [1870–75]

spell′ing pronuncia′tion, a pronunciation based on spelling, usually a variant of the traditional pronunciation. The spelling pronunciation of *waistcoat* is (wāst′-kōt′) rather than (wes′kət).

spell′ing reform′, an attempt to change the spelling of English words to make it conform more closely to pronunciation. [1870–75]

Spell·man (spel′mən), *n.* **Francis Joseph, Cardinal,** 1889–1967, U.S. Roman Catholic clergyman: archbishop of New York 1939–67.

spelt[1] (spelt), *v.* a pt. and pp. of **spell**[1].

spelt[2] (spelt), *n.* a wheat, *Triticum aestivum spelta,* native to southern Europe and western Asia, used chiefly for livestock feed. [bef. 1000; ME, OE < LL *spelta,* prob. < Gmc; cf. OHG *spelza* (G *Spelt*)]

spel·ter (spel′tər), *n.* zinc, esp. in the form of ingots. [1655–65; orig. uncert.; akin to MD *speauter,* G *spiauter* spelter]

spe·lunk (spi lungk′), *v.i.* to explore caves, esp. as a hobby. [back formation from SPELUNKER, *spelunking*]

spe·lunk·er (spi lung′kər), *n.* a person who explores caves, esp. as a hobby. [1940–45; < L *spēlunc(a)* cave (<< Gk *spēlynx,* s. *spēlyng-,* akin to *spélaion;* cf. SPELAEAN) + -ER[1]] —**spe·lunk′ing,** *n.*

Spe·mann (shpā′män), *n.* **Hans** (häns), 1869–1941, German zoologist: Nobel prize for medicine 1935.

spence (spens), *n. Brit. Dial.* a pantry. [1350–1400; ME *spense, spence* < MF *despense* pantry < ML *dispēnsa,* n. use of fem. of *dispēnsus,* ptp. of *dispendere* to weigh out; see DISPENSE]

Spence (spens), *n.* a male given name, form of **Spencer.**

spen·cer[1] (spen′sər), *n.* **1.** a short, close-fitting jacket, frequently trimmed with fur, worn in the 19th century by women and children. **2.** a man's close-fitting jacket, having a collar and lapels and reaching just below the waist, worn in the late 18th and early 19th centuries. **3.** an English wig of the 18th century. [1740–50; in defs. 1, 2 named after G. J. Spencer (1758–1834), English earl; in def. 3 named after Charles SPENCER]

spen·cer[2] (spen′sər), *n. Naut.* a large gaff sail used abaft a square-rigged foremast or abaft the mainmast of a ship or bark. [1830–40; orig. uncert.]

Spen·cer (spen′sər), *n.* **1. Charles, 3rd Earl of Sunderland,** 1674–1722, British statesman: prime minister 1718–21. **2. Herbert,** 1820–1903, English philosopher. **3. Platt Rogers** (plat), 1800–64, U.S. calligrapher and teacher of penmanship. **4.** a town in NW Iowa. 11,726. **5.** a town in central Massachusetts. 10,774. **6.** a male given name.

Spen·cer (spen′sər), *n. Mil.* a .52 caliber, lever-action repeating rifle and carbine patented in the U.S. in 1860 and used by the Union army and navy in the Civil War.

Spen·ce·ri·an (spen sēr′ē ən), *adj.* **1.** of Herbert Spencer or his philosophy. —*n.* **2.** a follower of Herbert Spencer. [1885–90; SPENCER + -IAN]

Spen·ce·ri·an (spen sēr′ē ən), *adj.* pertaining to or characteristic of a system of penmanship, characterized by clear, rounded letters slanting to the right. [1875–80; P. R. SPENCER + -IAN]

spend (spend), *v.,* **spent, spend·ing.** —*v.t.* **1.** to pay out, disburse, or expend; dispose of (money, wealth, resources, etc.): *resisting the temptation to spend one's money.* **2.** to employ (labor, thought, words, time, etc.), as on some object or in some proceeding: *Don't spend much time on it.* **3.** to pass (time) in a particular manner, place, etc.: *We spent a few days in Baltimore.* **4.** to use up, consume, or exhaust: *The storm had spent its fury.* **5.** to give (one's blood, life, etc.) for some cause. —*v.i.* **6.** to spend money, energy, time, etc. **7.** *Obs.* to be consumed or exhausted. [1125–75; ME *spenden,* con-

tinuing OE *-spendan* (in *āspendan, forspendan* to spend entirely or utterly) < WGmc < L *expendere* to pay out, EXPEND; cf. G *spenden*]
—**Syn. 1.** SPEND, DISBURSE, EXPEND, SQUANDER refer to paying out money. SPEND is the general word: *We spend more for living expenses now.* DISBURSE implies expending from a specific source or sum to meet specific obligations, or paying in definite allotments: *The treasurer has authority to disburse funds.* EXPEND is more formal, and implies spending for some definite and (usually) sensible or worthy object: *to expend most of one's salary on necessities.* SQUANDER suggests lavish, wasteful, or foolish expenditure: *to squander a legacy.* **2.** use, apply, devote. —**Ant. 1.** earn, keep.

spend•a•ble (spen′də bəl), *adj.* available for spending. [1490–1500; SPEND + -ABLE]

spend•er (spen′dər), *n.* a person who spends, esp. one who habitually spends excessively or lavishly; spendthrift. [1350–1400; ME; see SPEND, -ER[1]]

Spen•der (spen′dər), *n.* **Stephen,** 1909–96, English poet and critic.

spend′ing mon′ey, money for small personal expenses. [1590–1600]

spend•thrift (spend′thrift′), *n.* **1.** a person who spends possessions or money extravagantly or wastefully; prodigal. —*adj.* **2.** wastefully extravagant; prodigal. [1595–1605; SPEND + THRIFT]
—**Syn. 2.** wasteful, improvident, profligate.

spend′thrift trust′, *Law.* a trust that provides a fund for a beneficiary, as a minor, with the title vested so that the fund or its income cannot be claimed by others, as creditors of the beneficiary. Also called **sheltering trust.**

Spe•ner (shpā′nər), *n.* **Phi•lipp Ja•kob** (fē′lēp yä′kôp), 1635–1705, German theologian: founder of Pietism. —**Spe•ner•ism** (shpā′nə riz′əm, spā′-), *n.*

Speng•ler (speng′glər; *Ger.* shpeng′glər), *n.* **Os•wald** (oz′wôld; *Ger.* ôs′vält), 1880–1936, German philosopher. —**Speng•le•ri•an** (speng glēr′ē ən, shpeng-), *n., adj.*

Spen•ser (spen′sər), *n.* **Edmund,** c1552–99, English poet.

Spen•se•ri•an (spen sēr′ē ən), *adj.* **1.** of or characteristic of Spenser or his work. —*n.* **2.** an imitator of Spenser. **3.** See **Spenserian stanza. 4.** verse in Spenserian stanzas. [1810–20; SPENSER + -IAN]

Spense′rian son′net, a sonnet employing the rhyme scheme *abab, bcbc, cdcd, ee.*

Spense′rian stan′za, the stanza used by Spenser in his *Faerie Queene* and employed since by other poets, consisting of eight iambic pentameter lines and a final Alexandrine, with a rhyme scheme of *ababbcbcc.* [1810–20]

spent (spent), *v.* **1.** pt. and pp. of **spend. 2.** used up; consumed. **3.** tired; worn-out; exhausted.
—**Syn. 3.** weary, drained, fagged.

Spen•ta A•me•sha (spen′tə ä′me shə), *Zoroastrianism.* See **Amesha Spenta.**

Spen′ta Main′yu (mīn′yo͞o), *Zoroastrianism.* the good and creative spirit that is the offspring of Ahura Mazda.

spe•os (spē′os), *n.* a cavelike temple, tomb, or the like, cut in rock. [1835–45; < Gk *spéos* cave]

sperm[1] (spûrm), *n., pl.* **sperm, sperms** for 2. **1.** semen. **2.** a male reproductive cell; spermatozoon. [1350–1400; ME *sperme* < LL *sperma* < Gk *spérma* seed, equiv. to *sper-* (base of *speírein* to sow seeds) + *-ma* n. suffix of result]

sperm[2] (spûrm), *n.* **1.** spermaceti. **2.** See **sperm whale. 3.** See **sperm oil.** [1830–40; by shortening]

sperm-, var. of **spermo-** before a vowel: *spermine.*

-sperm, a combining form with the meaning "one having seeds" of the kind specified by the initial element: *gymnosperm.* [< Gk *-spermos;* see -SPERMOUS]

sper•ma•cet•i (spûr′mə set′ē, -sē′tē), *n. Chem., Pharm.* a pearly white, waxy, translucent solid, obtained from the oil in the head of the sperm whale: used chiefly in cosmetics and candles, and as an emollient. Also called **cetaceum.** [1425–75; late ME *sperma cete* < ML *sperma cētī* sperm of whale (see SPERM[1], CET-)] —**sper′ma•cet′i•like′,** *adj.*

sper•ma•go•ni•um (spûr′mə gō′nē əm), *n., pl.* **-ni•a** (-nē ə). *Bot., Mycol.* spermogonium.

-spermal, a combining form used to form adjectives corresponding to nouns ending in **-sperm:** *gymnospermal.* Also, **-spermic, -spermous.** [-SPERM + -AL[1]]

sper•ma•ry (spûr′mə rē), *n., pl.* **-ries.** an organ in which spermatozoa are generated; testis. [1860–65; < NL *spermārium,* equiv. to LL *sperm(a)* SPERM[1] + *-ārium* -ARY]

sper•ma•the•ca (spûr′mə thē′kə), *n., pl.* **-cae** (-sē). *Zool.* a small sac or cavity in female or hermaphroditic invertebrates used to store sperm for fertilizing eggs, as in the queen bee. [1820–30; *sperma-* (var. of SPERMATO-, SPERMO-) + THECA]

sper•mat•ic (spûr mat′ik), *adj.* **1.** of, pertaining to, or resembling sperm; seminal; generative. **2.** pertaining to a spermary. [1530–40; < LL *spermaticus* < Gk *spermatikós* relating to seed, equiv. to *spermat-* (s. of *spérma*) SPERM[1] + *-ikos* -IC] —**sper•mat′i•cal•ly,** *adv.*

spermat′ic cord′, *Anat.* the cord by which a testis is suspended in the scrotum, containing the vas deferens and the blood vessels and nerves of the testis. [1790–1800]

sper•mat•i•cide (spûr mat′ə sīd′, spûr′mə tə-), *n.* spermicide. —**sper•mat′i•cid′al,** *adj.*

sper•ma•tid (spûr′mə tid), *n. Cell Biol.* one of the cells that result from the meiotic divisions of a spermatocyte and mature into spermatozoa. [1885–90; SPERMAT- + -ID[3]]

sper•ma•ti•um (spûr mā′shē əm), *n., pl.* **-ti•a** (-shē ə). **1.** *Bot.* the nonmotile male gamete of a red alga. **2.** *Mycol.* a minute, colorless cell, of certain fungi and lichens, believed to be a male reproductive body, developed within spermogonia. [1855–60; < NL < Gk *spermátion,* equiv. to *spermat-* (s. of *spérma*) SPERM[1] + *-ion* -IUM]

spermato-, a combining form meaning "seed"; used with this meaning and as a combining form of **sperm**[1] in the formation of compound words: *spermatogonium.* Also, *esp. before a vowel,* **spermat-.** Cf. **sperm-, -sperm, -spermal, -spermic, spermo-, -spermous.** [< Gk *spermat-* (s. of *spérma;* see SPERM[1]) + -O-]

sper•mat•o•cide (spûr mat′ə sīd′, spûr′mə tə-), *n.* spermicide. —**sper•mat′o•cid′al,** *adj.*

sper•mat•o•cyte (spûr mat′ə sīt′, spûr′mə tə-), *n. Cell Biol.* a male germ cell **(primary spermatocyte)** that gives rise by meiosis to a pair of haploid cells **(secondary spermatocytes)** that give rise in turn to spermatids. [1885–90; SPERMATO- + -CYTE] —**sper′ma•to•cyt′al,** *adj.*

sper•mat•o•gen•e•sis (spûr mat′ə jen′ə sis, spûr′mə tə-), *n. Biol.* the origin and development of spermatozoa. [1880–85; < NL; see SPERMATO-, -GENESIS] —**sper•ma•to•ge•net•ic** (spûr′mə tō jə net′ik, spər mat′ō-), *adj.*

sper•ma•tog•e•nous (spûr′mə toj′ə nəs), *adj.* producing spermatozoa. [SPERMATO- + -GENOUS]

sper•mat•o•go•ni•um (spûr mat′ə gō′nē əm, spûr′mə tə-), *n., pl.* **-ni•a** (-nē ə). *Cell Biol.* one of the undifferentiated germ cells giving rise to spermatocytes. [1860–65; < NL; see SPERMATO-, -GONIUM] —**sper•mat′o•go′ni•al,** *adj.*

sper•ma•toid (spûr′mə toid′), *adj.* resembling sperm. [SPERMAT- + -OID]

sper•mat•o•phore (spûr mat′ə fôr′, -fōr′, spûr′mə tə-), *n. Zool.* a capsule surrounding a mass of spermatozoa, produced by the male of various animal species and transferred to the female. [1840–50; SPERMATO- + -PHORE] —**sper•ma•toph•or•al** (spûr′mə tof′ər əl), **sper•ma•toph•o•rous** (spûr′mə tof′ər əs), *adj.*

sper•mat•o•phyte (spûr mat′ə fīt′, spûr′mə tə-), *n.* any of the Spermatophyta, a primary division or group of plants comprising those that bear seeds. [1895–1900; < NL *Spermotophyta;* see SPERMATO-, -PHYTE] —**sper•ma•to•phyt•ic** (spûr′mə tə fit′ik, spûr mat′ə-), *adj.*

sper•ma•tor•rhe•a (spûr′mə tə rē′ə, spûr mat′ə-), *n. Pathol.* abnormally frequent and involuntary nonorgasmic emission of semen. Also, **sper′ma•tor•rhoe′a.** [1855–60; < NL; see SPERMATO-, -RRHEA]

sper•mat•o•tox•ic (spûr mat′ə tok′sik, spûr′mə tə-), *adj.* spermotoxic. Also, **sper•ma•tox•ic** (spûr′mə tok′sik).

sper•mat•o•tox•in (spûr mat′ə tok′sin, spûr′mə tə-), *n.* spermotoxin. Also, **sper•ma•tox•in** (spûr′mə tok′sin).

sper•ma•to•zo•id (spûr′mə tə zō′id, spûr mat′ə-), *n. Bot., Mycol.* a motile male gamete produced in an antheridium. [1855–60; SPERMATOZO(ON) + -ID[1]]

sper•ma•to•zo•on (spûr′mə tə zō′ən, -on, spûr mat′ə-), *n., pl.* **-zo•a** (-zō′ə). *Cell Biol.* one of the minute, usually actively motile gametes in semen, which serve to fertilize the ovum; a mature male reproductive cell. [1830–40; < NL; see SPERMATO-, -ZOON] —**sper′ma•to•zo′al, sper′ma•to•zo′an, sper′ma•to•zo′ic,** *adj.*

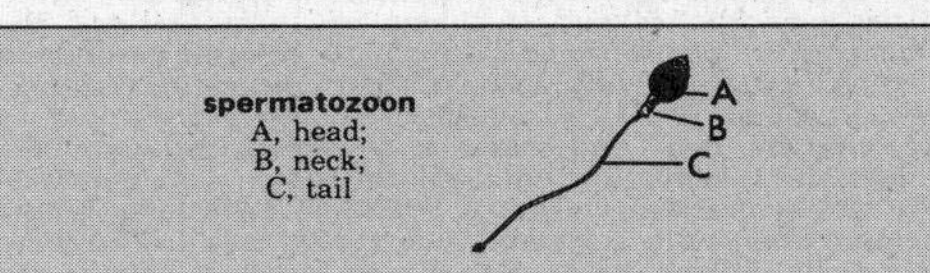

spermatozoon
A, head;
B, neck;
C, tail

sperm′ bank′, a repository for storing sperm and keeping it viable under scientifically controlled conditions prior to its use in artificial insemination. [1970–75]

sperm′ cell′, *Biol.* **1.** spermatozoon. **2.** any male gamete. [1850–55]

sper•mic (spûr′mik), *adj.* spermatic. [1855–60; SPERM- + -IC]

-spermic, var. of **-spermal:** *endospermic.* [< NL *-spermicus.* See -SPERM, -IC]

sper•mi•cide (spûr′mə sīd′), *n.* a sperm-killing agent, esp. a commercial birth-control preparation, usually a cream or jelly. [1925–30; SPERM[1] + -I- + -CIDE]

sper•mi•dine (spûr′mi dēn′, -din), *n. Biochem.* a biogenic polyamine, $H_2N(CH_2)_4NH(CH_2)_3NH_2$, formed from putrescine, occurring widely in nature and first identified in semen. [1925–30; SPERM- + -IDINE]

sper•mine (spûr′mēn, -min), *n. Biochem.* a polyamine, $H_2N(CH_2)_3NH(CH_2)_4NH(CH_2)_3NH_2$, formed from spermidine and occurring in all cells, esp. prevalent in semen, sputum, pancreatic tissue, and certain yeasts. [1890–95; SPERM- + -INE[2]]

sper•mi•o•gen•e•sis (spûr′mē ō jen′ə sis), *n. Cell Biol.* the development of a spermatozoon from a spermatid. [1915–20; < NL *spermi-,* comb. form of *sperma* SPERM[1] + -O- + GENESIS] —**sper•mi•o•ge•net•ic** (spûr′mē ō jə net′ik), *adj.*

spermo-, a combining form of **sperm**[1], used also with the meaning "seed," "germ," "semen," in the formation of compound words: *spermophyte.* Also, *esp. before a vowel,* **sperm-.**

sper•mo•go•ni•um (spûr′mə gō′nē əm), *n., pl.* **-ni•a** (-nē ə). *Bot., Mycol.* one of the cup-shaped or flask-shaped receptacles in which the spermatia of certain fungi and red algae are produced. Also, **spermagonium.** [1855–60; < NL; see SPERMO-, -GONIUM]

sperm′ oil′, *Chem.* a yellow, thin, water-insoluble liquid obtained from the sperm whale, used chiefly as a lubricant in light machinery, as watches, clocks, and scientific apparatus. [1820–30]

sper•mo•phile (spûr′mə fīl′, -fil), *n.* any of various burrowing rodents of the squirrel family, esp. of the genus *Spermophilus* (or *Citellus*), sometimes sufficiently numerous to do much damage to crops, as the ground squirrels and susliks. [1815–25; SPERMO- + -PHILE, modeled on NL *spermophilus*]

sper•mo•phyte (spûr′mə fīt′), *n. Bot.* spermatophyte. [1890–95; < NL *Spermophyta;* see SPERMO-, -PHYTE] —**sper•mo•phyt•ic** (spûr′mə fit′ik), *adj.*

sper•mo•tox•ic (spûr′mə tok′sik), *adj.* (of a substance) toxic to spermatozoa. Also, **spermatoxic, spermatotoxic.** [SPERMO- + TOXIC]

sper•mo•tox•in (spûr′mə tok′sin), *n.* a substance toxic to spermatozoa. Also, **spermatoxin, spermatotoxin.** [SPERMO- + TOXIN]

sper•mous (spûr′məs), *adj.* of the nature of or pertaining to sperm. [1815–25; SPERM[1] + -OUS]

-spermous, var. of **-spermal:** *gymnospermous.* [< Gk *-spermos,* adj. deriv. of *spérma;* see SPERM[1]]

sperm′ whale′, a large, square-snouted whale, *Physeter catodon,* valued for its oil and spermaceti: now reduced in number and rare in some areas. [1825–35]

sperm whale,
Physeter catodon,
length 60 ft. (18 m)

Sper•ry (sper′ē), *n.* **Elmer Ambrose,** 1860–1930, U.S. inventor and manufacturer.

sper•ry•lite (sper′ə līt′), *n.* a mineral, platinum arsenide, $PtAs_2$, occurring in minute tin-white crystals, usually cubes: a minor ore of platinum. [1905–10; named after F. L. *Sperry,* 19th-century Canadian chemist, who found it; see -LITE]

spes•sart•ite (spes′ər tīt′), *n. Mineral.* a yellow or red manganese-aluminum garnet, used as a semiprecious gem. Also called **spes•sart•ine** (spes′ər tēn′, -tin). [1885–90; named after *Spessart,* a district in Bavaria, where it is found; see -ITE[1]]

spew (spyo͞o), *v.i.* **1.** to discharge the contents of the stomach through the mouth; vomit. —*v.t.* **2.** to eject from the stomach through the mouth; vomit. **3.** to cast forth, gush, or eject, as in disgust or anger: *The angry sergeant spewed his charges at us.* —*n.* **4.** something that is spewed; vomit. Also, **spue.** [bef. 900; ME *spewen* to vomit, cast forth foul language, OE *spīwan* to vomit; c. G *speien,* ON *spȳja,* Goth *speiwan,* L *spuere*] —**spew′•er,** *n.*

Spey•er (shpī′ər), *n.* a city in SW West Germany, on the Rhine. 44,100. Also called **Spires.**

Spe•zia (*It.* spe′tsyä), *n.* See **La Spezia.**

SPF, sun protection factor: the effectiveness of suntanning preparations in protecting the skin from the harmful effects of the sun's ultraviolet radiation, as rated on a scale of increasing protectiveness from 2 to 15 or sometimes higher.

sp. gr., specific gravity.

sphae•ris•te•ri•um (sfēr′ə stēr′ē əm), *n., pl.* **sphae•ris•te•ri•a** (sfēr′ə stēr′ē ə). an ancient Roman handball court. [< L *sphaeristērium* < Gk *sphairistḗrion,* deriv. of *sphaîra* ball; see SPHERE]

sphaero-, var. of **sphero-:** *sphaerometer.*

sphag•nous (sfag′nəs), *adj.* pertaining to, abounding in, or consisting of sphagnum. [1820–30; SPHAGN(UM) + -OUS]

sphag•num (sfag′nəm), *n.* any soft moss of the genus *Sphagnum,* occurring chiefly in bogs, used for potting and packing plants, for dressing wounds, etc. [1745–55; < NL, alter. of Gk *sphágnos* a moss]

sphal•er•ite (sfal′ə rīt′, sfā′lə-), *n.* a very common mineral, zinc sulfide, ZnS, usually containing some iron and a little cadmium, occurring in yellow, brown, or black crystals or cleavable masses with resinous luster: the principal ore of zinc and cadmium; blackjack. [1865–70; < Gk *sphaler(ós)* slippery, deceptive + -ITE[1]]

S phase, *Cell Biol.* the period of the cell cycle prior to mitosis, during which the chromosomes are replicated. [1940–45]

sphe•cid (sfē′sid), *adj.* **1.** belonging or pertaining to the Sphecidae, a family of solitary wasps, including the mud daubers, sand wasps, etc. —*n.* **2.** a sphecid wasp. [< NL *Sphecidae,* equiv. to *Sphec-* (s. of *Sphex*) name of a genus (< Gk *sphḗx* wasp) + *-idae* -IDAE; see -ID[2]]

sphen-, var. of **spheno-** before a vowel: *sphenic.*

sphene (sfēn), *n.* a mineral, calcium titanium silicate, $CaTiSiO_5$, occurring as an accessory mineral in a variety of crystalline rocks, usually in small wedge-shaped crystals. Also called **titanite.** [1805–15; < Gk *sphḗn* wedge]

sphe•nic (sfē′nik), *adj.* wedge-shaped. [SPHEN- + -IC]

spheno-, a combining form meaning "wedge," used in the formation of compound words: *sphenography.* Also, *esp. before a vowel,* **sphen-.** [< NL < Gk *sphḗn* wedge + -O- -O-]

sphe•no•don (sfē′nə don′, sfen′ə-), *n.* tuatara. [1875–80; < NL: genus name (orig. *Sphaenodon*), equiv. to Gk *sphēn-* SPHEN- + *-odōn* -toothed (see -ODONT)]

sphe•no•gram (sfē′nə gram′), *n.* a cuneiform character. [1860–65; SPHENO- + -GRAM[1]]

sphe•nog•ra•phy (sfē nog′rə fē), *n.* **1.** the art of writing in cuneiform characters. **2.** the study of cuneiform writing. [1880–85; SPHENO- + -GRAPHY] —**sphe•nog′ra•pher, sphe•nog′ra•phist,** *n.* —**sphe•no•graph•ic** (sfē′nə graf′ik), *adj.*

sphe•noid (sfē′noid), *adj.* Also, **sphe•noi′dal. 1.** wedge-shaped. **2.** *Anat.* of or pertaining to the compound bone of the base of the skull, at the roof of the pharynx. See diag. under **skull.** —*n.* **3.** *Anat.* the sphenoid bone. [1725–35; < NL *sphēnoīdēs* < Gk *sphēnoeidḗs.* See SPHEN-, -OID]

sphe•nop•sid (sfi nop′sid), *n.* equisetoid. [1955–60; < NL *Sphenopsida* the order which includes horsetails; see SPHEN-, -OPSIS, -ID[2]]

spher•al (sfēr′əl), *adj.* **1.** of or pertaining to a sphere. **2.** spherical. **3.** symmetrical; perfect in form. [1565–75; < LL *sphaerālis.* See SPHERE, -AL[1]] —**sphe•ral•i•ty** (sfi ral′i tē), *n.*

sphere (sfēr), *n., v.,* **sphered, spher•ing.** —*n.* **1.** *Geom.* **a.** a solid geometric figure generated by the revolution of a semicircle about its diameter; a round body whose surface is at all points equidistant from the center. Equation: $x^2 + y^2 + z^2 = r^2$. **b.** the surface of such a figure; a spherical surface. **2.** any rounded body approximately of this form; a globular mass, shell, etc. **3.** *Astron.* **a.** a planet or star; heavenly body. **b.** See **celestial sphere. c.** any of the transparent, concentric, spherical shells, or layers, in which, according to ancient belief, the planets, stars, and other heavenly bodies were set. **4.** the place or environment within which a person or thing exists; a field of activity or operation: *to be out of one's professional sphere.* **5.** a particular social world, stratum of society, or walk of life: *His social sphere is small.* **6.** a field of something specified: *a sphere of knowledge.* —*v.t.* **7.** to enclose in or as if in a sphere. **8.** to form into a sphere. **9.** to place among the heavenly spheres. [1250–1300; < LL *sphēra,* L *sphaera* globe < Gk *sphaîra* ball; r. ME *spere* < OF *spere* < LL *spēra,* var. of *sphēra*] —**sphere′less,** *adj.* —**sphere′like′,** *adj.*
—**Syn. 4.** orbit, area, province, compass, realm, domain. **5.** class, rank.

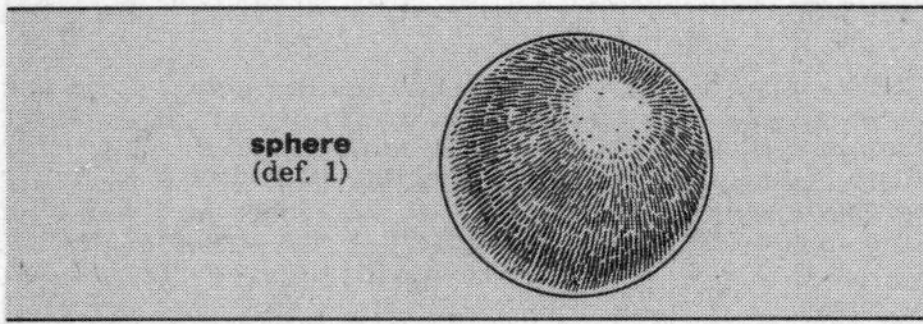
sphere (def. 1)

-sphere, a combining form of **sphere** (*planisphere*); having a special use in the names of the layers of gases and the like surrounding the earth and other celestial bodies (*ionosphere*).

sphere′ of in′fluence, any area in which one nation wields dominant power over another or others. [1880–85]

spher•i•cal (sfer′i kəl, sfēr′-), *adj.* **1.** having the form of a sphere; globular. **2.** formed in or on a sphere, as a figure. **3.** of or pertaining to a sphere or spheres. **4.** pertaining to the heavenly bodies, or to their supposed revolving spheres or shells. **5.** pertaining to the heavenly bodies regarded astrologically as exerting influence on humankind and events. Also, **spher′ic.** [1515–25; < LL *sphēric(us)* (see SPHERICS[1]) + -AL[1]] —**spher′i•cal′i•ty,** *n.* —**spher′i•cal•ly,** *adv.*
—**Syn. 1.** rounded.

spher′ical aberra′tion, variation in focal length of a lens or mirror from center to edge, due to its spherical shape. [1865–70]

spher′ical an′gle, *Geom.* an angle formed by arcs of great circles of a sphere. [1670–80]

spher′ical astron′omy, the branch of astronomy dealing with the determination of the positions of celestial bodies on the celestial sphere. Cf. **astrometry.**

spher′ical coor′dinates, *Math.* a system of coordinates for locating a point in space by the length of its radius vector and the angles this vector makes with two perpendicular polar planes. [1860–65]

spher′ical geom′etry, the branch of geometry that deals with figures on spherical surfaces. [1720–30]

spher′ical pol′ygon, *Geom.* a closed figure formed by arcs of great circles on a spherical surface. [1715–25]

spher′ical sail′ing, a method of navigation in which the curvature of the earth is taken into consideration. Also called **circular sailing.** Cf. **plane sailing.**

spher′ical tri′angle, *Geom.* a triangle formed by arcs of great circles of a sphere. [1575–85]

spher′ical trigonom′etry, the branch of trigonometry that deals with spherical triangles. [1720–30]

sphe•ric•i•ty (sfi ris′i tē), *n., pl.* **-ties.** a spherical state or form. [1615–25; < NL *sphēricitās,* equiv. to LL *sphēric(us)* (see SPHERICS[1]) + *-itās* -ITY]

spher•ics[1] (sfer′iks, sfēr′-), *n.* (*used with a singular v.*) the geometry and trigonometry of figures formed on the surface of a sphere. [1650–60; earlier *spheric,* n. use of the adj. < LL *sphēricus* < Gk *sphairikós.* See SPHERE, -IC, -ICS]

spher•ics[2] (sfer′iks, sfēr′-), *n.* **1.** Also, **sferics.** (*used with a singular v.*) a branch of meteorology in which electronic devices are used to forecast the weather and to study atmospheric conditions. **2.** (*used with a plural v.*) *Radio and Television.* atmospherics. **3.** (*used with a singular v.*) sferics (def. 3). [short for ATMOSPHERICS]

CONCISE ETYMOLOGY KEY: <, descended or borrowed from; >, whence; b., blend of, blended; c., cognate with; cf., compare; deriv., derivative; equiv., equivalent; imit., imitative; obl., oblique; r., replacing; s., stem; sp., spelling, spelled; resp., respelling, respelled; trans., translation; ?, origin unknown; *, unattested; ‡, probably earlier than. See the full key inside the front cover.

sphero-, a combining form representing **sphere** in compound words: *spherometer.* Also, **sphaero-, -sphere.**

sphe•roid (sfēr′oid), *Geom.* —*n.* **1.** a solid geometrical figure similar in shape to a sphere, as an ellipsoid. See diag. under **prolate.** —*adj.* **2.** spheroidal. [1655–65; < L *sphaeroīdēs* < Gk *sphairoeidḗs.* See SPHERE, -OID]

sphe•roi•dal (sfi roid′l), *adj.* **1.** pertaining to a spheroid or spheroids. **2.** shaped like a spheroid; approximately spherical. Also, **sphe•roi′dic.** [1775–85; SPHEROID + -AL[1]] —**sphe•roi′dal•ly, sphe•roi′di•cal•ly,** *adv.*

sphe•roi•dic•i•ty (sfēr′oi dis′i tē), *n.* a spheroidal state or form. Also, **sphe•roi•di•ty** (sfi roi′di tē). [1850–55; SPHEROID + -IC + -ITY]

sphe•rom•e•ter (sfi rom′i tər), *n.* an instrument for measuring the curvature of spheres and curved surfaces. [1820–30; < F *sphéromètre;* see SPHERO-, -METER]

sphe•ro•plast (sfēr′ə plast′, sfer′-), *n. Bacteriol.* a Gram-negative bacterial cell with a cell wall that has been altered or is partly missing, resulting in a spherical shape. [1915–20; SPHERO- + -PLAST]

spher•ule (sfer′o͞ol, -yo͞ol, sfēr′-), *n.* a small sphere or spherical body. [1655–65; < LL *sphaerula.* See SPHERE, -ULE] —**spher•u•lar** (sfer′yə lər, sfēr′-), *adj.* —**spher•u•late** (sfer′yo͝o lāt′, -lit, sfēr′-), *adj.*

spher•u•lite (sfer′o͝o līt′, -yo͝o-, sfēr′-), *n. Petrol.* a rounded aggregate of radiating crystals found in obsidian and other glassy igneous rocks. [1815–25; SPHERULE + -ITE[1]] —**spher•u•lit•ic** (sfer′o͝o lit′ik, -yo͝o-, sfēr′-), *adj.*

spher•y (sfēr′ē), *adj.* **1.** having the form of a sphere; spherelike. **2.** pertaining to or resembling a heavenly body; starlike. [1580–90; SPHERE + -Y[1]]

sphinc•ter (sfingk′tər), *n. Anat.* a circular band of voluntary or involuntary muscle that encircles an orifice of the body or one of its hollow organs. [1570–80; < LL < Gk *sphinktḗr,* equiv. to *sphing-,* base of *sphíngein* to hold tight + *-tēr* suffix denoting agent] —**sphinc′ter•al, sphinc•te•ri•al** (sfingk tēr′ē əl), **sphinc•ter•ic** (sfingk ter′ik), **sphinc•ter•ate** (sfingk′tər it, -tə rāt′), *adj.*

sphin•gid (sfin′jid), *n.* See **hawk moth.** [1905–10; < NL *Sphingidae* family name, equiv. to *sphing-* (s. of *Sphinx* type genus) + *-idae* -IDAE; see -ID[2]]

sphin•go•my•e•lin (sfing′gō mī′ə lin), *n. Biochem.* any of the class of phospholipids occurring chiefly in the brain and spinal cord, composed of phosphoric acid, choline, sphingosine, and a fatty acid. [< NL *sphingo-,* comb. form repr. Gk *sphíngein* to draw tight + MYELIN]

sphin•go•sine (sfing′gə sēn′, -sin), *n. Biochem.* a basic unsaturated amino alcohol, $C_{18}H_{33}(OH)_2NH_2$, produced by the hydrolysis of sphingomyelin or gangliosides. [1881; earlier *sphingosin,* equiv. to *sphingo-,* comb. form repr. Gk *sphínx* SPHINX + intrusive *-s-* + -IN[2]; so called in allusion to the enigmas it posed for its discoverer]

sphinx (sfingks), *n., pl.* **sphinx•es, sphin•ges** (sfin′jēz). **1.** (in ancient Egypt) **a.** a figure of an imaginary creature having the head of a man or an animal and the body of a lion. **b.** (*usually cap.*) the colossal recumbent stone figure of this kind near the pyramids of Giza. **2.** (*cap.*) *Class. Myth.* a monster, usually represented as having the head and breast of a woman, the body of a lion, and the wings of an eagle. Seated on a rock outside of Thebes, she proposed a riddle to travelers, killing them when they answered incorrectly, as all did before Oedipus. When he answered her riddle correctly the Sphinx killed herself. **3.** any similar monster. **4.** a mysterious, inscrutable person or thing, esp. one given to enigmatic questions or answers. [1375–1425; late ME < L < Gk *sphínx,* equiv. to *sphing-,* base of *sphíngein* to hold tight (cf. SPHINCTER) + *-s* nom. sing. ending]

sphinx (Egyptian)

sphinx′ moth′. See **hawk moth.** [1830–40]

sphra•gis•tic (sfrə jis′tik), *adj.* of or pertaining to seals or signet rings. [1830–40; < LGk *sphrāgistikós,* equiv. to Gk *sphrāgist(ós)* stamped, marked (deriv. of *sphrāgís* a seal) + *-ikos* -IC]

sphra•gis•tics (sfrə jis′tiks), *n.* (*used with a singular v.*) the scientific study of seals or signet rings. [1830–40; see SPHRAGISTIC, -ICS]

sp. ht., specific heat.

sphyg•mic (sfig′mik), *adj. Physiol., Med.* of or pertaining to the pulse. [1700–10; < Gk *sphygmikós,* equiv. to *sphygm(ós)* SPHYGMUS + *-ikos* -IC]

sphygmo-, a combining form representing **sphygmus** in compound words: *sphygmometer.*

sphyg•mo•gram (sfig′mə gram′), *n.* a tracing or diagram produced by a sphygmograph. [1885–90; SPHYGMO- + -GRAM[1]]

sphyg•mo•graph (sfig′mə graf′, -gräf′), *n.* an instrument for recording the rapidity, strength, and uniformity of the arterial pulse. [1855–60; SPHYGMO- + -GRAPH] —**sphyg•mo•graph•ic** (sfig′mə graf′ik), *adj.* —**sphyg•mog•ra•phy** (sfig mog′rə fē), *n.*

sphyg•moid (sfig′moid), *adj. Physiol., Med.* resembling the pulse; pulselike. [SPHYGM(O)- + -OID]

sphyg•mo•ma•nom•e•ter (sfig′mō mə nom′i tər), *n. Physiol.* an instrument, often attached to an inflatable air-bladder cuff and used with a stethoscope, for measuring blood pressure in an artery. [1860–65; SPHYGMO- + MANOMETER] —**sphyg•mo•man•o•met•ric** (sfig′mō man′ə me′trik), *adj.* —**sphyg′mo•ma•nom′e•try,** *n.*

sphyg•mus (sfig′məs), *n. Physiol.* the pulse. [1910–15; < NL < Gk *sphygmós* a throbbing, pulsation; cf. ASPHYXIA]

spic (spik), *n. Slang* (*disparaging and offensive*). a Spanish-American person. Also, **spik, spick.** [1910–15; earlier also *spig,* short for *spiggoty;* claimed, perh. correctly, to derive from an accented pron. of (*No*) *speak the* (*English*)]

spi•ca (spī′kə), *n., pl.* **-cae** (-sē), **-cas** for 1, 2. **1.** spike[2]. **2.** a type of bandage in the shape of a figure eight, extending from an extremity to the trunk. **3.** (*cap.*) *Astron.* a first-magnitude star in the constellation Virgo. [1350–1400; ME < L *spīca* lit., ear of grain; cf. SPIKE[2]]

spi•cate (spī′kāt), *adj. Bot.* **1.** having spikes, as a plant. **2.** arranged in spikes, as flowers. **3.** in the form of a spike, as in inflorescence. [1660–70; < L *spīcātus,* equiv. to *spīc(a)* SPICA + *-ātus* -ATE[1]]

spic•ca•to (spi kä′tō; *It.* spēk kä′tô), *adj.* (of violin music) performed with short, abrupt, rebounding motions of the bow. [1840–50; < It, equiv. to *spicc-* (s. of *spiccare* to detach) + *-ato* < L *-ātus* -ATE[1]]

spice (spīs), *n., v.,* **spiced, spic•ing.** —*n.* **1.** any of a class of pungent or aromatic substances of vegetable origin, as pepper, cinnamon, or cloves, used as seasoning, preservatives, etc. **2.** such substances collectively or as material: *Cookies without spice can be tasteless.* **3.** a spicy or aromatic odor or fragrance. **4.** something that gives zest: *a spice of humor in his solemnity.* **5.** a piquant, interesting element or quality; zest; piquancy: *The anecdotes lent spice to her talk.* **6.** *Archaic.* a small quantity of something; trace; bit. —*v.t.* **7.** to prepare or season with a spice or spices. **8.** to give zest, piquancy, or interest to by something added. [1175–1225; (n.) ME, aph. form of OF *espice* (F *épice*) < L *speciēs* appearance, sort, kind (see SPECIES), in LL (pl.): goods, wares, spices, drugs; (v.) ME *spicen,* in part deriv. of the n., in part < OF *espicer,* deriv. of *espice*] —**spice′a•ble,** *adj.* —**spice′less,** *adj.* —**spice′like′,** *adj.*
—**Syn. 5.** tang, gusto, zip.

spice•bush (spīs′bo͝osh′), *n.* **1.** Also called **spicewood.** a yellow-flowered, North American shrub, *Lindera benzoin,* of the laurel family, whose bark and leaves have a spicy odor. **2.** a North American shrub, *Calycanthus occidentalis,* having oblong leaves and fragrant, light-brown flowers. Also called **Benjamin-bush.** [1760–70, *Amer.;* SPICE + BUSH[1]]

spice′bush silk′ moth′. See **promethea moth.**

spice′bush swal′lowtail, a swallowtail butterfly, *Papilio troilus,* having a dark body with yellow spots on the forewings and greenish hind wings. Also called **troilus butterfly.** [1900–05]

Spice′ Is′lands, Moluccas.

spic•er•y (spī′sə rē), *n., pl.* **-er•ies** for 3. **1.** spices. **2.** spicy flavor or fragrance. **3.** *Archaic.* a storeroom or place for spices. [1250–1300; ME *spicerie* < OF *espicerie.* See SPICE, -ERY]

spice•wood (spīs′wo͝od′), *n.* spicebush (def. 1). [1750–60, *Amer.;* SPICE + WOOD[1]]

spice•y (spī′sē), *adj.,* **spic•i•er, spic•i•est.** spicy.

spick (spik), *n.* spic.

spick-and-span (spik′ən span′), *adj.* **1.** spotlessly clean and neat: *a spick-and-span kitchen.* **2.** perfectly new; fresh. —*adv.* **3.** in a spick-and-span manner. [1570–80; short for *spick-and-span-new,* alliterative extension of SPAN-NEW]

spic•u•la (spik′yə lə), *n., pl.* **-lae** (-lē′). a spicule. [1740–50; < NL *spicula,* ML, equiv. to L *spīc(a)* ear of grain + *-ula* -ULE]

spic•u•late (spik′yə lāt′, -lit), *adj.* **1.** having the form of a spicule. **2.** covered with or having spicules; consisting of spicules. Also, **spic•u•lar** (spik′yə lər). [1825–35; < L *spīculātus,* equiv. to *spīcul(um)* (see SPICULE) + *-ātus* -ATE[1]]

spic•ule (spik′yo͞ol), *n.* **1.** a small or minute, slender, sharp-pointed body or part; a small, needlelike crystal, process, or the like. **2.** *Zool.* one of the small, hard, calcareous or siliceous bodies that serve as the skeletal elements of various marine and freshwater invertebrates. **3.** *Astron.* a jet of gas several hundred miles in diameter rising from the sun's surface to heights of 3000 to 6000 miles (4800 to 9600 km). [1775–85; < L *spīculum* spearhead, arrowhead, bee stinger, equiv. to *spīc(a)* ear of grain (see SPICA) + *-ulum* -ULE]

spic•u•lum (spik′yə ləm), *n., pl.* **-la** (-lə). *Zool.* a small, needlelike body, part, process, or the like. [1740–50; < L *spīculum;* see SPICULE]

spic•y (spī′sē), *adj.,* **spic•i•er, spic•i•est. 1.** seasoned with or containing spice: *a spicy salad dressing.* **2.** characteristic or suggestive of spice. **3.** of the nature of or resembling spice. **4.** abounding in or yielding spices. **5.** aromatic or fragrant. **6.** piquant or pungent: *spicy criticism.* **7.** of a slightly improper or risqué nature; somewhat sexy: *a spicy novel.* **8.** *Informal.* full of spirit; lively. Also, **spicey.** [1555–65; SPICE + -Y[1]] —**spic′i•ly,** *adv.* —**spic′i•ness,** *n.*
—**Syn. 6.** hot, sharp, peppery. **7.** suggestive, racy, ribald, improper.

spi•der (spī′dər), *n.* **1.** any of numerous predaceous arachnids of the order Araneae, most of which spin webs that serve as nests and as traps for prey. **2.** (loosely) any of various other arachnids resembling or suggesting these. **3.** any of various things resembling or suggesting a spider. **4.** a frying pan, originally one with legs or feet. **5.** a trivet or tripod, as for supporting a pot or pan on a hearth. **6.** *Mach.* **a.** a part having a number of radiating spokes or arms, usually not connected at their outer ends. **b.** Also called **cross.** (in a universal joint) a crosslike part pivoted between the forked ends of two shafts to transmit motion between them. **7.** an evil person who entraps or lures others by wiles. **8.** a device attached to a cultivator, for pulverizing the soil. [bef. 1150; ME *spithre*, OE *spīthra*, akin to *spinnan* to SPIN; c. Dan *spinder*] **—spi′der·less,** *adj.* **—spi′der·like′,** *adj.*

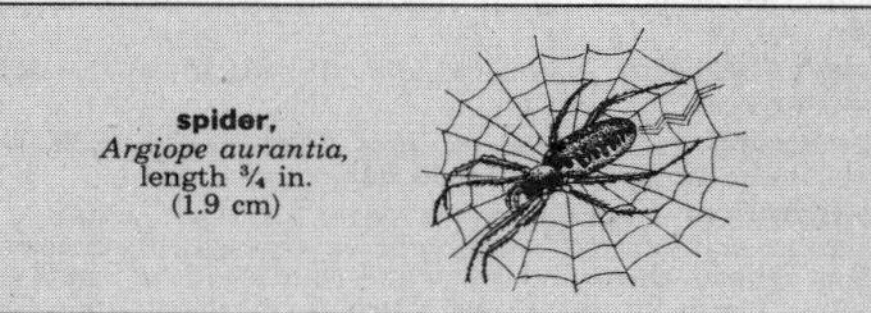
spider, *Argiope aurantia,* length ¾ in. (1.9 cm)

spi′der band′, *Naut.* See **futtock band.**

spi′der bug′. See **thread-legged bug.**

spi′der crab′, any of various crabs of the family Majidae, having long, slender legs and a comparatively small, triangular body. [1700–10]

spi′der fly′, *Angling.* an artificial fly having a hackle body, little or no tail, no wings, and unusually long legs, dressed to resemble a spider. [1780–90]

spi·der·hunt·er (spī′dər hun′tər), *n.* any of several sunbirds of the genus *Arachnothera,* of southern Asia and the East Indies, having dull-colored plumage and a long bill. [1855–60; SPIDER + HUNTER]

spi′der lil′y, any of several plants having lilylike flowers with narrow petals, as those belonging to the genera *Crinum, Hymenocallis,* and *Lycoris,* of the amaryllis family. [1885–90, *Amer.*]

spi·der·ling (spī′dər ling), *n.* the young of a spider. Also, **spi·der·let** (spī′dər lit). [1880–85; SPIDER + -LING[1]]

spi′der mite′, any of numerous, variously colored web-spinning mites of the family Tetranychidae, many of which are pests of garden plants and fruit trees. [1865–70]

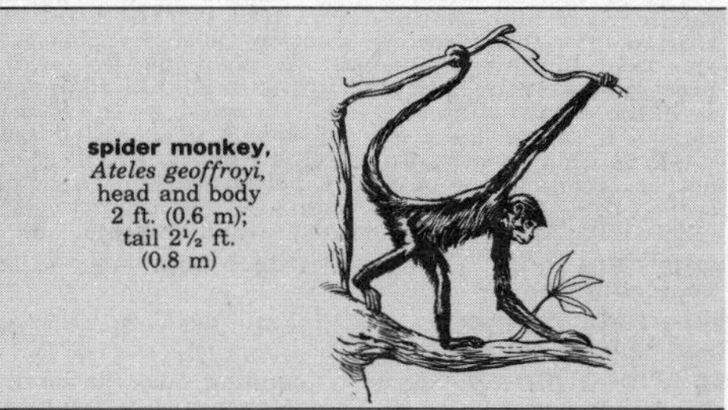
spider monkey, *Ateles geoffroyi,* head and body 2 ft. (0.6 m); tail 2½ ft. (0.8 m)

spi′der mon′key, any of several tropical American monkeys of the genus *Ateles,* having a slender body, long, slender limbs, and a long, prehensile tail: some are endangered. [1755–65]

spi′der plant′, 1. Also called **ribbon plant.** a plant, *Chlorophytum comosum,* of the lily family, native to southern Africa, that has long, narrow leaves and clusters of white flowers and is widely cultivated as a houseplant. **2.** cleome. [1850–55]

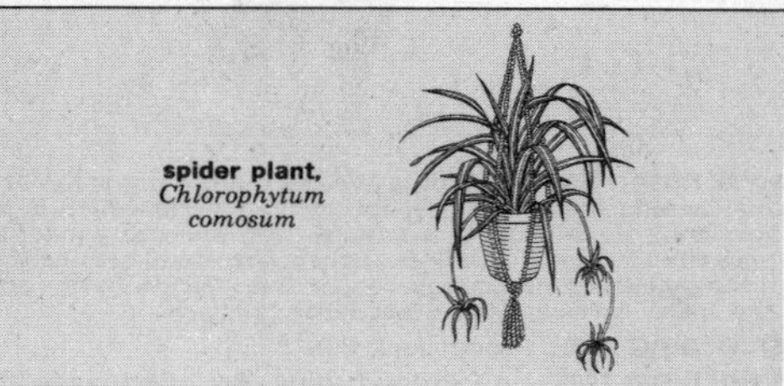
spider plant, *Chlorophytum comosum*

spi′der wasp′, any of certain wasps, esp. of the family Pompilidae, that provision their nests with paralyzed spiders. [1810–20]

spi′der web′, the web that is spun by a spider, made of interlaced threads of viscous fluid that harden on exposure to air. Also, **spi′der's web′.** [1525–35]

spi·der·web (spī′dər web′), *v.t.,* **-webbed, -web·bing.** to cover with a spider web or fine lines resembling a spider web. [1890–95; v. use of SPIDER WEB]

spi·der·wort (spī′dər wûrt′, -wôrt′), *n.* **1.** any plant of the genus *Tradescantia,* having blue, purple, or rose-colored flowers. **2.** any of several related plants. [1590–1600; SPIDER + WORT[2]]

spi·der·y (spī′də rē), *adj.* **1.** like a spider or a spider's web. **2.** full of spiders. [1830–40; SPIDER + -Y[1]]

spie·gel·ei·sen (spē′gəl ī′zən), *n.* a lustrous, crystalline pig iron containing a large amount of manganese, sometimes 15 percent or more, used in making steel. Also called **spie′gel, spie′gel i′ron.** [1865–70; < G, equiv. to *Spiegel* mirror + *Eisen* IRON]

spiel (spēl, shpēl), *Informal.* —*n.* **1.** a usually high-flown talk or speech, esp. for the purpose of luring people to a movie, a sale, etc.; pitch. —*v.i.* **2.** to speak extravagantly. [1890–95; (n.) < G *Spiel* or Yiddish *shpil* play, game; (v.) < G *spielen* or Yiddish *shpiln* to play, gamble]

Spiel·berg (spēl′bûrg), *n.* **Steven,** born 1947, U.S. film director, writer, and producer.

spiel·er (spē′lər), *n.* **1.** a barker, as at a circus sideshow. **2.** a person with an extravagant line of talk. **3.** *Austral.* a swindler. **4.** *Slang.* an announcer for radio or television, esp. one who gives commercials. [1885–90; < G; see SPIEL, -ER[1]]

spi·er[1] (spī′ər), *n.* a person who spies, watches, or discovers. [1225–75; ME; see SPY, -ER[1]]

spier[2] (spēr), *v.i., v.t.* speer.

spiff[1] (spif), *v.t. Informal.* to make spiffy (usually fol. by *up*): *Let's spiff up this office with new furniture.* [1875–80; perh. v. use of dial. *spiff* well-dressed; see SPIFFY]

spiff[2] (spif), *Slang.* —*n.* **1.** a bonus or other form of remuneration given to retail salespeople for promoting the products of a particular manufacturer. —*v.t.* **2.** to reward (a salesperson) with a spiff. [1855–60; orig. uncert.]

spiff·y (spif′ē), *adj.,* **spiff·i·er, spiff·i·est.** *Informal.* spruce; smart; fine. Also, **spif·fing** (spif′ing); *esp. Brit.,* **spivvy, spivving.** [1855–60; dial. *spiff* well-dressed (orig. uncert.) + -Y[1]] **—spiff′i·ly,** *adv.* **—spiff′i·ness,** *n.*

spig·ot (spig′ət), *n.* **1.** a small peg or plug for stopping the vent of a cask. **2.** a peg or plug for stopping the passage of liquid in a faucet or cock. **3.** a faucet or cock for controlling the flow of liquid from a pipe or the like. **4.** the end of a pipe that enters the enlarged end of another pipe to form a joint. [1350–1400; ME *spigot,* perh. < OF **espigot* < OPr *espig(a)* (< L *spīca* ear of grain; see SPICA) + OF *-ot* dim. suffix]
—Regional Variation. 3. See **faucet.**

spik (spik), *n.* spic.

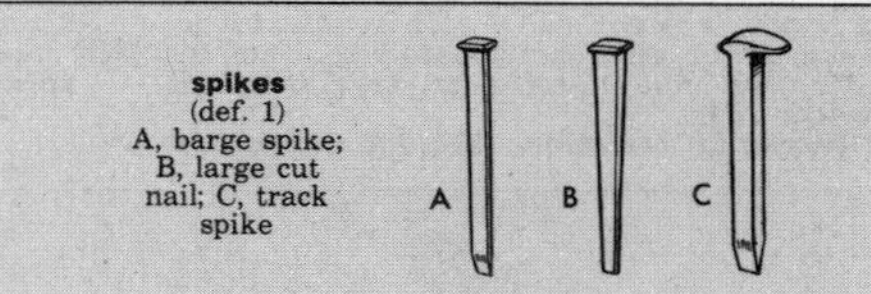

spikes (def. 1) A, barge spike; B, large cut nail; C, track spike

spike[1] (spīk), *n., v.,* **spiked, spik·ing.** —*n.* **1.** a naillike fastener, 3 to 12 in. (7.6 to 30.5 cm) long and proportionately thicker than a common nail, for fastening together heavy timbers or railroad track. **2.** something resembling such a nail; a stiff, sharp-pointed piece or part: *to set spikes in the top of a cement wall.* **3.** a sharp-pointed piece of metal set with the point outward, as on a weapon. **4.** an abrupt increase or rise: *a chart showing a spike of unusual activity in the stock market; a sudden spike of electrical current.* **5.** a rectangular or naillike metal projection on the heel and sole of a shoe for improving traction, as of a baseball player or a runner. **6. spikes,** a pair of shoes having such projections. **7.** the unbranched antler of a young deer. **8.** *Bot.* a flower stalk. See illus. under **inflorescence. 9.** a pointed portion of a continuous curve or graph, usually rising above the adjacent portion: *a spike in the value of the voltage.* **10.** *Volleyball.* a hard smash, hit close to the net, almost straight down into the opponent's court. **11.** *Slang.* a hypodermic needle. —*v.t.* **12.** to fasten or secure with a spike or spikes. **13.** to provide or set with a spike or spikes. **14.** to pierce with or impale on a spike. **15.** to set or stud with something suggesting spikes. **16.** to injure (another player or a competitor) with the spikes of one's shoe, as in baseball. **17.** *Volleyball.* to hit (a ball in the air) with a powerful, overarm motion from a position close to the net so as to cause it to travel almost straight down into the court of the opponents. **18.** *Football.* to slam (the ball) to the ground in the end zone, after scoring a touchdown. **19.** to render (a muzzle-loading gun) useless by driving a spike into the touchhole. **20.** to make ineffective; frustrate or thwart: *to spike a rumor; to spike someone's chances for promotion.* **21.** *Informal.* **a.** to add alcoholic liquor to (a drink). **b.** to add (a chemical, poison, or other substance) to: *The cocoa was spiked with cyanide.* **22.** *Journalism Slang.* to refuse (a story) by or as if by placing on a spindle. —*v.i.* **23.** to rise or increase sharply (often fol. by *up*): *Interest rates spiked up last week.* **24. spike someone's guns.** See **gun[1]** (def. 10). [1300–50; ME *spik(e)* (n.) < ON *spīkr* nail; akin to ON *spik,* MLG *spīker* nail] **—spike′like′,** *adj.*

spike[2] (spīk), *n.* **1.** an ear, as of wheat or other grain. **2.** *Bot.* an inflorescence in which the flowers are without a stalk, or apparently so, along an elongated, unbranched axis. See illus. under **inflorescence.** [1350–1400; ME; prob. special use of SPIKE[1], influenced by L *spīca* ear of grain]

spike·dace (spīk′dās′), *n., pl.* **-dac·es,** (*esp. collectively*) **-dace.** a scaleless, mottled, olive-brown fish, *Meda fulgida,* of the Gila River system in New Mexico and Arizona, having two dorsal spines. [SPIKE[1] + DACE]

spike′ heath′, a Eurasian evergreen shrub, *Bruckenthalia spiculifolia,* of the heath family, having narrow leaves and bell-shaped, pink flowers, growing in gritty soil.

spike′ heel′, a very high heel that tapers to a narrow base, used on women's shoes. [1925–30]

spike′ lav′ender, a lavender, *Lavandula latifolia,* having spikes of pale-purple flowers, and yielding an oil used in painting. [1890–95]

spike·let (spīk′lit), *n. Bot.* a small or secondary spike in grasses; one of the flower clusters, the unit of inflorescence, consisting of two or more flowers and subtended by one or more glumes variously disposed around a common axis. [1785–95; SPIKE[2] + -LET]

spike′ moss′, any of numerous plants of the genus *Selaginella,* allied to and resembling the club mosses.

spike·nard (spīk′nərd, -närd), *n.* **1.** an aromatic, Indian plant, *Nardostachys jatamansi,* of the valerian family, believed to be the nard of the ancients. **2.** an aromatic substance used by the ancients, supposed to be obtained from this plant. **3.** any of various other plants, esp. an American plant, *Aralia racemosa,* of the ginseng family, having an aromatic root. [1300–50; ME < ML *spīca nardī.* See SPIKE[2], NARD]

spik·er (spī′kər), *n.* **1.** a pointed, perforated tube connected to a garden hose, pushed into the soil for deep watering. **2.** *Volleyball.* a player who spikes the ball. [SPIKE[1] + -ER[1]]

spike′-tooth har′row (spīk′tōōth′), a harrow equipped with straight teeth on horizontal bars, usually employed to smooth and level plowed soil or seedbeds for planting or sowing. [1925–30]

spik·y (spī′kē), *adj.,* **spik·i·er, spik·i·est. 1.** having a spike or spikes. **2.** having the form of a spike; spikelike. **3.** acid or peevish in temper or mood; prickly. [1570–80; SPIKE[1] + -Y[1]] **—spik′i·ly,** *adv.* **—spik′i·ness,** *n.*

spile[1] (spīl), *n., v.,* **spiled, spil·ing.** —*n.* **1.** a peg or plug of wood, esp. one used as a spigot. **2.** a spout for conducting sap from the sugar maple. **3.** a heavy wooden stake or pile. **4.** *Mining.* forepole. —*v.t.* **5.** to stop up (a hole) with a spile or peg. **6.** to furnish with a spigot or spout, as for drawing off a liquid. **7.** to tap by means of a spile. **8.** to furnish, strengthen, or support with spiles or piles. [1505–15; < MD or MLG *spīle* splinter, peg; c. G *Speil*]

spile[2] (spīl), *v.t., v.i.,* **spiled, spil·ing,** *n. Dial.* spoil.

spil·ing (spī′ling), *n.* a group or mass of piles; spiles. [1835–45; SPILE[1] + -ING[1]]

spill[1] (spil), *v.,* **spilled** or **spilt, spill·ing,** *n.* —*v.t.* **1.** to cause or allow to run or fall from a container, esp. accidentally or wastefully: *to spill a bag of marbles; to spill milk.* **2.** to shed (blood), as in killing or wounding. **3.** to scatter: *to spill papers all over everything.* **4.** *Naut.* **a.** to let the wind out of (a sail). **b.** to lose (wind) from a sail. **5.** to cause to fall from a horse, vehicle, or the like: *His horse spilled him.* **6.** *Informal.* to divulge, disclose, or tell: *Don't spill the secret.* **7. spill the beans.** See **bean** (def. 9). —*v.i.* **8.** (of a liquid, loose particles, etc.) to run or escape from a container, esp. by accident or in careless handling. —*n.* **9.** a spilling, as of liquid. **10.** a quantity spilled. **11.** the mark made by something spilled. **12.** a spillway. **13.** Also called **spill′ light′.** superfluous or useless light rays, as from theatrical or photographic lighting units. **14.** *Theat.* an area of a stage illuminated by spill light. **15.** a throw or fall from a horse, vehicle, or the like: *She broke her arm in a spill.* [bef. 950; 1920–25 for def. 6; ME *spillen* to kill, destroy, shed (blood), OE *spillan* to kill; c. MHG, MD *spillen;* akin to SPOIL] **—spill′a·ble,** *adj., n.*

spill[2] (spil), *n.* **1.** a splinter. **2.** a slender piece of wood or of twisted paper, for lighting candles, lamps, etc. **3.** a peg made of metal. **4.** a small pin for stopping a cask; spile. **5.** *Mining.* forepole. [1250–1300; ME *spille* < ?]

spill·age (spil′ij), *n.* **1.** the act or process of spilling. **2.** an amount that spills or is spilled. [1920–25; SPILL[1] + -AGE]

spil·li·kin (spil′i kin), *n.* **1.** a jackstraw. **2. spillikins,** (*used with a singular v.*) the game of jackstraws. Also, **spilikin.** [1725–35; var. of *spellican* < obs. D *spelleken,* equiv. to *spelle* peg, pin + *-ken* -KIN]

spill·o·ver (spil′ō′vər), *n.* **1.** the act of spilling over. **2.** a quantity of something spilled over; overflow. [1940–45; n. use of v. phrase *spill over*]

spill·proof (spil′prōōf′), *adj.* (of a container) designed to prevent spilling. [SPILL[1] + -PROOF]

spill·way (spil′wā′), *n.* a passageway through which surplus water escapes from a reservoir, lake, or the like. [1885–90; SPILL[1] + WAY[1]]

spilt (spilt), *v.* a pt. and pp. of **spill[1].**

spilth (spilth), *n.* **1.** spillage (def. 1). **2.** something that is spilled. **3.** refuse; trash. [1600–10; SPILL[1] + -TH[1]]

spin (spin), *v.,* **spun** or (*Archaic*) **span, spun, spin·ning,** *n.* —*v.t.* **1.** to make (yarn) by drawing out, twisting, and winding fibers: *Pioneer women spun yarn on spinning wheels.* **2.** to form (the fibers of any material) into thread or yarn: *The machine spins nylon thread.* **3.** (of spiders, silkworms, etc.) to produce (a thread, cobweb, gossamer, silk, etc.) by extruding from the body a long, slender filament of a natural viscous matter that hardens in the air. **4.** to cause to turn around rapidly, as on an axis; twirl; whirl: *to spin a coin on a table.* **5.** *Informal.* to play (phonograph records): *a job spinning records on a radio show.* **6.** *Metalworking.* to shape (sheet metal) into a hollow, rounded form by pressure from a tool while rotating the metal on a lathe or wheel. **7.** to produce, fabricate, or evolve in a manner suggestive of spinning thread: *to spin a tale of sailing ships and bygone days.* **8.** *Rocketry.* to cause intentionally (a rocket or guided missile) to undergo a roll. **9.** to draw out, protract, or prolong (often fol. by *out*): *He spun the project out for over three years.* **10.** *Brit.* to flunk a student in an examination or a term's work. —*v.i.* **11.** to revolve or rotate rapidly, as the earth or a top. **12.** to produce a thread from the body, as spiders or silkworms. **13.** to produce yarn or thread by spinning. **14.** to move, go, run, ride, or travel rapidly. **15.** to have a sensation of whirling; reel: *My head began to spin and I fainted.* **16.** to fish with a spinning or revolving bait. **17. spin off, a.** to create something new, as a company or assets, without detracting from or affecting the relative size or stability of the original: *After the acquisition, the company was required to spin off about a third of its assets.* **b.** to derive from or base on something done previously: *They took the character of the maid and spun off an-*

other TV series. **18. spin one's wheels.** See **wheel** (def. 17). **19. spin out,** (of an automobile) to undergo a spinout. —*n.* **20.** the act of causing a spinning or whirling motion. **21.** a spinning motion given to a ball, wheel, axle, or other object. **22.** a downward movement or trend, esp. one that is sudden, alarming, etc.: *Steel prices went into a spin.* **23.** a rapid run, ride, drive, or the like, as for exercise or enjoyment: *They went for a spin in the car.* **24.** *Slang.* a particular viewpoint or bias, esp. in the media: slant: *They tried to put a favorable spin on the news coverage of the controversial speech.* **25.** Also called **tailspin, tail spin.** *Aeron.* a maneuver in which an airplane descends in a vertical direction along a helical path of large pitch and small radius at an angle of attack greater than the critical angle, dangerous when not done intentionally or under control. **26.** *Rocketry.* **a.** the act of intentionally causing a rocket or guided missile to undergo a roll. **b.** a roll so caused. **27.** *Physics.* the intrinsic angular momentum characterizing each kind of elementary particle, having one of the values 0, 1/2, 1, 3/2, . . . when measured in units of Planck's constant divided by 2π. **28.** *Australian.* a run of luck; fate. [bef. 900; ME *spinnen* to spin yarn, OE *spinnan;* c. D, G *spinnen,* ON *spinna,* Goth *spinnan*] **—spin′na·bil′i·ty,** *n.* **—spin′na·ble,** *adj.*
—Syn. 7. develop, narrate, relate. **9.** extend, lengthen. **11.** gyrate. See **turn.**

spi·na (spī′nə), *n., pl.* **-nae** (-nē). *Anat., Zool.* a spine or spinelike projection. [1350–1400; ME < L *spīna* thorn, backbone; see SPINE]

spi′na bif′i·da (bif′i də), *Pathol.* a congenital defect in which part of the meninges or spinal cord protrudes through the spinal column, often resulting in neurological impairment. [1710–20; < NL, L: cloven backbone]

spi·na·ceous (spi nā′shəs), *adj.* pertaining to or of the nature of spinach; belonging to the goosefoot family of plants. [1815–25; < NL *Spin(acia)* spinach + -ACEOUS]

spin·ach (spin′ich), *n.* **1.** a plant, *Spinacia oleracea,* cultivated for its edible, crinkly or flat leaves. **2.** the leaves. [1520–30; < MF *espinache, espinage* < OSp *espinaca,* alter. of Ar *isfānākh,* perh. < Pers] **—spin′·ach·like′,** *adj.*

spin′ach a′phid. See **green peach aphid.**

spin′ach dock′. See **herb patience.**

spin·ach-rhu·barb (spin′ich rōō′bärb), *n.* an Ethiopian plant, *Rumex abyssinicus,* of the buckwheat family, having leaves that are sometimes used as spinach and leafstalks sometimes used as rhubarb.

spi·nal (spīn′l), *adj.* **1.** of, pertaining to, or belonging to a spine or thornlike structure, esp. to the backbone. —*n.* **2.** *Med.* a spinal anesthetic. [1570–80; < LL *spīnālis,* equiv. to L *spīn(a)* SPINA + *-ālis* -AL[1]] **—spi′·nal·ly,** *adv.*

spi′nal acces′sory nerve′. See **accessory nerve.** [1880–85]

spi′nal anesthe′sia, *Med.* injection of an anesthetic into the lumbar region of the spinal canal to reduce sensitivity to pain without loss of consciousness.

spi′nal block′, **1.** See **spinal anesthesia. 2.** obstruction of the flow of spinal fluid by blockage of the spinal canal. Also called **subarachnoid block.**

spi′nal canal′, the tube formed by the vertebrae in which the spinal cord and its membranes are located. See diag. under **vertebra.** Also called **vertebral canal.** [1835–45]

spi′nal col′umn, the series of vertebrae in a vertebrate animal forming the axis of the skeleton and protecting the spinal cord; spine; backbone. Also called **vertebral column.** [1830–40]

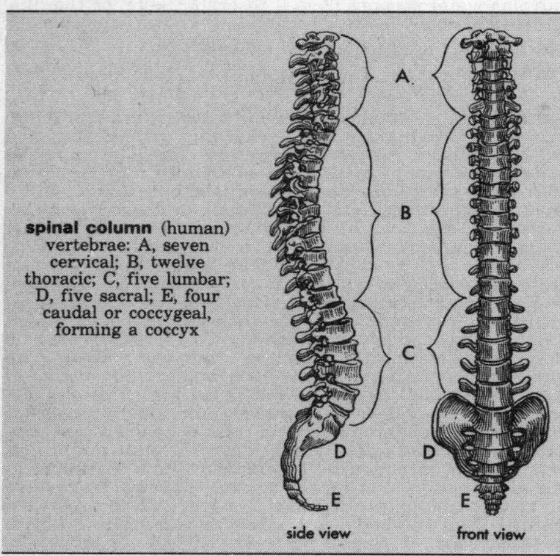

spinal column (human) vertebrae: A, seven cervical; B, twelve thoracic; C, five lumbar; D, five sacral; E, four caudal or coccygeal, forming a coccyx

spi′nal cord′, the cord of nerve tissue extending through the spinal canal of the spinal column. [1830–40]

spi′nal gan′glion, a ganglion on the dorsal root of each spinal nerve, containing the cell bodies of sensory nerves. [1855–60]

spi′nal nerve′, *Anat.* any of a series of paired nerves that originate in the nerve roots of the spinal cord and emerge from the vertebrae on both sides of the spinal column, each branching out to innervate a specific region of the neck, trunk, or limbs. [1785–95]

spi′nal tap′. See **lumbar puncture.**

spin′ cast′ing, spinning (def. 3). **—spin′ cast′er.**

spin′ control′, *Slang.* an attempt to give a bias to news coverage, esp. of a political candidate or event. [1985–90]

spin·dle (spin′dl), *n., adj., v.,* **-dled, -dling.** —*n.* **1.** a rounded rod, usually of wood, tapering toward each end, used in hand-spinning to twist into thread the fibers drawn from the mass on the distaff, and on which the thread is wound as it is spun. **2.** the rod on a spinning wheel by which the thread is twisted and on which it is wound. **3.** one of the rods of a spinning machine that bear the bobbins on which the spun thread is wound. **4.** any shaft, rod, or pin that turns around or on which something turns; an axle, axis, or shaft. **5.** a vertical shaft that serves to center a phonograph record on a turntable. **6.** either of two shafts or arbors that support the work on a lathe, one **(live spindle)** on the headstock, rotating with and imparting motion to the work, the other **(dead spindle)** on the tailstock, motionless. **7.** a small axis, arbor, or mandrel. **8.** an iron rod or the like, usually with a ball or cage at the top, fixed to a rock, sunken reef, etc., to serve as a guide in navigation. **9.** a measure of yarn, containing, for cotton, 15,120 yards (13,825 m), and for linen, 14,400 yards (13,267 m). **10.** a hydrometer. **11.** *Cell Biol.* a spindle-shaped structure, composed of microtubules, that forms near the cell nucleus during mitosis or meiosis and, as it divides, draws the chromosomes to opposite poles of the cell. **12.** a short, turned or circular ornament, as in a baluster or stair rail. **13.** See **spindle file. 14.** *Eastern New Eng.* a tassel on an ear of corn. **15.** *Chiefly New Jersey and Delaware Valley.* dragonfly. —*adj.* **16.** See **spindle side.** —*v.t.* **17.** to give the form of a spindle to. **18.** to provide or equip with a spindle or spindles. **19.** to impale (a card or paper) on a spindle, as for sorting purposes. —*v.i.* **20.** to shoot up, or grow, into a long, slender stalk or stem, as a plant. **21.** to grow tall and slender, often disproportionately so. [bef. 900; ME *spindel* (n.), OE *spin(e)l;* see SPIN, -LE; c. G *Spindel*] **—spin′·dle·like′,** *adj.*
—Regional Variation. 15. See **dragonfly.**

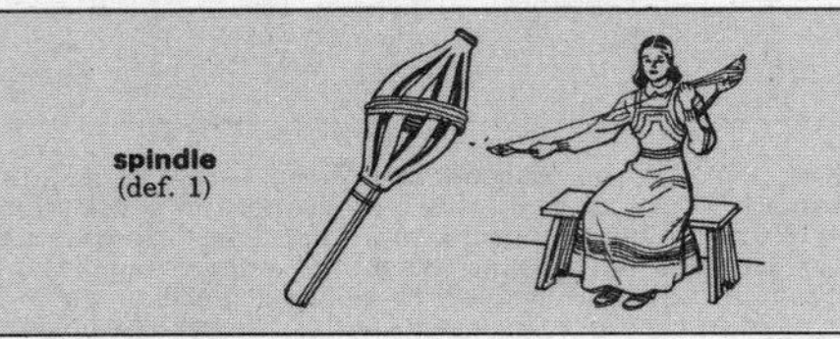
spindle (def. 1)

spin·dle·age (spin′dl ij), *n.* total number or capacity of spindles in a mill, area, etc. Also, **spin′dlage.** [SPINDLE + -AGE]

spin′dle file′, a device for holding bills, memos, etc., having a projecting metal spike or hooked object on which to stick papers. Also called **spindle.**

spin·dle·legs (spin′dl legz′), *n., pl.* **-legs** for 2. **1.** (*used with a plural v.*) long, thin legs. **2.** (*used with a singular v.*) *Informal.* a tall, thin person with such legs. [1640–50; SPINDLE + LEG + -S[3]] **—spin·dle-leg·ged** (spin′dl leg′id, -legd′), *adj.*

spin·dle·shanks (spin′dl shangks′), *n., pl.* **-shanks.** (*used with a singular or plural v.*) spindlelegs. [1560–70; SPINDLE + SHANK + -S[3]] **—spin·dle-shanked** (spin′dl shangkt′), *adj.*

spin′dle side′, the female side or line of descent of a family; distaff side (opposed to *spear side*). [1850–55]

spin·dling (spind′ling), *adj.* **1.** long or tall and slender, often disproportionately so. **2.** growing into a long, slender stalk or stem, often too slender or weak to remain upright. —*n.* **3.** a spindling person or thing. [1740–50; SPINDLE + -ING[2], -ING[1]]

spin·dly (spind′lē), *adj.,* **-dli·er, -dli·est.** long or tall, thin, and usually frail. [1645–55; SPINDLE + -Y[1]]

spin′ doc′tor, *Slang.* a press agent skilled at spin control. [1985–1990]

spin·drift (spin′drift′), *n.* spray swept by a violent wind along the surface of the sea. Also, **spoondrift.** [1590–1600; var. of Scots *speendrift* SPOONDRIFT]

spin-dry (spin′drī′), *v.t.,* **-dried, -dry·ing.** to remove moisture from (laundry) by centrifugal force, as in an automatic washing machine. **—spin′-dri′er, spin′-dry′er,** *n.*

spine (spīn), *n.* **1.** the spinal or vertebral column; backbone. **2.** any backbonelike part. **3.** a stiff, pointed process or appendage on an animal, as a quill of a porcupine, or a sharp ray in the fin of a fish. **4.** something, as a quality or trait, that constitutes a principal strength; resolution; backbone: *a situation that would test a person's spine.* **5.** a ridge, as of ground or rock. **6.** a sharp-pointed, hard or woody outgrowth on a plant; thorn. **7.** *Bookbinding.* the back of a book cover or binding, usually indicating the title and author. [1400–50; late ME < L *spīna* thorn, backbone] **—spined,** *adj.* **—spine′like′,** *adj.*

spine·bash (spīn′bash′), *v.i. Australian Slang.* to rest; loaf. [SPINE + BASH] **—spine′bash′er,** *n.*

spi·nel (spi nel′, spin′l), *n.* **1.** any of a group of minerals composed principally of oxides of magnesium, aluminum, iron, manganese, chromium, etc., characterized by their hardness and octahedral crystals. **2.** a mineral of this group, essentially magnesium aluminate, $MgAl_2O_4$, some varieties being used as gems. Also, **spi·nelle′.** [1520–30; < F *spinelle* < It *spinella,* equiv. to *spin(a)* thorn (< L *spīna*) + *-ella* -ELLE]

spine·less (spīn′lis), *adj.* **1.** having no spines or quills. **2.** having no spine or backbone. **3.** having a weak spine; limp. **4.** without moral force, resolution, or courage; feeble: *a spineless, lily-livered coward.* [1820–30; SPINE + -LESS] **—spine′less·ly,** *adv.* **—spine′less·ness,** *n.*
—Syn. 4. weak, irresolute, indecisive.

spinel′ ru′by. See **ruby spinel.** [1660–70]

spi·nes·cent (spī nes′ənt), *adj.* **1.** *Bot.* **a.** becoming spinelike. **b.** ending in a spine. **c.** bearing spines. **2.** *Zool.* somewhat spinelike; coarse, as hair. [1785–95; < LL *spīnēscent-* (s. of *spīnēscēns,* prp. of *spīnēscere* to grow thorny). See SPINE, -ESCENT] **—spi·nes′cence,** *n.*

spin·et (spin′it), *n.* **1.** a small upright piano. **2.** a small, square piano. **3.** any of various small harpsichords. **4.** Also called **spin′et or′gan.** a small electric organ. [1655–65; aph. var. of obs. *espinette* < F < It *spinetta,* prob. equiv. to *spin(a)* thorn (see SPINE) + *-etta* dim. suffix]

spin′ fish′ing, spinning (def. 3). [1945–50] **—spin′ fish′erman.**

Spin·garn (spin′gärn), *n.* **Joel Elias,** 1875–1939, U.S. literary critic, publisher, and editor.

spin·na·ker (spin′ə kər), *n. Naut.* a large, usually triangular sail carried by a yacht as a headsail when running before the wind or when the wind is abaft the beam. [1865–70; said to be alter. of *Sphinx,* name of the first yacht making regular use of this sail]

spin·ner (spin′ər), *n.* **1.** a person or thing that spins. **2.** *Angling.* a lure, as a spoon bait, that revolves in the water in trolling and casting. **3.** Also called **spin′ner play′.** *Football.* a play in which the player carrying the ball twirls about, to deceive the other team as to where the player intends to hit the line. **4.** *Aeron.* a streamlined fairing over a propeller hub. **5.** *Brit. Informal.* nightjar. **6.** *Slang.* a disc jockey. [1175–1225; ME *spinnere.* See SPIN, -ER[1]]

spin·ner·et (spin′ə ret′, spin′ə ret′), *n.* **1.** an organ or part by means of which a spider, insect larva, or the like spins a silky thread for its web or cocoon. **2.** a metal plate or cup with tiny holes through which a chemical solution is extruded to form continuous filaments, as of rayon, nylon, or polyester. [1820–30; SPINNER + -ET]

spin·ner·y (spin′ə rē), *n., pl.* **-ner·ies.** a spinning mill. [1830–40; SPIN + -ERY]

spin·ney (spin′ē), *n., pl.* **-neys.** *Brit.* a small wood or thicket. [1300–50; ME < MF *espinei* (masc.), *espinaie* (fem.) a place full of thorns, deriv. of *espine* SPINE; cf. LL *spīnētum* difficulty, equiv. to L *spīn(a)* thorn (see SPINE) + *-ētum* n. suffix (see ARBORETUM)]

spin·ning (spin′ing), *n.* **1.** *Textiles.* **a.** the act or process of converting staple or short lengths of fiber, as cotton or rayon, into continuous yarn or thread. **b.** the extrusion of a fiber-forming solution through holes in a spinneret to form filaments. **2.** *Entomol.* the act or process of secreting and placing silk or silklike filaments, as in the construction of a web by a spider or the formation of a cocoon by a caterpillar. **3.** Also called **spin casting, spin fishing, thread-line fishing.** *Angling.* the act or technique of casting a relatively light lure attached to a threadlike line wound on a stationary spool. [1250–1300; ME; see SPIN, -ING[1]] **—spin′ning·ly,** *adv.*

spin′ning box′. See **centrifugal box.** Also called **spin′ning pot′.**

spin′ning frame′, a machine for drawing, twisting, and winding yarn. [1815–25]

spin′ning jen′ny, an early spinning machine having more than one spindle, enabling a person to spin a number of yarns simultaneously. [1775–85]

spin′ning mule′, mule (def. 7). [1835–45]

spinning reel

spin′ning reel′, a fishing reel mounted on a spinning rod, having a stationary spool on the side of which is a revolving metal arm that catches the line and winds it onto the spool as a handle is turned, the metal arm being disengaged during casting so the line spirals freely off the spool, carried by the cast lure. [1945–50]

spin′ning ring′, ring[1] (def. 20).

spin′ning rod′, a flexible fishing rod, often made of fiberglass, used with a spinning reel. [1865–70]

spin′ning wheel′, a device formerly used for spinning wool, flax, etc., into yarn or thread, consisting essentially of a single spindle driven by a large wheel operated by hand or foot. [1375–1425; late ME]

spinning wheel

spi·node (spī′nōd), *n.* cusp (def. 3). [1850–55; irreg. < L *spīn(a)* SPINE + NODE]

spin-off (spin′ôf′, -of′), *n.* **1.** *Com.* a process of reorganizing a corporate structure whereby the capital stock

CONCISE ETYMOLOGY KEY: <, descended or borrowed from; >, whence; b., blend of, blended; c., cognate with; cf., compare; deriv., derivative; equiv., equivalent; imit., imitative; obl., oblique; r., replacing; s., stem; sp., spelling, spelled; resp., respelling, respelled; trans., translation; ?, origin unknown; *, unattested; ‡, probably earlier than. See the full key inside the front cover.

of a division or subsidiary of a corporation or of a newly affiliated company is transferred to the stockholders of the parent corporation without an exchange of any part of the stock of the latter. Cf. **split-off** (def. 3), **split-up** (def. 3). **2.** any product that is an adaption, outgrowth, or development of another similar product: *The paperback is a spin-off from the large hardcover encyclopedia.* **3.** a secondary or incidental product or effect derived from technological development in a somewhat unrelated area. Also, **spin′off′.** [1945–50; n. use of v. phrase *spin off*]
—Syn. 2, 3. by-product, issue, offshoot.

Spi·no·ne I·tal·i·an·o (spi nō′nē i tal′ē ä′nō, i tal-yä′), *pl.* **Spi·no·ni I·tal·i·an·i** (spi nō′nē i tal′ē ä′nē, ität yä′-). one of an Italian breed of large all-purpose hunting dogs having a short wiry coat, solid white or white with light brown or yellow patches in color. Also called **Italian pointer.** [< It]

spin·or (spin′ər), *n. Math., Physics.* a quantity resembling a vector or tensor that is used in physics to represent the spins of fermions. [1930–35; equiv. to SPIN + -OR[2], as in VECTOR, TENSOR]

spi·nose (spī′nōs, spī nōs′), *adj.* full of spines; spiniferous; spinous. [1650–60; < L *spīnōsus.* See SPINE, -OSE[1]] **—spi′nose·ly,** *adv.* **—spi·nos·i·ty** (spī nos′i tē), *n.*

spi·nous (spī′nəs), *adj.* **1.** covered with or having spines; thorny, as a plant. **2.** armed with or bearing sharp-pointed processes, as an animal. **3.** spinelike. [1630–40; < L *spīnōsus;* see SPINE, -OUS] **—spi′nous·ness,** *n.*

spi′nous proc′ess, *Anat., Zool.* a spinelike process of a bone, esp. the dorsal projection from the center of the arch of a vertebra. [1725–35]

spin-out (spin′out′), *n.* the spinning out of control into a rotating skid of a car or other vehicle. Also, **spin′out′.** [1950–55; n. use of v. phrase *spin out*]

Spi·no·za (spi nō′zə), *n.* **Ba·ruch** (bə ro͝ok′), or **Be·ne·dict de** (ben′ə dikt də), 1632–77, Dutch philosopher.

Spi·no·zism (spi nō′ziz əm), *n.* the philosophical system of Spinoza, which defines God as the unique substance, as an impersonal deity, and as possessing an infinite number of attributes, of which we know only thought and extension, and an infinite number of modes, each modifying all of the attributes, these attributes and modes being regarded both as proceeding necessarily from the nature of God and as constituents of God. [1720–30; SPINOZ(A) + -ISM] **—Spi·no′zist,** *n.* **—Spi·no·zis·tic** (spi nō zis′tik, spin′ō-), *adj.*

spin·proof (spin′pro͞of′), *adj.* (of an airplane) designed so as to be highly resistant to a tailspin. [SPIN + -PROOF]

spin′ quan′tum num′ber, *Physics.* the quantum number that designates the total angular momentum associated with electron spin and has a value of ½ in units of $h/2\pi$.

spin′ res′onance, *Physics.* See **electron spin resonance.**

spin·ster (spin′stər), *n.* **1.** a woman still unmarried beyond the usual age of marrying. **2.** *Chiefly Law.* a woman who has never married. **3.** a woman whose occupation is spinning. [1325–75; ME *spinnestere* a woman who spins. See SPIN, -STER] **—spin′ster·hood′,** *n.* **—spin′ster·ish,** *adj.* **—spin′ster·ish·ly,** *adv.* **—spin′ster·like′,** *adj.*

spin′ the bot′tle, a game in which someone spins a bottle and receives a kiss from the person at whom the bottle points on coming to rest. [1945–50, *Amer.*]

spin′ the plat′ter, a game in which one member of a group spins a platter on its edge and a designated member must catch it before it falls or pay a forfeit. Also called **spin′ the plate′.**

spin·to (spin′tō; *It.* spēn′tô), *adj.* having a lyric quality with a strong, dramatic element: *a spinto soprano voice.* [1940–45; < It: lit., excessive, pushed, ptp. of *spingere* to push < VL **expingere,* equiv. to L *ex-* EX-[1] + *-pingere,* comb. form of *pangere* to set, plant, arrange]

spi·nule (spī′nyo͞ol, spin′yo͞ol), *n. Zool., Bot.* a small spine. [1745–55; < L *spīnula.* See SPINE, -ULE] **—spin·u·lose** (spin′yə lōs′, spī′nyə-), *adj.*

spin·y (spī′nē), *adj.,* **spin·i·er, spin·i·est. 1.** abounding in or having spines; thorny, as a plant. **2.** covered with or having sharp-pointed processes, as an animal. **3.** in the form of a spine; resembling a spine; spinelike. **4.** troublesome or difficult to handle; thorny: *a spiny problem.* [1580–90; SPINE + -Y[1]] **—spin′i·ness,** *n.*

spin′y ant′eater, echidna (def. 1). [1820–30]

spin′y cock′lebur, a cocklebur, *Xanthium spinosum,* introduced into North America from Europe.

spin′y dog′fish, any of several dogfish sharks of the genus *Squalus,* having a spine in front of each of the two dorsal fins, esp. *S. acanthias,* inhabiting Atlantic coastal waters. [1840–50]

spin′y dor′mouse, a rat-sized rodent, *Platacanthomys lasiurus,* native to rocky hills of southern India, having reddish-brown fur and sharp, flat spines. Also called **pepper rat.**

spin·y-finned (spī′nē find′), *adj. Ichthyol.* having fins with sharp bony rays, as an acanthopterygian. [1880–85]

spin′y-head·ed worm′ (spī′nē hed′id), any of a small group of endoparasites of the phylum Acanthocephala, as larvae parasitic in insects and crustaceans and as adults in various vertebrates. [1945–50]

spin′y liz′ard, any of numerous iguanid lizards of the genus *Sceloporus,* common in North and Central America, usually having keeled scales that may end in a sharp point. [1850–55]

spin′y lob′ster, any of several edible crustaceans of the family Palinuridae, differing from the true lobsters in having a spiny shell and lacking the large pincers. Also called **crayfish, crawfish, sea crayfish, sea crawfish.** [1810–20]

spin′y rat′, any of various ratlike rodents of the genus *Echimys,* inhabiting forests of Central and South America, most having bristly fur.

spin′y-rayed fish′ (spī′nē rād′), any of various fishes, as basses and perches, that have sharp, often pointed and usually rigid fin spines. [1875–80]

spi·ra·cle (spī′rə kəl, spir′ə-), *n.* **1.** a breathing hole; an opening by which a confined space has communication with the outer air; air hole. **2.** *Zool.* **a.** an aperture or orifice through which air or water passes in the act of respiration, as the blowhole of a cetacean. **b.** an opening in the head of sharks and rays through which water is drawn and passed over gills. **c.** one of the external orifices of the tracheal respiratory system of certain invertebrates, usually on the sides of the body. See diag. under **insect.** [1300–50; ME < L *spīrāculum* air hole, equiv. to *spīrā(re)* to breathe + *-culum* -CLE[2]] **—spi·rac·u·lar** (spī rak′yə lər, spi-), *adj.*

spi·rae·a (spī rē′ə), *n.* spirea.

spi·ral (spī′rəl), *n., adj., v.,* **-raled, -ral·ing** or (*esp. Brit.*) **-ralled, -ral·ling.** **—n. 1.** *Geom.* a plane curve generated by a point moving around a fixed point while constantly receding from or approaching it. **2.** a helix. **3.** a single circle or ring of a spiral or helical curve or object. **4.** a spiral or helical object, formation, or form. **5.** *Aeron.* a maneuver in which an airplane descends in a helix of small pitch and large radius, with the angle of attack within that of the normal flight range. **6.** *Football.* a type of kick or pass in which the ball turns on its longer axis as it flies through the air. **7.** *Econ.* a continuous increase in costs, wages, prices, etc. **(inflationary spiral),** or a decrease in costs, wages, prices, etc. **(deflationary spiral).** **—adj. 8.** running continuously around a fixed point or center while constantly receding from or approaching it; coiling in a single plane: *a spiral curve.* **9.** coiling around a fixed line or axis in a constantly changing series of planes; helical. **10.** of or of the nature of a spire or coil. **11.** bound with a spiral binding; spiral-bound: *a spiral notebook.* **—v.i. 12.** to take a spiral form or course. **13.** to advance or increase steadily; rise: *Costs have been spiraling all year.* **14.** *Aeron.* to fly an airplane through a spiral course. **—v.t. 15.** to cause to take a spiral form or course. [1545–55; < ML *spīrālis,* equiv. to L *spīr(a)* coil (< Gk *speîra* anything coiled, wreathed, or twisted; see SPIRE[2]) + *-ālis* -AL[1]] **—spi·ral·i·ty** (spī ral′i tē), *n.* **—spi′ral·ly,** *adv.*

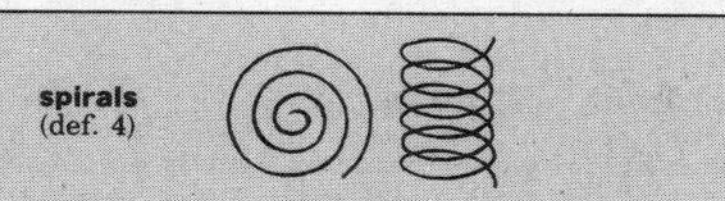

spi′ral arm′, *Astron.* any of the elongated and curved spiral sections that are connected to the center of a spiral galaxy. [1910–15]

spi′ral bev′el gear′, *Mach.* a bevel gear having curved teeth tending to converge on the axis of rotation. Also called **spiral gear.** [1930–35]

spi′ral bind′ing, a binding, as for a notebook or booklet, in which the pages are fastened together by a spiral of wire or plastic that coils through a series of holes punched along one side of each page and the front and back covers. [1940–45]

spi·ral-bound (spī′rəl bound′), *adj.* having a spiral binding. [1940–45]

spi′ral cas′ing, a spiral passage for directing the water from a penstock around a water turbine and into the rotor.

spi′ral gal′axy, *Astron.* a galaxy having a spiral structure. [1910–15]

spi′ral gear′, 1. a type of helical gear used for transmitting power between shafts that are at an angle to each other. **2.** See **spiral bevel gear.**

spi′ral neb′ula, *Astron.* (formerly) a spiral galaxy.

spi′ral of Archime′des, *Geom.* a curve that is the locus of a point that moves outward with uniform speed along a vector, beginning at the origin, while the vector rotates about the origin with uniform angular velocity. Equation (in polar coordinates): $r = a\theta$. [1650–60; named after ARCHIMEDES]

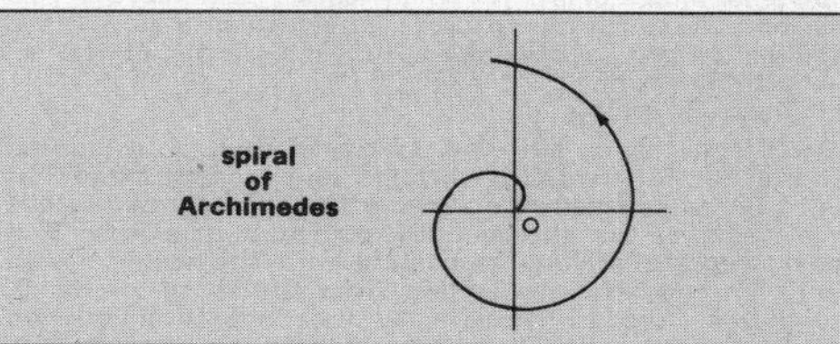

spi′ral spring′, a form of spring consisting of a wire coiled in a helix. See illus. under **spring.** [1680–90]

spi·rant (spī′rənt), *Phonet.* **—n. 1.** fricative (def. 2). **—adj. 2.** Also, **spi·ran·tal** (spī ran′tl). fricative. [1865–70; < L *spīrant-* (s. of *spīrāns,* prp. of *spīrāre* to breathe); see SPIRIT, -ANT]

spi·rant·ize (spī′rən tīz′), *v.t.,* **-ized, -iz·ing.** *Phonet.* to change into or pronounce as a spirant. Also, *esp. Brit.,* **spi′rant·ise′.** [1895–1900; SPIRANT + -IZE] **—spi′rant·i·za′tion,** *n.*

spire[1] (spīər), *n., v.,* **spired, spir·ing.** **—n. 1.** a tall, acutely pointed pyramidal roof or rooflike construction upon a tower, roof, etc. **2.** a similar construction forming the upper part of a steeple. See illus. under **steeple. 3.** a tapering, pointed part of something; a tall, sharp-pointed summit, peak, or the like: *the distant spires of the mountains.* **4.** the highest point or summit of something: *the spire of a hill; the spire of one's profession.* **5.** a sprout or shoot of a plant, as an acrospire of grain or a blade or spear of grass. **—v.i. 6.** to shoot or rise into spirelike form; rise or extend to a height in the manner of a spire. [bef. 1000; ME; OE *spīr* spike, blade; c. MD *spier,* MLG *spīr* shoot, sprout, sprig, ON *spíra* stalk] **—spire′less,** *adj.*

spire[2] (spīər), *n.* **1.** a coil or spiral. **2.** one of the series of convolutions of a coil or spiral. **3.** *Zool.* the upper, convoluted part of a spiral shell, above the aperture. [1565–75; < L *spīra* < Gk *speîra;* see SPIRAL] **—spire′less,** *adj.*

spi·re·a (spī rē′ə), *n.* any of various plants or shrubs belonging to the genus *Spiraea,* of the rose family, having clusters of small, white or pink flowers, certain species of which are cultivated as ornamentals. Also, **spiraea.** [1660–70; < NL, L *spīraea* < Gk *speiraía* privet]

spired (spīərd), *adj.* having a spire. [1600–10; SPIRE[1] + -ED[3]]

spire·let (spīər′lit), *n.* a small spire, as on a turret. [1840–50; SPIRE[1] + -LET]

spi·reme (spī′rēm), *n. Cell Biol.* the threadlike chromatin of a cell nucleus, present during early meiosis or mitosis. [1885–90; < Gk *speírēma* coil, equiv. to *speirē-,* var. s. of *speirâsthai* to be coiled around + *-ma* n. suffix of result]

Spires (spīərz), *n.* Speyer.

spi·ril·lum (spī ril′əm), *n., pl.* **-ril·la** (-ril′ə). *Bacteriol.* **1.** any of several spirally twisted, aerobic bacteria of the genus *Spirillum,* certain species of which are pathogenic for humans. See diag. under **bacteria. 2.** any of various similar microorganisms. [1870–75; < NL, equiv. to L *spīr(a)* (see SPIRE[2]) + *-illum* dim. suffix] **—spi·ril′lar,** *adj.*

spir·it (spir′it), *n.* **1.** the principle of conscious life; the vital principle in humans, animating the body or mediating between body and soul. **2.** the incorporeal part of humans: *present in spirit though absent in body.* **3.** the soul regarded as separating from the body at death. **4.** conscious, incorporeal being, as opposed to matter: *the world of spirit.* **5.** a supernatural, incorporeal being, esp. one inhabiting a place, object, etc., or having a particular character: *evil spirits.* **6.** a fairy, sprite, or elf. **7.** an angel or demon. **8.** an attitude or principle that inspires, animates, or pervades thought, feeling, or action: *the spirit of reform.* **9.** (*cap.*) the divine influence as an agency working in the human heart. **10.** a divine, inspiring, or animating being or influence. Num. 11:25; Is. 32:15. **11.** (*cap.*) the third person of the Trinity; Holy Spirit. **12.** the soul or heart as the seat of feelings or sentiments, or as prompting to action: *a man of broken spirit.* **13. spirits,** feelings or mood with regard to exaltation or depression: *low spirits; good spirits.* **14.** excellent disposition or attitude in terms of vigor, courage, firmness of intent, etc.; mettle: *That's the spirit!* **15.** temper or disposition: *meek in spirit.* **16.** an individual as characterized by a given attitude, disposition, character, action, etc.: *A few brave spirits remained to face the danger.* **17.** the dominant tendency or character of anything: *the spirit of the age.* **18.** vigorous sense of membership in a group: *college spirit.* **19.** the general meaning or intent of a statement, document, etc. (opposed to *letter*): *the spirit of the law.* **20.** *Chem.* the essence or active principle of a substance as extracted in liquid form, esp. by distillation. **21.** Often, **spirits.** a strong distilled alcoholic liquor. **22.** *Chiefly Brit.* alcohol. **23.** *Pharm.* a solution in alcohol of an essential or volatile principle; essence. **24.** any of certain subtle fluids formerly supposed to permeate the body. **25. out of spirits,** in low spirits; depressed: *We were feeling out of spirits after so many days of rain.* **26. the Spirit,** God. **—adj. 27.** pertaining to something that works by burning alcoholic spirits: *a spirit stove.* **28.** of or pertaining to spiritualist bodies or activities. **—v.t. 29.** to animate with fresh ardor or courage; inspirit. **30.** to encourage; urge on or stir up, as to action. **31.** to carry off mysteriously or secretly (often fol. by *away* or *off*): *His captors spirited him away.* [1200–50; ME (n.) < L *spīritus* orig., a breathing, equiv. to *spīri-,* comb. form repr. *spīrāre* to breathe + *-tus* suffix of v. action] **—spir′it·like′,** *adj.*
—Syn. 2. life, mind, consciousness, essence. **5.** apparition, phantom, shade. See **ghost. 6.** goblin, hobgoblin. **7.** genius. **14.** enthusiasm, energy, zeal, ardor, fire, enterprise. **15.** attitude, mood, humor. **17.** nature, drift, tenor, gist, essence, sense, complexion. **19.** intention, significance, purport.

Spir′it Cave′, an archaeological site in Thailand that has produced evidence of very early plant domestication in Southeast Asia, dated c7000 B.C.

spir′it com′pass, *Navig.* a wet compass filled with a mixture of alcohol and water.

spir·it·ed (spir′i tid), *adj.* having or showing mettle, courage, vigor, liveliness, etc.: *a spirited defense of poetry.* [1590–1600; SPIRIT + -ED[3]] **—spir′it·ed·ly,** *adv.* **—spir′it·ed·ness,** *n.*
—Syn. animated, vivacious, ardent, active, energetic, lively, vigorous, courageous, mettlesome.

spir′it gum′, a glue used in fastening false hair, as a beard or mustache, to an actor's skin. [1890–95]

spir·it·ism (spir′i tiz′əm), *n.* the doctrine or practices of spiritualism. [1860–65; SPIRIT + -ISM] **—spir′it·ist,** *n.* **—spir′it·is′tic,** *adj.*

Spir′it Lake′, a lake in SW Washington, at the N foot of Mount St. Helens: site of devastation during 1980 eruptions of Mount St. Helens.

spir·it·less (spir′it lis), *adj.* **1.** without spirit. **2.** without ardor, vigor, zeal, animation, etc.: *a spiritless reply to criticism.* [1560–70; SPIRIT + -LESS] **—spir′it·less·ly,** *adv.* **—spir′it·less·ness,** *n.*

spirit level
A, glass tube for determining horizontals; B, glass tube for determining verticals

spir′it lev′el, *Survey.* a device for determining true horizontal or vertical directions by the centering of a bubble in a slightly curved glass tube or tubes filled with alcohol or ether. Also called **level.** [1760–70]

spir′it lev′eling, *Survey.* leveling according to the indications of a spirit level. [1860–65]

spir′it of harts′horn, *Chem.* a colorless, pungent, suffocating, aqueous solution of about 28.5 percent ammonia gas: used chiefly as a detergent, for removing stains and extracting certain vegetable coloring agents, and in the manufacture of ammonium salts. Also, **spir′its of harts′horn.** [1675–85]

spir′it of ni′trous e′ther, *Pharm.* See **ethyl nitrite spirit.** [1855–60]

spi·ri·to·so (spir′i tō′sō; *It.* spē′rē tô′sô), *adj.* spirited; lively (used as a musical direction). [1715–25; < It; see SPIRIT, -OSE[1]]

spir·i·tous (spir′i təs), *adj. Archaic.* of the nature of spirit; immaterial, ethereal, or refined. [1595–1605; SPIRIT + -OUS]

spir′it rap′ping, *Spiritualism.* a form of communication between living persons and the spirits of deceased persons by tapping out messages on a table, board, or the like. [1850–55, *Amer.*] **—spir′it rap′per.**

spir′its of tur′pentine, *Chem.* See **oil of turpentine.** Also, **spir′it of tur′pentine.** [1785–95]

spir′its of wine′, alcohol (def. 1). [1745–55]

spir·it·u·al (spir′i cho͞o əl), *adj.* **1.** of, pertaining to, or consisting of spirit; incorporeal. **2.** of or pertaining to the spirit or soul, as distinguished from the physical nature: *a spiritual approach to life.* **3.** closely akin in interests, attitude, outlook, etc.: *the professor's spiritual heir in linguistics.* **4.** of or pertaining to spirits or to spiritualists; supernatural or spiritualistic. **5.** characterized by or suggesting predominance of the spirit; ethereal or delicately refined: *She is more of a spiritual type than her rowdy brother.* **6.** of or pertaining to the spirit as the seat of the moral or religious nature. **7.** of or pertaining to sacred things or matters; religious; devotional; sacred. **8.** of or belonging to the church; ecclesiastical: *lords spiritual and temporal.* **9.** of or relating to the mind or intellect. —*n.* **10.** a spiritual or religious song: *authentic folk spirituals.* **11. spirituals,** affairs of the church. **12.** a spiritual thing or matter. [1275–1325; ME < ML *spīrituālis,* equiv. to L *spīritu-* (s. of *spīritus* SPIRIT) + *-ālis* -AL[1]] **—spir′it·u·al·ly,** *adv.* **—spir′it·u·al·ness,** *n.*

spir′itual bouquet′, *Rom. Cath. Ch.* the spiritual presentation of a good work to another person. [1925–30]

spir′itual death′, death (def. 7).

spir·it·u·al·ism (spir′i cho͞o ə liz′əm), *n.* **1.** the belief or doctrine that the spirits of the dead, surviving after the mortal life, can and do communicate with the living, esp. through a person (a medium) particularly susceptible to their influence. **2.** the practices or phenomena associated with this belief. **3.** the belief that all reality is spiritual. **4.** *Metaphys.* any of various doctrines maintaining that the ultimate reality is spirit or mind. **5.** spiritual quality or tendency. **6.** insistence on the spiritual side of things, as in philosophy or religion. [1825–35; SPIRITUAL + -ISM] **—spir′it·u·al·is′tic,** *adj.* **—spir′it·u·al·is′ti·cal·ly,** *adv.*

spir·it·u·al·ist (spir′i cho͞o ə list), *n.* **1.** an adherent of spiritualism. **2.** a person who is concerned with or insists on the spiritual side of things. [1640–50; SPIRITUAL + -IST]

spir·it·u·al·i·ty (spir′i cho͞o al′i tē), *n., pl.* **-ties. 1.** the quality or fact of being spiritual. **2.** incorporeal or immaterial nature. **3.** predominantly spiritual character as shown in thought, life, etc.; spiritual tendency or tone. **4.** Often, **spiritualities.** property or revenue of the church or of an ecclesiastic in his or her official capacity. [1375–1425; late ME < ML *spīrituālitās.* See SPIRITUAL, -ITY]

spir·it·u·al·ize (spir′i cho͞o ə līz′), *v.t.,* **-ized, -iz·ing. 1.** to make spiritual. **2.** to invest with a spiritual meaning. Also, *esp. Brit.,* **spir′it·u·al·ise′.** [1625–35; SPIRITUAL + -IZE] **—spir′it·u·al·i·za′tion,** *n.* **—spir′i·tu·al·iz′er,** *n.*

spir·it·u·al·ty (spir′i cho͞o əl tē), *n., pl.* **-ties. 1.** Often, **spiritualties.** ecclesiastical property or revenue. **2.** the body of ecclesiastics; the clergy. [1350–1400; ME *spiritualte* < MF < ML *spīrituālitās;* see SPIRITUALITY]

spi·ri·tu·el (spir′i cho͞o el′; *Fr.* spē rē tyel′), *adj.* **1.** showing or having a refined and graceful mind or wit. **2.** light and airy in movement; ethereal. Also, **spi′ri·tu·elle′.** [1665–75; < F: lit., SPIRITUAL]

spir·it·u·ous (spir′i cho͞o əs), *adj.* **1.** containing, of the nature of, or pertaining to alcohol; alcoholic. **2.** (of alcoholic beverages) distilled, rather than fermented. [1590–1600; < L *spīritu-,* s. of *spīritus* SPIRIT + -OUS] **—spir′·it·u·ous·ly,** *adv.* **—spir′it·u·ous·ness,** *n.*

spir·i·tus as·per (spir′i təs as′pər; *Lat.* spē′ri to͞os äs′per). See **rough breathing.** [< LL *spiritus asper*]

spi·ri·tus fru·men·ti (spir′i təs fro͞o men′tī, -tē), whiskey. [< NL *spiritus frūmentī* lit., the spirit (or life) of grain]

spir·i·tus le·nis (spir′i təs lē′nis; *Lat.* spē′ri to͞os lā′nis). See **smooth breathing.** [< LL *spiritus lēnis*]

CONCISE ETYMOLOGY KEY: <, descended or borrowed from; >, whence; b., blend of, blended; c., cognate with; cf., compare; deriv., derivative; equiv., equivalent; imit., imitative; obl., oblique; r., replacing; s., stem; sp., spelling, spelled; resp., respelling, respelled; trans., translation; ?, origin unknown; *, unattested; ‡, probably earlier than. See the full key inside the front cover.

spir·i·tus vi·no·sus (spir′i təs vī nō′səs), (in prescriptions) spirits of wine; alcohol. [< L *spīritus vīnōsus*]

spir′it var′nish. See under **varnish** (def. 1). [1840–50]

Spir′it Wres′tler, a Doukhobor. [1895–1900]

spir′it writ′ing, writing allegedly produced by spirits or supernatural forces. [1870–75]

spiro-[1], a combining form meaning "respiration," used in the formation of compound words: *spirograph.* [comb. form of L *spīrāre* to breathe]

spiro-[2], a combining form meaning "coil," "spiral," used in the formation of compound words: *spirochete.* [comb. form of L *spīra* < Gk *speîra* coil]

spi·ro·chete (spī′rə kēt′), *n.* any of various spiral-shaped motile bacteria of the family Spirochaetaceae, certain species, as *Treponema, Leptospira,* and *Borrelia,* being pathogenic to humans and other animals, and other species being free-living, saprophytic, or parasitic. Also, **spi′ro·chaete′.** [1875–80; < NL *spirochaeta.* See SPIRO-[2], CHAETA-] **—spi′ro·chet′al, spi′ro·che′tic,** *adj.*

spi·ro·che·to·sis (spī′rə kē tō′sis), *n. Pathol.* a disease caused by infection with a spirochete. Also, **spi′ro·chae·to′sis.** [1920–25; SPIROCHETE + -OSIS] **—spi·ro·che·tot·ic, spi·ro·chae·tot·ic** (spī′rə kē tot′ik), *adj.*

spi·ro·graph (spī′rə graf′, -gräf′), *n.* an instrument for recording respiratory movements. [SPIRO-[1] + -GRAPH] **—spi·ro·graph·ic** (spī′rə graf′ik), *adj.*

spi·ro·gy·ra (spī′rə jī′rə), *n. Bot.* a widely distributed filamentous freshwater green alga of the genus *Spirogyra.* [1895–1900; < NL, equiv. to *spiro-* SPIRO-[2] + *-gyra,* alter. of Gk *gŷros* circle or *gŷrós* round]

spi·roid (spī′roid), *adj.* more or less spiral; resembling a spiral. [1840–50; < NL *spīroīdēs* < Gk *speiroeidḗs.* See SPIRO-[2], -OID]

spi·rom·e·ter (spī rom′i tər), *n.* an instrument for determining the capacity of the lungs. [1840–50; SPIRO-[1] + -METER] **—spi·ro·met·ric** (spī′rə me′trik), **spi′ro·met′ri·cal,** *adj.* **—spi·rom′e·try,** *n.*

spi·ro·no·lac·tone (spī′rə nō lak′tōn, spī rō′-, -ron′ə-), *n. Pharm.* a steroid, $C_{24}H_{32}O_4S$, used in combination with other drugs as a diuretic and antihypertensive. [1955–60; alter. of *spirolactone;* see SPIRO-[2], LACTONE]

spirt (spûrt), *v.i., v.t., n.* spurt.

spir·u·la (spir′yə lə, -o͝o lə), *n., pl.* **-lae** (-lē′). any cephalopod of the genus *Spirula,* having a flat, spiral shell that is partly inside and partly outside the posterior part of the body. [1825–35; < NL; LL *spīrula* twisted cake. See SPIRA, -ULE]

spi·ru·li·na (spī′rə lī′nə), *n.* any of the blue-green algae of the genus *Spirulina,* sometimes added to food for its nutrient value. [< NL, equiv. to *spīrul(a)* small coil (see SPIRAL, -ULE) + *-ina* -INA; so called from their corkscrew shape]

spir·y[1] (spīər′ē), *adj.* **1.** having the form of a spire, slender shoot, or tapering pointed body; tapering up to a point like a spire. **2.** abounding in spires or steeples. [1595–1605; SPIRE[1] + -Y[1]]

spir·y[2] (spī′rē), *adj.* spiral; coiled; coiling; helical. [1670–80; SPIRE[2] + -Y[1]]

spis·sa·tus (spi sā′təs), *adj. Meteorol.* (of a cloud) dense enough to obscure the sun. [< NL *spissātus,* ptp. of *spissāre* to thicken, pack tightly; see -ATE[1]]

spit[1] (spit), *v.,* **spit** or **spat, spit·ting,** *n.* —*v.i.* **1.** to eject saliva from the mouth; expectorate. **2.** to express hatred, contempt, etc., by or as if by ejecting saliva from the mouth. **3.** to sputter: *grease spitting on the fire.* **4.** to fall in scattered drops or flakes, as rain or snow. —*v.t.* **5.** to eject from the mouth: *The children were spitting watermelon seeds over the fence.* **6.** to throw out or emit like saliva: *The kettle spits boiling water over the stove.* **7.** to set a flame to. **8. spit up,** to vomit; throw up: *The wounded soldier spat up blood. If you jostle the baby, she'll spit up.* —*n.* **9.** saliva, esp. when ejected. **10.** the act of spitting. **11.** *Entomol.* spittle. **12.** a light fall of rain or snow. **13. spit and image.** Also, **spitting image, spit 'n' image.** *Informal.* exact likeness; counterpart: *Hunched over his desk, pen in hand, he was the spit and image of his father at work.* [bef. 950; (v.) ME *spitten,* OE *spittan;* c. G (dial.) *spitzen* to spit; akin to OE *spǣtan* to spit, *spātl* spittle; (n.) ME, deriv. of the v.] **—spit′like′,** *adj.*
—Syn. 3. spatter.

spit[2] (spit), *n., v.,* **spit·ted, spit·ting.** —*n.* **1.** a pointed rod or bar for thrusting through and holding meat that is to be cooked before or over a fire. **2.** any of various rods, pins, or the like used for particular purposes. **3.** a narrow point of land projecting into the water. **4.** a long, narrow shoal extending from the shore. —*v.t.* **5.** to pierce, stab, or transfix, as with a spit; impale on something sharp. **6.** to thrust a spit into or through. [bef. 1000; ME *spite,* OE *spitu;* c. MD, MLG *spit, spet,* OHG *spiz* spit; akin to ON *spita* peg]

spit·al (spit′l), *n. Archaic.* **1.** a hospital, esp. one for lazars. **2.** a shelter on a highway. [1625–35; alter. of *spittle,* ME *spitel* < ML *hospitāle;* see HOSPITAL]

spit′ and pol′ish, great care in maintaining smart appearance and crisp efficiency: *The commander was concerned more with spit and polish than with the company's morale.* **—spit-and-polish** (spit′n pol′ish), *adj.*

spit·ball (spit′bôl′), *n.* **1.** a small ball or lump of chewed paper used as a missile. **2.** Also called **spitter.** *Baseball.* a pitch, now illegal, made to curve by moistening one side of the ball with saliva or perspiration. [1840–50, *Amer.;* SPIT[1] + BALL[1]]

spit·ball·er (spit′bô′lər), *n. Baseball.* a pitcher who is known or believed to throw spitballs. [SPITBALL + -ER[1]]

spitch·cock (spich′kok′), *n.* **1.** an eel that is split, cut into pieces, and broiled or fried. —*v.t.* **2.** to split, cut up, and broil or fry (an eel). **3.** to treat severely. [1590–1600; orig. obscure]

spit′ curl′, a tight curl of hair, usually pressed against the forehead or cheek. [1825–35]

spite (spīt), *n., v.,* **spit·ed, spit·ing.** —*n.* **1.** a malicious, usually petty, desire to harm, annoy, frustrate, or humiliate another person; bitter ill will; malice. **2.** a particular instance of such an attitude or action; grudge. **3.** *Obs.* something that causes vexation; annoyance. **4. in spite of,** in disregard or defiance of; notwithstanding; despite: *She arrived at school on time in spite of the snowstorm.* —*v.t.* **5.** to treat with spite or malice. **6.** to annoy or thwart, out of spite. **7.** to fill with spite; vex; offend. **8. cut off one's nose to spite one's face.** See **nose** (def. 14). [1250–1300; ME; aph. var. of DESPITE] **—spite′less,** *adj.*
—Syn. 1. malevolence, maliciousness, rancor, venom, spleen. See **grudge. 4.** See **notwithstanding.**

spite′ fence′, a wall or fence erected solely to annoy one's neighbor or lower the value of his or her property. [1895–1900, *Amer.*]

spite·ful (spīt′fəl), *adj.* full of spite or malice; showing spite; malicious; malevolent; venomous: *a spiteful child.* [1400–50; late ME; see SPITE, -FUL] **—spite′ful·ly,** *adv.* **—spite′ful·ness,** *n.*
—Syn. vengeful, mean, cruel, rancorous. SPITEFUL, REVENGEFUL, VINDICTIVE refer to a desire to inflict a wrong or injury on someone, usually in return for one received. SPITEFUL implies a mean or malicious desire for (often petty) revenge: *a spiteful attitude toward a former friend.* REVENGEFUL implies a deep, powerful, and continued intent to repay a wrong: *a fierce and revengeful spirit.* VINDICTIVE does not imply action necessarily, but stresses the unforgiving nature of the avenger: *a vindictive look.* **—Ant.** benevolent.

spit·fire (spit′fīər′), *n.* **1.** a person, esp. a girl or woman, who is of fiery temper and easily provoked to outbursts. **2.** (*cap.*) a British fighter plane with a single in-line engine used by the R.A.F. throughout World War II. [1590–1600; SPIT[1] + FIRE]

Spit·head (spit′hed′), *n.* a roadstead off the S coast of England between Portsmouth and the Isle of Wight.

spit′ in the o′cean, *Cards.* a variety of poker in which four cards are dealt face down to each player and one card, forming the fifth for all hands, is dealt face up in the center of the table, the exposed card and others of its denomination being wild cards.

Spits·ber·gen (spits′bûr′gən), *n.* a group of islands in the Arctic Ocean, N of and belonging to Norway. 3431; 24,293 sq. mi. (62,920 sq. km). Also, **Spitzbergen.** Norwegian, **Svalbard.**

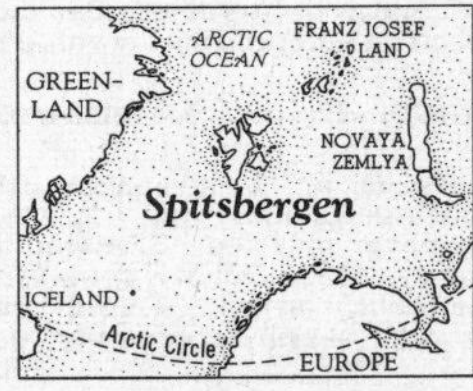

spit-shine (spit′shīn′), *n., v.,* **-shined, -shin·ing.** —*n.* **1.** a shoeshine in which a fluid, such as water, saliva, or lighter fluid, is used to impart a high gloss. —*v.t.* **2.** to give a spit-shine to.

Spit·te·ler (*Ger.* shpit′l ər), *n.* **Carl** (*Ger.* kärl), ("*Felix Tandem*"), 1845–1924, Swiss poet, novelist, and essayist: Nobel prize 1919.

spit·ter[1] (spit′ər), *n.* **1.** a person or thing that spits. **2.** *Baseball.* spitball (def. 2). [1350–1400; ME; see SPIT[1], -ER[1]]

spit·ter[2] (spit′ər), *n.* brocket (def. 2). [1555–65; SPIT[2] + -ER[1]]

spit′ting co′bra, any cobra or cobralike snake, esp. the ringhals, that sprays venom at the eyes of approaching animals. [1905–10]

spit′ting im′age, *Informal.* See **spit**[1] (def. 13). [1925–30; from the phrase *spit and image* (see SPIT[1]) by confusion of *spit and* with *spittin';* cf. earlier *the very spit of* the exact likeness of]

spit·tle (spit′l), *n.* **1.** saliva; spit. **2.** *Entomol.* the frothy secretion exuded by spittlebugs. [1470–80; b. ME *spit* (n.) (see SPIT[1]) and *spetil,* OE *spǣtl,* var. of *spātl* saliva]

spit·tle·bug (spit′l bug′), *n.* the nymph of the froghopper, which surrounds itself with a frothy mass. [1880–85, *Amer.;* SPITTLE + BUG[1]]

spit·toon (spi to͞on′), *n.* a cuspidor. [1815–25, *Amer.;* SPIT[1] + -OON]

spitz (spits), *n.* any of several dogs having a stocky body, a thick coat, erect, pointed ears, and a tail curved over the back, as a chow chow, Pomeranian, or Samoyed. [1835–45; < G *spitz* pointed]

Spitz (spits), *n.* **Mark (Andrew),** born 1950, U.S. swimmer: winner of seven gold medals in 1972 summer Olympic Games.

Spitz·ber·gen (spits′bûr′gən), *n.* Spitsbergen.

spitz·en·burg (spit′sən bûrg′), *n.* any of several red or yellow varieties of apple that ripen in the autumn. Also, **spitz′en·berg′.** [1795–1805, *Amer.;* short for *Esopus Spitzenberg,* after *Esopus,* N.Y. + D *spits* point + *berg* mountain; so called from its being found on a hill near Esopus]

spiv (spiv), *n. Brit. Informal.* a petty criminal, esp. a black marketeer, racetrack tout, or petty thief. [1885–90; back formation from dial. *spiving* smart; perh. akin to SPIFFY]

spiv·vy (spiv′ē), *adj.*, **-vi·er, -vi·est.** *Chiefly Brit.* spiffy. Also, **spiv·ving** (spiv′ing).

splad (splad), *n.* splat[1] (def. 1).

splake (splāk), *n., pl.* **splakes,** (*esp. collectively*) **splake.** the hybrid offspring of a lake trout and a brook trout. [1950–55; SP(ECKLED TROUT) + LAKE (TROUT)]

splanch·nic (splangk′nik), *adj.* **1.** of or pertaining to the viscera or entrails; visceral. **2.** of or pertaining to the splanchnic nerve. [1675–85; < NL *splanchnicus* < Gk *splanchnikós,* equiv. to *splánchn(a)* + *-ikos* -IC]

splanch′nic nerve′, *Anat.* any of several nerves to the viscera and blood vessels of the chest and pelvic areas. [1825–35]

splanchno-, a combining form meaning "viscera," used in the formation of compound words: *splanchnopleure.* [comb. form of Gk *splánchna* entrails (pl.)]

splanch·no·pleure (splangk′nə plo͝or′), *n. Embryol.* the double layer formed by the association of the lower layer of the lateral plate of mesoderm with the underlying entoderm, which develops into the embryonic viscera. Cf. **somatopleure.** [1870–75; < NL *splanchnopleura.* See SPLANCHNO-, PLEURA] —**splanch′no·pleu′ral, splanch′no·pleu′ric,** *adj.*

splash (splash), *v.t.* **1.** to wet or soil by dashing water, mud, or the like; spatter: *Don't splash her dress!* **2.** to fall upon (something) in scattered masses or particles, as a liquid does. **3.** to cause to appear spattered. **4.** to dash (water, mud, etc.) in scattered masses or particles. **5.** to make (one's way) with splashing: *He splashed his way across the pool.* **6.** *Logging.* to move (logs) by releasing a body of water from a splash dam. —*v.i.* **7.** to dash a liquid or semiliquid substance about. **8.** to fall, move, or go with a splash or splashes. **9.** (of liquid) to dash with force in scattered masses or particles. —*n.* **10.** the act of splashing. **11.** the sound of splashing. **12.** a quantity of a liquid or semiliquid substance splashed. **13.** a spot caused by something splashed. **14.** a patch, as of color or light. **15.** *Logging.* **a.** the act of splashing logs. **b.** water released, as from a splash dam, for splashing logs. **16.** a striking show or impression. [1705–15; perh. alter. of PLASH[1]] —**splash′ing·ly,** *adv.*
—**Syn. 16.** ado, impression, uproar, sensation.

splash·board (splash′bôrd′, -bōrd′), *n.* **1.** a board, guard, or screen to protect from splashing, as a dashboard of a vehicle or a guard placed over a wheel to intercept water, dirt, etc. **2.** *Naut.* washboard (def. 3). [1820–30; SPLASH + BOARD]

splash′ dam′, a flood dam built to contain water that is released for driving logs.

splash′ down′, 1. to land in a body of water in a returning spacecraft. **2.** (of a spacecraft) to land in a body of water. [1955–60, *Amer.*]

splash·down (splash′doun′), *n.* **1.** the landing of a space vehicle in a body of water, esp. the ocean. **2.** the exact place where such a landing is made. **3.** the time of such a landing. [1959; n. use of v. phrase *splash down*]

splash·er (splash′ər), *n.* **1.** a person or thing that splashes. **2.** something that protects from splashes. [1840–50; SPLASH + -ER[1]]

splash′ ero′sion, erosion caused by the impact of falling raindrops.

splash′ guard′, a large flap behind a rear tire to prevent mud, water, etc., from being splashed on the following vehicle. Also called **mudguard, mud flap.** [1925–30]

splash·y (splash′ē), *adj.*, **splash·i·er, splash·i·est. 1.** making a splash or splashes. **2.** making the sound of splashing. **3.** full of or marked by splashes, or irregular spots; spotty. **4.** making an ostentatious display; showy. [1825–35; SPLASH + -Y[1]] —**splash′i·ly,** *adv.* —**splash′i·ness,** *n.*

splat[1] (splat), *n.* **1.** Also, **splad.** a broad, flat piece of wood, either pierced or solid, forming the center upright part of a chair back or the like. **2.** a batten for covering joints between sheets of wallboard; panel strip. [1825–35; orig. uncert.; cf. OE *splātan* to split]

splat[2] (splat), *n.* a sound made by splattering or slapping. [1895–1900; back formation from SPLATTER]

splat·ter (splat′ər), *v.t., v.i.* **1.** to splash and scatter upon impact: *The paint splattered when I dropped the bucket.* —*n.* **2.** an act or instance of splattering. **3.** the quantity splattered: *to wipe up a splatter of ketchup on the rug.* —*adj.* **4.** characterized by gory imagery: *splatter films.* [1775–85; b. SPLASH and SPATTER]

splat′ter film′, *Slang.* **1.** a film containing many scenes of violent and gruesome murders. **2.** See **snuff film.** Also called **splat′ter mov′ie.**

splat·ter·punk (splat′ər pungk′), *n.* a form of fiction featuring extremely graphic violence. [1985–90]

splay (splā), *v.t.* **1.** to spread out, expand, or extend. **2.** to form with an oblique angle; make slanting; bevel. **3.** to make with a splay or splays. **4.** to disjoin; dislocate. —*v.i.* **5.** to have an oblique or slanting direction. **6.** to spread or flare. —*n.* **7.** *Archit.* a surface that makes an oblique angle with another, as where the opening through a wall for a window or door widens from the window or door proper toward the face of the wall. —*adj.* **8.** spread out; wide and flat; turned outward. **9.** clumsy or awkward. **10.** oblique or awry. [1300–50; ME; aph. form of DISPLAY]

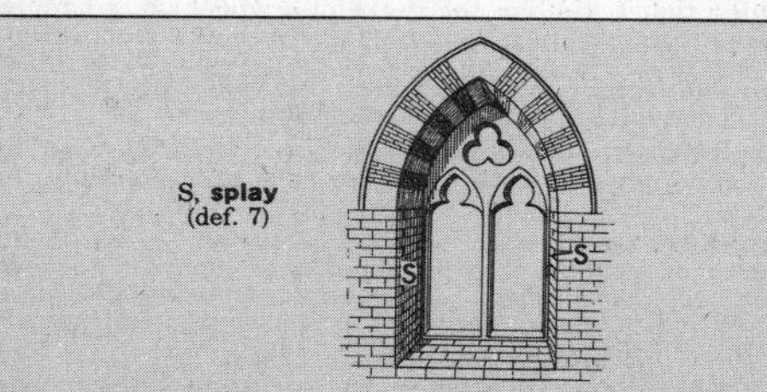

S, **splay** (def. 7)

splay·foot (splā′fo͝ot′), *n., pl.* **-feet,** *adj.* —*n.* **1.** a broad, flat foot, esp. one turned outward. **2.** *Pathol.* this condition as a deformity in which the arch is very low or absent and weight is borne on the entire sole; flatfoot. —*adj.* Also, **splay′foot′ed. 3.** of, pertaining to, or afflicted with splayfoot. **4.** clumsy or awkward. [1540–50; SPLAY + FOOT]

spleen (splēn), *n.* **1.** a highly vascular, glandular, ductless organ, situated in humans at the cardiac end of the stomach, serving chiefly in the formation of mature lymphocytes, in the destruction of worn-out red blood cells, and as a reservoir for blood. **2.** *Obs.* this organ conceived of as the seat of spirit and courage or of such emotions as mirth, ill humor, melancholy, etc. **3.** ill humor, peevish temper, or spite. **4.** *Archaic.* melancholy. **5.** *Obs.* caprice. [1250–1300; ME < L *splēn* < Gk *splḗn;* akin to Skt *plihan,* L *liēn* spleen] —**spleen′ish,** *adj.*
—**Syn. 3.** petulance, rancor, acrimoniousness; wrath, ire, anger.

spleen·ful (splēn′fəl), *adj.* **1.** full of or displaying spleen. **2.** ill-humored; irritable or peevish; spiteful; splenetic. [1580–90; SPLEEN + -FUL] —**spleen′ful·ly,** *adv.*

spleen·wort (splēn′wûrt′, -wôrt′), *n.* any of various temperate and tropical ferns of the genera *Asplenium* and *Diplazium,* certain species of which are grown as ornamentals. [1570–80; SPLEEN + WORT[2]]

spleen·y (splē′nē), *adj.*, **spleen·i·er, spleen·i·est.** abundant in or displaying spleen. [1595–1605; SPLEEN + -Y[1]]

splen-, var. of **spleno-** before a vowel: *splenectomy.*

splen·dent (splen′dənt), *adj.* **1.** shining or radiant, as the sun. **2.** gleaming or lustrous, as metal, marble, etc. **3.** brilliant in appearance, color, etc.; gorgeous; magnificent; splendid. **4.** eminent; illustrious. [1425–75; late ME < L *splendent-* (s. of *splendēns*), prp. of *splendēre* to shine; see -ENT] —**splen′dent·ly,** *adv.*

splen·did (splen′did), *adj.* **1.** gorgeous; magnificent; sumptuous. **2.** grand; superb, as beauty. **3.** distinguished or glorious, as a name, reputation, victory, etc. **4.** strikingly admirable or fine: *splendid talents.* **5.** excellent, fine, or very good: *to have a splendid time.* **6.** brilliant in appearance, color, etc. [1615–25; < L *splendidus* brilliant, equiv. to *splend(ēre)* to shine + *-idus* -ID[4]] —**splen′did·ly,** *adv.* —**splen′did·ness,** *n.*
—**Syn. 1.** luxurious, dazzling, imposing. See **magnificent. 3.** renowned, famed, famous, illustrious, eminent, conspicuous, celebrated, remarkable, brilliant; noble. —**Ant. 1.** squalid. **3.** ignoble.

splen·dif·er·ous (splen dif′ər əs), *adj.* splendid; magnificent; fine. [1425–75; late ME < LL *splendōrifer* brightness-bearing (see SPLENDOR, -FER, -OUS; loss of *-or* prob. by shift of stress, syncope, and dissimilation) + -OUS] —**splen·dif′er·ous·ly,** *adv.* —**splen·dif′er·ous·ness,** *n.*

splen·dor (splen′dər), *n.* **1.** brilliant or gorgeous appearance, coloring, etc.; magnificence: *the splendor of the palace.* **2.** an instance or display of imposing pomp or grandeur: *the splendor of the coronation.* **3.** grandeur; glory; brilliant distinction: *the splendor of ancient Greek architecture.* **4.** great brightness; brilliant light or luster. —*v.t.* **5.** to make splendid by decorating lavishly; adorn. —*v.i.* **6.** to move or proceed with splendor, grandeur, or pomp. Also, *esp. Brit.,* **splen′dour.** [1400–50; < L *splendor,* equiv. to *splend(ēre)* to shine + *-or* -OR[1]; r. late ME *splendure* < AF < L, as above] —**splen′dor·ous, splen·drous** (splen′drəs), *adj.*
—**Syn. 1.** show, dash. **3.** fame, eminence, renown, celebrity. **4.** dazzle, refulgence. —**Ant. 1.** squalor.

sple·nec·to·my (spli nek′tə mē), *n., pl.* **-mies.** *Surg.* excision or removal of the spleen. Also called **lienectomy.** [1855–60; SPLEN- + -ECTOMY]

sple·net·ic (spli net′ik), *adj.* Also, **sple·net′i·cal. 1.** of the spleen; splenic. **2.** irritable; peevish; spiteful. **3.** *Obs.* affected with, characterized by, or tending to produce melancholy. —*n.* **4.** a splenetic person. [1535–45; < LL *splēnēticus.* See SPLEN-, -ETIC] —**sple·net′i·cal·ly,** *adv.*
—**Syn. 2.** vexatious, irascible, testy, fretful, touchy, petulant, choleric.

splen·ic (splē′nik, splen′ik), *adj.* of, pertaining to, connected with, or affecting the spleen: *splenic nerves.* [1610–20; < L *splēnicus* < Gk *splēnikós.* See SPLEN-, -IC]

sple·ni·us (splē′nē əs), *n., pl.* **-ni·i** (-nē ī′). *Anat.* a broad muscle on each side of the back of the neck and the upper part of the thoracic region, the action of which draws the head backward and assists in turning it to one side. [1725–35; < NL, for L *splēnium* < Gk *splḗnion* plaster, patch] —**sple′ni·al,** *adj.*

spleno-, a combining form representing **spleen** in compound words: *splenomegaly.* Also, *esp. before a vowel,* **splen-.** [comb. form repr. Gk *splḗn* SPLEEN]

sple·no·meg·a·ly (splē′nə meg′ə lē, splen′ə-), *n. Pathol.* enlargement of the spleen. Also, **sple·no·me·ga·li·a** (splē′nō mə gā′lē ə, -gal′yə, splen′ō-). [1895–1900; SPLENO- + -MEGALY]

spleu·chan (splo͞o′khən), *n. Scot., Irish Eng.* a small pouch, esp. for carrying tobacco or money. Also, **spleughan** (splo͞o′khən). [1775–85; < ScotGael *spliùchan*]

splice (splīs), *v.,* **spliced, splic·ing,** *n.* —*v.t.* **1.** to join together or unite (two ropes or parts of a rope) by the interweaving of strands. **2.** to unite (timbers, spars, or the like) by overlapping and binding their ends. **3.** to unite (film, magnetic tape, or the like) by butting and cementing. **4.** to join or unite. **5.** *Genetics.* to join (segments of DNA or RNA) together. **6.** *Informal.* to unite in marriage. **7. splice the main brace,** *Naut.* **a.** to issue a ration of spirits, as grog, to all hands. **b.** to drink spirits. —*n.* **8.** a joining of two ropes or parts of a rope by splicing. **9.** the union or junction made by splicing. **10.** a joining or junction of two pieces of timber, spar, etc., by overlapping and fastening the ends. **11.** a joining of film, electromagnetic tape, or the like. [1515–25; < earlier D *splissen* (now *splitsen*)] —**splice′a·ble,** *adj.*

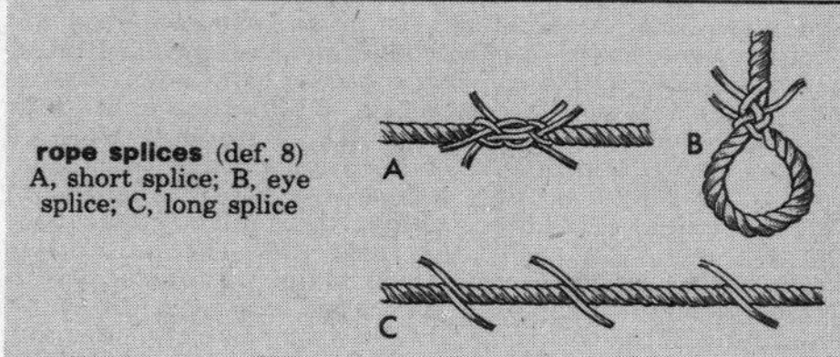

rope splices (def. 8)
A, short splice; B, eye splice; C, long splice

splic·er (splī′sər), *n.* a device used to hold two sections of motion-picture film, recording tape, etc., in proper alignment while they are being spliced together. [1925–30; SPLICE + -ER[1]]

spliff (splif), *n. Slang.* a marijuana cigarette, esp. a large or very potent one. [1935–40; orig. Jamaican E; of uncert. orig.]

spline (splīn), *n., v.,* **splined, splin·ing.** —*n.* **1.** a long, narrow, thin strip of wood, metal, etc.; slat. **2.** a long, flexible strip of wood or the like, used in drawing curves. **3.** *Mach.* **a.** any of a series of uniformly spaced ridges on a shaft, parallel to its axis and fitting inside corresponding grooves in the hub of a gear, etc., to transmit torque. **b.** See **feather key. 4.** *Building Trades.* a thin strip of material inserted into the edges of two boards, acoustic tiles, etc., to make a butt joint between them; a feather. **5.** *Math., Engineering.* a function that has specified values at a finite number of points and consists of segments of polynomial functions joined smoothly at these points, enabling it to be used for approximation and interpolation of functions. —*v.t. Mach.* **6.** to provide with a spline or key. **7.** to provide with a keyway. [1750–60; orig. East Anglian dial.; perh. akin to SPLINT; cf. OE *splin* spindle]

splint (splint), *n.* **1.** a thin piece of wood or other rigid material used to immobilize a fractured or dislocated bone, or to maintain any part of the body in a fixed position. **2.** one of a number of thin strips of wood woven together to make a chair seat, basket, etc. **3.** *Vet. Med.* an exostosis or bony enlargement of a splint bone of a horse or a related animal. **4.** *Armor.* **a.** any of a number of narrow plates or lames joined with rivets or a backing to form a piece of armor. **b.** a partial vambrace protecting only the outer part of the arm. **5.** *Brit. Dial.* a splinter of wood or stone. —*v.t.* **6.** to secure, hold in position, or support by means of a splint or splints, as a fractured bone. **7.** to support as if with splints. [1275–1325; ME < MD or MLG *splinte;* cf. SPLINTER] —**splint′like′,** *adj.*

splint′ bone′, one of the rudimentary, splintlike metacarpal or metatarsal bones of the horse or some allied animal, one on each side of the back of each cannon bone. [1695–1705]

splin·ter (splin′tər), *n.* **1.** a small, thin, sharp piece of wood, bone, or the like, split or broken off from the main body. **2.** See **splinter group.** —*v.t.* **3.** to split or break into splinters. **4.** to break off (something) in splinters. **5.** to split or break (a larger group) into separate factions or independent groups. **6.** *Obs.* to secure or support by a splint or splints, as a broken limb. —*v.i.* **7.** to be split or broken into splinters. **8.** to break off in splinters. [1350–1400; ME < MD or MLG; cf. SPLINT] —**splin′ter·less,** *adj.* —**splin′ter·y,** *adj.*
—**Syn. 1.** sliver. **8.** separate, part, split.

splin′ter group′, a small organization that becomes separated from or acts apart from an original larger group or a number of other small groups, with which it would normally be united, as because of disagreement.

split (split), *v.,* **split, split·ting,** *n., adj.* —*v.t.* **1.** to divide or separate from end to end or into layers: *to split a log in two.* **2.** to separate by cutting, chopping, etc., usually lengthwise: *to split a piece from a block.* **3.** to tear or break apart; rend or burst: *The wind split the sail.* **4.** to divide into distinct parts or portions (often fol. by *up*): *We split up our rations.* **5.** to separate (a part) by such division. **6.** to divide (persons) into different groups, factions, parties, etc., as by discord: *to split a political party.* **7.** to separate (a group, family, etc.) by such division. **8.** to cast (a ballot or vote) for candidates of more than one political party. **9.** to divide between two or more persons, groups, etc.; share: *We split a bottle of wine.* **10.** to separate into parts by interposing something: *to split an infinitive.* **11.** *Physics, Chem.* to divide (molecules or atoms) by cleavage into smaller parts. **12.** to issue additional shares of (stock) without charge to existing stockholders, thereby dividing their interest into a larger number of shares and reducing the price per share. **13.** *Slang.* leave; depart from: *Let's split this scene.* —*v.i.* **14.** to divide, break, or part lengthwise: *The board split in half.* **15.** to part, divide, or separate in any way (often fol. by *up*): *The group of children split up into two teams. We'll split up here and meet later.* **16.** to break asunder, as a ship by striking on a rock. **17.** to become separated, as a piece or part from a whole. **18.** to part or separate, as through disagreement; sever relations: *They split up after a year of marriage. He split with the company after a policy dispute.* **19.** to divide or share something with another or others; apportion. **20.** *Slang.* to leave; depart. **21. split hairs.** See **hair** (def. 11). **22. split the difference.** See **difference** (def. 11). —*n.* **23.** the act of splitting. **24.** a crack, tear, or fissure caused by splitting. **25.** a piece or part separated by or as by splitting. **26.** a breach or rupture, as between persons, in a party or organization, etc. **27.** a faction, party, etc., formed by a rupture or schism. **28.** an ice-cream dish made from sliced fruit, usually a banana, and ice cream, and covered with syrup and nuts. **29.** Also called, *esp. Brit.,* **nip.** a bottle for wine or, sometimes, another beverage, containing from 6 to 6½ oz. (170 to 184 g). **30.** a bottle, as of soda, liquor, etc., which is half the usual size. **31.** a strip split from an osier, used in basketmaking. **32.** *Masonry.* a brick of normal length and breadth but of half normal thickness, used to give level support to a course of bricks laid over one not level. **33.** Often, **splits.** the feat of separating the legs while sinking to the floor, until they extend at right angles to the body, as in stage performances or gymnastics. **34.** *Bowling.* an arrangement of the pins remaining after the first bowl in two separated groups, so that a spare is difficult. **35.** *Philately.* bisect (def. 5). **36.** one of the layers of leather into which a skin is cut. **37.** the act of splitting a stock. —*adj.* **38.** that has undergone splitting; parted lengthwise; cleft. **39.** disunited; divided: *a split opinion.* **40.** (of a stock quotation) given in sixteenths instead of eighths of a point. **41.** (of a stock) having undergone a split. [1570–80; 1950–55 for def. 13; < D *splitten;* akin to *splijten,* G *spleissen* to split] —**split′ta·ble,** *adj.*

Split (split), *n.* a seaport in S Croatia, on the Adriatic. Roman ruins. 180,571. Italian, **Spalato.**

split-brain (split′brān′), *adj.* having, involving, or pertaining to a severed corpus callosum. [1955–60]

split′ deci′sion, *Boxing.* a decision of a bout on whose outcome the referee and judges did not unanimously agree. [1945–50]

split′-dol′lar insur′ance (split′dol′ər), life insurance in which someone helps pay the premiums for another, as when an employer contributes to the premiums of an employee's policy.

split′ end′, *Football.* an offensive end who lines up some distance outside the formation on the line of scrimmage as a pass receiver. Also called **flanker, spread end.** [1950–55, *Amer.*]

split′-fin′gered fast′ball (split′fing′gərd), *Baseball.* a pitch, similar to the forkball but thrown with the same arm speed as a fastball, that drops suddenly as it nears the batter.

split′ flap′, *Aeron.* **1.** a flap that is located on the under surface of the trailing edge of an aircraft wing and that splits away from the wing structure when rotated downward, producing an increase in lift or drag or both. Cf. **landing flap. 2.** a flap that is located on the upper surface of the trailing edge of an aircraft wing and that acts as a spoiler when rotated upward.

split′ im′age range′ find′er, *Photog.* a range finder in which opposing halves of a split field move relative to each other and coincide when the object centered in the field is in focus.

split′ infin′itive, *Gram.* an expression in which there is a word or phrase, esp. an adverb or adverbial phrase, between *to* and its accompanying verb form in an infinitive, as in *to readily understand.* [1895–1900]
—**Usage.** The "rule" against placing a word, especially an adverb, between *to* and the verb in an English infinitive (*To really learn a language, you have to stay in a place where it is spoken*) is based on an analogy with Latin, in which infinitives are only one word and hence cannot be "split." The modeling of English style on Latin has in the past often been considered the epitome of good writing; the injunction against splitting the English infinitive is an example of the misguided application of this notion. Criticism of the split infinitive was especially strong in 19th-century usage guides. Nothing in the history of the infinitive in English, however, supports the so-called rule, and in many sentences, as in the example above, the only natural place for the modifying adverb is between *to* and the verb (*To really learn . . .*). Many modern speakers and writers depend on their ear for a natural sentence rather than on an arbitrary rule. Writers who ordinarily prefer not to split an infinitive will occasionally do so, to avoid awkward or stilted language.

split-lev·el (split′lev′əl), *adj.* **1.** noting a house having a room or rooms that are somewhat above or below adjacent rooms, with the floor levels usually differing by approximately half a story. —*n.* **2.** a split-level house. [1945–50]

split-off (split′ôf′, -of′), *n.* **1.** the act of separating or splitting away from something else. **2.** something that has split or has been split from something else. **3.** *Com.* a process of reorganizing a corporate structure whereby the capital stock of a division or subsidiary of a corporation or of a newly affiliated company is transferred to the stockholders of the parent corporation in exchange for part of the stock of the latter. Cf. **spin-off** (def. 1), **split-up** (def. 3). [1855–60; n. use of v. phrase *split off*]

split′ page′, 1. (in a newspaper) a page replacing one of an earlier edition and containing chiefly the same material in altered form. **2.** the first page of the second section of a newspaper.

split′ pea′, a dried green pea, split and used esp. for soup. [1730–40]

split′ personal′ity. See **multiple personality.** [1925–30]

split-phase (split′fāz′), *adj. Elect.* **1.** pertaining to or noting a current in one of two parallel circuits that have a single-phase current source but unequal impedances and that produce currents of different phase. **2.** pertaining to or noting a motor or system utilizing a split-phase current.

split′ rail′, a wooden rail split lengthwise from a log and commonly used in rustic rail and post fencing. [1820–30; *Amer.*]

split′ roll′, *Econ.* a taxation under which real-estate taxes on business and industrial buildings are levied at higher rates than on residential homes. Also called **split′-roll tax′.**

split′ run′, a pressrun, as that of a newspaper or magazine, which is interrupted after the running of a specified number of copies to permit the substitution of type or of a cut, as in a keyed advertisement: a device for testing the relative effectiveness of different versions of an advertisement.

split′ screen′, 1. Also called **composite shot.** *Motion Pictures, Television.* a type of process photography in which two or more shots are juxtaposed and projected simultaneously on the screen. **2.** *Computers.* a mode of operation that uses windows to enable simultaneous viewing of two or more displays on the same screen.

split′ sec′ond, 1. a fraction of a second. **2.** an infinitesimal amount of time; instant; twinkling. [1880–85] —**split′-sec′ond,** *adj.*

split′ spin′dle, *Furniture.* a turned piece halved lengthwise for use as applied ornament, as on a chest or cupboard, or as part of a chair back or the like. Also called **half-turning.**

splits·ville (splits′vil), *n. Slang.* the state or condition of being divorced or separated. [SPLIT + -s- + *-ville* (see SQUARESVILLE)]

split·tail (split′tāl′), *n.* a minnow, *Pogonichthys macrolepidotus,* of the Sacramento River, having the upper lobe of the tail much longer than the lower lobe: habitat changes have greatly reduced its numbers. [1880–85, *Amer.*; SPLIT + TAIL[1]]

split·ter (split′ər), *n.* **1.** a person or thing that splits. **2.** *Biol. Informal.* a taxonomist who believes that classifications should emphasize differences between organisms and therefore favors a multiplicity of taxa (opposed to *lumper*). [1615–25; SPLIT + -ER[1]]

split′ tick′et, *U.S. Politics.* **1.** a ballot on which not all votes have been cast for candidates of the same party. **2.** a ticket on which not all the candidates nominated by a party are members of the party. Cf. **straight ticket.** [1830–40, *Amer.*]

split-time (split′tīm′), *n.* a daylight-saving time based on a half-hour advance.

split·ting (split′ing), *adj.* **1.** being split or causing something to split. **2.** violent or severe, as a headache. **3.** very fast or rapid. —*n.* **4.** Usually, **splittings.** a part or fragment that has been split off from something: *Some cavemen made their smaller tools from the splittings of stone.* [1585–95; SPLIT + -ING[2], -ING[1]]

split′ting adz′, a heavy stone tool used by prehistoric peoples in northwestern North America and northeastern Asia.

split′ting field′, *Math.* a field containing a given field in which every polynomial can be written as the product of linear factors. Also called **root field.** [1960–65]

split-up (split′up′), *n.* **1.** a splitting or separating into two or more parts. **2.** a separation or dissociation of two groups or people. **3.** *Com.* a process of reorganizing a corporate structure whereby all the capital stock and assets are exchanged for those of two or more newly established companies, resulting in the liquidation of the parent corporation. Cf. **spin-off** (def. 1), **split-off** (def. 3). [1830–40; n. use of v. phrase *split up*]

splore (splôr, splōr), *n. Scot.* **1.** a frolic; revel; carousal. **2.** a commotion; disturbance. [1775–85; perh. aph. var. of EXPLORE]

splosh (splosh), *v.t., v.i., n.* splash.

splotch (sploch), *n.* **1.** a large, irregular spot; blot; stain; blotch. —*v.t.* **2.** to mark or cover with splotches. —*v.i.* **3.** to be susceptible to stains or blots; show or retain stains, blots, or spots of dirt or liquid: *Don't buy that tablecloth—the material splotches easily.* **4.** to cause or be liable to cause stains, blots, or spots: *Be careful of that paint—it splotches.* [1595–1605; orig. uncert.]

splotch·y (sploch′ē), *adj.,* **splotch·i·er, splotch·i·est.** marked or covered with splotches. [1805–15; SPLOTCH + -Y[1]]

splurge (splûrj), *v.,* **splurged, splurg·ing,** *n.* —*v.i.* **1.** to indulge oneself in some luxury or pleasure, esp. a costly one: *They splurged on a trip to Europe.* **2.** to show off. —*v.t.* **3.** to spend (money) lavishly or ostentatiously: *He splurged thousands on the party.* —*n.* **4.** an ostentatious display, esp. an extravagantly expensive one. [1820–30, *Amer.*; perh. b. SPLASH and SURGE] —**splurg′i·ly,** *adv.* —**splurg′y,** *adj.*
—**Syn. 4.** indulgence, spree.

splut·ter (splut′ər), *v.i.* **1.** to talk rapidly and somewhat incoherently, as when confused, excited, or embarrassed: *When pushed for an explanation, he always spluttered.* **2.** to make a sputtering sound, or emit particles of something explosively, as water dropped onto a hot griddle. **3.** to fly or fall in particles or drops; spatter, as a liquid. —*v.t.* **4.** to utter hastily and confusedly or incoherently; sputter: *Out of breath, she spluttered a poor excuse for her lateness.* **5.** to spatter (a liquid, small particles, etc.). **6.** to bespatter (someone or something). —*n.* **7.** spluttering utterance or talk; noise or fuss. **8.** a sputtering or spattering, as of liquid. [1670–80; b. SPLASH and SPUTTER] —**splut′ter·er,** *n.*

splut·ter·y (splut′ə rē), *adj.* tending to splutter: *spluttery fire sparks.* [1865–70; SPLUTTER + -Y[1]]

Spock (spok), *n.* **Benjamin (Mc·Lane)** (mə klān′), born 1903, U.S. physician and educator.

Spode (spōd), *Trademark.* china or porcelain manufactured by the Spodes or the firm they established. Also called **Spode′ chi′na.**

Spode (spōd), *n.* **Josiah,** 1733–97, and his son, **Josiah,** 1754–1827, English potters.

spod·o·sol (spod′ə sôl′, -sol′), *n.* an acidic forest soil of low fertility, common to the cool, humid areas of North America and Eurasia. [1955–60; < Gk *spodó(s)* wood ash + -SOL]

spod·u·mene (spoj′o͞o mēn′), *n.* a mineral, lithium aluminum silicate, $LiAlSi_2O_6$, occurring in prismatic crystals, transparent varieties being used as gems. [1795–1805; < F *spodumène* < G *Spodumen* < Gk *spodoúmenos,* prp. of *spodoûsthai* to be burned to ashes (deriv. of *spodós* wood ash)]

Spohr (shpōr), *n.* **Lud·wig** (lo͞ot′viKH, lo͞od′-) or **Lou·is** (lo͞o′ē), 1784–1859, German violinist and composer.

spoil (spoil), *v.,* **spoiled** or **spoilt, spoil·ing,** *n.* —*v.t.* **1.** to damage severely or harm (something), esp. with reference to its excellence, value, usefulness, etc.: *The water stain spoiled the painting. Drought spoiled the corn crop.* **2.** to diminish or impair the quality of; affect detrimentally: *Bad weather spoiled their vacation.* **3.** to impair, damage, or harm the character or nature of (someone) by unwise treatment, excessive indulgence, etc.: *to spoil a child by pampering him.* **4.** *Archaic.* to strip (persons, places, etc.) of goods, valuables, etc.; plunder; pillage; despoil. **5.** *Archaic.* to take or seize by force. —*v.i.* **6.** to become bad, or unfit for use, as food or other perishable substances; become tainted or putrid: *Milk spoils if not refrigerated.* **7.** to plunder, pillage, or rob. **8. be spoiling for,** *Informal.* to be very eager for; be desirous of: *It was obvious that he was spoiling for a fight.* —*n.* **9.** Often, **spoils.** booty, loot, or plunder taken in war or robbery. **10.** the act of plundering. **11.** an object of plundering. **12.** Usually, **spoils. a.** the emoluments and advantages of public office viewed as won by a victorious political party: *the spoils of office.* **b.** prizes won or treasures accumulated: *a child's spoils brought home from a party.* **13.** waste material, as that which is cast up in mining, excavating, quarrying, etc. **14.** an imperfectly made object, damaged during the manufacturing process. [1300–50; (v.) ME *spoilen* < OF *espoillier* < L *spoliāre* to despoil, equiv. to *spoli(um)* booty + *-āre* inf. suffix; (n.) deriv. of the v. or < OF *espoille,* deriv. of *espoillier*] —**spoil′a·ble,** *adj.* —**spoil′less,** *adj.*
—**Syn. 1.** disfigure, destroy, demolish, mar. SPOIL, RUIN, WRECK agree in meaning to reduce the value, quality, usefulness, etc., of anything. SPOIL is the general term: *to spoil a delicate fabric.* RUIN implies doing completely destructive or irreparable injury: *to ruin one's health.* WRECK implies a violent breaking up or demolition: *to wreck oneself with drink; to wreck a building.*

spoil·age (spoi′lij), *n.* **1.** the act of spoiling or the state of being spoiled. **2.** material or the amount of material that is spoiled or wasted: *The spoilage in today's shipment is much too great.* **3.** the decay of foodstuffs due to the action of bacteria; rotting: *He was concerned about the spoilage of fruit on the way to market.* [1590–1600; SPOIL + -AGE]

spoil′ bank′, a bank of excavated refuse or waste earth, as of shale from surface coal mining. [1820–30]

spoil·er (spoi′lər), *n.* **1.** a person or thing that spoils. **2.** a person who robs or ravages; despoiler; plunderer. **3.** *Aeron.* a device used to break up the airflow around an aerodynamic surface, as an aircraft wing, in order to slow the movement through the air or to decrease the lift on the surface and, as a result, provide bank or descent control. **4.** *Auto.* a similar device for changing the airflow past a moving vehicle, often having the form of a transverse fin or blade mounted at the front or rear to reduce lift and increase traction at high speeds. **5.** *Sports.* a team out of final contention that defeats a potential or favored contender and thereby thwarts its chances of winning a championship. **6.** any competitor, entrant, or candidate who has no chance of ultimate victory but does well enough to spoil the chances of another. [1525–35; SPOIL + -ER[1]]

spoil′er par′ty, *U.S. Politics.* a third political party formed to draw votes away from one of the two major parties, thus spoiling its chance of winning an election. [1965–70]

spoil·five (spoil′fīv′), *n. Cards.* a game played by two to ten persons having five cards each. [1830–40; SPOIL + FIVE]

spoil′ ground′, an area within a body of water, esp. in the sea, where dredged material is deposited.

spoils·man (spoilz′mən), *n., pl.* **-men. 1.** a person who seeks or receives a share in political spoils. **2.** an advocate of the spoils system in politics. [1835–45, *Amer.*; SPOILS + -MAN]

spoil·sport (spoil′spôrt′, -spōrt′), *n.* a person whose selfish or unsportsmanlike attitudes or actions spoil the pleasure of others, as in a game or social gathering. [1815–25; from phrase *spoil the sport*]

spoils′ sys′tem, the system or practice in which public offices with their emoluments and advantages are at the disposal of the victorious party for its own purposes. [1830–40, *Amer.*]

spoilt (spoilt), *v.* a pt. and pp. of **spoil.**

Spo·kane (spō kan′), *n.* a city in E Washington. 171,300.

spoke[1] (spōk), *v.* **1.** a pt. of **speak. 2.** *Nonstandard.* a pp. of **speak. 3.** *Archaic,* a pp. of **speak.**

spoke[2] (spōk), *n., v.,* **spoked, spok·ing.** —*n.* **1.** one of the bars, rods, or rungs radiating from the hub or nave of a wheel and supporting the rim or felloe. **2.** something that resembles the spoke of a wheel. **3.** a handlelike projection from the rim of a wheel, as a ship's steering wheel. **4.** a rung of a ladder. —*v.t.* **5.** to fit or furnish with or as with spokes. [bef. 900; ME; OE *spāca;* c. D *speek,* G *Speiche*] —**spoke′less,** *adj.*

spoke-dog (spōk′dôg′, -dog′), *n.* a stick used by wheelwrights to force the outer ends of spokes into the rim or felloe.

spo·ken (spō′kən), *v.* **1.** a pp. of **speak.** —*adj.* **2.** uttered or expressed by speaking; oral (opposed to *written*): *the spoken word.* **3.** speaking, or using speech, as specified (usually used in combination): *fair-spoken; plain-spoken; soft-spoken.*

spoke·shave (spōk′shāv′), *n.* a cutting tool having a

CONCISE ETYMOLOGY KEY: <, descended or borrowed from; >, whence; b., blend of, blended; c., cognate with; cf., compare; deriv., derivative; equiv., equivalent; imit., imitative; obl., oblique; r., replacing; s., stem; sp., spelling, spelled; resp., respelling, respelled; trans., translation; ?, origin unknown; *, unattested; ‡, probably earlier than. See the full key inside the front cover.

blade set between two handles, originally for shaping spokes, but now in general use for dressing curved edges of wood and forming round bars and shapes. [1500–10; SPOKE² + SHAVE]

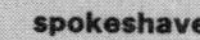

spokeshave

spokes•man (spōks′mən), *n., pl.* **-men.** **1.** a person who speaks for another or for a group. **2.** a public speaker. [1510–20; SPOKE¹ (irreg. as n.) + 's¹ + -MAN]
—Usage. See **-man.**

spokes•per•son (spōks′pûr′sən), *n.* a person who speaks for another or for a group. [1970–75; SPOKES(MAN) + -PERSON]
—Usage. See **-person.**

spokes•wom•an (spōks′wo͝om′ən), *n., pl.* **-wom•en.** a woman who speaks for another person or for a group. [1645–55; SPOKES(MAN) + -WOMAN]
—Usage. See **-woman.**

spoke•wise (spōk′wīz′), *adv.* **1.** in relation to, away from, or toward a center, as the spokes on a wheel: *The projections were arranged spokewise around the core.* —*adj.* **2.** having the parts placed as the spokes on a wheel; radiating from a center: *a spokewise structure.* [1835–45; SPOKE² + -WISE]

spo•li•a o•pi•ma (spō′lē ə ō pī′mə, -pē′-; *Lat.* spō′li-ä′ ô pē′mä), (in ancient Rome) the arms taken by a victorious general from the leader of a defeated army. [< L *spolia opīma* rich spoils]

spo•li•ate (spō′lē āt′), *v.t., v.i.,* **-at•ed, -at•ing.** to plunder, rob, or ruin. [1715–25; < L *spoliātus,* ptp. of *spoliāre* to spoil. See SPOIL, -ATE¹] **—spo′li•a′tor,** *n.*

spo•li•a•tion (spō′lē ā′shən), *n.* **1.** the act or an instance of plundering or despoiling. **2.** authorized plundering of neutrals at sea in time of war. **3.** *Law.* the destruction or material alteration of a bill of exchange, will, or the like. **4.** the act of spoiling or damaging something. [1350–1400; ME < L *spoliātiōn-* (s. of *spoliātiō*), equiv. to *spoliāt(us)* (ptp. of *spoliāre* to SPOIL; see -ATE¹) + *-iōn-* -ION]

spon•da•ic (spon dā′ik), *adj. Pros.* **1.** of or pertaining to a spondee. **2.** noting or constituting a spondee. **3.** consisting of spondees; characterized by a spondee or spondees. Also, **spon•da′i•cal.** [1715–25; < LL *spondaicus,* metathetic var. of *spondīacus* < Gk *spondeiakós,* equiv. to *spondeî(os)* SPONDEE + *-akos,* var. of *-ikos* -IC]

spon•dee (spon′dē), *n. Pros.* a foot of two syllables, both of which are long in quantitative meter or stressed in accentual meter. [1350–1400; ME *sponde* < L *spondēus* < Gk *spondeîos,* deriv. of *spondḗ* libation]

spon•du•licks (spon do͞o′liks), *n. Older Slang.* money; cash. Also, **spon•du′lix.** [1855–60, *Amer.*; orig. uncert.]

spon•dy•li•tis (spon′dl ī′tis), *n. Pathol.* inflammation of the vertebrae. [1840–50; < Gk *spóndyl(os)* vertebra, whorl, mussel + -ITIS] **—spon•dy•lit•ic** (spon′dl it′ik), *adj.*

spon•dy•lo•lis•the•sis (spon′dl ō lis thē′sis), *n. Pathol.* the forward displacement of a vertebra. [< NL (1853) < Gk *spóndyl(os)* vertebra + *olísthēsis* dislocation, equiv. to *olisthē-,* var. s. of *olisthánein* to slip, sprain (deriv. of *ólisthos* slipperiness) + *-sis* -SIS]

spon•dy•lo•sis (spon′dl ō′sis), *n. Pathol.* immobility and fusion of vertebral joints. [1895–1900; < Gk *spóndyl(os)* vertebra + -OSIS]

sponge (spunj), *n., v.,* **sponged, spong•ing.** —*n.* **1.** any aquatic, chiefly marine animal of the phylum Porifera, having a porous structure and usually a horny, siliceous or calcareous internal skeleton or framework, occurring in large, sessile colonies. **2.** the light, yielding, porous, fibrous skeleton or framework of certain animals or colonies of this group, esp. of the genera *Spongia* and *Hippospongia,* from which the living matter has been removed, characterized by readily absorbing water and becoming soft when wet while retaining toughness: used in bathing, in wiping or cleaning surfaces, etc. **3.** any of various other similar substances, often porous rubber or cellulose, used for washing or cleaning. **4.** See **sponge bath.** **5.** a person or thing that absorbs something freely: *His mind is a sponge gathering historical data.* **6.** a person who persistently borrows from or lives at the expense of others; sponger; parasite. **7.** *Informal.* a drunkard. **8.** *Metall.* a porous mass of metallic particles, as of platinum, obtained by the reduction of an oxide or purified compound at a temperature below the melting point. **9.** *Surg.* a sterile surgical dressing of absorbent material, usually cotton gauze, for wiping or absorbing pus, blood, or other fluids during a surgical operation. **10.** *Cookery.* **a.** dough raised with yeast, esp. before kneading, as for bread. **b.** a light, sweet pudding of a porous texture, made with gelatin, eggs, fruit juice or other flavoring material, etc. **11.** a disposable piece of polyurethane foam impregnated with a spermicide for insertion into the vagina as a contraceptive. **12. throw in the sponge,** *Informal.* to concede defeat; yield; give up: *The early election returns were heavily against him, but he wasn't ready to throw in the sponge.* —*v.t.* **13.** to wipe or rub with or as with a wet sponge, as to moisten or clean. **14.** to remove with or as with a wet sponge (usually fol. by *off, away,* etc.). **15.** to wipe out or efface with or as with a sponge (often fol. by *out*). **16.** to take up or absorb with or as with a sponge (often fol. by *up*): *to sponge up water.* **17.** to borrow, use, or obtain by imposing on another's good nature, friendship, hospitality, or the like: *He sponged 40 bucks from his friend and went to the city.* **18.** *Ceram.* to decorate (a ceramic object) by dabbing at it with a sponge soaked with color. —*v.i.* **19.** to take in or soak up liquid by absorption. **20.** to gather sponges. **21.** to live at the expense of others (often fol. by *on* or *off*): *He came back home and sponged off his family for a while.* [bef. 1000; (n.) ME, OE < L *spongia, spongea* < Gk *spongiā́;* (v.) ME *spongen* to clean with a sponge, deriv. of the n.] **—sponge′less,** *adj.* **—sponge′like′,** *adj.* **—spong′ing•ly,** *adv.*
—Syn. 6. leech. **13.** wash.

sponge′ bag′, *Brit.* a small, usually waterproof, case for carrying toilet articles. [1855–60]

sponge′ bath′, a bath in which the bather is cleaned by a wet sponge or washcloth dipped in water, without getting into a tub of water. [1855–60]

sponge′ cake′, a light, sweet cake made with a comparatively large proportion of eggs but no shortening. [1795–1805]

sponge′ cloth′, **1.** any cloth loosely woven of coarse yarn to produce a spongy look or texture, esp. one constructed in honeycomb weave. **2.** ratiné. [1860–65]

sponged′ ware′, spongeware.

sponge•fly (spunj′flī′), *n., pl.* **-flies.** any of several insects of the family Sisyridae, the aquatic larvae of which feed on freshwater sponges. Also, **spongillafly.** [SPONGE + FLY²]

sponge′ i′ron, finely divided, porous iron, reduced from an oxide at a temperature below the melting point. Also called **iron sponge.** [1870–75]

spong•er (spun′jər), *n.* **1.** a person or thing that sponges. **2.** a person who habitually borrows or lives at the expense of others; parasite. **3.** a person or boat engaged in gathering sponges. [1670–80; SPONGE + -ER¹]

sponge′ rub′ber, a light, spongy rubber, usually prepared by bubbling carbon dioxide through or whipping air into latex, used for padding, insulation, gaskets, etc.; foam rubber. [1885–90]

sponge′ tree′, huisache. [1890–95]

sponge•ware (spunj′wâr′), *n.* earthenware decorated with color applied with a sponge. [1940–45; SPONGE + WARE¹]

spon•gil•la•fly (spun jil′ə flī′, spon-), *n., pl.* **-flies.** spongefly. [< NL *spongilla* (L *spong(ia)* SPONGE + *-illa* dim. suffix) + FLY²]

spon•gin (spun′jin), *n.* a scleroprotein occurring in the form of fibers that form the skeleton of certain sponges. [1865–70; SPONGE + -IN²]

spon•gi•o•blast (spun′jē ō blast′, spon′-), *n. Embryol.* one of the primordial cells in the embryonic brain and spinal cord capable of developing into neuroglia. [1900–05; *spongio-* (comb. form of Gk *spongiā́* SPONGE) + -BLAST] **—spon′gi•o•blas′tic,** *adj.*

spon•go•coel (spong′gō sēl′), *n. Zool.* the central cavity in the body of a sponge. [< Gk *spongó(s),* var. of *spongiā́* SPONGE + E *-coel,* var. of -COELE]

spon•gy (spun′jē), *adj.,* **-gi•er, -gi•est.** **1.** of the nature of or resembling a sponge; light, porous, and elastic or readily compressible, as pith or bread. **2.** having the absorbent characteristics of a sponge; absorbing or holding liquid or yielding liquid when pressed. **3.** of or pertaining to a sponge. **4.** lacking in firmness or solidity: *spongy wood; a spongy feeling from the car brakes.* **5.** moist and soft; soggy: *spongy ground.* **6.** porous but hard, as bone. [1530–40; SPONGE + -Y¹] **—spon′gi•ly,** *adv.* **—spon′gi•ness,** *n.*

spon′gy paren′chyma, *Bot.* the lower layer of the ground tissue of a leaf, characteristically containing irregularly shaped cells with relatively few chloroplasts and large intercellular spaces. Also called **spon′gy mes′ophyll.** [1880–85]

spon•sion (spon′shən), *n.* **1.** an engagement or promise, esp. one made on behalf of another. **2.** *Internat. Law.* an engagement made on behalf of a government by an agent acting beyond his or her authority or without the required authorization and not binding on the government unless ratified. **3.** the act of becoming surety for another. [1670–80; < L *spōnsiōn-* (s. of *spōnsiō*) guarantee, equiv. to *spōns(us)* (ptp. of *spondēre* to pledge) + *-iōn-* -ION]

spon•son (spon′sən), *n.* **1.** a structure projecting from the side or main deck of a vessel to support a gun or the outer edge of a paddle box. **2.** a buoyant appendage at the gunwale of a canoe to resist capsizing. **3.** *Aeron.* a protuberance at the side of a flying-boat hull, designed to increase lateral stability in the water. [1825–35; var. of EXPANSION]

spon•sor (spon′sər), *n.* **1.** a person who vouches or is responsible for a person or thing. **2.** a person, firm, organization, etc., that finances and buys the time to broadcast a radio or television program so as to advertise a product, a political party, etc. **3.** a person who makes a pledge or promise on behalf of another. **4.** a person who answers for an infant at baptism, making the required professions and assuming responsibility for the child's religious upbringing; godfather or godmother. —*v.t.* **5.** to act as sponsor for; promise, vouch, or answer for. [1645–55; < L *spōnsor* guarantor, equiv. to *spond(ēre)* to pledge + *-tor* -TOR, with *dt* > *s*] **—spon•so•ri•al** (spon sôr′ē əl, -sōr′-), *adj.* **—spon′sor•ship′,** *n.*
—Syn. 1. patron, backer; guarantor. **2.** advertiser. **5.** guarantee, finance, back, underwrite.

spon•ta•ne•i•ty (spon′tə nē′i tē, -nā′-), *n., pl.* **-ties.** **1.** the state, quality, or fact of being spontaneous. **2.** spontaneous activity. **3. spontaneities,** spontaneous impulses, movements, or actions. [1645–55; < LL *spontāne(us)* SPONTANEOUS + -ITY]

spon•ta•ne•ous (spon tā′nē əs), *adj.* **1.** coming or resulting from a natural impulse or tendency; without effort or premeditation; natural and unconstrained; unplanned: *a spontaneous burst of applause.* **2.** (of a person) given to acting upon sudden impulses. **3.** (of natural phenomena) arising from internal forces or causes; independent of external agencies; self-acting. **4.** growing naturally or without cultivation, as plants and fruits; indigenous. **5.** produced by natural process. [1650–60; < LL *spontāneus,* equiv. to L *spont(e)* willingly + *-āneus* (*-ān(us)* -AN + *-eus* -EOUS)] **—spon•ta′ne•ous•ly,** *adv.* **—spon•ta′ne•ous•ness,** *n.*
—Syn. 1. unpremeditated, free. See **automatic, voluntary.** **—Ant. 1.** premeditated.

sponta′neous abor′tion, miscarriage (def. 1).

sponta′neous combus′tion, the ignition of a substance or body from the oxidation of its own constituents without heat from any external source. [1800–10]

sponta′neous genera′tion, *Biol.* abiogenesis. [1650–60]

spon•toon (spon to͞on′), *n.* a shafted weapon having a pointed blade with crossbar at its base, used by infantry officers in the 17th and 18th centuries. Also called **half-pike.** [1590–1600; < F *esponton* < It *spuntone,* equiv. to *s-* EX-¹ + *puntone* kind of weapon (lit., pointed object) (*punt(o)* POINT + *-one* aug. suffix)]

spoof (spo͞of), *n.* **1.** a mocking imitation of someone or something, usually light and good-humored; lampoon or parody: *The show was a spoof of college life.* **2.** a hoax; prank. —*v.t.* **3.** to mock (something or someone) lightly and good-humoredly; kid. **4.** to fool by a hoax; play a trick on, esp. one intended to deceive. —*v.i.* **5.** to scoff at something lightly and good-humoredly; kid: *The campus paper was always spoofing about the regulations.* [1885–90; after a game invented and named by Arthur Roberts (1852–1933), British comedian]

spoof•er•y (spo͞o′fə rē), *n.* good-humored mockery or teasing. [1925–30; SPOOF + -ERY]

spook (spo͝ok), *n.* **1.** *Informal.* a ghost; specter. **2.** *Slang.* a ghostwriter. **3.** *Slang.* an eccentric person. **4.** *Slang (disparaging and offensive).* a black person. **5.** *Slang.* an espionage agent; spy. —*v.t.* **6.** to haunt; inhabit or appear in or to as a ghost or specter. **7.** *Informal.* to frighten; scare. —*v.i.* **8.** *Informal.* to become frightened or scared: *The fish spooked at any disturbance in the pool.* [1795–1805, *Amer.*; < D; c. G *Spuk*] **—spook′er•y,** *n.* **—spook′ish,** *adj.*

spook•y (spo͞o′kē), *adj.,* **spook•i•er, spook•i•est.** *Informal.* **1.** like or befitting a spook or ghost; suggestive of spooks. **2.** eerie; scary. **3.** (esp. of horses) nervous; skittish. [1850–55, *Amer.*; SPOOK + -Y¹] **—spook′i•ly,** *adv.* **—spook′i•ness,** *n.*

spool (spo͞ol), *n.* **1.** any cylindrical piece or device on which something is wound. **2.** a small cylindrical piece of wood or other material on which yarn is wound in spinning; a bobbin. **3.** a small cylinder of wood or other material on which thread, wire, or tape is wound, typically expanded or with a rim at each end and having a hole lengthwise through the center. **4.** the material or quantity of material wound on such a device. **5.** *Angling.* the cylindrical drum in a reel that bears the line. —*v.t.* **6.** to wind on a spool. **7.** to unwind from a spool (usually fol. by *off* or *out*). **8.** *Computers.* to operate (an input/output device) by using buffers in main and secondary storage. —*v.i.* **9.** to wind. **10.** to unwind. [1275–1325; ME *spole* < MD *spoele* or MLG *spōle;* c. G *Spule*] **—spool′er,** *n.* **—spool′like′,** *adj.*

spoom (spo͞om), *n.* a kind of sherbet made from fruit juice or wine, mixed after freezing with uncooked meringue. [< It *spuma* foam, froth]

spoon (spo͞on), *n.* **1.** a utensil for use in eating, stirring, measuring, ladling, etc., consisting of a small, shallow bowl with a handle. **2.** any of various implements, objects, or parts resembling or suggesting this. **3.** a spoonful. **4.** Also called **spoon′ bait′.** *Angling.* a lure used in casting or trolling for fish, consisting of a bright spoon-shaped piece of metal or the like, swiveled above one or more fishhooks, and revolving as it is drawn through the water. **5.** Also called **number three wood.** *Golf.* a club with a wooden head whose face has a greater slope than the brassie or driver, for hitting long, high drives from the fairway. **6.** a curved piece projecting from the top of a torpedo tube to guide the torpedo horizontally and prevent it from striking the side of the ship from which it was fired. **7. born with a silver spoon in one's mouth,** born into a wealthy family; having an inherited fortune: *She was born with a silver spoon in her mouth and never worked a day in her life.* —*v.t.* **8.** to eat with, take up, or transfer in or as in a spoon. **9.** to hollow out or shape like a spoon. **10.** *Games.* **a.** to push or shove (a ball) with a lifting motion instead of striking it soundly, as in croquet or golf. **b.** to hit (a ball) up in the air, as in cricket. **11.** *Informal.* to show affection or love toward by kissing and caressing, esp. in an openly sentimental manner. —*v.i.* **12.** *Informal.* to show affection or love by kissing and caressing, esp. in an openly sentimental manner. **13.** *Games.* to spoon a ball. **14.** *Angling.* to fish with a spoon. [bef. 900; ME; OE *spōn;* c. LG *spon,* G *Span* chip, ON *spónn;* akin to Gk *sphḗn* wedge] **—spoon′less,** *adj.* **—spoon′like′,** *adj.*

spoon′ back′, a back of a chair or the like, having a splat curved outward at the bottom.

spoon•bill (spo͞on′bil′), *n.* **1.** any of several wading birds of the family Plataleidae, related to the ibises, having a long, flat bill with a spoonlike tip. **2.** any of various birds having a similar bill, as the shoveler duck. **3.** the paddlefish. [1670–80; SPOON + BILL²]

roseate spoonbill, *Ajaia ajaja,* length about 3 ft. (0.9 m)

CONCISE PRONUNCIATION KEY: act, cāpe, dâre, pärt; set, ēqual; if, īce; ox, ōver, ôrder, oil, bo͝ok, bo͞ot, out; up, ûrge; child; sing; shoe; thin, *th*at; zh as in *treasure.* ə = *a* as in *alone, e* as in *system, i* as in *easily, o* as in *gallop, u* as in *circus;* ᵊ as in *fire* (fīᵊr), *hour* (ouᵊr). l and n can serve as syllabic consonants, as in *cradle* (krād′l), and *button* (but′n). See the full key inside the front cover.

spoon′bill cat′fish. See **flathead catfish.** [1880–85]

spoon′ bow′ (bou), *Naut.* an overhanging bow having a convex, curved stem. [1900–05] **—spoon′-bowed′,** *adj.*

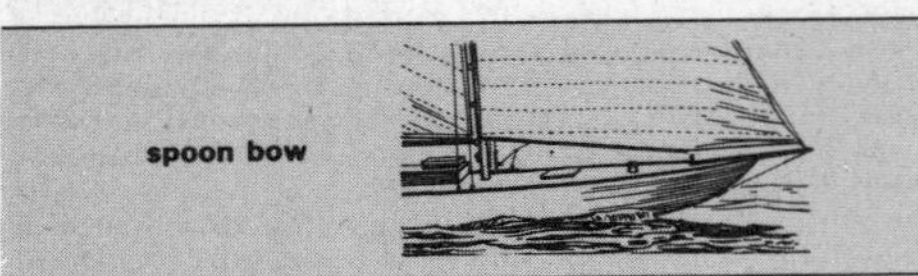
spoon bow

spoon′ bread′, 1. *Chiefly South Midland and Southern U.S.* a baked dish made with cornmeal, milk, eggs, and shortening, served as an accompaniment to meat. **2.** *Dial.* any of various types of biscuits shaped by dropping batter into a baking pan from a spoon. [1905–10, *Amer.*]

spoon·drift (spo͞on′drift′), *n.* spindrift. [1760–70; *spoon,* var. of obs. *spoom* (of a ship) to run or scud before the wind + DRIFT]

spoon·er·ism (spo͞o′nə riz′əm), *n.* the transposition of initial or other sounds of words, usually by accident, as in *a blushing crow* for *a crushing blow.* [1895–1900; after W. A. *Spooner* (1844–1930), English clergyman noted for such slips; see -ISM]

spoon·ey (spo͞o′nē), *adj.,* **spoon·i·er, spoon·i·est.** spoony.

spoon-fed (spo͞on′fed′), *adj.* **1.** fed with a spoon. **2.** treated with excessive solicitude; pampered. **3.** given no opportunity to act or think for oneself: *Having always been spoon-fed, I couldn't meet the challenge of college.* [1900–05]

spoon-feed (spo͞on′fēd′, -fēd′), *v.t.,* **-fed, -feed·ing.** to cause to be spoon-fed. [1605–15]

spoon·ful (spo͞on′fo͝ol), *n., pl.* **-fuls. 1.** as much as a spoon can hold. **2.** a small quantity. [1250–1300; ME *sponeful.* See SPOON, -FUL]
—Usage. See **-ful.**

spoon′ hook′, *Angling.* a fishhook equipped with a spoon lure. [1855–60]

spoon′ nail′, *Med.* an abnormal condition in which the outer surfaces of the nails are concave; koilonychia. [1895–1900]

spoon·worm (spo͞on′wûrm′), *n.* any of various unsegmented, burrowing marine worms of the phylum Echiura, of shallow waters worldwide, having a sausage-shaped body and a flattened head. [1835–45; SPOON + WORM]

spoon·y (spo͞o′nē), *adj.,* **spoon·i·er, spoon·i·est.** *Informal.* **1.** foolishly or sentimentally amorous. **2.** foolish; silly. [1805–15; SPOON + -Y[1]] **—spoon′i·ly,** *adv.* **—spoon′i·ness,** *n.*

spoor (spo͝or, spôr, spōr), *n.* **1.** a track or trail, esp. that of a wild animal pursued as game. **—***v.t., v.i.* **2.** to track by or follow a spoor. [1815–25; < Afrik *spoor* < D; c. OE, ON *spor,* G *Spur;* cf. SPEER] **—spoor′er,** *n.*

spor-, var. of **sporo-** before a vowel: *sporangium.*

Spor·a·des (spôr′ə dēz′; *Gk.* spô rä′thes), *n.pl.* two groups of Greek islands in the Aegean: the one **(Northern Sporades)** off the E coast of Greece; the other **(Southern Sporades),** including the Dodecanese, off the SW coast of Asia Minor.

spo·rad·ic (spə rad′ik), *adj.* **1.** (of similar things or occurrences) appearing or happening at irregular intervals in time; occasional: *sporadic renewals of enthusiasm.* **2.** appearing in scattered or isolated instances, as a disease. **3.** isolated, as a single instance of something; being or occurring apart from others. **4.** occurring singly or widely apart in locality: *the sporadic growth of plants.* Also, **spo·rad′i·cal.** [1680–90; < ML *sporadicus* < Gk *sporadikós,* equiv. to *sporad-* (s. of *sporás* strewn, akin to *sporá* SPORE) + *-ikos* -IC] **—spo·rad′i·cal·ly,** *adv.* **—spo·rad′i·cal·ness,** *n.* **—spo·ra·dic·i·ty** (spôr′ə dis′i tē, spōr′-), **spo′ra·dism,** *n.*
—Syn. 3. separate, unconnected. **—Ant. 1.** continuous.

spo·ran·gi·o·phore (spə ran′jē ə fôr′, -fōr′), *n. Bot., Mycol.* a structure bearing sporangia. [1870–75; SPORANGI(UM) + -O- + -PHORE]

spo·ran·gi·o·spore (spə ran′jē ə spôr′, -spōr′), *n. Bot., Mycol.* a spore that is produced within a sporangium. [1885–90; SPORANGI(UM) + -O- + SPORE]

spo·ran·gi·um (spə ran′jē əm), *n., pl.* **-gi·a** (-jē ə). *Bot., Mycol.* the case or sac in which spores are produced. Also called **spore′ case′.** [1815–25; < NL, equiv. to *spor-* SPOR- + Gk *angeîon* vessel] **—spo·ran′gi·al,** *adj.*

spore (spôr, spōr), *n., v.,* **spored, spor·ing.** **—***n.* **1.** *Biol.* a walled, single- to many-celled, reproductive body of an organism, capable of giving rise to a new individual either directly or indirectly. **2.** a germ, germ cell, seed, or the like. **—***v.i.* **3.** to bear or produce spores. [1830–40; < NL *spora* < Gk *sporá* sowing, seed, akin to *speírein* to sow; see SPERM[1]] **—spo′ral,** *adj.* **—spo′roid,** *adj.*

-spore, var. of **sporo-,** as final element of compound words: *teliospore.*

spore′ fruit′, *Bot., Mycol.* a spore-bearing structure, as an ascocarp; sporocarp. [1855–60]

spore·ling (spôr′ling, spōr′-), *n. Bot., Mycol.* the young individual developed from a spore. [1905–10; SPORE + -LING[1], as in SEEDLING]

spori-, var. of **sporo-** before elements of Latin origin: *sporiferous.*

CONCISE ETYMOLOGY KEY: <, descended or borrowed from; >, whence; b., blend of, blended; c., cognate with; cf., compare; deriv., derivative; equiv., equivalent; imit., imitative; obl., oblique; r., replacing; s., stem; sp., spelling, spelled; resp., respelling, respelled; trans., translation; ?, origin unknown; *, unattested; ‡, probably earlier than. See the full key inside the front cover.

spo·ri·cide (spôr′ə sīd′, spōr′-), *n.* a substance or preparation for killing spores. [SPOR- + -I- + -CIDE] **—spo′ri·cid′al,** *adj.*

spo·rif·er·ous (spə rif′ər əs), *adj.* bearing spores. [1830–40; SPOR- + -I- + -FEROUS]

Spork (spôrk), *Trademark.* an eating utensil combining features of a spoon and a fork.

sporo-, a combining form representing **spore** in compound words: *sporophyte.* Also, **spor-, -spore, spori-.** Cf. **-sporous.**

spo·ro·carp (spôr′ə kärp′, spōr′-), *n. Bot., Mycol.* (in higher fungi, lichens, and red algae) a multicellular structure in which spores form; a fruiting body. [1840–50; SPORO- + -CARP]

spo·ro·cyst (spôr′ə sist′, spōr′-), *n. Biol.* **1.** a walled body resulting from the multiple division of a sporozoan, which produces one or more sporozoites. **2.** a stage in development of trematodes that gives rise, asexually, to cercaria. [1860–65; SPORO- + -CYST] **—spo·ro·cys·tic** (spôr′ə sis′tik, spōr′-), *adj.*

spo·ro·cyte (spôr′ə sīt′, spōr′-), *n. Biol.* a diploid cell in certain spore-bearing plants, as liverworts, that produces four haploid spores through meiosis; a spore mother cell. [1890–95; SPORO- + -CYTE]

spo·ro·gen·e·sis (spôr′ə jen′ə sis, spōr′-), *n. Biol.* **1.** the production of spores; sporogony. **2.** reproduction by means of spores. [1885–90; SPORO- + -GENESIS]

spo·rog·e·nous (spə roj′ə nəs), *adj.* of or pertaining to spores or spore production. [1885–90; SPORO- + -GENOUS]

spo·ro·go·ni·um (spôr′ə gō′nē əm, spōr′-), *n., pl.* **-ni·a** (-nē ə). *Bot.* the sporangium of mosses and liverworts. [1870–75; SPORO- + -GONIUM] **—spo′ro·go′ni·al,** *adj.*

spo·rog·o·ny (spə rog′ə nē), *n. Biol.* (in certain sporozoans) the multiple fission of an encysted zygote or oocyte, resulting in the formation of sporozoites. [1885–90; SPORO- + -GONY]

spo·ront (spôr′ont, spōr′-), *n. Biol.* (in the sexual reproduction of certain sporozoans) an encysted spore developed from a zygote, which undergoes sporogony to form sporozoites. [1880–85; SPOR- + Gk *ont-* (see ONTO-)]

spo·ro·phore (spôr′ə fôr′, spōr′ə fōr′), *n. Mycol.* a fungus hypha specialized to bear spores. [1840–50; SPORO- + -PHORE] **—spo·ro·phor·ic** (spôr′ə fôr′ik, -for′-, spōr′-), **spo·roph·o·rous** (spə rof′ər əs), *adj.*

spo·ro·phyll (spôr′ə fil, spōr′-), *n. Bot.* a modified leaf that bears sporangia. Also, **spo′ro·phyl.** [1885–90; SPORO- + -PHYLL] **—spo·ro·phyl·la·ry** (spôr′ə fil′ə rē, spōr′-), *adj.*

spo·ro·phyte (spôr′ə fīt′, spōr′-), *n. Bot.* the form of a plant in the alternation of generations that produces asexual spores. Cf. **gametophyte.** [1885–90; SPORO- + -PHYTE] **—spo·ro·phyt·ic** (spôr′ə fit′ik, spōr′-), *adj.*

spo·ro·tri·cho·sis (spôr′ə tri kō′sis, spōr′-), *n. Pathol.* a widespread infectious disease marked by nodules or ulcers of the skin, chiefly affecting humans and domestic mammals and caused by the fungus *Sporothrix schenckii.* [1905–10; < NL; see SPORO-, TRICH-, -OSIS] **—spo·ro·tri·chot·ic** (spôr′ə tri kot′ik, spōr′-), *adj.*

-sporous, a combining form meaning "having spores" of the kind specified by the initial element: *helicosporous.* [< Gk *-sporos;* see SPORE, -OUS]

Spo·ro·zo·a (spôr′ə zō′ə, spōr′-), *n.* the protist phylum (or animal class) comprising the sporozoans. [< NL; see SPORO-, -ZOA]

spo·ro·zo·an (spôr′ə zō′ən, spōr′-), *n.* **1.** any parasitic spore-forming protozoan of the phylum (or class) Sporozoa, several species of which, as plasmodia, cause malaria. **—***adj.* **2.** Also, **spo′ro·zo′al.** belonging or pertaining to the Sporozoa. [1885–90; SPOROZO(A) + -AN]

spo·ro·zo·ite (spôr′ə zō′it, spōr′-), *n.* one of the minute, active bodies into which the spore of certain Sporozoa divides, each developing into an adult individual. [1885–90; SPOROZO(A) + -ITE[1]]

spor·ran (spor′ən), *n.* (in Scottish Highland costume) a large pouch for men, commonly of fur, worn, suspended from a belt, in front of the kilt. [1745–55; < ScotGael *sporan;* cf. Ir *sparán* purse]

S, sporran

sport (spôrt, spōrt), *n.* **1.** an athletic activity requiring skill or physical prowess and often of a competitive nature, as racing, baseball, tennis, golf, bowling, wrestling, boxing, hunting, fishing, etc. **2.** a particular form of this, esp. in the out of doors. **3.** diversion; recreation; pleasant pastime. **4.** jest; fun; mirth; pleasantry: *What he said in sport was taken seriously.* **5.** mockery; ridicule; derision: *They made sport of him.* **6.** an object of derision; laughingstock. **7.** something treated lightly or tossed about like a plaything. **8.** something or someone subject to the whims or vicissitudes of fate, circumstances, etc. **9.** a sportsman. **10.** *Informal.* a person who behaves in a sportsmanlike, fair, or admirable manner; an accommodating person: *He was a sport and took his defeat well.* **11.** *Informal.* a person who is interested in sports as an occasion for gambling; gambler. **12.** *Informal.* a flashy person; one who wears showy clothes, affects smart manners, pursues pleasurable pastimes, or the like; a bon vivant. **13.** *Biol.* an organism or part that shows an unusual or singular deviation from the normal or parent type; mutation. **14.** *Obs.* amorous dalliance. **—***adj.* **15.** of, pertaining to, or used in sports or a particular sport. **16.** suitable for outdoor or informal wear: *sport clothes.* **—***v.i.* **17.** to amuse oneself with some pleasant pastime or recreation. **18.** to play, frolic, or gambol, as a child or an animal. **19.** to engage in some open-air or athletic pastime or sport. **20.** to trifle or treat lightly: *to sport with another's emotions.* **21.** to mock, scoff, or tease: *to sport at suburban life.* **22.** *Bot.* to mutate. **—***v.t.* **23.** to pass (time) in amusement or sport. **24.** to spend or squander lightly or recklessly (often fol. by *away*). **25.** *Informal.* to wear, display, carry, etc., esp. with ostentation; show off: *to sport a new mink coat.* **26.** *Archaic.* to amuse (esp. oneself). **27. sport one's oak.** See **oak** (def. 5). [1350–1400; ME; aph. var. of DISPORT] **—sport′ful,** *adj.* **—sport′ful·ly,** *adv.* **—sport′ful·ness,** *n.* **—sport′less,** *adj.*
—Syn. 1. game. **3.** amusement, fun, entertainment. See **play. 18.** romp, caper. **20.** toy.

sport′ car′. See **sports car.**

sport·er (spôr′tər, spōr′-), *n.* **1.** a person or thing that sports, as a participant in a sport. **2.** an animal or piece of equipment for use in a sport, as a hunting dog or rifle. [1530–40; SPORT + -ER[1]]

sport′ fish′, a type of fish that is prized for the sport it gives the angler in its capture rather than for its value as food. [1940–45]

sport·fish·er·man (spôrt′fish′ər mən, spōrt′-), *n.* a motorboat fitted out for sportfishing. [1965–70; SPORT + FISHERMAN]

sport·fish·ing (spôrt′fish′ing), *n.* fishing with a rod and reel for sport, esp. for saltwater sport fish from a motorboat. [SPORT + FISHING]

sport·ing (spôr′ting, spōr′-), *adj.* **1.** engaging in, disposed to, or interested in open-air or athletic sports: *a rugged, sporting man.* **2.** concerned with or suitable for such sports: *sporting equipment.* **3.** sportsmanlike. **4.** interested in or connected with sports or pursuits involving betting or gambling: *the sporting life of Las Vegas.* **5.** involving or inducing the taking of risk, as in a sport. [1590–1600; SPORT + -ING[2]] **—sport′ing·ly,** *adv.*

sport′ing chance′, an even or fair opportunity for a favorable outcome in an enterprise, as winning in a game of chance or in any kind of contest: *They gave the less experienced players a sporting chance by handicapping the experts.* [1895–1900]

sport′ing dog′, one of any of several breeds of usually large dogs especially suited by size and training for hunting by pointing, flushing, and retrieving game and including the pointers, setters, retrievers, and spaniels. [1780–90]

sport′ing house′, 1. *Older Use.* a brothel. **2.** *Archaic.* an establishment, as a tavern, inn, or the like, catering to gamblers or sportsmen. [1855–60]

sport′ing la′dy, *Older Use.* a prostitute.

spor·tive (spôr′tiv, spōr′-), *adj.* **1.** playful or frolicsome; jesting, jocose, or merry: *a sportive puppy.* **2.** done in sport, rather than in earnest: *a sportive show of affection.* **3.** pertaining to or of the nature of a sport or sports. **4.** *Biol.* mutative. **5.** *Archaic.* ardent; wanton. [1580–90; SPORT + -IVE] **—spor′tive·ly,** *adv.* **—spor′tive·ness;** *Archaic.* **sport′a·bil′i·ty,** *n.*
—Syn. 1. jocular, gay, sprightly, frisky.

sports (spôrts, spōrts), *adj.* **1.** of or pertaining to a sport or sports, esp. of the open-air or athletic kind: *a sports festival.* **2.** (of garments, equipment, etc.) suitable for use in open-air sports, or for outdoor or informal use. [1910–15; SPORT + -S[3]]

sports′ car′, a small, high-powered automobile with long, low lines, usually seating two persons. Also, **sport car.** [1920–25]

sports·cast (spôrts′kast′, -käst′, spōrts′-), *n.* a radio or television program consisting of sports news or of a running description of a sports event. [1940–45; SPORTS + (BROAD)CAST] **—sports′cast′er,** *n.*

sports·cast·ing (spôrts′kas′ting, -kä′sting, spōrts′-), *n.* **1.** the reporting of a sports event by radio or television broadcast. **2.** the occupation of a sportscaster. [1965–70; SPORTSCAST + -ING[1]]

sports·dom (spôrts′dəm, spōrts′-), *n.* the world of professional and amateur competitive sports. [SPORTS + -DOM]

sport′ shirt′, a long- or short-sleeved soft shirt for informal wear by men, having a squared-off shirttail that may be left outside the trousers, usually worn without a tie. Also, **sports′ shirt′.** Cf. **dress shirt.** [1915–20]

sports′ jack′et, a jacket, often of textured wool or colorful pattern, with a collar, lapels, long sleeves, and buttons in the front, cut somewhat fuller than the jacket of a business suit, worn with slacks for informal occasions.

sports·man (spôrts′mən, spōrts′-), *n., pl.* **-men. 1.** a man who engages in sports, esp. in some open-air sport, as hunting, fishing, racing, etc. **2.** a person who exhibits qualities especially esteemed in those who engage in sports, as fairness, courtesy, good temper, etc. [1700–10; SPORTS + -MAN] **—sports′man·like′, sports′man·ly,** *adj.* **—sports′man·li·ness,** *n.*
—Usage. See **-man.**

sports·man·ship (spôrts′mən ship′, spōrts′-), *n.* **1.** the character, practice, or skill of a sportsman. **2.** sportsmanlike conduct, as fairness, courtesy, being a cheerful loser, etc. [1735–45; SPORTSMAN + -SHIP]

sports′ med′icine, a field of medicine concerned with the functioning of the human body during physical activity and with the prevention and treatment of athletic injuries. [1960–65]

sport·ster (spôrt′stər, spōrt′-), *n. Informal.* a sports car. [1960–65; SPORT(S CAR) + -STER, on the model of DRAGSTER, ROADSTER, etc.]

sports·wear (spôrts′wâr′, spōrts′-), *n.* **1.** clothing designed for wear while playing golf or tennis, hiking, bicycling, jogging, etc.; activewear. **2.** men's or women's clothing consisting of separate pieces, as jackets, trousers, sweaters, skirts, and shirts, that are casually styled and can be worn singly or in various combinations for business and informal activity. [1910–15; SPORTS + WEAR]

sports·wom·an (spôrts′wo͝om′ən, spōrts′-), *n., pl.* **-wom·en.** a woman who engages in sports. [1745–55; SPORTS + -WOMAN]
—Usage. See **-woman.**

sports·writ·er (spôrts′rī′tər, spōrts′-), *n.* a journalist who reports on sports and sporting events. [1900–05; SPORTS + WRITER] **—sports′writ′ing,** *n.*

sport·y (spôr′tē, spōr′-), *adj.,* **sport·i·er, sport·i·est.** *Informal.* **1.** flashy; showy. **2.** smart in dress, behavior, etc. **3.** like or befitting a sportsman. **4.** dissipated; fast: *a sporty crowd.* **5.** designed for or suitable for sport. [1885–90; SPORT + -Y[1]] **—sport′i·ly,** *adv.* **—sport′i·ness,** *n.*

spor·u·late (spôr′yə lāt′, spor′-), *v.i.,* **-lat·ed, -lat·ing.** *Biol.* to produce spores. [1880–85; SPORULE + -ATE[1]] **—spor′u·la′tion,** *n.*

spor·ule (spôr′yo͞ol, spor′-), *n. Biol.* a spore, esp. a small one. [1810–20; < NL *sporula.* See SPORE, -ULE] **—spor·u·lar** (spôr′yə lər, spor′-), *adj.*

spot (spot), *n., v.,* **spot·ted, spot·ting,** *adj.* **—***n.* **1.** a rounded mark or stain made by foreign matter, as mud, blood, paint, ink, etc.; a blot or speck. **2.** something that mars one's character or reputation; blemish; flaw. **3.** a small blemish, mole, or lesion on the skin or other surface. **4.** a small, circumscribed mark caused by disease, allergic reaction, decay, etc. **5.** a comparatively small, usually roundish, part of a surface differing from the rest in color, texture, character, etc.: *a bald spot.* **6.** a place or locality: *A monument marks the spot where Washington slept.* **7.** Usually, **spots.** places of entertainment or sightseeing interest: *We went to a few spots to dance and see the floor shows.* **8.** See **spot announcement. 9.** a specific position in a sequence or hierarchy: *The choral group has the second spot on the program, right after the dancers. He moved up from second spot to become president of the firm.* **10.** *Cards.* **a.** one of various traditional, geometric drawings of a club, diamond, heart, or spade on a playing card for indicating suit and value. **b.** any playing card from a two through a ten: *He drew a jack, a queen, and a three spot.* **11.** a pip, as on dice or dominoes. **12.** *Slang.* a piece of paper money, almost always indicated as a five- or ten-dollar bill: *Can you loan me a five spot until payday?* **13.** Also called **spot illustration.** a small drawing, usually black and white, appearing within or accompanying a text. **14.** *Chiefly Brit. Informal.* **a.** a small quantity of anything. **b.** a drink: *a spot of tea.* **15.** a small croaker, *Leiostomus xanthurus,* of the eastern coast of the U.S., used as a food fish. **16. spots,** *Informal.* commodities, as grain, wool, and soybeans, sold for immediate delivery. **17.** See **spot price. 18.** *Informal.* spotlight (def. 1). **19. hit the high spots,** *Informal.* to deal with or include only the major points of interest: *With but a limited amount of vacation time, he concentrated on hitting the high spots of Europe.* **20. hit the spot,** *Informal.* to satisfy a want or need, as to quench thirst: *Iced tea hits the spot during the hot summer months.* **21. in a (bad) spot,** in an uncomfortable or dangerous predicament: *The tourists found themselves in a bad spot after they lost their money in Las Vegas.* **22. knock spots off,** *Brit. Slang.* to outdo easily; beat. **23. on the spot, a.** without delay; at once; instantly. **b.** at the very place in question. **c.** in a difficult or embarrassing position. **d.** in a position of being expected to act or to respond in some way.
—*v.t.* **24.** to stain or mark with spots: *The grease spotted my dress.* **25.** to remove a spot or spots from (clothing), esp. before dry cleaning. **26.** to sully; blemish. **27.** to mark or diversify with spots or dots, as of color: *We spotted the wall with blue paint.* **28.** to detect or recognize; locate or identify by seeing: *to spot a hiding child.* **29.** to place or position on a particular place: *to spot a billiard ball.* **30.** to stop (a railroad car) at the exact place required. **31.** to scatter in various places: *to spot chairs here and there in the room.* **32.** *Informal.* spotlight (def. 5). **33.** *Mil.* **a.** to determine (a location) precisely on either the ground or a map. **b.** to observe (the results of gunfire at or near a target) for the purpose of correcting aim. **34.** *Photog.* to remove spots from (a negative or print) by covering with opaque color. **35.** *Sports.* to give or grant a certain margin or advantage to (an opponent): *He spotted the tyro 12 points a game. The champion won, although spotting the challenger twenty pounds.* **36.** (in gymnastics) to watch or assist (a performer) in order to prevent injury.
—*v.i.* **37.** to make a spot; cause a stain: *Ink spots badly.* **38.** to become spotted, as some fabrics when spattered with water. **39.** *Mil.* to serve or act as a spotter.
—*adj.* **40.** *Radio, Television.* **a.** pertaining to the point of origin of a local broadcast. **b.** broadcast between announced programs. **41.** made, paid, delivered, etc., at once: *a spot sale; spot goods.* [1150–1200; (n.) ME *spotte;* c. MD, LG *spot* speck, ON *spotti* bit; (v.) late ME *spotten* to stain, mark, deriv. of the n.] **—spot′like′,** *adj.* **—spot′ta·ble,** *adj.*
—Syn. 2. taint, stigma. **6.** locale, site, situation. **26.** stain, taint, stigmatize, soil, tarnish. **27.** speckle.

spot′ announce′ment, a brief radio or television announcement, usually an advertisement, made by an individual station during or after a network program.

spot′ card′, *Cards.* spot (def. 10b).

spot′ check′, a random sampling or quick sample investigation: *A spot check showed that at least ten percent of the items were defective.* [1940–45]

spot-check (spot′chek′), *v.t.* **1.** to examine or investigate by means of a spot check. **—***v.i.* **2.** to conduct a spot check. [1940–45] **—spot′-check′er,** *n.*

spot′ height′, 1. the elevation of a certain point. **2.** a figure on a map showing such an elevation.

spot′ illustra′tion, spot (def. 13).

spot·less (spot′lis), *adj.* **1.** free from any spot, stain, etc.; immaculately clean: *a spotless kitchen.* **2.** irreproachable; pure; undefiled: *a spotless reputation.* [1300–50; ME; see SPOT, -LESS] **—spot′less·ly,** *adv.* **—spot′less·ness,** *n.*
—Syn. 2. unblemished, flawless, untarnished, faultless.

spot·light (spot′līt′), *n., v.,* **-light·ed** or **-lit, -light·ing.** **—***n.* **1.** a strong, focused light thrown upon a particular spot, as on a small area of a stage or in a television studio, for making some object, person, or group especially conspicuous. **2.** a lamp for producing such a light. **3.** a brilliant light with a focused beam, mounted on the side of an automobile and used for illuminating objects not within range of the headlights. **4.** the area of immediate or conspicuous public attention: *Asia is in the spotlight now.* **—***v.t.* **5.** to direct the beam of a spotlight upon; light with a spotlight. **6.** to make conspicuous; call attention to: *Newspapers spotlighted the story for a week.* **7.** to hunt (animals) using a spotlight in order to temporarily blind or confuse them. **—***v.i.* **8.** to hunt by using a spotlight. [1910–15; SPOT + LIGHT[1]] **—spot′light′er,** *n.*

spot′ line′, *Theat.* a rope or wire hung from a specific place on the gridiron for flying a piece of scenery that could not be flied by the existing battens.

spot′ mar′ket, a market in which commodities, as grain, gold, or crude oil, are dealt in for cash and immediate delivery (distinguished from *futures market*). [1935–40]

spot′ me′ter, *Photog.* an exposure meter that measures light reflected from only a small area of a subject or scene. [1950–55]

spot′ news′, *Journalism.* **1.** the latest news, reported immediately. **2.** news that occurs unexpectedly.

spot′ pass′, *Basketball, Football.* a pass intentionally directed to a specific place in the court or field instead of a particular receiver, the receiver being expected to arrive at the place at the same time as the ball. [1945–50]

spot′ plate′, *Chem.* a flat ceramic or plastic plate containing small wells on which spot tests are made.

spot′ price′, the price of spot goods or of commodities on the spot market.

Spot·syl·va·ni·a (spot′sil vā′nē ə, -vān′yə), *n.* a village in NE Virginia: the scene of Civil War battles between the armies of Grant and Lee, May 8–21, 1864.

spot·ted (spot′id), *adj.* **1.** marked with or characterized by a spot or spots. **2.** sullied; blemished. [1200–50; ME; see SPOT, -ED[3]] **—spot′ted·ly,** *adv.* **—spot′ted·ness,** *n.*

spot′ted ad′der. See **milk snake.**

spot′ted alfal′fa a′phid, a pale yellowish aphid, *Therioaphis maculata,* of the southern U.S., esp. west of the Mississippi River, that is marked with black spots and has fine spines on its back: a pest mainly of alfalfa and some other legumes, as clover. [1955–60]

spot′ted ca′vy, paca. [1775–85]

spot′ted cow′bane, a North American water hemlock, *Cicuta maculata,* of the parsley family, having a purple-mottled stem, white flowers, and deadly poisonous, tuberlike roots. Also called **musquash root, spot′ted hem′lock.** [1840–50]

spot′ted crane's′-bill, the American wild geranium, *Geranium maculatum.*

spot′ted deer′. See **axis deer.** [1670–80]

spot′ted fe′ver, *Pathol.* **1.** any of several fevers characterized by spots on the skin, esp. as in cerebrospinal meningitis or typhus fever. **2.** See **tick fever.** [1640–50]

spot′ted hye′na, an African hyena, *Crocuta crocuta,* having a yellowish-gray coat with brown or black spots, noted for its distinctive howl. Also called **laughing hyena.** See illus. under **hyena.** [1775–85]

spot′ted joe-pye′ weed′. See **joe-pye weed** (def. 2).

spot′ted sand′piper, a North American sandpiper, *Actitis macularia,* that has brownish-gray upper parts and white underparts, and is spotted with black in the summer. See illus. under **sandpiper.** [1760–70]

spot′ted skunk′, either of two small, nocturnal skunks of the genus *Spilogale,* distinguished by a white forehead patch and a luxuriant coat of broken stripes and spots, including *S. putorius* of temperate North America and *S. pygmaea* of Mexico. [1915–20]

spot′ted sun′fish, a sunfish, *Lepomis punctatus,* inhabiting streams from South Carolina to Florida, having the body marked with longitudinal rows of spots. Also called **stumpknocker.** [1880–85]

Spot′ted Tail′, (*Sinte-galeshka*), 1833?–81, Brulé Sioux leader.

spot′ted wilt′, *Plant Pathol.* a viral disease of plants, characterized by wilting and by brown, sunken spots and streaks on the stems and leaves.

spot′ted win′tergreen, an evergreen plant, *Chimaphila maculata,* of central North America, having leaves with mottled-white veins and white, fragrant flowers. Also called **rheumatism-root.** [1840–50, *Amer.*]

spot·ter (spot′ər), *n.* **1.** a person employed to remove spots from clothing, esp. at a dry-cleaning establishment. **2.** (in civil defense) a civilian who watches for enemy airplanes. **3.** *Informal.* a person employed to watch the activity and behavior of others, esp. employees, as for evidence of dishonesty. **4.** *Mil.* an observer at a forward position who singles out targets for gunners. **5.** a person or thing that spots. **6.** (in small-arms practice firing) a small black disk attached to the target to make more prominent the places where a bullet has hit. **7.** an assistant to a sportscaster who provides the names of the players chiefly involved in each play of a game, esp. a football game. **8.** *Gymnastics, Tumbling.* a person who is stationed in the most effective place to guard against an injury to a performer in the act of executing a maneuver. [1605–15; SPOT + -ER[1]]

spot′ test′, 1. an informal test run without elaborate preparation in order to obtain an immediate sample response. **2.** *Chem.* a test for the identification of an element or compound by means of a reagent that produces a characteristic color change or precipitate. Cf. **spot plate.** [1925–30]

spot TV, *Slang.* the production or airing of television commercials.

spot·ty (spot′ē), *adj.* **-ti·er, -ti·est.** **1.** full of, having, or occurring in spots: *spotty coloring.* **2.** irregular or uneven in quality or character: *a spotty performance.* [1300–50; ME; see SPOT, -Y[1]] **—spot′ti·ly,** *adv.* **—spot′ti·ness,** *n.*
—Syn. 2. erratic, random, sporadic, episodic.

spot-weld (spot′weld′), *v.t.* **1.** to weld (two pieces of metal) together in a small area or spot by the application of heat and pressure. **—***n.* **2.** a welded joint made by this process.

spous·al (spou′zəl), *n.* **1.** Often, **spousals.** the ceremony of marriage; nuptials. **—***adj.* **2.** nuptial; matrimonial. [1250–1300; ME *spousaille,* aph. var. of *espousaille* ESPOUSAL] **—spous′al·ly,** *adv.*

spouse (*n.* spous, spouz; *v.* spouz, spous), *n., v.,* **spoused, spous·ing.** **—***n.* **1.** either member of a married pair in relation to the other; one's husband or wife. **—***v.t.* **2.** *Obs.* to join, give, or take in marriage. [1150–1200; (n.) ME < OF *spous* (masc.), *spouse* (fem.) (aph. for *espous, espouse*) < L *spōnsus, spōnsa* lit., pledged (man, woman) (n. uses of ptp. of *spondēre* to pledge), equiv. to *spond-* verb s. + *-tus, -ta* ptp. suffix; (v.) ME *spousen* < OF *esp(o)user;* cf. ESPOUSE] **—spouse′hood,** *n.* **—spouse′less,** *adj.*

spout (spout), *v.t.* **1.** to emit or discharge forcibly (a liquid, granulated substance, etc.) in a stream or jet. **2.** *Informal.* to state or declaim volubly or in an oratorical manner: *He spouted his theories on foreign policy for the better part of the night.* **—***v.i.* **3.** to discharge, as a liquid, in a jet or continuous stream. **4.** to issue forth with force, as liquid or other material through a narrow orifice. **5.** *Informal.* to talk or speak at some length or in an oratorical manner. **—***n.* **6.** a pipe, tube, or liplike projection through or by which a liquid is discharged, poured, or conveyed. **7.** a trough or shoot for discharging or conveying grain, flour, etc. **8.** a waterspout. **9.** a continuous stream of liquid, granulated substance, etc., discharged from or as if from a pipe, tube, shoot, etc. **10.** a spring of water. **11.** a downpour or fall, esp. of water, from a high place; waterfall. **12.** a dumbwaiter or chute, formerly common in pawnbrokers' shops, by which articles pawned were sent to another floor for storage. **13.** *Brit. Slang.* pawnshop. **14. up the spout,** *Brit. Slang.* **a.** pawned. **b.** in a desperate situation; beyond help: *His financial affairs are up the spout.* [1300–50; (v.) ME *spouten;* c. D *spuiten;* akin to ON *spȳta* to SPIT[1]; (n.) ME *spowt(e)* pipe, akin to the n.] **—spout′er,** *n.* **—spout′less,** *adj.* **—spout′like′,** *adj.*
—Syn. 3, 4. squirt, stream, pour. See **flow. 5.** declaim, rant, harangue, speechify. **6.** nozzle, nose.

spout′ cup′, a deep vessel used in feeding babies and invalids, having a long, curved, rising spout. Also called **feeding cup.** [1695–1705]

spout·ed (spou′tid), *adj.* fitted with a spout: *a spouted pitcher.* [1825–35; SPOUT + -ED[3]]

spout·ing (spou′ting), *n. Midland U.S.* guttering (defs. 1–3). [1870–75; SPOUT + -ING[1]]

spp., species (pl. of **specie**[1]).

S.P.Q.R., the Senate and People of Rome. Also, **SPQR** [< L *Senātus Populusque Rōmānus*]

S.P.R., Society for Psychical Research.

Sprach·ge·fühl (shpräkh′gə fyl′), *n. German.* a sensitivity to language, esp. for what is grammatically or idiomatically acceptable in a given language.

sprad·dle (sprad′l), *v.,* **-dled, -dling.** **—***v.t.* **1.** to straddle. **—***v.i.* **2.** to sprawl. [1625–35; orig. uncert.; cf. Norw dial. *spradla* squirm, flail]

sprad·dle-leg·ged (sprad′l leg′id, -legd′), *adj.* **1.** moving with or having the legs wide apart: *a spraddle-legged walk.* **—***adv.* **2.** with the legs sprawled, spread apart, etc.: *sitting spraddle-legged on the chair.*

sprag[1] (sprag), *n., v.,* **spragged, sprag·ging.** **—***n.* **1.** a pole or bar hinged to the rear axle of a cart or the like in such a way that it can brace the vehicle against a road to prevent it from rolling downhill. **2.** *Mining.* a short timber for propping up loose walls or spacing two sets. **—***v.t.* **3.** to prop, support, or immobilize (a vehicle) by means of a sprag. **—***v.i.* **4.** to slow a vehicle by means of a sprag or, sometimes, by bracing the feet against the ground. [1835–45; special use of dial. *sprag* twig (OE *spræcg* shoot, slip); akin to SPRIG]

sprag[2] (sprag), *n.* a young cod. [1700–10; special use of dial. *sprag* twig, lively young man; see SPRAG[1] and for meaning, cf. SPRIG]

Sprague (sprāg), *n.* **Frank Julian,** 1857–1934, U.S. electrical engineer and inventor.

sprain (sprān), *v.t.* **1.** to overstrain or wrench (the ligaments of an ankle, wrist, or other joint) so as to in-

CONCISE PRONUNCIATION KEY: act, cāpe, dâre, pärt; set, ēqual; if, īce; ox, ōver, ôrder, oil, bo͝ok, bo͞ot, out; up, ûrge; child; sing; shoe; thin, *th*at; zh as in *treasure.* ə = *a* as in *alone, e* as in *system, i* as in *easily, o* as in *gallop, u* as in *circus;* ᵊ as in *fire* (fīᵊr), *hour* (ouᵊr). l and n can serve as syllabic consonants, as in *cradle* (krād′l), and *button* (but′n). See the full key inside the front cover.

jure without fracture or dislocation. —*n.* **2.** a violent straining or wrenching of the parts around a joint, without dislocation. **3.** the condition of being sprained. [1595–1605; orig. uncert.]
—**Syn. 1.** twist. See **strain**[1].

sprang[1] (sprang), *v.* a pt. of **spring.**

sprang[2] (sprang), *n.* a technique of weaving in which the warp is interwoven and there is no weft. [1950–55; perh. < Norw: lace, tatting]

sprat (sprat), *n., pl.* **sprats,** (*esp. collectively*) **sprat** for 1. **1.** a species of herring, *Clupea sprattus,* of the eastern North Atlantic. **2.** a small or inconsequential person or thing. [1590–1600; var. of earlier *sprot,* ME, OE (c. G *Sprott*); appar. same word as OE *sprott* sprout, twig (for the two meanings cf. SPRAG[2]); akin to OE *spryttan* to SPROUT]

sprat·tle (sprat′l), *n. Scot.* a struggle; fight. [1815–25; metathetic var. of *spartle* to scatter, itself alter. of *sparple* (ME < OF *esparpeiller* < ?)]

sprawl (sprôl), *v.i.* **1.** to be stretched or spread out in an unnatural or ungraceful manner: *The puppy's legs sprawled in all directions.* **2.** to sit or lie in a relaxed position with the limbs spread out carelessly or ungracefully: *He sprawled across the bed.* **3.** to spread out, extend, or be distributed in a straggling or irregular manner, as vines, buildings, handwriting, etc. **4.** to crawl awkwardly with the aid of all the limbs; scramble. —*v.t.* **5.** to stretch out (the limbs) as in sprawling. **6.** to spread out or distribute in a straggling manner. —*n.* **7.** the act or an instance of sprawling; a sprawling posture. **8.** a straggling array of something. [bef. 1000; ME *spraulen* to move awkwardly, OE *spreawlian;* c. Fris (N dial.) *spraweli*] —**sprawl′er,** *n.* —**sprawl′ing·ly,** *adv.*
—**Syn. 3.** straggle, branch.

sprawl·y (sprô′lē), *adj.,* **sprawl·i·er, sprawl·i·est.** tending to sprawl; straggly: *The colt's legs were long and sprawly.* [1790–1800; SPRAWL + -Y[1]]

spray[1] (sprā), *n.* **1.** water or other liquid broken up into minute droplets and blown, ejected into, or falling through the air. **2.** a jet of fine particles of liquid, as medicine, insecticide, paint, perfume, etc., discharged from an atomizer or other device for direct application to a surface. **3.** a liquid to be discharged or applied in such a jet. **4.** an apparatus or device for discharging such a liquid. **5.** a quantity of small objects, flying or discharged through the air: *a spray of shattered glass.* —*v.t.* **6.** to scatter in the form of fine particles. **7.** to apply as a spray: *to spray an insecticide on plants.* **8.** to sprinkle or treat with a spray: *to spray plants with insecticide.* **9.** to direct a spray of particles, missiles, etc., upon: *to spray the mob with tear gas.* —*v.i.* **10.** to scatter spray; discharge a spray: *The hose sprayed over the flowers.* **11.** to issue as spray: *The water sprayed from the hose.* [1615–25; < earlier D *spraeyen;* c. MHG *spræjen*] —**spray′a·ble,** *adj.* —**spray′a·bil′i·ty,** *n.* —**spray′er,** *n.* —**spray′less,** *adj.* —**spray′like′,** *adj.*

spray[2] (sprā), *n.* **1.** a single, slender shoot, twig, or branch with its leaves, flowers, or berries. **2.** a group or bunch of cut flowers, leafy twigs, etc., arranged decoratively and for display, as in a vase. **3.** an ornament having a similar form. [1250–1300; ME; akin to SPRAG[1]] —**spray′like′,** *adj.*

spray′ can′, 1. a small can whose contents are in aerosol form. Cf. **aerosol bomb. 2.** the contents of such a can or the amount it holds: *She used two spray cans of white enamel to paint the cupboard.* —**spray′-can′,** *adj.*

spray′ gun′, a device consisting of a container from which paint or other liquid is sprayed through a nozzle by air pressure from a pump. Also called **squirt gun.** [1925–30]

spray′ mil′let, the seeds of millet left on the spike and sold in pet shops for cage birds.

spray′ paint′, paint that is packaged in an aerosol container for spraying directly onto a surface.

spray-paint (sprā′pānt′), *v.t.* to cover, mark, draw, or write with spray paint. [1965–70]

spray′ tank′, a closed tank into which air is pumped to force out a liquid, esp. for a spray.

spread (spred), *v.,* **spread, spread·ing,** *n., adj.* —*v.t.* **1.** to draw, stretch, or open out, esp. over a flat surface, as something rolled or folded (often fol. by *out*). **2.** to stretch out or unfurl in the air, as folded wings, a flag, etc. (often fol. by *out*). **3.** to distribute over a greater or a relatively great area of space or time (often fol. by *out*): *to spread out the papers on the table.* **4.** to display or exhibit the full extent of; set out in full: *He spread the pots on the ground and started hawking his wares.* **5.** to dispose or distribute in a sheet or layer: *to spread hay to dry.* **6.** to apply in a thin layer or coating: *to spread butter on a slice of bread.* **7.** to overlay or cover with something: *She spread the blanket over her knees.* **8.** to set or prepare (a table), as for a meal. **9.** to extend or distribute over a region, place, period of time, among a group, etc. **10.** to send out, scatter, or shed in various directions, as sound, light, etc. **11.** to scatter abroad; diffuse or disseminate, as knowledge, news, disease, etc.: *to spread the word of the gospel.* **12.** to move or force apart: *He spread his arms over his head in surrender.* **13.** to flatten out: *to spread the end of a rivet by hammering.* **14.** *Phonet.* **a.** to extend the aperture between (the lips) laterally, so as to reduce it vertically, during an utterance. **b.** to delabialize. Cf. **round** (def. 57c), **unround.**
—*v.i.* **15.** to become stretched out or extended, as a flag in the wind; expand, as in growth. **16.** to extend over a greater or a considerable area or period: *The factory spread along the river front.* **17.** to be or lie outspread or fully extended or displayed, as a landscape or scene. **18.** to admit of being spread or applied in a thin layer, as a soft substance: *Margarine spreads easily.* **19.** to become extended or distributed over a region, as population, animals, plants, etc. **20.** to become shed abroad, diffused, or disseminated, as light, influences, rumors, ideas, infection, etc. **21.** to be forced apart, as the rails of a railroad track; separate. **22. spread oneself thin,** to carry on so many projects simultaneously that none is done adequately, or that one's health suffers: *Many college students spread themselves thin by taking on too many activities during the semester.*
—*n.* **23.** an act or instance of spreading: *With a spread of her arms the actress acknowledged the applause.* **24.** expansion, extension, or diffusion: *the spread of consumerism.* **25.** the extent of spreading: *to measure the spread of branches.* **26.** *Finance.* **a.** the difference between the prices bid and asked of stock or a commodity for a given time. **b.** a type of straddle in which the call price is placed above and the put price is placed below the current market quotation. **c.** the difference between any two prices or rates for related costs: *the widening spread between lending and borrowing costs.* **d.** *Stock Exchange.* a broker's profit or the difference between his or her buying and selling price. **e.** any difference between return on assets and costs of liabilities. **27.** capacity for spreading: *the spread of an elastic material.* **28.** a distance or range, as between two points or dates: *The long-distance movers planned a five-day spread between pickup and delivery.* **29.** a stretch, expanse, or extent of something: *a spread of timber.* **30.** a cloth covering for a bed, table, or the like, esp. a bedspread. **31.** *Informal.* an abundance of food set out on a table; feast. **32.** any food preparation for spreading on bread, crackers, etc., as jam or peanut butter. **33.** *Aeron.* wingspan. **34.** Also called **layout.** *Journalism.* (in newspapers and magazines) an extensive, varied treatment of a subject, consisting primarily either of a number of cuts (**picture spread**) or of a major story and several supplementary stories, usually extending across three or more columns. Cf. **double truck. 35.** an advertisement, photograph, article, or the like, covering several columns, a full page, or two facing pages of a newspaper, magazine, book, etc.: *a full-page spread; a two-page spread.* **36.** two facing pages, as of a newspaper, magazine, or book. **37.** landed property, as a farm or ranch. **38.** lay[1] (def. 64). **39.** See **point spread.**
—*adj.* **40.** *Jewelry.* (of a gem) cut with the table too large and the crown too shallow for maximum brilliance; swindled. **41.** *Phonet.* (of the opening between the lips) extended laterally. Cf. **rounded** (def. 2), **unrounded.** [1150–1200; ME *spreden* (v.), OE *sprǣdan;* c. MD *spreden,* G *spreiten*]
—**Syn. 1.** unfold, unroll, expand. **10.** emit, diffuse, radiate. **11.** disperse, scatter, publish, circulate, promulgate, propagate. **15.** stretch, dilate. **25.** reach, compass.

spread·a·ble (spred′ə bəl), *adj.* capable of being spread; easily spread: *a soft, spreadable cheese.* [SPREAD + -ABLE] —**spread′a·bil′i·ty,** *n.*

spread′ ea′gle, 1. a representation of an eagle with outspread wings: used as an emblem of the U.S. **2.** an acrobatic figure in skating performed by making a glide with the skates touching heel-to-heel in a straight line and with the arms outstretched. **3.** an acrobatic stunt in ski jumping executed with the legs and arms widely outstretched to the sides. [1560–70]

spread-ea·gle (spred′ē′gəl), *adj., v.,* **-gled, -gling.** —*adj.* **1.** having or suggesting the form of a spread eagle. **2.** lying prone with arms and legs outstretched. **3.** boastful or bombastic, esp. in the display of patriotic or nationalistic pride in the U.S. —*v.t.* **4.** to stretch out (something) in the manner of a spread eagle. —*v.i.* **5.** to assume the position or perform the acrobatic figure of a spread eagle: *The skater spread-eagled across the rink.* [1820–30]

spread-ea·gle·ism (spred′ē′gə liz′əm), *n.* boastfulness or bombast, esp. in the display of patriotic or nationalistic pride in the U.S.; flag-waving. [1855–60, *Amer.;* SPREAD-EAGLE + -ISM] —**spread′-ea′gle·ist,** *n.*

spread′ end′, *Football.* See **split end.**

spread·er (spred′ər), *n.* **1.** a person or thing that spreads. **2.** a small, dull knife or spatula used for spreading butter, jelly, etc., on bread. **3.** a machine for dispersing bulk material: *manure spreader.* **4.** a device for spacing or keeping apart two objects, as electric wires. **5.** *Naut.* a strut for spreading shrouds on a mast. [1475–85; SPREAD + -ER[1]]

spread′er beam′, a crosspiece for spacing the chains or cables hanging from the boom of a crane. Also called **yoke.**

spread·er-ditch·er (spred′ər dich′ər), *n. Railroads.* a machine for shaping and cleaning roadbeds and ditches and for freeing tracks of ice and snow by plowing and digging.

spread′ing cen′ter, *Geol.* a linear zone in the sea floor along which magma rises and from which adjacent crustal plates are moving apart.

spread′ op′tion, spread (def. 26b).

spread·sheet (spred′shēt′), **1.** *Accounting.* a work sheet that is arranged in the manner of a mathematical matrix and contains a multicolumn analysis of related entries for easy reference on a single sheet. **2.** *Computers.* See **electronic spreadsheet.** Also, **spread′ sheet′.** [SPREAD + SHEET[1]]

sprech·ge·sang (*Ger.* shprekh′gə zäng′), *n.* a vocal style intermediate between speech and singing but without exact pitch intonation. [< G, equiv. to *sprech(en)* to SPEAK + *Gesang* song]

sprech·stim·me (*Ger.* shprekh′shtim′ə), *n.* sprechgesang. [< G, equiv. to *sprech(en)* to SPEAK + *Stimme* voice]

spree (sprē), *n.* **1.** a lively frolic or outing. **2.** a bout or spell of drinking to intoxication; binge; carousal. **3.** a period, spell, or bout of indulgence, as of a particular wish, craving, or whim: *an eating spree; a spending spree.* **4.** a period or outburst of extreme activity: *Our basketball team went on a scoring spree and won 114 to 78.* [1795–1805; orig. uncert.]

Spree (shprā), *n.* a river in East Germany, flowing N through Berlin to the Havel River. 220 mi. (354 km) long.

sprent (sprent), *adj. Archaic.* sprinkled. [1505–15; ptp. of obs. *sprenge* to sprinkle, ME *sprengen,* OE *sprengan;* c. OHG, MHG, G *sprengen,* ON *sprengja* to make jump; cf. SPRINKLE]

spri·er (sprī′ər), *adj.* a comparative of **spry.**

spri·est (sprī′ist), *adj.* a superlative of **spry.**

sprig (sprig), *n., v.,* **sprigged, sprig·ging.** —*n.* **1.** a small spray of some plant with its leaves, flowers, etc. **2.** an ornament having the form of such a spray. **3.** a shoot, twig, or small branch. **4.** *Facetious.* a scion, offspring, or heir of a family, class, etc. **5.** a youth or young fellow. **6.** See **glazier's point. 7.** a headless brad. **8.** *Metall.* **a.** a small peg for reinforcing the walls of a mold. **b.** a metal insert, used to chill certain portions of cast metal, that becomes an integral part of the finished casting. —*v.t.* **9.** to mark or decorate (fabrics, pottery, etc.) with a design of sprigs. **10.** to fasten with brads. **11.** *Hort.* to propagate a plant, esp. grass, by planting individual stolons. **12.** *Metall.* to reinforce the walls of (a mold) with sprigs. **13.** to remove a sprig or sprigs from (a plant). [1300–50; ME *sprigge* (n.); orig. uncert.; sense "peg" perh. of distinct orig.; cf. SPRAG[1], SPRAY[2]]

sprig·gy (sprig′ē), *adj.,* **-gi·er, -gi·est.** possessing sprigs or small branches. [1590–1600; SPRIG + -Y[1]]

spright·ful (sprīt′fəl), *adj.* sprightly. [1585–95; *spright* (sp. var. of SPRITE) + -FUL]

spright·ly (sprīt′lē), *adj.,* **-li·er, -li·est,** *adv.* —*adj.* **1.** animated, vivacious, or gay; lively. —*adv.* **2.** in a sprightly manner. [1590–1600; *spright* (sp. var. of SPRITE) + -LY] —**spright′li·ness,** *n.*
—**Syn. 1.** spirited, blithe, buoyant, spry.

sprig·tail (sprig′tāl′), *n.* **1.** the pintail, *Anas acuta.* **2.** See **ruddy duck. 3.** See **sharp-tailed grouse.** [1670–80; SPRIG + TAIL[1]]

spring (spring), *v.,* **sprang** or, often, **sprung; sprung; spring·ing;** *n., adj.* —*v.i.* **1.** to rise, leap, move, or act suddenly and swiftly, as by a sudden dart or thrust forward or outward, or being suddenly released from a coiled or constrained position: *to spring into the air; a tiger about to spring.* **2.** to be released from a constrained position, as by resilient or elastic force or from the action of a spring: *A trap springs. The door sprang open and in he walked.* **3.** to issue forth suddenly, as water, blood, sparks, fire, etc. (often fol. by *forth, out,* or *up*): *Blood sprang from the wound.* **4.** to come into being, rise, or arise within a short time (usually fol. by *up*): *Industries sprang up in the suburbs.* **5.** to come into being by growth, as from a seed or germ, bulb, root, etc.; grow, as plants. **6.** to proceed or originate from a specific source or cause. **7.** to have as one's birth or lineage; be descended, as from a person, family, stock, etc.; come from: *to spring from ancient aristocracy.* **8.** to rise or extend upward, as a spire. **9.** to take an upward course or curve from a point of support, as an arch. **10.** to come or appear suddenly, as if at a bound: *An objection sprang to mind.* **11.** to start or rise from cover, as a pheasant, woodcock, or the like. **12.** to become bent or warped, as boards. **13.** to shift or work loose, as parts of a mechanism, structure, etc.: *The board sprang from the fence during the storm.* **14.** to explode, as a mine. **15.** *Archaic.* to begin to appear, as day, light, etc.; dawn.
—*v.t.* **16.** to cause to spring. **17.** to cause to fly back, move, or act, as by resiliency, elastic force, a spring, etc.: *to spring a lock.* **18.** to cause to shift out of place, work loose, warp, split, or crack: *Moisture sprang the board from the fence.* **19.** to split or crack: *The ship sprang its keel on a rock.* **20.** to develop by or as by splitting or cracking: *The boat sprang a leak.* **21.** to bend by force, or force in by bending, as a resilient slat or bar. **22.** to stretch or bend (a spring or other resilient device) beyond its elastic tolerance: *This clip has been sprung.* **23.** to bring out, disclose, produce, make, etc., suddenly: *to spring a joke.* **24.** to leap over. **25.** *Slang.* to secure the release of (someone) from confinement, as of jail, military service, or the like. **26.** *Naut.* to move (a vessel) into or out of a berth by pulling on the offshore end of a warp made fast to the pier. **27.** to explode (a mine). **28. spring for,** *Informal.* to pay for; treat someone to.
—*n.* **29.** a leap, jump, or bound. **30.** a sudden movement caused by the release of something elastic. **31.** an elastic or bouncing quality: *There is a spring in his walk.* **32.** elasticity or resilience: *This board has spring in it.* **33.** a structural defect or injury caused by a warp, crack, etc. **34.** an issue of water from the earth, taking the form, on the surface, of a small stream or standing as a pool or small lake. **35.** the place of such an issue: *mineral springs.* **36.** a source or fountainhead of something: *a spring of inspiration.* **37.** an elastic contrivance or body, as a strip or wire of steel coiled spirally, that recovers its shape after being compressed, bent, or stretched. See illus. on next page. **38.** the season between winter and summer: in the Northern Hemisphere from the vernal equinox to the summer solstice; in the Southern Hemisphere from the autumnal equinox to the winter solstice. **39.** (in temperate zones) the season of the year following winter and characterized by the budding of trees, growth of plants, the onset of warmer weather, etc. **40.** the first stage and freshest period: *the spring of life.* **41.** *Naut.* **a.** warp (def. 16). **b.** a line from the quarter of a vessel to an anchor on the bottom, used to hold the vessel at its mooring, broadside to the current. **42.** Also called **springing.** *Archit.* **a.** the point at which an arch or dome rises from its support. **b.** the rise or the angle of the rise of an arch. **43.** *Archaic.* the dawn, as of day, light, etc.
—*adj.* **44.** of, pertaining to, characteristic of, or suitable for the season of spring: *spring flowers.* **45.** resting on or containing mechanical springs. [bef. 900; (v.) ME *springen,* OE *springan;* c. D, G *springen,* ON *springa;* (n.) ME *spring(e),* OE *spring, spryng* issue of a stream; cf. MLG, OHG, Dan, Sw *spring*] —**spring′like′,** *adj.*

—**Syn.** **1.** jump, bound, hop, vault. **2.** recoil, rebound. **3.** shoot, dart, fly. **4.** start, originate. **6.** emerge, emanate, issue, flow. **12.** bend, warp. **32.** resiliency, buoyancy. **36.** origin, head. **44.** vernal.

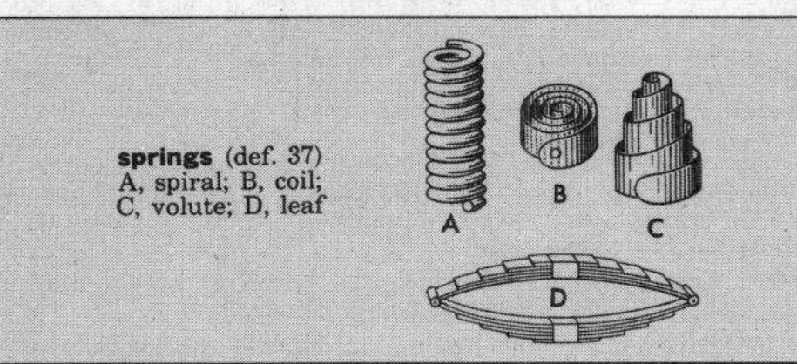

springs (def. 37) A, spiral; B, coil; C, volute; D, leaf

spring·ald (spring′əld), *n.* a youth; young fellow. [1400–50; late ME, alter. (by dissimilation) of **springard* leaper, jumper. See SPRING, -ARD]

spring′ beau′ty, any American spring plant belonging to the genus *Claytonia,* of the purslane family, esp. *C. virginica,* having an elongated cluster of white flowers tinged with pink. [1815–25, *Amer.*]

spring′ bind′er, a loose-leaf binder in which a single, long, clamplike spring, forming the spine, holds the leaves.

spring·board (spring′bôrd′, -bōrd′), *n.* **1.** a flexible board, projecting over water, from which divers leap or spring. **2.** a flexible board used as a takeoff in vaulting, tumbling, etc., to increase the height of leaps. **3.** something that supplies the impetus or conditions for a beginning, change, or progress; a point of departure: *a lecture to serve as a springboard for a series of seminars.* —*v.t., v.i.* **4.** to impel or launch on or as if on a springboard. [1865–70; SPRING + BOARD]

spring·bok (spring′bok′), *n., pl.* **-boks,** (*esp. collectively*) **-bok.** a gazelle, *Antidorcas marsupialis,* of southern Africa, noted for its habit of springing into the air when alarmed. [1765–75; < Afrik. See SPRING, BUCK¹]

springbok, *Antidorcas marsupialis,* 2½ ft. (0.8 m) high at shoulder; horns 15 in. (38 cm); length 5 ft. (1.5 m)

spring·buck (spring′buk′), *n., pl.* **-bucks,** (*esp. collectively*) **-buck.** springbok.

spring′ can′kerworm. See under **cankerworm.** [1885–90, *Amer.*]

spring′ catch′, a catch for an interior or cabinet door that has a bolt operated by a spring. [1835–45]

spring′ chick′en, 1. a young chicken, esp. a broiler or fryer. **2.** *Slang.* a young person: *I don't know his age, but he's no spring chicken.* [1835–45, *Amer.*]

spring-clean (spring′klēn′), *v.t.* to subject (a place) to a spring-cleaning. [1890–95]

spring-clean·ing (spring′klē′ning), *n.* **1.** a complete cleaning of a place, as a home, done traditionally in the spring of the year. **2.** the activity of giving a place a complete cleaning: *We've been involved in spring-cleaning and are exhausted.* [1855–60]

Spring·dale (spring′dāl′), *n.* **1.** a city in NW Arkansas. 23,458. **2.** a city in NE Ohio. 10,111.

springe (sprinj), *n., v.,* **springed, spring·ing.** —*n.* **1.** a snare for catching small game. —*v.t.* **2.** to catch in a springe. —*v.i.* **3.** to set a springe or springes. [1200–50; ME, var. of *sprenge* a snare, lit., something that is made to spring, deriv. of *sprengen* to make spring, OE *sprengan,* causative of *springan* to SPRING]

spring′ e′quinox, vernal equinox. See under **equinox.** [1580–90]

spring·er (spring′ər), *n.* **1.** a person or thing that springs. **2.** *Archit.* the first voussoir above the impost of an arch. See diag. under **arch¹.** [1350–1400; ME; see SPRING, -ER¹]

spring′er span′iel, a dog of either of two breeds of medium-sized spaniels, used for flushing and retrieving game. Cf. **English springer spaniel, Welsh springer spaniel.** [1880–85]

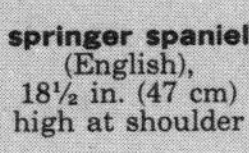

springer spaniel (English), 18½ in. (47 cm) high at shoulder

spring′ fe′ver, a listless, lazy, or restless feeling commonly associated with the beginning of spring. [1855–60, *Amer.*]

Spring·field (spring′fēld′), *n.* **1.** a city in S Massachusetts, on the Connecticut River. 152,319. **2.** a city in SW Missouri. 133,116. **3.** a city in and the capital of Illinois, in the central part. 99,637. **4.** a city in W Ohio. 72,563. **5.** a city in W Oregon. 41,621. **6.** a town in SE Pennsylvania, near Philadelphia. 25,326. **7.** a town in N Tennessee. 10,814. **8.** a town in SE Vermont. 10,190.

Spring′field ri′fle, 1. a single-shot, breechloading .45-caliber rifle used by the U.S. Army from 1867 to 1893. **2.** Also called **Springfield 1903.** a bolt-operated, magazine-fed, .30-caliber rifle adopted by the U.S. Army in 1903 and used during World War I. **3.** a single-shot, muzzleloading rifle of .58-inch caliber, used by the Union Army during the Civil War. [after SPRINGFIELD, Mass., site of a federal armory that made the rifles]

spring′form pan′ (spring′fôrm′), a metal cake pan with sides that can be unfastened to facilitate releasing the cake when done. [1925–30; SPRING + -FORM]

spring·halt (spring′hôlt′), *n. Vet. Pathol.* stringhalt. [1605–15; alter. by assoc. with SPRING]

spring·hare (spring′hâr′), *n.* a leaping and burrowing rodent, *Pedetes capensis,* native to southern Africa, having kangaroolike legs and long, pointed ears. Also called **jumping hare, spring·haas** (spring′häs′). [1815–25; trans. of Afrik *springhaas;* see SPRING, HARE]

spring·head (spring′hed′), *n.* **1.** a spring or fountainhead from which a stream flows. **2.** the source of something: *the springhead of desire.* [1545–55; SPRING + HEAD]

spring·house (spring′hous′), *n., pl.* **-hous·es** (-hou′ziz). a small storehouse built over a spring or part of a brook, for keeping such foods as meat and dairy products cool and fresh. [1745–55, *Amer.*; SPRING + HOUSE]

spring·ing (spring′ing), *n.* **1.** the act or process of a person or thing that springs. **2.** the mechanical springs or the type or arrangement of springs with which any of various devices are equipped, esp. a vehicle. **3.** *Archit.* spring (def. 42). [1250–1300; ME; see SPRING, -ING¹] —**spring′ing·ly,** *adv.*

spring′ lamb′, a lamb born in the late winter or early spring and sold for slaughter before July 1.

spring·less (spring′lis), *adj.* **1.** having no springs: *a springless bed.* **2.** lacking liveliness or resilience; lifeless: *His shoulders drooped and his walk had become springless.* [1675–85; SPRING + -LESS]

spring·let (spring′lit), *n.* a small spring of water. [1740–50; SPRING + -LET]

spring′ line′, *Naut.* warp (def. 16).

spring-load·ed (spring′lō′did), *adj.* (of a machine part) kept normally in a certain position by a spring: *a spring-loaded safety valve.*

spring·lock (spring′lok′), *n.* a lock that fastens automatically by a spring. [1475–85; SPRING + LOCK¹]

spring′ mold′ing, *Carpentry.* See **sprung molding.**

spring′ peep′er, a tree frog, *Hyla crucifer,* having an X-shaped mark on the back and voicing a shrill call commonly heard near ponds and swamps of eastern North America in the early spring. [1905–10, *Amer.*]

spring′ roll′, *Chinese Cookery.* an egg roll. [1965–70; trans. of Chin *chūn-juǎn*]

Springs (springz), *n.* a city in S Transvaal, in the E Republic of South Africa, E of Johannesburg. 110,000.

spring′ snow′. See **corn snow.** [1840–50, *Amer.*]

spring·tail (spring′tāl′), *n.* any of numerous minute, wingless primitive insects of the order Collembola, most possessing a special abdominal appendage for jumping that allows for the nearly perpetual jumping pattern characteristic of the group. [1790–1800; SPRING + TAIL¹]

spring′ tide′, 1. the large rise and fall of the tide at or soon after the new or the full moon. See diag. under **tide¹. 2.** any great flood or swelling rush: *a spring tide of compliments.* [1520–30]

spring·time (spring′tīm′), *n.* **1.** the season of spring. **2.** the first or earliest period: *the springtime of love.* Also called **spring·tide** (spring′tīd′). [1485–95; SPRING + TIME]

spring′ train′ing, 1. a program of physical exercise, practice, and exhibition games followed by a baseball team in the late winter and early spring, before the start of the regular season. **2.** the period during which such a program takes place, usually from the beginning of March until the middle of April. [1895–1900, *Amer.*]

Spring′ Val′ley, 1. a city in SW California, near San Diego. 40,191. **2.** a town in SE New York. 20,537.

spring′ vetch′. See under **vetch** (def. 1).

Spring·ville (spring′vil), *n.* a town in central Utah. 12,101.

spring·wood (spring′wŏŏd′), *n.* the part of an annual ring of wood, characterized by large, thin-walled cells, formed during the first part of the growing season. Also called **early wood.** Cf. **summerwood.** [1515–25; SPRING + WOOD¹]

spring·y (spring′ē), *adj.,* **spring·i·er, spring·i·est. 1.** characterized by spring or elasticity; flexible; resilient: *He walks with a springy step.* **2.** (of land) abounding in or having springs of water. [1585–95; SPRING + -Y¹] —**spring′i·ly,** *adv.* —**spring′i·ness,** *n.*
—**Syn. 1.** buoyant, bouncy; youthful.

sprin·kle (spring′kəl), *v.,* **-kled, -kling,** *n.* —*v.t.* **1.** to scatter (a liquid, powder, etc.) in drops or particles: *She sprinkled powder on the baby.* **2.** to disperse or distribute here and there. **3.** to overspread with drops or particles of water, powder, or the like: *to sprinkle a lawn.* **4.** to diversify or intersperse with objects scattered here and there. —*v.i.* **5.** to scatter or disperse liquid, a powder, etc., in drops or particles. **6.** to be sprinkled. **7.** to rain slightly (often used impersonally with *it* as subject): *It may sprinkle this evening.* —*n.* **8.** the act or an instance of sprinkling. **9.** something used for sprinkling. **10.** Usually, **sprinkles.** small particles of chocolate, candy, sugar, etc., used as a decorative topping for cookies, cakes, ice-cream cones, and the like. **11.** a light rain. **12.** a small quantity or number. [1350–1400; ME *sprenklen* (v.); c. D *sprenkelen,* G *sprenkeln;* akin to OE *sprengan* to sprinkle, make (something) spring, scatter, causative of *springan* to SPRING]
—**Syn. 1.** distribute, rain. SPRINKLE, SCATTER, STREW mean to fling, spread, or disperse. To SPRINKLE means to fling about small drops or particles: *to sprinkle water on clothes, powder on plants.* To SCATTER is to disperse or spread widely: *to scatter seeds.* To STREW is to scatter, esp. in such a way as to cover or partially cover a surface: *to strew flowers on a grave.*

sprin·kler (spring′klər), *n.* **1.** any of various devices for sprinkling, as a watering pot, a container of water with a perforated top used to sprinkle clothes before ironing, or esp. a perforated ring or small stand with a revolving nozzle to which a hose is attached for watering a lawn with a fine, even spray. **2.** a person who sprinkles. —*v.t.* **3.** to provide (a warehouse, school, office building, etc.) with a sprinkler system. [1525–35; SPRINKLE + -ER¹]

sprin·klered (spring′klərd), *adj.* having or protected by a sprinkler system. [1925–30; SPRINKLER + -ED³]

sprin′kler sys′tem, apparatus for automatically extinguishing fires in a building, consisting of a system of water pipes in or below the ceilings, with valves or sprinklers usually made to open automatically at a certain temperature. [1880–85]

sprin·kling (spring′kling), *n.* **1.** a small quantity or number scattered here and there. **2.** a small quantity sprinkled or to be sprinkled. [1400–50; late ME *sprenclyng.* See SPRINKLE, -ING¹] —**sprin′kling·ly,** *adv.*
—**Syn. 1, 2.** sprinkle, touch, dash, hint.

sprin′kling can′. See **watering pot.**

sprint (sprint), *v.i.* **1.** to race or move at full speed, esp. for a short distance, as in running, rowing, etc. —*v.t.* **2.** to traverse in sprinting: *to sprint a half mile.* —*n.* **3.** a short race at full speed. **4.** a burst of speed at any point during a long race, as near the finish line. **5.** a brief spell of great activity. [1560–70; perh. continuing OE **sprintan* (cf. *gesprintan* to emit); c. ON *spretta,* OHG *sprinzan* to jump up] —**sprint′er,** *n.*

sprint′ med′ley, *Track.* a medley relay in which the first member of a team runs 440 yards, the second and third members run 220 yards each, and the fourth member runs 880 yards. Cf. **distance medley.**

sprit (sprit), *n. Naut.* a small pole or spar crossing a fore-and-aft sail diagonally from the mast to the upper aftermost corner, serving to extend the sail. [bef. 900; ME *spret,* OE *sprēot;* c. D, G *Spriet;* akin to SPROUT]

S, **sprit**

sprite (sprīt), *n.* an elf, fairy, or goblin. [1250–1300; ME *sprit* < OF *esprit* < L *spīritus* SPIRIT] —**sprite′·hood,** *n.* —**sprite′less,** *adj.* —**sprite′like′,** *adj.*
—**Syn.** See **fairy.**

sprite′ crab′. See **ghost crab.**

sprit·sail (sprit′sāl′; *Naut.* sprit′səl), *n. Naut.* a sail extended by a sprit. [1425–75; late ME *sprete seyle* (see SPRIT, SAIL); cf. D *sprietzeil*]

spritz (sprits, shprits), *Informal.* —*v.t.* **1.** to spray briefly and quickly; squirt: *He spritzed a little soda in his drink.* —*n.* **2.** a quick, brief spray of liquid; squirt. [1915–20, *Amer.*; < G *spritzen* to squirt, spray]

spritz·er (sprit′sər, shprit′-), *n.* a tall drink made with chilled wine and soda. [1940–45; < G *Spritzer;* see SPRITZ, -ER¹]

sproat (sprōt), *n. Angling.* a fishhook having a circular bend. Also, **sproat′ hook′.** [1865–70; named after W. H. *Sproat,* 19th-century English angler]

sprock·et (sprok′it), *n.* **1.** *Mach.* **a.** Also called **chain-wheel, sprock′et wheel′.** a toothed wheel engaging with a conveyor or power chain. **b.** one tooth of such a wheel. **2.** *Carpentry.* a wedge-shaped piece of wood extending a sloping roof over the eaves with a flatter pitch. [1530–40; orig. uncert.]

sprockets (def. 1)

sprock′et hole′, any of a series of regular perforations along the edge of photographic film for engaging the drive sprockets in a motion-picture camera or projector. [1905–10]

sprout (sprout), *v.i.* **1.** to begin to grow; shoot forth, as a plant from a seed. **2.** (of a seed or plant) to put forth buds or shoots. **3.** to develop or grow quickly: *a boy*

CONCISE PRONUNCIATION KEY: act, cāpe, dâre, pärt; set, ēqual; *if,* īce; ox, ōver, ôrder, oil, bŏŏk, bōōt, out; up, ûrge; child; sing; shoe; thin, *that;* zh as in *treasure.* ə = *a* as in *alone, e* as in *system, i* as in *easily, o* as in *gallop, u* as in *circus;* ᵊ as in *fire* (fīᵊr), *hour* (ouᵊr). l and n can serve as syllabic consonants, as in *cradle* (krād′l), and *button* (but′n). See the full key inside the front cover.

awkwardly sprouting into manhood. —*v.t.* **4.** to cause to sprout. **5.** to remove sprouts from: *Sprout and boil the potatoes.* —*n.* **6.** a shoot of a plant. **7.** a new growth from a germinating seed, or from a rootstock, tuber, bud, or the like. **8.** something resembling or suggesting a sprout, as in growth. **9.** a young person; youth. **10. sprouts, a.** the young shoots of alfalfa, soybeans, etc., eaten as a raw vegetable. **b.** See **Brussels sprout.** [1150–1200; (v.) ME *spr(o)uten,* OE *-sprūtan,* in *āsproten* (ptp.; see A-[3]); c. MD *sprūten,* G *spriessen* to sprout; akin to Gk *speirein* to scatter; (n.) ME; cf. MD, MLG *sprute*]
—**Syn. 1.** spring, bud, burgeon, develop.

Spru·ance (sprōō′əns), *n.* **Raymond Ames** (āmz), 1886–1969, U.S. admiral.

spruce[1] (sprōōs), *n.* **1.** any evergreen, coniferous tree of the genus *Picea,* of the pine family, having short, angular, needle-shaped leaves attached singly around twigs and bearing hanging cones with persistent scales. **2.** any of various allied trees, as the Douglas fir and the hemlock spruce. **3.** the wood of any such tree. —*adj.* **4.** made from the wood of a spruce tree or trees. **5.** containing or abounding in spruce trees. [1350–1400; ME, special use of *Spruce,* sandhi var. of *Pruce* < OF *Pruce* < ML *Prussia* PRUSSIA, whence the timber came]

spruce[2] (sprōōs), *adj.,* **spruc·er, spruc·est,** *v.,* **spruced, spruc·ing.** —*adj.* **1.** trim in dress or appearance; neat; smart; dapper. —*v.t.* **2.** to make spruce or smart (often fol. by *up*): *Spruce up the children before the company comes.* —*v.i.* **3.** to make oneself spruce (usually fol. by *up*). [1580–90; obs. *spruce jerkin* orig., jerkin made of *spruce leather,* i.e., leather imported from Prussia (see SPRUCE[1]), hence fine, smart, etc.] —**spruce′ly,** *adv.* —**spruce′ness,** *n.*

spruce′ beer′, a fermented beverage made with spruce leaves and twigs, or an extract from them. [1490–1500]

spruce′ bee′tle, a beetle, *Dendroctonus rufipennis,* that feeds on and nests in spruce, pine, and other evergreen trees, sometimes causing extensive damage.

spruce′ bud′worm (bud′wûrm′), the larva of a common tortricid moth, *Choristoneura fumiferana,* that is a destructive pest primarily of spruce and balsam fir in the northern and northeastern U.S. and in Canada. [1880–85]

spruce′ gall′ a′phid. See under **adelgid.** Also called **spruce′ gall′ adel′gid.**

spruce′ grouse′, a grouse, *Canachites canadensis,* of coniferous forests of northern North America, that feeds on evergreen buds and needles. [1835–45, *Amer.*]

spruce′ pine′, 1. a tall coniferous tree, *Pinus glabra,* of the southeastern U.S., having smooth, gray bark and needles in bundles of two. **2.** any of several other pines, as *P. elliottii* or *P. virginiana.* [1675–85, *Amer.*]

spruce′ saw′fly, any of several sawflies of the family Diprionidae, esp. *Diprion hercyniae* **(European spruce sawfly),** the larvae of which feed on the foliage of spruce.

spruce-up (sprōōs′up′) *n.* an act of cleaning up, refurbishing, renovating, or the like. [n. use of v. phrase *spruce up*]

spruc·y (sprōō′sē), *adj.,* **spruc·i·er, spruc·i·est.** spruce[2] (def. 1). [1765–75; SPRUCE[2] + -Y[1]]

sprue[1] (sprōō), *n., v.,* **sprued, spru·ing.** —*n.* **1.** *Metall.* **a.** an opening through which molten metal is poured into a mold. **b.** the waste metal left in this opening after casting. **2.** *Metalworking.* a channel in a forging die permitting the die to clear that part of the rough piece not being forged. —*v.t.* **3.** to cut the sprues from (a casting). [1820–30; orig. uncert.]

sprue[2] (sprōō), *n. Pathol.* a chronic disease, occurring chiefly in the tropics, resulting from malabsorption of nutrients from the small intestine and characterized by diarrhea, ulceration of the mucous membrane of the digestive tract, and a smooth, shining tongue; psilosis. [1815–25; < D *spruw;* c. MLG *sprūwe* tumor]

spruik (sprōōk), *v.i. Australian Slang.* to make or give a speech, esp. extensively or elaborately; spiel; orate. [1915–20; orig. uncert.] —**spruik′er,** *n.*

spruit (sprōōt, sprāt), *n.* (in southern Africa) a small stream. [1860–65; < Afrik < D *spruit* SPROUT]

sprung (sprung), *v.* a pt. and pp. of **spring.**

sprung′ mold′ing, *Carpentry.* a molded board, as one forming part of a cornice, placed diagonally and secured at the ends to two surfaces intersecting at a right angle. Also called **spring molding.**

sprung′ rhythm′, a poetic rhythm characterized by the use of strongly accented syllables, often in juxtaposition, accompanied by an indefinite number of unaccented syllables in each foot, of which the accented syllable is the essential component. [term introduced by Gerard Manley Hopkins (1877)]

spry (sprī), *adj.,* **spry·er, spry·est** or **spri·er, spri·est.** active; nimble; agile; energetic; brisk. [1740–50; orig. uncert.] —**spry′ly,** *adv.* —**spry′ness,** *n.*

spt., seaport.

spud (spud), *n., v.,* **spud·ded, spud·ding.** —*n.* **1.** *Informal.* a potato. **2.** a spadelike instrument, esp. one with a narrow blade, as for digging up or cutting the roots of weeds. **3.** a chisellike tool for removing bark. **4.** a pointed leg or stake for staying or supporting dredging or earth-boring machinery. **5.** a short pipe, as for connecting a water pipe with a meter. **6.** *Surg.* an instrument having a dull flattened blade for removing substances or foreign bodies from certain parts of the body, as wax from the ear. —*v.t.* **7.** to remove with a spud. **8. spud in,** to set up earth-boring equipment, esp. for drilling an oil well. [1400–50; late ME *spudde* short knife < ?]

spud·der (spud′ər), *n.* **1.** a person who prepares and operates a rig for drilling oil wells. **2.** a light drilling rig used chiefly in beginning a well. **3.** spud (def. 3). [1920–25 for def. 2; SPUD + -ER[1]]

Spud′ Is′land, *Canadian Slang.* See **Prince Edward Island.**

spue (spyōō), *v.i., v.t.,* **spued, spu·ing,** *n.* spew.

spu·ky (spōō′kē), *n., pl.* **-kies.** *Chiefly Boston.* a hero sandwich. Also, **spu′kie.** [orig. uncert.]
—**Regional Variation.** See **hero sandwich.**

spu·man·te (*It.* spōō män′te; *Eng.* spə män′tē, -tā, spyə-), *n.* **1.** *Italian.* any sparkling wine. **2.** See **Asti spumante.** [< It: lit., foaming; see SPUME]

spume (spyōōm), *v.,* **spumed, spum·ing,** *n.* —*v.t.* **1.** to eject or discharge as or like foam or froth; spew (often fol. by *forth*). —*v.i.* **2.** to foam; froth. —*n.* **3.** foam, froth, or scum. [1300–50; ME < L *spūma* foam, froth; akin to FOAM] —**spu′mous, spum′y,** *adj.*

spu·mes·cent (spyōō mes′ənt), *adj.* foamy; foamlike; frothy. [1855–60; SPUME + -ESCENT] —**spu·mes′cence,** *n.*

spu·mo·ne (spə mō′nē, -nā; *It.* spōō mô′ne), *n.* an Italian style of ice cream of a very fine and smooth texture, usually containing layers of various colors and flavors and chopped fruit or nuts. Also, **spu·mo·ni** (spə-mō′nē). [1920–25; < It, equiv. to *spum(a)* SPUME + *-one* aug. suffix]

spun (spun), *v.* **1.** a pt. and pp. of **spin.** —*adj.* **2.** formed by or as by spinning.

spun·bond·ed (spun′bon′did), *adj.* being or designating a material or fiber produced by spun-bonding. Also, **spun′-bond′ed.** [1960–65; SPUN + BONDED]

spun-bond·ing (spun′bon′ding), *n.* a process for forming nonwoven fabrics, usually of limited durability, by bonding continuous-filament synthetic fibers immediately after extrusion.

spun′ glass′, 1. blown glass in which fine threads of glass form the surface texture. **2.** fiberglass. [1770–80]

spunk (spungk), *n.* **1.** pluck; spirit; mettle. **2.** touchwood, tinder, or punk. [1530–40; b. SPARK[1] and obs. *funk* spark, touchwood (c. D *vonk,* G *Funke*)] —**spunk′less,** *adj.*

spunk·ie (spung′kē), *n. Scot.* a will-o'-the-wisp. [1720–30; SPUNK + -IE]

spunk·y (spung′kē), *adj.,* **spunk·i·er, spunk·i·est.** plucky; spirited. [1780–90; SPUNK + -Y[1]] —**spunk′i·ly,** *adv.* —**spunk′i·ness,** *n.*

spun′ ray′on, 1. yarn produced by spinning short, uniform lengths of rayon filaments into a continuous strand. **2.** a fabric woven from this yarn. [1925–30]

spun′ silk′, 1. yarn produced by spinning silk waste and short, broken filaments from which the sericin has been removed. Cf. **reeled silk. 2.** a fabric woven from this yarn. [1750–60]

spun′ sug′ar, a confection resembling fluff or floss, made from hot boiled sugar that has threaded, used as a garnish, frosting, or in making cotton candy.

spun·ware (spun′wâr′), *n. Metalworking.* objects formed by spinning. [1910–15; SPUN + WARE[1]]

spun′ yarn′, 1. yarn produced by spinning fibers into a continuous strand. **2.** *Naut.* cord formed of rope yarns loosely twisted together, for serving ropes, bending sails, etc. [1350–1400; ME]

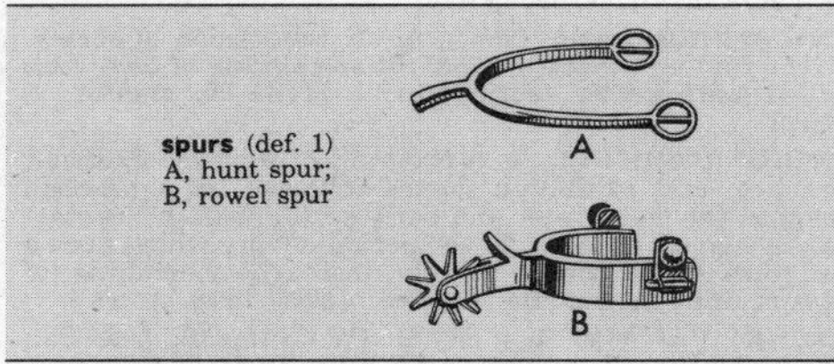

spurs (def. 1)
A, hunt spur;
B, rowel spur

spur[1] (spûr), *n., v.,* **spurred, spur·ring.** —*n.* **1.** a U-shaped device that slips over and straps to the heel of a boot and has a blunt, pointed, or roweled projection at the back for use by a mounted rider to urge a horse forward. **2.** anything that goads, impels, or urges, as to action, speed, or achievement. **3.** See **climbing iron. 4.** *Ornith.* a stiff, usually sharp, horny process on the leg of various birds, esp. the domestic rooster, or on the bend of the wing, as in jacanas and screamers. **5.** *Pathol.* a bony projection or exostosis. **6.** a sharp piercing or cutting instrument fastened to the leg of a gamecock in cockfighting; gaff. **7.** *Physical Geog.* a ridge or line of elevation projecting from or subordinate to the main body of a mountain or mountain range. **8.** something that projects and resembles or suggests a gaff; sharp projection. **9.** a short or stunted branch or shoot, as of a tree. **10.** *Typography.* a short, seriflike projection from the bottom of the short vertical stroke in the capital G in some fonts. **11.** See **wing dam. 12.** *Bot.* **a.** a slender, usually hollow, projection from some part of a flower, as from the calyx of the larkspur or the corolla of the violet. **b.** a short shoot bearing flowers, as in fruit trees. **13.** *Archit.* **a.** a short wooden brace, usually temporary, for strengthening a post or some other part. **b.** any offset from a wall, as a buttress. **c.** griffe[2]. **14.** *Ceram.* a triangular support of refractory clay for an object being fired. **15.** *Railroads.* See **spur track. 16. on the spur of the moment,** without deliberation; impulsively; suddenly: *We headed for the beach on the spur of the moment.* **17. win one's spurs,** to achieve distinction or success for the first time; prove one's ability or worth: *Our team hasn't won its spurs yet.* —*v.t.* **18.** to prick with or as if with a spur or spurs; incite or urge on: *The rider spurred his mount ruthlessly. Appreciation spurs ambition.* **19.** to strike or wound with the spur, as a gamecock. **20.** to furnish with spurs or a spur. —*v.i.* **21.** to goad or urge one's horse with spurs or a spur; ride quickly. **22.** to proceed hurriedly; press forward: *We spurred onward through the night.* [bef. 900; (n.) ME *spure,* OE *spura;* c. OHG *sporo,* ON *spori* spur; akin to SPURN; (v.) ME *spuren,* deriv. of the n.] —**spur′less,** *adj.* —**spur′like′,** *adj.* —**spur′rer,** *n.*
—**Syn. 1, 2.** goad. **2.** incitement, stimulus, incentive, inducement, provocation, instigation. **18.** goad, provoke, stimulate, impel, inspire, induce, instigate.
—**Ant. 18.** discourage.

spur[2] (spûr), *n. Papermaking.* a batch of newly made rag-paper sheets. [1880–85; orig. uncert.]

spur′ blight′, *Plant Pathol.* a disease of raspberries, characterized by reddish-brown spots on the stems, caused by a fungus, *Didymella applanata.*

spur′ gall′, a hairless and indurated area or gall on the side of a horse, caused by the irritation of a spur. [1545–55]

spurge (spûrj), *n.* any of numerous plants of the genus *Euphorbia,* having a milky juice and flowers with no petals or sepals. Cf. **spurge family.** [1350–1400; ME < MF *espurge,* n. deriv. of *espurgier* to cleanse < L *expurgāre.* See EX-[1], PURGE]

spur′ gear′, *Mach.* a gear having straight teeth cut on the rim parallel to the axis of rotation. Also called **spur wheel.** [1815–25]

spur gear

spur′ gear′ing. 1. a system of spur gears. **2.** any system of gears with parallel axes of rotation. [1835–45]

spurge′ fam′ily, the large plant family Euphorbiaceae, characterized by herbaceous plants, shrubs, and trees having milky juice, simple alternate leaves or no leaves, usually petalless flowers often with showy bracts, and capsular fruit, and including cassava, croton, crown-of-thorns, poinsettia, snow-on-the-mountain, spurge, and the plants that produce castor oil, rubber, and tung oil.

Spur·geon (spûr′jən), *n.* **Charles Had·don** (had′n), 1834–92, English Baptist preacher.

spu·ri·ous (spyŏŏr′ē əs), *adj.* **1.** not genuine, authentic, or true; not from the claimed, pretended, or proper source; counterfeit. **2.** *Biol.* (of two or more parts, plants, etc.) having a similar appearance but a different structure. **3.** of illegitimate birth; bastard. [1590–1600; < L *spurius* bastard, perh. < Etruscan; see -OUS] —**spu′ri·ous·ly,** *adv.* —**spu′ri·ous·ness,** *n.*
—**Syn. 1.** false, sham, bogus, mock, feigned, phony; meretricious, deceitful. —**Ant. 1.** genuine.

spu′rious wing′, alula (def. 1).

spurn (spûrn), *v.t.* **1.** to reject with disdain; scorn. **2.** to treat with contempt; despise. **3.** to kick or trample with the foot. —*v.i.* **4.** to show disdain or contempt; scorn something. —*n.* **5.** disdainful rejection. **6.** contemptuous treatment. **7.** a kick. [1250–1300; (v.) ME *spurnen,* OE *spurnan;* c. OS, OHG *spurnan,* ON *sporna* to kick; akin to L *spernere* to put away; (n.) ME: a kick, contemptuous stroke, deriv. of the n.] —**spurn′er,** *n.*
—**Syn. 1.** See **refuse**[1]. **6.** contumely. —**Ant. 1.** accept.

spur-of-the-mo·ment (spûr′əv *th*ə mō′mənt), *adj.* occurring or done without advance preparation or deliberation; extemporaneous; unplanned: *a spur-of-the-moment decision.* [1800–10]

spurred (spûrd), *adj.* **1.** having a spur or spurs. **2.** bearing spurs or spurlike spines. [1350–1400; ME; see SPUR[1], -ED[3]]

spur·rey (spûr′ē, spur′ē), *n., pl.* **-ries.** spurry.

spur·ri·er (spûr′ē ər, spur′-), *n.* a maker of spurs. [1350–1400; ME *sporier.* See SPUR[1], -IER[1]]

spur·ry (spûr′ē, spur′ē), *n., pl.* **-ries. 1.** any of several plants belonging to the genus *Spergula,* of the pink family, esp. *S. arvensis,* having white flowers and numerous linear leaves. **2.** any of various allied or similar plants. [1570–80; SPUR[1] + -Y[1]]

spurt (spûrt), *v.i.* **1.** to gush or issue suddenly in a stream or jet, as a liquid; spout. **2.** to show marked, usually increased, activity or energy for a short period: *The runners spurted forward in the last lap of the race.* —*v.t.* **3.** to expel or force out suddenly in a stream or jet, as a liquid; spout. —*n.* **4.** a sudden, forceful gush or jet. **5.** a marked increase of effort for a short period or distance, as in running, rowing, etc. **6.** a sudden burst or outburst, as of activity, energy, or feeling. Also, **spirt.** [1560–70; var. of *spirt;* orig. uncert.] —**spurt′er,** *n.* —**spur′tive,** *adj.* —**spur′tive·ly,** *adv.*
—**Syn. 1.** well, spring. See **flow. 4.** spout. —**Ant. 1.** drip, ooze.

spur·tle (spûr′tl), *n. Chiefly Scot.* a stick used to stir porridge. [1540–50; *spurt-* (by metathesis from SPRIT) + -LE]

spur′ track′, *Railroads.* a short branch track leading from the main track, and connected with it at one end only. Also called **spur, stub track.** [1880–85]

spur′ wheel′. See **spur gear.** [1725–35]

sput·nik (spŏŏt′nik, sput′-; *Russ.* spōōt′nyik), *n.* (*sometimes cap.*) any of a series of Soviet earth-orbiting

CONCISE ETYMOLOGY KEY: <, descended or borrowed from; >, whence; b., blend of, blended; c., cognate with; cf., compare; deriv., derivative; equiv., equivalent; imit., imitative; obl., oblique; r., replacing; s., stem; sp., spelling, spelled; resp., respelling, respelled; trans., translation; ?, origin unknown; *, unattested; ‡, probably earlier than. See the full key inside the front cover.

satellites: *Sputnik I was the world's first space satellite.* [1957; < Russ *spútnik* satellite, traveling companion, equiv. to *s-* together, with + *put'* way, route + *-nik* agent suffix (cf. -NIK)]

sput·ter (sput′ər), *v.i.* **1.** to make explosive popping or sizzling sounds. **2.** to emit particles, sparks, etc., forcibly or explosively, esp. accompanied by sputtering sounds. **3.** to eject particles of saliva, food, etc., from the mouth in a light spray, as when speaking angrily or excitedly. **4.** to utter or spit out words or sounds explosively or incoherently, as when angry or flustered. —*v.t.* **5.** to emit (anything) forcibly and in small particles, as if by spitting: *The fire sputtered cinders.* **6.** to eject (saliva, food, etc.) in small particles explosively and involuntarily, as in excitement. **7.** to utter explosively and incoherently. —*n.* **8.** the act or sound of sputtering. **9.** explosive, incoherent utterance. **10.** matter ejected in sputtering. [1590–1600; *sput-* (var. of SPOUT) + -ER[6]; c. D *sputteren*] —**sput′ter·er,** *n.* —**sput′ter·ing·ly,** *adv.*

sput·ter·ing (sput′ər ing), *n. Engin., Electronics.* a process that uses ions of an inert gas to dislodge atoms from the surface of a crystalline material, the atoms then being electrically deposited to form an extremely thin coating on a glass, metal, plastic, or other surface. [1900–05; SPUTTER + -ING[1]]

spu·tum (spyōō′təm), *n., pl.* **-ta** (-tə). matter, as saliva mixed with mucus or pus, expectorated from the lungs and respiratory passages. [1685–95; < L *spūtum,* n. use of neut. of *spūtus,* ptp. of *spuere* to spit, equiv. to *spū-* var. s. + *-tus* ptp. suffix]

Spuy′ten Duy′vil Creek′ (spīt′n dī′vəl), a channel in New York City at the north end of Manhattan Island, connecting the Hudson and Harlem rivers.

spy (spī), *n., pl.* **spies,** *v.,* **spied, spy·ing.** —*n.* **1.** a person employed by a government to obtain secret information or intelligence about another, usually hostile, country, esp. with reference to military or naval affairs. **2.** a person who keeps close and secret watch on the actions and words of another or others. **3.** a person who seeks to obtain confidential information about the activities, plans, methods, etc., of an organization or person, esp. one who is employed for this purpose by a competitor: *an industrial spy.* **4.** the act of spying. —*v.i.* **5.** to observe secretively or furtively with hostile intent (often fol. by *on* or *upon*). **6.** to act as a spy; engage in espionage. **7.** to be on the lookout; keep watch. **8.** to search for or examine something closely or carefully. —*v.t.* **9.** to catch sight of suddenly; espy; descry: *to spy a rare bird overhead.* **10.** to discover or find out by observation or scrutiny (often fol. by *out*). **11.** to observe (a person, place, enemy, etc.) secretively or furtively with hostile intent. **12.** to inspect or examine or to search or look for closely or carefully. [1200–50; (v.) ME *spien,* aph. var. of *espien* to ESPY; (n.) ME, aph. var. of *espy* a spy < OF *espie*] —**spy′ship,** *n.*

spy·glass (spī′glas′, -gläs′), *n.* a small telescope. [1700–10; SPY + GLASS]

spy·hop (spī′hop′), *n., v.,* **-hopped, -hop·ping.** *Animal Behav.* —*n.* **1. a.** a vertical half-rise out of the water performed by a whale in order to view the surroundings. **b.** a springing bounce in tall grasses performed by certain land mammals, as foxes and wolves, to view the surroundings. —*v.i.* **2.** to perform such a rise or bounce. [SPY + HOP[1]]

spy·mas·ter (spī′mas′tər, -mä′stər), *n.* an espionage agent who directs a network of subordinate agents. [1940–45; SPY + MASTER]

Spy·ri (shpē′rē, spē′-), *n.* **Jo·han·na** (*Ger.* yô hä′nä; *Eng.* jō han′ə, -an′ə), 1827–1901, Swiss author.

Sq., **1.** Squadron. **2.** Square (of a city or town).

sq., **1.** sequence. **2.** the following; the following one. [< L *sequēns*] **3.** squadron. **4.** square.

sq. cm, square centimeter; square centimeters.

sqd., squad.

sq. ft., square foot; square feet.

sq. in., square inch; square inches.

sq. km, square kilometer; square kilometers.

sq. m, square meter; square meters.

sq. mi., square mile; square miles.

sq. mm, square millimeter; square millimeters.

sqq., the following; the following ones. [< L *sequentia*]

sq. r., square rod; square rods.

squab (skwob), *n. pl.* **squabs,** (*esp. collectively for 1*) **squab,** *adj.* —*n.* **1.** a nestling pigeon, marketed when fully grown but still unfledged. **2.** a short, stout person. **3.** a thickly stuffed, soft cushion. —*adj.* **4.** short and thick or broad. **5.** (of a bird) unfledged or newly hatched. [1630–40; prob. < Scand; cf. Sw dial. *skvabb* loose, fat flesh, *skvabba* fat woman, Norw *skvabb* soft wet mass]

squab·ble (skwob′əl), *v.,* **-bled, -bling,** *n.* —*v.i.* **1.** to engage in a petty quarrel. —*v.t.* **2.** *Print.* to disarrange and mix (composed type). —*n.* **3.** a petty quarrel. [1595–1605; prob. < Scand; cf. Sw dial. *skvabbel* a quarrel, gossip, Norw dial. *skvabba* to prattle] —**squab′bler,** *n.* —**squab′bling·ly,** *adv.*
—**Syn. 1.** quarrel, wrangle, bicker, fight.

squab·by (skwob′ē), *adj.,* **-bi·er, -bi·est.** short and stout; squat. [1745–55; SQUAB + -Y[1]]

squad (skwod), *n., v.,* **squad·ded, squad·ding.** —*n.* **1.** a small number of soldiers, commonly 10 privates, a staff sergeant, and a corporal; the smallest military unit. **2.** a group of police officers, esp. one organized to deal with a particular area of law enforcement: *drug squad; fraud squad.* **3.** any small group or party of persons engaged in a common enterprise. **4.** a sports team or a group of players from which a team is selected. —*v.t.* **5.** to form into squads. **6.** to assign to a squad. [1640–50; < F *esquade,* alter. of *esquadre* < Sp *escuadra* SQUARE; so called from square shape of the formation]

squad′ car′, an automobile used by police officers, equipped with a radiotelephone for communicating with police headquarters. Also called **cruise car, patrol car, police car.** [1930–35, *Amer.*]

squad·der (skwod′ər), *n.* a member of a squad: *riot squadder; fire squadder.* [1580–90; SQUAD + -ER[1]]

squad·ron (skwod′rən), *n.* **1.** a portion of a naval fleet or a detachment of warships; a subdivision of a fleet. **2.** an armored cavalry or cavalry unit consisting of two or more troops, a headquarters, and various supporting units. **3.** (in the U.S. Air Force). **a.** the basic administrative and tactical unit, smaller than a group and composed of two or more flights. **b.** a flight formation. **4.** a number of persons grouped or united together for some purpose; group. —*v.t.* **5.** to form into a squadron or squadrons; marshal or array in or as if in squadrons. [1555–65; < It *squadrone,* equiv. to *squadr(a)* SQUARE + *-one* aug. suffix]

squad′ room′, **1.** a room in a police station where police officers assemble, as for inspection, roll call, or duty assignments. **2.** a room in a barracks in which a number of soldiers sleep. [1940–45]

squads·man (skwodz′mən), *n., pl.* **-men.** a member of a squad or team. [SQUAD + -'S[1] + -MAN]

squa·lene (skwā′lēn), *n. Biochem.* an oil, $C_{30}H_{50}$, intermediate in the synthesis of cholesterol, obtained for use in manufacturing pharmaceuticals. [1925–30; < NL *Squal(us)* name of a genus of sharks (the liver of which yields the oil), L: a kind of fish + -ENE]

squal·id (skwol′id, skwô′lid), *adj.* **1.** foul and repulsive, as from lack of care or cleanliness; neglected and filthy. **2.** wretched; miserable; degraded; sordid. [1585–95; < L *squālidus* dirty, equiv. to *squāl(ēre)* to be dirty, encrusted + *-idus* -ID[4]] —**squal′id·ly,** *adv.* —**squal′·id·ness, squa·lid·i·ty** (skwo lid′i tē), *n.*
—**Syn. 1.** unclean. See **dirty.**

squall[1] (skwôl), *n.* **1.** a sudden, violent gust of wind, often accompanied by rain, snow, or sleet. **2.** a sudden disturbance or commotion. —*v.i.* **3.** to blow as a squall. [1690–1700; perh. special use of SQUALL[2]] —**squall′ish,** *adj.*

squall[2] (skwôl), *v.i.* **1.** to cry or scream loudly and violently: *The hungry baby began to squall.* —*v.t.* **2.** to utter in a screaming tone. —*n.* **3.** the act or sound of squalling: *The baby's squall was heard next door.* [1625–35; perh. < ON *skvala* shriek, cry; cf. Sw, Norw *skvala* splash, stream] —**squall′er,** *n.*

squall′ line′, *Meteorol.* a line or extended narrow region within which squalls or thunderstorms occur, often several hundred miles long.

squal·ly (skwô′lē), *adj.,* **-li·er, -li·est.** **1.** characterized by squalls. **2.** stormy; threatening. [1710–20; SQUALL[1] + -Y[1]]

squal·or (skwol′ər, skwô′lər), *n.* the condition of being squalid; filth and misery. [1615–25; < L *squālor* dirtiness, equiv. to *squāl(ēre)* to be dirty, encrusted + *-or* -OR[1]]
—**Syn.** wretchedness. —**Ant.** splendor.

squam-, var. of **squamo-** before a vowel: *squamation.*

squa·ma (skwā′mə), *n., pl.* **-mae** (-mē). a scale or scalelike part, as of epidermis or bone. [1700–10; < L *squāma* scale]

squa·mate (skwā′māt), *adj.* provided or covered with squamae or scales; scaly. [1820–30; < LL *squāmātus.* See SQUAMA, -ATE[1]]

squa·ma·tion (skwā mā′shən), *n.* **1.** the state of being squamate. **2.** the arrangement of the squamae or scales of an animal. [1880–85; SQUAM- + -ATION]

squa·mi·form (skwā′mə fôrm′), *adj.* shaped like a scale. [1820–30; SQUAM- + -I- + -FORM]

Squa·mish (skwom′ish, skwô′mish), *n., pl.* **-mish·es,** (*esp. collectively*) **-mish** for 1. **1.** a member of a North American Indian people of the southwestern coast of British Columbia. **2.** the Salishan language of the Squamish. Also, **Squauwmish.**

squamo-, a combining form of **squama:** *squamocellular.* Also, *esp. before a vowel,* **squam-.**

squa·mo·sal (skwə mō′səl), *adj.* **1.** *Anat.* of or pertaining to the thin, scalelike portion of the temporal bone that is situated on the side of the skull above and behind the ear. **2.** *Zool.* pertaining to a corresponding bone in other vertebrates. **3.** squamous. —*n.* **4.** a squamosal bone. [1840–50; < L *squāmōs(us)* squamous + -AL[1]]

squa·mous (skwā′məs), *adj.* **1.** covered with or formed of squamae or scales. **2.** scalelike. Also, **squa·mosal, squa·mose** (skwā′mōs, skwə mōs′). [1535–45; < L *squāmōsus.* See SQUAMA, -OUS] —**squa′mous·ly, squa′mose·ly,** *adv.* —**squa′mous·ness, squa′mose·ness,** *n.*

squa′mous epithe′lium, *Biol.* epithelium consisting of one or more layers of scalelike cells.

squam·u·lose (skwam′yə lōs′, skwā′myə-), *adj.* furnished or covered with tiny scales. [1840–50; < L *squāmula* small scale (*squām(a)* scale + *-ula* -ULE) + -OSE[1]]

squan·der (skwon′dər), *v.t.* **1.** to spend or use (money, time, etc.) extravagantly or wastefully (often fol. by *away*). **2.** to scatter. —*n.* **3.** extravagant or wasteful expenditure. [1585–95; orig. uncert.] —**squan′der·er,** *n.* —**squan′der·ing·ly,** *adv.*
—**Syn. 1.** waste, dissipate, lavish. See **spend.** —**Ant. 1.** save.

Squan·to (skwon′tō), *n.* died 1622, North American Indian of the Narragansett tribe: interpreter for the Pilgrims. Also called **Tisquantum.**

square (skwâr), *n., v.,* **squared, squar·ing,** *adj.,* **squar·er, squar·est,** *adv.* —*n.* **1.** a rectangle having all four sides of equal length. **2.** anything having this form or a form approximating it, as a city block, rectangular piece of candy, etc. **3.** an open area or plaza in a city or town, formed by the meeting or intersecting of two or more streets and often planted with grass, trees, etc., in the center. **4.** a rectangularly shaped area on a game board, as in chess or checkers. **5.** a try square, T square, or the like. **6.** *Math.* **a.** the second power of a quantity, expressed as $a^2 = a \times a$, where a is the quantity. **b.** a quantity that is the second power of another: *Four is the square of two.* **7.** *Slang.* a person who is ignorant of or uninterested in current fads, ideas, manners, tastes, etc.; an old-fashioned, conventional, or conservative person. **8.** *Mil.* (formerly) a body of troops drawn up in quadrilateral form. **9.** *Building Trades.* a unit of measure for roofing materials, equal to 100 square feet (9.3 sq. m). **10.** a flower bud of the cotton plant. **11.** *Naut.* the area at the bottom of a hatchway. **12.** Usually, **squares.** *Informal.* a square meal: *to get three squares a day.* **13.** *Astrol.* a situation in which two heavenly bodies or groups of heavenly bodies have celestial longitudes differing by 90 degrees, an aspect indicative of internal tension with an equally strong and conflicting need for adjustment. **14.** *Obs.* a pattern, standard, or example. **15. on the square, a.** at right angles. **b.** *Informal.* straightforward; honest; just: *Their dealings with us have always been on the square.* **16. out of square, a.** not at right angles. **b.** not in agreement; incorrect; irregular: *The inspector's conclusions are out of square with his earlier report.*
—*v.t.* **17.** to reduce to square, rectangular, or cubical form (often fol. by *off*): *He squared off the log to make a timber for his house.* **18.** to mark out in one or more squares or rectangles. **19.** to test with measuring devices for deviation from a right angle, straight line, or plane surface. **20.** *Math.* **a.** to multiply (a number or quantity) by itself; raise to the second power. **b.** to describe or find a square that is equivalent in area to: *to square a circle.* **21.** to bring to the form of a right angle or right angles; set at right angles to something else. **22.** to even the score of (a contest): *to square a game.* **23.** to set (the shoulders and back) in an erect posture so they form an angle similar to a right angle. **24.** to make straight, level, or even: *Square the cloth on the table.* **25.** to regulate, as by a standard; adapt; adjust. **26.** to adjust harmoniously or satisfactorily (often fol. by *with*): *How could you square such actions with your conscience?* **27.** to balance; pay off; settle: *to square a debt.* **28.** *Slang.* to secure a desired action or attitude by means of bribery; bribe.
—*v.i.* **29.** to accord or agree (often fol. by *with*): *Your theory does not square with the facts.* **30.** to settle, even, or balance a matter, as by paying a bill, returning a favor, or tying a score. **31.** (of a cotton plant) to form buds. **32. square around,** *Baseball.* (of a bunter) to shift the feet and body from a conventional batting stance to a position facing the pitcher, with the bat held across and in front of the body. **33. square away, a.** *Naut.* to arrange the yards so as to sail before the wind. **b.** to prepare; get ready: *Square away for dinner.* **c.** to assume a position of defense or offense: *The wrestlers squared away for the first fall.* **d.** to organize or complete satisfactorily; put in order: *I want to square away the work before going on vacation.* **34. square off, a.** to assume a posture of defense or offense, as in boxing: *They squared off for a fight.* **b.** to prepare to dispute with another; show signs of opposition or resistance: *The governor and the legislature are squaring off over the landfill issue.* **35. square the circle,** to strive without chance of success; attempt the impossible. **36. square up,** to pay or settle an account, bill, etc.: *We squared up with the cashier and checked out of the hotel.*
—*adj.* **37.** formed by or as a right angle; having some part or parts rectangular: *a square corner.* **38.** having four sides and four right angles in two dimensions or three pairs of parallel sides meeting at right angles in three dimensions; having each dimension in the shape of a square or rectangle and all angles right angles: *a square box.* **39.** noting any unit of area measurement having the form of a square and designated by a unit of linear measurement forming a side of the square: *one square foot.* **40.** noting a system of area measurement in terms of such units. **41.** (of an area) equal to a square of a specified length on a side: *five miles square.* **42.** at right angles, or perpendicular. **43.** *Naut.* at right angles to the mast and the keel, as a yard. **44.** having a square or rectangular section: *a square bar.* **45.** having a solid, sturdy form, esp. when characterized by a rectilinear or angular outline. **46.** straight, level, or even, as a surface. **47.** leaving no balance of debt on either side; having all accounts settled: *I'm all square with my landlord.* **48.** just, fair, or honest. **49.** straightforward, direct, or unequivocal. **50.** *Slang.* conventional or conservative in style or outlook; not hip.
—*adv.* **51.** so as to be square; in square or rectangular form. **52.** at right angles. **53.** fairly or honestly. **54.** directly or straightforwardly. [1250–1300; (n.) ME < OF *esquar(r)e* < VL **exquadra,* deriv. of **exquadrāre* (L *ex-* EX-[1] + *quadrāre* to square; see QUADRATE); (v.) ME *squaren* < OF *esquarrer* < VL **exquadrāre;* (adj.) ME < OF *esquarré,* ptp. of *esquarrer;* (adv.) deriv. of the adj.] —**squar′a·ble,** *adj.* —**square′like′,** *adj.* —**square′·ness,** *n.* —**squar′er,** *n.*
—**Syn. 3.** place, park. **24.** straighten. **25.** rectify. **47.** balanced. **49.** downright, straight.

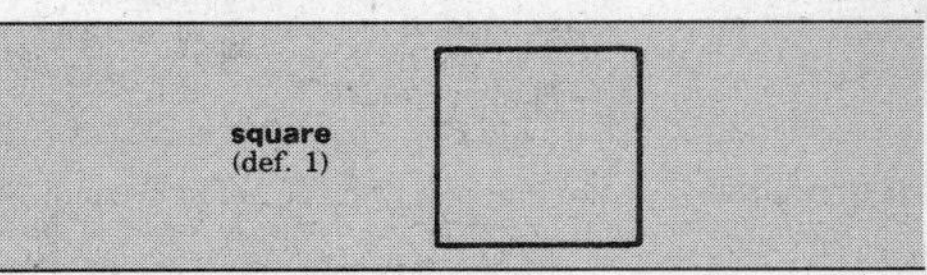
square (def. 1)

square′ and rab′bet, annulet (def. 1).

square′ brack′et, bracket (def. 3). [1885–90]

square′ cen′timeter, a unit of area measurement equal to a square measuring one centimeter on each side. *Abbr.:* cm^2, sq. cm

square′ dance′, 1. a dance by a set of four couples arranged in a square or in some set form. 2. hoedown (def. 1). [1865–70] —**square′ danc′er.** —**square′ danc′ing.**

square-dance (skwâr′dans′, -däns′), *v.i.,* **-danced, -danc•ing.** 1. to perform or participate in a square dance. 2. to participate in a hoedown. [1955–60]

square′ deal′, a fair and honest arrangement or transaction. [1880–85, *Amer.*]

Square′ Deal′, *U.S. Hist.* the stated policy of President Theodore Roosevelt, originally promising fairness in all dealings with labor and management and later extended to include other groups.

squared′ pa′per, graph paper with a pattern of squares formed by lines crossing at right angles. [1900–05]

squared′ ring′, *Informal.* See **boxing ring.** Also called **squared′ cir′cle.**

squared′ splice′. See **square splice.**

square′ foot′, a unit of area measurement equal to a square measuring one foot on each side; 0.0929 square meters. *Abbr.:* ft^2, sq. ft.

square•head (skwâr′hed′), *n. Slang.* 1. a stupid person. 2. *Disparaging and Offensive.* **a.** a German or Dutch person. **b.** a Scandinavian, esp. a Swede. [1905–10, *Amer.*; SQUARE + HEAD]

square′ inch′, a unit of area measurement equal to a square measuring one inch on each side; 6.452 square centimeters. *Abbr.:* in^2, sq. in.

square′ kilo′meter, a unit of area measurement equal to a square measuring one kilometer on each side. *Abbr.:* km^2, sq. km

square′ knot′, a common knot in which the ends come out alongside of the standing parts. See illus. under **knot.** [1865–70]

square-law (skwâr′lô′), *adj. Electronics.* of or pertaining to an electronic circuit or device that produces an output voltage proportional to the square of its input voltage over the range of input voltages for which it is designed to function: *square-law detector.* [1925–30]

square′ leg′, *Cricket.* 1. the position of a fielder on the left of the batsman and almost on the opposite side of the wicket. 2. the fielder occupying this position. Also, **square′-leg′.** [1850–55]

square•ly (skwâr′lē), *adv.* 1. in a square shape, form, or manner. 2. directly; without evasion; in a straight or straightforward manner: *to face a problem squarely.* 3. in an honest or open manner; straightforwardly; fairly. 4. firmly; solidly; unequivocally. [1550–60; SQUARE + -LY]

square′ ma′trix, *Math.* a matrix in which the number of rows is equal to the number of columns. [1930–35]

square′ meal′, a nourishing or filling meal: *You'll feel better after you've had a square meal.* [1830–40]

square′ meas′ure, a system of units for the measurement of surfaces or areas. [1720–30]

square′ me′ter, a unit of area measurement equal to a square measuring one meter on each side. *Abbr.:* m^2, sq. m

square′ mile′, a unit of area measurement equal to a square measuring one mile on each side; 2.59 square kilometers. *Abbr.:* mi^2, sq. mi.

square′ mil′limeter, a unit of area measurement equal to a square measuring one millimeter on each side. *Abbr.:* mm^2, sq. mm

square′ num′ber, a number that is the square of another integer, as 1 of 1, 4 of 2, 9 of 3, etc. [1550–60]

square′ of opposi′tion, *Logic.* a diagrammatic representation of the opposition of categorical propositions. [1860–65]

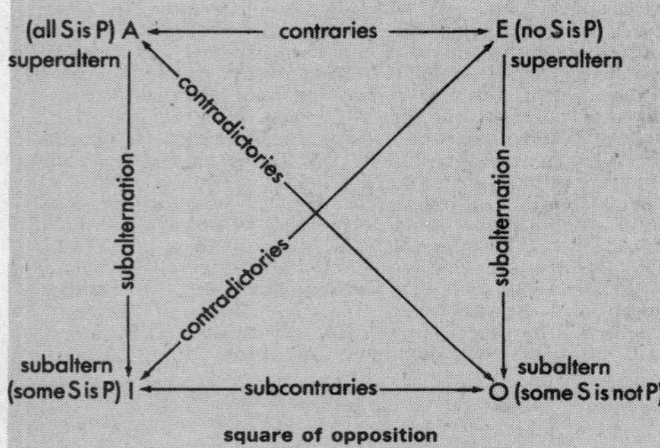

square of opposition

square′ one′, a starting point; initial stage or step: *If this plan fails, we'll have to go back to square one.* [1955–60; alluding to board games in which a player is penalized by being forced to return to the starting point]

square′ pian′o, a piano with a rectangular, horizontal body.

square-rigged (skwâr′rigd′), *adj. Naut.* having square sails as the principal sails. [1760–70] —**square′-rig′ger,** *n.*

CONCISE ETYMOLOGY KEY: <, descended or borrowed from; >, whence; b., blend of, blended; c., cognate with; cf., compare; deriv., derivative; equiv., equivalent; imit., imitative; obl., oblique; r., replacing; s., stem; sp., spelling, spelled; resp., respelling, respelled; trans., translation; ?, origin unknown; *, unattested; ‡, probably earlier than. See the full key inside the front cover.

square′ rod′, a unit of area measurement equal to a square measuring one rod on each side.

square′ root′, a quantity of which a given quantity is the square: *The quantities* +6 *and* −6 *are square roots of 36 since* $(+6)\times(+6)=36$ *and* $(-6)\times(-6)=36$. [1550–60]

square′ sail′, *Naut.* a sail set beneath a horizontal yard, the normal position of which, when not trimmed to the wind, is directly athwartships. See diag. under **sail.** [1590–1600]

square′ ser′if, *Typography.* a font of type having serifs with a weight equal to or greater than that of the main strokes. Cf. **Egyptian** (def. 5).

square′ set′, *Mining.* a set having 12 timbers joined to form eight 90° solid angles. [1815–25, *Amer.*]

square′ shake′. See **square deal.**

square′ shoot′er, *Informal.* an honest, fair person. [1915–20] —**square′ shoot′ing.**

square-shoul•dered (skwâr′shōl′dərd), *adj.* having the shoulders held back, giving a straight form to the upper part of the back. [1815–25]

square′ splice′, *Carpentry.* a scarf joint between two pieces, having the form of a half-lap joint with a thicker and a thinner section for each piece, the thicker one being at the end: used to resist tension.

squares•ville (skwârz′vil), *n. Slang.* a thing, place, etc., regarded as conventional, unfashionable, or conservative. [1955–60, *Amer.*; SQUARE + -s- + *-ville,* formed by analogy with placenames ending in possessive *-s* (see *'s*[1]) and the suffix *-ville*]

square•tail (skwâr′tāl′), *n.* any of several fishes of the genus *Tetragonurus,* inhabiting deep waters of tropical and temperate seas, having a squarish tail and an armor of tough, bony scales. [1835–45; SQUARE + TAIL[1]]

square•toed (skwâr′tōd′), *adj.* 1. having a broad, square toe, as a shoe. 2. old-fashioned or conservative in habits, ideas, etc.; prim. [1775–85; SQUARE + TOED] —**square′-toed′ness,** *n.*

square-toes (skwâr′tōz′), *n.* (*used with a singular v.*) an old-fashioned or strait-laced person. [1765–75]

square′ wave′, *Math., Physics.* a graph, function, vibration, etc., that is periodic and equal to one constant on one half of the period and a different constant, which may be zero, on the other half. [1930–35]

square′ yard′, a unit of area measurement equal to a square measuring one yard on each side; 0.8361 square meters. *Abbr.:* yd^2, sq. yd.

squar′ing the cir′cle. See **quadrature of the circle.**

squar•ish (skwâr′ish), *adj.* approximately square. [1735–45; SQUARE + -ISH[1]] —**squar′ish•ly,** *adv.* —**squar′ish•ness,** *n.*

s quark, *Physics.* See **strange quark.** [1975–80]

squar•rose (skwar′ōs, skwo rōs′), *adj. Biol.* denoting any rough or ragged surface. [1750–60; < L *squarrōsus* scurfy, scaly] —**squar′rose•ly,** *adv.*

squash[1] (skwosh, skwôsh), *v.t.* 1. to press into a flat mass or pulp; crush: *She squashed the flower under her heel.* 2. to suppress or put down; quash. 3. to silence or disconcert (someone), as with a crushing retort or emotional or psychological pressure. 4. to press forcibly against or cram into a small space; squeeze. —*v.i.* 5. to be pressed into a flat mass or pulp. 6. (of a soft, heavy body) to fall heavily. 7. to make a splashing sound; splash. 8. to be capable of being or likely to be squashed: *Tomatoes squash easily.* 9. to squeeze or crowd; crush. —*n.* 10. the act or sound of squashing. 11. the fact of squashing or of being squashed. 12. something squashed or crushed. 13. something soft and easily crushed. 14. Also called **squash′ rac′quets.** a game for two or four persons, similar to racquets but played on a smaller court and with a racket having a round head and a long handle. See illus. under **racket**[2]. 15. Also called **squash′ ten′nis.** a game for two persons, resembling squash racquets except that the ball is larger and livelier and the racket is shaped like a tennis racket. 16. *Brit.* a beverage made from fruit juice and soda water: *lemon squash.* [1555–65; < MF *esquasser* < VL **exquassāre.* See EX-[1], QUASH] —**squash′er,** *n.*
—**Syn. 2, 3.** quell, crush, repress.

squash[2] (skwosh, skwôsh), *n., pl.* **squash•es,** (*esp. collectively*) **squash.** 1. the fruit of any of various vinelike, tendril-bearing plants belonging to the genus *Curcurbita,* of the gourd family, as *C. moschata* or *C. pepo,* used as a vegetable. 2. any of these plants. [1635–45, *Amer.*; < Narragansett (E sp.) *askútasquash* (pl.)]

squash-blos•som (skwosh′blos′əm, skwôsh′-), *adj.* indicating or pertaining to a design or configuration resembling the flower of the squash plant, esp. as found in jewelry made by various American Indians. [1920–25]

squash′ bug′, a dark-brown bug, *Anasa tristis,* that sucks the sap from the leaves of squash, pumpkin, and other plants of the gourd family. [1840–50, *Amer.*]

squash′ vine′ bor′er, the larva of a clearwing moth, *Melittia satyriniformis,* that bores into the stems of squash and related plants.

squash•y (skwosh′ē, skwô′shē), *adj.,* **squash•i•er, squash•i•est.** 1. easily squashed; pulpy. 2. soft and wet, as the ground after rain. 3. having a squashed appearance. [1690–1700; SQUASH[1] + -Y[1]] —**squash′i•ly,** *adv.* —**squash′i•ness,** *n.*

squas•sa•tion (skwo sā′shən), *n.* a form of strappado in which the victim, with arms bound behind and feet heavily weighted, was jerked up and down at the end of a rope passed under the arms. [1725–35; < It *squassare* (to shake severely (< VL **exquassāre;* see SQUASH[1]) + -ATION]

squat (skwot), *v.,* **squat•ted** or **squat, squat•ting,** *adj.,* **squat•ter, squat•test,** *n.* —*v.i.* 1. to sit in a low or crouching position with the legs drawn up closely beneath or in front of the body; sit on one's haunches or heels. 2. to crouch down or cower, as an animal. 3. to settle on or occupy property, esp. otherwise unoccupied property, without any title, right, or payment of rent. 4. to settle on public land under government regulation, in order to acquire title. 5. *Naut.* (of a vessel, esp. a power vessel) to draw more water astern when in motion forward than when at rest. —*v.t.* 6. to cause to squat. 7. to occupy (property) as a squatter. —*adj.* 8. (of a person, animal, the body, etc.) short and thickset. 9. low and thick or broad: *The building had a squat shape.* 10. seated or being in a squatting position; crouching. —*n.* 11. the act or fact of squatting. 12. a squatting position or posture. 13. *Naut.* the tendency of a vessel to draw more water astern when in motion than when stationary. 14. *Slang.* doodly-squat. 15. a place occupied by squatters. [1250–1300; (v.) ME *squatten* < OF *esquater, esquatir,* equiv. to *es-* EX-[1] + *quatir* < VL **coactire* to compress, equiv. to L *coāct(us),* ptp. of *cōgere* to compress (*co-* co- + *ag(ere)* to drive + *-tus* ptp. suffix) + *-ire* inf. suffix; (n.) ME, deriv. of the v.; (adj.) ME: in a squatting position, orig., ptp. of the v.] —**squat′ly,** *adv.* —**squat′ness,** *n.*
—**Syn. 8.** dumpy, stocky, square.

squat•ter (skwot′ər), *n.* 1. a person or thing that squats. 2. a person who settles on land or occupies property without title, right, or payment of rent. 3. a person who settles on land under government regulation, in order to acquire title. [1775–85; SQUAT + -ER[1]] —**squat′ter•dom,** *n.*

squat′ter sov′ereignty, *U.S. Hist.* (used contemptuously by its opponents) See **popular sovereignty** (def. 2). [1850–55, *Amer.*]

squat′ter's right′, *Law Informal.* a claim to real property, esp. public land, that may be granted to a person who has openly possessed and continuously occupied it without legal authority for a prescribed period of years. [1855–60, *Amer.*]

squat•ty (skwot′ē), *adj.,* **-ti•er, -ti•est.** short and thick; low and broad. [1880–85; SQUAT + -Y[1]] —**squat′ti•ly,** *adv.* —**squat′ti•ness,** *n.*

squaw (skwô), *n.* 1. *Often Offensive.* a North American Indian woman, esp. a wife. 2. *Slang (disparaging and offensive).* **a.** a wife. **b.** any woman or girl. [1625–35, *Amer.*; < Massachusett (E sp.) *squa, ussqua* woman, younger woman < Proto-Algonquian **eθkwe·wa*]

squaw•bush (skwô′bo͝osh′), *n.* a rank-smelling, sprawling shrub, *Rhus trilobata malacophylla,* of the cashew family, native to California, having spikes of greenish flowers. [1825–35, *Amer.*; SQUAW + BUSH[1], so called from its use by the Indians]

squaw•fish (skwô′fish′), *n., pl.* (*esp. collectively*) **-fish,** (*esp. referring to two or more kinds or species*) **-fish•es.** 1. any of several large, voracious cyprinid fishes of the genus *Ptychocheilus,* inhabiting rivers of the western U.S. and Canada: the Colorado squawfish, *P. lucius,* is endangered. 2. a viviparous perch, *Embiotoca lateralis,* living off the Pacific Coast of the U.S. [1880–85, *Amer.*; SQUAW + FISH]

squaw′ huck′leberry, deerberry. [1855–60]

squawk (skwôk), *v.i.* 1. to utter a loud, harsh cry, as a duck or other fowl when frightened. 2. *Informal.* to complain loudly and vehemently. —*v.t.* 3. to utter or give forth with a squawk. —*n.* 4. a loud, harsh cry or sound. 5. *Informal.* a loud, vehement complaint. 6. the black-crowned night heron. See under **night heron.** [1815–25; b. SQUALL[2] and HAWK[3]] —**squawk′er,** *n.*
—**Syn. 2.** grumble, gripe, complain, yelp.

squawk′ box′, *Informal.* 1. the speaker of a public-address system or an intercom system; loudspeaker. 2. an intercom system. [1940–45]

squawk•y (skwô′kē), *adj.,* **squawk•i•er, squawk•i•est.** unpleasantly discordant or harsh in sound; cacophonous. [1895–1900; SQUAWK + -Y[1]]

squaw′ man′, *Offensive.* a white or other non-Indian man married to a North American Indian woman. [1865–70, *Amer.*]

Squauw•mish (skwô′mish), *n., pl.* **-mish•es,** (*esp. collectively*) **-mish.** Squamish.

squaw•root (skwô′ro͞ot′, -ro͝ot′), *n.* 1. a fleshy, leafless plant, *Conopholis americana,* of the broomrape family, native to eastern North America, having a stout, yellowish, conelike stalk of lipped flowers, and growing in clusters, esp. under oaks. 2. the blue cohosh. See under **cohosh.** [1805–15; SQUAW + ROOT[1], from its former use by Indians in treating women]

squeak (skwēk), *n.* 1. a short, sharp, shrill cry; a sharp, high-pitched sound. 2. *Informal.* opportunity; chance: *their last squeak to correct the manuscript.* 3. an escape from defeat, danger, death, or destruction (usually qualified by *narrow* or *close*). —*v.i.* 4. to utter or emit a squeak or squeaky sound. 5. *Slang.* to confess or turn informer; squeal. —*v.t.* 6. to utter or sound with a squeak or squeaks. 7. **squeak by** or **through,** to succeed, survive, pass, win, etc., by a very narrow margin: *They can barely squeak by on their income. The team managed to squeak through.* [1350–1400; ME *squeken,* perh. < Scand; cf. Sw *skväka* to croak] —**squeak′ing•ly,** *adv.*

squeak•er (skwē′kər), *n.* 1. a person or thing that squeaks. 2. *Informal.* a contest or game won by a very small margin. 3. *Informal.* a dangerous situation. [1635–45; SQUEAK + -ER[1]]

squeak•y (skwē′kē), *adj.,* **squeak•i•er, squeak•i•est.** squeaking; tending to squeak: *His squeaky shoes could be heard across the lobby.* [1860–65; SQUEAK + -Y[1]] —**squeak′i•ly,** *adv.* —**squeak′i•ness,** *n.*

squeak•y-clean (skwē′kē klēn′), *adj. Informal.* 1. scrupulously clean. 2. virtuous, wholesome, and above reproach: *a squeaky-clean reputation.*

squeal (skwēl), *n.* 1. a somewhat prolonged, sharp, shrill cry, as of pain, fear, or surprise. 2. *Slang.* **a.** an instance of informing against someone. **b.** a protest or complaint; beef. —*v.i.* 3. to utter or emit a squeal or squealing sound. 4. *Slang.* **a.** to turn informer; inform. **b.** to protest or complain; beef. —*v.t.* 5. to utter or produce with a squeal. [1250–1300; ME *squelen;* imit.] **—squeal′er,** *n.*

squeam·ish (skwē′mish), *adj.* **1.** fastidious or dainty. **2.** easily shocked by anything slightly immodest; prudish. **3.** excessively particular or scrupulous as to the moral aspect of things. **4.** easily nauseated or disgusted: *to get squeamish at the sight of blood.* [1400–50; late ME *squemish,* alter. (conformed to -ISH[1]) of *squemes, squaymes,* alter. of *squaymous* < AF *escoymous;* ulterior orig. uncert.] **—squeam′ish·ly,** *adv.* **—squeam′ish·ness,** *n.*
—Syn. 1. modest. **3.** finical, finicky, delicate, exacting. **—Ant. 1–3.** bold.

squee·gee (skwē′jē, skwē jē′), *n., v.,* **-geed, -gee·ing.** *—n.* **1.** an implement edged with rubber or the like, for removing water from windows after washing, sweeping water from wet decks, etc. **2.** a similar and smaller device, as for removing excess water from photographic negatives or prints or for forcing paint, ink, etc., through a porous surface, as in serigraphy. *—v.t.* **3.** to sweep, scrape, or press with or as if with a squeegee. **4.** to force (paint, ink, etc.) through a screen in making a silk-screen print. Also, **squilgee, squillagee.** [1835–45; orig. a nautical term; of obscure orig.]

squeez·a·ble (skwē′zə bəl), *adj.* **1.** easily squeezed, compressed, or the like. **2.** (of a person) susceptible to intimidation or pressure, esp. by blackmail. [1805–15; SQUEEZE + -ABLE] **—squeez′a·bil′i·ty, squeez′a·ble·ness,** *n.* **—squeez′a·bly,** *adv.*

squeeze (skwēz), *v.,* **squeezed, squeez·ing,** *n.* *—v.t.* **1.** to press forcibly together; compress. **2.** to apply pressure to in order to extract juice, sap, or the like: *to squeeze an orange.* **3.** to force out, extract, or procure by pressure: *to squeeze juice from an orange.* **4.** to thrust forcibly; force by pressure; cram: *to squeeze three suits into a small suitcase.* **5.** to fit into a small or crowded space or timespan: *The doctor will try to squeeze you in between appointments.* **6.** to enclose (another person's hand, arm, etc.) in one's hand and apply pressure as a token of affection, friendship, sympathy, or the like: *His father squeezed his hand and wished him luck.* **7.** to give (someone) a hug. **8.** to threaten, intimidate, harass, or oppress (a person) in order to obtain a favor, money, or an advantageous attitude or action. **9.** to cause financial hardship to: *manufacturers squeezed by high tariffs.* **10.** to obtain a facsimile impression of. **11.** to cause to merge, as two or more lines of traffic into fewer lanes. **12.** *Baseball.* **a.** to enable (a runner on third base) to score on a squeeze play (often fol. by *in*): *He squeezed him in with a perfect bunt.* **b.** to score (a run) in this way (often fol. by *in*): *The Dodgers squeezed in a run in the eighth inning.* **13.** *Bridge.* to force (an opponent) to play a potentially winning card on a trick he or she cannot win. *—v.i.* **14.** to exert a compressing force. **15.** to force a way through some narrow or crowded place (usually fol. by *through, in, out,* etc.). **16.** to merge or come together. *—n.* **17.** the act or fact of squeezing or the fact of being squeezed. **18.** a clasping of one's hand around another's hand, arm, etc., as a token of affection, friendship, sympathy, or the like. **19.** a hug or close embrace. **20.** a troubled financial condition, esp. caused by a shortage or restriction, as of credit or funds. **21.** a small quantity or amount of anything obtained by squeezing. **22.** squeak (def. 3). **23.** *Slang.* a sweetheart: *his main squeeze.* **24.** a facsimile impression of an inscription or the like, obtained by pressing some plastic substance over or around it. **25.** See **squeeze play. 26.** *Bridge.* a play or circumstance whereby an opponent is forced to waste or discard a potentially winning card. **27.** an act of threatening, intimidating, harassing, or oppressing a person or persons to obtain a favor, money, or an advantageous attitude or action: *gangsters putting the squeeze on small businesses.* **28.** money or a favor obtained in such a way. [1590–1600; perh. var. of obs. *squize* (OE *cwȳsan*) to squeeze, with initial *s* by false division of words in sandhi] **—squeez′er,** *n.* **—squeez′ing·ly,** *adv.*
—Syn. 4. crowd, pack, jam, stuff.

squeeze′ bot′tle, a flexible plastic bottle the contents of which can be forced out by squeezing. [1945–50]

squeeze·box (skwēz′boks′), *n. Informal.* a concertina or accordion. [1905–10; SQUEEZE + BOX[1]]

squeezed′ joint′, *Building Trades.* a joint between two members cemented or glued together under pressure. Also, **squeeze′ joint′.**

squeeze′ play′, **1.** *Baseball.* **a.** Also called **suicide squeeze, suicide squeeze play.** a play executed when there is a runner on third base and usually not more than one out, in which the runner starts for home as soon as the pitcher makes a motion to pitch, and the batter bunts. **b.** Also called **safety squeeze, safety squeeze play.** a similar play in which the runner on third base waits until the batter has successfully bunted before trying to score. **2.** the application of pressure or influence on a person or group in order to force compliance or gain an advantage. Also called **squeeze.** [1900–05, *Amer.*]

squeg (skweg), *v.i.,* **squegged, squeg·ging.** (of an electronic circuit or component) to produce an output that oscillates between a certain maximum and zero, esp. when due to the effect of a grid. [1940–45; b. SQUEEZE and PEG]

squelch (skwelch), *v.t.* **1.** to strike or press with crushing force; crush down; squash. **2.** to put down, suppress, or silence, as with a crushing retort or argument. *—v.i.* **3.** to make a splashing sound. **4.** to tread heavily in water, mud, wet shoes, etc., with such a sound. *—n.* **5.** a squelched or crushed mass of anything. **6.** a splashing sound. **7.** an act of squelching or suppressing, as by a crushing retort or argument. **8.** Also called **squelch′ cir′cuit, noise suppressor.** *Electronics.* a circuit in a receiver, as a radio receiver, that automatically reduces or eliminates noise when the receiver is tuned to a frequency at which virtually no carrier wave occurs. [1610–20; var. of *quelch* in same sense (perh. b. QUELL and QUASH); initial *s* perh. from SQUASH[1]] **—squelch′er,** *n.* **—squelch′ing·ly,** *adv.* **—squelch′ing·ness,** *n.*

sque·teague (skwē tēg′), *n., pl.* **-teagues,** (*esp. collectively*) **-teague. 1.** an Atlantic food fish, *Cynoscion regalis,* of the croaker family. **2.** any of several other Atlantic fishes of the same genus; sea trout. [1795–1805, *Amer.;* < southeastern New England Algonquian, orig. pl. (cf. obs. E dial. *chickwit, squit,* etc. < sing. of the same word, c. Mohegan (E sp.) *cheegut*)]

squib (skwib), *n., v.,* **squibbed, squib·bing.** *—n.* **1.** a short and witty or sarcastic saying or writing. **2.** *Journalism.* a short news story, often used as a filler. **3.** a small firework, consisting of a tube or ball filled with powder, that burns with a hissing noise terminated usually by a slight explosion. **4.** a firecracker broken in the middle so that it burns with a hissing noise but does not explode. **5.** *Australian.* a coward. **6.** an electric, pyrotechnic device for firing the igniter of a rocket engine, esp. a solid-propellant engine. **7.** *Obs.* a mean or paltry fellow. *—v.i.* **8.** to write squibs. **9.** to shoot a squib. **10.** to explode with a small, sharp sound. **11.** to move swiftly and irregularly. **12.** *Australian.* **a.** to be afraid. **b.** to flee; escape. *—v.t.* **13.** to assail in squibs or lampoons. **14.** to toss, shoot, or utilize as a squib. [1515–25; orig. uncert.] **—squib′bish,** *adj.*

Squibb (skwib), *n.* **Edward Robinson,** 1819–1900, U.S. pharmaceutical manufacturer and medical reformer.

squid (skwid), *n., pl.* (*esp. collectively*) **squid,** (*esp. referring to two or more kinds or species*) **squids.** any of several ten-armed cephalopods, as of the genera *Loligo* and *Ommastrephes,* having a slender body and a pair of rounded or triangular caudal fins and varying in length from 4–6 in. (10–15 cm) to 60–80 ft. (18–24 m). [1605–15; orig. uncert.]

squid, *Loligo pealeii,* length 8 in. (20 cm); mantle 5 in. (13 cm)

squiffed (skwift), *adj. Slang.* intoxicated. [1870–75; orig. uncert.]

squig·gle (skwig′əl), *n., v.,* **-gled, -gling.** *—n.* **1.** a short, irregular curve or twist, as in writing or drawing. *—v.i.* **2.** to move in or appear as squiggles: *His handwriting squiggled across the page.* *—v.t.* **3.** to form in or cause to appear as squiggles; scribble. [1830–40; b. SQUIRM and WRIGGLE] **—squig′gly,** *adj.*

squil·gee (skwil′jē, skwil jē′), *n., v.t.,* **-geed, -gee·ing.** squeegee.

squill (skwil), *n.* **1.** the bulb of the sea onion, *Urginea maritima,* of the lily family, cut into thin slices and dried, and used in medicine chiefly as an expectorant. **2.** the plant itself. **3.** any related plant of the genus *Scilla.* [1350–1400; ME < L *squilla,* var. of *scilla* < Gk *skílla*] **—squill′-like′,** *adj.*

squil·la (skwil′ə), *n., pl.* **squil·las, squil·lae** (skwil′ē). See **mantis shrimp.** [1650–60; < L; see SQUILL]

squil·la·gee (skwil′ə jē′), *n., v.t.,* **-geed, -gee·ing.** squeegee.

squin·an·cy (skwin′ən sē, -ə sē), *n.* a prostrate Eurasian plant, *Asperula cynanchica,* of the madder family, having smooth, weak stems and sparse white or pink flowers, formerly believed to be a cure for quinsy. [1350–1400; ME *squynancy* quinsy < ML *squinancia, -antia* < Gk *synánchē, kynánchē,* diseases of the throat]

squinch[1] (skwinch), *n. Archit.* a small arch, corbeling, or the like, built across the interior angle between two walls, as in a square tower for supporting the side of a superimposed octagonal spire. [1490–1500; var. of *scunch,* short for *scuncheon,* ME *sconch(e)on* < MF *escoinson, esconchon;* see SCONCHEON]

squinch

squinch[2] (skwinch), *v.t.* **1.** to contort (the features) or squint. **2.** to squeeze together or contract. *—v.i.* **3.** to squeeze together or crouch down, as to fit into a smaller space. [1830–40; orig. uncert.; cf. SQUINT]

squin·ny (skwin′ē), *v.,* **-nied, -ny·ing,** *n., pl.* **-nies.** *—v.i.* **1.** to squint. *—n.* **2.** a squint. [1595–1605; perh. equiv. to *squin-* (< D *schuin* oblique, aslant) + *-y* EYE]

squint (skwint), *v.i.* **1.** to look with the eyes partly closed. **2.** *Ophthalm.* to be affected with strabismus; be cross-eyed. **3.** to look or glance obliquely or sidewise; look askance. **4.** to make or have an indirect reference to or bearing on; tend or incline toward (usually fol. by *toward, at,* etc.). *—v.t.* **5.** to close (the eyes) partly in looking: *The baby squinted its eyes at the bright lights.* **6.** to cause to squint; cause to look obliquely. *—n.* **7.** an act or instance of squinting. **8.** *Ophthalm.* a condition of the eye consisting in noncoincidence of the optic axes; strabismus. **9.** *Informal.* a quick glance: *Let me have a squint at that paper.* **10.** a looking obliquely or askance. **11.** an indirect reference. **12.** an inclination or tendency, esp. an oblique or perverse one. **13.** Also called **hagioscope.** (in a church) a small opening in a wall giving a view of the altar. *—adj.* **14.** looking obliquely; looking with a side glance; looking askance. **15.** *Ophthalm.* (of the eyes) affected with strabismus. [1350–1400 for earlier adv. sense; 1570–80 for adj. senses; ME; aph. var. of ASQUINT] **—squint′er,** *n.* **—squint′ing·ly,** *adv.* **—squint′ing·ness,** *n.*

squint-eyed (skwint′īd′), *adj.* **1.** affected with or characterized by strabismus. **2.** looking obliquely or askance. **3.** manifesting a malicious, envious, or spiteful attitude or disposition: *squint-eyed with vengefulness and blind to reason.* [1580–90]

squint′ing mod′ifier, *Gram.* a word or phrase that can modify either the words that precede it or those that follow, as *frequently* in the sentence *Studying frequently is tedious.* Also called **squint′ing construc′tion.**

squint·y (skwin′tē), *adj.* characterized by or having a squint. [1590–1600; SQUINT + -Y[1]] **—squint′i·ness,** *n.*

squir·ar·chy (skwīər′är kē), *n., pl.* **-chies.** squirearchy. **—squir·ar′chal, squir·ar′chi·cal,** *adj.*

squire (skwīər), *n., v.,* **squired, squir·ing.** *—n.* **1.** (in England) a country gentleman, esp. the chief landed proprietor in a district. **2.** (in the Middle Ages) a young man of noble birth who as an aspirant to knighthood served a knight. **3.** a personal attendant, as of a person of rank. **4.** a man who accompanies or escorts a woman. **5.** a title applied to a justice of the peace, local judge, or other local dignitary of a rural district or small town. *—v.t.* **6.** to attend as, or in the manner of, a squire. **7.** to escort (a woman), as to a dance or social gathering. [1250–1300; ME *squier;* aph. var. of ESQUIRE] **—squire′less,** *adj.* **—squire′like′,** *adj.*

squire·arch (skwīər′ärk), *n.* a member of the squirearchy. Also, **squir′arch.** [1825–35; back formation from SQUIREARCHY]

squire·ar·chy (skwīər′är kē), *n., pl.* **-chies. 1.** the collective body of squires or landed gentry of a country. **2.** the social, economic, and political class formed by the landed gentry. Also, **squirarchy.** [1795–1805; SQUIRE + -ARCHY] **—squire·ar′chal, squire·ar′chi·cal,** *adj.*

squire·dom (skwīər′dəm), *n.* **1.** the squirearchy. **2.** the position or status of a squire. [1640–50; SQUIRE + -DOM]

squi·reen (skwī rēn′), *n. Chiefly Irish Eng.* the landowner of a small estate; a squire of a small domain. [1800–10; SQUIRE + *-een* dim. suffix < Ir *-ín*]

squire·ling (skwīər′ling), *n.* **1.** a landowner of a small estate. **2.** a petty squire. [1675–85; SQUIRE + -LING[1]]

squirm (skwûrm), *v.i.* **1.** to wriggle or writhe. **2.** to feel or display discomfort or distress, as from reproof, embarrassment, pain, etc.: *He squirmed under the judge's questioning.* *—n.* **3.** the act of squirming; a squirming or wriggling movement. [1685–95; of expressive orig., perh. echoing WORM] **—squirm′er,** *n.* **—squirm′ing·ly,** *adv.*
—Syn. 1. turn, twist.

squirm·y (skwûr′mē), *adj.,* **squirm·i·er, squirm·i·est.** characterized by squirming. [1830–40; SQUIRM + -Y[1]] **—squirm′i·ness,** *n.*

gray squirrel, *Sciurus carolinensis,* head and body 11 in. (28 cm); tail 10 in. (25 cm)

squir·rel (skwûr′əl, skwur′- or, *esp. Brit.,* skwir′əl), *n., pl.* **-rels,** (*esp. collectively*) **-rel,** *v.,* **-reled, -rel·ing** or (*esp. Brit.*) **-relled, -rel·ling.** *—n.* **1.** any of numerous arboreal, bushy-tailed rodents of the genus *Sciurus,* of the family Sciuridae. **2.** any of various other members of the family Sciuridae, as the chipmunks, flying squirrels, and woodchucks. **3.** the meat of such an animal. **4.** the pelt or fur of such an animal: *a coat trimmed with squirrel.* *—v.t.* **5.** to store or hide (money, valuables, etc.), usually for the future (often fol. by *away*): *I've squirreled away a few dollars for an emergency.* [1325–75; ME *squirel* < AF *esquirel* (OF *escureul*) << VL **scūrellus,* **scūriolus,* repr. L *sciurus* (< Gk *skíouros* lit., shadow-tailed (*ski(á)* shadow + *-ouros,* adj. deriv. of *ourá* tail); appar. so called because the tail was large enough to provide shade for the rest of the animal) with dim. suffixes *-ellus, -olus*] **—squir′rel·ish, squir′rel·like′,** *adj.*

squir′rel cage′, **1.** a cage containing a cylindrical framework that is rotated by a squirrel or other small animal running inside of it. **2.** any situation that seems to be endlessly without goal or achievement. [1815–25]

squir′rel corn′, an American plant, *Dicentra canadensis,* of the fumitory family, having yellow roots resembling kernels of corn, finely dissected leaves, and clusters of drooping, heart-shaped, cream-colored flowers. [1835–45, *Amer.*]

squir·rel·fish (skwûr′əl fish′, skwur′- or, *esp. Brit.,* skwir′-), *n., pl.* (*esp. collectively*) **-fish,** (*esp. referring to two or more kinds or species*) **-fish·es.** any of several brightly colored, nocturnal fishes of the family Holocentridae, inhabiting shallow waters of tropical reefs, esp. the reddish *Holocentrus ascensionis* of the West Indies, armed with sharp spines and scales. [1795–1805; perh. after the sound it makes out of water, likened to a squirrel's bark]

squir′rel mon′key, either of two small, long-tailed monkeys, *Saimiri oerstedii* of Central America and *S. sciureus* of South America, having a small white face with black muzzle and gold, brown, or greenish fur: *S. oerstedii* is endangered. [1765–75]

squir′rel's-foot fern′ (skwûr′əlz fo͝ot′, skwur′- *or, esp. Brit.,* skwir′-). See **ball fern.**

squir′rel-tail grass′ (skwûr′əl tāl′, skwur′- *or, esp. Brit.,* skwir′-), any of various grasses having long fruiting stalks. [1770–80]

squir·rel·y (skwûr′ə lē, skwur′- *or, esp. Brit.,* skwir′-), *adj. Slang.* eccentric; flighty. Also, **squir′rel·ly.** [1930–35; SQUIRREL + -Y[1]]

squirt (skwûrt), *v.i.* **1.** to eject liquid in a jet from a narrow orifice: *The hose squirted all over us.* **2.** to eject a spurt of liquid: *The lemon squirted in my eye.* —*v.t.* **3.** to cause (liquid or a viscous substance) to spurt or issue in a jet, as from a narrow orifice: *Squirt the water over that way!* **4.** to wet or bespatter with a liquid or viscous substance so ejected: *to squirt someone with a hose.* —*n.* **5.** the act of squirting. **6.** a spurt or jetlike stream, as of water. **7.** a small quantity of liquid or viscous substance squirted: *Put a squirt of chocolate sauce on my ice cream.* **8.** *Informal.* **a.** a youngster, esp. a meddlesome or impudent one. **b.** a short person. **c.** an insignificant, self-assertive person, esp. one who is small or young. **9.** an instrument for squirting, as a syringe. **10.** Usually, **squirts.** *Dial.* diarrhea. [1425–75; (v.) late ME *squirten,* appar. var. of *swirten;* c. LG *swirtjen* in same sense; perh. akin to SWIRL; (n.) late ME *sqwyrt* diarrhea, deriv. of the v.] —**squirt′er,** *n.* —**squirt′ing·ly,** *adv.*
—**Syn. 6.** jet, spray, stream.

squirt′ can′, an oilcan with a flexible body that ejects oil when compressed.

squirt′ gun′, **1.** See **spray gun. 2.** See **water pistol.** [1795–1805, *Amer.*]

squirt′ing cu′cumber, a Mediterranean plant, *Ecballium elaterium,* of the gourd family, whose ripened fruit forcibly ejects the seeds and juice. [1795–1805]

squish (skwish), *v.t.* **1.** to squeeze or squash. —*v.i.* **2.** (of water, soft mud, etc.) to make a gushing or splashing sound when walked in or on. —*n.* **3.** a squishing sound: *the squish of footsteps on wet leaves.* [1640–50; alter. of SQUASH[1]]

squish·y (skwish′ē), *adj.,* **squish·i·er, squish·i·est. 1.** soft and wet: *The ground was squishy from the rain.* **2.** softly gurgling or splashing: *The sponge made a squishy sound when it was squeezed.* **3.** emotional or sentimental. [1840–50; SQUISH + -Y[1]] —**squish′i·ness,** *n.*

squiz (skwiz), *v.,* **squizzed, squiz·zing,** *n. Australian Informal.* —*v.t.* **1.** to peer at quickly and closely. —*n.* **2.** a quick, close look. [1905–10; expressive formation, perh. b. SQUINT and QUIZ]

sqush·y (skwush′ē, skwo͝osh′ē), *adj.,* **sqush·i·er, sqush·i·est.** squishy.

squush (skwush, skwo͝osh), *v.t., v.i., n.* squish. Also, **sqush.**

squush·y (skwush′ē, skwo͝osh′ē), *adj.,* **squush·i·er, squush·i·est.** squishy.

sq. yd., square yard; square yards.

Sr, *Symbol, Chem.* strontium.

sr, steradian.

Sr., 1. Senhor. **2.** Senior. **3.** Señor. **4.** Sir. **5.** *Eccles.* Sister. [< L *Soror*]

S.R., Sons of the Revolution.

Sra., 1. Senhora. **2.** Señora.

Sra·nan (srä′nən), *n.* an English-based creole widely spoken in Suriname. Also called **Sranan Tongo, Taki-Taki.** [1950–55; < Sranan: lit., Suriname (tongue)]

Sra′nan Ton′go (tong′gō), Sranan.

SRB, See **solid rocket booster.**

SRBM, short-range ballistic missile.

S. Rept., Senate report.

S. Res., Senate resolution.

sri (srē, shrē), *n.* **1.** a Hindu title of address prefixed to the name of a deity, holy person, etc. **2.** a respectful title of address prefixed to a man's name in India; Mr.

Sri Lan·ka (srē′ läng′kə, lang′kə, shrē′), an island republic in the Indian Ocean, S of India: a member of the Commonwealth of Nations. 14,200,000; 25,332 sq. mi. (65,610 sq. km). *Cap.:* Colombo. Formerly, **Ceylon.** Arabic, **Serendip.** —**Sri′ Lan′kan,** *adj., n.*

Sri·na·gar (srē nug′ər), *n.* a city in and the summer capital of Kashmir, on the Jhelum River. 403,000.

Śri-Vaish·na·vism (shrē′vīsh′nə viz′əm), *n.* a Hindu sect advocating theistic devotion as a philosophically and scripturally valid way to achieve salvation. —**Śri′-Vaish′na·vite′,** *n., adj.*

SRO, 1. single-room occupancy. **2.** standing room only. Also, **S.R.O.**

SRS, air bag. [1985–90; *s(upplemental) r(estraint) s(ystem)*]

Srta., 1. Senhorita. **2.** Señorita.

sru·ti (shro͝ot′ē), *n. Hinduism.* the Vedas and some of the Upanishads, regarded as divinely revealed. [< Skt *śruti*]

SS, 1. Schutzstaffel. **2.** social security. **3.** steamship. **4.** supersonic.

ss, (in prescriptions) a half. Also, **ss.** [< L *sēmis*]

SS., 1. Saints. [< L *sānctī*] **2.** Schutzstaffel. **3.** See **ss.** (def. 1).

ss., 1. to wit; namely (used esp. on legal documents, as an affidavit, pleading, etc., to verify the place of action). [< L *scilicet*] **2.** sections. **3.** *Baseball.* shortstop.

S.S., 1. Schutzstaffel. **2.** (in prescriptions) in the strict sense. [< L *sēnsū strictō*] **3.** steamship. **4.** Sunday School.

SSA, 1. Social Security Act. **2.** See **Social Security Administration.**

SSAE, stamped self-addressed envelope.

SSB, Social Security Board.

SSBN, the U.S. Navy designation for the fleet ballistic missile submarine. [1965–70; *S(trategic) S(ubmarine) B(allistic) N(uclear)*]

SSC, small-saver certificate.

S.Sc.D., Doctor of Social Science.

S-scroll (es′skrōl′), *n.* an ornamental motif in the form of the letter S.

SS.D., Most Holy Lord: a title of the pope. [< L *Sānctissimus Dominus*]

S.S.D., Doctor of Sacred Scripture. [< L *Sacrae Scriptūrae Doctor*]

SSE, south-southeast. Also, **S.S.E., s.s.e.**

SSI, *Electronics.* **1.** small-scale integration: the technology for concentrating up to ten semiconductor devices in a single integrated circuit. Cf. **MSI, LSI. 2.** See **Supplemental Security Income.**

S sleep. See **slow-wave sleep.** [1970–75]

SSM, surface-to-surface missile.

SSPE, subacute sclerosing panencephalitis.

SSR, Soviet Socialist Republic. Also, **S.S.R.**

SSS, Selective Service System.

SST, supersonic transport.

S star, *Astron.* a relatively cool red giant having a surface temperature of about 2500 K and an absorption spectrum with strong lines of zirconium oxide. Cf. **spectral type.**

SSW, south-southwest. Also, **S.S.W., s.s.w.**

ST, *Real Estate.* septic tank.

st, stere.

-st[1], var. of **-est**[1]: *first; least.*

-st[2], var. of **-est**[2]: *hadst; wouldst; dost.*

St., 1. Saint. **2.** statute; statutes. **3.** Strait. **4.** Street.

st., 1. stanza. **2.** state. **3.** statute; statutes. **4.** stet. **5.** stitch. **6.** stone (weight). **7.** strait. **8.** street.

s.t., short ton.

Sta., 1. Santa. **2.** Station.

sta., 1. station. **2.** stationary.

stab (stab), *v.,* **stabbed, stab·bing,** *n.* —*v.t.* **1.** to pierce or wound with or as if with a pointed weapon: *She stabbed a piece of chicken with her fork.* **2.** to thrust, plunge, or jab (a knife, pointed weapon, or the like) into something: *He stabbed the knife into the man's chest.* **3.** to penetrate sharply or painfully: *Their misery stabbed his conscience.* **4.** to make a piercing, thrusting, or pointing motion at or in: *He stabbed me in the chest with his finger. The speaker stabbed the air in anger.* —*v.i.* **5.** to thrust with or as if with a knife or other pointed weapon: *to stab at an attacker.* **6.** to deliver a wound, as with a pointed weapon. **7. stab (someone) in the back,** to do harm to (someone), esp. to a friend or to a person who is unsuspecting or in a defenseless position. —*n.* **8.** the act of stabbing. **9.** a thrust or blow with, or as if with, a pointed weapon. **10.** an attempt; try: *Make a stab at an answer before giving up.* **11.** a wound made by stabbing. **12.** a sudden, brief, and usually painful, sensation: *He felt a stab of pain in his foot. A stab of pity ran through her.* **13. stab in the back,** an act of treachery. [1325–75; (v.) ME (Scots) *stabben* < ?; (n.) late ME, akin to or deriv. of the v.; cf. Scots *stob* STUB[1]]
—**Syn. 1.** spear, penetrate, pin, transfix.

stab., 1. stabilization. **2.** stabilizer. **3.** stable.

Sta·bat Ma·ter (stä′bät mä′ter, stä′bat mā′tər), **1.** (*italics*) a Latin hymn, composed in the 13th century, commemorating the sorrows of the Virgin Mary at the Cross. **2.** a musical setting for this. [lit., the mother was standing, the first words of the hymn]

stab·bing (stab′ing), *adj.* **1.** penetrating; piercing: *a stabbing pain.* **2.** emotionally wounding: *a stabbing remark.* **3.** incisive or trenchant: *a stabbing, satirical phrase.* [1590–1600; STAB + -ING[2]] —**stab′bing·ly,** *adv.*

sta·bile (*adj.* stā′bil, -bəl *or, esp. Brit.,* -bīl; *n.* stā′bēl *or, esp. Brit.,* -bīl), *adj.* **1.** fixed in position; stable. **2.** *Med.* resistant to physical or chemical changes. —*n.* **3.** a piece of abstract sculpture having immobile units constructed of sheet metal, wire, or other material and attached to fixed supports. Cf. **mobile** (def. 9). [1790–1800; < L: neut. of *stabilis,* equiv. to *sta-* (s. of *stāre* to STAND) + *-bilis* -BLE]

sta·bi·lim·e·ter (stā′bə lim′i tər, stab′ə-), *n.* stabilograph. [1905–10; < L *stabil(is)* STABILE + -I- + -METER]

sta·bil·i·ty (stə bil′i tē), *n., pl.* **-ties. 1.** the state or quality of being stable. **2.** firmness in position. **3.** continuance without change; permanence. **4.** *Chem.* resistance or the degree of resistance to chemical change or disintegration. **5.** resistance to change, esp. sudden change or deterioration: *The stability of the economy encourages investment.* **6.** steadfastness; constancy, as of character or purpose: *The job calls for a great deal of emotional stability.* **7.** *Aeron.* the ability of an aircraft to return to its original flying position when abruptly displaced. **8.** *Rom. Cath. Ch.* a vow taken by a Benedictine monk, binding him to residence for life in the same monastery in which he made the vow. [1400–50; < L *stabilitās,* equiv. to *stabili(s)* STABILE + *-tās* -TY; r. late ME *stablete* < OF < L, as above]
—**Syn. 6.** steadiness, strength, soundness, poise, solidity, balance.

sta·bi·li·za·tion (stā′bə li zā′shən), *n.* **1.** the act or process of stabilizing or the state of being stabilized. **2.** Also called **stabiliza′tion proc′ess.** *Photog.* a process for making temporary black-and-white prints using special sensitized paper **(stabiliza′tion pa′per)** that can be rapidly processed through one or two solutions that quickly develop and stabilize the nonpermanent image. [1920–25; STABILIZE + -ATION]

stabiliza′tion fund′, a monetary reserve established by a country to provide funds for maintaining the official exchange rates of its currency by equalizing the buying and selling of foreign exchange. Also called **equalization fund, exchange equalization fund, exchange stabilization fund.**

stabiliza′tion print′, *Photog.* a print made by the stabilization process.

sta·bi·lize (stā′bə līz′), *v.,* **-lized, -liz·ing.** —*v.t.* **1.** to make or hold stable, firm, or steadfast. **2.** to maintain at a given or unfluctuating level or quantity: *The government will try to stabilize the cost of living.* **3.** *Aeron.* to put or keep (an aircraft) in stable equilibrium, as by some special device. —*v.i.* **4.** to become stabilized. Also, *esp. Brit.,* **sta′bi·lise′.** [1860–65; STABILE + -IZE; cf. F *stabiliser*]

sta·bi·liz·er (stā′bə lī′zər), *n.* **1.** a person or thing that stabilizes. **2.** *Aeron.* a device for stabilizing an aircraft, as the fixed, horizontal tail surface on an airplane. Cf. **horizontal stabilizer, vertical stabilizer. 3.** *Naut.* **a.** a mechanical device for counteracting the roll of a vessel, consisting of a pair of retractable fins so pivoted as to oppose a downward force with an upward one, and vice versa. **b.** a gyrostabilizer. **4.** any of various substances added to foods, chemical compounds, etc., to prevent deterioration, the breaking down of an emulsion, or the loss of desirable properties. **5.** any compound that, when included with an explosive, decreases the ability of the latter to decompose spontaneously. **6.** a substance, as beeswax or aluminum stearate, added to a fast-drying oil paint to improve the dispersion of pigment. **7.** a comparatively large shock absorber for motor vehicles. **8.** *Mil.* **a.** any of various devices or systems that keep a gun mounted on a moving ship, tank, or plane automatically aimed at its target. **b.** any of various mechanical devices, such as fins, or electronic systems that keep a shell, bomb, rocket, etc., aligned with its target. **9.** *Navy.* any of various devices or systems used to keep a submarine or a torpedo at the proper depth or in the proper position. [1905–10; STABILIZE + -ER[1]]

sta′bilizer bar′, a horizontal metal bar linking the two front suspension systems of an automobile, used to reduce swaying or rolling. Also called **antiroll bar, antisway bar, sway bar.** [1930–35]

sta·bi·lo·graph (stā′bə lə graf′, -gräf′, stab′ə-), *n.* an instrument for measuring body sway. Also called **stabilimeter.** [< L *stabil(is)* STABILE + -O- + -GRAPH]

sta·ble[1] (stā′bəl), *n., v.,* **-bled, -bling.** —*n.* **1.** a building for the lodging and feeding of horses, cattle, etc. **2.** such a building with stalls. **3.** a collection of animals housed in such a building. **4.** *Horse Racing.* **a.** an establishment where racehorses are kept and trained. **b.** the horses belonging to, or the persons connected with, such an establishment. **5.** *Informal.* **a.** a number of people, usually in the same profession, who are employed, trained, or represented by the same company, agency, manager, etc.: *a comedy show with a large stable of writers.* **b.** the establishment that trains or manages such a group of people: *two boxers from the same stable.* **c.** a collection of items produced by or belonging to an establishment, industry, profession, or the like: *The American auto industry has some new small cars in its stable.* —*v.t.* **6.** to put or lodge in or as if in a stable. —*v.i.* **7.** to live in or as if in a stable. [1200–50; ME *stable* < OF *estable* < L *stabulum* standing room, equiv. to *sta-,* s. of *stāre* to STAND + *-bulum* n. suffix denoting place] —**sta′ble·like′,** *adj.*
—**Syn. 1.** barn, mews.

sta·ble[2] (stā′bəl), *adj.,* **-bler, -blest. 1.** not likely to fall or give way, as a structure, support, foundation, etc.; firm; steady. **2.** able or likely to continue or last; firmly established; enduring or permanent: *a stable government.* **3.** resistant to sudden change or deterioration: *A stable economy is the aim of every government.* **4.** steadfast; not wavering or changeable, as in character or purpose; dependable. **5.** not subject to emotional instability or illness; sane; mentally sound. **6.** *Physics.* having the ability to react to a disturbing force by maintaining or reestablishing position, form, etc. **7.** *Chem.* not readily decomposing, as a compound; resisting molecular or chemical change. **8.** (of a patient's condition) exhibiting no significant change. [1225–75; ME < OF *estable* < L *stabilis* STABILE] —**sta′ble·ness,** *n.* —**sta′bly,** *adv.*
—**Syn. 1.** fixed, strong, sturdy. **4.** invariable, unvarying, staunch, constant, reliable, steady, solid.

sta·ble·boy (stā′bəl boi′), *n.* a person who works in a stable. [1720–30; STABLE[1] + BOY]

sta′ble equa′tion, *Math.* a differential equation each solution of which tends to zero as the independent variable increases to infinity. Cf. **transient** (def. 6).

CONCISE ETYMOLOGY KEY: <, descended or borrowed from; >, whence; b., blend of, blended; c., cognate with; cf., compare; deriv., derivative; equiv., equivalent; imit., imitative; obl., oblique; r., replacing; s., stem; sp., spelling, spelled; resp., respelling, respelled; trans., translation; ?, origin unknown; *, unattested; ‡, probably earlier than. See the full key inside the front cover.

sta′ble fly′, a two-winged fly, *Stomoxys calcitrans,* having the mouthparts adapted for biting, and commonly a household and stable pest. Also called **biting housefly.** [1860–65]

sta·ble·man (stā′bəl mən, -man′), *n., pl.* **-men** (-mən, -men′). a person who works in a stable. [1720–30; STABLE[1] + MAN[1]]

sta·ble·mate (stā′bəl māt′), *n.* **1.** a horse sharing a stable with another. **2.** one of several horses owned by the same person. **3.** *Informal.* a person or thing originating from or belonging to the same establishment, field, etc., as another. [1925–30; STABLE[1] + MATE[1]]

sta·bler (stā′blər), *n.* a person who runs a horse stable. [1400–50; late ME; see STABLE[1], -ER[1]]

sta·bling (stā′bling), *n.* **1.** accommodation for horses or other draft or farm animals in a stable. **2.** stables collectively. [1475–85; STABLE[1] + -ING[1]]

stab·lish (stab′lish), *v.t. Archaic.* establish. [1250–1300; ME *stablissen,* aph. var. of ESTABLISH]

stacc., *Music.* staccato.

stac·ca·to (stə kä′tō), *adj., adv., n., pl.* **-tos, -ti** (-tē). —*adj.* **1.** shortened and detached when played or sung: *staccato notes.* **2.** characterized by performance in which the notes are abruptly disconnected: *a staccato style of playing.* Cf. **legato. 3.** composed of or characterized by abruptly disconnected elements; disjointed: *rapid-fire, staccato speech.* —*adv.* **4.** in a staccato manner. —*n.* **5.** performance in a staccato manner. **6.** a staccato passage. [1715–25; < It: disconnected, ptp. of *staccare* (deriv. of *stacca* pole < Goth, but taken as a var. of *distaccare* to DETACH)]

staccato notes

stacca′to mark′, (in music notation) a dot, wedge, or vertical stroke over or under a note to indicate that it should be played staccato. [1900–05]

Sta·cey (stā′sē), *n.* a male or female given name.

Sta·cia (stā′shə), *n.* a female given name.

stack (stak), *n.* **1.** a more or less orderly pile or heap: *a precariously balanced stack of books; a neat stack of papers.* **2.** a large, usually conical, circular, or rectangular pile of hay, straw, or the like. **3.** Often, **stacks.** a set of shelves for books or other materials ranged compactly one above the other, as in a library. **4. stacks,** the area or part of a library in which the books and other holdings are stored or kept. **5.** a number of chimneys or flues grouped together. **6.** smokestack. **7.** a vertical duct for conveying warm air from a leader to a register on an upper story of a building. **8.** a vertical waste pipe or vent pipe serving a number of floors. **9.** *Informal.* a great quantity or number. **10.** *Radio.* an antenna consisting of a number of components connected in a substantially vertical series. **11.** *Computers.* a linear list arranged so that the last item stored is the first item retrieved. **12.** *Mil.* a conical, free-standing group of three rifles placed on their butts and hooked together with stacking swivels. **13.** Also called **air stack, stackup.** *Aviation.* a group of airplanes circling over an airport awaiting their turns to land. **14.** an English measure for coal and wood, equal to 108 cubic feet (3 cu. m). **15.** *Geol.* a column of rock isolated from a shore by the action of waves. **16.** *Games.* **a.** a given quantity of chips that can be bought at one time, as in poker or other gambling games. **b.** the quantity of chips held by a player at a given point in a gambling game. **17. blow one's stack,** *Slang.* to lose one's temper or become uncontrollably angry, esp. to display one's fury, as by shouting: *When he came in and saw the mess he blew his stack.* —*v.t.* **18.** to pile, arrange, or place in a stack: *to stack hay; to stack rifles.* **19.** to cover or load with something in stacks or piles. **20.** to arrange or select unfairly in order to force a desired result, esp. to load (a jury, committee, etc.) with members having a biased viewpoint: *The lawyer charged that the jury had been stacked against his client.* **21.** to keep (a number of incoming airplanes) flying nearly circular patterns at various altitudes over an airport where crowded runways, a low ceiling, or other temporary conditions prevent immediate landings. —*v.i.* **22.** to be arranged in or form a stack: *These chairs stack easily.* **23. stack the deck, a.** to arrange cards or a pack of cards so as to cheat: *He stacked the deck and won every hand.* **b.** to manipulate events, information, etc., esp. unethically, in order to achieve an advantage or desired result. **24. stack up, a.** *Aviation.* to control the flight patterns of airplanes waiting to land at an airport so that each circles at a designated altitude. **b.** *Informal.* to compare; measure up (often fol. by *against*): *How does the movie stack up against the novel?* **c.** *Informal.* to appear plausible or in keeping with the known facts: *Your story just doesn't stack up.* [1250–1300; (n.) ME *stak* < ON *stakkr* haystack; (v.) ME *stakken,* deriv. of the v.] —**stack′er,** *n.* —**stack′less,** *adj.*

stack·a·ble (stak′ə bəl), *adj.* capable of being stacked, esp. easily: *stackable chairs.* [1960–65; STACK + -ABLE] —**stack′a·bil′i·ty,** *n.*

stacked (stakt), *adj. Slang.* (of a woman) having a voluptuous figure. [1940–45; STACK (v.) + -ED[2]]

stacked′ heel′, a shoe heel constructed from several layers of material. Also, **stack′ heel′.** [1955–60]

stack′ing swiv′el, a metal swivel attached to the stock of a military rifle for use in hooking three rifles together to form a stack. [1870–75]

stack′ ta′ble. See **nesting table.**

stack·up (stak′up′), *n. Aviation.* stack (def. 13). [n. use of v. phrase *stack up*]

stac·te (stak′tē), *n.* one of the sweet spices used in the holy incense of the ancient Hebrews. Ex. 30:34. [1350–1400; ME < L *stactē* myrrh < Gk *staktḗ,* fem. of *staktós* trickling (verbid of *stázein* to fall in drops)]

stac·tom·e·ter (stak tom′i tər), *n.* stalagmometer. [1835–45; *stacto-* (see STACTE) + -METER]

Sta·cy (stā′sē), *n.* a male or female given name.

stad·dle (stad′l), *n.* **1.** the lower part of a stack of hay or the like. **2.** a supporting frame for a stack, or a platform on which a stack is placed. **3.** any supporting framework or base. [bef. 900; ME *stathel,* OE *stathol* base, support, tree trunk; c. OHG *stadal* barn, ON *stǫthull* milking place; akin to STEAD]

stade (stād), *n. Geol.* a period of time represented by a glacial deposit. Also, **stadial.** [1530–40; < MF (earlier *estade*) < L *stadium;* see STADIUM]

Sta′der splint′ (stā′dər), *Med.* a splint consisting of an adjustable metal rod with a steel pin at either end for insertion in the bone above and below a fracture. [named after Otto *Stader,* (1894–1962), American veterinary surgeon]

stad·hold·er (stad′hōl′dər), *n.* **1.** the chief magistrate of the former republic of the United Provinces of the Netherlands. **2.** (formerly, in the Netherlands) the viceroy or governor of a province. Also, **stadtholder.** [1585–95; partial trans. of D *stadhouder,* equiv. to *stad* place + *houder* HOLDER; trans. of ML *locum tenēns*] —**stad′·hold′er·ate, stad′hold′er·ship′,** *n.*

sta·di·a[1] (stā′dē ə), *n.* **1.** a method of surveying in which distances are read by noting the interval on a graduated rod intercepted by two parallel cross hairs (**sta′dia hairs′** or **sta′dia wires′**) mounted in the telescope of a surveying instrument, the rod being placed at one end of the distance to be measured and the surveying instrument at the other. —*adj.* **2.** pertaining to such a method of surveying. [1860–65; prob. special use of STADIA[2]]

sta·di·a[2] (stā′dē ə), *n.* a pl. of **stadium.**

sta·di·al (stā′dē əl), *Geol.* —*n.* **1.** stade. —*adj.* **2.** of or pertaining to a stade or stades. [1350–1400; ME. See STADE, -IAL]

sta′dia rod′, *Survey.* rod (def. 19).

sta·dim·e·ter (stə dim′i tər), *n.* an instrument for determining the distance between an observer and an object of known height by measurement of the angle subtended by the object. [STADI(A)[1] + -METER]

sta·di·um (stā′dē əm), *n., pl.* **-di·ums, -di·a** (-dē ə). **1.** a sports arena, usually oval or horseshoe-shaped, with tiers of seats for spectators. **2.** an ancient Greek course for foot races, typically semicircular, with tiers of seats for spectators. **3.** an ancient Greek and Roman unit of length, the Athenian unit being equal to about 607 feet (185 m). **4.** a stage in a process or in the life of an organism. **5.** *Entomol.* stage (def. 11b). [1350–1400; ME < L < Gk *stádion* unit of distance, racecourse]

sta′dium jack′et, an insulated, parkalike jacket that reaches to the mid thigh or the knees and often has a drawstring around the bottom edge, worn outdoors in cold weather. Also called **sta′dium coat′.**

stad·le (stad′l), *n.* staddle.

stadt·hold·er (stat′hōl′dər), *n.* stadholder. —**stadt′·hold′er·ate, stadt′hold′er·ship′,** *n.*

Staël-Hol·stein (stäl′ôl sten′), *n.* **Anne Louise Germaine Neck·er** (ᴀɴ lwēz zher men′ ne kᴇʀ′), **Baronne de,** (*Madame de Staël*) 1766–1817, French writer.

staff[1] (staf, stäf), *n., pl.* **staffs** for 1–4, 8; **staves** (stāvz) or **staffs** for 5–7, 9, 10; *adj., v.* —*n.* **1.** a group of persons, as employees, charged with carrying out the work of an establishment or executing some undertaking. **2.** a group of assistants to a manager, superintendent, or executive. **3.** *Mil.* **a.** a body of officers without command authority, appointed to assist a commanding officer. **b.** the parts of any army concerned with administrative matters, planning, etc., rather than with actual participation in combat. **4.** those members of an organization serving only in an auxiliary or advisory capacity on a given project. Cf. **line**[1] (def. 38). **5.** a stick, pole, or rod for aid in walking or climbing, for use as a weapon, etc. **6.** a rod or wand serving as a symbol of office or authority, as a crozier, baton, truncheon, or mace. **7.** a pole on which a flag is hung or displayed. **8.** something that supports or sustains. **9.** Also, **stave.** *Music.* a set of horizontal lines, now five in number, with the corresponding four spaces between them, on which music is written. **10.** *Archaic.* the shaft of a spear, lance, etc. —*adj.* **11.** of or pertaining to a military or organizational staff: *a staff officer; staff meetings.* **12.** (of a professional person) employed on the staff of a corporation, publication, institution, or the like rather than being self-employed or practicing privately: *a staff writer; staff physicians at the hospital.* —*v.t.* **13.** to provide with a staff of assistants or workers: *She staffed her office with excellent secretaries.* **14.** to serve on the staff of. **15.** to send to a staff for study or further work (often fol. by *out*): *The White House will staff out the recommendations before making a decision.* —*v.i.* **16.** to hire employees, as for a new office or project (sometimes fol. by *up*): *Next month we'll begin staffing up for the reelection campaign.* [bef. 900; ME *staf* (n.), OE *stæf;* c. D *staf,* G *Stab,* ON *stafr* staff, Skt *stabh-* support] —**staff′less,** *adj.*
—**Usage.** See **collective noun.**

staff[2] (staf, stäf), *n.* a composition of plaster and fibrous material used for a temporary finish and in ornamental work, as on exposition buildings. [1890–95, *Amer.*; perh. < G *Stoff* STUFF]

Staf·fa (staf′ə), *n.* an island in W Scotland, in the Hebrides: site of Fingal's Cave.

staff′ cap′tain, a person who assists the master of a large ocean passenger vessel, being especially responsible for safety apparatus, fire and lifeboat drills, etc. [1865–70]

staff·er (staf′ər, stä′fər), *n.* **1.** a member of a staff of employees or coworkers. **2.** *Journalism.* an editorial employee, esp. a writer. Cf. **stringer** (def. 6). [1680–90; STAFF[1] + -ER[1]]

staff·man (staf′man′, stäf′-), *n., pl.* **-men.** staffer. [1650–60; STAFF[1] + MAN[1]]

staff′ of Aescula′pius, a representation of a forked staff with an entwining serpent, used as a symbol of the medical profession and as the insignia of the American Medical Association and other medical organizations. Cf. **caduceus** (def. 2).

staff′ of′ficer, *Mil.* a commissioned officer who is a member of a staff. [1695–1705]

staff′ of life′, bread, considered as the mainstay of the human diet. [1630–40]

Staf·ford (staf′ərd), *n.* **1. Sir Edward William,** 1819–1901, New Zealand political leader, born in Scotland: prime minister 1856–61, 1865–69, 1872. **2.** a city in and the county seat of Staffordshire, in central England. 114,300. **3.** Staffordshire.

Staf·ford·shire (staf′ərd shēr′, -shər), *n.* a county in central England. 988,400; 1154 sq. mi. (2715 sq. km). *Co. seat:* Stafford. Also called **Stafford, Staffs** (stafs).

Staf′fordshire bull′ ter′rier, one of an English breed of strong, stocky, muscular dogs having a broad skull and a smooth coat, in combinations of red, white, black, or blue, originally raised for bullbaiting and later dogfighting, but now bred as a companion dog. [1935–40]

Staf′fordshire ter′rier, former name of **American Staffordshire terrier.** [1935–40]

staff′ sec′tion, *Mil.* section (def. 10b).

staff′ ser′geant, 1. *U.S. Air Force.* a noncommissioned officer ranking below a technical sergeant and above an airman first class. **2.** *U.S. Army.* a noncommissioned officer ranking below a sergeant first class and above a sergeant. **3.** *U.S. Marine Corps.* a noncommissioned officer ranking below a gunnery sergeant and above a sergeant. [1805–15]

staff′ ser′geant ma′jor, *U.S. Army.* a noncommissioned officer equivalent in rank to a command sergeant major but having no command responsibility.

stag (stag), *n., v.,* **stagged, stag·ging,** *adj., adv.* —*n.* **1.** an adult male deer. **2.** the male of various other animals. **3.** a man who attends a social gathering unaccompanied by a woman. **4.** *Informal.* See **stag party. 5.** a swine or bull castrated after maturation of the sex organs. **6.** *Brit.* a speculator who buys securities of a new issue in the hope of selling them quickly at a higher price. —*v.i.* **7.** *Informal.* (of a man) to attend a social function without a female companion. —*adj.* **8.** of or for men only: *a stag dinner.* **9.** intended for male audiences and usually pornographic in content: *a stag show.* —*adv.* **10.** without a companion or date: *to go stag to a dance.* [1150–1200; ME *stagge;* akin to ON *steggi, steggr* male bird (>E (north dial.) *steg* gander), Icel *steggur* male fox, tomcat] —**stag′like′,** *adj.*

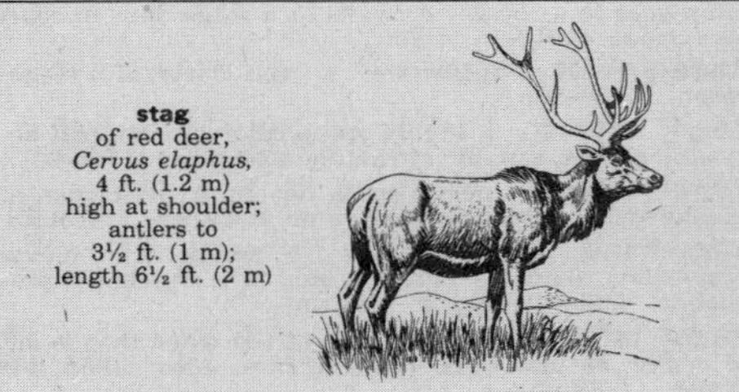
stag
of red deer,
Cervus elaphus,
4 ft. (1.2 m)
high at shoulder;
antlers to
3½ ft. (1 m);
length 6½ ft. (2 m)

stag′ bee′tle, any of numerous lamellicorn beetles of the family Lucanidae, some of the males of which have mandibles resembling the antlers of a stag. [1675–85]

stage (stāj), *n., v.,* **staged, stag·ing.** —*n.* **1.** a single step or degree in a process; a particular phase, period, position, etc., in a process, development, or series. **2.** a raised platform or floor, as for speakers, performers, etc. **3.** *Theat.* **a.** the platform on which the actors perform in a theater. **b.** this platform with all the parts of the theater and all the apparatus back of the proscenium. **4. the stage,** the theater, esp. acting, as a profession: *He plans to make the stage his career.* **5.** *Motion Pictures.* See **sound stage. 6.** the scene of any action. **7.** a stagecoach. **8.** a place of rest on a journey; a regular stopping place of a stagecoach or the like, for the change of horses, mules, etc. **9.** the distance between two places of rest on a journey; each of the portions of a journey. **10.** a portion or period of a course of action, of life, etc.: *the adolescent stage of human development.* **11.** *Entomol.* **a.** any one of the major time periods in the development of an insect, as the embryonic, larval, pupal, and imaginal stages. **b.** Also called **stadium.** any one of the periods of larval growth between molts. **12.** *Econ., Sociol.* a major phase of the economic or sociological life of human beings or society: *the patriarchal stage.* **13.** *Geol.* a division of stratified rocks corresponding to a single geologic age. **14.** the small platform of a microscope on which the object to be examined is placed. See illus. under **microscope. 15.** *Radio.* an element in a complex mechanism, as a tube and its accessory structures in a multiple amplifier. **16.** *Rocketry.* a section of a rocket containing a rocket engine or cluster of rocket engines, usually separable from other such sections when its propellant is exhausted. **17. by easy stages,** working, traveling, etc., slowly, with frequent pauses; unhurriedly, with many stops; gradually. **18. go on the stage,** to

CONCISE PRONUNCIATION KEY: *act, cāpe, dâre, pärt; set, ēqual; if, ice; ox, ōver, ôrder, oil, bo͝ok, bo͞ot, out; up, ûrge; child; sing; shoe; thin,* t͟h*at;* zh *as in treasure.* ə = *a as in alone, e as in system, i as in easily, o as in gallop, u as in circus;* ə *as in fire* (fīər), *hour* (ouər). l *and* n *can serve as syllabic consonants, as in cradle* (krād′l), *and button* (but′n). *See the full key inside the front cover.*

become an actor, esp. in the theater. **19. hold the stage, a.** to continue to be produced, as a play or other theatrical production. **b.** to be the center of attention. **20. on stage,** performing, esp. as an actor. —*v.t.* **21.** to represent, produce, or exhibit on or as if on a stage: *The drama class staged a play during Christmas vacation.* **22.** to furnish with a stage, staging, stage set, etc. **23.** to write, direct, or produce (a play) with the action taking place as if in a specified locale or time: *He staged the fantasy on Mars in the year 2500.* **24.** to plan, organize, or carry out (an activity), esp. for dramatic or public effect: *Workers staged a one-day strike.* **25.** to classify the natural progression of (a disease, esp. cancer). —*v.i.* **26.** to be suitable for presentation or performance on the stage: *The script didn't stage well.* **27.** to travel by stagecoach. [1250–1300; ME (n.) < OF *estage* (F *étage*) < VL **staticum* standing place, equiv. to *stat(us)* STATUS + *-icum,* neut. of *-icus* -IC] —**stage′a·ble,** *adj.* —**stage′a·bil′i·ty,** *n.* —**stage′a·bly,** *adv.*
—**Syn. 6.** spot, setting, locale.

stage′ brace′, a brace for supporting upright pieces of theatrical scenery.

stage′ busi′ness, business (def. 10). [1815–25]

stage·coach (stāj′kōch′), *n.* a horse-drawn coach that formerly traveled regularly over a fixed route with passengers, parcels, etc. [1630–40; STAGE + COACH]

stagecoach

stage·craft (stāj′kraft′, -kräft′), *n.* skill in or the art of writing, adapting, or staging plays. [1880–85; STAGE + CRAFT]

staged (stājd), *adj.* **1.** adapted for or produced on the stage. **2.** contrived for a desired impression: *It was a staged, rather than spontaneous, demonstration of affection.* **3.** occurring or planned to occur in stages: *a staged increase in wages.* [1560–70; STAGE + -ED[3]]

stage′ direc′tion, 1. an instruction written into the script of a play, indicating stage actions, movements of performers, or production requirements. **2.** the art or technique of a stage director. [1780–90]

stage′ direc′tor, 1. a person who directs a theatrical production. **2.** (formerly) a stage manager. [1905–10]

stage′ door′, a door at the back or side of a theater, used by performers and theater personnel. [1770–80]

stage′-door John′ny (stāj′dôr′, -dōr′), a man who often goes to a theater or waits at a stage door to court an actress. [1910–15, *Amer.*]

stage-driv·er (stāj′drī′vər), *n.* the driver of a stagecoach. [1780–90]

stage′ effect′, a highly spectacular or artificial device or means, esp. for attracting attention. [1785–95]

stage′ fright′, nervousness felt by a performer or speaker when appearing before an audience. [1875–80]

stage·hand (stāj′hand′), *n.* a person who moves properties, regulates lighting, etc., in a theatrical production. [1900–05; STAGE + HAND]

stage′ left′, *Theat.* the part of the stage that is left of center as one faces the audience. Also called **left stage.** [1930–35]

stage-man·age (stāj′man′ij), *v.,* **-aged, -ag·ing.** —*v.t.* **1.** to work as a stage manager for: *to stage-manage a repertory theater.* **2.** to arrange or stage in order to produce a theatrical or spectacular effect: *The clients were most impressed with the way she stage-managed the whole presentation.* **3.** to arrange or direct unobtrusively or in secret: *He stage-managed Mediterranean black-market operations from his secluded villa on the Riviera.* —*v.i.* **4.** to work as a stage manager. [1875–80; back formation from STAGE MANAGER]

stage′ man′ager, a person responsible for the technical details of a theatrical production, assisting the director during rehearsal, supervising the lighting, costuming, setting, prompting, etc., and assuming full responsibility for the stage during a performance of a play. [1810–20] —**stage′ man′agership.**

stage′ pock′et, *Theat.* one of several metal boxes placed backstage in the floor **(floor pocket)** or wall of a theater and containing jacks for electric cables used in lighting units.

stag·er (stā′jər), *n.* **1.** a person of experience in some profession, way of life, etc. **2.** *Archaic.* an actor. [1560–70; STAGE + -ER[1]]

stage′ right′, *Theat.* the part of the stage that is right of center as one faces the audience. Also called **right stage.** [1930–35]

stage′ screw′, a large, tapered screw fitted with a handle, used to secure braces for scenery to the floor of a stage. Also called **stage′ peg′.**

stage′ set′ting, setting (def. 6). Also, **stage′ set′.**

stage·struck (stāj′struk′), *adj.* **1.** obsessed with the desire to become an actor or actress. **2.** enthralled by the theater and the people, customs, traditions, etc., associated with it. Also, **stage′-struck′.** [1805–15]

CONCISE ETYMOLOGY KEY: <, descended or borrowed from; >, whence; b., blend of, blended; c., cognate with; cf., compare; deriv., derivative; equiv., equivalent; imit., imitative; obl., oblique; r., replacing; s., stem; sp., spelling, spelled; resp., respelling, respelled; trans., translation; ?, origin unknown; *, unattested; ‡, probably earlier than. See the full key inside the front cover.

stage′ wait′, *Theat.* an unintentional pause during a performance, usually caused by a performer's or stagehand's missing a cue. [1860–65]

stage′ whis′per, 1. a loud whisper on a stage, meant to be heard by the audience. **2.** any whisper loud enough to be overheard. [1860–65]

stage·y (stā′jē), *adj.,* **stag·i·er, stag·i·est.** stagy.

stag·fla·tion (stag flā′shən), *n.* an inflationary period accompanied by rising unemployment and lack of growth in consumer demand and business activity. [1965–70; b. STAGNATION and INFLATION]

Stagg (stag), *n.* **Amos Alonzo,** 1862–1965, U.S. football coach.

stag·gard (stag′ərd), *n.* a four-year-old male red deer. Also, **stag·gart** (stag′ərt). [1350–1400; ME; see STAG, -ARD]

stag·ger (stag′ər), *v.i.* **1.** to walk, move, or stand unsteadily. **2.** to falter or begin to give way, as in an argument or fight. **3.** to waver or begin to doubt, as in purpose or opinion; hesitate: *After staggering momentarily, he recognized that he had to make a decision.* —*v.t.* **4.** to cause to reel, totter, or become unsteady: *This load would stagger an elephant.* **5.** to shock; render helpless with amazement or the like; astonish: *The vastness of outer space staggers the mind.* **6.** to cause to waver or falter: *The news staggered her belief in the triumph of justice.* **7.** to arrange in a zigzag order or manner on either side of a center: *The captain staggered the troops along the road.* **8.** to arrange otherwise than at the same time, esp. in a series of alternating or continually overlapping intervals: *They planned to stagger lunch hours so that the cafeteria would not be rushed.* **9.** *Aeron.* to arrange (the wings of a biplane or the like) so that the entering edge of an upper wing is either in advance of or behind that of a corresponding lower wing. —*n.* **10.** the act of staggering; a reeling or tottering movement or motion. **11.** a staggered order or arrangement. **12.** *Aeron.* **a.** a staggered arrangement of wings. **b.** the amount of staggering. **13. staggers.** (*used with a singular v.*) *Vet. Pathol.* **a.** Also called **blind staggers.** acute selenium poisoning of livestock characterized by a staggering gait usually followed by respiratory failure and death. **b.** a condition of unknown cause, occurring in pregnant sheep, cattle, and other animals during or just following extended transport, characterized by a staggering gait and progressive paralysis. [1520–30; earlier *stacker* to reel, ME *stakeren* < ON *stakra* to reel, equiv. to *stak(a)* to stagger + *-ra* freq. suffix] —**stag′ger·er,** *n.*
—**Syn. 1.** STAGGER, REEL, TOTTER suggest an unsteady manner of walking. To STAGGER is successively to lose and regain one's equilibrium and the ability to maintain one's direction: *to stagger with exhaustion, a heavy load, or intoxication.* To REEL is to sway dizzily and be in imminent danger of falling: *to reel when faint with hunger.* To TOTTER is to move in a shaky, uncertain, faltering manner and suggests the immediate likelihood of falling from weakness or feebleness: *An old man tottered along with a cane.* **3.** vacillate. **5.** astound, confound, dumfound. **7.** alternate.

stag′ger head′, dropline. Also, **stag′gered head′.**

stag·ger·ing (stag′ə ring), *adj.* tending to stagger or overwhelm: *a staggering amount of money required in the initial investment.* [1555–65; STAGGER + -ING[2]] —**stag′ger·ing·ly,** *adv.*

stag′gering bob′, *Brit., Australian.* **1.** a newborn calf. **2.** any newborn or young animal. [1770–80]

stag·gy (stag′ē), *n., pl.* **-gies.** *Scot.* a colt. Also, **stag′·gie.** [1780–90; STAG + -Y[2]]

stag·horn (stag′hôrn′), *n.* **1.** a piece of a stag's antler, esp. when used to form objects, decorations, or the like. **2.** See **sea staghorn.** —*adj.* **3.** made of or decorated with staghorn: *a knife with a staghorn handle.* [1655–65; STAG + HORN]

stag′horn cor′al, any of several stony corals of the genus *Acropora,* having the skeleton branched like the antlers of a stag. Also, **stag's-horn coral.** [1880–85, *Amer.*]

stag′horn fern′, any of several epiphytic Old World ferns of the genus *Platycerium,* having broad, often antlerlike leaves and cultivated as a houseplant. [1880–85]

stag′horn su′mac, a sumac, *Rhus typhina,* of eastern North America, having leaves that turn scarlet, orange, and purple in the autumn. [1655–65]

stag·hound (stag′hound′), *n.* a hound trained to hunt stags and other large animals. [1700–10; STAG + HOUND[1]]

stag·ing (stā′jing), *n.* **1.** the act, process, or manner of presenting a play on the stage. **2.** a temporary platform or structure of posts and boards for support, as in building; scaffolding. **3.** *Rocketry.* the in-flight separation of a rocket stage from the remaining stages of a multistage missile or launch vehicle. **4.** the business of running stagecoaches. **5.** the act of traveling by stages or by stagecoach. [1275–1325; ME; see STAGE, -ING[1]]

stag′ing ar′ea, 1. an area, as a port of embarkation, where troops are assembled and readied for transit to a new field of operations. **2.** any area or place serving as a point of assembly or preparation on the way to a destination. Also called **stag′ing post′.** [1940–45]

Sta·gi·ra (stə jī′rə), *n.* an ancient town in NE Greece, in Macedonia on the E Chalcidice peninsula: birthplace of Aristotle. Also, **Sta·gi·ros** (stə jī′rəs, -ros).

Stag·i·rite (staj′ə rīt′), *n.* **1.** a native or inhabitant of Stagira. **2. the Stagirite,** Aristotle. Also, **Stagyrite.** [1610–20; < L *Stagīrītēs* < Gk *Stagirī́tēs.* See STAGIRA, -ITE[1]] —**Stag·i·rit·ic** (staj′ə rit′ik), *adj.*

stag′ line′, the men at a social gathering who are not accompanied by a date or dancing partner. [1915–20, *Amer.*]

stag′ mov′ie, a pornographic film intended primarily for male audiences.

stag·nant (stag′nənt), *adj.* **1.** not flowing or running, as water, air, etc. **2.** stale or foul from standing, as a pool of water. **3.** characterized by lack of development, advancement, or progressive movement: *a stagnant economy.* **4.** inactive, sluggish, or dull. [1660–70; < L *stāgnant-* (s. of *stāgnāns*), prp. of *stāgnāre* to STAGNATE; see -ANT] —**stag′nan·cy, stag′nance,** *n.* —**stag′·nant·ly,** *adv.*
—**Syn. 4.** dormant, lifeless, dead, inert, lazy.

stag·nate (stag′nāt), *v.i.,* **-nat·ed, -nat·ing. 1.** to cease to run or flow, as water, air, etc. **2.** to be or become stale or foul from standing, as a pool of water. **3.** to stop developing, growing, progressing, or advancing: *My mind is stagnating from too much TV.* **4.** to be or become sluggish and dull: *When the leading lady left, the show started to stagnate.* —*v.t.* **5.** to make stagnant. [1660–70; < L *stāgnātus* (ptp. of *stāgnāre*), equiv. to *stāgn(um)* pool of standing water + *-ātus* -ATE[1]] —**stag·na′tion,** *n.* —**stag·na·to·ry** (stag′nə tôr′ē, -tōr′ē), *adj.*

stagna′tion masti′tis, *Pathol.* See **caked breast.**

stag′ par′ty, 1. a social gathering or outing for men only. **2.** a party given a bachelor by his male friends before his marriage, often on the night before the wedding, ranging from a formal gathering to a night of carousing. **3.** a gathering for men only, esp. one for the purpose of watching sexually titillating movies or exhibitions. [1850–55, *Amer.*]

stag's′-horn cor′al (stagz′hôrn′). See **staghorn coral.** [1880–85]

stag·y (stā′jē), *adj.,* **stag·i·er, stag·i·est. 1.** of, pertaining to, or suggestive of the stage. **2.** theatrical; unnatural. Also, **stagey.** [1855–60; STAGE + -Y[1]] —**stag′i·ly,** *adv.* —**stag′i·ness,** *n.*

Stag·y·rite (staj′ə rīt′), *n.* Stagirite.

Stahl (shtäl), *n.* **Ge·org Ernst** (gā ōʀk′ ernst), 1660–1734, German chemist and physician.

staid (stād), *adj.* **1.** of settled or sedate character; not flighty or capricious. **2.** fixed, settled, or permanent. —*v.* **3.** *Archaic.* a pt. and pp. of **stay**[1]. [1535–45 for adj. use] —**staid′ly,** *adv.* —**staid′ness,** *n.*
—**Syn. 1.** proper, serious, decorous, solemn. STAID, SEDATE, SETTLED indicate a sober and composed type of conduct. STAID indicates an ingrained seriousness and propriety that shows itself in complete decorum; a colorless kind of correctness is indicated: *a staid and uninteresting family.* SEDATE applies to one who is noticeably quiet, composed, and sober in conduct: *a sedate and dignified young man.* One who is SETTLED has become fixed, esp. in a sober or determined way, in manner, judgments, or mode of life: *He is young to be so settled in his ways.* —**Ant. 1.** wild, frivolous.

stain (stān), *n.* **1.** a discoloration produced by foreign matter having penetrated into or chemically reacted with a material; a spot not easily removed. **2.** a natural spot or patch of color different from that of the basic color, as on the body of an animal. **3.** a cause of reproach; stigma; blemish: *a stain on one's reputation.* **4.** coloration produced by a dye that penetrates a substance, as wood. **5.** a dye made into a solution for coloring woods, textiles, etc. **6.** a reagent or dye used in treating a specimen for microscopic examination. —*v.t.* **7.** to discolor with spots or streaks of foreign matter. **8.** to bring reproach or dishonor upon; blemish. **9.** to sully with guilt or infamy; corrupt. **10.** to color or dye (wood, cloth, etc.) by any of various processes that change or react with the substance chemically. **11.** to color with something that penetrates the substance. **12.** to treat (a microscopic specimen) with some reagent or dye in order to color the whole or parts and so give distinctness, contrast of tissues, etc. —*v.i.* **13.** to produce a stain. **14.** to become stained; take a stain: *This fabric stains easily.* [1350–1400; ME *steynen* < ON *steina* to paint; in some senses aph. form of DISTAIN] —**stain′a·ble,** *adj.* —**stain′a·bil′i·ty, stain′a·ble·ness,** *n.* —**stain′a·bly,** *adv.* —**stain′er,** *n.*
—**Syn. 1, 3.** mark, imperfection, blot. **3.** taint. **7.** spot, streak, soil, dirty. **8.** sully, taint, tarnish, disgrace, dishonor, debase, defile, contaminate, pollute.

stained′ glass′, glass that has been colored, enameled, painted, or stained, esp. by having pigments baked onto its surface or by having various metallic oxides fused into it, as used in church windows, decorative lampshades, etc. [1785–95] —**stained′-glass′,** *adj.*

stain·less (stān′lis), *adj.* **1.** having no stain; spotless. **2.** made of stainless steel. **3.** resistant to staining, rusting, the corrosive effect of chemicals, etc. —*n.* **4.** flatware made of stainless steel. **5.** See **stainless steel.** [1580–90; STAIN + -LESS] —**stain′less·ly,** *adv.* —**stain′·less·ness,** *n.*

stain′less steel′, alloy steel containing 12 percent or more chromium, so as to be resistant to rust and attack from various chemicals. Also called **stainless.** [1915–20]

stair (stâr), *n.* **1.** one of a flight or series of steps for going from one level to another, as in a building. **2. stairs,** such steps collectively, esp. as forming a flight or a series of flights: *I was so excited I ran all the way up the stairs.* **3.** a series or flight of steps; stairway: *a winding stair.* [bef. 1000; ME *stey(e)r,* OE *stǣger;* c. D, LG *steiger* landing; akin to STY[1]] —**stair′less,** *adj.* —**stair′like′,** *adj.*

stair·case (stâr′kās′), *n.* a flight of stairs with its framework, banisters, etc., or a series of such flights. [1615–25; STAIR + CASE[2]]

stair·head (stâr′hed′), *n.* the top of a staircase; top landing. [1525–35; STAIR + HEAD]

Stair·Mas·ter (stâr′mas′tər, -mä′stər), *Trademark.* an exercise machine that allows the user to go through the motions of climbing stairs.

stair′ rod′, a rod for holding a stair carpet in place against the bottom of a riser. [1855–60]

stair·step (stâr′step′), *n., v.,* **-stepped, -step·ping,** *adj.* —*n.* **1.** a step in a staircase. **2. stairsteps,** stairs; a staircase. **3.** a person or thing whose position, status, behavior, or the like suggests the shape or rise of the steps in a staircase: *Their six children are stairsteps* *ranging from ages two to twelve.* —*v.i.* **4.** to occur or move in a regular pattern suggesting the steps of a staircase: *housing units stairstepping down the hill to the edge of the lake.* —*adj.* **5.** suggesting or resembling the steps of a staircase, as in movement or shape: *stairstep progress in improved appliance sales.* Also, **stair′-step′.** [1825–35; STAIR + STEP]

stair•way (stâr′wā′), *n.* a passageway from one level, as of a building, to another by a series of stairs; staircase. [1790–1800; STAIR + WAY[1]]

stair•well (stâr′wel′), *n.* the vertical shaft or opening containing a stairway. Also, **stair′ well′.** [1915–20; STAIR + WELL[2]]

stake[1] (stāk), *n., v.,* **staked, stak•ing.** —*n.* **1.** a stick or post pointed at one end for driving into the ground as a boundary mark, part of a fence, support for a plant, etc. **2.** a post to which a person is bound for execution, usually by burning. **3. the stake,** the punishment of death by burning: *Joan of Arc was sentenced to the stake.* **4.** one of a number of vertical posts fitting into sockets or staples on the edge of the platform of a truck or other vehicle, as to retain the load. **5.** *Mormon Ch.* a division of ecclesiastical territory, consisting of a number of wards presided over by a president and two counselors. **6.** sett (def. 2). **7. pull up stakes,** *Informal.* to leave one's job, place of residence, etc.; move: *They pulled up stakes and went to California.* —*v.t.* **8.** to mark with or as if with stakes (often fol. by *off* or *out*): *We staked out the boundaries of the garden.* **9.** to possess, claim, or reserve a share of (land, profit, glory, etc.) as if by marking or bounding with stakes (usually fol. by *out* or *off*): *I'm staking out ten percent of the profit for myself.* **10.** to separate or close off by a barrier of stakes. **11.** to support with a stake or stakes, as a plant: *to stake tomato vines.* **12.** to tether or secure to a stake, as an animal: *They staked the goat in the back yard.* **13.** to fasten with a stake or stakes. **14. stake out, a.** to keep (a suspect) under police surveillance. **b.** to appoint (a police officer) to maintain constant watch over a suspect or place. [bef. 900; (n.) ME; OE *staca* pin; c. D *staak,* G *Stake,* ON *-staki* (in *lȳsistaki* candlestick); akin to STICK[1]; (v.) ME *staken* to mark (land) with stakes, deriv. of the n.]
—**Syn. 1.** pale, picket, pike.

stake[2] (stāk), *n., v.,* **staked, stak•ing.** —*n.* **1.** something that is wagered in a game, race, or contest. **2.** a monetary or commercial interest, investment, share, or involvement in something, as in hope of gain: *I have a big stake in the success of the firm.* **3.** a personal or emotional concern, interest, involvement, or share: *Parents have a big stake in their children's happiness.* **4.** the funds with which a gambler operates. **5.** Often, **stakes.** a prize, reward, increase in status, etc., in or as if in a contest. **6. stakes.** *Poker.* the cash values assigned to the various colored chips, various bets, and raises: *Our stakes are 5, 10, and 25 cents: you can bet out 10 cents on a pair and reraise twice at 25 cents.* **7.** a grubstake. **8. at stake,** in danger of being lost, as something that has been wagered; critically involved. —*v.t.* **9.** to risk (something), as upon the result of a game or the occurrence or outcome of any uncertain event, venture, etc.: *He staked his reputation on the success of the invention.* **10.** to furnish (someone) with necessaries or resources, esp. money: *They staked me to a good meal and a train ticket.* [1520–30; orig. uncert.]
—**Syn. 1.** wager, bet. **5.** winnings, purse. **9.** bet, gamble, hazard; jeopardize.

stake′ boat′, **1.** an anchored boat to which barges or other boats are temporarily moored. **2.** an anchored boat used as a turning point in races. [1880–85]

stake′ bod′y, an open truck body having a platform with sockets at the edge into which upright stakes may be placed to form a fence around a load. [1930–35]

Staked′ Plain′. See **Llano Estacado.**

stake•hold•er (stāk′hōl′dər), *n.* **1.** the holder of the stakes of a wager. **2.** a person or group that has an investment, share, or interest in something, as a business or industry. **3.** *Law.* a person holding money or property to which two or more persons make rival claims. [1700–10; STAKE[2] + HOLDER]

stake′ horse′, a horse that is regularly entered in stake races. [1890–95, *Amer.*]

stake•out (stāk′out′), *n.* **1.** the surveillance of a location by the police, as in anticipation of a crime or the arrival of a wanted person. **2.** the place from which such surveillance is carried out. **3.** something that is bounded or separated by or as if by stakes, esp. property, territory, or the like that one identifies or claims as one's own. [1940–45; n. use of v. phrase *stake out*]

stake′ race′, *Horse Racing.* a race in which part of the prize or purse is put up by the owners of the horses nominated to run in the race. Also, **stakes′ race′.** [1905–10]

stake′ truck′, a truck or trailer with a stake body, as for hauling farm animals or feed bags. Cf. **flatbed.** [1925–30]

Sta•kha•nov (stu KHä′nəf), *n.* a city in E Ukraine, W of Lugansk. 108,000. Formerly, **Kadiyevka.**

Sta•kha•nov•ism (stə kä′nə viz′əm, stä hä′no-), *n.* a method for increasing production by rewarding individual initiative, developed in the Soviet Union in 1935. [1935–40; STAKHANOV(ITE) + -ISM]

Sta•kha•nov•ite (stə kä′nə vit′, -kan′ə-), *n.* **1.** a worker in the Soviet Union who regularly surpasses production quotas and is specially honored and rewarded. —*adj.* **2.** of or pertaining to a Stakhanovite or to Stakhanovism. [trans. of Russ *stakhánovets* (1935), after Alekseĭ Grigor′evich *Stakhanov* (1906–77), Soviet coal miner, whose productivity was the focus of a propaganda campaign; see -ITE[1]]

sta•lac•ti•form (stə lak′tə fôrm′), *adj.* resembling or shaped like a stalactite. [1830–40; STALACT(ITE) + -I- + -FORM]

sta•lac•tite (stə lak′tīt, stal′ək tīt′), *n.* a deposit, usually of calcium carbonate, shaped like an icicle, hanging from the roof of a cave or the like, and formed by the dripping of percolating calcareous water. [1670–80; < NL *stalactites* < Gk *stalakt(ós)* dripping (*stalag-,* s. of *stalássein* to drip + *-tos* verbid suffix) + NL *-ites* -ITE[1]] —**stal•ac•tit•ic** (stal′ək tit′ik), **stal′ac•tit′i•cal,** *adj.* —**stal′ac•tit′i•cal•ly,** *adv.*

A, **stalactite;**
B, stalagmite

stalac′tite work′, (in Islamic architecture) intricate decorative corbeling in the form of brackets, squinches, and portions of pointed vaults. Also called **honeycomb work.** [1900–05]

sta•lag (stal′əg; *Ger.* shtä′läk), *n.* a World War II German military camp housing prisoners of war of enlisted ranks. [1940–45; < G, short for *Sta(mm)lag(er),* equiv. to *Stamm* cadre, main body + *Lager* camp]

sta•lag•mite (stə lag′mīt, stal′əg mīt′), *n.* a deposit, usually of calcium carbonate, more or less resembling an inverted stalactite, formed on the floor of a cave or the like by the dripping of percolating calcareous water. See illus. under **stalactite.** [1675–85; < NL *stalagmites* < Gk *stálagm(a)* a drop (*stalag-,* s. of *stalássein* to drip + *-ma* n. suffix of result) + NL *-ites* -ITE[1]] —**stal•ag•mit•ic** (stal′əg mit′ik), **stal′ag•mit′i•cal,** *adj.* —**stal′ag•mit′i•cal•ly,** *adv.*

stal•ag•mom•e•ter (stal′əg mom′i tər), *n. Chem., Physics.* an instrument for determining the number of drops, or the weight of each drop, in a given volume of liquid. Also called **stactometer.** [1860–65; < Gk *stalagmó(s)* dripping + -METER] —**sta•lag•mo•met•ric** (stə-lag′mə me′trik), *adj.* —**stal′ag•mom′e•try,** *n.*

St. Al•bans (ôl′bənz), **1.** a city in W Hertfordshire, in SE England: Norman cathedral; battles of Wars of the Roses 1455, 1461. 123,500. **2.** a city in W West Virginia, near Charleston. 12,402.

St. Albert, a town in central Alberta, in W Canada, near Edmonton. 31,996.

stale[1] (stāl), *adj.,* **stal•er, stal•est,** *v.,* **staled, stal•ing.** —*adj.* **1.** not fresh; vapid or flat, as beverages; dry or hardened, as bread. **2.** musty; stagnant: *stale air.* **3.** having lost novelty or interest; hackneyed; trite: *a stale joke.* **4.** having lost freshness, vigor, quick intelligence, initiative, or the like, as from overstrain, boredom, or surfeit: *He had grown stale on the job and needed a long vacation.* **5.** *Law.* having lost force or effectiveness through absence of action, as a claim. —*v.t., v.i.* **6.** to make or become stale. [1250–1300; ME; akin to MD *stel* in same sense; perh. akin to STAND or to STALE[2]] —**stale′ly,** *adv.* —**stale′ness,** *n.*
—**Syn. 1.** hard, tasteless, sour, insipid. **3.** uninteresting, stereotyped, old, common. —**Ant. 1.** fresh.

stale[2] (stāl), *v.i.,* **staled, stal•ing.** (of livestock, esp. horses) to urinate. [1400–50; late ME *stalen* to urinate; c. G *stallen,* Dan *stalle,* Norw, Sw *stalla*]

stale•mate (stāl′māt′), *n., v.,* **-mat•ed, -mat•ing.** —*n.* **1.** *Chess.* a position of the pieces in which a player cannot move any piece except the king and cannot move the king without putting it in check. **2.** any position or situation in which no action can be taken or progress made; deadlock: *Talks between union and management resulted in a stalemate.* —*v.t.* **3.** to subject to a stalemate. **4.** to bring to a standstill. —*v.i.* **5.** to be or result in a stalemate or standoff: *Negotiations stalemated when new salary demands were introduced.* [1755–65; late ME *stale* stalemate (whence AF *estale*) (appar. special use of STALE[1]) + MATE[2]]
—**Syn. 2.** impasse, standoff, standstill.

Sta•lin (stä′lin, -lēn, stal′in; *Russ.* stä′lyin), *n.* **1. Joseph V.** (*Iosif Vissarionovich Dzhugashvili* or *Dzugashvili*), 1879–1953, Soviet political leader: secretary general of the Communist party 1922–53; premier of the U.S.S.R. 1941–53. **2.** a former name of **Donetsk. 3.** former name of **Varna. 4.** former name of **Braşov.**

Sta•li•na•bad (stä′lə nə bäd′; *Russ.* stə lyi nu bät′), *n.* a former name of **Dushanbe.**

Sta•lin•grad (stä′lin grad′; *Russ.* stə lyin grät′), *n.* former name of **Volgograd.**

Sta•lin•ism (stä′lə niz′əm), *n.* the principles of communism associated with Joseph Stalin, characterized esp. by the extreme suppression of dissident political or ideological views, the concentration of power in one person, and an aggressive international policy. [1925–30; STALIN + -ISM]

Sta•lin•ist (stä′lə nist), *adj.* **1.** of or pertaining to Joseph Stalin or Stalinism. —*n.* **2.** an advocate or supporter of Stalin or Stalinism. [1925–30; STALIN + -IST]

Sta•li•no (stä′lə nō′; *Russ.* stä′lyi nə), *n.* a former name of **Donetsk.**

Sta′lin Peak′, former name of **Communism Peak.**

Sta•linsk (stä′linsk; *Russ.* stä′lyinsk), *n.* former name of **Novokuznetsk.**

stalk[1] (stôk), *n.* **1.** the stem or main axis of a plant. **2.** any slender supporting or connecting part of a plant, as the petiole of a leaf, the peduncle of a flower, or the funicle of an ovule. **3.** a similar structural part of an animal. **4.** a stem, shaft, or slender supporting part of anything. **5.** *Auto.* a slender lever, usually mounted on or near the steering wheel, that is used by the driver to control a signal or function: *The horn button is on the turn-signal stalk.* [1275–1325; ME *stalke,* appar. equiv. to OE *stal(u)* stave + *-k* dim. suffix] —**stalk′like′,** *adj.*

stalk[2] (stôk), *v.i.* **1.** to pursue or approach prey, quarry, etc., stealthily. **2.** to walk with measured, stiff, or haughty strides: *He was so angry he stalked away without saying goodbye.* **3.** to proceed in a steady, deliberate, or sinister manner: *Famine stalked through the nation.* **4.** *Obs.* to walk or go stealthily along. —*v.t.* **5.** to pursue (game, a person, etc.) stealthily. **6.** to proceed through (an area) in search of prey or quarry: *to stalk the woods for game.* **7.** to proceed or spread through in a steady or sinister manner: *Disease stalked the land.* —*n.* **8.** an act or course of stalking quarry, prey, or the like: *We shot the mountain goat after a five-hour stalk.* **9.** a slow, stiff stride or gait. [1250–1300; ME *stalken* (v.), repr. the base of OE *bestealcian* to move stealthily, *stealcung* stalking (ger.); akin to STEAL] —**stalk′a•ble,** *adj.* —**stalk′er,** *n.* —**stalk′ing•ly,** *adv.*

stalked (stôkt), *adj.* having a stalk or stem. [1725–35; STALK[1] + -ED[3]]

stalked′ puff′ball, a puffball-like mushroom of the genus *Tulestoma,* maturing in early winter.

stalk-eyed (stôk′īd′), *adj. Anat.* having the eyes located on pedicels, as some crustaceans and dipterans. [1850–55]

stalk•ing-horse (stô′king hôrs′), *n.* **1.** a horse, or a figure of a horse, behind which a hunter hides in stalking game. **2.** anything put forward to mask plans or efforts; pretext. **3.** a political candidate used to conceal the candidacy of a more important figure or to draw votes from and cause the defeat of a rival. [1510–20]

stalk•less (stôk′lis), *adj.* **1.** having no stalk. **2.** *Bot.* sessile. [1690–1700; STALK[1] + -LESS]

stalk•y (stô′kē), *adj.,* **stalk•i•er, stalk•i•est. 1.** abounding in stalks. **2.** stalklike; long and slender. [1545–55; STALK[1] + -Y[1]] —**stalk′i•ly,** *adv.* —**stalk′i•ness,** *n.*

stall[1] (stôl), *n.* **1.** a compartment in a stable or shed for the accommodation of one animal. **2.** a stable or shed for horses or cattle. **3.** a booth or stand in which merchandise is displayed for sale, or in which some business is carried on (sometimes used in combination): *a butcher's stall; a bookstall.* **4.** carrel (def. 1). **5.** one of a number of fixed enclosed seats in the choir or chancel of a church for the use of the clergy. **6.** a pew. **7.** any small compartment or booth for a specific activity or housing a specific thing: *a shower stall.* **8.** a rectangular space marked off or reserved for parking a car or other vehicle, as in a parking lot. **9.** an instance or the condition of causing an engine, or a vehicle powered by an engine, to stop, esp. by supplying it with a poor fuel mixture or by overloading it. **10.** *Aeron.* an instance or the condition of causing an airplane to fly at an angle of attack greater than the angle of maximum lift, causing loss of control and a downward spin. Cf. **critical angle** (def. 2). **11.** a protective covering for a finger or toe, as various guards and sheaths or one finger of a glove. **12.** *Brit.* a chairlike seat in a theater, separated from others by arms or rails, esp. one in the front section of the parquet. —*v.t.* **13.** to assign to, put, or keep in a stall or stalls, as an animal or a car. **14.** to confine in a stall for fattening, as cattle. **15.** to cause (a motor or the vehicle it powers) to stop, esp. by supplying it with a poor fuel mixture or overloading it. **16.** *Aeron.* **a.** to put (an airplane) into a stall. **b.** to lose control of or crash (an airplane) from so doing. **17.** to bring to a standstill; check the progress or motion of, esp. unintentionally. **18.** to cause to stick fast, as in mire or snow. —*v.i.* **19.** (of an engine, car, airplane, etc.) to be stalled or go through the process of stalling (sometimes fol. by *out*). **20.** to come to a standstill; be brought to a stop. **21.** to stick fast, as in mire. **22.** to occupy a stall, as an animal. [bef. 900; ME; OE *steall;* c. G *Stall,* ON *stallr;* akin to OE *stellan,* G *stellen* to put, place] —**stall′-like′,** *adj.*

stall[2] (stôl), *v.i.* **1.** to delay, esp. by evasion or deception. **2.** *Sports.* to prolong holding the ball as a tactic to prevent the opponent from scoring, as when one's team has the lead. Cf. **freeze** (def. 31). —*v.t.* **3.** to delay or put off, esp. by evasion or deception (often fol. by *off*): *He stalled the police for 15 minutes so his accomplice could get away.* —*n.* **4.** a pretext, as a ruse, trick, or the like, used to delay or deceive. **5.** *Underworld Slang.* the member of a pickpocket's team who distracts the victim long enough for the theft to take place. **6.** *Sports.* slowdown (def. 3). [1490–1500; earlier *stale* decoy bird (> AF *estale* decoy pigeon), OE *stæl-* decoy (in *stælhrān* decoy reindeer); akin to STALL[1]]

stall•age (stô′lij), *n. Eng. Law.* **1.** the right to set up a stall in a fair or market. **2.** rent paid for such a stall. [1350–1400; ME < AL *stallāgium,* AF *estalage.* See STALL[1], -AGE]

stall-fed (stôl′fed′), *adj.* (of animals) confined to and fed in a stall, esp. for fattening. [1545–55]

stall-feed (stôl′fēd′), *v.t.,* **-fed, -feed•ing. 1.** to keep and feed (an animal) in a stall. **2.** to fatten (an animal) for slaughter by stall-feeding. [1755–65]

stall′ing an′gle, *Aeron.* See **critical angle** (def. 2).

stal•lion (stal′yən), *n.* an uncastrated adult male horse, esp. one used for breeding. [1275–1325; ME *stalon* < OF *estalon,* equiv. to *stal-* (< Gmc; see STALL[1]) + *-on* n. suffix]

stal•wart (stôl′wərt), *adj.* **1.** strongly and stoutly built; sturdy and robust. **2.** strong and brave; valiant: *a stalwart knight.* **3.** firm, steadfast, or uncompromising:

a stalwart supporter of the U.N. —*n.* **4.** a physically stalwart person. **5.** a steadfast or uncompromising partisan: *They counted on the party stalwarts for support in the off-year campaigns.* [1325–75; ME (Scots), var. of *stalward,* earlier *stalwurthe;* see STALWORTH] —**stal′wart·ly,** *adv.* —**stal′wart·ness,** *n.*

Stal·wart (stôl′wərt), *n.* a conservative Republican in the 1870's and 1880's, esp. one opposed to civil service and other reforms during the administrations of presidents Rutherford B. Hayes and James A. Garfield.

stal·worth (stôl′wərth), *adj. Archaic.* stalwart. [bef. 900; ME *stalwurthe,* OE *stǣlwirthe* serviceable, equiv. to *stǣl* (contr. of *stathol* STADDLE) + *weorth* WORTH]

stam·ba (stam′bä), *n.* (in India) a memorial pillar. [< Skt *stambha* pillar, column]

Stam·bul (stäm bo͝ol′), *n.* **1.** the oldest part and principal Turkish residential section of Istanbul, south of the Golden Horn. **2.** Istanbul. Also, **Stam·boul** (stäm bo͝ol′; *Fr.* stän bo͝ol′).

sta·men (stā′mən), *n., pl.* **sta·mens, stam·i·na** (stam′ə nə). *Bot.* the pollen-bearing organ of a flower, consisting of the filament and the anther. See diag. under **flower.** [1640–50; < L *stāmen* warp in upright loom, thread, filament, equiv. to *stā(re)* to STAND + *-men* n. suffix; akin to Gk *stḗmōn* warp, Skt *sthāman* place] —**sta′mened,** *adj.*

sta′men blight′, *Plant Pathol.* a disease of blackberries, characterized by a gray, powdery mass of spores covering the anthers, caused by a fungus, *Hapalosphaeria deformans.*

Stam·ford (stam′fərd), *n.* **1.** a city in SW Connecticut. 102,453. **2.** a male given name.

stam·in (stam′in), *n.* a coarse woolen fabric, used in the manufacture of garments. [1175–1225; ME < MF *estamine* << L *stāminea,* fem. of *stāmineus* consisting of threads, equiv. to *stāmin-* (see STAMEN) + *-eus* -EOUS]

stamin-, var. of **stamini-** before a vowel: *staminate.*

stam·i·na[1] (stam′ə nə), *n.* strength of physical constitution; power to endure disease, fatigue, privation, etc. [1535–45; < L, pl. of *stāmen* thread (see STAMEN); i.e., the life-threads spun by the Fates]

stam·i·na[2] (stam′ə nə), *n.* a pl. of **stamen.**

stam·i·nal[1] (stam′ə nl), *adj. Bot.* of or pertaining to stamens. Also, **sta·min·e·al** (stə min′ē əl). [1835–45; STAMIN- + -AL[1]]

stam·i·nal[2] (stam′ə nl), *adj.* of or pertaining to stamina or endurance. [1775–85; STAMIN(A)[1] + -AL[1]]

stam·i·nate (stam′ə nit, -nāt′), *adj. Bot.* **1.** having a stamen or stamens. **2.** having stamens but no pistils. See illus. under **monoecious.** [1835–45; STAMIN- + -ATE[1]]

stamini-, a combining form representing **stamen** in compound words: *staminiferous.* Also, *esp. before a vowel,* **stamin-.** [comb. form repr. L *stāmin-* (s. of *stāmen*); see -I-]

stam·i·nif·er·ous (stam′ə nif′ər əs), *adj. Bot.* bearing or having a stamen or stamens. [1755–65; STAMINI- + -FEROUS]

stam·i·no·di·um (stam′ə nō′dē əm), *n., pl.* **-di·a** (-dē ə). *Bot.* **1.** a sterile or abortive stamen. **2.** a part resembling such a stamen. Also, **stam·i·node** (stam′ə-nōd′). [1815–25; STAMIN- + -ODE[1] + -IUM]

stam·i·no·dy (stam′ə nō′dē), *n. Bot.* the metamorphosis of any of various flower organs, as a sepal or a petal, into a stamen. [1865–70; alter. of STAMINODIUM, with -Y[3] r. -IUM]

stam·mer (stam′ər), *v.i.* **1.** to speak with involuntary breaks and pauses, or with spasmodic repetitions of syllables or sounds. —*v.t.* **2.** to say with a stammer (often fol. by *out*). —*n.* **3.** a stammering mode of utterance. **4.** a stammered utterance. [bef. 1000; ME *stameren* (v.), OE *stamerian* (c. G *stammern*), equiv. to *stam* stammering + *-erian* -ER[6]; akin to ON *stamma* to stammer, Goth *stams* stammering] —**stam′mer·er,** *n.* —**stam′mer·ing·ly,** *adv.*

—**Syn. 1.** pause, hesitate, falter. STAMMER, STUTTER mean to speak with some form of difficulty. STAMMER, the general term, suggests a speech difficulty that results in broken or inarticulate sounds and sometimes in complete stoppage of speech; it may be temporary, caused by sudden excitement, confusion, embarrassment, or other emotion, or it may be so deep-seated as to require special treatment for its correction. STUTTER, the parallel term preferred in technical usage, designates a broad range of defects that produce spasmodic interruptions of the speech rhythm, repetitions, or prolongations of sounds or syllables: *The child's stutter was no mere stammer of embarrassment.*

stamm·rel (stam′rəl), *adj., n. Scot.* staumrel.

stam·nos (stam′nos), *n., pl.* **-noi** (-noi). *Gk. and Rom. Antiq.* a storage jar having an oval body tapering at the base and two horizontal handles set on the shoulder. Cf. **amphora, pelike.** [1835–45; < Gk *stámnos;* akin to *histánai* to cause to stand; see STAND]

stamp (stamp), *v.t.* **1.** to strike or beat with a forcible, downward thrust of the foot. **2.** to bring (the foot) down forcibly or smartly on the ground, floor, etc. **3.** to extinguish, crush, etc., by striking with a forcible downward thrust of the foot (fol. by *out*): *to stamp out a fire.* **4.** to suppress or quell (a rebellion, uprising, etc.) quickly through the use of overwhelming force (usually fol. by *out*). **5.** to crush or pound with or as with a pestle. **6.** to impress with a particular mark or device, as to indicate genuineness, approval, or ownership: *to stamp a document with a seal.* **7.** to mark or impress with a design, word, mark, etc.: *Age stamped his face with lines.* **8.** to impress (a design, word, mark, etc.) on: *to stamp one's initials on a document.* **9.** to affix a postage stamp to (a letter, envelope, etc.). **10.** to characterize, distinguish, or reveal: *His ingenuity with words stamped him as a potential poet.* —*v.i.* **11.** to bring the foot down forcibly or smartly, as in crushing something, expressing rage, etc. **12.** to walk with forcible or heavy, resounding steps: *He stamped out of the room in anger.* —*n.* **13.** See **postage stamp. 14.** an act or instance of stamping. **15.** a die or block for impressing or imprinting. **16.** a design or legend made with such a die or block. **17.** an official mark indicating genuineness, validity, etc., or payment of a duty or charge. **18.** a peculiar or distinctive impression or mark: *a great man who left his stamp on legal procedure.* **19.** character, kind, or type: *a woman of serious stamp.* **20.** an official seal or device appearing on a business or legal document to show that a tax has been paid. **21.** Also called **local, local stamp.** such a device, often similar to a postage stamp, issued by a private organization to show that the charges for mail carrying have been paid. **22.** See **trading stamp. 23.** See **food stamp. 24.** an instrument for stamping, crushing, or pounding. **25.** a heavy piece of iron or the like, as in a stamp mill, for crushing ore or other material. [1150–1200; (v.) early ME *stampen* to pound, crush, prob. continuing OE **stampian* (c. MD, MLG *stampen,* OHG *stampfōn,* ON *stappa*); sense development appar. influenced by OF *estamper* to stamp < Gmc; (n.) late ME: instrument for stamping an impression; partly deriv. of the v., partly < OF *estampe,* deriv. of *estamper*] —**stamp′a·ble,** *adj.* —**stamp′less,** *adj.*

—**Syn. 4.** eliminate, quash. See **abolish.**

Stamp′ Act′, *Amer. Hist.* an act of the British Parliament for raising revenue in the American Colonies by requiring the use of stamps and stamped paper for official documents, commercial writings, and various articles: it was to go into effect on November 1, 1765, but met with intense opposition and was repealed in March, 1766.

stam·pede (stam pēd′), *n., v.,* **-ped·ed, -ped·ing.** —*n.* **1.** a sudden, frenzied rush or headlong flight of a herd of frightened animals, esp. cattle or horses. **2.** any headlong general flight or rush. **3.** *Western U.S., Canada.* a celebration, usually held annually, combining a rodeo, contests, exhibitions, dancing, etc. —*v.i.* **4.** to scatter or flee in a stampede: *People stampeded from the burning theater.* **5.** to make a general rush: *On hearing of the sale, they stampeded to the store.* —*v.t.* **6.** to cause to stampede. **7.** to rush or overrun (a place): *Customers stampeded the stores.* [1815–25, *Amer.*; < AmerSp *estampida,* Sp, equiv. to *estamp(ar)* to stamp + *-ida* n. suffix] —**stam·ped′er,** *n.*

stamp·er (stam′pər), *n.* **1.** a person or thing that stamps. **2.** (in a post office) an employee who applies postmarks and cancels postage stamps. **3.** a pestle, esp. one in a stamp mill. **4.** a mold, usually of metal, from which disk recordings are pressed. [1350–1400; ME *stampere.* See STAMP, -ER[1]]

stamp′ing ground′, a habitual or favorite haunt. [1780–90]

stamp′ mill′, *Mining.* a mill or machine in which ore is crushed to powder by means of heavy stamps or pestles. Also, **stamp′ing mill′.** [1740–50]

stamp′ tax′, a tax whose revenue is derived from the sale of stamps that are required to be affixed to certain retail merchandise and legal documents. [1815–25]

Stan (stan), *n.* a male given name, form of **Stanley.**

stance (stans), *n.* **1.** the position or bearing of the body while standing: *legs spread in a wide stance; the threatening stance of the bull.* **2.** a mental or emotional position adopted with respect to something: *They assumed an increasingly hostile stance in their foreign policy.* **3.** *Sports.* the relative position of the feet, as in addressing a golf ball or in making a stroke. [1525–35; < OF *estance* (standing) position < VL **stantia,* deriv. of L *stant-* (s. of *stāns*), prp. of *stāre* to STAND]

stanch[1] (stônch, stanch, stänch), *v.t.* **1.** to stop the flow of (a liquid, esp. blood). **2.** to stop the flow of blood or other liquid from (a wound, leak, etc.). **3.** *Archaic.* to check, allay, or extinguish. —*v.i.* **4.** to stop flowing, as blood; be stanched. —*n.* **5.** Also called **flash-lock, navigation weir.** a lock that, after being partially emptied, is opened suddenly to send a boat over a shallow place with a rush of water. Also, **staunch.** [1275–1325; ME *stanchen, staunchen* (v.) < OF *estanchier* to close, stop, slake (thirst) < VL **stanticāre,* equiv. to L *stant-* (s. of *stāns,* prp. of *stāre* to STAND) + *-icāre* causative suffix] —**stanch′a·ble,** *adj.* —**stanch′er,** *n.*

stanch[2] (stônch, stänch, stanch), *adj.,* **-er, -est.** staunch[2]. —**stanch′ly,** *adv.* —**stanch′ness,** *n.*

stan·chion (stan′shən), *n.* **1.** an upright bar, beam, post, or support, as in a window, stall, ship, etc. —*v.t.* **2.** to furnish with stanchions. **3.** to secure by or to a stanchion or stanchions. [1375–1425; late ME *stanchon* < OF *estanchon,* equiv. to *estanche* (var. of *estance,* prob. < VL **stantia,* equiv. to L *stant-* (s. of *stāns*), prp. of *stāre* to STAND + *-ia* -Y[3]) + *-on* n. suffix]

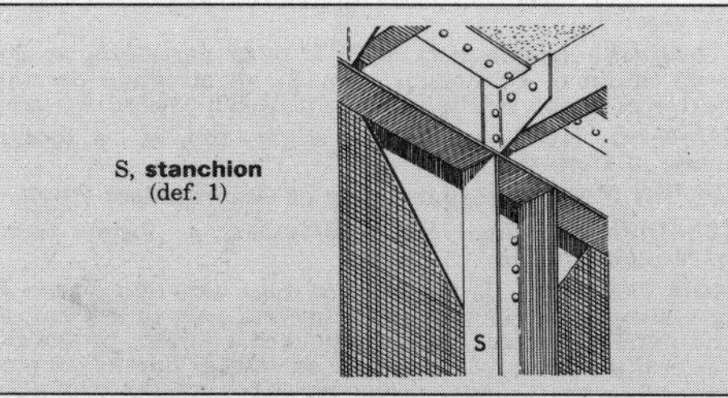

S, stanchion (def. 1)

stanch·less (stônch′lis, stänch′-, stanch′-), *adj.* **1.** not to be stanched. **2.** incessant: *a stanchless torrent of words.* [1595–1605; STANCH[1] + -LESS] —**stanch′less·ly,** *adv.*

stand (stand), *v.,* **stood, stand·ing,** *n., pl.* **stands** for 43–63, **stands, stand** for 64. —*v.i.* **1.** (of a person) to be in an upright position on the feet. **2.** to rise to one's feet (often fol. by *up*). **3.** to have a specified height when in this position: *a basketball player who stands six feet seven inches.* **4.** to stop or remain motionless or steady on the feet. **5.** to take a position or place as indicated: *to stand aside.* **6.** to remain firm or steadfast, as in a cause. **7.** to take up or maintain a position or attitude with respect to a person, issue, or the like: *to stand as sponsor for a person.* **8.** to have or adopt a certain policy, course, or attitude, as of adherence, support, opposition, or resistance: *He stands for free trade.* **9.** (of things) to be in an upright or vertical position, be set on end, or rest on or as on a support. **10.** to be set, placed, fixed, located, or situated: *The building stands at 34th Street and 5th Avenue.* **11.** (of an account, score, etc.) to show, be, or remain as indicated; show the specified position of the parties concerned: *The score stood 18 to 14 at the half.* **12.** to remain erect or whole; resist change, decay, or destruction (often fol. by *up*): *The ruins still stand. The old building stood up well.* **13.** to continue in force or remain valid: *The agreement stands as signed.* **14.** to remain still, stationary, or unused: *The bicycle stood in the basement all winter.* **15.** to be or become stagnant, as water. **16.** (of persons or things) to be or remain in a specified state, condition, relation, relative position, etc.: *He stood in jeopardy of losing his license.* **17.** to have the possibility or likelihood: *He stands to gain a sizable profit through the sale of the house.* **18.** *Chiefly Brit.* to become or be a candidate, as for public office (usually fol. by *for*). **19.** *Naut.* **a.** to take or hold a particular course at sea. **b.** to move in a certain direction: *to stand offshore.* **20.** (of a male domestic animal, esp. a stud) to be available as a sire, usually for a fee: *Three Derby winners are now standing in Kentucky.* —*v.t.* **21.** to cause to stand; set upright; set: *Stand the chair by the lamp.* **22.** to face or encounter: *to stand an assault.* **23.** to undergo or submit to: *to stand trial.* **24.** to endure or undergo without harm or damage or without giving way: *His eyes are strong enough to stand the glare.* **25.** to endure or tolerate: *She can't stand her father.* **26.** to treat or pay for: *I'll stand you to a drink when the manuscript is in.* **27.** to perform the duty of or participate in as part of one's job or duty: *to stand watch aboard ship.* **28. stand a chance** or **show,** to have a chance or possibility, esp. of winning or surviving: *He's a good shortstop but doesn't stand a chance of making the major leagues because he can't hit.* **29. stand by, a.** to uphold; support: *She stood by him whenever he was in trouble.* **b.** to adhere to (an agreement, promise, etc.); affirm: *She stood by her decision despite her sister's arguments.* **c.** to stand ready; wait: *Please stand by while I fix this antenna.* **d.** to get ready to speak, act, etc., as at the beginning of a radio or television program. **e.** to be ready to board a plane, train, or other transport if accommodations become available at the last minute. **30. stand down, a.** *Law.* to leave the witness stand. **b.** to step aside; withdraw, as from a competition: *I agreed to stand down so that she could run for the nomination unopposed.* **c.** to leave or take out of active work or service: *to stand down some of the ships in the fleet.* **31. stand for, a.** to represent; symbolize: *P.S. stands for "postscript."* **b.** to advocate; favor: *He stands for both freedom and justice.* **c.** *Informal.* to tolerate; allow: *I won't stand for any nonsense!* **32. stand in with, a.** to be in association or conspiracy with. **b.** to enjoy the favor of; be on friendly terms with. **33. stand off, a.** to keep or stay at a distance. **b.** to put off; evade. **34. stand on, a.** to depend on; rest on: *The case stands on his testimony.* **b.** to be particular about; demand: *to stand on ceremony.* **c.** *Naut.* to maintain a course and speed. **35. stand out, a.** to project; protrude: *The piers stand out from the harbor wall.* **b.** to be conspicuous or prominent: *She stands out in a crowd.* **c.** to persist in opposition or resistance; be inflexible. **d.** *Naut.* to maintain a course away from shore. **36. stand over, a.** to supervise very closely; watch constantly: *He won't work unless someone stands over him.* **b.** to put aside temporarily; postpone: *to let a project stand over until the following year.* **37. stand pat.** See **pat**[2] (def. 6). **38. stand to, a.** to continue to hold; persist in: *to stand to one's statement.* **b.** to keep at steadily: *Stand to your rowing, men!* **c.** to wait in readiness; stand by: *Stand to for action.* **39. stand to reason.** See **reason** (def. 11). **40. stand up, a.** to come to or remain in a standing position: *to stand up when being introduced.* **b.** to remain strong, convincing, or durable: *The case will never stand up in court. Wool stands up better than silk.* **c.** *Slang.* to fail to keep an appointment with (someone, esp. a sweetheart or date): *I waited for Kim for an hour before I realized I'd been stood up.* **41. stand up for, a.** to defend the cause of; support: *No one could understand why he stood up for an incorrigible criminal.* **b.** to serve a bridegroom or bride, as best man or maid (matron) of honor. **42. stand up to,** to meet or deal with fearlessly; confront: *to stand up to a bully.*

—*n.* **43.** the act of standing; an assuming of or a remaining in an upright position. **44.** a cessation of motion; halt or stop. **45.** a determined effort for or against something, esp. a final defensive effort: *Custer's last stand.* **46.** a determined policy, position, attitude, etc., taken or maintained: *We must take a stand on political issues.* **47.** the place in which a person or thing stands; station. **48.** See **witness stand. 49.** a raised platform, as for a speaker, a band, or the like. **50. stands,** a raised section of seats for spectators; grandstand. **51.** a framework on or in which articles are placed for support, exhibition, etc.: *a hat stand.* **52.** a piece of furniture of various forms, on or in which to put articles (often used in combination): *a nightstand; a washstand.* **53.** a small, light table. **54.** a stall, booth, counter, or the like, where articles are displayed for sale or where some business is carried on: *a fruit stand.* **55.** newsstand: *The papers usually hit the stands at 5 A.M.* **56.** a site or location for business: *After 20 years the ice-cream vendor was still at the same stand.* **57.** a place or station oc-

CONCISE ETYMOLOGY KEY: <, descended or borrowed from; >, whence; b., blend of, blended; c., cognate with; cf., compare; deriv., derivative; equiv., equivalent; imit., imitative; obl., oblique; r., replacing; s., stem; sp., spelling, spelled; resp., respelling, respelled; trans., translation; ?, origin unknown; *, unattested; ‡, probably earlier than. See the full key inside the front cover.

cupied by vehicles available for hire: *a taxicab stand.* **58.** the vehicles occupying such a place. **59.** the growing trees, or those of a particular species or grade, in a given area. **60.** a standing growth, as of grass, wheat, etc. **61.** a halt of a theatrical company on tour, to give a performance or performances: *a series of one-night stands on the strawhat trail.* **62.** the town at which a touring theatrical company gives a performance. **63.** hive (def. 2). **64.** *Metalworking.* a rolling unit in a rolling mill. **65.** *Chiefly Brit.* a complete set of arms or accoutrements for one soldier. **66. take the stand,** to testify in a courtroom. [bef. 900; ME *standen* (v.), OE *standan;* c. OS *standan,* MD *standen,* OHG *stantan, standa, standan;* akin to L *stāre* to stand, *sistere,* Gk *histánai* to make stand, Skt *sthā* to stand, OIr *at-tá* (he) is]
—Syn. 25. abide, stomach. See **bear**[1].

stand-a•lone (stand′ə lōn′), *Computers.* —*adj.* **1.** self-contained and able to operate without other hardware or software. —*n.* **2.** a device or program with these characteristics. [1965–70]

stand•ard (stan′dərd), *n.* **1.** something considered by an authority or by general consent as a basis of comparison; an approved model. **2.** an object that is regarded as the usual or most common size or form of its kind: *We stock the deluxe models as well as the standards.* **3.** a rule or principle that is used as a basis for judgment: *They tried to establish standards for a new philosophical approach.* **4.** an average or normal requirement, quality, quantity, level, grade, etc.: *His work this week hasn't been up to his usual standard.* **5. standards,** those morals, ethics, habits, etc., established by authority, custom, or an individual as acceptable: *He tried to live up to his father's standards.* **6.** a grade of beef immediately below good. **7.** the authorized exemplar of a unit of weight or measure. **8.** a certain commodity in or by which a basic monetary unit is stated. Cf. **gold standard, silver standard, bimetallism, monometallism. 9.** the legally established content of full-weight coins. **10.** the prescribed degree of fineness for gold or silver. **11.** *Brit.* a class or grade in elementary schools. **12.** a musical piece of sufficiently enduring popularity to be made part of a permanent repertoire, esp. a popular song. **13.** a flag indicating the presence of a sovereign or public official. **14.** a flag, emblematic figure, or other object raised on a pole to indicate the rallying point of an army, fleet, etc. **15.** *Mil.* **a.** any of various military or naval flags. **b.** the colors of a mounted unit. **c.** (*cap.*) a U.S. Navy radar-guided surface-to-air missile with a range of 10–30 miles (16–48 km). **16.** *Heraldry.* a long, tapering flag or ensign, as of a monarch or a nation. **17.** something that stands or is placed upright. **18.** a long candlestick or candelabrum used in a church. **19.** an upright support or supporting part. **20.** *Armor.* a standing collar of mail. **21.** *Hort.* a plant trained or grafted to have a single, erect, treelike stem. **22.** *Bot.* a distinct petal, larger than the rest, of certain flowers; a vexillum. —*adj.* **23.** serving as a basis of weight, measure, value, comparison, or judgment. **24.** of recognized excellence or established authority: *a standard reference on medieval history.* **25.** usual, common, or customary: *Chairs are standard furniture in American households.* **26.** manual; not electric or automatic: *standard transmission.* **27.** conforming in pronunciation, grammar, vocabulary, etc., to the usage of most educated native speakers, esp. those having prestige, and widely considered acceptable or correct: *Standard American English; standard pronunciation.* Cf. **nonstandard** (def. 2). **28.** authorized or approved: *The program was broadcast on the standard broadcast band.* [1125–75; ME < OF, prob. < Frankish **standord* (cf. G *Standort* standing-point), conformed to *-ard* -ARD]
—Syn. 1, 3. gauge, basis, pattern, guide. STANDARD, CRITERION refer to the basis for making a judgment. A STANDARD is an authoritative principle or rule that usually implies a model or pattern for guidance, by comparison with which the quantity, excellence, correctness, etc., of other things may be determined: *She could serve as the standard of good breeding.* A CRITERION is a rule or principle used to judge the value, suitability, probability, etc., of something, without necessarily implying any comparison: *Wealth is no criterion of a person's worth.*

stand′ard at′mosphere, **1.** an arbitrarily determined vertical distribution of atmospheric pressure, temperature, and density, assumed to have physical constants and conforming to parametric equations, used for calculations in ballistics, the design of pressure altimeters, etc. **2.** a standard unit of atmospheric pressure, having a value of 1013.2 millibars or 29.9213 in. (760 mm) of mercury.

stand•ard-bear•er (stan′dərd bâr′ər), *n.* **1.** an officer or soldier of an army or military unit who bears a standard. **2.** a conspicuous leader of a movement, political party, or the like. [1400–50; late ME] —**stand′ard-bear′er•ship′,** *n.*

Stan′dard Book′ Num′ber. See **International Standard Book Number.** *Abbr.:* SBN

stand•ard-bred (stan′dərd bred′), *adj.* pertaining to a horse of the Standardbred breed. [1890–95]

Stand•ard•bred (stan′dərd bred′), *n.* one of an American breed of trotting and pacing horses used chiefly for harness racing. [1890–95; STANDARD + BRED]

stand′ard cell′, *Elect.* a primary electric cell, as the Weston cell, that produces an accurately known constant voltage: used in scientific measurements. [1870–75]

stand′ard coin′, a coin having value in bullion at least equal to its face value.

stand′ard condi′tions. See **standard temperature and pressure.**

stand′ard cost′, a predetermined cost of material, labor, etc., based on specifications prepared from time-and-motion studies, accounting records, and the like. Cf. **actual cost.** [1930–35]

stand′ard devia′tion, *Statistics.* a measure of dispersion in a frequency distribution, equal to the square root of the mean of the squares of the deviations from the arithmetic mean of the distribution. [1920–25]

stand′ard dol′lar, the basic monetary unit of the U.S., since January 31, 1934, containing $15\frac{5}{21}$ grains of gold, 0.900 fine: previously contained 25.8 grains of gold, 0.900 fine. [1875–80, *Amer.*]

Stand′ard Eng′lish, the English language in its most widely accepted form, as written and spoken by educated people in both formal and informal contexts, having universal currency while incorporating regional differences. [1870–75]

stand′ard er′ror, *Statistics.* the standard deviation of a distribution of a sample statistic, esp. when the mean is used as the statistic. [1895–1900]

stand′ard gauge′. See under **gauge** (def. 13). Also, *esp. in technical use,* **stand′ard gage′.** [1870–75] —**stand′ard-gauge′, stand′ard-gauged′,** *adj.*

stand•ard•ize (stan′dər dīz′), *v.,* **-ized, -iz•ing.** —*v.t.* **1.** to bring to or make of an established standard size, weight, quality, strength, or the like: *to standardize manufactured parts.* **2.** to compare with or test by a standard. **3.** to choose or establish a standard for. —*v.i.* **4.** to become standardized. Also, *esp. Brit.,* **stand′ard•ise′.** [1870–75; STANDARD + -IZE] —**stand′ard•iz′a•ble,** *adj.* —**stand′ard•i•za′tion,** *n.* —**stand′ard•iz′er,** *n.*

stand′ard lin′ing, *Print.* **1.** a system for aligning type so that all fonts of the same point size have a common baseline. **2.** a design of type that provides room on the body for accommodation of descenders of all standard type of the same point size. Cf. **art lining, title lining.**

stand′ard mon′ey, money made of a metal that has utility and value apart from its use as a unit of monetary exchange. [1955–60]

stand′ard of liv′ing, a grade or level of subsistence and comfort in everyday life enjoyed by a community, class, or individual: *The well-educated generally have a high standard of living.* Also called **living standard.** [1900–05]

stand′ard op′erating proce′dure, a set of fixed instructions or steps for carrying out usually routine operations. *Abbr.:* SOP Also called **standing operating procedure.** [1950–55]

stand′ard schnau′zer, schnauzer. [1930–35]

stand′ard score′, *Statistics.* the test score of a participant expressed as the deviation of the score from the mean score of the sample in units of standard deviation. [1925–30]

stand′ard tem′perature and pres′sure, the temperature of 0°C and pressure of 1 atmosphere, usually taken as the conditions when stating properties of gases. Also called **standard conditions.** *Abbr.:* STP

stand′ard time′, the civil time officially adopted for a country or region, usually the civil time of some specific meridian lying within the region. The standard time zones in the U.S. (**Atlantic time, Eastern time, Central time, Mountain time, Pacific time, Yukon time, Alaska-Hawaii time,** and **Bering time**) use the civil times of the 60th, 75th, 90th, 105th, 120th, 135th, 150th, and 165th meridians respectively, the difference of time between one zone and the next being exactly one hour. See diag. under **time zone.** [1880–85, *Amer.*]

stand•a•way (stand′ə wā′), *adj.* (of a garment) designed or constructed to stand upright or extend outward from the body: *a standaway collar.* [1935–40; adj. use of v. phrase *stand away*]

stand•by (stand′bī′), *n., pl.* **-bys,** *adj.* —*n.* **1.** a staunch supporter or adherent; one who can be relied upon. **2.** something upon which one can rely and therefore choose or use regularly. **3.** something or someone held ready to serve as a substitute, esp. a radio or television program used as a filler in case of cancellation of a regularly scheduled program. **4.** a traveler who is waiting for last-minute accommodations to become available on a plane, train, or other transport as a result of a cancellation. **5. on standby,** in a state of readiness to act, respond, or be used immediately when needed. —*adj.* **6.** kept readily available for use in an emergency, shortage, or the like: *a standby player.* **7.** of or pertaining to last-minute accommodations, the transport that offers them, or a traveler who is waiting for them: *a standby flight.* **8.** of or pertaining to a waiting period. Also, **stand′ by′.** [1790–1800; n., adj. use of v. phrase *stand by*]

stand-down (stand′doun′), *n.* **1.** *Mil.* a temporary cessation of offensive actions; cease-fire; truce: *a stand-down for the Christmas holidays.* **2.** a work stoppage or layoff. Also, **stand′down′.** [1920–25; n. use of v. phrase *stand down*]

stand•ee (stan dē′), *n.* a person who stands, as a passenger in a train, a spectator at a theater, etc., either because all the seats are taken or because standing room is cheaper than a seat. [1820–30, *Amer.;* STAND + -EE]

stand•fast (stand′fast′, -fäst′), *n.* a rigid or unyielding position. [1710–20; n. use of v. phrase *stand fast*]

stand-in (stand′in′), *n.* **1.** a substitute for a motion-picture star during the preparation of lighting, cameras, etc., or in dangerous scenes. **2.** any substitute. [1930–35; n. use of v. phrase *stand in*]

stand•ing (stan′ding), *n.* **1.** rank or status, esp. with respect to social, economic, or personal position, reputation, etc.: *He had little standing in the community.* **2.** good position, reputation, or credit: *He is a merchant of standing in the community.* **3.** length of existence, continuance, residence, membership, experience, etc.: *a friend of long standing.* **4. standings,** *Sports.* a list of teams or contestants arranged according to their past records: *According to the standings, the White Sox are leading the division by three games.* **5.** the act of a person or thing that stands. **6.** a place where a person or thing stands. **7.** *Law.* the right to initiate or participate in a legal action: *having standing as a friend of the court.* —*adj.* **8.** having an erect or upright position: *a standing lamp.* **9.** performed in or from an erect position: *a standing jump.* **10.** still; not flowing or stagnant, as water; stationary. **11.** continuing without cessation or change; lasting or permanent. **12.** continuing in operation, force, use, etc.: *a standing rule.* **13.** customary or habitual; generally understood: *We have a standing bridge game every Friday night.* **14.** *Print.* kept for use in subsequent printings: *standing type.* **15.** out of use; idle: *a standing engine.* **16.** *Naut.* noting any of various objects or assemblages of objects fixed in place or position, unless moved for adjustment or repairs: *standing bowsprit.* **17.** *Knots.* noting the part of a rope that is in use and terminates in a knot or the like. [1300–50; ME; see STAND, -ING[1], -ING[2]]
—Syn. 2. See **credit.**

stand′ing ar′my, a permanently organized military force maintained by a nation. [1595–1605]

stand′ing broad′ jump′, *Track.* a jump for distance from a standing position.

stand′ing commit′tee, **1.** a permanent committee, as of a legislature, society, etc., intended to consider all matters pertaining to a designated subject. **2.** (*caps.*) the highest policymaking body of the Chinese Communist party, composed of top party leaders from the Politburo. [1900–05]

stand′ing cup′, a tall decorative cup of the Middle Ages and Renaissance, having a raised cover.

stand′ing cy′press, a plant, *Ipomopsis rubra,* of the southern U.S., having feathery leaves and clusters of red and yellow flowers. [1860–65, *Amer.*]

stand′ing mar′tingale, martingale (def. 1).

stand′ing op′erating proce′dure, *Mil.* See **standard operating procedure.**

stand′ing or′der, **1.** *Mil.* (formerly) a general order always in force in a command and establishing uniform procedures for it; standard operating procedure. **2. standing orders,** *Parl. Proc.* the rules ensuring continuity of procedure during the meetings of an assembly. [1730–40]

stand′ing rib′ roast′. See **rib roast.**

stand′ing rig′ging, *Naut.* rigging remaining permanently in position as a means of steadying various spars, shrouds, stays, etc. (contrasted with *running rigging*). [1740–50]

stand′ing room′, **1.** space in which to stand, as in a theater, stadium, or the like. **2.** accommodation for standing. [1595–1605]

stand′ing wave′, *Physics.* a wave in a medium in which each point on the axis of the wave has an associated constant amplitude ranging from zero at the nodes to a maximum at the antinodes. Also called **stationary wave.** [1905–10]

stand•ish (stan′dish), *n. Archaic.* a stand for ink, pens, and other writing materials. [1425–75; late ME; orig. uncert.; perh. STAND + DISH]

Stan•dish (stan′dish), *n.* **1. Burt L.,** pseudonym of Gilbert Patten. **2. Myles** or **Miles** (mīlz), c1584–1656, American settler, born in England: military leader in Plymouth Colony.

stand•off (stand′ôf′, -of′), *n.* **1.** a standing off or apart; aloofness. **2.** a tie or draw, as in a game. **3.** something that counterbalances. **4.** a prop for holding the top of a ladder away from the vertical surface against which it is leaning. **5.** *Elect.* an insulator that supports a conductor above a surface. —*adj.* **6.** standing off or apart; aloof; reserved: *an uncordial and standoff manner.* Also, **stand′-off′.** [1830–40; n., adj. use of v. phrase *stand off*]

stand•off•ish (stand′ô′fish, -of′ish), *adj.* somewhat aloof or reserved; cold and unfriendly. Also, **stand′-off′•ish.** [1855–60; STANDOFF + -ISH[1]] —**stand′off′ish•ly,** *adv.* —**stand′off′ish•ness,** *n.*

stand′ oil′, a thick oil made by heating linseed oil to temperatures of 600°F and higher, used chiefly as a medium in paints. [1920–25]

stand•out (stand′out′), *n.* **1.** something or someone, as a person, performance, etc., remarkably superior to others: *Evans was a standout in the mixed doubles.* **2.** someone who is conspicuous in an area because of his or her refusal to conform with the actions, opinions, desires, etc., of the majority. —*adj.* **3.** outstanding; superior. Also, **stand′-out′.** [1895–1900; n., adj. use of v. phrase *stand out*]

stand•pat (stand′pat′), *n.* **1.** standpatter. —*adj.* **2.** characterized by refusal to consider or accept change. [1900–05; n., adj. use of v. phrase *stand pat*]

stand•pat•ter (stand′pat′ər, -pat′-), *n.* a person who refuses to consider or accept change. [1900–05, *Amer.;* STANDPAT + -ER[1]]

stand•pat•tism (stand′pat′iz əm), *n.* belief in or the practice of resisting or refusing to accept change, esp. in politics. Also, **stand′pat′ism.** [1900–05, *Amer.;* STANDPAT + -ISM]

stand•pipe (stand′pīp′), *n.* **1.** a vertical pipe or tower into which water is pumped to obtain a required head. **2.** a water pipe for supplying the fire hoses of a building, connected with the water supply of the building and usually with a siamese outside the building. [1840–50; STAND + PIPE[1]]

stand•point (stand′point′), *n.* **1.** the point or place at which a person stands to view something. **2.** the mental position, attitude, etc., from which a person views and judges things: *From the lawyer's standpoint, her client is right.* [1820–30; STAND + POINT, modeled on G *Standpunkt*]

St. An•drews (an′dro͞oz), a seaport in the Fife region, in E Scotland: resort; golf courses. 11,468.

St. Andrew's cross, a cross composed of four diagonal arms of equal length; saltire. See illus. under **cross.**

CONCISE PRONUNCIATION KEY: act, cāpe, dâre, pärt; set, ēqual; *if,* īce; ox, ōver, ôrder, oil, bo͝ok, bo͞ot, out; up, ûrge; child; sing; shoe; thin, *th*at; zh as in *treasure.* ə = *a* as in *alone, e* as in *system, i* as in *easily, o* as in *gallop, u* as in *circus;* ᵊ as in *fire* (fīᵊr), *hour* (ouᵊr). l and n can serve as syllabic consonants, as in *cradle* (krād′l), and *button* (but′n). See the full key inside the front cover.

St. An·drew's-cross (an′dro͞oz krôs′, -kros′), a low evergreen shrub, *Ascyrum hypericoides,* native to temperate and subtropical America, having flowers in clusters of three: often cultivated.

stand·still (stand′stil′), *n.* a state of cessation of movement or action; halt; stop: *The ball rolled to a standstill.* [1695–1705; n. use of v. phrase *stand still*]

stand-up (stand′up′), *adj.* **1.** standing erect or upright, as a collar. **2.** performed, taken, etc., while one stands: *a stand-up meal.* **3.** designed for or requiring a standing position: *a stand-up lunch counter.* **4.** (of a fight) characterized by the rapid exchange of many blows with little attention given to defensive maneuvering. **5.** characterized by an erect or bold stance: *a stand-up batter who hits many doubles.* **6.** *Baseball.* (of a double or triple) pertaining to a hit that allows the hitter to reach the base safely without having to slide. **7.** (of a comedian) delivering a comic monologue while alone on the stage. Also, **stand′up′.** [1580–90; adj. use of v. phrase *stand up*]

stane (stān), *n., adj., adv., v.t.,* **staned, stan·ing.** *Scot. and North Eng.* stone.

Stan·ford (stan′fərd), *n.* **1. (Amasa) Leland,** 1824–93, U.S. railroad developer, politician, and philanthropist: governor of California 1861–63; senator 1885–93. **2.** a male given name.

Stan′ford-Bi·net′ test′ (stan′fərd bi nā′), *Psychol.* a revised version of the Binet-Simon scale, prepared at Stanford University for use in the U.S. [1916; named after *Stanford* University, Palo Alto, California, and A. BINET]

stang (stang), *v. Obs.* pt. of **sting.**

stan·hope (stan′hōp′, stan′əp), *n.* a light, open, one-seated, horse-drawn carriage with two or four wheels. [1795–1805; named after Fitzroy *Stanhope* (1787–1864), British clergyman]

Stan·hope (stan′hōp′, stan′əp), *n.* **1. James, 1st Earl Stanhope,** 1673–1721, British soldier and statesman: prime minister 1717–18. **2. Philip Dor·mer** (dôr′mər). See **Chesterfield, 4th Earl of.**

Stan·is·laus (stan′is lôs′, -lous′), *n.* a male given name.

Stanislaus I, (*Stanislaus Leszczynski*) 1677–1766, king of Poland 1704–09, 1733–35. Also, **Stan·is·las I** (stan′is-ləs, -läs′).

Sta·ni·slav (stan′ə släf′, stan′ə släf′; *Russ.* stə nyi-släf′), *n.* former name of **Ivano-Frankovsk.**

Stan·i·slav·ski (stan′ə släv′skē, -släf′-; *Russ.* stə nyi-släf′skyē), *n.* **Kon·stan·tin** (kon′stən tēn′; *Russ.* kən-stun tyēn′), (*Konstantin Sergeevich Alekseev*), 1863–1938, Russian actor, producer, and director. Also, **Stan′i·slav′sky.**

Stanislav′ski Meth′od, method (def. 5). Also called **Stanislav′ski Sys′tem.** [1940–45; named after K. STANISLAVSKI]

Sta·ni·sla·wów (*Pol.* stä′nē slä′vo͝of), *n.* Polish name of **Ivano-Frankovsk.**

stank (stangk), *v.* a pt. of **stink.**

Stan·ley (stan′lē), *n.* **1. Arthur Pen·rhyn** (pen′rin), (*Dean Stanley*) 1815–81, English clergyman and author. **2. Edward George Geoffrey Smith, 14th Earl of Derby,** 1799–1869, British statesman: prime minister 1852, 1858–59, 1866–68. **3. Francis Edgar,** 1849–1918, and his twin brother **Free·lan** (frē′lən), 1849–1940, U.S. inventors and manufacturers: developed steam-powered car. **4. Sir Henry Morton,** (*John Rowlands*) 1841–1904, British journalist and explorer in Africa: led successful search for David Livingstone. **5. Wendell M(eredith),** 1904–71, U.S. biochemist: Nobel prize 1946. **6.** the capital and principal harbor of the Falkland Islands, in the E part. 1000. **7. Mount,** former name of **Ngaliema, Mount. 8.** a male given name: an Old English family name taken from a placename meaning "stone field."

Stan′ley Cup′, *Ice Hockey.* **1.** a trophy emblematic since 1926 of the championship of the National Hockey League, composed of Canadian and U.S. professional teams. **2.** the best-of-seven-games series in which the champion of the Prince of Wales Conference and that from the Clarence S. Campbell Conference oppose each other for this trophy. [named after Frederick Arthur, Lord *Stanley* of Preston (1841–1908), governor general of Canada, who donated the trophy for the best amateur team of the 1893–94 season]

Stan′ley Falls′, seven cataracts of the Zaire (Congo) River, in NE Zaire, on the equator.

Stan′ley Pool′. See **Malebo Pool.**

Stan·ley·ville (stan′lē vil′), *n.* former name of **Kisangani.**

St. Ann, a city in E Missouri. 15,523.

stan·na·ry (stan′ə rē), *n., pl.* **-ries.** *Brit.* **1.** a tin-mining region or district. **2.** a place where tin is mined or smelted. [1425–75; late ME < ML *stannāria* tin mine, equiv. to LL *stann(um)* STANNUM + *-āria* -ARY]

stan·nate (stan′āt), *n. Chem.* a salt of a stannic acid. [1830–40; STANN(IC ACID) + -ATE[2]]

stan·nic (stan′ik), *adj. Chem.* of or containing tin, esp. in the tetravalent state. [1780–90; STANN(UM) + -IC]

stan′nic ac′id, *Chem.* any of the series of acids usually occurring as amorphous powders and varying in composition from H_2SnO_3 **(alpha-stannic acid)** to H_4SnO_4. [1780–90]

stan′nic chlo′ride, *Chem.* a colorless fuming and caustic liquid, $SnCl_4$, soluble in water and alcohol, that converts with water to a crystalline solid: used for electrically conductive and electroluminescent coatings and in ceramics. Also called **tin chloride, tin tetrachloride.**

stan′nic ox′ide, *Chem.* a white, amorphous, water-insoluble powder, SnO_2, used chiefly in the manufacture of ceramic glazes and glass, and of polishing powders for metal, glass, and marble. Also called **tin ash.** [1840–50]

stan′nic sul′fide, *Chem.* a yellowish or brownish, water-insoluble powder, SnS_2, usually used suspended in lacquer or varnish for gilding and bronzing metals, wood, paper, etc.; mosaic gold.

stan·nite (stan′īt), *n.* a mineral, iron-black to steel-gray in color, with a metallic luster, copper iron tin sulfide, Cu_2FeSnS_4: an ore of tin. Also called **tin pyrites.** [1850–55; STANN(UM) + -ITE[1]]

stan·nous (stan′əs), *adj. Chem.* containing tin, esp. in the bivalent state. [1840–50; STANN(UM) + -OUS]

stan′nous chlo′ride, *Chem.* a white, crystalline, water-soluble solid, $SnCl_2{\cdot}2H_2O$, used chiefly as a reducing and tinning agent, and as a mordant in dyeing with cochineal. [1865–70]

stan′nous fluo′ride, a white, crystalline powder, SnF_2, slightly soluble in water: used as a source of fluorine in the prevention of dental caries, esp. as a toothpaste additive. Also called **tin difluoride, tin fluoride.**

stan·num (stan′əm), *n.* tin. [1775–85; < LL: tin, L *stannum, stagnum* alloy of silver and lead]

Sta·no·voi (stan′ə voi′; *Russ.* stə nu voi′), *n.* a mountain range in the E Russian Federation in Asia: a watershed between the Pacific and Arctic oceans; highest peak, 8143 ft. (2480 m).

Stans (shtäns), *n.* a town in and the capital of Nidwalden, in central Switzerland. 5700.

St. Anthony's cross. See **tau cross.** [1880–85]

Stan·ton (stan′tn), *n.* **1. Edwin Mc·Mas·ters** (mək-mas′tərz, -mä′stərz), 1814–69, U.S. statesman: Secretary of War 1862–67. **2. Elizabeth Ca·dy** (kā′dē), 1815–1902, U.S. social reformer. **3.** a city in SW California. 21,144. **4.** a male given name.

stan·za (stan′zə), *n. Pros.* an arrangement of a certain number of lines, usually four or more, sometimes having a fixed length, meter, or rhyme scheme, forming a division of a poem. [1580–90; < It: room, station, stopping-place (pl. *stanze*) < VL **stantia,* equiv. to L *stant-* (s. of *stāns*), prp. of *stāre* to STAND + *-ia* -Y[3]] **—stan′zaed,** *adj.* **—stan·za·ic** (stan zā′ik), **stan·za′i·cal,** *adj.* **—stan·za′i·cal·ly,** *adv.*
—Syn. See **verse.**

sta·pe·dec·to·my (stā′pi dek′tə mē), *n., pl.* **-mies.** a microsurgical procedure to relieve deafness by replacing the stapes of the ear with a prosthetic device. [1890–95; < NL *staped-,* s. of *stapēs* STAPES + -ECTOMY]

sta·pe·li·a (stə pē′lē ə), *n.* any of various plants of the genus *Stapelia,* of the milkweed family, native to southern Africa, having short, fleshy, leafless stems, and flowers that are oddly colored or mottled and in most species emit a fetid, carrionlike odor. [1775–85; < NL, after J. B. van *Stapel* (d. 1636), Dutch botanist; see -IA]

sta·pes (stā′pēz), *n., pl.* **sta·pes, sta·pe·des** (stə pē′-dēz). *Anat.* the innermost, stirrup-shaped bone of a chain of three small bones in the middle ear of humans and other mammals, involved in the conduction of sound vibrations to the inner ear. Also called **stirrup.** Cf. **incus** (def. 1), **malleus.** See diag. under **ear.** [1660–70; < NL *stapēs,* ML: stirrup, perh. etymologizing alter. of It *staffa* stirrup (< Gmc) by assoc. with L *stāre* to stand, and *pēs,* s. *ped-* FOOT] **—sta·pe·di·al** (stə pē′dē əl), *adj.*

staph (staf), *n. Informal.* staphylococcus. [1930–35; by shortening]

staph·y·lin·id (staf′ə lin′id, -lī′nid), *n.* See **rove beetle.** [1840–50; < NL *Staphylinidae* family name, equiv. to *Staphylin(us)* genus name (< Gk *staphylînos* kind of insect) + *-idae* -ID[2]]

staphylo-, a combining form borrowed from Greek, where it meant "bunch of grapes," "uvula," used with these meanings, and also with reference to the palate and to staphylococci, in the formation of compound words: *staphyloplasty.* [comb. form repr. Gk *staphylḗ*]

staph·y·lo·coc·cus (staf′ə lə kok′əs), *n., pl.* **-coc·ci** (-kok′sī). *Bacteriol.* any of several spherical bacteria of the genus *Staphylococcus,* occurring in pairs, tetrads, and irregular clusters, certain species of which, as *S. aureus,* can be pathogenic for humans. [1885–90; < NL; see STAPHYLO-, COCCUS] **—staph·y·lo·coc·cal** (staf′ə lə-kok′əl), **staph·y·lo·coc·cic** (staf′ə lə kok′sik), *adj.*

sta·ple[1] (stā′pəl), *n., v.,* **-pled, -pling.** —*n.* **1.** a short piece of wire bent so as to bind together papers, sections of a book, or the like, by driving the ends through the sheets and clinching them on the other side. **2.** a similar, often U-shaped piece of wire or metal with pointed ends for driving into a surface to hold a hasp, hook, pin, bolt, wire, or the like. —*v.t.* **3.** to secure or fasten by a staple or staples: *to staple three sheets together.* [bef. 900; ME *stapel* orig., support, post, OE *stapol*; c. MD *stapel* foundation, G *Stapel* pile, ON *stopull* pillar]

sta·ple[2] (stā′pəl), *n., adj., v.,* **-pled, -pling.** —*n.* **1.** a principal raw material or commodity grown or manufactured in a locality. **2.** a principal commodity in a mercantile field; goods in steady demand or of known or recognized quality. **3.** a basic or necessary item of food: *She bought flour, sugar, salt, and other staples.* **4.** a basic or principal item, thing, feature, element, or part: *Cowboy dramas are a staple on television.* **5.** the fiber of wool, cotton, flax, rayon, etc., considered with reference to length and fineness. **6.** *Textiles.* a standard length of textile fibers, representing the average of such fibers taken collectively, as short-staple or long-staple cotton. **7.** *Hist.* a town or place appointed by royal authority as the seat of a body of merchants having the exclusive right of purchase of certain classes of goods for export. —*adj.* **8.** chief or prominent among the products exported or produced by a country or district; chiefly or largely dealt in or consumed. **9.** basic, chief, or principal: *staple industries.* **10.** principally used: *staple subjects of conversation.* —*v.t.* **11.** to sort or classify according to the staple or fiber, as wool. [1375–1425; late ME: place where merchants have trading rights < MD *stapel*]

sta·pler[1] (stā′plər), *n.* **1.** a machine for fastening together sheets of paper or the like, with wire staples. **2.** a wire-stitching machine, esp. one used in bookbinding. **3.** Also called **sta′ple gun′.** a hand-powered tool used for driving heavy-duty wire staples into wood and other materials. [1905–10; STAPLE[1] + -ER[1]]

sta·pler[2] (stā′plər), *n.* **1.** a person who staples wool. **2.** a merchant who deals in a staple or staples. [1505–15; STAPLE[2] + -ER[1]]

sta·pling (stā′pling), *n. Shipbuilding.* a collar formed of angle iron surrounding a structural member passing through a deck or bulkhead to make a seal that is watertight, oiltight, etc. Also called **angle collar.** [STAPLE[1] + -ING[1]]

star (stär), *n., adj., v.,* **starred, star·ring.** —*n.* **1.** any of the heavenly bodies, except the moon, appearing as fixed luminous points in the sky at night. **2.** *Astron.* any of the large, self-luminous, heavenly bodies, as the sun, Polaris, etc. **3.** any heavenly body. **4.** *Astrol.* a heavenly body, esp. a planet, considered as influencing humankind and events. **5.** a person's destiny, fortune, temperament, etc., regarded as influenced and determined by the stars. **6.** a conventionalized figure usually having five or six points radiating from or disposed about a center. **7.** this figure used as an ornament, award, badge, mark of excellence, etc.: *The movie was awarded three stars.* **8.** *Jewelry.* **a.** a gem having the star cut. **b.** the asterism in a crystal or a gemstone, as in a star sapphire. **c.** a crystal or a gemstone having such asterism. **d.** See **star facet. 9.** *Print.* an asterisk. **10.** a person who is celebrated or distinguished in some art, profession, or other field. **11.** a prominent actor, singer, or the like, esp. one who plays the leading role in a performance. **12.** *U.S. Mil.* See **battle star. 13.** *U.S. Navy.* **a.** a gold or bronze star worn on the ribbon of a decoration or medal to represent a second or subsequent award of the same decoration or medal. **b.** a silver star worn in place of five gold or bronze stars. **14.** a white spot on the forehead of a horse. **15.** *Heraldry.* a mullet. **16. make someone see stars,** to deal someone a severe blow causing the illusion of brilliant streaks of light before the eyes: *The blow on the head made him see stars, and the next thing he knew he was in the hospital.* **17. thank one's lucky stars,** to acknowledge one's good fortune; be grateful: *Instead of complaining about hospital bills she should thank her lucky stars she's still alive.* Also, **thank one's stars.** —*adj.* **18.** celebrated, prominent, or distinguished; preeminent: *a star basketball player; a star reporter.* **19.** of or pertaining to a star or stars. —*v.t.* **20.** to set with or as with stars; spangle. **21.** to feature as a star: *an old movie starring Rudolph Valentino* . **22.** to mark with a star or asterisk, as for special notice. —*v.i.* **23.** to shine as a star; be brilliant or prominent. **24.** (of a performer) to appear as a star: *He starred in several productions of Shaw's plays.* [bef. 900; ME *sterre,* OE *steorra*; c. OHG *sterro*; akin to OHG *sterno,* ON *stjarna,* Goth *stairno,* L *stella,* Gk *astḗr,* Skt *stṛ*] **—star′less,** *adj.*

star′ an′ise, a shrub or small tree, *Illicium verum,* of China, having white flowers that turn purple and bearing anise-scented, star-shaped clusters of carminative fruit. Also called **Chinese anise.** [1830–40]

star′ ap′ple, 1. the edible fruit of a West Indian tree, *Chrysophyllum cainito,* of the sapodilla family, which when cut across exhibits a star-shaped figure within. **2.** the tree itself. [1675–85]

Sta·ra Za·go·ra (stä′rä zä gô′rä), a city in central Bulgaria. 121,505.

star·board (stär′bərd, -bôrd′, -bōrd′), *n.* **1.** the right-hand side of or direction from a vessel or aircraft, facing forward. —*adj.* **2.** of or pertaining or located to the starboard. —*adv.* **3.** toward the right side. —*v.t., v.i.* **4.** to turn (the helm) to starboard. [bef. 900; ME *sterbord* (n.), OE *stēorbord,* equiv. to *stēor* steering (see STEER[1]) + *bord* side (see BOARD)]

Star′ Carr′ (kär), an archaeological site in Yorkshire, England, that was the lakeside camp of a Neolithic hunting, fishing, and gathering culture, 9000–7000 B.C.

starch (stärch), *n.* **1.** a white, tasteless, solid carbohydrate, $(C_6H_{10}O_5)_n$, occurring in the form of minute granules in the seeds, tubers, and other parts of plants, and forming an important constituent of rice, corn, wheat, beans, potatoes, and many other vegetable foods. **2.** a commercial preparation of this substance used to stiffen textile fabrics in laundering. **3. starches,** foods rich in natural starch. **4.** stiffness or formality, as of manner: *He is so full of starch he can't relax.* **5.** *Informal.* vigor; energy; stamina; boldness. —*v.t.* **6.** to stiffen or treat with starch. **7.** to make stiff or rigidly formal (sometimes fol. by *up*). [1375–1425; (v.) late ME *sterchen* orig., to stiffen, OE *stercean* to make stiff, strengthen, deriv. of *stearc* STARK; c. G *stärken* to strengthen; (n.) late ME *starch(e), sterche,* deriv. of the v.] **—starch′less,** *adj.* **—starch′like′,** *adj.*

Star′ Cham′ber, 1. a former court of inquisitorial and criminal jurisdiction in England that sat without a jury and that became noted for its arbitrary methods and severe punishments, abolished 1641. **2.** any tribunal, committee, or the like, which proceeds by arbitrary or unfair methods. [1350–1400; ME]

star′ chart′, *Astron.* a chart or map showing the relative apparent positions of the stars, as seen from the earth, in a particular area of the sky. Also called **star map.** [1865–70]

starch′ block′er, a substance ingested in the belief that it inhibits the body's ability to metabolize starch and thereby promotes weight loss: declared illegal in the U.S. by the FDA. Also, **starch′block′.** [1980–85] **—starch′-block′ing,** *adj.*

starch′ syr′up, glucose (def. 2).

starch·y (stär′chē), *adj.,* **starch·i·er, starch·i·est. 1.** of, pertaining to, or of the nature of starch. **2.** containing starch. **3.** stiffened with starch. **4.** stiff and formal,

CONCISE ETYMOLOGY KEY: <, descended or borrowed from; >, whence; b., blend of, blended; c., cognate with; cf., compare; deriv., derivative; equiv., equivalent; imit., imitative; obl., oblique; r., replacing; s., stem; sp., spelling, spelled; resp., respelling, respelled; trans., translation; ?, origin unknown; *, unattested; ‡, probably earlier than. See the full key inside the front cover.

as in manner. [1795–1805; STARCH + -Y[1]] **—starch′i·ly,** *adv.* **—starch′i·ness,** *n.*

star′ cloud′, *Astron.* a cloudlike patch of light on the celestial sphere, consisting of a multitude of stars. [1930–35]

star′ clus′ter, *Astron.* a number of stars of common origin held together as a group by gravitational attraction. Cf. **globular cluster, open cluster, stellar association.**

star-crossed (stär′krôst′, -krost′), *adj.* thwarted or opposed by the stars; ill-fated: *star-crossed lovers.* [1585–95]

star′ cut′, a gem cut having a hexagonal table surrounded by six facets in the form of equilateral triangles. [1695–1705]

star·dom (stär′dəm), *n.* **1.** the world or class of professional stars, as of the stage. **2.** the status of a star or preeminent performer. [1860–65; STAR + -DOM]

star′ drill′, a chisellike drill for masonry or plasterwork, having a pointed head faceted in alternately projecting and reentering angles.

star·dust (stär′dust′), *n.* **1.** (not in technical use) a mass of distant stars appearing as tiny particles of dust. **2.** a naively romantic quality: *There was stardust in her eyes.* Also, **star′ dust′.** [1835–45; STAR + DUST]

stare (stâr), *v.,* **stared, star·ing,** *n.* **—***v.i.* **1.** to gaze fixedly and intently, esp. with the eyes wide open. **2.** to be boldly or obtrusively conspicuous: *The bright modern painting stares out at you in the otherwise conservative gallery.* **3.** (of hair, feathers, etc.) to stand on end; bristle. **—***v.t.* **4.** to stare at: *to stare a person up and down.* **5.** to effect or have a certain effect on by staring: *to stare one out of countenance.* **6. stare down,** to cause to become uncomfortable by gazing steadily at one; overcome by staring: *A nonsmoker at the next table tried to stare me down.* **7. stare one in the face,** to be urgent or impending; confront: *The income-tax deadline is staring us in the face.* **—***n.* **8.** a staring gaze; a fixed look with the eyes wide open: *The banker greeted him with a glassy stare.* [bef. 900; ME *staren,* OE *starian;* c. D *staren,* G *starren,* ON *stara;* akin to STARK, STARVE] **—star′er,** *n.* **—star′ing·ly,** *adv.*
—Syn. 1. See **gaze.**

sta·re de·ci·sis (stâr′ē di sī′sis), *Law.* the doctrine that rules or principles of law on which a court rested a previous decision are authoritative in all future cases in which the facts are substantially the same. [1855–60; < L *stāre dēcīsis* to stand by things (that have been) settled]

sta·rets (stär′its, -yits), *n., pl.* **star·tsy** (stärt′sē). *Russ. Orth. Ch.* a religious teacher or counselor. [1915–20; < Russ *stárets* elder, deriv. of *stáryĭ* old]

star′ fac′et, *Jewelry.* (in a brilliant) any of the eight small facets of the crown immediately below the table. [1745–55]

star·fish (stär′fish′), *n., pl.* (*esp. collectively*) **-fish,** (*esp. referring to two or more kinds or species*) **-fish·es.** any echinoderm of the class Asteroidea, having the body radially arranged, usually in the form of a star, with five or more rays or arms radiating from a central disk; asteroid. Also called **sea star.** [1530–40; STAR + FISH]

starfish, *Asterias rubens,* diameter 3½ in. (8.9 cm)

star′fish flow′er. See **carrion flower** (def. 2). [1880–85]

star·flow·er (stär′flou′ər), *n.* any of several plants having starlike flowers, as the star-of-Bethlehem or a plant belonging to the genus *Trientalis* of the primrose family. [1620–30; STAR + FLOWER]

star′ fruit′, carambola (def. 2). [1855–60]

star·gaze (stär′gāz′), *v.i.,* **-gazed, -gaz·ing. 1.** to gaze at or observe the stars. **2.** to daydream. [1620–30; back formation from STARGAZER]

star·gaz·er (stär′gā′zər), *n.* **1.** a person who stargazes, as an astronomer or astrologer. **2.** a daydreamer. **3.** an impractical idealist. **4.** any of several marine fishes of the family Uranoscopidae, having the eyes at the top of the head. **5.** See **sand stargazer.** [1550–60; STAR + GAZER]

star′ grass′, any of various grasslike plants having star-shaped flowers or a starlike arrangement of leaves, as the North American plant, *Hypoxis hirsuta,* of the amaryllis family. [1680–90]

star′ jas′mine, a shrubby, evergreen vine, *Trachelospermum jasminoides,* of the dogbane family, native to China, having small clusters of fragrant, white flowers, often cultivated as an ornamental. Also called **Confederate jasmine.**

stark (stärk), *adj.,* **-er, -est,** *adv.* **—***adj.* **1.** sheer, utter, downright, or complete: *stark madness.* **2.** harsh, grim, or desolate, as a view, place, etc.: *a stark landscape.* **3.** extremely simple or severe: *a stark interior.* **4.** bluntly or sternly plain; not softened or glamorized: *the stark reality of the schedule's deadline.* **5.** stiff or rigid in substance, muscles, etc. **6.** rigid in death. **7.** *Archaic.* strong; powerful; massive or robust. **—***adv.* **8.** utterly, absolutely, or quite: *stark mad.* **9.** *Chiefly Scot. and North Eng.* in a stark manner; stoutly or vigorously. [bef. 900; (adj.) ME; OE *stearc* stiff, firm; c. G *stark* strong; akin to ON *sterkr* strong; akin to STARCH, STARE; (adv.) ME *sterke,* deriv. of the adj.] **—stark′ly,** *adv.* **—stark′ness,** *n.*
—Syn. 2, 3. See **austere, bare.**

Stark (stärk; *for 2 also Ger.* shtärk), *n.* **1. Harold Rayns·ford** (rānz′fərd), 1880–1972, U.S. admiral. **2. Jo·han·nes** (yō hä′nəs), 1874–1957, German physicist: Nobel prize 1919. **3. John,** 1728–1822, American Revolutionary War general.

Stark′ effect′, *Physics.* (*often l.c.*) the splitting into two or more components of the spectral lines of atoms in an electric field. [named after J. STARK, who described it in 1913]

Star·ker (shtär′kər), *n.* **Ja·nos** (yä′nôsh), born 1924, U.S. cellist, born in Hungary.

stark·ers (stär′kərz), *adj., adv. Brit. Informal.* wearing no clothes; naked. [1905–10; STARK-(NAKED) + -ERS]

stark-nak·ed (stärk′nā′kid), *adj.* absolutely naked. [1520–30; STARK + NAKED; r. *start-naked* (*start,* ME; OE *steort* tail; c. D *staart,* OHG *sterz,* ON *stertr*)]

Stark·ville (stärk′vil), *n.* a town in E Mississippi. 15,169.

star·let (stär′lit), *n.* **1.** a young actress promoted and publicized as a future star, esp. in motion pictures. **2.** a small star or other heavenly body. [1820–30; STAR + -LET]

star·light (stär′līt′), *n.* the light emanating from the stars. [1325–75; ME; see STAR, LIGHT[1]]

star·like (stär′līk′), *adj.* **1.** of the shape of or like a star. **2.** shining like a star. **3.** Also, **star-shaped.** *Math.* (of a set with respect to a point) having the property that the line segment connecting a given point and any other point in a region lies completely within the region. [1585–95; STAR + -LIKE]

star′ lil′y, a lily, *Lilium concolor,* of China, having erect, somewhat fragrant, bright-red flowers.

star·ling[1] (stär′ling), *n.* **1.** a chunky, medium-sized European passerine bird, *Sturnus vulgaris,* of iridescent black plumage with seasonal speckles, that nests in colonies: introduced into North America. **2.** any of various similar Old World birds of the family Sturnidae. [bef. 1050; ME; OE *stærling,* equiv. to *stær* starling (c. OHG *stara,* ON *stari*) + *-ling* -LING[1]; akin to OE *stearn* kind of bird, L *sturnus* starling]

starling, *Sturnus vulgaris,* length 8½ in. (22 cm)

star·ling[2] (stär′ling), *n.* a pointed cluster of pilings for protecting a bridge pier from drifting ice, debris, etc. [1675–85; orig. uncert.]

star·lit (stär′lit), *adj.* lighted by the stars: *a starlit night.* Also, **star′light′ed.** [1820–30; STAR + LIT[1]]

star′ map′. See **star chart.** [1865–70]

star′ net′work, *Elect.* a circuit with three or more branches all of which have one common terminal.

star′-nosed mole′ (stär′nōzd′), a North American mole, *Condylura cristata,* having a starlike ring of fleshy processes around the end of the snout. Also, **star′nose mole′.** Also called **star′nose′.** [1820–30, *Amer.*]

Star′ of Beth′lehem, the star that guided the Magi to the manger of the infant Jesus in Bethlehem. Matt. 2:1–10.

star-of-Beth·le·hem (stär′əv beth′lē əm, -li hem′), *n., pl.* **stars-of-Beth·le·hem.** any of several plants belonging to the genus *Ornithogalum,* of the lily family, having grasslike leaves and clusters of white flowers. Also called **summer snowflake.** [1565–75]

Star′ of Da′vid, a hexagram used as a symbol of Judaism. Also called **Magen David, Mogen David, Shield of David.** See illus. under **hexagram.**

star-of-Je·ru·sa·lem (stär′əv jə ro͞o′sə ləm), *n., pl.* **stars-of-Je·ru·sa·lem.** See **meadow salsify.** [1565–75]

star·quake (stär′kwāk′), *n. Astron.* a rapid change in the mass distribution or shape of a pulsar, resulting in a fluctuation of the pulsar's pulse rate or radiation intensity. [1965–70; STAR + (EARTH)QUAKE]

Starr (stär), *n.* a male or female given name.

starred (stärd), *adj.* **1.** set or studded with or as with stars. **2.** decorated with a star, as of an order. **3.** marked with a starlike figure or spot, esp. an asterisk. **4.** *Ling.* (of a form or construction) ungrammatical or otherwise unacceptable: so called because of the convention of placing an asterisk before such a form. Cf. **asterisk** (def. 2). **5.** *Historical Ling.* (of a form) hypothetical or reconstructed, but unattested. Cf. **asterisk** (def. 3). [1175–1225; ME; see STAR, -ED[3]]

star′ route′, former name for **highway contract route.** [1815–25]

star·ry (stär′ē), *adj.,* **-ri·er, -ri·est. 1.** abounding with stars: *a starry night.* **2.** of, pertaining to, or proceeding from the stars. **3.** of the nature of or consisting of stars: *starry worlds.* **4.** resembling a star; star-shaped or stellate. **5.** shining like stars: *starry reflections on the dark water.* [1325–75; ME; see STAR, -Y[1]] **—star′ri·ness,** *n.*

star·ry-eyed (stär′ē īd′), *adj.* overly romantic or idealistic: *He was a starry-eyed dreamer.* [1900–05]

star′ry grass′wort (gras′wûrt′, -wôrt′), a weedy plant, *Cerastium arvense,* of the pink family, native to the North Temperate Zone, having narrow leaves and white flowers. Also called **field chickweed.** [GRASS + WORT[2]]

Star′ry Night′, The, a painting (1889) by Vincent van Gogh.

Stars′ and Bars′, *U.S. Hist.* the flag adopted by the Confederate States of America, consisting of two broad horizontal bars of red separated by one of white, with a blue union marked with a circle of white stars, one for each Confederate state. Cf. **Southern Cross** (def. 2). [1861, *Amer.*]

Stars′ and Stripes′, the national flag of the U.S., consisting of 13 horizontal stripes that are alternately red and white, representing the original states, and of a blue field containing 50 white stars, representing the present states. Also called **Old Glory, The Star-Spangled Banner.**

star′ sap′phire, a sapphire, cut cabochon, exhibiting asterism in the form of a colorless six-rayed star. [1795–1805]

star-shaped (stär′shāpt′), *adj.* **1.** of the shape of or like a star. **2.** *Math.* starlike (def. 3). [1805–15]

star′ shell′, a shell that bursts in the air and produces a bright light to illuminate enemy positions. [1875–80]

star·ship (stär′ship′), *n.* a spaceship designed for intergalactic travel. [STAR + SHIP]

star-span·gled (stär′spang′gəld), *adj.* **1.** spangled with stars. **2.** *Informal.* made up of or attended by celebrities, distinguished or illustrious persons, etc.: *a star-spangled reception.* [1585–95]

Star′-Spangled Ban′ner, The, 1. See **Stars and Stripes. 2.** (*italics*) the national anthem of the United States of America, based on a poem written by Francis Scott Key on September 14, 1814, and set by him to the melody of the English song *To Anacreon in Heaven:* officially adopted by the U.S. Congress in 1931.

star-stud·ded (stär′stud′id), *adj.* **1.** lighted by or full of stars; bright: *a star-studded night.* **2.** exhibiting or characterized by the presence of many preeminent performers: *a star-studded Hollywood party.* [1950–55]

star′ sys′tem, the practice of casting and promoting star performers for their ability to draw at the box office. [1900–05]

start (stärt), *v.i.* **1.** to begin or set out, as on a journey or activity. **2.** to appear or come suddenly into action, life, view, etc.; rise or issue suddenly forth. **3.** to spring, move, or dart suddenly from a position or place: *The rabbit started from the bush.* **4.** to be among the entrants in a race or the initial participants in a game or contest. **5.** to give a sudden, involuntary jerk, jump, or twitch, as from a shock of surprise, alarm, or pain: *The sudden clap of thunder caused everyone to start.* **6.** to protrude: *eyes seeming to start from their sockets.* **7.** to spring, slip, or work loose from place or fastenings, as timbers or other structural parts. **—***v.t.* **8.** to set moving, going, or acting; to set in operation: *to start an automobile; to start a fire.* **9.** to establish or found: *to start a new business.* **10.** to begin work on: *to start a book.* **11.** to enable or help (someone) set out on a journey, a career, or the like: *The record started the young singer on the road to stardom.* **12.** to cause or choose to be an entrant in a game or contest: *He started his ace pitcher in the crucial game.* **13.** to cause (an object) to work loose from place or fastenings. **14.** to rouse (game) from its lair or covert; flush. **15.** to draw or discharge (liquid or other contents) from a vessel or container; empty (a container). **16.** *Archaic.* to cause to twitch, jump, or flinch involuntarily; startle. **—***n.* **17.** a beginning of an action, journey, etc. **18.** a signal to move, proceed, or begin, as on a course or in a race. **19.** a place or time from which something begins. **20.** the first part or beginning segment of anything: *The start of the book was good but the last half was dull.* **21.** an instance of being a participant in a race or an initial participant in a game or contest: *The horse won his first two starts.* **22.** a sudden, springing movement from a position. **23.** a sudden, involuntary jerking movement of the body: *to awake with a start.* **24.** a lead or advance of specified amount, as over competitors or pursuers. **25.** the position or advantage of one who starts first: *The youngest child should have the start over the rest.* **26.** a chance, opportunity, aid, or encouragement given to one starting on a course or career: *The bride's parents gave the couple a start by buying them a house.* **27.** a spurt of activity. **28.** a starting of parts from their place or fastenings in a structure. **29.** the resulting break or opening. **30.** an outburst or sally, as of emotion, wit, or fancy. [bef. 1150; (v.) ME *sterten* to rush out, leap (c. MHG *sterzen*); r. OE *styrtan* (attested once), c. G *stürzen;* (n.) ME *stert(e)* sudden jerk, leap, deriv. of the v.]
—Syn. 9. institute. **10.** See **begin. 17.** commencement, onset. **23.** twitch, jump. **—Ant. 10.** end, terminate.

START (stärt), Strategic Arms Reduction Talks.

start·er (stär′tər), *n.* **1.** a person or thing that starts. **2.** a person who gives the signal to begin, as for a race, the running of a train, bus, elevator, etc. **3.** a device that starts an internal-combustion engine without a need for cranking by hand. **4.** a person or thing that starts in a race or contest: *Only five starters finished the race.* **5.** a culture of bacteria used to start a particular fermentation, as in the manufacture of cheese, buttermilk, sour cream, etc. **6.** *Cookery.* sourdough (def. 1). **7.** *Slang.* a shill, as at a gaming table in a casino. **8.** *Cribbage.* the card turned face up on the stack before the play. **9. for starters,** *Informal.* as the first step or part; initially; first: *We will have soup for starters. For starters, he doesn't even know how to drive.* **—***adj.* **10.** constituting a basis or beginning: *a starter set of dishes; a starter home.* [1530–40; START + -ER[1]]

start′ing block′, *Track.* a device used by runners, esp. sprinters, for increasing their speed off the mark, consisting of a metal or wooden frame, usually secured to the ground at both ends, with adjustable, triangular-shaped blocks on each side for bracing the feet. [1945–50]

CONCISE PRONUNCIATION KEY: act, cāpe, dâre, pärt; set, ēqual; *if,* ice; ox, ōver, ôrder, oil, bo͝ok, bo͞ot, out; up, ûrge; child; sing; shoe; thin, *th*at; zh as in *treasure.* ə = *a* as in *alone, e* as in *system, i* as in *easily, o* as in *gallop, u* as in *circus;* ᵊ as in *fire* (fīᵊr), *hour* (ouᵊr). l and n can serve as syllabic consonants, as in *cradle* (krād′l), and *button* (but′n). See the full key inside the front cover.

start′ing gate′, any of various types of movable barriers for lining up and giving an equal start to the entries in a horse or dog race. [1895–1900]

start′ing han′dle, *Brit.* a crank used to start the motor of an automobile. [1885–90]

star•tle (stär′tl), *v.*, **-tled, -tling,** *n.* —*v.t.* **1.** to disturb or agitate suddenly as by surprise or alarm. **2.** to cause to start involuntarily, or as by a sudden shock. —*v.i.* **3.** to start involuntarily, as from a shock of surprise or alarm. —*n.* **4.** a sudden shock of surprise, alarm, or the like. **5.** something that startles. [bef. 1100; ME *stertlen* to rush, caper, equiv. to *stert(en)* to START + -*(e)len* -LE, or continuing OE *steartlian* to kick, struggle] —**star′•tle•ment,** *n.* —**star′tler,** *n.*
—**Syn. 1.** scare, frighten, astonish. See **shock**[1].

star•tling (stärt′ling, stär′tl ing), *adj.* creating sudden alarm, surprise, or wonder; astonishing. [STARTLE + -ING[2]] —**star′tling•ly,** *adv.*

start-up (stärt′up′), *n.* **1.** the act or fact of starting something; a setting in motion. —*adj.* **2.** of or pertaining to the beginning of a new project or venture, esp. to an investment made to initiate such a project, as in a commercial or industrial enterprise: *high start-up costs.* Also, **start′up′.** [1550–60; n. use of v. phrase *start up*]

star′ turn′, **1.** the leading performer or act in a play, review, film, or the like. **2.** a bravura performance by a featured player or act. [1905–10]

star•va•tion (stär vā′shən), *n.* **1.** the act or state of starving; condition of being starved. —*adj.* **2.** liable or seeming to cause starving: *a starvation diet.* [1770–80; STARVE + -ATION]

starva′tion wag′es, wages below the level necessary for subsistence. [1885–90]

starve (stärv), *v.*, **starved, starv•ing.** —*v.i.* **1.** to die or perish from lack of food or nourishment. **2.** to be in the process of perishing or suffering severely from hunger. **3.** to suffer from extreme poverty and need. **4.** to feel a strong need or desire: *The child was starving for affection.* **5.** *Chiefly Brit. Dial.* to perish or suffer extremely from cold. **6.** *Obs.* to die. —*v.t.* **7.** to cause to starve; kill, weaken, or reduce by lack of food. **8.** to subdue, or force to some condition or action, by hunger: *to starve a besieged garrison into a surrender.* **9.** to cause to suffer for lack of something needed or craved. **10.** *Chiefly Brit. Dial.* to cause to perish, or to suffer extremely, from cold. [bef. 1000; ME *sterven,* OE *steorfan* to die; c. G *sterben*]

starve•ling (stärv′ling), *n.* **1.** a person, animal, or plant that is starving. —*adj.* **2.** starving; suffering from lack of nourishment. **3.** pining with want. **4.** poverty-stricken. **5.** poor in condition or quality. **6.** such as to entail or suggest starvation. [1540–50; STARVE + -LING[1]]

CONCISE ETYMOLOGY KEY: <, descended or borrowed from; >, whence; b., blend of, blended; c., cognate with; cf., compare; deriv., derivative; equiv., equivalent; imit., imitative; obl., oblique; r., replacing; s., stem; sp., spelling, spelled; resp., respelling, respelled; trans., translation; ?, origin unknown; *, unattested; ‡, probably earlier than. See the full key inside the front cover.

Star′ Wars′, a U.S. weapons research program begun in 1984 to explore technologies, including ground- and space-based lasers, for destroying attacking missiles and warheads. Also called **Strategic Defense Initiative.**

star•wort (stär′wûrt′, -wôrt′), *n.* **1.** any of several chickweeds of the genus *Stellaria.* **2.** any of several plants of the genera *Aster* and *Arenaria.* [1350–1400; ME; see STAR, WORT[2]]

Sta•ry O•skol (stä′rē u skôl′; *Eng.* stär′ē ə skōl′), a city in the W RSFSR, in the central Soviet Union in Europe, NE of Kharkov. 115,000.

stash (stash), *v.t.* **1.** to put by or away as for safekeeping or future use, usually in a secret place (usually fol. by *away*): *The squirrel stashes away nuts for winter.* —*n.* **2.** something put away or hidden: *a stash of gold coins buried in the garden.* **3.** a place in which something is stored secretly; hiding place; cache. **4.** *Slang.* a supply of hidden drugs. [1775–85; b. STOW and CACHE]

sta•sid•i•on (stə sid′ē ən), *n.*, *pl.* **-sid•i•a** (-sid′ē ə). a choir stall in an Orthodox church. [< MGk *stasídion* station, seat in a church, prob. equiv. to Gk *stás(is)* position, station (see STASIS) + -*idion* dim. suffix]

stas•i•mon (stas′ə mon′), *n.*, *pl.* **-ma** (-mə). (in ancient Greek drama) a choral ode, esp. in tragedy, divided into strophe and antistrophe: usually alternating with the episodion and, in the final ode, preceding the exodos. [1860–65; < Gk *stásimon,* neut. of *stásimos* stopping, stationary, equiv. to *stási(s)* a standing (see STASIS) + -*mos* adj. suffix]

sta•sis (stā′sis, stas′is), *n.*, *pl.* **sta•ses** (stā′sēz, stas′ēz). **1.** the state of equilibrium or inactivity caused by opposing equal forces. **2.** *Pathol.* stagnation in the flow of any of the fluids of the body, as of the blood in an inflamed area or the intestinal contents proximal to an obstruction. [1735–45; < Gk *stásis* state of standing, equiv. to *sta-* (s. of *histánai* to make stand; see STAND) + -*sis* -SIS]

Stas•sen (stas′ən), *n.* **Harold Edward,** born 1907, U.S. politician.

stat[1] (stat), *Informal.* —*n.* **1.** Also, **'stat.** thermostat. **2.** photostat. [1955–60; by shortening]

stat[2] (stat), *Informal.* —*n.* **1.** statistic. **2.** Usually, **stats.** statistics. —*adj.* **3.** of, pertaining to, or containing statistics: *Some sports fans memorize all the stat sheets published about a team.* [shortening of STATISTICS, STATISTIC]

stat[3] (stat), *adv. Med. Informal.* immediately. [< L *statim*]

-stat, a combining form used in the names of devices that stabilize or make constant what is specified by the initial element: *thermostat; rheostat.* [< Gk -*statēs,* equiv. to *sta-* (s. of *histánai* to make stand; see STAND) + -*tēs* agent n. suffix]

stat., **1.** (in prescriptions) immediately. [< L *statim*] **2.** statuary. **3.** statue. **4.** statute.

stat•am•pere (stat am′pēr, stat′am pēr′), *n. Elect.* the electrostatic unit of current, equivalent to 3.3356 $\times$ 10^{-10} ampere and equal to the current produced by an electromotive force of one statvolt acting through a resistance of one statohm. [*stat-* (comb. form representing ELECTROSTATIC; see -STAT) + AMPERE]

sta•tant (stāt′nt), *adj. Heraldry.* (of an animal) represented as standing with all feet on the ground: *a bear statant.* [1490–1500; < L *stat(us)* (ptp. of *stāre* to STAND) + -ANT]

stat•cou•lomb (stat ko͞o′lom, -lōm), *n. Elect.* the electrostatic unit of a quantity of electricity, equivalent to 3.3356 $\times$ 10^{-10} coulomb and equal to the quantity of charge transferred in one second across a conductor in which there is a constant current of one statampere. [*stat-* (see STATAMPERE) + COULOMB]

state (stāt), *n., adj., v.,* **stat•ed, stat•ing.** —*n.* **1.** the condition of a person or thing, as with respect to circumstances or attributes: *a state of health.* **2.** the condition of matter with respect to structure, form, constitution, phase, or the like: *water in a gaseous state.* **3.** status, rank, or position in life; station: *He dresses in a manner befitting his state.* **4.** the style of living befitting a person of wealth and high rank: *to travel in state.* **5.** a particular condition of mind or feeling: *to be in an excited state.* **6.** an abnormally tense, nervous, or perturbed condition: *He's been in a state since hearing about his brother's death.* **7.** a politically unified people occupying a definite territory; nation. **8.** the territory, or one of the territories, of a government. **9.** (*sometimes cap.*) any of the bodies politic which together make up a federal union, as in the United States of America. See table below. **10.** the body politic as organized for civil rule and government (distinguished from *church*). **11.** the operations or activities of a central civil government: *affairs of state.* **12.** (*cap.*) Also called **State Department.** *Informal.* the Department of State. **13.** *Print.* a set of copies of an edition of a publication which differ from others of the same printing because of additions, corrections, or transpositions made during printing or at any time before publication. **14. lie in state,** (of a corpse) to be exhibited publicly with honors before burial: *The president's body lay in state for two days.* **15. the States,** *Informal.* the United States (usually used outside its borders): *After a year's study in Spain, he returned to the States.*
—*adj.* **16.** of or pertaining to the central civil government or authority. **17.** made, maintained, or chartered by or under the authority of one of the commonwealths that make up a federal union: *a state highway; a state bank.* **18.** characterized by, attended with, or involving

STATES OF THE UNITED STATES

State	Capital	Population	Total Area Sq. Mi.	Total Area Sq. Km	State Flower	State Nickname
Alabama	Montgomery	3,890,061	51,609	133,670	Camellia	Cotton State
Alaska	Juneau	400,481	586,400	1,519,000	Forget-me-not	Last Frontier
Arizona	Phoenix	2,717,866	113,909	295,025	Giant Cactus	Grand Canyon State
Arkansas	Little Rock	2,285,513	53,103	137,537	Apple Blossom	Land of Opportunity
California	Sacramento	23,668,562	158,693	411,015	Golden Poppy	Golden State
Colorado	Denver	2,888,834	104,247	270,000	Columbine	Centennial State
Connecticut	Hartford	3,107,576	5009	12,975	Mountain Laurel	Constitution State
Delaware	Dover	595,225	2057	5330	Peach Blossom	First State
Florida	Tallahassee	9,739,992	58,560	151,670	Orange Blossom	Sunshine State
Georgia	Atlanta	5,464,265	58,876	152,489	Cherokee Rose	Empire State of the South
Hawaii	Honolulu	965,000	6424	16,638	Hibiscus	Aloha State
Idaho	Boise	943,935	83,557	216,415	Mock Orange	Gem State
Illinois	Springfield	11,418,461	56,400	146,075	Native Violet	Land of Lincoln
Indiana	Indianapolis	5,490,179	36,291	93,995	Peony	Hoosier State
Iowa	Des Moines	2,913,387	56,290	145,790	Wild Rose	Hawkeye State
Kansas	Topeka	2,363,208	82,276	213,094	Sunflower	Sunflower State
Kentucky	Frankfort	3,661,433	40,395	14,625	Goldenrod	Bluegrass State
Louisiana	Baton Rouge	4,203,972	48,522	125,672	Magnolia	Pelican State
Maine	Augusta	1,124,660	33,215	86,027	Pine Cone and Tassel	Pine Tree State
Maryland	Annapolis	4,216,446	10,577	27,395	Black-eyed Susan	Old Line State
Massachusetts	Boston	5,737,037	8257	21,385	Trailing Arbutus	Bay State
Michigan	Lansing	9,258,344	58,216	150,760	Apple Blossom	Wolverine State
Minnesota	St. Paul	4,077,148	84,068	217,735	Lady's-slipper	Gopher State
Mississippi	Jackson	2,520,638	47,716	129,585	Magnolia	Magnolia State
Missouri	Jefferson City	4,917,444	69,674	180,455	Hawthorn	Show Me State
Montana	Helena	786,690	147,138	381,085	Bitterroot	Treasure State
Nebraska	Lincoln	1,570,006	77,237	200,044	Goldenrod	Cornhusker State
Nevada	Carson City	799,184	110,540	286,300	Sagebrush	Silver State
New Hampshire	Concord	920,610	9304	24,100	Purple Lilac	Granite State
New Jersey	Trenton	7,364,158	7836	20,295	Purple Violet	Garden State
New Mexico	Santa Fe	1,299,968	121,666	315,115	Yucca	Land of Enchantment
New York	Albany	17,557,288	49,576	128,400	Rose	Empire State
North Carolina	Raleigh	5,874,429	52,586	136,198	Dogwood	Tarheel State
North Dakota	Bismarck	652,695	70,665	183,020	Prairie Rose	Flickertail State
Ohio	Columbus	10,797,419	41,222	106,765	Scarlet Carnation	Buckeye State
Oklahoma	Oklahoma City	3,025,266	69,919	181,090	Mistletoe	Sooner State
Oregon	Salem	2,632,663	96,981	251,180	Oregon Grape	Beaver State
Pennsylvania	Harrisburg	11,886,728	45,333	117,410	Mountain Laurel	Keystone State
Rhode Island	Providence	947,154	1214	3145	Violet	Ocean State
South Carolina	Columbia	3,119,208	31,055	80,430	Carolina Jessamine	Palmetto State
South Dakota	Pierre	690,178	77,047	199,550	American Pasqueflower	Sunshine State
Tennessee	Nashville	4,590,750	42,246	109,415	Iris	Volunteer State
Texas	Austin	14,228,383	267,339	692,410	Bluebonnet	Lone Star State
Utah	Salt Lake City	1,461,037	84,916	219,930	Sego Lily	Beehive State
Vermont	Montpelier	511,456	9609	24,885	Red Clover	Green Mountain State
Virginia	Richmond	5,346,279	40,815	105,710	American Dogwood	Old Dominion State
Washington	Olympia	3,553,231	68,192	176,615	Rhododendron	Evergreen State
West Virginia	Charleston	1,949,644	24,181	62,629	Rosebay Rhododendron	Mountain State
Wisconsin	Madison	4,705,335	56,154	145,440	Wood Violet	Badger State
Wyoming	Cheyenne	470,816	97,914	253,595	Indian Paintbrush	Equality State
FEDERAL DISTRICT:						
Dist. of Columbia	Washington	637,651	69	179	American Beauty Rose	

ceremony: *a state dinner.* **19.** used on or reserved for occasions of ceremony. —*v.t.* **20.** to declare definitely or specifically: *She stated her position on the case.* **21.** to set forth formally in speech or writing: *to state a hypothesis.* **22.** to set forth in proper or definite form: *to state a problem.* **23.** to say. **24.** to fix or settle, as by authority. [1175–1225; ME *stat* (n.), partly aph. var. of *estat* ESTATE, partly < L *status* condition (see STATUS); in defs. 7–11 < L *status* (*rērum*) state (of things) or *status* (*reī pūblicae*) state (of the republic)] —**stat′a·ble, state′a·ble,** *adj.*
—**Syn. 1.** STATE, CONDITION, SITUATION, STATUS are terms for existing circumstances or surroundings. STATE is the general word, often with no concrete implications or material relationships: *the present state of affairs.* CONDITION carries an implication of a relationship to causes and circumstances: *The conditions made flying impossible.* SITUATION suggests an arrangement of circumstances, related to one another and to the character of a person: *He was master of the situation.* STATUS carries official or legal implications; it suggests a complete picture of interrelated circumstances as having to do with rank, position, standing, a stage reached in progress, etc.: *the status of negotiations.* **3.** standing. **18.** stately, ceremonial, imposing, dignified. **20.** aver, assert, asseverate, affirm, See **maintain. 24.** determine.

state′ aid′, financial support extended by a state government to a local institution serving the public, as a school or library. [1855–60, *Amer.*]

state′ attor′ney. See **state's attorney.**

state′ bank′, a bank chartered by a state and operated under the banking laws of that state. [1805–15, *Amer.*]

state′ bird′, a bird chosen as an official symbol of a U.S. state. [1905–10, *Amer.*]

state′ cap′italism, a form of capitalism in which the central government controls most of the capital, industry, natural resources, etc. [1925–30]

state′ cham′ber, a room for public ceremonies and celebrations.

state′ church′. See **established church.** [1720–30]

State′ Col′lege, a city in central Pennsylvania. 36,130.

state′ coor′dinate sys′tem, *Survey.* a system of right-angled planar coordinates established by the U.S. Coast and Geodetic Survey for each state in the United States.

state·craft (stāt′kraft′, -kräft′), *n.* the art of government and diplomacy. [1635–45; STATE + CRAFT]

stat·ed (stā′tid), *adj.* **1.** fixed or settled: *a stated price.* **2.** explicitly set forth; declared as fact. **3.** recognized or official. [1635–45; STATE + -ED[2]] —**stat′ed·ly,** *adv.*

State′ Depart′ment, state (def. 12).

state′ flow′er, a flower chosen as an official symbol of a U.S. state. See table under **state.** [1895–1900, *Amer.*]

state·hood (stāt′ho͝od), *n.* the status or condition of being a state, esp. a state of the U.S. [1865–70, *Amer.*; STATE + -HOOD]

state·hood·er (stāt′ho͝od ər), *n.* a person who supports or advocates the attainment of statehood for a territory, colony, or the like, esp. for Puerto Rico. [STATEHOOD + -ER[1]]

state·house (stāt′hous′), *n., pl.* **-hous·es** (-hou′ziz). the building in which the legislature of a state sits; the capitol of a state. [1585–95; STATE + HOUSE]

state·less (stāt′lis), *adj.* **1.** lacking nationality. **2.** *Finance.* of, pertaining to, or consisting of any currency deposited in banks outside the country of original issue. [1600–10; STATE + -LESS] —**state′less·ness,** *n.*

state·ly (stāt′lē), *adj.,* **-li·er, -li·est,** *adv.* —*adj.* **1.** majestic; imposing in magnificence, elegance, etc.: *a stately home.* **2.** dignified. —*adv.* **3.** in a stately manner. [1350–1400; ME *statly.* See STATE, -LY] —**state′li·ness,** *n.*

state′ly home′, *Brit.* a country mansion, usually of architectural interest and often open to the public.

state′ med′icine. See **socialized medicine.** [1920–25]

state·ment (stāt′mənt), *n.* **1.** something stated. **2.** a communication or declaration in speech or writing, setting forth facts, particulars, etc. **3.** a single sentence or assertion: *I agree with everything you said except for your last statement.* **4.** *Com.* an abstract of an account, as one rendered to show the balance due. **5.** an appearance of a theme, subject, or motif within a musical composition. **6.** the act or manner of stating something. **7.** the communication of an idea, position, mood, or the like through something other than words: *The furniture in the room makes a statement about the occupant's love of color. Walking out of the meeting will be a statement of our refusal to submit.* **8.** *Computers.* an instruction or other elementary component in a high-level programming language. [1765–75; STATE (v.) + -MENT]

state′ment sav′ings account′, a savings account in which transactions are confirmed periodically by a bank statement. Cf. **passbook savings account.**

Stat′en Is′land (stat′n), **1.** an island facing New York Bay. **2.** Formerly, **Richmond.** a borough of New York City including this island. 352,121; 64½ sq. mi. (167 sq. km).

State′ of A′den, Aden (def. 2).

state′ of grace′, grace (def. 8d).

state′ of the art′, the latest and most sophisticated or advanced stage of a technology, art, or science. [1960–65] —**state′-of-the-art′,** *adj.*

State′ of the Un′ion mes′sage, *U.S. Govt.* an annual message to Congress in which the President reports on the state of the nation and outlines a legislative program: required by the Constitution (Article II, Section 3). Also called **State′ of the Un′ion address′.**

state′ of war′, **1.** a condition marked by armed conflict between or among states, existing whether or not war has been declared formally by any of the belligerents. **2.** a legal condition initiated and concluded by formal declaration, and not necessarily involving armed conflict. **3.** the duration of such a condition. [1945–50]

state′ police′, a police force under state authority rather than under the authority of a city or county in the state.

state′ pris′on, a prison maintained by a state for the confinement of felons. [1715–25]

sta·ter (stā′tər), *n.* any of various gold or silver or electrum coin units or coins of the ancient Greek states or cities. [1350–1400; ME < LL *statēr* < Gk *statḗr,* akin to *histánai* to place in the balance, lit., to make stand]

state′ reli′gion, the official religion of a state as established by law. [1820–30]

state′ rights′. See **states' rights.**

state·room (stāt′ro͞om′, -ro͝om′), *n.* a private room or compartment on a ship, train, etc. [1695–1705; STATE + ROOM]

state's′ attor′ney, (in judicial proceedings) the legal representative of the state. Also, **state attorney.** [1770–80, *Amer.*]

States·bor·o (stāts′bûr ō, -bur ō), *n.* a town in E Georgia. 14,866.

state's′ ev′idence, **1.** evidence given by an accomplice in a crime who becomes a voluntary witness against the other defendants: *The defendants' case was lost when one of them turned state's evidence.* **2.** evidence for the state, esp. in criminal trials. [1790–1800]

States-Gen·er·al (stāts′jen′ər əl), *n.* **1.** the parliament of the Netherlands, consisting of an upper chamber **(First Chamber)** and a lower chamber **(Second Chamber). 2.** *Fr. Hist.* the legislative body in France before the French Revolution. [1575–85]

state·side (stāt′sīd′), *adj.* **1.** being in or toward the continental U.S. —*adv.* **2.** in or toward the continental U.S. Also, **State′side′.** [1940–45; (the) STATES + SIDE[1]]

state·sid·er (stāt′sī′dər), *n.* a person who lives in one of the forty-eight contiguous states of the U.S. Also, **state′ sid′er.** [STATESIDE + -ER[1]]

states·man (stāts′mən), *n., pl.* **-men. 1.** a person who is experienced in the art of government or versed in the administration of government affairs. **2.** a person who exhibits great wisdom and ability in directing the affairs of a government or in dealing with important public issues. [1585–95; STATE + 'S[1] + -MAN, modeled on *steersman;* cf. the phrase *ship of state*] —**states′man·like′, states′man·ly,** *adj.*
—**Syn. 1.** See **politician.**
—**Usage.** See **-man.**

states·man·ship (stāts′mən ship′), *n.* the ability, qualifications, or practice of a statesman; wisdom and skill in the management of public affairs. [1755–65; STATESMAN + -SHIP]

state′ so′cialism, the theory, doctrine, and movement advocating a planned economy controlled by the state, with state ownership of all industries and natural resources. [1875–80] —**state′ so′cialist.**

States′ of the Church′. See **Papal States.**

states′ right′er, a person who opposes U.S. federal intervention in affairs of the separate states, supporting this position by a strict interpretation of the Constitution of the U.S. [1940–45; STATES' RIGHT(S) + -ER[1]]

states′ rights′, the rights belonging to the various states, esp. with reference to the strict interpretation of the Constitution, by which all rights not delegated by the Constitution to the federal government belong to the states. [1790–1800, *Amer.*]

States′ Rights′ Dem′ocratic par′ty, a political party formed by dissident southern Democrats who opposed the candidacy of Harry Truman in 1948 and campaigned on a platform of states' rights.

States·ville (stāts′vil), *n.* a city in central North Carolina. 18,622.

states·wom·an (stāts′wo͝om′ən), *n., pl.* **-wom·en. 1.** a woman who is experienced in the art of government. **2.** a woman who exhibits great wisdom and ability in directing the affairs of a government. [1600–10; STATES(MAN) + -WOMAN]
—**Usage.** See **-woman.**

state′ tree′, a tree chosen as an official symbol of a U.S. state. [1915–20, *Amer.*]

state′ troop′er, a member of a U.S. state police force.

state′ univer′sity, a university maintained by the government of a state. [1825–35, *Amer.*]

state′ vis′it, an official visit of the chief of state of one country to that of another.

state·wide (stāt′wīd′), *adj.* **1.** extending throughout all parts of a state in the U.S.: *a statewide search.* —*adv.* **2.** throughout a state: *It was applauded statewide.* [1910–15, *Amer.*; STATE + -WIDE]

stat·far·ad (stat′far′əd, -ad), *n. Elect.* the electrostatic unit of capacitance, equivalent to 1.1126×10^{-12} farad and equal to the capacitance of a condenser in which one statcoulomb is transferred from one conductor of the condenser to the other per volt of potential difference between the conductors. [*stat-* (see STATAMPERE) + FARAD]

stat·hen·ry (stat′hen′rē), *n., pl.* **-ries, -rys.** *Elect.* the electrostatic unit of inductance, equivalent to 8.9876×10^{11} henries and equal to the inductance of a circuit in which an electromotive force of one statvolt is produced by a current in the circuit which varies at the rate of one statampere per second. [*stat-* (see STATAMPERE) + HENRY]

Sta·tia (stā′shə), *n.* See **St. Eustatius.**

stat·ic (stat′ik), *adj.* Also, **stat′i·cal. 1.** pertaining to or characterized by a fixed or stationary condition. **2.** showing little or no change: *a static concept; a static relationship.* **3.** lacking movement, development, or vitality: *The novel was marred by static characterizations, especially in its central figures.* **4.** *Sociol.* referring to a condition of social life bound by tradition. **5.** *Elect.* pertaining to or noting static electricity. **6.** noting or pertaining to atmospheric electricity interfering with radar, radio, the sending and receiving of wireless messages, etc. **7.** *Physics.* acting by mere weight without producing motion: *static pressure.* **8.** *Econ.* pertaining to fixed relations, or different combinations of fixed quantities: *static population.* —*n.* **9.** *Elect.* **a.** static or atmospheric electricity. **b.** interference due to such electricity. **10.** *Informal.* difficulty; trouble: *Will your dad give you any static on using the car?* [1560–70; < NL *staticus* < Gk *statikós,* equiv. to *sta-* (s. of *histánai* to make STAND) + *-tikos* -TIC] —**stat′i·cal·ly,** *adv.*

stat′ic cling′, the adhering of clothing to other clothing or a person's body, caused by an accumulation of static electricity in the materials, esp. those containing synthetic fibers.

stat·ice (stat′is, -ə sē′), *n.* any of various plants belonging to the genus *Limonium,* of the leadwort family, having clusters of variously colored flowers that retain their color when dried. [1725–35; < NL (orig. a genus name), L < Gk *statikḗ* an astringent herb, n. use of fem. of *statikós* astringent, lit., causing to stand; see STATIC]

stat′ic electric′ity, *Elect.* a stationary electric charge built up on an insulating material. Cf. **electrostatics.** [1875–80]

stat′ic line′, *Mil.* a line attached to a parachute pack and to a cable in an aircraft for the purpose of automatically opening the parachute after it is dropped. [1925–30]

stat·ics (stat′iks), *n.* (*used with a singular v.*) the branch of mechanics that deals with bodies at rest or forces in equilibrium. [1650–60; see STATIC, -ICS]

stat′ic tube′, a tube for measuring the static pressure of a fluid in motion, so placed in the fluid as not to be affected by the pressure changes caused by the motion of the fluid. [1930–35]

stat′ic wa′ter, *Brit.* water collected and stored in reservoirs, tanks, etc., as for urban use.

sta·tion (stā′shən), *n.* **1.** a place or position in which a person or thing is normally located. **2.** a stopping place for trains or other land conveyances, for the transfer of freight or passengers. **3.** the building or buildings at such a stopping place. **4.** the district or municipal headquarters of certain public services: *police station; fire station; postal station.* **5.** a place equipped for some particular kind of work, service, research, or the like: *gasoline station; geophysical station.* **6.** the position, as of persons or things, in a scale of estimation, rank, or dignity; standing: *the responsibility of persons of high station.* **7.** a position, office, rank, calling, or the like. **8.** *Radio and Television.* **a.** a studio or building from which broadcasts originate. **b.** a person or organization originating and broadcasting messages or programs. **c.** a specific frequency or band of frequencies assigned to a regular or special broadcaster: *Tune to the Civil Defense station.* **d.** the complete equipment used in transmitting and receiving broadcasts. **9.** *Mil.* **a.** a military place of duty. **b.** a semipermanent army post. **10.** *Navy.* a place or region to which a ship or fleet is assigned for duty. **11.** (formerly in India) the area in which the British officials of a district or the officers of a garrison resided. **12.** *Biol.* a particular area or type of region where a given animal or plant is found. **13.** *Australian.* a ranch with its buildings, land, etc., esp. for raising sheep. **14.** *Survey.* **a.** Also called **instrument station, set-up.** a point where an observation is taken. **b.** a precisely located reference point. **c.** a length of 100 ft. (30 m) along a survey line. **15.** a section or area assigned to a waiter, soldier, etc.; post: *The waiter says this isn't his station.* **16.** See **stations of the cross. 17.** *Archaic.* the fact or condition of standing still. —*v.t.* **18.** to assign a station to; place or post in a station or position. [1350–1400; < L *statiōn-* (s. of *statiō*) a standing still, standing-place, equiv. to *stat(us)* (ptp. of *stāre* to STAND) + *-iōn-* -ION; r. ME *stacioun* < AF < L, as above] —**sta′tion·al,** *adj.*
—**Syn. 1.** situation, location. **3.** depot, terminal. **7.** metier, occupation, trade, business, employment. **15.** See **appointment. 18.** position, locate, establish, set, fix.

sta′tion a′gent, a person who manages a small railroad station. [1850–55, *Amer.*]

sta·tion·ar·y (stā′shə ner′ē), *adj., n., pl.* **-ar·ies.** —*adj.* **1.** standing still; not moving. **2.** having a fixed position; not movable. **3.** established in one place; not itinerant or migratory. **4.** remaining in the same condition or state; not changing: *The market price has remained stationary for a week.* —*n.* **5.** a person or thing that is stationary. [1400–50; late ME < L *statiōnārius.* See STATION, -ARY]

sta′tionary bi′cycle. See **exercise bicycle.**

sta′tionary en′gine, an engine mounted in a fixed position, as one used for driving generators, compressors, etc. [1830–40]

sta′tionary engineer′, a person who runs or is licensed to run a stationary engine. —**sta′tionary engineer′ing.**

sta′tionary front′, *Meteorol.* a front between warm and cold air masses that is moving very slowly or not at all. [1935–40]

sta′tionary state′, *Physics.* any of several energy states an atom may occupy without emitting electromagnetic radiation.

CONCISE PRONUNCIATION KEY: act, cāpe, dâre, pärt; set, ēqual; *if,* īce; ox, ōver, ôrder, oil, bo͝ok, bo͞ot, out; up, ûrge; child; sing; shoe; thin, *th*at; zh as in *treasure.* ə = *a* as in *alone,* e as in *system,* i as in *easily,* o as in *gallop,* u as in *circus;* ə as in *fire* (fīər), *hour* (ouər). l and n can serve as syllabic consonants, as in *cradle* (krād′l), and *button* (but′n). See the full key inside the front cover.

sta′tionary wave′. See **standing wave.** [1895–1900]

sta′tion break′, *Radio and Television.* an interval between or during programs for identifying the station, making announcements, etc. [1935–40]

sta·tion·er (stā′shə nər), *n.* **1.** a person who sells the materials used in writing, as paper, pens, pencils, and ink. **2.** *Archaic.* **a.** a bookseller. **b.** a publisher. [1350–1400; ME *stacio(u)ner* < ML *statiōnārius,* n. use of the adj.: STATIONARY, i.e., pertaining to dealers with permanent shops as distinguished from itinerant vendors]

Sta′tioners' Com′pany, a company or guild of the city of London composed of booksellers, printers, dealers in writing materials, etc., incorporated in 1557.

sta·tion·er·y (stā′shə ner′ē), *n.* **1.** writing paper. **2.** writing materials, as pens, pencils, paper, and envelopes. [1670–80; STATIONER + -Y[3]]

sta′tion house′, a police station or fire station. [1825–35]

sta·tion·mas·ter (stā′shən mas′tər, -mä′stər), *n.* a person in charge of a railroad station; station agent. [1855–60, *Amer.*; STATION + MASTER]

sta′tions of the cross′, *Eccles.* a series of 14 representations of successive incidents from the Passion of Christ, each with a wooden cross, or a series of wooden crosses alone, set up in a church, or sometimes outdoors, and visited in sequence, for prayer and meditation. Also, **Sta′tions of the Cross′.** [1885–90]

sta·tion-to-sta·tion (stā′shən tə stā′shən), *adj.* **1.** (of a long-distance telephone call) chargeable upon speaking with anyone at the number called: *a station-to-station call to his home in Dallas.* —*adv.* **2.** from one station to another. **3.** by telephone at station-to-station rates. Cf. **person-to-person** (defs. 1, 3).

sta′tion wag′on, an automobile with one or more rows of folding or removable seats behind the driver and no luggage compartment but an area behind the seats into which suitcases, parcels, etc., can be loaded through a tailgate. Also called, *esp. Brit.,* **estate car.** [1925–30, *Amer.*]

stat·ism (stā′tiz əm), *n.* **1.** the principle or policy of concentrating extensive economic, political, and related controls in the state at the cost of individual liberty. **2.** support of or belief in the sovereignty of a state, usually a republic. [1600–10; STATE + -ISM]

stat·ist[1] (stā′tist), *n.* **1.** an advocate of statism. —*adj.* **2.** of, pertaining to, or characteristic of a statist or statism. [1575–85; STATE + -IST]

stat·ist[2] (stat′ist), *n.* statistician. [shortened form]

sta·tis·tic (stə tis′tik), *n. Statistics.* a numerical fact or datum, esp. one computed from a sample. [1780–90; < NL *statisticus.* See STATUS, -ISTIC]

sta·tis·ti·cal (stə tis′ti kəl), *adj.* of, pertaining to, consisting of, or based on statistics. [1590–1600; STATISTIC(S) + -AL[1]] —**sta·tis′ti·cal·ly,** *adv.*

statis′tical independ′ence, *Statistics.* the condition or state of events or values of being statistically independent. Also called **stochastic independence.**

statis′tically independ′ent, *Statistics.* (of events or values) having the probability of their joint occurrence equal to the product of their individual probabilities. Also, **independent, stochastically independent.**

statis′tical mechan′ics, *Physics, Chem.* (*used with a singular v.*) the science that deals with average properties of the molecules, atoms, or elementary particles in random motion in a system of many such particles and relates these properties to the thermodynamic and other macroscopic properties of the system. Also called **statis′tical phys′ics, statis′tical thermodynam′ics.** Cf. **Maxwell-Boltzmann statistics, quantum statistics.** [1880–85]

stat·is·ti·cian (stat′i stish′ən), *n.* an expert in or compiler of statistics. Also, **statist.** [1815–25; STATISTIC(ICS) + -ICIAN]

sta·tis·tics (stə tis′tiks), *n.* **1.** (*used with a singular v.*) the science that deals with the collection, classification, analysis, and interpretation of numerical facts or data, and that, by use of mathematical theories of probability, imposes order and regularity on aggregates of more or less disparate elements. **2.** (*used with a plural v.*) the numerical facts or data themselves. [1780–90; see STATISTIC, -ICS]

Sta·ti·us (stā′shē əs), *n.* **Pub·li·us Pa·pin·i·us** (pub′lē əs pə pin′ē əs), A.D. c45–c96, Roman poet.

sta·tive (stā′tiv), *adj. Gram.* (of a verb) expressing a state or condition, as *like, want,* or *believe,* and usually used in simple, not progressive, tenses: *I liked them. I want some. I will never believe it.* Cf. **nonstative.** [1625–35; < NL *statīvus,* L, equiv. to *stat(us)* (ptp. of *stāre* to STAND) + *-īvus* -IVE]

Stat·ler (stat′lər), *n.* **Ellsworth Milton,** 1863–1928, U.S. hotel-chain developer.

stat·o·blast (stat′ə blast′), *n. Zool.* (in certain bryozoans) an asexually produced group of cells encased in a chitinous covering that can survive unfavorable conditions, as freezing or drought, and germinate to produce a new colony. [1850–55; *stato-* (comb. form of Gk *statós* standing; akin to STATUS, STATIC) + -BLAST]

stat·o·cyst (stat′ə sist′), *n. Zool.* (in certain invertebrates) a sense organ consisting of a sac enclosing sensory hairs and particles of sand, lime, etc., that functions in maintaining equilibrium, serving to indicate position in space. [1900–05; *stato-* (see STATOBLAST) + -CYST]

stat·ohm (stat′ōm′), *n. Elect.* the electrostatic unit of resistance, equivalent to 8.9876×10^{11} ohms and equal to the resistance in a conductor in which one statvolt of potential difference produces a current of one statampere. [*stat-* (see STATAMPERE) + -OHM]

stat·o·lith (stat′l ith), *n.* **1.** *Zool.* any of the granules of lime, sand, etc., contained within a statocyst. **2.** *Bot.* an inclusion, as a starch grain, that by a change in position within the cells of an organ or part is assumed to cause a corresponding change in position of the organ or part. [1895–1900; *stato-* (see STATOBLAST) + -LITH] —**stat′o·lith′ic,** *adj.*

sta·tor (stā′tər), *n.* **1.** *Elect., Mach.* a portion of a machine that remains fixed with respect to rotating parts, esp. the collection of stationary parts in the magnetic circuits of a machine. Cf. **rotor** (def. 1). **2.** *Aeron.* the system of stationary airfoils in the compressor of a jet engine. [1900–05; < NL, L: lit., one that stands. See STATUS, -TOR]

stat·o·scope (stat′ə skōp′), *n.* **1.** an aneroid barometer for registering minute variations of atmospheric pressure. **2.** *Aeron.* an instrument for detecting a small rate of rise or fall of an aircraft. [1895–1900; *stato-* (see STATOBLAST) + -SCOPE]

stat·u·ar·y (stach′o͞o er′ē), *n., pl.* **-ar·ies,** *adj.* —*n.* **1.** statues collectively. **2.** a group or collection of statues. —*adj.* **3.** of, pertaining to, or suitable for statues. [1535–45; < L *statuārius.* See STATUE, -ARY]

stat·ue (stach′o͞o), *n.* a three-dimensional work of art, as a representational or abstract form, carved in stone or wood, molded in a plastic material, cast in bronze, or the like. [1300–50; ME < MF < L *statua,* n. deriv. of *statuere* to set up, itself deriv. of *status* (see STATUS)] —**stat′ue·like′,** *adj.*

stat·ued (stach′o͞od), *adj.* having or ornamented with statues: *a statued avenue.* [1800–10; STATUE + -ED[3]]

Stat′ue of Lib′erty, 1. a large copper statue, on Liberty Island, in New York harbor, depicting a woman holding a burning torch: designed by F. A. Bartholdi and presented to the U.S. by France; unveiled 1886. **2.** Also called **Stat′ue of Lib′erty play′.** *Football.* a play in which a back, usually the quarterback, fakes a pass, and a back or end running behind him takes the ball from his upraised hand and runs with it.

stat·u·esque (stach′o͞o esk′), *adj.* like or suggesting a statue, as in massive or majestic dignity, grace, or beauty. [1825–35; STATUE + -ESQUE] —**stat′u·esque′·ly,** *adv.* —**stat′u·esque′ness,** *n.*

stat·u·ette (stach′o͞o et′), *n.* a small statue. [1835–45; < F; see STATUE, -ETTE]

stat·ure (stach′ər), *n.* **1.** the height of a human or animal body. **2.** the height of any object. **3.** degree of development attained; level of achievement: *a minister of great stature.* [1250–1300; ME < OF *estature* < L *statūra,* equiv. to *stat(us)* ptp. of *stāre* to STAND + *-ūra* -URE]

stat·ured (stach′ərd), *adj.* of or having a stature of a certain kind (usually used in combination): *the short-statured inhabitants of the Malay Peninsula.* [1600–10; STATURE + -ED[3]]

sta·tus (stā′təs, stat′əs), *n.* **1.** the position of an individual in relation to another or others, esp. in regard to social or professional standing. **2.** state or condition of affairs: *Arbitration has failed to change the status of the disagreement.* **3.** *Law.* the standing of a person before the law. —*adj.* **4.** conferring or believed to confer elevated status: *a status car; a status job.* [1665–75; < L: the condition of standing, stature, status, equiv. to *sta-* (var. s. of *stāre* to STAND) + *-tus* suffix of v. action]
—**Syn. 2.** See **state.**

sta′tus group′, *Sociol.* a social stratum sharing the same lifestyle or occupation and having the same level of prestige. [1905–10]

sta′tus quo′ (kwō), the existing state or condition. Also called **sta′tus in quo′.** [1825–35; < L *status quō* lit., state in which]

sta′tus sym′bol, an object, habit, etc., by which the social or economic status of the possessor may be judged.

stat·u·ta·ble (stach′o͝o tə bəl), *adj.* **1.** (of an offense) recognized by statute; legally punishable. **2.** prescribed, authorized, or permitted by statute: *the statutable age of a voter.* [1630–40; STATUTE + -ABLE]

stat·ute (stach′o͞ot, -o͝ot), *n.* **1.** *Law.* **a.** an enactment made by a legislature and expressed in a formal document. **b.** the document in which such an enactment is expressed. **2.** *Internat. Law.* an instrument annexed or subsidiary to an international agreement, as a treaty. **3.** a permanent rule established by an organization, corporation, etc., to govern its internal affairs. [1250–1300; ME *statut* < OF *estatut* < LL *statūtum,* n. use of neut. of L *statūtus* (ptp. of *statuere* to make stand, set up, deriv. of *status* STATUS), equiv. to *statū-,* verb. s. + *-tus* ptp. suffix]

stat′ute book′, a book containing the laws enacted by the legislature of a state or nation. [1585–95]

stat′ute law′. See **statutory law.** [1605–15]

stat′ute mile′, mile (def. 1). [1860–65]

stat′ute of limita′tions, *Law.* a statute defining the period within which legal action may be taken. [1760–70]

stat·u·to·ry (stach′o͝o tôr′ē, -tōr′ē), *adj.* **1.** of, pertaining to, or of the nature of a statute. **2.** prescribed or authorized by statute. **3.** conforming to statute. **4.** (of an offense) recognized by statute; legally punishable. [1710–20; STATUTE + -ORY[1]] —**stat′u·to′ri·ly,** *adv.*

stat′utory crime′. See **statutory offense.**

stat′utory law′, the written law established by enactments expressing the will of the legislature, as distinguished from the unwritten law or common law. Also called **statute law.** [1875–80]

stat′utory offense′, *Law.* a wrong punishable under a statute, rather than at common law. Also called **statutory crime.** [1930–35]

stat′utory rape′, *U.S. Law.* sexual intercourse with a girl under the age of consent, which age varies in different states. [1930–35]

stat·volt (stat′vōlt′), *n. Elect.* the electrostatic unit of electromotive force or potential difference, approximately equivalent to 300 volts and equal to the electromotive force or potential difference that will cause a current of one statampere to flow through a conductor with a resistance of one statohm. [*stat-* (see STATAMPERE) + VOLT[1]]

Stau·ding·er (shtou′ding ər), *n.* **Her·mann** (her′män), 1881–1965, German chemist: Nobel prize 1953.

St. Au·gus·tine (ô′gə stēn′), a seacoast city in NE Florida: founded by the Spanish 1565; oldest city in the U.S.; resort. 11,985.

St. Augustine grass, a low, mat-forming grass, *Stenotaphrum secundatum,* of the southern U.S. and tropical America, that is cultivated as a lawn grass. Also called **buffalo grass.** [1930–35; after ST. AUGUSTINE, Florida]

staum·rel (stam′rəl, stôm′-), *Scot.* —*adj.* **1.** stupid; half-witted. —*n.* **2.** a stupid person. Also, **stammrel, staume·ral** (stam′rəl, stam′ə rəl, stôm′rəl, stô′mə rəl). [1780–90; *staumer,* Scots var. of STAMMER + -REL]

staunch[1] (stônch), *v.t., v.i., n.* stanch[1].

staunch[2] (stônch, stänch), *adj.,* **-er, -est. 1.** firm or steadfast in principle, loyalty, etc., as a person: *a staunch Republican; a staunch friend.* **2.** characterized by firmness, steadfastness, or loyalty: *He delivered a staunch defense of the government.* **3.** strong; substantial: *a staunch little hut in the woods.* **4.** impervious to water or other liquids; watertight: *a staunch vessel.* Also, **stanch.** [1375–1425; late ME *sta(u)nch* < MF *estanche* (fem.), *estanc* (masc.), deriv. of *estancher* to STANCH[1]]
—**Syn. 1.** constant, true, faithful. See **steadfast. 2.** resolute. **3.** stout, sound.

Staun·ton (stan′tn), *n.* a city in N Virginia. 21,857.

stau·ro·lite (stôr′ə līt′), *n.* a mineral, basic iron aluminum silicate, $Fe_2Al_2O_7(SiO_4)_4(OH)$, occurring in brown to black prismatic crystals, which are often twinned in the form of a cross. [1790–1800; < Gk *stauró(s)* a cross + -LITE] —**stau·ro·lit·ic** (stôr′ə lit′ik), *adj.*

stau·ro·pe·gi·on (stäv′rô pē′yē ôn; *Eng.* stav′rō pē′jē on′), *n., pl.* **-gi·a** (-yē ä; *Eng.* -jē ə). *Gk. Orth. Ch.* (in an autocephalous church) a monastery subject directly to the primate. [< MGk *stauropḗgion,* equiv. to Gk *stauró(s)* a cross + *pēg(nýnai)* to fix, fasten + *-ion* n. suffix] —**stau·ro·pe·gi·al** (stav′rō pē′jē əl), *adj.*

Sta·vang·er (stä väng′ər), *n.* a seaport in SW Norway. 86,643.

stave (stāv), *n., v.,* **staved** or **stove, stav·ing.** —*n.* **1.** one of the thin, narrow, shaped pieces of wood that form the sides of a cask, tub, or similar vessel. **2.** a stick, rod, pole, or the like. **3.** a rung of a ladder, chair, etc. **4.** *Pros.* **a.** a verse or stanza of a poem or song. **b.** the alliterating sound in a line of verse, as the *w*-sound in *wind in the willows.* **5.** *Music.* staff[1] (def. 9). —*v.t.* **6.** to break in a stave or staves of (a cask or barrel) so as to release the wine, liquor, or other contents. **7.** to release (wine, liquor, etc.) by breaking the cask or barrel. **8.** to break or crush (something) inward (often fol. by *in*). **9.** to break (a hole) in, esp. in the hull of a boat. **10.** to break to pieces; splinter; smash. **11.** to furnish with a stave or staves. **12.** to beat with a stave or staff. —*v.i.* **13.** to become staved in, as a boat; break in or up. **14.** to move along rapidly. **15. stave off, a.** to put, ward, or keep off, as by force or evasion. **b.** to prevent in time; forestall: *to stave off bankruptcy.* [1125–75; (n.) ME, back formation from STAVES; (v.) deriv. of the n.]
—**Syn. 4.** See **verse.**

staves (stāvz), *n.* **1.** a pl. of **staff**[1]. **2.** pl. of **stave.**

staves·a·cre (stāvz′ā′kər), *n.* **1.** a larkspur, *Delphinium staphisagria,* of Europe and Asia Minor, having violently emetic and cathartic poisonous seeds. **2.** the seeds themselves. [1350–1400; ME *staphisagre* < L *staphis agria* < Gk *staphìs agría* lit., wild raisin]

Stav·ro·pol (stav rō′pəl; *Russ.* stä′vrə pəl), *n.* **1.** a territory of the Russian Federation in Europe, N of the Caucasus. 2,306,000; 29,600 sq. mi. (76,960 sq. km). **2.** the capital of this territory. 306,000. **3.** former name of **Tolyatti.**

staw (stô), *n., v.t., v.i. Chiefly Scot.* stall[1].

stay[1] (stā), *v.,* **stayed** or **staid, stay·ing,** *n.* —*v.i.* **1.** to spend some time in a place, in a situation, with a person or group, etc.: *He stayed in the army for ten years.* **2.** to continue to be as specified, as to condition or state: *to stay clean.* **3.** to hold out or endure, as in a contest or task (fol. by *with* or *at*): *Please stay with the project as long as you can.* **4.** to keep up, as with a competitor (fol. by *with*). **5.** *Poker.* to continue in a hand by matching an ante, bet, or raise. **6.** to stop or halt. **7.** to pause or wait, as for a moment, before proceeding or continuing; linger or tarry. **8.** *Archaic.* to cease or desist. **9.** *Archaic.* to stand firm. —*v.t.* **10.** to stop or halt. **11.** to hold back, detain, or restrain, as from going further. **12.** to suspend or delay (actions, proceedings, etc.). **13.** to appease or satisfy temporarily the cravings of (the stomach, appetite, etc.). **14.** to remain through or during (a period of time): *We stayed two days in San Francisco.* **15.** to remain to the end of; remain beyond (usually fol. by *out*). **16.** *Archaic.* to await. **17. stay the course,** to persevere; endure to completion. —*n.* **18.** the act of stopping or being stopped. **19.** a stop, halt, or pause; a standstill. **20.** a sojourn or temporary residence: *a week's stay in Miami.* **21.** *Law.* a stoppage or arrest of action; suspension of a judicial proceeding: *The governor granted a stay of execution.* **22.** *Informal.* staying power; endurance. [1400–50; late ME *staien* < AF *estaier,* OF *estai-,* s. of *ester* < L *stāre* to STAND]

stay[2] (stā), *n., v.,* **stayed, stay·ing.** —*n.* **1.** something used to support or steady a thing; prop; brace. **2.** a flat strip of steel, plastic, etc., used esp. for stiffening corsets, collars, etc. **3.** a long rod running between opposite walls, heads or sides of a furnace, boiler, tank, or the like, to strengthen them against internal pressures. **4. stays,** *Chiefly Brit.* a corset. —*v.t.* **5.** to support, prop, or hold up (sometimes fol. by *up*). **6.** to sustain or

CONCISE ETYMOLOGY KEY: <, descended or borrowed from; >, whence; b., blend of, blended; c., cognate with; cf., compare; deriv., derivative; equiv., equivalent; imit., imitative; obl., oblique; r., replacing; s., stem; sp., spelling, spelled; resp., respelling, respelled; trans., translation; ?, origin unknown; *, unattested; ‡, probably earlier than. See the full key inside the front cover.

strengthen mentally or spiritually. **7.** to rest on (something, as a foundation or base) for support. **8.** to cause something to become fixed or to rest on (a support, foundation, base, etc.) [1505–15; appar. same as STAY^3 (cf. OF *estayer* to hold in place, support, perh. deriv. of ME *steye* STAY^3)]

stay^3 (stā), *n., v.,* **stayed, stay•ing.** *Chiefly Naut.* —*n.* **1.** any of various strong ropes or wires for steadying masts, funnels, etc. **2. in stays,** (of a fore-and-aft-rigged vessel) heading into the wind with sails shaking, as in coming about. —*v.t.* **3.** to support or secure with a stay or stays: *to stay a mast.* **4.** to put (a ship) on the other tack. —*v.i.* **5.** (of a ship) to change to the other tack. [bef. 1150; ME *stey(e),* OE *stæg;* c. G *Stag*]

stay-at-home (stā′ət hōm′), *adj.* **1.** not inclined to travel or seek diversions or pastimes outside one's residence, area, or country. **2.** of or pertaining to time spent at home: *a stay-at-home evening.* —*n.* **3.** a person who stays at home a good deal; a person not inclined to travel; homebody. [1800–10]

stay•bolt (stā′bōlt′), *n.* a long rod with threaded ends, used as a stay for a boiler, tank, etc. [1830–40; STAY^2 + BOLT^1]

stay′ing pow′er, ability or strength to last or endure; endurance; stamina. [1855–60]

stay′-in strike′ (stā′in′), *Brit.* See **sit-down strike.** Also called **stay′-in′.**

Stay•man (stā′mən), *n., pl.* **-mans.** a variety of apple grown chiefly in the Shenandoah Valley of Virginia.

stay-press (stā′pres′), *adj.* (of fabric or clothing) treated so as to retain a freshly ironed look after washing.

stay•sail (stā′sāl′; *Naut.* stā′səl), *n. Naut.* any sail set on a stay, as a triangular sail between two masts. See diag. under **ship.** [1660–70; STAY^3 + SAIL]

S.T.B., 1. Bachelor of Sacred Theology. [< NL *Sacrae Theologiae Baccalaureus*] **2.** Bachelor of Theology. [< NL *Scientiae Theologicae Baccalaureus*]

stbd., starboard.

St. Ber•nard (sānt′ bər närd′; *for 1, 2 also Fr.* saN ber nar′), **1. Great,** a mountain pass between SW Switzerland and NW Italy, in the Pennine Alps: Napoleon led his army through it in 1800; location of a hospice. 8108 ft. (2470 m) high. See map under **Simplon. 2. Little,** a mountain pass between SE France and NW Italy, in the Alps, S of Mont Blanc. 7177 ft. (2185 m) high. **3.** one of a breed of very large dogs having a massive head and a dense coat, bred in the Swiss Alps as guide dogs and used to rescue lost, snowbound travelers.

St. Bernard (def. 3), 28 in. (71 cm) high at shoulder

St. Bri•euc (saN brē œ′), a city in and the capital of the Côtes-du-Nord, in W France. 56,282.

St.-Bru•no-de-Mon•tar•ville (sānt′bro͞o′nō də mon′tər vil′; *Fr.* saN bRY nō də môN taR vēl′), *n.* a town in S Quebec, in E Canada, near Montreal. 22,880.

St. Cath•ar•ines (kath′ər inz, kath′rinz), a city in SE Ontario, in SE Canada. 123,351.

St. Charles, 1. a city in E Missouri, on the Missouri River. 37,379. **2.** a town in NE Illinois. 17,492.

St. Christopher. See **St. Kitts.**

St. Chris•to•pher-Ne•vis (kris′tə fər nē′vis, -nev′is). See **St. Kitts-Nevis.**

St. Clair (sānt′ klâr′; *for 1 also* sing′klâr, sin′-), **1. Arthur,** 1736–1818, American Revolutionary War general, born in Scotland: 1st governor of the Northwest Territory, 1787–1802. **2.** a river in the N central U.S. and S Canada, flowing S from Lake Huron to Lake St. Clair, forming part of the boundary between Michigan and Ontario. 41 mi. (66 km) long. **3. Lake,** a lake between SE Michigan and Ontario, Canada. 26 mi. (42 km) long; 460 sq. mi. (1190 sq. km).

St. Clair Shores, a city in SE Michigan, near Detroit. 76,210.

St. Cloud (sānt′ kloud′ *for 1;* saN klo͞o′ *for 2*). **1.** a city in central Minnesota, on the Mississippi. 42,566. **2.** a suburb of Paris in N France, on the Seine: former royal palace. 28,350.

St. Crispin's Day, October 25: anniversary of the Battle of Agincourt (1415).

St. Croix (kroi), **1.** Also called **Santa Cruz.** a U.S. island in the N Lesser Antilles: the largest of the Virgin Islands. 51,570; 82 sq. mi. (212 sq. km). **2.** a river flowing from NW Wisconsin along the boundary between Wisconsin and Minnesota into the Mississippi. 164 mi. (264 km) long. **3.** a river in the NE United States and SE Canada, forming a part of the boundary between Maine and New Brunswick, flowing into Passamaquoddy Bay. 75 mi. (121 km) long.

St. Cyr-l'É•cole (saN sēr lā kôl′), a town in N France, W of Versailles: military academy. 17,795.

STD, sexually transmitted disease.

std., standard.

S.T.D., Doctor of Sacred Theology. [< NL *Sacrae Theologiae Doctor*]

St. Den•is (sānt′ den′is; *for 2, 3 also Fr.* saN də nē′), **1. Ruth,** 1880?–1968, U.S. dancer. **2.** a suburb of Paris in N France: famous abbey, the burial place of many French kings. 96,759. **3.** a seaport in and the capital of Réunion island, in the Indian Ocean. 94,000.

Ste., (referring to a woman) Saint. [< F *Sainte*]

stead (sted), *n.* **1.** the place of a person or thing as occupied by a successor or substitute: *The nephew of the queen came in her stead.* **2.** *Obs.* a place or locality. **3. stand in good stead,** to be useful to, esp. in a critical situation: *Your experience will stand you in good stead.* —*v.t.* **4.** to be of service, advantage, or avail to. [bef. 900; (n.) ME, OE *stede;* c. G *Stätte* place; akin to G *Stadt,* ON *stathr,* Goth *staths,* Gk *stásis* (see STASIS); (v.) ME *steden,* deriv. of the n.]

stead•fast (sted′fast′, -fäst′, -fəst), *adj.* **1.** fixed in direction; steadily directed: *a steadfast gaze.* **2.** firm in purpose, resolution, faith, attachment, etc., as a person: *a steadfast friend.* **3.** unwavering, as resolution, faith, adherence, etc. **4.** firmly established, as an institution or a state of affairs. **5.** firmly fixed in place or position. Also, **stedfast.** [bef. 1000; ME *stedefast,* OE *stedefæst.* See STEAD, FAST^1] —**stead′fast′ly,** *adv.* —**stead′fast′ness,** *n.*

—**Syn. 2.** sure, dependable, reliable, constant, unwavering. STEADFAST, STAUNCH, STEADY imply a sureness and continuousness that may be depended upon. STEADFAST literally means fixed in place, but is chiefly used figuratively to indicate undeviating constancy or resolution: *steadfast in one's faith.* STAUNCH literally means watertight, as of a vessel, and therefore strong and firm; figuratively, it is used of loyal support that will endure strain: *a staunch advocate of free trade.* Literally, STEADY is applied to that which is relatively firm in position or continuous in movement or duration: *a steady flow;* figuratively, it implies sober regularity or persistence: *a steady worker.* **4, 5.** stable. —**Ant. 2.** capricious, variable.

stead•ing (sted′ing), *n. Scot. and North Eng.* a farm, esp. its buildings. [1425–75; late ME (north and Scots); see STEAD, -ING^1]

stead•y (sted′ē), *adj.,* **stead•i•er, stead•i•est,** *interj., n., pl.* **stead•ies,** *v.,* **stead•ied, stead•y•ing,** *adv.* —*adj.* **1.** firmly placed or fixed; stable in position or equilibrium: *a steady ladder.* **2.** even or regular in movement: *the steady swing of the pendulum.* **3.** free from change, variation, or interruption; uniform; continuous: *a steady diet of meat and potatoes; a steady wind.* **4.** constant, regular, or habitual: *a steady job.* **5.** free from excitement or agitation; calm: *steady nerves.* **6.** firm; unfaltering: *a steady gaze; a steady hand.* **7.** steadfast or unwavering; resolute: *a steady purpose.* **8.** settled, staid, or sober, as a person, habits, etc. **9.** *Naut.* (of a vessel) keeping nearly upright, as in a heavy sea. **10. go steady,** *Informal.* to date one person exclusively: *Her father didn't approve of her going steady at such an early age.* —*interj.* **11.** (used to urge someone to calm down or be under control.) **12.** *Naut.* (a helm order to keep a vessel steady on its present heading.) —*n.* **13.** *Informal.* a person of the opposite sex whom one dates exclusively; sweetheart; boyfriend or girlfriend. **14.** *Informal.* a steady visitor, customer, or the like; habitué. —*v.t.* **15.** to make or keep steady, as in position, movement, action, character, etc.: *His calm confidence steadied the nervous passengers.* —*v.i.* **16.** to become steady. —*adv.* **17.** in a firm or steady manner: *Hold the ladder steady.* **18.** *Informal.* steadily, regularly, or continuously: *Is she working steady now?* [1520–30; 1905–10 for def. 13; STEAD + -Y^1] —**stead′i•ly,** *adv.* —**stead′i•ness,** *n.*

—**Syn. 1.** balanced. **3.** undeviating, invariable. **7.** See **steadfast.**

stead•y-go•ing (sted′ē gō′ing), *adj.* **1.** steadfast; faithful; unchanging: *steady-going service to the cause of justice.* **2.** regular and dependable, as in habits of living: *a steady-going family man.* [1815–25]

stead•y-hand•ed (sted′ē han′did), *adj.* having steady hands; having self-control; calm. [1605–15]

stead′y state′ the′ory, *Astron.* a theory in which the universe is assumed to have average properties that are constant in space and time so that new matter must be continuously and spontaneously created to maintain average densities as the universe expands. Also called **stead′y state′ mod′el.** Cf. **big bang theory.** [1950–55]

steak (stāk), *n.* **1.** a slice of meat or fish, esp. beef, cooked by broiling, frying, etc. **2.** chopped meat prepared in the same manner as a steak. [1400–50; late ME *steike* < ON *steik* meat roasted on a stick]

steak au poivre (stek ō pwav′R^{ə}; *Eng.* stāk′ ō pwä′vrə, pwäv′), *French.* See **pepper steak** (def. 2).

steak•house (stāk′hous′), *n., pl.* **-hous•es** (-hou′ziz). a restaurant specializing in beefsteak. [1865–70; STEAK + HOUSE]

steak′ knife′, a sharp dinner knife the blade of which is made of steel and usually serrated, used in cutting meat. [1925–30]

steak′ set′, a carving set for steaks.

steak′ tartare′. See **tartar steak.** [1950–55]

steal (stēl), *v.,* **stole, sto•len, steal•ing,** *n.* —*v.t.* **1.** to take (the property of another or others) without permission or right, esp. secretly or by force: *A pickpocket stole his watch.* **2.** to appropriate (ideas, credit, words, etc.) without right or acknowledgment. **3.** to take, get, or win insidiously, surreptitiously, subtly, or by chance: *He stole my girlfriend.* **4.** to move, bring, convey, or put secretly or quietly; smuggle (usually fol. by *away, from, in, into,* etc.): *They stole the bicycle into the bedroom to surprise the child.* **5.** *Baseball.* (of a base runner) to gain (a base) without the help of a walk or batted ball, as by running to it during the delivery of a pitch. **6.** *Games.* to gain (a point, advantage, etc.) by strategy, chance, or luck. **7.** to gain or seize more than one's share of attention in, as by giving a superior performance: *The comedian stole the show.* —*v.i.* **8.** to commit or practice theft. **9.** to move, go, or come secretly, quietly, or unobserved: *She stole out of the house at midnight.* **10.** to pass, happen, etc., imperceptibly, gently, or gradually: *The years steal by.* **11.** *Baseball.* (of a base runner) to advance a base without the help of a walk or batted ball. **12. steal someone's thunder,** to appropriate or use another's idea, plan, words, etc. —*n.* **13.** *Informal.* an act of stealing; theft. **14.** *Informal.* the thing stolen; booty. **15.** *Informal.* something acquired at a cost far below its real value; bargain: *This dress is a steal at $40.* **16.** *Baseball.* the act of advancing a base by stealing. [bef. 900; 1860–65 for def. 5; ME *stelen,* OE *stelan;* c. G *stehlen,* ON *stela,* Goth *stilan*] —**steal′a•ble,** *adj.* —**steal′er,** *n.*

steal•age (stē′lij), *n.* **1.** the act of stealing. **2.** losses due to theft. [1860–65; STEAL + -AGE]

steal•ing (stē′ling), *n.* **1.** the act of a person who steals. **2.** Usually, **stealings.** something that is stolen. —*adj.* **3.** given to or characterized by theft. [1300–50; ME *steling* (ger.). See STEAL, -ING^1, -ING^2] —**steal′ing•ly,** *adv.*

stealth (stelth), *n.* **1.** secret, clandestine, or surreptitious procedure. **2.** a furtive departure or entrance. **3.** *Obs.* **a.** an act of stealing; theft. **b.** the thing stolen; booty. **4.** *(cap.) Mil.* a U.S. Air Force project involving a range of technologies, with the purpose of developing aircraft that are difficult to detect by sight, sound, radar, and infrared energy. [1200–50; ME *stelthe;* cf. OE *stælthing* theft. See STEAL, -TH^1] —**stealth′ful,** *adj.* —**stealth′ful•ly,** *adv.* —**stealth′less,** *adj.*

stealth•y (stel′thē), *adj.,* **stealth•i•er, stealth•i•est.** done, characterized, or acting by stealth; furtive: *stealthy footsteps.* [1595–1605; STEALTH + -Y^1] —**stealth′i•ly,** *adv.* —**stealth′i•ness,** *n.*

steam (stēm), *n.* **1.** water in the form of an invisible gas or vapor. **2.** water changed to this form by boiling, extensively used for the generation of mechanical power, for heating purposes, etc. **3.** the mist formed when the gas or vapor from boiling water condenses in the air. **4.** an exhalation of a vapor or mist. **5.** *Informal.* power or energy. **6. blow off** or **let off steam,** *Informal.* to give vent to one's repressed emotions, esp. by talking or behaving in an unrestrained manner: *Don't take her remarks too seriously—she was just blowing off steam.* —*v.i.* **7.** to emit or give off steam or vapor. **8.** to rise or pass off in the form of steam or vapor. **9.** to become covered with condensed steam, as a window or other surface (often fol. by *up*). **10.** to generate or produce steam, as in a boiler. **11.** to move or travel by the agency of steam. **12.** to move rapidly or evenly: *He steamed out of the room.* **13.** *Informal.* to be angry or show anger. —*v.t.* **14.** to expose to or treat with steam, as in order to heat, cook, soften, renovate, or the like. **15.** to emit or exhale (steam or vapor). **16.** *Slang.* to cause to become irked or angry (often fol. by *up*). **17.** to convey by the agency of steam: *to steam the ship safely into port.* —*adj.* **18.** heated by or heating with steam: *a steam radiator.* **19.** propelled by or propelling with a steam engine. **20.** operated by steam. **21.** conducting steam: *a steam line.* **22.** bathed with or affected by steam. **23.** of or pertaining to steam. [bef. 1000; ME *steme,* OE *stēam;* c. D *stoom*] —**steam′less,** *adj.*

steam′ bath′, **1.** a bath of steam, usually in a specially equipped room or enclosure, for cleansing or refreshing oneself. **2.** a special room or enclosure, or an establishment containing it, for such a bath. **3.** a bath of steam used in laboratories for sterilizing equipment, utensils, etc. [1820–30]

steam′ beer′, a naturally carbonated, malt-flavored beer brewed esp. in the western U.S. [1895–1900; named after the steamlike pressure released when the cask is tapped]

steam•boat (stēm′bōt′), *n.* a steam-driven vessel, esp. a small one or one used on inland waters. [1775–85, *Amer.;* STEAM + BOAT]

Steam′boat Goth′ic, a florid architectural style suggesting the gingerbread-decorated construction of river boats of the Victorian period. Also, **steam′boat goth′ic.** [1940–45]

Steam′boat Springs′, a town in NW Colorado: ski resort. 5098.

steam′ boil′er, a receptacle in which water is boiled to generate steam. [1795–1805]

steam′ chest′, the chamber from which steam enters the cylinder of an engine. Also called **steam′ box′.** [1790–1800]

steam′ coal′, coal with relatively high sulfur content, suited for generating steam but not for coking. [1840–50]

steam′ en′gine, an engine worked by steam, typically one in which a sliding piston in a cylinder is moved by the expansive action of the steam generated in a boiler. [1745–55] —**steam′-en′gine,** *adj.*

steam•er (stē′mər), *n.* **1.** something propelled or operated by steam, as a steamship. **2.** a person or thing that steams. **3.** a device, pot, or container in which something is steamed. **4.** See **soft-shell clam.** —*v.i.* **5.** to travel by steamship. [1805–15; STEAM + -ER^1]

steam′er bas′ket, a gift basket of fruit, sweets, and the like, often including champagne, sent to a person departing on a trip, esp. by ship. [1905–10]

steam′er chair′. See **deck chair.** [1885–90]

steam′er clam′. See **soft-shell clam.**

steam′er rug′, a coarse, heavy lap robe used by ship passengers sitting in deck chairs. [1885–90]

steam′er trunk′, a rectangular traveling trunk low enough to slide under a bunk on a ship. [1890–95]

steam′ fit′ter, a person who installs and repairs

CONCISE PRONUNCIATION KEY: act, cāpe, dâre, pärt; set, ēqual; *if,* ice; ox, ōver, ôrder, oil, bo͝ok, bo͞ot, out; up, ûrge; child; sing; shoe; thin, *th*at; zh as in *treasure.* ə = *a* as in *alone, e* as in *system, i* as in *easily, o* as in *gallop, u* as in *circus;* ᵊ as in *fire* (fīᵊr), *hour* (ouᵊr). l and n can serve as syllabic consonants, as in *cradle* (krād′l), and *button* (but′n). See the full key inside the front cover.

steampipes and their accessories. [1885–90] **—steam′ fit′ting.**

steam′ fog′, *Meteorol.* fog caused by cold air flowing over a body of comparatively warm water, the vapor condensing in small convective columns near the water surface and giving the appearance of smoke or steam. Also called **sea smoke.**

steam′ ham′mer, a hammer for forging, operated by steam. [1835–45]

steam′ heat′, heat obtained by the circulation of steam in pipes, radiators, etc. [1815–25]

steam-heat·ed (stēm′hē′tid), *adj.* heated by steam. [1880–85, *Amer.*]

steam′ heat′ing, a heating system utilizing steam circulated through radiators and pipes. [1875–80]

steam′ i′ron, an electric iron with a water chamber, which emits steam onto the fabric or garment being ironed. [1940–45]

steam′ jack′et, a casing, as on the cylinder of a steam engine, filled with live steam to keep the interior hot. [1830–40] **—steam′-jack′et·ed,** *adj.*

steam′ locomo′tive, a locomotive moved by steam power generated in its own boiler: still in commercial use in nations that have not yet converted entirely to diesel and electric locomotives. See table under **Whyte classification.**

steam′ or′gan, calliope (def. 1). [1785–95]

steam·pipe (stēm′pīp′), *n.* a pipe for conveying steam from a boiler. [1855–60; STEAM + PIPE[1]]

steam′ point′, the temperature at which water vapor condenses at a pressure of one atmosphere, represented by 100°C and 212°F. Cf. **ice point.** [1900–05]

steam·roll (stēm′rōl′), *v.t., v.i.* steamroller. [1910–15; by back formation]

steam·roll·er (stēm′rō′lər), *n.* **1.** a heavy steam-powered vehicle having a roller for crushing, compacting, or leveling materials used for a road or the like. **2.** (not in technical use) any similar vehicle with a roller. **3.** an overpowering force, esp. one that crushes all opposition with ruthless disregard for individual rights. —*v.t.* **4.** to crush or flatten with a steamroller. **5.** to overcome with superior force: *to steamroller the competition.* **6.** to bring about the adoption of by overwhelming pressure: *to steamroller the resolution through.* —*v.i.* **7.** to proceed with implacable force. —*adj.* **8.** suggestive of a steamroller; ruthlessly overpowering: *steamroller tactics.* [1865–70; STEAM + ROLLER[1]]

steam′ room′, a steam-filled and heated room to induce sweating, as in a Turkish bath. [1870–75]

steam·ship (stēm′ship′), *n.* a large commercial vessel, esp. one driven by steam. [1780–90; STEAM + SHIP]

steam′ shov′el, a machine for digging or excavating, operated by its own engine and boiler. [1875–80, *Amer.*]

steam shovel

steam′ ta′ble, a boxlike table or counter, usually of stainless steel, with receptacles in the top into which containers of food may be fitted to be kept warm by steam or hot water in the compartment below. [1860–65]

steam·tight (stēm′tīt′), *adj.* impervious to steam. [1865–70; STEAM + TIGHT] **—steam′tight′ness,** *n.*

steam′ tur′bine, a turbine driven by steam pressure. [1890–95] **—steam′-tur′bine,** *adj.*

steam·y (stē′mē), *adj.,* **steam·i·er, steam·i·est. 1.** consisting of or resembling steam. **2.** full of or abounding in steam; emitting steam. **3.** covered with or as if with condensed steam: *a steamy bathroom mirror.* **4.** hot and humid. **5.** *Informal.* passionate or erotic. [1635–45; STEAM + -Y[1]] **—steam′i·ly,** *adv.* **—steam′i·ness,** *n.*

Ste. Anne de Beau·pré (sānt an′ də bō prā′; *Fr.* saɴ tan də bō prā′), a village in S Quebec, in SE Canada, on the St. Lawrence, NE of Quebec: Roman Catholic shrine. 3284.

ste·ap·sin (stē ap′sin), *n. Biochem.* the lipase present in pancreatic juice. [1895–1900; STEA(R)- + (PE)PSIN]

stear-, var. of **stearo-** before a vowel: *stearate.*

ste·a·rate (stē′ə rāt′, stēr′āt), *n. Chem.* a salt or ester of stearic acid. [1835–45; STEAR(IC ACID) + -ATE[2]]

ste·ar·ic (stē ar′ik, stēr′ik), *adj.* **1.** of or pertaining to suet or fat. **2.** of or derived from stearic acid. [1825–35; STEAR- + -IC]

stear′ic ac′id, *Chem.* a colorless, waxlike, sparingly water-soluble, odorless solid, $C_{18}H_{36}O_2$, the most common fatty acid, occurring as the glyceride in tallow and other animal fats and in some animal oils: used chiefly in the manufacture of soaps, stearates, candles, cosmetics, and in medicine in suppositories and pill coatings. Also called **octadecanoic acid.** [1825–35]

CONCISE ETYMOLOGY KEY: <, descended or borrowed from; >, whence; b., blend of, blended; c., cognate with; cf., compare; deriv., derivative; equiv., equivalent; imit., imitative; obl., oblique; r., replacing; s., stem; sp., spelling, spelled; resp., respelling, respelled; trans., translation; ?, origin unknown; *, unattested; ‡, probably earlier than. See the full key inside the front cover.

ste·a·rin (stē′ə rin, stēr′in), *n.* **1.** *Chem.* any of the three glyceryl esters of stearic acid, esp. $C_3H_5(C_{18}H_{35}O_2)_3$, a soft, white, odorless solid found in many natural fats. **2.** the crude commercial form of stearic acid, used chiefly in the manufacture of candles. Also, **ste·a·rine** (stē′ər in, -ə rēn′, stēr′in). [1810–20; < F *stéarine* < Gk *stéar* fat, grease + F *-ine* -INE[2]; see -IN[2]]

stearo-, a combining form borrowed from Greek, where it meant "fat", used with this meaning, and with reference to stearic acid and its related compounds, in the formation of compound words: *stearoptene; stearoyl.* Also, *esp. before a vowel,* **stear-.** [comb. form repr. Gk *stéar* fat, grease; cf. STEATO-]

ste·a·rop·tene (stē′ə rop′tēn), *n. Chem.* the oxygenated solid part of an essential oil (opposed to *eleoptene*). [1830–40; STEARO- + *-ptene* < Gk *ptēnós* winged, volatile; cf. ELEOPTENE]

ste·a·tite (stē′ə tīt′), *n.* soapstone. [1595–1605; < L *steatītēs* < Gk *steat-* (s. of *stéar*) fat, tallow + *-ītēs* -ITE[1]] **—ste·a·tit·ic** (stē′ə tit′ik), *adj.*

steato-, a combining form meaning "fat," "tallow"; used in the formation of compound words: *steatopygia.* Also, *esp. before a vowel,* **steat-.** [< Gk *steat-* (s. of *stéar* fat) + -O-]

ste·at·o·py·gi·a (stē at′ə pī′jē ə, stē′ə tə-), *n.* extreme accumulation of fat on and about the buttocks, esp. of women. [1855–60; STEATO- + Gk *pȳg(ḗ)* buttocks + *-ia* -IA] **—ste·at·o·pyg·ic** (stē at′ə pij′ik, stē′ə tə-), **ste·at·o·py·gous** (stē at′ə pī′gəs, stē′ə top′ə gəs, stē′ə-tə pī′-), *adj.*

ste·at·or·rhe·a (stē at′ə rē′ə, stē′ə tə-), *n. Pathol.* the presence of excess fat in the stools, usually caused by disease of the pancreas or intestine, and characterized by chronic diarrhea and weight loss. Also, **ste·at′or·rhoe′·a.** [1855–60; STEATO- + -RRHEA]

stech (stekн), *Scot. and North Eng.* —*v.t.* **1.** to fill or gorge (one's stomach) with food. —*v.i.* **2.** to eat voraciously. [1715–25; appar. var. of STACK]

Stech·helm (stek′helm′), *n.* a heavy German jousting helm of the 15th and 16th centuries, having a bluntly pointed front with a V-shaped vision slit. [< G, equiv. to *stech(en)* to pierce (see STICK[2]) + *Helm* HELM[2]]

sted·fast (sted′fast′, -fäst′, -fəst), *adj.* steadfast.

steed (stēd), *n.* a horse, esp. a high-spirited one. [bef. 900; ME *stēde,* OE *stēda* stallion; akin to *stōd* STUD[2]; cf. G *Stute*] **—steed′like′,** *adj.*

steek (stēk, stāk), *v.t. Scot.* to shut, close, fasten or lock (a window, door, or the like). [1150–1200; ME (north) *steken* (v.), OE *stician* to prick, stab]

steel (stēl), *n.* **1.** any of various modified forms of iron, artificially produced, having a carbon content less than that of pig iron and more than that of wrought iron, and having qualities of hardness, elasticity, and strength varying according to composition and heat treatment: generally categorized as having a high, medium, or low-carbon content. **2.** a thing or things made of this metal. **3.** a flat strip of this metal used for stiffening, esp. in corsets; stay. **4.** a bar of this metal that has one end formed to hold a bit for driving through rock. **5. steels,** stocks or bonds of companies producing this metal. **6.** a sword. **7.** a rounded rod of ridged steel, fitted with a handle and used esp. for sharpening knives. —*adj.* **8.** pertaining to or made of steel. **9.** like steel in color, hardness, or strength. —*v.t.* **10.** to fit with steel, as by pointing, edging, or overlaying. **11.** to cause to resemble steel in some way. **12.** to render insensible, inflexible, unyielding, determined, etc.: *He steeled himself to perform the dangerous task.* [bef. 900; (n.) ME *stele,* OE (north) *stēle;* c. D *staal,* G *Stahl,* ON *stāl;* (v.) ME *stelen,* OE *styled* edged with steel, deriv. of the n.] **—steel′·like′,** *adj.*

steel′ band′, *Music.* a band, native to Trinidad and common in other of the Caribbean islands, using steel oil drums cut to various heights and tuned to specific pitches. [1945–50]

steel′ blue′, dark bluish gray. [1810–20]

Steele (stēl), *n.* **Sir Richard,** 1672–1729, English essayist, journalist, dramatist, and political leader; born in Ireland.

steel′ engrav′ing, *Print.* **1.** a method of incising letters, designs, etc., on steel. **2.** the imprint, as on paper, from a plate of engraved steel. [1815–25]

steel-faced (stēl′fāst′), *adj.* having the front or outer surfaces covered with or characterized by steel. [1870–75]

steel′ gray′, dark metallic gray with a bluish tinge. [1835–45]

steel′ guitar′, 1. an acoustic, hand-held guitar having a metal resonator and producing a wailing, variable sound. **2.** a pedal steel guitar. **3.** a Hawaiian guitar. [1925–30]

steel·head (stēl′hed′), *n., pl.* **-heads,** (*esp. collectively*) **-head.** a silvery rainbow trout that migrates to the sea before returning to fresh water to spawn. [1580–90; STEEL + HEAD]

steel·ie[1] (stē′lē), *n.* a playing marble made of steel. [1920–25; STEEL + -IE]

steel·ie[2] (stē′lē), *n. Informal.* steelhead. [1920–25; STEEL(HEAD) + -IE]

steel′ lum′ber, metal lumber composed of sheet steel.

steel·mak·er (stēl′mā′kər), *n.* a manufacturer of steel. [1830–40; STEEL + MAKER]

steel·mak·ing (stēl′mā′king), *n.* the manufacture of steel. [1805–15; STEEL + MAKING]

steel·man (stēl′mən), *n., pl.* **-men.** a person engaged in the steelmaking business. [STEEL + -MAN]

steel′ mill′, a steelworks. [1640–50]

steel′ square′, *Carpentry.* See **framing square.**

steel′ trap′, a trap for catching animals, consisting of spring-operated steel jaws with sharp projections that clamp shut. [1725–35]

steel′ wool′, a tangled or matted mass of stringlike steel shavings, used for scouring, polishing, smoothing, etc. [1895–1900]

steel·work (stēl′wûrk′), *n.* **1.** steel parts or articles. **2.** the steel frame or superstructure of a building, bridge, etc. [1675–85; STEEL + WORK]

steel·work·er (stēl′wûr′kər), *n.* a person employed in the process of manufacturing steel and steel products. [1880–85; STEEL + WORKER]

steel·works (stēl′wûrks′), *n., pl.* **-works.** (*used with a singular or plural v.*) an establishment where steel is made and often manufactured into girders, rails, etc. [STEEL + WORKS]

steel·y (stē′lē), *adj.,* **steel·i·er, steel·i·est. 1.** consisting or made of steel. **2.** resembling or suggesting steel, as in color, strength, or hardness. [1500–10; STEEL + -Y[1]] **—steel′i·ness,** *n.*

steel·yard (stēl′yärd′, stil′yərd), *n.* a portable balance with two unequal arms, the longer one having a movable counterpoise and the shorter one bearing a hook or the like for holding the object to be weighed. [1630–40; STEEL + YARD[1]]

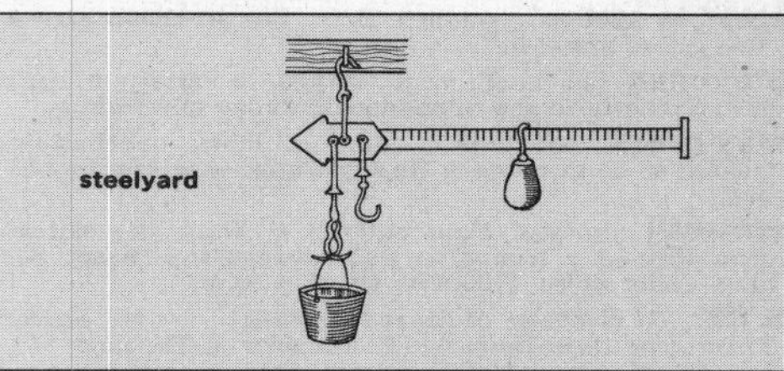
steelyard

Steen (stān), *n.* **Jan** (yän), 1626–79, Dutch painter.

steen·bok (stēn′bok′, stān′-), *n., pl.* **-boks,** (*esp. collectively*) **-bok.** a small antelope, *Raphicerus campestris,* of grassy areas of eastern and southern Africa. Also, **steinbok.** [1765–75; < Afrik < D *steen* STONE + *bok* BUCK[1]]

steep[1] (stēp), *adj.,* **-er, -est,** *n.* —*adj.* **1.** having an almost vertical slope or pitch, or a relatively high gradient, as a hill, an ascent, stairs, etc. **2.** (of a price or amount) unduly high; exorbitant: *Those prices are too steep for me.* **3.** extreme or incredible, as a statement or story. **4.** high or lofty. —*n.* **5.** a steep place; declivity, as of a hill. [bef. 900; ME *stepe* (adj.), OE *stēap;* akin to STOOP[1]] **—steep′ly,** *adv.* **—steep′ness,** *n.*

steep[2] (stēp), *v.t.* **1.** to soak in water or other liquid, as to soften, cleanse, or extract some constituent: *to steep tea in boiling-hot water; to steep reeds for basket weaving.* **2.** to wet thoroughly in or with a liquid; drench; saturate; imbue. **3.** to immerse in or saturate or imbue with some pervading, absorbing, or stupefying influence or agency: *an incident steeped in mystery.* —*v.i.* **4.** to lie soaking in a liquid. —*n.* **5.** the act or process of steeping or the state of being steeped. **6.** a liquid in which something is steeped. [1350–1400; (v.) ME *stepen* < ?; cf. Sw *stöpa;* (n.) late ME *stepe,* deriv. of the v.] **—steep′·er,** *n.*
—Syn. 1. infuse. **2.** permeate. **3.** bury, engulf.

steep·en (stē′pən), *v.t., v.i.* to make or become steeper. [1840–50; STEEP[1] + -EN[1]]

stee·ple (stē′pəl), *n., v.,* **-pled, -pling.** —*n.* **1.** an ornamental construction, usually ending in a spire, erected on a roof or tower of a church, public building, etc. **2.** a tower terminating in such a construction. **3.** (loosely) a spire. —*v.t.* **4.** to provide with or form into a steeple or steeplelike configuration. [bef. 1000; ME *stepel* steeple, tower, OE *stēpel* tower. See STEEP[1], -LE] **—stee′pled,** *adj.* **—stee′ple·less,** *adj.* **—stee′ple·like′,** *adj.*

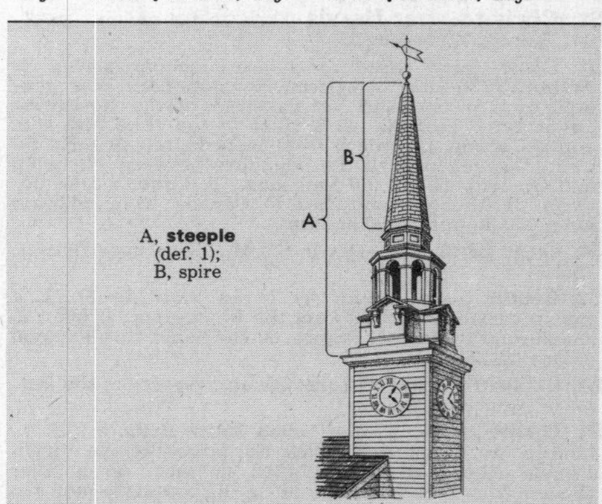

A, **steeple** (def. 1); B, spire

stee·ple·bush (stē′pəl bo͝osh′), *n.* the hardhack. [1810–20, *Amer.;* STEEPLE + BUSH[1]; so called because of its steeplelike blossom shoots]

stee·ple·chase (stē′pəl chās′), *n., v.,* **-chased, -chasing.** —*n.* **1.** a horse race over a turf course furnished with artificial ditches, hedges, and other obstacles over which the horses must jump. **2.** a point-to-point race. **3.** a foot race run on a cross-country course or over a course having obstacles, as ditches, hurdles, or the like, which the runners must clear. —*v.i.* **4.** to ride or run in a steeplechase. [1795–1805; STEEPLE + CHASE[1]; so called because the course was kept by sighting a church steeple] **—stee′ple·chas′er,** *n.*

stee•ple•chas•ing (stē′pəl chā′sing), *n.* the sport of riding or running in a steeplechase. [STEEPLECHASE + -ING[1]]

stee′ple cup′, a standing cup of the 17th century having a cover with a tall finial. [1905–10]

stee′ple head′dress, hennin.

stee•ple•jack (stē′pəl jak′), *n.* a person who climbs steeples, towers, or the like, to build or repair them. [1880–85; STEEPLE + JACK[1]]

steer[1] (stēr), *v.t.* **1.** to guide the course of (something in motion) by a rudder, helm, wheel, etc.: *to steer a bicycle.* **2.** to follow or pursue (a particular course). **3.** to direct the course of; guide: *I can steer you to the best restaurant in town.* —*v.i.* **4.** to direct the course of a vessel, vehicle, airplane, or the like, by the use of a rudder or other means. **5.** to pursue a course of action. **6.** (of a vessel, vehicle, airplane, etc.) to be steered or guided in a particular direction or manner. **7. steer clear of,** to stay away from purposely; avoid: *She steered clear of any deep emotional involvements.* —*n.* **8.** *Informal.* a suggestion about a course of action; tip: *He got a good steer about finding the right job.* [bef. 900; ME *steren,* OE *stēoran,* akin to *stēor* steering, guidance; c. G *steuern,* ON *stȳra,* Goth *stiurjan*] —**steer′a•ble,** *adj.* —**steer′•a•bil′i•ty,** *n.*

steer[2] (stēr), *n., pl.* **steers,** (*esp. collectively*) **steer.** a male bovine that is castrated before sexual maturity, esp. one raised for beef. [bef. 900; ME; OE *stēor;* c. D, G *Stier,* ON *stjórr,* Goth *stiur*]

steer[3] (stēr), *v.t., v.i., n. Brit. Dial.* stir[1].

steer•age (stēr′ij), *n.* **1.** a part or division of a ship, formerly the part containing the steering apparatus. **2.** (in a passenger ship) the part or accommodations allotted to the passengers who travel at the cheapest rate. [1400–50; late ME *sterage.* See STEER[1], -AGE]

steer•age•way (stēr′ij wā′), *n. Naut.* sufficient speed to permit a vessel to be maneuvered. [1710–20; STEERAGE + WAY[1]]

steer•er (stēr′ər), *n.* **1.** a person or thing that steers. **2.** *Informal.* a confederate who directs potential customers to a gambling game, brothel, drug seller, etc. [STEER[1] + -ER[1]]

steer•hide (stēr′hīd′), *n.* **1.** the hide of a steer. **2.** the leather made from this hide. [STEER[2] + HIDE[2]]

steer•ing (stēr′ing), *n.* the discriminatory practice by a real estate agent of maneuvering a client from a minority group away from considering a home in a white neighborhood. [1975–80]

steer′ing col′umn, the shaft that connects the steering wheel to the steering gear assembly of an automotive vehicle. [1900–05]

steer′ing commit′tee, a committee, esp. of a deliberative or legislative body, charged with preparing the agenda of a session. [1885–90, *Amer.*]

steer′ing gear′, the apparatus or mechanism for steering a ship, automobile, airplane, etc. [1865–70]

steer′ing wheel′, a wheel used by a driver, pilot, or the like, to steer an automobile, ship, etc. [1740–50]

steers•man (stērz′mən), *n., pl.* **-men. 1.** a person who steers a ship; helmsman. **2.** a person who drives a machine. [bef. 1000; ME *steresman,* OE *stēoresmann,* equiv. to *stēor* steering, helm (see STEER[1]) + *-es* 's[1] + *man* MAN[1]] —**steers′man•ship′,** *n.*

steeve[1] (stēv), *v.,* **steeved, steev•ing,** *n.* —*v.t.* **1.** to stuff (cotton or other cargo) into a ship's hold. —*n.* **2.** a long derrick or spar, with a block at one end, used in stowing cargo in a ship's hold. [1475–85; prob. < Sp *estibar* to cram < L *stīpāre* to stuff, pack tightly; akin to OE *stīf* STIFF]

steeve[2] (stēv), *v.,* **steeved, steev•ing,** *n. Naut.* —*v.i.* **1.** (of a bowsprit or the like) to incline upward at an angle instead of extending horizontally. —*v.t.* **2.** to set (a spar) at an upward inclination. [1635–45; orig. uncert.]

Ste′fan-Boltz′mann law′ (stef′ən bōlts′mən; *Ger.* shte′fän bôlts′män), *Physics.* the law stating that the total energy radiated from a blackbody is proportional to the fourth power of its absolute temperature. Also called **Ste′fan's law′ of radia′tion.** [1895–1900; named after Josef *Stefan* (1835–93) and Ludwig E. *Boltzmann* (1844–1906), Austrian physicists, who independently formulated the law]

Stef•a•nie (stef′ə nē; *Fr.* ste fA nē′), *n.* a female given name.

Stef•ans•son (stef′ən sən), *n.* **Vil•hjal•mur** (vil′-hyoul′mər), 1879–1962, U.S. arctic explorer and author, born in Canada.

Stef•fens (stef′ənz), *n.* **(Joseph) Lincoln,** 1866–1936, U.S. author, journalist, and editor.

Ste.-Foy (sānt′fwä′; *Fr.* sant fwA′), *n.* a city in S Quebec, in E Canada, near Quebec. 68,883.

stego-, a combining form meaning "cover," used in the formation of compound words: *stegosaur.* [comb. form of Gk *stégos* roof]

steg•o•don (steg′ə don′), *n.* any extinct elephantlike mammal of the genus *Stegodon,* from the late Pliocene and Pleistocene epochs, usually considered to be directly ancestral to the modern elephant. [< NL, equiv. to *stego-* STEGO- + GK + *-odōn* toothed; see -ODONT]

steg•o•saur (steg′ə sôr′), *n.* a plant-eating dinosaur of the genus *Stegosaurus,* from the Jurassic and Cretaceous periods, having a heavy, bony armor and a row of bony plates along its back, and growing to a length of 20 to 40 ft. (6–12 m). [< NL *Stegosaurus* (1877); see STEGO-, -SAUR]

stegosaur,
Stegosaurus stenops,
length 18 ft. (5.5 m)

Stei•chen (stī′kən), *n.* **Edward,** 1879–1973, U.S. photographer.

Stei•er•mark (shtī′ər märk′), *n.* German name of **Styria.**

Steig (stīg), *n.* **William,** born 1907, U.S. artist.

stein (stīn), *n.* **1.** a mug, usually earthenware, esp. for beer. **2.** the quantity of beer or other liquid contained in a stein. [1900–05; < G: lit., STONE]

Stein (stīn *for 1, 3;* shtīn *for 2*), *n.* **1. Gertrude,** 1874–1946, U.S. author in France. **2. Hein•rich Frie•drich Karl** (hīn′rikh frē′drikh kärl), **Baron vom und zum** (fôm o͝ont tso͞om), 1757–1831, German statesman. **3. William Howard,** 1911–80, U.S. biochemist: Nobel prize for chemistry 1972.

Stein•am•ang•er (shtīn′äm äng′ər), *n.* German name of **Szombathely.**

Stein•beck (stīn′bek), *n.* **John (Ernst)** (ûrnst), 1902–68, U.S. novelist: Nobel prize 1962.

Stein•berg (stīn′bûrg), *n.* **1. Saul,** born 1914, U.S. painter, cartoonist, and illustrator; born in Rumania. **2. William,** 1899–1978, U.S. conductor, born in Germany.

stein•bok (stīn′bok), *n., pl.* **-boks,** (*esp. collectively*) **-bok.** steenbok. [1675–85]

Stein•em (stī′nəm), *n.* **Gloria,** born 1934, U.S. women's-rights activist, journalist, and editor.

Stei•ner (stī′nər; *Ger.* shtī′nər), *n.* **1. Ja•kob** (yä′-kôp), 1796–1863, Swiss mathematician. **2. Ru•dolf** (ro͞o′-dôlf), 1861–1925, Austrian social philosopher: teacher of the spiritual doctrines of anthroposophy.

Stein′heim man′ (shtīn′hīm, stīn′-), a human of the middle Pleistocene Epoch known from a skull found in West Germany and considered to be archaic *Homo sapiens.* [after *Steinheim* am Murr, Germany]

Stei•nitz (stī′nits, shtī′-), *n.* **William** (*Wilhelm Steinitz*), 1836–1900, U.S. chess player, born in Czechoslovakia.

stein•kern (shtīn′kern′, -kûrn′, stīn′-), *n. Archaeol.* the fossilized outline of a hollow organic structure, as a skull or a mollusk shell, formed when mud or sediment consolidated within the structure and the structure itself disintegrated or dissolved. Also called **endocast.** [< G *Steinkern* lit., stone, pit (of a fruit), equiv. to *Stein* STONE + *Kern* core, KERNEL]

Stein•man (stīn′mən), *n.* **David Barnard,** 1886–1960, U.S. civil engineer: specialist in bridge design and construction.

Stein•metz (stīn′mets), *n.* **Charles Pro•te•us** (prō′tē-əs), 1865–1923, U.S. electrical engineer, born in Germany.

Stein•way (stīn′wā′), *n.* **Henry En•gel•hard** (eng′gəl-härd′, -härt′), (*Heinrich Engelhard Steinweg*), 1797–1871, U.S. piano manufacturer, born in Germany.

ste•la (stē′lə), *n., pl.* **ste•lae** (stē′lē). stele (defs. 1–3).

Stel•a•zine (stel′ə zēn′), *Pharm., Trademark.* a brand of trifluoperazine.

ste•le (stē′lē, stēl *for 1–3;* stēl, stē′lē *for 4*), *n., pl.* **ste•lai** (stē′lī), **ste•les** (stē′lēz, stēlz). **1.** an upright stone slab or pillar bearing an inscription or design and serving as a monument, marker, or the like. **2.** *Archit.* a prepared surface on the face of a building, a rock, etc., bearing an inscription or the like. **3.** (in ancient Rome) a burial stone. **4.** *Bot.* the central cylinder or cylinders of vascular and related tissue in the stem, root, petiole, leaf, etc., of the higher plants. Also, **stela** (for defs. 1–3). [1810–20; < Gk *stḗlē,* akin to *histánai* to make stand, L *stāre* to STAND] —**ste•lar** (stē′lər), *adj.*

St. Elias, Mount, a mountain on the boundary between Alaska and Canada, a peak of the St. Elias Mountains. 18,008 ft. (5490 m).

St. Elias Mountains, a mountain range between SE Alaska and the SW Yukon territory. Highest peak, Mount Logan, 19,850 ft. (6050 m).

stel•la (stel′ə), *n.* a four-dollar pattern coin of the U.S. having a metal content based on the metric system, issued 1879–80.

Stel•la (stel′ə), *n.* **1. Frank (Philip),** born 1936, U.S. painter. **2.** a female given name: from a Latin word meaning "star."

Stel′la Polar′is, Polaris.

stel•lar (stel′ər), *adj.* **1.** of or pertaining to the stars; consisting of stars. **2.** like a star, as in brilliance. **3.** pertaining to a preeminent performer, athlete, etc. [1650–60; < LL *stellāris,* equiv. to *stell(a)* STAR + *-āris* -AR[1]]

stel′lar associa′tion, *Astron.* a sparsely populated group of between 10 and 1000 young stars of similar spectral type and common origin that are moving too fast to form a permanent, gravitationally bound system. Also called **association of stars, association.** Cf. **globular cluster, open cluster.**

stel•lar•a•tor (stel′ə rā′tər), *n. Physics.* an experimental plasma-physics device in which magnetic fields confine the plasma within a tube shaped like a figure eight. [1951; STELLAR + (GENER)ATOR, so named because the reactions produced resemble those in stars]

stel′lar wind′, *Astron.* the radial outflow of ionized gas from a star. [1960–65]

stel•late (stel′it, -āt), *adj.* like the form of a conventionalized figure of a star; star-shaped. Also, **stel′lat•ed.** [1490–1500; < L *stellātus* starry, equiv. to *stell(a)* STAR + *-ātus* -ATE[1]] —**stel′late•ly,** *adv.*

Stel′ler's jay′ (stel′ərz), a common jay, *Cyanocitta stelleri,* of western North America, having blackish-brown and dusky-blue plumage. [1820–30, *Amer.;* after George W. Steller (1709–46), German naturalist]

Stel′ler's sea′ li′on. See under **sea lion.** [see STELLER'S JAY]

stel•lif•er•ous (ste lif′ər əs), *adj.* having or abounding with stars. [1575–85; < L *stellifer* star-bearing (*stell(a)* STAR + *-i-* -I- + *-fer* -FER) + -OUS; see -FEROUS]

stel•li•form (stel′ə fôrm′), *adj.* star-shaped. [1790–1800; *stelli-* (see STELLIFEROUS) + -FORM]

stel•lion•ate (stel′yə nit, -nāt′), *n. Civil Law, Scots Law.* any crime of unspecified class that involves fraud, esp. one that involves the selling of the same property to different people. [1615–25; < L *stelliōnātus* deceit, underhandedness, equiv. to *stelliōn-* (s. of *stelliō*) lizard, crafty person + *-ātus* -ATE[3]]

stel•lu•lar (stel′yə lər), *adj.* **1.** having the form of a small star or small stars. **2.** spotted with stars. [1790–1800; < LL *stellul(a)* (*stell(a)* STAR + *-ula* -ULE) + -AR[1]]

St. El•mo's fire (el′mōz). See **corona discharge.** Also called **St. Elmo's light, St. Ulmo's fire, St. Ulmo's light.** [named after *St. Elmo* (d. A.D. 303), patron saint of sailors]

stem[1] (stem), *n., v.,* **stemmed, stem•ming.** —*n.* **1.** the ascending axis of a plant, whether above or below ground, which ordinarily grows in an opposite direction to the root or descending axis. **2.** the stalk that supports a leaf, flower, or fruit. **3.** the main body of that portion of a tree, shrub, or other plant which is above ground; trunk; stalk. **4.** a cut flower: *We bought roses at the flower market for 50¢ a stem.* **5.** a petiole; peduncle; pedicel. **6.** a stalk of bananas. **7.** something resembling or suggesting a leaf or flower stalk. **8.** a long, slender part: *the stem of a tobacco pipe.* **9.** the slender, vertical part of a goblet, wineglass, etc., between the bowl and the base. **10.** *Informal.* a drinking glass having a stem. **11.** the handle of a spoon. **12.** a projection from the rim of a watch, having on its end a knob for winding the watch. **13.** the circular rod in some locks about which the key fits and rotates. **14.** the rod or spindle by which a valve is operated from outside. **15.** the stock or line of descent of a family; ancestry or pedigree. **16.** *Gram.* the underlying form, often consisting of a root plus an affix, to which the inflectional endings of a word are added, as *tend-,* the stem in Latin *tendere* "to stretch," the root of which is *ten-.* Cf. **base**[1] (def. 18), **theme** (def. 5). **17.** *Music.* the vertical line forming part of a note. **18. stems,** *Slang.* the legs of a human being. **19.** the main or relatively thick stroke of a letter in printing. —*v.t.* **20.** to remove the stem from (a leaf, fruit, etc.): *to stem cherries.* —*v.i.* **21.** to arise or originate: *This project stems from last week's lecture.* [bef. 900; ME; OE *stemn, stefn,* equiv. to *ste-* (var. of *sta-,* base of *standan* to STAND) + *-mn-* suffix; akin to G *Stamm* stem, tribe; see STAFF[1]] —**stem′less,** *adj.* —**stem′like′,** *adj.*

stem[2] (stem), *v.,* **stemmed, stem•ming,** *n.* —*v.t.* **1.** to stop, check, or restrain. **2.** to dam up; stop the flow of (a stream, river, or the like). **3.** to tamp, plug, or make tight, as a hole or joint. **4.** *Skiing.* to maneuver (a ski or skis) in executing a stem. **5.** to stanch (bleeding). —*v.i.* **6.** *Skiing.* to execute a stem. —*n.* **7.** *Skiing.* the act or instance of a skier pushing the heel of one or both skis outward so that the heels are far apart, as in making certain turns or slowing down. [1400–50; late ME *stemmen* < ON *stemma* to dam or MLG *stemmen*]

stem[3] (stem), *v.t.,* **stemmed, stem•ming. 1.** to make headway against (a tide, current, gale, etc.). **2.** to make progress against (any opposition). [1585–95; v. use of STEM[4]]

stem[4] (stem), *n. Naut.* **1.** (at the bow of a vessel) an upright into which the side timbers or plates are jointed. **2.** the forward part of a vessel (often opposed to *stern*). [bef. 900; continuing OE *stefn, stemn* end-timber; special use of STEM[1]; ME *stampne, stamyn(e)* appar. < the c. ON *stamn, stafn* in same sense]

stem[5] (stem), *v.t.,* **stemmed, stem•ming.** to arrange the loading of (a merchant vessel) within a specified time. [1895–1900; var. of *steven* to direct one's course < ON *stefna* to sail directly, aim, deriv. of *stafn* STEM[4]]

stem′ cab′bage, kohlrabi.

stem′ can′ker, *Plant Pathol.* a disease of plants characterized by cankers on the stems and twigs and caused by any of several fungi.

stem′ cell′, *Cell Biol.* a cell that upon division replaces its own numbers and also gives rise to cells that differentiate further into one or more specialized types, as various B cells and T cells. [1880–85]

stem′ duch′y, (in medieval Germany) any of the independent duchies corresponding in part to areas of tribal settlement and preserving some elements of tribal social structure.

stem′-end rot′ (stem′end′), *Plant Pathol.* a disease of fruits characterized by discoloration, shriveling, and decay of the stem and adjacent parts of the fruit and caused by any of several fungi of the genera *Diplodia* and *Phomopsis.*

St.-É•mi•li•on (sānt′ə mē′lē ən, -ə mēl′yən; *Fr.* san-tā mē lyôn′), *n.* a dry claret wine from the parish of St.-Émilion in the Bordeaux region of France.

stem•ma (stem′ə), *n., pl.* **stem•ma•ta** (stem′ə tə). ocellus (def. 1). [1650–60; < NL < Gk *stémma* wreath, garland, deriv. (with *-ma* n. suffix of result) from root of *stéphos* garland, *stéphein* to crown; from the crownlike appearance of ocelli in certain insects]

stemmed (stemd), *adj.* **1.** having a stem or a specified kind of stem (often used in combination): *a long-stemmed rose.* **2.** having the stem or stems removed: *stemmed cherries.* [1570–80; STEM[1] + -ED[2]]

stem•mer[1] (stem′ər), *n.* **1.** a person who removes stems. **2.** a device for removing stems, as from tobacco, grapes, etc. [1890–95; STEM[1] + -ER[1]]

stem•mer[2] (stem′ər), *n.* an implement for stemming or tamping. [1855–60; STEM[2] + -ER[1]]

stem•mer•y (stem′ə rē), *n., pl.* **-mer•ies.** a factory or other place where tobacco leaves are stripped. [1855–60, *Amer.*; STEM[1] + -ERY]

stem′ rot′, *Plant Pathol.* **1.** a symptom or phase of many diseases of plants, characterized by decay of the stem tissues. **2.** any disease so characterized.

stem′ rust′, *Plant Pathol.* **1.** any of several fungal diseases of plants affecting the stems, esp. a disease of wheat and other grasses characterized by pustules of red and then black spores. **2.** any of the fungi causing such a disease. [1915–20]

stem•son (stem′sən), *n. Naut.* a curved timber in a wooden bow, scarfed at its lower end to the keelson. [1760–70; STEM[4] + (KEEL)SON]

stem′ turn′, *Skiing.* a turn in which a skier stems one ski in the direction to be turned and brings the other ski around so that both skis are parallel. [1930–35]

stem•ware (stem′wâr′), *n.* glass or crystal vessels, esp. for beverages and desserts, having rounded bowls mounted on footed stems. [1925–30; STEM[1] + WARE[1]]

stem•wind•er (stem′wīn′dər), *n.* **1.** a stemwinding watch. **2.** *Older Slang.* **a.** something remarkable of its kind. **b.** a rousing speech, esp. a stirring political address. **c.** a stirring orator. Also, **stem′-wind′er.** [1865–70, *Amer.*; STEM[1] + WINDER]

stem•wind•ing (stem′wīn′ding), *adj.* wound by turning a knob at the stem. Also, **stem′-wind′ing.** [1865–70; STEM[1] + WINDING]

stench (stench), *n.* **1.** an offensive smell or odor; stink. **2.** a foul quality. [bef. 900; ME; OE *stenc* odor (good or bad); akin to STINK] **—stench′ful,** *adj.*
—Syn. See **odor.**

stench′ bomb′. See **stink bomb.**

sten•cil (sten′səl), *n., v.,* **-ciled, -cil•ing** or (*esp. Brit.*) **-cilled, -cil•ling.** **—***n.* **1.** a device for applying a pattern, design, words, etc., to a surface, consisting of a thin sheet of cardboard, metal, or other material from which figures or letters have been cut out, a coloring substance, ink, etc., being rubbed, brushed, or pressed over the sheet, passing through the perforations and onto the surface. **2.** the letters, designs, etc., produced on a surface by this method. **—***v.t.* **3.** to mark or paint (a surface) by means of a stencil. **4.** to produce (letters, figures, designs, etc.) by means of a stencil. [1375–1425; earlier *stanesile,* late ME *stansele* to ornament with diverse colors or spangles < MF *estanceler,* deriv. of *estencele* a spark, ornamental spangle < VL **stincilla,* metathetic var. of L *scintilla* SCINTILLA] **—sten′cil•er;** *esp. Brit.,* **sten′cil•ler,** *n.*

stencil (def. 1)

sten•cil•ize (sten′sə līz′), *v.t.,* **-ized, -iz•ing.** **1.** to make into a stencil. **2.** stencil (def. 3). Also, *esp. Brit.,* **sten′cil•ise′.** [STENCIL + -IZE]

Sten•dhal (sten däl′, stan-; *Fr.* stän dal′), *n.* (*Marie Henri Beyle*) 1783–1842, French novelist and critic.

Steng•el (steng′gəl), *n.* **Charles Dillon** (*"Casey"*), 1891–1975, U.S. baseball player and manager.

Sten′ gun′, a British light submachine gun. Also called **Sten.** [1940–45; R.V. *S*(*hepherd*) + H.J. *T*(*urpin*), the designers + *En*(*field*), England]

sten•o (sten′ō), *n., pl.* **sten•os** for 1. **1.** a stenographer. **2.** the art or practice of a stenographer; stenography. [1910–15; by shortening; see STENO-]

steno-, a combining form meaning "narrow," "close," used in the formation of compound words: *stenopetalous.* [< Gk *stenós*]

steno., **1.** stenographer. **2.** stenographic. **3.** stenography. Also, **stenog.** [1905–10, *Amer.*; by shortening]

sten•o•bath (sten′ə bath′), *n.* a stenobathic organism. [back formation from STENOBATHIC]

sten•o•bath•ic (sten′ə bath′ik), *adj. Ecol.* of or pertaining to marine or freshwater life that can tolerate only limited changes in depth (opposed to *eurybathic*). [1900–05; STENO- + Gk *báth*(*os*) depth (see BATHO-) + -IC]

sten•o•graph (sten′ə graf′, -gräf′), *n.* **1.** any of various keyboard instruments, somewhat resembling a typewriter, used for writing in shorthand, as by means of phonetic or arbitrary symbols. **2.** a character written in shorthand. **—***v.t.* **3.** to write in shorthand. [1815–25; STENO- + -GRAPH]

ste•nog•ra•pher (stə nog′rə fər), *n.* a person who specializes in taking dictation in shorthand. Also, **ste•nog′ra•phist.** [1790–1800, *Amer.*; STENOGRAPH + -ER[1]]

ste•nog•ra•phy (stə nog′rə fē), *n.* the art of writing in shorthand. [1595–1605; STENO- + -GRAPHY] **—sten•o•graph•ic** (sten′ə graf′ik), **sten′o•graph′i•cal,** *adj.* **—sten′o•graph′i•cal•ly,** *adv.*

sten•o•pe•ic (sten′ə pē′ik), *adj.* **1.** pertaining to or containing a narrow slit or minute opening: *a stenopeic device to aid vision after eye surgery.* **—***n.* **2.** a device, as of wood, metal, or cardboard, with a narrow horizontal slit, worn over the eyes for protection against sunlight. Also, **sten′o•pae′ic, sten•o•pa•ic** (sten′ə pā′ik). [1860–65; STEN(O)- + Gk *opaî*(*os*) having a hole + -IC]

CONCISE ETYMOLOGY KEY: <, descended or borrowed from; >, whence; b., blend of, blended; c., cognate with; cf., compare; deriv., derivative; equiv., equivalent; imit., imitative; obl., oblique; r., replacing; s., stem; sp., spelling, spelled; resp., respelling, respelled; trans., translation; ?, origin unknown; *, unattested; ‡, probably earlier than. See the full key inside the front cover.

sten•o•pet•al•ous (sten′ō pet′l əs), *adj. Bot.* having narrow petals. [1830–40; STENO- + PETALOUS]

ste•noph•a•gous (sti nof′ə gəs), *adj. Ecol.* (of an animal) feeding on a limited variety of foods (opposed to *euryphagous*). [1875–80; STENO- + -PHAGOUS]

sten•o•phyl•lous (sten′ō fil′əs), *adj. Bot.* having narrow leaves. [1875–80; STENO- + -PHYLLOUS]

ste•nosed (sti nōst′, -nōzd′), *adj. Med.* characterized by stenosis; abnormally narrowed. [1895–1900; STENOS(IS) + -ED[2], as if deriv. of a v. *stenose* (cf. METAMORPHOSE, DIAGNOSE)]

ste•no•sis (sti nō′sis), *n. Pathol.* a narrowing or stricture of a passage or vessel. [1855–60; < NL < Gk *sténōsis.* See STENO-, -OSIS] **—ste•not•ic** (sti not′ik), *adj.*

sten•o•ther•mo•phile (sten′ə thûr′mə fīl′, -fil), *n.* a stenothermophilic bacterium. [STENO- + THERMO- + -PHILE]

sten•o•ther•mo•phil•ic (sten′ə thûr′mə fil′ik), *adj.* growing best within a narrow temperature range. [1955–60; STENO- + THERMO- + -PHILIC]

sten•o•type (sten′ə tīp′), *n.* **1.** a keyboard machine resembling a typewriter, used in a system of phonetic shorthand. **2.** the symbols typed in one stroke on this machine. [formerly a trademark]

sten•o•typ•y (sten′ə tī′pē), *n.* shorthand in which alphabetic letters or types are used to produce shortened forms of words or groups of words. [1890–95; STENOTYPE + -Y[3]] **—sten•o•typ•ic** (sten′ə tip′ik), *adj.* **—sten′o•typ′ist,** *n.*

stent (stent), *n. Med.* a small, expendable tube used for inserting in a blocked vessel or other part. [1960–65; orig. uncert.]

Sten•tor (sten′tôr), *n.* **1.** (in the *Iliad*) a Greek herald with a loud voice. **2.** (*l.c.*) a person having a very loud or powerful voice. **3.** (*l.c.*) a trumpet-shaped, ciliate protozoan of the genus *Stentor.*

sten•to•ri•an (sten tôr′ē ən, -tōr′-), *adj.* very loud or powerful in sound: *a stentorian voice.* [1595–1605; STENTOR + -IAN] **—sten•to′ri•an•ly,** *adv.*

sten•to•ri•ous (sten tôr′ē əs, -tōr′-), *adj.* stentorian. [1540–50; STENTOR + -IOUS] **—sten•to′ri•ous•ly,** *adv.*

step (step), *n., v.,* **stepped, step•ping.** **—***n.* **1.** a movement made by lifting the foot and setting it down again in a new position, accompanied by a shifting of the weight of the body in the direction of the new position, as in walking, running, or dancing. **2.** such a movement followed by a movement of equal distance of the other foot: *The soldier took one step forward and stood at attention.* **3.** the space passed over or the distance measured by one such movement of the foot. **4.** the sound made by the foot in making such a movement. **5.** a mark or impression made by the foot on the ground; footprint. **6.** the manner of walking; gait; stride. **7.** pace in marching: *double-quick step.* **8.** a pace uniform with that of another or others, or in time with music. **9.** **steps,** movements or course in walking or running: *to retrace one's steps.* **10.** a move, act, or proceeding, as toward some end or in the general course of some action; stage, measure, or period: *the five steps to success.* **11.** rank, degree, or grade, as on a vertical scale. **12.** a support for the foot in ascending or descending: *a step of a ladder; a stair of 14 steps.* **13.** a very short distance: *She was never more than a step away from her children.* **14.** a repeated pattern or unit of movement in a dance formed by a combination of foot and body motions. **15.** *Music.* **a.** a degree of the staff or of the scale. **b.** the interval between two adjacent scale degrees; second. Cf. **semitone, whole step.** **16.** **steps,** *Brit.* a stepladder. **17.** an offset part of anything. **18.** *Naut.* a socket, frame, or platform for supporting the lower end of a mast. **19.** *Mining.* a flat-topped ledge on the face of a quarry or a mine working. **20.** **break step,** to interrupt or cease walking or marching in step: *The marching units were allowed to break step after they had passed the reviewing stand.* **21.** **in step, a.** moving in time to a rhythm or with the corresponding step of others. **b.** in harmony or conformity with: *They are not in step with the times.* **22.** **keep step,** to keep pace; stay in step: *The construction of classrooms have not kept step with population growth.* **23.** **out of step, a.** not in time to a rhythm or corresponding to the step of others. **b.** not in harmony or conformity with: *They are out of step with the others in their group.* **24.** **step by step, a.** from one stage to the next in sequence. **b.** gradually and steadily: *We were shown the steelmaking process step by step.* **25.** **take steps,** to set about putting something into operation; begin to act: *I will take steps to see that your application is processed.* **26.** **watch one's step,** to proceed with caution; behave prudently: *If she doesn't watch her step, she will be fired from her job.*
—*v.i.* **27.** to move, go, etc., by lifting the foot and setting it down again in a new position, or by using the feet alternately in this manner: *to step forward.* **28.** to walk, or go on foot, esp. for a few strides or a short distance: *Step over to the bar.* **29.** to move with measured steps, as in a dance. **30.** to go briskly or fast, as a horse. **31.** to obtain, find, win, come upon, etc., something easily and naturally, as if by a mere step of the foot: *to step into a good business opportunity.* **32.** to put the foot down; tread by intention or accident: *to step on a cat's tail.* **33.** to press with the foot, as on a lever, spring, or the like, in order to operate some mechanism.
—*v.t.* **34.** to take (a step, pace, stride, etc.). **35.** to go through or perform the steps of (a dance). **36.** to move or set (the foot) in taking a step. **37.** to measure (a distance, ground, etc.) by steps (sometimes fol. by *off* or *out*). **38.** to make or arrange in the manner of a series of steps. **39.** *Naut.* to fix (a mast) in its step. **40.** **step down, a.** to lower or decrease by degrees. **b.** to relinquish one's authority or control; resign: *Although he was past retirement age, he refused to step down and let his son take over the business.* **41.** **step in,** to become involved; intervene, as in a quarrel or fight: *The police stepped in to stop the brawl.* **42.** **step on it,** *Informal.* to hasten one's activity or steps; hurry up: *If we don't step on it, we'll miss the show.* **43.** **step out, a.** to leave a place, esp. for a brief period of time. **b.** to walk or march at a more rapid pace. **c.** to go out to a social gathering or on a date. **44.** **step up, a.** to raise or increase by degrees: *to step up production.* **b.** to be promoted; advance. **c.** to make progress; improve. [bef. 900; (v.) ME *steppen,* OE *steppan;* c. OHG *stepfen;* akin to STAMP; (n.) ME; OE *stepe*] **—step′less,** *adj.* **—step′like′,** *adj.*

step-, a prefix denoting connection between members of a family by the remarriage of a parent and not by blood: *stepbrother.* [ME; OE *stēop-;* c. G *stief-,* ON *stjūp-* step-; akin to OE *āstēpan* to bereave, *bestēpan* to deprive (of children)]

Ste•pa•na•kert (step′ə nə kert′; *Russ.* styi pə nu kyert′), *n.* a city in and the capital of the Nagorno-Karabakh Autonomous Region, within Azerbaijan. 33,000.

step-and-re•peat (step′ən ri pēt′), *adj. Print.* noting or pertaining to a process by which successive photo-offset plates are produced automatically or semiautomatically with great precision: used esp. in making plates for multicolor printing.

step•broth•er (step′bruth′ər), *n.* one's stepfather's son or stepmother's son by a previous marriage. [1400–50; late ME; see STEP-, BROTHER]

step•chair (step′châr′), *n.* a set of steps folding into a chair. [1870–75; STEP + CHAIR]

step•child (step′chīld′), *n., pl.* **-child•ren.** **1.** a child of one's husband or wife by a previous marriage. **2.** any person, organization, affiliate, project, etc., that is not properly treated, supported, or appreciated: *This agency is the stepchild when appropriations are handed out.* [bef. 1000; ME; OE *stēopcild.* See STEP-, CHILD]

step′ cut′, *Jewelry.* a cut consisting of a rectangular girdle, often faceted, with two or more tiers of narrow facets running parallel to the girdle on both the crown and the pavilion: used esp. in stones in which color is more important than brilliance. Also called **trap cut.** [1860–65] **—step′-cut′,** *adj.*

step•dame (step′dām′), *n. Archaic.* a stepmother. [1350–1400; ME; see STEP-, DAME]

step•dance (step′dans′, -däns′), *n.* a dance in which the steps are the most important characteristic, specifically a solo dance with intricate, vigorous steps, often performed with the hands kept in the pockets. [1885–90; STEP + DANCE] **—step′danc′er,** *n.* **—step′danc′ing,** *n.*

step•daugh•ter (step′dô′tər), *n.* a daughter of one's husband or wife by a previous marriage. [bef. 900; ME *stepdohter,* OE *stēopdohtor.* See STEP-, DAUGHTER]

step-down (step′doun′), *adj. Elect.* serving to reduce or decrease voltage: *a step-down transformer.* [1890–95; adj. use of v. phrase *step down*]

step•fam•i•ly (step′fam′ə lē, -fam′lē), *n., pl.* **-lies.** a family composed of a parent, a stepparent, and a child or children by a previous marriage. [STEP- + FAMILY]

step•fa•ther (step′fä′thər), *n.* the husband of one's mother by a later marriage. [bef. 900; ME *stepfader,* OE *stēopfæder.* See STEP-, FATHER] **—step′fa′ther•ly,** *adv.*

step′ func′tion, *Math.* a function that is constant on each of a finite set of subintervals of its domain, the union of the subintervals being the domain. [1925–30]

Steph•a•nie (stef′ə nē), *n.* a female given name.

steph•an•ite (stef′ə nīt′), *n.* a mineral, silver antimony sulfide, Ag_5SbS_4: an ore of silver. [1840–50; named after *Stephan,* Archduke of Austria (d. 1867); see -ITE[1]]

steph•a•no•tis (stef′ə nō′tis), *n.* any vine belonging to the genus *Stephanotis,* of the milkweed family, having fragrant, waxy, white flowers and leathery leaves. [1865–70; < NL < Gk *stephanōtís* (fem. adj.) fit for a crown, deriv. of *stéphanos* (masc.) crown]

step•head (step′hed′), *n.* dropline. [STEP + HEAD]

Ste•phen (stē′vən), *n.* **1.** **Saint,** died A.D. c35, first Christian martyr. **2.** **Saint,** c975–1038, first king of Hungary 997–1038. **3.** (*Stephen of Blois*) 1097?–1154, king of England 1135–54. **4.** **Sir Leslie,** 1832–1904, English critic, biographer, and philosopher. **5.** a male given name.

Stephen I, **Saint,** died A.D. 257?, pope 254–257.

Stephen II, died A.D. 757, pope 752–757.

Stephen III, died A.D. 772, pope 768–772.

Stephen IV, died A.D. 817, pope 816–817.

Stephen V, died A.D. 891, pope 885–891.

Stephen VI, died A.D. 897, pope 896–897.

Stephen VII, died A.D. 931, pope 928–931.

Stephen VIII, died A.D. 942, pope 939–942.

Stephen IX, died 1058, pope 1057–58.

Ste•phens (stē′vənz), *n.* **1.** **Alexander Hamilton,** 1812–83, U.S. statesman: vice-president of the Confederacy 1861–65. **2.** **James,** 1882–1950, Irish poet and novelist.

Ste•phen•son (stē′vən sən), *n.* **1.** **George,** 1781–1848, English inventor and engineer. **2.** his son **Robert,** 1803–59, English engineer.

Ste•phen•ville (stē′vən vil′), *n.* a town in central Texas. 11,881.

step-in (step′in′), *adj.* **1.** (of garments, shoes, etc.) put on by being stepped into. **—***n.* **2.** **step-ins,** panties, esp. bias-cut panties with wide legs worn by women in the 1920's and 1930's. **3.** any step-in garment. [1920–25; adj., n. use of v. phrase *step in*]

step•lad•der (step′lad′ər), *n.* **1.** a ladder having flat steps or treads in place of rungs. **2.** any ladder, esp. a tall one with a hinged frame opening up to form four supporting legs. [1745–55; STEP + LADDER]

step•moth•er (step′muth′ər), *n.* the wife of one's father by a later marriage. [bef. 900; ME *stepmoder,* OE *stēopmōdor.* See STEP-, MOTHER[1]] **—step′moth′er•ly,** *adv.* **—step′moth′er•li•ness,** *n.*

Step•ney (step′nē), *n.* a former borough of Greater London, England, now part of Tower Hamlets.

step-off (step′ôf′, -of′), *n.* an abrupt drop, as from a shoreline into deep water. [n. use of v. phrase *step off*]

step-on (step′on′, -ôn′), *adj.* made to open by the operation of a pedal, as a can for kitchen garbage. [adj. use of v. phrase *step on*]

step•par•ent (step′pâr′ənt, -par′-), *n.* a stepfather or stepmother. [1885–90; STEP- + PARENT] **—step′par′•ent•ing,** *n.*

steppe (step), *n.* **1.** an extensive plain, esp. one without trees. **2. The Steppes, a.** the vast grasslands in the S and E European and W and SW Asian parts of Russia. **b.** See **Kirghiz Steppe.** [1665–75; < Russ *step′* or Ukrainian *step;* ulterior orig. uncert.]

stepped′ line′, dropline.

stepped-up (stept′up′), *adj.* increased; augmented; expanded; heightened: *a stepped-up fundraising campaign.* [1900–05]

Step•pen•wolf (*Ger.* shtep′ən vôlf′; *Eng.* step′ən-wo͝olf′), *n.* a novel (1927) by Hermann Hesse.

step•per (step′ər), *n.* **1.** a person or animal that steps, esp. a horse that lifts its front legs high at the knee. **2.** *Informal.* a dancer. [1825–35; STEP + -ER[1]]

step′ping-off′ place′ (step′ing ôf′, -of′). See **jumping-off place** (def. 2). [1890–95]

step•ping•stone (step′ing stōn′), *n.* **1.** a stone, or one of a line of stones, in shallow water, a marshy place, or the like, that is stepped on in crossing. **2.** a stone for use in mounting or ascending. **3.** any means or stage of advancement or improvement: *She looked on the governorship as a steppingstone to the presidency.* [1275–1325; ME]

step′ rock′et, *Rocketry.* a multistage rocket that discards burned-out stages.

step•sis•ter (step′sis′tər), *n.* one's stepfather's or stepmother's daughter by a previous marriage. [1400–50; late ME; see STEP-, SISTER]

step•son (step′sun′), *n.* a son of one's husband or wife by a previous marriage. [bef. 900; ME *stepsone,* OE *stēopsunu.* See STEP-, SON]

step•stool (step′sto͞ol′), *n.* a low set of hinged steps, often folding into or under a stool, used typically in a kitchen for reaching high shelves. [1945–50; STEP + STOOL]

step•toe (step′tō′), *n. Western U.S.* an isolated hill or mountain surrounded by lava. [STEP + TOE]

step′ turn′, *Skiing.* a turn in which a skier lifts one ski from the snow, faces the ski slightly outward in the direction to be turned, sets it down, and brings the other ski around so that both skis are parallel. [1940–45]

step-up (step′up′), *adj.* **1.** effecting an increase. **2.** *Elect.* serving to increase voltage: *a step-up transformer.* **3.** (of a lease) allowing for gradual rent increases to the highest amount permissible. **—***n.* **4.** an increase or rise in the rate or quantity of something. Also, **step′up′.** [1890–95; adj., n. use of v. phrase *step up*]

step•wise (step′wīz′), *adv.* **1.** in a steplike arrangement. **2.** *Music.* from one adjacent tone to another: *The melody ascends stepwise.* **—***adj.* **3.** *Music.* moving from one adjacent tone to another: *stepwise melodic progression.* [1885–90; STEP + -WISE]

-ster, a suffix used in forming nouns, often derogatory, referring especially to occupation, habit, or association: *gamester; songster; trickster.* [ME; OE *-estre;* c. D *-ster,* MLG *-(e)ster*]

ster., sterling.

ste•ra•di•an (stə rā′dē ən), *n. Geom.* a solid angle at the center of a sphere subtending a section on the surface equal in area to the square of the radius of the sphere. *Abbr.:* sr [1880–85; STE(REO)- + RADIAN]

ster•co•ra•ceous (stûr′kə rā′shəs), *adj. Physiol.* consisting of, resembling, or pertaining to dung or feces. Also, **ster•co•rous** (stûr′kər əs). [1725–35; < L *stercor-* (s. of *stercus*) dung + -ACEOUS]

ster•cu•li•a (stûr kyo͞o′lē ə), *n.* any of various tropical trees of the genus *Sterculia,* of which some species are grown as ornamentals and some are the source of commercially valuable wood. [1765–75; < NL, equiv. to L *Stercul(us)* a Roman deity supposed to have invented manuring (deriv. of *stercus* manure, excrement) + *ia* -IA; from the fetid odor of the blossoms of certain species]

stercu′lia gum′. See **karaya gum.** [1940–45]

stere (stēr), *n.* a cubic meter equivalent to 35.315 cubic feet or 1.3080 cubic yards, used to measure cordwood. *Abbr.:* st [1790–1800; < F *stère* < Gk *stereós* solid]

ster•e•o (ster′ē ō′, stēr′-), *n., pl.* **ster•e•os,** *adj., v.* **—***n.* **1.** stereoscopic photography. **2.** a stereoscopic photograph. **3.** stereophonic sound reproduction. **4.** a system or the equipment for reproducing stereophonic sound. **5.** *Print.* stereotype (defs. 1, 2). **—***adj.* **6.** pertaining to stereophonic sound, stereoscopic photography, etc. **—***v.t.* **7.** *Print.* stereotype (def. 5). [1815–25; by shortening]

stereo-, a combining form borrowed from Greek, where it meant "solid", used with reference to hardness, solidity, three-dimensionality in the formation of compound words: *stereochemistry; stereogram; stereoscope.* Also, *esp. before a vowel,* **stere-.** [< Gk *stereós*]

stereo., stereotype.

ster•e•o•bate (ster′ē ə bāt′, stēr′-), *n. Archit.* **1.** the foundation or base upon which a building or the like is erected. **2.** the solid platform forming the floor and substructure of a classical temple; crepidoma; podium. Cf. **stylobate.** [1830–40; < L *stereobatēs* < Gk *stereobatēs,* equiv. to *stereo-* STEREO- + *-batēs* walker (see STYLOBATE)] **—ster•e•o•bat•ic** (ster′ē ə bat′ik, stēr′-), *adj.*

ster•e•o•cam•er•a (ster′ē ō kam′ər ə, -kam′rə, stēr′-), *n.* a stereoscopic camera. [STEREO- + CAMERA]

ster•e•o•chem•is•try (ster′ē ō kem′ə strē, stēr′-), *n.* the branch of chemistry that deals with the determination of the relative positions in space of the atoms or groups of atoms in a compound and with the effects of these positions on the properties of the compound. [1885–90; STEREO- + CHEMISTRY] **—ster•e•o•chem•ic** (ster′ē ō kem′ik, stēr′-), **ster′e•o•chem′i•cal,** *adj.* **—ster′e•o•chem′i•cal•ly,** *adv.*

ster•e•o•chrome (ster′ē ə krōm′, stēr′-), *n.* a picture produced by a process in which water glass is used as a vehicle or as a preservative coating. [1850–55; back formation from STEREOCHROMY]

ster•e•o•chro•my (ster′ē ə krō′mē, stēr′-), *n.* the stereochrome process. Also called **waterglass painting.** [1835–45; STEREO- + *-chromy* (see -CHROME, -Y[3])] **—ster′e•o•chro′mic, ster•e•o•chro•mat•ic** (ster′ē ō-krə mat′ik, -krō-, stēr′-), *adj.* **—ster′e•o•chro′mi•cal•ly, ster′e•o•chro•mat′i•cal•ly,** *adv.*

ster•e•o•cil•i•um (ster′ē ə sil′ē əm, stēr′-), *n., pl.* **-cil•i•a** (-sil′ē ə). *Anat.* any of the long, flexible microvilli that superficially resemble cilia and occur as a brush border or series of tufts on the surface of various epithelial tissues. [< NL; see STEREO-, CILIUM]

ster•e•og•no•sis (ster′ē og nō′sis, stēr′-), *n.* the ability to determine the shape and weight of an object by touching or lifting it. [1900–05; < NL; see STEREO-, -GNOSIS] **—ster•e•og•nos•tic** (ster′ē og nos′tik, stēr′-), *adj.*

ster•e•o•gram (ster′ē ə gram′, stēr′-), *n.* **1.** a diagram or picture representing objects in a way to give the impression of solidity. **2.** a stereograph. [1865–70; STEREO- + -GRAM[1]]

ster•e•o•graph (ster′ē ə graf′, -gräf′, stēr′-), *n.* **1.** a single or double picture for a stereoscope. **—***v.t.* **2.** to make a stereograph of. [1855–60; STEREO- + -GRAPH]

ster•e•og•ra•pher (ster′ē og′rə fər, stēr′-), *n.* a person who takes stereoscopic photographs. [1930–35; STEREOGRAPH + -ER[1]]

ster′eograph′ic projec′tion, *Math.* a one-to-one correspondence between the points on a sphere and the extended complex plane where the north pole on the sphere corresponds to the point at infinity of the plane. Cf. **extended complex plane.** [1695–1705]

ster•e•og•ra•phy (ster′ē og′rə fē, stēr′-), *n.* **1.** the art of delineating the forms of solid bodies on a plane. **2.** a branch of solid geometry dealing with the construction of regularly defined solids. [1690–1700; STEREO- + -GRAPHY] **—ster•e•o•graph•ic** (ster′ē ə graf′ik, stēr′-), **ster′e•o•graph′i•cal,** *adj.* **—ster′e•o•graph′i•cal•ly,** *adv.*

ster•e•o•im•age (ster′ē ō im′ij, stēr′-), *n.* the single three-dimensional image perceived in the brain by the coordination of the two slightly different views seen by the eyes. [STEREO- + IMAGE]

ster•e•o•i•so•mer (ster′ē ō ī′sə mər, stēr′-), *n. Chem.* any of two or more isomers exhibiting stereoisomerism. [1895–1900; STEREO- + ISOMER]

ster•e•o•i•so•mer•ic (ster′ē ō ī′sə mer′ik, stēr′-), *adj. Chem.* pertaining to or exhibiting stereoisomerism. [1895–1900; STEREOISOMER(ISM) + -IC]

ster•e•o•i•som•er•ism (ster′ē ō ī som′ə riz′əm, stēr′-), *n. Chem.* the isomerism ascribed to different relative positions of the atoms or groups of atoms in the molecules of organic compounds. [1890–95; STEREO- + ISOMERISM]

ster•e•ol•o•gy (ster′ē ol′ə jē, stēr′-), *n.* a branch of science dealing with the determination of the three-dimensional structure of objects based on two-dimensional views of them. [1960–65; STEREO- + -LOGY]

ster•e•om•e•try (ster′ē om′i trē, stēr′-), *n.* the measurement of volumes. [1560–70; < NL *stereometria.* See STEREO-, -METRY] **—ster•e•o•met•ric** (ster′ē ə me′-trik, stēr′-), **ster′e•o•met′ri•cal,** *adj.* **—ster′e•o•met′-ri•cal•ly,** *adv.*

ster•e•o•mi•cro•scope (ster′ē ō mī′krə skōp′, stēr′-), *n.* See **stereoscopic microscope.** [1945–50; STEREO- + MICROSCOPE] **—ster•e•o•mi•cros•co•py** (ster′ē ō mī kros′kə pē, -mī′krə skō′pē, stēr′-), *n.*

ster•e•o•pair (ster′ē ō pâr′, stēr′-), *n. Photogrammetry.* a pair of photographs of the same area taken from slightly different positions so as to give a stereoscopic effect when properly mounted and viewed. [STEREO- + PAIR]

ster•e•o•phon•ic (ster′ē ə fon′ik, stēr′-), *adj.* pertaining to a system of sound recording or reproduction using two or more separate channels to produce a more realistic effect by capturing the spatial dimensions of a performance (the location of performers as well as their acoustic surroundings), used esp. with high-fidelity recordings and reproduction systems (opposed to *monophonic*). Cf. **quadraphonic.** [1935–40; STEREO- + PHON(O)- + -IC] **—ster′e•o•phon′i•cal•ly,** *adv.*

ster•e•oph•o•ny (ster′ē of′ə nē, stēr′-, ster′ē ə fō′nē, stēr′-), *n.* the state or condition of being stereophonic. [STEREO- + -PHONY]

ster•e•o•pho•tog•ra•phy (ster′ē ō fə tog′rə fē, stēr′-), *n.* photography producing stereoscopic images. [1900–05; STEREO- + PHOTOGRAPHY] **—ster•e•o•pho•to•graph** (ster′ē ō fō′tə graf′, -gräf′, stēr′-), *n.* **—ster•e•o•pho•to•graph•ic** (ster′ē ō fō′tə graf′ik, stēr′-), *adj.*

ster•e•op•sis (ster′ē op′sis, stēr′-), *n.* stereoscopic vision; the ability to perceive depth. [1925–30; STERE(O)- + -OPSIS]

ster•e•op•ti•con (ster′ē op′ti kən, -kon′, stēr′-), *n. Optics.* a projector usually consisting of two complete lanterns arranged so that one picture appears to dissolve while the next is forming. [1860–65, *Amer.;* STERE(O)- + Gk *optikón* (neut.) OPTIC] **—ster′e•op′ti•can,** *adj.* **—ster•e•op•ti•cian** (ster′ē op tish′ən, stēr′-), *n.*

ster•e•o•reg•u•lar•i•ty (ster′ē ō reg′yə lar′i tē, stēr′-), *n. Chem.* (of a polymer) the degree to which successive configurations in space along the chain follow a simple rule. Also called **tacticity.** Cf. **configuration** (def. 4). [1955–60; STEREO- + REGULARITY]

ster•e•o•scope (ster′ē ə skōp′, stēr′-), *n.* an optical instrument through which two pictures of the same object, taken from slightly different points of view, are viewed, one by each eye, producing the effect of a single picture of the object, with the appearance of depth or relief. [1830–40; STEREO- + -SCOPE]

ster•e•o•scop•ic (ster′ē ə skop′ik, stēr′-), *adj.* **1.** noting or pertaining to three-dimensional vision or any of various processes and devices for giving the illusion of depth from two-dimensional images or reproductions, as of a photograph or motion picture. **2.** of, pertaining to, or characterized by a stereoscope or stereoscopy. Also, **ster′e•o•scop′i•cal.** [1850–55; STEREOSCOPE + -IC] **—ster′e•o•scop′i•cal•ly,** *adv.*

ster′eoscop′ic mi′croscope, a microscope that produces a three-dimensional image of an object by focusing on the object from slightly different positions in each of two lenses. Also, **stereomicroscope.**

ster•e•os•co•py (ster′ē os′kə pē, stēr′-), *n.* **1.** the study of the stereoscope and its techniques. **2.** three-dimensional vision. [1860–65; STEREO- + -SCOPY] **—ster′e•os′co•pist,** *n.*

ster•e•o•spe•cif•ic (ster′ē ō spə sif′ik, stēr′-), *adj. Chem.* **1.** (of a reaction) producing a simple stereoisomer. **2.** (of a polymer) having a regular sequence of configurations in space along the chain, resulting in the potential for close-packing of molecules and for partial or complete crystallinity. Also, **ster•e•o•reg•u•lar** (ster′-ē ō reg′yə lər, stēr′-). [STEREO- + SPECIFIC] **—ster•e•o•spec•i•fic•i•ty** (ster′ē ō spes′ə fis′i tē, stēr′-), *n.*

ster•e•o•tape (ster′ē ō tāp′, stēr′-), *n.* magnetic tape used for recording and reproducing sound stereophonically. [1955–60; STEREO- + TAPE]

ster•e•o•tax•ic (ster′ē ə tak′sik, stēr′-), *adj. Anat.* of, pertaining to, or based on three-dimensional studies of the brain, esp. as an adjunct to brain surgery. [1905–10; see STEREO-, -TAXIS, -IC]

ster•e•o•tax•is (ster′ē ə tak′sis, stēr′-), *n. Biol.* movement of an organism in response to contact with a solid. [1915–20; STEREO- + -TAXIS] **—ster•e•o•tac•tic** (ster′ē ə tak′tik, stēr′-), *adj.* **—ster′e•o•tac′ti•cal•ly,** *adv.*

ster•e•ot•o•my (ster′ē ot′ə mē, stēr′-), *n.* the technique of cutting solids, as stones, to specified forms and dimensions. [1720–30; STEREO- + -TOMY] **—ster•e•o•tom•ic** (ster′ē ə tom′ik, stēr′-), **ster′e•o•tom′i•cal,** *adj.* **—ster′e•ot′o•mist,** *n.*

ster•e•ot•ro•pism (ster′ē o′trə piz′əm, stēr′-), *n. Biol.* a tropism determined by contact with a solid. [1895–1900; STEREO- + TROPISM]

ster•e•o•type (ster′ē ə tīp′, stēr′-), *n., v.,* **-typed, -typ•ing.** **—***n.* **1.** a process, now often replaced by more advanced methods, for making metal printing plates by taking a mold of composed type or the like in papier-mâché or other material and then taking from this mold a cast in type metal. **2.** a plate made by this process. **3.** a set form; convention. **4.** *Sociol.* a simplified and standardized conception or image invested with special meaning and held in common by members of a group: *The cowboy and Indian are American stereotypes.* **—***v.t.* **5.** to make a stereotype of. **6.** to characterize or regard as a stereotype: *The actor has been stereotyped as a villain.* **7.** to give a fixed form to. [1790–1800; STEREO- + -TYPE] **—ster′e•o•typ′er, ster′e•o•typ′ist,** *n.* **—ster•e•o•typ•ic** (ster′ē ə tip′ik, stēr′-), **ster′e•o•typ′i•cal,** *adj.*
—Syn. 6. categorize, type, identify.

ster•e•o•typed (ster′ē ə tīpt′, stēr′-), *adj.* **1.** reproduced in or by stereotype plates. **2.** fixed or settled in form; hackneyed; conventional. [1810–20; STEREOTYPE + -ED[2]]
—Syn. 2. lifeless, stale, worn, dull. See **commonplace. —Ant. 2.** rare, unusual.

ster•e•o•typ•y (ster′ē ə tī′pē, stēr′-), *n.* **1.** the stereotype process. **2.** Also called **ster′eotyped behav′ior.** *Psychiatry.* persistent mechanical repetition of speech or movement, sometimes occurring as a symptom of schizophrenia, autism, or other mental disorder. [1860–65; STEREOTYPE + -Y[3]]

ster•e•o•vi•sion (ster′ē ə vizh′ən, stēr′-), *n.* visual perception in three dimensions. [STEREO- + VISION]

ster•ic (ster′ik, stēr′-), *adj. Chem.* of or pertaining to the spatial relationships of atoms in a molecule. Also, **ster′i•cal.** [1895–1900; STER(EO)- + -IC] **—ster′i•cal•ly,** *adv.*

ster′ic hin′drance, *Chem.* the prevention or retardation of inter- or intramolecular interactions as a result of the spatial structure of a molecule. [1900–05]

ste•rig•ma (stə rig′mə), *n., pl.* **-ma•ta** (-mə tə). *Mycol.* a small stalk that bears a sporangium, a conidium, or esp. a basidiospore. [1865–70; < NL < Gk *stērigma* a support, equiv. to *stērig-,* base of *stērízein* to support + *-ma* n. suffix] **—ster•ig•mat•ic** (ster′ig mat′ik, stēr′-), *adj.*

ster•i•lant (ster′ə lənt), *n. Chem.* a sterilizing agent. [1940–45; STERILE + -ANT]

ster•ile (ster′il *or, esp. Brit.,* -īl), *adj.* **1.** free from living germs or microorganisms; aseptic: *sterile surgical instruments.* **2.** incapable of producing offspring; not producing offspring. **3.** barren; not producing vegetation: *sterile soil.* **4.** *Bot.* **a.** noting a plant in which reproductive structures fail to develop. **b.** bearing no stamens or pistils. **5.** not productive of results, ideas, etc.; fruitless. [1545–55; < L *sterilis* unfruitful] **—ster′ile•ly,** *adv.* **—ste•ril•i•ty** (stə ril′i tē), **ster′ile•ness,** *n.*
—Syn. 2. infecund, unfruitful. **—Ant. 2, 3.** fertile.

ster•i•li•za•tion (ster′ə lə zā′shən), *n.* **1.** the act of sterilizing. **2.** the condition of being sterilized. **3.** the

CONCISE PRONUNCIATION KEY: act, cāpe, dâre, pärt; set, ēqual; if, īce; ox, ōver, ôrder, oil, bo͝ok, bo͞ot, out; up, ûrge; child; sing; shoe; thin, *th*at; zh as in *treasure.* ə = *a* as in *alone, e* as in *system, i* as in *easily, o* as in *gallop, u* as in *circus;* ᵊ as in *fire* (fīᵊr), *hour* (ouᵊr). l and n can serve as syllabic consonants, as in *cradle* (krād′l), and *button* (but′n). See the full key inside the front cover.

destruction of all living microorganisms, as pathogenic or saprophytic bacteria, vegetative forms, and spores. [1870–75; STERILE + -IZATION]

ster·i·lize (ster′ə līz′), *v.t.*, **-lized, -liz·ing.** **1.** to destroy microorganisms in or on, usually by bringing to a high temperature with steam, dry heat, or boiling liquid. **2.** to destroy the ability of (a person or animal) to reproduce by removing the sex organs or inhibiting their functions. **3.** to make (land) barren or unproductive. **4.** *Informal.* to delete or remove anything comprising or damaging from: *to sterilize a government document before releasing it to the press.* **5.** *Informal.* to isolate or completely protect from unwanted, unauthorized, or unwholesome activities, attitudes, influences, etc.: *You can't sterilize children against violence.* Also, *esp. Brit.,* **ster′i·lise′.** [1685–95; STERILE + -IZE] **—ster′i·liz′a·ble,** *adj.* **—ster′i·liz′a·bil′i·ty,** *n.* **—ster′i·liz′er,** *n.*

ster·let (stûr′lit), *n.* a small sturgeon, *Acipenser ruthenus,* of the Black and Caspian seas, valued as a source of caviar. [1585–95; < Russ *stérlyad′,* ORuss *sterlyagi* (pl.) < G *Störling* a small sturgeon, equiv. to *Stör* sturgeon (MHG *stör(e), stür(e),* OHG *stur(i)o;* cf. STURGEON) + *-ling* -LING[1]]

ster·ling (stûr′ling), *adj.* **1.** of, pertaining to, or noting British money: *The sterling equivalent is £5.50.* **2.** (of silver) having the standard fineness of 0.925. **3.** made of silver of this fineness: *a sterling teapot.* **4.** thoroughly excellent: *a man of sterling worth.* —*n.* **5.** British currency. **6.** the standard of fineness for gold and silver coin in the United Kingdom, 0.91666 for gold and 0.500 for silver. **7.** Also called **ster′ling sil′ver.** silver having a fineness of 0.925, now used esp. in the manufacture of table utensils, jewelry, etc. **8.** manufactured articles of sterling silver. **9.** sterling flatware. [1250–1300; ME: name of a silver coin (see STAR, -LING[1]), with reference to the little star on some of the mintages] **—ster′ling·ly,** *adv.* **—ster′ling·ness,** *n.*
—Syn. 4. noble, honorable, worthy, first-rate.

Ster·ling (stûr′ling), *n.* **1.** a city in NW Illinois. 16,273. **2.** a city in NE Colorado. 11,385. **3.** a male given name.

ster′ling bloc′, those countries having currencies whose values tend to vary directly with the rise and fall of the value of the pound sterling. Also called **ster′ling ar′ea.**

Ster′ling Heights′, a city in SE Michigan, near Detroit. 108,999.

Ster·li·ta·mak (stûr′lit ə mak′; *Russ.* styiR lyi tumäk′), *n.* a city in the Russian Federation in Europe, W of the Southern Urals. 220,000.

stern[1] (stûrn), *adj.,* **-er, -est.** **1.** firm, strict, or uncompromising: *stern discipline.* **2.** hard, harsh, or severe: *a stern reprimand.* **3.** rigorous or austere; of an unpleasantly serious character: *stern times.* **4.** grim or forbidding in aspect: *a stern face.* [bef. 1000; ME; OE *styrne*] **—stern′ly,** *adv.* **—stern′ness,** *n.*
—Syn. 1, 2. adamant, unrelenting, unsympathetic, cruel, unfeeling. STERN, SEVERE, HARSH agree in referring to methods, aspects, manners, or facial expressions. STERN implies uncompromising, inflexible firmness, and sometimes a hard, forbidding, or withdrawn aspect or nature: *a stern parent.* SEVERE implies strictness, lack of sympathy, and a tendency to impose a hard discipline on others: *a severe judge.* HARSH suggests a great severity and roughness, and cruel, unfeeling treatment of others: *a harsh critic.* **—Ant. 1.** lenient.

stern[2] (stûrn), *n.* **1.** the after part of a vessel (often opposed to *stem*). **2.** the back or rear of anything. **3.** (*cap.*) *Astron.* the constellation Puppis. **4.** *Fox Hunting.* the tail of a hound. [1250–1300; ME *sterne,* prob. < ON *stjórn* steering (done aft; see STERNPOST)]

Stern (stûrn), *n.* **1. Isaac,** born 1920, U.S. violinist, born in Russia. **2. Otto,** 1888–1969, U.S. physicist, born in Germany: Nobel prize 1943.

stern-, var. of **sterno-** before a vowel: *sternite.*

ster·nal (stûr′nl), *adj.* of or pertaining to the sternum. [1750–60; < NL *sternālis.* See STERNUM, -AL[1]]

Stern·berg (stûrn′bûrg), *n.* **1. George Miller,** 1838–1915, U.S. bacteriologist and medical researcher. **2. Josef von** (jō′zəf, -səf). See **von Sternberg, Josef.**

stern′ chas′er, a cannon mounted at or near the stern of a sailing ship, facing aft. [1805–15]

stern′ drive′, *Naut.* inboard-outboard (def. 2). [1965–70]

stern-drive (stûrn′drīv′), *adj. Naut.* inboard-outboard (def. 1). [1965–70]

Sterne (stûrn), *n.* **Laurence,** 1713–68, English clergyman and novelist.

stern·fore·most (stûrn′fôr′mōst, -fōr′- *or, esp. Brit.,* -məst), *adv.* **1.** *Naut.* with the stern foremost. **2.** awkwardly; with difficulty. [1830–40; STERN[2] + FOREMOST]

ster·nite (stûr′nīt), *n. Entomol.* a sclerite of the sternum of an insect, esp. a ventral sclerite of an abdominal segment. [1865–70; STERN- + -ITE[1]] **—ster·nit·ic** (stərnit′ik), *adj.*

stern·most (stûrn′mōst *or, esp. Brit.,* -məst), *adj. Naut.* **1.** farthest aft. **2.** nearest the stern. [1615–25; STERN[2] + -MOST]

Sterno (stûr′nō), *Trademark.* flammable hydrocarbon jelly packaged in a small can for use as a portable heat source for cooking.

sterno-, a combining form representing **sternum** in compound words: *sternocostal.* Also, *esp. before a vowel,* **stern-.**

ster·no·clei·do·mas·toid (stûr′nō klī′də mas′toid), *Anat.* —*adj.* **1.** of, pertaining to, or involving the sternum, the clavicle, and the mastoid process. —*n.* **2.** a thick muscle on each side of the neck, the action of which assists in bending the head and neck forward and sideways. [1820–30; STERNO- + Gk *kleido-,* comb. form of *kleís* key, clavicle + MASTOID]

ster·no·cos·tal (stûr′nō kos′tl, -kô′stl), *adj. Anat., Zool.* of, pertaining to, or situated between the sternum and ribs. [1775–85; STERNO- + COSTAL]

stern·post (stûrn′pōst′), *n. Naut.* an upright member rising from the after end of a keel; a rudderpost or propeller post. Also called **body post.** [1570–80; STERN[2] + POST[1]]

stern′ sheets′, *Naut.* the after part of an open boat, occupied by the person in command or by passengers. [1475–85]

stern·son (stûrn′sən), *n.* a knee in a timber-framed vessel, reinforcing the angle between the keelson and the sternpost. [1840–50; STERN[2] + (KEEL)SON]

ster·num (stûr′nəm), *n., pl.* **-na** (-nə), **-nums.** **1.** *Anat., Zool.* a bone or series of bones extending along the middle line of the ventral portion of the body of most vertebrates, consisting in humans of a flat, narrow bone connected with the clavicles and the true ribs; breastbone. See diag. under **skeleton.** **2.** the ventral surface of a body segment of an arthropod. [1660–70; < NL < Gk *stérnon* chest, breastbone]

ster·nu·ta·tion (stûr′nyə tā′shən), *n.* the act of sneezing. [1535–45; < L *sternūtātiōn-* (s. of *sternūtātiō*), equiv. to *sternūtāt(us)* (ptp. of *sternūtāre,* freq. of *sternuere* to sneeze) + *-iōn-* -ION]

ster·nu·ta·tor (stûr′nyə tā′tər), *n. Chemical Warfare.* a chemical agent causing nose irritation, coughing, etc. [1920–25; back formation from STERNUTATORY]

ster·nu·ta·to·ry (stər nōō′tə tôr′ē, -tōr′ē, -nyōō′-), *adj., n., pl.* **-ries.** —*adj.* **1.** Also, **ster·nu′ta·tive.** causing or tending to cause sneezing. —*n.* **2.** a sternutatory substance. [1610–20; < LL *sternūtātōrius,* equiv. to *sternūtā(re)* (see STERNUTATION) + *-tōrius* -TORY[1]]

stern·ward (stûrn′wərd), *adv.* toward the stern; astern. [1825–35; STERN[2] + -WARD]

stern·way (stûrn′wā′), *n. Naut.* the movement of a vessel backward, or stern foremost. [1760–70; STERN[2] + WAY[1]]

stern-wheel (stûrn′hwēl′, -wēl′), *adj.* (of a vessel) propelled by a paddle wheel at the stern. [1855–60]

stern·wheel (stûrn′hwēl, -wēl′), *n. Naut.* a paddle wheel at the stern of a vessel. [1810–20; STERN[2] + WHEEL]

stern·wheel·er (stûrn′hwē′lər, -wē′-), *n.* a boat propelled by a paddle wheel at the stern. [1850–55; *Amer.;* STERNWHEEL + -ER[1]]

ste·roid (stēr′oid, ster′-), *Biochem.* —*n.* **1.** any of a large group of fat-soluble organic compounds, as the sterols, bile acids, and sex hormones, most of which have specific physiological action. —*adj.* **2.** Also, **ste·roi·dal** (sti roid′l, ste-). pertaining to or characteristic of a steroid. [1925–30; STER(OL) + -OID]

ste·roi·do·gen·e·sis (sti roi′də jen′ə sis, ste-), *n.* the formation of steroids, as by the adrenal cortex, testes, and ovaries. [1950–55; STEROID + -O- + -GENESIS]

ste·rol (stēr′ôl, -ol, ster′-), *n. Biochem.* any of a group of solid, mostly unsaturated, polycyclic alcohols, as cholesterol and ergosterol, derived from plants or animals. [1910–15; extracted from such words as CHOLESTEROL, ERGOSTEROL, etc.]

ster·tor (stûr′tər), *n. Pathol.* a heavy snoring sound accompanying respiration in certain diseases. [1795–1805; < L *stert(ere)* to snore + -OR[1]]

ster·to·rous (stûr′tər əs), *adj.* **1.** characterized by stertor or heavy snoring. **2.** breathing in this manner. [1795–1805; STERTOR + -OUS] **—ster′to·rous·ly,** *adv.* **—ster′to·rous·ness,** *n.*

stet (stet), *v.,* **stet·ted, stet·ting.** —*v.i.* **1.** let it stand (used imperatively as a direction on a printer's proof, manuscript, or the like, to retain material previously cancelled, usually accompanied by a row of dots under or beside the material). —*v.t.* **2.** to mark (a manuscript, printer's proof, etc.) with the word "stet" or with dots as a direction to let cancelled material remain. [1815–25; < L *stet,* pres. subj. 3rd pers. sing. of *stāre* to STAND]

Ste.-Thé·rèse (sānt′tə rēz′, -rāz′; *Fr.* saNt tā rez′), *n.* a town in S Quebec, in E Canada. 18,750.

stetho-, a combining form meaning "chest," used in the formation of compound words: *stethoscope.* [comb. form of Gk *stêthos*]

ste·thom·e·ter (ste thom′i tər), *n.* an instrument for measuring the expansion of the chest and abdomen during respiration. [1840–50; STETHO- + -METER] **—steth·o·met·ric** (steth′ə me′trik), *adj.* **—ste·thom′e·try,** *n.*

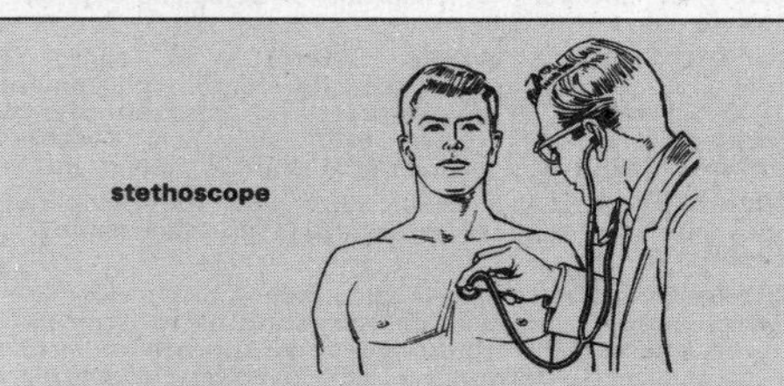

steth·o·scope (steth′ə skōp′), *n. Med.* an instrument used in auscultation to convey sounds in the chest or other parts of the body to the ear of the examiner. [1810–20; STETHO- + -SCOPE] **—steth′o·scoped′,** *adj.* **—ste·thos·co·pist** (ste thos′kə pist), *n.* **—ste·thos·co·py** (ste thos′kə pē, steth′ə skō′-), *n.*

steth·o·scop·ic (steth′ə skop′ik), *adj.* pertaining to the stethoscope or to stethoscopy. Also, **steth′o·scop′i·cal.** [1820–30; STETHOSCOPE + -IC] **—steth′o·scop′i·cal·ly,** *adv.*

St.-É·tienne (saN tā tyen′), *n.* a city in and the capital of Loire, in SE France. 221,775.

Stet·son (stet′sən), *Trademark.* a brand of felt hat with a broad brim and high crown, esp. one worn as part of a cowboy's outfit.

Stet·tin (shte tēn′), *n.* German name of **Szczecin.**

Stet·tin·i·us (stə tin′ē əs), *n.* **Edward Reil·ley** (rī′lē), 1900–49, U.S. industrialist: Secretary of State 1944–45.

Steu·ben (stōō′bən, styōō′-, stōō ben′, styōō-; *Ger.* shtoi′bən), *n.* **Frie·drich Wil·helm Lu·dolf Ger·hard Au·gus·tin von** (frē′drikH vil′helm lōō′dôlf gār′härt ou′gōōs tēn′ fən), 1730–94, Prussian major general in the American Revolutionary army.

Steu′ben glass′, *Trademark.* a brand of handmade heavy lead crystal made in the U.S. by Steuben Glass Works, Corning, New York.

Steu·ben·ville (stōō′bən vil′, styōō′-), *n.* a city in E Ohio, on the Ohio River. 26,400.

St.-Eus·tache (*Fr.* saN tœs tash′), *n.* a town in S Quebec, in E Canada. 29,716.

St. Eu·sta·ti·us (yōō stā′shē əs, -shəs), an island in the Netherlands Antilles, in the E West Indies. 1421; 7 sq. mi. (18 sq. km). Also called **Statia.**

Steve (stēv), *n.* a male given name, form of **Steven** or **Stephen.**

ste·ve·dore (stē′vi dôr′, -dōr′), *n., v.,* **-dored, -dor·ing.** —*n.* **1.** a firm or individual engaged in the loading or unloading of a vessel. —*v.t.* **2.** to load or unload the cargo of (a ship). —*v.i.* **3.** to load or unload a vessel. [1780–90, *Amer.;* < Sp *estibador,* equiv. to *estib(ar)* to pack, stow (see STEEVE[1]) + *-ador* -ATOR]

ste′vedore's knot′, a knot that forms a lump in a line to prevent it from passing through a hole or grommet. [1860–65]

Ste·ven (stē′vən), *n.* a male given name.

Ste·ven·age (stē′və nij), *n.* a town in N Hertfordshire, in SE England. 73,300.

Ste·ven·graph (stē′vən graf′, -gräf′), *n.* a small picture woven in colored silk thread: introduced in 1879 and mass-produced on a Jacquard-type loom. Also, **Ste·vens·graph** (stē′vənz graf′, -gräf′). [after Thomas *Stevens* (1828–88), English silk-weaver, who developed a mechanical technique to produce the pictures; see -GRAPH]

Ste·vens (stē′vənz), *n.* **1. Alfred,** 1817–75, English painter and sculptor. **2. George (Cooper),** 1905–75, U.S. film director. **3. John Cox** (koks), 1749–1838, and his son **Robert Livingston,** 1787–1856, U.S. engineers and inventors. **4. John Paul,** born 1920, U.S. jurist: associate justice of the U.S. Supreme Court since 1975. **5. Thaddeus,** 1792–1868, U.S. abolitionist and political leader. **6. Wallace,** 1879–1955, U.S. poet.

Ste·ven·son (stē′vən sən), *n.* **1. Ad·lai Ew·ing** (ad′lā yōō′ing), 1835–1914, vice president of the U.S. 1893–97. **2.** his grandson, **Adlai E(wing),** 1900–65, U.S. statesman and diplomat: ambassador to the U.N. 1960–65. **3. Andrew,** 1784–1857, U.S. politician: Speaker of the House 1827–34. **4. Robert Louis** (*Robert Lewis Balfour*), 1850–94, Scottish novelist, essayist, and poet.

Ste′vens Point′, a city in central Wisconsin. 22,970.

Ste·vin (stə vīn′), *n.* **Si·mon** (sē′môn), 1548–1620, Dutch mathematician and physicist.

Stev·i·nus (sti vē′nəs), *n.* See **Stevin, Simon.**

stew[1] (stōō, styōō), *v.t.* **1.** to cook (food) by simmering or slow boiling. —*v.i.* **2.** to undergo cooking by simmering or slow boiling. **3.** *Informal.* to fret, worry, or fuss: *He stewed about his chaotic state of affairs all day.* **4.** to feel uncomfortable due to a hot, humid, stuffy atmosphere, as in a closed room; swelter. **5. stew in one's own juice,** to suffer the consequences of one's own actions. —*n.* **6.** a preparation of meat, fish, or other food cooked by stewing, esp. a mixture of meat and vegetables. **7.** *Informal.* a state of agitation, uneasiness, or worry. **8.** a brothel; whorehouse. **9. stews,** a neighborhood occupied chiefly by brothels. **10.** *Obs.* a vessel for boiling or stewing. [1350–1400; ME *stewen, stuwen* to take a sweat bath < MF *estuver,* v. deriv. of *estuve* sweat room of a bath; see STOVE[1]] **—stew′a·ble,** *adj.*
—Syn. 1. See **boil[1]. 6.** ragout.

stew[2] (stōō, styōō), *n. Slang.* **1.** steward; **2.** stewardess. [by shortening]

stew·ard (stōō′ərd, styōō′-), *n.* **1.** a person who manages another's property or financial affairs; one who administers anything as the agent of another or others. **2.** a person who has charge of the household of another, buying or obtaining food, directing the servants, etc. **3.** an employee who has charge of the table, wine, servants, etc., in a club, restaurant, or the like. **4.** a person who attends to the domestic concerns of persons on board a vessel, as in overseeing maids and waiters. **5.** an employee on a ship, train, or bus who waits on and is responsible for the comfort of passengers, takes orders for or distributes food, etc. **6.** a flight attendant. **7.** a person appointed by an organization or group to supervise the affairs of that group at certain functions. **8.** *U.S. Navy.* a petty officer in charge of officer's quarters and mess. —*v.t.* **9.** to act as steward of; manage. —*v.i.* **10.** to act or serve as steward. [bef. 900; ME; OE *stīweard, stigweard,* equiv. to *stig-* (sense uncert.; prob. "house, hall"; see STY[1]) + *weard* WARD[2]] **—stew′ard·ship′,** *n.*

stew·ard·ess (stōō′ər dis, styōō′-), *n.* **1.** a woman flight attendant. **2.** a woman who attends to the comfort of passengers on a ship, train, or bus. [1625–35 for earlier sense "female steward"; 1930–35 for def. 1; STEWARD + -ESS]
—Usage. See **-ess.**

Stew·art (stōō′ərt, styōō′-), *n.* **1.** Also, **Stuart.** See **Darnley, Lord Henry.** **2. Du·gald** (dōō′gəld, dyōō′-), 1753–1828, Scottish philosopher. **3. Potter,** 1915–85,

CONCISE ETYMOLOGY KEY: <, descended or borrowed from; >, whence; b., blend of, blended; c., cognate with; cf., compare; deriv., derivative; equiv., equivalent; imit., imitative; obl., oblique; r., replacing; s., stem; sp., spelling, spelled; resp., respelling, respelled; trans., translation; ?, origin unknown; *, unattested; ‡, probably earlier than. See the full key inside the front cover.

U.S. jurist: associate justice of the U.S. Supreme Court 1958–81. **4.** a male given name.

Stew′art Is′land, one of the islands of New Zealand, S of South Island. 329; 670 sq. mi. (1735 sq. km).

stew•bum (sto͞o′bum′, styo͞o′-), *n. Slang.* a drunken bum. [1915–20; STEW[1] + BUM]

stewed (sto͞od, styo͞od), *adj.* **1.** cooked by simmering or slow boiling, as food. **2.** *Slang.* intoxicated; drunk. [1400–50; late ME; see STEW[1], -ED[2]]

stew•pan (sto͞o′pan′, styo͞o′-), *n.* a pan for stewing; saucepan. [1625–35; STEW[1] + PAN[1]]

stew•pot (sto͞o′pot′, styo͞o′-), *n.* a large, heavy, covered pot used for making stews. [1535–45; STEW[1] + POT[1]]

St. Ex., Stock Exchange.

St. Francis, a city in SE Wisconsin. 10,066.

stg., sterling.

St. Gal•len (gä′lən), **1.** a canton in NE Switzerland. 384,800; 777 sq. mi. (2010 sq. km). **2.** a city in and the capital of this canton. 77,800. French, **St. Gall** (saN gal′). German, **Sankt Gallen.**

stge., storage.

St. George, a town in SW Utah. 11,350.

St. George's (jôr′jiz), a seaport on and the capital of Grenada, in the SW part. 6657.

St. George's Channel, a channel between Wales and Ireland, connecting the Irish Sea and the Atlantic. 100 mi. (160 km) long; 50–90 mi. (81–145 km) wide.

St.-Ger•main (saN zher maN′), *n.* St.-Germain-en-Laye.

St.-Ger•main-des-Prés (saN zher maN dā prā′), *n.* an area in Paris, on the Left Bank.

St.-Ger•main-en-Laye (saN zher ma näN lā′), *n.* a city in N France, near Paris: royal château and forest; treaties 1570, 1632, 1679, 1919. 40,471. Also called **St.-Germain.**

St. Got•thard (sänt′ got′ərd; *Ger.* zängkt′ gôt′härt), **1.** a mountain range in S Switzerland; a part of the Alps; highest peak, 10,490 ft. (3195 m). **2.** a mountain pass over this range. 6935 ft. (2115 m) high. **3.** a railway tunnel under this pass. 9¼ mi. (15 km) long. French, **St. Gothard** (saN gô tar′).

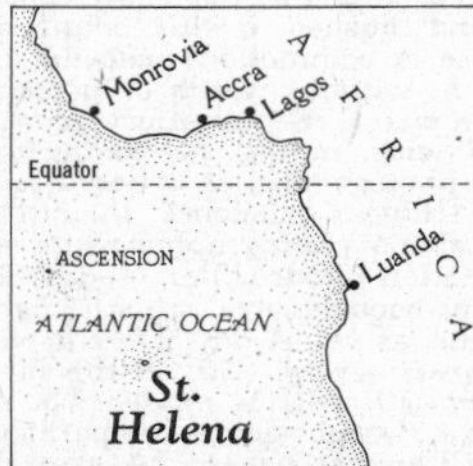

St. He•le•na (hə lē′nə), **1.** a British island in the S Atlantic: Napoleon's place of exile 1815–21. 5147; 47 sq. mi (122 sq. km). **2.** a British colony comprising this island, Ascension Island, and the Tristan da Cunha group. 5147; 126 sq. mi. (326 sq. km). *Cap.:* Jamestown.

St. Hel•ens (hel′ənz), **1.** a city in Merseyside, in NW England, near Liverpool. 194,700. **2. Mount,** an active volcano in SW Washington, part of the Cascade Range: seven major eruptions during 1980, the first since 1854–57. 8364 ft. (2549 m).

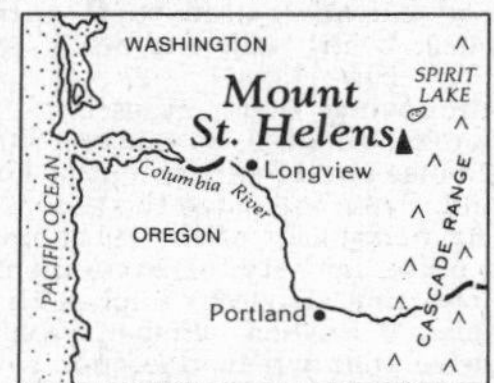

St. Hel•ier (sänt′ hel′yər; *Fr.* saN te lyā′), a seaport on the island of Jersey in the English Channel: resort. 28,135.

sthe•ni•a (sthə nī′ə, sthē′nē ə), *n.* strength; excessive vital force. Cf. **asthenia.** [1780–90; < NL, extracted from ASTHENIA]

sthen•ic (sthen′ik), *adj.* sturdy; heavily and strongly built. [1780–90; extracted from ASTHENIC]

stib•i•al (stib′ē əl), *adj.* of or resembling antimony. [1660–70; STIBI(UM) + -AL[1]]

stib•ine (stib′ēn, -in), *n. Chem.* **1.** a colorless, slightly water-soluble, poisonous gas, SbH_3, usually produced by the reaction of dilute hydrochloric acid with an alloy of antimony and either zinc or magnesium. **2.** any derivative of this compound in which the hydrogen atoms are replaced by one or more organic groups. Also called **antimony hydride.** [1835–45; STIB(IUM) + -INE[2]; cf. ARSINE, PHOSPHINE]

stib•i•um (stib′ē əm), *n. Chem.* antimony. [1350–1400; ME < L *stibi(s), stibium* < Gk *stíbi* (var. of *stímmi* < Egyptian *sdm*)]

stib•nite (stib′nīt), *n.* a soft mineral, antimony sulfide, Sb_2S_3, lead-gray in color with a metallic luster, occurring in crystals, often acicular, or in bladed masses: the most important ore of antimony. [1850–55; STIB(I)NE (in obs. sense "stibnite") + -ITE[1]]

stich[1] (stik), *n.* a verse or line of poetry. [1715–25; < Gk *stíchos* row, line, verse]

stich[2] (stik), *n. Cards.* the last trick, being of special scoring value in certain games, as pinochle or klaberjass. [< G: lit., sting; OHG *stih* prick; see STITCH]

sti•cha•ri•on (stē KHä′RE ôn; *Eng.* sti kâr′ē on′), *n., pl.* **-cha•ri•a** (-KHä′RE ä; *Eng.* -kâr′ē ə). *Gk. Orth. Ch.* a white tunic of silk or linen, corresponding to the alb, worn by deacons, priests, and bishops. [1765–75; < Gk *stichárion,* dim. of *stíchē* tunic]

stich•ic (stik′ik), *adj.* **1.** pertaining to or consisting of stichs or verses. **2.** composed of lines of the same metrical form throughout. [1860–65; < Gk *stichikós.* See STICH[1], -IC] **—stich′i•cal•ly,** *adv.*

sti•chom•e•try (sti kom′i trē), *n.* the practice of writing a prose text in lines, often of slightly differing lengths, that correspond to units of sense and indicate phrasal rhythms. [1745–55; < Gk *stích(os)* (see STICH[1]) + -O- + -METRY] **—stich•o•met•ric** (stik′ə me′trik), **stich′o•met′ri•cal,** *adj.* **—stich′o•met′ri•cal•ly,** *adv.*

sti•cho•myth•i•a (stik′ə mith′ē ə), *n.* dramatic dialogue, as in a Greek play, characterized by brief exchanges between two characters, each of whom usually speaks in one line of verse during a scene of intense emotion or strong argumentation. Also, **sti•chom•y•thy** (sti kom′ə thē). [1860–65; < Gk *stichomȳthía,* equiv. to *stícho(s)* (see STICH[1]) + *-mythia* (*mȳth(os)* speech, story + *-ia* -IA)] **—stich′o•myth′ic,** *adj.*

-stichous, *Bot., Zool.* a combining form meaning "having rows" of the kind or number specified by the initial element: *distichous.* [< LL *-stichus* < Gk *-stichos,* adj. deriv. of *stíchos* STICH[1]]

stick[1] (stik), *n., v.,* **sticked, stick•ing.** **—n. 1.** a branch or shoot of a tree or shrub that has been cut or broken off. **2.** a relatively long and slender piece of wood. **3.** a long piece of wood for use as fuel, in carpentry, etc. **4.** a rod or wand. **5.** a baton. **6.** *Chiefly Brit.* a walking stick or cane. **7.** a club or cudgel. **8.** something that serves to goad or coerce: *The threat of unemployment was the stick that kept the workers toiling overtime.* Cf. **carrot** (def. 3). **9.** a long, slender piece or part of anything: *a stick of candy; sticks of celery.* **10.** any of four equal parts in a pound of butter or margarine. **11.** *Sports.* an implement used to drive or propel a ball or puck, as a crosse or a hockey stick. **12.** *Aeron.* a lever, usually with a handle, by which the longitudinal and lateral motions of an airplane are controlled. **13.** *Naut.* a mast or spar. **14.** *Print.* See **composing stick. 15. the sticks,** *Informal.* any region distant from cities or towns, as rural districts; the country: *Having lived in a large city all his life, he found it hard to adjust to the sticks.* **16.** *Mil.* **a.** a group of bombs so arranged as to be released in a row across a target. **b.** the bomb load. **17.** *Informal.* See **stick shift. 18.** *Slang.* a marijuana cigarette. **19.** *Informal.* an unenthusiastic or uninteresting person. **20.** *Informal.* a portion of liquor, as brandy, added to a nonalcoholic drink. **21. short** or **dirty end of the stick,** *Slang.* the least desirable assignment, decision, or part of an arrangement. **—v.t. 22.** to furnish (a plant, vine, etc.) with a stick or sticks in order to prop or support. **23.** *Print.* to set (type) in a composing stick. [bef. 1000; ME *stikke,* OE *sticca;* akin to OHG *stehho,* ON *stik* stick; akin to STICK[2]] **—stick′less,** *adj.* **—stick′like′,** *adj.*

stick[2] (stik), *v.,* **stuck, stick•ing,** *n.* **—v.t. 1.** to pierce or puncture with something pointed, as a pin, dagger, or spear; stab: *to stick one's finger with a needle.* **2.** to kill by this means: *to stick a pig.* **3.** to thrust (something pointed) in, into, through, etc.: *to stick a needle into a pincushion.* **4.** to fasten in position by thrusting a point or end into something: *to stick a peg in a pegboard.* **5.** to fasten in position by or as if by something thrust through: *to stick a painting on the wall.* **6.** to put on or hold with something pointed; impale: *to stick a marshmallow on a fork.* **7.** to decorate or furnish with things piercing the surface: *to stick a cushion full of pins.* **8.** to furnish or adorn with things attached or set here and there: *to stick shelves full of knickknacks.* **9.** to place upon a stick or pin for exhibit: *to stick butterflies.* **10.** to thrust or poke into a place or position indicated: *to stick one's head out of the window.* **11.** to place or set in a specified position; put: *Stick the chair in the corner.* **12.** to fasten or attach by causing to adhere: *to stick a stamp on a letter.* **13.** to bring to a standstill; render unable to proceed or go back (usually used in the passive): *The car was stuck in the mud.* **14.** *Carpentry.* to start (a nail). **15.** *Ceram.* to join (pieces of partially hardened clay) together, using slip as an adhesive. **16.** *Chiefly Brit. Informal.* to tolerate; endure: *He couldn't stick the job more than three days.* **17.** to confuse or puzzle; bewilder; perplex; nonplus: *He was stuck by the very first problem on the test.* **18.** *Informal.* to impose something disagreeable upon (a person or persons), as a large bill or a difficult task: *The committee persistently stuck him with fund collection.* **19.** *Informal.* to cheat. **20.** *Slang (often vulgar).* to go to hell with: often used imperatively.
—v.i. 21. to have the point piercing or embedded in something: *The arrow stuck in the tree.* **22.** to remain attached by adhesion. **23.** to hold, cleave, or cling: *The young rider stuck to the back of his terrified horse.* **24.** to remain persistently or permanently: *a fact that sticks in the mind.* **25.** to remain firm, as in resolution, opinion, statement, or attachment; hold faithfully, as to a promise or bargain. **26.** to keep or remain steadily or unremittingly, as to a task, undertaking, or the like: *to stick to a job until it is finished.* **27.** to become fastened, hindered, checked, or stationary by some obstruction: *Her zipper stuck halfway up.* **28.** to be at a standstill, as from difficulties: *I'm stuck on this problem.* **29.** to be embarrassed or puzzled; hesitate or scruple (usually fol. by *at*). **30.** to be thrust or placed so as to extend, project, or protrude (usually fol. by *through, from, out, up,* etc.). **31. stick around,** *Informal.* to wait in the vicinity; linger: *If you had stuck around, you'd have seen the fireworks.* **32. stick by** or **to,** to maintain one's attachment or loyalty to; remain faithful to: *They vowed to stick by one another no matter what happened.* **33. stick it,** *Slang (often vulgar).* See **shove**[1] (def. 5). **34. stick it to (someone),** *Slang.* to take advantage of; treat unfairly. **35. stick it out,** to endure something patiently to the end or its completion: *It was a long, dusty trip but we stuck it out.* **36. stick it up your** or **one's ass,** *Slang (vulgar).* See **shove**[1] (def. 6). **37. stick one's neck out.** See **neck** (def. 20). **38. stick out,** to extend; protrude: *Stick out your tongue. Your shirttail is sticking out.* **39. stick to one's guns.** See **gun**[1] (def. 11). **40. stick to the** or **one's ribs,** to be substantial and nourishing, as a hearty meal: *Hot cereal sticks to your ribs on those cold winter mornings.* **41. stick up,** *Informal.* to rob, esp. at gunpoint: *A lone gunman stuck up the gas station.* **42. stick up for,** to speak in favor of; come to the defense of; support: *She always sticks up for him, even though he doesn't deserve it.* **—n. 43.** a thrust with a pointed instrument; stab. **44.** a stoppage or standstill. **45.** something causing delay or difficulty. **46.** the quality of adhering or of causing things to adhere. **47.** something causing adhesion. [bef. 900; ME *stiken,* OE *stician* to pierce, thrust; akin to G *stechen* to sting, L *-stig-* in *instigāre* (see INSTIGATE), Gk *stízein* (see STIGMA)] **—stick′a•ble,** *adj.* **—stick′a•bil′i•ty** *n.*
—Syn. 1. penetrate, spear. **6.** transfix. **9.** pin. **12.** glue, cement, paste. **22.** STICK, ADHERE, COHERE mean to cling to or be tightly attached to something. ADHERE implies that one kind of material clings tenaciously to another; COHERE adds the idea that a thing is attracted to and held by something like itself: *Particles of sealing wax cohere and form a mass that will adhere to tin.* STICK, a more colloquial and general term, is used particularly when a third kind of material is involved: *A gummed label will stick to a package.* **29.** stickle, waver, doubt.

stick-at-it-ive (stik′at′it iv, -i tiv), *adj. Informal.* stick-to-it-ive. **—stick′-at′-it-ive•ness,** *n.*

stick•ball (stik′bôl′), *n.* a form of baseball played in the streets, on playgrounds, etc., in which a rubber ball and a broomstick or the like are used in place of a baseball and bat. [1815–25, *Amer.*; (BROOM)STICK + BALL[1]] **—stick′ball′er,** *n.*

stick-built (stik′bilt′), *adj.* (of a house or other structure) built piece-by-piece at the construction site, as opposed to factory-built. [1835–45]

stick•er (stik′ər), *n.* **1.** a person or thing that sticks. **2.** an adhesive label. **3.** *Informal.* See **sticker price. 4.** something, as a problem or riddle, that puzzles or nonpluses one. **5.** *Slang.* a knife, esp. one used as a weapon by a criminal. **6.** a worker who kills animals in a slaughterhouse by piercing the jugular vein with a pointed instrument. **7.** a bur, thorn, or the like. **—adj. 8.** of or pertaining to the sticker price of an automobile: *Customers are experiencing sticker shock at the high price of new cars.* **—v.t. 9.** to place a sticker on. [1575–85; STICK[2] + -ER[1]]

stick′er price′, 1. the dealer's full asking price of a new automobile as shown on a sticker attached to it and accompanied by an itemized list of the cost of its basic and optional equipment and other charges. **2.** the retailer's full asking price of various other manufactured consumer items; list price.

stick′ fig′ure, a diagrammatic drawing representing a human or animal, usually made with one line each for the torso and appendages, and often a circle for the head. Also called **stick′ draw′ing.** [‡1945–50]

stick•ful (stik′fo͝ol′), *n., pl.* **-fuls.** *Print.* as much set type as a composing stick will hold, usually about two column inches. [1675–85; STICK[1] + -FUL]
—Usage. See **-ful.**

stick•han•dler (stik′hand′lər), *n.* a hockey or lacrosse player, esp. one who is talented at stickhandling. Also, **stick′ han′dler.** [1910–15; STICK[1] + HANDLER]

stick•han•dling (stik′hand′ling), *n.* (in hockey and lacrosse) the art of controlling and skillfully maneuvering the ball or puck with the stick. Also, **stick′ han′•dling.** [1900–05; STICK[1] + HANDLING]

stick′ing place′, 1. Also called **sticking point.** the place or point at which something stops and holds firm. **2.** the place in the lower part of an animal's neck where the knife is thrust in slaughtering. [1570–80]

stick′ing plas′ter, an adhesive cloth or other material for covering and closing superficial wounds, holding bandages in place, etc. [1645–55]

stick′ing point′, 1. a point, detail, or circumstance causing or likely to cause a stalemate or impasse: *The bill would have gone through the Senate quickly but for one sticking point.* **2.** See **sticking place** (def. 1). [1820–30]

stick′ in′sect. See **walking stick** (def. 2). [1850–55]

stick-in-the-mud (stik′in *th*ə mud′), *n.* someone who avoids new activities, ideas, or attitudes; old fogy. [1725–35]

stick•it (stik′it), *adj. Scot.* **1.** (of a task or product) imperfect; ruined. **2.** (of a person) unsuccessful, esp. in a chosen occupation. [1780–90; var. of *sticked.* See STICK[2], -ED[2]]

stick•le (stik′əl), *v.i.,* **-led, -ling. 1.** to argue or haggle insistently, esp. on trivial matters. **2.** to raise objections; scruple; demur. [1520–30; var. of obs. *stightle* to set in order, freq. of *stight* to set in order, ME *stighten,* OE *stihtan* to arrange; c. G *stiften,* ON *stētta* to set up]

stick•le•back (stik′əl bak′), *n.* any of the small, pugnacious, spiny-backed fishes of the family Gastero-

CONCISE PRONUNCIATION KEY: act, cāpe, dâre, pärt; set, ēqual; *if,* īce; ox, ōver, ôrder, oil, bo͝ok, bo͞ot, out; up, ûrge; child; sing; shoe; thin, *th*at; zh as in *treasure.* ə = a as in *alone,* e as in *system,* i as in *easily,* o as in *gallop,* u as in *circus;* ə as in *fire* (fīər), *hour* (ouər). l and n can serve as syllabic consonants, as in *cradle* (krād′l), and *button* (but′n). See the full key inside the front cover.

steidae, inhabiting northern fresh waters and sea inlets, the male of which builds and guards the nest. Also called **prickleback.** [1400–50; late ME *stykylbak,* equiv. to OE *sticol* scaly + *bæc* BACK[1]]

stickleback, *Culaea inconstans,* length 2½ in. (6.4 cm)

stick•ler (stik′lər), *n.* **1.** a person who insists on something unyieldingly (usually fol. by *for*): *a stickler for ceremony.* **2.** any puzzling or difficult problem. [1530–40; STICKLE + -ER[1]]
—Syn. 1. fanatic, purist, perfectionist. **2.** puzzle, riddle, mystery.

stick•man (stik′man′, -mən), *n., pl.* **-men** (-men′, -mən). croupier (def. 1). [1930–35, *Amer.*; STICK[1] + MAN[1]]

stick-on (stik′on′, -ôn′), *n.* a label, sticker, or the like, that has an adhesive backing. [n. use of the v. phrase *stick on*]

stick•out (stik′out′), *Informal.* **—n. 1.** a person who is outstanding or conspicuous, usually for superior endowments, talents, etc.: *Jimmy Brown is the stickout among running backs.* **—adj. 2.** outstanding; conspicuous: *a stickout actor.* [1840–50; n., adj. use of v. phrase *stick out*]

stick•pin (stik′pin′), *n.* a decorative straight pin with a jeweled or ornamented head and a long shaft with a sheath for encasing the point, used for holding an ascot or necktie in place. [1900–05, *Amer.*; STICK[2] + PIN]

stick•seed (stik′sēd′), *n.* any of the weedy plants belonging to the genus *Lappula,* having prickly seeds that adhere to clothing. [1835–45, *Amer.*; STICK[2] + SEED]

stick′ shift′, a manually operated transmission for an automotive vehicle, with the shift lever set either in the floor or on the steering column. [1955–60]

Stick′ Style′, a style in mid-Victorian American wooden architecture characterized by the use of vertical board siding with battens or grids of boards over horizontal siding to express the framing beneath.

stick•tight (stik′tīt′), *n.* **1.** any of several composite plants of the genus *Bidens,* having barbed achenes that adhere to clothing or fur. **2.** any of various other plants having seeds that adhere to clothing or fur. **3.** a seed of any of these plants. [n. use of v. phrase *stick tight*]

stick-to-it-ive (stik′to͞o′i tiv, -it iv), *adj. Informal.* tenaciously resolute; persevering: *Stick-to-it-ive people get ahead in life.* [1865–70, *Amer.*; *stick to it* + -IVE] **—stick′-to′-it-ive-ness,** *n.*

stick•um (stik′əm), *n. Informal.* any adhesive substance. [1905–10; STICK[2] + *-um* (sp. var. of 'EM)]

stick•up (stik′up′), *n. Informal.* a holdup; robbery. Also, **stick′-up′.** [1855–60; n. use of v. phrase *stick up*]

stick′up man′, *Informal.* a man who commits a stickup. [1930–35]

stick•weed (stik′wēd′), *n.* the ragweed. [1735–45, *Amer.*; STICK[2] + WEED[1]]

stick•work (stik′wûrk′), *n. Sports.* a player's degree of competence or proficiency as a baseball batter, hockey or lacrosse player, etc.: *Frequent practice improved his stickwork.* [1900–05; STICK[1] + WORK]

stick•y (stik′ē), *adj.,* **stick•i•er, stick•i•est. 1.** having the property of adhering, as glue; adhesive. **2.** covered with adhesive or viscid matter: *sticky hands.* **3.** (of the weather or climate) hot and humid: *It was an unbearably sticky day.* **4.** requiring careful treatment; awkwardly difficult: *a rather sticky diplomatic problem; Breaking the news is going to be sticky.* **5.** *Informal.* unpleasant; unfortunate; nasty: *The villain of the story meets a sticky end.* [1720–30; 1910–15 for def. 4; STICK[2] + -Y[1]] **—stick′i•ly,** *adv.* **—stick′i•ness,** *n.*
—Syn. 3. muggy, sultry, damp, steamy.

stick•y•beak (stik′ē bēk′), *n. Australian Slang.* a busybody; meddler. [1925–30; STICKY + BEAK]

stick′y bun′, *Chiefly Northern and Western U.S.* See **honey bun** (def. 1).

stick′y end′, *Genetics, Biotech.* a single-stranded end of DNA or RNA having a nucleotide base sequence complementary to that of another strand, enabling the two strands to be connected by base pairing: produced in the laboratory with the use of restriction enzymes for genetic engineering purposes. [1970–75]

stick′y fin′gers, *Informal.* a propensity to steal. [1930–35] **—stick•y-fin•gered** (stik′ē fing′gərd), *adj.*

stick′y wick′et, 1. *Cricket.* the area of ground around a wicket when it is tacky because of recent rain and therefore does not allow the ball to bounce well. **2.** *Chiefly Brit.* a situation requiring delicate treatment; an awkward situation: *In telling his wife that he has to be away for a month in Cannes, he'll be batting on a sticky wicket.* [1925–30]

Stie•gel (stē′gəl; *Ger.* shtē′gəl), *n.* **Henry William,** 1729–85, German iron and glass manufacturer in America.

Stieg•litz (stēg′lits), *n.* **Alfred,** 1864–1946, U.S. photographer and editor (husband of Georgia O'Keeffe).

CONCISE ETYMOLOGY KEY: <, descended or borrowed from; >, whence; b., blend of, blended; c., cognate with; cf., compare; deriv., derivative; equiv., equivalent; imit., imitative; obl., oblique; r., replacing; s., stem; sp., spelling, spelled; resp., respelling, respelled; trans., translation; ?, origin unknown; *, unattested; ‡, probably earlier than. See the full key inside the front cover.

stiff (stif), *adj.,* **-er, -est,** *n., adv., v.* **—adj. 1.** rigid or firm; difficult or impossible to bend or flex: *a stiff collar.* **2.** not moving or working easily: *The motor was a little stiff from the cold weather.* **3.** (of a person or animal) not supple; moving with difficulty, as from cold, age, exhaustion, or injury. **4.** strong; forceful; powerful: *stiff winds; The fighter threw a stiff right to his opponent's jaw.* **5.** strong or potent to the taste or system, as a beverage or medicine: *He was cold and wanted a good stiff drink.* **6.** resolute; firm in purpose; unyielding; stubborn. **7.** stubbornly continued: *a stiff battle.* **8.** firm against any tendency to decrease, as stock-market prices. **9.** rigidly formal; cold and unfriendly, as people, manners, or proceedings. **10.** lacking ease and grace; awkward: *a stiff style of writing.* **11.** excessively regular or formal, as a design; not graceful in form or arrangement. **12.** laborious or difficult, as a task. **13.** severe or harsh, as a penalty or demand. **14.** excessive; unusually high or great: *$50 is pretty stiff to pay for that.* **15.** firm from tension; taut: *to keep a stiff rein.* **16.** relatively firm in consistency, as semisolid matter; thick: *a stiff jelly; a stiff batter.* **17.** dense or compact; not friable: *stiff soil.* **18.** *Naut.* (of a vessel) having a high resistance to rolling; stable (opposed to *crank*). **19.** *Scot. and North Eng.* sturdy, stout, or strongly built. **20.** *Australian Slang.* out of luck; unfortunate. **—n. 21.** *Slang.* **a.** a dead body; corpse. **b.** a formal or priggish person. **c.** a poor tipper; tightwad. **d.** a drunk. **22.** *Slang.* **a.** a fellow: *lucky stiff; poor stiff.* **b.** a tramp; hobo. **c.** a laborer. **23.** *Slang.* **a.** a forged check. **b.** a promissory note or bill of exchange. **c.** a letter or note, esp. if secret or smuggled. **24.** *Slang.* a contestant, esp. a racehorse, sure to lose. **—adv. 25.** in or to a firm or rigid state: *The wet shirt was frozen stiff.* **26.** completely, intensely, or extremely: *I'm bored stiff by these lectures. We're scared stiff.* **—v.t. 27.** *Slang.* to fail or refuse to tip (a waiter, porter, etc.). **28.** *Slang.* to cheat; gyp; do out of: *The company stiffed me out of a week's pay.* [bef. 1000; ME (adj. and adv.); OE *stīf;* c. G *steif;* akin to STIFLE[1], STEEVE[1]] **—stiff′ish,** *adj.* **—stiff′ly,** *adv.* **—stiff′ness,** *n.*
—Syn. 1. unbending, unyielding. See **firm**[1]. **6.** unrelenting, resolved, obstinate, pertinacious. **9.** reserved, constrained, starched, prim. **10.** graceless, inelegant.

stiff-arm (stif′ärm′), *v.t., n.* straight-arm. [1905–10]

stiff•en (stif′ən), *v.t.* **1.** to make stiff. **—v.i. 2.** to become stiff. **3.** to become suddenly tense, rigid, or taut, as in bracing oneself for or drawing back from shock, fear, or displeasure: *He stiffened, expecting to hear the worst.* [1490–1500; STIFF + -EN[1]]

stiff•en•er (stif′ə nər, stif′nər), *n.* **1.** a person or thing that stiffens. **2.** any substance, as starch or buckram, that serves to stiffen fabric. [1690–1700; STIFFEN + -ER[1]]

stiff-necked (stif′nekt′), *adj.* **1.** having a stiff neck; having torticollis. **2.** haughty and obstinate; refractory. [1520–30] **—stiff•neck•ed•ly** (stif′nek′id lē, -nekt′lē), *adv.* **—stiff′neck′ed•ness,** *n.*
—Syn. 2. stubborn, obstinate, intractable, willful, pigheaded.

sti•fle[1] (stī′fəl), *v.,* **-fled, -fling.** **—v.t. 1.** to quell, crush, or end by force: *to stifle a revolt; to stifle free expression.* **2.** to suppress, curb, or withhold: *to stifle a yawn.* **3.** to kill by impeding respiration; smother. **—v.i. 4.** to suffer from difficulty in breathing, as in a close atmosphere. **5.** to become stifled or suffocated. [1350–1400; ME < ON *stifla* to stop up, dam, akin to *stīfr* stiff] **—sti′fler,** *n.*
—Syn. 1. prevent, preclude, put down. **2.** check. **3.** suffocate, strangle, choke. **—Ant. 1, 2.** encourage.

sti•fle[2] (stī′fəl), *n.* (in a horse or other quadruped) the joint between the femur and the tibia, corresponding anatomically to the human knee. Also called **sti′fle joint′.** See diag. under **horse.** [1275–1325; ME < ?]

sti•fling (stī′fling), *adj.* suffocating; oppressively close: *the stifling atmosphere of the cavern.* [1550–60; STIFLE[1] + -ING[2]] **—sti′fling•ly,** *adv.*

stig•ma (stig′mə), *n., pl.* **stig•ma•ta** (stig′mə tə, stig mä′tə, -mat′ə), **stig•mas. 1.** a mark of disgrace or infamy; a stain or reproach, as on one's reputation. **2.** *Med.* **a.** a mental or physical mark that is characteristic of a defect or disease: *the stigmata of leprosy.* **b.** a place or point on the skin that bleeds during certain mental states, as in hysteria. **3.** *Zool.* **a.** a small mark, spot, or pore on an animal or organ. **b.** the eyespot of a protozoan. **c.** an entrance into the respiratory system of insects. **4.** *Bot.* the part of a pistil that receives the pollen. See diag. under **flower. 5. stigmata,** marks resembling the wounds of the crucified body of Christ, said to be supernaturally impressed on the bodies of certain persons, esp. nuns, tertiaries, and monastics. **6.** *Archaic.* a mark made by a branding iron on the skin of a criminal or slave. [1580–90; < L < Gk *stígma* tattoo mark, equiv. to *stig-* (s. of *stízein* to tattoo) + *-ma* n. suffix denoting result of action; see STICK[2]]
—Syn. 1. blot, blemish, tarnish.

stig•mas•ter•ol (stig mas′tə rôl′, -rōl′), *n. Biochem.* a crystalline, water-insoluble steroid, $C_{29}H_{48}O$, present in soybeans or calabar beans, used chiefly as a raw material in the manufacture of progesterone. [1920–25; < NL (*Physo*)*stigma* (see PHYSOSTIGMINE) + STEROL]

stig•mat•ic (stig mat′ik), *adj.* Also, **stig•mat′i•cal. 1.** pertaining to a stigma, mark, spot, or the like. **2.** *Bot.* pertaining to or having the character of a stigma. **3.** *Optics.* converging to a point; anastigmatic. **—n. 4.** a person marked with supernatural stigmata. [1585–95; < ML *stigmaticus,* equiv. to *stigmat-* (s. of *stigma* STIGMA) + *-icus* -IC] **—stig•mat′i•cal•ly,** *adv.* **—stig•mat′i•cal•ness,** *n.*

stig•ma•tism (stig′mə tiz′əm), *n.* **1.** *Optics.* the property of a lens that is stigmatic. **2.** *Pathol.* a condition in which stigmata are present. [1655–65; *stigmat-* (see STIGMATIC) + -ISM]

stig•ma•tist (stig′mə tist), *n.* a person who bears stigmata. [1600–10; STIGMAT(A) + -IST]

stig•ma•tize (stig′mə tīz′), *v.t.,* **-tized, -tiz•ing. 1.** to set some mark of disgrace or infamy upon: *The crime of the father stigmatized the whole family.* **2.** to mark with a stigma or brand. **3.** to produce stigmata, marks, spots, or the like, on. Also, *esp. Brit.,* **stig′ma•tise′.** [1575–85; < ML *stigmatizāre,* equiv. to *stigmat-* (see STIGMATIC) + *-izāre* -IZE] **—stig′ma•ti•za′tion,** *n.* **—stig′ma•tiz′er,** *n.*

Stijl, De (də stīl), *Dutch.* a group of Dutch artists of the early 20th century whose theories and works influenced the development of contemporary architecture and applied arts. Cf. **neoplasticism.** [lit., *The Style,* title of a periodical associated with the group]

stilb (stilb), *n. Optics.* a unit of luminance, equal to one candle per square centimeter. [< Gk *stílbē* lamp]

stil•bene (stil′bēn), *n. Chem.* a colorless to slightly yellow, crystalline, water-insoluble solid, $C_{14}H_{12}$, used chiefly in the manufacture of dyes **(stil′bene dyes′).** [1865–70; < Gk *stilb-* (s. of *stílbein* to shine) + -ENE]

stil•bite (stil′bīt), *n.* a white-to-brown or red zeolite mineral, a hydrous silicate of calcium and aluminum, occurring in sheaflike aggregates of crystals and in radiated masses. [1805–15; < Gk *stilb-* (s. of *stílbein* to shine) + -ITE[1]]

stile[1] (stīl), *n.* **1.** a series of steps or rungs by means of which a person may pass over a wall or fence that remains a barrier to sheep or cattle. **2.** a turnstile. [bef. 900; ME; OE *stigel,* deriv. of *stīgan* to climb, c. G *steigen*]

stile[2] (stīl), *n. Carpentry, Furniture.* any of various upright members framing panels or the like, as in a system of paneling, a paneled door, window sash, or chest of drawers. Cf. **rail**[1] (def. 8). [1670–80; perh. < D *stijl* (door-, bed-) post, strut]

sti•let•to (sti let′ō), *n., pl.* **-tos, -toes,** *v.,* **-toed, -to•ing. —n. 1.** a short dagger with a blade that is thick in proportion to its width. **2.** a pointed instrument for making eyelet holes in needlework. **—v.t. 3.** to stab or kill with a stiletto. [1605–15; < It, equiv. to *stil(o)* dagger (< L *stilus* STYLUS) + *-etto* -ETTE] **—sti•let′to•like′,** *adj.*

stilet′to heel′. See **spike heel.** [1950–55]

Stil•i•cho (stil′i kō′), *n.* **Fla•vi•us** (flā′vē əs), A.D. 359?–408, Roman general and statesman.

still[1] (stil), *adj.,* **-er, -est,** *n., adv., conj., v.* **—adj. 1.** remaining in place or at rest; motionless; stationary: *to stand still.* **2.** free from sound or noise, as a place or persons; silent: *to keep still about a matter.* **3.** subdued or low in sound; hushed: *a still, small voice.* **4.** free from turbulence or commotion; peaceful; tranquil; calm: *the still air.* **5.** without waves or perceptible current; not flowing, as water. **6.** not effervescent or sparkling, as wine. **7.** *Photog.* noting, pertaining to, or used for making single photographs, as opposed to a motion picture. **—n. 8.** stillness or silence: *the still of the night.* **9.** *Photog.* a single photographic print, as one of the frames of a motion-picture film. **—adv. 10.** at this or that time; as previously: *Are you still here?* **11.** up to this or that time; as yet: *A day before departure we were still lacking an itinerary.* **12.** in the future as in the past: *Objections will still be made.* **13.** even; in addition; yet (used to emphasize a comparative): *still more complaints; still greater riches.* **14.** even then; yet; nevertheless: *to be rich and still crave more.* **15.** without sound or movement; quietly: *Sit still!* **16.** at or to a greater distance or degree. **17.** *Archaic.* steadily; constantly; always. **—conj. 18.** and yet; but yet; nevertheless: *It was futile, still they fought.* **19. still and all,** nonetheless; even with everything considered: *Even though you dislike us, still and all you should be polite.* **—v.t. 20.** to silence or hush (sounds, voices, etc.). **21.** to calm, appease, or allay: *to still a craving.* **22.** to quiet, subdue, or cause to subside (waves, winds, commotion, tumult, passion, pain, etc.). **—v.i. 23.** to become still or quiet. [bef. 900; (adj. and adv.) ME *still(e),* OE *stille;* (n.) ME: a calm, deriv. of the adj.; (v.) ME *styllen,* OE *stillan;* (conj.) deriv. of the adv.; akin to G *still* (adj.), *stille* (adv.), *stillen* (v.), D *stil* (adj. and adv.), *stillen* (v.); see STALL[1]]
—Syn. 1. unmoving, inert, quiescent. **2.** soundless, mute. STILL, QUIET, HUSHED, NOISELESS, SILENT indicate the absence of noise and of excitement or activity accompanied by sound. STILL indicates the absence of sound or movement: *The house was still.* QUIET implies relative freedom from noise, activity, or excitement: *a quiet engine; a quiet vacation.* HUSHED implies the suppression of sound or noise: *a hushed whisper.* NOISELESS and SILENT characterize that which does not reveal its presence or movement by any sound: *a noiseless footstep; silent dissent.* **4.** pacific, placid, serene. **8.** quiet, hush, calm. **18.** See **but**[1]. **20.** quiet, mute, stifle, muffle, smother. **21.** soothe, pacify.

still[2] (stil), *n.* **1.** a distilling apparatus, consisting of a vessel in which a liquid is heated and vaporized and a cooling device or coil for condensing the vapor. **2.** a distillery. **—v.t., v.i. 3.** to distill. [1250–1300; (v.) ME *stillen,* aph. var. of *distillen* to DISTILL; (n.) deriv. of the v.]

Still (stil), *n.* **1. Andrew Taylor,** 1828–1917, U.S. founder of osteopathy. **2. William Grant,** 1895–1978, U.S. composer.

stil•lage (stil′ij), *n.* a low platform on which goods are stored in a warehouse or factory to keep them off the floor, to aid in handling, etc. Cf. **skid** (def. 3). [1590–1600; < D *stellage,* equiv. to *stell(en)* to place + *-age* -AGE]

still′ alarm′, a burglar alarm, fire alarm, or the like, that is activated silently and transmits a warning signal, usually by telephone. [1870–75, *Amer.*]

still•birth (stil′bûrth′), *n.* **1.** the birth of a dead child or organism. **2.** a fetus dead at birth. [1745–55; STILL[1] + BIRTH]

still•born (stil′bôrn′), *adj.* **1.** dead when born. **2.** ineffectual from the beginning; abortive; fruitless: *a stillborn plan of escape.* [1590–1600; STILL[1] + BORN]

still′ hunt′, 1. a hunt for game carried on stealthily,

as by stalking, or under cover, as in ambush. **2.** *Informal.* a quiet or secret pursuit of any object. [1820–30]

still-hunt (stil′hunt′), *v.t.* **1.** to pursue or ambush by a still hunt. —*v.i.* **2.** to carry on a still hunt. [1855–60, *Amer.*] —**still′-hunt′er,** *n.*

stil·li·form (stil′ə fôrm′), *adj.* drop-shaped; globular. [*stilli-* (comb. form of L *stilla* drop) + -FORM]

still′ life′, *pl.* **still lifes. 1.** a representation chiefly of inanimate objects, as a painting of a bowl of fruit. **2.** the category of subject matter in which inanimate objects are represented, as in painting or photography. [1635–45] —**still′-life′,** *adj.*

still·ness (stil′nis), *n.* **1.** silence; quiet; hush. **2.** the absence of motion. [bef. 1000; ME *stilnesse,* OE *stilnes.* See STILL[1], -NESS]

still′ pack′, *Cards.* the pack not in play in a game in which two packs are used alternately.

still·room (stil′ro͞om′, -ro͝om′), *n.* **1.** (in a large house) a room for distilling or for the preparation of special foods and drinks. **2.** a room off a kitchen for making tea, coffee, etc., and for storing liquors, tea, preserves, jams, wine, etc. [1700–10; STILL[2] + ROOM]

Still′son wrench′ (stil′sən), *Trademark.* a monkey wrench with a pivoted, adjustable jaw that grips pipes, bars, etc., more tightly when pressure is exerted on the handle.

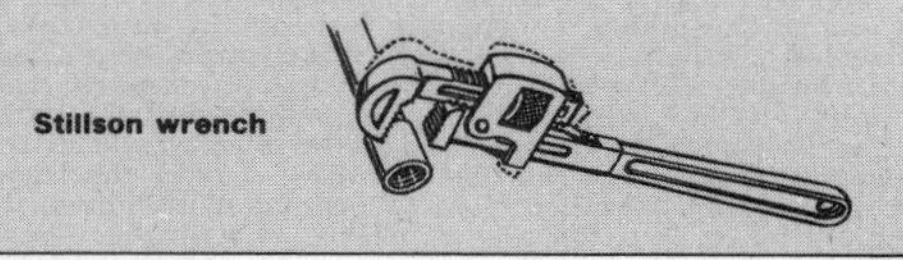
Stillson wrench

still′ trail′er, any dog that follows the trail of its quarry silently. Cf. **open trailer.**

still′ wa′ter, a part of a stream that is level or where the level of inclination is so slight that no current is visible. [1620–30]

Still·wa·ter (stil′wô′tər, -wot′ər), *n.* **1.** a city in N Oklahoma. 38,268. **2.** a town in E Minnesota. 12,290.

still′ wine′, any nonsparkling table wine.

stil·ly (*adv.* stil′lē; *adj.* stil′ē), *adv.* **1.** quietly; silently. —*adj.* **2.** *Chiefly Literary.* still; quiet. [bef. 1000; ME (adv.); OE *stillice.* See STILL[1], -LY]

stilt (stilt), *n.* **1.** one of two poles, each with a support for the foot at some distance above the bottom end, enabling the wearer to walk with his or her feet above the ground. **2.** one of several posts supporting a structure built above the surface of land or water. **3.** *Ceram.* a three-armed support for an object being fired. **4.** any of several white-and-black wading birds, esp. *Cladorhynchus leucocephalus* and *Himantopus himantopus,* having long, bright pink legs and a long, slender black bill. **5.** *Brit. Dial.* **a.** a plow handle. **b.** a crutch. —*v.t.* **6.** to raise on or as if on stilts. [1275–1325; ME *stilte;* c. LG *stilte* pole, G *Stelze*] —**stilt′like′,** *adj.*

stilt′ bug′, any of various slender, long-legged, brownish bugs of the family Berytidae, inhabiting dense vegetation: sometimes classified with the leaf-footed bugs. [1890–95]

stilt·ed (stil′tid), *adj.* **1.** stiffly dignified or formal, as speech or literary style; pompous. **2.** *Archit.* (of an arch) resting on imposts treated in part as downward continuations of the arch. See illus. under **arch**[1]. [1610–20; STILT + -ED[3]]
—**Syn. 1.** wooden, mannered, stuffy, constrained.

Stil·ton (stil′tn), *Trademark.* a rich, waxy, white cheese, veined with mold: made principally in England. Also called **Stil′ton cheese′.** [1730–40; after *Stilton,* England, where it was first sold]

Stil·well (stil′wel, -wəl), *n.* **Joseph W.** (*"Vinegar Joe"*), 1883–1946, U.S. general.

sti·lya·ga (styi lyä′gə; *Eng.* stil yä′gə), *n., pl.,* **-gi** (-gyi; *Eng.* -gē). *Russian.* (in the Soviet Union) a person, usually young, who adopts the unconventional manner and dress of some Western youth groups, as rockers or punk-rock fans.

stime (stīm), *n. Scot., Irish Eng.* the smallest bit; a drop, taste, or glimpse. [1250–1300; ME (Scots); perh. < ON *skimi* a glimpse]

Stim·son (stim′sən), *n.* **Henry L(ewis),** 1867–1950, U.S. statesman: Secretary of War 1911–13, 1940–45; Secretary of State 1929–33.

stim·u·lant (stim′yə lənt), *n.* **1.** *Physiol., Med.* something that temporarily quickens some vital process or the functional activity of some organ or part: *Adrenalin is a stimulant for the heart.* **2.** any food or beverage that stimulates, esp. coffee, tea, or, in its initial effect, alcoholic liquor. **3.** a stimulus or incentive. —*adj.* **4.** *Physiol., Med.* temporarily quickening some vital process or functional activity. **5.** stimulating. Cf. **depressant.** [1720–30; < L *stimulant-* (s. of *stimulāns,* prp. of *stimulāre* to goad). See STIMULUS, -ANT]

stim·u·late (stim′yə lāt′), *v.,* **-lat·ed, -lat·ing.** —*v.t.* **1.** to rouse to action or effort, as by encouragement or pressure; spur on; incite: *to stimulate his interest in mathematics.* **2.** *Physiol., Med.* to excite (a nerve, gland, etc.) to its functional activity. **3.** to invigorate (a person) by a food or beverage containing a stimulant, as coffee, tea, or alcoholic liquor. —*v.i.* **4.** to act as a stimulus or stimulant. [1540–50; < L *stimulātus* (ptp. of *stimulāre* to goad). See STIMULUS, -ATE[1]] —**stim′u·la·ble,** *adj.* —**stim·u·la·bil·i·ty** (stim′yə lə bil′i tē), *n.* —**stim′u·lat′ing·ly,** *adv.* —**stim′u·la′tion,** *n.* —**stim′u·la′tor, stim′u·lat′er,** *n.*
—**Syn. 1.** arouse, activate, excite. See **animate.**

stim·u·la·tive (stim′yə lā′tiv), *adj.* **1.** serving to stimulate. —*n.* **2.** a stimulating agency. [1740–50; STIMULATE + -IVE] —**stim′u·la′tive·ly,** *adv.* —**stim′u·la′tive·ness,** *n.*

stim·u·lus (stim′yə ləs), *n., pl.* **-li** (-lī′). **1.** something that incites to action or exertion or quickens action, feeling, thought, etc.: *The approval of others is a potent stimulus.* **2.** *Physiol., Med.* something that excites an organism or part to functional activity. [1605–15; < L: a goad]
—**Syn. 1.** incitement, enticement, motive, provocation. **2.** stimulant. —**Ant. 1.** discouragement.

stim′ulus generaliza′tion, *Psychol.* generalization (def. 4a).

sti·my (stī′mē), *n., pl.* **-mies,** *v.t.,* **-mied, -my·ing.** stymie.

sting (sting), *v.,* **stung** or (*Obs.*) **stang; stung; sting·ing;** *n.* —*v.t.* **1.** to prick or wound with a sharp-pointed, often venom-bearing organ. **2.** to affect painfully or irritatingly as a result of contact, as certain plants do: *to be stung by nettles.* **3.** to cause to smart or to cause a sharp pain: *The blowing sand stung his eyes.* **4.** to cause mental or moral anguish: *to be stung with remorse.* **5.** to goad or drive, as by sharp irritation. **6.** *Slang.* to cheat or take advantage of, esp. to overcharge; soak. —*v.i.* **7.** to use, have, or wound with a sting, as bees. **8.** to cause a sharp, smarting pain, as some plants, an acrid liquid or gas, or a slap or hit. **9.** to cause acute mental pain or irritation, as annoying thoughts or one's conscience: *The memory of that insult still stings.* **10.** to feel acute mental pain or irritation: *He was stinging from the blow to his pride.* **11.** to feel a smarting pain, as from a blow or the sting of an insect. —*n.* **12.** an act or an instance of stinging. **13.** a wound, pain, or smart caused by stinging. **14.** any sharp physical or mental wound, hurt, or pain. **15.** anything or an element in anything that wounds, pains, or irritates: *to feel the sting of defeat; Death, where is thy sting?* **16.** capacity to wound or pain: *Satire has a sting.* **17.** a sharp stimulus or incitement: *driven by the sting of jealousy; the sting of ambition.* **18.** *Bot.* a glandular hair on certain plants, as nettles, that emits an irritating fluid. **19.** *Zool.* any of various sharp-pointed, often venom-bearing organs of insects and other animals capable of inflicting painful or dangerous wounds. **20.** *Slang.* **a.** See **confidence game. b.** an ostensibly illegal operation, as the buying of stolen goods or the bribing of public officials, used by undercover investigators to collect evidence of wrongdoing. [bef. 900; (v.) ME *stingen,* OE *stingan* to pierce; c. ON *stinga* to pierce, Goth *-stangan* (in *usstangan* to pull out); (n.) ME *sting(e),* OE: act of stinging, deriv. of the v.] —**sting′ing·ly,** *adv.* —**sting′less,** *adj.*

sting·a·ree (sting′ə rē′, sting′ə rē′), *n.* a stingray. [1830–40]

sting·er (sting′ər), *n.* **1.** a person or thing that stings. **2.** an animal or plant having a stinging organ. **3.** the sting or stinging organ of an insect or other animal. **4.** *Informal.* a stinging blow, remark, or the like. **5.** a cocktail made of brandy and crème de menthe. **6.** (*cap.*) *Mil.* a U.S. Army shoulder-launched, heat-seeking antiaircraft missile, with a range of 3 miles (5 km). **7.** *Brit. Informal.* a highball of whiskey and soda. [1545–55; STING + -ER[1]]

sting′ing cap′sule, *Zool.* a nematocyst. Also called **sting′ing cell′.** [1880–85]

sting′ing hair′, *Bot.* sting (def. 18).

sting′ing net′tle, a bristly, stinging Eurasian nettle, *Urtica dioica,* naturalized in North America, having forked clusters of greenish flowers, the young foliage sometimes cooked and eaten like spinach by the Scots. [1515–25]

sting′less bee′, any of certain social, honey-producing tropical bees of the family Apidae, as of the genus *Melipona,* having a nonfunctional stinger. [1855–60]

stin·go (sting′gō), *n. Chiefly Brit. Slang.* strong beer. [1625–35; STING + -O; cf. BLOTTO, STINKO]

sting·ray (sting′rā′), *n.* any of the rays, esp. of the family Dasyatidae, having a long, flexible tail armed near the base with a strong, serrated bony spine with which they can inflict painful wounds. [1605–15; STING + RAY[2]]

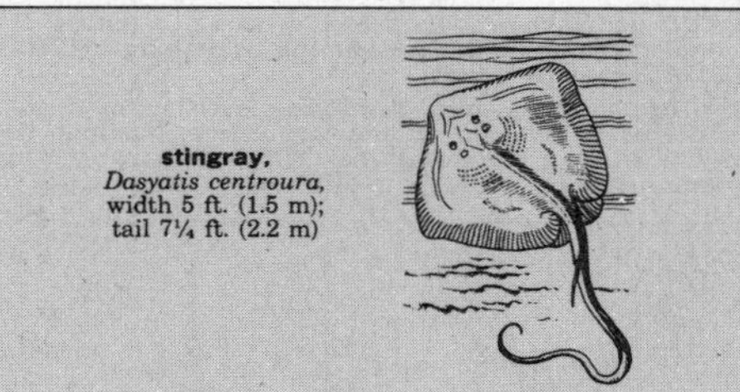
stingray, *Dasyatis centroura,* width 5 ft. (1.5 m); tail 7¼ ft. (2.2 m)

stin·gy[1] (stin′jē), *adj.,* **-gi·er, -gi·est. 1.** reluctant to give or spend; not generous; niggardly; penurious: *He's a stingy old miser.* **2.** scanty or meager: *a stingy little income.* [1650–60; perh. deriv. of STING; see -Y[1]] —**stin′·gi·ly,** *adv.* —**stin′gi·ness,** *n.*
—**Syn. 1.** tight. STINGY, PARSIMONIOUS, MISERLY, MEAN, CLOSE all mean reluctant to part with money or goods. STINGY, the most general of these terms, means unwilling to share, give, or spend possessions or money: *children who are stingy with their toys; a stingy, grasping skinflint.* PARSIMONIOUS describes an extreme stinginess arising from unusual or excessive frugality: *a sternly parsimonious, penny-pinching existence.* MISERLY stresses a pathological pleasure in acquiring and hoarding money that is so powerful that even necessities are only grudgingly purchased: *a wretched, miserly way of life.* MEAN suggests a small-minded, ignoble, petty stinginess leading to miserable, cheerless living: *depressingly mean with his money; mean surroundings; a mean repast.* CLOSE implies extreme caution in spending money, even an aversion to spending: *a close dealer, buying only at rock bottom prices; generous with advice, but very close with his money.* **2.** sparse, paltry, poor. —**Ant. 1.** generous.

sting·y[2] (sting′ē), *adj.* having a sting. [1605–15; STING + -Y[1]]

stink (stingk), *v.,* **stank** or, often, **stunk; stunk; stink·ing;** *n.* —*v.i.* **1.** to emit a strong offensive smell. **2.** to be offensive to honesty or propriety; to be in extremely bad repute or disfavor. **3.** *Informal.* to be disgustingly inferior: *That book stinks.* **4.** *Slang.* to have a large quantity of something (usually fol. by *of* or *with*): *They stink of money. She stinks with jewelry.* —*v.t.* **5.** to cause to stink or be otherwise offensive (often fol. by *up*): *an amateurish performance that really stank up the stage.* **6. stink out,** to repel or drive out by means of a highly offensive smell. —*n.* **7.** a strong offensive smell; stench. **8.** *Informal.* an unpleasant fuss; scandal: *There was a big stink about his accepting a bribe.* **9. stinks,** (*used with a singular v.*) *Brit. Slang.* chemistry as a course of study. [bef. 900; (v.) ME *stinken,* OE *stincan;* (n.) ME, deriv. of the v.; c. G *stinken.* (v.); cf. STENCH]
—**Syn. 1.** reek.

stink·ard (sting′kərd), *n.* a despicable person; stinker. [1590–1600; STINK + -ARD] —**stink′ard·ly,** *adv.*

stink·a·roo (sting′kə ro͞o′, sting′kə ro͞o′), *n., pl.* **-roos.** *Slang.* something markedly inferior in quality: *a stinkaroo of a motion picture.* Also, **stink′er·oo′.** [STINK(ER) + *-aroo,* sp. var. of -EROO]

stink′ bomb′, a small bomb made to emit a foul smell on exploding. Also called **stench bomb.** [1910–15]

stink′ bug′, 1. any of numerous broad, flat bugs of the family Pentatomidae, that emit a disagreeable odor. **2.** any of various other malodorous bugs. [1875–80, *Amer.*]

stink·er (sting′kər), *n.* **1.** a person or thing that stinks. **2.** *Informal.* a mean or despicable person; louse. **3.** *Informal.* something, esp. some form of entertainment, of inferior quality. **4.** *Informal.* something difficult: *a real stinker of a crossword puzzle.* **5.** any device emitting an offensive odor, as a stink bomb or stinkpot. **6.** *Dial.* any of several large petrels. [1600–10; 1920–25 for def. 2; STINK + -ER[1]]

stink·horn (stingk′hôrn′), *n.* any of various rank-smelling, brown-capped mushrooms of the genus *Phallus,* esp. *P. impudicus.* [1715–25; STINK + HORN]

stink·ing (sting′king), *adj.* **1.** foul-smelling. **2.** *Slang.* very drunk; plastered. **3.** *Slang.* very rich: *His father left him so much money he's stinking.* **4.** contemptible; disgusting: *a stinking shame.* —*adv.* **5.** completely or extremely: *stinking drunk.* [bef. 1000; ME *stinkinge,* OE *stincende.* See STINK, -ING[2]] —**stink′ing·ly,** *adv.* —**stink′ing·ness,** *n.*
—**Syn. 1.** smelly, putrid, rotten, putrescent, foul, miasmal, rank.

stink′ing ce′dar, an evergreen tree, *Torreya taxifolia,* of the yew family, native to Florida, having rank-smelling foliage and dark-green, egg-shaped fruit. [1865–70]

stink′ing cham′omile, mayweed.

stink′ing clo′ver. See **Rocky Mountain beeplant.**

stink′ing Rog′er, any of various plants having an unpleasant odor. [1895–1900]

stink′ing smut′, *Plant Pathol.* bunt[3]. [1890–95]

stink·o (sting′kō), *adj. Slang.* **1.** drunk. **2.** wretched; abysmal: *It was a great book but a stinko movie.* [1925–30; STINK + -O]

stink·pot (stingk′pot′), *n.* **1.** a jar containing combustibles or other materials that generate offensive and suffocating vapors, formerly used in warfare. **2.** *Informal.* a stinker; meany. **3.** a common musk turtle, *Sternotherus odoratus,* of the eastern and southern U.S., that sometimes climbs trees along the water's edge. [1655–65; STINK + POT[1]]

stink·weed (stingk′wēd′), *n.* **1.** any of various rank-smelling plants, as the jimson weed. **2.** See **tree of heaven.** [1745–55, *Amer.*; STINK + WEED[1]]

stink·wood (stingk′wo͝od′), *n.* **1.** any of several trees yielding fetid wood. **2.** the wood of any of these trees. [1725–35; STINK + WOOD[1]]

stink·y (sting′kē), *adj.,* **stink·i·er, stink·i·est. 1.** foul smelling; stinking. **2.** *Informal.* mean-spirited; nasty. [STINK + -Y[1]]

stink′y pink′y, an oral word game in which one player provides a definition to which the others are to supply a rhyming phrase, as "a mighty nightie" for "a powerful pair of pajamas." Also, **stink′y pink′ie.**

Stin·nes (shtin′əs), *n.* **Hu·go** (ho͞o′gō; *Eng.* hyo͞o′gō), 1870–1924, German industrialist.

stint[1] (stint), *v.i.* **1.** to be frugal; get along on a scanty allowance: *Don't stint on the food. They stinted for years in order to save money.* **2.** *Archaic.* to cease action; desist. —*v.t.* **3.** to limit to a certain amount, number, share, or allowance, often unduly; set limits to; restrict. **4.** *Archaic.* to bring to an end; check. —*n.* **5.** a period of time spent doing something: *a two-year stint in the army.* **6.** an allotted amount or piece of work: *to do one's daily stint.* **7.** limitation or restriction, esp. as to amount: *to give without stint.* **8.** a limited, prescribed, or expected quantity, share, rate, etc.: *to exceed one's stint.* **9.** *Obs.* a pause; halt. [1150–1200; (v.) ME *stinten,* OE *styntan* to make blunt, dull; (n.) ME, deriv. of the v.; c. ON *stytta* to shorten; cf. STUNT[1]] —**stint′ed·ly,** *adv.*

—stint′ed·ness, *n.* **—stint′er,** *n.* **—stint′ing·ly,** *adv.* **—stint′less,** *adj.*
—Syn. **3.** confine, restrain. **7.** restraint, constraint. **8.** allotment, portion.

stint[2] (stint), *n.* any of various small sandpipers of the genus *Calidris,* as the least sandpiper. [1425–75; late ME *stynte* < ?]

stipe (stīp), *n.* **1.** *Bot., Mycol.* a stalk or slender support, as the petiole of a fern frond, the stem supporting the pileus of a mushroom, or a stalklike elongation of the receptacle of a flower. **2.** *Zool.* a stemlike part, as a footstalk; stalk. [1775–85; < F < L *stīpes* post, tree trunk or branch, log]

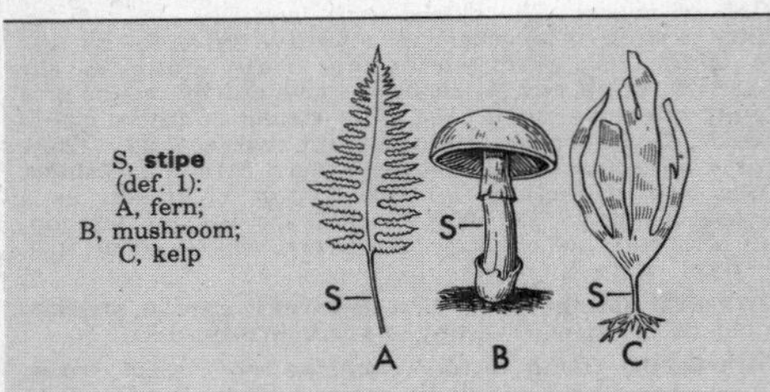

S, **stipe** (def. 1): A, fern; B, mushroom; C, kelp

sti·pel (stī′pəl), *n. Bot.* a secondary stipule situated at the base of a leaflet of a compound leaf. [1815–25; < NL *stipella,* for L *stipula* (see STIPULE), with *-ella* r. *-ula* -ULE] **—sti·pel·late** (stī pel′it, -āt, stī′pə lit, -lāt′), *adj.*

sti·pend (stī′pend), *n.* **1.** a periodic payment, esp. a scholarship or fellowship allowance granted to a student. **2.** fixed or regular pay; salary. [1400–50; late ME *stipendie* < L *stīpendium* soldier's pay, syncopated var. of **stipipendium,* equiv. to *stipi-,* comb. form of *stips* a coin + *pend(ere)* to weigh out, pay (see PEND) + *-ium* -IUM] **—sti′pend·less,** *adj.*
—Syn. **1, 2.** See **pay.**[1]

sti·pen·di·ar·y (stī pen′dē er′ē), *adj., n., pl.* **-ar·ies.** *—adj.* **1.** receiving a stipend; performing services for regular pay. **2.** paid for by a stipend: *stipendiary services.* **3.** pertaining to or of the nature of a stipend. *—n.* **4.** a person who receives a stipend. [1535–45; < L *stīpendiārius,* equiv. to *stīpendi(um)* STIPEND + *-ārius* -ARY]

sti·pes (stī′pēz), *n., pl.* **stip·i·tes** (stip′i tēz′). **1.** *Zool.* the second joint in a maxilla of crustaceans and insects. **2.** *Bot., Mycol.* a stipe. [1750–60; < L *stīpes;* see STIPE]

stip·i·tate (stip′i tāt′), *adj.* having or supported by a stipe: *a stipitate ovary.* [1775–85; < NL *stīpitātus,* equiv. to *stīpit-* (s. of *stīpes*) STIPE + *-ātus* -ATE[1]]

stip·i·ti·form (stip′i tə fôrm′), *adj.* having the form of a stipe. [1855–60; *stipit-* (see STIPITATE) + -I- + -FORM]

sti·po (stē′pō), *n., pl.* **-pos.** a tall, ornate, Italian desk with a drop lid. [< It, prob. deriv. of *stipare* to pack closely]

stip·ple (stip′əl), *v.,* **-pled, -pling,** *n.* *—v.t.* **1.** to paint, engrave, or draw by means of dots or small touches. *—n.* Also, **stip′pling. 2.** the method of painting, engraving, etc., by stippling. **3.** stippled work; a painting, engraving, or the like, executed by means of dots or small spots. [1660–70; < D *stippelen,* freq. of *stippen* to dot, deriv. of *stip* dot] **—stip′pler,** *n.*

stip·u·late[1] (stip′yə lāt′), *v.,* **-lat·ed, -lat·ing.** *—v.i.* **1.** to make an express demand or arrangement as a condition of agreement (often fol. by *for*). *—v.t.* **2.** to arrange expressly or specify in terms of agreement: *to stipulate a price.* **3.** to require as an essential condition in making an agreement: *Total disarmament was stipulated in the peace treaty.* **4.** to promise, in making an agreement. **5.** *Law.* to accept (a proposition) without requiring that it be established by proof: *to stipulate the existence of certain facts or that an expert witness is qualified.* [1615–25; < L *stipulātus* (ptp. of *stipulārī* to demand a formal agreement), appar. equiv. to *stipul-* (see STIPULE) + *-ātus* -ATE[1]] **—stip·u·la·ble** (stip′yə lə bəl), *adj.* **—stip′u·la′tor,** *n.* **—stip·u·la·to·ry** (stip′yə lə tôr′ē, -tōr′ē), *adj.*
—Syn. **2, 3.** specify, designate, indicate, cite.

stip·u·late[2] (stip′yə lit, -lāt′), *adj. Bot.* having stipules. [1770–80; < NL *stipulātus.* See STIPULE, -ATE[1]]

stip·u·la·tion (stip′yə lā′shən), *n.* **1.** a condition, demand, or promise in an agreement or contract. **2.** the act of stipulating. [1545–55; < L *stipulātiōn-* (s. of *stipulātiō*). See STIPULATE[1], -ION]

stip·ule (stip′yo͞ol), *n. Bot.* one of a pair of lateral appendages, often leaflike, at the base of a leaf petiole in many plants. [1785–95; < L *stipula* stalk, n. use of fem. of **stipulus* firm (recorded in LL); akin to STIPES] **—stip′u·lar,** *adj.*

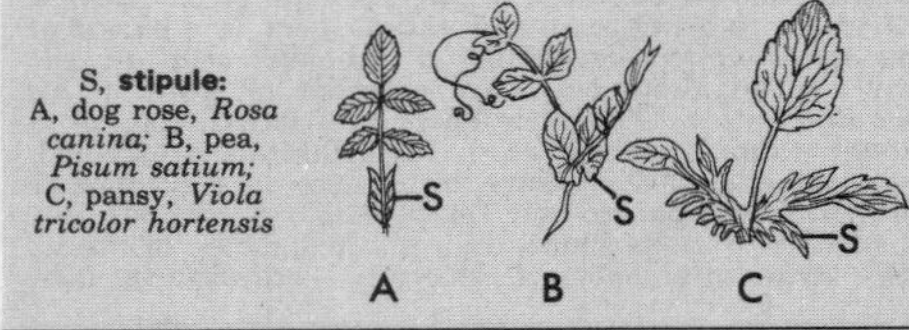

S, **stipule:** A, dog rose, *Rosa canina;* B, pea, *Pisum sativum;* C, pansy, *Viola tricolor hortensis*

CONCISE ETYMOLOGY KEY: <, descended or borrowed from; >, whence; b., blend of, blended; c., cognate with; cf., compare; deriv., derivative; equiv., equivalent; imit., imitative; obl., oblique; r., replacing; s., stem; sp., spelling, spelled; resp., respelling, respelled; trans., translation; ?, origin unknown; *, unattested; ‡, probably earlier than. See the full key inside the front cover.

stip·u·li·form (stip′yə lə fôrm′), *adj. Bot.* shaped like a stipule. [1865–70; STIPULE + -I- + -FORM]

stir[1] (stûr), *v.,* **stirred, stir·ring,** *n.* *—v.t.* **1.** to move one's hand or an implement continuously or repeatedly through (a liquid or other substance) in order to cool, mix, agitate, dissolve, etc., any or all of the component parts: *to stir one's coffee with a spoon.* **2.** to set in tremulous, fluttering, or irregular motion: *A soft breeze stirred the leaves.* **3.** to affect strongly; excite: *to stir pity; to stir one's heart.* **4.** to incite, instigate, or prompt (usually fol. by *up*): *to stir up a people to rebellion.* **5.** to move briskly; bestir: *to stir oneself.* **6.** to move, esp. in a slight way: *He would not stir a finger to help them.* **7.** to rouse from inactivity, quiet, contentment, indifference, etc. (usually fol. by *up*): *to stir up his potential.* **8.** to bring up for notice or discussion. **9.** to disturb; trouble. *—v.i.* **10.** to move, esp. slightly or lightly: *Not a leaf stirred.* **11.** to move around, esp. briskly; be active: *Everyone in the house was stirring.* **12.** to become active, as from some rousing or quickening impulse. **13.** to be emotionally moved or strongly affected. **14.** to be in circulation, current, or afoot: *Is there any news stirring?* *—n.* **15.** the act of stirring or moving. **16.** the sound made by stirring or moving slightly. **17.** a state or occasion of general excitement; commotion: *The news created a stir.* **18.** a mental impulse, sensation, or feeling: *a stir of hope.* **19.** a jog, poke, or thrust: *He gave the refuse a stir with his foot.* **20.** movement, esp. brisk and busy movement: *There was too much clamor and stir for her.* [bef. 900; ME *stiren* (v.), OE *styrian;* c. G *stören;* akin to ON *styrr* disturbance; see STORM] **—stir′ra·ble,** *adj.* **—stir′less,** *adj.* **—stir′less·ly,** *adv.*
—Syn. **1.** disturb. **4.** rouse, foment, arouse, provoke, stimulate, goad, spur. **17.** fuss, pother, agitation, disorder, uproar. See **ado. 20.** bustle, **—Ant. 17.** quiet.

stir[2] (stûr), *n. Slang.* prison. [1850–55; argot word of obscure orig; cf. earlier argot *start* in same sense]

stir·a·bout (stûr′ə bout′), *n. Brit.* porridge. [1675–85; n. use of v. phrase *stir about* to stir up]

stir-cra·zy (stûr′krā′zē), *adj. Slang.* **1.** *Informal.* restless or frantic because of confinement, routine, etc.: *I was stir-crazy after just two months of keeping house.* **2.** mentally ill because of long imprisonment. [1935–40; STIR[2] + CRAZY] **—stir′-cra′zi·ness,** *n.*

stir-fried (stûr′frīd′), *adj.* (of food) prepared by cooking quickly in a small amount of oil over high heat: *stir-fried shrimp and snow peas.* [1955–60]

stir-fry (stûr′frī′), *v.,* **-fried, -fry·ing,** *n., adj.* *—v.t.* **1.** to cook (food) quickly by cutting into small pieces and stirring constantly in a lightly oiled wok or frying pan over high heat: a common method of Chinese cookery. *—n.* **2.** a dish of stir-fried meat, vegetables, etc. *—adj.* **3.** stir-fried. [1955–60]

stirk (stûrk), *n. Brit.* a young bull or cow, esp. one in its second year. [bef. 900; ME; OE *stirc* calf, equiv. to *stir-* (akin to STEER[2]) + suffixal *-c* (see -OCK)]

Stir·ling (stûr′ling), *n.* **1.** Also called **Stir·ling·shire** (stûr′ling shēr′, -shər). a historic county in central Scotland. **2.** a city in and the administrative center of the Central region, in central Scotland, on the Forth River. 29,769.

Stir′ling en′gine, an external-combustion engine in which heat from outside the cylinders causes air confined in the cylinders to expand and drive the pistons. [1895–1900; after Robert *Stirling* (d. 1878), Scottish engineer]

Stir′ling's for′mula (stûr′lingz), *Math.* a relation that approximates the value of *n* factorial (*n!*), expressed as $(n/e)^n\sqrt{2\pi n}$. [1925–30; after James *Stirling* (d. 1770), Scottish mathematician]

stirp (stûrp), *n. Anthropol.* a line of descendants from a common ancestor. [1495–1505; < L *stirp-,* s. of *stirps* STIRPS]

stir·pi·cul·ture (stûr′pi kul′chər), *n.* the production of special stocks or strains by careful breeding. [1865–70, *Amer.;* < L *stirpi-* (s. of *stirps*) stock, stem + CULTURE] **—stir′pi·cul′tur·al,** *adj.* **—stir′pi·cul′tur·ist,** *n.*

stirps (stûrps), *n., pl.* **stir·pes** (stûr′pēz). **1.** a stock; family or branch of a family; line of descent. **2.** *Law.* a person from whom a family is descended. **3.** *Biol. Now Rare.* a family, superfamily, or permanent variety. [1675–85; < L: rootstock, trunk]

stir·rer (stûr′ər), *n.* **1.** a person or thing that stirs. **2.** an implement or device for stirring something. [1350–1400; ME; see STIR[1], -ER[1]]

stir·ring (stûr′ing), *adj.* **1.** rousing, exciting, or thrilling: *a stirring speech.* **2.** moving, active, bustling, or lively: *a stirring business.* [bef. 900; ME *stiringe,* OE *styriende.* See STIR[1], -ING[2]] **—stir′ring·ly,** *adv.*

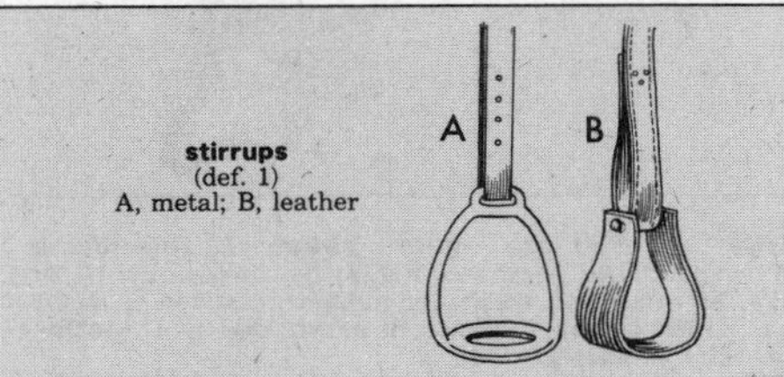

stirrups (def. 1) A, metal; B, leather

stir·rup (stûr′əp, stir′-, stur′-), *n.* **1.** a loop, ring, or other contrivance of metal, wood, leather, etc., suspended from the saddle of a horse to support the rider's foot. **2.** any of various similar supports or clamps used for special purposes. **3.** *Naut.* a short rope with an eye at the end hung from a yard to support a footrope, the footrope being rove through the eye. **4.** Also called **binder.** (in reinforced-concrete constructions) a U-shaped or W-shaped bent rod for supporting longitudinal reinforcing rods. **5.** *Anat.* stapes. [bef. 1000; ME; OE *stigrāp* (*stige* ascent + *rāp* ROPE); c. G *Stegreif*] **—stir′rup·less,** *adj.* **—stir′rup·like′,** *adj.*

stir′rup cup′, 1. farewell drink, esp. one offered to a rider already mounted for departure. **2.** an ornamental cup or bowl for such a drink. [1675–85]

stir′rup jar′, pseudamphora. Also called **stir′rup vase′.** [1900–05]

stir′rup leath′er, the strap that holds the stirrup of a saddle. Also called **stir′rup strap′.** See diag. under **saddle.** [1350–1400; ME]

stir′rup pump′, a small hand pump held steady by a stirruplike foot bracket, often used in firefighting. [1935–40]

stish·ov·ite (stish′ə vīt′), *n. Mineral.* a rare polymorph of quartz, SiO_2, formed under very high pressure, as by meteorite impact. Cf. **coesite.** [1960–65; named after S. M. *Stishov,* 20th-century Russian mineralogist; see -ITE[1]]

stitch (stich), *n.* **1.** one complete movement of a threaded needle through a fabric or material such as to leave behind it a single loop or portion of thread, as in sewing, embroidery, or the surgical closing of wounds. **2.** a loop or portion of thread disposed in place by one such movement in sewing: *to rip out stitches.* **3.** a particular mode of disposing the thread in sewing or the style of work produced by one such method. **4.** one complete movement of the needle or other implement used in knitting, crocheting, netting, tatting, etc. **5.** the portion of work produced. **6.** a thread, bit, or piece of any fabric or of clothing: *to remove every stitch of clothes.* **7.** the least bit of anything: *He wouldn't do a stitch of work.* **8.** a sudden, sharp pain, esp. in the intercostal muscles: *a stitch in the side.* **9. in stitches,** convulsed with laughter: *The comedian had us in stitches all evening.* *—v.t.* **10.** to work upon, join, mend, or fasten with or as if with stitches; sew (often fol. by *together*): *to stitch together flour sacks to make curtains; a plan that was barely stitched together.* **11.** to ornament or embellish with stitches: *to stitch a shirt with a monogram.* *—v.i.* **12.** to make stitches, join together, or sew. [bef. 900; (n.) ME *stiche,* OE *stice* a thrust, stab; c. G *Stich* prick; akin to STICK[2]; (v.) ME *stichen* to stab, pierce, deriv. of the n.] **—stitch′er,** *n.* **—stitch′like′,** *adj.*

stitch·er·y (stich′ə rē), *n.* needlework. [1600–10; STITCH + -ERY]

stitch·ing (stich′ing), *n.* **1.** the act of a person or thing that stitches. **2.** a series or line of stitches. **3.** mending by means of sewing. [1515–25; STITCH + -ING[1]]

stitch·work (stich′wûrk′), *n.* embroidery or needlework. [1840–50; STITCH + WORK]

stitch·wort (stich′wûrt′, -wôrt′), *n.* any of several plants belonging to the genus *Stellaria,* of the pink family, having white flowers. [1225–75; ME *stichewort,* OE *sticwyrt* agrimony. See STITCH, WORT[2]]

stith·y (stith′ē, stith′ē), *n., pl.* **stith·ies,** *v.,* **stith·ied, stith·y·ing.** *—n.* **1.** an anvil. **2.** a forge or smithy. *—v.t.* **3.** *Obs.* to forge. [1250–1300; ME *stithie, stethie* < ON *stethi* anvil]

sti·ver (stī′vər), *n.* **1.** Also, **stuiver.** a former nickel coin of the Netherlands, equal to five Dutch cents. **2.** the smallest possible amount: *not worth a stiver; not a stiver of work.* [1495–1505; < D *stuiver*]

St. James, a town on N Long Island, in SE New York. 12,122.

St. James-As·sin·i·boi·a (sānt′ jāmz′ə sin′ə boi′ə), a city in SE Manitoba, in S central Canada: suburb of Winnipeg. 71,431.

St. James's Palace (sānt′ jām′ziz, sənt), a palace in London, England: the royal residence from the time of Henry VIII until the accession of Victoria. Also called **St. James's.** Cf. **Court of St. James's.**

St.-Jean (saN zhäN′), *n.* French name of **St. Johns.**

St.-Jé·rôme (sānt′jə rōm′; *Fr.* saN zhā rōm′), *n.* a city in S Quebec, in E Canada, NW of Montreal. 25,123.

St. Joe, *Informal.* St. Joseph, Missouri.

St. John (sānt′ jon′; *for 1 also* sin′jən), **1. Henry, 1st Viscount Bolingbroke.** See **Bolingbroke, 1st Viscount. 2.** an island of the Virgin Islands of the United States, in the E West Indies. 2300; ab. 20 sq. mi. (52 sq. km). **3. Lake,** a lake in SE Canada, in Quebec province, draining into the Saguenay River. 365 sq. mi. (945 sq. km). **4.** a river in the NE United States and SE Canada, flowing NE and E from Maine to New Brunswick province and then S to the Bay of Fundy. 450 mi. (725 km) long. **5.** a seaport in S New Brunswick, in SE Canada, on the Bay of Fundy, at the mouth of the St. John River. 80,521. **6.** See **St. John's.**

St.-John Perse (sin′jən pûrs′), (*Alexis Saint-Léger Léger*), 1887–1975, French diplomat and poet: Nobel prize for literature 1960.

St. Johns, 1. a river flowing N and E through NE Florida into the Atlantic. 276 mi. (444 km) long. **2.** French, **St.-Jean.** a city in S Quebec, in E Canada. 35,640.

St. John's, 1. a seaport in and the capital of Newfoundland, on the SE part of the island. 86,576. **2.** a seaport on and the capital of Antigua and Barbuda, in the E West Indies. 13,000. Also, **St. John.**

St. John's-bread (jonz′bred′), carob (def. 2). [1885–90]

St. John's Day. See **Midsummer Day.**

St. John's Eve. See **Midsummer Eve.** Also called **St. John's Night.**

St.-John's-wort (sānt′jonz′wûrt′, -wôrt′), *n.* any of various plants or shrubs of the genus *Hypericum,* having yellow flowers and transparently dotted leaves. [1745–55; so named because gathered on St. John's Eve to ward off evil]

St. Joseph, a city in NW Missouri, on the Missouri River. 76,691.

stk., stock.

St. Kitts (kits), one of the Leeward Islands, in the E West Indies: part of St. Kitts-Nevis; formerly a British colony. 68 sq. mi. (176 sq. km). Also called **St. Christopher.** Cf. **St. Kitts-Nevis-Anguilla.**

St. Kitts-Ne·vis (kits′nē′vis, -nev′is), a twin-island state in the Leeward Islands, in the E West Indies, consisting of the islands of St. Kitts and Nevis: formerly a British colony and member of the West Indies Associated States; gained independence 1983. 44,400; 104 sq. mi. (269 sq. km). *Cap.:* Basseterre. Also called **St. Christopher-Nevis.**

St. Kitts-Ne·vis-An·guil·la (kits′nē′vis ang gwil′ə, -nev′is), a former British colony (1967–71) in the Leeward Islands, in the E West Indies: comprising St. Kitts, Nevis, Anguilla, and adjacent small islands: a member of the former West Indies Associated States. Cf. **St. Kitts-Nevis.**

S.T.L., Licentiate in Sacred Theology.

St.-Lam·bert (sānt′lam′bərt; *Fr.* saɴ län beʀ′), *n.* a city in S Quebec, in E Canada, across from Montreal, on the St. Lawrence. 20,557.

St. Lau·rent (saɴ lô ʀäɴ′), **1. Louis Ste·phen** (lwē ste fen′),1882–1973, prime minister of Canada 1948–57. **2. Yves (Ma·thieu)** (ēv mᴀ tyœ′), born 1936, French fashion designer. **3.** a city in S Quebec, in E Canada, W of Montreal. 65,900.

St. Lawrence, 1. a river in SE Canada, flowing NE from Lake Ontario, forming part of the boundary between New York and Ontario, and emptying into the Gulf of St. Lawrence. 760 mi. (1225 km) long. **2. Gulf of,** an arm of the Atlantic between SE Canada and Newfoundland.

St. Lawrence Seaway, a series of channels, locks, and canals between Montreal and the mouth of Lake Ontario, a distance of 182 miles (293 km), enabling most deep-draft vessels to travel from the Atlantic Ocean, up the St. Lawrence River, to all the Great Lakes ports: developed jointly by the U.S. and Canada.

St.-Lé·o·nard (sānt′len′ərd; *Fr.* saɴ lā ô nᴀʀ′), *n.* a city in S Quebec, in E Canada: suburb of Montreal. 79,429.

stlg., sterling.

St. Lô (saɴ lō′), a city in and the capital of Manche, in NW France: World War II battle June–July 1944. 25,037.

St. Lou·is (sānt′ lo͞o′is), a port in E Missouri, on the Mississippi. 453,085.

St. Louis Park, a city in E Minnesota, near Minneapolis. 42,931.

St. Lu·cia (lo͞o′shə, -sē ə), **1.** one of the Windward Islands, in the E West Indies. **2.** an independent country comprising this island: a former British colony; gained independence 1979. 120,000;238 sq. mi. (616 sq. km). *Cap.:* Castries. —**St. Lucian.**

St. Lu·cie cherry (lo͞o′sē), mahaleb.

STM, scanning tunneling microscope.

S.T.M., Master of Sacred Theology.

St. Ma·lo (saɴ mᴀ lō′), **1.** a seaport in NW France, on the Gulf of St. Malo: resort; surrendered by German forces August 1944. 46,270. **2. Gulf of,** an arm of the English Channel in NW France. 60 mi. (97 km) wide.

St. Mar·tin (sānt′ mär′tn, -tin; *Fr.* saɴ mᴀʀ taɴ′), an island in the N Leeward Islands, in the E West Indies, divided in two parts: the N section is a dependency of Guadeloupe. 5061; 20 sq. mi. (52 sq. km); the S section is an administrative part of the Netherlands Antilles. 6881. 17 sq. mi. (44 sq. km). Dutch, **Sint Maarten.**

St. Mar·ys (mâr′ēz), a river in the north-central U.S. and S Canada, forming the boundary between NE Michigan and Ontario, flowing SE from Lake Superior into Lake Huron. 63 mi. (101 km) long. Cf. **Sault Ste. Marie.**

St. Matthews, a town in N Kentucky. 13,354.

St.-Mi·hiel (saɴ mē yel′), *n.* a town in NE France, on the Meuse River, NW of Nancy: captured by American forces 1918. 5382.

St. Mo·ritz (mō rits′, mô-, mə-; môr′its, mōr′-), a resort town in SE Switzerland: a popular center for winter sports. 5699; 6037 ft. (1840 m) high. German, **Sankt Moritz.**

stmt, statement.

St. Na·zaire (saɴ nᴀ zᴀʀ′), a seaport in W France, on the Loire estuary. 69,769.

sto·a (stō′ə), *n., pl.* **sto·as, sto·ai** (stō′ī), **sto·ae** (stō′ē). *Gk. Archit.* a portico, usually a detached portico of considerable length, that is used as a promenade or meeting place. [1595–1605; < Gk *stoá*]

stoat (stōt), *n.* the ermine, *Mustela erminea,* esp. when in brown summer pelage. [1425–75; late ME *stote* < ?]

stoa·ting (stō′ting), *n. Tailoring.* the process or technique of finishing a facing, collar, or the like, or of mending material with concealed stitching. Also, **stoting.** [1955–60; orig. uncert.]

stob (stob), *n. Chiefly South Midland U.S.* a post, stump, or stake. [1275–1325; ME; var. of STUB¹]

stoc·ca·do (stə kä′dō), *n., pl.* **-dos.** *Archaic.* a thrust with a rapier or other pointed weapon. Also, **stoc·ca·ta** (stə kä′tə). [1575–85; alter. of It *stoccata,* equiv. to *stocc(o)* swordpoint, dagger (< Gmc; cf. OE *stocc* stake) + *-ata* -ADE¹; *-ado* < Sp, as in *renegado*]

sto·chas·tic (stə kas′tik), *adj. Statistics.* of or pertaining to a process involving a randomly determined sequence of observations each of which is considered as a sample of one element from a probability distribution. [1655–65; < Gk *stochastikós,* equiv. to *stochas-* (var. s. of *stocházesthai* to aim at) + *-tikos* -TIC] —**sto·chas′ti·cal·ly,** *adv.*

stochas′tically independ′ent, *Statistics.* See **statistically independent.**

stochas′tic independ′ence, *Statistics.* See **statistical independence.**

stochas′tic ma′trix, *Math.* a square matrix with positive entries totaling 1 in each row.

stochas′tic var′iable, *Statistics.* a random variable.

stock (stok), *n.* **1.** a supply of goods kept on hand for sale to customers by a merchant, distributor, manufacturer, etc.; inventory. **2.** a quantity of something accumulated, as for future use: *a stock of provisions.* **3.** livestock. **4.** *Theat.* a stock company: *a job in summer stock.* **5.** *Finance.* **a.** the outstanding capital of a company or corporation. **b.** the shares of a particular company or corporation. **c.** the certificate of ownership of such stock; stock certificate. **d.** (formerly) a tally or stick used in transactions between a debtor and a creditor. **6.** *Hort.* **a.** Also called **understock.** in grafting, a stem in which the bud or scion is inserted. **b.** a stem, tree, or plant that furnishes slips or cuttings; stock plant. **7.** the trunk or main stem of a tree or other plant, as distinguished from roots and branches. **8.** the type from which a group of animals or plants has been derived. **9.** a race or other related group of animals or plants. **10.** the person from whom a given line of descent is derived; the original progenitor. **11.** a line of descent; a tribe, race, or ethnic group. **12.** *Ling.* a category consisting of language families that, because of resemblances in grammatical structure and vocabulary, are considered likely to be related by common origin. Cf. **family** (def. 14), **phylum** (def. 2). **13.** any grouping of related languages. **14.** the handle of a whip, fishing rod, etc. **15.** *Firearms.* **a.** the wooden or metal piece to which the barrel and mechanism of a rifle are attached. **b.** a part of an automatic weapon, as a machine gun, similar in position or function. **16.** the trunk or stump of a tree, left standing. **17.** a dull or stupid person. **18.** something lifeless or senseless. **19.** the main upright part of anything, esp. a supporting structure. **20. stocks, a.** a former instrument of punishment consisting of a framework with holes for securing the ankles and, sometimes, the wrists, used to expose an offender to public derision. Cf. **pillory** (def. 1). **b.** a frame in which a horse or other animal is secured in a standing position for shoeing or for a veterinary operation. **c.** the frame on which a boat rests while under construction. **21.** *Naut.* **a.** a vertical shaft forming part of a rudder and controlling the rudder's movement. **b.** a transverse piece of wood or metal near the ring on some anchors. See diag. under **anchor. 22.** the metal or wooden body of a carpenter's plane. **23.** *Metall.* **a.** material being smelted in a blast furnace. **b.** a metal piece to be forged. **24.** *Printing.* **a.** a specified quality or kind of paper: *glossy stock; card stock; offset stock.* **b.** the paper for printing a particular job: *We don't have enough stock for that large a run.* **25.** the raw material from which something is made. **26.** *Papermaking.* stuff (def. 15). **27.** *Cookery.* the liquor or broth prepared by boiling meat, fish, chicken, etc., with or without vegetables or seasonings, and used esp. as a foundation for soups and sauces. **28.** any of several plants belonging to the genus *Matthiola,* of the mustard family, esp. *M. incana,* having fragrant white, blue, purple, reddish, or yellowish flowers. **29.** a rhizome or rootstock. **30.** *Zool.* a compound organism, as a colony of corals. **31.** a collar or a neckcloth fitting like a band around the neck. **32.** *Cards.* the portion of a pack of cards that, in certain games, is not dealt out to the players, but is left on the table, to be drawn from as occasion requires. **33.** an adjustable wrench for holding dies for cutting screws. **34.** *Railroads.* See **rolling stock. 35.** *Dominoes.* boneyard (def. 3). **36.** *Informal.* See **stock car** (def. 1). **37.** *Rom. Cath. Ch.* one of a set of three metal containers for holy oil. **38.** *Geol., Mining.* an irregular igneous intrusion, usually an offshoot of a batholith, often mineralized. **39.** *Archaic.* a stocking. **40.** *Obs.* the frame of a plow to which the share, handles, etc., are attached. **41. in stock,** on hand for use or sale: *There are no more blue skirts in stock.* **42. lock, stock, and barrel.** See **lock**¹ (def. 12). **43. on the stocks, a.** under construction, as esp. a ship. **b.** in progress or preparation: *a new novel on the stocks.* **44. out of stock,** lacking a supply of, esp. temporarily: *We are out of stock in this item.* **45. take** or **put stock in,** to put confidence in or attach importance to; believe; trust: *Considering his general unreliability, I can't take stock in what he has told you.* **46. take stock, a.** to make an inventory of stock on hand. **b.** to make an appraisal of resources or prospects: *She took stock of her decorating scheme and decided it was time for a change.*
—*adj.* **47.** kept regularly on hand, as for use or sale; staple; standard: *stock articles.* **48.** having as one's job the care of a concern's goods: *a stock clerk.* **49.** of the common or ordinary type; in common use: *a stock argument.* **50.** banal; commonplace: *a stock remark.* **51.** pertaining to or designating the breeding and raising of livestock: *stock farming.* **52.** *Southern U.S.* (*chiefly Southern Appalachian and South Atlantic States*). (of farm animals) being a fully grown male: *a stock-hog.* **53.** of or pertaining to the stock of a company or corporation: *a stock report.* **54.** *Theat.* **a.** pertaining to a stock company. **b.** appearing together in a repertoire, as a company. **c.** forming part of a repertoire, as a play. **d.** being a character type fixed by convention, as in the commedia dell'arte, a harlequinade, minstrel show, or the like. **55.** *Informal.* of, pertaining to, or characteristic of a stock car.
—*v.t.* **56.** to furnish with a stock or supply. **57.** to furnish with stock, as a farm with horses, cattle, etc. **58.** to lay up in store, as for future use. **59.** to fasten to or provide with a stock, as a rifle, plow, bell, anchor, etc. **60.** to put in the stocks as a punishment.
—*v.i.* **61.** to lay in a stock of something (often fol. by *up*). [bef. 900; (n.) ME; OE *stoc(c)* stump, stake, post, log; c. G *Stock,* ON *stokkr* tree-trunk; (v.) deriv. of the n.] —**stock′like′,** *adj.*
—**Syn. 1.** store, provision, reserve. **11.** lineage, family. **14.** haft. **49.** usual.

stocks (def. 20a)

stock·ade (sto kād′), *n., v.,* **-ad·ed, -ad·ing.** —*n.* **1.** *Fort.* a defensive barrier consisting of strong posts or timbers fixed upright in the ground. **2.** an enclosure or pen made with posts and stakes. **3.** *U.S. Mil.* a prison for military personnel. —*v.t.* **4.** to protect, fortify, or encompass with a stockade. [1605–15; < MF *estocade,* var. of *estacade* < Sp *estacada.* See STAKE¹, -ADE¹]

stockade′ fence′, a fence of closely fitted vertical boards with pointed tops.

stock′ book′, 1. See **stock ledger** (def. 1). **2.** See **stores ledger.** [1825–35, *Amer.*]

stock′ boy′, a boy or man responsible for replenishing stock, as on the shelves of a grocery store. Also, **stock′-boy′.**

stock·breed·ing (stok′brē′ding), *n.* the breeding and raising of livestock for marketing or exhibition. [1935–40; STOCK + BREEDING] —**stock′breed′er,** *n.*

stock·brok·er (stok′brō′kər), *n.* a broker, esp. one employed by a member firm of a stock exchange, who buys and sells stocks and other securities for customers. Also called **broker.** [1700–10; STOCK + BROKER] —**stock·brok·er·age** (stok′brō′kər ij), *n.* —**stock′brok′erage.** —**stock′brok′ing, stock′brok′er·ing,** *n.*

stock′ buy′back, buyback (def. 3).

stock′ car′, 1. a standard model of automobile changed in various ways for racing purposes. **2.** Also called **cattle car.** *Railroads.* a boxcar for carrying livestock. [1855–60, *Amer.* for def. 2] —**stock′-car′,** *adj.*

stock′ certif′icate, a certificate evidencing ownership of one or more shares of stock in a corporation. [1860–65]

stock′ char′acter, a character in literature, theater, or film of a type quickly recognized and accepted by the reader or viewer and requiring no development by the writer. [1860–65]

stock′ clerk′, 1. a worker in a stockroom who is in charge of the materials and goods stored there. **2.** a clerk responsible for replenishing the stock displayed in a grocery store, hardware store, etc.

stock′ com′pany, 1. *Finance.* a company or corporation whose capital is divided into shares represented by stock. **2.** *Theat.* a company acting a repertoire of plays, more or less permanently together, usually at its own theater. [1820–30]

stock′ div′idend, *Finance.* **1.** a form of dividend collected by a stockholder in extra shares of the corporation's stock rather than in cash. **2.** the stock received in such a dividend. [1900–05]

stock′ dove′ (duv), a cosmopolitan wild pigeon, *Columba oenas,* of Europe. [1300–50; ME *stokdove;* cf. G *Stocktaube;* so called because it nests in hollow tree trunks]

stock·er (stok′ər), *n.* **1.** a person or thing that stocks. **2.** a young steer or heifer that is fed chiefly pasture or other roughage prior to more intensive feeding. Cf. **feeder** (def. 4). **3.** *Informal.* See **stock car.** [1635–45; STOCK + -ER¹]

stock′ exchange′, 1. a building or place where stocks and other securities are bought and sold. **2.** an association of brokers and dealers in stocks and bonds who meet together and transact business according to fixed rules. [1765–75]

stock′ farm′, a farm devoted to breeding livestock. [1800–10] —**stock′ farm′er.** —**stock′ farm′ing.**

stock·fish (stok′fish′), *n., pl. (esp. collectively)* **-fish,** *(esp. referring to two or more kinds or species)* **-fish·es.** fish, as the cod or haddock, cured by splitting and drying in the air without salt. [1250–1300; ME *stocfish* < MD *stocvisch.* See STOCK, FISH]

stock′ foot′age, *Motion Pictures, Television.* film containing stock shots.

stock′ guard′, *Railroad.* a barrier for keeping cattle and other animals off the tracks or right of way. [1895–1900, *Amer.*]

Stock·hau·sen (shtôk′hou′zən), *n.* **Karl·heinz** (kärl′hīnts′), born 1928, German composer.

stock·hold·er (stok′hōl′dər), *n.* **1.** a holder or owner of stock in a corporation. **2.** *Australian.* an owner of livestock, as a rancher. [1745–55; STOCK + HOLDER]

stock′holder of rec′ord, a stockholder or his or her agent whose name is registered on the books of the issuing corporation at the close of a business day set for determining that stockholders shall receive dividends or vote on an issue.

stock′holders' eq′uity, the net assets of a corporation as owned by stockholders in capital stock, capital surplus, and undistributed earnings.

Stock·holm (stok′hōm, -hōlm; *Swed.* stôk′hôlm′), *n.* the chief seaport in and the capital of Sweden, in the SE part. 647,214; with suburbs 1,493,546.

Stock′holm syn′drome, *Psychiatry.* an emotional attachment to a captor formed by a hostage as a result of continuous stress, dependence, and a need to cooperate for survival. [after an incident in STOCKHOLM in 1973, during which a bank employee became romantically attached to a robber who held her hostage]

stock·horn (stok′hôrn′), *n.* pibgorn. [STOCK + HORN]

stock′ horse′, *Western U.S.* a horse or pony used in herding cattle. [1860–65]

stock·i·nette (stok′ə net′), *n.* **1.** Also, **stock′i·net′.** a stretchy, machine-knitted fabric used for making undergarments, infants' wear, etc. **2.** Also called **stockinette′ stitch′.** a knitting pattern made by alter-

CONCISE PRONUNCIATION KEY: act, cāpe, dâre, pärt; set, ēqual; *if,* ice; ox, ōver, ôrder, oil, bo͝ok, bo͞ot, out; up, ûrge; child; sing; shoe; thin, *that;* zh as in *treasure.* ə = *a* as in *alone, e* as in *system, i* as in *easily, o* as in *gallop, u* as in *circus;* ᵊ as in *fire* (fīᵊr), *hour* (ouᵊr). l and n can serve as syllabic consonants, as in *cradle* (krād′l), and *button* (but′n). See the full key inside the front cover.

nating single rows of knit stitches and of purl stitches in such a way that all the knit stitches show on one side of the fabric and all the purl stitches on the other. [1775–85; earlier *stocking-net*]

stock·ing (stok′ing), *n.* **1.** a close-fitting covering for the foot and part of the leg, usually knitted, of wool, cotton, nylon, silk, or similar material. **2.** something resembling such a covering. **3. in one's stocking feet,** wearing stockings, but without shoes: *Be careful of glass splinters if you walk through here in your stocking feet.* [1575–85; STOCK + -ING[1]] **—stock′inged,** *adj.* **—stock′ing·less,** *adj.*

stock′ing cap′, a long, conical, knitted cap, usually with a tassel or pompon at the tip.

stock′ing stitch′, *Chiefly Brit.* stockinette (def. 2).

stock′ing stuff′er, 1. a small, usually inexpensive gift that is placed with others in a Christmas stocking. **2.** any small, inexpensive gift given during the Christmas holidays.

stock′ in trade′, 1. the requisites for carrying on a business, esp. goods kept on hand for sale in a store. **2.** resources or abilities peculiar to an individual or group or employed for a specific purpose: *A feeling for language should be part of the stock in trade of any writer.* Also, **stock′-in-trade′.** [1660–70]

stock·ish (stok′ish), *adj.* like a block of wood; stupid. [1590–1600; STOCK + -ISH[1]] **—stock′ish·ly,** *adv.* **—stock′ish·ness,** *n.*

stock·ist (stok′ist), *n. Brit.* a wholesale or retail establishment that stocks merchandise. [1905–10; STOCK + -IST]

stock·job·ber (stok′job′ər), *n.* **1.** a stock salesperson, esp. one who sells or promotes worthless securities. **2.** *Brit.* a stock-exchange operator who acts as an intermediary between brokers. [1620–30; STOCK + JOBBER] **—stock′job′ber·y, stock′job′bing,** *n.*

stock′ ledg′er, 1. a permanent record of the capital stock of a corporation, listing the names and addresses of the stockholders, the number of the shares owned, the serial numbers of their stock certificates, etc. **2.** See **stores ledger.** Also, **stock book.**

stock·less (stok′lis), *adj.* having no stock, as an anchor. [1885–90; STOCK + -LESS]

stock·man (stok′mən *or, for 3,* -man′), *n., pl.* **-men** (-mən *or, for 3,* -men′). **1.** *U.S. and Australia.* a person who raises livestock. **2.** a person employed on a stock farm. **3.** a person in charge of a stock of goods, as in a warehouse. [1800–10; STOCK + MAN[1]]

stock′ mar′ket, 1. a particular market where stocks and bonds are traded; stock exchange. **2.** the market for stocks throughout a nation: *The stock market reacted strongly to the president's speech.* [1800–10]

stock′ op′tion, an option giving the holder, usually an officer or employee, the right to buy stock of the issuing corporation at a specific price within a stated period. [1940–45]

stock·out (stok′out′), *n.* a state or instance of being out of stock of goods. [STOCK + OUT]

stock·pile (stok′pīl′), *n., v.,* **-piled, -pil·ing.** *—n.* **1.** a supply of material, as a pile of gravel in road maintenance. **2.** a large supply of some metal, chemical, food, etc., gathered and held in reserve for use during a shortage or during a period of higher prices. **3.** a quantity, as of munitions or weapons, accumulated for possible future use. *—v.t.* **4.** to accumulate (material, goods, or the like) for future use; put or store in a stockpile. *—v.i.* **5.** to accumulate in a stockpile. [1915–20; STOCK + PILE[1]] **—stock′pil′er,** *n.*

Stock·port (stok′pôrt′, -pōrt′), *n.* borough of Greater Manchester, in NW England. 293,400.

stock·pot (stok′pot′), *n.* a pot in which stock for soup, sauces, etc., is made and kept. [1850–55; STOCK + POT[1]]

stock′ pow′er, a power of attorney permitting a person other than the owner of stock in a corporation to transfer the title of ownership to a third party.

stock′ rais′ing, the breeding and raising of livestock. [1790–1800] **—stock′ rais′er.**

stock′ rec′ord. See **stores ledger.**

stock·rid·er (stok′rī′dər), *n. Australian.* a cowboy. [1860–65; STOCK + RIDER]

stock·room (stok′ro͞om′, -ro͝om′), *n.* a room in which a stock of materials or goods is kept for use or sale. [1815–25; STOCK + ROOM]

stock·route (stok′ro͞ot′, -rout′), *n. Australian.* a public trail having right of way across private properties and over which cattle and sheep may be herded to grazing grounds or to market. [1885–90]

stock′ sad′dle. See **Western saddle.** [1885–90]

stock′ shot′, *Motion Pictures.* any of various prefilmed shots, as from newsreels or travelogues, available from specialized film libraries for inserting into a film to establish locale, atmosphere, etc.

stock′ solu′tion, *Photog.* a concentrated chemical solution, diluted before using.

stock-still (stok′stil′), *adj.* completely still; motionless. [1425–75; late ME *stok still.* See STOCK, STILL[1]]

stock·tak·ing (stok′tā′king), *n.* **1.** the examination or counting over of materials or goods on hand, as in a stockroom or store. **2.** the act of appraising a present situation, condition, degree of progress, etc., in terms of accomplishments and ultimate goals. [1855–60; STOCK + TAKING]

stock′ tick′er, ticker (def. 1). [1885–90, *Amer.*]

CONCISE ETYMOLOGY KEY: <, descended or borrowed from; >, whence; b., blend of, blended; c., cognate with; cf., compare; deriv., derivative; equiv., equivalent; imit., imitative; obl., oblique; r., replacing; s., stem; sp., spelling, spelled; resp., respelling, respelled; trans., translation; ?, origin unknown; *, unattested; ‡, probably earlier than. See the full key inside the front cover.

Stock·ton (stok′tən), *n.* **1. Frank R.** (*Francis Richard Stockton*), 1834–1902, U.S. novelist and short-story writer. **2.** a city in central California, on the San Joaquin River. 149,779.

Stock·ton-on-Tees (stok′tən on tēz′, -ôn-), *n.* a seaport in Cleveland, in NE England, near the mouth of the Tees River. 164,000.

stock·y (stok′ē), *adj.,* **stock·i·er, stock·i·est. 1.** of solid and sturdy form or build; thick-set and, usually, short. **2.** having a strong, stout stem, as a plant. [1350–1400; ME *stokky.* See STOCK, -Y[1]] **—stock′i·ly,** *adv.* **—stock′i·ness,** *n.*

stock·yard (stok′yärd′), *n.* **1.** an enclosure with pens, sheds, etc., connected with a slaughterhouse, railroad, market, etc., for the temporary housing of cattle, sheep, swine, or horses. **2.** a yard for livestock. [1795–1805; STOCK + YARD[2]]

stodge (stoj), *v.,* **stodged, stodg·ing,** *n.* *—v.t.* **1.** to stuff full, esp. with food or drink; gorge. *—v.i.* **2.** to trudge: *to stodge along through the mire.* *—n.* **3.** food that is particularly filling. [1665–75; orig. uncert.; in some senses perh. b. *stoff* (earlier form of STUFF) and GORGE]

stodg·y (stoj′ē), *adj.,* **stodg·i·er, stodg·i·est. 1.** heavy, dull, or uninteresting; tediously commonplace; boring: *a stodgy Victorian novel.* **2.** of a thick, semisolid consistency; heavy, as food. **3.** stocky; thick-set. **4.** old-fashioned; unduly formal and traditional: *a stodgy old gentleman.* **5.** dull; graceless; inelegant: *a stodgy business suit.* [1815–25; STODGE + -Y[1]] **—stodg′i·ly,** *adv.* **—stodg′i·ness,** *n.*
—Syn. 1. tiresome, stuffy, prosaic. **—Ant. 1.** lively, exciting.

sto·gy (stō′gē), *n., pl.* **-gies. 1.** a long, slender, roughly made, inexpensive cigar. **2.** a coarse, heavy boot or shoe. Also, **stogie.** [1840–50, *Amer.*; *stog*(*a*) (short for *Conestoga,* town in Pennsylvania) + -Y[2]]

Sto·ic (stō′ik), *adj.* **1.** of or pertaining to the school of philosophy founded by Zeno, who taught that people should be free from passion, unmoved by joy or grief, and submit without complaint to unavoidable necessity. **2.** (*l.c.*) stoical. *—n.* **3.** a member or adherent of the Stoic school of philosophy. **4.** (*l.c.*) a person who maintains or affects the mental attitude advocated by the Stoics. [1350–1400; ME < L *Stōicus* < Gk *Stōikós,* equiv. to *stō-* (var. s. of *stoá* STOA) + *-ikos* -IC]

sto·i·cal (stō′i kəl), *adj.* **1.** impassive; characterized by a calm, austere fortitude befitting the Stoics: *a stoical sufferer.* **2.** (*cap.*) of or pertaining to the Stoics. [1400–50; ME; see STOIC, -AL[1]] **—sto′i·cal·ly,** *adv.* **—sto′i·cal·ness,** *n.*
—Syn. 1. imperturbable, cool, indifferent. **—Ant. 1.** sympathetic, warm, demonstrative, effusive.

stoi·chi·o·met·ric (stoi′kē ə me′trik), *adj. Chem.* **1.** of or pertaining to stoichiometry. **2.** pertaining to or involving substances that are in the exact proportions required for a given reaction. Also, **stoi′chi·o·met′ri·cal.** [1890–95; < Gk *stoicheîo*(*n*) component (akin to *stíchos* STICH[1]) + METRIC[2]] **—stoi′chi·o·met′ri·cal·ly,** *adv.*

stoi·chi·om·e·try (stoi′kē om′i trē), *n.* **1.** the calculation of the quantities of chemical elements or compounds involved in chemical reactions. **2.** the branch of chemistry dealing with relationships of combining elements, esp. quantitatively. Also, **stoi·chei·om·e·try** (stoi′kī om′i trē). [1800–10; < Gk *stoicheîo*(*n*) (see STOICHIOMETRIC) + -METRY]

Sto·i·cism (stō′ə siz′əm), *n.* **1.** a systematic philosophy, dating from around 300 B.C., that held the principles of logical thought to reflect a cosmic reason instantiated in nature. **2.** (*l.c.*) conduct conforming to the precepts of the Stoics, as repression of emotion and indifference to pleasure or pain. [1620–30; STOIC + -ISM]
—Syn. 2. See **patience.**

stoke[1] (stōk), *v.,* **stoked, stok·ing.** *—v.t.* **1.** to poke, stir up, and feed (a fire). **2.** to tend the fire of (a furnace, esp. one used with a boiler to generate steam for an engine); supply with fuel. *—v.i.* **3.** to shake up the coals of a fire. **4.** to tend a fire or furnace. [1675–85; < D *stoken* to feed or stock a fire; see STOCK]

stoke[2] (stōk), *n. Physics.* a unit of kinematic viscosity, equal to the viscosity of a fluid in poises divided by the density of the fluid in grams per cubic centimeter. [after Sir G. STOKES]

stoked (stōkt), *adj. Slang.* **1.** exhilarated; excited. **2.** intoxicated or stupefied with a drug; high. [STOKE[1] + -ED[2]]

stoke·hole (stōk′hōl′), *n.* **1.** Also, **stoke·hold** (stōk′-hōld′). See **fire room. 2.** a hole in a furnace through which the fire is stoked. [1650–60; STOKE[1] + HOLE]

Stoke-on-Trent (stōk′on trent′, -ôn-), *n.* a city in N Staffordshire, in central England, on the Trent River: pottery and china. 255,800. Also, **Stoke′-up·on-Trent′.** Cf. **Potteries.**

Stoke Po·ges (stōk′ pō′jis), a village in S Buckinghamshire, in S England, W of London: the churchyard here is believed to be the setting of Gray's *Elegy Written in a Country Churchyard.*

stok·er (stō′kər), *n.* **1.** a person or thing that stokes. **2.** a laborer employed to tend and fuel a furnace, esp. a furnace used to generate steam, as on a steamship. **3.** *Chiefly Brit.* the fireman on a locomotive. **4.** a mechanical device for supplying coal or other solid fuel to a furnace. [1650–60; < D, equiv. to *stok*(*en*) to STOKE[1] + *-er* -ER[1]] **—stok′er·less,** *adj.*

Sto·ker (stō′kər), *n.* **Bram** (bram) (*Abraham Stoker*), 1847–1912, British novelist, born in Ireland: creator of Dracula.

Stokes (stōks), *n.* **1. Carl B(urton),** born 1927, U.S. politician: the first black mayor of a major U.S. city (Cleveland, Ohio, 1967–71). **2. Sir Frederick Wilfrid Scott,** 1860–1927, British inventor and engineer. **3. Sir George Gabriel,** 1819–1903, British physicist and mathematician, born in Ireland.

Stokes′-Ad′ams syn′drome (stōks′ad′əmz), *Med.* unconsciousness accompanying atrioventricular heart block, sometimes characterized by weakness, irregular pulse, and intermittent convulsive or nonconvulsive seizures. Also, **Stokes′-Ad′ams disease′, Adams-Stokes syndrome, Adams-Stokes disease.** [named after W. *Stokes* (1804–78), and R. *Adams* (1791–1875), Irish physicians]

Stokes′ as′ter (stōks), a composite plant, *Stokesia laevis,* having lavender-blue, asterlike flowers. [1885–90; named after J. *Stokes* (d. 1831), English botanist]

Stokes′ law′, *Physics.* **1.** the law that the force that retards a sphere moving through a viscous fluid is directly proportional to the velocity of the sphere, the radius of the sphere, and the viscosity of the fluid. **2.** the law that the frequency of luminescence induced by radiation is usually less than the frequency of the radiation. [named after Sir G. STOKES]

Sto·kow·ski (stə kou′skē, -kôf′-, -kôv′-), *n.* **Le·o·pold An·to·ni Sta·ni·slaw** (lē′ə pōld′ än tō′nē stä nē′släf), 1882–1977, U.S. orchestra conductor, born in England.

STOL (es′tôl′), *n.* a convertiplane that can become airborne after a short takeoff run and has forward speeds comparable to those of conventional aircraft. [*s*(*hort*) *t*(*ake*)*o*(*ff and*) *l*(*anding*)]

sto·la (stō′lə), *n., pl.* **-lae** (-lē), **-las.** a long, loose tunic or robe, with or without sleeves, worn by women of ancient Rome. [1720–30; < L < Gk *stolḗ*; see STOLE[2]]

stole[1] (stōl), *v.* pt. of **steal.**

stole[2] (stōl), *n.* **1.** an ecclesiastical vestment consisting of a narrow strip of silk or other material worn over the shoulders or, by deacons, over the left shoulder only, and arranged to hang down in front to the knee or below. Cf. **tippet** (def. 2). **2.** a woman's shoulder scarf of fur, marabou, silk, or other material. Cf. **tippet** (def. 1). **3.** a long robe, esp. one worn by the matrons of ancient Rome. [bef. 950; ME, OE < L *stola* < Gk *stolḗ* clothing, robe; akin to Gk *stéllein* to array, OE *stellan* to place, put]

sto·len (stō′lən), *v.* pp. of **steal.**

stol·id (stol′id), *adj.* not easily stirred or moved mentally; unemotional; impassive. [1590–1600; < L *stolidus* inert, dull, stupid] **—sto·lid·i·ty** (stə lid′i tē), **stol′id·ness,** *n.* **—stol′id·ly,** *adv.*
—Syn. apathetic, lethargic, phlegmatic.

stol·len (stō′lən; *Ger.* shtô′lən), *n. German Cookery.* a sweetened bread made from raised dough, usually containing nuts, raisins, and citron. [1925–30; < G *Stolle*(*n*), lit., post, support; so called from its shape]

sto·lon (stō′lən), *n.* **1.** *Bot.* a prostrate stem, at or just below the surface of the ground, that produces new plants from buds at its tips or nodes. **2.** *Zool.* a rootlike extension of the body wall in a compound organism, as a bryozoan, usually giving rise to new members by budding. [1595–1605; < L *stolōn-* (s. of *stolō*) branch, shoot, twig] **—sto·lon·ic** (stō lon′ik), *adj.*

sto·lon·ate (stō′lə nit, -nāt′), *adj.* having stolons; developing from a stolon. [< NL *stolōnātus*; see STOLON, -ATE[1]]

sto·lo·nif·er·ous (stō′lə nif′ər əs), *adj.* producing or bearing stolons. [1770–80; STOLON + -I- + -FEROUS] **—sto′lon·if′er·ous·ly,** *adv.*

sto·lon·i·za·tion (stō′lə nə zā′shən), *n.* the production of stolons. [STOLON + -IZE + -ATION]

sto·ma (stō′mə), *n., pl.* **sto·ma·ta** (stō′mə tə, stom′ə-, stō mä′tə), **sto·mas. 1.** Also, **stomate.** *Bot.* any of various small apertures, esp. one of the minute orifices or slits in the epidermis of leaves, stems, etc., through which gases are exchanged. **2.** *Zool.* a mouth or ingestive opening, esp. when in the form of a small or simple aperture. **3.** *Med.* an artificial opening between two hollow organs or between one hollow organ and the outside of the body, constructed to permit the passage of body fluids or waste products. [1675–85; < NL < Gk *stóma* mouth] **—sto′mal,** *adj.*

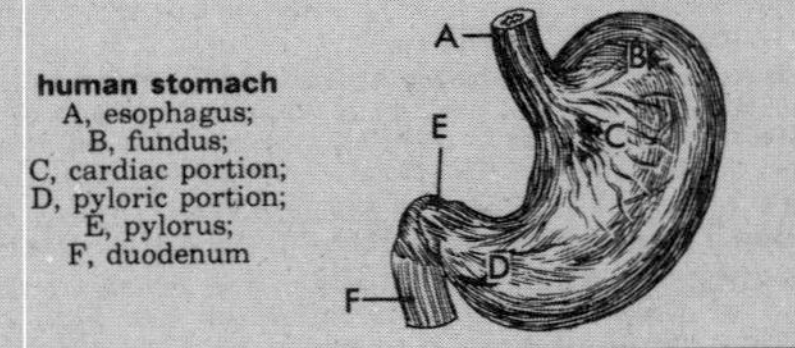

human stomach
A, esophagus;
B, fundus;
C, cardiac portion;
D, pyloric portion;
E, pylorus;
F, duodenum

stom·ach (stum′ək), *n.* **1.** *Anat., Zool.* **a.** a saclike enlargement of the alimentary canal, as in humans and certain animals, forming an organ for storing, diluting, and digesting food. **b.** such an organ or an analogous portion of the alimentary canal when divided into two or more sections or parts. **c.** any one of these sections. **2.** *Zool.* any analogous digestive cavity or tract in invertebrates. **3.** the part of the body containing the stomach; belly or abdomen. **4.** appetite for food. **5.** desire, inclination, or liking: *I have no stomach for this trip.* **6.** *Obs.* **a.** spirit; courage. **b.** pride; haughtiness. **c.** resentment; anger. *—v.t.* **7.** to endure or tolerate (someone or something): *I can't stomach your constant nagging.* **8.** *Obs.* to be offended at or resent. [1300–50; ME *stomak* < L *stomachus* gullet, stomach < Gk *stómachos* orig., opening; akin to STOMA]
—Syn. 7. bear, stand, abide, countenance.

stom·ach·ache (stum′ək āk′), *n.* pain in the stomach or abdomen; colic. Also, **stom′ach ache′.** [1755–65; STOMACH + ACHE] **—stom′ach-ach′y,** *adj.*

stom·ach·er (stum′ə kər), *n.* a richly ornamented garment covering the stomach and chest, worn by both sexes in the 15th and 16th centuries, and later worn under a bodice by women. See illus. on next page. [1400–50; late ME; see STOMACH, -ER[1]]

stomacher

sto•mach•ic (stō mak′ik), *adj.* Also, **sto•mach′i•cal. 1.** of or pertaining to the stomach; gastric. **2.** beneficial to the stomach; stimulating gastric digestion; sharpening the appetite. —*n.* **3.** a stomachic agent or drug. [1650–60; < L *stomachicus* < Gk *stomachikós.* See STOMACH, -IC] —**sto•mach′i•cal•ly,** *adv.*

stom′ach pump′, *Med.* a suction pump for removing the contents of the stomach, used esp. in cases of poisoning. [1815–25]

stom′ach sweet′bread, sweetbread (def. 1).

stom′ach tooth′, a lower canine milk tooth of infants. [1870–75, *Amer.;* so called because its appearance is often accompanied by gastric disturbance]

stom′ach worm′, a nematode, *Haemonchus contortus,* parasitic in the stomach of sheep, cattle, and related animals. Also called **twisted stomach worm, wireworm.** [1640–50]

stom•ach•y (stum′ə kē), *adj.* **1.** paunchy; having a prominent stomach. **2.** *Brit. Dial.* irritable; quick to take offense. [1815–25; STOMACH + -Y[1]]

stomat-, var. of **stomato-** before a vowel: *stomatitis.*

sto•ma•ta (stō′mə tə, stom′ə-, stō mä′tə), *n.* a pl. of **stoma.**

stom•a•tal (stom′ə tl, stō′mə-), *adj.* **1.** of, pertaining to, or of the nature of a stoma. **2.** having stomata. [1860–65; STOMAT- + -AL[1]]

sto•mate (stō′māt), *n.* stoma (def. 1). [perh. by back formation from STOMATA, based on an assumed NL sing. *stomatum; see -ATE[1]]

sto•mat•ic (stō mat′ik), *adj.* **1.** pertaining to the mouth. **2.** stomatal. [1650–60; < Gk *stomatikós.* See STOMAT-, -IC]

sto•ma•ti•tis (stō′mə tī′tis, stom′ə-), *n. Pathol.* inflammation of the mouth. [1855–60; STOMAT- + -ITIS] —**sto•ma•tit•ic** (stō′mə tit′ik, stom′ə-), *adj.*

stomato-, a combining form meaning "mouth," used in the formation of compound words: *stomatoplasty.* Also, *esp. before a vowel,* **stomat-.** Cf. **-stome, -stomous, -stomy.** [< Gk *stomat-,* s. of *stóma;* see STOMA]

sto•ma•tol•o•gy (stō′mə tol′ə jē, stom′ə-), *n.* the science dealing with the mouth and its diseases. [1890–95; STOMATO- + -LOGY] —**sto•mat•o•log•ic** (stō mat′l oj′ik, stō′mə tl-), **sto•mat′o•log′i•cal,** *adj.* —**sto′ma•tol′o•gist,** *n.*

sto•mat•o•my (stō mat′ə mē), *n., pl.* **-mies.** *Surg.* stomatotomy.

sto•mat•o•plas•ty (stō mat′ə plas′tē, stō′mə tə-), *n.* plastic surgery of the mouth or the cervix. [1855–60; STOMATO- + -PLASTY] —**sto•mat′o•plas′tic,** *adj.*

sto•mat•o•pod (stō mat′ə pod′, stō′mə tə-), *n.* any crustacean of the order Stomatopoda, having a carapace that does not cover the posterior thorax and a broad abdomen bearing gills on the appendages. [1875–80; STOMATO- + -POD]

sto•ma•tot•o•my (stō′mə tot′ə mē, stom′ə-), *n., pl.* **-mies.** *Surg.* incision of the cervix to facilitate labor. Also, **stomatomy.** [STOMATO- + -TOMY]

stom•a•tous (stom′ə təs, stō′mə-), *adj.* stomatal. [1875–80; STOMAT- + -OUS]

-stome, a combining form meaning "organism having a mouth or mouthlike organ" (*cyclostome*), "mouthlike organ" (*cytostome*), as specified by the initial element. Cf. **-stomous, -stomy.** [comb. form repr. Gk *stóma* mouth, and *stómion* little mouth]

sto•mo•dae•um (stō′mə dē′əm, stom′ə-), *n., pl.* **-dae•a** (-dē′ə). stomodeum. —**sto′mo•dae′al,** *adj.*

sto•mo•de•um (stō′mə dē′əm, stom′ə-), *n., pl.* **-de•a** (-dē′ə). *Embryol.* a depression in the ectoderm of the oral region of a young embryo, which develops into the mouth and oral cavity. [1875–80; < NL < Gk *stóm(a)* STOMA + *hodaîon* (neut. sing.) on the way; akin to -ODE[2]] —**sto′mo•de′al,** *adj.*

-stomous, a combining form meaning "having a mouth" of the kind or number specified by the initial element: *monostomous.* [< Gk *-stomos* -mouthed, adj. deriv. of *stóma* mouth; see -STOME, -OUS]

stomp (stomp), *v.t.* **1.** stamp (defs. 1–3). —*v.i.* **2.** stamp (defs. 11, 12). **3.** to dance the stomp. —*n.* **4.** stamp (def. 14). **5.** a jazz composition, esp. in early jazz, marked by a driving rhythm and a fast tempo. **6.** a dance to this music, usually marked by heavy stamping of the feet. [1820–30; var. of STAMP] —**stomp′er,** *n.*

-stomy, a combining form used in the names of surgical operations that involve the establishment of an artificial opening into or between the part or parts specified by the initial element: *gastrostomy.* [< Gk *-stomia,* deriv. of *stóma* mouth. See -STOME, -Y[3]]

stone (stōn), *n., pl.* **stones** for 1–5, 7–19, **stone** for 6, *adj., adv., v.,* **stoned, ston•ing.** —*n.* **1.** the hard substance, formed of mineral matter, of which rocks consist. **2.** a rock or particular piece or kind of rock, as a boulder or piece of agate. **3.** a piece of rock quarried and worked into a specific size and shape for a particular purpose: *paving stone; building stone.* **4.** a small piece of rock, as a pebble. **5.** See **precious stone. 6.** one of various units of weight, esp. the British unit equivalent to 14 pounds (6.4 kg). **7.** something resembling a small piece of rock in size, shape, or hardness. **8.** any small, hard seed, as of a date; pit. **9.** *Bot.* the hard endocarp of a drupe, as of a peach. **10.** *Pathol.* **a.** a calculous concretion in the body, as in the kidney, gallbladder, or urinary bladder. **b.** a disease arising from such a concretion. **11.** a gravestone or tombstone. **12.** a grindstone. **13.** a millstone. **14.** a hailstone. **15.** *Building Trades.* any of various artificial materials imitating cut stone or rubble. **16.** *Print.* a table with a smooth surface, formerly made of stone, on which page forms are composed. **17.** (in lithography) any surface on which an artist draws or etches a picture or design from which a lithograph is made. **18.** a playing piece in the game of dominoes, checkers, or backgammon. **19.** Usually, **stones.** testes. **20. cast the first stone,** to be the first to condemn or blame a wrongdoer; be hasty in one's judgment: *What right has she to cast the first stone?* **21. leave no stone unturned,** to exhaust every possibility in attempting to achieve one's goal; spare no effort: *We will leave no stone unturned in our efforts to find the culprit.* —*adj.* **22.** made of or pertaining to stone. **23.** made of stoneware: *a stone mug or bottle.* —*adv.* **24.** completely; totally (usually used in combination): *stone cold.* —*v.t.* **25.** to throw stones at; drive by pelting with stones. **26.** to put to death by pelting with stones. **27.** to provide, fit, pave, line, face or fortify with stones. **28.** to rub (something) with or on a stone, as to sharpen, polish, or smooth. **29.** to remove stones from, as fruit. **30.** *Obs.* to make insensitive or unfeeling. [bef. 900; (n.) ME *stan, sto(o)n,* OE *stān;* c. D *steen,* G *Stein,* ON *steinn,* Goth *stains;* akin to Gk *stía* pebble, L *stiria* icicle; (v.) ME *stanen, stonen,* deriv. of the n.; (adj. and adv.) ME, deriv. of the n.] —**ston′a•ble, stone′a•ble,** *adj.* —**stone′less,** *adj.* —**stone′less•ness,** *n.* —**stone′•like′,** *adj.* —**ston′er,** *n.*

Stone (stōn), *n.* **1. Edward Du•rell** (do͝o rel′, dyo͝o-), 1902–78, U.S. architect. **2. Har•lan Fiske** (här′lən), 1872–1946, U.S. jurist: Chief Justice of the U.S. 1941–46. **3. Irving,** born 1903, U.S. author. **4. I(sidor) F(einstein)** (fīn′stīn), born 1907, U.S. political journalist. **5. Lucy,** 1818–93, U.S. suffragist (wife of Henry Brown Blackwell).

Stone′ Age′, the period in the history of humankind, preceding the Bronze Age and the Iron Age, and marked by the use of stone implements and weapons: subdivided into the Paleolithic, Mesolithic, and Neolithic periods. [1860–65]

stone′ bass′ (bas), wreckfish. [1690–1700]

stone-blind (stōn′blīnd′), *adj.* completely blind. [1325–75; ME (north) *staneblynde;* see STONE, BLIND] —**stone′blind′ness,** *n.* —**Syn.** See **blind.**

stone-broke (stōn′brōk′), *adj.* having no money whatsoever. [1885–90]

stone′ bruise′, a bruise on the sole of the foot, caused by walking on or striking against a small stone or other hard object. [1795–1805, *Amer.*]

stone′ canal′, (in certain echinoderms) a tube lined with calcareous deposits, connecting the madreporite with a circular canal around the mouth. [1885–90]

stone•cat (stōn′kat′), *n.* a yellowish-brown, freshwater catfish, *Noturus flavus,* of the Mississippi River valley and Great Lakes, having poisonous pectoral spines. Also called **beadeye.** [1870–75, *Amer.;* STONE + CAT[1]]

stone•chat (stōn′chat′), *n.* any of several small Old World birds, esp. of the genus *Saxicola,* as *S. torquata.* [1775–85; STONE + CHAT, so called from its warning cry which sounds like a clash of stones]

stone′ chi′na, hard earthenware containing china stone. [1815–25]

stone′ crab′, an edible crab, *Menippe mercenaria,* of rocky shores from the southern U.S. to Mexico and certain areas of the Caribbean, prized for the meat of its claws. [1700–10, *Amer.*]

stone•crop (stōn′krop′), *n.* **1.** any plant of the genus *Sedum,* esp. a mosslike herb, *S. acre,* having small, fleshy leaves and yellow flowers, frequently growing on rocks and walls. **2.** any of various related plants. [bef. 1000; ME *stooncrop,* OE *stāncrop.* See STONE, CROP]

stone′crop fam′ily, the plant family Crassulaceae, characterized by succulent herbaceous plants and shrubs with simple, fleshy leaves, clusters of small flowers, and dry, dehiscent fruit, and including hen-and-chickens, houseleek, kalanchoe, live-forever, orpine, sedum, and stonecrop.

stone′ cur′lew, thick-knee. [1670–80]

stone•cut•ter (stōn′kut′ər), *n.* **1.** a person who cuts or carves stone. **2.** a machine for cutting or dressing stone. [1530–40; STONE + CUTTER] —**stone′cut′ting,** *n.*

stoned (stōnd), *adj. Slang.* **1.** drunk. **2.** intoxicated or dazed from drugs; high (sometimes fol. by *out*): *to be stoned out on pot.* [1475–85 for sense "pelted with stones"; 1950–55 for current senses; STONE + -ED[2]]

stone-dead (stōn′ded′), *adj.* undeniably dead; completely lifeless. [1250–1300; ME (north) *standed.* See STONE, DEAD]

stone-deaf (stōn′def′), *adj.* totally deaf. [1830–40; STONE + DEAF]

stone•face (stōn′fās′), *n.* See **living stones.** [STONE + FACE]

stone•fish (stōn′fish′), *n., pl.* **-fish•es,** (*esp. collectively*) **-fish.** a tropical scorpion fish, *Synanceja verrucosa,* having dorsal-fin spines from which a deadly poison is discharged. [1660–70; STONE + FISH]

stone•fly (stōn′flī′), *n., pl.* **-flies.** any of numerous dull-colored primitive aquatic insects of the order Plecoptera, having a distinctive flattened body shape: a major food source for game fish, esp. bass and trout, which makes them popular as models for fishing flies. [1400–50; late ME *ston flie.* See STONE, FLY[2]]

stone′ fruit′, a fruit with a stone or hard endocarp, as a peach or plum; drupe. [1515–25]

stone′ fun′gus, the Canadian tuckahoe, *Polyporus tuberaster,* an irregularly spherical mass of fungus mycelium and earth, forming a pseudosclerotium. Also called **fungus stone.**

stone-ground (stōn′ground′), *adj.* (of wheat or other grain) ground between millstones, esp. those made of burstone, so as to retain the whole of the grain and preserve nutritional content. [1900–05]

Stone•ham (stō′nəm), *n.* a town in E Massachusetts, near Boston. 21,424.

Stone•henge (stōn′henj), *n.* a prehistoric monument on Salisbury Plain, Wiltshire, England, consisting of a large circle of megaliths surrounding a smaller circle and four massive trilithons; dating to late Neolithic and early Bronze Age times (c1700–1200 B.C.) and believed to have been connected with a sun cult or used for astronomical observations. [cf. HENGE]

stone′ lan′tern, 1. (in Japan) an intricately carved lantern of stone, often placed in a garden or before a shrine. **2.** a usually inexpensive reproduction of this, often made of cast metal.

stone′ lil′y, a fossil crinoid. [1800–10]

stone•man (stōn′mən), *n., pl.* **-men.** a stonecutter or stoneworker. [1870–75; STONE + -MAN]

stone′ mar′ten, a marten, *Mustela foina,* of Europe and Asia, having a white mark on the throat and breast. Also called **beech marten.** [1835–45]

stone•ma•son (stōn′mā′sən), *n.* a person who builds with or dresses stone. [1750–60; STONE + MASON] —**stone′ma′son•ry,** *n.*

stone′ mint′, dittany (def. 2). [1850–55; so called because it grows in rocky woodlands]

Stone′ Moun′tain, 1. a massive, dome-shaped granite outcrop in NW Georgia, near Atlanta: sculptures of Confederate heroes: 825 ft. (252 m) high. **2.** a town in NW Georgia, near the sculpted Stone Mountain. 4867.

stone′ pars′ley, a parsley, *Sison amomum,* of Eurasia, bearing aromatic seeds that are used as a condiment. [1540–50]

stone′ pine′, 1. Also called **umbrella pine, parasol pine.** a tree, *Pinus pinea,* native to southern Europe, having branches forming an umbrellalike crown and bearing edible, nutlike seeds. **2.** any of several piñons. [1750–60]

stone′ plant′. See **living stones.** [1670–80]

Stone′ Riv′er, a river in central Tennessee, flowing NW to the Cumberland River. Cf. **Murfreesboro** (def. 1).

stone•roll•er (stōn′rō′lər), *n.* **1.** an American minnow, *Campostoma anomalum,* named from its habit of moving stones as it feeds. **2.** any of several other minnows or suckers with similar habits, as *Hypentelium nigricans.* [1795–1805; STONE + ROLLER]

stone's′ throw′, a short distance: *The railroad station is only a stone's throw from our house.* [1575–85]

stone•wall (stōn′wôl′), *v.i.* **1.** to engage in stonewalling. **2.** *Brit.* filibuster (def. 3). **3.** *Cricket.* (of a batsman) to play a defensive game, as by persistently blocking the ball instead of batting it for distance and runs. —*v.t.* **4.** *Informal.* to block, stall, or resist intentionally: *lobbying efforts to stonewall passage of the legislation.* **5.** *Brit.* to obstruct (the passage of a legislative bill) in Parliament, esp. by excessive or prolonged debate. —*adj.* **6.** pertaining to or characteristic of stonewalling: *a new round of stonewall tactics.* [v. and adj. use of n. phrase *stone wall*] —**stone′wall′er,** *n.*

stone•wall•ing (stōn′wô′ling), *n.* the act of stalling, evading, or filibustering, esp. to avoid revealing politically embarrassing information. [1875–80; STONEWALL + -ING[1]]

Stone′wall Jack′son (stōn′wôl′), nickname of Thomas Jonathan Jackson.

stone•ware (stōn′wâr′), *n.* a hard, opaque, vitrified ceramic ware. [1675–85; STONE + WARE[1]]

stone•wash (stōn′wosh′, -wôsh′), *v.t.* to wash (cloth) with pebbles or stones so as to give the appearance of wear. [STONE + WASH]

stone•work (stōn′wûrk′), *n.* **1.** any construction, as walls or the like, of stone; stone masonry. **2.** the techniques, processes, work, or art of dressing, setting, or designing in stone. **3.** Usually, **stoneworks.** (*usually used with a singular v.*) a place where stone is dressed, as for building. [bef. 1000; ME *stoonwerk,* OE *stānweorc.* See STONE, WORK] —**stone′work′er,** *n.*

stone•wort (stōn′wûrt′, -wôrt′), *n.* any of a plantlike group of green algae constituting the class Charophyceae, having a jointed body frequently encrusted with lime and usually attached to the bottom in fresh water. [1575–85; STONE + WORT[2]]

ston•ey (stō′nē), *adj.,* **ston•i•er, ston•i•est.** stony.

Ston′ey Creek′, a town in SE Ontario, in S Canada. 36,762.

Ston•ing•ton (stō′ning tən), *n.* a town in NE Connecticut. 16,220.

stonk•er (stong′kər), *v.t. Australian Informal.* **1.** to hit hard; knock unconscious. **2.** to defeat decisively. **3.** to baffle; confuse. [1910–15; orig. uncert.]

ston•y (stō′nē), *adj.,* **ston•i•er, ston•i•est. 1.** full of or abounding in stones or rock: *a stony beach.* **2.** pertaining to or characteristic of stone. **3.** resembling or suggesting stone, esp. in its hardness. **4.** unfeeling; merciless; obdurate: *a stony heart.* **5.** motionless or rigid; without expression, as the eyes or a look: *a hard, stony stare.* **6.** petrifying; stupefying: *stony fear.* **7.** having a stone or stones, as fruit. **8.** *Slang.* stone-broke. Also,

CONCISE PRONUNCIATION KEY: act, cāpe, dâre, pärt; set, ēqual; if, ice; ox, ōver, ôrder, oil, bo͝ok, bo͞ot, out; up, ûrge; child; sing; shoe; thin, *th*at; zh as in *treasure.* ə = *a* as in *alone, e* as in *system, i* as in *easily, o* as in *gallop, u* as in *circus;* ᵊ as in *fire* (fīᵊr), *hour* (ouᵊr). l and n can serve as syllabic consonants, as in *cradle* (krād′l), and *button* (but′n). See the full key inside the front cover.

stoney. [bef. 1000; ME; OE *stānig.* See STONE, -Y[1]] **—ston′i·ly,** *adv.* **—ston′i·ness,** *n.*
—Syn. 1. rocky, pebbly. **4.** adamant, hard, flinty, pitiless, inflexible, unbending.

Ston′y Brook′, a town in N Long Island, in SE New York. 16,155.

ston′y cor′al, a true coral consisting of numerous anthozoan polyps embedded in the calcareous material that they secrete. [1610–20]

ston·y-faced (stō′nē fāst′), *adj.* having a rigid, expressionless face. [1930–35]

ston·y-heart·ed (stō′nē här′tid), *adj.* hard-hearted. [1560–70] **—ston′y-heart′ed·ly,** *adv.* **—ston′y-heart′ed·ness,** *n.*

ston′y pit′, *Plant Pathol.* a disease of pears, caused by a virus and characterized by deformed, pitted fruit.

Ston′y Point′, a village in SE New York, on the Hudson: site of a strategic fort in the Revolutionary War. 12,838.

stood (stŏŏd), *v.* pt. and pp. of **stand.**

stooge (stōōj), *n., v.,* **stooged, stoog·ing.** *—n.* **1.** an entertainer who feeds lines to the main comedian and usually serves as the butt of his or her jokes. **2.** any underling, assistant, or accomplice. *—v.i.* **3.** to act as a stooge. [1910–15, *Amer.*; orig. uncert.]

stook (stŏŏk, stōōk), *Chiefly Brit. and Canadian.* *—n.* **1.** shock[2] (def. 1). *—v.t.* **2.** shock[2] (def. 2). *—v.i.* **3.** to stack sheaves of grain; form a pile of straw. [1400–50; late ME *stouk,* OE *stūc* heap; c. MLG *stūke,* G *Stauche;* akin to STOCK] **—stook′er,** *n.*

stool (stōōl), *n.* **1.** a single seat on legs or a pedestal and without arms or a back. **2.** a short, low support on which to stand, step, kneel, or rest the feet while sitting. **3.** *Hort.* the stump, base, or root of a plant from which propagative organs are produced, as shoots for layering. **4.** the base of a plant that annually produces new stems or shoots. **5.** a cluster of shoots or stems springing up from such a base or from any root, or a single shoot or layer. **6.** a bird fastened to a pole or perch and used as a decoy. **7.** an artificial duck or other bird, usually made from wood, used as a decoy by hunters. **8.** a privy. **9.** the fecal matter evacuated at each movement of the bowels. **10.** the sill of a window. See diag. under **double-hung. 11.** a bishop's seat considered as symbolic of his authority; see. **12.** the sacred chair of certain African chiefs, symbolic of their kingship. **13. fall between two stools,** to fail, through hesitation or indecision, to select either of two alternatives. *—v.i.* **14.** to put forth shoots from the base or root, as a plant; form a stool. **15.** *Slang.* to turn informer; serve as a stool pigeon. [bef. 900; ME; OE *stōl;* c. G *Stuhl,* ON *stóll,* Goth *stols* chair; all < Gmc **stō-* (< IE root of STAND) + *-*l-* suffix; akin to OCS *stolŭ* throne] **—stool′like′,** *adj.*

stool′ pi′geon, 1. a pigeon used as a decoy. **2.** Also called **stool·ie** (stōō′lē), **stooly.** *Slang.* a person employed or acting as a decoy or informer, esp. for the police. [1820–30, *Amer.*]

stool·y (stōō′lē), *n., pl.* **stool·ies.** *Slang.* See **stool pigeon** (def. 2). [STOOL (PIGEON) + -Y[2]]

stoop[1] (stōōp), *v.i.* **1.** to bend the head and shoulders, or the body generally, forward and downward from an erect position: *to stoop over a desk.* **2.** to carry the head and shoulders habitually bowed forward: *to stoop from age.* **3.** (of trees, precipices, etc.) to bend, bow, or lean. **4.** to descend from one's level of dignity; condescend; deign: *Don't stoop to argue with him.* **5.** to swoop down, as a hawk at prey. **6.** to submit; yield. **7.** *Obs.* to come down from a height. *—v.t.* **8.** to bend (oneself, one's head, etc.) forward and downward. **9.** *Archaic.* to abase, humble, or subdue. *—n.* **10.** the act or an instance of stooping. **11.** a stooping position or carriage of body: *The elderly man walked with a stoop.* **12.** a descent from dignity or superiority. **13.** a downward swoop, as of a hawk. [bef. 900; ME *stoupen* (v.), OE *stūpian;* c. MD *stūpen* to bend, bow; akin to STEEP[1]] **—stoop′er,** *n.* **—stoop′ing·ly,** *adv.*
—Syn. 1. lean, crouch. See **bend[1]**.

stoop[2] (stōōp), *n.* a small raised platform, approached by steps and sometimes having a roof and seats, at the entrance of a house; a small porch. [1670–80, *Amer.*; < D *stoep;* c. MLG *stōpe,* G *Stufe* step in a stair. See STEP]

stoop[3] (stōōp), *n.* stoup.

stoop′ ball′, a game resembling baseball, played in a street, schoolyard, or other confined paved area, in which a ball is thrown forcibly against a stairway or wall so that it rebounds into the air, bases and runs being awarded depending on the number of bounces the ball takes before being caught by the opposing player or team. [1940–45]

stoop′ la′bor, the physical labor associated with the cultivation or picking of crops in farm fields, esp. as performed by poorly paid, unskilled workers. [1945–50]

stop (stop), *v.,* **stopped** or (*Archaic*) **stopt; stop·ping;** *n.* *—v.t.* **1.** to cease from, leave off, or discontinue: *to stop running.* **2.** to cause to cease; put an end to: *to stop noise in the street.* **3.** to interrupt, arrest, or check (a course, proceeding, process, etc.): *Stop your work just a minute.* **4.** to cut off, intercept, or withhold: *to stop supplies.* **5.** to restrain, hinder, or prevent (usually fol. by *from*): *I couldn't stop him from going.* **6.** to prevent from proceeding, acting, operating, continuing, etc.: *to stop a speaker; to stop a car.* **7.** to block, obstruct, or close (a passageway, channel, opening, duct, etc.) (usually fol. by *up*): *He stopped up the sink with a paper towel. He stopped the hole in the tire with a patch.* **8.** to fill the hole or holes in (a wall, a decayed tooth, etc.). **9.** to close (a container, tube, etc.) with a cork, plug, bung, or the like. **10.** to close the external orifice of (the ears, nose, mouth, etc.). **11.** *Sports.* **a.** to check (a stroke, blow, etc.); parry; ward off. **b.** to defeat (an opposing player or team): *The Browns stopped the Colts.* **c.** *Boxing.* to defeat by a knockout or technical knockout: *Louis stopped Conn in the 13th round.* **12.** *Banking.* to notify a bank to refuse payment of (a check) upon presentation. **13.** *Bridge.* to have an honor card and a sufficient number of protecting cards to keep an opponent from continuing to win in (a suit). **14.** *Music.* **a.** to close (a fingerhole) in order to produce a particular note from a wind instrument. **b.** to press down (a string of a violin, viola, etc.) in order to alter the pitch of the tone produced from it. **c.** to produce (a particular note) by so doing. *—v.i.* **15.** to come to a stand, as in a course or journey; halt. **16.** to cease moving, proceeding, speaking, acting, operating, etc.; to pause; desist. **17.** to cease; come to an end. **18.** to halt for a brief visit (often fol. by *at, in,* or *by*): *He is stopping at the best hotel in town.* **19. stop by,** to make a brief visit on one's way elsewhere: *I'll stop by on my way home.* **20. stop down,** *Photog.* (on a camera) to reduce (the diaphragm opening of a lens). **21. stop in,** to make a brief, incidental visit: *If you're in town, be sure to stop in.* **22. stop off,** to halt for a brief stay at some point on the way elsewhere: *On the way to Rome we stopped off at Florence.* **23. stop out, a.** to mask (certain areas of an etching plate, photographic negative, etc.) with varnish, paper, or the like, to prevent their being etched, printed, etc. **b.** to withdraw temporarily from school: *Most of the students who stop out eventually return to get their degrees.* **24. stop over,** to stop briefly in the course of a journey: *Many motorists were forced to stop over in that town because of floods.* *—n.* **25.** the act of stopping. **26.** a cessation or arrest of movement, action, operation, etc.; end: *The noise came to a stop. Put a stop to that behavior!* **27.** a stay or sojourn made at a place, as in the course of a journey: *Above all, he enjoyed his stop in Trieste.* **28.** a place where trains or other vehicles halt to take on and discharge passengers: *Is this a bus stop?* **29.** a closing or filling up, as of a hole. **30.** a blocking or obstructing, as of a passage or channel. **31.** a plug or other stopper for an opening. **32.** an obstacle, impediment, or hindrance. **33.** any piece or device that serves to check or control movement or action in a mechanism. **34.** *Archit.* a feature terminating a molding or chamfer. **35.** *Com.* **a.** an order to refuse payment of a check. **b.** See **stop order. 36.** *Music.* **a.** the act of closing a fingerhole or pressing a string of an instrument in order to produce a particular note. **b.** a device or contrivance, as on an instrument, for accomplishing this. **c.** (in an organ) a graduated set of pipes of the same kind and giving tones of the same quality. **d.** Also called **stop knob.** a knob or handle that is drawn out or pushed back to permit or prevent the sounding of such a set of pipes or to control some other part of the organ. **e.** (in a reed organ) a group of reeds functioning like a pipe-organ stop. **37.** *Sports.* an individual defensive play or act that prevents an opponent or opposing team from scoring, advancing, or gaining an advantage, as a catch in baseball, a tackle in football, or the deflection of a shot in hockey. **38.** *Naut.* a piece of small line used to lash or fasten something, as a furled sail. **39.** *Phonet.* **a.** an articulation that interrupts the flow of air from the lungs. **b.** a consonant sound characterized by stop articulation, as *p, b, t, d, k,* and *g.* Cf. **continuant. 40.** *Photog.* the diaphragm opening of a lens, esp. as indicated by an f- number. **41.** *Building Trades.* **a.** See **stop bead. b.** doorstop (def. 2). **42.** any of various marks used as punctuation at the end of a sentence, esp. a period. **43.** the word "stop" printed in the body of a telegram or cablegram to indicate a period. **44. stops,** (*used with a singular v.*) a family of card games whose object is to play all of one's cards in a predetermined sequence before one's opponents. **45.** *Zool.* a depression in the face of certain animals, esp. dogs, marking the division between the forehead and the projecting part of the muzzle. See diag. under **dog. 46. pull out all the stops, a.** to use every means available. **b.** to express, do, or carry out something without reservation. [bef. 1000; ME *stoppen* (v.), OE *-stoppian* (in *forstoppian* to stop up); c. D, LG *stoppen,* G *stopfen;* all << VL **stuppāre* to plug with oakum, deriv. of L *stuppa* coarse hemp or flax < Gk *stýppē*] **—stop′less,** *adj.* **—stop′less·ness,** *n.*
—Syn. 3. STOP, ARREST, CHECK, HALT imply causing a cessation of movement or progress (literal or figurative). STOP is the general term for the idea: *to stop a clock.* ARREST usually refers to stopping by imposing a sudden and complete restraint: *to arrest development.* CHECK implies bringing about an abrupt, partial, or temporary stop: *to check a trotting horse.* To HALT means to make a temporary stop, esp. one resulting from a command: *to halt a company of soldiers.* **5.** thwart, obstruct, impede. **16.** quit. **26.** halt; termination. **28.** terminal. **33.** governor. **—Ant. 1–3.** start.

stop′-ac′tion photog′raphy (stop′ak′shən), *Motion Pictures.* See **stop motion** (def. 1).

stop-and-go (stop′ən gō′), *adj.* characterized by periodically enforced stops, as caused by heavy traffic or traffic signals: *stop-and-go traffic.* [1920–25]

stop′ bath′, *Photog.* an acid bath or rinse for stopping the action of a developer before fixing a negative or print. Also called **shortstop, shortstop bath.** [1915–20]

stop′ bead′, a strip of molding along the inside of a window frame for holding a sliding sash. Also called **stop.**

stop′ clause′, a clause by which a contract or other agreement may be terminated, esp. between theatrical producers and theater owners in whose agreements it is often stipulated that when weekly receipts fall below a certain minimum usually for two consecutive weeks, the production must vacate the theater. Also called **eviction clause.**

stop·cock (stop′kok′), *n.* cock[1] (def. 3). [1575–85; STOP + COCK[1]]

stope (stōp), *n., v.,* **stoped, stop·ing.** *—n.* **1.** any excavation made in a mine, esp. from a steeply inclined vein, to remove the ore that has been rendered accessible by the shafts and drifts. *—v.i., v.t.* **2.** to mine or work by stopes. [1740–50; appar. < LG *stope;* see STOOP[2]]

stop·er (stō′pər), *n.* a machine for drilling rock from below. [1870–75; STOPE + -ER[1]]

stop·gap (stop′gap′), *n.* **1.** something that fills the place of something else that is lacking; temporary substitute; makeshift: *Candles are a stopgap when the electricity fails.* *—adj.* **2.** makeshift: *This is only a stopgap solution.* [1525–35; n., adj. use of v. phrase *stop a gap*]
—Syn. 2. improvised, temporary, substitute, impromptu.

stop·ing (stō′ping), *n. Geol.* a process by which magmas move upward in the earth by breaking off and engulfing blocks of overlying rocks. [1770–80; STOPE + -ING[1]]

stop′ knob′, stop (def. 36d). [1885–90]

stop·light (stop′līt′), *n.* **1.** a taillight that lights up as the driver of a vehicle steps on the brake pedal to slow down or stop. **2.** See **traffic light.** [1925–30; STOP + LIGHT[1]]

stop′-lim′it or′der (stop′lim′it). See **stop order.**

stop-loss (stop′lôs′, -los′), *adj.* designed or planned to prevent continued loss, as a customer's order to a broker to sell a stock if its price declines to a specific amount. [1900–05]

stop′-loss clause′, *Insurance.* a limitation on the amount of loss sustained by the insured without compensation in a given period.

stop′-loss or′der, See **stop order.**

stop′ mo′tion, *Motion Pictures.* **1.** Also called **stop-action photography, stop′-motion cinematog′raphy.** a special effect, carried out while shooting, in which the performers stop their motion and the camera is stopped while an object or performer is added to or removed from the scene, with camera movement and action then resumed for the remainder of the scene: used to create an illusion of sudden appearance or disappearance of persons or objects. **2.** See **freeze frame** (def. 1). **—stop′-mo′tion,** *adj.*

stop′ num′ber, f-number.

stop-off (stop′ôf′, -of′), *n.* stopover. Also, **stop′off′.** [1865–70; n. use of v. phrase *stop off*]

stop′ or′der, an order from a customer to a broker to sell a security if the market price drops below a designated level. Also called **stop-limit order, stop-loss order.** Cf. **limit order, market order.** [1870–75]

stop-out (stop′out′), *n.* **1.** a temporary withdrawal from school or a delay in the pursuit of one's education. **2.** a student who withdraws from school temporarily. Also, **stop′out′.** [1970–75; STOP + (DROP)OUT]

stop·o·ver (stop′ō′vər), *n.* **1.** a brief stop in the course of a journey, as to eat, sleep, or visit friends. **2.** such a stop made with the privilege of proceeding later on the ticket originally issued. [1860–65; n. use of v. phrase *stop over*]

stop·pa·ble (stop′ə bəl), *adj.* capable of being stopped. [1930–35; STOP + -ABLE] **—stop′pa·bil′i·ty, stop′pa·ble·ness,** *n.* **—stop′pa·bly,** *adv.*

stop·page (stop′ij), *n.* **1.** an act or instance of stopping; cessation of activity: *the stoppage of all work at the factory.* **2.** the state of being stopped: *During the stoppage of bus service he drove to work.* [1400–50; late ME; see STOP, -AGE]

Stop·pard (stop′ərd), *n.* **Tom** (*Thomas Straussler*), born 1937, British playwright, born in Czechoslovakia.

stop′ pay′ment, an order by the drawer of a check to his or her bank not to pay a specified check. [1915–20]

stopped′ diapa′son. See under **diapason** (def. 4). [1895–1900]

stop·per (stop′ər), *n.* **1.** a person or thing that stops. **2.** a plug, cork, bung, or other piece for closing a bottle, tube, drain, or the like. **3.** *Informal.* something or someone that commands attention, as an unusual window display or a flamboyant person. **4.** *Cards.* a card in a suit that prevents the successive taking of all tricks in the suit by the opponents. **5.** *Baseball Slang.* a formidably and consistently effective pitcher counted on to win, as a team's best starting pitcher or a superior reliever often called on to preserve a victory; pitching ace. *—v.t.* **6.** to close, secure, or fit with a stopper. [1470–80; STOP + -ER[1]] **—stop′per·less,** *adj.*

stop·ping (stop′ing), *n. Mining.* a barrier erected to prevent the flow of air or gas. [1700–05; special use of *stopping,* verbal n. of STOP; see -ING[1]]

Stop′ping by Woods′ on a Snow′y Eve′ning, a poem (1923) by Robert Frost.

stop·ple (stop′əl), *n., v.,* **-pled, -pling.** *Chiefly Northern U.S.* *—n.* **1.** a stopper, esp. for a bottle. *—v.t.* **2.** to close or fit with a stopple. [1350–1400; ME *stoppel.* See STOP, -LE]

stop′ price′, the price at which a stop order is activated.

stop′ sign′, a traffic sign requiring a motorist to stop before continuing. [1930–35]

stop′ street′, a street at the intersections of which all traffic must stop before continuing. Cf. **through street.** [1925–30]

stopt (stopt), *v. Archaic.* a pt. and pp. of **stop.**

stop′ vol′ley, *Tennis.* a softly hit volley that barely falls over the net and cannot be reached for a return. [1915–20]

stop·watch (stop′woch′), *n.* a watch with a hand or hands that can be stopped or started at any instant, used for precise timing, as in races. [1730–40; STOP + WATCH]

stor·a·ble (stôr′ə bəl, stōr′-), *adj.* **1.** capable of being stored for considerable time without loss of freshness or usability. *—n.* **2.** Usually, **storables.** articles that are storable. [1865–70; STORE + -ABLE] **—stor′a·bil′i·ty,** *n.*

CONCISE ETYMOLOGY KEY: <, descended or borrowed from; >, whence; b., blend of, blended; c., cognate with; cf., compare; deriv., derivative; equiv., equivalent; imit., imitative; obl., oblique; r., replacing; s., stem; sp., spelling, spelled; resp., respelling, respelled; trans., translation; ?, origin unknown; *, unattested; ‡, probably earlier than. See the full key inside the front cover.

stor·age (stôr′ij, stōr′-), *n.* **1.** the act of storing; state or fact of being stored: *All my furniture is in storage.* **2.** capacity or space for storing. **3.** a place, as a room or building, for storing. **4.** *Computers.* memory (def. 11). **5.** the price charged for storing goods. [1605–15; STORE + -AGE]

stor′age bat′tery, *Elect.* **1.** a voltaic battery consisting of two or more storage cells. **2.** See **storage cell.** [1880–85]

stor′age cell′, *Elect.* a cell whose energy can be renewed by passing a current through it in the direction opposite to that of the flow of current generated by the cell. Also called **secondary cell, storage battery.** [1880–85]

stor′age disease′, *Pathol.* a metabolic disorder characterized by excessive storage in certain cells of normal metabolic intermediates, as fats, iron, and carbohydrates.

stor′age life′. See **shelf life.**

stor′age or′gan, *Bot.* any swollen plant part in which food is stored, as fruit, root, or tuber.

stor′age ring′, *Physics.* a device for storing charged particles fed from an accelerator, consisting of a set of magnets placed in a ring and adjusted to keep the particles circulating until they are used. [1955–60]

stor′age wall′, a set of shelves, cabinets, or the like that covers or forms a wall. [1955–60]

sto·rax (stôr′aks, stōr′-), *n.* **1.** a solid resin with a vanillalike odor, obtained from a small tree, *Styrax officinalis:* formerly used in medicine and perfumery. **2.** a liquid balsam **(liquid storax)** obtained from species of liquidambar, esp. from the wood and inner bark of *Liquidambar orientalis* **(Levant storax),** a tree of Asia Minor: used chiefly in medicine and perfumery. **3.** any shrub or tree of the genus *Styrax,* of the storax family, having elongated clusters of showy, white flowers. [1350–1400; ME < L, var. of *styrax* < Gk *stýrax*]

sto′rax fam′ily, the plant family Styracaceae, characterized by trees and shrubs having simple, alternate leaves, clusters of bell-shaped white flowers, and fleshy or dry fruit, and including the silver bell, snowbell, and storax.

store (stôr, stōr), *n., v.,* **stored, stor·ing,** *adj.* —*n.* **1.** an establishment where merchandise is sold, usually on a retail basis. **2.** a grocery: *We need bread and milk from the store.* **3.** a stall, room, floor, or building housing or suitable for housing a retail business. **4.** a supply or stock of something, esp. one for future use. **5. stores,** supplies of food, clothing, or other requisites, as for a household, inn, or naval or military forces. **6.** *Chiefly Brit.* a storehouse or warehouse. **7.** quantity, esp. great quantity; abundance, or plenty: *a rich store of grain.* **8. in store, a.** in readiness or reserve. **b.** about to happen; imminent: *There is a great deal of trouble in store for them if they persist in their ways.* **9. set** or **lay store by,** to have high regard for; value; esteem: *She sets great store by good character.* —*v.t.* **10.** to supply or stock with something, as for future use. **11.** to accumulate or put away, for future use (usually fol. by *up* or *away*). **12.** to deposit in a storehouse, warehouse, or other place for keeping. **13.** *Computers.* to put or retain (data) in a memory unit. —*v.i.* **14.** to take in or hold supplies, goods, or articles, as for future use. **15.** to remain fresh and usable for considerable time on being stored: *Flour stores well.* —*adj.* **16.** bought from a store; commercial: *a loaf of store bread.* [1225–75; (v.) ME *storen,* aph. var. of *astoren* < OF *estorer* < L *instaurāre* to set up, renew, equiv. to *in-* IN-[2] + *staur-* (akin to Gk *staurós* across and to STEER[1]) + *-āre* inf. suffix; (n.) ME, aph. var. of *astore* < OF *estore,* deriv. of *estorer*] —**stor′er,** *n.*
—**Syn. 11.** amass, save, husband; hoard, stockpile.

store-bought (stôr′bôt′, stōr′-), *adj. Chiefly Midland and Southern U.S.* commercially made rather than homemade. [1900–05]

store′ brand′, an item offered for sale under a store's own label.

store′ card′, a token bearing the name of a business, often exchangeable for a particular item.

store·front (stôr′frunt′, stōr′-), *n.* **1.** the side of a store facing a street, usually containing display windows. **2.** a store or other establishment that has frontage on a street or thoroughfare: *After the fire the family took shelter temporarily in an abandoned storefront.* —*adj.* **3.** of or pertaining to the frontage of a store, esp. the display windows: *a storefront sign.* **4.** located or operating in a storelike area, room, or set of rooms fronting on a street: *a storefront community center.* [1935–40; STORE + FRONT]

store·house (stôr′hous′, stōr′-), *n., pl.* **-hous·es** (-hou′ziz). **1.** a building in which things are stored. **2.** any repository or source of abundant supplies, as of facts or knowledge. [1300–50; ME *storhous.* See STORE, HOUSE]
—**Syn. 1.** warehouse, depot.

store·keep·er (stôr′kē′pər, stōr′-), *n.* **1.** a person who owns a store. **2.** a person who has charge of or operates a store or stores. **3.** *U.S. Navy.* a petty officer in charge of a supply office afloat or ashore. [1610–20; STORE + KEEPER] —**store′keep′ing,** *n.*

store·room (stôr′ro͞om′, -ro͝om′, stōr′-), *n.* **1.** a room in which stores are kept. **2.** room or space for storage. [1740–50; STORE + ROOM]

stores′ ledg′er, a record kept of the amount, type, etc., of raw materials and supplies on hand, as in a manufacturing plant. Also called **stock book, stock ledger, stock record.**

store·wide (stôr′wīd′, stōr′-), *adj.* applying to all the merchandise or all the departments within a store: *the annual storewide clearance sale.* [STORE + -WIDE]

sto·rey (stôr′ē, stōr′ē), *n., pl.* **-reys.** *Chiefly Brit.* story[2].

sto·ried[1] (stôr′ēd, stōr′-), *adj.* **1.** recorded or celebrated in history or story: *the storied cities of ancient Greece.* **2.** ornamented with designs representing historical, legendary, or similar subjects. [1475–85; STORY[1] + -ED[3]]

sto·ried[2] (stôr′ēd, stōr′-), *adj.* having stories or floors (often used in combination): *a two-storied house.* Also, *esp. Brit.,* **sto′reyed.** [1615–25; STORY[2] + -ED[3]]

stork (stôrk), *n., pl.* **storks,** *(esp. collectively)* **stork. 1.** any of several wading birds of the family Ciconiidae, having long legs and a long neck and bill. Cf. **adjutant stork, jabiru, marabou** (def. 1), **white stork, wood ibis. 2. the stork,** this bird as the mythical or symbolic deliverer of a new baby: *My brother and his wife are expecting the stork in July.* [bef. 900; ME; OE *storc;* c. G *Storch,* ON *storkr;* akin to STARK] —**stork′like′,** *adj.*

white stork, *Ciconia ciconia,* length 3½ ft. (1 m)

stork's-bill (stôrks′bil′), *n.* **1.** Also called **heron's-bill.** any of various plants belonging to the genus *Erodium,* of the geranium family, having deeply lobed leaves, loose clusters of pink, purple, white, or yellow flowers, and long, slender fruit. **2.** geranium (def. 2). [1555–65]

storm (stôrm), *n.* **1.** a disturbance of the normal condition of the atmosphere, manifesting itself by winds of unusual force or direction, often accompanied by rain, snow, hail, thunder, and lightning, or flying sand or dust. **2.** a heavy fall of rain, snow, or hail, or a violent outbreak of thunder and lightning, unaccompanied by strong winds. **3.** Also called **violent storm.** *Meteorol.* a wind of 64–72 mph (29–32 m/sec). **4.** a violent military assault on a fortified place, strong position, or the like. **5.** a heavy or sudden volley or discharge: *a storm of criticism; a storm of bullets.* **6.** a violent disturbance of affairs, as a civil, political, social, or domestic commotion. **7.** a violent outburst or outbreak of expression: *a storm of applause.* **8.** *Informal.* See **storm window. 9. storm in a teacup.** See **teacup** (def. 3). —*v.i.* **10.** (of the wind or weather) to blow with unusual force, or to rain, snow, hail, etc., esp. with violence (usually used impersonally with *it* as subject): *It stormed all day.* **11.** to rage or complain with violence or fury: *He stormed angrily at me.* **12.** to deliver a violent attack or fire, as with artillery: *The troops stormed against the garrison.* **13.** to rush to an assault or attack: *The tanks stormed towards the city.* **14.** to rush angrily: *to storm out of a room.* —*v.t.* **15.** to subject to or as if to a storm: *The salesman stormed them with offers.* **16.** to utter or say with angry vehemence: *The strikers stormed their demands.* **17.** to attack or assault (persons, places, or things): *to storm a fortress.* [bef. 900; (n.) ME, OE; c. D *storm,* G *Sturm,* ON *stormr;* (v.) ME *stormen,* deriv. of the n. (cf. obs. *sturme,* ME *sturmen,* OE *styrman,* denominative v. from the same Gmc base as *storm*); akin to STIR[1]] —**storm′like′,** *adj.*
—**Syn. 1.** gale, hurricane, tempest, tornado, cyclone, squall, wind, blizzard.

Storm (shtôrm), *n.* **The·o·dore Wold·sen** (tā′ô dôr′ vôlt′sən), 1817–88, German poet and novelist.

Storm′ and Stress′. See **Sturm und Drang.** [1850–55]

storm′ boat′. See **assault boat.** [1940–45]

storm·bound (stôrm′bound′), *adj.* confined, detained, or isolated by storms: *a stormbound ship; a stormbound village.* [1820–30; STORM + -BOUND[1]]

storm′ cel′lar, a cellar or underground chamber for refuge during violent storms; cyclone cellar. [1900–05]

storm′ cen′ter, 1. the center of a cyclonic storm, the area of lowest pressure and of comparative calm. **2.** a center of disturbance, tumult, or trouble: *South Africa has been a storm center of racial conflict.* [1890–95]

storm′ coat′, an overcoat, usually of a water-repellent fabric, lined with material serving as insulation against very cold weather, often having a fur collar. Also, **storm′coat′.** [1895–1900]

storm′ door′, a supplementary outside door, usually glazed, for protecting the entrance door against drafts, driving rain, etc. [1875–80, *Amer.*]

storm′ house′, *Midland U.S. and Gulf States.* a storm cellar. [1830–40, *Amer.*]

storm·less (stôrm′lis), *adj.* without storms. [1490–1500; STORM + -LESS] —**storm′less·ly,** *adv.* —**storm′less·ness,** *n.*

storm′ pet′rel, any of several small, tube-nosed seabirds of the family Hydrobatidae, usually having black or sooty-brown plumage with a white rump. Also, **storm′-pet′rel.** Cf. **stormy petrel.** [1795–1805]

storm′ pit′, *Southern U.S.* a storm cellar.

storm·proof (stôrm′pro͞of′), *adj.* protected from or not affected by storms. [1585–95; STORM + -PROOF]

storm′ sew′er, a sewer for carrying off rainfall drained from paved surfaces, roofs, etc. Also called **storm′ drain′.**

storm′ sig′nal, 1. a visual signal, as a flag, giving advance notice of a heavy storm, used esp. along coastal areas. **2.** See **storm warning** (def. 2). [1860–65]

storm′ surge′, an abnormal rise in the level of the sea along a coast caused by the onshore winds of a severe cyclone. Also called **storm′tide′, surge.**

storm′ track′, the path followed by the center of a cyclonic storm. [1830–40]

storm′ troop′er, 1. a member of the storm troops. **2.** a member of the Sturmabteilung of Nazi Germany. [1920–25]

storm′ troops′, *Mil.* (formerly) German troops specially chosen and equipped for carrying out assault operations. [1915–20; trans. of G *Sturmtruppen*]

storm′ warn′ing, 1. a showing of storm signals. **2.** *Meteorol.* a National Weather Service warning of winds having speeds of 48 knots (55 mph, 25 m/sec) or greater. Cf. **hurricane warning, warning** (def. 3). **3.** any sign of approaching trouble: *The troops on the border were a storm warning, and we prepared for war. His angry look was a storm warning.* [1865–70]

storm′ watch′, *Meteorol.* watch (def. 23).

storm′ win′dow, a supplementary window sash for protecting a window against drafts, driving rain, etc. Also called **storm′ sash′.** [1885–90]

storm·y (stôr′mē), *adj.,* **storm·i·er, storm·i·est. 1.** affected, characterized by, or subject to storms; tempestuous: *a stormy sea.* **2.** characterized by violent commotion, actions, speech, passions, etc.: *a stormy debate.* [1150–1200; ME; OE *stormig.* See STORM, -Y[1]] —**storm′i·ly,** *adv.* —**storm′i·ness,** *n.*

storm′y pet′rel, 1. the British storm petrel, *Hydrobates pelagicus,* of the eastern Atlantic Ocean, Mediterranean Sea, and Indian Ocean. **2.** a person who causes or likes trouble or strife. [1770–80]

Stor·no·way (stôr′nə wā′), *n.* a city in NW Scotland, in the Hebrides. 5247.

Storrs (stôrz), *n.* a town in NE Connecticut 11,394.

Stor·ting (stôr′ting′, stōr′-), *n.* the parliament of Norway, elected by popular vote, which is divided into the upper house **(Lagting),** comprising one quarter of the members, and the lower house **(Odelsting),** comprising the rest. Also, **Stor′thing.** [1825–35; < Norw, equiv. to *stor* great + *ting* assembly, court; c. THING[2]]

sto·ry[1] (stôr′ē, stōr′ē), *n., pl.* **-ries,** *v.,* **-ried, -ry·ing.** —*n.* **1.** a narrative, either true or fictitious, in prose or verse, designed to interest, amuse, or instruct the hearer or reader; tale. **2.** a fictitious tale, shorter and less elaborate than a novel. **3.** such narratives or tales as a branch of literature: *song and story.* **4.** the plot or succession of incidents of a novel, poem, drama, etc.: *The characterizations were good, but the story was weak.* **5.** a narration of an incident or a series of events or an example of these that is or may be narrated, as an anecdote, joke, etc. **6.** a narration of the events in the life of a person or the existence of a thing, or such events as a subject for narration: *the story of medicine; the story of his life.* **7.** a report or account of a matter; statement or allegation: *The story goes that he rejected the offer.* **8.** See **news story. 9.** a lie or fabrication: *What he said about himself turned out to be a story.* **10.** *Obs.* history. —*v.t.* **11.** to ornament with pictured scenes, as from history or legend. **12.** *Obs.* to tell the history or story of. [1175–1225; ME *storie* < AF *estorie* < L *historia* HISTORY] —**sto′ry·less,** *adj.*
—**Syn. 1.** legend, fable, romance; anecdote, record, history, chronicle. **5.** recital. **7.** description.

sto·ry[2] (stôr′ē, stōr′ē), *n., pl.* **-ries. 1.** a complete horizontal section of a building, having one continuous or practically continuous floor. **2.** the set of rooms on the same floor or level of a building. **3.** any major horizontal architectural division, as of a façade or the wall of a nave. **4.** a layer. Also, *esp. Brit.,* **storey.** [1350–1400; ME *storie* < AL *historia* picture decorating a building, a part of the building so decorated, hence floor, story < L *historia* HISTORY]

Sto·ry (stôr′ē, stōr′ē), *n.* **1. Joseph,** 1779–1845, U.S. jurist. **2. William Wet·more** (wet′môr′, -mōr′), 1819–95, U.S. sculptor and poet.

sto·ry·board (stôr′ē bôrd′, stōr′ē bōrd′), *n.* a panel or panels on which a sequence of sketches depict the significant changes of action and scene in a planned film, as for a movie, television show, or advertisement. [‡1945–50; STORY[1] + BOARD]

sto·ry·book (stôr′ē bo͝ok′, stōr′-), *n.* a book that contains a story or stories, esp. for children. [1705–15; STORY[1] + BOOK]

sto′ry line′, 1. plot (def. 2). **2.** a detailed description of the plot of a motion picture, TV series, etc., for use by writers, producers, prospective investors, or the like: *The story line runs to 125 pages.* Also, **sto′ry·line′.** [1945–50]

sto·ry·tell·er (stôr′ē tel′ər, stōr′-), *n.* **1.** a person who tells or writes stories or anecdotes. **2.** a person who tells more or less trivial falsehoods; fibber. [1700–10; STORY[1] + TELLER[1]]

sto·ry·tell·ing (stôr′ē tel′ing, stōr′-), *n.* the telling or writing of stories. [1700–10; STORY[1] + TELLING]

Sto·ry·ville (stôr′ē vil′, stōr′-), *n.* a red-light district of New Orleans known as a wellspring of jazz before World War I.

sto·ry·writ·er (stôr′ē rī′tər, stōr′-), *n.* **1.** a person who writes stories, tales, fables, etc. **2.** a person who writes news items for radio, television, or newspapers. [1475–85 in sense "historiographer"; STORY[1] + WRITER]

stoss (stōs; *Ger.* shtōs), *adj. Geol.* noting or pertaining to the side, as of a hill or dale, that receives or has received the thrust of a glacier or other impulse. [1875–80; < G: thrust, push]

Stoss (shtōs), *n.* **Veit** (fīt), c1440–1533, German sculptor and painter.

stot (stot), *n., v.,* **stot·ted, stot·ting.** —*n.* **1.** a springing gait of certain bovids, as gazelles and antelopes, used esp. when running in alarm from a predator. —*v.i.* **2.** to

CONCISE PRONUNCIATION KEY: *act, cāpe, dâre, pärt; set, ēqual; if, īce; ox, ōver, ôrder, oil, bo͝ok, bo͞ot, out; up, ûrge; child; sing; shoe; thin, that;* zh as in *treasure.* ə = *a* as in *alone, e* as in *system, i* as in *easily, o* as in *gallop, u* as in *circus;* ə as in *fire* (fīər), *hour* (ouər). l and n can serve as syllabic consonants, as in *cradle* (krād′l), and *button* (but′n). See the full key inside the front cover.

run with such a gait. [special use of Scots, N England dial. *stot* bound, go by leaps, bounce; perh. akin to ME *stuten* to STUTTER]

sto·ting (stō′ting), *n.* stoating.

sto·tin·ka (stô ting′kä), *n., pl.* **-ki** (-kē). a minor coin of Bulgaria, the 100th part of a lev. [< Bulg *stotínka,* deriv. of *sto,* OCS *sŭto* HUNDRED]

St.-Ouen (san twän′), *n.* a suburb of Paris in N France. 43,695.

Stough·ton (stōt′n), *n.* a city in E Massachusetts. 26,710.

stound (stound, sto͞ond), *n.* **1.** *Archaic.* a short time; short while. —*v.t., v.i.* **2.** *Chiefly Scot.* to pain; hurt. [bef. 1000; (n.) ME *sto(u)nd,* OE *stund* space of time; c. G *Stunde,* ON *stund* hour; (v.) ME *stunden* to stay, remain for a stound, deriv. of the n.; akin to STAND]

stoup (sto͞op), *n.* **1.** a basin for holy water, as at the entrance of a church. **2.** *Scot.* a pail or bucket. **3.** *Scot. and North Eng.* **a.** a drinking vessel, as a cup or tankard. **b.** the amount it holds. [1350–1400; ME *stowp* < ON *staup* drinking vessel; c. OE *stēap* flagon]

stoup (def. 1)

stour (sto͝or), *n.* **1.** *Brit. Dial.* **a.** tumult; confusion. **b.** a storm. **2.** *Brit. Dial.* blowing dust or a deposit of dust. **3.** *Archaic.* armed combat; battle. **4.** *Brit. Dial.* a time of tumult. [1250–1300; ME < OF *estour* battle < Gmc; akin to STORM]

stoush (stoush), *Australian Informal.* —*v.t.* **1.** stonker (defs. 1, 2). —*n.* **2.** a fight or brawl. [1890–95; perh. imit.]

stout (stout), *adj.* **-er, -est,** *n.* —*adj.* **1.** bulky in figure; heavily built; corpulent; thickset; fat: *She is getting too stout for her dresses.* **2.** bold, brave, or dauntless: *a stout heart; stout fellows.* **3.** firm; stubborn; resolute: *stout resistance.* **4.** forceful; vigorous: *a stout argument; a stout wind.* **5.** strong of body; hearty; sturdy: *stout seamen.* **6.** having endurance or staying power, as a horse. **7.** strong in substance or body, as a beverage. **8.** strong and thick or heavy: *a stout cudgel.* —*n.* **9.** a dark, sweet brew made of roasted malt and having a higher percentage of hops than porter. **10.** porter of extra strength. **11.** a stout person. **12.** a garment size designed for a stout man. **13.** a garment, as a suit or overcoat, in this size. [1250–1300; ME (adj.) < OF *estout* bold, proud < Gmc; cf. MD *stout* bold, MLG *stolt,* MHG *stolz* proud] —**stout′ly,** *adv.* —**stout′ness,** *n.*
—**Syn. 1.** portly, fleshy. STOUT, FAT, PLUMP imply corpulence of body. STOUT describes a heavily built but usually strong and healthy body: *a handsome stout lady.* FAT, an informal word with unpleasant connotations, suggests an unbecoming fleshy stoutness; it may, however, apply also to a hearty fun-loving type of stout person: *a fat old man; fat and jolly.* PLUMP connotes a pleasing roundness and is often used as a complimentary or euphemistic equivalent for stout, fleshy, etc.: *a plump figure attractively dressed.* **2.** valiant, gallant, intrepid, fearless, indomitable, courageous. **3.** obstinate. **5.** brawny, sinewy. —**Ant. 1.** thin, lean.

Stout (stout), *n.* **Robert,** 1844–1930, New Zealand jurist and statesman: prime minister 1884–87.

stout·en (stout′n), *v.t.* **1.** to make stout. —*v.i.* **2.** to grow stout. [1825–35; STOUT + -EN[1]]

stout-heart·ed (stout′här′tid), *adj.* brave and resolute; dauntless. [1645–55] —**stout′-heart′ed·ly,** *adv.* —**stout′-heart′ed·ness,** *n.*

stout·ish (stou′tish), *adj.* rather stout. [1825–35; STOUT + -ISH[1]]

stove[1] (stōv), *n., v.,* **stoved, stov·ing.** —*n.* **1.** a portable or fixed apparatus that furnishes heat for warmth, cooking, etc., commonly using coal, oil, gas, wood, or electricity as a source of power. **2.** a heated chamber or box for some special purpose, as a drying room or a kiln for firing pottery. —*v.t.* **3.** to treat with or subject to heat, as in a stove. [1425–75; (n.) late ME: sweat bath, heated room, prob. < MD, MLG, c. OE *stofa, stofu* heated room for bathing, OHG *stuba* (G *Stube* room; cf. BIERSTUBE), ON *stofa;* early Gmc borrowing < VL **extupa,* **extūpa* (> F *étuve* sweat room of a bath; cf. STEW[1]), n. deriv. of **extūpāre,* **extūfāre* to fill with vapor, equiv. to L *ex-* EX-[1] + VL **-tūfāre* < Gk *tȳphein* to raise smoke, smoke, akin to *tȳphos* fever (see TYPHUS); alternatively explained as a native Gmc base, borrowed into Rom (cf. IZBA); (v.) late ME *stoven* to subject to hot-air bath, deriv. of the n.]

stove[2] (stōv), *v.* a pt. and pp. of **stave.**

stove′ bolt′, a small bolt, similar to a machine screw but with a coarser thread. See diag. under **bolt.**

stove′ coal′, anthracite in sizes ranging from 2⁷⁄₁₆ to 1⅝ in. (6 to 4 cm), intermediate between egg coal and chestnut coal. [1880–85]

stove·pipe (stōv′pīp′), *n.* **1.** a pipe, as of sheet metal, serving as a stove chimney or to connect a stove with a chimney flue. **2.** See **stovepipe hat.** [1690–1700; STOVE[1] + PIPE[1]]

stove′pipe hat′, *Older Slang.* a tall silk hat. [1850–55, *Amer.*]

sto·ver (stō′vər), *n.* **1.** coarse roughage used as feed for livestock. **2.** stalks and leaves, not including grain, of such forages as corn and sorghum. **3.** *Brit. Dial.* fodder minus the grain portion of the plant. [1300–50; ME; aph. var. of *estover;* see ESTOVERS]

stove·top (stōv′top′), *n.* **1.** the upper surface of a stove, esp. the area used for cooking: *a stovetop cluttered with unwashed pots and pans.* —*adj.* **2.** pertaining to or suitable for use or preparation on the top of a cooking stove: *stovetop meals; stovetop utensils.* [STOVE[1] + TOP[1]]

stow (stō), *v.t.* **1.** *Naut.* **a.** to put (cargo, provisions, etc.) in the places intended for them. **b.** to put (sails, spars, gear, etc.) in the proper place or condition when not in use. **2.** to put in a place or receptacle, as for storage or reserve; pack: *He stowed the potatoes in our cellar.* **3.** to fill (a place or receptacle) by packing: *to stow a carton with books.* **4.** to have or afford room for; hold. **5.** *Slang.* to stop; break off: *Stow it! Stow the talk!* **6.** to put away, as in a safe or convenient place (often fol. by *away*). **7.** to lodge or quarter. **8. stow away,** to conceal oneself aboard a ship or other conveyance in order to obtain free transportation or to elude pursuers. [1300–50; ME *stowen,* OE *stōwigan* to keep, hold back (lit., to place), deriv. of *stōw* place; akin to ON *eldstō* fireplace, Goth *stojan* to judge (lit., to place)] —**stow′a·ble,** *adj.*

Stow (stō), *n.* a city in NE Ohio. 25,303.

stow·age (stō′ij), *n.* **1.** an act or operation of stowing. **2.** the state or manner of being stowed. **3.** room or accommodation for stowing something. **4.** a place in which something is or may be stowed. **5.** something that is stowed or to be stowed. **6.** a charge for stowing something. [1350–1400; ME; see STOW, -AGE]

stow·a·way (stō′ə wā′), *n.* a person who hides aboard a ship or airplane in order to obtain free transportation or elude pursuers. [1850–55; n. use of v. phrase *stow away*]

Stowe (stō), *n.* **1. Harriet (Elizabeth) Beecher,** 1811–96, U.S. abolitionist and novelist. **2.** a town in N Vermont: ski resort. 531.

stown·lins (stoun′linz), *adv. Scot.* secretly; stealthily. [1780–90; *stown* (var. of *stoln* STOLEN) + *-lins* (see -LING[2], -S[1])]

stowp (stōp), *n. Scot.* stoup.

STP, See **standard temperature and pressure.**

STP, *Slang.* a potent long-acting hallucinogen. [1965–70; prob. after *STP,* trademark of a motor-oil additive]

St. Paul, a port in and the capital of Minnesota, in the SE part, on the Mississippi. 270,230.

St. Paul's, a cathedral in London, England: designed by Sir Christopher Wren.

St. Peters, a town in E central Missouri. 15,700.

St. Peter's, a basilica in Vatican City: dome designed by Michelangelo.

St. Petersburg, 1. Formerly, **Leningrad** (1924–91); **Petrograd** (1914–24). a seaport in the NW Russian Federation in Europe, in the Gulf of Finland, off the Baltic Sea: founded 1703 by Peter the Great; capital of the Russian Empire (1712–1917). 5,020,000. **2.** a city in W Florida, on Tampa Bay: 238,629.

St. Peter's Square, a square surrounded by colonnades, forming a boundary of and an entrance to Vatican City, leading to St. Peter's: designed by Giovanni Bernini and built during the 17th century.

St. Pierre (sānt′ pyâr′; *Fr.* san pyer′), **1.** a city on Réunion Island, in the Indian Ocean. 45,000. **2.** a former city on Martinique, in the French West Indies: destroyed 1902, with the entire population of 26,000, by an eruption of the volcano Mt. Pelée.

St. Pierre and Miq·ue·lon (mik′ə lon′; *Fr.* mēk-lôn′), two small groups of islands off the S coast of Newfoundland: an overseas territory of France; fishing center. 5232; 93 sq. mi. (240 sq. km). *Cap.:* St. Pierre.

St. Quen·tin (sānt′ kwen′tn; *Fr.* san kän tan′), a city in N France, on the Somme: retaken from the Germans 1918. 69,153.

str., 1. steamer. **2.** strait. **3.** *Music.* string; strings.

stra·bis·mus (strə biz′məs), *n. Ophthalm.* a disorder of vision due to a deviation from normal orientation of one or both eyes so that both cannot be directed at the same object at the same time; squint; crossed eyes. [1675–85; < NL < Gk *strabismós,* equiv. to *strab(ós)* squinting + *-ismos* -ISM] —**stra·bis′mal, stra·bis′mic, stra·bis′mi·cal,** *adj.* —**stra·bis′mal·ly,** *adv.*

Stra·bo (strā′bō), *n.* 63? B.C.–A.D. 21?, Greek geographer and historian.

stra·bot·o·my (strə bot′ə mē), *n., pl.* **-mies.** *Surg.* the operation of cutting one or more of the muscles of the eye to correct strabismus. [1855–60; < Gk *strabó(s)* (see STRABISMUS) + -TOMY]

Stra·chey (strā′chē), *n.* **(Giles) Lyt·ton** (jīlz lit′n), 1880–1932, English biographer and literary critic.

strad·dle (strad′l), *v.,* **-dled, -dling,** *n.* —*v.i.* **1.** to walk, stand, or sit with the legs wide apart; stand or sit astride. **2.** to stand wide apart, as the legs. **3.** to favor or appear to favor both of two opposite sides; maintain an equivocal position. —*v.t.* **4.** to walk, stand, or sit with one leg on each side of; stand or sit astride of: *to straddle a horse.* **5.** to spread (the legs) wide apart. **6.** to favor or appear to favor both sides of (an issue, political division, etc.). —*n.* **7.** an act or instance of straddling. **8.** the distance straddled over. **9.** the taking of a noncommittal position. **10.** *Finance.* **a.** an option consisting of a put and a call combined, both at the same current market price and for the same specified period. **b.** a similar transaction in securities or futures in which options to buy and sell the same security or commodity are purchased simultaneously in order to hedge one's risk. [1555–65; appar. freq. (with -LE) of var. s. of STRIDE] —**strad′dler,** *n.* —**strad′dling·ly,** *adv.*

strad′dle truck′, a self-propelled vehicle, having a chassis far above the ground, for carrying loads of lumber or the like beneath the chassis and between the wheels. Also called **strad′dle car′rier.**

Stra·del·la (strä del′lä), *n.* **A·les·san·dro** (ä′les sän′-drô), 1645?–82?, Italian composer.

Stra·di·va·ri (strad′ə vâr′ē; *It.* strä′dē vä′rē), *n.* **Antonio** (an tō′nē ō; *It.* än tô′nyô), 1644?–1737, Italian violinmaker of Cremona (pupil of Nicolò Amati). Latin, **Stradivarius.**

Strad·i·var·i·us (strad′ə vâr′ē əs), *n.* **1.** a violin or other instrument made by Stradivari or his family. **2.** See **Stradivari, Antonio.** [1825–35]

strafe (strāf, sträf), *v.,* **strafed, straf·ing,** *n.* —*v.t.* **1.** to attack (ground troops or installations) by airplanes with machine-gun fire. **2.** *Slang.* to reprimand viciously. —*n.* **3.** a strafing attack. [1910–15; < G *strafen* to punish] —**straf′er,** *n.*

Straf·ford (straf′ərd), *n.* **1st Earl of** (*Thomas Wentworth*), 1593–1641, English statesman: chief adviser of Charles I of England.

strag·gle (strag′əl), *v.i.,* **-gled, -gling. 1.** to stray from the road, course, or line of march. **2.** to wander about in a scattered fashion; ramble. **3.** to spread or be spread in a scattered fashion or at irregular intervals: *The trees straggle over the countryside.* [1350–1400; ME *straglen* < ?] —**strag′gler,** *n.* —**strag′gling·ly,** *adv.*

strag·gly (strag′lē), *adj.,* **-gli·er, -gli·est.** straggling; rambling. [1865–70; STRAGGLE + -Y[1]]

straight (strāt), *adj.* **-er, -est,** *adv., n.* —*adj.* **1.** without a bend, angle, or curve; not curved; direct: *a straight path.* **2.** exactly vertical or horizontal; in a perfectly vertical or horizontal plane: *a straight table.* **3.** (of a line) generated by a point moving at a constant velocity with respect to another point. **4.** evenly or uprightly formed or set: *straight shoulders.* **5.** without circumlocution; frank; candid: *straight speaking.* **6.** honest, honorable, or upright, as conduct, dealings, methods, or persons. **7.** *Informal.* reliable, as a report or information. **8.** right or correct, as reasoning, thinking, or a thinker. **9.** in the proper order or condition: *Things are straight now.* **10.** continuous or unbroken: *in straight succession.* **11.** thoroughgoing or unreserved: *a straight Republican.* **12.** supporting or cast for all candidates of one political party: *to vote a straight ticket.* **13.** unmodified or unaltered: *a straight comedy.* **14.** without change in the original melody or tempo: *She does straight songs, with just the piano backing her.* **15.** *Informal.* **a.** heterosexual. **b.** traditional; conventional. **c.** free from using narcotics. **d.** not engaged in crime; law-abiding; reformed. **16.** undiluted, as whiskey. **17.** *Theat.* (of acting) straightforward; not striving for effect. **18.** *Journalism.* written or to be written in a direct and objective manner, with no attempt at individual styling, comment, etc.: *She gave me a straight story. Treat it as straight news.* **19.** *Cards.* containing cards in consecutive denominations, as a two, three, four, five, and six, in various suits. —*adv.* **20.** in a straight line: *to walk straight.* **21.** in an even form or position: *pictures hung straight.* **22.** in an erect posture: *to stand up straight.* **23.** directly: *to go straight to a place.* **24.** without circumlocution; frankly; candidly (often fol. by *out*). **25.** honestly, honorably, or virtuously: *to live straight.* **26.** without intricate involvement; not in a roundabout way; to the point. **27.** in a steady course (often fol. by *on*): *to keep straight on after the second traffic light.* **28.** into the proper form or condition; in order: *to put a room straight.* **29.** in possession of the truth or of true ideas: *I want to set you straight before you make mistakes.* **30.** sold without discount regardless of the quantity bought: *Candy bars are twenty cents straight.* **31.** *Journalism.* directly and objectively: *Write the circus story straight.* **32.** without personal embellishments, additions, etc.: *Tell the story straight. Sing the song straight.* **33.** (of liquor) served or drunk without ice, a mixer, or water; neat: *He drank his whiskey straight.* **34. go straight,** *Informal.* to live a law-abiding life; no longer engage in crime. **35. play it straight,** *Informal.* to do something without jokes, tricks, subterfuge, distortions, or the like: *a comedian who plays it straight when he crusades against drug abuse.* **36. straight off,** without delay; immediately: *I told him straight off what I thought about the matter.* Also, **straight away. 37. straight up,** (of a cocktail) served without ice: *a gin martini straight up.* —*n.* **38.** the condition of being straight. **39.** a straight form or position. **40.** a straight line. **41.** a straight part, as of a racecourse. **42.** *Informal.* **a.** a heterosexual. **b.** a person who follows traditional or conventional mores. **c.** a person who is free from narcotics. **43.** *Chiefly Games.* a succession of strokes, plays, etc., which gives a perfect score. [1250–1300; (adj.) ME; orig. ptp. of *strecchen* to STRETCH; (adv. and n.) ME, deriv. of the adj.] —**straight′ly,** *adv.* —**straight′ness,** *n.*
—**Syn. 5.** open, direct. **6.** virtuous, just, fair, equitable. —**Ant. 1.** crooked. **5.** devious.

straight A, achieving or showing the highest grade or superior accomplishment, esp. scholastically: *a straight A report card.* Also, **straight-A.** [1945–50]

straight-a·head (strāt′ə hed′), *adj.* not deviating from what is usual or expected; conventional or traditional; standard: *a straight-ahead novel with a happy ending.* [1830–40]

straight′ and nar′row, the way of virtuous or proper conduct: *After his release from prison, he resolved to follow the straight and narrow.* [1945–50]

straight′ an′gle, the angle formed by two radii of a

CONCISE ETYMOLOGY KEY: <, descended or borrowed from; >, whence; b., blend of, blended; c., cognate with; cf., compare; deriv., derivative; equiv., equivalent; imit., imitative; obl., oblique; r., replacing; s., stem; sp., spelling, spelled; resp., respelling, respelled; trans., translation; ?, origin unknown; *, unattested; ‡, probably earlier than. See the full key inside the front cover.

circle that are drawn to the extremities of an arc equal to one half of the circle; an angle of 180°. [1595–1605]

straight-arm (strāt′ärm′), *v.t.* **1.** *Football.* to push (a potential tackler) away by holding the arm out straight; stiff-arm. **2.** to force, push, or fend off by or as if by holding out a stiff arm against obstacles: *He straight-armed his way into the middle of the crowded room.* —*n.* **3.** *Football.* an act or instance of straight-arming. Also, **stiff-arm.**

straight′ ar′row, *Informal.* a person who manifests high-minded devotion to clean living and moral righteousness. [1965–70] —**straight′-ar′row,** *adj.*

straight·a·way (strāt′ə wā′), *adj.* **1.** straight onward, without turn or curve, as a racecourse. —*n.* **2.** a straightaway course or part. —*adv.* **3.** immediately; right away. [1870–75; from phrase *straight away*]

straight-backed (strāt′bakt′), *adj.* having a straight, usually high, back: *a straight-backed chair.* Also, **straight′-back′.**

straight′ bill′ of lad′ing, a bill of lading that is issued to a specified consignee for the delivery of the goods and that cannot be endorsed to another party. Cf. **order bill of lading.**

straight-chain (strāt′chān′), *n. Chem.* an open chain of atoms, usually carbon, with no side chains attached to it. Also called **straight′ chain′.** Cf. **branched chain.** [1925–30]

straight′ chair′, a chair with a straight back, esp. one that is unupholstered and has straight legs and straight arms or no arms.

straight-edge (strāt′ej′), *adj.* advocating abstinence from alcohol, cigarettes, drugs, and sex and sometimes advocating vegetarianism. [1980–85]

straight·edge (strāt′ej′), *n.* a bar or strip of wood, plastic, or metal having at least one long edge of sufficiently reliable straightness for use in drawing or testing straight lines, plane surfaces, etc. [1805–15; STRAIGHT + EDGE]

straight·en (strāt′n), *v.t., v.i.* to make or become straight in direction, form, position, character, conduct, condition, etc. (often fol. by *up* or *out*). [1535–45; STRAIGHT + -EN[1]] —**straight′en·er,** *n.*

straight′ face′, a serious or impassive facial expression that conceals one's true feelings about something, esp. a desire to laugh. [1890–95] —**straight′-faced′,** *adj.* —**straight-fac·ed·ly** (strāt′fā′sid lē, -fāst′lē), *adv.*

straight′ flush′, *Poker.* a sequence of five consecutive cards of the same suit. [1860–65]

straight·for·ward (strāt′fôr′wərd), *adj.* **1.** going or directed straight ahead: *a straightforward gaze.* **2.** direct; not roundabout: *a straightforward approach to a problem.* **3.** free from deceit; honest: *straightforward in one's dealings.* —*adv.* **4.** Also, **straight′for′wards.** straight ahead; directly or continuously forward. [1800–10; STRAIGHT + FORWARD] —**straight′for′ward·ly,** *adv.* —**straight′for′ward·ness,** *n.*
—**Syn. 1.** undeviating, unswerving. —**Ant. 1, 2.** devious.

straight-from-the-shoul·der (strāt′frəm thə shōl′dər), *adj.* direct, honest, and forceful in expression; outspoken.

straight-jack·et (strāt′jak′it), *n., v.t.* straitjacket.

straight-laced (strāt′lāst′), *adj.* strait-laced. —**straight-lac·ed·ly** (strāt′lā′sid lē, -lāst′lē), *adv.* —**straight′-lac′ed·ness,** *n.*

straight′ life′ insur′ance. See **ordinary life insurance.**

straight-line (strāt′līn′), *adj.* **1.** *Mach.* **a.** noting a machine or mechanism the working parts of which act or are arranged in a straight line. **b.** noting a mechanism for causing one part to move along a straight line. **2.** *Accounting.* denoting uniform allocation, as in calculating the total depreciation over the life of a depreciable asset, dividing that into equal parts, and depreciating each segment at regular intervals. [1835–45]

straight′ man′, an entertainer who plays the part of a foil for a comic partner. [1925–30]

straight′ mat′ter, *Print.* **1.** the body text of an article, story, etc., as distinguished from the title, subhead, and other display matter. **2.** editorial text as distinguished from advertising.

straight·neck (strāt′nek′), *n.* a variety of summer squash related to the crookneck but not having a recurved neck. [STRAIGHT + NECK]

straight-out (strāt′out′), *adj. Informal.* **1.** thoroughgoing: *a straight-out Democrat.* **2.** frank; aboveboard. [1830–40, *Amer.*; from phrase *straight out*]

straight′ pok′er, one of the original forms of poker in which players are dealt five cards face down, upon which they bet and then have the showdown without drawing any cards. [1860–65, *Amer.*]

straight′ ra′zor, a razor having a stiff blade made of steel that is hinged to a handle into which it folds. [1715–25]

straight′ shoot′er, a person who is forthright and upstanding in behavior.

straight′ stall′, a narrow, oblong stall in which a horse or other animal cannot turn around. Cf. **box stall.** [1855–60]

straight′ tick′et, *U.S. Politics.* **1.** a ballot on which all votes have been cast for candidates of the same party. **2.** a ticket on which all the candidates nominated by a party are members of the party. Cf. **split ticket.** [1855–60, *Amer.*]

straight′ time′, **1.** the time or number of hours standard for a specific work period in a particular industry, usually computed on the basis of a workweek and fixed variously from 35 to 40 hours. **2.** the rate of pay established for the period (distinguished from *overtime*). [1855–60, *Amer.*] —**straight′-time′,** *adj.*

straight·way (strāt′wā′), *adv.* straightaway. [1425–75; late ME; see STRAIGHT, WAY[1]]

straight′ whis′key, pure, unblended whiskey of 80 to 110 proof. [1860–65, *Amer.*]

strain[1] (strān), *v.t.* **1.** to draw tight or taut, esp. to the utmost tension; stretch to the full: *to strain a rope.* **2.** to exert to the utmost: *to strain one's ears to catch a sound.* **3.** to impair, injure, or weaken (a muscle, tendon, etc.) by stretching or overexertion. **4.** to cause mechanical deformation in (a body or structure) as the result of stress. **5.** to stretch beyond the proper point or limit: *to strain the meaning of a word.* **6.** to make excessive demands upon: *to strain one's luck; to strain one's resources.* **7.** to pour (liquid containing solid matter) through a filter, sieve, or the like in order to hold back the denser solid constituents: *to strain gravy.* **8.** to draw off (clear or pure liquid) by means of a filter or sieve: *to strain the water from spinach; to strain broth.* **9.** to hold back (solid particles) from liquid matter by means of a filter or sieve: *to strain seeds from orange juice; to strain rice.* **10.** to clasp tightly in the arms, the hand, etc.: *The mother strained her child close to her breast.* **11.** *Obs.* to constrain, as to a course of action. —*v.i.* **12.** to pull forcibly: *a dog straining at a leash.* **13.** to stretch one's muscles, nerves, etc., to the utmost. **14.** to make violent physical efforts; strive hard. **15.** to resist forcefully; balk: *to strain at accepting an unpleasant fact.* **16.** to be subjected to tension or stress; suffer strain. **17.** to filter, percolate, or ooze. **18.** to trickle or flow: *Sap strained from the bark.* —*n.* **19.** any force or pressure tending to alter shape, cause a fracture, etc. **20.** strong muscular or physical effort. **21.** great or excessive effort or striving after some goal, object, or effect. **22.** an injury to a muscle, tendon, etc., due to excessive tension or use; sprain. **23.** *Mech., Physics.* deformation of a body or structure as a result of an applied force. **24.** condition of being strained or stretched. **25.** a task, goal, or effect accomplished only with great effort: *Housecleaning is a real strain.* **26.** severe, trying, or fatiguing pressure or exertion; taxing onus: *the strain of hard work.* **27.** a severe demand on or test of resources, feelings, a person, etc.: *a strain on one's hospitality.* **28.** a flow or burst of language, eloquence, etc.: *the lofty strain of Cicero.* **29.** Often, **strains.** a passage of melody, music, or songs as rendered or heard: *the strains of the nightingale.* **30.** *Music.* a section of a piece of music, more or less complete in itself. **31.** a passage or piece of poetry. **32.** the tone, style, or spirit of an utterance, writing, etc.: *a humorous strain.* **33.** a particular degree, height, or pitch attained: *a strain of courageous enthusiasm.* [1250–1300; ME *streinen* (v.) < OF *estrein-,* s. of *estreindre* to press tightly, grip < L *stringere* to bind, tie, draw tight. See STRINGENT] —**strain′ing·ly,** *adv.* —**strain′less,** *adj.* —**strain′less·ly,** *adv.*
—**Syn. 1.** tighten. **3.** STRAIN, SPRAIN imply a wrenching, twisting, and stretching of muscles and tendons. To STRAIN is to stretch tightly, make taut, wrench, tear, cause injury to, by long-continued or sudden and too violent effort or movement: *to strain one's heart by overexertion, one's eyes by reading small print.* To SPRAIN is to strain excessively (but without dislocation) by a sudden twist or wrench, the tendons and muscles connected with a joint, esp. those of the ankle or wrist: *to sprain an ankle.* **7.** filter, sieve. **10.** hug, embrace, press. **17.** seep. **20.** exertion. **22.** wrench.

strain[2] (strān), *n.* **1.** the body of descendants of a common ancestor, as a family or stock. **2.** any of the different lines of ancestry united in a family or an individual. **3.** a group of plants distinguished from other plants of the variety to which it belongs by some intrinsic quality, such as a tendency to yield heavily; race. **4.** an artificial variety of a species of domestic animal or cultivated plant. **5.** a variety, esp. of microorganisms. **6.** ancestry or descent. **7.** hereditary or natural character, tendency, or trait: *a strain of insanity in a family.* **8.** a streak or trace. **9.** a kind or sort. **10.** *Obs.* procreation. [bef. 950; ME *strene,* OE *strēon* lineage, race, stock, tribe; akin to *strienan* to beget]
—**Syn. 7.** streak, vein, predisposition.

strained (strānd), *adj.* affected or produced by effort; not natural or spontaneous; forced: *strained hospitality.* [1350–1400; ME; see STRAIN[1], -ED[2]] —**strained·ly** (strānd′lē, strā′nid-), *adv.* —**strained′ness,** *n.*

strain·er (strā′nər), *n.* **1.** a person or thing that strains. **2.** a filter, sieve, or the like for straining liquids. **3.** a stretcher or tightener. [1300–50; ME; see STRAIN[1], -ER[1]]

strain′ gauge′, *Geol.* a type of extensometer designed for geophysical use. Also called **strain·me·ter** (strān′mē′tər), **strain·om·e·ter** (strā nom′i tər). [1905–10]

strain′ing arch′, an arch for resisting thrusts, as in a flying buttress. Also, **strain′er arch′.** [1840–50]

strain′ing piece′, (in a queen-post roof) a horizontal beam uniting the tops of the two queen posts, and resisting the thrust of the roof. Also called **strain′ing beam′.** See diag. under **queen post.** [1795–1805]

strain′ing sill′, (in a roof with a queen post) a compression member lying along the tie beam and separating the feet of the struts.

strait (strāt), *n.* **1.** Often, **straits.** (*used with a singular v.*) a narrow passage of water connecting two large bodies of water. **2.** Often, **straits.** a position of difficulty, distress, or need: *in sad straits.* **3.** *Archaic.* a narrow passage or area. **4.** an isthmus. —*adj. Archaic.* **5.** narrow. **6.** affording little space; confined in area. **7.** strict, as in requirements or principles. [1150–1200; ME *streit* < OF *estreit* < L *strictus* ptp. of *stringere* to bind; see STRAIN[1]] —**strait′ly,** *adv.* —**strait′ness,** *n.*
—**Syn. 2.** exigency, pinch, dilemma, predicament, plight. See **emergency.** —**Ant. 2.** ease.

strait·en (strāt′n), *v.t.* **1.** to put into difficulties, esp. financial ones: *His obligations had straitened him.* **2.** to restrict in range, extent, amount, etc: *Poverty straitens one's way of living.* **3.** *Archaic.* **a.** to make narrow. **b.** to confine within narrow limits. [1515–25; STRAIT + -EN[1]]

strait·jack·et (strāt′jak′it), *n.* **1.** a garment made of strong material and designed to bind the arms, as of a violently disoriented person. **2.** anything that severely confines, constricts, or hinders: *Conventional attitudes can be a straitjacket, preventing original thinking.* —*v.t.* Also, **strait′-jack′et. 3.** to put in or as in a straitjacket: *Her ambition was straitjacketed by her family.* Also, **straightjacket.** [1805–15; STRAIT + JACKET]

strait-lace (strāt′lās′), *v.t.,* **-laced, -lac·ing.** to bind, confine, or restrain with or as if with laces. [1630–40; back formation from STRAIT-LACED]

strait-laced (strāt′lāst′), *adj.* **1.** excessively strict in conduct or morality; puritanical; prudish: *strait-laced censors.* **2.** tightly laced, as a bodice. **3.** wearing tightly laced garments. Also, **straight-laced.** [1400–50; late ME] —**strait-lac′ed·ly** (strāt′lā′sid lē, -lāst′lē), *adv.* —**strait′-lac′ed·ness,** *n.*

Straits′ dol′lar (strāts), a former silver coin and monetary unit of the Straits Settlements. [1905–10]

Straits′ Set′tlements, a former British crown colony in SE Asia: included the settlements of Singapore, Penang, Malacca, and Labuan.

strake (strāk), *n. Naut.* a continuous course of planks or plates on a ship forming a hull shell, deck, etc. [1300–50; ME; appar. akin to STRETCH] —**straked,** *adj.*

Stral·sund (shträl′zo͝ont), *n.* a seaport in N East Germany: a member of the medieval Hanseatic League; besieged by Wallenstein 1628. 74,105.

stra·mash (strə mash′, stram′əsh), *n. Scot.* an uproar; disturbance. [1795–1805; orig. uncert.]

stra·min·e·ous (strə min′ē əs), *adj.* **1.** of or resembling straw. **2.** straw-colored; yellowish. [1615–25; < L *strāmineus* of straw, equiv. to *strāmin-* (s. of *strāmen* straw; akin to STRATUM) + *-eus* -EOUS]

stra·mo·ni·um (strə mō′nē əm), *n.* **1.** See **jimson weed. 2.** the dried leaves of the jimson weed, used in medicine as an analgesic, antispasmodic, etc. [1655–65; < NL < ?]

strand[1] (strand), *v.t.* **1.** to drive or leave (a ship, fish, etc.) aground or ashore. **2.** (usually used in the passive) to bring into or leave in a helpless position: *He was stranded in the middle of nowhere.* —*v.i.* **3.** to be driven or left ashore; run aground. **4.** to be halted or struck by a difficult situation: *He stranded in the middle of his speech.* —*n.* **5.** the land bordering the sea, a lake, or a river; shore; beach. [bef. 1000; ME (n.), OE; c. D *strand,* G *Strand,* ON *strǫnd;* akin to STREW]

strand[2] (strand), *n.* **1.** one of a number of fibers or threads that are twisted together to form a rope, cord, etc. **2.** a similar part of a wire rope. **3.** a rope made of such twisted or plaited fibers. **4.** a fiber or filament, as in animal or plant tissue. **5.** a thread or threadlike part of anything: *the strands of a plot.* **6.** a tress of hair. **7.** a string of pearls, beads, etc. —*v.t.* **8.** to form (a rope, cable, etc.) by twisting strands together. **9.** to break one or more strands of (a rope). [1490–1500; orig. uncert.]

Strand (strand), *n.* **1. Mark,** born 1934, U.S. poet, born in Canada: U.S. poet laureate 1990–91. **2. Paul,** 1890–1976, U.S. photographer and documentary-film producer. **3. the,** a street parallel to the Thames, in W central London, England: famous for hotels and theaters.

strand·ed (stran′did), *adj.* composed of a specified number or kind of strands (usually used in combination): *a five-stranded rope.* [1805–15; STRAND[2] + -ED[3]] —**strand′ed·ness,** *n.*

strand′ line′, a shoreline, esp. one from which the sea or a lake has receded. [1900–05]

strand′ wolf′. See **brown hyena.** [1820–30]

strange (strānj), *adj.,* **strang·er, strang·est,** *adv.* —*adj.* **1.** unusual, extraordinary, or curious; odd; queer: *a strange remark to make.* **2.** estranged, alienated, etc., as a result of being out of one's natural environment: *In Bombay I felt strange.* **3.** situated, belonging, or coming from outside of one's own locality; foreign: *to move to a strange place; strange religions.* **4.** outside of one's previous experience; hitherto unknown; unfamiliar: *strange faces; strange customs.* **5.** unaccustomed to or inexperienced in; unacquainted (usually fol. by *to*): *I'm strange to this part of the job.* **6.** distant or reserved; shy. —*adv.* **7.** in a strange manner. [1250–1300; ME < OF *estrange* < L *extrāneus;* see EXTRANEOUS] —**strange′ly,** *adv.*
—**Syn. 1.** bizarre, singular, abnormal, anomalous. STRANGE, PECULIAR, ODD, QUEER refer to that which is out of the ordinary. STRANGE implies that the thing or its cause is unknown or unexplained; it is unfamiliar and unusual: *a strange expression.* That which is PECULIAR mystifies, or exhibits qualities not shared by others: *peculiar behavior.* That which is ODD is irregular or unconventional, and sometimes approaches the bizarre: *an odd custom.* QUEER sometimes adds to ODD the suggestion of something abnormal and eccentric: *queer in the head.* **6.** aloof. —**Ant. 4–6.** familiar.

strange′ attrac′tor, *Physics.* a stable, nonperiodic state or behavior exhibited by some dynamic systems, esp. turbulent ones, that can be represented as a nonrepeating pattern in the system's phase space.

Strange′ In′terlude, a play (1928) by Eugene O'Neill.

strange·ness (strānj′nis), *n.* **1.** the quality or condition of being strange. **2.** *Physics.* a quantum number assigned the value −1 for one kind of quark, +1 for its antiquark, and 0 for all other quarks; the strangeness of a hadron is the sum of the values for the strangeness of its constituent quarks and antiquarks. *Symbol:* S Cf. **strange quark.** [1350–1400; ME; see STRANGE, -NESS]

strange′ par′ticle, *Physics.* any elementary particle

with a strangeness quantum number other than zero. [1955–60; originally so called because of the anomalously long decay time of such particles]

strange′ quark′, *Physics.* a quark having electric charge −⅓ times the elementary charge and strangeness −1; it is more massive than the up and down quarks. Also called **s quark.** [1970–75]

stran·ger (strān′jər), *n.* **1.** a person with whom one has had no personal acquaintance: *He is a perfect stranger to me.* **2.** a newcomer in a place or locality: *a stranger in town.* **3.** an outsider: *They want no strangers in on the club meetings.* **4.** a person who is unacquainted with or unaccustomed to something (usually fol. by *to*): *He is no stranger to poverty.* **5.** a person who is not a member of the family, group, community, or the like, as a visitor or guest: *Our town shows hospitality to strangers.* **6.** *Law.* one not privy or party to an act, proceeding, etc. [1325–75; ME < MF *estrangier,* equiv. to *estrange* STRANGE + *-ier* -IER²] **—stran′ger·like′,** *adj.*
—Syn. 1, 5. STRANGER, ALIEN, FOREIGNER all refer to someone regarded as outside of or distinct from a particular group. STRANGER may apply to one who does not belong to some group—social, professional, national, etc.—or may apply to a person with whom one is not acquainted. ALIEN emphasizes a difference in political allegiance and citizenship from that of the country in which one is living. FOREIGNER emphasizes a difference in language, customs, and background. **—Ant. 1.** acquaintance.

Stranger, The, (French, *L'Étranger*), a novel (1942) by Albert Camus.

stran·gle (strang′gəl), *v.,* **-gled, -gling.** **—***v.t.* **1.** to kill by squeezing the throat in order to compress the windpipe and prevent the intake of air, as with the hands or a tightly drawn cord. **2.** to kill by stopping the breath in any manner; choke; stifle; suffocate. **3.** to prevent the continuance, growth, rise, or action of; suppress: *Censorship strangles a free press.* **—***v.i.* **4.** to be choked, stifled, or suffocated. [1250–1300; ME *strangelen* < OF *estrangler* < L *strangulāre* < Gk *strangalân,* deriv. of *strangálē* halter, akin to *strangós* twisted] **—stran′·gler,** *n.* **—stran′gling·ly,** *adv.*
—Syn. 1. garrote, throttle, choke. **2.** smother. **3.** check, repress, gag, muzzle.

stran·gle·hold (strang′gəl hōld′), *n.* **1.** *Wrestling.* an illegal hold by which an opponent's breath is choked off. **2.** any force or influence that restricts the free actions or development of a person or group: *the stranglehold of superstition.* [1890–95; STRANGLE + HOLD¹]

stran·gles (strang′gəlz), *n.* (*used with a singular v.*) *Vet. Pathol.* distemper¹ (def. 1b). [1590–1600; obs. *strangle* act of strangling + -S³]

stran·gu·late (strang′gyə lāt′), *v.t.,* **-lat·ed, -lat·ing.** **1.** *Pathol., Surg.* to compress or constrict (a duct, intestine, vessel, etc.) so as to prevent circulation or suppress function. **2.** to strangle. [1655–65; < L *strangulātus,* ptp. of *strangulāre* to STRANGLE; see -ATE¹] **—stran·gu·la·ble** (strang′gyə lə bəl), *adj.* **—stran′gu·la′tion,** *n.* **—stran′gu·la′tive,** *adj.* **—stran·gu·la·to·ry** (strang′gyə lə tôr′ē, -tōr′ē), *adj.*

stran′gulated her′nia, a hernia, esp. of the intestine, that swells and constricts the blood supply of the herniated part, resulting in obstruction and gangrene.

stran·gu·ry (strang′gyə rē), *n. Pathol.* painful urination in which the urine is emitted drop by drop owing to muscle spasms of the urethra or urinary bladder. [1350–1400; ME < L *strangūria* < Gk *strangouríā,* equiv. to *strang(ós)* flowing drop by drop + *oûr(on)* URINE + *-ia* -Y³]

strap (strap), *n., v.,* **strapped, strap·ping.** **—***n.* **1.** a narrow strip of flexible material, esp. leather, as for fastening or holding things together. **2.** a looped band by which an item may be held, pulled, lifted, etc., as a bootstrap or a ring that standing passengers may hold on to in a bus, subway, or the like. **3.** a strop for a razor. **4.** a long, narrow object or piece of something; strip; band. **5.** an ornamental strip or band. **6.** See **shoulder strap. 7.** watchband. **8.** *Mach.* a shallow metal fitting surrounding and retaining other parts, as on the end of a rod. See diag. under **exploded view. 9.** *Naut., Mach.* strop (def. 2). **—***v.t.* **10.** to fasten or secure with a strap or straps. **11.** to fasten (a thing) around something in the manner of a strap. **12.** to sharpen on a strap or strop: *to strap a razor.* **13.** to beat or flog with a strap. [1565–75; var. of STROP] **—strap′pa·ble,** *adj.* **—strap′·like′,** *adj.*

strap·hang (strap′hang′), *v.i.* to travel as a straphanger. [1905–10; STRAP + HANG]

strap·hang·er (strap′hang′ər), *n.* **1.** a passenger who stands in a crowded bus or subway train and holds onto a strap or other support suspended from above. **2.** any user of such public transportation. [1900–05; STRAP + HANGER]

strap-hinge (strap′hinj′), *n.* a hinge having a flap, esp. a long one, attached to one face of a door or the like. See illus. under **hinge.** [1730–40]

strap-laid (strap′lād′), *adj. Ropemaking.* noting a type of flat cordage made by stitching strands together side by side. [1830–40]

strap·less (strap′lis), *adj.* **1.** without a strap or straps. **2.** designed and made without shoulder straps: *a strapless evening gown; a strapless bra.* [1840–50; STRAP + -LESS]

strap·pa·do (strə pā′dō, -pä′-), *n., pl.* **-does. 1.** an old form of punishment or torture in which the victim, with arms bound behind, was raised from the ground by a rope fastened to the wrists, abruptly released, then arrested with a painful jerk just before reaching the ground. **2.** the instrument used for this purpose. [1550–60; alter. of MF *strapade* or its source, It *strappata* a sharp pull or tug, equiv. to *strapp-* (s. of *strappare* to snatch (< Goth *strappan* to stretch) + *-ata* -ADE¹]

strapped (strapt), *adj.* needy; wanting: *The company is rather strapped for funds.* [1775–85; STRAP + -ED²]

strap·per (strap′ər), *n.* **1.** a person or thing that straps. **2.** *Informal.* a large, robust person. [1665–75; STRAP + -ER¹]

strap·ping¹ (strap′ing), *adj.* **1.** powerfully built; robust. **2.** large; whopping. [1650–60; STRAP + -ING²]

strap·ping² (strap′ing), *n.* **1.** straps collectively. **2.** material used to make a strap or straps: *manufacturers of plastic strapping.* [1800–10; STRAP + -ING¹]

Stras·berg (sträs′bərg, stras′-), *n.* **Lee,** 1901–82, U.S. theatrical director, teacher, and actor, born in Austria.

Stras·bourg (stras′bûrg, sträz′bo͝org; *Fr.* strаz-bo͞or′), *n.* a fortress city in and the capital of Bas-Rhin, in NE France, near the Rhine: cathedral; taken by Allied forces November 1944. 257,303. German, **Strass·burg** (shträs′bo͝ork).

strass¹ (stras), *n.* a flint glass with a high lead content, used to imitate gemstones. [1810–20; < G, named after J. *Strasser,* 18th-century German jeweler who invented it]

strass² (stras), *n.* silk waste produced in making skeins. [1855–60; < F *strasse* < It *straccio,* n. deriv. of *stracciare* to tear < VL **extractiare,* deriv. of L *extractus* (see EXTRACT)]

stra·ta (strā′tə, strat′ə, strä′tə), *n.* **1.** a pl. of **stratum. 2.** (*usually considered nonstandard*) stratum.
—Usage. See **stratum.**

strat·a·gem (strat′ə jəm), *n.* **1.** a plan, scheme, or trick for surprising or deceiving an enemy. **2.** any artifice, ruse, or trick devised or used to attain a goal or to gain an advantage over an adversary or competitor: *business stratagems.* [1480–90; (< MF *stratageme*) < It *stratagemma* war ruse < L *stratēgēma* < Gk *stratḗgēma* instance of generalship, deriv. of *stratēgeîn* to be in command, deriv. of *stratēgós* military commander (see STRATEGY)] **—strat·a·gem·i·cal** (strat′ə jem′i kəl), *adj.* **—strat′a·gem′i·cal·ly,** *adv.*
—Syn. 1, 2. See **trick. 2.** deception, intrigue, device, maneuver, contrivance.

stra·tal (strāt′l), *adj.* of a stratum or strata. [1870–75; STRAT(UM) + -AL¹]

stra·te·gic (strə tē′jik), *adj.* **1.** pertaining to, characterized by, or of the nature of strategy: *strategic movements.* **2.** important in or essential to strategy. **3.** (of an action, as a military operation or a move in a game) forming an integral part of a stratagem: *a strategic move in a game of chess.* **4.** *Mil.* **a.** intended to render the enemy incapable of making war, as by the destruction of materials, factories, etc.: *a strategic bombing mission.* **b.** essential to the conduct of a war: *Copper is a strategic material.* Also, **stra·te′gi·cal.** [1815–25; < Gk *stratēgikós,* equiv. to *stratēg(ós)* general (see STRATEGY + *-ikos* -IC] **—stra·te′gi·cal·ly,** *adv.*
—Syn. 2. opportune, critical, key, principal, crucial.

Strate′gic Air′ Command′, a U.S. Air Force command charged with intercontinental air strikes, especially nuclear attacks.

Strate′gic Arms′ Limita′tion Trea′ty, either of two preliminary five-year agreements between the U.S. and the Soviet Union for the control of certain nuclear weapons, the first concluded in 1972 (**Salt I**) and the second drafted in 1979 (**Salt II**) but not ratified.

Strate′gic Defense′ Ini′tiative. See **Star Wars.**

stra·te·gics (strə tē′jiks), *n.* (*used with a singular v.*) strategy (def. 1). [1850–55; see STRATEGIC, -ICS]

strat·e·gist (strat′i jist), *n.* an expert in strategy, esp. in warfare: *Julius Caesar was a great military strategist.* [1830–40; STRATEG(Y) + -IST]

strat·e·gize (strat′i jīz′), *v.i.,* **-gized, -giz·ing.** to make up or determine strategy; plan. Also, *esp. Brit.,* **strat′e·gise′.** [1970–75; STRATEG(Y) + -IZE]

strat·e·gy (strat′i jē), *n., pl.* **-gies. 1.** Also, **strategics.** the science or art of combining and employing the means of war in planning and directing large military movements and operations. **2.** the use or an instance of using this science or art. **3.** skillful use of a stratagem: *The salesperson's strategy was to seem always to agree with the customer.* **4.** a plan, method, or series of maneuvers or stratagems for obtaining a specific goal or result: *a strategy for getting ahead in the world.* [1680–90; < Gk *stratēgía* generalship, equiv. to *stratēg(ós)* military commander, general (*strat(ós)* army + *-ēgos* n. deriv. of *ágein* to lead) + *-ia* -Y³]
—Syn. 1. In military usage, a distinction is made between STRATEGY and TACTICS. STRATEGY is the utilization, during both peace and war, of all of a nation's forces, through large-scale, long-range planning and development, to ensure security or victory. TACTICS deals with the use and deployment of troops in actual combat.

Strat·ford (strat′fərd), *n.* **1.** a town in SW Connecticut, near Bridgeport: Shakespeare theater. 50,541. **2.** a city in SE Ontario, in S Canada: Shakespeare theater. 25,657. **3.** a male given name.

Strat′ford de Red′cliffe (də red′klif), **1st Viscount** (*Stratford Canning*), 1786–1880, English diplomat.

Strat·ford-on-A·von (strat′fərd on ā′vən, -ôn-), *n.* a town in SW Warwickshire, in central England, on the Avon River: birthplace and burial place of Shakespeare. 99,400. Also, **Strat′ford-up·on-A′von.**

strath (strath; *Scot.* sträth), *n. Scot.* a wide valley. [1530–40; < Ir, ScotGael *srath;* akin to STRATUM]

Strath·clyde (strath klīd′), *n.* a region in SW Scotland. 2,504,909; 5300 sq. mi. (13,727 sq. km).

strath·spey (strath′spā′, strath′spā′), *n.* **1.** a slow Scottish dance in quadruple meter. **2.** the music for this dance. [1645–55; after *Strath Spey,* the valley of the river Spey in Scotland]

strati-, a combining form representing **stratum** in compound words: *stratiform.* [STRAT(UM) + -I-]

strat·i·fi·ca·tion (strat′ə fi kā′shən), *n.* **1.** the act or an instance of stratifying. **2.** a stratified state or appearance: *the stratification of ancient ruins from eight different periods.* **3.** *Sociol.* the hierarchical or vertical division of society according to rank, caste, or class: *stratification of feudal society.* **4.** *Geol.* **a.** formation of strata; deposition or occurrence in strata. **b.** a stratum. [1610–20; < ML *strātificātiōn-* (s. of *strātificātiō*). See STRATI-, -FICATION]

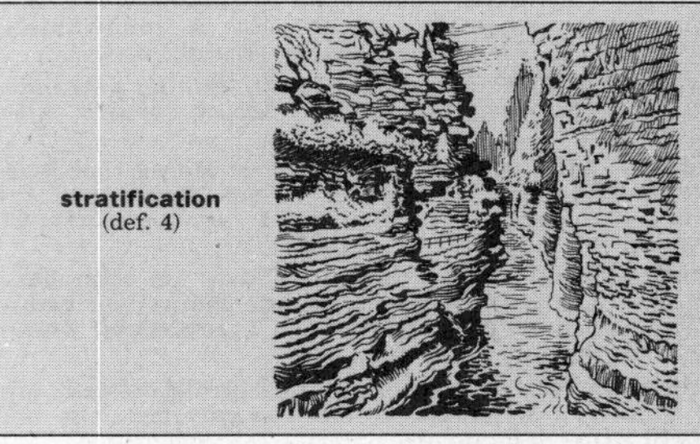
stratification (def. 4)

strat·i·fi·ca′tion·al gram′mar, (strat′ə fi kā′shənl), a grammar based upon the theory that language is made up of successive strata that are interconnected by established rules. [1960–65]

strat′ified charge′ en′gine, an internal-combustion engine in which a small charge of a rich fuel mixture is ignited first and used to improve combustion of a larger charge of a lean fuel mixture. Also, **strat′·ified-charge en′gine.** [1960–65]

strat′ified ran′dom sam′ple, *Statistics.* a random sample of a population in which the population is first divided into distinct subpopulations, or strata, and random samples are then taken separately from each stratum.

strat·i·form (strat′ə fôrm′), *adj.* **1.** *Geol.* occurring as a bed or beds; arranged in strata. **2.** *Anat.* noting arrangement in thin layers, as in bone. **3.** *Meteorol.* (of a cloud) having predominantly horizontal development. Cf. **cumuliform.** [1795–1805; STRATI- + -FORM]

strat·i·for·mis (strat′ə fôr′mis), *adj. Meteorol.* (of a cloud with cumuliform elements) occurring in a very extensive horizontal layer. [< NL: STRATIFORM]

strat·i·fy (strat′ə fī′), *v.,* **-fied, -fy·ing.** **—***v.t.* **1.** to form or place in strata or layers. **2.** to preserve or germinate (seeds) by placing them between layers of earth. **3.** *Sociol.* to arrange in a hierarchical order, esp. according to graded status levels. **—***v.i.* **4.** to form strata. **5.** *Geol.* to lie in beds or layers. **6.** *Sociol.* to develop hierarchically, esp. as graded status levels. [1655–65; modeled on NL *strātificāre,* equiv. to *strāti-* STRATI- + *-ficāre* -FY]

stratig., stratigraphy.

stra·tig·ra·phy (strə tig′rə fē), *n.* a branch of geology dealing with the classification, nomenclature, correlation, and interpretation of stratified rocks. [1860–65; STRATI- + -GRAPHY] **—stra·tig′ra·pher, stra·tig′ra·phist,** *n.* **—strat·i·graph·ic** (strat′i graf′ik), **strat′i·graph′i·cal,** *adj.* **—strat′i·graph′i·cal·ly,** *adv.*

strato-, a combining form representing **stratus** (*stratocumulus*) or specialized as a combining form of **stratosphere** (*stratovision*). [STRAT(US) + -O-]

stra·toc·ra·cy (strə tok′rə sē), *n., pl.* **-cies.** government by the military. [1645–55; < Gk *stratō(s)* army + -CRACY]

stra·to·cu·mu·lus (strā′tō kyo͞o′myə ləs, strat′ō-), *n., pl.* **-lus.** a cloud of a class characterized by large dark, rounded masses, usually in groups, lines, or waves, the individual elements being larger than those in altocumulus and the whole being at a lower altitude, usually below 8000 feet (2400 m). [1890–95; STRATO- + -CUMULUS]

strat·o·pause (strat′ə pôz′), *n. Meteorol.* the boundary or transition layer between the stratosphere and mesosphere. [STRATO- + PAUSE]

strat·o·sphere (strat′ə sfēr′), *n.* **1.** the region of the upper atmosphere extending upward from the tropopause to about 30 miles (50 km) above the earth, characterized by little vertical change in temperature. **2.** (formerly) all of the earth's atmosphere lying outside the troposphere. **3.** any great height or degree, as the highest point of a graded scale. [1905–10; STRAT(UM) + -O- + SPHERE] **—strat·o·spher·ic** (strat′ə sfer′ik, -sfēr′-), **strat′o·spher′i·cal,** *adj.*

Strat·ton (strat′n), *n.* **Charles Sherwood** (*"General Tom Thumb"*), 1838–83, U.S. midget who performed in the circus of P. T. Barnum.

stra·tum (strā′təm, strat′əm), *n., pl.* **stra·ta** (strā′tə, strat′ə), **stra·tums. 1.** a layer of material, naturally or artificially formed, often one of a number of parallel layers one upon another: *a stratum of ancient foundations.* **2.** one of a number of portions or divisions likened to layers or levels: *an allegory with many strata of meaning.* **3.** *Geol.* a single bed of sedimentary rock, generally consisting of one kind of matter representing continuous deposition. **4.** *Biol.* a layer of tissue; lamella. **5.** *Ecol.* (in a plant community) a layer of vegetation, usually of the same or similar height. **6.** a layer of the ocean or the atmosphere distinguished by natural or arbitrary limits. **7.** *Sociol.* a level or grade of a people or population with reference to social position, education, etc.: *the lowest stratum of society.* **8.** *Ling.* (in stratificational grammar) a major subdivision of linguistic structure. Cf. **level** (def. 18). [1590–1600; < L *strātum* lit., a cover, n.

CONCISE ETYMOLOGY KEY: <, descended or borrowed from; >, whence; b., blend of, blended; c., cognate with; cf., compare; deriv., derivative; equiv., equivalent; imit., imitative; obl., oblique; r., replacing; s., stem; sp., spelling, spelled; resp., respelling, respelled; trans., translation; ?, origin unknown; *, unattested; ‡, probably earlier than. See the full key inside the front cover.

use of neut. of *strātus,* ptp. of *sternere* to spread, STREW, equiv. to *strā-* var. s. + *-tus* ptp. suffix] **—stra′tous,** *adj.*

—Usage. STRATA, historically the plural of STRATUM, is occasionally used as a singular: *The lowest economic strata consists of the permanently unemployable.* Less frequently, a plural STRATAS occurs: *Several stratas of settlement can be seen in the excavation.* At present, these uses are not well established, and they are condemned in usage guides. STRATA may eventually become part of a group of borrowed plurals that are now used as singulars in English, such as *agenda* and *candelabra,* but it is not yet in that category. See also **agenda, criterion, media, phenomenon.**

stra•tus (strā′təs, strat′əs), *n., pl.* **stra•ti** (strā′tī, strat′ī). a cloud of a class characterized by a gray, horizontal layer with a uniform base, found at a lower altitude than altostratus, usually below 8000 feet (2400 m). [1795–1805; < L *strātus;* see STRATUM]

Straus (strous; *Ger.* shtrous), *n.* **1. Isidor,** 1845–1912, U.S. retail merchant and politician, born in Bavaria: congressman 1894–95 (brother of Nathan and Oscar Solomon Straus). **2. Nathan,** 1848–1931, U.S. retail merchant, born in Bavaria. **3. Os•car** (os′kər; *Ger.* ôs′kär), 1870–1954, Austrian composer. **4. Oscar Solomon,** 1850–1926, U.S. diplomat, jurist, and government official, born in Bavaria: Secretary of Commerce and Labor 1906–09.

Strauss (strous *or, for 1–3, 5, Ger.* shtrous), *n.* **1. Da•vid Frie•drich** (dä′vēt frē′driKH), 1808–74, German theologian, philosopher, and author. **2. Jo•hann** (yō′hän), 1804–49, Austrian orchestra conductor and composer. **3.** his son **Johann** (*"The Waltz King"*), 1825–99, Austrian orchestra conductor and composer. **4. Levi,** 1829?–1902, U.S. pants manufacturer: developed Levis. **5. Ri•chard** (riKH′ärt), 1864–1949, German orchestra conductor and composer.

stra•vage (strə vāg′), *v.i.,* **-vaged, -vag•ing. 1.** *Scot., Irish, and North Eng.* to wander aimlessly. **2.** to saunter; stroll. Also, **stra•vaig** (strə vāg′). [1765–75; by aphesis < ML *extrāvagārī* to wander out of bounds. See EXTRAVAGANT] **—stra•vaig′er,** *n.*

Stra•vin•ski•an (strə vin′skē ən), *adj.* of, pertaining to, or suggesting the composer Igor Stravinsky or his works. [1920–25; STRAVINSKY + -AN]

Stra•vin•sky (strə vin′skē; *Russ.* stru vyen′skyə), *n.* **I•gor Fë•do•ro•vich** (ē′gôr fyô′də rō′vich; *Russ.* ē′gər fyô′də rə vyich), 1882–1971, U.S. composer, born in Russia.

straw (strô), *n.* **1.** a single stalk or stem, esp. of certain species of grain, chiefly wheat, rye, oats, and barley. **2.** a mass of such stalks, esp. after drying and threshing, used as fodder. **3.** material, fibers, etc., made from such stalks, as used for making hats or baskets. **4.** the negligible value of one such stalk; trifle; least bit: *not to care a straw.* **5.** a tube, usually of paper or glass, for sucking up a beverage from a container: *to sip lemonade through a straw.* **6.** anything of possible but dubious help in a desperate circumstance. **7.** See **straw man** (def. 2). **8.** a straw hat. **9. catch, clutch,** or **grasp at a straw, at straws,** or **at any straw** or **straws,** to seize at any chance, no matter how slight, of saving oneself from calamity. **10. draw straws,** to decide by lottery using straws or strawlike items of different lengths, usually with the short straw or straws determining the person chosen or the loser. **—adj. 11.** of, pertaining to, containing, or made of straw: *a straw hat.* **12.** of the color of straw; pale yellow. **13.** of little value or consequence; worthless. **14.** sham; fictitious. [bef. 950; ME; OE *strēaw;* c. G *Stroh;* akin to STREW] **—straw′less,** *adj.* **—straw′like′,** *adj.*

straw•ber•ry (strô′ber′ē, -bə rē), *n., pl.* **-ries. 1.** the fruit of any stemless plant belonging to the genus *Fragaria,* of the rose family, consisting of an enlarged fleshy receptacle bearing achenes on its exterior. See illus. under **achene. 2.** the plant itself. [bef. 1000; ME; OE *strēawberige.* See STRAW, BERRY]

straw′berry bass′ (bas), the black crappie. See under **crappie.** [1865–70, *Amer.*]

straw′berry blite′, a plant, *Chenopodium capitatum,* having dense, rounded clusters of minute reddish flowers.

straw′berry blond′, 1. reddish blond. **2.** a person with reddish-blond hair. [1875–80, *Amer.*]

—Usage. See **blonde.**

straw′berry dish′, a shallow, circular fruit dish with a fluted or pierced border.

straw′berry gera′nium, a plant, *Saxifraga stolonifera* (or *S. sarmentosa*), of the saxifrage family, native to eastern Asia, that has rounded, variegated leaves and numerous threadlike stolons and is frequently cultivated as a houseplant. Also called **mother-of-thousands.** [1875–80]

straw′berry gua′va, a shrub or small tree, *Psidium littorale,* of the myrtle family, native to Brazil, having smooth, grayish-brown bark, leathery leaves, white flowers, and edible, white-fleshed, purplish-red fruit.

straw′berry mark′, a small, reddish, slightly raised birthmark. [1840–50]

straw•ber•ry-rasp•ber•ry (strô′ber′ē raz′ber′ē, strô′bə rē raz′bə rē), *n.* an arching, prickly, Japanese plant, *Rubus illecebrosus,* of the rose family, having an herbaceous stem, white, fragrant flowers, and large, edible, scarlet fruit. Also called **balloon-berry.**

straw′berry roan′, a horse with a reddish coat that is liberally flecked with white hairs. [1930–35]

straw′berry toma′to, 1. the small, edible, tomato-like fruit of the plant *Physalis pruinosa,* of the nightshade family. **2.** the plant itself. [1840–50, *Amer.*]

straw′berry tree′, an evergreen shrub or tree, *Arbutus unedo,* of the heath family, native to southern Europe, bearing a scarlet, strawberrylike fruit. [1400–50; late ME]

straw•board (strô′bôrd′, -bōrd′), *n.* coarse, yellow paperboard made of straw pulp, used in packing, for making boxes, etc. [1840–50; STRAW + BOARD]

straw′ boss′, a member of a work crew, as in a factory or logging camp, who acts as a boss; assistant foreman. [1890–95, *Amer.*]

straw-boss (strô′bôs′, -bos′), *v.t.* to act as a straw boss to: *She was assigned to straw-boss the night shift.*

straw′ col′or, a pale yellow similar to the color of straw. [1580–90] **—straw′-col′ored,** *adj.*

straw•flow•er (strô′flou′ər), *n.* **1.** any of several everlasting flowers, esp. an Australian composite plant, *Helichrysum bracteatum,* having heads of chaffy yellow, orange, red, or white flowers. **2.** Also called **cornflower.** a bellwort, *Uvularia grandiflora,* of the lily family, having yellow flowers. [1920–25; STRAW + FLOWER]

straw•hat (strô′hat′), *adj.* of or pertaining to a summer theater situated outside an urban or metropolitan area: *strawhat theater; strawhat circuit.* [1935–40; so called from the wearing of straw hats in summer]

straw′ man′, 1. a mass of straw formed to resemble a man, as for a doll or scarecrow. **2.** a person whose importance or function is only nominal, as to cover another's activities; front. **3.** a fabricated or conveniently weak or innocuous person, object, matter, etc., used as a seeming adversary or argument: *The issue she railed about was no more than a straw man.* [1585–95]

straw′ mite′, a mite, *Pyemotes ventricosus,* that often occurs in straw and normally feeds on the larvae of insects but opportunistically bites humans, causing an itching dermatitis. Also called **grain itch mite.**

straw′ mush′room, a small brown mushroom, *Volvariella volvacea,* used in Asian cookery.

straw′ vote′, an unofficial vote taken to obtain an indication of the general trend of opinion on a particular issue. Also called **straw′ poll′.** [1885–90, *Amer.*]

straw′ wine′, a usually rich or sweet wine produced from grapes partially dried on the vine or picked and dried in the sun on a bed of straw or reeds. [1815–25]

straw•worm (strô′wûrm′), *n.* **1.** caddisworm. **2.** jointworm. [1645–55; STRAW + WORM]

straw•y (strô′ē), *adj.,* **straw•i•er, straw•i•est. 1.** of, containing, or resembling straw. **2.** strewn or thatched with straw. [1545–55; STRAW + -Y[1]]

stray (strā), *v.i.* **1.** to deviate from the direct course, leave the proper place, or go beyond the proper limits, esp. without a fixed course or purpose; ramble: *to stray from the main road.* **2.** to wander; roam: *The new puppy strayed from room to room.* **3.** to go astray; deviate, as from a moral, religious, or philosophical course: *to stray from the teachings of the church.* **4.** to digress or become distracted. **—n. 5.** a domestic animal found wandering at large or without an owner. **6.** any homeless or friendless person or animal. **7.** a person or animal that strays: *the strays of a flock.* **8. strays,** *Radio.* static. **—adj. 9.** straying or having strayed, as a domestic animal. **10.** found or occurring apart from others or as an isolated or casual instance; incidental or occasional. **11.** *Radio.* undesired: *stray capacitance.* [1250–1300; (v.) ME *strayen,* aph. var. of *astraien, estraien* < MF *estraier* < VL **extrāvagāre* to wander out of bounds (see EXTRAVAGANT); (n.) ME, in part deriv. of the v., in part < AF *stray,* MF *estrai,* deriv. of *estraier*] **—stray′er,** *n.*

—Syn. 1. rove, range. **2.** meander. **3.** err.

streak (strēk), *n.* **1.** a long, narrow mark, smear, band of color, or the like: *streaks of mud.* **2.** a portion or layer of something, distinguished by color or nature from the rest; a vein or stratum: *streaks of fat in meat.* **3.** a vein, strain, or admixture of anything: *a streak of humor.* **4.** *Informal.* **a.** a spell or run: *a streak of good luck.* **b.** an uninterrupted series: *The team had a losing streak of ten games.* **5.** a flash leaving a visible line or aftereffect, as of lightning; bolt. **6.** *Mineral.* the line of powder obtained by scratching a mineral or rubbing it upon a hard, rough white surface, often differing in color from the mineral in the mass, and serving as an important distinguishing character. **7.** *Plant Pathol.* **a.** an elongated, narrow, superficial lesion on stems or leaf veins, becoming brown and necrotic. **b.** any disease characterized by such lesions. **8. blue streak.** See **blue streak. —v.t. 9.** to mark with a streak or streaks; form streaks on: *sunlight streaking the water with gold; frost streaking the windows.* **10.** to lighten or color (strands of hair) for contrastive effect. **11.** to dispose, arrange, smear, spread, etc., in the form of a streak or streaks: *to streak cold germs on a slide for microscopic study.* **—v.i. 12.** to become streaked. **13.** to run, go, or work rapidly. **14.** to flash, as lightning. **15.** to make a sudden dash in public while naked, esp. as a prank. [bef. 1000; (n.) ME *streke,* akin to *strike,* OE *strica* stroke, line, mark; c. G *Strich,* Goth *striks* stroke, L *strigil* STRIGIL; (v.) late ME *streken* to cross out, deriv. of the n. (akin to STRIKE, STROKE[1])] **—streaked•ly** (strēkt′lē, strē′kid lē), *adv.* **—streaked′ness,** *n.* **—streak′er,** *n.* **—streak′like′,** *adj.*

—Syn. 3. cast, touch, element, trace.

streak•y (strē′kē), *adj.,* **streak•i•er, streak•i•est. 1.** occurring in streaks or a streak. **2.** marked with or characterized by streaks. **3.** varying or uneven in quality. [1660–70; STREAK + -Y[1]] **—streak′i•ly,** *adv.* **—streak′i•ness,** *n.*

stream (strēm), *n.* **1.** a body of water flowing in a channel or watercourse, as a river, rivulet, or brook. **2.** a steady current in water, as in a river or the ocean: *to row against the stream; the Gulf Stream.* **3.** any flow of water or other liquid or fluid: *streams of blood.* **4.** a current or flow of air, gas, or the like. **5.** a beam or trail of light: *A stream of moonlight fell from the clouds.* **6.** a continuous flow or succession of anything: *a stream of words.* **7.** prevailing direction; drift: *the stream of opinion.* **8. on stream,** in or into operation: *The factory will be on stream in a month.* **—v.i. 9.** to flow, pass, or issue in a stream, as water, tears, or blood. **10.** to send forth or throw off a stream; run or flow (often fol. by *with*): *eyes streaming with tears.* **11.** to extend in a beam or in rays, as light: *Sunlight streamed in through the windows.* **12.** to move or proceed continuously like a flowing stream, as a procession. **13.** to wave or float outward, as a flag in the wind. **14.** to hang in a loose, flowing manner, as long hair. **—v.t. 15.** to send forth or discharge in a stream: *The wound streamed blood.* **16.** to cause to stream or float outward, as a flag. **17.** *Naut.* to place (an object) in the water at the end of a line attached to a vessel. [bef. 900; (n.) ME *streem,* OE *strēam;* c. G *Strom,* ON *straumr;* akin to Gk *rhein* to flow (see RHEUM); (v.) ME *streamen,* deriv. of the n.] **—stream′less,** *adj.* **—stream′like′,** *adj.*

—Syn. 1. rill, run, streamlet, runnel. STREAM, CURRENT refer to a steady flow. In this use they are interchangeable. In the sense of running water, however, a STREAM is a flow that may be as small as a brook or as large as a river: *A number of streams have their sources in mountains.* CURRENT refers to the most rapidly moving part of the stream: *This river has a swift current.* **2.** flow, tide. **6.** torrent, rush. **9.** pour.

stream•bed (strēm′bed′), *n.* the channel in which a stream flows or formerly flowed. [1855–60; STREAM + BED]

stream′ cap′ture, *Geol.* piracy (def. 3).

stream•er (strē′mər), *n.* **1.** something that streams: *streamers of flame.* **2.** a long, narrow flag or pennant. **3.** a long, flowing ribbon, feather, or the like used for ornament, as in dress. **4.** any long, narrow piece or thing, as a spray of a plant or a strip of cloud. **5.** a stream of light, esp. one appearing in some forms of the aurora borealis. **6.** *Elect.* an electric discharge in a narrow stream from a point of high potential on a charged body. **7.** *Astron.* a long extension of the solar corona, several solar radii long. **8.** *Journalism.* banner (def. 7). **9.** a parachute that comes out of its packing in a long stream but does not expand. [1250–1300; ME *stremer.* See STREAM, -ER[1]]

stream′er fly′, *Angling.* an artificial fly having a wing or wings extending beyond the crook of the fishhook.

stream•flow (strēm′flō′), *n.* the water that flows in a specific stream site, esp. its volume and rate of flow. [STREAM + FLOW]

stream•ing (strē′ming), *n.* **1.** an act or instance of flowing. **2.** Also called **protoplasmic streaming.** *Biol.* rapid flowing of cytoplasm within a cell; cyclosis. [1350–1400; ME *streming.* See STREAM, -ING[1]] **—stream′ing•ly,** *adv.*

stream′ing poten′tial, *Physical Chem.* the potential produced in the walls of a porous membrane or a capillary tube by forcing a liquid through it.

stream•let (strēm′lit), *n.* a small stream; rivulet. [1545–55; STREAM + -LET]

stream•line (strēm′līn′), *n., v.,* **-lined, -lin•ing.** *adj.* **—n. 1.** a teardrop line of contour offering the least possible resistance to a current of air, water, etc. **2.** the path of a particle that is flowing steadily and without turbulence in a fluid past an object. **—v.t. 3.** to make streamlined. **4.** to alter in order to make more efficient or simple. **—adj. 5.** streamlined. [1870–75; STREAM + LINE[1]]

stream•lined (strēm′līnd′), *adj.* **1.** having a contour designed to offer the least possible resistance to a current of air, water, etc.; optimally shaped for motion or conductivity. **2.** designed or organized to give maximum efficiency; compact. **3.** modernized; up-to-date. [1890–95; STREAMLINE + -ED[2]]

stream′line flow′, the flow of a fluid past an object such that the velocity at any fixed point in the fluid is constant or varies in a regular manner. Cf. **turbulent flow.** [1905–10]

stream•lin•er (strēm′lī′nər), *n.* something that is streamlined, esp. a locomotive or passenger train. [1930–35; STREAMLINE + -ER[1]]

stream′ of con′sciousness, 1. *Psychol.* thought regarded as a succession of ideas and images constantly moving forward in time. **2.** See **interior monologue.** [1885–90]

stream-of-con•scious•ness (strēm′əv kon′shəs nis), *adj.* of, pertaining to, or characterized by a manner of writing in which a character's thoughts or perceptions are presented as occurring in random form, without regard for logical sequences, syntactic structure, distinctions between various levels of reality, or the like: *a stream-of-consciousness novel; a stream-of-consciousness technique.* Cf. **interior monologue.**

stream•way (strēm′wā′), *n.* the bed of a stream. [1815–25; STREAM + WAY[1]]

Stream•wood (strēm′wŏŏd′), *n.* a city in NE Illinois. 23,456.

stream•y (strē′mē), *adj.,* **stream•i•er, stream•i•est. 1.** abounding in streams or watercourses: *streamy meadows.* **2.** flowing in a stream; streaming. [1400–50; late ME *stremy.* See STREAM, -Y[1]] **—stream′i•ness,** *n.*

Stre•ator (strē′tər), *n.* a city in N Illinois. 14,769.

streek (strēk), *Brit. Dial.* **—v.t. 1.** to stretch (one's limbs), as on awakening or by exercise. **2.** to extend (one's hand or arm), as in reaching for or offering an object. **3.** to stretch out or prepare (a corpse) for burial. **—v.i. 4.** to fall or lie prostrate. **5.** to move quickly, esp. to advance. [1200–50; ME (north) *streken,* var. of *strecchen* to STRETCH] **—streek′er,** *n.*

streek•ing (strē′king), *n. Brit. Dial.* the act of stretching one's limbs, as on awakening or by exercise. [1300–50; ME *streekynge.* See STREEK, -ING[1]]

street (strēt), *n.* **1.** a public thoroughfare, usually paved, in a village, town, or city, including the sidewalk or sidewalks. **2.** such a thoroughfare together with adjacent buildings, lots, etc.: *Houses, lawns, and trees composed a very pleasant street.* **3.** the roadway of such a thoroughfare, as distinguished from the sidewalk: *to cross a street.* **4.** a main way or thoroughfare, as distinguished from a lane, alley, or the like. **5.** the inhabitants or frequenters of a street: *The whole street gossiped about the new neighbors.* **6. the Street,** *Informal.* **a.** the section of a city associated with a given profession or trade, esp. when concerned with business or finance, as Wall Street. **b.** the principal theater and entertainment district of any of a number of U.S. cities. **7. on** or **in the street, a.** without a home. **b.** without a job or occupation; idle. **c.** out of prison or police custody; at liberty. **8. up one's street,** *Brit.* See **alley**[1] (def. 7). —*adj.* **9.** of, on, or adjoining a street: *a street door.* **10.** taking place or appearing on the street: *street fight; street musicians.* **11.** coarse; crude; vulgar: *street language.* **12.** suitable for everyday wear: *street clothes; street dress.* **13.** retail: *the street price of a new computer; the street value of a drug.* [bef. 900; ME; OE *strēt, strǣt;* c. D *straat,* G *Strasse;* all << L (*via*) *strāta* paved (road); see STRATUM] —**street′less,** *adj.* —**street′like′,** *adj.*

—**Syn. 1.** roadway, concourse. STREET, ALLEY, AVENUE, BOULEVARD all refer to public ways or roads in municipal areas. A STREET is a road in a village, town, or city, esp. a road lined with buildings. An ALLEY is a narrow street or footway, esp. at the rear of or between rows of buildings or lots. An AVENUE is properly a prominent street, often one bordered by fine residences and impressive buildings, or with a row of trees on each side. A BOULEVARD is a beautiful, broad street, lined with rows of stately trees, esp. used as a promenade. In some cities STREET and AVENUE are used interchangeably, the only difference being that those running one direction (say, north and south) are given one designation and those crossing them are given the other.

street′ ar′ab, (*sometimes offensive*) a person, esp. a child, who lives a homeless, vagabond life on the streets; urchin. Also, **street′ Ar′ab.** [1860–65]

street·car (strēt′kär′), *n.* a public vehicle running regularly along certain streets, usually on rails, as a trolley car or trolley bus. [1860–65, *Amer.*; STREET + CAR[1]]

Street′car Named′ Desire′, A, a play (1947) by Tennessee Williams.

street′ certif′icate, a certificate showing ownership of a specified number of shares of stock: endorsed by the owner and guaranteed by a broker, it may be traded without formal transfer on the books of the corporation issuing the stock.

street′ Chris′tian, (esp. in the 1960's) a Christian whose religious life centers more in social or communal groups than in institutional churches. [1965–70]

street′ clean′er, a sanitation worker who cleans streets or sidewalks.

street′ fight′er, 1. a person whose style of fistfighting was learned in the streets, as opposed to a trained or proficient boxer. **2.** a person who deals with others in an aggressive, cunning manner. Also, **street′-fight′er.** —**street′-fight′ing,** *n., adj.*

street′ hock′ey, *Canadian.* See **road hockey.** [1960–65]

street·light (strēt′līt′), *n.* a light, usually supported by a lamppost, for illuminating a street or road. [1615–25; STREET + LIGHT[1]]

street′ min′istry, the vocation of a church worker, clergyman, or the like who frequents public places in an attempt to help runaways, prostitutes, or others on the margins of society.

street′ mon′ey, *Slang.* See **walking-around money.** [1975–80]

street′ name′, *Stock Exchange.* **1.** a broker who holds securities registered in his or her name instead of in the name of the customer, esp. for convenience in executing transfers and in pledging for borrowing in margin accounts. **2.** a familiar or slang name of a narcotic drug: *"angel dust" is a street name for phencyclidine.*

street′ or′derly, *Brit.* See **street cleaner.** [1850–55]

street′ peo′ple, 1. persons whose home is in the streets of a city; the homeless. **2.** people who make their living in the streets, esp. of large cities, as vendors or performers. **3.** the people of a neighborhood, esp. a crowded big-city neighborhood or ghetto, who frequent the streets of their area. [1965–70]

street′ rail′way, a company that operates streetcars or buses. [1860–65, *Amer.*]

street′ rod′, an old automobile that has been well maintained and typically has been provided with a powerful, modern engine and modern interior fittings.

street·scape (strēt′skāp′), *n.* **1.** a pictorial view of a street. **2.** an environment of streets: *The little park provides a tranquil refuge so uncharacteristic of the urban streetscape.* [1920–25; STREET + -SCAPE]

street-smart (strēt′smärt′), *adj.* possessing or showing street smarts. [1965–70]

street′ smarts′, *Informal.* shrewd awareness of how to survive or succeed in any situation, esp. as a result of living or working in a difficult environment, as a city ghetto neighborhood. [1970–75]

street′ the′ater, the presentation of plays or other entertainments by traveling companies on the streets, in parks, etc., often with the use of temporary or mobile stages. [1955–60, *Amer.*]

street′ vi′rus, a virus, as rabies, obtained from a naturally infected animal and usually virulent, as opposed to a laboratory-attenuated strain. [1910–15]

street·walk·er (strēt′wô′kər), *n.* a prostitute who solicits on the streets. [1585–95; STREET + WALKER] —**street′walk′ing,** *n.*

street·wise (strēt′wīz′), *adj.* street-smart. Also, **street′-wise′.** [1960–65, *Amer.*; STREET + WISE[1]]

street·work·er (strēt′wûr′kər), *n.* a social worker who works with youths of a neighborhood. [1960–65; STREET + WORKER]

Stre·ga (strā′gə), *Trademark.* a brand of spicy, orange-flavored liqueur made in Italy.

strength (strengkth, strength, strenth), *n.* **1.** the quality or state of being strong; bodily or muscular power; vigor. **2.** mental power, force, or vigor. **3.** moral power, firmness, or courage. **4.** power by reason of influence, authority, resources, numbers, etc. **5.** number, as of personnel or ships in a force or body: *a regiment with a strength of 3000.* **6.** effective force, potency, or cogency, as of inducements or arguments: *the strength of his plea.* **7.** power of resisting force, strain, wear, etc. **8.** vigor of action, language, feeling, etc. **9.** the effective or essential properties characteristic of a beverage, chemical, or the like: *The alcoholic strength of brandy far exceeds that of wine.* **10.** a particular proportion or concentration of these properties; intensity, as of light, color, sound, flavor, or odor: *coffee of normal strength.* **11.** something or someone that gives one strength or is a source of power or encouragement; sustenance: *The Bible was her strength and joy.* **12.** power to rise or remain firm in prices: *The pound declined in strength.* **13. on the strength of,** on the basis of; relying on: *He was accepted by the college on the strength of ardent personal recommendations.* [bef. 900; ME *strengthe,* OE *strengthu;* see STRONG, -TH[1]]

—**Syn. 4.** STRENGTH, POWER, FORCE, MIGHT suggest capacity to do something. STRENGTH is inherent capacity to manifest energy, to endure, and to resist. POWER is capacity to do work and to act. FORCE is the exercise of power: *One has the power to do something. He exerts force when he does it. He has sufficient strength to complete it.* MIGHT is power or strength in a great or overwhelming degree: *the might of an army.* **9.** potency. **10.** brightness, loudness, vividness, pungency.

strength·en (strengk′thən, streng′-, stren′-), *v.t.* **1.** to make stronger; give strength to. **2.** *Phonet.* to change (a speech sound) to an articulation requiring more effort, as from fricative to stop or nongeminate to geminate. —*v.i.* **3.** to gain strength; grow stronger. [1250–1300; ME *strengthnen.* See STRENGTH, -EN[1]] —**strength′en·er,** *n.* —**strength′en·ing·ly,** *adv.*

—**Syn. 1.** buttress, reinforce, fortify, support.

strength·less (strengkth′lis, strength′-, strenth′-), *adj.* lacking strength. [1150–1200; ME; see STRENGTH, -LESS] —**strength′less·ly,** *adv.* —**strength′less·ness,** *n.*

stren·u·ous (stren′yo͞o əs), *adj.* **1.** characterized by vigorous exertion, as action, efforts, life, etc.: *a strenuous afternoon of hunting.* **2.** demanding or requiring vigorous exertion; laborious: *To think deeply is a strenuous task.* **3.** vigorous, energetic, or zealously active: *a strenuous person; a strenuous intellect.* [1590–1600; < L *strēnuus;* see -OUS] —**stren′u·ous·ly,** *adv.* —**stren′u·ous·ness, stren·u·os·i·ty** (stren′yo͞o os′i tē), *n.*

—**Syn. 3.** forceful. See **active.** —**Ant. 2.** easy.

strep (strep), *Informal.* —*n.* **1.** streptococcus. —*adj.* **2.** streptococcal. [1930–35; by shortening]

strep·i·tous (strep′i təs), *adj.* boisterous; noisy. Also, **strep′i·tant.** [1675–85; < L *strepit(us)* noise + -OUS]

strep·sip·ter·an (strep sip′tər ən), *adj.* **1.** strepsipterous. —*n.* **2.** strepsipteron. [1835–45; < NL *Strepsipter(a)* (see STREPSIPTEROUS) + -AN]

strep·sip·ter·on (strep sip′tər ən, -tə ron′), *n.* a strepsipterous insect. Also, **strepsipteran.** [< NL: sing. of *Strepsiptera* (see STREPSIPTEROUS)]

strep·sip·ter·ous (strep sip′tər əs), *adj.* belonging or pertaining to the order Strepsiptera, comprising minute insects that are closely related to the beetles, the twisted-winged male being free-living and the wingless female parasitic in various insect hosts. [1810–20; < NL *Strepsipter(a)* order name (< Gk *strepsi-* (s. of *strépsis* a turning round, equiv. to *strep-* (var. s. of *stréphein* to twist, turn; cf. STREPTO-) + *-sis* -SIS) + *-ptera,* neut. pl. of *-pteros* -PTEROUS) + -OUS]

strep′ throat′, *Pathol.* an acute sore throat caused by hemolytic streptococci and accompanied by fever and prostration. [1925–30]

strepto-, a combining form meaning "twisted," used in the formation of compound words: *streptococcus.* [comb. form of Gk *streptós* pliant, twisted, twined, equiv. to *strep-* (var. s. of *stréphein* to twist) + *-tos* verbid suffix]

strep·to·ba·cil·lus (strep′tō bə sil′əs), *n., pl.* **-cil·li** (-sil′ī). *Bacteriol.* **1.** any of various bacilli that form in chains. **2.** any of the Gram-negative bacteria of the genus *Streptobacillus,* common in rat saliva and a cause of ratbite fever. [1895–1900; < NL; see STREPTO-, BACILLUS]

strep·to·car·pus (strep′tə kär′pəs), *n.* any of various plants belonging to the genus *Streptocarpus,* of the gesneria family, native to Africa and Asia, having showy white, pink, or purplish flowers and often cultivated as a houseplant. Also called **Cape primrose.** [< NL (1828); see STREPTO-, -CARPOUS; so named in reference to the tight spirals formed by the ruptured seed capsules]

strep·to·coc·cus (strep′tə kok′əs), *n., pl.* **-coc·ci** (-kok′sī, -sē). *Bacteriol.* any of several spherical or oval bacteria of the genus *Streptococcus,* occurring in pairs or chains, certain species of which are pathogenic for humans, causing scarlet fever, tonsillitis, etc. [1875–80; < NL; see STREPTO-, COCCUS] —**strep·to·coc·cal** (strep′tə-kok′əl), **strep·to·coc·cic** (strep′tə kok′sik), *adj.*

strep·to·dor·nase (strep′tō dôr′nās, -nāz), *n. Biochem., Pharm.* a deoxyribonuclease, obtained from hemolytic streptococci, used in medicine for decomposing blood clots and fibrinous and purulent matter. [STREPTO- + D(E)O(XY)R(IBO)N(UCLE)ASE]

strep·to·ki·nase (strep′tō kī′nās, -nāz, -kin′ās, -āz), *n. Pharm.* an enzyme used to dissolve blood clots. [1945–50; STREPTO- + KINASE]

strep·to·ly·sin (strep′tə lī′sin), *n. Bacteriol.* a type of hemolysin produced by certain species of streptococcus. [1900–05; STREPTO- (repr. generic names which begin with this element, as *Streptococcus*) + (HEMO)LYSIN]

strep·to·my·ces (strep′tə mī′sēz), *n., pl.* **-ces.** *Bacteriol.* any of several aerobic bacteria of the genus *Streptomyces,* certain species of which produce antibiotics. [< NL (1943), equiv. to *strepto-* STREPTO- + Gk *mýkēs* mushroom, fungus]

strep·to·my·cin (strep′tə mī′sin), *n. Pharm.* an antibiotic, $C_{21}H_{39}N_7O_{12}$, produced by a soil actinomycete, *Streptomyces griseus,* and used in medicine in the form of its white, water-soluble sulfate salt, chiefly in the treatment of tuberculosis. Cf. **dihydrostreptomycin.** [1944; < NL *Streptomyc(es)* STREPTOMYCES + -IN[2]]

strep·to·thri·cin (strep′tə thrī′sin), *n. Pharm.* an antibacterial substance produced by a soil fungus, *Actinomyces lavendulae.* [1925–30; STREPTO- + *thric-* (var. of TRICH-) + -IN[2]]

Stre·se·mann (shtrā′zə män′), *n.* **Gus·tav** (go͝os′täf), 1878–1929, German statesman: Nobel peace prize 1926.

stress (stres), *n.* **1.** importance or significance attached to a thing; emphasis: *to lay stress upon good manners.* **2.** *Phonet.* emphasis in the form of prominent relative loudness of a syllable or a word as a result of special effort in utterance. **3.** *Pros.* accent or emphasis on syllables in a metrical pattern; beat. **4.** emphasis in melody, rhythm, etc.; beat. **5.** the physical pressure, pull, or other force exerted on one thing by another; strain. **6.** *Mech.* **a.** the action on a body of any system of balanced forces whereby strain or deformation results. **b.** the amount of stress, usually measured in pounds per square inch or in pascals. **c.** a load, force, or system of forces producing a strain. **d.** the internal resistance or reaction of an elastic body to the external forces applied to it. **e.** the ratio of force to area. **7.** *Physiol.* a specific response by the body to a stimulus, as fear or pain, that disturbs or interferes with the normal physiological equilibrium of an organism. **8.** physical, mental, or emotional strain or tension: *Worry over his job and his wife's health put him under a great stress.* **9.** a situation, occurrence, or factor causing this: *The stress of being trapped in the elevator gave him a pounding headache.* **10.** *Archaic.* strong or straining exertion. —*v.t.* **11.** to lay stress on; emphasize. **12.** *Phonet.* to pronounce (a syllable or a word) with prominent loudness: *Stress the first syllable of "runner." Stress the second word in "put up with."* Cf. **accent** (def. 18). **13.** to subject to stress or strain. **14.** *Mech.* to subject to stress. [1275–1325; (n.) ME *stresse,* aph. var. of *distresse* DISTRESS; (v.) deriv. of the n.] —**stress′less,** *adj.* —**stress′less·ness,** *n.*

—**Syn. 8.** anxiety, burden, pressure, worry.

-stress, a feminine equivalent of **-ster:** *seamstress; songstress.* [-ST(E)R + -ESS]

stressed-out (strest′out′), *adj.* afflicted with or incapacitated by stress.

stress′ frac′ture, *Pathol.* a hairline crack in a bone, esp. of a foot or leg, caused by repeated or prolonged stress and often occurring in runners, dancers, and soldiers **(march fracture).**

stress·ful (stres′fəl), *adj.* full of stress or tension: *the stressful days before a war.* [1850–55; STRESS + -FUL] —**stress′ful·ly,** *adv.*

stress′ mark′, a mark placed before, after, or over a syllable to indicate stress in pronunciation; accent mark.

stres·sor (stres′ər, -ôr), *n.* an activity, event, or other stimulus that causes stress. [1950–55; STRESS + -OR[2]]

stress′ test′, 1. a test, esp. one conducted in a laboratory, to determine how much pressure, tension, wear, etc., a product or material can withstand. **2.** *Med.* a test of cardiovascular health made by recording heart rate, blood pressure, electrocardiogram, and other parameters while a person undergoes physical exertion. [1970–75]

stress-test (stres′test′), *v.t.* to subject to a stress test.

stress-timed (stres′tīmd′), *adj. Phonet.* (of a language) having a rhythm in which stressed syllables tend to occur at regular intervals of time, regardless of the number of intervening unstressed syllables. Cf. **syllable-timed.**

stretch (strech), *v.t.* **1.** to draw out or extend (oneself, a body, limbs, wings, etc.) to the full length or extent (often fol. by *out*): *to stretch oneself out on the ground.* **2.** to hold out, reach forth, or extend (one's arm, head, etc.). **3.** to extend, spread, or place (something) so as to reach from one point or place to another: *to stretch a rope across a road.* **4.** to draw tight or taut: *to stretch the strings of a violin.* **5.** to lengthen, widen, distend, or enlarge by tension: *to stretch a rubber band.* **6.** to draw out, extend, or enlarge unduly: *The jacket was stretched at the elbows.* **7.** to extend, force, or make serve beyond the normal or proper limits; strain: *to stretch the imagination; to stretch the facts; to stretch food to feed extra guests; to stretch money to keep within a budget.* **8.** to extend or strain (oneself) to the utmost, as by intense exertion; tax. **9.** to increase the quantity of (a beverage, food, paint, etc.) by dilution or admixing: *They caught the bartender stretching the gin with water.* **10.** *Radio and Television.* to prolong or slow down (action or pace) in order not to end too early: *to stretch a show; to stretch the action two minutes.* —*v.i.* **11.** to recline at full length (usually fol. by *out*): *to stretch out on a couch.* **12.** to extend the hand or to reach, as for something. **13.** to extend over a distance or area or in a particular direction: *The forest stretches for miles.* **14.** to extend in time: *His memory stretches back to his early childhood.* **15.** to stretch oneself by extending the limbs and lengthening the muscles to the utmost: *to stretch and yawn.* **16.** to become stretched, or admit of being stretched, to greater length, width, etc., as any elastic or ductile mate-

CONCISE ETYMOLOGY KEY: <, descended or borrowed from; >, whence; b., blend of, blended; c., cognate with; cf., compare; deriv., derivative; equiv., equivalent; imit., imitative; obl., oblique; r., replacing; s., stem; sp., spelling, spelled; resp., respelling, respelled; trans., translation; ?, origin unknown; *, unattested; ‡, probably earlier than. See the full key inside the front cover.

rial. **17.** *Radio and Television.* to reduce the pace or slow down the action of a radio or television program. —*n.* **18.** an act or instance of stretching. **19.** the state of being stretched. **20.** a continuous length, distance, tract, or expanse: *a stretch of meadow.* **21.** *Horse Racing.* the backstretch or homestretch of a racetrack. **22.** *Baseball.* a short windup, usually used to keep base runners from taking too long a lead, in which the pitcher starts the pitching motion with hands together at the waist, raises them to or above the head, brings them back to the waist, and, after a momentary pause, delivers the ball. **23.** an extent in time; duration: *for a stretch of ten years.* **24.** elasticity or capacity for extension. **25.** *Slang.* a term of imprisonment: *He's doing a stretch in the pen.* **26.** (*cap.*) a nickname for a tall, lanky person. —*adj.* **27.** made of synthetic or composite yarn having a sufficiently low denier or having been subjected to any of several special mechanical treatments to permit increased elasticity: *stretch girdle; stretch pants.* **28.** (of yarn) modified or twisted so as to afford high elasticity. **29.** Also, **stretched.** of or pertaining to a conveyance, as a limousine or airliner, whose seating area is expanded to carry more passengers or afford greater legroom and to allow space for other comforts and amenities. [bef. 900; ME *strecchen* (v.), OE *streccan;* c. D *strekken,* G *strecken;* akin to OE *stræc* firm, hard, MD *strac* stiff. See STARE, STARK] —**stretch′a·ble,** *adj.* —**stretch′a·bil′i·ty,** *n.*

—**Syn. 5.** See **lengthen. 11.** lie down. **20.** range, reach, compass. —**Ant. 5, 16.** shorten, shrink.

stretch·er (strech′ər), *n.* **1.** *Med.* **a.** a kind of litter, often of canvas stretched on a frame, for carrying the sick, wounded, or dead. **b.** a similar litter on wheels, adapted for use in ambulances and hospitals. **2.** a person or thing that stretches. **3.** any of various instruments for extending, widening, distending, etc. **4.** a bar, beam, or fabricated material, serving as a tie or brace. **5.** *Masonry.* a brick or stone laid in a wall so that its longer edge is exposed or parallel to the surface. Cf. **header** (def. 5a). **6.** a simple wooden framework on which the canvas for an oil painting is stretched. **7.** *Furniture.* **a.** a framework connecting and bracing the legs of a piece of furniture. **b.** one member of this framework. **8.** a crosspiece that is set athwart and near the bottom in a small boat, and against which the feet of a rower are braced. **9.** one of the thin, sliding rods connecting the canopy and handle of an umbrella. —*v.t.* **10.** to stretch (canvas for a painting) on a stretcher. [1375–1425; late ME *stretcher.* See STRETCH, -ER[1]]

stretch·er-bear·er (strech′ər bâr′ər), *n.* a person who helps carry a stretcher, as in removing wounded from a battlefield. [1875–80]

stretch′er bond′, *Masonry.* See **running bond.**

stretch′ing course′, (in brickwork) a course of stretchers. Cf. **heading course.** [1685–95]

stretch′ mark′, a silvery streak occurring typically on the abdomen or thighs and caused by stretching of the skin over a short period of time, as during pregnancy or rapid weight gain.

stretch′ mill′, *Metalworking.* a mill for rolling and stretching seamless tubes, the rolls of each successive stand operating more quickly than those of the preceding. Also called **stretch′ reduc′ing mill′.**

stretch·out (strech′out′), *n.* **1.** a deliberate extension of time for meeting a production quota. **2.** a method of labor management by which employees do additional work without a commensurate increase in wages. Also **stretch′-out′** [1925–30; n. use of v. phrase *stretch out*]

stretch′ recep′tor, *Anat., Physiol.* See **muscle spindle.** [1935–40]

stretch′ run′ner, an athlete or horse that is especially strong or fast in the final stage of a race. [1920–25]

stretch·y (strech′ē), *adj.,* **stretch·i·er, stretch·i·est. 1.** having a tendency to stretch, esp. excessively or unduly. **2.** capable of being stretched; elastic. **3.** (esp. of a pig) having a long body. [1850–55; STRETCH + -Y[1]] —**stretch′i·ness,** *n.*

stret·ta (stret′ə), *n., pl.* **stret·te** (stret′ā), **stret·tas.** *Music.* a concluding passage played at a faster tempo. [1875–80; < It; fem. of STRETTO]

stret·to (stret′ō), *n., pl.* **stret·ti** (stret′ē), **stret·tos.** *Music.* the close overlapping of statements of the subject in a fugue, each voice entering immediately after the preceding one. [1745–55; < It: lit., narrow < L *strictus.* See STRICT, STRAIT]

streu·sel (*Ger.* shtroi′zəl; *Eng.* stro͞o′zəl, stroi′-), *n.* a topping for coffeecake, consisting of crumbs of blended sugar, cinnamon, flour, butter, and chopped nutmeats. [1925–30; < G: lit., a sprinkling; see STREW]

streu·sel·ku·chen (*Ger.* shtroi′zəl ko͞o′кнən; *Eng.* stro͞o′zəl ko͞o′кнən, -kən, stroi′-), *n.* coffeecake topped with streusel. [< G; see STREUSEL, KUCHEN]

strew (stro͞o), *v.t.,* **strewed, strewn** (stro͞on) or **strewed, strew·ing. 1.** to let fall in separate pieces or particles over a surface; scatter or sprinkle: *to strew seed in a garden bed.* **2.** to cover or overspread (a surface, place, etc.) with something scattered or sprinkled: *to strew a floor with sawdust.* **3.** to be scattered or sprinkled over (a surface): *Sawdust strewed the floor.* **4.** to spread widely; disseminate: *to strew rumors among the troops.* [bef. 1000; ME *strewen,* OE *strewian;* c. G *streuen,* ON *strā,* Goth *straujan;* akin to L *sternere* to spread (see STRATUM)] —**strew′er,** *n.*

—**Syn. 1.** broadcast. See **sprinkle.** —**Ant. 1.** gather, reap.

strew·ment (stro͞o′mənt), *n.* something strewed or intended for strewing, as flowers. [1595–1605; STREW + -MENT]

stri·a (strī′ə), *n., pl.* **stri·ae** (strī′ē). **1.** a slight or narrow furrow, ridge, stripe, or streak, esp. one of a number in parallel arrangement: *striae of muscle fiber.* **2.** *Mineral.* any of a series of parallel lines or tiny grooves on the surface of a crystal, indicative of the mode of growth. **3.** *Archit.* a flute on the shaft of a column. [1555–65; < L: furrow, channel]

stri·ate (*v.* strī′āt; *adj.* strī′it, -āt), *v.,* **-at·ed, -at·ing,** *adj.* —*v.t.* **1.** to mark with striae; furrow; stripe; streak. —*adj.* **2.** striated. [1660–70; < L *striātus* furrowed, fluted, equiv. to *stri(a)* (see STRIA) + *-ātus* -ATE[1]]

stri·at·ed (strī′ā tid), *adj.* marked with striae; furrowed; striped; streaked. [1640–50; STRIATE + -ED[2]]

stri·a·tion (strī ā′shən), *n.* **1.** striated condition or appearance. **2.** a stria; one of many parallel striae. **3.** *Geol.* any of a number of scratches or parallel grooves on the surface of a rock, resulting from the action of moving ice, as of a glacier. **4.** *Cell Biol.* any of the alternating light and dark crossbands that are visible in certain muscle fibers, esp. of voluntary muscles, and are produced by the distribution of contractile proteins. [1840–50; STRIATE + -ION]

strick (strik), *n.* **1.** a group of any of the major bast fibers, as flax or jute, prepared for conversion into sliver form. **2.** any of the pieces cut from a layer of carded and combed silk. [1375–1425; late ME *strik* bundle of hemp or flax, stick for leveling heaping measures; cf. STRICKLE]

strick·en (strik′ən), *v.* **1.** a pp. of **strike.** —*adj.* **2.** hit or wounded by a weapon, missile, or the like. **3.** beset or afflicted, as with disease, trouble, or sorrow: *stricken areas; a stricken family.* **4.** deeply affected, as with grief, fear, or other emotions. **5.** characterized by or showing the effects of affliction, trouble, misfortune, a mental blow, etc.: *stricken features.* —**strick′en·ly,** *adv.*

Strick·land (strik′lənd), *n.* **William,** 1787–1854, U.S. architect and engineer.

strick·le (strik′əl), *n., v.,* **-led, -ling.** —*n.* **1.** a straightedge used for sweeping off heaped-up grain to the level of the rim of a measure. **2.** *Metall.* a template rotated to generate a mold surface symmetrical about one axis. **3.** an implement for sharpening scythes, composed typically of a piece of wood smeared with grease and sand. —*v.t.* **4.** to sweep off or remove with a strickle. [1400–50; late ME *strikyll;* perh. continuing OE *stricel* teat (perh. also "leveling stick"); see STRIKE, -LE]

strict (strikt), *adj.,* **-er, -est. 1.** characterized by or acting in close conformity to requirements or principles: *a strict observance of rituals.* **2.** stringent or exacting in or in enforcing rules, requirements, obligations, etc.: *strict laws; a strict judge.* **3.** closely or rigorously enforced or maintained: *strict silence.* **4.** exact or precise: *a strict statement of facts.* **5.** extremely defined or conservative; narrowly or carefully limited: *a strict construction of the Constitution.* **6.** close, careful, or minute: *a strict search.* **7.** absolute, perfect, or complete; utmost: *told in strict confidence.* **8.** stern; severe; austere: *strict parents.* **9.** *Obs.* drawn tight or close. [1570–80; < L *strictus,* equiv. to *strig-,* var. s. of *stringere* to draw tight + *-tus* ptp. suffix] —**strict′ness,** *n.*

—**Syn. 1.** narrow, illiberal, harsh, austere. STRICT, RIGID, RIGOROUS, STRINGENT imply inflexibility, severity, and an exacting quality. STRICT implies great exactness, esp. in the observance or enforcement of rules: *strict discipline.* RIGID, literally stiff or unbending, applies to that which is (often unnecessarily or narrowly) inflexible: *rigid economy.* RIGOROUS, with the same literal meaning, applies to that which is severe, exacting, and uncompromising, esp. in action or application: *rigorous self-denial.* STRINGENT applies to that which is vigorously exacting and severe: *stringent measures to suppress disorder.* **4.** accurate, scrupulous. —**Ant. 1.** flexible, lax.

stric·tion (strik′shən), *n.* the act of constricting. [1870–75; < LL *strictiōn-* (s. of *strictiō*), equiv. to L *strict(us)* (see STRICT) + *-iōn-* -ION]

strict·ly (strikt′lē), *adv.* **1.** in a strict manner; rigorously; stringently: *strictly enforced.* **2.** precisely or candidly; factually: *strictly speaking.* [1480–90; STRICT + -LY]

strict′ly decreas′ing func′tion, *Math.* a function having the property that for any two points in the domain such that one is larger than the other, the image of the larger point is less than the image of the smaller point. Cf. **strictly increasing function.**

strict′ly increas′ing func′tion, *Math.* a function having the property that for any two points in the domain such that one is larger than the other, the image of the larger point is greater than the image of the smaller point. Cf. **strictly decreasing function.**

stric·ture (strik′chər), *n.* **1.** a remark or comment, esp. an adverse criticism: *The reviewer made several strictures upon the author's style.* **2.** an abnormal contraction of any passage or duct of the body. **3.** a restriction. **4.** *Archaic.* the act of enclosing or binding tightly. **5.** *Obs.* strictness. [1350–1400; ME < LL *strictūra* tightening, equiv. to L *strict(us)* (see STRICT) + *-ūra* -URE] —**stric′tured,** *adj.*

stride (strīd), *v.,* **strode, strid·den** (strid′n), **strid·ing,** *n.* —*v.i.* **1.** to walk with long steps, as with vigor, haste, impatience, or arrogance. **2.** to take a long step: *to stride across a puddle.* **3.** to straddle. —*v.t.* **4.** to walk with long steps along, on, through, over, etc.: *to stride the deck.* **5.** to pass over or across in one long step: *to stride a ditch.* **6.** to straddle. —*n.* **7.** a striding manner or a striding gait. **8.** a long step in walking. **9.** (in animal locomotion) the act of progressive movement completed when all the feet are returned to the same relative position as at the beginning. **10.** the distance covered by such a movement: *He was walking a stride or two ahead of the others.* **11.** a regular or steady course, pace, etc. **12.** a step forward in development or progress: *rapid strides in mastering algebra.* **13. hit one's stride, a.** to achieve a regular or steady pace or course. **b.** to reach the point or level at which one functions most competently and consistently: *The quarterback didn't hit his stride until the second half of the game.* **14. strides,** (*used with a plural v.*) *Australian Informal.* trousers. **15. take in stride,** to deal with calmly; cope with successfully: *She was able to take her sudden rise to fame in stride.* [bef. 900; (v.) ME *striden,* OE *strīdan;* c. D *strijden,* LG *strīden* to stride; (n.) ME *stride,* deriv. of the v.; akin to STRADDLE] —**strid′er,** *n.* —**strid′ing·ly,** *adv.*

—**Syn. 12.** advance, progress, headway, improvement.

stri·dent (strīd′nt), *adj.* **1.** making or having a harsh sound; grating; creaking: *strident insects; strident hinges.* **2.** having a shrill, irritating quality or character: *a strident tone in his writings.* **3.** *Ling.* (in distinctive feature analysis) characterized acoustically by noise of relatively high intensity, as sibilants, labiodental and uvular fricatives, and most affricates. [1650–60; < L *strīdent-* (s. of *strīdēns*), prp. of *strīdēre* to make a harsh noise; see -ENT] —**stri′dence, stri′den·cy,** *n.* —**stri′dent·ly,** *adv.*

stride′ pian′o, a style of jazz piano playing in which the right hand plays the melody while the left hand plays a single bass note or octave on the strong beat and a chord on the weak beat, developed in Harlem during the 1920's, partly from ragtime piano playing. [1950–55]

stri·dor (strī′dər), *n.* **1.** a harsh, grating, or creaking sound. **2.** *Pathol.* a harsh respiratory sound due to any of various forms of obstruction of the breathing passages. [1625–35; < L *strīdor,* equiv. to *strīd(ēre)* (see STRIDENT) + *-or* -OR[1]]

strid·u·late (strij′ə lāt′), *v.i.,* **-lat·ed, -lat·ing.** to produce a shrill, grating sound, as a cricket does, by rubbing together certain parts of the body; shrill. [1830–40; back formation from *stridulation.* See STRIDULOUS, -ATE[1], -ION] —**strid′u·la′tion,** *n.* —**strid·u·la·to·ry** (strij′ə lə tôr′ē, -tōr′ē), *adj.*

strid·u·lous (strij′ə ləs), *adj.* **1.** Also, **strid′u·lant.** making or having a harsh or grating sound. **2.** *Pathol.* pertaining to or characterized by stridor. [1605–15; < L *strīdulus,* equiv. to *strīd-* (see STRIDENT) + *-ulus* -ULOUS] —**strid′u·lous·ly,** *adv.* —**strid′u·lous·ness,** *n.*

strife (strīf), *n.* **1.** vigorous or bitter conflict, discord, or antagonism: *to be at strife.* **2.** a quarrel, struggle, or clash: *armed strife.* **3.** competition or rivalry: *the strife of the marketplace.* **4.** *Archaic.* strenuous effort. [1175–1225; ME *strif* < OF *estrif,* akin to *estriver* to STRIVE] —**strife′ful,** *adj.* —**strife′less,** *adj.*

—**Syn. 1.** difference, disagreement, contrariety, opposition. **2.** fight, conflict. —**Ant. 1, 2.** peace.

strig·i·form (strij′ə fôrm′), *adj.* of, pertaining, or belonging to the order Strigiformes, comprising the owls. [< NL *Strigiformes* name of the order, equiv. to L *strig-,* s. of *strix* kind of owl (< Gk *strínx*) + NL *-iformes* -IFORMES]

strig·il (strij′əl), *n.* an instrument with a curved blade, used esp. by the ancient Greeks and Romans for scraping the skin at the bath and in the gymnasium. [1575–85; < L *strigilis,* akin to *stringere* to touch lightly; see STREAK, STRIKE] —**strig·il·ate** (strij′ə lit, -lāt′), *adj.*

stri·gose (strī′gōs), *adj.* **1.** *Bot.* set with stiff bristles of hairs; hispid. **2.** *Zool.* marked with fine, closely set ridges, grooves, or points. [1785–95; < L *strig(a)* furrow, row of bristles (akin to *stria* STRIA) + -OSE[1]]

strik·a·ble (strī′kə bəl), *adj.* being cause for a strike, as by union members: *strikable labor issues.* [1900–05; STRIKE + -ABLE]

strike (strīk), *v.,* **struck** or (*Obs.*) **strook; struck** or (*esp. for 31–34*) **strick·en** or (*Obs.*) **strook; strik·ing;** *n., adj.* —*v.t.* **1.** to deal a blow or stroke to (a person or thing), as with the fist, a weapon, or a hammer; hit. **2.** to inflict, deliver, or deal (a blow, stroke, attack, etc.). **3.** to drive so as to cause impact: *to strike the hands together.* **4.** to thrust forcibly: *Brutus struck a dagger into the dying Caesar.* **5.** to produce (fire, sparks, light, etc.) by percussion, friction, etc. **6.** to cause (a match) to ignite by friction. **7.** (of some natural or supernatural agency) to smite or blast: *Lightning struck the spire. May God strike you dead!* **8.** to come into forcible contact or collision with; hit into or against: *The ship struck a rock.* **9.** to reach or fall upon (the senses), as light or sound: *A shrill peal of bells struck their ears.* **10.** to enter the mind of; occur to: *A happy thought struck him.* **11.** to catch or arrest (the sight, hearing, etc.): *the first object that strikes one's eye.* **12.** to impress strongly: *a picture that strikes one's fancy.* **13.** to impress in a particular manner: *How does it strike you?* **14.** to come across, meet with, or encounter suddenly or unexpectedly: *to strike the name of a friend in a newspaper.* **15.** to come upon or find (oil, ore, etc.) in drilling, prospecting, or the like. **16.** to send down or put forth (a root), as a plant or cutting. **17.** to arrive at or achieve by or as by balancing: *to strike a balance; to strike a compromise.* **18.** to take apart or pull down (a structure or object, as a tent). **19.** to remove from the stage (the scenery and properties of an act or scene): *to strike a set.* **20.** *Naut.* **a.** to lower or take down (a sail, mast, etc.). **b.** to lower (a sail, flag, etc.) as a salute or as a sign of surrender. **c.** to lower (something) into the hold of a vessel by means of a rope and tackle. **21.** *Falconry.* to loosen (a hood) from the head of a hawk so that it may be instantly removed. **22.** *Angling.* **a.** to hook (a fish that has taken the bait) by making a sharp jerk on the line. **b.** (of a fish) to snatch at (the bait). **23.** to harpoon (a whale). **24.** (in technical use) to make level or smooth. **25.** to make level or even, as a measure of grain or salt, by drawing a strickle across the top. **26.** to efface, cancel, or cross out, with or as with the stroke of a pen (usually fol. by *out*): *to strike a passage out of a book.* **27.** to impress or stamp (a coin, medal, etc.) by printing or punching: *to strike a medal in commemoration.* **28.** to remove or separate with or as if with a cut (usually fol. by *off*): *Illness struck him off from social contacts. The butcher struck off a chop.* **29.** *Masonry.* to finish (a mortar joint) with a stroke of the trowel. **30.** to indicate (the hour of day) by a stroke or strokes, as a clock: *to strike 12.* **31.** to afflict suddenly, as with disease, suffering, or death

(often fol. by *down*): *The plague struck Europe. Apoplexy struck him down.* **32.** to overwhelm emotionally, as with terror or fear; affect deeply. **33.** to make blind, dumb, etc., suddenly, as if by a blow. **34.** to implant or induce (a feeling): *to strike fear into a person.* **35.** to start or move suddenly into (vigorous movement): *The horse struck a gallop.* **36.** to assume (an attitude or posture): *He likes to strike a noble pose.* **37.** to cause (chill, warmth, etc.) to pass or penetrate quickly. **38.** to come upon or reach in traveling or in a course of procedure: *We struck Rome before dark.* **39.** to make, conclude, or ratify (an agreement, treaty, etc.). **40.** to estimate or determine (a mean or average). **41.** to leave off (work) or stop (working) as a coercive measure, or as at the close of the day. **42.** (of a union or union member) **a.** to declare or engage in a suspension of (work) until an employer grants certain demands, such as pay increases, an improved pension plan, etc. **b.** to declare or engage in a suspension of work against (a factory, employer, industry, etc.) until certain demands are met. **43.** to draw (a straight line); paint the edge of an area with (a regular, usually straight line). **44.** *Law.* to choose (a jury) from a panel by striking off names until only the required number remains.
—*v.i.* **45.** to deal or aim a blow or stroke, as with the fist, a weapon, or a hammer. **46.** to make an attack, esp. a planned military assault: *Our troops struck at dawn.* **47.** to knock, rap, or tap. **48.** to hit or dash on or against something, as a moving body does; come into forcible contact; collide. **49.** to run upon a bank, rock, or other obstacle, as a ship does. **50.** to fall, as light or sound does (fol. by *on* or *upon*). **51.** to make an impression on the mind, senses, etc., as something seen or heard. **52.** to come suddenly or unexpectedly (usually fol. by *on* or *upon*): *to strike on a new way of doing a thing.* **53.** to sound by percussion: *The clock strikes.* **54.** to be indicated by or as by such percussion: *The hour has struck.* **55.** to ignite or be ignited by friction, as a match. **56.** to make a stroke, as with the arms or legs in swimming or with an oar in rowing. **57.** to produce a sound, music, etc., by touching a string or playing upon an instrument. **58.** to take root, as a slip of a plant. **59.** to go, proceed, or advance, esp. in a new direction: *They struck out at dawn. They struck toward a new town.* **60. a.** *U.S. Army.* to act as a voluntary paid servant to a commissioned officer. **b.** *U.S. Navy.* to work hard: strive (followed by *for*): *He is striking for yeoman.* **61.** (of a union or union member) to engage in a suspension of work until an employer or industry meets certain demands. **62.** *Naut.* **a.** to lower the flag or colors, esp. as a salute or as a sign of surrender. **b.** to run up the white flag of surrender. **63.** *Angling.* (of fish) to swallow or take the bait. **64. strike camp,** to dismantle and pack up equipment; prepare to move on; break camp: *The army struck camp and moved on.* **65. strike hands,** to conclude a bargain, as by shaking or joining hands; confirm an agreement: *They reached a price satisfactory to both of them, and struck hands on it.* **66. strike home, a.** to deal an effective blow, hit a vulnerable part, or wound critically or mortally: *The second arrow struck home.* **b.** to have the intended effect; hit the mark: *The sermon on Christian charity struck home.* **67. strike in,** to interrupt suddenly; intervene: *I struck in with a suggestion.* **68. strike it rich, a.** to come upon a valuable mineral or oil deposit. **b.** to have sudden or unexpected financial success: *She struck it rich in real estate.* **69. strike off, a.** *Print.* to print: *They struck off 300 copies of the book.* **b.** to remove or cancel, as from a record, list, etc.: *His name was struck off the waiting list.* **c.** to produce rapidly and easily: *She struck off several letters and had no more work to do.* **d.** to depart rapidly: *We struck off for the country.* **70. strike oil.** See **oil** (def. 9). **71. strike out, a.** *Baseball.* to put out or be put out by a strike-out: *The pitcher walked two and struck out three. He struck out twice in three times at bat.* **b.** (of a person or effort) to fail: *His next two business ventures struck out.* **c.** to lose favor. **d.** to erase; cross out. **e.** to set forth; venture forth: *She struck out on her own at the age of 18.* **72. strike up, a.** to begin to play or to sing: *The orchestra struck up a waltz.* **b.** to set in operation; begin: *Strike up the band!* **c.** to bring into being; commence; begin: *to strike up an acquaintance with new neighbors.*
—*n.* **73.** an act or instance of striking. **74.** a concerted stopping of work or withdrawal of workers' services, as to compel an employer to accede to workers' demands or in protest against terms or conditions imposed by an employer. **75.** a temporary stoppage of something. **76.** Also called **strike plate.** a metal plate on a jamb holding the bolt of the lock on a door when closed. **77.** *Baseball.* **a.** a pitch that is swung at and missed by the batter. **b.** a pitch that passes through the strike zone and is not swung at by the batter. **c.** a foul tip caught by the catcher when there are already two strikes against the batter. **d.** a foul bunt when there are already two strikes against the batter. **e.** a ball hit foul and not caught on the fly when there are less than two strikes against the batter. **78.** *Bowling.* **a.** the knocking down of all of the pins with the first bowl. **b.** the score so made. Cf. **spare** (def. 22). **79.** *Horol.* the striking mechanism of a timepiece. **80.** *Brewing.* the degree of excellence or strength of beer, ale, etc. **81.** *Angling.* **a.** a sharp jerk on the line, made in order to set the hook in the mouth of the fish. **b.** a pull on the line, made by the fish in the process of taking the bait. **82.** *Coining.* a quantity of coins struck at one time. **83.** *Geol.* **a.** the direction of the line formed by the intersection of the bedding plane of a bed or stratum of sedimentary rock with a horizontal plane. **b.** the direction or trend of a structural feature, as an anticlinal axis or the lineation resulting from metamorphism. **84.** the discovery of a rich vein or ore in mining, of petroleum in boring, etc. **85.** *Mil.* a planned attack, esp. by aircraft, on a target. **86. have two strikes against one,** to be in an unfavorable or a critical position: *His age and his lack of education are two strikes against him in his search for a job.* **87. on strike,** engaged in a stoppage of work, services, or other activities, as by union workers to get better wages.
—*adj.* **88.** *Mil.* describing a fighter-bomber aircraft designed to carry large payloads at high speeds and low altitudes and also to engage in air-to-air combat. [bef. 1000; 1768 for def. 74; (v.) ME *striken* to stroke, beat, cross out, OE *strīcan* to stroke, make level; c. G *streichen;* (n.) ME: unit of dry measure (i.e., something leveled off; see STRICK), deriv. of the v.; akin to STREAK, STROKE[1]] **—strike′less,** *adj.*
—Syn. 1. STRIKE, HIT, KNOCK imply suddenly bringing one body in contact with another. STRIKE suggests such an action in a general way: *to strike a child.* HIT is less formal than STRIKE, and often implies giving a single blow, but usually a strong one and definitely aimed: *to hit a baseball.* To KNOCK is to strike, often with a tendency to displace the object struck; it also means to strike repeatedly: *to knock someone down; to knock at a door.* See also **beat. —Ant. 1.** miss.

strike′ ben′efit, money paid to strikers by a union to enable them to subsist during a strike. Also called **strike pay.**

strike·bound (strīk′bound′), *adj.* closed by a strike: *a strikebound factory.* [1940–45; STRIKE + -BOUND[1]]

strike·break·er (strīk′brā′kər), *n.* a person who takes part in breaking up a strike of workers, either by working or by furnishing workers. [1900–05; STRIKE + BREAKER[1]]

strike·break·ing (strīk′brā′king), *n.* action directed at breaking up a strike of workers. [1915–20; STRIKE + BREAKING[1]]

strike′ fault′, *Geol.* a fault that trends parallel to the strike of the strata that it offsets.

strike′ force′, 1. a military force armed and trained for attack. **2.** a group or team, as of law-enforcement agents, who are assigned to one special problem: *the FBI's strike force against organized crime.* [1960–65]

strike·out (strīk′out′), *n. Baseball.* an out made by a batter to whom three strikes have been charged, or as recorded by the pitcher who accomplishes this. [1885–90, *Amer.*; n. use of v. phrase *strike out*]

strike·o·ver (strīk′ō′vər), *n.* **1.** an act or instance of typing over a character, as one typed in error, without erasing it. **2.** the typed-over character: *The letter was full of strikeovers.* [1935–40; n. use of v. phrase *strike over*]

strike′ pay′. See **strike benefit.** [1875–80]

strike′ plate′, strike (def. 76).

strik·er (strī′kər), *n.* **1.** a person or thing that strikes. **2.** a worker who is on strike. **3.** manhelper. **4.** the clapper in a clock that strikes the hours or rings an alarm. **5.** *U.S. Army.* a private who acts as a voluntary paid servant to a commissioned officer. **6.** *U.S. Navy.* an enlisted person in training for a specific technical rating. **7.** a person who strikes fish, whales, etc., with a spear or harpoon. **8.** *Whaling.* a harpoon. **9.** *Soccer.* one of the attacking forwards. [1350–1400; 1840–50 for def. 2; ME; see STRIKE, -ER[1]]

strike′ slip′, *Geol.* the component of slip on a fault parallel with the linear extension or strike of the fault. [1910–15] **—strike′-slip′,** *adj.*

strike′ zone′, *Baseball.* the area above home plate extending from the batter's knees to his or her shoulders. [1945–50]

strik·ing (strī′king), *adj.* **1.** attractive; impressive: *a scene of striking beauty.* **2.** noticeable; conspicuous: *a striking lack of enthusiasm.* **3.** being on strike, as workers. **4. a.** capable of attacking an enemy, esp. by air: *striking power.* **b.** within the extent of space through which it is possible to attack a target effectively: *striking distance.* [1605–15; STRIKE + -ING[2]] **—strik′ing·ly,** *adv.* **—strik′ing·ness,** *n.*
—Syn. 1. remarkable, noteworthy.

strik′ing price′, *Finance.* the fixed price at which a person can exercise an option to buy or sell something, esp. in a call or put option. Also called **exercise price.** [1960–65]

strik′ing train′, *Horol.* the gear train of the striking mechanism of a timepiece. Cf. **going train.** [1880–85]

Strind·berg (strind′bûrg, strin′-; *Swed.* strin′bar′yə), *n.* **Jo·han Au·gust** (yōō′hän ou′gŏŏst), 1849–1912, Swedish novelist, dramatist, and essayist.

strine (strīn), *n. Informal.* Australian English. [1964; jocular representation of the supposed pron. of AUSTRALIAN by uneducated Australian speakers]

string (string), *n., v.,* **strung; strung** or (*Rare*) **stringed; string·ing.** —*n.* **1.** a slender cord or thick thread used for binding or tying; line. **2.** something resembling a cord or thread. **3.** *Physics.* a mathematical entity used to represent elementary particles, as gravitons, quarks, or leptons, in terms of a small but finite stringlike object existing in the four dimensions of space-time and in additional, hypothetical, spacelike dimensions. The theory of such objects **(string theory)** avoids the many mathematical difficulties that arise from treating particles as points. **4.** a narrow strip of flexible material, as cloth or leather, for tying parts together: *the strings of a bonnet.* **5.** a necklace consisting of a number of beads, pearls, or the like threaded or strung on a cord; strand: *She wore a double string of pearls.* **6.** any series of things arranged or connected in a line or following closely one after another: *a string of islands; a string of questions.* **7.** a series of railroad cars coupled together but not constituting an entire train. **8.** *Journalism.* a compilation of clippings of a stringer's published writings, submitted in request of payment according to an agreed space rate. **9.** a group of animals, esp. saddle horses, owned or used by one person: *a string of polo ponies.* **10.** (in a musical instrument) a tightly stretched cord or wire that produces a tone when caused to vibrate, as by plucking, striking, or friction of a bow. **11. strings, a.** stringed instruments, esp. those played with a bow. **b.** players on such instruments in an orchestra or band. **12.** a bowstring. **13.** a cord or fiber in a plant. **14.** the tough piece uniting the two parts of a pod: *the strings of beans.* **15.** *Archit.* **a.** a stringcourse. **b.** Also called **stringer.** one of the sloping sides of a stair, supporting the treads and risers. **16.** *Computers, Ling.* a linear sequence of symbols, words, characters, or bits that is treated as a unit. **17.** *Billiards, Pool.* **a.** a stroke made by each player from the head of the table to the opposite cushion and back, to determine, by means of the resultant positions of the cue balls, who shall open the game. **b.** Also called **string line.** a line from behind which the cue ball is placed after being out of play. **18.** a complement of contestants or players grouped as a squad in accordance with their skill: *He made the second string on the football team.* **19.** Usually, **strings.** conditions or limitations on a proposal: *a generous offer with no strings attached.* **20.** *Obs.* a ligament, nerve, or the like in an animal body. **21. on a** or **the string,** *Informal.* subject to the whim of another; in one's power; dependent: *After keeping me on a string for two months, they finally hired someone else.* **22. pull strings** or **wires, a.** to use one's influence or authority, usually in secret, in order to bring about a desired result. **b.** to gain or attempt to gain one's objectives by means of influential friends, associates, etc.: *He had his uncle pull strings to get him a promotion.*
—*v.t.* **23.** to furnish with or as with a string or strings: *to string a bonnet; to string a bow.* **24.** to extend or stretch (a cord, thread, etc.) from one point to another. **25.** to thread on or as on a string: *to string beads.* **26.** to connect in or as in a line; arrange in a series or succession: *She knows how to string words together.* **27.** *Music.* **a.** to adjust the string of (a bow) or tighten the strings of (a musical instrument) to the required pitch. **b.** to equip (a bow or instrument) with new strings. **28.** to provide or adorn with something suspended or slung: *a room strung with festoons.* **29.** to deprive of a string or strings; strip the strings from: *to string beans.* **30.** to make tense, as the sinews, nerves, mind, etc. **31.** to kill by hanging (usually fol. by *up*). **32.** *Slang.* to fool or hoax.
—*v.i.* **33.** to form into or move in a string or series: *The ideas string together coherently.* **34.** to form into a string or strings, as a glutinous substance does when pulled: *Good taffy doesn't break—it strings.* **35. string along,** *Informal.* **a.** to be in agreement; follow with confidence: *He found he couldn't string along with all their modern notions.* **b.** to keep (a person) waiting or in a state of uncertainty. **c.** to deceive; cheat; trick. **36. string out, a.** to extend; stretch out: *The parade strung out for miles.* **b.** to prolong: *The promised three days strung out to six weeks.* [bef. 900; (n.) ME *string, streng,* OE *streng;* c. D *streng,* G *Strang;* akin to L *stringere* to bind; (v.) late ME *stringen* to string a bow, deriv. of the n.] **—string′less,** *adj.* **—string′like′,** *adj.*

string′ bag′, an openwork bag made of string, esp. one with handles.

string′ bass′ (bās). See **double bass.** [1935–40]

string′ bean′, 1. any of various kinds of bean, as the green bean, the unripe pods of which are used as food, usually after stripping off the fibrous thread along the side. **2.** the pod itself. **3.** *Informal.* a tall, thin person. [1750–60, *Amer.*]

string·board (string′bôrd′, -bōrd′), *n.* a board or facing covering the ends of the steps in a staircase. [1695–1705; STRING + BOARD]

string′ correspond′ent, stringer (def. 6).

string·course (string′kôrs′, -kōrs′), *n. Archit.* a horizontal band or course, as of stone, projecting beyond or flush with the face of a building, often molded and sometimes richly carved. Also called **belt course.** [1815–25; STRING + COURSE]

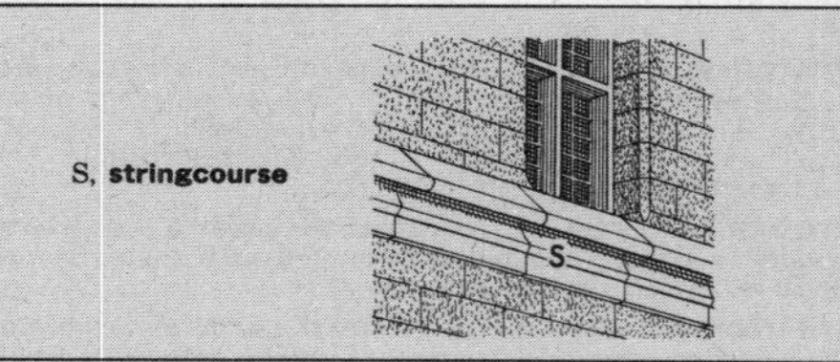

S, **stringcourse**

stringed (stringd), *adj.* **1.** fitted with strings (often used in combination): *a five-stringed banjo.* **2.** produced or sounded by strings: *stringed melodies.* [bef. 1000; ME; OE *strængede;* see STRING, -ED[3]]

stringed′ in′strument, a musical instrument having strings as the medium of sound production, played with the fingers or with a plectrum or a bow: *The guitar, the harp, and the violin are stringed instruments.*

strin·gen·cy (strin′jən sē), *n., pl.* **-cies. 1.** stringent character or condition: *the stringency of poverty.* **2.** strictness; closeness; rigor: *the stringency of school discipline.* **3.** tightness; straitness: *stringency in the money market.* [1835–45; STRING(ENT) + -ENCY]

strin·gen·do (strin jen′dō; *It.* strēn jen′dô), *adj., adv. Music.* (of a musical direction) progressively quickening in tempo. [1850–55; < It, ger. of *stringere* to tighten < L (see STRICT)]

strin·gent (strin′jənt), *adj.* **1.** rigorously binding or exacting; strict; severe: *stringent laws.* **2.** compelling, constraining, or urgent: *stringent necessity.* **3.** convincing or forcible: *stringent arguments.* **4.** (of the money market) characterized by a shortage in money for loan or investment purposes; tight. [1595–1605; < L *stringent-* (s. of *stringēns*), prp. of *stringere* to draw tight; see -ENT] **—strin′gent·ly,** *adv.*
—Syn. 1. restrictive. See **strict. 3.** forceful, powerful, effective. **—Ant. 1.** flexible.

string·er (string′ər), *n.* **1.** a person or thing that strings. **2.** a long horizontal timber connecting upright posts. **3.** *Archit.* string (def. 15b). **4.** *Civ. Engin.* a lon-

CONCISE ETYMOLOGY KEY: <, descended or borrowed from; >, whence; b., blend of, blended; c., cognate with; cf., compare; deriv., derivative; equiv., equivalent; imit., imitative; obl., oblique; r., replacing; s., stem; sp., spelling, spelled; resp., respelling, respelled; trans., translation; ?, origin unknown; *, unattested; ‡, probably earlier than. See the full key inside the front cover.

gitudinal bridge girder for supporting part of a deck or railroad track between bents or piers. **5.** a longitudinal reinforcement in the fuselage or wing of an airplane. **6.** Also called **string correspondent.** *Journalism.* a part-time newspaper correspondent covering a local area for a paper published elsewhere: *The Los Angeles paper has a correspondent in San Francisco but only a stringer in Seattle.* Cf. **staffer** (def. 2). **7.** a stout string, rope, etc., strung through the gills and mouth of newly caught fish, so that they may be carried or put back in the water to keep them alive or fresh. **8.** a contestant, player, or other person ranked according to skill or accomplishment (used in combination): *Most of the conductors at the opera house were third-stringers.* **9.** *Mining.* a small vein or seam of ore, coal, etc. [1375–1425; late ME; see STRING, -ER[1]]

string′er bead′, *Welding.* See under **bead** (def. 13).

string•halt (string′hôlt′), *n. Vet. Pathol.* a nerve disorder in horses, causing exaggerated flexing movements of the hind legs in walking. Also, **springhalt.** [1515–25; STRING + HALT[2]] —**string′halt′ed, string′halt′y,** *adj.* —**string′halt′ed•ness,** *n.*

string•hold•er (string′hōl′dər), *n.* an oblong piece of wood at the lower end of the body of a viol or other stringed instrument to which the strings are attached. [STRING + HOLDER]

string•ing (string′ing), *n.* a narrow band of inlay, as in a piece of furniture. [1610–20; STRING + -ING[1]]

string′ line′, *Billiards, Pool.* string (def. 17b). [1865–70, *Amer.*]

string•piece (string′pēs′), *n.* a long, usually horizontal piece of timber, beam, etc., for strengthening, connecting, or supporting a framework. [1780–90; STRING + PIECE]

string′ play′er, a person who plays an instrument of the violin family.

string′ quartet′, 1. a musical composition, usually in three or four movements, for four stringed instruments, typically two violins, viola, and cello. **2.** a first violinist, second violinist, violist, and cellist forming a group for the performance of string quartets and similar music. [1870–75]

string′ the′ory, *Physics.* See under **string** (def. 3).

string′ tie′, a short, very narrow, and unflared necktie, usually tied in a bow. [1915–20]

string′ trim′mer. See **line trimmer.**

string•y (string′ē), *adj.*, **string•i•er, string•i•est. 1.** resembling a string or strings; consisting of strings or stringlike pieces: *stringy weeds; a stringy fiber.* **2.** coarsely or toughly fibrous, as meat. **3.** sinewy or wiry, as a person. **4.** ropy, as a glutinous liquid. [1660–70; STRING + -Y[1]] —**string′i•ness,** *n.*

strip[1] (strip), *v.*, **stripped** or **stript, strip•ping,** *n.* —*v.t.* **1.** to deprive of covering: *to strip a fruit of its rind.* **2.** to deprive of clothing; make bare or naked. **3.** to take away or remove: *to strip sheets from the bed.* **4.** to deprive or divest: *to strip a tree of its bark; to strip him of all privileges.* **5.** to clear out or empty: *to strip a house of its contents.* **6.** to deprive of equipment; dismantle: *to strip a ship of rigging.* **7.** to dispossess, rob, or plunder: *to strip a man of his possessions.* **8.** to remove varnish, paint, wax, or the like from: *The wood should be stripped and then refinished.* **9.** to separate the leaves from the stalks of (tobacco). **10.** to remove the midrib, as from tobacco leaves. **11.** *Mach.* to break off the thread of (a screw, bolt, etc.) or the teeth of (a gear), as by applying too much force. **12.** to remove the mold from (an ingot). **13.** to draw the last milk from (a cow), esp. by a stroking and compressing movement. **14.** to draw out (milk) in this manner. **15.** *Photoengraving.* to remove (the emulsion from a film base) in order to place it on a glass plate for exposure to the metal plate. **16.** *Textiles.* **a.** to clean (a carding roller) by removing waste fibers. **b.** to transfer (fibers) from one carding roller to another. **c.** to remove (color) from a cloth or yarn in order to redye it another color. **d.** to remove color from (a cloth or yarn). **17.** *Bridge.* to lead successively winning cards from (a hand) in order to dispose of as many cards as necessary preparatory to surrendering the lead to an opponent so that any card the opponent plays will be to his or her disadvantage. **18.** *Mining.* to strip-mine. **19.** *Chem.* to remove the most volatile components from, as by distillation or evaporation. **20.** *Finance.* to split (a bond) for selling separately as a principal certificate and as interest coupons. **21.** *Surg.* to remove (a vein) by pulling it inside out through a small incision, using a long, hooked instrument. —*v.i.* **22.** to strip something. **23.** to remove one's clothes. **24.** to perform a striptease. **25.** to become stripped: *Bananas strip easily.* —*n.* **26.** a striptease. [1175–1225; (v.) ME *strippe,* OE **stryppan* (cf. MHG *strupfen* to strip off); r. ME *stripen, strepen, strupen* (cf. OE *bestrȳpan* to rob, plunder)]
—**Syn. 1.** uncover, peel, decorticate. **2.** denude. **7.** despoil. STRIP, DEPRIVE, DISPOSSESS, DIVEST imply more or less forcibly taking something away from someone. To STRIP is to take something completely (often violently) from a person or thing so as to leave in a destitute or powerless state: *to strip a man of all his property; to strip the bark from a tree.* To DEPRIVE is to take away forcibly or coercively what one has, or to withhold what one might have: *to deprive workers of their livelihood.* To DISPOSSESS is to deprive of the holding or use of something: *to dispossess the renters of a house.* DIVEST usually means depriving of rights, privileges, powers, or the like: *to divest a king of authority.* —**Ant. 6.** supply, furnish.

strip[2] (strip), *n.*, *v.*, **stripped, strip•ping.** —*n.* **1.** a narrow piece, comparatively long and usually of uniform width: *a strip of cloth, metal, land, etc.* **2.** a continuous series of drawings or pictures illustrating incidents, conversation, etc., as a comic strip. **3.** *Aeron.* **a.** an airstrip; runway. **b.** See **landing strip. 4.** *Philately.* three or more stamps joined either in a horizontal or vertical row. **5.** *Informal.* striplight. **6.** (*sometimes cap.*) a road, street, or avenue, usually in a city or a main thoroughfare between outlying suburbs, densely lined on both sides by a large variety of retail stores, gas stations, restaurants, bars, etc.: *Sunset Strip in Los Angeles.* **7.** See **strip steak. 8.** See **drag strip.** —*v.t.* **9.** to cut, tear, or form into strips. **10.** *Print.* to combine (a piece of film) with another, esp. for making a combination plate of lines and halftones. **11.** to broadcast (a television series) in multiple related segments, as daily from Monday through Friday. [1425–75; late ME, c. or < MLG *strippe* strap; see STRIPE[1]]

strip′ bond′, *Finance.* a bond that has been stripped into its principal certificate and interest coupons, each part to be sold separately.

strip′ cit′y, a continuous area of urban development lying between or embracing two or more large cities and having a population of at least one million; megalopolis. [1965–70]

strip′ crop′ping, the growing of different crops on alternate strips of ground that usually follow the contour of the land, a recourse to minimize erosion. Also called **strip farming, strip planting.** [1935–40]

stripe[1] (strīp), *n.*, *v.*, **striped, strip•ing.** —*n.* **1.** a relatively long, narrow band of a different color, appearance, weave, material, or nature from the rest of a surface or thing: *the stripes of a zebra.* **2.** a fabric or material containing such a band or bands. **3.** a strip of braid, tape, or the like. **4. stripes, a.** a number or combination of such strips, worn on a military, naval, or other uniform as a badge of rank, service, good conduct, combat wounds, etc. **b.** *Informal.* status or recognition as a result of one's efforts, experience, or achievements: *She earned her stripes as a traveling sales representative and then moved up to district manager.* **5.** a strip, or long, narrow piece of anything: *a stripe of beach.* **6.** a streak or layer of a different nature within a substance. **7.** style, variety, sort, or kind: *a man of quite a different stripe.* **8.** Also called **magnetic stripe.** *Motion Pictures.* a strip of iron oxide layer on the edge of a film that is used for recording and reproducing a magnetic sound track. —*v.t.* **9.** to mark or furnish with a stripe or stripes. [1620–30; < MD or MLG *strīpe;* see STRIP[2], STRIPE[2]] —**stripe′less,** *adj.*

stripe[2] (strīp), *n.* a stroke with a whip, rod, etc., as in punishment. [1400–50; late ME; obscurely akin to STRIPE[1]]

striped (strīpt, strī′pid), *adj.* having stripes or bands. [1610–20; STRIPE[1] + -ED[3]]

striped′ bass′ (bas), an important American game fish, *Morone saxatilis,* having blackish stripes along each side. Also called **striper.** [1810–20, *Amer.*]

striped′ go′pher, a ground squirrel marked with stripes, esp. the thirteen-lined ground squirrel. [1940–45, *Amer.*]

striped′ hye′na, a hyena, *Hyaena hyaena,* of northern Africa, Arabia, and India, having a grayish coat with distinct blackish stripes.

striped′ kil′lifish, a killifish, *Fundulus majalis,* of the Atlantic coast of the U.S., the female of which is marked with black stripes. Also called **mayfish.**

striped′ ma′ple, a maple, *Acer pensylvanicum,* of northeastern North America, having white-striped bark. Also called **moosewood.** [1775–85, *Amer.*]

striped′ mar′lin, a marlin, *Tetrapturus audax,* of the Pacific Ocean, having the sides of the body marked with dark blue vertical stripes, valued for sport and food.

striped′ sper′mophile. See **thirteen-lined ground squirrel.**

striped′ squir′rel, any squirrel with stripes on its back, as a chipmunk. [1785–95]

strip•er (strī′pər), *n. Informal.* **1.** *Mil.* **a.** a naval officer whose uniform sleeve displays stripes: *a four-striper.* **b.** an enlisted person of any of the armed services whose sleeve displays stripes denoting years of service: *a six-striper.* **2.** See **striped bass.** [STRIPE[1] + -ER[1]]

stripe′ rust′, *Plant Pathol.* a disease of wheat, barley, rye, and other grasses, characterized by elongated rows of yellow spores on the affected parts, caused by a rust fungus, *Puccinia glumarum.* Also called **yellow rust.**

stripe′ smut′, *Plant Pathol.* a disease of grasses, characterized by stripes of black spores on the leaves, caused by any of several smut fungi of the genera *Urocystis* and *Ustilago.*

strip′ farm′, a tract of land where strip cropping is done. [1905–10]

strip′ farm′ing. See **strip cropping.**

strip•ing (strī′ping), *n.* **1.** the act of decorating or otherwise providing with stripes: *The striping of the boat proceeded slowly.* **2.** a striped pattern: *the striping of the zebra; striping of different colors.* [1670–80; STRIPE[1] + -ING[1]]

strip•light (strip′līt′), *n. Theat.* a row of lamps, provided with a reflector for floodlighting the stage, used as border lights, footlights, backing lights, etc. [1670–80; STRIP[2] + LIGHT[1]]

strip•ling (strip′ling), *n.* a youth. [1350–1400; ME; see STRIP[2], -LING[1]]

strip′ map′, a map charting only the immediate territory to be traversed, which appears as a long, narrow strip. [1900–05]

strip-mine (strip′mīn′), *v.t., v.i.*, **-mined, -min•ing.** to excavate by open-cut methods. Also, **strip.** [1925–30] —**strip′ mine′.**

strip′ min′ing, mining in an open pit after removal of the overburden.

strip•pa•ble (strip′ə bəl), *adj.* **1.** *Mining.* of or pertaining to ore or coal that can be produced by strip mining. **2.** capable of being stripped off: *strippable wallpaper.* [1970–75; STRIP[1] + -ABLE]

stripped (stript), *adj.* **1.** having had a covering, clothing, equipment, or furnishings removed: *trees stripped of their leaves by the storm; a stripped bed ready for clean sheets.* **2.** having had usable parts or items removed, as for reuse or resale: *the hulk of a stripped car.* **3.** having or containing the bare essentials, with no added features or accessories: *a stripped new car, with no radio or air conditioning.* [1925–30; STRIP[1] + -ED[2]]

stripped-down (stript′doun′), *adj.* having only essential features; lacking any special appointments or accessories.

strip•per (strip′ər), *n.* **1.** a person who strips. **2.** a thing that strips, as an appliance or machine for stripping. **3.** Also called **ecdysiast, exotic dancer, stripteaser.** a person who performs a striptease. **4.** a harvesting machine for stripping the seed heads from the stalks of grain. **5.** a machine used in harvesting cotton to strip the bolls from the plants. **6.** a chemical solution that removes varnish, paint, wax, etc., from a surface, as of furniture or flooring. **7.** any of several rollers covered with card clothing that operate in combination with the worker rollers and the cylinder in the carding of fibers. **8.** *Print.* a worker who assembles and strips photographic negatives or positives for platemaking. Cf. **strip**[2] (def. 10). [1575–85; STRIP[1] + -ER[1]]

strip′ plant′ing. See **strip cropping.**

strip′ pok′er, a game of poker in which the losers in a hand remove an article of clothing. [1915–20]

strip′ search′, an act or instance of strip-searching. Also called **skin search.**

strip-search (strip′sûrch′), *v.t.* to search (a suspect who has been required to remove all clothing) esp. for concealed weapons, contraband, or evidence of drug abuse.

strip′ steak′, a steak cut from the upper part of the short loin. Also called **New York strip.**

stript (stript), *v.* a pt. and pp. of **strip**[1].

strip•tease (strip′tēz′), *n.*, *v.*, **-teased, -teas•ing.** —*n.* **1.** a burlesque act in which a dancer removes garments one at a time to the accompaniment of music. —*v.i.* **2.** to do a striptease. [1935–40, *Amer.*; STRIP[1] + TEASE]

strip•teas•er (strip′tē′zər), *n.* stripper (def. 3). [1935–40; STRIPTEASE + -ER[1]]

strip•y (strī′pē), *adj.*, **strip•i•er, strip•i•est.** having or marked with stripes. [1505–15; STRIPE[1] + -Y[1]]

strive (strīv), *v.i.*, **strove** or **strived, striv•en** (striv′ən), or **strived, striv•ing. 1.** to exert oneself vigorously; try hard: *He strove to make himself understood.* **2.** to make strenuous efforts toward any goal: *to strive for success.* **3.** to contend in opposition, battle, or any conflict; compete. **4.** to struggle vigorously, as in opposition or resistance: *to strive against fate.* **5.** to rival; vie. [1175–1225; ME *striven* < OF *estriver* to quarrel, compete, strive < Gmc; cf. obs. D *strijven,* G *streben* to strive] —**striv′er,** *n.* —**striv′ing•ly,** *adv.*
—**Syn. 1.** See **try. 2.** toil. **3.** struggle, fight.

strobe (strōb), *Photog. Informal.* —*n.* **1.** Also called **strobe′ light′.** stroboscope (def. 2a). —*adj.* **2.** stroboscopic. [1940–45; shortened form]

stro•bi•la (strō bī′lə), *n.*, *pl.* **-lae** (-lē). *Zool.* **1.** the body of a tapeworm exclusive of the head and neck region. Cf. **scolex. 2.** the chain of segments of the larva of a jellyfish in the class Scyphozoa, each segment of which gives rise to a free-swimming medusa. [1835–45; < NL, orig. coined as a genus name < Gk *strobilē* a plug of lint shaped like a fir cone; see STROBILUS]

strob•i•la•ceous (strob′ə lā′shəs), *adj.* **1.** resembling a strobilus; conelike. **2.** bearing strobili. [1795–1805; < NL *strobilāceus;* see STROBILUS, -ACEOUS]

stro•bi•lus (strō bī′ləs), *n.*, *pl.* **-li** (-lī). *Bot.* **1.** a reproductive structure characterized by overlapping scalelike parts, as a pine cone or the fruit of the hop. **2.** a conelike structure composed of sporophylls, as of the club mosses and horsetails. Also called **stro•bile** (strō′bil, -bīl). [1700–10; < NL *strobilus,* LL: pine cone < Gk *stróbīlos* pine cone, whirlwind, whirling dance, deriv. of *stróbos* whirling around]

stro•bo•ra•di•o•graph (strō′bə rā′dē ə graf′, -gräf′, strob′ə-), *n.* a stroboscopic radiograph. [< Gk *stróbo*(s) action of whirling + RADIOGRAPH]

stro•bo•scope (strō′bə skōp′, strob′ə-), *n.* **1.** a device for studying the motion of a body, esp. a body in rapid revolution or vibration, by making the motion appear to slow down or stop, as by periodically illuminating the body or viewing it through widely spaced openings in a revolving disk. **2.** *Photog.* **a.** Also called **strobe, strobe light, stro′boscop′ic lamp′.** a lamp capable of producing an extremely short, brilliant burst of light, for synchronization with a camera having a high shutter speed, in order to photograph a rapidly moving object, as a bullet, for such a short duration that it will appear to be standing still. **b.** the device and equipment for holding and firing such a lamp. **3.** such a lamp used for creating special lighting effects, as in a theater or discotheque or at a rock concert. [1830–40; < Gk *stróbo*(s) action of whirling + -SCOPE] —**stro•bo•scop•ic** (strō′bə skop′ik, strob′ə-), **stro′bo•scop′i•cal,** *adj.* —**stro•bos•co•py** (strə bos′kə pē), *n.*

stro•bo•tron (strō′bə tron′, strob′ə-), *n. Electronics.* a glow lamp, used in stroboscopes, that gives very bright flashes of light in response to voltage pulses. [1935–40; *strobo-* (see STROBOSCOPE) + -TRON]

strode (strōd), *v.* pt. of **stride.**

Stroess•ner (stres′nər; *Sp.* STRES′NER), *n.* **Al•fre•do** (al frā′dō; *Sp.* äl fre′thō), born 1912, Paraguayan general and statesman: president since 1954.

stro•ga•noff (strô′gə nôf′, strō′-), *n. Cookery.* a dish

CONCISE PRONUNCIATION KEY: act, cāpe, dâre, pärt; set, ēqual; if, īce; ox, ōver, ôrder, oil, bŏŏk, bōōt, out; up, ûrge; child; sing; shoe; thin, *th*at; zh as in *treasure.* ə = *a* as in *alone, e* as in *system, i* as in *easily, o* as in *gallop, u* as in *circus;* ᵊ as in *fire* (fīᵊr), *hour* (ouᵊr). l and n can serve as syllabic consonants, as in *cradle* (krād′l), and *button* (but′n). See the full key inside the front cover.

of meat sautéed with onion and cooked in a sauce of sour cream, seasonings, and, usually, mushrooms: *beef stroganoff.* [named after P. *Stroganov,* 19th-century Russian count and diplomat]

stroke[1] (strōk), *n., v.,* **stroked, strok•ing.** —*n.* **1.** the act or an instance of striking, as with the fist, a weapon, or a hammer; a blow. **2.** a hitting of or upon anything. **3.** a striking of a clapper or hammer, as on a bell. **4.** the sound produced by this. **5.** a throb or pulsation, as of the heart. **6.** Also called **apoplexy, cerebrovascular accident.** *Pathol.* a blockage or hemorrhage of a blood vessel leading to the brain, causing inadequate oxygen supply and, depending on the extent and location of the abnormality, such symptoms as weakness, paralysis of parts of the body, speech difficulties, and, if severe, loss of consciousness or death. **7.** something likened to a blow in its effect, as in causing pain, injury, or death; an attack of apoplexy or paralysis. **8.** a destructive discharge of lightning. **9.** a vigorous movement, as if in dealing a blow. **10.** *Sports.* a hitting of a ball, as by the swing of a racquet in tennis or the controlled jabbing or thrusting with the cue in pool and billiards. **11.** a single complete movement, esp. one continuously repeated in some process. **12.** *Mach.* **a.** one of a series of alternating continuous movements of something back and forth over or through the same line. **b.** the complete movement of a moving part, esp. a reciprocating part, in one direction. **c.** the distance traversed in such a movement. **d.** a half revolution of an engine during which the piston travels from one extreme of its range to the other. **13.** *Swimming.* **a.** a type or method of swimming: *The crawl is a rapid stroke.* **b.** each of the successive movements of the arms and legs in propelling the body through the water. **14.** *Rowing.* **a.** a single pull of the oar. **b.** the manner or style of moving the oars. **c.** Also called **stroke oar.** the crew member nearest to the stern of the boat, to whose strokes those of the other crew members must conform. **15.** a movement of a pen, pencil, brush, graver, or the like. **16.** a mark traced by or as if by one movement of a pen, pencil, brush, or the like. **17.** a distinctive or effective touch in a literary composition: *His style revealed the stroke of a master.* **18.** a single or minimal act, piece, or amount of work, activity, etc.: *to refuse to do a stroke of work.* **19.** an attempt to attain some object: *a bold stroke for liberty.* **20.** a measure adopted for a particular purpose. **21.** a keystroke: *no more than 65 strokes to the line for business letters.* **22.** a feat or achievement: *a stroke of genius.* **23.** a sudden or chance happening, as of luck or fortune. —*v.t.* **24.** to mark with a stroke or strokes, as of a pen; cancel, as by a stroke of a pen. **25.** *Rowing.* **a.** to row as a stroke oar of (a boat or crew). **b.** to set the stroke for the crew of (a boat). **26.** *Sports.* to hit (a ball), as with a deliberate, smooth swing of a bat or club. [1250–1300; ME *strok, strak* (n.), prob. continuing OE **strāc* (whence *strācian* to STROKE[2]); c. G *Streich;* akin to STRIKE]
—**Syn. 1.** rap, tap, knock, pat. **1, 7.** See **blow**[1]. **5.** beat, thump; rhythm.

stroke[2] (strōk), *v.,* **stroked, strok•ing,** *n.* —*v.t.* **1.** to pass the hand or an instrument over (something or somebody) lightly or with little pressure; rub gently, as in soothing or caressing. **2.** *Informal.* to promote feelings of self-approval in; flatter. —*n.* **3.** an act or instance of stroking; a stroking movement. [bef. 900; ME *stroken* (v.), OE *strācian;* c. G *streichen;* akin to STRIKE]

stroke′ hole′, *Golf.* (in a handicap match) a hole at which players with a handicap deduct a stroke from the number taken to play the hole.

stroke′ oar′, *Rowing.* **1.** the oar nearest to the stern of the boat. **2.** stroke[1] (def. 14c). [1825–35]

stroke′ play′, *Golf.* See **medal play.** [1750–60]

stroll (strōl), *v.i.* **1.** to walk leisurely as inclination directs; ramble; saunter; take a walk: *to stroll along the beach.* **2.** to wander or rove from place to place; roam: *strolling troubadours.* —*v.t.* **3.** to saunter along or through: *to stroll the countryside.* —*n.* **4.** a leisurely walk; ramble; saunter: *a short stroll before supper.* [1595–1605; of uncert. orig.]
—**Syn. 1.** stray, meander. **4.** promenade.

stroll•er (strō′lər), *n.* **1.** a person who takes a leisurely walk; saunterer. **2.** a wanderer; vagrant. **3.** an itinerant performer. **4.** a four-wheeled, often collapsible, chairlike carriage in which small children are pushed. [1600–10; STROLL + -ER[1]]

stro•ma (strō′mə), *n., pl.* **-ma•ta** (-mə tə). **1.** *Cell Biol.* the supporting framework or matrix of a cell. **2.** *Anat.* the supporting framework, usually of connective tissue, of an organ, as distinguished from the parenchyma. **3.** *Mycol.* (in certain fungi) a compact, somatic mass of fungous tissue, in or on which the fructifications may be developed. **4.** *Bot.* the matrix of a chloroplast, containing various molecules and ions. [1825–35; < LL *strōma* mattress < Gk *strôma* bed-covering; akin to L *sternere* to spread, STREW, *strātum* (see STRATUM)] —**stro•mat•ic** (strō mat′ik), **stro′mal, stro′ma•tous,** *adj.*

stro•ma•te•id (strō′mə tē′id), *n.* **1.** any of numerous small marine fishes of the family Stromateidae, having a laterally compressed body and an expanded muscular esophagus, often lined with teeth. —*adj.* **2.** belonging or pertaining to the Stromateidae. [< NL *Stromateidae* name of the family, equiv. to *Stromate(us)* a genus < Gk *strōmateús* bed-covering of patchwork, a kind of fish, (deriv. of *strôma,* s. *strōmat-* mattress; see STROMA) + NL *-idae* -ID[2]]

stro•ma•te•oid (strō′mə tē′oid), *adj.* **1.** resembling or related to the Stromateidae. —*n.* **2.** a stromateoid fish. [1880–85; < NL *Stromate(idae)* (see STROMATEID) + -OID]

stro•mat•o•lite (strō mat′l īt′), *n. Geol.* a laminated calcareous fossil structure built by marine algae and having a rounded or columnar form. [< G *Stromatolith* (1908) < NL *stromat-,* s. of *stroma* STROMA + -o- -o- + G *-lith* -LITH; see -LITE] —**stro•mat•o•lit•ic** (strō mat′l-it′ik), *adj.*

Strom•bo•li (strom′bə lē; *It.* strôm′bô lē), *n.* **1.** an island off the NE coast of Sicily, in the Lipari group. **2.** an active volcano on this island. 3040 ft. (927 m).

strong (strông, strong), *adj.,* **strong•er** (strông′gər, strong′-), **strong•est** (strông′gist, strong′-), *adv.* —*adj.* **1.** having, showing, or able to exert great bodily or muscular power; physically vigorous or robust: *a strong boy.* **2.** accompanied or delivered by great physical, mechanical, etc., power or force: *a strong handshake; With one strong blow the machine stamped out a fender.* **3.** mentally powerful or vigorous: *He may be old, but his mind is still strong.* **4.** especially able, competent, or powerful in a specific field or respect: *She's very strong in mathematics. He's weak at bat, but he's a strong fielder.* **5.** of great moral power, firmness, or courage: *strong under temptation.* **6.** powerful in influence, authority, resources, or means of prevailing or succeeding: *a strong nation.* **7.** aggressive; willful: *a strong personality.* **8.** of great force, effectiveness, potency, or cogency; compelling: *strong reasons; strong arguments.* **9.** clear and firm; loud: *He has a strong voice.* **10.** solid or stable; healthy; thriving: *The banker predicted a strong economy.* **11.** well-supplied or rich in something specific: *a strong hand in trumps.* **12.** having powerful means to resist attack, assault, or aggression: *a strong fortress; a strong defense.* **13.** able to resist strain, force, wear, etc.: *strong walls; strong cloth.* **14.** decisively unyielding; firm or uncompromising: *She has strong views about the United Nations. He has a strong sense of duty.* **15.** fervent; zealous; thoroughgoing: *He's a strong Democrat.* **16.** strenuous or energetic; vigorous: *strong efforts.* **17.** moving or acting with force or vigor: *strong winds.* **18.** distinct or marked; vivid, as impressions, resemblance or contrast: *He bears a strong resemblance to his grandfather.* **19.** intense, as light or color. **20.** having a large proportion of the effective or essential properties or ingredients; concentrated: *strong tea.* **21.** (of a beverage or food) containing much alcohol: *strong drink; The fruitcake was too strong.* **22.** having a high degree of flavor or odor: *strong cheese; strong perfume.* **23.** having an unpleasant or offensive flavor or odor, esp. in the process of decay: *strong butter.* **24.** of a designated number: *Marines 20,000 strong.* **25.** *Com.* characterized by steady or advancing prices: *The market resumed its strong pace after yesterday's setback.* **26.** *Gram.* **a.** (of Germanic verbs) having vowel change in the root in inflected forms, as the English verbs *sing, sang, sung; ride, rode, ridden.* **b.** (of Germanic nouns and adjectives) inflected with endings that are generally distinctive of case, number, and gender, as German *alter Mann* "old man." **c.** belonging to the morphophonemically less regular of two inflectional subtypes. **27.** (of a word or syllable) stressed. **28.** *Optics.* having great magnifying or refractive power: *a strong microscope.* —*adv.* **29.** strongly. **30. come on strong,** *Slang.* to behave in an aggressive, ardent, or flamboyant manner: *When you're interviewed for the job, don't come on too strong.* [bef. 900; (adj.) ME *strang, strong,* OE; c. MD *stranc,* ON *strangr;* (adv.) ME *strange, stronge,* OE; c. OHG *strango;* akin to STRING] —**strong′ish,** *adj.* —**strong′ly,** *adv.* —**strong′ness,** *n.*
—**Syn. 1.** mighty, sturdy, brawny, sinewy, hardy, muscular, stout, stalwart. **4.** potent, capable, efficient. **5.** valiant, brave. **7.** bold, intense. **8.** persuasive, cogent, impressive, conclusive. **10.** steady, firm, secure. **14.** unwavering, resolute. **15.** fervid, vehement. **18.** stark, sharp. **19.** brilliant, vivid. **22.** pungent, aromatic, sharp, piquant, hot, spicy, biting. **23.** smelly, rank. —**Ant. 1.** weak.

strong′ accumula′tion point′, *Math.* a point such that every neighborhood of the point contains infinitely many points of a given set. Cf. **accumulation point, strong derived set.**

strong-arm (strông′ärm′, strong′-), *adj.* **1.** using, involving, or threatening the use of physical force or violence to gain an objective: *strong-arm methods.* —*v.t.* **2.** to use violent methods upon; assault. **3.** to rob by force. **4.** to coerce by threats or intimidation; bully: *They strong-armed me into voting for the plan.* [1820–30, *Amer.*]

strong•bark (strông′bärk′, strong′-), *n.* any of the several tropical American shrubs or small trees belonging to the genus *Bourreria,* of the borage family, esp. *B. ovata,* of southern Florida and the West Indies, having elliptic leaves and fragrant, white flowers. Also called **strong•back** (strông′bak′, strong′-). [1860–65; STRONG + BARK[2]]

strong•box (strông′boks′, strong′-), *n.* a strongly made, lockable box or chest for safeguarding valuable possessions, as money, jewels, or documents. [1675–85; STRONG + BOX[1]]

strong′ breeze′, *Meteorol.* a wind of 25–30 mph (11–13 m/sec). [1795–1805]

strong′ derived′ set′, *Math.* the set of all strong accumulation points of a given set.

strong′ force′, *Physics.* **1.** the short-range attractive force between baryons that holds together the nucleus of the atom. **2.** Also called **color force.** the force between quarks. Cf. **gluon, strong interaction.** [1965–70]

strong′ gale′, *Meteorol.* a wind of 47–54 mph (21–24 m/sec). [1795–1805]

strong•hold (strông′hōld′, strong′-), *n.* **1.** a well-fortified place; fortress. **2.** a place that serves as the center of a group, as of militants or of persons holding a controversial viewpoint: *The campus was a stronghold of liberalism.* [1375–1425; late ME; see STRONG, HOLD[1]]
—**Syn. 1, 2.** bulwark, bastion. **2.** home, refuge.

strong′ interac′tion, *Physics.* the interaction between gluons and between gluons and quarks that is responsible for the strong force. [1945–50]

strong•man (strông′man′, strong′-), *n., pl.* **-men. 1.** a person who performs remarkable feats of strength, as in a circus. **2.** a political leader who controls by force; dictator. **3.** the most powerful or influential person in an organization or business, by reason of skill in the formulation and execution of plans, work, etc. Also, **strong′ man′.** [1855–60; STRONG + MAN[1]]

strong-mind•ed (strông′mīn′did, strong′-), *adj.* **1.** having a forceful and independent mind. **2.** determined or obstinate; strong-willed. [1785–95]

strong•room (strông′ro͞om′, -ro͝om′, strong′-), *n.* a fireproof, burglarproof room in which valuables are kept. Also, **strong′ room′.** [1755–65; STRONG + ROOM]

strong′ safe′ty, *Football.* the defensive back assigned to cover the area across from the strong side of the opponent's offensive line and primarily responsible for defending against pass plays.

strong′ side′, *Football.* the side of the offensive line where the tight end is positioned, thereby the side having the greater number of players. [1950–55]

strong′ suit′, **1.** *Bridge.* a long suit that contains high cards. **2.** one's most highly developed characteristic, talent, or skill; forte: *Patience is not his strong suit.* [1860–65]

Strongs•ville (strôngz′vil, strongz′-), *n.* a town in N Ohio. 28,577.

strong-willed (strông′wild′, strong′-), *adj.* **1.** having a powerful will; resolute. **2.** stubborn; obstinate. [1895–1900]

stron•gyle (stron′jil), *n.* any nematode of the family Strongylidae, parasitic as an adult in the intestine of mammals, esp. horses. Also, **stron′gyl.** [1840–50; < NL *Strongylus* name of type genus < Gk *strongýlos* round, spherical] —**stron•gy•late** (stron′jə lāt′), *adj.*

stron•gy•lo•sis (stron′jə lō′sis), *n. Vet. Pathol.* a disease, esp. of horses, caused by an infestation by strongyles and characterized in serious cases by weakness and anemia. [1910–15; < NL, equiv. to *Strongyl(us)* STRONGYLE + *-ōsis* -OSIS]

stron•ti•a (stron′shē ə, -shə), *n. Chem.* **1.** Also called **stron′tium ox′ide.** a white or grayish-white, amorphous powder, SrO, resembling lime in its general character: used chiefly in the manufacture of strontium salts. **2.** See **strontium hydroxide.** [1795–1805; STRONTI(AN) + -A[4]]

stron•ti•an (stron′shē ən, -shən), *n.* **1.** strontianite. **2.** strontia. **3.** strontium. [1780–90; short for *Strontian earth* mineral first found in *Strontian* parish, Argyllshire, Scotland]

stron•ti•an•ite (stron′shē ə nīt′, -shə nīt′), *n.* a mineral, strontium carbonate, $SrCO_3$, occurring in radiating, fibrous, or granular aggregates and crystals, varying from white to yellow and pale green: a minor ore of strontium. [1785–95; STRONTIAN + -ITE[1]]

stron•ti•um (stron′shē əm, -shəm, -tē əm), *n. Chem.* a bivalent, metallic element whose compounds resemble those of calcium, found in nature only in the combined state, as in strontianite: used in fireworks, flares, and tracer bullets. *Symbol:* Sr; *at. wt.:* 87.62; *at. no.:* 38; *sp. gr.:* 2.6. [1800–10; STRONT(IA) + -IUM] —**stron•tic** (stron′tik), *adj.*

stron′tium hydrox′ide, *Chem.* a white, slightly water-soluble powder, $Sr(OH)_2$, or its crystalline octahydrate (**stron′tium hy′drate**): used chiefly in the refining of beet sugar. Also called **strontia.**

strontium 90, *Chem.* a harmful radioactive isotope of strontium, produced in certain nuclear reactions and present in their fallout. Also called **radiostrontium.** [1950–55]

strook (stro͝ok), *v. Scot. and North Eng.* a pt. and pp. of **strike.**

strop (strop), *n., v.,* **stropped, strop•ping.** —*n.* **1.** any of several devices for sharpening razors, esp. a strip of leather or other flexible material. **2.** Also, **strap.** *Naut., Mach.* **a.** a rope or a band of metal surrounding and supporting a block, deadeye, etc. **b.** a metal band surrounding the pulley of a block to transmit the load on the pulley to its hook or shackle. **c.** a rope sling, as for handling cargo. **d.** a ring or grommet of rope. —*v.t.* **3.** to sharpen on or as if on a strop. [bef. 1050; ME (n.), OE; c. D, LG *strop;* all prob. < L *stroppus,* var. of *struppus* strap] —**strop′per,** *n.*

stro•phan•thin (strō fan′thin), *n. Pharm.* a very poisonous, bitter glycoside or mixture of glycosides obtained from the dried, ripe seeds of a strophanthus, esp. *Strophanthus kombe,* used as a cardiac stimulant. [1875–80; STROPHANTH(US) + -IN[2]]

stro•phan•thus (strō fan′thəs), *n., pl.* **-thus•es. 1.** any of various shrubs or small trees belonging to the genus *Strophanthus,* of the dogbane family, chiefly of tropical Africa. **2.** the dried, ripe seed of any of these plants, which yields the drug strophanthin. [< NL (1802) < Gk *stróph(os)* twine + *ánthos* flower]

stro•phe (strō′fē), *n.* **1.** the part of an ancient Greek choral ode sung by the chorus when moving from right to left. **2.** the movement performed by the chorus during the singing of this part. **3.** the first of the three series of lines forming the divisions of each section of a Pindaric ode. **4.** (in modern poetry) any separate section or extended movement in a poem, distinguished from a stanza in that it does not follow a regularly repeated pattern. [1595–1605; < Gk *strophḗ* a twist, turning about, akin to *stréphein* to turn; see STREPTO-]
—**Syn. 3.** See **verse.**

stroph•ic (strof′ik, strō′fik), *adj.* **1.** Also, **stroph′i•cal.** consisting of, pertaining to, or characterized by a strophe or strophes. **2.** *Music.* (of a song) having the same music for each successive stanza. Cf. **through-composed.** [1840–50; STROPH(E) + -IC] —**stroph′i•cal•ly,** *adv.*

stroph•oid (strof′oid, strō′foid), *n. Geom.* a plane curve generated by the loci of points *p* and *p′* on a straight line that intersects the y-axis at a point *n* and

CONCISE ETYMOLOGY KEY: <, descended or borrowed from; >, whence; b., blend of, blended; c., cognate with; cf., compare; deriv., derivative; equiv., equivalent; imit., imitative; obl., oblique; r., replacing; s., stem; sp., spelling, spelled; resp., respelling, respelled; trans., translation; ?, origin unknown; *, unattested; ‡, probably earlier than. See the full key inside the front cover.

the minus x-axis at a fixed point q, such that $pn = np' = on$, as on changes, where o is the origin. Equation: $y^2 = x^2(x+a)/(a-x)$. [1875–80; < Gk *stróph(os)* twine + -OID, modeled on F *strophoïde*]

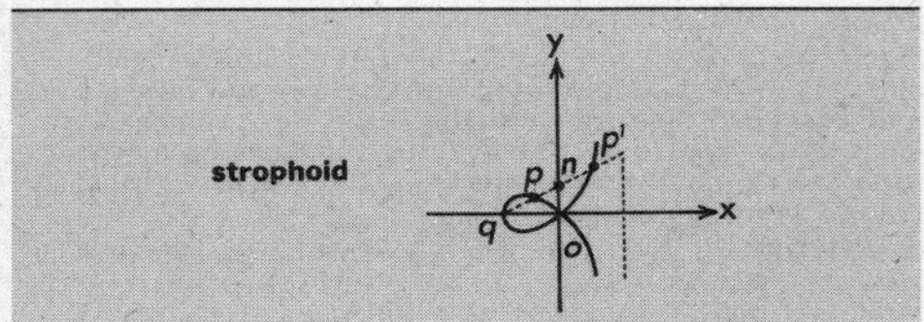

stroph·u·lus (strof′yə ləs), *n. Pathol.* a papular eruption of the skin, esp. in infants, occurring in several forms and usually harmless. Also called **red gum, tooth rash.** [1800–10; < NL < Gk *stróph(os)* twine + L *-ulus* -ULE]

strop·per (strop′ər), *n.* **1.** a person who strops. **2.** a mechanical instrument for honing double-edged blades for safety razors. [1700–10; STROP + -ER[1]]

strop·py (strop′ē), *adj.*, **-pi·er, -pi·est.** *Brit. Informal.* bad-tempered or hostile; quick to take offense. [1950–55; perh. (OB)STREP(EROUS) + -Y[1], though *o* is unexplained]

Stro·ther (strô′thər, struth′ər), *n.* a male given name.

stroud (stroud), *n.* a coarse woolen cloth, blanket, or garment formerly used by the British in bartering with the North American Indians. [1670–80; named after *Stroud* in Gloucestershire, England, where woolens are made]

strove (strōv), *v.* pt. of **strive.**

strow (strō), *v.*, **strowed, strown** or **strowed, strow·ing.** *Archaic.* strew. [1300–50; ME *strowen,* var. of *strewen* to STREW]

stroy (stroi), *v.t. Archaic.* to destroy. [1400–50; late ME *stroyen,* aph. var. of *destroyen* to DESTROY] —**stroy′·er,** *n.*

Stroz·zi (strôt′tsē), *n.* **Ber·nar·do** (ber när′dô), (*"Il Cappuccino"*), 1581–1644, Italian painter and engraver. Also, **Stroz·za** (strôt′tsä).

struck (struk), *v.* **1.** pt. and a pp. of **strike.** —*adj.* **2.** (of a factory, industry, etc.) closed or otherwise affected by a strike of workers. [1890–95 for def. 2]

struck′ ju′ry, *Law.* a jury obtained by special agreement between the opposing attorneys, each taking turns in eliminating a member of the impaneled group until 12 members remain. [1855–60]

struck′ meas′ure, a measure, esp. of grain, level with the top of a receptacle. [1930–35]

struc·tur·al (struk′chər əl), *adj.* **1.** of or pertaining to structure; pertaining or essential to a structure. **2.** *Biol.* pertaining to organic structure; morphological. **3.** *Geol.* of or pertaining to geological structure, as of rock or strata. **4.** *Chem.* pertaining to or showing the arrangement or mode of attachment of the atoms that constitute a molecule of a substance. Cf. **structural formula. 5.** resulting from or pertaining to political or economic structure. **6.** of, pertaining to, or based on the assumption that the elements of a field of study are naturally arranged in a systematic structure: *structural grammar.* —*n.* **7.** *Building Trades.* **a.** a part of a structure that carries a load. **b.** the structural member used for such a part. [1825–35; STRUCTURE + -AL[1]] —**struc′tur·al·ly,** *adv.*

struc′tural anthropol′ogy, a school of anthropology founded by Claude Lévi-Strauss and based loosely on the principles of structural linguistics.

struc′tural for′mula, *Chem.* a chemical formula showing the linkage of the atoms in a molecule diagrammatically, as H–O–H. Cf. **empirical formula, molecular formula.** [1885–90]

struc′tural func′tionalism, *Sociol.* functionalism (def. 3). [1955–60]

struc′tural gene′, *Genetics.* cistron. [1955–60]

struc′tural geol′ogy, the branch of geology dealing with the structure and distribution of the rocks that make up the crust of the earth. Also called **tectonics.** Cf. **structure** (def. 7a). [1880–85]

struc′tural i′ron, iron shaped for use in construction. [1890–95]

struc·tur·al·ism (struk′chər ə liz′əm), *n.* **1.** any theory that embodies structural principles. **2.** See **structural anthropology. 3.** See **structural linguistics. 4.** See **structural psychology.** [1945–50; STRUCTURAL + -ISM] —**struc′tur·al·ist,** *n., adj.* —**struc′tur·al·is′tic,** *adj.*

struc′tural isom′erism, *Chem.* See under **isomerism** (def. 1). [1925–30]

struc·tur·al·ize (struk′chər ə līz′), *v.t.*, **-ized, -iz·ing.** to form into or make part of a structure. Also, *esp. Brit.,* **struc′tur·al·ise′.** [1930–35; STRUCTURAL + -IZE] —**struc′tur·al·i·za′tion,** *n.*

struc′tural linguis′tics, 1. a usually synchronic approach to language study in which a language is analyzed as an independent network of formal systems, each of which is composed of elements that are defined in terms of their contrasts with other elements in the system. **2.** a school of linguistics that developed in the U.S. during the 1930's–1950's, characterized by such an approach and by an emphasis on the overt formal features of language, esp. of phonology, morphology, and syntax. Also called **structuralism.**

struc′tural psychol′ogy, psychology centering on the analysis of the structure or content of conscious mental states by introspective methods. Also called **structuralism.**

struc′tural shop′, *Shipbuilding.* See **plate shop.**

struc′tural steel′, 1. the variety of steel shapes rolled for use in construction. **2.** a steel having a composition suitable for such shapes. [1890–95]

struc′tural unemploy′ment, unemployment caused by basic changes in the overall economy, as in demographics, technology, or industrial organization. [1960–65]

struc·ture (struk′chər), *n., v.*, **-tured, -tur·ing.** —*n.* **1.** mode of building, construction, or organization; arrangement of parts, elements, or constituents: *a pyramidal structure.* **2.** something built or constructed, as a building, bridge, or dam. **3.** a complex system considered from the point of view of the whole rather than of any single part: *the structure of modern science.* **4.** anything composed of parts arranged together in some way; an organization. **5.** the relationship or organization of the component parts of a work of art or literature: *the structure of a poem.* **6.** *Biol.* mode of organization; construction and arrangement of tissues, parts, or organs. **7.** *Geol.* **a.** the attitude of a bed or stratum or of beds or strata of sedimentary rocks, as indicated by the dip and strike. **b.** the coarser composition of a rock, as contrasted with its texture. **8.** *Chem.* the manner in which atoms in a molecule are joined to each other, esp. in organic chemistry where molecular arrangement is represented by a diagram or model. **9.** *Sociol.* **a.** the system or complex of beliefs held by members of a social group. **b.** the system of relations between the constituent groups of a society. **c.** the relationship between or the interrelated arrangement of the social institutions of a society or culture, as of mores, marriage customs, or family. **d.** the pattern of relationships, as of status or friendship, existing among the members of a group or society. **10.** the pattern of organization of a language as a whole or of arrangements of linguistic units, as phonemes, morphemes or tagmemes, within larger units. —*v.t.* **11.** to give a structure, organization, or arrangement to; construct a systematic framework for. [1400–50; late ME < L *structūra,* equiv. to *struct(us)* (ptp. of *struere* to put together) + *-ūra* -URE]
—**Syn. 1.** system, form, configuration. **2.** See **building.**

struc·tured (struk′chərd), *adj.* having and manifesting a clearly defined structure or organization. [1870–75; STRUCTURE + -ED[3]]

struc′tured pro′gramming, *Computers.* the design and coding of programs by a methodology **(top-down)** that successively breaks problems into smaller, nested subunits. [1970–75]

struc·ture·less (struk′chər lis), *adj.* without structure, organization, or arrangement; formless. [1840–50; STRUCTURE + -LESS] —**struc′ture·less·ness,** *n.*

stru·del (strōōd′l; *Ger.* shtrōōd′l), *n.* a pastry, usually consisting of a fruit, cheese, or other mixture, rolled in a paper-thin sheet of dough and baked. [1925–30; < G: lit., eddy, whirlpool]

strug·gle (strug′əl), *v.*, **-gled, -gling,** *n.* —*v.i.* **1.** to contend with an adversary or opposing force. **2.** to contend resolutely with a task, problem, etc.; strive: *to struggle for existence.* **3.** to advance with violent effort: *to struggle through the snow.* **4.** (of athletes and competitors) to be coping with inability to perform well or to win; contend with difficulty: *After struggling for the whole month of June, he suddenly caught fire and raised his batting average 30 points.* —*v.t.* **5.** to bring, put, etc., by struggling: *She struggled the heavy box into a corner.* **6.** to make (one's way) with violent effort. —*n.* **7.** the process or an act or instance of struggling. **8.** a war, fight, conflict, or contest of any kind. **9.** a task or goal requiring much effort to accomplish or achieve. [1350–1400; ME *struglen, stroglen,* freq. v. (see -LE) formed on a base of obscure orig.] —**strug′gler,** *n.* —**strug′gling·ly,** *adv.*
—**Syn. 1.** oppose, contest, fight, conflict. **7.** endeavor, exertion. **8.** encounter, skirmish. STRUGGLE, BRUSH, CLASH refer to a hostile meeting of opposing persons, parties, or forces. STRUGGLE implies vigorous bodily effort or violent exertion: *a hand-to-hand struggle.* A BRUSH is a brief, but smart, and often casual combat: *a brush between patrols.* CLASH implies a direct and sharp collision between opposing parties, efforts, interests, etc.: *a clash of opinions.*

strug′gle for exist′ence, the competition in nature among organisms of a population to maintain themselves in a given environment and to survive to reproduce others of their kind. [1820–30]

strum[1] (strum), *v.*, **strummed, strum·ming,** *n.* —*v.t.* **1.** to play on (a stringed musical instrument) by running the fingers lightly across the strings. **2.** to produce (notes, a melody, etc.) by such playing: *to strum a tune.* —*v.i.* **3.** to play on a stringed musical instrument by running the fingers lightly across the strings. —*n.* **4.** the act of strumming. **5.** the sound produced by strumming. [1765–75; perh. b. STRING and THRUM[1]] —**strum′·mer,** *n.*

strum[2] (strum), *n.* a strainer, as at the inlet of a system of tubing. [orig. uncert.]

stru·ma (strōō′mə), *n., pl.* **-mae** (-mē). **1.** *Pathol.* goiter. **2.** *Bot.* a cushionlike swelling on an organ, as that at one side of the base of the capsule in many mosses. [1555–65; < NL; L *strūma* scrofulous tumor]

Stru·ma (strōō′mä), *n.* a river in S Europe, flowing SE through SW Bulgaria and NE Greece into the Aegean. 225 mi. (362 km) long.

stru·mec·to·my (strōō mek′tə mē), *n., pl.* **-mies.** *Surg.* excision of part or all of a goiter. [1890–95; STRUM(A) + -ECTOMY]

stru·mose (strōō′mōs, strōō mōs′), *adj.* having a struma or strumae. [1835–45; < L *strūmōsus,* equiv. to *strūm(a)* STRUMA + *-ōsus* -OSE[1]]

stru·mous (strōō′məs), *adj.* strumose. [1580–90; STRUM(A) + -OUS] —**stru′mous·ness,** *n.*

strum·pet (strum′pit), *n.* a prostitute; harlot. [1300–50; ME < ?] —**strum′pet·like′,** *adj.*

strung (strung), *v.* pt. and pp. of **string.**

strung-out (strung′out′), *adj. Slang.* **1.** severely debilitated from alcohol or drugs. **2.** physically or emotionally exhausted.

strunt (strunt, strŏŏnt), *Scot. and North Eng.* —*n.* **1.** the fleshy part or stump of a tail, esp. of a horse's tail. —*v.t.* **2.** to cut short, esp. to dock (the tail of a horse or sheep). [1600–10; nasalized var. of STRUT[2]; cf. Norw *strunta* to walk stiffly]

strut[1] (strut), *v.*, **strut·ted, strut·ting,** *n.* —*v.i.* **1.** to walk with a vain, pompous bearing, as with head erect and chest thrown out, as if expecting to impress observers. —*v.t.* **2. strut one's stuff,** to dress, behave, perform, etc., one's best in order to impress others; show off. —*n.* **3.** the act of strutting. **4.** a strutting walk or gait. [bef. 1000; ME *strouten* to protrude stiffly, swell, bluster, OE *strūtian* to struggle, deriv. of **strūt* (whence ME *strut* strife)] —**strut′ter,** *n.*
—**Syn. 1.** parade, flourish. STRUT and SWAGGER refer especially to carriage in walking. STRUT implies swelling pride or pompousness; to STRUT is to walk with a stiff, pompous, seemingly affected or self-conscious gait: *A turkey struts about the barnyard.* SWAGGER implies a domineering, sometimes jaunty, superiority or challenge, and a self-important manner: *to swagger down the street.*

strut[2] (strut), *n., v.*, **strut·ted, strut·ting.** —*n.* **1.** any of various structural members, as in trusses, primarily intended to resist longitudinal compression. See diags. under **king post, queen post.** —*v.t.* **2.** to brace or support by means of a strut or struts. [1565–75; obscurely akin to STRUT[1]]

Struth·ers (struth′ərz), *n.* a city in NE Ohio, near Youngstown. 13,624.

stru·thi·ous (strōō′thē əs), *adj.* resembling or related to the ostriches or other ratite birds. [1765–75; < LL *strūthi(ō)* ostrich (< LGk *strouthíōn,* deriv. of Gk *strouthós* sparrow, bird; cf. *strouthòs ho mégas* ostrich, lit., the big bird) + -OUS]

strut·ting (strut′ing), *adj.* walking or moving with a strut; walking pompously; pompous. [1350–1400; ME; see STRUT[1], -ING[2]] —**strut′ting·ly,** *adv.*

Stru·ve (strōō′və; *Ger.* shtrōō′və), *n.* **1. Frie·drich Ge·org Wil·helm von** (frē′drĭkh gā ôrk′ vil′helm fən), 1793–1864, Russian astronomer, born in Germany. **2. Otto,** 1897–1963, U.S. astronomer, born in Russia (great-grandson of Friedrich Georg Wilhelm von Struve).

strych·nine (strik′nin, -nēn, -nīn), *n.* **1.** *Pharm.* a colorless, crystalline poison, $C_{21}H_{22}N_2O_2$, obtained chiefly by extraction from the seeds of nux vomica, formerly used as a central nervous system stimulant. **2.** an Indian tree, *Strychnos nux-vomica,* of the logania family, having small, yellowish-white flowers in clusters, berrylike fruit, and seeds that yield strychnine. Also, **strych·ni·a** (strik′nē ə), **strych·ni·na** (strik′ni nə). [1810–20; < F, equiv. to NL *Strychn(os)* genus name (< Gk *strýchnos* a kind of nightshade) + F *-ine* -INE[2]] —**strych′nic,** *adj.*

strych·nin·ism (strik′ni niz′əm), *n. Pathol.* a condition induced by an overdose or by excessive use of strychnine. [1855–60; STRYCHNINE + -ISM]

St. Swith·in's Day (swith′ənz), July 15, superstitiously regarded as a day that, should it rain or be fair, will be followed by 40 consecutive days of like weather.

St. Thomas, 1. an island in the Virgin Islands of the U.S., in the E West Indies. 47,260; 32 sq. mi. (83 sq. km). **2.** a city in SE Ontario, in S Canada. 28,165. **3.** former name of **Charlotte Amalie. 4.** See **São Tomé.**

Stu (stōō, styōō), *n.* a male given name, form of **Stewart** or **Stuart.**

Stu·art (stōō′ərt, styōō′-), *n.* **1.** a member of the royal family that ruled in Scotland from 1371 to 1714 and in England from 1603 to 1714. **2. Charles Edward** (*"the Young Pretender"* or *"Bonnie Prince Charlie"*), 1720–80, grandson of James II. **3.** Also, **Stewart.** See **Darnley, Lord Henry. 4. Gilbert,** 1755–1828, U.S. painter. **5. James Ewell Brown** (*"Jeb"*), 1833–64, Confederate general in the Civil War. **6. James Francis Edward.** Also called **James III.** (*"the Old Pretender"*), 1688–1766, English prince. **7. Jesse Hilton,** 1907–84, U.S. writer. **8. John, 3rd Earl of Bute,** 1713–92, British statesman: prime minister 1762–63. **9. Mary.** See **Mary, Queen of Scots. 10.** former name of **Alice Springs. 11.** a male given name: from an Old English word meaning "steward."

stub[1] (stub), *n., v.*, **stubbed, stub·bing.** —*n.* **1.** a short projecting part. **2.** a short remaining piece, as of a pencil, candle, or cigar. **3.** (in a checkbook, receipt book, etc.) the inner end of each leaf, for keeping a record of the content of the part filled out and torn away. **4.** the returned portion of a ticket. **5.** the end of a fallen tree, shrub, or plant left fixed in the ground; stump. **6.** something having a short, blunt shape, esp. a short-pointed, blunt pen. **7.** See **stub nail. 8.** something having the look of incomplete or stunted growth, as a horn of an animal. **9.** *Bridge.* a part-score. —*v.t.* **10.** to strike accidentally against a projecting object: *I stubbed my toe against the step.* **11.** to extinguish the burning end of (a cigarette or cigar) by crushing it against a solid object (often fol. by *out*): *He stubbed out the cigarette in the ashtray.* **12.** to clear of stubs, as land. **13.** to dig up by the roots; grub up (roots). [bef. 1000; (n.) ME *stubb(e),* OE *stubb* tree stump; c. MLG, MD *stubbe,* ON *stubbi;* akin to ON *stūfr* stump; (v.) late ME *stubben* to dig up by the roots, clear stumps from (land), deriv. of the n.] —**stub′ber,** *n.*

stub[2] (stub), *adj.* stocky; squat. [1705–15; special use of STUB[1]]

stub·bed (stub′id, stubd), *adj.* **1.** reduced to or resembling a stub; short and thick; stumpy. **2.** abounding in or rough with stubs. [1520–30; STUB[1] + -ED[3]] **—stub′·bed·ness,** *n.*

stub·ble (stub′əl), *n.* **1.** Usually, **stubbles.** the stumps of grain and other stalks left in the ground when the crop is cut. **2.** such stumps collectively. **3.** any short, rough growth, as of beard. [1250–1300; ME *stuble* < OF *estuble* < VL **stupula,* L *stipula* STIPULE] **—stub′bled, stub′bly,** *adj.*

stub·born (stub′ərn), *adj.* **1.** unreasonably obstinate; obstinately unmoving: *a stubborn child.* **2.** fixed or set in purpose or opinion; resolute: *a stubborn opponent of foreign aid.* **3.** obstinately maintained, as a course of action: *a stubborn resistance.* **4.** difficult to manage or suppress: *a stubborn horse; a stubborn pain.* **5.** hard, tough, or stiff, as stone or wood; difficult to shape or work. [1350–1400; ME *stiborn(e), styborne, stuborn* < ?] **—stub′born·ly,** *adv.* **—stub′born·ness,** *n.*
—Syn. 1. contrary, intractable, refractory, unyielding, headstrong, obdurate. **2.** persevering. STUBBORN, DOGGED, OBSTINATE, PERSISTENT imply fixity of purpose or condition and resistance to change. STUBBORN and OBSTINATE both imply resistance to advice, entreaty, remonstrance, or force; but STUBBORN implies more of innate quality and is the more frequently used when referring to inanimate things: *stubborn disposition; stubborn difficulties.* DOGGED implies pertinacity and grimness in doing something, esp. in the face of discouragements: *dogged determination.* PERSISTENT implies having staying or lasting qualities, resoluteness, and perseverance: *persistent questioning.* **—Ant. 1.** tractable. **2.** irresolute.

Stubbs (stubz), *n.* **William,** 1825–1901, English historian and bishop.

stub·by (stub′ē), *adj.,* **-bi·er, -bi·est. 1.** of the nature of or resembling a stub. **2.** short and thick or broad; thick-set or squat: *stubby fingers.* **3.** consisting of or abounding in stubs. **4.** bristly, as the hair or beard. [1565–75; STUB[1] + -Y[1]] **—stub′bi·ly,** *adv.* **—stub′bi·ness,** *n.*

stub′ nail′, 1. a short, thick nail. **2.** an old or worn horseshoe nail. Also called **stub.** [1630–40]

stub′ track′. See **spur track.**

stuc·co (stuk′ō), *n., pl.* **-coes, -cos,** *v.,* **-coed, -co·ing.** **—***n.* **1.** an exterior finish for masonry or frame walls, usually composed of cement, sand, and hydrated lime mixed with water and laid on wet. **2.** any of various fine plasters for decorative work, moldings, etc. **3.** any of various finishes made with cement, plaster, or mortar, as albarium. **4.** a wall, facing, molding, or other work made of such materials. **—***v.t.* **5.** to cover or ornament with stucco. [1590–1600; < It < Langobardic; cf. OHG *stucki* crust, piece (G *Stück*)]

stuc·co·work (stuk′ō wûrk′), *n.* moldings, decorative work, or a finish made of stucco. [1680–90; STUCCO + WORK] **—stuc′co·work′er,** *n.*

stuck (stuk), *v.* **1.** pt. and pp. of **stick[2]. 2. stuck on.** *Informal.* infatuated with: *He met her only once and is already stuck on her.*

stuck-up (stuk′up′), *adj. Informal.* snobbishly conceited. [1820–30] **—stuck′-up′ness,** *n.*
—Syn. vain, arrogant, snobbish, snooty.

stud[1] (stud), *n., v.,* **stud·ded, stud·ding,** *adj.* **—***n.* **1.** a boss, knob, nailhead, or other protuberance projecting from a surface or part, esp. as an ornament. **2.** any of various buttonlike, usually ornamental objects, mounted on a shank that is passed through an article of clothing to fasten it: *a collar stud.* **3.** any of a number of slender, upright members of wood, steel, etc., forming the frame of a wall or partition and covered with plasterwork, siding, etc. **4.** any of various projecting pins, lugs, or the like, on machines or other implements. **5.** *Auto.* any of a large number of small projecting lugs embedded in an automobile tire **(studded tire)** to improve traction on snowy or icy roads. **6.** an earring consisting of a small, buttonlike ornament mounted on a metal post designed to pass through a pierced ear lobe. **7.** *Horol.* the piece to which the fixed end of a hairspring is attached. **—***v.t.* **8.** to set with or as if with studs, bosses, or the like: *The leather-covered door was studded with brass nails.* **9.** (of things) to be scattered over the expanse or surface of: *Stars stud the sky.* **10.** to set or scatter (objects) at intervals over an expanse or surface: *to stud raisins over a cake.* **11.** to furnish with or support by studs. **—***adj.* **12.** ornamented with rivets, nailheads, or other buttonlike, usually metallic objects: *a stud belt.* [bef. 900; ME *stude* knob, post, OE *studu* post; c. MHG *stud,* ON *stoth* post]

stud[2] (stud), *n.* **1.** a studhorse or stallion. **2.** an establishment, as a farm, in which horses are kept for breeding. **3.** a number of horses, usually for racing or hunting, bred or kept by one owner. **4.** a male animal, as a bull or ram, kept for breeding. **5.** a herd of animals kept for breeding. **6.** *Slang.* a man, esp. one who is notably virile and sexually active. **7.** *Poker.* See **stud poker. 8. at** or **in stud,** (of a male animal) offered for the purpose of breeding. **—***adj.* **9.** of, associated with, or pertaining to a studhorse or studhorses. **10.** retained for breeding purposes. [bef. 1000; 1920–25 for def. 6; ME; OE *stōd;* c. ON *stōth;* akin to STAND]

stud., student.

stud′ bolt′, a headless bolt threaded at each end. [1885–90]

stud·book (stud′bo͝ok′), *n.* a genealogical register of a stud or studs; a book giving the pedigree of animals, esp. horses. [1795–1805; STUD[2] + BOOK]

stud′ded tire′, *Auto.* See under **stud[1]** (def. 5).

stud·die (stud′ē, sto͝od′ē), *n. Scot.* stithy.

CONCISE ETYMOLOGY KEY: <, descended or borrowed from; >, whence; b., blend of, blended; c., cognate with; cf., compare; deriv., derivative; equiv., equivalent; imit., imitative; obl., oblique; r., replacing; s., stem; sp., spelling, spelled; resp., respelling, respelled; trans., translation; ?, origin unknown; *, unattested; ‡, probably earlier than. See the full key inside the front cover.

stud·ding (stud′ing), *n.* **1.** a number of studs, as in a wall or partition. **2.** timbers or manufactured objects for use as studs. [1580–90; STUD[1] + -ING[1]]

stud·ding·sail (stud′ing sāl′; *Naut.* stun′səl), *n. Naut.* a light sail, sometimes set outboard of either of the leeches of a square sail and extended by booms. Also, **stunsail, stuns'l.** [1540–50; *studding* (< ?) + SAIL]

Stu·de·ba·ker (sto͞o′də bā′kər, styo͞o′-), *n.* **Clement,** 1831–1901, U.S. wagon maker and pioneer automobile designer.

stu·dent (sto͞od′nt, styo͞od′-), *n.* **1.** a person formally engaged in learning, esp. one enrolled in a school or college; pupil: *a student at Yale.* **2.** any person who studies, investigates, or examines thoughtfully: *a student of human nature.* [1350–1400; ME < L *student-* (s. of *studēns*), prp. of *studēre* to take pains; see -ENT; r. ME *studiant,* aph. var. of *estudiant* < OF, n. use of prp. of *estudier* to STUDY] **—stu′dent·less,** *adj.* **—stu′dent·like′,** *adj.*
—Syn. 1, 2. See **pupil[1].**
—Pronunciation. See **new.**

stu′dent bod′y, all the students enrolled at an educational institution. [1920–25]

stu′dent coun′cil, a representative body composed chiefly of students chosen by their classmates to organize social and extracurricular activities and to participate in the government of a school or college.

stu′dent lamp′, a table lamp whose light source can be adjusted in height. [1870–75, *Amer.*]

Stu′dent Loan′ Mar′keting Associa′tion, a U.S. government-chartered private company whose chief function is to make available to qualified students low-cost loans backed by government agencies through lending institutions. *Abbr.:* SLMA Also called **Sallie Mae.**

Stu′dent Na′tional Coor′dinating Commit′tee. See **SNCC.** Formerly, **Stu′dent Nonvi′olent Coor′dinating Commit′tee.**

stu′dent nurse′, a person who is training to be a nurse at a nursing school or hospital. [1930–35]

Stu′dents for a Democrat′ic Soci′ety. See **SDS.**

stu·dent·ship (sto͞od′nt ship′, styo͞od′-), *n.* **1.** the state or condition of being a student. **2.** *Chiefly Brit.* a financial grant from a college or university for advanced academic study; scholarship or fellowship. [1775–85; STUDENT + -SHIP]

Student's t distribution, *Statistics.* a bell-shaped probability distribution that is flatter or more stretched out than the normal distribution. Also, **Student t distribution.** Also called **t distribution.** [1925–30; after *Student,* pseudonym of William Sealy Gosset (1876–1937), English statistician; *t* represents a random variable in the equation describing this type of distribution]

Student's t-test (tē′test′), *Statistics.* a test for determining whether or not an observed sample mean differs significantly from a hypothetical normal population mean. [1945–50; see STUDENT'S T DISTRIBUTION]

stu′dent teach′er, a student who is studying to be a teacher and who, as part of the training, observes classroom instruction or does closely supervised teaching in an elementary or secondary school. Also called **intern, practice teacher.** [1905–10] **—stu′dent teach′ing.**

stu′dent un′ion, a building or rooms on a college or university campus, set aside for recreational, social, and governmental activities of the students. [1945–50]

stud′ fee′, the charge for the service of a male animal, as a horse, in breeding.

stud·fish (stud′fish′), *n., pl.* (*esp. collectively*) **-fish,** (*esp. referring to two or more kinds or species*) **-fish·es.** either of two killifishes marked with orange spots, *Fundulus catenatus* **(northern studfish),** of the Tennessee and Cumberland rivers and Ozark Mountains region, or *F. stellifer* **(southern studfish),** of the Alabama River. [1880–85, *Amer.;* STUD[1] + FISH]

stud·horse (stud′hôrs′), *n.* a stallion kept for breeding. [bef. 1000; OE *stōdhors* (not recorded in ME). See STUD[2], HORSE]

stud′horse pok′er, *Older Use.* See **stud poker.** Also, **stud′-horse pok′er.**

stud·ied (stud′ēd), *adj.* **1.** marked by or suggestive of conscious effort; not spontaneous or natural; affected: *studied simplicity.* **2.** carefully deliberated: *a studied approval.* **3.** learned. [1520–30; STUDY + -ED[2]] **—stud′ied·ly,** *adv.* **—stud′ied·ness,** *n.*
—Syn. 1. deliberate. **1, 2.** considered. See **elaborate.**

stu·di·o (sto͞o′dē ō′, styo͞o′-), *n., pl.* **-di·os. 1.** the workroom or atelier of an artist, as a painter or sculptor. **2.** a room or place for instruction or experimentation in one of the performing arts: *a dance studio.* **3.** a room or set of rooms specially equipped for broadcasting radio or television programs, making phonograph records, filming motion pictures, etc. **4.** all the buildings and adjacent land required or used by a company engaged in the production of motion pictures. **5.** See **studio apartment.** [1800–10; 1910–15 for def. 4; < It < L *studium;* see STUDY]

stu′dio apart′ment, 1. an apartment consisting of one main room, a kitchen or kitchenette, and a bathroom. Cf. **efficiency apartment. 2.** (formerly) a one-room apartment having a high ceiling and large windows. [1920–25]

stu′dio couch′, an upholstered couch, usually without a back, convertible into a double bed by sliding a bed frame out from beneath it and covering the frame with the mattress that forms the upper thickness of the upholstery. [1935–40, *Amer.*]

stu′dio glass′, art glass produced by an independent artisan in the studio.

stu·di·ous (sto͞o′dē əs, styo͞o′-), *adj.* **1.** disposed or given to diligent study: *a studious boy.* **2.** concerned with, characterized by, or pertaining to study: *studious tastes.* **3.** zealous, assiduous, or painstaking: *studious care.* **4.** carefully planned or maintained; studied: *a studious program to maintain peace.* **5.** devoted to or favorable for study. [1350–1400; ME < L *studiōsus,* equiv. to *studi(um)* (see STUDY) + *-ōsus* -OUS] **—stu′di·ous·ly,** *adv.* **—stu′di·ous·ness,** *n.*

stud′ pok′er, *Cards.* **1.** a variety of poker in which each player is dealt one card face down in the first round and one card face up in each of the next four rounds, each of the last four rounds being followed by a betting interval. Cf. **seven-card stud. 2.** any similar variety of poker. [1860–65, *Amer.*]

stud·work (stud′wûrk′), *n.* **1.** the act or process of building with studding. **2.** structural work containing studding. [1780–90; STUD[1] + WORK]

stud·y (stud′ē), *n., pl.* **stud·ies,** *v.,* **stud·ied, stud·y·ing. —***n.* **1.** application of the mind to the acquisition of knowledge, as by reading, investigation, or reflection: *long hours of study.* **2.** the cultivation of a particular branch of learning, science, or art: *the study of law.* **3.** Often, **studies.** a personal effort to gain knowledge: *to pursue one's studies.* **4.** something studied or to be studied: *Balzac's study was human nature.* **5.** research or a detailed examination and analysis of a subject, phenomenon, etc.: *She made a study of the transistor market for her firm.* **6.** a written account of such research, examination, or analysis: *He published a study of Milton's poetry.* **7.** a well-defined, organized branch of learning or knowledge. **8.** zealous endeavor or assiduous effort. **9.** the object of such endeavor or effort. **10.** deep thought, reverie, or a state of abstraction: *He was lost in study and did not hear us come in.* **11.** a room, in a house or other building, set apart for private study, reading, writing, or the like. **12.** Also called **étude.** *Music.* a composition that combines exercise in technique with a greater or lesser amount of artistic value. **13.** *Literature.* **a.** a literary composition executed for exercise or as an experiment in a particular method of treatment. **b.** such a composition dealing in detail with a particular subject, as a single main character. **14.** *Art.* something produced as an educational exercise, as a memorandum or record of observations or effects, or as a guide for a finished production: *She made a quick pencil sketch of his hands as a study for the full portrait in oils.* **15.** a person, as an actor, considered in terms of his or her quickness or slowness in memorizing lines: *a quick study.* **—***v.i.* **16.** to apply oneself to the acquisition of knowledge, as by reading, investigation, or practice. **17.** to apply oneself; endeavor. **18.** to think deeply, reflect, or consider. **19.** to take a course of study, as at a college. **—***v.t.* **20.** to apply oneself to acquiring a knowledge of (a subject). **21.** to examine or investigate carefully and in detail: *to study the political situation.* **22.** to observe attentively; scrutinize: *to study a person's face.* **23.** to read carefully or intently: *to study a book.* **24.** to endeavor to learn or memorize, as a part in a play. **25.** to consider, as something to be achieved or devised. **26.** to think out, as the result of careful consideration or devising. [1250–1300; (n.) ME *studie* < OF *estudie* < L *studium,* equiv. to *stud(ēre)* to be busy with, devote oneself to, concentrate on + *-ium* -IUM; (v.) ME *studien* < OF *estudier* < ML *studiāre,* deriv. of *studium*] **—stud′i·a·ble,** *adj.* **—stud′i·er,** *n.*
—Syn. 1. inquiry, research, reading, thought, consideration. **7.** subject, field, area. **11.** library, den. **21.** STUDY, CONSIDER, REFLECT, WEIGH imply fixing the mind upon something, generally doing so with a view to some decision or action. STUDY implies an attempt to obtain a grasp of something by methodical or exhaustive thought: *to study a problem.* To CONSIDER is to fix the thought upon something and give it close attention before making a decision concerning it, or beginning an action connected with it: *to consider ways and means.* REFLECT implies looking back quietly over past experience and giving it consideration: *to reflect on similar cases in the past.* WEIGH implies a deliberate and judicial estimate, as by a balance: *to weigh a decision.*

stud′y group′, an informal gathering of people who convene regularly to exchange ideas and information on a specific subject.

stud′y hall′, 1. (in some schools) a room used solely or chiefly for studying. **2.** a period of time in a school day, set aside for study and doing homework, usually under the supervision of a teacher and in a room designated for this purpose. [1840–50]

stuff (stuf), *n.* **1.** the material of which anything is made: *a hard, crystalline stuff.* **2.** material to be worked upon or to be used in making something: *wood, steel, and other stuff for building.* **3.** material of some unspecified kind: *a cushion filled with some soft stuff.* **4.** *Chiefly Brit.* woven material or fabric, esp. wool. **5.** property, as personal belongings or equipment; things. **6.** something to be swallowed, as food, drink, or medicine. **7.** inward character, qualities, or capabilities: *to have good stuff in one.* **8.** *Informal.* action or talk of a particular kind: *kid stuff; Cut out the rough stuff.* **9.** worthless things or matter: *to clean the stuff out of a closet.* **10.** worthless or foolish ideas, talk, or writing: *a lot of stuff and nonsense.* **11.** *Sports.* **a.** *Baseball.* the assortment of pitches that a pitcher uses in a game together with the ability to deliver them in the proper manner at the right speed to the desired spot: *He saved his best stuff for the tougher hitters in the lineup.* **b.** spin or speed imparted to a ball, as by a baseball pitcher, a bowler, or a tennis player: *a pitch with plenty of stuff.* **12.** *Informal.* journalistic, literary, artistic, dramatic, musical, or other compositions or performances: *Bach composed some splendid stuff.* **13.** *Informal.* one's trade, skill, field, facts, etc.: *She knows her stuff.* **14.** *Slang.* any kind of drug, esp. an illicit one. **15.** Also called **stock.** *Papermaking.* refined and beaten wet pulp ready for spreading on the wire. **—***v.t.* **16.** to fill (a receptacle), esp. by packing the contents closely together; cram full. **17.** to fill (an aperture, cavity, etc.) by forcing something into it. **18.** to fill or line with some kind of material as a padding or packing. **19.** to fill or cram (oneself, one's stomach, etc.) with food. **20.** to fill (meat, vegetables, etc.) with seasoned bread crumbs or other savory matter. **21.** to fill the preserved skin of (a dead

animal) with material, retaining its natural form and appearance for display. **22.** to put fraudulent votes into (a ballot box). **23.** to thrust or cram (something) into a receptacle, cavity, or the like. **24.** to pack tightly in a confined place; crowd together. **25.** to crowd (a vehicle, room, etc.) with persons. **26.** to clutter or fill (the mind) with facts, details, etc. **27.** (in leather manufacturing) to treat (a skin, hide, etc.) with a composition of tallow and other ingredients. **28.** to stop up or plug; block or choke (usually fol. by *up*). —*v.i.* **29.** to cram oneself with food; eat gluttonously; gorge. [1300–50; (v.) late ME *stuffen* to equip, furnish < OF *estoffer* lit., to stuff < Frankish **stopfōn,* **stoppōn* (see STOP); (n.) ME < OF *estoffe,* deriv. of the v.] —**stuff′less,** *adj.*
—**Syn. 1, 2, 3.** See **matter. 9.** waste, rubbish, trash. **10.** nonsense, twaddle, claptrap, balderdash. **23.** press, stow. **28.** obstruct.

stuffed′ der′ma, kishke.

stuffed′ shirt′, a pompous, self-satisfied, and inflexible person. [1910–15, *Amer.*]

stuff•er (stuf′ər), *n.* **1.** a person or thing that stuffs. **2.** a small printed advertisement, announcement, or reminder that is inserted in an envelope and mailed with something else, as a bill or bank statement. [1605–15; STUFF + -ER[1]]

stuff•ing (stuf′ing), *n.* **1.** the act of a person or thing that stuffs. **2.** a material or substance used to stuff something. **3.** seasoned bread crumbs or other filling used to stuff a chicken, turkey, etc., before cooking. **4.** *Informal.* internal parts; insides: *to beat the stuffing out of an opponent.* [1520–30; STUFF + -ING[1]]

stuff′ing box′, *Mach.* a device for preventing leakage of gases or liquids along a moving rod or shaft at the point at which it leaves a cylinder, tank, ship hull, etc. Also called **gland.** [1790–1800]

stuff′ing nut′, *Mach.* a nut that serves to condense packing and so to tighten its seal. Also called **packing nut.** See diag. under **valve.**

stuff′ shot′, *Basketball.* See **dunk shot.** [1965–70]

stuff•y (stuf′ē), *adj.,* **stuff•i•er, stuff•i•est. 1.** close; poorly ventilated: *a stuffy room.* **2.** oppressive from lack of freshness: *stuffy air; a stuffy odor.* **3.** lacking in interest, as writing or discourse. **4.** affected with a sensation of obstruction in the respiratory passages: *a stuffy nose.* **5.** dull or tedious; boring. **6.** self-important; pompous. **7.** rigid or strait-laced in attitudes, esp. in matters of personal behavior. **8.** old-fashioned; conservative. **9.** ill-tempered; sulky. [1545–55; STUFF + -Y[1]] —**stuff′i•ly,** *adv.* —**stuff′i•ness,** *n.*
—**Syn. 3, 5, 8.** stodgy. **6.** smug. **7.** priggish.

stui•ver (stī′vər), *n.* stiver (def. 1).

Stu•ka (sto͞o′kə; *Ger.* shto͞o′kä), *n.* a German two-seated dive bomber with a single in-line engine, used by the Luftwaffe in World War II. [1940–45; < G *Stu(rz)-ka(mpfflugzeug)* dive bomber, equiv. to *Sturz* dive + *Kampfflugzeug* combat plane]

stull (stul), *n. Mining.* **1.** a timber prop. **2.** a timber wedged in between two walls of a stope as part of a protective covering or platform. [1770–80; orig. uncert.; cf. G *Stollen* prop, STOLLEN]

St. Ul•mo's fire (ul′mōz). See **St. Elmo's fire.** Also called **St. Ulmo's light.**

stul•ti•fy (stul′tə fī′), *v.t.,* **-fied, -fy•ing. 1.** to make, or cause to appear, foolish or ridiculous. **2.** to render absurdly or wholly futile or ineffectual, esp. by degrading or frustrating means: *Menial work can stultify the mind.* **3.** *Law.* to allege or prove (oneself or another) to be of unsound mind. [1760–70; < LL *stultificāre,* equiv. to L *stult(us)* stupid + *-i-* -I- + *-ficāre* -FY] —**stul′ti•fi•ca′tion,** *n.* —**stul′ti•fi′er,** *n.* —**stul′ti•fy′ing•ly,** *adv.*
—**Syn. 2.** cripple, impede, frustrate, hinder, thwart.

stum (stum), *n., v.,* **stummed, stum•ming.** —*n.* **1.** unfermented or partly fermented grape juice. **2.** wine in which increased fermentation has taken place because of the addition of stum. —*v.t.* **3.** to increase the fermentation of (wine) by adding stum. [1650–60; < D *stom* dumb, dull; cf. F *vin muet,* G *stummer Wein,* in the same sense]

stum•ble (stum′bəl), *v.,* **-bled, -bling,** *n.* —*v.i.* **1.** to strike the foot against something, as in walking or running, so as to stagger or fall; trip. **2.** to walk or go unsteadily: *to stumble down a dark passage.* **3.** to make a slip, mistake, or blunder, esp. a sinful one: *to stumble over a question; to stumble and fall from grace.* **4.** to proceed in a hesitating or blundering manner, as in action or speech (often fol. by *along*). **5.** to discover or meet with accidentally or unexpectedly (usually fol. by *on, upon,* or *across*): *They stumbled on a little village.* **6.** to falter or hesitate, as at an obstacle to progress or belief. —*v.t.* **7.** to cause to stumble; trip. **8.** to give pause to; puzzle or perplex. —*n.* **9.** the act of stumbling. **10.** a moral lapse or error. **11.** a slip or blunder. [1275–1325; ME *stumblen;* c. Norw *stumla* to grope and stumble in the dark; akin to STAMMER] —**stum′bler,** *n.* —**stum′bling•ly,** *adv.*

stum•ble•bum (stum′bəl bum′), *n. Informal.* **1.** a clumsy, second-rate prizefighter. **2.** a clumsy, incompetent person. [1930–35; STUMBLE + BUM[1]]

stum′bling block′, an obstacle or hindrance to progress, belief, or understanding. [1580–90]
—**Syn.** hurdle, barrier, impediment, block, bar.

stu•mer (sto͞o′mər, styo͞o′-), *n. Brit. Slang.* **1.** something bogus or fraudulent. **2.** a counterfeit coin or bill. **3.** See **rubber check.** [1885–90; orig. uncert.]

stump (stump), *n.* **1.** the lower end of a tree or plant left after the main part falls or is cut off; a standing tree trunk from which the upper part and branches have been removed. **2.** the part of a limb of the body remaining after the rest has been cut off. **3.** a part of a broken or decayed tooth left in the gum. **4.** a short remnant, as of a candle; stub. **5.** any basal part remaining after the main or more important part has been removed. **6.** an artificial leg. **7.** Usually, **stumps.** *Informal.* legs: *Stir your stumps and get out of here.* **8.** a short, stocky person. **9.** a heavy step or gait, as of a wooden-legged or lame person. **10.** the figurative place of political speechmaking: *to go on the stump.* **11.** *Furniture.* a support for the front end of the arm of a chair, sofa, etc. Cf. **post**[1] (def. 2). **12.** a short, thick roll of paper, soft leather, or some similar material, usually having a blunt point, for rubbing a pencil, charcoal, or crayon drawing in order to achieve subtle gradations of tone in representing light and shade. **13.** *Cricket.* each of the three upright sticks that, with the two bails laid on top of them, form a wicket. **14. up a stump,** *Informal.* at a loss; embarrassed; perplexed: *Sociologists are up a stump over the sharp rise in juvenile delinquency and crime.* —*v.t.* **15.** to reduce to a stump; truncate; lop. **16.** to clear of stumps, as land. **17.** *Chiefly Southern U.S.* to stub, as one's toe. **18.** to nonplus, embarrass, or render completely at a loss: *This riddle stumps me.* **19.** to challenge or dare to do something. **20.** to make political campaign speeches to or in: *to stump a state.* **21.** *Cricket.* (of the wicketkeeper) to put (a batsman) out by knocking down a stump or by dislodging a bail with the ball held in the hand at a moment when the batsman is off his ground. **22.** to tone or modify (a crayon drawing, pencil rendering, etc.) by means of a stump. —*v.i.* **23.** to walk heavily or clumsily, as if with a wooden leg: *The captain stumped across the deck.* **24.** to make political campaign speeches; electioneer. [1200–50; (n.) ME *stompe,* c. or < MLG *stump(e),* MD *stomp* (cf. G *Stumpf*); (v.) ME *stumpen* to stumble (as over a stump), deriv. of the n.] —**stump′less,** *adj.* —**stump′like′,** *adj.*

stump•age (stum′pij), *n.* **1.** standing timber with reference to its value. **2.** the value of such timber. [1815–25; STUMP + -AGE]

stump′ bed′, a bed without posts. [1835–45]

stump•er (stum′pər), *n.* **1.** a person or thing that stumps. **2.** an extremely difficult question, task, or problem. **3.** a person who makes stump speeches. [1725–35; STUMP + -ER[1]]

stump′ farm′, a farm that was started on previously forested land covered with the stumps of felled trees.

stump′ foot′, *Furniture.* a foot continuing the surfaces of a square leg in an outward flare.

stump•knock•er (stump′nok′ər), *n.* See **spotted sunfish.** [STUMP + KNOCKER]

stump′ speech′, a political campaign speech, esp. one made on a campaign tour. [1810–20, *Amer.*]

stump•suck•er (stump′suk′ər), *n.* **1.** windsucker; cribber. **2.** a shoot developing from a tree stump. [1805–15, *Amer.;* STUMP + SUCKER]

stump•work (stump′wûrk′), *n.* a type of embroidery popular in the 17th century, consisting of intricate, colorful designs padded with horsehair to make them stand out in relief. [1900–05; STUMP + WORK]

stump•y (stum′pē), *adj.,* **stump•i•er, stump•i•est. 1.** of the nature of or resembling a stump. **2.** short and thick; stubby; stocky. **3.** abounding in stumps: *a stumpy field.* [1590–1600; STUMP + -Y[1]] —**stump′i•ly,** *adv.* —**stump′i•ness,** *n.*

stun (stun), *v.,* **stunned, stun•ning,** *n.* —*v.t.* **1.** to deprive of consciousness or strength by or as if by a blow, fall, etc.: *The blow to his jaw stunned him for a moment.* **2.** to astonish; astound; amaze: *Her wit stunned the audience.* **3.** to shock; overwhelm: *The world was stunned by the attempted assassination.* **4.** to daze or bewilder by noise. —*n.* **5.** the act of stunning. **6.** the condition of being stunned. [1250–1300; ME *stonen, stunen* (v.) < OF *estoner* to shake, make resound; see ASTONISH]
—**Syn. 2, 3.** See **shock**[1]. **4.** stupefy.

stung (stung), *v.* a pt. and pp. of **sting.**

stun′ gun′, 1. a battery-powered, hand-held weapon that fires an electric charge when held against a person and activated by a trigger or button, used, esp. by police, to immobilize a person briefly and without injury. **2.** any of various hand-held weapons that shoot small pellet-filled bags, tranquilizer darts, darts attached to electric wires, or the like to immobilize a person or animal briefly and without injury. [1965–70]

stunk (stungk), *v.* a pt. and pp. of **stink.**

stun•ner (stun′ər), *n.* **1.** a person or thing that stuns. **2.** *Informal.* a person or thing of striking excellence, beauty, achievement, etc. [1840–50; STUN + -ER[1]]

stun•ning (stun′ing), *adj.* **1.** causing, capable of causing, or liable to cause astonishment, bewilderment, or a loss of consciousness or strength: *a stunning blow.* **2.** of striking beauty or excellence: *What a stunning dress you're wearing!* [1660–70; STUN + -ING[2]] —**stun′ning•ly,** *adv.*
—**Syn. 1.** stupefying, numbing, dumbfounding, astounding.

stun•sail (stun′səl), *n.* studdingsail. Also, **stun′s'l.** [1755–65; syncopated var. of STUDDINGSAIL]

stunt[1] (stunt), *v.t.* **1.** to stop, slow down, or hinder the growth or development of; dwarf: *A harsh climate stunted the trees. Brutal treatment in childhood stunted his personality.* —*n.* **2.** a stop or hindrance in growth or development. **3.** arrested development. **4.** a plant or animal hindered from attaining its proper growth. **5.** *Plant Pathol.* a disease of plants, characterized by a dwarfing or stunting of the plant. [1575–85; v. use of dial. *stunt* dwarfed, stubborn (ME; OE: stupid); c. MHG *stunz,* ON *stuttr* short; akin to STINT[1]] —**stunt′ing•ly,** *adv.* —**stunt′y,** *adj.*

stunt[2] (stunt), *n.* **1.** a performance displaying a person's skill or dexterity, as in athletics; feat: *an acrobatic stunt.* **2.** any remarkable feat performed chiefly to attract attention: *The kidnapping was said to be a publicity stunt.* —*v.i.* **3.** to do a stunt or stunts. **4.** *Television Slang.* to add specials, miniseries, etc., to a schedule of programs, esp. so as to increase ratings. —*v.t.* **5.** to use in doing stunts: *to stunt an airplane.* [1890–95, *Amer.;* orig. uncert.]

stunt•ed (stun′tid), *adj.* slowed or stopped abnormally in growth or development. [1650–60; STUNT[1] + -ED[2]] —**stunt′ed•ness,** *n.*

stunt′ man′, *Motion Pictures, Television.* a man who substitutes for an actor in scenes requiring hazardous or acrobatic feats. [1925–30, *Amer.*]

stunt′ per′son, a stunt man or stunt woman.

stunt′ wom′an, *Motion Pictures, Television.* a woman who substitutes for an actor in scenes requiring hazardous or acrobatic feats. [1945–50]

stu•pa (sto͞o′pə), *n.* a monumental pile of earth or other material, in memory of Buddha or a Buddhist saint, and commemorating some event or marking a sacred spot. [1875–80; < Skt *stūpa*]

stupe[1] (sto͞op, styo͞op), *n.* two or more layers of flannel or other cloth soaked in hot water and applied to the skin as a counterirritant. [1350–1400; ME < L *stūpa,* var. of *stuppa* < Gk *stýppē* flax, hemp, tow]

stupe[2] (sto͞op), *n. Slang.* a stupid person. [1755–65; by shortening of STUPID]

stu•pe•fa•cient (sto͞o′pə fā′shənt, styo͞o′-), *adj.* **1.** stupefying; producing stupor. —*n.* **2.** a drug or agent that produces stupor. [1660–70; < L *stupefacient-* (s. of *stupefaciēns*) prp. of *stupefacere* to benumb; see STUPEFY, -FACIENT]

stu•pe•fac•tion (sto͞o′pə fak′shən, styo͞o′-), *n.* **1.** the state of being stupefied; stupor. **2.** overwhelming amazement. [1535–45; < NL *stupefactiōn-* (s. of *stupefactiō*) senseless state, equiv. to *stupefact(us),* ptp. of *stupefacere* to STUPEFY + *-iōn-* -ION]

stu•pe•fac•tive (sto͞o′pə fak′tiv, styo͞o′-), *adj.* serving to stupefy. [1520–30; < ML *stupefactīvus,* equiv. to L *stupefact(us)* (see STUPEFACTION) + *-īvus* -IVE]

stu•pe•fy (sto͞o′pə fī′, styo͞o′-), *v.t.,* **-fied, -fy•ing. 1.** to put into a state of little or no sensibility; benumb the faculties of; put into a stupor. **2.** to stun, as with a narcotic, a shock, or a strong emotion. **3.** to overwhelm with amazement; astound; astonish. [1590–1600; < MF *stupefier* << L *stupefacere* to benumb, equiv. to *stupe-,* s. of *stupēre* to be numb or stunned + *facere* to make, DO[1]; see -FY] —**stu•pe•fied•ness** (sto͞o′pə fīd′nis, -fī′id-, styo͞o′-), *n.* —**stu′pe•fi′er,** *n.* —**stu′pe•fy′ing•ly,** *adv.*

stu•pen•dous (sto͞o pen′dəs, styo͞o-), *adj.* **1.** causing amazement; astounding; marvelous: *stupendous news.* **2.** amazingly large or great; immense: *a stupendous mass of information.* [1965–70; < L *stupendus,* ger. of *stupēre* to be stunned; see -OUS] —**stu•pen′dous•ly,** *adv.* —**stu•pen′dous•ness,** *n.*
—**Syn. 1.** extraordinary. **2.** colossal, vast, gigantic, prodigious.

stu•pid (sto͞o′pid, styo͞o′-), *adj.,* **-er, -est,** *n.* —*adj.* **1.** lacking ordinary quickness and keenness of mind; slow-thinking; dull. **2.** characterized by, indicative of, or proceeding from mental dullness; foolish; senseless: *a stupid act.* **3.** tediously dull or uninteresting, esp. due to lack of meaning or sense: *to read a stupid book; to go to a stupid party.* **4.** annoying or irritating; troublesome: *stupid rules and regulations.* **5.** in a state of stupor; stupefied: *to be stupid from fatigue.* **6.** *Slang.* excellent; terrific. —*n.* **7.** *Informal.* a stupid person. [1535–45; < L *stupidus,* equiv. to *stup(ēre)* to be numb or stunned + *-idus* -ID[4]] —**stu′pid•ly,** *adv.* —**stu′pid•ness,** *n.*
—**Syn. 1.** witless, dumb. See **foolish. 3.** prosaic, tedious, pointless, inane, asinine. See **dull. 4.** vexatious; exasperating. —**Ant. 1.** bright, clever.

stu•pid•i•ty (sto͞o pid′i tē, styo͞o-), *n., pl.* **-ties** for 2. **1.** the state, quality, or fact of being stupid. **2.** a stupid act, notion, speech, etc. [1535–45; < L *stupiditās,* equiv. to *stupid(us)* STUPID + *-itās* -ITY]

stu•por (sto͞o′pər, styo͞o′-), *n.* **1.** suspension or great diminution of sensibility, as in disease or as caused by narcotics, intoxicants, etc.: *He lay there in a drunken stupor.* **2.** mental torpor; apathy; stupefaction. [1350–1400; ME < L: astonishment, insensibility, equiv. to *stup(ēre)* to be numb or stunned + *-or* -OR[1]] —**stu′por•ous,** *adj.*
—**Syn. 2.** inertia, lethargy, daze.

Stur•bridge (stûr′brij′), *n.* a town in central Massachusetts: reconstruction of early American village. 5976.

stur•dy[1] (stûr′dē), *adj.,* **-di•er, -di•est. 1.** strongly built; stalwart; robust: *sturdy young athletes.* **2.** strong, as in substance, construction, or texture: *sturdy walls.* **3.** firm; courageous; indomitable: *the sturdy defenders of the Alamo.* **4.** of strong or hardy growth, as a plant. [1250–1300; ME *stourdi* < OF *estourdi* dazed, stunned, violent, reckless (ptp. of *estourdir* < ?)] —**stur′di•ly,** *adv.* —**stur′di•ness,** *n.*
—**Syn. 1.** hardy, muscular, brawny, sinewy, stout, strong, powerful. **3.** resolute, vigorous, determined, unconquerable. —**Ant. 1.** weak.

stur•dy[2] (stûr′dē), *n. Vet. Pathol.* gid. [1560–70; n. use of STURDY[1] in obs. sense "giddy"] —**stur′died,** *adj.*

stur•geon (stûr′jən), *n., pl.* (*esp. collectively*) **-geon,** (*esp. referring to two or more kinds or species*) **-geons.** any of various large fishes of the family Acipenseridae, inhabiting fresh and salt North Temperate waters, valued for their flesh and as a source of caviar and isinglass: *A. brevirostrum,* of the Atlantic coast, is endangered. [1250–1300; ME < AF, OF *esturgeon* < Gmc; cf. OE *styria,* OHG *sturio* (G *Stör*), ON *styrja*]

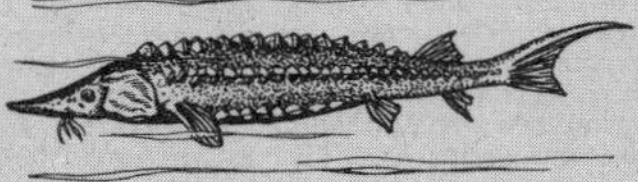

sturgeon, *Acipenser oxyrhynchus,* length to 12 ft. (3.7 m)

CONCISE PRONUNCIATION KEY: act, cāpe, dâre, pärt; set, ēqual; if, īce; ox, ōver, ôrder, oil, bo͝ok, bo͞ot, out; up, ûrge; child; sing; shoe; thin, *that;* zh as in *treasure.* ə = a as in *alone,* e as in *system,* i as in *easily,* o as in *gallop,* u as in *circus;* ° as in *fire* (fī°r), *hour* (ou°r). l and n can serve as syllabic consonants, as in *cradle* (krād′l), and *button* (but′n). See the full key inside the front cover.

Stur·gis (stûr′jis), *n.* **Russell,** 1836–1909, U.S. architect and author.

Stur·lu·son (stûr′lə sən), *n.* See **Snorri Sturluson.**

Sturm·ab·tei·lung (shto͝orm′äp′tī′lo͝ong), *n.* a political militia of the Nazi party, organized about 1923 and notorious for its violence and terrorism up to 1934, when it was purged and reorganized as an instrument of physical training and political indoctrination of German men; Brown Shirts. [< G, equiv. to *Sturm* storm, troop of storm troopers + *Abteilung* division, department]

Sturm und Drang (shto͝orm′ o͝ont dräng′), **1.** a style or movement of German literature of the latter half of the 18th century: characterized chiefly by impetuosity of manner, exaltation of individual sensibility and intuitive perception, opposition to established forms of society and thought, and extreme nationalism. **2.** tumult; turmoil; upheaval. [< G: lit., storm and stress]

sturt (stûrt), *n., Scot.* violent quarreling. [1325–75; ME; metathetic var. of STRUT[1]] —**sturt·y,** *adj.*

stut·ter (stut′ər), *v.t., v.i.* **1.** to speak in such a way that the rhythm is interrupted by repetitions, blocks or spasms, or prolongations of sounds or syllables, sometimes accompanied by contortions of the face and body. —*n.* **2.** distorted speech characterized principally by blocks or spasms interrupting the rhythm. [1520–30; earlier *stut* (ME *stutten* to stutter) + -ER[6]; cf. D *stotteren,* MLG *stotern* in same sense] —**stut′ter·er,** *n.* —**stut′ter·ing·ly,** *adv.*
—**Syn. 1.** See **stammer.**

Stutt·gart (stut′gärt, shto͝ot′-; *for 1 also Ger.* shto͝ot′gärt), *n.* **1.** a city in and the capital of Baden-Württemberg, in SW Germany. 594,100. **2.** a town in central Arkansas. 10,941.

Stutt′gart disease′, *Pathol.* See **canine leptospirosis.** Also, **Stutt′gart's disease′.**

Stutz (stuts), *n.* **Harry Clayton,** 1876–1930, U.S. automobile manufacturer.

Stuy·ve·sant (stī′və sənt), *n.* **Peter,** 1592–1672, Dutch colonial administrator in the Americas: last governor of New Netherlands 1646–64.

STV, subscription television. See **pay television.**

St. Vincent, 1. an island in the S Windward Islands, in the SE West Indies: part of the state of St. Vincent and the Grenadines; a member of the former West Indies Associated States. 133 sq. mi. (345 sq. km). **2.** a former British colony comprising this island and the N Grenadines. **3. Cape,** the SW tip of Portugal: naval battle 1797.

St. Vin′cent and the Gren′adines, an island state in the S Windward Islands, in the SE West Indies comprising St. Vincent island and the N Grenadines: gained independence 1979. 100,000; 150 sq. mi. (389 sq. km). *Cap.:* Kingstown.

St. Vi·tus's dance (vī′tə siz), *Pathol.* chorea (def. 2). Also, **St. Vi·tus dance** (vī′təs), **St. Vi·tus' dance** (vī′təs, -tə siz), **Saint Vitus's dance.** [1955–60; named after *St. Vitus* (3rd century), patron saint of those afflicted with chorea]

S twist, a direction of the twist in yarns, from top left to bottom right, resembling the long stroke of the letter *S.* Cf. **Z twist.**

sty[1] (stī), *n., pl.* **sties,** *v.,* **stied, sty·ing.** —*n.* **1.** a pen or enclosure for swine; pigpen. **2.** any filthy place or abode. **3.** a place of bestial debauchery. —*v.t.* **4.** to keep or lodge in or as if in a sty. —*v.i.* **5.** to live in or as if in a sty. [bef. 1000; (n.) ME; OE **stī* in *stī-fearh* sty-pig; prob. identical with *stig-* in *stigweard* STEWARD; c. ON *stī,* D *stijg,* G *Steige*]

sty[2] (stī), *n., pl.* **sties.** *Ophthalm.* a circumscribed abscess caused by bacterial infection of the glands on the edge of the eyelid; hordeolum. Also, **stye.** [1610–20; by false division of ME *styanye* sty (*styan* (OE *stīgend* sty, lit., rising) + *ye* EYE), taken to be *sty on eye*]

Styg·i·an (stij′ē ən), *adj.* **1.** of or pertaining to the river Styx or to Hades. **2.** dark or gloomy. **3.** infernal; hellish. Also, **styg′i·an** (for defs. 2, 3). [1560–70; < L *Stygi(us)* < Gk *Stýgios* (*Styg-,* s. of *Stýx* STYX + *-ios* adj. suffix) + -AN]

sty·lar (stī′lər), *adj.* having the shape of an ancient style; resembling a pen, pin, or peg. [1605–15; STYL(US) + -AR[1]]

sty·late (stī′lāt, -lit), *adj. Biol.* having a style. [1865–70; < NL *stylātus;* see STYLE, -ATE[1]]

style (stīl), *n., v.* **styled, styl·ing.** —*n.* **1.** a particular kind, sort, or type, as with reference to form, appearance, or character: *the baroque style; The style of the house was too austere for their liking.* **2.** a particular, distinctive, or characteristic mode of action or manner of acting: *They do these things in a grand style.* **3.** a mode of living, as with respect to expense or display. **4.** an elegant, fashionable, or luxurious mode of living: *to live in style.* **5.** a mode of fashion, as in dress, esp. good or approved fashion; elegance; smartness. **6.** the mode of expressing thought in writing or speaking by selecting and arranging words, considered with respect to clearness, effectiveness, euphony, or the like, that is characteristic of a group, period, person, personality, etc.: *to write in the style of Faulkner; a familiar style; a pompous, pedantic style.* **7.** those components or features of a literary composition that have to do with the form of expression rather than the content of the thought expressed: *His writing is all style and no substance.* **8.** manner or tone adopted in discourse or conversation: *a patronizing style of addressing others.* **9.** a particular, distinctive, or characteristic mode or form of construction or execution in any art or work: *Her painting is beginning to show a personal style.* **10.** a descriptive or distinguishing appellation, esp. a legal, official, or recognized title: *a firm trading under the style of Smith, Jones, & Co.* **11.** stylus (defs. 1, 2). **12.** the gnomon of a sundial. **13.** a method of reckoning time. Cf. **New Style, old style** (def. 2). **14.** *Zool.* a small, pointed process or part. **15.** *Bot.* a narrow, usually cylindrical and more or less filiform extension of the pistil, which, when present, bears the stigma at its apex. See diag. under **flower. 16.** the rules or customs of typography, punctuation, spelling, and related matters used by a newspaper, magazine, publishing house, etc., or in a specific publication. **17. go out of style,** to become unfashionable: *The jacket he's wearing went out of style ten years ago.* **18. in style,** fashionable. —*v.t.* **19.** to call by a given title or appellation; denominate; name; call: *The pope is styled His or Your Holiness.* **20.** to design or arrange in accordance with a given or new style: *to style an evening dress; to style one's hair.* **21.** to bring into conformity with a specific style or give a specific style to: *Please style this manuscript.* —*v.i.* **22.** to do decorative work with a style or stylus. [1250–1300; ME (n.) < L *stylus,* sp. var. of *stilus* tool for writing, hence, written composition, style; see STYLUS] —**style′less,** *adj.* —**style′less·ness,** *n.* —**style′like′,** *adj.*
—**Syn. 2.** method, approach. **5.** chic. See **fashion. 9.** touch, characteristic, mark. **18.** designate, address.

-style[1], a combining form of **style** (defs. 14, 15): *blastostyle.* Cf. **stylo-**[1].

-style[2], a combining form with the meanings "column," "columned," "having columns (of the kind specified)" used in the formation of compound words: *orthostyle; urostyle.* Cf. **stylo-**[2]. [< Gk *stŷlos* column or *-stylos* -columned, adj. deriv. of *stŷlos*]

style·book (stīl′bo͝ok′), *n.* **1.** a book containing rules of usage in typography, punctuation, etc., employed by printers, editors, and writers. **2.** a book featuring styles, fashions, or the rules of style. [1700–10; STYLE + BOOK]

styl·er (stī′lər), *n.* **1.** a person or thing that styles. **2.** an electric appliance for setting or styling the hair. [STYLE + -ER[1]]

style′ sheet′, a listing of the rules of usage in style employed by a publishing house or in a publishing project. Cf. **stylebook** (def. 1). [1930–35, *Amer.*]

sty·let (stī′lit), *n.* **1.** a stiletto or dagger. **2.** any similar sharp-pointed instrument. **3.** *Med.* **a.** a probe. **b.** a wire run through the length of a catheter, cannula, or needle to make it rigid or to clear it. [1690–1700; < F < MF *stilet* < It *stiletto* STILETTO; *-y-* < L *stylus.* See STYLE, STYLUS]

sty·li (stī′lī), *n.* a pl. of **stylus.**

sty·li·form (stī′lə fôrm′), *adj.* having the shape of an ancient style; stylar. [1570–80; < NL *stiliformis,* equiv. to L *stil(us)* STYLUS + -I- + *-formis* -FORM]

styl·ish (stī′lish), *adj.* characterized by or conforming to style or the fashionable standard; fashionably elegant; smart or chic: *She wore a very stylish gown to the inaugural ball.* [1775–85; STYLE + -ISH[1]] —**styl′ish·ly,** *adv.* —**styl′ish·ness,** *n.*

styl·ist (stī′list), *n.* **1.** a writer or speaker who is skilled in or who cultivates a literary style. **2.** a designer or consultant in a field subject to changes in style, esp. hairdressing, clothing, or interior decoration. **3.** a person who cultivates or maintains any particular style. [1785–95; STYLE + -IST]

sty·lis·tic (stī lis′tik), *adj.* of or pertaining to style. Also, **sty·lis′ti·cal.** [1855–60; STYLE + -ISTIC] —**sty·lis′ti·cal·ly,** *adv.*

sty·lis·tics (stī lis′tiks), *n.* (*used with a singular v.*) the study and description of the choices of linguistic expression that are characteristic of a group or an individual in specific communicative settings, esp. in literary works. [1840–50; see STYLISTIC, -ICS] —**sty·lis·ti·cian** (stī′li stish′ən), *n.*

sty·lite (stī′līt), *n. Eccles. Hist.* one of a class of solitary ascetics who lived on the top of high pillars or columns. [1630–40; < LGk *stylī́tēs,* equiv. to *stŷl(os)* pillar + *-ītēs* -ITE[1]] —**sty·lit·ic** (stī lit′ik), *adj.*

styl·ize (stī′līz), *v.t.,* **-ized, -iz·ing.** to design in or cause to conform to a particular style, as of representation or treatment in art; conventionalize. Also, *esp. Brit.,* **styl′ise.** [1895–1900; STYLE + -IZE] —**styl′i·za′tion,** *n.* —**styl′iz·er,** *n.*

stylo-[1], a combining form representing **style** or **styloid** in the formation of compound words: *stylography.* [comb. form repr. L *stilus.* See STYLUS, -O-]

stylo-[2], a combining form meaning "column," "pillar," "tube," used in the formation of compound words: *stylolite.* [< Gk, comb. form of *stŷlos* pillar]

sty·lo·bate (stī′lə bāt′), *n. Archit.* (in a classical temple) a course of masonry, part of the stereobate, forming the foundation for a colonnade, esp. the outermost colonnade. [1555–65; < L *stylobatēs, stylobata* < Gk *stylobátēs,* equiv. to *stylo-* STYLO-[2] + *-batēs* (*ba-* (base of *baínein* to step) + *-tēs* agent suffix)]

sty·lo·graph (stī′lə graf′, -gräf′), *n.* a fountain pen in which the writing point is a fine, hollow tube instead of a nib. Also called **sty′lograph′ic pen′.** [1865–70; STYLO-[1] + -GRAPH]

sty·lo·graph·ic (stī′lə graf′ik), *adj.* **1.** of or pertaining to a stylograph. **2.** of, pertaining to, or used in stylography. Also, **sty′lo·graph′i·cal.** [1800–10; STYLO-[1] + GRAPHIC] —**sty′lo·graph′i·cal·ly,** *adv.*

sty·log·ra·phy (stī log′rə fē), *n.* the art of writing, tracing, drawing, etc., with a style. [1830–40; STYLO-[1] + -GRAPHY]

sty·lo·hy·oid (stī′lō hī′oid), *adj., Anat.* of, pertaining to, or situated between the styloid process of the temporal bone and the hyoid bone. [1700–10; < NL *stylohyoīdeus.* See STYLO-[1], HYOID]

sty·loid (stī′loid), *adj.* **1.** *Bot.* resembling a style; slender and pointed. **2.** *Anat.* pertaining to a styloid process. [1605–15; < NL *styloidēs.* See STYLE, -OID]

sty′loid proc′ess, *Anat.* a long, spinelike process of a bone, esp. the projection from the base of the temporal bone. See diag. under **skull.** [1700–10]

sty·lo·lite (stī′lə līt′), *n. Geol.* an irregular columnar structure in certain limestones, the columns being approximately at right angles to the bedding planes. [1865–70; STYLO-[2] + -LITE] —**sty·lo·lit·ic** (stī′lə lit′ik), *adj.*

sty·lo·po·di·um (stī′lə pō′dē əm), *n., pl.* **-di·a** (-dē ə). *Bot.* a glandular disk or expansion surmounting the ovary and supporting the styles in plants of the parsley family. [1825–35; < NL; see STYLO-[1], -PODIUM]

sty·lus (stī′ləs), *n., pl.* **-li** (-lī), **-lus·es. 1.** an instrument of metal, bone, or the like, used by the ancients for writing on waxed tablets, having one end pointed for incising the letters and the other end blunt for rubbing out writing and smoothing the tablet. **2.** any of various pointed, pen-shaped instruments used in drawing, artwork, etc. **3.** *Audio.* **a.** Also called **cutting stylus.** a needle used for cutting grooves in making a disk recording to be played on a phonograph. **b.** a needle for reproducing the sounds of a phonograph record. **4.** any of various pointed wedges used to punch holes in paper or other material, as in writing Braille. **5.** any of various kinds of pens for tracing a line automatically, as on a recording seismograph or electrocardiograph. Also, **style** (for defs. 1, 2). [1720–30; < L: sp. var. of *stilus* stake, pointed writing instrument; sp. with *-y-* from fancied derivation < Gk *stŷlos* column]

sty·mie (stī′mē), *n., v.,* **-mied, -mie·ing.** —*n.* **1.** *Golf.* (on a putting green) an instance of a ball's lying on a direct line between the cup and the ball of an opponent about to putt. **2.** a situation or problem presenting such difficulties as to discourage or defeat any attempt to deal with or resolve it. —*v.t.* **3.** to hinder, block, or thwart. Also, **stymy, stimy.** [1855–60; orig. uncert.]
—**Syn. 3.** stump, mystify, frustrate, confound.

Stym·pha′li·an birds′ (stim fā′lē ən, -fāl′yən), *Class. Myth.* a flock of predacious birds of Arcadia that were driven away and killed by Hercules as one of his labors.

sty·my (stī′mē), *n., pl.* **-mies,** *v.t.,* **-mied, -my·ing.** stymie.

styp·sis (stip′sis), *n.* the employment or application of styptics. [1885–90; < LL *stypsis* < Gk *stŷpsis,* equiv. to *stŷp-* (var. s. of *stýphein* to contract) + *-sis* -SIS]

styp·tic (stip′tik), *adj.* Also, **styp′ti·cal. 1.** serving to contract organic tissue; astringent; binding. **2.** serving to check hemorrhage or bleeding, as a drug; hemostatic. —*n.* **3.** a styptic agent or substance. [1350–1400; ME < LL *stypticus* < Gk *stypikós* contractile, equiv. to *stŷp-* (see STYPSIS) + *-tikos* -TIC] —**styp·tic·i·ty** (stip tis′i tē), **styp′ti·cal·ness,** *n.*

styp′tic pen′cil, a pencil-shaped stick of a paste containing alum or a similar styptic agent, used to stanch the bleeding of minor cuts. [1930–35]

Styr (stēr; *Russ.* stir), *n.* a river in NW Ukraine, flowing N to the Pripet River. 300 mi. (480 km) long.

sty·ra·ca·ceous (stī′rə kā′shəs), *adj.* belonging to the Styracaceae, the storax family of plants. Cf. **storax family.** [< NL *Styracace(ae)* (see STORAX, -ACEAE) + -OUS]

sty′ra·lyl ac′etate (stī′rə lil, stēr′ə-), *Chem.* See **methylphenylcarbinyl acetate.** [< NL *styrax* (see STORAX) + -AL[3] + -YL]

sty·rene (stī′rēn, stēr′ēn), *n. Chem.* a colorless, water-insoluble liquid, C_8H_8, having a penetrating aromatic odor, usually prepared from ethylene and benzene or ethylbenzene, that polymerizes to a clear transparent material and copolymerizes with other materials to form synthetic rubbers. Also called **cinnamene, phenylethylene, vinylbenzene.** Cf. **polystyrene.** [1880–85; *styr-* (shortened s. of STYRAX) + -ENE]

sty′rene res′in, *Chem.* a transparent thermoplastic resin formed by polymerizing styrene.

Styr·i·a (stēr′ē ə), *n.* a province in SE Austria: formerly a duchy. 1,187,512; 6327 sq. mi. (16,385 sq. km). *Cap.:* Graz. German, **Steiermark.**

Sty·ro·foam (stī′rə fōm′), *Trademark.* a brand of expanded plastic made from polystyrene.

Sty·ron (stī′rən), *n.* **William,** born 1925, U.S. author.

stythe (stīth, stīth), *n. Brit. Mining.* chokedamp. [1700–10; orig. uncert.]

Styx (stiks), *n. Class. Myth.* a river in the underworld, over which the souls of the dead were ferried by Charon, and by which the gods swore their most solemn oaths.

su-, var. of **sub-** before *sp: suspect.*

su·a·ble (so͞o′ə bəl), *adj.* liable to be sued; capable of being sued. [1615–25; SUE + -ABLE] —**su′a·bil′i·ty,** *n.* —**su′a·bly,** *adv.*

Suá·rez (swär′ez; *Sp.* swä′reth, -res), *n.* **Fran·cis·co** (fran sis′kō; *Sp.* främ thēs′kô, -sēs′-), 1548–1617, Spanish theologian and philosopher.

sua·sion (swā′zhən), *n.* **1.** the act of advising, urging, or attempting to persuade; persuasion. **2.** an instance of this; a persuasive effort. [1325–75; ME < L *suāsiōn-* (s. of *suāsiō*), equiv. to *suās(us),* ptp. of *suādēre* to advise (*suād-,* verb s. + *-tus* ptp. suffix, with *dt* > *s*) + *-iōn-* -ION] —**sua·sive** (swā′siv), **sua·so·ry** (swā′sə rē), *adj.* —**sua′sive·ly,** *adv.* —**sua′sive·ness,** *n.*

suave (swäv), *adj.,* **suav·er, suav·est.** (of persons or their manner, speech, etc.) smoothly agreeable or polite; agreeably or blandly urbane. [1495–1505; < F < L *suāvis* SWEET] —**suave′ly,** *adv.* —**suave′ness,** *n.*
—**Syn.** sophisticated, worldly.

sua·vi·ter in mo·do, for·ti·ter in re (swä′wi ter′ in mō′dō, fôr′ti ter′ in rā′; *Eng.* swav′i tər in mō′dō, fôr′ti tər in rē′, fôr′-, swä′vi tər), *Latin.* gently in manner, firmly in action.

suav·i·ty (swä′vi tē, swav′i-), *n., pl.* **-ties. 1.** a suave or smoothly agreeable quality. **2. suavities,** suave or courteous actions or manners; amenities. Also, **suave′-**

CONCISE ETYMOLOGY KEY: <, descended or borrowed from; >, whence; b., blend of, blended; c., cognate with; cf., compare; deriv., derivative; equiv., equivalent; imit., imitative; obl., oblique; r., replacing; s., stem; sp., spelling, spelled; resp., respelling, respelled; trans., translation; ?, origin unknown; *, unattested; ‡, probably earlier than. See the full key inside the front cover.

ness. [1400–50; late ME < L *suāvitās* pleasantness, equiv. to *suāv(is)* SWEET + *-itās* -ITY]

sub (sub), *n., v.,* **subbed, sub·bing.** *Informal.* —*n.* **1.** a submarine. **2.** a substitute. **3.** a submarine sandwich. See **hero sandwich. 4.** a subcontractor. **5.** a sublieutenant. **6.** a subordinate. **7.** a subaltern. **8.** *Brit.* an advance against one's wages, esp. one granted as a subsistence allowance. **9.** *Photog.* a substratum. —*v.i.* **10.** to act as a substitute for another. —*v.t.* **11.** *Photog.* to coat (a film or plate) with a substratum. [by shortening of words prefixed with SUB-]
—**Regional Variation. 3.** See **hero sandwich.**

SUB, supplemental unemployment benefits.

sub-, **1.** a prefix occurring originally in loanwords from Latin (*subject; subtract; subvert; subsidy*); on this model, freely attached to elements of any origin and used with the meaning "under," "below," "beneath" (*subalpine; substratum*), "slightly," "imperfectly," "nearly" (*subcolumnar; subtropical*), "secondary," "subordinate" (*subcommittee; subplot*). **2.** *Chem.* **a.** a prefix indicating a basic compound: *subacetate; subcarbonate; subnitrate.* **b.** a prefix indicating that the element is present in a relatively small proportion, i.e., in a low oxidation state: *subchloride; suboxide.* Also, **su-, suc-, suf-, sug-, sum-, sup-, sur-, sus-.** [< L, comb. form repr. *sub* (prep.); akin to Gk *hypó*; see HYPO-]
—**Note.** The lists at the bottom of this and following pages provide the spelling, syllabification, and stress for words whose meanings may be easily inferred by combining the meanings of SUB- and an attached base word, or base word plus a suffix. Appropriate parts of speech are also shown. Words prefixed by SUB- that have special meanings or uses are entered in their proper alphabetical places in the main vocabulary or as derived forms run on at the end of a main vocabulary entry.

sub., **1.** subordinated. **2.** subscription. **3.** substitute. **4.** suburb. **5.** suburban. **6.** subway.

sub·ac·e·tate (sub as′i tāt′), *n. Chem.* a basic salt of acetic acid. [1810–20; SUB- + ACETATE]

sub·ac·id (sub as′id), *adj.* **1.** slightly or moderately acid or sour: *a subacid fruit.* **2.** (of a person or a person's speech, temper, etc.) somewhat biting or sharp. [1660–70; SUB- + ACID] —**sub·a·cid·i·ty** (sub′ə sid′i tē), **sub·ac′id·ness,** *n.* —**sub·ac′id·ly,** *adv.*

sub·a·cute (sub′ə kyōōt′), *adj.* somewhat or moderately acute. [1745–55; SUB- + ACUTE] —**sub′a·cute′ly,** *adv.*

sub′acute scle·ros′ing pan′en·ceph·a·li′tis (skli rō′sing pan′en sef′ə lī′tis, pan′-), *Pathol.* a rare infection of the central nervous system caused by the measles virus, occurring in children and adolescents several years after a measles attack and characterized by progressive personality changes, seizures, and muscular incoordination. *Abbr.:* SSPE [1965–70; SCLEROS(IS) + -ING²; PAN- + ENCEPHALITIS]

su·ba·dar (sōō′bə där′), *n.* (formerly, in India) **1.** a provincial governor of the Mogul empire. **2.** the chief native officer of a company of native troops in the British Indian Service. Also, **su′bah·dar′.** [1665–75; < Urdu < Pers, equiv. to *ṣūba* province + *dār* holding, holder]

sub·aer·i·al (sub âr′ē əl, -ā ēr′ē əl), *adj.* located or occurring on the surface of the earth. [1825–35; SUB- + AERIAL] —**sub·aer′i·al·ly,** *adv.*

sub·a·gent (sub ā′jənt), *n.* **1.** a person whose duties as an agent are delegated to him or her by another agent. **2.** a person who works for or under the supervision of an agent. [1810–20, *Amer.*; SUB- + AGENT]

sub·al·i·men·ta·tion (sub′al ə men tā′shən), *n. Pathol.* hypoalimentation. [SUB- + ALIMENTATION]

sub·al·pine (sub al′pīn, -pin), *adj.* **1.** pertaining to the regions at the foot of the Alps. **2.** *Bot.* growing on mountains below the limit of tree growth, and above the foothill, or montane, zone. [1650–60; SUB- + ALPINE]

sub·al·tern (sub ôl′tərn *or, esp. for 3, 6,* sub′əl tûrn′), *adj.* **1.** lower in rank; subordinate: *a subaltern employee.* **2.** *Brit. Mil.* noting a commissioned officer below the rank of captain. **3.** *Logic.* **a.** denoting the relation of one proposition to another when the first proposition is implied by the second but the second is not implied by the first. **b.** (in Aristotelian logic) denoting the relation of a particular proposition to a universal proposition having the same subject, predicate, and quality. **c.** of or pertaining to a proposition having either of these relations to another. —*n.* **4.** a person who has a subordinate position. **5.** *Brit. Mil.* a commissioned officer below the rank of captain. **6.** *Logic.* a subaltern proposition. [1575–85; < LL *subalternus,* equiv. to *sub-* SUB- + *alternus* ALTERNATE] —**sub′al·ter′ni·ty,** *n.*

sub·al·ter·nate (sub ôl′tər nit, -al′-), *adj.* **1.** subordinate. **2.** *Bot.* placed singly along an axis, but tending to become grouped oppositely. [1400–50; late ME < ML *subalternātus* (ptp. of *subalternāre* to subordinate), equiv. to *subaltern(us)* SUBALTERN + *-ātus* -ATE¹] —**sub·al·ter·na·tion** (sub ôl′tər nā′shən, -al′-), *n.*

sub·ant·arc·tic (sub′ant ärk′tik, -är′tik), *adj.* of, pertaining to, similar to, or being the region immediately north of the Antarctic Circle; subpolar. [1870–75; SUB- + ANTARCTIC]

sub·ap·i·cal (sub ap′i kəl, -ā′pi-), *adj. Anat.* located below the apex. [1840–50; SUB- + APICAL] —**sub·ap′i·cal·ly,** *adv.*

sub·a·quat·ic (sub′ə kwat′ik, -ə kwot′-), *adj.* **1.** living or growing partly on land, partly in water. **2.** under water. [1780–90; SUB- + AQUATIC]

sub·a·que·ous (sub ā′kwē əs, -ak′wē-), *adj.* **1.** existing or situated under water; underwater. **2.** occurring or performed under water. **3.** used under water. [1670–80; SUB- + AQUEOUS]

sub·a·rach·noid (sub′ə rak′noid), *adj. Anat.* of, pertaining to, or situated below the arachnoid membrane. [1830–40; SUB- + ARACHNOID]

subarach′noid block′. See **spinal block.**

sub·arc·tic (sub ärk′tik, -är′tik), *adj.* of, pertaining to, similar to, or being the region immediately south of the Arctic Circle; subpolar. [1850–55; SUB- + ARCTIC]

Subarc′tic Cur′rent. See **Aleutian Current.**

sub·ar·e·a (sub′âr′ē ə), *n.* a subsidiary area, field, study, or the like. [SUB- + AREA] —**sub·ar′e·al,** *adj.*

sub·ar·id (sub ar′id), *adj.* moderately arid. [1910–15; SUB- + ARID]

sub·as·sem·ble (sub′ə sem′bəl), *v.t.,* **-bled, -bling.** to assemble a basic unit of (a larger assembly). [back formation from SUBASSEMBLY]

sub·as·sem·bly (sub′ə sem′blē), *n., pl.* **-blies.** a structural assembly, as of electronic or machine parts, forming part of a larger assembly. [1925–30; SUB- + ASSEMBLY]

sub·as·trin·gent (sub′ə strin′jənt), *adj.* slightly astringent. [1685–95; SUB- + ASTRINGENT]

sub·at·mos·pher·ic (sub′at məs fer′ik, -fēr′-), *adj.* (of a quantity) having a value lower than that of the atmosphere: *subatmospheric temperatures.* [1940–45; SUB- + ATMOSPHERIC]

sub·at·om (sub at′əm), *n. Chem.* any component of an atom. [1875–80; SUB- + ATOM]

sub·a·tom·ic (sub′ə tom′ik), *adj. Physics.* **1.** of or pertaining to a process that occurs within an atom. **2.** noting or pertaining to a particle or particles contained in an atom, as electrons, protons, or neutrons. [1900–05; SUB- + ATOMIC]

sub·au·di·tion (sub′ô dish′ən), *n.* **1.** an act or instance of understanding or mentally supplying something not expressed. **2.** something mentally supplied; understood or implied meaning. [1650–60; < LL *subauditiōn-* (s. of *subauditiō*) understanding, i.e., supplying an omitted word. See SUB-, AUDITION]

sub·au·ric·u·lar (sub′ô rik′yə lər), *adj. Anat.* situated below the ear. [SUB- + AURICULAR]

sub·ax·il·la·ry (sub ak′sə ler′ē), *adj. Bot.* situated or placed beneath an axil. [1760–70; SUB- + AXILLARY]

sub·base (sub′bās′), *n.* **1.** *Archit.* the lowest part of a base, as of a column, that consists of two or more horizontal members. **2.** *Math.* a collection of subsets of a topological space having the property that every open set of a given topology can be written as the union of intersections of finite numbers of sets in the collection. Cf. **base¹** (def. 13b). [1820–30; SUB- + BASE¹] —**sub·ba′sal,** *adj.*

sub·base·ment (sub′bās′mənt), *n.* a basement or one of a series of basements below the main basement of a building. [1900–05; SUB- + BASEMENT]

sub·bing (sub′ing), *n. Photog.* **1.** the act or process of applying a substratum. **2.** the material used for a substratum. [SUB + -ING¹]

sub·branch (sub′branch′, -bränch′), *n.* a subordinate branch or a branch of a branch, as of a bank, business, or the like. [1855–60; SUB- + BRANCH]

sub·cab·i·net (sub kab′ə nit, sub′kab′-), *n.* **1.** a group of advisers ranking below the cabinet level, chosen by a chief executive usually from members of the various executive departments. —*adj.* **2.** of or pertaining to a subcabinet. [1950–55; SUB- + CABINET]

sub·car·bide (sub kär′bīd), *n. Chem.* a carbide containing less than the normal proportion of carbon. [SUB- + CARBIDE]

sub·car·ti·lag·i·nous (sub′kär tl aj′ə nəs), *adj. Anat., Zool.* **1.** partially or incompletely cartilaginous. **2.** situated below or beneath cartilage. [1535–45; SUB- + CARTILAGINOUS]

sub·cas·ing (sub kā′sing, sub′kā′-), *n. Carpentry.* a rough casing for a doorway or window. [SUB- + CASING]

sub·cat·e·go·ry (sub kat′ə gôr′ē, -gōr′ē), *n., pl.* **-ries.** a subordinate category or a division of a category. [SUB- + CATEGORY]

sub·ce·les·tial (sub′sə les′chəl), *adj.* **1.** being beneath the heavens; terrestrial. **2.** mundane; worldly. —*n.* **3.** a subcelestial being. [1555–65; SUB- + CELESTIAL]

sub·cel·lar (sub′sel′ər), *n.* a cellar below the main cellar. [1850–55; SUB- + CELLAR]

sub·cel·lu·lar (sub sel′yə lər), *adj. Biol.* **1.** contained within a cell. **2.** at a level of organization lower than the cellular. [1945–50; SUB- + CELLULAR]

sub·cen·ter (sub′sen′tər), *n.* a secondary or subordinate center, as in the location of a business. [1920–25; SUB- + CENTER]

sub·cen·tral (sub sen′trəl), *adj.* near or almost to the center. [1815–25; SUB- + CENTRAL] —**sub·cen′tral·ly,** *adv.*

subch., subchapter.

sub·chair·man (sub châr′mən), *n., pl.* **-men.** a subordinate or substitute chairman. [SUB- + CHAIRMAN]
—**Usage.** See **chairperson.**

sub·chap·ter (sub′chap′tər), *n.* a subdivision esp. of a body of laws. [SUB- + CHAPTER]

sub·chas·er (sub′chā′sər), *n.* See **submarine chaser.** [1915–20; SUB + CHASER¹]

sub·chlo·ride (sub klôr′īd, -id, -klōr′-), *n. Chem.* a chloride containing a relatively small proportion of chlorine, as mercurous chloride. [SUB- + CHLORIDE]

sub·cinc·to·ri·um (sub′singk tôr′ē əm, -tōr′-), *n., pl.* **-to·ri·a** (-tôr′ē ə, -tōr′-). *Rom. Cath. Ch.* an embroidered silk vestment resembling, but somewhat broader than, a maniple, worn by the pope on solemn occasions. Also, **succinctorium.** [1680–90; < LL *subcinctōrium, succinctōrium,* equiv. to *sub-* or *suc-* SUB- + *cing(ere)* to gird + *-tōrium* -TORY²; see -IUM]

sub·class (sub′klas′, -kläs′), *n.* **1.** a primary division of a class. **2.** a subordinate class, esp. one of persons who lack the rights and privileges of the primary class: *a subclass of alien workers.* **3.** *Biol.* a category of related orders within a class. —*v.t.* **4.** to place in a subclass. [1810–20; SUB- + CLASS]

sub·clas·si·fy (sub klas′ə fī′), *v.t.,* **-fied, -fy·ing.** to arrange in subclasses. [1905–10; SUB- + CLASSIFY] —**sub′clas·si·fi·ca′tion,** *n.*

sub·cla·vate (sub klā′vāt), *adj. Zool.* somewhat clubshaped. [1820–30; SUB- + CLAVATE]

sub·cla·vi·an (sub klā′vē ən), *Anat.* —*adj.* **1.** situated or extending beneath the clavicle, as certain arteries or veins. **2.** pertaining to such an artery, vein, or the like. [1640–50; < NL *subclāvi(us)* SUBCLAVIUS + -AN]

subcla′vian ar′tery, *Anat.* either of a pair of arteries, one on each side of the body, that carry the main supply of blood to the arms. [1680–90]

subcla′vian vein′, *Anat.* either of a pair of veins, one on each side of the body, that return blood from the arms to the heart. [1760–70]

sub·cla·vi·us (sub klā′vē əs), *n., pl.* **-vi·i** (-vē ī′). *Anat.* a small shoulder muscle, the action of which assists in depressing the shoulder. [1695–1705; < NL *subclāvius* (*musculus*) subclavian (muscle), equiv. to L *sub-* SUB- + *clāvi(s)* key (see CLAVICLE) + *-us* adj. suffix]

sub·cli·max (sub klī′maks), *n. Ecol.* the development of an ecological community to a stage short of the expected climax because of some factor, as repeated fires in a forest, that arrests the normal succession. [1930–35; SUB- + CLIMAX]

CONCISE PRONUNCIATION KEY: act, cāpe, dâre, pärt; set, ēqual; *if,* ice; ox, ōver, ôrder, oil, bŏŏk, bōōt, out; up, ûrge; child; sing; shoe; thin, *th*at; zh as in *treasure.* ə = *a* as in *alone, e* as in *system, i* as in *easily, o* as in *gallop, u* as in *circus;* ᵊ as in *fire* (fīᵊr), *hour* (ouᵊr). l and n can serve as syllabic consonants, as in *cradle* (krād′l), and *button* (but′n). See the full key inside the front cover.

sub·ab′bot, *n.*
sub′a·bil′i·ty, *n., pl.* **-ties.**
sub·ab′so·lute′, *adj.*
sub′ac·a·dem′ic, *adj.*
sub′ac·a·dem′i·cal, *adj.;* **-ly,** *adv.*
sub′ac·count′, *n.*
sub′ac·e·tab′u·lar, *adj.*
sub′a·cid′u·lous, *adj.*
sub·ac′rid, *adj.;* **-ly,** *adv.;* **-ness,** *n.*
sub′a·crid′i·ty, *n.*
sub′a·cro·drome′, *adj.*
sub′a·crod′ro·mous, *adj.*
sub′a·cro′mi·al, *adj.*
sub′a·cu′mi·nate, *adj.*
sub′a·cu′mi·na′tion, *n.*
sub·ad′di·tive, *adj.;* **-ly,** *adv.*
sub′ad·ja′cent, *adj.;* **-ly,** *adv.*
sub′ad·min′is·trate′, *v.t.,* **-trat·ed, -trat·ing.**
sub′ad·min′is·tra′tion, *n.*
sub′ad·min′is·tra′tive, *adj.;* **-ly,** *adv.*
sub′ad·min′is·tra′tor, *n.*
sub′ad·o·les′cent, *adj., n.*
sub′a·dult′, *adj., n.;* **-ness,** *n.*
sub·ad′vo·cate, *n.*
sub·aer′ate, *v.t.,* **-at·ed, -at·ing.**
sub′aer·a′tion, *n.*
sub·af′flu·ence, *n.*
sub·af′flu·ent, *adj.;* **-ly,** *adv.*
sub′age′, *n.*
sub·a′gen·cy, *n., pl.* **-cies.**
sub·ag′gre·gate, *adj., n.;* **-ly,** *adv.*
sub′ag·gre·ga′tion, *n.*
sub·ag′gre·ga′tive, *adj.*
sub·a′la·ry, *adj.*
sub·a′late, *adj.*
sub·a′lat·ed, *adj.*
sub′al·ge·bra′ic, *adj.*
sub′al·ge·bra′i·cal, *adj.;* **-ly,** *adv.*
sub·al′ge·bra′ist, *n.*
sub′al·li′ance, *n.*
sub′al·lo·ca′tion, *n.*
sub·al′mon·er, *n.*
sub·a′nal, *adj.*
sub′an·co′ne·al, *adj.*
sub-An′de·an, *adj.*
sub·an′gu·lar, *adj.;* **-ly,** *adv.;* **-ness,** *n.*
sub′an·gu·lar′i·ty, *n., pl.* **-ties.**
sub·an′gu·late, *adj.;* **-ly,** *adv.*
sub·an′gu·lat′ed, *adj.*
sub·an·gu·la′tion, *n.*
sub′an·tique′, *adj.;* **-ly,** *adv.;* **-ness,** *n.*
sub′an·tiq′ui·ty, *n., pl.* **-ties.**
sub′ap·par′ent, *adj.;* **-ly,** *adv.;* **-ness,** *n.*
sub′ap·pear′ance, *n.*
sub′ap·pressed′, *adj.*
sub′ap·pro·ba′tion, *n.*
sub·ap′pro·ba′tive, *adj.;* **-ness,** *n.*
sub′ap·pro′ba·to′ry, *adj.*
sub′ar·bo′re·al, *adj.*
sub′ar·bo′re·ous, *adj.*
sub′ar·bo·res′cence, *n.*
sub′ar·bo·res′cent, *adj.*
sub′ar·che·spo′ri·al, *adj.*
sub·ar′chi·tect′, *n.*
sub·ar′cu·ate, *adj.*
sub·ar′cu·at′ed, *adj.*
sub·ar′mor, *n.*
sub′a·rous′al, *n.*
sub′ar·te′sian, *adj.*
sub·ar′ti·cle, *n.*
sub′ar·tic′u·late, *adj.;* **-ly,** *adv.;* **-ness,** *n.*
sub′ar·tic′u·la′tion, *n.*
sub′ar·tic′u·la′tive, *adj.*
sub′ar·y·te′noid, *adj.*
sub′ar·y·te·noi′dal, *adj.*
sub′as·cend′ing, *adj.*
sub′as·sem′blage, *n.*
sub′as·so′ci·a′tion, *n.*
sub′as·so′ci·a′tion·al, *adj.*
sub′as·so′ci·a′tive, *adj.;* **-ly,** *adv.*
sub′as·trag′a·lar, *adj.*
sub·as′tral, *adj.*
sub′-At·lan′tic, *adj.*
sub′at·ten′u·ate, *adj.*
sub′at·ten′u·at′ed, *adj.*
sub′at·ten′u·a′tion, *n.*
sub·at′tor′ney, *n., pl.* **-neys.**
sub·at·tor′ney·ship′, *n.*
sub′au·di·bil′i·ty, *n.*
sub·au′di·ble, *adj.;* **-ble·ness,** *n.;* **-bly,** *adv.*
sub·au′di·tor, *n.*
sub·au′ral, *adj.;* **-ly,** *adv.*
sub·au·ric′u·late, *adj.*
sub′au·to·mat′ic, *adj.*
sub′au·to·mat′i·cal·ly, *adv.*
sub·av′er·age, *adj.;* **-ly,** *adv.*
sub·ax′i·al, *adj.;* **-ly,** *adv.*
sub·ax′ile, *adj.*
sub·bail′ie, *n.*
sub·bail′iff, *n.*
sub·bail′i·wick, *n.*
sub·bal′last, *n.*
sub′band′, *n.*
sub′bank′, *n.*

sub·clin·i·cal (sub klin′i kəl), *adj. Med.* pertaining to an early stage of a disease; having no noticeable clinical symptoms. [1930–35; SUB- + CLINICAL]

sub·co·lum·nar (sub′kə lum′nər), *adj.* almost or imperfectly columnar. [SUB- + COLUMNAR]

sub·com·mit·tee (sub′kə mit′ē), *n.* a secondary committee appointed out of a main committee. [1600–10; SUB- + COMMITTEE]

sub·com·mu·ni·ty (sub′kə myo͞o′ni tē, sub′kə-myo͞o′-), *n., pl.* **-ties.** a self-contained community usually within the suburbs of a large urban area. [1965–70; SUB- + COMMUNITY]

sub·com·pact (sub kom′pakt), *n.* an automobile that is smaller than a compact. Also called **sub′compact car′.** [1965–70; SUB- + COMPACT[1]]

sub·com·pa·ny (sub′kum′pə nē), *n., pl.* **-nies.** See **subsidiary company.** [SUB- + COMPANY]

sub·con·scious (sub kon′shəs), *adj.* **1.** existing or operating in the mind beneath or beyond consciousness: *the subconscious self.* Cf. **preconscious, unconscious. 2.** imperfectly or not wholly conscious: *subconscious motivations.* —*n.* **3.** the totality of mental processes of which the individual is not aware; unreportable mental activities. [1825–35; SUB- + CONSCIOUS] —**sub·con′·scious·ly,** *adv.* —**sub·con′scious·ness,** *n.*

sub·con·tig·u·ous (sub′kən tig′yo͞o əs), *adj.* almost touching; nearly contiguous. [SUB- + CONTIGUOUS]

sub·con·ti·nent (sub kon′tn ənt, sub′kon′-), *n.* **1.** a large, relatively self-contained landmass forming a subdivision of a continent: *the subcontinent of India.* **2.** a large landmass, as Greenland, that is smaller than any of the usually recognized continents. [1860–65; SUB- + CONTINENT] —**sub·con·ti·nen·tal** (sub′kon tn en′tl), *adj.*

sub·con·tract (*n.* sub kon′trakt, sub′kon′-; *v.* sub′kən trakt′), *Law.* —*n.* **1.** a contract by which one agrees to render services or to provide materials necessary for the performance of another contract. —*v.t.* **2.** to make a subcontract for. —*v.i.* **3.** to make a subcontract. [1595–1605; SUB- + CONTRACT]

sub·con·trac·tor (sub kon′trak tər, sub′kon′-, sub′kən trak′tər), *n.* **1.** *Law.* a person who or business that contracts to provide some service or material necessary for the performance of another's contract. **2.** a person or business firm contracted to do part of another's work. [1835–45; SUB- + CONTRACTOR]

sub·con·tra·ry (sub kon′trer ē), *n., pl.* **-ries.** *Logic.* one of two propositions that can both be true but cannot both be false. [1595–1605; < ML *subcontrārius,* LL (see SUB-, CONTRARY), orig. as trans. of Gk *hypenantíos*]

sub·cor·ti·cal (sub kôr′ti kəl), *adj. Anat.* situated beneath the cortex. [1805–15; SUB- + CORTICAL] —**sub·cor′ti·cal·ly,** *adv.*

sub·cos·ta (sub kos′tə, -kô′stə), *n., pl.* **-cos·tae** (-kos′tē, -kô′stē). a longitudinal vein in the anterior portion of the wing of an insect. [1860–65; < NL; see SUB-, COSTA] —**sub·cos′tal,** *adj.*

sub·cov·er (sub′kuv′ər), *n. Math.* a set of subsets of a cover of a given set that also is a cover of the set. [SUB- + COVER]

sub·crit·i·cal (sub krit′i kəl), *adj.* **1.** *Physics.* pertaining to a state, value, or quantity that is less than critical, esp. to a mass of radioactive material. **2.** being of less than critical importance. [1940–45; SUB- + CRITICAL]

sub·crus·tal (sub krus′tl), *adj. Geol.* situated or occurring below the crust of the earth. [1895–1900; SUB- + CRUSTAL]

sub·cul·ture (*v.* sub kul′chər; *n.* sub′kul′chər), *v.,* **-tured, -tur·ing,** *n.* —*v.t.* **1.** *Bacteriol.* to cultivate (a bacterial strain) again on a new medium. —*n.* **2.** *Bacteriol.* a culture derived in this manner. **3.** *Sociol.* **a.** the cultural values and behavioral patterns distinctive of a particular group in a society. **b.** a group having social, economic, ethnic, or other traits distinctive enough to distinguish it from others within the same culture or society. [1895–1900; SUB- + CULTURE] —**sub·cul′tur·al,** *adj.* —**sub·cul′tur·al·ly,** *adv.*

sub·cur·rent (sub′kûr′ənt, -kur′-), *n.* a not clearly revealed or formulated direction of thought, intention, action, etc., underlying what is manifested: *His words, though ostensibly friendly, betrayed a subcurrent of hostility.* [1900–05; SUB- + CURRENT]

sub·cu·ta·ne·ous (sub′kyo͞o tā′nē əs), *adj.* **1.** situated or lying under the skin, as tissue. **2.** performed or introduced under the skin, as an injection by a syringe. **3.** living below the several layers of the skin, as certain parasites. Also, **sub·der·mal** (sub dûr′məl), **sub·der′·mic.** [1645–55; < LL *subcutāneus.* See SUB-, CUTANEOUS] —**sub′cu·ta′ne·ous·ly,** *adv.* —**sub′cu·ta′ne·ous·ness,** *n.*

sub·cu·tis (sub kyo͞o′tis), *n. Anat.* the deeper layer of the dermis, containing mostly fat and connective tissue. [1895–1900; SUB- + CUTIS]

sub·dea·con (sub dē′kən, sub′dē′-), *n.* a member of the clerical order next below that of deacon. [1275–1325; ME *subdecon, -dekene* < LL *subdiāconus.* See SUB-, DEACON]

sub·dea·con·ate (sub dē′kə nit, -nāt′), *n.* subdiaconate. [1875–80; SUBDEACON + -ATE[3]]

sub·deb (sub′deb′), *n. Informal.* **1.** a subdebutante. **2.** any girl in her teens. [1915–20; shortened form]

sub·deb·u·tante (sub deb′yo͝o tänt′, -yə-), *n.* a young woman who has not yet made her debut into society. [1915–20; SUB- + DEBUTANTE]

sub·de·lir·i·um (sub′di lēr′ē əm), *n., pl.* **-lir·i·ums, -lir·i·a** (-lēr′ē ə). *Med.* a mild delirium with lucid intervals. [SUB- + DELIRIUM]

sub·de·riv·a·tive (sub′di riv′ə tiv), *n.* a word derived from a derivative. [SUB- + DERIVATIVE]

sub·di·ac·o·nal (sub′dī ak′ə nl), *adj.* of or pertaining to a subdeacon. [1840–50; SUB- + DIACONAL]

sub·di·ac·o·nate (sub′dī ak′ə nit, -nāt′), *n.* **1.** the office or dignity of a subdeacon. **2.** a body of subdeacons. Also, **subdeaconate.** [1715–25; SUB- + DIACONATE]

sub·dis·trict (sub′dis′trikt), *n.* **1.** a division of a district. —*v.t.* **2.** to divide into subdistricts. [1810–20; SUB- + DISTRICT]

sub·di·vide (sub′di vīd′, sub′di vīd′), *v.,* **-vid·ed, -vid·ing.** —*v.t.* **1.** to divide (that which has already been divided) into smaller parts; divide again after a first division. **2.** to divide into parts. **3.** to divide (a plot, tract of land, etc.) into building lots. —*v.i.* **4.** to become separated into divisions. [1400–50; late ME < LL *subdividere.* See SUB-, DIVIDE] —**sub′di·vid′a·ble,** *adj.* —**sub′di·vid′er,** *n.*

sub·di·vi·sion (sub′di vizh′ən), *n.* **1.** the act or fact of subdividing. **2.** a product of subdividing, as a section of a department. **3.** a portion of land divided into lots for real-estate development. **4.** *Bot., Mycol.* a category of related classes within a division or phylum. [1545–55; < LL *subdīvisiōn-* (s. of *subdīvisiō*), equiv. to *subdīvis(us)* (ptp. of *subdīvidere* to SUBDIVIDE) + *-iōn-* -ION]

sub·dom·i·nant (sub dom′ə nənt), *n.* **1.** *Music.* the fourth tone of a diatonic scale, next below the dominant. —*adj.* **2.** less than or not quite dominant. [1785–95; SUB- + DOMINANT]

sub·du·al (səb do͞o′əl, -dyo͞o′-), *n.* **1.** an act or instance of subduing. **2.** the state of being subdued. [1665–75; SUBDUE + -AL[2]]

sub·duct (səb dukt′), *v.t.* **1.** to take away; subtract. **2.** to withdraw; remove. [1565–75; < L *subductus,* ptp. of *subdūcere* to draw up, withdraw (*sub-* SUB- + *dūcere* to lead), equiv. to *subduc-* ptp. s. + *-tus* ptp. suffix]

sub·duc·tion (səb duk′shən), *n.* **1.** an act or instance of subducting; subtraction or withdrawal. **2.** *Geol.* the process by which collision of the earth's crustal plates results in one plate's being drawn down or overridden by another, localized along the juncture (**subduc′tion zone′**) of two plates. [1570–80; < L *subductiōn-,* s. of *subductiō* pulling up, computation; see SUBDUCT, -ION]

sub·due (səb do͞o′, -dyo͞o′), *v.t.,* **-dued, -du·ing. 1.** to conquer and bring into subjection: *Rome subdued Gaul.* **2.** to overpower by superior force; overcome. **3.** to bring under mental or emotional control, as by persuasion or intimidation; render submissive. **4.** to repress (feelings, impulses, etc.). **5.** to bring (land) under cultivation: *to subdue the wilderness.* **6.** to reduce the intensity, force, or vividness of (sound, light, color, etc.); tone down; soften. **7.** to allay (inflammation, infection, etc.). [1350–1400; ME *so(b)duen, so(b)dewen* < AF **soduer* to overcome, OF *soduire* to deceive, seduce < L *subdūcere* to withdraw (see SUBDUCT); meaning in E (and AF) < L *subdere* to place beneath, subdue] —**sub·du′a·ble,** *adj.* —**sub·du′a·ble·ness,** *n.* —**sub·du′a·bly,** *adv.* —**sub·du′er,** *n.* —**sub·du′ing·ly,** *adv.*
—**Syn. 1.** subjugate, vanquish. See **defeat. 3.** tame, break, discipline. **3, 4.** suppress. —**Ant. 4.** awaken, arouse. **6.** intensify.

sub·dued (səb do͞od′, -dyo͞od′), *adj.* **1.** quiet; inhibited; repressed; controlled: *After the argument he was much more subdued.* **2.** lowered in intensity or strength; reduced in fullness of tone, as a color or voice; muted: *subdued light; wallpaper in subdued greens.* **3.** (of land) not marked by any striking features, as mountains or cliffs: *a subdued landscape.* [1595–1605; SUBDUE + -ED[2]] —**sub·dued′ly,** *adv.* —**sub·dued′ness,** *n.*

sub·ed·it (sub ed′it), *v.t., v.i. Brit.* to copyedit. [1860–65; back formation from SUBEDITOR]

sub·ed·i·tor (sub ed′i tər), *n.* **1.** a subordinate or junior editor. **2.** *Brit.* a copyeditor. [1825–35; SUB- + EDITOR] —**sub·ed·i·to·ri·al** (sub′ed i tôr′ē əl, -tōr′-), *adj.* —**sub·ed′i·tor·ship′,** *n.*

sub·em·ploy·ment (sub′em ploi′mənt), *n.* insufficient employment in the labor force of a country, area, or industry, including unemployment and underemployment. [1965–70; SUB- + EMPLOYMENT]

sub·en·try (sub′en′trē), *n., pl.* **-tries.** an item shown or listed under a main entry, as in bookkeeping. [1890–95; SUB- + ENTRY]

sub·e·qua·to·ri·al (sub′ē kwə tôr′ē əl, -tōr′-, -ek-wə-), *adj.* of, pertaining to, or being a region near the equatorial region. [SUB- + EQUATORIAL]

su·ber (so͞o′bər), *n.* cork (def. 6). [1790–1800; < NL, L *sūber* cork oak, its outer bark]

su·be·re·ous (so͞o bēr′ē əs), *adj.* of the nature of or resembling cork; suberose. [1820–30; < L *sūbereus;* see SUBER, -EOUS]

su·ber·ic (so͞o ber′ik), *adj.* of or pertaining to cork. [1790–1800; < L *sūber* cork + -IC]

suber′ic ac′id, *Chem.* a crystalline dibasic acid, $C_8H_{14}O_4$, obtained esp. from suberin, castor oil, and cork: used chiefly in the preparation of plastics and plasticizers. [1800–10]

su·ber·in (so͞o′bər in), *n. Bot.* a waxlike, fatty substance, occurring in cork cell walls and in or between other cells, that on alkaline hydrolysis yields chiefly suberic acid. [1820–30; < L *sūber* cork + -IN[2]; cf. F *subérine*]

su·ber·i·za·tion (so͞o′bər ə zā′shən), *n. Bot.* the impregnation of cell walls with suberin, causing the formation of cork. [1880–85; SUBERIZE + -ATION]

su·ber·ize (so͞o′bə rīz′), *v.t.,* **-ized, -iz·ing.** *Bot.* to convert into cork tissue. Also, *esp. Brit.,* **su′ber·ise′.** [1880–85; < L *sūber* cork + -IZE]

su·ber·ose (so͞o′bə rōs′), *adj.* of the nature of cork; corklike; corky. Also, **su·ber·ous** (so͞o′bər əs). [1835–45; < NL *sūberōsus;* see SUBER, -OSE[1]]

sub·fam·i·ly (sub fam′ə lē, -fam′lē, sub′fam′ə lē, -fam′lē), *n., pl.* **-lies. 1.** *Biol.* a category of related genera within a family. **2.** *Ling.* (in the classification of related languages within a family) a category of a higher order than a branch. Cf. **branch** (def. 8), **family** (def. 14). [1825–35; SUB- + FAMILY]

sub·fe·brile (sub fē′brəl, -feb′rəl *or, esp. Brit.,* -fē′-bril), *adj.* pertaining to or marked by a temperature slightly above normal. [1895–1900; SUB- + FEBRILE]

sub·field (sub′fēld′), *n. Math.* a field that is a subset of a given field. [1945–50; SUB- + FIELD]

sub·fix (sub′fiks), *n.* subscript (def. 4). [1890–95; SUB- + *-fix,* extracted from PREFIX, SUFFIX, etc.]

sub·floor (sub′flôr′, -flōr′), *n.* a rough floor beneath a finished floor. Also called **blind floor.** [SUB- + FLOOR]

sub·freez·ing (sub′frē′zing), *adj.* below the freezing point. [1945–50; SUB- + FREEZING]

sub·fusc (sub fusk′), *adj.* **1.** subfuscous; dusky. **2.** dark and dull; dingy; drab: *a subfusc mining town.* [1755–65; < L *subfuscus* SUBFUSCOUS]

sub·fus·cous (sub fus′kəs), *adj.* slightly dark, dusky, or somber. [1750–60; < L *subfuscus,* equiv. to *sub-* SUB- + *fuscus* FUSCOUS]

sub·gen·re (sub′zhän′rə, -zhäN′Rᵊ), *n.* a lesser or subordinate genre: *a subgenre of popular fiction.* [SUB- + GENRE]

sub·ge·nus (sub jē′nəs), *n., pl.* **-gen·er·a** (-jen′ər ə), **-ge·nus·es.** *Anthropol., Biol.* a category of related species within a genus. [1805–15; < NL; see SUB-, GENUS] —**sub·ge·ner·ic** (sub′jə ner′ik), *adj.*

sub·gin·gi·val (sub′jin jī′vəl, sub jin′jə-), *adj.* being or occurring under the gums; esp., being or occurring in

CONCISE ETYMOLOGY KEY: <, descended or borrowed from; >, whence; b., blend of, blended; c., cognate with; cf., compare; deriv., derivative; equiv., equivalent; imit., imitative; obl., oblique; r., replacing; s., stem; sp., spelling, spelled; resp., respelling, respelled; trans., translation; ?, origin unknown; *, unattested; ‡, probably earlier than. See the full key inside the front cover.

sub′ba·sal′tic, *adj.*
sub′ba′sin, *n.*
sub′bat·tal′i·on, *n.*
sub·bea′dle, *n.*
sub·bi′as, *n.*
sub′block′, *n.*
sub·bran′chi·al, *adj.*
sub′breed′, *n.*
sub′bri·gade′, *n.*
sub·bro′ker, *n.*
sub·bro′mide, *n.*
sub·bron′chi·al, *adj.;* **-ly,** *adv.*
sub′bu′reau, *n., pl.* **-reaus, -reaux.**
sub·cae′cal, *adj.*
sub·cal·car′e·ous, *adj.*
sub′cal·lo′sal, *adj.*
sub·cam·pan′u·late, *adj.*
sub·can′cel·late′, *adj.*
sub·can′cel·lous, *adj.*
sub·can′did, *adj.;* **-ly,** *adv.;* **-ness,** *n.*
sub·cap′su·lar, *adj.*
sub·cap′tain, *n.*
sub·cap′tain·cy, *n., pl.* **-cies.**
sub·cap′tain·ship′, *n.*
sub·cap′tion, *n.*
sub·car·bo·na′ceous, *adj.*
sub·car′di·nal, *adj.;* **-ly,** *adv.*
sub·car′i·nate′, *adj.*
sub·car′i·nat′ed, *adj.*
sub′-Car·pa′thi·an, *adj.*
sub′case′, *n.*
sub′cash′, *n.*
sub′cash·ier′, *n.*
sub′ca·si′no, *n., pl.* **-nos.**
sub′cast′, *n.*
sub′caste′, *n.*
sub′cat·e·go·ri·za′tion, *n.*
sub′cause′, *n.*
sub·cav′i·ty, *n., pl.* **-ties.**
sub·ce′cal, *adj.*
sub′ceil′ing, *n.*
sub′cell′, *n.*
sub′cer·e·bel′lar, *adj.*
sub·cer′e·bral, *adj.*
sub·cham′ber·er, *n.*
sub·chan′cel, *n.*
sub′char′ter, *n., v.*
sub·che′li·form′, *adj.*
sub′chief′, *n.*
sub·chon′dral, *adj.*
sub′cho′ri·oid′, *adj.*
sub′cho·ri·oi′dal, *adj.*
sub′cho·ri·on′ic, *adj.*
sub·cho′roid, *adj.*
sub′cho·roi′dal, *adj.*
sub-Chris′tian, *adj.*
sub′chron′ic, *adj.*
sub·chron′i·cal, *adj.;* **-ly,** *adv.*
sub·cir′cuit, *n.*
sub·cir′cu·lar, *adj.;* **-ly,** *adv.*
sub′cir·cu·lar′i·ty, *n.*
sub·cit′y, *n., pl.* **-cit·ies.**
sub′civ·i·li·za′tion, *n.*
sub·civ′i·lized′, *adj.*
sub′clan′, *n.*
sub·claus′al, *adj.*
sub′clause′, *n.*
sub′cla·vic′u·lar, *adj.*
sub′clerk′, *n.*
sub·clerk′ship, *n.*
sub·cli′mate, *n.*
sub′cli·mat′ic, *adj.*
sub′clique′, *n.*
sub·clus′ter, *n.*
sub′code′, *n.*
sub′col·lec′tion, *n.*
sub′col·lec′tor, *n.*
sub′col·lec′tor·ship′, *n.*
sub′col′lege, *n.*
sub′col·le′gi·al, *adj.*
sub′col·le′giate, *adj.*
sub′col′o·ny, *n., pl.* **-nies.**
sub′com·mand′er, *n.*
sub′com·mand′er·ship′, *n.*
sub′com·men·da′tion, *n.*
sub′com·mend′a·to′ry, *adj.*
sub′com·mend′ed, *adj.*
sub′com·mis·sar′i·al, *adj.*
sub′com′mis·sar′y, *n., pl.* **-sar·ies.**
sub′com·mis′sion, *n.*
sub′com·mis′sion·er, *n.*
sub′com·mis′sion·er·ship′, *n.*
sub·com′pen·sate′, *v.t.,* **-sat·ed, -sat·ing.**
sub′com·pen·sa′tion, *n.*
sub′com·pen·sa′tion·al, *adj.*
sub′com·pen′sa·tive, *adj.*
sub′com·pen′sa·to′ry, *adj.*
sub′com·plete′, *adj.;* **-ly,** *adv.;* **-ness,** *n.*
sub′com·ple′tion, *n.*
sub′com·po′nent, *n.*
sub′com·pressed′, *adj.*
sub′con·cave′, *adj.;* **-ly,** *adv.;* **-ness,** *n.*
sub′con·cav′i·ty, *n., pl.* **-ties.**
sub′con·cealed′, *adj.*
sub′con·ces′sion, *n.*
sub′con·ces′sion·aire′, *n.*
sub′con·ces′sion·ar′y, *adj., n., pl.* **-ar·ies.**
sub′con·ces′sion·er, *n.*
sub′con·choi′dal, *adj.*
sub·con·den·sa′tion, *n.*
sub·con′fer·ence, *n.*

the crevice between the gum margin and the neck or root of a tooth. [SUB- + GINGIVAL]

sub•gla•cial (sub glā′shəl), *adj.* **1.** beneath a glacier: *a subglacial stream.* **2.** formerly beneath a glacier: *a subglacial deposit.* [1810–20; SUB- + GLACIAL] —**sub•gla′cial•ly,** *adv.*

sub•grade (sub′grād′), *Civ. Engin., Building Trades.* —*n.* **1.** the prepared earth surface on which a pavement or the ballast of a railroad track is placed or upon which the foundation of a structure is built. —*adj.* **2.** beneath the finished ground level of a project. [1895–1900; SUB- + GRADE]

sub•group (sub′gro͞op′), *n.* **1.** a subordinate group; a division of a group. **2.** *Chem.* a division of a group in the periodic table. **3.** *Math.* a subset of a group that is closed under the group operation and in which every element has an inverse in the subset. [1835–45; SUB- + GROUP]

sub•gum (sub′gum′), *adj. Chinese or Chinese-American Cookery.* prepared with mixed vegetables, as with water chestnuts, mushrooms, and bean sprouts. [1935–40; < dial. Chin (Guangdong) *sahp-gám,* akin to Chin *shíjǐn* lit., ten brocades]

sub•hal•ide (sub hal′īd, -hā′līd), *n. Chem.* a halide containing a relatively small proportion of the halogen, as mercurous chloride. [SUB- + HALIDE]

sub•har•mon•ic (sub′här mon′ik), *n. Physics.* an oscillation that has a frequency which is an integral submultiple of the frequency of a related oscillation. [SUB- + HARMONIC]

sub•head (sub′hed′), *n.* **1.** a title or heading of a subdivision, as in a chapter, essay, or newspaper article. **2.** a subordinate division of a title or heading. **3.** the immediate subordinate of the president or other head of an educational institution. Also, **sub′head′ing** (for defs. 1, 2). [1580–90; SUB- + HEAD]

sub•he•dral (sub hē′drəl), *adj. Petrog.* (of mineral grains comprising igneous rocks) having a partial or incomplete crystal face or form. [SUB- + -HEDRAL]

sub•hu•man (sub hyo͞o′mən *or, often,* -yo͞o′-), *adj.* **1.** less than or not quite human. **2.** almost human: *In some respects, the porpoise is subhuman.* [1785–95; SUB- + HUMAN]

sub•in•ci•sion (sub′in sizh′ən), *n.* the slitting of the underside of the penis to the urethra, performed as a puberty rite among some tribal peoples, esp. in Australia. [1895–1900; SUB- + INCISION]

sub•in•dex (sub in′deks), *n., pl.* **-dex•es, -di•ces** (-də sēz′). **1.** an index to a part or subdivision of a larger category. **2.** inferior (def. 11). [1920–25; SUB- + INDEX]

sub•in•feu•date (sub′in fyo͞o′dāt), *v.t., v.i.,* **-dat•ed, -dat•ing.** to grant subinfeudation (to). Also, **sub′in•feud′.** [1830–40; back formation from SUBINFEUDATION]

sub•in•feu•da•tion (sub′in fyo͞o dā′shən), *n. Feudal Law.* **1.** secondary infeudation; the granting of a portion of an estate by a feudal tenant to a subtenant, held from the tenant on terms similar to those of the grant to the tenant. **2.** the tenure established. **3.** the estate or fief so created. [1720–30; SUB- + *infeudation* enfeoffment < ML *infeudātiōn-,* s. of *infeudātiō* (see IN-[2], FEUD[2], -ATION)]

sub•in•feu•da•to•ry (sub′in fyo͞o′də tôr′ē, -tōr′ē), *n., pl.* **-ries.** a person who holds by subinfeudation. [1885–90; SUBINFEUDAT(ION) + -ORY[1]]

sub•in•flu•ent (sub in′flo͞o ənt), *n. Ecol.* an organism that has a lesser effect than an influent on the ecological processes within a community. [SUB- + INFLUENT]

sub•in•ter•val (sub in′tər vəl), *n. Math.* an interval that is a subset of a given interval. [1925–30; SUB- + INTERVAL]

sub•ir•ri•gate (sub ir′i gāt′), *v.t.,* **-gat•ed, -gat•ing.** to irrigate beneath the surface of the ground, as with water passing through a system of underground porous pipes or transmitted through the subsoil from ditches, etc. [1900–05, *Amer.*; SUB- + IRRIGATE] —**sub′ir•ri•ga′tion,** *n.*

su•bi•tize (so͞o′bi tīz′), *v.i.,* **-tized, -tiz•ing.** *Psychol.* to perceive at a glance the number of items presented, the limit for humans being about seven. Also, *esp. Brit.,* **su′bi•tise′.** [1949; < L *subit(us)* sudden or LL *subit(āre)* to appear suddenly (see SUBITO) + -IZE]

su•bi•to (so͞o′bi tō′; *It.* so͞o′bē tô), *adv.* (as a musical direction) suddenly; abruptly: *subito pianissimo.* [1715–25; < It < L *subitō* orig., abl. sing. neut. of *subitus* sudden, equiv. to *sub-* SUB- + *-i-* (base of *ire* to go) + *-tus* ptp. suffix]

subj., **1.** subject. **2.** subjective. **3.** subjectively. **4.** subjunctive.

sub•ja•cent (sub jā′sənt), *adj.* **1.** situated or occurring underneath or below; underlying. **2.** forming a basis. **3.** lower than but not directly under something. [1590–1600; < L *subjacent-* (s. of *subjacēns*), prp. of *subjacēre* to underlie, equiv. to *sub-* SUB- + *jac(ēre)* to lie + *-ent-* -ENT] —**sub•ja′cen•cy,** *n.* —**sub•ja′cent•ly,** *adv.*

sub•ject (*n., adj.* sub′jikt; *v.* səb jekt′), *n.* **1.** that which forms a basic matter of thought, discussion, investigation, etc.: *a subject of conversation.* **2.** a branch of knowledge as a course of study: *He studied four subjects in his first year at college.* **3.** a motive, cause, or ground: *a subject for complaint.* **4.** the theme of a sermon, book, story, etc. **5.** the principal melodic motif or phrase in a musical composition, esp. in a fugue. **6.** an object, scene, incident, etc., chosen by an artist for representation, or as represented in art. **7.** a person who is under the dominion or rule of a sovereign. **8.** a person who owes allegiance to a government and lives under its protection: *four subjects of Sweden.* **9.** *Gram.* (in English and many other languages) a syntactic unit that functions as one of the two main constituents of a simple sentence, the other being the predicate, and that consists of a noun, noun phrase, or noun substitute which often refers to the one performing the action or being in the state expressed by the predicate, as *He* in *He gave notice.* **10.** a person or thing that undergoes or may undergo some action: *As a dissenter, he found himself the subject of the group's animosity.* **11.** a person or thing under the control or influence of another. **12.** a person as an object of medical, surgical, or psychological treatment or experiment. **13.** a cadaver used for dissection. **14.** *Logic.* that term of a proposition concerning which the predicate is affirmed or denied. **15.** *Philos.* **a.** that which thinks, feels, perceives, intends, etc., as contrasted with the objects of thought, feeling, etc. **b.** the self or ego. **16.** *Metaphysics.* that in which qualities or attributes inhere; substance.
—*adj.* **17.** being under domination, control, or influence (often fol. by *to*). **18.** being under dominion, rule, or authority, as of a sovereign, state, or some governing power; owing allegiance or obedience (often fol. by *to*). **19.** open or exposed (usually fol. by *to*): *subject to ridicule.* **20.** being dependent or conditional upon something (usually fol. by *to*): *His consent is subject to your approval.* **21.** being under the necessity of undergoing something (usually fol. by *to*): *All beings are subject to death.* **22.** liable; prone (usually fol. by *to*): *subject to headaches.*
—*v.t.* **23.** to bring under domination, control, or influence (usually fol. by *to*). **24.** to bring under dominion, rule, or authority, as of a conqueror or a governing power (usually fol. by *to*). **25.** to cause to undergo the action of something specified; expose (usually fol. by *to*): *to subject metal to intense heat.* **26.** to make liable or vulnerable; lay open; expose (usually fol. by *to*): *to subject oneself to ridicule.* **27.** *Obs.* to place beneath something; make subjacent. [1275–1325; (adj.) < L *subjectus* placed beneath, inferior, open to inspection, orig. ptp. of *subicere* to throw or place beneath, make subject, equiv. to *sub-* SUB- + *-jec-,* comb. form of *jacere* to throw + *-tus* ptp. suffix; r. ME *suget* < OF < L, as above; (n.) < LL *subjectum* grammatical or dialectical subject, n. use of neut. of *subjectus;* r. ME *suget,* as above; (v.) < L *subjectāre,* freq. of *subicere;* r. ME *suget(t)en* < OF *sugetter* < L, as above] —**sub•ject′a•ble,** *adj.* —**sub•ject′a•bil′i•ty,** *n.* —**sub•ject′ed•ly,** *adv.* —**sub•ject′ed•ness,** *n.* —**sub′ject•less,** *adj.* —**sub′ject•like′,** *adj.*
—**Syn. 1, 4.** SUBJECT, THEME, TOPIC are often interchangeable to express the material being considered in a speech or written composition. SUBJECT is a broad word for whatever is treated in writing, speech, art, etc.: *the subject for discussion.* THEME and TOPIC are usually narrower and apply to some limited or specific part of a general subject. A THEME is often the underlying conception of a discourse or composition, perhaps not put into words but easily recognizable: *The theme of a need for reform runs throughout her work.* A TOPIC is the statement of what is to be treated in a section of a composition: *The topic is treated fully in this section.* **3.** reason, rationale. **17.** subordinate, subservient. **20.** contingent.

sub′ject cat′alog, *Library Science.* a catalog having entries listed by subject only. [1885–90]

sub′ject com′plement, *Gram.* a word or a group of words, usually functioning as an adjective or noun, that is used in the predicate following a copula and describes or is identified with the subject of the sentence, as *sleepy* in *The travelers became sleepy.* Also called **subjective complement.** [1935–40]

sub•jec•ti•fy (səb jek′tə fī′), *v.t.,* **-fied, -fy•ing. 1.** to make subjective. **2.** to identify with (a subject) or interpret subjectively. Cf. **objectify.** [1865–70; SUBJECT + -IFY] —**sub•jec′ti•fi•ca′tion,** *n.*

sub•jec•tion (səb jek′shən), *n.* **1.** the act of subjecting. **2.** the state or fact of being subjected. [1300–50; ME < L *subjectiōn-* (s. of *subjectiō*) a throwing under, equiv. to *subject-* (see SUBJECT) + *-iōn-* -ION] —**sub•jec′tion•al,** *adj.*

sub•jec•tive (səb jek′tiv), *adj.* **1.** existing in the mind; belonging to the thinking subject rather than to the object of thought (opposed to *objective*). **2.** pertaining to or characteristic of an individual; personal; individual: *a subjective evaluation.* **3.** placing excessive emphasis on one's own moods, attitudes, opinions, etc.; unduly egocentric. **4.** *Philos.* relating to or of the nature of an object as it is known in the mind as distinct from a thing in itself. **5.** relating to properties or specific conditions of the mind as distinguished from general or universal experience. **6.** pertaining to the subject or substance in which attributes inhere; essential. **7.** *Gram.* **a.** pertaining to or constituting the subject of a sentence. **b.** (in English and certain other languages) noting a case specialized for that use, as *He* in *He hit the ball.* **c.** similar to such a case in meaning. Cf. **nominative. 8.** *Obs.* characteristic of a political subject; submissive. [1400–50; late ME: pertaining to a subject of a ruler < L *subjectivus;* see SUBJECT, -IVE] —**sub•jec′tive•ly,** *adv.* —**sub•jec′tive•ness,** *n.*
—**Syn. 1.** mental. **6.** substantial, inherent.

subjec′tive com′plement. See **subject complement.** [1920–25]

subjec′tive ide′alism, *Philos.* a doctrine that the world has no existence independent of sensations or ideas. Cf. **objective idealism.** [1875–80] —**subjec′tive ide′alist.**

subjec′tive spir′it, *Hegelianism.* spirit, insofar as it falls short of the attainments of objective spirit.

sub•jec•tiv•ism (səb jek′tə viz′əm), *n.* **1.** *Epistemology.* the doctrine that all knowledge is limited to experiences by the self, and that transcendent knowledge is impossible. **2.** *Ethics.* **a.** any of various theories maintaining that moral judgments are statements concerning the emotional or mental reactions of the individual or the community. **b.** any of several theories holding that certain states of thought or feeling are the highest good. [1855–60; SUBJECTIVE + -ISM] —**sub•jec′tiv•ist,** *n.* —**sub•jec′ti•vis′tic,** *adj.* —**sub•jec′ti•vis′ti•cal•ly,** *adv.*

sub•jec•tiv•i•ty (sub′jek tiv′i tē), *n., pl.* **-ties** for 2. **1.** the state or quality of being subjective; subjectiveness. **2.** a subjective thought or idea. **3.** intentness on internal thoughts. **4.** internal reality. [1805–15; SUBJECTIVE + -ITY; as a philosophical term < F *subjectivité*]

sub′ject mat′ter, 1. the substance of a discussion, book, writing, etc., as distinguished from its form or style. **2.** the matter that is subject to some action. **3.** the matter out of which a thing is formed. [1590–1600]

sub•join (səb join′), *v.t.* **1.** to add at the end, as of something said or written; append. **2.** to place in sequence or juxtaposition to something else. [1565–75; < MF *subjoindre.* See SUB-, JOIN]

sub•join•der (səb join′dər), *n.* something subjoined, as an additional comment. [1825–35; SUB- + *-joinder,* as in *rejoinder*]

sub ju•di•ce (sub jo͞o′di sē′; *Lat.* so͝ob yo͞o′di ke′), before a judge or court; awaiting judicial determination. [1605–15; < L *sub jūdice*]

sub•ju•gate (sub′jə gāt′), *v.t.,* **-gat•ed, -gat•ing. 1.** to bring under complete control or subjection; conquer; master. **2.** to make submissive or subservient; enslave. [1400–50; late ME < LL *subjugātus,* ptp. of *subjugāre* to subjugate, equiv. to *sub-* SUB- + *jug(um)* YOKE[1] + *-ātus* -ATE[1]] —**sub•ju•ga•ble** (sub′jə gə bəl), *adj.* —**sub′ju•ga′tion,** *n.* —**sub′ju•ga′tor,** *n.*
—**Syn. 1, 2.** overcome, vanquish, reduce, overpower.

sub•junc•tion (səb jungk′shən), *n.* **1.** an act of subjoining. **2.** the state of being subjoined. **3.** something subjoined. [1625–35; < LL *subjunctiōn-* (s. of *subjunctiō*) a subjoining. See SUB-, JUNCTION]

sub•junc•tive (səb jungk′tiv), *Gram.* —*adj.* **1.** (in English and certain other languages) noting or pertaining to a mood or mode of the verb that may be used for

CONCISE PRONUNCIATION KEY: act, cāpe, dâre, pärt; set, ēqual; if, īce; ox, ōver, ôrder, oil, bo͝ok, bo͞ot, out; up, ûrge; child; sing; shoe; thin, *th*at; zh as in *treasure.* ə = *a* as in *alone, e* as in *system, i* as in *easily, o* as in *gallop, u* as in *circus;* ᵊ as in *fire* (fīᵊr), *hour* (ouᵊr). l and n can serve as syllabic consonants, as in *cradle* (krād′l), and *button* (but′n). See the full key inside the front cover.

sub′con•fer•en′tial, *adj.*
sub′con•form′a•bil′i•ty, *n.*
sub′con•form′a•ble, *adj.;* **-ble•ness,** *n.;* **-bly,** *adv.*
sub•con′ic, *adj.*
sub•con′i•cal, *adj.;* **-ly,** *adv.*
sub′con•junc•ti′val, *adj.*
sub′con•junc′tive, *adj.;* **-ly,** *adv.*
sub•con′nate, *adj.*
sub′con•na′tion, *n.*
sub′con•nect′, *v.*
sub′con•nect′ed•ly, *adv.*
sub′con•niv′ent, *adj.*
sub•con′science, *n.*
sub′con•ser•va′tor, *n.*
sub′con•sid′er•a′tion, *n.*
sub′con•stel•la′tion, *n.*
sub•con′sul, *n.*
sub•con′su•lar, *adj.*
sub•con′sul•ship′, *n.*
sub′con•tained′, *adj.*
sub•con′test, *n.*
sub′con•trol′, *v.t.,* **-trolled, -trol•ling.**
sub′con•vex′, *adj.*
sub•con′vo•lute′, *adj.;* **-ly,** *adv.*
sub•cool′, *v.t.*
sub•cor′a•coid′, *adj.*
sub•cor′date, *adj.;* **-ly,** *adv.*
sub•cor′di•form′, *adj.*
sub′co•ri•a′ceous, *adj.*
sub•cor′ne•ous, *adj.*
sub•cor′nu•al, *adj.*
sub′cor•po•ra′tion, *n.*
sub•cor′tex, *n., pl.* **-ti•ces.**
sub′co•rym′bose, *adj.;* **-ly,** *adv.*
sub•coun′cil, *n.*
sub•coun′ty, *n., pl.* **-ties.**
sub•cra′ni•al, *adj.;* **-ly,** *adv.*
sub•cre′a•tive, *adj.;* **-ly,** *adv.;* **-ness,** *n.*
sub′creek′, *n.*
sub•cre′nate, *adj.;* **-ly,** *adv.*
sub•cre′nat•ed, *adj.*
sub′crep•i•ta′tion, *n.*
sub′cres•cen′tic, *adj.*
sub′crest′, *n.*
sub•crim′i•nal, *adj.;* **-ly,** *adv.*
sub•cross′ing, *n.*
sub•cru′ci•form′, *adj.*
sub•crys′tal•line, *adj.*
sub•cu′bic, *adj.*
sub•cu′bi•cal, *adj.*
sub•cu′boid, *adj.*
sub′cu•boi′dal, *adj.*
sub•cul′trate, *adj.*
sub•cul′trat•ed, *adj.*
sub•cu′ne•us, *n., pl.* **-ne•i.**
sub•cu′rate, *n.*
sub•cur′a•tive, *n., adj.*
sub′cu•ra′tor, *n.*
sub′cu•ra•to′ri•al, *adj.*
sub′cu•ra′tor•ship′, *n.*
sub′cu•tic′u•lar, *adj.*
sub′cy•an′e•ous, *adj.*
sub•cy′a•nid, *n.*
sub•cy′a•nide′, *n.*
sub′cy•lin′dric, *adj.*
sub′cy•lin′dri•cal, *adj.*
sub•da′ta•ry, *n., pl.* **-ries.**
sub•date′, *v.t.,* **-dat•ed, -dat•ing.**
sub•deal′er, *n.*
sub′de•ci′sion, *n.*
sub′de•duc′i•ble, *adj.*
sub′def•i•ni′tion, *n.*
sub•del′e•gate, *n.*
sub•del′e•gate′, *v.t.,* **-gat•ed, -gat•ing.**
sub′del•e•ga′tion, *n.*
sub′del•ta′ic, *adj.*
sub•del′toid, *adj.*
sub′del•toi′dal, *adj.*
sub•dem′on•strate′, *v.t.,* **-strat•ed, -strat•ing.**
sub′dem•on•stra′tion, *n.*
sub•den′droid, *adj.*
sub′den•droi′dal, *adj.*
sub•den′tate, *adj.*
sub•den′tat•ed, *adj.*
sub′den•ta′tion, *n.*
sub′den•tic′u•late, *adj.*
sub′den•tic′u•lat′ed, *adj.*
sub′de•part′ment, *n.*
sub′de•part•men′tal, *adj.*
sub′de•pos′it, *n.*
sub′de•pos′i•to′ry, *n., pl.* **-ries.**
sub•de′pot, *n.*
sub′de•pressed′, *adj.*
sub•dep′u•ty, *n., pl.* **-ties.**
sub′de•vel′op•ment, *n.*
sub•dev′il, *n.*
sub•di′a•lect′, *n.*
sub′di•a•lec′tal, *adj.;* **-ly,** *adv.*
sub′di•a•pa′son, *n.*
sub′di•a•pa′son•al, *adj.*
sub′di•a•phrag•mat′ic, *adj.*
sub′di•a•phrag•mat′i•cal•ly, *adv.*
sub′di•chot′o•my, *n., pl.* **-mies.**
sub′die′, *n.*
sub′di•lat′ed, *adj.*
sub′di•rec′tor, *n.*
sub′di•rec′tor•ship′, *n.*
sub•dis′ci•pline, *n.*
sub•dis′coid, *adj.*
sub′dis•coi′dal, *adj.*
sub•dis′tich, *n.*
sub•dis′ti•chous, *adj.;* **-ly,** *adv.*
sub′dis•tinc′tion, *n.*
sub′dis•tinc′tive, *adj.;* **-ly,** *adv.;* **-ness,** *n.*
sub′dis•trib′u•tor, *n.*

subjective, doubtful, hypothetical, or grammatically subordinate statements or questions, as the mood of *be* in *if this be treason.* Cf. **imperative** (def. 3), **indicative** (def. 2). —*n.* **2.** the subjunctive mood or mode. **3.** a verb in the subjunctive mood or form. [1520–30; < LL *subjunctivus,* equiv. to *subjunct(us)* (ptp. of *subjungere* to subjoin, equiv. to *sub-* SUB- + *jung(ere)* to JOIN + *-tus* ptp. suffix) + *-īvus* -IVE] —**sub·junc′tive·ly,** *adv.*

—**Usage.** The subjunctive mood of the verb, once used extensively in English, has largely disappeared today. The subjunctive survives, though by no means consistently, in sentences with conditional clauses contrary to fact and in subordinate clauses after verbs like *wish: If the house were nearer to the road, we would hear more traffic noise. I wish I were in Florida.* The subjunctive also occurs in subordinate *that* clauses after a main clause expressing recommendation, resolution, demand, etc.: *We ask that each tenant take* (not *takes*) *responsibility for keeping the front door locked. It is important that only fresh spinach be* (not *is*) *used.* The subjunctive occurs too in some established or idiomatic expressions: *So be it. Heaven help us. God rest ye merry, gentlemen.* Were in the phrase *as it were,* meaning "in a way," is a subjunctive: *His apology, as it were, sounded more like an insult.*

sub·king·dom (sub king′dəm, sub′king′-), *n. Biol.* a category of related phyla within a kingdom. [1815–25; SUB- + KINGDOM]

sub·lan·guage (sub′lang′gwij), *n.* a subvariety of language used in a particular field or by a particular social group and characterized esp. by distinctive vocabulary. [1930–35; SUB- + LANGUAGE]

sub·lap·sar·i·an·ism (sub′lap sâr′ē ə niz′əm), *n. Theol.* infralapsarianism. [1860–65; < NL *sublāpsāri(us)* (L *sub-* SUB- + *lāps(us)* a slip, LAPSE + *-ārius* -ARY) + -AN + -ISM] —**sub′lap·sar′i·an,** *adj., n.*

sub·lat·tice (sub′lat′is), *n. Math.* a set of elements of a lattice, in which each subset of two elements has a least upper bound and a greatest lower bound contained in the given set. [SUB- + LATTICE]

sub·lease (*n.* sub′lēs′; *v.* sub lēs′), *n., v.,* **-leased, -leas·ing.** —*n.* **1.** a lease granted by one who is already a lessee of a property, as an apartment. —*v.t.* **2.** to grant a sublease of. **3.** to take or hold a sublease of. [1820–30; SUB- + LEASE] —**sub·les·see** (sub′le sē′), *n.* —**sub·les·sor** (sub les′ôr, sub′le sôr′), *n.*

sub·let (*v.* sub let′; *n.* sub′let′, sub let′), *v.,* **-let, -let·ting,** *n.* —*v.t.* **1.** to sublease. **2.** to let under a subcontract. —*n.* **3.** a sublease. **4.** a property obtained by subleasing, as an apartment. [1760–70; SUB- + LET[1]]

sub·le·thal (sub lē′thəl), *adj.* almost lethal or fatal: *a sublethal dose of poison.* [1890–95; SUB- + LETHAL]

sub·lev·el (sub′lev′əl), *n. Mining.* a drift, dug through ore, into which overlying material, esp. from an upper layer of ore, is caved.

sub·li·cense (sub lī′səns), *n., v.,* **-censed, -cens·ing.** —*n.* **1.** a license or contract granted to a third party by a licensee for specified rights or uses of a product, brand name, logo, etc. —*v.t.* **2.** to grant a sublicense for. [SUB- + LICENSE]

sub·li·cen·see (sub′lī sən sē′), *n.* a person, company, etc., to whom a sublicense is granted. [SUBLICENSE + -EE]

sub·lieu·ten·ant (sub′loo ten′ənt), *n. Brit.* a navy officer ranking next below a lieutenant. [1695–1705; SUB- + LIEUTENANT] —**sub′lieu·ten′an·cy,** *n.*

sub·li·mate (*v.* sub′lə māt′; *n., adj.* sub′lə mit, -māt′), *v.,* **-mat·ed, -mat·ing,** *n., adj.* —*v.t.* **1.** *Psychol.* to divert the energy of (a sexual or other biological impulse) from its immediate goal to one of a more acceptable social, moral, or aesthetic nature or use. **2.** *Chem.* **a.** to sublime (a solid substance); extract by this process. **b.** to refine or purify (a substance). **3.** to make nobler or purer. —*v.i.* **4.** to become sublimated; undergo sublimation. —*n.* **5.** *Chem.* the crystals, deposit, or material obtained when a substance is sublimated. —*adj.* **6.** purified or exalted; sublimated. [1425–75; late ME: exalted, sublimated < L *sublīmātus* (ptp. of *sublīmāre* to elevate), equiv. to *sublīm(is)* SUBLIME + *-ātus* -ATE[1]] —**sub·li·ma·ble** (sub′lə mə bəl), *adj.* —**sub′li·ma·ble·ness,** *n.* —**sub′li·ma′tion,** *n.* —**sub′li·ma′tion·al,** *adj.*

CONCISE ETYMOLOGY KEY: <, descended or borrowed from; >, whence; b., blend of, blended; c., cognate with; cf., compare; deriv., derivative; equiv., equivalent; imit., imitative; obl., oblique; r., replacing; s., stem; sp., spelling, spelled; resp., respelling, respelled; trans., translation; ?, origin unknown; *, unattested; ‡, probably earlier than. See the full key inside the front cover.

sub·lime (sə blīm′), *adj., n., v.,* **-limed, -lim·ing.** —*adj.* **1.** elevated or lofty in thought, language, etc.: *Paradise Lost is sublime poetry.* **2.** impressing the mind with a sense of grandeur or power; inspiring awe, veneration, etc.: *Switzerland has sublime scenery.* **3.** supreme or outstanding: *a sublime dinner.* **4.** complete; absolute; utter: *sublime stupidity.* **5.** *Archaic.* **a.** of lofty bearing. **b.** haughty. **6.** *Archaic.* raised high; high up. —*n.* **7.** **the sublime, a.** the realm of things that are sublime: *the sublime in art.* **b.** the quality of sublimity. **c.** the greatest or supreme degree. —*v.t.* **8.** to make higher, nobler, or purer. **9.** *Chem.* **a.** to convert (a solid substance) by heat into a vapor, which on cooling condenses again to solid form, without apparent liquefaction. **b.** to cause to be given off by this or some analogous process. —*v.i.* **10.** *Chem.* to volatilize from the solid state to a gas, and then condense again as a solid without passing through the liquid state. [1350–1400; (n. and adj.) < L *sublīmis* high, equiv. to *sub-* SUB- + an element of uncert. orig., variously identified with *līmis, līmus* oblique or *līmen* lintel, threshold; (v.) ME *sublimen* < OF *sublimer* < L *sublīmāre* to raise, deriv. of *sublīmis*] —**sub·lime′ly,** *adv.* —**sub·lime′ness,** *n.* —**sub·lim′er,** *n.*

—**Syn. 1.** exalted, noble. **2.** magnificent, superb, august, grand, gorgeous, resplendent, imposing, majestic.

Sublime′ Porte′ (pôrt, pōrt), official name of **Porte.**

sub·lim·i·nal (sub lim′ə nl), *adj. Psychol.* existing or operating below the threshold of consciousness; being or employing stimuli insufficiently intense to produce a discrete sensation but often being or designed to be intense enough to influence the mental processes or the behavior of the individual: *a subliminal stimulus; subliminal advertising.* [1885–90; SUB- + L *līmin-* (s. of *līmen*) threshold + -AL[1]] —**sub·lim′i·nal·ly,** *adv.*

sub·lim·i·ty (sə blim′i tē), *n., pl.* **-ties** for 2. **1.** the state or quality of being sublime. **2.** a sublime person or thing. [1520–30; < L *sublīmitās* height, equiv. to *sublīm(is)* SUBLIME + *-itās* -ITY]

sub·lin·gual (sub ling′gwəl), *Anat.* —*adj.* **1.** situated under the tongue, or on the underside of the tongue. —*n.* **2.** a sublingual gland, artery, or the like. [1655–65; < NL *sublinguālis;* see SUB-, LINGUAL]

sub·lit·er·ate (sub lit′ər it), *adj.* less than fully literate. [1945–50; SUB- + LITERATE]

sub·lit·er·a·ture (sub′lit′ər ə chər, -chŏŏr′, -li′trə-), *n.* **1.** writing below the standards of literature as an art form. **2.** a report or similar material written for immediate use and reproduced in an impermanent form. [1950–55; SUB- + LITERATURE] —**sub·lit′er·ar′y,** *adj.*

sub·lit·to·ral (sub lit′ər əl), *adj.* **1.** of or pertaining to the biogeographic region of the ocean bottom between the littoral and bathyal zones, from the low water line to the edge of the continental shelf, or to a depth of approximately 660 ft. (200 m). **2.** being or situated in the zone of a lake extending from the lowest depth of rooted photosynthetic plants to the level at which the photosynthetic rate of flora equals the respiration rate. —*n.* **3.** a sublittoral zone or region. [1840–50; SUB- + LITTORAL]

sub·lu·nar·y (sub′lŏŏ ner′ē, sub lŏŏ′nə rē), *adj.* **1.** situated beneath the moon or between the earth and the moon. **2.** characteristic of or pertaining to the earth; terrestrial. **3.** mundane or worldly: *fleeting, sublunary pleasure.* Also, **sub·lu·nar** (sub lŏŏ′nər). [1585–95; < LL *sublūn(āris)* (see SUB-, LUNAR) + -ARY]

sub·lux·a·tion (sub′luk sā′shən), *n. Med.* a partial dislocation, as of a joint; sprain. [1680–90; < NL *subluxātiōn-,* s. of *subluxātiō;* see SUB-, LUXATION]

sub·ma·chine′ gun′ (sub′mə shēn′), a lightweight automatic or semiautomatic gun, fired from the shoulder or hip. [1915–20; SUB- + MACHINE GUN]

sub·man·dib′u·lar gland′ (sub′man dib′yə lər), either of a pair of salivary glands located one on each side of and beneath the lower jaw. Also called **submaxillary gland.** [SUB- + MANDIBULAR]

sub·mar·gin·al (sub mär′jə nl), *adj.* **1.** *Biol.* near the margin. **2.** below the margin. **3.** not worth cultivating, as land; less than satisfactory; unproductive. [1820–30; SUB- + MARGINAL] —**sub·mar′gin·al·ly,** *adv.*

sub·ma·rine (*n.* sub′mə rēn′, sub′mə rēn′; *adj., v.* sub′mə rēn′), *n., adj., v.,* **-rined, -rin·ing.** —*n.* **1.** a vessel that can be submerged and navigated under water, usually built for warfare and armed with torpedoes or guided missiles. **2.** something situated or living under the surface of the sea, as a plant or animal. **3.** *Chiefly Northeastern and North Midland U.S.* a hero sandwich. —*adj.* **4.** situated, occurring, operating, or living under the surface of the sea: *a submarine mountain.* **5.** of, pertaining to, or carried on by a submarine or submarines: *submarine warfare.* —*v.i.* **6.** to participate in the operating of a submarine. **7.** to move or slide under something. **8.** *Slang.* **a.** to be thrown under the steering wheel of the vehicle one is driving during a frontal crash. **b.** to be thrown out of one's seat belt in such a crash. —*v.t.* **9.** to attack or sink by submarine. [1640–50; 1895–1900 for def. 1; SUB- + MARINE]

—**Regional Variation. 3.** See **hero sandwich.**

sub′marine chas′er, a small patrol vessel, 100–200 ft. (30–60 m) long, designed for military operations against submarines. Also called **subchaser.**

sub·ma·rin·er (sub′mə rē′nər, səb mar′ə nər), *n.* a member of the crew of a submarine. [1910–15; SUBMARINE + -ER[1]]

sub·ma·rin·ing (sub′mə rē′ning), *n. Computers.* the disappearance or flickering of a cursor on a computer screen. [1991]

sub·ma·trix (sub mā′triks, -ma′triks), *n., pl.* **-tri·ces** (-tri sēz′), **-trix·es.** *Math.* a set of certain rows and columns of a given matrix. [SUB- + MATRIX]

sub·max·il·la (sub′mak sil′ə), *n., pl.* **-max·il·lae** (-mak sil′ē). *Anat.* mandible. [1895–1900; SUB- + MAXILLA]

sub·max·il·lar·y (sub mak′sə ler′ē, sub′mak sil′ə rē), *adj.* of or pertaining to the lower jaw or lower jawbone. [1780–90; SUB- + MAXILLARY]

submax′illary gland′, *Anat.* See **submandibular gland.** [1780–90]

sub·me·di·ant (sub mē′dē ənt), *n. Music.* the sixth tone of a diatonic scale, being midway between the subdominant and the upper tonic. Also called **superdominant.** [1800–10; SUB- + MEDIANT]

sub·merge (səb mûrj′), *v.,* **-merged, -merg·ing.** —*v.t.* **1.** to put or sink below the surface of water or any other enveloping medium. **2.** to cover or overflow with water; immerse. **3.** to cover; bury; subordinate; suppress: *His aspirations were submerged by the necessity of making a living.* —*v.i.* **4.** to sink or plunge under water or beneath the surface of any enveloping medium. **5.** to be covered or lost from sight. [1600–10; < L *submergere,* equiv. to *sub-* SUB- + *mergere* to dip, immerse; see MERGE] —**sub·mer′gence,** *n.*

—**Syn. 1.** submerse. **2.** flood, inundate, engulf.

sub·merged (səb mûrjd′), *adj.* **1.** under the surface of water or any other enveloping medium; inundated. **2.** hidden, covered, or unknown: *There are many submerged facts which could have a bearing on the case.* **3.** poverty-stricken; destitute; impoverished: *submerged socioeconomic groups.* [1790–1800; SUBMERGE + -ED[2]]

sub·mer·gi·ble (səb mûr′jə bəl), *adj.* submersible. [1865–70; SUBMERGE + -IBLE] —**sub·mer′gi·bil′i·ty,** *n.*

sub·merse (səb mûrs′), *v.t.,* **-mersed, -mers·ing.** to submerge. [1830–40; prob. back-formation from *submersion* < LL *submersiōn-,* s. of *submersiō* a sinking, equiv. to L *submers(us)* ptp. of *submergere* to SUBMERGE + *-iōn-* -ION] —**sub·mer·sion** (səb mûr′zhən, -shən), *n.*

sub·mersed (səb mûrst′), *adj.* **1.** submerged. **2.** *Bot.* growing under water. [1720–30; < L *submers(us)* (see SUBMERSE) + -ED[2]]

sub·mers·i·ble (səb mûr′sə bəl), *adj.* **1.** capable of being submersed. **2.** capable of functioning while submersed: *a submersible pump.* —*n.* **3.** a ship capable of submerging and operating under water; submarine. **4.** a device designed for underwater work or exploration, as a bathyscaphe or diving bell. [1865–70; SUBMERSE + -IBLE] —**sub·mers′i·bil′i·ty,** *n.*

sub·me·tal·lic (sub′mə tal′ik), *adj.* somewhat or imperfectly metallic. [SUB- + METALLIC]

sub·mi·cron (sub mī′kron), *adj.* (of particles) being less than a micron in overall dimensions. [1945–50; SUB- + MICRON]

sub·mi·cro·scop·ic (sub′mī krə skop′ik), *adj.* too small to be seen through a microscope. Also, **sub′mi·cro·scop′i·cal.** [SUB- + MICROSCOPIC] —**sub′mi·cro·scop′i·cal·ly,** *adv.*

sub·mil·li·me·ter (sub mil′ə mē′tər), *adj.* less than a millimeter in size: *a submillimeter wave.* [1950–55; SUB- + MILLIMETER]

sub·min·i·a·ture (sub min′ē ə chər, -chŏŏr′, -min′ə-chər), *n.* **1.** See **subminiature camera.** —*adj.* **2.** noting or pertaining to subminiature cameras, their accessories, or systems of photography. **3.** smaller than miniature, as certain electronic components; ultraminiature. [1945–50; SUB- + MINIATURE]

submin′iature cam′era, a very small, palm-sized still camera for taking photographs on 16-millimeter or similar film. Also called **subminiature.**

sub′di·vine′, *adj.;* **-ly,** *adv.;* **-ness,** *n.*
sub·doc′tor, *n.*
sub′dol·i·cho·ce·phal′ic, *adj.*
sub′dol·i·cho·ceph′a·lism, *n.*
sub′dol·i·cho·ceph′a·lous, *adj.*
sub′dol·i·cho·ceph′a·ly, *n.*
sub·dor′sal, *adj.;* **-ly,** *adv.*
sub·dru′id, *n.*
sub·du′ral, *adj.*
sub·ech′o, *n., pl.* **-ech·oes.**
sub′ec·o·nom′ic, *adj.*
sub′e·con′o·my, *n., pl.* **-mies.**
sub′ec·to·der′mal, *adj.*
sub′ec·to·der′mic, *adj.*
sub′ef·fec′tive, *adj.;* **-ly,** *adv.;* **-ness,** *n.*
sub′e·lec′tion, *n.*
sub·el′e·ment, *n.*
sub′el·e·men′tal, *adj.;* **-ly,** *adv.*
sub′el·lip′tic, *adj.*
sub′el·lip′ti·cal, *adj.*
sub′e·lon′gate, *adj.*
sub′e·lon′gat·ed, *adj.*
sub′e·mar′gi·nate, *adj.*
sub′e·mar′gi·nat′ed, *adj.*
sub′en·do·car′di·al, *adj.*
sub′en·dorse′, *v.t.,* **-dorsed, -dors·ing.**
sub′en·dorse′ment, *n.*
sub′en·do·the′li·al, *adj.*
sub′en·gi·neer′, *n.*
sub′en·tire′, *adj.*
sub′en·ti′tle, *v.t.,* **-tled, -tling.**
sub′ep·i·glot′tal, *adj.*
sub′ep·i·glot′tic, *adj.*
sub′ep·i·the′li·al, *adj.*
sub′ep′och, *n.*
sub·e′qual, *adj.;* **-ly,** *adv.*
sub′e·qual′i·ty, *n., pl.* **-ties.**
sub′e·qui·lat′er·al, *adj.*
sub′e·rect′, *adj.;* **-ly,** *adv.;* **-ness,** *n.*
sub′es·cheat′or, *n.*
sub′e·soph′a·ge′al, *adj.*
sub′es·sen′tial, *adj.;* **-ly,** *adv.;* **-ness,** *n.*
sub·es′tu·a·rine′, *adj.*
sub′et·y·mol′o·gy, *n., pl.* **-gies.**
sub·ev′er·green′, *adj.*
sub′ex·am′in·er, *n.*
sub′ex·ec′u·tor, *n.*
sub′ex·ten′si·bil′i·ty, *n.*
sub′ex·ten′si·ble, *adj.;* **-ness,** *n.*
sub′ex·ter′nal, *adj.;* **-ly,** *adv.*
sub′face′, *n.*
sub·fa′ci·es′, *n., pl.* **-fa·ci·es.**
sub·fac′tor, *n.*
sub·fac′to·ry, *n., pl.* **-ries.**
sub·fal′cate, *adj.*
sub·fal′cial, *adj.*
sub·fal′ci·form′, *adj.*
sub·fas′ci·al, *adj.*
sub′fas·tig′i·ate, *adj.*
sub′fas·tig′i·at′ed, *adj.*
sub·fer′ry·man, *n., pl.* **-men.**
sub·fes′tive, *adj.;* **-ly,** *adv.;* **-ness,** *n.*
sub·fi′brous, *adj.*
sub·fig′ure, *n.*
sub′file′, *n.*
sub·fis′sure, *n.*
sub·flex′u·ose′, *adj.*
sub·flex′u·ous, *adj.;* **-ly,** *adv.*
sub·flo′ra, *n., pl.* **-flo·ras, -flo·rae.**
sub·fo′li·ar, *adj.*
sub′fo′li·ate, *adj.*
sub′fo·li·a′tion, *n.*
sub′fore′man, *n., pl.* **-men.**
sub′fore′man·ship′, *n.*
sub′form′, *n.*
sub′for·ma′tion, *n.*
sub·form′a·tive, *adj.;* **-ly,** *adv.;* **-ness,** *n.*
sub·fos′sil, *n.*
sub′fos·so′ri·al, *adj.*
sub·frac′tion, *n.*
sub·frac′tion·al, *adj.;* **-ly,** *adv.*
sub·frac′tion·ar′y, *adj.*
sub′frame′, *n.*
sub·fran′chise, *n., v.t.,* **-chised, -chis·ing.**
sub·fresh′man, *n., pl.* **-men.**
sub·fron′tal, *adj.;* **-ly,** *adv.*
sub·ful′gent, *adj.;* **-ly,** *adv.*
sub′fu·mi·ga′tion, *n.*
sub·func′tion, *n.*
sub·func′tion·al, *adj.;* **-ly,** *adv.*
sub·fu′si·form′, *adj.*
sub·gan′oid, *adj.*
sub·gape′, *v.i.,* **-gaped, -gap·ing.**
sub′ge·lat′i·ni·za′tion, *n.*
sub′ge·lat′i·noid′, *adj.*
sub′ge·lat′i·nous, *adj.;* **-ly,** *adv.;* **-ness,** *n.*
sub′gen·er·a′tion, *n.*
sub′ge·nic′u·late, *adj.*
sub′ge·nic′u·la′tion, *n.*
sub·gen′i·tal, *adj.*
sub′gens′, *n., pl.* **-gen·tes.**
sub′ge·o·met′ric, *adj.*
sub′ge·o·met′ri·cal, *adj.;* **-ly,** *adv.*
sub·ger′mi·nal, *adj.;* **-ly,** *adv.*
sub·gla′brous, *adj.*
sub·gle′noid, *adj.*
sub·glo′boid, *adj.*
sub·glo′bose, *adj.;* **-ly,** *adv.;* **-ness,** *n.*
sub′glo·bos′i·ty, *n.*
sub·glob′u·lar, *adj.;* **-ly,** *adv.*

sub•min•i•a•tur•ize (sub min′ē ə chə rīz′, -min′ə-chə-), *v.t.*, **-ized, -iz•ing.** to design or manufacture (equipment, esp. electronic equipment) of a greatly reduced scale. Also, *esp. Brit.*, **sub•min′i•a•tur•ise′.** [SUB- + MINIATURIZE] —**sub•min′i•a•tur•i•za′tion,** *n.*

sub•min•i•mum (sub min′ə məm), *adj.* **1.** being below a minimum standard, rate, quota, etc.: *a subminimum wage for teenagers.* —*n.* **2.** something that is below a minimum standard or rate. [SUB- + MINIMUM]

sub•miss (səb mis′), *adj. Archaic.* submissive. [1560–70; < L *submissus* (ptp. of *submittere* to SUBMIT)]

sub•mis•sion (səb mish′ən), *n.* **1.** an act or instance of submitting. **2.** the condition of having submitted. **3.** submissive conduct or attitude. **4.** something that is submitted, as an application. **5.** *Law.* an agreement between parties involved in a dispute, to abide by the decision of an arbitrator or arbitrators. [1375–1425; late ME < L *submissiōn-* (s. of *submissiō*) a letting down. See SUB-, MISSION]

sub•mis•sive (səb mis′iv), *adj.* **1.** inclined or ready to submit; unresistingly or humbly obedient: *submissive servants.* **2.** marked by or indicating submission: *a submissive reply.* [1580–90; SUBMISS + -IVE] —**sub•mis′sive•ly,** *adv.* —**sub•mis′sive•ness,** *n.*
—**Syn. 1.** tractable, compliant, pliant, amenable. **2.** passive, resigned, patient, docile, tame, subdued. —**Ant. 1.** rebellious, disobedient.

sub•mit (səb mit′), *v.*, **-mit•ted, -mit•ting.** —*v.t.* **1.** to give over or yield to the power or authority of another (often used reflexively). **2.** to subject to some kind of treatment or influence. **3.** to present for the approval, consideration, or decision of another or others: *to submit a plan; to submit an application.* **4.** to state or urge with deference; suggest or propose (usually fol. by a clause): *I submit that full proof should be required.* —*v.i.* **5.** to yield oneself to the power or authority of another: *to submit to a conqueror.* **6.** to allow oneself to be subjected to some kind of treatment: *to submit to chemotherapy.* **7.** to defer to another's judgment, opinion, decision, etc.: *I submit to your superior judgment.* [1325–75; ME *submitten* < L *submittere* to lower, reduce, yield, equiv. to *sub-* SUB- + *mittere* to send] —**sub•mit′ta•ble, sub•mis•si•ble** (səb mis′ə bəl), *adj.* —**sub•mit′tal,** *n.* —**sub•mit′ter,** *n.* —**sub•mit′ting•ly,** *adv.*
—**Syn. 1.** comply, bow, obey, agree, resign. See **yield.** —**Ant. 1.** fight.

sub•mon•tane (sub mon′tān), *adj.* **1.** under or beneath a mountain or mountains. **2.** at or near the foot of mountains. **3.** pertaining or belonging to the lower slopes of mountains. [1810–20; < LL *submontānus;* see SUB-, MONTANE] —**sub•mon′tane•ly,** *adv.*

sub•mu•co•sa (sub′myōō kō′sə, -zə), *n. Anat.* the layer of connective tissue located beneath the mucous membrane. [1880–85; NL; see SUB-, MUCOSA] —**sub′mu•co′sal,** *adj.*

sub•mul•ti•ple (sub mul′tə pəl), *n.* **1.** a number that is contained by another number an integral number of times without a remainder: *The number 3 is a submultiple of 12.* —*adj.* **2.** pertaining to or noting a quantity that is a submultiple. [1690–1700; SUB- + MULTIPLE]

sub•net (sub′net′), *n. Math.* the abstraction, in topology, of a subsequence. [SUB- + NET[1]]

sub•ni•trate (sub nī′trāt), *n. Chem.* a basic salt of nitric acid. [1795–1805; SUB- + NITRATE] —**sub•ni′trat•ed,** *adj.*

sub•nor•mal (sub nôr′məl), *adj.* **1.** below the normal; less than or inferior to the normal: *a subnormal amount of rain.* **2.** being less than average in any psychological trait, as intelligence or emotional adjustment. —*n.* **3.** a subnormal person. **4.** *Geom.* that part of the x-axis of a curve cut off between the ordinate and a normal. [1700–10; SUB- + NORMAL] —**sub′nor•mal′i•ty,** *n.*

sub•nu′cle•ar par′ticle (sub nōō′klē ər, -nyōō′- *or, by metathesis,* -kyə lər) *Physics.* any of the elementary particles, including those that do not exist in stable matter but appear as a result of high-energy collisions of other particles or nuclei. [1960–65; SUB- + NUCLEAR]
—**Pronunciation.** See **nuclear.**

sub•oc•cip•i•tal (sub′ok sip′i tl), *adj.* situated below the occipital bone or the occipital lobe of the brain. [1725–35; < NL *suboccipitālis;* see SUB-, OCCIPITAL]

sub•o•ce•an•ic (sub′ō shē an′ik), *adj.* **1.** occurring or existing below the floor of the ocean: *suboceanic oil.* **2.** of, pertaining to, or on the floor of the ocean: *suboceanic plants.* Also, **sub•o•cean** (sub ō′shən). [1855–60; SUB- + OCEANIC]

sub•op•ti•mal (sub op′tə məl), *adj.* being below an optimal level or standard. Also, **sub•op•ti•mum** (sub-op′tə məm). [1930–35; SUB- + OPTIMAL]

sub•or•bit•al (sub ôr′bi tl), *adj.* **1.** (of a spacecraft) not in orbit; not achieving an altitude and velocity resulting in a ballistic trajectory circling the earth at least once. **2.** *Anat.* situated below the orbit of the eye. [1815–25; SUB- + ORBITAL]

sub•or•der (sub′ôr′dər), *n. Biol.* a category of related families within an order. [1820–30; SUB- + ORDER]

sub•or•di•nal (sub ôr′dn l), *adj.* of, pertaining to, or ranked as a suborder. [1865–70; SUB- + ORDINAL[1]]

sub•or•di•nate (*adj., n.* sə bôr′dn it; *v.* sə bôr′dn āt′), *adj., n., v.,* **-nat•ed, -nat•ing.** —*adj.* **1.** placed in or belonging to a lower order or rank. **2.** of less importance; secondary. **3.** subject to or under the authority of a superior. **4.** subservient or inferior. **5.** subject; dependent. **6.** *Gram.* **a.** acting as a modifier, as *when I finished,* which is subordinate to *They were glad* in *They were glad when I finished.* **b.** noting or pertaining to a subordinating conjunction. **7.** *Obs.* submissive. —*n.* **8.** a subordinate person or thing. —*v.t.* **9.** to place in a lower order or rank. **10.** to make secondary (usually fol. by *to*): *to subordinate work to pleasure.* **11.** to make subject, subservient, or dependent (usually fol. by *to*): *to subordinate passion to reason.* [1425–75; late ME (adj.) < ML *subōrdinātus* ptp. of *subōrdināre* to subordinate, equiv. to L *sub-* SUB- + *ōrdin-* (s. of *ōrdō*) rank, order + *-ātus* -ATE[1]] —**sub•or′di•nate•ly,** *adv.* —**sub•or′di•nate•ness,** *n.* —**sub•or′di•na′tion, sub•or•di•na•cy** (sə bôr′dn ə sē), *n.* —**sub•or•di•na•tive** (sə bôr′dn-ā′tiv, -bôr′dn ə-), *adj.*
—**Syn. 2.** ancillary. **8.** inferior, subject. **9.** lower, reduce. —**Ant. 2.** superior; primary.

subor′dinate clause′, *Gram.* a clause that modifies the principal clause or some part of it or that serves a noun function in the principal clause, as *when she arrived* in the sentence *I was there when she arrived* or *that she has arrived* in the sentence *I doubt that she has arrived.* Cf. **main clause.**

sub•or•di•nat•ed (sə bôr′dn ā′tid), *adj. Finance.* noting or designating a debt obligation whose holder is placed in precedence below secured and general creditors: *subordinated debentures.* [SUBORDINATE + -ED[2]]

subor′dinating conjunc′tion, *Gram.* a conjunction introducing a subordinate clause, as *when* in *They were glad when I finished.* Also, **subor′dinate conjunc′tion.** Also called **sub•or′di•na′tor.** Cf. **coordinating conjunction.** [1870–75; SUBORDINATE + -ING[2]]

sub•or•di•na•tion•ism (sə bôr′dn ā′shə niz′əm), *n. Theol.* the doctrine that the first person of the Holy Trinity is superior to the second, and the second superior to the third. [1835–45; SUBORDINATION + -ISM] —**sub•or′di•na′tion•ist,** *n.*

sub•orn (sə bôrn′), *v.t.* **1.** to bribe or induce (someone) unlawfully or secretly to perform some misdeed or to commit a crime. **2.** *Law.* **a.** to induce (a person, esp. a witness) to give false testimony. **b.** to obtain (false testimony) from a witness. [1525–35; < L *subornāre* to instigate secretly, orig., to supply, equiv. to *sub-* SUB- + *ornāre* to equip; see ADORN] —**sub•or•na•tion** (sub′ôr nā′shən), *n.* —**sub•or•na•tive** (sə bôr′nə tiv), *adj.* —**sub•orn′er,** *n.*

suborna′tion of per′jury, *Crim. Law.* the offense of bribing or otherwise persuading another to commit perjury. [1580–90]

sub•os•cine (sub os′in, -īn), *Ornith.* —*adj.* **1.** of or pertaining to birds of the suborder Suboscines, of the order Passeriformes, comprising the supposedly more primitive members of the order, with less well developed vocal organs than the oscine birds. —*n.* **2.** a suboscine bird. [SUB- + OSCINE]

Su•bo•ti•ca (*Serbo-Croatian.* sōō′bô ti tsä), *n.* a city in N Vojvodina, in N Yugoslavia. 88,787. Hungarian, **Szabadka.**

sub•ox•ide (sub ok′sīd, -sid), *n. Chem.* the oxide of an element that contains the smallest proportion of oxygen. [1795–1805; SUB- + OXIDE]

sub•phy•lum (sub fī′ləm), *n., pl.* **-la** (-lə). *Biol.* a category of related classes within a phylum. [1930–35; < NL; see SUB-, PHYLUM] —**sub•phy′lar,** *adj.*

sub•pleu•ral (sub plŏŏr′əl), *adj.* situated under the pleura. [1860–65; SUB- + PLEURAL]

sub•plot (sub′plot′), *n.* a secondary or subordinate plot, as in a play, novel, or other literary work; underplot. Cf. **counterplot** (def. 2). [1915–20; SUB- + PLOT]

sub•poe•na (sə pē′nə, səb-), *n., v.,* **-naed, -na•ing.** *Law.* —*n.* **1.** the usual writ for the summoning of witnesses or the submission of evidence, as records or documents, before a court or other deliberative body. —*v.t.* **2.** to serve with a subpoena. Also, **sub•pe′na.** [1375–1425; late ME < L *sub poenā* under penalty (the first words of the writ)]

sub•poe•na du•ces te•cum (sə pē′nə dōō′sēz tē′-kəm, dōō′säz tā′kəm, səb-), *Law.* a writ directing a person to appear in court and to bring some document described in the writ. Also called **duces tecum.** [1755–65; < NL: lit., under penalty you shall bring with you]

sub•po•lar (sub pō′lər), *adj.* **1.** subantarctic. **2.** subarctic. [1820–30; SUB- + POLAR]

sub•pri•mal (sub prī′məl), *adj.* **1.** (of meat) being a cut of meat larger than a steak, roast, or other single cut but smaller than a side of beef: shipped by the packer to local markets for final cutting to reduce processing costs and to retard spoilage. —*n.* **2.** such a cut of meat. [SUB- + PRIMAL]

sub•prime (sub prīm′), *adj.* **1.** being of less than top quality: *a subprime grade of steel.* **2.** being below a prime rate: *banks engaging in subprime lending.* [SUB- + PRIME]

sub•prin•ci•pal (sub prin′sə pəl, sub′prin′-), *n.* **1.** an assistant or deputy principal. **2.** *Music.* (in an organ) a subbass of the open diapason class. [1590–1600; SUB- + PRINCIPAL]

sub•pro•fes•sion•al (sub′prə fesh′ə nl), *adj.* **1.** being below professional standards: *subprofessional health care.* **2.** paraprofessional. —*n.* **3.** a paraprofessional. [1940–45; SUB- + PROFESSIONAL] —**sub′pro•fes′sion•al•ly,** *adv.*

sub•pro•gram (sub′prō′gram, -grəm), *n. Computers.* procedure (def. 4b). [1955–60]

sub•pur•lin (sub pûr′lin), *n.* a light structural member for carrying roofing materials, supported by and running at right angles to purlins. [SUB- + PURLIN]

sub•quar•ter (sub′kwôr′tər, -kwô′-), *n. Heraldry.* one of the quarterings of a grand quarter. [SUB- + QUARTER]

sub•quar•ter•ly (sub kwôr′tər lē, -kwô′-), *adv. Heraldry.* as one of the quarterings of a grand quarter: *a coat of arms borne subquarterly.* [SUB- + QUARTERLY]

sub•ra•tion•al (sub rash′ə nl), *adj.* less than or almost rational. [1860–65; SUB- + RATIONAL]

sub•re•gion (sub′rē′jən), *n.* a division or subdivision of a region, esp. a division of a zoogeographical region. [1860–65; SUB- + REGION] —**sub•re′gion•al,** *adj.*

sub•rep•tion (səb rep′shən), *n.* **1.** *Canon Law.* a concealment of the pertinent facts in a petition, as for dispensation or favor, that in certain cases nullifies the grant. Cf. **obreption** (def. 1.). **2.** *Scots Law.* the act of obtaining something, as an escheat, by concealing pertinent facts. Cf. **obreption** (def. 2). **3.** a fallacious representation or an inference from it. [1590–1600; < L *subreptiōn-* (s. of *subreptiō*) a stealing, equiv. to *subrept(us)* (ptp. of *subripere* to steal, itself equiv. to *sub-* -SUB + *-rep-* (comb. form of *rapere* to seize, RAPE[1]) + *-tus* ptp. suffix) + *-iōn-* -ION] —**sub•rep•ti•tious** (sub′rep tish′-əs), *adj.*

sub•right (sub′rīt′), *n.* Usually, **subrights.** subsidiary rights, as for a literary or dramatic property. [SUB- + RIGHT]

sub•ring (sub′ring′), *n. Math.* a subset of a ring that is a subgroup under addition and that is closed under multiplication. Cf. **ring**[1] (def. 22). [1950–55; SUB- + RING[1]]

Sub•roc (sub′rok′), *n. Mil.* a rocket that contains a nuclear depth charge and that can be launched underwater from a submarine torpedo tube. Also, **SUBROC** [*sub(marine) roc(ket)*]

sub•ro•gate (sub′rə gāt′), *v.t.*, **-gat•ed, -gat•ing. 1.** to put into the place of another; substitute for another. **2.** *Civil Law.* to substitute (one person) for another with reference to a claim or right. [1400–50; 1540–50 for def. 1; late ME (ptp.) < L *subrogātus* (ptp. of *subrogāre* to nominate (someone) as a substitute), equiv. to *sub-* SUB- + *rogā(re)* to request + *-tus* ptp. suffix] —**sub′ro•ga′tion,** *n.*

sub ro•sa (sub rō′zə), confidentially; secretly; privately. [1920–25; < L *sub rosā* lit., under the rose, from the ancient use of the rose at meetings as a symbol of the sworn confidence of the participants]

CONCISE PRONUNCIATION KEY: act, cāpe, dâre, pärt; set, ēqual; if, ice; ox, ōver, ôrder, oil, bŏŏk, bōōt, out; up, ûrge; child; sing; shoe; thin, *th*at; zh as in *treasure.* ə = a as in *alone,* e as in *system,* i as in *easily,* o as in *gallop,* u as in *circus;* ᵊ as in *fire* (fīᵊr), *hour* (ouᵊr). l and n can serve as syllabic consonants, as in *cradle* (krād′l), and *button* (but′n). See the full key inside the front cover.

sub′glob•u•lar′i•ty, *n.*
sub•glos′sal, *adj.*
sub•glot′tal, *adj.;* **-ly,** *adv.*
sub•glot′tic, *adj.*
sub′glu•ma′ceous, *adj.*
sub′goal′, *n.*
sub′god′, *n.*
sub•gov′ern•ess, *n.*
sub•gov′ern•ment, *n.*
sub•gov′er•nor, *n.*
sub•gov′er•nor•ship′, *n.*
sub•gran′u•lar, *adj.;* **-ly,** *adv.*
sub•gran•u•lar′i•ty, *n.*
sub′grin′, *n.*
sub•gu′lar, *adj.*
sub•gyre′, *n.*
sub•gy′rus, *n., pl.* **-gy•ri.**
sub′hall′, *n.*
sub•hatch′er•y, *n., pl.* **-er•ies.**
sub•head′quar′ters, *n., pl.* **-ters.**
sub′head′wait′er, *n.*
sub•health′, *n.*
sub′hem•i•spher′ic, *adj.*
sub′hem•i•spher′i•cal, *adj.;* **-ly,** *adv.*
sub′he•pat′ic, *adj.*
sub′herd′, *n.*
sub•he′ro, *n., pl.* **-roes.**
sub′hex•ag′o•nal, *adj.*
sub′-Him•a•la′yan, *adj.*
sub•hir′sute, *adj.;* **-ness,** *n.*
sub•hooked′, *adj.*
sub′hor•i•zon′tal, *adj.;* **-ly,** *adv.;* **-ness,** *n.*
sub′house′, *n.*
sub•hu′mer•al, *adj.*
sub•hu′mid, *adj.*
sub•hy′a•lin, *adj.*
sub•hy′a•line, *adj.*
sub•hy′a•loid′, *adj.*
sub′hy•me′ni•al, *adj.*
sub′hy•me′ni•um, *n., pl.* **-ni•a.**
sub•hy′oid, *adj.*
sub′hy•oid′e•an, *adj.*
sub′hy•poth′e•sis, *n., pl.* **-ses.**
sub′hys•te′ri•a, *n.*
sub′ic•ter′ic, *adj.*
sub′ic•ter′i•cal, *adj.*
sub′i•de′a, *n.*
sub′i•de′al, *adj., n.*
sub•il′i•um, *n., pl.* **-il•i•a.**
sub•im′bri•cate, *adj.;* **-ly,** *adv.*
sub•im′bri•cat′ed, *adj.*
sub•im′bri•ca′tive, *adj.*
sub′im•posed′, *adj.*
sub′im•pressed′, *adj.*
sub′in•com•plete′, *adj.*
sub•in′dus•try, *n., pl.* **-tries.**
sub′in•fec′tion, *n.*
sub′in•fer′, *v.,* **-ferred, -fer•ring.**
sub′in•fe′ri•or, *adj.*
sub′in•flam•ma′tion, *n.*
sub′in•flam′ma•to′ry, *adj.*
sub′in•form′, *v.t*
sub′in•hib′i•to′ry, *adj.*
sub′in•i′tial, *v.t.,* **-tialed, -tial•ing** or (*esp. Brit.*) **-tialled, -tial•ling.**
sub′in•sert′, *v.t*
sub′in•ser′tion, *n.*
sub′in•spec′tor, *n.*
sub′in•spec′tor•ship′, *n.*
sub′in•teg′u•men′tal, *adj.*
sub′in•teg′u•men′ta•ry, *adj.*
sub′in•ten′tion, *n.*
sub′in•ten′tion•al, *adj.;* **-ly,** *adv.*
sub•in•ter•ces′sor, *n.*
sub′in•ter′nal, *adj.;* **-ly,** *adv.*
sub′in•tes′ti•nal, *adj.*
sub•in′ti•mal, *adj.*
sub′in•tro•duce′, *v.t.,* **-duced, -duc•ing.**
sub′in•tro•duc′tion, *n.*
sub′in•tro•duc′tive, *adj.*
sub′in•tro•duc′to•ry, *adj.*
sub•in′vo•lute′, *adj.*
sub•in′vo•lut′ed, *adj.*
sub•i′o•dide′, *n.*
sub•i′tem, *n.*
sub′jack′, *n.*
sub′joint′, *n.*
sub′judge′, *n.*
sub•judge′ship, *n.*
sub′ju•di′cial, *adj.;* **-ly,** *adv.*
sub′ju•di′ci•ar′y, *adj., n., pl.* **-ar•ies.**
sub•ju′gal, *adj.*
sub•jug′u•lar, *adj.*
sub•jun′ior, *adj.*
sub′king′, *n.*
sub•la′bi•al, *adj.;* **-ly,** *adv.*
sub′la•cin′i•ate′, *adj.*
sub′la•cu′nose, *adj.*
sub′la•cus′trine, *adj.*
sub•la′nate, *adj.*
sub•lan′ce•o•late′, *adj.*
sub′la•ryn′gal, *adj.*
sub′la•ryn′ge•al, *adj.;* **-ly,** *adv.*
sub•lead′er, *n.*
sub•lec′tur•er, *n.*
sub′leg•is•la′tion, *n.*
sub•leg′is•la′ture, *n.*
sub′len•tic′u•lar, *adj.*
sub′len•tic′u•late, *adj.*
sub′li•brar′i•an, *n.*
sub′li•brar′i•an•ship′, *n.*
sub′lid′, *n.*
sub•light′ed, *adj.*
sub•lin′e•ar, *adj.*
sub•lob′u•lar, *adj.*
sub•long′, *adj.*
sub•lo′ral, *adj.*

sub•round (sub round′), *adj.* somewhat round or rounded. [1780–90; SUB- + ROUND[1]]

sub•rou•tine (sub′ro͞o tēn′), *n. Computers.* an instruction sequence in a machine or assembly language program that can be prewritten and referred to as often as needed. Cf. **procedure** (def. 4a). [1945–50; SUB- + ROUTINE]

sub-Sa•har•an (sub′sə har′ən, -hâr′ən, -här′ən), *adj.* of, pertaining to, or in Africa south of the Sahara Desert: *a sub-Saharan country; sub-Saharan peoples.* [1960–65]

sub•sam•ple (*n.* sub′sam′pəl; *v.* sub sam′pəl), *n., v.,* **-pled, -pling.** —*n.* **1.** a specimen from or a small part of a sample. —*v.t.* **2.** to take a subsample of. [1895–1900; SUB- + SAMPLE]

sub•sat•el•lite (sub′sat′l īt′), *n.* a satellite designed to be released into orbit from another spacecraft. [1890–95; SUB- + SATELLITE]

subsc, subscription.

sub•scap•u•lar (sub skap′yə lər), *Anat.* —*adj.* **1.** situated beneath or on the deep surface of the scapula, as a muscle. —*n.* **2.** a subscapular muscle, artery, etc. Also, **sub•scap•u•lar•y** (sub skap′yə ler′ē). [1825–35; < NL *subscapulāris,* equiv. to *sub-* SUB- + *scapulāris* SCAPULAR]

sub•scribe (səb skrīb′), *v.,* **-scribed, -scrib•ing.** —*v.t.* **1.** to pledge, as by signing an agreement, to give or pay (a sum of money) as a contribution, gift, or investment: *He subscribed $6,000 for the new church.* **2.** to give or pay in fulfillment of such a pledge. **3.** to append one's signature or mark to (a document), as in approval or attestation of its contents. **4.** to attest by or as by signing. **5.** to append, as one's signature, at the bottom of a document or the like; sign. **6.** to agree or assent to. —*v.i.* **7.** to pledge, as by signing an agreement, to give or pay money as a contribution, gift, or investment. **8.** to give or pay money in fulfillment of such a pledge. **9.** to obtain a subscription to a magazine, newspaper, etc. **10.** to give one's consent; sanction: *I will not subscribe to popular fallacies.* **11.** to sign one's name to a document. **12.** to give approval to the contents of a document by signing one's name. [1375–1425; late ME *subscriben* < L *subscribere,* equiv. to *sub-* SUB- + *scribere* to write] —**sub•scrib′a•ble,** *adj.* —**sub•scrib′er•ship′,** *n.*

sub•scrib•er (səb skrī′bər), *n.* **1.** a person, company, etc., that subscribes, as to a publication or concert series. **2.** a homeowner, apartment dweller, business, etc., that pays a monthly charge to be connected to a television cable service. **3.** a person who promises to donate a sum of money, purchase stock, etc. [1590–1600; SUBSCRIBE + -ER[1]]

sub•script (sub′skript), *adj.* **1.** written below (distinguished from *adscript, superscript*). **2.** inferior (def. 9). —*n.* **3.** inferior (def. 11). **4.** Also called **subfix.** any character, number, or symbol written next to and slightly below another. [1695–1705; < L *subscriptus* (ptp. of *subscribere* to SUBSCRIBE), equiv. to *sub-* SUB- + *scrib(ere)* to write + *-tus* ptp. suffix]

sub•scrip•tion (səb skrip′shən), *n.* **1.** a sum of money given or pledged as a contribution, payment, investment, etc. **2.** the right to receive a periodical for a sum paid, usually for an agreed number of issues. **3.** an arrangement for presenting a series of concerts, plays, etc., that one may attend by the payment of a membership fee: *to purchase a 10-concert subscription.* **4.** *Chiefly Brit.* the dues paid by a member of a club, society, etc. **5.** a fund raised through sums of money subscribed. **6.** a sum subscribed. **7.** the act of appending one's signature or mark, as to a document. **8.** a signature or mark thus appended. **9.** something written beneath or at the end of a document or the like. **10.** a document to which a signature is attached. **11.** assent, agreement, or approval expressed verbally or by signing one's name. **12.** *Eccles.* assent to or acceptance of a body of principles or doctrines, the purpose of which is to establish uniformity. **13.** *Ch. of Eng.* formal acceptance of the Thirty-nine Articles of 1563 and the Book of Common Prayer. [1400–50; late ME < L *subscriptiōn-* (s. of *subscriptiō*) a writing beneath, equiv. to *subscript(us)* (see SUBSCRIPT) + *-iōn-* -ION] —**sub•scrip•tive** (səb skrip′tiv), *adj.* —**sub•scrip′tive•ly,** *adv.*

subscrip′tion edi′tion, **1.** an edition of one or more volumes for which a number of prospective purchasers place orders, usually in advance of publication. **2.** a specially designed edition offered to subscribers, usually on an installment or deferred payment plan, or on an installment or deferred delivery plan, or both.

subscrip′tion tel′evision. See **pay television.** Also called **subscription TV** [1950–55]

sub•sea (sub sē′, sub′sē′), *adj.* occurring, working, etc., under the sea or ocean: *a subsea specialist in oil rigs.* [SUB- + SEA]

sub•sec•re•tar•i•at (sub sek′ri târ′ē it, sub′sek-), *n.* an administrative department that assists and is subordinate to a secretariat. [SUB- + SECRETARIAT]

sub•sec•tion (sub sek′shən, sub′sek′-), *n.* **1.** a part or division of a section. —*v.t.* **2.** to divide or partition into subsections. [1615–25; SUB- + SECTION]

sub•seg•ment (sub seg′mənt, sub′seg′-), *n.* a part or division of a segment. [SUB- + SEGMENT]

sub•sel•li•um (sub sel′ē əm), *n., pl.* **-sel•li•a** (-sel′ē ə). misericord (def. 2). [1695–1705; < L: low seat, bench, equiv. to *sub-* SUB- + *sell(a)* seat + *-ium* -IUM]

sub•se•quence[1] (sub′si kwəns), *n.* **1.** the state or fact of being subsequent. **2.** a subsequent occurrence, event, etc.; sequel. [1490–1500; SUBSEQU(ENT) + -ENCE]

sub•se•quence[2] (sub′sē′kwəns), *n. Math.* a sequence obtained from a given sequence by selecting terms from it and placing them in the order in which they occur in it. [1940–45; SUB- + SEQUENCE]

sub•se•quent (sub′si kwənt), *adj.* **1.** occurring or coming later or after: *subsequent events.* **2.** following in order or succession; succeeding: *a subsequent section in a treaty.* [1425–75; late ME < L *subsequent-* (s. of *subsequēns*), prp. of *subsequi* to follow close behind, equiv. to *sub-* SUB- + *sequ(i)* to follow + *-ent-* -ENT] —**sub′se•quent•ly,** *adv.*

sub•se•rous (sub sēr′əs), *adj.* situated or occurring under a serous membrane. [1825–35; SUB- + SEROUS]

sub•serve (səb sûrv′), *v.t.,* **-served, -serv•ing.** **1.** to be useful or instrumental in promoting (a purpose, action, etc.): *Light exercise subserves digestion.* **2.** *Obs.* to serve as a subordinate. [1610–20; < L *subservire,* equiv. to *sub-* SUB- + *servire* to SERVE]

sub•ser•vi•ent (səb sûr′vē ənt), *adj.* **1.** serving or acting in a subordinate capacity; subordinate. **2.** servile; excessively submissive; obsequious: *subservient persons; subservient conduct.* **3.** useful in promoting a purpose or end. [1625–35; < L *subservient-* (s. of *subserviēns,* prp. of *subservire* to SUBSERVE), equiv. to *sub-* SUB- + *servi-,* s. of *servire* to SERVE + *-ent* -ENT] —**sub•ser′vi•ence, sub•ser′vi•en•cy,** *n.* —**sub•ser′vi•ent•ly,** *adv.*

sub•set (sub′set′), *n.* **1.** a set that is a part of a larger set. **2.** *Math.* a set consisting of elements of a given set that can be the same as the given set or smaller. [1900–05; SUB- + SET]

sub•shell (sub′shel′), *n. Physics.* a group of electrons in an atom belonging to the same shell and also having the same azimuthal quantum number. [1965–70; SUB- + SHELL]

sub•shrub (sub′shrub′), *n.* a plant consisting of a woody, perennial base with annual, herbaceous shoots. [1850–55; SUB- + SHRUB] —**sub′shrub′by,** *adj.*

sub•side (səb sīd′), *v.i.,* **-sid•ed, -sid•ing.** **1.** to sink to a low or lower level. **2.** to become quiet, less active, or less violent; abate: *The laughter subsided.* **3.** to sink or fall to the bottom; settle; precipitate: *to cause coffee grounds to subside.* [1640–50; < L *subsidere,* equiv. to *sub-* SUB- + *sidere* to sit, settle; akin to *sedēre* to be seated; see SIT[1]] —**sub•sid•ence** (səb sīd′ns, sub′si dns), *n.* —**sub•sid′er,** *n.*
—**Syn. 1.** decline, descend, settle. **2.** diminish, lessen, wane, ebb. —**Ant. 1.** rise. **2.** increase.

sub•sid•i•ar•y (səb sid′ē er′ē), *adj., n., pl.* **-ar•ies.** —*adj.* **1.** serving to assist or supplement; auxiliary; supplementary. **2.** subordinate or secondary: *subsidiary issues.* **3.** of or pertaining to a subsidiary. —*n.* **4.** a subsidiary thing or person. **5.** See **subsidiary company. 6.** *Music.* a subordinate theme or subject. [1535–45; < L *subsidiārius,* equiv. to *subsidi(um)* (see SUBSIDY) + *-ārius* -ARY] —**sub•sid•i•ar•i•ly** (səb sid′ē âr′ə lē, -sid′ē er′-), *adv.* —**sub•sid′i•ar′i•ness,** *n.*

subsid′iary coin′, a coin, esp. one made of silver, having a value less than that of the monetary unit. Cf. **minor coin.** [1885–90, *Amer.*]

subsid′iary com′pany, a company whose controlling interest is owned by another company. [1915–20]

subsid′iary ledg′er, (in accounting) a ledger containing a group of detailed and related accounts the total of which is summarized in the control account.

subsid′iary rights′, rights to publish or produce in different formats works based on the original work under contract, as a paperback edition of an original hardcover book or a motion picture based on a novel.

sub•si•dize (sub′si dīz′), *v.t.,* **-dized, -diz•ing.** **1.** to furnish or aid with a subsidy. **2.** to purchase the assistance of by the payment of a subsidy. **3.** to secure the cooperation of by bribery; buy over. Also, *esp. Brit.,* **sub′si•dise′.** [1785–95; SUBSID(Y) + -IZE] —**sub′si•diz′a•ble,** *adj.* —**sub′si•di•za′tion,** *n.* —**sub′si•diz′er,** *n.*

sub•si•dy (sub′si dē), *n., pl.* **-dies.** **1.** a direct pecuniary aid furnished by a government to a private industrial undertaking, a charity organization, or the like. **2.** a sum paid, often in accordance with a treaty, by one government to another to secure some service in return. **3.** a grant or contribution of money. **4.** money formerly granted by the English Parliament to the crown for special needs. [1325–75; ME *subsidie* < AF < L *subsidium* auxiliary force, reserve, help, equiv. to *sub-* SUB- + *sid-,* comb. form of *sedēre* to SIT[1] + *-ium* -IUM]
—**Syn. 1.** SUBSIDY, SUBVENTION are both grants of money, especially governmental, to aid private undertakings. A SUBSIDY is usually given to promote commercial enterprise: *a subsidy to manufacturers during a war.* A SUBVENTION is usually a grant to stimulate enterprises connected with science and the arts: *a subvention to a research chemist by a major company.*

sub•sist (səb sist′), *v.i.* **1.** to exist; continue in existence. **2.** to remain alive; live, as on food, resources, etc. **3.** to have existence in, or by reason of, something. **4.** to reside, lie, or consist (usually fol. by *in*). **5.** *Philos.* **a.** to have timeless or abstract existence, as a number, relation, etc. **b.** to have existence, esp. independent existence. —*v.t.* **6.** to provide sustenance or support for; maintain. [1540–50; < L *subsistere* to remain, equiv. to *sub-* SUB- + *sistere* to stand, make stand; see STAND] —**sub•sist′ing•ly,** *adv.*

sub•sist•ence (səb sis′təns), *n.* **1.** the state or fact of subsisting. **2.** the state or fact of existing. **3.** the providing of sustenance or support. **4.** means of supporting life; a living or livelihood. **5.** the source from which food and other items necessary to exist are obtained. **6.** *Philos.* **a.** existence, especially of an independent entity. **b.** the quality of having timeless or abstract existence. **c.** mode of existence or that by which a substance is individualized. [1400–50; late ME < LL *subsistentia;* see SUBSIST, -ENCE]
—**Syn. 3.** survival, maintenance, nourishment.

subsist′ence allow′ance, **1.** money given in advance to a new soldier, employee, etc., to buy food, clothing, and pay for other necessities while awaiting a first pay. **2.** money paid a worker in addition to salary to cover expenses that may be incurred in the performance of the job. **3.** money paid to members of the armed forces in lieu of meals; an allowance for food.

subsist′ence farm′ing, **1.** farming whose products are intended to provide for the basic needs of the farmer, with little surplus for marketing. **2.** farming that brings little or no profit to the farmer, allowing only for a marginal livelihood. Also, **subsist′ence ag′riculture.** [1935–40]

sub•sist•ent (səb sis′tənt), *adj.* **1.** subsisting, existing, or continuing in existence. **2.** inherent: *subsistent qualities of character.* —*n.* **3.** *Philos.* something that exists necessarily as opposed to contingent existence in space and time. [1520–30; < L *subsistent-* (s. of *subsistēns*), prp. of *subsistere* to remain; see SUBSIST, -ENT]

sub•so•cial (sub sō′shəl), *adj.* without a definite social structure. [1905–10; SUB- + SOCIAL] —**sub•so′cial•ly,** *adv.*

sub•soil (sub′soil′), *n.* the bed or stratum of earth or earthy material immediately under the surface soil. Also called **undersoil.** [1790–1800; SUB- + SOIL[1]]

sub•soil•er (sub′soi′lər), *n.* **1.** one who operates a subsoil plow. **2.** See **subsoil plow.** [1850–55; SUBSOIL + -ER[1]]

sub′soil plow′, a plow for stirring the subsoil, usually without disturbing the surface. [1825–35]

sub•so•lar (sub sō′lər), *adj.* **1.** situated beneath the sun or between the earth and the sun. **2.** between the tropics. [1650–60; SUB- + SOLAR[1]]

sub•song (sub′sông′, -song′), *n.* an unstructured, often rambling vocalization of low volume heard in young birds and, at the start of the breeding season, in adult birds of certain species. [SUB- + SONG]

CONCISE ETYMOLOGY KEY: <, descended or borrowed from; >, whence; b., blend of, blended; c., cognate with; cf., compare; deriv., derivative; equiv., equivalent; imit., imitative; obl., oblique; r., replacing; s., stem; sp., spelling, spelled; resp., respelling, respelled; trans., translation; ?, origin unknown; *, unattested; ‡, probably earlier than. See the full key inside the front cover.

sub′lot′, *n.*
sub•lum′bar, *adj.*
sub•lu′nate, *adj.*
sub•lu′nat•ed, *adj.*
sub•lus′trous, *adj.;* **-ly,** *adv.;* **-ness,** *n.*
sub′maid′, *n.*
sub•mam′ma•ry, *adj.*
sub•man′ag•er, *n.*
sub•man′ag•er•ship′, *n.*
sub•ma′ni•a, *n.*
sub′ma•ni′a•cal, *adj.;* **-ly,** *adv.*
sub•man′ic, *adj.*
sub•man′or, *n.*
sub′mar′ket, *n.*
sub•mar′shal, *n.*
sub•mas′ter, *n.*
sub•max′i•mal, *adj.*
sub•max′i•mum, *adj.*
sub•mean′ing, *n.*
sub•me′di•al, *adj.;* **-ly,** *adv.*
sub•me′di•an, *adj.*
sub′me•di•a′tion, *n.*
sub′me•di•o′cre, *adj.*
sub•meet′ing, *n.*
sub•mem′ber, *n.*
sub′mem•bra•na′ceous, *adj.*
sub•mem′bra•nous, *adj.*
sub′me•nin′ge•al, *adj.*
sub•men′tal, *adj.*
sub′met•a•phor′ic, *adj.*
sub′met•a•phor′i•cal, *adj.;* **-ly,** *adv.*
sub•mil′i•ar′y, *adj.*
sub′mind′, *n.*
sub•min′i•mal, *adj.*
sub•min′is•ter, *n.*
sub•min′is•trant, *adj.*
sub′mo•lec′u•lar, *adj.*
sub•mol′e•cule′, *n.*
sub•mort′gage, *n.*
sub•moun′tain, *adj.*
sub•mu′cous, *adj.*
sub•mu′cro•nate, *adj.*
sub•mu′cro•nat′ed, *adj.*
sub′mun•dane′, *adj.*
sub•mu′ri•ate′, *n.*
sub•mus′cu•lar, *adj.;* **-ly,** *adv.*
sub•na′cre•ous, *adj.*
sub′nar•cot′ic, *adj.*
sub•na′tion•al, *adj.*
sub•nat′u•ral, *adj.;* **-ly,** *adv.;* **-ness,** *n.*
sub•net′work′, *n.*
sub•neu′ral, *adj.*
sub•nod′u•lose′, *adj.*
sub•nod′u•lous, *adj.*
sub′no•ta′tion, *n.*
sub′no•ta′tion•al, *adj.*
sub′note′, *n.*
sub•no•to•chord′al, *adj.*
sub•nu′cle•us, *n., pl.* **-cle•i, -cle•us•es.**
sub•nude′, *adj.*
sub•num′ber, *n.*
sub′nu•tri′tious, *adj.;* **-ly,** *adv.;* **-ness,** *n.*
sub′o•blique′, *adj.;* **-ly,** *adv.;* **-ness,** *n.*
sub′ob•scure′, *adj.;* **-ly,** *adv.;* **-ness,** *n.*
sub•ob′so•lete′, *adj.;* **-ly,** *adv.;* **-ness,** *n.*
sub′ob•tuse′, *adj.;* **-ly,** *adv.;* **-ness,** *n.*
sub•oc′u•lar, *adj.;* **-ly,** *adv.*
sub′oe•soph′a•ge′al, *adj.*
sub•of′fice, *n.*
sub•of′fi•cer, *n.*
sub′of•fi′cial, *n., adj.;* **-ly,** *adv.*
sub•ol′ive, *adj.*
sub′o•paque′, *adj.;* **-ly,** *adv.;* **-ness,** *n.*
sub•op′er•a′tion, *n.*
sub•op′po•site, *adj.;* **-ly,** *adv.;* **-ness,** *n.*
sub•op′tic, *adj.*
sub•op′ti•cal, *adj.;* **-ly,** *adv.*
sub•o′ral, *adj.*
sub′or•bic′u•lar, *adj.;* **-ly,** *adv.*
sub′or•bic′u•lar′i•ty, *n.*
sub′or•bic′u•late, *adj.*
sub′or•bic′u•lat′ed, *adj.*
sub′or•gan′ic, *adj.*
sub′or•gan′i•cal•ly, *adv.*
sub•or′gan•i•za′tion, *n.*
sub′o•var′i•an, *adj.*
sub•o′vate, *adj.*
sub•o′ver•se′er, *n.*
sub•o′void, *adj.*
sub•pack′age, *n.*
sub′pa•go′da, *n.*
sub•pal′li•al, *adj.*
sub•pal′mate, *adj.*
sub•pal′mat•ed, *adj.*
sub•pan′el, *n.*
sub•par′, *adj.*
sub•par′a•graph′, *n.*
sub•par′al•lel′, *adj.*
sub•par′a•lyt′ic, *adj.*
sub′pa•ri′e•tal, *adj.*
sub•par′lia•ment, *n.*
sub′part′, *n.*
sub•par•ti′tion, *n.*
sub′par•ti′tioned, *adj.*
sub•par•ti′tion•ment, *n.*
sub′par′ty, *n., pl.* **-ties.**
sub′pass′, *n.*
sub•pas′tor, *n.*
sub•pas′tor•ship′, *n.*
sub′pa•tel′lar, *adj.*
sub•pa′tron, *n.*
sub•pa′tron•al, *adj.*
sub•pa′tron•ess, *n.*
sub•pat′tern, *n.*

sub·son·ic (sub son′ik), *adj.* **1.** noting or pertaining to a speed less than that of sound in air at the same height above sea level. **2.** infrasonic. [1940–45; SUB- + -SONIC] **—sub·son′i·cal·ly,** *adv.*

sub·space (sub′spās′), *n.* **1.** a smaller space within a main area that has been divided or subdivided: *The jewelry shop occupies a subspace in the hotel's lobby.* **2.** *Math.* **a.** a subset of a given space. **b.** Also called **linear manifold.** a subset of a vector space which is itself a vector space. **c.** a subset of a topological space, having the relative topology. [1925–30; SUB- + SPACE]

sub′space topol′ogy, *Math.* See **relative topology.**

sub·spe·cial·ty (sub spesh′əl tē, sub′spesh′-), *n., pl.* **-ties.** a lesser or minor specialty: *a cinematographer with a subspecialty of portrait photography.* [1925–30; SUB- + SPECIALTY]

sub·spe·cies (sub′spē′shēz, sub spē′-), *n., pl.* **-cies.** a subdivision of a species, esp. a geographical or ecological subdivision. [1690–1700; SUB- + SPECIES]

sub·spe·cif·ic (sub′spə sif′ik), *adj.* **1.** of, pertaining to, or of the nature of a subspecies. **2.** less than specific. [1865–70; SUB- + SPECIFIC] **—sub′spe·cif′i·cal·ly,** *adv.*

subst., **1.** substantive. **2.** substantively. **3.** substitute.

sub·stage (sub′stāj′), *n.* the component part of a microscope below the stage, for supporting a condenser, mirror, or other accessories. [1855–60; SUB- + STAGE]

sub·stance (sub′stəns), *n.* **1.** that of which a thing consists; physical matter or material: *form and substance.* **2.** a species of matter of definite chemical composition: *a chalky substance.* **3.** See **controlled substance.** **4.** the subject matter of thought, discourse, study, etc. **5.** the actual matter of a thing, as opposed to the appearance or shadow; reality. **6.** substantial or solid character or quality: *claims lacking in substance.* **7.** consistency; body: *soup without much substance.* **8.** the meaning or gist, as of speech or writing. **9.** something that has separate or independent existence. **10.** *Philos.* **a.** something that exists by itself and in which accidents or attributes inhere; that which receives modifications and is not itself a mode; something that is causally active; something that is more than an event. **b.** the essential part of a thing; essence. **c.** a thing considered as a continuing whole. **11.** possessions, means, or wealth: *to squander one's substance.* **12.** *Ling.* the articulatory or acoustic reality or the perceptual manifestation of a word or other construction (distinguished from *form*). **13.** a standard of weights for paper. **14. in substance, a.** concerning the essentials; substantially. **b.** actually; really: *That is in substance how it appeared to me.* [1250–1300; ME < L *substantia* substance, essence (lit., that which stands under, i.e., underlies), equiv. to *sub-* SUB- + *-stant-* (s. of *stāns,* prp. of *stāre* to STAND) + *-ia* -IA (see -ANCE)] **—sub′stance·less,** *adj.*
—Syn. 1. See **matter. 4.** theme, subject. **4, 5, 8.** essence. **8.** significance, import, pith.

sub′stance abuse′, long-term, pathological use of alcohol or drugs, characterized by daily intoxication, inability to reduce consumption, and impairment in social or occupational functioning; broadly, alcohol or drug addiction.

substance P, a small peptide released upon stimulation in the nervous system and involved in regulation of the pain threshold. [earlier *standard preparation P* (1931); the initial is unexplained by the substance's discoverers]

sub·stand·ard (sub stan′dərd), *adj.* **1.** below standard or less than adequate: *substandard housing conditions.* **2.** noting or pertaining to a dialect or variety of a language or a feature of usage that is often considered by others to mark its user as uneducated; nonstandard. **3.** *Insurance.* **a.** not measuring up to an insurer's regular standards in undertaking risks: *a substandard risk.* **b.** pertaining to insurance written to cover substandard risks. [1895–1900; SUB- + STANDARD]

sub·stan·tial (səb stan′shəl), *adj.* **1.** of ample or considerable amount, quantity, size, etc.: *a substantial sum of money.* **2.** of a corporeal or material nature; tangible; real. **3.** of solid character or quality; firm, stout, or strong: *a substantial physique.* **4.** basic or essential; fundamental: *two stories in substantial agreement.* **5.** wealthy or influential: *one of the substantial men of the town.* **6.** of real worth, value, or effect: *substantial reasons.* **7.** pertaining to the substance, matter, or material of a thing. **8.** of or pertaining to the essence of a thing; essential, material, or important. **9.** being a substance; having independent existence. **10.** *Philos.* pertaining to or of the nature of substance rather than an accident or attribute. **—***n.* **11.** something substantial. [1300–50; ME *substancial* < LL *substantiālis,* equiv. to L *substanti(a)* SUBSTANCE + *-ālis* -AL[1]] **—sub·stan′ti·al′i·ty, sub·stan′tial·ness,** *n.* **—sub·stan′tial·ly,** *adv.*
—Syn. 3. stable, sound. **6.** valid, important. **—Ant. 2.** immaterial, ethereal.

sub·stan·tial·ism (səb stan′shə liz′əm), *n. Philos.* the doctrine that substantial noumena exist as a basis for phenomena. [1880–85; SUBSTANTIAL + -ISM] **—sub·stan′tial·ist,** *n.*

sub·stan·ti·a ni·gra (səb stan′shē ə nī′grə, nig′rə), *pl.* **sub·stan·ti·ae ni·grae** (sub stan′shē ē′ nī′grē, nig′rē), **substantia nigras.** a deeply pigmented area of the midbrain containing dopamine-producing nerve cells. [1880–85; < NL: black substance]

sub·stan·ti·ate (səb stan′shē āt′), *v.t.,* **-at·ed, -at·ing. 1.** to establish by proof or competent evidence: *to substantiate a charge.* **2.** to give substantial existence to: *to substantiate an idea through action.* **3.** to affirm as having substance; give body to; strengthen: *to substantiate a friendship.* [1650–60; < NL *substantiātus* (ptp. of *substantiāre*), equiv. to L *substanti(a)* SUBSTANCE + *-ātus* -ATE[1]] **—sub·stan′ti·a·ble,** *adj.* **—sub·stan′·ti·a′tion,** *n.* **—sub·stan′ti·a′tive,** *adj.* **—sub·stan′ti·a′tor,** *n.*
—Syn. 1. prove, confirm, verify, validate.

sub·stan·ti·val (sub′stən tī′vəl), *adj.* noting, of, or pertaining to a substantive. [1825–35; SUBSTANTIVE + -AL[1]] **—sub′stan·ti′val·ly,** *adv.*

sub·stan·tive (sub′stən tiv), *n. Gram.* **1.** a noun. **2.** a pronoun or other word or phrase functioning or inflected like a noun. **—***adj.* **3.** *Gram.* **a.** pertaining to substantives. **b.** used in a sentence like a noun: *a substantive adjective.* **c.** expressing existence: *"to be" is a substantive verb.* **4.** having independent existence; independent. **5.** belonging to the real nature or essential part of a thing; essential. **6.** real or actual. **7.** of considerable amount or quantity. **8.** possessing substance; having practical importance, value, or effect: *substantive issues under discussion.* **9.** *Law.* pertaining to the rules of right which courts are called on to apply, as distinguished from rules of procedure (opposed to *adjective*). **10.** (of dye colors) attaching directly to the material without the aid of a mordant (opposed to *adjective*). [1350–1400; ME < LL *substantīvus,* equiv. to L *substant(ia)* SUBSTANCE + *-īvus* -IVE] **—sub′stan·tive·ly,** *adv.* **—sub′stan·tive·ness,** *n.*

sub′stantive right′, a right, as life, liberty, or property, recognized for its own sake and as part of the natural legal order of society. [1935–40]

sub·stan·tiv·ize (sub′stən tə vīz′), *v.t.,* **-ized, -iz·ing.** to use (an adjective, verb, etc.) as a substantive; convert into a substantive: *a substantivized participle.* Also, *esp. Brit.,* **sub′stan·tiv·ise′.** [1865–70; SUBSTANTIVE + -IZE] **—sub′stan·tiv·i·za′tion,** *n.*

sub·sta·tion (sub′stā′shən), *n.* **1.** a branch of a main post office. **2.** an auxiliary power station where electrical current is converted, as from AC to DC, voltage is stepped up or down, etc. [1885–90; SUB- + STATION]

sub·stit·u·ent (sub stich′o͞o ənt), *n.* **1.** *Chem.* an atom or atomic group that takes the place of another atom or group present in the molecule of the original compound. **—***adj.* **2.** having been or capable of being substituted. [1890–95; < L *substituent-* (s. of *substituēns*), prp. of *substituere* to SUBSTITUTE, equiv. to *sub-* SUB- + *-stitu-,* comb. form of *statuere* to set up, erect (see STATUE) + *-ent-* -ENT]

sub·sti·tute (sub′sti to͞ot′, -tyo͞ot′), *n., v.,* **-tut·ed, -tut·ing,** *adj.* **—***n.* **1.** a person or thing acting or serving in place of another. **2.** (formerly) a person who, for payment, served in an army or navy in the place of a conscript. **3.** *Gram.* a word that functions as a replacement for any member of a class of words or constructions, as *do* in *He doesn't know but I do.* **—***v.t.* **4.** to put (a person or thing) in the place of another. **5.** to take the place of; replace. **6.** *Chem.* to replace (one or more elements or groups in a compound) by other elements or groups. **—***v.i.* **7.** to act as a substitute. **—***adj.* **8.** of or pertaining to a substitute or substitutes. **9.** composed of substitutes. [1350–1400; ME < L *substitūtus* (ptp. of *substituere* to put in place of), equiv. to *sub-* SUB- + *-stitū-,* comb. form of *statū-,* ptp. s. of *statuere* (see SUBSTITUENT) + *-tus* ptp. suffix] **—sub′sti·tut′a·ble,** *adj.* **—sub′sti·tut′a·bil′i·ty,** *n.* **—sub′sti·tut′er,** *n.* **—sub′·sti·tut′ing·ly,** *adv.* **—sub′sti·tu′tion,** *n.* **—sub′·sti·tu′tion·al, sub·sti·tu·tion·ar·y** (sub′sti to͞o′shə ner′ē, -tyo͞o′-), *adj.* **—sub′sti·tu′tion·al·ly,** *adv.*
—Syn. 1. alternative, replacement, equivalent.

substitu′tion ci′pher, *Cryptography.* a cipher that replaces letters of the plain text with another set of letters or symbols. Cf. **transposition cipher.** [1935–40]

substitu′tion reac′tion, *Chem.* the replacement of an atom or group of atoms in a compound by another atom or group.

sub·sti·tu·tive (sub′sti to͞o′tiv, -tyo͞o′-), *adj.* **1.** serving as or capable of serving as a substitute. **2.** pertaining to or involving substitution. [1590–1600; SUBSTITUTE + -IVE] **—sub′sti·tu′tive·ly,** *adv.*

sub·strate (sub′strāt), *n.* **1.** a substratum. **2.** *Biochem.* the substance acted upon by an enzyme. **3.** *Electronics.* a supporting material on which a circuit is formed or fabricated. [1570–80; var. of SUBSTRATUM]

sub·strat·o·sphere (sub strat′ə sfēr′), *n.* (not used technically) the upper troposphere. [1915–20; SUB- + STRATOSPHERE] **—sub·strat·o·spher·ic** (sub′strat ə sfer′ik, -sfēr′-), *adj.*

sub·stra·tum (sub′strā′təm, -strat′əm, sub strā′təm, -strat′əm), *n., pl.* **-stra·ta** (-strā′tə, -strat′ə, -strā′tə, -strat′ə), **-stra·tums. 1.** something that is spread or laid under something else; a stratum or layer lying under another. **2.** something that underlies or serves as a basis or foundation. **3.** *Agric.* the subsoil. **4.** *Biol.* the base or material on which a nonmotile organism lives or grows. **5.** *Philos.* substance, considered as that which supports accidents or attributes. **6.** *Photog.* a layer of material placed directly on a film or plate as a foundation for the sensitive emulsion. **7.** *Historical Ling.* a set of features of a language traceable to the influence of an earlier language that it has replaced, esp. among a subjugated population: *The French word for 80, quatre-vingts ("four twenties"), may reflect a Celtic substratum.* Cf. **superstratum.** [1625–35; < NL; see SUB-, STRATUM] **—sub·stra′tive, sub·stra′tal,** *adj.*

sub·struc·tion (sub struk′shən), *n.* a foundation or substructure. [1615–25; < L *substructiōn-* (s. of *substructiō*) foundation, equiv. to *substruct(us),* ptp. of *substruere* to lay a foundation (*sub-* SUB- + *struc-,* var. s. of *struere* to arrange, put in order + *-tus* ptp. suffix) + *-iōn-* -ION] **—sub·struc′tion·al,** *adj.*

sub·struc·ture (sub struk′chər, sub′struk′-), *n.* **1.** a structure forming the foundation of a building or other construction. **2.** the foundations, piers, and abutments upon which the trusses or girders of the spans of a bridge rest. **3.** any basic structure or organization. [1720–30; SUB- + STRUCTURE] **—sub·struc′tur·al,** *adj.*

sub·sul·fate (sub sul′fāt), *n. Chem.* a basic salt of sulfuric acid. Also, **sub·sul′phate.** [1795–1805; SUB- + SULFATE]

sub·sume (səb so͞om′), *v.t.,* **-sumed, -sum·ing. 1.** to consider or include (an idea, term, proposition, etc.) as part of a more comprehensive one. **2.** to bring (a case, instance, etc.) under a rule. **3.** to take up into a more inclusive classification. [1525–35; < ML *subsūmere,* equiv. to L *sub-* SUB- + *sūmere* to take; see CONSUME] **—sub·sum′a·ble,** *adj.*

sub·sump·tion (səb sump′shən), *n.* **1.** an act of subsuming. **2.** the state of being subsumed. **3.** something that is subsumed. **4.** a proposition subsumed under another. [1630–40; < ML *subsūmptiōn-* (s. of *subsūmptiō*) a subjoining, equiv. to *subsūmpt(us)* (ptp. of *subsūmere* to SUBSUME + L *-iōn-* -ION] **—sub·sump′tive,** *adj.*

sub·sur·face (sub sûr′fəs, sub′sûr′-), *adj.* below the surface, esp. of a body of water. [1770–80; SUB- + SURFACE]

sub·sys·tem (sub′sis′təm, sub sis′-), *n.* a secondary or subordinate system. [SUB- + SYSTEM]

sub·tan·gent (sub tan′jənt), *n. Geom.* the part of the x-axis cut off between the ordinate of a given point of a curve and the tangent at that point. [1705–15; SUB- + TANGENT]

sub·teen (sub′tēn′), *n.* **1.** a young person approaching the teens or adolescence. **2.** a range of even-numbered garment sizes, chiefly from 6 to 14, designed for girls under 13. **—***adj.* **3.** of, pertaining to, or designed for subteens: *subteen clothes.* [1950–55; SUB- + TEEN[2]]

sub·tem·per·ate (sub tem′pər it), *adj.* of, pertaining to, or occurring in the colder parts of the Temperate Zone. [1850–55; SUB- + TEMPERATE]

sub·ten·ant (sub ten′ənt), *n.* a person who rents land, a house, or the like, from a tenant. [1400–50; late ME. See SUB-, TENANT] **—sub·ten′an·cy,** *n.*

CONCISE PRONUNCIATION KEY: *act, cāpe, dâre, pärt; set, ēqual; if, īce; ox, ōver, ôrder, oil, bo͝ok, bo͞ot, out; up, ûrge; child; sing; shoe; thin, that;* zh as in *treasure.* ə = *a* as in *alone, e* as in *system, i* as in *easily, o* as in *gallop, u* as in *circus;* ᵊ as in *fire* (fīᵊr), *hour* (ouᵊr). l and n can serve as syllabic consonants, as in *cradle* (krād′l), and *button* (but′n). See the full key inside the front cover.

sub′pave′ment, *n.*
sub·pec′ti·nate′, *adj.*
sub′pec′ti·nat′ed, *adj.*
sub′pec·ti·na′tion, *n.*
sub·pec′to·ral, *adj.*
sub′pe·dun′cle, *n.*
sub′pe·dun′cled, *adj.*
sub′pe·dun′cu·lar, *adj.*
sub′pe·dun′cu·late, *adj.*
sub′pe·dun′cu·lat′ed, *adj.*
sub′pel·lu′cid, *adj.;* **-ly,** *adv.;* **-ness,** *n.*
sub′pel·lu·cid′i·ty, *n.*
sub·pel′tate, *adj.;* **-ly,** *adv.*
sub′pen·tag′o·nal, *adj.*
sub′per·i·car′di·ac′, *adj.*
sub′per·i·car′di·al, *adj.*
sub′per·i·cra′ni·al, *adj.*
sub·pe′ri·od, *n.*
sub′per·i·os′te·al, *adj.;* **-ly,** *adv.*
sub′per·i·to·ne′al, *adj.*
sub·per′ma·nent, *adj.;* **-ly,** *adv.*
sub·pet′i·o·late′, *adj.*
sub·pet′i·o·lat′ed, *adj.*
sub′pe·tro′sal, *adj.*
sub′pha·ryn′gal, *adj.*
sub′pha·ryn′ge·al, *adj.;* **-ly,** *adv.*
sub′phase′, *n.*
sub·phos′phate, *n.*
sub·phra′try, *n., pl.* **-tries.**
sub·phren′ic, *adj.*
sub·pi′al, *adj.*
sub·pi′lose, *adj.*
sub′pi·los′i·ty, *n.*
sub·pis′ton, *n.*
sub′pla·cen′ta, *n., pl.* **-tas, -tae.**
sub′pla·cen′tal, *adj.*
sub′plant′, *n.*
sub·plan′ti·grade′, *adj.*
sub·plex′al, *adj.*
sub′plow′, *n.*
sub·plow′, *v.*
sub′po·lit′i·cal, *adj.;* **-ly,** *adv.*
sub′po·lyg′o·nal, *adj.;* **-ly,** *adv.*
sub-Pon′tine, *adj.*
sub′pool′, *n.*
sub·pop′u·lar, *adj.*
sub′pop·u·la′tion, *n.*
sub′por·phy·rit′ic, *adj.*
sub′port′, *n.*
sub′post′, *n.*
sub·post′mas′ter, *n.*
sub·post′mas′ter·ship′, *n.*
sub·post′script′, *n.*
sub′pre·cep′tor, *n.*
sub′pre·cep′to·ral, *adj.*
sub′pre·cep′tor·ate, *n.*
sub′pre·cep·to′ri·al, *adj.*
sub·pred′i·cate, *n.*
sub′pred·i·ca′tion, *n.*
sub·pred′i·ca′tive, *adj.*
sub·pre′fect, *n.*
sub′pre·fec·to′ri·al, *adj.*
sub·pre′fec·ture, *n.*
sub′pre·hen′sile, *adj.*
sub′pre·hen·sil′i·ty, *n.*
sub′pre·pu′tial, *adj.*
sub·pri′ma·ry, *adj.*
sub·pri′or, *n.*
sub·pri′or·ess, *n.*
sub·pri′or·ship′, *n.*
sub·prob′lem, *n.*
sub·proc′tor, *n.*
sub′proc·to′ri·al, *adj.*
sub·proc′tor·ship′, *n.*
sub′prod′uct, *n.*
sub′pro·fes′sor, *n.*
sub′pro·fes′sor·ate, *n.*
sub′pro·fes·so′ri·ate, *n.*
sub′pro·fes′sor·ship′, *n.*
sub·prof′it·a·ble, *adj.;* **-ble·ness,** *n.;* **-bly,** *adv.*
sub′proj′ect, *n.*
sub′pro·por′tion·al, *adj.;* **-ly,** *adv.*
sub′pro·stat′ic, *adj.*
sub′pro·tec′tor, *n.*
sub′pro·tec′tor·ship′, *n.*
sub·prov′ince, *n.*
sub′pro·vin′cial, *adj., n.*
sub′pu·bes′cent, *adj.*
sub·pu′bic, *adj.*
sub·pul′mo·nar′y, *adj.*
sub·pul′ver·iz′er, *n.*
sub′py·ram′i·dal, *adj.*
sub′pyr·a·mid′ic, *adj.*
sub′pyr·a·mid′i·cal, *adj.*
sub′-Pyr·e·ne′an, *adj.*
sub·pyr′i·form′, *adj.*
sub′quad·ran′gu·lar, *adj.*
sub·quad′rate, *adj.*
sub·qual′i·ty, *n., pl.* **-ties.**
sub·ques′tion, *n.*
sub·quin′que·fid, *adj.*
sub′race′, *n.*
sub·ra′di·ance, *n.*
sub·ra′di·an·cy, *n.*
sub·ra′di·ate, *adj.*
sub·ra′di·a′tive, *adj.*
sub·rad′i·cal, *adj.;* **-ness,** *n.*
sub·rad′u·lar, *adj.*
sub·ra′mose, *adj.*
sub·ra′mous, *adj.*
sub′range′, *n.*
sub·read′er, *n.*
sub·rea′son, *n.*
sub′re·bel′lion, *n.*
sub·rec′tal, *adj.*
sub′rec·tan′gu·lar, *adj.*
sub·rec′tor, *n.*
sub·rec′to·ry, *n., pl.* **-ries.**
sub·ref′er·ence, *n.*
sub·re′gent, *n.*

sub·tend (səb tend′, sub-), *v.t.* **1.** *Geom.* to extend under or be opposite to: *a chord subtending an arc.* **2.** *Bot.* (of a leaf, bract, etc.) to occur beneath or close to. **3.** to form or mark the outline or boundary of. [1560–70; < L *subtendere* to stretch beneath, equiv. to *sub-* SUB- + *tendere* to stretch; see TEND¹]

chord AC **subtends** (def. 1) arc ABC

sub·ten·ure (sub ten′yər), *n.* the tenancy of a subtenant. [1830–40; SUB- + TENURE]

sub·ter·fuge (sub′tər fyo͞oj′), *n.* an artifice or expedient used to evade a rule, escape a consequence, hide something, etc. [1565–75; < LL *subterfugium,* equiv. to L *subterfug(ere)* to evade (*subter* below + *fugere* to flee) + *-ium* -IUM] —**Syn.** deception, scheme, trick, dodge, ruse.

sub·ter·rane (sub′tə rān′, sub′tə rān′), *n.* a cave or subterranean room. Also, **sub′ter·rain′, sub·ter·rene** (sub′tə rēn′, sub′tə rēn′). [1605–15, in sense "subterranean"; 1765–75 for current sense; < L *subterrāneus* subterranean, equiv. to *sub-* SUB- + *terr(a)* earth + *-āneus* composite adj. suffix, equiv. to *-ān(us)* -AN + *-eus* -EOUS]

sub·ter·ra·ne·an (sub′tə rā′nē ən), *adj.* Also, **sub′·ter·ra′ne·ous. 1.** existing, situated, or operating below the surface of the earth; underground. **2.** existing or operating out of sight or secretly; hidden or secret. —*n.* **3.** a person or thing that is subterranean. **4.** a subterrane. [1595–1605; < L *subterrāne(us)* (see SUBTERRANE) + -AN] —**sub′ter·ra′ne·an·ly, sub′ter·ra′ne·ous·ly,** *adv.*

sub·ter·res·tri·al (sub′tə res′trē əl), *adj.* underground; subterranean. [1605–15; SUB- + TERRESTRIAL]

sub·text (sub′tekst′), *n.* the underlying or implicit meaning, as of a literary work. [1945–50; trans. of Russ *podtékst;* see SUB-, TEXT] —**sub·tex′tu·al,** *adj.*

sub·ther·a·peu·tic (sub′ther ə pyo͞o′tik), *adj.* indicating a dosage, as of a drug or vitamin, less than the amount required for a therapeutic effect. —**sub′ther·a·peu′ti·cal·ly,** *adv.* [SUB- + THERAPEUTIC]

sub·thresh·old (sub thresh′ōld, -thresh′hōld), *adj.* *Psychol., Physiol.* (of a stimulus) too weak to produce a response. [1940–45; SUB- + THRESHOLD]

sub·tile (sut′l, sub′til), *adj.,* **-til·er, -til·est.** subtle. [1325–75; ME < L *subtīlis* fine (orig. of fabric), equiv. to *sub-* SUB- + *-tīlis,* akin to *tēla* cloth on a loom, loom (< **tekslā,* deriv. of *texere* to weave; see TEXT)] —**sub′tile·ly,** *adv.* —**sub′tile·ness,** *n.*

sub·til·i·sin (sub til′ə sin), *n. Biochem.* a proteolytic enzyme produced by the bacterium *Bacillus subtilis,* used as an active ingredient in detergents and also in research to help reveal protein structure. [1953; < NL *subtilis* specific epithet (see SUBTILE) + -IN²]

sub·til·ize (sut′l īz′, sub′tə līz′), *v.,* **-ized, -iz·ing.** —*v.t.* **1.** to elevate in character; sublimate. **2.** to make (the mind, senses, etc.) keen or discerning; sharpen. **3.** to introduce subtleties into or argue subtly about. **4.** to make thin, rare, or more fluid or volatile; refine. —*v.i.* **5.** to make subtle distinctions or to argue subtly. Also, *esp. Brit.,* **sub′til·ise′.** [1585–95; < ML *subtilizāre,* equiv. to *subtīl(is)* SUBTLE + *-izāre* -IZE] —**sub′til·i·za′·tion,** *n.* —**sub′til·iz′er,** *n.*

sub·til·ty (sut′l tē, sub′til-), *n., pl.* **-ties.** *Archaic.* subtlety. Also, **sub·til·i·ty** (sub til′i tē).

sub·ti·tle (sub′tīt′l), *n., v.,* **-tled, -tling.** —*n.* **1.** a secondary or subordinate title of a literary work, usually of explanatory character. **2.** a repetition of the leading words in the full title of a book at the head of the first page of text. **3.** *Motion Pictures, Television.* **a.** the text of dialogue, speeches, operas, etc., translated into another language and projected on the lower part of the screen. **b.** (in silent motion pictures) a title or caption. —*v.t.* **4.** to give a subtitle to. [1875–80; SUB- + TITLE] —**sub·tit·u·lar** (sub tich′ə lər, -tit′yə-), *adj.*

sub·tle (sut′l), *adj.,* **-tler, -tlest. 1.** thin, tenuous, or rarefied, as a fluid or an odor. **2.** fine or delicate in meaning or intent; difficult to perceive or understand: *subtle irony.* **3.** delicate or faint and mysterious: *a subtle smile.* **4.** requiring mental acuteness, penetration, or discernment: *a subtle philosophy.* **5.** characterized by mental acuteness or penetration: *a subtle understanding.* **6.** cunning, wily, or crafty: *a subtle liar.* **7.** insidious in operation: *subtle poison.* **8.** skillful, clever, or ingenious: *a subtle painter.* [1250–1300; ME *sotil* < OF < L *subtilis* SUBTILE (*b* of mod. sp. < L)] —**sub′tle·ness,** *n.* —**sub′tly,** *adv.*
—**Syn. 6.** sly, tricky, foxy, slick.

CONCISE ETYMOLOGY KEY: <, descended or borrowed from; >, whence; b., blend of, blended; c., cognate with; cf., compare; deriv., derivative; equiv., equivalent; imit., imitative; obl., oblique; r., replacing; s., stem; sp., spelling, spelled; resp., respelling, respelled; trans., translation; ?, origin unknown; *, unattested; ‡, probably earlier than. See the full key inside the front cover.

sub·tle·ty (sut′l tē), *n., pl.* **-ties. 1.** the state or quality of being subtle. **2.** delicacy or nicety of character or meaning. **3.** acuteness or penetration of mind; delicacy of discrimination. **4.** a fine-drawn distinction; refinement of reasoning: *the subtleties of logic.* **5.** something subtle. **6.** *Hist.* an elaborate confection, ornate in construction and ornamentation, sometimes edible but more often made and used as a decoration for a table or buffet. [1300–50; ME *subtelte, sutilte* < OF *sutilte* < L *subtīlitāt-* (s. of *subtīlitās*) fineness, equiv. to *subtīli(s)* SUBTILE + *-tāt-* -TY²]

sub·ton·ic (sub ton′ik), *n.* the seventh tone of a scale, being the next below the upper tonic. [1825–35; SUB- + TONIC]

sub·top·ic (sub′top′ik, sub top′-), *n.* a topic that is included within another topic. [SUB- + TOPIC]

sub·tor·rid (sub tôr′id, -tor′-), *adj.* subtropical (def. 2). [1850–55; SUB- + TORRID]

sub·to·tal (sub′tōt′l, sub tōt′-), *n., adj., v.,* **-taled, -tal·ing** or (*esp. Brit.*) **-talled, -tal·ling.** —*n.* **1.** the sum or total of a part of a group or column of figures, as in an accounting statement. —*adj.* **2.** somewhat less than complete; not total: *subtotal commitment.* —*v.t.* **3.** to determine a subtotal for, as figures. —*v.i.* **4.** to determine a subtotal. [1905–10; SUB- + TOTAL]

sub·tract (səb trakt′), *v.t.* **1.** to withdraw or take away, as a part from a whole. **2.** *Math.* to take (one number or quantity) from another; deduct. —*v.i.* **3.** to take away something or a part, as from a whole. [1530–40; < L *subtractus* (ptp. of *subtrahere* to draw away from underneath), equiv. to *sub-* SUB- + *trac-* (ptp. s. of *trahere* to draw) + *-tus* ptp. suffix] —**sub·tract′er,** *n.*
—**Syn. 1, 3.** SUBTRACT, DEDUCT express diminution in sum or quantity. To SUBTRACT suggests taking a part from a whole or a smaller from a larger: *to subtract the tax from one's salary.* To DEDUCT is to take away an amount or quantity from an aggregate or total so as to lessen or lower it: *to deduct a discount.* SUBTRACT is both transitive and intransitive, and has general or figurative uses; DEDUCT is always transitive and usually concrete and practical in application. —**Ant. 1–3.** add.

sub·trac·tion (səb trak′shən), *n.* **1.** an act or instance of subtracting. **2.** *Math.* the operation or process of finding the difference between two numbers or quantities, denoted by a minus sign (−). [1350–1400; ME < LL *subtractiōn-* (s. of *subtractiō*) a withdrawing, equiv. to *subtract(us)* (see SUBTRACT) + *-iōn-* -ION]

sub·trac·tive (səb trak′tiv), *adj.* **1.** tending to subtract; having power to subtract. **2.** *Math.* (of a quantity) that is to be subtracted; having the minus sign (−). [1680–90; SUBTRACT + -IVE]

subtrac′tive col′or, *Photog.* cyan, yellow, or magenta, as used in the subtractive process of color photography. Also called **subtrac′tive pri′mary.**

subtrac′tive proc′ess, a process of color photography in which the colors are formed by combination of cyan, yellow, and magenta lights. Cf. **additive process.** [1925–30]

sub·tra·hend (sub′trə hend′), *n. Arith.* a number that is subtracted from another. Cf. **minuend.** [1665–75; < L *subtrahendum,* neut. ger. of *subtrahere;* see SUBTRACT]

sub·treas·ur·y (sub trezh′ə rē, sub′trezh′-), *n., pl.* **-ur·ies. 1.** a subordinate or branch treasury. **2.** (formerly) any of the branch treasuries maintained by the U.S. government. [1830–40, *Amer.;* SUB- + TREASURY] —**sub·treas′ur·er,** *n.* —**sub·treas′ur·er·ship′,** *n.*

sub·trop·i·cal (sub trop′i kəl), *adj.* **1.** bordering on the tropics; nearly tropical. **2.** pertaining to or occurring in a region between tropical and temperate; subtorrid; semitropical. —*n.* **3.** a subtropical plant. [1835–45; SUB- + TROPICAL]

subtrop′ical high′, *Meteorol.* one of several highs, as the Azores and Pacific highs, that prevail over the oceans at latitudes of about 30 degrees N and S. Also called **subtrop′ical anticy′clone.** Cf. **high** (def. 41).

sub·trop·ics (sub trop′iks), *n.pl.* subtropical regions. [1895–90; SUB- + TROPICS]

sub·type (sub′tīp′), *n.* **1.** a subordinate type. **2.** a special type included within a more general type. [1860–65; SUB- + TYPE] —**sub·typ·i·cal** (sub tip′i kəl), *adj.*

su·bu·late (so͞o′byə lit, -lāt′), *adj. Biol.* slender, somewhat cylindrical, and tapering to a point; awlshaped. [1750–60; < NL *sūbulātus,* equiv. to L *sūbul(a)* awl + *-ātus* -ATE¹]

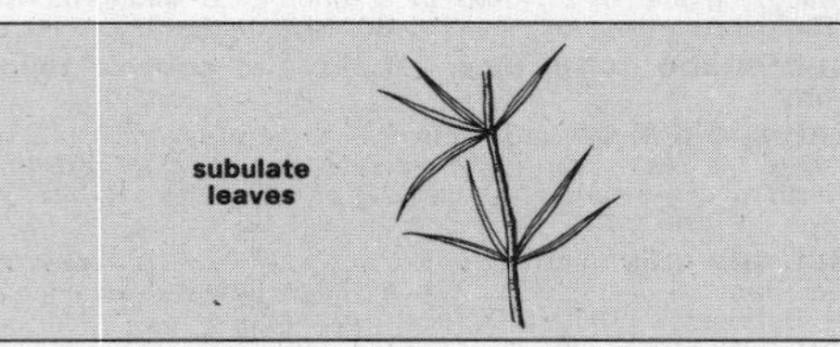

sub·um·brel·la (sub′um brel′ə), *n. Zool.* the concave undersurface of a coelenterate medusa, as a jellyfish. [1875–80; SUB- + UMBRELLA] —**sub′um·brel′lar,** *adj.*

sub·urb (sub′ûrb), *n.* **1.** a district lying immediately outside a city or town, esp. a smaller residential community. **2. the suburbs,** the area composed of such districts. **3.** an outlying part. [1350–1400; ME < L *suburbium,* equiv. to *sub-* SUB- + *urb(s)* city + *-ium* -IUM] —**sub′urbed,** *adj.*

sub·ur·ban (sə bûr′bən), *adj.* **1.** pertaining to, inhabiting, or being in a suburb or the suburbs of a city or town. **2.** characteristic of a suburb or suburbs. —*n.* **3.** a suburbanite. **4.** a short overcoat for casual wear. **5.** See **station wagon.** [1615–25; < L *suburbānus,* equiv. to *sub-* SUB- + *urb(s)* city + *-ānus* -AN] —**sub·ur′ban·ism,** *n.*

sub·ur·ban·ite (sə bûr′bə nīt′), *n.* a person who lives in a suburb of a city or large town. [1885–90; SUBURBAN + -ITE¹]

sub·ur·ban·ize (sə bûr′bə nīz′), *v.t.,* **-ized, -iz·ing.** to give suburban characteristics to: *to suburbanize a rural area.* Also, *esp. Brit.,* **sub·ur′ban·ise′.** [1890–95; SUBURBAN + -IZE] —**sub·ur′ban·i·za′tion,** *n.*

sub·ur·bi·a (sə bûr′bē ə), *n.* **1.** suburbs collectively. **2.** suburbanites collectively. **3.** the social or cultural aspects of life in suburbs. [1895–1900; SUBURB + -IA]

sub·ur·bi·car·i·an (sə bûr′bi kâr′ē ən), *adj.* **1.** being near the city of Rome. **2.** designating any of the dioceses surrounding the city of Rome, each of which is under the jurisdiction of a cardinal-bishop. [1645–55; < LL *suburbicāri(us)* (L *suburb(ium)* SUBURB + *-ic(us)* -IC + *-ārius* -ARY) + -AN]

sub·vene (səb vēn′), *v.i.,* **-vened, -ven·ing.** to arrive or occur as a support or relief. [1750–60; < L *subvenīre,* equiv. to *sub-* SUB- + *venīre* to COME]

sub·ven·tion (səb ven′shən), *n.* **1.** a grant of money, as by a government or some other authority, in aid or support of some institution or undertaking, esp. in connection with science or the arts. **2.** the furnishing of aid or relief. [1400–50; late ME < LL *subventiōn-* (s. of *subventiō*) official grant in aid, equiv. to *subvent(us)* (ptp. of *subvenīre* to SUBVENE) + *-iōn-* -ION] —**sub·ven′tion·ar′y,** *adj.*
—**Syn. 1.** See **subsidy.**

sub ver·bo (so͝ob wer′bō; *Eng.* sub vûr′bō), *Latin.* (used as a direction to a reference) under the word or heading.

sub·ver·sion (səb vûr′zhən, -shən), *n.* **1.** an act or instance of subverting. **2.** the state of being subverted; destruction. **3.** something that subverts or overthrows. [1350–1400; ME < LL *subversiōn-* (s. of *subversiō*) an overthrowing. See SUB-, VERSION]

sub·ver·sive (səb vûr′siv), *adj.* **1.** Also, **sub·ver·sion·ar·y** (səb vûr′zhə ner′ē, -shə-). tending to subvert or advocating subversion, esp. in an attempt to overthrow or cause the destruction of an established or legally constituted government. —*n.* **2.** a person who adopts subversive principles or policies. [1635–45; < L *subvers(us)* (ptp. of *subvertere* to SUBVERT) + -IVE] —**sub·ver′sive·ly,** *adv.* —**sub·ver′siv·ism, sub·ver′sive·ness,** *n.*
—**Syn. 1.** traitorous, treacherous, seditious, destructive.

sub·vert (səb vûrt′), *v.t.* **1.** to overthrow (something established or existing). **2.** to cause the downfall, ruin, or destruction of. **3.** to undermine the principles of; corrupt. [1325–75; ME *subverten* < L *subvertere* to over-

sub·reg′u·lar, *adj.*
sub′reg·u·lar′i·ty, *n.*
sub′re·la′tion, *n.*
sub′re·li′gion, *n.*
sub·ren′i·form′, *adj.*
sub′re·pand′, *adj.*
sub′re·pent, *adj.*
sub′re·port′, *n.*
sub·rep′u·ta·ble, *adj.;* **-bly,** *adv.*
sub·ret′i·nal, *adj.*
sub′re·trac′tile, *adj.*
sub·rhom′bic, *adj.*
sub·rhom′bi·cal, *adj.*
sub·rhom′boid, *adj.*
sub′rhom·boi′dal, *adj.*
sub·ric′tal, *adj.*
sub·rig′id, *adj.;* **-ly,** *adv.;* **-ness,** *n.*
sub′ri·gid′i·ty, *n.*
sub′root′, *n.*
sub·ros′tral, *adj.*
sub′ro·tund′, *adj.;* **-ly,** *adv.;* **-ness,** *n.*
sub′ro·tun′di·ty, *n.*
sub′rule′, *n.*
sub·rul′er, *n.*
sub·sa′cral, *adj.*
sub′sale′, *n.*
sub·sa′line, *adj.*
sub′sa·lin′i·ty, *n.*
sub′sa·tir′ic, *adj.*
sub′sa·tir′i·cal, *adj.;* **-ly,** *adv.;* **-ness,** *n.*
sub·sat′u·rat′ed, *adj.*
sub′sat·u·ra′tion, *n.*
sub′scale′, *n.*
sub·sched′ule, *n.*
sub′scheme′, *n.*
sub′school′, *n.*
sub·sci′ence, *n.*
sub·scle′ral, *adj.*
sub′scle·rot′ic, *adj.*
sub·scrip′ture, *n.*
sub′sec·re·tar′i·al, *adj.*
sub·sec′re·tar′y, *n., pl.* **-tar·ies.**
sub·sec′re·tar′y·ship′, *n.*
sub′sect′, *n.*
sub′sec′tor, *n.*
sub′se·cu′ri·ty, *n., pl.* **-ties.**
sub′sen·sa′tion, *n.*
sub·sen′su·al, *adj.;* **-ly,** *adv.*
sub·sen′su·ous, *adj.;* **-ly,** *adv.;* **-ness,** *n.*
sub′sept′, *n.*
sub·sep′tate, *adj.*
sub·se′ries, *n., pl.* **-ries.**
sub·ser′rate, *adj.*
sub·ser′rat·ed, *adj.*
sub·ses′sile, *adj.*
sub·sew′er, *n.*
sub′shaft′, *n.*
sub·sher′iff, *n.*
sub′shire′, *n.*
sub·sib′i·lance, *n.*
sub·sib′i·lan·cy, *n.*
sub·sib′i·lant, *adj., n.;* **-ly,** *adv.*
sub·sil′i·cate, *n.*
sub·sim′i·an, *adj.*
sub·sim′i·ous, *adj.*
sub·sim′ple, *adj.*
sub·sin′u·ous, *adj.*
sub·siz′ar, *n.*
sub·siz′ar·ship′, *n.*
sub·smile′, *n.*
sub·sneer′, *n.*
sub′so·ci′e·ty, *n., pl.* **-ties.**
sub·sol′id, *n.*
sub′sort′, *n.*
sub·sort′, *v.*
sub·sort′er, *n.*
sub·sov′er·eign, *n., adj.*
sub·spat′u·late, *adj.*
sub·spe′cial·ist, *n.*
sub′spe′cial·i·za′tion, *n.*
sub·spe′cial·ize′, *v.,* **-ized, -iz·ing.**
sub·spe′cial·ty, *n., pl.* **-ties.**
sub·sphe′noid, *adj.*
sub′sphe·noi′dal, *adj.*
sub′sphere′, *n.*
sub·spher′ic, *adj.*
sub·spher′i·cal, *adj.*
sub·spi′nose, *adj.*
sub·spi′nous, *adj.*
sub·spi′ral, *adj.;* **-ly,** *adv.*
sub·sple′ni·al, *adj.*
sub′spon·ta′ne·ous, *adj.;* **-ly,** *adv.;* **-ness,** *n.*
sub·squad′ron, *n.*
sub′stand·ard·i·za′tion, *n.*
sub·stand′ard·ize′, *v.t.,* **-ized, -iz·ing.**
sub′state′, *n.*
sub·ster′nal, *adj.*
sub′stock′, *n.*
sub′store′, *n.*
sub·store′room′, *n.*
sub·sto′ry, *n., pl.* **-ries.**
sub·stri′ate, *adj.*
sub·stri′at·ed, *adj.*
sub·sul′cus, *n., pl.* **-ci.**
sub·sul′fide, *n.*
sub·sul′phide, *n.*
sub′su·per·fi′cial, *adj.;* **-ly,** *adv.;* **-ness,** *n.*
sub·sur′e·ty, *n., pl.* **-ties.**
sub·syn′di·cate, *n.*
sub′syn·di·ca′tion, *n.*
sub·syn′od, *n.*
sub′syn·od′al, *adj.*
sub′syn·od′ic, *adj.*
sub′syn·od′i·cal, *adj.;* **-ly,** *adv.*
sub′syn·o·vi′al, *adj.*
sub·tar′sal, *adj.*
sub′task′, *n.*

throw, equiv. to *sub-* SUB- + *vertere* to turn] —**sub·vert′er,** *n.*
—**Syn. 1.** upset, disrupt, undermine, overturn, sabotage.

sub·vi·ral (sub vī′rəl), *adj. Microbiol.* **1.** of or pertaining to any macromolecule smaller in size or possessing a lesser degree of organization than a comparable intact viral particle. **2.** of or pertaining to a component or precursor particle of an intact infective virus. [1960–65; SUB- + VIRAL]

sub·vis·i·ble (sub viz′ə bəl), *adj.* invisible unless viewed through a microscope. [SUB- + VISIBLE]

sub·vo·cal (sub vō′kəl), *adj.* mentally formulated as words, esp. without vocalization. [1920–25; SUB- + VOCAL]

sub vo·ce (so͝ob wō′ke; *Eng.* sub vō′sē), *Latin.* (used as a direction to a reference) under the specified word.

sub·way (sub′wā′), *n.* **1.** Also called, *esp. Brit.,* **tube, underground.** an underground electric railroad, usually in a large city. **2.** *Chiefly Brit.* a short tunnel or underground passageway for pedestrians, automobiles, etc.; underpass. —*v.i.* **3.** to be transported by a subway: *We subwayed uptown.* [1820–30; SUB- + WAY[1]]

sub·woof·er (sub′wo͝of′ər), *n.* a loudspeaker component designed to reproduce only extremely low bass frequencies, generally below 125 Hz. [SUB- + WOOFER]

sub-ze·ro (sub zēr′ō), *adj.* **1.** indicating or recording lower than zero on some scale, esp. on the Fahrenheit scale: *a week of sub-zero temperatures.* **2.** characterized by or appropriate for sub-zero temperatures: *sub-zero climates; sub-zero clothing for the exploration.* [SUB- + ZERO]

sub·zone (sub′zōn′), *n.* a subdivision of a zone. [1885–90; SUB- + ZONE] —**sub·zon′al, sub·zon′a·ry,** *adj.*

suc, successor.

suc-, var. of **sub-** before *c: succeed.*

suc·cah (*Seph.* so͞o kä′; *Ashk., Eng.* so͝ok′ə), *n., pl.* ***suc·coth, suc·cot, suc·cos*** (*Seph.* so͞o kōt′; *Ashk.* so͞o-kōs′), *Eng.* **suc·cahs.** *Hebrew.* sukkah.

suc·ce·da·ne·um (suk′si dā′nē əm), *n., pl.* **-ne·a** (-nē ə). a substitute. [1635–45; < NL *succēdāneum,* n. use of neut. sing. of L *succēdāneus* substituted, equiv. to *suc-* SUC- + *cēd(ere)* to come, go (see CEDE) + *-āneus* composite adj. suffix, equiv. to *-ān(us)* -AN + *-eus* -EOUS] —**suc′ce·da′ne·ous,** *adj.*

suc·ce·dent (sək sēd′nt) *adj.* **1.** following or succeeding; subsequent. —*n.* **2.** *Astrol.* See **succedent house.** [1350–1400; ME < L *succēdent-,* s. of *succēdēns,* prp. of *succēdere* to SUCCEED]

succe′dent house′, *Astrol.* any of the four houses that fall between the angular and cadent houses: the second, fifth, eighth, and eleventh houses, which correspond, respectively, to possessions and values, love and creation, shared possessions and resources, and friends and social concerns. Also called **succedent.** Cf. **angular house, cadent house.** [1585–95]

suc·ceed (sək sēd′), *v.i.* **1.** to happen or terminate according to desire; turn out successfully; have the desired result: *Our efforts succeeded.* **2.** to thrive, prosper, grow, or the like: *Grass will not succeed in this dry soil.* **3.** to accomplish what is attempted or intended: *We succeeded in our efforts to start the car.* **4.** to attain success in some popularly recognized form, as wealth or standing: *The class voted him the one most likely to succeed.* **5.** to follow or replace another by descent, election, appointment, etc. (often fol. by *to*). **6.** to come next after something else in an order or series. —*v.t.* **7.** to come after and take the place of, as in an office or estate. **8.** to come next after in an order or series, or in the course of events; follow. [1325–75; ME *succeden* < L *succēdere* to go (from) under, follow, prosper, equiv. to *suc-* SUC- + *cēdere* to go (see CEDE)] —**suc·ceed′a·ble,** *adj.* —**suc·ceed′er,** *n.*
—**Syn. 1–4.** SUCCEED, FLOURISH, PROSPER, THRIVE mean to do well. To SUCCEED is to turn out well, to attain a goal: *It is everyone's wish to succeed in life.* To FLOURISH is to give evidence of success or a ripe development of power, reputation, etc.: *Culture flourishes among free people.* To PROSPER is to achieve and enjoy material success: *He prospered but was still discontented.* THRIVE suggests vigorous growth and development such as results from natural vitality or favorable conditions: *The children thrived in the sunshine.* **5.** See **follow.**
—**Ant. 1–4.** fail. **8.** precede.

suc·ceed·ing (sək sē′ding), *adj.* being that which follows; subsequent; ensuing: *laws to benefit succeeding generations.* [1555–65; SUCCEED + -ING[2]] —**suc·ceed′ing·ly,** *adv.*

suc·cen·tor (sək sen′tər), *n. Eccles.* a precentor's deputy. [1600–10; < LL, equiv. to L *suc-* SUC- + *-cen-,* comb. form of *canere* to sing + *-tor* -TOR]

suc·cès de scan·dale (syk sedᵊ skän dal′), *French.* success won by reason of topical, usually scandalous, subject matter rather than by merit and critical respect.

suc·cès d'es·time (syk se des tēm′), *French.* success won by reason of merit and critical respect rather than by popularity.

suc·cès fou (syk se fo͞o′), *French.* an extraordinarily great success.

suc·cess (sək ses′), *n.* **1.** the favorable or prosperous termination of attempts or endeavors. **2.** the attainment of wealth, position, honors, or the like. **3.** a successful performance or achievement: *The play was an instant success.* **4.** a person or thing that is successful: *She was a great success on the talk show.* **5.** *Obs.* outcome. [1530–40; < L *successus,* equiv. to *succēd-,* s. of *succēdere* to SUCCEED + *-tus* suffix of v. action, with *dt* > *ss*] —**suc·cess′less,** *adj.* —**suc·cess′less·ly,** *adv.* —**suc·cess′less·ness,** *n.*
—**Syn. 2.** achievement, fame, triumph.

suc·cess·ful (sək ses′fəl), *adj.* **1.** achieving or having achieved success. **2.** having attained wealth, position, honors, or the like. **3.** resulting in or attended with success. [1580–90; SUCCESS + -FUL] —**suc·cess′ful·ly,** *adv.* —**suc·cess′ful·ness,** *n.*

suc·ces·sion (sək sesh′ən), *n.* **1.** the coming of one person or thing after another in order, sequence, or in the course of events: *many troubles in succession.* **2.** a number of persons or things following one another in order or sequence. **3.** the right, act, or process, by which one person succeeds to the office, rank, estate, or the like, of another. **4.** the order or line of those entitled to succeed one another. **5.** the descent or transmission of a throne, dignity, estate, or the like. **6.** Also called **ecological succession.** *Ecol.* the progressive replacement of one community by another until a climax community is established. [1275–1325; ME < L *successiōn-* (s. of *successiō*) a following (someone) in office, equiv. to *success(us),* ptp. of *succēdere* to SUCCEED + *-iōn-* -ION] —**suc·ces′sion·al,** *adj.* —**suc·ces′sion·al·ly,** *adv.*
—**Syn. 2.** See **series.**

succes′sion of crops′, **1.** the continuous cultivation of a crop throughout a season by successive plantings or by the use of varieties with different rates of growth. **2.** the successive cultivation of short-lived crops. [1770–80]

suc·ces·sive (sək ses′iv), *adj.* **1.** following in order or in uninterrupted sequence; consecutive: *three successive days.* **2.** following another in a regular sequence: *the second successive day.* **3.** characterized by or involving succession. [1400–50; late ME < ML *successīvus,* equiv. to *success(us),* ptp. of *succēdere* to SUCCEED + *-īvus* -IVE] —**suc·ces′sive·ly,** *adv.* —**suc·ces′sive·ness,** *n.*

suc·ces·sor (sək ses′ər), *n.* **1.** a person or thing that succeeds or follows. **2.** a person who succeeds another in an office, position, or the like. [1250–1300; < L, equiv. to *succed-,* var. s. of *succēdere* to SUCCEED + *-tor* -TOR, with *dt* > *ss;* r. ME *successour* < AF < L, as above] —**suc·ces′sor·al,** *adj.*

success′ sto′ry, an account of the achievement of success, fortune, or fame by someone or some enterprise.

suc·ci·nate (suk′sə nāt′), *n. Chem.* a salt or ester of succinic acid. [1780–90; < F; see SUCCINIC, -ATE[2]]

suc·cinct (sək singkt′), *adj.* **1.** expressed in few words; concise; terse. **2.** characterized by conciseness or verbal brevity. **3.** compressed into a small area, scope, or compass. **4.** *Archaic.* **a.** drawn up, as by a girdle. **b.** close-fitting. **c.** encircled, as by a girdle. [1400–50; late ME < L *succinctus,* ptp. of *succingere* to gird, gather up (one's clothes), prepare for action, equiv. to *suc-* SUC- + *cing(ere)* to gird, equip + *-tus* ptp. suffix] —**suc·cinct′ly,** *adv.* —**suc·cinct′ness,** *n.*
—**Syn. 1, 2.** See **concise.**

suc·cinc·to·ri·um (suk′singk tôr′ē əm, -tōr′), *n., pl.* **-to·ri·a** (-tôr′ē ə, -tōr′ē ə). *Rom. Cath. Ch.* subcinctorium.

suc·cin·ic (sək sin′ik), *adj.* **1.** pertaining to or obtained from amber. **2.** *Chem.* of or derived from succinic acid. [1780–90; < F *succinique* < L *succin(um), sūcinum* amber + F *-ique* -IC]

succin′ic ac′id, *Chem.* a colorless, crystalline, water-soluble solid, $C_4H_6O_4$, used chiefly in the manufacture of lacquers, dyes, and perfume. [1780–90]

suc′ci·nyl·cho·line chlo′ride (suk′sə nil kō′lēn, -kol′ēn, -sə nl-), *Pharm.* a crystalline compound, $C_{14}H_{30}Cl_2N_2O_4$, used as a skeletal muscle relaxant in surgical procedures. [SUCCIN(IC) + -YL + CHOLINE]

suc·cor (suk′ər), *n.* **1.** help; relief; aid; assistance. **2.** a person or thing that gives help, relief, aid, etc. —*v.t.* **3.** to help or relieve. Also, *esp. Brit.,* **suc′cour.** [1250–1300; (v.) ME *sucuren* < OF *suc(c)urre, socorre* < L *succurrere* to go beneath, run to help, equiv. to *suc-* SUC- + *currere* to run (see CURRENT); (n.) ME *soc(o)ur,* back formation from *sucurs* (taken as pl.) < OF < ML *succursus,* equiv. to L *succur(rere)* + *-sus,* var of *-tus* suffix of v. action] —**suc′cor·a·ble,** *adj.* —**suc′cor·er,** *n.*
—**Syn. 1, 3.** support. **3.** See **help.**
—**Usage.** See **-or**[1].

suc·cor·ance (suk′ər əns), *n.* the act of seeking out affectionate care and social support. [1935–40; SUCCOR + -ANCE] —**suc′cor·ant,** *adj.*

suc·co·ry (suk′ə rē), *n., pl.* **-ries.** chicory. [1525–35; < MLG *suckerie,* perh. < ML, b. L *succus* juice and *cichorium* CHICORY; the plant's roots are full of sap]

suc·co·tash (suk′ə tash′), *n.* a cooked dish of kernels of corn mixed with shell beans, esp. lima beans, and, often, with green and sweet red peppers. [1745–55, *Amer.;* < Narragansett (E sp.) *msickquatash* boiled whole kernels of corn (c. Eastern Abenaki (F sp.) *mesikoutar,* equiv. to Proto-Algonquian **mes-* whole + **-i·nkw-* eye (hence, kernel) + **-ete·-* be cooked (+ *-w-*) + **-ali* pl. suffix)]

suc·coth (*Seph.* so͞o kōt′; *Ashk.* so͝o kōs′), *n. Hebrew.* a pl. of ***succah.*** Also, ***suc·cot′, suc·cos′.***

Suc·coth (*Seph. Heb.* so͞o kōt′; *Ashk. Heb., Eng.* so͝o′-kəs, so͞o kōs′), *n. Judaism.* Sukkoth. Also, **Suc·cot′, Suc·cos′.**

suc·cu·ba (suk′yə bə), *n.* a succubus. [1550–60; < L: paramour, equiv. to *succub(āre)* to lie beneath (*suc-* SUC- + *cubāre* to lie down; cf. CONCUBINE) + *-a* fem. n. suffix]

suc·cu·bous (suk′yə bəs), *adj. Bot.* (of leaves) overlapping, with the base of each leaf covering part of that under it. Cf. **incubous.** [1855–60; < L *succub(āre)* to lie under (see SUCCUBA) + -OUS]

suc·cu·bus (suk′yə bəs), *n., pl.* **-bi** (-bī′). **1.** a demon in female form, said to have sexual intercourse with men in their sleep. Cf. **incubus** (def. 1). **2.** any demon or evil spirit. **3.** a strumpet or prostitute. [1350–1400; ME < ML, var. of L *succuba* SUCCUBA; cf. INCUBUS]

suc·cu·lent (suk′yə lənt), *adj.* **1.** full of juice; juicy. **2.** rich in desirable qualities. **3.** affording mental nourishment. **4.** (of a plant) having fleshy and juicy tissues. —*n.* **5.** a succulent plant, as a sedum or cactus. [1595–1605; < LL *sūculentus,* equiv. to L *sūc(us),* *succus* juice + *-ulentus* -ULENT] —**suc′cu·lence, suc′cu·len·cy,** *n.* —**suc′cu·lent·ly,** *adv.*

suc·cumb (sə kum′), *v.i.* **1.** to give way to superior force; yield: *to succumb to despair.* **2.** to yield to disease, wounds, old age, etc.; die. [1480–90; < L *succumbere,* equiv. to *suc-* SUC- + *-cumbere,* transit. deriv. of *cubāre* to lie, recline; cf. INCUMBENT] —**suc·cumb′er,** *n.*
—**Syn. 1.** submit, accede, surrender.

suc·cur·sal (sə kûr′səl), *adj.* subsidiary, esp. noting a religious establishment that is dependent upon a principal one. [1835–45; < F *succursale* < L *succurs(us)* (see SUCCOR) + *-ale* -AL[1]]

suc·cuss (sə kus′), *v.t.* **1.** to shake up; shake. **2.** *Med.* to shake (a patient) in order to determine if a fluid is present in the thorax or elsewhere. [1860–65; < L *succussus* (ptp. of *succutere* to toss up), equiv. to *suc-* SUC- + *-cut(ere),* comb. form of *quatere* to shake + *-tus* ptp. suffix, with *tt* > *ss*] —**suc·cus·sion** (sə kush′ən), *n.* —**suc·cus′sive,** *adj.*

such (such), *adj.* **1.** of the kind, character, degree, extent, etc., of that or those indicated or implied: *Such a man is dangerous.* **2.** of that particular kind or character: *The food, such as it was, was plentiful.* **3.** like or similar: *tea, coffee, and such commodities.* **4.** (used with omission of an indication of comparison) of so extreme a kind; so great, good, bad, etc.: *He is such a liar.* **5.** being as stated or indicated: *Such is the case.* **6.** being the person or thing or the persons or things indicated: *If any member be behind in his dues, such member shall be suspended.* **7.** definite but not specified; such and such: *Allow such an amount for food and such an amount for*

CONCISE PRONUNCIATION KEY: act, cāpe, dâre, pärt; set, ēqual; *if,* ice; ox, ōver, ôrder, oil, bo͝ok, bo͞ot, out; up, ûrge; child; sing; shoe; thin, *th*at; zh as in *treasure.* ə = *a* as in *alone,* e as in *system,* i as in *easily,* o as in *gallop,* u as in *circus;* ᵊ as in *fire* (fīᵊr), *hour* (ouᵊr). l and n can serve as syllabic consonants, as in *cradle* (krād′l), and *button* (but′n). See the full key inside the front cover.

sub·tax′er, *n.*
sub·teg′mi·nal, *adj.*
sub′teg·u·men′tal, *adj.*
sub′teg·u·men′ta·ry, *adj.*
sub·tem′po·ral, *adj.*
sub′ten·tac′u·lar, *adj.*
sub·tep′id, *adj.;* **-ly,** *adv.;* **-ness,** *n.*
sub′te·pid′i·ty, *n.*
sub′te·rete′, *adj.*
sub·ter′mi·nal, *adj.;* **-ly,** *adv.*
sub′ter·ra′que·ous, *adj.*
sub′ter·ri·to′ri·al, *adj.*
sub·ter′ri·to′ry, *n., pl.* **-ries.**
sub·ter′tian, *adj.*
sub′test′, *n.*
sub′te·tan′ic, *adj.*
sub′te·tan′i·cal, *adj.*
sub′tha·lam′ic, *adj.*
sub′theme′, *n.*
sub·tho′ra·cal, *adj.*
sub′tho·rac′ic, *adj.*
sub′thrill′, *n.*
sub·to′tem, *n.*
sub′to·tem′ic, *adj.*
sub·tow′er, *n.*
sub′trans·lu′cence, *n.*
sub′trans·lu′cen·cy, *n.*
sub′trans·lu′cent, *adj.*
sub′trans·par′ent, *adj.;* **-ly,** *adv.;* **-ness,** *n.*
sub′trans·ver′sal, *adj.;* **-ly,** *adv.*
sub′trans·verse′, *adj.;* **-ly,** *adv.*
sub·trap′e·zoid′, *adj.*
sub′trap·e·zoi′dal, *adj.*
sub′tread′, *n.*
sub′trench′, *n.*
sub′trend′, *n.*
sub′tri·an′gu·lar, *adj.*
sub′tri·an′gu·lar′i·ty, *n.*
sub′tri·an′gu·late, *adj.*
sub·trib′al, *adj.*
sub′tribe′, *n.*
sub·tri′fid, *adj.*
sub·trig′o·nal, *adj.*
sub′tri·he′dral, *adj.*
sub·trip′li·cate, *adj.*
sub·trip′li·cat′ed, *adj.*
sub′trip·li·ca′tion, *n.*
sub′tri·que′trous, *adj.*
sub′tro·chan·ter′ic, *adj.*
sub′troch′le·ar, *adj.*
sub′troch·le·ar′i·form′, *adj.*
sub·trun′cate, *adj.*
sub·trun′cat·ed, *adj.*
sub′trun·ca′tion, *n.*
sub′trunk′, *n.*
sub·tu′bi·form′, *adj.*
sub·tu′nic, *n.*
sub·tun′nel, *n.*
sub′tur·ric′u·late, *adj.*
sub′tur·ric′u·lat′ed, *adj.*
sub·tu′tor, *n.*
sub·tu′tor·ship′, *n.*
sub′twined′, *adj.*
sub′tym·pa·nit′ic, *adj.*
sub·ul′ti·mate, *adj.*
sub·um′bel·lar, *adj.*
sub·um′bel·late, *adj.*
sub·um′bel·lat′ed, *adj.*
sub′um·bel·lif′er·ous, *adj.*
sub′um·bil′i·cal, *adj.*
sub·um′bo·nal, *adj.*
sub·um′bo·nate, *adj.*
sub·un′ci·nal, *adj.*
sub·un′ci·nate, *adj.*
sub·un′ci·nat′ed, *adj.*
sub′un·e′qual, *adj.;* **-ly,** *adv.;* **-ness,** *n.*
sub·un′gual, *adj.*
sub′u′nit, *n.*
sub′u·ni·ver′sal, *adj.*
sub′u′ni·verse′, *n.*
sub′u·re′thral, *adj.*
sub·ur′sine, *adj.*
sub′va·ri′e·ty, *n., pl.* **-ties.**
sub·vas′sal, *n.*
sub·vas′sal·age, *n.*
sub′vein′, *n.*
sub·ven′tral, *adj.;* **-ly,** *adv.*
sub·ven′tri·cose′, *adj.*
sub′ven·tric′u·lar, *adj.*
sub·ver′bal, *adj.*
sub·ver′mi·form′, *adj.*
sub·ver′te·bral, *adj.*
sub·ver′te·brate′, *n., adj.*
sub·ver′ti·cal, *adj.;* **-ly,** *adv.;* **-ness,** *n.*
sub′ver·tic′il·late, *adj.*
sub′ver·tic′il·lat′ed, *adj.*
sub′ve·sic′u·lar, *adj.*
sub·vest′ment, *n.*
sub·vic′ar, *n.*
sub·vic′ar·ship′, *n.*
sub·vil′lain, *n.*
sub·vir′ile, *adj.*
sub·vis′u·al, *adj.,* **-ly,** *adv.*
sub′vi·tal·i·za′tion, *n.*
sub·vi′tal·ized′, *adj.*
sub·vit′re·ous, *adj.;* **-ly,** *adv.;* **-ness,** *n.*
sub·vo′cal·ize′, *v.,* **-ized, -iz·ing.**
sub′war′, *n.*
sub·war′den, *n.*
sub·war′den·ship′, *n.*
sub·wealth′y, *adj.*
sub′wink′, *n.*
sub·work′er, *n.*
sub·work′man, *n., pl.* **-men.**
sub′zy·go·mat′ic, *adj.*

rent. —*adv.* **8.** so; very; to such a degree: *such pleasant people.* **9.** in such a way or manner. —*pron.* **10.** such a person or thing or such persons or things: *kings, princes, and such.* **11.** someone or something indicated or exemplified: *He claims to be a friend but is not such.* **12. as such.** See **as**[1] (def. 26). **13. such as, a.** of the kind specified: *A plan such as you propose will never succeed.* **b.** for example: *He considers quiet pastimes, such as reading and chess, a bore.* [bef. 900; ME *such, swulch, suilch,* OE *swilc, swelc* < Gmc **swa* SO[1] + **līko-* LIKE[1]; c. G *solch,* ON *slīkr,* Goth *swaleiks*]

such′ and such′, **1.** definite or particular, but not named or specified: *They turned out to be such and such kind of people.* **2.** something or someone not specified: *if such and such should happen.* Also, **such′-and-such′.** [1400–50; late ME]

such·like (such′līk′), *adj.* **1.** of any such kind; similar. —*pron.* **2.** persons or things of such a kind. [1375–1425; late ME; see SUCH, LIKE[1]]

such·ness (such′nis), *n.* **1.** a fundamental, intrinsic, or characteristic quality or condition: *seraphic indifference to the suchness of his surroundings.* **2.** *Buddhism.* Tathata. [bef. 1000; OE *swilcnesse* (not recorded in ME); see SUCH, -NESS]

Su·chou (*Chin.* sy′jō′), *n. Wade-Giles.* Suzhou.

Sü·chow (*Chin.* sy′jō′), *n. Older Spelling.* Xuzhou.

suck (suk), *v.t.* **1.** to draw into the mouth by producing a partial vacuum by action of the lips and tongue: *to suck lemonade through a straw.* **2.** to draw (water, moisture, air, etc.) by or as if by suction: *Plants suck moisture from the earth. The pump sucked water from the basement.* **3.** to apply the lips or mouth to and draw upon by producing a partial vacuum, esp. for extracting fluid contents: *to suck an orange.* **4.** to put into the mouth and draw upon: *to suck one's thumb.* **5.** to take into the mouth and dissolve by the action of the tongue, saliva, etc.: *to suck a piece of candy.* **6.** to render or bring to a specified condition by or as if by sucking. —*v.i.* **7.** to draw something in by producing a partial vacuum in the mouth, esp. to draw milk from the breast. **8.** to draw or be drawn by or as if by suction. **9.** (of a pump) to draw air instead of water, as when the water is low or a valve is defective. **10.** *Slang.* to behave in a fawning manner (usually fol. by *around*). **11.** *Slang.* to be repellent or disgusting: *Poverty sucks.* **12. suck face,** to engage in soul-kissing. **13. suck in,** *Slang.* to deceive; cheat; defraud: *The confidence man sucked us all in.* **14. suck off,** *Slang* (*vulgar*). to fellate. **15. suck up,** *Slang.* to be obsequious; toady: *The workers are all sucking up to him because he's the one who decides who'll get the bonuses.* —*n.* **16.** an act or instance of sucking. **17.** a sucking force. **18.** the sound produced by sucking. **19.** that which is sucked; nourishment drawn from the breast. **20.** a small drink; sip. **21.** a whirlpool. [bef. 900; (v.) ME *souken,* OE *sūcan,* c. L *sūgere;* (n.) ME *souke* act of suckling, deriv. of the n.; akin to SOAK] —**suck′less,** *adj.*

sucker, *Catostomus commersoni,* length 12 in. (30 cm)

suck·er (suk′ər), *n.* **1.** a person or thing that sucks. **2.** *Informal.* a person easily cheated, deceived, or imposed upon. **3.** an infant or a young animal that is suckled, esp. a suckling pig. **4.** a part or organ of an animal adapted for sucking nourishment, or for adhering to an object as by suction. **5.** any of several freshwater, mostly North American food fishes of the family Catostomidae, having thick lips: some are now rare. **6.** *Informal.* a lollipop. **7.** the piston of a pump that works by suction, or the valve of such a piston. **8.** a pipe or tube through which something is drawn or sucked. **9.** *Bot.* a shoot rising from a subterranean stem or root. **10.** *Informal.* a person attracted to something as indicated: *He's a sucker for new clothes.* **11.** *Slang.* any person or thing: *He's one of those smart, handsome suckers everybody likes. They're good boots, but the suckers pinch my feet.* —*v.t.* **12.** *Slang.* to make a sucker of; fool; hoodwink: *another person suckered by a con artist.* —*v.i.* **13.** to send out suckers or shoots, as a plant. [1350–1400; 1835–45 for def. 2; ME; see SUCK, -ER[1]] —**suck′er-like′,** *adj.*

suck′er bait′, *Slang.* an enticement calculated to lure a person into a scheme in which he or she may be victimized.

suck·er·fish (suk′ər fish′), *n., pl.* **-fish·es,** (*esp. collectively*) **-fish.** remora. [1835–45, *Amer.;* SUCKER + FISH]

suck′er list′, *Informal.* a list of names and addresses of persons considered by a business, charity organization, etc., to be likely purchasers or donors. [1945–50, *Amer.*]

suck·er-punch (suk′ər punch′), *v.t. Slang.* to strike (someone) with an unexpected blow. —**suck′er punch′.**

suck′et fork′ (suk′it), a utensil for sweetmeats of the 16th, 17th, and early 18th centuries, having fork tines at one end and a spoon bowl at the other end of a common stem. [*sucket,* alter. of *succade* candied fruit < AF *sukade,* diff. OF (northeast) *succade*]

suck·fish (suk′fish′), *n., pl.* (*esp. collectively*) **-fish,** (*esp. referring to two or more kinds or species*) **-fish·es.** **1.** remora (def. 1). **2.** a clingfish. [1745–55; SUCK + FISH]

CONCISE ETYMOLOGY KEY: <, descended or borrowed from; >, whence; b., blend of, blended; c., cognate with; cf., compare; deriv., derivative; equiv., equivalent; imit., imitative; obl., oblique; r., replacing; s., stem; sp., spelling, spelled; resp., respelling, respelled; trans., translation; ?, origin unknown; *, unattested; ‡, probably earlier than. See the full key inside the front cover.

suck·ing (suk′ing), *adj.* **1.** not weaned. **2.** very young. [bef. 1000; ME *souking(e),* OE *sūcende;* see SUCK, -ING[2]]

suck′ing louse′. See under **louse** (def. 1). [1905–10]

suck·le (suk′əl), *v.,* **-led, -ling.** —*v.t.* **1.** to nurse at the breast or udder. **2.** to nourish or bring up. **3.** to put to suck. —*v.i.* **4.** to suck at the breast or udder. [1375–1425; late ME *sucklen;* see SUCK, -LE]

suck·ler (suk′lər), *n.* **1.** an animal that suckles its young; mammal. **2.** a suckling. [1425–75; late ME; see SUCKLE, -ER[1]]

suck·ling (suk′ling), *n.* an infant or a young animal that is not yet weaned. [1400–50; late ME; see SUCK, -LING[1]]

Suck·ling (suk′ling), *n.* **Sir John,** 1609–42, English poet.

suck·y (suk′ē), *adj.,* **suck·i·er, suck·i·est.** *Slang.* disagreeable; unpleasant. [SUCK + -Y[1]]

su·cral·fate (so͞o′krəl fāt′), *n. Pharm.* a sugar-aluminum complex, $C_{12}H_{54}Al_{16}O_{75}S_8$, used for the treatment of duodenal ulcer. [prob. SUCR(OSE) + AL(UMINUM) + (SUL)FATE]

su·crase (so͞o′krās, -krāz), *n. Biochem.* invertase. [1895–1900; < F *sucre* SUGAR + -ASE]

Su·cre (so͞o′kre), *n.* **1. An·to·nio Jo·sé de** (än tô′nyô hô se′ the), 1793–1830, Venezuelan general and South American liberator: 1st president of Bolivia 1826–28. **2.** a city in and the official capital of Bolivia, in the S part. 57,090. **3.** (*l.c.*) a cupronickel coin and monetary unit of Ecuador, equal to 100 centavos. *Abbr.:* S.

su·crose (so͞o′krōs), *n. Chem.* a crystalline disaccharide, $C_{12}H_{22}O_{11}$, the sugar obtained from the sugarcane, the sugar beet, and sorghum, and forming the greater part of maple sugar; sugar. [1855–60; < F *sucre* SUGAR + -OSE[2]]

suc·tion (suk′shən), *n.* **1.** the act, process, or condition of sucking. **2.** the force that, by a pressure differential, attracts a substance or object to the region of lower pressure. **3.** the act or process of producing such a force. —*v.t.* **4.** to draw out or remove by aspiration. [1605–15; < LL *suctiōn-* (s. of *suctiō*) a sucking, equiv. to L *suct(us)* (ptp. of *sūgere* to SUCK) + *-iōn-* -ION] —**suc′tion·al,** *adj.*

suc′tion and curet′tage, *Surg.* a technique involving extraction of the fetus through a suction tube, used to perform abortions during the early stages of pregnancy.

suc′tion cup′, a cup-shaped object of rubber, glass, plastic, etc., which, by producing a partial vacuum, can be made to adhere to or draw something to a surface.

suc′tion lipec′tomy, the removal of fatty tissue by making a small incision in the skin, loosening the fat layer, and withdrawing it by suction. Cf. **lipectomy.** [1980–85]

suc′tion pump′, a pump for raising water or other fluids by suction, consisting essentially of a vertical cylinder in which a piston works up and down, both the cylinder and the pump having valves that control the flow of the fluid. [1815–25]

suc′tion stop′, *Phonet.* click (def. 3). [1885–90]

suc·to·ri·al (suk tôr′ē əl, -tōr′-), *adj.* **1.** adapted for sucking or suction, as an organ; functioning as a sucker for imbibing or adhering. **2.** having sucking organs; imbibing or adhering by suckers. **3.** pertaining to or characterized by suction. [1825–35; < NL *suctōri(us)* (see SUCTORIAN) + -AL[1]]

suc·to·ri·an (suk tôr′ē ən, -tōr′-), *n.* **1.** a suctorial animal. **2.** a protozoan of the class or order Suctoria, which live, as adults, attached by a stalk to the substrate and feed by means of long, suctorial tentacles. —*adj.* **3.** belonging or pertaining to the Suctoria. [1835–45; < NL *Suctori(a),* n. use of neut. pl. of *suctōrius* sucking (< L *sūg(ere)* to SUCK + *-tōrius* -TORY[1]) + -AN]

Su·da·fed (so͞o′də fed′), *Pharm., Trademark.* a brand of pseudoephedrine.

Su·dan (so͞o dan′), *n.* **1.** a region in N Africa, S of the Sahara and Libyan deserts, extending from the Atlantic to the Red Sea. **2. Republic of the.** Formerly, **Anglo-Egyptian Sudan.** a republic in NE Africa, S of Egypt and bordering on the Red Sea: a former condominium of Egypt and Great Britain. 16,400,000; 967,500 sq. mi. (2,505,825 sq. km). *Cap.:* Khartoum.

Su·da·nese (so͞od′n ēz′, -ēs′), *n., pl.* **-nese,** *adj.* —*n.* **1.** a native or inhabitant of Sudan. —*adj.* **2.** of or pertaining to Sudan or its inhabitants. [1880–85; SUDAN + -ESE]

Sudan′ grass′, a sorghum, *Sorghum sudanense,* introduced into the U.S. from Africa, grown for hay and pasture. [1910–15]

Su·dan·ic (so͞o dan′ik), *adj.* **1.** (esp. in former systems of classification) of or pertaining to a residual category of African languages including most of the non-Bantu and non-Hamitic languages of northern and central Africa: most now reclassified as part of the Niger-Congo subfamily. **2.** of or pertaining to the Sudan or the Sudanese. [1920–25; SUDAN + -IC]

su·dar·i·um (so͞o dâr′ē əm), *n., pl.* **-dar·i·a** (-dâr′ē ə). **1.** (in ancient Rome) a cloth, usually of linen, for wiping the face; handkerchief. **2.** (*sometimes cap.*) veronica[1] (def. 3). [1595–1605; < L *sūdārium,* equiv. to *sūd(āre)* to SWEAT + *-ārium* -ARY]

su·da·ti·o (so͞o dā′shē ō′), *n., pl.* **-da·ti·o·nes** (-dā′shē ō′nēz). (in an ancient Roman bath) a chamber, between the sudatorium and the calidarium, where sweat was removed. [< L *sūdātiō* orig., act of sweating, equiv. to *sūdā(re)* to SWEAT + *-tiō* n. suffix]

su·da·to·ri·um (so͞o′də tôr′ē əm, -tōr′-), *n., pl.* **-to·ri·a** (-tôr′ē ə, -tōr′-). a hot-air bath for inducing sweating. Also, **sudatory.** [1750–60; < L *sūdātōrium,* n. use of neut. of *sūdātōrius* SUDATORY; see -TORY[2]]

su·da·to·ry (so͞o′də tôr′ē, -tōr′ē), *adj., n., pl.* **-ries.** —*adj.* **1.** pertaining to or causing sweating. **2.** pertaining to a sudatorium. —*n.* **3.** sudatorium. [1590–1600; < L *sūdātōrius* inducing sweat, equiv. to *sūdā(re)* to SWEAT + *-tōrius* —TORY[1]]

Sud·bur·y (sud′ber′ē, -bə rē), *n.* **1.** a city in S Ontario, in S Canada. 97,604. **2.** a city in NE Massachusetts. 14,027 —**Sud·bu·ri·an** (sud byo͝or′ē ən), *adj.*

sudd (sud), *n.* (in the White Nile) floating vegetable matter that often obstructs navigation. [1870–75; < Ar: lit., obstruction]

sud·den (sud′n), *adj.* **1.** happening, coming, made, or done quickly, without warning, or unexpectedly: *a sudden attack.* **2.** occurring without transition from the previous form, state, etc.; abrupt: *a sudden turn.* **3.** impetuous; rash. **4.** *Archaic.* quickly made or provided. **5.** *Obs.* unpremeditated. —*adv.* **6.** *Literary.* suddenly. —*n.* **7.** *Obs.* an unexpected occasion or occurrence. **8. all of a sudden,** without warning; unexpectedly; suddenly. Also, **on a sudden.** [1250–1300; ME *sodain* (adj. and adv.) < MF < L *subitāneus* going or coming stealthily, equiv. to *subit(us)* sudden, taking by surprise (see SUBITO) + *-āneus* composite adj. suffix, equiv. to *-ān(us)* -AN + *-eus* -EOUS] —**sud′den·ly,** *adv.* —**sud′den·ness,** *n.*

—**Syn. 1, 2.** unforeseen, unanticipated. SUDDEN, UNEXPECTED, ABRUPT describe acts, events, or conditions for which there has been no preparation or gradual approach. SUDDEN refers to the quickness of an occurrence, although the event may have been expected: *a sudden change in the weather.* UNEXPECTED emphasizes the lack of preparedness for what occurs or appears: *an unexpected crisis.* ABRUPT characterizes something involving a swift adjustment; the effect is often unpleasant, unfavorable, or the cause of dismay: *He had an abrupt change in manner. The road came to an abrupt end.* —**Ant. 1, 2.** gradual, foreseen.

sud′den death′, *Sports.* an overtime period in which a tied contest is won and play is stopped immediately after one of the contestants scores, as in football, or goes ahead, as in golf. [1825–35] —**sud′den-death′,** *adj.*

sud′den in′fant death′ syn′drome, *Pathol.* death from the sudden cessation of breathing (apnea) of a seemingly healthy infant, almost always during sleep, sometimes traceable to a chronic oxygen deficiency. *Abbr.:* SIDS Also called **crib death;** *esp. Brit.,* **cot death.** [1970–75]

Su·der·mann (zo͞o′dər män′), *n.* **Hermann** (her′män), 1857–1928, German dramatist and novelist.

Su·de·ten (so͞o dāt′n; *Ger.* zo͞o dāt′n), *n.* **1.** Also, **Su·de·tes** (so͞o dē′tēz), Czech, **Su·de·ty** (so͝o′de ti). a mountain range in E central Europe, extending along the N boundary of the Czech Republic between the Elbe and Oder rivers. Highest peak, 5259 ft. (1603 m). **2.** a native or inhabitant of the Sudetenland. **3.** Sudetenland.

Su·de·ten·land (so͞o dāt′n land′; *Ger.* zo͞o dāt′n länt′), *n.* a mountainous region in the N Czech Republic, including the Sudeten and the Erz gebirge: annexed by Germany 1938; returned to Czechoslovakia 1945. Also called **Sudeten.**

su·dor·if·er·ous (so͞o′də rif′ər əs), *adj.* bearing or secreting sweat. [1590–1600; < LL *sūdōrifer* (L *sūdōr-,* s. of *sūdor* sweat (*sūd(āre)* to SWEAT + *-ōr-* -OR[1]) + *-i-* -I- + *-fer* -FER) + -OUS] —**su′dor·if′er·ous·ness,** *n.*

su·dor·if·ic (so͞o′də rif′ik), *adj.* **1.** causing sweat; diaphoretic. **2.** sudoriparous. —*n.* **3.** a sudorific agent. [1620–30; < NL *sūdōrificus,* equiv. to L *sūdōr-,* s. of *sūdor* sweat (see SUDORIFEROUS) + *-i-* -I- + *-ficus* -FIC]

su·dor·ip·a·rous (so͞o′də rip′ər əs), *adj.* producing or secreting sweat. [1850–55; < L *sūdor* sweat (see SUDORIFEROUS) + -I- + -PAROUS]

Su·dra (so͞o′drə), *n.* Shudra. [< Skt *śūdra*]

suds (sudz), *n.* (*used with a plural v.*) **1.** soapy water. **2.** foam; lather. **3.** *Slang.* beer. —*v.t.* **4.** to wash with soap or detergent (often fol. by *out*): *to suds out a pair of socks.* [1540–50; 1900–05 for def. 3; perh. < MD *sudse* puddle, marsh; akin to SODDEN] —**suds′a·ble,** *adj.*

suds·er (sud′zər), *n. Informal.* **1.** a soap opera. **2.** any movie, play, or the like that is designed to provoke a tearful response. [1965–70; SUDS + -ER[1]]

suds·y (sud′zē), *adj.,* **suds·i·er, suds·i·est.** **1.** consisting of, containing, or producing foamy lather. **2.** resembling or suggesting suds. **3.** *Slang.* soapy (def. 5). [1865–70, *Amer.;* SUDS + -Y[1]]

sue (so͞o), *v.,* **sued, su·ing.** —*v.t.* **1.** to institute a process in law against; bring a civil action against: *to sue someone for damages.* **2.** to woo or court. **3.** *Obs.* to make petition or appeal to. —*v.i.* **4.** to institute legal proceedings, or bring suit: *She threatened to sue.* **5.** to make petition or appeal: *to sue for peace.* **6.** to court a woman. **7. sue out,** to make application for or apply for and obtain (a writ or the like) from a court of law. [1150–1200; ME *suen, siwen* < OF *sivre* < VL **sequere* to follow, for L *sequī*] —**su′er,** *n.*

—**Syn. 5.** beg, petition, plead, pray.

Sue (so͞o; *Fr.* sy), *n.* **1. Eu·gène** (œ zhen′), (*Marie Joseph Sue*), 1804–57, French novelist. **2.** a female given name, form of **Susan, Susanna, Susannah.**

suede (swād), *n., v.,* **sued·ed, sued·ing.** —*n.* **1.** kid or other leather finished with a soft, napped surface, on the flesh side or on the outer side after removal of a thin outer layer. **2.** Also called **suede′ cloth′.** a fabric with a napped surface suggesting this. —*v.t.* **3.** to treat so as to raise a nap on (leather, cloth, etc.). —*v.i.* **4.** to raise a nap on leather, cloth, etc. Also, **suède.** [1855–60; < F (*gants de*) *Suède* (gloves from) Sweden]

su•et (so͞o′it), *n.* the hard fatty tissue about the loins and kidneys of beef, sheep, etc., used in cooking or processed to yield tallow. [1350–1400; ME *sewet* < AF **suet,* equiv. to *su-*, *sew* (< L *sēbum* tallow) + *-et* -ET] —**su′•et•y,** *adj.*

Sue•to•ni•us (swi tō′nē əs), *n.* (*Gaius Suetonius Tranquillus*) A.D. 75–150, Roman historian.

su′et pud′ding, a pudding made of chopped beef suet and flour, boiled or steamed in a cloth, often with other ingredients, as raisins, spices, etc. [1750–60]

Sue•vi•an (swā′vē ən), *n.* **1.** a member of an ancient Germanic people of uncertain origin, mentioned in the writings of Caesar and Tacitus. **2.** a member of a Germanic people that invaded France and Spain in the 5th century A.D. —*adj.* **3.** of or pertaining to the Suevians. [1610–20; < L *Suēb*(*i*), *Suēv*(*i*) (of Gmc orig.; cf. G *Schwaben,* OE *Swǣfe*) + -IAN]

Su•ez (so͞o ez′, so͞o′ez), *n.* **1.** a seaport in NE Egypt, near the S end of the Suez Canal. 275,000. **2. Gulf of,** a NW arm of the Red Sea, W of the Sinai Peninsula. **3. Isthmus of,** an isthmus in NE Egypt, joining Africa and Asia. 72 mi. (116 km) wide.

Su′ez Canal′, a canal in NE Egypt, cutting across the Isthmus of Suez and connecting the Mediterranean and the Red Sea. 107 mi. (172 km) long.

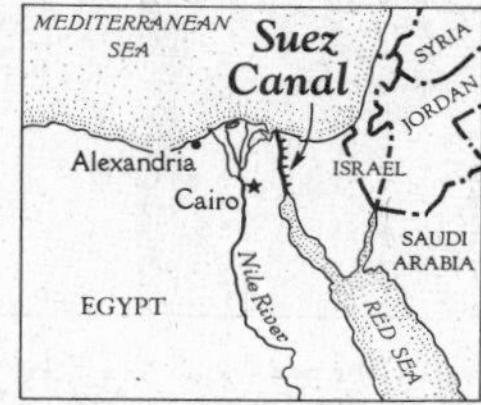

suf-, var. of **sub-** before *f*: *suffer.*

suf., suffix. Also, **suff.**

Suff., **1.** Suffolk. **2.** suffragan.

suff., **1.** sufficient. **2.** suffix.

suf•fer (suf′ər), *v.i.* **1.** to undergo or feel pain or distress: *The patient is still suffering.* **2.** to sustain injury, disadvantage, or loss: *One's health suffers from overwork. The business suffers from lack of capital.* **3.** to undergo a penalty, as of death: *The traitor was made to suffer on the gallows.* **4.** to endure pain, disability, death, etc., patiently or willingly. —*v.t.* **5.** to undergo, be subjected to, or endure (pain, distress, injury, loss, or anything unpleasant): *to suffer the pangs of conscience.* **6.** to undergo or experience (any action, process, or condition): *to suffer change.* **7.** to tolerate or allow: *I do not suffer fools gladly.* [1200–50; ME *suff*(*e*)*ren* < L *sufferre,* equiv. to *suf-* SUF- + *ferre* to BEAR[1]; cf. OF *sofrir* < VL **sufferire*] —**suf′fer•a•ble,** *adj.* —**suf′fer•a•ble•ness,** *n.* —**suf′fer•a•bly,** *adv.* —**suf′fer•er,** *n.*
—**Syn. 5.** sustain. **7.** stomach, stand, abide.

suf•fer•ance (suf′ər əns, suf′rəns), *n.* **1.** passive permission resulting from lack of interference; tolerance, esp. of something wrong or illegal (usually prec. by *on* or *by*). **2.** capacity to endure pain, hardship, etc.; endurance. **3.** *Archaic.* suffering; misery. **4.** *Archaic.* patient endurance. [1250–1300; ME *suffrance* < OF *soufrance,* < LL *sufferentia,* equiv. to *suffer*(*re*) to SUFFER + *-entia* -ENCE, -ANCE]

suf•fer•ing (suf′ər ing, suf′ring), *n.* **1.** the state of a person or thing that suffers. **2.** Often, **sufferings.** something suffered by a person or a group of people; pain: *the sufferings of the slaves.* [1300–50; ME; see SUFFER, -ING[1]] —**suf′fer•ing•ly,** *adv*
—**Syn. 1.** agony, torment, torture; pain, distress.

Suf•fern (suf′ərn), *n.* a town in SE New York. 10,794.

suf•fice (sə fīs′, -fīz′), *v.,* **-ficed, -fic•ing.** —*v.i.* **1.** to be enough or adequate, as for needs, purposes, etc. —*v.t.* **2.** to be enough or adequate for; satisfy. [1275–1325; ME *sufficen* < L *sufficere* to supply, suffice, equiv. to *suf-* SUF- + *-ficere,* comb. form of *facere* to make, DO[1]; r. ME *suffisen* < OF < L, as above]

suf•fi•cien•cy (sə fish′ən sē), *n.* **1.** the state or fact of being sufficient; adequacy. **2.** a sufficient number or amount; enough. **3.** adequate provision or supply, esp. of wealth. [1485–95; < LL *sufficientia;* see SUFFICIENT, -ENCY]

suf•fi•cient (sə fish′ənt), *adj.* **1.** adequate for the purpose; enough: *sufficient proof; sufficient protection.* **2.** *Logic.* (of a condition) such that its existence leads to the occurrence of a given event or the existence of a given thing. Cf. **necessary** (def. 4c). **3.** *Archaic.* competent. [1350–1400; ME < L *sufficient-* (s. of *sufficiēns*), prp. of *sufficere* to SUFFICE, equiv. to *suf-* SUF- + *-fici-,* pres. s. of *-ficere,* comb. form of *facere* to make, DO[1] + *-ent-* -ENT] —**suf•fi′cient•ly,** *adv.*
—**Ant. 1.** meager, scant, inadequate.

suf•fix (*n.* suf′iks; *v.* suf′iks, sə fiks′), *n.* **1.** *Gram.* an affix that follows the element to which it is added, as *-ly* in *kindly.* **2.** something added to the end of something else. —*v.t.* **3.** *Gram.* to add as a suffix. **4.** to affix at the end of something. **5.** to fix or put under. —*v.i.* *Gram.* **6.** to admit a suffix. **7.** to add a suffix. [1595–1605; < NL *suffixum,* n. use of neut. of L *suffixus* (ptp. of *suffigere* to attach on top of), equiv. to *suf-* SUF- + *fixus* (see FIX)] —**suf•fix•al** (suf′ik səl, sə fik′-), *adj.* —**suf•fix•a•tion** (suf′ik sā′shən), **suf•fix•ion** (sə fik′shən), *n.*

suf•flate (sə flāt′), *v.t.,* **-flat•ed, -flat•ing.** to inflate. [1610–20; < L *sufflātus* (ptp. of *sufflāre* to blow from below, blow up, inflate), equiv. to *suf-* SUF- + *flā*(*re*) to BLOW[2] + *-tus* ptp. suffix] —**suf•fla′tion,** *n.*

suf•fo•cate (suf′ə kāt′), *v.,* **-cat•ed, -cat•ing.** —*v.t.* **1.** to kill by preventing the access of air to the blood through the lungs or analogous organs, as gills; strangle. **2.** to impede the respiration of. **3.** to discomfort by a lack of fresh or cool air. **4.** to overcome or extinguish; suppress. —*v.i.* **5.** to become suffocated; stifle; smother. **6.** to be uncomfortable due to a lack of fresh or cool air. [1520–30; < L *suffōcātus* (ptp. of *suffōcāre* to choke, stifle), equiv. to *suf-* SUF- + *-fōc-* (comb. form of *fauc-,* s. of *faucēs* throat) + *-ātus* -ATE[1]] —**suf′fo•cat′ing•ly,** *adv.* —**suf′fo•ca′tion,** *n.* —**suf′fo•ca′tive,** *adj.*

Suf•folk (suf′ək), *n.* **1.** a county in E England. 570,000; 1470 sq. mi. (3805 sq. km). **2.** one of an English breed of sheep having a black face and legs, noted for mutton of high quality. **3.** one of an English breed of chestnut draft horses having a deep body and short legs. **4.** one of an English breed of small, black hogs. **5.** a city in SE Virginia. 47,621.

Suffr., suffragan.

suf•fra•gan (suf′rə gən), *adj.* **1.** assisting or auxiliary to, as applied to any bishop in relation to the archbishop or metropolitan who is his superior, or as applied to an assistant or subsidiary bishop who performs episcopal functions in a diocese but has no ordinary jurisdiction, as, in the Church of England, a bishop consecrated to assist the ordinary bishop of a see in part of his diocese. **2.** (of a see or diocese) subordinate to an archiepiscopal or metropolitan see. —*n.* **3.** a suffragan bishop. [1350–1400; ME *suffragane* < ML *suffrāgāneus* voting, equiv. to *suffrāg*(*ium*) SUFFRAGE + *-āneus,* composite adj. suffix, equiv. to *-ān*(*us*) -AN + *-eus* -EOUS]

suf•frage (suf′rij), *n.* **1.** the right to vote, esp. in a political election. **2.** a vote given in favor of a proposed measure, candidate, or the like. **3.** *Eccles.* a prayer, esp. a short intercessory prayer or petition. [1350–1400; ME < L *suffrāgium* voting tablet, vote, equiv. to L *suffrā-g*(*āri*) to vote for, support + *-ium* -IUM]

suf•fra•gette (suf′rə jet′), *n.* a woman advocate of female suffrage. [1900–05; SUFFRAGE + -ETTE] —**suf′•fra•get′tism,** *n.*
—**Usage.** See **-ette.**

suf•fra•gist (suf′rə jist), *n.* an advocate of the grant or extension of political suffrage, esp. to women. [1815–25; SUFFRAGE + -IST] —**suf′fra•gism,** *n.* —**suf′fra•gis′ti•cal•ly,** *adv.*

suf•fru•tes•cent (suf′ro͞o tes′ənt), *adj.* partially or slightly woody; subshrubby. [1810–20; < NL *suffrutēscent-* (s. of *suffrutēscēns*), equiv. to L *suf-* SUF- + NL *frut-* (shortened s. of L *frutex* shrub, bush) + L *-ēscent-* -ESCENT]

suf•fru•ti•cose (sə fro͞o′ti kōs′), *adj.* woody at the base and herbaceous above. [1785–95; < NL *suffruticōsus,* equiv. to L *suf-* SUF- + *frutic-* (s. of *frutex* shrub, bush) + *-ōsus* -OSE[1]]

suf•fu•mi•gate (sə fyo͞o′mi gāt′), *v.t.,* **-gat•ed, -gat•ing.** to fumigate from below; apply fumes or smoke to. [1580–90; < L *suffūmigātus;* see SUF-, FUMIGATE] —**suf•fu′mi•ga′tion,** *n.*

suf•fuse (sə fyo͞oz′), *v.t.,* **-fused, -fus•ing.** to overspread with or as with a liquid, color, etc. [1580–90; < L *suffūsus* (ptp. of *suffundere*). See SUF-, FUSE[2]] —**suf•fused•ly** (sə fyo͞o′zid lē, -fyo͞ozd′-), *adv.* —**suf•fu•sion** (sə fyo͞o′zhən), *n.* —**suf•fu•sive** (sə fyo͞o′siv), *adj.*
—**Syn.** cover, pervade, diffuse, bathe, flood.

Su•fi (so͞o′fē), *n., pl.* **-fis.** **1.** a member of an ascetic, mystical Muslim sect. —*adj.* **2.** of or pertaining to Sufis or Sufism. [< Ar *Ṣūfī,* perh. equiv. to *ṣūf* wool + *-ī* suffix of appurtenance; so called from their garb]

Su•fism (so͞o′fiz əm), *n.* the ascetic and mystical system of the Sufis. Also, **Su•fi•ism** (so͞o′fē iz′əm). [1810–20; SUFI + -ISM] —**Su•fis′tic,** *adj.*

sug-, var. of **sub-** before *g*: *suggest.*

sug•ar (sho͝og′ər), *n.* **1.** a sweet, crystalline substance, $C_{12}H_{22}O_{11}$, obtained chiefly from the juice of the sugarcane and the sugar beet, and present in sorghum, maple sap, etc.: used extensively as an ingredient and flavoring of certain foods and as a fermenting agent in the manufacture of certain alcoholic beverages; sucrose. Cf. **beet sugar, cane sugar.** **2.** *Chem.* a member of the same class of carbohydrates, as lactose, glucose, or fructose. **3.** (*sometimes cap.*) an affectionate or familiar term of address (sometimes offensive when used to strangers, casual acquaintances, subordinates, etc., esp. by a male to a female). **4.** a word formerly used in communications to represent the letter *S.* **5.** *Slang.* money. **6.** *Slang.* LSD —*v.t.* **7.** to cover, sprinkle, mix, or sweeten with sugar. **8.** to make agreeable. —*v.i.* **9.** to form sugar or sugar crystals. **10.** to make maple sugar. **11. sugar off,** (in making maple sugar) to complete the boiling down of the syrup in preparation for granulation. [1250–1300; ME *sugre, sucre* (n.) < MF *sucre* < ML *succārum* < It *zucchero* < Ar *sukkar;* obscurely akin to Pers *shakar,* Gk *sákcharon* (see SACCHAR-)] —**sug′ar•less,** *adj.* —**sug′ar•like′,** *adj.*

Sug′ar Act′, *Amer. Hist.* a law passed by the British Parliament in 1764 raising duties on foreign refined sugar imported by the colonies so as to give British sugar growers in the West Indies a monopoly on the colonial market. Cf. **Navigation Act.**

sug′ar ap′ple, sweetsop. [1730–40]

sug′ar ba′sin, *Brit.* See **sugar bowl.** [1850–55]

sug′ar beet′, a beet, *Beta vulgaris,* having a white root, cultivated for the sugar it yields. [1810–20]

sug•ar•ber•ry (sho͝og′ər ber′ē), *n., pl.* **-ries.** a hackberry, *Celtis laevigata,* of the southern U.S. [1830–40, *Amer.*; SUGAR + BERRY]

sug•ar•bird (sho͝og′ər bûrd′), *n.* any of various honeycreepers that feed on nectar. [1680–90; SUGAR + BIRD]

sug′ar bowl′, a small bowl, usually having a cover, for serving granulated sugar or sugar cubes. [1765–75, *Amer.*]

sug•ar•bush (sho͝og′ər bo͝osh′), *n.* **1.** an evergreen shrub, *Rhus ovata,* of the cashew family, native to the desert regions of the southwestern U.S., having light yellow flowers in short, dense spikes and hairy, dark-red fruit. **2.** an orchard or grove of sugar maples. [1795–1805; SUGAR + BUSH[1]]

sug′ar camp′, *Chiefly North Midland U.S., esp. Indiana and Ohio.* a grove of sugar maples. [1770–80, *Amer.*]

sug′ar can′dy, **1.** a confection made by boiling pure sugar until it hardens. **2.** a person or thing that is pleasing. [1350–1400; ME]

sug•ar-can•dy (sho͝og′ər kan′dē), *adj.* **1.** excessively sweet; saccharine: *sugar-candy stories in family magazines.* **2.** pertaining to or characteristic of someone or something that is pleasing.

sug•ar•cane (sho͝og′ər kān′), *n.* a tall grass, *Saccharum officinarum,* of tropical and warm regions, having a stout, jointed stalk, and constituting the chief source of sugar. Also, **su′gar cane′.** [1560–70; SUGAR + CANE]

sug′arcane bor′er, the larva of the pyralid moth, *Diatraea saccharalis,* a serious pest of sugarcane, corn, rice, and sorghums. [1890–95, *Amer.*]

sug•ar•coat (sho͝og′ər kōt′), *v.t.* **1.** to cover with sugar: *to sugarcoat a pill.* **2.** to make (something difficult or distasteful) appear more pleasant or acceptable: *There was no way to sugarcoat the bad news.* [1865–70; SUGAR + COAT]

sug•ar•coat•ing (sho͝og′ər kō′ting), *n.* **1.** the act or process of covering something with sugar. **2.** a coating or layer of sugar or a sugary substance. **3.** a thing used to make something else considered unpleasant or disagreeable seem attractive or palatable. [1905–10; SUGAR + COAT + -ING[1]]

sug′ar corn′. See **sweet corn.**

sug′ar dad′dy, *Informal.* a wealthy, middle-aged man who spends freely on a young woman in return for her companionship or intimacy. [1915–20]

sug•ared (sho͝og′ərd), *adj.* **1.** covered, mixed, or sweetened with sugar. **2.** sweetened as if with sugar; made agreeable; honeyed, as words, speech, etc. [1325–75; ME *sugred.* See SUGAR, -ED[3]]

sug•ar-free (sho͝og′ər frē′), *adj.* containing no sugar: *a sugar-free cola.*

sug′ar glid′er, a gliding possum, *Petaurus breviceps,* inhabiting open forests of New Guinea, Tasmania, and Australia.

sug′ar grove′, sugarbush (def. 2). [1785–95, *Amer.*]

sug•ar•house (sho͝og′ər hous′), *n., pl.* **-hous•es** (-hou′ziz). a shed or other building where maple syrup or maple sugar is made. [1590–1600; SUGAR + HOUSE]

sug•ar•loaf (sho͝og′ər lōf′), *n., pl.* **-loaves** (-lōvz′). **1.** a large, usually conical loaf or mass of hard refined sugar: the common form of household sugar until the mid-19th century. **2.** anything resembling this in shape. [1375–1425; late ME]

sug•ar-loaf (sho͝og′ər lōf′), *adj.* resembling a sugarloaf. Also, **sug′ar-loafed′.** [1600–10]

Sug′arloaf Moun′tain, a mountain in SE Brazil in Rio de Janeiro, at the entrance to Guanabara Bay. 1280 ft. (390 m). Portuguese, **Pão de Açúcar.**

sug′ar ma′ple, any of several maples having a sweet sap, esp. *Acer saccharum* (the state tree of New York, Vermont, West Virginia, and Wisconsin), having a short trunk and long, curving branches, yielding a hard wood used for making furniture and being the chief source of maple sugar. [1725–35, *Amer.*] —**sug′ar-ma′ple,** *adj.*

sug′ar of lead′ (led), *Chem.* See **lead acetate.** [1655–65]

sug′ar of milk′, lactose. [1745–55]

sug′ar or′chard, *Chiefly New England and South Midland U.S.* sugarbush (def. 2). [1825–35, *Amer.*]

sug′ar palm′, gomuti (def. 1).

sug′ar pea′. See **snow pea.** [1700–10]

sug′ar pine′, a tall pine, *Pinus lambertiana,* of California, Oregon, etc., having cones 20 in. (51 cm) long. [1840–50, *Amer.*]

sug•ar•plum (sho͝og′ər plum′), *n.* a small sweetmeat made of sugar with various flavoring and coloring ingredients; a bonbon. [1600–10; SUGAR + PLUM[1]]

sug′ar sift′er. See **berry spoon.**

sug′ar snap′ pea′. See **snap pea.** [1975–80]

sug′ar sor′ghum, sorgo.

sug′ar spoon′, a small spoon for serving granulated sugar, resembling but having a wider bowl than a teaspoon. [1700–10]

sug•ar•tit (sho͝og′ər tit′), *n.* a piece of cloth containing moist sugar, wrapped to resemble a nipple and used to pacify an infant. Also, **sug•ar•teat** (sho͝og′ər tēt′). [1840–50]

sug′ar tongs′, small tongs used for serving cubed sugar. [1700–10]

CONCISE PRONUNCIATION KEY: act, cāpe, dâre, pärt; set, ēqual; if, īce; ox, ōver, ôrder, oil, bo͝ok, bo͞ot, out; up, ûrge; child; sing; shoe; thin, *th*at; zh as in *treasure.* ə = *a* as in *alone, e* as in *system, i* as in *easily, o* as in *gallop, u* as in *circus;* ə as in *fire* (fīər), *hour* (ouər). l and n can serve as syllabic consonants, as in *cradle* (krād′l), and *button* (but′n). See the full key inside the front cover.

sug′ar tree′, *Chiefly South Midland U.S.* a sugar maple. [1695–1705, *Amer.*]

sug·ar·y (shŏŏg′ə rē), *adj.* **1.** of, containing, or resembling sugar. **2.** sweet; excessively sweet. **3.** honeyed; cloying; deceitfully agreeable: *sugary words of greeting.* [1585–95; SUGAR + -Y[1]] **—sug′ar·i·ness,** *n.*

sug·gest (səg jest′, sə-), *v.t.* **1.** to mention or introduce (an idea, proposition, plan, etc.) for consideration or possible action: *The architect suggested that the building be restored.* **2.** to propose (a person or thing) as suitable or possible for some purpose: *We suggested him for president.* **3.** (of things) to prompt the consideration, making, doing, etc., of: *The glove suggests that she was at the scene of the crime.* **4.** to bring before a person's mind indirectly or without plain expression: *I didn't tell him to leave, I only suggested it.* **5.** to call (something) up in the mind through association or natural connection of ideas: *The music suggests a still night.* [1520–30; < L *suggestus* (ptp. of *suggerere* to build up, supply, hint, suggest), equiv. to *sug-* SUG- + *ges-* (ptp. s. of *gerere* to carry, do, display) + *-tus* ptp. suffix] **—sug·gest′ed·ness,** *n.* **—sug·gest′er,** *n.* **—sug·gest′ing·ly,** *adv.*
—Syn. 2. recommend, advise. **4.** indicate, imply. See **hint.**

sug·gest·i·ble (səg jes′tə bəl, sə-), *adj.* **1.** subject to or easily influenced by suggestion. **2.** that may be suggested. [1885–90; SUGGEST + -IBLE] **—sug·gest′i·bil′i·ty, sug·gest′i·ble·ness,** *n.* **—sug·gest′i·bly,** *adv.*

sug·ges·tion (səg jes′chən, sə-), *n.* **1.** the act of suggesting. **2.** the state of being suggested. **3.** something suggested, as a piece of advice: *We made the suggestion that she resign.* **4.** a slight trace: *He speaks with a suggestion of a foreign accent.* **5.** the calling up in the mind of one idea by another by virtue of some association or of some natural connection between the ideas. **6.** the idea thus called up. **7.** *Psychol.* **a.** the process of inducing a thought, sensation, or action in a receptive person without using persuasion and without giving rise to reflection in the recipient. **b.** the thought, sensation, or action induced in this way. [1300–50; ME *suggestio(u)n* incitement to evil < ML *suggestiōn-* (s. of *suggestiō*), L: act of supplying an answer or hint, equiv. to *suggest(us)* (see SUGGEST) + *-iōn-* -ION]
—Syn. 1, 3. See **advice.**

sug·ges·tive (səg jes′tiv, sə-), *adj.* **1.** that suggests; referring to other thoughts, persons, etc.: *His recommendation was suggestive of his boss's thinking.* **2.** rich in suggestions or ideas: *a suggestive critical essay.* **3.** evocative; presented partially rather than in detail. **4.** that suggests or implies something improper or indecent; risqué: *suggestive remarks.* [1625–35; SUGGEST + -IVE] **—sug·ges′tive·ly,** *adv.* **—sug·ges′tive·ness,** *n.*
—Syn. 1. See **expressive.**

sugh (sŏŏKH, sŏŏf, sōō), *n., v.t. Scot.* sough[2].

su·gi (sōō′gē), *n., pl.* **-gi, -gis.** See **Japan cedar.** [< Japn]

Su·har·to (sōō här′tō), *n.* born 1921, Indonesian army officer and political leader: president since 1968. Also, **Soeharto.**

Sui (swē), *n.* a dynasty ruling in China A.D. 589–618.

su·i·cid·al (sōō′ə sīd′l), *adj.* **1.** pertaining to, involving, or suggesting suicide. **2.** tending or leading to suicide. **3.** foolishly or rashly dangerous: *He drives at a suicidal speed.* [1770–80; SUICIDE + -AL[1]] **—su′i·cid′al·ly,** *adv.*

su·i·cide (sōō′ə sīd′), *n., v.,* **-cid·ed, -cid·ing.** **—*n.*** **1.** the intentional taking of one's own life. **2.** destruction of one's own interests or prospects: *Buying that house was financial suicide.* **3.** a person who intentionally takes his or her own life. **—*v.i.*** **4.** to commit suicide. **—*v.t.*** **5.** to kill (oneself). [1645–55; < NL *suicīdium, -cīda,* equiv. to L *suī* of oneself, gen. sing. of reflexive pron. + *-cīdium, -cīda* -CIDE]

su′icide clause′, a clause in a life-insurance policy stating that the insurer is required to pay only the reserve or the total premiums paid if the policyholder should commit suicide within a stated period.

su′icide machine′, a device designed to permit a terminally ill person to commit suicide, as by the automatic injection of a lethal drug. [1985–90]

su′icide pact′, an agreement between two or more people to commit suicide together. [1910–15]

su′icide squeeze′. See **squeeze play** (def. 1a). Also called **su′icide squeeze′ play′.**

su·i·cid·ol·o·gy (sōō′ə sī dol′ə jē), *n.* the study of the causes and prevention of suicide. [1925–30; SUICIDE + -O- + -LOGY] **—su′i·ci·dol′o·gist,** *n.*

su·i ge·ne·ris (sōō′ī ge′ne Ris; *Eng.* sōō′ī jen′ər is, sōō′ē), *Latin.* of his, her, its, or their own kind; unique.

su·i ju·ris (sōō′ī jŏŏr′is, sōō′ē), *Law.* capable of managing one's affairs or assuming legal responsibility. Cf. **alieni juris.** [1605–15; < L *suī jūris* of one's own right]

su·i·mate (sōō′ī māt′, sōō′ē-), *n. Chess.* self-mate. [1865–70; < L *suī* of oneself + MATE[1]]

su·int (sōō′int, swint), *n.* the natural grease of the wool of sheep, consisting of a mixture of fatty matter and potassium salts, used as a source of potash and in the preparation of ointments. [1785–95; < F, MF, equiv. to *su(er)* to sweat (< L *sūdāre;* see SWEAT) + *-in* suffix of mass nouns (as in *crottin* dung); *-t* after *oint,* ptp. of *oindre* to rub with oil, ANOINT]

Suisse (swēs), *n.* French name of **Switzerland.**

Sui·sun′ Cit′y (sə sōōn′), a town in central California. 11,087.

CONCISE ETYMOLOGY KEY: <, descended or borrowed from; >, whence; b., blend of, blended; c., cognate with; cf., compare; deriv., derivative; equiv., equivalent; imit., imitative; obl., oblique; r., replacing; s., stem; sp., spelling, spelled; resp., respelling, respelled; trans., translation; ?, origin unknown; *, unattested; ‡, probably earlier than. See the full key inside the front cover.

suit (sōōt), *n.* **1.** a set of clothing, armor, or the like, intended for wear together. **2.** a set of men's garments of the same color and fabric, consisting of trousers, a jacket, and sometimes a vest. **3.** a similarly matched set consisting of a skirt and jacket, and sometimes a topcoat or blouse, worn by women. **4.** any costume worn for some special activity: *a running suit.* **5.** *Slang.* a business executive. **6.** *Law.* the act, the process, or an instance of suing in a court of law; legal prosecution; lawsuit. **7.** *Cards.* **a.** one of the four sets or classes (spades, hearts, diamonds, and clubs) into which a common deck of playing cards is divided. **b.** the aggregate of cards belonging to one of these sets held in a player's hand at one time: *Spades were his long suit.* **c.** one of various sets or classes into which less common decks of cards are divided, as lances, hammers, etc., found in certain decks formerly used or used in fortune telling. **8.** suite (defs. 1–3, 5). **9.** the wooing or courting of a woman: *She rejected his suit.* **10.** the act of making a petition or an appeal. **11.** a petition, as to a person of rank or station. **12.** Also called **set.** *Naut.* a complete group of sails for a boat. **13.** one of the seven classes into which a standard set of 28 dominoes may be divided by matching the numbers on half the face of each: a three suit contains the 3-blank, 3-1, 3-2, 3-3, 3-4, 3-5, and 3-6. Since each such suit contains one of each of the other possible suits, only one complete suit is available per game. **14. follow suit, a.** *Cards.* to play a card of the same suit as that led. **b.** to follow the example of another: *The girl jumped over the fence, and her playmates followed suit.* **—*v.t.*** **15.** to make appropriate, adapt, or accommodate, as one thing to another: *to suit the punishment to the crime.* **16.** to be appropriate or becoming to: *Blue suits you very well.* **17.** to be or prove satisfactory, agreeable, or acceptable to; satisfy or please: *The arrangements suit me.* **18.** to provide with a suit, as of clothing or armor; clothe; array. **—*v.i.*** **19.** to be appropriate or suitable; accord. **20.** to be satisfactory, agreeable, or acceptable. **21. suit up,** to dress in a uniform or special suit. [1250–1300; ME *siute, sute, suite* (n.) < AF, OF, akin to *sivre* to follow. See SUE, SUITE] **—suit′like′,** *adj.*

Su·i·ta (sōō ē′tä), *n.* a city on S Honshu, in Japan: a suburb of Osaka. 332,413.

suit·a·ble (sōō′tə bəl), *adj.* such as to suit; appropriate; fitting; becoming. [1505–15; SUIT + -ABLE] **—suit′·a·bil′i·ty, suit′a·ble·ness,** *n.* **—suit′a·bly,** *adv.*
—Syn. proper, befitting, seemly, apt.

suit·case (sōōt′kās′), *n.* a usually rectangular piece of luggage esp. for carrying clothes while traveling. [1900–05; SUIT + CASE[2]]

suit-dress (sōōt′dres′), *n.* a costume ensemble for women, consisting of a dress and matching coat or jacket.

suite (swēt *or, for 3 often,* sōōt), *n.* **1.** a number of things forming a series or set. **2.** a connected series of rooms to be used together: *a hotel suite.* **3.** a set of furniture, esp. a set comprising the basic furniture necessary for one room: *a bedroom suite.* **4.** a company of followers or attendants; a train or retinue. **5.** *Music.* **a.** an ordered series of instrumental dances, in the same or related keys, commonly preceded by a prelude. **b.** an ordered series of instrumental movements of any character. [1665–75; < F, appar. metathetic var. of OF *siute* (see SUIT); akin to SUE, SUITOR]

suit·ed (sōō′tid), *adj.* **1.** appropriate: *She is suited to such a job.* **2.** compatible or consistent with: *a prose style suited to the subject.* [1615–25; SUIT + -ED[2]]

suit·ing (sōō′ting), *n.* fabric for making suits. [1530–40; SUIT + -ING[1]]

Suit′land-Sil′ver Hill′ (sōōt′lənd sil′vər), a city in central Maryland, near Washington, D.C. 32,164.

suit·or (sōō′tər), *n.* **1.** a man who courts or woos a woman. **2.** *Law.* a petitioner or plaintiff. **3.** a person who sues or petitions for anything. **4.** *Informal.* an individual who seeks to buy a business. [1250–1300; ME *s(e)utor, suitour* < AF < L *secūtor,* equiv. to *secū-,* var. s. of *sequī* to follow + *-tor* -TOR]

suk (sŏŏk), *n.* (esp. in the Arab countries) the market, esp. the traditional bazaar. Also, **suq, souk.** [1820–30; < Ar *sūq*]

Su·kar·no (sōō kär′nō), *n.* **Ach·med** (äk′med), 1901–1970, Indonesian statesman: president of the Republic of Indonesia 1945–67. Also, **Soekarno.**

Su·khu·mi (sŏŏ kōō′mē; *Russ.* sōō KHŏŏ′myi), *n.* a city in and the capital of Abkhazia, in the NW Georgian Republic, on the Black Sea. 122,000. Formerly, **Su·khum** (sōō KHōōm′).

su·ki·ya·ki (sōō′kē yä′kē, sŏŏk′ē-, skē yä′kē), *n.* a Japanese dish made with beef, chicken, or pork and usually containing soy sauce, bean curd, and greens, often cooked over direct heat at the table. [1920–25; < Japn, equiv. to *suki* slice + *yaki* broil]

suk·kah (*Seph.* sōō kä′; *Ashk., Eng.* sŏŏk′ə), *n., pl.* ***suk·koth, suk·kot, suk·kos*** (*Seph.* sōō kôt′; *Ashk.* sŏŏ-kōs′), *Eng.* **suk·kahs.** *Hebrew.* a booth or hut roofed with branches, built against or near a house or synagogue and used during the Jewish festival of Sukkoth as a temporary dining or living area. Also, ***succah.*** [*sukkāh* lit., booth]

Suk·koth (*Seph. Heb.* sōō kôt′; *Ashk. Heb., Eng.* sŏŏk′əs, sōō kōs′), *n.* a Jewish festival beginning on the 15th day of the month of Tishri and celebrated for nine days by Orthodox and Conservative Jews outside of Israel and for eight days by Reform Jews and by Jews in Israel that celebrates the harvest and commemorates the period during which the Jews wandered in the wilderness after the Exodus, marked by the building of *sukkoth.* Also, **Suk·kot′, Suk·kos′, Succoth, Succot, Succos.** Also called **Feast of Booths, Feast of Tabernacles.** Cf. **Hoshana Rabbah, Shemini Atzereth, Simhath Torah.** [< Heb *sukkōth* lit., booths]

Suk·kur (sŏŏk′ər), *n.* a city in SE Pakistan, on the Indus River. 158,876.

Su·ku·ma (sŏŏ kōō′mə), *n., pl.* **-mas,** (*esp. collectively*) **-ma** for 1. **1.** a member of an agricultural people of northwestern Tanzania, near Lake Victoria, who constitute the country's largest population group. **2.** the Bantu language of the Sukuma.

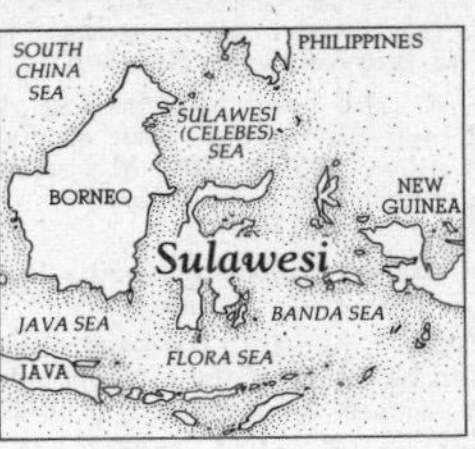

Su·la·we·si (sōō′lä wä′sē), *n.* an island in central Indonesia. 8,925,000 with adjacent islands; 72,986 sq. mi. (189,034 sq. km). Formerly, **Celebes.**

sul·cate (sul′kāt), *adj.* having long, narrow grooves or channels, as plant stems, or being furrowed or cleft, as hoofs. Also, **sul′cat·ed.** [1750–60; < L *sulcātus* (ptp. of *sulcāre* to plow). See SULCUS, -ATE[1]] **—sul·ca′tion,** *n.*

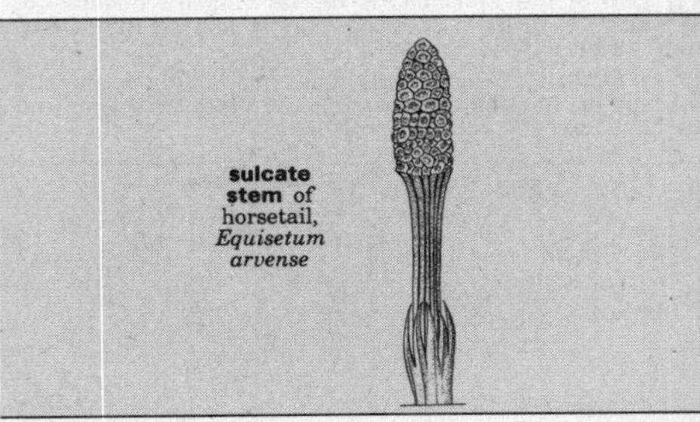
sulcate stem of horsetail, *Equisetum arvense*

sul·cus (sul′kəs), *n., pl.* **-ci** (-sī). **1.** a furrow or groove. **2.** *Anat.* a groove or fissure, esp. a fissure between two convolutions of the brain. [1655–65; L: furrow]

Su·lei·man I (sōō′lə män′, -lā-, sōō′lā män′), *("the Magnificent")* 1495?–1566, sultan of the Ottoman Empire 1520–66. Also, **Soliman I, Solyman I.**

sulf-, a combining form representing **sulfur** in compound words: *sulfarsphenamine.* Also, **sulfo-;** *esp. Brit.,* **sulph-.**

sul·fa (sul′fə), *Pharm.* **—*adj.*** **1.** related chemically to sulfanilamide. **2.** pertaining to, consisting of, or involving a sulfa drug or drugs. **—*n.*** **3.** See **sulfa drug.** [1935–40; short for SULFANILAMIDE]

sul·fa·di·a·zine (sul′fə dī′ə zēn′, -zin), *n. Pharm.* a sulfanilamide derivative, $C_{10}H_{10}N_4O_2S$, used chiefly in the treatment of urinary tract infections, meningitis, and malaria. [1935–40; SULFA(NILAMIDE) + DIAZINE]

sul′fa drug′, *Pharm.* any of a group of drugs closely related in chemical structure to sulfanilamide, having a bacteriostatic rather than a bactericidal effect: used in the treatment of various wounds, burns, and infections. Also called **sulfa.** [1935–40]

sul·fa·meth·ox·a·zole (sul′fə meth ok′sə zōl′), *n. Pharm.* an antimicrobial substance, $C_{10}H_{11}N_3O_3S$, used against a variety of susceptible Gram-positive and Gram-negative organisms, as in the treatment of certain urinary tract infections and skin infections. [1955–60; SULFA(NILAMIDE) + METH(YL) + (*is*)*oxazole;* see IS-, OX-, AZOLE]

Sul·fa·my·lon (sul′fə mī′lon), *Pharm., Trademark.* a brand of mafenide acetate.

sul·fa·nil·a·mide (sul′fə nil′ə mīd′, -mid), *n. Pharm.* a white, crystalline amide of sulfanilic acid, $C_6H_8N_2O_2S$, formerly used in the treatment of bacterial infections: replaced by its derivatives and by antibiotics. [1935–40; SULFANIL(IC ACID) + AMIDE]

sul′fa·nil′ic ac′id (sul′fə nil′ik, sul′-), *Chem.* a grayish-white, crystalline, slightly water-soluble solid, the para form of $C_6H_7NO_3S$, used chiefly as an intermediate in the manufacture of dyes. [1855–60; SULF- + *anilic* (see ANIL, -IC)]

sul·fan·i·lyl (sul fan′ə lil), *adj. Chem.* containing the sulfanilyl group. [SULFANIL(IC ACID) + -YL]

sulfan′ilyl group′, *Chem.* the para form of the group $C_6H_6NO_2S$–, derived from sulfanilic acid. Also called **sulfan′ilyl rad′ical.**

sulf·an·ti·mo·nide (sul fan′tə mə nīd′, -nid), *n. Chem.* any compound containing an antimonide and a sulfide. [SULF- + *antimonide;* see ANTIMONY, -IDE]

sul·fa·pyr·i·dine (sul′fə pir′i dēn′, -din), *n. Pharm.* a sulfanilamide derivative, $C_{11}H_{11}N_3O_2S$, formerly used for infections caused by pneumococci, now used primarily for a particular dermatitis. [SULFA(NILAMIDE) + PYRIDINE]

sulf·ar·se·nide (sul fär′sə nīd′, -nid), *n. Chem.* any compound containing an arsenide and a sulfide. [SULF- + ARSENIDE]

sulf·ars·phen·a·mine (sulf′ärs fen′ə mēn′, -min), *n. Pharm.* a yellow, water-soluble, arsenic-containing powder, $C_{14}H_{14}As_2N_2Na_2O_8S_2$, formerly used in the treatment of syphilis. [SULF- + ARSPHENAMINE]

sul·fa·sal·a·zine (sul′fə sal′ə zēn′), *n. Pharm.* a substance, $C_{18}H_{14}N_4O_5S$, used in the treatment of ulcerative colitis. [1960–65; SULFA(NILAMIDE) + SAL(ICYLIC ACID) + AZINE]

sul·fa·tase (sul′fə tās′, -tāz′), *n. Biochem.* any of a class of enzymes that catalyze the hydrolysis of sulfuric acid esters. [< G *Sulfatase* (1924); see SULFATE, -ASE]

sul•fate (sul′fāt), *n., v.,* **-fat•ed, -fat•ing.** —*n.* **1.** *Chem.* a salt or ester of sulfuric acid. —*v.t.* **2.** to combine, treat, or impregnate with sulfuric acid, a sulfate, or sulfates. **3.** to convert into a sulfate. **4.** *Elect.* to form a deposit of lead-sulfate compound on (the lead electrodes of a storage battery). —*v.i.* **5.** to become sulfated. [1780–90; < NL *sulphātum.* See SULFUR, -ATE²] —**sul•fa′tion,** *n.*

sul′fate pa′per, paper made from sulfate pulp.

sul′fate proc′ess, *Chem.* a process for making wood pulp by digesting wood chips in an alkaline liquor consisting chiefly of caustic soda together with sodium sulfate. Also called **kraft process.**

sul′fate pulp′, wood pulp made by the sulfate process.

sul•fa•thi•a•zole (sul′fə thī′ə zōl′), *n. Pharm.* a sulfanilamide derivative, $C_9H_9N_3O_2S_2$, formerly used in the treatment of pneumonia and staphylococcal infections, but now largely replaced because of its toxicity. [SULFA(NILAMIDE) + THIAZOLE]

sul•fat•ize (sul′fə tīz′), *v.t.,* **-ized, -iz•ing.** to convert into a sulfate, as by the roasting of ores. Also, *esp. Brit.,* **sulphatise.** [SULFATE + -IZE] —**sul′fat•i•za′tion,** *n.*

sulf•hy•dryl (sulf hī′dril), *adj. Chem.* mercapto. [1930–35; SULF- + HYDR-² + -YL]

sul•fide (sul′fīd, -fid), *n. Chem.* a compound of sulfur with a more electropositive element or, less often, a group. [1830–40; SULF(UR) + -IDE]

sul′fide dye′, *Chem.* See **sulfur dye.**

sul•fin•pyr•a•zone (sul′fin pir′ə zōn′), *n. Pharm.* a substance, $C_{23}H_{20}N_2O_3S$, used in the treatment of chronic gout. [1955–60; SULFIN(YL) + PYRAZ(OLE) + -ONE]

sul•fi•nyl (sul′fə nil), *adj. Chem.* containing the sulfinyl group; thionyl. [1930–35; SULF- + -IN² + -YL]

sul′finyl group′, *Chem.* the bivalent group >SO. Also called **sul′finyl rad′ical.**

sul•fi•sox•a•zole (sul′fi sok′sə zōl′), *n. Pharm.* a white to yellowish, crystalline, slightly bitter sulfonamide, $C_{11}H_{13}N_3O_3S$, used chiefly in the treatment of infections of the urinary tract. [1960–65; SULF(ONAMIDE) + *isoxazole;* see IS-, OX-, AZOLE]

sul•fite (sul′fīt), *n. Chem.* **1.** a salt or ester of sulfurous acid. **2.** any sulfite-containing compound, esp. one that is used in foods or drug products as a preservative and that can cause severe allergic reactions in susceptible individuals: use in fresh fruits and vegetables banned by the FDA in 1986. [1780–90; SULF(UR) + -ITE¹] —**sul•fit•ic** (sul fit′ik), *adj.*

sul′fite pa′per, paper made from sulfite pulp.

sul′fite proc′ess, *Chem.* a process for making wood pulp by digesting wood chips in an acid liquor consisting of sulfurous acid and a salt, usually calcium bisulfite. [1900–05]

sul′fite pulp′, wood pulp made by the sulfite process. [1905–10]

sul′fit•ing a′gent (sul′fī ting), sulfite (def. 2).

sul•fo (sul′fō), *adj. Chem.* containing the sulfo group; sulfonic. [shortening of SULFONIC OR SULFONYL]

sulfo-, var. of **sulf-,** esp. before a consonant: *sulfocarbanilide.*

sul•fo•car•ba•nil•ide (sul′fō kär′bə nil′īd, -id, -kär-ban′l īd, -id), *n. Chem.* thiocarbanilide. [SULFO- + CARBANIL + -IDE]

sul′fo group′, *Chem.* the univalent group SO_3H–, derived from sulfuric acid. Also called **sulfo radical.** [1870–75]

sul•fon•a•mide (sul fon′ə mīd′, -mid, sul′fə nam′īd, -id), *n. Pharm.* See **sulfa drug.** [1900–05; SULFON(IC ACID) + AMIDE]

sul•fo•nate (sul′fə nāt′), *n., v.,* **-nat•ed, -nat•ing.** *Chem.* —*n.* **1.** an ester or salt derived from a sulfonic acid. —*v.t.* **2.** to make into a sulfonic acid, as by treating an aromatic hydrocarbon with concentrated sulfuric acid. **3.** to introduce the sulfonic group into (an organic compound). [1875–80; SULFON(IC ACID) + -ATE¹ or -ATE²]

sul•fo•na•tion (sul′fə nā′shən), *n. Chem.* the process of attaching the sulfonic acid group, $–SO_3H$, directly to carbon in an organic compound. [1885–90; SULFONATE + -ION]

sul•fone (sul′fōn), *n. Chem.* any of a class of organic compounds containing the bivalent group $–SO_2–$, united with two hydrocarbon groups. [1870–75; < G *Sulfon;* see SULFUR, -ONE]

sul•fon•ic (sul fon′ik), *adj. Chem.* sulfo. [1870–75; SULFONE + -IC]

sulfon′ic ac′id, *Chem.* any of a large group of organic compounds of the structure RSO_2OH, which are strong acids that give neutral sodium salts: used in the synthesis of phenols, dyes, and other substances. [1870–75]

sul•fo•ni•um (sul fō′nē əm), *n. Chem.* the positively charged group H_3S^+, its salts, or their substitute products. [1890–95; SULF(UR) + (AMM)ONIUM]

sul•fo•nyl (sul′fə nil), *adj. Chem.* sulfuryl. [1915–20; SULFONE + -YL]

sul′fonyl chlo′ride, *Chem.* See **sulfuryl chloride.**

sul′fo rad′ical. See **sulfo group.**

sulf•ox•ide (sul fok′sīd) *n. Chem.* **1.** a brown liquid, $C_{18}H_{28}O_3S$, insoluble in water, used as an insecticide synergist. **2.** any of the compounds with the radical =SO, as dimethyl sulfoxide, $(CH_3)_2SO$. [1890–95; SULF- + OXIDE]

sul•fur (sul′fər), *n.* **1.** Also, *esp. Brit.,* **sulphur.** *Chem.* a nonmetallic element that exists in several forms, the ordinary one being a yellow rhombic crystalline solid, and that burns with a blue flame and a suffocating odor: used esp. in making gunpowder and matches, in medicine, in vulcanizing rubber, etc. *Symbol:* S; *at. wt.:* 32.064; *at. no.:* 16; *sp. gr.:* 2.07 at 20° C. **2.** sulphur (def. 2). [1300–50; ME *sulphur* < L *sulpur, sulphur, sulfur* brimstone, sulfur]

sul•fu•rate (sul′fyə rāt′, -fə-), *v.t.,* **-rat•ed, -rat•ing.** to combine, treat, or impregnate with sulfur, the fumes of burning sulfur, etc. [1750–60; < L *sulphurātus.* See SULFUR, -ATE¹] —**sul′fu•ra′tion,** *n.* —**sul′fu•ra′tor,** *n.*

sul′furated pot′ash, *Vet. Med.* a yellowish-brown mixture consisting mainly of potassium polysulfides and potassium thiosulfate, used in treating mange. Also called **liver of sulfur.** [1865–70]

sul′fur bacte′ria, several species of bacteria, esp. of the genera *Beggiatoa* and *Thiobacillus,* that have the ability to utilize sulfur or inorganic sulfur compounds as an energy source. [1900–05]

sul•fur-bot•tom (sul′fər bot′əm), *n.* See **blue whale.**

sul′fur but′terfly, any of various yellow or orange butterflies of the family Pieridae. [1875–80]

sul′fur diox′ide, *Chem.* a colorless, nonflammable, water-soluble, suffocating gas, SO_2, formed when sulfur burns: used chiefly in the manufacture of chemicals such as sulfuric acid, in preserving fruits and vegetables, and in bleaching, disinfecting, and fumigating. [1865–70]

sul′fur dye′, *Chem.* any of the class of dyes produced by heating an organic compound, as an indophenol, with sulfur or sodium polysulfide, used chiefly in dyeing cotton. Also, **sulfide dye.**

sul•fu•re•ous (sul fyŏŏr′ē əs), *adj.* **1.** consisting of, containing, or pertaining to sulfur. **2.** like sulfur, esp. in color. [1545–55; < L *sulfureus.* See SULFUR, -EOUS] —**sul•fu′re•ous•ly,** *adv.* —**sul•fu′re•ous•ness,** *n.*

sul•fu•ret (sul′fyə ret′), *n., v.,* **-ret•ed, -ret•ing** or (*esp. Brit.*) **-ret•ted, -ret•ting.** —*n.* **1.** *Chem.* a sulfide. —*v.t.* **2.** to treat or combine with sulfur. [1780–90; < NL *sulfurētum.* See SULF-, -URET]

sul′fureted hy′drogen, *Chem.* See **hydrogen sulfide.** [1795–1805]

sul•fur-flow•er (sul′fər flou′ər), *n.* sulphur-flower.

sul•fu•ric (sul fyŏŏr′ik), *adj. Chem.* of, pertaining to, or containing sulfur, esp. in the hexavalent state. [1780–90; < F *sulfurique;* see SULFUR, -IC]

sulfu′ric ac′id, *Chem.* a clear, colorless to brownish, dense, oily, corrosive, water-miscible liquid, H_2SO_4, usually produced from sulfur dioxide: used chiefly in the manufacture of fertilizers, chemicals, explosives, and dyestuffs and in petroleum refining. Also called **oil of vitriol.** [1780–90]

sulfu′ric anhy′dride, *Chem.* See **sulfur trioxide.** [1860–65]

sulfu′ric e′ther, *Chem.* ether (def. 1). [1805–15]

sul•fu•rize (sul′fyə rīz′, -fə-), *v.t.,* **-rized, -riz•ing. 1.** to combine, treat, or impregnate with sulfur. **2.** to fumigate with sulfur dioxide. Also, *esp. Brit.,* **sulphurise.** [1785–95; < F *sulfuriser.* See SULFUR, -IZE] —**sul′fu•ri•za′tion,** *n.*

sul•fur•ous (sul′fər əs, sul fyŏŏr′əs), *adj.* **1.** of, pertaining to, or containing sulfur, esp. in the tetravalent state. **2.** of the yellow color of sulfur. **3.** sulphurous (defs. 2, 3). [1520–30; < L *sulfurōsus.* See SULFUR, -OUS] —**sul′fur•ous•ly,** *adv.* —**sul′fur•ous•ness,** *n.*

sul′furous ac′id, *Chem.* a colorless liquid, H_2SO_3, having a suffocating odor, obtained by dissolving sulfur dioxide in water, known mainly by its salts, which are sulfites: used chiefly in organic synthesis and as a bleach. [1780–90]

sul′fur pol′ypore. See **chicken mushroom.**

sul′fur shelf′. See **chicken mushroom.**

sul′fur spring′, a spring the water of which contains naturally occurring sulfur compounds. [1870–75]

sul′fur triox′ide, *Chem.* an irritant, corrosive, low-melting solid, SO_3, obtained by the oxidation of sulfur dioxide, used as an intermediate in the manufacture of sulfuric acid. Also called **sulfuric anhydride.** [1865–70]

sul•fur•yl (sul′fə ril, -fyə ril), *adj. Chem.* containing the sulfuryl group, SO_2, as sulfuryl chloride; sulfonyl. [1865–70; SULFUR + -YL]

sul′furyl chlo′ride, *Chem.* a colorless liquid, SO_2Cl_2, having a very pungent odor and corrosive to the skin and mucous membranes: used as a chlorinating or sulfonating agent. Also, **sulfonyl chloride.** [1865–70]

sul′furyl group′, *Chem.* the bivalent group, SO_2, derived from sulfuric acid. Also called **sul′furyl rad′ical.** [1865–70]

su•lin•dac (sə lin′dak), *n. Pharm.* a yellow crystalline substance, $C_{20}H_{17}FO_3S$, that is used as an analgesic, antipyretic, and anti-inflammatory in the treatment of certain rheumatic diseases. [SUL(FINYL) + IND(ENE) + AC(ETIC ACID)]

sulk (sulk), *v.i.* **1.** to remain silent or hold oneself aloof in a sullen, ill-humored, or offended mood: *Promise me that you won't sulk if I want to leave the party early.* —*n.* **2.** a state or fit of sulking. **3. sulks,** ill-humor shown by sulking: *to be in the sulks.* **4.** Also, **sulk′er.** a person who sulks. [1775–85; back formation from SULKY]

sulk•y (sul′kē), *adj.,* **sulk•i•er, sulk•i•est,** *n., pl.* **sulk•ies.** —*adj.* **1.** marked by or given to sulking; sullen. **2.** gloomy or dull: *sulky weather.* —*n.* **3.** a light, two-wheeled, one-horse carriage for one person. [1735–45; akin to OE *solcen-* lazy (in *solcennes* laziness), Fris (N dial.) *sulkig* sulky] —**sulk′i•ly,** *adv.* —**sulk′i•ness,** *n.*
—**Syn. 1.** moody, surly, morose, churlish. —**Ant. 1.** good-humored, good-natured.

sulky (def. 3)

Sul•la (sul′ə), *n.* (*Lucius Cornelius Sulla Felix*) 138–78 B.C., Roman general and statesman: dictator 82–79.

sul•lage (sul′ij), *n.* **1.** refuse or waste; sewage. **2.** silt; sediment. [1545–55; orig. uncert.]

sul•len (sul′ən), *adj.* **1.** showing irritation or ill humor by a gloomy silence or reserve. **2.** persistently and silently ill-humored; morose. **3.** indicative of gloomy ill humor. **4.** gloomy or dismal, as weather or a sound. **5.** sluggish, as a stream. **6.** *Obs.* malignant, as planets or influences. [1565–75; earlier *solein,* ME < ?] —**sul′len•ly,** *adv.* —**sul′len•ness,** *n.*
—**Syn. 1.** See **cross. 1, 2.** See **glum. 2.** sulky, moody, sour, bad-tempered. **4.** cheerless, clouded, overcast, somber, mournful, dark. **5.** slow, stagnant. —**Ant. 1, 2.** cheerful.

Sul•li•van (sul′ə vən), *n.* **1. Annie** (*Anne Mansfield Sullivan Macy*), 1866–1936, U.S. teacher of Helen Keller. **2. Sir Arthur (Seymour),** 1842–1900, English composer: collaborator with Sir William Gilbert. **3. Ed(ward Vincent),** 1902–74, U.S. journalist and television host. **4. Harry Stack** (stak), 1892–1949, U.S. psychiatrist. **5. John L(awrence),** 1858–1918, U.S. boxer: world heavyweight champion 1882–92. **6. Louis Hen•ri** (hen′rē), 1856–1924, U.S. architect.

sul•ly (sul′ē), *v.,* **-lied, -ly•ing,** *n., pl.* **-lies.** —*v.t.* **1.** to soil, stain, or tarnish. **2.** to mar the purity or luster of; defile: *to sully a reputation.* —*v.i.* **3.** to become sullied, soiled, or tarnished. —*n.* **4.** *Obs.* a stain; soil. [1585–95; orig. uncert.] —**sul′li•a•ble,** *adj.*
—**Syn. 1.** taint, blemish, contaminate. **2.** dirty, disgrace, dishonor.

Sul•ly (sul′ē; *for 1 also Fr.* SY lē′), *n.* **1. Ma•xi•mi•lien de Bé•thune** (mAk sē mē lyaN′ də bā tyn′), **Duc de,** 1560–1641, French statesman. **2. Thomas,** 1783–1872, U.S. painter, born in England.

Sul•ly-Pru•dhomme (SY lē′PRY dôm′), *n.* **Re•né Fran•çois Ar•mand** (Rə nā′ FRÄN SWA′ AR mäN′), 1839–1907, French poet: Nobel prize 1901.

sulph-, *Chiefly Brit.* var. of **sulf-.**

sul•phat•ise (sul′fə tīz′), *v.t.,* **-ised, -is•ing.** *Chiefly Brit.* sulfatize.

sul•phur (sul′fər), *n.* **1.** *Chiefly Brit.* sulfur (def. 1). **2.** Also, **sulfur.** yellow with a greenish tinge; lemon color. [var. of SULFUR]

Sul•phur (sul′fər), *n.* a city in SW Louisiana. 19,709.

sul•phur-bot•tom (sul′fər bot′əm), *n.* See **blue whale.** [1775–85]

sul′phur but′terfly. See **sulfur butterfly.** [1875–80]

sul•phur-flow•er (sul′fər flou′ər), *n.* a plant, *Eriogonum umbellatum,* of the buckwheat family, native to the western coast of the U.S., having leaves with white, woolly hairs on the underside and golden-yellow flowers. Also, **sulfur-flower.**

sul•phu•rise (sul′fyə rīz′, -fə-), *v.t.,* **-rised, -ris•ing.** *Chiefly Brit.* sulfurize.

sul•phur•ous (sul′fər əs, sul fyŏŏr′əs), *adj.* **1.** sulfurous (defs. 1, 2). **2.** pertaining to the fires of hell; hellish or satanic. **3.** fiery or heated. [1520–30; sp. var. of SULFUROUS] —**sul′phur•ous•ly,** *adv.* —**sul′phur•ous•ness,** *n.*

Sul′phur Springs′, a town in NE Texas. 12,804.

Sul•pi•cian (sul pish′ən), *n. Rom. Cath. Ch.* a member of a society of secular priests founded in France in 1642, engaged chiefly in training men to teach in seminaries. [1780–90; < F *sulpicien,* after *la Campagnie de Saint Sulpice* the Society of St. Sulpice, named after the church where its founder was pastor; see -IAN]

sul•tan (sul′tn), *n.* **1.** the sovereign of an Islamic country. **2.** (*often cap.*) any of the former sovereigns of Turkey. **3.** any absolute ruler or despot. [1545–55; < MF < Turk < Ar *sulṭān* sovereign] —**sul•tan•ic** (sul tan′ik), *adj.* —**sul′tan•like′,** *adj.* —**sul′tan•ship′,** *n.*

sul•tan•a (sul tan′ə, -tä′nə), *n.* **1.** a small, seedless raisin. **2.** a wife or a concubine of a sultan. **3.** a sister, daughter, or mother of a sultan. **4.** a mistress, esp. of a king or other royal personage. **5.** Also called **old amethyst.** a deep purplish-red color. [1575–85; < It, fem. of *sultano* SULTAN]

sul•tan•ate (sul′tn āt′), *n.* **1.** the office or rule of a sultan. **2.** the territory ruled over by a sultan. [1815–25; SULTAN + -ATE³]

sul•tan•ess (sul′tn is), *n.* sultana (defs. 2, 3). [1605–15; SULTAN + -ESS]
—**Usage.** See **-ess.**

sul•try (sul′trē), *adj.,* **-tri•er, -tri•est. 1.** oppressively hot and close or moist; sweltering: *a sultry day.* **2.** oppressively hot; emitting great heat: *the sultry sun.* **3.** characterized by or associated with sweltering heat: *sultry work in the fields.* **4.** characterized by or arousing

CONCISE PRONUNCIATION KEY: act, cāpe, dâre, pärt; set, ēqual; *if,* īce; ox, ōver, ôrder, oil, bŏŏk, bōōt, out; up, ûrge; child; sing; shoe; thin, *that;* zh as in *treasure.* ə = *a* as in *alone, e* as in *system, i* as in *easily, o* as in *gallop, u* as in *circus;* ᵊ as in *fire* (fīᵊr), *hour* (ouᵊr). l and n can serve as syllabic consonants, as in *cradle* (krād′l), and *button* (but′n). See the full key inside the front cover.

passion: *sultry eyes.* [1585–95; *sult(e)r* (var. of SWELTER) + -Y[1]] —**sul′tri·ly,** *adv.* —**sul′tri·ness,** *n.*
—**Syn. 1.** oppressive, stifling, humid.

Su·lu (so͞o′lo͞o), *n., pl.* **-lus,** (*esp. collectively*) **-lu.** a member of the most numerous tribe of Moros, living chiefly in the Sulu Archipelago.

Su′lu Archipel′ago, an island group in the SW Philippines, separating the Sulawesi Sea from the Sulu Sea. 555,239; 1086 sq. mi. (2813 sq. km). *Cap.:* Jolo.

Su′lu Sea′, a sea in the W Pacific, between the SW Philippines and Borneo.

Sulz·ber·ger (sulz′bûr gər), *n.* **Arthur Hays,** 1891–1968, U.S. newspaper publisher.

sum (sum), *n., v.,* **summed, sum·ming.** —*n.* **1.** the aggregate of two or more numbers, magnitudes, quantities, or particulars as determined by or as if by the mathematical process of addition: *The sum of 6 and 8 is 14.* **2.** a particular aggregate or total, esp. with reference to money: *The expenses came to an enormous sum.* **3.** an indefinite amount or quantity, esp. of money: *to lend small sums.* **4.** a series of numbers or quantities to be added up. **5.** an arithmetical problem to be solved, or such a problem worked out and having the various steps shown. **6.** the full amount, or the whole. **7.** the substance or gist of a matter, comprehensively or broadly viewed or expressed: *the sum of his opinions.* **8.** concise or brief form: *in sum.* **9.** *Math.* **a.** the limit of the sequence of partial sums of a given infinite series. **b.** union (def. 10a). **10.** a summary. —*v.t.* **11.** to combine into an aggregate or total (often fol. by *up*). **12.** to ascertain the sum of, as by addition. **13.** to bring into or contain in a small compass (often fol. by *up*). —*v.i.* **14.** to amount (usually fol. by *to* or *into*): *Their expenses summed into the thousands.* **15. sum up, a.** to reckon: *We summed up our assets and liabilities.* **b.** to bring into or contain in a brief and comprehensive statement; summarize: *to sum up the case for the prosecution.* **c.** to form a quick estimate of: *I summed him up in a minute.* [1250–1300; (n.) ME *summe* < L *summa* sum, n. use of fem. of *summus* highest, superl. of *superus* (see SUPERIOR); (v.) ME *summen* (< OF *summer*) < ML *summāre,* deriv. of *summa*] —**sum′less,** *adj.* —**sum′less·ness,** *n.*
—**Syn. 1.** See **number.**

sum-, var. of **sub-** before *m: summon.*

SUM, surface-to-underwater missile.

su·mac (so͞o′mak, sho͞o′-), *n.* **1.** any of several shrubs or small trees belonging to the genus *Rhus* of the cashew family, having milky sap, compound leaves, and small, fleshy fruit. **2.** a preparation of the dried and powdered leaves, bark, etc., of certain species of *Rhus,* esp. *R. coriaria* of southern Europe, used esp. in tanning. **3.** the wood of these trees. Also, **su′mach.** [1250–1300; ME < ML < Ar *summāq*]

su′mac wax′. See **Japan wax.**

sum′ and sub′stance, main idea, gist, or point: *the sum and substance of an argument.* [1585–95]

Su·ma·tra (so͝o mä′trə), *n.* a large island in the W part of Indonesia. 20,800,000; 164,147 sq. mi. (425,141 sq. km). —**Su·ma′tran,** *adj., n.*

Suma′tra cam′phor, borneol. [1840–50]

Sum·ba (so͞om′bä), *n.* one of the Lesser Sunda Islands, in Indonesia, S of Flores. 4306 sq. mi. (11,153 sq. km). Also called **Sandalwood Island.** Dutch, **Soemba.**

Sum·ba·wa (so͞om bä′wä), *n.* one of the Lesser Sunda Islands, in Indonesia: destructive eruption in 1815 of Mt. Tambora. 5965 sq. mi. (15,449 sq. km). Dutch, **Soembawa.**

Su·mer (so͞o′mər), *n.* an ancient region in southern Mesopotamia that contained a number of independent cities and city-states of which the first were established possibly as early as 5000 B.C.: conquered by the Elamites and, about 2000 B.C., by the Babylonians; a number of its cities, as Ur, Uruk, Kish, and Lagash, are major archaeological sites in southern Iraq.

Su·me·ri·an (so͞o mer′ē ən, -mer′-), *adj.* **1.** of or pertaining to Sumer, its people, or their language. —*n.* **2.** a native or inhabitant of Sumer. **3.** a language of unknown affinities that was the language of the Sumerians and had, in the late 4th and 3rd millenniums B.C., a well-developed literature that is preserved in pictographic and cuneiform writing and represents the world's oldest extant written documents. [1870–75; SUMER + -IAN]

Su·me·rol·o·gy (so͞o′mə rol′ə jē), *n.* the study of the history, language, and culture of the Sumerians. [1895–1900; SUMER + -O- + -LOGY] —**Su′me·rol′o·gist,** *n.*

Sum·ga·it (so͞om gu yēt′; *Eng.* so͞om′gä ēt′), *n.* a city in SE Azerbaijan, on the Caspian Sea. 234,000.

su·mi (so͞o′mē), *n. Japanese.* black ink made from a mixture of plant soot and glue solidified into sticks or cakes the ends of which are scraped or ground into water on an ink slab, much used by calligraphers and painters.

su·mi-e (so͞o′mē e′), *n., pl.* ***su·mi-e.*** *Japanese.* (in fine arts) a monochrome painting executed in ink: *Zen painters were masters of sumi-e.*

sum·ma (so͝om′ə, sum′ə), *n., pl.* **sum·mae** (so͝om′ī, sum′ē), **sum·mas. 1.** a comprehensive work or series of works covering, synthesizing, or summarizing a particular field or subject. **2.** a work or series of works that is a summary of all human knowledge. [1400–50; late ME < ML; L: SUM]

sum·ma·ble (sum′ə bəl), *adj. Math.* **1.** capable of being added. **2.** (of an infinite series, esp. a divergent one) capable of having a sum assigned to it by a method other than the usual one of taking the limit of successive partial sums. **3.** (of a function) possessing a finite Lebesgue integral. [1775–85; SUM + -ABLE] —**sum′ma·bil′i·ty,** *n.*

sum·ma cum lau·de (so͝om′ə ko͝om lou′dā, -də, -dē; sum′ə kum lô′dē), with highest praise: used in diplomas to grant the highest of three special honors for grades above the average. Cf. **cum laude, magna cum laude.** [1895–1900; < L *summā cum laude*]

sum·mand (sum′and, sum and′, sə mand′), *n.* a part of a sum. [1890–95; < ML *summandus,* ger. of *summāre* to SUM]

sum·mar·i·ly (sə mâr′ə lē, sum′ər ə-), *adv.* **1.** in a prompt or direct manner; immediately; straightaway. **2.** without notice; precipitately: *to be dismissed summarily from one's job.* [1520–30; SUMMARY + -LY]

sum·ma·rize (sum′ə rīz′), *v.t.,* **-rized, -riz·ing. 1.** to make a summary of; state or express in a concise form. **2.** to constitute a summary of. Also, *esp. Brit.,* **sum′ma·rise′.** [1870–75; SUMMAR(Y) + -IZE] —**sum′ma·riz′a·ble,** *adj.* —**sum′ma·ri·za′tion,** *n.* —**sum′ma·riz′er,** **sum′mar·ist,** *n.*

sum·ma·ry (sum′ə rē), *n., pl.* **-ries,** *adj.* —*n.* **1.** a comprehensive and usually brief abstract, recapitulation, or compendium of previously stated facts or statements. —*adj.* **2.** brief and comprehensive; concise. **3.** direct and prompt; unceremoniously fast: *to treat someone with summary dispatch.* **4.** (of legal proceedings, jurisdiction, etc.) conducted without, or exempt from, the various steps and delays of a formal trial. [1400–50; late ME < L *summārium,* equiv. to *summ(a)* SUM + *-ārium* -ARY] —**sum·mar·i·ness** (sə mâr′ i nis), *n.*
—**Syn. 1.** outline, précis. SUMMARY, BRIEF, DIGEST, SYNOPSIS are terms for a short version of a longer work. A SUMMARY is a brief statement or restatement of main points, esp. as a conclusion to a work: *a summary of a chapter.* A BRIEF is a detailed outline, by heads and subheads, of a discourse (usually legal) to be completed: *a brief for an argument.* A DIGEST is an abridgement of an article, book, etc., or an organized arrangement of material under heads and titles: *a digest of a popular novel; a digest of Roman law.* A SYNOPSIS is usually a compressed statement of the plot of a novel, play, etc.: *a synopsis of* Hamlet. **2.** short, condensed, compact, succinct. **3.** curt, terse, peremptory.

sum′mary court′-martial, *U.S. Mil.* a court-martial composed of one commissioned officer, authorized to try minor offenses against military law.

sum′mary judg′ment, *Law.* a judgment, as in an action for debt, that is entered without the necessity of jury trial, based on affidavits of the creditor and debtor that convince the court that there is no arguable issue.

sum′mary proceed′ing, *Law.* a mode of trial authorized by statute to be held before a judge without the usual full hearing.

sum·mate (sum′āt), *v.t.,* **-mat·ed, -mat·ing.** to add together; total; sum up. [1895–1900; back formation from SUMMATION]

Sum·ma The·o·lo·gi·ca (so͝om′ə thē′ə loj′i kə, sum′ə), a philosophical and theological work (1265–74) by St. Thomas Aquinas, consisting of an exposition of Christian doctrine.

sum·ma·tion (sə mā′shən), *n.* **1.** the act or process of summing. **2.** the result of this; an aggregate or total. **3.** a review or recapitulation of previously stated facts or statements, often with a final conclusion or conclusions drawn from them. **4.** *Law.* the final arguments of opposing attorneys before a case goes to the jury. **5.** *Physiol.* the arousal of impulses by a rapid succession of stimuli, carried either by separate sensory neurons (**spatial summation**) or by the same sensory neuron (**temporal summation**). [1750–60; < ML *summātiōn-* (s. of *summātiō*), equiv. to *summāt(us)* (ptp. of *summāre* to SUM; see -ATE[1]) + *-iōn-* -ION] —**sum·ma′tion·al,** *adj.*

summa′tion meth′od, *Math.* a method for associating a sum with a divergent series.

sum·ma·tive (sum′ə tiv), *adj.* additive. [1880–85; < ML *summāt(us)* (see SUMMATION) + -IVE]

sum·mer[1] (sum′ər), *n.* **1.** the season between spring and autumn, in the Northern Hemisphere from the summer solstice to the autumnal equinox, and in the Southern Hemisphere from the winter solstice to the vernal equinox. **2.** the period comprising the months of June, July, and August in the U.S., and from the middle of May to the middle of August in Great Britain. **3.** a period of hot, usually sunny weather: *We had no real summer last year.* **4.** the hotter half of the year (opposed to *winter*): *They spend the summers in New Hampshire and the winters in Florida.* **5.** the period of finest development, perfection, or beauty previous to any decline: *the summer of life.* **6.** a whole year as represented by this season: *a girl of fifteen summers.* —*adj.* **7.** of, pertaining to, or characteristic of summer: *Iced tea is a summer drink.* **8.** appropriate for or done during the summer: *summer clothes; summer sports.* **9.** having the weather or warmth of summer: *summer days in late October.* —*v.i.* **10.** to spend or pass the summer: *They summered in Maine.* —*v.t.* **11.** to keep, feed, or manage during the summer: *Sheep are summered in high pastures.* **12.** to make summerlike. [bef. 900; ME *sumer,* OE *sumor;* c. D *zomer,* G *Sommer,* ON *sumar* summer; akin to Skt *samā* half-year, year, OIr *sam-,* Welsh *haf* summer] —**sum′mer·less,** *adj.*

sum·mer[2] (sum′ər), *n.* **1.** a principal beam or girder, as one running between girts to support joists. **2.** a stone laid upon a pier, column, or wall, from which one or more arches spring: usually molded or otherwise treated like the arch or arches springing from it. **3.** a beam or lintel. [1275–1325; ME *somer* < AF; OF *somier* packhorse, beam < VL **saumārius,* equiv. to L *sagm(a)* packsaddle (< Gk *ságma*) + *-ārius* -ARY; see -ER[2]]

sum′mer camp′, a camp, esp. one for children during the summer, providing facilities for sleeping and eating, and usually for handicrafts, sports, etc. Cf. **day camp.**

sum′mer complaint′, an acute condition of diarrhea, occurring during the hot summer months chiefly in infants and children, caused by bacterial contamination of food and associated with poor hygiene. Also called **sum′mer diarrhe′a.** [1840–50, *Amer.*]

sum′mer cy′press. See **burning bush** (def. 2). [1760–70]

sum′mer floun′der, a flounder, *Paralichthys dentatus,* inhabiting shallow waters from Cape Cod to South Carolina, valued as food. [1805–15, *Amer.*]

Sum′mer Games′, Olympic Games held every fourth summer and including swimming, diving, track and field, boxing, and basketball. Compare **Winter Games.**

sum′mer grape′, a high-climbing vine, *Vitis aestivalis,* of the eastern U.S., having leaves that are dull above and rusty beneath, and bearing black, edible fruit. Also called **pigeon grape.** [1700–10, *Amer.*]

sum·mer·house (sum′ər hous′), *n., pl.* **-hous·es** (-hou′ziz). a simple, often rustic structure in a park or garden, intended to provide shade in the summer. [1350–1400; ME *sumer hous.* See SUMMER[1], HOUSE]

sum·mer·ize (sum′ə rīz′), *v.t.,* **-ized, -iz·ing. 1.** to prepare (a house, car, etc.) so as to counteract the hot weather of summer: *to summerize a house by adding air conditioning.* **2.** to protect in hot weather for future use: *to summerize a snowmobile.* Also, *esp. Brit.,* **sum′mer·ise′.** [SUMMER[1] + -IZE]

sum′mer kitch′en, an extra kitchen, usually detached from a house, for use in warm weather. [1870–75, *Amer.*]

sum·mer·like (sum′ər līk′), *adj.* like or characteristic of summer; summery. [1520–30; SUMMER[1] + -LIKE]

sum·mer·ly (sum′ər lē), *adj.* summerlike; summery. [bef. 1000; ME *sumerly,* OE *sumorlic.* See SUMMER[1], -LY] —**sum′mer·li·ness,** *n.*

sum·mer·sault (sum′ər sôlt′), *n., v.i.* somersault.

sum′mer sau′sage, dried or smoked sausage that keeps without refrigeration.

sum′mer sa′vory. See under **savory**[2]. [1565–75]

sum′mer school′, 1. study programs offered by a school, college, or university during the summer to those who wish to obtain their degrees more quickly, who must make up credits, or who wish to supplement their education. **2.** a school offering such programs. [1870–75, *Amer.*]

sum·mer·set (sum′ər set′), *n., v.i.* somersault.

sum′mer snow′flake, star-of-Bethlehem.

sum′mer sol′stice, *Astron.* the solstice on or about June 21st that marks the beginning of summer in the Northern Hemisphere. [1540–50]

sum′mer squash′, any of several squashes of the variety *Cucurbita pepo melopepo,* that mature in the late summer or early autumn and are used as a vegetable in an unripe state, before the rind and seeds become hard. [1745–55]

sum′mer stock′, 1. the production of plays, musical comedy, etc., during the summer, esp. in a suburban or resort area, often by a repertory company. **2.** summer theaters collectively or their productions. [1925–30]

sum·mer-sweet (sum′ər swēt′), *n.* See **sweet pepperbush.**

sum′mer tan′ager, a tanager, *Piranga rubra,* of the south and central U.S., the male of which is rose-red, the female olive-green above and yellow below. [1775–85, *Amer.*]

sum′mer the′ater, 1. a theater that operates during the summer, esp. in a suburban or resort area, usually offering a different play or musical comedy each week. **2.** See **summer stock.** [1945–50]

sum′mer time′, *Chiefly Brit.* See **daylight-saving time.**

sum·mer·time (sum′ər tīm′), *n.* the summer season. [1350–1400; ME *somertime.* See SUMMER[1], TIME]

sum·mer·tree (sum′ər trē′), *n.* summer[2] (def. 1). [1425–75; ME *somere tre.* See SUMMER[2], TREE]

sum·mer·wood (sum′ər wo͝od′), *n.* the part of an annual ring of wood, characterized by compact, thick-walled cells, formed during the later part of the growing season. Also called **late wood.** Cf. **springwood.** [1900–05; SUMMER[1] + WOOD[1]]

sum·mer·y (sum′ə rē), *adj.* of, like, or appropriate for summer: *summery weather; a summery dress.* [1815–25; SUMMER[1] + -Y[1]] —**sum′mer·i·ness,** *n.*

sum·ming-up (sum′ing up′), *n., pl.* **sum·mings-up.** a summation or statement made for the purpose of reviewing the basic concepts or principles of an argument, story, explanation, testimony, or the like, and usually presented at the end. [1780–90; *sum up* + -ING[1]]

sum·mit (sum′it), *n.* **1.** the highest point or part, as of a hill, a line of travel, or any object; top; apex. **2.** the highest point of attainment or aspiration: *the summit of one's ambition.* **3.** the highest state or degree. **4.** the highest level of diplomatic or other governmental officials: *a meeting at the summit.* **5.** See **summit meeting.** —*adj.* **6.** of or pertaining to a summit meeting: *summit talks.* —*v.i.* **7.** to take part in a summit meeting. [1425–75; late ME *somete* < OF, equiv. to *som* top (< L *summum,* n. use of neut. of *summus* highest; see SUM) + *-ete* -ET] —**sum′mit·al,** *adj.* —**sum′mit·less,** *adj.*
—**Syn. 1.** peak, pinnacle. **2, 3.** acme, zenith, culmination. —**Ant. 1.** base.

Sum·mit (sum′it), *n.* **1.** a city in NE New Jersey. 21,071. **2.** a city in NE Illinois. 10,110.

CONCISE ETYMOLOGY KEY: <, descended or borrowed from; >, whence; b., blend of, blended; c., cognate with; cf., compare; deriv., derivative; equiv., equivalent; imit., imitative; obl., oblique; r., replacing; s., stem; sp., spelling, spelled; resp., respelling, respelled; trans., translation; ?, origin unknown; *, unattested; ‡, probably earlier than. See the full key inside the front cover.

sum•mit•eer (sum′i tēr′), *n.* a participant in a summit meeting. [1955–60; SUMMIT + -EER]

sum′mit meet′ing, 1. a meeting or conference of heads of state, esp. to conduct diplomatic negotiations and ease international tensions. **2.** any meeting or conference of top-level officials, executives, etc. Also called **summit, sum′mit con′ference.** [1950–55]

sum•mit•ry (sum′i trē), *n.* **1.** the act or practice of holding a summit meeting, esp. to conduct diplomatic negotiations. **2.** the art or technique of conducting summit meetings. **3.** summit meetings collectively. [1955–60; SUMMIT + -RY]

sum•mon (sum′ən), *v.t.* **1.** to call upon to do something specified. **2.** to call for the presence of, as by command, message, or signal; call. **3.** to call or notify to appear at a specified place, esp. before a court: *to summon a defendant.* **4.** to authorize or order a gathering of; call together by authority, as for deliberation or action: *to summon parliament.* **5.** to call into action; rouse; call forth (often. fol. by *up*): *to summon all one's courage.* [1175–1225; < ML *summonēre* to summon, L: to remind unofficially, suggest, equiv. to *sum-* SUM- + *monēre* to remind, warn; r. ME *somonen* < OF *semondre, somondre* < VL **summonere,* L *summonēre,* as above] **—sum′•mon•a•ble,** *adj.* **—sum′mon•er,** *n.*
—Syn. 1-3. See **call.**

sum•mons (sum′ənz), *n., pl.* **-mons•es,** *v.* **—n. 1.** an authoritative command, message, or signal by which one is summoned. **2.** a request, demand, or call to do something: *a summons to surrender.* **3.** *Law.* **a.** a call or citation by authority to appear before a court or a judicial officer. **b.** the writ by which the call is made. **4.** an authoritative call or notice to appear at a specified place, as for a particular purpose or duty. **5.** a call issued for the meeting of an assembly or parliament. **—v.t. 6.** to serve with a summons; summon. [1250–1300; ME *somons* < AF; OF *somonse* < VL **summonsa,* for L *summonita,* fem. ptp. of *summonēre;* see SUMMON]

sum•mum bo•num (so͝om′o͝om bō′no͝om; *Eng.* sum′əm bō′nəm), *Latin.* the highest or chief good.

Sum•ner (sum′nər), *n.* **1. Charles,** 1811–74, U.S. statesman. **2. James Batch•el•ler** (bach′ə lər), 1887–1955, U.S. biochemist: Nobel prize 1946. **3. William Graham,** 1840–1910, U.S. sociologist and economist. **4.** a male given name.

su•mo (so͞o′mō), *n.* a form of wrestling in Japan in which a contestant wins by forcing his opponent out of the ring or by causing him to touch the ground with any part of his body other than the soles of his feet, contestants usually being men of great height and weight. [1895–1900; < Japn *sumō,* earlier *suma(f)u* to wrestle] **—su′mo•ist,** *n.*

sump (sump), *n.* **1.** a pit, well, or the like in which water or other liquid is collected. **2.** *Mach.* a chamber at the bottom of a machine, pump, circulation system, etc., into which a fluid drains before recirculation or in which wastes gather before disposal. **3.** *Mining.* **a.** a space where water is allowed to collect at the bottom of a shaft or below a passageway. **b.** a pilot shaft or tunnel pushed out in front of a main bore. **4.** *Brit.* crankcase. **5.** *Brit. Dial.* a swamp, bog, or muddy pool. [1375–1425; late ME *sompe* < MLG or MD *sump;* c. G *Sumpf;* akin to SWAMP]

sump′ pump′, a pump for removing liquid or wastes from a sump. [1895–1900]

sump•si•mus (sump′sə məs), *n., pl.* **-mus•es** for 2. **1.** adherence to or persistence in using a strictly correct term, holding to a precise practice, etc., as a rejection of an erroneous but more common form (opposed to *mumpsimus*). **2.** a person who is obstinate or zealous about such strict correctness (opposed to *mumpsimus*). [1540–50; see MUMPSIMUS]

sump•ter (sump′tər), *n.* a packhorse or mule. [1275–1325; ME *sompter* < OF *sometier* pack-horse driver < VL **saumatārius,* equiv. to L *sagmat-* (s. of *sagma;* see SUMMER[2]) + *-ārius* -ARY]

sump•tu•ary (sump′cho͞o er′ē), *adj.* **1.** pertaining to, dealing with, or regulating expense or expenditure. **2.** intended to regulate personal habits on moral or religious grounds. [1590–1600; < L *sūmptuārius,* equiv. to *sūmptu(s)* spending, expense (*sūm(ere)* to take, procure (see CONSUME) + intrusive *-p-* + *-tus* suffix of v. action) + *-ārius* -ARY]

sump′tuary law′, 1. a law regulating personal habits that offend the moral beliefs of the community. **2.** a law regulating personal expenditures designed to restrain extravagance, esp. in food and dress. [1590–1600]

sump•tu•ous (sump′cho͞o əs), *adj.* **1.** entailing great expense, as from choice materials, fine work, etc.; costly. **2.** luxuriously fine or large; lavish; splendid: *a sumptuous feast.* [1475–85; < L *sūmptuōsus,* equiv. to *sūmptu(s)* expense (see SUMPTUARY) + *-ōsus* -OUS] **—sump′•tu•ous•ly,** *adv.* **—sump′tu•ous•ness,** *n.*
—Syn. 2. magnificent, luxurious, munificent.

Sum•ter (sum′tər, sump′-), *n.* **1.** a city in central South Carolina. 24,890. **2.** See **Fort Sumter.**

sum′ to′tal, 1. complete numerical total: *the sum total of my savings.* **2.** essence; substance: *The sum total of research in the field.* [1350–1400; ME]

sum-up (sum′up′), *n.* the act or result of summing up; summary. Also, **sum′up′.** [1890–95; n. use of v. phrase *sum up*]

Su•my (so͞o′mē; *Russ.* so͞o′mi), *n.* a city in the NE Ukraine, in the S Soviet Union in Europe. 228,000.

sun (sun), *n., v.,* **sunned, sun•ning.** **—n. 1.** (*often cap.*) the star that is the central body of the solar system, around which the planets revolve and from which they receive light and heat: its mean distance from the earth is about 93 million miles (150 million km), its diameter about 864,000 miles (1.4 million km), and its mass about 330,000 times that of the earth; its period of surface rotation is about 26 days at its equator but longer at higher latitudes. **2.** the sun considered with reference to its position in the sky, its visibility, the season of the year, the time at which it is seen, etc. **3.** a self-luminous heavenly body; star. **4.** sunshine; the heat and light from the sun: *exposed to the sun.* **5.** a figure or representation of the sun, as a heraldic bearing usually surrounded with rays and marked with the features of a human face. **6.** something likened to the sun in brightness, splendor, etc. **7.** *Chiefly Literary.* **a.** clime; climate. **b.** glory; splendor. **8.** sunrise or sunset: *from sun to sun.* **9.** *Archaic.* **a.** a day. **b.** a year. **10. against the sun,** *Naut.* counterclockwise. **11. place in the sun,** a favorable or advantageous position; prominence; recognition: *to achieve a place in the sun.* **12. under the sun,** on earth; anywhere: *the most beautiful city under the sun.* **13. with the sun,** *Naut.* clockwise. **—v.t. 14.** to expose to the sun's rays. **15.** to warm, dry, etc., in the sunshine. **16.** to put, bring, make, etc., by exposure to the sun. **—v.i. 17.** to be exposed to the rays of the sun: *to sun in the yard.* [bef. 900; ME *sun, sonne,* OE *sunne;* c. G *Sonne,* ON *sunna,* Goth *sunno;* akin to ON *sōl,* Goth *sauil,* L *sōl* (see SOLAR), Gk *hḗlios* (see HELIO-), Welsh *haul,* Lith *saũlė,* Pol *słońce*] **—sun′like′,** *adj.*

Sun., Sunday. Also, **Sund.**

Sun′ Al′so Ris′es, The, a novel (1926) by Ernest Hemingway.

sun′-and-plan′et gear′ (sun′ən plan′it), *Mach.* a planetary epicyclic gear train. [1900–05]

sun-and-planet gear

sun′ animal′cule, a heliozoan. [1865–70]

sun•back (sun′bak′), *adj.* (of a garment) cut low to expose the back for sunbathing or coolness. [SUN + BACK[1]]

sun•baked (sun′bākt′), *adj.* **1.** baked by exposure to the sun, as bricks. **2.** heated, dried, or hardened by the heat of the sun. [1620–30; SUN + BAKED]

sun•bath (sun′bath′, -bäth′), *n., pl.* **-baths** (-baṯẖz′, -bäṯẖz′, -baths′, -bäths′). deliberate exposure of the body to the direct rays of the sun or a sunlamp. [1870–75; SUN + BATH[1]]

sun•bathe (sun′bāṯẖ′), *v.i.,* **-bathed, -bath•ing.** to take a sunbath. [1590–1600; SUN + BATHE] **—sun′•bath′er,** *n.*

sun•beam (sun′bēm′), *n.* **1.** a beam or ray of sunlight. **2.** *Australian Slang.* a dish or utensil that has not been used during a meal and so does not have to be washed. [bef. 1000; ME *sunnebem,* OE *sun(ne)bēam.* See SUN, BEAM] **—sun′beamed′, sun′beam′y,** *adj.*

sun′ bear′, a small, black bear, *Ursus (Helarctos) malayanus,* of Southeast Asian forests, having a light muzzle and yellow chest markings. Also called **honey bear, Malay bear.** [1835–45]

Sun•belt (sun′belt′), *n.* (*sometimes l.c.*) the southern and southwestern region of the U.S. Also, **Sun′ Belt′.** [1950–55]

sun•ber•ry (sun′ber′ē, -bə rē), *n., pl.* **-ries.** wonderberry. [SUN + BERRY]

sun•bird (sun′bûrd′), *n.* any of various small, brilliantly colored Old World birds of the family Nectariniidae. [1790–1800; SUN + BIRD]

sun′ bit′tern, a graceful South American wading bird, *Eurypyga helias,* related to the cranes and rails, having variegated plumage. [1865–70]

sun•block (sun′blok′), *n.* **1.** a substance that provides a high degree of protection against sunburn, often preventing most tanning as well as burning, as by obstructing the penetration of ultraviolet rays. **2.** a lotion, cream, etc., containing such a substance. Also, **sun′ block′.** [1975–80; SUN + BLOCK]

sun•bon•net (sun′bon′it), *n.* a bonnet with a large brim shading the face and sometimes a piece projecting over the neck, worn by women and children. [1815–25; SUN + BONNET] **—sun′bon′net•ed,** *adj.*

sun•bow (sun′bō′), *n.* a bow or arc of prismatic colors like a rainbow, appearing in the spray of cataracts, waterfalls, fountains, etc. [1810–20; SUN + BOW[2]]

sun•break (sun′brāk′), *n.* a projection from the side of a building for intercepting part of the sunlight falling upon the adjacent surface. Also, **sun′break′er.** [1820–30; SUN + BREAK]

sun•burn (sun′bûrn′), *n., v.,* **-burned** or **-burnt, -burn•ing.** **—n. 1.** inflammation of the skin caused by overexposure to the sun or a sunlamp. **—v.t., v.i. 2.** to affect or be affected with sunburn: *I sunburn easily.* [1520–30; SUN + BURN[1]]

sun•burst (sun′bûrst′), *n.* **1.** a burst of sunlight; a sudden shining of the sun through rifted clouds. **2.** a firework, piece of jewelry, ornament, or the like, resembling the sun with rays issuing in all directions. **—adj. 3.** *Sewing.* sewn or made to resemble a sunburst; having the lines of design flared from a central point: *sunburst pleats; sunburst tucks.* [1810–20; SUN + BURST]

Sun•bur•y (sun′ber′ē, -bə rē), *n.* a city in E central Pennsylvania. 12,292.

sun•choke (sun′chōk′), *n.* See **Jerusalem artichoke** (def. 2). [1980–85; SUN(FLOWER) + (ARTI)CHOKE]

sun-cured (sun′kyo͝ord′), *adj.* cured or preserved by exposure to the rays of the sun, as meat, fish, fruit, tobacco, etc. [1875–80, *Amer.*]

Sund., Sunday

sun•dae (sun′dā, -dē), *n.* ice cream served with syrup poured over it, and often other toppings, as whipped cream, chopped nuts, or fruit. [1890–95, *Amer.;* perh. special use of *Sunday* (with distinctive sp.)]

Sun′da Is′lands (sun′də; *Du.* so͞on′dä), a chain of islands in Indonesia, in the Malay Archipelago, including Borneo, Sumatra, Java, and Sulawesi **(Greater Sunda Islands);** and a group of smaller islands extending E from Java to Timor **(Lesser Sunda Islands).** Also, **Soenda Islands.**

sun′ dance′, a religious ceremony associated with the sun, practiced by North American Indians of the Plains, consisting of dancing attended with various symbolic rites and commonly including self-torture. [1840–50]

Sun•da•nese (sun′də nēz′, -nēs′), *n., pl.* **-nese,** *adj.* **—n. 1.** a member of a people of western Java. **2.** the Austronesian language of the Sundanese. **—adj. 3.** of or pertaining to the Sunda Islands, the Sundanese, or their language. [1875–80; SUNDA (ISLANDS) + *-n-* (as in JAPANESE, JAVANESE, etc.) + -ESE]

Sun′da Strait′, a strait between Sumatra and Java, connecting the Java Sea and the Indian Ocean. 20–65 mi. (32–105 km) wide.

Sun•day (sun′dā, -dē), *n.* **1.** the first day of the week, observed as the Sabbath by most Christian sects. **2. a month of Sundays,** an indeterminately great length of time: *She hadn't taken a vacation in a month of Sundays.* **—adj. 3.** of, pertaining to, or characteristic of Sunday. **4.** used, done, taking place, or being as indicated only on or as if on Sundays: *a Sunday matinée.* [bef. 900; ME *sun(nen)day,* OE *sunnandæg,* trans. of L *diēs sōlis,* itself trans. of Gk *hēméra helíou* day of the sun; c. G *Sonntag*] **—Sun′day•like′,** *adj.*

Sun•day (sun′dā, -dē), *n.* **1. William Ashley** (ash′lē), ("*Billy Sunday*"), 1862–1935, U.S. evangelist. **2.** a female given name.

Sun′day ba′by, *South Atlantic States* (*chiefly North Carolina*). an illegitimate child. Also called **Sun′day child′.**

Sun′day clothes′, a person's best or newest clothing, as saved for Sundays and special occasions. Also called **Sun′day best′.** [1635–45]

Sun′day driv′er, a person who drives a car inexpertly, esp. slowly or overcautiously, in the manner of one who drives infrequently. [1915–20]

Sun•day-go-to-meet•ing (sun′dā gō′tə mēt′n, -mē′ting, -dē-). *adj. Informal.* most presentable; best: *Sunday-go-to-meeting clothes.* [1825–35, *Amer.*]

Sun′day Morn′ing, a poem (1923) by Wallace Stevens.

Sun′day paint′er, *Fine Arts.* a nonprofessional painter, usually unschooled and generally painting during spare time.

Sun′day punch′, 1. *Boxing.* the most powerful and effective punch of a boxer, esp. the punch used in trying to gain a knockout. **2.** anything, as an armed force, line of argument, etc., capable of inflicting a powerful blow on a hostile or opposing person or thing. [1930–35]

Sun•days (sun′dāz, -dēz), *adv.* on Sundays.

Sun′day school′, 1. a school, now usually in connection with a church, for religious instruction on Sunday. **2.** the members of such a school. Also called **Sabbath school.** [1775–85]

Sun′day sup′plement, a special section incorporated in the Sunday editions of many newspapers, often containing features on books, celebrities, home entertainment, gardening, and the like. [1925–30, *Amer.*]

sun′ deck′, a raised, open area, as a roof, terrace, or ship's deck, that is exposed to the sun. Also, **sun′deck′.** [1905–10]

sun•der (sun′dər), *v.t.* **1.** to separate; part; divide; sever. **—v.i. 2.** to become separated; part. [bef. 900; ME *sundren,* OE *sundrian;* c. G *sondern,* ON *sundra;* see SUNDRY] **—sun′der•a•ble,** *adj.* **—sun′der•ance,** *n.* **—sun′der•er,** *n.*

Sun•der•land (sun′dər lənd), *n.* a seaport in Tyne and Wear, in NE England. 298,000.

sun•dew (sun′do͞o′, -dyo͞o′), *n.* any of several small, carnivorous bog plants of the genus *Drosera,* having sticky hairs that trap insects. Also called **dew plant, rosa solis.** [1570–80; < D *sondauw* (cf. G *Sonnentau*), trans. of L *rōs sōlis* dew of the sun]

sun•di•al (sun′dī′əl, -dīl′), *n.* an instrument that indicates the time of day by means of the position, on a graduated plate or surface, of the shadow of the gnomon as it is cast by the sun. [1570–80; SUN + DIAL]

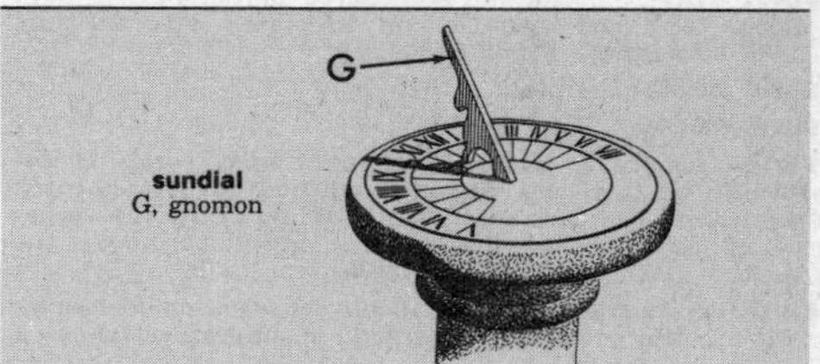

sundial
G, gnomon

CONCISE PRONUNCIATION KEY: act, cāpe, dâre, pärt; set, ēqual; *if,* ice; ox, ōver, ôrder, oil, bo͝ok, bo͞ot, out; up, ûrge; child; sing; shoe; thin, ṯẖat; zh as in *treasure.* ə = *a* as in *alone, e* as in *system, i* as in *easily, o* as in *gallop, u* as in *circus;* ᵊ as in *fire* (fīᵊr), *hour* (ouᵊr). l and n can serve as syllabic consonants, as in *cradle* (krād′l), and *button* (but′n). See the full key inside the front cover.

sun disk (def. 2) (ancient Egyptian)

sun′ disk′, 1. the disk of the sun. 2. a representation of this, esp. in religious symbolism. [1875–80]

sun·dog (sun′dôg′, -dog′), *n.* 1. parhelion. 2. a small or incomplete rainbow. [1625–35; orig. uncert.]

sun·down (sun′doun′), *n.* 1. sunset, esp. the time of sunset. —*v.i.* 2. *Psychiatry.* to experience confusion or hallucinations at night as a result of strange surroundings, drug effects, decreased sensory input, or reduction of oxygen supply to the brain. [1610–20; SUN + DOWN[1]]

sun·down·er (sun′dou′nər), *n.* 1. *Chiefly Brit.* an alcoholic drink taken after completing the day's work, usually at sundown. 2. *Australian.* a tramp or hobo, esp. one who arrives at a homestead near sundown in order to avoid having to work in exchange for shelter. [1870–75; SUNDOWN + -ER[1]]

sun·dress (sun′dres′), *n.* a dress with a bodice styled to expose the arms, shoulders, and back, for wear during hot weather. [1940–45; SUN + DRESS]

sun-dried (sun′drīd′), *adj.* 1. dried in the sun, as bricks or raisins. 2. dried up or withered by the sun. [1590–1600]

sun·dries (sun′drēz), *n.pl.* sundry things or items, esp. small, miscellaneous items of little value. Cf. **notion** (def. 6). [1805–15; n. pl. use of SUNDRY]

sun·drops (sun′drops′), *n., pl.* **-drops.** any of various plants of the genus *Oenothera,* of the evening primrose family, having flowers that bloom during the day. [1775–85, *Amer.*; SUN + DROP + -S[3]]

sun·dry (sun′drē), *adj.* 1. various or diverse: *sundry persons.* 2. **all and sundry,** everybody, collectively and individually: *Free samples were given to all and sundry.* [bef. 900; ME; OE *syndrig* private, separate, equiv. to *syndr-* (mutated form of *sundor* ASUNDER) + *-ig* -Y[1]; akin to SUNDER] —**sun′dri·ly,** *adv.* —**sun′dri·ness,** *n.*

Sunds·vall (sunts′väl), *n.* a seaport in E Sweden, on the Gulf of Bothnia. 94,742.

sun·fast (sun′fast′, -fäst′), *adj.* not subject to fading in sunlight, as a dye, fabric, or garment. [1925–30; SUN + FAST[1]]

sun·fish (sun′fish′), *n., pl. (esp. collectively)* **-fish,** *(esp. referring to two or more kinds or species)* **-fish·es.** 1. the ocean sunfish, *Mola mola.* 2. any of various other fishes of the family Molidae. 3. any of several small, brightly colored, spiny-rayed freshwater fishes of the genus *Lepomis,* of North America, having a deep, compressed body. [1620–30; SUN + FISH]

sun·flow·er (sun′flou′ər), *n.* 1. any of various composite plants of the genus *Helianthus,* as *H. annuus,* having showy, yellow-rayed flower heads often 12 in. (30 cm) wide, and edible seeds that yield an oil with a wide variety of uses: the state flower of Kansas. 2. Also called **aster.** *Furniture.* a conventionalized flower motif carved in the center panels of a Connecticut chest. [1555–65; trans. of L *flōs sōlis* flower of the sun]

sun′flower chest′. See **Connecticut chest.**

Sun′flower State′, Kansas (used as a nickname).

sung (sung), *v.* a pt. and pp. of **sing.**

Sung (sŏŏng), *n.* a dynasty in China, A.D. 960–1279, characterized by a high level of achievement in painting, ceramics, and philosophy: overthrown by the Mongols. Also, **Song.**

Sun·ga·ri (sŏŏng′gə rē), *n.* Songhua.

sun′ gear′, *Mach.* (in an epicyclic train) the central gear around which the planet gears revolve. Also called **sun wheel.**

Sung·hua (*Chin.* sŏŏng′hwä′), *n. Wade-Giles.* Songhua. Also called **Sung′hua Chiang′** (jyäng).

Sung·kiang (sŏŏng′gyäng′), *n. Older Spelling.* Songjiang. Also, **Sung·chiang** (sŏŏng′jyäng′).

sun·glass[1] (sun′glas′, -gläs′), *n.* See **burning glass.** [1800–10; SUN + GLASS]

sun·glass[2] (sun′glas′, -gläs′), *adj.* of or pertaining to sunglasses: *a new concept in sunglass design.*

sun·glass·es (sun′glas′iz, -glä′siz), *n.pl.* eyeglasses with colored or tinted lenses that protect the eyes from the glare of sunlight. [1800–10; SUN + GLASSES]

sun·glow (sun′glō′), *n.* a diffused, hazy light seen around the sun, caused by atmospheric dust. [1835–45; SUN + GLOW]

sung′ Mass′, a Mass in which parts of the proper and the ordinary are sung rather than recited; missa cantata. [1520–30]

sun′ god′, 1. the sun considered or personified as a deity. 2. a god identified or associated with the sun. Also, **sun′-god′.** [1585–95]

sun′ grebe′, finfoot. [1915–20]

sun′ hemp′, sunn.

sunk (sungk), *v.* 1. a pt. and pp. of **sink.** —*adj.* 2. *Informal.* beyond help; done for; washed up: *If they catch you cheating, you're really sunk.* 3. *Naut.* (of a forecastle or poop) raised less than a full deck above the weather deck of a ship. [1925–30 for def. 2]

sunk·en (sung′kən), *adj.* 1. having sunk or been sunk beneath the surface; submerged. 2. having settled to a lower level, as walls. 3. situated or lying on a lower level: *a sunken living room.* 4. hollow; depressed: *sunken cheeks.* —*v.* 5. *Obs.* a pp. of **sink.** [1325–75; ME, ptp. of *sinken* to SINK]

CONCISE ETYMOLOGY KEY: <, descended or borrowed from; >, whence; b., blend of, blended; c., cognate with; cf., compare; deriv., derivative; equiv., equivalent; imit., imitative; obl., oblique; r., replacing; s., stem; sp., spelling, spelled; resp., respelling, respelled; trans., translation; ?, origin unknown; *, unattested; ‡, probably earlier than. See the full key inside the front cover.

sunk′en gar′den, a formal garden set below the main level of the ground surrounding it. Also, **sunk′ gar′den.**

sun·ket (sung′kit, sŏŏng′-), *n. Scot. and North Eng.* 1. something, esp. something to eat. 2. a table delicacy; fancy tidbit of food. [1680–90; alter. of SOMEWHAT]

sunk′ fence′, a wall or other barrier set in a ditch to divide lands without marring the landscape. [1755–65]

sunk′ relief′, cavo-relievo. [1930–35]

sun·lamp (sun′lamp′), *n.* 1. a lamp that generates ultraviolet rays, used as a therapeutic device, for obtaining an artificial suntan, etc. 2. a lamp used in motion-picture photography, having parabolic mirrors arranged to direct and concentrate the light. [1925–30]

sun·less (sun′lis), *adj.* 1. lacking sun or sunlight; dark: *a sunless room.* 2. dismal; gloomy; cheerless: *a sunless smile.* [1580–90; SUN + -LESS] —**sun′less·ly,** *adv.* —**sun′less·ness,** *n.*

sun′ let′ter, *Arabic Gram.* any letter, as tā or sīn, representing a consonant that assimilates the *l* of a prefixed definite article. Cf. **moon letter.** [trans. of Ar *al-hurūf ash-shamsīyah,* so called from the use of *ash-shams* "the sun" to illustrate assimilation of *l* to *sh* in *al* the]

sun·light (sun′līt′), *n.* the light of the sun; sunshine. [1175–1225; ME *sonneliht.* See SUN, LIGHT[1]]

sun·lit (sun′lit′), *adj.* lighted by the sun. [1815–25; SUN + LIT[1]]

sun′ moss′. See **rose moss.**

sunn (sun), *n.* 1. a tall East Indian shrub, *Crotalaria juncea,* of the legume family, having slender branches and yellow flowers, and an inner bark that yields a hemplike fiber used for making ropes, sacking, etc. 2. the fiber. Also called **sunn′ hemp′, sun hemp, Bombay hemp, Madras hemp.** [1580–90; < Hindi *san* < Skt *śāṇa*]

Sun·na (sŏŏn′ə), *n. Islam.* the traditional portion of Muslim law, based on the words and acts of Muhammad, and preserved in the traditional literature. Also, **Sun′·nah.** [1620–30; < Ar *sunnah* lit., way, path, rule]

Sun·ni (sŏŏn′ē), *n. Islam.* 1. Also called **Sunnite.** a member of one of the two great religious divisions of Islam, regarding the first four caliphs as legitimate successors of Muhammad and stressing the importance of Sunna as a basis for law. Cf. **Shi′ite.** 2. *(used with a plural v.)* the Sunni Muslims. [1620–30; < Ar *sunnī,* deriv. of *sunnah* SUNNA] —**Sun′nism,** *n.*

Sun·nite (sŏŏn′īt), *n.* Sunni (def. 1). [see SUNNI, -ITE[1]]

sun·ny (sun′ē), *adj.,* **-ni·er, -ni·est.** 1. abounding in sunshine: *a sunny day.* 2. exposed to, lighted, or warmed by the direct rays of the sun: *a sunny room.* 3. pertaining to or proceeding from the sun; solar. 4. resembling the sun. 5. cheery, cheerful, or joyous: *a sunny disposition.* [1250–1300 ME; see SUN, -Y[1]] —**sun′·ni·ly,** *adv.* —**sun′ni·ness,** *n.*

sun′ny side′, 1. the part upon which sunlight falls: *the sunny side of the house.* 2. a pleasant or hopeful aspect or part: *the sunny side of life.* 3. some age less than one specified: *You're still on the sunny side of thirty.* [1825–35]

sun′ny-side up′ (sun′ē sīd′), (of an egg) fried without breaking the yolk or being turned over, with the yolk remaining visible and somewhat liquid inside. Cf. **over easy.** [1900–05]

Sun·ny·vale (sun′ē vāl′), *n.* a city in central California, south of San Francisco. 106,618.

sun′ pan′, *Ceram.* a vat for drying slip, sometimes artificially heated. [1715–25]

sun′ par′lor, a porch or room with many windows exposed to sunshine; sun porch; solarium. [1915–20, *Amer.*]

sun′ pil′lar, *Astron.* a halo phenomenon in which a vertical streak of light appears above and below the sun, believed to be caused by the reflection of sunlight by ice crystals with vertical axes. Cf. **moon pillar.** [1900–05]

sun′ porch′, 1. a windowed porch or porchlike room having more window than wall area, intended to receive large amounts of sunlight. 2. an open pen, raised above the ground, for giving poultry light and air under sanitary conditions. [1915–20, *Amer.*]

Sun′ Prai′rie, a town in S Wisconsin. 12,931.

sun·proof (sun′prōōf′), *adj.* impervious to sunlight or damage by the rays of the sun. [1600–10; SUN + -PROOF]

sun′ protec′tion fac′tor. See **SPF.** [1975–80]

sun·ray (sun′rā′), *n.* a ray of sunlight; sunbeam. [1820–30; SUN + RAY[1]]

sun·rise (sun′rīz′), *n.* 1. the rise or ascent of the sun above the horizon in the morning. 2. the atmospheric and scenic phenomena accompanying this. 3. the time when half the sun has risen above the horizon. 4. the open or beginning stage of any period. —*adj.* 5. (of an industry, technology, etc.) new and growing; developing; emerging: *high-technology sunrise industries.* [1300–50; ME, short for *sunrising* (see SUN, RISE, -ING[1])]

Sun·rise (sun′rīz′), *n.* a city in SE Florida. 39,681.

sun′rise serv′ice, *(sometimes caps.)* an outdoor religious service held at dawn on Easter morning.

sun′rise watch′, dogwatch (def. 2).

sun·roof (sun′rōōf′, -rŏŏf′), *n., pl.* **roofs.** a section of an automobile roof that can be slid or lifted open. Cf. **moonroof.** [1950–55; SUN + ROOF]

sun·room (sun′rōōm′, -rŏŏm′), *n.* a room designed to admit a large amount of sunlight; sun parlor or sun porch. [1920–25, *Amer.*; SUN + ROOM]

sun·scald (sun′skôld′), *n.* injury to the leaves, bark, or underlying tissues of woody plants due to the combined effects of heat, humidity, and intense sunshine. [1850–55; SUN + SCALD[1]]

sun·screen (sun′skrēn′), *n.* 1. a substance formulated to prevent sunburn, skin cancers, and other conditions caused by excessive exposure to the sun, usually by absorbing and reflecting ultraviolet radiation. Cf. **SPF.** 2. a lotion, cream, etc., containing such a substance. 3. a latticework or similar construction to shield a patio, atrium, or the like, from direct sunlight. Also, **sun′screen′.** [1730–40; SUN + SCREEN]

sun·seek·er (sun′sē′kər), *n.* a person who travels to a warm and sunny climate, esp. during cold months. [1950–55; SUN + SEEKER]

sun·set (sun′set′), *n.* 1. the setting or descent of the sun below the horizon in the evening. 2. the atmospheric and scenic phenomena accompanying this. 3. the time when the sun sets. 4. the close or final stage of any period. —*adj.* 5. (of an industry, technology, etc.) old; declining: *sunset industries.* 6. of, pertaining to, or characteristic of a sunset law: *to add sunset restrictions to a bill.* [1350–1400; ME; see SUN, SET]

sun′set law′, a statute that includes provision for automatic termination of a government program, agency, etc., at the end of a specified time period unless it is reauthorized by the legislature. [1975–80, *Amer.*]

Sun′set State′, Oregon (used as a nickname).

sun·shade (sun′shād′), *n.* something used as a protection from the rays of the sun, as an awning or a parasol. [1835–45; SUN + SHADE]

sun·shine (sun′shīn′), *n.* 1. the shining of the sun; direct light of the sun. 2. brightness or radiance; cheerfulness or happiness. 3. a source of cheer or happiness. 4. the effect of the sun in lighting and heating a place. 5. a place where the direct rays of the sun fall. —*adj.* 6. of or pertaining to sunshine laws: *sunshine rules.* 7. fair-weather (def. 2). [1200–50; ME *sunnesin;* see SUN, SHINE] —**sun′shine′less,** *adj.* —**sun′shin′y,** *adj.*

sun′shine law′, a law requiring a government agency to open its official meetings and records to the general public. Also called **sun′shine act′.** [1970–75, *Amer.*]

Sun′shine State′, Florida (used as a nickname).

sun·sick (sun′sik′), *adj.* suffering from mild heat exhaustion. [SUN + SICK[1]]

sun′ sign′, *Astrol.* the sign of the zodiac through which the sun moves for approximately 30 days each year as the signs rotate through the heavens along the elliptic. [1890–95]

sun′ spi′der, any predatory, scorpionlike arachnid of the order Solifugae (or Solpugida), having enormously developed mouth pincers and a long body covered with tactile hairs, inhabiting deserts and plains regions in all warm parts of the world except Australia. Also called **wind scorpion, solifugid, solpugid.**

sun·spot (sun′spot′), *n.* one of the relatively dark patches that appear periodically on the surface of the sun and affect terrestrial magnetism and certain other terrestrial phenomena. [1805–15; SUN + SPOT] —**sun′·spot′ted,** *adj.* —**sun′spot′ted·ness,** *n.*

sun′spot cy′cle, *Astron.* the cycle, averaging in duration slightly more than 11 years, in which the frequency of sunspots varies from a maximum to a minimum and back to a maximum again. Cf. **solar cycle.**

sun′spot num′ber, *Astron.* See **Wolf number.**

sun′ star′, any starfish of the genus *Solaster,* inhabiting cold and temperate waters off both U.S. coasts. [1835–45]

sun·stone (sun′stōn′), *n.* a reddish variety of oligoclase feldspar, used as a gem, having a red and bright-yellow play of color. [1350–1400; ME; see SUN, STONE]

sun·stroke (sun′strōk′), *n. Pathol.* a sudden and sometimes fatal affection due to exposure to the sun's rays or to excessive heat, marked by prostration with or without fever, convulsion, and coma. Also called **insolation, siriasis, thermic fever.** [1850–55; SUN + STROKE[1]]

sun·struck (sun′struk′), *adj.* affected with sunstroke. [1830–40; SUN + STRUCK]

sun·suit (sun′sōōt′), *n.* any of various brief garments or outfits worn by women and children for leisure or play in warm weather, as shorts and a halter. [1925–30; SUN + SUIT]

sun·tan (sun′tan′), *n., v.,* **-tanned, -tan·ning.** —*n.* 1. a browning or a brown color of the skin resulting from exposure to sunlight or a sunlamp; tan. 2. Also called **mayfair tan, merida.** a light to medium yellow-brown. 3. Also called **pastel orange.** a medium orange color. —*v.t., v.i.* 4. tan[1] (defs. 2, 4). [1900–05; SUN + TAN[1]]

sun·tanned (sun′tand′), *adj.* having a suntan: *suntanned strollers on the boardwalk.* [SUNTAN + -ED[2]]

sun·tans (sun′tanz′), *n. (used with a plural v.)* a tan military uniform for summer wear. [1935–40, *Amer.*; see SUNTAN, -S[3]]

sun·up (sun′up′), *n.* sunrise, esp. the time of sunrise. [1705–15, *Amer.*; SUN + UP, on the model of SUNDOWN]

Sun′ Val′ley, a village in S central Idaho: winter resort. 545.

sun′ vi′sor, a flap, usually of padded cardboard, acetate, or the like, that is attached inside a vehicle above the windshield and can be swung down to protect the eyes from the sun's glare.

sun·ward (sun′wərd), *adv.* 1. Also, **sun′wards.** toward the sun. —*adj.* 2. directed toward the sun. [1605–15; SUN + -WARD]

sun′ wheel′, *Mach.* See **sun gear.** [1810–20]

sun·wise (sun′wīz′), *adv.* 1. in the direction of the sun's apparent daily motion. 2. in a clockwise direction. [1860–65; SUN + -WISE]

Sun·ya·ta (shōōn′yə tä′), *n. Buddhism.* that which

exists absolutely and without predication. Also, **Sun·ya** (sho͞on′yə). [< Skt *śūnyatā*, n. deriv. of *śūnya* empty]

Sun Yat-sen (so͝on′ yät′sen′), 1866–1925, Chinese political and revolutionary leader. Also, *Pinyin,* **Sun Yi·xian** (so͝on′ yē′shyän′).

su·o ju·re (so͞o′ō yo͞o′re; *Eng.* so͞o′ō jo͝or′ē), *Latin.* in one's own right.

su·o lo·co (so͞o′ō lô′kō; *Eng.* so͞o′ō lō′kō), *Latin.* in one's own or rightful place.

Suo·mi (swô′mi), *n.* Finnish name of **Finland.**

suo·ve·tau·ril·i·a (swō′vi tô ril′ē ə), *n.* (in ancient Rome) a sacrifice of a hog, a ram, and a bull. [< L *suovetaurīlia,* equiv. to *sū(s)* swine + *ove-,* comb. form of *ovis* sheep + *taur(us)* bull + *-īlia* n. use of neut. pl. of *-īlis* denominal adj. suffix)]

sup[1] (sup), *v.,* **supped, sup·ping.** —*v.i.* **1.** to eat the evening meal; have supper. —*v.t.* **2.** to provide with or entertain at supper. [1250–1300; ME *s(o)upen* < OF *souper* to take supper < Gmc; cf. OE *sūpan* to swallow, taste, sip. See SUP[2]]

sup[2] (sup), *v.,* **supped, sup·ping,** *n.* —*v.t.* **1.** to take (liquid food, or any liquid) into the mouth in small quantities, as from a spoon or cup; sip. —*v.i.* **2.** to take liquid into the mouth in small quantities, as by spoonfuls or sips. —*n.* **3.** a mouthful or small portion of drink or liquid food; sip. [bef. 900; ME *suppen,* var. of *supen,* OE *sūpan;* c. G *saufen* to drink. Cf. SIP, SOP, SOUP, SUP[1]]

sup[3] (so͞op), *n. Math.* supremum.

sup-, var. of **sub-** before *p: suppose.*

sup., 1. superior. **2.** superlative. **3.** supine. **4.** supplement. **5.** supplementary. **6.** supply. **7.** supra.

Sup. Ct., 1. Superior Court. **2.** Supreme Court.

supe (so͞op), *n. Theat. Informal.* a supernumerary. [by shortening]

su·per (so͞o′pər), *n.* **1.** *Informal.* **a.** a superintendent, esp. of an apartment house. **b.** supermarket. **c.** supernumerary. **d.** supervisor. **2.** an article of a superior quality, grade, size, etc. **3.** (in beekeeping) the portion of a hive in which honey is stored. **4.** *Printing.* supercalendered paper. **5.** *Television.* an additional image superimposed on the original video image. —*adj.* **6.** of the highest degree, power, etc. **7.** of an extreme or excessive degree. **8.** *Informal.* very good; first-rate; excellent. **9.** (of measurement) superficial. **10.** superfine. —*adv.* **11.** *Slang.* very; extremely or excessively: *super classy; a super large portion of food.* [1620–30; 1920–25 for def. 8; independent use of SUPER- (construed as an adj. or adv.), or shortening of words prefixed with it]

super-, a prefix occurring originally in loanwords from Latin, with the basic meaning "above, beyond." Words formed with **super-** have the following general senses: "to place or be placed above or over" (*superimpose; supersede*), "a thing placed over or added to another" (*superscript; superstructure; supertax*), "situated over" (*superficial; superlunary*) and, more figuratively, "an individual, thing, or property that exceeds customary norms or levels" (*superalloy; superconductivity; superman; superstar*), "an individual or thing larger, more powerful, or with wider application than others of its kind" (*supercomputer; superhighway; superpower; supertanker*), "exceeding the norms or limits of a given class" (*superhuman; superplastic*), "having the specified property to a great or excessive degree" (*supercritical; superfine; supersensitive*), "to subject to (a physical process) to an extreme degree or in an unusual way" (*supercharge; supercool; supersaturate*), "a category that embraces a number of lesser items of the specified kind" (*superfamily; supergalaxy*), "a chemical compound with a higher proportion than usual of a given constituent" (*superphosphate*). [< L *super* (prep. and v. prefix) above, beyond, in addition, to an especially high degree; akin to Gk *hypér* (see HYPER-), Skt *upari;* see OVER]
—**Note.** The lists at the bottom of this and following pages provide the spelling, syllabification, and stress for words whose meanings may be easily inferred by combining the meanings of SUPER- and an attached base word, or base word plus a suffix. Appropriate parts of speech are also shown. Words prefixed by SUPER- that have special meanings or uses are entered in their proper alphabetical places in the main vocabulary or as derived forms run on at the end of a main vocabulary entry.

super., 1. superintendent. **2.** superior.

su·per·a·ble (so͞o′pər ə bəl), *adj.* capable of being overcome; surmountable. [1620–30; < L *superābilis,* equiv. to *superā(re)* to overcome (deriv. of *super;* see SUPER-) + *-bilis* -BLE] —**su′per·a·bil′i·ty, su′per·a·ble·ness,** *n.* —**su′per·a·bly,** *adv.*

su·per·a·bound (so͞o′pər ə bound′), *v.i.* **1.** to abound beyond something else. **2.** to be very abundant or too abundant (usually fol. by *in* or *with*). [1400–50; late ME *superabounden* < LL *superabundāre,* equiv. to *super-* SUPER- + *abundāre* to ABOUND]

su·per·ab·sorb·ent (so͞o′pər ab sôr′bənt, -zôr′-), *adj.* **1.** extremely or unusually absorbent: *superabsorbent fibers.* —*n.* **2.** a superabsorbent material. [SUPER- + ABSORBENT] —**su′per·ab·sorb′en·cy,** *n.*

su·per·a·bun·dant (so͞o′pər ə bun′dənt), *adj.* exceedingly or excessively abundant; more than sufficient; excessive. [1375–1425; late ME < LL *superabundant-* (s. of *superabundāns*), prp. of *superabundāre* to SUPERABOUND; see ABUNDANT] —**su′per·a·bun′dance,** *n.* —**su′per·a·bun′dant·ly,** *adv.*

su·per·add (so͞o′pər ad′), *v.t.* to add over and above; join as a further addition; add besides. [1425–75; late ME *superadden* < L *superaddere,* equiv. to *super-* SUPER- + *addere* to ADD] —**su·per·ad·di·tion** (so͞o′pər ə dish′ən), *n.* —**su′per·ad·di′tion·al,** *adj.*

su·per·aer·o·dy·nam·ics (so͞o′pər âr′ō dī nam′iks, -di-), *n.* (*used with a singular v.*) the branch of aerodynamics that deals with gases at very low densities. [SUPER- + AERODYNAMICS]

su·per·a·gen·cy (so͞o′pər ā′jən sē), *n., pl.* **-cies.** a very large agency, esp. a large government agency that oversees smaller ones. [1890–95; SUPER- + AGENCY]

su·per·al·loy (so͞o′pər al′oi), *n.* an alloy, often with a nickel, nickel-iron, or cobalt base, capable of withstanding very high temperatures, used in jet engines, rockets, etc. [1945–50; SUPER- + ALLOY]

su·per·al·tern (so͞o′pər ôl′tərn), *n. Logic.* a universal proposition that is the basis for the immediate inference of a corresponding particular proposition. [1920–25; SUPER- + (SUB)ALTERN]

su·per·an·nu·ate (so͞o′pər an′yo͞o āt′), *v.,* **-at·ed, -at·ing.** —*v.t.* **1.** to allow to retire from service or office on a pension because of age or infirmity. **2.** to set aside as out of date; remove as too old. —*v.i.* **3.** to be or become old, out of date, or retired. [1640–50; back formation from SUPERANNUATED]

su·per·an·nu·at·ed (so͞o′pər an′yo͞o ā′tid), *adj.* **1.** retired because of age or infirmity. **2.** too old for use, work, service, or a position. **3.** antiquated or obsolete: *superannuated ideas.* [1625–35; alter. (with *-u-* of ANNUAL) of ML *superannātus* over a year old (said of cattle), equiv. to *super ann(um)* beyond a year + *-ātus* -ATE[1]; see -ED[2]]

su·per·an·nu·a·tion (so͞o′pər an′yo͞o ā′shən), *n.* **1.** the act of superannuating. **2.** the state of being superannuated. **3.** a pension or allowance to a superannuated person. [1650–60; SUPERANNUATE + -ION]

su·perb (so͝o pûrb′, sə-), *adj.* **1.** admirably fine or excellent; extremely good: *a superb performance.* **2.** sumptuous; rich; grand: *superb jewels.* **3.** of a proudly imposing appearance or kind; majestic: *superb mountain vistas.* [1540–50; < L *superbus* proud, superior, excellent, equiv. to *super-* SUPER- + *-bus* adj. suffix (akin to BE)] —**su·perb′ly,** *adv.* —**su·perb′ness,** *n.*
—**Syn. 2.** elegant. See **magnificent.**

su·per·ba·by (so͞o′pər bā′bē), *n., pl.* **-bies.** an infant whose mental development and language acquisition are stimulated and presumably accelerated by certain teaching methods. [1980–85]

su·per·block (so͞o′pər blok′), *n.* an area of city land larger than the usual block, treated according to a unified plan and generally closed to vehicular through traffic. [1925–30; SUPER- + BLOCK]

su·per·bomb (so͞o′pər bom′), *n.* a highly destructive bomb, esp. a hydrogen bomb. [1945–50; SUPER- + BOMB]

Su′per Bowl′, the annual championship football game between the best team of the National Football Conference and that of the American Football Conference.

su·per·cal·en·der (so͞o′pər kal′ən dər), *n.* **1.** a roll or set of rolls for giving a high, smooth finish to paper. —*v.t.* **2.** to finish (paper) in a supercalender. [1885–90; SUPER- + CALENDER]

su·per·cal·i·frag·i·lis·tic·ex·pi·al·i·do·cious (so͞o′pər kal′ə fraj′ə lis′tik ek′spē al′i dō′shəs), *adj.* (used as a nonsense word by children to express approval.)

su·per·cap·i·tal (so͞o′pər kap′i tl), *n. Archit.* a member situated between a capital and the spring of an arch, as a dosseret. [SUPER- + CAPITAL[2]]

su·per·car·go (so͞o′pər kär′gō, so͞o′pər kär′-), *n., pl.* **-goes, -gos.** a merchant-ship officer who is in charge of the cargo and the commercial concerns of the voyage. [1690–1700; < Sp *sobrecargo,* with *sobre-* over (< L *super*) Latinized; r. *supracargo* (with *supra-* for Sp *sobre-*); see CARGO]

su·per·cede (so͞o′pər sēd′), *v.t.,* **-ced·ed, -ced·ing.** supersede.

su·per·charge (so͞o′pər chärj′), *v.t.,* **-charged, -charg·ing. 1.** to charge with an abundant or excessive amount, as of energy, emotion, or tension. **2.** to supply air to (an internal-combustion engine) at greater than atmospheric pressure. **3.** pressurize (def. 3). [1760–70; SUPER- + CHARGE]

su·per·charged (so͞o′pər chärjd′), *adj.* **1.** equipped with a supercharger. **2.** (of a gas or liquid) subjected to pressurization. **3.** full of energy, emotion, tension, etc. [1885–90; SUPERCHARGE + -ED[2]]

su·per·charg·er (so͞o′pər chär′jər), *n.* a mechanism for forcing air into an internal-combustion engine in order to increase engine power. [1920–25; SUPERCHARGE + -ER[1]]

su·per·cil·i·ar·y (so͞o′pər sil′ē er′ē), *adj. Anat., Zool.* **1.** of or pertaining to the eyebrow. **2.** having a conspicuous line or marking over the eye, as certain birds. **3.** situated on the frontal bone at the level of the eyebrow. [1725–35; SUPERCILI(UM) + -ARY]

supercil′iary ridge′, *Anat.* browridge. [1725–35]

su·per·cil·i·ous (so͞o′pər sil′ē əs), *adj.* haughtily disdainful or contemptuous, as a person or a look. [1520–30; < L *superciliōsus.* See SUPERCILIUM, -OUS] —**su′per·cil′i·ous·ly,** *adv.* —**su′per·cil′i·ous·ness,** *n.*
—**Syn.** arrogant, scornful. —**Ant.** humble.

su·per·cil·i·um (so͞o′pər sil′ē əm), *n., pl.* **-cil·i·a** (-sil′ē ə). *Archit.* **1.** the fillet above the cyma of a cornice. **2.** (on an Attic base) either of the fillets above and below the scotia. [1555–65; < L: eyebrow, haughtiness, equiv. to *super-* SUPER- + *-cilium* eyelid, akin to *cēlāre* to CONCEAL, E HULL, Gk *kaliá* hut, shrine; cf. -IUM]

su·per·cit·y (so͞o′pər sit′ē), *n., pl.* **-cit·ies. 1.** a large, heavily populated urban area that includes several cities; megalopolis. **2.** a very large city. [1920–25, *Amer.;* SUPER- + CITY]

su·per·class (so͞o′pər klas′, -kläs′), *n. Biol.* **1.** a category of related classes within a phylum or subphylum. **2.** a subphylum. [1890–95; SUPER- + CLASS]

su·per·clus·ter (so͞o′pər klus′tər), *n. Astron.* a cluster of open clusters. [1925–30; SUPER- + CLUSTER]

su·per·coil (so͞o′pər koil′), *n. Biochem.* superhelix. [1965–70; SUPER- + COIL[1]] —**su′per·coiled′,** *adj.*

su·per·co·lum·nar (so͞o′pər kə lum′nər), *adj. Archit.* **1.** existing above a column or columns: *a supercolumnar*

CONCISE PRONUNCIATION KEY: act, cāpe, dâre, pärt; set, ēqual; *if,* ice; ox, ōver, ôrder, oil, bo͝ok, bo͞ot, out; up, ûrge; child; sing; shoe; thin, *th*at; zh as in *treasure.* ə = *a* as in *alone, e* as in *system, i* as in *easily, o* as in *gallop, u* as in *circus;* ° as in *fire* (fī°r), *hour* (ou°r). l and n can serve as syllabic consonants, as in *cradle* (krād′l), and *button* (but′n). See the full key inside the front cover.

su′per·ab·hor′, *v.t.,* **-horred, -hor·ring.**
su′per·ab·nor′mal, *adj.;* **-ly,** *adv.*
su′per·a·bom′i·na·ble, *adj.;* **-ble·ness,** *n.;* **-bly,** *adv.*
su′per·a·bom′i·na′tion, *n.*
su′per·ab·stract′, *adj.;* **-ly,** *adv.;* **-ness,** *n.*
su′per·ab·surd′, *adj.;* **-ly,** *adv.;* **-ness,** *n.*
su′per·ab·surd′i·ty, *n., pl.* **-ties.**
su′per·ac·com′mo·dat′ing, *adj.*
su′per·ac·com′plished, *adj.*
su′per·ac·crue′, *v.i.,* **-crued, -cru·ing.**
su′per·ac·cu′mu·late′, *v.i.,* **-lat·ed, -lat·ing.**
su′per·ac·cu′mu·la′tion, *n.*
su′per·ac′cu·rate, *adj.;* **-ly,** *adv.;* **-ness,** *n.*
su′per·a·chieve′ment, *n.*
su′per·a·chiev′er, *n.*
su′per·a·cid′i·ty, *n.*
su′per·a·cid′u·lat′ed, *adj.*
su′per·ac·knowl′edg·ment, *n.*
su′per·ac′qui·si′tion, *n.*
su′per·a·cro′mi·al, *adj.*
su′per·ac′ti·vate′, *v.t.,* **-vat·ed, -vat·ing.**
su′per·ac′tive, *adj.;* **-ly,** *adv.;* **-ness,** *n.*
su′per·ac·tiv′i·ty, *n., pl.* **-ties.**
su′per·a·cute′, *adj.;* **-ly,** *adv.;* **-ness,** *n.*
su′per·a·dapt′a·ble, *adj.;* **-ble·ness,** *n.;* **-bly,** *adv.*
su′per·ad′e·quate, *adj.;* **-ly,** *adv.;* **-ness,** *n.*
su′per·ad·ja′cent, *adj.;* **-ly,** *adv.*
su′per·ad·min′is·tra′tion, *n.*
su′per·ad′mi·ra·ble, *adj.;* **-ble·ness,** *n.;* **-bly,** *adv.*
su′per·ad′mi·ra′tion, *n.*
su′per·a·dorn′, *v.t.*
su′per·a·dorn′ment, *n.*
su′per·aer′i·al, *adj.;* **-ly,** *adv.*
su′per·aes·thet′i·cal, *adj.;* **-ly,** *adv.*
su′per·af·fil′i·a′tion, *n.*
su′per·af′flu·ence, *n.*
su′per·af′flu·ent, *adj.;* **-ly,** *adv.*
su′per·af·fu′sion, *n.*
su′per·a′gent, *n.*
su′per·ag′gra·va′tion, *n.*
su′per·ag·gres′sive, *adj.*
su′per·ag′i·ta′tion, *n.*
su′per·a·grar′i·an, *adj.*
su′per·al′i·men·ta′tion, *n.*
su′per·al′ka·lin′i·ty, *n.*
su′per·al·low′ance, *n.*
su′per·am·bi′tion, *n.*
su′per·am·bi′tious, *adj.;* **-ly,** *adv.;* **-ness,** *n.*
su′per·an·gel′ic, *adj.*
su′per·an·gel′i·cal·ly, *adv.*
su′per·an′i·mal, *adj.*
su′per·an′i·mal′i·ty, *n.*
su′per·an·nu′i·ty, *n., pl.* **-ties.**
su′per·a·pol′o·gy, *n., pl.* **-gies.**
su′per·ap·pre′ci·a′tion, *n.*
su′per·a′que·ous, *adj.*
su′per·ar′bi·ter, *n.*
su′per·arc′tic, *adj.*
su′per·ar′du·ous, *adj.;* **-ly,** *adv.;* **-ness,** *n.*
su′per·ar′ro·gance, *n.*
su′per·ar′ro·gant, *adj.;* **-ly,** *adv.*
su′per·ar′ti·fi′cial, *adj.;* **-ly,** *adv.*
su′per·ar′ti·fi′ci·al′i·ty, *n., pl.* **-ties.**
su′per·as′pi·ra′tion, *n.*
su′per·as·ser′tion, *n.*
su′per·as·so′ci·ate, *n.*
su′per·as·sume′, *v.t.,* **-sumed, -sum·ing.**
su′per·as·sump′tion, *n.*
su′per·as·ton′ish, *v.*
su′per·as·ton′ish·ment, *n.*
su′per·ath′lete, *n.*
su′per·at·tach′ment, *n.*
su′per·at·tain′a·ble, *adj.;* **-ble·ness,** *n.;* **-bly,** *adv.*
su′per·at·tend′ant, *n., adj.*
su′per·at·trac′tion, *n.*
su′per·at·trac′tive, *adj.;* **-ly,** *adv.;* **-ness,** *n.*
su′per·au′di·tor, *n.*
su′per·av′er·age, *adj.;* **-ness,** *n.*
su′per·a·ward′, *n.*
su′per·ax′il·lar′y, *adj.*
su′per·be′ing, *n.*
su′per·be·lief′, *n.*
su′per·be·liev′a·ble, *adj.;* **-ble·ness,** *n.;* **-bly,** *adv.*
su′per·be·lov′ed, *adj.*
su′per·ben′e·fit, *n.*
su′per·be·nev′o·lence, *n.*
su′per·be·nev′o·lent, *adj.;* **-ly,** *adv.*
su′per·be·nign′, *adj.;* **-ly,** *adv.*
su′per·bi′as, *n.*
su′per·bitch′, *n.*
su′per·blessed′, *adj.*
su′per·bless′ed·ness, *n.*
su′per·blun′der, *n.*
su′per·bold′, *adj.;* **-ly,** *adv.;* **-ness,** *n.*
su′per·bomb′er, *n.*
su′per·boss′, *n.*
su′per·brain′, *n.*
su′per·brave′, *adj.;* **-ly,** *adv.;* **-ness,** *n.*
su′per·bright′, *adj.*
su′per·brute′, *n.*
su′per·build′, *v.,* **-built, -build·ing.**
su′per·bull′ish, *adj.;* **-ly,** *adv.;* **-ness,** *n.*
su′per·bus′i·ly, *adv.*
su′per·bus′y, *adj.*
su′per·cab′i·net, *n.*
su′per·can′did, *adj.;* **-ly,** *adv.;* **-ness,** *n.*
su′per·ca′nine, *adj., n.*
su′per·ca·non′i·cal, *adj.*
su′per·can′on·i·za′tion, *n.*
su′per·can′o·py, *n., pl.* **-pies.**
su′per·ca′pa·bil′i·ty, *n., pl.* **-ties.**
su′per·ca′pa·ble, *adj.;* **-ble·ness,** *n.;* **-bly,** *adv.*
su′per·cap′tion, *n.*
su′per·car′, *n.*
su′per·car′pal, *adj.*
su′per·car′ri·er, *n.*
su′per·ca·tas′tro·phe, *n.*
su′per·cat′a·stroph′ic, *adj.*
su′per·cath′o·lic, *adj.*
su′per·ca·thol′i·cal·ly, *adv.*
su′per·caus′al, *adj.*
su′per·cau′tion, *n.*
su′per·cau′tious, *adj.*
su′per·ce·les′tial, *adj.;* **-ly,** *adv.*
su′per·cen′sure, *n.*
su′per·cen′ter, *n.*
su′per·cer′e·bel′lar, *adj.*
su′per·ce·re′bral, *adj.;* **-ly,** *adv.*

feature. **2.** of, pertaining to, or characterized by supercolumniation: *a supercolumnar composition.* [SUPER- + COLUMNAR]

su·per·co·lum·ni·a·tion (so͞o′pər kə lum′nē ā′shən), *n. Archit.* the placing of one order of columns above another. [1830–40; SUPER- + COLUMNIATION]

su·per·com·put·er (so͞o′pər kəm pyo͞o′tər, so͞o′pər-kəm pyo͞o′tər), *n.* a very fast, powerful mainframe computer, used in advanced military and scientific applications. [SUPER- + COMPUTER]

su·per·con·duc·tiv·i·ty (so͞o′pər kon′dək tiv′i tē), *n. Physics.* the phenomenon of almost perfect conductivity shown by certain substances at temperatures approaching absolute zero. The recent discovery of materials that are superconductive at temperatures hundreds of degrees above absolute zero raises the possibility of revolutionary developments in the production and transmission of electrical energy. [1915–20; SUPER- + CONDUCTIVITY] **—su·per·con·duc·tion** (so͞o′pər kən duk′shən), *n.* **—su·per·con·duc·tive** (so͞o′pər kən duk′tiv), **su′per·con·duct′ing,** *adj.* **—su·per·con·duc·tor** (so͞o′pər kən-duk′tər), *n.*

su·per·con·ti·nent (so͞o′pər kon′tn ənt), *n. Geol.* a hypothetical protocontinent of the remote geologic past that rifted apart to form the continents of today. Cf. **Pangaea.** [1955–60; SUPER- + CONTINENT]

su·per·cool (so͞o′pər ko͞ol′), *v.t.* **1.** to cool (a liquid) below its freezing point without producing solidification or crystallization; undercool. *—v.i.* **2.** to become supercooled. *—adj.* **3.** very cool in temperature, esp. of the maximum coolness possible: used as a setting on air conditioners. **4.** *Slang.* very cool; very sophisticated, up-to-date, unemotional, etc. [1905–10; SUPER- + COOL]

su·per·crat (so͞o′pər krat′), *n. Informal.* a high-ranking bureaucrat, esp. one of cabinet rank. [1970–75; SUPER- + (BUREAU)CRAT]

su·per·crit·i·cal (so͞o′pər krit′i kəl), *adj.* **1.** extremely critical. **2.** *Physics.* pertaining to a mass of radioactive material in which the rate of a chain reaction increases with time. [1600–10; SUPER- + CRITICAL] **—su′per·crit′i·cal·ly,** *adv.* **—su′per·crit′i·cal·ness,** *n.*

su·per·cur·rent (so͞o′pər kûr′ənt, -kur′-), *n. Physics.* an electric current that flows without resistance in a superconducting material. [SUPER- + CURRENT]

su·per·del·e·gate (so͞o′pər del′i git, -gāt′), *n.* a party leader or elected public official chosen as an uncommitted delegate to a national political convention. Also, **su′per-del′e·gate.** [1984]

su·per·dom·i·nant (so͞o′pər dom′ə nənt), *n. Music.* submediant. [1825–35; SUPER- + DOMINANT]

su·per·du·per (so͞o′pər do͞o′pər), *adj. Informal.* extremely good, powerful, large, etc.; very super; marvelous or colossal. [1935–40; rhyming compound with invented second element]

su·per·e·go (so͞o′pər ē′gō, -eg′ō), *n., pl.* **-gos.** *Psychoanal.* the part of the personality representing the conscience, formed in early life by internalization of the standards of parents and other models of behavior. [1890–95; trans. of G *Über-Ich* (Freud); see SUPER-, EGO]

su·per·el·e·vat·ed (so͞o′pər el′ə vā′tid), *adj. Civ. Engin.* (of a curve in a road, railroad track, etc.) banked. [SUPER- + ELEVATED]

su·per·el·e·va·tion (so͞o′pər el′ə vā′shən), *n.* bank[1] (def. 6). [1645–55, in sense "elevation to a higher rank"; 1885–90 for current sense; SUPER- + ELEVATION]

su·per·em·i·nent (so͞o′pər em′ə nənt), *adj.* of superior rank or dignity; distinguished or conspicuous above others. [1545–55; < L *superēminent-* (s. of *superēminēns*), prp. of *superēminēre* to stand out. See SUPER-, EMINENT] **—su′per·em′i·nence,** *n.* **—su′per·em′i·nent·ly,** *adv.*

CONCISE ETYMOLOGY KEY: <, descended or borrowed from; >, whence; b., blend of, blended; c., cognate with; cf., compare; deriv., derivative; equiv., equivalent; imit., imitative; obl., oblique; r., replacing; s., stem; sp., spelling, spelled; resp., respelling, respelled; trans., translation; ?, origin unknown; *, unattested; ‡, probably earlier than. See the full key inside the front cover.

su·per·en·ci·pher (so͞o′pər en sī′fər), *v.t. Cryptography.* to encode (a message) that is already a cryptogram. [1960–65; SUPER- + ENCIPHER]

su·per·er·o·gate (so͞o′pər er′ə gāt′), *v.i.,* **-gat·ed, -gat·ing.** to do more than duty requires. [1730–40; < LL *superērogātus* (ptp. of *superērogāre* to pay out in addition), equiv. to *super-* SUPER- + *ērogātus* ptp. of *ērogāre* to pay out, equiv. to *ē-* E- + *rog(ere)* to ask + *-ātus* -ATE[1]] **—su′per·er′o·ga′tion,** *n.* **—su′per·er′o·ga′tor,** *n.*

su·per·e·rog·a·to·ry (so͞o′pər ə rog′ə tôr′ē, -tōr′ē), *adj.* **1.** going beyond the requirements of duty. **2.** greater than that required or needed; superfluous. [1585–95; < ML *superērogātōrius.* See SUPEREROGATE, -TORY[1]] **—su′per·e·rog′a·to′ri·ly,** *adv.*

su·per·ette (so͞o′pə ret′), *n.* a grocery store with some of the self-service features of a supermarket. [SUPER(MARKET) + -ETTE]

su·per·fam·i·ly (so͞o′pər fam′ə lē, -fam′lē), *n., pl.* **-lies.** *Biol.* a category of related families within an order or suborder. [1870–75; SUPER- + FAMILY]

su·per·fect·a (so͞o′pər fek′tə), *n.* **1.** a type of bet, esp. on horse races, in which the bettor must select the first four finishers in exact order. **2.** a race in which such bets are made. Cf. **trifecta.** [1970–75, *Amer.*; b. SUPER and PERFECTA]

su·per·fe·cun·da·tion (so͞o′pər fē′kən dā′shən, -fek′ən-), *n.* the fertilization of two or more ova discharged at the same ovulation by successive acts of sexual intercourse. [1850–55; SUPER- + FECUNDATION]

su·per·fe·ta·tion (so͞o′pər fē tā′shən), *n.* the fertilization of an ovum in a female mammal already pregnant. [1595–1605; < L *superfētāt(us)* (ptp. of *superfētāre* to conceive again while still pregnant, equiv. to *super-* SUPER- + *fēta(re)* to breed (see FETUS) + *-tus* ptp. suffix) + -ION] **—su′per·fe′tate,** *adj.*

su·per·fi·cial (so͞o′pər fish′əl), *adj.* **1.** being at, on, or near the surface: *a superficial wound.* **2.** of or pertaining to the surface: *superficial measurement.* **3.** external or outward: *a superficial resemblance.* **4.** concerned with or comprehending only what is on the surface or obvious: *a superficial observer.* **5.** shallow; not profound or thorough: *a superficial writer.* **6.** apparent rather than real. **7.** insubstantial or insignificant: *superficial improvements.* [1375–1425; late ME *superficiall* < LL *superficiālis,* equiv. to L *superfici(ēs)* SUPERFICIES + *-ālis* -AL[1]] **—su·per·fi·ci·al·i·ty** (so͞o′pər fish′ē al′i tē), **su′per·fi′cial·ness,** *n.* **—su′per·fi′cial·ly,** *adv.*

su·per·fi·ci·es (so͞o′pər fish′ē ēz′, -fish′ēz), *n., pl.* **-ci·es. 1.** the surface, outer face, or outside of a thing. **2.** the outward appearance, esp. as distinguished from the inner nature. [1520–30; < L *superficiēs,* equiv. to *super-* SUPER- + *-ficiēs,* comb. form of *faciēs* FACE]

su·per·fine (so͞o′pər fīn′), *adj.* **1.** extra fine, as in grain or texture; unusually fine: *superfine sugar.* **2.** extra fine in quality. **3.** excessively refined; overnice: *superfine manners.* [1400–50; late ME; see SUPER-, FINE[1]]

su·per·fix (so͞o′pər fiks′), *n.* a suprasegmental feature having an identifiable meaning or grammatical function, as the stress pattern that distinguishes the noun *record* from the verb *record* or the parallel falling stress patterns of *blackbird* and *highchair,* reflecting a parallel relationship between the elements. [1945–50; SUPER- + *-fix,* extracted from AFFIX, INFIX, etc.]

su·per·flu·id (so͞o′pər flo͞o′id), *Physics.* *—n.* **1.** a fluid that exhibits frictionless flow, very high heat conductivity, and other unusual physical properties, helium below 2.186 K being the only known example. *—adj.* **2.** of or pertaining to a superfluid. [1940–45; SUPER- + FLUID] **—su′per·flu·id′i·ty,** *n.*

su·per·flu·i·ty (so͞o′pər flo͞o′i tē), *n., pl.* **-ties. 1.** the state of being superfluous. **2.** a superabundant or excessive amount. **3.** something superfluous, as a luxury. [1350–1400; ME *superfluite* < OF < L *superfluitās.* See SUPERFLUOUS, -ITY]

su·per·flu·ous (so͝o pûr′flo͞o əs), *adj.* **1.** being more than is sufficient or required; excessive. **2.** unnecessary or needless. **3.** *Obs.* possessing or spending more than enough or necessary; extravagant. [1400–50; late ME < L *superfluus,* equiv. to *super-* SUPER- + *flu-* (s. of *fluere* to flow) + *-us* -OUS] **—su·per′flu·ous·ly,** *adv.* **—su·per′flu·ous·ness,** *n.*
—Syn. 1. extra; redundant.

Su·per·for·tress (so͞o′pər fôr′tris), *n. U.S. Mil.* a heavy, long-range, four-engined bomber used during World War II. Also called **B-29, Su·per·fort** (so͞o′pər-fôrt′, -fōrt′). [SUPER- + (FLYING) FORTRESS]

su·per·fund (so͞o′pər fund′), *n.* (*sometimes cap.*) a large fund set up to finance an expensive program or project. [1980–85; SUPER- + FUND]

su·per·fuse (so͞o′pər fyo͞oz′), *v.t.,* **-fused, -fus·ing.** *Obs.* to pour. [1650–60; < L *superfūsus,* ptp. of *superfundere* to pour over, equiv. to *super-* SUPER- + *fundere* to pour] **—su·per·fu·sion** (so͞o′pər fyo͞o′zhən), *n.*

su·per·gal·ax·y (so͞o′pər gal′ək sē), *n., pl.* **-ax·ies.** *Astron.* a system of galaxies. [1925–30; SUPER- + GALAXY] **—su·per·ga·lac·tic** (so͞o′pər gə lak′tik), *adj.*

su·per·gene[1] (so͞o′pər jēn′), *adj. Geol.* formed by descending waters, as mineral or ore deposits (opposed to *hypogene*). [1945–50; SUPER- + *-gene,* as in HYPOGENE]

su·per·gene[2] (so͞o′pər jēn′), *n. Genetics.* a portion of a chromosome consisting of linked genes that act as a single unit of inheritance. [1945–50; SUPER- + GENE]

su·per·gi·ant (so͞o′pər jī′ənt), *n.* **1.** *Astron.* See **supergiant star. 2.** an extremely large or powerful person, company, thing, etc. *—adj.* **3.** extremely large; immense. [1925–30; SUPER- + GIANT]

su′per gi′ant sla′lom, a slalom race in which the course is longer and has more widely spaced gates than in a giant slalom. Also called **super G.** [1980–85]

su′pergiant star′, *Astron.* an exceptionally luminous star whose diameter is more than 100 times that of the sun, as Betelgeuse. Also called **supergiant.** [1925–30]

su·per·gla·cial (so͞o′pər glā′shəl), *adj.* **1.** on the surface of a glacier. **2.** believed to have been formerly on the surface of a glacier: *superglacial debris.* [1885–90; SUPER- + GLACIAL]

Su′per glue′, *Trademark.* a brand of glue, containing a cyanoacrylate adhesive, that is quick-drying and strong. Also, **su′per·glue′.**

su·per·gov·ern·ment (so͞o′pər guv′ərn mənt, -guv′ər-), *n.* **1.** a centralized organization formed by a group of governments to enforce justice or maintain peace. **2.** an internationally organized body designed to regulate the relations of its member states. **3.** any government having far-reaching powers. [SUPER- + GOVERNMENT]

su·per·grade (so͞o′pər grād′), *n. U.S. Govt.* **1.** a high-level rank, Grade 16, 17, or 18, in the federal civil service. **2.** a government employee having such a rank. *—adj.* **3.** of, pertaining to, or characteristic of such a rank or employee. [SUPER- + GRADE]

su·per·gran·u·la·tion cell′ (so͞o′pər gran′yə lā′-shən), *Astron.* one of a number of large convection cells in the photosphere and chromosphere of the sun, each having a diameter of 10,000–20,000 mi. (16,000–32,000 km) and lasting longer than a day. Also called **su′per·gran′u·la′tion.** [1970–75; SUPER- + GRANULATION]

su·per·graph·ics (so͞o′pər graf′iks), *n.* (*used with a singular or plural v.*) large-scale painted or applied art in bold colors and geometric or typographic designs, used over walls and sometimes floors and ceilings to create an illusion of expanded or altered space. [1965–70; SUPER- + GRAPHICS] **—su′per·graph′ic,** *adj.*

su·per·grav·i·ty (so͞o′pər grav′i tē), *n. Physics.* See under **supersymmetry.** [1975–80; SUPER- + GRAVITY]

su·per·hard·en (so͞o′pər här′dn), *v.t. Mil.* harden (def. 6). [SUPER- + HARDEN]

su·per·heat (*n.* so͞o′pər hēt′; *v.* so͞o′pər hēt′), *n.* **1.** the state of being superheated. **2.** the amount of superheating. *—v.t.* **3.** to heat to an extreme degree or to a very high temperature. **4.** to heat (a liquid) above its boiling point without the formation of bubbles of vapor. **5.** to heat (a gas, as steam not in contact with water) to

su′per·cer′e·mo′ni·ous, *adj.;* **-ly,** *adv.;* **-ness,** *n.*
su′per·chem′i·cal, *adj., n.;* **-ly,** *adv.*
su′per·chic′, *adj.*
su′per·chiv′al·rous, *adj.;* **-ly,** *adv.;* **-ness,** *n.*
su′per·civ′il, *adj.;* **-ly,** *adv.*
su′per·civ′i·li·za′tion, *n.*
su′per·civ′i·lized′, *adj.*
su′per·claim′, *n.*
su′per·clas′si·fied′, *adj.*
su′per·clean′, *adj.*
su′per·club′, *n.*
su′per·co·in′ci·dence, *n.*
su′per·co·in′ci·dent, *adj.;* **-ly,** *adv.*
su′per·co·los′sal, *adj.;* **-ly,** *adv.*
su′per·com′bi·na′tion, *n.*
su′per·com′fort·a·ble, *adj.*
su′per·com′men·da′tion, *n.*
su′per·com′men·tar′y, *n., pl.* **-tar·ies.**
su′per·com′men·ta′tor, *n.*
su′per·com·mer′cial, *adj.;* **-ly,** *adv.*
su′per·com·mer′cial·ism, *n.*
su′per·com′pe·ti′tion, *n.*
su′per·com·pet′i·tive, *adj.*
su′per·com·plex′, *adj.*
su′per·com·plex′i·ty, *n., pl.* **-ties.**
su′per·com′pre·hen′sion, *n.*
su′per·com·pres′sion, *n.*
su′per·con′cen·trat′ed, *adj.*
su′per·con′fi·dence, *n.*
su′per·con′fi·dent, *adj.;* **-ly,** *adv.*
su′per·con′fir·ma′tion, *n.*
su′per·con·form′a·ble, *adj.;* **-ble·ness,** *n.;* **-bly,** *adv.*
su′per·con·form′ist, *n.*
su′per·con·form′i·ty, *n.*
su′per·con·fused′, *adj.*
su′per·con·fu′sion, *n.*
su′per·con·gest′ed, *adj.*
su′per·con·ges′tion, *n.*
su′per·con·glom′er·ate, *n.*
su′per·con′se·crat′ed, *adj.*
su′per·con′se·quence′, *n.*
su′per·con·serv′a·tive, *adj.;* **-ly,** *adv.;* **-ness,** *n.*
su′per·con′sti·tu′tion·al, *adj.;* **-ly,** *adv.*
su′per·con′test, *n.*
su′per·con·test′, *v.t.*
su′per·con′tri·bu′tion, *n.*
su′per·con·trol′, *n.*
su′per·con·ven′ient, *adj.*
su′per·cop′, *n.*
su′per·cor′dial, *adj.;* **-ly,** *adv.;* **-ness,** *n.*
su′per·cor′po·ra′tion, *n.*
su′per·cred′it, *n.*
su′per·cre·ta′ceous, *adj.*
su′per·crime′, *n.*
su′per·crim′i·nal, *adj., n.;* **-ly,** *adv.*
su′per·crit′ic, *n.*
su′per·crowned′, *adj.*
su′per·cul′ti·vat′ed, *adj.*
su′per·cul′ture, *n.*
su′per·cu′ri·ous, *adj.;* **-ly,** *adv.;* **-ness,** *n.*
su′per·cy′cle, *n.*
su′per·cyn′i·cal, *adj.;* **-ly,** *adv.;* **-ness,** *n.*
su′per·dain′ty, *adj.*
su′per·dan′ger, *n.*
su′per·debt′, *n.*
su′per·de·clam′a·to′ry, *adj.*
su′per·dec′o·rat′ed, *adj.*
su′per·dec′o·ra′tion, *n.*
su′per·def′i·cit, *n.*
su′per·de′i·ty, *n., pl.* **-ties.**
su′per·de·jec′tion, *n.*
su′per·del′e·gate, *n.*
su′per·del′i·cate, *adj.;* **-ly,** *adv.;* **-ness,** *n.*
su′per·de·luxe′, *adj.*
su′per·de·mand′, *n.*
su′per·dem′o·crat′ic, *adj.*
su′per·dem′o·crat′i·cal·ly, *adv.*
su′per·de·mon′ic, *adj.*
su′per·dem′on·stra′tion, *n.*
su′per·dense′, *adj.*
su′per·den′si·ty, *n.*
su′per·de·pos′it, *n.*
su′per·de·sir′ous, *adj.;* **-ly,** *adv.*
su′per·de·vel′op·ment, *n.*
su′per·dev′il·ish, *adj.;* **-ly,** *adv.;* **-ness,** *n.*
su′per·de·vo′tion, *n.*
su′per·di′a·bol′i·cal, *adj.;* **-ly,** *adv.;* **-ness,** *n.*
su′per·dif′fi·cult′, *adj.;* **-ly,** *adv.*
su′per·di·plo′ma·cy, *n.*
su′per·di·rec′tion, *n.*
su′per·dis′count, *n.*
su′per·dis·ten′tion, *n.*
su′per·dis′tri·bu′tion, *n.*
su′per·div′i·dend′, *n.*
su′per·di·vine′, *adj.*
su′per·di·vi′sion, *n.*
su′per·doc′tor, *n.*
su′per·dom′i·neer′ing, *adj.*
su′per·do·na′tion, *n.*
su′per·dose′, *n.*
su′per·dram′a·tist, *n.*
su′per·du′bi·ous, *adj.;* **-ly,** *adv.;* **-ness,** *n.*
su′per·du′pli·ca′tion, *n.*
su′per·du′ral, *adj.*
su′per·earth′ly, *adj.*
su′per·e·con′o·my, *n., pl.* **-mies.**
su′per·ed′u·cat′ed, *adj.*
su′per·ed′u·ca′tion, *n.*
su′per·ef·fec′tive, *adj.;* **-ly,** *adv.;* **-ness,** *n.*
su′per·ef·fi′cien·cy, *n., pl.* **-cies.**
su′per·ef·fi′cient, *adj.*
su′per·ef′flu·ence, *n.*
su′per·ef′flu·ent, *adj.*
su′per·e·lab′o·rate, *adj.;* **-ly,** *adv.;* **-ness,** *n.*
su′per·e·las′tic, *adj.*
su′per·e·las′ti·cal·ly, *adv.*
su′per·e·lat′ed, *adj.*
su′per·el′e·gance, *n.*
su′per·el′e·gan·cy, *n., pl.* **-cies.**
su′per·el′e·gant, *adj.;* **-ly,** *adv.*
su′per·el′e·men′ta·ry, *adj.*
su′per·el′i·gi·bil′i·ty, *n.*
su′per·el′i·gi·ble, *adj.;* **-ble·ness,** *n.;* **-bly,** *adv.*
su′per·e·lite′, *n.*
su′per·el′o·quence, *n.*
su′per·el′o·quent, *adj.;* **-ly,** *adv.*
su′per·em′pha·sis, *n., pl.* **-ses.**
su′per·em′pha·size′, *v.t.,* **-sized, -siz·ing.**
su′per·en·dorse′, *v.t.,* **-dorsed, -dors·ing.**
su′per·en·dorse′ment, *n.*
su′per·en·dow′, *v.t.*
su′per·en′er·get′ic, *adj.*
su′per·en′er·get′i·cal·ly, *adv.*
su′per·en′er·gized′, *adj.*
su′per·en·force′ment, *n.*
su′per·en·grave′, *v.t.,* **-graved, -grav·ing.**
su′per·en·roll′ment, *n.*
su′per·ep′ic, *adj., n.*
su′per·ep′och, *n.*
su′per·e·quiv′a·lent, *adj., n.*

such a degree that its temperature may be lowered or its pressure increased without the conversion of any of the gas into liquid. [1855–60; SUPER- + HEAT] **—su′per·heat′er,** *n.*

su·per·he·lix (so͞o′pər hē′liks), *n., pl.* **-hel·i·ces** (-hel′ə sēz′), **-he·lix·es.** *Biochem.* a coil formed by intertwined helical DNA or by protein chains. Also called **supercoil.** [SUPER- + HELIX] **—su·per·hel·i·cal** (so͞o′pər hel′i kəl, -hē′li-), *adj.* **—su·per·he·lic·i·ty** (so͞o′pər hə lis′i tē), *n.*

su·per·he·ro (so͞o′pər hēr′ō), *n., pl.* **-roes.** a hero, esp. in children's comic books and television cartoons, possessing extraordinary, often magical powers. [1960–65]

su·per·het (so͞o′pər het′), *adj., n. Radio Informal.* superheterodyne. [1925–30; by shortening]

su·per·het·er·o·dyne (so͞o′pər het′ər ə dīn′), *Radio.* *—adj.* **1.** denoting, pertaining to, or using a method of processing received radio or video signals in which an incoming modulated wave is changed by the heterodyne process into a lower-frequency wave and then subjected to amplification and subsequent detection. *—n.* **2.** a superheterodyne receiver. [1920–25; SUPER(SONIC) + HETERODYNE]

su′per·high fre′quency (so͞o′pər hī′), *Radio.* any frequency between 3000 and 30,000 megahertz. *Abbr.:* SHF [1940–45; SUPER- + HIGH FREQUENCY]

su·per·high·way (so͞o′pər hī′wā, so͞o′pər hī′wā′), *n.* a highway designed for travel at high speeds, having more than one lane for each direction of traffic, a safety strip dividing the two directions, and cloverleaves to route the traffic on and off the highway. Cf. **expressway.** [1925–30; SUPER- + HIGHWAY]

su·per·hive (so͞o′pər hīv′), *n. Entomol. Now Rare.* super (def. 3). [1850–55; SUPER- + HIVE]

su·per·hu·man (so͞o′pər hyo͞o′mən *or, often,* -yo͞o′-), *adj.* **1.** above or beyond what is human; having a higher nature or greater powers than humans have: *a superhuman being.* **2.** exceeding ordinary human power, experience, etc.: *a superhuman effort.* [1625–35; < NL *superhūmānus.* See SUPER-, HUMAN] **—su·per·hu·man·i·ty** (so͞o′pər hyo͞o man′i tē *or, often,* -yo͞o-), **su′per·hu′man·ness,** *n.* **—su′per·hu′man·ly,** *adv.*

Su·pe·ri (so͞o′pə rī′, -rē′), *n.pl.* (in ancient Rome) the gods.

su·per·im·pose (so͞o′pər im pōz′), *v.t.,* **-posed, -pos·ing. 1.** to impose, place, or set over, above, or on something else. **2.** to put or join as an addition (usually fol. by *on* or *upon*). **3.** *Motion Pictures, Television.* to print (an image) over another image so that both are seen at once: *The credits were superimposed over the opening scene.* [1785–95; SUPER- + IMPOSE] **—su·per·im·po·si·tion** (so͞o′pər im′pə zish′ən), *n.*

su·per·im·posed (so͞o′pər im pōzd′), *adj. Geol.* (of a stream or drainage system) having a course not adjusted to the structure of the rocks presently undergoing erosion but determined rather by a prior erosion cycle or by formerly overlying rocks or sediments. [1795–1805; SUPERIMPOSE + -ED[2]]

su·per·in·cum·bent (so͞o′pər in kum′bənt), *adj.* **1.** lying or resting on something else. **2.** situated above; overhanging. **3.** exerted from above, as pressure. [1655–65; < L *superincumbent-* (s. of *superincumbēns*), prp. of *superincumbere* to lean over; see SUPER-, INCUMBENT] **—su′per·in·cum′bence, su′per·in·cum′ben·cy,** *n.* **—su′per·in·cum′bent·ly,** *adv.*

su·per·in·duce (so͞o′pər in do͞os′, -dyo͞os′), *v.t.,* **-duced, -duc·ing.** to bring in or induce as an added feature, circumstance, etc.; superimpose. [1545–55; < L *superindūcere.* See SUPER-, INDUCE] **—su·per·in·duc·tion** (so͞o′pər in duk′shən), *n.*

su·per·in·fec·tion (so͞o′pər in fek′shən), *n. Pathol.* marked proliferation of a parasitic microorganism during antimicrobial treatment for another infection. [1920–25; SUPER- + INFECTION]

su·per·in·fla·tion (so͞o′pər in flā′shən), *n.* hyperinflation. [SUPER- + INFLATION]

su·per·in·tend (so͞o′pər in tend′, so͞o′prin-), *v.t.* **1.** to oversee and direct (work, processes, etc.). **2.** to exercise supervision over (an institution, district, place, etc.). [1605–15; < LL *superintendere.* See SUPER-, INTEND]
—Syn. supervise, manage, conduct, run; control.

su·per·in·tend·en·cy (so͞o′pər in ten′dən sē, so͞o′prin-), *n., pl.* **-cies. 1.** a district or place under a superintendent. **2.** the position or work of a superintendent. **3.** Also, **su′per·in·tend′ence.** the act or process of superintending; direction; supervision; oversight. [1590–1600; < ML *superintendentia,* equiv. to *superintend(ere)* to SUPERINTEND + *-entia* -ENCY]

su·per·in·tend·ent (so͞o′pər in ten′dənt, so͞o′prin-), *n.* **1.** a person who oversees or directs some work, enterprise, establishment, organization, district, etc.; supervisor. **2.** a person who is in charge of maintenance and repairs of an apartment house; custodian. **3.** a high-ranking police officer, esp. a chief of police or an officer ranking next above an inspector. *—adj.* **4.** superintending. [1545–55; < ML *superintendent-* (s. of *superintendēns*), prp. of *superintendere* to SUPERINTEND; see -ENT]

superintend′ent engineer′. See **port engineer.**

su·pe·ri·or (sə pēr′ē ər, so͝o-), *adj.* **1.** higher in station, rank, importance, etc.: *a superior officer.* **2.** above the average in excellence, intelligence, etc.: *superior math students.* **3.** of higher grade or quality: *superior merchandise.* **4.** greater in quantity or amount: *superior numbers.* **5.** showing a consciousness or feeling of being better than or above others: *superior airs.* **6.** not yielding or susceptible (usually fol. by *to*): *superior to temptation.* **7.** higher in place or position: *superior ground.* **8.** *Bot.* **a.** situated above some other organ. **b.** (of a calyx) seeming to originate from the top of the ovary. **c.** (of an ovary) free from the calyx. **9.** *Anat.* (of an organ or part) **a.** higher in place or position; situated above another. **b.** toward the head. Cf. **inferior** (def. 7). **10.** *Print.* written or printed high on a line of text, as the "2" in a^2b; superscript. Cf. **inferior** (def. 9). *—n.* **11.** one superior to another. **12.** Also called **superscript.** *Print.* a superior letter, number, or symbol. Cf. **inferior** (def. 11). **13.** *Eccles.* the head of a monastery, convent, or the like. [1350–1400; ME (adj.) < L, equiv. to *super(us)* situated above (adj. deriv. of *super;* see SUPER-) + *-ior* comp. suffix; see -ER[4]] **—su·pe′ri·or·ly,** *adv.*
—Syn. 2. excellent, distinguished, unrivaled, first-rate, matchless. **5.** haughty, arrogant, snobbish.

Su·pe·ri·or (sə pēr′ē ər, so͝o-), *n.* **1. Lake,** a lake in the N central United States and S Canada: the northernmost of the Great Lakes; the largest body of fresh water in the world. 350 mi. (564 km) long; 31,820 sq. mi. (82,415 sq. km); greatest depth, 1290 ft. (393 m); 602 ft. (183 m) above sea level. **2.** a port in NW Wisconsin, on Lake Superior. 29,571.

supe′rior conjunc′tion, *Astron.* the alignment of an inferior planet and the sun in which the planet is at the far side of the sun from the earth. Cf. **inferior conjunction.** [1825–35]

supe′rior court′, 1. the court of general jurisdiction found in many states of the United States. **2.** any court that has general jurisdiction above other courts. [1680–90, *Amer.*]

supe′rior gen′eral, *pl.* **superiors general.** *Eccles.* the superior of an order or congregation. [1765–75]

supe′rior goods′, *Econ.* commodities that are more in demand as consumer income rises. Cf. **inferior goods.**

su·pe·ri·or·i·ty (sə pēr′ē ôr′i tē, -or′-, so͝o-), *n.* the quality or condition of being superior. [1520–30; < ML *superiōritāt-* (s. of *superiōritās*). See SUPERIOR, -ITY]

superior′ity com′plex, an exaggerated feeling of one's own superiority. [1920–25]

supe′rior o′vary, *Bot.* an ovary positioned above a receptacle of a flower, as in members of the mint family.

supe′rior plan′et, *Astron.* any of the six planets whose orbits are outside the orbit of the earth: Mars, Jupiter, Saturn, Uranus, Neptune, and Pluto. Cf. **inferior planet, outer planet.** [1575–85; i.e., superior in distance from the sun]

supe′rior ve′na ca′va, *pl.* **superior venae cavae.** See under **vena cava.** See illus. under **heart.** Also called **precava.** [1905–10]

su·per·ja·cent (so͞o′pər jā′sənt), *adj.* lying above or upon something else. [1600–10; < L *superjacent-* (s. of *superjacēns*), prp. of *superjacēre* to rest upon. See SUPER-, SUBJACENT]

su·per·jet (so͞o′pər jet′), *n.* a jet aircraft, esp. a large one, capable of supersonic flight. [1960–65; SUPER- + JET[1]]

superl., superlative.

su·per·la·tive (sə pûr′lə tiv, so͝o-), *adj.* **1.** of the highest kind, quality, or order; surpassing all else or others; supreme; extreme: *superlative wisdom.* **2.** *Gram.* of, pertaining to, or noting the highest degree of the comparison of adjectives and adverbs, as *smallest, best,* and *most carefully,* the superlative forms of *small, good,* and *carefully.* Cf. **comparative** (def. 4), **positive** (def. 20). **3.** being more than is proper or normal; exaggerated in language or style. *—n.* **4.** a superlative person or thing. **5.** the utmost degree; acme. **6.** *Gram.* **a.** the superlative degree. **b.** a form in the superlative. [1350–1400; ME < LL *superlātīvus,* equiv. to L *superlāt(us)* hyperbolical (*super-* SUPER- + *-lātus,* suppletive ptp. of *ferre* to BEAR[1]) + *-īvus* -IVE; r. ME *superlatif* < OF < LL, as above] **—su·per′la·tive·ly,** *adv.* **—su·per′la·tive·ness,** *n.*
—Syn. 1. surpassing, excellent, preeminent.

su·per·lin·er (so͞o′pər lī′nər), *n.* **1.** an ocean liner of relatively great size or speed. **2.** a railroad car or train providing express service and usually deluxe passenger accommodations. [1915–20; SUPER- + LINER[1]]

su·per·lu·mi·nal (so͞o′pər lo͞o′mə nl), *adj. Astron.* appearing to travel faster than the speed of light. [SUPER- + L *lūmin-,* s. of *lūmen* light + -AL[1]]

su·per·lu·na·ry (so͞o′pər lo͞o′nə rē), *adj.* **1.** situated above or beyond the moon. **2.** celestial, rather than earthly. Also, **su′per·lu′nar.** [1605–15; SUPER- + (SUB)LUNARY]

su·per·ma·jor·i·ty (so͞o′pər mə jôr′i tē, -jor′-), *n., pl.,* **-ties.** a majority that must represent some percentage more than a simple majority. [SUPER- + MAJORITY]

su·per·man (so͞o′pər man′), *n., pl.* **-men. 1.** a person of extraordinary or superhuman powers. **2.** an ideal superior being conceived by Nietzsche who attains happiness, dominance, and creativity. **3.** a superior being conceived as the product of human evolution. **4.** one who prevails by virtue of being a ruthless egoist of superior strength, cunning, and force of will. [1900–05; SUPER- + MAN[1], trans. of G *Übermensch*]
—Usage. See **-man.**

su·per·mar·ket (so͞o′pər mär′kit), *n.* **1.** a large retail market that sells food and other household goods and that is usually operated on a self-service basis. **2.** any business or company offering an unusually wide range of goods or services: *a financial supermarket that sells stocks, bonds, insurance, and real estate.* [1920–25, *Amer.;* SUPER- + MARKET]

su·per·mar·ket·er (so͞o′pər mär′ki tər), *n.* a person who owns or operates a supermarket. [SUPERMARKET + -ER[1]] **—su′per·mar′ket·ing,** *n.*

su′per·mas′sive star′ (so͞o′pər mas′iv, so͞o′-), *Astron.* a star with a mass more than fifty times the mass of the sun. [SUPER- + MASSIVE]

su·per·max·il·la (so͞o′pər mak sil′ə), *n., pl.* **-max·il·lae** (-mak sil′ē). the upper jaw. [< NL; see SUPER-, MAXILLA] **—su·per·max·il·lar·y** (so͞o′pər mak′sə ler′ē, -mak sil′ə rē), *adj.*

su·per·mi·cro (so͞o′pər mī′krō), *n., pl.* **-cros.** *Computers.* the fastest and most powerful type of microcomputer, with capabilities more commonly associated with

CONCISE PRONUNCIATION KEY: act, cāpe, dâre, pärt; set, ēqual; *if,* īce; ox, ōver, ôrder, oil, bo͝ok, bo͞ot, out; up, ûrge; child; sing; shoe; thin, *th*at; zh as in *treasure.* ə = *a* as in *alone, e* as in *system, i* as in *easily, o* as in *gallop, u* as in *circus;* ᵊ as in *fire* (fīᵊr), *hour* (ouᵊr). l and n can serve as syllabic consonants, as in *cradle* (krād′l), and *button* (but′n). See the full key inside the front cover.

su′per·es·tab′lish, *v.t.*
su′per·es·tab′lish·ment, *n.*
su′per·e′ther, *n.*
su′per·eth′i·cal, *adj.;* **-ly,** *adv.;* **-ness,** *n.*
su′per·e′van·gel′i·cal, *adj.;* **-ly,** *adv.*
su′per·e·vent′, *n.*
su′per·ev′i·dence, *n.*
su′per·ev′i·dent, *adj.;* **-ly,** *adv.*
su′per·ex·act′ing, *adj.*
su′per·ex·alt′, *v.t.*
su′per·ex′al·ta′tion, *n.*
su′per·ex·am′in·er, *n.*
su′per·ex·ceed′, *v.i.*
su′per·ex′cel·lence, *n.*
su′per·ex′cel·len·cy, *n., pl.* **-cies.**
su′per·ex′cel·lent, *adj.;* **-ly,** *adv.*
su′per·ex·cep′tion·al, *adj.;* **-ly,** *adv.*
su′per·ex′ci·ta′tion, *n.*
su′per·ex·cit′ed, *adj.*
su′per·ex·cite′ment, *n.*
su′per·ex·cres′cence, *n.*
su′per·ex·cres′cent, *adj.;* **-ly,** *adv.*
su′per·ex·ert′, *v.t.*
su′per·ex·er′tion, *n.*
su′per·ex·pand′, *v.*
su′per·ex·pan′sion, *n.*
su′per·ex′pec·ta′tion, *n.*
su′per·ex·pend′i·ture, *n.*
su′per·ex·plic′it, *adj.;* **-ly,** *adv.*
su′per·ex′port, *n.*
su′per·ex·port′, *v.t.*
su′per·ex·press′, *n.*
su′per·ex·pres′sion, *n.*
su′per·ex·pres′sive, *adj.;* **-ly,** *adv.;* **-ness,** *n.*
su′per·ex·qui′site, *adj.;* **-ly,** *adv.;* **-ness,** *n.*
su′per·ex·tend′, *v.*
su′per·ex·ten′sion, *n.*
su′per·ex·tol′, *v.t.,* **-tolled, -tol·ling.**
su′per·ex·toll′, *v.t.*
su′per·ex·treme′, *adj.;* **-ly,** *adv.;* **-ness,** *n.*
su′per·ex·trem′i·ty, *n., pl.* **-ties.**
su′per·fan·tas′tic, *adj.*
su′per·fan·tas′ti·cal·ly, *adv.*
su′per·farm′, *n.*
su′per·fast′, *adj.*
su′per·fe·cun′di·ty, *n.*
su′per·fee′, *n.*
su′per·fem′i·nine, *adj.*
su′per·fem′i·nin′i·ty, *n.*
su′per·fer′vent, *adj.;* **-ly,** *adv.*
su′per·fi′bri·na′tion, *n.*
su′per·fi·nance′, *n., v.,* **-nanced, -nanc·ing.**
su′per·fin′ick·y, *adj.*
su′per·fi′nite, *adj.;* **-ly,** *adv.;* **-ness,** *n.*
su′per·firm′, *adj.*
su′per·fis′sure, *n.*
su′per·fit′, *n., adj., v.,* **-fit** or **-fit·ted, -fit·ting.**
su′per·fleet′, *n.*
su′per·flex′ion, *n.*
su′per·flux′, *n.*
su′per·fo′li·a′ceous, *adj.*
su′per·fo′li·a′tion, *n.*
su′per·fol′ly, *n., pl.* **-lies.**
su′per·for′mal, *adj.;* **-ly,** *adv.;* **-ness,** *n.*
su′per·for·ma′tion, *n.*
su′per·for′mi·da·ble, *adj.;* **-ble·ness,** *n.;* **-bly,** *adv.*
su′per·for′tu·nate, *adj.;* **-ly,** *adv.*
su′per·fruc′ti·fied′, *adj.*
su′per·ful·fill′, *v.t.*
su′per·ful·fill′ment, *n.*
su′per·func′tion, *n.*
su′per·func′tion·al, *adj.*
su′per·gai′e·ty, *n.*
su′per·gal′lant, *adj.;* **-ly,** *adv.;* **-ness,** *n.*
su′per·ge·ner′ic, *adj.*
su′per·ge·ner′i·cal·ly, *adv.*
su′per·gen′er·os′i·ty, *n.*
su′per·gen′er·ous, *adj.;* **-ly,** *adv.*
su′per·ge′nu·al, *adj.*
su′per·glo′ri·ous, *adj.;* **-ly,** *adv.;* **-ness,** *n.*
su′per·glot′tal, *adj.;* **-ly,** *adv.*
su′per·glot′tic, *adj.*
su′per·god′dess, *n.*
su′per·good′ness, *n.*
su′per·gov′ern, *v.t.*
su′per·grad′u·ate, *n.*
su′per·grain′, *n.*
su′per·grant′, *n.*
su′per·grat′i·fi·ca′tion, *n.*
su′per·grat′i·fy, *v.t.,* **-fied, -fy·ing.**
su′per·grav′i·tate′, *v.i.,* **-tat·ed, -tat·ing.**
su′per·grav′i·ta′tion, *n.*
su′per·group′, *n.*
su′per·growth′, *n., adj.*
su′per·guar′an·tee′, *n., v.,* **-teed, -tee·ing.**
su′per·gun′, *n.*
su′per·gyre′, *n.*
su′per·hand′some, *adj.*
su′per·hawk′, *n.*
su′per·heart′i·ly, *adv.*
su′per·heart′i·ness, *n.*
su′per·heart′y, *adj.*
su′per·her′e·sy, *n., pl.* **-sies.**
su′per·he′ro, *n., pl.* **-roes.**
su′per·he·ro′ic, *adj.*
su′per·he·ro′i·cal·ly, *adv.*
su′per·his·tor′ic, *adj.*
su′per·his·tor′i·cal, *adj.;* **-ly,** *adv.*
su′per·her′o·ine, *n.*
su′per·hu′man·ize′, *v.t.,* **-ized, -iz·ing.**
su′per·hyp′o·crite, *n.*
su′per·i·de′al, *adj., n.;* **-ly,** *adv.*
su′per·i·de′al·ist, *n., adj.*
su′per·ig′no·rant, *adj.;* **-ly,** *adv.*
su′per·il′lus·trate′, *v.t.,* **-trat·ed, -trat·ing.**
su′per·il′lus·tra′tion, *n.*
su′per·im·pend′, *v.i.*
su′per·im·per′son·al, *adj.;* **-ly,** *adv.*
su′per·im·ply′, *v.t.,* **-plied, -ply·ing.**
su′per·im·por′tant, *adj.;* **-ly,** *adv.*
su′per·im·prob′a·ble, *adj.;* **-ble·ness,** *n.;* **-bly,** *adv.*
su′per·im·proved′, *adj.*
su′per·in·cen′tive, *n., adj.*
su′per·in′cli·na′tion, *n.*
su′per·in·clu′sive, *adj.;* **-ly,** *adv.;* **-ness,** *n.*
su′per·in′com·pre·hen′si·ble, *adj.;* **-ble·ness,** *n.;* **-bly,** *adv.*
su′per·in·crease′, *v.t.,* **-creased, -creas·ing.**
su′per·in′crease, *n.*
su′per·in′de·pend′ence, *n.*
su′per·in′de·pend′ent, *adj.;* **-ly,** *adv.*
su′per·in·dict′ment, *n.*
su′per·in·dif′fer·ence, *n.*
su′per·in·dif′fer·ent, *adj.;* **-ly,** *adv.*

minicomputers. Also called **su·per·mi·cro·com·put·er** (sōō′pər mī′krō kəm pyōō′tər). [SUPER- + MICRO(COMPUTER)]

su·per·min·i (sōō′pər min′ē), *n. Computers.* the fastest and most powerful type of minicomputer, with capabilities more commonly associated with mainframes. Also called **su·per·min·i·com·put·er** (sōō′pər min′ē-kəm pyōō′tər). [SUPER- + MINI(COMPUTER)]

su·per·mun·dane (sōō′pər mun dān′), *adj.* above and beyond the nature or character of the worldly or terrestrial. [1670–80; < ML *supermundānus.* See SUPER-, MUNDANE]

su·per·nal (sŏŏ pûr′nl), *adj.* **1.** being in or belonging to the heaven of divine beings; heavenly, celestial, or divine. **2:** lofty; of more than earthly or human excellence, powers, etc. **3.** being on high or in the sky or visible heavens. [1475–85; < MF < L *supern(us)* upper + *-ālis* -AL[1]] **—su·per′nal·ly,** *adv.*

su·per·na·tant (sōō′pər nāt′nt), *adj.* floating above or on the surface. [1655–65; < L *supernatant-* (s. of *supernatāns*), prp. of *supernatāre* to swim or float above. See SUPER-, NATANT]

su·per·na·tion·al (sōō′pər nash′ə nl), *adj.* tending to involve, or extending authority over, more than one nation; international; supranational. [1910–15; SUPER- + NATIONAL] **—su′per·na′tion·al·ly,** *adv.*

su·per·na·tion·al·ism (sōō′pər nash′ə nl iz′əm), *n.* **1.** an extreme or fanatical loyalty or devotion to a nation. **2.** advocacy of the establishment of governments composed of more than one nation, each nation agreeing to surrender at least part of its national sovereignty to a superior governmental authority. **3.** advocacy of the establishment of organizations composed of groups from more than one nation, each of which agrees to surrender at least part of its authority to a superior, centralized authority. [1915–20; SUPER- + NATIONALISM] **—su′per·na′tion·al·ist,** *n., adj.*

su·per·nat·u·ral (sōō′pər nach′ər əl, -nach′rəl), *adj.* **1.** of, pertaining to, or being above or beyond what is natural; unexplainable by natural law or phenomena; abnormal. **2.** of, pertaining to, characteristic of, or attributed to God or a deity. **3.** of a superlative degree; preternatural: *a missile of supernatural speed.* **4.** of, pertaining to, or attributed to ghosts or other unearthly beings; eerie; occult. **—***n.* **5.** a being, place, object, occurrence, etc., considered as supernatural or of supernatural origin; that which is outside the natural order. **6.** behavior supposedly caused by the intervention of supernatural beings. **7.** direct influence or action of a deity on earthly affairs. **8. the supernatural, a.** supernatural beings, behavior, and occurrences collectively. **b.** supernatural forces and the supernatural plane of existence: *a deep fear of the supernatural.* [1520–30; < ML *supernātūrālis.* See SUPER-, NATURAL] **—su′per·nat′u·ral·ly,** *adv.* **—su′per·nat′u·ral·ness,** *n.*
—Syn. 1. See **miraculous.**

su·per·nat·u·ral·ism (sōō′pər nach′ər ə liz′əm, -nach′rə liz′əm), *n.* **1.** supernatural character or agency. **2.** belief in the doctrine of supernatural or divine agency as manifested in the world, in human events, religious revelation, etc. [1790–1800; SUPERNATURAL + -ISM] **—su′per·nat′u·ral·ist,** *n., adj.* **—su′per·nat′u·ral·is′tic,** *adj.*

su·per·nat·u·ral·i·ty (sōō′pər nach′ə ral′i tē), *n., pl.* **-ties. 1.** the quality or state of being supernatural; supernaturalism. **2.** a supernatural thing, act, or occurrence. [1630–40; SUPERNATURAL + -ITY]

su·per·nat·u·ral·ize (sōō′pər nach′ər ə līz′, -nach′rə līz′), *v.t.,* **-ized, -iz·ing. 1.** to make supernatural; give supernatural character or qualities to. **2.** to consider or interpret as supernatural. Also, *esp. Brit.,* **su′per·nat′u·ral·ise′.** [1635–45; SUPERNATURAL + -IZE]

CONCISE ETYMOLOGY KEY: <, descended or borrowed from; >, whence; b., blend of, blended; c., cognate with; cf., compare; deriv., derivative; equiv., equivalent; imit., imitative; obl., oblique; r., replacing; s., stem; sp., spelling, spelled; resp., respelling, respelled; trans., translation; ?, origin unknown; *, unattested; ‡, probably earlier than. See the full key inside the front cover.

su′pernat′ural vir′tue. See **theological virtue.**

su·per·nor·mal (sōō′pər nôr′məl), *adj.* **1.** in excess of the normal or average: *supernormal faculties.* **2.** lying beyond normal or natural powers of comprehension: *supernormal intimations.* [1865–70; SUPER- + NORMAL] **—su′per·nor·mal′i·ty,** *n.* **—su′per·nor′mal·ly,** *adv.*

su·per·no·va (sōō′pər nō′və), *n., pl.* **-vas, -vae** (-vē). *Astron.* **1.** the explosion of a star, possibly caused by gravitational collapse, during which the star's luminosity increases by as much as 20 magnitudes and most of the star's mass is blown away at very high velocity, sometimes leaving behind a dense core. **2.** the star undergoing such an explosion. Cf. **supernova remnant, black hole, neutron star, nova.** [1925–30; SUPER- + NOVA]

superno′va rem′nant, *Astron.* an expanding shell of gas, with accompanying strong radio and x-ray emissions, produced by a supernova.

su·per·nu·mer·ar·y (sōō′pər nōō′mə rer′ē, -nyōō′-), *adj., n., pl.* **-ar·ies. —***adj.* **1.** being in excess of the usual, proper, or prescribed number; additional; extra. **2.** associated with a regular body or staff as an assistant or substitute in case of necessity. **—***n.* **3.** a supernumerary or extra person or thing. **4.** a supernumerary official or employee. **5.** a person who appears in a play or film without speaking lines or as part of a crowd; walk-on; extra. [1595–1605; < LL *supernumerārius.* See SUPER-, NUMERARY]

su·per·or·der (sōō′pər ôr′dər), *n. Biol.* a category of related orders within a class or subclass. [1885–90; SUPER- + ORDER]

su·per·or·di·nate (*adj., n.* sōō′pər ôr′dn it; *v.* sōō′-pər ôr′dn āt′), *adj., n., v.,* **-nat·ed, -nat·ing. —***adj.* **1.** of higher degree in condition or rank. **2.** *Logic.* (of a universal proposition) related to a particular proposition of the same quality and containing the same terms in the same order. **—***n.* **3.** a superordinate person or thing. **4.** *Ling.* a term that denotes a general class under which a set of subcategories is subsumed: *"Child" is the superordinate of "girl" and "boy."* Cf. **hyponym. —***v.t.* **5.** to elevate to superordinate position. [1610–20; SUPER- + (SUB)ORDINATE]

su·per·or·di·na·tion (sōō′pər ôr′dn ā′shən), *n.* **1.** *Logic.* the relation between a universal proposition and a particular proposition of the same quality containing the same terms in the same order. **2.** *Eccles.* the ordination by an official of his or her successor. [1645–55; < LL *superōrdinātiōn-* (s. of *superōrdinātiō*), equiv. to *superōrdināt(us)* (ptp. of *superōrdināre;* see SUPER-, ORDAIN, -ATE[1]) + *-iōn-* -ION]

su·per·or·gan·ic (sōō′pər ôr gan′ik), *adj. Sociol., Anthropol.* of or pertaining to the structure of cultural elements within society conceived as independent of and superior to the individual members of society. [SUPER- + ORGANIC] **—su′per·or·gan′i·cism,** *n.* **—su′per·or·gan′i·cist,** *n.*

su·per·ov·u·late (sōō′pər ov′yə lāt′, -ō′vyə-), *v.,* **-lat·ed, -lat·ing.** (of humans, domestic animals, etc.) **—***v.i.* **1.** to produce more than the normal number of ova at one time, as through hormone treatment. **—***v.t.* **2.** to cause to superovulate. [1960–65; SUPER- + OVULATE] **—su′per·ov′u·la′tion,** *n.*

su·per·ox·ide (sōō′pər ok′sīd, -sid), *n. Chem.* **1.** a compound containing the univalent ion O_2^-. **2.** peroxide (def. 1a, b). Also called **hyperoxide.** [1840–50; SUPER- + OXIDE]

su·per·par·a·site (sōō′pər par′ə sīt′), *n. Biol.* hyperparasite. [1875–80; SUPER- + PARASITE] **—su·per·par·a·sit·ic** (sōō′pər par′ə sit′ik), *adj.* **—su′per·par′a·sit′·ism,** *n.*

su·per·pa·tri·ot (sōō′pər pā′trē ət, sōō′pər pā′-; *esp. Brit.,* sōō′pər pa′trē ət, sōō′pər pa′-), *n.* a person who is patriotic to an extreme. [SUPER- + PATRIOT] **—su·per·pa·tri·ot·ic** (sōō′pər pā′trē ot′ik; *esp. Brit.,* sōō′pər-pa′trē ot′ik), *adj.* **—su′per·pa′tri·ot′i·cal·ly,** *adv.* **—su′per·pa′tri·ot·ism,** *n.*

su·per·phos·phate (sōō′pər fos′fāt), *n. Chem.* **1.** Also called **acid phosphate.** a mixture of calcium acid phosphate and calcium sulfate prepared by treating phosphate rock with sulfuric acid: used chiefly as a fertilizer. **2.** Also called **triple superphosphate.** a mixture prepared with phosphoric acid and containing about 45 percent of soluble phosphates, used as a fertilizer. [1790–1800; SUPER- + PHOSPHATE]

su·per·phy·lum (sōō′pər fī′ləm), *n., pl.* **-la** (-lə). *Biol.* a category of related phyla within a kingdom. [SUPER- + PHYLUM]

su·per·phys·i·cal (sōō′pər fiz′i kəl), *adj.* above or beyond what is physical; hyperphysical. [1595–1605; SUPER- + PHYSICAL]

su·per·plas·tic (sōō′pər plas′tik), *adj.* (of some metals and alloys) having the capacity to undergo extreme deformation at high temperatures. [1945–50; SUPER- + PLASTIC; cf. Russ *sverkhplastíchnost′* (1945) superplasticity] **—su·per·plas·tic·i·ty** (sōō′pər plas tis′i tē), *n.*

su·per·port (sōō′pər pôrt′, -pōrt′), *n.* a deepwater port, often one built offshore, capable of accommodating very large ships, esp. supertankers of 100,000 tons or more. [1965–70; SUPER- + PORT[1]]

su·per·pose (sōō′pər pōz′), *v.t.,* **-posed, -pos·ing. 1.** to place above or upon something else, or one upon another. **2.** *Geom.* to place (one figure) in the space occupied by another, so that the two figures coincide throughout their whole extent. [1815–25; < F *superposer.* See SUPER-, POSE[1]] **—su′per·pos′a·ble,** *adj.*

su·per·po·si·tion (sōō′pər pə zish′ən), *n. Geol.* the order in which sedimentary strata are superposed one above another. Cf. **law of superposition.** [1790–1800; < F *superposition;* see SUPER-, POSITION]

superposi′tion prin′ciple, *Physics.* See **principle of superposition.** [1820–30]

su·per·pow·er (sōō′pər pou′ər), *n.* **1.** an extremely powerful nation, esp. one capable of influencing international events and the acts and policies of less powerful nations. **2.** power greater in scope or magnitude than that which is considered natural or has previously existed. **3.** power, esp. mechanical or electric power, on an extremely large scale secured by the linking together of a number of separate power systems, with a view to more efficient generation and distribution. [1920–25; SUPER- + POWER] **—su′per·pow′ered,** *adj.*

su·per·race (sōō′pər rās′), *n.* a race, class, or people considered superior to others. [SUPER- + RACE[2]]

su·per·ra·tion·al (sōō′pər rash′ə nl), *adj.* **1.** beyond the scope or range of reason; intuitional. **2.** extremely rational. [1675–85; SUPER- + RATIONAL] **—su′per·ra′·tion·al′i·ty,** *n.* **—su′per·ra′tion·al·ly,** *adv.*

su·per·re·al·ism (sōō′pər rē′ə liz′əm), *n.* (*sometimes cap.*) **1.** photorealism. **2.** surrealism. [1930–35; orig. as trans. of F *surréalisme* SURREALISM] **—su′per·re′al·ist,** *n., adj.*

su·per·re·gen·er·a·tion (sōō′pər ri jen′ə rā′shən), *n. Electronics.* regeneration in which a signal is alternately amplified and quenched at a frequency slightly above the audible range to achieve high sensitivity with a single tube. [SUPER- + REGENERATION] **—su·per·re·gen·er·a·tive** (sōō′pər ri jen′ə rā′tiv, -ər ə tiv), *adj.*

su·per·sales·man (sōō′pər sālz′mən, sōō′pər sālz′-), *n., pl.* **-men. 1.** an extremely skillful and effective salesperson. **2.** a person who is extremely skillful and effective at persuading others to agree to something. [SUPER- + SALESMAN] **—su′per·sales′man·ship′,** *n.*

su·per·sat·u·rate (sōō′pər sach′ə rāt′), *v.t.,* **-rat·ed, -rat·ing.** to increase the concentration of (a solution) beyond saturation; saturate abnormally. [1750–60; SUPER- + SATURATE] **—su′per·sat′u·ra′tion,** *n.*

su·per·saur (sōō′pər sôr′), *n.* a huge sauropod dinosaur of the genus *Supersaurus,* of W North America, that reached a length of about 130 ft. (40 m). [1985–90; < NL; see SUPER-, -SAUR]

su·per·sav·er (sōō′pər sā′vər), *n.* **1.** a specially reduced fare, as for passengers reserving tickets in advance or traveling during off-peak periods. **2.** any item

su′per·in·dig′nant, *adj.;* **-ly,** *adv.*
su′per·in′di·vid′u·al, *adj., n.;* **-ly,** *adv.*
su′per·in′di·vid′u·al·ism, *n.*
su′per·in′di·vid′u·al·ist, *n.*
su′per·in·dul′gence, *n.*
su′per·in·dul′gent, *adj.;* **-ly,** *adv.*
su′per·in·dus′tri·ous, *adj.;* **-ly,** *adv.;* **-ness,** *n.*
su′per·in′dus·try, *n., pl.* **-tries.**
su′per·in·fer′, *v.t.,* **-ferred, -fer·ring.**
su′per·in′fer·ence, *n.*
su′per·in′fi·nite, *adj.;* **-ly,** *adv.;* **-ness,** *n.*
su′per·in·fir′mi·ty, *n., pl.* **-ties.**
su′per·in′flu·ence, *n., v.t.,* **-enced, -enc·ing.**
su′per·in·for′mal, *adj.;* **-ly,** *adv.*
su′per·in·for·mal′i·ty, *n., pl.* **-ties.**
su′per·in·fuse′, *v.t.,* **-fused, -fus·ing.**
su′per·in·gen′ious, *adj.;* **-ly,** *adv.;* **-ness,** *n.*
su′per·in′ge·nu′i·ty, *n., pl.* **-ties.**
su′per·in·i′ti·a·tive, *n.*
su′per·in·jec′tion, *n.*
su′per·in·jus′tice, *n.*
su′per·in′no·cence, *n.*
su′per·in′no·cent, *adj.;* **-ly,** *adv.*
su′per·in·quis′i·tive, *adj.;* **-ly,** *adv.;* **-ness,** *n.*
su′per·in·scribe′, *v.t.,* **-scribed, -scrib·ing.**
su′per·in·scrip′tion, *n.*
su′per·in·sist′, *v.i.*
su′per·in·sist′ence, *n.*
su′per·in·sist′ent, *adj.;* **-ly,** *adv.*
su′per·in′su·lat′ed, *adj.*
su′per·in′tel·lec′tu·al, *adj., n.;* **-ly,** *adv.*
su′per·in·tel′li·gence, *n.*
su′per·in·tel′li·gent, *adj.*
su′per·in·tense′, *adj.;* **-ly,** *adv.;* **-ness,** *n.*
su′per·in·ten′si·ty, *n.*
su′per·in·tol′er·a·ble, *adj.;* **-ble·ness,** *n.;* **-bly,** *adv.*
su′per·in′un·da′tion, *n.*
su′per·in′vo·lu′tion, *n.*
su′per·ir′ri·ta·bil′i·ty, *n.*
su′per·jock′, *n.*
su′per·ju·di′cial, *adj.;* **-ly,** *adv.*
su′per·ju′ris·dic′tion, *n.*
su′per·jus′ti·fi·ca′tion, *n.*
su′per·knowl′edge, *n.*
su′per·la·bo′ri·ous, *adj.;* **-ly,** *adv.;* **-ness,** *n.*
su′per·lac·ta′tion, *n.*
su′per·la·ryn′ge·al, *adj.;* **-ly,** *adv.*
su′per·lean′, *adj.*
su′per·le′ni·ent, *adj.;* **-ly,** *adv.*
su′per·lie′, *v.,* **-lied, -ly·ing.**
su′per·light′, *adj.*
su′per·like′li·hood′, *n.*
su′per·line′, *n.*
su′per·lo′cal, *adj.;* **-ly,** *adv.*
su′per·log′i·cal, *adj.;* **-ly,** *adv.*
su′per·log′i·cal′i·ty, *n.*
su′per·loy′al, *adj.;* **-ly,** *adv.*
su′per·luck′y, *adj.*
su′per·lux·u′ri·ous, *adj.;* **-ly,** *adv.;* **-ness,** *n.*
su′per·lux′u·ry, *n., adj.*
su′per·ma′cho, *n., pl.* **-chos.**
su′per·mag·nif′i·cent, *adj.;* **-ly,** *adv.*
su′per·mal′ate, *n.*
su′per·male′, *n.*
su′per·man′i·fest′, *v.t.*
su′per·mar′gin·al, *adj.;* **-ly,** *adv.*
su′per·ma·rine′, *adj.*
su′per·mar′vel·ous, *adj.;* **-ly,** *adv.;* **-ness,** *n.*
su′per·mas′cu·line, *adj.*
su′per·mas′cu·lin′i·ty, *n.*
su′per·ma·te′ri·al, *n.*
su′per·math′e·mat′i·cal, *adj.;* **-ly,** *adv.*
su′per·me·chan′i·cal, *adj.;* **-ly,** *adv.*
su′per·me′di·al, *adj.;* **-ly,** *adv.*
su′per·med′i·cine, *n.*
su′per·me′di·o′cre, *adj.*
su′per·men′tal, *adj.;* **-ly,** *adv.*
su′per·men·tal′i·ty, *n.*
su′per·met′ro·pol′i·tan, *adj.*
su′per·mil′i·tant, *adj.*
su′per·mil′i·tar′y, *adj., n.*
su′per·min′i·a·ture, *adj.*
su′per·min′i·a·tur·ize′, *v.t.,* **-ized, -iz·ing.**
su′per·mix′ture, *n.*
su′per·mod′el, *n.*
su′per·mod′ern, *adj.*
su′per·mod′est, *adj.;* **-ly,** *adv.*
su′per·mois′ten, *v.t.*
su′per·mol′e·cule′, *n.*
su′per·mol′ten, *adj.*
su′per·mor′al, *adj.;* **-ly,** *adv.*
su′per·mo·rose′, *adj.;* **-ly,** *adv.;* **-ness,** *n.*
su′per·mo·til′i·ty, *n.*
su′per·mu·nic′i·pal, *adj.*
su′per·mys′ter·y, *n., pl.* **-ter·ies.**
su′per·na′tion, *n.*
su′per·ne·ces′si·ty, *n., pl.* **-ties.**
su′per·neg′li·gence, *n.*
su′per·neg′li·gent, *adj.;* **-ly,** *adv.*
su′per·net′work, *n.*
su′per·no′ta·ble, *adj.;* **-ble·ness,** *n.;* **-bly,** *adv.*
su′per·nu′mer·ous, *adj.;* **-ly,** *adv.;* **-ness,** *n.*
su′per·nu·tri′tion, *n.*
su′per·o·be′di·ence, *n.*
su′per·o·be′di·ent, *adj.;* **-ly,** *adv.*
su′per·o·bese′, *adj.*
su′per·ob·ject′, *v.i.*
su′per·ob·jec′tion, *n.*
su′per·ob·jec′tion·a·ble, *adj.;* **-bly,** *adv.*
su′per·ob′li·ga′tion, *n.*
su′per·ob′sti·nate, *adj.;* **-ly,** *adv.;* **-ness,** *n.*
su′per·oc·cip′i·tal, *adj.*
su′per·oc′u·lar, *adj.;* **-ly,** *adv.*
su′per·of·fen′sive, *adj., n.;* **-ly,** *adv.;* **-ness,** *n.*
su′per·of·fi′cious, *adj.;* **-ly,** *adv.;* **-ness,** *n.*
su′per·op′po·si′tion, *n.*
su′per·op′ti·mal, *adj.*
su′per·op′ti·mist, *n.*
su′per·op′ti·mis′tic, *adj.*
su′per·o′ra·tor′i·cal, *adj.;* **-ly,** *adv.*

on which there is a specially reduced price: *The grocery's supersavers this week include oranges, canned peas, and sugar.* —*adj.* **3.** of or at a specially reduced fare or price. [1975–80, *Amer.*; SUPER- + SAVER]

su·per·scribe (so͞o′pər skrīb′, so͞o′pər skrīb′), *v.t.,* **-scribed, -scrib·ing. 1.** to write (words, letters, one's name, address, etc.) above or on something. **2.** to inscribe or mark with writing at the top or on the outside or surface of: *to superscribe the cover of a text with corrections.* [1590–1600; < L *superscrībere,* equiv. to *super-* SUPER- + *scrībere* to write; see SCRIBE[1]]

su·per·script (so͞o′pər skript′), *adj.* **1.** *Print.* superior (def. 10). —*n.* **2.** *Print.* superior (def. 12). **3.** *Obs.* an address on a letter; superscription. [1580–90; < L *superscrīptus* (ptp. of *superscrībere* to SUPERSCRIBE), equiv. to *super-* SUPER- + *scrīptus* written; see SCRIPT]

su·per·scrip·tion (so͞o′pər skrip′shən), *n.* **1.** the act of superscribing. **2.** something that is superscribed. **3.** an address on a letter, parcel, or the like. **4.** *Pharm.* the sign ℞, meaning "take," at the beginning of a prescription. [1350–1400; ME *superscripcioun* < LL *superscrīptiōn-* (s. of *superscrīptiō*) a writing above. See SUPERSCRIPT, -ION]

su·per·sede (so͞o′pər sēd′), *v.t.,* **-sed·ed, -sed·ing. 1.** to replace in power, authority, effectiveness, acceptance, use, etc., as by another person or thing. **2.** to set aside or cause to be set aside as void, useless, or obsolete, usually in favor of something mentioned; make obsolete: *They superseded the old statute with a new one.* **3.** to succeed to the position, function, office, etc., of; supplant. [1485–95; < L *supersedēre* to sit above or upon, forbear, equiv. to *super-* SUPER- + *sedēre* to SIT[1]] —**su′per·sed′a·ble,** *adj.* —**su′per·sed′er,** *n.*
—**Syn. 1.** See **replace. 2.** void, overrule, annul, revoke, rescind.

su·per·se·de·as (so͞o′pər sē′dē əs, -as′), *n., pl.* **-de·as.** *Law.* a writ ordering a stoppage or suspension of a judicial proceeding, of the execution of a judgment, or of the enforcement of another writ. [< L *supersedeās,* 2nd person sing. pres. subj. of *supersedēre* to SUPERSEDE, the writ being so named because *supersedeās,* i.e., you shall desist, occurs in it]

su·per·se·dure (so͞o′pər sē′jər), *n.* supersession. [1780–90, *Amer.*; SUPERSEDE + -URE]

su·per·sen·ior·i·ty (so͞o′pər sēn yôr′i tē, -yor′-), *n.* seniority that is granted or held without regard to age or service. [SUPER- + SENIORITY]

su·per·sen·si·ble (so͞o′pər sen′sə bəl), *adj.* being above or beyond perception by the senses; beyond the reach of the senses. [1790–1800; SUPER- + SENSIBLE] —**su′per·sen′si·bly,** *adv.*

su·per·sen·si·tive (so͞o′pər sen′si tiv), *adj.* **1.** extremely or excessively sensitive; hypersensitive: *a supersensitive smoke detector.* **2.** *Elect.* of or pertaining to relays that operate on very small currents, below about 250 microamperes. **3.** hypersensitive (def. 2). [1830–40; SUPER- + SENSITIVE] —**su′per·sen′si·tive·ness,** *n.* —**su′per·sen′si·tiv′i·ty,** *n.*

su·per·sen·si·tize (so͞o′pər sen′si tīz′), *v.t.,* **-tized, -tiz·ing.** to render or make supersensitive. Also, *esp. Brit.,* **su′per·sen′si·tise′.** [SUPER- + SENSIT(IVE) + -IZE] —**su′per·sen′si·ti·za′tion,** *n.* —**su′per·sen′si·tiz′er,** *n.*

su·per·sen·so·ry (so͞o′pər sen′sə rē), *adj.* **1.** supersensible. **2.** independent of the organs of sense. [1880–85; SUPER- + SENSORY]

su·per·sen·su·al (so͞o′pər sen′sho͞o əl), *adj.* **1.** beyond the range of the senses. **2.** spiritual. **3.** extremely sensual. [1675–85; SUPER- + SENSUAL] —**su′per·sen′su·al·ism,** *n.* —**su′per·sen′su·al·ist,** *n.* —**su′per·sen′su·al·is′tic,** *adj.* —**su′per·sen′su·al′i·ty,** *n.* —**su′per·sen′su·al·ly,** *adv.*

su·per·serv·ice·a·ble (so͞o′pər sûr′vi sə bəl), *adj.* overly disposed to be of service; officious. [1595–1605; SUPER- + SERVICEABLE] —**su′per·serv′ice·a·ble·ness,** *n.* —**su′per·serv′ice·a·bly,** *adv.*

su·per·ses·sion (so͞o′pər sesh′ən), *n.* **1.** the act of superseding. **2.** the state of being superseded. [1650–60; < ML *supersessiōn-* (s. of *supersessiō*), equiv. to L *supersess(us)* (ptp. of *supersedēre* to SUPERSEDE) + *-iōn-* -ION; see SESSION]

su·per·smooth (so͞o′pər smo͞oth′), *adj.* (of a metal file) dead-smooth.

su·per·son·ic (so͞o′pər son′ik), *adj.* **1.** greater than the speed of sound through air. **2.** capable of achieving such speed: *a supersonic plane.* **3.** ultrasonic. [1915–20; SUPER- + SONIC] —**su′per·son′i·cal·ly,** *adv.*

su·per·son·ics (so͞o′pər son′iks), *n.* (*used with a singular v.*) the branch of science that deals with supersonic phenomena. [1925–30; see SUPERSONIC, -ICS]

su′person′ic trans′port, a commercial jet airplane that can fly faster than the speed of sound. *Abbr.:* SST [1965–70]

su·per·speed (so͞o′pər spēd′), *adj.* intended to function at a very high speed. [SUPER- + SPEED]

su·per·star (so͞o′pər stär′), *n.* **1.** a person, as a performer or athlete, who enjoys wide recognition, is esteemed for exceptional talent, and is eagerly sought after for his or her services. **2.** any very prominent or successful person or thing. [1920–25, *Amer.*; SUPER- + STAR] —**su′per·star′dom,** *n.*

su·per·state (so͞o′pər stāt′), *n.* **1.** a state or a governing power presiding over states subordinated to it. **2.** an extremely powerful centralized government maintaining close control or supervision over its member states and their inhabitants. [SUPER- + STATE]

su·per·sta·tion (so͞o′pər stā′shən), *n.* an independent television station whose signal is transmitted by satellite to subscribers on a cable system. [SUPER- + STATION]

su·per·sti·tion (so͞o′pər stish′ən), *n.* **1.** a belief or notion, not based on reason or knowledge, in or of the ominous significance of a particular thing, circumstance, occurrence, proceeding, or the like. **2.** a system or collection of such beliefs. **3.** a custom or act based on such a belief. **4.** irrational fear of what is unknown or mysterious, esp. in connection with religion. **5.** any blindly accepted belief or notion. [1375–1425; late ME < L *superstitiōn-* (s. of *superstitiō*), equiv. to *superstit-* (s. of *superstes*) standing beyond, outliving (*super-* SUPER- + *-stit-,* comb. form of *stat-,* adj. deriv. of *stāre* to STAND) + *-iōn-* -ION]

su·per·sti·tious (so͞o′pər stish′əs), *adj.* **1.** of the nature of, characterized by, or proceeding from superstition: *superstitious fears.* **2.** pertaining to or connected with superstition: *superstitious legends.* **3.** believing in, full of, or influenced by superstition. [1350–1400; ME *supersticious* < L *superstitiōsus,* equiv. to *superstiti(ō)* SUPERSTITION + *-ōsus* -OUS] —**su′per·sti′tious·ly,** *adv.* —**su′per·sti′tious·ness,** *n.*

su·per·stra·tum (so͞o′pər strā′təm, -strat′əm), *n., pl.* **-stra·ta** (-strā′tə, -strat′ə), **-stra·tums. 1.** an overlying layer. **2.** *Historical Ling.* a set of features of a language traceable to the influence of a language formerly spoken within the same society by a dominant group: *English has a Norman-French superstratum.* Cf. **substratum.** [1800–10; SUPER- + STRATUM; cf. SUBSTRATUM]

su·per·string (so͞o′pər string′), *n. Physics.* an elementary particle treated as a string in any string theory of supersymmetry. [SUPER- + STRING]

su′perstring the′ory (so͞o′pər string′), *Physics.* any supersymmetric string theory in which each type of elementary particle is treated as a vibration of a single fundamental string **(superstring)** at a particular frequency.

su·per·struc·ture (so͞o′pər struk′chər), *n.* **1.** the part of a building or construction entirely above its foundation or basement. **2.** any structure built on something else. **3.** the overlying framework or features of an organization, institution, or system, built or superimposed on a more fundamental base. **4.** *Naut.* any construction built above the main deck of a vessel as an upward continuation of the sides. Cf. **deckhouse. 5.** the part of a bridge that rests on the piers and abutments. **6.** anything based on or rising from some foundation or basis: *a complex ideological superstructure based on two hypotheses.* [1635–45; SUPER- + STRUCTURE] —**su′per·struc′tur·al,** *adj.*

su·per·sub·tle (so͞o′pər sut′l), *adj.* extremely or excessively subtle; oversubtle. [1590–1600; SUPER- + SUBTLE] —**su′per·sub′tle·ty,** *n.*

su·per·sym·me·try (so͞o′pər sim′i trē), *n. Physics.* a hypothetical symmetry among groups of particles containing fermions and bosons, esp. in theories of gravity **(supergravity)** that unify electromagnetism, the weak force, and the strong force with gravity into a single unified force. [1970–75; SUPER- + SYMMETRY]

su·per·tank·er (so͞o′pər tang′kər), *n.* a tanker with a deadweight capacity of over 75,000 tons. [SUPER- + TANKER]

su·per·task (so͞o′pər task′, -täsk′), *n. Logic.* a paradox resulting from the notion that a task requiring an infinite number of steps could be performed in a finite time by halving the duration of each step. [1970–75; SUPER- + TASK]

su·per·tax (so͞o′pər taks′), *n.* **1.** *Chiefly Brit.* a tax in addition to a normal tax, as one upon income above a certain amount. **2.** a surtax. [1905–10; SUPER- + TAX]

su·per·ti·tle (so͞o′pər tīt′l), *n., v.,* **-tled, -tling.** —*n.* **1.** (esp. in opera production) a translation of a segment of the libretto or other text or sometimes a brief summary of the plot projected onto a screen above the stage during a performance. —*v.t.* **2.** to provide supertitles for. Also, **surtitle.** [SUPER- + TITLE]

su·per·ton·ic (so͞o′pər ton′ik), *n. Music.* the second tone of a diatonic scale, being the next above the tonic. [1800–10; SUPER- + TONIC]

su·per·u·ni·fi·ca·tion (so͞o′pər yo͞o′nə fi kā′shən), *n. Physics.* a theory intended to describe the electromagnetic force, the strong force, the weak force, and gravity as a single, unified force. [SUPER- + UNIFICATION]

su·per·vene (so͞o′pər vēn′), *v.i.,* **-vened, -ven·ing. 1.** to take place or occur as something additional or extraneous (sometimes fol. by *on* or *upon*). **2.** to ensue. [1640–50; < L *supervenīre,* equiv. to *super-* SUPER- + *venīre* to COME] —**su·per·ven·ience** (so͞o′pər vēn′yəns), **su·per·ven·tion** (so͞o′pər ven′shən), *n.* —**su·per·ven·ient** (so͞o′pər vēn′yənt), *adj.*

su·per·vise (so͞o′pər vīz′), *v.t.,* **-vised, -vis·ing.** to oversee (a process, work, workers, etc.) during execution or performance; superintend; have the direction of. [1580–90; < ML *supervīsus* (ptp. of *supervidēre* to oversee), equiv. to *super-* SUPER- + *vid-,* s. of *vidēre* to see + *-tus* ptp. suffix, with *dt* > *s*; see VISION, WIT[2]]
—**Syn.** manage, direct, control, guide.

su·per·vi·sion (so͞o′pər vizh′ən), *n.* the act or function of supervising; superintendence. [1615–25; < ML *supervīsiōn-* (s. of *supervīsiō*) oversight, equiv. to *super-* SUPER- + *vīsiōn-* VISION]

su·per·vi·sor (so͞o′pər vī′zər), *n.* **1.** a person who supervises workers or the work done by others; superintendent. **2.** *Educ.* an official responsible for assisting teachers in the preparation of syllabuses, in devising teaching methods, etc., in a department of instruction, esp. in public schools. **3.** (in some U.S. states) the chief elected administrative officer of a township, who is often also a member of the governing board of the county. [1425–75; late ME < ML *supervīsor,* equiv. to *supervid-,* s. of *supervidēre* to SUPERVISE + *-tor* -TOR, with *dt* > *s*] —**su′per·vi′sor·ship′,** *n.*

su·per·vi·so·ry (so͞o′pər vī′zə rē), *adj.* of, pertaining to, or having supervision. [1840–50; SUPERVISE + -ORY[1]]

CONCISE PRONUNCIATION KEY: act, cāpe, dâre, pärt; set, ēqual; if, īce; ox, ōver, ôrder, oil, bo͝ok, bo͞ot, out; up, ûrge; child; sing; shoe; thin, *th*at; zh as in *treasure.* ə = *a* as in *alone,* *e* as in *system,* *i* as in *easily,* *o* as in *gallop,* *u* as in *circus;* ə as in *fire* (fīər), *hour* (ouər). l and n can serve as syllabic consonants, as in *cradle* (krād′l), and *button* (but′n). See the full key inside the front cover.

su′per·or′bit·al, *adj.*
su′per·or·dain′, *v.i.*
su′per·or′di·nar′y, *adj.*
su′per·or′gan·ism, *n.*
su′per·or′gan·i·za′tion, *n.*
su′per·or′gasm, *n.*
su′per·or′na·ment, *n.*
su′per·or′na·ment′, *v.t.*
su′per·or′na·men′tal, *adj.*; **-ly,** *adv.*
su′per·out′put′, *n.*
su′per·ox′a·late′, *n.*
su′per·ox′y·gen·ate′, *v.t.,* **-at·ed, -at·ing.**
su′per·ox′y·gen·a′tion, *n.*
su′per·par′a·mount′, *adj.*
su′per·park′, *n.*
su′per·par′lia·men′ta·ry, *adj.*
su′per·pas′sage, *n.*
su′per·pas′teur·ized′, *adj.*
su′per·pa′tience, *n.*
su′per·pa′tient, *adj.*; **-ly,** *adv.*
su′per·per′fect, *adj.*; **-ly,** *adv.*
su′per·per·fec′tion, *n.*
su′per·per′son, *n.*
su′per·per′son·al, *adj.*; **-ly,** *adv.*
su′per·pe·tro′sal, *adj.*
su′per·pet′rous, *adj.*
su′per·pi′e·ty, *n.,pl.* **-ties.**
su′per·pi′ous, *adj.*; **-ly,** *adv.*; **-ness,** *n.*
su′per·plane′, *n.*
su′per·plau′si·ble, *adj.*; **-ble·ness,** *n.*; **-bly,** *adv.*
su′per·play′er, *n.*
su′per·po·lite′, *adj.*; **-ly,** *adv.*; **-ness,** *n.*
su′per·pol′y·mer, *n.*
su′per·pop′u·lat′ed, *adj.*
su′per·pop′u·la′tion, *n.*
su′per·pos′i·tive, *adj.*; **-ly,** *adv.*; **-ness,** *n.*
su′per·pow′er·ful, *adj.*
su′per·praise′, *n., v.t.,* **-praised, -prais·ing.**
su′per·pre·car′i·ous, *adj.*; **-ly,** *adv.*; **-ness,** *n.*
su′per·pre·cise′, *adj.*; **-ly,** *adv.*; **-ness,** *n.*
su′per·pre′mi·um, *adj., n.*
su′per·prep′a·ra′tion, *n.*
su′per·pre·pared′, *adj.*
su′per·pres′sure, *n., adj.*
su′per·prize′, *n.*
su′per·prob′a·bil′i·ty, *n., pl.* **-ties.**
su′per·pro·duce′, *v.,* **-duced, -duc·ing.**
su′per·pro′duce, *n.*
su′per·pro·duc′tion, *n.*
su′per·pro·por′tion, *n.*
su′per·pros′per·ous, *adj.*
su′per·pru′dent, *adj.*
su′per·pub·lic′i·ty, *n.*
su′per·pure′, *adj.*
su′per·pur·ga′tion, *n.*
su′per·pu′ri·ty, *n.*
su′per·qual′i·fy′, *v.,* **-fied, -fy·ing.**
su′per·quote′, *v.,* **-quot·ed, -quot·ing,** *n.*
su′per·ra′di·ance, *n.*
su′per·ra′di·ant, *adj.*
su′per·rad′i·cal, *adj.*; **-ly,** *adv.*; **-ness,** *n.*
su′per·re·ac′tion, *n.*
su′per·re·fine′, *v.t.,* **-fined, -fin·ing.**
su′per·re·fined′, *adj.*
su′per·re·fine′ment, *n.*
su′per·re·flec′tion, *n.*
su′per·re·form′, *n., v.t.*
su′per·ref′or·ma′tion, *n.*
su′per·re′gal, *adj.*; **-ly,** *adv.*
su′per·reg′is·tra′tion, *n.*
su′per·reg′u·la′tion, *n.*
su′per·re·li′ance, *n.*
su′per·re·mu′ner·a′tion, *n.*
su′per·re′nal, *adj.*
su′per·re·quire′ment, *n.*
su′per·re·spect′a·bil′i·ty, *n.*
su′per·re·spect′a·ble, *adj.*; **-ble·ness,** *n.*; **-bly,** *adv.*
su′per·re·spon′si·bil′i·ty, *n., pl.* **-ties.**
su′per·re·spon′si·ble, *adj.*; **-ble·ness,** *n.*; **-bly,** *adv.*
su′per·re·stric′tion, *n.*
su′per·re·ward′, *v.t., n.*
su′per·rich′, *adj., n.*
su′per·right′eous, *adj.*; **-ly,** *adv.*; **-ness,** *n.*
su′per·ro·man′tic, *adj.*
su′per·ro·man′ti·cal·ly, *adv.*
su′per·ro·man′ti·cism, *n.*
su′per·sac′er·do′tal, *adj.*; **-ly,** *adv.*
su′per·sa′cral, *adj.*
su′per·sa′cred, *adj.*
su′per·sac′ri·fice′, *n., v.t.,* **-ficed, -fic·ing.**
su′per·safe′, *adj.*; **-ly,** *adv.*; **-ness,** *n.*
su′per·safe′ty, *n.*
su′per·sa·ga′cious, *adj.*; **-ly,** *adv.*; **-ness,** *n.*
su′per·saint′, *n.*
su′per·saint′ly, *adj.*
su′per·sanc′tion, *v.t., n.*
su′per·san′guine, *adj.*
su′per·san·guin′i·ty, *n.*
su′per·san′i·ty, *n.*
su′per·sar′casm, *n.*
su′per·sar·cas′tic, *adj.*
su′per·sar·cas′ti·cal·ly, *adv.*
su′per·sat′is·fac′tion, *n.*
su′per·sat′is·fy′, *v.t.,* **-fied, -fy·ing.**
su′per·scale′, *n.*
su′per·scan′dal, *n.*
su′per·scan′dal·ous, *adj.*; **-ly,** *adv.*
su′per·schol′ar·ly, *adj.*
su′per·school′, *n.*
su′per·sci′en·tif′ic, *adj.*
su′per·sci′en·tif′i·cal·ly, *adv.*
su′per·scout′, *n.*
su′per·screen′, *n., adj.*
su′per·sea′man, *n., pl.* **-men.**
su′per·se′cre·cy, *n., pl.* **-cies.**
su′per·se′cret, *n.*
su′per·se·cre′tion, *n.*
su′per·se·cre′tive, *adj.*; **-ly,** *adv.*; **-ness,** *n.*
su′per·sec′u·lar, *adj.*; **-ly,** *adv.*
su′per·se·cure′, *adj.*; **-ly,** *adv.*; **-ness,** *n.*
su′per·se·lec′tion, *n.*
su′per·sell′, *n.*
su′per·sell′er, *n.*
su′per·sen′su·ous, *adj.*; **-ly,** *adv.*; **-ness,** *n.*
su′per·sen′ti·men′tal, *adj.*; **-ly,** *adv.*
su′per·sep′tal, *adj.*
su′per·se·raph′ic, *adj.*
su′per·se·raph′i·cal, *adj.*; **-ly,** *adv.*
su′per·se′ries, *n., pl.* **-ries.**
su′per·se′ri·ous, *adj.*; **-ly,** *adv.*; **-ness,** *n.*
su′per·serv′ice, *n.*

su·per·wom·an (so͞o′pər wo͝om′ən), *n., pl.* **-wom·en. 1.** a woman of extraordinary or superhuman powers. **2.** a woman who copes successfully with the simultaneous demands of a career, marriage, and motherhood. [SUPER- + WOMAN]
—Usage. See **-woman.**

su·pi·nate (so͞o′pə nāt′), *v.,* **-nat·ed, -nat·ing.** *—v.t.* **1.** to turn to a supine position; rotate (the hand or foot) so that the palm or sole is upward. *—v.i.* **2.** to become supinated. [1825–35; < L *supīnātus* (ptp. of *supīnāre* to lay face up). See SUPINE, -ATE[1]]

su·pi·na·tion (so͞o′pə nā′shən), *n.* **1.** rotation of the hand or forearm so that the palmar surface is facing upward (opposed to *pronation*). **2.** a comparable motion of the foot, consisting of adduction followed by inversion. **3.** the position assumed as the result of this rotation. [1660–70; SUPINATE + -ION]

su·pi·na·tor (so͞o′pə nā′tər), *n. Anat.* a muscle used in supination. [1605–15; < NL; see SUPINATE, -TOR]

su·pine (*adj.* so͞o pīn′; *n.* so͞o′pīn), *adj.* **1.** lying on the back, face or front upward. **2.** inactive, passive, or inert, esp. from indolence or indifference. **3.** (of the hand) having the palm upward. *—n.* **4.** (in Latin) a noun form derived from verbs, appearing only in the accusative and the dative-ablative, as *dictū* in *mīrābile dictū,* "wonderful to say." **5.** (in English) the simple infinitive of a verb preceded by *to.* **6.** an analogous form in some other language. [1490–1500; < L *supīnus* lying face up, inactive] **—su·pine′ly,** *adv.* **—su·pine′ness,** *n.*

supp., 1. supplement. **2.** supplementary. Also, **suppl.**

sup·pawn (sə pôn′), *n. Hudson Valley.* cornmeal mush. [1785–95, *Amer.*; < New York D *suppaen, sapaen* < Munsee Delaware *nsá·pa·n*; see SAMP]

Sup·pé (so͞o′pā; *Ger.* zo͝op′ā), *n.* **Franz von** (fränts fən), 1819–95, Austrian composer.

sup·pe·da·ne·um (sup′i dā′nē əm), *n., pl.* **-ne·a** (-nē ə). a shelf affixed to a cross for supporting the feet of the crucified. [1860–65; < ML, n. use of neut. of LL *suppedāneus* under the feet, equiv. to *sup-* SUP- + *ped-* (s. of *pēs*) FOOT + *-āneus* (*-ān(us)* -AN + *-eus* -EOUS)]

sup·per (sup′ər), *n.* **1.** the evening meal, often the principal meal of the day. **2.** any light evening meal, esp. one taken late in the evening: *an after-the-theater supper.* *—adj.* **3.** of or pertaining to supper: *the supper dishes.* **4.** for, during, or including supper: *a supper party.* [1225–75; ME *sup(p)er* < OF *souper,* n. use of *souper* to SUP[1]] **—sup′per·less,** *adj.*

sup′per club′, a nightclub, esp. a small, luxurious one. [1920–25]

sup·per·time (sup′ər tīm′), *n.* the time at which supper is served, usually between the hours of 5 and 7 P.M. [1325–75; ME *soper tyme.* See SUPPER, TIME]

sup·plant (sə plant′, -plänt′), *v.t.* **1.** to take the place of (another), as through force, scheming, strategy, or the like. **2.** to replace (one thing) by something else. [1250–1300; ME *supplanten* < L *supplantāre* to trip up, overthrow. See SUP-, PLANT] **—sup·plan·ta·tion** (sup′lən tā′shən), *n.* **—sup·plant′er,** *n.*
—Syn. 1. remove, succeed. See **replace.**

sup·ple (sup′əl), *adj.,* **-pler, -plest,** *v.,* **-pled, -pling.** *—adj.* **1.** bending readily without breaking or becoming deformed; pliant; flexible: *a supple bough.* **2.** characterized by ease in bending; limber; lithe: *supple movements.* **3.** characterized by ease, responsiveness, and adaptability in mental action. **4.** compliant or yielding. **5.** obsequious; servile. *—v.t., v.i.* **6.** to make or become supple. [1250–1300; (adj.) ME *souple* flexible, compliant < OF: soft, yielding, lithe < L *supplic-* (s. of *supplex*) submissive, suppliant, equiv. to *sup-* SUP- + *-plic-,* variously explained as akin to *plicāre* to FOLD[1], bend (thus meaning "bent over"; cf. COMPLEX), or to *plācāre* to PLACATE (thus meaning "in the attitude of a suppliant"); (v.) ME *supplen* to soften, deriv. of the n. (cf. OF *asoplir*)] **—sup′ple·ness,** *n.*

CONCISE ETYMOLOGY KEY: <, descended or borrowed from; >, whence; b., blend of, blended; c., cognate with; cf., compare; deriv., derivative; equiv., equivalent; imit., imitative; obl., oblique; r., replacing; s., stem; sp., spelling, spelled; resp., respelling, respelled; trans., translation; ?, origin unknown; *, unattested; ‡, probably earlier than. See the full key inside the front cover.

sup·ple·jack (sup′əl jak′), *n.* **1.** a strong, pliant cane or walking stick. **2.** any of various climbing shrubs with strong stems suitable for making walking sticks. [1715–25; SUPPLE + JACK[1]]

sup·ple·ly (sup′ə lē, sup′lē), *adv.* supply[2].

sup·ple·ment (*n.* sup′lə mənt; *v.* sup′lə ment′), *n.* **1.** something added to complete a thing, supply a deficiency, or reinforce or extend a whole. **2.** a part added to a book, document, etc., to supply additional or later information, correct errors, or the like. **3.** a part, usually of special character, issued as an additional feature of a newspaper or other periodical. **4.** *Geom.* the quantity by which an angle or an arc falls short of 180° or a semicircle. *—v.t.* **5.** to complete, add to, or extend by a supplement. **6.** to form a supplement or addition to. **7.** to supply (a deficiency). [1350–1400; ME < L *supplēmentum* that by which anything is made full, equiv. to *sup-* SUP- + *plē-* (s. of *plēre* to fill; see FULL[1]) + *-mentum* -MENT] **—sup′ple·ment′er,** *n.*
—Syn. 2. addendum, epilogue, postscript. See **appendix. 5.** See **complement.**

sup·ple·men·tal (sup′lə men′tl), *adj.* **1.** supplementary. **2.** nonscheduled (def. 2). **3.** (of a pleading, an affidavit, etc.) added to furnish what is lacking or missing. *—n.* **4.** anything that is supplemental: *supplementals attached to the bill in committee.* [1595–1605; SUPPLEMENT + -AL[1]] **—sup′ple·men′tal·ly,** *adv.*

sup′plemen′tal plum′age, *Ornith.* the third plumage assumed by certain birds having three different plumages in their annual cycle of molts.

Supplemen′tal Secu′rity In′come, income provided by the U.S. government to needy aged, blind, and disabled persons. *Abbr.:* SSI

sup·ple·men·ta·ry (sup′lə men′tə rē), *adj., n., pl.* **-ries.** *—adj.* **1.** Also, **supplemental.** of the nature of or forming a supplement; additional. *—n.* **2.** a person or thing that is supplementary. [1660–70; SUPPLEMENT + -ARY]

sup′plemen′tary an′gle, *Math.* either of two angles that added together produce an angle of 180°. Cf. **complementary angle.** [1830–40]

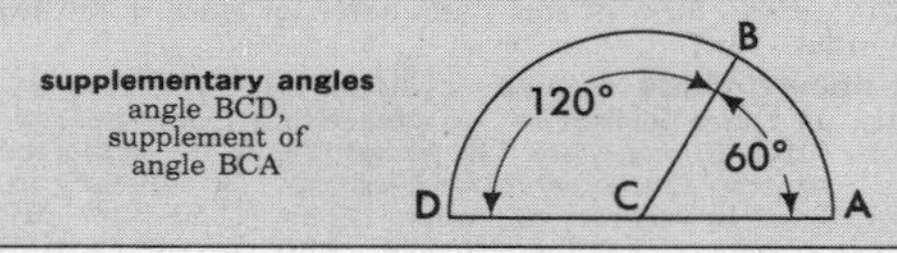

supplementary angles
angle BCD, supplement of angle BCA

sup′plemen′tary stor′y, *Journalism.* follow-up (def. 3b).

sup·ple·men·ta·tion (sup′lə men tā′shən, -mən-), *n.* **1.** the act or process of supplementing. **2.** the state of being supplemented. **3.** something that supplements. [1850–55; SUPPLEMENT + -ATION]

sup·ple·tion (sə plē′shən), *n. Gram.* the use in inflection or derivation of an allomorph that is not related in form to the primary allomorph of a morpheme, as the use of *better* as the comparative of *good.* [1275–1325; ME: supplementation, supplement < ML *supplētiōn-* (s. of *supplētiō*) a filling up, equiv. to *supplēt(us),* ptp. of *supplēre* to make complete, (*sup-* SUP- + *plē-,* s. of *plēre* to fill (see FULL[1]) + *-tus* ptp. suffix) + *-iōn-* -ION]

sup·ple·tive (sə plē′tiv, sup′li tiv), *adj. Gram.* **1.** serving as an inflected form of a word with a totally different stem, as *went,* the suppletive past of *go.* **2.** including one or more such forms: *a suppletive paradigm.* **3.** characterized by the use of such forms: *suppletive inflection.* [1810–20; < ML *supplētīvus,* equiv. to L *supplēt(us)* (ptp. of *supplēre* to fill up; see SUPPLETION) + *-īvus* -IVE]

sup·ple·to·ry (sup′li tôr′ē, -tōr′ē), *adj.* supplying a deficiency. [1620–30; < LL *supplētōrius,* equiv. to *supplē(re)* (see SUPPLETION) + *-tōrius* -TORY[1]] **—sup′ple·to′ri·ly,** *adv.*

sup·pli·ance[1] (sə plī′əns), *n.* the act, method, or process of supplying. [1590–1600; SUPPLY[1] + -ANCE]

sup·pli·ance[2] (sup′lē əns), *n.* appeal; entreaty; plea; supplication: *He knelt in an attitude of suppliance.* Also, **suppliancy.** [1605–15; SUPPLI(ANT) + -ANCE]

sup·pli·an·cy (sup′lē ən sē), *n., pl.* **-cies.** suppliance[2]. [1830–40; SUPPLI(ANT) + -ANCY]

sup·pli·ant (sup′lē ənt), *n.* **1.** a person who supplicates; petitioner. *—adj.* **2.** supplicating. **3.** expressive of supplication, as words, actions, etc. [1400–50; late ME < MF, prp. of *supplier* < L *supplicāre* to beseech, SUPPLICATE. See -ANT] **—sup′pli·ant·ly,** *adv.* **—sup′pli·ant·ness,** *n.*

Suppliants, The, **1.** a tragedy (c463 B.C.) by Aeschylus. **2.** a tragedy (c420 B.C.) by Euripides.

sup·pli·cant (sup′li kənt), *adj.* **1.** supplicating. *—n.* **2.** a suppliant. [1590–1600; < L *supplicant-* (s. of *supplicāns*), prp. of *supplicāre* to SUPPLICATE; see -ANT; doublet of SUPPLIANT]

sup·pli·cate (sup′li kāt′), *v.,* **-cat·ed, -cat·ing.** *—v.i.* **1.** to pray humbly; make humble and earnest entreaty or petition. *—v.t.* **2.** to pray humbly to; entreat or petition humbly. **3.** to seek or ask for by humble entreaty. [1375–1425; late ME < L *supplicātus* (ptp. of *supplicāre* to kneel), equiv. to *supplic-,* s. of *supplex* submissive, suppliant (see SUPPLE) + *-ātus* -ATE[1]] **—sup′pli·cat′ing·ly,** *adv.* **—sup·pli·ca·to·ry** (sup′li kə tôr′ē, -tōr′ē), *adj.*
—Syn. 2. implore, crave, solicit, beseech. See **appeal.**

sup·pli·ca·tion (sup′li kā′shən), *n.* an act or instance of supplicating; humble prayer, entreaty, or petition. [1350–1400; ME < L *supplicātiōn-* (s. of *supplicātiō*). See SUPPLICATE, -ION]

sup·ply[1] (sə plī′), *v.,* **-plied, -ply·ing,** *n., pl.* **-plies.** *—v.t.* **1.** to furnish or provide (a person, establishment, place, etc.) with what is lacking or requisite: *to supply someone clothing; to supply a community with electricity.* **2.** to furnish or provide (something wanting or requisite): *to supply electricity to a community.* **3.** to make up, compensate for, or satisfy (a deficiency, loss, need, etc.): *The TVA supplied the need for cheap electricity.* **4.** to fill or occupy as a substitute, as a vacancy, a pulpit, etc.: *During the summer local clergymen will supply the pulpit.* *—v.i.* **5.** to fill the place of another, esp. the pulpit of a church, temporarily or as a substitute: *Who will supply until the new minister arrives?* *—n.* **6.** the act of supplying, furnishing, providing, satisfying, etc.: *to begin the supply of household help.* **7.** something that is supplied: *The storm cut off our water supply.* **8.** a quantity of something on hand or available, as for use; a stock or store: *Did you see our new supply of shirts?* **9.** Usually, **supplies.** a provision, stock, or store of food or other things necessary for maintenance: *to lay in supplies for the winter.* **10.** *Econ.* the quantity of a commodity that is in the market and available for purchase or that is available for purchase at a particular price. **11. supplies,** *Mil.* **a.** all items necessary for the equipment, maintenance, and operation of a military command, including food, clothing, arms, ammunition, fuel, materials, and machinery. **b.** procurement, distribution, maintenance, and salvage of supplies. **12.** a person who fills a vacancy or takes the place of another, esp. temporarily. **13. supplies.** *Obs.* reinforcements. **14.** *Obs.* aid. [1325–75; (v.) ME *sup(p)lien* < MF *souplier,* var. of *soupleer* << L *supplēre* to fill up, equiv. to *sup-* SUP- + *plēre* to fill (see FULL[1]); (n.) late ME: aid, succor, deriv. of the v.] **—sup·pli′er,** *n.*

sup·ply[2] (sup′lē), *adv.* in a supple manner or way; supplely. [1525–35; SUPPLE + -LY]

sup·ply-side (sə plī′sīd′), *adj. Econ.* of or pertaining to a theory that stresses the reduction of taxes, esp. for those of higher income, as a means of encouraging business investment and growth and stabilizing the economy. [1975–80]

sup·ply-sid·er (sə plī′sī′dər), *n.* a person, esp. an economist, who advocates supply-side economics. [1975–80; SUPPLY-SIDE + -ER[1]]

sup·port (sə pôrt′, -pōrt′), *v.t.* **1.** to bear or hold up (a load, mass, structure, part, etc.); serve as a foundation for. **2.** to sustain or withstand (weight, pressure, strain,

su′per·se·vere′, *adj.;* **-ly,** *adv.;* **-ness,** *n.*
su′per·se·ver′i·ty, *n.*
su′per·sex′u·al′i·ty, *n.*
su′per·sharp′, *adj.*
su′per·ship′ment, *n.*
su′per·show′, *n.*
su′per·sig·nif′i·cant, *adj.;* **-ly,** *adv.*
su′per·si′lent, *adj.;* **-ly,** *adv.*
su′per·sim·plic′i·ty, *n.*
su′per·sim′pli·fy′, *v.t.,* **-fied, -fy·ing.**
su′per·sin·cer′i·ty, *n.*
su′per·sin′gu·lar, *adj.*
su′per·size′, *n., adj.*
su′per·sized′, *adj.*
su′per·sleuth′, *n.*
su′per·slick′, *adj.*
su′per·smart′, *adj.;* **-ly,** *adv.;* **-ness,** *n.*
su′per·soft′, *adj.*
su′per·soil′, *n.*
su′per·so′lar, *adj.*
su′per·sol′emn, *adj.;* **-ly,** *adv.;* **-ness,** *n.*
su′per·so·lem′ni·ty, *n.*
su′per·so·lic′it, *v.*
su′per·so·lic′i·ta′tion, *n.*
su′per·so·phis′ti·cat′ed, *adj.*
su′per·sov′er·eign, *adj., n.*
su′per·sov′er·eign·ty, *n.*
su′per·spe′cial, *adj., n.*
su′per·spe′cial·i·za′tion, *n.*
su′per·spe′cial·ize′, *v.i.,* **-ized, -iz·ing.**
su′per·spe′cies, *n., pl.* **-cies.**
su′per·spec′i·fi·ca′tion, *n.*
su′per·spec′ta·cle, *n.*
su′per·sphe′noid, *adj.*
su′per·sphe·noi′dal, *adj.*
su′per·spir′it·u·al, *adj.;* **-ly,** *adv.*
su′per·spir′it·u·al′i·ty, *n.*
su′per·spy′, *n., pl.* **-spies.**
su′per·squa·mo′sal, *adj.*
su′per·stage′, *n.*
su′per·stamp′, *n., v.t.*
su′per·stand′ard, *n., adj.*
su′per·states′man, *n., pl.* **-men.**
su′per·stim′u·late′, *v.t.,* **-lat·ed, -lat·ing.**
su′per·stim·u·la′tion, *n.*
su′per·sto′i·cal, *adj.;* **-ly,** *adv.*
su′per·store′, *n.*
su′per·straight′, *adj.*
su′per·strain′, *n., v.t.*
su′per·strength′, *n.*
su′per·stren′u·ous, *adj.;* **-ly,** *adv.;* **-ness,** *n.*
su′per·strict′, *adj.;* **-ly,** *adv.;* **-ness,** *n.*
su′per·strong′, *adj.*
su′per·styl′ish, *adj.;* **-ly,** *adv.;* **-ness,** *n.*
su′per·sub′li·mat′ed, *adj.*
su′per·sub·sist′, *v.i.*
su′per·sub·stan′tial, *adj.;* **-ly,** *adv.*
su′per·sub′til·ized′, *adj.*
su′per·suf·fi′cien·cy, *n.*
su′per·suf·fi′cient, *adj.;* **-ly,** *adv.*
su′per·sul′fate, *n.*
su′per·sul′fu·ret′ed, *adj.*
su′per·sul′fu·rize′, *v.t.,* **-rized, -riz·ing.**
su′per·sul′phate, *n.*
su′per·sul′phu·ret′ed, *adj.*
su′per·sul′phu·rize′, *v.t.,* **-rized, -riz·ing.**
su′per·sur·prise′, *n.*
su′per·sus·pi′cion, *n.*
su′per·sus·pi′cious, *adj.;* **-ly,** *adv.;* **-ness,** *n.*
su′per·sweet′, *adj.;* **-ly,** *adv.;* **-ness,** *n.*
su′per·sym′pa·thet′ic, *adj.*
su′per·sym′pa·thy, *n., pl.* **-thies.**
su′per·syn′di·cate, *n.*
su′per·sys′tem, *n.*
su′per·tar′trate, *n.*
su′per·tech·nol′o·gy, *n., pl.* **-gies.**
su′per·tem′po·ral, *adj.*
su′per·tempt′, *v.t.*
su′per·temp·ta′tion, *n.*
su′per·ten′sion, *n.*
su′per·ter·res′tri·al, *adj.*
su′per·thank′ful, *adj.;* **-ly,** *adv.;* **-ness,** *n.*
su′per·thick′, *adj.*
su′per·thin′, *adj.*
su′per·thor′ough, *adj.;* **-ly,** *adv.;* **-ness,** *n.*
su′per·tol′er·a′tion, *n.*
su′per·to′tal, *n.*
su′per·tough′, *adj.*
su′per·tow′er, *n.*
su′per·trag′e·dy, *n., pl.* **-dies.**
su′per·trag′ic, *adj.*
su′per·trag′i·cal·ly, *adv.*
su′per·train′, *v.*
su′per·tran·scend′ent, *adj.;* **-ly,** *adv.;* **-ness,** *n.*
su′per·trea′son, *n.*
su′per·triv′i·al, *adj.*
su′per·tu′nic, *n.*
su′per·tu′te·lar′y, *adj.*
su′per·ug′ly, *adj.*
su′per·u′nit, *n.*
su′per·u′ni·ty, *n.*
su′per·u′ni·ver′sal, *adj.;* **-ly,** *adv.;* **-ness,** *n.*
su′per·u′ni·verse′, *n.*
su′per·ur′gen·cy, *n.*
su′per·ur′gent, *adj.;* **-ly,** *adv.*
su′per·val′ue, *n., v.t.,* **-ued, -u·ing.**
su′per·vast′, *adj.;* **-ly,** *adv.;* **-ness,** *n.*
su′per·ve·nos′i·ty, *n.*
su′per·vest′ment, *n.*
su′per·vex·a′tion, *n.*
su′per·vic·to′ri·ous, *adj.;* **-ly,** *adv.;* **-ness,** *n.*
su′per·vic′to·ry, *n., pl.* **-ries.**
su′per·vig′i·lance, *n.*
su′per·vig′i·lant, *adj.;* **-ly,** *adv.*
su′per·vig′or·ous, *adj.;* **-ly,** *adv.;* **-ness,** *n.*
su′per·vir′u·lent, *adj.;* **-ly,** *adv.*
su′per·vis′u·al, *adj.;* **-ly,** *adv.*
su′per·vi′tal, *adj.;* **-ly,** *adv.;* **-ness,** *n.*
su′per·vi·tal′i·ty, *n.*
su′per·vo·li′tion, *n.*
su′per·vo·lu′mi·nous, *adj.;* **-ly,** *adv.*
su′per·wa′ger, *n.*
su′per·wealth′y, *adj.*
su′per·weap′on, *n.*
su′per·wide′, *adj.*
su′per·wise′, *adj.*
su′per·world′li·ness, *n.*
su′per·world′ly, *adj.*
su′per·wrought′, *adj.*
su′per·yacht′, *n.*
su′per·zeal′ous, *adj.;* **-ly,** *adv.;* **-ness,** *n.*

etc.) without giving way; serve as a prop for. **3.** to undergo or endure, esp. with patience or submission; tolerate. **4.** to sustain (a person, the mind, spirits, courage, etc.) under trial or affliction: *They supported him through his ordeal.* **5.** to maintain (a person, family, establishment, institution, etc.) by supplying with things necessary to existence; provide for: *to support a family.* **6.** to uphold (a person, cause, policy, etc.) by aid, countenance, one's vote, etc.; back; second. **7.** to maintain or advocate (a theory, principle, etc.). **8.** to corroborate (a statement, opinion, etc.): *Leading doctors supported his testimony.* **9.** to act with or second (a lead performer): *The star was supported by a talented newcomer.* —*n.* **10.** the act or an instance of supporting. **11.** the state of being supported. **12.** something that serves as a foundation, prop, brace, or stay. **13.** maintenance, as of a person or family, with necessaries, means, or funds: *to pay for support of an orphan.* **14.** a person or thing that supports, as financially: *The pension was his only support.* **15.** a person or thing that gives aid or assistance. **16.** an actor, actress, or group performing with a lead performer. **17.** the material, as canvas or wood, on which a picture is painted. **18.** *Stock Exchange.* See **support level.** —*adj.* **19.** (of hosiery) made with elasticized fibers so as to fit snugly on the legs, thereby aiding circulation, relieving fatigue, etc. [1350–1400; (v.) ME *supporten* < MF *supporter* < ML *supportāre* to endure (L: to convey), equiv. to *sup-* SUP- + *portāre* to carry (see PORT[5]); (n.) ME, deriv. of the v.] —**sup·port′ing·ly,** *adv.*
—**Syn. 1, 6.** SUPPORT, MAINTAIN, SUSTAIN, UPHOLD all mean to hold up and to preserve. To SUPPORT is to hold up or add strength to, literally or figuratively: *The columns support the roof.* To MAINTAIN is to support so as to preserve intact: *to maintain an attitude of defiance.* To SUSTAIN, a rather elevated word, suggests completeness and adequacy in supporting: *The court sustained his claim.* UPHOLD applies esp. to supporting or backing another, as in a statement, opinion, or belief: *to uphold the rights of a minority.* **3.** suffer, bear, stand, stomach. **13.** sustenance, subsistence, keep. See **living.**

sup·port·a·ble (sə pôr′tə bəl, -pōr′-), *adj.* capable of being supported; endurable; maintainable. [1525–35; SUPPORT + -ABLE] —**sup·port′a·bil′i·ty,** *n.*

sup·port·er (sə pôr′tər, -pōr′-), *n.* **1.** a person or thing that supports. **2.** an adherent, follower, backer, or advocate. **3.** a device, usually of elastic cotton webbing, for supporting some part of the body, esp. a jockstrap. **4.** a garter, esp. one attached to a garter belt or girdle. **5.** *Heraldry.* either of two human or animal figures flanking and supporting an escutcheon in an achievement of arms. [1400–50; late ME; see SUPPORT, -ER[1]]

support′ group′, a group of people who meet regularly to support or sustain each other by discussing problems affecting them in common, as alcoholism or bereavement. [1985–90]

sup·port·ive (sə pôr′tiv, -pōr′-), *adj.* **1.** giving support. **2.** providing sympathy or encouragement: *His family was supportive of his attempts to be a writer.* **3.** providing additional help, information, etc.; auxiliary: *manufacturers of supportive materials.* **4.** *Med.* helping to maintain a normal physiological balance, as by the intravenous administration of required nutriment. [1585–95; SUPPORT + -IVE] —**sup·port′ive·ness,** *n.*

support′ive psychother′apy, a type of psychotherapy that seeks to reduce psychological conflict and strengthen a patient's defenses through the use of various techniques, as reassurance, suggestion, counseling, and reeducation. [1960–65]

support′ lev′el, *Stock Exchange.* a minimum price below which a specific stock is not supposed to fall, as because of the stock's inherent worth. Also called **support, support′ ar′ea, support′ zone′.** Cf. **resistance level.** [1950–55]

support′ mis′sion, assistance given by one military unit to another in the accomplishment of a mission.

support′ price′, the price at which the government will purchase commodities, esp. farm produce, in order to maintain a certain price level. [1940–45]

support′ sys′tem, people who provide support: *a family support system to help a troubled youth.*

sup·pos·al (sə pō′zəl), *n.* **1.** the act of supposing. **2.** something that is supposed; conjecture or notion. [1350–1400; ME < MF *supposaille.* See SUPPOSE, -AL[2]]

sup·pose (sə pōz′), *v.,* **-posed, -pos·ing.** —*v.t.* **1.** to assume (something), as for the sake of argument or as part of a proposition or theory: *Suppose the distance to be one mile.* **2.** to consider (something) as a possibility suggested or an idea or plan proposed: *Suppose we wait until tomorrow.* **3.** to believe or assume as true; take for granted: *It is supposed that his death was an accident.* **4.** to think or hold as an opinion: *What do you suppose he will do?* **5.** to require logically; imply; presuppose: *The evidence supposes his presence near the scene.* **6.** (used in the passive) to expect or design; require or permit (fol. by an infinitive verb): *I'm not supposed to run fast.* —*v.i.* **7.** to assume something; presume; think. [1275–1325; ME *supposen* < OF *supposer,* equiv. to *sup-* SUP- + *poser* to POSE[1]; cf. ML *suppōnere* to suppose, L: to substitute, place below] —**sup·pos′a·ble,** *adj.* —**sup·pos′a·bly,** *adv.* —**sup·pos′er,** *n.*

sup·posed (sə pōzd′, -pō′zid), *adj.* **1.** assumed as true, regardless of fact; hypothetical: *a supposed case.* **2.** accepted or believed as true, without positive knowledge: *the supposed site of an ancient temple.* **3.** merely thought to be such; imagined: *supposed gains.* [1560–70; SUPPOSE + -ED[2]] —**sup·pos·ed·ly** (sə pō′zid lē), *adv.*

sup·pos·ing (sə pō′zing), *conj.* upon the supposition that; in the event that. [1835–45; see SUPPOSE, -ING[2]]

sup·po·si·tion (sup′ə zish′ən), *n.* **1.** the act of supposing. **2.** something that is supposed; assumption; hypothesis. [1400–50; late ME < L *suppositiōn-* (s. of *suppositiō*) substitution (E meaning by assoc. with SUPPOSE), equiv. to *supposit(us)* (ptp. of *suppōnere* to substitute) + *-iōn-* -ION. See SUP-, POSITION] —**sup′po·si′tion·al,** *adj.* —**sup′po·si′tion·al·ly,** *adv.*

sup·po·si·tious (sup′ə zish′əs), *adj.* **1.** formed from or growing out of supposition: *suppositious evidence.* **2.** supposititious. [1615–25; shortened form of SUPPOSITITIOUS]

sup·pos·i·ti·tious (sə poz′i tish′əs), *adj.* **1.** fraudulently substituted or pretended; spurious; not genuine. **2.** hypothetical. [1605–15; < L *suppositīcius,* equiv. to *supposit(us)* (ptp. of *suppōnere;* see SUPPOSITION) + *-īcius* -ITIOUS] —**sup·pos′i·ti′tious·ly,** *adv.* —**sup·pos′i·ti′tious·ness,** *n.*

sup·pos·i·tive (sə poz′i tiv), *adj.* **1.** of the nature of or involving supposition; suppositional. **2.** supposititious or false. **3.** *Gram.* expressing or noting supposition, as the words *if, granting,* or *provided.* —*n.* **4.** *Gram.* a suppositive word. [1595–1605; < LL *suppositīvus,* equiv. to *supposit(us)* (see SUPPOSITION) + *-īvus* -IVE] —**sup·pos′i·tive·ly,** *adv.*

sup·pos·i·to·ry (sə poz′i tôr′ē, -tōr′ē), *n., pl.* **-ries.** a solid, conical mass of medicinal substance that melts upon insertion into the rectum or vagina. [1350–1400; ME < ML *suppositōrium,* equiv. to *supposi-,* var. s. of *suppōnere* (see SUPPOSE) + *-tōrium* -TORY[1]]

sup·press (sə pres′), *v.t.* **1.** to put an end to the activities of (a person, body of persons, etc.): *to suppress the Communist party.* **2.** to do away with by or as by authority; abolish; stop (a practice, custom, etc.). **3.** to keep in or repress (a feeling, smile, groan, etc.). **4.** to withhold from disclosure or publication (truth, evidence, a book, names, etc.). **5.** to stop or arrest (a flow, hemorrhage, cough, etc.). **6.** to vanquish or subdue (a revolt, rebellion, etc.); quell; crush. **7.** *Elect.* to reduce or eliminate (an irregular or undesired oscillation or frequency) in a circuit. [1375–1425; late ME *suppressen* < L *suppressus* (ptp. of *supprimere* to press down), equiv. to *sup-* SUP- + *pressus* (see PRESS[1])] —**sup·press·ed·ly** (sə prest′lē, -pres′id-), *adv.* —**sup·press′i·ble,** *adj.* —**sup·pres′sive,** *adj.* —**sup·pres′sive·ly,** *adv.* —**sup·pres′sor, sup·press′er,** *n.*

sup·pres·sant (sə pres′ənt), *n.* a substance that suppresses an undesirable action or condition: *an appetite suppressant.* [1940–45; SUPRESS + -ANT]

sup·pres·sion (sə presh′ən), *n.* **1.** the act of suppressing. **2.** the state of being suppressed. **3.** *Psychoanal.* conscious inhibition of an impulse. **4.** *Bot.* the absence of parts normally or usually present due to the action of frost, disease, or insects. **5.** *Radio, Electronics.* the elimination of a component of a varying emission, as the elimination of a frequency or group of frequencies from a signal. **6.** *Elect.* the reduction or elimination of irregular current oscillations or frequencies in a circuit. [1520–30; < L *suppressiōn-* (s. of *suppressiō*) a pressing under. See SUPPRESS, -ION]

suppressor T cell, *Immunol.* a T cell capable of inhibiting the activity of B cells and other T cells. Also called **T suppressor cell.**

Supp. Rev. Stat., Supplement to the Revised Statutes.

sup·pu·rate (sup′yə rāt′), *v.i.,* **-rat·ed, -rat·ing.** to produce or discharge pus, as a wound; maturate. [1555–65; < L *suppūrātus* (ptp. of *suppūrāre*), equiv. to *sup-* SUP- + *pūr-* (s. of *pūs*) PUS + *-ātus* -ATE[1]]

sup·pu·ra·tion (sup′yə rā′shən), *n.* **1.** the process of suppurating. **2.** the matter produced by suppuration; pus. [1535–45; < L *suppūrātiōn-* (s. of *suppūrātiō*) a forming of pus. See SUPPURATE, -ION]

sup·pu·ra·tive (sup′yə rā′tiv), *adj.* **1.** suppurating; characterized by suppuration. **2.** promoting suppuration. —*n.* **3.** a medicine or application that promotes suppuration. [1535–45; < ML *suppūrātīvus.* See SUPPURATE, -IVE]

supr., **1.** superior. **2.** supreme.

su·pra (so͞o′prə), *adv.* above, esp. when used in referring to parts of a text. Cf. **infra.** [1400–50; late ME < L *suprā* (prep.) on top of, above, exceeding, (adv.) on top, higher up; akin to SUPER-]

supra-, a prefix meaning "above, over" (*supraorbital*) or "beyond the limits of, outside of" (*supramolecular; suprasegmental*). Cf. **super-.** [see SUPRA]

su·pra·lap·sar·i·an·ism (so͞o′prə lap sâr′ē ə niz′əm), *n. Theol.* the doctrine that the decree of election preceded human creation and the Fall (opposed to *infralapsarianism*). [1765–75; SUPRA- + *lapsarian,* as in INFRALAPSARIAN + -ISM] —**su′pra·lap·sar′i·an,** *n., adj.*

su·pra·lim·i·nal (so͞o′prə lim′ə nl), *adj. Psychol.* being above the threshold of perception of a stimulus. [1890–95; SUPRA- + LIMINAL] —**su′pra·lim′i·nal·ly,** *adv.*

su·pra·lit·to·ral (so͞o′prə lit′ər əl), *adj.* **1.** of or pertaining to the biogeographic region of a shore of a lake, sea, or ocean permanently above water but made damp by spray from waves or by capillarity of the substrate. —*n.* **2.** a supralittoral zone or region. [1905–10; SUPRA- + LITTORAL]

su·pra·mo·lec·u·lar (so͞o′prə mə lek′yə lər), *adj.* **1.** having an organization more complex than that of a molecule. **2.** composed of an aggregate of molecules. [1905–10; SUPRA- + MOLECULAR]

su·pra·na·tion·al (so͞o′prə nash′ə nl), *adj.* outside or beyond the authority of one national government, as a project or policy that is planned and controlled by a group of nations. [1905–10; SUPRA- + NATIONAL] —**su′pra·na′tion·al·ism,** *n.* —**su′pra·na′tion·al′i·ty,** *n.*

su·pra·nat·u·ral (so͞o′prə nach′ər əl, -nach′rəl), *adj.* beyond what is natural; supernatural. [1855–60; SUPRA- + NATURAL] —**su′pra·nat′u·ral·ism,** *n.* —**su′pra·nat′u·ral·ist,** *n., adj.* —**su′pra·nat′u·ral·is′tic,** *adj.*

su·pra·or·bit·al (so͞o′prə ôr′bi tl), *adj.* situated above the eye socket. [1820–30; < NL *suprāorbitālis* equiv. to L *suprā-* SUPRA- + *orbit(a)* ORBIT + *-ālis* -AL[1]]

su′praor′bital ridge′, *Anat.* browridge. [1835–45]

su·pra·pro·test (so͞o′prə prō′test), *n. Law.* an acceptance or a payment of a bill by a third person after protest for nonacceptance or nonpayment by the drawee. [1855–60; part Latinization, part trans. of It *sopra protesto* upon protest]

su·pra·ra·tion·al (so͞o′prə rash′ə nl), *adj.* not understandable by reason alone; beyond rational comprehension. [1815–25; SUPRA- + RATIONAL]

su·pra·re·nal (so͞o′prə rēn′l), *Anat.* —*adj.* **1.** situated above or on the kidney. —*n.* **2.** a suprarenal part, esp. the adrenal gland. [1820–30; < NL *suprārēnālis.* See SUPRA-, RENAL]

suprare′nal gland′. See **adrenal gland.** [1875–80]

su·pra·seg·men·tal (so͞o′prə seg men′tl), *adj.* **1.** above, beyond, or in addition to a segment. **2.** *Ling.* pertaining to or noting features of speech, as stress, pitch, and length, that accompany individual consonants and vowels and may extend over more than one such segmental element; pertaining to junctural and prosodic features. —*n.* **3.** a suprasegmental feature. [1940–45; SUPRA- + SEGMENTAL]

su·pra·tem·po·ral (so͞o′prə tem′pər əl), *adj. Anat.* situated above the upper part of the temporal bone or region. [1840–50; SUPRA- + TEMPORAL[2]]

su·pra·vi·tal (so͞o′prə vīt′l), *adj. Histol.* pertaining to or involving a staining method for a preparation of living cells. [1915–20; SUPRA- + VITAL]

su·prem·a·cist (sə prem′ə sist, so͝o-), *n.* a person who believes in or advocates the supremacy of a particular group, esp. a racial group: *a white supremacist.* [1945–50; SUPREMAC(Y) + -IST]

su·prem·a·cy (sə prem′ə sē, so͝o-), *n.* **1.** the state of being supreme. **2.** supreme authority or power. [1540–50; SUPREME[1] + -ACY]

su·prem·a·tism (sə prem′ə tiz′əm, so͝o-), *n.* (*sometimes cap.*) *Fine Arts.* a nonrepresentational style of art developed in Russia in the early 20th century, characterized by severely simple geometric shapes or forms and an extremely limited palette. [< Russ *suprematízm* (1913) < F *suprémat(ie)* SUPREMACY + Russ *-izm* -ISM]

su·preme[1] (sə prēm′, so͝o-), *adj.* **1.** highest in rank or authority; paramount; sovereign; chief. **2.** of the highest quality, degree, character, importance, etc.: *supreme courage.* **3.** greatest, utmost, or extreme: *supreme disgust.* **4.** last or final; ultimate. [1510–20; < L *suprēmus,* superl. of *superus* upper, adj. deriv. of *super* (see SUPER-)] —**su·preme′ly,** *adv.* —**su·preme′ness,** *n.*

su·preme[2] (sə prēm′, -prām′, so͝o-), *n.* suprême (def. 3).

su·prême (sə prēm′, -prām′, so͝o-; *Fr.* SY PREM′), *n.* **1.** Also called **sauce suprême.** a velouté made with a rich chicken stock. **2.** a dish prepared or served with this sauce, esp. boned chicken breast. **3.** Also, **supreme. a.** a bowl or the like designed for the serving of cold foods in an inner container that is nestled in cracked ice. **b.** a dessert or appetizer served in such a container. [< F < L *suprēmus* SUPREME[1]]

Supreme′ Be′ing, God. [1690–1700]

supreme′ command′er, the military officer commanding all allied forces in a theater of war. [1940–45]

Supreme′ Coun′cil. See **Supreme Soviet.**

Supreme′ Court′, **1.** the highest court of the U.S. **2.** (in many states) the highest court of the state. **3.** (*l.c.*) (in some states) a court of general jurisdiction subordinate to an appeals court. Also called **High Court** (for defs. 1, 2).

CHIEF JUSTICES OF THE UNITED STATES SUPREME COURT

Name	Born	Died	Term
John Jay	1745	1829	1789–1795
John Rutledge	1739	1800	1795
Oliver Ellsworth	1745	1807	1796–1800
John Marshall	1755	1835	1801–1835
Roger B. Taney	1777	1864	1836–1864
Salmon P. Chase	1808	1873	1864–1873
Morrison R. Waite	1816	1888	1874–1888
Melville W. Fuller	1833	1910	1888–1910
Edward D. White	1845	1921	1910–1921
William H. Taft	1857	1930	1921–1930
Charles E. Hughes	1862	1948	1930–1941
Harlan F. Stone	1872	1946	1941–1946
Frederick M. Vinson	1890	1953	1946–1953
Earl Warren	1891	1974	1953–1969
Warren E. Burger	1907		1969–1986
William H. Rehnquist	1924		1986–

Supreme′ Court′ of Ju′dicature, an English court formed in 1873 from several superior courts and consisting of a court of original jurisdiction **(High Court of Justice)** and an appellate court **(Court of Appeal).**

supreme′ judi′cial court′, (*often caps.*) the highest court in some states, as Massachusetts and Maine.

supreme′ sac′rifice, the sacrifice of one's own life: *Many made the supreme sacrifice during the war.*

Supreme′ So′viet, (formerly) the legislature of the Soviet Union, consisting of an upper house **(Soviet of the Union** or **Council of the Union),** whose delegates are elected on the basis of population, and a lower house **(Soviet of Nationalities** or **Council of Nationalities),** whose delegates are elected to represent the various nationalities. Also called **Supreme Council.** [trans. of Russ *Vérkhniĭ sovét*]

CONCISE PRONUNCIATION KEY: act, cāpe, dâre, pärt; set, ēqual; if, īce; ox, ōver, ôrder, oil, bo͝ok, bo͞ot, out; up, ûrge; child; sing; shoe; thin, *th*at; zh as in *treasure.* ə = *a* as in *alone, e* as in *system, i* as in *easily, o* as in *gallop, u* as in *circus;* ᵊ as in *fire* (fīᵊr), *hour* (ouᵊr). l and n can serve as syllabic consonants, as in *cradle* (krād′l), and *button* (but′n). See the full key inside the front cover.

su·pre·mo (sə prē′mō, so͝o-), *n., pl.* **-mos.** *Chiefly Brit. Informal.* **1.** the person in charge; chief. **2.** a person of supreme or complete power, authority, ability, etc.: *His victory makes him the new chess supremo.* [1935–40; < Sp or It *supremo,* both < L *suprēmus* SUPREME[1]; E sense perh. esp. < Sp *El Supremo* as the title of Latin-American dictators, e.g., J. G. Rodríguez Francia (1766–1840), Paraguayan dictator]

su·pre·mum (sə prē′məm, so͝o-), *n. Math.* See **least upper bound.** Also called **sup.** [< NL *suprēmum,* n. use of neut. of L *suprēmus* SUPREME[1]]

Supt., superintendent. Also, **supt.**

supvr., supervisor.

suq (so͞ok, sho͞ok), *n.* suk.

Su·qua·mish (sə kwom′ish, -kwô′mish), *n., pl.* **-mish·es,** (*esp. collectively*) **-mish.** a member of a Salishan-speaking North American Indian people of Washington, near Puget Sound.

sur (sûr), *prep. Law.* upon; on the basis of: *sur mortgage.* [< F < L *super* SUPER-]

Sur (so͝or), *n.* a town in S Lebanon, on the Mediterranean Sea: site of ancient port of Tyre.

sur-[1], a prefix meaning "over, above," "in addition," occurring mainly in loanwords from French and partial calques of French words: *surcharge; surname; surrender; survive.* Cf. **super-.** [ME < OF < L *super-* SUPER-]

sur-[2], var. of **sub-** before *r: surrogate.*

su·ra (so͝or′ə), *n. Islam.* any of the 114 chapters of the Koran. Also, **surah.** [1655–65; < Ar *sūrah* lit., row, step, rung]

Su·ra·ba·ya (so͝or′ə bä′yə), *n.* a seaport on NE Java: second largest city in Indonesia; naval base. 1,556,255. Also, **Su′ra·ba′ja.** Dutch, **Soerabaja.**

su·rah[1] (so͝or′ə), *n.* a soft, twilled silk or rayon fabric. [1880–85; appar. var. of SURAT]

su·rah[2] (so͝or′ə), *n. Islam.* sura.

Su·ra·jah Dow·lah (sə rä′jə dou′lə), Siraj-ud-daula.

Su·ra·kar·ta (so͝or′ə kär′tə), *n.* a city on central Java, in central Indonesia. 414,285. Formerly, **Solo.**

su·ral (so͝or′əl), *adj. Anat.* of or pertaining to the calf of the leg. [1605–15; < NL *sūrālis,* equiv. to L *sūr(a)* calf of the leg + *-ālis* -AL[1]]

Su·rat (so͝o rat′, so͝or′ət), *n.* a seaport in S Gujarat, in W India: first British settlement in India 1612. 471,815.

sur·base (sûr′bās′), *n. Archit.* a molding above a base, as that immediately above a baseboard, the crowning molding of a pedestal, etc. [1670–80; SUR-[1] + BASE[1]]

sur·based (sûr′bāst′), *adj. Archit.* **1.** having a surbase. **2.** depressed; flattened. **3.** (of an arch) having a rise of less than half the span. [1755–65; SUR-[1] + (A)BASED lowered; modeled on F *surbaissé,* equiv. to *sur-* (intensive) + *baissé* lowered]

sur′based arch′. See **drop arch** (def. 2). [1755–65]

sur·cease (sûr sēs′), *v.,* **-ceased, -ceas·ing.** *n.* —*v.i.* **1.** to cease from some action; desist. **2.** to come to an end. —*v.t.* **3.** *Archaic* to cease from; leave off. —*n.* **4.** cessation; end. [1400–50; SUR-[1] + CEASE; r. late ME *sursesen* (v.) < MF *sursis* (ptp. of *surseoir*) < L *supersessus* (ptp. of *supersedēre* to forbear; see SUPERSEDE), equiv. to *super-* SUPER- + *sed(ēre)* SIT[1] + *-tus* ptp. suffix, with *dt > ss*]

sur·charge (*n.* sûr′chärj′; *v.* sûr chärj′, sûr′chärj′), *n., v.,* **-charged, -charg·ing.** —*n.* **1.** an additional charge, tax, or cost. **2.** an excessive sum or price charged. **3.** an additional or excessive load or burden. **4.** *Philately.* **a.** an overprint that alters or restates the face value or denomination of a stamp to which it has been applied. **b.** a stamp bearing such an overprint. **5.** act of surcharging. —*v.t.* **6.** to subject to an additional or extra charge, tax, cost, etc. (for payment). **7.** to overcharge for goods. **8.** to show an omission in (an account) of something that operates as a charge against the accounting party; to omit a credit toward (an account). **9.** *Philately.* to print a surcharge on (a stamp). **10.** to put an additional or excessive burden upon. [1400–50; late ME *surchargen* (v.) < OF *surcharger.* See SUR-[1], CHARGE] —**sur·charg′er,** *n.*

sur·cin·gle (sûr′sing′gəl), *n.* **1.** a belt or girth that passes around the belly of a horse and over the blanket, pack, saddle, etc., and is buckled on the horse's back. **2.** a beltlike fastening for a garment, esp. a cassock. [1350–1400; ME *surcengle* < MF, equiv. to *sur-* SUR-[1] + *cengle* belt < L *cingulum;* see CINGULUM]

sur·coat (sûr′kōt′), *n.* **1.** a garment worn over medieval armor, often embroidered with heraldic arms. **2.** an outer coat or other outer garment. [1300–50; ME *surcote* < MF. See SUR-[1], COAT]

surcoat (def. 1) (13th century)

CONCISE ETYMOLOGY KEY: <, descended or borrowed from; >, whence; b., blend of, blended; c., cognate with; cf., compare; deriv., derivative; equiv., equivalent; imit., imitative; obl., oblique; r., replacing; s., stem; sp., spelling, spelled; resp., respelling, respelled; trans., translation; ?, origin unknown; *, unattested; ‡, probably earlier than. See the full key inside the front cover.

sur·cu·lose (sûr′kyə lōs′), *adj. Bot.* producing suckers. [1835–45; < L *surculōsus* twiggy, equiv. to *surcul(us)* shoot, twig + *-ōsus* -OSE[1]]

surd (sûrd), *adj.* **1.** *Phonet.* voiceless (opposed to *sonant*). **2.** *Math.* (of a quantity) not capable of being expressed in rational numbers; irrational. —*n.* **3.** *Phonet.* a voiceless consonant (opposed to *sonant*). **4.** *Math.* a surd quantity. [1545–55; < L *surdus* dull-sounding, mute, deaf]

sure (sho͝or, shûr), *adj.,* **sur·er, sur·est,** *adv.* —*adj.* **1.** free from doubt as to the reliability, character, action, etc., of something: *to be sure of one's data.* **2.** confident, as of something expected: *sure of success.* **3.** convinced, fully persuaded, or positive: *to be sure of a person's guilt.* **4.** assured or certain beyond question: *a sure victory.* **5.** worthy of confidence; reliable; stable: *a sure messenger.* **6.** unfailing; never disappointing expectations: *a sure cure.* **7.** unerring; never missing, slipping, etc.: *a sure aim.* **8.** admitting of no doubt or question: *sure proof.* **9.** destined; bound inevitably; certain: *sure death.* **10.** *Obs.* secure; safe. **11. be sure,** to take care (to be or do as specified); be certain: *Be sure to close the windows.* **12. for sure,** as a certainty; surely: *It's going to be a good day, for sure.* **13. make sure,** to be or become absolutely certain: *I'm calling to make sure that you remember to come.* **14. sure enough,** *Informal.* as might have been supposed; actually; certainly: *Sure enough, the picnic was rained out.* **15. to be sure, a.** without doubt; surely; certainly. **b.** admittedly: *She sings well, to be sure, but she can't act.* —*adv.* **16.** *Informal.* certainly; surely: *It sure is cold out. Sure, I'll come.* [1300–50; ME *sur(e)* < MF *sur,* OF *seur* < L *sēcūrus* SECURE] —**sure′ness,** *n.*

—**Syn. 1.** SURE, CERTAIN, CONFIDENT, POSITIVE indicate full belief and trust that something is true. SURE, CERTAIN, and POSITIVE are often used interchangeably. SURE, the simplest and most general, expresses mere absence of doubt. CERTAIN suggests that there are definite reasons that have freed one from doubt. CONFIDENT emphasizes the strength of the belief or the certainty of expectation felt. POSITIVE implies emphatic certainty, which may even become overconfidence or dogmatism.

—**Usage.** Both SURE and SURELY are used as intensifying adverbs with the sense "undoubtedly, certainly." In this use, SURE is generally informal and occurs mainly in speech and written representations of speech: *She sure dazzled the audience with her acceptance speech. It was sure hot enough in the auditorium.* SURELY is used in this sense in all varieties of speech and writing, even the most formal: *The court ruled that the law was surely meant to apply to both profit-making and nonprofit organizations.* See also **quick, slow.**

sure-e·nough (sho͝or′i nuf′, shûr′-), *adj. Older Use.* real; genuine. [1535–45]

sure-fire (sho͝or′fīᵊr′, shûr′-), *adj.* sure to work; foolproof: *a surefire moneymaking scheme.* [1915–20; SURE + FIRE]

sure-foot·ed (sho͝or′fo͝ot′id, shûr′-), *adj.* **1.** not likely to stumble, slip, or fall. **2.** proceeding surely; unerring: *his surefooted pursuit of success.* [1625–35; SURE + FOOT + -ED[3]] —**sure′-foot′ed·ly,** *adv.* —**sure′-foot′ed·ness,** *n.*

sure-hand·ed (sho͝or′han′did, shûr′-), *adj.* **1.** using the hands with skill and confidence; dexterous. **2.** done with skill and proficiency: *a sure-handed sketch of a proposed building.* **3.** displaying the skill and experience of an expert: *a sure-handed politician.* [1945–50] —**sure′-hand′ed·ly,** *adv.* —**sure′-hand′ed·ness,** *n.*

sure·ly (sho͝or′lē, shûr′-), *adv.* **1.** firmly; unerringly; without missing, slipping, etc. **2.** undoubtedly, assuredly, or certainly: *The results are surely encouraging.* **3.** (in emphatic utterances that are not necessarily sustained by fact) assuredly: *Surely you are mistaken.* **4.** inevitably or without fail: *Slowly but surely the end approached.* **5.** yes, indeed: *Surely, I'll go with you!* [1300–50; ME *surliche.* See SURE, -LY]

—**Usage. 2.** See **sure.**

Sûre·té (SYR tā′), *n.* **la** (lä), the criminal investigation department of the French government.

sure′ thing′, 1. something that is or is supposed to be a certain success, as a bet or a business venture: *He thinks that real estate is a sure thing.* **2.** something assured; certainty: *It's a sure thing that he'll refuse to cooperate.* **3.** surely; for sure; O.K.; roger (often used as an interjection). [1830–40, *Amer.*]

sur·e·ty (sho͝or′i tē, sho͝or′tē, shûr′i tē, shûr′tē), *n., pl.* **-ties. 1.** security against loss or damage or for the fulfillment of an obligation, the payment of a debt, etc.; a pledge, guaranty, or bond. **2.** a person who has made himself or herself responsible for another, as a sponsor, godparent, or bondsman. **3.** the state or quality of being sure. **4.** certainty. **5.** something that makes sure; ground of confidence or safety. **6.** a person who is legally responsible for the debt, default, or delinquency of another. **7.** assurance, esp. self-assurance. [1300–50; ME *surte* < MF; OF *seurte* < L *sēcūritāt-,* s. of *sēcūritās* SECURITY]

sur·e·ty·ship (sho͝or′i tē ship′, sho͝or′tē-, shûr′i tē-, shûr′tē-), *n. Law.* the relationship between the surety, the principal debtor, and the creditor. [1525–35; SURETY + -SHIP]

surf (sûrf), *n.* **1.** the swell of the sea that breaks upon a shore or upon shoals. **2.** the mass or line of foamy water caused by the breaking of the sea upon a shore, esp. a shallow or sloping shore. —*v.i.* **3.** to ride a surfboard. **4.** to float on the crest of a wave toward shore. **5.** to swim, play, or bathe in the surf. —*v.t.* **6.** to ride a surfboard on: *We surfed every big wave in sight.* [1675–85; earlier *suff;* of uncert. orig.] —**surf′a·ble,** *adj.*—**surf′er,** *n.* —**surf′like′,** *adj.*

—**Syn. 1.** See **wave.**

sur·face (sûr′fis), *n., adj., v.,* **-faced, -fac·ing.** —*n.* **1.** the outer face, outside, or exterior boundary of a thing; outermost or uppermost layer or area. **2.** any face of a body or thing: *the six surfaces of a cube.* **3.** extent or area of outer face; superficial area. **4.** the outward appearance, esp. as distinguished from the inner nature: *to look below the surface of a matter.* **5.** *Geom.* any figure having only two dimensions; part or all of the boundary of a solid. **6.** land or sea transportation, rather than air, underground, or undersea transportation. **7.** *Aeron.* an airfoil. —*adj.* **8.** of, on, or pertaining to the surface; external. **9.** apparent rather than real; superficial: *to be guilty of surface judgments.* **10.** of, pertaining to, or via land or sea: *surface mail.* **11.** *Ling.* belonging to a late stage in the transformational derivation of a sentence; belonging to the surface structure. —*v.t.* **12.** to finish the surface of; give a particular kind of surface to; make even or smooth. **13.** to bring to the surface; cause to appear openly: *Depth charges surfaced the sub. So far we've surfaced no applicants.* —*v.i.* **14.** to rise to the surface: *The submarine surfaced after four days.* **15.** to work on or at the surface. [1605–15; < F, equiv. to *sur-* SUR-[1] + *face* FACE, appar. modeled on L *superficies* SUPERFICIES] —**sur′face·less,** *adj.* —**sur′fac·er,** *n.*

sur·face-ac·tive a′gent (sûr′fis ak′tiv), *Chem.* any substance that when dissolved in water or an aqueous solution reduces its surface tension or the interfacial tension between it and another liquid. Also called **surfactant.**

sur′face bound′ary lay′er, *Meteorol.* the thin layer of air adjacent to the earth's surface, usually considered to be less than 300 ft. (91 m) high. Also called **sur′face lay′er, atmospheric boundary layer, friction layer, ground layer.**

sur′face condens′er, a device condensing steam or vapor by passing it over a cool surface. [1860–65]

sur′face den′sity, *Physics.* quantity, as of electric charge, per unit surface area.

sur′face effect′ ship′, a large, ship-size air cushion vehicle operated over water. [1940–45]

sur′face effect′ ve′hicle. See **ACV** (def. 2).

sur′face in′tegral, *Math.* the limit, as the norm of the partition of a given surface into sections of area approaches zero, of the sum of the product of the areas times the value of a given function of three variables at some point on each section. [1870–75]

sur′face noise′, *Audio.* extraneous noise caused by physical wear or a physical flaw on a phonograph record or in a pickup system, rather than by a flaw in the equipment. [1930–35]

sur′face of light′ and shade′, (in architectural shades and shadows) a surface in a plane tangent to the parallel rays from the theoretical light source, treated as a shade surface. Also called **light and shade surface.**

sur′face of projec′tion, the surface upon which an image or a set of points is projected.

sur′face of revolu′tion, *Math.* a surface formed by revolving a plane curve about a given line. [1830–40]

sur′face plate′, *Mach.* a flat plate used by machinists for testing surfaces that are to be made perfectly flat. Also called **planometer.** [1840–50]

sur·face-print·ing (sûr′fis prin′ting), *n.* planography. [1830–40]

sur·face-rip·ened (sûr′fis rī′pənd), *adj.* (of cheese) ripened on the surface by molds or other microorganisms. [1940–45]

sur′face road′, a road or street level with its surroundings: *surface roads and elevated highways.* [1900–05, *Amer.*]

sur′face struc′ture, *Ling.* (in transformational-generative grammar) **1.** a structural representation of the final syntactic form of a sentence, as it exists after the transformational component has modified a deep structure. Cf. **deep structure. 2.** the string of words that is actually produced. [1960–65]

sur′face ten′sion, *Physics.* the elasticlike force existing in the surface of a body, esp. a liquid, tending to minimize the area of the surface, caused by asymmetries in the intermolecular forces between surface molecules. [1875–80]

sur·face-to-air (sûr′fis to͞o âr′), *adj.* **1.** (of a missile, message, etc.) capable of traveling from the surface of the earth to a target in the atmosphere. —*adv.* **2.** from the surface of the earth to a target in the atmosphere: *an antimissile missile fired surface-to-air.* [1945–50]

sur·face-to-sur·face (sûr′fis tə sûr′fis), *adj.* **1.** (of a missile, message, etc.) capable of traveling from a base on the surface of the earth to a target also on the surface. —*adv.* **2.** from a base on the surface of the earth to a target on the surface.

sur·face-to-un·der·wa·ter (sûr′fis to͞o un′dər wô′tər, -wot′ər), *adj.* **1.** (of a missile, message, etc.) traveling from the surface of the earth to a target underwater. —*adv.* **2.** from the surface of the earth to a target underwater.

sur′face wave′, *Geol.* a seismic wave that travels along or parallel to the earth's surface (distinguished from *body wave*).

sur′face yeast′. See **top yeast.**

sur·fac·ing (sûr′fə sing), *n.* **1.** the action or process of giving a finished surface to something. **2.** the material with which something is surfaced. **3.** the act or an instance of rising to the surface of a body of water. [1855–60; SURFACE + -ING[1]]

sur·fac·tant (sər fak′tənt), *n. Chem.* See **surface-active agent.** [1945–50; shortening of *surf(ace)-act(ive) a(ge)nt*]

surf′ and turf′, a steak served with seafood or fish, esp. filet mignon and lobster. Also, **surf-'n'-turf.**

surf·bird (sûrf′bûrd′), *n.* a sandpiperlike shorebird, *Aphriza virgata,* of the Pacific coast, breeding in Alaska and wintering in South America. [1830–40, *Amer.*; SURF + BIRD]

surf·board (sûrf′bôrd′, -bōrd′), *n.* **1.** a long, narrow board on which a person stands or lies prone in surfboarding. See illus. on next page. —*v.i.* **2.** to ride a surfboard. [1820–30; SURF + BOARD]

surfboard (def. 1)

surf•board•ing (sûrf′bôr′ding, -bōr′-), *n.* a sport in which a person stands or lies prone on a surfboard and rides the crest of a breaking wave toward the shore; surfing. [SURFBOARD + -ING[1]] **—surf′board′er,** *n.*

surf′ boat′, a strong, buoyant rowboat with high ends, adapted for beaching and passing through surf. [1855–60; SURF + BOAT]

surf′ cast′ing, *Angling.* the act, technique, or sport of fishing by casting from the shoreline into the sea, usually using heavy-duty tackle. [1930–35] **—surf′ cast′er.**

surf′ clam′, any of several typically large common clams of the family Mactridae, inhabiting the zone of breaking surf in coastal waters. [1880–90; *Amer.*]

surf′ duck′, a scoter, esp. the surf scoter. [1800–10]

sur•feit (sûr′fit), *n.* **1.** excess; an excessive amount: *a surfeit of speechmaking.* **2.** excess or overindulgence in eating or drinking. **3.** an uncomfortably full or crapulous feeling due to excessive eating or drinking. **4.** general disgust caused by excess or satiety. *—v.t.* **5.** to bring to a state of surfeit by excess of food or drink. **6.** to supply with anything to excess or satiety; satiate. *—v.i.* **7.** to eat or drink to excess. **8.** to suffer from the effects of overindulgence in eating or drinking. **9.** to indulge to excess in anything. [1250–1300; (n.) ME *sorfete, surfait* < MF *surfait, surfet* (n. use of ptp. of *surfaire* to overdo), equiv. to *sur-* SUR-[1] + *fait* < L *factus,* ptp. of *facere* to do (see FACT); (v.) *sorfeten,* deriv. of the n.] **—Syn. 1.** superabundance, superfluity. **5, 6.** stuff, gorge. **6.** fill. **—Ant. 1.** lack.

surf′er's knot′, a tumorlike nodule below a surfer's knee or on the upper area of the foot, caused by pressure on the skin and tissue exerted by the surfboard. Also called **surf′er's knob′.**

surf•fish (sûrf′fish′), *n., pl.* (*esp. collectively*) **-fish,** (*esp. referring to two or more kinds or species*) **-fish•es. 1.** surfperch. **2.** any of several sciaenoid fishes, as *Umbrina roncador,* inhabiting waters along the Pacific coast of North America. **3.** See **surf smelt.** [1880–85, *Amer.*; SURF + FISH]

sur•fi•cial (sər fish′əl), *adj.* of or pertaining to a surface, esp. the land surface: *a surficial geologic deposit.* [1890–95; b. SURFACE and SUPERFICIAL] **—sur•fi′cial•ly,** *adv.*

surf•ing (sûr′fing), *n.* the act or sport of riding the surf, as on a surfboard. Also called **surfriding.** [1915–20; SURF + -ING[1]]

surf′ing mu′sic, rock-'n'-roll music from California in the early 1960's, characterized by close treble harmonies and with lyrics emphasizing the exhilaration of surfing and beach life. Also called **surf′ mu′sic.**

surf-'n'-turf (sûrf′ən tûrf′), *n.* See **surf and turf.**

surf•perch (sûrf′pûrch′), *n., pl.* (*esp. collectively*) **-perch,** (*esp. referring to two or more kinds or species*) **-perch•es.** any of several fishes of the family Embiotocidae, inhabiting shallow waters along the Pacific coast of North America. Also called **seaperch, surffish.** [1880–85, *Amer.*; SURF + PERCH[2]]

surf•rid•ing (sûrf′rī′ding), *n.* surfing. [1965–70; SURF + RIDING[1]] **—surf′rid′er,** *n.*

surf′ sco′ter, *Ornith.* a large, North American scoter, *Melanitta perspicillata,* the adult male of which is black with two white patches on the head. [1825–35]

surf′ smelt′, a smelt, *Hypomesus pretiosus,* inhabiting shallow waters from southern California to Alaska, and spawning in the surf. [1880–85]

surf•y (sûr′fē), *adj.,* **surf•i•er, surf•i•est.** abounding with surf; forming or like surf. [1805–15; SURF + -Y[1]]

surg., 1. surgeon. **2.** surgery. **3.** surgical.

surge (sûrj), *n., v.,* **surged, surg•ing.** *—n.* **1.** a strong, wavelike, forward movement, rush, or sweep: *the onward surge of an angry mob.* **2.** a strong, swelling, wavelike volume or body of something: *a billowing surge of smoke.* **3.** the rolling swell of the sea. **4.** the swelling and rolling sea: *The surge crashed against the rocky coast.* **5.** a swelling wave; billow. **6.** *Meteorol.* **a.** a widespread change in atmospheric pressure that is in addition to cyclonic and normal diurnal changes. **b.** See **storm surge. 7.** *Elect.* **a.** a sudden rush or burst of current or voltage. **b.** a violent oscillatory disturbance. **8.** *Naut.* a slackening or slipping back, as of a rope or cable. **9.** *Mach.* **a.** an uneven flow and strong momentum given to a fluid, as water in a tank, resulting in a rapid, temporary rise in pressure. **b.** pulsating unevenness of motion in an engine or gas turbine. *—v.i.* **10.** (of a ship) to rise and fall, toss about, or move along on the waves: *to surge at anchor.* **11.** to rise, roll, move, or swell forward in or like waves: *The sea surged against the shore. The crowd surged back and forth.* **12.** to rise as if by a heaving or swelling force: *Blood surged to his face.* **13.** *Elect.* **a.** to increase suddenly, as current or voltage. **b.** to oscillate violently. **14.** *Naut.* **a.** to slack off or loosen a rope or cable around a capstan or windlass. **b.** to slip back, as a rope. **15.** *Mach.* to move with pulsating unevenness, as something driven by an engine or gas turbine. *—v.t.* **16.** to cause to surge or roll in or as in waves. **17.** *Naut.* to slacken (a rope). [1480–90; perh. < L *surgere* to spring up, arise, stand up]

surge′ cham′ber, *Mach.* a chamber for absorbing surge from a liquid or gas.

sur•geon (sûr′jən), *n.* a physician who specializes in surgery. [1250–1300; ME *surgien* < AF, alter. of OF *cirurgien* CHIRURGEON]

sur•geon•fish (sûr′jən fish′), *n., pl.* (*esp. collectively*) **-fish,** (*esp. referring to two or more kinds or species*) **-fish•es.** any tropical, coral-reef fish of the family Acanthuridae, with one or more sharp spines near the base of the tail fin. [1870–75, *Amer.*; SURGEON + FISH; so called from the resemblance of its spines to a surgeon's instruments]

sur′geon gen′eral, *pl.,* **surgeons general. 1.** the chief of medical services in one of the armed forces. **2.** (*caps.*) the head of the U.S. Bureau of Public Health or, in some states, of a state health agency. [1770–80]

sur′geon's knot′, a knot resembling a reef knot, used by surgeons for tying ligatures and the like. [1805–15]

sur•ger•y (sûr′jə rē), *n., pl.* **-ger•ies** for 3–5. **1.** the art, practice, or work of treating diseases, injuries, or deformities by manual or operative procedures. **2.** the branch of medicine concerned with such treatment. **3.** treatment, as an operation, performed by a surgeon. **4.** a room or place for surgical operations. **5.** *Brit.* a doctor's or dentist's office or office hours. [1250–1300; ME *surgerie* < OF *cirurgerie* CHIRURGERY]

surge′ tank′, a large surge chamber.

Surg. Gen., Surgeon General.

sur•gi•cal (sûr′ji kəl), *adj.* **1.** pertaining to or involving surgery or surgeons. **2.** used in surgery. **3.** characterized by extreme precision or incisiveness: *a surgical air strike against enemy targets.* [1760–70; SURG(EON) + -ICAL] **—sur′gi•cal•ly,** *adv.*

sur′gical nee′dle, a needle for suturing.

sur•gi•cen•ter (sûr′jə sen′tər), *n.* a facility where minor surgery is performed on an outpatient basis. [1970–75; SURGI(CAL) + CENTER]

surg•y (sûr′jē), *adj.* billowy; surging or swelling. [1575–85; SURGE + -Y[1]]

Su•ri•ba•chi (so͝or′ə bä′chē), *n.* an extinct volcano on Iwo Jima island: World War II battle 1945.

su•ri•cate (so͝or′i kāt′), *n.* a small, burrowing South African carnivore, *Suricata suricatta,* of a grayish color with dark bands across the back. [1775–85; earlier *surikate* < F < D *surikat* macaque]

suricate, *Suricata suricatta,* head and body 12½ in. (32 cm); tail 8½ in. (22 cm)

su•ri•mi (so͞o rē′mē), *n.* a paste of inexpensive fish shaped, colored, and flavored in imitation of lobster meat, crabmeat, etc. Also called **sea legs.** [1980–85; < Japn: minced flesh]

Su′rinam cher′ry, 1. a tropical American tree, *Eugenia uniflora,* of the myrtle family, having ovate leaves and fragrant, white flowers. **2.** the yellow or red cherrylike fruit of this tree. Also called **pitanga.**

Su•ri•na•me (so͝or′ə näm′, -nam′; *Du.* SY′RĒ nä′mə), *n.* a republic on the NE coast of South America: formerly a territory of the Netherlands; gained independence 1975. 414,000; 60,230 sq. mi. (155,995 sq. km). *Cap.:* Paramaribo. Also, **Su•ri•nam** (so͝or′ə näm′, -nam′). Formerly, **Dutch Guiana, Netherlands Guiana.**

Su•ri•na•mese (so͝or′ə nə mēz′, -mēs′), *n., pl.* **-mese,** *adj.* *—n.* **1.** a native or inhabitant of Suriname. *—adj.* **2.** of or pertaining to Suriname or its inhabitants. [SURINAM + -ESE]

Su′rinam toad′, a South American aquatic frog, *Pipa pipa,* the female of which carries the eggs and tadpoles in small depressions on its back. [1765–75]

sur•jec•tion (sər jek′shən), *n. Math.* See **onto function.** [1960–65; SUR-[1] + *-jection,* as in INJECTION]

sur•jec•tive (sər jek′tiv), *adj. Math.* onto (def. 3). [1960–65; SURJECT(ION) + -IVE]

sur•ly (sûr′lē), *adj.,* **-li•er, -li•est. 1.** churlishly rude or bad-tempered: *a surly waiter.* **2.** unfriendly or hostile; menacingly irritable: *a surly old lion.* **3.** dark or dismal; menacing; threatening: *a surly sky.* **4.** *Obs.* lordly; arrogant. [1560–70; sp. var. of obs. *sirly* lordly, arrogant, equiv. to SIR + -LY] **—sur′li•ly,** *adv.* **—sur′li•ness,** *n.* **—Syn. 1.** sullen, irascible, cross, grumpy. See **glum.**

sur•mise (*v.* sər mīz′; *n.* sər mīz′, sûr′mīz), *v.,* **-mised, -mis•ing,** *n.* *—v.t.* **1.** to think or infer without certain or strong evidence; conjecture; guess. *—v.i.* **2.** to conjecture or guess. *—n.* **3.** a matter of conjecture. **4.** an idea or thought of something as being possible or likely. **5.** a conjecture or opinion. [1350–1400; ME *surmisen* < AF *surmis(e),* MF (ptp. of *surmettre* to accuse < L *supermittere* to throw upon), equiv. to *sur-* SUR-[1] + *mis* (masc.), *mise* (fem.) < L *missus, missa,* equiv. to *mit(tere)* to send + *-tus, -ta* ptp. suffix] **—sur•mis′a•ble,** *adj.* **—sur•mised•ly** (sər mīzd′lē, -mī′zid-), *adv.* **—sur•mis′er,** *n.* **—Syn. 1.** imagine, suppose, suspect. See **guess.**

sur•mount (sər mount′), *v.t.* **1.** to mount upon; get on the top of; mount upon and cross over: *to surmount a hill.* **2.** to get over or across (barriers, obstacles, etc.). **3.** to prevail over: *to surmount tremendous difficulties.* **4.** to be on top of or above: *a statue surmounting a pillar.* **5.** to furnish with something placed on top or above: *to surmount a tower with a spire.* **6.** *Obs.* **a.** to surpass in excellence. **b.** to exceed in amount. [1325–75; ME *surmounten* < AF *surmounter,* MF. See SUR-[1], MOUNT[1]] **—sur•mount′a•ble,** *adj.* **—sur•mount′a•ble•ness,** *n.* **—sur•mount′er,** *n.*

sur•mul•let (sər mul′it), *n.* a goatfish, esp. one of the European species used for food. [1665–75; < F *surmulet,* MF *sormulet,* equiv. to *sor* reddish brown (see SORREL[1]) + *mulet* MULLET]

sur•name (*n.* sûr′nām′; *v.* sûr′nām′, sûr nām′), *n., v.,* **-named, -nam•ing.** *—n.* **1.** the name that a person has in common with other family members, as distinguished from a Christian name or given name; family name. **2.** a name added to a person's name, as one indicating a circumstance of birth or some characteristic or achievement; epithet. *—v.t.* **3.** to give a surname to; call by a surname. [1300–50; ME (n.); see SUR-[1], NAME; modeled on OF *surnom*]

sur•pass (sər pas′, -päs′), *v.t.* **1.** to go beyond in amount, extent, or degree; be greater than; exceed. **2.** to go beyond in excellence or achievement; be superior to; excel: *He surpassed his brother in sports.* **3.** to be beyond the range or capacity of; transcend: *misery that surpasses description.* [1545–55; < MF *surpasser,* equiv. to *sur-* SUR-[1] + *passer* to PASS] **—sur•pass′a•ble,** *adj.* **—sur•pass′er,** *n.*
—Syn. 2. beat, outstrip. See **excel.**

sur•pass•ing (sər pas′ing, -pä′sing), *adj.* **1.** of a large amount or high degree; exceeding, excelling, or extraordinary: *structures of surpassing magnificence.* *—adv.* **2.** in a surpassing manner; extraordinarily. [1570–80; SURPASS + -ING[2]] **—sur•pass′ing•ly,** *adv.*

sur•plice (sûr′plis), *n.* **1.** a loose-fitting, broad-sleeved white vestment, worn over the cassock by clergy and choristers. **2.** a garment in which the two halves of the front cross diagonally. [1250–1300; ME *surplis* < AF *surpliz,* syncopated var. of OF *surpeliz* < ML *superpellicium (vestimentum)* over-pelt (garment), neut. of *superpellicius* (adj.), equiv. to L *super-* SUPER- + *pellit(us)* clothed with skins + *-ius* adj. suffix] **—sur′pliced,** *adj.*

surplice (def. 1)

sur•plus (sûr′plus, -pləs), *n., adj., v.,* **-plussed** or **-plused, -plus•sing** or **-plus•ing.** *—n.* **1.** something that remains above what is used or needed. **2.** an amount, quantity, etc., greater than needed. **3.** agricultural produce or a quantity of food grown by a nation or area in excess of its needs, esp. such a quantity of food purchased and stored by a governmental program of guaranteeing farmers a specific price for certain crops. **4.** *Accounting.* **a.** the excess of assets over liabilities accumulated throughout the existence of a business, excepting assets against which stock certificates have been issued; excess of net worth over capital-stock value. **b.** an amount of assets in excess of what is requisite to meet liabilities. *—adj.* **5.** being a surplus; being in excess of what is required: *surplus wheat.* *—v.t.* **6.** to treat as surplus; sell off; retire: *The government surplussed some of its desert lands.* [1325–75; ME (n.) < OF < ML *superplus,* equiv. to *super-* SUPER- + *plus* PLUS] **—Syn. 1.** superabundance. See **remainder.**

sur•plus•age (sûr′plus ij), *n.* **1.** something that is surplus; an excess amount. **2.** an excess of words. [1375–1425; late ME; see SURPLUS, -AGE]

sur′plus val′ue, (in Marxian economics) the part of the value of a commodity that exceeds the cost of labor, regarded as the profit of the capitalist. [1885–90]

sur•print (sûr′print′), *v.t.* **1.** to print over with additional marks or matter; overprint. **2.** to print (additional marks, a new address, etc.) over something already printed. *—n.* **3.** something surprinted. [1915–20; SUR-[1] + PRINT]

sur•pris•al (sər prī′zəl), *n.* **1.** the act of surprising. **2.** the state of being surprised. **3.** a surprise. [1585–95; SURPRISE + -AL[2]]

sur•prise (sər prīz′, sə-), *v.,* **-prised, -pris•ing,** *n.* *—v.t.* **1.** to strike or occur to with a sudden feeling of wonder or astonishment, as through unexpectedness: *Her beauty surprised me.* **2.** to come upon or discover suddenly and unexpectedly: *We surprised the children raiding the cookie jar.* **3.** to make an unexpected assault on (an unprepared army, fort, person, etc.). **4.** to elicit or bring out suddenly and without warning: *to surprise the facts from the witness.* **5.** to lead or bring unawares, as into doing something not intended: *to surprise a witness into telling the truth.* *—n.* **6.** an act or instance of surprising or being surprised. **7.** something that surprises someone; a completely unexpected occurrence, appearance, or statement: *His announcement was a surprise to all.* **8.** an assault, as on an army or a fort, made without warning. **9.** a coming upon unexpectedly; detecting in the act; taking unawares. **10. take by surprise, a.** to come upon unawares. **b.** to astonish; amaze: *The amount of the donation took us completely by surprise.* [1425–75; (n.) late ME < AF *surpris(e),* MF, ptp. of *surprendre,* equiv. to *sur-* SUR-[1] + *pris* (masc.), *prise* (fem.) < L *prēnsus, -sa,* equiv. to *prēnd(ere),* contracted var. of *prehendere* to take (see PREHENSION) + *-tus, -ta* ptp. suffix; (v.) late ME *surprisen* < AF *surpris(e)* (ptp.),

CONCISE PRONUNCIATION KEY: *act, cāpe, dâre, pärt; set, ēqual; if, ice; ox, ōver, ôrder, oil, bo͝ok, bo͞ot, out; up, ûrge; child; sing; shoe; thin, that;* zh as in *treasure.* ə = *a* as in *alone, e* as in *system, i* as in *easily, o* as in *gallop, u* as in *circus;* ə as in *fire* (fīər), *hour* (ouər). l and n can serve as syllabic consonants, as in *cradle* (krād′l), and *button* (but′n). See the full key inside the front cover.

MF, as above] **—sur·pris·ed·ly** (sər prī′zid lē, -prīzd′-, sə-), *adv.* **—sur·pris′er,** *n.*
—Syn. 1. SURPRISE, ASTONISH, AMAZE, ASTOUND mean to strike with wonder because of unexpectedness, strangeness, unusualness, etc. To SURPRISE is to take unawares or to affect with wonder: *surprised at receiving a telegram.* To ASTONISH is to strike with wonder by something unlooked for, startling, or seemingly inexplicable: *astonished at someone's behavior.* To AMAZE is to astonish so greatly as to disconcert or bewilder: *amazed at such an evidence of stupidity.* To ASTOUND is to so overwhelm with surprise that one is unable to think or act: *astounded by the news.*

surprise′ par′ty, 1. a party or celebration planned for someone as a surprise. **2.** something that surprises someone. [1835–45]

Surprise′ Sym′phony, the Symphony No. 94 in G major (1791) by Franz Joseph Haydn.

sur·pris·ing (sər prī′zing, sə-), *adj.* **1.** causing surprise, wonder, or astonishment. **2.** unexpected. [1570–80; SURPRISE + -ING²] **—sur·pris′ing·ly,** *adv.*

sur·ra (sŏŏr′ə), *n. Vet. Pathol.* an often fatal infectious disease of horses, camels, elephants, and dogs caused by a blood-infecting protozoan parasite, *Trypanosoma evansi,* transmitted by the bite of horseflies, characterized by fever, anemia, and emaciation. [1885–90; < Marathi *sūra* heavy breathing sound]

Sur·ratt (sə rat′), *n.* **Mary Eugenia (Jenkins),** 1820–'65, alleged conspirator: boardinghouse owner hanged as accomplice in assassination of President Lincoln.

sur·re·al (sə rē′əl, -rēl′), *adj.* **1.** of, pertaining to, or characteristic of surrealism; surrealistic. **2.** having the disorienting, hallucinatory quality of a dream; unreal; fantastic: *surreal complexities of the bureaucracy.* [1935–40; back formation from SURREALISM; see SUR-¹, REAL¹] **—sur·re′al·ly,** *adv.* **—sur·re·al·i·ty** (sə rē al′i tē), *n.*

sur·re·al·ism (sə rē′ə liz′əm), *n.* (*sometimes cap.*) a style of art and literature developed principally in the 20th century, stressing the subconscious or nonrational significance of imagery arrived at by automatism or the exploitation of chance effects, unexpected juxtapositions, etc. [1920–25; < F *surréalisme.* See SUR-¹, REALISM] **—sur·re′al·ist,** *n., adj.*

sur·re·al·is·tic (sə rē′ə lis′tik), *adj.* **1.** of, pertaining to, or characteristic of surrealism; surreal. **2.** having features typical or reminiscent of those depicted in surrealistic painting or drawing: *the moon's surrealistic landscape.* [1925–30; SURREALIST + -IC] **—sur·re′al·is′ti·cal·ly,** *adv.*

sur·re·but·tal (sûr′ri but′l), *n. Law.* the giving of evidence to meet a defendant's rebuttal. [1885–90; SUR-¹ + REBUTTAL]

sur·re·but·ter (sûr′ri but′ər), *n. Law.* a plaintiff's reply to a defendant's rebutter. [1595–1605; SUR-¹ + REBUTTER]

sur·re·join·der (sûr′ri join′dər), *n. Law.* a plaintiff's reply to a defendant's rejoinder. [1535–45; SUR-¹ + REJOINDER]

sur·ren·der (sə ren′dər), *v.t.* **1.** to yield (something) to the possession or power of another; deliver up possession of on demand or under duress: *to surrender the fort to the enemy; to surrender the stolen goods to the police.* **2.** to give (oneself) up, as to the police. **3.** to give (oneself) up to some influence, course, emotion, etc.: *He surrendered himself to a life of hardship.* **4.** to give up, abandon, or relinquish (comfort, hope, etc.). **5.** to yield or resign (an office, privilege, etc.) in favor of another. *—v.i.* **6.** to give oneself up, as into the power of another; submit or yield. *—n.* **7.** the act or an instance of surrendering. **8.** *Insurance.* the voluntary abandonment of a life-insurance policy by the owner for any of its nonforfeiture values. **9.** the deed by which a legal surrendering is made. [1425–75; (v.) late ME *surrendren* < AF *surrender,* OF *surrendre* to give up, equiv. to *sur-* SUR-¹ + *rendre* to RENDER; (n.) < AF; OF *surrendre,* n. use of the inf.] **—sur·ren′der·er,** *n.*
—Syn. 1. See **yield. 4.** renounce. **5.** waive, cede, abandon, forgo. **6.** capitulate. **7.** capitulation, relinquishment.

surren′der val′ue, *Insurance.* See **cash value.** [1875–80]

sur·rep·ti·tious (sûr′əp tish′əs), *adj.* **1.** obtained, done, made, etc., by stealth; secret or unauthorized; clandestine: *a surreptitious glance.* **2.** acting in a stealthy way. **3.** obtained by subreption; subreptitious. [1400–50; late ME < L *surrepticius* stolen, clandestine, equiv. to *surrept(us),* ptp. of *surripere* to steal, (*sur-* SUR-² + *rep-,* comb. form of *rapere* to snatch, RAPE¹ + *-tus* ptp. suffix) + *-īcius* -ITIOUS] **—sur′rep·ti′tious·ly,** *adv.* **—sur′rep·ti′tious·ness,** *n.*

sur·rey (sûr′ē, sur′ē), *n., pl.* **-reys.** a light, four-wheeled, two-seated carriage, with or without a top, for four persons. [1890–95; after SURREY, England]

surrey

CONCISE ETYMOLOGY KEY: <, descended or borrowed from; >, whence; b., blend of, blended; c., cognate with; cf., compare; deriv., derivative; equiv., equivalent; imit., imitative; obl., oblique; r., replacing; s., stem; sp., spelling, spelled; resp., respelling, respelled; trans., translation; ?, origin unknown; *, unattested; ‡, probably earlier than. See the full key inside the front cover.

Sur·rey (sûr′ē, sur′ē), *n.* **1. Earl of** (*Henry Howard*), 1517?–47, English poet. **2.** a county in SE England, bordering S London. 1,000,700; 648 sq. mi. (1680 sq. km).

sur·ro·gate (*n., adj.* sûr′ə gāt′, -git, sur′-; *v.* sûr′ə-gāt′, sur′-), *n., adj., v.,* **-gat·ed, -gat·ing.** *—n.* **1.** a person appointed to act for another; deputy. **2.** (in some states) a judicial officer having jurisdiction over the probate of wills, the administration of estates, etc. **3.** the deputy of an ecclesiastical judge, esp. of a bishop or a bishop's chancellor. **4.** a substitute. **5.** a surrogate mother. *—adj.* **6.** regarded or acting as a surrogate: *a surrogate father.* **7.** involving or indicating the use of a surrogate mother to conceive or carry an embryo: *surrogate parenting.* *—v.t.* **8.** to put into the place of another as a successor, substitute, or deputy; substitute for another. **9.** to subrogate. [1525–35; < L *surrogātus,* assimilated var. of *subrogātus;* see SUBROGATE] **—sur′ro·gate·ship′,** *n.* **—sur′ro·ga′tion,** *n.*

sur′rogate moth′er, 1. a person who acts in the place of another person's biological mother. **2.** an animal that is given another's offspring to raise. **3.** *Med.* a woman who helps a couple to have a child by carrying to term an embryo conceived by the couple and transferred to her uterus, or by being inseminated with the man's sperm and either donating the embryo for transfer to the woman's uterus or carrying it to term. Cf. **embryo transfer.** [1975–80]

sur·round (sə round′), *v.t.* **1.** to enclose on all sides; encompass: *She was surrounded by reporters.* **2.** to form an enclosure round; encircle: *A stone wall surrounds the estate.* **3.** to enclose (a body of troops, a fort or town, etc.) so as to cut off communication or retreat. *—n.* **4.** something that surrounds, as the area, border, etc., around an object or central space: *a tile surround for the shower stall.* **5.** environment or setting: *The designer created a Persian surround for the new restaurant.* **6.** *Hunting.* **a.** a means of hunting in which wild animals are encircled and chased into a special spot that makes their escape impossible. **b.** the act of hunting by this means. **c.** the location encircled by hunters using this means. [1400–50; late ME *surounden* to inundate, submerge < AF *surounder,* MF *s(o)ronder* < LL *superundāre* to overflow, equiv. to L *super-* SUPER- + *undāre* to flood, deriv. of *unda* wave (see UNDULATE); current sp. by analysis as SUR-¹ + ROUND¹ (v.)]

sur·round·ing (sə roun′ding), *n.* **1.** something that surrounds. **2. surroundings,** environing things, circumstances, conditions, etc.; environment: *He was too sick to be aware of his surroundings.* **3.** the act of encircling or enclosing. *—adj.* **4.** enclosing or encircling. **5.** being the environment or adjacent area. [1400–50; late ME: inundation; see SURROUND, -ING¹, -ING²]
—Syn. 2. See **environment.**

surround′ the′ater, a theater, concert hall, or the like, in which seats are arranged around or on all four sides of a central stage. Cf. **arena theater.**

sur·roy·al (sûr roi′əl), *n.* See **crown antler.** [1350–1400; ME *surryal.* See SUR-¹, ROYAL]

sur·sum cor·da (sŏŏr′sŏŏm kôr′dä, kōr′-), *Eccles.* the words "Lift up your hearts," addressed by the celebrant of the Mass to the congregation just before the preface. [1550–60; < L]

Surt (sûrt, sŏŏrt), *n. Scand. Myth.* the guardian and ruler of Muspelheim, destined to defeat Frey at Ragnarok and destroy the world with fire. [< ON *Surtr,* perh. akin to *svartr* black, with regularly changed vowel (see SWART)]

sur·tax (*n.* sûr′taks′; *v.* sûr′taks′, sûr taks′), *n.* **1.** an additional or extra tax on something already taxed. **2.** one of a graded series of additional taxes levied on incomes exceeding a certain amount. *—v.t.* **3.** to put an additional or extra tax on; charge with a surtax. [1880–85; SUR-¹ + TAX; cf. SUPERTAX, F *surtaxe*]

Sur·tees (sûr′tēz), *n.* **Robert Smith,** 1805–64, English editor and writer.

sur·ti·tle (sûr′tīt′l), *n., v.t.,* **-tled, -tling.** supertitle. [SUR-¹ + TITLE]

sur·tout (sər tōō′, -tōōt′; *Fr.* SYR tōō′), *n., pl.* **-touts** (-tōōz′, -tōōts′; *Fr.* -tōō′). **1.** a man's close-fitting overcoat, esp. a frock coat. **2.** a hood with a mantle, worn by women. [1680–90; < F: lit., over all, equiv. to *sur* upon, on (see SUR-¹) + *tout* everything]

Surt·sey (sûrt′sē; *Icel.* sœRt′sā), *n.* an island S of and belonging to Iceland: formed by an undersea volcano 1963. ab. one mi. (1.5 km) in diameter; ab. 500 ft. (150 m) high.

surv., 1. survey. **2.** surveying. **3.** surveyor.

sur·veil (sər vāl′), *v.t.,* **-veilled, -veil·ling.** to place under surveillance. [1965–70; back formation from SURVEILLANCE]

sur·veil·lance (sər vā′ləns, -vāl′yəns), *n.* **1.** a watch kept over a person, group, etc., esp. over a suspect, prisoner, or the like: *The suspects were under police surveillance.* **2.** supervision or superintendence. [1790–1800; < F, equiv. to *surveill(er)* to watch over (*sur-* SUR-¹ + *veiller* < L *vigilāre* to watch; see VIGIL) + *-ance* -ANCE]

sur·veil·lant (sər vā′lənt, -vāl′yənt), *adj.* **1.** exercising surveillance. *—n.* **2.** a person who exercises surveillance. [1810–20; < F, prp. of *surveiller* (see SURVEILLANCE, -ANT)]

sur·vey (*v.* sər vā′; *n.* sûr′vā, sər vā′), *v., n., pl.* **-veys.** *—v.t.* **1.** to take a general or comprehensive view of or appraise, as a situation, area of study, etc. **2.** to view in detail, esp. to inspect, examine, or appraise formally or officially in order to ascertain condition, value, etc. **3.** to conduct a survey of or among: *to survey TV viewers.* **4.** to determine the exact form, boundaries, position, extent, etc., of (a tract of land, section of a country, etc.) by linear and angular measurements and the application of the principles of geometry and trigonometry. *—v.i.* **5.** to survey land; practice surveying. *—n.* **6.** an act or instance of surveying or of taking a comprehensive view of something: *The course is a survey of Italian painting.* **7.** a formal or official examination of the particulars of something, made in order to ascertain condition, character, etc. **8.** a statement or description embodying the result of this: *They presented their survey to the board of directors.* **9.** a sampling, or partial collection, of facts, figures, or opinions taken and used to approximate or indicate what a complete collection and analysis might reveal: *The survey showed the percentage of the population that planned to vote.* **10.** the act of determining the exact form, boundaries, position, etc., as of a tract of land or section of a country, by linear measurements, angular measurements, etc. **11.** the plan or description resulting from such an operation. **12.** an agency for making determinations: *U.S. Geological Survey.* [1425–75; late ME *surveien* (v.) < AF *surveier,* MF *surv(e)ier, surveoir* to oversee, equiv. to *sur-* SUR-¹ + *v(e)ier* < L *vidēre* to see] **—sur·vey′a·ble,** *adj.*

survey., surveying.

sur′vey course′, *Educ.* an introductory course of study that provides a general view of an academic subject. [1915–20]

sur·vey·ing (sər vā′ing), *n.* **1.** the science or scientific method of making surveys of land. **2.** the occupation of one who makes land surveys. **3.** the act of one who surveys: *The surveying required nearly two days.* [1425–75; late ME: act of examining closely; see SURVEY, -ING¹]

sur·vey·or (sər vā′ər), *n.* **1.** a person whose occupation is surveying. **2.** an overseer or supervisor. **3.** *Chiefly Brit.* a person who inspects something officially for the purpose of ascertaining condition, value, etc. **4.** (formerly) a U.S. customs official responsible for ascertaining the quantity and value of imported merchandise. **5.** (*cap.*) *U.S. Aerospace.* one of a series of space probes (1966–68) that analyzed lunar soil and obtained other scientific information after soft-landing on the moon. [1375–1425; late ME *surveio(u)r* < AF *surveiour;* MF *surve(i)our,* equiv. to *surve(i)-* (see SURVEY) + *-our* -OR²] **—sur·vey′or·ship′,** *n.*

survey′or's chain′. See under **chain** (def. 8a).

survey′or's com′pass, an instrument used by surveyors for measuring azimuths. Also called **survey′or's di′al.**

survey′or's lev′el, level (def. 9a).

survey′or's meas′ure, a system of units of length used in surveying land, based on the surveyor's chain of 66 ft. (20.12 m) and its 100 links of 7.92 in. (20.12 cm).

sur·viv·a·ble (sər vī′və bəl), *adj.* **1.** able to be survived: *Would an atomic war be survivable?* **2.** capable of withstanding attack or countermeasures: *a bomber survivable against fighter planes.* [1950–55; SURVIVE + -ABLE] **—sur·viv′a·bil′i·ty,** *n.*

sur·viv·al (sər vī′vəl), *n.* **1.** the act or fact of surviving, esp. under adverse or unusual circumstances. **2.** a person or thing that survives or endures, esp. an ancient custom, observance, belief, or the like. **3.** *Anthropol.* (no longer in technical use) the persistence of a cultural trait, practice, or the like long after it has lost its original meaning or usefulness. *—adj.* **4.** of, pertaining to, or for use in surviving, esp. under adverse or unusual circumstances: *survival techniques.* [1590–1600; SURVIVE + -AL²]

surviv′al curve′, a line or curve plotted on a graph indicating survival rates of a specific population, as breast-cancer patients, over a period of time. [1935–40]

sur·viv·al·ist (sər vī′və list), *n.* a person who makes preparations to survive a widespread catastrophe, as an atomic war or anarchy, esp. by storing food and weapons in a safe place. [1965–70; SURVIVAL + -IST] **—sur·viv′al·ism,** *n.*

surviv′al kit′, 1. *Mil.* a package containing medical supplies, rations, and other vital equipment for use by a person forced to land in or parachute into the ocean, jungle, or other isolated or hostile territory. **2.** a similar emergency kit for campers, hikers, etc.

surviv′al of the fit′test, 1. (not in technical use) natural selection. **2.** a 19th-century concept of human society, inspired by the principle of natural selection, postulating that those who are eliminated in the struggle for existence are the unfit. [1860–65]

surviv′al val′ue, the utility of a behavioral trait or of a physical feature of an organism in aiding the survival and reproduction of the organism.

sur·vive (sər vīv′), *v.,* **-vived, -viv·ing.** *—v.i.* **1.** to remain alive after the death of someone, the cessation of something, or the occurrence of some event; continue to live: *Few survived after the holocaust.* **2.** to remain or continue in existence or use: *Ancient farming methods still survive in the Middle East.* **3.** to get along or remain healthy, happy, and unaffected in spite of some occurrence: *She's surviving after the divorce.* *—v.t.* **4.** to continue to live or exist after the death, cessation, or occurrence of: *His wife survived him. He survived the operation.* **5.** to endure or live through (an affliction, adversity, misery, etc.): *She's survived two divorces.* [1425–75; late ME < MF *survivre* < L *supervīvere,* equiv. to *super-* SUPER- + *vīvere* to live; see SUR-¹, VIVID]
—Syn. 1. persist, succeed. SURVIVE, OUTLIVE refer to remaining alive longer than someone else or after some event. SURVIVE usually means to succeed in keeping alive against odds, to live after some event that has threatened one: *to survive an automobile accident.* It is also used of living longer than another person (usually a relative), but, today, mainly in the passive, as in the fixed expression: *The deceased is survived by his wife and children.* OUTLIVE stresses capacity for endurance, the time element, and sometimes a sense of competition: *He outlived all his enemies.* It is also used, however, of a person or object that has lived or lasted beyond a certain point: *He has outlived his usefulness.*

sur·vi·vor (sər vī′vər), *n.* **1.** a person or thing that survives. **2.** *Law.* the one of two or more designated persons, as joint tenants or others having a joint interest, who outlives the other or others. **3.** a person who continues to function or prosper in spite of opposition, hardship, or setbacks. [1495–1505; SURVIVE + -OR²]

survi′vor guilt′, *Psychiatry.* feelings of guilt for having survived a catastrophe in which others died. Cf. **survivor syndrome.** [1970–75]

sur•vi•vor•ship (sər vī′vər ship′), *n.* **1.** the state of being a survivor. **2.** *Law.* a right of a person to property on the death of another having a joint interest: in the case of more than two joint tenants, the property passes to successive survivors. [1615–25; SURVIVOR + -SHIP]

survi′vor syn′drome, *Psychiatry.* a characteristic group of symptoms, including recurrent images of death, depression, persistent anxiety, and emotional numbness, occurring in survivors of disaster. Cf. **survivor guilt.** [1965–70]

sus-, var. of **sub-** before *c, p, t: susceptible.*

Su•sa (so͞o′sə, -sä), *n.* a ruined city in W Iran: the capital of ancient Elam; palaces of Darius and Artaxerxes I; stele containing the Code of Hammurabi discovered here. Biblical name, **Shushan.**

Su•san (so͞o′zən), *n.* a female given name, form of **Susanna** or **Susannah.**

Su•san•na (so͞o zan′ə), *n.* **1.** a book of the Apocrypha, constituting the 13th chapter of Daniel in the Douay Bible. **2.** Also, **Su•san′nah.** a female given name: from a Hebrew word meaning "lily."

Su•sanne (so͞o zan′), *n.* a female given name, form of **Susanna** or **Susannah.**

sus•cep•tance (sə sep′təns), *n. Elect.* the imaginary component of admittance, equal to the quotient of the negative of the reactance divided by the sum of the squares of the reactance and resistance. *Symbol:* B [1905–10; SUSCEPT(IBILITY) + -ANCE]

sus•cep•ti•bil•i•ty (sə sep′tə bil′i tē), *n., pl.* **-ties. 1.** state or character of being susceptible: *susceptibility to disease.* **2.** capacity for receiving mental or moral impressions; tendency to be emotionally affected. **3. susceptibilities,** capacities for emotion; feelings: *His susceptibilities are easily wounded.* **4.** *Elect.* **a.** See **electric susceptibility. b.** See **magnetic susceptibility.** [1635–45; < ML *susceptibilitās,* equiv. to *susceptibil(is)* SUSCEPTIBLE + *-itās* -ITY]
—Syn. 2. See **sensibility.**

sus•cep•ti•ble (sə sep′tə bəl), *adj.* **1.** admitting or capable of some specified treatment: *susceptible of a high polish; susceptible to various interpretations.* **2.** accessible or especially liable or subject to some influence, mood, agency, etc.: *susceptible to colds; susceptible to flattery.* **3.** capable of being affected emotionally; impressionable. [1595–1605; < LL *susceptibilis,* equiv. to *suscept(us),* ptp. of *suscipere* to take up, support (*sus-* SUS- + *-cep-,* comb form of *capere* to take, CAPTURE + *-tus* ptp. suffix) + *-ibilis* -IBLE] **—sus•cep′ti•ble•ness,** *n.* **—sus•cep′ti•bly,** *adv.*

sus•cep•tive (sə sep′tiv), *adj.* **1.** receptive. **2.** susceptible. [1545–55; < LL *susceptīvus,* equiv. to *suscept(us)* (see SUSCEPTIBLE) + *-īvus* -IVE] **—sus•cep•tiv•i•ty** (sus′ep tiv′i tē), **sus•cep′tive•ness,** *n.*

Su•sette (so͞o zet′), *n.* a female given name, form of **Susanna** or **Susannah.**

su•shi (so͞o′shē), *n. Japanese Cookery.* cold boiled rice moistened with rice vinegar, usually shaped into bite-size pieces and topped with raw seafood **(nigiri-zushi)** or formed into a long seaweed-wrapped roll, often around strips of vegetable or raw fish, and sliced into bite-size pieces **(maki-zushi).** Cf. **sashimi.** [1895–1900; < literary Japn: lit., it is sour]

Su•si•an (so͞o′zē ən), *n.* **1.** a native or inhabitant of Susa or Susiana. **2.** Elamite (def. 2). —*adj.* **3.** of or pertaining to Susa or Susiana. [1560–70; SUS(A), SUS(IANA) + -IAN]

Su•si•a•na (so͞o′zē ä′nə, -an′ə), *n.* Elam.

Su•sie (so͞o′zē), *n.* a female given name, form of **Susanna** or **Susannah.** Also, **Su′si.**

sus•lik (sus′lik), *n.* **1.** a common ground squirrel or spermophile, *Spermophilus (Citellus) citellus,* of Europe and Asia. **2.** the fur of this animal. Also, **souslik.** [1765–75; < Russ *súslik,* ORuss *susolŭ,* akin to Czech, Slovak *sysel,* Pol *susel,* Bulg *sŭsel* ground squirrel, rat, perh. ult. from an imit. v. base *sys-, *sus- whistle, hiss]

Su•slov (so͞os′lôf, -lof; *Russ.* so͞o′sləf), *n.* **Mi•kha•il An•dre•e•vich** (myi KHU yēl′ un drye′yi vyich), 1902–82, Soviet government official.

sus•pect (*v.* sə spekt′; *n.* sus′pekt; *adj.* sus′pekt, sə spekt′), *v.t.* **1.** to believe to be guilty, false, counterfeit, undesirable, defective, bad, etc., with little or no proof: *to suspect a person of murder.* **2.** to doubt or mistrust: *I suspect his motives.* **3.** to believe to be the case or to be likely or probable; surmise: *I suspect his knowledge did not amount to much.* **4.** to have some hint or foreknowledge of: *I think she suspected the surprise.* —*v.i.* **5.** to believe something, esp. something evil or wrong, to be the case; have suspicion. —*n.* **6.** a person who is suspected, esp. one suspected of a crime, offense, or the like. —*adj.* **7.** suspected; open to or under suspicion. [1250–1300; ME (adj.) < L *suspectāre,* equiv. to *su-* SU- + *spectāre,* freq. of *specere* to look at] **—sus•pect′i•ble,** *adj.*
—Syn. 3. guess, conjecture, suppose.

sus•pend (sə spend′), *v.t.* **1.** to hang by attachment to something above: *to suspend a chandelier from the ceiling.* **2.** to attach so as to allow free movement: *to suspend a door on a hinge.* **3.** to keep from falling, sinking, forming a deposit, etc., as if by hanging: *to suspend solid particles in a liquid.* **4.** to hold or keep undetermined; refrain from forming or concluding definitely: *to suspend one's judgment.* **5.** to defer or postpone: *to suspend sentence on a convicted person.* **6.** to cause to cease or bring to a stop or stay, usually for a time: *to suspend payment.* **7.** to cause to cease for a time from operation or effect, as a law, rule, privilege, service, or the like: *to suspend ferry service.* **8.** to debar, usually for a limited time, from the exercise of an office or function or the enjoyment of a privilege: *The student was suspended from school.* **9.** to keep in a mood or feeling of expectation or incompleteness; keep waiting in suspense: *Finish the story; don't suspend us in midair.* **10.** *Music.* to prolong (a note or tone) into the next chord. —*v.i.* **11.** to come to a stop, usually temporarily; cease from operation for a time. **12.** to stop payment; be unable to meet financial obligations. **13.** to hang or be suspended, as from another object: *The chandelier suspends from the ceiling.* **14.** to be suspended, as in a liquid, gas, etc. [1250–1300; ME *suspenden* < L *suspendere* to hang up, equiv. to *sus-* SUS- + *pendere* (transit.) to hang (see PEND, SUSPENSE)] **—sus•pend′i•ble,** *adj.* **—sus•pend′i•bil′i•ty,** *n.*
—Syn. 6. hold up, intermit. See **interrupt.**

suspend′ed anima′tion, a state of temporary cessation of the vital functions. [1810–20]

sus•pend•er (sə spen′dər), *n.* **1.** Usually, **suspenders.** Also called, *esp. Brit.,* **braces.** adjustable straps or bands worn over the shoulders with the ends buttoned or clipped to the waistband of a pair of trousers or a skirt to support it. **2.** *Brit.* garter. **3.** a hanging cable or chain in a suspension bridge connecting the deck with the suspension cable or chain. **4.** a person or thing that suspends. [1515–25; 1800–10, *Amer.* for def. 1; SUSPEND + -ER[1]] **—sus•pend′er•less,** *adj.*

suspend′er belt′, *Brit.* See **garter belt.**

sus•pense (sə spens′), *n.* **1.** a state or condition of mental uncertainty or excitement, as in awaiting a decision or outcome, usually accompanied by a degree of apprehension or anxiety. **2.** a state of mental indecision. **3.** undecided or doubtful condition, as of affairs: *For a few days matters hung in suspense.* **4.** the state or condition of being suspended. [1375–1425; late ME < ML *suspēnsum* deferment, suspension, uncertainty, n. use of neut. of L *suspēnsus* hung up, doubtful, in suspense (ptp. of *suspendere* to hang up, leave undecided), equiv. to *sus-* SUS- + *pēnsus* (*pend-,* s. of *pendere* (trans.) to hang (see PEND) + *-tus* ptp. suffix, with *dt* > *s*)] **—suspense′ful,** *adj.*

suspense′ account′, *Bookkeeping.* an account in which items are temporarily entered until their final disposition is determined. [1875–80]

sus•pen•si•ble (sə spen′sə bəl), *adj.* capable of being suspended. [1785–95; < L *suspēns(us)* (see SUSPENSE) + -IBLE] **—sus•pen′si•bil′i•ty,** *n.*

sus•pen•sion (sə spen′shən), *n.* **1.** the act of suspending. **2.** the state of being suspended. **3.** temporary abrogation or withholding, as of a law, privilege, decision, belief, etc. **4.** stoppage of payment of debts or claims because of financial inability or insolvency. **5.** *Chem.* **a.** the state in which the particles of a substance are mixed with a fluid but are undissolved. **b.** a substance in such a state. **6.** *Physical Chem.* a system consisting of small particles kept dispersed by agitation **(mechanical suspension)** or by the molecular motion in the surrounding medium **(colloidal suspension). 7.** something on or by which something else is suspended or hung. **8.** something that is suspended or hung. **9.** Also called **suspen′sion sys′tem.** the arrangement of springs, shock absorbers, hangers, etc., in an automobile, railway car, etc., connecting the wheel-suspension units or axles to the chassis frame. **10.** *Elect.* a wire, filament, or group of wires by which the conducting part of an instrument or device is suspended. **11.** *Music.* **a.** the prolongation of a tone in one chord into the following chord, usually producing a temporary dissonance. **b.** the tone so prolonged. **12.** *Rhet.* the heightening of interest by delay of the main subject or clause, especially by means of a series of parallel preceding elements. [1520–30; < L *suspēnsiōn-* (s. of *suspēnsiō*), equiv. to *suspēns(us)* (see SUSPENSE) + *-iōn-* -ION]
—Syn. 1–3. intermission, interruption, discontinuance, cessation, abeyance, hiatus.

suspen′sion bridge′, a bridge having a deck suspended from cables anchored at their extremities and usually raised on towers. [1815–25]

suspen′sion points′, *Print.* a series of periods used as an ellipsis. Also called **breaks.** [1915–20]

sus•pen•sive (sə spen′siv), *adj.* **1.** pertaining to or characterized by suspension. **2.** undecided in mind. **3.** pertaining to or characterized by suspense. **4.** (of words, phrases, etc.) characterized by or expressing suspense; keeping the reader or listener in suspense. **5.** having the effect of suspending the operation of something. [1540–50; < ML *suspēnsīvus,* equiv. to *suspēns(us)* (see SUSPENSE) + *-īvus* -IVE] **—sus•pen′sive•ly,** *adv.* **—sus•pen′sive•ness,** *n.*

sus•pen•soid (sə spen′soid), *n. Physical Chem.* a sol having a solid disperse phase. Cf. **emulsoid.** [1920–25; SUSPENS(ION) + (COLL)OID]

sus•pen•sor (sə spen′sər), *n.* **1.** a suspensory ligament, bandage, etc. **2.** *Bot.* a cellular structure, developed along with the embryo in seed-bearing plants, that bears the embryo at its apex and by elongation carries the embryo to its food source. [1740–50; < NL *suspēnsor,* equiv. to *suspend-,* s. of *suspendere* to SUSPEND + *-tor* -TOR, with *dt* > *s*]

sus•pen•so•ry (sə spen′sə rē), *n., pl.* **-ries,** *adj.* —*n.* **1.** a supporting bandage, muscle, ligament, etc. —*adj.* **2.** serving as a suspensory. **3.** suspending the operation of something. [1535–45; < L *suspēns(us)* (see SUSPENSE) + -ORY]

suspen′sory lig′ament, *Anat.* any of several tissues that suspend certain organs or parts of the body, esp. the transparent, delicate web of fibrous tissue that supports the crystalline lens. See diag. under **eye.** [1825–35]

sus•pi•cion (sə spish′ən), *n.* **1.** act of suspecting. **2.** the state of mind or feeling of one who suspects: *Suspicion kept him awake all night long.* **3.** an instance of suspecting something or someone. **4.** state of being suspected: *under suspicion; above suspicion.* **5.** imagination of anything to be the case or to be likely; a vague notion of something. **6.** a slight trace, hint, or suggestion: *a suspicion of a smile.* —*v.t.* **7.** *Nonstandard.* to suspect. [1250–1300; ME < L *suspiciōn-* (s. of *suspiciō*), equiv. to *suspic-* (var. s. of *suspicere* to look from below, SUSPECT) + *-iōn-* -ION]
—Syn. 2. doubt, mistrust, misgiving. SUSPICION, DISTRUST are terms for a feeling that appearances are not reliable. SUSPICION is the positive tendency to doubt the trustworthiness of appearances and therefore to believe that one has detected possibilities of something unreliable, unfavorable, menacing, or the like: *to feel suspicion about the honesty of a prominent man.* DISTRUST may be a passive want of trust, faith, or reliance in a person or thing: *to feel distrust of one's own ability.*

sus•pi•cion•al (sə spish′ə nl), *adj.* of or pertaining to suspicion, esp. morbid or insane suspicions. [1885–90; SUSPICION + -AL[1]]

sus•pi•cious (sə spish′əs), *adj.* **1.** tending to cause or excite suspicion; questionable: *suspicious behavior.* **2.** inclined to suspect, esp. inclined to suspect evil; distrustful: *a suspicious tyrant.* **3.** full of or feeling suspicion. **4.** expressing or indicating suspicion: *a suspicious glance.* [1300–50; ME < L *suspiciōsus,* equiv. to *suspici-* (see SUSPICION) + *-ōsus* -OUS] **—sus•pi′cious•ly,** *adv.* **—sus•pi′cious•ness,** *n.*
—Syn. 1. suspect, dubious, doubtful. **2.** mistrustful, wary, disbelieving.

sus•pi•ra•tion (sus′pə rā′shən), *n.* a long, deep sigh. [1475–85; < L *suspīrātiōn-* (s. of *suspīrātiō*), equiv. to *suspīrāt(us)* (ptp. of *suspīrāre* to SUSPIRE) + *-iōn-* -ION]

sus•pire (sə spīər′), *v.,* **-pired, -pir•ing.** —*v.i.* **1.** to sigh. **2.** to breathe. —*v.t.* **3.** to sigh; utter with long, sighing breaths. [1400–50; late ME < L *suspīrāre,* equiv. to *su-* SU- + *spīrāre* to breathe]

Sus•que•han•na (sus′kwə han′ə), *n.* a river flowing S from central New York through E Pennsylvania and NE Maryland into Chesapeake Bay. 444 mi. (715 km) long.

suss (sus), *v.t. Chiefly Brit. Slang.* to investigate or figure out (usually fol. by *out*). [1965–70; earlier, to suspect, a suspect, shortening of SUSPECT]

Sus•sex (sus′iks), *n.* **1.** a former county in SE England: divided into East Sussex and West Sussex. **2.** one of an English breed of red beef cattle. **3.** one of an English breed of chickens, raised chiefly for marketing as roasters. **4.** a kingdom of the Anglo-Saxon heptarchy in SE England. See map under **Mercia.**

Sus′sex span′iel, one of an English breed of short-legged spaniels having a golden liver-colored coat. [1855–60]

sus•tain (sə stān′), *v.t.* **1.** to support, hold, or bear up from below; bear the weight of, as a structure. **2.** to bear (a burden, charge, etc.). **3.** to undergo, experience, or suffer (injury, loss, etc.); endure without giving way or yielding. **4.** to keep (a person, the mind, the spirits, etc.) from giving way, as under trial or affliction. **5.** to keep up or keep going, as an action or process: *to sustain a conversation.* **6.** to supply with food, drink, and other necessities of life. **7.** to provide for (an institution or the like) by furnishing means or funds. **8.** to support (a cause or the like) by aid or approval. **9.** to uphold as valid, just, or correct, as a claim or the person making it: *The judge sustained the lawyer's objection.* **10.** to confirm or corroborate, as a statement: *Further investigation sustained my suspicions.* [1250–1300; ME *suste(i)nen* < AF *sustenir,* OF < L *sustinēre* to uphold, equiv. to *sus-* SUS- + *-tinēre,* comb. form of *tenēre* to hold] **—sus•tain′a•ble,** *adj.* **—sus•tain′a•bil′i•ty,** *n.* **—sus•tain•ed•ly** (sə stā′nid lē, -stānd′-), *adv.* **—sus•tain′ing•ly,** *adv.* **—sus•tain′ment,** *n.*
—Syn. 1. carry. See **support. 3.** bear. **5.** maintain.

sus•tained-re•lease (sə stānd′ri lēs′), *adj. Chem., Pharm.* (of a drug or fertilizer) capable of gradual release of an active agent over a period of time, allowing for a sustained effect; timed-release; long-acting; prolonged-action; slow-release. [1955–60]

sus•tain•er (sə stā′nər), *n.* **1.** a person or thing that sustains. **2.** *Rocketry.* **a.** any stage of a multistage rocket or guided missile that sustains flight after the burnout of the booster. **b.** the rocket engine or cluster of engines contained in such a stage. [1350–1400; ME *sosteynere.* See SUSTAIN, -ER[1]]

sustain′ing pro′gram, a radio or television program without a commercial sponsor. [1930–35, *Amer.*]

sus•te•nance (sus′tə nəns), *n.* **1.** means of sustaining life; nourishment. **2.** means of livelihood. **3.** the process of sustaining. **4.** the state of being sustained. [1250–1300; ME *sustena(u)nce* < AF; OF *sostenance.* See SUSTAIN, -ANCE] **—sus′te•nance•less,** *adj.*

sus•ten•tac•u•lar (sus′tən tak′yə lər), *adj. Anat.* supporting. [1885–90; < NL *sustentācul(um)* a support (L *sustentā(re),* freq. of *sustinēre* to SUSTAIN + *-culum* -CULE[2]) + -AR[1]]

sus•ten•ta•tion (sus′tən tā′shən), *n.* **1.** maintenance in being or activity; the sustaining of life through vital processes. **2.** provision with means or funds for upkeep. **3.** means of sustaining life; sustenance. [1350–1400; ME < L *sustentātiōn-* (s. of *sustentātiō*) an upholding, equiv. to *sustentāt(us)* (ptp. of *sustentāre,* freq. of *sustinēre* to SUSTAIN) + *-iōn-* -ION] **—sus′ten•ta′tion•al,** *adj.* **—sus•ten•ta•tive** (sus′tən tā′tiv, sə sten′tə tiv), *adj.*

sus•ten•tion (sə sten′shən), *n.* **1.** the act of sustaining. **2.** the state or quality of being sustained. [1865–70; *susten-* (see SUSTAIN) + -TION, modeled on *detain: detention, retain: retention*] **—sus•ten•tive** (sə sten′tiv), *adj.*

sus•ti•ne•o a•las (so͞os tin′e ō′ ä′läs; *Eng.* sə stin′ē ō′ ā′ləs), *Latin.* I sustain the wings: motto of the U.S. Air Force.

su•su (so͞o′so͞o′), *n.* an institutionalized kinship group among the Dobuans, composed of a woman, her brother, and the woman's children. [1915–20; < Dobuan, said to mean lit., milk of the mother]

su•sur•rant (so͝o sûr′ənt), *adj.* softly murmuring; whispering. [1785–95; < L *susurrant-* (s. of *susurrāns*) (prp. of *susurrāre* to whisper). See SUSURRUS, -ANT]

CONCISE PRONUNCIATION KEY: *act, cāpe, dâre, pärt; set, ēqual; if, īce; ox, ōver, ôrder, oil, bo͝ok, bo͞ot, out; up, ûrge; child; sing; shoe; thin, that;* zh as in *treasure.* ə = *a* as in *alone, e* as in *system, i* as in *easily, o* as in *gallop, u* as in *circus;* ə as in *fire* (fīər), *hour* (ouər). l and n can serve as syllabic consonants, as in *cradle* (krād′l), and *button* (but′n). See the full key inside the front cover.

su·sur·ra·tion (so͞o′sə rā′shən), *n.* a soft murmur; whisper. [1350–1400; ME < LL *susurrātiōn-* (s. of *susurrātiō*), equiv. to *susurrāt(us)* (ptp. of *susurrāre*; see SUSURRUS, -ATE[1]) + *-iōn-* -ION]

su·sur·rous (so͝o sûr′əs), *adj.* full of whispering or rustling sounds. [1855–60; SUSURR(US) + -OUS]

su·sur·rus (so͝o sûr′əs), *n., pl.* **-rus·es.** a soft murmuring or rustling sound; whisper. [1825–35; < L: a whisper]

Su·sy (so͞o′zē), *n.* a female given name, form of **Susanna** or **Susannah.**

Suth·er·land (suth′ər lənd), *n.* **1. Earl Wilbur, Jr.,** 1915–74, U.S. biochemist: Nobel prize for medicine 1971. **2. George,** 1862–1942, U.S. politician and jurist: associate justice of the U.S. Supreme Court 1922–38. **3. Dame Joan,** born 1926, Australian soprano. **4.** Also called **Suth·er·land·shire** (suth′ər lənd shēr′, -shər). a historic county in N Scotland.

Suth′erland Falls′, a waterfall in New Zealand, on SW South Island. 1904 ft. (580 m) high.

Sut·lej (sut′lej), *n.* a river in S Asia, flowing W and SW from SW Tibet through NW India into the Indus River in Pakistan. 900 mi. (1450 km) long.

sut·ler (sut′lər), *n.* (formerly) a person who followed an army or maintained a store on an army post to sell provisions to the soldiers. [1580–90; < early D *soeteler* (now *zoetelaar*), equiv. to *soetel(en)* to do dirty work, work poorly (akin to SOOT) + *-er* -ER[1]] **—sut′ler·ship′,** *n.*

su·tra (so͞o′trə), *n.* **1.** *Hinduism.* a collection of aphorisms relating to some aspect of the conduct of life. **2.** Pali, **sut·ta** (so͝ot′ə). *Buddhism.* any of the sermons of Buddha. **3.** one of the approximately 4000 rules or aphorisms that constitute Panini's grammar of Sanskrit. [1795–1805; < Skt *sūtra*]

Sut′ta Pit′aka (so͝ot′ə), *Buddhism.* See under **Pali Canon.**

sut·tee (su tē′, sut′ē), *n.* sati. **—sut·tee′ism,** *n.*

Sut·ter (sut′ər, so͞o′tər), *n.* **John Augustus,** 1803–80, U.S. frontiersman: owner of Sutter's Mill.

Sut′ter's Mill′, the location in California, NE of Sacramento, near which gold was discovered in 1848, precipitating the gold rush of 1849. [after J. SUTTER, its owner]

Sutt·ner (zo͝ot′nər, so͝ot′-; *Ger.* zo͝ot′nər), *n.* **Ber·tha von** (bûr′thə von; *Ger.* ber′tə fən), 1843–1914, Austrian writer: Nobel peace prize 1905.

Sut·ton (sut′n), *n.* a borough of Greater London, England. 165,800.

Sut′ton Hoo′ (ho͞o), an archaeological site in Suffolk, England: a rowing boat, 80 feet (24 m) long, discovered here and believed to have been buried A.D. c670 by Anglo-Saxons, possibly as a cenotaph in honor of a king.

Sut·tung (so͝ot′to͝ong), *n. Scand. Myth.* one of the Jotun, who for a time was the owner of the mead of poetry, guarded by his daughter Gunnlod, who lost a portion of it to Odin when he seduced her.

su·ture (so͞o′chər), *n., v.,* **-tured, -tur·ing.** —*n.* **1.** *Surg.* **a.** a joining of the lips or edges of a wound or the like by stitching or some similar process. **b.** a particular method of doing this. **c.** one of the stitches or fastenings employed. **2.** *Anat.* **a.** the line of junction of two bones, esp. of the skull, in an immovable articulation. **b.** the articulation itself. **3.** *Zool., Bot.* the junction or line of junction of contiguous parts, as the line of closure between the valves of a bivalve shell, a seam where carpels of a pericarp join, etc. **4.** a seam as formed in sewing; a line of junction between two parts. **5.** a sewing together or a joining as by sewing. —*v.t.* **6.** to unite by or as by a suture. [1535–45; < L *sūtūra* seam, suture, equiv. to *sūt(us)* (ptp. of *suere* to SEW[1]) + *-ūra* -URE] **—su′tur·al,** *adj.* **—su′tur·al·ly,** *adv.*

su·um cui·que (so͞o′o͝om ko͞oi′kwe; *Eng.* so͞o′əm ki′kwē, kwī′-, kwē′kwe), *Latin.* to each his own; to each what rightfully belongs to him.

Su·va (so͞o′vä), *n.* a seaport in and the capital of Fiji, on Viti Levu island. 96,000.

Su·vo·rov (so͞o vôr′ôf, -of; *Russ.* so͞o vô′rəf), *n.* **A·le·ksan·dr Va·si·le·vich** (u lyi ksän′dr vu syē′lyi vyich), *(Count Suvorov Rumnikski, Prince Itliski),* 1729–1800, Russian field marshal.

Su·wan·nee (sə won′ē, -wô′nē, swon′ē, swô′nē), *n.* a river in SE Georgia and N Florida, flowing SW to the Gulf of Mexico. 240 mi. (386 km) long. Also, **Swanee.**

Su·wŏn (so͞o′wun′) *n.* a city in NW South Korea, S of Seoul. 167,201.

Su·zanne (so͞o zan′) *n.* a female given name, French form of **Susanna** or **Susannah.** Also, **Su·zann′.**

su·ze·rain (so͞o′zə rin, -rān′), *n.* **1.** a sovereign or a state exercising political control over a dependent state. **2.** *Hist.* a feudal overlord. —*adj.* **3.** characteristic of or being a suzerain. [1800–10; < F, equiv. to *sus* above (< L *sūsum,* var. of *sursum,* contr. of *subversum,* neut. of *subversus* upturned; see SUB-, VERSE) + *(souv)erain* SOVEREIGN]

su·ze·rain·ty (so͞o′zə rin tē, -rān′-), *n., pl.* **-ties. 1.** the position or authority of a suzerain. **2.** the domain or area subject to a suzerain. [1815–25; < F *suzeraineté,* MF *suserenete,* equiv. to *suseren* SUZERAIN + *-ete* -ITY]

Su·zhou (sy′jō′), *n. Pinyin.* **1.** Formerly, **Wuxian.** a city in S Jiangsu province, in E China. 1,300,000. **2.** former name of **Yibin.** Also, **Soochow, Suchou.**

Su·zie (so͞o′zē), *n.* a female given name, form of **Susanna** or **Susannah.** Also, **Su′zy.**

Sv, *Physics.* sievert; sieverts.

S.V., Holy Virgin. [< L *Sāncta Virgō*]

s.v., 1. sub verbo. **2.** sub voce.

Sval·bard (sväl′bär), *n.* Norwegian name of **Spitsbergen.**

sva·ra·bhak·ti (sfär′ä bäk′tē; *Skt.* svə rə buk′ti), *n. Ling.* the process of inserting vowel sounds into a consonant cluster, as in a loanword to make it conform to the pattern of the speaker's language and, hence, more easily pronounceable, as in the Italian pronunciation (län′tsē ke nek′kô) for German *Landsknecht* (länts′-knekht′). Cf. **epenthesis.** [1875–80; < Skt: vowel segment (inserted in particular environments)]

svc., service. Also, **svce.**

Sved·berg (sved′bar′yə), *n.* **The(o·dor)** (tā′ō dôr′), 1884–1971, Swedish chemist: Nobel prize 1926.

svelte (svelt, sfelt), *adj.,* **svelt·er, svelt·est. 1.** slender, esp. gracefully slender in figure; lithe. **2.** suave; blandly urbane. [1810–20; < F < It *svelto* < VL **exvellitus* pulled out (r. L *ēvulsus,* ptp. of *ēvellere*), equiv. to L *ex-* EX- + *velli-,* var. s. of *vellere* to pull, pluck + *-tus* ptp. suffix]

Sven·ga·li (sven gä′lē, sfen-), *n.* a person who completely dominates another, usually with selfish or sinister motives. [1940–45; after the evil hypnotist of the same name in the novel *Trilby* (1894) by George Du Maurier]

Sverd·lovsk (sverd lôfsk′, -lofsk′, sferd-; *Russ.* svyir-dlôfsk′), *n.* former name (1924–91) of **Ekaterinburg.**

Sver·drup (sver′drəp, sfer′-; *Norw.* svar′dro͝op), *n.* **1. Ot·to Neu·mann** (ôt′tō noi′män), 1855?–1930, Norwegian explorer of the Arctic. **2.** Also called **Sver′drup Is′lands.** a group of islands in the N Northwest Territories of Canada, in the Arctic, W of Ellesmere Island: named after Otto Neumann Sverdrup.

Sve·ri·ge (sve′rē ye), *n.* Swedish name of **Sweden.**

Sve·tam·ba·ra (shve täm′bər ə), *n.* one of the two principal Jain sects, whose members wear white and believe that women can attain salvation. Cf. **Digambara.** [< Skt *śvetāmbara* white-clad]

Svet·la·na (svet lä′nə, sfet-; *Russ.* svyi tlä′nə), *n.* a female given name.

SV 40, simian virus 40; a virus of the Papovaviridae family, originally isolated from kidney cells of healthy monkeys, and important in recombinant DNA and cancer research. Also, **SV-40, SV40**

svgs., savings.

Sviz·ze·ra (zvēt′tse rä), *n.* Italian name of **Switzerland.**

SVO language, *Ling.* a type of language that has basic subject-verb-object word order, as English, Chinese, or Spanish. Cf. **SOV language, VO language, VSO language.**

S.V.R., (in prescriptions) rectified spirit of wine (alcohol). [< L *spīritus vīnī rēctificātus*]

SVS, still-camera video system.

SW, 1. shipper's weight. **2.** southwest. **3.** southwestern. Also, **Sw** (for defs. 2, 3).

Sw., 1. Sweden. **2.** Swedish. Also, **Swed**

S/W, *Computers.* software.

S.W., 1. South Wales. **2.** southwest. **3.** southwestern.

S.W.A., South West Africa.

swab (swob), *n., v.,* **swabbed, swab·bing.** —*n.* **1.** a large mop used on shipboard for cleaning decks, living quarters, etc. **2.** a bit of sponge, cloth, cotton, or the like, sometimes fixed to a stick, for cleansing the mouth of a sick person or for applying medicaments, drying areas, etc. **3.** the material collected with a swab as a specimen for microscopic study. **4.** a brush or wad of absorbent material for cleaning the bore of a firearm. **5.** *Slang.* a sailor; swabby. **6.** *Slang.* a clumsy fellow. —*v.t.* **7.** to clean with or as if with a swab: *His first assignment on board was to swab the decks.* **8.** to take up or apply, as moisture, with or as if with a swab: *to swab soapy water from the decks.* **9.** to pass over a surface: *to swab a mop over the decks.* Also, **swob.** [1645–55; back formation from SWABBER]

Swab., 1. Swabia. **2.** Swabian.

swab·ber (swob′ər), *n.* **1.** a person who uses a swab. **2.** *Slang.* swab (def. 6). **3.** a swab; mop. [1585–95; < D *zwabber;* cf. MLG *swabben* to splash in water or filth]

swab·by (swob′ē), *n., pl.* **-bies.** *Slang.* (in the Navy or Coast Guard) a sailor; gob. Also, **swab′bie.** [1940–45; SWAB + -Y[2]]

Swa·bi·a (swā′bē ə), *n.* a region and medieval duchy in SW Germany: it constituted the area presently included in the states of Baden-Württemberg and Bavaria in S Germany. German, **Schwaben. —Swa′bi·an,** *n., adj.*

swad·dle (swod′l), *v.,* **-dled, -dling,** *n.* —*v.t.* **1.** to bind (an infant, esp. a newborn infant) with long, narrow strips of cloth to prevent free movement; wrap tightly with clothes. **2.** to wrap (anything) round with bandages. —*n.* **3.** a long, narrow strip of cloth used for swaddling or bandaging. [1375–1425; late ME, in *suadiling* (ger.); akin by gradation to ME *swethel* (n.), OE; see SWATHE, -LE]

swad′dling clothes′, 1. clothes consisting of long, narrow strips of cloth for swaddling an infant. **2.** long garments for an infant. **3.** the period of infancy or immaturity, as of a person, or incipience, as of a thing: *Nuclear energy is still in its swaddling clothes.* **4.** rigid supervision or restriction of actions or movements, as of the immature: *new nations that are freeing themselves of their swaddling clothes.* Also called **swad′dling bands′** (for defs. 1, 2). [1525–35]

Swa·de·shi (swə dā′shē), *n.* a political movement in British India that encouraged domestic production and the boycott of foreign, esp. British, goods as a step toward home rule. [1900–05; < Hindi or Bengali *svadeśī,* equiv. to *sva-* self, own + *deśī* native]

swag[1] (swag), *n., v.,* **swagged, swag·ging.** —*n.* **1.** a suspended wreath, garland, drapery, or the like, fastened up at or near each end and hanging down in the middle; festoon. **2.** a wreath, spray, or cluster of foliage, flowers, or fruit. **3.** a festoon, esp. one very heavy toward the center. **4.** a swale. **5.** a swaying or lurching movement. —*v.i.* **6.** to move heavily or unsteadily from side to side or up and down; sway. **7.** to hang loosely and heavily; sink down. —*v.t.* **8.** to cause to sway, sink, or sag. **9.** to hang or adorn with swags. [1520–30; perh. < Scand; cf. Norw *svaga, svagga* to sway, rock]

swag[2] (swag), *n., v.,* **swagged, swag·ging.** —*n.* **1.** *Slang.* **a.** plunder; booty. **b.** money; valuables. **2.** *Australian.* a traveler's bundle containing personal belongings, cooking utensils, food, or the like. —*v.i.* **3.** *Australian.* to travel about carrying one's bundle of personal belongings. [1860–65; special uses of SWAG[1]]

swage (swāj), *n., v.,* **swaged, swag·ing.** —*n.* **1.** a tool for bending cold metal to a required shape. **2.** a tool, die, or stamp for giving a particular shape to metal on an anvil, in a stamping press, etc. **3.** See **swage block.** —*v.t.* **4.** to bend or shape by means of a swage. **5.** to reduce or taper (an object), as by forging or squeezing. [1325–75; ME *souage* < MF] **—swag′er,** *n.*

swage′ block′, an iron block containing holes and grooves of various sizes, used for heading bolts and shaping objects not easily worked on an anvil. [1835–45]

swag·ger (swag′ər), *v.i.* **1.** to walk or strut with a defiant or insolent air. **2.** to boast or brag noisily. —*v.t.* **3.** to bring, drive, force, etc., by blustering. —*n.* **4.** swaggering manner, conduct, or walk; ostentatious display of arrogance and conceit. [1580–90; SWAG[1] + -ER[6]] **—swag′ger·er,** *n.*
—Syn. 1. See **strut**[1].

swag′ger coat′, a woman's pyramid-shaped coat with a full flared back and usually raglan sleeves, first popularized in the 1930's. [1930–35]

swag·ger·ing (swag′ər ing), *adj.* pertaining to, characteristic of, or behaving in the manner of a person who swaggers. [1590–1600; SWAGGER + -ING[2]] **—swag′ger·ing·ly,** *adv.*

swag′ger stick′, a short, batonlike stick, usually leather-covered, sometimes carried by army officers, soldiers, etc. [1885–90]

swag·man (swag′mən), *n., pl.* **-men.** *Australian.* **1.** a tramp, hobo, or vagabond. **2.** anyone who carries a swag while traveling, as a camper or prospector. [1875–80; SWAG[2] + -MAN]

Swa·hi·li (swä hē′lē), *n., pl.* **-lis,** *(esp. collectively)* **-li** for 1. **1.** a member of a Bantu people of Zanzibar and the neighboring coast of Africa. **2.** Also, **Kiswahili, Ki-Swahili.** the Bantu language of the Swahili people, used also as a lingua franca in Tanzania, Kenya, and parts of Zaire. **—Swa·hi′li·an,** *adj.*

swain (swān), *n.* **1.** a male admirer or lover. **2.** a country lad. **3.** a country gallant. [bef. 1150; ME *swein* servant < ON *sveinn* boy, servant; c. OE *swān*] **—swain′ish,** *adj.* **—swain′ish·ness,** *n.*

Swain′son's hawk′ (swān′sənz), a migratory hawk, *Buteo swainsoni,* of western North America, that winters in southern South America. [1890–95, *Amer.*; named after William *Swainson* (1789–1855), English naturalist]

Swain′son's thrush′, a North American thrush, *Catharus ustulatus,* having olive upper parts and wintering south to Argentina. Also called **olive-backed thrush.** [see SWAINSON'S HAWK]

S.W.A.K., sealed with a kiss (written at the end of a love letter or on the back of its envelope). Also, **SWAK** (swak). [1925–30]

swa·ka·ra (swä′kər ə), *n.* the fur of Karakul sheep raised in Namibia; Persian lamb. [1965–70; *S(outh) W(est) A(frica)* + KARA(KUL)]

swale (swāl), *n. Chiefly Northeastern U.S.* **1.** a low place in a tract of land, usually moister and often having ranker vegetation than the adjacent higher land. **2.** a valleylike intersection of two slopes in a piece of land. [1400–50; late ME; orig. a cool, shady spot, perh. < ON *svalr* cool, or *svalir* a covered porch]

swal·let (swol′it), *n. Brit.* **1.** an underground stream. **2.** an opening through which a stream descends underground. [1660–70; SWALL(OW)[1] + -ET]

swal·low[1] (swol′ō), *v.t.* **1.** to take into the stomach by drawing through the throat and esophagus with a voluntary muscular action, as food, drink, or other substances. **2.** to take in so as to envelop; withdraw from sight; assimilate or absorb: *He was swallowed by the crowd.* **3.** to accept without question or suspicion. **4.** to accept without opposition; put up with: *to swallow an insult.* **5.** to accept for lack of an alternative: *Consumers will have to swallow new price hikes.* **6.** to suppress (emotion, a laugh, a sob, etc.) as if by drawing it down one's throat. **7.** to take back; retract: *to swallow one's words.* **8.** to enunciate poorly; mutter: *He swallowed his words.* —*v.i.* **9.** to perform the act of swallowing. —*n.* **10.** the act or an instance of swallowing. **11.** a quantity swallowed at one time; a mouthful: *Take one swallow of brandy.* **12.** capacity for swallowing. **13.** Also called **crown, throat.** *Naut., Mach.* the space in a block, between the groove of the sheave and the shell, through which the rope runs. [bef. 1000; (v.) ME *swalwen,* var. of *swelwen,* OE *swelgan;* c. G *schwelgen;* akin to ON *svelgja;* (n.) ME *swalwe, swolgh* throat, abyss, whirlpool, OE *geswelgh* (see Y-); akin to MLG *swelch,* OHG *swelgo* glutton, ON *svelgr* whirlpool, devourer] —**swal′low·a·ble,** *adj.* —**swal′low·er,** *n.*
—**Syn. 1.** eat, gulp, drink. **2.** engulf, devour. **10.** gulp, draught, drink.

swal·low[2] (swol′ō), *n.* **1.** any of numerous small, long-winged passerine birds of the family Hirundinidae, noted for their swift, graceful flight and for the extent and regularity of their migrations. Cf. **bank swallow, barn swallow, martin. 2.** any of several unrelated, swallow-like birds, as the chimney swift. [bef. 900; ME *swalwe,* OE *swealwe;* c. G *Schwalbe,* ON *svala*]

swal′low dive′, *Chiefly Brit.* See **swan dive.** [1895–1900]

swal·low·tail (swol′ō tāl′), *n.* **1.** the tail of a swallow or a deeply forked tail like that of a swallow. **2.** any of several butterflies of the genus *Papilio,* characterized by elongated hind wings that resemble the tail of a swallow, as *P. polyxenes* **(black swallowtail).** Cf. **spicebush swallowtail, tiger swallowtail, zebra swallowtail. 3.** See **tail coat.** [1535–45; SWALLOW[2] + TAIL[1]]

tiger swallowtail, *Papilio glaucus,* wingspread to 4 in. (10 cm)

swal·low-tailed (swol′ō tāld′), *adj.* **1.** having a deeply forked tail like that of a swallow, as various birds. **2.** having an end or part suggesting a swallow's tail. **3.** (of a flag) having a triangular indentation in the fly so as to create two tails. [1690–1700]

swal′low-tailed coat′. See **tail coat.** [1825–35]

swal′low-tailed kite′, an American kite, *Elanoides forficatus,* having black upper parts, white head and underparts, and a long, deeply forked tail. [1870–75]

swal·low-tan·a·ger (swol′ō tan′ə jər), *n.* a tropical American bird, *Tersina viridis,* related to the true tanagers but with longer, swallowlike wings.

swal·low·wort (swol′ō wûrt′, -wôrt′), *n.* **1.** celandine (def. 1). **2.** any of several plants of the milkweed family, esp. a climbing vine, *Cynanchum nigrum* **(black swallowwort),** native to Europe, having small, brownish flowers. [1540–50; SWALLOW[2] + WORT[2]]

swam (swam), *v.* pt. of **swim.**

swa·mi (swä′mē), *n., pl.* **-mies. 1.** an honorific title given to a Hindu religious teacher. **2.** a person resembling a swami, esp. in authority, critical judgment, etc.; pundit: *The swamis are saying the stock market is due for a drop.* Also, **swamy.** [1765–75; < Skt *svāmī,* nom. sing. of *svāmin* master, owner]

Swam·mer·dam (sväm′ər däm′), *n.* **Jan** (yän), 1637–80, Dutch anatomist and entomologist.

swamp (swomp), *n.* **1.** a tract of wet, spongy land, often having a growth of certain types of trees and other vegetation, but unfit for cultivation. —*v.t.* **2.** to flood or drench with water or the like. **3.** *Naut.* to sink or fill (a boat) with water. **4.** to plunge or cause to sink in or as if in a swamp. **5.** to overwhelm, esp. to overwhelm with an excess of something: *He swamped us with work.* **6.** to render helpless. **7.** to remove trees and underbrush from (a specific area), esp. to make or cleave a trail (often fol. by *out*). **8.** to trim (felled trees) into logs, as at a logging camp or sawmill. —*v.i.* **9.** to fill with water and sink, as a boat. **10.** to sink or be stuck in a swamp or something likened to a swamp. **11.** to be plunged into or overwhelmed with something, esp. something that keeps one busy, worried, etc. [1615–25; < D *zwamp* creek, fen; akin to SUMP and to MLG *swamp,* ON *svǫppr* sponge] —**swamp′ish,** *adj.*

swamp′ androm′eda, a spreading shrub, *Lyonia ligustrina,* of the eastern U.S., having leafless, white flowers in terminal clusters. Also called **he-huckleberry, maleberry, privet andromeda.**

swamp′ azal′ea, an azalea, *Rhododendron viscosum,* of the eastern U.S., having fragrant, white to pink or sometimes red flowers. [1790–1800]

swamp′ bug′gy, an amphibious vehicle for use in and around swamps, typically having an automobile engine, four-wheel drive, large wheels with deep treads, and a raised chassis. Also called **marsh buggy.** [1940–45, *Amer.*]

swamp′ but′tonwood, the buttonbush. [1745–55, *Amer.*]

swamp′ cab′bage. See **skunk cabbage.** [1785–95, *Amer.*]

swamp′ cy′press. See **bald cypress.** [1875–80]

swamp·er (swom′pər), *n.* **1.** *Informal.* a person who inhabits, works in, or is exceptionally familiar with swamps. **2.** a general assistant or laborer; menial. **3.** a person who trims felled trees into logs at a logging camp or sawmill. **4.** *CB Slang.* a motorist or truck driver, esp. one using a CB radio. [1715–25; SWAMP + -ER[1]]

swamp′ fe′ver, *Pathol., Vet. Pathol.* **1.** leptospirosis. **2.** Also called **infectious anemia of horses.** an equine viral disease characterized by weakness and recurring fever, transmitted by contaminated food and water. **3.** malaria. [1840–50, *Amer.*]

swamp·fish (swomp′fish′), *n., pl.* **-fish·es,** (*esp. collectively*) **-fish.** a small fish, *Chologaster cornuta,* related to the cavefishes, inhabiting swamps and streams of the Atlantic coastal plain, having small but functional eyes and almost transparent skin. [SWAMP + FISH]

swamp′ gas′. See **marsh gas.**

swamp·hen (swomp′hen′), *n. Ornith.* any of several large Old World gallinules varying from purple to white, all possibly belonging to the single species *Porphyrio porphyrio.* [SWAMP + HEN]

swamp·land (swomp′land′), *n.* land or an area covered with swamps. [1655–65, *Amer.*; SWAMP + LAND]

swamp′ lo′cust. See **water locust.** [1820–30]

swamp′ mal′low, a rose mallow, *Hibiscus moscheutos.*

swamp′ ma′ple. See **red maple.** [1660–70, *Amer.*]

swamp′ milk′weed, a coarse milkweed, *Asclepias incarnata,* growing in swampy places from eastern North America to Colorado, having ball-like clusters of rose-purple flowers. [1855–60, *Amer.*]

swamp′ pink′, **1.** a bog plant, *Helonias bullata,* of the lily family, native to the eastern U.S., having a dense spike of small, fragrant pink flowers. **2.** See **arethusa** (def. 1). **3.** any of several other pink-flowered plants that grow in wet places. [1775–85, *Amer.*]

swamp′ rab′bit, any of several southern cottontails, esp. *Sylvilagus aquaticus,* of swamps and lowlands. Also called **canecutter.** See illus. under **rabbit.** [1840–50, *Amer.*]

swamp′ rose′, a shrub, *Rosa palustris,* of eastern North America, having pink flowers nearly 2 in. (5 cm) wide. [1775–85, *Amer.*]

Swamp·scott (swomp′skət), *n.* a city in NE Massachusetts. 13,837.

swamp′ spar′row, a North American sparrow, *Melospiza georgiana,* inhabiting marshy areas. [1805–15, *Amer.*]

swamp′ white′ oak′, an oak, *Quercus bicolor,* of eastern North America, yielding a hard, heavy wood used in shipbuilding, for making furniture, etc. [1715–25, *Amer.*]

swamp·y (swom′pē), *adj.,* **swamp·i·er, swamp·i·est. 1.** of the nature of, resembling, or abounding in swamps. **2.** found in swamps. [1640–50; SWAMP + -Y[1]] —**swamp′i·ness,** *n.*

swa·my (swä′mē), *n., pl.* **-mies.** swami.

swan[1] (swon), *n.* **1.** any of several large, stately aquatic birds of the subfamily Anserinae, having a long, slender neck and usually pure-white plumage in the adult. Cf. **mute swan, trumpeter swan, whistling swan, whooper swan. 2.** a person or thing of unusual beauty, excellence, purity, or the like. **3.** *Literary.* a person who sings sweetly or a poet. **4.** (*cap.*) *Astron.* the constellation Cygnus. [bef. 900; ME, OE; c. G *Schwan,* ON *svanr*] —**swan′like′,** *adj.*

mute swan, *Cygnus olor,* length 5 ft. (1.5 m)

swan[2] (swon), *v.i. Midland and Southern U.S. Older Use.* to swear or declare (used with *I*): *Well, I swan, I never expected to see you here!* [1775–85, *Amer.*; prob. continuing dial. (N England) *I s'wan,* shortening of *I shall warrant*]

Swan (swon), *n.* **Sir Joseph Wilson,** 1828–1914, British chemist, electrical engineer, and inventor.

swan′ dive′, *Diving.* a forward dive in which the diver while in the air assumes a position with the arms outstretched at shoulder height and the legs straight and together, and enters the water with the arms stretched above the head. Also called, *esp. Brit.,* **swallow dive.** [1895–1900, *Amer.*]

swan-dive (swon′dīv′), *v.i.,* **-dived, -div·ing. 1.** to perform a swan dive. **2.** to decrease suddenly and decisively; plummet: *Stock prices swan-dived overnight.*

Swa·nee (swon′ē, swô′nē), *n.* Suwannee.

swang (swang), *v. Chiefly Scot. and North Eng.* pt. of **swing**[1].

swan·herd (swon′hûrd′), *n.* a person who tends swans. [1475–85; SWAN[1] + HERD[2]]

swank[1] (swangk), *n., adj.,* **-er, -est,** *v.* —*n.* **1.** dashing smartness, as in dress or appearance; style. **2.** a swagger. —*adj.* **3.** stylish or elegant. **4.** pretentiously stylish. —*v.i.* **5.** to swagger in behavior; show off. [1800–10; cf. Scots *swank* lively, perh. ult. repr. back formation from OE *swancor* lithe; akin to MD *swanc* supple, MHG *swanken* to sway]

swank[2] (swangk), *v.* a pt. of **swink.**

swank·y (swang′kē), *adj.,* **swank·i·er, swank·i·est.** elegant or ostentatious; swank. [1835–45; SWANK[1] + -Y[1]] —**swank′i·ly,** *adv.* —**swank′i·ness,** *n.*
—**Syn.** stylish, chic, smart, fashionable.

Swan′ Lake′, The, a ballet (1876) by Tchaikovsky.

swan′ maid′en, any of a class of folkloric maidens, in many Indo-European and Asian tales, capable of being transformed into swans, as by magic or sorcery. [1865–70]

swan·ner·y (swon′ə rē), *n., pl.* **-ner·ies.** a place where swans are raised. [1560–70; SWAN[1] + -ERY]

Swans′combe man′ (swonz′kəm), a primitive human, *Homo sapiens steinheimensis,* of the middle Pleistocene Epoch, known from a fossil skull fragment found at Swanscombe, England. [1935–40]

swans·down (swonz′doun′), *n.* **1.** the down or under plumage of a swan, used for trimming, powder puffs, etc. **2.** a fine, soft, thick woolen cloth. **3.** a sturdy cotton flannel with a thickly napped face. [1600–10; SWAN[1] + 'S[1] + DOWN[2]]

Swan·sea (swon′sē, -zē), *n.* **1.** a seaport in West Glamorgan, in S Wales. 190,500. **2.** a city in SE Massachusetts. 15,461.

swan·skin (swon′skin′), *n.* **1.** the skin of a swan, with the feathers on. **2.** a closely woven twill-weave flannel for work clothes. [1600–10; SWAN[1] + SKIN]

swan's′ neck′, a shallow S-curve used in decorative work. Also, **swan′ neck′.**

swan's′ neck′ ped′iment, *Archit., Furniture.* a broken pediment, the outline of which consists of a pair of S-curves tangent to the cornice level at the ends of the pediment, rising to a pair of scrolls on either side of the center, where a finial often rises between the scrolls. Also, **swan′ neck′ ped′iment.**

Swan·son (swon′sən), *n.* **Gloria** (*Gloria Josephine May Swenson*), 1899–1983, U.S. film actress.

swan′ song′, the last act or manifestation of someone or something; farewell appearance: *This building turned out to be the swan song of Victorian architecture.* [1825–35; so called from the belief that the dying swan sings]

swan-up·ping (swon′up′ing), *n. Brit.* **1.** the taking up of young swans to mark them with nicks on the beak for identification. **2.** an annual expedition for this purpose on the Thames. [1800–10; SWAN[1] + *upping* (UP + -ING[1])]

swap (swop), *v.,* **swapped, swap·ping,** *n.* —*v.t.* **1.** to exchange, barter, or trade, as one thing for another: *He swapped his wrist watch for the radio.* —*v.i.* **2.** to make an exchange. —*n.* **3.** an exchange: *He got the radio in a swap.* Also, **swop.** [1300–50; ME *swappen* to strike, strike hands (in bargaining); c. dial. G *schwappen* to box (the ears)] —**swap′per,** *n.*

swap′ meet′, a fair or bazaar where objects, usually secondhand, are bartered or sold. [1960–65]

swap′ shop′, a store or shop where items, esp. secondhand ones, are traded or sold.

swa·raj (swə räj′), *n.* **1.** (in India) self-government. **2.** (*cap.*) (formerly, in British India) the political party supporting this principle over British rule. [1905–10; < Hindi, presumably equiv. to Skt *sva* own + Hindi *rāj* RAJ] —**swa·raj′ism,** *n.* —**swa·raj′ist,** *n., adj.*

sward (swôrd), *n.* **1.** the grassy surface of land; turf. **2.** a stretch of turf; a growth of grass. —*v.t.* **3.** to cover with sward or turf. —*v.i.* **4.** to become covered with sward. [bef. 900; ME (n.); OE *sweard* skin, rind; c. G *Schwarte* rind, OFris *swarde* scalp, MD *swaerde* skin]

sware (swâr), *v. Archaic.* pt. of **swear.**

swarf (swôrf), *n.* an accumulation of fine particles of metal or abrasive cut or ground from work by a machine tool or grinder. [1560–70; < ON *svarf,* akin to *sverfa* to file, or continuing OE *geswearf, gesweorf*]

swarm[1] (swôrm), *n.* **1.** a body of honeybees that emigrate from a hive and fly off together, accompanied by a queen, to start a new colony. **2.** a body of bees settled together, as in a hive. **3.** a great number of things or persons, esp. in motion. **4.** *Biol.* a group or aggregation of free-floating or free-swimming cells or organisms. **5.** *Geol.* a cluster of earthquakes or other geologic phenomena or features. —*v.i.* **6.** to fly off together in a swarm, as bees. **7.** to move about, along, forth, etc., in great numbers, as things or persons. **8.** to congregate, hover, or occur in groups or multitudes; be exceedingly numerous, as in a place or area. **9.** (of a place) to be thronged or overrun; abound or teem: *The beach swarms with children on summer weekends.* **10.** *Biol.* to move or swim about in a swarm. —*v.t.* **11.** to swarm about, over, or in; throng; overrun. **12.** to produce a swarm of. [bef. 900; (n.) ME; OE *swearm;* c. G *Schwarm* swarm, ON *svarmr* tumult; (v.) ME *swarmen,* deriv. of the n.] —**swarm′er,** *n.*
—**Syn. 3.** horde, host, mass. See **crowd**[1].

swarm[2] (swôrm), *v.t., v.i.* to climb by clasping with the legs and hands or arms and drawing oneself up; shin. [1540–50; orig. uncert.]

swarm′ cell′, *Mycol.* the amebalike germinated spore cell of myxomycetes. [1880–85]

swart (swôrt), *adj.* swarthy. [bef. 900; ME; OE *sweart* black, dark; c. G *schwarz,* ON *svartr,* Goth *swarts;* akin to L *sordēs* filth] —**swart′ness,** *n.*

Swart (swôrt), *n.* **Charles Rob·berts** (rob′ərts), 1894–1982, South African statesman: president 1961–67.

CONCISE PRONUNCIATION KEY: act, cāpe, dâre, pärt; set, ēqual; if, ice; ox, ōver, ôrder, oil, bo͝ok, bo͞ot, out; up, ûrge; child; sing; shoe; thin, *th*at; zh as in *treasure.* ə = *a* as in *alone, e* as in *system, i* as in *easily, o* as in *gallop, u* as in *circus;* ə as in *fire* (fīər), *hour* (ouər). l and n can serve as syllabic consonants, as in *cradle* (krād′l), and *button* (but′n). See the full key inside the front cover.

swarth[1] (swôrth), *n.* sward; greensward. [bef. 900; ME; OE *swearth,* var. of *sweard* skin, rind; see SWARD]

swarth[2] (swôrth), *adj.* swarthy. [unexplained var. of SWART] —**swarth′ness,** *n.*

Swar•thout (swôr′thout), *n.* **Gladys,** 1904–69, U.S. soprano.

swarth•y (swôr′thē, -thē), *adj.,* **swarth•i•er, swarth•i•est.** (of skin color, complexion, etc.) dark. [1570–80; unexplained var. of obs. *swarty* (SWART + -Y[1])] —**swarth′i•ness,** *n.*

Swart′krans ape′-man (sfärt′kränz), the fossil remains of the extinct hominid *Australopithecus robustus,* found at Swartkrans, Republic of South Africa: formerly classified in the genus *Paranthropus.*

swartz•ite (swôrt′sīt), *n. Mineral.* a hydrous carbonate of calcium, magnesium, and uranium, occurring in green crystals: an ore of uranium. [named after C. K. *Swartz* (1861–1949), American geologist; see -ITE[1]]

swash (swosh, swôsh), *v.i.* **1.** to splash, as things in water, or as water does: *Waves were swashing against the piers.* **2.** to dash around, as things in violent motion. **3.** to swagger. —*v.t.* **4.** to dash or cast violently, esp. to dash (water or other liquid) around, down, etc. —*n.* **5.** the surging or dashing, sometimes violent, of water, waves, etc. **6.** the sound made by such dashing: *the thunderous swash of the waves.* **7.** the ground over which water washes. **8.** *Chiefly Southeastern U.S.* a channel of water through or behind a sandbank. **9.** *Print.* an extending ornamental flourish, as on letters of certain fonts of italic or cursive type. —*adj.* **10.** *Print.* noting or pertaining to a character having a swash: *a swash letter.* [1520–30; imit.]

swash•buck•le (swosh′buk′əl, swôsh′-), *v.i.,* **-led, -ling.** to work, behave, or perform as a swashbuckler. [1895–1900; back formation from SWASHBUCKLER]

swash•buck•ler (swosh′buk′lər, swôsh′-), *n.* a swaggering swordsman, soldier, or adventurer; daredevil. Also, **swash′er.** [1550–60; SWASH + BUCKLER]

swash•buck•ling (swosh′buk′ling, swôsh′-), *adj.* **1.** characteristic of or behaving in the manner of a swashbuckler. —*n.* **2.** the activities, deeds, or adventures of a swashbuckler. Also, **swash′buck′ler•ing.** [1685–95; SWASHBUCKL(ER) + -ING[2], -ING[1]]

swash•ing (swosh′ing, swô′shing), *adj.* **1.** tending to swash: *swashing water.* **2.** swashbuckling. [1550–60; SWASH + -ING[2]] —**swash′ing•ly,** *adv.*

swash′ let′ter, an ornamental italic capital letter having a flourish extending beyond the body of the type. [1675–85]

swash′ plate′, *Mach.* an inclined circular plate on a rotating shaft for transferring force and motion to or from parts reciprocating in a direction parallel to the axis of shaft rotation. Also, **swash′plate′.**

swas•ti•ka (swos′ti kə *or, esp. Brit.,* swas′-), *n.* **1.** a figure used as a symbol or an ornament in the Old World and in America since prehistoric times, consisting of a cross with arms of equal length, each arm having a continuation at right angles. **2.** this figure as the official emblem of the Nazi party and the Third Reich. [1850–55; < Skt *svastika,* equiv. to *su-* good, well (c. Gk *eu-* EU-) + *as-* be (see IS) + *-ti-* abstract n. suffix + *-ka* secondary n. suffix] —**swas′ti•kaed,** *adj.*

swastika (def. 1)

swastika (def. 2)

swat[1] (swot), *v.,* **swat•ted, swat•ting,** *n.* —*v.t.* **1.** to hit; slap; smack. **2.** *Baseball.* to hit (a ball) powerfully, usually for a long distance. —*n.* **3.** a smart blow; slap; smack. **4.** *Baseball.* a powerfully hit ball. Also, **swot.** [1790–1800; orig. var. of SQUAT]

swat[2] (swot), *v. Dial.* pt. and pp. of **sweat.**

swat[3] (swot), *v.i.,* **swat•ted, swat•ting,** *n. Brit. Slang.* swot[2].

Swat (swät), *n.* **1.** a former princely state in NW India: now a part of Pakistan. **2.** Also, **Swati.** a Muslim inhabitant of Swat.

SWAT (swot), *n.* a special section of some law enforcement agencies trained and equipped to deal with especially dangerous or violent situations, as when hostages are being held (often used attributively): *a SWAT team.* Also, **S.W.A.T.** [*S*(*pecial*) *W*(*eapons*) *a*(*nd*) *T*(*actics*)]

swatch (swoch), *n.* **1.** a sample of cloth or other material. **2.** a sample, patch, or characteristic specimen of anything. [1505–15; akin to SWITCH]

swath (swoth, swôth), *n.* **1.** the space covered by the stroke of a scythe or the cut of a mowing machine. **2.** the piece or strip so cut. **3.** a line or ridge of grass, grain, or the like, cut and thrown together by a scythe or mowing machine. **4.** a strip, belt, or long and relatively narrow extent of anything. **5. cut a swath,** to make a pretentious display; attract notice: *The new doctor cut a swath in the small community.* Also, **swathe.** [bef. 900; ME; OE *swæth* footprint; c. G *Shwade*]

CONCISE ETYMOLOGY KEY: <, descended or borrowed from; >, whence; b., blend of, blended; c., cognate with; cf., compare; deriv., derivative; equiv., equivalent; imit., imitative; obl., oblique; r., replacing; s., stem; sp., spelling, spelled; resp., respelling, respelled; trans., translation; ?, origin unknown; *, unattested; ‡, probably earlier than. See the full key inside the front cover.

swathe[1] (swoth, swāth), *v.,* **swathed, swath•ing,** *n.* —*v.t.* **1.** to wrap, bind, or swaddle with bands of some material; wrap up closely or fully. **2.** to bandage. **3.** to enfold or envelop, as wrappings do. **4.** to wrap (cloth, rope, etc.) around something. —*n.* **5.** a band of linen or the like in which something is wrapped; wrapping; bandage. [bef. 1050; (n.) ME; OE *swæth* or *swath* (in *swathum* dat. pl.); cf. SWADDLE; (v.) ME *swathen,* late OE *swathian,* deriv. of the n.; c. ON *svatha*]

swathe[2] (swoth, swāth), *n.* swath.

Swa•ti (swä′tē), *n., pl.* **-tis,** (*esp. collectively*) **-ti.** Swat (def. 2).

Swa•tow (swä′tou′), *n. Older Spelling.* Shantou.

swats (swats), *n.* (*used with a plural v.*) *Scot.* sweet, new beer or ale. [1500–10; cf. OE *swatan* beer (pl.)]

swat•ter (swot′ər), *n.* **1.** a person or thing that swats. **2.** See **fly swatter.** [1910–15; SWAT[1] + -ER[1]]

S wave, *Geol.* a transverse earthquake wave that travels through the interior of the earth and is usually the second conspicuous wave to reach a seismograph. Also called **secondary wave.** Cf. **L wave, P wave.**

sway (swā), *v.i.* **1.** to move or swing to and fro, as something fixed at one end or resting on a support. **2.** to move or incline to one side or in a particular direction. **3.** to incline in opinion, sympathy, tendency, etc.: *She swayed toward conservatism.* **4.** to fluctuate or vacillate, as in opinion: *His ideas swayed this way and that.* **5.** to wield power; exercise rule. —*v.t.* **6.** to cause to move to and fro or to incline from side to side. **7.** to cause to move to one side or in a particular direction. **8.** *Naut.* to hoist or raise (a yard, topmast, or the like) (usually fol. by *up*). **9.** to cause to fluctuate or vacillate. **10.** to cause (the mind, emotions, etc., or a person) to incline or turn in a specified way; influence. **11.** to cause to swerve, as from a purpose or a course of action: *He swayed them from their plan.* **12.** to dominate; direct. **13.** to wield, as a weapon or scepter. **14.** to rule; govern. —*n.* **15.** the act of swaying; swaying movement. **16.** rule; dominion: *He held all Asia in his sway.* **17.** dominating power or influence: *Many voters were under his sway.* [1300–50; (v.) ME *sweyen* < ON *sveigja* to bend, sway (transit.); (n.) ME, deriv. of the v.] —**sway′a•ble,** *adj.* —**sway′er,** *n.* —**sway′ing•ly,** *adv.*
—**Syn. 1.** wave. See **swing**[1]. **3.** lean, bend, tend.

sway•back (swā′bak′), *Vet. Pathol.* —*n.* **1.** an excessive downward curvature of the spinal column in the dorsal region, esp. of horses. —*adj.* **2.** swaybacked. [1865–70, *Amer.;* SWAY + BACK[1]]

sway•backed (swā′bakt′), *adj. Vet. Pathol.* having the back sagged to an unusual degree; having a swayback. Also, **swayback.** [1670–80; SWAY + BACKED]

sway′ bar′, *Auto.* See **stabilizer bar.** [1945–50]

swayed (swād), *adj. Vet. Pathol.* swaybacked. [1570–80; SWAY + -ED[2]]

Swa•zi (swä′zē), *n., pl.* **-zis,** (*esp. collectively*) **-zi** for 1. **1.** a member of a Nguni people of Swaziland and the Republic of South Africa. **2.** the Bantu language of the Swazi.

Swa•zi•land (swä′zē land′), *n.* a kingdom in SE Africa between S Mozambique and the E Republic of South Africa: formerly a British protectorate. 480,000; 6704 sq. mi. (17,363 sq. km). *Cap.:* Mbabane.

SWbS, See **southwest by south.**

SWbW, See **southwest by west.**

swear (swâr), *v.,* **swore** or (*Archaic*) **sware; sworn; swear•ing.** —*v.i.* **1.** to make a solemn declaration or affirmation by some sacred being or object, as a deity or the Bible. **2.** to bind oneself by oath. **3.** to give evidence or make a statement on oath. **4.** to use profane oaths or language: *Don't swear in front of the children.* —*v.t.* **5.** to declare, affirm, attest, etc., by swearing by a deity, some sacred object, etc. **6.** to affirm, assert, or say with solemn earnestness. **7.** to promise or undertake on oath or in a solemn manner; vow. **8.** to testify or state on oath: *He swore it on the witness stand.* **9.** to take (an oath), as in order to give solemnity or force to a declaration, promise, etc. **10.** to bind by an oath: *to swear someone to secrecy.* **11. swear by, a.** to name (a sacred being or thing) as one's witness or guarantee in swearing. **b.** *Informal.* to have great confidence in; rely on: *He swears by his dentist.* **c.** to have certain knowledge of: *I thought I saw him leaving, but I couldn't swear by it.* **12. swear in,** to admit to office or service by administering an oath: *A new president will be sworn in today.* **13. swear off,** to promise or resolve to give up something, esp. intoxicating beverages. **14. swear out,** to secure (a warrant for arrest) by making an accusation under oath. [bef. 900; ME *sweren,* OE *swerian;* c. G *schwören,* ON *sverja;* akin to Goth *swaran* to swear; see ANSWER] —**swear′er,** *n.* —**swear′ing•ly,** *adv.*
—**Syn. 1.** declare, affirm, avow. **3.** depose, testify. **4.** imprecate. See **curse.**

swear•ing-in (swâr′ing in′), *n.* an official ceremony where a person takes an oath of office, allegiance, etc. [1890–95; from v. phrase *swear in;* see -ING[1]]

swear•word (swâr′wûrd′), *n.* a word used in swearing or cursing; a profane or obscene word. [1880–85, *Amer.;* SWEAR + WORD]

sweat (swet), *v.,* **sweat** or **sweat•ed, sweat•ing,** *n., adj.* —*v.i.* **1.** to perspire, esp. freely or profusely. **2.** to exude moisture, as green plants piled in a heap or cheese. **3.** to gather moisture from the surrounding air by condensation. **4.** (of moisture or liquid) to ooze or be exuded. **5.** *Informal.* to work hard. **6.** *Informal.* to experience distress, as from anxiety. **7.** (of tobacco) to ferment.
—*v.t.* **8.** to excrete (perspiration, moisture, etc.) through the pores of the skin. **9.** to exude in drops or small particles: *The drying figs sweat tiny drops of moisture.* **10.** to send forth or get rid of with or like perspiration (often fol. by *out* or *off*). **11.** to wet or stain with perspiration. **12.** to cause (a person, a horse, etc.) to perspire. **13.** to cause to exude moisture, esp. as a step in an industrial drying process: *to sweat wood.* **14.** to earn, produce, or obtain (a result, promotion, compliment, etc.) by hard work. **15.** to cause to lose (weight) as by perspiring or hard work: *The hard week's work sweated five pounds off him.* **16.** to cause, force, or bring pressure on (a person, an animal, etc.) to work hard. **17.** to employ (workers) at low wages, for long hours, or under other unfavorable conditions. **18.** to labor with meticulous care over: *The manufacturer of this beautiful car has really sweated the details.* **19.** *Slang.* **a.** to obtain or extort (money) from someone. **b.** to extort money from; fleece. **20.** *Slang.* to subject to severe questioning; give the third degree to. **21.** *Metall.* **a.** to heat (an alloy) in order to remove a constituent melting at a lower temperature than the alloy as a whole. **b.** to heat (solder or the like) to melting. **c.** to join (metal objects) by heating and pressing together, usually with solder. **22.** to remove bits of metal from (gold coins) by shaking them against one another, as in a bag. Cf. **clip**[1] (def. 4). **23.** to cause (tobacco or cocoa) to ferment. **24. no sweat,** *Informal.* with no difficulty or problem. **25. sweat blood,** *Informal.* **a.** to be under a strain; work strenuously. **b.** to wait anxiously; worry: *He was sweating blood while she was in the operating room.* **26. sweat it,** *Informal.* **a.** to wait anxiously; endure the best way one can: *There was no news of survivors, so all we could do was sweat it.* **b.** to worry; be apprehensive: *You'll do OK, so don't sweat it.* **27. sweat out,** *Informal.* **a.** to await anxiously the outcome of; endure apprehensively: *The accused sweated out the jury's deliberation.* **b.** to work arduously at or toward: *The director sweated out a camera angle with the cinematographer.*
—*n.* **28.** the process of sweating or perspiring. **29.** that which is secreted from sweat glands; perspiration. **30.** a state or a period of sweating. **31.** hard work. **32.** *Informal.* a state of anxiety or impatience. **33.** a process of inducing sweating or perspiration, or of being sweated, as in medical treatment. **34.** moisture exuded from something or gathered on a surface. **35.** an exuding of moisture, as by a substance. **36.** an inducing of such exudation, as in some industrial process. **37.** a run given to a horse for exercise, as before a race. **38. sweats,** *Informal.* sweatpants, sweatshirts, sweat suits, or the like.
—*adj.* **39.** *Informal.* **a.** (of clothes) made to be worn for exercise, sports, or other physical activity. **b.** made of the absorbent fabric used for such clothes: *sweat dresses.* **c.** of, for, or associated with such clothes: *the sweat look in sportswear.* [bef. 900; 1970–75 for def. 6; (v.) ME *sweten,* OE *swǣtan* to sweat, deriv. of *swāt* (n.) (> obs. E *swote*); (n.) ME, alter. of *swote,* influenced by the v.; c. D *zweet,* G *Schweiss,* ON *sveiti,* Skt *svedas;* akin to L *sūdor,* Gk *hidrōs*] —**sweat′less,** *adj.*
—**Syn. 29.** See **perspiration.**

sweat•band (swet′band′), *n.* **1.** a band lining the inside of a hat or cap to protect it against sweat from the head. **2.** a band of fabric worn around the head to absorb sweat. [1890–95; SWEAT + BAND[2]]

sweat′ bee′, any of several bees of the family Halictidae that are attracted by perspiration. [1890–95]

sweat•box (swet′boks′), *n.* **1.** a sauna or other enclosure for sweating. **2.** any uncomfortably warm room or environment. **3.** a box or cell in which a prisoner is punished or given the third degree. **4.** a device for removing moisture from tobacco leaves, figs, raisins, etc. [1870–75; SWEAT + BOX[1]]

sweat•ed (swet′id), *adj.* **1.** made by underpaid workers. **2.** underpaid and overworked. **3.** having poor working conditions. [1645–55 for earlier sense "saturated with sweat"; 1880–85 for def. 2; SWEAT + -ED[2]]

sweat′ eq′uity, unreimbursed labor that results in the increased value of property or that is invested to establish or expand an enterprise. [1965–70]

sweat•er (swet′ər), *n.* **1.** a knitted jacket or jersey, in pullover or cardigan style, with or without sleeves. **2.** a person or thing that sweats. **3.** an employer who underpays and overworks employees. —*adj.* **4.** of, for, or pertaining to a sweater: *sweater yarn; sweater fashions.* **5.** made like a sweater: *a sweater dress.* [1520–30 for def. 2; 1880–85 for def. 1; SWEAT + -ER[1]]

sweat•er•coat (swet′ər kōt′), *n.* a coat knitted like a bulky sweater. [1910–15; SWEATER + COAT]

sweat′er girl′, a young woman with a shapely bosom, esp. one who wears tight sweaters. [1940–45]

sweat′ gland′, *Anat.* one of the minute, coiled, tubular glands of the skin that secrete sweat. [1835–45]

sweat′ing sick′ness, a febrile epidemic disease that appeared in the 15th and 16th centuries: characterized by profuse sweating and frequently fatal in a few hours. [1495–1505]

sweat′ing sys′tem, the practice of employing workers in sweatshops. [1850–55]

sweat•pants (swet′pants′), *n.* (*used with a plural v.*) loose-fitting pants of soft, absorbent fabric, as cotton jersey, usually with a drawstring at the waist and close-fitting or elastic cuffs at the ankles, commonly worn during athletic activity for warmth or to induce sweating. Also, **sweat′ pants′.** [1920–25; SWEAT + PANTS]

sweat•shirt (swet′shûrt′), *n.* a loose, long-sleeved, collarless pullover of soft, absorbent fabric, as cotton jersey, with close-fitting or elastic cuffs and sometimes a drawstring at the waist, commonly worn during athletic activity for warmth or to induce sweating. Also, **sweat′ shirt′.** [1920–25; SWEAT + SHIRT]

sweat•shop (swet′shop′), *n.* a shop employing workers at low wages, for long hours, and under poor conditions. [1865–70; SWEAT + SHOP]

sweat′ socks′, socks made of thick, absorbent cotton, wool, or other material and worn during exercise, sports, leisure activity, etc.

sweat′ suit′, a set of garments consisting of sweatpants and a sweatshirt. [1945–50]

sweat•weed (swet′wēd′), *n.* See **marsh mallow.** [1885–90; SWEAT + WEED[1]]

sweat·y (swet′ē), *adj.,* **sweat·i·er, sweat·i·est.** **1.** covered, moist, or stained with sweat. **2.** causing sweat. **3.** laborious. [1325–75; ME *swety.* See SWEAT, -Y[1]] —**sweat′i·ly,** *adv.* —**sweat′i·ness,** *n.*

Swed., **1.** Sweden. **2.** Swedish.

Swede (swēd), *n.* **1.** a native or inhabitant of Sweden. **2.** (*l.c.*) *Chiefly Brit.* a rutabaga. [1580–90; < MD or MLG; c. G *Schwede;* cf. OE *Swēon* (pl.), ON *Svēar, Svīar,* ML *Suiōnes*]

Swe·den (swēd′n), *n.* a kingdom in N Europe, in the E part of the Scandinavian Peninsula. 8,317,937; 173,394 sq. mi. (449,090 sq. km). *Cap.:* Stockholm. Swedish, **Sverige.**

Swe·den·borg (swēd′n bôrg′; *Sw.* svād′n bôʀ′yᵊ), *n.* **E·ma·nu·el** (i man′yo͞o əl; *Sw.* e mä′no͞o əl), (*Emanuel Swedberg*), 1688–1772, Swedish scientist, philosopher, and mystic.

Swe·den·bor·gi·an (swēd′n bôr′jē ən, -gē-), *adj.* **1.** of or pertaining to Emanuel Swedenborg, his religious doctrines, or the body of followers adhering to these doctrines and constituting the Church of the New Jerusalem, or New Church. —*n.* **2.** a believer in the religious doctrines of Swedenborg. [1795–1805; SWEDENBORG + -IAN] —**Swe′den·bor′gi·an·ism, Swe′den·borg′·ism,** *n.*

Swed·ish (swē′dish), *adj.* **1.** of or pertaining to Sweden, its inhabitants, or their language. —*n.* **2.** the people of Sweden collectively. **3.** a Germanic language, the language of Sweden and parts of Finland, closely related to Danish and Norwegian. *Abbr.:* Sw [SWEDE + -ISH[1]]

Swed′ish i′vy, any of various plants belonging to the genus *Plectranthus,* of the mint family, native to the Old World tropics, having rounded, scalloped or toothed leaves and widely cultivated as a houseplant.

Swed′ish massage′, a massage employing techniques of manipulation and muscular exercise systematized in Sweden in the 19th century. [1910–15]

Swed′ish Night′ingale, nickname of Jenny Lind.

Swed′ish tur′nip, rutabaga. [1800–10; so called because introduced into Great Britain from Sweden]

Swee·linck (svā′lingk), *n.* **Jan Pie·ters** (yän pē′təʀs) or **Jan Pie·ters·zoon** (yän pē′təʀ sōn′), 1562–1621, Dutch organist and composer. Also, **Swelinck.**

swee·ny (swē′nē), *n. Vet. Pathol.* atrophy of the shoulder muscles in horses. Also, **swinney.** [1820–30, *Amer.*; cf. dial. G *Schweine,* PaG *Schwinne* atrophy, OE *swindan* to pine away, disappear]

sweep[1] (swēp), *v.,* **swept, sweep·ing,** *n.* —*v.t.* **1.** to move or remove (dust, dirt, etc.) with or as if with a broom, brush, or the like. **2.** to clear or clean (a floor, room, chimney, etc.) of dirt, litter, or the like, by means of a broom or brush. **3.** to drive or carry by some steady force, as of a wind or wave: *The wind swept the snow into drifts.* **4.** to pass or draw (something) over a surface with a continuous stroke or movement: *The painter swept a brush over his canvas.* **5.** to make (a path, opening, etc.) by clearing a space with or as if with a broom. **6.** to clear (a surface, place, etc.) of something on or in it (often fol. by *of*): *to sweep a sea of enemy ships.* **7.** to pass over (a surface, region, etc.) with a steady, driving movement or unimpeded course, as winds, floods, etc.: *sandstorms sweeping the plains.* **8.** to search (an area or building) thoroughly: *Soldiers swept the town, looking for deserters.* **9.** to pass the gaze, eyes, etc., over (a region, area, etc.): *His eyes swept the countryside.* **10.** to direct (the eyes, gaze, etc.) over a region, surface, or the like: *He swept his eyes over the countryside.* **11.** to examine electronically, as to search for a hidden listening device. **12.** to win a complete or overwhelming victory in (a contest): *Johnson swept the presidential election of 1964.* **13.** to win (every game, round, hand, etc., of a series of contests): *The Yankees swept the three-game series.* **14.** *Music.* **a.** to pass the fingers or bow over (a musical instrument, its strings or keys, etc.), as in playing. **b.** to bring forth (music) thus. —*v.i.* **15.** to sweep a floor, room, etc., with or as if with a broom: *The new broom sweeps well.* **16.** to move steadily and strongly or swiftly (usually fol. by *along, down, by, into,* etc.). **17.** to move or pass in a swift but stately manner: *Proudly, she swept from the room.* **18.** to move, pass, or extend in a continuous course, esp. a wide curve or circuit: *His glance swept around the room.* **19.** to conduct an underwater search by towing a drag under the surface of the water. **20.** *Aeron.* (of an airfoil or its leading or trailing edge) to project from the fuselage at an angle rearward or forward of a line perpendicular to the longitudinal axis of the aircraft. —*n.* **21.** the act of sweeping, esp. a moving, removing, clearing, etc., by or as if by the use of a broom: *to give the house a good sweep.* **22.** the steady, driving motion or swift onward course of something moving with force or without interruption: *the sweep of the wind and the waves.* **23.** an examination by electronic detection devices of a room or building to determine the presence of hidden listening devices. **24.** a swinging or curving movement or stroke, as of the arm, a weapon, an oar, etc. **25.** reach, range, or compass, as of something sweeping about: *the sweep of a road about a marsh.* **26.** a continuous extent or stretch: *a broad sweep of sand.* **27.** a curving, esp. widely or gently curving, line, form, part, or mass. **28.** matter removed or gathered by sweeping. **29.** Also called **well sweep.** a leverlike device for raising or lowering a bucket in a well. **30.** a large oar used in small vessels, sometimes to assist the rudder or to propel the craft. **31.** an overwhelming victory in a contest. **32.** a winning of all the games, rounds, hands, prizes, etc., in a contest by one contestant. **33.** *Football.* See **end run. 34.** one of the sails of a windmill. **35.** *Agric.* any of the detachable triangular blades on a cultivator. **36.** *Chiefly Brit.* a person employed to clean by sweeping, esp. a chimney sweeper. **37.** *Cards.* **a.** *Whist.* the winning of all the tricks in a hand. Cf. **slam**[2] (def. 1). **b.** *Casino.* a pairing or combining, and hence taking, of all the cards on the board. **38.** *Physics.* an irreversible process tending towards thermal equilibrium. [1250–1300; ME *swepen* (v.); cf. OE *geswēpa* sweepings, deriv. of *swāpan* to sweep (> obs. E *swope*); c. G *schweifen*] —**sweep′a·ble,** *adj.*

sweep[2] (swēp), *n. Slang.* a sweepstakes. Also, **sweeps.** [by shortening]

sweep′ account′, *Finance.* a checking account from which money in excess of a specified amount is automatically transferred to another account or to an investment that earns a higher rate of return.

sweep·back (swēp′bak′), *n. Aeron.* the shape of, or the angle formed by, an airplane wing or other airfoil the leading or trailing edge of which slopes backward from the fuselage. [1915–20; n. use of v. phrase *sweep back*]

sweep′ check′, *Ice Hockey.* a maneuver for depriving an opponent of the puck by seizing it in the crook of one's stick and pulling it away with a movement in a long arc, the stick being held level or nearly level with the ice. Cf. **check**[1] (def. 42). [1960–65]

sweep·er (swē′pər), *n.* **1.** a person or thing that sweeps. **2.** See **carpet sweeper. 3.** a janitor. **4.** any of several fishes of the family Pempheridae, of tropical and warm, temperate seas, having an oblong, compressed body. [1400–50; late ME; see SWEEP[1], -ER[1]]

sweep′ hand′, *Horol.* a hand, usually a second hand, centrally mounted with the minute and hour hands of a timepiece and reaching to the edge of the dial. [1940–45]

sweep·ing (swē′ping), *adj.* **1.** of wide range or scope. **2.** moving or passing about over a wide area: *a sweeping glance.* **3.** moving, driving, or passing steadily and forcibly on. **4.** (of the outcome of a contest) decisive; overwhelming; complete: *a sweeping victory.* —*n.* **5.** the act of a person or thing that sweeps. **6. sweepings,** matter swept out or up, as dust, refuse, etc. [1470–80; SWEEP[1] + -ING[2], -ING[1]] —**sweep′ing·ly,** *adv.*
—**Syn. 1.** extensive, broad, comprehensive.

sweep′ing score′, *Curling.* a line at each end of the rink parallel to the foot score and extending through the center of the tee.

sweeps (swēps), *n.* (*used with a singular or plural v.*) *Slang.* sweep[2].

sweep-sec·ond (swēp′sek′ənd), *n.* (on a timepiece) a second hand that is a sweep hand. [1935–40]

sweep·stake (swēp′stāk′), *n.* a sweepstakes.

sweep·stakes (swēp′stāks′), *n.* (*used with a singular or plural v.*) **1.** a race or other contest for which the prize consists of the stakes contributed by the various competitors. **2.** the prize itself. **3.** a lottery in which winning tickets are selected at random, each winning-ticket number then being matched to one of the horses nominated for or entered in a specific race, and the amounts paid the winners being determined by the finishing order of the horses that run. **4.** lottery (def. 2). **5.** any gambling transaction in which each of a number of persons contributes a stake, and the stakes are awarded to one or several winners. **6.** a risky venture that promises large rewards: *the high-tech sweepstakes.* [1485–95; earlier *sweepestake* orig., a person who won all the stakes in a game; see SWEEP[1], STAKE[2], -S[3]]

sweep·y (swē′pē), *adj.,* **sweep·i·er, sweep·i·est.** sweeping. [1690–1700; SWEEP[1] + -Y[1]]

sweer (swēr), *adj. Scot. and North Eng.* **1.** slothful; indolent. **2.** unwilling; reluctant. [bef. 900; ME *swer(e),* OE *swǣr(e)* heavy, sluggish; c. G *schwer*]

sweet (swēt), *adj.,* **-er, -est,** *adv., n.* —*adj.* **1.** having the taste or flavor characteristic of sugar, honey, etc. **2.** producing the one of the four basic taste sensations that is not bitter, sour, or salt. **3.** not rancid or stale; fresh: *This milk is still sweet.* **4.** not salt or salted: *sweet butter.* **5.** pleasing to the ear; making a delicate, pleasant, or agreeable sound; musical. **6.** pleasing or fresh to the smell; fragrant; perfumed. **7.** pleasing or agreeable; delightful. **8.** amiable; kind or gracious, as a person, action, etc. **9.** dear; beloved; precious. **10.** easily managed; done or effected without effort. **11.** (of wine) not dry; containing unfermented, natural sugar. **12.** (of a cocktail) made with a greater proportion of vermouth than usual. **13.** sentimental, cloying, or unrealistic: *a sweet painting of little kittens.* **14.** (of air) fresh; free from odor, staleness, excess humidity, noxious gases, etc. **15.** free from acidity or sourness, as soil. **16.** *Chem.* **a.** devoid of corrosive or acidic substances. **b.** (of fuel oil or gas) containing no sulfur compounds. **17.** (of jazz or big band music) performed with a regular beat, moderate tempo, lack of improvisation, and an emphasis on warm tone and clearly outlined melody. **18. sweet on,** *Informal.* infatuated with; in love with: *He's sweet on her.* —*adv.* **19.** in a sweet manner; sweetly. —*n.* **20.** a sweet flavor, smell, or sound; sweetness. **21.** something that is sweet or causes or gives a sweet flavor, smell, or sound. **22. sweets,** *Informal.* **a.** candied sweet potatoes. **b.** (in direct address) sweetheart. **23. sweets,** pie, cake, candy, and other foods high in sugar content. **24.** *Chiefly Brit.* **a.** a piece of candy; sweetmeat or bonbon. **b.** a sweet dish or dessert, as a pudding or tart. **25.** something pleasant to the mind or feelings. **26.** a beloved person. **27.** (in direct address) darling; sweetheart. [bef. 900; (adj. and adv.) ME *swet(e),* OE *swēte* (adj.); (n.) ME *swet(e),* deriv. of the adj.; c. OS *swōti,* OHG *swuozi* (G *süss*); akin to D *zoet,* ON *sætr,* Goth *suts,* Gk *hēdýs* sweet, L *suādēre* to recommend, *suāvis* pleasant] —**sweet′ly,** *adv.* —**sweet′·ness,** *n.*
—**Syn. 1.** sugary. **5.** melodious, mellifluous. **6.** redolent, aromatic, scented. **8.** winning, lovable, charming.

Sweet (swēt), *n.* **Henry,** 1845–1912, English philologist and linguist.

sweet′ al′mond. See under **almond** (def. 1). [1710–20]

sweet′ al′mond oil′. See **almond oil** (def. 1).

sweet′ alys′sum, a garden plant, *Lobularia maritima,* of the mustard family, having narrow leaves and small, white or violet flowers. [1825–35]

sweet-and-sour (swēt′n souᵊr′, -sou′ər), *adj.* cooked with sugar and vinegar or lemon juice and often other seasonings. [1925–30]

sweet′ bas′il. See under **basil.** [1640–50]

sweet′ bay′, **1.** laurel (def. 1). **2.** an American magnolia, *Magnolia virginiana,* having large oblong leaves and fragrant, white flowers, common on the Atlantic coast. [1710–20]

sweet′ birch′, a North American tree, *Betula lenta,* having smooth, blackish bark and twigs that are a source of methyl salicylate. Also called **black birch, cherry birch.** [1775–85, *Amer.*]

sweet′ birch′ oil′. See **methyl salicylate.**

sweet·bread (swēt′bred′), *n.* **1.** Also called **stomach sweetbread.** the pancreas of an animal, esp. a calf or a lamb, used for food. **2.** Also called **neck sweetbread, throat sweetbread.** the thymus gland of such an animal, used for food. [1555–65; SWEET + BREAD]

sweet·bri·er (swēt′brī′ər), *n.* a rose, *Rosa eglanteria,* of Europe and central Asia, having a tall stem, stout, hooked prickles often mixed with bristles, and single, pink flowers. Also, **sweet′bri′ar.** [1530–40; SWEET + BRIER[1]]

sweet′ cal′amus. See **sweet flag.**

sweet′ cassa′va. See under **cassava** (def. 1).

sweet′ cher′ry, **1.** a cherry tree, *Prunus avium,* characterized by reddish-brown bark and a pyramidal manner of growth. **2.** the red, purplish-black, or yellow, edible, sweet fruit of this tree. [1900–05]

sweet′ cic′ely, any of several plants, as a European plant, *Myrrhis odorata,* of the parsley family, used as a potherb, or certain related North American plants of the genus *Osmorhiza.* [1660–70]

sweet′ ci′der. See under **cider.**

sweet′ clo′ver, melilot. [1865–70]

sweet′ corn′, **1.** any of several varieties of corn, esp. *Zea mays rugosa,* the grain or kernels of which are sweet and suitable for eating. **2.** *Chiefly Northern, North Midland, and Western U.S.* the young and tender ears of corn, esp. when used as a table vegetable. Also called **green corn.** [1640–50, *Amer.*]

sweet′ crab′ ap′ple. See **American crab apple.**

sweet·en (swēt′n), *v.t.* **1.** to make sweet, as by adding sugar. **2.** to make mild or kind; soften. **3.** to lessen the acridity or pungency of (a food) by prolonged cooking. **4.** to reduce the saltiness of (a food or dish) by diluting with water, milk, or other liquid. **5.** to make (the breath, room air, etc.) sweet or fresh, as with a mouthwash, spray, etc. **6.** (in musical recording) to add musical instruments to (an arrangement), esp. strings for a lusher sound. **7.** *Chem.* **a.** to make (the stomach, soil, etc.) less acidic, as by means of certain preparations, chemicals, etc. **b.** to remove sulfur and its compounds from (oil or gas). **8.** *Informal.* **a.** to enhance the value of (loan collateral) by including additional or especially valuable securities. **b.** to add to the value or attractiveness of (any proposition, holding, etc.). **9.** to add more liquor to (an alcoholic drink). **10.** *Poker.* to add stakes to (a pot) before opening. —*v.i.* **11.** to become sweet or sweeter. [1545–55; SWEET + -EN[1]]

sweet·en·er (swēt′n ər), *n.* **1.** something that sweetens, as sugar or a low-calorie synthetic product used instead of sugar. **2.** an added inducement: *such sweeteners as tax breaks and low-cost loans.* [1640–50; SWEETEN + -ER[1]]

sweet·en·ing (swēt′n ing, swēt′ning), *n.* **1.** something that sweetens food, beverages, etc., as sugar, saccharine, etc. **2.** the process of causing something to be or become sweet. [1585–95; SWEETEN + -ING[1]]

sweet′ flag′, a plant, *Acorus calamus,* of the arum family, having long, sword-shaped leaves and a pungent, aromatic rootstock. Also called **sweet calamus.** [1775–85]

sweet′ gale′, an aromatic shrub, *Myrica gale,* of marshes, having lance-shaped leaves and yellowish fruit. Also called **bog myrtle, moor myrtle.** [1630–40]

sweet′ grass′, any of several fragrant plants, as manna grass or the sweet flag. [1570–80]

sweet′ gum′, **1.** a tall, aromatic tree, *Liquidambar styraciflua,* of the eastern U.S., having star-shaped leaves and fruits in rounded, burlike clusters. **2.** the hard reddish-brown wood of this tree, used for making furniture. **3.** the amber balsam exuded by this tree, used in the manufacture of perfumes and medicines. Also called **red gum** (for defs. 1, 2). [1690–1700, *Amer.*]

sweet•heart (swēt′härt′), *n.* **1.** either of a pair of lovers in relation to the other. **2.** (*sometimes cap.*) an affectionate or familiar term of address. **3.** a beloved person. **4.** *Informal.* a generous, friendly person. **5.** *Informal.* anything that arouses loyal affection: *My old car was a real sweetheart.* [1250–1300; ME *swete herte.* See SWEET, HEART]

sweet′heart con′tract, a contract made through collusion between management and labor representatives containing terms beneficial to management and detrimental to union workers. Also called **sweet′heart agree′ment.** [1945–50]

sweet′heart neck′line, a neckline on a woman's garment, as a dress, with a high back and a low-cut front with two curved edges resembling the conventionalized shape of a heart. Also called **sweet′heart neck′.** [1940–45]

sweet•ie (swē′tē), *n.* **1.** *Informal.* sweetheart. **2.** Usually, **sweeties.** *Brit.* candy; sweets. [1695–1705; SWEET + -IE]

sweet′ie pie′, *Informal.* sweetheart (used esp. as a term of endearment). [1935–40]

sweet•ing (swē′ting), *n.* **1.** a sweet variety of apple. **2.** *Archaic.* sweetheart. [1250–1300; ME *sweting.* See SWEET, -ING[3]]

sweet•ish (swē′tish), *adj.* somewhat sweet. [1570–80; SWEET + -ISH[1]] —**sweet′ish•ly,** *adv.* —**sweet′ish•ness,** *n.*

sweet•leaf (swēt′lēf′), *n., pl.* **-leaves.** a shrub or small tree, *Symplocos tinctoria,* of the eastern coast of the U.S., having lance-shaped leaves, yellowish, fragrant flowers, and orange or brown fruit. [1805–15, *Amer.*; SWEET + LEAF]

sweet′ mar′joram. See under **marjoram.** [1555–65]

sweet′ mar′ten, the European pine marten, *Martes martes:* trapped for its fur and now greatly reduced in number. [1780–90]

sweet•meat (swēt′mēt′), *n.* **1.** a sweet delicacy, prepared with sugar, honey, or the like, as preserves, candy, or, formerly, cakes or pastry. **2.** Usually, **sweetmeats.** any sweet delicacy of the confectionery or candy kind, as candied fruit, sugar-covered nuts, sugarplums, bonbons, or balls or sticks of candy. [bef. 1150; OE *swētmete* (not recorded in ME); see SWEET, MEAT]

sweet′ mock′ or′ange, the syringa, *Philadelphus coronarius.*

sweet′ness and light′, **1.** extreme or excessive pleasantness or amiability. **2.** decorous charm combined with intelligence. [1695–1705]

sweet′ oil′. See **olive oil.** [1575–85]

sweet′ or′ange. See under **orange** (def. 2). [1790–1800]

sweet′ pea′, a climbing plant, *Lathyrus odoratus,* of the legume family, having sweet-scented flowers. [1725–35]

sweet′ pep′per, **1.** a variety of pepper, *Capsicum annuum grossum,* having a mild-flavored, bell-shaped or somewhat oblong fruit. **2.** the fruit itself, used as a vegetable. Also called **bell pepper.** [1830–40]

sweet′ pep′per•bush (pep′ər bo͝osh′), a shrub, *Clethra alnifolia,* of the eastern and southern coastal U.S., having numerous erect clusters of white or pinkish flowers. Also called **summer-sweet, white alder.** [1830–40, *Amer.*]

sweet′ pota′to, **1.** a plant, *Ipomoea batatas,* of the morning glory family, grown for its sweet, edible, tuberous roots. **2.** the root itself, used as a vegetable. **3.** *Informal.* ocarina. [1740–50, *Amer.*]

sweet′ roll′, a roll made of sweet dough, often containing spices, raisins, nuts, candied fruit, etc., and sometimes iced on top.

sweet′ sca′bious, a plant, *Scabiosa atropurpurea,* native to Europe, cultivated for its purple, reddish, or white flowers. Also called **mourning bride.** [1790–1800]

sweet-scent•ed (swēt′sen′tid), *adj.* having a pleasant and sweet smell; fragrant. [1585–95]

sweet-shop (swēt′shop′), *n. Brit.* a store that sells candy. [1875–80]

sweet′ shrub′. See **Carolina allspice.** [1800–10, *Amer.*]

sweet•sop (swēt′sop′), *n.* **1.** a sweet, pulpy fruit having a thin, tuberculate rind, borne by a tropical American tree or shrub, *Annona squamosa,* of the annona family. **2.** the tree or shrub. Also called **sugar apple.** [1690–1700; SWEET + SOP]

sweet′ sor′ghum, sorgo. [1865–70]

sweet′ spire′. See **Virginia willow.**

CONCISE ETYMOLOGY KEY: <, descended or borrowed from; >, whence; b., blend of, blended; c., cognate with; cf., compare; deriv., derivative; equiv., equivalent; imit., imitative; obl., oblique; r., replacing; s., stem; sp., spelling, spelled; resp., respelling, respelled; trans., translation; ?, origin unknown; *, unattested; ‡, probably earlier than. See the full key inside the front cover.

sweet′ spir′it of ni′tre, *Pharm.* See **ethyl nitrite spirit.** Also, **sweet′ spir′it of ni′ter.**

sweet′ talk′, *Informal.* cajolery; soft soap. [1925–30]

sweet-talk (swēt′tôk′), *Informal.* —*v.i.* **1.** to use cajoling words. —*v.t.* **2.** to use cajoling words on in order to persuade; soft-soap: *They tried to sweet-talk the boss into giving them raises.* [1925–30]

sweet-tem•pered (swēt′tem′pərd), *adj.* having a gentle and equable disposition; pleasant. [1625–35] —**sweet′-tem′pered•ness,** *n.*

sweet′ tooth′, a liking or craving for candy and other sweets. [1350–1400; ME]

sweet′ ver′nal grass′, a Eurasian meadow grass, *Anthoxanthum odoratum,* found throughout North America, having clusters of brownish-green flowers. [1835–45]

sweet′ vibur′num, the sheepberry, *Viburnum lentago.* [1835–45, *Amer.*]

sweet′ vi′olet, a plant, *Viola odorata,* of the violet family, native to the Old World, having fragrant, usually purple flowers that are the source of an oil used in perfumery.

Sweet•wa•ter (swēt′wô′tər, -wot′ər), *n.* a city in NW Texas. 12,242.

sweet′ wil′liam, a pink, *Dianthus barbatus,* having clusters of small, variously colored flowers. Also, **sweet′ Wil′liam.** Also called **bunch pink.** [1555–65]

sweet′ wil′liam catch′fly, a southern European plant, *Silene armeria,* of the pink family, having a flat-topped cluster of pink flowers. Also called **none-so-pretty.**

sweet′ wood′ruff. See under **woodruff.** [1790–1800]

sweet′ worm′wood, a widely distributed plant, *Artemisia annua,* having scented leaves and loose, nodding clusters of yellow flowers.

sweet•wort (swēt′wûrt′, -wôrt′), *n. Brit.* an infusion of unfermented malt. [1560–70; SWEET + WORT[1]]

Swe•linck (svā′lingk), *n.* **Jan Pie•ters** (yän pē′tərs) or **Jan Pie•ters•zoon** (yän pē′tər sōn′). See **Sweelinck, Jan Pieters** or **Jan Pieterszoon.**

swell (swel), *v.,* **swelled, swol•len** or **swelled, swell•ing,** *n., adj.* —*v.i.* **1.** to grow in bulk, as by the absorption of moisture or the processes of growth. **2.** *Path.* to increase abnormally in size, as by inflation, distention, accumulation of fluids, or the like: *Her ankles swelled from standing.* **3.** to rise in waves, as the sea. **4.** to well up, as a spring or as tears. **5.** to bulge out, as a sail or the middle of a cask. **6.** to grow in amount, degree, force, etc. **7.** to increase gradually in volume or intensity, as sound: *The music swelled.* **8.** to arise and grow within one, as a feeling or emotion. **9.** to become puffed up with pride. —*v.t.* **10.** to cause to grow in bulk. **11.** to cause to increase gradually in loudness: *to swell a musical tone.* **12.** to cause (a thing) to bulge out or be protuberant. **13.** to increase in amount, degree, force, etc. **14.** to affect with a strong, expansive emotion. **15.** to puff up with pride. —*n.* **16.** the act of swelling or the condition of being swollen. **17.** inflation or distention. **18.** a protuberant part. **19.** a wave, esp. when long and unbroken, or a series of such waves. **20.** a gradually rising elevation of the land. **21.** an increase in amount, degree, force, etc. **22.** a gradual increase in loudness of sound. **23.** *Music.* **a.** a gradual increase (crescendo) followed by a gradual decrease (diminuendo) in loudness or force of musical sound. **b.** the sign (< >) for indicating this. **c.** a device, as in an organ, by which the loudness of tones may be varied. **24.** a swelling of emotion within one. **25.** *Slang.* **a.** a fashionably dressed person; dandy. **b.** a socially prominent person. —*adj. Informal.* **26.** (of things) stylish; elegant: *a swell hotel.* **27.** (of persons) fashionably dressed or socially prominent. **28.** first-rate; fine: *a swell party.* [bef. 900; ME *swellen* (v.), OE *swellan;* c. D *zwellen,* G *schwellen,* ON *svella;* akin to Goth *ufswalleins* pride]
—**Syn. 1.** distend, expand. **5.** protrude. **10.** inflate, expand. **17.** swelling. **18.** bulge. **19.** billow. **27, 28.** grand. —**Ant. 1.** contract. **13.** decrease, diminish.

swell′ box′, a chamber containing a set of pipes in a pipe organ or of reeds in a reed organ, and having movable slats or shutters that can be opened or closed to increase or diminish tonal volume. [1795–1805]

swelled′ head′, an inordinately grand opinion of oneself; conceit. [1890–95] —**swelled′-head′ed,** *adj.* —**swelled′-head′ed•ness,** *n.*

swell•fish (swel′fish′), *n., pl.* (*esp. collectively*) **-fish,** (*esp. referring to two or more kinds or species*) **-fish•es.** puffer (def. 2). [1800–10, *Amer.*; SWELL + FISH]

swell′ front′, *Furniture.* a horizontally convex front, as of a chest of drawers. Also called **bow front.** Cf. **bombé.** [1855–60]

swell•head (swel′hed′), *n.* a vain or arrogant person. [1835–45, *Amer.*; SWELL + HEAD] —**swell′head′ed,** *adj.* —**swell′head′ed•ness,** *n.*

swell•ing (swel′ing), *n.* **1.** the act of a person or thing that swells. **2.** the condition of being or becoming swollen. **3.** a swollen part; a protuberance or prominence. **4.** *Pathol.* an abnormal enlargement or protuberance, as that resulting from edema. [bef. 900; ME, OE; see SWELL, -ING[1]]

swel•ter (swel′tər), *v.i.* **1.** to suffer from oppressive heat. —*v.t.* **2.** to oppress with heat. **3.** *Archaic.* to exude, as venom. —*n.* **4.** a sweltering condition. [1375–1425; late ME *swelt(e)ren* (v.), equiv. to *swelt(en)* to be overcome with heat (OE *sweltan* to die; c. ON *svelta,* Goth *swiltan*) + *-eren* -ER[6]]

swel•ter•ing (swel′tər ing), *adj.* **1.** suffering oppressive heat. **2.** characterized by oppressive heat; sultry. [1565–75; SWELTER + -ING[2]] —**swel′ter•ing•ly,** *adv.*

swel•try (swel′trē), *adj.,* **-tri•er, -tri•est.** hot, sizzling, roasting; sweltering. [1570–80; SWELT(E)R + -Y[1]; cf. SULTRY]

swept (swept), *v.* **1.** pt. and pp. of **sweep.** —*adj.* **2.** (of a sword guard) made up of curved bars.

swept•back (swept′bak′), *adj. Aeron.* **1.** (of the leading edge of an airfoil) forming a markedly obtuse angle with the fuselage. **2.** (of an aircraft or winged missile) having wings of this type. [1915–20; adj. use of v. phrase *swept back*]

swept•wing (swept′wing′), *adj. Aeron.* (of an aircraft, winged missile, etc.) having sweptback wings. [SWEPT(BACK) + WING]

swerve (swûrv), *v.,* **swerved, swerv•ing,** *n.* —*v.i.* **1.** to turn aside abruptly in movement or direction; deviate suddenly from the straight or direct course. —*v.t.* **2.** to cause to turn aside: *Nothing could swerve him.* —*n.* **3.** an act of swerving; turning aside. [1175–1225; ME *swerven* (v.); OE *sweorfan* to rub, file; c. D *zwerven* to rove, OHG *swerban,* ON *sverfa* to file, Goth *afswairban* to wipe off]
—**Syn. 1.** See **deviate.**

swev•en (swev′ən), *n. Archaic.* a vision; dream. [bef. 900; ME; OE *swefn;* akin to ON *sofa* to sleep, L *somnus,* Gk *hýpnos* sleep]

S.W.G., standard wire gauge.

swid•den (swid′n), *n.* a plot of land cleared for farming by burning away vegetation. [1951; special use of dial. (N England) *swidden* area of moor from which vegetation has been burned off, n. use of *swidden, swithen* to singe < ON *svithna* to be singed, deriv. of *svītha* to singe (cf. dial. *swithe,* ME *swithen*)]

swift (swift), *adj.,* **-er, -est,** *adv., n.* —*adj.* **1.** moving or capable of moving with great speed or velocity; fleet; rapid: *a swift ship.* **2.** coming, happening, or performed quickly or without delay: *a swift decision.* **3.** quick or prompt to act or respond: *swift to jump to conclusions.* **4.** *Slang.* quick to perceive or understand; smart; clever: *You can't cheat him, he's too swift.* —*adv.* **5.** swiftly. —*n.* **6.** any of numerous long-winged, swallowlike birds of the family Apodidae, related to the hummingbirds and noted for their rapid flight. **7.** See **tree swift. 8.** See **spiny lizard. 9.** Also called **swift′ moth′, ghost moth.** any of several brown or gray moths, the males of which are usually white, of the family Hepialidae, noted for rapid flight. **10.** an adjustable device upon which a hank of yarn is placed in order to wind off skeins or balls. **11.** the main cylinder on a machine for carding flax. [bef. 900; ME (adj. and adv.), OE (adj.); akin to OE *swīfan* to revolve, ON *svīfa* to rove; see SWIVEL] —**swift′ly,** *adv.* —**swift′ness,** *n.*
—**Syn. 1.** speedy. See **quick. 2.** expeditious.

Swift (swift), *n.* **1. Gustavus Franklin,** 1839–1903, U.S. meat packer. **2. Jonathan** (*"Isaac Bickerstaff"*), 1667–1745, English satirist and clergyman, born in Ireland.

Swift′ Cur′rent, a city in SW Saskatchewan, in S Canada. 14,264.

swift-foot•ed (swift′fo͝ot′id), *adj.* swift in running. [1590–1600]

swift•let (swift′lit), *n.* any of several swifts of the genus *Collocalia,* of southeastern Asia, the East Indies, and Australia, certain species of which use saliva to construct nests, which are used in making bird's-nest soup. [1890–95; SWIFT + -LET]

swig (swig), *n., v.,* **swigged, swig•ging.** *Informal.* —*n.* **1.** an amount of liquid, esp. liquor, taken in one swallow; draught: *He took a swig from the flask.* —*v.t., v.i.* **2.** to drink heartily or greedily. [1540–50; orig. uncert.] —**swig′ger,** *n.*

swill (swil), *n.* **1.** liquid or partly liquid food for animals, esp. kitchen refuse given to swine; hogwash. **2.** kitchen refuse in general; garbage. **3.** any liquid mess, waste, or refuse; slop. **4.** a deep draught of liquor. **5.** contemptibly worthless utterance or writing; drivel. —*v.i.* **6.** to drink greedily or excessively. —*v.t.* **7.** to drink (something) greedily or to excess; guzzle. **8.** to feed (animals) with swill: *to swill hogs.* **9.** *Chiefly Brit.* to wash by rinsing or flooding with water. [bef. 900; ME *swilen* (v.), OE *swilian, swillan*] —**swill′er,** *n.*

swim (swim), *v.,* **swam, swum, swim•ming,** *n.* —*v.i.* **1.** to move in water by movements of the limbs, fins, tail, etc. **2.** to float on the surface of water or some other liquid. **3.** to move, rest, or be suspended in air as if swimming in water. **4.** to move, glide, or go smoothly over a surface. **5.** to be immersed or steeped in or overflowing or flooded with a liquid: *eyes swimming with tears.* **6.** to be dizzy or giddy; seem to whirl: *My head began to swim.* —*v.t.* **7.** to move along in or cross (a body of water) by swimming: *to swim a lake.* **8.** to perform (a particular stroke) in swimming: *to swim a sidestroke.* **9.** to cause to swim or float, as on a stream. **10.** to furnish with sufficient water to swim or float. —*n.* **11.** an act, instance, or period of swimming. **12.** a motion as of swimming; a smooth, gliding movement. **13. in the swim,** alert to or actively engaged in events; in the thick of things: *Despite her age, she is still in the swim.* [bef. 900; ME *swimmen,* OE *swimman;* c. D *zwemmen,* G *schwimmen,* ON *svimma*] —**swim′ma•ble,** *adj.* —**swim′mer,** *n.*

swim′ blad′der. See **air bladder** (def. 2). [1830–40]

swim′ fin′, one of a pair of flippers. [1945–50]

swim′ mask′, mask (def. 3).

swim•mer•et (swim′ə ret′), *n.* (in many crustaceans) one of a number of abdominal limbs or appendages, usually adapted for swimming and for carrying eggs, as distinguished from other limbs adapted for walking or seizing. [1830–40; SWIMMER + -ET]

swim′mer's ear′, *Pathol.* an inflammation of the outer ear occurring in persons who swim for long periods or fail to dry the ears.

swim′mer's itch′, *Pathol.* an inflammation of the skin, resembling insect bites, caused by burrowing larval forms of schistosomes. [1925–30; so called because the schistosomes enter the skin from untreated water]

swim•ming (swim′ing), *n.* **1.** the act of a person or thing that swims. **2.** the skill or technique of a person who swims. **3.** the sport of swimming. —*adj.* **4.** pertaining to, characterized by, or capable of swimming. **5.** used in or for swimming: *swimming trunks.* **6.** immersed in or overflowing with water or some other liquid. **7.** dizzy or giddy: *a swimming head.* [bef. 1000; ME; OE *swimmende* (adj.). See SWIM, -ING[2], -ING[1]] —**swim′ming•ness,** *n.*

swim′ming bath′, *Brit.* See **swimming pool.** [1735–45]

swim′ming crab′, any of numerous, chiefly marine crabs, esp. of the family Portunidae, having the legs adapted for swimming.

swim′ming hole′, a place, as in a stream or creek, where there is water deep enough to use for swimming. [1865–70, *Amer.*]

swim•ming•ly (swim′ing lē), *adv.* without difficulty; with great success; effortlessly: *She passed the exam swimmingly.* [1615–25; SWIMMING (in sense "progressing smoothly") + -LY]

swim′ming pool′, a tank or large artificial basin, as of concrete, for filling with water for swimming. [1895–1900]

swim•suit (swim′so͞ot′), *n.* See **bathing suit.** [1925–30; SWIM + SUIT]

swim•wear (swim′wâr′), *n.* clothing designed to be worn for swimming or at a beach. [1930–35; SWIM + WEAR]

Swin•burne (swin′bərn), *n.* **Algernon Charles,** 1837–1909, English poet and critic.

swin•dle (swin′dl), *v.,* **-dled, -dling,** *n.* —*v.t.* **1.** to cheat (a person, business, etc.) out of money or other assets. **2.** to obtain by fraud or deceit. —*v.i.* **3.** to put forward plausible schemes or use unscrupulous trickery to defraud others; cheat. —*n.* **4.** an act of swindling or a fraudulent transaction or scheme. **5.** anything deceptive; a fraud: *This advertisement is a real swindle.* [1775–85; back formation from *swindler* < G *Schwindler* irresponsible person, promoter of wildcat schemes, cheat, deriv. of *schwindeln* to be dizzy (hence dizzy-minded, irresponsible), defraud, equiv. to *schwind-* (akin to OE *swindan* to languish) + -*(e)l-* -LE + -*er* -ER[1]] —**swin′dle•a•ble,** *adj.* —**swin′dler,** *n.* —**swin′dling•ly,** *adv.*
—**Syn. 1.** cozen, dupe, trick, gull.

swin•dled (swin′dld), *adj. Jewelry.* (of a gem) cut so as to retain the maximum weight of the original stone or to give a false impression of size, esp. by having the table too large. [SWINDLE + -ED[2]]

swin′dle sheet′, *Slang.* **1.** an expense account. **2.** a log sheet, as kept by a trucker, cab driver, hourly worker, or the like. [1945–50]

swine (swīn), *n., pl.* **swine. 1.** any stout, cloven-hoofed artiodactyl of the Old World family Suidae, having a thick hide sparsely covered with coarse hair, a disklike snout, and an often short, tasseled tail: now of worldwide distribution and hunted or raised for its meat and other products. Cf. **hog, pig, wild boar. 2.** the domestic hog, *Sus scrofa.* **3.** a coarse, gross, or brutishly sensual person. **4.** a contemptible person. [bef. 900; ME; OE *swīn;* c. G *Schwein* hog, L *suīnus* (adj.) porcine; akin to SOW[2]] —**swine′like′,** *adj.*

swine′ erysip′elas, *Vet. Pathol.* erysipelas (def. 2). Cf. **erysipeloid.**

swine′ fe′ver, *Vet. Pathol.* See **hog cholera.** [1895–1900]

swine′ flu′, *Pathol.* a highly contagious form of influenza caused by infection with a filterable virus first isolated from swine. [1920–25]

swine•herd (swīn′hûrd′), *n.* a person who tends swine. [bef. 1100; ME; late OE *swȳnhyrde.* See SWINE, HERD[2]] —**swine′herd′ship,** *n.*

swine′ plague′, *Vet. Pathol.* hemorrhagic septicemia of hogs, caused by the bacterium *Pasteurella suiseptica,* characterized by an accompanying infection of pneumonia. [1890–95]

swine•pox (swīn′poks′), *n.* **1.** a variety of chicken pox. **2.** *Vet. Pathol.* a mild pox disease of swine, caused by a virus related to that of cowpox, characterized by the appearance of pustules in the skin, esp. of the abdomen. [1520–30]

swing[1] (swing), *v.,* **swung, swing•ing,** *n., adj.* —*v.t.* **1.** to cause to move to and fro, sway, or oscillate, as something suspended from above: *to swing one's arms in walking.* **2.** to cause to move in alternate directions or in either direction around a fixed point, on an axis, or on a line of support, as a door on hinges. **3.** to move (the hand or something held) with an oscillating or rotary movement: *to swing one's fists; to swing a club around one's head.* **4.** *Aeron.* to pull or turn (a propeller) by hand, esp. in order to start the engine. **5.** to turn in a new direction in a curve, as if around a central point: *to swing the car into the driveway.* **6.** to suspend so as to hang freely, as a hammock or a door. **7.** *Informal.* to influence or win over; manage or arrange as desired: *to swing votes; to swing a business deal.* **8.** to direct, change, or shift (one's interest, opinion, support, etc.). **9.** to turn (a ship or aircraft) to various headings in order to check compass deviation.
—*v.i.* **10.** to move or sway to and fro, as a pendulum or other suspended object. **11.** to move to and fro in a swing, as for recreation. **12.** to move in alternate directions or in either direction around a point, an axis, or a line of support, as a gate on its hinges. **13.** to move in a curve, as around a corner or central point: *The highway swings to the east.* **14.** to move with a free, swaying motion, as soldiers on the march. **15.** to be suspended so as to hang freely, as a bell or hammock. **16.** to move by grasping a support with the hands and drawing up the arms or using the momentum of the swaying body: *a monkey swinging through trees.* **17.** to change or shift one's attention, interest, opinion, condition, etc.: *He swung from mere indifference to outright scorn.* **18.** to hit at someone or something, with the hand or something grasped in the hand: *The batter swung and struck out.* **19.** *Slang.* **a.** to be characterized by a modern, lively atmosphere: *Las Vegas swings all year.* **b.** to be stylish, trendy, hip, etc., esp. in pursuing enjoyment. **c.** to engage uninhibitedly in sexual activity. **d.** (of married couples) to exchange partners for sexual activity. **20.** *Informal.* to suffer death by hanging: *He'll swing for the crime.* **21. swing round the circle,** to tour an area on a political campaign.
—*n.* **22.** the act, manner, or progression of swinging; movement in alternate directions or in a particular direction. **23.** the amount or extent of such movement: *to correct the swing of a pendulum.* **24.** a curving movement or course. **25.** a moving of the body with a free, swaying motion, as in walking. **26.** a blow or stroke with the hand or an object grasped in the hands: *His swing drove the ball over the fence.* **27.** a change or shift in attitude, opinion, behavior, etc. **28.** a steady, marked rhythm or movement, as of verse or music. **29.** a regular upward or downward movement in the price of a commodity or of a security, or in any business activity. **30.** *Informal.* **a.** a work period coming between the regular day and night shifts. **b.** a change by a group of workers from working one shift to working another. **31.** freedom of action: *to have free swing in carrying out a project.* **32.** active operation; progression: *to get into the swing of things.* **33.** something that is swung or that swings. **34.** a seat suspended from above by means of a loop of rope or between ropes or rods, on which one may sit and swing to and fro for recreation. **35.** the maximum diameter of the work machinable in a certain lathe or other machine tool. **36. in full swing,** operating at the highest speed or level of activity; in full operation: *Automobile production is in full swing.* **37. take a swing at,** to strike or attempt to strike with the fist: *to take a swing at a rude waiter.*
—*adj.* **38.** of or pertaining to a swing. **39.** capable of determining the outcome, as of an election; deciding: *the swing vote.* **40.** designed or constructed to permit swinging or hanging. **41.** acting to relieve other workers when needed, as at night. [bef. 900; ME *swingen* (v.), OE *swingan;* c. G *schwingen*] —**swing′a•ble,** *adj.*
—**Syn. 10.** SWING, SWAY, OSCILLATE, ROCK suggest a movement back and forth. SWING expresses the comparatively regular motion to and fro of a body supported from the end or ends, esp. from above: *A lamp swings from the ceiling.* To SWAY is to swing gently and is used esp. of fixed objects or of persons: *Young oaks sway in the breeze.* OSCILLATE refers to the smooth, regular, alternating movement of a body within certain limits between two fixed points. ROCK indicates the slow and regular movement back and forth of a body, as on curved supports: *A cradle rocks.* **22.** sway, vibration, oscillation. **23.** range, scope, sweep, play.

swing[2] (swing), *n., adj., v.,* **swung, swing•ing.** —*n.* **1.** Also called **Big Band music, swing music.** a style of jazz, popular esp. in the 1930's and often arranged for a large dance band, marked by a smoother beat and more flowing phrasing than Dixieland and having less complex harmonies and rhythms than modern jazz. **2.** the rhythmic element that excites dancers and listeners to move in time to jazz music. —*adj.* **3.** of, pertaining to, or characteristic of swing: *a swing record.* —*v.t.* **4.** to play (music) in the style of swing. [special use of SWING[1]]

swing•back (swing′bak′), *n.* (esp. in political affairs) a return or reversion, as to previous opinion, custom, or ideology: *We must fight any swingback to isolationism.* [1860–65; n. use of v. phrase *swing back*]

swing′ bridge′, a bridge that can open by pivoting on a central pier to let vessels pass. [1700–10]

swing′ by′, *Aerospace.* a trajectory that uses the gravitational field of one celestial body to alter the course of a spacecraft destined for another body. [1960–65, *Amer.;* n. use of v. phrase *swing by*]

swinge[1] (swinj), *v.t.,* **swinged, swinge•ing.** *Brit. Dial.* to thrash; punish. [1250–1300; ME *swengen* to shake, smite, OE *swengan,* causative of *swingan* to swing, or denominative deriv. of OE *sweng* a blow] —**swing•er** (swin′jər), *n.*

swinge[2] (swinj), *v.t.,* **swinged, swinge•ing.** to singe. [1580–90; obscurely akin to SINGE]

swinge•ing (swin′jing), *adj. Chiefly Brit.* **1.** enormous; thumping. **2.** *Slang.* swinging (def. 3). [1560–70; SWINGE[1] + -ING[2]] —**swinge′ing•ly,** *adv.*

swing•er (swing′ər), *n.* **1.** a person or thing that swings. **2.** *Slang.* a lively, active, and modern person whose activities are fashionable or trendy. **3.** *Slang.* **a.** a person who indulges in promiscuous sex. **b.** a person who engages in the exchanging of spouses for sexual activities. [1535–45 for def. 1; 1955–60 for def. 2; SWING[1] + -ER[1]]

swing•ing (swing′ing), *adj., superl.* **-ing•est,** *n.* —*adj.* **1.** characterized by or capable of swinging, being swung, or causing to swing. **2.** intended for swinging upon, by, from, or in: *the swinging devices in a playground.* **3.** *Slang.* excellent; first-rate. **4.** *Slang.* lively, active, and modern; hip. **5.** *Slang.* **a.** free and uninhibited sexually: *a swinging bachelor.* **b.** exchanging spouses for sex: *swinging married couples.* —*n.* **6.** the activity or act of a person who swings. **7.** *Slang.* **a.** the act or practice of being free and uninhibited sexually. **b.** the exchanging of spouses for sex. [1550–60; SWING[1] + -ING[2]] —**swing′ing•ly,** *adv.*

swing′ing door′, a door that swings open on being pushed or pulled from either side and then swings closed by itself. Also called **swing′ door′.** [1795–1805]

swin•gle[1] (swing′gəl), *n., v.,* **-gled, -gling.** —*n.* **1.** a swipple. **2.** a wooden instrument shaped like a large knife, for beating flax or hemp and scraping from it the woody or coarse portions. —*v.t.* **3.** to clean (flax or hemp) by beating and scraping with a swingle. [1275–1325; ME *swingel,* OE *swingell* rod (c. MD *swinghel*), equiv. to *swing-* (see SWING[1]) + -*el* instrumental suffix (see -LE)]

swin•gle[2] (swing′gəl), *n. Slang.* a single person who swings, esp. one who is highly active socially and sexually. [1965–70, *Amer.;* b. SWING[1] and SINGLE]

swin•gle•bar (swing′gəl bär′), *n.* a whiffletree. [1840–50; SWINGLE[1] + BAR[1]]

swing′ leg′, *Furniture.* a leg at the end of a hinged rail, swinging out to support a drop leaf. Cf. **gate leg.**

swin•gle•tree (swing′gəl trē′), *n. Chiefly Midland and Southern U.S.* a whiffletree. Also called **swiveltree.** [1425–75; late ME; see SWINGLE[1], TREE]

swing′ loan′, a bridge loan.

swing•man (swing′man′), *n., pl.* **-men.** *Basketball.* a player who can play either of two positions, usually guard and forward. [1965–70; SWING[1] + MAN[1]]

swing′ mu′sic, swing[2] (def. 1).

swing•o•ver (swing′ō′vər), *n.* a shift or transfer in attitude, opinion, or the like. [1925–30; n. use of v. phrase *swing over*]

swing′ shift′, **1.** a work shift in industry from midafternoon until midnight. **2.** the group of workers on such a shift. [1935–40] —**swing′ shift′er.**

swing•tree (swing′trē′), *n.* a whiffletree. [1350–1400; ME; appar. syncopated var. of SWINGLETREE]

swing-wing (swing′wing′), *adj.* (of an airplane) having wings whose horizontal angle to the fuselage centerline can be adjusted fore and aft to optimize aerodynamic performance at widely differing speeds. [1965–70]

swing•y (swing′ē), *adj.,* **swing•i•er, swing•i•est.** characterized by swing; lively; swinging: *swingy dance tunes.* [1910–15; SWING[1] + -Y[1]]

swin•ish (swī′nish), *adj.* **1.** like or befitting swine; hoggish. **2.** brutishly coarse, gross, or sensual. [1150–1200; ME; see SWINE, -ISH[1]] —**swin′ish•ly,** *adv.* —**swin′ish•ness,** *n.*

swink (swingk), *v.i.,* **swank** or **swonk, swonk•en, swink•ing,** *n. Brit. Archaic.* labor; toil. [bef. 900; ME *swinken,* OE *swincan;* akin to SWING[1]] —**swink′er,** *n.*

Swin•ner•ton (swin′ər tən), *n.* **Frank (Arthur),** 1884–1982, English novelist and critic.

swin•ney (swin′ē), *n. Vet. Pathol.* sweeny.

swipe (swīp), *n., v.,* **swiped, swip•ing.** —*n.* **1.** a strong, sweeping blow, as with a cricket bat or golf club. **2.** *Informal.* a swing of the arm in order to strike somebody; punch. **3.** a sideswipe. **4.** *Informal.* a critical or cutting remark. **5.** a leverlike device for raising or lowering a weight, esp. a bucket in a well; sweep. **6.** *Horse Racing.* a person who rubs down horses in a stable; groom. —*v.t.* **7.** to strike with a sweeping blow. **8.** *Informal.* to steal: *He'll swipe anything that isn't nailed down.* —*v.i.* **9.** to make a sweeping stroke. [1730–40; akin to SWEEP[1]; c. G *schweifen*]

swipes (swīps), *n.* (*used with a plural v.*) *Brit. Informal.* **1.** poor, watery, or spoiled beer. **2.** malt liquor in general, esp. beer and small beer. [1780–90; n. pl. use of *swipe* to drink down at one gulp, var. of SWEEP[1]]

swip•ple (swip′əl), *n.* the freely swinging part of a flail, which falls upon the grain in threshing; swingle. Also, **swi′ple.** [1400–50; late ME *swipyl,* var. of *swepyl,* equiv. to *swep(en)* to SWEEP[1] + -*yl* instrumental suffix (see -LE)]

swirl (swûrl), *v.i.* **1.** to move around or along with a whirling motion; whirl; eddy. **2.** to be dizzy or giddy, as the head. —*v.t.* **3.** to cause to whirl; twist. —*n.* **4.** a swirling movement; whirl; eddy. **5.** a twist, as of hair around the head or of trimming on a hat. **6.** any curving, twisting line, shape, or form. **7.** confusion; disorder. [1375–1425; late ME (north) < Scand; cf. Norw *svirla;* c. D *zwirrelen* to whirl, G (dial.) *schwirrlen* to totter; all < a root **swir-* (whence Dan *svirre* to whirl, G *schwirren* to whir) + -*l-* freq. suffix] —**swirl′ing•ly,** *adv.*
—**Syn. 2.** reel, spin.

swirl•y (swûr′lē), *adj.,* **swirl•i•er, swirl•i•est.** swirling, whirling, or twisted. [1775–85; SWIRL + -Y[1]]

swish (swish), *v.i.* **1.** to move with or make a sibilant sound, as a slender rod cutting sharply through the air or as small waves washing on the shore. **2.** to rustle, as silk. **3.** to move or behave in an exaggeratedly effeminate manner. —*v.t.* **4.** to flourish, whisk, etc., with a swishing movement or sound: *to swish a cane.* **5.** to bring, take, cut, etc., with such a movement or sound: *to swish off the tops of plants with a cane.* **6.** to flog or whip. —*n.* **7.** a swishing movement or sound. **8.** a stock or rod for flogging or a stroke with this. **9.** *Slang (disparaging and offensive).* an effeminate male homosexual. —*adj.* **10.** *Slang.* swishy (def. 2). **11.** *Chiefly Brit. Informal.* stylishly elegant; fashionable. [1750–60; imit.] —**swish′er,** *n.* —**swish′ing•ly,** *adv.*

swish•y (swish′ē), *adj.,* **swish•i•er, swish•i•est. 1.** causing, giving rise to, or characterized by a swishing sound or motion. **2.** Also, **swish.** *Slang.* exhibiting effeminate tendencies or characteristics. [1820–30; SWISH + -Y[1]]

Swiss (swis), *adj.* **1.** of, pertaining to, associated with, or characteristic of Switzerland or its inhabitants. —*n.* **2.** a native or inhabitant of Switzerland. **3.** (*sometimes l.c.*) See **Swiss muslin. 4.** See **Swiss cheese.** [1505–15; < MF *suisse* < MHG *Swiz*]

Swiss′ chard′, chard. [1825–35]

Swiss′ cheese′, a firm, pale-yellow cheese made originally in Switzerland, typically made from cow's milk and having many holes. Also called **Swiss.** Cf. **Emmenthaler, Gruyère.** [1815–25]

Swiss·er (swis′ər), *n.* Swiss (def. 2). [1520–30; SWISS + -ER[1], modeled on SWITZER]

Swiss′ Guard′, a member of a corps of bodyguards protecting the pope, with membership restricted to natives of Switzerland. [1690–1700]

Swiss′ la′pis, *Jewelry.* cracked quartz, stained blue in imitation of lapis lazuli.

Swiss′ mus′lin, a crisp, sheer muslin that is constructed in plain weave, bleached white or dyed, and often ornamented with raised dots or figures **(dotted swiss),** used chiefly in the manufacture of curtains and women's summer clothes. Also called **Swiss.** [1880–85]

Swiss′ steak′, a thick slice of steak dredged in flour and pounded, browned, and braised with tomatoes, onions, and other vegetables. [1920–25]

Swiss·vale (swis′vāl′), *n.* a city in SW Pennsylvania, on the Monongahela River. 11,345.

Swit., Switzerland.

switch (swich), *n.* **1.** a slender, flexible shoot, rod, etc., used esp. in whipping or disciplining. **2.** an act of whipping or beating with or as with such an object; a stroke, lash, or whisking movement. **3.** a slender growing shoot, as of a plant. **4.** a hairpiece consisting of a bunch or tress of long hair or some substitute, fastened together at one end and worn by women to supplement their own hair. **5.** *Elect.* a device for turning on or off or directing an electric current or for making or breaking a circuit. **6.** *Railroads.* a track structure for diverting moving trains or rolling stock from one track to another, commonly consisting of a pair of movable rails. **7.** a turning, shifting, or changing: *a switch of votes to another candidate.* **8.** *Bridge.* a change to a suit other than the one played or bid previously. **9.** *Basketball.* a maneuver in which two teammates on defense shift assignments so that each guards the opponent usually guarded by the other. **10.** a tuft of hair at the end of the tail of some animals, as of the cow or lion. **11. asleep at the switch,** *Informal.* failing to perform one's duty, missing an opportunity, etc., because of negligence or inattention: *He lost the contract because he was asleep at the switch.* —*v.t.* **12.** to whip or beat with a switch or the like; lash: *He switched the boy with a cane.* **13.** to move, swing, or whisk (a cane, a fishing line, etc.) with a swift, lashing stroke. **14.** to shift or exchange: *The two girls switched their lunch boxes.* **15.** to turn, shift, or divert: *to switch conversation from a painful subject.* **16.** *Elect.* to connect, disconnect, or redirect (an electric circuit or the device it serves) by operating a switch (often fol. by *off* or *on*): *I switched on a light.* **17.** *Railroads.* **a.** to move or transfer (a train, car, etc.) from one set of tracks to another. **b.** to drop or add (cars) or to make up (a train). **18.** *Motion Pictures, Television.* to shift rapidly from one camera to another in order to change camera angles or shots. —*v.i.* **19.** to strike with or as with a switch. **20.** to change direction or course; turn, shift, or change. **21.** to exchange or replace something with another: *He used to smoke this brand of cigarettes, but he switched.* **22.** to move or sway back and forth, as a cat's tail. **23.** to be shifted, turned, etc., by means of a switch. **24.** *Basketball.* to execute a switch. **25.** *Bridge.* to lead a card of a suit different from the suit just led by oneself or one's partner. [1585–95; earlier *swits, switz* slender riding whip, flexible stick; cf. LG (Hanoverian) *schwutsche* long, thin stick] —**switch′a·ble,** *adj.* —**switch′er,** *n.* —**switch′like′,** *adj.*
—**Syn. 7.** change, shift, alternation, substitution.

switch·back (swich′bak′), *n.* **1.** a highway, as in a mountainous area, having many hairpin curves. **2.** *Railroads.* a zigzag track arrangement for climbing a steep grade. **3.** *Brit.* See **roller coaster.** —*v.i.* **4.** (of a road, railroad track, etc.) to progress through a series of hairpin curves; zigzag: *The road switchbacks up the mountain.* [1860–65, *Amer.*; SWITCH + BACK[2]]

switch·blade (swich′blād′), *n.* a pocketknife, the blade of which is held by a spring and can be released suddenly, as by pressing a button. Also called **switch′·blade knife′.** [1905–10; SWITCH + BLADE]

switch·board (swich′bôrd′, -bōrd′), *n. Elect.* **1.** a structural unit on which are mounted switches and instruments necessary to complete telephone circuits manually. **2.** Also called **lightboard.** a panel of switches, dimmers, etc., for controlling the lighting on a stage or in an auditorium. [1870–75, *Amer.*; SWITCH + BOARD]

switch′ box′, a box, usually of metal, containing one or more electric switches.

switch′ cane′. See under **cane** (def. 5). [1835–45, *Amer.*]

switched-on (swicht′on′, -ôn′), *adj. Slang.* turned-on (def. 1).

switch′ en′gine, *Railroads.* a locomotive for switching rolling stock in a yard. Also called **switcher, switch′ing locomo′tive.** [1865–70, *Amer.*]

switch·er·oo (swich′ə rōō′, swich′ə rōō′), *n., pl.* **-oos.** *Slang.* an unexpected or sudden change or reversal in attitude, character, position, action, etc. [1930–35; SWITCH + -EROO]

switch·gear (swich′gēr′), *n. Elect.* switching equipment used in an electric power station. Also, **switch′ gear′.** [1900–05; SWITCH + GEAR]

switch′ grass′, a North American grass, *Panicum virgatum,* having an open, branching inflorescence. [1830–40, *Amer.*; alter. of QUITCH (GRASS)]

switch-hit (swich′hit′), *v.i.,* **-hit, -hit·ting.** *Baseball.* to be able to bat from either side of the plate, or both as a left-handed and as a right-handed batter. [1950–55] —**switch′ hit′ter.** —**switch′-hit′ter,** *n.*

CONCISE ETYMOLOGY KEY: <, descended or borrowed from; >, whence; b., blend of, blended; c., cognate with; cf., compare; deriv., derivative; equiv., equivalent; imit., imitative; obl., oblique; r., replacing; s., stem; sp., spelling, spelled; resp., respelling, respelled; trans., translation; ?, origin unknown; *, unattested; ‡, probably earlier than. See the full key inside the front cover.

switch·man (swich′mən), *n., pl.* **-men. 1.** a person who has charge of a switch on a railroad. **2.** a person who assists in moving cars in a railway yard or terminal. [1835–45; SWITCH + -MAN]

switch-off (swich′ôf′, -of′), *n.* the act or process of switching off a power supply, light source, appliance, etc. [n. use of v. phrase *switch off*]

switch-on (swich′on′, -ôn′), *n.* the act or process of switching on an ignition, light, appliance, etc. [n. use of v. phrase *switch on*]

switch·o·ver (swich′ō′vər), *n.* **1.** the act or process of changing from one power source, system, etc., to another. **2.** an act or an instance of changing from one job, belief, style, etc., to another. [1925–30; n. use of v. phrase *switch over*]

switch′ plate′, a plate, usually of metal, ceramic, or plastic, covering a switch so that the knob or toggle protrudes. Also, **switch′plate′.** Also called **wall plate.**

switch′ plug′, a plug, as for an electric iron, equipped with an on-off switch. [1900–05]

switch·yard (swich′yärd′), *n.* a railroad yard in which rolling stock is distributed or made up into trains. [1885–90, *Amer.*; SWITCH + YARD[2]]

swith (swith), *adv.* **1.** *Chiefly Brit. Dial.* immediately; quickly. —*v.t.* **2.** *Scot.* to hurry; hasten. Also, **swithe.** [bef. 900; ME (adv.), OE *swīthe* strongly, equiv. to *swīth* strong (c. G *geschwind,* ON *svinnr* fast, Goth *swinths* strong) + *-e* adv. suffix] —**swith′ly,** *adv.*

swith·er (swith′ər), *n. Brit. Dial.* a state of confusion, excitement, or perplexity. [1495–1505; orig. uncert.; cf. OE *geswithrian* to retire, dwindle, fail]

Swith·in (swith′in, swith′-), *n.* **Saint,** died A.D. 862, English ecclesiastic: bishop of Winchester 852?–862. Also, **Swith′un.**

Switz., Switzerland.

Switz·er (swit′sər), *n.* Swiss (def. 2). [1540–50; << MHG, equiv. to *Switz* Switzerland + *-er* -ER[1]]

Switz·er·land (swit′sər lənd), *n.* a republic in central Europe. 6,333,200; 15,944 sq. mi. (41,295 sq. km). *Cap.:* Bern. French, **Suisse.** German, **Schweiz.** Italian, **Svizzera.**

swive (swīv), *v.,* **swived, swiv·ing.** *Obs.* —*v.t.* **1.** to copulate with. —*v.i.* **2.** to copulate. [1350–1400; ME *swiven;* appar. special use of OE *swīfan* to move, wend, sweep; cf. SWIFT, SWIVEL]

swiv·el (swiv′əl), *n., v.,* **-eled, -el·ing** or (*esp. Brit.*) **-elled, -el·ling.** —*n.* **1.** a fastening device that allows the thing fastened to turn around freely upon it, esp. to turn in a full circle. **2.** such a device consisting of two parts, each of which turns around independently, as a compound link of a chain, one part of which turns freely in the other by means of a headed pin or the like. **3.** a pivoted support allowing a gun to turn around in a horizontal plane. **4.** a swivel gun. **5.** a device attached to a loom and used as a shuttle to weave extra threads in the production of small figures, esp. dots. —*v.t.* **6.** to turn or pivot on or as if on a swivel: *He swiveled his chair around.* **7.** to fasten by a swivel; furnish with a swivel. —*v.i.* **8.** to turn on or if as on a swivel. [1275–1325; ME (n.), equiv. to *swiv-* (weak s. of OE *swīfan* to revolve; c. ON *svīfa* to turn) + *-el* instrumental suffix] —**swiv′el·like′,** *adj.*

swiv′el chair′, a chair whose seat turns around horizontally on a swivel. [1850–55, *Amer.*]

swiv′el gun′, a gun mounted on a pedestal so that it can be turned from side to side or up and down. [1705–15]

swiv·el-hipped (swiv′əl hipt′), *adj.* characterized by an exaggeratedly swinging or extremely free motion of the hips. [1945–50]

swiv·el·tree (swiv′əl trē′), *n. Dial.* swingletree. [SWIVEL + TREE]

swiv′el weav′ing, the process of weaving on a loom equipped with a swivel. [1890–95]

swiv·et (swiv′it), *n.* a state of nervous excitement, haste, or anxiety; flutter: *I was in such a swivet that I could hardly speak.* [1890–95; orig. obscure]

swiz·zle (swiz′əl), *n., v.,* **-zled, -zling.** —*n.* **1.** a tall drink, originating in Barbados, composed of full-flavored West Indian rum, lime juice, crushed ice, and sugar: typically served with a swizzle stick. —*v.t.* **2.** to agitate (a beverage) with a swizzle stick. **3.** to gulp down; guzzle. [1805–15; orig. uncert.] —**swiz′zler,** *n.*

swiz′zle stick′, a rod for stirring highballs and cocktails in the glass. [1875–80]

swob (swob), *n., v.t.,* **swobbed, swob·bing.** swab.

swol·len (swō′lən), *v.* **1.** a pp. of **swell.** —*adj.* **2.** enlarged by or as by swelling; puffed up; tumid. **3.** turgid or bombastic. —**swol′len·ly,** *adv.* —**swol′len·ness,** *n.*

swoln (swōln), *adj. Archaic.* swollen.

swonk (swongk), *v.* a pt. of **swink.**

swonk·en (swong′kən), *v.* pp. of **swink.**

swoon (swōōn), *v.i.* **1.** to faint; lose consciousness. **2.** to enter a state of hysterical rapture or ecstasy: *The teenagers swooned at the sight of the singing star.* —*n.* **3.** a faint or fainting fit; syncope. [1250–1300; (v.) ME *swo(w)nen* to faint, orig. as ger. *swowening, swoghning* act of swooning, ult. continuing OE *-swōgan* (in compounds) to rush, overrun, choke; (n.) ME, partly deriv. of the v., partly extracted from *in (a) swoune, on swoune,* alter. of *a swoune, aswoune* in a swoon, as if equiv. to *a* A-[1] + *swoon* (n.), but prob. continuing OE *āswōgen,* ptp. of *āswōgan* to overcome (see A-[3]), or *geswōgen* (ptp.) senseless, dead] —**swoon′ing·ly,** *adv.*

swoop (swōōp), *v.i.* **1.** to sweep through the air, as a bird or a bat, esp. down upon prey. **2.** to come down upon something in a sudden, swift attack (often fol. by *down* and *on* or *upon*): *The army swooped down on the town.* —*v.t.* **3.** to take, lift, scoop up, or remove with or as with one sweeping motion (often fol. by *up, away,* or *off*): *He swooped her up in his arms.* —*n.* **4.** an act or instance of swooping; a sudden, swift descent. **5. at** or **in one fell swoop,** all at once or all together, as if by one blow: *The quake flattened the houses at one fell swoop.* [1535–45; var. (with close ō) of ME *swopen,* OE *swāpan* to SWEEP[1]; c. G *schweifen*]
—**Syn. 4.** dive, plunge, sweep, drop.

swoosh (swŏŏsh), *v.i.* **1.** to move with or make a rustling, swirling, or brushing sound. **2.** to pour out swiftly. —*v.t.* **3.** to cause to make or move with a rustling, swirling, or brushing sound. —*n.* **4.** a swirling or rustling sound or movement. [1865–70; imit.]

swop (swop), *v.t., v.i.,* **swopped, swop·ping,** *n.* swap.

sword (sôrd, sōrd), *n.* **1.** a weapon having various forms but consisting typically of a long, straight or slightly curved blade, sharp-edged on one or both sides, with one end pointed and the other fixed in a hilt or handle. **2.** this weapon as the symbol of military power, punitive justice, authority, etc.: *The pen is mightier than the sword.* **3.** a cause of death or destruction. **4.** war, combat, slaughter, or violence, esp. military force or aggression: *to perish by the sword.* **5.** (*cap.*) *Mil.* the code name for one of the five D-Day invasion beaches on France's Normandy coast, assaulted by British forces. **6. at swords' points,** mutually antagonistic or hostile; opposed: *Father and son are constantly at swords' point.* **7. cross swords, a.** to engage in combat; fight. **b.** to disagree violently; argue: *The board members crossed swords in the selection of a president.* **8. put to the sword,** to slay; execute: *The entire population of the town was put to the sword.* [bef. 900; ME; OE *sweord;* c. D *zwaard,* G *Schwert,* ON *sverth*] —**sword′less,** *adj.* —**sword′like′,** *adj.*

sword′ bay′onet, a short sword that may be attached to the muzzle of a gun and used as a bayonet. [1835–45]

sword′ bean′, a twining vine, *Canavalia gladiata,* of the legume family, found in the tropics of the Eastern Hemisphere, having large, showy, pealike flowers and reddish-brown seeds. [1880–85]

sword-bear·er (sôrd′bâr′ər), *n. Brit.* an official who carries the sword of state on ceremonial occasions, as before the sovereign, a magistrate, or the like. [1400–50; late ME *swerd berer.* See SWORD, BEARER]

sword′ belt′, a military belt from which a sword may be hung. [1515–25]

sword·bill (sôrd′bil′, sōrd′-), *n.* a South American hummingbird, *Ensifera ensifera,* having a slender bill that is longer than its body. [1860–65; SWORD + BILL[2]]

sword′ cane′, a cane or walking stick having a hollow shaft that serves as a sheath for a sword or dagger. [1830–40]

sword·craft (sôrd′kraft′, -kräft′, sōrd′-), *n.* **1.** skill in or the art of swordplay. **2.** military skill or power. [1850–55; SWORD + CRAFT]

sword′ dance′, any of various dances, usually performed by men, in which swords are ceremonially flourished or are laid on the ground and danced around. [1595–1605] —**sword′ danc′er.**

sword′ fern′, any fern of the genus *Nephrolepis,* esp. *N. exaltata,* characterized by sword-shaped, pinnate fronds, a common houseplant. [1820–30]

sword·fish (sôrd′fish′, sōrd′-), *n., pl.* **-fish·es,** (*esp. collectively*) **-fish** for 1. **1.** a large, marine food fish, *Xiphias gladius,* having the upper jaw elongated into a swordlike structure. **2.** (*cap.*) *Astron.* the constellation Dorado. [1350–1400; ME; see SWORD, FISH]

swordfish, *Xiphias gladius,* length to 15 ft. (4.6 m)

sword′ grass′, any of various grasses or plants having swordlike or sharp leaves, as the sword lily. [1590–1600]

sword′ knot′, a looped strap, ribbon, or the like attached to the hilt of a sword as a support or ornament. [1685–95]

sword′ lil′y, a gladiolus. [1780–90]

sword·man (sôrd′mən, sōrd′-), *n., pl.* **-men.** swordsman. [1350–1400; ME *swerdman.* See SWORD, -MAN] —**sword′man·ship′,** *n.*

sword′ of Dam′ocles. See **Damocles** (def. 2). [1810–20]

sword·play (sôrd′plā′, sōrd′-), *n.* the action or technique of wielding a sword; fencing. [1620–30; SWORD + PLAY] —**sword′play′er,** *n.*

swords·man (sôrdz′mən, sōrdz′-), *n., pl.* **-men. 1.** a person who uses or is skilled in the use of a sword. **2.** a fencer. **3.** a soldier. Also, **swordman.** [1670–80; SWORD + 's[1] + -MAN] —**swords′man·ship′,** *n.*

sword·tail (sôrd′tāl′, sōrd′-), *n.* any of several small, brightly colored, viviparous, freshwater fishes of the genus *Xiphophorus,* native to Central America, having the lower part of the caudal fin elongated into a swordlike structure: often kept in aquariums. Also called **helleri.** [1925–30; SWORD + TAIL[1]]

swore (swôr, swōr), *v.* a pt. of **swear.**

sworn (swôrn, swōrn), *v.* **1.** pp. of **swear.** —*adj.* **2.** having taken an oath: *a duly elected and sworn official.* **3.** bound by or as if by an oath or pledge. **4.** avowed; affirmed: *He is my sworn enemy.*

swot[1] (swot), *v.t.* **swot·ted, swot·ting,** *n.* swat[1]. —**swot′ter,** *n.*

swot[2] (swot), *v.,* **swot·ted, swot·ting,** *n. Brit. Slang.* —*v.i.* **1.** to study or work hard. —*n.* **2.** a student who studies assiduously, esp. to the exclusion of other activities or interests; grind. **3.** hard study or hard work; concentrated effort. [1840–50; dial. var. of SWEAT]

swot·ter (swot′ər), *n. Brit. Slang.* swot[2] (def. 2).

swound (swound, swōōnd), *v.i., n. Archaic.* swoon. [1400–50; late ME *swounde* (v.), var. (with excrescent *d*) of *swoune* to SWOON]

'swounds (zwoundz, zoundz, zwōōndz), *interj. Obs.* zounds. [1580–90; 's[3] + WOUND[1] + -s[3]]

Swtz., Switzerland.

swum (swum), *v.* pp. of **swim.**

swung (swung), *v.* pt. and pp. of **swing.**

swung′ dash′, a mark of punctuation (~) used in place of a word or part of a word previously spelled out. [1950–55]

swy (swī), *n. Australian.* the game of two-up. [< G *zwei* TWO]

Sy (sī), *n.* a male given name, form of **Seymour, Simon,** or **Silas.**

sy-, var. of **syn-** before *s* followed by a consonant and before *z: systaltic; syzygy.*

-sy, a suffix forming nouns or adjectives, sometimes a diminutive of the base word and usually confined to informal and jocular use (*bitsy; footsie; halvsies*); adjectives formed with **-sy** may be ironic, implying that the quality in question is self-consciously assumed or feigned (*artsy; cutesy; folksy*). The combination of **-s**[3] and **-y**[1] or **-y**[2] in certain words (*antsy; gutsy*) should perhaps be considered further instances of this suffix. [perh. orig. two distinct suffixes, one diminutive (as in *Betsy, popsy, tootsy*) and the other adjectival; sources of both are uncert.]

Syb·a·ris (sib′ə ris), *n.* an ancient Greek city in S Italy: noted for its wealth and luxury; destroyed 510 B.C.

Syb·a·rite (sib′ə rīt′), *n.* **1.** (*usually l.c.*) a person devoted to luxury and pleasure. **2.** an inhabitant of Sybaris. [1590–1600; < L *Sybarīta* < Gk *Sybarī́tēs.* See SYBARIS, -ITE[1]] —**syb′a·rit·ism** (sib′ə rī tiz′əm), *n.*
—**Syn. 1.** sensualist.

Syb·a·rit·ic (sib′ə rit′ik), *adj.* **1.** (*usually l.c.*) pertaining to or characteristic of a sybarite; characterized by or loving luxury or sensuous pleasure: *to wallow in sybaritic splendor.* **2.** of, pertaining to, or characteristic of Sybaris or its inhabitants. Also, **Syb′a·rit′i·cal.** [< L *Sybarīticus* < Gk *Sybarītikós,* equiv. to *Sybarī́t(ēs)* SYBARITE + *-ikos* -IC] —**Syb′a·rit′i·cal·ly,** *adv.*

Syb·il (sib′əl), *n.* a female given name.

syc·a·mine (sik′ə min, -mīn′), *n.* a tree mentioned in the New Testament, probably the black mulberry. [1520–30; < L *sycaminus* < Gk *sȳkáminos* < Sem; cf. Heb *shiqmāh* mulberry tree, sycamore (Gk form with *ȳ* influenced by *sȳkon* fig)]

syc·a·more (sik′ə môr′, -mōr′), *n.* **1.** Also called **buttonwood.** any of several North American plane trees, esp. *Platanus occidentalis,* having shallowly lobed ovate leaves, globular seed heads, and wood valued as timber. **2.** *Brit.* the sycamore maple. **3.** a tree, *Ficus sycomorus,* of the Near East, related to the common fig, bearing an edible fruit. [1300–50; ME *sicomore* < OF < L *sȳcomorus* < Gk *sykómoros,* equiv. to *sŷko(n)* fig + *mór(on)* mulberry + *-os* n. suffix, appar. by folk etymology < Sem; cf. Heb *shiqmāh* sycamore]

syc′amore ma′ple, a maple, *Acer pseudoplatanus,* of Europe and western Asia, having gray bark and opposite, lobed leaves: grown as a shade tree. [1790–1800]

syce (sīs), *n.* (in India) a groom; stable attendant. Also, **saice, sice.** [1645–55; < Urdu *sā′is* < Ar]

sy·cee (sī sē′), *n.* fine uncoined silver in lumps of various sizes usually bearing a banker's or assayer's stamp or mark, formerly used in China as a medium of exchange. Also called **sycee′ sil′ver.** [1705–15; < Chin dial. (Guangdong) *sai-si,* akin to Chin *xìsī* silk floss; so called because it can be made into wire as fine as silk thread]

sy·con (sī′kon), *n.* a type of sponge having a thick body wall that is folded to form many short canals leading to the spongocoel. Cf. **ascon, leucon.** [1885–90; < NL < Gk *sŷkon* fig]

sy·co·ni·um (sī kō′nē əm), *n., pl.* **-ni·a** (-nē ə). *Bot.* a multiple fruit developed from a hollow fleshy receptacle containing numerous flowers, as in the fig. [1855–60; < NL < Gk *sŷkon* fig + NL *-ium* -IUM]

sy·co·noid (sī′kə noid′), *adj.* pertaining to or resembling a sycon. [SYCON + -OID]

syc·o·phan·cy (sik′ə fən sē, -fan′-, sī′kə-), *n.* **1.** self-seeking or servile flattery. **2.** the character or conduct of a sycophant. [1615–25; < L *sȳcophantia* trickery < Gk *sȳkophantía* dishonest prosecution, equiv. to *sȳkophant-* (see SYCOPHANT) + *-ia* -Y[3]; see -CY]

syc·o·phant (sik′ə fənt, -fant′, sī′kə-), *n.* a self-seeking, servile flatterer; fawning parasite. [1530–40; < L *sȳcophanta* < Gk *sȳkophántēs* informer, equiv. to *sŷko(n)* fig + *phan-* (s. of *phaínein* to show) + *-tēs* agentive suffix] —**syc′o·phan′tic, syc′o·phan′ti·cal, syc′o·phant′ish,** *adj.* —**syc′o·phan′ti·cal·ly, syc′o·phant′·ish·ly,** *adv.* —**syc′o·phant·ism,** *n.*
—**Syn.** toady, yes man, flunky, fawner, flatterer.

sy·co·sis (sī kō′sis), *n. Pathol.* an inflammatory disease of the hair follicles, characterized by a pustular eruption. [1570–80; < NL < Gk *sȳ́kōsis,* equiv. to *sȳ́k(on)* fig + *-ōsis* -OSIS]

Syd·ney (sid′nē), *n.* **1. Sir Philip.** See **Sidney, Sir Philip. 2.** a seaport in and the capital of New South Wales, in SE Australia. 2,876,508. **3.** a seaport on NE Cape Breton Island, Nova Scotia, in SE Canada. 30,645. **4.** a male or female given name.

Syd′ney silk′y. See **silky terrier.** [1940–45; after SYDNEY, Australia]

Sy·e·ne (sī ē′nē), *n.* ancient name of **Aswan.**

sy·e·nite (sī′ə nīt′), *n.* a granular igneous rock consisting chiefly of orthoclase and oligoclase with hornblende, biotite, or augite. [1790–1800; < L *syēnītēs* (*lapis*) (stone) of SYENE < Gk *syēnī́tēs* (*líthos*); see -ITE[1]] —**sy·e·nit·ic** (sī′ə nit′ik), *adj.*

syke (sīk), *n. Scot. and North Eng.* sike.

Syk·tyv·kar (sik tif kär′), *n.* a city in and the capital of the Komi Autonomous Republic in the NW Russian Federation in Europe. 233,000. Formerly, **Ust Sysolsk.**

syl-, var. of **syn-** before *l: syllepsis.*

Syl·a·cau·ga (sil′ə kô′gə), *n.* a city in central Alabama. 12,708.

sy·li (sē′lē), *n.* an aluminum coin and monetary unit of Guinea, equal to 100 cauris: replaced the franc in 1972.

syll., 1. syllable. **2.** syllabus.

syl·la·bar·i·um (sil′ə bâr′ē əm), *n., pl.* **-bar·i·a** (-bâr′ē ə). syllabary. [< NL; see SYLLABARY]

syl·la·bar·y (sil′ə ber′ē), *n., pl.* **-bar·ies. 1.** a list or catalog of syllables. **2.** a set of written symbols, each of which represents a syllable, used to write a given language: *the Japanese syllabary.* [1580–90; < NL *syllabārium.* See SYLLABLE, -ARY]

syl·la·bi (sil′ə bī′), *n.* a pl. of **syllabus.**

syl·lab·ic (si lab′ik), *adj.* **1.** of, pertaining to, or consisting of a syllable or syllables. **2.** pronounced with careful distinction of syllables. **3.** of, pertaining to, or noting poetry based on a specific number of syllables, as distinguished from poetry depending on stresses or quantities. **4.** (of chanting) having each syllable sung to one note only. **5.** *Phonet.* **a.** (of a consonant) forming a syllable by itself, as the (n) in *button* (but′n) or the (l) in *bottle* (bot′l). **b.** (of a vowel) dominating the other sounds in a syllable; sonantal. —*n.* **6.** *Phonet.* a syllabic sound. [1720–30; < LL *syllabicus* < Gk *syllabikós.* See SYLLABLE, -IC] —**syl·lab′i·cal·ly,** *adv.*

syl·lab·i·cate (si lab′i kāt′), *v.t.,* **-cat·ed, -cat·ing.** to syllabify. [1765–75; back formation from *syllabication* < ML *syllabicātiōn-* (s. of *syllabicātiō*). See SYLLABIC, -ATION] —**syl·lab′i·ca′tion,** *n.*

syl·la·bic·i·ty (sil′ə bis′i tē), *n.* the state of being syllabic; the ability to form a syllable. [1930–35; SYLLABIC + -ITY]

syl·lab·i·fy (si lab′ə fī′), *v.t.,* **-fied, -fy·ing.** to form or divide into syllables. [1860–65; < NL *syllabificāre.* See SYLLABLE, -IFY] —**syl·lab′i·fi·ca′tion,** *n.*

syl·la·bism (sil′ə biz′əm), *n.* **1.** the use of syllabic characters, as in writing. **2.** division into syllables. [1880–85; < L *syllab(a)* SYLLABLE + -ISM]

syl·la·bize (sil′ə bīz′), *v.t.,* **-bized, -biz·ing.** to syllabify. Also, *esp. Brit.,* **syl′la·bise′.** [1650–60; < ML *syllabizāre* < Gk *syllabízein.* See SYLLABLE, -IZE]

syl·la·ble (sil′ə bəl), *n., v.,* **-bled, -bling.** —*n.* **1.** an uninterrupted segment of speech consisting of a center of relatively great sonority with or without one or more accompanying sounds of relatively less sonority: *"Man," "eye," "strength," and "sixths" are English words of one syllable.* **2.** one or more written letters or characters representing more or less exactly such an element of speech. **3.** the slightest portion or amount of speech or writing; the least mention: *Do not breathe a syllable of all this.* —*v.t.* **4.** to utter in syllables; articulate. **5.** to represent by syllables. —*v.i.* **6.** to utter syllables; speak. [1350–1400; ME *sillable* < AF; MF *sillabe* < L *syllaba* < Gk *syllabḗ,* equiv. to *syl-* SYL- + *lab-* (base of *lambánein* to take) + *-ē* n. suffix]

syl·la·ble-timed (sil′ə bəl tīmd′), *adj. Phonet.* (of a language) having a rhythm in which syllables are approximately equal in duration and thus tend to follow each other at regular intervals of time. Cf. **stress-timed.**

syl·la·bub (sil′ə bub′), *n.* **1.** a drink of milk or cream sweetened, flavored, and mixed with wine or cider. **2.** a dessert of beaten cream that is thickened with gelatin, sweetened, and flavored with wine or liquor. **3.** a glass or punch cup in which syllabub is served. [1530–40; earlier *sollybubbe, sillabub,* of obscure orig.]

syl·la·bus (sil′ə bəs), *n., pl.* **-bus·es, -bi** (-bī′). **1.** an outline or other brief statement of the main points of a discourse, the subjects of a course of lectures, the contents of a curriculum, etc. **2.** *Law.* **a.** a short summary of the legal basis of a court's decision appearing at the beginning of a reported case. **b.** a book containing summaries of the leading cases in a legal field, used esp. by students. **3.** (*often cap.*) Also called **Syl′labus of Er′·rors.** *Rom. Cath. Ch.* the list of 80 propositions condemned as erroneous by Pope Pius IX in 1864. [1650–60; < NL *syllabus, syllabos,* prob. a misreading (in mss. of Cicero) of Gk *sittybās,* acc. pl. of *síttyba* label for a papyrus roll]

syl·lep·sis (si lep′sis), *n., pl.* **-ses** (-sēz). *Gram.* the use of a word or expression to perform two syntactic functions, esp. to modify two or more words of which at least one does not agree in number, case, or gender, as the use of *are* in *Neither he nor we are willing.* Cf. **zeugma.** [1570–80; < ML *syllēpsis* < Gk *sýllēpsis,* equiv. to *syl-* SYL- + *lēb-* (var. s. of *lambánein* to take) + *-sis* -SIS] —**syl·lep·tic** (si lep′tik), *adj.* —**syl·lep′ti·cal·ly,** *adv.*

syl·lo·gism (sil′ə jiz′əm), *n.* **1.** *Logic.* an argument the conclusion of which is supported by two premises, of which one **(major premise)** contains the term **(major term)** that is the predicate of the conclusion, and the other **(minor premise)** contains the term **(minor term)** that is the subject of the conclusion; common to both premises is a term **(middle term)** that is excluded from the conclusion. A typical form is "All A is C; all B is A; therefore all B is C." **2.** deductive reasoning. **3.** an extremely subtle, sophisticated, or deceptive argument. [1350–1400; < L *syllogismus* < Gk *syllogismós,* equiv. to *syllog-* (see SYLLOGIZE) + *-ismos* -ISM; r. ME *silogime* < OF < L, as above]

syl·lo·gist (sil′ə jist), *n.* a person who engages in syllogistic argument. [1790–1800; SYLLOG(ISM) + -IST]

syl·lo·gis·tic (sil′ə jis′tik), *adj.* Also, **syl′lo·gis′ti·cal. 1.** of or pertaining to a syllogism. **2.** like or consisting of syllogisms. —*n.* **3.** the part of logic that deals with syllogisms. **4.** syllogistic reasoning. [1660–70; < L *syllogisticus* < Gk *syllogistikós,* equiv. to *syllogist(ós),* verbid of *syllogízesthai* (see SYLLOGIZE) + *-ikos* -IC] —**syl′lo·gis′·ti·cal·ly,** *adv.*

syl·lo·gize (sil′ə jīz′), *v.i., v.t.,* **-gized, -giz·ing.** to argue or reason by syllogism. Also, *esp. Brit.,* **syl′lo·gise′.** [1375–1425; late ME *silogysen* < LL *syllogizāre* < Gk *syllogízesthai* to reason, equiv. to *syl-* SYL- + *logízesthai* to reckon, infer, equiv. to *lóg(os)* discourse (see LOGOS) + *-izesthai* -IZE] —**syl′lo·gi·za′tion,** *n.* —**syl′·lo·giz′er,** *n.*

sylph (silf), *n.* **1.** a slender, graceful woman or girl. **2.** (in folklore) one of a race of supernatural beings supposed to inhabit the air. [1650–60; < NL *sylphēs* (pl.), coined by Paracelsus; appar. b. *sylva* (var. sp. of L *silva* forest) and Gk *nýmphē* NYMPH] —**sylph′ic,** *adj.* —**sylph′like′,** *adj.*
—**Syn. 2.** SYLPH, SALAMANDER, UNDINE (NYMPH), GNOME were imaginary beings inhabiting the four elements once believed to make up the physical world. All except the GNOMES were female. SYLPHS dwelt in the air and were light, dainty, and airy beings. SALAMANDERS dwelt in fire: *"a salamander that . . . lives in the midst of flames"* (Addison). UNDINES were water spirits: *By marrying a man, an undine could acquire a mortal soul.* (They were also called NYMPHS, though nymphs were ordinarily minor divinities of nature who dwelt in woods, hills, and meadows as well as in waters.) GNOMES were little old men or dwarfs, dwelling in the earth: *ugly enough to be king of the gnomes.*

sylph·id (sil′fid), *n.* **1.** a little or young sylph. —*adj.* **2.** Also, **sylph·id·ine** (sil′fi din, -dīn′). of, pertaining to, or characteristic of a sylph. [1670–80; < F *sylphide.* See SYLPH, -ID[1]]

syl·va (sil′və), *n.* silva. [< L]

Syl·va (sil′və; *Rum.* sēl′vä), *n.* **Car·men** (kär′mən; *Rum.* kär′men), pen name of Elizabeth, queen of Rumania.

syl·van (sil′vən), *adj.* **1.** of, pertaining to, or inhabiting the woods. **2.** consisting of or abounding in woods or trees; wooded; woody: *a shady, sylvan glade.* **3.** made of trees, branches, boughs, etc. —*n.* **4.** a person dwelling in a woodland region. **5.** a mythical deity or spirit of the woods. Also, **silvan.** [1555–65; < L *sylvānus,* sp. var. of *silvānus,* equiv. to *silv(a)* forest + *-ānus* -AN]

Syl·va·ner (sil vä′nər, -van′ər), *n.* **1.** a white grape grown in the Alsace region of France and in Switzerland, Germany, and Austria. **2.** a mild white wine made from this grape. [< G; see SYLVAN, -ER[1]]

Syl·va·ni·a (sil vā′nē ə, -vān′yə), *n.* a town in NW Ohio. 15,527.

syl·van·ite (sil′və nīt′), *n.* a mineral, gold silver telluride, $(AuAg)Te_2$, silver-white with metallic luster, often occurring in crystals so arranged as to resemble written characters: an ore of gold. [1790–1800; named after TRANSYLVANIA; see -ITE[1]]

Syl·va·nus (sil vā′nəs), *n., pl.* **-ni** (-nī). Silvanus.

syl·vat·ic (sil vat′ik), *adj.* sylvan. [1650–60; < L *silvāticus,* equiv. to *silv(a)* SILVA + *-āticus* (see -ATE[1], -IC)]

Syl·ves·ter (sil ves′tər), *n.* a male given name.

Sylvester I, Saint, died A.D. 335, pope 314–335. Also, **Silvester I.**

Sylvester II, (*Gerbert*) died 1003, French ecclesiastic: pope 999–1003. Also, **Silvester II.**

Syl·vi·a (sil′vē ə), *n.* a female given name.

Syl′vi·an fis′sure (sil′vē ən), *Anat.* See **lateral fissure.** [1870–75; named after *Sylvius,* Latinized form of Jacques *Dubois* (d. 1555), French anatomist; see -AN]

syl′vic ac′id (sil′vik), *Chem.* See **abietic acid.** [1830–40; < F *sylvique* < L *silv(a)* a wood + F *-ique* -IC]

syl·vi·cul·ture (sil′vi kul′chər), *n.* silviculture. [< L *sylv(a)* (var. sp. of *silva*) forest + -I- + CULTURE]

syl·vite (sil′vīt), *n.* a common mineral, potassium chloride, KCl, colorless to milky-white or red, occurring in crystals, usually cubes, and masses with cubic cleavage, bitter in taste: the most important source of potassium. Also, **syl·vin, syl·vine** (sil′vin). [1965–70; < L (*sal digestīvus*) *Sylvi(i)* digestive salt of *Sylvius* (see SYLVIAN FISSURE) + -ITE[1]; r. *sylvine* < F]

sym-, var. of **syn-** before *b, p, m: symbol; symphony; symmetry.*

sym., 1. symbol. **2.** *Chem.* symmetrical. **3.** symphony. **4.** symptom.

Sym·bi·o·nese (sim′bē ə nēz′, -nēs′), *adj.* of, pertaining to, or characteristic of the Symbionese Liberation

Army or its adherents. [1973; according to the group's manifesto, "taken from the word symbiosis . . . a body of dissimilar bodies and organisms living in deep and loving harmony . . .; *-nese* prob. after CHINESE, JAPANESE, etc.]

Symbionese′ Libera′tion Ar′my, a group of urban guerrillas, active in the early 1970's in the U.S. Also called **Sym′bionese Ar′my.**

sym·bi·ont (sim′bē ont′, -bī-), *n. Biol.* an organism living in a state of symbiosis. Also, **sym·bi·ote** (sim′bē ōt′, -bī-). [1885–90; < Gk *symbiont-* (s. of *symbiṓn*), prp. of *symbioûn* to live together; see SYMBIOSIS, ONTO-] —**sym·bi·on·tic** (sim′bē on′tik, -bī-), *adj.*

sym·bi·o·sis (sim′bē ō′sis, -bī-), *n., pl.* **-ses** (-sēz). **1.** *Biol.* **a.** the living together of two dissimilar organisms, as in mutualism, commensalism, amensalism, or parasitism. **b.** (formerly) mutualism (def. 1). **2.** *Psychiatry.* a relationship between two people in which each person is dependent upon and receives reinforcement, whether beneficial or detrimental, from the other. **3.** *Psychoanal.* the relationship between an infant and its mother in which the infant is dependent on the mother both physically and emotionally. **4.** any interdependent or mutually beneficial relationship between two persons, groups, etc. [1615–25; < Gk *symbíōsis,* equiv. to *sym-* SYM- + *biō-* (var. s. of *bioûn* to live) + *-sis* -SIS] —**sym·bi·ot·ic** (sim′bē ot′ik, -bī-) **sym′bi·ot′i·cal,** *adj.* —**sym′bi·ot′i·cal·ly,** *adv.*

sym·bol (sim′bəl), *n., v.,* **-boled, -bol·ing** or (*esp. Brit.*) **-bolled, -bol·ling.** —*n.* **1.** something used for or regarded as representing something else; a material object representing something, often something immaterial; emblem, token, or sign. **2.** a letter, figure, or other character or mark or a combination of letters or the like used to designate something: *the algebraic symbol* x; *the chemical symbol Au.* **3.** a word, phrase, image, or the like having a complex of associated meanings and perceived as having inherent value separable from that which is symbolized, as being part of that which is symbolized, and as performing its normal function of standing for or representing that which is symbolized: usually conceived as deriving its meaning chiefly from the structure in which it appears, and generally distinguished from a sign. —*v.t.* **4.** to symbolize. [1400–50; late ME < L *symbolum* < Gk *sýmbolon* sign, equiv. to *sym-* SYM- + *-bolon,* neut. for *bolḗ* (fem.) a throw]

sym·bol·ic (sim bol′ik), *adj.* **1.** serving as a symbol of something (often fol. by *of*). **2.** of, pertaining to, or expressed by a symbol. **3.** characterized by or involving the use of symbols: *a highly symbolic poem.* **4.** (in semantics, esp. formerly) pertaining to a class of words that express only relations. Cf. **notional** (def. 7). **5.** *Computers.* expressed in characters, usually nonnumeric, that require translation before they can be used (opposed to *absolute*). Also, **sym·bol′i·cal** (for defs. 1–4). [1650–60; < LL *symbolicus* < Gk *symbolikós.* See SYMBOL, -IC] —**sym·bol′i·cal·ly,** *adv.* —**sym·bol′i·cal·ness,** *n.*

symbol′ical books′, *Eccles.* the books of a religion containing the creeds, beliefs, etc. Also, **symbol′ic books′.** [1735–45]

symbol′ic code′, *Computers.* pseudo-code.

symbol′ic interac′tionism, *Sociol.* a theory that human interaction and communication is facilitated by words, gestures, and other symbols that have acquired conventionalized meanings. [1965–70] —**symbol′ic interac′tionist.**

symbol′ic lan′guage, a specialized language dependent upon the use of symbols for communication and created for the purpose of achieving greater exactitude, as in symbolic logic or mathematics.

symbol′ic log′ic, a modern development of formal logic employing a special notation or symbolism capable of manipulation in accordance with precise rules. Also called **mathematical logic.** [1880–85]

sym·bol·ics (sim bol′iks), *n.* (*used with a singular v.*) the branch of theology dealing with the study of the history and meaning of church creeds and confessions. [see SYMBOLIC, -ICS]

sym·bol·ism (sim′bə liz′əm), *n.* **1.** the practice of representing things by symbols, or of investing things with a symbolic meaning or character. **2.** a set or system of symbols. **3.** symbolic meaning or character. **4.** the principles and practice of symbolists in art or literature. **5.** (*cap.*) a movement of the late 19th century in French art and literature. Cf. **symbolist** (defs. 3b, 4b). **6.** the use of any of certain special figures or marks of identification to signify a religious message or divine being, as the cross for Christ and the Christian faith. [1645–55; SYMBOL + -ISM]

sym·bol·ist (sim′bə list), *n.* **1.** a person who uses symbols or symbolism. **2.** a person versed in the study or interpretation of symbols. **3.** *Literature.* **a.** a writer who seeks to express or evoke emotions, ideas, etc., by stressing the symbolic value of language, to which is ascribed a capacity for communicating otherwise inexpressible visions of reality. **b.** (*usually cap.*) a member of a group of chiefly French and Belgian poets of the latter part of the 19th century who sought to evoke aesthetic emotions by emphasizing the associative character of verbal, often private, images or by using synesthetic devices, as vowel sounds, presumably evocative of color. **4.** *Fine Arts.* **a.** an artist who seeks to symbolize or suggest ideas or emotions by the objects represented, the colors used, etc. **b.** (*usually cap.*) a member of a group of late 19th-century artists who rejected realism and sought to express subjective visions rather than objective reality through the use of evocative images. **5.** (*often cap.*) *Eccles.* a person who rejects the doctrine of transubstantiation and views the Eucharist symbolically. **6.** a person who favors the use of symbols in religious services. —*adj.* **7.** of or pertaining to symbolists or symbolism. [1575–85; SYMBOL + -IST] —**sym′bol·is′tic,** *adj.* —**sym′bol·is′ti·cal·ly,** *adv.*

sym·bol·i·za·tion (sim′bə lə zā′shən), *n.* **1.** the act or process of symbolizing. **2.** *Psychoanal.* an unconscious mental process whereby one object or idea comes to stand for another through some part, quality, or aspect that the two share in common, with the symbol carrying the emotional feelings vested in the initial object or idea. [1595–1605; SYMBOLIZE + -ATION]

sym·bol·ize (sim′bə līz′), *v.,* **-ized, -iz·ing.** —*v.t.* **1.** to be a symbol of; stand for or represent in the manner of a symbol. **2.** to represent by a symbol or symbols. **3.** to regard or treat as symbolic. —*v.i.* **4.** to use symbols. Also, *esp. Brit.,* **sym′bol·ise′.** [1580–90; < NL *symbolizāre.* See SYMBOL, -IZE]

sym·bol·o·gy (sim bol′ə jē), *n.* **1.** the study of symbols. **2.** the use of symbols; symbolism. [1830–40; by haplology, *symbolo-* (comb. form of SYMBOL) + -LOGY] —**sym·bo·log·i·cal** (sim′bə loj′i kəl), *adj.* —**sym·bol′o·gist,** *n.*

Sy·ming·ton (sī′ming tən), *n.* **(William) Stuart,** born 1901, U.S. politician: senator 1952–77.

Sym·ma·chus (sim′ə kəs), *n.* **Saint,** died A.D. 514, pope 498–514.

sym·met·al·ism (sim met′l iz′əm), *n.* the use of two or more metals, such as gold and silver, combined in assigned proportions as a monetary standard. [1890–95; SYM- + *-metallism,* as in BIMETALLISM]

Sym·me·trel (sim′i trəl), *Pharm., Trademark.* a brand of amantadine.

sym·met·ri·cal (si me′tri kəl), *adj.* **1.** characterized by or exhibiting symmetry; well-proportioned, as a body or whole; regular in form or arrangement of corresponding parts. **2.** *Geom.* **a.** noting two points in a plane such that the line segment joining the points is bisected by an axis: *Points (1, 1) and (1, −1) are symmetrical with respect to the x-axis.* **b.** noting a set consisting of pairs of points having this relation with respect to the same axis. **c.** noting two points in a plane such that the line segment joining the points is bisected by a point or center: *The points (1, 1) and (−1, −1) are symmetrical with respect to (0, 0).* **d.** noting a set consisting of pairs of points having this relation with respect to the same center. **3.** Often, **symmetric.** *Math.* **a.** noting a square matrix that is equal to its transpose. **b.** noting a dyad or dyadic that is equal to its conjugate. **c.** noting a relation in which one element in relation to a second implies the second in relation to the first. **4.** *Bot.* **a.** divisible into two similar parts by more than one plane passing through the center; actinomorphic. **b.** (of a flower) having the same number of parts in each whorl. **5.** *Chem.* **a.** having a structure that exhibits a regular repeated pattern of the component parts. **b.** noting a benzene derivative in which three substitutions have occurred at alternate carbon atoms. **6.** affecting corresponding parts simultaneously, as certain diseases. Also, **sym·met′ric.** [1745–55; SYMMETR(Y) + -ICAL] —**sym·met′ri·cal·ly,** *adv.* —**sym·met′ri·cal·ness,** *n.*

—**Syn. 1.** balanced, orderly, regular, congruent.

symmet′ric dif′ference, *Math.* the union of the relative complements of two sets. Also called **Boolean sum.**

symmet′ric func′tion, *Math.* a polynomial in several indeterminates that stays the same under any permutation of the indeterminates. Also called **symmet′ric polyno′mial.** [1850–55]

symmet′ric group′, *Math.* the group of all permutations of a finite set. Cf. **alternating group.** [1905–10]

sym·me·trize (sim′i trīz′), *v.t.,* **-trized, -triz·ing.** to reduce to symmetry; make symmetrical. Also, *esp. Brit.,* **sym′me·trise′.** [1780–90; SYMMETR(Y) + -IZE] —**sym′·me·tri·za′tion,** *n.*

sym·me·try (sim′i trē), *n., pl.* **-tries.** **1.** the correspondence in size, form, and arrangement of parts on opposite sides of a plane, line, or point; regularity of form or arrangement in terms of like, reciprocal, or corresponding parts. **2.** the proper or due proportion of the parts of a body or whole to one another with regard to size and form; excellence of proportion. **3.** beauty based on or characterized by such excellence of proportion. **4.** *Math.* **a.** a geometrical or other regularity that is possessed by a mathematical object and is characterized by the operations that leave the object invariant: *A circle has rotational symmetry and reflection symmetry.* **b.** a rotation or translation of a plane figure that leaves the figure unchanged although its position may be altered. **5.** *Physics.* a property of a physical system that is unaffected by certain mathematical transformations as, for example, the work done by gravity on an object, which is not affected by any change in the position from which the potential energy of the object is measured. [1535–45; < L *symmetria* < Gk *symmetría* commensurateness. See SYM-, -METRY]

—**Syn. 1.** consonance, concord, correspondence. SYMMETRY, BALANCE, PROPORTION, HARMONY are terms used, particularly in the arts, to denote qualities based upon a correspondence or agreement, usually pleasing, among the parts of a whole. SYMMETRY implies either a quantitative equality of parts (*the perfect symmetry of pairs of matched columns*) or a unified system of subordinate parts: *the symmetry of a well-ordered musical composition.* BALANCE implies equality of parts, often as a means of emphasis: *Balance in sentences may emphasize the contrast in ideas.* PROPORTION depends less upon equality of parts than upon that agreement among them that is determined by their relation to a whole: *The dimensions of the room gave a feeling of right proportion.* HARMONY, a technical term in music, may also suggest the pleasing quality that arises from a just ordering of parts in other forms of artistic composition: *harmony of line, color, mass, phrase, ideas.* —**Ant. 1.** asymmetry.

sym′metry ax′is of ro′tary inver′sion, *Crystall.* See **rotation-inversion axis.**

sym′metry ax′is of rota′tion, *Crystall.* See **rotation axis.**

sym′metry class′, *Crystall.* See **point group.**

sym′metry el′ement, *Crystall.* any of four points, lines, or planes of a crystal: a center of symmetry, a reflection plane, a rotation axis, or a rotation-inversion axis.

sym′metry plane′, *Crystall.* See **reflection plane.** [1875–80]

Sym·onds (sim′əndz), *n.* **John Add·ing·ton** (ad′ing-tən), 1840–93, English poet, essayist, and critic.

Sy·mons (sī′mənz), *n.* **Arthur,** 1865–1945, English poet and critic, born in Wales.

sym·pa·thec·to·my (sim′pə thek′tə mē), *n., pl.* **-mies.** *Med.* **1.** surgery that interrupts a nerve pathway of the sympathetic or involuntary nervous system. **2.** Also called **chemical sympathectomy.** a like interruption by chemical means. [1895–1900; SYMPATH(ETIC) + -ECTOMY]

sym·path·e·tec·to·my (sim path′i tek′tə mē), *n., pl.* **-mies.** *Med.* sympathectomy.

sym·pa·thet·ic (sim′pə thet′ik), *adj.* **1.** characterized by, proceeding from, exhibiting, or feeling sympathy; sympathizing; compassionate: *a sympathetic listener.* **2.** acting or affected by, of the nature of, or pertaining to a special affinity or mutual relationship; congenial: *With their many similar tastes, he found her a most sympathetic companion.* **3.** looking upon with favor (often fol. by *to* or *toward*): *She is sympathetic to the project.* **4.** *Anat., Physiol.* **a.** pertaining to that part of the autonomic nervous system consisting of nerves that arise from the thoracic and lumbar regions of the spinal cord, and functioning in opposition to the parasympathetic system, as in stimulating heartbeat, dilating the pupil of the eye, etc. **b.** *Obs.* pertaining to the autonomic nervous system in its entirety. **5.** *Physics.* noting or pertaining to vibrations, sounds, etc., produced by a body as the direct result of similar vibrations in a different body. [1635–45; < NL *sympatheticus* < Gk *sympathētikós.* See SYM-, PATHETIC] —**sym′pa·thet′i·cal·ly,** *adv.*

—**Syn. 1.** commiserating, kind, tender, affectionate.

sym′pathet′ic con′tact, *Sociol.* behavior toward an individual based on the individual's personal makeup rather than on his or her group membership. Cf. **categoric contact.**

sym′pathet′ic ink′, a fluid for producing writing that is invisible until brought out by heat, chemicals, etc.; invisible ink. [1715–25]

sympathet′ic introspec′tion, *Sociol.* a study of human conduct in which the investigator imagines himself or herself engaged in that conduct.

sym′pathet′ic mag′ic, magic predicated on the belief that one thing or event can affect another at a distance as a consequence of a sympathetic connection between them. Cf. **contagious magic, imitative magic.** [1900–05]

sympathet′ic ophthal′mia, *Ophthalm.* inflammation of one eye due to injury or disease of the other eye. [1870–75]

sym′pathet′ic strike′. See **sympathy strike.** [1890–95]

sym′pathet′ic string′, a thin wire string, as in various obsolete musical instruments, designed to vibrate sympathetically with the bowed or plucked strings to reinforce the sound.

sympathet′ic vibra′tion, *Physics.* a vibration induced by resonance. [1895–1900]

sym·pa·thize (sim′pə thīz′), *v.i.,* **-thized, -thiz·ing.** **1.** to be in sympathy or agreement of feeling; share in a feeling (often fol. by *with*). **2.** to feel a compassionate sympathy, as for suffering or trouble (often fol. by *with*). **3.** to express sympathy or condole (often fol. by *with*). **4.** to be in approving accord, as with a person or cause: *to sympathize with a person's aims.* **5.** to agree, correspond, or accord. Also, *esp. Brit.,* **sym′pa·thise′.** [1580–90; < MF *sympathiser,* equiv. to *sympath(ie)* SYMPATHY + *-iser* -IZE] —**sym′pa·thiz′ing·ly,** *adv.*

—**Syn. 4.** understand, approve, favor, back, support.

sym·pa·thiz·er (sim′pə thī′zər), *n.* **1.** a person who sympathizes. **2.** *Ophthalm.* an eye that exhibits ophthalmia because of disease or injury of the other. [1805–15; SYMPATHIZE + -ER[1]]

sym·pa·tho·lyt·ic (sim′pə thō lit′ik), *adj. Physiol., Pharm.* opposing the effects of stimulation of the sympathetic nervous system. Cf. **cholinolytic.** [1940–45; SYMPATH(ETIC) + -O- + -LYTIC]

sym·pa·tho·mi·met·ic (sim′pə thō mi met′ik, -mī-), *Physiol., Pharm.* —*adj.* **1.** mimicking stimulation of the sympathetic nervous system. —*n.* **2.** an agent that mimics the stimulation of the sympathetic nervous system. [1905–10; SYMPATH(ETIC) + -O- + -MIMETIC]

sym·pa·thy (sim′pə thē), *n., pl.* **-thies,** *adj.* —*n.* **1.** harmony of or agreement in feeling, as between persons or on the part of one person with respect to another. **2.** the harmony of feeling naturally existing between persons of like tastes or opinion or of congenial dispositions. **3.** the fact or power of sharing the feelings of another, esp. in sorrow or trouble; fellow feeling, compassion, or commiseration. **4.** **sympathies, a.** feelings or impulses of compassion. **b.** feelings of favor, support, or loyalty: *It's hard to tell where your sympathies lie.* **5.** favorable or approving accord; favor or approval: *He viewed the plan with sympathy and publicly backed it.* **6.** agreement, consonance, or accord. **7.** *Psychol.* a relationship between persons in which the condition of one induces a parallel or reciprocal condition in another. **8.** *Physiol.* the relation between parts or organs whereby a condition or disorder of one part induces some effect in another. —*adj.* **9.** expressing sympathy: *a sympathy card; a sympathy vote.* [1560–70; < L *sympathia* < Gk *sympátheia,* equiv. to *sympathēs* sympathetic (*sym-* SYM- + *páth(os)* suffering, sensation + *-ēs* adj. suffix) + *-ia* -Y[3]]

—**Syn. 1.** concord, understanding, rapport, affinity. SYMPATHY, COMPASSION, PITY, EMPATHY all denote the tendency, practice, or capacity to share in the feelings of

CONCISE ETYMOLOGY KEY: <, descended or borrowed from; >, whence; b., blend of, blended; c., cognate with; cf., compare; deriv., derivative; equiv., equivalent; imit., imitative; obl., oblique; r., replacing; s., stem; sp., spelling, spelled; resp., respelling, respelled; trans., translation; ?, origin unknown; *, unattested; ‡, probably earlier than. See the full key inside the front cover.

others, especially their distress, sorrow, or unfulfilled desires. SYMPATHY is the broadest of these terms, signifying a general kinship with another's feelings, no matter of what kind: *in sympathy with her yearning for peace and freedom; to extend sympathy to the bereaved.* COMPASSION implies a deep sympathy for the sorrows or troubles of another coupled to a powerful urge to alleviate the pain or distress or to remove its source: *to show compassion for homeless refugees.* PITY usually suggests a kindly, but sometimes condescending, sorrow aroused by the suffering or ill fortune of others, often leading to a show of mercy: *tears of pity for war casualties; to have pity on a thief driven by hunger.* EMPATHY most often refers to a vicarious participation in the emotions, ideas, or opinions of others, the ability to imagine oneself in the condition or predicament of another: *empathy with those striving to improve their lives; to feel empathy with Hamlet as one watches the play.*

sym′pathy strike′, a strike by a body of workers, not because of grievances against their own employer, but by way of endorsing and aiding another group of workers who are on strike or have been locked out. Also called **sympathetic strike.** [1900–05]

sym·pat·ric (sim pa′trik, -pā′-), *adj. Biol., Ecol.* originating in or occupying the same geographical area. [1900–05; SYM- + Gk *pátr(ā)* fatherland (*patr-*, s. of *patḗr* FATHER + *-ā* fem. n. suffix) + -IC]

sym·pet·al·ous (sim pet′l əs), *adj. Bot.* gamopetalous. [1875–80; SYM- + PETALOUS]

sym·pho·nette (sim′fə net′), *n.* a small symphony orchestra that usually specializes in playing short, familiar classical works or salon music. [SYMPHON(Y) + -ETTE]

sym·pho·ni·a (sim fō′nē ə), *n.* any of various medieval musical instruments, as the hurdy-gurdy. [1570–80; < LL, L *symphōnia* SYMPHONY]

sym·phon·ic (sim fon′ik), *adj.* **1.** *Music.* of, for, pertaining to, or having the character of a symphony or symphony orchestra. **2.** of or pertaining to symphony or harmony of sounds. **3.** characterized by similarity of sound, as words. [1855–60; SYMPHON(Y) + -IC] —**sym·phon′i·cal·ly,** *adv.*

symphon′ic po′em, *Music.* a form of tone poem, scored for a symphony orchestra, in which a literary or pictorial "plot" is treated with considerable program detail: originated by Franz Liszt in the mid-19th century and developed esp. by Richard Strauss. [1860–65]

Sym·pho·nie Fan·tas·tique (*Fr.* saN fô nē fän tas-tēk′), a programmatic symphony (1830–31) in five movements by Hector Berlioz.

sym·pho·ni·ous (sim fō′nē əs), *adj.* harmonious; in harmonious agreement or accord. [1645–55; SYMPHONY + -OUS] —**sym·pho′ni·ous·ly,** *adv.*

sym·pho·nist (sim′fə nist), *n.* a composer who writes symphonies. [1650–60; SYMPHON(Y) + -IST]

sym·pho·nize (sim′fə nīz′), *v.i.,* **-nized, -niz·ing.** to play or sound together harmoniously. Also, *esp. Brit.,* **sym′pho·nise′.** [1485–95; SYMPHON(Y) + -IZE] —**sym′·pho·ni·za′tion,** *n.*

sym·pho·ny (sim′fə nē), *n., pl.* **-nies. 1.** *Music.* **a.** an elaborate instrumental composition in three or more movements, similar in form to a sonata but written for an orchestra and usually of far grander proportions and more varied elements. **b.** an instrumental passage occurring in a vocal composition, or between vocal movements in a composition. **c.** an instrumental piece, often in several movements, forming the overture to an opera or the like. **2.** See **symphony orchestra. 3.** a concert performed by a symphony orchestra. **4.** anything characterized by a harmonious combination of elements, esp. an effective combination of colors. **5.** harmony of sounds. **6.** *Archaic.* agreement; concord. [1250–1300; ME *symfonye* < OF *symphonie* < L *symphōnia* concert < Gk *symphōnía* harmony. See SYM-, -PHONY]

sym′phony or′chestra, a large orchestra composed of wind, string, and percussion instruments and organized to perform symphonic compositions. [1880–85]

sym·phys·i·al (sim fiz′ē əl), *adj.* of, pertaining to, or noting a symphysis. Also, **sym·phys′e·al.** [1825–35; SYMPHYSI(S) + -AL[1]]

sym·phy·sis (sim′fə sis), *n., pl.* **-ses** (-sēz′). *Anat., Zool.* **1.** the growing together, or the fixed or nearly fixed union, of bones, as that of the two halves of the lower jaw in humans or of the pubic bones in the anterior part of the pelvic girdle. **2.** a line of junction or articulation so formed. [1570–80; < NL < Gk *sýmphysis* a growing together, equiv. to *sym-* SYM- + *phýsis,* equiv. to *phy-,* s. of *phýein* to grow (see BE) + *-sis* -SIS] —**sym·phys·tic** (sim fis′tik), *adj.*

Sym·pleg·a·des (sim pleg′ə dēz′), *n.pl. Class. Myth.* a pair of rocky islands, at the entrance to the Black Sea, that often clashed together: Athena helped the Argonauts navigate them, after which they became fixed.

sym·plo·ce (sim′plō sē), *n. Rhet.* the simultaneous use of anaphora and epistrophe. [1570–80; < NL *symplocē* < Gk *symplokḗ* intertwining, combination, equiv. to *sym-* SYM- + *plokḗ,* n. deriv. of *plékein* to plait, twine; akin to L *plectere* (see -PLEX)]

sym·po·di·um (sim pō′dē əm), *n., pl.* **-di·a** (-dē ə). *Bot.* an axis or stem that simulates a simple stem but is made up of the bases of a number of axes that arise successively as branches, one from another, as in the grapevine. Cf. **monopodium.** [1860–65; < NL < Gk *sym-* SYM- + *pódion* small foot, base; see PODIUM] —**sym·po′di·al,** *adj.* —**sym·po′di·al·ly,** *adv.*

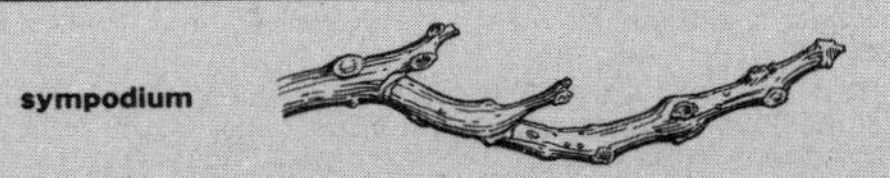
sympodium

sym·po·si·ac (sim pō′zē ak′), *adj.* **1.** of, pertaining to, or suitable for a symposium. —*n.* **2.** a symposium. [1575–85; < L *symposiacus* < Gk *symposiakós.* See SYMPOSIUM, -AC]

sym·po·si·arch (sim pō′zē ärk′), *n.* **1.** the president, director, or master of a symposium. **2.** a toastmaster. [1595–1605; < Gk *symposíarchos.* See SYMPOSIUM, -ARCH]

sym·po·si·ast (sim pō′zē ast′, -əst), *n.* a person who attends or participates in a symposium. [1650–60; orig. < assumed Gk **symposiastḗs,* deriv. of *symposiázein* to drink together (with agentive suffix *-tēs*), v. deriv. of *sympósion* drinking party (see SYMPOSIUM); in recent use prob. recoinage: SYMPOSI(UM) + -AST]

sym·po·si·um (sim pō′zē əm), *n., pl.* **-si·ums, -si·a** (-zē ə). **1.** a meeting or conference for the discussion of some subject, esp. a meeting at which several speakers talk on or discuss a topic before an audience. **2.** a collection of opinions expressed or articles contributed by several persons on a given subject or topic. **3.** an account of a discussion meeting or of the conversation at it. **4.** (in ancient Greece and Rome) a convivial meeting, usually following a dinner, for drinking and intellectual conversation. **5.** (*cap., italics*) a philosophical dialogue (4th century B.C.) by Plato, dealing with ideal love and the vision of absolute beauty. [1580–90; < L < Gk *sympósion* drinking party, equiv. to *sym-* SYM- + *po-* (var. s. of *pínein* to drink) + *-sion* n. suffix]

symp·tom (simp′təm), *n.* **1.** any phenomenon or circumstance accompanying something and serving as evidence of it. **2.** a sign or indication of something. **3.** *Pathol.* a phenomenon that arises from and accompanies a particular disease or disorder and serves as an indication of it. [1350–1400; ME < LL *symptōma* < Gk *sýmptōma* occurrence, that which falls together with something, equiv. to *sym-* SYM- + *ptō-* (var. s. of *píptein* to fall) + *-ma* n. suffix of result]
—**Syn. 2.** signal, token, mark.

symp·to·mat·ic (simp′tə mat′ik), *adj.* **1.** pertaining to a symptom or symptoms. **2.** of the nature of or constituting a symptom; indicative (often fol by *of*): *a condition symptomatic of cholera; a disagreement that was symptomatic of the deterioration in their relationship.* **3.** according to symptoms: *a symptomatic classification of disease.* Also, **symp′to·mat′i·cal.** [1690–1700; < ML *symptōmaticus,* equiv. to LL *symptōmat-* (s. of *symptōma*) SYMPTOM + *-icus* -IC] —**symp′to·mat′i·cal·ly,** *adv.*

symp′tomat′ic an′thrax, *Vet. Pathol.* blackleg.

symp·tom·a·tol·o·gy (simp′tə mə tol′ə jē), *n.* **1.** the branch of medical science dealing with symptoms. **2.** the collective symptoms of a patient or disease. Cf. **syndrome.** [1790–1800; < NL *symptōmatologia,* equiv. to LL *symptōmat-* (s. of *symptōma*) SYMPTOM + *-o-* -O- + *-logia* -LOGY]

symp·tom·less (simp′təm lis), *adj.* having or showing no symptoms. [1885–90; SYMPTOM + -LESS]

symp·to·sis (simp tō′sis), *n. Pathol.* **1.** local or general atrophy. **2.** wasting away; emaciation. [< Gk *sýmptōsis* a falling together, collapse, equiv. to *symptō-* (see SYMPTOM) + *-sis* -SIS]

syn-, a prefix occurring in loanwords from Greek, having the same function as **co-** (*synthesis; synoptic*); used, with the meaning "with," "together," in the formation of compound words (*synsepalous*) or "synthetic" in such compounds (*syngas*). Also, **sy-, syl-, sym-, sys-.** [< Gk, comb. form repr. *sýn* with, together with]

syn., 1. synonym. **2.** synonymous. **3.** synonymy.

syn·aer·e·sis (si ner′ə sis), *n. Phonet.* **1.** the contraction of two syllables or two vowels into one, esp. the contraction of two vowels so as to form a diphthong. **2.** synizesis. Also, **syneresis.** [1570–80; < LL < Gk *synaíresis* act of taking together, equiv. to *syn-* SYN- + *(h)aire-* (s. of *haireîn* to take) + *-sis* -SIS]

syn·aes·the·sia (sin′is thē′zhə, -zhē ə, -zē ə), *n.* synesthesia. —**syn·aes·thet·ic** (sin′is thet′ik), *adj.*

syn·a·gogue (sin′ə gog′, -gôg′), *n.* **1.** a Jewish house of worship, often having facilities for religious instruction. **2.** an assembly or congregation of Jews for the purpose of religious worship. **3.** the Jewish religion; Judaism. Also, **syn′a·gog′.** [1125–75; ME *synagoge* < LL *synagōga* < Gk *synagōgḗ* assembly, meeting, equiv. to *syn-* SYN- + *agōgḗ,* n. use of fem. of *agōgós* (adj.) gathering, deriv. of *ágein* to bring, lead; akin to L *agere* to drive] —**syn·a·gog·i·cal** (sin′ə goj′i kəl), **syn·a·gog·al** (sin′ə gog′əl, -gô′gəl), *adj.*

syn·al·gia (sin al′jə, -jē ə), *n.* See **referred pain.** [1885–90; SYN- + -ALGIA] —**syn·al′gic,** *adj.*

syn·a·loe·pha (sin′l ē′fə), *n.* the blending of two successive vowels into one, esp. the coalescence of a vowel at the end of one word with a vowel at the beginning of the next. Also, **syn′a·le′pha, syn·a·le·phe** (sin′l ē′fē). [1530–40; < NL < Gk *synaloiphḗ, synaliphḗ,* equiv. to *syn-* SYN- + *aloiph-, aliph-* (var. stems of *aleíphein* to smear) + *-ē* fem. n. suffix]

syn·apse (sin′aps, si naps′), *n., v.,* **-apsed, -aps·ing.** *Physiol.* —*n.* **1.** a region where nerve impulses are transmitted and received, encompassing the axon terminal of a neuron that releases neurotransmitters in response to an impulse, an extremely small gap across which the neurotransmitters travel, and the adjacent membrane of an axon, dendrite, or muscle or gland cell with the appropriate receptor molecules for picking up the neurotransmitters. —*v.i.* **2.** *Cell Biol.; Physiol.* to form a synapse or a synapsis. [1895–1900; back formation from *synapses,* pl. of SYNAPSIS]

syn·ap·sis (si nap′sis), *n., pl.* **-ses** (-sēz). **1.** Also called **syndesis.** *Cell Biol.* the pairing of homologous chromosomes, one from each parent, during early meiosis. **2.** *Physiol.* synapse. [1645–55; < NL < Gk *sýnapsis* junction, equiv. to *synap-* (s. of *synáptein* to make contact, equiv. to *syn-* SYN- + *(h)áptein* to touch) + *-sis* -SIS] —**syn·ap·tic** (si nap′tik), **syn·ap′ti·cal,** *adj.* —**syn·ap′ti·cal·ly,** *adv.*

sy·nap·te (sē′näp tē′, sin′ap tē), *n. Eastern Ch.* a litany. [< MGk *synaptḗ,* n. use of fem. of Gk *synaptós* (adj.) joined together; see SYNAPSIS]

synap′tic cleft′, *Physiol.* the small gap, measured in nanometers, between an axon terminal and any of the cell membranes in the immediate vicinity. [1975–80]

syn·ar·thro·di·a (sin′är thrō′dē ə), *n., pl.* **-di·ae** (-dē-ē′). synarthrosis. [< NL; see SYN-, ARTHRODIA] —**syn′·ar·thro′di·al,** *adj.* —**syn′ar·thro′di·al·ly,** *adv.*

syn·ar·thro·sis (sin′är thrō′sis), *n., pl.* **-ses** (-sēz). *Anat.* immovable articulation; a fixed or immovable joint; suture. [1570–80; < NL < Gk *synárthrōsis,* equiv. to *synarthrō-* (var. s. of *synarthroûsthai* to be joined by articulation, equiv. to *syn-* SYN- + *árthro(n)* joint + *-esthai* inf. suffix) + *-sis* -SIS]

syn·as·try (si nas′trē, sin′ə strē), *n. Astrol.* the comparison of two or more natal charts in order to analyze or forecast the interaction of the individuals involved. [1650–60; < LL *synastria* favorable conjunction of the stars < LGk, equiv. to Gk *syn-* SYN- + *ástr(on)* star + *-ía* -Y[3]]

sy·na·xa·ri·on (sē′nä ksä′rē ôn; *Eng.* sin′ak sâr′ē-on′), *n., pl.* **sy·na·xa·ri·a** (sē′nä ksä′rē ä; *Eng.* sin′ak-sâr′ē ə). *Gk. Orth. Ch.* **1.** a summary of the life of a saint or of the particulars of a feast, read at the orthros. **2.** a book containing such summaries. [1840–50; < MGk *synaxárion,* equiv. to *sýnax(is)* SYNAXIS + *-arion* -ARY]

syn·ax·a·ri·um (sin′ak sâr′ē əm), *n., pl.* **-ax·a·ri·a** (-ak sâr′ē ə). synaxarion. [1910–15; < NL < MGk *synaxárion* SYNAXARION]

syn·ax·a·ry (si nak′sə rē), *n., pl.* **-ries.** synaxarion.

syn·ax·is (si nak′sis), *n., pl.* **syn·ax·es** (si nak′sēz). an assembly for religious worship, esp. for the celebration of the Eucharist. [1615–25; < LL < MGk *sýnaxis,* equiv. to *synág(ein)* to meet together (see SYNAGOGUE) + *-sis* -SIS]

sync (singk), *Informal.* —*n.* (used esp. in the phrases *in sync* and *out of sync*) **1.** Also, **synch** (singk). synchronization: *The picture and the soundtrack were out of sync.* **2.** harmony or harmonious relationship: *Management wants to be in sync with the client's wishes.* —*v.i., v.t.* **3.** to synchronize; harmonize. [1930–35; shortened form]

syn·carp (sin′kärp), *n. Bot.* **1.** an aggregate fruit. **2.** a collective fruit. [1820–30; < NL *syncarpium,* equiv. to *syncarp(us)* SYNCARPOUS + *-ium* -IUM]

syn·car·pous (sin kär′pəs), *adj. Bot.* **1.** of the nature of or pertaining to a syncarp. **2.** composed of or having united carpels. [1820–30; < NL *syncarpus.* See SYN-, -CARPOUS] —**syn·car·py** (sin′kär pē), *n.*

syn·cat·e·gor·e·mat·ic (sin kat′i gôr′ə mat′ik, -gor′-), *adj.* **1.** *Traditional Logic.* of or pertaining to a word that is part of a categorical proposition but is not a term, as *all, some, is.* **2.** *Contemporary Logic.* of or pertaining to a word or symbol that has no independent meaning and acquires meaning only in the context of other words or symbols, as the symbol (or the word *of.* Cf. **term** (def. 9). [1820–30; < LL *syncatēgorēmat-,* s. of *syncatēgorēma* part of a discourse that needs another word to become fully intelligible (see SYN-, CATEGOREMATIC) + -IC]

sync-gen·er·a·tor (singk′jen′ə rā′tər), *n. Television.* an electronic generator that supplies synchronizing pulses to television scanning and transmitting equipment. [SYNC + GENERATOR]

synchro-, a combining form representing **synchronized** or **synchronous** in compound words: *synchroscope; synchrotron.*

syn·chro·cy·clo·tron (sing′krō sī′klə tron′, -sik′lə-), *n. Physics.* a type of cyclotron that synchronizes its accelerating voltage with particle velocity in order to compensate for the relativistic mass increase of the particle as it approaches the speed of light. Also called **FM cyclotron.** Cf. **synchrotron.** [1945–50; SYNCHRO- + CYCLOTRON]

syn·chro·flash (sing′krə flash′), *adj.* of or pertaining to photography employing a device that synchronizes the photoflash with the shutter. [1935–40; SYNCHRO- + FLASH]

syn·chro·mesh (sing′krə mesh′), *Auto.* —*adj.* **1.** noting or pertaining to a synchronized shifting mechanism. —*n.* **2.** a synchronized shifting mechanism. **3.** any of the gears of such a mechanism. [1925–30; SYNCHRO- + MESH]

syn·chro·mism (sing′krə miz′əm), *n.* (*sometimes cap.*) a movement of the early 20th century led by American artists and manifested in their experimentation with nonfigurative or entirely abstract paintings containing shapes and volumes of pure color. Cf. **Orphism** (def. 2). [1910–15; SYN- + CHROM- + -ISM] —**syn′chro·mist,** *n., adj.*

syn·chro·nal (sing′krə nl), *adj.* synchronous. [1650–60; < NL *synchron(us)* SYNCHRONOUS + -AL[1]]

syn·chro·ne·i·ty (sing′krə nē′i tē, -nā′-), *n.* the state of being synchronous; synchronism. [1905–10; SYNCHRON(OUS) + *-eity,* as in SIMULTANEITY, SPONTANEITY]

syn·chron·ic (sin kron′ik, sing-), *adj. Ling.* having reference to the facts of a linguistic system as it exists at one point in time without reference to its history: *synchronic analysis; synchronic dialectology.* Also, **syn·chron′i·cal.** Cf. **diachronic.** [1825–35; < LL *synchron(us)* SYNCHRONOUS + -IC] —**syn·chron′i·cal·ly,** *adv.*

synchron′ic linguis′tics. See **descriptive linguistics.**

syn·chro·nism (sing′krə niz′əm), *n.* **1.** coincidence in

CONCISE PRONUNCIATION KEY: act, cāpe, dâre, pärt; set, ēqual; *if,* īce; ox, ōver, ôrder, oil, bo͝ok, bo͞ot, out; up, ûrge; child; sing; shoe; thin, *th*at; zh as in *treasure.* ə = *a* as in *alone, e* as in *system, i* as in *easily, o* as in *gallop, u* as in *circus;* ə as in *fire* (fīər), *hour* (ouər). l and n can serve as syllabic consonants, as in *cradle* (krād′l), and *button* (but′n). See the full key inside the front cover.

time; contemporaneousness; simultaneousness. **2.** the arrangement or treatment of synchronous things or events in conjunction, as in a history. **3.** a tabular arrangement of historical events or personages, grouped according to their dates. **4.** *Physics, Elect.* the state of being synchronous. **5.** *Psychoanal.* the simultaneous occurrence of causally unrelated events and the belief that the simultaneity has meaning beyond mere coincidence. [1580–90; < ML *synchronismus* < Gk *synchronismós,* equiv. to *sýnchron(os)* SYNCHRONOUS + *-ismos* -ISM] —**syn′chro·nis′tic, syn′chro·nis′ti·cal,** *adj.* —**syn′·chro·nis′ti·cal·ly,** *adv.*

syn·chro·nize (sing′krə nīz′), *v.,* **-nized, -niz·ing.** —*v.t.* **1.** to cause to indicate the same time, as one timepiece with another: *Synchronize your watches.* **2.** to cause to go on, move, operate, work, etc., at the same rate and exactly together: *They synchronized their steps and walked on together.* **3.** *Motion Pictures, Television.* **a.** to cause (sound and action) to match precisely: *to synchronize the sound of footsteps with the actor's movements.* **b.** to match the sound and action in (a scene). **4.** to cause to agree in time of occurrence; assign to the same time or period, as in a history. **5.** to adjust the periodicities of (two or more electrical or mechanical devices) so that the periods are equal or integral multiples or fractions of each other. —*v.i.* **6.** to occur at the same time or coincide or agree in time. **7.** to go on, move, operate, work, etc., at the same rate and exactly together; recur together. Also, *esp. Brit.,* **syn′chro·nise′.** [1615–25; < Gk *synchronízein* to be contemporary with, equiv. to *sýnchron(os)* SYNCHRONOUS + *-izein* -IZE] —**syn′·chro·ni·za′tion,** *n.* —**syn′chro·niz′er,** *n.*

syn′chronized shift′ing, *Auto.* gear shifting in which the gears to be meshed are made to rotate at the same speed.

syn′chronized swim′ming, 1. a sport growing out of water ballet in which swimmers, in solo, duet, and team efforts, complete various required figures by performing motions in relatively stationary positions, along with a freestyle competition, with the contestants synchronizing movements to music and being judged for body position, control, and the degree of difficulty of the moves. **2.** a swimming exercise or exhibition derived from the competitive sport. [1945–50]

syn·chron·o·scope (sin kron′ə skōp′, sing-), *n.* synchroscope. [< NL *synchron(us)* SYNCHRONOUS + -O- + -SCOPE]

syn·chro·nous (sing′krə nəs), *adj.* **1.** occurring at the same time; coinciding in time; contemporaneous; simultaneous. **2.** going on at the same rate and exactly together; recurring together. **3.** *Physics, Elect.* having the same frequency and zero phase difference. **4.** *Computers, Telecommunications.* of, pertaining to, or operating using fixed-time intervals controlled by a clock (opposed to *asynchronous*). **5.** *Aerospace.* geostationary. [1660–70; < LL *synchronus* < Gk *sýnchronos,* equiv. to *syn-* SYN- + *chrón(os)* time + *-os* adj. suffix; see -OUS] —**syn′chro·nous·ly,** *adv.* —**syn′chro·nous·ness,** *n.*

syn′chronous convert′er, *Elect.* a synchronous machine for converting alternating current to direct current, or vice versa, in which the armature winding is connected to collector rings and to a commutator. Also called **rotary, rotary converter.**

syn′chronous machine′, *Elect.* an alternating-current machine in which the average speed of normal operation is exactly proportional to the frequency of the system to which it is connected.

Syn′chronous Meteorolog′ical Sat′ellite, former name of **Geostationary Operational Environmental Satellite.** *Abbr.:* SMS

syn′chronous mo′tor, *Elect.* a synchronous machine that acts as a motor. [1900–05]

syn′chronous rota′tion, *Astron.* rotation of a satellite in which the period of rotation is equal to the period of orbit around its primary, leaving the same face always pointing toward the primary: *The moon is in synchronous rotation about the earth.* [1970–75]

syn′chronous speed′, *Elect.* the speed at which an alternating-current machine must operate to generate electromotive force at a given frequency.

syn·chro·ny (sing′krə nē), *n., pl.* **-nies. 1.** simultaneous occurrence; synchronism. **2.** *Ling.* a synchronic approach to language study. [1840–50; SYNCHRON(OUS) + -Y[3]]

syn·chro·scope (sing′krə skōp′), *n.* an instrument for determining the difference in phase between two related motions, as those of two aircraft engines or two electric generators. Also, **synchronoscope.** [SYNCHRO- + -SCOPE]

syn·chro·tron (sing′krə tron′), *n. Physics.* a type of cyclotron consisting of magnetic sections alternately spaced with sections in which particles are electrostatically accelerated. [1945–50; SYNCHRO- + -TRON]

syn′chrotron radia′tion, electromagnetic radiation emitted by charged particles as they pass through magnetic fields. [1960–65]

syn′chro u′nit (sing′krō), *Elect.* a type of alternating-current motor designed to maintain continuously, at some remote location, the same rotational angle that may be imposed by force upon the electrically connected rotating element of a similar motor. [*synchro,* shortened form of SYNCHRONOUS]

syn·clas·tic (sin klas′tik, sing-), *adj. Math.* (of a surface) having principal curvatures of similar sign at a given point. Cf. **anticlastic.** [1865–70; SYN- + Gk *klastós* broken + -IC]

CONCISE ETYMOLOGY KEY: <, descended or borrowed from; >, whence; b., blend of, blended; c., cognate with; cf., compare; deriv., derivative; equiv., equivalent; imit., imitative; obl., oblique; r., replacing; s., stem; sp., spelling, spelled; resp., respelling, respelled; trans., translation; ?, origin unknown; *, unattested; ‡, probably earlier than. See the full key inside the front cover.

syn·cli·nal (sin klīn′l, sing-, sing′kli nl), *adj.* **1.** sloping downward from opposite directions so as to meet in a common point or line. **2.** *Geol.* **a.** inclining upward on both sides from a median line or axis, as a downward fold of rock strata. **b.** pertaining to such a fold. [1825–35; SYN- + Gk *klīn(ein)* to LEAN[1] + -AL[1]] —**syn·cli′nal·ly,** *adv.*

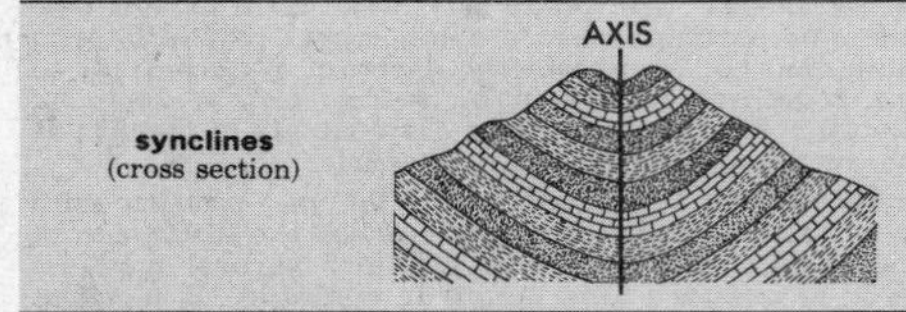

synclines (cross section)

syn·cline (sing′klīn, sin′-), *n. Geol.* a synclinal fold. [1870–75; back formation from SYNCLINAL]

syn·cli·no·ri·um (sing′klə nôr′ē əm, -nōr′-), *n., pl.* **-no·ri·a** (-nôr′ē ə, -nōr′ē ə), **-no·ri·ums.** *Geol.* a regional structure of general synclinal form that includes a series of smaller folds. Cf. **anticlinorium.** [1875–80; < NL; see SYNCLINE, -ORY[2]] —**syn′cli·no′ri·al, syn′cli·no′ri·an,** *adj.*

Syn·com (sin′kom), *n. U.S. Aerospace.* one of a series of experimental communications satellites that were the first to be placed in geostationary orbit. [*syn(chronous) com(munications satellite)*]

syn·co·pate (sing′kə pāt′, sin′-), *v.t.,* **-pat·ed, -pat·ing. 1.** *Music.* **a.** to place (the accents) on beats that are normally unaccented. **b.** to treat (a passage, piece, etc.) in this way. **2.** *Gram.* to contract (a word) by omitting one or more sounds from the middle, as in reducing *Gloucester* to *Gloster.* [1595–1605; < ML *syncopātus* (ptp. of *syncopāre* to shorten by syncope). See SYNCOPE, -ATE[1]] —**syn′co·pa′tor,** *n.*

syn·co·pat·ed (sing′kə pā′tid, sin′-), *adj.* **1.** marked by syncopation: *syncopated rhythm.* **2.** cut short; abbreviated. [1655–65; < LL *syncopāt(us)* (see SYNCOPATE) + -ED[2]]

syn·co·pa·tion (sing′kə pā′shən, sin′-), *n.* **1.** *Music.* a shifting of the normal accent, usually by stressing the normally unaccented beats. **2.** something, as a rhythm or a passage of music, that is syncopated. **3.** Also called **counterpoint, counterpoint rhythm.** *Pros.* the use of rhetorical stress at variance with the metrical stress of a line of verse, as the stress on *and* and *of* in *Come praise Colonus' horses and come praise/The wine-dark of the wood's intricacies.* **4.** *Gram.* syncope. [1525–35; < ML *syncopātiōn-* (s. of *syncopātiō*), equiv. to LL *syncopāt(us)* (see SYNCOPATE) + *-iōn-* -ION]

syncopation (def. 1)

syn·co·pe (sing′kə pē′, sin′-), *n.* **1.** *Gram.* the contraction of a word by omitting one or more sounds from the middle, as in the reduction of *never* to *ne'er.* **2.** *Pathol.* brief loss of consciousness associated with transient cerebral anemia, as in heart block, sudden lowering of the blood pressure, etc.; fainting. [1350–1400; ME < LL *syncopē* < Gk *synkopḗ* a cutting short, equiv. to *syn-* SYN- + *kop-* (s. of *kóptein* to cut) + *-ē* fem. n. suffix] —**syn·cop·ic** (sin kop′ik), **syn′co·pal,** *adj.*

syn·cre·tism (sing′kri tiz′əm, sin′-), *n.* **1.** the attempted reconciliation or union of different or opposing principles, practices, or parties, as in philosophy or religion. **2.** *Gram.* the merging, as by historical change in a language, of two or more categories in a specified environment into one, as, in nonstandard English, the use of *was* with both singular and plural subjects, while in standard English *was* is used with singular subjects (except for *you* in the second person singular) and *were* with plural subjects. [1610–20; < NL *syncretismus* < Gk *synkrētismós* union of Cretans, i.e., a united front of two opposing parties against a common foe, deriv. of *synkrēt(ízein)* to SYNCRETIZE + *-ismos* -ISM] —**syn·cret·ic** (sin kret′ik), **syn·cret′i·cal, syn·cre·tis·tic** (sing′kri tis′tik, sin′-), *adj.* —**syn′cre·tist,** *n.*

syn·cre·tize (sing′kri tīz′, sin′-), *v.t., v.i.,* **-tized, -tiz·ing.** to attempt to combine or unite, as different or opposing principles, parties, etc. Also, *esp. Brit.,* **syn′cre·tise′.** [1665–75; < NL *syncrētizāre* < Gk *synkrētízein* to form a confederation, equiv. to *syn-* SYN- + *Krēt-* (s. of *Krḗs*) a Cretan + *-izein* -IZE; see SYNCRETISM]

syn·cri·sis (sing′krə sis, sin′-), *n. Rhet. Obs.* the comparison of opposites. [1650–60; < LL < Gk *sýnkrisis* combination, comparison, equiv. to *syn-* SYN- + *kri-* (s. of *krínein* to separate) + *-sis* -SIS]

syn·cy·tium (sin sish′əm, -ē əm), *n., pl.* **-cy·tia** (-sish′ə, -ē ə). *Biol.* a multinucleate mass of cytoplasm that is not separated into cells. [1875–80; < NL; see SYN-, CYTO-, -IUM] —**syn·cy·tial** (sin sish′əl), *adj.*

synd., 1. syndicate. **2.** syndicated.

syn·dac·tyl (sin dak′til), *adj.* **1.** having certain digits joined together. —*n.* **2.** a syndactyl animal. [1830–40; var. of SYNDACTYLUS] —**syn·dac·tyl·ism** (sin dak′tə liz′əm), **syn·dac·tyl·y** (sin dak′tə lē), *n.*

syn·dac·ty·lus (sin dak′tə ləs), *n., pl.* **-li** (-lī′, -lē′). *Med.* a person having united or webbed fingers or toes. [< NL, n. use of the adj.: having webbed digits; see SYN-, -DACTYLOUS]

syn·de·re·sis (sin′də rē′sis), *n.* **1.** innate knowledge of the basic principles of morality. **2.** *Christian Mysticism.* the essence of the soul that unites with God. Also, **synteresis.** [1350–1400; ME < ML *synderēsis, syntērēsis* < Gk *syntḗrēsis* a guarding, equiv. to *syntērē-,* var. s. of *syntēreîn* to guard closely (*syn-* SYN- + *tēreîn* to guard) + *-sis* -SIS]

syn·de·sis (sin′də sis, sin dē′-), *n., pl.* **-ses** (-sēz′, -sēz). *Cell Biol.* synapsis (def. 1). [< NL < Gk *sýndesis* equiv. to *syn-* SYN- + *désis* a binding together, equiv. to *de-* (s. of *deîn* to bind) + *-sis* -SIS]

syn·des·mec·to·my (sin′dez mek′tə mē, -des-), *n., pl.* **-mies.** *Surg.* excision of part of a ligament. [< Gk *sýndesm(os)* bond, fastening (*syn-* SYN- + *des-,* var. s. of *deîn* to bind (see SYNDESIS) + *-mos* n. suffix) + -ECTOMY]

syn·des·mo·sis (sin′dez mō′sis, -des-), *n., pl.* **-ses** (-sēz). *Anat.* a connection of bones by ligaments, fasciae, or membranes other than in a joint. [1720–30; < Gk *sýndesm(os)* bond (see SYNDESMECTOMY) + -OSIS] —**syn·des·mot·ic** (sin′dez mot′ik, -des-), *adj.*

syn·det·ic (sin det′ik), *adj.* **1.** serving to unite or connect; connective; copulative. **2.** *Gram.* **a.** conjunctive (def. 3c). **b.** connected by a conjunction. Also, **syn·det′i·cal.** [1615–25; < Gk *syndetikós,* equiv. to *sýndet(os)* bound together (*syn-* SYN- + *de-* (see SYNDESIS) + *-tos* verbid suffix) + *-ikos* -IC] —**syn·det′i·cal·ly,** *adv.*

syn·dic (sin′dik), *n.* **1.** a person chosen to represent and transact business for a corporation, as a university. **2.** a civil magistrate having different powers in different countries. [1595–1605; < F < LL *syndicus* city official < Gk *sýndikos* counsel for defendant, equiv. to *syn-* SYN- + *dik-* (s. of *díkē*) justice + *-os* n. suffix] —**syn′dic·ship′,** *n.*

syn·di·cal (sin′di kəl), *adj.* **1.** of or pertaining to a union of persons engaged in a particular trade. **2.** of or pertaining to syndicalism. [1860–65; < F; see SYNDIC, -AL[1]]

syn·di·cal·ism (sin′di kə liz′əm), *n.* **1.** a form or development of trade unionism, originating in France, that aims at the possession of the means of production and distribution, and ultimately at the control of society, by federated bodies of industrial workers, and that seeks to realize its purposes through general strikes, terrorism, sabotage, etc. **2.** an economic system in which workers own and manage industry. [1905–10; < F *syndicalisme.* See SYNDICAL, -ISM] —**syn′di·cal·ist,** *adj., n.* —**syn′di·cal·is′tic,** *adj.*

syn·di·cate (*n.* sin′di kit; *v.* sin′di kāt′), *n., v.,* **-cat·ed, -cat·ing.** —*n.* **1.** a group of individuals or organizations combined or making a joint effort to undertake some specific duty or carry out specific transactions or negotiations: *The local furniture store is individually owned, but is part of a buying syndicate.* **2.** a combination of bankers or capitalists formed for the purpose of carrying out some project requiring large resources of capital, as the underwriting of an issue of stock or bonds. **3.** *Journalism.* **a.** an agency that buys articles, stories, columns, photographs, comic strips, or other features and distributes them for simultaneous publication in a number of newspapers or periodicals in different localities. Cf. **boiler plate** (def. 2). **b.** a business organization owning and operating a number of newspapers; newspaper chain. **4.** a group, combination, or association of gangsters controlling organized crime or one type of crime, esp. in one region of the country. **5.** a council or body of syndics. **6.** a local organization of employers or employees in Italy during the Fascist regime. —*v.t.* **7.** to combine into a syndicate. **8.** to publish simultaneously, or supply for simultaneous publication, in a number of newspapers or other periodicals in different places: *Her column is syndicated in 120 papers.* **9.** *Television.* to sell (a program, series, etc.) directly to independent stations. **10.** to sell shares in or offer participation in the financial sharing of (a risk venture, loan, or the like): *to syndicate a racehorse among speculators; to syndicate a loan among several banks.* —*v.i.* **11.** to combine to form a syndicate. [1600–10; < MF *syndicat* office of syndic, board of syndics < ML *syndicātus.* See SYNDIC, -ATE[3]] —**syn′di·cat′a·ble,** *adj.* —**syn′di·ca′·tion,** *n.*

syn·di·o·tac·tic (sin dī′ō tak′tik, sin′dī-), *adj. Chem.* (of a polymer molecule) having a regular alternation of opposite configurations at successive regularly spaced positions along the chain. Cf. **configuration** (def. 4). [1955–60; irreg. < Gk *sýndyo* two together (see SYN-, DUO-) + TACTIC] —**syn·di·o·tac·tic·i·ty** (sin dī′ō tak-tis′i tē, sin′dī-), *n.*

syn·drome (sin′drōm, -drəm), *n.* **1.** *Pathol., Psychiatry.* a group of symptoms that together are characteristic of a specific disorder, disease, or the like. **2.** a group of related or coincident things, events, actions, etc. **3.** the pattern of symptoms that characterize or indicate a particular social condition. **4.** a predictable, characteristic pattern of behavior, action, etc., that tends to occur under certain circumstances: *the retirement syndrome of endless golf and bridge games; the feast-or-famine syndrome of big business.* [1535–45; < NL < Gk *syndromḗ* concurrence, combination, equiv. to *syn-* SYN- + *drom-,* base meaning "run" (see -DROME) + *-ē* fem. n. suffix] —**syn·drom·ic** (sin drom′ik), *adj.*

syne (sīn), *adv., prep., conj. Scot. and North Eng.* since. [1300–50; ME (north) *seine, syn,* contraction of *sethen* since; see SITH]

syn·ec·do·che (si nek′də kē), *n. Rhet.* a figure of speech in which a part is used for the whole or the whole for a part, the special for the general or the general for the special, as in *ten sail* for *ten ships* or a *Croesus* for *a rich man.* [1350–1400; < ML < Gk *synekdochḗ,* equiv. to *syn-* SYN- + *ekdochḗ* act of receiving from another, equiv. to *ek-* EC- + *-dochē,* n. deriv. of *dechesthai* to receive] —**syn·ec·doch·ic** (sin′ik dok′ik), **syn′ec·doch′·i·cal,** *adj.* —**syn′ec·doch′i·cal·ly,** *adv.*

syn·ech·i·a (si nek′ē ə, -nē′kē ə, sin′i kī′ə), *n., pl.* **syn·ech·i·ae** (si nek′ē ē′, -nē′kē ē′, sin′i kī′ē). *Med., Pathol.* any adhesion of parts of the body, as of the iris to the cornea. [1835–45; < NL < Gk *synécheia* continuity, coherence, equiv. to *syneche-,* s. of *synechḗs* (adj.) holding together (*syn-* SYN- + *ech(ein)* to hold + *-ēs* adj. suffix) + *-ia* -IA]

syn·e·chism (sin′i kiz′əm), *n.* a doctrine of philosophical thinking stressing the importance of the idea of continuity: named and advocated by C. S. Peirce. [SYNECH(IA) + -ISM] —**syn′e·chist,** *n., adj.*

syn•e•cious (si nē′shəs), *adj.* synoicous. [SYN- + *eci-* (< Gk *oikía* house) + -OUS]

syn•e•col•o•gy (sin′i kol′ə jē), *n.* the branch of ecology dealing with the relations between natural communities and their environments. Cf. **autecology.** [1910–15; SYN- + ECOLOGY] —**syn•ec•o•log•ic** (sin′ek ə loj′ik), **syn′ec•o•log′i•cal,** *adj.* —**syn′ec•o•log′i•cal•ly,** *adv.*

syn•ec•tics (si nek′tiks), *n.* (*used with a singular v.*) the study of creative processes, esp. as applied to the solution of problems by a group of diverse individuals. [1960–65; *synect(ic)* continuous, (of a cause) direct (< LL *synecticus* coherent < Gk *synektikós,* equiv. to *synéch(ein)* (see SYNECHIA) + *-tikos* -TIC) + -ICS] —**syn•ec′•tic,** *adj.* —**syn•ec′ti•cal•ly,** *adv.*

synec′tics group′, a group of people of varied background that meets to attempt creative solutions of problems through the unrestricted exercise of imagination and the correlation of disparate elements.

syn•er•e•sis (si ner′ə sis), *n.* **1.** synaeresis. **2.** *Physical Chem.* the contraction of a gel accompanied by the exudation of liquid. [1570–80; var. of SYNAERESIS]

syn•er•get•ic (sin′ər jet′ik), *adj.* working together; cooperative. [1675–85; < Gk *synergētikós,* equiv. to *syn-* SYN- + *-ergētikos;* see ENERGETIC]

syn•er•gism (sin′ər jiz′əm, si nûr′jiz-), *n.* **1.** the interaction of elements that when combined produce a total effect that is greater than the sum of the individual elements, contributions, etc. **2.** the joint action of agents, as drugs, that when taken together increase each other's effectiveness (contrasted with *antagonism*). **3.** *Theol.* the doctrine that the human will cooperates with the Holy Ghost in the work of regeneration. Cf. **monergism.** [1755–65; < NL *synergismus* < Gk *synerg(ós)* working together (*syn-* SYN- + *érg(on)* WORK + *-os* adj. suffix) + NL *-ismus* -ISM]

syn•er•gist (sin′ər jist, si nûr′-), *n.* **1.** *Physiol., Med.* a body organ, medicine, etc., that cooperates with another or others to produce or enhance an effect. **2.** *Chem., Pharm.* any admixture to a substance for increasing the effectiveness of one or more of its properties. **3.** *Theol.* a person who holds the doctrine of synergism. [1650–60; < NL *synergista* < Gk *synerg(ós)* (see SYNERGISM) + NL *-ista* -IST]

syn•er•gis•tic (sin′ər jis′tik), *adj.* **1.** pertaining to, characteristic of, or resembling synergism: *a synergistic effect.* **2.** acting as a synergist; producing synergism; interacting. **3.** of or pertaining to theological synergism or synergists. [1810–20; SYNERG(ISM) or SYNERG(IST) + -ISTIC] —**syn′er•gis′ti•cal•ly,** *adv.*

syn•er•gy (sin′ər jē), *n., pl.* **-gies. 1.** combined action or functioning; synergism. **2.** the cooperative action of two or more muscles, nerves, or the like. **3.** the cooperative action of two or more stimuli or drugs. [1650–60; < NL *synergia* < Gk *synergía,* equiv. to *synerg(ós)* (see SYNERGISM) + *-ia* -Y[3]] —**syn•er•gic** (si nûr′jik), *adj.*

syn•e•sis (sin′ə sis), *n. Gram.* a construction in which an expected grammatical agreement in form is replaced by an agreement in meaning, as in *The crowd rose to their feet,* where a plural pronoun is used to refer to a singular noun. [1890–95; < NL < Gk *sýnesis* understanding, intelligence, equiv. to *syn-* SYN- + *(h)e-* (s. of *hiénai* to throw, send) + *-sis* -SIS]

syn•es•the•sia (sin′əs thē′zhə, -zhē ə, -zē ə), *n.* a sensation produced in one modality when a stimulus is applied to another modality, as when the hearing of a certain sound induces the visualization of a certain color. Also, **synaesthesia.** [1890–95; < NL; see SYN-, ESTHESIA] —**syn•es•thete** (sin′əs thēt′), *n.* —**syn•es•thet•ic** (sin′əs thet′ik), *adj.*

syn•fu•el (sin′fyo͞o′əl), *n.* See **synthetic fuel.** [1970–75, *Amer.;* SYN(THETIC) + FUEL]

syn•ga•my (sing′gə mē), *n. Biol.* union of gametes, as in fertilization or conjugation; sexual reproduction. [1900–05; SYN- + -GAMY] —**syn•gam•ic** (sin gam′ik), **syn•ga•mous** (sing′gə məs), *adj.*

syn•gas (sin′gas′), *n.* synthetic natural gas. See under **synthetic fuel.** [1970–75; SYN(THETIC) + GAS]

Synge (sing), *n.* **1. John Mil•ling•ton** (mil′ing tən), 1871–1909, Irish dramatist. **2. Richard Laurence Millington,** 1914–96, English biochemist: Nobel prize for chemistry 1952.

syn•gen•e•sis (sin jen′ə sis), *n. Biol.* sexual reproduction. [1830–40; < NL; see SYN-, -GENESIS] —**syn•ge•net•ic** (sin′jə net′ik), *adj.*

syn•graft (sin′graft′, -gräft′), *n. Surg.* a tissue or organ transplanted from one member of a species to another, genetically identical member of the species, as a kidney transplanted from one identical twin to the other. Also called **isograft, isoplastic graft, syn•ge•ne′ic graft′** (sin′jə nē′ik). Cf. **allograft, autograft, xenograft.** [SYN- + GRAFT[1]]

syn•i•ze•sis (sin′ə zē′sis), *n. Phonet.* the combination into one syllable of two vowels (or of a vowel and a diphthong) that do not form a diphthong. Also called **synaeresis.** [1840–50; < LL < Gk *synízēsis,* equiv. to *syn-* SYN- + *(h)iz-* (s. of *hízein* to SIT[1]) + *-ēsis* -ESIS]

syn•kar•y•on (sin kar′ē on′, -ən), *n., pl.* **-kar•y•a** (-kar′ē ə). *n. Cell Biol.* a nucleus formed by the fusion of two preexisting nuclei. [1900–05; SYN- + Gk *káryon* nut, kernel; cf. KARYO-]

syn•ne•ma (si nē′mə), *n., pl.* **-ma•ta** (-mə tə). *Mycol.* a spore-bearing structure having very compact conidiophores. [< NL, equiv. to *syn-* SYN- + Gk *nêma* thread]

syn•od (sin′əd), *n.* **1.** an assembly of ecclesiastics or other church delegates, convoked pursuant to the law of the church, for the discussion and decision of ecclesiastical affairs; ecclesiastical council. **2.** any council. [1350–1400; ME < L *synodus* < Gk *sýnodos* meeting, equiv. to *syn-* SYN- + *(h)odós* way] —**syn′od•al,** *adj.*

syn•od•ic (si nod′ik), *adj.* **1.** *Astron.* pertaining to a conjunction, or to two successive conjunctions of the same bodies. **2.** of or pertaining to a synod; synodal. Also, **syn•od′i•cal.** [1555–65; < LL *synodicus* < Gk *synodikós.* See SYNOD, -IC] —**syn•od′i•cal•ly,** *adv.*

synod′ic month′. See under **month** (def. 5). [1645–55]

syn•oi•cous (si noi′kəs), *adj. Bot.* having male and female flowers on one head, as in many composite plants. Also, **synecious, syn•oe•cious** (si nē′shəs). [1860–65; < Gk *sýnoikos* dwelling in the same house, equiv. to *syn-* SYN- + *oik-* (base of *oîkos, oikía* house, *oikeîn* to dwell) + *-os* adj. suffix; see -OUS] —**syn•oi′cous•ly, syn•oe′cious•ly,** *adv.* —**syn•oi′cous•ness, syn•oe′cious•ness,** *n.*

syn•o•nym (sin′ə nim), *n.* **1.** a word having the same or nearly the same meaning as another in the language, as *joyful, elated, glad.* **2.** a word or expression accepted as another name for something, as *Arcadia* for *pastoral simplicity;* metonym. **3.** *Biol.* one of two or more scientific names applied to a single taxon. [1400–50; < L *synōnymum* < Gk *synṓnymon,* n. use of neut. of *synṓnymos* SYNONYMOUS; r. ME *sinonyme* < MF < L, as above] —**syn′o•nym′ic, syn′o•nym′i•cal,** *adj.* —**syn•o•nym•i•ty** (sin′ə nim′i tē), *n.*

syn•on•y•mist (si non′ə mist), *n.* a specialist in the study or compiling of synonyms. [1745–55; SYNONYM + -IST]

syn•on•y•mize (si non′ə mīz′), *v.t.,* **-mized, -miz•ing.** to give synonyms for (a word, name, etc.); furnish with synonyms. Also, *esp. Brit.,* **syn•on′y•mise′.** [1585–95; SYNONYM + -IZE]

syn•on•y•mous (si non′ə məs), *adj.* having the character of synonyms or a synonym; equivalent in meaning; expressing or implying the same idea. [1600–10; < ML *synōnymus* < Gk *synṓnymos,* equiv. to *syn-* SYN- + *-ōnym-* -ONYM + *-os* adj. suffix; see -OUS] —**syn•on′y•mous•ly,** *adv.* —**syn•on′y•mous•ness,** *n.*

syn•on•y•my (si non′ə mē), *n., pl.* **-mies** for 3, 4. **1.** the quality of being synonymous; equivalence in meaning. **2.** the study of synonyms. **3.** a set, list, or system of synonyms. **4.** *Biol.* a list of the scientific names, with explanatory matter and location of type or types, for a particular taxonomic group. [1600–10; < LL *synōnymia* < Gk *synōnymía.* See SYNONYMOUS, -Y[3]]

synop., synopsis.

syn•oph•thal•mi•a (sin′of thal′mē ə), *n. Med.* cyclopia. [SYN- + OPHTHALMIA]

syn•op•sis (si nop′sis), *n., pl.* **-ses** (-sēz). **1.** a brief or condensed statement giving a general view of some subject. **2.** a compendium of heads or short paragraphs giving a view of the whole. **3.** a brief summary of the plot of a novel, motion picture, play, etc. [1605–15; < LL < Gk *sýnopsis,* equiv. to *syn-* SYN- + *op-* (suppletive s. of *horân* to see; cf. AUTOPSY) + *-sis* -SIS]

—**Syn.** condensation, epitome, abstract, abridgment, précis. See **summary.**

syn•op•size (si nop′sīz), *v.t.,* **-sized, -siz•ing.** to make a synopsis of; summarize. Also, *esp. Brit.,* **syn•op′sise.** [1880–85; SYNOPS(IS) + -IZE]

syn•op•tic (si nop′tik), *adj.* **1.** pertaining to or constituting a synopsis; affording or taking a general view of the principal parts of a subject. **2.** (*often cap.*) taking a common view: used chiefly in reference to the first three Gospels **(synop′tic Gos′pels),** Matthew, Mark, and Luke, from their similarity in content, order, and statement. **3.** (*often cap.*) pertaining to the synoptic Gospels. Also, **syn•op′ti•cal.** [1755–65; < Gk *synoptikós,* equiv. to *synop-* (see SYNOPSIS) + *-tikos* -TIC] —**syn•op′ti•cal•ly,** *adv.*

synop′tic chart′, a chart showing the distribution of meteorological conditions over a wide region at a given moment. [1885–90]

synop′tic meteorol′ogy, a branch of meteorology analyzing data collected simultaneously over a wide region, for the purpose of weather forecasting.

syn•op•tist (si nop′tist), *n.* (*often cap.*) one of the authors (Matthew, Mark, or Luke) of the synoptic Gospels. [1855–60; SYNOPT(IC) + -IST] —**syn′op•tis′tic,** *adj.*

syn•os•te•o•sis (si nos′tē ō′sis), *n., pl.* **-ses** (-sēz). *Anat.* synostosis.

syn•os•to•sis (sin′o stō′sis), *n., pl.* **-ses** (-sēz). *Anat.* union of separate bones into a single bone. [1840–50; < NL; see SYN-, OSTOSIS] —**syn•os•tot•ic** (sin′o stot′ik), **syn′os•tot′i•cal,** *adj.* —**syn′os•tot′i•cal•ly,** *adv.*

syn•o•vi•a (si nō′vē ə), *n. Physiol.* a lubricating fluid resembling the white of an egg, secreted by certain membranes, as those of the joints. [1640–50; < NL, equiv. to *syn-* SYN- + L *ōv-* (s. of *ōvum* EGG[1]) + *-ia* -IA] —**syn•o′vi•al,** *adj.* —**syn•o′vi•al•ly,** *adv.*

syn•o•vi•tis (sin′ə vī′tis), *n. Pathol.* inflammation of a synovial membrane. [1825–35; SYNOV(IA) + -ITIS] —**syn•o•vit•ic** (sin′ə vit′ik), *adj.*

syn•sac•rum (sin sak′rəm, -sā′krəm), *n., pl.* **-sac•ra** (-sak′rə, -sā′krə). *Ornith.* a dorsal ridge of bone in the pelvic region of birds, formed by the fusion of certain thoracic, lumbar, sacral, and caudal vertebrae. [1900–05; SYN- + SACRUM] —**syn•sa′cral,** *adj.*

syn•sep•al•ous (sin sep′ə ləs), *adj. Bot.* gamosepalous. [1840–50; SYN- + -SEPALOUS]

syn•tac•tic (sin tak′tik), *adj.* **1.** of or pertaining to syntax. **2.** consisting of or noting morphemes that are combined in the same order as they would be if they were separate words in a corresponding construction: *The word* blackberry, *which consists of an adjective followed by a noun, is a syntactic compound.* Also, **syn•tac′ti•cal.** [1570–80; < NL *syntacticus* < Gk *syntaktikós,* equiv. to *syntakt(ós)* ordered, arranged together, verbid of *syntássein* to arrange together (*syn-* SYN- + *tag-,* base of *tássein* to arrange + *-tos* adj. suffix) + *-ikos* -IC; see TACTIC] —**syn•tac′ti•cal•ly,** *adv.*

syntac′tic construc′tion, *Gram.* **1.** a construction that has no bound forms among its immediate constituents. Cf. **morphologic construction. 2.** any phrase or sentence.

syn•tac•tics (sin tak′tiks), *n.* (*used with a singular v.*) *Ling.* the branch of semiotics dealing with the formal properties of languages and systems of symbols. Also called **logical syntax.** [1820–30; see SYNTACTIC, -ICS]

syn•tag•ma (sin tag′mə), *n., pl.* **-mas, -ma•ta** (-mə tə). *Ling.* an element that enters into a syntagmatic relationship. Also, **syn•tagm** (sin′tam). [1635–45; < Gk *sýntagma* something put together, equiv. to *syntag-* (see SYNTACTIC) + *-ma* resultative n. suffix]

syn•tag•mat•ic (sin′tag mat′ik), *adj. Ling.* pertaining to a relationship among linguistic elements that occur sequentially in the chain of speech or writing, as the relationship between *the sun* and *is shining* or *the* and *sun* in the sentence *The sun is shining.* Also, **syn′•tag•mat′i•cal.** Cf. **paradigmatic.** [1935–40; < Gk *syntagmatikós* of a syntagma, equiv. to *syntagmat-* s. of *sýntagma* SYNTAGMA + *-ikos* -IC] —**syn′tag•mat′i•cal•ly,** *adv.*

syn•tal•i•ty (sin tal′i tē), *n.* behavioral characteristics of a group perceived as parallel to or inferable from the personality structure of an individual. [SYN- + intrusive *-t-* + *-ality,* as in *personality*]

syn•tax (sin′taks), *n.* **1.** *Ling.* **a.** the study of the rules for the formation of grammatical sentences in a language. **b.** the study of the patterns of formation of sentences and phrases from words. **c.** the rules or patterns so studied: *English syntax.* **d.** a presentation of these: *a syntax of English.* **e.** an instance of these: *the syntax of a sentence.* **2.** *Logic.* **a.** that branch of modern logic that studies the various kinds of signs that occur in a system and the possible arrangements of those signs, complete abstraction being made of the meaning of the signs. **b.** the outcome of such a study when directed upon a specified language. **3.** a system or orderly arrangement. [1565–75; short for earlier *syntaxis* < LL < Gk *sýntaxis* an arranging in order, equiv. to *syntag-* (see SYNTACTIC) + *-sis* -SIS]

syn′tax lan′guage, *Philos.* a metalanguage used to refer to the grammatical or other formal features of an object language.

syn•te•re•sis (sin′tə rē′sis), *n.* synderesis.

syn•the•sis (sin′thə sis), *n., pl.* **-ses** (-sēz′). **1.** the combining of the constituent elements of separate material or abstract entities into a single or unified entity (opposed to *analysis*). **2.** a complex whole formed by combining. **3.** *Chem.* the forming or building of a more complex substance or compound from elements or simpler compounds. **4.** *Philos.* See under **Hegelian dialectic. 5.** *Biol.* See **modern synthesis. 6.** *Psychol., Psychiatry.* the integration of traits, attitudes, and impulses to create a total personality. [1580–90; < L < Gk *sýnthesis,* equiv. to *syn-* SYN- + *the-* (s. of *tithénai* to put, place) + *-sis* -SIS] —**syn′the•sist,** *n.*

syn′thesis gas′, *Chem.* any of several gaseous mixtures consisting essentially of carbon monoxide and hydrogen, used in the synthesis of chemical compounds, as ammonia and alcohols. [1940–45]

syn•the•size (sin′thə sīz′), *v.,* **-sized, -siz•ing.** —*v.t.* **1.** to form (a material or abstract entity) by combining parts or elements (opposed to *analyze*): *to synthesize a statement.* **2.** *Chem.* to combine (constituent elements) into a single or unified entity. **3.** to treat synthetically. —*v.i.* **4.** to make or form a synthesis. Also, **synthetize;** *esp. Brit.,* **syn′the•sise′.** [1820–30; SYNTHES(IS) + -IZE] —**syn′the•si•za′tion,** *n.*

syn•the•siz•er (sin′thə sī′zər), *n.* **1.** a person or thing that synthesizes. **2.** *Music.* any of various electronic, sometimes portable consoles or modules, usually computerized, for creating, modifying, and combining tones or reproducing the sounds of musical instruments by controlling voltage patterns, operated by means of keyboards, joysticks, sliders, or knobs. [1865–70; 1905–10, for def. 2; SYNTHESIZE + -ER[1]]

syn•the•tase (sin′thə tās′, -tāz′), *n. Biochem.* ligase. [1947; SYNTHET(IC) + -ASE]

syn•thet•ic (sin thet′ik), *adj.* **1.** of, pertaining to, proceeding by, or involving synthesis (opposed to *analytic*). **2.** noting or pertaining to compounds formed through a chemical process by human agency, as opposed to those of natural origin: *synthetic vitamins; synthetic fiber.* **3.** (of a language) characterized by a relatively widespread use of affixes, rather than separate words, to express syntactic relationships: *Latin is a synthetic language, while English is analytic.* Cf. **analytic** (def. 3), **polysynthetic** (def. 1). **4.** Also, **syn•thet′i•cal.** *Logic.* of or pertaining to a noncontradictory proposition in which the predicate is not included in, or entailed by, the subject. **5.** not real or genuine; artificial; feigned: *a synthetic chuckle at a poor joke.* **6.** *Jewelry.* **a.** noting a gem mineral manufactured so as to be physically, chemically, and optically identical with the mineral as found in nature. **b.** (not in technical use) noting a gem mineral manufactured and pigmented in imitation of a natural gemstone of that name. —*n.* **7.** something made by a synthetic, or chemical, process. **8. synthetics. a.** substances or products made by chemical synthesis, as plastics or artificial fibers. **b.** the science or industry concerned with such products. [1690–1700; < NL *syntheticus* < Gk *synthetikós,* equiv. to *synthet(ós)* placed together, verbid of *syntithénai* to put together (*syn-* SYN- + *the-,* s. of *tithénai* to put, place + *-tos* verbid suffix) + *-ikos* -IC] —**syn•thet′i•cal•ly,** *adv.*

—**Syn. 5.** fake, phony, counterfeit, sham.

synthet′ic cub′ism, (*sometimes caps.*) *Fine Arts.* the late phase of cubism, characterized chiefly by an increased use of color and the imitation or introduction of

CONCISE PRONUNCIATION KEY: act, cāpe, dâre, pärt; set, ēqual; *if,* ice; ox, ōver, ôrder, oil, bo͝ok, bo͞ot, out; up, ûrge; child; sing; shoe; thin, *that;* zh as in *treasure.* ə = *a* as in *alone, e* as in *system, i* as in *easily, o* as in *gallop, u* as in *circus;* ᵊ as in *fire* (fīᵊr), *hour* (ouᵊr). l and n can serve as syllabic consonants, as in *cradle* (krād′l), and *button* (but′n). See the full key inside the front cover.

a wide range of textures and material into painting. Cf. **analytical cubism.**

synthet′ic deter′gent, any synthetic substance, other than soap, that is an effective cleanser and functions equally well in hard or soft water.

synthet′ic divi′sion, a simplified procedure for dividing a polynomial by a linear polynomial. [1900–05]

synthet′ic fu′el, fuel in the form of liquid or gas **(synthet′ic nat′ural gas′)** manufactured from coal or in the form of oil extracted from shale or tar sands. Also called **synfuel.**

synthet′ic geom′etry, elementary geometry, as distinct from analytic geometry. [1885–90]

synthet′ic philos′ophy, the philosophy of Herbert Spencer, intended as a synthesis of all the sciences.

synthet′ic rub′ber, any of several substances similar to natural rubber in properties and uses, produced by the polymerization of an unsaturated hydrocarbon, as butylene or isoprene, or by the copolymerization of such hydrocarbons with styrene, butadiene, or the like.

syn•the•tize (sin′thi tīz′), *v.t., v.i.,* **-tized, -tiz•ing.** to synthesize. Also, *esp. Brit.,* **syn′the•tise′.** [1820–30; < Gk *synthetízesthai;* see SYNTHETIC, -IZE] **—syn′the•ti•za′tion,** *n.* **—syn′the•tiz′er,** *n.*

syn•thol (sin′thôl, -thol), *n. Chem.* a synthetic motor fuel produced by heating, under pressure, hydrogen and carbon monoxide in the presence of a catalyst. [SYNTH(ETIC) + -OL[1]]

synth•pop (sinth′pop′), *n.* popular music played with synthesizers and having light upbeat melodies and lyrics. [1980–85; SYNTH(ESIZER) + POP[2]]

syn•ton•ic (sin ton′ik), *adj.* **1.** *Elect.* adjusted to oscillations of the same or a particular frequency. **2.** *Psychiatry.* of or denoting a personality characterized by normal emotional responsiveness to the environment. Also, **syn•ton′i•cal, syntonous.** [1890–95; < Gk *sýnton(os)* attuned to, lit., stretched together (verbid of *synteínein* to harmonize, equiv. to *syn-* SYN- + *ton-* (deriv. of *teínein* to stretch; see TONE) + *-os* adj. suffix) + -IC] **—syn•ton′i•cal•ly,** *adv.*

syn•to•nize (sin′tn īz′), *v.t.,* **-nized, -niz•ing.** to render syntonic; tune to the same frequency. Also, *esp. Brit.,* **syn′to•nise′.** [1890–95; SYNTON(Y) + -IZE] **—syn′to•ni•za′tion,** *n.* **—syn′to•niz′er,** *n.*

syn•to•nous (sin′tn əs), *adj.* syntonic. [1780–90; < Gk *sýntonos.* See SYNTONIC, -OUS]

syn•to•ny (sin′tn ē), *n. Elect.* the state or condition of being syntonic. [1890–95; < Gk *syntonía,* equiv. to *sýnton(os)* (see SYNTONIC) + *-ia* -Y[3]]

syn•type (sin′tīp′), *n. Biol.* a type specimen other than the holotype used in the description of a species. [1905–10; SYN- + TYPE] **—syn•typ•ic** (sin tip′ik), *adj.*

syph (sif), *n. Slang.* syphilis (often prec. by *the*). [by shortening]

sy•pher (sī′fər), *v.t.* to join (boards having beveled edges) so as to make a flush surface. [1835–45; sp. var. of CIPHER]

syph•i•lis (sif′ə lis), *n. Pathol.* a chronic infectious disease, caused by a spirochete, *Treponema pallidum,* usually venereal in origin but often congenital, and affecting almost any body organ, esp. the genitals, skin, brain, and nervous tissue. Cf. **primary syphilis, secondary syphilis, tertiary syphilis.** [< NL, coined by Giovanni Fracastoro (1478–1553), Italian physician and poet, in his 1530 Latin poem *Syphilis, sive morbus Gallicus* ("Syphilis, or the French Disease"), an early account of syphilis]

syph•i•lit•ic (sif′ə lit′ik), *adj.* **1.** pertaining to, noting, or affected with syphilis. —*n.* **2.** a person affected with syphilis. [1780–90; < NL *syphiliticus,* equiv. to *syphili(s)* SYPHILIS + *-ticus* -TIC] **—syph′i•lit′i•cal•ly,** *adv.*

syph•i•loid (sif′ə loid′), *adj.* resembling syphilis. [1805–15; SYPHIL(IS) + -OID]

sy•phon (sī′fən), *n., v.t., v.i.* siphon.

Syr., **1.** Syria. **2.** Syriac. **3.** Syrian.

syr, *Pharm.* syrup.

Syr•a•cuse (sir′ə kyo͞os′, -kyo͞oz′), *n.* **1.** a city in central New York. 170,105. **2.** Italian, **Siracusa.** a seaport in SE Sicily: ancient city founded by the Carthaginians 734 B.C.; battles 413 B.C., 212 B.C. 121,134. **—Syr′a•cu′•san,** *adj., n.*

Syr Dar•ya (sēr′ där′yə; *Russ.* sɪʀ′ du ʀyä′), a river in central Asia, flowing NW from the Tien Shan Mountains in Kyrgyzstan, through Uzbekistan and Kazakhstan to the Aral Sea. 1300 mi. (2100 km) long. Ancient name, **Jaxartes.**

Syr•i•a (sēr′ē ə), *n.* **1.** Official name, **Syr′ian Ar′ab Repub′lic.** a republic in SW Asia at the E end of the Mediterranean. 7,200,000; 71,227 sq. mi. (184,478 sq. km). *Cap.:* Damascus. **2.** a territory mandated to France in 1922, including the present republics of Syria and Lebanon (Latakia and Jebel ed Druz were incorporated into Syria 1942): the French mandatory powers were nominally terminated as of January 1, 1944. **3.** an ancient country in W Asia, including the present Syria, Lebanon, Israel, and adjacent areas: a part of the Roman Empire 64 B.C.–A.D. 636.

Syr•i•ac (sēr′ē ak′), *n.* a form of Aramaic used by various Eastern Churches. [< L *Syriacus* < Gk *Syriakós.* See SYRIA, -AC]

Syr•i•an (sēr′ē ən), *adj.* **1.** of or pertaining to Syria or its inhabitants. —*n.* **2.** a native or inhabitant of Syria. [1350–1400; ME *Sirien* < MF. See SYRIA, -AN]

Syr′ian Des′ert, a desert in N Saudi Arabia, SE Syria, W Iraq, and NE Jordan. ab. 125,000 sq. mi. (323,750 sq. km).

Syr′ian ham′ster. See **golden hamster.** [1945–50]

sy•rin•ga (sə ring′gə), *n.* **1.** See **mock orange** (def. 1). **2.** any shrub or tree of the genus *Syringa,* including the lilacs. [1655–65; < NL < Gk *sȳring-* (s. of *sŷrinx* SYRINX) + NL *-a* -A[2]; name first given to mock orange, the stems of which were used in pipe-making]

sy•ringe (sə rinj′, sir′inj), *n., v.,* **-ringed, -ring•ing.** —*n.* **1.** a small device consisting of a glass, metal, or hard rubber tube, narrowed at its outlet, and fitted with either a piston or a rubber bulb for drawing in a quantity of fluid or for ejecting fluid in a stream, for cleaning wounds, injecting fluids into the body, etc. **2.** any similar device for pumping and spraying liquids through a small aperture. —*v.t.* **3.** to cleanse, wash, inject, etc., by means of a syringe. [1375–1425; new singular formed from LL *sȳringēs,* pl. of *sŷrinx* SYRINX; r. late ME *syring* < ML *syringa*] **—sy•ringe′ful,** *adj.*

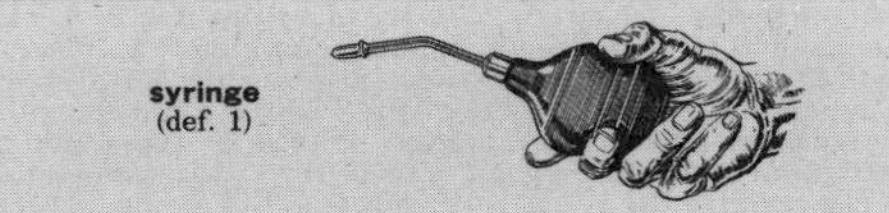

syringe (def. 1)

sy•rin•ge•al (sə rin′jē əl), *adj. Ornith.* of, pertaining to, or connected with the syrinx. [1870–75; *syringe-* (var. s. of SYRINX) + -AL[1]]

sy•rin•go•my•e•li•a (sə ring′gō mī ē′lē ə), *n. Pathol.* a disease of the spinal cord in which the nerve tissue is replaced by a cavity filled with fluid. [1875–80; *syringo-* (comb. form of Gk *sŷrinx* SYRINX) + *myelia* (MYEL- + -IA)] **—sy•rin•go•my•el•ic** (sə ring′gō mī el′ik), *adj.*

syr•inx (sir′ingks), *n., pl.* **sy•rin•ges** (sə rin′jēz), **syr•inx•es. 1.** *Ornith.* the vocal organ of birds, situated at or near the bifurcation of the trachea into the bronchi. **2.** (*cap.*) *Class. Myth.* a mountain nymph of Arcadia who was transformed, in order to protect her chastity from Pan, into the reed from which Pan then made the panpipe. **3.** a panpipe. **4.** a narrow corridor in an ancient Egyptian tomb. [1600–10; (< L) < Gk *sŷrinx* pipe, pipelike object]

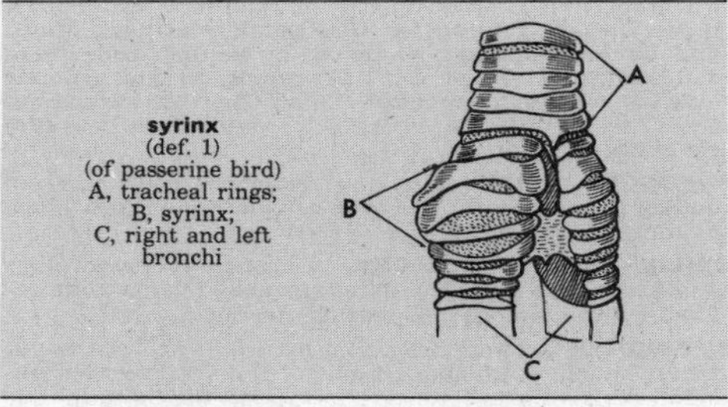

syrinx (def. 1) (of passerine bird) A, tracheal rings; B, syrinx; C, right and left bronchi

syr•phid (sûr′fid), *n.* **1.** See **syrphid fly.** —*adj.* **2.** belonging or pertaining to the family Syrphidae. Also, **syr•phi•an** (sûr′fē ən). [1890–95; < NL *Syrphidae* family name, equiv. to *Syrph(us)* a genus (< Gk *sýrphos* gnat) + NL *-idae* -ID[2]]

syr′phid fly′, any of numerous beelike or wasplike flies of the family Syrphidae that feed on the nectar and pollen of flowers and have larvae that feed on decaying vegetation or prey on aphids. Also, **syr′phus fly′** (sûr′fəs). Also called **flower fly.**

syrphid fly, *Didea fuscipes,* length ½ in. (1.3 cm)

Syr′tis Ma′jor (sûr′tis), an area in the northern hemisphere and near the equator of Mars, appearing as a dark region when viewed telescopically from the earth.

syr•up (sir′əp, sûr′-), *n.* **1.** any of various thick, sweet liquids prepared for table use from molasses, glucose, etc. **2.** any of various preparations consisting of fruit juices, water, etc., boiled with sugar: *raspberry syrup.* **3.** *Pharm.* a concentrated sugar solution that contains medication or flavoring. **4.** See **simple syrup.** —*v.t.* **5.** to bring to the form or consistency of syrup. **6.** to cover, fill, or sweeten with syrup. Also, **sirup.** [1350–1400; < ML *syrupus* < Ar *sharāb* a drink; r. ME *sirop* < MF < ML, as above] **—syr′up•like′,** *adj.*

syr′up of ip′ecac, *Pharm.* See **ipecac syrup.**

syr•up•y (sir′ə pē, sûr′-), *adj.* **1.** having the appearance or quality of syrup; thick or sweet: *syrupy coffee.* **2.** sentimental or saccharine; mawkish: *a syrupy manner; a syrupy poem.* Also, **sirupy.** [1700–10; SYRUP + -Y[1]]

sys-, var. of **syn-** before *s: syssarcosis.*

sys•op (sis′op′), *n. Computers Informal.* a person who operates a computer bulletin board. [*sys(tems) op(erator)*]

sys•sar•co•sis (sis′är kō′sis), *n., pl.* **-ses** (-sēz). *Anat.* the joining or attachment of bones by means of muscle. [1670–80; < NL < Gk *syssárkōsis;* see SYS-, SARC-, -OSIS]

syst., system.

sys•tal•tic (si stôl′tik, -stal′-), *adj. Physiol.* **1.** rhythmically contracting. **2.** of the nature of contraction. **3.** characterized by alternate contraction and dilation, as the action of the heart. [1670–80; < LL *systalticus* < Gk *systaltikós,* equiv. to *systalt(ós)* contracted, verbid of *systéllein* to put together (*sy-* SY- + *stal-,* var. s. of *stéllein* to place + *-tos* verbid suffix) + *-ikos* -IC]

sys•tem (sis′təm), *n.* **1.** an assemblage or combination of things or parts forming a complex or unitary whole: *a mountain system; a railroad system.* **2.** any assemblage or set of correlated members: *a system of currency; a system of shorthand characters.* **3.** an ordered and comprehensive assemblage of facts, principles, doctrines, or the like in a particular field of knowledge or thought: *a system of philosophy.* **4.** a coordinated body of methods or a scheme or plan of procedure; organizational scheme: *a system of government.* **5.** any formulated, regular, or special method or plan of procedure: *a winning system at bridge.* **6.** due method or orderly manner of arrangement or procedure: *There is no system in his work.* **7.** the world or universe. **8.** *Astron.* **a.** a number of heavenly bodies associated and acting together according to certain natural laws: *the solar system.* **b.** a hypothesis or theory of the disposition and arrangements of the heavenly bodies by which their phenomena, motions, changes, etc., are explained: *the Ptolemaic system; the Copernican system.* **9.** *Biol.* **a.** an assemblage of organs or related tissues concerned with the same function: *the nervous system; the digestive system.* **b.** the entire human or animal body considered as a functioning unit: *an ingredient toxic to the system.* **10.** one's psychological makeup, esp. with reference to desires or preoccupations: *to get something out of one's system.* **11.** a method or scheme of classification: *the Linnean system of plants.* **12.** (*sometimes cap.*) the prevailing structure or organization of society, business, or politics or of society in general; establishment (usually prec. by *the*): *to work within the system instead of trying to change it.* **13.** *Geol.* a major division of rocks comprising sedimentary deposits and igneous masses formed during a single geologic period. **14.** *Physical Chem.* a combination of two or more phases, as a binary system, each of which consists of one or more substances, that is attaining or is in equilibrium. **15.** *Computers.* a working combination of hardware, software, and data communications devices. **16.** *Checkers.* either of the two groups of 16 playing squares on four alternate columns. [1610–20; < LL *systēma* < Gk *sýstēma* whole compounded of several parts, equiv. to *sy-* SY- + *stē-* (var. s. of *histánai* to cause to stand; akin to L *stāre* to STAND) + *-ma* n. suffix denoting result of action] **—sys′tem•less,** *adj.*
—Syn. 1. organization. **7.** cosmos. **9b.** organism.

sys•tem•at•ic (sis′tə mat′ik), *adj.* **1.** having, showing, or involving a system, method, or plan: *a systematic course of reading; systematic efforts.* **2.** given to or using a system or method; methodical: *a systematic person.* **3.** arranged in or comprising an ordered system: *systematic theology.* **4.** concerned with classification: *systematic botany.* **5.** pertaining to, based on, or in accordance with a system of classification: *the systematic names of plants.* Also, **sys′tem•at′i•cal.** [1670–80; < LL *systēmaticus* < Gk *systēmatikós,* equiv. to *systēmat-* (s. of *sýstēma*) SYSTEM + *-ikos* -IC] **—sys′tem•at′ic•ness,** *n.* **—sys′tem•at′i•cal•ly,** *adv.*
—Syn. 2. See **orderly.**

sys′temat′ic er′ror, *Statistics.* a persistent error that cannot be attributed to chance. Cf. **random error.** [1890–95]

sys′temat′ic pho′neme, *Ling.* a phonological unit in generative phonology representing an underlying form that takes into account the relationship between phonological patterns and morphological variation, as the unit underlying the second vowel in both *derive* and *derivative.* Cf. **autonomous phoneme.**

sys•tem•at•ics (sis′tə mat′iks), *n.* (*used with a singular v.*) **1.** the study of systems or of classification. **2.** *Biol.* **a.** the study and classification of organisms with the goal of reconstructing their evolutionary histories and relationships. **b.** phylogenetic classification. [1885–90; see SYSTEMATIC, -ICS]

sys•tem•a•tism (sis′tə mə tiz′əm), *n.* **1.** the practice of systematizing. **2.** adherence to system or method. [1840–50; SYSTEMAT(IZE) + -ISM]

sys•tem•a•tist (sis′tə mə tist), *n.* **1.** a person who constructs a system. **2.** a naturalist engaged in classification. **3.** a person who adheres to a system, order, or method. [1690–1700; < Gk *systēmat-* (s. of *sýstēma*) SYSTEM + -IST]

sys•tem•a•tize (sis′tə mə tīz′), *v.t.,* **-tized, -tiz•ing.** to arrange in or according to a system; reduce to a system; make systematic. Also, **systemize;** *esp. Brit.,* **sys′•tem•a•tise′.** [1755–65; < Gk *systēmat-* (s. of *sýstēma*) SYSTEM + -IZE] **—sys′tem•a•ti•za′tion,** *n.* **—sys′tem•a•tiz′er,** *n.*
—Syn. organize, order, articulate.

sys•tem•a•tol•o•gy (sis′tə mə tol′ə jē), *n.* the science of systems or their formation. [< Gk *systēmat-* (s. of *sýstēma*) SYSTEM + -O- + -LOGY]

sys•tem•ic (si stem′ik), *adj.* **1.** of or pertaining to a system. **2.** *Physiol., Pathol.* **a.** pertaining to or affecting the body as a whole. **b.** pertaining to or affecting a particular body system. **3.** (of a pesticide) absorbed and circulated by a plant or other organism so as to be lethal to pests that feed on it. [1795–1805; SYSTEM + -IC] **—sys·tem′i·cal·ly,** *adv.*

system′ic circula′tion, *Anat.* **1.** the circulatory system in general. **2.** (in mammals and birds) the circulatory system excluding the pulmonary circulation.

system′ic linguis′tics, a school of linguistics of British origin that emphasizes the social functions of language and describes grammar in terms of hierarchically organized structures and of systems of mutually exclusive choices available to the speaker under specified conditions.

system′ic lu′pus erythemato′sus, *Pathol.* an autoimmune inflammatory disease of the connective tissues, occurring mainly among middle-aged women, chiefly characterized by skin eruptions, joint pain, recurrent pleurisy, and kidney disease. *Abbr.:* SLE

sys·tem·ize (sis′tə mīz′), *v.t.,* **-ized, -iz·ing.** systematize. Also, *esp. Brit.,* **sys′tem·ise′.** [1770–80; SYSTEM + -IZE] **—sys′tem·i·za′tion,** *n.* **—sys′tem·iz′er,** *n.*

sys′tem pro′gram, *Computers.* a program, as an operating system, compiler, or utility program, that controls some aspect of the operation of a computer (opposed to *application program*). Also, **sys′tems pro′·gram.** **—sys′tem pro′grammer.** **—sys′tem pro′·gramming.**

sys′tems anal′ysis, **1.** the evaluation of an activity to identify its desired objectives and determine procedures for efficiently attaining them. **2.** *Computers.* the methodical study of the data-processing needs of a business or department, together with recommendations for specific hardware and software installations. [1950–55] **—sys′tems an′alyst.**

sys′tems engineer′, an engineer who specializes in the implementation of production systems. **—sys′tems engineer′ing.**

sys′tems soft′ware, *Computers.* a collection of system programs for use with a particular computer system. [1975–80]

sys·to·le (sis′tə lē′, -lē), *n.* **1.** *Physiol.* the normal rhythmical contraction of the heart, during which the blood in the chambers is forced onward. Cf. **diastole.** **2.** *Class. Pros.* the shortening of a syllable regularly long. [1570–80; < Gk *systolḗ* a drawing up, contraction, equiv. to *sy-* SY- + *stolḗ* pressure, orig., garment, equipment, equiv. to *stol-* (n. deriv. of *stéllein* to send, place) + *-ē* fem. n. suffix; cf. DIASTOLE, SYSTALTIC]

sys·tol·ic (si stol′ik), *adj.* (of blood pressure) indicating the maximum arterial pressure occurring during contraction of the left ventricle of the heart. Cf. **diastolic.** [1685–95; SYSTOLE + -IC]

sys·tyle (sis′tīl), *adj. Archit.* having an intercolumniation of two diameters. See illus. under **intercolumniation.** [1695–1705; < L *systȳlos* < Gk *sýstȳlos,* equiv. to *sy-* SY- + *-stȳlos* -STYLE[2]]

Syz·ran (siz′rən; *Russ.* si′zʀən), *n.* a city in the E Russian Federation in Europe, on the Volga. 174,000.

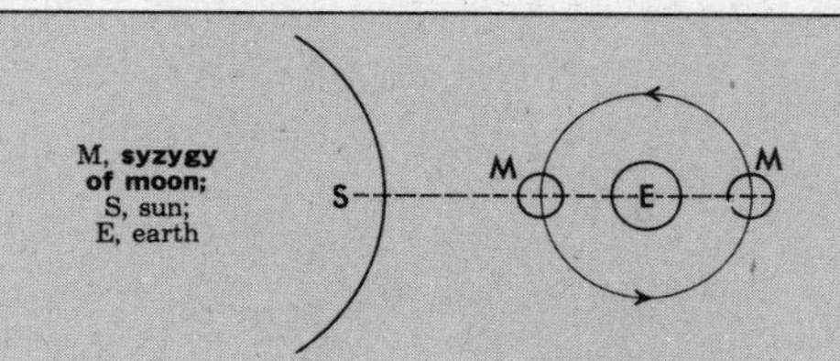

syz·y·gy (siz′i jē), *n., pl.* **-gies.** **1.** *Astron.* an alignment of three celestial objects, as the sun, the earth, and either the moon or a planet: *Syzygy in the sun-earth-moon system occurs at the time of full moon and new moon.* **2.** *Class. Pros.* a group or combination of two feet, sometimes restricted to a combination of two feet of different kinds. **3.** any two related things, either alike or opposite. [1650–60; < LL *syzygia* < Gk *syzygía* union, pair, equiv. to *sýzyg(os)* yoked together (*sy-* SY- + *zyg-,* base of *zeugnýnai* to YOKE[1] + *-os* adj. suffix) + *-ia* -Y[3]] **—sy·zyg·i·al** (si zij′ē əl), **syz·y·get·ic** (siz′i jet′ik), **syz·y·gal** (siz′i gəl), *adj.*

Sza·bad·ka (so′bot ko), *n.* Hungarian name of **Subotica.**

Szcze·cin (shche′ chēn), *n.* a seaport in NW Poland: formerly in Germany. 370,000. German, **Stettin.**

Sze·chwan (sech′wän′, sech′o͞o än′; *Chin.* su′-chwän′), *n.* Sichuan. Also, **Sze′chuan.**

Sze·ged (se′ged), *n.* a city in S Hungary, on the Tisza River. 166,040. German, **Sze·ge·din** (se′gə din).

Szé·kes·fe·hér·vár (sā′kesh fe′hâʀ väʀ), *n.* a city in W central Hungary. 102,000.

Szell (sel), *n.* **George,** 1897–1970, U.S. pianist and conductor, born in Hungary.

Szent-Györ·gyi (sent jûr′jē; *Hung.* sent dyœʀ′dyi), *n.* **Al·bert** (al′bərt; *Hung.* ol′beʀt), 1893–1986, U.S. biochemist, born in Hungary: Nobel prize for medicine 1937.

Szi·ge·ti (sig′i tē, si get′ē; *Hung.* si′ge tē), *n.* **Joseph,** 1892–1973, U.S. violinist, born in Hungary.

Szi·lard (sil′ärd), *n.* **Leo,** 1898–1964, U.S. physicist, born in Hungary.

Szold (zōld), *n.* **Henrietta,** 1860–1945, U.S. Zionist: founded Hadassah in 1912.

Szom·bat·hely (sôm′bot hā′), *n.* a city in W Hungary: founded A.D. 48. 76,000. German, **Steinamanger.**

Szy·ma·now·ski (shē′mä nôf′skē), *n.* **Ka·rol** (kä′ʀôl), 1882?–1937, Polish composer.

CONCISE PRONUNCIATION KEY: *act, cāpe, dâre, pärt; set, ēqual; if, īce; ox, ōver, ôrder, oil, bo͝ok, bo͞ot, out; up, ûrge; child; sing; shoe; thin, that;* zh as in *treasure.* ə = *a* as in *alone, e* as in *system, i* as in *easily, o* as in *gallop, u* as in *circus;* ᵊ as in *fire* (fīᵊr), *hour* (ouᵊr). l and n can serve as syllabic consonants, as in *cradle* (krād′l), and *button* (but′n). See the full key inside the front cover.

DEVELOPMENT OF MAJUSCULE								
NORTH SEMITIC	GREEK		ETR	LATIN		MODERN		
						GOTHIC	ITALIC	ROMAN
+	×	T	Ƭ	T	T	𝔗	*T*	T

T

DEVELOPMENT OF MINUSCULE					
ROMAN CURSIVE	ROMAN UNCIAL	CAROL MIN	MODERN		
			GOTHIC	ITALIC	ROMAN
ꞇ	T	ꞇ	t	*t*	t

The twentieth letter of the English alphabet developed from North Semitic *taw.* The symbol has hardly changed in its long history, and its minuscule (t) is only a slight variant of the capital.

T, t (tē), *n., pl.* **T's** or **Ts, t's** or **ts. 1.** the 20th letter of the English alphabet, a consonant. **2.** any spoken sound represented by the letter *T* or *t,* as in *tub, but,* or *butter.* **3.** something having the shape of a T. **4.** a written or printed representation of the letter *T* or *t.* **5.** a device, as a printer's type, for reproducing the letter *T* or *t.* **6. to a T,** exactly; perfectly: *That job would suit you to a T.* Also, **to a tee.**

T (tē), *n.* (*sometimes l.c.*) T-shirt.

T, 1. tera-. **2.** *Elec.* tesla; teslas. **3.** *Physics.* temperature.

T, *Symbol.* **1.** the 20th in order or in a series, or, when *I* is omitted, the 19th. **2.** (*sometimes l.c.*) the medieval Roman numeral for 160. Cf. **Roman numerals. 3.** surface tension. **4.** *Biochem.* **a.** threonine. **b.** thymine. **5.** *Photog.* See **T number. 6.** *Physics.* **a.** tau lepton. **b.** time reversal. **7.** the launching time of a rocket or missile: *T minus two.*

T_3, triiodothyronine.

T_4, thyroxine.

t, *Statistics.* **1.** a random variable having Student's t distribution. **2.** the statistic employed in Student's t-test.

't, a shortened form of *it,* before or after a verb, as in *'twas, 'tis, do't, see't.*

T-, *U.S. Mil.* (in designations of aircraft) trainer: *T-11.*

t-, *Chem.* tertiary.

-t, var. of **-ed** used in forming the past tense or past participle of certain verbs, usually occurring when the final consonant of the stem is voiceless, a lateral, or a nasal and there is internal vowel change in the root: *slept; felt; dreamt.*

T., 1. tablespoon; tablespoonful. **2.** Territory. **3.** Township. **4.** Tuesday.

t., 1. *Football.* tackle. **2.** taken from. **3.** tare. **4.** teaspoon; teaspoonful. **5.** temperature. **6.** in the time of. [< L *tempore*] **7.** tenor. **8.** *Gram.* tense. **9.** territory. **10.** time. **11.** tome. **12.** ton. **13.** town. **14.** township. **15.** transit. **16.** transitive. **17.** troy.

ta (tä), *interj. Brit. Slang.* thank you. [1765–75; by infantile shortening and alter.]

tā (tä), *n.* the third letter of the Arabic alphabet. [< Ar]

ṭā (tä), *n.* the 16th letter of the Arabic alphabet. [< Ar]

TA, 1. See **transactional analysis. 2.** transit authority.

Ta, *Symbol, Chem.* tantalum.

Taal (täl), *n.* Afrikaans (usually prec. by *the*). [1895–1900; < Afrik < D *taal* language, speech; c. TALE]

Ta•al (tä äl′), *n.* an active volcano in the Philippines, on SW Luzon, on an island in Taal Lake: eruptions 1749, 1873, 1911. 1050 ft. (320 m).

Ta•a•nith Es•ther (tä′nit′ es′tər, -nis; *Seph. Heb.* tä′ä nēt′ es tεr′; *Ashk. Heb.* tä′ä nis es′tər), a Jewish fast day observed on the 13th day of the month of Adar in memory of Esther's fast of three days before petitioning her husband, King Ahasuerus of Persia, to spare the Jews from destruction by Haman. Also, **Ta′a•nit Es′ther, Ta′a•nis Es′ther.** Also called **Fast of Esther.** [< Heb *ta'anīth estēr* fast of Esther]

tab[1] (tab), *n., v.,* **tabbed, tab•bing.** *—n.* **1.** a small flap, strap, loop, or similar appendage, as on a garment, used for pulling, hanging, or decoration. **2.** a tag or label. **3.** a small projection from a card, paper, or folder, used as an aid in filing. **4.** *Informal.* a bill, as for a meal in a restaurant; check. **5.** a small piece attached or intended to be attached, as to an automobile license plate. **6.** a small flap or tongue of material used to seal or close the opening of a container. **7.** Also called **tabulator.** a stop on a typewriter, actuated by a key, that moves the carriage, typing element, etc., a predetermined number of spaces, used for typing material in columns, for fixed indentations, etc. **8.** a programmed command on a computer, actuated by a key, that moves the cursor or printhead a predetermined number of spaces, used for keying material in columns, for fixed indentations, etc. **9.** *Theat.* **a.** a small, often narrow, drop curtain, for masking part of the stage. **b.** See **tableau curtain. 10.** *Aeron.* a small airfoil hinged to the rear portion of a control surface, as to an elevator, aileron, or rudder. Cf. **trim tab. 11. keep tabs** or **tab on,** *Informal.* to keep an account of; check on; observe: *The police kept tabs on the suspect's activities.* *—v.t.* **12.** to furnish or ornament with a tab or tabs. **13.** to name or designate. *—v.i.* **14.** Also, **tabulate.** to operate the tab function on a typewriter or computer. [1600–10; (in defs. 1–3, 5) < ?; (in defs. 7 and 8) short for TABULATOR; (in def. 9) short for TABLEAU; (in defs. 4 and 11) partly from shortening of TABLE, partly in sense of def. 1]

tab[2] (tab), *n. Informal.* **1.** tabloid (def. 1). **2.** *Slang.* a tablet, as of a drug or medication. [by shortening]

tab., 1. tables. **2.** (in prescriptions) tablet. [< L *tabella*]

tab•a•nid (tab′ə nid, tə bā′nid, -ban′id), *n.* **1.** any of numerous bloodsucking flies of the family Tabanidae, comprising the deer flies and horse flies. *—adj.* **2.** belonging or pertaining to the family Tabanidae. [1890–95; < NL *Tabanidae* name of the family, equiv. to *Tabanus* a genus (L *tabānus* gadfly) + *-idae* -ID[2]]

tab•ard (tab′ərd), *n.* **1.** a loose outer garment, sleeveless or with short sleeves, esp. one worn by a knight over his armor and usually emblazoned with his arms. **2.** an official garment of a herald, emblazoned with the arms of his master. **3.** a coarse, heavy, short coat, with or without sleeves, formerly worn outdoors. [1250–1300; ME < OF *tabart*] **—tab′ard•ed,** *adj.*

tabard (def. 2)

tab•a•ret (tab′ə rit), *n.* **1.** a durable silk or acetate fabric having alternating stripes of satin and moiré, for drapery and upholstery. **2.** tambour (def. 3). [1850–55; perh. akin to TABBY[1]]

Ta•bas•co (tə bas′kō; *Sp.* tä väs′kô), *n.* a state in SE Mexico, on the Gulf of Campeche. 1,054,000; 9783 sq. mi. (25,338 sq. km). *Cap.:* Villahermosa.

Ta•bas•co (tə bas′kō), *Trademark.* a brand name for a pungent condiment sauce prepared from the fruit of a variety of capsicum.

tab•bi•net (tab′ə net′), *n.* tabinet.

tab•bou•leh (tə bo͞o′lə, -lē), *n. Middle Eastern Cookery.* a salad of fine-ground bulgur, parsley, tomatoes, green onions, mint, olive oil, and lemon juice. Also, **tabouli, tabouleh, tabooli.** [1960–65; (< F) < Levantine Ar *tabbule,* deriv. of *tābil* spice]

tab•by[1] (tab′ē), *n., pl.* **-bies,** *adj., v.,* **-bied, -by•ing.** *—n.* **1.** a cat with a striped or brindled coat. **2.** a domestic cat, esp. a female one. **3.** a spinster. **4.** a spiteful female gossip or tattler. **5.** See **plain weave. 6.** a watered silk fabric, or any other watered material, as moreen. *—adj.* **7.** striped or brindled. **8.** made of or resembling tabby. *—v.t.* **9.** to give a wavy or watered appearance to, as silk. [1630–40; back formation from F *tabis* (taken as pl.), MF *(a)tabis* silk cloth < ML *attābi* < Ar *'attābi,* deriv. of *(al-)'Attābiyah,* quarter of Baghdad where the silk was first made, lit., the quarter of (Prince) 'Attāb]

tab•by[2] (tab′ē), *n.* (in the southeastern U.S.) a building material composed of ground oyster shells, lime, and sand, mixed with salt water. [1765–75, *Amer.*; said to be of West African orig.]

ta•ber (tā′bər), *n. Music.* tabor.

tab•er•nac•le (tab′ər nak′əl), *n., v.,* **-led, -ling.** *—n.* **1.** any place or house of worship, esp. one designed for a large congregation. **2.** (*often cap.*) the portable sanctuary in use by the Israelites from the time of their wandering in the wilderness after the Exodus from Egypt to the building of the Temple in Jerusalem by Solomon. Ex. 25–27. **3.** *Eccles.* an ornamental receptacle for the reserved Eucharist, now generally found on the altar. **4.** a canopied niche or recess, as for an image or icon. **5.** a temporary dwelling or shelter, as a tent or hut. **6.** a dwelling place. **7.** the human body as the temporary abode of the soul. *—v.t., v.i.* **8.** to place or dwell in, or as if in, a tabernacle. [1200–50; ME < LL *tabernāculum,* L: tent, equiv. to *tabern(a)* hut, stall, inn (cf. TAVERN) + *-āculum,* prob. extracted from *hibernāculum* winter quarters (see HIBERNACULUM)] **—tab•er•nac•u•lar** (tab′ər nak′yə lər), *adj.*

tab′ernacle frame′, a frame, esp. of the 18th century, around a doorway, niche, etc., that suggests a small building, characteristically one with a pediment and two pilasters on a base.

tab′ernacle mir′ror, a mirror of c1800, having columns and a cornice, usually gilt, with a painted panel over the mirror.

ta•bes (tā′bēz), *n. Pathol.* **1.** a gradually progressive emaciation. **2.** See **tabes dorsalis.** [1645–55; < L *tābēs* wasting, decay, akin to *tābēre* to waste away]

ta•bes•cent (tə bes′ənt), *adj.* wasting away; becoming emaciated or consumed. [1885–90; < L *tābēscent-* (s. of *tābēscēns*), prp. of *tābēscere* to waste away. See TABES, -ESCENT] **—ta•bes′cence,** *n.*

ta′bes dor•sal′is (dôr sal′is, -sā′lis), *Pathol.* syphilis of the spinal cord and its appendages, characterized by shooting pains and other sensory disturbances, and, in the later stages, by paralysis. Also called **locomotor ataxia.** [1675–85; < NL *tābēs dorsālis* lit., tabes of the back; see DORSAL]

ta•bet•ic (tə bet′ik), *Pathol.* *—adj.* **1.** Also, **tab•id** (tab′id). pertaining to or affected with tabes. *—n.* **2.** a person affected with tabes. [TABE(S) + -TIC]

ta•bi (tä′bē), *n., pl.* **-bi, -bis.** a covering for the foot, similar to a sock, having a separate pouchlike stall for the large toe, worn esp. in Japan, often with zoris. [1890–95; < Japn, perh. < MChin, equiv. to Chin *dānpí* single-skin]

tab•i•net (tab′ə net′), *n.* a fabric resembling poplin, made of silk and wool and usually given a watered finish. Also, **tabbinet.** [1770–80; obs. *tabine* (perh. TABB(Y)[1] + -INE[2]) + -ET]

tab′ key′, a key on a typewriter, computer terminal, or other keyboard, that is pressed in order to indent what will be typed next to a predetermined position.

ta•bla (tä′blə, tub′lə), *n.* a small drum or pair of drums of India tuned to different pitches and played with the hands. [1860–65; earlier *tubla* < Hindi *tablā* < Ar *ṭabla,* deriv. of *ṭabl* drum]

CONCISE ETYMOLOGY KEY: <, descended or borrowed from; >, whence; b., blend of, blended; c., cognate with; cf., compare; deriv., derivative; equiv., equivalent; imit., imitative; obl., oblique; r., replacing; s., stem; sp., spelling, spelled; resp., respelling, respelled; trans., translation; ?, origin unknown; *, unattested; ‡, probably earlier than. See the full key inside the front cover.

tab•la•ture (tab′lə chər, -cho͝or′), *n.* **1.** *Music.* any of various systems of music notation using letters, numbers, or other signs to indicate the strings, frets, keys, etc., to be played. **2.** a tabular space, surface, or structure. [1565–75; < MF, Latinization (influenced by L *tabula* board) of It *intavolatura*, deriv. of *intavolare* to put on a board, score]

ta•ble (tā′bəl), *n., v.,* **-bled, -bling,** *adj.* —*n.* **1.** an article of furniture consisting of a flat, slablike top supported on one or more legs or other supports: *a kitchen table; an operating table; a pool table.* **2.** such a piece of furniture specifically used for serving food to those seated at it. **3.** the food placed on a table to be eaten: *She sets a good table.* **4.** a group of persons at a table, as for a meal, game, or business transaction. **5.** a gaming table. **6.** a flat or plane surface; a level area. **7.** a tableland or plateau. **8.** a concise list or guide: *a table of contents.* **9.** an arrangement of words, numbers, or signs, or combinations of them, as in parallel columns, to exhibit a set of facts or relations in a definite, compact, and comprehensive form; a synopsis or scheme. **10.** (*cap.*) *Astron.* the constellation Mensa. **11.** a flat and relatively thin piece of wood, stone, metal, or other hard substance, esp. one artificially shaped for a particular purpose. **12.** *Archit.* **a.** a course or band, esp. of masonry, having a distinctive form or position. **b.** a distinctively treated surface on a wall. **13.** a smooth, flat board or slab on which inscriptions may be put. **14. tables, a.** the tablets on which certain collections of laws were anciently inscribed: *the tables of the Decalogue.* **b.** the laws themselves. **15.** *Anat.* the inner or outer hard layer or any of the flat bones of the skull. **16.** *Music.* a sounding board. **17.** *Jewelry.* **a.** the upper horizontal surface of a faceted gem. **b.** a gem with such a surface. **18. on the table,** *Parl. Proc.* **a.** *U.S.* postponed. **b.** *Brit.* submitted for consideration. **19. turn the tables,** to cause a reversal of an existing situation, esp. with regard to gaining the upper hand over a competitor, rival, antagonist, etc.: *Fortune turned the tables and we won. We turned the tables on them and undersold them by 50 percent.* **20. under the table, a.** drunk. **b.** as a bribe; secretly: *She gave money under the table to get the apartment.* **21. wait (on) table,** to work as a waiter or waitress: *He worked his way through college by waiting table.* Also, **wait tables.** —*v.t.* **22.** to place (a card, money, etc.) on a table. **23.** to enter in or form into a table or list. **24.** *Parl. Proc.* **a.** *Chiefly U.S.* to lay aside (a proposal, resolution, etc.) for future discussion, usually with a view to postponing or shelving the matter indefinitely. **b.** *Brit.* to present (a proposal, resolution, etc.) for discussion. —*adj.* **25.** of, pertaining to, or for use on a table: *a table lamp.* **26.** suitable for serving at a table or for eating or drinking: *table grapes.* [bef. 900; (n.) ME; OE *tabule,* var. of *tabula* < L: plank, tablet; (v.) late ME: to record on a table, entertain at table, deriv. of the n.] —**ta′ble•less,** *adj.*

tab•leau (ta blō′, tab′lō), *n., pl.* **tab•leaux** (ta blōz′, tab′lōz), **tab•leaus. 1.** a picture, as of a scene. **2.** a picturesque grouping of persons or objects; a striking scene. **3.** a representation of a picture, statue, scene, etc., by one or more persons suitably costumed and posed. **4.** *Solitaire.* the portion of a layout to which one may add cards according to suit or denomination. [1690–1700; < F: board, picture, MF *tablel,* dim. of *table* TABLE]

tableau′ cur′tain, *Theat.* a curtain, often used as an act curtain, designed to be drawn aside and up to give a festooned or draped effect. [1945–50]

ta•bleau vi•vant (tᴀ blō vē väN′), *pl.* ***ta•bleaux vi•vants*** (tᴀ blō vē väN′). *French.* tableau (def. 3). [lit., living picture]

ta′ble board′, daily meals provided for pay. [1475–85]

ta•ble•cloth (tā′bəl klôth′, -kloth′), *n., pl.* **-cloths** (-klôthz′, -klothz′, -klôths′, -kloths′). a cloth for covering the top of a table, esp. during a meal. [1425–75; late ME; see TABLE, CLOTH]

ta′ble corn′, *Chiefly Eastern U.S.* sweet corn.

ta′ble cut′, *Jewelry.* **1.** a variety of step cut in which a very large table is joined to the girdle with a bevel. **2.** (formerly) a diamond cut in which the natural octahedral crystal of the diamond is used intact, the only cutting being in the formation of the table and culet. [1680–90]

ta•ble d'hôte (tä′bəl dōt′, tab′əl; *Fr.* tᴀblᵊ dōt′), *pl.* **ta•bles d'hôte** (tä′bəlz dōt′, tab′əlz; *Fr.* tᴀblᵊ dōt′). a meal of preselected courses served at a fixed time and price to the guests at a hotel or restaurant. Cf. **à la carte, prix fixe.** [1610–20; < F: lit., the host's table]

ta•ble•ful (tā′bəl fo͝ol′), *n., pl.* **-fuls. 1.** the number of persons that can be seated at a table. **2.** the amount of food, dishes, etc., that a table can hold. [1525–35; TABLE + -FUL]
—**Usage.** See **-ful.**

ta•ble-hop (tā′bəl hop′), *v.i.,* **-hopped, -hop•ping.** *Informal.* to move about in a restaurant, nightclub, or the like, chatting with people at various tables. [1940–45; TABLE + HOP¹] —**ta′ble-hop′per,** *n.*

ta•ble•land (tā′bəl land′), *n.* an elevated and generally level region of considerable extent; plateau. [1690–1700; TABLE + -LAND]

ta′ble lin′en, tablecloths, napkins, etc., used in setting a table. [1670–80]

Ta′ble Moun′tain, a mountain in the Republic of South Africa, near Cape Town. 3550 ft. (1080 m).

ta′ble salt′, salt (def. 1). [1875–80]

ta•ble•spoon (tā′bəl spo͞on′), *n.* **1.** a spoon larger than a teaspoon or a dessert spoon, used in serving food at the table and as a standard measuring unit in recipes. **2.** a tablespoonful. [1755–65; TABLE + SPOON]

ta•ble•spoon•ful (tā′bəl spo͞on fo͝ol′), *n., pl.* **-fuls. 1.** the amount a tablespoon can hold. **2.** a volumetric measure equal to ½ fluid ounce (14.8 ml), or three teaspoonfuls. *Abbr.:* T., tbs., tbsp. [1765–75; TABLESPOON + -FUL]
—**Usage.** See **-ful.**

ta′ble stake′, *Poker.* **1.** a stake that a player places on the table at the beginning of a game that may not be changed once the deal begins. **2. table stakes,** the limiting of a bet to the amount remaining in a player's table stake during a game.

tab•let (tab′lit), *n., v.,* **-let•ed, -let•ing** or **-let•ted, -let•ting.** —*n.* **1.** a number of sheets of writing paper, business forms, etc., fastened together at the edge; pad. **2.** a flat slab or surface, esp. one bearing or intended to bear an inscription, carving, or the like. **3.** a thin, flat leaf or sheet of slate, wax-coated wood, or other rigid material, used for writing or marking on, esp. one of a pair or set hinged or otherwise fastened together. **4. tablets,** the set as a whole. **5.** a small, flat, or flattish cake or piece of some solid or solidified substance, as a drug, chemical, or soap. —*v.t.* **6.** to furnish or mark with a tablet or plaque. **7.** to mark or inscribe (memoranda, notes, etc.) on a tablet. **8.** to form into tablets, cakes, pellets, etc. [1275–1325; ME *tablette* < MF *tablete.* See TABLE, -ET]
—**Syn. 2.** plaque.

ta′ble talk′, 1. informal conversation at meals. **2.** a subject that is considered appropriate for conversation at meals. [1560–70]

tab′let chair′, a chair with one arm extending and expanding into a writing surface.

ta′ble ten′nis, a game resembling tennis, played on a table with small paddles and a hollow celluloid or plastic ball. See illus. under **racket².** [1900–05]

ta•ble•top (tā′bəl top′), *n.* **1.** a surface forming or suggesting the top of a table. **2.** a photograph of an arrangement of objects on top of a table. —*adj.* **3.** intended for use on the top of a table or the like. **4.** noting or pertaining to an arrangement of objects, esp. miniatures or models, as would be appropriate to the top of a table. [1800–10; TABLE + TOP¹]

ta′ble tri′pod, *Motion Pictures, Television.* a low mount or stand for a camera.

ta•ble•ware (tā′bəl wâr′), *n.* the dishes, utensils, etc., used at the table. [1825–35; TABLE + WARE¹]

ta′ble wine′, a wine that contains not more than 14 percent alcohol and is usually served as an accompaniment to food. [1820–30]

tab•li•num (ta blī′nəm), *n., pl.* **-na** (-nə). (in an ancient Roman house) a large, open room at the side of the peristyle farthest from the main entrance. [1820–30; < L *tab(u)līnum,* equiv. to *tabula* (see TABLE) + *-inum,* neut. of *-inus* -INE¹]

tab•loid (tab′loid), *n.* **1.** a newspaper whose pages, usually five columns wide, are about one-half the size of a standard-sized newspaper page. **2.** a newspaper this size concentrating on sensational and lurid news, usually heavily illustrated. **3.** a short form or version; condensation; synopsis; summary. —*adj.* **4.** compressed or condensed in or as if in a tabloid: *a tabloid article; a tabloid account of the adventure.* **5.** luridly or vulgarly sensational. [1905–10; TABL(ET) + -OID] —**tab′loid•ism,** *n.*

ta•boo (tə bo͞o′, ta-), *adj., n., pl.* **-boos,** *v.,* **-booed, -boo•ing.** —*adj.* **1.** proscribed by society as improper or unacceptable: *taboo words.* **2.** (among the Polynesians and other peoples of the South Pacific) separated or set apart as sacred; forbidden for general use; placed under a prohibition or ban. —*n.* **3.** a prohibition or interdiction of anything; exclusion from use or practice. **4.** (among the Polynesians and other peoples of the South Pacific) **a.** the system, practice, or act whereby things are set apart as sacred, forbidden for general use, or placed under a prohibition or interdiction. **b.** the condition of being so set apart, forbidden, or interdicted. **5.** exclusion from social relations; ostracism. —*v.t.* **6.** to put under a taboo; prohibit or forbid. **7.** to ostracize (a person, group, etc.). Also, **tabu.** [1770–80; < Tongan *tapu* or Fijian *tabu* forbidden, prohibited]
—**Syn. 1.** prohibited, banned. **3.** ban, proscription, embargo. **6.** See **forbid.**

ta•boo•li (tə bo͞o′lē), *n.* tabbouleh.

ta•bor (tā′bər), *n.* **1.** a small drum formerly used to accompany oneself on a pipe or fife. —*v.i.* **2.** to play upon or as if upon a tabor; drum. —*v.t.* **3.** to strike or beat, as on a tabor. Also, **taber, ta′bour.** [1250–1300; (n.) ME < OF *tab(o)ur;* see TAMBOUR; (v.) ME *tabouren,* deriv. of the n. or < OF *taborer,* deriv. of *tab(o)ur*] —**ta′bor•er, ta′bour•er,** *n.*

T, **tabor** (def. 1)

Ta•bor (tā′bər), *n.* **Mount,** a mountain in N Israel, E of Nazareth. 1929 ft. (588 m).

Ta•bo•ra (tə bôr′ə, -bōr′ə), *n.* a city in NW Tanzania. 21,012.

tab•o•ret (tab′ər it, tab′ə ret′, -rā′), *n.* **1.** a low seat without back or arms, for one person; stool. **2.** a frame for embroidery. **3.** a small, usually portable stand, cabinet, or chest of drawers, as for holding work supplies. **4.** a small tabor. Also, **tab′ou•ret.** [1650–60; < F *tabouret* lit., small drum. See TABOR, -ET]

tab•o•rin (tab′ər in), *n.* a small tabor. [1490–1500; < MF *tabourin.* See TABOR, -IN¹]

Ta•bor•ite (tā′bə rīt′), *n.* (in the 15th century) a member of the militant body of Hussites maintaining a strict literal interpretation of the Scriptures. [1640–50; named after *Tabor,* city in Bohemia where the radical party of Hussites had its headquarters; see -ITE¹]

ta•bou•leh (tə bo͞o′lə, -lē), *n.* tabbouleh. Also, **ta•bou′•li.**

tab•ret (tab′rit, tā′brit), *n.* **1.** a small tabor. **2.** *Obs.* a person who plays upon this instrument. [1350–1400; ME *taberett,* equiv. to *taber* (var. of TABOR) + *-ett* -ET]

Ta•briz (tä brēz′, tə-), *n.* a city in and the capital of Eastern Azerbaijan province, in NW Iran. 403,413.

ta•bu (tə bo͞o′, ta-), *adj., n., v.t.* taboo.

tab•u•lar (tab′yə lər), *adj.* **1.** of, pertaining to, or arranged in a table or systematic arrangement by columns, rows, etc., as statistics. **2.** ascertained from or computed by the use of tables. **3.** having the form of a table, tablet, or tablature. **4.** flat and expansive, as tableland or a plateau. [1650–60; < L *tabulāris* pertaining to a board or tablet. See TABLE, -AR¹] —**tab′u•lar•ly,** *adv.*

ta•bu•la ra•sa (tab′yə lə rä′sə, -zə, rā′-; *Lat.* tä′bo͞o-lä′ rä′sä), *pl.* **ta•bu•lae ra•sae** (tab′yə lē′ rä′sē, -zē, rā′-; *Lat.* tä′bo͞o lī′ rä′sī). **1.** a mind not yet affected by experiences, impressions, etc. **2.** anything existing undisturbed in its original pure state. [1525–35; < L *tabula rāsa* scraped tablet, clean slate]

tab•u•lar•ize (tab′yə lə rīz′), *v.t.,* **-ized, -iz•ing.** to tabulate. Also, *esp. Brit.,* **tab′u•lar•ise′.** [1850–55; TABULAR + -IZE] —**tab′u•lar•i•za′tion,** *n.*

tab•u•late (*v.* tab′yə lāt′; *adj.* tab′yə lit, -lāt′), *v.,* **-lat•ed, -lat•ing,** *adj.* —*v.t.* **1.** to put or arrange in a tabular, systematic, or condensed form; formulate tabularly. —*v.i.* **2.** tab¹ (def. 14). —*adj.* **3.** shaped like a table or tablet; tabular. **4.** having transverse septae, as certain corals. [1590–1600; (adj.) < LL *tabulātus,* ptp. of *tabulāre* to fit with planks, floor; see TABLE, -ATE¹; (v.) < L *tabul(a),* for TABLE + -ATE¹] —**tab′u•la•ble,** *adj.* —**tab′u•la′tion,** *n.*
—**Syn. 1.** order, rank, sort, group, classify.

tab•u•la•tor (tab′yə lā′tər), *n.* **1.** a person or thing that tabulates. **2.** tab¹ (def. 7). [1880–85; TABULATE + -OR²]

tac•a•ma•hac (tak′ə mə hak′), *n.* **1.** any of several resinous substances, used in incenses, ointments, etc. **2.** any tree, as of the genera *Bursera* and *Populus,* yielding such a product. **3.** See **balsam poplar.** Also, **tac•a•ma•hac•a** (tak′ə mə hak′ə), **tacmahack.** [1570–80; < MexSp *tecama(ha)ca* < Nahuatl *tecamac* resin used in medicine]

tace (tas, tās), *n. Armor.* tasset. [var. of *tasse;* see TASSET]

ta•cet (tä′ket, tas′it, tā′sit), *v. imperative. Music.* be silent (directing an instrument or voice not to play or sing). [1715–25; < L: lit., (it) is silent]

tach (tak), *n. Informal.* tachometer. [1925–30; by shortening]

tache (tach), *n. Archaic.* a buckle; clasp. [1400–50; late ME < MF < Gmc. See TACK¹]

tach′i•na fly′ (tak′ə nə), any of numerous dipterous insects of the family Tachinidae, the larvae of which are parasitic on caterpillars, beetles, and other insects. [< NL *Tachina* genus of flies, n. use of Gk *tachinē,* fem. of *tachinós* swift, equiv. to *tach(ýs)* swift + *-inē,* fem. of *-inos* -INE¹]

Ta Ch'ing (dä′ ching′), Ch'ing.

tach•i•ol (tak′ē ôl′, -ol′), *n. Chem.* See **silver fluoride.** [TACHY- + -OL¹]

tach•ism (tash′iz əm), *n.* (*sometimes cap.*) See **action painting** (def. 1). Also, **ta•chisme** (*Fr.* tᴀ shēs′mᵊ). [1950–55; < F *tachisme,* equiv. to *tache* spot, (< VL **tacca,* prob. < Goth *taikns* mark, akin to TOKEN) + *-isme* -ISM] —**tach′ist, ta•chiste** (*Fr.* tᴀ shēst′), *n., adj.*

ta•chis•to•scope (tə kis′tə skōp′), *n. Psychol.* an apparatus for use in exposing visual stimuli, as pictures, letters, or words, for an extremely brief period, used chiefly to assess visual perception or to increase reading speed. [1905–10; < Gk *táchist(os),* superl. of *tachýs* swift + -O- + SCOPE] —**ta•chis•to•scop•ic** (tə kis′tə skop′ik), *adj.*

tacho-, a combining form meaning "speed," used in the formation of compound words: *tachometer.* Cf. **tachy-.** [comb. form repr. Gk *táchos;* akin to *tachýs* swift]

tach•o•gram (tak′ə gram′), *n.* the record produced by the action of a tachometer. Also, **tachograph.** [TACHO- + -GRAM¹]

tach•o•graph (tak′ə graf′, -gräf′), *n.* **1.** a recording tachometer. **2.** tachogram. [TACHO- + -GRAPH]

ta•chom•e•ter (ta kom′i tər, tə-), *n.* **1.** any of various instruments for measuring or indicating velocity or speed, as of a machine, a river, or the blood. **2.** an instrument measuring revolutions per minute, as of an engine. [1800–10; TACHO- + -METER] —**tach•o•met•ri•cal•ly** (tak′ə me′trik lē), *adv.* —**ta•chom′e•try,** *n.*

tachy-, a combining form meaning "swift," used in the formation of compound words: *tachygraphy.* Cf. **tacho-.** [< Gk, comb. form of *tachýs*]

tach•y•car•di•a (tak′i kär′dē ə), *n. Med.* excessively rapid heartbeat. [1885–90; TACHY- + -CARDIA]

tach•y•graph (tak′i graf′, -gräf′), *n.* **1.** tachygraphic writing. **2.** a person who writes or is skilled in writing tachygraphy. [1800–10; TACHY- + -GRAPH]

ta•chyg•ra•phy (ta kig′rə fē, tə-), *n.* shorthand, esp. the ancient Greek and Roman handwriting used for rapid stenography and writing. [1635–45; TACHY- + -GRAPHY] —**ta•chyg′ra•pher, ta•chyg′ra•phist,** *n.* —**tach•y•graph•ic** (tak′i graf′ik), **tach′y•graph′i•cal,** *adj.* —**tach′y•graph′i•cal•ly,** *adv.*

CONCISE PRONUNCIATION KEY: *act, cāpe, dâre, pärt; set, ēqual; if, īce; ox, ōver, ôrder, oil, bo͝ok, bo͞ot, out; up, ûrge; child; sing; shoe; thin, that;* zh as in *treasure.* ə = *a* as in *alone, e* as in *system, i* as in *easily, o* as in *gallop, u* as in *circus;* ᵊ as in *fire* (fīᵊr), *hour* (ouᵊr). l and n can serve as syllabic consonants, as in *cradle* (krād′l), and *button* (but′n). See the full key inside the front cover.

tach·y·lyte (tak′ə līt′), *n. Petrog.* a black, glassy form of basalt, readily fusible and of a high luster. Also, **tach′y·lite′.** [1865–70; TACHY- + -LYTE[2]] —**tach·y·lit·ic** (tak′ə lit′ik), *adj.*

ta·chym·e·ter (ta kim′i tər, tə-), *n. Survey.* any of several instruments for rapidly determining distances, directions, and differences of elevation. [1855–60; TACHY- + -METER] —**ta·chym′e·try,** *n.*

tach·y·on (tak′ē on′), *n. Physics.* a hypothetical particle that travels faster than the speed of light. [1967; TACHY- + -ON[1]]

tach·y·phy·lax·is (tak′ə fi lak′sis), *n.* **1.** *Med.* immediate, temporary immunization against the effects of injection of a toxic extract owing to previous small injections of the same extract. **2.** a decreased response to a medicine given over a period of time so that larger doses are required to produce the same response. Also, **tach·y·phy·lax·i·a** (tak′ə fi lak′sē ə). [TACHY- + Gk *phýlaxis* a guarding, equiv. to *phylak-* (s. of *phylássein* to guard) + *-sis* -SIS] —**tach·y·phy·lac·tic** (tak′ə fi lak′tik), *adj.*

tach·yp·ne·a (tak′ip nē′ə, tak′i nē′ə), *n. Med.* excessively rapid respiration. Also, **tach′yp·noe′a.** [1895–1900; TACHY- + -PNEA] —**tach′yp·ne′ic,** *adj.*

tach·y·tel·ic (tak′i tel′ik), *adj. Biol.* of or pertaining to evolution at a rate faster than the standard for a given group of plants or animals. Cf. **bradytelic, horotelic.** [TACHY- + TELIC] —**tach·y·tel·y** (tak′i tel′ē), *n.*

tac·it (tas′it), *adj.* **1.** understood without being openly expressed; implied: *tacit approval.* **2.** silent; saying nothing: *a tacit partner.* **3.** unvoiced or unspoken: *a tacit prayer.* [1595–1605; < L *tacitus* silent, ptp. of *tacēre* to be silent (c. Goth *thahan;* akin to ON *thegja*)] —**tac′·it·ly,** *adv.* —**tac′it·ness,** *n.*
—**Syn. 1.** unexpressed, unspoken, unsaid, implicit.
—**Ant. 1.** expressed.

Tac·i·te·an (tas′i tē′ən), *adj.* of, pertaining to, or characteristic of Publius Cornelius Tacitus. [1885–90; TACIT(US) + -EAN]

tac·i·turn (tas′i tûrn′), *adj.* **1.** inclined to silence; reserved in speech; reluctant to join in conversation. **2.** dour, stern, and silent in expression and manner. [1765–75; < L *taciturnus,* quiet, maintaining silence, equiv. to *tacit(us)* silent (see TACIT) + *-urnus* adj. suffix of time] —**tac′i·turn′ly,** *adv.*
—**Syn. 1.** silent, uncommunicative, reticent, quiet.

tac·i·tur·ni·ty (tas′i tûr′ni tē), *n.* **1.** the state or quality of being reserved or reticent in conversation. **2.** *Scots Law.* the relinquishing of a legal right through an unduly long delay, as by the silence of the creditor. [1400–50; late ME < L *taciturnitās,* equiv. to *taciturn(us)* TACITURN + *-itās* -ITY]

Tac·i·tus (tas′i təs), *n.* **Pub·li·us Cornelius** (pub′lē-əs), A.D. c55–c120, Roman historian.

tack[1] (tak), *n.* **1.** a short, sharp-pointed nail, usually with a flat, broad head. **2.** *Naut.* **a.** a rope for extending the lower forward corner of a course. **b.** the lower forward corner of a course or fore-and-aft sail. See diag. under **sail. c.** the heading of a sailing vessel, when sailing close-hauled, with reference to the wind direction. **d.** a course run obliquely against the wind. **e.** one of the series of straight runs that make up the zigzag course of a ship proceeding to windward. **3.** a course of action or conduct, esp. one differing from some preceding or other course. **4.** one of the movements of a zigzag course on land. **5.** a stitch, esp. a long stitch used in fastening seams, preparatory to a more thorough sewing. **6.** a fastening, esp. of a temporary kind. **7.** stickiness, as of nearly dry paint or glue or of a printing ink or gummed tape; adhesiveness. **8.** the gear used in equipping a horse, including saddle, bridle, martingale, etc. **9. on the wrong tack,** under a misapprehension; in error; astray: *His line of questioning began on the wrong tack.* —*v.t.* **10.** to fasten by a tack or tacks: *to tack a rug to the floor.* **11.** to secure by some slight or temporary fastening. **12.** to join together; unite; combine. **13.** to attach as something supplementary; append; annex (often fol. by *on* or *onto*). **14.** *Naut.* **a.** to change the course of (a sailing vessel) to the opposite tack. **b.** to navigate (a sailing vessel) by a series of tacks. **15.** to equip (a horse) with tack. —*v.i.* **16.** *Naut.* **a.** to change the course of a sailing vessel by bringing the head into the wind and then causing it to fall off on the other side: *He ordered us to tack at once.* **b.** (of a sailing vessel) to change course in this way. **c.** to proceed to windward by a series of courses as close to the wind as the vessel will sail. **17.** to take or follow a zigzag course or route. **18.** to change one's course of action, conduct, ideas, etc. **19.** to equip a horse with tack (usually fol. by *up*): *Please tack up quickly.* [1300–50; (n.) ME *tak* buckle, clasp, nail (later, tack); c. G *Zacke* prong, D *tak* twig; (v.) ME *tacken* to attach, deriv. of the n.; see TACHE, ATTACH] —**tack′·er,** *n.* —**tack′less,** *adj.*
—**Syn. 13.** affix, fasten, add.

tack[2] (tak), *n.* food; fare. [1740–50; orig. uncert.]

tack[3] (tak), *n. Scot. and North Eng.* **1.** a lease, esp. on farmland. **2.** a rented pasture. **3.** a catch, haul, or take of fish. [1250–1300; ME *tak* < ON *tak* goods, seizure, grasp. See TAKE]

tack·board (tak′bôrd′, -bōrd′), *n.* a large board, usually made of cork or soft wood, on which notices can be tacked. Also, **tack′ board′.** [1905–10; TACK[1] + BOARD]

tack′ claw′, a small hand tool having a handle with a claw at one end for removing tacks. [1875–80]

tack·et (tak′it), *n. Brit. Dial.* a nail or tack, esp. a hobnail. [1275–1325; ME *taket.* See TACK[1], -ET] —**tack′·et·ed,** *adj.*

tack′ ham′mer, a light hammer for driving tacks, often magnetized to hold the tack to the head. See illus. under **hammer.** [1885–90]

tack·le (tak′əl *or, for 2–4,* tā′kəl), *n., v.,* **-led, -ling.** —*n.* **1.** equipment, apparatus, or gear, esp. for fishing: *fishing tackle.* **2.** a mechanism or apparatus, as a rope and block or a combination of ropes and blocks, for hoisting, lowering, and shifting objects or materials; purchase. **3.** any system of leverage using several pulleys. **4.** *Naut.* the gear and running rigging for handling a ship or performing some task on a ship. **5.** an act of tackling, as in football; a seizing, grasping, or bringing down. **6.** *Football.* **a.** either of the linemen stationed between a guard and an end. **b.** the position played by this lineman. **7.** (formerly) tack[1] (def. 8). —*v.t.* **8.** to undertake to handle, master, solve, etc.: *to tackle a difficult problem.* **9.** to deal with (a person) on some problem, issue, etc. **10.** to harness (a horse). **11.** *Football.* to seize, stop, or throw down (a ball-carrier). **12.** *Soccer, Field Hockey.* to block or impede the movement or progress of (an opponent having the ball) with the result of depriving the opponent of the ball. **13.** to seize suddenly, esp. in order to stop. —*v.i.* **14.** *Football.* to tackle an opponent having the ball. [1200–50; ME *takel* gear, apparatus < MLG; akin to TAKE] —**tack′ler,** *n.*

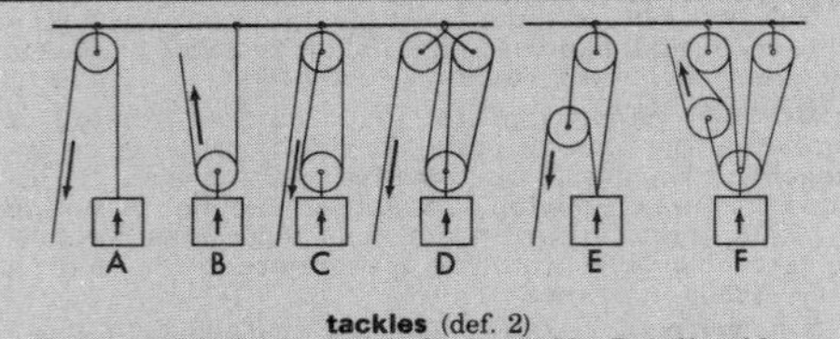

tackles (def. 2)
A, single whip; B, runner; C, gun tackle; D, luff tackle; E, single Spanish burton; F, double Spanish burton

tack·ling (tak′ling), *n. Archaic.* equipment; tackle. [1375–1425; late ME; see TACKLE, -ING[1]]

tack′ room′, a room in or near a stable for storing saddles, harnesses, and other tack. [1955–60]

tack-weld (tak′weld′), *v.t.* to join (pieces of metal) with a number of small welds spaced some distance apart.

tack·y[1] (tak′ē), *adj.,* **tack·i·er, tack·i·est.** sticky to the touch; adhesive. [1780–90; TACK[1] + -Y[1]] —**tack′i·ness,** *n.*

tack·y[2] (tak′ē), *adj.,* **tack·i·er, tack·i·est. 1.** not tasteful or fashionable; dowdy. **2.** shabby in appearance; shoddy: *a tacky, jerry-built housing development.* **3.** crass; cheaply vulgar; tasteless; crude. **4.** gaudy; flashy; showy. [1880–85, *Amer.*; appar. identical with earlier *tack(e)y* small horse, pony, poor farmer; of obscure orig.] —**tack′i·ness,** *n.*

Ta·clo·ban (tä klō′bän), *n.* a seaport on NE Leyte, in the central Philippines. 102,523.

tac·ma·hack (tak′mə hak′), *n.* tacamahac.

Tac·na-A·ri·ca (tak′nə ə rē′kə; *Sp.* täk′nä ä Rē′kä), *n.* a maritime region in W South America: long in dispute between Chile and Peru; annexed by Chile 1883; divided as a result of arbitration 1929 into a Peruvian department **(Tac′na)** and a Chilean department **(Arica).**

ta·co (tä′kō; *Sp.* tä′kô), *n., pl.* **-cos** (-kōz; *Sp.* -kôs). *Mexican Cookery.* an often crisply fried tortilla folded over and filled, as with seasoned chopped meat, lettuce, tomatoes, and cheese. [1930–35; < MexSp; Sp: wadding, plug, prob. of expressive origin]

Ta·co·ma (tə kō′mə), *n.* **1.** a seaport in W Washington, on Puget Sound. 158,501. **2. Mount.** See **Rainier, Mount.** —**Ta·co′man,** *n.*

tac·o·nite (tak′ə nīt′), *n.* a low-grade iron ore, containing about 27 percent iron and 51 percent silica, found as a hard rock formation in the Lake Superior region. [1890–95, *Amer.*; named after the *Taconic* mountain range (east of the Hudson River); see -ITE[1]]

tact (takt), *n.* **1.** a keen sense of what to say or do to avoid giving offense; skill in dealing with difficult or delicate situations. **2.** a keen sense of what is appropriate, tasteful, or aesthetically pleasing; taste; discrimination. **3.** touch or the sense of touch. [1150–1200; < L *tāctus* sense of touch, equiv. to *tag-,* var. s. of *tangere* to touch + *-tus* suffix of v. action]
—**Syn. 1.** perception, sensitivity; diplomacy, poise.

tact·ful (takt′fəl), *adj.* having or manifesting tact: *a tactful person; a tactful reply.* [1860–65; TACT + -FUL] —**tact′ful·ly,** *adv.* —**tact′ful·ness,** *n.*
—**Syn.** See **diplomatic.**

tac·tic (tak′tik), *n.* **1.** tactics (def. 1). **2.** a system or a detail of tactics. **3.** a plan, procedure, or expedient for promoting a desired end or result. —*adj.* **4.** of or pertaining to arrangement or order; tactical. [1560–70; NL *tacticus* < Gk *taktikós* fit for arranging or ordering, equiv. to *tak-* (base of *tássein* (Attic *táttein*) to arrange, put in order) + *-tikos* -TIC]

tac·ti·cal (tak′ti kəl), *adj.* **1.** of or pertaining to tactics, esp. military or naval tactics. **2.** characterized by skillful tactics or adroit maneuvering or procedure: *tactical movements.* **3.** of or pertaining to a maneuver or plan of action designed as an expedient toward gaining a desired end or temporary advantage. **4.** expedient; calculated. **5.** prudent; politic. [1560–70; TACTIC + -AL[1]] —**tac′ti·cal·ly,** *adv.*

Tac′tical Air′ Command′, a U.S. Air Force command supplying direct air support to U.S. Army ground combat units.

tac′tical u′nit, *Mil.* a group organized to function in combat as a self-contained unit. [1875–80]

tac′tical wire′, *Mil.* wire entanglements used to break up attacking enemy formations or to keep them within the field of defensive fire.

tac·ti·cian (tak tish′ən), *n.* a person who is adept in planning tactics. [1790–1800; TACTIC + -IAN]

tac·tic·i·ty (tak tis′i tē), *n. Chem.* stereoregularity. [1955–60; TACTIC + -ITY]

tac·tics (tak′tiks), *n.* **1.** (*usually used with a singular v.*) the art or science of disposing military or naval forces for battle and maneuvering them in battle. **2.** (*used with a plural v.*) the maneuvers themselves. **3.** (*used with a singular v.*) any mode of procedure for gaining advantage or success. **4.** (*usually used with a singular v.*) *Ling.* **a.** the patterns in which the elements of a given level or stratum in a language may combine to form larger constructions. **b.** the study and description of such patterns. [1620–30; see TACTIC, -ICS]
—**Syn. 1.** See **strategy.**

tac·tile (tak′til, -tīl), *adj.* **1.** of, pertaining to, endowed with, or affecting the sense of touch. **2.** perceptible to the touch; tangible. [1605–15; < L *tāctilis* tangible, equiv. to *tāct(us)* (ptp. of *tangere* to touch) + *-ilis* -ILE] —**tac·til·i·ty** (tak til′i tē), *n.*

tac′tile cor′puscle, an oval sense organ made of flattened cells and encapsulated nerve endings, occurring in hairless skin, as the tips of the fingers and toes, and functioning as a touch receptor. Also called **Meissner's corpuscle.** [1870–75]

tac·tion (tak′shən), *n.* touch; contact. [1615–25; < L *tāctiōn-* (s. of *tāctiō*) a touching, equiv. to *tāct(us)* (ptp. of *tangere* to touch) + *-iōn-* -ION]

tact·less (takt′lis), *adj.* lacking tact; showing no tact; undiplomatic; offendingly blunt: *a tactless remark.* [1840–50; TACT + -LESS] —**tact′less·ly,** *adv.* —**tact′·less·ness,** *n.*
—**Syn.** rude, inconsiderate, thoughtless, brash, boorish.

tac·tu·al (tak′cho͞o əl), *adj.* **1.** of or pertaining to the sense of touch. **2.** communicating or imparting the sensation of contact; arising from or due to touch. [1635–45; < L *tāctu(s)* touch (see TACT) + -AL[1]] —**tac′tu·al·ly,** *adv.*

tac·tus (täk′to͝os), *n.* the basic metrical unit in medieval music. [< L *tāctus* touch; see TACT]

Ta·cu·ba·ya (tä′ko͞o vä′yä), *n.* a former city in the Federal District of Mexico: now a SW district of Mexico City; national observatory.

tad (tad), *n. Informal.* **1.** a small child, esp. a boy. **2.** a very small amount or degree; bit: *Please shift your chair a tad to the right. The frosting could use a tad more vanilla.* [1875–80, *Amer.*, for def. 1; 1935–40, *Amer.*, for def. 2; perh. shortening of TADPOLE]

Tad (tad), *n.* a male given name, form of **Thaddeus** or **Theodore.**

ta-da (tə dä′), *interj.* (used as a jovial interjection in making an announcement, taking a bow, etc.). Also, **ta-dah′.**

Tad·e·ma (tad′ə mə), *n.* **Sir Lawrence Alma-.** See **Alma-Tadema, Sir Lawrence.**

Ta·djik (tä jik′, -jēk′; *Russ.* tu jik′), *n.* Tajik.

Tad·mor (tad′môr, täd′-), *n.* Biblical name of **Palmyra.**

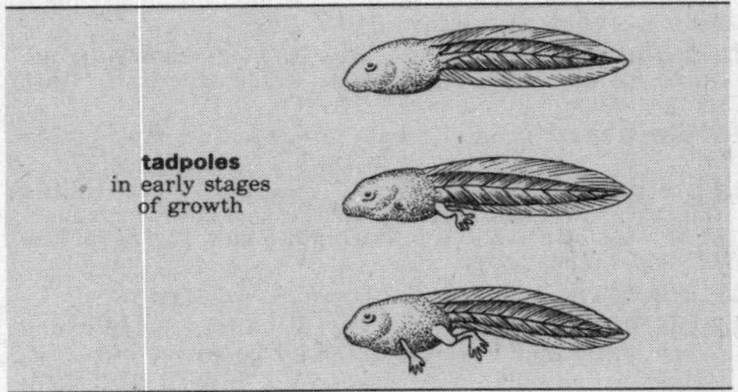
tadpoles in early stages of growth

tad·pole (tad′pōl), *n.* the aquatic larva or immature form of frogs and toads, esp. after the development of the internal gills and before the appearance of the forelimbs and the resorption of the tail. [1400–50; late ME *tad(de)pol,* equiv. to *tad(de)* TOAD + *pol* POLL[1] (head)]

Ta·dzhik (tä jik′, -jēk′; *Russ.* tu jik′), *n.* Tajik.

Ta·dzhik·i·stan (tə jik′ə stan′, -stän′, -jē′kə-, tä-; *Russ.* tə ji kyi stän′), *n.* a republic in central Asia, N of Afghanistan. 5,112,000; 55,240 sq. mi. (143,100 sq. km). *Cap.:* Dushanbe. Also, **Tajikistan.** Formerly, **Tadzhik So′viet So′cialist Repub′lic.**

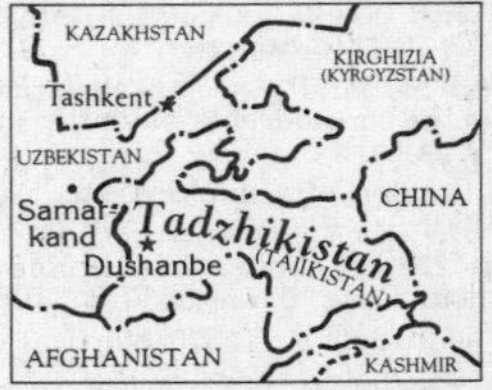

tae (tā), *prep. Scot.* to.

Tae·gu (tī′go͞o′), *n.* a city in SE South Korea: commercial center. 1,311,078.

Tae·jon (tī′jon′), *n.* a city in W South Korea. 506,703.

tae kwon do (tī′ kwon′ dō′), a Korean martial art, a particularly aggressive form of karate, that utilizes punches, jabs, chops, blocking and choking moves, and especially powerful, leaping kicks. Also, **tae′kwon′do′.**

CONCISE ETYMOLOGY KEY: <, descended or borrowed from; >, whence; b., blend of, blended; c., cognate with; cf., compare; deriv., derivative; equiv., equivalent; imit., imitative; obl., oblique; r., replacing; s., stem; sp., spelling, spelled; resp., respelling, respelled; trans., translation; ?, origin unknown; *, unattested; ‡, probably earlier than. See the full key inside the front cover.

[1965–70; < Korean *t'aekwŏndo,* equiv. to *t'ae-* trample (< MChin, akin to Chin *tái*) + *kwŏn* fist (< MChin, akin to Chin *quán*) + *-do,* comb. form of *to* way (< MChin, akin to Chin *dào*)]

tael (tāl), *n.* **1.** liang. **2.** any of various other similar units of weight in the Far East. **3.** a former Chinese money of account, being the value of this weight of standard silver. [1580–90; < Pg < Malay *tahil* liang]

ta'en (tān), *v. Archaic.* taken. [ME *ytan, tane, tain,* contraction of TAKEN]

tae·ni·a (tē′nē ə), *n., pl.* **-ni·ae** (-nē ē′). **1.** *Class. Antiq.* a headband or fillet. **2.** *Archit.* (on a Doric entablature) a fillet or band separating the frieze from the architrave. **3.** *Anat.* a ribbonlike structure, as certain bands of white nerve fibers in the brain. **4.** any tapeworm of the genus *Taenia,* parasitic in humans and other mammals. Also, **tenia.** [1555–65; < L < Gk *tainía* band, ribbon; (in def. 4) < NL, L, as above]

tae·ni·a·cide (tē′nē ə sīd′), *n. Pharm.* an agent that destroys tapeworms. Also, **teniacide.** [1855–60; TAENIA + -CIDE] **—tae′ni·a·cid′al,** *adj.*

tae·ni·a·fuge (tē′nē ə fyo͞oj′), *n. Med.* an agent or medicine for expelling tapeworms from the body. Also, **teniafuge.** [1855–60; TAENIA + -FUGE]

tae·ni·a·sis (tē nī′ə sis), *n. Pathol.* infestation with tapeworms. Also, **teniasis.** [1885–90; TAENI(A) + -ASIS]

taf·fa·rel (taf′ər əl, -ə rel′), *n. Archaic.* taffrail. Also, **taf′fe·rel.** [1615–25; < MD *tafereel,* var. (by dissimilation) of *tafeleel* < F (dial.) *tavlel* TABLEAU]

taf·fe·ta (taf′i tə), *n.* **1.** a medium-weight or lightweight fabric of acetate, nylon, rayon, or silk, usually smooth, crisp, and lustrous, plain-woven, and with a fine crosswise rib effect. **2.** any of various other fabrics of silk, linen, wool, etc., in use at different periods. —*adj.* **3.** of or resembling taffeta. [1325–75; ME *taffata* < ML << Pers *tāftah* silken or linen cloth, n. use of ptp. of *tāftan* to twist, spin]

taf′feta weave′. See **plain weave.**

taff·rail (taf′rāl′, -rəl), *n. Naut.* **1.** the upper part of the stern of a ship. **2.** a rail above the stern of a ship. [1805–15; syncopated var. of TAFFAREL; *-ai-* sp. D *-ee-*]

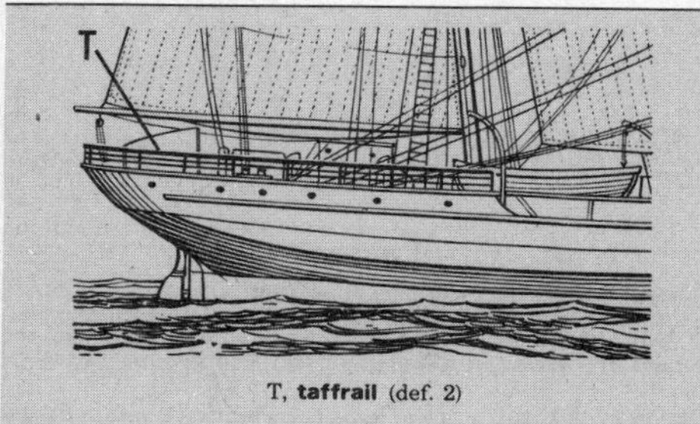

T, **taffrail** (def. 2)

taf·fy (taf′ē), *n.* **1.** a chewy candy made of sugar or molasses boiled down, often with butter, nuts, etc. **2.** *Informal.* flattery. Also, **toffee, toffy.** [1810–20; var. of TOFFEE]

taf′fy ap′ple. See **candy apple.**

taf·i·a (taf′ē ə), *n.* a type of rum made in Haiti from lower grades of molasses, refuse sugar, or the like. Also, **taf′fi·a.** [1755–65, *Amer.*; < West Indian F; aph. var. of *ratafia* RATAFIA]

Ta·fi·lelt (tä fē′lelt, tä′fē lelt′), *n.* an oasis in SE Morocco, ab. 200 sq. mi. (520 sq. km). Also, **Ta·fi·la·let** (tä′fē lä′let).

Taft (taft), *n.* **1. Lo·ra·do** (lə rā′dō), 1860–1936, U.S. sculptor. **2. Robert A(l·phon·so)** (al fon′sō), 1889–1953, U.S. lawyer and political leader (son of William Howard). **3. William Howard,** 1857–1930, 27th president of the U.S. 1909–13; Chief Justice of the U.S. Supreme Court 1921–30.

Taft′-Hart′ley Act′ (taft′härt′lē), an act of the U.S. Congress (1947) that supersedes but continues most of the provisions of the National Labor Relations Act and that, in addition, provides for an eighty-day injunction against strikes that endanger public health and safety and bans closed shops, featherbedding, secondary boycotts, jurisdictional strikes, and certain other union practices.

tag[1] (tag), *n., v.,* **tagged, tag·ging.** —*n.* **1.** a piece or strip of strong paper, plastic, metal, leather, etc., for attaching by one end to something as a mark or label: *The price is on the tag.* **2.** any small hanging or loosely attached part or piece; tatter. **3.** a loop of material sewn on a garment so that it can be hung up. **4.** a metal or plastic tip at the end of a shoelace, cord, or the like. **5.** a license plate for a motor vehicle. **6.** *Angling.* a small piece of tinsel or the like tied to the shank of a hook at the body of an artificial fly. **7.** the tail end or concluding part, as of a proceeding. **8.** the last words of a speech, scene, act, etc., as in a play; a curtain line. **9.** *Computers.* sentinel (def. 3). **10.** an addition to a speech or writing, as the moral of a fable. **11.** a quotation added for special effect. **12.** a descriptive word or phrase applied to a person, group, organization, etc., as a label or means of identification; epithet. **13.** a trite phrase or saying; cliché. **14.** *Slang.* a person's name, nickname, initials, monogram, or symbol. **15.** See **tag question** (def. 1). **16.** a traffic ticket. **17.** a curlicue in writing. **18.** a lock of hair. **19.** a matted lock of wool on a sheep. **20.** *Fox Hunting.* the white tip of the tail of a fox. **21.** *Obs.* the rabble. —*v.t.* **22.** to furnish with a tag or tags; attach a tag to. **23.** to append as a tag, addition, or afterthought to something else. **24.** to attach or give an epithet to; label. **25.** to accuse of a violation, esp. of a traffic law; give a traffic ticket to: *He was tagged for speeding. The police officer tagged the cars for overtime parking.* **26.** to hold answerable or accountable for something; attach blame to: *The pitcher was tagged with the loss of the game.* **27.** to set a price on; fix the cost of: *The dealer tagged the boat at $500 less than the suggested retail price.* **28.** *Informal.* to follow closely: *I tagged him to an old house on the outskirts of town.* **29.** to remove the tags of wool from (a sheep). —*v.i.* **30.** to follow closely; go along or about as a follower: *to tag after someone; to tag along behind someone.* [1375–1425; late ME *tagge* (n.); c. MLG, Norw *tagge,* Sw *tagg* pointed protruding part; akin to TACK[1]] **—tag′ger,** *n.* **—tag′like′,** *adj.*

tag[2] (tag), *n., v.,* **tagged, tag·ging.** —*n.* **1.** a children's game in which one player chases the others in an effort to touch one of them, who then takes the role of pursuer. **2.** *Baseball.* an act or instance of tagging a base runner. —*v.t.* **3.** to touch in or as if in the game of tag. **4.** *Baseball.* **a.** to touch (a base runner) with the ball held in the hand or glove. **b.** to hit (a pitched ball) solidly. **c.** to make a number of hits or runs as specified in batting against (a pitcher): *They tagged him for two hits in the first and three hits and two runs in the third.* **5.** *Boxing.* to strike (an opponent) with a powerful blow. **6. tag up,** *Baseball.* (of a base runner) to touch the base occupied before attempting to advance a base, after the catch of a fly ball: *He tagged up and scored from third on a long fly to center.* [1730–40; perh. special use of TAG[1]]

Ta·gāb (tə gäb′), *n.* a city in E Afghanistan. 106,777.

Ta·ga·log (tə gä′ləg, -lôg, tä-), *n., pl.* **-logs,** (*esp. collectively*) **-log** for 1. **1.** a member of a Malayan people native to Luzon, in the Philippines. **2.** the principal language of the Philippines, an Indonesian language of the Austronesian family.

tag·a·long (tag′ə lông′, -long′), *n.* a person or thing that follows the lead or initiative of another. [1930–35; n. use of v. phrase *tag along*]

Tag·a·met (tag′ə met′), *Pharm., Trademark.* a brand of cimetidine.

Ta·gan·rog (tag′ən rog′; *Russ.* tə gun rôk′), *n.* **1.** a seaport in the S Russian Federation in Europe, on the Gulf of Taganrog. 295,000. **2. Gulf of,** an arm of the Sea of Azov.

tag·board (tag′bôrd′, -bōrd′), *n.* a strong cardboard suitable for tags or posters. Also called **oaktag.** [1900–05; TAG[1] + BOARD]

tag′ boat′, a small rowboat usually towed astern of a larger vessel. [1890–95, *Amer.*]

tag′ day′, a day on which contributions to a fund are solicited, each contributor receiving a tag. [1905–10]

tag′ end′, 1. the last or final part of something: *They came in at the tag end of the performance.* **2.** a random scrap, fragment, or remnant. [1810–20]

Tag·gard (tag′ərd), *n.* **Genevieve,** 1894–1948, U.S. poet.

ta·glia·ri·ni (tal′yə rē′nē; *It.* täl′lyä rē′nē), *n.* egg noodles cut in long, flat, slender pieces, narrower than tagliatelle. [< It, equiv. to *tagliar(e)* to cut (< LL *tāliāre;* see TAILOR[1]) + It *-ini,* masc. pl. dim. suffix < L *-īnus* -INE[1]]

ta·glia·tel·le (täl′yə tel′ē, *It.* täl′lyä tel′le), *n.* egg noodles cut in long, flat pieces. [< It: flat noodles, equiv. to *tagliat-* (ptp. s. of *tagliare* to cut < LL *tāliāre;* see TAILOR[1]) + *-elle,* pl. of *-ella* -ELLE]

Ta·glia·vi·ni (täl′yä vē′nē), *n.* **Fer·ruc·cio** (fer ro͞ot′chō), born 1913, Italian tenor.

tag′ line′, 1. the last line of a play, story, speech, etc., used to clarify or dramatize a point. **2.** a phrase or catchword that becomes identified or associated with a person, group, product, etc., through repetition: *Entertainers often develop tag lines, like Ted Lewis's "Is everybody happy?"* **3.** *Mach.* (on a crane) a cable for steadying a suspended bucket at the rear. Also, **tag′line′.** [1935–40]

tag·lock (tag′lok′), *n.* a matted lock of wool or hair. [1605–15; TAG[1] + LOCK[2]]

tag·meme (tag′mēm), *n. Ling.* the basic unit of grammatical analysis in tagmemics, consisting of a correlation between a grammatical function and the class of items that can occur in that function. Cf. **filler** (def. 9), **slot**[1] (def. 3). [1930–35; < Gk *tágm(a)* arrangement (equiv. to *tag-,* base of *tássein* to arrange + *-ma* n. suffix of result) + -EME]

tag·me·mic (tag mē′mik), *adj. Ling.* **1.** of or pertaining to tagmemes. **2.** of or pertaining to tagmemics. [1955–60; TAGMEME + -IC]

tag·me·mics (tag mē′miks), *n.* (*used with a singular v.*) *Ling.* a school of linguistics deriving from American structuralism based on the work of Kenneth Lee Pike and using the tagmeme as the basic unit of grammatical analysis. [1945–50; TAGMEME + -ICS] **—tag·me·mi·cist** (tag mē′mə sist), *n.*

Ta·gore (tə gôr′, -gōr′, tä′gôr), *n.* **Sir Ra·bin·dra·nath** (rə bēn′drə nät′), 1861–1941, Indian poet: Nobel prize 1913.

tag′ ques′tion, *Gram.* **1.** Also called **tag.** a short interrogative structure appended to a statement or command, as *isn't it* in *It's raining, isn't it?, are you* in *You're not going, are you?,* or German *nicht wahr.* **2.** a question formed by appending such a structure to a declarative sentence or command, often inviting confirmation or assent, as *She lives nearby, doesn't she?* or *Sit down, won't you?* [1960–65]

tag·rag (tag′rag′), *n.* **1.** riffraff; rabble. **2.** a tatter. [1575–85; TAG[1] + RAG[1]]

tag′rag and bob′tail. See **ragtag and bobtail.** Also, **tag′, rag′, and bob′tail.**

tag′ sale′. See **garage sale.** [1950–55]

T/Agt, transfer agent. Also, **T. Agt.**

tag′ team′, *Professional Wrestling.* a team of two wrestlers who compete one at a time against either member of another such team, the wrestlers in the ring changing places with those outside by tagging them. [1950–55]

Ta·gus (tā′gəs), *n.* a river in SW Europe, flowing W through central Spain and Portugal to the Atlantic at Lisbon. 566 mi. (910 km) long. Spanish, **Tajo.** Portuguese, **Tejo.**

ta·hi·ni (tə hē′nē, tä-), *n. Middle Eastern Cookery.* a paste made of ground sesame seeds. [1895–1900; < Levantine Ar *ṭaḥīne,* deriv. of *ṭaḥan* grind]

Ta·hi·ti (tə hē′tē, tä-), *n.* the principal island of the Society Islands, in the S Pacific. 79,494; 402 sq. mi. (1041 sq. km). *Cap.:* Papeete.

Ta·hi·tian (tə hē′shən, -tē ən, tä-), *adj.* **1.** of or pertaining to Tahiti, its inhabitants, or their language. —*n.* **2.** a native or inhabitant of Tahiti. **3.** the Polynesian language of Tahiti. [1815–25; TAHITI + -AN]

Ta·hoe (tä′hō), *n.* **Lake,** a lake in E California and W Nevada, in the Sierra Nevada Mountains: resort. ab. 200 sq. mi. (520 sq. km); 6225 ft. (1897 m) above sea level.

tahr (tär), *n.* any of several Old World wild goats of the genus *Hemitragus,* as *H. jemlahicus* **(Himalayan tahr),** introduced into New Zealand, having a long mane and short, stout, recurving horns: most are endangered or threatened in their native regions. Also, **thar.** [1832; < Nepali *thār*]

tah·sil·dar (tə sēl där′), *n.* (in India) a collector for, or official of, the revenue department. Also, **tah·seel·dar′.** [1790–1800; < Urdu < Pers, equiv. to *tahṣīl* collection (< Ar) + *-dār* agent suffix]

tai (tī), *n., pl.* **tai.** any of several sparoid fishes of the Pacific Ocean, as *Pagrus major* **(red tai),** a food fish of Japan. [1615–25; < Japn *ta(w)i,* earlier *tafi*]

Tai (tī, tä′ē), *n.* **1.** a group of languages spoken in SE Asia, including Thai, Lao, and Shan, and thought by some to be related to the Sino-Tibetan languages. **2.** Thai. —*adj.* **3.** of, pertaining to, or characteristic of Tai. **4.** Thai.

Tai·bei (tī′bā′), *n. Pinyin.* Taipei.

t'ai chi ch'uan (tī′ jē′ chwän′, chē′), a Chinese martial art and form of stylized, meditative exercise, characterized by methodically slow circular and stretching movements and positions of bodily balance. Also, **tai′ chi′ chuan′;** *Pinyin,* **tai ji quan** (tī′ jē′ chyän′). Also called **t'ai′ chi′, tai′ chi′, tai′ ji′.** [1960–65; < Chin *tàijí quán* lit., fist of the Great Absolute]

Tai·chow (*Chin.* tī′jō′), *n. Older Spelling.* Taizhou. Also, *Wade-Giles,* **T'ai′chou′.**

Tai·chung (tī′jo͝ong′), *n. Wade-Giles.* a city in and the provincial capital of Taiwan, in the W part. 575,000. Also, **Taizhong.**

Ta·if (tä′if), *n.* a city in W Saudi Arabia. 100,000.

tai·ga (tī′gə, tī gä′), *n.* the coniferous evergreen forests of subarctic lands, covering vast areas of northern North America and Eurasia. [1885–90; < Russ *taigá* < one or more Turkic languages of the Altai Mountain region; cf. Altai, Shor *tayya* forest-covered mountain]

taig·lach (tāg′ləкн, -läкн, tig′-), *n.* (*used with a singular or plural v.*) teiglach.

tail[1] (tāl), *n.* **1.** the hindmost part of an animal, esp. that forming a distinct, flexible appendage to the trunk. **2.** something resembling or suggesting this in shape or position: *the tail of a kite.* **3.** *Astron.* the luminous stream extending from the head of a comet. **4.** the reverse of a coin (opposed to *head*). **5.** *Aeron.* the after portion of an airplane or the like. **6. tails, a.** See **tail coat. b.** the tapering skirts or ends at the back of a coat, esp. a tail coat. **c.** men's full-dress attire. **d.** *Distilling.* alcohol obtained in the final distillation. Cf. **head** (def. 22). **7.** *Slang.* the buttocks or rump. **8.** *Informal.* a person who trails or keeps a close surveillance of another, as a detective or spy: *The police decided to put a tail on the suspect.* **9.** *Informal.* the trail of a fleeing person or animal: *They put a detective on his tail.* **10.** *Slang* (*vulgar*). **a.** coitus. **b.** a woman considered as a sexual object. **11.** the hinder, bottom, or end part of anything; the rear. **12.** a final or concluding part of a sentence, conversation, social gathering, etc.; conclusion; end: *The tail of the speech was boring. Toward the tail of the concert I'd begun to get tired.* **13.** the inferior or unwanted part of anything. **14.** a long braid or tress of hair. **15.** an arrangement of objects or persons extending as or as if a tail. **16.** a line of persons awaiting their turns at something; queue. **17.** a retinue; train. **18.** the lower part of a pool or stream. **19.** the exposed portion of a piece of roofing, as a slate. **20.** *Print., Bookbinding.* the bottom of a page or book. **21.** *Print.* the lower portion of a type, as of *g, y,* or *Q.* **22. turn tail, a.** to turn one's back on, as in aversion or fright. **b.** to run away from difficulty, opposition, etc.; flee: *The sight of superior forces made the attackers turn tail.* **23. with one's tail between one's legs,** utterly humiliated; defeated;

cowed: *They were forced to retreat with their tails between their legs.* —*adj.* **24.** coming from behind: *a tail breeze.* **25.** being in the back or rear: *the tail section of a plane.* —*v.t.* **26.** *Informal.* to follow in order to hinder escape of or to observe: *to tail a suspect.* **27.** to form or furnish with a tail. **28.** to form or constitute the tail or end of (a procession, retinue, etc.). **29.** to terminate; come after or behind; follow like a tail. **30.** to join or attach (one thing) at the tail or end of another. **31.** *Building Trades.* to fasten (a beam, stone, etc.) by one end (usually fol. by *in* or *into*). **32.** to dock the tail of (a horse, dog, etc.). —*v.i.* **33.** to follow close behind: *She always tails after her sister.* **34.** to disappear gradually or merge into: *The path tails off into the woods.* **35.** to form, or move or pass in, a line or column suggestive of a tail: *The hikers tailed up the narrow path.* **36.** (of a boat) to have or take a position with the stern in a particular direction. **37.** *Building Trades.* (of a beam, stone, etc.) to be fastened by one end (usually fol. by *in* or *into*). [bef. 900; ME; OE *tægl*; c. ON *tagl* horse's tail, Goth *tagl* hair, MHG *zagel* tail, MLG *tagel* rope-end] —**tail′er,** *n.* —**tail′less,** *adj.* —**tail′less•ly,** *adv.* —**tail′less•ness,** *n.* —**tail′like′,** *adj.*

tail[2] (tāl), *Law.* —*n.* **1.** the limitation of an estate to a person and the heirs of his or her body, or some particular class of such heirs. —*adj.* **2.** limited to a specified line of heirs; being in tail. [1200–50; (n.) ME *taille* < OF, deriv. of *taillier* to cut < LL *tāliāre* (see TAILOR[1]); (adj.) late ME *taille* < AF *tailé* cut, shaped, limited, ptp. of *taillier*] —**tail′less,** *adj.*

tail•back (tāl′bak′), *n. Football.* **1.** the offensive back who lines up farthest behind the line of scrimmage, as in a single wingback or double wingback formation. **2.** the position played by this back. [1935–40; TAIL[1] + BACK[1]]

tail•band (tāl′band′), *n.* a band sewn or glued to the tail of a book. Cf. **headband** (def. 3). [1475–85; TAIL[1] + BAND[2]]

tail•board (tāl′bôrd′, -bōrd′), *n.* the tailgate, esp. of a wagon or truck. Also called **endgate.** [1795–1805; TAIL[1] + BOARD]

tail•bone (tāl′bōn′), *n. Anat.* the coccyx. [1540–50; TAIL[1] + BONE]

tail′ coat′. a man's fitted coat, cut away over the hips and descending in a pair of tapering skirts behind, usually black and worn as part of full evening dress. Also, **tail′coat′.** Also called **tails, dress coat, swallow-tailed coat.** [1840–50]

tail′ cone′, *Rocketry.* a cone-shaped component at the rear of a jet engine, rocket, or missile, usually serving as an exhaust pipe.

tail′ cov′ert, any of the feathers concealing the bases of a bird's tail feathers. [1805–15]

tailed (tāld), *adj.* **1.** having a tail. **2.** having a tail of a specified kind (usually used in combination): *a ring-tailed monkey.* [1250–1300; ME; see TAIL[1], -ED[3]]

tailed′ frog′, a frog, *Ascaphus truei,* of the northwestern U.S. and adjacent Canada, the male of which has its cloaca modified into a taillike copulatory organ. Also called **bell toad, ribbed toad, tailed′ toad′.**

tail′ end′, **1.** the hinder or rear part of anything. **2.** the concluding or final part or section; tag end: *the tail end of a lecture.* [1350–1400; ME]

tail′ fan′, *Zool.* the fanlike posterior appendage of crayfish and lobsters, consisting of a telson and two uropods, used for rapid backward propulsion. [1890–95]

tail′ fin′. **1.** See **caudal fin.** **2.** *Auto.* See under **fin**[1] (def. 7). [1675–85]

tail•first (tāl′fûrst′), *adv.* with the tail or rear part foremost. [1885–90; TAIL[1] + FIRST]

tail•gate[1] (tāl′gāt′), *n., v.,* **-gat•ed, -gat•ing,** *adj.* —*n.* **1.** the board or gate at the back of a wagon, truck, station wagon, etc., which can be removed or let down for convenience in loading or unloading. —*v.i.* **2.** to follow or drive hazardously close to the rear of another vehicle. —*v.t.* **3.** to follow or drive hazardously close to the rear of (another vehicle). —*adj.* **4.** pertaining to or set up on a tailgate: *a tailgate picnic before the football game.* [1850–55, *Amer.*; TAIL[1] + GATE]

tail•gate[2] (tāl′gāt′), *n. Jazz.* a style of playing the trombone, esp. in Dixieland jazz, distinguished esp. by the use of melodic counterpoint and long glissandi. [1945–50; so called from the usual seat of trombonists in trucks carrying musicians during a parade]

tail•gat•er[1] (tāl′gā′tər), *n.* **1.** a person who drives hazardously close to the rear of another moving vehicle. **2.** a person who participates in a tailgate picnic. [TAILGATE[1] + -ER[1]]

tail•gat•er[2] (tāl′gā′tər), *n.* a musician who plays trombone in tailgate style. [TAILGATE[2] + -ER[1]]

tail•ing (tā′ling), *n.* **1.** the part of a projecting stone or brick tailed or inserted in a wall. **2. tailings, a.** *Building Trades.* gravel, aggregate, etc., failing to pass through a given screen. **b.** the residue of any product, as in mining; leavings. [1640–50; TAIL[1] + -ING[1]]

taille (tāl; *Fr.* tä′yᵊ), *n., pl.* **tailles** (tālz; *Fr.* tä′yᵊ). **1.** *French Hist.* a tax that was levied by a king or seigneur on his subjects or on lands held under him and that became solely a royal tax in the 15th century from which the lords and later the clergy were exempt. **2.** (in dressmaking) the waist or bodice of a garment. **3.** *Obs.* the shape of one's body from shoulders to waist; figure; build. [1545–55; < F: lit., a cutting; see TAIL[2]]

tail•leur (tä yûr′), *n.* a tailored or tailor-made costume for women. [1920–25; F: lit., tailor; see TAILOR[1], -EUR]

tail•light (tāl′līt′), *n.* a light, usually red, at the rear of an automobile, train, etc. Also called **tail′ lamp′.** [1835–45; TAIL[1] + LIGHT[1]]

tai•lor[1] (tā′lər), *n.* **1.** a person whose occupation is the making, mending, or altering of clothes, esp. suits, coats, and other outer garments. —*v.t.* **2.** to make by tailor's work. **3.** to fashion or adapt to a particular taste, purpose, need, etc.: *to tailor one's actions to those of another.* **4.** to fit or furnish with clothing. **5.** *Chiefly U.S. Mil.* to make (a uniform) to order; cut (a ready-made uniform) so as to cause to fit more snugly; taper. —*v.i.* **6.** to do the work of a tailor. [1250–1300; ME (n.) < AF *tailour,* OF *tailleor,* equiv. to *taill(ier)* to cut (< LL *tāliāre,* deriv. of L *tālea* a cutting, lit., heel-piece; see TALLY) + *-or* -OR[2]]

tai•lor[2] (tā′lər), *n. Brit. Dial.* a stroke of a bell indicating someone's death; knell. [alter. by folk etym. of TELLER]

tai•lor•a•ble (tā′lər ə bəl), *adj.* **1.** capable of being made into clothing: *tailorable fabrics.* **2.** capable of being adapted to a given purpose or function. [TAILOR[1] + -ABLE] —**tai′lor•a•bil′i•ty,** *n.*

tai•lor•bird (tā′lər bûrd′), *n.* any of several small Asian passerine birds, esp. of the genus *Orthotomus,* that stitch leaves together to form and conceal their nests. [1760–70; TAILOR[1] + BIRD]

tai•lored (tā′lərd), *adj.* **1.** (of a woman's garment) in a simple or plain style with fitted lines. Cf. **dressmaker** (def. 2). **2.** having simple, straight lines and a neat appearance: *tailored slipcovers.* [1855–60; TAILOR[1] + -ED[2]]

tai•lor•ing (tā′lər ing), *n.* **1.** the business or work of a tailor. **2.** the skill or craftsmanship of a tailor. [1655–65; TAILOR[1] + -ING[1]]

tai•lor-made (*adj.* tā′lər mād′; *n.* tā′lər mād′, -mād′), *adj.* **1.** tailored. **2.** custom-made; made-to-order; made-to-measure: *an expensive tailor-made suit.* **3.** fashioned to a particular taste, purpose, demand, etc.: *a musical comedy tailor-made for the popular audience.* —*n.* **4.** something, as a garment, that is tailor-made. [1825–35]

tai•lor-make (tā′lər māk′), *v.t.,* **-made, -mak•ing.** to make or adjust to meet the needs of the particular situation, individual, object, etc.: *to tailor-make a tour.* [1895–1900]

tai′lor's bun′ion, bunionette.

tai′lor's chalk′, hardened chalk or soapstone used to make temporary guide marks on a garment that is being altered. [1880–85]

tail•piece (tāl′pēs′), *n.* **1.** a piece added at the end; an appendage. **2.** *Print.* a small decorative design at the end of a chapter or at the bottom of a page. **3.** (in a musical instrument of the viol family) a triangular piece of wood, usually of ebony, to which the lower ends of the strings are fastened. **4.** *Building Trades.* a relatively short beam or rafter inserted in a wall by tailing and supported by a header. [1595–1605; TAIL[1] + PIECE]

tail•pipe (tāl′pīp′), *n.* an exhaust pipe located at the rear of a motor vehicle or aircraft powered by an internal-combustion engine. Also, **tail pipe.** [1880–85, in sense, "suction pipe of a pump"; 1905–10 for current sense; TAIL[1] + PIPE[1]]

tail′ plane′, *Aeron. Chiefly Brit.* See **horizontal stabilizer.** [1905–10]

tail•race (tāl′rās′), *n.* **1.** the race, flume, or channel leading away from a waterwheel or the like. **2.** *Mining.* the channel for conducting tailings or refuse away in water. [1770–80; TAIL[1] + RACE[1]]

tails (tālz), *adj., adv.* **1.** (of a coin) with the reverse facing up: *On the next toss, the coin came up tails.* Cf. **heads.** —*n.* **2.** tail (def. 6). [1675–85; TAIL[1] + -S[1]]

tail′ skid′, *Aeron.* a runner under the tail of an airplane. [1915–20]

tail•spin (tāl′spin′), *n., v.,* **-spinned, -spin•ning.** —*n.* Also, **tail′ spin′.** **1.** spin (def. 24). **2.** a sudden and helpless collapse into failure, confusion, or the like. —*v.i.* **3.** to take or experience a sudden and dramatic downturn: *After the mill closes, the local economy may tailspin.* [1910–15; TAIL[1] + SPIN]

tail•stock (tāl′stok′), *n.* a movable or sliding support for the dead center of a lathe or grinder. See illus. under **lathe.** [1860–65; TAIL[1] + STOCK]

tail•wa•ter (tāl′wô′tər, -wot′ər), *n.* the water in a tailrace. [1750–60; TAIL[1] + WATER]

tail•wind (tāl′wind′), *n.* a wind coming from directly behind a moving object, esp. an aircraft or other vehicle (opposed to *headwind*). [1895–1900; TAIL[1] + WIND[1]]

Tai•myr′ Penin′sula (tī mēr′; *Russ.* tī mɪʀ′), a peninsula in the N Russian Federation in Asia, between the Kara and Laptev seas. Also, **Tai•mir′ Penin′sula.**

tain (tān), *n.* **1.** a thin tin plate. **2.** tin foil for the backs of mirrors. [1855–60; < F: silvering, foil, aph. var. of *étain* tin]

Tai•nan (tī′nän′), *n. Wade-Giles, Pinyin.* a city in SW Taiwan. 550,000.

Taine (tān; *Fr.* ten), *n.* **Hip•po•lyte A•dolphe** (ē pô lēt′ ᴀ dôlf′), 1828–93, French literary critic and historian.

Tai•no (tī′nō), *n., pl.* **-nos,** (*esp. collectively*) **-no** for 1. **1.** a member of an extinct Arawakan Indian tribe of the West Indies. **2.** the language of the Taino.

taint (tānt), *n.* **1.** a trace of something bad, offensive, or harmful. **2.** a trace of infection, contamination, or the like. **3.** a trace of dishonor or discredit. **4.** *Obs.* color; tint. —*v.t.* **5.** to modify by or as if by a trace of something offensive or deleterious. **6.** to infect, contaminate, corrupt, or spoil. **7.** to sully or tarnish (a person's name, reputation, etc.). **8.** *Obs.* to color or tint. —*v.i.* **9.** to become tainted; spoil. [1325–75; conflation of ME *taynt,* aph. var. of *attaint* struck, attainted, ptp. of *attainten* to ATTAINT; late ME *taynt* hue, TINT < AF *teint* (< L *tinctus,* equiv. to *ting(ere)* to dye, TINGE + *-tus* suffix of v. action); and *teinte* < LL *tincta* inked stroke, n. use of fem. of ptp. of *tingere*]
—**Syn.** **1.** defect, spot, flaw, fault. **1, 7.** blemish, stain.

taint•less (tānt′lis), *adj.* free from or without taint; pure; innocent. [1580–90; TAINT + -LESS] —**taint′less•ly,** *adv.* —**taint′less•ness,** *n.*

tai•pan[1] (tī′pan), *n.* (in China) the head or owner of a foreign business establishment. [1895–1900; < dial. Chin (cf. Guangdong dial. *daaih-bāan*), akin to Chin *dàbǎn* (*dà* great + *bǎn* company, class)]

tai•pan[2] (tī′pan), *n.* a highly venomous elapid snake, *Oxyuranus scutellatus,* of New Guinea and northern Australia, that grows to a length of from 10 to 12 ft. (3.1 to 3.7 m). [1930–35; < Wik-Munkan (Australian Aboriginal language spoken around the Archer River, N Queensland), recorded as *tay-pan*]

Tai•pei (tī′pā′; *Chin.* tī′bā′), *n. Wade-Giles.* a city in and the capital of Taiwan, in the N part. 2,100,000. Also, **Taibei;** *Older Spelling,* **Tai′peh′.**

Tai•ping (tī′ping′), *n.* a person who participated in the unsuccessful rebellion (**Tai′ping′ Rebel′lion**), 1850–64, led by Hung Hsiu-ch'üan (Hong Xiuquan), who attempted to overthrow the Manchu dynasty. [< Chin *tàipíng* lit., great peace]

Tai•ra (tī′rä′), *n.* **1.** a member of a powerful family in Japan that ruled the country 1160–85. **2.** former name of **Iwaki.**

Tai•sho (tī′shō′), *n. Japanese Hist.* the designation of the period of the reign of Emperor Yoshihito, 1912–26. [< Japn *taishō* < MChin, equiv. to Chin *dà* great + *zhèng* right(ness)]

T'ai Tsu (tī′ dzo͞o′). See **Chao K'uang-yin.** Also, *Pinyin,* **Tai Zu** (tī′zo͞o′).

T'ai Tsung (tī′dzo͝ong′), (*Li Shih-min*), ᴀ.ᴅ. 597–649, Chinese emperor of the T'ang dynasty 627–649. Also, *Pinyin,* **Tai Zong** (tī′ zông′).

Tai•wan (tī′wän′), *n. Wade-Giles, Pinyin.* a Chinese island separated from the SE coast of China by Taiwan Strait: a possession of Japan 1895–1945; restored to China 1945; seat of the Republic of China since 1949. *Cap.:* Taipei. Also called **Formosa.**

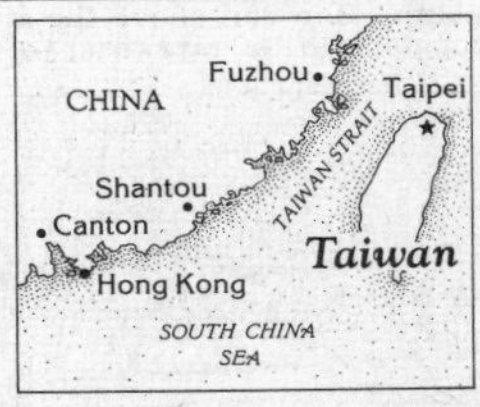

Tai•wan•ese (tī′wä nēz′, -nēs′), *adj., n., pl.* **-ese** for 2. —*adj.* **1.** of or pertaining to Taiwan or its people. —*n.* **2.** a native or inhabitant of Taiwan. **3.** the Chinese language of Taiwan, a member of the Min group. [TAIWAN + -ESE]

Tai′wan Strait′, an arm of the Pacific Ocean between China and Taiwan, connecting the East and South China Seas. Formerly, **Formosa Strait.**

Tai•yuan (tī′yyän′), *n. Pinyin, Wade-Giles.* a city in and the capital of Shanxi province, in N China; a walled city. 1,350,000. Also, *Wade-Giles,* **Tai′yüan′, T'ai′•yüan′.** Formerly, **Yangqu.**

Ta•iz (ta iz′), *n.* a city in S Yemen. 178,043. Also, **Ta'izz′.**

Tai•zhong (tī′zhông′), *n. Pinyin.* Taichung.

Tai•zhou (tī′jō′), *n. Pinyin.* a city in central Jiangsu province, in E China. 275,000. Also, **T'aichou, Taichow.**

taj (täzh, täj), *n.* a high, conical cap worn in Muslim countries. [1850–55; < Ar *tāj* < Pers]

Ta•jik (tä jik′, -jēk′; *Russ.* tu jik′), *n., pl.* **-jiks,** (*esp. collectively*) **-jik** for 1. **1.** a member of a people living mainly in Tadzhikistan, as well as parts of Afghanistan and China. **2.** Also, **Ta•ji•ki** (tä′ji kē, tä jē′-). the Iranian language spoken by the Tajiks, closely related to Persian but in Tadzhikistan written in the Cyrillic alphabet. Also, **Tadjik, Tadzhik.**

Ta•jik•i•stan (tə jik′ə stan′, -stän′, -jē′kə-), *n.* Tadzhikistan.

Taj Ma•hal (täzh′ mə häl′, täj′), a white marble mausoleum built at Agra, India, by the Mogul emperor Shah Jahan (fl. 1628–58) for his favorite wife.

Ta•jo (tä′hô), *n.* Spanish name of **Tagus.**

Taj•rish (täj ʀēsh′), *n.* a city in NW Iran, near Teheran. 157,486.

ta•ka (tä′kə), *n, pl.* **-ka.** a paper money, cupronickel coin, and monetary unit of Bangladesh, equal to 100 poisha. [< Bengali *ṭākā*]

ta•ka•he (tə kī′, -kä′ē), *n.* notornis. [1850–55; < Maori *takahē*]

Ta•ka•ma•tsu (tä′kä mä′tso͞o), *n.* a seaport on NE Shikoku, in SW Japan. 316,662.

Ta•ka•tsu•ki (tä′kət so͞o′kē, tə kät′so͞o kē; *Japn.* tä′kä tso͞o′kē), *n.* a city on S Honshu, in Japan: a suburb of Osaka. 340,722.

take (tāk), *v.,* **took, tak•en, tak•ing,** *n.* —*v.t.* **1.** to get into one's hold or possession by voluntary action: *to take a cigarette out of a box; to take a pen and begin to write.* **2.** to hold, grasp, or grip: *to take a book in one's hand; to take a child by the hand.* **3.** to get into one's hands, possession, control, etc., by force or artifice: *to take a bone from a snarling dog.* **4.** to seize or capture: *to take an enemy town; to take a prisoner.* **5.** to catch or get (fish, game, etc.), esp. by killing: *to take a dozen trout on a good afternoon.* **6.** to pick from a number; select: *Take whichever you wish.* **7.** to receive and accept willingly (something given or offered): *to take a compliment with a smile; to take a bribe.* **8.** to receive or be the recipient of (something bestowed, administered, etc.): *to take first*

CONCISE ETYMOLOGY KEY: <, descended or borrowed from; >, whence; b., blend of, blended; c., cognate with; cf., compare; deriv., derivative; equiv., equivalent; imit., imitative; obl., oblique; r., replacing; s., stem; sp., spelling, spelled; resp., respelling, respelled; trans., translation; ?, origin unknown; *, unattested; ‡, probably earlier than. See the full key inside the front cover.

prize. **9.** to accept and act upon or comply with: *to take advice; to take a dare.* **10.** to receive or accept (a person) into some relation: *to take someone in marriage; to take new members once a year.* **11.** to receive, react, or respond to in a specified manner: *Although she kept calm, she took his death hard.* **12.** to receive as a payment or charge: *He refused to take any money for the use of his car.* **13.** to gain for use by payment, lease, etc.: *to take a box at the opera; to take a beach house for a month.* **14.** to secure regularly or periodically by payment: *to take a magazine.* **15.** to get or obtain from a source; derive: *The book takes its title from Dante.* **16.** to extract or quote: *He took whole passages straight from Dickens.* **17.** to obtain or exact as compensation for some wrong: *to take revenge.* **18.** to receive into the body or system, as by swallowing or inhaling: *to take a pill; to take a breath of fresh air.* **19.** to have for one's benefit or use: *to take a meal; to take a nap; to take a bath.* **20.** to use as a flavoring agent in a food or beverage: *to take sugar in one's coffee.* **21.** to be subjected to; undergo: *to take a heat treatment.* **22.** to endure or submit to with equanimity or without an appreciable weakening of one's resistance: *to take a joke; unable to take punishment.* **23.** to enter into the enjoyment of (recreation, a holiday, etc.): *to take a vacation.* **24.** to carry off without permission: *to take something that belongs to another.* **25.** to remove: *to take the pins out of one's hair.* **26.** to remove by death: *The flood took many families.* **27.** to end (a life): *She took her own life.* **28.** to subtract or deduct: *If you take 2 from 5, that leaves 3.* **29.** to carry with one: *Take your lunch with you. Are you taking an umbrella?* **30.** to convey in a means of transportation: *We took them for a ride in the country.* **31.** (of a vehicle) to convey or transport: *Will this bus take me across town?* **32.** (of a road, path, etc.) to serve as a means of conducting to or through some place or region: *Fifth Avenue took us through the center of town. These stairs will take you up to the attic.* **33.** to bring about a change in the state or condition of: *Her ambition and perseverance took her quickly to the top of her field.* **34.** to conduct or escort: *to take someone out for dinner.* **35.** to set about or succeed in getting over, through, or around (some obstacle); clear; negotiate: *The horse took the hedge easily. He took the corner at top speed.* **36.** to come upon suddenly; catch: *to take someone by surprise.* **37.** to get or contract; catch: *He took cold over the weekend. I took a chill.* **38.** to attack or affect, as with a disease: *suddenly taken with a fit of coughing.* **39.** to be capable of attaining as a result of some action or treatment: *Most leathers take a high polish.* **40.** to absorb or become impregnated with; be susceptible to: *Waxed paper will not take ink. This cloth takes dye.* **41.** to attract and hold: *The red sweater took his eye. The urgent voice took her attention.* **42.** to captivate or charm: *The kitten took my fancy.* **43.** to require: *It takes courage to do that. The climb took all our strength.* **44.** to employ for some specified or implied purpose: *to take measures to curb drugs.* **45.** to use as a means of transportation: *to take a bus to the ferry.* **46.** to get on or board (a means of transportation) at a given time or in a given place: *She takes the train at Scarsdale.* **47.** to proceed to occupy: *to take a seat.* **48.** to occupy; fill (time, space, etc.): *His hobby takes most of his spare time. The machine takes a lot of room.* **49.** to use up; consume: *This car takes a great deal of oil. He took ten minutes to solve the problem.* **50.** to avail oneself of: *He took the opportunity to leave. She took the time to finish it properly.* **51.** to do, perform, execute, etc.: *to take a walk.* **52.** to go into or enter: *Take the next road to the left.* **53.** to adopt and enter upon (a way, course, etc.): *to take the path of least resistance.* **54.** to act or perform: *to take the part of the hero.* **55.** to make (a reproduction, picture, or photograph): *to take home movies of the children.* **56.** to make a picture, esp. a photograph, of: *The photographer took us sitting down.* **57.** to write down: *to take a letter in shorthand; to take notes at a lecture.* **58.** to apply oneself to; study: *to take ballet; She took four courses in her freshman year.* **59.** to deal with; treat: *to take things in their proper order.* **60.** to proceed to handle in some manner: *to take a matter under consideration.* **61.** to assume or undertake (a function, duty, job, etc.): *The mayor took office last month.* **62.** to assume or adopt (a symbol, badge, or the like) as a token of office: *to take the veil; to take the throne.* **63.** to assume the obligation of; be bound by: *to take an oath.* **64.** to assume or adopt as one's own: *to take someone's part in an argument; He took the side of the speaker.* **65.** to assume or appropriate as if by right: *to take credit for someone else's work.* **66.** to accept the burden of: *She took the blame for his failure.* **67.** to determine by inquiry, examination, measurement, scientific observation, etc.: *to take someone's pulse; to take a census.* **68.** to make or carry out for purposes of yielding such a determination: *to take someone's measurements; to take a seismographic reading.* **69.** to begin to have; experience (a certain feeling or state of mind): *to take pride in one's appearance.* **70.** to form and hold in the mind: *to take a gloomy view.* **71.** to grasp or apprehend mentally; understand; comprehend: *Do you take my meaning, sir?* **72.** to understand in a specified way: *You shouldn't take the remark as an insult.* **73.** to grasp the meaning of (a person): *if we take him correctly.* **74.** to accept the statements of: *to take him at his word.* **75.** to assume as a fact: *I take it that you will be there.* **76.** to regard or consider: *They were taken to be wealthy.* **77.** to capture or win (a piece, trick, etc.) in a game. **78.** *Informal.* to cheat, swindle, or victimize: *They really take people in that shop. The museum got taken on that painting.* **79.** to win or obtain money from: *He took me for $10 in the poker game.* **80.** (of a man) to have sexual intercourse with. **81.** *Gram.* to be used with (a certain form, accent, case, mood, etc.): *a verb that always takes an object.* **82.** *Law.* to acquire property, as on the happening of an event: *They take a fortune under the will.* **83.** *Baseball.* (of a batter) to allow (a pitch) to go by without swinging at it: *He took a third strike.*
—*v.i.* **84.** to catch or engage, as a mechanical device: *She turned the key and heard a click as the catch took.* **85.** to strike root or begin to grow, as a plant. **86.** to adhere, as ink, dye, or color. **87.** (of a person or thing) to win favor or acceptance: *a new TV show that took with the public.* **88.** to have the intended result or effect, as a medicine, inoculation, etc.: *The vaccination took.* **89.** to enter into possession, as of an estate. **90.** to detract (usually fol. by *from*). **91.** to apply or devote oneself: *He took to his studies.* **92.** to make one's way; proceed; go: *to take across the meadow.* **93.** to fall or become: *She took sick and had to go home.* **94.** to admit of being photographed in a particular manner: *a model who takes exceptionally well.* **95.** to admit of being moved or separated: *This crib takes apart for easy storage.* **96.** **take after, a.** to resemble (another person, as a parent) physically, temperamentally, etc.: *The baby took after his mother.* **b.** Also, **take off after, take out after.** to follow; chase: *The detective took after the burglars.* **97.** **take back, a.** to regain possession of: *to take back one's lawn mower.* **b.** to return, as for exchange: *It was defective, so I took it back to the store.* **c.** to allow to return; resume a relationship with: *She said she would never take him back again.* **d.** to cause to remember: *It takes one back to the old days.* **e.** to retract: *to take back a statement.* **98.** **take down, a.** to move from a higher to a lower level or place. **b.** to pull apart or take apart; dismantle; disassemble. **c.** to write down; record. **d.** to diminish the pride or arrogance of; humble: *to take someone down a notch or two.* **99.** **take for, a.** to assume to be: *I took it for the truth.* **b.** to assume falsely to be; mistake for: *to be taken for a foreigner.* **100.** **take for granted.** See **grant** (def. 6). **101.** **take in, a.** to permit to enter; admit. **b.** to alter (an article of clothing) so as to make smaller. **c.** to provide lodging for. **d.** to include; encompass. **e.** to grasp the meaning of; comprehend. **f.** to deceive; trick; cheat. **g.** to observe; notice. **h.** to visit or attend: *to take in a show.* **i.** to furl (a sail). **j.** to receive as proceeds, as from business activity. **k.** *Chiefly Brit.* to subscribe to: *to take in a magazine.* **102.** **take it, a.** to accept or believe something; aquiesce: *I'll take it on your say-so.* **b.** *Informal.* to be able to resist or endure hardship, abuse, etc. **c.** to understand: *I take it that you're not interested.* **103.** **take it out in,** to accept as payment for services or as an equivalent of monetary compensation: *He takes it out in goods instead of cash.* **104.** **take it out of, a.** to exhaust; enervate: *Every year the winter takes it out of me.* **b.** to exact payment from; penalize: *They took it out of your pay.* **105.** **take it out on,** *Informal.* to cause (someone else) to suffer for one's own misfortune or dissatisfaction: *Just because you're angry with him you don't have to take it out on me!* **106.** **take off, a.** to remove: *Take off your coat.* **b.** to lead away: *The child was taken off by kidnappers.* **c.** *Informal.* to depart; leave: *They took off yesterday for California.* **d.** to leave the ground, as an airplane. **e.** to move onward or forward with a sudden or intense burst of speed: *The police car took off after the drunken driver.* **f.** to withdraw or remove from: *She was taken off the night shift.* **g.** to remove by death; kill: *Millions were taken off by the Black Plague.* **h.** to make a likeness or copy of; reproduce. **i.** to subtract, as a discount; deduct: *Shop early and we'll take off 20 percent.* **j.** *Informal.* to imitate; mimic; burlesque. **k.** *Informal.* to achieve sudden, marked growth, success, etc.: *Sales took off just before Christmas. The actor's career took off after his role in that movie.* **107.** **take on, a.** to hire; employ. **b.** to undertake; assume: *to take on new responsibilities.* **c.** to acquire: *The situation begins to take on a new light.* **d.** to accept as a challenge; contend against: *to take on a bully.* **e.** *Informal.* to show great emotion; become excited: *There's no need to take on so.* **108.** **take out, a.** to withdraw; remove: *to take out a handkerchief.* **b.** to procure by application: *to take out an insurance policy.* **c.** to carry out for use or consumption elsewhere: *to take a book out of the library; to get food to take out.* **d.** to escort; invite: *He takes out my sister now and then.* **e.** to set out; start: *They took out for the nearest beach.* **f.** *Slang.* to kill; destroy. **109.** **take over,** to assume management or possession of or responsibility for: *The first officer took over the ship when the captain suffered a heart attack.* **110.** **take to, a.** to devote or apply oneself to; become habituated to: *to take to drink.* **b.** to respond favorably to; begin to like: *They took to each other at once.* **c.** to go to: *to take to one's bed.* **d.** to have recourse to; resort to: *She took to getting up at five to go jogging before work.* **111.** **take up, a.** to occupy oneself with the study or practice of: *She took up painting in her spare time.* **b.** to lift or pick up: *He took up the fallen leaves with a rake.* **c.** to occupy; cover: *A grand piano would take up half of our living room.* **d.** to consume; use up; absorb: *Traveling to her job takes up a great deal of time.* **e.** to begin to advocate or support; sponsor: *He has taken up another struggling artist.* **f.** to continue; resume: *We took up where we had left off.* **g.** to reply to in order to reprove: *The author takes up his critics in the preface of his latest book.* **h.** to assume: *He took up the duties of the presidency.* **i.** to absorb: *Use a sponge to take up the spilled milk.* **j.** to make shorter, as by hemming: *to take up the sleeves an inch.* **k.** to make tighter, as by winding in: *to take up the slack in a reel of tape.* **l.** to deal with in discussion: *to take up the issue of mass transit.* **m.** to adopt seriously: *to take up the idea of seeking public office.* **n.** to accept, as an offer or challenge. **o.** to buy as much as is offered: *The sale was taken up in a matter of days.* **p.** *Chiefly Brit.* to clear by paying off, as a loan. **q.** *Obs.* to arrest (esp. a runaway slave). **112.** **take up a collection,** to ask for or gather donations, usually of money, from a number of people. **113.** **take upon oneself,** to assume as a responsibility or obligation: *She has taken it upon herself to support the family.* **114.** **take up with,** *Informal.* to become friendly with; keep company with: *He took up with a bad crowd.*
—*n.* **115.** the act of taking. **116.** something that is taken. **117.** the quantity of fish, game, etc., taken at one time. **118.** *Informal.* money taken in, esp. profits. **119.** *Journalism.* a portion of copy assigned to a Linotype operator or compositor, usually part of a story or article. **120.** *Motion Pictures.* **a.** a scene, or a portion of a scene, photographed without any interruption or break. **b.** an instance of such continuous operation of the camera. **121.** *Informal.* a visual and mental response to something typically manifested in a stare expressing total absorption or wonderment: *She did a slow take on being asked by reporters the same question for the third time.* **122.** a recording of a musical performance. **123.** *Med.* a successful inoculation. **124.** **on the take,** *Slang.* **a.** accepting bribes. **b.** in search of personal profit at the expense of others. [bef. 1100; ME *taken* to take, strike, lay hold of, grasp, late OE *tacan* to grasp, touch < ON *taka* to take; c. MD *taken* to grasp, Goth *tekan* to touch] —**tak′a·ble, take′a·ble,** *adj.* —**tak′er,** *n.*
—**Syn. 1.** acquire, secure, procure. See **bring. 6.** choose. **22.** bear, stand, tolerate. **42.** delight, attract, interest, engage. **43.** need, demand. **44.** use. **67.** ascertain. **75.** suppose, presume. —**Ant. 1.** give.

take-all (tāk′ôl′), *n. Plant Pathol.* a disease of wheat, rye, barley and oats, characterized by the blackening and decaying of the base of the stems, caused by a fungus, *Ophiobolus graminis.* [1875–80]

take-a-long (tāk′ə lông′, -ə long′), *adj. Informal.* **1.** intended or suitable for taking along, as on a trip: *take-along snacks for long car trips.* **2.** sized, built, or adapted to be carried easily; portable: *a take-along TV set.* —*n.* **3.** something that is or can be taken along or carried. [adj., n. use of the v. phrase *take along*]

take·a·way (tāk′ə wā′), *n.* **1.** something taken back or away, esp. an employee benefit that is eliminated or substantially reduced by the terms of a union contract. —*adj.* **2.** of or pertaining to what is or can be taken away: *a list of takeaway proposals presented by management.* **3.** *Chiefly Brit.* takeout (def. 7). Also, **take′-a·way′.** [1930–35 for earlier sense "train car for carrying logs"; 1960–65 for def. 2; TAKE + AWAY]

take·back (tāk′bak′), *n.* **1.** something taken back or withdrawn, esp. an employee benefit previously gained in a union contract; takeaway. —*adj.* **2.** of or pertaining to what is taken back: *a takeback agreement.* [n. use of v. phrase *take back*]

take-charge (tāk′chärj′), *adj.* able or seemingly able to take charge: *She is a take-charge management type.*

take·down (tāk′doun′), *adj.* **1.** made or constructed so as to be easily dismantled or disassembled. **2.** *Finance.* takeout (def. 8). —*n.* **3.** the act of taking down. **4.** a firearm designed to be swiftly disassembled or assembled. **5.** the point of separation of two or more of the parts of a takedown firearm or other device. **6.** *Informal.* the act of being humbled. **7.** *Wrestling.* a move or series of maneuvers that succeeds in bringing a standing opponent down onto the mat. **8.** *Finance.* takeout (def. 5). Also, **take′-down′.** [1890–95; adj., n. use of v. phrase *take down*]

take′-home pay′ (tāk′hōm′), the amount of salary remaining after deductions, as of taxes, have been made. [1940–45]

take-in (tāk′in′), *n. Informal.* a deception, fraud, or imposition. [1770–80; n. use of v. phrase *take in*]

Ta·kel·ma (tə kel′mə), *n.* **1.** a member of a North American Indian people of southwestern Oregon, extinct since the early 20th century. **2.** the Penutian language of the Takelma.

tak·en (tā′kən), *v.* **1.** pp. of **take. 2.** *Nonstandard.* a pt. of **take.** —*adj.* **3.** **taken with,** charmed or captivated by: *He was quite taken with your niece.*

take·off (tāk′ôf′, -of′), *n.* **1.** a taking or setting off; the leaving of the ground, as in leaping or in beginning a flight in an airplane. **2.** a taking off from a starting point, as in beginning a race. **3.** the place or point at which a person or thing takes off. **4.** a humorous or satirical imitation; burlesque. **5.** *Mach.* a shaft geared to a main shaft for running auxiliary machinery. **6.** a branch connection to a pipe, electric line, etc. Also, **take′-off′.** [1820–30; n. use of v. phrase *take off*]

take·out (tāk′out′), *n.* **1.** the act or fact of taking out. **2.** something made to be taken out, esp. food prepared in a store or restaurant to be carried out for consumption elsewhere. **3.** *Informal.* a store, restaurant, or counter specializing in preparing food meant to be carried out for consumption elsewhere. **4.** a section, as of a magazine, that may be removed intact, usually consisting of a story, article, or set of illustrations. **5.** Also called **takedown, take′out loan′, take′out mort′gage.** *Finance.* a long-term real-estate mortgage arranged for a building the construction of which is financed by an interim short-term loan **(construction loan). 6.** *Cards.* **a.** *Bridge.* a bid in a suit or denomination different from the one bid by one's partner. **b.** *Poker.* the minimum with which a player can begin. —*adj.* **7.** pertaining to or supplying food and drink to be taken out and consumed elsewhere: *the takeout window of a restaurant.* **8.** Also, **takedown.** of, pertaining to, or providing a takeout mortgage: *The high-rise developer has found a takeout commitment from a large insurance company.* Also, **take′-out′.** [1915–20; n. use of v. phrase *take out*]

take′out dou′ble, *Bridge.* See **informatory double.** [1940–45]

take·o·ver (tāk′ō′vər), *n.* **1.** the act of seizing, appropriating, or arrogating authority, control, management, etc. **2.** an aquisition or gaining control of a corporation through the purchase or exchange of stock. Also, **take′-o′ver.** [1940–45; n. use of v. phrase *take over*]

tak·er-in (tā′kər in′), *n.* licker-in. [1830–40]

take-up (tāk′up′), *n.* **1.** the act of taking up. **2.** *Mach.* **a.** uptake (def. 3). **b.** any of various devices for taking up slack, winding in, or compensating for the looseness of parts due to wear. **3.** the contraction of fabric resulting from the wet operations in the finishing process, esp. fulling. [1815–25; n. use of v. phrase *take up*]

take′-up reel′, *Motion Pictures.* (on a projector) the reel onto which the film is wound after it has been projected.

ta·kin (tä′kin, -kēn), *n.* a mountain-dwelling bovid, *Budorcas taxicolor,* native to the eastern Himalayas, China, and northern Burma, that resembles a cross between a goat and a musk ox. [1840–50; alleged to be < Mishmi (Tibeto-Burman language of a tribal people of Arunachal Pradesh, NE India)]

tak•ing (tā′king), *n.* **1.** the act of a person or thing that takes. **2.** the state of being taken. **3.** something that is taken. **4. takings,** receipts, esp. of money earned or gained. **5.** *Archaic.* a state of agitation or distress. —*adj.* **6.** captivating, winning, or pleasing. **7.** *Archaic.* infectious or contagious. [1300–50; ME *takyng* (ger.). See TAKE, -ING[1], -ING[2]] —**tak′ing•ly,** *adv.*

tak′ing lens′, *Photog.* See under **reflex camera.** [1950–55]

Ta•ki-Ta•ki (tä′kē tä′kē), *n.* Sranan.

Ta•kla•ma•kan (tä′klə mə kän′), *n.* a desert in S central Xingjiang Uygur Autonomous Region, China. ab. 125,000 sq. mi. (323,750 sq. km). Also, **Ta′kli•ma•kan′.**

Ta•ko′ma Park′ (tə kō′mə), a city in central Maryland. 16,231.

Ta•ku (tä′kōō′), *n.* *Wade-Giles.* Dagu.

tal., (in prescriptions) such; like this. [< L *tālis*]

ta•la[1] (tä′lə), *n.* a repeated rhythmic pattern of stressed and unstressed beats played on a percussion instrument in Indian music. [1890–95; < Skt *tāla;* cf. Hindi *tāl*]

ta•la[2] (tä′lə), *n, pl.* **-la.** a paper money, cupronickel or silver coin, and monetary unit of Western Samoa, equal to 100 sene. [1965–70; < Samoan *tālā* < E DOLLAR]

tal•a•poin (tal′ə poin′), *n.* a small, yellowish guenon monkey, *Micropithecus* (*Cercopithecus*) *talapoin,* of western Africa. [1580–90; < F, special use (orig. jocular) of *talapoin* Buddhist monk < Mon *təlaʔ p n* (written *tila puin*) Buddha, lit., the Lord of Merit (Old Mon *tirlaa′* lord + Pali *puñña* merit)]

Ta•la•ra (tä lä′rä), *n.* a seaport in NW Peru. 38,200.

ta•lar•i•a (tə lâr′ē ə), *n.pl. Class. Myth.* the wings or winged sandals on the feet of Hermes, or Mercury. [< L *tālāria,* n. use of neut. pl. of *tālāris* attached to the ankles, equiv. to *tāl(us)* ankle + *-āris* -AR[1]]

Ta•las•si•o (tə las′ē ō′), *n.* a god invoked at ancient Roman weddings, esp. in epithalamions.

Ta•la•ve•ra de la Rei•na (tä′lä ve′rä the lä rā′nä), a city in central Spain, on the Tagus River: British and Spanish defeat of the French 1809. 45,327.

ta•la•yot (tə lä′yōt), *n.* any of the round or square prehistoric stone towers found in the Balearic Islands, possibly modeled after the nuraghi in Sardinia. [1870–75; < Catalan *talaiot* < Ar *ṭalāyi′,* pl. of *ṭali‘ah* sentinel]

tal•bot (tôl′bət, tal′-), *n.* a hound with long pendent ears. [1350–1400; ME: dog's name, orig. man's nickname < OF]

Tal•bot (tôl′bət *or, for 3,* tal′-), *n.* **1. Charles, Duke of Shrewsbury,** 1660–1718, British statesman: prime minister 1714. **2. William Henry Fox,** 1800–77, English pioneer in photography. **3.** a male given name.

Tal•bo•type (tôl′bə tīp′, tal′-), *n. Photog.* calotype. [1840–50; W.F.H. TALBOT + -TYPE, on the model of DAGUERREOTYPE]

talc (talk), *n., v.,* **talcked** or **talced** (talkt), **talck•ing** or **talc•ing** (tal′king). —*n.* **1.** Also, **tal•cum** (tal′kəm). a green-to-gray, soft mineral, hydrous magnesium silicate, $Mg_3(Si_4O_{10})(OH)_2$, unctuous to the touch, and occurring usually in foliated or compact masses, used in making lubricants, talcum powder, electrical insulation, etc. **2.** See **talcum powder.** —*v.t.* **3.** to treat or rub with talc. [1595–1605; < ML *talcum* < Ar *ṭalq* mica < Pers *talk*]

Tal•ca (täl′kä), *n.* a city in central Chile. 115,130.

Tal•ca•hua•no (täl′kä wä′nô), *n.* a seaport in central Chile. 183,591.

talc•ose (tal′kōs, tal kōs′), *adj.* containing or composed largely of talc. Also, **talc•ous** (tal′kəs). [1790–1800; TALC + -OSE[1]]

tal′cum pow′der (tal′kəm), a powder made of purified, usually perfumed talc, for toilet purposes. [1885–90; < ML *talcum* TALC]

tale (tāl), *n.* **1.** a narrative that relates the details of some real or imaginary event, incident, or case; story: *a tale about Lincoln's dog.* **2.** a literary composition having the form of such a narrative. **3.** a falsehood; lie. **4.** a rumor or piece of gossip, often malicious or untrue. **5.** the full number or amount. **6.** *Archaic.* enumeration; count. **7.** *Obs.* talk; discourse. [bef. 900; ME; OE *talu* series, list, narrative, story; c. D *taal* speech, language, G *Zahl* number, ON *tala* number, speech. See TELL[1]]

tale•bear•er (tāl′bâr′ər), *n.* a person who spreads gossip, secrets, etc., that may cause trouble or harm. [1470–80; TALE + BEARER] —**tale′bear′ing,** *adj., n.*

tal•ent (tal′ənt), *n.* **1.** a special natural ability or aptitude: *a talent for drawing.* **2.** a capacity for achievement or success; ability: *young men of talent.* **3.** a talented person: *The cast includes many of the theater's major talents.* **4.** a group of persons with special ability: *an exhibition of watercolors by the local talent.* **5.** *Motion Pictures and Television.* professional actors collectively, esp. star performers. **6.** a power of mind or body considered as given to a person for use and improvement: so called from the parable in Matt. 25:14–30. **7.** any of various ancient units of weight, as a unit of Palestine and Syria equal to 3000 shekels, or a unit of Greece equal to 6000 drachmas. **8.** any of various ancient Hebrew or Attic monetary units equal in value to that of a talent weight of gold, silver, or other metal. **9.** *Obs.* inclination or disposition. [bef. 900; ME, OE *talente* < L *talenta,* pl. of *talentum* < Gk *tálanton* balance, weight, monetary unit]
—**Syn. 1.** capability, gift, genius. See **ability.**

tal•ent•ed (tal′ən tid), *adj.* having talent or special ability; gifted. [1375–1425; late ME: inclined, disposed; see TALENT, -ED[3]]

tal′ent scout′, a person whose business it is to recognize and recruit persons of marked aptitude for a certain field or occupation, esp. in entertainment or sports. [1935–40]

tal′ent show′, a theatrical show in which a series of usually amateur or aspiring singers, dancers, comedians, instrumentalists, etc., perform in the hope of gaining recognition.

Tale′ of Gen′ji, The, (Japanese, *Genji Monogatari*), a novel (1001–20?) by Lady Murasaki, dealing with Japanese court life.

Tale′ of Two′ Cit′ies, A, a historical novel (1859) by Dickens.

ta•ler (tä′lər), *n., pl.* **-ler, -lers.** thaler.

tales (tālz, tā′lēz), *n. Law.* **1.** (*used with a plural v.*) persons chosen to serve on the jury when the original panel is insufficiently large: originally selected from among those present in court. **2.** (*used with a singular v.*) the order or writ summoning such jurors. [1300–50; ME < ML *tālēs* (*dē circumstantibus*) such (of the bystanders)]

tales•man (tālz′mən, tā′lēz mən), *n., pl.* **-men.** a person summoned as one of the tales. [1670–80; TALES + MAN[1]]

tale•tell•er (tāl′tel′ər), *n.* **1.** a telltale; talebearer. **2.** a person who tells falsehoods. **3.** a person who tells tales or stories; narrator. [1350–1400; ME; see TALE, TELLER] —**tale′tell′ing,** *adj., n.*

tali-, a combining form meaning "ankle," used in the formation of compound words: *taligrade.* [comb. form repr. L *tālus*]

Ta•lien (dä′lyen′), *n.* *Wade-Giles.* Dalian.

Tal•i•es•in (tal′ē es′in), *n.* fl. A.D. c550, Welsh bard.

tal•i•grade (tal′i grād′), *adj. Zool.* walking on the outer side of the foot. [TALI- + -GRADE]

tal•i•on (tal′ē ən), *n.* See **lex talionis.** [1375–1425; < L *tāliōn-* (s. of *tāliō*) exaction of compensation in kind; r. late ME *talioun* < AF < L, as above]

tal•i•ped (tal′ə ped′), *adj.* **1.** (of a foot) twisted or distorted out of shape or position. **2.** (of a person) clubfooted. —*n.* **3.** a taliped person or animal. [1895–1900; TALI- + -PED]

tal•i•pes (tal′ə pēz′), *n.* **1.** a clubfoot. **2.** the condition of being clubfooted. [1835–45; TALI- + L *pēs* FOOT]

tal•i•pot (tal′ə pot′), *n.* a tall palm, *Corypha umbraculifera,* of southern India and Ceylon, having large fronds used for making fans and umbrellas, for covering houses, and in place of writing paper: also grown as an ornamental. Also called **tal′ipot palm′.** [1675–85; < Malay *talipat* << Skt *tālapattra,* equiv. to *tāla* fan palm + *pattra* leaf]

tal•is•man (tal′is mən, -iz-), *n., pl.* **-mans. 1.** a stone, ring, or other object, engraved with figures or characters supposed to possess occult powers and worn as an amulet or charm. **2.** any amulet or charm. **3.** anything whose presence exercises a remarkable or powerful influence on human feelings or actions. [1630–40; < F or Sp << Ar *ṭilasm* < Gk *télesma* payment, equiv. to *teles-* (var. s. of *teleîn* to complete, perform) + *-ma* n. suffix of result] —**tal•is•man•ic** (tal′is man′ik, -iz-), **tal′is•man′i•cal,** *adj.* —**tal′is•man′i•cal•ly,** *adv.*

talk (tôk), *v.i.* **1.** to communicate or exchange ideas, information, etc., by speaking: *to talk about poetry.* **2.** to consult or confer: *Talk with your adviser.* **3.** to spread a rumor or tell a confidence; gossip. **4.** to chatter or prate. **5.** to employ speech; perform the act of speaking: *to talk very softly; to talk into a microphone.* **6.** to deliver a speech, lecture, etc.: *The professor talked on the uses of comedy in the tragedies of Shakespeare.* **7.** to give or reveal confidential or incriminating information: *After a long interrogation, the spy finally talked.* **8.** to communicate ideas by means other than speech, as by writing, signs, or signals. **9.** *Computers.* to transmit data, as between computers or between a computer and a terminal. **10.** to make sounds imitative or suggestive of speech. —*v.t.* **11.** to express in words; utter: *to talk sense.* **12.** to use (a specified language or idiom) in speaking or conversing: *They talk French together for practice.* **13.** to discuss: *to talk politics.* **14.** to bring, put, drive, influence, etc., by talk: *to talk a person to sleep; to talk a person into doing something.* **15. talk around,** to bring (someone) over to one's way of thinking; persuade: *She sounded adamant over the phone, but I may still be able to talk her around.* **16. talk at, a.** to talk to in a manner that indicates that a response is not expected or wanted. **b.** to direct remarks meant for one person to another person present; speak indirectly to. **17. talk away,** to spend or consume (time) in talking: *We talked away the tedious hours in the hospital.* **18. talk back,** to reply to a command, request, etc., in a rude or disrespectful manner: *Her father never allowed them to talk back.* **19. talk big,** *Informal.* to speak boastingly; brag: *He always talked big, but never amounted to anything.* **20. talk down, a.** to overwhelm by force of argument or by loud and persistent talking; subdue by talking. **b.** to speak disparagingly of; belittle. **c.** Also, **talk in.** to give instructions to by radio for a ground-controlled landing, esp. to a pilot who is unable to make a conventional landing because of snow, fog, etc. **21. talk down to,** to speak condescendingly to; patronize: *Children dislike adults who talk down to them.* **22. talk of,** to debate as a possibility; discuss: *The two companies have been talking of a merger.* **23. talk out, a.** to talk until conversation is exhausted. **b.** to attempt to reach a settlement or understanding by discussion: *We arrived at a compromise by talking out the problem.* **c.** *Brit. Politics.* to thwart the passage of (a bill, motion, etc.) by prolonging discussion until the session of Parliament adjourns. Cf. **filibuster** (def. 5). **24. talk over, a.** to weigh in conversation; consider; discuss. **b.** to cause (someone) to change an opinion; convince by talking: *He became an expert at talking people over to his views.* **25. talk someone's head** or **ear off,** to bore or weary someone by excessive talk; talk incessantly: *All I wanted was a chance to read my book, but my seatmate talked my ear off.* **26. talk to death, a.** to impede or prevent the passage of (a bill) through filibustering. **b.** to talk to incessantly or at great length. **27. talk up, a.** to promote interest in; discuss enthusiastically. **b.** to speak without hesitation; speak distinctly and openly: *If you don't talk up now, you may not get another chance.*
—*n.* **28.** the act of talking; speech; conversation, esp. of a familiar or informal kind. **29.** an informal speech or lecture. **30.** a conference or negotiating session: *peace talks.* **31.** report or rumor; gossip: *There is a lot of talk going around about her.* **32.** a subject or occasion of talking, esp. of gossip: *Your wild escapades are the talk of the neighborhood.* **33.** mere empty speech: *That's just a lot of talk.* **34.** a way of talking: *a halting, lisping talk.* **35.** language, dialect, or lingo. **36.** signs or sounds imitative or suggestive of speech, as the noise made by loose parts in a mechanism. [1175–1225; ME *talk(i)en* to converse, speak, deriv. (with *-k* suffix) of *tale* speech, discourse, TALE; c. Fris (E dial.) *talken*] —**talk′•a•ble,** *adj.* —**talk′a•bil′i•ty,** *n.* —**talk′er,** *n.*
—**Syn. 1.** See **speak. 4, 33.** prattle. **28.** discourse. **30.** colloquy, dialogue, parley, confabulation.

talk•a•thon (tô′kə thon′), *n.* an unusually long speech or discussion, esp. on a matter of public interest, as a Congressional filibuster or a televised question-and-answer session with a political candidate. [1930–35; TALK + -ATHON]

talk•a•tive (tô′kə tiv), *adj.* inclined to talk a great deal: *One drink and she became very talkative.* [1400–50; late ME; see TALK, -ATIVE] —**talk′a•tive•ly,** *adv.* —**talk′a•tive•ness,** *n.*
—**Syn.** wordy, verbose, prolix. TALKATIVE, GARRULOUS, LOQUACIOUS characterize a person who talks a great deal. TALKATIVE is a neutral or mildly unfavorable word applied to a person who is inclined to talk a great deal, sometimes without significance: *a talkative child.* The GARRULOUS person talks with wearisome persistence, usually about personal and trivial things: *a garrulous old man.* A LOQUACIOUS person, intending to be sociable, talks continuously and at length: *a loquacious host.*

talk-back (tôk′bak′), *n. Radio and Television.* a communications system enabling those in the studio to hear control-room personnel through a loudspeaker or headphones. [n. use of v. phrase *talk back*]

talk′ between′ ships′. See **TBS.**

talk•fest (tôk′fest), *n.* a lengthy conversation, discussion, or debate. [1905–10, *Amer.;* TALK + -FEST]

talk•ie (tô′kē), *n. Older Use.* See **talking picture.** [1910–15, *Amer.;* TALK + (MOV)IE]

talk′ing book′, a phonograph record or tape recording of readings of a book, magazine, etc., made esp. for use by the blind. [1935–40]

talk′ing chief′, a noble who serves as public spokesperson for the chief in some Polynesian tribes.

talk′ing head′, 1. *Television Slang.* a closeup picture of a person who is talking, esp. as a participant in a talk show. **2.** *Slang.* a person whose talk is empty and pretentious. [1965–70]

talk′ing machine′, *Older Use.* a phonograph. [1835–45, *Amer.*]

talk′ing pic′ture, *Older Use.* a motion picture with accompanying synchronized speech, singing, etc.

talk′ing point′, a fact or feature that aids or supports one side, as in an argument or competition. [1910–15]

talk•ing-to (tô′king tōō′), *n., pl.* **-tos.** a scolding. [1875–80]

talk′ ra′dio, a radio format featuring talk shows and listener call-ins. [1985–90]

talk′ show′, a radio or television show in which a host interviews or chats with guests, esp. celebrity guests.

talk•y (tô′kē), *adj.,* **talk•i•er, talk•i•est. 1.** having or containing superfluous or purposeless talk, conversation, or dialogue, esp. so as to impede action or progress: *a talky play that bored the audience.* **2.** inclined to talk a great deal; talkative. [1835–45; TALK + -Y[1]] —**talk′i•ness,** *n.*

tall (tôl), *adj.,* **-er, -est,** *adv.* —*adj.* **1.** having a relatively great height; of more than average stature: *a tall woman; tall grass.* **2.** having stature or height as specified: *a man six feet tall.* **3.** large in amount or degree; considerable: *a tall price; Swinging that deal is a tall order.* **4.** extravagant; difficult to believe: *a tall tale.* **5.** high-flown; grandiloquent: *He engages in so much tall talk, one never really knows what he's saying.* **6.** having more than usual length; long and relatively narrow: *He carried a tall walking stick.* **7.** *Archaic.* valiant. **8.** *Obs.* **a.** seemly; proper. **b.** fine; handsome. —*adv.* **9.** in a proud, confident, or erect manner: *to stand tall; to walk tall.* [bef. 1000; ME: big, bold, comely, proper, ready, OE *getæl* (pl. *getale*) quick, ready, competent; c. OHG *gizal* quick] —**tall′ness,** *n.*
—**Syn. 2.** See **high.** —**Ant. 1.** short.

Tal•la•de•ga (tal′ə dē′gə), *n.* a city in central Alabama, E of Birmingham. 19,128.

tal•lage (tal′ij), *n.* **1.** *Medieval Hist.* a tax paid by peasants to the lord of their manor. **2.** a compulsory tax levied by the Norman and early Angevin kings of England upon the demesne lands of the crown and upon all royal towns. [1250–1300; ME *taillage* < OF *taill(ier)* to cut, tax (see TAIL[2]) + ME *-age* -AGE]

Tal•la•has•see (tal′ə has′ē), *n.* a city in and the capital of Florida, in the N part. 81,548.

tall•boy (tôl′boi′), *n.* **1.** *Eng. Furniture.* **a.** a chest of drawers supported by a low stand. Cf. **highboy. b.** a chest-on-chest. **2.** a tall chimney pot. **3.** a tall-stemmed goblet. **4.** (*cap.*) *Mil.* a 12,000-pound (5400 kg) British bomb of World War II, designed to penetrate the target

CONCISE ETYMOLOGY KEY: <, descended or borrowed from; >, whence; b., blend of, blended; c., cognate with; cf., compare; deriv., derivative; equiv., equivalent; imit., imitative; obl., oblique; r., replacing; s., stem; sp., spelling, spelled; resp., respelling, respelled; trans., translation; ?, origin unknown; *, unattested; ‡, probably earlier than. See the full key inside the front cover.

or plunge deep into the ground before detonating. [1670–80; TALL + BOY]

tall′ but′tercup, a Eurasian buttercup, *Ranunculus acris,* naturalized in North American fields and meadows, having a tall stem and shiny yellow flowers.

tall′-case clock′ (tôl′kās′), a pendulum clock tall enough to stand on the floor; a grandfather's or grandmother's clock. Also called **long-case clock.**

Tall•chief (tôl′chēf′), *n.* **Maria,** born 1925, U.S. ballet dancer.

tall′ drink′, a beverage consisting of liquor and a sparkling soda, fruit juice, or the like, to which may be added other ingredients, served in a tall glass, usually with ice. [1955–60]

Tal•ley•rand-Pé•ri•gord (tal′ə rand′per′i gôr′; *Fr.* tᴀ le ʀᴀɴ pā ʀē gôʀ′), *n.* **Charles Mau•rice de** (sʜᴀʀl mō ʀēs′ də), **Prince de Bé•né•vent** (də bā nā vᴀɴ′), 1754–1838, French statesman.

Tal•linn (tä′lin, tal′in), *n.* a seaport in and the capital of Estonia, on the Gulf of Finland. 499,800. Also, **Tal′lin.** Formerly, Russian, **Revel;** German, **Reval.**

Tal•lis (tal′is), *n.* **Thomas,** c1505–85, English organist and composer, esp. of church music. Also, **Tallys, Talys.**

tall•ish (tô′lish), *adj.* rather tall. [1740–50; TALL + -ISH[1]]

tal•lith (*Ashk. Heb., Eng.* tä′lis; *Seph. Heb.* tä lēt′), *n., pl.* **tal•li•thim, tal•li•tim, tal•li•sim** (*Ashk. Heb., Eng.* tä-le′sim, -lā′-, tä′lə sim′; *Seph. Heb.* tä lē tēm′). *Judaism.* a shawllike garment of wool, silk, or the like, with fringes, or zizith, at the four corners, worn around the shoulders by Orthodox and Conservative (sometimes also Reform) Jews, as during the morning service. Also, **tal′•lit, tal′lis.** [1605–15; < Heb *ṭallīth* lit., cover, cloak]

tallith

tal•lith ka•tan (*Seph.* tä lēt′ kä tän′; *Ashk.* tä′lis kô′tôn), *Hebrew.* See **arba kanfoth.** [*ṭallīth qāṭān* lit., little tallith]

Tall•madge (tal′mij), *n.* a city in NE Ohio. 15,269.

tall′ mead′ow rue′, a meadow rue, *Thalictrum polygamum.*

tall′ oil′ (täl), a resinous secondary product resulting from the manufacture of chemical wood pulp: used in the manufacture of soaps, paints, etc. [1925–30; < Sw *tallolja,* equiv. to *tall* pine (c. ON *thǫll* young pine tree) + *olja* oil]

tall′ one′, *Informal.* a beverage, esp. an alcoholic drink, in a tall glass. Also called **long one.**

tal•low (tal′ō), *n.* **1.** the fatty tissue or suet of animals. **2.** the harder fat of sheep, cattle, etc., separated by melting from the fibrous and membranous matter naturally mixed with it, and used to make candles, soap, etc. **3.** any of various similar fatty substances: *vegetable tallow.* —*v.t.* **4.** to smear with tallow. [1300–50; ME *talow, talgh;* c. G *Talg*]

tal′low tree′, a small tree, *Sapium sebiferum,* of the spurge family, cultivated in China and the tropics, having popcorn-shaped seeds with a waxy coating that is used for soap, candles, and oil. [1695–1705]

tal•low•y (tal′ō ē), *adj.* resembling tallow in consistency, color, etc.; fatty: *a tallowy mass of moistened powder; tallowy skin.* Also, **tal′low•like′.** [1400–50; late ME *talwy.* See TALLOW, -Y[1]] —**tal′low•i•ness,** *n.*

tall′ sun′flower. See **giant sunflower.**

Tal•lu•lah (tə lo͞o′lə), *n.* **1.** a town in NE Louisiana. 10,392. **2.** a female given name.

tal•ly (tal′ē), *n., pl.* **-lies,** *v.,* **-lied, -ly•ing.** —*n.* **1.** an account or reckoning; a record of debit and credit, of the score of a game, or the like. **2.** Also called **tal′ly stick′.** a stick of wood with notches cut to indicate the amount of a debt or payment, often split lengthwise across the notches, the debtor retaining one piece and the creditor the other. **3.** anything on which a score or account is kept. **4.** a notch or mark made on or in a tally. **5.** a number or group of items recorded. **6.** a mark made to register a certain number of items, as four consecutive vertical lines with a diagonal line through them to indicate a group of five. **7.** a number of objects serving as a unit of computation. **8.** a ticket, label, or mark used as a means of identification, classification, etc. **9.** anything corresponding to another thing as a counterpart or duplicate. —*v.t.* **10.** to mark or enter on a tally; register; record. **11.** to count or reckon up. **12.** to furnish with a tally or identifying label. **13.** to cause to correspond or agree. —*v.i.* **14.** to correspond, as one part of a tally with the other; accord or agree: *Does his story tally with hers?* **15.** to score a point or make a goal, as in a game. [1275–1325; (n.) ME *taly* < ML *talia,* var. of L *tālea* rod, cutting, lit., heel-piece, deriv. of *tālus* heel; (v.) late ME *talyen,* deriv. of the n.] —**tal′li•er,** *n.*
—**Syn. 1.** inventory, count, enumeration. **10.** enroll, list. **11.** enumerate, calculate.

tal•ly•ho (tal′ē hō′ *for 1;* tal′ē hō′ *for 2–5*), *n., pl.* **-hos,** *interj., v.* **-hoed** or **-ho′d, -ho•ing.** —*n.* **1.** *Chiefly Brit.* a mail coach or a four-in-hand pleasure coach. **2.** a cry of "tallyho." —*interj.* **3.** the cry of a hunter on first sighting the fox. —*v.t.* **4.** to arouse by crying "tallyho," as to the hounds. —*v.i.* **5.** to utter a cry of "tallyho." [1750–60; cf. F *tayau* hunter's cry]

tal•ly•man (tal′ē mən), *n., pl.* **-men. 1.** a person who tallies or keeps account of something. **2.** *Brit.* a person who sells merchandise on the hire-purchase system. [1645–55; TALLY + -MAN]

Tal•lys (tal′is), *n.* **Thomas.** See **Tallis, Thomas.**

tal′ly sheet′, a sheet for checking, counting, or scoring, as of cargo loaded or unloaded. Also called **tal′ly card′.** [1885–90, *Amer.*]

tal•ly•shop (tal′ē shop′), *n. Brit.* a store specializing in selling merchandise on the hire-purchase system. [1850–55; TALLY + SHOP]

Tal′mi gold′ (täl′mē), a metal made by rolling gold on brass, used in making costume jewelry. Also called **Abyssinian gold.** [1865–70; < G *Talmigold* counterfeit gold, partial trans. of F *Tal. mi-or,* shortening of *Tallois demi-or* lit., Tallois half-gold, a copper-zinc alloy with a thin gold coating, named after a 19th-century Parisian inventor]

Tal•mud (täl′mo͝od, -məd, tal′-), *n.* **1.** the collection of Jewish law and tradition consisting of the Mishnah and the Gemara and being either the edition produced in Palestine A.D. c400 or the larger, more important one produced in Babylonia A.D. c500. **2.** the Gemara. [1525–35; < Heb *talmūdh* lit., instruction] —**Tal•mud•ic** (täl-mo͞o′dik, -myo͞o′-, -mo͝od′ik, -mud′-, tal-), **Tal•mud′i•cal,** *adj.* —**Tal′mud•ism,** *n.*

Tal•mud•ist (täl′mo͝o dist, -mə-, tal′-), *n.* **1.** a person versed in the Talmud. **2.** one of the writers or compilers of the Talmud. **3.** a person who accepts or supports the doctrines of the Talmud. [1560–70; TALMUD + -IST]

Tal•mud To•rah (*Seph.* täl mo͞od′ tô rä′; *Ashk.* täl′-mo͝od tō′ʀə, -məd; *Eng.* täl′məd tôr′ə, tōr′ə, tal′-), *Hebrew.* **1.** (in Europe) a community-supported Jewish elementary school for teaching children Hebrew, Bible, and the fundamentals of Judaism. **2.** (in the U.S.) a Jewish religious school for children, holding classes at the end of the secular school day.

tal•on (tal′ən), *n.* **1.** a claw, esp. of a bird of prey. **2.** the shoulder on the bolt of a lock against which the key presses in sliding the bolt. **3.** *Cards.* the cards left over after the deal; stock. [1350–1400; ME *taloun* < AF; OF *talon* < VL **tālōn-,* s. of **tālō,* for L *tālus* heel] —**tal′•oned,** *adj.*

Ta•los (tā′los), *n. Class. Myth.* a man of brass made by Hephaestus for Minos as a guardian of Crete.

tal. qual., of ordinary or average quality. [< L *tālis quālis*]

ta•luk (tä′lo͝ok, tä lo͝ok′), *n.* (in India) **1.** a hereditary estate. **2.** a subdivision of a revenue district. Also, **ta•lu•ka, ta•loo•ka** (tä lo͞o′kə). [1790–1800; < Urdu *ta'alluq* estate < Ar]

ta•lus[1] (tā′ləs), *n., pl.* **-li** (-lī). *Anat.* the uppermost bone of the proximal row of bones of the tarsus; anklebone. [1685–95; < L *tālus* ankle, anklebone, die. See TASSEL[1]]

ta•lus[2] (tā′ləs, tal′əs), *n., pl.* **-lus•es. 1.** a slope. **2.** *Geol.* a sloping mass of rocky fragments at the base of a cliff. **3.** *Fort.* the slope of the face of a work. [1635–45; < F: pseudo-learned alter. of OF *talu* slope < L *talūtium* gold-bearing slope or talus (VL: slope), perh. of Iberian origin]

Ta•lys (tal′is), *n.* **Thomas.** See **Tallis, Thomas.**

tam (tam), *n.* tam-o'-shanter. [by shortening]

tam•a•ble (tā′mə bəl), *adj.* able to be tamed. Also, **tameable.** [1545–55; TAME + -ABLE] —**tam′a•bil′i•ty, tam′a•ble•ness,** *n.*

ta•ma•le (tə mä′lē), *n.* a Mexican dish made of minced and seasoned meat packed in cornmeal dough, wrapped in corn husks, and steamed. [1605–15, *Amer.;* construed as sing. of MexSp *tamales,* pl. of *tamal* < Nahuatl *tamalli*]

Ta•ma•le (tə mä′lē), *n.* a city in N Ghana. 90,000.

ta•man•du•a (tə man′do͞o ə, tə man′do͞o ä′), *n.* a tree-dwelling, tropical American anteater, *Tamandua tetradactyla,* having a prehensile tail, four-clawed forelimbs, and coarse, tan hair with black markings on the trunk. Also, **tam•an•du** (tam′ən do͞o′). [1605–15; < Pg < Tupi: lit., ant-trapper]

Ta•mar (tā′mər, tā′-), *n.* the daughter of David and half-sister of Absalom. II Sam. 13.

ta•ma•ra (tə mär′ə), *n. Italian Cookery.* a powdered mixture of cinnamon, cloves, coriander, aniseed, and fennel seed. [orig. uncert.]

Tam•a•ra (tam′ər ə, tə mar′ə, -mär′ə), *n.* a female given name.

Tam•a•rac (tam′ə rak′), *n.* a city in SE Florida. 29,142.

tam•a•rack (tam′ə rak′), *n.* **1.** an American larch, *Larix laricina,* of the pine family, having a reddish-brown bark and crowded clusters of blue-green needles and yielding a useful timber. **2.** any of several related, very similar trees. **3.** the wood of these trees. [1795–1805, *Amer.*; cf. CanF *tamarac;* assumed to be of Algonquian orig.]

ta•ma•rao (tä′mə rou′, tam′ə-), *n., pl.* **-raos.** tamarau.

ta•ma•rau (tä′mə rou′, tam′ə-), *n.* a small wild buffalo, *Bubalus (Anoa) mindorensis,* of Mindoro in the Philippines, having thick, brown hair and short, massive horns. Also, **tamarao, timarau.** [1895–1900; < Tagalog]

ta•ma•ril•lo (tam′ə ril′ō, -rē′yō), *n., pl.* **-los. 1.** the edible, plumlike fruit of a tree, *Cyphomandra betacea,* of the nightshade family, native to the Peruvian Andes. **2.** the tree itself. Also called **tree tomato.** [1965–70; pseudo-Sp commercial name (originated in New Zealand); cf. Sp *tomatillo,* dim. of *tomate* TOMATO]

tam•a•rin (tam′ə rin, -ran′), *n.* any South American marmoset of the genera *Saguinus* and *Leontopithecus* (*Leontideus*), having silky fur and a nonprehensile tail: several species are threatened or endangered. [1735–45; < F < Carib]

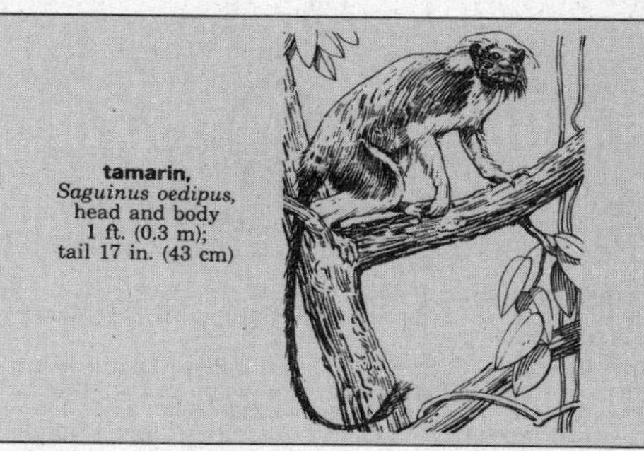
tamarin, *Saguinus oedipus,* head and body 1 ft. (0.3 m); tail 17 in. (43 cm)

tam•a•rind (tam′ə rind), *n.* **1.** the pod of a large, tropical tree, *Tamarindus indica,* of the legume family, containing seeds enclosed in a juicy acid pulp that is used in beverages and food. **2.** the tree itself. [1525–35; < ML *tamarindus* << Ar *tamr hindī* lit., Indian date]

tam•a•risk (tam′ə risk), *n.* **1.** any Old World tropical plant of the genus *Tamarix,* esp. *T. gallica,* an ornamental Mediterranean shrub or small tree having slender, feathery branches. **2.** a shrub or small tree, *Tamarix chinensis,* of Eurasia, having scalelike leaves and clusters of pink flowers, naturalized in the southwestern U.S., where it has become a troublesome weed. [1350–1400; ME *tamariscus* < LL, var. of L *tamarix,* perh. of Hamitic orig.]

tam′arisk ger′bil, gerbil (def. 2).

ta•mas (tum′əs), *n. Hinduism.* See under **guna.** [< Skt: darkness] —**ta•mas•ic** (tə mas′ik), *adj.*

ta•ma•sha (tə mä′shə), *n.* (in the East Indies) a spectacle; entertainment. [1680–90; < Urdu < Pers *tamāshā* a stroll < Ar]

Ta•ma•tave (tä′mä täv′, -mə-), *n.* a seaport on E Madagascar. 59,503.

Ta•mau•li•pas (tä′mou lē′päs), *n.* a state in NE Mexico, bordering on the Gulf of Mexico. 1,901,000; 30,731 sq. mi. (79,595 sq. km). *Cap.:* Ciudad Victoria.

Ta•ma•yo (tä mä′yô), *n.* **Ru•fi•no** (ro͞o fē′nô), 1899–1991, Mexican painter.

Ta•ma•zight (tä′mə zit′, tam′ə-), *n.* a Berber language spoken in Morocco.

tam•bac (tam′bak), *n.* tombac.

tam•ba•la (täm bä′lə), *n.* a bronze coin and monetary unit of Malawi, the 100th part of a kwacha.

Tam•bo (tam′bō), *n.* See **Mr. Tambo.**

Tam•bo•ra (täm′bô rä′, -bō-, -bə-), *n.* an active volcano in Indonesia, on N Sumbawa: eruption 1815. 9042 ft. (2756 m).

tam•bour (tam′bo͝or, tam bo͝or′), *n.* **1.** *Music.* a drum. **2.** a drum player. **3.** Also called **tabaret.** a circular frame consisting of two hoops, one fitting within the other, in which cloth is stretched for embroidering. **4.** embroidery done on such a frame. **5.** *Furniture.* a flexible shutter used as a desk top or in place of a door, composed of a number of closely set wood strips attached to a piece of cloth, the whole sliding in grooves along the sides or at the top and bottom. **6.** *Archit.* drum[1] (def. 10). **7.** *Court Tennis.* a sloping buttress opposite the penthouse, on the hazard side of the court. —*v.t., v.i.* **8.** to embroider on a tambour. [1475–85; < MF: drum << Ar *tanbūr* lute < MGk *pandoúra;* cf. BANDORE]

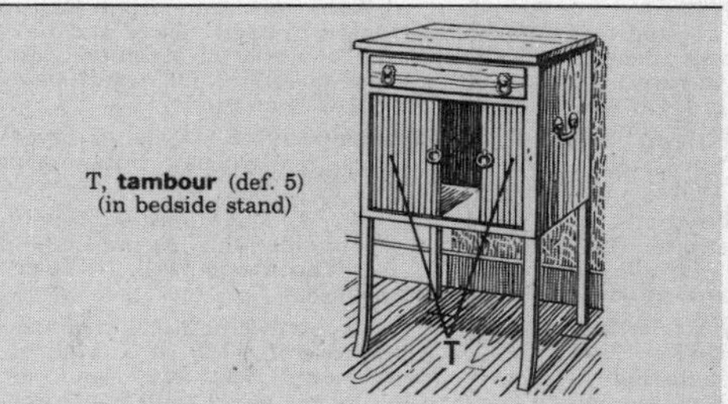

T, **tambour** (def. 5) (in bedside stand)

tam•bou•rin (tam′bo͞o rin; *Fr.* tän bo͞o ʀᴀɴ′), *n., pl.* **-rins** (-rinz; *Fr.* -ʀᴀɴ′). **1.** a long narrow drum of Provence. **2.** an old Provençal dance in duple meter, accompanied by a drone bass or by a steady drumbeat. **3.** the music for this dance. [1790–1800; < F < Pr *tamborin,* dim. of *tambor* TAMBOUR]

tam•bou•rine (tam′bə rēn′), *n.* a small drum consisting of a circular frame with a skin stretched over it and several pairs of metal jingles attached to the frame, played by striking with the knuckles, shaking, and the like. [1570–80; earlier *tamboryne* < MD *tamborijn* small drum < MF *tambourin* or ML *tamborinum.* See TAMBOUR, -INE[1]] —**tam′bou·rin′ist,** *n.*

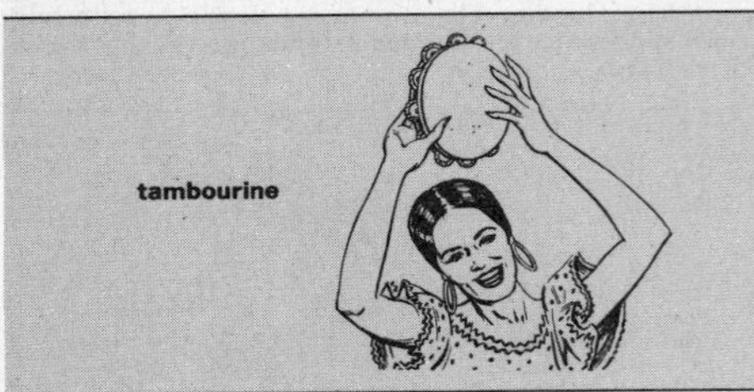
tambourine

Tam·bov (täm bôf′, -bôv′; *Russ.* tum bôf′), *n.* a city in the Russian Federation in Europe, SE of Moscow. 305,000.

tam·bu·ra (tam bŏŏr′ə), *n.* an Asian musical instrument of the lute family having a small, round body and a long neck. Also, **tam·bou′ra, tam·bur** (tam bŏŏr′), **tampur, tanbur.** [< Hindi < Ar *ṭanbūr* (see TAMBOUR)]

tam·bu·rit·za (tam bŏŏr′it sə, tam′bə rit′sə), *n.* one of a family of mandolinlike stringed instruments of southern Slavic regions. [1925–30; < Serbo-Croatian *tàmburica,* dim. of *tàmbura* a stringed instrument < Turk *tambura* < Pers *ṭanbūr;* see TAMBURA]

Tam·bur·laine (tam′bər lān′), *n.* Tamerlane.

tame (tām), *adj.,* **tam·er, tam·est,** *v.,* **tamed, tam·ing.** —*adj.* **1.** changed from the wild or savage state; domesticated: *a tame bear.* **2.** without the savageness or fear of humans normal in wild animals; gentle, fearless, or without shyness, as if domesticated: *That lion acts as tame as a house cat.* **3.** tractable, docile, or submissive, as a person or the disposition. **4.** lacking in excitement; dull; insipid: *a very tame party.* **5.** spiritless or pusillanimous. **6.** not to be taken very seriously; without real power or importance; serviceable but harmless: *They kept a tame scientist around.* **7.** brought into service; rendered useful and manageable; under control, as natural resources or a source of power. **8.** cultivated or improved by cultivation, as a plant or its fruit. —*v.t.* **9.** to make tame; domesticate; make tractable. **10.** to deprive of courage, ardor, or zest. **11.** to deprive of interest, excitement, or attractiveness; make dull. **12.** to soften; tone down. **13.** to harness or control; render useful, as a source of power. **14.** to cultivate, as land or plants. —*v.i.* **15.** to become tame. [bef. 900; (adj.) ME; OE *tam;* c. D *tam,* G *zahm,* ON *tamr;* (v.) ME *tamen,* deriv. of the adj.; r. ME *temen* to tame, OE *temian,* deriv. of *tam;* c. ON *temja,* Goth *gatamjan;* akin to L *domāre* to tame] —**tame′ly,** *adv.* —**tame′ness,** *n.* —**tam′er,** *n.*
—**Syn. 3.** meek, subdued. **4.** flat, empty, vapid, boring, tedious, uninteresting. **5.** cowardly, dastardly. **9.** break, subdue. **12.** calm, mollify. —**Ant. 1.** wild.

tame·a·ble (tā′mə bəl), *adj.* tamable.

tame·less (tām′lis), *adj.* untamed or untamable. [1590–1600; TAME + -LESS] —**tame′less·ly,** *adv.* —**tame′less·ness,** *n.*

Tam·er·lane (tam′ər lān′), *n.* (*Timur Lenk*) 1336?–1405, Tartar conqueror in southern and western Asia: ruler of Samarkand 1369–1405. Also, **Tamburlaine.** Also called **Timour, Timur.**

Tam·il (tam′əl, tum′-, tä′məl), *n., pl.* **-ils,** (*esp. collectively*) **-il,** *adj.* —*n.* **1.** a member of a people of Dravidian stock of S India and Sri Lanka. **2.** the Dravidian language of the Tamils, spoken in India principally in Tamil Nadu state and in Sri Lanka on the N and E coasts. —*adj.* **3.** of or pertaining to the Tamils or their language.

Tam′il Na′du (nä′do͞o), a large state in S India: formerly a presidency; boundaries readjusted on a linguistic basis 1956. 41,200,000; 50,110 sq. mi. (129,785 sq. km). Formerly, **Madras.**

Tam′ing of the Shrew′, The, a comedy (1594?) by Shakespeare.

tam·is (tam′ē, -is), *n., pl.* **tam·ises** (tam′ēz, -ə siz). a worsted cloth mesh constructed in open weave and having a corded face, used as a sieve or strainer. Also, **tammy.** [1595–1605; < F: sieve < ?; cf. OE *temes* sieve, c. MLG *temes,* MD *temse,* OHG *zemisa*]

Tamm (täm), *n.* **I·gor Ev·ge·nie·vich** (ē′gər yiv gye′-nyi vyich), 1895–1971, Russian physicist: Nobel prize 1958.

Tam·ma·ny (tam′ə nē), *adj.* **1.** pertaining to, involving, or characteristic of the membership or methods of Tammany Hall. —*n.* **2.** See **Tammany Hall.** —**Tam′·ma·ny·ism,** *n.* —**Tam′ma·ny·ite′,** *n.*

Tam′many Hall′, 1. a Democratic political organization in New York City, founded in 1789 as a fraternal benevolent society (**Tam′many Soci′ety**) and associated esp. in the late 1800's and early 1900's with corruption and abuse of power. **2.** the building in which the Tammany organization had its headquarters. [named after *Tammany* (var. of *Tamanen, Tammenund*), 17th-century Delaware Indian chief, later facetiously canonized as patron saint of U.S.]

Tam·mer·fors (täm′mər fôrs′), *n.* Swedish name of **Tampere.**

Tam·muz (tä′mo͝oz; *for 1 also* tä mo͞oz′; *for 2 also* tam′uz), *n.* **1.** the tenth month of the Jewish calendar. Cf. **Jewish calendar. 2.** a Sumerian and Babylonian shepherd god, originally king of Erech, confined forever in the afterworld as a substitute for his consort Inanna or Ishtar. [< Heb *tammūz*]

tam·my[1] (tam′ē), *n.* a fabric of mixed fibers, constructed in plain weave and often heavily glazed, used in the manufacture of linings and undergarments. Also, **tam′mie.** [1630–40; perh. back formation from obs. F *tamise* kind of glossy cloth (taken as pl.)]

tam·my[2] (tam′ē), *n., pl.* **-mies.** tamis.

Tam·my (tam′ē), *n.* a female given name.

ta·mo (tä′mō), *n., pl.* **-mos.** the light, yellowish-brown wood of a Japanese ash, *Fraxinus mandschurica,* used for making furniture. [< Japn *tamo(-no-ki), tamu-(no-ki)* name of the tree]

tam-o'-shan·ter (tam′ə shan′tər, tam′ə shan′ter), *n.* a cap of Scottish origin, usually made of wool, having a round, flat top that projects all around the head and has a pompon at its center. Also called **tam.** [1880–85; named after the hero of *Tam O'Shanter* (1791), poem by Robert Burns]

tam-o'-shanter

ta·mox·i·fen (tə mok′sə fən), *n. Pharm.* an antineoplastic drug, $C_{26}H_{29}NO$, that blocks the estrogen receptors on cancer cells, used in the treatment of breast cancer. [1970–75; perh. T(RANS)- + AM(INO)- + OXY-[2] + PHEN(YL), with resp. of *y* and *ph*]

tamp (tamp), *v.t.* **1.** to force in or down by repeated, rather light, strokes: *He tamped the tobacco in his pipe.* **2.** (in blasting) to fill (a drilled hole) with earth or the like after the charge has been inserted. [1810–20; perh. alter of TAMPION]

Tam·pa (tam′pə), *n.* a seaport in W Florida, on Tampa Bay: fishing resort. 271,523. —**Tam′pan,** *n., adj.*

Tam′pa Bay′, an inlet of the Gulf of Mexico, in W Florida. ab. 27 mi. (43 km) long.

tam·pal·a (tam pal′ə), *n.* a branching tropical plant, *Amaranthus tricolor,* of the amaranth family, cultivated in Asia as a green vegetable. Cf. **Joseph's-coat.** [perh. < Sinhalese]

tam·per[1] (tam′pər), *v.i.* **1.** to meddle, esp. for the purpose of altering, damaging, or misusing (usually fol. by *with*): *Someone has been tampering with the lock.* **2.** to make changes in something, esp. in order to falsify (usually fol. by *with*): *to tamper with official records.* **3.** to engage secretly or improperly in something. **4.** to engage in underhand or corrupt dealings, esp. in order to influence improperly (usually fol. by *with*): *Any lawyer who tries to tamper with a jury should be disbarred.* [1560–70; prob. var. of TEMPER (v.)] —**tam′per·er,** *n.*
—**Syn. 1.** interfere.

tam·per[2] (tam′pər), *n.* a person or thing that tamps. [TAMP + -ER[1]]

Tam·pe·re (täm′pe re), *n.* a city in SW Finland. 167,000. Swedish, **Tammerfors.**

tam·per·proof (tam′pər pro͞of′), *adj.* that cannot be tampered with; impervious to tampering: *a tamper-proof lock.* Also, **tam′per-proof′.** [1885–90; TAMPER[1] + -PROOF]

tam·per-re·sist·ant (tam′pər ri zis′tənt), *adj.* difficult to tamper with: *a tamper-resistant cap on a medicine bottle.*

Tam·pi·co (tam pē′kō; *Sp.* täm pē′kô), *n.* a seaport in SE Tamaulipas, in E Mexico. 240,500. —**Tam·pi′can,** *n.*

Tampi′co hemp′, a stiff fiber obtained from the leaves of various species of *Agave,* as *A. falcata* or *A. sisalana.* Also called **Tampi′co fi′ber.** [1930–35]

tam·pi·on (tam′pē ən), *n.* a plug or stopper placed in the muzzle of a piece of ordnance when not in use, to keep out dampness and dust. Also, **tompion.** [1425–75; late ME *tampyon,* var. of *tampon* < MF, nasalized var. of OF *tapon,* deriv. of *tape* plug < Gmc. See TAP[2]]

tam·pon (tam′pon), *n.* **1.** a plug of cotton or the like for insertion into an orifice, wound, etc., chiefly for absorbing blood or stopping hemorrhages. **2.** such a plug used for absorbing menstrual flow, esp. one that is manufactured commercially. **3.** a two-headed drumstick for playing rolls. —*v.t.* **4.** to fill or plug with a tampon. [1855–60; < F; see TAMPION]

tam·pon·ade (tam′pə nād′), *n.* **1.** *Med.* the use of a tampon, as to stop a hemorrhage. **2.** Also called **cardiac tamponade, heart tamponade.** *Pathol.* a condition in which the heart is compressed because of an accumulation of fluid in the pericardium. Also, **tam·pon·age** (tam′pə nij). [1885–90; TAMPON + -ADE[1]]

tam·pur (täm po͝or′), *n.* tambura.

tam-tam (tum′tum′, tam′tam′), *n.* **1.** a gong with indefinite pitch. **2.** tom-tom. [1775–85; var. of TOM-TOM]

Tam·worth (tam′wûrth′), *n.* one of an English breed of red hogs, raised chiefly for bacon. [after *Tamworth,* in Staffordshire, England where the breed was developed]

Tam·worth (tam′wûrth′), *n.* a city in E Australia. 29,657.

tan[1] (tan), *v.,* **tanned, tan·ning,** *n., adj.,* **tan·ner, tan·nest.** —*v.t.* **1.** to convert (a hide) into leather, esp. by soaking or steeping in a bath prepared from tanbark or synthetically. **2.** to make brown by exposure to ultraviolet rays, as of the sun. **3.** *Informal.* to thrash; spank. —*v.i.* **4.** to become tanned. **5. tan someone's hide,** *Informal.* to beat someone soundly: *She threatened to tan our hides if she found us on her property again.* —*n.* **6.** the brown color imparted to the skin by exposure to the sun or open air. **7.** yellowish brown; light brown. **8.** tanbark. —*adj.* **9.** of the color of tan; yellowish-brown. **10.** used in or relating to tanning processes, materials, etc. [bef. 1000; 1920–25 for def. 2; ME *tannen* to make hide into leather, late OE **tannian* (in ptp. *getanned;* cf. TANNER[1]) < ML *tannāre,* deriv. of *tannum* oak bark, tanbark < Gmc; cf. OHG *tanna* oak, fir, akin to D *den* fir] —**tan′na·ble,** *adj.*

tan[2] (tan), *n.* tangent (def. 5b). [by shortening]

TAN (tan), *n.* tax-anticipation note.

tan^{-1}, *Symbol, Trig.* arc tangent.

ta·na (tä′nə), *n.* thana.

Ta·na (tä′nä, -nə), *n.* **1.** a river in E Africa, in Kenya, flowing SE to the Indian Ocean. 500 mi. (800 km) long. **2. Lake.** Also, **Tsana.** a lake in NW Ethiopia: the source of the Blue Nile. 1100 sq. mi. (2850 sq. km).

Ta·nach (tä näkh′), *n. Hebrew.* the three Jewish divisions of the Old Testament, comprising the Law or Torah, the Prophets or *Neviim,* and the Hagiographa or *Ketuvim,* taken as a whole. [vocalization of Heb *TNK,* for *Tōrāh* law + *Nəbhī′īm* prophets + *Kəthūbhīm* (other) writings]

tan·a·ger (tan′ə jər), *n.* any of numerous songbirds of the New World family Thraupidae, the males of which are usually brightly colored. [1605–15; < NL *tanagra,* metathetic var. of Tupi *tangara*]

scarlet tanager, *Piranga olivacea,* length to 7 in. (18 cm)

Tan·a·gra (tan′ə grə, tə nag′rə), *n.* a town in ancient Greece, in Boeotia: Spartan victory over the Athenians 457 B.C.

Tan′agra figurine′, a small terra-cotta statuette produced from the late 4th to the 3rd century B.C. in Tanagra, Boeotia, and found chiefly in tombs. Also, **Tan′agra fig′ure.** [1890–95]

tan·a·grine (tan′ə grin), *adj.* of or pertaining to the tanagers; belonging to the tanager family. [1885–90; < NL *tanagr(a)* TANAGER + -INE[1]]

Ta·nai·na (tə nī′nə), *n., pl.* **-nas,** (*esp. collectively*) **-na** for 1. **1.** a member of a North American Indian people of the Cook Inlet area of Alaska. **2.** the Athabaskan language of the Tanaina.

Ta·na·ka (tə nä′kə; *Japn.* tä′nä kä′), *n.* **Baron Gi·i·chi** (gē ē′chē), 1863–1929, Japanese military and political leader: prime minister 1927–29.

Ta·na·na (tan′ə nä′, -nô′), *n., pl.* **-nas,** (*esp. collectively*) **-na** for 2. **1.** a river flowing NW from E Alaska to the Yukon River. ab. 650 mi. (1045 km) long. **2.** a member of a North American Indian people of the Tanana River drainage basin in east-central Alaska. **3.** the Athabaskan language of the Tanana.

Ta·na·na·rive (*Fr.* TA NA NA RĒV′; *Eng.* tə nan′ə rēv′), *n.* former name of **Antananarivo.**

Tan·a·quil (tan′ə kwil), *n.* a legendary queen of Rome who prophesied the future greatness of Servius Tullius and helped him to gain the throne after the murder of her husband by a political faction.

tan·bark (tan′bärk′), **1.** the bark of the oak, hemlock, etc., bruised and broken by a mill and used esp. in tanning hides. **2.** a surface covered with pieces of tanbark, esp. a circus ring. [1790–1800; TAN[1] + BARK[2]]

tan′bark oak′, any oak that yields tanbark, esp. an evergreen oak, *Lithocarpus densiflora,* of the Pacific coast of North America. [1880–85, *Amer.*]

tan·bur (tän bo͝or′), *n.* tambura.

Tan·cred (tang′krid), *n.* 1078?–1112, Norman leader in the first Crusade.

T&A, 1. *Slang.* See **tits and ass. 2.** tonsillectomy and adenoidectomy. Also, **T and A**

T&E, travel and entertainment. Also, **T and E**

tan·dem (tan′dəm), *adv.* **1.** one following or behind the other: *to drive horses tandem.* **2. in tandem, a.** in single file: *They swam in tandem.* **b.** in association or partnership. —*adj.* **3.** having animals, seats, parts, etc., arranged tandem or one behind another. —*n.* **4.** a vehicle, as a truck, tractor, or trailer, in which a pair or pairs of axles are arranged in tandem. **5.** See **tandem bicycle. 6.** See **tandem trailer** (def. 1). **7.** a team of horses harnessed one behind the other. **8.** a two-wheeled carriage with a high driver's seat, drawn by two or more horses so harnessed. **9.** any of various mechanisms having a tandem arrangement. [1735–45; special use (orig. facetious) of L *tandem* at length, finally, equiv. to *tam* so far + *-dem* demonstrative suffix]

tandem (def. 8)

tan′dem bi′cycle, a bicycle for two or more persons, having seats and corresponding sets of pedals arranged in tandem, esp. popular in the 19th century. [1885–90]

tan·dem-com·pound (tan′dəm kom′pound), *adj.* (of a compound engine or turbine) having high-pressure and low-pressure units in tandem. Cf. **cross-compound.**

tan′dem trail′er, 1. Also called **double-bottom, double-trailer truck, tandem.** a very long rig consisting of a tractor pulling two trailers hooked up one behind another. **2.** a semitrailer designed to be hooked up to another part of such a rig.

tan·door (tän do͝or′), *n., pl.* **-doors, -door·i** (-do͝or′ē). *Indian Cookery.* a cylindrical clay oven, fired to a high heat by wood or charcoal, in which foods, esp. meats, are cooked and bread is baked. [1655–65; < Hindi, Urdu *tandūr* < Pers *tanūr*]

tan·door·i (tän do͝or′ē), *adj.* **1.** baked or cooked in a tandoor: *tandoori chicken.* —*n.* **2.** a pl. of **tandoor.** [1965–70; < Hindi *tandūrī*, adj. deriv. of *tandūr* TANDUR]

Ta·ne (tä′nā), *n.* a Polynesian god of fertility.

Ta·nen Taung·gyi (tə nin′ toun′jē), a mountain range in NW Thailand and SE Burma, rising to a height of 7000 ft. (2134 m).

Ta·ney (tô′nē), *n.* **Roger Brooke,** 1777–1864, U.S. jurist: Chief Justice of the U.S. 1836–64.

tang[1] (tang), *n.* **1.** a strong taste or flavor. **2.** the distinctive flavor or quality of a thing. **3.** a pungent or distinctive odor. **4.** a touch or suggestion of something; slight trace. **5.** a long and slender projecting strip, tongue, or prong forming part of an object, as a chisel, file, or knife, and serving as a means of attachment for another part, as a handle or stock. **6.** a surgeonfish. —*v.t.* **7.** to furnish with a tang. [1300–50; ME *tange* tongue of a snake, projection on a tool, perh. < ON *tangi* projection, headland]
—**Syn. 1.** savor. **4.** taste, hint.

tang[2] (tang), *n.* **1.** a sharp ringing or twanging sound; clang. —*v.t., v.i.* **2.** to ring or twang; clang. [1550–60; imit.; see TING[1]]

T'ang (täng), *n.* a dynasty in China, A.D. 618–907, marked by territorial expansion, the invention of printing, and the high development of poetry. Also, **Tang.**

tan·ga (təng gä′), *n.* **1.** either of two former coins of India, one gold and one silver, issued by various Muslim rulers. **2.** a former coin of Portuguese India, equal to the 10th part of a rupee. **3.** a former silver coin of Tibet of varying weight and fineness. Also, **tangka.** [1590–1600; < Hindi *taṅgā*]

Tan·ga (tang′gə), *n.* a seaport in NE Tanzania. 61,000.

Tan·gan·yi·ka (tan′gən yē′kə, -gə nē′-, tang′-), *n.* **1.** a former country in E Africa: formed the larger part of German East Africa; British trusteeship **(Tan′ganyi′ka Ter′ritory)** 1946–61; became independent 1961; now the mainland part of Tanzania. 361,800 sq. mi. (937,062 sq. km). **2. Lake,** a lake in central Africa, between Zaire and Tanzania: the longest freshwater lake in the world. ab. 450 mi. (725 km) long; 30–40 mi. (48–64 km) wide; 12,700 sq. mi. (32,893 sq. km). —**Tan′gan·yi′kan,** *adj., n.*

Tanganyi′ka and Zan′zibar, United Republic of, former name of **Tanzania.**

tan·ge·lo (tan′jə lō′), *n., pl.* **-los.** a hybrid citrus fruit, *Citrus tangelo*, that is a cross between the grapefruit and the tangerine and is cultivated in several varieties. [1900–05; TANG(ERINE) + (POM)ELO]

tan·gen·cy (tan′jən sē), *n.* the state of being tangent. [1810–20; TANG(ENT) + -ENCY]

tan·gent (tan′jənt), *adj.* **1.** in immediate physical contact; touching. **2.** *Geom.* **a.** touching at a single point, as a tangent in relation to a curve or surface. **b.** in contact along a single line or element, as a plane with a cylinder. **3.** tangential (def. 3). —*n.* **4.** *Geom.* a line or a plane that touches a curve or a surface at a point so that it is closer to the curve in the vicinity of the point than any other line or plane drawn through the point. **5.** *Trig.* **a.** (in a right triangle) the ratio of the side opposite a given angle to the side adjacent to the angle. **b.** Also called **tan.** (of an angle) a trigonometric function equal to the ratio of the ordinate of the end point of the arc to the abscissa of this end point, the origin being at the center of the circle on which the arc lies and the initial point of the arc being on the x-axis. *Abbr.:* tg, tgn **c.** (originally) a straight line perpendicular to the radius of a circle at one end of an arc and extending from this point to the produced radius which cuts off the arc at its other end. **6.** the upright metal blade, fastened on the inner end of a clavichord key, that rises and strikes the string when the outer end of the key is depressed. **7. off on** or **at a tangent,** digressing suddenly from one course of action or thought and turning to another: *The speaker flew off on a tangent.* [1585–90; < L *tangent-* (s. of *tangēns*, prp. of *tangere* to touch) in phrase *līnea tangēns* touching line; see -ENT]
—**Syn. 1.** meeting, abutting.

tangent (defs. 5a, b) ACB being the angle, the ratio of AB to AC is the tangent, or AC being taken equal to unity, the tangent is AB

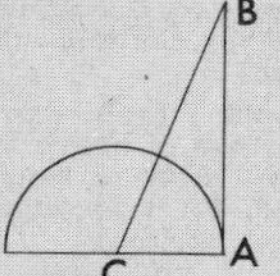

tan·gen·tial (tan jen′shəl), *adj.* **1.** pertaining to or of the nature of a tangent; being or moving in the direction of a tangent. **2.** merely touching; slightly connected: *tangential information.* **3.** divergent or digressive, as from a subject under consideration: *tangential remarks.* **4.** tending to digress or to reply to questions obliquely. Also, **tan·gen·tal** (tan jen′tl). [1620–30; TANGENT + -IAL] —**tan·gen′ti·al′i·ty,** *n.* —**tan·gen′tial·ly, tan·gen′tal·ly,** *adv.*

tangen′tial mo′tion, *Astron.* the component of the linear motion of a star with respect to the sun, measured along a line perpendicular to its line of sight and expressed in miles or kilometers per second. Also called **tangen′tial veloc′ity.** Cf. **proper motion, radial motion.** [1760–70]

tan·ge·rine (tan′jə rēn′, tan′jə rēn′), *n.* **1.** Also called **mandarin, mandarin orange.** any of several varieties of mandarin, cultivated widely, esp. in the U.S. **2.** deep orange; reddish orange. —*adj.* **3.** of the color tangerine; reddish-orange. [TANG(I)ER + -INE[1]]

tan·gi·ble (tan′jə bəl), *adj.* **1.** capable of being touched; discernible by the touch; material or substantial. **2.** real or actual, rather than imaginary or visionary: *the tangible benefits of sunshine.* **3.** definite; not vague or elusive: *no tangible grounds for suspicion.* **4.** (of an asset) having actual physical existence, as real estate or chattels, and therefore capable of being assigned a value in monetary terms. —*n.* **5.** something tangible, esp. a tangible asset. [1580–90; < LL *tangibilis*, equiv. to L *tang(ere)* to touch + *-ibilis* -IBLE] —**tan′gi·bil′i·ty, tan′gi·ble·ness,** *n.* —**tan′gi·bly,** *adv.*
—**Syn. 1.** palpable, corporeal. **2.** certain, genuine, perceptible. **3.** specific.

Tan·gier (tan jēr′), *n.* a seaport in N Morocco, on the W Strait of Gibraltar: capital of the former Tangier Zone. 243,600. Also, **Tan·giers** (tan jērz′). French, **Tanger** (täN zhā′).

Tangier′ Zone′, a former internationalized zone on the Strait of Gibraltar: became a part of Morocco 1956. Cf. **Morocco** (def. 1).

tang·ka (təng kä′), *n.* tanga.

tan·gle[1] (tang′gəl), *v.,* **-gled, -gling,** *n.* —*v.t.* **1.** to bring together into a mass of confusedly interlaced or intertwisted threads, strands, or other like parts; snarl. **2.** to involve in something that hampers, obstructs, or overgrows: *The bushes were tangled with vines.* **3.** to catch and hold in or as if in a net or snare. —*v.i.* **4.** to be or become tangled. **5.** *Informal.* to come into conflict; fight or argue: *I don't want to tangle with him over the new ruling.* —*n.* **6.** a tangled condition or situation. **7.** a tangled or confused mass or assemblage of something. **8.** a confused jumble: *a tangle of contradictory statements.* **9.** *Informal.* a conflict; disagreement: *He got into a tangle with the governor.* [1300–50; ME *tangilen, tagilen* to entangle < Scand; cf. Sw (dial.) *taggla* to disarrange] —**tan′gle·ment,** *n.* —**tan′gler,** *n.* —**tan′gly,** *adv.*
—**Syn. 8.** snarl, net, labyrinth, maze.

tan·gle[2] (tang′gəl), *n.* any of several large seaweeds of the genus *Laminaria*. [1530–40; < Scand; cf. ON *þǫngull* strand of tangle, Norw *tang*]

tan·gle·ber·ry (tang′gəl ber′ē), *n., pl.* **-ries.** a huckleberry, *Gaylussacia frondosa*, of the eastern U.S. Also called **blue huckleberry, dangleberry.** [TANGLE[1] + BERRY]

tan·gled (tang′gəld), *adj.* **1.** snarled, interlaced, or mixed up: *tangled thread.* **2.** very complicated, intricate, or involved: *tangled bureaucratic procedures.* [1580–90; TANGLE[1] + -ED[2]]

Tan·gle·wood (tang′gəl wo͝od′), *n.* See under **Lenox.**

tan·go (tang′gō), *n., pl.* **-gos,** *v.,* **-goed, -go·ing.** —*n.* **1.** a ballroom dance of Latin-American origin, danced by couples, and having many varied steps, figures, and poses. **2.** music for this dance. **3.** a word used in communications to represent the letter *T.* —*v.i.* **4.** to dance the tango. [1910–15; < AmerSp < ?]

tan·gor (tan′jôr, tang′gôr), *n.* See **temple orange.** [TANG(ERINE) + OR(ANGE)]

tan·go·re·cep·tor (tang′gō ri sep′tər), *n. Physiol., Biol.* a receptor stimulated by touch. [< L *tang(ere)* to touch + -o- + RECEPTOR]

tan·gram (tang′grəm), *n.* a Chinese puzzle consisting of a square cut into five triangles, a square, and a rhomboid, which can be combined so as to form a great variety of other figures. [1860–65; *tang-*, perh. < Chin *Táng* TANG, i.e., Chinese + -GRAM]

Tang·shan (täng′shän′), *n. Pinyin, Wade-Giles.* a city in NE Hebei province, in NE China. 1,200,000. Also, **T'ang′shan′.**

Tan·guy (täN gē′), *n.* **Yves** (ēv), 1900–55, French painter, in the U.S. after 1939.

tang·y (tang′ē), *adj.,* **tang·i·er, tang·i·est.** having a tang. [1870–75; TANG[1] + -Y[1]] —**tang′i·ness,** *n.*

tanh, *Symbol, Math.* hyperbolic tangent. [TAN(GENT) + H(YPERBOLIC)]

Ta·nis (tā′nis), *n.* an ancient city in Lower Egypt, in the Nile delta. Biblical, **Zoan.**

tan·ist (tan′ist, thô′nist), *n. Hist.* the successor apparent to a Celtic chief, usually the oldest or worthiest of his kin, chosen by election among the tribe during the chief's lifetime. [1530–40; < Ir *tánaiste* second, substitute, heir by election]

tan·ist·ry (tan′ə strē, thô′nə-), *n.* the system among various Celtic tribes of choosing a tanist. [1590–1600; TANIST + -RY]

Ta·ni·za·ki (tä′nē zä′kē), *n.* **Ju·ni·chi·ro** (jo͞o′nē chē′rô), 1886–1965, Japanese novelist.

Tan·jore (tan jôr′, -jōr′), *n.* former name of **Thanjavur.**

Tan·jung·pan·dan (tän′jo͝ong pän′dän), *n.* a town on NW Billiton, in central Indonesia.

tank (def. 3)

tank (tangk), *n.* **1.** a large receptacle, container, or structure for holding a liquid or gas: *tanks for storing oil.* **2.** a natural or artificial pool, pond, or lake. **3.** *Mil.* an armored, self-propelled combat vehicle, armed with cannon and machine guns and moving on a caterpillar tread. **4.** *Slang.* a prison cell or enclosure for more than one occupant, as for prisoners awaiting a hearing. **5.** See **tank top. 6. go in the tank,** *Boxing Slang.* to go through the motions of a match but deliberately lose because of an illicit prearrangement or fix; throw a fight. —*v.t.* **7.** to put or store in a tank. **8. tank up, a.** to fill the gas tank of an automobile or other motor vehicle. **b.** *Slang.* to drink a great quantity of alcoholic beverage, esp. to intoxication. [1610–20; perh. jointly < Gujarati *ṭā̃kh* reservoir, lake, and Pg *tanque*, contr. of *estanque* pond, lit., something dammed up, deriv. of *estancar* (< VL **stanticāre*) to dam up, weaken; adopted as a cover name for the military vehicle during the early stages of its manufacture in England (December, 1915)] —**tank′less,** *adj.* —**tank′like′,** *adj.*

tan·ka (täng′kə), *n., pl.* **-kas, -ka.** *Pros.* a Japanese poem consisting of 31 syllables in 5 lines, with 5 syllables in the first and third lines and 7 in the others. [1915–20; < Japn < MChin, equiv. to Chin *duǎn* short + *gē* song; cf. RENGA]

tank·age (tang′kij), *n.* **1.** the capacity of a tank or tanks. **2.** the act or process of storing liquid in a tank. **3.** the fee charged for such storage. **4.** the residue from tanks in which carcasses and other offal have been steamed and the fat has been rendered, used as a fertilizer. [1865–70; TANK + -AGE]

tan·kard (tang′kərd), *n.* a large drinking cup, usually with a handle and a hinged cover. [1275–1325; ME: bucket; cf. MD *tanckaert*, MF *tanquart*]

tankard (18th century)

tank′ car′, *Railroads.* a car containing one or more tanks for the transportation of liquids, gases, or granular solids. [1870–75, *Amer.*]

tank′ destroy′er, a high-speed, self-propelled, armored combat vehicle with antitank cannon. [1940–45]

tanked (tangkt), *adj.* **1.** put or stored in a tank. **2.** Also, **tanked′ up′.** *Slang.* drunk. [1895–1900; TANK + -ED[2]]

tank·er (tang′kər), *n.* **1.** a ship, airplane, or truck designed for bulk shipment of liquids or gases. **2.** a tank trailer or tank truck. —*v.t.* **3.** to transport by tanker. [1895–1900; TANK + -ER[1]]

tank′ farm′, an area or expanse of land used for holding oil-storage tanks. [1920–25]

tank′ farm′ing, hydroponics.

tank′ fight′er, *Boxing.* a boxer known for false shows of being knocked down or out in bouts the results of which have been prearranged.

tank·ful (tangk′fo͝ol), *n., pl.* **-fuls.** the amount a tank can hold. [1885–90; TANK + -FUL]
—**Usage.** See **-ful.**

tank′ locomo′tive, a steam locomotive carrying its own fuel and water without the use of a tender.

tank·ship (tangk′ship′), *n.* a ship for carrying bulk cargoes of liquids; tanker. [TANK + -SHIP]

tank′ suit′, a simple one-piece bathing suit for women, having a scoop neck and shoulder straps and usually no lining or inner construction; maillot. [1935–40]

tank′ top′, a close-fitting, low-cut top having shoulder straps and often made of lightweight, knitted fabric. Also called **tank.** [1945–50]

tank′ town′, **1.** a town where trains stop to take on a supply of water. **2.** any small, unimportant, or uninteresting town. [1910–15, *Amer.*]

tank′ trail′er, a trailer truck or tractor-trailer with a tank body, suitable for transporting gases or liquids, as oil, gasoline, or milk, in bulk. [1940–45]

tank′ truck′, a truck with a tank body, suitable for transporting gases or liquids, as oil, gasoline, or milk, in bulk.

tan·na (*Seph. Heb.* tä nä′; *Ashk. Heb., Eng.* tä′nä), *n., pl.* **tan·na·im** (*Seph. Heb.* tä nä ēm′; *Ashk. Heb., Eng.* tä nä′im). (*often cap.*) *Judaism.* one of a group of Jewish scholars, active in Palestine during the 1st and 2nd centuries A.D., whose teachings are found chiefly in the Mishnah. Cf. **amora, sabora.** [< Heb *tannā teacher*] **—tan·na·i·tic** (tä′nə it′ik), *adj.*

tan·nage (tan′ij), *n.* **1.** the act or process of tanning. **2.** the product of tanning; something that is tanned. [1655–65; TAN + -AGE]

tan·nate (tan′āt), *n. Chem.* a salt of tannic acid. [1795–1805; TANN(IN) + -ATE[2]]

Tan·nen·baum (tä′nən boum′; *Eng.* tan′ən boum′), *n., pl.* ***-bäu·me*** (-boi′mə), *Eng.* **-baums.** *German.* a Christmas tree. [lit., fir tree]

Tan·nen·berg (*Ger.* tän′ən berk), *n.* a village formerly in East Prussia, now in N Poland: major German victory over the Russians 1914. Polish, **Stębark.**

tan·ner[1] (tan′ər), *n.* a person whose occupation it is to tan hides. [bef. 1000; ME, OE *tannere.* See TAN[1], -ER[1]]

tan·ner[2] (tan′ər), *adj.* comparative of **tan**[1].

tan·ner[3] (tan′ər), *n. Brit. Slang.* a sixpenny piece. [1805–15; orig. uncert.]

Tan·ner (tan′ər), *n.* **Henry Os·sa·wa** (os′ə wə), 1859–1937, U.S. painter, in France after 1891.

tan·ner·y (tan′ə rē), *n., pl.* **-ner·ies.** a place where tanning is carried on. [1400–50; late ME; see TAN[1], -ERY]

Tann·häu·ser (tan′hoi′zər, -hou′-; *Ger.* tän′hoi′zər), *n.* **1.** a German lyric poet of the 13th century: a well-known legend tells of his stay with Venus in the Venusberg and his later repentance. **2.** (*italics*) an opera (1845) by Richard Wagner.

tan·nic (tan′ik), *adj.* **1.** *Chem.* of, pertaining to, or derived from tan or tannin. **2.** (of wine) having an astringent taste imparted by the presence of tannin. [1825–35; TAN[1] or TANN(IN) + -IC]

tan′nic ac′id, *Chem.* See under **tannin.** [1830–40]

tan·nin (tan′in), *n.* **1.** *Chem.* any of a group of astringent vegetable principles or compounds, chiefly complex glucosides of catechol and pyrogallol, as the reddish compound that gives the tanning properties to oak bark or the whitish compound that occurs in large quantities in nutgalls (**common tannin, tannic acid**). **2.** any of these compounds occurring in wine and imparting an astringent taste, esp. in red wine. [1795–1805; earlier *tanin* < F. See TAN[1], -IN[2]]

tan·ning (tan′ing), *n.* **1.** the process or art of converting hides or skins into leather. **2.** a browning or darkening of the skin, as by exposure to the sun. **3.** *Informal.* a thrashing; whipping. [1475–85; TAN[1], + -ING[1]]

tan′ning bed′, a boxlike bed having a hinged cover and equipped with sunlamps to produce a suntan. [1980–85, *Amer.*]

tan·nish (tan′ish), *adj.* somewhat tan: *a tannish belt.* [1935–40; TAN[1] + -ISH[1]]

Tan′nu Tu′va Peo′ple's Repub′lic (tan′o͞o to͞o′-və), former name of **Tuva Autonomous Republic.** Also called **Tan′nu Tu′va.** **—Tan′nu Tu′van.**

tan′ oak′. See **tanbark oak.** [1920–25]

Ta·no·an (tä′nō ən), *n.* an American Indian language family of which the three surviving languages are spoken in several pueblos, including Taos, in northern New Mexico near the Rio Grande. [1891; coined by J.W. Powell as *Tañoan,* based on AmerSp *Tagno* (see -AN; *gn* misinterpreted as equiv. to Sp *ñ*), var. of *Tano,* ethnic name of Southern Tewa subgroup of Tanoans < Southern Tewa *tʰá·nu*]

tan·rec (tan′rek), *n.* tenrec.

tan·sy (tan′zē), *n., pl.* **-sies.** any of several composite plants of the genus *Tanacetum,* esp. a strong-scented, weedy, Old World herb, *T. vulgare,* having flat-topped clusters of tubular yellow flowers. [1225–75; ME < OF *tanesie,* aph. var. of *atanesie* < ML *athanasia* < Gk *athanasía* immortality, equiv. to *a-* A-[6] + *thánat(os)* death (see THANATOS) + *-ia* -Y[3], with *ti* < *si*]

tan′sy rag′wort, a European composite plant, *Senecio jacobaea,* naturalized in North America, having numerous yellow flowers. [1895–1900]

Tan·ta (tän′tä), *n.* a city in N Egypt, in the Nile delta. 240,500.

tan·ta·late (tan′tl āt′), *n. Chem.* a salt of any tantalic acid. [1840–50; TANTAL(IC ACID) + -ATE[2]]

tan·tal·ic (tan tal′ik), *adj. Chem.* of or pertaining to tantalum, esp. in the pentavalent state. [1835–45; TANTAL(UM) + -IC]

tantal′ic ac′id, *Chem.* an acid, $HTaO_3$, that forms complex salts or tantalates. [1835–45]

tan·ta·lite (tan′tl īt′), *n.* a black, crystalline mineral, iron tantalate, (Fe, Mn) Ta_2O_6, the principal ore of tantalum and an end member of a series of solid solutions in which manganese and niobium combine to form columbite. [1795–1805; TANTAL(UM) + -ITE[1]]

tan·ta·lize (tan′tl īz′), *v.t.,* **-lized, -liz·ing.** to torment with, or as if with, the sight of something desired but out of reach; tease by arousing expectations that are repeatedly disappointed. Also, *esp. Brit.,* **tan′ta·lise′.** [1590–1600; TANTAL(US) + -IZE] **—tan′ta·li·za′tion,** *n.* **—tan′ta·liz′er,** *n.*
—Syn. provoke, taunt, tempt; frustrate. **—Ant.** satisfy.

tan·ta·liz·ing (tan′tl ī′zing), *adj.* having or exhibiting something that provokes or arouses expectation, interest, or desire, esp. that which remains unobtainable or beyond one's reach: *a tantalizing taste of success.* [1650–60; TANTALIZE + -ING[2]] **—tan′ta·liz′ing·ly,** *adv.*

tan·ta·lous (tan′tl əs), *adj. Chem.* containing trivalent tantalum. [1865–70; TANTAL(UM) + -OUS]

tan·ta·lum (tan′tl əm), *n. Chem.* a gray, hard, rare, metallic element occurring in columbite and tantalite and usually associated with niobium: used, because of its resistance to corrosion by most acids, for chemical, dental, and surgical instruments and apparatus. *Symbol:* Ta; *at. wt.:* 180.948; *at. no.:* 73; *sp. gr.:* 16.6. [1795–1805; < NL; named after TANTALUS]

Tan·ta·lus (tan′tl əs), *n., pl.* **-lus·es** for 2. **1.** *Class. Myth.* a Phrygian king who was condemned to remain in Tartarus, chin deep in water, with fruit-laden branches hanging above his head: whenever he tried to drink or eat, the water and fruit receded out of reach. **2.** (*l.c.*) *Chiefly Brit.* a stand or rack containing visible decanters, esp. of wines or liquors, secured by a lock.

tan′ta·lus mon′key (tan′tl əs), a long-tailed African monkey, *Cercopithecus tantalus* (or *C. aethiops tantalus*), of central African grasslands, having a long face framed by upswept whiskers. Cf. **savanna monkey.**

tan·ta·mount (tan′tə mount′), *adj.* equivalent, as in value, force, effect, or signification: *His angry speech was tantamount to a declaration of war.* [1635–45; adj. use of obs. n.: that which amounts to as much, itself n. use of obs. v.: to amount to as much < AF *tant amunter* or It *tanto montare* to amount to as much. See TANTO, AMOUNT]
—Syn. See **equal.**

tan·ta·ra (tan′tər ə, tan tar′ə, -tär′ə), *n.* **1.** a blast of a trumpet or horn. **2.** any similar sound. [1530–40; imit.; cf. L *taratantara*]

tan·tiv·y (tan tiv′ē), *adv., adj., n., pl.* **-tiv·ies,** *interj.* **—***adv.* **1.** at full gallop: *to ride tantivy.* **—***adj.* **2.** swift; rapid. **—***n.* **3.** a gallop; rush **—***interj.* **4.** (used as a hunting cry when the chase is at full speed.) [1635–45; orig. uncert.]

tant mieux (tän myœ′), *French.* so much the better.

tan·to (tän′tō; *It.* tän′tô), *adv. Music.* (of a musical direction) too much; so much. [1875–80; It < L *tantum* so much]

tant pis (tän pē′), *French.* so much the worse.

Tan·tra (tun′trə, tan′-), *n.* **1.** (*italics*) *Hinduism.* any of several books of esoteric doctrine regarding rituals, disciplines, meditation, etc., composed in the form of dialogues between Shiva and his Shakti; Agama. **2.** Also called **Tan·trism** (tun′triz əm, tan′-). the philosophy or doctrine of these books, regarding the changing, visible world as the creative dance or play of the Divine Mother and regarding enlightenment as the realization of the essential oneness of one's self and of the visible world with Shiva-Shakti, the Godhead: influential in some schools of Mahayana Buddhism, esp. in Tibet. [< Skt]

Tan·tri·ka (tun′tri kə, tan′-), *n.* **1.** Also called **Tan·trist** (tun′trist, tan′-). an adherent of Tantra. **—***adj.* **2.** of or pertaining to Tantra. Also, **Tan·tric, Tan·trik** (tun′trik, tan′-). [var. of *Tantric.* See TANTRA, -IC]

tan·trum (tan′trəm), *n.* a violent demonstration of rage or frustration; a sudden burst of ill temper. [1740–50; orig. uncert.]

Tan·ya (tan′yə, tän′-), *n.* a female given name.

tan·yard (tan′yärd′), *n.* an area of a tannery set aside for the operation of tanning vats. [TAN[1] + YARD[2]]

Tan·za·ni·a (tan′zə nē′ə; *Swahili.* tän zä nē′ä), *n.* a republic in E Africa formed in 1964 by the merger of the republic of Tanganyika and the former island sultanate of Zanzibar (including Pemba and adjacent small islands). 24,800,000; 364,881 sq. mi. (945,037 sq. km). *Cap.:* Dodoma. Official name, **United Republic of Tanzania.** **—Tan′za·ni′an,** *n., adj.*

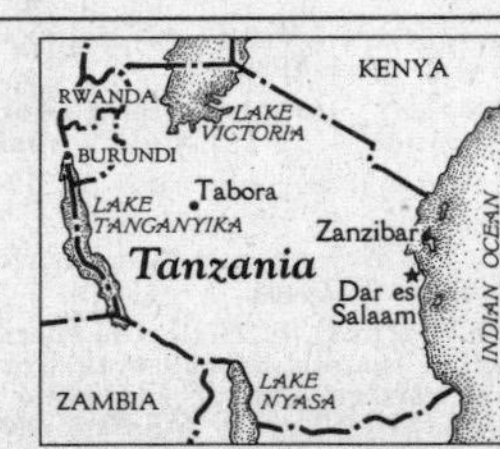

tan·za·nite (tan′zə nīt′), *n. Mineral.* a variety of zoisite valued as a gem for its purplish-blue color and strong pleochroism. [1965–70; named after TANZANIA, where found; see -ITE[1]]

Tao (dou, tou), *n.* (*sometimes l.c.*) **1.** (in philosophical Taoism) that in virtue of which all things happen or exist. **2.** the rational basis of human activity or conduct. **3.** a universal, regarded as an ideal attained to a greater or lesser degree by those embodying it. [< Chin (Wade-Giles) *Tao*[4], (pinyin) *dào* lit., way]

Tao·ism (dou′iz əm, tou′-), *n.* **1.** the philosophical system evolved by Lao-tzu and Chuang-tzu, advocating a life of complete simplicity and naturalness and of noninterference with the course of natural events, in order to attain a happy existence in harmony with the Tao. **2.** Also called **Hsüan Chiao.** a popular Chinese religion, originating in the doctrines of Lao-tzu but later highly eclectic in nature and characterized by a pantheon of many gods and by the practice of alchemy, divination, and magic. [TAO + -ISM] **—Tao′ist,** *n., adj.* **—Tao·is′tic,** *adj.*

Taos (tous), *n., pl.* **Taos** for 2. **1.** a Tanoan language spoken in two villages in New Mexico. **2.** a member of an American Indian people occupying a pueblo in New Mexico. **3.** a town in N New Mexico: resort; art colony. 3369.

Tao Te Ching (dou′ de jing′), the philosophical book in verse supposedly written by Lao-tzu. Also called ***Lao-tzu, Lao-tse.***

t'ao t'ieh (tou′ tye′), the face of a mythical animal with a gaping mouth appearing as a motif in ancient Chinese art. Also, *Pinyin,* **tao tie** (tou′ tyoe′). [< Chin *tāotiè*]

tap[1] (tap), *v.,* **tapped, tap·ping,** *n.* **—***v.t.* **1.** to strike with a light but audible blow or blows; hit with repeated, slight blows: *He tapped the door twice.* **2.** to make, put, etc., by tapping: *to tap a nail into a wall.* **3.** to strike (the fingers, a foot, a pencil, etc.) upon or against something, esp. with repeated light blows: *Stop tapping your feet!* **4.** *Basketball.* to strike (a ball in the air) in the direction of a teammate or of the basket. **5.** to enter information or produce copy by tapping on a keyboard: *to tap data into a computer; to tap out a magazine article.* **6.** to add a thickness of leather to the sole or heel of (a boot or shoe), as in repairing. **—***v.i.* **7.** to strike lightly but audibly, as to attract attention. **8.** to strike light blows. **9.** to tap-dance. **—***n.* **10.** a light but audible blow: *a tap on the shoulder.* **11.** the sound made by this. **12.** a piece of metal attached to the toe or heel of a shoe, as for reinforcement or for making the tapping of a dancer more audible. **13.** *Basketball.* an act or instance of tapping the ball: *Hanson got the tap from our center, who, 6′9″ tall, couldn't lose a jump ball.* **14.** a thickness of leather added to the sole or heel of a boot or shoe, as in repairing. [1175–1225; (v.) ME *tappen,* var. of early ME *teppen,* prob. imit.; (n.) ME, deriv. of the v.] **—tap′pa·ble,** *adj.*

tap[2] (tap), *n., v.,* **tapped, tap·ping.** **—***n.* **1.** a cylindrical stick, long plug, or stopper for closing an opening through which liquid is drawn, as in a cask; spigot. **2.** a faucet or cock. **3.** the liquor drawn through a particular tap. **4.** *Brit.* a taphouse or taproom. **5.** a tool for cutting screw threads into the cylindrical surface of a round opening. **6.** *Surg.* the withdrawal of fluid: *spinal tap.* **7.** a hole made in tapping, as one in a pipe to furnish connection for a branch pipe. **8.** *Elect.* a connection brought out of a winding at some point between its extremities, for controlling the voltage ratio. **9.** *Informal.* an act or instance of wiretapping. **10.** *Archaic.* a particular kind or quality of drink. **11. on tap, a.** ready to be drawn and served, as liquor from a cask. **b.** furnished with a tap or cock, as a barrel containing liquor. **c.** *Informal.* ready for immediate use; available: *There are numerous other projects on tap.* **—***v.t.* **12.** to draw liquid from (a vessel or container). **13.** to draw off (liquid) by removing or opening a tap or by piercing a container. **14.** to draw the tap or plug from or pierce (a cask or other container). **15.** to penetrate, open up, reach into, etc., for the purpose of using something or drawing something off; begin to use: *to tap one's resources.* **16.** to connect into secretly so as to receive the message or signal being transmitted: *to tap a telephone wire or telephone.* **17.** to furnish (a cask, container, pipe, etc.) with a tap. **18.** to cut a screw thread into the surface of (an opening). **19.** to open outlets from (power lines, highways, pipes, etc.). **20. tap into,** *Informal.* to gain access to; become friendly with: *The candidate tapped into some wealthy supporters.* **21. tap off,** to remove (liquid, molten metal, etc.) from a keg, furnace, or the like: *to tap off slag from a blast furnace.* [bef. 1050; (n.) ME *tappe,* OE *tæppa;* c. D *tap,* OHG *zapfo,* ON *tappi;* (v.) ME *tappen,* OE *tæppian;* c. MLG, MD *tappen,* G *zapfen,* ON *tappa*] **—tap′pa·ble,** *adj.*

ta·pa[1] (tä′pä), *n.* Usually, **tapas.** (esp. in Spain) a snack or appetizer, typically served with wine or beer. [< Sp: lit., cover, lid (prob. < Gmc; see TAP[2])]

ta·pa[2] (tä′pə, tap′ə), *n.* **1.** the bark of the paper mulberry. **2.** Also called **ta′pa cloth′.** a cloth of the Pacific islands made by pounding this or similar barks flat and thin, used for clothing and floor covering. [1815–25; < Polynesian]

tap·a·de·ra (tap′ə dâr′ə), *n. Southwestern U.S.* a hoodlike piece of heavy leather around the front of the stirrup of a stock or range saddle to protect the rider's foot. [1835–45; < Sp, equiv. to *tapad(o),* ptp. of *tapar* to cover, stop up, deriv. of *tapa* cover, lid (see TAPA[1]) + *-era,* fem. of *-ero* -ARY]

tap·a·de·ro (tap′ə dâr′ō), *n., pl.* **-de·ros.** tapadera.

Ta·pa·jós (tä′pə zhôs′), *n.* a river flowing NE through central Brazil to the Amazon. 500 mi. (800 km) long.

ta·pas (tup′əs), *n. Yoga.* the conditioning of the body through the proper kinds and amounts of diet, rest, bodily training, meditation, etc., to bring it to the greatest possible state of creative power. [1930–35; < Skt: penance, lit., heat]

CONCISE ETYMOLOGY KEY: <, descended or borrowed from; >, whence; b., blend of, blended; c., cognate with; cf., compare; deriv., derivative; equiv., equivalent; imit., imitative; obl., oblique; r., replacing; s., stem; sp., spelling, spelled; resp., respelling, respelled; trans., translation; ?, origin unknown; *, unattested; ‡, probably earlier than. See the full key inside the front cover.

tap′ bell′, a signal bell giving a single ring, as one announcing the approach to a certain floor of an elevator.

tap′ bolt′, a bolt for driving into a tapped hole in metal and that can be held in place without a nut. [1860–65]

tap′ dance′, a dance in which the rhythm or rhythmical variation is audibly tapped out with the toe or heel by a dancer wearing shoes with special hard soles or with taps. [‡1925–30]

tap-dance (tap′dans′, -däns′), *v.i.*, **-danced, -danc·ing.** to perform a tap dance. [1925–30] **—tap′-danc′·er,** *n.*

tape (tāp), *n., v.,* **taped, tap·ing.** **—***n.* **1.** a long, narrow strip of linen, cotton, or the like, used for tying garments, binding seams or carpets, etc. **2.** a long, narrow strip of paper, metal, etc. **3.** a strip of cloth, paper, or plastic with an adhesive surface, used for sealing, binding, or attaching items together; adhesive tape or masking tape. **4.** See **tape measure. 5.** a string stretched across the finishing line in a race and broken by the winning contestant on crossing the line. **6.** See **ticker tape. 7.** See **magnetic tape. 8.** a magnetic tape carrying prerecorded sound: *a tape of a rock concert.* **—***v.t.* **9.** to furnish with a tape or tapes. **10.** to tie up, bind, or attach with tape. **11.** to measure with or as if with a tape measure. **12.** to record or prerecord on magnetic tape. **—***v.i.* **13.** to record something on magnetic tape. [bef. 1000; ME; unexplained var. of *tappe,* OE *tæppe* strip (of cloth), lit., part torn off; akin to MLG *teppen* to tear, pluck] **—tape′less,** *adj.* **—tape′like′,** *adj.*

tape′ deck′, a component of an audio system for playing tapes, using an external amplifier and speakers. Also called **deck.** [1955–60]

tape′ drive′, *Computers.* a program-controlled device that reads data from or writes data on a magnetic tape which moves past a read-write head. [1950–55]

tape′ ed′iting, the process of putting the various segments of a master video or audio tape into a predetermined sequence: usually done electronically.

tape′ grass′, a freshwater plant, *Vallisneria spiralis,* that has long, ribbonlike leaves and grows under water. Also called **eelgrass, wild celery.** [1810–20]

tape′ machine′, a tape recorder. [1890–95]

tape·man (tāp′mən), *n., pl.* **-men.** *Survey.* a person who holds and positions a tape in taking measurements. [1895–1900; TAPE + -MAN]

tape′ meas′ure, a long, flexible strip or ribbon, as of cloth or metal, marked with subdivisions of the foot or meter and used for measuring. Also called **tape·line** (tāp′līn′). [1835–45]

tape′ play′er, a small device for playing magnetic tape recordings. [1950–55]

ta·per[1] (tā′pər), *v.i.* **1.** to become smaller or thinner toward one end. **2.** to grow gradually lean. **—***v.t.* **3.** to make gradually smaller toward one end. **4.** to reduce gradually. **5. taper off, a.** to become gradually more slender toward one end. **b.** to cease by degrees; decrease; diminish: *The storm is beginning to taper off now. I haven't stopped smoking entirely, but I'm tapering off to three cigarettes a day.* **—***n.* **6.** gradual diminution of width or thickness in an elongated object. **7.** gradual decrease of force, capacity, etc. **8.** anything having a tapering form, as a spire or obelisk. **9.** a candle, esp. a very slender one. **10.** a long wick coated with wax, tallow, or the like, as for use in lighting candles or gas. [bef. 900; ME: wax candle, OE, var. of *tapur,* dissimilated var. of **papur* PAPER] **—ta′per·er,** *n.* **—ta′per·ing·ly,** *adv.*

tap·er[2] (tā′pər), *n.* a person who records or edits magnetic tape, videotape, etc. [TAPE + -ER[1]]

tape-re·cord (tāp′ri kôrd′), *v.t.* to record (speech, music, etc.) on magnetic tape. [1945–50]

tape′ record′er, an electrical device for recording or playing back sound, video, or data on magnetic tape. [1940–45]

tape′ record′ing, 1. a magnetic tape on which speech, music, etc., have been recorded. **2.** the act of recording on magnetic tape. [1940–45]

ta′per jack′. See **wax jack.**

ta·per·stick (tā′pər stik′), *n.* a candlestick designed to hold tapers. [1540–50; TAPER + STICK[1]]

tap·es·tried (tap′ə strēd), *adj.* **1.** furnished or covered with tapestries. **2.** represented in tapestry, as a story. [1620–30; TAPESTRY + -ED[2], -ED[3]]

tap·es·try (tap′ə strē), *n., pl.* **-tries,** *v.,* **-tried, -try·ing.** **—***n.* **1.** a fabric consisting of a warp upon which colored threads are woven by hand to produce a design, often pictorial, used for wall hangings, furniture coverings, etc. **2.** a machine-woven reproduction of this. **—***v.t.* **3.** to furnish, cover, or adorn with tapestry. **4.** to represent or depict in a tapestry. [1400–50; late ME *tapst(e)ry, tapistry* < MF *tapisserie* carpeting. See TAPIS, -ERY] **—tap′es·try·like′,** *adj.*

tap′estry Brus′sels. See under **Brussels carpet.**

tap′estry moth′. See **carpet moth.** [1805–15]

tape′ trans′port, *Recording.* transport (def. 12). [1950–55]

ta·pe·tum (tə pē′təm), *n., pl.* **-ta** (-tə). **1.** *Bot.* a layer of cells often investing the archespore in a developing sporangium and absorbed as the spores mature. **2.** *Anat., Zool.* any of certain membranous layers or layered coverings, as in the choroid of the eyes of certain animals. [1705–15; < NL, special use of ML *tapētum* coverlet (L, only pl.) < Gk *tapēt-* (s. of *tápēs*) carpet, rug] **—ta·pe′tal,** *adj.*

tape·worm (tāp′wûrm′), *n.* any of various flat or tapelike worms of the class Cestoidea, lacking an alimentary canal, and parasitic when adult in the alimentary canal of humans and other vertebrates: the larval and adult stages are usually in different hosts. [1745–55; TAPE + WORM]

taph·e·pho·bi·a (taf′ə fō′bē ə), *n. Psychiatry.* an abnormal fear of being buried alive. [< Gk *taphḗ* grave + -PHOBIA]

Ta·phi·ae (tā′fē ī′), *n.* (*used with a plural v.*) (in ancient geography) a group of islands in the Ionian Sea. Also called **Teleboides.**

tap·hole (tap′hōl′), *n. Metall.* a hole in a blast furnace, steelmaking furnace, etc., through which molten metal or slag is tapped off. [1585–95; TAP[2] + HOLE]

ta·phon·o·my (tə fon′ə mē), *n. Paleontol., Anthropol.* **1.** the circumstances and processes of fossilization. **2.** the study of the environmental conditions affecting the preservation of animal or plant remains. [1965–70; < Gk *táph(ē)* grave + -o- + -NOMY] **—taph·o·nom·ic** (taf′ə nom′ik), *adj.* **—ta·phon′o·mist,** *n.*

tap·house (tap′hous′), *n., pl.* **-hous·es** (-hou′ziz). *Brit.* an inn or tavern where liquor is kept on tap for sale. [1490–1500; TAP[1] + HOUSE]

Tà·pies (tä′pyes), *n.* **An·to·ni** (än′tô nē′) or **An·to·nio** (än tô′nyô), born 1923, Spanish painter.

tap-in (tap′in′), *n. Basketball.* a field goal made by striking a ball in the air into the basket, usually from close range. Also called **tip-in.** [n. use of v. phrase *tap in*]

tap·i·o·ca (tap′ē ō′kə), *n.* a food substance prepared from cassava in granular, flake, pellet (**pearl tapioca**), or flour form, used in puddings, as a thickener, etc. [1605–15; < Pg < Tupi *tipioca* lit., juice (of cassava) squeezed out, i.e., pulp after squeezing]

tap·i·o·ca-plant (tap′ē ō′kə plant′, -plänt′), *n.* the cassava, *Manihot esculenta.*

tapio′ca snow′. See **snow pellets.**

ta·pir (tā′pər, tə pēr′), *n., pl.* **-pirs,** (*esp. collectively*) **-pir.** any of several large, stout, three-toed ungulates of the family Tapiridae, of Central and South America, the Malay Peninsula, and Sumatra, somewhat resembling swine and having a long, flexible snout: all species are threatened or endangered. [1560–70; << Tupi *tapira*]

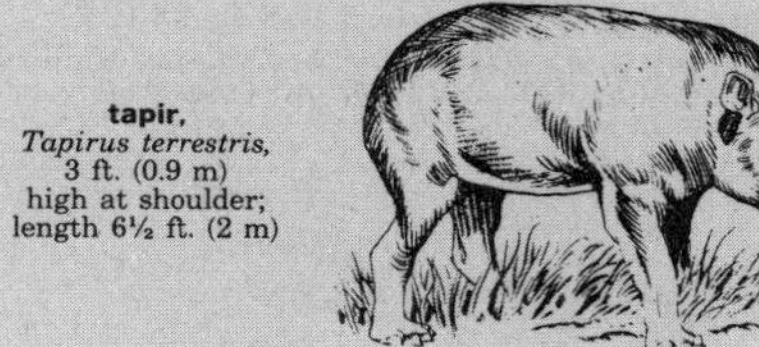
tapir, *Tapirus terrestris,* 3 ft. (0.9 m) high at shoulder; length 6½ ft. (2 m)

tap·is (tap′ē, tap′is, ta pē′), *n., pl.* **tap·is. 1.** *Obs.* a carpet, tapestry, or other covering. **2. on the tapis,** under consideration or discussion: *A new housing development for that area is on the tapis.* [1485–95; < MF; OF *tapiz* << Gk *tapḗtion* little carpet, equiv. to *tapēt-* (s. of *tápēs*) carpet + *-ion* dim. suffix]

ta·pis vert (tᴀ pē vᴇʀ′), *pl.* ***ta·pis verts*** (tᴀ pē vᴇʀ′). *French.* an unbroken expanse of lawn used as a major element of a landscape design. [lit., green carpet]

tap′ loop′ jump′. See **toe loop.**

ta·pote·ment (tə pōt′mənt), *n.* the use of various light, quick chopping, slapping, or beating strokes on the body during massage. [1885–90; < F, equiv. to *tapot(er)* to tap, drum on, with the fingers or edge of the hand (*tap(er)* to tap, strike (expressive v. akin to TAP[1]) + *-oter* freq. or attenuating suffix) + *-ment* -MENT]

Tap·pan (tap′ən), *n.* **Arthur,** 1786–1865, and his brother **Lewis,** 1788–1873, U.S. businessmen, philanthropists, and abolitionists.

tap′ pants′, 1. women's loose-fitting underpants. **2.** women's loose-fitting shorts worn for exercising or other physical activity, as dancing. [1975–80; after the earlier use of such shorts for tap dancing]

tap·per[1] (tap′ər), *n.* **1.** a person or thing that taps or strikes lightly. **2.** a telegraph key. [1800–10; TAP[1] + -ER[1]]

tap·per[2] (tap′ər), *n.* **1.** a person or thing that taps, as trees for the sap or juice, a blast furnace, cask, or other container for their contents, etc. **2.** a person who cuts screw threads into the surface of a circular opening, as of a pipe, nut, etc. [bef. 1000; OE *tæppere* (not recorded in ME); see TAP[2], -ER[1]]

tap·pet (tap′it), *n. Mach.* a sliding rod, intermittently struck by a cam, for moving another part, as a valve. [1735–45; TAP[1] + -ET]

tap·ping[1] (tap′ing), *n.* **1.** the act of a person or thing that taps or strikes lightly. **2.** the sound produced by this. [1400–50; late ME; see TAP[1], -ING[1]]

tap·ping[2] (tap′ing), *n.* **1.** the act of tapping casks, telephone conversations, etc. **2.** something that is drawn by tapping. **3.** paracentesis. [1590–1600; TAP[2] + -ING[1]]

tap′ping screw′. See **self-tapping screw.**

tap·pit-hen (tap′it hen′), *n. Scot.* **1.** a hen with a crest or topknot. **2.** a tankard, esp. a large one, with a knob or ornament projecting from the top of its lid. [1715–25; *tappit* (Scots var. of *topped;* see TOP[1], -ED[3]) + HEN]

tap·room (tap′ro͞om′, -ro͝om′), *n.* a barroom, esp. in an inn or hotel; bar. [1800–10; TAP[1] + ROOM]

tap·root (tap′ro͞ot′, -ro͝ot′), *n. Bot.* a main root descending downward from the radicle and giving off small lateral roots. See illus. under **root**[1]. [1595–1605; TAP[2] + ROOT[1]]

taps (taps), *n.* (*used with a singular or plural v.*) *Mil.* a signal by bugle or drum, sounded at night as an order to extinguish all lights, and sometimes performed as a postlude to a military funeral. [1815–25, *Amer.;* prob. *tap(too),* var. of TATTOO[1] + -S[3]]

tap·sal-tee·rie (tap′səl tēr′ē), *adv. Scot.* topsy-turvy. Also, **tap·sie-tee·rie** (tap′sē tēr′ē).

tap·ster (tap′stər), *n.* a bartender. [bef. 1000; ME; OE *tæppestre.* See TAP[2], -STER]

tap′ wa′ter, water, obtained directly from a faucet or tap, that has not been purified, distilled, or otherwise treated. [1880–85]

ta·qi·yah (tə kē′yə), *n.* (in Shi'ite Islam) the practice of denying one's religion, permissible when one is faced with persecution, esp. by Sunnites: regarded as a means of protecting the religion. Also, **ta·qi′ya.** [< Ar *taqiyyah* lit., caution, prudence]

taq·lid (tak lēd′), *n. Islam.* the acceptance of authority in religious matters. [< Ar *taqlīd* lit., imitation]

tar[1] (tär), *n., v.,* **tarred, tar·ring,** *adj.* **—***n.* **1.** any of various dark-colored viscid products obtained by the destructive distillation of certain organic substances, as coal or wood. **2.** coal-tar pitch. **3.** smoke solids or components: *cigarette tar.* **4. beat, knock,** or **whale the tar out of,** *Informal.* to beat mercilessly: *The thief had knocked the tar out of the old man and left him for dead.* **—***v.t.* **5.** to smear or cover with or as if with tar. **6. tar and feather, a.** to coat (a person) with tar and feathers as a punishment or humiliation. **b.** to punish severely: *She should be tarred and feathered for what she has done.* **—***adj.* **7.** of or characteristic of tar. **8.** covered or smeared with tar; tarred. **9. tarred with the same brush,** possessing the same shortcomings or guilty of the same misdeeds: *The whole family is tarred with the same brush.* [bef. 900; (n.) ME *tarr(e), ter(re),* OE *teru;* c. D, G *teer,* ON *tjara;* akin to TREE; (v.) ME *terren,* OE *tierwian,* deriv. of the n.]

tar[2] (tär), *n. Informal.* a sailor. [1740–50; perh. short for TARPAULIN]
—Syn. seafarer, gob. See **sailor.**

Tar·a (tar′ə), *n.* a village in the NE Republic of Ireland, NW of Dublin: home of the ancient Irish kings (**Hill′ of Tar′a**).

tar·a·did·dle (tar′ə did′l), *n. Informal.* **1.** a small lie; fib. **2.** pretentious nonsense. Also, **tarradiddle.** [1790–1800; orig. uncert.]

Ta·ra·hu·ma·ra (tär′ə ho͞o mär′ə, tar′-), *n., pl.* **-ras,** (*esp. collectively*) **-ra** for 1. **1.** a member of an American Indian people of the Sierra Madre region of the state of Chihuahua, Mexico. **2.** the Uto-Aztecan language of the Tarahumara.

Ta·rai (tə rī′), *n.* Terai.

ta·ran·tass (tär′ən täs′), *n.* a large, four-wheeled Russian carriage mounted without springs on two parallel longitudinal wooden bars. Also, **ta′ran·tas′.** [1840–50; < Russ *tarantás,* said to be < Tatar *tarıntas*]

tar·an·tel·la (tar′ən tel′ə), *n.* **1.** a rapid, whirling southern Italian dance in very quick sextuple, originally quadruple, meter, usually performed by a single couple, and formerly supposed to be a remedy for tarantism. **2.** a piece of music either for the dance or in its rhythm. [1775–85; < It, equiv. to *Tarant(o)* TARANTO + *-ella* -ELLE]

tar·ant·ism (tar′ən tiz′əm), *n.* a mania characterized by an uncontrollable impulse to dance, esp. as prevalent in southern Italy from the 15th to the 17th century, popularly attributed to the bite of the tarantula. Also, **tarentism.** Cf. **tarantula** (def. 3). [1630–40; < NL *tarantismus.* See TARANTO, -ISM] **—tar′ant·ist,** *n.*

Ta·ran·to (tä′rᴀn tô; *Eng.* tär′ən tō′, tar′-, tə ran′tō), *n.* **1.** Ancient, **Tarentum.** a fortified seaport in SE Italy, on the Gulf of Taranto: founded by the Greeks in the 8th century B.C.; naval base. 244,249. **2. Gulf of,** an arm of the Ionian Sea, in S Italy. 85 mi. (137 km) long.

ta·ran·tu·la (tə ran′chə lə), *n., pl.* **-las, -lae** (-lē′). **1.** any of several large, hairy spiders of the family Theraphosidae, as *Aphonopelma chalcodes,* of the southwestern U.S., having a painful but not highly venomous bite. **2.** any of various related spiders. **3.** a large wolf spider, *Lycosa tarantula,* of southern Europe, having a bite once thought to be the cause of tarantism. [1555–65; < ML < It *tarantola.* See TARANTO, -ULE]

tarantula, *Aphonopelma chalcodes,* body length 2 in. (5 cm)

Ta·ra·po·to (tä′rᴀ pô′tô), *n.* a city in N Peru. 15,000.

Ta·ras·can (tə ras′kən, -räs′-), *n., pl.* **-cans,** (*esp. collectively*) **-can** for 1. **—***n.* Also, **Tarasco. 1.** a member of an American Indian people of Michoacán state, in southwestern Mexico. **2.** the language of the Tarascans. **—***adj.* **3.** of or pertaining to the Tarascans or their language.

Ta·ras·co (tə ras′kō, -räs′-), *n., pl.* **-cos,** (*esp. collectively*) **-co.** Tarascan.

ta·ra·ta (tə rä′tə), *n.* a tree, *Pittosporum eugenioides,* of New Zealand, having elliptic leaves and fragrant, yellow flowers, grown as an ornamental. [1875–80; < Maori]

ta′ra vine′ (tär′ə, tar′ə), a leafy, woody vine, *Actinidia arguta,* of Japan and eastern Asia, having white flowers and yellowish, sweet, edible fruit. [appar.

misapplication of Japn *tara(-no-ki)* name for *Aralia elata,* an araliaceous shrub]

Ta·ra·wa (tə rä′wə, tar′ə wä′, tä′rä wä′), *n.* one of the Gilbert Islands, in the central Pacific; capital, since 1979, of the independent nation of Kiribati: U.S. victory over Japanese forces after severe fighting, November, 1943. 19,000; 14 sq. mi. (36 sq. km).

ta·rax·a·cum (tə rak′sə kəm), *n. Pharm.* the dried roots of any of several composite plants of the genus *Taraxacum,* as the dandelion, *T. officinale* or *T. laevigatum,* used in medicine in powdered or fluidextract form chiefly as a tonic and aperient. [1700–10; < NL < Ar *ṭarakhshaqūn* wild chicory < Pers *tarkhashqūn* wild endive]

tar′ ba′by, a situation, problem, or the like, that is almost impossible to solve or to break away from. Also, **tar′ba′by.** [after the tar doll used to trap Brer Rabbit in an Uncle Remus story (1881) of Joel Chandler Harris]

tar′ ball′, a lump or blob of solidified tar resulting from an oil spill, natural seepage from the sea, or other source, that resists biodegradation and often washes up on beaches. [1725–35]

Tar·bell (tär′bel′), *n.* **Ida Minerva,** 1857–1944, U.S. author.

Tarbes (tarb), *n.* a city in and the capital of Hautes-Pyrénées, in SW France. 57,765.

tar·boosh (tär bo͞osh′), *n.* a tasseled cap of cloth or felt, usually red, that is worn by Muslim men either by itself or as the inner part of the turban. Also, **tar·bush′.** [1695–1705; < Ar *ṭarbūsh* < Ottoman Turk *terposh,* prob. < Pers *sarposh* headdress (equiv. to *sar* head + *pūsh* covering), by assoc. with Turk *ter* sweat]

tar·brush (tär′brush′), *n.* **1.** a brush for applying tar. **2.** *Slang (disparaging and offensive).* black ancestry. [1705–15; TAR[1] + BRUSH[1]]

Tarde (tard), *n.* **Ga·bri·el** (ga brē el′), 1843–1904, French sociologist.

Tar·dieu (tar dyœ′), *n.* **An·dré Pierre Ga·bri·el A·mé·dée** (än drā′ pyer ga brē el′ a mā dā′), 1876–1945, French statesman.

tar·di·grade (tär′di grād′), *n.* **1.** Also called **bear animalcule, water bear.** any microscopic, chiefly herbivorous invertebrate of the phylum Tardigrada, living in water, on mosses, lichens, etc. —*adj.* **2.** belonging or pertaining to the phylum Tardigrada. **3.** slow in pace or movement. [1615–25; < L *tardigradus* slow-paced. See TARDY, -GRADE]

tar·dive (tär′div), *adj.* appearing or tending to appear late, as in human development or in the treatment of a disease. [1960–65; < F *tardive,* fem. of *tardif* TARDY]

tar′dive dyskine′sia, *Pathol.* a disorder characterized by restlessness and involuntary rolling of the tongue or twitching of the face, trunk, or limbs, usually occurring as a complication of long-term therapy with antipsychotic drugs. [1965–70]

tar·do (tär′dō; *It.* tär′dô), *adj.* slow (used as a musical direction). [1840–50; < It: slow < L *tardus*]

tar·dy (tär′dē), *adj.,* **-di·er, -di·est.** **1.** late; behind time; not on time: *How tardy were you today?* **2.** moving or acting slowly; slow; sluggish. **3.** delaying through reluctance. [1475–85; earlier *tardive, tardif* < OF < VL **tardīvus,* equiv. to L *tard(us)* slow + *-īvus* -IVE] —**tar′di·ly,** *adv.* —**tar′di·ness,** *n.*
—**Syn. 1.** slack. **3.** dilatory. —**Ant. 1.** prompt.

tare[1] (târ), *n.* **1.** any of various vetches, esp. *Vicia sativa.* **2.** the seed of a vetch. **3.** *Bible.* a noxious weed, probably the darnel. [1300–50; ME: vetch; akin to D *tarwe* wheat]

tare[2] (târ), *n., v.,* **tared, tar·ing.** —*n.* **1.** the weight of the wrapping, receptacle, or conveyance containing goods. **2.** a deduction from the gross weight to allow for this. **3.** the weight of a vehicle without cargo, passengers, etc. **4.** a counterweight used in chemical analysis to balance the weight of a container. **5.** a word formerly used in communications to represent the letter *T.* —*v.t.* **6.** to ascertain, note, or allow for the tare of. [1480–90; < MF (equiv. to ML, It, Pr, Sp, Pg *tara,* Sp *atara*) << Ar *ṭarḥah* what one throws away, deriv. of *ṭaraḥa* to throw away]

tare[3] (târ), *v. Archaic.* pt. and pp. of **tear**[2].

tar·ent·ism (tar′ən tiz′əm), *n.* tarantism.

Ta·ren·tum (tə ren′təm), *n.* ancient name of **Taranto.**

targe (tärj), *n. Archaic.* a small, round shield; a target or buckler. [bef. 1000; ME < OF < ON *targa* round shield; c. OHG *zarga* rim, ring; r. OE *targe, targa* < ON]

tar·get (tär′git), *n.* **1.** an object, usually marked with concentric circles, to be aimed at in shooting practice or contests. **2.** any object used for this purpose. **3.** anything fired at. **4.** a goal to be reached. **5.** an object of abuse, scorn, derision, etc.; butt. **6.** *Fencing.* the portion of a fencer's body where a touch can be scored. **7.** a disk-shaped signal, as at a railroad switch, indicating the position of a switch. **8.** *Survey.* **a.** the sliding sight on a leveling rod. **b.** any marker on which sights are taken. **9.** a small shield, usually round, carried by a foot soldier; buckler. **10. on target, a.** properly aimed or on the right course toward a target. **b.** accurate, correct, or valid: *Their description of the event was on target.* **c.** filling or meeting a requirement or expectations: *The amount of supplies we took was right on target.* —*adj.* **11.** that is or may be a target or goal: *The target group consisted of college graduates who earned more than $50,000 a year.* —*v.t.* **12.** to use, set up, or designate as a target or goal. **13.** to direct toward a target: *The new warheads can be targeted with great precision.* **14.** to make a target of (an object, person, city, etc.) for attack or bombardment. **15. target on** or **in on,** to establish or use as a target or goal: *The club is targeting on September for the move to larger quarters.* [1350–1400; ME (n.) < MF *targuete,* var. of *targete* small shield. See TARGE, -ET] —**tar′get·a·ble,** *adj.* —**tar′get·less,** *adj.*
—**Syn. 4.** aim, end, purpose.

CONCISE ETYMOLOGY KEY: <, descended or borrowed from; >, whence; b., blend of, blended; c., cognate with; cf., compare; deriv., derivative; equiv., equivalent; imit., imitative; obl., oblique; r., replacing; s., stem; sp., spelling, spelled; resp., respelling, respelled; trans., translation; ?, origin unknown; *, unattested; ‡, probably earlier than. See the full key inside the front cover.

tar′get date′, the date set or aimed at for the commencement, fulfillment, or completion of some effort: *The target date for the book is next May.* [1940–45]

tar·get·eer (tär′gi tēr′), *n.* a soldier armed with a sword and buckler. [1580–90; TARGET + -EER]

tar′get lan′guage, 1. the language into which a text is to be translated from another language. Cf. **source language** (def. 1). **2.** a language, esp. a foreign language, that one is in the process of learning. Cf. **source language** (def. 2). [1950–55]

tar′get ri′fle, a rifle designed esp. for shooting at targets. [1900–05]

Tar·gum (tär′go͝om; *Seph. Heb.* tär go͞om′; *Ashk. Heb.* tär′go͝om), *n., pl.* **Tar·gums,** *Heb.* **Tar·gu·mim** (*Seph.* tär go͞o mēm′; *Ashk.* tär go͞o′mim). a translation or paraphrase in Aramaic of a book or division of the Old Testament. [< Aram *targūm* lit., paraphrase, interpretation] —**Tar·gum′ic,** *adj.* —**Tar′gum·ist,** *n.*

Târ·gu-Mu·reș (tir′go͞o mo͞o′resh), *n.* a city in central Rumania. 129,284.

Tar′ Heel′, a native or inhabitant of North Carolina (used as a nickname). [1860–65, *Amer.*]

Tar′ Heel′ State′, North Carolina (used as a nickname).

tar·iff (tar′if), *n.* **1.** an official list or table showing the duties or customs imposed by a government on imports or exports. **2.** the schedule or system of duties so imposed. **3.** any duty or rate of duty in such a list or schedule. **4.** any table of charges, as of a railroad, bus line, etc. **5.** bill; cost; charge. —*v.t.* **6.** to subject to a tariff. **7.** to put a valuation on according to a tariff. [1585–95; earlier *tariffa* < It < Ar *ta'rīfah,* deriv. of *'arrafa* to make known] —**tar′iff·less,** *adj.*

Ta·ri·ja (tä rē′hä), *n.* a city in S Bolivia. 66,120.

Ta·rim (tä′rēm′), *n.* a river in NW China, in Xinjiang Uygur region. ab. 1300 mi. (2090 km) long. Also called **Ta′rim′ He′** (hu).

Ta′rim′ Ba′sin, a region in W China between the Tien Shan and Kunlun mountain ranges. ab. 350,000 sq. mi. (906,000 sq. km).

ta·ri·qah (tə rē′kə), *n. Islam.* **1.** a system of rites for the spiritual training of a Sufi order. **2.** any of the Sufi orders. Also, **ta·ri′qa.** [< Ar *ṭarīqah* lit., path]

Tar·king·ton (tär′king tən), *n.* **(Newton) Booth,** 1869–1946, U.S. novelist and playwright.

Tar·lac (tär′läk), *n.* a city on N central Luzon, in the N Philippines. 175,691.

tar·la·tan (tär′lə tn, -tən), *n.* a thin, plain-weave, open-mesh cotton fabric finished with stiffening agents and sometimes glazed. [1720–30; < F *tarlatane,* dissimilated var. of *tarnatane* kind of cloth orig. imported from India < ?]

Tarl·ton (tärl′tn), *n.* **Richard,** died 1588, English actor.

Tar·mac (tär′mak), **1.** *Trademark.* a brand of bituminous binder, similar to tarmacadam, for surfacing roads, airport runways, parking areas, etc. —*n.* **2.** (*l.c.*) a road, airport runway, parking area, etc., paved with Tarmac, tarmacadam, or a layer of tar. **3.** (*l.c.*) a layer or covering of Tarmac, tarmacadam, or tar.

tar·mac·ad·am (tär′mə kad′əm), *n.* a paving material consisting of coarse crushed stone covered with a mixture of tar and bitumen. [1880–85; TAR[1] + MACADAM]

tarn (tärn), *n.* a small mountain lake or pool, esp. one in a cirque. [1300–50; ME *terne* < ON *tjǫrn* pond, pool]

Tarn (tarn), *n.* a department in S France. 338,024; 2232 sq. mi. (5780 sq. km). *Cap.:* Albi.

tar·na·tion (tär nā′shən), *Older Use.* —*interj.* **1.** damnation. —*n.* **2.** damnation; hell (used as a euphemism): *Where in tarnation is that boy?* —*adv.* **3.** damned. [1775–85; b. *'tarnal,* dial. form of ETERNAL and DAMNATION]

Tar·ne (tär′nē), *n.* (in the *Iliad*) Sardis.

Tarn-et-Ga·ronne (tar′nā ga rôn′), *n.* a department in S France. 183,314; 1440 sq. mi. (3730 sq. km). *Cap.:* Montauban.

tar·nish (tär′nish), *v.t.* **1.** to dull the luster of (a metallic surface), esp. by oxidation; discolor. **2.** to diminish or destroy the purity of; stain; sully: *The scandal tarnished his reputation.* —*v.i.* **3.** to grow dull or discolored; lose luster. **4.** to become sullied. —*n.* **5.** a tarnished coating. **6.** tarnished condition; discoloration; alteration of the luster of a metal. **7.** a stain or blemish. [1590–1600; < MF *terniss-,* long s. of *ternir* to dull, deaden, deriv. of *terne* dull, wan < Gmc; cf. OHG *tarni,* c. OS *derni,* OE *dierne* hidden, obscure; see -ISH[2]] —**tar′nish·a·ble,** *adj.*
—**Syn. 2.** taint, blemish, soil. —**Ant. 1.** brighten.

tar′nished plant′ bug′, a bug, *Lygus lineolaris,* of the family Miridae, that is a common and widely distributed pest of alfalfa and other legumes and of peach and other fruit trees. [1885–90]

Tar·no·pol (*Pol.* tär nô′pôl), *n.* Ternopol.

Tar·nów (tär′no͞of), *n.* a city in SE Poland, E of Cracow. 85,500.

ta·ro (tär′ō, târ′ō, tar′ō), *n., pl.* **-ros. 1.** a stemless plant, *Colocasia esculenta,* of the arum family, cultivated in tropical regions, in the Pacific islands and elsewhere, for the edible tuber. **2.** the tuber itself. Cf. **dasheen.** [1770–80; < Polynesian]

ta·rok (tə rok′), *n.* a card game dating probably from the Renaissance and still popular in central Europe, originally played with a special pack of 78 cards but now usually played with 32 cards of a regular pack together with 22 tarots. [1605–15; < obs. It *tarocco;* see TAROT]

ta·rot (tar′ō, ta rō′), *n.* any of a set of 22 playing cards bearing allegorical representations, used for fortunetelling and as trump cards in tarok. [1590–1600; back formation from *taros* (pl.) < MF < It *tarocchi,* pl. of *tarocco*]

tarp (tärp), *n. Informal.* tarpaulin. [1905–10, *Amer.;* by shortening]

tar·pan (tär pan′), *n.* a small, dun-colored wild horse chiefly of southern Russia, having a flowing mane and tail: extinct since the early 20th century but somewhat restored by selective breeding of mixed-breed domestic horses, and sustained in zoos. [1835–45; < Russ *tarpán,* said to be < Kazakh or Kirghiz]

tar·pa·per (tär′pā′pər), *n.* a heavy, tar-coated paper used as a waterproofing material in building construction. [1890–95, *Amer.;* TAR[1] + PAPER]

tar·pau·lin (tär pô′lin, tär′pə lin), *n.* **1.** a protective covering of canvas or other material waterproofed with tar, paint, or wax. **2.** a hat, esp. a sailor's, made of or covered with such material. **3.** *Rare.* a sailor. [1595–1605; earlier *tarpauling.* See TAR[1], PALL[1], -ING[1]]

Tar·pe·ia (tär pē′ə), *n. Class. Myth.* a vestal virgin who betrayed Rome to the Sabines and was crushed under their shields when she claimed a reward.

Tar·pe′ian Rock′ (tär pē′ən), a rock on the Capitoline Hill in Rome, from which criminals and traitors were hurled. [1600–10; < L (*mōns*) *Tarpēi(us)* Tarpeian (hill) + -AN]

tar·pit (tär′pit′), *n.* seepage of natural tar or asphalt, esp. an accumulation that has acted as a natural trap into which animals have fallen and sunk and had their bones preserved. Also, **tar′ pit′.** [1830–40; TAR[1] + PIT[1]]

tar·pon (tär′pən), *n., pl.* **-pons,** (*esp. collectively*) **-pon.** a large, powerful game fish, *Megalops atlantica,* inhabiting the warmer waters of the Atlantic Ocean, having a compressed body and large, silvery scales. [1675–85; earlier *tarpum, trapham, terbum,* of uncert. orig.; cf. D *tarpoen;* words in various Indian languages of Central America (Miskito *tapam,* Sumo *tahpam,* Rama *tāpum,* Paya *ta'pam*) prob. ult. < E]

tarpon, *Megalops atlantica,* length to 8 ft. (2.4 m)

Tar′pon Springs′, a town in W Florida. 13,251.

Tar·quin·i·us (tär kwin′ē əs), *n.* **1.** (*Lucius Tarquinius Priscus*) died 578 B.C., king of Rome 616–578. **2.** (*Lucius Tarquinius Superbus*) ("*the Proud*") died 498 B.C., king of Rome 534–510. Also, **Tar′quin.**

tar·ra·did·dle (tar′ə did′l), *n.* taradiddle.

tar·ra·gon (tar′ə gon′, -gən), *n.* **1.** an Old World plant, *Artemisia dracunculus,* having aromatic leaves used for seasoning. **2.** the leaves themselves. Also called **estragon.** [1530–40; earlier *taragon* < MF *targon,* var. of *tarc(h)on* < ML < MGk *tarchṓn* < Ar *ṭarkhūn* < Gk *drákōn* lit., dragon; cf. L *dracunculus* tarragon]

Tar·ra·sa (tär rä′sä), *n.* a city in NE Spain, N of Barcelona. 138,697.

tar·ri·ance (tar′ē əns), *n. Archaic.* **1.** delay. **2.** sojourn. [1425–75; late ME; see TARRY[1], -ANCE]

tar·ry[1] (tar′ē), *v.,* **-ried, -ry·ing,** *n., pl.* **-ries.** —*v.i.* **1.** to remain or stay, as in a place; sojourn: *He tarried in Baltimore on his way to Washington.* **2.** to delay or be tardy in acting, starting, coming, etc.; linger or loiter. **3.** to wait. —*v.t.* **4.** *Archaic.* to wait for. —*n.* **5.** a stay; sojourn. [1275–1325; ME *taryen* to delay, *tary* a delay < ?] —**tar′ri·er,** *n.*
—**Syn. 1.** rest, lodge, stop, abide. **3.** See **wait.** —**Ant. 1.** leave.

tar·ry[2] (tär′ē), *adj.,* **-ri·er, -ri·est.** of or like tar; smeared with tar. [1545–55; TAR[1] + -Y[1]] —**tar′ri·ness,** *n.*

Tar·ry·town (tar′ē toun′), *n.* a village in SE New York, on the Hudson River: restored home of Washington Irving. 10,648.

tars-, var. of **tarso-** before a vowel: *tarsal.*

tar·sal (tär′səl), *adj.* **1.** of or pertaining to the tarsus of the foot. **2.** pertaining to the tarsi of the eyelids. —*n.* **3.** a tarsal bone, joint, or the like. [1810–20; TARS(US) + -AL[1]]

tar′ sand′, *Geol.* bituminous sand or sandstone from which asphalt can be obtained. [1895–1900]

Tar·shish (tär′shish), *n.* an ancient country, of uncertain location, mentioned in the Bible. I Kings 10:22.

tar•si•a (tär′sē ə, tär sē′ə), *n.* intarsia. [< It < Ar *tarṣī*ʿ inlay]

tar•si•er (tär′sē ər, -sē ā′), *n.* a small, arboreal, nocturnal primate of the genus *Tarsius,* of Indonesia and the Philippines, having a long thin tail, very large immobile eyes, and prominent pads on the fingers and toes. [1765–75; < F, equiv. to *tarse* TARSUS + *-ier* -IER²]

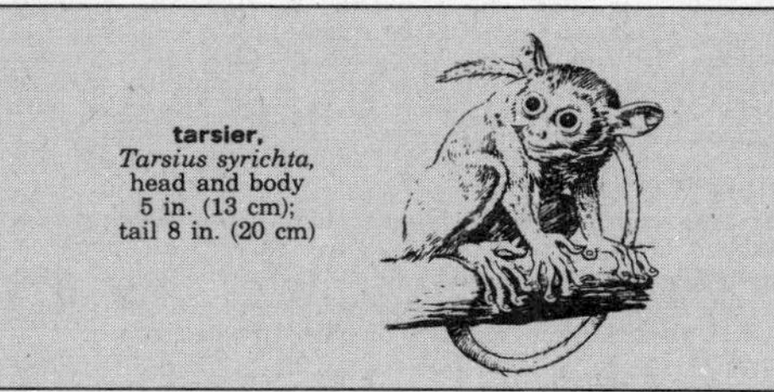
tarsier, *Tarsius syrichta,* head and body 5 in. (13 cm); tail 8 in. (20 cm)

Tar•ski (tär′skē), *n.* **Alfred,** born 1902, U.S. mathematician and logician, born in Poland.

tarso-, a combining form of **tarsus:** *tarsometatarsus.*

tar•so•met•a•tar•sus (tär′sō met′ə tär′səs), *n., pl.* **-si** (-sī, -sē). *Ornith.* the large bone in the lower leg of a bird with which the toe bones articulate, formed by the fusion of tarsal and metatarsal bones. [1850–55; TARSO- + METATARSUS] —**tar′so•met′a•tar′sal,** *adj.*

tar•sus (tär′səs), *n., pl.* **-si** (-sī, -sē). **1.** *Anat., Zool.* the bones of the proximal segment of the foot; the bones between the tibia and the metatarsus, contributing to the construction of the ankle joint. See diag. under **skeleton. 2.** the small plate of connective tissue along the border of an eyelid. **3.** tarsometatarsus. **4.** the distal part of the leg of an insect, usually subdivided in the adult into two to five segments. See diag. under **coxa.** [1670–80; < NL < Gk *tarsós* flat of the foot]

Tar•sus (tär′səs), *n.* a city in S Turkey, near the Mediterranean, on the Cydnus River: important seaport of ancient Cilicia; birthplace of Saint Paul. 74,510.

tart¹ (tärt), *adj.,* **-er, -est. 1.** sharp to the taste; sour or acid: *tart apples.* **2.** sharp in character, spirit, or expression; cutting; caustic: *a tart remark.* [bef. 1000; ME; OE *teart* sharp, rough; akin to D *tarten* to defy, MHG *traz* defiance] —**tart′ish,** *adj.* —**tart′ish•ly,** *adv.* —**tart′•ly,** *adv.* —**tart′ness,** *n.*

tart² (tärt), *n.* **1.** a small pie filled with cooked fruit or other sweetened preparation, usually having no top crust. **2.** a covered pie containing fruit or the like. **3.** *Slang.* a prostitute or promiscuous woman. —*v.t.* **4. tart up,** *Slang.* to adorn, dress, or decorate, esp. in a flamboyant manner: *The old restaurant was tarted up to look like a Viennese café.* [1350–1400; 1905–10 for def. 3; ME *tarte* < MF; cf. ML *tarta*]

tar•tan (tär′tn), *n.* **1.** a woolen or worsted cloth woven with stripes of different colors and widths crossing at right angles, worn chiefly by the Scottish Highlanders, each clan having its own distinctive plaid. **2.** a design of such a plaid known by the name of the clan wearing it. **3.** any plaid. —*adj.* **4.** of, pertaining to, or resembling tartan. **5.** made of tartan. [1490–1500; var. of *tertane* < MF *tertaine* (OF *tiretaine*) linsey-woolsey]

tartan (defs. 1, 2)

tar•tar (tär′tər), *n.* **1.** *Dentistry.* calculus (def. 3). **2.** the deposit from wines, potassium bitartrate. **3.** the intermediate product of cream of tartar, obtained from the crude form, argol. [1350–1400; ME < ML *tartarum* < LGk *tártaron;* r. ME *tartre* < MF < ML, as above]

Tar•tar (tär′tər), *n.* **1.** a member of any of the various tribes, chiefly Mongolian and Turkish, who, originally under the leadership of Genghis Khan, overran Asia and much of eastern Europe in the Middle Ages. **2.** a member of the descendants of this people variously intermingled with other peoples and tribes, now inhabiting parts of the European and W and central Asian Russian Federation. **3.** Tatar (defs. 1–3). **4.** (*often l.c.*) a savage, intractable person. **5.** (*often l.c.*) an ill-tempered person. **6. catch a Tartar,** to deal with someone or something that proves unexpectedly troublesome or powerful. Also, **catch a tartar.** —*adj.* **7.** of or pertaining to a Tartar or Tartars; Tartarian. **8.** Tatar (def. 5). Also, **Tatar** (for defs. 1, 2, 4–6). [1350–1400; ME < ML *Tartarus,* perh. var. of **Tātārus* < Pers *Tātār,* by assoc. with TARTARUS; r. ME *Tartre* < MF < ML, as above] —**Tar′tar•ly,** *adv.*

Tar•tar (tär′tər), *n. Obs.* Tartarus.

tar•tar•at•ed (tär′tə rā′tid), *adj. Chem.* tartrated.

Tar′tar Auton′omous Repub′lic. See **Tatar Autonomous Republic.**

Tar•tar•e•an (tär târ′ē ən), *adj.* of or pertaining to Tartarus; infernal. [1615–25; < L *Tartare(us)* of TARTARUS (see -EOUS) + -AN]

tar′tar emet′ic, *Chem., Pharm.* a white, water-soluble, sweet and metallic-tasting, poisonous powder or granules, $C_4H_4KO_7Sb$, used as a mordant for dyeing textiles and leather, and in medicine as an expectorant, for inducing vomiting, and for infections by schistosomes. Also called **antimony potassium tartrate, potassium antimonyl tartrate.** [1695–1705]

Tar•tar•i•an (tär târ′ē ən), *adj.* of, pertaining to, or characteristic of a Tartar or the Tartars; Tartar. [1350–1400; ME. See TARTAR, -IAN]

Tartar′ian as′ter, a Siberian aster, *Aster tataricus,* having large blue to purple flower heads.

Tartar′ian hon′eysuckle, an Asian honeysuckle, *Lonicera tatarica,* having fragrant, white to pink flowers. [1805–15]

tar•tar•ic (tär tar′ik, -tär′-), *adj.* pertaining to or derived from tartar. [1780–90; TARTAR + -IC]

tartar′ic ac′id, *Chem.* an organic compound, $C_4H_6O_6$, existing in four isomeric forms, the common or dextrorotatory isomer being a white, crystalline, water-soluble powder or transparent crystals: used in effervescent beverages, baking powders, confections, photography, and tanning. [1800–10]

tar•tar•ize (tär′tə rīz′), *v.t.,* **-ized, -iz•ing.** *Chem.* to impregnate, combine, or treat with tartar or potassium bitartrate. Also, *esp. Brit.,* **tar′tar•ise′.** [1700–10; TARTAR + -IZE] —**tar′tar•i•za′tion,** *n.*

tar•tar•ous (tär′tər əs), *adj.* consisting of or containing tartar. [1595–1605; TARTAR + -OUS]

tar′tar sauce′, a mayonnaise dressing for fish and seafood, usually with chopped pickles, onions, olives, capers, and green herbs added. Also, **tar′tare sauce′.** [1895–1900; < F *sauce tartare*]

tar′tar steak′, ground beefsteak seasoned with salt and pepper and served uncooked, often mixed with a raw egg and garnished with capers, onions, etc. Also, **tar•tare′ steak′** (tär tär′, tär′tər). Also called **steak tartare.** [1950–55]

Tar•ta•rus (tär′tər əs), *n. Class. Myth.* **1.** a sunless abyss, below Hades, in which Zeus imprisoned the Titans. **2.** a place in Hades for the punishment of the wicked.

Tar•ta•ry (tär′tə rē), *n.* the historical name of a region of indefinite extent in E Europe and Asia: designates the area overrun by the Tartars in the Middle Ages, from the Dnieper River to the Pacific. Also, **Tatary.** [1350–1400; ME *Tartarye* < MF *Tartarie* < ML *Tartaria.* See TARTAR, -Y³]

Tar•ti•ni (tär tē′nē), *n.* **Giu•sep•pe** (jo͞o zep′pe), 1692–1770, Italian violinist and composer.

tart•let (tärt′lit), *n.* a small pie. [1375–1425; late ME *tartlote.* See TART², -LET]

tar•trate (tär′trāt), *n. Chem.* a salt or ester of tartaric acid. [*tartr-* (comb. form repr. TARTAR) + -ATE²]

tar•trat•ed (tär′trā tid), *adj. Chem.* formed into a tartrate; combined with tartaric acid. Also, **tartarated.** [1875–80; TARTRATE + -ED³]

tar•tra•zine (tär′trə zēn′, -zin), *n.* See **Yellow No. 5.** [1890–95; *tartr-* (comb. form repr. TARTAR) + AZINE]

Tar•tu (tär′to͞o), *n.* a city in SE Estonia. 115,000. Formerly, German, **Dorpat;** Russian, **Yurev.**

Tar•tuffe (tär to͝of′, -to͞of′; *Fr.* TAR TYF′), *n., pl.* **-tuffes** (-to͝ofs′, -to͞ofs′; *Fr.* -TYF′) for 2. **1.** (*italics*) a comedy (1664–69) by Molière. **2.** Also, **Tar•tufe′.** (*often l.c.*) a hypocritical pretender to piety.

Tar•tuf•fer•y (tär to͝of′ə rē, -to͞o′fə-), *n.* behavior or character of a Tartuffe, esp. hypocritical piety. [1850–55; < F *tartufferie.* See TARTUFFE, -RY]

tart•y¹ (tär′tē), *adj.,* **tart•i•er, tart•i•est.** tart; somewhat sour. [TART¹ + -Y¹]

tart•y² (tär′tē), *adj.,* **tart•i•er, tart•i•est.** of, pertaining to, or suggesting a prostitute. [1915–20; TART² + -Y¹]

Ta•run•tius (tə run′shəs), *n.* a crater in the first quadrant of the face of the moon: about 38 miles (61 km) in diameter.

Tar•vi•a (tär′vē ə), *Trademark.* a brand of road-surfacing material made with asphalt.

tar•weed (tär′wēd′), *n.* any of several resinous or gummy, composite plants of the genus *Grindelia,* having solitary flower heads. [1865–70, *Amer.;* TAR¹ + WEED¹]

Tar•zan (tär′zən, -zan), *n.* **1.** the hero of a series of jungle stories by Edgar Rice Burroughs. **2.** a person of superior or superhuman physical strength, agility, and prowess.

Ta•sa•day (tä′sə dī′), *n., pl.* **-days,** (*esp. collectively*) **-day.** a member of a very small group of forest-dwelling people of southern Mindanao.

ta•sa•jil•lo (tä′sə hē′ō), *n., pl.* **-los.** a bushy or treelike cactus, *Opuntia leptocaulis,* of the southwestern U.S., having slender, spiny branches, greenish-yellow flowers, and red berrylike fruit. [1890–95, *Amer.;* < MexSp, dim. of Sp *tasajo* piece of meat]

Ta•ser (tā′zər), *Trademark.* a small gunlike device that fires electric darts to incapacitate a person temporarily.

Ta•shi La•ma (tä′shē lä′mə), any of a succession of Tibetan monks and spiritual leaders, second in importance only to the Dalai Lama. Also called **Bainquen Lama, Panchen Lama, Panchen Rimpoche.** [after *Tashi* (*Lumpo*) name of monastery of which this Lama is abbot]

Tash•kent (täsh kent′, tash-; *Russ.* tu shkyent′), *n.* a city in and the capital of Uzbekistan, in the NE part. 2,073,000.

Tash•likh (*Seph.* täsh lēkh′; *Ashk.* täsh′likh), *n. Hebrew.* a Jewish rite, performed on the afternoon usually of the first day of Rosh Hashanah, in which the participants symbolically cast off their sins by gathering along the banks of a river, stream, or the like and reciting prayers of repentance. Also, ***Tash′lik, Tash′lich.*** [*tashlikh* lit., you will cast]

task (task, täsk), *n.* **1.** a definite piece of work assigned to, falling to, or expected of a person; duty. **2.** any piece of work. **3.** a matter of considerable labor or difficulty. **4.** *Obs.* a tax or impost. **5. take to task,** to call to account; blame; censure: *The teacher took them to task for not doing their homework.* —*v.t.* **6.** to subject to severe or excessive labor or exertion; put a strain upon (powers, resources, etc.). **7.** to impose a task on. **8.** *Obs.* to tax. —*adj.* **9.** of or pertaining to a task or tasks: *A task chart will help organize the department's work.* [1250–1300; ME (n.) < ML *tasca,* metathetic var. of *taxa* TAX] —**task′less,** *adj.*

—**Syn. 1, 2.** job, assignment. TASK, CHORE, JOB, ASSIGNMENT refer to a definite and specific instance or act of work. TASK and CHORE and, to a lesser extent, JOB often imply work that is tiresome, arduous, or otherwise unpleasant. TASK usually refers to a clearly defined piece of work, sometimes of short or limited duration, assigned to or expected of a person: *the task of pacifying angry customers; a difficult, time-consuming task.* A CHORE is a minor task, usually one of several performed as part of a routine, as in farming, and often more tedious than difficult: *the daily chore of taking out the garbage; early morning chores of feeding the livestock.* JOB is the most general of these terms, referring to almost any work or responsibility, including a person's means of earning a living: *the job of washing the windows; a well-paying job in advertising.* ASSIGNMENT refers to a specific task allocated to a person by someone in a position of authority: *a homework assignment; a reporter's assignment to cover international news.*

task′ force′, 1. *Navy, Mil.* a temporary grouping of units under one commander, formed for the purpose of carrying out a specific operation or mission. **2.** a group or committee, usually of experts or specialists, formed for analyzing, investigating, or solving a specific problem. [1940–45]

task•mas•ter (task′mas′tər, täsk′mä′stər), *n.* **1.** a person whose function it is to assign tasks, esp. burdensome ones, to others. **2.** a person who supervises rigorously the work of others. [1520–30; TASK + MASTER] —**task′mas′ter•ship′,** *n.*

task•mis•tress (task′mis′tris, täsk′-), *n.* **1.** a woman whose function it is to assign tasks, esp. burdensome ones, to others. **2.** a woman who supervises others' work rigorously. [1595–1605; TASK + MISTRESS] —**Usage.** See **-ess.**

task•work (task′wûrk′, täsk′-), *n.* **1.** work assigned or imposed as a task. **2.** unpleasant or disagreeable work. **3.** work paid for by the job; piecework. [1480–90; TASK + WORK]

Tasm., Tasmania.

Tas•man (taz′mən; *Du.* täs′män′), *n.* **A•bel Jans•zoon** (ä′bəl yän′sōn), 1602?–59, Dutch navigator and explorer.

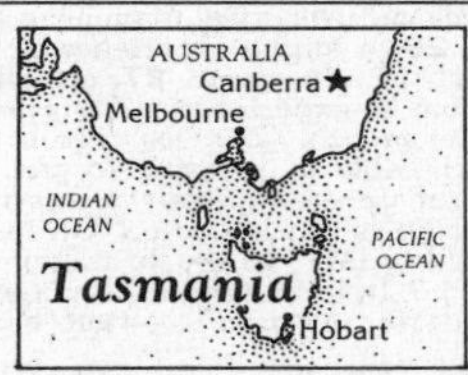

Tas•ma•ni•a (taz mā′nē ə, -mān′yə), *n.* an island S of Australia: a state of the commonwealth of Australia. 418,957; 26,382 sq. mi. (68,330 sq. km). *Cap.:* Hobart. Formerly, **Van Diemen's Land.** —**Tas•ma′ni•an,** *adj., n.*

Tasma′nian dev′il, a small, predacious marsupial, *Sarcophilus harrisii,* of Tasmania, having a black coat with white patches: its dwindling population is now confined to isolated areas. [1885–90]

Tasmanian devil, *Sarcophilus harrisii,* head and body 2 ft. (0.6 m); tail 10½ in. (27 cm)

Tasma′nian wolf′, thylacine. Also called **Tasma′•nian ti′ger.** [1885–90]

Tas′man Sea′ (taz′mən), a part of the Pacific Ocean between SE Australia and New Zealand.

tass (tas), *n. Chiefly Scot.* **1.** a cup or small goblet, esp. an ornamental one. **2.** the contents of a cup or goblet; a small draught, as of liquor. Also, **tassie.** [1475–85; earlier *tasse* < MF < Ar *ṭass, ṭassah* basin < Pers *tasht;* see TAZZA]

Tass (tas, täs), *n.* a news-gathering agency of the former Soviet Union: merged with an alternative news service to form Itar-Tass (Russian Information Telegraph Agency). Also, **TASS** [< Russ, acronym from *T(elegráfnoe) a(géntstvo) S(ovétskogo) S(oyúza)* Telegraph Agency of the Soviet Union]

tas•sel (tas′əl), *n., v.,* **-seled, -sel•ing** or (*esp. Brit.*) **-selled, -sel•ling.** —*n.* **1.** a pendent ornament consisting commonly of a bunch of threads, small cords, or other strands hanging from a roundish knob or head, used on clothing, in jewelry, on curtains, etc. **2.** something resembling this, as the inflorescence of certain plants, esp. that at the summit of a stalk of corn. —*v.t.* **3.** to furnish or adorn with tassels. **4.** to form into a tassel or tassels. **5.** to remove the tassel from (growing corn) in order to improve the crop. —*v.i.* **6.** (of corn) to

CONCISE PRONUNCIATION KEY: *act, cāpe, dâre, pärt; set, ēqual; if, īce; ox, ōver, ôrder, oil, bo͝ok, bo͞ot, out; up, ûrge; child; sing; shoe; thin, that;* zh as in *treasure.* ə = *a* as in *alone, e* as in *system, i* as in *easily, o* as in *gallop, u* as in *circus;* ᵊ as in *fire* (fīᵊr), *hour* (ouᵊr). l and n can serve as syllabic consonants, as in *cradle* (krād′l), and *button* (but′n). See the full key inside the front cover.

put forth tassels (often fol. by *out*). [1250–1300; ME (n.) < OF *tas(s)el* fastening for cloak < VL **tassellus*, b. L *tessella* (dim. of *tessera* die for gaming) and *taxillus* (dim. of *tālus* die for gaming). See TESSELLATE, TALUS[1]] —**tas′sel·er;** *esp. Brit.,* **tas′sel·ler,** *n.* —**tas′sel·ly;** *esp. Brit.,* **tas′sel·ly,** *adj.*

tas′sel flow′er, love-lies-bleeding. [1830–40, *Amer.*]

tas·set (tas′it), *n. Armor.* either of two pieces of plate armor hanging from the fauld to protect the upper parts of the thighs. Also, **tace, tasse** (tas). [1825–35; < F *tassette,* MF *tassete,* equiv. to *tasse* pouch (< MHG *tasche* lit., pendent object) + *-ete* -ET]

tass·ie (tas′ē), *n. Chiefly Scot.* tass. [TASS + -IE]

Tas·so (tas′ō; *It.* täs′sô), *n.* **Tor·qua·to** (tôʀ kwä′tô), 1544–95, Italian poet.

taste (tāst), *v.,* **tast·ed, tast·ing,** *n.* —*v.t.* **1.** to try or test the flavor or quality of (something) by taking some into the mouth: *to taste food.* **2.** to eat or drink a little of: *She barely tasted her dinner.* **3.** to eat or drink (often used in negative constructions): *He hadn't tasted food for three days.* **4.** to perceive or distinguish the flavor of: *to taste the wine in a sauce.* **5.** to have or get experience, esp. a slight experience: *these young men who had only begun to taste life.* **6.** to perceive in any way. **7.** *Archaic.* to enjoy or appreciate. **8.** *Obs.* **a.** to examine by touch; feel. **b.** to test or try. **9. taste blood.** See **blood** (def. 22). —*v.i.* **10.** to try the flavor or quality of something. **11.** to eat or drink a little (usually fol. by *of*): *She tasted of the cake.* **12.** to perceive or distinguish the flavor of anything. **13.** to have experience of something, however limited or slight. **14.** to have a particular flavor (often fol. by *of*): *The coffee tastes bitter. The bread tastes of mold.* **15.** to smack or savor (usually fol. by *of*): *The story tastes of treason.* —*n.* **16.** the act of tasting food or drink. **17.** the sense by which the flavor or savor of things is perceived when they are brought into contact with the tongue. **18.** the sensation or quality as perceived by this sense; flavor. **19.** a small quantity tasted; a morsel, bit, or sip. **20.** a relish, liking, or partiality for something: *a taste for music.* **21.** the sense of what is fitting, harmonious, or beautiful; the perception and enjoyment of what constitutes excellence in the fine arts, literature, fashion, etc. **22.** the sense of what is seemly, polite, tactful, etc., to say or do in a given social situation. **23.** one's personal attitude or reaction toward an aesthetic phenomenon or social situation, regarded as either good or bad. **24.** the ideas of aesthetic excellence or of aesthetically valid forms prevailing in a culture or personal to an individual: *a sample of Victorian taste; I consulted only my own taste in decorating this room.* **25.** the formal idiom preferred by a certain artist or culture; style; manner: *a façade in the Baroque taste.* **26.** a slight experience or a sample of something: *a taste of adventure.* **27.** a feeling or sensation resulting from an experience: *a compromise that left a bad taste in her mouth.* **28.** *Obs.* test or trial. **29. to one's taste,** agreeable or pleasing to one: *He couldn't find any ties that were completely to his taste.* [1250–1300; (v.) ME *tasten* to touch, taste < OF *taster* to touch, explore by touching (MF: to touch, taste); c. It *tastare,* Pr, OSp *tastar* < ?; (n.) ME *tast* sense of touch, a trying, tasting < OF, deriv. of *taster*] —**tast′a·ble, taste′a·ble,** *adj.*

—**Syn. 1.** savor. **18.** TASTE, FLAVOR, SAVOR refer to a quality that is perceived when a substance is placed upon the tongue. TASTE is the general word: *the taste of roast beef.* FLAVOR is a characteristic taste, usually of a pleasing kind, and as of some ingredient put into the food: *lemon flavor.* SAVOR, much less common than TASTE or FLAVOR, implies pleasing scent as well as taste or flavor, and connotes enjoyment in tasting: *The sauce has an excellent savor.* **20.** fondness, disposition, appreciation, predisposition. **21.** discernment, perception, judgment. —**Ant. 20.** antipathy.

taste′ bud′, one of numerous small, flask-shaped bodies, chiefly in the epithelium of the tongue, which are the end organs for the sense of taste. [1885–90]

taste·ful (tāst′fəl), *adj.* having, displaying, or in accordance with good taste: *tasteful clothing; a tasteful room.* [1605–15; TASTE + -FUL] —**taste′ful·ly,** *adv.* —**taste′ful·ness,** *n.*

—**Syn.** elegant, chic, refined, suitable, becoming.

taste·less (tāst′lis), *adj.* **1.** having no taste or flavor; insipid. **2.** dull; uninteresting. **3.** lacking in aesthetic quality or capacity; devoid of good taste: *a houseful of tasteless furnishings; a tasteless director of stale, dreary films.* **4.** lacking in politeness, seemliness, tact, etc.; unmannerly; insensitive: *a tasteless remark.* **5.** lacking the physical sense of taste. [1585–95; TASTE + -LESS] —**taste′less·ly,** *adv.* —**taste′less·ness,** *n.*

taste·mak·er (tāst′mā′kər), *n.* a person or thing that establishes or strongly influences what is considered to be stylish, acceptable, or worthwhile in a given sphere of interest, as the arts. [1950–55; TASTE + MAKER]

tast·er (tā′stər), *n.* **1.** a person who tastes, esp. one skilled in distinguishing the qualities of liquors, tea, etc., by the taste. **2.** a container for taking samples or tasting. **3.** a wide shallow cup, usually metal, for holding wine to be tasted, as by a professional taster. **4.** a person employed or ordered to taste the food and drink prepared for a king, dictator, etc., to ascertain the presence of poison. **5.** *Genetics.* a person able to taste phenylthiourea or some other test substance. [1350–1400; ME *tastour* < AF. See TASTE, -ER[1]]

tast·y (tā′stē), *adj.,* **tast·i·er, tast·i·est. 1.** good-tasting; savory: *a tasty canapé.* **2.** *Informal.* having or showing good taste; tasteful. [1610–20; TASTE + -Y[1]] —**tast′i·ly,** *adv.* —**tast′i·ness,** *n.*

—**Syn. 1.** delicious, delectable, toothsome, appetizing. See **palatable.**

CONCISE ETYMOLOGY KEY: <, descended or borrowed from; >, whence; b., blend of, blended; c., cognate with; cf., compare; deriv., derivative; equiv., equivalent; imit., imitative; obl., oblique; r., replacing; s., stem; sp., spelling, spelled; resp., respelling, respelled; trans., translation; ?, origin unknown; *, unattested; ‡, probably earlier than. See the full key inside the front cover.

tat (tat), *v.i., v.t.,* **tat·ted, tat·ting.** to do, or make by, tatting. [1900–05; back formation from TATTING]

TAT, See **Thematic Apperception Test.**

ta ta (tä tä′), *Chiefly Brit.* good-bye. [1830–40; orig. uncert.]

ta·ta·mi (tə tä′mē), *n., pl.* **-mi, -mis.** (in Japanese houses) any of a number of thick, woven straw mats of uniform dimensions, about three feet by six feet (91 cm by 183 cm), the placing of which determines the dimensions of an interior. [1895–1900; < Japn, n. use of v.: to fold up]

Ta·tar (tä′tər), *n.* **1.** a member of a modern Turkic people living in the Tatar Autonomous Republic and adjacent regions of eastern European Russia and in widely scattered communities in western Siberia and central Asia. **2.** the language of this people, including the literary language of the Tatar Autonomous Republic, the dialects of the Tatar Autonomous Republic and adjacent regions of the Volga basin **(Volga Tatar),** and numerous other dialects, some transitional to other Turkic languages. **3.** See **Crimean Tatar. 4.** Tartar (defs. 1, 2, 4–6). —*adj.* **5.** of or pertaining to the Tatars or their language. **6.** Tartar (def. 7). Also, **Tartar** (for defs. 1–3, 5). [1805–15; see TARTAR] —**Ta·tar·i·an** (tä târ′ē ən), **Ta·tar·ic** (tä tar′ik), *adj.*

Ta′tar Auton′omous Repub′lic, an autonomous republic in the E Russian Federation in Europe. 3,640,000; ab. 26,255 sq. mi. (68,000 sq. km). *Cap.:* Kazan. Also, **Tartar Autonomous Republic.**

Ta·ta·ry (tä′tə rē), *n.* Tartary.

Tate (tāt), *n.* **1. Sir Henry,** 1819–99, English merchant and philanthropist: founder of an art gallery **(Tate′ Gal′lery)** in London, England. **2. (John Or·ley) Allen** (ôr′lē), 1899–1979, U.S. poet, critic, and editor. **3. Na·hum** (nā′əm, -həm), 1652–1715, English poet and playwright, born in Ireland: poet laureate 1692–1715.

ta·ter (tā′tər), *n. Dial.* potato. [1750–60; by aphesis, and dial. substitution of *-er* for final *-o;* see FELLER[1]]

Ta·tha·ga·ta (tə tä′gə tə), *n.* one of the names of Buddha. [< Skt, Pali *tathāgata*]

Ta·tha·ta (tut′ə tä′), *n. Buddhism.* the absoluteness of Sunya. Also called **Bhutatathata.** [< Pali *tathatā,* n. deriv of *tathā* thus < Skt]

Ta·tia·na (tä tyä′nə), *n.* a female given name.

Ta·tin (tä taɴ′), *adj.* caramelized and baked in the manner of an upside-down cake: *an apple tart Tatin.* [< F *(tarte) tatin, à la Tatin, des desmoiselles Tatin;* said to be after two (or more) Tatin sisters, who developed the recipe]

Ta·tius (tā′shəs), *n. Rom. Legend.* a Sabine king who, following the rape of the Sabine women, attacked Rome and eventually ruled with Romulus. Also, **Titus.**

Tat·ler, The (tat′lər), a triweekly periodical (1709–11) written, edited, and published by Richard Steele with the collaboration of Joseph Addison.

tat·ou·ay (tat′o͞o ā′, tä′to͞o ī′), *n.* a naked-tailed armadillo, *Cabassous unicintus,* of tropical South America. [1825–35; < Sp *tatuay* < Pg < Guarani *tatu-ai,* equiv. to *tatu* armadillo + *ai* worthless, lazy]

tat·pur·u·sha (tat po͝or′ə shə, tut-), *n. Ling.* a compound of two words in which the first is an attributive noun and the second a substantive, as *bookcase, aircraft,* or *flowerpot.* [< Skt *tatpuruṣa* lit., his man, his servant; equiv. to the two words *tasya* + *puruṣaḥ;* an example of the compound used to name the compound type]

Ta′tra Moun′tains (tä′trə), a mountain range in N Slovakia and S Poland: a part of the central Carpathian Mountains. Highest peak, Gerlachovka, 8737 ft. (2663 m). Also called **High Tatra.**

tat·ter[1] (tat′ər), *n.* **1.** a torn piece hanging loose from the main part, as of a garment or flag. **2.** a separate torn piece; shred. **3. tatters,** torn or ragged clothing: *dressed in rags and tatters.* —*v.t.* **4.** to tear or wear to tatters. —*v.i.* **5.** to become ragged. [1375–1425; (n.) late ME < ON *tǫturr* rag, tatter; akin to OE *tætteca* rag, shred; (v.) back formation from TATTERED]

tat·ter[2] (tat′ər), *n.* a person who does tatting, esp. as an occupation. [1880–85; TAT + -ER[1]]

tat·ter·de·mal·ion (tat′ər di māl′yən, -mal′-), *n.* **1.** a person in tattered clothing; a shabby person. —*adj.* **2.** ragged; unkempt or dilapidated. [1600–10; first written *tatter-de-mallian* and rhymed with *Italian;* see TATTER[1]; *-de-mallian* < ?]

tat·tered (tat′ərd), *adj.* **1.** torn to tatters; ragged: *a tattered flag.* **2.** wearing ragged clothing: *a tattered old man.* [1300–50; ME; see TATTER[1] (n.), -ED[3]]

tat·ter·sall (tat′ər sôl′, -səl), *n.* **1.** a pattern of squares formed by colored crossbars on a solid-color, usually light background. **2.** a fabric with this pattern. —*adj.* **3.** having this pattern or made of such fabric: *a tattersall vest.* [1890–95; after *Tattersall's,* London horse market; such patterns were common on horse blankets]

tat·tie (tat′ē), *n.* tatty[2].

tat·ting (tat′ing), *n.* **1.** the act or process of making a kind of knotted lace of cotton or linen thread with a shuttle. **2.** such lace. [1835–45; orig. uncert.]

tat·tle (tat′l), *v.,* **-tled, -tling,** *n.* —*v.i.* **1.** to let out secrets. **2.** to chatter, prate, or gossip. —*v.t.* **3.** to utter idly; disclose by gossiping. —*n.* **4.** the act of tattling. **5.** idle talk; chatter; gossip. [1475–85; < D *tatelen;* c. MLG *tatelen*] —**tat′tling·ly,** *adv.*

tat·tler (tat′lər), *n.* **1.** a person who tattles; telltale. **2.** either of two shorebirds of the genus *Heteroscelus,* having a loud, whistling cry. **3.** any of various related shorebirds having shrill cries, as the yellowlegs. **4.** a small bass, *Serranus phoebe,* of the West Indies and Florida. [1540–50; TATTLE + -ER[1]]

tat·tle·tale (tat′l tāl′), *n.* **1.** a talebearer or informer, esp. among children. —*adj.* **2.** telltale; revealing: *a tattletale smear of lipstick on his collar.* [1885–90, *Amer.;* TATTLE + TALE]

tat′tletale gray′, a dirty or grayish white. [1940–45]

tat·too[1] (ta to͞o′), *n., pl.* **-toos. 1.** a signal on a drum, bugle, or trumpet at night, for soldiers or sailors to go to their quarters. **2.** a knocking or strong pulsation: *My heart beat a tattoo on my ribs.* **3.** *Brit.* an outdoor military pageant or display. [1570–80; earlier *taptoo* < D *taptoe* lit., the tap(room) is to (i.e., shut)]

tat·too[2] (ta to͞o′), *n., pl.* **-toos,** *v.,* **-tooed, -too·ing.** —*n.* **1.** the act or practice of marking the skin with indelible patterns, pictures, legends, etc., by making punctures in it and inserting pigments. **2.** a pattern, picture, legend, etc., so made. —*v.t.* **3.** to mark (the skin) with tattoos. **4.** to put (tattoos) on the skin. [1760–70; < Marquesan *tatu;* r. *tattow* < Tahitian *tatau*] —**tat·too′er, tat·too′ist,** *n.*

tat·tva (tut′və), *n.* (in Hindu philosophy) essence. [< Skt]

tat tvam as·i (tat′ tvam′ as′ē, tut′ twum′ us′ē), *Sanskrit.* Thou art That (the statement, in the Upanishads, that Atman is identical with Brahman).

tat·ty[1] (tat′ē), *adj.,* **-ti·er, -ti·est. 1.** cheap or tawdry; vulgar: *a tatty production of a Shakespearean play.* **2.** shabby or ill-kempt; ragged; untidy: *an old house with dirty windows and tatty curtains.* [1505–15; *tat* rag (prob. back formation from TATTER[1]) + -Y[1]] —**tat′ti·ly,** *adv.* —**tat′ti·ness,** *n.*

tat·ty[2] (tat′ē), *n., pl.* **-ties.** (in India) a screen, usually made of coarse, fragrant fibers, placed over a window or door and kept moistened with water in order to cool and deodorize the room. Also, **tattie.** [1785–95; < Hindi *ṭaṭṭī*]

Ta·tum (tā′təm), *n.* **1. Art,** 1910–56, U.S. jazz pianist. **2. Edward Law·rie** (lôr′ē), 1909–75, U.S. biochemist: Nobel prize for medicine 1958.

Ta·tung (*Chin.* dä′to͝ong′), *n. Wade-Giles.* Datong.

tau (tou, tô *for 1, 2, 4;* täv, tôv *for 3*), *n.* **1.** the 19th letter of the Greek alphabet (Τ, τ). **2.** the consonant sound represented by this letter. **3.** tav. **4.** Also, **tauon.** *Physics.* See **tau lepton.** [1250–1300; ME < L < Gk *taû* < Sem; cf. TAV]

Tau·ber (tou′bər), *n.* **Richard,** 1892–1948, Austrian tenor, in England after 1940.

Tauch·nitz (toukн′nits), *n.* **Karl Chri·stoph Trau·gott** (kärl′ kris′tôf trou′gôt), 1761–1836, and his son, **Karl Chri·sti·an Phi·lipp** (kris′tē än′ fē′lip, fil′ip), 1798–1884, German printers and publishers.

tau′ cross′, a T-shaped cross. Also called **St. Anthony's cross.** See illus. under **cross.** [1425–75; late ME]

taught (tôt), *v.* pt. and pp. of **teach.**

tau′ lep′ton, *Physics.* an unstable lepton with a mass approximately 3500 times that of the electron. *Symbol:* T Also called **tau, tauon.** [1975–80]

tau′ neutri′no, *Physics.* a hypothetical type of neutrino that would obey a conservation law together with the tau lepton, with the total number of tau leptons and tau neutrinos minus the total number of their antiparticles remaining constant. Also called **tau·on′ic neutri′no** (tô on′ik, tou-). Cf. **lepton**[2].

taunt[1] (tônt, tänt), *v.t.* **1.** to reproach in a sarcastic, insulting, or jeering manner; mock. **2.** to provoke by taunts; twit. —*n.* **3.** an insulting gibe or sarcasm; scornful reproach or challenge. **4.** *Obs.* an object of insulting gibes or scornful reproaches. [1505–15; orig. uncert.] —**taunt′er,** *n.* —**taunt′ing·ly,** *adv.*

—**Syn. 1.** censure, upbraid, flout, insult. **2, 3.** jeer. See **ridicule. 3.** scoff, derision, insult, censure, ridicule.

taunt[2] (tônt, tänt), *adj. Naut.* tall, as a mast. [1490–1500; orig. uncert.]

Taun·ton (tôn′tn, tän′-), *n.* **1.** a city in SE Massachusetts. 45,001. **2.** former name of **Taunton Deane.**

Taun′ton Deane′ (dēn), a city in Somersetshire, in SW England. 82,600. Formerly, **Taunton.**

tau·on (tô′on, tou′-), *n. Physics.* See **tau lepton.** [TAU + -ON[1]]

taupe (tōp), *n.* a moderate to dark brownish gray, sometimes slightly tinged with purple, yellow, or green. [1910–15; < F < L *talpa* mole]

Tau·po (tou′pō), *n.* **Lake,** a lake in N New Zealand, in the central part of North Island: largest lake in New Zealand. ab. 234 sq. mi. (605 sq. km).

taur-, var. of **tauro-** before a vowel: *taurine.*

Tau·rang·a (tou räng′ə), *n.* a city on the N coast of North Island, in N New Zealand. 48,153.

tauri-, var. of **tauro-.**

Tau·rids (tôr′idz), *n.* (*used with a plural v.*) *Astron.* a collection of meteors constituting a meteor shower **(Tau′rid me′teor show′er)** visible during the period of October 26 to November 16 and having its apparent origin in the constellation Taurus. [1885–90; TAUR(US) + -ID[1] + -S[3]]

tau·ri·form (tôr′ə fôrm′), *adj.* shaped like a bull or the head or horns of a bull. [1715–25; < L *tauriformis.* See TAURI-, -FORM]

tau·rine[1] (tôr′īn, -in), *adj.* **1.** of, pertaining to, or resembling a bull. **2.** pertaining to the zodiacal sign Taurus. [1605–15; < L *taurinus.* See TAUR-, -INE[1]]

tau·rine[2] (tôr′ēn, -in), *n. Chem.* a neutral crystalline substance, $C_2H_7NO_3S$, obtained from bile. [1835–45; TAUR(OCHOLIC) + -INE[2]]

tauro-, a combining form meaning "bull," used in the formation of compound words: *taurocholic.* Also, **taur-, tauri-.** [comb. form repr. L *taurus,* Gk *taûros*]

tau·ro·bo·li·um (tôr′ə bō′lē əm), *n., pl.* **-li·a** (-lē ə). **1.** the sacrifice of a bull, followed by the baptism of neophytes in the blood, as practiced in the ancient rites of Mithras or Cybele. **2.** *Fine Arts.* a representation of the killing of a bull, as in Mithraic art. [1690–1700; < LL < Gk *taurobólion,* equiv. to *tauroból(os)* bull sacrifice (*taûro(s)* bull + *bólos* a cast, throw, akin to *bolḗ* a wound, *bállein* to throw) + *-ion* dim. suffix]

tau·ro·cho·lic (tôr′ə kō′lik, -kol′ik), *adj. Chem.* of or derived from taurocholic acid. [1855–60; TAURO- + CHOLIC]

tau′rocho′lic ac′id, *Chem.* an acid, $C_{26}H_{45}NO_7S$, occurring as a sodium salt in the bile of carnivorous animals, which on hydrolysis yields taurine and cholic acid.

tau·rom·a·chy (tô rom′ə kē), *n.* the art or technique of bullfighting. [1840–50; (< Sp *tauromaquia*) < Gk *tauromachía.* See TAURO-, -MACHY] **—tau·ro·ma·chi·an** (tôr′ə mā′kē ən), *adj.*

Tau·rus (tôr′əs), *n., gen.* **Tau·ri** (tôr′ī) for 1. **1.** *Astron.* the Bull, a zodiacal constellation between Gemini and Aries, containing the bright star Aldebaran. **2.** *Astrol.* **a.** the second sign of the zodiac: the fixed earth sign. See illus. under **zodiac. b.** a person born under this sign, usually between April 20th and May 20th. [1350–1400; ME < L]

Tau·rus (tôr′əs), *n.* a mountain range in S Turkey: highest peak, 12,251 ft. (3734 m).

Taus·sig (tou′sig), *n.* **Frank William,** 1859–1940, U.S. economist.

taut (tôt), *adj.,* **-er, -est. 1.** tightly drawn; tense; not slack. **2.** emotionally or mentally strained or tense: *taut nerves.* **3.** in good order or condition; tidy; neat. [1275–1325; earlier *taught,* ME *tought;* akin to TOW[1]] **—taut′ly,** *adv.* **—taut′ness,** *n.*
—Syn. 3. trim, trig, spruce, smart.

Tau′ta·vel man′ (tô′tə vel′). See **Arago man.** [after *Tautavel,* village in the E French Pyrenees]

taut·ed (tä′tid), *adj. Scot.* (esp. of wood or hair) tangled or matted together. [1775–85; *taut* (var. of dial. *tate* small tuft of wool, hair, or grass) + -ED[3]]

taut·en (tôt′n), *v.t., v.i.* to make or become taut. [1805–15; TAUT + -EN[1]]

tauto-, a combining form meaning "same," used in the formation of compound words: *tautomerism.* [< Gk, comb. form of *tautó,* contr. of *tò autó* the same]

tau·tog (tô tog′, -tôg′), *n.* a black food and game fish, *Tautoga onitis,* inhabiting waters along the North Atlantic coast of the U.S. [1635–45, *Amer.;* < Narragansett (E sp.) *tautaŭog,* pl. of *taut*]

tau·tol·o·gism (tô tol′ə jiz′əm), *n.* **1.** the use of tautology. **2.** a tautology. [1805–15; TAUTOLOG(Y) + -ISM]

tau·tol·o·gize (tô tol′ə jīz′), *v.i.,* **-gized, -giz·ing.** to use tautology. Also, *esp. Brit.,* **tau·tol′o·gise′.** [1600–10; TAUTOLOG(Y) + -IZE]

tau·tol·o·gy (tô tol′ə jē), *n., pl.* **-gies. 1.** needless repetition of an idea, esp. in words other than those of the immediate context, without imparting additional force or clearness, as in "widow woman." **2.** an instance of such repetition. **3.** *Logic.* **a.** a compound propositional form all of whose instances are true, as "A or not A." **b.** an instance of such a form, as "This candidate will win or will not win." [1570–80; < LL *tautologia* < Gk *tautología.* See TAUTO-, -LOGY] **—tau·to·log·i·cal** (tôt′l oj′i kəl), **tau·to·log′ic, tau·tol·o·gous** (tô tol′ə gəs), *adj.* **—tau′to·log′i·cal·ly, tau·tol′o·gous·ly,** *adv.* **—tau·tol′o·gist,** *n.*

tau·to·mer (tô′tə mər), *n. Chem.* a compound that exhibits tautomerism. [1900–05; back formation from TAUTOMERISM]

tau·tom·er·ism (tô tom′ə riz′əm), *n. Chem.* the ability of certain organic compounds to react in isomeric structures that differ from each other in the position of a hydrogen atom and a double bond. [1880–85; TAUTO- + (ISO)MERISM] **—tau·to·mer·ic** (tô′tə mer′ik), *adj.*

tau·tom·er·ize (tô tom′ə rīz′), *v.,* **-ized, -iz·ing.** *—v.i.* **1.** to undergo tautomerism. *—v.t.* **2.** to cause to undergo tautomerism. Also, *esp. Brit.,* **tau·tom′er·ise′.** [TAUTOMER(ISM) + -IZE] **—tau·tom′er·iz′a·ble,** *adj.* **—tau·tom′er·i·za′tion,** *n.*

tau·to·nym (tô′tə nim), *n. Biol.* a scientific name in which the generic and the specific names are the same, as *Chloris chloris* (the greenfinch). [1895–1900; < Gk *tautṓnymos* of the same name, equiv. to *tauto-* TAUTO- + *-ōnymos* named; see -ONYM] **—tau′to·nym′ic, tau·ton·y·mous** (tô ton′ə məs), *adj.* **—tau·ton′y·my,** *n.*

tau·to·syl·lab·ic (tô′tō si lab′ik), *adj. Phonet.* occurring within the same syllable: *The* (s) *and* (t) *are tautosyllabic in the word* disturb, *but not in* distaste. [TAUTO- + SYLLABIC]

tav (täv, tôv, täf, tôf), *n.* **1.** the 23rd letter of the Hebrew alphabet. **2.** the consonant sound represented by this letter. Also, **tau, taw.** [< Heb *tāw* lit., mark]

Ta·vel (tä vel′), *n.* a dry rosé wine from the Rhone region of France.

tav·ern (tav′ərn), *n.* **1.** a place where liquors are sold to be consumed on the premises. **2.** a public house for travelers and others; inn. [1250–1300; ME *taverne* < OF < L *taberna* hut, inn, wine shop] **—tav′ern·less,** *adj.*
—Syn. 1. bar; pub. **2.** hostelry. See **hotel.**

ta·ver·na (tə vûr′nə, -vär′-; *Gk.* tä ver′nä), *n.* a small, unpretentious café or restaurant in Greece. [1945–50; < ModGk *tabérna* (pron. *taverna*), MGk, LGk < L. See TAVERN]

tav·ern·er (tav′ər nər), *n.* **1.** the owner of a tavern. **2.** *Obs.* a frequenter of taverns. [1300–50; ME < AF; OF *tavernier.* See TAVERN, -ER[2]]

tav′ern nuts′, shelled peanuts with the skins left on and lightly salted and sugared.

tav′ern ta′ble, a short table having a narrow, deep apron and legs connected by a box stretcher.

taw[1] (tô), *n.* **1.** a choice or fancy marble used as a shooter. **2.** a game in which marbles are arranged in the center of a circle drawn or scratched on the ground, the object being to knock out as many as possible from the circle; ringer. **3.** Also, **taw′ line′.** the line from which the players shoot. *—v.i.* **4.** to shoot a marble. [1700–10; orig. uncert.]

taw[2] (tô), *v.t.* **1.** to prepare or dress (some raw material) for use or further manipulation. **2.** to transform the skin of an animal into white leather by the application of minerals, emulsions, etc. **3.** *Archaic.* to flog; thrash. [bef. 900; ME *tawen,* OE *tawian;* c. D *touwen,* Goth *taujan*] **—taw′er,** *n.*

taw[3] (täv, tôv, täf, tôf), *n.* tav.

taw·dry (tô′drē), *adj.,* **-dri·er, -dri·est,** *n.* *—adj.* **1.** (of finery, trappings, etc.) gaudy; showy and cheap. **2.** low or mean; base: *tawdry motives.* *—n.* **3.** cheap, gaudy apparel. [1605–15; short for (*Sain*)*t Audrey lace,* i.e., neck lace bought at St. Audrey's Fair in Ely, England; so called after *St. Audrey* (OE *Aethelthrȳth,* d. 679), Northumbrian queen and patron saint of Ely, who, according to tradition, died of a throat tumor which she considered just punishment of her youthful liking for neck laces] **—taw′dri·ly,** *adv.* **—taw′dri·ness,** *n.*
—Syn. 1. flashy, meretricious. **—Ant. 1.** elegant.

taw·ie (tô′ē), *adj. Scot.* docile; easy to manage. [1780–90; TAW[2] (in obs. sense "to mistreat, abuse") + *-ie* -Y[1]]

taw·ney (tô′nē), *adj.,* **-ni·er, -ni·est,** *n.* tawny.

Taw·ney (tô′nē, tä′-), *n.* **Richard Henry,** 1880–1962, English historian, born in Calcutta.

taw·ny (tô′nē), *adj.,* **-ni·er, -ni·est,** *n.* *—adj.* **1.** of a dark yellowish or dull yellowish-brown color. *—n.* **2.** a shade of brown tinged with yellow; dull yellowish brown. [1350–1400; ME *tauny* < AF *taune* < MF *tané,* ptp. of *taner* to TAN] **—taw′ni·ly,** *adv.* **—taw′ni·ness,** *n.*

taw·pie (tô′pē), *n. Scot.* a foolish or thoughtless young person. [1720–30; *tawp-* (< Scand; cf. Norw, *tåpe,* Sw *tåp,* Dan *tåbe* simpleton, fool) + -IE]

taws (tôz, täz), *n., pl.* **taws.** *Chiefly Scot.* **1.** a whip or leather thong used to drive a spinning top. **2.** a leather whip having its tip divided into smaller strips, used to punish schoolchildren. [1505–15; pl. of obs. *taw* < ON *taug* rope; c. OE *tēag* TIE]

tax (taks), *n.* **1.** a sum of money demanded by a government for its support or for specific facilities or services, levied upon incomes, property, sales, etc. **2.** a burdensome charge, obligation, duty, or demand. *—v.t.* **3.** (of a government) **a.** to demand a tax from (a person, business, etc.). **b.** to demand a tax in consideration of the possession or occurrence of (income, goods, sales, etc.), usually in proportion to the value of money involved. **4.** to lay a burden on; make serious demands on: *to tax one's resources.* **5.** to take to task; censure; reprove; accuse: *to tax one with laziness.* **6.** *Informal.* to charge: *What did he tax you for that?* **7.** *Archaic.* to estimate or determine the amount or value of. *—v.i.* **8.** to levy taxes. [1250–1300; (v.) ME *taxen* < ML *taxāre* to tax, appraise, L: to appraise, handle, freq. of *tangere* to touch; (n.) ME, deriv. of the v.] **—tax′er,** *n.* **—tax′ing·ly,** *adv.* **—tax′less,** *adj.* **—tax′less·ly,** *adv.* **—tax′less·ness,** *n.*
—Syn. 1. duty, impost, levy. **4.** strain, tire, stretch.

tax-, var. of **taxo-** before a vowel: *taxeme.*

tax·a (tak′sə), *n.* pl. of **taxon.**

tax·a·ble (tak′sə bəl), *adj.* **1.** capable of being taxed; subject to tax: *a taxable gain.* *—n.* **2.** Usually, **taxables.** persons, items of property, etc., that are subject to tax. [1425–75; late ME; see TAX, -ABLE] **—tax′a·bil′i·ty, tax′a·ble·ness,** *n.* **—tax′a·bly,** *adv.*

tax·a·ceous (tak sā′shəs), *adj.* belonging to the Taxaceae, the yew family of plants. Cf. **yew family.** [1840–50; < NL *Taxace(ae)* name of the family (*Tax(us)* a genus (L: yew) + *-aceae* -ACEAE) + -OUS]

tax·a·tion (tak sā′shən), *n.* **1.** the act of taxing. **2.** the fact of being taxed. **3.** a tax imposed. **4.** the revenue raised by taxes. [1250–1300; < ML *taxātiōn-* (s. of *taxātiō*) an appraising (see TAX, -ATION); r. ME *taxacioun* < AF < ML, as above] **—tax·a′tion·al,** *adj.*

taxa′tion without′ representa′tion, *Amer. Hist.* a phrase, generally attributed to James Otis about 1761, that reflected the resentment of American colonists at being taxed by a British Parliament to which they elected no representatives and became an anti-British slogan before the American Revolution; in full, "Taxation without representation is tyranny."

tax′-brack·et creep′ (taks′brak′it). See **bracket creep.**

tax′ certif′icate, a document issued to the purchaser of property sold for unpaid taxes attesting to the holder's right to eventual receipt of the title deed. Cf. **tax deed.**

tax-de·duct·i·ble (taks′di duk′tə bəl), *adj.* noting an item the value or cost of which is deductible from the gross amount on which a tax is calculated.

tax′ deduc′tion, an expenditure that is deducted from taxable income.

tax′ deed′, a title deed issued by a public authority to the purchaser of property sold for the nonpayment of taxes. Cf. **tax certificate. —tax′-deed′ed,** *adj.*

tax-de·ferred (taks′di fûrd′), *adj.* noting or providing income that is not taxed until a later time.

tax·eme (tak′sēm), *n. Ling.* a feature of the arrangement of elements in a construction, as selection, order, phonetic modification, or modulation. [1930–35; TAX- + -EME] **—tax·e′mic,** *adj.*

tax′ eva′sion, the nonpayment of taxes, as through the failure to report taxable income. [1920–25]

tax-ex·empt (taks′ig zempt′), *adj.* **1.** not subject or liable to taxation: *tax-exempt imports.* **2.** providing income that is not taxable: *tax-exempt municipal bonds.* *—n.* **3.** a tax-exempt security. [1920–25]

tax′ ex′ile, a person who moves outside the jurisdiction of a country to avoid paying taxes. Also called **tax′ expa′triate.** [1960–65]

tax′ expend′iture, any reduction in government revenue through preferential tax treatment, as deductions or credits.

tax·fla·tion (taks flā′shən), *n.* See **bracket creep.** [TAX + (IN)FLATION]

tax-free (taks′frē′), *adj.* tax-exempt (def. 1).

tax·gath·er·er (taks′gath′ər ər), *n.* a person who collects taxes. [1545–55; TAX + GATHERER] **—tax′gath′er·ing,** *n.*

tax′ ha′ven, a foreign country or corporation used to avoid or reduce income taxes, esp. by investors from another country.

tax·i (tak′sē), *n., pl.* **tax·is** or **tax·ies,** *v.,* **tax·ied, tax·i·ing** or **tax·y·ing.** *—n.* **1.** a taxicab. *—v.i.* **2.** to ride or travel in a taxicab. **3.** (of an airplane) to move over the surface of the ground or water under its own power. *—v.t.* **4.** to cause (an airplane) to taxi. [1905–10, *Amer.;* short for TAXICAB]

taxi-, var. of **taxo-:** *taxidermy.*

tax·i·cab (tak′sē kab′), *n.* a public passenger vehicle, esp. an automobile, usually fitted with a taximeter. [1905–10; TAXI(METER) + CAB]

tax′i danc′er, a girl or woman employed, as by a dance hall, to dance with patrons who pay a fee for each dance or for a set period of time. [1925–30; so called because such a dancer, like a taxi, is hired for the occasion]

tax·i·der·my (tak′si dûr′mē), *n.* the art of preparing and preserving the skins of animals and of stuffing and mounting them in lifelike form. [1810–20; TAXI- + Gk *dérm(a)* skin (see DERMA) + -Y[3]] **—tax′i·der′mal, tax′i·der′mic,** *adj.* **—tax′i·der′mist,** *n.*

Tax·i·la (tak′sə lə), *n.* an archaeological site near Rawalpindi, Pakistan: ruins of three successive cities on the same site, dating from about the 7th century B.C. to about the 7th century A.D.; Buddhist center.

tax·i·man (tak′sē mən), *n., pl.* **-men.** *Chiefly Brit.* a taxi driver. [1920–25; TAXI + -MAN]

tax·i·me·ter (tak′sē mē′tər), *n.* a device fitted to a taxicab or other vehicle, for automatically computing and indicating the fare due. [1885–90; < F *taximètre,* equiv. to *taxe* TAX + *-i-* -I- + *-mètre* -METER; r. earlier *taxameter* < G, equiv. to *Taxa* (< ML: tax, charge) + *-meter* -METER]

tax·ing (tak′sing), *adj.* wearingly burdensome: *the day-to-day, taxing duties of a supervisor.* [1790–1800; TAX + -ING[2]] **—tax′ing·ly,** *adv.*

tax·i·plane (tak′sē plān′), *n.* an airplane available for chartered or unscheduled trips. [1915–20; TAXI(CAB) + (AIR)PLANE]

tax·is[1] (tak′sis), *n., pl.* **tax·es** (tak′sēz). **1.** arrangement or order, as in one of the physical sciences. **2.** *Biol.* oriented movement of a motile organism in response to an external stimulus, as toward or away from light. **3.** *Surg.* the replacing of a displaced part, or the reducing of a hernia or the like, by manipulation without cutting. **4.** *Archit.* the adaptation to the purposes of a building of its various parts. [1720–30; < NL < Gk *táxis,* equiv. to *tak-* (base of *tássein* to arrange, put in order) + *-sis* -SIS]

tax·is[2] (tak′sēz), *n.* a pl. of **taxi.**

-taxis, a combining form representing **taxis**[1] in compound words: *heterotaxis.* Cf. **tax-, taxi-, taxo-, -taxy.**

tax′i squad′, *Football.* **1.** (formerly) a group of players under contract to and practicing with a professional team who are not on the team's roster as playing members and therefore are ineligible to play in official games. **2.** the four extra players on a professional football team's roster who are not allowed to suit up for an official game but who are ready to join the team at any time to replace injured or unsuccessful players. [1945–50, *Amer.*] **—tax′i-squad′,** *adj.* **—tax′i-squad′der,** *n.*

tax′i strip′, *Aeron.* a narrow taxiway.

tax·i·way (tak′sē wā′), *n.* any surface area of an airport used for taxiing airplanes to and from a runway, parking apron, terminal, etc. [1930–35; TAXI (v.) + WAY]

taxo-, a combining form representing **taxis**[1] in compound words: *taxonomy.* Also, **tax-, taxi-.**

Tax·ol (tak′sōl, -sol), *Trademark.* a chemical substance derived from a yew tree of the Pacific Coast: used experimentally as a drug in the treatment of cancer.

tax·on (tak′son), *n., pl.* **tax·a** (tak′sə). a taxonomic category, as a species or genus. [1945–50; < Gk *táx(is)* TAXIS[1] + *-on* neut. n. ending; see -ON[1]]

tax′onom′ic pho′neme. See **autonomous phoneme.**

tax·on·o·my (tak son′ə mē), *n.* **1.** the science or technique of classification. **2.** *Biol.* the science dealing with the description, identification, naming, and classification of organisms. [1805–15; F *taxonomie.* See TAXO-, -NOMY] **—tax·o·nom·ic** (tak′sə nom′ik), **tax′o·nom′i·cal,** *adj.* **—tax′o·nom′i·cal·ly,** *adv.* **—tax·on′o·mist, tax·on′o·mer,** *n.*

TAXONOMIC CLASSIFICATION

Taxon	Animal	Plant
	human being	white oak
Kingdom	Animalia	Plantae
Phylum	Chordata	Magnoliophyta
Class	Mammalia	Magnoliopsida
Order	Primates	Fagales
Family	Hominidae	Fagaceae (beech)
Genus	*Homo*	*Quercus*
Species	*Homo sapiens*	*Quercus alba*

tax·paid (taks′pād′), *adj.* salaried or paid for by taxes: *taxpaid teachers; taxpaid highways.* [TAX + PAID]

tax·pay·er (taks′pā′ər), *n.* **1.** a person who pays a tax or is subject to taxation. **2.** a temporary building that yields rent sufficient only to pay the taxes on the property on which it stands. [1810–20; TAX + PAYER] **—tax′pay′ing,** *n.*

tax′ rate′, the percentage of the value of a property to be paid as a tax. [1875–80]

tax′ return′, return (def. 24). [1885–90]

tax′ sale′, the sale of real property, as land, usually at auction by a public authority, in order to pay delinquent taxes assessed upon its owner. [1825–35, *Amer.*]

tax′ shar′ing. See **revenue sharing.**

tax′ shel′ter, any financial arrangement (as a certain kind of investment or allowance) that results in a reduction or elimination of taxes due. **—tax′-shel′tered,** *adj.*

tax′ stamp′, a stamp required to be affixed to certain products, documents, etc., before they change hands to indicate that a tax has been paid.

tax′ ti′tle, *Law.* a title, acquired by the purchaser at a forced sale of property for nonpayment of taxes. [1825–35, *Amer.*]

-taxy, var. of **-taxis:** *heterotaxy.* [< Gk *-taxia.* See TAXIS[1], -Y[3]]

Tay (tā), *n.* **1.** a river flowing through central Scotland into the Firth of Tay. 118 mi. (190 km) long. **2. Firth of,** an estuary of the North Sea, off the coast of central Scotland. 25 mi. (40 km) long.

Tay·lor (tā′lər), *n.* **1. A(lan) J(ohn) P(ercivale),** 1906–90, English historian. **2. Bay·ard** (bī′ərd, bā′-), (*James Bayard*), 1825–78, U.S. poet, novelist, and travel writer. **3. Brook,** 1685–1731, English mathematician. **4. Cecil (Percival),** born 1933, U.S. jazz pianist and composer. **5. David Watson,** 1864–1940, U.S. naval architect. **6. Edward,** 1644?–1729, American physician, clergyman, and poet; born in England. **7. Edward Thompson** (*"Father Taylor"*), 1793–1871, U.S. Methodist clergyman. **8. Frederick Winslow,** 1856–1915, U.S. inventor. **9. Jeremy,** 1613–67, English prelate and theological writer. **10. John W.,** 1784–1854, U.S. politician: Speaker of the House 1820–21, 1825–27. **11. (Joseph) Deems,** 1885–1966, U.S. composer, music critic, and author. **12. Maxwell (Davenport),** 1901–87, U.S. army general and diplomat: chief of staff 1955–59; chairman of Joint Chiefs of Staff 1962–64. **13. Myron Charles,** 1874–1959, U.S. lawyer, industrialist, and diplomat. **14. Paul (Bel·ville)** (bel′vil), born 1930, U.S. dancer and choreographer. **15. Tom,** 1817–80, English playwright and editor. **16. Zachary** (*"Old Rough and Ready"*), 1784–1850, 12th president of the U.S. 1849–50: major general during the Mexican War and commander of the army of the Rio Grande 1846. **17.** a city in SE Michigan. 77,568. **18.** a town in central Texas. 10,619. **19.** a male or female given name.

Tay·lor·ism (tā′lə riz′əm), *n.* a modified form of Calvinism that maintains that every person has a free will, and that makes a distinction between depravity, as the tendency to commit sins, and sin, as a voluntary choice of evil actions. Also called **New Haven theology.** [after Nathaniel William *Taylor* (1786–1858), U.S. theologian; see -ISM] **—Tay·lor·ite** (tā′lə rit′), *n.*

Tay·lor·ism (tā′lə riz′əm), *n.* the application of scientific methods to the problem of obtaining maximum efficiency in industrial work or the like. [1925–30; after Frederick W. TAYLOR; see -ISM]

Tay′lor se′ries, *Math.* an approximation of a given function f at a particular point x, in terms of values of the function and its derivatives at a neighboring point x_0, by a power series in which the terms are given by $f^{(n)}(x_0)\,(x-x_0)^n/n!$, where $f^{(n)}(x_0)$ is the derivative of order n evaluated at point x_0. Cf. **Maclaurin series.** [1905–10; after BROOK TAYLOR]

Tay·lor·ville (tā′lər vil′), *n.* a town in central Illinois. 11,386.

tay·ra (tī′rə), *n.* a small animal, *Eira barbara,* of the weasel family, ranging from Mexico to tropical South America. [1850–55; < Pg, Sp, *taira* < Tupi]

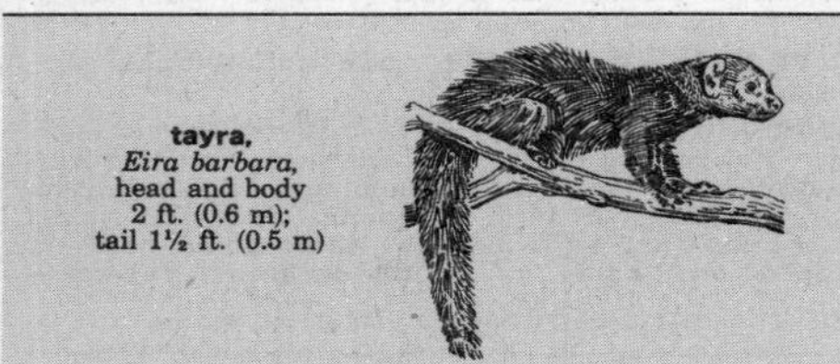

tayra, *Eira barbara,* head and body 2 ft. (0.6 m); tail 1½ ft. (0.5 m)

Tay′-Sachs′ disease′ (tā′saks′), *Pathol.* a rare fatal hereditary disease, occurring chiefly in infants and children, esp. of eastern European Jewish origin, characterized by a red spot on the retina, gradual blindness, and paralysis. [1920–25; named after W. *Tay* (1843–1927), English physician, and B. *Sachs* (1858–1944), American neurologist]

Tay·side (tā′sīd′), *n.* a region in E Scotland. 401,987; 1100 sq. mi. (2849 sq. km).

ta·ʻzi·yah (tə zē′yə), *n.* (in Shiʻite Islam) a passion play commemorating the martyrdom of Hussein, grandson of Muhammad and son of Ali and Fatima, on the tenth of Muharram, A.D. 680. [< Ar *taʻziyah* lit., consolation]

CONCISE ETYMOLOGY KEY: <, descended or borrowed from; >, whence; b., blend of, blended; c., cognate with; cf., compare; deriv., derivative; equiv., equivalent; imit., imitative; obl., oblique; r., replacing; s., stem; sp., spelling, spelled; resp., respelling, respelled; trans., translation; ?, origin unknown; *, unattested; ‡, probably earlier than. See the full key inside the front cover.

taz·za (tät′sə; *It.* tät′tsä), *n., pl.* **-zas,** *It.* **-ze** (-tse). a shallow, saucerlike, ornamental bowl, often having handles and usually on a high base or pedestal. [1835–45; < It < Ar *ṭassah* basin. See TASS]

TB, 1. tubercle bacillus. **2.** tuberculosis. Also **T.B.**

Tb, 1. tubercle bacillus. **2.** tuberculosis.

Tb, *Symbol, Chem.* terbium.

t.b., 1. trial balance. **2.** tubercle bacillus. **3.** tuberculosis.

T.B.A., to be announced. Also, **t.b.a.**

T-bar (tē′bär′), *n. Building Trades.* a rolled metal bar or beam with a cross section resembling a T. Also called **tee.** See illus. under **shape.**

T-bar lift, a ski lift having an upside-down T-shaped bar against which two skiers may lean while being pulled uphill. Also called **T-bar.** [1885–90]

TBI, *Auto.* See **throttle-body injection.**

Tbi·li·si (tə bə lē′sē; *Russ.* tbyi lyē′syi), *n.* a city in and the capital of the Georgian Republic, in the SE part, on the Kura. 1,194,000. Formerly, **Tiflis.**

T-bill (tē′bil′), *n.* a U.S. Treasury bill. [1970–75, *Amer.*]

T.B.O., *Theat.* total blackout.

T-bond (tē′bond′), *n.* a U.S. Treasury bond.

T-bone steak (tē′bōn′), a loin steak having some tenderloin, characterized by its T-shaped bone. [1920–25]

TBS, *Naut.* talk between ships: a radiotelephone for short-range communication between vessels.

tbs., 1. tablespoon; tablespoons. **2.** tablespoonful; tablespoonfuls. Also, **tbsp.**

TC, 1. Teachers College. **2.** Trusteeship Council (of the United Nations).

Tc, *Symbol, Chem.* technetium.

TCA, *Chem.* See **trichloroacetic acid.**

TCBM, transcontinental ballistic missile.

TCDD, *Pharm.* dioxin.

TCE, *Chem.* trichloroethylene.

T cell, *Immunol.* any of several closely related lymphocytes, developed in the thymus, that circulate in the blood and lymph and orchestrate the immune system's response to infected or malignant cells, either by lymphokine secretions or by direct contact: helper T cells recognize foreign antigen on the surfaces of other cells, then they stimulate B cells to produce antibody and signal killer T cells to destroy the antigen-displaying cells; subsequently suppressor T cells return the immune system to normal by inactivating the B cells and killer T cells. Also called **T lymphocyte.** [1965–70; *T(hymus-derived)*]

Tchad (*Fr.* chad), *n.* Chad.

Tchai·kov·sky (chī kôf′skē, -kof′-, chi-), *n.* **Peter Il·yich** (il′yich) or **Pëtr Il·ich** (*Russ.* pyôtʀ′ ē lyĕch′), 1840–93, Russian composer. Russian, **Chaikovski.** Also, **Tschaikovsky, Tschaikowsky.**

Tcham·bu·li (chäm bo͞o′lē), *n., pl.* **-lis,** (*esp. collectively*) **-li.** a member of an indigenous people of Papua New Guinea.

Tche·by·cheff′ equa′tion (chə bə shôf′), *Math.* a differential equation of the form $(1 - x^2)\, d^2y/dx^2 - x\, dy/dx + n^2y = 0$, where n is any nonnegative integer. Also called **Chebyshev equation.** [named after Pafnutiĭ L. *Chebyshev* (1821–94), Russian mathematician]

Tchebycheff′ polyno′mial, *Math.* a polynomial solution of the Tchebycheff equation, of the form $T_n(x) = \cos(n\cos^{-1}x)$, where n is an integer. Also called **Chebyshev polynomial.** [see TCHEBYCHEFF EQUATION]

Tche·khov (chek′ôf, -of; *Russ.* chye′khəf), *n.* **An·ton Pa·vlo·vich** (an′ton pav lō′vich; *Russ.* un tôn′ pu vlô′-vyich). See **Chekhov, Anton.**

Tche·rep·nin (chə rep′nin; *Russ.* chyi ʀyip nyēn′), *n.* **1. Alexander** (*Aleksandr Nikolaevich*), 1899–1977, Russian pianist and composer, in the U.S. **2.** his father, **Nicholas** (*Nikolai Nickolaevich*), 1873–1945, Russian composer and conductor.

tcher·no·sem (cher′no zem′), *n.* chernozem.

tcher·vo·netz (chər vō′nits, -nets; *Russ.* chyiʀ vô′-nyits), *n., pl.* **-von·tzi** (-vōnt′sē; *Russ.* -vôn′tsi). chervonets.

tchotch·ke (chäch′kə), *n. Slang.* an inexpensive souvenir, trinket, or ornament. Also, **chotchke.** [1965–70, *Amer.*; < Yiddish *tshatshke* < Pol *czaczko* bibelot, knickknack (now obs.; cf. mod. *cacko* with same sense, orig. dial.); of expressive orig.]

tchr., teacher.

TCP theorem, *Physics.* See **CPT theorem.**

TCS, traffic control station.

TD, 1. touchdown; touchdowns. **2.** trust deed.

T/D, time deposit.

T.D., 1. Traffic Director. **2.** Treasury Department.

TDD, telecommunications device for the deaf.

t distribution. See **Student's t distribution.** [1955–60]

TDN, totally digestible nutrients. Also, **t.d.n.**

TDRS, Tracking and Data Relay Satellite.

TDY, temporary duty.

te (tā), *n. Music.* ti[1].

Te (de), *n.* (in philosophical Taoism) the virtue or power inherent in a person or thing existing in harmony with the Tao. Also, **Teh.** [< Chin (Wade-Giles) *te*[2], (pinyin) *dé*]

Te, *Symbol, Chem.* tellurium.

tea (tē), *n.* **1.** the dried and prepared leaves of a shrub, *Camellia sinensis,* from which a somewhat bitter, aromatic beverage is prepared by infusion in hot water. **2.** the shrub itself, extensively cultivated in China, Japan, India, etc., and having fragrant white flowers. Cf. **tea family. 3.** the beverage so prepared, served hot or iced. **4.** any kind of leaves, flowers, etc., so used, or any plant yielding them. **5.** any of various infusions prepared from the leaves, flowers, etc., of other plants, and used as beverages or medicines. **6.** See **beef bouillon. 7.** *Brit.* any meal, whether a light snack or one consisting of several courses, eaten in the late afternoon or in the evening; any meal other than dinner, eaten after the middle of the afternoon. **8.** an afternoon reception at which tea is served. **9.** *Slang.* marijuana. **10. one's cup of tea,** something suitable, appropriate, or attractive to one: *Horror movies and westerns are just not my cup of tea.* [1590–1600; 1940–45 for def. 9; < dial. Chin (Xiamen) *t'e,* akin to Chin *chá*] **—tea′less,** *adj.*

Tea′ Act′, *Amer. Hist.* an act of the British Parliament (1773) that created a monopoly unfair to American tea merchants: the chief cause of the Boston Tea Party.

tea′ bag′, a container of thin paper or cloth holding a measured amount of tea leaves for making an individual serving of tea. [1900–05]

tea′ ball′, a small ball of perforated metal or other material in which tea leaves are placed to be immersed in hot water to make tea. [1900–05]

tea′ bas′ket, *Brit.* a lunch basket or picnic hamper. [1900–05]

tea·ber·ry (tē′ber′ē, -bə rē), *n., pl.* **-ries.** the spicy red fruit of the American wintergreen, *Gaultheria procumbens.* [1790–1800; TEA + BERRY]

tea′ bis′cuit, a small, round, soft biscuit, usually shortened and sweetened.

tea′ break′, *Chiefly Brit.* an intermission from work, usually in the middle of the morning or afternoon, for a cup of tea, a snack, etc.

tea′ cad′dy, a small box, can, or chest for holding tea leaves. [1830–40; prob. orig. CATTY[2], the box that held the measure being confused with the measure itself]

tea·cake (tē′kāk′), *n.* **1.** a small cake, cookie, tart, or the like, for serving with tea or punch. **2.** (in England) a light, flat, sweet cake with raisins, usually buttered and served hot with tea. [1820–30, *Amer.*; TEA + CAKE]

tea·cart (tē′kärt′), *n.* See **tea wagon.** [1925–30; TEA + CART]

teach (tēch), *v.,* **taught, teach·ing,** *n.* **—*v.t.* 1.** to impart knowledge of or skill in; give instruction in: *She teaches mathematics.* **2.** to impart knowledge or skill to; give instruction to: *He teaches a large class.* **—*v.i.* 3.** to impart knowledge or skill; give instruction. **—*n.* 4.** *Informal.* teacher. [bef. 900; ME *techen,* OE *tǣcan*; akin to TOKEN]
—Syn. 1–3. coach. **2, 3.** inform, enlighten, discipline, drill, school, indoctrinate. TEACH, INSTRUCT, TUTOR, TRAIN, EDUCATE share the meaning of imparting information, understanding, or skill. TEACH is the broadest and most general of these terms and can refer to almost any practice that causes others to develop skill or knowledge: *to teach children to write; to teach marksmanship to soldiers; to teach tricks to a dog.* INSTRUCT almost always implies a systematic, structured method of teaching: *to instruct paramedics in techniques of cardiopulmonary resuscitation.* TUTOR refers to the giving of usually private instruction or coaching in a particular subject or skill: *to tutor a child in (a foreign language, algebra, history, or the like).* TRAIN lays stress on the development of desired behaviors through practice, discipline, or the use of rewards or punishments: *to train a child to be polite; to train recruits in military skills; to train a dog to heel.* EDUCATE, with a root sense of "to lead forth from," refers to the imparting of a specific body of knowledge, esp. one that equips a person to practice a profession: *to educate a person for a high-school diploma; to educate someone for the law.*

Teach (tēch), *n.* **Edward** (*"Blackbeard"*), died 1718, English pirate and privateer in the Americas. Also, **Thatch, Thach.**

teach·a·ble (tē′chə bəl), *adj.* **1.** capable of being instructed, as a person; docile. **2.** capable of being taught, as a subject. [1475–85; TEACH + -ABLE] **—teach′a·bil′i·ty, teach′a·ble·ness,** *n.* **—teach′a·bly,** *adv.*

teach·er (tē′chər), *n.* a person who teaches or instructs, esp. as a profession; instructor. [1250–1300; ME *techer.* See TEACH, -ER[1]] **—teach′er·less,** *adj.* **—teach′er·ship′,** *n.*

teach·er·age (tē′chər ij), *n.* a building serving as a combination school and living quarters, as on certain government reservations and in remote, sparsely settled areas. [1930–35, *Amer.*; TEACHER + -AGE]

teach′er bird′, the ovenbird, *Seiurus aurocapillus,* a songbird that builds a nest shaped like a dome. [1930–35, *Amer.*; *teacher* fancifully repr. the bird's note]

teach′ers col′lege, a four-year college offering courses for the training of primary and secondary school teachers and granting the bachelor's degree and often advanced degrees. [1905–10]

teach′er's pet′, a pupil who is a favorite of a teacher. [1925–30]

teach-in (tēch′in′), *n., pl.* **teach-ins.** a prolonged period of lectures, speeches, etc., conducted without interruption by members of the faculty and invited guests at a college or university as a technique of social protest. [1960–65; see -IN[3]]

teach·ing (tē′ching), *n.* **1.** the act or profession of a person who teaches. **2.** something that is taught. **3.** Often, **teachings.** doctrines or precepts: *the teachings of Lao-tzu.* [1125–75; ME *teching.* See TEACH, -ING[1]]

teach′ing aid′, material used by a teacher to supplement classroom instruction or to stimulate the interest of students.

teach′ing el′der, a minister in a Presbyterian church. [1635–45, *Amer.*]

teach′ing fel′low, a holder of a teaching fellowship.

teach′ing fel′lowship, a fellowship providing a student in a graduate school with free tuition and expenses and stipulating that the student assume some teaching duties in return.

teach′ing hos′pital, a hospital associated with a medical college and offering clinical and other facilities to those in various areas of medical study, as students, interns, and residents.

teach′ing machine′, a mechanical, electrical, or other automatic device that presents the user with items of information in planned sequence, registers his or her response to each item, and immediately indicates the acceptability of each response.

tea′ co′zy, cozy (def. 5). [1870–75]

tea•cup (tē′kup′), *n.* **1.** a cup in which tea is served, usually of small or moderate size. **2.** a teacupful. **3.** **tempest in a teacup** or **teapot,** a disturbance or uproar about little or nothing: *The fight over who should become the next assistant treasurer of the organization is just a tempest in a teacup.* Also, **storm in a teacup.** [1690–1700; TEA + CUP]

tea•cup•ful (tē′kup fo͝ol′), *n., pl.* **-fuls.** as much as a teacup will hold, equal to 4 fluid ounces (113 grams). [1695–1705; TEACUP + -FUL]
—Usage. See **-ful.**

tea′ dance′, a dance held at teatime. [1880–85]

tea′ fam′ily, the plant family Theaceae, characterized by shrubs and trees having simple, alternate leaves, often showy flowers, and capsular, berrylike, or dry fruit, and including the camellia, franklinia, and tea.

tea′ gar′den, a tea plantation. [1795–1805]

Tea•gar•den (tē′gär′dn), *n.* **Wel•don John** (wel′dn), (*Jack*), 1905–64, U.S. jazz trombonist and singer.

tea′ gown′, a semiformal gown of fine material, esp. one styled with soft, flowing lines, worn for afternoon social occasions. [1875–80]

tea•house (tē′hous′), *n., pl.* **-hous•es** (-hou′ziz). a restaurant or other establishment, esp. in the Far East, where tea and refreshments are served. [1680–90; TEA + HOUSE]

teak (tēk), *n.* **1.** a large East Indian tree, *Tectona grandis,* of the verbena family, yielding a hard, durable, resinous, yellowish-brown wood used for shipbuilding, making furniture, etc. **2.** the wood of this tree. **3.** any of various similar trees or woods. [1665–75; earlier *teke* < Pg *teca* < Malayalam *tēkka*]

tea•ket•tle (tē′ket′l), *n.* a portable kettle with a cover, spout, and handle, used for boiling water. [1695–1705; TEA + KETTLE]

teak•wood (tēk′wo͝od′), *n.* the wood of the teak. [1775–85; TEAK + WOOD[1]]

teal (tēl), *n., pl.* **teals,** (*esp. collectively*) **teal** for 1. **1.** any of several species of small dabbling ducks, of worldwide distribution, usually traveling in tight flocks and frequenting ponds and marshes. **2.** Also called **teal′ blue′.** a medium to dark greenish blue. [1275–1325; ME *tele;* akin to D *taling,* MLG *telink*]

tea′ lead′ (led), hard, stiff sheet lead, originally used as a lining for tea chests. [1805–15]

team (tēm), *n.* **1.** a number of persons forming one of the sides in a game or contest: *a football team.* **2.** a number of persons associated in some joint action: *a team of advisers.* **3.** two or more horses, oxen, or other animals harnessed together to draw a vehicle, plow, or the like. **4.** one or more draft animals together with the harness and vehicle drawn. **5.** a family of young animals, esp. ducks or pigs. **6.** *Obs.* offspring or progeny; race or lineage. *—v.t.* **7.** to join together in a team. **8.** *Chiefly Northern U.S. Older Use.* to convey or transport by means of a team; haul. *—v.i.* **9.** to drive a team. **10.** to gather or join in a team, a band, or a cooperative effort (usually fol. by *up, together,* etc.). *—adj.* **11.** of, pertaining to, or performed by a team: *a team sport; team effort.* [bef. 900; ME *teme* (n.), OE *tēam* child-bearing, brood, offspring, set of draft beasts; c. D *toom* bridle, reins, G *Zaum,* ON *taumr*]
—Syn. 10. combine, unite, ally, merge.
—Usage. See **collective noun.**

tea′ mak′er, a perforated, spoonlike object used as a tea strainer and having a hinged, convex lid. [1835–45]

team•er (tē′mər), *n.* a teamster. [1835–45; TEAM + -ER[1]]

team•mate (tēm′māt′), *n.* a member of the same team. [1910–15; TEAM + MATE[1]]

tea′ mon′ey, (esp. in parts of China) a bribe used to facilitate any business dealing.

team′ play′er, a person who willingly works in cooperation with others. [1885–90, *Amer.*]

team•ster (tēm′stər), *n.* **1.** a person who drives a team or a truck for hauling, esp. as an occupation. **2.** a member of the Teamsters Union. [1770–80, *Amer.*; TEAM + -STER]

Team′sters U′nion, the unofficial name of the International Brotherhood of Teamsters, Chauffeurs, Warehousemen, and Helpers of America.

team′ teach′ing, *Educ.* a program in which two or more teachers integrate their subjects, such as literature and history, into one course, which they teach as a team, to create a broader perspective for the student. [1955–60]

team•work (tēm′wûrk′), *n.* **1.** cooperative or coordinated effort on the part of a group of persons acting together as a team or in the interests of a common cause. **2.** work done with a team. [1820–30; TEAM + WORK]

Tea•neck (tē′nek′), *n.* a township in NE New Jersey. 39,007.

tea-of-heav•en (tē′əv hev′ən), *n.* a shrub, *Hydrangea macrophylla serrata,* of the saxifrage family, native to Japan and Korea, having hairy, ovate leaves and flat or slightly arched clusters of blue or white flowers.

tea′ par′ty, a social gathering, usually in the afternoon, at which tea and light refreshments are served. [1770–80]

tea•pot (tē′pot′), *n.* a container with a lid, spout, and handle, in which tea is made and from which it is poured. [1610–20; TEA + POT[1]]

Tea′pot Dome′, *U.S. Hist.* a federal oil reserve in Wyoming, leased to private producer Harry F. Sinclair by Secretary of the Interior Albert B. Fall in 1922, leading to a major government scandal and the tarnishing of the reputation of President Warren G. Harding's administration (1921–23).

tea•poy (tē′poi), *n.* **1.** a small three-legged table or stand. **2.** a small table for use in serving tea. [1820–30; < Hindi *tipāi,* alter. (with *t-* from *tir-* three < Skt *tri*) of Pers *si-pāya* three-legged stand]

tear[1] (tēr), *n.* **1.** a drop of the saline, watery fluid continually secreted by the lacrimal glands between the surface of the eye and the eyelid, serving to moisten and lubricate these parts and keep them clear of foreign particles. **2.** this fluid appearing in or flowing from the eye as the result of emotion, esp. grief. **3.** something resembling or suggesting a tear, as a drop of a liquid or a tearlike mass of a solid substance, esp. having a spherical or globular shape at one end and tapering to a point at the other. **4.** *Glassmaking.* a decorative air bubble enclosed in a glass vessel; air bell. **5.** **tears,** grief; sorrow. **6.** **in tears,** weeping: *He was in tears over the death of his dog.* *—v.i.* **7.** to fill up and overflow with tears, as the eyes. [bef. 900; (n.) ME *teer,* OE *tēar, tehher, taeher;* c. OHG *zahar,* ON *tār,* Goth *tagr,* Gk *dákry,* L *lacrima* (see LACHRYMAL); (v.) ME *teren,* OE *teheran,* in *teherende* (ger.), deriv. of the n.]

tear[2] (târ), *v.,* **tore** or (*Archaic*) **tare, torn** or (*Archaic*) **tare, tear•ing;** *n.* *—v.t.* **1.** to pull apart or in pieces by force, esp. so as to leave ragged or irregular edges. **2.** to pull or snatch violently; wrench away with force: *to tear wrappings from a package; to tear a book from someone's hands.* **3.** to distress greatly: *anguish that tears the heart.* **4.** to divide or disrupt: *a country torn by civil war.* **5.** to wound or injure by or as if by rending; lacerate. **6.** to produce or effect by rending: *to tear a hole in one's coat.* **7.** to remove by force or effort: *to be unable to tear oneself from a place.* *—v.i.* **8.** to become torn. **9.** to make a tear or rent. **10.** to move or behave with force, violent haste, or energy: *The wind tore through the trees; cars tearing up and down the highway; I was tearing around all afternoon trying to find sandals for the beach.* **11.** **tear at, a.** to pluck violently at; attempt to tear: *She tore at the bandages until they loosened.* **b.** to distress; afflict: *remorse that tears at one's soul.* **12.** **tear down, a.** to pull down; destroy; demolish. **b.** to disparage or discredit: *to tear down one's friends behind their backs.* **13.** **tear into,** *Informal.* **a.** to attack impulsively and heedlessly: *He tore into the food with a will.* **b.** to attack verbally: *She tore into him for being late for dinner.* **14.** **tear it,** *Slang.* to ruin all hope; spoil everything. **15.** **tear off,** *Slang.* to perform or do, esp. rapidly or casually: *to tear off a poem; to tear off a set of tennis.* **16.** **tear one's hair,** to tug at one's hair, as with anger or sorrow. Also, **tear one's hair out. 17.** **tear up, a.** to tear into small shreds: *He tore up the drawings because she had criticized them.* **b.** to cancel or annul: *to tear up a contract.* *—n.* **18.** the act of tearing. **19.** a rent or fissure. **20.** a rage or passion; violent flurry or outburst. **21.** *Informal.* a spree. [bef. 900; ME *teren* (v.), OE *teran;* c. D *teren,* G *zehren* to consume, Goth *distairan* to destroy, Gk *dérein* to flay] **—tear′a•ble,** *adj.* **—tear′a•ble•ness,** *n.* **—tear′er,** *n.*
—Syn. 1. TEAR, REND, RIP mean to pull apart. To TEAR is to split the fibers of something by pulling apart, usually so as to leave ragged or irregular edges: *to tear open a letter.* REND implies force or violence in tearing apart or in pieces: *to rend one's clothes in grief.* RIP implies vigorous tearing asunder, esp. along a seam or line: *to rip the sleeves out of a coat.* **3.** shatter, afflict. **4.** split. **5.** cut, mangle. **19.** rip.

tear•a•way (târ′ə wā′), *adj.* **1.** designed to be easily separated or opened by tearing: *a box with a tearaway seal.* *—n.* **2.** *Brit.* a wild, reckless person. [1825–35; adj., n. use of v. phrase *tear away*]

tear′ bomb′ (tēr), a bomb or grenade containing tear gas. Also called **tear shell, tear′ grenade′.**

tear•down (târ′doun′), *n.* a taking apart; disassembly. [1925–30; n. use of v. phrase *tear down*]

tear•drop (tēr′drop′), *n.* **1.** a tear or something suggesting a tear: *A single teardrop rolled down her face.* **2.** something shaped like a drop of a thin liquid, having a globular form at the bottom, tapering to a point at the top. [1790–1800; TEAR[1] + DROP]

tear•ful (tēr′fəl), *adj.* **1.** full of tears; weeping. **2.** causing tears: *the tearful story of his poverty.* [1580–90; TEAR[1] + -FUL] **—tear′ful•ly,** *adv.* **—tear′ful•ness,** *n.*

tear′ gas′ (tēr), a gas that makes the eyes smart and water, thus producing a temporary blindness, used in modern warfare, to quell riots, etc. [1915–20]

tear-gas (tēr′gas′), *v.t.,* **-gassed, -gas•sing.** to subject to tear gas. [1945–50]

tear•ing[1] (tēr′ing), *adj.* shedding tears. [bef. 1000; OE *tæherende* (not recorded in ME); see TEAR[1], -ING[2]]

tear•ing[2] (târ′ing), *adj.* violent or hasty: *with tearing speed.* [1600–10; TEAR[2] + -ING[2]] **—tear′ing•ly,** *adv.*

tear•jerk•er (tēr′jûr′kər), *n. Informal.* a pathetic story, play, movie, or the like; an excessively sentimental tale. [1930–35; TEAR[1] + JERK[1] + -ER[1]] **—tear′jerk′ing,** *adj.*

tear•less (tēr′lis), *adj.* **1.** not weeping or shedding tears. **2.** unable to shed tears. [1585–95; TEAR[1] + -LESS] **—tear′less•ly,** *adv.* **—tear′less•ness,** *n.*

tear-off (târ′ôf′, -of′), *adj.* designed to be easily removed by tearing, usually along a perforated line: *a sales letter with a tear-off order blank.* [1885–90; adj., n. use of v. phrase *tear off*]

tea•room (tē′ro͞om′, -ro͝om′), *n.* a room or shop where tea and other refreshments are served to customers. [1770–80; TEA + ROOM]

tea′ rose′, *Hort.* any of several cultivated varieties of roses having a scent resembling that of tea. [1840–50]

tear-out (târ′out′), *adj.* designed to be easily torn out, as from bound matter: *a tear-out children's section of games and puzzles.* [adj. use of v. phrase *tear out*]

tear′ sheet′ (târ), a sheet or page torn from a magazine, journal, or the like, as one containing an advertisement and sent to the advertiser as proof of publication. [1920–25]

tear′ shell′ (tēr). See **tear bomb.** [1915–20]

tear-stained (tēr′stānd′), *adj.* **1.** marked or wet with tears: *a tear-stained letter.* **2.** showing traces of tears or signs of having wept: *tear-stained cheeks.* [1585–95]

tear′ strip′ (târ), a strip or string that is pulled to open a can, box, candy wrapper, etc.

tear•y (tēr′ē), *adj.,* **tear•i•er, tear•i•est. 1.** of or like tears. **2.** tearful. [1325–75; ME *tery.* See TEAR[1], -Y[1]] **—tear′i•ly,** *adv.* **—tear′i•ness,** *n.*

tear•y-eyed (tēr′ē īd′), *adj.* with tears welling up in one's eyes: *teary-eyed mourners.*

Teas•dale (tēz′dāl′), *n.* **Sara,** 1884–1933, U.S. poet.

tease (tēz), *v.,* **teased, teas•ing,** *n.* *—v.t.* **1.** to irritate or provoke with persistent petty distractions, trifling raillery, or other annoyance, often in sport. **2.** to pull apart or separate the adhering fibers of (wool or the like), as in combing or carding; comb or card, as wool; shred. **3.** to ruffle (the hair) by holding it at the ends and combing toward the scalp so as to give body to a hairdo. **4.** to raise a nap on (cloth) with teasels; teasel. **5.** Also, **teaser.** *Television Slang.* a short scene or highlight shown at the beginning of a film or television show to attract the audience's attention. *—v.i.* **6.** to provoke or disturb a person or animal by importunity or persistent petty annoyances. *—n.* **7.** a person who teases or annoys. **8.** the act of teasing or the state of being teased. [bef. 1000; ME *tesen* (v.), OE *tǣsan* to pull, tear, comb; c. MLG *tesen,* OHG *zeisan* to pluck] **—teas′a•ble,** *adj.* **—teas′a•ble•ness,** *n.* **—teas′ing•ly,** *adv.*
—Syn. 1. trouble, disturb, vex; harass. See **bother.**
—Ant. 1. mollify.

tea•sel (tē′zəl), *n., v.,* **-seled, -sel•ing** or (*esp. Brit.*) **-selled, -sel•ling.** *—n.* **1.** any of several plants of the genus *Dipsacus,* having prickly leaves and flower heads. Cf. **teasel family. 2.** the dried flower head or bur of the plant *D. fullonum,* used for teasing or teaseling cloth. **3.** any mechanical contrivance used for teaseling. *—v.t.* **4.** to raise a nap on (cloth) with teasels; dress by means of teasels. Also, **teazel, teazle.** [bef. 1000; ME *tesel,* OE *tǣsel;* akin to TEASE] **—tea′sel•er;** *esp. Brit.,* **tea′sel•ler,** *n.*

tea′sel fam′ily, the plant family Dipsacaceae, characterized by herbaceous plants having opposite or whorled leaves, dense flower heads surrounded by an involucre, and small, dry fruit, and including the scabious and teasel.

tea′sel gourd′, a prickly-stemmed Arabian vine, *Cucumis dipsaceus,* of the gourd family, having burlike, bristly fruit. Also called **hedgehog gourd.**

teas•er (tē′zər), *n.* **1.** a person or thing that teases. **2.** *Theat.* a drapery or flat piece across the top of the proscenium arch that masks the flies and that, together with the tormentors, forms a frame for the stage opening. **3.** *Print., Journ.* kicker (def. 9). **4.** an advertisement that lures customers or clients by offering a bonus, gift, or the like. **5.** *Television Slang.* tease (def. 5). [1350–1400; ME *teser* machine for teasing wool; see TEASE, -ER[1]]

tea′ serv′ice, 1. a set of chinaware for preparing and drinking hot beverages, esp. tea. **2.** a set of silver or other metalware for preparing and serving hot beverages, esp. tea. Also called **tea′ set′.** [1855–60]

tea′ shop′, 1. a tearoom. **2.** *Brit.* a café or tearoom that specializes in serving light meals and snacks; lunchroom. [1735–45]

tea•spoon (tē′spo͞on′), *n.* **1.** a small spoon generally used to stir tea, coffee, etc. **2.** a teaspoonful. [1680–90; TEA + SPOON]

tea•spoon•ful (tē′spo͞on fo͝ol′), *n., pl.* **-fuls. 1.** the amount a teaspoon can hold. **2.** a volumetric measure equal to ⅙ fluid ounce (4.9 ml); ⅓ tablespoonful. *Abbr.:* t., tsp. [1725–35; TEASPOON + -FUL]
—Usage. See **-ful.**

teat (tēt, tit), *n.* **1.** the protuberance on the breast or udder in female mammals, except the monotremes, through which the milk ducts discharge; nipple or mammilla. **2.** something resembling a teat. [1250–1300; ME *tete* < OF < Gmc; see TIT[2]]

tea′ ta′ble, a small table for holding a tea service and cups, plates, etc., for several people. [1680–90] **—tea′-ta′ble,** *adj.*

tea•tast•er (tē′tā′stər), *n.* a person whose profession is tasting and grading samples of tea. [1855–60; TEA + TASTER]

tea•time (tē′tīm′), *n.* the time at which tea is served or taken, usually in the late afternoon. [1750–60; TEA + TIME]

tea′ tow′el, a dishtowel. [1870–75]

tea′ tray′, a tray for carrying or holding articles used in serving tea. [1765–75]

tea′ tree′, a tall shrub or small tree, *Leptospermum scoparium,* of the myrtle family, native to New Zealand and Australia, having silky foliage when young, and bell-shaped, white flowers: often planted to prevent beach erosion. [1750–60; so called from the use of its leaves as an infusion]

tea′ wag′on, a small table on wheels for carrying articles for use in serving tea. Also called **teacart.**

tea·zel (tē′zəl), *n., v.t.,* **-zeled, -zel·ing** or (*esp. Brit.*) **-zelled, -zel·ling.** teasel.

tea·zle (tē′zəl), *n., v.t.,* **-zled, -zling.** teasel.

Te·bal·di (tə bäl′dē, -bôl′-; *It.* te bäl′dē), *n.* **Re·na·ta** (rə nä′tə; *It.* re nä′tä), born 1922, Italian soprano.

Te·bet (*Seph. Heb.* te vet′; *Ashk. Heb.* tā′vās, -vəs; *Eng.* tā′vās, -vät, -vəs), *n.* Tevet.

tec (tek), *n. Slang.* detective. [by aphesis and shortening]

tech (tek), *Informal.* —*adj.* **1.** technical: *The engineers sat together exchanging tech talk.* —*n.* **2.** a technician: *He's a tech for a film crew.* **3.** technology: *She has a good grasp of computer tech.* [by shortening]

tech., **1.** technic. **2.** technical. **3.** technology.

teched (techt), *adj.* tetched.

tech·ie (tek′ē), *n. Informal.* **1.** a technical expert, student, or enthusiast, esp. in the field of electronics. **2.** a technician, as for a stage crew. Also, **tekkie.** [1980–85; TECH(NICAL) + -IE]

tech·ne·ti·um (tek nē′shē əm, -shəm), *n. Chem.* an element of the manganese family, not found in nature, but obtained in the fission of uranium or by the bombardment of molybdenum. *Symbol:* Tc; *at. wt.:* 99; *at. no.:* 43; *sp. gr.:* 11.5. [1945–50; < Gk *technēt(ós)* artificial (lit., made, verbid of *technâsthai;* see TECHNO-) + -IUM]

tech·ne·tron·ic (tek′ni tron′ik), *adj.* pertaining to or characterized by cultural changes brought about by advances in technology, electronics, and communications: *a technetronic era.* [coinage based on TECHNOLOGY and ELECTRONIC; current from its use in a 1968 article "America in the Technetronic Age" by U.S. political scientist Zbigniew Brzezinski (b. 1928)]

tech·nic (tek′nik *or, for 1,* tek nēk′), *n.* **1.** technique. **2.** a technicality. **3. technics,** (*used with a singular or plural v.*) the study or science of an art or of arts in general, esp. the mechanical or industrial arts. —*adj.* **4.** technical. [1605–15; (n.) earlier *technica* < Gk *technikā́,* neut. pl. of *technikós* of art and craft, equiv. to *téchn(ē)* art, craft + *-ikos* -IC; (adj.) < Gk *technikós*]

tech·ni·cal (tek′ni kəl), *adj.* **1.** belonging or pertaining to an art, science, or the like: *technical skill.* **2.** peculiar to or characteristic of a particular art, science, profession, trade, etc.: *technical details.* **3.** using terminology or treating subject matter in a manner peculiar to a particular field, as a writer or a book: *a technical report.* **4.** skilled in or familiar in a practical way with a particular art, trade, etc., as a person. **5.** of, pertaining to, or showing technique. **6.** pertaining to or connected with the mechanical or industrial arts and the applied sciences: *a technical school.* **7.** so considered from a point of view in accordance with a stringent interpretation of the rules: *a military engagement ending in a technical defeat.* **8.** concerned with or dwelling on technicalities: *You're getting too technical for me.* **9.** noting a market in which prices are determined largely by supply and demand and other such internal factors rather than by general business, economic, or psychological factors that influence market activity: *technical weakness or strength.* [1610–20; TECHNIC + -AL] —**tech′ni·cal·ly,** *adv.* —**tech′ni·cal·ness,** *n.*

tech′nical foul′, *Basketball.* a foul committed by a player or coach, usually not involving physical contact with an opponent, called often for unsportsmanlike conduct, as holding on to the basket or using profanity, that gives the opposing team one or two free throws and sometimes, if the foul was flagrant, requires the ejection of the offending player or coach from the game.

tech·ni·cal·i·ty (tek′ni kal′i tē), *n., pl.* **-ties** for 2, 3. **1.** technical character. **2.** the use of technical methods or terms. **3.** something that is technical; a technical point, detail, or expression. [1805–15; TECHNICAL + -ITY]

tech′nical knock′out, *Boxing.* the termination of a bout by the referee when it is the judgment of the attending physician, a boxer's seconds, or the referee that a boxer cannot continue fighting without sustaining severe or disabling injury. *Abbr.:* TKO, T.K.O. [1945–50]

tech′nical ser′geant, *U.S. Air Force.* a noncommissioned officer ranking below a master sergeant and above a staff sergeant. [1955–60]

tech·ni·cian (tek nish′ən), *n.* **1.** a person who is trained or skilled in the technicalities of a subject. **2.** a person who is skilled in the technique of an art, as music or painting. [1825–35; TECHNIC + -IAN; see -ICIAN]

Tech·ni·col·or (tek′ni kul′ər), *Trademark.* a brand name for a system of making color motion pictures by means of superimposing the three primary colors to produce a final colored print.

tech·nique (tek nēk′), *n.* **1.** the manner and ability with which an artist, writer, dancer, athlete, or the like employs the technical skills of a particular art or field of endeavor. **2.** the body of specialized procedures and methods used in any specific field, esp. in an area of applied science. **3.** method of performance; way of accomplishing. **4.** technical skill; ability to apply procedures or methods so as to effect a desired result. **5.** *Informal.* method of projecting personal charm, appeal, etc.: *He has the greatest technique with customers.* [1810–20; < F: technical (adj.), technic (n.) < Gk *technikós, technikā́;* see TECHNIC]

tech·no (tek′nō), *n.* a style of disco music characterized by very fast synthesizer rhythms, heavy use of samples, and a lack of melody. [1985–90]

CONCISE ETYMOLOGY KEY: <, descended or borrowed from; >, whence; b., blend of, blended; c., cognate with; cf., compare; deriv., derivative; equiv., equivalent; imit., imitative; obl., oblique; r., replacing; s., stem; sp., spelling, spelled; resp., respelling, respelled; trans., translation; ?, origin unknown; *, unattested; ‡, probably earlier than. See the full key inside the front cover.

techno-, a combining form borrowed from Greek where it meant "art," "skill," used in the formation of compound words with the meaning "technique," "technology," etc.: *technography.* [comb. form repr. Gk *téchnē* art, skill. See TECHNIC]

tech·no·ban·dit (tek′nə ban′dit), *n. Informal.* a person who steals technological secrets, as from the government or a place of employment, and sells them to agents of foreign governments or to competing firms. [1980–85; TECHNO- + BANDIT]

tech·noc·ra·cy (tek nok′rə sē), *n., pl.* **-cies** for 2, 3. **1.** a theory and movement, prominent about 1932, advocating control of industrial resources, reform of financial institutions, and reorganization of the social system, based on the findings of technologists and engineers. **2.** a system of government in which this theory is applied. **3.** any application of this theory. [1919; TECHNO- + -CRACY]

tech·no·crat (tek′nə krat′), *n.* **1.** a proponent, adherent, or supporter of technocracy. **2.** a technological expert, esp. one concerned with management or administration. [1930–35; TECHNO- + -CRAT]

tech·no·crat·ic (tek′nə krat′ik), *adj.* of, pertaining to, or designating a technocrat or technocracy. [TECHNOCRAT + -IC]

tech·nog·ra·phy (tek nog′rə fē), *n.* the description and study of the arts and sciences in their geographical and ethnic distribution and historical development. [1880–85; TECHNO- + -GRAPHY]

technol., technology.

tech·no·log·i·cal (tek′nə loj′i kəl), *adj.* **1.** of or pertaining to technology; relating to science and industry. **2.** *Econ.* caused by technical advances in production methods. Also, **tech′no·log′ic.** [1620–30; TECHNOLOG(Y) + -ICAL] —**tech′no·log′i·cal·ly,** *adv.*

technolog′ical unemploy′ment, unemployment caused by technological changes or new methods of production in an industry or business. [1925–30]

tech·nol·o·gist (tek nol′ə jist), *n.* a person who specializes in technology. [1855–60; TECHNOLOG(Y) + -IST]

tech·nol·o·gy (tek nol′ə jē), *n.* **1.** the branch of knowledge that deals with the creation and use of technical means and their interrelation with life, society, and the environment, drawing upon such subjects as industrial arts, engineering, applied science, and pure science. **2.** the terminology of an art, science, etc.; technical nomenclature. **3.** a technological process, invention, method, or the like. **4.** the sum of the ways in which social groups provide themselves with the material objects of their civilization. [1605–15; < Gk *technología* systematic treatment. See TECHNO-, -LOGY]

tech·no·pho·bi·a (tek′nə fō′bē ə), *n.* abnormal fear of or anxiety about the effects of advanced technology. [1960–65; TECHNO- + -PHOBIA] —**tech′no·phobe′,** *n.*

tech·no·pop (tek′nō pop′), *n.* synthpop. [1980–85]

tech·no·struc·ture (tek′nō struk′chər), *n.* the group or class of technically skilled administrators, scientists, and engineers who manage and influence business, the economy, and government affairs. [1965–70; TECHNO- + STRUCTURE]

tech·no-thrill·er (tek′nō thril′ər), *n.* a suspense novel in which the manipulation of sophisticated technology, as of aircraft or weapons systems, plays a prominent part. [1985–90]

tech. sgt., technical sergeant.

tech·y (tech′ē), *adj.,* **tech·i·er, tech·i·est.** tetchy. —**tech′i·ly,** *adv.* —**tech′i·ness,** *n.*

tec·ti·form (tek′tə fôrm′), *adj.* **1.** having the shape of a roof. —*n.* **2.** *Archaeol.* a design found in Paleolithic cave art and believed to represent a structure or dwelling. [< L *tēct(um)* roof (see TECTUM) + -I- + -FORM]

tec·ton·ic (tek ton′ik), *adj.* **1.** of or pertaining to building or construction; constructive; architectural. **2.** *Geol.* **a.** pertaining to the structure of the earth's crust. **b.** referring to the forces or conditions within the earth that cause movements of the crust. **c.** designating the results of such movements: *tectonic valleys.* [1650–60; < LL *tectonicus* < Gk *tektonikós* pertaining to construction, equiv. to *tekton-* (s. of *téktōn*) carpenter + *-ikos* -IC] —**tec·ton′i·cal·ly,** *adv.*

tec·ton·ics (tek ton′iks), *n.* (*used with a singular v.*) **1.** the science or art of assembling, shaping, or ornamenting materials in construction; the constructive arts in general. **2.** See **structural geology.** [1625–35; see TECTONIC, -ICS]

tec·to·nism (tek′tə niz′əm), *n. Geol.* diastrophism (def. 1). [1945–50; TECTON(IC) + -ISM]

tec·to·sil·i·cate (tek′tō sil′i kit, -kāt′), *n. Mineral.* tektosilicate.

tec·trix (tek′triks), *n., pl.* **tec·tri·ces** (tek′trə sēz′, tek trī′sēz). *Ornith.* covert (def. 8). [1760–70; < NL *tēctrix,* equiv. to L *teg(ere)* to cover + *-trix* -TRIX] —**tec·tri·cial** (tek trish′əl), *adj.*

tec·tum (tek′təm), *n., pl.* **-tums, -ta** (-tə). *Anat., Zool.* a rooflike structure. [1900–05; < NL, L *tēctum* roof, special use of neut. of *tēctus,* ptp. of *tegere* to cover; cf. PROTECT] —**tec′tal, tec·to·ri·al** (tek tôr′ē əl, -tōr′-), *adj.*

Te·cum·seh (ti kum′sə), *n.* 1768?–1813, American Indian chief of the Shawnee tribe. Also, **Te·cum·tha** (ti kum′thə).

ted (ted), *v.t.,* **ted·ded, ted·ding.** to spread out for drying, as newly mown hay. [1400–50; late ME *tedde;* c. ON *tethja* to manure, OHG *zettan* to spread, Gk *dateîsthai* to divide]

Ted (ted), *n.* **1.** *Brit. Slang.* See **Teddy boy. 2.** a male given name, form of **Edward** or **Theodore.**

ted·der (ted′ər), *n.* **1.** a person who teds. **2.** an implement that turns and loosens hay after mowing in order to hasten drying. [1400–50; late ME *teddere.* See TED, -ER[1]]

Ted·der (ted′ər), *n.* **Arthur William, 1st Baron,** 1890–1967, British Royal Air Force marshal and educator, born in Scotland.

ted·dy (ted′ē), *n., pl.* **-dies. 1.** Often, **teddies.** a woman's one-piece undergarment combining a chemise and underpants, sometimes having a snap crotch. **2.** *Informal.* See **teddy bear.** [(in def. 1) 1920–25, *Amer.*]

Ted·dy (ted′ē), *n.* **1.** a male given name, form of **Edward** or **Theodore. 2.** a female given name, form of **Theodora.** Also, **Ted′die.**

ted′dy bear′, a toy bear, esp. a stuffed one. [1905–10, *Amer.;* after Theodore Roosevelt, called *Teddy,* who is said to have saved the life of a bear cub while hunting]

Ted′dy boy′, (*often l.c.*) *Informal.* a rebellious British youth who, in the 1950's and early 1960's, affected the dress of the reign of Edward VII.

Ted′dy girl′, (*often l.c.*) *Informal.* **1.** a rebellious British girl who, in the 1950's and early 1960's, affected the dress of the reign of Edward VII. **2.** a girl companion of Teddy boys.

Te De·um (tā dā′o͝om, -əm, tē dē′əm), **1.** (*italics*) an ancient Latin hymn of praise to God, in the form of a psalm, sung regularly at matins in the Roman Catholic Church and, usually, in an English translation, at Morning Prayer in the Anglican Church, as well as on special occasions as a service of thanksgiving. **2.** a musical setting of this hymn. **3.** a service of thanksgiving in which this hymn forms a prominent part. [< LL, first two words of the hymn, which begins: *Tē Deum laudāmus* we praise thee God]

te·di·ous (tē′dē əs, tē′jəs), *adj.* **1.** marked by tedium; long and tiresome: *tedious tasks; a tedious journey.* **2.** wordy so as to cause weariness or boredom, as a speaker or writer; prolix. [1375–1425; late ME < ML *tēdiōsus,* LL *taediōsus.* See TEDIUM, -OUS] —**te′di·ous·ly,** *adv.* —**te′di·ous·ness,** *n.*
—**Syn. 1.** wearing, boring, tiring, monotonous, dull.

te·di·um (tē′dē əm), *n.* the quality or state of being wearisome; irksomeness; tediousness. [1655–65; < L *taedium*]
—**Syn.** monotony, sameness, dullness.

tee[1] (tē), *n.* **1.** the letter *T* or *t.* **2.** something shaped like a T, as a three-way joint used in fitting pipes together. **3.** T-bar. **4.** T-shirt. **5.** the mark aimed at in various games, as curling. **6. to a tee.** See **T, t** (def. 6). —*adj.* **7.** having a crosspiece at the top; shaped like a T. [sp. form of the letter name]

tee[2] (tē), *n., v.,* **teed, tee·ing.** —*n.* **1.** *Golf.* **a.** Also called **teeing ground.** the starting place, usually a hard mound of earth, at the beginning of play for each hole. **b.** a small wooden, plastic, metal, or rubber peg from which the ball is driven, as in teeing off. **2.** *Football.* a device on which the ball may be placed to raise it off the ground preparatory to kicking. —*v.t.* **3.** *Golf.* to place (the ball) on a tee. **4. tee off, a.** *Golf.* to strike the ball from a tee. **b.** *Slang.* to reprimand severely; scold: *He teed off on his son for wrecking the car.* **c.** *Informal.* to begin: *They teed off the program with a medley of songs.* **d.** *Baseball, Softball.* to make many runs and hits, esp. extra-base hits: *teeing off for six runs on eight hits, including three doubles and a home run.* **e.** *Baseball, Softball.* to hit (a pitched ball) hard and far: *He teed off on a fastball and drove it into the bleachers.* **f.** *Boxing.* to strike with a powerful blow, esp. to the head: *He teed off on his opponent with an overhand right.* **g.** *Slang.* to make angry, irritated, or disgusted: *She was teed off because her guests were late.* [1665–75; orig. uncert.]

TEE, Trans-Europe Express. Also, **T-E-E**

tee′ing ground′, *Golf.* tee[2] (def. 1a). [1885–90]

teel (tēl), *n.* til.

teem[1] (tēm), *v.i.* **1.** to abound or swarm; be prolific or fertile (usually fol. by *with*). **2.** *Obs.* to be or become pregnant; bring forth young. —*v.t.* **3.** *Obs.* to produce (offspring). [bef. 900; ME *temen,* OE *tēman, tieman* to produce (offspring), deriv. of *tēam* TEAM] —**teem′er,** *n.*
—**Syn. 1.** overflow, brim, overrun, bristle.

teem[2] (tēm), *v.t., v.i.* to empty or pour out; discharge. [1250–1300; ME *temen* < ON *tæma* to empty, deriv. of *tōmr* empty, c. OE *tōm* free from]

teem·ing[1] (tē′ming), *adj.* **1.** abounding or swarming with something, as with people: *We elbowed our way through the teeming station.* **2.** prolific or fertile. [1525–35; TEEM[1] + -ING[2]] —**teem′ing·ly,** *adv.* —**teem′ing·ness,** *n.*

teem·ing[2] (tē′ming), *adj.* falling in torrents: *a teeming rain.* [1685–95; TEEM[2] + -ING[2]]

teen[1] (tēn), *n.* **1.** *Archaic.* suffering; grief. **2.** *Obs.* injury; harm. [bef. 1000; ME *tene,* OE *tēona;* c. OFris *tiona,* OS *tiono,* ON *tjōn*]

teen[2] (tēn), *adj.* **1.** teenage. —*n.* **2.** a teenager. [1940–45; by shortening]

-teen, a suffix used to form cardinal numerals from 13 to 19. [ME, OE *-tēne,* comb. form of TEN; c. D *-tien,* G *-zehn*]

Tee·na (tē′nə), *n.* a female given name, form of **Albertina, Bettina,** or **Christina.**

teen·age (tēn′āj′), *adj.* of, pertaining to, or characteristic of a teenager. Also, **teen′aged′.** [1920–25; *teen* (see TEENS) + AGE]

teen·ag·er (tēn′ā′jər), *n.* a person in his or her teens. [1935–40; TEENAGE + -ER[1]]

teen·er (tē′nər), *n.* a teenager. [1890–95; TEEN[2] + -ER[1]]

teens (tēnz), *n.pl.* the numbers 13 through 19, esp. in a progression, as the 13th through the 19th years of a lifetime or of a given century. [1595–1605; *teen* (extracted from numbers with -TEEN as final element) + -S[3]]

teen·sy (tēn′sē), *adj.,* **-si·er, -si·est.** teeny; tiny. [see TEENY, -SY]

teen·sy-ween·sy (tēn′sē wēn′sē), *adj. Baby Talk.*

tiny; small. Also, **teent·sy-weent·sy** (tēnt′sē wēnt′sē), **teen′sie-ween′sie.** [alter. of TEENY-WEENY; see -SY]

teen·ter (tēn′tər), *n.* tinter[2].
—**Regional Variation.** See **seesaw.**

tee·ny (tē′nē), *adj.*, **-ni·er, -ni·est.** tiny. [1815–25; b. TINY and WEE]

tee·ny·bop·per (tē′nē bop′ər), *n. Slang.* **1.** a teenage girl, esp. a young one. **2.** a young teenage girl who is devoted to teenage fads, rock music, etc. [1960–65; TEEN[2] + -Y[2] + BOPPER]

tee·ny-wee·ny (tē′nē wē′nē), *adj. Baby Talk.* tiny; small. Also, **tee′nie-wee′nie.** [1875–80; TEENY + *weeny* tiny; see WEENIE]

tee·pee (tē′pē), *n.* tepee.

Tees (tēz), *n.* a river in N England, flowing E along the boundary between Durham and Yorkshire to the North Sea. 70 mi. (113 km) long.

tee′ shirt′, T-shirt.

tee·ter (tē′tər), *Chiefly Northern U.S.* —*v.i.* **1.** to move unsteadily. **2.** to ride a seesaw; teetertotter. —*v.t.* **3.** to tip (something) up and down; move unsteadily. —*n.* **4.** a seesaw motion; wobble. **5.** a seesaw; teetertotter. [1835–45; var. of dial. *titter*, ME *titeren* < ON *titra* tremble; c. G *zittern* to tremble, quiver]

tee·ter·board (tē′tər bôrd′, -bōrd′), *n.* **1.** a seesaw; teeter. **2.** a similar board used by acrobats and tumblers that propels a person into the air when another person jumps onto the opposite end. [1835–45, *Amer.*; TEETER + BOARD]

tee·ter·tot·ter (tē′tər tot′ər), *Chiefly Northern, North Midland, and Western U.S.* —*n.* **1.** a seesaw. —*v.i.* **2.** to ride a seesaw. Also, **tee′ter-tot′ter.** [gradational formation based on TOTTER]
—**Regional Variation. 1.** See **seesaw.**

teeth (tēth), *n.* pl. of **tooth.** —**teeth′less,** *adj.*

teethe (tēth), *v.i.*, **teethed, teeth·ing.** to grow teeth; cut one's teeth. [1375–1425; late ME *tethen*, deriv. of *teth* TEETH]

teeth·er (tē′thər), *n.* **1.** a device for a baby to bite on during teething. Cf. **teething ring. 2.** a baby who is teething. [1945–50; TEETHE + -ER[1]]

teeth′ grind′ing, *Pathol.* habitual, purposeless clenching and grinding of the teeth, esp. during sleep. Also called **bruxism.**

teeth·ing (tē′thing), *n. Dentistry.* eruption of the deciduous teeth, esp. the phenomena associated with their eruption. [1725–35; TEETHE + -ING[1]]

teeth′ing ring′, a circular ring, usually of plastic, ivory, bone, etc., on which a teething baby can bite. [1890–95, *Amer.*]

teeth·ridge (tēth′rij′), *n. Phonet.* See **alveolar ridge.** [1925–30; TEETH + RIDGE]

tee·to·tal (tē tōt′l, tē′tōt′l), *adj.*, *v.* **-taled, -tal·ing** or (*esp. Brit.*) **-talled, -tal·ling.** —*adj.* **1.** of or pertaining to, advocating, or pledged to total abstinence from intoxicating drink. **2.** *Informal.* absolute; complete. —*v.i.* **3.** to practice teetotalism. [reduplicated var. of TOTAL, coined by R. Turner, of Preston, England, in 1833, in a speech advocating total abstinence from alcoholic drinks] —**tee·to′tal·ly,** *adv.*

tee·to·tal·er (tē tōt′lər, tē′tōt′-), *n.* a person who abstains totally from intoxicating drink. Also, **tee·to′tal·ist;** *esp. Brit.*, **tee·to′tal·ler.** [1825–35; TEETOTAL + -ER[1]]

tee·to·tal·ism (tē tōt′l iz′əm, tē′tōt′-), *n.* the principle or practice of total abstinence from intoxicating drink. [1825–35; TEETOTAL + -ISM]

tee·to·tum (tē tō′təm), *n.* **1.** any small top spun with the fingers. **2.** a kind of die having four sides, each marked with a different initial letter, spun with the fingers in an old game of chance. [1710–20; earlier *T totum*, alter. of *totum* name of toy (< L *tōtum*, neut. of *tōtus* all) by prefixing its initial letter, which appeared on one side of the toy]

tee·vee (tē′vē′, tē′-), *n. Informal.* television. [TEE[1] + VEE, repr. pron. of TV]

teff (tef), *n.* a grass, *Eragrostis tef*, native to northern Africa, where it is cultivated for its edible seeds. [1780–90; < Amharic *t'ef*; cf. Geez *t'ah'əf, t'ayəf*]

te·fil·lin (*Ashk. Heb., Eng.* tə fil′in; *Seph. Heb.* tə fē lēn′), *n.pl. Judaism.* the phylacteries. Also, **tephillin.** [1605–15; < Heb *təphillīn*, akin to *təphillāh* prayer]

TEFL, teaching English as a foreign language. Cf. **EFL.**

Tef·lon (tef′lon), **1.** *Trademark.* a fluorocarbon polymer with slippery, nonsticking properties; polytetrafluoroethylene. —*adj.* **2.** characterized by imperviousness to blame or criticism: *a Teflon politician.*

teg (teg), *n.* **1.** *Animal Husb.* **a.** a two-year-old sheep that has not been shorn. **b.** the wool shorn from such a sheep. **2.** *Chiefly Brit.* a two-year-old doe. **3.** *Brit. Dial.* a yearling sheep. Also, **tegg.** [1520–30; orig. uncert.]

Te·ge·a (tē′jē ə), *n.* an ancient city in SE Arcadia, Greece.

teg·men (teg′mən), *n.*, *pl.* **-mi·na** (-mə nə). **1.** a cover, covering, or integument. **2.** *Bot.* the delicate inner integument or coat of a seed. **3.** (of certain orthopterous insects) one of a pair of leathery forewings that forms a protective covering for the hind wings. [1800–10; < L: covering (also *tegumen, tegimen* with anaptyctic vowel), equiv. to *teg*(*ere*) to cover + *-men* n. suffix] —**teg·mi·nal** (teg′mə nl), *adj.*

Te·gu·ci·gal·pa (tə gōō′si gal′pə; *Sp.* te gōō′sē gäl′pä), *n.* a city in and the capital of Honduras, in the S part. 270,645.

teg·u·la (teg′yə lə), *n.*, *pl.* **-lae** (-lē′). (in certain insects) a scalelike lobe at the base of the forewing. [1820–30; < L *tēgula* tile]

teg·u·lar (teg′yə lər), *adj.* **1.** pertaining to or resembling a tile. **2.** consisting of or arranged like tiles. **3.** of or pertaining to a tegula. [1790–1800; < L *tēgul*(*a*) tile + -AR[1]] —**teg′u·lar·ly,** *adv.*

teg·u·ment (teg′yə mənt), *n.* a covering or vestment; integument. [1400–50; late ME < L *tegumentum*, equiv. to *tegu-* (see TEGMEN) + *-mentum* -MENT] —**teg·u·men·tal** (teg′yə men′tl), **teg·u·men·ta·ry** (teg′yə men′tə rē, -trē), *adj.*

Teh (de), *n.* Te.

te-hee (tē hē′), *interj.*, *n.*, *v.*, **-heed, -hee·ing.** —*interj.* **1.** (used as an exclamation or representation of laughter, as in expressing amusement or derision.) —*n.* **2.** a titter; snicker. —*v.i.* **3.** to titter; snicker. [1250–1300; ME (interj.); imit.]

Te·he·ran (te ran′, -rän′, te′hə-, tā′ə-; *Pers.* te hRän′), *n.* a city in and the capital of Iran, in the N part: wartime conference of Roosevelt, Churchill, and Stalin 1943. 3,150,000. Also, **Teh·ran′.**

Te·hil·lim (*Seph.* tə hē lēm′; *Ashk.* tə hē′lim), *n. Hebrew.* the Book of Psalms.

Te·hua·cán′ Val′ley (tā′wä kän′, -wə kan′), a desert valley site in Puebla, Mexico, where aridity has preserved the vegetable remains of communities from 9000 B.C. to historic times, thus documenting the transition from hunting and gathering to the largely agricultural subsistence of the full Neolithic phase (1500–900 B.C.).

Te·huan·te·pec (tə wän′tə pek′; *Sp.* te wän′te pek′), *n.* **1. Isthmus of,** an isthmus in S Mexico, between the Gulf of Tehuantepec and the Gulf of Campeche. 125 mi. (200 km) wide at its narrowest point. **2. Gulf of,** an inlet of the Pacific, off the S coast of Mexico. ab. 300 mi. (485 km) wide.

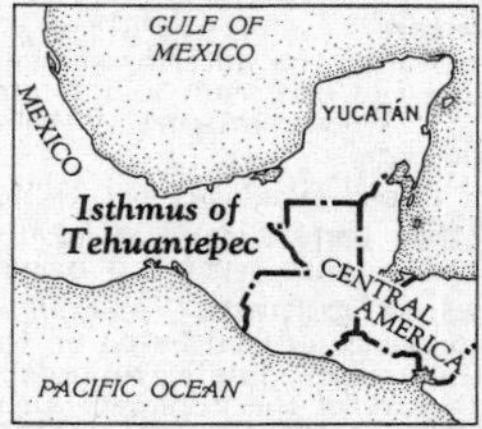

Te·huel·che (tə wel′chē, -chā), *n.*, *pl.* **-ches,** (*esp. collectively*) **-che** for 1. **1.** a member of an Indian people of Patagonia. **2.** the language of these people. [< Araucanian *cheu*(*ù*)*lche*, said to mean lit. "fearless and elusive"] —**Te·huel′che·an,** *adj.*

Teich′mann's crys′tals (tīk′mənz), *Biochem.* hemin. [named after L. *Teichmann*-Stawiarski (d. 1895), German anatomist]

Tei·de (tā′the), *n.* **Pi·co de** (pē′kô the), a volcanic peak in the Canary Islands, on Tenerife. 12,190 ft. (3716 m). Also called **Pico de Tenerife, Pico de Teneriffe, Pico de Teyde.**

teig·lach (tāg′ləKH, -läKH, tīg′-), *n.* (*used with a singular or plural v.*) a confection consisting of small balls of dough boiled in a syrup of honey, sugar, and spices. Also, **taiglach.** [< Yiddish *teyglekh*, pl. of *teygl*, dim. of *teyg* dough < MHG *teig*, OHG *teic*]

tei·id (tē′id), *n.* **1.** any of a large group of chiefly tropical New World lizards of the family Teiidae, as the racerunner or whiptail, characterized by large rectangular scales on the belly and a long tail. —*adj.* **2.** belonging or pertaining to the Teiidae. [1955–60; < NL *Teiidae*, equiv. to *Tei*(*us*) genus name (< Pg *tejú* lizard of the genus *Tupinambis* < Tupi *tejú, teyú*) + *-idae* -ID[2]]

teil (tēl), *n. Archaic.* the European linden, *Tilia europaea.* [1350–1400; < MF (OF *til*); r. ME *tilia* < L *tilia* linden]

Teil·hard de Char·din (te yar də shar dan′), **Pierre** (pyer), 1881–1955, French Jesuit priest, paleontologist, and philosopher.

Tei·re·si·as (tī rē′sē əs), *n.* Tiresias.

Te·jo (te′zhōō), *n.* Tagus.

Tek·a·kwith·a (tek′ə kwith′ə), *n.* **Ka·te·ri** (kä′tə rē) or **Catherine,** 1656–80, North American Indian ascetic; convert to Roman Catholicism.

tek·kie (tek′ē), *n. Informal.* techie.

tek·non·y·my (tek non′ə mē), *n.* the practice among certain peoples of renaming a parent after a child. [< Gk *tékn*(*on*) child + *ónym*(*a*) NAME + -Y[3]] —**tek·non′y·mous,** *adj.* —**tek·non′y·mous·ly,** *adv.*

tek·tite (tek′tīt), *n. Geol.* any of several kinds of small glassy bodies, in various forms, occurring in Australia and elsewhere, now believed to have been produced by the impact of meteorites on the earth's surface. [1920–25; < Gk *tēkt*(*ós*) molten + -ITE[1]]

tek·to·sil·i·cate (tek′tō sil′i kit, -kāt′), *n. Mineral.* any silicate in which each tetrahedral group shares all its oxygen atoms with neighboring groups, the ratio of silicon to oxygen being 1 to 2. Also, **tectosilicate.** Cf. **cyclosilicate, inosilicate, nesosilicate, sorosilicate.** [< Gk *tēktó*(*s*) molten + SILICATE]

TEL, *Chem.* See **tetraethyl lead.**

tel-[1], var. of **tele-**[1]: *telesthesia.*

tel-[2], var. of **tele-**[2]: *telencephalon.*

tel., **1.** telegram. **2.** telegraph. **3.** telephone.

Te·la (te′lä), *n.* a seaport in N Honduras. 9658.

tel·aes·the·sia (tel′əs thē′zhə, -zhē ə, -zē ə), *n.* telesthesia.

Tel A·mar·na (tel′ ə mär′nə). See **Tell el Amarna.**

tel·a·mon (tel′ə mən, -mon′), *n.*, *pl.* **tel·a·mo·nes** (tel′ə mō′nēz). *Archit.* atlas (def. 5). [1700–10; < L *telamōn* < Gk *telamṓn* bearer, support; identified with TELAMON]

Tel·a·mon (tel′ə mən, -mon′), *n. Class. Myth.* an Argonaut and friend of Hercules, and the father of Ajax and Teucer.

Tel·a·mo′ni·an A′jax (tel′ə mō′nē ən), *Class. Myth.* Ajax (def. 1).

Te·la·nai·pu·ra (tel′ə nī pŏŏr′ə), *n.* former name of **Jambi** (def. 2).

tel·an·gi·ec·ta·sis (tel an′jē ek′tə sis), *n.*, *pl.* **-ses** (-sēz′). *Pathol.* chronic dilatation of the capillaries and other small blood vessels. [1825–35; < NL < Gk *tél*(*os*) end + *angeî*(*on*) receptacle + *éktasis* extension] —**tel·an·gi·ec·tat·ic** (tel an′jē ek tat′ik), *adj.*

Tel·an·thro·pus (tə lan′thrə pəs, tel′an thrō′pəs), *n.* a genus of fossil hominids, known from two fragmentary lower jaws found in the region of Swartkrans, near Johannesburg, South Africa. [1890–95; < NL; see TEL-[2], ANTHROPO-]

Tel A·viv (tel′ ə vēv′), a city in W central Israel: one of the centers of Jewish immigration following World War II. 334,900. Official name, **Tel A·viv-Jaf·fa** (tel′ ə vēv′yä′fə), **Tel A·viv-Ya·fo** (tel′ ə vēv′yä′fō). —**Tel′ A·viv′i·an.**

Tel·chi·nes (tel kī′nēz), *n.pl. Class. Myth.* nine dog-headed sea monsters who as great artisans crafted the sickle of Cronus and the trident of Poseidon.

tel·e (tel′ē), *n. Brit. Informal.* television. Also, **telly.** [by shortening]

tele-[1], a combining form meaning "distant," esp. "transmission over a distance," used in the formation of compound words: *telegraph.* Also, **tel-, telo-.** [comb. form repr. Gk *têle* far, akin to *télos* end (see TELE-[2])]

tele-[2], a combining form meaning "end," "complete," used in the formation of compound words: *telestich.* Also, **tel-, teleo-, telo-.** [comb. form repr. Gk *télos* end, and *téleios* perfected; akin to *teleîn* to fulfill]

tele., television.

Tel·e·boi·des (tel′ə boi′dēz), *n.* (*used with a plural v.*) Taphiae.

tel·e·cam·er·a (tel′i kam′ər ə, -kam′rə), *n.* a television camera. [1905–10; TELE(VISION) + CAMERA]

tel·e·cast (tel′i kast′, -käst′), *v.*, **-cast** or **-cast·ed, -cast·ing,** *n.* —*v.t.*, *v.i.* **1.** to broadcast by television. —*n.* **2.** a television broadcast. [1935–40; TELE(VISION) + (BROAD)CAST] —**tel′e·cast′er,** *n.*

tel·e·cin·e (tel′ə sin′ē, tel′ə sin′ē), *n.* **1.** equipment used mainly by television studios for converting film images to signals suitable for television transmission. **2.** the transmission of a motion picture by television. **3.** a motion picture so transmitted. [TELE-[1] + CINE(MATOGRAPH)]

tel·e·com (tel′i kom′), *n. Informal.* telecommunications. [by shortening]

tel·e·com·mu·ni·cate (tel′i kə myōō′ni kāt′), *v.t.*, **-cat·ed, -cat·ing.** to transmit (data, sound, images, etc.) by telecommunications. [back formation from TELECOMMUNICATIONS] —**tel′e·com·mu′ni·ca′tor,** *n.*

tel·e·com·mu·ni·ca·tions (tel′i kə myōō′ni kā′shənz), *n.* **1.** Sometimes, **telecommunication.** (*used with a singular v.*) the transmission of information, as words, sounds, or images, usually over great distances, in the form of electromagnetic signals, as by telegraph, telephone, radio, or television. **2.** Sometimes, **telecommunication.** (*used with a singular v.*) the science and technology of such communication. **3. telecommunication,** a message so transmitted. —*adj.* **4.** of or pertaining to telecommunications. [1930–35; TELE-[1] + COMMUNICATION + -S[3]]

tel·e·com·mute (tel′i kə myōōt′), *v.i.*, **-mut·ed, -mut·ing.** to engage in telecommuting. [1970–75; TELE-[1] + COMMUTE] —**tel′e·com·mut′er,** *n.*

tel·e·com·mut·ing (tel′i kə myōō′ting), *n.* working at home by using a computer terminal electronically linked to one's place of employment. [1970–75; TELECOMMUTE + -ING[1]]

tel·e·com·put·ing (tel′i kəm pyōō′ting), *n. Computers.* teleprocessing. [1980–85; TELE-[1] + COMPUTING] —**tel′e·com·put′er,** *n.*

tel·e·con·fer·ence (tel′i kon′fər əns, -frəns), *n.*, *v.*, **-enced, -enc·ing.** —*n.* **1.** a business meeting, educational session, etc., conducted among participants in different locations via telecommunications equipment. Cf. **videoconference.** —*v.i.* **2.** to participate in such a meeting or meetings. [1950–55; TELE-[1] + CONFERENCE]

tel·e·con·fer·enc·ing (tel′i kon′fər ən sing, -frən-), *n.* **1.** the holding of teleconferences. Cf. **conferencing, videoconferencing.** —*adj.* **2.** pertaining to or suitable for holding such meetings. [1970–75; TELECONFERENCE + -ING[1]]

tel·e·con·vert·er (tel′i kən vûr′tər), *n. Photog.* See under **converter** (def. 8). Also called **teleconvert′er lens′.** [1965–70; TELE-[1] + CONVERTER]

Tel·e·cop·i·er (tel′i kop′ē ər), *Trademark.* a brand name for a device used in facsimile transmission to transmit and reproduce documents, drawings, etc. Cf. **facsimile** (def. 2).

tel·e·course (tel′i kôrs′, -kōrs′), *n.* a course of study presented on television, as for local home viewers receiv-

CONCISE PRONUNCIATION KEY: act, cāpe, dâre, pärt; set, ēqual; if, īce; ox, ōver, ôrder, oil, bŏŏk, bōōt, out; up, ûrge; child; sing; shoe; thin, that; zh as in *treasure.* ə = *a* as in *alone, e* as in *system, i* as in *easily, o* as in *gallop, u* as in *circus;* ə as in *fire* (fīər), *hour* (ouər). l and n can serve as syllabic consonants, as in *cradle* (krād′l), and *button* (but′n). See the full key inside the front cover.

ing credit at a community college. [1945–50; TELE(VISION) + COURSE]

tel·e·di·ag·no·sis (tel′i dī′ag nō′sis), *n., pl.* **-ses** (-sēz). the detection of a disease by evaluating data transmitted to a receiving station from instruments monitoring a distant patient, as someone in a spacecraft. [1960–65; TELE-^{1} + DIAGNOSIS]

tel·e·dra·ma (tel′i drä′mə, -dram′ə), *n. Television.* a drama written esp. for broadcast on television. [1950–55; TELE(VISION) + DRAMA]

tel·e·du (tel′i do͞o′), *n.* a small, dark-brown, badgerlike mammal, *Mydaus javensis,* of the mountains of Java, Sumatra, and Borneo, having a white stripe down the back, and ejecting a foul-smelling secretion when alarmed. [1815–25; < Sumatran Malay *tələdu* (sp. *teledu*)]

tel·e·fea·ture (tel′ə fē′chər), *n. Television.* a major dramatic television film, usually of a length comparable to a theatrical feature film. [TELE(VISION) + FEATURE]

tel·e·fer·ic (tel′ə fer′ik), *n. Transp.* telpher. Also, **tel·e·fe·rique** (tel′ə fə rēk′). [1915–20; < F *téléférique, téléphérique* or It *teleferica,* both ult. < E TELPHER with restoration of Gk *tele-;* see -IC]

tel·e·film (tel′ə film′), *n.* a motion picture intended primarily to be shown on television. [1935–40; TELE(VISION) + FILM]

tel·e·fo·to (tel′ə fō′tō), *adj. Informal.* telephoto.

teleg., 1. telegram. **2.** telegraph. **3.** telegraphy.

te·le·ga (tə leg′ə; *Russ.* tyi lye′gə), *n.* a Russian cart of rude construction, having four wheels and no springs. [1550–60; < Russ *teléga,* prob. ult. < Mongolian; cf. classical Mongolian *telege(n)* carriage]

tel·e·gen·ic (tel′i jen′ik), *adj.* having physical qualities or characteristics that televise well; videogenic. [1935–40; TELE(VISION) + -GENIC] **—tel′e·gen′i·cal·ly,** *adv.*

tel·eg·no·sis (tel′ə nō′sis, tel′ig-), *n.* supernatural or occult knowledge; clairvoyance. [1910–15; TELE-^{1} + -GNOSIS] **—tel·eg·nos·tic** (tel′ə nos′tik, tel′ig-), *adj.*

Te·leg·o·nus (tə leg′ə nəs), *n. Class. Myth.* **1.** a son of Odysseus and Circe who unknowingly killed his father and eventually married Penelope. **2.** a son of Proteus and the husband of Io who was killed by Hercules in a wrestling match.

te·leg·o·ny (tə leg′ə nē), *n.* a former belief that a sire can influence the characteristics of the progeny of the female parent and subsequent mates. [1890–95; TELE-^{1} + -GONY] **—tel·e·gon·ic** (tel′i gon′ik), *adj.*

tel·e·gram (tel′i gram′), *n., v.,* **-grammed, gram·ming.** *—n.* **1.** a message or communication sent by telegraph; a telegraphic dispatch. *—v.t., v.i.* **2.** to telegraph. [1850–55, *Amer.;* TELE-^{1} + -GRAM^1] **—tel′e·gram′mic, tel·e·gram·ma·tic** (tel′i grə mat′ik), *adj.*

tel·e·graph (tel′i graf′, -gräf′), *n.* **1.** an apparatus, system, or process for transmitting messages or signals to a distant place, esp. by means of an electric device consisting essentially of a sending instrument and a distant receiving instrument connected by a conducting wire or other communications channel. **2.** *Naut.* an apparatus, usually mechanical, for transmitting and receiving orders between the bridge of a ship and the engine room or some other part of the engineering department. **3.** a telegraphic message. *—v.t.* **4.** to transmit or send (a message) by telegraph. **5.** to send a message to (a person) by telegraph. **6.** *Informal.* to divulge or indicate unwittingly (one's intention, next offensive move, etc.), as to an opponent or to an audience; broadcast: *The fighter telegraphed his punch and his opponent was able to parry it. If you act nervous too early in the scene, you'll telegraph the character's guilt.* *—v.i.* **7.** to send a message by telegraph. [< F *télégraphe* (1792) a kind of manual signaling device; see TELE-^{1}, -GRAPH] **—te·leg·ra·pher** (tə leg′rə fər); *esp. Brit.,* **te·leg′ra·phist,** *n.*

tel′egraph bu′oy, a buoy placed over an underwater telegraph cable.

tel·e·graph·ese (tel′i gra fēz′, -fēs′, tel′i gra fēz′, -fēs′), *n.* a style of writing or speaking distinguished by the omissions, abbreviations, and combinations that are characteristic of telegrams, as in "EXPECT ARRIVE SIX EVENING." [1880–85; TELEGRAPH + -ESE]

tel·e·graph·ic (tel′i graf′ik), *adj.* **1.** of or pertaining to the telegraph. **2.** concise, clipped, or elliptical in style: *telegraphic speech.* [1785–95; TELEGRAPH + -IC] **—tel′e·graph′i·cal·ly,** *adv.*

te·leg·ra·phone (tə leg′rə fōn′), *n.* an early magnetic sound-recording device for use with wire, tape, or disks. [1885–90; < Dan *telegraphon.* See TELE-^{1}, GRAPHO-, -PHONE]

tel′egraph plant′, a tick trefoil, *Desmodium motorium,* of the legume family, native to tropical Asia, noted for the spontaneous, jerking, signallike motions of its leaflets. [1880–85]

te·leg·ra·phy (tə leg′rə fē), *n.* the art or practice of constructing or operating telegraphs. [1785–95; TELE-^{1} + -GRAPHY]

Tel·e·gu (tel′i go͞o′), *n., pl.* **-gus,** (*esp. collectively*) **-gu,** *adj.* Telugu.

tel·e·ki·ne·sis (tel′i ki nē′sis, -kī-), *n.* psychokinesis. [1885–90; TELE-^{1} + -KINESIS] **—tel·e·ki·net·ic** (tel′i ki net′ik, -kī-), *adj.*

Tel el A·mar·na (tel′ el ə mär′nə). See **Tell el Amarna.**

Te·lem·a·chus (tə lem′ə kəs), *n. Class. Myth.* the son of Odysseus and Penelope who helped Odysseus to kill the suitors of Penelope.

CONCISE ETYMOLOGY KEY: <, descended or borrowed from; >, whence; b., blend of, blended; c., cognate with; cf., compare; deriv., derivative; equiv., equivalent; imit., imitative; obl., oblique; r., replacing; s., stem; sp., spelling, spelled; resp., respelling, respelled; trans., translation; ?, origin unknown; *, unattested; ‡, probably earlier than. See the full key inside the front cover.

Te·le·mann (tā′lə män′), *n.* **Ge·org Phi·lipp** (gā ôrk′ fē′lip, fil′ip), 1681–1767, German composer.

tel·e·mark (tel′ə märk′), *n.* (*sometimes cap.*) *Skiing.* a turn in which a skier places one ski far forward of the other and gradually angles the tip of the forward ski inward in the direction to be turned. [1905–10; named after *Telemark,* a Norwegian county]

tel·e·mar·ket·ing (tel′ə mär′ki ting), *n.* selling or advertising by telephone. [TELE-^{1} + MARKETING] **—tel′e·mar′ket·er,** *n.*

tel·e·me·chan·ics (tel′ə mi kan′iks), *n.* (*used with a singular v.*) the science or practice of operating mechanisms by remote control. [TELE-^{1} + MECHANICS]

tel·e·med·i·cine (tel′ə med′ə sin *or, esp. Brit.,* -med′sin), *n.* the diagnosis and treatment of patients in remote areas using medical information, as x-rays or television pictures, transmitted over long distances, esp. by satellite. [1965–70; TELE-^{1} + MEDICINE]

te·lem·e·ter (tə lem′i tər, tel′ə mē′tər), *n.* **1.** any of certain devices or attachments for determining distances by measuring the angle subtending a known distance. **2.** *Elect.* the complete measuring, transmitting, and receiving apparatus for indicating, recording, or integrating at a distance, by electrical translating means, the value of a quantity. *—v.t.* **3.** to transmit (radio signals, data, etc.) automatically and at a distance, as between a ground station and an artificial satellite, space probe, or the like, esp. in order to record information, operate guidance apparatus, etc. *—v.i.* **4.** to telemeter radio signals, data, etc. [1855–60; TELE-^{1} + -METER] **—tel·e·met·ric** (tel′ə me′trik), *adj.* **—tel′e·met′ri·cal·ly,** *adv.* **—te·lem·e·try** (tə lem′i trē), *n.*

tel·e·mo·tor (tel′ə mō′tər), *n.* a mechanical, electrical, or hydraulic system by which power is applied at or controlled from a distant point, esp. such a system actuating a ship's rudder. [1885–90; TELE-^{1} + MOTOR]

tel·en·ceph·a·lon (tel′en sef′ə lon′, -lən), *n., pl.* **-lons, -la** (-lə). *Anat.* the anterior section of the forebrain comprising the cerebrum and related structures. [1900–05; TEL-^{2} + ENCEPHALON] **—tel·en·ce·phal·ic** (tel′en sə fal′ik), *adj.*

teleo-, var. of **tele-^{2}**: *teleology.*

tel′e·ob·jec′tive lens′ (tel′ē əb jek′tiv, tel′-), *Photog.* See **telephoto lens.** [TELE-^{1} + OBJECTIVE]

tel′eolog′ical ar′gument, *Metaphys.* the argument for the existence of God based on the assumption that order in the universe implies an orderer and cannot be a natural feature of the universe. Also called **argument from design, tel′eolog′ical proof′.**

tel·e·ol·o·gy (tel′ē ol′ə jē, tē′lē-), *n. Philos.* **1.** the doctrine that final causes exist. **2.** the study of the evidences of design or purpose in nature. **3.** such design or purpose. **4.** the belief that purpose and design are a part of or are apparent in nature. **5.** (in vitalist philosophy) the doctrine that phenomena are guided not only by mechanical forces but that they also move toward certain goals of self-realization. [1730–40; < NL *teleologia.* See TELEO-, -LOGY] **—tel·e·o·log·i·cal** (tel′ē ə loj′i kəl, tē′lē-), **tel′e·o·log′ic,** *adj.* **—tel′e·o·log′i·cal·ly,** *adv.* **—tel′e·ol′o·gism,** *n.* **—tel′e·ol′o·gist,** *n.*

tel·e·ost (tel′ē ost′, tē′lē-), *adj.* **1.** belonging or pertaining to the Teleostei, a group of bony fishes including most living species. *—n.* **2.** Also called **tel·e·o·stome** (tel′ē ə stōm′, tē′lē-). a teleost fish. Also, **tel′e·os′te·an.** [1860–65; < NL *Teleostei* infraclass name (designating fish with completely ossified skeletons), pl. of *teleosteus,* equiv. to Gk *tele-* TELE-^{2} + *-osteos* -boned, adj. deriv. of *ostéon* bone; see OSTEO-, -OUS]

te·lep·a·thist (tə lep′ə thist), *n.* **1.** a student of or believer in telepathy. **2.** a person having telepathic power. [1890–95; TELEPATH(Y) + -IST]

te·lep·a·thize (tə lep′ə thīz′), *v.,* **-thized, -thiz·ing.** *—v.t.* **1.** to communicate with by telepathy. *—v.i.* **2.** to practice or conduct telepathy. Also, *esp. Brit.,* **te·lep′a·thise′.** [1890–95; TELEPATH(Y) + -IZE]

te·lep·a·thy (tə lep′ə thē), *n.* communication between minds by some means other than sensory perception. Also called **mental telepathy.** [1880–85; TELE-^{1} + -PATHY] **—tel·e·path·ic** (tel′ə path′ik), *adj.* **—tel′e·path′i·cal·ly,** *adv.*

teleph., telephony.

tel·e·phone (tel′ə fōn′), *n., v.,* **-phoned, -phon·ing.** *—n.* **1.** an apparatus, system, or process for transmission of sound or speech to a distant point, esp. by an electric device. *—v.t.* **2.** to speak to or summon (a person) by telephone. **3.** to send (a message) by telephone. *—v.i.* **4.** to send a message by telephone. Also, **phone.** [1825–35; TELE-^{1} + -PHONE] **—tel′e·phon′er,** *n.*

tel′ephone an′swering machine′. See **answering machine.** [1960–65]

tel′ephone bank′, an array of telephones used in large-scale telephoning operations, as for a political campaign.

tel′ephone book′, a book, directory, or the like, usually containing an alphabetical list of telephone subscribers in a city or other area, together with their addresses and telephone numbers. Also called **tel′ephone direc′tory.** [1910–15]

tel′ephone booth′, a more or less soundproof booth containing a public telephone. Also called, *esp. Brit.,* **tel′ephone box′.** [1895–1900, *Amer.*]

tel′ephone exchange′, a telecommunications facility to which subscribers' telephones connect, that switches calls among subscribers or to other exchanges for further routing.

tel′ephone pole′, a utility pole for supporting telephone wires. [1880–85, *Amer.*]

tel′ephone receiv′er, a device, as in a telephone, that converts changes in an electric current into sound.

tel′ephone tag′, repeated unsuccessful attempts by two persons to connect with one another by telephone.

tel·e·phon·ic (tel′ə fon′ik), *adj.* **1.** of, pertaining to, or happening by means of a telephone system. **2.** carrying sound to a distance by artificial means. [1825–35; TELE-^{1} + -PHONE + -IC] **—tel′e·phon′i·cal·ly,** *adv.*

te·leph·o·nist (tə lef′ə nist, tel′ə fō′-), *n. Chiefly Brit.* a telephone switchboard operator. [TELEPHONE + -IST]

te·leph·o·ny (tə lef′ə nē), *n.* **1.** the construction or operation of telephones or telephonic systems. **2.** a system of telecommunications in which telephonic equipment is employed in the transmission of speech or other sound between points, with or without the use of wires. [1825–35; TELEPHONE + -Y^3]

tel·e·pho·to (tel′ə fō′tō), *adj.* noting or pertaining to telephotography. [1890–95; short for *telephotographic;* see TELEPHOTOGRAPH, -IC]

Tel·e·pho·to (tel′ə fō′tō), *Trademark.* **1.** a brand of apparatus for electrical transmission of photographs. **2.** a photograph transmitted by this apparatus.

tel·e·pho·to·graph (tel′ə fō′tə graf′, -gräf′), *n.* a photograph taken with a telephoto lens. [1880–85; TELE-^{1} + PHOTOGRAPH]

tel·e·pho·tog·ra·phy (tel′ə fə tog′rə fē), *n.* photography of distant objects, using a telephoto lens. [1880–85; TELE-^{1} + PHOTOGRAPHY] **—tel·e·pho·to·graph·ic** (tel′ə fō′tə graf′ik), *adj.*

tel′epho′to lens′, *Photog.* a lens constructed so as to produce a relatively large image with a focal length shorter than that required by an ordinary lens producing an image of the same size: used to photograph small or distant objects. Also called **tel′ephotograph′ic lens′, teleobjective lens.** [1940–45]

tel·e·pho·tom·e·ter (tel′ə fō tom′i tər), *n.* an instrument for measuring the amount of light emanating from a distant object. [1925–30; TELE-^{1} + PHOTOMETER]

tel·e·plasm (tel′ə plaz′əm), *n. Parapsychol.* a hypothetical emanation from the body of a medium that serves as the means for telekinesis. [1925–30; TELE-^{1} + -PLASM] **—tel′e·plas′mic,** *adj.*

tel·e·play (tel′ə plā′), *n.* a play written or adapted for broadcast on television. Also called **videoplay, video drama.** [1950–55; TELE(VISION) + PLAY]

tel·e·port^1 (tel′ə pôrt′, -pōrt′), *v.t.* to transport (a body) by telekinesis. [1950–55; back formation from *teleportation,* equiv. to TELE-^{1} + (TRANS)PORTATION] **—tel′e·por·ta′tion, tel′e·por′tage,** *n.*

tel·e·port^2 (tel′ə pôrt′, -pōrt′), *n.* a regional telecommunications network that provides access to communications satellites and other long-distance media; telecommunications hub. [1980–1985; TELE-^{1} + PORT^1]

tel·e·print·er (tel′ə prin′tər), *n.* a teletypewriter. [1925–30; TELE(TYPE) + PRINTER]

tel·e·proc·ess·ing (tel′ə pros′es ing, -ə sing *or, esp. Brit.,* -prō′ses ing, -prō′sə sing), *n. Computers.* computerized processing and transmission of data over the telephone or other long-distance communications systems. Also, **telecomputing.** [1960–65; TELE-^{1} + PROCESSING]

Tel·e·Promp·Ter (tel′ə promp′tər), *Trademark.* a brand name for an off-camera device that displays a magnified script so that it is visible to the performers or speakers on a television program.

tel·e·ran (tel′ə ran′), *n.* (*sometimes cap.*) a navigational aid that uses radar to map the sky above an airfield, which, together with a map of the airfield itself, is transmitted by television to aircraft approaching the field. [*Tele(vision) R(adar) A(ir) N(avigation)*]

tel·e·scope (tel′ə skōp′), *n., adj., v.,* **-scoped, -scop·ing.** *—n.* **1.** an optical instrument for making distant objects appear larger and therefore nearer. One of the two principal forms **(refracting telescope)** consists essentially of an objective lens set into one end of a tube and an adjustable eyepiece or combination of lenses set into the other end of a tube that slides into the first and through which the enlarged object is viewed directly; the other form **(reflecting telescope)** has a concave mirror that gathers light from the object and focuses it into an adjustable eyepiece or combination of lenses through which the reflection of the object is enlarged and viewed. Cf. **radio telescope. 2.** (*cap.*) *Astron.* the constellation Telescopium. *—adj.* **3.** consisting of parts that fit and slide one within another. *—v.t.* **4.** to force together, one into another, or force into something else, in the manner of the sliding tubes of a jointed telescope. **5.** to shorten or condense; compress: *to telescope the events of five hundred years into one history lecture.* *—v.i.* **6.** to slide together, or into something else, in the manner of the tubes of a jointed telescope. **7.** to be driven one into another, as railroad cars in a collision. **8.** to be or become shortened or condensed. [1610–20; TELE-^{1} + -SCOPE; r. *telescopium* (< NL; see -IUM) and *telescopio* (< It)]

tel′escope eyes′, protruding orbits, as on certain goldfish. **—tel′e·scope′-eyed′,** *adj.*

tel·e·scop·ic (tel′ə skop′ik), *adj.* **1.** of, pertaining to, or of the nature of a telescope. **2.** capable of magnifying distant objects: *a telescopic lens.* **3.** obtained by means of a telescope: *a telescopic view of the moon.* **4.** seen by a telescope; visible only through a telescope. **5.** capable of viewing objects from a distance; farseeing: *a telescopic eye.* **6.** consisting of parts that slide one within another like the tubes of a jointed telescope and are thus capable of being extended or shortened. Also, **tel′e·scop′i·cal.** [TELESCOPE + -IC] **—tel′e·scop′i·cal·ly,** *adv.*

Tel·e·sco·pi·um (tel′ə skō′pē əm), *n., gen.* **-pi·i** (-pē ī′). *Astron.* the Telescope, a small southern constellation between Ara and Corona Austrinus. [< NL]

te·les·co·py (tə les′kə pē), *n.* **1.** the use of the telescope. **2.** telescopic investigation. [1860–65; TELESCOPE + -Y^3] **—te·les′co·pist,** *n.*

tel·e·screen (tel′ə skrēn′), *n.* a television screen, esp. a large one suitable for viewing by large numbers of people. [1940–45; TELE(VISION) + SCREEN]

tel·e·seism (tel′ə sī′zəm), *n. Geol.* a tremor caused by an earthquake originating a great distance from the seismographic station that records it. [TELE-^{1} + SEISM]

tel·e·shop (tel′ə shop′), *v.i.,* **-shopped, -shop·ping.** to engage in teleshopping. [1980–85; TELE-[1] + SHOP] —**tel′e·shop′per,** *n.*

tel·e·shop·ping (tel′ə shop′ing), *n.* electronic shopping via videotex or other interactive information service. [1980–85; TELE-[1] + SHOPPING]

tel·e·sis (tel′ə sis), *n. Sociol.* deliberate, purposeful utilization of the processes of nature and society to obtain particular goals. [1895–1900; < Gk *télesis* completion]

Te·les·pho·rus (tə les′fər əs), *n.* pope A.D. 125?–136?.

tel·e·ster·e·o·scope (tel′ə ster′ē ə skōp′, -stēr′-), *n.* a binocular optical instrument used for stereoscopic viewing of distant objects; a small range finder. [1860–65; TELE-[1] + STEREOSCOPE]

tel·es·te·ri·on (tel′ə stēr′ē on′), *n., pl.* **tel·es·te·ri·a** (tel′i stēr′ē ə). (in ancient Greece) a building in which religious mysteries were celebrated. [< Gk *telestḗrion* place for initiation, equiv. to *teles-*, s. of *teleîn* to fulfill, initiate (see TELE-[2]) + *-tērion* neut. n. suffix denoting place]

tel·es·the·sia (təl′əs thē′zhə, -zhē ə, -zē ə), *n.* sensation or perception received at a distance without the normal operation of the recognized sense organs. Also, **telaesthesia.** [1880–85; TEL-[1] + ESTHESIA] —**tel·es·thet·ic** (tel′əs thet′ik), *adj.*

te·les·tich (tə les′tik, tel′ə stik′), *n. Pros.* a poem in which the last letters of successive lines form a word, a phrase, or the consecutive letters of the alphabet. Cf. **acrostic.** [1630–40; TELE-[2] + STICH[1]]

tel·e·text (tel′i tekst′), *n. Television.* a system that allows viewers having television sets with special decoders to receive signals that display printed information as well as graphics on their screens. Cf. **videotex.** [TELE-[1] + TEXT]

tel·e·ther·a·py (tel′ə ther′ə pē), *n.* **1.** treatment in which the source of therapy is some distance from the body, as certain radiation therapies. **2.** psychological counseling by telephone. [TELE-[1] + THERAPY]

tel·e·ther·mom·e·ter (tel′ə thər mom′i tər), *n.* any of various thermometers that indicate or record temperatures at a distance, as by means of an electric current. Also called **tel·e·ther·mo·scope** (tel′ə thûr′mə skōp′). [1890–95; TELE-[1] + THERMOMETER] —**tel′e·ther·mom′e·try,** *n.*

tel·e·thon (tel′ə thon′), *n.* a television broadcast lasting several hours, esp. one soliciting support for a charity. [1945–50; TELE-[1] + -THON]

Tel·e·type (tel′i tīp′), *n., v.,* **-typed, -typ·ing.** **1.** *Trademark.* a brand of teletypewriter. —*n.* **2.** (*l.c.*) a network of teletypewriters with their connecting lines, switchboards, etc. —*v.t.* **3.** (*l.c.*) to send by Teletype. —*v.i.* **4.** (*l.c.*) to operate a Teletype.

Tel·e·type·set·ter (tel′i tīp′set′ər, tel′i tīp′-), *Trademark.* a brand name for an apparatus, actuated by punched paper tape, that fits over the keyboard of a slugcasting machine, as the Linotype, for operating it automatically. *Abbr.:* TTS —**tel′e·type′set′ting,** *n.*

tel·e·type·writ·er (tel′i tīp′rī′tər, tel′i tīp′-), *n.* a telegraphic apparatus by which signals are sent by striking the letters and symbols of the keyboard of an instrument resembling a typewriter and are received by a similar instrument that automatically prints them in type corresponding to the keys struck. *Abbr.:* TTY [1900–05; TELE-[1] + TYPEWRITER]

tel·e·typ·ist (tel′i tī′pist), *n.* a person who operates a teletypewriter. [TELE-[1] + TYPIST]

tel·e·van·ge·list (tel′i van′jə list), *n.* an evangelist who regularly conducts religious services on television. [1980–85; b. TELEVISION and EVANGELIST]

tel·e·view (tel′ə vyōō′), *v.t., v.i.* to view with a television receiver. [1935–40; TELE-[1] + VIEW] —**tel′e·view′er,** *n.*

tel·e·vise (tel′ə vīz′), *v.t., v.i.,* **-vised, -vis·ing.** to send or receive by television. [1925–30; back formation from TELEVISION]

tel·e·vi·sion (tel′ə vizh′ən), *n.* **1.** the broadcasting of a still or moving image via radiowaves to receivers that project a view of the image on a picture tube. **2.** the process involved. **3.** a set for receiving television broadcasts. **4.** the field of television broadcasting. [1905–10; TELE-[1] + VISION] —**tel·e·vi·sion·al** (tel′ə vizh′ə nl), *adj.* —**tel′e·vi′sion·al·ly,** *adv.* —**tel·e·vi·sion·ar·y** (tel′ə-vizh′ə ner′ē), *adj.*

tel′evision sta′tion. See **station** (def. 8).

tel·e·vi·sor (tel′ə vī′zər), *n.* an apparatus for transmitting or receiving television. [1925–30; TELEVISE + -OR[2]]

tel·ex (tel′eks), *n.* **1.** (*sometimes cap.*) a two-way teletypewriter service channeled through a public telecommunications system for instantaneous, direct communication between subscribers at remote locations. **2.** a teletypewriter used to send or receive on such a service. **3.** a message transmitted by telex. —*v.t.* **4.** to send (a message) by telex: *We telex instructions to the agent.* **5.** to send a message by telex to: *They telexed the Paris office.* [1930–35; TEL(EPRINTER) + EX(CHANGE)]

tel·fer (tel′fər), *n., adj., v.t.* telpher. —**tel′fer·age,** *n.*

tel·ford (tel′fərd), *adj.* noting a form of road pavement composed of compacted and rolled stones of various sizes. [1895–1900; after Thomas *Telford* (1757–1834), Scottish engineer]

tel·har·mo·ni·um (tel′här mō′nē əm), *n.* a musical keyboard instrument operating by alternating currents of electricity which, on impulse from the keyboard, produce music at a distant point via telephone lines. [TEL-[1] + HARMONIUM]

tel·ic (tel′ik, tē′lik), *adj.* **1.** *Gram.* expressing end or purpose: *a telic conjunction.* **2.** tending to a definite end. [1840–50; < Gk *telikós* pertaining to an end or cause. See TEL-[2], -IC] —**tel′i·cal·ly,** *adv.*

te·li·o·spore (tē′lē ə spôr′, -spōr′, tel′ē-), *n. Mycol.* a spore of certain rust fungi, which carries the fungus through the winter and which, on germination, produces the promycelium. [1870–75; *telio-* (comb. form of TELIUM) + -SPORE] —**te′li·o·spor′ic,** *adj.*

te·li·um (tē′lē əm, tel′ē-), *n., pl.* **te·li·a** (tē′lē ə, tel′ē ə). *Mycol.* the cluster of spore cases of the rust and smut fungi, bearing teliospores. [1905–10; < NL < Gk *téleion*, neut. of *téleios* finished] —**te′li·al,** *adj.*

tell[1] (tel), *v.,* **told, tell·ing.** —*v.t.* **1.** to give an account or narrative of; narrate; relate (a story, tale, etc.): *to tell the story of Lincoln's childhood.* **2.** to make known by speech or writing (a fact, news, information, etc.); communicate. **3.** to announce or proclaim. **4.** to utter (the truth, a lie, etc.). **5.** to express in words (thoughts, feelings, etc.). **6.** to reveal or divulge (something secret or private). **7.** to say plainly or positively: *I cannot tell just what was done.* **8.** to discern or recognize (a distant person or thing) so as to be able to identify or describe: *Can you tell who that is over there?* **9.** to distinguish; discriminate; ascertain: *You could hardly tell the difference between them.* **10.** to inform (a person) of something: *He told me his name.* **11.** to assure emphatically: *I won't, I tell you!* **12.** to bid, order, or command: *Tell him to stop.* **13.** to mention one after another, as in enumerating; count or set one by one or in exact amount: *to tell the cattle in a herd; All told there were 17 if we are correct.* —*v.i.* **14.** to give an account or report: *Tell me about your trip.* **15.** to give evidence or be an indication: *The ruined temples told of an ancient culture, long since passed from existence.* **16.** to disclose something secret or private; inform; tattle: *She knows who did it, but she won't tell.* **17.** to say positively; determine; predict: *Who can tell?* **18.** to have force or effect; operate effectively: *a contest in which every stroke tells.* **19.** to produce a marked or severe effect: *The strain was telling on his health.* **20.** *Brit. Dial.* to talk or chat. **21. tell it like it is,** *Informal.* to tell the complete, unadulterated truth; be forthright: *He may be crude but he tells it like it is.* **22. tell off, a.** to separate from the whole and assign to a particular duty. **b.** *Informal.* to rebuke severely; scold: *It was about time that someone told him off.* **23. tell on,** to tattle on (someone). [bef. 900; ME *tellen*, OE *tellan* to relate, count; c. D *tellen* to reckon, count, ON *telja* to count, say, OHG *zellēn;* akin to TALE]
—**Syn. 1.** recount, describe, report. **2.** impart. **4.** speak. **6.** disclose, betray; acknowledge, own, confess; declare.

tell[2] (tel), *n.* an artificial mound consisting of the accumulated remains of one or more ancient settlements (often used in Egypt and the Middle East as part of a place name). [1860–65; < Ar *tall* hillock]

Tell (tel), *n.* **Wil·helm** (vil′helm). See **William Tell.**

tell·a·ble (tel′ə bəl), *adj.* **1.** capable of being told. **2.** worthy of being told. [1475–85; TELL[1] + -ABLE] —**tell′a·ble·ness,** *n.*

Tell el A·mar·na (tel′ el ə mär′nə), a village in central Egypt, on the Nile: site of the ancient Egyptian city of Akhetaton; extensive excavations. Also, **Tell′-el-A·mar′na, Tel el Amarna, Tel Amarna.**

tell·er (tel′ər), *n.* **1.** a person or thing that tells, relates, or communicates; narrator. **2.** a person employed in a bank to receive or pay out money over the counter. **3.** a person who tells, counts, or enumerates, as one appointed to count votes in a legislative body. [1300–50; ME; see TELL[1], -ER[1]] —**tell′er·ship′,** *n.*

Tel·ler (tel′ər), *n.* **Edward,** born 1908, U.S. physicist, born in Hungary.

Tél·lez (*Sp.* te′lyeth), *n.* **Ga·bri·el** (*Sp.* gä′vʀē el′). See **Tirso de Molina.**

tel·lin (tel′in), *n.* any marine bivalve mollusk of the genus *Tellina*, having a thin, rounded shell of white, yellow, pink, or purple. [1895–1900; < NL *Tellina* name of the genus < Gk *tellī́nē* a shellfish]

tell·ing (tel′ing), *adj.* **1.** having force or effect; effective; striking: *a telling blow.* **2.** revealing; indicative of much otherwise unnoticed: *a telling analysis of motivation in business.* [1850–55; TELL[1] + -ING[2]] —**tell′ing·ly,** *adv.*
—**Syn. 1.** powerful, forceful, potent, weighty.

Tel·loh (te lō′), *n.* a village in SE Iraq, between the lower Tigris and Euphrates: site of the ancient Sumerian city of Lagash. Also, **Tel·lo′.**

tell·tale (tel′tāl′), *n.* **1.** a person who heedlessly or maliciously reveals private or confidential matters; tattler; talebearer. **2.** a thing serving to reveal or disclose something. **3.** any of various indicating or registering devices, as a time clock. **4.** *Music.* a gauge on an organ for indicating the air pressure. **5.** an indicator showing the position of a ship's rudder. **6.** a row of strips hung over a track to warn train crew members on freight trains that a low bridge, tunnel, or the like is approaching. **7.** *Yachting.* (on a sailboat) a feather, string, or similar device, often attached to the port and starboard shrouds and to the backstay, to indicate the relative direction of the wind. **8.** *Squash.* a narrow piece of metal across the front wall of a court, parallel to and extending 17 inches (43.2 cm) above the base: a ball striking this is an out. —*adj.* **9.** that reveals or betrays what is not intended to be known: *a telltale blush.* **10.** giving notice or warning of something, as a mechanical device. [1540–50; TELL[1] + TALE] —**tell′tale′ly,** *adv.*

tel·lu·rate (tel′yə rāt′), *n. Chem.* a salt of a telluric acid, as of H_2TeO or H_6TeO_6. [1820–30; TELLUR(IC ACID) + -ATE[2]]

tel·lu·ri·an[1] (te lŏŏr′ē ən), *adj.* **1.** of or characteristic of the earth or its inhabitants; terrestrial. —*n.* **2.** an inhabitant of the earth. [1840–50; < L *tellūr-* (s. of *tellūs*) earth + -IAN]

tel·lu·ri·an[2] (te lŏŏr′ē ən), *n.* tellurion.

tel·lu·ric[1] (te lŏŏr′ik), *adj.* **1.** of or pertaining to the earth; terrestrial. **2.** of or proceeding from the earth or soil. [1830–40; < L *tellūr-* (s. of *tellūs*) earth + -IC]

tel·lu·ric[2] (te lŏŏr′ik), *adj. Chem.* **1.** of or containing tellurium, esp. in the hexavalent state. **2.** containing tellurium in a higher valence state than the corresponding tellurous compound. [1790–1800; TELLUR(IUM) + -IC]

tellur′ic ac′id, *Chem.* a white, crystalline compound, H_6TeO_6, slightly soluble in cold water, soluble in hot water and alkalis: used as an analytical agent. [1835–45]

tel·lu·ride (tel′yə rīd′, -rid), *n. Chem.* a binary compound of tellurium with an electropositive element or group. [1840–50; TELLUR(IUM) + -IDE]

tel·lu·ri·on (te lŏŏr′ē on′), *n.* an apparatus for showing the manner in which the diurnal rotation and annual revolution of the earth and the obliquity of its axis produce the alternation of day and night and the changes of the seasons. Also, **tellurian.** [1825–35; < L *tellūr-* (s. of *tellūs*) earth + Gk *-ion* dim. suffix]

tel·lu·rite (tel′yə rīt′), *n.* **1.** *Chem.* a salt of tellurous acid, as sodium tellurite, Na_2TeO_3. **2.** a rare mineral, tellurium dioxide, TeO_2. [1790–1800; TELLUR(IUM) or TELLUR(OUS) + -ITE[1]]

tel·lu·ri·um (te lŏŏr′ē əm), *n. Chem.* a rare, lustrous, brittle, crystalline, silver-white element resembling sulfur in its properties, and usually occurring in nature combined with gold, silver, or other metals of high atomic weight: used in the manufacture of alloys and as a coloring agent in glass and ceramics. *Symbol:* Te; *at. wt.:* 127.60; *at. no.:* 52; *sp. gr.:* 6.24. [< NL (1798), equiv. to L *tellūr-* (s. of *tellūs*) earth + -IUM]

tel·lu·rize (tel′yə rīz′), *v.t.,* **-rized, -riz·ing.** to mix or cause to combine with tellurium. Also, *esp. Brit.,* **tel′lu·rise′.** [TELLUR(IUM) + -IZE]

tel·lu·rous (tel′yər əs, te lŏŏr′əs), *adj. Chem.* containing tetravalent tellurium. [1835–45; TELLUR(IUM) + -OUS]

Tel·lus (tel′əs), *n.* an ancient Roman goddess of the earth, marriage, and fertility, identified with the Greek goddess Gaea.

tel·ly (tel′ē), *n., pl.* **-lies.** *Brit. Informal.* **1.** television. **2.** a television receiving set. [1935–40; TEL(EVISION) + -Y[2]]

telo-[1], var. of **tele-**[1]: *telodynamic.*

telo-[2], var. of **tele-**[2]: *telophase.*

tel·o·cen·tric (tel′ə sen′trik), *adj. Genetics.* of or pertaining to any chromosome or chromatid whose centromere is positioned at its end, creating one chromosome arm. Cf. **acentric** (def. 2), **acrocentric, metacentric** (def. 2). [1940–45; TELO-[2] + -CENTRIC]

tel·o·dy·nam·ic (tel′ō dī nam′ik, tē′lō-), *adj.* pertaining to the transmission of mechanical power over considerable distances, as by means of endless cables on pulleys. [1865–70; TELO-[1] + DYNAMIC]

tel·o·lec·i·thal (tel′ō les′ə thəl, tē′lō-), *adj. Embryol.* having an accumulation of yolk near the vegetal pole, as the large-yolked eggs or ova of reptiles and birds. [1875–80; TELO-[2] + Gk *lékith(os)* yolk + -AL[1]]

tel·o·phase (tel′ə fāz′, tē′lə-), *n. Biol.* the final stage of meiosis or mitosis, in which the separated chromosomes reach the opposite poles of the dividing cell and the nuclei of the daughter cells form around the two sets of chromosomes. [1895–1900; TELO-[2] + PHASE] —**tel′o·pha′sic,** *adj.*

te·los (tel′os, tē′los), *n., pl.* **te·loi** (tel′oi, tē′loi). the end term of a goal-directed process; esp., the Aristotelian final cause. [1900–05; < Gk *télos;* cf. TELE-[2]]

tel·o·tax·is (tel′ə tak′sis), *n. Biol.* orientation or movement, by an organism with sensory receptors, toward or away from a particular source of stimulation. [1935–40; TELO-[2] + -TAXIS]

tel·pher (tel′fər), *n.* **1.** Also, **teleferic.** a traveling unit, car, or carrier in a telpherage. —*adj.* **2.** of or pertaining to a system of telpherage. —*v.t.* **3.** to transport by means of a telpherage. Also, **telfer.** [1880–85; alter. of *telephore.* See TELE-[1], -PHORE]

tel·pher·age (tel′fər ij), *n.* a transportation system in which cars or other carriers are suspended from or run on wire cables or the like, esp. one operated by electricity. Also, **telferage.** [1880–85; TELPHER + -AGE]

tel·son (tel′sən), *n.* the last segment, or an appendage of the last segment, of certain arthropods, as the middle flipper of a lobster's tail. [1850–55; < Gk *télson* boundary, limit] —**tel·son·ic** (tel son′ik), *adj.*

tel·son·tail (tel′sən tāl′), *n.* any of several minute, wingless, primitive insects of the order Protura, having a cone-shaped head with sucking and piercing mouthparts and no eyes or antennae, inhabiting damp soil or decaying organic matter. [TELSON + TAIL[1]]

Tel·star (tel′stär′), *Trademark.* **1.** one of an early series of privately financed, low-orbit, active communications satellites, the first of which was launched July 10, 1962. **2.** one of a later series of privately financed, geosynchronous communications satellites that provide domestic television, telephone, and data exchange transmission to the U.S.

Tel·u·gu (tel′ə gōō′), *n., pl.* **-gus,** (*esp. collectively*) **-gu,** *adj.* —*n.* **1.** a Dravidian language spoken mainly in Andhra Pradesh state, SE India. **2.** a member of the people speaking this language. —*adj.* **3.** of Telugu or the Telugu. Also, **Telegu.**

Te·luk·be·tung (tə lŏŏk′bə tŏŏng′), *n.* a port on SE Sumatra, in Indonesia. 198,986.

tem·blor (tem′blər, -blôr; *Sp.* tem blôr′), *n., pl.* **-blors,** *Sp.* **-blo·res** (-blô′ʀes). a tremor; earthquake. [1895–1900, *Amer.;* < Sp: lit., a quaking, equiv. to *tembl(ar)* to quake (perh. << L *timēre* to fear and LL *tremulāre* to quake; see TREMBLE) + *-or* -OR[1]]

Tem•e•nus (tem′ə nəs), *n. Class. Myth.* **1.** a son of Aristomachus who was allotted the city of Argos for his participation in the Heraclidae invasion of Peloponnesus. **2.** a son of Pelasgus believed to have reared Hera.

tem•er•ar•i•ous (tem′ə râr′ē əs), *adj.* reckless; rash. [1525–35; < L *temerārius,* equiv. to *temer(e)* blindly, heedlessly + *-ārius* -ARY] —**tem′er•ar′i•ous•ly,** *adv.* —**tem′er•ar′i•ous•ness,** *n.*

te•mer•i•ty (tə mer′i tē), *n.* reckless boldness; rashness. [1400–50; late ME *temeryte* < L *temeritās* hap, chance, rashness, equiv. to *temer(e)* by chance, rashly + *-itās* -ITY]
—**Syn.** audacity, effrontery, foolhardiness.

Te•mes•vár (te′mesh vär), *n.* Hungarian name of **Timişoara.**

Tem•in (tem′in), *n.* **Howard M(artin),** 1934–94, U.S. virologist: Nobel prize for medicine 1975.

Te•mir•tau (tä′mər tou′; *Russ.* tyĭ myir tä′o͞o), *n.* a city in E central Kazakhstan, NW of Karaganda. 228,000.

Tem•ne (tem′nē), *n., pl.* **-nes,** (*esp. collectively*) **-ne** for 1. **1.** a member of a people living mainly in Sierra Leone. **2.** the West Atlantic language of the Temne people.

temp (temp), *n. Informal.* temporary (def. 2). [1930–35; by shortening]

temp., **1.** temperature. **2.** temporary. **3.** in the time of. [< L *tempore*]

Tem•pe (tem′pē), *n.* **1. Vale of,** a valley in E Greece, in Thessaly, between Mounts Olympus and Ossa. **2.** a city in central Arizona, near Phoenix. 106,743.

tem•peh (tem′pā), *n. Indonesian Cookery.* a fermented soybean cake. [1960–65; < Javanese *témpé*]

Tem•pel•hof (tem′pəl hōf′), *n.* a district of S West Berlin: international airport.

tem•per (tem′pər), *n.* **1.** a particular state of mind or feelings. **2.** habit of mind, esp. with respect to irritability or patience, outbursts of anger, or the like; disposition: *an even temper.* **3.** heat of mind or passion, shown in outbursts of anger, resentment, etc. **4.** calm disposition or state of mind: *to be out of temper.* **5.** a substance added to something to modify its properties or qualities. **6.** *Metall.* **a.** the degree of hardness and strength imparted to a metal, as by quenching, heat treatment, or cold working. **b.** the percentage of carbon in tool steel. **c.** the operation of tempering. **7.** *Archaic.* a middle course; compromise. **8.** *Obs.* the constitution or character of a substance. —*v.t.* **9.** to moderate or mitigate: *to temper justice with mercy.* **10.** to soften or tone down. **11.** to bring to a proper, suitable, or desirable state by or as by blending or admixture. **12.** to moisten, mix, and work up into proper consistency, as clay or mortar. **13.** *Metall.* to impart strength or toughness to (steel or cast iron) by heating and cooling. **14.** to produce internal stresses in (glass) by sudden cooling from low red heat; toughen. **15.** to tune (a keyboard instrument, as a piano, organ, or harpsichord) so as to make the tones available in different keys or tonalities. **16.** to modify (color) by mixing with a medium. **17.** *Archaic.* to combine or blend in due proportions. **18.** *Archaic.* to pacify. —*v.i.* **19.** to be or become tempered. [bef. 1000; (v.) ME *tempren,* OE *temprian* < L *temperāre* to divide or proportion duly, temper; (n.) ME: proportion, deriv. of the v.] —**tem′per•a•ble,** *adj.* —**tem′per•a•bil′i•ty,** *n.* —**tem′per•er,** *n.*
—**Syn. 1.** nature, condition. **2.** humor. See **disposition. 3.** irritation. **4.** equanimity, coolness, composure. **10.** See **modify.**

tem•per•a (tem′pər ə), *n.* **1.** a technique of painting in which an emulsion consisting of water and pure egg yolk or a mixture of egg and oil is used as a binder or medium, characterized by its lean film-forming properties and rapid drying rate. **2.** a painting executed in this technique. **3.** a water paint used in this technique in which the egg-water or egg-oil emulsion is used as a binder. Cf. **distemper**[2] (defs. 1, 2). [1825–35; < It, short for (*pingere a*) *tempera* (painting in) distemper, deriv. of *temperare* to mingle, temper; see TEMPER]

tem•per•a•ment (tem′pər ə mənt, -prə mənt, -pər-mənt), *n.* **1.** the combination of mental, physical, and emotional traits of a person; natural predisposition. **2.** unusual personal attitude or nature as manifested by peculiarities of feeling, temper, action, etc., often with a disinclination to submit to conventional rules or restraints. **3.** (old physiology) the combination of the four cardinal humors, the relative proportions of which were supposed to determine physical and mental constitution. **4.** *Music.* **a.** the tuning of a keyboard instrument, as the piano, organ, or harpsichord, so that the instrument may be played in all keys without further tuning. **b.** a particular system of doing this. **5.** *Archaic.* an act of tempering or moderating. **6.** *Archaic.* climate. [1375–1425; late ME < L *temperāmentum* due mixture, equiv. to *temperā(re)* to mix properly + *-mentum* -MENT]
—**Syn. 1.** nature, makeup. See **disposition.**

tem•per•a•men•tal (tem′pər ə men′tl, -prə men′-, -pər men′-), *adj.* **1.** having or exhibiting a strongly marked, individual temperament. **2.** moody, irritable, or sensitive: *a temperamental artist.* **3.** given to erratic behavior; unpredictable. **4.** of or pertaining to temperament; constitutional: *temperamental differences.* [1640–50; TEMPERAMENT + -AL[1]] —**tem′per•a•men′tal•ly,** *adv.*
—**Syn. 2.** excitable, volatile, emotional.

tem•per•ance (tem′pər əns, tem′prəns), *n.* **1.** moderation or self-restraint in action, statement, etc.; self-control. **2.** habitual moderation in the indulgence of a natural appetite or passion, esp. in the use of alcoholic liquors. **3.** total abstinence from alcoholic liquors. [1200–50; ME *temperaunce* < AF < L *temperantia* self-control. See TEMPER, -ANCE]

tem•per•ate (tem′pər it, tem′prit), *adj.* **1.** moderate or self-restrained; not extreme in opinion, statement, etc.: *a temperate response to an insulting challenge.* **2.** moderate as regards indulgence of appetite or passion, esp. in the use of alcoholic liquors. **3.** not excessive in degree, as things, qualities, etc. **4.** moderate in respect to temperature; not subject to prolonged extremes of hot or cold weather. **5.** *Microbiol.* (of a virus) existing in infected host cells but rarely causing lysis. [1350–1400; ME *temperat* < L *temperātus,* ptp. of *temperāre* to exercise restraint, control. See TEMPER, -ATE[1]] —**tem′per•ate•ly,** *adv.* —**tem′per•ate•ness,** *n.*
—**Syn. 1.** sober, dispassionate. See **moderate.**

Tem′perate Zone′, *Geog.* the part of the earth's surface lying between the tropic of Cancer and the Arctic Circle in the Northern Hemisphere or between the tropic of Capricorn and the Antarctic Circle in the Southern Hemisphere, and characterized by having a climate that is warm in the summer, cold in the winter, and moderate in the spring and fall. Also called **Variable Zone.**

tem•per•a•ture (tem′pər ə chər, -cho͝or′, -prə-, -pər-chər, -cho͝or′), *n.* **1.** a measure of the warmth or coldness of an object or substance with reference to some standard value. The temperature of two systems is the same when the systems are in thermal equilibrium. **2.** *Physiol., Pathol.* **a.** the degree of heat in a living body, normally about 98.6°F (37°C) in humans. **b.** the excess of this above the normal. **3.** *Obs.* mildness, as of the weather. **4.** *Obs.* temperament. [1525–35; < L *temperātūra* a tempering. See TEMPERATE, -URE]

tem′perature gra′dient, *Meteorol.* rate of change of temperature with distance.

tem′per•a•ture-hu•mid′i•ty in′dex (tem′pər ə-chər hyo͞o mid′i tē *or, often,* -yo͞o-, -prə-, -pər chər-, -cho͝or′), a number representing an estimate of the effect of temperature and moisture on humans, computed by multiplying the sum of dry-bulb and wet-bulb temperature readings by 0.4 and adding 15, with 65 assumed as the highest comfortable index. *Abbr.:* T.H.I. Cf. **heat index.**

tem′perature inver′sion, *Meteorol.* inversion (def. 12). [1940–45]

tem′perature spot′, *Physiol.* a sensory area in the skin that selectively responds to increased or decreased temperature; a warm spot or a cold spot.

tem′per col′or, *Metall.* any of the colors appearing on the surface of clean, unoxidized steel heated in air, from pale yellow at the coolest to dark blue at the hottest: used as an approximate indication of temperature.

tem•pered (tem′pərd), *adj.* **1.** having a temper or disposition of a specified character (usually used in combination): *a good-tempered child.* **2.** *Music.* tuned in accordance with some other temperament than just or pure temperament, esp. tuned in equal temperament. **3.** made less intense or violent, esp. by the influence of something good or benign: *justice tempered with mercy.* **4.** properly moistened or mixed, as clay. **5.** *Metall.* of or pertaining to steel or cast iron that has been tempered. [1325–75; ME; see TEMPER, -ED[2], -ED[3]]

tem′per tan′trum, tantrum. [1925–30]

tem•pest (tem′pist), *n.* **1.** a violent windstorm, esp. one with rain, hail, or snow. **2.** a violent commotion, disturbance, or tumult. **3. tempest in a teacup.** See **teacup** (def. 3). —*v.t.* **4.** to affect by or as by a tempest; disturb violently. [1200–50; ME *tempeste* < OF < VL **tempesta,* for L *tempestās* season, weather, storm, equiv. to *tempes-* (var. s. of *tempus* time) + *-tās* -TY[2]]

Tempest, The, a comedy (1611) by Shakespeare.

tem•pest-tossed (tem′pist tôst′, -tost′), *adj.* buffeted about, as by adversities. Also, **tem′pest-tost′.** [1585–95]

tem•pes•tu•ous (tem pes′cho͞o əs), *adj.* **1.** characterized by or subject to tempests: *the tempestuous ocean.* **2.** of the nature of or resembling a tempest: *a tempestuous wind.* **3.** tumultuous; turbulent: *a tempestuous period in history.* [1500–10; < LL *tempestuōsus,* deriv. of *tempestus,* var. of *tempestās* TEMPEST (see -OUS); r. earlier *tempeste(u)ous, tempestious* (see -EOUS, -IOUS)] —**tem•pes′tu•ous•ly,** *adv.* —**tem•pes′tu•ous•ness,** *n.*
—**Syn. 2.** violent, stormy.

tem•pi (tem′pē), *n.* a pl. of **tempo.**

Tem•plar (tem′plər), *n.* **1.** a member of a religious military order founded by Crusaders in Jerusalem about 1118, and suppressed in 1312. **2.** a barrister or other person occupying chambers in the Temple, London. **3.** a member of the Masonic order, Knights Templars. Also called **Knight Templar.** [1250–1300; < ML *templārius* (see TEMPLE[1], -AR[2]); r. ME *templer* < AF (see -ER[2])]

tem•plate (tem′plit), *n.* **1.** a pattern, mold, or the like, usually consisting of a thin plate of wood or metal, serving as a gauge or guide in mechanical work. **2.** *Building Trades.* a horizontal piece, as of timber or stone, in a wall, to receive and distribute the pressure of a girder, beam, or the like. **3.** *Shipbuilding.* either of two wedges in each of the temporary blocks forming the support for the keel of a ship while building. **4.** *Aerial Photogrammetry.* any object having lines, slots, or straightedges to represent lines radiating from the center of a photograph, used for graphic triangulation. **5.** *Genetics.* a strand of DNA or RNA that serves as a pattern for the synthesis of a complementary strand of nucleic acid or protein. **6.** *Computers.* a small sheet or strip of cardboard, plastic, or the like, that fits over a portion of the keyboard and provides ready reference to the keystroke commands of a particular software program. **7.** Also called **safe.** a marble base for a toilet. Also, **templet.** [1670–80; alter. of TEMPLET, appar. by falsely etymologizing final syllable as PLATE[1]]

tem•ple[1] (tem′pəl), *n.* **1.** an edifice or place dedicated to the service or worship of a deity or deities. **2.** (*usually cap.*) any of the three successive houses of worship in Jerusalem in use by the Jews in Biblical times, the first built by Solomon, the second by Zerubbabel, and the third by Herod. **3.** a synagogue, usually a Reform or Conservative one. **4.** an edifice erected as a place of public worship; a church, esp. a large or imposing one. **5.** any place or object in which God dwells, as the body of a Christian. I Cor. 6:19. **6.** (in France) a Protestant church. **7.** *Mormonism.* a building devoted to administering sacred ordinances, principally that of eternal marriage. **8.** a building, usually large or pretentious, devoted to some public use: *a temple of music.* **9.** (*cap.*) either of two establishments of the medieval Templars, one in London and the other in Paris. **10.** (*cap.*) either of two groups of buildings (**Inner Temple** and **Middle Temple**) on the site of the Templars' former establishment in London, occupied by two of the Inns of Court. **11.** a building used by the Templars in the U.S. **12.** a building used by any of various fraternal orders. [bef. 900; ME, var. of *tempel,* OE < L *templum* space demarcated by an augur for taking auspices, temple] —**tem′-pled,** *adj.* —**tem′ple•like′,** *adj.*

tem•ple[2] (tem′pəl), *n.* **1.** *Anat.* the flattened region on either side of the forehead in human beings. **2.** *Zool.* a corresponding region in certain animals. **3.** *Ophthalm.* either of the sidepieces of a pair of eyeglasses extending back above and often around the ears. [1275–1325; ME < MF < VL **tempula,* for L *tempora* the temples, pl. (taken as fem. sing.) of *tempus* temple]

tem•ple[3] (tem′pəl), *n.* a device in a loom for keeping the cloth stretched to the proper width during the weaving. [1475–85; earlier *tempylle* < MF *temple* < L *templum* purlin, small piece of timber. See TEMPLE[1]]

Tem•ple (tem′pəl), *n.* **1. Shirley** (*Shirley Temple Black*), born 1928, U.S. film actress, famous for child roles during the 1930's, and diplomat. **2. Sir William,** 1628–99, English essayist and diplomat. **3.** a city in central Texas. 42,483.

Tem′ple Cit′y, a town in SW California, near Los Angeles. 28,972.

Tem′ple of Ar′temis, the temple at Ephesus dedicated to Artemis. Cf. **Seven Wonders of the World.**

tem′ple or′ange, a hybrid fruit, *Citrus nobilis,* that is a cross between the sweet orange and the tangerine. Also called **tangor.**

tem•plet (tem′plit), *n.* template. [1670–80; perh. < F, dim. of *temple* TEMPLE[3] (see -ET), but semantic link is unclear]

Tem′ple Ter′race, a town in W Florida. 11,097.

tem•po (tem′pō), *n., pl.* **-pos, -pi** (-pē). **1.** *Music.* relative rapidity or rate of movement, usually indicated by such terms as *adagio, allegro,* etc., or by reference to the metronome. **2.** characteristic rate, rhythm, or pattern of work or activity: *the tempo of city life.* **3.** *Chess.* the gaining or losing of time and effectiveness relative to one's continued mobility or developing position, esp. with respect to the number of moves required to gain an objective: *Black gained a tempo.* [1680–90; < It < L *tempus* time]

tem•po•ral[1] (tem′pər əl, tem′prəl), *adj.* **1.** of or pertaining to time. **2.** pertaining to or concerned with the present life or this world; worldly: *temporal joys.* **3.** enduring for a time only; temporary; transitory (opposed to *eternal*). **4.** *Gram.* **a.** of, pertaining to, or expressing time: *a temporal adverb.* **b.** of or pertaining to the tenses of a verb. **5.** secular, lay, or civil, as opposed to ecclesiastical. —*n.* Usually, **temporals. 6.** a temporal possession, estate, or the like; temporality. **7.** something that is temporal; a temporal matter or affair. [1300–50; ME (adj. and n.) < L *temporālis,* equiv. to *tempor-* (s. of *tempus*) time + *-ālis* -AL[1]] —**tem′po•ral•ly,** *adv.* —**tem′-po•ral•ness,** *n.*

tem•po•ral[2] (tem′pər əl, tem′prəl), *Anat., Zool.* —*adj.* **1.** of, pertaining to, or situated near the temple or a temporal bone. —*n.* **2.** any of several parts in the temporal region, esp. the temporal bone. [1535–45; < LL *temporālis,* equiv. to *tempor-* (s. of *tempus*) TEMPLE[2] + *-ālis* -AL[1]]

tem′poral bone′, *Anat., Zool.* either of a pair of thick compound bones forming the part of the skull that encases the inner ear. See diag. under **skull.** [1765–75]

tem′poral hour′, *Horol.* a unit of time used in the Roman and Ottoman empires that divided the daylight into an equal number of hours, resulting in long summer hours and short winter hours. [1585–95]

tem•po•ral•i•ty (tem′pə ral′i tē), *n., pl.* **-ties. 1.** temporal character or nature; temporariness. **2.** something temporal. **3.** Usually, **temporalities.** a worldly or secular possession, revenue, or the like, as of the church or clergy. [1350–1400; ME *temporalite* < LL *temporālitās.* See TEMPORAL[1], -ITY]

tem•po•ral•ize (tem′pər ə līz′, tem′prə-), *v.t.,* **-ized, -iz•ing. 1.** to make temporal in time; place in time. **2.** to make concerned with the present life; secularize. Also, *esp. Brit.,* **tem′po•ral•ise′.** [1820–30; TEMPORAL[1] + -IZE]

tem′poral lobe′, *Anat., Zool.* the lateral lobe of each cerebral hemisphere, in front of the occipital lobe. [1890–95]

tem′po•ral-lobe ep′ilepsy (tem′pər əl lōb′), *Pathol.* a type of seizure disorder produced by abnormal electric discharges in the temporal lobe of the brain, characterized by the occurrence of any of a variety of auras followed by a brief loss of consciousness with accompanying repetitive, automatic movements. Also called **psychomotor epilepsy.**

tem′poral summa′tion. See under **summation.** [1945–50]

tem•po•ra mu•tan•tur, nos et mu•ta•mur in il•lis (tem′pô rä′ mo͞o tän′to͝or, nōs et mo͞o tä′mo͝or in il′lēs; *Eng.* tem′pər ə myo͞o tan′tər, nos et myo͞o tā′mər in il′is), *Latin.* the times change and we change with them.

tem•po•rar•y (tem′pə rer′ē), *adj., n., pl.* **-rar•ies.** —*adj.* **1.** lasting, existing, serving, or effective for a time only; not permanent: *a temporary need; a temporary job.* —*n.* **2.** an office worker hired, usually through an agency on a per diem basis, for a short period of time. [1540–50; < L *temporārius,* equiv. to *tempor-* (s. of *tempus*) time + *-ārius* -ARY] —**tem•po•rar•i•ly** (tem′pə râr′ə lē, tem′pə rer′-), *adv.* —**tem′po•rar′i•ness,** *n.*
—**Syn. 1.** impermanent, passing. TEMPORARY, TRANSIENT, TRANSITORY agree in referring to that which is not lasting or permanent. TEMPORARY implies an arrangement established with no thought of continuance but with the idea of being changed soon: *a temporary structure.* TRANSIENT describes that which is in the process of passing by, and which will therefore last or stay only a short time: *a transient condition.* TRANSITORY describes an innate characteristic by which a thing, by its very nature, lasts only a short time: *Life is transitory.* —**Ant. 1.** permanent.

tem′porary du′ty, duty of limited duration performed with an organization other than the one to which a person is normally attached or assigned. *Abbr.:* TDY [1940–45]

tem′porary life′ annu′ity, *Insurance.* an annuity that ceases upon the death of the annuitant or upon the expiration of a period of time, whichever occurs first.

tem•po•rize (tem′pə rīz′), *v.i.,* **-rized, -riz•ing. 1.** to be indecisive or evasive to gain time or delay acting. **2.** to comply with the time or occasion; yield temporarily or ostensibly to prevailing opinion or circumstances. **3.** to treat or parley so as to gain time (usually fol. by *with*). **4.** to come to terms (usually fol. by *with*). **5.** to effect a compromise (usually fol. by *between*). Also, *esp. Brit.,* **tem′po•rise′.** [1570–80; < ML *temporizāre* to hang back, delay, equiv. to L *tempor-* (s. of *tempus*) time + ML *-izāre* -IZE] —**tem′po•ri•za′tion,** *n.* —**tem′po•riz′er,** *n.* —**tem′po•riz′ing•ly,** *adv.*
—**Syn. 1.** hedge, stall, equivocate.

temporo-, a combining form representing **temple**[2] in compound words: *temporomandibular.* [< L *tempor-* (s. of *tempus*) TEMPLE[2] + -O-]

tem•po•ro•man•dib•u•lar (tem′pə rō man dib′yə lər), *adj. Anat.* of, pertaining to, or situated near the hinge joint formed by the lower jaw and the temporal bone of the skull. [1885–90; TEMPORO- + MANDIBULAR]

tem′poromandib′ular joint′ syn′drome, *Pathol.* a condition attributed to tension in or faulty articulation of the temporomandibular joint, having a wide range of symptoms that include dizziness, ringing in the ears, and pain in the head, neck, and shoulders. Also called **TMJ syndrome.**

temps (*Fr.* täN), *n., pl.* **temps** (*Fr.* täN). *Ballet.* part of a dance step in which there is no transfer of weight. [1885–90; < F: lit., time < L *tempus*]

temps le•vé (*Fr.* täN lə vā′), *pl.* **temps le•vés** (*Fr.* täN lə vā′). *Ballet.* a small hop on one foot, with the other foot raised off the floor. [< F]

temps li•é (*Fr.* täN lē ā′), *pl.* **temps li•és** (*Fr.* täN lē ā′). *Ballet.* a series of systematized and connected arm and leg movements done for practice. [< F]

tempt (tempt), *v.t.* **1.** to entice or allure to do something often regarded as unwise, wrong, or immoral. **2.** to attract, appeal strongly to, or invite: *The offer tempts me.* **3.** to render strongly disposed to do something: *The book tempted me to read more on the subject.* **4.** to put (someone) to the test in a venturesome way; provoke: *to tempt one's fate.* **5.** *Obs.* to try or test. [1175–1225; ME < L *temptāre* to probe, feel, test, tempt] —**tempt′a•ble,** *adj.*
—**Syn. 1.** TEMPT, SEDUCE may both mean to allure or entice to something unwise or wicked. To TEMPT is to attract by holding out the probability of gratification or advantage, often in the direction of that which is wrong or unwise: *to tempt a man with a bribe.* To SEDUCE is literally to lead astray, sometimes from that which absorbs one or demands attention, but oftener, in a moral sense, from rectitude, chastity, etc.: *to seduce a person away from loyalty.* **2.** inveigle, induce, lure, incite, persuade.

temp•ta•tion (temp tā′shən), *n.* **1.** the act of tempting; enticement or allurement. **2.** something that tempts, entices, or allures. **3.** the fact or state of being tempted, esp. to evil. **4.** an instance of this. **5.** (*cap.*) the temptation of Christ by Satan. Matt. 4. [1175–1225; ME *temptacion* < L *temptātiōn-* (s. of *temptātiō*) a testing. See TEMPT, -ATION] —**temp•ta′tion•al,** *adj.*
—**Syn. 1.** lure, attraction, pull, seduction, inducement.

tempt•er (temp′tər), *n.* **1.** a person or thing that tempts, esp. to evil. **2. the Tempter,** Satan; the devil. [1350–1400; TEMPT + -ER[1]; r. ME *temptour* < OF *tempteur, temptēor* < LL *temptātōr-,* s. of *temptātor* tempter (to sin), L: one who makes an attempt; see TEMPT, -TOR]

tempt•ing (temp′ting), *adj.* that tempts; enticing or inviting. [1540–50; TEMPT + -ING[2]] —**tempt′ing•ly,** *adv.* —**tempt′ing•ness,** *n.*
—**Syn.** attractive, alluring, seductive. —**Ant.** repellent.

tempt•ress (temp′tris), *n.* a woman who tempts, entices, or allures. [1585–95; TEMPT(E)R + -ESS]
—**Usage.** See **-ess.**

tem•pu•ra (tem po͝or′ə), *n. Japanese Cookery.* seafood or vegetables dipped in batter and deep-fried. [1935–40; < Japn *tenpura,* allegedly < Pg *tempêro* seasoning, taste (deriv. of *temperar* to season < L *temperāre*; see TEMPER)]

tem•pus e•dax re•rum (tem′po͝os e′däks rā′ro͝om; *Eng.* tem′pəs ē′daks rēr′əm), *Latin.* time, devourer of all things.

tem•pus fu•git (tem′po͝os fo͞o′git; *Eng.* tem′pəs fyo͞o′jit), *Latin.* time flies.

Tem•pyō (tem′pyô′), *adj.* of or pertaining to the period of Japanese art history, A.D. 725–794, characterized by the flowering of Buddhist architecture and statuary: combined T'ang Chinese influences and emerging native traits. [< Japn, imperial era name < MChin, equiv. to Chin *tiān píng* heaven is peaceful]

Te•mu•co (te mo͞o′kô), *n.* a city in S Chile. 138,430.

ten (ten), *n.* **1.** a cardinal number, nine plus one. **2.** a symbol for this number, as 10 or X. **3.** a set of this many persons or things. **4.** a playing card with ten pips. **5.** *Informal.* a ten-dollar bill: *She had two tens and a five in her purse.* **6.** Also called **ten's place.** *Math.* **a.** (in a mixed number) the position of the second digit to the left of the decimal point. **b.** (in a whole number) the position of the second digit from the right. **7. take ten,** *Informal.* to rest from what one is doing, esp. for ten minutes. —*adj.* **8.** amounting to ten in number. [bef. 900; ME *ten(e), tenn(e),* OE *tēn(e), tien(e)*; c. D *tien,* G *zehn,* ON *tīu,* Goth *taihun,* L *decem,* Gk *déka,* Skt *daśa*]

10, the upper end of a rating scale, with 10 indicating the best or a perfect score: *That new novel is wonderful —I'd rate it a 10.*

ten., **1.** tenor. **2.** *Music.* tenuto.

Ten•a (ten′ə), *n.* Koyukon.

ten•a•ble (ten′ə bəl), *adj.* **1.** capable of being held, maintained, or defended, as against attack or dispute: *a tenable theory.* **2.** capable of being occupied, possessed, held, or enjoyed, as under certain conditions: *a research grant tenable for two years.* [1570–80; < F: that can be held, equiv. to *ten(ir)* to hold (<< L *tenēre*) + *-able* -ABLE] —**ten′a•bil′i•ty, ten′a•ble•ness,** *n.* —**ten′a•bly,** *adv.*
—**Syn. 1.** workable, viable, maintainable, warrantable.

ten•ace (ten′ās′), *n. Whist, Bridge.* a sequence of two high cards of the same suit that lack an intervening card to be in consecutive order, as the ace and queen. Cf. **major tenace, minor tenace.** [1645–55; < Sp *tenazas* tongs, tenace (in card games), deriv. of *tenaz* << L *tenāx* TENACIOUS; cf. ML *tenācēs* forceps]

te•na•cious (tə nā′shəs), *adj.* **1.** holding fast; characterized by keeping a firm hold (often fol. by *of*): *a tenacious grip on my arm; tenacious of old habits.* **2.** highly retentive: *a tenacious memory.* **3.** pertinacious, persistent, stubborn, or obstinate. **4.** adhesive or sticky; viscous or glutinous. **5.** holding together; cohesive; not easily pulled asunder; tough. [1600–10; TENACI(TY) + -OUS] —**te•na′cious•ly,** *adv.* —**te•na′cious•ness,** *n.*
—**Syn. 3.** opinionated, dogged. **4.** clinging.

te•nac•i•ty (tə nas′i tē), *n.* the quality or property of being tenacious. [1520–30; < L *tenācitās* equiv. to *tenāc-* (s. of *tenāx*) holding fast, deriv. of *tenēre* to hold + *-itās* -ITY[2]]
—**Syn.** See **perseverance.**

te•nac•u•lum (tə nak′yə ləm), *n., pl.* **-la** (-lə). **1.** *Surg.* a small sharp-pointed hook set in a handle, used for seizing and picking up parts in operations and dissections. **2.** *Entomol.* a clasplike appendage on the abdomen of a springtail, which holds the springing device in place. [1685–95; < L *tenāculum* instrument for gripping, equiv. to *ten(ēre)* to hold + *-ā-* (from v. stems ending in *-ā-*; see GUBERNACULUM) + *-culum* -CULE[2]]

Ten•a•fly (ten′ə flī′), *n.* a borough in NE New Jersey. 13,552.

te•na•im (*Yiddish, Ashk. Heb., Eng.* tə nä′yim, -nô′-; *Seph. Heb.* tə nä ēm′), *n.* (*used with a singular or plural v.*) *Judaism.* the terms of a Jewish marriage, as the wedding date, amount of the bride's dowry, etc., or an agreement containing such terms, made by the parents of an engaged couple at the engagement party. [lit., agreements]

ten•an•cy (ten′ən sē), *n., pl.* **-cies. 1.** a holding, as of lands, by any kind of title; occupancy of land, a house, or the like, under a lease or on payment of rent; tenure. **2.** the period of a tenant's occupancy. **3.** occupancy or enjoyment of a position, post, situation, etc.: *her tenancy as professor of history at the state university.* **4.** *Archaic.* a piece of land held by a tenant; holding. [1570–80; TEN(ANT) + -ANCY; cf. ML *tenantia,* var. of *tenentia*]

ten′ancy in com′mon, *Law.* a holding of property, usually real, by two or more persons with each owning an undivided share and with no right of survivorship. Cf. **joint tenancy.** [1760–70]

ten•ant (ten′ənt), *n.* **1.** a person or group that rents and occupies land, a house, an office, or the like, from another for a period of time; lessee. **2.** *Law.* a person who holds or possesses for a time lands, tenements, or personalty of another, usually for rent. **3.** an occupant or inhabitant of any place. —*v.t.* **4.** to hold or occupy as a tenant; dwell in; inhabit. —*v.i.* **5.** to dwell or live (usually fol. by *in*). [1250–1300; ME *tena(u)nt* < AF; MF *tenant,* n. use of prp. of *tenir* to hold << L *tenēre.* See -ANT] —**ten′ant•a•ble,** *adj.* —**ten′ant•less,** *adj.* —**ten′ant•like′,** *adj.*

ten′ant farm′er, a person who farms the land of another and pays rent with cash or with a portion of the produce. [1855–60]

ten′ant in chief′, a feudal vassal who holds land directly from the king. Also, **ten′ant-in-chief′.** Also called **ten′ant in cap′i•te** (kap′i tē). [1600–10]

ten′ant in com′mon, *Law.* one of two or more persons who hold property by tenancy in common. Cf. **joint tenant.** [1600–10]

ten•ant•ry (ten′ən trē), *n.* **1.** tenants collectively; the body of tenants on an estate. **2.** the state or condition of being a tenant. [1350–1400; ME; see TENANT, -RY]

ten′-cent store′ (ten′sent′, -sent′), five-and-ten (def. 1). [1900–05, *Amer.*]

tench (tench), *n., pl.* **tench•es,** (*esp. collectively*) **tench.** a freshwater food fish, *Tinca tinca,* of Europe and Asia that can survive short periods out of water. [1350–1400; ME *tenche* < MF, OF < LL *tinca*]

ten′ code′, *Radio.* a set of code numbers each beginning with the number ten and used as a code to describe different situations: originally used by the police, now used in CB and other radio communications. Cf. **ten-four.**

Ten′ Command′ments, the precepts spoken by God to Israel, delivered to Moses on Mount Sinai; the Decalogue. Ex. 20; 24:12,34; Deut. 5. Though the numbering of these commandments may differ in some religions, that which has been followed in this dictionary is based on the King James Version of the Bible.

tend[1] (tend), *v.i.* **1.** to be disposed or inclined in action, operation, or effect to do something: *The particles tend to unite.* **2.** to be disposed toward an idea, emotion, way of thinking, etc.: *He tends to be overly optimistic. Her religious philosophy tends toward pantheism.* **3.** to lead or conduce, as to some result or resulting condition: *measures tending to improved working conditions; Governments are tending toward democracy.* **4.** to be inclined to or have a tendency toward a particular quality, state, or degree: *This wine tends toward the sweet side.* **5.** (of a journey, course, road, etc.) to lead or be directed in a particular direction (usually fol. by *to, toward,* etc.): *a path tending toward the beach.* [1300–50; ME *tenden* < MF *tendre* < L *tendere* to stretch, extend, proceed]

tend[2] (tend), *v.t.* **1.** to attend to by work or services, care, etc.: *to tend a fire.* **2.** to look after; watch over and care for; minister to or wait on with service: *to tend the sick.* **3.** *Naut.* to handle or attend to (a rope). —*v.i.* **4.** to attend by action, care, etc. (usually fol. by *to*). **5. tend on** or **upon,** *Archaic.* to attend or wait upon; minister to; serve: *She tended on the sick and dying with infinite compassion.* [1300–50; ME *tenden,* aph. var. of ATTEND]

tend•ance (ten′dəns), *n.* **1.** attention; care; ministration, as to the sick. **2.** *Archaic.* servants or attendants. [1565–75; aph. var. of ATTENDANCE]

ten•den•cy (ten′dən sē), *n., pl.* **-cies. 1.** a natural or prevailing disposition to move, proceed, or act in some direction or toward some point, end, or result: *the tendency of falling bodies toward the earth.* **2.** an inclination, bent, or predisposition to something: *a tendency to talk too much.* **3.** a special and definite purpose in a novel or other literary work. [1620–30; < ML *tendentia.* See TEND[1], -ENCY]
—**Syn. 1.** TENDENCY, DIRECTION, TREND, DRIFT refer to inclination or line of action or movement. A TENDENCY is an inclination toward a certain line of action (whether or not the action follows), and is often the result of inherent qualities, nature, or habit: *a tendency to procrastinate.* DIRECTION is the line along which an object or course of action moves, often toward some set point or intended goal: *The change is in the direction of improvement.* TREND emphasizes simultaneous movement in a certain direction of a number of factors, although the course or goal may not be clear for any single feature: *Business indicators showed a downward trend.* DRIFT emphasizes gradual development as well as direction: *the drift of his argument.* **2.** proclivity, leaning.

ten′dency tone′, a tone that is harmonically or melodically unstable and tends naturally to resolve itself either upward or downward.

ten•den•tious (ten den′shəs), *adj.* having or showing a definite tendency, bias, or purpose: *a tendentious novel.* Also, **ten•den′cious, ten•den•tial** (ten den′shəl). [1895–1900; < ML *tendenti(a)* TENDENCY + -OUS] —**ten•den′tious•ly,** *adv.* —**ten•den′tious•ness,** *n.*

ten•der[1] (ten′dər), *adj.,* **-er, -est,** *v.* —*adj.* **1.** soft or delicate in substance; not hard or tough: *a tender steak.* **2.** weak or delicate in constitution; not strong or hardy. **3.** (of plants) unable to withstand freezing temperatures. **4.** young or immature: *children of tender age.* **5.** delicate or soft in quality: *tender blue.* **6.** delicate, soft, or gentle: *the tender touch of her hand.* **7.** easily moved to sympathy or compassion; kind: *a tender heart.* **8.** affectionate or loving; sentimental or amatory: *a tender glance.* **9.** considerate or careful; chary or reluctant (usually fol. by *of*). **10.** acutely or painfully sensitive: *a tender bruise.* **11.** easily distressed; readily made uneasy: *a tender conscience.* **12.** yielding readily to force or pressure; easily broken; fragile. **13.** of a delicate or ticklish nature; requiring careful or tactful handling: *a tender subject.* **14.** *Naut.* crank[2] (def. 1). —*v.t.* **15.** to make tender. **16.** *Archaic.* to regard or treat tenderly. [1175–1225; ME, var. of *tendre* < OF < L *tenerum,* acc. of *tener* tender] —**ten′der•ly,** *adv.* —**ten′der•ness,** *n.*

ten•der[2] (ten′dər), *v.t.* **1.** to present formally for acceptance; make formal offer of: *to tender one's resignation.* **2.** to offer or proffer. **3.** *Law.* to offer, as money or goods, in payment of a debt or other obligation, esp. in exact accordance with the terms of the law and of the obligation. —*v.i.* **4.** to make or submit a bid (often fol. by *for*). —*n.* **5.** the act of tendering; an offer of something for acceptance. **6.** something tendered or offered, esp. money, as in payment. **7.** *Com.* an offer made in writing by one party to another to execute certain work, supply certain commodities, etc., at a given cost; bid. **8.** *Law.* an offer, as of money or goods, in payment or satisfaction of a debt or other obligation. [1535–45; earlier *tendre,* n. use of AF *tendre* to extend, offer. See TEND[1]] —**ten′der•er,** *n.*
—**Syn. 1.** See **offer. 5.** proposal, proffer.

tend•er[3] (ten′dər), *n.* **1.** a person who tends; a person who attends to or takes charge of someone or something. **2.** an auxiliary ship employed to attend one or more other ships, as for supplying provisions. **3.** a dinghy carried or towed by a yacht. **4.** *Railroads.* a car attached to a steam locomotive for carrying fuel and water. [1425–75; late ME; orig. aph. var. of *attender;* see TEND[2], -ER[1]]

ten•der•a•ble (ten′dər ə bəl), *adj.* capable of being tendered or offered in payment, as money or goods. [1880–85; TENDER[2] + -ABLE] —**ten′der•a•bil′i•ty,** *n.*

ten·der·foot (ten′dər fo͝ot′), *n., pl.* **-foots, -feet** (-fēt′). **1.** a raw, inexperienced person; novice. **2.** a newcomer to the ranching and mining regions of the western U.S., unused to hardships. **3.** one in the lowest rank of the Boy Scouts of America or Girl Scouts of America. [1840–50, *Amer.*; TENDER[1] + FOOT]

ten·der-heart·ed (ten′dər här′tid), *adj.* soft-hearted; sympathetic. [1530–40] **—ten′der-heart′ed·ly,** *adv.* **—ten′der-heart′ed·ness,** *n.*
—Syn. compassionate.

Ten′der Is′ the Night′, a novel (1934) by F. Scott Fitzgerald.

ten·der·ize (ten′də rīz′), *v.t.,* **-ized, -iz·ing.** to make (meat) tender, as by pounding or by a chemical process or treatment. Also, *esp. Brit.,* **ten′der·ise′.** [1725–35; TENDER[1] + -IZE] **—ten′der·i·za′tion,** *n.* **—ten′der·iz′·er,** *n.*

ten·der·loin (ten′dər loin′), *n.* **1.** (in beef or pork) the tender meat of the muscle running through the sirloin and terminating before the ribs. **2.** a cut of beef lying between the sirloin and ribs. **3.** (*cap.*) **a.** (formerly) a district in New York City noted for corruption and vice: so called because police there could eat well from their bribes. **b.** a similar district in any U.S. city. [1820–30, *Amer.*; TENDER[1] + LOIN]

tend·er·man (ten′dər mən), *n., pl.* **-men.** *n. Canadian Fishery.* any member of the crew of a vessel engaged in conveying fish from a trap or pound to the shore. [TENDER[3] + -MAN]

ten·der-mind·ed (ten′dər mīn′did), *adj.* compassionate and idealistic. [1595–1605]

ten′der of′fer, a public offer to purchase stock of a corporation from its shareholders at a certain price within a stated time limit, often in an effort to win control of the company. [1960–65]

ten·di·ni·tis (ten′də nī′tis), *n. Pathol.* inflammation of a tendon. Also, **ten′do·ni′tis, tenonitis.** [1895–1900; < NL *tendin-* (see TENDINOUS) + -ITIS]

ten·di·nous (ten′də nəs), *adj.* **1.** of the nature of or resembling a tendon. **2.** consisting of tendons. [1650–60; < NL *tendin-* (r. ML *tendōn-*), s. of *tendō* TENDON + -OUS]

ten·don (ten′dən), *n.* **1.** *Anat.* a cord or band of dense, tough, inelastic, white, fibrous tissue, serving to connect a muscle with a bone or part; sinew. **2.** a reinforcing strand in prestressed concrete. [1535–45; < ML *tendōn-* (s. of *tendō*) < Gk *ténōn* sinew (sp. with *-d-* by association with L *tendere* to stretch)]

ten·dril (ten′dril), *n. Bot.* a threadlike, leafless organ of climbing plants, often growing in spiral form, which attaches itself to or twines round some other body, so as to support the plant. [1530–40; earlier *tendrel,* var. (perh. by dissimilation) of ME *tendren, tendron* < MF *tendron* shoot, sprout, cartilage] **—ten′dril·lar, ten′·dril·ous,** *adj.* **—ten′dril·ly,** *adj.*

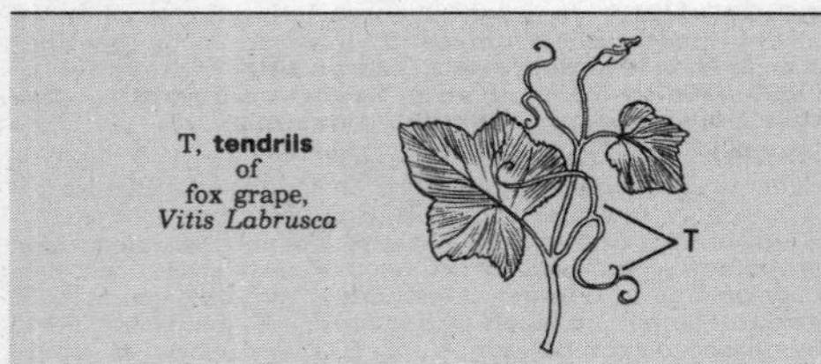

T, **tendrils** of fox grape, *Vitis Labrusca*

ten·du (tän do͞o′; *Fr.* tän dy′), *adj. Ballet.* of or pertaining to a movement that is stretched or held. [1920–25; < F: stretched, ptp. of *tendre* to stretch, extend]

-tene, a combining form meaning "ribbon," used in biology to form compound nouns that refer to the shape or number of chromosomes involved in meiosis: *leptotene; pachytene; diplotene.* [< F *-tène* (in scientific compounds) < L *taenia* TAENIA]

Ten·e·brae (ten′ə brā′), *n.* (*used with a singular or plural v.*) *Rom. Cath. Ch.* the office of matins and lauds for Thursday, Friday, and Saturday of Holy Week, sung respectively on the afternoon of Wednesday, Thursday, and Friday of that week, at which the Crucifixion is commemorated by the gradual extinguishment of candles. [1645–55; < L: lit., darkness]

ten·e·brif·ic (ten′ə brif′ik), *adj.* producing darkness. [1640–50; < L *tenebr(ae)* darkness + -I- + -FIC]

te·neb·ri·o·nid (tə neb′rē ə nid), *n.* See **darkling beetle.** [1900–05; < NL *Tenebrionidae* family name, equiv. to *Tenebrion-,* s. of *Tenebrio* type genus (< L *tenebriō,* s. *tenebriōn-* one who operates in the dark) + *-idae* -ID[2]]

ten·e·brous (ten′ə brəs), *adj.* dark; gloomy; obscure. Also, **te·neb·ri·ous** (tə neb′rē əs). [1375–1425; late ME < L *tenebrōsus.* See TENEBRAE, -OUS] **—ten′e·brous·ness,** *n.*

Ten·e·dos (ten′i dos′, -dōs′; *Gk.* ten′e thôs), *n.* an island in the Aegean, near the entrance to the Dardanelles, belonging to Turkey. Also called **Bozcaada.**

1080 (ten′ā′tē). See **sodium fluoroacetate.** Also, **ten′-eight′y.**

ten·e·ment (ten′ə mənt), *n.* **1.** Also called **ten′ement house′.** a run-down and often overcrowded apartment house, esp. in a poor section of a large city. **2.** *Law.* **a.** any species of permanent property, as lands, houses, rents, an office, or a franchise, that may be held of another. **b. tenements,** freehold interests in things immovable considered as subjects of property. **3.** *Brit.* an apartment or room rented by a tenant. **4.** *Archaic.* any abode or habitation. [1250–1300; ME < ML *tenēmentum,* equiv. to L *tenē(re)* to hold + *-mentum* -MENT] **—ten·e·men·tal** (ten′ə men′tl), **ten·e·men·ta·ry** (ten′ə men′tə rē), *adj.* **—ten′e·ment·ed,** *adj.*

Ten·er·ife (ten′ə rif′, -rēf′; *Sp.* te′ne rē′fe), *n.* **1.** the largest of the Canary Islands, off the NW Coast of Africa. 500,381; 794 sq. mi. (2055 sq. km). *Cap.:* Santa Cruz de Tenerife. **2. Pi·co de** (pē′kō dā; *Sp.* pē′kô the). See **Teide, Pico de.** Also, **Ten′er·iffe′.**

te·nes·mus (tə nez′məs, -nes′-), *n. Pathol.* a straining to urinate or defecate, without the ability to do so. [1520–30; < ML, var. of L *tēnesmos* < Gk *teinesmós,* equiv. to *teín(ein)* to stretch + *-esmos* n. suffix]

ten·et (ten′it; *Brit. also* tē′nit), *n.* any opinion, principle, doctrine, dogma, etc., esp. one held as true by members of a profession, group, or movement. [1590–1600; < L: he holds]
—Syn. belief, position.

ten·fold (*adj.* ten′fōld′; *adv.* ten′fōld′), *adj.* **1.** comprising ten parts or members. **2.** ten times as great or as much. **—*adv.*** **3.** in tenfold measure: *good deeds rewarded tenfold.* [1150–1200; ME; OE *tienfeald.* See TEN, -FOLD]

ten-four (ten′fôr′, -fōr′), *interj. CB Radio Slang.* (used to express affirmation or confirmation). Cf. **ten code.** [1960–65]

ten′-gal·lon hat′ (ten′gal′ən), a broad-brimmed hat with a high crown, worn esp. in the western and southwestern U.S.; cowboy hat. Cf. **sombrero.** [1925–30; said to be < Sp *galón* braid, GALLOON (rows of which were wrapped above the brim)]

10-gauge (ten′gāj′), *n.* **1.** Also called **10-gauge shotgun.** a shotgun using a shell of approx. 0.775 in. (1.97 cm) in diameter. **2.** the shell itself.

Teng Hsiao-ping (*Chin.* dung′ shyou′ping′), *Wade-Giles.* See **Deng Xiaoping.** Also, **Teng′ Hsiao′-p'ing′.**

Ten·gri Khan (teng′grē kän′, KHän′), a mountain in central Asia, on the boundary between Kirghizia (Kyrgyzstan) and China: highest peak of the Tien Shan Mountains. ab. 23,950 ft. (7300 m). Also called **Khan Tengri.**

Ten·gri Nor (teng′grē nôr′, nōr′), a salt lake in E Tibet, NW of Lhasa. ab. 700 sq. mi. (1813 sq. km); 15,186 ft. (4629 m) above sea level.

te·ni·a (tē′nē ə), *n., pl.* **-ni·ae** (-nē ē′). taenia.

te·ni·a·cide (tē′nē ə sīd′), *n. Med.* taeniacide. **—te′·ni·a·cid′al,** *adj.*

te·ni·a·fuge (tē′nē ə fyo͞oj′), *adj., n. Med.* taeniafuge.

te·ni·a·sis (tē nī′ə sis), *n. Pathol.* taeniasis.

Ten·iers (ten′yərz, tə nērz′; *Flem.* tə nērs′; *Fr.* te nyā′), *n.* **1. Da·vid** (dā′vid; *Flem.* dä′vit; *Fr.* dä vēd′) (*"the Elder"*), 1582–1649, Flemish painter and engraver. **2.** his son, **David** (*"the Younger"*), 1610–90, Flemish painter.

Tenn., Tennessee.

Ten·nant (ten′ənt), *n.* **Smithson,** 1761–1815, English chemist: discoverer of osmium and iridium.

ten·nant·ite (ten′ən tīt′), *n.* a mineral, copper arsenic sulfide, approximately Cu_3AsS_3: a copper ore and an end member of a series of solid solutions into which antimony enters to form tetrahedrite. [1830–40; after S. TENNANT; see -ITE[1]]

ten·ner (ten′ər), *n. Informal.* **1.** a 10-dollar bill. **2.** *Brit.* a 10-pound note. [1840–50; TEN + -ER[1]]

Ten·nes·se·an (ten′ə sē′ən), *adj.* **1.** of, pertaining to, or characteristic of the state of Tennessee or its inhabitants. **—*n.*** **2.** a native or inhabitant of the state of Tennessee. Also, **Ten′nes·see′an.** [1805–15, *Amer.*; TENNESSEE + -AN]

Ten·nes·see (ten′ə sē′), *n.* **1.** a state in the SE United States. 4,590,750; 42,246 sq. mi. (109,415 sq. km). *Cap.:* Nashville. *Abbr.:* TN (for use with zip code), Tenn. **2.** a river flowing from E Tennessee through N Alabama, W Tennessee, and SW Kentucky into the Ohio near Paducah. 652 mi. (1050 km) long.

Ten′nessee Val′ley Author′ity. See **TVA.**

Ten′nessee walk′ing horse′, one of a breed of saddle horses developed largely from Standardbred and Morgan stock. Also called **Plantation walking horse.** [1940–45, *Amer.*]

Ten′nessee war′bler, a North American wood warbler, *Vermivora peregrina,* having a gray head, a greenish back, and white underparts. [1805–15, *Amer.*]

Ten·niel (ten′yəl), *n.* **Sir John,** 1820–1914, English caricaturist and illustrator.

ten·nis (ten′is), *n.* a game played on a rectangular court by two players or two pairs of players equipped with rackets, in which a ball is driven back and forth over a low net that divides the court in half. Cf. **lawn tennis.** See illus. under **racket**[2]. [1350–1400; ME *tenetz, ten(e)ys* < AF: take!, impv. pl. of *tenir* to hold, take, receive, appar. used as a server's call]

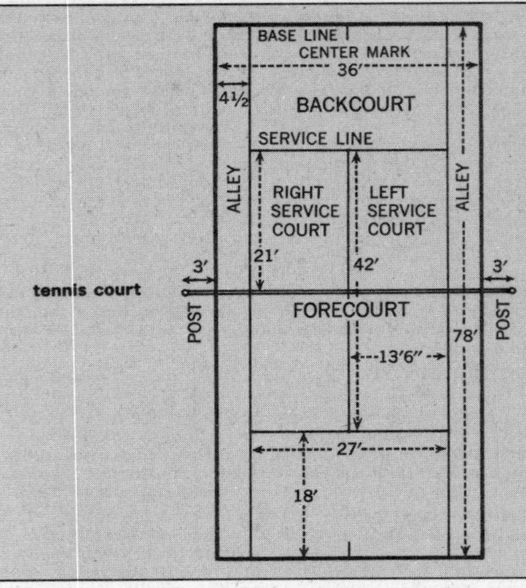

tennis court

ten′nis ball′, a hollow ball used in tennis, made of rubber with a fuzzy covering of woven Dacron, nylon, or wool. [1400–50; late ME]

ten′nis el′bow, irritation of the synovial membrane, or joint rotary area, of the elbow, caused by immoderate motions while playing tennis or other sports; epicondylitis. [1880–85]

ten′nis shoe′, a sports shoe with a rubber sole (usually pebbled) and a stitched canvas upper that laces over the instep. [1890–95]

Ten·ny·son (ten′ə sən), *n.* **Alfred, Lord** (*1st Baron*), 1809–92, English poet: poet laureate 1850–92.

Ten·ny·so·ni·an (ten′ə sō′nē ən), *adj.* of, pertaining to, or characteristic of Tennyson or his writings. [1835–45; TENNYSON + -IAN]

teno-, a combining form meaning "tendon," used in the formation of compound words: *tenotomy.* [comb. form repr. Gk *ténōn*]

Te·noch·ti·tlán (te nôch′tē tlän′), *n.* the capital of the Aztec empire: founded in 1325; destroyed by the Spaniards in 1521; now the site of Mexico City.

ten·on (ten′ən), *n.* **1.** a projection formed on the end of a timber or the like for insertion into a mortise of the same dimensions. See illus. under **mortise.** **—*v.t.*** **2.** to provide with a tenon. **3.** to join by or as by a tenon. **4.** to join securely. [1400–50; late ME < MF, equiv. to *ten(ir)* to hold (< L *tenēre*) + *-on* n. suffix] **—ten′on·er,** *n.*

ten·o·ni·tis (ten′ə nī′tis), *n. Pathol.* tendinitis. [1885–90; < Gk *ténōn* TENDON + -ITIS]

ten·or (ten′ər), *n.* **1.** the course of thought or meaning that runs through something written or spoken; purport; drift. **2.** continuous course, progress, or movement. **3.** *Rhet.* the subject of a metaphor, as "she" in "She is a rose." Cf. **vehicle** (def. 8). **4.** *Music.* **a.** the adult male voice intermediate between the bass and the alto or countertenor. **b.** a part sung by or written for such a voice, esp. the next to the lowest part in four-part harmony. **c.** a singer with such a voice. **d.** an instrument corresponding in compass to this voice, esp. the viola. **e.** the lowest-toned bell of a peal. **5.** quality, character, or condition. **—*adj.*** **6.** *Music.* of, pertaining to, or having the compass of a tenor. [1250–1300; < ML, L: course, continuity, tone, equiv. to *ten(ēre)* to hold + *-or* -OR[1]; r. ME *ten(o)ur* < AF < L, as above] **—ten′or·less,** *adj.*
—Syn. 1. sense, import, content, substance, gist.

ten′or clef′, *Music.* a sign locating middle C on the next to the top line of the staff. See illus. under **C clef.** [1800–10]

ten′or cor′, mellophone. [1925–30]

ten′or horn′, *n.* a musical brass wind instrument with valves; the tenor member of the cornet family.

ten·or·ist (ten′ə rist), *n.* **1.** a person who sings tenor. **2.** a person who plays a tenor instrument. [1715–25; TENOR + -IST]

ten·o·rite (ten′ə rīt′), *n.* a mineral, cupric oxide, CuO, occurring in veins of copper in black, minute scales. [1860–65; named after G. *Tenore* (d. 1861), president of Naples Academy; see -ITE[1]]

te·nor·rha·phy (tə nôr′ə fē, -nor′-), *n., pl.* **-phies.** *Surg.* suture of a tendon. [1885–90; TENO- + -RRHAPHY]

ten·o·syn·o·vi·tis (ten′ō sin′ə vī′tis), *n. Pathol.* inflammation of a tendon sheath, as from trauma, repeated strain, or systemic disease. [1885–90; TENO- + SYNOVITIS]

te·not·o·my (tə not′ə mē), *n., pl.* **-mies.** *Surg.* the cutting of a tendon. [1835–45; TENO- + -TOMY]

ten·pen·ny (ten′pen′ē, -pə nē), *adj.* **1.** noting a nail 3 in. (7.6 cm) in length. *Symbol:* 10d. **2.** worth or costing 10 cents. [1400–50; late ME; see TEN, PENNY]

ten′ percent′er, *Informal.* an agent, esp. an actor's agent, whose fee is 10 percent of a client's salary. Also, **ten′-per·cent′er.** [1900–05; *ten percent* + -ER[1]]

ten·pins (ten′pinz′), *n.* **1.** (*used with a singular v.*) a form of bowling, played with ten wooden pins at which a ball is bowled to knock them down. **2. tenpin,** a pin used in this game. [1590–1600; TEN + PIN + -S[3]]

ten·pound·er (ten′poun′dər), *n.* **1.** ladyfish. **2.** the machete, *Elops affinis,* a common food fish of warm seas. [1685–95; *ten pound(s)* + -ER[1]]

CONCISE ETYMOLOGY KEY: <, descended or borrowed from; >, whence; b., blend of, blended; c., cognate with; cf., compare; deriv., derivative; equiv., equivalent; imit., imitative; obl., oblique; r., replacing; s., stem; sp., spelling, spelled; resp., respelling, respelled; trans., translation; ?, origin unknown; *, unattested; ‡, probably earlier than. See the full key inside the front cover.

tenrec, *Tenrec ecaudatus,* length 14 in. (36 cm)

ten•rec (ten′rek), *n.* any of several insectivorous mammals of the family Tenrecidae, of Madagascar, having a long, pointed snout, certain species of which are spiny and tailless. Also, **tanrec.** [1720–30; < F < Malagasy *tàndraka*]

TENS (tenz), *n. Med.* a self-operated portable device used to treat chronic pain by sending electrical impulses through electrodes placed over the painful area. [*t*(*ranscutaneous*) *e*(*lectrical*) *n*(*erve*) *s*(*timulator*)]

tense[1] (tens), *adj.,* **tens•er, tens•est,** *v.,* **tensed, tens•ing.** —*adj.* **1.** stretched tight, as a cord, fiber, etc.; drawn taut; rigid. **2.** in a state of mental or nervous strain; high-strung; taut: *a tense person.* **3.** characterized by a strain upon the nerves or feelings: *a tense moment.* **4.** *Phonet.* pronounced with relatively tense tongue muscles; narrow. Cf. **lax** (def. 7). —*v.t., v.i.* **5.** to make or become tense. [1660–70; < L *tēnsus* ptp. of *tendere* to stretch; see TEND[1]] —**tense′ly,** *adv.* —**tense′•ness,** *n.*

tense[2] (tens), *n.* **1.** a category of verbal inflection that serves chiefly to specify the time of the action or state expressed by the verb. **2.** a set of such categories or constructions in a particular language. **3.** the time, as past, present, or future, expressed by such a category. **4.** such categories or constructions, or their meanings collectively. [1275–1325; ME *tens* < MF < L *tempus* time] —**tense′less,** *adj.* —**tense′less•ly,** *adv.* —**tense′less•ness,** *n.*

ten•seg•ri•ty (ten seg′ri tē), *n. Archit.* **1.** the property of skeleton structures that employ continuous tension members and discontinuous compression members in such a way that each member operates with the maximum efficiency and economy. —*adj.* **2.** noting any of a series of structures developed by R. Buckminster Fuller that embody this property. [TENS(ION) + (INT)EGRITY]

ten•si•ble (ten′sə bəl), *adj.* capable of being stretched; tensile. [1620–30; < NL *tēnsibilis.* See TENSE[1], -IBLE] —**ten′si•bil′i•ty, ten′si•ble•ness,** *n.* —**ten′si•bly,** *adv.*

ten•sile (ten′səl, -sil *or, esp. Brit.,* -sīl), *adj.* **1.** of or pertaining to tension: *tensile strain.* **2.** capable of being stretched or drawn out; ductile. [1620–30; < NL *tēnsilis.* See TENSE[1], -ILE] —**ten•sil•i•ty** (ten sil′i tē), **ten′sile•ness,** *n.* —**ten′sile•ly,** *adv.*

ten′sile strength′, the resistance of a material to longitudinal stress, measured by the minimum amount of longitudinal stress required to rupture the material. [1860–65]

ten•sim•e•ter (ten sim′i tər), *n.* manometer. [1900–05; TENSI(ON) (def. 5) + -METER]

ten•si•om•e•ter (ten′sē om′i tər), *n.* **1.** an instrument for measuring longitudinal stress in wires, structural beams, etc. **2.** an instrument for measuring the surface tension of a liquid. [1910–15; TENSIO(N) + -METER]

ten•sion (ten′shən), *n.* **1.** the act of stretching or straining. **2.** the state of being stretched or strained. **3.** mental or emotional strain; intense, suppressed suspense, anxiety, or excitement. **4.** a strained relationship between individuals, groups, nations, etc. **5.** (not in current use) pressure, esp. of a vapor. **6.** *Mech.* **a.** the longitudinal deformation of an elastic body that results in its elongation. **b.** the force producing such deformation. **7.** *Elect.* electromotive force; potential. **8.** *Mach.* a device for stretching or pulling something. **9.** a device to hold the proper tension on the material being woven in a loom. —*v.t.* **10.** to subject (a cable, belt, tendon, or the like) to tension, esp. for a specific purpose. [1525–35; < L *tēnsiōn-* (s. of *tēnsiō*) a stretching. See TENSE[1], -ION] —**ten′sion•al,** *adj.* —**ten′sion•less,** *adj.*

ten•si•ty (ten′si tē), *n.* the state of being tense; tenseness. [1650–60; < ML *tēnsitās.* See TENSE[1], -ITY]

ten•sive (ten′siv), *adj.* stretching or straining. [1695–1705; TENS(ION) + -IVE; cf. F *tensif*]

ten•son (ten sōn′), *n.* a Provençal poem taking the form of a dialogue or debate between two rival troubadours. [1830–40; < F; OF *tençon* < Pr *tensoun, tenso* contest, dispute < L *tēnsiōn-* (s. of *tēnsiō*); see TENSION]

ten•sor (ten′sər, -sôr), *n.* **1.** *Anat.* a muscle that stretches or tightens some part of the body. **2.** *Math.* a mathematical entity with components that change in a particular way in a transformation from one coordinate system to another. [1695–1705; < NL: stretcher, equiv. to L *tend(ere)* to stretch (see TEND[1]) + *-tor* -TOR, with *dt* > *s*] —**ten•so•ri•al** (ten sôr′ē əl, -sōr′-), *adj.*

ten′sor anal′ysis, the branch of mathematics dealing with the calculus of tensors, esp. the study of properties that are unaffected by a change of coordinate system.

ten-speed (ten′spēd′), *n.* **1.** a system of gears having ten forward gear ratios, esp. on a bicycle. **2.** a bicycle having such a system of gears. —*adj.* **3.** having ten forward gear ratios. [1970–75]

ten′s′ place′, *Math.* ten (def. 6). [1935–40]

ten-spot (ten′spot′), *n.* **1.** a playing card the face of which bears ten pips. **2.** *Slang.* a ten-dollar bill. [1835–45]

ten-strike (ten′strīk′), *n.* **1.** *Tenpins.* a strike. **2.** *Informal.* any stroke or act that is completely successful. [1830–40]

tent[1] (tent), *n.* **1.** a portable shelter of skins, canvas, plastic, or the like, supported by one or more poles or a frame and often secured by ropes fastened to pegs in the ground. **2.** something that resembles a tent. **3.** tent dress. —*v.t.* **4.** to lodge in tents. **5.** to cover with or as if with a tent: *In winter the tennis courts are tented in plastic.* —*v.i.* **6.** to live in a tent; encamp. [1250–1300; ME *tente* < OF < L *tenta,* fem. of *tentus* ptp. of *tendere* to extend, stretch; cf. *tentōrium* tent] —**tent′less,** *adj.* —**tent′like′,** *adj.*

tent[2] (tent), *v.t. Chiefly Scot.* to give or pay attention to; heed. [1250–1300; ME, deriv. of *tent* (n.) attention, aph. var. of *attent* < OF *atente* attention, intention < L *attenta,* fem. of *attentus,* ptp. of *attendere* to ATTEND]

tent[3] (tent), *Surg.* —*n.* **1.** a probe. **2.** a roll or pledget, usually of soft absorbent material, as lint or gauze, for dilating an orifice, keeping a wound open, etc. —*v.t.* **3.** to keep (a wound) open with a tent. [1325–75; ME *tente* a probe < MF, n. deriv. of *tenter* < L *tentāre,* var. of *temptāre* to probe, test. See TEMPT]

ten•ta•cle (ten′tə kəl), *n.* **1.** *Zool.* any of various slender, flexible processes or appendages in animals, esp. invertebrates, that serve as organs of touch, prehension, etc.; feeler. **2.** *Bot.* a sensitive filament or process, as one of the glandular hairs of the sundew. [1755–65; < NL *tentāculum,* equiv. to L *tentā(re)* (var. of *temptāre* to feel, probe) + *-culum* -CULE[2]] —**ten•tac•u•lar** (ten tak′yə lər), *adj.* —**ten′ta•cle•like′, ten•tac′u•loid′,** *adj.*

ten•ta•cled (ten′tə kəld), *adj.* having tentacles. Also, **ten•tac•u•lat•ed** (ten tak′yə lā′tid). [1855–60; TENTACLE + -ED[3]]

tent•age (ten′tij), *n.* tents collectively; equipment or supply of tents. [1595–1605; TENT[1] + -AGE]

ten•ta•tion (ten tā′shən), *n.* a method of making mechanical adjustments or the like by a succession of trials. [1875–80; < L *tentātiōn-* (s. of *tentātiō*) trial, var. of *temptātiō.* See TEMPTATION]

ten•ta•tive (ten′tə tiv), *adj.* **1.** of the nature of or made or done as a trial, experiment, or attempt; experimental: *a tentative report on her findings.* **2.** unsure; uncertain; not definite or positive; hesitant: *a tentative smile on his face.* [1580–90; < ML *tentātīvus,* equiv. to L *tentāt(us)* (ptp. of *tentāre,* var. of *temptāre* to test; see TEMPT) + *-īvus* -IVE] —**ten′ta•tive•ly,** *adv.* —**ten′ta•tive•ness,** *n.*

tent′ bed′, a field bed having a canopy in the form of a tent. [1745–55]

tent′ cat′erpillar, 1. any of the larvae of several moths of the genus *Malacosoma,* which feed on the leaves of orchard and shade trees and live colonially in a tentlike silken web. **2.** the North American larva of *M. disstria* **(forest tent caterpillar),** which spins a dense net. [1850–55, *Amer.*]

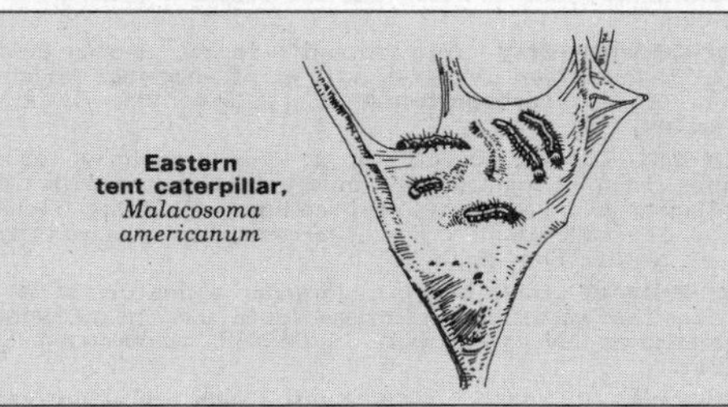

Eastern tent caterpillar, *Malacosoma americanum*

tent′ cir′cus, a circus performed in tents rather than in an arena. [1945–50, *Amer.*]

tent′ cit′y, an area set up with tents, esp. as to house homeless or displaced persons.

tent′ dress′, a loose-fitting dress that gradually flares outward or grows fuller from the shoulder to the hem and has no waistline. Also called **tent.**

tent•ed (ten′tid), *adj.* **1.** covered with or living in a tent or tents. **2.** shaped like a tent. [1595–1605; TENT[1] + -ED[3]]

ten•ter (ten′tər), *n.* **1.** a framework on which cloth in the process of manufacture is stretched so it may set or dry evenly. **2.** *Obs.* a tenterhook. —*v.t.* **3.** to stretch (cloth) on a tenter or tenters. —*v.i.* **4.** to be capable of being tentered. [1300–50; ME *tente* to stretch (< L *tentus,* var. of *tēnsus* TENSE[1]) + -ER[1]; r. ME *teyntur,* of unclear derivation]

ten•ter•hook (ten′tər ho͝ok′), *n.* **1.** one of the hooks or bent nails that hold cloth stretched on a tenter. **2. on tenterhooks,** in a state of uneasy suspense or painful anxiety: *The movie keeps one on tenterhooks until the very last moment.* [1470–80; TENTER + HOOK]

tent′ fly′, fly[1] (def. 28). [1840–50, *Amer.*]

tenth (tenth), *adj.* **1.** next after ninth; being the ordinal number for ten. **2.** being one of ten equal parts. —*n.* **3.** one of ten equal parts, esp. of one (1/10). **4.** the member of a series preceding the eleventh and following the ninth. **5.** *Music.* **a.** a tone distant from another tone by an interval of an octave and a third. **b.** the interval between such tones. **c.** the harmonic combination of such tones. **6.** Also called **tenth's′ place′.** (in decimal notation) the position of the first digit to the right of the decimal point. —*adv.* **7.** in the tenth place; tenthly. [bef. 1150; ME *tenthe,* OE. See TEN, -TH[2], TITHE]

Tenth′ Amend′ment, an amendment to the U.S. Constitution, ratified in 1791 as part of the Bill of Rights, guaranteeing to the states and the people those rights that are not delegated to the federal government by the Constitution.

Tenth′ Command′ment, "Thou shalt not covet thy neighbour's house, thou shalt not covet thy neighbour's wife, nor his manservant, nor his maidservant, nor his ox, nor his ass, nor any thing that is thy neighbour's": tenth of the Ten Commandments. Cf. **Ten Commandments.**

tenth•ly (tenth′lē), *adv.* in the tenth place; tenth. [TENTH + -LY]

tent•ie (ten′tē), *adj.,* **tent•i•er, tent•i•est.** *Scot.* tenty.

tent•mak•er (tent′mā′kər), *n.* a person who makes tents. [1555–65; TENT[1] + MAKER]

tent′ meet′ing. See **camp meeting.** [1865–70, *Amer.*] —**tent′-meet′ing,** *adj.*

ten•to•ri•um (ten tôr′ē əm, -tōr′-), *n., pl.* **-to•ri•a** (-tôr′ē ə, -tōr′-). **1.** *Anat.* an extension of one of the membranes covering the cerebrum which, with the transverse fissure, separates the cerebrum from the cerebellum. **2.** *Zool.* (of an insect) the internal skeleton of the head. [1655–65; < NL *tentōrium,* L: tent, equiv. to *ten(dere)* to extend, stretch + *-tōrium* -TORY[2]] —**ten•to′ri•al,** *adj.*

tent′ show′, an exhibition or performance, esp. a circus, presented in a tent.

tent′ stitch′, a short, slanting stitch used in embroidery. Cf. **gros point** (def. 1), **petit point** (def. 1). [1630–40]

tent′ trail′er, an automobile-drawn recreational trailer with a folding canvas or other fabric shelter that makes the vehicle suitable for outdoor camping. Cf. **camper** (def. 3), **trailer** (def. 2). [1960–65]

tent•y (ten′tē), *adj.,* **tent•i•er, tent•i•est.** *Scot.* watchful; attentive. Also, **tentie.** [1545–55; TENT[2] + -Y[1]]

ten•u•is (ten′yo͞o is), *n., pl.* **ten•u•es** (ten′yo͞o ēz′). an unaspirated, voiceless plosive. [1640–50; < L: thin, fine, slender; akin to THIN]

te•nu•i•ty (tə no͞o′i tē, -nyo͞o′-, te-), *n.* **1.** the state of being tenuous. **2.** slenderness. **3.** thinness of consistency; rarefied condition. [1525–35; < L *tenuitās* thinness, equiv. to *tenui(s)* (see TENUIS) + *-tās* -TY[2]]

ten•u•ous (ten′yo͞o əs), *adj.* **1.** thin or slender in form, as a thread. **2.** lacking a sound basis, as reasoning; unsubstantiated; weak: *a tenuous argument.* **3.** thin in consistency; rare or rarefied. **4.** of slight importance or significance; unsubstantial: *He holds a rather tenuous position in history.* **5.** lacking in clarity; vague: *He gave a rather tenuous account of his past life.* [1590–1600; TENU(ITY) + -OUS] —**ten′u•ous•ly,** *adv.* —**ten′u•ous•ness,** *n.*

—**Syn. 1.** attenuated. **4.** insignificant, unimportant, trivial, trifling. —**Ant. 1.** thick. **4.** important, substantial.

ten•ure (ten′yər), *n.* **1.** the holding or possessing of anything: *the tenure of an office.* **2.** the holding of property, esp. real property, of a superior in return for services to be rendered. **3.** the period or term of holding something. **4.** status granted to an employee, usually after a probationary period, indicating that the position or employment is permanent. —*v.t.* **5.** to give tenure to: *After she served three years on probation, the committee tenured her.* [1250–1300; ME < AF; OF *teneure* < VL **tenitura,* equiv. to **tenit(us)* held (for L *tentus,* ptp. of *tenēre*) + *-ura* -URE] —**ten•u•ri•al** (ten yo͝or′ē əl), *adj.* —**ten•u′ri•al•ly,** *adv.*

ten•ured (ten′yərd), *adj.* **1.** of, having, or eligible for tenure, esp. in a college or university: *There are three tenured professors in the history department.* **2.** granting, allowing, or leading to tenure: *None of the advertised jobs is a tenured position.* [1960–65; TENURE + -ED[3]]

te•nu•to (tə no͞o′tō; *It.* te no͞o′tô), *adj. Music.* (of a note, chord, or rest) held to the full time value. [1890–95; < It: held (ptp. of *tenere*) < VL **tenūtus,* for L *tentus*]

ten′-weeks′ stock′ (ten′wēks′), a stock, *Matthiola incana annua,* of the mustard family, having spikes of white, lilac, or crimson flowers. [1775–85]

Ten-Wheel•er (ten′hwē′lər, -wē′-), *n.* a steam locomotive having a four-wheeled front truck, six driving wheels, and no rear truck. See table under **Whyte classification.** [1900–05]

Ten′ Years′ War′, a popular insurrection in Cuba (1868–78) against Spanish rule.

Ten•zing (ten′zing), *n.* (*Norgay*) 1913?–86, Nepalese mountain climber who scaled Mt. Everest 1953.

te•o•cal•li (tē′ə kal′ē, tā′ə kä′lē; *Sp.* te′ô kä′yē), *n., pl.* **-cal•lis** (-kal′ēz, -kä′lēz; *Sp.* -kä′yēs). a ceremonial structure of the Aztecs, consisting of a truncated terraced pyramid supporting a temple. [1605–15; < Nahuatl, equiv. to *teō(tl)* god + *calli* house]

Te•ó•fi•lo O•to•ni (ti ô′fi lo͝o o͞o tô′nē), a city in E central Brazil. 134,476. Also, **Theophilo Ottoni.**

te•o•sin•te (tē′ə sin′tē, tā′-), *n.* a tall grass, *Zea mexicana,* of Mexico and Central America, closely related to corn, and sometimes cultivated as a fodder plant. [1875–80; < MexSp < Nahuatl *teōcintli,* equiv. to *teō(tl)* god + *cintli* dried ear of maize]

Te•o•ti•hua•cán (te′ô tē′wä kän′), *n.* the ruins of an ancient Mesoamerican city in central Mexico, near Mexico City, that flourished A.D. c200–c750 and is the site of the pyramids of the Sun and Moon and of many temples, palaces, and dwellings.

te•pal (tē′pəl, tep′əl), *n. Bot.* one of the divisions of a flower perianth, esp. one that is not clearly differentiated into petals and sepals, as in lilies and tulips. [< F *tépale* (1827), alter. of *pétale* petal, on the model of *sépale* sepal; coined by Augustin-Pierre de Candolle (1778–1841), Swiss botanist]

tep′a•ry bean′ (tep′ə rē), a twining or bushy plant, *Phaseolus acutifolius latifolius,* of the legume family, native to Mexico and Arizona, having white or violet-colored flowers, grown as a food plant in dry regions. [1910–15, *Amer.*; orig. uncert.]

te•pe (tep′ē; *Turk.* te′pe), *n.* (in Turkey, Iran, and Iraq) tell[2]. [< Turk: hill]

te·pee (tē′pē), *n.* a tent of the American Indians, made usually from animal skins laid on a conical frame of long poles and having an opening at the top for ventilation and a flap door. Also, **teepee, tipi.** Cf. **lodge** (def. 9), **wigwam.** [1735–45, *Amer.*; < Dakota *tʰípi,* equiv. to *tʰí-* to dwell + *-pi* pl. indefinite abstract n. suffix]

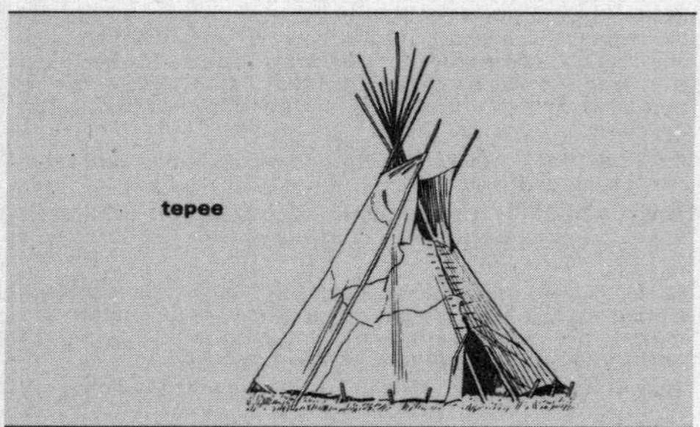

Te·pe Gaw·ra (*Turk.* te′pe gou rä′), an archaeological site in N Iraq, near Mosul: excavations have revealed that numerous settlements have occupied this site since c5000 B.C.

Te′pex·pán man′ (tep′ə spän′, tep′ə spän′), an early human known from skeletal remains found near Tepexpán, Mexico, and dating c10,000–8000 B.C.

te·phil·lin (*Ashk. Heb., Eng.* tə fil′in; *Seph. Heb.* tə fē lēn′), *n.pl. Judaism.* tefillin.

teph·ra (tef′rə), *n.* (*used with a plural v.*) clastic volcanic material, as scoria, dust, etc., ejected during an eruption. [1960–65; < Gk *téphra* (sing.) ashes]

teph·rite (tef′rīt), *n. Petrog.* a basaltic rock consisting essentially of pyroxene and plagioclase with nepheline or leucite. [1875–80; < Gk *tephr(ós)* ash-colored + -ITE[1]] **—teph·rit·ic** (tef rit′ik), *adj.*

teph·ro·chro·nol·o·gy (tef′rō krə nol′ə jē), *n. Geol.* a geochronologic technique based on the dating of layers of volcanic ash. Cf. **tephra.** [1940–45; < Sw *tefrokronologi,* equiv. to *tefr(a)* volcanic ejecta (< Gk *téphra* ash) + *-o-* -O- + *kronologi* CHRONOLOGY] **—teph·ro·chron·o·log·i·cal** (tef′rō kron′l oj′i kəl), *adj.*

teph·ro·ite (tef′rō īt′), *n.* a mineral, silicate of manganese, Mn_2SiO_4, occurring in orthorhombic crystals. [< G *Tephroit* < Gk *tephró(s)* ash gray + G *-it* -ITE[1]]

Te·pic (te pēk′), *n.* a city in and the capital of Nayarit, W central Mexico. 114,512.

tep·id (tep′id), *adj.* **1.** moderately warm; lukewarm: *tepid water.* **2.** characterized by a lack of force or enthusiasm: *tepid prose; the critics' tepid reception for the new play.* [1350–1400; ME < L *tepidus* lukewarm, equiv. to *tep(ēre)* to be lukewarm + *-idus* -ID[4]] **—te·pid′i·ty, tep′id·ness,** *n.* **—tep′id·ly,** *adv.*
—Syn. 1 moderate, mild. **2.** unemotional, half-hearted, apathetic.

TEPP, *Chem.* See **tetraethyl pyrophosphate.**

te·qui·la (tə kē′lə), *n.* **1.** a strong liquor from Mexico, distilled from fermented mash of an agave. **2.** the plant itself, *Agave tequilana.* [1840–50; after *Tequila,* a town in Jalisco, Mexico, a center for its production]

ter (tûr), *adv.* (in prescriptions) three times. [< L]

ter-, a combining form meaning "thrice," used in the formation of compound words: *tercentennial.* [< L, comb. form of *ter;* akin to *trēs* THREE]

ter., **1.** (in prescriptions) rub. [< L *tere*] **2.** terrace. **3.** territorial. **4.** territory.

tera-, **1.** a combining form used in the names of units of measure equal to one trillion of a given base unit: *terahertz.* **2.** *Computers.* a combining form of like function with the value 2^{40} (=1,099,511,627,766). *Abbr.:* T [< Gk *téras* monster. See TERATO-]

ter·a·flops (ter′ə flops′), *n.* a measure of computer speed, equal to one trillion floating-point operations per second. [1985–90; see FLOPS]

Te·rah (tēr′ə, ter′ä), *n.* the father of Abraham. Gen. 11:25–32.

ter·a·hertz (ter′ə hûrts′), *n., pl.* **-hertz, -hertz·es.** one trillion (10^{12}) hertz. *Abbr:* THz [TERA- + HERTZ]

Te·rai (tə rī′), *n.* **1.** a marshy lowland area in N India and S Nepal, between the Ganges and the foothills of the Himalayas. **2.** (*l.c.*) See **terai hat.** Also, **Tarai.**

terai′ hat′, a felt sun helmet with a high crown and wide brim, worn esp. in the subtropics. [1895–1900; named after TERAI]

ter·a·phim (ter′ə fim), *n.pl., sing.* **ter·aph** (ter′əf). idols or images reverenced by the ancient Hebrews and kindred peoples, apparently as household gods. [1350–1400; < Heb *tərāphīm;* r. ME *theraphym* < LL *theraphim* (Vulgate) < Gk *theraphín* (Septuagint) < Heb]

terat-, var. of **terato-** before a vowel: *teratoid.*

ter·a·tism (ter′ə tiz′əm), *n.* **1.** love or worship of the monstrous. **2.** *Biol.* a monstrosity. [TERAT- + -ISM]

terato-, a combining form meaning "monster," used in the formation of compound words: *teratology.* Also, *esp. before a vowel,* **terat-.** [< Gk *terat-* (s. of *téras*) monster, marvel + -O-]

te·rat·o·gen (tə rat′ə jən, -jen′, ter′ə tə-), *n. Biol.* a drug or other substance capable of interfering with the development of a fetus, causing birth defects. [1900–05; TERATO- + -GEN] **—te·rat′o·gen′ic,** *adj.*

te·rat·o·gen·e·sis (tə rat′ə jen′ə sis, ter′ə tə-), *n. Biol.* the production or induction of malformations or monstrosities, esp. of a developing embryo or fetus. Also called **ter·a·tog·e·ny** (ter′ə toj′ə nē), **te·rat·o·ge·nic·i·ty** (tə rat′ō jə nis′i tē, ter′ə tō-). [1900–05; TERATO- + -GENESIS] **—te·rat·o·ge·net·ic** (tə rat′ō jə net′ik, ter′ə tō-), *adj.*

ter·a·toid (ter′ə toid′), *adj. Biol.* resembling a monster. [1875–80; TERAT- + -OID]

ter·a·tol·o·gy (ter′ə tol′ə jē), *n. Biol.* the science or study of monstrosities or abnormal formations in organisms. [1670–80; TERATO- + -LOGY] **—ter·a·to·log·i·cal** (ter′ə tl oj′i kəl), *adj.* **—ter′a·tol′o·gist,** *n.*

ter·a·to·ma (ter′ə tō′mə), *n., pl.* **-mas, -ma·ta** (-mə tə). *Pathol.* a tumor made up of different types of tissue. [1885–90; TERAT- + -OMA]

ter·a·to·sis (ter′ə tō′sis), *n. Biol.* teratism (def. 2). [< NL; see TERAT-, -OSIS]

ter·bi·a (tûr′bē ə), *n. Chem.* an amorphous white powder, Tb_2O_3. Also called **ter′bium ox′ide.** [1905–10; < NL; see TERBIUM, -IA]

ter·bi·um (tûr′bē əm), *n. Chem.* a rare-earth, metallic element present in certain minerals and yielding colorless salts. *Symbol:* Tb; *at. no.:* 65; *at. wt.:* 158.924; *sp. gr.:* 8.25. [1835–45; *(Yt)terb(y),* name of Swedish town where found + -IUM. See YTTERBIUM] **—ter′bic,** *adj.*

ter′bium met′al, *Chem.* any of a subgroup of rare-earth metals, of which the cerium and yttrium metals comprise the other two subgroups.

Ter Borch (tər bôrkh′), *n.* **Ge·rard** (khä′rärt), 1617–81, Dutch painter. Also, **Ter·borch′, Ter·burg** (tər bo͝orkh′).

ter·bu·ta·line (tər byo͞ot′l ēn′), *n. Pharm.* a selective beta-adrenergic receptor agonist substance, $C_{12}H_{19}NO_3$, used in the treatment of asthma. [TER- + BUT(YL) + -AL[3] + -INE[2]]

terce (tûrs), *n. Eccles.* tierce (def. 3).

Ter·cei·ra (tər sā′rə), *n.* an island in the Azores, in the N Atlantic. 153 sq. mi. (395 sq. km). *Cap.:* Angra do Heroismo.

ter·cel (tûr′səl), *n. Falconry.* the male of a hawk, esp. of a gyrfalcon or peregrine. Also, **terce·let** (tûrs′lit), **tiercel.** [1350–1400; ME < MF *terçuel* < VL **tertiolus,* equiv. to L *terti(us)* third + *-olus* -OLE[1]; prob. so called because the male is about one third smaller than the female]

ter·cen·ten·ar·y (tûr′sen ten′ə rē, tûr sen′tn er′ē; *esp. Brit.* tûr′sen tē′nə rē), *adj., n., pl.* **-nar·ies.** tricentennial. Also, **ter′cen·ten′ni·al.** [1835–45; TER- + CENTENARY]

ter·cet (tûr′sit, tûr set′), *n.* **1.** *Pros.* a group of three lines rhyming together or connected by rhyme with the adjacent group or groups of three lines. **2.** *Music.* triplet (def. 5). [1590–1600; < F < It *terzetto,* dim. of *terzo* third < L *tertius.* See -ET]

ter·e·bene (ter′ə bēn′), *n. Pharm.* a mixture of terpenes that occurs as a colorless liquid, used in medicine chiefly as an expectorant. [1855–60; TEREB(INTH) + -ENE]

te·reb·ic (tə reb′ik, -rē′bik), *adj. Chem.* of or derived from terebic acid. Also, **ter·e·bin·ic** (ter′ə bin′ik). [1855–60; TEREB(INTH) + -IC]

tereb′ic ac′id, *Chem.* an acid, $C_7H_{10}O_4$, formed by the oxidation of certain terpenes and historically important in the discovery of the structures of many terpenes. Also, **ter′ebin′ic ac′id.** [1855–60]

ter·e·binth (ter′ə binth), *n.* a Mediterranean tree, *Pistacia terebinthus,* of the cashew family, yielding Chian turpentine. [1350–1400; < L *terebinthus* < Gk *terébinthos* turpentine tree; r. ME *therebinte* < MF < L, as above]

ter·e·bin·thi·nate (ter′ə bin′thə nāt′), *adj.* of, pertaining to, or resembling turpentine. [1670–80; TEREBINTHINE + -ATE[1]]

ter·e·bin·thine (ter′ə bin′thin, -thīn), *adj.* **1.** terebinthinate. **2.** of or pertaining to the terebinth. [1505–15; TEREBINTH + -INE[1]]

te·re·do (tə rē′dō), *n., pl.* **-re·dos, -red·i·nes** (-red′n-ēz′). a shipworm of the genus *Teredo.* [1350–1400; ME < L *terēdō* < Gk *terēdṓn* wood-boring worm]

te·re·fah (tə rä′fə, trā′-), *n. Judaism.* tref.

Ter·ence (ter′əns), *n.* **1.** (*Publius Terentius Afer*) c190–159? B.C., Roman playwright. **2.** a male given name: taken from a Roman family name.

Te·reng·ga·nu (tə reng gä′no͞o), *n.* Trengganu.

ter·eph·thal·ate (ter′ef thal′āt, -it, tə ref′thə lāt′), *n. Chem.* a salt or ester of terephthalic acid. [1865–70; TEREPHTHAL(IC ACID) + -ATE[2]]

ter′eph·thal′ic ac′id (ter′ef thal′ik, ter′-), *Chem.* a white, crystalline, water-insoluble solid, $C_8H_6O_2$, the para isomer of phthalic acid: used chiefly in the manufacture of resins and textile fibers. [1855–60; TERE(BIC) + PHTHALIC]

Te·re·sa (tə rē′sə, -zə, -rā′-; *for 2 also Sp.* te re′sä), *n.* **1. Mother** (*Agnes Gonxha Bojaxhiu*), born 1910, Albanian nun: Nobel peace prize 1979 for work in the slums of Calcutta, India. **2. Saint.** See **Theresa, Saint. 3.** a female given name, form of **Theresa.**

Te·resh·ko·va (ter′əsh kō′və; *Russ.* tyi ryi shkô′və), *n.* **Va·len·ti·na Vla·di·mi·rov·na** (və lyin tyē′nə vlə dyi myē′rəv nə), born 1937, Soviet cosmonaut: first woman in space 1963.

Te·re·sian (tə rē′zhən), *n.* **1.** a member of the reformed order of barefooted Carmelites, founded in Spain in 1562. —*adj.* **2.** of or pertaining to St. Theresa or the Teresians. [1620–30; Saint TERES(A) + -IAN]

Te·re·si·na (ti ri zē′nä), *n.* a port in NE Brazil, on the Parnahiba River. 388,922. Formerly, **Therezina.**

te·rete (tə rēt′, ter′ēt), *adj.* **1.** slender and smooth, with a circular transverse section. **2.** cylindrical or slightly tapering. [1610–20; earlier *teret* < L *teret-* (s. of *teres*) smooth and round, akin to *terere* to rub]

Te·re·us (tēr′ē əs, tēr′yo͞os), *n. Class. Myth.* a Thracian prince, the husband of Procne, who raped his sister-in-law Philomela and was changed into a hoopoe as a punishment.

ter·gal (tûr′gəl), *adj.* of or pertaining to the tergum. [1855–60; TERG(UM) + -AL[1]]

ter·gite (tûr′jīt), *n.* the dorsal sclerite of an abdominal segment of an insect. [1880–85; TERG(UM) + -ITE[1]]

ter·gi·ver·sate (tûr′ji vər sāt′), *v.i.,* **-sat·ed, -sat·ing. 1.** to change repeatedly one's attitude or opinions with respect to a cause, subject, etc.; equivocate. **2.** to turn renegade. [1645–55; < L *tergiversātus* (ptp. of *tergiversārī* to turn one's back), equiv. to *tergi-* (comb. form of *tergum* back) + *versātus,* ptp. of *versāre,* freq. of *vertere* to turn; see -ATE[1]] **—ter′gi·ver·sa′tion,** *n.* **—ter′gi·ver·sa′tor, ter·gi·ver·sant** (tûr′ji vûr′sənt), *n.* **—ter·gi·ver·sa·to·ry** (tûr′ji vûr′sə tôr′ē, -tōr′ē), *adj.*

ter·gum (tûr′gəm), *n., pl.* **-ga** (-gə). *Zool.* the dorsal surface of a body segment of an arthropod. [1820–30; < L: the back]

Ter·hune (tər hyo͞on′), *n.* **Albert Pay·son** (pā′sən), 1872–1942, U.S. novelist and short-story writer.

ter·i·ya·ki (ter′ə yä′kē), *n. Japanese Cookery.* **1.** a dish of grilled slices of beef, chicken, or fish that have been marinated in soy sauce seasoned with sake, ginger, and sugar. —*adj.* **2.** prepared in this manner: *chicken teriyaki.* [1960–65; < Japn, equiv. to *teri* glaze + *yaki* broil]

term (tûrm), *n.* **1.** a word or group of words designating something, esp. in a particular field, as *atom* in physics, *quietism* in theology, *adze* in carpentry, or *district leader* in politics. **2.** any word or group of words considered as a member of a construction or utterance. **3.** the time or period through which something lasts. **4.** a period of time to which limits have been set: *elected for a term of four years.* **5.** one of two or more divisions of a school year, during which instruction is regularly provided. **6.** an appointed or set time or date, as for the payment of rent, interest, wages, etc. **7. terms, a.** conditions with regard to payment, price, charge, rates, wages, etc.: *reasonable terms.* **b.** conditions or stipulations limiting what is proposed to be granted or done: *the terms of a treaty.* **c.** footing or standing; relations: *on good terms with someone.* **d.** *Obs.* state, situation, or circumstances. **8.** *Algebra, Arith.* **a.** each of the members of which an expression, a series of quantities, or the like, is composed, as one of two or more parts of an algebraic expression. **b.** a mathematical expression of the form ax^p, ax^py^q, etc., where *a, p,* and *q* are numbers and *x* and *y* are variables. **9.** *Logic.* **a.** the subject or predicate of a categorical proposition. **b.** the word or expression denoting the subject or predicate of a categorical proposition. **10.** Also called **terminus.** a figure, esp. of Terminus, in the form of a herm, used by the ancient Romans as a boundary marker; terminal figure. **11.** *Law.* **a.** an estate or interest in land or the like, to be enjoyed for a fixed period. **b.** the duration of an estate. **c.** each of the periods during which certain courts of law hold their sessions. **12.** completion of pregnancy; parturition. **13.** *Archaic.* **a.** end, conclusion, or termination. **b.** boundary or limit. **14. bring to terms,** to force to agree to stated demands or conditions; bring into submission: *After a long struggle, we brought them to terms.* **15. come to terms, a.** to reach an agreement; make an arrangement: *to come to terms with a creditor.* **b.** to become resigned or accustomed: *to come to terms with one's life.* **16. eat one's terms,** *Brit. Informal.* to study for the bar; be a law student. **17. in terms of,** with regard to; concerning: *The book offers nothing in terms of a satisfactory conclusion.* —*v.t.* **18.** to apply a particular term or name to; name; call; designate. [1175–1225; ME *terme* < OF < L *terminus* boundary, limit, end; akin to Gk *térmōn* limit] **—term′ly,** *adv.*

term., **1.** terminal. **2.** termination.

ter·ma·gant (tûr′mə gənt), *n.* **1.** a violent, turbulent, or brawling woman. **2.** (*cap.*) a mythical deity popularly believed in the Middle Ages to be worshiped by the Muslims and introduced into the morality play as a violent, overbearing personage in long robes. —*adj.* **3.** violent; turbulent; brawling; shrewish. [1175–1225; ME *Termagaunt,* earlier *Tervagaunt,* alter. of OF *Tervagan* name of the imaginary deity] **—ter′ma·gant·ly,** *adv.*
—Syn. 1. shrew, virago, harridan, scold.

term′ day′, a fixed or appointed day, as for the payment of money due; a quarter day. [1250–1300; ME]

term·er (tûr′mər), *n.* a person who is serving a term, esp. in prison (usually used in combination): *a first-termer.* [1625–35; TERM + -ER[1]]

ter·mi·na·ble (tûr′mə nə bəl), *adj.* **1.** capable of being terminated. **2.** (of an annuity) coming to an end after a certain term. [1375–1425; late ME, equiv. to *termin(en)* to end (< L *termināre*) + -ABLE] **—ter′mi·na·bil′i·ty, ter′mi·na·ble·ness,** *n.* **—ter′mi·na·bly,** *adv.*

ter·mi·nal (tûr′mə nl), *adj.* **1.** situated at or forming the end or extremity of something: *a terminal feature of a vista.* **2.** occurring at or forming the end of a series, succession, or the like; closing; concluding. **3.** pertaining to or lasting for a term or definite period; occurring at fixed terms or in every term: *terminal payments.* **4.** pertaining to, situated at, or forming the terminus of a railroad. **5.** *Bot.* growing at the end of a branch or stem, as a bud or inflorescence. **6.** *Archit.* noting a figure, as a herm or term, in the form of a bust upon a gaine. **7.** pertaining to or placed at a boundary, as a landmark. **8.** occurring at or causing the end of life: *a terminal disease.* **9.** *Informal.* utterly beyond hope, rescue, or saving: *The undercapitalized project is a terminal problem.* —*n.* **10.** a terminal part of a structure; end or extremity. **11.** *Railroads.* a major assemblage of station, yard, maintenance, and repair facilities, as at a terminus, at which trains originate or terminate, or at which they are distributed or combined. **12.** *Computers.* any device for

entering information into a computer or receiving information from it, as a keyboard with video display unit, either adjoining the computer or at some distance from it. **13.** a station on the line of a public carrier, as in a city center or at an airport, where passengers embark or disembark and where freight is received or discharged. **14.** *Elect.* **a.** the mechanical device by means of which an electric connection to an apparatus is established. **b.** the point of current entry to, or point of current departure from, any conducting component in an electric circuit. **15.** *Archit.* **a.** a herm or term. **b.** a carving or the like at the end of something, as a finial. [1480–90; late ME < L *terminālis,* equiv. to *termin(us)* end, limit + *-ālis* -AL[1]] —**ter′mi·nal·ly,** *adv.*
—**Syn. 1, 2.** final, ending, ultimate. **8.** fatal, mortal, lethal.

ter′minal junc′ture, *Phonet.* a form of juncture consisting of a change in pitch before a pause, marking the end of an utterance or a break between utterances, as between clauses. Cf. **close juncture, juncture** (def. 7), **open juncture.** [1955–60]

ter′minal leave′, the final leave granted to a member of the armed forces just before discharge, equal to the total unused leave accumulated during active service. [1940–45]

ter′minal mar′ket, an organized market in a city into which large quantities of agricultural produce, livestock, etc., are shipped for distribution and sale. [1890–95]

ter′minal moraine′, *Geol.* a moraine marking the farthest advance of a glacier or ice sheet. [1855–60]

ter′minal veloc′ity, 1. *Physics.* **a.** the velocity at which a falling body moves through a medium, as air, when the force of resistance of the medium is equal in magnitude and opposite in direction to the force of gravity. **b.** the maximum velocity of a body falling through a viscous fluid. **2.** *Rocketry, Ballistics.* **a.** the greatest speed that a rocket, missile, etc., attains after burnout or after leaving the barrel of a gun. **b.** the speed of a missile or projectile on impact with its target.

ter·mi·nate (tûr′mə nāt′), *v.,* **-nat·ed, -nat·ing.** —*v.t.* **1.** to bring to an end; put an end to: *to terminate a contract.* **2.** to occur at or form the conclusion of: *The countess's soliloquy terminates the play.* **3.** to bound or limit spatially; form or be situated at the extremity of. **4.** to dismiss from a job; fire: *to terminate employees during a recession.* —*v.i.* **5.** to end, conclude, or cease. **6.** (of a train, bus, or other public conveyance) to end a scheduled run at a certain place: *This train terminates in New York.* **7.** to come to an end (often fol. by *at, in,* or *with*). **8.** to issue or result (usually fol. by *in*). [1580–90; v. use of late ME *terminate* (adj.) limited < L *terminātus,* ptp. of *termināre.* See TERM, -ATE[1]] —**ter′mi·na′tive,** *adj.* —**ter′mi·na′tive·ly,** *adv.*
—**Syn. 1, 2.** end, finish, conclude, close, complete.

ter′minating dec′imal, *Math.* a decimal numeral in which, after a finite number of decimal places, all succeeding place values are 0, as ⅛ = 0.125 (contrasted with *nonterminating decimal*). Also called **finite decimal.** [1905–10]

ter·mi·na·tion (tûr′mə nā′shən), *n.* **1.** the act of terminating **2.** the fact of being terminated. **3.** the place or part where anything terminates; bound or limit. **4.** an end or extremity; close or conclusion. **5.** an issue or result. **6.** *Gram.* a suffix or ending. **7.** an ending of employment with a specific employer. [1400–50; late ME *terminacion* < L *terminātiōn-* (s. of *terminātiō*) decision. See TERMINATE, -ION] —**ter′mi·na′tion·al,** *adj.*

ter·mi·na·tor (tûr′mə nā′tər), *n.* **1.** a person or thing that terminates. **2.** *Astron.* the dividing line between the illuminated and the unilluminated part of a satellite or planet, esp. the moon. [1760–70; < LL *terminātor,* equiv. to *termina(re)* to TERMINATE + *-tor* -TOR]

ter·mi·na·to·ry (tûr′mə nə tôr′ē, -tōr′ē), *adj.* pertaining to or forming the extremity or boundary; terminal; terminating. [1750–60; TERMINATE + -ORY[1]]

ter·mi·nol·o·gy (tûr′mə nol′ə jē), *n., pl.* **-gies. 1.** the system of terms belonging or peculiar to a science, art, or specialized subject; nomenclature: *the terminology of botany.* **2.** the science of terms, as in particular sciences or arts. [1795–1805; < ML *termin(us)* TERM + -O- + -LOGY] —**ter·mi·no·log·i·cal** (tûr′mə nl oj′i kəl), *adj.* —**ter′mi·no·log′i·cal·ly,** *adv.* —**ter′mi·nol′o·gist,** *n.*

term′ insur′ance. an insurance policy that provides coverage for a limited period, the value payable only if a loss occurs within the term, with nothing payable upon its expiration. [1895–1900]

ter·mi·nus (tûr′mə nəs), *n., pl.* **-ni** (-nī′), **-nus·es. 1.** the end or extremity of anything. **2.** either end of a railroad line. **3.** *Brit.* the station or the town at the end of a railway or bus route. **4.** the point toward which anything tends; goal or end. **5.** a boundary or limit. **6.** a boundary post or stone. **7.** (*cap.*) the ancient Roman god of boundaries and landmarks. **8.** term (def. 10). [1545–55; < L: boundary, limit, end]

ter·mi·nus ad quem (teʀ′mi no͝os′ äd kwem′; *Eng.* tûr′mə nəs ad kwem′), *Latin.* the end to which; aim; goal; final or latest limiting point.

ter·mi·nus a quo (teʀ′mi no͝os′ ä kwō′; *Eng.* tûr′mə nəs ā kwō′), *Latin.* the end from which; beginning; starting point; earliest limiting point.

ter·mi·tar·i·um (tûr′mi târ′ē əm), *n., pl.* **-tar·i·a** (-târ′ē ə). a termites' nest. [1860–65; < NL *termit(ēs),* pl. of *termes* TERMITE + -ARIUM]

ter·mi·ta·ry (tûr′mi ter′ē), *n., pl.* **-ries.** termitarium. [1900–05; TERMITE + -ARY]

ter·mite (tûr′mīt), *n.* any of numerous pale-colored, soft-bodied, chiefly tropical social insects, of the order Isoptera, that feed on wood, some being highly destructive to buildings, furniture, etc. Also called **white ant.** [1775–85; taken as sing. of NL *termites,* pl. of *termes* white ant, L *tarmes* wood-eating worm]

termite (worker), *Reticulitermes flavipes,* length ¼ in. (0.6 cm)

ter·mit·ic (tər mit′ik), *adj.* of, pertaining to, produced by, or infested with termites. [1880–85; TERMITE + -IC]

ter·mit·ing (tûr′mī ting), *n.* the poking of a twig down the opening of a termite's nest, performed by certain chimpanzees to collect termites for food. [TERMITE + -ING[1]]

term·less (tûrm′lis), *adj.* **1.** not limited; unconditional. **2.** boundless; endless. [1530–40; TERM + -LESS]

term′ life′ insur′ance, life insurance for which premiums are paid over a limited time and that covers a specific term, the face value payable only if death occurs within that term. Cf. **ordinary life insurance, term insurance.**

ter·mor (tûr′mər), *n. Law.* a person who has an estate for a term of years or for life. [1250–1300; TERM + -OR[2]; r. ME *termur* < AF *termer* (see -ER[2])]

term′ pa′per, a long essay, report, or the like, written by a student as an assignment over the course of a term or semester. [1925–30]

term′ pol′icy, *Insurance.* a policy whose period of coverage is in excess of one year, usually paying a reduced premium rate, as in fire insurance. [1895–1900]

term·wise (tûrm′wīz′), *adv. Math.* term by term: *The series can be integrated termwise. Two series are added termwise.* [1910–15; TERM + -WISE]

tern[1] (tûrn), *n.* any of numerous aquatic birds of the subfamily Sterninae of the family Laridae, related to the gulls but usually having a more slender body and bill, smaller feet, a long, deeply forked tail, and a more graceful flight, esp. those of the genus *Sterna,* as *S. hirundo* **(common tern),** of Eurasia and America, having white, black, and gray plumage. [1670–80; < Dan *terne* or Norw *terna;* c. ON *therna*]

common tern, *Sterna hirundo,* length 15 in. (38 cm); wingspread 2½ ft. (0.8 m)

tern[2] (tûrn), *n.* **1.** a set of three. **2.** three winning numbers drawn together in a lottery. **3.** a prize won by drawing these. [1300–50; ME *terne* < MF < It *terno* < L *ternus,* sing. of *ternī* three each, triad, akin to *ter* thrice; see THREE]

ter·na (ter′nə, tûr′-), *n. Rom. Cath. Ch.* a list of three names submitted to the pope as recommended to fill a vacant bishopric or benefice. [1880–85; short for NL *terna nōmina* three names together, fem. of *ternus.* See TERN[2]]

ter·na·ry (tûr′nə rē), *adj., n., pl.* **-ries.** —*adj.* **1.** consisting of or involving three; threefold; triple. **2.** third in order or rank. **3.** based on the number three. **4.** *Chem.* **a.** consisting of three different elements or groups. **b.** (formerly) consisting of three atoms. **5.** *Math.* having three variables. **6.** *Metall.* (of an alloy) having three principal constituents. —*n.* **7.** a group of three. [1400–50; late ME < L *ternārius* made up of three. See TERN[2], -ARY]

ter′nary form′, a musical form in three sections, with the third usually an exact repetition of the first. [1895–1900]

ter′nary opera′tion, an operation in a mathematical system by which three elements are combined to yield a single result. Cf. **binary operation, unary operation.**

ter·nate (tûr′nit, -nāt), *adj.* **1.** consisting of three; arranged in threes. **2.** *Bot.* **a.** consisting of three leaflets, as a compound leaf. **b.** having leaves arranged in whorls of three, as a plant. [1745–55; < NL *ternātus.* See TERN[2], -ATE[1]] —**ter′nate·ly,** *adv.*

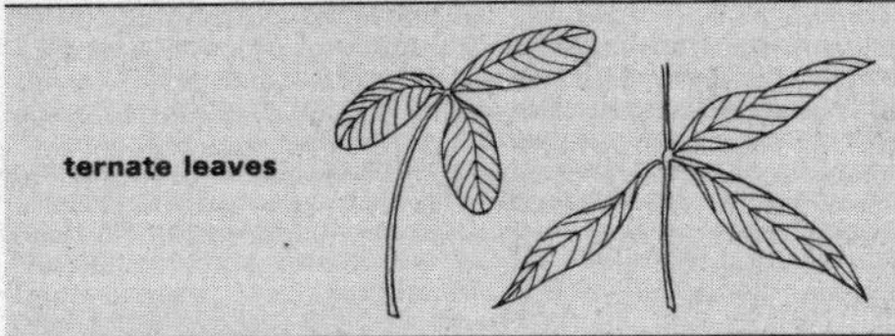
ternate leaves

Ter·na·te (teʀ nä′te; *Eng.* tər nä′tē), *n.* an island in E Indonesia, W of Halmahera: important source of spices. 53 sq. mi. (137 sq. km).

terne′ met′al (tûrn), an alloy of lead and tin used for plating. [see TERNEPLATE]

terne·plate (tûrn′plāt′), *n.* steel plate coated with terne metal. [1855–60; obs. *terne* (< F: dull; see TARNISH) + PLATE[1]]

tern′ foot′, *Furniture.* a foot ending in three scrolls.

Ter·ni (teʀ′nē), *n.* a city in central Italy. 112,534.

ter·ni·on (tûr′nē ən), *n.* a set or group of three; triad. [1580–90; < L *terniōn-* (s. of *terniō*) triad. See TERN[2], -ION]

Ter·no·pol (tər nō′pəl; *Russ.* tyiʀ nô′pəl), *n.* a city in W Ukraine: formerly in Poland. 175,000. Polish, **Tarnopol.**

ter·pene (tûr′pēn), *n. Chem.* **1.** (originally) any of a class of monocyclic hydrocarbons of the formula $C_{10}H_{16}$, obtained from plants. **2.** this class or any of its oxygenated derivatives, any hydrocarbon from the same source having the formula C_5H_8 **(hemiterpene),** the formula $C_{10}H_{16}$ with an aliphatic structure **(acyclic terpene)** or two-ringed structure **(bicyclic terpene),** the formula $C_{15}H_{24}$ **(sesquiterpene),** etc., and any of their oxygenated derivatives. [1865–70; alter. of TEREBENE, with *p* from TURPENTINE] —**ter′pene·less,** *adj.* —**ter·pe·nic** (tûr pē′nik), *adj.*

ter·pin·e·ol (tûr pin′ē ôl′, -ol′), *n. Chem.* any of several unsaturated, cyclic, tertiary alcohols having the formula $C_{10}H_{18}O$, occurring in nature in many essential oils or prepared synthetically: used chiefly in the manufacture of perfumes. [1840–50; *terpine* (TERP(ENE) + -INE[2]) + -OL[2]]

ter′pin hy′drate (tûr′pin), *Pharm.* a white, crystalline powder, $C_{10}H_{20}O_2 \cdot H_2O$, usually used in combination with codeine, as an expectorant. [1865–70; TERP(ENE) + -IN[2]]

ter·pol·y·mer (tər pol′ə mər), *n. Chem.* a polymer consisting of three different monomers, as ABS resin. [1945–50; TER- + POLYMER]

Terp·sich·o·re (tûrp sik′ə rē′), *n.* **1.** *Class. Myth.* the Muse of dancing and choral song. **2.** (*l.c.*) choreography; the art of dancing. [< L *Terpsichorē* < Gk *Terpsichórē,* n. use of fem. of *terpsíchoros* dance-liking; see CHORUS]

terp·si·cho·re·an (tûrp′si kə rē′ən, tûrp′si kôr′ē ən, -kōr′-), *adj.* **1.** pertaining to dancing. **2.** (*cap.*) of or pertaining to Terpsichore. —*n.* **3.** a dancer. [TERPSICHORE + -AN]

terr., 1. terrace. **2.** territorial. **3.** territory.

ter·ra (ter′ə), *n.* earth; land. [1605–15; < L]

ter′ra al′ba (al′bə, ôl′-), any of various white, earthy or powdery substances, as pipe clay, gypsum, kaolin, or magnesia. [1870–75; < L: white earth]

ter·race (ter′əs), *n., v.,* **-raced, -rac·ing.** —*n.* **1.** a raised level with a vertical or sloping front or sides faced with masonry, turf, or the like, esp. one of a series of levels rising one above another. **2.** the top of such a construction, used as a platform, garden, road, etc. **3.** a nearly level strip of land with a more or less abrupt descent along the margin of the sea, a lake, or a river. **4.** the flat roof of a house. **5.** an open, often paved area connected to a house or an apartment house and serving as an outdoor living area; deck. **6.** an open platform, as projecting from the outside wall of an apartment; a large balcony. **7.** a row of houses on or near the top of a slope. **8.** a residential street following the top of a slope. —*v.t., v.i.* **9.** to form into or furnish with a terrace or terraces. [1505–15; earlier *terrasse* < MF < OPr *terrassa* < VL **terrācea,* fem. of **terrāceus.* See TERRA, -ACEOUS] —**ter′race·less,** *adj.*

ter·ra·chlor (ter′ə klôr′, -klōr′), *n. Chem.* pentachloronitrobenzene. [perh. < L *terra* earth (as in TERRAMYCIN) + CHLOR-[2]]

ter·rac·ing (ter′ə sing), *n.* **1.** something formed as a terrace. **2.** a system of terraces. **3.** the act or process of making terraces. [1780–90; TERRACE + -ING[1]]

ter′ra cot′ta (kot′ə), **1.** a hard, fired clay, brownish-red in color when unglazed, that is used for architectural ornaments and facings, structural units, pottery, and as a material for sculpture. **2.** something made of terra cotta. **3.** a brownish-orange color like that of unglazed terra cotta. [1715–25; < It: lit., baked earth < L *terra cocta*]

ter·ra-cot·ta (ter′ə kot′ə), *adj.* made of or having the color of terra cotta. [1865–70]

ter′ra fir′ma (fûr′mə), firm or solid earth; dry land (as opposed to water or air). [1595–1605; < L]

ter·ra·form (ter′ə fôrm′), *v.t.* to alter the environment of (a celestial body) in order to make capable of supporting terrestrial life forms. [1975–80; TERRA + FORM; perh. taken as v. use of an adj. with -FORM as second element]

ter·rain (tə rān′), *n.* **1.** a tract of land, esp. as considered with reference to its natural features, military advantages, etc. **2.** *Geol.* terrane. [1720–30; < F << VL **terrānum,* n. use of neut. of **terrānus* of land. See TERRA, -AN]

ter·ra in·cog·ni·ta (ter′ə in kog′ni tə, in′kog nē′-; *Lat.* teʀ′rä in kôg′ni tä). an unknown or unexplored land, region, or subject.

ter·ra·ma·ra (ter′ə mär′ə), *n., pl.* **-ma·re** (-mär′ē). a lake dwelling or settlement of lake dwellings, esp. those whose remains survive in mounds in the Po valley of N Italy. [1865–70; < It dial., prob. assimilation of L *terra mala* bad earth]

Ter·ra Ma·ter (ter′ə mā′tər), *Rom. Religion.* Tellus.

Ter·ra·my·cin (ter′ə mī′sin), *Pharm., Trademark.* a brand of oxytetracycline.

ter·rane (tə rān′, ter′ān), *n. Geol.* any rock formation or series of formations or the area in which a particular formation or group of rocks is predominant. Also, **terrain.** [1815–25; sp. var. of TERRAIN]

CONCISE PRONUNCIATION KEY: *act, cāpe, dâre, pärt; set, ēqual; if, ice; ox, ōver, ôrder, oil, bo͝ok, bo͞ot, out; up, ûrge; child; sing; shoe; thin, that;* zh as in *treasure.* ə = *a* as in *alone, e* as in *system, i* as in *easily, o* as in *gallop, u* as in *circus;* ᵊ as in *fire* (fīᵊr), *hour* (ouᵊr). l and n can serve as syllabic consonants, as in *cradle* (krād′l), and *button* (but′n). See the full key inside the front cover.

ter·ra·pin (ter′ə pin), *n.* **1.** any of several edible North American turtles of the family Emydidae, inhabiting fresh or brackish waters, esp. the diamondback terrapin: some are threatened or endangered. **2.** any of various similar turtles. [1605–15; earlier *torope* (< Virginia Algonquian < Eastern Algonquian **to·rəpe·w* variety of turtle > Munsee Delaware *tò·lpe·w*) + *-in,* of uncert. orig.]

ter·ra·que·ous (ter ā′kwē əs, -ak′wē-), *adj.* consisting of land and water, as the earth. [1650–60; TERR(A) + AQUEOUS]

ter·rar·i·um (tə râr′ē əm), *n., pl.* **-rar·i·ums, -rar·i·a** (-râr′ē ə). **1.** a vivarium for land animals (distinguished from *aquarium*). **2.** a glass container, chiefly or wholly enclosed, for growing and displaying plants. [1885–90; TERR(A) + -ARIUM]

ter′ra sig·il·la′ta (sig′ə lä′tə, sij′ə lā′tə), **1.** See **Arretine ware. 2.** See **Samian ware.** [< NL or It, explained as "earth (i.e., earthenware) with incised decoration" (see TERRA COTTA, SIGILLATE), but appar. orig. an adaptation of an earlier and ML name for Lemnian earth (a clay mineral used as an astringent), perh. associated with the pottery because of its red color]

ter·ra ver·de (ter′ə ver′dä; *It.* teʀ′ʀä veʀ′de). See **green earth.** [1895–1900; < It]

ter·raz·zo (tə raz′ō, -räz′ō, -rät′sō; *It.* teʀ ʀät′tsô), *n.* a mosaic flooring or paving composed of chips of broken stone, usually marble, and cement, polished when in place. [1895–1900; < It: balcony, terraced or flat roof < VL **terrāceus,* deriv. of L *terra* ground]

Terre·bonne (*Fr.* teʀ bôn′), *n.* a town in S Quebec, in E Canada, near Montreal. 11,769.

Ter·re Haute (ter′ə hōt′, hut′, hôt′), a city in W Indiana, on the Wabash River. 61,125.

Ter·rell (ter′əl), *n.* a city in NE Texas. 13,225.

Ter·rence (ter′əns), *n.* a male given name.

ter·rene (te rēn′, tə-, ter′ēn), *adj.* **1.** earthly; worldly. **2.** earthy. —*n.* **3.** the earth. **4.** a land or region. [1300–50; ME < L *terrēnus* pertaining to earth. See TERRA] **—ter·rene′ly,** *adv.*

terre·plein (ter′plān′, ter′ə-), *n. Fort.* the top platform or horizontal surface of a rampart where guns are mounted. [1585–95; < F < It *terrapieno,* deriv. of *terrapienare* to fill with earth; see TERRA, PLENUM]

ter·res·tri·al (tə res′trē əl), *adj.* **1.** pertaining to, consisting of, or representing the earth as distinct from other planets. **2.** of or pertaining to land as distinct from water. **3.** *Bot.* **a.** growing on land; not aquatic. **b.** growing in the ground; not epiphytic or aerial. **4.** *Zool.* living on or in the ground; not aquatic, arboreal, or aerial. **5.** of or pertaining to the earth or this world; worldly; mundane. —*n.* **6.** an inhabitant of the earth, esp. a human being. [1400–50; late ME < L *terrestri(s)* pertaining to earth (deriv. of *terra* earth) + -AL[1]] **—ter·res′tri·al·ly,** *adv.*
—Syn. 1. terrene. See **earthly. —Ant. 1.** celestial.

terres′trial globe′. See under **globe** (def. 3). [1550–60]

terres′trial plan′et. *Astron.* See **inner planet.** [1885–90]

terres′trial tel′escope, a refracting telescope having inverting lenses or an eyepiece that presents an erect image. [1805–15]

ter·ret (ter′it), *n.* one of the round loops or rings on the saddle of a harness, through which the driving reins pass. See illus. under **harness.** [1480–90; earlier *teret,* unexplained var. of ME *toret* < MF, OF *tor* ring (see TOUR) + *-et* -ET]

terre verte (ter′ vert′), **1.** a grayish-green color. **2.** See **green earth.** [1650–60; < F: lit., green earth]

Ter·ri (ter′ē), *n.* a female given name, form of **Theresa.**

ter·ri·ble (ter′ə bəl), *adj.* **1.** distressing; severe: *a terrible winter.* **2.** extremely bad; horrible: *terrible coffee; a terrible movie.* **3.** exciting terror, awe, or great fear; dreadful; awful. **4.** formidably great: *a terrible responsibility.* [1400–50; late ME < L *terribilis,* equiv. to *terr(ēre)* to frighten + *-ibilis* -IBLE] **—ter′ri·ble·ness,** *n.*
—Syn. 3. fearful, frightful, appalling, dire, horrible, horrifying, terrifying, horrendous, horrid.

ter·ri·bly (ter′ə blē), *adv.* **1.** in a terrible manner. **2.** *Informal.* extremely; very: *It's terribly late. I'm terribly sorry.* [1520–30; TERRIBLE + -LY]

ter·ric·o·lous (te rik′ə ləs), *adj. Biol.* living on or in the ground. [1825–35; < L *terri-* (comb. form of *terra* earth) + -COLOUS]

ter·ri·er[1] (ter′ē ər), *n.* **1.** any of several breeds of usually small dogs, used originally to pursue game and drive it out of its hole or burrow. **2.** (*cap.*) *U.S. Mil.* a surface-to-air, two-stage antiaircraft missile. [1400–50; < MF, short for *chien terrier* lit., dog of the earth (< ML *terrārius;* see TERRA, -IER[2]); so called because used to start badgers from their burrows; r. late ME *terrere* < AF (see -ER[2])]

ter·ri·er[2] (ter′ē ər), *n. Law.* a book or document in which are described the site, boundaries, acreage, tenants, etc., of certain lands. [1470–80; < MF, short for *registre terrier* register of land (< ML *terrārius;* see TERRA, -IER[2]). r. earlier *terrere* < AF (see -ER[2])]

ter·rif·ic (tə rif′ik), *adj.* **1.** extraordinarily great or intense: *terrific speed.* **2.** extremely good; wonderful: *a terrific vacation.* **3.** causing terror; terrifying. [1660–70; < L *terrificus* frightening, equiv. to *terr(ēre)* to frighten + *-i-* -I- + *-ficus* -FIC] **—ter·rif′i·cal·ly,** *adv.*
—Syn. 1, 2. extraordinary, remarkable. **2.** fine, excellent.

ter·ri·fy (ter′ə fī′), *v.t.,* **-fied, -fy·ing.** to fill with terror or alarm; make greatly afraid. [1565–75; < L *terrificāre,* equiv. to *terr(ēre)* to frighten + *-ificāre* -IFY] **—ter′ri·fi′er,** *n.* **—ter′ri·fy′ing·ly,** *adv.*
—Syn. See **frighten.**

ter·rig·e·nous (te rij′ə nəs), *adj.* **1.** produced by the earth. **2.** *Geol.* noting or pertaining to sediments on the sea bottom derived directly from the neighboring land, or to the rocks formed primarily by the consolidation of such sediments. [1675–85; < L *terrigenus,* equiv. to *terr(a)* earth + *-i-* -I- + *-genus* -GENOUS]

ter·rine (tə rēn′), *n.* **1.** a casserole dish made of pottery. **2.** a paté or similar dish of chopped meat, game, fish, or vegetables baked in such a dish and served cold. **3.** a tureen. [1700–10; < F; see TUREEN]

ter·ri·to·ri·al (ter′i tôr′ē əl, -tōr′-), *adj.* **1.** of or pertaining to territory or land. **2.** of, pertaining to, associated with, or restricted to a particular territory or district; local. **3.** pertaining or belonging to the territory of a state or ruler. **4.** (of an animal) characterized by territoriality; defending an area against intruders, esp. of the same species. **5.** (*often cap.*) of or pertaining to a territory of the U.S. **6.** (*cap.*) *Mil.* organized on a local basis for home defense: *the British Territorial Army.* —*n.* **7.** (*cap.*) a member of the British Territorial Army. **8.** a soldier in a territorial army. [1615–25; < LL *territōriālis.* See TERRITORY, -AL[1]] **—ter′ri·to′ri·al·ly,** *adv.*

territo′rial court′, a court established in U.S. territories that is empowered to hear local and federal cases. [1855–60]

ter·ri·to·ri·al·ism (ter′i tôr′ē ə liz′əm, -tōr′-), *n.* **1.** a principle or system that gives predominance to the landed classes. **2.** Also called **territo′rial sys′tem.** a theory of church policy according to which the supreme ecclesiastical authority is vested in the civil power. [1870–75; TERRITORIAL + -ISM] **—ter′ri·to′ri·al·ist,** *n.*

ter·ri·to·ri·al·i·ty (ter′i tôr′ē al′i tē, -tōr′-), *n.* **1.** territorial quality, condition, or status. **2.** the behavior of an animal in defining and defending its territory. **3.** attachment to or protection of a territory or domain. [1890–95; TERRITORIAL + -ITY]

ter·ri·to·ri·al·ize (ter′i tôr′ē ə līz′, -tōr′-), *v.t.,* **-ized, -iz·ing. 1.** to extend by adding new territory. **2.** to reduce to the status of a territory. **3.** to make territorial. Also, *esp. Brit.,* **ter′ri·to′ri·al·ise′.** [1810–20; TERRITORIAL + -IZE] **—ter′ri·to′ri·al·i·za′tion,** *n.*

territo′rial wa′ters, the waters of a littoral state that are regarded as under the jurisdiction of the state: traditionally those waters within three miles (4.8 km) of the shore, but in the 20th century claims by coastal nations have extended to 12 or even 200 miles (19.3 or 321.8 km). Also called **marine belt.** Cf. **high sea.** [1870–75]

ter·ri·to·ry (ter′i tôr′ē, -tōr′ē), *n., pl.* **-ries. 1.** any tract of land; region or district. **2.** the land and waters belonging to or under the jurisdiction of a state, sovereign, etc. **3.** any separate tract of land belonging to a state. **4.** (*often cap.*) *Govt.* **a.** a region or district of the U.S. not admitted to the Union as a state but having its own legislature, with a governor and other officers appointed by the President and confirmed by the Senate. **b.** some similar district elsewhere, as in Canada and Australia. **5.** a field or sphere of action, thought, etc.; domain or province of something. **6.** the region or district assigned to a representative, agent, or the like, as for making sales. **7.** the area that an animal defends against intruders, esp. of the same species. [1400–50; late ME < L *territōrium* land round a town, district, equiv. to *terr(a)* land + *-i-* -I- + *-tōrium* -TORY[2]]
—Syn. 2. domain, dominion, sovereignty.

ter′ritory wool′, the wool of sheep raised west of the Mississippi River, esp. in Washington and the Rocky Mountain States. Also called **modock wool, range wool, western wool.** Cf. **bright wool.** [1915–20, *Amer.*]

ter·ror (ter′ər), *n.* **1.** intense, sharp, overmastering fear: *to be frantic with terror.* **2.** an instance or cause of intense fear or anxiety; quality of causing terror: *to be a terror to evildoers.* **3.** any period of frightful violence or bloodshed likened to the Reign of Terror in France. **4.** violence or threats of violence used for intimidation or coercion; terrorism. **5.** *Informal.* a person or thing that is especially annoying or unpleasant. [1325–75; < L, equiv. to *terr(ēre)* to frighten + *-or* -OR[1]; r. ME *terrour* < AF < L, as above] **—ter′ror·ful,** *adj.* **—ter′ror·less,** *adj.*
—Syn. 1. alarm, dismay, consternation. TERROR, HORROR, PANIC, FRIGHT all imply extreme fear in the presence of danger or evil. TERROR implies an intense fear that is somewhat prolonged and may refer to imagined or future dangers: *frozen with terror.* HORROR implies a sense of shock at a danger that is also evil, and the danger may be to others rather than to oneself: *to recoil in horror.* PANIC and FRIGHT both imply a sudden shock of fear. FRIGHT is usually of short duration: *a spasm of fright.* PANIC is uncontrolled and unreasoning fear, often groundless, that may be prolonged: *The mob was in a panic.* **—Ant. 1.** calm.

ter·ror·ism (ter′ə riz′əm), *n.* **1.** the use of violence and threats to intimidate or coerce, esp. for political purposes. **2.** the state of fear and submission produced by terrorism or terrorization. **3.** a terroristic method of governing or of resisting a government. [1785–95; TERROR + -ISM]

ter·ror·ist (ter′ər ist), *n.* **1.** a person, usually a member of a group, who uses or advocates terrorism. **2.** a person who terrorizes or frightens others. **3.** (formerly) a member of a political group in Russia aiming at the demoralization of the government by terror. **4.** an agent or partisan of the revolutionary tribunal during the Reign of Terror in France. —*adj.* **5.** of, pertaining to, or characteristic of terrorism or terrorists: *terrorist tactics.* [1785–95; TERROR + -IST; cf. F *terroriste*] **—ter′ror·is′tic,** *adj.*

ter·ror·ize (ter′ə rīz′), *v.t.,* **-ized, -iz·ing. 1.** to fill or overcome with terror. **2.** to dominate or coerce by intimidation. **3.** to produce widespread fear by acts of violence, as bombings. Also, *esp. Brit.,* **ter′ror·ise′.** [1815–25; TERROR + -IZE] **—ter′ror·i·za′tion,** *n.* **—ter′ror·iz′er,** *n.*
—Syn. 1, 2. See **frighten.**

ter·ror-strick·en (ter′ər strik′ən), *adj.* overwhelmed by terror; terrified. Also, **ter·ror-struck** (ter′ər struk′). [1835–45]

ter·ry (ter′ē), *n., pl.* **-ries,** *adj.* —*n.* **1.** the loop formed by the pile of a fabric when left uncut. **2.** Also called **ter′ry cloth′.** a pile fabric, usually of cotton, with loops on both sides, as in a Turkish towel. —*adj.* **3.** made of such a fabric: *a terry bathrobe.* **4.** having the pile loops uncut: *terry velvet.* [1775–85; perh. var. of TERRET]

Ter·ry (ter′ē), *n.* **1. Ellen (Alicia** or **Alice),** 1848?–1928, English actress. **2.** a male given name, form of **Terrence** or **Theodore. 3.** a female given name, form of **Theresa.**

Ter·sanc·tus (tûr sangk′təs, ter-), *n.* Sanctus (def. 1). [< NL: lit., thrice holy (trans. of LGk *triságios*), equiv. to L *ter* thrice + *sānctus* holy; see SAINT]

terse (tûrs), *adj.* **ters·er, ters·est. 1.** neatly or effectively concise; brief and pithy, as language. **2.** abruptly concise; curt; brusque. [1595–1605; < L *tersus,* ptp. of *tergēre* to rub off, wipe off, clean, polish] **—terse′ly,** *adv.* **—terse′ness,** *n.*
—Syn. 1. succinct, compact, neat, concentrated. **1, 2.** See **concise.**

ter·tial (tûr′shəl), *Ornith.* —*adj.* **1.** pertaining to any of a set of flight feathers situated on the basal segment of a bird's wing. —*n.* **2.** a tertial feather. [1830–40; < L *terti(us)* THIRD + -AL[1]]

ter·tian (tûr′shən), *adj.* **1.** *Pathol.* (of a malarial fever, etc.) characterized by paroxysms that recur every other day. —*n.* **2.** *Pathol.* a tertian fever. **3.** a Jesuit during the period of tertianship. [1325–75; ME *terciane* < L *(febris) tertiāna* tertian (fever), equiv. to *terti(us)* THIRD + *-āna,* fem. of *-ānus* -AN]

ter·tian·ship (tûr′shən ship′), *n.* (in the Jesuit order) a period of strict discipline before the taking of final vows, beginning one or two years after ordination. [1850–55; TERTIAN + -SHIP]

ter·ti·ar·y (tûr′shē er′ē, tûr′shə rē), *adj., n., pl.* **-ar·ies.** —*adj.* **1.** of the third order, rank, stage, formation, etc.; third. **2.** *Chem.* **a.** noting or containing a carbon atom united to three other carbon atoms. **b.** formed by replacement of three atoms or groups. **3.** (*cap.*) *Geol.* noting or pertaining to the period forming the earlier part of the Cenozoic Era, occurring from 65 million to 2 million years ago, characterized by the development and proliferation of mammals. See table under **geologic time. 4.** *Ornith.* tertial. **5.** *Eccles.* noting or pertaining to a branch, or third order, of certain religious orders that consists of lay members living in community (**regular tertiaries**) or living in the world (**secular tertiaries**). —*n.* **6.** (*cap.*) *Geol.* the Tertiary Period or System. **7.** *Ornith.* a tertial feather. **8.** (*often cap.*) *Eccles.* a member of a tertiary branch of a religious order. **9.** See **tertiary color.** [1540–50; < L *tertiārius* of third part or rank, equiv. to *terti(us)* THIRD + *-ārius* -ARY]

ter′tiary care′, *Med.* the aspect of in-patient care dealing with illnesses or conditions requiring specialized techniques, as coronary artery bypass surgery, renal hemodialysis, and treatment of severe burns.

ter′tiary col′or, a color, as brown, produced by mixing two secondary colors. [1860–65]

ter′tiary syph′ilis, *Pathol.* the third stage of syphilis, characterized by involvement of the internal organs, esp. the brain, spinal cord, heart, and liver. [1870–75]

ter·ti·um quid (tûr′shē əm kwid′; *Lat.* teʀ′ti o͝om′ kwid′), something related in some way to two things, but distinct from both; something intermediate between two things. [1715–25; < L, trans. of Gk *tríton ti* some third thing]

Ter·tul·li·an (tər tul′ē ən, -tul′yən), *n.* (*Quintus Septimius Florens Tertullianus*) A.D. c160–c230, Carthaginian theologian.

ter·va·lent (tûr vā′lənt), *adj. Chem.* **1.** trivalent. **2.** possessing three different valences, as cobalt with valences 2, 3, and 4. [1900–05; TER- + VALENT] **—ter·va′lence, ter·va′len·cy,** *n.*

Ter·y·lene (ter′ə lēn′), *Brit. Trademark.* Dacron.

ter·za ri·ma (tert′sə rē′mə; *It.* teʀ′tsä ʀē′mä), *Pros.* an Italian form of iambic verse consisting of eleven-syllable lines arranged in tercets, the middle line of each tercet rhyming with the first and last lines of the following tercet. [1810–20; < It: third rhyme]

tesch·en·ite (tesh′ə nīt′), *n.* a coarse-grained igneous rock consisting of plagioclase, olivine, and augite. [1865–70; *Teschen* (German name of Czech *Těšín,* town in Czechoslovakia) + -ITE[1]]

TESL, teaching English as a second language. Cf. **ESL.**

tes·la (tes′lə), *n.* a unit of magnetic induction equal to one weber per square meter. *Abbr.:* T [named after N. TESLA]

Tes·la (tes′lə), *n.* **Ni·ko·la** (nik′ō lə), 1856–1943, U.S. physicist, electrical engineer, and inventor, born in Croatia.

Tes′la coil′, *Elect.* an air-core transformer used to produce high voltages of high-frequency alternating currents. Also called **Tes′la transform′er.** [1900–05; named after its inventor, N. TESLA]

TESOL (tē′sôl, tes′əl), *n.* **1.** teaching English to speakers of other languages. Cf. **ESOL. 2.** Teachers of English to Speakers of Other Languages.

Tess (tes), *n.* a female given name, form of **Theresa.** Also, **Tes·sa** (tes′ə).

tes·se·late (tes′ə lāt′), *v.t.,* **-lat·ed, -lat·ing,** *adj.* tessellate.

tes·sel·late (*v.* tes′ə lāt′; *adj.* tes′ə lit, -lāt′), *v.,* **-lat·ed, -lat·ing,** *adj.* —*v.t.* **1.** to form of small squares or blocks, as floors or pavements; form or arrange in a checkered or mosaic pattern. —*adj.* **2.** tessellated. [1785–95; < L *tessellātus* mosaic, equiv. to *tessell*(*a*) small square stone (dim. of *tessera* TESSERA) + *-ātus* -ATE[1]]

tes·sel·lat·ed (tes′ə lā′tid), *adj.* **1.** of, pertaining to, or like a mosaic. **2.** arranged in or having the appearance of a mosaic; checkered. Also, **tes′se·lat′ed.** [1685–95; TESSELLATE + -ED[2]]

tes·sel·la·tion (tes′ə lā′shən), *n.* **1.** the art or practice of tessellating. **2.** tessellated form or arrangement. **3.** tessellated work. Also, **tes′se·la′tion.** [1650–60; TESSELLATE (V.) + -ION]

tes·ser·a (tes′ər ə), *n., pl.* **tes·ser·ae** (tes′ə rē′). **1.** one of the small pieces used in mosaic work. **2.** a small square of bone, wood, or the like, used in ancient times as a token, tally, ticket, etc. [1640–50; < L < Gk (Ionic) *tésseres* FOUR]

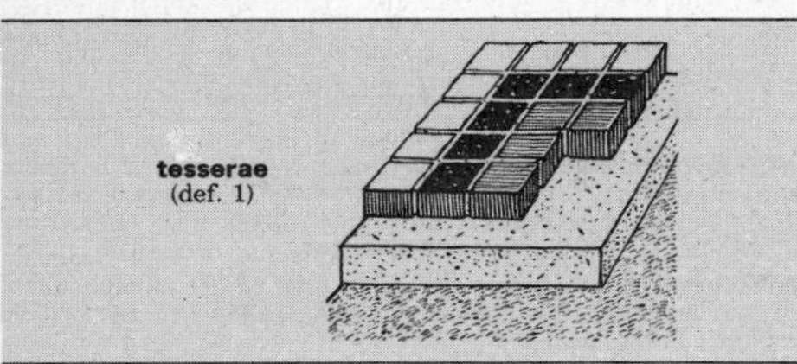
tesserae (def. 1)

tes·ser·act (tes′ə rakt′), *n.* the generalization of a cube to four dimensions. [1885–90; < Gk *tésser*(*es*) FOUR + *aktís* ray]

Tes·sie (tes′ē), *n.* a female given name, form of **Theresa.**

Tes·sin (*Fr.* te saN′; *Ger.* te sēn′), *n.* French and German name of **Ticino.**

tes·si·tu·ra (tes′i to͝or′ə; *It.* tes′sē to͞o′Rä), *n., pl.* **-tu·ras,** **-tu·re** (-to͝or′ā; *It.* -to͞o′Re). the general pitch level or average range of a vocal or instrumental part in a musical composition: *an uncomfortably high tessitura.* [1890–95; < It: lit., texture < L *textūra;* see TEXTURE]

Tess′ of the D'Ur′ber·villes (dûr′bər vilz′), a novel (1891) by Thomas Hardy.

test[1] (test), *n.* **1.** the means by which the presence, quality, or genuineness of anything is determined; a means of trial. **2.** the trial of the quality of something: *to put to the test.* **3.** a particular process or method for trying or assessing. **4.** a set of questions, problems, or the like, used as a means of evaluating the abilities, aptitudes, skills, or performance of an individual or group; examination. **5.** *Psychol.* a set of standardized questions, problems, or tasks designed to elicit responses for use in measuring the traits, capacities, or achievements of an individual. **6.** *Chem.* **a.** the process of identifying or detecting the presence of a constituent of a substance, or of determining the nature of a substance, commonly by the addition of a reagent. **b.** the reagent used. **c.** an indication or evidence of the presence of a constituent, or of the nature of a substance, obtained by such means. **7.** an oath or other confirmation of one's loyalty, religious beliefs, etc. **8.** *Brit.* a cupel for refining or assaying metals. —*v.t.* **9.** to subject to a test of any kind; try. **10.** *Chem.* to subject to a chemical test. **11.** *Metall.* to assay or refine in a cupel. —*v.i.* **12.** to undergo a test or trial; try out. **13.** to perform on a test: *People test better in a relaxed environment.* **14.** to conduct a test: *to test for diabetes.* [1350–1400; ME: cupel < MF < L *testū, testum* earthen pot; akin to TEST[2]] —**test′a·ble,** *adj.* —**test′a·bil′i·ty,** *n.* —**test′ing·ly,** *adv.*
—**Syn. 1.** proof, assay. See **trial. 9.** assay, prove, examine.

test[2] (test), *n.* **1.** *Zool.* the hard, protective shell or covering of certain invertebrates, as echinoderms or tunicates. **2.** *Bot.* testa. [1535–45; < L *testa* tile, shell, covering; akin to TEST[1]]

Test., Testament.

test., **1.** testator. **2.** testimony.

tes·ta (tes′tə), *n., pl.* **-tae** (-tē). *Bot.* the outer, usually hard, integument or coat of a seed. [1790–1800; < NL, L; see TEST[2]]

tes·ta·cean (te stā′shən), *adj. Zool.* having a shell or test. [1835–45; < L *testāce*(*us*) shell-covered, TESTACEOUS + -AN]

tes·ta·ceous (te stā′shəs), *adj.* **1.** of, pertaining to, or derived from shells. **2.** having a test or shell-like covering. **3.** of a brick-red, brownish-red, or brownish-yellow color. [1640–50; < L *testāceus* shell-covered, equiv. to *test*(*a*) (see TEST[2]) + *-āceus* -ACEOUS]

test′ act′, **1.** any law requiring a person to belong to the established church of a country as a condition for holding public office. **2.** (*caps.*) *Eng. Hist.* the statute (1673) requiring all military officers and public officials to take an oath of allegiance to the Crown, receive the sacraments of the Church of England, and reject the doctrine of transubstantiation: repealed in 1828. [1700–10]

tes·ta·cy (tes′tə sē), *n.* the state of being testate. [1860–65; TEST(ATE) + -ACY]

tes·ta·ment (tes′tə mənt), *n.* **1.** *Law.* **a.** a will, esp. one that relates to the disposition of one's personal property. **b.** will[2] (def. 8). **2.** either of the two major portions of the Bible: the Mosaic or old covenant or dispensation, or the Christian or new covenant or dispensation. **3.** (*cap.*) the New Testament, as distinct from the Old Testament. **4.** (*cap.*) a copy of the New Testament. **5.** a covenant, esp. between God and humans. [1250–1300; ME: will, covenant < L *testāmentum,* equiv. to *testā*(*rī*) to bear witness (see TESTATE) + *-mentum* -MENT]

tes·ta·men·ta·ry (tes′tə men′tə rē, -men′trē), *adj.* **1.** of, pertaining to, or of the nature of a testament or will. **2.** given, bequeathed, done, or appointed by will. **3.** set forth or contained in a will. Also, **tes′ta·men′tal.** [1425–75; late ME < L *testāmentārius.* See TESTAMENT, -ARY]

testamen′tary trust′, *Law.* a trust set up under the terms of a will. Cf. **living trust.**

tes·tate (tes′tāt), *adj.* having made and left a valid will. [1425–75; late ME < L *testātus,* ptp. of *testārī* to bear witness, make a will, deriv. of *testis* witness; see -ATE[1]]

tes·ta·tor (tes′tā tər, te stā′tər), *n. Law.* **1.** a person who makes a will. **2.** a person who has died leaving a valid will. [1275–1325; < L *testātor;* see TESTATE, -TOR; r. ME *testatour* < AF]

tes·ta·trix (te stā′triks), *n., pl.* **tes·ta·tri·ces** (te stā′trə sēz′, tes′tə trī′sēz), *Law.* **1.** a woman who makes a will. **2.** a woman who has died leaving a valid will. [1585–95; < LL *testātrīx;* see TESTATOR, -TRIX]
—**Usage.** See **-trix.**

test′ ban′, an agreement by nations producing nuclear weapons to refrain from testing them in the atmosphere. [1955–60] —**test′-ban′,** *adj.*

test′ blank′, a typed or printed test form containing questions or tasks to be responded to.

test′ case′, **1.** a typical case whose court decision may be interpreted as a precedent for application in future similar cases. **2.** a legal action taken, sometimes deliberately by agreement of both parties, with a special view to determining the position of the law on some matter, as the constitutionality of a statute. [1890–95]

test·cross (test′krôs′, -kros′), *n.* a genetic test for heterozygosity in which an organism of dominant phenotype, but unknown genotype, is crossed to an organism recessive for all markers in question. [1930–35; TEST[1] + CROSS]

test-drive (test′drīv′), *v.t.,* **-drove, -driv·en, -driv·ing.** to drive (a vehicle) on the highway or a special track or route in order to evaluate performance and reliability. [1945–50]

test·ee (te stē′), *n.* a person who is tested, as by a scholastic examination. [1930–35; TEST[1] + -EE]

test·er[1] (tes′tər), *n.* a person or thing that tests. [1655–65; TEST[1] + -ER[1]]

tes·ter[2] (tes′tər, tēs′-), *n.* a canopy, as over a bed or altar. [1350–1400; ME < ML *testrum* canopy of a bed; akin to L *testa* covering. See TEST[2]]

tes·ter[3] (tes′tər), *n.* the teston of Henry VIII. [1540–50; earlier *testorn,* var. of TESTON, with *-r-* from MF *testart* teston]

tes·tes (tes′tēz), *n.* pl. of **testis.**

test′ flight′, a flight made to observe the performance characteristics of a new aircraft or spacecraft. [1910–15]

test-fly (test′flī′), *v.t.,* **-flew, -flown, -fly·ing.** to fly (an aircraft or spacecraft) for the evaluation of performance. [1935–40]

tes·ti·cle (tes′ti kəl), *n.* testis. [1375–1425; late ME < L *testiculus.* See TESTIS, -CLE[1]]

tes·tic·u·lar (te stik′yə lər), *adj.* **1.** of or pertaining to the testes. **2.** testiculate. [1650–60; < L *testicul*(*us*) TESTICLE + -AR[1]]

tes·tic·u·late (te stik′yə lit), *adj. Bot.* **1.** shaped like a testis. **2.** having tubers shaped like testes, as certain orchids. [1715–25; < LL *testiculātus.* See TESTICLE, -ATE[1]]

tes·ti·fi·ca·tion (tes′tə fi kā′shən), *n.* the act of testifying or giving testimony. [1400–50; late ME < L *testificātiōn-* (s. of *testificātiō*) a bearing witness. See TESTIFY, -FICATION]

tes·ti·fy (tes′tə fī′), *v.,* **-fied, -fy·ing.** —*v.i.* **1.** to bear witness; give or afford evidence. **2.** *Law.* to give testimony under oath or solemn affirmation, usually in court. **3.** to make solemn declaration. —*v.t.* **4.** to bear witness to; affirm as fact or truth; attest. **5.** to give or afford evidence of in any manner. **6.** *Law.* to state or declare under oath or affirmation, usually in court. **7.** to declare, profess, or acknowledge openly. [1350–1400; ME *testifyen* < L *testificārī* to bear witness, equiv. to *testi*(*s*) witness + *-ficārī* -FY] —**tes′ti·fi′er,** *n.*
—**Syn. 5.** indicate, show, signify, prove.

tes·ti·mo·ni·al (tes′tə mō′nē əl), *n.* **1.** a written declaration certifying to a person's character, conduct, or qualifications, or to the value, excellence, etc., of a thing; a letter or written statement of recommendation. **2.** something given or done as an expression of esteem, admiration, or gratitude. —*adj.* **3.** pertaining to or serving as a testimonial: *a testimonial dinner for the retiring dean.* [1375–1425; late ME < LL *testimōniālis.* See TESTIMONY, -AL[1]]

tes·ti·mo·ni·al·ize (tes′tə mō′nē ə līz′), *v.t.,* **-ized, -iz·ing.** to honor (someone) by giving or doing something testimonial. Also, *esp. Brit.,* **tes′ti·mo′ni·al·ise′.** [1850–55; TESTIMONIAL + -IZE]

tes·ti·mo·ny (tes′tə mō′nē, *or, esp. Brit.,* -mə nē), *n., pl.* **-nies.** **1.** *Law.* the statement or declaration of a witness under oath or affirmation, usually in court. **2.** evidence in support of a fact or statement; proof. **3.** open declaration or profession, as of faith. **4.** Usually, **testimonies.** the precepts of God. **5.** the Decalogue as inscribed on the two tables of the law, or the ark in which the tables were kept. Ex. 16:34; 25:16. **6.** *Archaic.* a declaration of disapproval; protest. [1350–1400; ME < L *testimōnium,* equiv. to *testi*(*s*) witness + *-mōnium* -MONY]
—**Syn. 1.** deposition, attestation. See **evidence. 2.** corroboration. **3.** affirmation.

tes′timony meet′ing, a meeting at which persons give testimonies of religious faith and related religious experiences. Also called **experience meeting.**

tes·tis (tes′tis), *n., pl.* **-tes** (-tēz). *Anat., Zool.* the male gonad or reproductive gland, either of two oval glands located in the scrotum. [1675–85; < L]

test-mar·ket (test′mär′kit), *v.t.* to offer (a new product) for sale, usually in a limited area, in order to ascertain and evaluate consumer response. [1950–55]

test′ match′, **1.** a group of cricket games played between all-star teams of Australia and England to determine the champion. **2.** a similar game or group of games played between all-star teams of other countries. [1895–1900]

tes·ton (tes′tən, -ton, te sto͞on′), *n.* **1.** a former silver coin of France, equal at various times to between 10 and 14½ sols, bearing on the obverse a bust of the reigning king. **2.** a former silver coin of England, issued by Henry VII, Henry VIII, and Edward VI, and bearing on the obverse the bust of the reigning king: equal originally to 12 pence, later to sixpence. **3.** Also, **tes·to·ne** (te stō′nā). a former silver coin of Milan, first issued in 1468, bearing on the obverse a bust of the Duke of Milan. Also, **tes·toon** (te sto͞on′). [1535–45; < F < It *testone,* aug. of *testa* head < LL; see TESTA]

tes·tos·ter·one (tes tos′tə rōn′), *n.* **1.** *Biochem.* the sex hormone, $C_{19}H_{28}O_2$, secreted by the testes, that stimulates the development of male sex organs, secondary sexual traits, and sperm. **2.** *Pharm.* a commercially prepared form of this compound, originally isolated from bull's testes and now also produced synthetically, used in medicine chiefly for treatment of testosterone deficiency and for certain gynecological conditions. [1930–35; *testo-* (comb. form of TESTIS) + STER(OL) + -ONE]

test′ pa′per, **1.** the paper bearing a student's answers on an examination. **2.** *Chem.* paper impregnated with a reagent, as litmus, that changes color when acted upon by certain substances. [1820–30]

test′ pat′tern, *Television.* a geometric design broadcast to receivers for testing the quality of transmission, often identifying the transmitting station and channel. [1945–50]

test′ pi′lot, a pilot employed to test-fly newly-built aircraft. [1925–30]

test′ stand′, *Rocketry.* a device that restrains a missile or rocket during a captive test. [1840–50]

test′ statis′tic, a statistic used to test a hypothesis.

test′ tube′, a hollow cylinder of thin glass with one end closed, used in chemical and biological experimentation and analysis. [1840–50]

test-tube (test′to͞ob′, -tyo͞ob′), *adj.* produced in or as if in a test tube; synthetic or experimental. [1885–90]

test′-tube ba′by, an infant developed from an ovum fertilized in vitro and implanted into a woman's uterus, usually that of the biological mother. [1930–35]

test′-tube skin′, *Med.* skin that has been grown in the laboratory from a patch of a person's skin, used for autografting, esp. in the treatment of extensive burns.

tes·tu·di·nal (te sto͞od′n l, -styo͞od′-), *adj.* pertaining to or resembling a tortoise or tortoise shell. Also, **tes·tu·di·nar·i·an** (te sto͞od′n âr′ē ən, -styo͞od′-). [1815–25; < L *testūdin-* (s. of *testūdō*) tortoise (see TESTUDO) + -AL[1]]

tes·tu·di·nate (te sto͞od′n it, -āt′, -styo͞od′-), *adj.* **1.** formed like the carapace of a tortoise; arched; vaulted. **2.** chelonian. —*n.* **3.** a turtle. **4.** any member of the order Testudines, comprising turtles, tortoises, and terrapins. [1720–30; < L *testūdinātus.* See TESTUDINAL, -ATE[1]]

tes·tu·do (te sto͞o′dō, -styo͞o′-), *n., pl.* **tes·tu·di·nes** (te sto͞od′n ēz′, -styo͞od′-). **1.** (among the ancient Romans) a movable shelter with a strong and usually fireproof arched roof, used for protection of soldiers in siege operations. **2.** a shelter formed by overlapping oblong shields, held by soldiers above their heads. [1350–1400 for earlier sense "tumor"; 1600–10 for def. 1; ME < L *testūdō* tortoise, tortoise shell, siege engine; akin to TEST[2]]

testudo (def. 2)

tes·ty (tes′tē), *adj.,* **-ti·er, -ti·est.** irritably impatient; touchy. [1325–75; late ME *testi,* alter. of MF *testu* headstrong; r. ME *testif* < MF. See TEST[2], -IVE] —**tes′ti·ly,** *adv.* —**tes′ti·ness,** *n.*
—**Syn.** tetchy, edgy, snappish, cross, irascible. See **irritable.** —**Ant.** composed.

Tet (tet), *n.* the Vietnamese New Year celebration, occurring during the first seven days of the first month of the lunar calendar. [< Vietnamese *têt*]

te·tan·ic (tə tan′ik), *adj.* **1.** *Pathol.* pertaining to, of the nature of, or characterized by tetanus. **2.** *Med.* noting a medicine or poison that can cause tetanic spasms of the muscles. Cf. **tetany.** Also, **te·tan′i·cal.** [1720–30; < L *tetanicus* < Gk *tetanikós,* equiv. to *tétan*(*os*) spasm, TETANUS + *-ikos* -IC] —**te·tan′i·cal·ly,** *adv.*

tet·a·nize (tet′n īz′), *v.t.,* **-nized, -niz·ing.** *Physiol.* to

CONCISE PRONUNCIATION KEY: act, cāpe, dâre, pärt; set, ēqual; *if,* īce; ox, ōver, ôrder, oil, bo͝ok, bo͞ot, out; up, ûrge; child; sing; shoe; thin, *th*at; zh as in *treasure.* ə = *a* as in *alone, e* as in *system, i* as in *easily, o* as in *gallop, u* as in *circus;* ᵊ as in *fire* (fīᵊr), *hour* (ouᵊr). l and n can serve as syllabic consonants, as in *cradle* (krād′l), and *button* (but′n). See the full key inside the front cover.

induce tetanus in (a muscle). Also, *esp. Brit.,* **tet′a•nise′.** [1840–50; TETAN(US) + -IZE] —**tet′a•ni•za′tion,** *n.*

tet•a•nus (tet′n əs), *n.* **1.** *Pathol.* an infectious, often fatal disease caused by a specific bacterium that enters the body through wounds and characterized by respiratory paralysis and tonic spasms and rigidity of the voluntary muscles, esp. those of the neck and lower jaw. Cf. **lockjaw.** **2.** Also called **tet′anus bacil′lus.** *Bacteriol.* the bacterium, *Clostridium tetani,* causing this disease. **3.** *Physiol.* a state of sustained contraction of a muscle during which the muscle does not relax to its initial length or tension, induced by a rapid succession of stimuli. [1350–1400; < L < Gk *tétanos* spasm (of muscles), tetanus; r. ME *tetane* < L, as above] —**tet′a•nal,** *adj.* —**tet′a•noid′,** *adj.*

tet′anus tox′oid, *Pharm.* an inactivated form of tetanus toxin obtained from *Clostridium tetani,* used to produce an active immunity to the toxin.

tet•a•ny (tet′n ē), *n. Pathol.* a state marked by severe, intermittent tonic contractions and muscular pain, due to abnormal calcium metabolism. [1880–85; < NL *tetania.* See TETANUS, -Y[3]]

te•tar•to•he•dral (ti tär′tō hē′drəl), *adj.* (of a crystal) having one fourth the planes or faces required by the maximum symmetry of the system to which it belongs. [1855–60; < Gk *tétarto(s)* one fourth + -HEDRAL] —**te•tar′to•he′dral•ly,** *adv.* —**te•tar′to•he′drism,** *n.*

tetched (techt), *adj.* touched; slightly crazy. Also, **teched.** [1925–30; var. of TOUCHED; perh. repr. earlier *tached* (ME *techyd*) in the compounds (*well-*)*tached,* (*evil-*)*tached* having the (specified) quality or disposition (ME *tach(e), tech(e)* trait, spot, stain < OF *tache* spot (see TACHISM) + -ED[3])]

tetch•y (tech′ē), *adj.* **tetch•i•er, tetch•i•est.** irritable; touchy. Also, **techy.** [1585–95; orig. uncert.; cf. TETCHED, -Y[1]] —**tetch′i•ly,** *adv.* —**tetch′i•ness,** *n.*

Te•te (tā′tā), *n.* a city in W Mozambique, on the Zambezi River. 38,196.

tête-à-tête (tāt′ə tāt′, tet′ə tet′; *Fr.* te tᴀ tet′), *n., pl.* **tête-à-têtes,** *Fr.* ***tête-à-tête,*** *adj., adv.* —*n.* **1.** a private conversation or interview, usually between two people. **2.** Also called **vis-à-vis.** a sofa shaped like an S so two people are able to converse face to face. —*adj.* **3.** of, between, or for two persons together without others. —*adv.* **4.** (of two persons) together in private: *to sit tête-à-tête.* [1690–1700; < F: lit., head to head]

tête-bêche (tet besh′), *adj. Philately.* of or pertaining to a pair of stamps that have been printed with one stamp inverted. [1880–85; < F, equiv. to *tête* head + *bêche,* reduced from *béchevet* placed with the head of one against the foot of the other]

teth (tet, tes), *n.* **1.** the ninth letter of the Hebrew alphabet. **2.** the consonant sound represented by this letter. [< Heb]

teth•er (teth′ər), *n.* **1.** a rope, chain, or the like, by which an animal is fastened to a fixed object so as to limit its range of movement. **2.** the utmost length to which one can go in action; the utmost extent or limit of ability or resources. **3. at the end of one's tether,** at the end of one's resources, patience, or strength. —*v.t.* **4.** to fasten or confine with or as if with a tether. [1350–1400; ME (n.); cf. ON *tjóthr,* D *tuier*]

teth•er•ball (teth′ər bôl′), *n.* a game for two persons, in which each player, standing on each side of a post from the top of which a ball is suspended by a cord, hits the ball with the hand or a paddle in a direction opposite to that in which the other player hits it, the object being to coil the cord completely around the post. [1895–1900; TETHER + BALL[1]]

Te•thys (tē′this), *n.* **1.** *Class. Myth.* a Titan, a daughter of Uranus and Gaea, the wife of Oceanus and mother of the Oceanids and river gods. **2.** *Astron.* one of the moons of Saturn. **3.** *Geol.* the Mesozoic ocean or seaway of which the Mediterranean Sea is a greatly shrunken remnant.

Tet′ offen′sive, an offensive by Vietcong and North Vietnamese forces against South Vietnamese and U.S. positions in South Vietnam, beginning on Jan. 31, 1968, the start of Tet.

Te•ton (tē′ton), *n., pl.* **-tons,** (*esp. collectively*) **-ton** for 2. **1.** the westernmost branch of the Dakota Indians. **2.** a member of any of the tribes belonging to this branch, as the Brulé, Hunkpapa, Miniconjou, and Oglala. **3.** a dialect of the Dakota language. Also called **Lakhota, Lakota.**

Te′ton Range′, a mountain range in NW Wyoming and SE Idaho: a part of the Rocky Mountains. Highest peak, Grand Teton, ab. 13,700 ft (4175 m).

Té•touan (tā twän′), *n.* Tetuán.

tetr-, var. of **tetra-** before a vowel: *tetryl.*

tet•ra (te′trə), *n.* any of several tropical, freshwater fishes of the family Characidae, often kept in aquariums. [1930–35; shortening of NL *Tetragonopterus* former genus name. See TETRAGON, -O-, -PTEROUS]

tetra-, a combining form meaning "four," used in the formation of compound words: *tetrabranchiate.* Also, *esp. before a vowel,* **tetr-.** [< Gk, comb. form of *téttara,* neut. of *téttares* FOUR]

tet•ra•ba•sic (te′trə bā′sik), *adj. Chem.* **1.** (of an acid) having four atoms of hydrogen replaceable by basic atoms or groups. **2.** containing four basic atoms or groups having a valence of one. [1860–65; TETRA- + BASIC] —**tet•ra•ba•sic•i•ty** (te′trə bā sis′i tē), *n.*

tet•ra•brach (te′trə brak′), *n. Class. Pros.* a metrical foot or word of four short syllables. [< Gk *tetrábrachys* having four short syllables. See TETRA-, BRACHY-]

CONCISE ETYMOLOGY KEY: <, descended or borrowed from; >, whence; b., blend of, blended; c., cognate with; cf., compare; deriv., derivative; equiv., equivalent; imit., imitative; obl., oblique; r., replacing; s., stem; sp., spelling, spelled; resp., respelling, respelled; trans., translation; ?, origin unknown; *, unattested; ‡, probably earlier than. See the full key inside the front cover.

tet•ra•bran•chi•ate (te′trə brang′kē it, -āt′), *adj.* belonging or pertaining to the Nautiloidea (Tetrabranchiata), a subclass or order of cephalopods with four gills, including the pearly nautilus and numerous fossil forms. [1825–35; TETRA- + BRANCHIATE]

tet•ra•bro•mo•fluo•res•ce•in (te′trə brō′mō flŏŏ res′ē in, -flô-, -flō-), *n. Chem.* eosin (def. 1). [TETRA- + BROMO- + FLUORESCEIN]

tet•ra•caine (te′trə kān′), *n. Pharm.* a white, water-soluble, crystalline solid, $C_{15}H_{24}N_2O_2$, used chiefly as an anesthetic. [1930–35; TETRA- + (PRO)CAINE]

tet•ra•cene (te′trə sēn′), *n. Chem.* naphthacene. [alter. of TETRAZENE]

tet•ra•chlo•ride (te′trə klôr′īd, -id, -klōr′-), *n. Chem.* a chloride containing four atoms of chlorine. [1865–70; TETRA- + CHLORIDE]

tet•ra•chlo•ro•eth•yl•ene (te′trə klôr′ō eth′ə lēn′, -klōr′-), *n. Chem.* a colorless, nonflammable, nonexplosive liquid, C_2Cl_4, used as a solvent, esp. in dry cleaning. Also called **perchloroethylene.** [1910–15; TETRA- + CHLOROETHYLENE]

tet•ra•chlo•ro•meth•ane (te′trə klôr′ō meth′ān, -klōr′-), *n. Chem.* See **carbon tetrachloride.** [TETRA- + CHLOROMETHANE]

tet•ra•chord (te′trə kôrd′), *n. Music.* a diatonic series of four tones, the first and last separated by a perfect fourth. [1595–1605; < Gk *tetráchordos* having four strings. See TETRA-, CHORD[1]] —**tet′ra•chor′dal,** *adj.*

te•trac•id (te tras′id), *n. Chem.* a base or alcohol containing four hydroxyl groups. [TETR- + ACID]

tet•ra•coc•cus (te′trə kok′əs), *n., pl.* **-coc•ci** (-kok′sī, -sē), *Bacteriol.* a spherical bacterium occurring in square groups of four. [1895–1900; TETRA- + -COCCUS]

tet•ra•cy•cline (te′trə sī′klēn, -klin), *n. Pharm.* an antibiotic, $C_{22}H_{24}N_2O_8$, derived from chlortetracycline, used in medicine to treat a broad variety of infections. [1950–55; TETRA- + CYCL- + -INE]

Tet•ra•cyn (te′trə sin), *Pharm., Trademark.* a brand name for a form of tetracycline.

tet•rad (te′trad), *n.* **1.** a group of four. **2.** the number four. **3.** *Cell Biol.* a group of four chromatids formed by synapsis at the beginning of meiosis. **4.** *Chem.* a tetravalent or quadrivalent element, atom, or group. [1645–55; < Gk *tetrad-* (s. of *tetrás*) group of four]

tet•ra•drach•ma (te′trə drak′mə), *n.* a silver coin of ancient Greece, equal to four drachmas. Also, **tet•ra•drachm** (te′trə dram′). [1570–80; TETRA- + DRACHMA] —**tet′ra•drach′mal,** *adj.*

te•trad•y•mite (te trad′ə mīt′), *n.* a mineral, bismuth telluride and sulfide, Bi_2Te_2S, occurring in soft-gray to black foliated masses. [1840–50; < Gk *tetrádym(os)* fourfold (see TETRA-, DIDYMOUS) + -ITE[1]; modeled on G *Tetradymit*]

tet•ra•dy•na•mous (te′trə dī′nə məs), *adj. Bot.* having four long and two short stamens, as a cruciferous flower. [1820–30; TETRA- + Gk *-dynamos* -powered (*dýnam(is)* power + *-os* adj. suffix; see -OUS)]

tet•ra•eth•yl (te′trə eth′əl), *adj. Chem.* containing four ethyl groups. [TETRA- + ETHYL]

tet•ra•eth•yl•lead (te′trə eth′əl led′), *n. Chem.* a colorless, oily, water-insoluble, poisonous liquid, $(C_2H_5)_4Pb$, used as an antiknock agent in gasoline. Also, **tet′raeth′yl lead′.** Also called **lead tetraethyl, TEL** [1920–25; TETRAETHYL + LEAD[2]]

tetraeth′yl pyrophos′phate, *Chem.* a colorless to amber, hygroscopic, poisonous liquid, $(C_2H_5)_4P_2O_7$, used as an insecticide and as a rodenticide. Also called **TEPP**

tet•ra•fluor•ide (te′trə flŏŏr′īd, -flôr′-, -flōr′-), *n. Chem.* a fluoride containing four fluorine atoms. [1905–10; TETRA- + FLUORIDE]

tet•ra•fluo•ro•eth•yl•ene (te′trə flŏŏr′ō eth′ə lēn′, -flôr′-, -flōr′-), *n. Chem.* a colorless, water-insoluble, flammable gas, C_2F_4, used in the synthesis of certain polymeric resins, as Teflon. [1930–35; TETRA- + FLUORO- + ETHYLENE]

tet•ra•func•tion•al (te′trə fungk′shə nl), *adj. Chem.* pertaining to molecules or groups that can bond at four sites. [TETRA- + FUNCTIONAL]

tet•ra•gon (te′trə gon′), *n.* a polygon having four angles or sides; a quadrangle or quadrilateral. [1620–30; < Gk *tetrágōnon.* See TETRA-, -GON]

te•trag•o•nal (te trag′ə nl), *adj.* **1.** pertaining to or having the form of a tetragon. **2.** *Crystall.* noting or pertaining to a system of crystallization in which all three axes are at right angles to one another, two being equal in length and the third being of a different length. Cf. **crystal system.** [1565–75; TETRAGON + -AL[1]] —**te•trag′o•nal•ly,** *adv.* —**te•trag′o•nal•ness,** *n.*

tetrag′onal trisoctahe′dron, *Geom.* a trisoctahedron the faces of which are quadrilaterals; trapezohedron.

tet•ra•gram (te′trə gram′), *n.* a word of four letters. [1860–65; < Gk *tetrágrammon,* n. use of neut. of *tetrágrammos* having four letters, equiv. to *tetra-* TETRA- + *grámm(a)* letter (see -GRAM[1]) + *-os* adj. suffix]

Tet•ra•gram•ma•ton (te′trə gram′ə ton′), *n.* the Hebrew word for God, consisting of the four letters *yod, he, vav,* and *he,* transliterated consonantally usually as *YHVH,* now pronounced as *Adonai* or *Elohim* in substitution for the original pronunciation forbidden since the 2nd or 3rd century B.C. Cf. **Yahweh.** [1350–1400; ME < Gk *tetragrámmaton,* n. use of neut. of *tetragrámmatos* having four letters, equiv. to *tetra-* TETRA- + *grammat-* (s. of *grámma*) letter + *-os* adj. suffix]

tet•ra•he•dral (te′trə hē′drəl), *adj.* **1.** pertaining to or having the form of a tetrahedron. **2.** having four lateral planes in addition to the top and bottom. [1785–95; TETRAHEDR(ON) + -AL[1]] —**tet′ra•he′dral•ly,** *adv.*

tet•ra•he•drite (te′trə hē′drīt), *n.* a steel-gray or blackish mineral with a brilliant metallic luster, essentially copper and antimony sulfide, $(Cu, Fe, Zn, Ag)_{12}Sb_4S_{13}$, an end member of a series of solid solutions into which arsenic enters to form tennantite: mined as an ore of copper and silver. [1865–70; TETRAHEDR(ON) + -ITE[1], modeled on G *Tetraedrit*]

tet•ra•he•dron (te′trə hē′drən), *n., pl.* **-drons, -dra** (-drə). **1.** *Geom.* a solid contained by four plane faces; a triangular pyramid. **2.** any of various objects resembling a tetrahedron in the distribution of its faces or apexes. [1560–70; TETRA- + -HEDRON, modeled on LGk *tetráedron,* n. use of neut. of *tetráedros* four-sided]

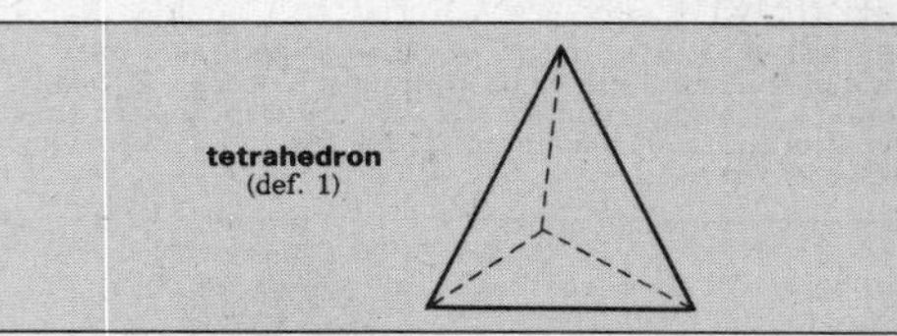

tet•ra•hy•drate (te′trə hī′drāt), *n. Chem.* a hydrate that contains four molecules of water, as potassium sodium tartrate, $KNaC_4H_4O_6 \cdot 4H_2O$. [1885–90; TETRA- + HYDRATE] —**tet′ra•hy′drat•ed,** *adj.*

tet•ra•hy•dric (te′trə hī′drik), *adj. Chem.* (esp. of alcohols and phenols) tetrahydroxy. [1885–90; TETRA- + -HYDRIC]

tet•ra•hy•dro•can•nab•i•nol (te′trə hī′drə kə nab′ə nôl′, -nol′), *n. Pharm.* a compound, $C_{21}H_{30}O_2$, that is the physiologically active component in cannabis preparations (marijuana, hashish, etc.) derived from the Indian hemp plant or produced synthetically. *Abbr.:* THC [1965–70; TETRA- + HYDRO-[2] + CANNABINOL]

tet•ra•hy•dro•fu•ran (te′trə hī′drə fyŏŏr′an), *n. Chem.* a clear liquid, C_4H_8O, soluble in water and organic solvents, used as a solvent for resins, in polymerizations and as a chemical intermediate. [1940–45; TETRA- + HYDRO-[2] + FURAN]

tet•ra•hy•drox•y (te′trə hī drok′sē), *adj. Chem.* (of a molecule) containing four hydroxyl groups. [TETRA- + HYDROXY]

tet•ra•hy•droz•o•line (te′trə hī droz′ə lēn′), *n. Pharm.* a compound, $C_{13}H_{16}N_2$, used in the treatment of nasal congestion and certain conditions of eye irritation. [TETRA- + HYDRO-[2] + (IMIDA)ZOL + -INE[2]]

tet•ra•hy•me•na (te′trə hī′mə nə), *n. Biol.* any ciliated protozoan of the genus *Tetrahymena,* a relative of the paramecium: often used in genetics research. [< NL (1940); see TETRA-, HYMEN, -A[2]; so named from the four membranous ciliary organelles that characterized a cytostomal pattern exemplified by this genus]

tet•ra•lite (te′trə līt′), *n. Chem.* tetryl. [TETRA- + -LITE]

te•tral•o•gy (te tral′ə jē, -träl′ə-), *n., pl.* **-gies.** **1.** a series of four related dramas, operas, novels, etc. **2.** a group of four dramas, three tragedies and one satyr play, performed consecutively at the festival of Dionysus in ancient Athens. [1650–60; < Gk *tetralogía.* See TETRA-, -LOGY]

tetral′ogy of Fal•lot′ (fa lō′), *Pathol.* a congenital malformation of the heart characterized by an abnormal opening in the septum dividing the ventricles, misplacement of the aorta so that it receives blood from both ventricles instead of only the left ventricle, narrowing of the pulmonary artery, and enlargement of the right ventricle. [after Étienne *Fallot,* French physician who named the disease in 1888]

tet•ra•mer (te′trə mər), *n.* **1.** a molecule composed of four identical, simpler molecules. **2.** a polymer derived from four identical monomers. Cf. **oligomer.** [1905–10; TETRA- + -MER]

te•tram•er•ous (te tram′ər əs), *adj.* **1.** consisting of or divided into four parts. **2.** *Bot.* (of flowers) having the parts of a whorl arranged in fours or multiples of four. [1820–30; < NL *tetramerus* < Gk *tetramerés* having four parts. See TETRA-, -MEROUS] —**te•tram′er•ism,** *n.*

te•tram•e•ter (te tram′i tər), *n.* **1.** *Pros.* a verse of four feet. *n.* **2.** *Class Pros.* a line consisting of four dipodies in trochaic, iambic, or anapestic meter. —*adj.* **3.** *Pros.* consisting of four metrical feet. [1605–15; < L *tetrametrus* < Gk *tetrámetros* having four measures. See TETRA-, METER[2]]

tet•ra•meth•yl•lead (te′trə meth′əl led′), *n. Chem.* a colorless liquid, $(CH_3)_4Pb$, insoluble in water, slightly soluble in alcohol and benzene, used as an antiknock agent in gasoline. Also called **TML** [1960–65; TETRA- + METHYL + LEAD[2]]

te•tran•drous (te tran′drəs), *adj. Bot.* having four stamens. [1800–10; TETR- + -ANDROUS]

tet•ra•ni•trate (te′trə nī′trāt), *n. Chem.* a compound containing four nitrate groups. [TETRA- + NITRATE]

tet•ra•pet•al•ous (te′trə pet′l əs), *adj. Bot.* having four petals. [1690–1700; TETRA- + PETALOUS]

tet·ra·ple·gi·a (te′trə plē′jē ə, -jə), *n. Pathol.* quadriplegia. [1910–15; TETRA- + -PLEGIA]

tet·ra·ploid (te′trə ploid′), *adj. Biol.* **1.** having a chromosome number that is four times the basic or haploid number. —*n.* **2.** a tetraploid cell or organism. [1925–30; TETRA- + -PLOID] —**tet′ra·ploi′dy,** *n.*

tet·ra·pod (te′trə pod′), *n.* **1.** any vertebrate having four limbs or, as in the snake and whale, having had four-limbed ancestors. **2.** an object, as a caltrop, having four projections radiating from one central node, with each forming an angle of 120° with any other, so that no matter how the object is placed on a relatively flat surface, three of the projections will form a supporting tripod and the fourth will point directly upward. —*adj.* **3.** having four limbs or descended from four-limbed ancestors. [< NL *tetrapodus* < Gk *tetrapod-* (s. of *tetrápous*) four-footed. (see TETRA-, -POD) + NL *-us* adj. suffix]

te·trap·o·dy (te trap′ə dē), *n., pl.* **-dies.** *Pros.* a measure consisting of four feet. [1840–50; < Gk *tetrapodía.* See TETRA-, -POD, -Y[3]] —**tet·ra·pod·ic** (te′trə-pod′ik), *adj.*

te·trap·ter·ous (te trap′tər əs), *adj.* **1.** *Zool.* having four wings or winglike appendages. **2.** *Bot.* having four winglike appendages. [1820–30; < Gk *tetrápteros.* See TETRA-, -PTEROUS] —**te·trap′ter·an,** *adj., n.*

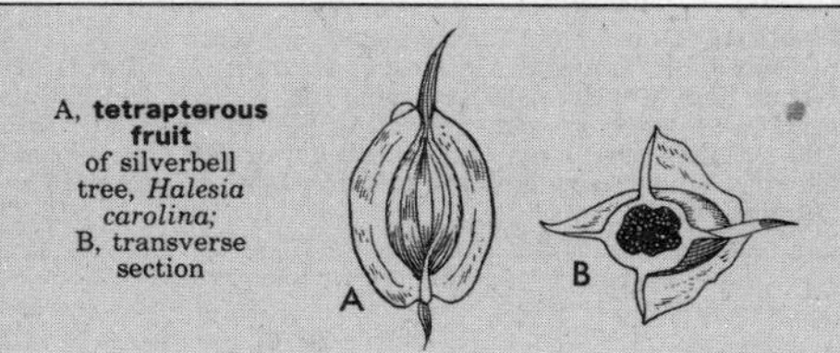

A, **tetrapterous fruit** of silverbell tree, *Halesia carolina;* B, transverse section

tet·ra·py·lon (te′trə pī′lon), *n., pl.* **-la** (-lə). a structure having four gateways as features of an architectural composition. [1900–05; < Gk, *tetrápylon,* n. use of neut. of *tetrápylos* having four gates. See TETRA-, PYLON]

te·trarch (te′trärk, tē′-), *n.* **1.** any ruler of a fourth part, division, etc. **2.** a subordinate ruler. **3.** one of four joint rulers or chiefs. **4.** the ruler of the fourth part of a country or province in the ancient Roman Empire. [1350–1400; ME, *tetrarcha, tetrarke* < LL *tetrarcha,* var. of L *tetrarchēs* < Gk *tetrárchēs.* See TETR-, -ARCH] —**te′trar·chy, te·trarch·ate** (te′trär kāt′, -kit, tē′-), *n.* —**te·trar·chic** (te trär′kik, ti-), **te·trar′chi·cal,** *adj.*

tet·ra·spo·ran·gi·um (te′trə spô ran′jē əm, -spō-), *n., pl.* **-gi·a** (-jē ə). *Bot.* a sporangium containing four asexual spores. [1885–90; TETRA- + SPORANGIUM]

tet·ra·spore (te′trə spôr′, -spōr′), *n. Bot.* one of the four asexual spores produced within a tetrasporangium. [1855–60; TETRA- + SPORE] —**tet·ra·spor·ic** (te′trə-spôr′ik, -spor′-), **tet·ra·spor·ous** (te′trə spôr′əs, -spōr′-, ti tras′pər-), *adj.*

tet·ra·stich (te′trə stik, te tras′tik), *n. Pros.* a strophe, stanza, or poem consisting of four lines. [1570–80; < L *tetrastichon* < Gk *tetrástichon,* n. use of neut. of *tetrástichos.* See TETRASTICHOUS] —**tet·ra·stich·ic** (te′-trə stik′ik), **te·tras·ti·chal** (ti tras′ti kəl), *adj.*

te·tras·ti·chous (ti tras′ti kəs), *adj. Bot.* **1.** arranged in a spike of four vertical rows, as flowers. **2.** having four such rows of flowers, as a spike. [1865–70; < NL *tetrastichus* < Gk *tetrástichos* having four lines or rows. See TETRA-, STICH[1], -OUS]

tet·ra·style (te′trə stīl′), *adj. Archit.* having four columns. [< L *tetrastȳlon* < Gk *tetrástȳlon,* n. use of neut. of *tetrástȳlos* having four pillars; see TETRA-, -STYLE[2]]

tet·ra·syl·la·ble (te′trə sil′ə bəl, te′trə sil′-), *n.* a word or line of verse of four syllables. [1580–90; TETRA- + SYLLABLE] —**tet·ra·syl·lab·ic** (te′trə si lab′ik), **tet′ra·syl·lab′i·cal,** *adj.*

tet·ra·va·lent (te′trə vā′lənt, te trav′ə-), *adj. Chem.* **1.** having a valence of four, as Pt^{+4}. **2.** quadrivalent. [1865–70; TETRA- + -VALENT] —**tet′ra·va′lence, tet′ra·va′len·cy,** *n.*

tet·ra·zene (te′trə zēn′), *n. Chem.* **1.** either of two isomeric compounds with the formula N_4H_4, known only in the form of their derivatives. **2.** naphthacene. [TETR- + AZ- + -ENE]

Te·traz·zi·ni (te′trə zē′nē; *It.* te′trät tsē′nē), *n.* **Lu·i·sa** (lo͞o ē′zä), **1.** 1874–1940, Italian operatic soprano. —*adj.* **2.** (often l.c.) served over pasta with a cream sauce, often flavored with sherry, sprinkled with cheese, and browned in the oven: *chicken Tetrazzini.* [(in def. 2) after L. *Tetrazzini,* for whom it was first made]

tet·rode (te′trōd), *n. Electronics.* a vacuum tube containing four electrodes, usually a plate, two grids, and a cathode. [1900–05; TETR- + -ODE[1]]

te·tro·do·tox·in (te trō′də tok′sin), *n. Pharm.* a neurotoxin, $C_{11}H_{17}N_3O_8$, occurring in a species of puffer fish: ingestion of the toxin is usually rapidly fatal due to heart failure or asphyxiation; used experimentally to block impulse conduction potential in excitable cells. [1910–15; < NL *Tetrodo(n)* genus name of the puffer fish (see TETR-, -ODONT) + TOXIN]

te·trox·ide (te trok′sīd, -sid), *n. Chem.* an oxide whose molecule contains four atoms of oxygen. [1865–70; TETR- + OXIDE]

tet·ryl (te′tril), *n. Chem.* a yellow, crystalline, water-insoluble solid, $C_7H_5N_5O_8$, used as a chemical indicator and as a detonator and bursting charge in small-caliber shells. Also, **tetralite.** Also called **nitramine, trinitrophenylmethylnitramine.** [1855–60; TETR- + -YL]

tet·ry·tol (te′tri tôl′, -tol′), *n.* an explosive consisting of tetryl and TNT. [TETRY(L) + TOL(UENE)]

tet·ter (tet′ər), *n.* (not in technical use) any of various eruptive skin diseases, as herpes, eczema, and impetigo. [bef. 900; ME; OE *teter;* c. Skt *dadru* kind of skin disease]

tet·ti·go·ni·id (tet′i gō′nē id), *n.* See **long-horned grasshopper.** [1920–25; < NL *Tettigoniidae* family name, equiv. to *Tettigoni(a)* genus name (formed on Gk *tettig-,* s. of *téttix* cicada) + *-idae* -ID[2]]

Te·tuán (te twän′), *n.* a seaport in N Morocco, on the Mediterranean: former capital of the Spanish zone of Morocco. 844,000. Also, **Tétouan.**

Tet·zel (tet′səl), *n.* **Jo·hann** (yō′hän), 1465?–1519, German monk: antagonist of Martin Luther. Also, **Tezel.**

Teu·cri·an (to͞o′krē ən, tyo͞o′-), *adj.* **1.** of or pertaining to the ancient Trojans. —*n.* **2.** one of the ancient Trojans. [< Gk *Teûkr(os)* Teucer, first king of Troy]

Teut., **1.** Teuton. **2.** Teutonic.

Teu·to·bur·ger Wald (toi′tō bo͝or′gər vält′), a chain of wooded hills in NW Germany, in Westphalia: Romans defeated by German tribes A.D. 9.

Teu·ton (to͞ot′n, tyo͞ot′n), *n.* **1.** a member of a Germanic people or tribe first mentioned in the 4th century B.C. and supposed to have dwelt in Jutland. **2.** a native of Germany or a person of German origin. —*adj.* **3.** Teutonic. [< L *Teutonī* (pl.) tribal name < Gmc]

Teu·ton·ic (to͞o ton′ik, tyo͞o-), *adj.* **1.** of or pertaining to the ancient Teutons. **2.** of, pertaining to, or characteristic of the Teutons or Germans; German. **3.** noting or pertaining to the northern European stock that includes the German, Dutch, Scandinavian, British, and related peoples. **4.** (of languages) Germanic. **5.** Nordic. —*n.* **6.** Germanic. [1580–90; TEUTON + -IC] —**Teu·ton′i·cal·ly,** *adv.*

Teuton′ic Or′der, a religious military order founded c1190 in the Holy Land by German crusaders that originally did charitable work among the sick and later fought against the Slavic and Baltic peoples in the eastward expansion of medieval Germany. Also called **Teuton′ic Knights′.**

Teu·ton·ism (to͞ot′n iz′əm, tyo͞ot′-), *n.* the character, spirit, or culture of the Teutons, esp. the Germans. **1.** a Teutonic or German characteristic. **2.** Germanism. Also, **Teu·ton·i·cism** (to͞o ton′ə siz′əm, tyo͞o-). [1850–55; TEUTON + -ISM] —**Teu′ton·ist,** *n.*

Teu·ton·ize (to͞ot′n īz′, tyo͞ot′-), *v.t., v.i.,* **-ized, -iz·ing.** to make or become Teutonic or German; Germanize. Also, *esp. Brit.,* **Teu′ton·ise′.** [1835–45; TEUTON + -IZE] —**Teu′ton·i·za′tion,** *n.*

TeV, trillion electron-volts. Also, **Tev, tev.**

tev·a·tron (tev′ə tron′), *n.* an accelerator in which protons or antiprotons are raised to energies of a few trillion electron-volts. [1980–85; TEV + *-atron,* as in BETATRON, BEVATRON]

Te·ve·re (te′ve re), *n.* Italian name of the **Tiber.**

Te·vet (te vet′, tā-, tā′väs), *n.* the fourth month of the Jewish calendar. Also, **Tebet.** Cf. **Jewish calendar.** [< Heb *tēbhēth*]

Te·wa (tā′wə, tē′-), *n., pl.* **-was,** (*esp. collectively*) **-wa** for 1. **1.** a member of a cluster of pueblo-dwelling North American Indian peoples of New Mexico and Arizona. **2.** the Tanoan language of the Tewa.

Tewkes·bur·y (to͞oks′ber′ē, -bə rē, -brē, tyo͞oks′-), *n.* a town in N Gloucestershire, in W England: final defeat of the Lancastrians in the Wars of the Roses 1471. 79,500.

Tewks·bur·y (to͞oks′bə rē, -brē, tyo͞oks′-), *n.* a city in NE Massachusetts. 24,635.

Tex., **1.** Texan. **2.** Texas.

Tex·ar·kan·a (tek′sär kan′ə), *n.* **1.** a city in NE Texas. 31,271. **2.** a city in SW Arkansas: contiguous with but politically independent of Texarkana, Texas. 21,459. **3.** Texarkana, Arkansas, and Texarkana, Texas, considered as a unit.

tex·as (tek′səs), *n. U.S. Naut.* **1.** a deckhouse on a texas deck for the accommodation of officers. **2.** See **texas deck.** [1855–60; after TEXAS, from the fact that the officers' accommodation was the most spacious on the Mississippi steamboats, on which cabins were named after states]

Tex·as (tek′səs), *n.* a state in the S United States. 14,228,383; 267,339 sq. mi. (692,410 sq. km). *Cap.:* Austin. *Abbr.:* Tex., TX (for use with zip code). —**Tex′an, Tex·i·an** (tek′sē ən), *adj., n.*

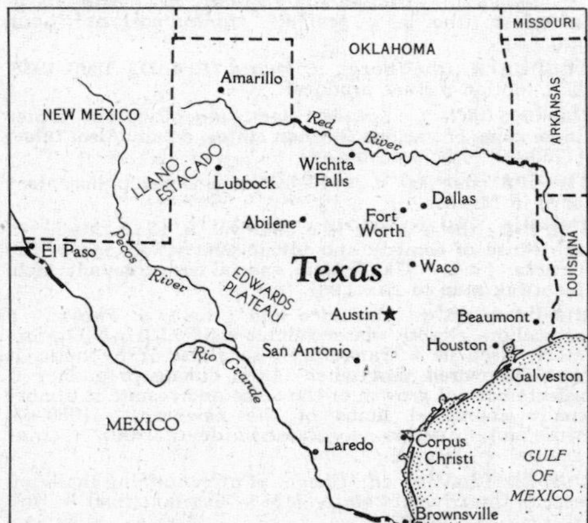

Tex′as armadil′lo. See **nine-banded armadillo.**

Tex′as Cit′y, a city in SE Texas, on Galveston Bay. 41,403.

tex′as deck′, *U.S. Naut.* the uppermost deck of an inland or western river steamer. [1850–55, *Amer.;* see TEXAS]

Tex′as fe′ver, babesiosis of cattle. [1815–25, *Amer.*]

Tex′as Independ′ence Day′, March 2, observed in Texas as the anniversary of the declaration in 1836 of the independence of Texas from Mexico and also as the birthday of Sam Houston.

Tex′as lea′guer, *Baseball.* a pop fly that falls safely between converging infielders and outfielders. [1900–05]

Tex′as long′horn, one of a breed of long-horned beef cattle of the southwestern U.S., developed from cattle introduced into North America from Spain and valued for disease resistance, fecundity, and a historical association with the old West: now rare. [1905–10, *Amer.*]

Tex′as Rang′er, **1.** a member of the Texas state police force or, esp. formerly, of the mounted state police. **2.** a member of a semiofficial group of settlers organized to fight Indians and maintain order.

Tex′as Revolu′tion, *U.S. Hist.* a revolutionary movement, 1832–36, in which U.S. settlers asserted their independence from Mexico and established the republic of Texas.

Tex′as sage′, a slightly woody, hairy plant, *Salvia coccinea,* of the mint family, native to the southeastern U.S. and tropical America, having elongated clusters of scarlet flowers.

Tex′as tow′er, an offshore radar-equipped platform supported by foundations sunk into the floor of the ocean, formerly used as part of a system for warning against air attacks.

Tex-Mex (teks′meks′), *adj.* **1.** of or pertaining to aspects of culture that combine Mexican and Texan or southwestern U.S. features, esp. aspects of culture developed in southern Texas based on or influenced by Mexican elements: *Tex-Mex cooking; Tex-Mex music.* —*n.* **2.** a form of Mexican Spanish having elements of English and spoken near the border of Texas and Mexico, esp. Mexican Spanish as spoken in Texas. **3.** *Music.* norteña. [1945–50, *Amer.;* by shortening]

text (tekst), *n.* **1.** the main body of matter in a manuscript, book, newspaper, etc., as distinguished from notes, appendixes, headings, illustrations, etc. **2.** the original words of an author or speaker, as opposed to a translation, paraphrase, commentary, or the like: *The newspaper published the whole text of the speech.* **3.** the actual wording of anything written or printed: *You have not kept to the text of my remarks.* **4.** any of the various forms in which a writing exists: *The text is a medieval transcription.* **5.** the wording adopted by an editor as representing the original words of an author: *the authoritative text of Catullus.* **6.** any theme or topic; subject. **7.** the words of a song or the like. **8.** a textbook. **9.** a short passage of Scripture, esp. one chosen in proof of a doctrine or as the subject of a sermon: *The text he chose was the* Sermon on the Mount. **10.** the letter of the Holy Scripture, or the Scriptures themselves. **11.** *Print.* **a.** See **black letter. b.** type, as distinguished from illustrations, margins, etc. **12.** *Ling.* a unit of connected speech or writing, esp. composed of more than one sentence, that forms a cohesive whole. [1300–50; ME < ML *textus* text, terms, L: text, structure, orig., pattern of weaving, texture (of cloth), equiv. to *tex(ere)* to weave + *-tus* suffix of v. action] —**text′less,** *adj.*

text·book (tekst′bo͝ok′), *n.* **1.** a book used by students as a standard work for a particular branch of study. —*adj.* **2.** pertaining to, characteristic of, or seemingly suitable for inclusion in a textbook; typical; classic: *a textbook case.* [1720–30; TEXT + BOOK]

text·book·ish (tekst′bo͝ok′ish), *adj.* suggesting a textbook, esp. in literary style or composition. [1925–30; TEXTBOOK + -ISH[1]]

text′ edi′tion, a special edition of a book for distribution to schools or colleges, subject to a special rate of discount, sometimes without a dust jacket (distinguished from *trade edition*). Also called **school edition**

text′ ed′itor, *Computers.* a program for editing stored documents, performing such functions as adding, deleting, or moving text. [1970–75] —**text′-ed′it·ing,** *adj.*

text′ hand′, handwriting characterized by large neat letters. [1535–45]

tex·tile (teks′tīl, -til), *n.* **1.** any cloth or goods produced by weaving, knitting, or felting. **2.** a material, as a fiber or yarn, used in or suitable for weaving: *Glass can be used as a textile.* —*adj.* **3.** woven or capable of being woven: *textile fabrics.* **4.** of or pertaining to weaving. **5.** of or pertaining to textiles or the production of textiles: *the textile industry.* [1520–30; < L *textilis* woven, *textile* (n. use of neut.) woven fabric, equiv. to *text(us),* ptp. of *texere* to weave + *-ilis, -ile* -ILE]

tex·tu·al (teks′cho͞o əl), *adj.* **1.** of or pertaining to a text: *textual errors.* **2.** based on or conforming to the text, as of the Scriptures: *a textual interpretation of the Bible.* [1350–1400; ME < ML *textu(s)* (see TEXT) + -AL[1]; r. ME *textuel* < MF < ML, as above] —**tex′tu·al·ly,** *adv.*

tex′tual crit′icism. See **lower criticism.** [1870–75] —**tex′tual crit′ic.**

tex·tu·al·ism (teks′cho͞o ə liz′əm), *n.* strict adherence to a text, esp. of the Scriptures. [1860–65; TEXTUAL + -ISM]

tex·tu·al·ist (teks′cho͞o ə list), *n.* **1.** a person who ad-

CONCISE PRONUNCIATION KEY: act, cāpe, dâre, pärt; set, ēqual; if, īce; ox, ōver, ôrder, oil, bo͝ok, bo͞ot, out; up, ûrge; child; sing; shoe; thin, *th*at; zh as in *treasure.* ə = *a* as in *alone, e* as in *system, i* as in *easily, o* as in *gallop, u* as in *circus;* ᵊ as in *fire* (fīᵊr), *hour* (ouᵊr). l and n can serve as syllabic consonants, as in *cradle* (krād′l), and *button* (but′n). See the full key inside the front cover.

heres closely to a text, esp. of the Scriptures. **2.** a person who is well versed in the text of the Scriptures. [1620–30; TEXTUAL + -IST]

tex·tu·ar·y (teks′cho͞o er′ē), *adj., n., pl.* **-ar·ies.** —*adj.* **1.** of or pertaining to a text; textual. —*n.* **2.** a textualist. [1600–10; < ML *textu(s)* (see TEXT) + -ARY]

tex·ture (teks′chər), *n., v.,* **-tured, -tur·ing.** —*n.* **1.** the visual and esp. tactile quality of a surface: *rough texture.* **2.** the characteristic structure of the interwoven or intertwined threads, strands, or the like, that make up a textile fabric: *coarse texture.* **3.** the characteristic physical structure given to a material, an object, etc., by the size, shape, arrangement, and proportions of its parts: *soil of a sandy texture; a cake with a heavy texture.* **4.** an essential or characteristic quality; essence. **5.** *Fine Arts.* **a.** the characteristic visual and tactile quality of the surface of a work of art resulting from the way in which the materials are used. **b.** the imitation of the tactile quality of represented objects. **6.** the quality given, as to a musical or literary work, by the combination or interrelation of parts or elements. **7.** a rough or grainy surface quality. **8.** anything produced by weaving; woven fabric. —*v.t.* **9.** to give texture or a particular texture to. **10.** to make by or as if by weaving. [1400–50; late ME < L *textūra* web, equiv. to *text(us)* (ptp. of *texere* to weave) + *-ūra* -URE] —**tex′tur·al,** *adj.* —**tex′tur·al·ly,** *adv.* —**tex′ture·less,** *adj.*

tex′ture paint′, a finish paint having an insoluble additive, as sand, for giving a slightly rough textural effect.

tex·tur·ize (teks′chə rīz′), *v.t.,* **-ized, -iz·ing.** to give texture or a particular texture to: *texturized yarn.* Also, *esp. Brit.,* **tex′tur·ise′.** [1945–50; TEXTURE + -IZE] —**tex′tur·iz′er,** *n.*

tex·tus re·cep·tus (tek′stəs ri sep′təs), a text of a work that is generally accepted as being genuine or original. [1855–60; < NL: received text]

Tey·de (*Sp.* tā′t͟hе), *n.* **Pi·co de** (pē′kô t͟hе). See **Teide, Pico de.**

Tez·cat·li·po·ca (tes kät′li pō′kä), *n.* an Aztec god. [< Nahuatl *Tēzcatlepōca,* perh. equiv. to *tēzca(tl)* mirror + *tle(tl)* fire + *(po)pōca* smokes (3d sing. v.)]

Te·zel (tet′səl), *n.* **Johann.** See **Tetzel, Johann.**

T formation, *Football.* an offensive formation in which the quarterback lines up directly behind the center with the fullback about three yards behind the quarterback and the halfbacks on opposite sides of and about one yard from the fullback. [1930–35]

tfr., transfer.

TFX, *Mil.* (in designations of fighter aircraft) tactical fighter experimental.

TG, **1.** transformational-generative (grammar). **2.** transformational grammar.

tg, *Trigonom.* tangent.

t.g., *Biol.* type genus.

TGG, transformational-generative grammar.

TGIF, *Informal.* thank God it's Friday. Also, **T.G.I.F.**

tgn, *Trigonom.* tangent.

T-group (tē′gro͞op′), *n.* See **sensitivity group.** [1960–65; *T(raining) group*]

TGV, a high-speed French passenger train that runs on a separate track and is capable of a top speed of over 200 mph (320 km/h). [< F *t(rain à) g(rande) v(itesse)* high-speed train]

Th, *Symbol, Chem.* thorium.

Th 227, *Symbol, Chem.* radioactinium. Also, **Th-227**

-th[1], a suffix forming nouns of action (*birth*) or abstract nouns denoting quality or condition (*depth; length; warmth*). [ME *-th(e),* OE *-thu, -tho, -th* (var. *-t* after a velar, *f,* or *s*); c. Goth *-itha,* L *-tus,* Gk *-tos*]

-th[2], a suffix used in the formation of ordinal numbers (*fourth, tenth*), in some cases, added to altered stems of the cardinal (*fifth; twelfth*). [ME *-the, -te,* OE *-tha, -the* (var. *-ta* after *f* or *s*); c. ON *-thi, -di,* L *-tus,* Gk *-tos;* see -ETH]

-th[3], var. of **-eth**[1]: *doth.*

Th., Thursday.

T.H., Territory of Hawaii.

thā (thä), *n.* the fourth letter of the Arabic alphabet. [< Ar]

Thach (thach), *n.* **Edward.** See **Teach, Edward.**

Thack·er·ay (thak′ə rē), *n.* **William Make·peace** (māk′pēs′), 1811–63, English novelist, born in India. —**Thack′er·ay·an,** *adj., n.*

Thad·de·us (thad′ē əs), *n.* **1.** one of the twelve apostles. Matt. 10:3. **2.** a male given name: from an Aramaic word meaning "praise."

thae (t͟hā), *pron., adj. Scot. and North Eng.* **1.** those. **2.** these. [1575–85; repr. north and Scots development of ME, OE *thā,* pl. of *thæt* THAT]

Thai (tī), *n.* **1.** Also called **Thai·land·er** (tī′lan′dər, -lən-). a native or descendant of a native of Thailand. **2.** the language of Thailand, a member of the Tai group of languages. —*adj.* **3.** of or pertaining to Thailand, its people, or their language; Siamese. Also, **Tai.**

Thai·land (tī′land′, -lənd), *n.* **1.** Formerly, **Siam.** a kingdom in SE Asia: official name of Siam 1939–45 and since 1949. 40,000,000; 198,242 sq. mi. (513,445 sq. km). *Cap.:* Bangkok. **2. Gulf of.** Also called **Gulf of Siam.** an arm of the South China Sea, S of Thailand.

CONCISE ETYMOLOGY KEY: <, descended or borrowed from; >, whence; b., blend of, blended; c., cognate with; cf., compare; deriv., derivative; equiv., equivalent; imit., imitative; obl., oblique; r., replacing; s., stem; sp., spelling, spelled; resp., respelling, respelled; trans., translation; ?, origin unknown; *, unattested; ‡, probably earlier than. See the full key inside the front cover.

Tha·ïs (thā′is), *n.* fl. late 4th century B.C., Athenian courtesan: mistress of Alexander the Great and Ptolemy I.

Thai′ stick′, *Slang.* a cigar-shaped stick of highly potent marijuana from Thailand. [1975–80]

Tha·kur (tä′ko͝or), *n.* chief or master (used as a term of respectful address among the Kshatriya caste in India). [1790–1800; < Hindi *ṭhākur* master, chief < Prakrit *ṭhakkura* village headman < Skt: a title]

thal·a·men·ceph·a·lon (thal′ə men sef′ə lon′, -lən), *n., pl.* **-lons, -la** (-lə). *Anat.* the diencephalon. [1870–75; THALAM(US) + ENCEPHALON] —**thal·a·men·ce·phal·ic** (thal′ə men′sə fal′ik), *adj.*

tha·la·mi·um (thə lā′mē əm), *n., pl.* **-mi·a** (-mē ə). thalamus (def. 3). [< NL, dim. of THALAMUS; see -IUM]

thal·a·mus (thal′ə məs), *n., pl.* **-mi** (-mī′). **1.** *Anat.* the middle part of the diencephalon through which sensory impulses pass to reach the cerebral cortex. **2.** *Bot.* a receptacle or torus. **3.** Also called **thalamium.** an apartment for women in an ancient Greek house. [1695–1705; < NL; L: bedroom < Gk *thálamos*] —**tha·lam·ic** (thə lam′ik), *adj.* —**tha·lam′i·cal·ly,** *adv.*

Tha·las·sa (thə las′ə), *n. Class. Myth.* the personification of the sea.

thal·as·se·mi·a (thal′ə sē′mē ə), *n. Pathol.* a hereditary form of anemia, occurring chiefly in people of Mediterranean origin, marked by the abnormal synthesis of hemoglobin and a consequent shortened life span of red blood cells. Also called **Cooley's anemia.** [1932; < Gk *thálass(a)* sea (alluding to the Mediterranean Sea; the anemia was first reported among children in Mediterranean countries) + -EMIA]

tha·las·sic (thə las′ik), *adj.* **1.** of or pertaining to seas and oceans. **2.** of or pertaining to smaller bodies of water, as seas and gulfs, as distinguished from large oceanic bodies. **3.** growing, living, or found in the sea; marine. [1855–60; < Gk *thálass(a)* sea + -IC]

thalasso-, a combining form meaning "sea," used in the formation of compound words: *thalassocracy.* [comb. form repr. Gk *thálassa* sea]

thal·as·soc·ra·cy (thal′ə sok′rə sē), *n., pl.* **-cies.** dominion over the seas, as in exploration, trade, or colonization. [1840–50; THALASSO- + -CRACY]

tha·las·so·crat (thə las′ə krat′), *n.* a nation that has dominion over the seas. [1940–45; THALASSO- + -CRAT]

thal·as·sog·ra·phy (thal′ə sog′rə fē), *n.* oceanography, esp. that branch dealing with smaller bodies of water, as bays, sounds, and gulfs. [1885–90; THALASSO- + -GRAPHY] —**thal′as·sog′ra·pher,** *n.* —**tha·las·so·graph·ic** (thə las′ə graf′ik), **tha·las′so·graph′i·cal,** *adj.*

Thal·berg (thôl′bûrg), *n.* **Irving (Grant),** 1899–1936, U.S. motion-picture producer.

tha·ler (tä′lər), *n., pl.* **-ler, -lers.** any of various former large coins of various German states; dollar. Also, **taler.** [1780–90; < G; see DOLLAR]

Tha·les (thā′lēz), *n.* c640–546? B.C., Greek philosopher, born in Miletus.

Tha·li·a (thə lī′ə, thā′lē ə, thāl′yə), *n. Class. Myth.* **1.** the Muse of comedy and idyllic poetry. **2.** one of the Graces. [< L < Gk *Tháleia,* special use of the adj.: rich, plentiful; akin to THALLUS]

tha·lid·o·mide (thə lid′ə mīd′, tha-), *n. Pharm.* a crystalline, slightly water-soluble solid, $C_{13}H_{10}N_2O_4$, formerly used as a tranquilizer, sedative, or hypnotic: it was discovered that when taken during pregnancy it affects normal growth of the fetus and results in abnormally shortened limbs of the newborn. [1960–65; THAL(IC) + (IM)IDO- + *(glutari)mide* (GLUT(EN) + (TART)AR(IC) + -IMIDE)]

thal·lic (thal′ik), *adj. Chem.* of or containing thallium, esp. in the trivalent state. [1865–70; THALL(IUM) + -IC]

thal·li·um (thal′ē əm), *n. Chem.* a soft, malleable, rare, bluish-white metallic element: used in the manufacture of alloys and, in the form of its salts, in rodenticides. *Symbol:* Tl; *at. wt.:* 204.37; *at. no.:* 81; *sp. gr.:* 11.85 at 20°C. [1860–65; < NL, equiv. to *thall-* (< Gk *thallós* green stalk) + *-ium* -IUM; named after green line in its spectrum]

thal′lium sul′fate, *Chem.* a colorless, crystalline, water-soluble, poisonous solid, Tl_2SO_4, used chiefly as an insecticide and rodenticide. Also, **thal′lous sul′fate.**

thal·loid (thal′oid), *adj. Bot. Mycol.* resembling or consisting of a thallus. [1855–60; THALL(US) + -OID]

thal·lo·phyte (thal′ə fīt′), *n.* any of the Thallophyta, a plant division in some older classification schemes, comprising algae, fungi, and lichens. [1850–55; < NL *Thallophyta* group name. See THALLUS, -O-, -PHYTE] —**thal·lo·phyt·ic** (thal′ə fit′ik), *adj.*

thal·lous (thal′əs), *adj. Chem.* containing univalent thallium. Also, **thal·li·ous** (thal′ē əs). [1885–90; THALL(IUM) + -OUS]

thal·lus (thal′əs), *n., pl.* **thal·li** (thal′ī), **thal·lus·es.** *Bot., Mycol.* a simple vegetative body undifferentiated into true leaves, stem, and root, ranging from an aggregation of filaments to a complex plantlike form. [1820–30; < NL < Gk *thallós* young shoot, twig]

thal·weg (täl′veg, -väk), *n.* **1.** a line, as drawn on a map, connecting the lowest points of a valley. **2.** *Chiefly Internat. Law.* the middle of the main navigable channel of a waterway that serves as a boundary line between states. [1860–65; < G, equiv. to *Thal,* now obs. sp. of *Tal* valley (c. DALE) + *Weg* WAY[1]]

Tha·mar (thā′mər), *n. Douay Bible.* Tamar.

Thames (temz *for 1, 2;* thāmz, tāmz, temz *for 3*), *n.* **1.** a river in S England, flowing E through London to the North Sea. 209 mi. (336 km) long. **2.** a river in SE Canada, in Ontario province, flowing SW to Lake St. Clair. 160 mi. (260 km) long. **3.** an estuary in SE Connecticut, flowing S past New London to Long Island Sound. 15 mi. (24 km) long.

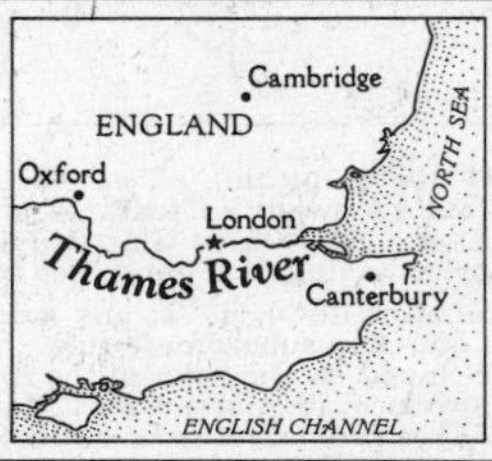

tha·min (thä′min), *n.* a small deer, *Cervus eldi,* of southeastern Asia, having long, curved antlers: now reduced in numbers throughout its range. [said to be < Burmese]

than (t͟han, t͟hen; *unstressed* t͟hən, ən), *conj.* **1.** (used, as after comparative adjectives and adverbs, to introduce the second member of an unequal comparison): *She's taller than I am.* **2.** (used after some adverbs and adjectives expressing choice or diversity, such as *other, otherwise, else, anywhere,* or *different,* to introduce an alternative or denote a difference in kind, place, style, identity, etc.): *I had no choice other than that. You won't find such freedom anywhere else than in this country.* **3.** (used to introduce the rejected choice in expressions of preference): *I'd rather walk than drive there.* **4.** except; other than: *We had no choice than to return home.* **5.** when: *We had barely arrived than we had to leave again.* —*prep.* **6.** in relation to; by comparison with (usually fol. by a pronoun in the objective case): *He is a person than whom I can imagine no one more courteous.* [bef. 900; ME, OE *than(ne)* than, then, when, var. (in special senses) of *thonne* THEN; c. G *dann* then, *denn* than, D *dan* then, than]

—**Usage.** Whether THAN is to be followed by the objective or subjective case of a pronoun is much discussed in usage guides. When, as a conjunction, THAN introduces a subordinate clause, the case of any pronouns following THAN is determined by their function in that clause: *He is younger than I am. I like her better than I like him.* When THAN is followed only by a pronoun or pronouns, with no verb expressed, the usual advice for determining the case is to form a clause mentally after THAN to see whether the pronoun would be a subject or an object. Thus, the sentences *He was more upset than I* and *She gave him more sympathy than I* are to be understood, respectively, as *He was more upset than I was* and *She gave him more sympathy than I gave him.* In the second sentence, the use of the objective case after THAN (*She gave him more sympathy than me*) would produce a different meaning (*She gave him more sympathy than she gave me*). This method of determining the case of pronouns after THAN is generally employed in formal speech and writing.

THAN occurs as a preposition in the old and well-established construction THAN WHOM: *a musician than whom none is more expressive.* In informal, especially uneducated, speech and writing, THAN is usually treated as a preposition and followed by the objective case of the pronoun: *He is younger than me. She plays better poker than him, but you play even better than her.* See also **but**[1], **different, me.**

tha·na (tä′nə), *n.* **1.** a police station in India. **2.** (formerly) a military base in India. Also, **tana.** [< Hindi *thānā* < Skt *sthāna* a place]

Tha·na (tä′nə), *n.* a city in W Maharashtra, in W India: suburb of Bombay. 170,675.

than·age (thā′nij), *n.* **1.** the tenure by which lands were held by a thane. **2.** the land so held. **3.** the office, rank, or jurisdiction of a thane. [1350–1400; ME < AL *thanāgium.* See THANE, -AGE]

thanato-, a combining form meaning "death," used in the formation of compound words: *thanatophobia.* [comb. form repr. Gk *thánatos*]

than·a·tol·o·gy (than′ə tol′ə jē), *n.* **1.** the study of death and its surrounding circumstances, as in forensic medicine. **2.** *Psychiatry.* the study of the effects of death and dying, esp. the investigation of ways to lessen the suffering and address the needs of the terminally ill and their survivors. [1835–45; THANATO- + -LOGY] **—than·a·to·log·i·cal** (than′ə tl oj′i kəl), *adj.* **—than′a·tol′o·gist,** *n.*

than·a·to·pho·bi·a (than′ə tə fō′bē ə), *n. Psychiatry.* an abnormal fear of death. [1855–60; THANATO- + -PHOBIA]

than·a·top·sis (than′ə top′sis), *n.* **1.** a view or contemplation of death. **2.** (*cap., italics*) a poem (1817) by William Cullen Bryant. [THANAT(O)- + -OPSIS]

Than·a·tos (than′ə tos′, -tōs), *n.* **1.** an ancient Greek personification of death. **2.** *Psychoanal.* (*usually l.c.*) the death instinct, esp. as expressed in violent aggression. **—Than·a·tot·ic** (than′ə tot′ik), *adj.*

thane (thān), *n.* **1.** *Early Eng. Hist.* a member of any of several aristocratic classes of men ranking between earls and ordinary freemen, and granted lands by the king or by lords for military service. **2.** *Scot. Hist.* a person, ranking with an earl's son, holding lands of the king; the chief of a clan, who became one of the king's barons. Also, **thegn.** [bef. 900; late ME, sp. var. (Scots) of ME *thain, thein,* OE *thegn;* c. ON *thegn* subject, G *Degen* warrior, hero, Gk *téknon* child]

thane·ship (thān′ship), *n.* thanage. [1760–70; THANE + -SHIP; in reference to English history repr. OE *theg(e)nscipe*]

Than·et (than′it), *n.* **1. Oc·tave** (ok′tiv, -tāv), pen name of Alice French. **2. Isle of,** an island in SE England, forming the NE tip of Kent county. 42 sq. mi. (109 sq. km).

Than·ja·vur (tun′jə vo͝or′), *n.* a city in E Tamil Nadu, in SE India. 140,470. Formerly, **Tanjore.**

thank (thangk), *v.t.* **1.** to express gratitude, appreciation, or acknowledgment to: *She thanked them for their hospitality.* **2. have oneself to thank,** to be personally to blame; have the responsibility: *The citizens have only themselves to thank for corruption in government.* **3. thank God,** (used interjectionally to express relief, thankfulness, etc.) Also, **thank goodness, thank heaven. 4. thank you,** (used interjectionally to express gratitude, appreciation, or acknowledgment, as for a gift, favor, service, or courtesy). **—***n.* **5.** Usually, **thanks.** a grateful feeling or acknowledgment of a benefit, favor, or the like, expressed by words or otherwise: *to return a borrowed book with thanks.* **6. thanks to,** because of; owing to: *Thanks to good organization and hard work, the benefit concert was a great success.* **—***interj.* **7. thanks,** (used as an informal expression of gratitude, appreciation, or acknowledgment). [bef. 900; (n.) ME: favorable thought, goodwill, gratitude, (in sing. and pl.) expression of thanks; OE *thanc* (in sing.) expression of thanks, orig., thought, thoughtfulness; (v.) ME *thanken,* OE *thancian* (c. D, G *danken*); akin to THINK[1]] **—thank′er,** *n.*

thank·ee (thang′kē), *interj. Chiefly Dial.* thank you. [1815–25; by alter.]

thank·ful (thangk′fəl), *adj.* feeling or expressing gratitude; appreciative. [bef. 900; ME; OE *thancful.* See THANK, -FUL] **—thank′ful·ly,** *adv.* **—thank′ful·ness,** *n.*
—Syn. beholden, obliged. See **grateful.**

thank·less (thangk′lis), *adj.* **1.** not likely to be appreciated or rewarded; unappreciated: *a thankless job.* **2.** not feeling or expressing gratitude or appreciation; ungrateful: *a thankless child.* [1530–40; THANK + -LESS] **—thank′less·ly,** *adv.* **—thank′less·ness,** *n.*
—Syn. 1. unacknowledged, vain, unrewarding, profitless.

thanks·giv·er (thangks′giv′ər), *n.* a person who gives thanks. [1615–25; THANK + -S[3] + GIVER]

thanks·giv·ing (thangks′giv′ing), *n.* **1.** the act of giving thanks; grateful acknowledgment of benefits or favors, esp. to God. **2.** an expression of thanks, esp. to God. **3.** a public celebration in acknowledgment of divine favor or kindness. **4.** a day set apart for giving thanks to God. **5.** (*cap.*) See **Thanksgiving Day.** [1525–35; THANK + -S[3] + GIVING]

Thanksgiv′ing cac′tus. See **crab cactus.**

Thanksgiv′ing Day′, a national holiday celebrated as a day of feasting and giving thanks for divine favors or goodness, observed on the fourth Thursday of November in the U.S. and in Canada on the second Monday of October. [1665–75, *Amer.*]

thank·wor·thy (thangk′wûr′thē), *adj.* deserving gratitude. [1350–1400; ME; see THANK, WORTHY]

thank-you (thangk′yo͞o′), *adj.* **1.** expressing one's gratitude or thanks: *a thank-you note.* **—***n.* **2.** an expression of thanks, as by saying "thank you": *I never got so much as a thank-you for helping him.* [1785–95 for def. 2; n. and adj. use of v. phrase *thank you*]

thank-you-ma'am (thangk′yo͞o mam′), *n.* a bump or depression in a road that jars a person riding over it. [1840–50, *Amer.*]

Thant (thant, thont), *n.* **U.** See **U Thant.**

Thap·sus (thap′səs), *n.* an ancient town on the coast of Tunisia: decisive victory of Caesar 46 B.C.

thar (tär), *n.* tahr.

Thar′ Des′ert (tûr, tär), a desert in NW India and S Pakistan. ab. 100,000 sq. mi. (259,000 sq. km). Also called **Indian Desert.**

Thar·e (thâr′ə), *n. Douay Bible.* Terah.

Thar·sis (thär′sis), *n. Douay Bible.* Tarshish.

Tha·sos (thā′sôs; *Eng.* thā′sos, -sōs), *n.* a Greek island in the N Aegean. 13,316; ab. 170 sq. mi. (440 sq. km). **—Tha·si·an** (thā′shē ən, -shən, -sē ən), *adj., n.*

that (that; *unstressed* thət), *pron. and adj., pl.* **those;** *adv.; conj.* **—***pron.* **1.** (used to indicate a person, thing, idea, state, event, time, remark, etc., as pointed out or present, mentioned before, supposed to be understood, or by way of emphasis): *That is her mother. After that we saw each other.* **2.** (used to indicate one of two or more persons, things, etc., already mentioned, referring to the one more remote in place, time, or thought; opposed to *this*): *This is my sister and that's my cousin.* **3.** (used to indicate one of two or more persons, things, etc., already mentioned, implying a contrast or contradistinction; opposed to *this*): *This suit fits better than that.* **4.** (used as the subject or object of a relative clause, esp. one defining or restricting the antecedent, sometimes replaceable by *who, whom,* or *which*): *the horse that he bought.* **5.** (used as the object of a preposition, with the preposition standing at the end of a relative clause): *the farm that I spoke of.* **6.** (used in various special or elliptical constructions): *fool that he is.* **7. at that, a.** in spite of something; nevertheless: *Although perhaps too elaborate, it seemed like a good plan at that.* **b.** in addition; besides: *It was a long wait, and an exasperating one at that.* **8. that is,** (by way of explanation, clarification, or an example); more accurately: *I read the book, that is, I read most of it.* Also, **that is to say. 9. that's that,** *Informal.* there is no more to be said or done; that is finished: *I'm not going, and that's that!* **10. with that,** following that; thereupon: *With that, he turned on his heel and fled.* **—***adj.* **11.** (used to indicate a person, place, thing, or degree as indicated, mentioned before, present, or as well-known or characteristic): *That woman is her mother. Those little mannerisms of hers make me sick.* **12.** (used to indicate the more remote in time, place, or thought of two persons, things, etc., already mentioned; opposed to *this*): *This room is his and that one is mine.* **13.** (used to imply mere contradistinction; opposed to *this*): *not this house, but that one.* **14. that way,** *Informal.* in love or very fond of (usually fol. by *about* or *for*): *The star and the director are that way. I'm that way about coffee.* **—***adv.* **15.** (used with adjectives and adverbs of quantity or extent) to the extent or degree indicated: *that much; The fish was that big.* **16.** to a great extent or degree; very: *It's not that important.* **17.** *Dial.* (used to modify an adjective or another adverb) to such an extent: *He was that weak he could hardly stand.* **—***conj.* **18.** (used to introduce a subordinate clause as the subject or object of the principal verb or as the necessary complement to a statement made, or a clause expressing cause or reason, purpose or aim, result or consequence, etc.): *I'm sure that you'll like it. That he will come is certain. Hold it up so that everyone can see it.* **19.** (used elliptically to introduce an exclamation expressing desire, a wish, surprise, indignation, or other strong feeling): *Oh, that I had never been born!* [bef. 900; ME; OE *thæt* (pronoun, adj., adv. and conj.), orig., neut. of *se* the; c. D *dat,* G *das(s),* ON *that,* Gk *tó,* Skt *tad*]
—Usage. 4. When THAT introduces a relative clause, the clause is usually restrictive; that is, essential to the complete meaning of the sentence because it restricts or specifies the noun or pronoun it modifies. In the sentence *The keys that I lost last month have been found,* it is clear that keys referred to are a particular set. Without the THAT clause, the sentence *The keys have been found* would be vague and probably puzzling. THAT is used to refer to animate and inanimate nouns and thus can substitute in most uses for *who(m)* and *which: Many of the workers that* (or *who*) *built the pyramids died while working. The negotiator made an offer that* (or *which*) *was very attractive to the union.* Experienced writers choose among these forms not only on the basis of grammar and the kind of noun referred to but also on the basis of sound of the sentence and their own personal preference.
The relative pronoun THAT is sometimes omitted. Its omission as a subject is usually considered nonstandard, but the construction is heard occasionally even from educated speakers: *A fellow (that) lives near here takes people rafting.* Most often it is as an object that the relative pronoun is omitted. The omission almost always occurs when the dependent clause begins with a personal pronoun or a proper name: *The mechanic (that) we take our car to is very competent. The films (that) Chaplin made have become classics.* The omission of the relative pronoun as in the two preceding examples is standard in all varieties of speech and writing.
18. The conjunction THAT, which introduces a noun clause, is, like the relative pronoun THAT, sometimes omitted, often after verbs of thinking, saying, believing, etc.: *She said (that) they would come in separate cars. He dismissed the idea (that) he was being followed.* As with the omission of the relative pronoun, the omission of the conjunction almost always occurs when the dependent clause begins with a personal pronoun or with a proper name. This omission of the conjunction THAT occurs most frequently in informal speech and writing, but it is a stylistic option often chosen in more formal speech and writing.

that·a·way (that′ə wā′), *adv. Older Use.* **1.** in or toward the direction pointed out: *The outlaws went thataway when they rode out of town.* **2.** in the manner indicated: *You'll get an electric shock if you do it thataway.* [1830–40, *Amer.*; alter. of *that way*]

thatch (thach), *n.* **1.** Also, **thatching.** a material, as straw, rushes, leaves, or the like, used to cover roofs, grain stacks, etc. **2.** a covering of such a material. **3.** the leaves of various palms that are used for thatching. **4.** something resembling thatch on a roof, esp. thick hair covering the head: *a thatch of unruly red hair.* **5.** *Hort.* a tightly bound layer of dead grass, including leaves, stems, and roots, that builds up on the soil surface at the base of the living grass of a lawn. **—***v.t.* **6.** to cover with or as if with thatch. **7.** *Hort.* to remove thatch from (a lawn); dethatch. [bef. 900; (v.) ME *thacchen,* var. (with *a* from *thak* >dial. *thack*) of *thecchen,* OE *theccan* to cover, hide; c. D *dekken* (see DECK), G *decken,* ON *thekja;* (n.) ME *thacche,* var. (with *ch* from the v.) of *thak*] **—thatch′less,** *adj.* **—thatch′y,** *adj.*

Thatch (thach), *n.* **Edward.** See **Teach, Edward.**

thatch·er (thach′ər), *n.* **1.** a person who thatches. **2.** a rake or other tool designed to remove thatch from a lawn. [1400–50; late ME. See THATCH, -ER[1]]

Thatch·er (thach′ər), *n.* **Margaret (Hilda),** born 1925, British political leader: prime minister 1979–90.

thatch·ing (thach′ing), *n.* thatch (def. 1). [1350–1400; ME *thecchyng.* See THATCH, ING[1]]

thatch′ palm′, any of several fan palms, esp. of the genera *Sabal, Thrinax,* or *Coccothrinax,* the leaves of which are used for thatching. [1865–70]

that's (thats; *unstressed* thəts), **1.** contraction of *that is: That's mine.* **2.** contraction of *that has: That's got more leaves.*
—Usage. See **contraction.**

thaub (tōb), *n.* tobe.

thaumato-, a combining form meaning "miracle," "wonder," used in the formation of compound words: *thaumatology.* [< Gk, comb. form of *thaumat-* (s. of *thaûma*)]

thau·ma·tol·o·gy (thô′mə tol′ə jē), *n.* the study or description of miracles. [1850–55; THAUMATO- + -LOGY]

thau·ma·trope (thô′mə trōp′), *n.* a card with different pictures on opposite sides, as a horse on one side and a rider on the other, which appear as if combined when the card is twirled rapidly, thus illustrating the persistence of visual impressions. [1820–30; THAUMA(TO)- + -TROPE] **—thau·ma·trop·i·cal** (thô′mə trop′i kəl), *adj.*

thau·ma·turge (thô′mə tûrj′), *n.* a worker of wonders or miracles; magician. Also, **thau′ma·tur′gist.** [1705–15; back formation from THAUMATURGIC]

thau·ma·tur·gic (thô′mə tûr′jik), *adj.* **1.** pertaining to a thaumaturge or to thaumaturgy. **2.** having the powers of a thaumaturge. Also, **thau′ma·tur′gi·cal.** [1560–70; < NL *thaumatūrgicus,* equiv. to *thaumatūrg(us)* wonder worker (< Gk *thaumatourgós,* equiv. to *thaumat-* THAUMATO- + *-ourgos;* see -URGY, -OUS) + *-icus* -IC]

thau·ma·tur·gy (thô′mə tûr′jē), *n.* the working of wonders or miracles; magic. [1720–30; < Gk *thaumatourgía.* See THAUMATO-, -URGY]

thaw (thô), *v.i.* **1.** to pass or change from a frozen to a liquid or semiliquid state; melt. **2.** to be freed from the physical effect of frost or extreme cold (sometimes fol. by *out*): *Sit by the fire and thaw out.* **3.** (of the weather) to become warm enough to melt ice and snow: *It will probably thaw today.* **4.** to become less formal, reserved, or aloof: *He thawed at their kindness.* **5.** to become less hostile or tense: *International relations thawed.* **—***v.t.* **6.** to cause to change from a frozen to a liquid or semiliquid state; melt. **7.** to free from the physical effect of frost or extreme cold; bring to a more normal temperature, esp. to room temperature: *I took the steaks out of the freezer and thawed them.* **8.** to make less cold, formal, or reserved. **9.** to make less tense or hostile. **—***n.* **10.** the act or process of thawing. **11.** the act or fact of becoming less formal, reserved, or aloof. **12.** a reduction or easing in tension or hostility. **13.** (in winter or in areas where freezing weather is the norm) weather warm enough to melt ice and snow. **14.** a period of such weather: *We had a two-week thaw in January.* **15. the thaw,** the first day in the year when ice in harbors, rivers, etc., breaks up or loosens enough to begin flowing to the sea, allowing navigation: *The Anchorage thaw came on May 18th.* [bef. 1000; (v.) ME *thawen,* OE *thawian;* c. D *dooien,* ON *theyja;* (n.) late ME, deriv. of the v.] **—thaw′less,** *adj.*
—Syn. 1. See **melt. 2, 8.** warm. **—Ant. 1.** freeze.

Thay·er (thā′ər, thâr), *n.* **1. Sylvanus,** 1785–1872, U.S. army officer and educator. **2. William Roscoe,** 1859–1923, U.S. historian and author.

Th.B., Bachelor of Theology. [< NL *Theologicae Baccalaureus*]

THC, *Pharm.* tetrahydrocannabinol.

Th.D., Doctor of Theology. [< NL *Theologicae Doctor*]

the[1] (*stressed* thē; *unstressed before a consonant* thə; *unstressed before a vowel* thē), *definite article.* **1.** (used, esp. before a noun, with a specifying or particularizing effect, as opposed to the indefinite or generalizing force of the indefinite article *a* or *an*): *the book you gave me; Come into the house.* **2.** (used to mark a proper noun, natural phenomenon, ship, building, time, point of the compass, branch of endeavor, or field of study as something well-known or unique): *the sun; the Alps; the* Queen Elizabeth; *the past; the West.* **3.** (used with or as part of a title): *the Duke of Wellington; the Reverend John Smith.* **4.** (used to mark a noun as indicating the best-known, most approved, most important, most satisfying, etc.): *the skiing center of the U.S.; If you're going to work hard, now is the time.* **5.** (used to mark a noun as being used generically): *The dog is a quadruped.* **6.** (used in place of a possessive pronoun, to note a part of the body or a personal belonging): *He won't be able to play football until the leg mends.* **7.** (used before adjectives that are used substantively, to note an individual, a class or number of individuals, or an abstract idea): *to visit the sick; from the sublime to the ridiculous.* **8.** (used before a modifying adjective to specify or limit its modifying effect): *He took the wrong road and drove miles out of his way.* **9.** (used to indicate one particular decade of a lifetime or of a century): *the sixties; the gay nineties.* **10.** (one of many of a class or type, as of a manufactured item, as opposed to an individual one): *Did you listen to the radio last night?* **11.** enough: *He saved until he had the money for a new car. She didn't have the courage to leave.* **12.** (used distributively, to note any one separately) for, to, or in each; a or an: *at one dollar the pound.* [bef. 900; ME, OE, uninflected s. of the demonstrative pronoun. See THAT]
—Pronunciation. As shown above, the pronunciation

of the definite article THE changes, primarily depending on whether the following sound is a consonant or a vowel. Before a consonant sound the pronunciation is (thə): *the book, the mountain* (thə bo͝ok, thə moun′tn). Before a vowel sound it is usually (thē), sometimes (thi): *the apple, the end* (thē *or* thi ap′əl, thē *or* thi end). As an emphatic form ("I didn't say *a* book—I said *the* book.") or a citation form ("The word *the* is a definite article."), the usual pronunciation is (thē), although in both of these uses of the stressed form, (thē) is often replaced by (thu), especially among younger speakers.

the² (*before a consonant* thə; *before a vowel* thē), *adv.* **1.** (used to modify an adjective or adverb in the comparative degree and to signify "in or by that," "on that account," "in or by so much," or "in some or any degree"): *He's been on vacation and looks the better for it.* **2.** (used in correlative constructions to modify an adjective or adverb in the comparative degree, in one instance with relative force and in the other with demonstrative force, and signifying "by how much . . . by so much" or "in what degree . . . in that degree"): *the more the merrier; The bigger they are, the harder they fall.* [bef. 900; ME; OE *thē, thȳ,* instrumental case of demonstrative pronoun. See THAT, LEST]

the-, var. of **theo-** before a vowel: *thearchy.*

The•a (thē′ə), *n.* a female given name.

the•a•ceous (thē ā′shəs), *adj.* belonging to the Theaceae, the tea family of plants. Cf. **tea family.** [< NL *the(a)* tea + -ACEOUS]

the•an•throp•ic (thē′an throp′ik), *adj.* of or pertaining to both God or a god and human beings; both divine and human. [1645–55; THE- + ANTHROP- + -IC]

the•an•thro•pism (thē an′thrə piz′əm), *n.* **1.** the doctrine of the union of the divine and human natures, esp. the manifestation of God as man in Christ. **2.** the attribution of human nature to the gods. [1810–20; THE- + ANTHROP- + -ISM] **—the•an′thro•pist,** *n.*

the•ar•chy (thē′är kē), *n., pl.* **-chies. 1.** the rule or government of God or of a god. **2.** an order or system of deities. [1635–45; < LGk *thearchía.* See THE-, -ARCHY] **—the•ar′chic,** *adj.*

theat., 1. theater. **2.** theatrical.

the•a•ter (thē′ə tər, thēᵊ′-), *n.* **1.** a building, part of a building, or outdoor area for housing dramatic presentations, stage entertainments, or motion-picture shows. **2.** the audience at a theatrical or motion-picture performance: *The theater wept.* **3.** a theatrical or acting company. **4.** a room or hall, fitted with tiers of seats rising like steps, used for lectures, surgical demonstrations, etc.: *Students crowded into the operating theater.* **5. the theater,** dramatic performances as a branch of art; the drama: *an actress devoted to the theater.* **6.** dramatic works collectively, as of literature, a nation, or an author (often prec. by *the*): *the theater of Ibsen.* **7.** the quality or effectiveness of dramatic performance: *good theater; bad theater; pure theater.* **8.** a place of action; field of operations. **9.** a natural formation of land rising by steps or gradations. Also, **theatre.** [1325–75; ME *theatre* < L *theātrum* < Gk *théātron* seeing place, theater, equiv. to *theā-,* s. of *theâsthai* to view + *-tron* suffix denoting means or place]
—Syn. 8. arena, site, stage, setting, scene.
—Pronunciation. THEATER, an early Middle English borrowing from French, originally had its primary stress on the second syllable: (*Fr.* tā ä′trᵊ). As with many early French borrowings (*beauty, carriage, marriage*), the stress moved to the first syllable, in conformity with a common English pattern of stress, and this pattern remains the standard one for THEATER today: (thē′ə tər, thēᵊ′-). A pronunciation with stress on the second syllable and the (ā) vowel: (thē ā′tər) or sometimes (thē′ā′tər) is characteristic chiefly of uneducated speech.

the•a•ter•go•er (thē′ə tər gō′ər, thēᵊ′-), *n.* a person who goes to the theater, esp. often or habitually. Also, **the′a•tre•go′er.** [1870–75; THEATER + GOER]

the•a•ter-in-the-round (thē′ə tər in thə round′, thēᵊ′-), *n.* **1.** See **arena theater. 2.** a style of theatrical presentation in which the audience is seated on all sides of the performance area. [1945–50]

the′ater of cru′elty, a form of surrealist theater originated by Antonin Artaud and emphasizing the cruelty of human existence by portraying sadistic acts and intense suffering. [1950–55; trans. of F *théâtre de la cruauté*]

the′ater of opera′tions, the part of the theater of war, including a combat zone and a communications zone, that is engaged in military operations and their support. [1875–80]

the′ater of the absurd′, theater in which standard or naturalistic conventions of plot, characterization, and thematic structure are ignored or distorted in order to convey the irrational or fictive nature of reality and the essential isolation of humanity in a meaningless world. [1960–65]

the′ater of war′, the entire area in which ground, sea, and air forces may become directly employed in war operations, including the theater of operations and the zone of interior. [1885–90]

The•a•tine (thē′ə tin, -tīn′, -tēn′), *n.* **1.** a member of a congregation of regular clerics, founded in Italy in 1524 to combat Protestantism and promote higher morality among Roman Catholics. **2.** a member of a congregation of nuns, founded in Italy in 1583 under the direction of the Theatine fathers. [1590–1600; < NL *Theatīnus* of Chieti, Italy, where one of the founders held the archbishopric]

CONCISE ETYMOLOGY KEY: <, descended or borrowed from; >, whence; b., blend of, blended; c., cognate with; cf., compare; deriv., derivative; equiv., equivalent; imit., imitative; obl., oblique; r., replacing; s., stem; sp., spelling, spelled; resp., respelling, respelled; trans., translation; ?, origin unknown; *, unattested; ‡, probably earlier than. See the full key inside the front cover.

the•a•tre (thē′ə tər, thēᵊ′-), *n.* theater.

Thé•â•tre-Fran•çais (*Fr.* tā ä trᵊ frän se′), *n.* See **Comédie Française.**

the•at•ri•cal (thē a′tri kəl), *adj.* Also, **the•at′ric. 1.** of or pertaining to the theater or dramatic presentations: *theatrical performances.* **2.** suggestive of the theater or of acting; artificial, pompous, spectacular, or extravagantly histrionic: *a theatrical display of grief.* **—*n.* 3. theatricals, a.** dramatic performances, now esp. as given by amateurs. **b.** artificial or histrionic actions. **4.** a professional actor: *a family of renowned theatricals.* [1550–60; < LL *theātric(us)* < Gk *theātrikós,* equiv. to *theātr(on)* THEATER + *-ikos* -IC + -AL¹] **—the•at•ri•cal•i•ty** (thē a′tri kal′i tē), **the•at′ri•cal•ness,** *n.* **—the•at′ri•cal•ly,** *adv.*
—Syn. 2. exaggerated, melodramatic, stagy, extravagant.

theat′rical film′, *Motion Pictures.* a film made for exhibition in theaters, as distinguished from one made for television.

the•at•ri•cal•ism (thē a′tri kə liz′əm), *n.* conduct suggesting theatrical actions or mannerisms, esp. of an extravagant or exhibitionist sort. [1850–55; THEATRICAL + -ISM]

the•at•ri•cal•ize (thē a′tri kə līz′), *v.t.,* **-ized, -iz•ing. 1.** to put into dramatic or theatrical form; dramatize. **2.** to express or represent in a spectacular or extravagantly histrionic manner. [1770–80; THEATRICAL + -IZE] **—the•at′ri•cal•i•za′tion,** *n.*

the•at•ri•cism (thē a′trə siz′əm), *n.* theatricalism. [1870–75; THEATRIC(S) + -ISM]

the•at•rics (thē a′triks), *n.* **1.** (*used with a singular v.*) the art of staging plays and other stage performances. **2.** (*used with a plural v.*) exaggerated, artificial, or histrionic mannerisms, actions, or words. [1800–10; THEATR(IC) + -ICS]

The•ba•id (thē′bā id, -bē-), *n.* the ancient region surrounding Thebes, in Egypt.

the•ba•ine (thē′bə ēn′, thi bā′ēn, -in), *n. Chem.* a white, crystalline, slightly water-soluble, poisonous alkaloid, $C_{19}H_{21}NO_3$, present in opium in small quantities, but having a strychninelike rather than a narcotic effect. [1890–95; < NL *thēba(ia)* (opium) of Thebes, Egypt (alter. of L *Thēbaea,* fem. of *Thēbaeus* Theban) + -INE²]

the•be (te′be), *n.* an aluminum coin and monetary unit of Botswana, the 100th part of a pula.

Thebes (thēbz), *n.* **1.** an ancient city in Upper Egypt, on the Nile, whose ruins are located in the modern towns of Karnak and Luxor: a former capital of Egypt. **2.** a city of ancient Greece, in Boeotia: a rival of ancient Athens. **—The•ba•ic** (thi bā′ik), *adj.* **—The•ban** (thē′bən), *adj., n.*

the•ca (thē′kə), *n., pl.* **-cae** (-sē). **1.** a case or receptacle. **2.** *Bot., Mycol.* **a.** a sac, cell, or capsule. **b.** a sporangium. **3.** *Anat., Zool.* a case or sheath enclosing an organ, structure, etc., as the horny covering of an insect pupa. [1655–65; < L *thēca* < Gk *thḗkē* case, cover, akin to *tithénai* to place, put] **—the′cal,** *adj.*

the•cate (thē′kit, -kāt), *adj.* having or being contained in a theca. [1890–95; THEC(A) + -ATE¹]

the•ci•um (thē′shē əm, -sē əm), *n., pl.* **-ci•a** (-shē ə, -sē ə). *Mycol.* hymenium. [1880–85; < NL < Gk *thēkíon,* dim. of *thḗkē* THECA; see -IUM] **—the′ci•al,** *adj.*

the•co•dont (thē′kə dont′), *n.* **1.** any of various reptiles of the extinct order Thecodontia, occurring in the late Permian to late Triassic periods and characterized by teeth set in sockets. **—*adj.* 2.** having the teeth set in sockets. **3.** belonging to or pertaining to the Thecodontia. [1830–40; < NL, equiv. to Gk *thḗk(ē)* case, chest (see THECA) + *-odont-* -ODONT; so named from the sockets in which the marginal teeth were implanted]

thé dan•sant (tā dän sän′), *pl.* ***thés dan•sants*** (tā dän sän′). *French.* a tea dance.

thee (thē), *pron.* **1.** the objective case of **thou:** *With this ring, I thee wed. I shall bring thee a mighty army.* **2.** thou (now used chiefly by the Friends). [bef. 900; ME; OE *thē* (orig. dat.; later dat. and acc.); c. LG *di,* G *dir,* ON *thēr.* See THOU]

theft (theft), *n.* **1.** the act of stealing; the wrongful taking and carrying away of the personal goods or property of another; larceny. **2.** an instance of this. **3.** *Archaic.* something stolen. [bef. 900; ME; OE *thēfth, thēofth;* see THIEF, -TH¹; c. ON *thȳfth,* obs. D *diefte*]

theft′ insur′ance, insurance against loss or damage of property resulting from theft.

theft•proof (theft′pro͞of′), *n.* safe from theft. [THEFT + PROOF]

thegn (thān), *n.* thane. [1840–50; < OE: THANE]

Thei•ler (tī′lər), *n.* **Max,** 1899–1972, South African medical scientist, in the U.S. after 1922: Nobel prize for medicine 1951.

the•ine (thē′ēn, -in), *n.* caffeine, esp. in tea. [1830–40; < NL *the(a)* TEA + -INE²]

their (thâr; *unstressed* thər), *pron.* **1.** a form of the possessive case of **they** used as an attributive adjective, before a noun: *their home; their rights as citizens; their departure for Rome.* **2.** (used after an indefinite singular antecedent in place of the definite masculine form *his* or the definite feminine form *her*): *Someone left their book on the table. Did everyone bring their lunch?* Cf. **theirs.** [1150–1200; ME < ON *theirra* their; r. OE *thāra, thǣra;* cf. THEY]
—Usage. See **he¹, me, they.**

theirn (thârn), *pron. Nonstandard.* theirs. Also, **their'n.** [THEIR + *-n,* as in *mine, thine*]

theirs (thârz), *pron.* **1.** a form of the possessive case of **they** used as a predicate adjective, after a noun or without a noun: *Are you a friend of theirs? It is theirs.* **2.** (used after an indefinite singular antecedent in place of the definite masculine form *his* or the definite feminine form *hers*): *I have my book; does everyone else have theirs?* **3.** that which belongs to them: *Theirs is the largest house on the block.* [1150–1200; ME; see THEIR, -S¹]

their•self (thâr′self′), *pron. Nonstandard.* themselves. Also, **their•selves** (thâr′selvz′). [1250–1300; ME; formed on analogy of MYSELF]

the•ism (thē′iz əm), *n.* **1.** the belief in one God as the creator and ruler of the universe, without rejection of revelation (distinguished from *deism*). **2.** belief in the existence of a god or gods (opposed to *atheism*). [1670–80; THE- + -ISM] **—the•ist** (thē′ist), *n., adj.* **—the•is′tic, the•is′ti•cal,** *adj.* **—the•is′ti•cal•ly,** *adv.*

Theiss (tīs), *n.* German name of **Tisza.**

the•li•tis (thi lī′tis), *n. Pathol.* inflammation of the nipple. [1840–50; < Gk *thēl(ḗ)* nipple + -ITIS]

Thel•ma (thel′mə), *n.* a female given name.

The•lon (thē′lon), *n.* a river in the SE Northwest Territories, in central Canada, flowing NE into Hudson Bay. ab. 550 mi. (885 km) long.

T helper cell, *Immunol.* See **helper T cell.**

the•lyt•o•kous (thi lit′ə kəs), *adj.* pertaining to or produced by thelytoky. Also, **thel•y•ot•o•kous** (thel′ē ot′ə kəs). [1875–80; < Gk *thēlytókos.* See THELYTOKY, -OUS]

the•lyt•o•ky (thi lit′ə kē), *n.* parthenogenesis in which only females are produced. Also, **thel•y•ot•o•ky** (thel′ē ot′ə kē). [1890–95; < Gk *thēlytokía,* equiv. to *thêly(s)* female + *tók(os)* parturition, offspring + *-ia* -Y³]

them (them; *unstressed* thəm, əm), *pron.* **1.** the objective case of **they,** used as a direct or indirect object: *We saw them yesterday. I gave them the books.* **2.** *Informal.* (used instead of the pronoun *they* in the predicate after the verb *to be*): *It's them, across the street. It isn't them.* **3.** *Informal.* (used instead of the pronoun *their* before a gerund): *The boys' parents objected to them hiking without adult supervision.* **—*adj.* 4.** *Nonstandard.* those: *He don't want them books.* [1150–1200; ME *theym* < ON *theim* them (dat.); r. ME *tham(e),* OE *thǣm, thām;* cf. THEY]
—Usage. See **he¹, me, they.**

the•ma (thē′mə), *n., pl.* **-ma•ta** (-mə tə). theme (def. 7). [< L < Gk *théma;* see THEME]

the•mat•ic (thē mat′ik), *adj.* **1.** of or pertaining to a theme. **2.** *Gram.* **a.** (of a word or words) of, pertaining to, or producing a theme or themes. **b.** (of a vowel) pertaining to the theme or stem: the thematic vowel ends the stem and precedes the inflectional ending of a word form, as *i* in Latin *audiō* "I hear." [1690–1700; < Gk *thematikós, equiv. to themat-* (s. of *théma*) THEME + *-ikos* -IC] **—the•mat′i•cal•ly,** *adv.*

Themat′ic Appercep′tion Test′, *Psychol.* a projective technique in which stories told by a subject about each of a series of pictures are assumed to reveal dominant needs or motivations. *Abbr.:* TAT

theme (thēm), *n., adj., v.,* **themed, them•ing. —*n.* 1.** a subject of discourse, discussion, meditation, or composition; topic: *The need for world peace was the theme of the meeting.* **2.** a unifying or dominant idea, motif, etc., as in a work of art. **3.** a short, informal essay, esp. a school composition. **4.** *Music.* **a.** a principal melodic subject in a musical composition. **b.** a short melodic subject from which variations are developed. **5.** *Gram.* the element common to all or most of the forms of an inflectional paradigm, often consisting of a root with certain formative elements or modifications. Cf. **stem¹** (def. 16). **6.** *Ling.* topic (def. 4). **7.** Also, **thema.** an administrative division of the Byzantine Empire. **—*adj.* 8.** having a unifying theme: *a theme restaurant decorated like a spaceship.* **—*v.t.* 9.** to provide with a theme. [1250–1300; ME *teme, theme* (< OF *teme*) < ML *thema,* L < Gk *théma* proposition, deposit, akin to *tithénai* to put, set down] **—theme′less,** *adj.*
—Syn. 1. thesis, text. See **subject. 3.** paper.

theme′ park′, an amusement park in which landscaping, buildings, and attractions are based on one or more specific themes, as jungle wildlife, fairy tales, or the Old West. [1955–60, *Amer.*]

theme′ song′, 1. a melody in an operetta or musical comedy so emphasized by repetition as to dominate the presentation. **2.** a melody identifying or identified with a radio or television program, dance band, etc., usually played at the beginning of each program. **3.** an expression, comment, or subject of conversation that a person or group uses habitually. [1925–30, *Amer.*]

The•mis•to•cles (thə mis′tə klēz′), *n.* 527?–460? B.C., Athenian statesman.

them•selves (thəm selvz′, them′-), *pron.pl.* **1.** an emphatic form of **them** or **they:** *The authors themselves left the theater. The contract was written by the partners themselves.* **2.** a reflexive form of **they** (used as the direct or indirect object of a verb or the object of a preposition): *They washed themselves quickly. The painters gave themselves a week to finish the work. The noisy passengers drew attention to themselves.* **3.** (used after an indefinite singular antecedent in place of the definite

masculine *himself* or the definite feminine *herself*): *No one who ignores the law can call themselves a good citizen.* **4.** (used in place of *they* or *them* after *as, than,* or *but*): *no soldiers braver than themselves; As for the entertainers, everyone got paid but themselves.* **5.** their usual, normal, characteristic selves: *After a hot meal and a few hours' rest, they were themselves again.* [1300–50; THEM + SELVES; r. *themself,* ME *thamself;* see SELF]
—Usage. See **myself.**

then (then), *adv.* **1.** at that time: *Prices were lower then.* **2.** immediately or soon afterward: *The rain stopped and then started again.* **3.** next in order of time: *We ate, then we started home.* **4.** at the same time: *At first the water seemed blue, then gray.* **5.** next in order of place: *Standing beside Charlie is my uncle, then my cousin, then my brother.* **6.** in addition; besides; also: *I love my job, and then it pays so well.* **7.** in that case; as a consequence; in those circumstances: *If you're sick, then you should stay in bed.* **8.** since that is so; as it appears; therefore: *You have, then, found the mistake? You are leaving tonight then.* **9. but then,** but on the other hand: *I found their conversation very dull, but then I have different tastes.* **10. then and there,** at that precise time and place; at once; on the spot: *I started to pack my things right then and there.* Also, **there and then.** —*adj.* **11.** being; being such; existing or being at the time indicated: *the then prime minister.* —*n.* **12.** that time: *We have not been back since then. Till then, farewell.* [bef. 900; ME *then(ne), than(n)e,* OE *thonne, thanne, thænne;* cf. THAN; akin to THAT]
—Syn. 8. See **therefore.**

the•nar (thē′när), *n. Anat.* **1.** the fleshy mass of the outer side of the palm of the hand. **2.** the fleshy prominence or ball of muscle at the base of the thumb. —*adj.* **3.** of or pertaining to the thenar. [1665–75; < NL < Gk *thénar* palm of hand or sole of foot]

the•nard•ite (thə när′dīt, tə-), *n.* a mineral, sodium sulfate, Na_2SO_4, occurring in white crystals and masses, esp. in salt lakes and arid regions. [1835–45; named after L. J. *Thénard* (1777–1857), French chemist; see -ITE[1]]

The•nard's′ blue′ (thə närdz′, tə-). See **cobalt blue.** [see THENARDITE]

thence (thens), *adv.* **1.** from that place: *I went first to Paris and thence to Rome.* **2.** from that time; thenceforth: *He fell ill and thence was seldom seen.* **3.** from that source: *Thence came all our troubles.* **4.** from that fact or reason; therefore: *We were young, and thence optimistic.* [1250–1300; ME *thennes,* equiv. to *thenne* (earlier *thenene,* OE *thanon(e)* thence) + *-es* -S[1]]
—Usage. See **whence.**

thence•forth (thens′fôrth′, -fōrth′, thens′fôrth′, -fōrth′), *adv.* from that time or place onward. Also, **thence•for•ward** (thens′fôr′wərd), **thence′for′wards.** [1325–75; ME *thennes forth* (cf. OE *thanonforth*). See THENCE, FORTH]

theo-, a combining form meaning "god," used in the formation of compound words: *theocrat.* Also, *esp. before a vowel,* **the-.** [< Gk, comb. form of *theós*]

The•o•bald (thē′ə bôld′), *n.* **Lewis, 1.** 1688–1744, English author. **2.** Also, **The•o•bold** (thē′ə bōld′). a male given name.

the•o•bro•mine (thē′ə brō′mēn, -min), *n. Pharm.* a white, crystalline, water-insoluble, poisonous powder, $C_7H_8N_4O_2$, an isomer of theophylline and lower homologue of caffeine, occurring in tea and obtained from the cacao bean: used chiefly as a diuretic, myocardial stimulant, and vasodilator. [1835–45; < NL *Theobrom(a)* genus of trees typified by cacao (< Gk *theo-* THEO- + *brôma* food) + -INE[2]]

the•o•cen•tric (thē′ə sen′trik), *adj.* having God as the focal point of thoughts, interests, and feelings: *theocentric philosophy.* [1885–90; THEO- + -CENTRIC] **—the•o•cen•tric•i•ty** (thē′ō sen tris′i tē), *n.* **—the′o•cen′trism, the•o•cen•tri•cism** (thē′ə sen′trə siz′əm), *n.*

The•o•cly•me•nus (thē′ə klī′mə nəs), *n. Class. Myth.* **1.** (in the *Odyssey*) a seer who foretold the return of Odysseus and the death of Penelope's suitors. **2.** a son of Proteus and Psamathe who succeeded his father as king of Egypt.

the•oc•ra•cy (thē ok′rə sē), *n., pl.* **-cies. 1.** a form of government in which God or a deity is recognized as the supreme civil ruler, the God's or deity's laws being interpreted by the ecclesiastical authorities. **2.** a system of government by priests claiming a divine commission. **3.** a commonwealth or state under such a form or system of government. [1615–25; < Gk *theokratía.* See THEO-, -CRACY] **—the•o•crat•ic** (thē′ə krat′ik), **the′o•crat′i•cal,** *adj.* **—the′o•crat′i•cal•ly,** *adv.*

the•oc•ra•sy (thē ok′rə sē), *n.* **1.** a mixture of religious forms and deities by worshipers. **2.** union of the personal soul with God, as in Neoplatonism. [1810–20; < Gk *theokrāsía,* equiv. to *theo-* THEO- + *krâs(is)* a mingling + *-ia* -Y[3]]

the•o•crat (thē′ə krat′), *n.* **1.** a person who rules, governs as a representative of God or a deity, or is a member of the ruling group in a theocracy, as a divine king or a high priest. **2.** a person who favors theocracy. [1820–30; back formation from *theocratic* < Gk *theokrat(ía)* THEOCRACY + -IC]

The•oc•ri•tus (thē ok′ri təs), *n.* fl. c270 B.C., Greek poet. **—The•oc•ri•te•an** (thē ok′ri tē′ən), **The•oc′ri•tan,** *adj.*

the•od•i•cy (thē od′ə sē), *n., pl.* **-cies.** a vindication of the divine attributes, particularly holiness and justice, in establishing or allowing the existence of physical and moral evil. [1790–1800; THEO- + Gk *dík(ē)* justice + -Y[3], modeled on F *théodicée,* a coinage of Leibniz] **—the•od′i•ce′an,** *adj.*

the•od•o•lite (thē od′l īt′), *n.* **1.** *Survey.* a precision instrument having a telescopic sight for establishing horizontal and sometimes vertical angles. Cf. **transit** (def. 6). **2.** phototheodolite. [1565–75; < NL *theodolitus* < ?] **—the•od•o•lit•ic** (thē od′l it′ik), *adj.*

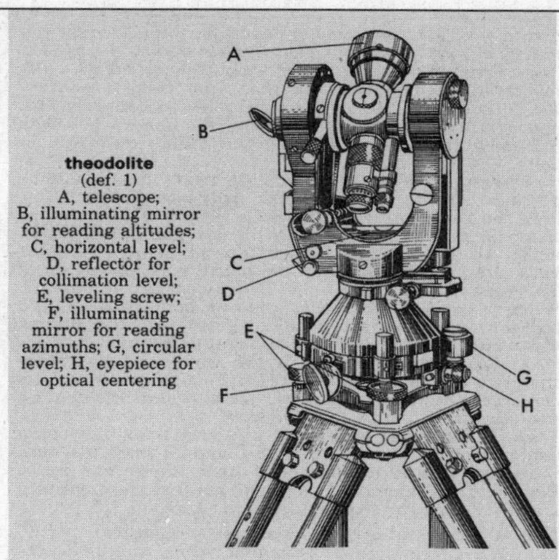

theodolite (def. 1) A, telescope; B, illuminating mirror for reading altitudes; C, horizontal level; D, reflector for collimation level; E, leveling screw; F, illuminating mirror for reading azimuths; G, circular level; H, eyepiece for optical centering

The•o•do•ra (thē′ə dôr′ə, -dōr′ə), *n.* **1.** A.D. 508–548, Byzantine empress: consort of Justinian I. **2.** a female given name: derived from *Theodore.*

The•o•dore (thē′ə dôr′, -dōr′), *n.* a male given name: from a Greek word meaning "gift of God."

Theodore I, died A.D. 649, pope 642–649.

Theodore II, pope A.D. 897.

The•od•o•ric (thē od′ə rik), *n.* A.D. 454?–526, king of the Ostrogoths and founder of the Ostrogothic monarchy in Italy: ruler of Italy 493–526.

The•o•do•si•a (thē′ə dō′shē ə, -shə), *n.* a female given name: from a Greek word meaning "god-given."

The•o•do•sian (thē′ə dō′shən, -shē ən), *adj.* **1.** of or pertaining to Theodosius I, who made Christianity the official state religion of the Roman Empire. **2.** of or pertaining to Theodosius II, who issued the earliest collection of the imperial laws **(Theodo′sian Code′).** [1755–65; THEODOSI(US) + -AN]

The•o•do•si•us I (thē′ə dō′shē əs, -shəs), *("the Great")* A.D. 346?–395, Roman emperor of the Eastern Roman Empire 379–395.

Theodosius II, A.D. 401–450, emperor of the Eastern Roman Empire 408–450.

the•og•o•ny (thē og′ə nē), *n., pl.* **-nies. 1.** the origin of the gods. **2.** an account of this; a genealogical account of the gods. [1605–15; < Gk *theogonía.* See THEO-, -GONY] **—the•o•gon•ic** (thē′ə gon′ik), *adj.* **—the•og′o•nist,** *n.*

theol., 1. theologian. **2.** theological. **3.** theology.

the•ol•a•try (thē ol′ə trē), *n.* worship of a deity. [1800–10; < Gk *theolatreía.* See THEO-, -LATRY]

the•o•lo•gian (thē′ə lō′jən, -jē ən), *n.* a person versed in theology, esp. Christian theology; divine. [1475–85; THEOLOGY + -AN; r. earlier *theologien* < MF]

the•o•log•i•cal (thē′ə loj′i kəl), *adj.* **1.** of, pertaining to, or involved with theology: *a theological student.* **2.** based upon the nature and will of God as revealed to humans. Also, **the′o•log′ic.** [1520–30; < ML *theologicālis,* equiv. to *theologic(us)* (< Gk *theologikós;* see THEOLOGY, -IC) + *-ālis* -AL[1]] **—the′o•log′i•cal•ly,** *adv.*

theolog′ical vir′tue, one of the three graces: faith, hope, or charity, infused into the human intellect and will by a special grace of God . Also called **supernatural virtue.** Cf. **natural virtue.** [1520–30]

the•ol•o•gize (thē ol′ə jīz′), *v.,* **-gized, -giz•ing.** —*v.i.* **1.** to theorize or speculate upon theological subjects. —*v.t.* **2.** to make theological; treat theologically. Also, *esp. Brit.,* **the•ol′o•gise′.** [1640–50; < ML *theologizāre.* See THEOLOGY, -IZE] **—the•ol′o•gi•za′tion,** *n.* **—the•ol′o•giz′er,** *n.*

the•o•logue (thē′ə lôg′, -log′), *n.* a theological student. Also, **the′o•log′.** [1375–1425; late ME < L *theologus* < Gk *theológos.* See THEO-, LOGUE]

the•ol•o•gy (thē ol′ə jē), *n., pl.* **-gies. 1.** the field of study and analysis that treats of God and of God's attributes and relations to the universe; study of divine things or religious truth; divinity. **2.** a particular form, system, branch, or course of this study. [1325–75; ME *theologie* < OF < LL *theologia* < Gk *theología.* See THEO-, -LOGY]

theol′ogy of cri′sis. See **crisis theology.**

the•om•a•chy (thē om′ə kē), *n., pl.* **-chies.** a battle with or among the gods. [1560–70; < LL *theomachia* < Gk *theomachia.* See THEO-, -MACHY]

the•o•ma•ni•a (thē′ō mā′nē ə, -mān′yə), *n.* a delusional mental illness in which a person believes himself or herself to be God or specially chosen by God, as to found a religious order. [1855–60; < NL; see THEO-, -MANIA] **—the•o•ma•ni•ac** (thē′ō mā′nē ak′), *n.*

the•o•mor•phic (thē′ə môr′fik), *adj.* having the form or likeness of God or a deity. [1865–70; < Gk *theómorph(os)* (see THEO-, -MORPHOUS) + -IC; see -MORPHIC] **—the′o•mor′phism,** *n.*

the•on•o•my (thē on′ə mē), *n.* the state of an individual or society that regards its own nature and norms as being in accord with the divine nature. Cf. **heteronomy.** [1885–90; < G *Theonomie;* see THEO-, -NOMY] **—the•on′o•mous,** *adj.*

the•op•a•thy (thē op′ə thē), *n.* religious emotion excited by the contemplation of God. [1740–50; THEO- + (SYM)PATHY] **—the•o•pa•thet•ic** (thē′ō pə thet′ik), **the•o•path•ic** (thē′ə path′ik), *adj.*

the•oph•a•ny (thē of′ə nē), *n., pl.* **-nies.** a manifestation or appearance of God or a god to a person. [1625–35; < LL *theophania* < LGk *theopháneia.* See THEO-, -PHANY] **—the•o•phan•ic** (thē′ə fan′ik), **the•oph′a•nous,** *adj.*

The•o•phi•lo Ot•to•ni (ti ô′fi lŏŏ ŏŏ tô′nē). See **Teófilo Otoni.**

The•oph•i•lus (thē of′ə ləs), *n.* **1.** a walled plain in the 4th quadrant of the face of the moon: about 65 mi. (105 km) in diameter. **2.** a male given name.

The•o•phras•tus (thē′ə fras′təs), *n.* 372?–287 B.C., Greek philosopher. **—The•o•phras•tian** (thē′ə fras′chən), *adj.*

the•o•phyl•line (thē′ə fil′ēn, -in), *n. Pharm.* a white, crystalline, poisonous alkaloid, $C_7H_8N_4O_2$, an isomer of theobromine, extracted from tea leaves or produced synthetically: used to relieve bronchial spasms, in the treatment of certain heart conditions, and as a diuretic. [1890–95; *theo-,* irreg. comb. form repr. NL *thea* tea + -PHYLL + -INE[2]]

theophyl′line eth′yl•ene•di′a•mine (eth′ə lēn-dī′ə mēn′, -dī am′in), *Pharm.* aminophylline. [ETHYLENE + DIAMINE]

theor., theorem.

the•or•bo (thē ôr′bō), *n., pl.* **-bos.** an obsolete bass lute with two sets of strings attached to separate peg boxes, one above the other, on the neck. [1595–1605; < It *teorba,* var. of *tiorba,* special use of Venetian *tiorba,* var. of *tuorba* traveling bag << Turk *torba* bag; so called from the bag it was carried in] **—the•or′bist,** *n.*

theorbo

The•o•rell (tā′ō rel′), *n.* **Ax•el Hu•go Te•o•dor** (äk′səl hōō′gō te′ō dôr′), 1903–82, Swedish biochemist: Nobel prize for medicine 1955.

the•o•rem (thē′ər əm, thēr′əm), *n.* **1.** *Math.* a theoretical proposition, statement, or formula embodying something to be proved from other propositions or formulas. **2.** a rule or law, esp. one expressed by an equation or formula. **3.** *Logic.* a proposition that can be deduced from the premises or assumptions of a system. **4.** an idea, belief, method, or statement generally accepted as true or worthwhile without proof. [1545–55; < LL *theōrēma* < Gk *theṓrēma* spectacle, hence, subject for contemplation, thesis (to be proved), equiv. to *theōrē-,* var. s. of *theōreîn* to view + *-ma* n. suffix] **—the•o•re•mat•ic** (thē′ər ə mat′ik, thēr′ə-), *adj.* **—the′o•re•mat′i•cal•ly,** *adv.*

the′orem of the mean′, *Math.* See **mean value theorem.**

the•o•ret•i•cal (thē′ə ret′i kəl), *adj.* **1.** of, pertaining to, or consisting in theory; not practical (distinguished from *applied*). **2.** existing only in theory; hypothetical. **3.** given to, forming, or dealing with theories; speculative. Also, **the′o•ret′ic.** [1610–20; *theoretic* (< LL *theōrēticus* < Gk *theōrētikós,* equiv. to *theōrēt(ós)* to be seen (verbid of *theōreîn* to view) + *-ikos* -IC) + -AL[1]] **—the′o•ret′i•cal•ly,** *adv.*

theoret′ical arith′metic, arithmetic (def. 2).

the•o•re•ti•cian (thē′ər i tish′ən, thēr′i-), *n.* a person who deals with or is expert in the theoretical side of a subject: *a military theoretician.* [1885–90; THEORETIC(S) + -IAN]

the•o•ret•ics (thē′ə ret′iks), *n.* (*used with a singular v.*) the theoretical or speculative part of a science or subject. [1650–60; *theoret(ic)* (see THEORETICAL) + -ICS]

the•o•rist (thē′ər ist, thēr′-), *n.* **1.** a person who theorizes. **2.** a person who deals mainly with the theory of a subject: *a theorist in medical research.* [1585–95; THEOR(Y) + -IST]

the•o•rize (thē′ə rīz′, thēr′īz), *v.,* **-rized, -riz•ing.** —*v.i.* **1.** to form a theory or theories. —*v.t.* **2.** to form a theory or theories about. Also, *esp. Brit.,* **the′o•rise′.** [1630–40; < ML *theorizāre.* See THEORY, -IZE] **—the′o•ri•za′tion,** *n.* **—the′o•riz′er,** *n.*

the•o•ry (thē′ə rē, thēr′ē), *n., pl.* **-ries. 1.** a coherent group of general propositions used as principles of explanation for a class of phenomena: *Einstein's theory of relativity.* **2.** a proposed explanation whose status is still conjectural, in contrast to well-established propositions that are regarded as reporting matters of actual fact. **3.** *Math.* a body of principles, theorems, or the like, belonging to one subject: *number theory.* **4.** the branch of a science or art that deals with its principles or methods, as distinguished from its practice: *music theory.* **5.** a particular conception or view of something to be done or of the method of doing it; a system of rules or principles. **6.** contemplation or speculation. **7.** guess or conjecture. [1590–1600; < LL *theōria* < Gk *theōría* a viewing, contemplating, equiv. to *theōr(eîn)* to view + *-ia* -Y[3]]

CONCISE PRONUNCIATION KEY: act, cāpe, dâre, pärt; set, ēqual; *if,* īce; ox, ōver, ôrder, oil, bŏŏk, bōōt, out; up, ûrge; child; sing; shoe; thin, *that;* zh as in *treasure.* ə = *a* as in *alone, e* as in *system, i* as in *easily, o* as in *gallop, u* as in *circus;* ə as in *fire* (fīər), *hour* (ouər). l and n can serve as syllabic consonants, as in *cradle* (krād′l), and *button* (but′n). See the full key inside the front cover.

—**Syn.** **1.** THEORY, HYPOTHESIS are used in non-technical contexts to mean an untested idea or opinion. A THEORY in technical use is a more or less verified or established explanation accounting for known facts or phenomena: *the theory of relativity.* A HYPOTHESIS is a conjecture put forth as a possible explanation of phenomena or relations, which serves as a basis of argument or experimentation to reach the truth: *This idea is only a hypothesis.*

the′ory of equa′tions, *Math.* the branch of mathematics dealing with methods of finding the solutions to algebraic equations. [1790–1800]

The′ory of Ev′erything, a theory intended to show that the electroweak, strong, and gravitational forces are components of a single quantized force. [1985–90]

the′ory of games′. See **game theory.** [1950–55]

the′ory of num′bers. See **number theory.**

the′ory of relativ′ity, *Physics.* relativity (def. 2).

theos., **1.** theosophical. **2.** theosophy.

Theosoph′ical Soci′ety, a society founded by Madame Blavatsky and others, in New York in 1875, advocating a worldwide eclectic religion based largely on Brahmanic and Buddhistic teachings.

the•os•o•phy (thē os′ə fē), *n.* **1.** any of various forms of philosophical or religious thought based on a mystical insight into the divine nature. **2.** (*often caps.*) the system of belief and practice of the Theosophical Society. [1640–50; < ML *theosophia* < LGk *theosophía.* See THEO-, -SOPHY] —**the•o•soph•i•cal** (thē′ə sof′i kəl), **the′•o•soph′ic,** *adj.* —**the′o•soph′i•cal•ly,** *adv.* —**the•os′•o•phism,** *n.* —**the•os′o•phist,** *n.*

The•o•to•co•pou•los (*Gk.* the′ô tô kô′po͞o lôs), *n.* **Do•men•i•kos** (t͟hô men′ē kôs). See **El Greco.**

The•o•to•kos (thē′ə tok′əs), *n.* a title of the Virgin Mary as the Mother of the incarnate Son of God. Also, **The′o•to′cos.** [1870–75; < LGk *Theotókos,* equiv. to *theo-* THEO- + *-tokos* giving birth to]

The•ra (thēr′ə), *n.* a Greek island in the S Aegean, in the Cyclades group. 30 sq. mi. (78 sq. km). Also, **Thira.** Also called **Santorin, Santorini.**

the•ra•lite (thēr′ə līt′), *n.* a coarse-grained, phaneritic rock composed of labradorite, nepheline, and augite. [< Gk *théra* hunting + -LITE; so called because success in hunting it down was thought to be certain]

ther•a•peu•tic (ther′ə pyo͞o′tik), *adj.* Also, **ther′a•peu′ti•cal.** **1.** of or pertaining to the treating or curing of disease; curative. —*n.* **2.** a therapeutic substance. [1535–45; < NL *therapeuticus* < Gk *therapeutikós,* equiv. to *therapeú(ein)* to attend, treat medically (akin to *therápōn* attendant) + *-tikos* -TIC] —**ther′a•peu′ti•cal•ly,** *adv.*

therapeu′tic abor′tion, abortion performed when a woman's pregnancy endangers her health.

ther′apeu′tic in′dex, *Pharm.* the ratio between the dosage of a drug that causes a lethal effect and the dosage that causes a therapeutic effect. Also called **margin of safety.** [1925–30]

ther•a•peu•tics (ther′ə pyo͞o′tiks), *n.* (*used with a singular v.*) the branch of medicine concerned with the remedial treatment of disease. [1665–75; see THERAPEUTIC, -ICS]

ther•a•pist (ther′ə pist), *n.* **1.** a person trained in the use of physical methods, as exercises, heat treatments, etc., in treating or rehabilitating the sick or wounded or helping patients overcome physical defects. **2.** a person trained in the use of psychological methods for helping patients overcome psychological problems. **3.** Also, **ther•a•peu•tist** (ther′ə pyo͞o′tist). a person, as a doctor, skilled in therapeutics. [1885–90; THERAP(Y) + -IST]

the•rap•sid (thə rap′sid), *n.* **1.** any of various groups of mammallike reptiles of the extinct order Therapsida, inhabiting all continents from mid-Permian to late Triassic times, some of which were probably warm-blooded and directly ancestral to mammals. —*adj.* **2.** of or pertaining to the Therapsida. [< NL *The*-*apsida* (1905), equiv. to Gk *thēr-* (s. of *thḗr* wild beast) + *apsid-* (s. of *apsís* arch, vault, referring to the temporal arch of the skull) + NL *-a* neut. pl. ending (see -A[1])]

ther•a•py (ther′ə pē), *n., pl.* **-pies.** **1.** the treatment of disease or disorders, as by some remedial, rehabilitating, or curative process: *speech therapy.* **2.** a curative power or quality. **3.** psychotherapy. **4.** any act, hobby, task, program, etc., that relieves tension. [1840–50; < NL *therapia* < Gk *therapeía* healing (akin to *therápōn* attendant)]

Ther•a•va•da (ther′ə vä′də), *n. Buddhism.* Hinayanist name for **Hinayana.**

Ther•a•va•din (ther′ə väd′n), *n. Buddhism.* Hinayanist.

ther•blig (thûr′blig), *n.* (in time and motion study) any of the basic elements involved in completing a given manual operation or task that can be subjected to analysis. [1930–35, *Amer.*; anagram of F. B. Gilbreth (1868–1924), American engineer]

there (t͟hâr; *unstressed* t͟hər), *adv.* **1.** in or at that place (opposed to *here*): *She is there now.* **2.** at that point in an action, speech, etc.: *He stopped there for applause.* **3.** in that matter, particular, or respect: *His anger was justified there.* **4.** into or to that place; thither: *We went there last year.* **5.** (used by way of calling attention to something or someone): *There they go.* **6.** in or at that place where you are: *Well, hi there.* —*pron.* **7.** (used to introduce a sentence or clause in which the verb comes before its subject or has no complement): *There is no hope.* **8.** that place: *He comes from there, too.* **9.** that point. —*n.* **10.** that state or condition: *I'll introduce you to her, but you're on your own from there on.* —*adj.* **11.** (used for emphasis, esp. after a noun modified by a demonstrative adjective): *Ask that man there.* —*interj.* **12.** (used to express satisfaction, relief, encouragement, approval, consolation, etc.): *There! It's done.* [bef. 900; ME (adv.), OE *thǣr thēr,* c. D *daar,* OHG *dār;* akin to Goth, ON *thar;* cf. THAT]

—**Usage.** **7.** The verb following THERE is singular or plural according to the number of the subject that follows the verb: *There is a message for you. There are patients in the waiting room.* With compound subjects in which all the coordinate words are singular, a singular verb often occurs, although the plural may also be used: *There was* (or *were*) *a horse and a cow in the pasture.* When a compound subject contains both singular and plural words, the verb usually agrees with the subject closest to the verb, although a plural verb sometimes occurs regardless, especially if the compound has more than two elements: *There were staff meetings and a press conference daily. There was* (or *were*) *a glass, two plates, two cups, and a teapot on the shelf.*

11. It is nonstandard usage to place THERE between a demonstrative adjective and the noun it modifies: *that there car.* The same is true of HERE: *these here nails.* Placed after the noun, both THERE and HERE are entirely standard: *that car there; these nails here.*

-there a combining form meaning "wild animal, beast," used in the formation of compound words, usually denoting extinct mammals, as adaptions of zoological taxa ending in *-therium* or *-theria: baluchithere.* [< NL *-therium* (sing.), *-theria* (pl.) < Gk *thēríon,* deriv. of *thḗr* beast of prey; akin to FERAL[1], FIERCE]

there•a•bout (t͟hâr′ə bout′, t͟hâr′ə bout′), *adv.* **1.** about or near that place or time: *last June or thereabout.* **2.** about that number, amount, etc. Also, **there′a•bouts′.** [bef. 950; ME *ther aboute,* OE *thǣr abūtan.* See THERE, ABOUT]

there•af•ter (t͟hâr′af′tər, -äf′-), *adv.* **1.** after that in time or sequence; afterward: *Thereafter they did not speak.* **2.** *Obs.* accordingly. [bef. 900; ME *ther after,* OE *thǣr æfter.* See THERE, AFTER]

—**Syn.** **1.** later, subsequently, thenceforth.

there•at (t͟hâr′at′), *adv.* **1.** at that place or time; there: *Seeing the gate, they entered thereat.* **2.** because of that; thereupon. [bef. 900; ME *ther at,* OE *thǣr æt.* See THERE, AT[1]]

there•by (t͟hâr′bī′, t͟hâr′bī′), *adv.* **1.** by that; by means of that. **2.** in that connection or relation: *Thereby hangs a tale.* **3.** by or near that place. **4.** *Scot.* about that number, quantity, or degree. [bef. 900; ME *therby,* OE *thǣrbī.* See THERE, BY[1]]

there•for (t͟hâr′fôr′), *adv.* for or in exchange for that or this; for it: *a refund therefor.* [1125–75; ME *therfor.* See THERE, FOR]

there•fore (t͟hâr′fôr′, -fōr′), *adv.* in consequence of that; as a result; consequently: *I think; therefore I am.* [1125–75; ME *ther(e)fore,* var. of *therfor* THEREFOR]

—**Syn.** hence, whence. THEREFORE, WHEREFORE, ACCORDINGLY, CONSEQUENTLY, SO, THEN all introduce a statement resulting from, or caused by, what immediately precedes. THEREFORE (for this or that reason) and WHEREFORE (for which reason) imply exactness of reasoning; they are esp. used in logic, law, mathematics, etc., and in a formal style of speaking or writing. ACCORDINGLY (in conformity with the preceding) and CONSEQUENTLY (as a result, or sequence, or effect of the preceding), although also somewhat formal, occur mainly in less technical contexts. So (because the preceding is true or this being the case) and THEN (since the preceding is true) are informal or conversational in tone.

there•from (t͟hâr′frum′, -from′), *adv.* from that place, thing, etc. [1200–50; ME; see THERE, FROM]

there•in (t͟hâr′in′), *adv.* **1.** in or into that place or thing. **2.** in that matter, circumstance, etc. [bef. 1000; ME *therin,* OE *thǣrin.* See THERE, IN]

there•in•af•ter (t͟hâr′in af′tər, -äf′-), *adv.* afterward in that document. [1810–20; THEREIN + AFTER]

there•in•to (t͟hâr′in′to͞o, t͟hâr′in to͞o′), *adv.* **1.** into that place or thing. **2.** into that matter, circumstance, etc. [1250–1300; ME *thar into.* See THERE, INTO]

ther•e•min (ther′ə min), *n.* a musical instrument with electronic tone generation, the pitch and tone volume being controlled by the distance between the player's hands and two metal rods serving as antennas. [1925–30; named after Leo *Theremin* (b. 1896), Russian inventor] —**ther′e•min′ist,** *n.*

there•of (t͟hâr′uv′, -ov′), *adv.* **1.** of that or it. **2.** from or out of that origin or cause. [bef. 1000; ME *therof,* OE *thǣrof.* See THERE, OF[1]]

there•on (t͟hâr′on′, -ôn′), *adv.* **1.** on or upon that or it. **2.** immediately after that; thereupon. [bef. 900; ME *ther on,* OE *thǣron.* See THERE, ON]

there's (t͟hârz), **1.** contraction of *there is: There's the hotel we were looking for.* **2.** contraction of *there has: There's been entirely too much said on the subject.*

—**Usage.** See **contraction.**

The•re•sa (tə rē′sə, -zə; *Sp.* te re′sä), *n.* **1.** **Saint.** Also, **Teresa.** Also called **There′sa of A′vi•la** (ä′vē lä′). 1515–82, Spanish Carmelite nun, mystic, and writer. **2.** a female given name.

Thé•rèse de Li•sieux (tā rez də lē zyœ′), *n.* **Saint** (*Marie Françoise Thérèse Martin*) ("*the Little Flower*"), 1873–97, French Carmelite nun.

there•to (t͟hâr′to͞o′), *adv.* **1.** to that place, thing, etc. **2.** to that matter, circumstance, etc. Also, **there•un•to** (t͟hâr′un to͞o′, t͟hâr′un′to͞o). [bef. 900; ME *therto,* OE *thǣrtō.* See THERE, TO]

there•to•fore (t͟hâr′tə fôr′, -fōr′), *adv.* before or until that time. [1300–50; ME *ther tofore.* See THERE, HERETOFORE]

there•un•der (t͟hâr′un′dər), *adv.* **1.** under or beneath that. **2.** under the authority of or in accordance with that. [bef. 900; ME *therunder,* OE *thǣrunder.* See THERE, UNDER]

there•up•on (t͟hâr′ə pon′, -pôn′, t͟hâr′ə pon′, -pôn′), *adv.* **1.** immediately following that. **2.** in consequence of that. **3.** upon that or it. **4.** with reference to that. [1125–75; ME *ther uppon.* See THERE, UPON]

there•with (t͟hâr′with′, -wit͟h′), *adv.* **1.** with that. **2.** in addition to that. **3.** following upon that; thereupon. [bef. 900; ME *ther(e)with,* OE *thǣrwith.* See THERE, WITH]

there•with•al (t͟hâr′wit͟h ôl′, -with-, t͟hâr′wit͟h ôl′, -with-), *adv.* **1.** together with that; in addition to that. **2.** following upon that. [1250–1300; ME *ther withal.* See THERE, WITHAL]

The•re•zi•na (*Port.* ti ʀi zē′nä), *n.* former name of **Teresina.**

the•ri•ac (thēr′ē ak′), *n.* **1.** molasses; treacle. **2.** a paste formerly used as an antidote to poison, esp. snake venom, made from 60 or 70 different drugs pulverized and mixed with honey. Also, **the•ri•a•ca** (thə rī′ə kə). [bef. 1000; < L *thēriaca* antidote to poison < Gk *thēriakḗ,* fem. of *thēriakós,* equiv. to *thērí(on)* wild beast + *-akos* -AC; r. ME *tiriake,* OE *tȳriaca* < ML, var. of *thēriaca*] —**the•ri′a•cal,** *adj.*

the•ri•an (thēr′ē ən), *adj.* **1.** (in some classification systems) belonging or pertaining to the group Theria, comprising the marsupial and placental mammals and their extinct ancestors. —*n.* **2.** a therian animal. [< NL *Theri(a)* name of the group (< Gk *thēría,* pl. of *thēríon* wild beast) + -AN]

the•ri•an•throp•ic (thēr′ē an throp′ik), *adj.* **1.** being partly bestial and partly human in form. **2.** of or pertaining to deities conceived or represented in such form. [1885–90; < Gk *thērí(on)* beast + ANTHROP- + -IC] —**the•ri•an•thro•pism** (thēr′ē an′thrə piz′əm), *n.*

the•ri•at•rics (thēr′ē a′triks), *n.* (*used with a singular v.*) the study and practice of veterinary medicine. [< Gk *thēr-,* comb. form of *thḗr* beast, carnivore + -IATRICS]

the•rid•i•id (thə rid′ē id, ther′i dī′id), *n.* **1.** a spider of the family Theridiidae, comprising the comb-footed spiders. —*adj.* **2.** belonging or pertaining to the family Theridiidae. [< NL *Theridiidae* name of the family, equiv. to *Theridi(um)* a genus (< Gk *thērídion,* dim of *thēríon* beast) + NL *-idae* -ID[2]]

the•ri•o•ge•nol•o•gy (thēr′ē ō jə nol′ə jē), *n.* the branch of veterinary medicine encompassing all aspects of reproduction. [< Gk *thērí(on)* beast + -O- + Gk *gén(os)* offspring, sex + -O- + -LOGY]

the•ri•o•mor•phic (thēr′ē ə môr′fik), *adj.* (of deities) thought of or represented as having the form of beasts. Also, **the′ri•o•mor′phous.** [1880–85; < Gk *thēriómorph(os)* beast-shaped (*thērío(n)* wild beast + *-morphos* -MORPHOUS) + -IC] —**the′ri•o•morph′,** *n.*

therm (thûrm), *n. Physics.* any of several units of heat, as one equivalent to 1000 large calories or 100,000 British thermal units. Also, **therme.** [1885–90; < Gk *thérmē* heat]

therm-, var. of **thermo-** before a vowel: *thermesthesia.*

-therm, var. of **thermo-** as final element in compound words: *isotherm.*

therm., thermometer.

Ther•ma (thûr′mə), *n.* ancient name of **Salonika.**

ther•mae (thûr′mē), *n.* (*used with a plural v.*) **1.** hot springs; hot baths. **2.** a public bathing establishment of the ancient Greeks or Romans. [1590–1600; < L < Gk *thérmai;* n. use of pl. of *thérmē* heat; see THERMO-]

therm•aes•the•sia (thûrm′is thē′zhə, -zhē ə, -zē ə), *n.* thermesthesia.

ther•mal (thûr′məl), *adj.* **1.** Also, **thermic.** of, pertaining to, or caused by heat or temperature: *thermal capacity.* **2.** of, pertaining to, or of the nature of thermae: *thermal waters.* **3.** designed to aid in or promote the retention of body heat: *a thermal blanket.* —*n.* **4.** *Meteorol.* a rising air current caused by heating from the underlying surface, esp. such a current when not producing a cloud. **5.** **thermals.** See **thermal underwear.** [1750–60; THERM- + -AL[1]] —**ther′mal•ly,** *adv.*

ther′mal anal′ysis, *Chem.* any analysis of materials in which properties relating to heat, such as freezing and boiling temperatures, the heat of fusion, the heat of vaporization, etc., are measured. Also called **thermoanalysis.** [1920–25]

ther′mal bar′rier, *Aeron., Rocketry.* the high temperatures produced by the friction between a supersonic object and the earth's atmosphere that limit the speed of an airplane or rocket. Also called **heat barrier.** [1950–55]

ther′mal con′ductiv′ity, *Physics.* the amount of heat per unit time per unit area that can be conducted through a plate of unit thickness of a given material, the faces of the plate differing by one unit of temperature.

ther′mal diffu′sion, *Physical Chem.* the separation of constituents, often isotopes, of a fluid under the influence of a temperature gradient. Also, **thermodiffusion.**

ther′mal effi′ciency, *Thermodynam.* the ratio of the work output of a heat engine to the heat input expressed in the same units of energy. [1905–10]

ther′mal e′quilib′rium, *Thermodynam.* **1.** the relationship between two systems connected only by a diathermic wall. **2.** the relationship between two isolated systems the states of which are such that no net transfer of energy would occur between them if they were connected by a diathermic wall.

therm•al•ge•si•a (thûrm′al jē′zē ə, -sē ə), *n. Med.* pain caused by heat. [THERM- + ALGESIA]

ther′mal noise′, *Thermodynam., Elect.* a wide spectrum of electromagnetic noise appearing in electronic circuits and devices as a result of the temperature-dependent random motions of electrons and other charge carriers. Cf. **shot effect.** [1925–30]

CONCISE ETYMOLOGY KEY: <, descended or borrowed from; >, whence; b., blend of, blended; c., cognate with; cf., compare; deriv., derivative; equiv., equivalent; imit., imitative; obl., oblique; r., replacing; s., stem; sp., spelling, spelled; resp., respelling, respelled; trans., translation; ?, origin unknown; *, unattested; ‡, probably earlier than. See the full key inside the front cover.

ther′mal pollu′tion, a rise in the temperature of rivers or lakes that is injurious to water-dwelling life and is caused by the disposal of heated industrial waste water or water from the cooling towers of nuclear power plants.

ther′mal print′er, *Computers.* a printer that produces output by selectively heating a heat-sensitive paper (**ther′mal pa′per**) in patterns corresponding to the characters to be produced. [1980–85]

ther′mal radia′tion, *Thermodynam.* electromagnetic radiation emitted by all matter above a temperature of absolute zero because of the thermal motion of atomic particles. [1930–35]

ther′mal spring′, a spring whose temperature is higher than the mean temperature of ground water in the area. [1790–1800]

ther′mal un′derwear, underwear designed to retain body heat in cold temperatures. Also called **thermals.**

ther′mal u′nit, a unit of heat energy or of the equivalent of heat energy in work. [1875–80]

therm•an•es•the•sia (thûrm′an is thē′zhə), *n. Pathol.* loss of ability to feel cold or heat; loss of the sense or feeling of temperature. Also, **thermoanesthesia.** [1880–85; THERM- + ANESTHESIA]

ther•mate (thûr′māt), *n.* a mixture of thermite and other oxidizing agents used as filling for incendiary munitions. [THERM(ITE) + -ATE²]

therme (thûrm), *n. Physics.* therm.

therm•el (thûr′mel), *n.* thermocouple. [THERM- + EL(ECTRIC)]

therm•es•the•sia (thûrm′is thē′zhə, -zhē ə, -zē ə), *n. Pathol.* ability to perceive or sense cold or heat; sensitiveness to heat. Also, **thermaesthesia.** [THERM- + ESTHESIA]

ther•mic (thûr′mik), *adj.* thermal (def. 1). [1840–50; THERM- + -IC]

ther′mic fe′ver, *Pathol.* sunstroke. [1885–90]

Ther•mi•dor (thûr′mi dôr′; *Fr.* ter mē dôr′), *n.* **1.** Also called **Fervidor.** (in the French Revolutionary calendar) the 11th month of the year, extending from July 19 to August 17. **2.** *(sometimes l.c.)* See **lobster Thermidor.** [1820–30; < F < Gk *thérm(ē)* heat + *dôr(on)* gift; cf. -I-]

Ther•mi•do•ri•an (thûr′mi dôr′ē ən, -dōr′-), *n.* **1.** a member of the French moderate group who participated in the downfall of Robespierre and his followers on the 9th Thermidor (July 27th), 1794. **2.** a supporter of the reactionary movement following this coup d'état. Also, **Ther′mi•do′re•an.** [1820–30; < F *thermidorien.* See THERMIDOR, -IAN]

therm•i•on (thûrm′ī′ən, -on; thûr′mē ən), *n. Physics.* an ion emitted by incandescent material. [1910–15; THERM- + ION] —**therm′i•on′ic,** *adj.* —**therm′i•on′i•cal•ly,** *adv.*

therm′ion′ic cur′rent, an electric current produced by the flow of thermions. [1910–15]

therm•i•on•ics (thûrm′ī on′iks, thûr′mē-), *n.* (*used with a singular v.*) the branch of physics that deals with thermionic phenomena. [1925–30; see THERMIONIC, -ICS]

therm′ion′ic tube′, *Electronics.* a vacuum tube in which the cathode is heated electrically to cause the emission of electrons by thermal agitation. Also called **hot-cathode tube.** [1925–30]

therm′ion′ic valve′, *Brit.* See **vacuum tube.** [1915–20]

therm•is•tor (thər mis′tər, thûr′mə stər), *n. Electronics.* a resistor whose action depends upon changes of its resistance material with changes in temperature. [1935–40; THERM- + (RES)ISTOR]

Ther•mit (thûr′mit), *Trademark.* a brand of thermite.

ther•mite (thûr′mīt), *n.* a mixture of finely-divided metallic aluminum and ferric oxide that when ignited produces extremely high temperatures as the result of the union of the aluminum with the oxygen of the oxide: used in welding, incendiary bombs, etc. [1895–1900; THERM- + -ITE¹]

thermo-, a combining form meaning "heat," "hot," used in the formation of compound words: *thermoplastic.* Also, **therm-, -therm.** [< Gk, comb. form of *thermós* hot, *thérmē* heat]

ther•mo•a•cid•o•phile (thûr′mō ə sid′ə fīl′, -as′-i də-), *n.* any organism, esp. a type of archaebacterium, that thrives in strongly acidic environments at high temperatures. [THERMO- + ACIDOPHILE]

ther•mo•am•me•ter (thûr′mō am′mē′tər), *n. Elect.* an ammeter that measures amperage by means of a thermocouple. [1890–95; THERMO- + AMMETER]

ther•mo•a•nal•y•sis (thûr′mō ə nal′ə sis), *n., pl.* **-ses** (-sēz′). See **thermal analysis.** [THERMO- + ANALYSIS]

ther•mo•an•es•the•sia (thûr′mō an′is thē′zhə), *n. Pathol.* thermanesthesia.

ther•mo•ba•rom•e•ter (thûr′mō bə rom′i tər), *n.* **1.** Also called **hypsometer.** an instrument for measuring atmospheric pressure, and sometimes altitude, from its effect upon the boiling point of a liquid. **2.** a form of barometer so constructed that it may also be used as a thermometer. [1860–65; THERMO- + BAROMETER]

ther•mo•chem•is•try (thûr′mō kem′ə strē), *n.* the branch of chemistry dealing with the relationship between chemical action and heat. [1835–45; THERMO- + CHEMISTRY] —**ther•mo•chem•i•cal** (thûr′mō kem′i-kəl), *adj.* —**ther′mo•chem′i•cal•ly,** *adv.* —**ther′mo•chem′ist,** *n.*

ther•mo•cline (thûr′mə klīn′), *n.* a layer of water in an ocean or certain lakes, where the temperature gradient is greater than that of the warmer layer above and the colder layer below. Cf. **epilimnion, hypolimnion.** [1895–1900; THERMO- + Gk *klínē* bed] —**ther′mo•clin′•al,** *adj.*

ther•mo•co•ag•u•la•tion (thûr′mō kō ag′yə lā′shən), *n. Surg.* the coagulation of tissue by heat-producing high-frequency electric currents, used therapeutically to remove small growths or to create specific lesions in the brain. [1920–25; THERMO- + COAGULATION]

ther•mo•cou•ple (thûr′mə kup′əl), *n. Physics.* a device that consists of the junction of two dissimilar metallic conductors, as copper and iron, in which an electromotive force is induced when the conductors are maintained at different temperatures, the force being related to the temperature difference: used to determine the temperature of a third substance by connecting it to the junction of the metals and measuring the electromotive force produced. Also called **thermoelectric couple, thermoelectric thermometer.** [1885–90; THERMO- + COUPLE]

ther•mo•cur•rent (thûr′mō kûr′ənt, -kur′-), *n.* a thermoelectric current. [1840–50; THERMO- + CURRENT]

ther•mo•dif•fu•sion (thûr′mō di fyōō′zhən), *n. Physical Chem.* See **thermal diffusion.** [1895–1900; THERMO- + DIFFUSION]

ther•mo•dur•ic (thûr′mə dŏŏr′ik, -dyŏŏr′ik), *adj. Bacteriol.* (of certain microorganisms) able to survive high temperatures, as during pasteurization. [1930–35; THERMO- + L *dūr(āre)* to last + -IC]

thermodynam., thermodynamics.

ther•mo•dy•nam•ic (thûr′mō dī nam′ik), *adj.* **1.** of or pertaining to thermodynamics. **2.** using or producing heat. Also, **ther′mo•dy•nam′i•cal.** [1840–50; THERMO- + DYNAMIC] —**ther′mo•dy•nam′i•cal•ly,** *adv.*

ther′modynam′ic poten′tial, *Thermodynam.* See **Gibbs function.**

ther•mo•dy•nam•ics (thûr′mō dī nam′iks), *n.* (*used with a singular v.*) the science concerned with the relations between heat and mechanical energy or work, and the conversion of one into the other: modern thermodynamics deals with the properties of systems for the description of which temperature is a necessary coordinate. [1850–55; THERMO- + DYNAMICS] —**ther′mo•dy•nam′i•cist,** *n.*

ther′modynam′ic sys′tem, *Physics.* a system whose states of equilibrium can be specified by a few macroscopic properties.

ther•mo•e•las•tic (thûr′mō i las′tik), *adj. Physics.* pertaining to the thermodynamic effects produced by deformation of an elastic substance. [1900–05; THERMO- + ELASTIC]

ther•mo•e•lec•tric (thûr′mō i lek′trik), *adj.* of, pertaining to, or involving the direct relationship between heat and electricity. Also, **ther′mo•e•lec′tri•cal.** [1815–25; THERMO- + ELECTRIC] —**ther′mo•e•lec′tri•cal•ly,** *adv.*

ther′moelec′tric cou′ple, *Physics.* thermocouple. [1860–65]

thermoelec′tric effect′, *Physics.* the production of an electromotive force in a thermocouple. Also called **Seebeck effect.**

ther•mo•e•lec•tric•i•ty (thûr′mō i lek tris′i tē, -ē′lek-), *n.* electricity generated by heat or temperature difference, as in a thermocouple. [1815–25; THERMO- + ELECTRICITY]

ther′moelec′tric thermom′eter, *Physics.* thermocouple.

ther•mo•e•lec•trom•e•ter (thûr′mō i lek trom′i tər, -ē′lek-), *n. Elect.* an instrument for measuring a charge or voltage by means of the heat it produces in a resistance. [1835–45; THERMO- + ELECTROMETER]

ther′mo•e•lec•tro•mo′tive force′ (thûr′mō i-lek′trə mō′tiv, thûr′-), the electromotive force developed by the thermoelectric effect. [1885–90; THERMO- + ELECTROMOTIVE]

ther•mo•e•lec•tron (thûr′mō i lek′tron), *n. Physics.* an electron emitted by an incandescent material. [1925–30; THERMO- + ELECTRON] —**ther•mo•e•lec•tron•ic,** (thûr′mō i lek tron′ik, -ē′lek-), *adj.*

ther•mo•form (thûr′mə fôrm′), *v.t.* to shape (esp. plastic) by the use of heat and pressure. [1955–60; THERMO- + FORM] —**ther′mo•form′a•ble,** *adj.*

ther•mo•gal•va•nom•e•ter (thûr′mō gal′və nom′i-tər), *n. Elect.* a thermoammeter for measuring small currents, consisting of a thermocouple connected to a direct-current galvanometer. [1865–70; THERMO- + GALVANOMETER]

ther•mo•gen•e•sis (thûr′mō jen′ə sis), *n.* the production of heat, esp. in an animal body by physiological processes. [1890–95; THERMO- + -GENESIS] —**ther•mo•ge•net•ic** (thûr′mō jə net′ik), *adj.*

ther•mo•gen•ic (thûr′mə jen′ik), *adj.* causing or pertaining to the production of heat. [1875–80; THERMO- + -GENIC]

ther•mo•ge•og•ra•phy (thûr′mō jē og′rə fē), *n.* the study of the geographical variation and distribution of temperature. [1895–1900; THERMO- + GEOGRAPHY]

ther•mo•gram (thûr′mə gram′), *n. Med.* a graphic or visual record produced by thermography. [1880–85; THERMO- + -GRAM¹]

ther•mo•graph (thûr′mə graf′, -gräf′), *n.* a thermometer that records the temperatures it measures. [1830–40; THERMO- + -GRAPH]

ther•mog•ra•phy (thər mog′rə fē), *n.* **1.** a technique for imitating an embossed appearance, as on business cards, stationery, or the like, by dusting printed areas with a powder that adheres only to the wet ink, and fusing the ink and powder to the paper by heat. **2.** *Med.* a technique for measuring regional skin temperatures, used esp. as a screening method for detection of breast cancer. [1830–40; THERMO- + -GRAPHY] —**ther•mog′•ra•pher,** *n.* —**ther•mo•graph•ic** (thûr′mə graf′ik), *adj.* —**ther′mo•graph′i•cal•ly,** *adv.*

ther•mo•la•bile (thûr′mō lā′bil, -bīl), *adj. Biochem.* subject to destruction or loss of characteristic properties by the action of moderate heat, as certain toxins and enzymes (opposed to *thermostable*). [1900–05; THERMO- + LABILE] —**ther•mo•la•bil•i•ty** (thûr′mō lə bil′i tē), *n.*

ther•mo•lu•mi•nes•cence (thûr′mō lōō′mə nes′əns), *n. Physics.* phosphorescence produced by the heating of a substance. [1895–1900; THERMO- + LUMINESCENCE] —**ther′mo•lu′mi•nes′cent,** *adj.*

thermolumines′cence dat′ing, *Archaeol.* a method of dating archaeological specimens, chiefly pottery, by measuring the radiation given off by ceramic materials as they are heated. [1965–70]

ther•mol•y•sis (thər mol′ə sis), *n.* **1.** *Physiol.* the dispersion of heat from the body. **2.** *Chem.* dissociation by heat. [1870–75; THERMO- + -LYSIS] —**ther•mo•lyt•ic** (thûr′mə lit′ik), *adj.*

ther•mo•mag•net•ic (thûr′mō mag net′ik), *adj. Physics.* **1.** of or pertaining to the effect of heat on the magnetic properties of a substance. **2.** of or pertaining to the effect of a magnetic field on a conductor of heat. [1815–25; THERMO- + MAGNETIC]

ther•mom•e•ter (thər mom′i tər), *n.* an instrument for measuring temperature, often a sealed glass tube that contains a column of liquid, as mercury, that expands and contracts, or rises and falls, with temperature changes, the temperature being read where the top of the column coincides with a calibrated scale marked on the tube or its frame. [1615–25; THERMO- + -METER] —**ther•mo•met•ric** (thûr′mə me′trik), **ther′mo•met′ri•cal,** *adj.* —**ther′mo•met′ri•cal•ly,** *adv.*

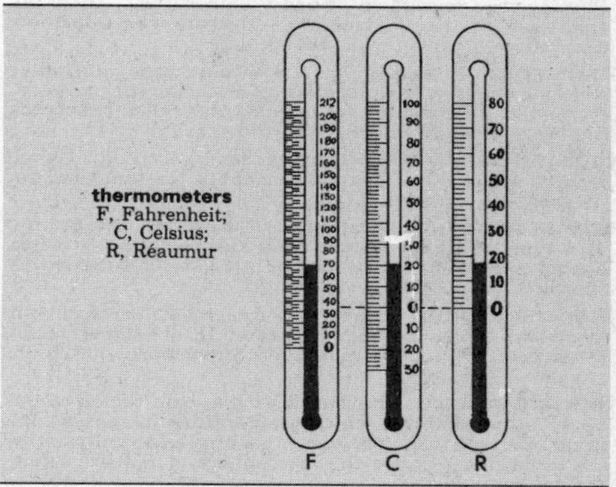

thermometers
F, Fahrenheit;
C, Celsius;
R, Réaumur

thermomet′ric titra′tion, *Chem.* titration in which the end point is determined by measuring the temperature of a solution.

ther•mom•e•try (thər mom′i trē), *n.* **1.** the branch of physics dealing with the measurement of temperature. **2.** the science of the construction and use of thermometers. [1855–60; THERMO- + -METRY]

ther•mo•mo•tive (thûr′mə mō′tiv), *adj.* pertaining to motion produced by heat. [THERMO- + MOTIVE]

ther•mo•mo•tor (thûr′mə mō′tər), *n.* a heat engine. [THERMO- + MOTOR]

ther•mo•nu•cle•ar (thûr′mō nōō′klē ər, -nyōō′- *or, by metathesis,* -kyə lər), *adj.* of, pertaining to, or involving a thermonuclear reaction: *thermonuclear power.* [1935–40; THERMO- + NUCLEAR] —**Pronunciation.** See **nuclear.**

thermonu′clear bomb′. See **hydrogen bomb.** [1945–50]

thermonu′clear reac′tion, *Chem., Physics.* a nuclear-fusion reaction that takes place between the nuclei of a gas, esp. hydrogen, heated to a temperature of several million degrees.

Ther•mo•pane (thûr′mə pān′), *Trademark.* a brand name for a hermetically sealed double glazing.

ther•mo•pe•ri•od•ic (thûr′mō pēr′ē od′ik), *adj. Biol.* responding to or affected by periodic differences in temperatures. [THERMO- + PERIODIC¹]

ther•mo•pe•ri•o•dic•i•ty (thûr′mō pēr′ē ə dis′i tē), *n. Biol.* the effect on an organism of rhythmic fluctuations in temperature. Also, **ther•mo•pe•ri•o•dism** (thûr′-mō pēr′ē ə diz′əm). [1940–45; THERMO- + PERIODICITY]

ther•mo•phile (thûr′mə fīl′, -fil), *n.* a thermophilic organism. [1895–1900; THERMO- + -PHILE]

ther•mo•phil•ic (thûr′mə fil′ik), *adj.* **1.** growing best in a warm environment. **2.** (of bacteria) growing best at temperatures between 50° and 60°C. [1895–1900; THERMO- + -PHILIC]

ther•mo•phone (thûr′mə fōn′), *n.* an electroacoustic transducer that forms sound waves by the expansion and contraction of the air adjacent to a conductor that varies in temperature according to the magnitude of the current passing through it; formerly used to calibrate microphones. [1875–80; THERMO- + -PHONE]

ther•mo•phos•pho•res•cence (thûr′mō fos′fə res′-əns), *n. Physics.* thermoluminescence. [THERMO- + PHOSPHORESCENCE] —**ther′mo•phos′pho•res′cent,** *adj.*

ther•mo•pile (thûr′mə pīl′), *n. Physics.* a device consisting of a number of thermocouples joined in series, used for generating thermoelectric current or for detecting and measuring radiant energy, as from a star. [1840–50; THERMO- + PILE¹]

ther•mo•plas•tic (thûr′mə plas′tik), *adj.* **1.** soft and pliable when heated, as some plastics, without any change of the inherent properties. —*n.* **2.** a plastic of this type. [1880–85; THERMO- + PLASTIC] —**ther·mo·plas·tic·i·ty** (thûr′mō pla stis′i tē), *n.*

Ther·mop·y·lae (thər mop′ə lē′), *n.* a pass in E Greece, between the cliffs of Mt. Oeta and the Gulf of Lamia: Persian defeat of the Spartans 480 B.C.

ther·mo·re·cep·tor (thûr′mō ri sep′tər), *n. Physiol.* a receptor stimulated by changes in temperature. [1945–50; THERMO- + RECEPTOR]

ther·mo·reg·u·la·tion (thûr′mō reg′yə lā′shən), *n. Physiol.* the regulation of body temperature. [1925–30; THERMO- + REGULATION] —**ther·mo·reg·u·la·to·ry** (thûr′mō reg′yə lə tôr′ē, -tōr′ē), *adj.*

ther·mos (thûr′məs), *n.* a vacuum bottle or similar container lined with an insulating material, such as polystyrene, to keep liquids hot or cold. Also called **ther′mos bot′tle.** [1905–10; formerly a trademark]

ther·mo·sen·si·tive (thûr′mō sen′si tiv), *adj. Chem.* readily affected by heat or a change in temperature. [THERMO- + SENSITIVE]

ther·mo·set·ting (thûr′mō set′ing), *adj.* pertaining to a type of plastic, as the urea resins, that sets when heated and cannot be remolded. [1935–40; THERMO- + SETTING]

ther·mo·si·phon (thûr′mə sī′fən), *n.* an arrangement of siphon tubes that enables water in a heating apparatus to circulate by means of convection. [1825–35; THERMO- + SIPHON]

ther·mo·sphere (thûr′mə sfēr′), *n.* the region of the upper atmosphere in which temperature increases continuously with altitude, encompassing essentially all of the atmosphere above the mesosphere. [1950–55; THERMO- + SPHERE]

ther·mo·sta·ble (thûr′mō stā′bəl), *adj. Biochem.* capable of being subjected to a moderate degree of heat without loss of characteristic properties, as certain toxins and enzymes (opposed to *thermolabile*). [1900–05; THERMO- + STABLE[2]] —**ther′mo·sta·bil′i·ty,** *n.*

ther·mo·stat (thûr′mə stat′), *n., v.,* **-stat·ted** or **-stat·ed; -stat·ting** or **-stat·ing.** —*n.* **1.** a device, including a relay actuated by thermal conduction or convection, that functions to establish and maintain a desired temperature automatically or signals a change in temperature for manual adjustment. —*v.t.* **2.** to equip or control with a thermostat. [1825–35; THERMO- + -STAT] —**ther′mo·stat′ic,** *adj.* —**ther′mo·stat′i·cal·ly,** *adv.*

ther·mo·tax·is (thûr′mə tak′sis), *n.* **1.** *Biol.* movement of an organism toward or away from a source of heat. **2.** *Physiol.* the regulation of the bodily temperature. [1890–95; THERMO- + -TAXIS] —**ther·mo·tac·tic** (thûr′mə tak′tik), **ther′mo·tax′ic,** *adj.*

ther·mo·ther·a·py (thûr′mō ther′ə pē), *n.* treatment of disease by means of moist or dry heat. [1855–60; THERMO- + THERAPY]

ther·mot·ro·pism (thər mo′trə piz′əm), *n. Biol.* oriented growth of an organism in response to heat. [1885–90; THERMO- + -TROPISM] —**ther·mo·trop·ic** (thûr′mə trop′ik, -trō′pik), *adj.*

-thermy, a combining form meaning "heat," "heat generation," used in the formation of compound words: *diathermy.* [< NL *-thermia;* see -THERM, -Y[3]]

the·ro·phyte (thēr′ə fīt′), *n. Bot.* a plant living only one year or one growing season. [< Gk *théro(s)* summer + -PHYTE]

the·ro·pod (thēr′ə pod′), *n.* any member of the suborder Theropoda, comprising carnivorous dinosaurs that had short forelimbs and walked or ran on their hind legs. Also called **bird-footed dinosaur.** [< NL *Theropoda* (1881) suborder name; see -THERE, -O-, -PODA]

Ther·si·tes (thər sī′tēz), *n.* (in the *Iliad*) a Greek who accused Agamemnon of greed and Achilles of cowardice during the Trojan War.

ther·sit·i·cal (thər sit′i kəl), *adj.* scurrilous; foul-mouthed; grossly abusive. [1640–50; THERSIT(ES) + -ICAL]

Thes., Thessalonians.

the·sau·ris·mo·sis (thə sôr′əz mō′sis, -əs-), *n. Pathol.* See **storage disease.** [< Gk *thēsaúrism(a)* store, treasure, deriv., with *-ma* resultative n. suffix, of *thēsaurízein* to store up (deriv. of *thēsaurós* treasure) + -OSIS]

the·sau·rus (thi sôr′əs), *n., pl.* **-sau·rus·es, -sau·ri** (-sôr′ī). **1.** a dictionary of synonyms and antonyms. **2.** any dictionary, encyclopedia, or other comprehensive reference book. **3.** a storehouse, repository, or treasury. **4.** *Computers.* **a.** an index to information stored in a computer, consisting of a comprehensive list of subjects concerning which information may be retrieved by using the proper key terms. **b.** a dictionary of synonyms and antonyms stored in memory for use in word processing. [1730–40; < L *thēsaurus* < Gk *thēsaurós* treasure, treasury]

CONCISE ETYMOLOGY KEY: <, descended or borrowed from; >, whence; b., blend of, blended; c., cognate with; cf., compare; deriv., derivative; equiv., equivalent; imit., imitative; obl., oblique; r., replacing; s., stem; sp., spelling, spelled; resp., respelling, respelled; trans., translation; ?, origin unknown; *, unattested; ‡, probably earlier than. See the full key inside the front cover.

these (thēz), *pron., adj.* pl. of **this.**

The·seus (thē′sē əs, -syōōs), *n. Class. Myth.* an Attic hero, the husband of Phaedra, father of Hippolytus, and slayer of the Minotaur and the robber Procrustes. —**The·se·an** (thi sē′ən), *adj.*

the·sis (thē′sis), *n., pl.* **-ses** (-sēz). **1.** a proposition stated or put forward for consideration, esp. one to be discussed and proved or to be maintained against objections: *He vigorously defended his thesis on the causes of war.* **2.** a subject for a composition or essay. **3.** a dissertation on a particular subject in which one has done original research, as one presented by a candidate for a diploma or degree. **4.** *Music.* the downward stroke in conducting; downbeat. Cf. **arsis** (def. 1). **5.** *Pros.* **a.** a part of a metrical foot that does not bear the ictus or stress. **b.** (less commonly) the part of a metrical foot that bears the ictus. Cf. **arsis** (def. 2). **6.** *Philos.* See under **Hegelian dialectic.** [1350–1400; ME < L < Gk *thésis* a setting down, something set down, equiv. to *the-* (s. of *tithénai* to put, set down) + *-sis* -SIS]
—**Syn. 1.** theory, contention, proposal.

the′sis play′, a play that develops or defends a particular thesis. [1900–05]

Thes·pi·ae (thes′pē ē′), *n.* a city at the foot of Mount Helicon where, according to mythology, the Muses performed their games.

Thes·pi·an (thes′pē ən), *adj.* **1.** (*often l.c.*) pertaining to tragedy or to the dramatic art in general. **2.** of or characteristic of Thespis. **3.** of or pertaining to Thespiae. —*n.* **4.** (*sometimes l.c.*) a tragedian; an actor or actress. [1665–75; THESPI(S) + -AN]

Thes′pian Li′on, *Class. Myth.* a lion that attacked the flocks of Amphitryon and was killed by Hercules.

Thes·pis (thes′pis), *n.* fl. 6th century B.C., Greek poet.

Thes·pi·us (thes′pē əs), *n. Class. Myth.* the founder of the city of Thespiae and the father, by Megamede, of 50 daughters, all of whom bore sons to Hercules.

Thes·pro·ti (thes prō′tī), *n. pl.* the first inhabitants of ancient Epirus. Also, **Thes·pro·tians** (thes prō′shənz).

Thes·pro·tia (thes prō′shə), *n.* an ancient coastal district in SW Epirus. Also, **Thes·pro·tis** (thes prō′tis).

Thess., Thessalonians.

Thes·sa·lo·ni·an (thes′ə lō′nē ən), *adj.* **1.** of or pertaining to Thessalonike or its inhabitants. —*n.* **2.** a native or inhabitant of Thessalonike. [THESSALONI(KE) + -AN]

Thes·sa·lo·ni·ans (thes′ə lō′nē ənz), *n.* (*used with a singular v.*) either of two books of the New Testament, I Thessalonians or II Thessalonians, written by Paul. *Abbr.:* Thes., Thess.

Thes·sa·lo·ni·ke (*Gk.* the′sä lô nē′kē), *n.* official name of **Salonika.** Also, **Thes·sa·lon·i·ca** (thes′ə lon′i kə, -ə lō nī′kə).

Thes·sa·ly (thes′ə lē), *n.* a region in E Greece: a former division of ancient Greece. 659,913; 5208 sq. mi. (14,490 sq. km). —**Thes·sa·li·an** (the sā′lē ən, -sāl′yən), *adj., n.*

the·ta (thā′tə, thē′-), *n.* **1.** the eighth letter of the Greek alphabet (Θ, θ). **2.** the consonant sound represented by this letter. [1595–1605; < Gk *thêta* < Sem. See TETH]

the′ta rhythm′, *Physiol.* a pattern of brain waves having a regular frequency of 4 to 7 cycles per second as recorded by an electroencephalograph, observed during various states of light sleep or arousal. [1945–50]

the′ta wave′, *Physiol.* any of the brain waves constituting theta rhythm. [1965–70]

Thet′ford Mines′ (thet′fərd), a city in S Quebec, in E Canada: asbestos mining. 19,965.

thet·ic (thet′ik, thē′tik), *adj.* positive; dogmatic. Also, **thet′i·cal.** [1670–80; < Gk *thetikós,* equiv. to *thet(ós)* placed, set (verbid of *tithénai* to lay down) + *-ikos* -IC] —**thet′i·cal·ly,** *adv.*

The·tis (thē′tis), *n. Class. Myth.* a Nereid, the wife of Peleus and the mother of Achilles.

the·ur·gy (thē′ûr jē), *n., pl.* **-gies. 1.** a system of beneficent magic practiced by the Egyptian Platonists and others. **2.** the working of a divine or supernatural agency in human affairs. [1560–70; < LL *theūrgia* < Gk *theourgeía* magic. See THE-, -URGY] —**the·ur′gic, the·ur′gi·cal,** *adj.* —**the′ur·gist,** *n.*

thew (thyōō), *n.* **1.** Usually, **thews.** muscle or sinew. **2. thews,** physical strength. [bef. 900; ME; OE *thēaw* custom, usage; c. OHG *thau* (later *dau*) discipline; akin to L *tuērī* to watch] —**thew′y,** *adj.*

thew·less (thyōō′lis), *adj.* cowardly; timid. [1300–50; ME *theweles.* See THEW, -LESS]

they (thā), *pron. pl., poss.* **their** or **theirs,** *obj.* **them. 1.** nominative plural of **he, she,** and **it. 2.** people in general: *They say he's rich.* **3.** (used with an indefinite singular antecedent in place of the definite masculine *he* or the definite feminine *she*): *Whoever is of voting age, whether they are interested in politics or not, should vote.* [1150–1200; ME < ON *their* they (r. OE *hī(e)*); c. OE *thā,* pl. of *thæt* THAT]
—**Usage.** Long before the use of generic HE was condemned as sexist, the pronouns THEY, THEIR, and THEM were used in educated speech and in all but the most formal writing to refer to indefinite pronouns and to singular nouns of general personal reference, probably because such nouns are often not felt to be exclusively singular: *If anyone calls, tell them I'll be back at six. Everyone began looking for their books at once.* Such use is not a recent development, nor is it a mark of ignorance. Shakespeare, Swift, Shelley, Scott, and Dickens, as well as many other English and American writers, have used THEY and its forms to refer to singular antecedents. Already widespread in the language (though still rejected as ungrammatical by some), this use of THEY, THEIR, and THEM is increasing in all but the most conservatively edited American English. This increased use is at least partly impelled by the desire to avoid the sexist implications of HE as a pronoun of general reference. See also **he**[1].

they'd (thād), **1.** contraction of *they had.* **2.** contraction of *they would.*
—**Usage.** See **contraction.**

they'll (thāl), contraction of *they will.*
—**Usage.** See **contraction.**

they're (thâr; *unstressed* thər), contraction of *they are.*
—**Usage.** See **contraction.**

they've (thāv), contraction of *they have.*
—**Usage.** See **contraction.**

thi-, var. of **thio-** before a vowel: *thiazine.*

T.H.I., temperature-humidity index.

thi′a·ce′tic ac′id (thī′ə sē′tik, -ə set′ik, thī′-), *Chem.* See **thioacetic acid.** [1850–55]

thi·a·mine (thī′ə min, -mēn′), *n. Biochem.* a white, crystalline, water-soluble compound of the vitamin-B complex, containing a thiazole and a pyrimidine group, $C_{12}H_{17}ClN_4OS$, essential for normal functioning of the nervous system, a deficiency of which results chiefly in beriberi and other nerve disorders: occurring in many natural sources, as green peas, liver, and esp. the seed coats of cereal grains, the commercial product of which is chiefly synthesized in the form of its chloride (**thi′amine chlo′ride** or **thi′amine hydrochlo′ride**) for therapeutic administration, or in nitrate form (**thiamine mononitrate**) for enriching flour mixes. Also, **thi·a·min** (thī′ə min). Also called **vitamin B$_1$, aneurin, aneurine.** [1905–10; THI- + AMINE]

thi′amine mon·o·ni′trate (mon′ə nī′trāt). See under **thiamine.**

thi·a·zide (thī′ə zīd′, -zid), *n. Pharm.* a member of a class of diuretic substances that inhibit the reabsorption of sodium chloride in the distal convoluted tubule of the kidneys: used principally to treat hypertension. [1955–60; THI- + AZIDE]

thi·a·zine (thī′ə zēn′, -zin), *n. Chem.* any of a class of compounds containing a ring composed of one atom each of sulfur and nitrogen and four atoms of carbon. [1895–1900; THI- + AZINE]

thi·a·zole (thī′ə zōl′), *n. Chem.* **1.** a colorless, slightly water-miscible liquid, C_3H_3NS, having a disagreeable odor. **2.** any of various derivatives of this substance, used as dyes or reagents. [1885–90; THI- + AZOLE]

Thi·bet (ti bet′), *n.* Tibet. —**Thi·bet′an,** *adj., n.*

Thib·o·daux (tib′ə dō′), *n.* a city in SE Louisiana. 15,810.

thick (thik), *adj.,* **-er, -est,** *adv.,* **-er, -est,** *n.* —*adj.* **1.** having relatively great extent from one surface or side to the opposite; not thin: *a thick slice.* **2.** measured, as specified, between opposite surfaces, from top to bottom, or in a direction perpendicular to that of the length and breadth; (of a solid having three general dimensions) measured across its smallest dimension: *a board one inch thick.* **3.** composed of or containing objects, particles, etc., close together; dense: *a thick fog; a thick forest.* **4.** filled, covered, or abounding (usually fol. by *with*): *tables thick with dust.* **5.** husky or hoarse; not distinctly articulated: *The patient's speech is still quite thick.* **6.** markedly so (as specified): *a thick German accent.* **7.** deep or profound: *thick darkness.* **8.** (of a liquid) heavy or viscous: *a thick syrup.* **9.** *Informal.* close in friendship; intimate. **10.** mentally slow; stupid; dull. **11.** disagreeably excessive or exaggerated: *They thought it a bit thick when he called himself a genius.* —*adv.* **12.** in a thick manner. **13.** close together; closely packed: *The roses grew thick along the path.* **14.** in a manner to produce something thick: *Slice the cheese thick.* **15. lay it on thick,** *Informal.* to praise excessively; flatter: *He's laying it on thick because he wants you to do him a favor.* —*n.* **16.** the thickest, densest, or most crowded part: *in the thick of the fight.* **17. through thick and thin,** under favorable and unfavorable conditions; steadfastly: *We have been friends for 20 years, through thick and thin.* [bef. 900; (adj. and adv.) ME *thikke,* OE *thicce;* c. D *dik,* G *dick;* akin to ON *thykkr* (n.) ME, deriv. of the adj.] —**thick′ish,** *adj.* —**thick′ly,** *adv.*
—**Syn. 6.** strong, pronounced, decided.

thick·en (thik′ən), *v.t., v.i.* **1.** to make or become thick or thicker. **2.** to make or grow more intense, profound, intricate, or complex: *The plot thickens.* [1375–1425; late ME *thiknen* < ON *thykkna.* See THICK, -EN[1]]

thick·en·er (thik′ə nər), *n.* **1.** something that thickens. **2.** an apparatus for the sedimentation and removal of solids suspended in various liquids. [1645–55; THICKEN + -ER[1]]

thick·en·ing (thik′ə ning), *n.* **1.** a making or becoming thick. **2.** a thickened part or area; swelling. **3.** something used to thicken; thickener. [1570–80; THICKEN + -ING[1]]

thick·et (thik′it), *n.* a thick or dense growth of shrubs, bushes, or small trees; a thick coppice. [bef. 1000; OE *thiccet* (not recorded in ME), equiv. to *thicce* THICK + *-et* n. suffix] —**thick′et·ed, thick′et·y,** *adj.*

thick·head (thik′hed′), *n.* **1.** a stupid person; blockhead. **2.** Also called **whistler.** any of several Old World birds of the genus *Pachycephala,* chiefly of various islands in the Pacific Ocean, related to the flycatchers, and having a melodious whistling call. [1830–40; THICK + HEAD]

thick·head·ed (thik′hed′id), *adj.* **1.** (of a person) dull-witted; stupid. **2.** (of an animal) having a thick head. [1700–10; THICK + HEADED] —**thick′head′ed·ly,** *adv.* —**thick′head′ed·ness,** *n.*

thick-knee (thik′nē′), *n.* any of several crepuscular or nocturnal wading birds of the family Burhinidae, of the Old World and tropical America, having a thickened joint between the femoral and tibiotarsal bones. Also called **stone curlew.** [1810–20]

thick′ milk′, *Hudson Valley and North Midland U.S.* clabber.
—**Regional Variation.** See **clabber.**

thick·ness (thik′nis), *n.* **1.** the state or quality of being thick. **2.** the measure of the smallest dimension of a solid figure: *a board of two-inch thickness.* **3.** the thick part or body of something: *the thickness of the leg.* **4.** a layer, stratum, or ply: *three thicknesses of cloth.* —*v.t.* **5.** to bring (a piece, as a board) to a uniform thickness. [bef. 900; ME *thiknesse,* OE *thicnes.* See THICK, -NESS]

thick′ness piece′, *Theat.* a narrow flat or board used in scenic construction to give the illusion of depth or solidity to a door, wall, window, or the like.

thick′ reg′ister, *Music.* See **chest register.** [1900–05]

thick·set (*adj.* thik′set′; *n.* thik′set′), *adj.* **1.** set thickly or in close arrangement; dense: *a thickset hedge.* **2.** studded, or furnished thickly; closely packed: *a sky thickset with stars.* **3.** heavily or solidly built; stocky: *a thickset young man.* —*n.* **4.** a thicket. [1325–75; ME *thikke sette.* See THICK (adv.), SET]

thick-skinned (thik′skind′), *adj.* **1.** having a thick skin. **2.** insensitive or hardened to criticism, reproach, rebuff, etc. [1535–45]

thick-skulled (thik′skuld′), *adj.* stupid; dull. [1645–55]

thick′-tailed ray′ (thik′tāld′), *Ichthyol.* any ray of the order Rajiformes, having a relatively thick, fleshy tail, including the guitarfishes and the skates.

thick-wit·ted (thik′wit′id), *adj.* lacking intelligence; thickheaded; dull; stupid. [1625–35] —**thick′-wit′ted·ly,** *adv.* —**thick′-wit′ted·ness,** *n.*

thief (thēf), *n., pl.* **thieves.** a person who steals, esp. secretly or without open force; one guilty of theft or larceny. [bef. 900; ME; OE *thēof;* c. D *dief,* G *Dieb,* ON *thjōfr,* Goth *thiufs*]
—**Syn.** burglar, pickpocket, highwayman. THIEF, ROBBER refer to one who steals. A THIEF takes the goods or property of another by stealth without the latter's knowledge: *like a thief in the night.* A ROBBER trespasses upon the house, property, or person of another, and makes away with things of value, even at the cost of violence: *A robber held up two women on the street.*

thief′ ant′, a small red ant, *Solenopsis molesta,* of North America, that nests in the walls of the nest of a larger species from which it steals eggs and young larvae. [1900–05]

Thiers (tyer′), *n.* **Louis A·dolphe** (lwē A dôlf′), 1797–1877, French statesman: president 1871–73.

Thieu (tyo͞o), *n.* **Ngu·yen Van** (ngo͞o′yen′ vän, no͞o′-). See **Nguyen Van Thieu.**

thieve (thēv), *v.,* **thieved, thiev·ing.** —*v.t.* **1.** to take by theft; steal. —*v.i.* **2.** to act as a thief; commit theft; steal. [bef. 950; OE *thēofian,* deriv. of *thēof* THIEF (not recorded in ME)] —**thiev′ing·ly,** *adv.*

thiev·er·y (thē′və rē), *n., pl.* **-er·ies.** **1.** the act or practice of thieving; theft. **2.** something taken by theft. [1560–70; THIEVE + -ERY]

thiev·ish (thē′vish), *adj.* **1.** given to thieving. **2.** of, pertaining to, or characteristic of a thief; stealthy: *a furtive, thievish look.* [1400–50; late ME *thevisch;* see THIEF, -ISH[1]] —**thiev′ish·ly,** *adv.* —**thiev′ish·ness,** *n.*

thigh (thī), *n.* **1.** the part of the lower limb in humans between the hip and the knee. **2.** the corresponding part of the hind limb of other animals; the femoral region. **3.** (in birds) **a.** the true femoral region that is hidden by the skin or feathers of the body. **b.** the segment below, containing the fibula and tibia. **4.** *Entomol.* the femur. [bef. 900; ME *thi, thigh(e), the(h),* OE *thīoh, thēoh;* c. D *dij,* OHG *dioh,* ON *thjō*]

thigh·bone (thī′bōn′), *n.* femur (def. 1). [1400–50; late ME *the bane.* See THIGH, BONE]

thigh-slap·per (thī′slap′ər), *n. Informal.* a very funny joke, remark, story, or incident. [1960–65]

thig·mo·tax·is (thig′mə tak′sis), *n. Biol.* movement of an organism toward or away from any object that provides a mechanical stimulus. [1895–1900; < Gk *thígm(a)* touch + -o- + -TAXIS] —**thig·mo·tac·tic** (thig′mə-tak′tik), *adj.*

thig·mot·ro·pism (thig mo′trə piz′əm), *n. Biol.* oriented growth of an organism in response to mechanical contact, as a plant tendril coiling around a string support. [1895–1900; < Gk *thígm(a)* touch + -o- + -TROPISM] —**thig·mo·trop·ic** (thig′mə trop′ik, -trō′pik), *adj.*

thill (thil), *n.* either of the pair of shafts of a vehicle between which a draft animal is harnessed. [1275–1325; ME *thille* shaft < ?]

thim·ble (thim′bəl), *n.* **1.** a small cap, usually of metal, worn over the fingertip to protect it when pushing a needle through cloth in sewing. **2.** *Mech.* any of various similar devices or attachments. **3.** *Naut.* a metal ring with a concave groove on the outside, used to line the outside of a ring of rope forming an eye. **4.** a sleeve of sheet metal passing through the wall of a chimney, for holding the end of a stovepipe or the like. **5.** a thimble-shaped printing element with raised characters on the exterior: used in a type of electronic typewriter or computer printer (**thim′ble print′er**). [bef. 1000; ME *thym(b)yl,* OE *thȳmel;* akin to ON *thumall* thumb of a glove. See THUMB, -LE] —**thim′ble·like′,** *adj.*

thim·ble·ber·ry (thim′bəl ber′ē), *n., pl.* **-ries.** any of several American raspberries bearing a thimble-shaped fruit, esp. the black raspberry, *Rubus occidentalis.* [1780–90, *Amer.;* THIMBLE + BERRY]

thim·ble·ful (thim′bəl fo͝ol′), *n., pl.* **-fuls.** **1.** the amount that a thimble will hold. **2.** a small quantity, esp. of liquid. [1600–10; THIMBLE + -FUL]
—**Usage.** See **-ful.**

thim·ble·rig (thim′bəl rig′), *n., v.,* **-rigged, -rig·ging.** —*n.* **1.** a sleight-of-hand swindling game in which the operator palms a pellet or pea while appearing to cover it with one of three thimblelike cups, and then, moving the cups about, offers to bet that no one can tell under which cup the pellet or pea lies. —*v.t.* **2.** to cheat by or as by the thimblerig. [1815–25; THIMBLE + RIG] —**thim′ble·rig′ger,** *n.*

thim·ble·weed (thim′bəl wēd′), *n.* any of several plants having a thimble-shaped fruiting head, esp. either of two white-flowered North American plants, *Anemone riparia* or *A. virginiana.* [1825–35, *Amer.;* THIMBLE + WEED[1]]

thi·mer·o·sal (thī mûr′ə sal′, -mer′-), *n. Pharm.* a cream-colored, crystalline, water-soluble powder, $C_9H_9HgNaO_2S$, used chiefly as an antiseptic. [1945–50; perh. THI- + MER(CURY) + -o- + SAL(ICYLATE)]

Thim·phu (tim po͞o′), *n.* a city in and the capital of Bhutan, in the W part. 20,000. Also, **Thim·bu** (tim bo͞o′).

thin (thin), *adj.,* **thin·ner, thin·nest,** *adv., v.,* **thinned, thin·ning.** —*adj.* **1.** having relatively little extent from one surface or side to the opposite; not thick: *thin ice.* **2.** of small cross section in comparison with the length; slender: *a thin wire.* **3.** having little flesh; spare; lean: *a thin man.* **4.** composed of or containing objects, particles, etc., widely separated; sparse: *thin vegetation.* **5.** scant; not abundant or plentiful. **6.** of relatively slight consistency or viscosity: *thin soup.* **7.** rarefied, as air. **8.** without solidity or substance; flimsy: *a very thin plot for such a long book.* **9.** lacking fullness or volume; weak and shrill: *a thin voice.* **10.** without force or a sincere effort: *a thin smile.* **11.** lacking body, richness, or strength: *a thin wine.* **12.** lacking in chroma; of light tint. **13.** *Photog.* (of a developed negative) lacking in density or contrast through underdevelopment or underexposure. —*adv.* **14.** in a thin manner. **15.** sparsely; not densely. **16.** so as to produce something thin: *Slice the ham thin.* —*v.t.* **17.** to make thin or thinner (often fol. by *down, out,* etc.). —*v.i.* **18.** to become thin or thinner; become reduced or diminished (often fol. by *down, out, off,* etc.): *The crowd is thinning out.* [bef. 900; (adj. and adv.) ME *thyn(ne),* OE *thynne;* c. D *dun,* G *dünn,* ON *thunnr;* (v.) ME *thynnen,* OE *thynnian,* deriv. of the adj.; cf. MD *dunnen,* ON *thynna;* akin to OIr *tana,* L *tenuis* thin, Gk *tany-* long] —**thin′ly,** *adv.* —**thin′ness,** *n.*
—**Syn.** **3.** slim, slender, skinny, lank, scrawny. THIN, GAUNT, LEAN, SPARE agree in referring to one having little flesh. THIN applies often to one in an unnaturally reduced state, as from sickness, overwork, lack of food, or the like: *a thin, dirty little waif.* GAUNT suggests the angularity of bones prominently displayed in a thin face and body: *to look ill and gaunt.* LEAN usually applies to a person or animal that is naturally thin: *looking lean but healthy after an outdoor vacation.* SPARE implies a muscular leanness with no diminution of vitality: *Lincoln was spare in body.* **5.** meager. **8.** weak.

thine (thīn), *pron.* **1.** the possessive case of **thou** used as a predicate adjective, after a noun or without a noun. **2.** the possessive case of **thou** used as an attributive adjective before a noun beginning with a vowel or vowel sound: *thine eyes; thine honor.* Cf. **thy.** **3.** that which belongs to thee: *Thine is the power and the glory.* [bef. 900; ME, OE *thīn;* c. ON *thinn,* Goth *theins;* see THOU]

thin′ film′, a film of material only a few microns thick, deposited on a substrate, as in the technology for making integrated circuits. [1955–60] —**thin′-film′,** *adj.*

thing[1] (thing), *n.* **1.** a material object without life or consciousness; an inanimate object. **2.** some entity, object, or creature that is not or cannot be specifically designated or precisely described: *The stick had a brass thing on it.* **3.** anything that is or may become an object of thought: *things of the spirit.* **4.** **things,** matters; affairs: *Things are going well now.* **5.** a fact, circumstance, or state of affairs: *It is a curious thing.* **6.** an action, deed, event, or performance: *to do great things; His death was a horrible thing.* **7.** a particular, respect, or detail: *perfect in all things.* **8.** aim; objective: *The thing is to reach this line with the ball.* **9.** an article of clothing: *I don't have a thing to wear.* **10.** **things, a.** implements, utensils, or other articles for service: *I'll wash the breakfast things.* **b.** personal possessions or belongings: *Pack your things and go!* **11.** a task; chore: *I've got a lot of things to do today.* **12.** a living being or creature: *His baby's a cute little thing.* **13.** a thought or statement: *I have just one thing to say to you.* **14.** *Informal.* a peculiar attitude or feeling, either positive or negative, toward something; mental quirk: *She has a thing about cats.* **15.** something signified or represented, as distinguished from a word, symbol, or idea representing it. **16.** *Law.* anything that may be the subject of a property right. **17.** **do** or **find one's own thing,** *Informal.* to pursue a lifestyle that expresses one's self. Also, **do** or **find one's thing.** **18.** **make a good thing of,** *Informal.* to turn (a situation, experience, etc.) to one's own profit; benefit by: *She made a good thing of her spare-time hobbies.* **19.** **new thing,** *Jazz.* See **free jazz.** **20.** **not to get a thing out of, a.** to be unable to obtain information or news from: *The police couldn't get a thing out of him.* **b.** to fail to appreciate, understand, or derive aesthetic pleasure from: *My wife likes opera, but I don't get a thing out of it.* **21.** **see** or **hear things,** *Informal.* to have hallucinations. **22.** **the thing, a.** something that is correct or fashionable: *That café is the thing now.* **b.** that which is expedient or necessary: *The thing to do is to tell them the truth.* [bef. 900; ME; OE: orig., meeting; see THING[2]]

thing[2] (thing, ting), *n.* (in Scandinavian countries) a public meeting or assembly, esp. a legislative assembly or a court of law. Also, **ting.** Cf. **thingstead.** [1830–40; < ON: assembly; c. THING[1], D *ding,* G *Ding* thing, orig., meeting; akin to Goth *theihs* time]

thing·a·ma·bob (thing′ə mə bob′), *n. Informal.* thingamajig. Also, **thing′u·ma·bob′, thing·um·bob** (thing′-əm bob′) [1835–45; see THINGAMAJIG, BOB[2]]

thing·a·ma·jig (thing′ə mə jig′), *n. Informal.* a gadget or other thing for which the speaker does not know or has forgotten the name. Also, **thing′u·ma·jig′.** [1870–75; *thingum* or *thingummy* + JIG[1], metrically patterned like GOBBLEDYGOOK, RIGAMAROLE; *thingum* perh. orig. from the gradational compound *thingum-thangum* (based on THING[1]) with the same terminal syllable as in CRINKUM-CRANKUM, HARUM-SCARUM, *trinkum-trankum,* the ult. orig. of which is unclear]

T hinge, cross-garnet. [1835–45]

thing-in-it·self (thing′in it self′), *n., pl.* **things-in-them·selves** (thingz′in t͟həm selvz′). *Kantianism.* reality as it is apart from experience; what remains to be postulated after space, time, and all the categories of the understanding are assigned to consciousness. Cf. **noumenon** (def. 3). [1650–60; trans. of G *Ding an sich*]

thing·ness (thing′nis), *n.* objective reality. Also, **thing·hood** (thing′ho͝od′). [1895–1900; THING[1] + -NESS]

thing·stead (thing′sted, ting′-), *n.* the meeting place of a Scandinavian assembly. Cf. **thing**[2]. [THING[2] + STEAD]

thing·y (thing′ē), *n., pl.* **thing·ies,** *adj.* —*n.* **1.** *Facetious.* any small item whose name is unknown or forgotten. —*adj.* **2.** of, pertaining to, or characteristic of inanimate objects. [1885–90 for def. 1; 1890–95 for def. 2; THING[1] + -Y[2], -Y[1]]

think[1] (thingk), *v.,* **thought, think·ing,** *adj., n.* —*v.i.* **1.** to have a conscious mind, to some extent of reasoning, remembering experiences, making rational decisions, etc. **2.** to employ one's mind rationally and objectively in evaluating or dealing with a given situation: *Think carefully before you begin.* **3.** to have a certain thing as the subject of one's thoughts: *I was thinking about you. We could think of nothing else.* **4.** to call something to one's conscious mind: *I couldn't think of his phone number.* **5.** to consider something as a possible action, choice, etc.: *She thought about cutting her hair.* **6.** to invent or conceive of something: *We thought of a new plan.* **7.** to have consideration or regard for someone: *Think of others first.* **8.** to esteem a person or thing as indicated: *to think badly of someone.* **9.** to have a belief or opinion as indicated: *I think so.* **10.** (of a device or machine, esp. a computer) to use artificial intelligence to perform an activity analogous to human thought. —*v.t.* **11.** to have or form in the mind as an idea, conception, etc. **12.** to consider for evaluation or for possible action upon: *Think the deal over.* **13.** to regard as specified: *He thought me unkind.* **14.** to believe to be true of someone or something: *to think evil of the neighbors.* **15.** to analyze or evolve rationally: *to think the problem out.* **16.** to have as a plan or intention: *I thought that I would go.* **17.** to anticipate or expect: *I did not think to find you here.* **18.** **think better of,** to change one's mind about; reconsider: *She considered emigrating to Australia, but thought better of it.* **19.** **think fit,** to consider advisable or appropriate: *By all means, take a vacation if you think fit.* **20.** **think nothing of.** See **nothing** (def. 17). **21.** **think of, a.** to conceive of; imagine. **b.** to have an opinion or judgment of. **c.** to consider; anticipate: *When one thinks of what the future may bring, one is both worried and hopeful.* **22.** **think out** or **through, a.** to think about until a conclusion is reached; understand or solve by thinking. **b.** to devise by thinking; contrive: *He thought out a plan for saving time.* **23.** **think twice,** to weigh carefully before acting; consider: *I would think twice before taking on such a responsibility.* **24.** **think up,** to devise or contrive by thinking: *Can you think up an arrangement of furniture for this room?* —*adj.* **25.** of or pertaining to thinking or thought. **26.** *Informal.* stimulating or challenging to the intellect or mind: *the think book of the year.* Cf. **think piece.** —*n.* **27.** *Informal.* the act or a period of thinking: *I want to sit down and give it a good think.* [bef. 900; ME *thinken,* var. of *thenken,* OE *thencan;* c. D, G *denken,* ON *thekkja,* Goth *thagkjan;* akin to THANK]

think[2] (thingk), *v.i.,* **thought, think·ing.** *Obs.* to seem or appear (usually used impersonally with a dative as the subject). Cf. **methinks.** [bef. 900; ME *thinken,* OE *thyncan;* c. D *dunken,* G *dünken,* ON *thykkja,* Goth *thugkjan*]

think·a·ble (thing′kə bəl), *adj.* **1.** capable of being thought; conceivable. **2.** that may be considered as possible or likely. [1850–55; THINK[1] + -ABLE] —**think′a·ble·ness,** *n.* —**think′a·bly,** *adv.*

think·er (thing′kər), *n.* **1.** a person who thinks, as in a specified way or manner: *a slow thinker.* **2.** a person who has a well-developed faculty for thinking, as a philosopher, theorist, or scholar: *the great thinkers.* [1400–50; late ME *thenkare.* See THINK[1], -ER[1]]

Thinker, The, (French, *Le Penseur*), a bronze statue (1879–89) by Rodin.

think·ing (thing′king), *adj.* **1.** rational; reasoning: *People are thinking animals.* **2.** thoughtful; reflective: *Any thinking person would reject that plan.* —*n.* **3.** thought; judgment, reflection: *clear thinking.* [1250–1300; ME *thenking* (n.). See THINK[1], -ING[2], -ING[1]] —**think′ing·ly,** *adv.*

think′ing cap′, a state of mind marked by reflection or concentration: *If we put on our thinking caps, we may come up with the answer.* [1870–75]

think′ piece′, *Journalism.* an article analyzing and giving the background of a news event, often with the author's opinions and forecast for the future. Also called **dope story.** Cf. **editorial, news story.** [1940–45]

think′ tank′, a research institute or organization employed to solve complex problems or predict or plan future developments, as in military, political, or social areas. Also called **think′ fac′tory.** [1900–05 for earlier sense "brain"; 1955–60 for current sense]

thin′-lay′er chromatog′raphy, (thin′lā′ər), *Chem.* chromatography in which glass plates coated with thin layers of alumina, silica gel, or cellulose are used as an adsorbent. [1955–60; trans. of G *dünnschicht-chromatographie*]

thin•ner[1] (thin′ər), *n.* **1.** a volatile liquid, as turpentine, used to dilute paint, varnish, rubber cement, etc., to the desired or proper consistency. **2.** a person who adds thinners to paints, varnishes, etc. **3.** a person who specializes in weeding plants, pruning shrubbery, thinning fruit, etc. [1825–35; THIN + -ER[1]]

thin•ner[2] (thin′ər), *adj.* comparative of **thin.**

thin•nish (thin′ish), *adj.* somewhat thin. [1535–45; THIN + -ISH[1]]

thin′ reg′ister, *Music.* See **head register.**

thin-skinned (thin′skind′), *adj.* **1.** having a thin skin. **2.** sensitive to criticism, reproach, or rebuff; easily offended; touchy: *a thin-skinned poet.* [1590–1600] **—Syn. 2.** squeamish, soft, susceptible.

thi•o (thī′ō), *adj. Chem.* containing sulfur, esp. in place of oxygen. [independent use of THIO-]

thio-, a combining form meaning "sulfur," used in chemical nomenclature in the names of compounds in which part or all of the oxygen atoms have been replaced by sulfur; often used to designate sulfur analogues of oxygen compounds. Also, *esp. before a vowel,* **thi-.** [comb. form repr. Gk *theîon*]

thi•o•ac•et•am•ide (thī′ō as′i tam′īd, -id, -ə set′ə-mīd′, -mid), *n. Chem.* a colorless, crystalline, water-soluble solid, C_2H_5NS, used chiefly in analytical chemistry as a source of hydrogen sulfide. [THIO- + ACETAMIDE]

thi•o•a•ce•tic (thī′ō ə sē′tik, -set′ik), *adj. Chem.* of or derived from thioacetic acid. [1850–55; THIO- + ACETIC]

thi′oace′tic ac′id, *Chem.* a yellow, fuming, pungent liquid, C_2H_4SO, used as a reagent and tear gas. Also, **thiacetic acid.** [1850–55]

thi′o ac′id, *Chem.* an acid in which part or all of the oxygen has been replaced by sulfur. [1890–95]

thi•o•al•de•hyde (thī′ō al′də hīd′), *n. Chem.* any of a class of compounds formed by the action of hydrogen sulfide on aldehydes, and regarded as aldehydes with the oxygen replaced by sulfur. [THIO- + ALDEHYDE]

thi′o•al′lyl e′ther (thī′ō al′il, thī′-). See **allyl sulfide.** [THIO- + ALLYL]

thi•o•ba•cil•lus (thī′ō bə sil′əs), *n., pl.* **-cil•li** (-sil′ī). *Bacteriol.* any of several rod-shaped bacteria of the genus *Thiobacillus*, inhabiting soil, sewage, etc., that derive energy from oxidation of sulfur or sulfur compounds. [1975–80; NL; see THIO-, BACILLUS]

thi•o•car•bam•ide (thī′ō kär bam′īd, -id, -kär′bə-mīd′, -mid), *n. Chem.* thiourea. [1875–80; THIO- + CARBAMIDE]

thi•o•car•ba•nil•ide (thī′ō kär′bə nil′īd, -id, -kär-ban′l īd′, -id), *n. Chem.* a gray powder, $C_{13}H_{12}N_2S$, used as an intermediate in dyes and as an accelerator in vulcanization. Also called **sulfocarbonilide.** [THIO- + CARB- + ANILIDE]

thi•oc′tic ac′id (thī ok′tik), **1.** *Biochem.* an organic acid, $C_8H_{14}O_2S_2$, that occurs as a coenzyme in hydrogen transfer reactions in certain plants, microorganisms, and animals and functions as a growth factor for many species of bacteria and protozoa. **2.** *Pharm.* a preparation of thioctic acid used to treat liver disease and poisoning from amanita mushrooms. [THI- + OCT- + -IC]

thi•o•cy•a•nate (thī′ō sī′ə nāt′), *n. Chem.* a salt or ester of thiocyanic acid, as sodium thiocyanate, NaSCN. Also, **thi•o•cy•a•nide** (thī′ō sī′ə nīd′), [1875–80; THIO- + CYANATE]

thi′o•cy•an′ic ac′id, (thī′ō sī an′ik, thī′-), *Chem.* an unstable acid, HSCN, known chiefly in the form of its salts. [1875–80; THIO- + CYANIC ACID]

Thi•o•dan (thī′ə dan′), *Trademark.* (*sometimes l.c.*) a brand of endosulfan.

Thi•o•kol (thī′ə kôl′, -kol′), *n. Trademark.* a brand name for any of a group of durable synthetic rubber products derived from an organic halide, as ethylene dichloride, $C_2H_4Cl_2$, and an alkaline polysulfide, as sodium polysulfide: used chiefly in the manufacture of sealants, adhesives, and hoses for gasoline and oil.

thi•ol (thī′ôl, -ol), *Chem.* **—n. 1.** mercaptan. **—adj. 2.** mercapto. [1885–90; THI- + -OL[1]] **—thi•ol•ic** (thī ol′ik), *adj.*

thi•on•ic (thī on′ik), *adj. Chem.* of or pertaining to sulfur. [1875–80; < Gk *theîon* sulfur + -IC]

thion′ic ac′id, *Chem.* any of the five acids of sulfur of the type $H_2S_nO_6$, where *n* is from two to six. [1875–80]

thi•o•nyl (thī′ə nil), *adj. Chem.* sulfinyl. [1870–75; < Gk *theîon* sulfur + -YL]

thi′onyl chlo′ride, *Chem.* a clear, pale yellow or red, fuming, corrosive liquid, $SOCl_2$, used chiefly in organic synthesis. [1870–75]

thi′o•pen′tal so′dium (thī′ə pen′tl, -tal, -tôl, thī′-), *Pharm.* a barbiturate, $C_{11}H_{18}N_2NaO_2S$, used as an anesthetic in surgery and, in psychiatry, for narcoanalysis and to stimulate recall of past events. [1945–50; THIO- + PENT- + -AL[3]]

thi•o•phene (thī′ə fēn′), *n. Chem.* a water-insoluble, colorless liquid, C_4H_4S, resembling benzene, occurring in crude coal-tar benzene: used chiefly as a solvent and in organic synthesis. Also, **thi•o•phen** (thī′ə fen′). [1880–85; THIO- + *-phene*, word-final var. of PHEN-]

thi•o•phe•nol (thī′ə fē′nôl, -nol), *n. Chem.* a colorless, foul-smelling liquid, C_6H_6S, used chiefly in organic synthesis. [1895–1900; THIO- + PHENOL]

thi•o•phos•phate (thī′ō fos′fāt), *n. Chem.* a salt or ester of thiophosphoric acid. [THIO- + PHOSPHATE]

thi•o•phos•phor•ic ac′id (thī′ō fos fôr′ik, -for′-), *Chem.* an acid derived from phosphoric acid by substituting one or more sulfur atoms for oxygen atoms. [THIO- + PHOSPHORIC ACID]

thi•o•rid•a•zine (thī′ə rid′ə zēn′, -zin), *n. Pharm.* a phenothiazine, $C_{21}H_{26}N_2S_2$, used as an antipsychotic chiefly in the treatment of acute psychoses and schizophrenia. [1955–60; THIO- + (PIPE)RID(INE) + AZINE]

thi′o salt′, *Chem.* a salt of a thio acid.

thi•o•sin•am•ine (thī′ə si nam′in, -sin′ə mēn′), *n. Chem.* a white, crystalline, water-soluble, bitter-tasting powder, $C_4H_8N_2S$, occurring in mustard oil: used chiefly in organic synthesis. Also called **allylthiourea.** [1850–55; THIO- + Gk *sín(āpi)* mustard + -AMINE]

thi•o•sul•fate (thī′ō sul′fāt), *n. Chem.* a salt or ester of thiosulfuric acid. [1870–75; THIO- + -SULFATE]

thi•o•sul•fu•ric (thī′ō sul fyŏŏr′ik), *adj. Chem.* of or derived from thiosulfuric acid. [1870–75; THIO- + SULFURIC]

thi′osulfu′ric ac′id, *Chem.* an acid, $H_2S_2O_3$, that may be regarded as sulfuric acid with one oxygen atom replaced by sulfur. [1870–75]

thi•o•thix•ene (thī′ō thik′sēn), *n. Pharm.* a potent antipsychotic, $C_{23}H_{29}N_3O_2S_2$, used in the management of schizophrenia and related psychoses. [1960–65; THIO- + THI(O)X(ANTH)ENE]

thi•o•u•ra•cil (thī′ō yŏŏr′ə sil), *n. Pharm.* a white, slightly water-soluble, bitter, crystalline powder $C_4H_4N_2OS$, used chiefly in treating hyperthyroidism by reducing the activity of the thyroid gland. [1940–45; THIO- + URACIL]

thi•o•u•re•a (thī′ō yŏŏ rē′ə, -yŏŏr′ē ə), *n. Chem.* a colorless, crystalline, bitter-tasting, water-soluble solid, CH_4N_2S, derived from urea by replacement of the oxygen with sulfur: used chiefly in photography, inorganic synthesis, and to accelerate the vulcanization of rubber. Also called **thiocarbamide.** [1890–95; < NL; see THIO-, UREA]

thi•o•xan•thene (thī′ə zan′thēn), *n. Pharm.* any of a class of antipsychotics, as thiothixene, used to relieve symptoms of severe psychiatric disorders. [THIO- + XANTH- + -ENE]

thir (thûr, thėr), *pron. Scot. and North Eng.* these. [1300–50; ME (north) < ?]

Thi•ra (thēr′ə; *Gk.* thē′rä), *n.* Thera.

thi•ram (thī′ram), *n. Chem.* a white, crystalline compound, $C_6H_{12}N_2S_4$, insoluble in water, slightly soluble in alcohol, soluble in benzene and acetone, used as a vulcanizer and accelerator for rubber and as a fungicide, bacteriostat, and seed disinfectant. [1945–50; alter. of *thiuram*, equiv. to THI(O)UR(EA) + *-am*, as in CARBAMYL or CARBAMIC]

third (thûrd), *adj.* **1.** next after the second; being the ordinal number for three. **2.** being one of three equal parts. **3.** *Auto.* of, pertaining to, or operating at the gear transmission ratio at which the drive shaft speed is greater than that of second gear for a given engine crankshaft speed, but not as great as that of fourth gear, if such exists: *third gear.* **4.** rated, graded, or ranked one level below the second: *He's third engineer on the ship.* **—n. 5.** a third part, esp. of one (⅓). **6.** the third member of a series. **7.** *Auto.* third gear: *Don't try to start a car when it's in third.* **8.** a person or thing next after second in rank, precedence, order: *The writer of the best essay will receive a gold medal, the second a silver, and the third a bronze.* **9.** Usually, **thirds.** *Law.* **a.** the third part of the personal property of a deceased husband, which in certain circumstances goes absolutely to the widow. **b.** a widow's dower. **10.** *Music.* **a.** a tone on the third degree from a given tone (counted as the first). **b.** the interval between such tones. **c.** the harmonic combination of such tones. **11.** *Baseball.* See **third base. 12.** Usually, **thirds.** *Com.* a product or goods below second quality. Cf. **first** (def. 19), **second**[1] (def. 23). **—adv. 13.** in the third place; thirdly. [bef. 900; ME *thirde*, OE (north) *thirda*, var. of *thridda;* c. D *derde*, G *dritte*, ON *thrithi*, Goth *thridja*, Gk *trítos*, L *tertius*, Skt *tṛtīya*. See THREE] **—third′ly,** *adv.*

Third′ Amend′ment, an amendment to the U.S. Constitution, ratified in 1791 as part of the Bill of Rights, guaranteeing that the forced quartering of soldiers in private homes would be prohibited in peacetime and allowed only by prescribed law during wartime.

third′ base′, *Baseball.* **1.** the third in counterclockwise order of the bases from home plate. **2.** the playing position of the fielder covering the area of the infield near this base. [1835–45, *Amer.*]

third′ base′man, *Baseball.* the player whose position is third base. [1855–60, *Amer.*]

third′ class′, **1.** the class, grade, or rank immediately below the second. **2.** the least costly class of accommodations on trains, in hotels, etc. Cf. **tourist class. 3.** (in the U.S. Postal Service) the class of mail consisting of merchandise weighing up to 16 ounces, and written or printed material, as books, manuscripts, or circulars, not sealed against postal inspection. **4.** the lowest of three honors degrees conferred by a British university. [1835–45]

third-class (thûrd′klas′, -kläs′), *adj.* **1.** of the lowest or poorest class or quality; inferior. **2.** least costly and luxurious: *a third-class coach.* **—adv. 3.** by third-class mail or passenger accommodations: *to travel third-class.* [1830–40]

Third′ Command′ment, "Thou shalt not take the name of the Lord thy God in vain": third of the Ten Commandments. Cf. **Ten Commandments.**

third′ degree′, **1.** intensive questioning or rough treatment, esp. by the police, in order to get information or a confession. **2.** the degree of master mason in Freemasonry. [1860–65]

third-de•gree (thûrd′di grē′), *v.,* **-greed, -gree•ing,** *adj.* **—v.t. 1.** to subject to the third degree. **—adj. 2.** of or pertaining to the third degree. [1895–1900, *Amer.*]

third′-degree burn′, *Pathol.* See under **burn**[1] (def. 47). [1940–45]

third′ dimen′sion, **1.** the additional dimension by which a solid object is distinguished from a planar projection of itself or from any planar object. **2.** something that heightens the reality, vividness, or significance of a factual account, sequence of happenings, etc.: *The illustrations added a third dimension to the story.* [1855–60]

third′ ear′, intuition.

third′ estate′, the third of the three estates or political orders: the commons in France or England. Cf. **estate** (def. 5). [1595–1605]

third′ eye′, **1.** See **pineal eye. 2.** intuition. [1800–10]

third′ eye′lid. See **nictitating membrane.**

third′ fin′ger, the finger next to the little finger; ring finger.

third′ force′, a political faction or party, etc., occupying an intermediate position between two others representing opposite extremes. [1945–50]

third•hand (thûrd′hand′), *adj.* **1.** previously used or owned by two successive people. **2.** (loosely) secondhand, esp. in poor condition. **3.** obtained through two intermediates successively; twice removed from the original source. **—adv. 4.** after two other users or owners: *He bought the guitar thirdhand.* **5.** by way of several intermediate sources; indirectly. [1545–55; THIRD + HAND]

third′ house′, (*sometimes caps.*) *Informal.* a legislative lobby. [1850–55, *Amer.*]

Third′ Interna′tional, an international organization (1919–43), founded in Moscow, uniting Communist groups of various countries and advocating the attainment of their ends by violent revolution. Also called **Comintern, Communist International.** Cf. **international** (def. 6).

third′ law′ of mo′tion, *Physics.* See under **law of motion.**

third′ law′ of thermodynam′ics. See under **law of thermodynamics** (def. 1).

third′ man′, **1.** *Cricket.* **a.** the position of a fielder on the off side between slip and point. **b.** the fielder occupying this position. **2.** *Lacrosse.* **a.** the position of a player, first in the line of defense between center and goal. **b.** the player occupying this position. [1870–75]

third′ mate′, the officer of a merchant vessel next in command beneath the second mate. Also called **third′ of′ficer.**

Third′ Or′der, *Rom. Cath. Ch.* **1.** a branch of a religious order whose members are lay people following the avocations of a secular life. **2.** a member of a Third Order who follows its rule in the community under ordinary simple vows.

third′ par′ty, **1.** any party to an incident, case, quarrel, etc., who is incidentally involved. **2.** (in a two-party system) a political party formed as a dissenting or independent group from members of one or both of the two prevailing major parties. [1795–1805, *Amer.*]

third′-par′ty insur′ance (thûrd′pär′tē), insurance that compensates for a loss to a party other than the insured for which the insured is liable. [1900–05] **—third′-par′ty insur′er.**

third′ par′ty proce′dure, *Law.* impleader. [1880–85]

third′-par′ty soft′ware, *Computers.* software created by programmers or publishers independent of the manufacturer of the hardware for which it is intended.

third′ per′son, *Gram.* **1.** the person that is used by the speaker of an utterance in referring to anything or to anyone other than the speaker or the one or ones being addressed. **2.** a linguistic form or the group of linguistic forms referring to this grammatical person, as certain verb forms, pronouns, etc.: *"He goes" contains a pronoun and a verb form in the third person.* **3.** in or referring to such a grammatical person or linguistic form: *"He," "she," "it," and "they" are third person pronouns, singular and plural, nominative case.* [1580–90]

third′ posi′tion, *Ballet.* a position in which the feet overlap at the heels with the toes pointing out in opposite directions to the left and right. See illus. under **first position.**

third′ quar′tile, (in a frequency distribution) the largest quartile; the 75th percentile; the value of the variable below which three quarters of the elements are located.

third′ rail′, *Railroads.* **1.** a rail laid parallel and adjacent to the running rails of an electrified railroad to provide electric current to the motors of a car or locomotive through contact shoes. **2.** an additional running rail laid on the same ties as the two regular rails of a railroad track to provide a multigauge capability. [1865–70, *Amer.*]

CONCISE ETYMOLOGY KEY: <, descended or borrowed from; >, whence; b., blend of, blended; c., cognate with; cf., compare; deriv., derivative; equiv., equivalent; imit., imitative; obl., oblique; r., replacing; s., stem; sp., spelling, spelled; resp., respelling, respelled; trans., translation; ?, origin unknown; *, unattested; ‡, probably earlier than. See the full key inside the front cover.

third-rate (thûrd′rāt′), *adj.* **1.** of the third rate, quality, or class. **2.** distinctly inferior: *a third-rate performance.* [1640–50] —**third′-rat′er,** *n.*

third′ read′ing, the final step in the consideration of a legislative bill before it is put to a vote. [1565–75]

Third′ Reich′, Germany during the Nazi regime 1933–45. Cf. **Reich.**

Third′ Repub′lic, the republic established in France in 1870 and terminating with the Nazi occupation in 1940.

third′ sec′tor, the segment of a nation's economy that is made up of neither public nor business concerns, as nonprofit health or educational institutions. —**third′-sec′tor,** *adj.*

third′ stream′, a style of music that uses features of both jazz and classical music in an attempt to develop a new and distinctive musical idiom. [1960–65]

Third′ World′, (*sometimes l.c.*) **1.** the underdeveloped nations of the world, esp. those with widespread poverty. **2.** the group of developing nations, esp. of Asia and Africa, that do not align themselves with the policies of either the U.S. or the former Soviet Union. **3.** the minority groups within a nation or predominant culture. Cf. **First World, Second World, Fourth World.**

Third′ World′er (wûrl′dər), (*sometimes l.c.*) a citizen of a Third World country. [1965–70; THIRD WORLD + -ER[1]]

thirl (thûrl), *v.t. Brit. Dial.* **1.** to pierce. **2.** to thrill. [bef. 1000; ME *thirlen,* OE *thyrlian,* deriv. of *thyrel* hole. See NOSTRIL]

thirst (thûrst), *n.* **1.** a sensation of dryness in the mouth and throat caused by need of liquid. **2.** the physical condition resulting from this need, in any of various degrees: *They almost died of thirst.* **3.** strong or eager desire; craving: *a thirst for knowledge.* —*v.i.* **4.** to feel thirst; be thirsty. **5.** to have a strong desire. [bef. 900; ME *thirsten* (v.), OE *thyrstan,* deriv. of *thurst* (n.); c. D *dorst,* G *Durst,* ON *thorsti,* Goth *thaurstei;* n. has *-i-* from the v. or from THIRSTY; see TOAST[1]] —**thirst′er,** *n.*

thirst·y (thûr′stē), *adj.,* **thirst·i·er, thirst·i·est. 1.** feeling or having thirst; craving liquid. **2.** needing moisture, as land; parched; dry or arid: *the thirsty soil.* **3.** eagerly desirous; eager: *thirsty for news.* **4.** causing thirst: *Digging is thirsty work.* [bef. 950; ME *thirsti,* OE *thyrstig;* akin to D *dorstig,* G *durstig,* Skt *tṛṣita* thirsty] —**thirst′i·ly,** *adv.* —**thirst′i·ness,** *n.*

thir·teen (thûr′tēn′), *n.* **1.** a cardinal number, 10 plus 3. **2.** a symbol for this number, as 13 or XIII. **3.** a set of this many persons or things. —*adj.* **4.** amounting to 13 in number. [bef. 900; late ME *thirttene,* var. of ME *thrittene,* OE *thrēotēne;* c. D *dertien,* G *dreizehn,* ON *threttān.* See THREE, -TEEN]

thir′teen-lined′ ground′ squir′rel (thûr′tēn′-līnd′), a brownish ground squirrel, *Citellus tridecemlineatus,* of prairie regions of the U.S., having cream-colored stripes extending along its back and sides. Also called **thir′teen-lined′ go′pher, striped spermophile.**

thir·teenth (thûr′tēnth′), *adj.* **1.** next after the twelfth; being the ordinal number for 13. **2.** being one of 13 equal parts. —*n.* **3.** a thirteenth part, esp. of one (1/13). **4.** the thirteenth member of a series. [bef. 900; THIRTEEN + -TH[2]; r. ME *thrittenthe* (see THREE, TENTH), OE *thrytteotha* (see TITHE)]

Thir′teenth Amend′ment, an amendment to the U.S. Constitution, ratified in 1865, abolishing slavery.

thir·ti·eth (thûr′tē ith), *adj.* **1.** next after the twenty-ninth; being the ordinal number for 30. **2.** being one of 30 equal parts. —*n.* **3.** a thirtieth part, esp. of one (1/30). **4.** the thirtieth member of a series. [bef. 900; THIRTY + -ETH[2]; r. ME *thrittythe,* OE *thrītegtha*]

thir·ty (thûr′tē), *n., pl.* **-ties,** *adj.* —*n.* **1.** a cardinal number, 10 times 3. **2.** a symbol for this number, as 30 or XXX. **3.** a set of this many persons or things. **4.** *Print., Journalism.* 30-dash. **5. thirties,** the numbers, years, degrees, or the like, from 30 through 39, as in referring to numbered streets, indicating the years of a lifetime or of a century, or referring to degrees of temperature: *He works in the East Thirties. She must be in her thirties. The temperature was in the thirties yesterday.* —*adj.* **6.** amounting to 30 in number. [bef. 900; ME *thritty,* OE *thrītig,* equiv. to *thrī* THREE + *-tig* -TY[1]; c. D *dertig,* G *dreissig,* ON *thrjātiu*]

30-dash (thûr′tē dash′), *n. Print., Journalism.* the symbol —30—, —XXX—, —O—, etc., often used to mark the end of a piece of copy, story, etc.

thir·ty-eight (thûr′tē āt′), *n.* **1.** a cardinal number, 30 plus 8. **2.** a symbol for this number, as 38 or XXXVIII. **3.** a set of this many persons or things. —*adj.* **4.** amounting to 38 in number.

.38 (thûr′tē āt′), *n., pl.* **.38s, 38's. 1.** a pistol or revolver using a cartridge approximately .38 inch in diameter. **2.** the cartridge itself. Also, **thirty-eight.**

thir·ty-eighth (thûr′tē ātth′, -āth′), *adj.* **1.** next after the thirty-seventh; being the ordinal number for 38. **2.** being one of 38 equal parts. —*n.* **3.** a thirty-eighth part, esp. of one (1/38). **4.** the thirty-eighth member of a series.

thir·ty-fifth (thûr′tē fifth′ *or, often,* -fith′), *adj.* **1.** next after the thirty-fourth; being the ordinal number for 35. **2.** being one of 35 equal parts. —*n.* **3.** a thirty-fifth part, esp. of one (1/35). **4.** the thirty-fifth member of a series.

thir·ty-first (thûr′tē fûrst′), *adj.* **1.** next after the thirtieth; being the ordinal number for 31. **2.** being one of 31 equal parts. —*n.* **3.** a thirty-first part, esp. of one (1/31). **4.** the thirty-first member of a series.

thir·ty-five (thûr′tē fīv′), *n.* **1.** a cardinal number, 30 plus 5. **2.** a symbol for this number, as 35 or XXXV. **3.** a set of this many persons or things. —*adj.* **4.** amounting to 35 in number.

thir·ty-four (thûr′tē fôr′, -fōr′), *n.* **1.** a cardinal number, 30 plus 4. **2.** a symbol for this number, as 34 or XXXIV. **3.** a set of this many persons or things. —*adj.* **4.** amounting to 34 in number.

thir·ty-fourth (thûr′tē fôrth′, -fōrth′), *adj.* **1.** next after the thirty-third; being the ordinal number for 34. **2.** being one of 34 equal parts. —*n.* **3.** a thirty-fourth part, esp. of one (1/34). **4.** the thirty-fourth member of a series.

thir·ty-nine (thûr′tē nīn′), *n.* **1.** a cardinal number, 30 plus 9. **2.** a symbol for this number, as 39 or XXXIX. **3.** a set of this many persons or things. —*adj.* **4.** amounting to 39 in number.

thir·ty-ninth (thûr′tē ninth′), *adj.* **1.** next after the thirty-eighth; being the ordinal number for 39. **2.** being one of 39 equal parts. —*n.* **3.** a thirty-ninth part, esp. of one (1/39). **4.** the thirty-ninth member of a series.

thir·ty-one (thûr′tē wun′), *n.* **1.** a cardinal number, 30 plus 1. **2.** a symbol for this number, as 31 or XXXI. **3.** a set of this many persons or things. —*adj.* **4.** amounting to 31 in number.

thir·ty-sec·ond (thûr′tē sek′ənd), *adj.* **1.** next after the thirty-first; being the ordinal number for 32. **2.** being one of 32 equal parts. —*n.* **3.** a thirty-second part, esp. of one (1/32). **4.** the thirty-second member of a series.

thir′ty-sec′ond note′, *Music.* a note having 1/32 of the time value of a whole note; demi-semiquaver. See illus. under **note.** [1885–90]

thir′ty-sec′ond rest′, *Music.* a rest equal in value to a thirty-second note. See illus. under **rest**[1]. [1900–05]

thir·ty-sev·en (thûr′tē sev′ən), *n.* **1.** a cardinal number, 30 plus 7. **2.** a symbol for this number, as 37 or XXXVII. **3.** a set of this many persons or things. —*adj.* **4.** amounting to 37 in number.

thir·ty-sev·enth (thûr′tē sev′ənth), *adj.* **1.** next after the thirty-sixth; being the ordinal number for 37. **2.** being one of 37 equal parts. —*n.* **3.** a thirty-seventh part, esp. of one (1/37). **4.** the thirty-seventh member of a series.

thir·ty-six (thûr′tē siks′), *n.* **1.** a cardinal number, 30 plus 6. **2.** a symbol for this number, as 36 or XXXVI. **3.** a set of this many persons or things. —*adj.* **4.** amounting to 36 in number.

thir·ty-sixth (thûr′tē siksth′), *adj.* **1.** next after the thirty-fifth; being the ordinal number for 36. **2.** being one of 36 equal parts. —*n.* **3.** a thirty-sixth part, esp. of one (1/36). **4.** the thirty-sixth member of a series.

thir·ty-third (thûr′tē thûrd′), *adj.* **1.** next after the thirty-second; being the ordinal number for 33. **2.** being one of 33 equal parts. —*n.* **3.** a thirty-third part, esp. of one (1/33). **4.** the thirty-third member of a series.

.30-30 (thûr′tē thûr′tē), *n.* **1.** a rifle using a cartridge approximately .30 inch in diameter, originally having a powder charge of 30 grains but now of various charges. **2.** the cartridge itself.

thir·ty-three (thûr′tē thrē′), *n.* **1.** a cardinal number, 30 plus 3. **2.** a symbol for this number, as 33 or XXXIII. **3.** a set of this many persons or things. —*adj.* **4.** amounting to 33 in number.

thir·ty-two (thûr′tē to͞o′), *n.* **1.** a cardinal number, 30 plus 2. **2.** a symbol for this number, as 32 or XXXII. **3.** a set of this many persons or things. —*adj.* **4.** amounting to 32 in number.

thir·ty-two·mo (thûr′tē to͞o′mō), *n., pl.* **-mos,** *adj.* —*n.* **1.** a book size of about 3¼ × 5½ in. (8.3 × 14 cm), determined by printing on sheets that are folded to form 32 leaves or 64 pages. *Symbol:* 32mo, 32° **2.** a book of this size. —*adj.* **3.** printed, folded, or bound as a thirty-twomo. [1765–75; THIRTY-TWO + -MO]

Thir′ty Years′ War′, the war, often regarded as a series of wars (1618–48), in central Europe, initially involving a conflict between German Protestants and Catholics and later including political rivalries with France, Sweden, and Denmark opposing the Holy Roman Empire and Spain.

this (t͟his), *pron. and adj., pl.* **these** (t͟hēz); *adv.* —*pron.* **1.** (used to indicate a person, thing, idea, state, event, time, remark, etc., as present, near, just mentioned or pointed out, supposed to be understood, or by way of emphasis): *This is my coat.* **2.** (used to indicate one of two or more persons, things, etc., referring to the one nearer in place, time, or thought; opposed to *that*): *This is Liza and that is Amy.* **3.** (used to indicate one of two or more persons, things, etc., implying a contrast or contradistinction; opposed to *that*): *I'd take that instead of this.* **4.** what is about to follow: *Now hear this! Watch this!* **5. with this,** following this; hereupon: *With this, he threw down his glass and left the table.* —*adj.* **6.** (used to indicate a person, place, thing, or degree as present, near, just indicated or mentioned, or as well-known or characteristic): *These people are my friends. This problem has worried me for a long time.* **7.** (used to indicate the nearer in time, place, or thought of two persons, things, etc.; opposed to *that*). **8.** (used to imply mere contradistinction; opposed to *that*). **9.** (used in place of an indefinite article for emphasis): *I was walking down the street when I heard this explosion.* —*adv.* **10.** (used with adjectives and adverbs of quantity or extent) to the extent or degree indicated: *this far; this softly.* [bef. 900; (pronoun and adj.) ME; OE: nom. and acc. neut. sing. of the demonstrative pronoun *thes* (masc.), *thēos* (fem.); c. G *dies,* ON *thissi;* (adv.) ME, special use of the OE instrumental sing. *thȳs, this,* acc. sing. neut. *this,* perh. by association with THUS]

This·be (thiz′bē), *n. Class. Myth.* See **Pyramus and Thisbe.**

this·tle (this′əl), *n.* **1.** any of various prickly, composite plants having showy, purple flower heads, esp. of the genera *Cirsium, Carduus,* or *Onopordum.* **2.** any of various other prickly plants. [bef. 900; ME *thistel,* OE; c. D *distel,* G *Distel,* ON *thistill*] —**this′tle·like′,** *adj.*

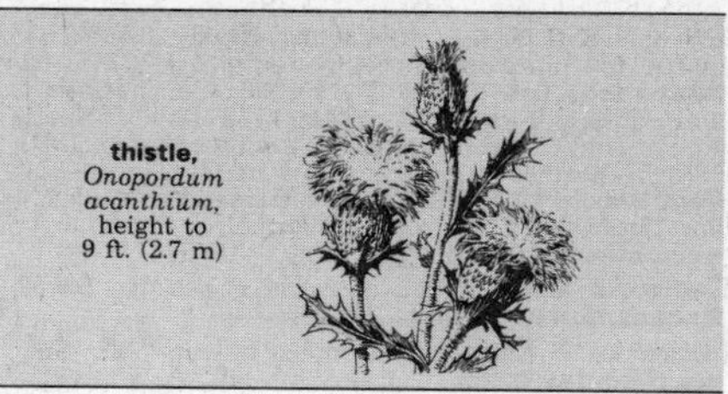

thistle, *Onopordum acanthium,* height to 9 ft. (2.7 m)

this′tle but′terfly, any nymphalid butterfly of the genus *Vanessa,* as the red admiral or painted lady.

this·tle·down (this′əl doun′), *n.* the mature, silky pappus of a thistle. [1555–65; THISTLE + DOWN[2]]

this′tle tube′, a glass funnel consisting of a long narrow tube with a thistle-shaped head. Also called **this′tle fun′nel.** [1890–95]

this·tly (this′lē, -ə lē), *adj.* **1.** filled with or having many thistles. **2.** suggesting a growth of thistles, esp. in being difficult or painful to handle: *a thistly set of problems.* [1590–1600; THISTLE + -Y[1]]

this-world·li·ness (this′wûrld′lē nis), *n.* concern or preoccupation with worldly things and values. [1870–75] —**this′-world′ly,** *adj.*

thith·er (thith′ər, t͟hith′-), *adv.* **1.** Also, **thith·er·ward** (thith′ər wərd, t͟hith′-), **thith′er·wards.** to or toward that place or point; there. —*adj.* **2.** on the farther or other side or in the direction away from the person speaking; farther; more remote. [bef. 900; ME, var. of ME *thider,* OE, alter. of *thæder* (i from *hider* HITHER); akin to ON *thathra* there, Goth *thathro* thence, Skt *tátra* there, thither]

thith·er·to (thith′ər to͞o′, t͟hith′-, thith′ər to͞o′, t͟hith′-), *adv.* up to that time; until then. [1400–50; late ME *thidir to.* See THITHER, TO]

thix·ot·ro·py (thik so′trə pē), *n. Chem.* the property exhibited by certain gels of becoming liquid when stirred or shaken. [1925–30; < Gk *thix(is)* touch + -o- + -TROPY] —**thix·o·trop·ic** (thik′sə trop′ik, -trō′pik), *adj.*

Thjal·fi (thyäl′vē), *n. Scand. Myth.* the fastest of men and the servant of Thor.

Thja·zi (thyät′sē), *n. Scand. Myth.* a giant who carried away Idun and the apples of youth from Asgard.

Thjórs·á (thyôr′sou, thyōr′-; *Icel.* thyōrs′ou), *n.* a river in central Iceland, flowing SW to the Atlantic Ocean. ab. 143 mi. (230 km) long.

Th.M., Master of Theology.

tho (t͟hō), *conj., adv.* an informal, simplified spelling of **though.** Also, **tho′.**

Tho·hoy·an·dou (tō hoi′an do͞o′), *n.* a city in and the capital of Venda, in NE South Africa. 40,000.

Thokk (thôk), *n. Scand. Myth.* an old giantess, possibly Loki in disguise, who was the only being to refuse to weep for the dead Balder, thus condemning him to eternity in Niflheim. [< ON *Thǫkk,* appar. same word as *thǫkk* thanks; see THANK]

thole[1] (thōl), *n.* a pin, or either of two pins, inserted into a gunwale to provide a fulcrum for an oar. Also called **thole·pin** (thōl′pin′). [ME *tholle,* OE *tholl;* c. LG *dolle,* ON *thollr;* akin to ON *thǫll* young fir-tree]

thole[1]

thole[2] (thōl), *v.t.,* **tholed, thol·ing.** *Chiefly Scot.* to suffer; bear; endure. [bef. 900; ME *tholen,* OE *tholian;* c. ON *thola,* Goth *thulan;* akin to L *tolerāre* (see TOLERATE), Gk *tlênai* to bear, endure]

thol·o·bate (thol′ə bāt′), *n. Archit.* the substructure supporting a dome or cupola. [1825–35; < Gk *thólo(s)* THOLOS + *-batēs* one that goes; cf. STYLOBATE]

tho·los (thō′los, -lōs), *n., pl.* **-loi** (-loi). **1.** (in classical architecture) **a.** a circular building. **b.** a small, round structure, as a lantern. **c.** a circular subterranean tomb, lined with masonry. **2.** a subterranean domed tomb chamber of the Mycenaean age. [1895–1900; < Gk *thólos* lit., rotunda]

tho·lus (thō′ləs), *n., pl.* **-li** (-lī). tholos. [1635–45; < L < Gk *thólos*]

Thom·as (tom′əs *for 1, 2, 4–14;* tô mä′ *for 3*), *n.* **1.** an apostle who demanded proof of Christ's Resurrection. John 20:24–29. **2. Augustus,** 1857–1934, U.S. playwright, journalist, and actor. **3. (Charles Louis) Ambroise** (shärl lwē äN brwaz′), 1811–96, French composer. **4. Clarence,** born 1948, U.S. jurist: associate justice of the U.S. Supreme Court since 1991. **5. Dyl·an (Mar·lais)** (dil′ən mär′lā), 1914–53, Welsh poet and short-story writer. **6. George Henry,** 1816–70, Union general in the U.S. Civil War. **7. John,** 1724–76, American physician and general in the American Revolution. **8. Lowell (Jackson),** 1892–1981, U.S. newscaster, world traveler, and writer. **9. Martha Carey,** 1857–1935, U.S. educator and women's-rights advocate. **10. Norman (Mat·toon)** (mə to͞on′), 1884–1968, U.S. socialist leader and political writer. **11. Seth,** 1785–1859, U.S. clock designer and manufacturer. **12. Theodore,** 1835–1905, U.S. orchestra conductor, born in Germany. **13. William Isaac,** 1863–1947, U.S. sociologist. **14.** See **doubting Thomas. 15.** a male given name: from an Aramaic word meaning "twin."

Thom·as à Beck·et (tom′əs ə bek′it), **Saint.** See **Becket, Saint Thomas à.**

Thom·as à Kem·pis (tom′əs ə kem′pis). See **Kempis, Thomas à.**

Thom′as Aqui′nas (tom′əs), **Saint.** See **Aquinas, Saint Thomas.**

Thom·a·si·na (tom′ə sē′nə), *n.* a female given name. Also, **Thom·a·sine** (tom′ə sēn′).

Thom·as of Er·cel·doune (tom′əs əv ûr′səl do͞on′), (*"Thomas the Rhymer"*), c1220–97?, Scottish poet.

Thom·as of Wood·stock (tom′əs əv wo͝od′stok′), **Duke of Gloucester,** 1355–97, English prince (son of Edward III).

Thom·as·ville (tom′əs vil′), *n.* **1.** a city in S Georgia. 18,463. **2.** a city in central North Carolina. 14,144.

tho·mi·sid (thō′mə sid), *n.* **1.** a spider of the family Thomisidae, comprising the crab spiders. —*adj.* **2.** belonging or pertaining to the family Thomisidae. [1930–35; < NL *Thomisidae* name of the family, irreg. < Gk *thômînx* string + NL *-idae* -ID[2]]

Tho·mism (tō′miz əm), *n.* the theological and philosophical system of Thomas Aquinas. [THOM(AS AQUINAS) + -ISM] —**Tho′mist,** *n., adj.* —**Tho·mis′tic,** *adj.*

Thomp·son (tomp′sən, tom′-), *n.* **1. Benjamin, Count Rumford,** 1753–1814, English physicist and diplomat, born in the U.S. **2. Dorothy,** 1894–1961, U.S. journalist. **3. Francis,** 1859–1907, English poet. **4. J(ames) Walter,** 1847–1928, U.S. advertising executive. **5. Sir John Sparrow David,** 1844–94, Canadian statesman: prime minister 1892–94. **6. Randall,** (ran′dl), 1899–1984, U.S. composer and teacher. **7. Sylvia,** 1902–68, English novelist, born in Scotland. **8.** a city in N central Manitoba, in central Canada: nickel mining. 14,288. **9.** a town in NE Connecticut. 8141.

Thomp′son seed′less, 1. a yellow, seedless variety of grape used in producing raisins. **2.** the vine bearing this fruit, grown in California. Also called **Thomp′son seed′less grape′.** [1890–95, *Amer.*; named after W. B. *Thompson* (1869–1930), American horticulturist]

Thomp′son submachine′ gun′, a portable, .45-caliber, automatic weapon designed to be fired from the shoulder or hip. Also called **Tommy gun.** [1920–25; named after J. T. *Thompson* (1860–1940), American army officer who aided in its invention]

Thom·sen (tom′sən), *n.* **Chris·tian Jür·gen·sen** (kris′tyän yo͞or′gən sən), 1788–1865, Danish archaeologist.

Thom·son (tom′sən), *n.* **1. Elihu,** 1853–1937, U.S. inventor, born in England. **2. Sir George Paget,** 1892–1975, English physicist (son of Sir Joseph John): Nobel prize 1937. **3. James,** 1700–48, English poet, born in Scotland. **4. James** (*"B.V."*), 1834–82, English poet. **5. John Arthur,** 1861–1933, Scottish scientist and author. **6. Sir Joseph John,** 1856–1940, English physicist: Nobel prize 1906. **7. Virgil,** born 1896, U.S. composer and music critic. **8. Sir William.** See **Kelvin, 1st Baron.**

Thom′son effect′, *Physics.* the tendency of unevenly heated segments of a strip of a conductor to increase or decrease in temperature differences when an electric current is passed through the strip. [named after Sir W. THOMSON]

Thom′son's gazelle′, a medium-sized antelope, *Gazella thomsoni,* abundant on the grassy steppes and dry bush of the East African plains. [1910–15; named after Joseph *Thomson* (1858–95), British explorer, who collected the type specimen]

Thon Bu·ri (tôn′ bo͝o rē′), a city in S Thailand, near Bangkok. 627,989.

thong (thông, thong), *n.* **1.** a strip of material, esp. of leather or hide, used to fasten or secure something. **2.** a strip of leather or hide used for whipping; whiplash. **3.** a shoe or slipper fastened to the foot chiefly by a strip of leather or other material passing between the first and second toes and often attaching to another strip of material, as a strap across the instep or around the ankle. [bef. 950; ME; OE *thwong;* akin to ON *thvengr* strap, *thvinga* to compel] —**thonged,** *adj.*

Thon·ga (tong′gə), *n.* Tsonga.

thong′ leath′er, whang[2] (def. 2).

Thor (thôr), *n.* **1.** *Scand. Myth.* the god of thunder, rain, and farming, represented as riding a chariot drawn by goats and wielding the hammer Mjolnir: the defender of the Aesir, destined to kill and be killed by the Midgard Serpent. **2.** a medium-range U.S. Air Force ballistic missile developed in the early 1950's and powered by a single liquid-propellant rocket engine. **3.** a male given name. [bef. 1050; OE *Thōr* < ON *Thōrr* lit., THUNDER]

thorac-, var. of **thoraco-** before a vowel: *thoracic.*

tho·ra·cen·te·sis (thôr′ə sen tē′sis, thōr′-), *n., pl.* **-ses** (-sēz). insertion of a hollow needle or similar instrument into the pleural cavity of the chest in order to drain pleural fluid. [1855–60; THORA(C)- + CENTESIS]

tho·rac·ic (thô ras′ik, thō-), *adj.* of or pertaining to the thorax. Also, **tho·ra·cal** (thôr′ə kəl, thōr′-). [1650–60; < ML *thōrācicus* < Gk *thōrākikós.* See THORAC-, -IC]

CONCISE ETYMOLOGY KEY: <, descended or borrowed from; >, whence; b., blend of, blended; c., cognate with; cf., compare; deriv., derivative; equiv., equivalent; imit., imitative; obl., oblique; r., replacing; s., stem; sp., spelling, spelled; resp., respelling, respelled; trans., translation; ?, origin unknown; *, unattested; ‡, probably earlier than. See the full key inside the front cover.

thorac′ic ar′tery, *Anat.* any of several arteries that distribute blood to the muscles and organs of the thorax: used as a replacement artery in coronary bypass surgery. Also called **mammary artery.** [1720–30]

thorac′ic duct′, *Anat.* the main trunk of the lymphatic system, passing along the spinal column in the thoracic cavity, and conveying a large amount of lymph and chyle into the venous circulation. [1720–30]

thoraco-, a combining form representing **thorax** in compound words: *thoracoplasty.* Also, *esp. before a vowel,* **thorac-.** [comb. form repr. Gk *thōrāk-* (s. of *thṓrāx*) chest; see -O-]

tho·ra·co·plas·ty (thôr′ə kō plas′tē, thōr′-), *n., pl.* **-ties.** *Surg.* the operation removing selected portions of the ribs to collapse part of the underlying lung or an abnormal pleural space, usually in the treatment of tuberculosis. [1885–90; THORACO- + -PLASTY]

tho·ra·cos·to·my (thôr′ə kos′tə mē, thōr′-), *n., pl.* **-mies.** *Surg.* **1.** the construction of an artificial opening through the chest wall, usually for the drainage of fluid or the release of an abnormal accumulation of air. **2.** the opening so constructed. [THORACO- + -STOMY]

tho·ra·cot·o·my (thôr′ə kot′ə mē, thōr′-), *n., pl.* **-mies.** *Surg.* incision into the chest cavity. [1855–60; THORACO- + -TOMY]

tho·rax (thôr′aks, thōr′-), *n., pl.* **tho·rax·es, tho·ra·ces** (thôr′ə sēz′, thōr′-). **1.** *Anat.* the part of the trunk in humans and higher vertebrates between the neck and the abdomen, containing the cavity, enclosed by the ribs, sternum, and certain vertebrae, in which the heart, lungs, etc., are situated; chest. **2.** *Zool.* a corresponding part in other animals. **3.** (in insects) the portion of the body between the head and the abdomen. See diag. under **insect.** [1350–1400; ME < L *thōrāx* < Gk *thṓrāx* breastplate, part of body which this covers]

Tho·ra·zine (thôr′ə zēn′, thōr′-), *Pharm., Trademark.* a brand of chlorpromazine.

Tho·reau (thə rō′, thôr′ō, thōr′ō), *n.* **Henry David,** 1817–62, U.S. naturalist and author. —**Tho·reau·vi·an** (thə rō′vē ən), *adj.*

Tho·rez (tô rez′), *n.* **Mau·rice** (mô rēs′), 1900–64, French Communist party leader.

tho·ri·a (thôr′ē ə, thōr′-), *n. Chem.* a white, heavy, water-insoluble powder, ThO_2, used chiefly in incandescent mantles, as the Welsbach gas mantle. Also called **tho′rium ox′ide, tho′rium diox′ide.** [1835–45; THORI(UM) + -A[4]]

tho·ri·a·nite (thôr′ē ə nīt′, thōr′-), *n.* a rare mineral, mainly thoria, ThO_2, but also containing uranium, cerium, and other rare-earth metals, occurring in small, black, cubic crystals: notable for its radioactivity and used as a minor source of thorium. [1900–05; *thorian* (THORI(A) + -AN) + -ITE[1]]

tho·rite (thôr′īt, thōr′-), *n.* a rare mineral, thorium silicate, $ThSiO_4$, occurring in the form of yellow or black crystals. [1825–35; *thor-* (as in THORIA, THORIUM) + -ITE[1], modeled on Sw *thorit*]

tho·ri·um (thôr′ē əm, thōr′-), *n. Chem.* a grayish-white, lustrous, somewhat ductile and malleable, radioactive metallic element present in monazite: used as a source of nuclear energy, as a coating on sun-lamp and vacuum-tube filament coatings, and in alloys. *Symbol:* Th; *at. wt.:* 232.038; *at. no.:* 90; *sp. gr.:* 11.7. Cf. **thoria.** [< NL (1829); see THOR, -IUM] —**thor·ic** (thôr′ik, thor′-), *adj.*

tho′rium se′ries, *Chem.* the radioactive series that starts with thorium and ends with a stable isotope of lead of mass number 208.

thorn (thôrn), *n.* **1.** a sharp excrescence on a plant, esp. a sharp-pointed aborted branch; spine; prickle. **2.** any of various thorny shrubs or trees, esp. the hawthorns belonging to the genus *Crataegus,* of the rose family. **3.** the wood of any of these trees. **4.** a runic character (þ), borrowed into the Latin alphabet and representing the initial *th* sounds in *thin* and *they* in Old English, or *thin* in modern Icelandic. **5.** something that wounds, annoys, or causes discomfort. **6. thorn in one's side** or **flesh,** a source of continual irritation or suffering: *That child is a thorn in the teacher's side.* —*v.t.* **7.** to prick with a thorn; vex. [bef. 900; ME (n.), OE; c. D *doorn,* G *Dorn,* ON *thorn,* Goth *thaurnus*] —**thorn′less,** *adj.* —**thorn′like′,** *adj.*

Thorn (tôrn), *n.* German name of **Torun.**

thorn′ ap′ple (thôrn), **1.** any poisonous plant belonging to the genus *Datura,* of the nightshade family, the species of which bear capsules covered with prickly spines, esp. the jimson weed, *D. stramonium.* **2.** the fruit of certain hawthorns of the genus *Crataegus.* [1570–80]

thorn·back (thôrn′bak′), *n.* **1.** a skate, *Raja clavata,* of European waters, having short spines on the back and tail. **2.** a California ray, *Platyrhinoidis triseriatus,* belonging to the guitarfish group. [1250–1300; ME; see THORN, BACK[1]]

thorn·bush (thôrn′bo͝osh′), *n.* any of various shrubs or bushes having spines or thorns. [1300–50; ME. See THORN, BUSH[1]]

Thorn·dike (thôrn′dīk′), *n.* **1. Ashley Horace,** 1871–1933, U.S. literary historian and teacher. **2. Edward Lee,** 1874–1949, U.S. psychologist and lexicographer. **3. (Everett) Lynn,** 1882–1965, U.S. historian and scholar (brother of Ashley Horace Thorndike). **4. Dame Sybil,** 1882–1976, English actress.

Thorn·ton (thôrn′tn), *n.* **1. William,** 1759–1828, U.S. architect, born in the British Virgin Islands. **2.** a town in NE Colorado. 40,343. **3.** a male given name.

thorn·y (thôr′nē), *adj.,* **thorn·i·er, thorn·i·est. 1.** abounding in or characterized by thorns; spiny; prickly. **2.** thornlike. **3.** overgrown with thorns or brambles. **4.** painful; vexatious: *a thorny predicament.* **5.** full of difficulties, complexities, or controversial points: *a thorny question.* [bef. 1000; ME; OE *thornig.* See THORN, -Y[1]] —**thorn′i·ly,** *adv.* —**thorn′i·ness,** *n.*
—**Syn. 5.** tough, sticky, ticklish, perplexing.

thor·o (thûr′ō, thur′ō), *adj., adv.* an informal, simplified spelling of **thorough.**

Thor·old (thôr′əld, thor′-), *n.* a city in SE Ontario, in S Canada. 15,412.

tho·ron (thôr′on, thōr′-), *n. Chem.* a radioactive isotope of radon, produced by the disintegration of thorium. *Symbol:* Tn; *at. wt.:* 220; *at. no.:* 86. [1925–30; THOR(IUM) + -ON[2]]

thor·ough (thûr′ō, thur′ō), *adj.* **1.** executed without negligence or omissions: *a thorough search.* **2.** complete; perfect; utter: *thorough enjoyment.* **3.** extremely attentive to accuracy and detail; painstaking: *a thorough worker; a thorough analysis.* **4.** having full command or mastery of an art, talent, etc.: *a thorough actress.* **5.** extending or passing through. —*adv., prep.* **6.** *Archaic.* through. —*n.* **7.** (*cap.*) *Eng. Hist.* the administrative policies of the Earl of Stafford and Archbishop Laud during the reign of Charles I: so called because they were uncompromisingly carried out. [bef. 900; ME (prep. and adv.); OE *thuruh,* var. of *thurh* THROUGH] —**thor′ough·ly,** *adv.* —**thor′ough·ness,** *n.*
—**Syn. 1.** unqualified, total. —**Ant. 1.** partial.

thor′ough bass′ (bās), *Music.* **1.** See **figured bass. 2.** continuo. [1655–65]

thor′ough brace′, either of two strong braces or bands of leather supporting the body of a coach or other vehicle and connecting the front and back springs. [1830–40, *Amer.*]

thor·ough·bred (thûr′ō bred′, -ə bred′, thur′-), *adj.* **1.** of pure or unmixed breed, stock, or race, as a horse or other animal; bred from the purest and best blood. **2.** (*sometimes cap.*) of or pertaining to the Thoroughbred breed of horses. **3.** (of a person) having good breeding or education. —*n.* **4.** (*cap.*) one of a breed of horses, to which all racehorses belong, originally developed in England by crossing Arabian stallions with European mares. **5.** a thoroughbred animal. **6.** a well-bred or well-educated person. [1695–1705; THOROUGH + BRED] —**thor′ough·bred′ness,** *n.*

thor·ough·fare (thûr′ō fâr′, -ə fâr′, thur′-), *n.* **1.** a road, street, or the like, that leads at each end into another street. **2.** a major road or highway. **3.** a passage or way through: *no thoroughfare.* **4.** a strait, river, or the like, affording passage. [1350–1400; ME *thurghfare.* See THOROUGH, FARE]

thor·ough·go·ing (thûr′ō gō′ing, -ə gō′-, thur′-), *adj.* **1.** doing things thoroughly. **2.** carried out to the full extent; thorough. **3.** complete; unqualified: *a thoroughgoing knave.* [1810–20; THOROUGH + GOING] —**thor′ough·go′ing·ly,** *adv.* —**thor′ough·go′ing·ness,** *n.*

thor·ough·paced (thûr′ō pāst′, -ə pāst′, thur′-), *adj.* **1.** trained to go through all the possible paces, as a horse. **2.** thoroughgoing, complete, or perfect. [1640–50; THOROUGH + PACED]

thor·ough·pin (thûr′ō pin′, -ə pin′, thur′-), *n. Vet. Pathol.* an abnormal swelling just above the hock of a horse, usually appearing on both sides of the leg and sometimes causing lameness. [1780–90; THOROUGH + PIN]

thor·ough·wort (thûr′ō wûrt′, -wôrt′, -ə wûrt′, -ə wôrt′, thur′-), *n.* boneset. [1805–15, *Amer.*; THOROUGH + WORT[2]]

thorp (thôrp), *n. Archaic.* a hamlet; village. Also, **thorpe.** [bef. 900; ME, OE; c. G *Dorf,* ON *thorp* village, Goth *thaurp* field]

Thorpe (thôrp), *n.* **James Francis** (*"Jim"*), 1888–1953, U.S. track-and-field athlete and football and baseball player.

Thors·havn (tôrs houn′), *n.* a city in and the capital of the Faeroe Islands, in the N Atlantic. 9738.

thort·veit·ite (tôrt vī′tīt, thôrt-), *n.* a scandium yttrium silicate mineral occurring in grayish-green orthorhombic crystals. [1910–15; < G *Thortveitit,* named after Olaus *Thortveit,* 20th-century Norwegian mineralogist; see -ITE[1]]

Thor·vald·sen (to͞or′väl′sən), *n.* **Albert Ber·tal** (äl′-bert bar′təl), 1770–1844, Danish sculptor. Also, **Thor·wald·sen** (to͞or′väl′sən).

those (t͟hōz), *pron., adj.* pl. of **that.** [1300–50; ME *those, thoos, thas(e),* var. of *tho* (ME, OE *thā*), pl. of THAT, by association with ME *thees, thas(e)* (OE *thās*), pl. of THIS]

Thoth (thōth, tōt), *n. Egyptian Religion.* the god of wisdom, learning, and magic represented as a man with the head either of an ibis or of a baboon.

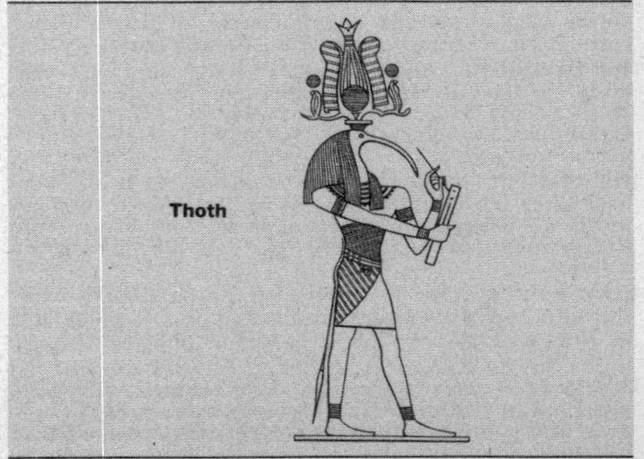
Thoth

Thot·mes I (thōt′mes). See **Thutmose I.** Also, **Thoth·mes I** (thoth′mēz, -mes, tōt′-, thōth′-).

Thotmes II. See **Thutmose II.** Also, **Thothmes II.**

Thotmes III. See **Thutmose III.** Also, **Thothmes III.**

thou[1] (thou), *pron., sing., nom.* **thou;** *poss.* **thy** or **thine;** *obj.* **thee;** *pl., nom.* **you** or **ye;** *poss.* **your** or **yours;** *obj.* **you** or **ye;** *v.* —*pron.* **1.** *Archaic (except in some elevated or ecclesiastical prose)* the personal pronoun of the second person singular in the nominative case (used to denote the person or thing addressed): *Thou shalt not kill.* **2.** (used by the Friends) a familiar form of address of the second person singular. —*v.t.* **3.** to address as "thou." —*v.i.* **4.** to use "thou" in discourse. [bef. 900; ME; OE *thū;* c. G, MD *du,* ON *thū,* Goth *thu,* OIr *tú,* Welsh, Cornish *ti,* L *tū,* Doric Gk *tý,* Lith *tù,* OCS *ty;* akin to Skt *tvam;* (v.) late ME *thowen,* deriv. of the pronoun]

thou[2] (thou), *n., pl.* **thous,** *(as after a numeral)* **thou.** *Slang.* one thousand dollars, pounds, etc. [1865–70; by shortening]

though (thō), *conj.* **1.** (used in introducing a subordinate clause, which is often marked by ellipsis) notwithstanding that; in spite of the fact that; although: *Though he tried very hard, he failed the course.* **2.** even if; granting that (often prec. by *even*). **3. as though,** as if: *It seems as though the place is deserted.* —*adv.* **4.** for all that; however. [1150–1200; ME *thoh* < ON *thō* (earlier **thauh*); r. OE *thēah;* c. G *doch,* Goth *thauh*]
—**Usage.** Among some conservatives there is a traditional objection to the use of THOUGH in place of ALTHOUGH as a conjunction. However, the latter (earlier *all though*) was originally an emphatic form of the former, and there is nothing in contemporary English usage to justify such a distinction.

thought[1] (thôt), *n.* **1.** the product of mental activity; that which one thinks: *a body of thought.* **2.** a single act or product of thinking; idea or notion: *to collect one's thoughts.* **3.** the act or process of thinking; mental activity: *Thought as well as action wearies us.* **4.** the capacity or faculty of thinking, reasoning, imagining, etc.: *All her thought went into her work.* **5.** a consideration or reflection: *Thought of death terrified her.* **6.** meditation, contemplation, or recollection: *deep in thought.* **7.** intention, design, or purpose, esp. a half-formed or imperfect intention: *We had some thought of going.* **8.** anticipation or expectation: *I had no thought of seeing you here.* **9.** consideration, attention, care, or regard: *She took no thought of her appearance.* **10.** a judgment, opinion, or belief: *According to his thought, all violence is evil.* **11.** the intellectual activity or the ideas, opinions, etc., characteristic of a particular place, class, or time: *Greek thought.* **12.** a very small amount; a touch; bit; trifle: *The steak is a thought underdone.* [bef. 900; ME *thoght,* OE *(ge)thōht;* c. D *gedachte;* akin to THANK, THINK[1]]
—**Syn. 2.** See **idea. 3.** reflection, cogitation.

thought[2] (thôt), *v.* pt. and pp. of **think.**

thought′ disor′der, *Psychiatry.* disorganized speech, as flight of ideas or loosening of associations, thought to reflect disorganized thinking and occurring as a symptom of some types of mental illness, as manic disorder or schizophrenia.

thought′ exper′iment *Physics.* a demonstration or calculation that is based on the postulates of a theory, as relativity, and that demonstrates or clarifies the consequences of the postulates. Also called **Gedanken experiment.** [1940–45]

thought·ful (thôt′fəl), *adj.* **1.** showing consideration for others; considerate. **2.** characterized by or manifesting careful thought: *a thoughtful essay.* **3.** occupied with or given to thought; contemplative; meditative; reflective: *in a thoughtful mood.* **4.** careful, heedful, or mindful: *to be thoughtful of one's safety.* [1150–1200; ME; see THOUGHT[1], -FUL] —**thought′ful·ly,** *adv.* —**thought′ful·ness,** *n.*
—**Syn. 1.** attentive, solicitous. THOUGHTFUL, CONSIDERATE mean taking thought for the comfort and the good of others. THOUGHTFUL implies providing little attentions, offering services, or in some way looking out for the comfort or welfare of others: *It was thoughtful of you to send the flowers.* CONSIDERATE implies sparing others annoyance or discomfort, and being careful not to hurt their feelings: *not considerate of his family.*

thought·less (thôt′lis), *adj.* **1.** lacking in consideration for others; inconsiderate; tactless: *a thoughtless remark.* **2.** characterized by or showing lack of thought: *a shallow, thoughtless book.* **3.** not thinking enough; careless or heedless: *thoughtless of his health.* **4.** devoid of or lacking capacity for thought. [1585–95; THOUGHT[1] + -LESS] —**thought′less·ly,** *adv.* —**thought′less·ness,** *n.*
—**Syn. 1.** negligent, neglectful. **3.** inattentive, remiss.

thought-out (thôt′out′), *adj.* produced by or showing the results of much thought: *a carefully thought-out argument.* [1865–70]

thought′ transfer′ence, transference of thought by extrasensory means from the mind of one individual to another; telepathy. [1880–85]

thought·way (thôt′wā′), *n.* a habitual manner of thought in a particular group of people. [1940–45; THOUGHT[1] + WAY[1]]

thou·sand (thou′zənd), *n., pl.* **-sands,** *(as after a numeral)* **-sand,** *adj.* —*n.* **1.** a cardinal number, 10 times 100. **2.** a symbol for this number, as 1000 or M. **3. thousands.** the numbers between 1000 and 999,999, as in referring to an amount of money: *Property damage was in the thousands.* **4.** a great number or amount. **5.** Also, **thou′sand's place′. a.** (in a mixed number) the position of the fourth digit to the left of the decimal point. **b.** (in a whole number) the position of the fourth digit from the right. —*adj.* **6.** amounting to 1000 in number. [bef. 900; ME; OE *thūsend;* c. D *duizend,* OHG *dūsunt,* ON *thūsund,* Goth *thūsindi*]

Thou′sand and One′ Nights′, The. See **Arabian Nights' Entertainments.**

thou′sand days′, *(sometimes caps.)* the presidential administration of John F. Kennedy, which lasted 1037 days (January 20, 1961, to November 22, 1963).

thou·sand·fold (*adj.* thou′zənd fōld′; *adv.* thou′zənd-fōld′), *adj.* **1.** having a thousand elements or parts. **2.** a thousand times as great or as much. —*adv.* **3.** in a thousandfold manner or measure. [bef. 1000; ME *thowsand folde,* OE *thūsendfealde.* See THOUSAND, -FOLD]

Thou′sand Is′land dress′ing, a seasoned mayonnaise, often containing chopped pickles, pimientos, sweet peppers, hard-boiled eggs, etc. [1920–25]

Thou′sand Is′lands, a group of about 1500 islands in S Canada and the N United States, in the St. Lawrence River at the outlet of Lake Ontario: summer resorts.

Thou′sand Oaks′, a town in S California. 77,797.

thou·sandth (thou′zəndth, -zəntth, -zənth), *adj.* **1.** last in order of a series of a thousand. **2.** being one of a thousand equal parts. —*n.* **3.** a thousandth part, esp. of one (1/1000). **4.** the thousandth member of a series. **5.** Also, **thou′sandth's place′.** (in decimal notation) the position of the third digit to the right of the decimal point. [1545–55; THOUSAND + -TH[2]]

Thr, *Biochem.* threonine.

Thrace (thrās), *n.* **1.** an ancient region of varying extent in the E part of the Balkan Peninsula: later a Roman province; now in Bulgaria, Turkey, and Greece. **2.** a modern region corresponding to the S part of the Roman province: now divided between Greece **(Western Thrace)** and Turkey **(Eastern Thrace).**

Thra·cian (thrā′shən), *adj.* **1.** of or pertaining to Thrace or its inhabitants. —*n.* **2.** a native or inhabitant of Thrace. **3.** an Indo-European language of ancient Thrace. [1560–70; < L *Thrāci(us)* of Thrace (< Gk *Thrāíkios,* equiv. to *Thrāík(ē)* THRACE + *-ios* adj. suffix) + -AN]

Thra·co-Phryg·i·an (thrā′kō frij′ē ən), *n.* **1.** a hypothetical branch of Indo-European implying a special genetic affinity between the meagerly attested Thracian and Phrygian languages. —*adj.* **2.** of, belonging to, or pertaining to Thraco-Phrygian. [*Thraco-* (< Gk *Thrāiko-,* comb. form of *Thrāíkē* Thrace) + PHRYGIAN]

Thrale (thrāl), *n.* **Hester Lynch** (*Hester Lynch Piozzi*), 1741–1821, Welsh writer and friend of Samuel Johnson.

thrall (thrôl), *n.* **1.** a person who is in bondage; slave. **2.** a person who is morally or mentally enslaved by some power, influence, or the like: *He was the thrall of morbid fantasies.* **3.** slavery; thralldom. —*v.t.* **4.** *Archaic.* to put or hold in thralldom; enslave. —*adj.* **5.** *Archaic.* subjected to bondage; enslaved. [bef. 950; ME; OE *thrǣl* < ON *thrǣll* slave]

thrall·dom (thrôl′dəm), *n.* the state of being a thrall; bondage; slavery; servitude. Also, **thral′dom.** [1125–75; ME *thraldom.* See THRALL, -DOM]

thrash (thrash), *v.t.* **1.** to beat soundly in punishment; flog. **2.** to defeat thoroughly: *The home team thrashed the visitors.* **3.** *Naut.* to force (a close-hauled sailing ship under heavy canvas) against a strong wind or sea. **4.** thresh. —*v.i.* **5.** to toss, or plunge about. **6.** *Naut.* to make way against the wind, tide, etc.; beat. **7.** thresh. **8. thrash out** or **over,** to talk over thoroughly and vigorously in order to reach a decision, conclusion, or understanding; discuss exhaustively. —*n.* **9.** an act or instance of thrashing; beating; blow. **10.** thresh. **11.** *Swimming.* the upward and downward movement of the legs, as in the crawl. **12.** *Brit. Slang.* a party, usually with drinks. [bef. 900; ME *thrasshen,* var. of *thresshen* to THRESH]
—**Syn. 1.** maul, drub. See **beat.**

thrash·er (thrash′ər), *n.* **1.** a person or thing that thrashes. **2.** any of several long-tailed, thrushlike birds, esp. of the genus *Toxostoma,* related to the mockingbirds. Cf. **brown thrasher. 3.** thresher (def. 2). [1350–1400; ME; see THRASH, -ER[1]]

thrash·ing (thrash′ing), *n.* **1.** a flogging; whipping. **2.** the act of a person or thing that thrashes. **3.** a pile or quantity of threshed grain or the grain threshed at one time. [1350–1400; ME; see THRASH, -ING[1]]

thra·son·i·cal (thrā son′i kəl), *adj.* boastful; vainglorious. [1555–65; < L *Thrasōn-* (s. of *Thrasō,* braggart in Terence's *Eunuchus*) + -ICAL] —**thra·son′i·cal·ly,** *adv.*

Thras·y·bu·lus (thras′ə byōō′ləs), *n.* died c389 B.C., Athenian patriot and general.

thraw (thrô, thrä), *v.t.* **1.** *Brit. Dial.* to throw. **2.** *Scot.* **a.** to twist; distort. **b.** to oppose; thwart; vex. —*v.i.* **3.** *Scot.* to disagree; object. —*adj.* **4.** *Scot.* thrawn (def. 1). [(v.) Scots, N England dial. form of THROW (retaining in part earliest sense of the word); (adj.) appar. shortened from THRAWN]

thra·wart (thrä′wərt), *adj. Scot.* **1.** obstinate or intractable. **2.** twisted or crooked. Also, **thra·ward** (thrä′wərd). [1425–75; late ME (Scots), alter. of *fraward, froward,* perh. under influence of THRAW, THRAWN]

thrawn (thrôn, thrän), *adj. Scot.* **1.** twisted; crooked; distorted. **2.** contrary; peevish; perverse. **3.** unpleasant; sullen. [1400–50; late ME (north and Scots), var. of THROWN; see THRAW] —**thrawn′ly,** *adv.* —**thrawn′·ness,** *n.*

thread (thred), *n.* **1.** a fine cord of flax, cotton, or other fibrous material spun out to considerable length, esp. when composed of two or more filaments twisted together. **2.** twisted filaments or fibers of any kind used for sewing. **3.** one of the lengths of yarn forming the warp or weft of a woven fabric. **4.** a filament or fiber of glass or other ductile substance. **5.** *Ropemaking.* **a.** any of a number of fibers twisted into a yarn. **b.** a yarn, esp. as enumerated in describing small stuff. **6.** something having the fineness or slenderness of a filament, as a thin continuous stream of liquid, a fine line of color, or a thin seam of ore: *a thread of smoke.* **7.** the helical ridge of a screw. **8.** that which runs through the whole course of something, connecting successive parts: *I lost the thread of the story.* **9.** something conceived as being spun or continuously drawn out, as the course of life fabled to be spun, measured, and cut by the Fates. **10. threads,** *Slang.* clothes. —*v.t.* **11.** to pass the end of a thread through the eye of (a needle). **12.** to fix (beads, pearls, etc.) upon a thread that is passed through; string. **13.** to pass continuously through the whole course of (something); pervade: *A joyous quality threaded the whole symphony.* **14.** to make one's way through (a narrow passage, forest, crowd, etc.). **15.** to make (one's way) thus: *He threaded his way through the crowd.* **16.** to form a thread on or in (a bolt, hole, etc.). **17.** to place and arrange thread, yarn, etc., in position on (a sewing machine, loom, textile machine, etc.). —*v.i.* **18.** to thread one's way, as through a passage or between obstacles: *They threaded carefully along the narrow pass.* **19.** to move in a threadlike course; wind or twine. **20.** *Cookery.* (of boiling syrup) to form a fine thread when poured from a spoon. [bef. 900; (n.) ME *threed,* OE *thrǣd;* c. D *draad,* G *Draht,* ON *thrathr* wire; (v.) ME *threeden,* deriv. of the n. See THROW] —**thread′er,** *n.* —**thread′less,** *adj.* —**thread′like′,** *adj.*

thread·bare (thred′bâr′), *adj.* **1.** having the nap worn off so as to lay bare the threads of the warp and woof, as a fabric, garment, etc. **2.** wearing threadbare clothes; shabby or poor: *a threadbare old man.* **3.** meager, scanty, or poor: *a threadbare emotional life.* **4.** hackneyed; trite; ineffectively stale: *threadbare arguments.* [1325–75; ME *thredbare.* See THREAD, BARE[1]] —**thread′bare′ness,** *n.*

thread′ blight′, *Plant Pathol.* a fungal disease of woody plants, characterized by thick, threadlike strands of mycelium on the undersides of the leaves and branches.

thread·ed (thred′id), *adj.* interwoven or ornamented with threads: *silk threaded with gold.* [1535–45; THREAD + -ED[3]]

thread′ed glass′, glass decorated with a pattern produced by variegated glass filaments.

thread′ escutch′eon, a raised metal rim around a keyhole.

thread·fin (thred′fin′), *n.* any spiny-rayed fishes of the family Polynemidae, having the lower part of the pectoral fin composed of numerous, separate, filamentous rays. [1885–90; THREAD + FIN]

thread·fish (thred′fish′), *n., pl. (esp. collectively)* **-fish,** *(esp. referring to two or more kinds or species)* **-fish·es.** any of several jacks of the genus *Alectis,* esp. *A. ciliaris,* having the front rays of the dorsal and anal fins greatly elongated. [1835–45; THREAD + FISH]

thread′-leg·ged bug′ (thred′leg′id, -legd′), any of certain insects of the family Reduviidae, characterized by an elongated, slender body and long frail legs, the front pair of which are raptorial. Also called **spider bug.**

thread′-line fish′ing (thred′līn′), *Angling.* spinning (def. 3).

thread′ mark′, a thin threading in paper currency to make counterfeiting difficult.

thread′ rope′, cordage ½ in. (1.3 cm) or less in thickness.

thread′ silk′, silk yarn produced by a silk throwster.

thread·worm (thred′wûrm′), *n.* any of various nematode worms, esp. a pinworm. [1795–1805; THREAD + WORM]

thread·y (thred′ē), *adj.,* **thread·i·er, thread·i·est. 1.** consisting of or resembling a thread or threads; fibrous; filamentous. **2.** stringy or viscid, as a liquid. **3.** (of the pulse) thin and feeble. **4.** (of sound, the voice, etc.) lacking fullness; weak; feeble. [1375–1425; late ME; see THREAD, -Y[1]] —**thread′i·ness,** *n.*

threap (thrēp), *Scot. and North Eng.* —*n.* **1.** an argument; quarrel. **2.** a hostile charge; accusation. —*v.t.* **3.** to rebuke; scold. —*v.i.* **4.** to argue; bicker. [bef. 900; (v.) ME *threpen,* OE *thrēapian* to blame; (n.) ME *threp(e),* deriv. of the v.] —**threap′er,** *n.*

threat (thret), *n.* **1.** a declaration of an intention or determination to inflict punishment, injury, etc., in retaliation for, or conditionally upon, some action or course; menace: *He confessed under the threat of imprisonment.* **2.** an indication or warning of probable trouble: *The threat of a storm was in the air.* **3.** a person or thing that threatens. —*v.t., v.i.* **4.** *Archaic.* to threaten. [bef. 900; (n.) ME *threte,* OE *thrēat* pressure, oppression; c. ON *thraut* hardship, bitter end; (v.) ME *threten,* OE *thrēatian* to press, threaten]

threat·en (thret′n), *v.t.* **1.** to utter a threat against; menace: *He threatened the boy with a beating.* **2.** to be a menace or source of danger to: *Sickness threatened her peace of mind.* **3.** to offer (a punishment, injury, etc.) by way of a threat: *They threatened swift retaliation.* **4.** to give an ominous indication of: *The clouds threaten rain.* —*v.i.* **5.** to utter or use threats. **6.** to indicate impending evil or mischief. [bef. 1000; ME *thretnen,* OE *thrēat-*

CONCISE PRONUNCIATION KEY: act, cāpe, dâre, pärt; set, ēqual; *if,* īce; ox, ōver, ôrder, oil, bŏŏk, bōōt, out; up, ûrge; child; sing; shoe; thin, *that;* zh as in *treasure.* ə = *a* as in *alone, e* as in *system, i* as in *easily, o* as in *gallop, u* as in *circus;* ˚ as in *fire* (fī˚r), *hour* (ou˚r). l and n can serve as syllabic consonants, as in *cradle* (krād′l), and *button* (but′n). See the full key inside the front cover.

nian, deriv. of *thrēat* pressure, oppression. See THREAT, -EN[1]] —**threat′en·er,** *n.*
—**Syn. 2.** endanger. —**Ant. 2.** protect, defend.

threat′ened spe′cies, a species likely, in the near future, to become an endangered species within all or much of its range. [1965–70]

threat·en·ing (thret′n ing), *adj.* **1.** tending or intended to menace: *threatening gestures.* **2.** causing alarm, as by being imminent; ominous; sinister: *threatening clouds.* [1520–30; THREATEN + -ING[2]] —**threat′·en·ing·ly,** *adv.*
—**Syn. 2.** See **imminent, ominous.**

three (thrē), *n.* **1.** a cardinal number, 2 plus 1. **2.** a symbol for this number, as 3 or III. **3.** a set of this many persons or things. **4.** a playing card, die face, or half of a domino face with three pips. —*adj.* **5.** amounting to three in number. **6. three sheets in the wind.** See **sheet**[2] (def. 2). [bef. 900; ME; OE *thrēo, thrīo,* fem. and neut. of *thrī(e);* c. D *drie,* G *drei,* ON *thrír,* Goth *threis,* Gk *treîs,* L *trēs* three, *ter* thrice, Ir *trí,* OCS *tri,* Skt *tri, tráyas*]

three-a-cat (thrē′ə kat′), *n. Games.* two-a-cat played with three bases and three batters. [1850–55]

three-bag·ger (thrē′bag′ər), *n. Baseball Informal.* triple (def. 7). [1870–75, *Amer.*]

three′-ball match′ (thrē′bôl′), *Golf.* a match among three players each of whom plays a ball. [1885–90]

three′-base hit′ (thrē′bās′), *Baseball.* triple (def. 7). [1870–75, *Amer.*]

three-birds (thrē′bûrdz′), *n., pl.* **-birds.** (*used with a singular or plural v.*) See **nodding pogonia.**

three′-bod′y prob′lem (thrē′bod′ē), *Astron., Mech.* the problem of calculating the motions of three bodies in space moving under the influence of only their mutual gravitational attraction. Cf. **two-body problem.**

three′-card mon′te (thrē′kärd′), *Cards.* **1.** a gambling game in which the players are shown three cards and bet that they can identify one particular card of the three, as stipulated by the dealer, after the cards have been moved around face down by the dealer. **2.** a form of three-card stud poker. [1850–55, *Amer.*]

three-col·or (thrē′kul′ər), *adj.* **1.** having or characterized by the use of three colors. **2.** noting or pertaining to a photomechanical process for making reproductions of paintings, artwork, etc., usually by making three printing plates, each corresponding to a primary color, by the halftone process, and printing superimposed impressions from these plates in three correspondingly colored inks. [1890–95]

three-cor·nered (thrē′kôr′nərd), *adj.* **1.** having three corners: *a three-cornered hat.* **2.** pertaining to or involving three persons, parties, or things: *The candidates were deadlocked in a three-cornered tie.* [1350–1400; ME *thre cornerid.* See THREE, CORNERED]

3-D (thrē′dē′), *adj.* **1.** of, pertaining to, or representing something in three dimensions; three-dimensional: *3-D movies.* —*n.* **2.** a three-dimensional form or appearance: *My dreams are always in 3-D.* [1930–35, *Amer.*]

three-deck·er (thrē′dek′ər), *n.* **1.** any ship having three decks, tiers, etc. **2.** (formerly) one of a class of sailing warships that carried guns on three decks. **3.** a sandwich made of three slices of bread interlaid with two layers of filling; club sandwich. **4.** something having three layers, levels, or tiers. Also called **triple-decker** (for defs. 3, 4). [1785–95]

three-di·men·sion·al (thrē′di men′shə nl, -dī-), *adj.* **1.** having, or seeming to have, the dimension of depth as well as width and height. **2.** (esp. in a literary work) fully developed: *The story came alive chiefly because the characters were vividly three-dimensional.* [1890–95] —**three′di·men′sion·al′i·ty,** *n.*

Three′ Fires′, *Buddhism.* the three causes of suffering, or dukkha, given as hate, greed or restlessness, and dullness of mind: they are extinguished in Nirvana.

three-fold (thrē′fōld′), *n.* a unit of stage scenery consisting of three flats hinged together.

three·fold (thrē′fōld′), *adj.* **1.** comprising three parts, members, or aspects; triple: *a threefold program.* **2.** three times as great or as much; treble: *a threefold return on an investment.* —*adv.* **3.** in threefold manner or measure; trebly. [bef. 1000; ME *threfold,* OE *thrifeald.* See THREE, -FOLD]

three-gait·ed (thrē′gā′tid), *adj. Manège.* noting a horse trained to walk, trot, and canter, as for pleasure riding and showing. Cf. **five-gaited.** [1945–50]

three-hand·ed (thrē′han′did), *adj.* involving three hands or players, as a game at cards. [1710–20]

Three′ Hours′, *Rom. Cath. Ch.* a religious observance practiced between noon and three o'clock on the afternoon of Good Friday.

three-leg·ged (thrē′leg′id, -legd′), *adj.* **1.** having three legs: *a three-legged stool.* **2.** *Informal.* (of a schooner) having three masts. [1590–1600]

three′-legged race′, a race among a number of paired contestants, each contestant having one leg tied to the adjacent leg of his or her partner. [1900–05]

three-mast·er (thrē′mas′tər, -mä′stər), *n. Naut.* a sailing ship with three masts. [1880–85] —**three′-mast′ed,** *adj.*

Three′ Mile′ Is′land, an island in the Susquehanna River, near Middletown, Pennsylvania, SE of Harrisburg: scene of a near-disastrous accident at a nuclear plant in 1979 that raised the issue of nuclear-energy safety.

CONCISE ETYMOLOGY KEY: <, descended or borrowed from; >, whence; b., blend of, blended; c., cognate with; cf., compare; deriv., derivative; equiv., equivalent; imit., imitative; obl., oblique; r., replacing; s., stem; sp., spelling, spelled; resp., respelling, respelled; trans., translation; ?, origin unknown; *, unattested; ‡, probably earlier than. See the full key inside the front cover.

three′-mile lim′it (thrē′mīl′), *Internat. Law.* the limit of the marine belt of three mi. (4.8 km), which is included within the jurisdiction of the state possessing the coast. [1890–95]

Three′ Musketeers′, The, (French, *Les Trois Mousquetaires*), a historical novel (1844) by Alexandre Dumas père.

three′ of a kind′, *Poker.* a set of three cards of the same denomination.

three old cat (thrē′ ə kat′), three-a-cat. Also, **three′ o′ cat′.**

three·pence (thrip′əns, threp′-, thrup′-; thrē′pens′), *n.* **1.** (*used with a singular or plural v.*) *Brit.* a sum of three pennies. **2.** a former cupronickel coin of the United Kingdom, a quarter of a shilling, equal to three pennies: use phased out after decimalization in 1971. Also, **thrippence, thruppence.** [1580–90; THREE + PENCE]

three·pen·ny (thrip′ə nē, threp′-, thrup′-; thrē′pen′-ē), *adj.* **1.** of the amount or value of threepence. **2.** of little worth. [1400–50; late ME; see THREE, PENNY]

three-phase (thrē′fāz′), *adj. Elect.* **1.** of or pertaining to a circuit, system, or device that is energized by three electromotive forces that differ in phase by one third of a cycle or 120°. **2.** having three phases. [1890–95]

three-piece (thrē′pēs′), *adj.* **1.** *Clothing.* consisting of three matching or harmonious pieces, as an ensemble of coat, skirt, and blouse for a woman or a suit of a jacket, vest, and pair of trousers for a man. **2.** having three parts. —*n.* **3.** a three-piece ensemble or suit. Cf. **coordinate** (def. 7). [1905–10]

three-ply (thrē′plī′), *adj.* consisting of three thicknesses, laminations, strands, or the like. [1865–70]

three′-point land′ing (thrē′point′), *Aeron.* an aircraft landing in which the two wheels of the main landing gear and the tail or nose wheel touch the ground simultaneously. [1925–30]

three′-point play′, *Basketball.* a play in which a player sinks the free throw that was awarded when the player was fouled while scoring a basket.

three-quar·ter (thrē′kwôr′tər), *adj.* **1.** consisting of or involving three quarters of a whole or of the usual length: *a blouse with a three-quarter sleeve.* **2.** (of a portrait) showing the face as seen from in front and somewhat to the side: *a three-quarter view.* Also, **three′-quar′ters.** [1400–50; late ME]

three′-quarter ar′mor, plate armor that leaves the legs exposed below the knees.

three′-quarter bind′ing, *Bookbinding.* a binding in which the material used for the back extends further over the covers than in half binding. [1895–1900]

three′-quarter nel′son, *Wrestling.* a hold in which a wrestler, from a kneeling position behind a prone opponent, applies a half nelson with one arm, passes the other arm under the opponent's body on the near side, and locks the arms at the fingers or wrist on the back of the opponent's neck. Cf. **nelson.**

three′-quar′ter time′, *Music.* the meter of a musical composition having a time signature of 3/4 and three quarter notes or their equivalent in each measure. Also called **waltz time.**

three′-quar′ter turn′ stair′, a staircase requiring a three-quarter turn at each landing for continued ascent or descent. [1960–65]

three′-ring cir′cus (thrē′ring′), **1.** a circus having three adjacent rings in which performances take place simultaneously. **2.** something spectacular, tumultuous, entertaining, or full of confused action: *Our family reunions are always three-ring circuses.* Also, **three′-ringed′ cir′cus.** [1880–85, *Amer.*]

Three′ Riv′ers, a city in S Quebec, in SE Canada, on the St. Lawrence. 55,240. French, **Trois-Rivières.**

three R's, **1.** reading, 'riting, and 'rithmetic, regarded as the fundamentals of education. **2.** the fundamentals, basic knowledge, or skills of any system or field: *the three R's of good government.* [1820–30]

threes′ and eights′, *CB Slang.* best wishes; good luck: used as a sign-off.

three·score (thrē′skôr′, -skōr′), *adj.* being or containing three times twenty; sixty. [1350–1400; ME *thre scoor.* See THREE, SCORE]

Three′ Signs′ of Be′ing, *Buddhism.* the three characteristics of every living thing, which are anicca, or impermanence, dukkha, or suffering, and anatta, or the absence of a personal and immortal soul.

Three′ Sis′ters, a play (1901) by Anton Chekhov.

three·some (thrē′səm), *adj.* **1.** consisting of three; threefold. **2.** performed or played by three persons. —*n.* **3.** three forming a group. **4.** something in which three persons participate, as certain games. **5.** *Golf.* a match in which two players, playing alternately with one ball, compete against a third player who also plays one ball. [1325–75; ME *thresum.* See THREE -SOME[2]]

three-speed (thrē′spēd′), *n.* **1.** a system of gears having three forward gear ratios, esp. on a bicycle. **2.** a bicycle having such a system of gears. —*adj.* **3.** having three forward gear ratios.

three′spine stick′leback (thrē′spīn′), a widely distributed stickleback, *Gasterosteus aculeatus,* occurring in marine, brackish, or fresh waters throughout the northern hemisphere. Also, **three′-spined stick′leback.** [1890–95]

three-spot (thrē′spot′), *n.* a playing card, an upward face of a die, or a domino half bearing three pips.

three-square (thrē′skwâr′), *adj.* having an equilateral triangular cross section, as certain files. [1400–50; late ME *thre square* threefold, modeled on FOURSQUARE]

three-star (thrē′stär′), *adj.* of or being a lieutenant general, as indicated by three stars on an insignia.

three-suit·er (thrē′sōō′tər), *n.* a man's suitcase or garment bag of a size to hold three suits. [*three suit(s)* + -ER[1]]

three′-thorned aca′cia (thrē′thôrnd′). See **honey locust.** [1815–25]

three′-toed sloth′ (thrē′tōd′), a small sloth of the genus *Bradypus,* having three claws on each limb and very long forelimbs.

three′-toed wood′pecker, **1.** either of two woodpeckers of the genus *Picoides,* of the Northern Hemisphere, having only three toes on each foot. **2.** any of various similar, tropical, Old World woodpeckers. [1765–75]

three′ u′nities, the. See under **unity** (def. 8).

three-val·ued (thrē′val′yōōd), *adj. Logic.* of or pertaining to propositions having a value other than truth or falsity.

three′-wat·tled bell′bird (thrē′wot′ld). See under **bellbird.**

three′-way bulb′ (thrē′wā′), a light bulb that can be switched to three successive degrees of illumination.

three-wheel·er (thrē′hwē′lər, -wē′-), *n.* a vehicle equipped with three wheels, as a tricycle, a motorcycle with a sidecar, or some small, experimental, or early-model cars. [1885–90; *three wheel(s)* + -ER[1]]

threm·ma·tol·o·gy (threm′ə tol′ə jē), *n. Biol.* the science of breeding or propagating animals and plants under domestication. [1885–90; < Gk *thremmato-* (comb. form of *thrémma* nursling) + -LOGY]

thre·node (thrē′nōd, thren′ōd), *n.* threnody. [1855–60; by alter.; see ODE]

thren·o·dy (thren′ə dē), *n., pl.* **-dies.** a poem, speech, or song of lamentation, esp. for the dead; dirge; funeral song. [1615–25; < Gk *thrēnōidía,* equiv. to *thrên(os)* dirge + *-ōid(ē)* song (see ODE) + *-ia* -Y[3]] —**thre·no·di·al** (thri nō′dē əl), **thre·nod·ic** (thri nod′ik), *adj.* —**thren·o·dist** (thren′ə dist), *n.*

thre·o·nine (thrē′ə nēn′, -nin), *n. Biochem.* an essential amino acid, $CH_3CHOHCH(NH_2)COOH$, obtained by the hydrolysis of proteins. *Abbr.:* Thr; *Symbol:* T [1925–30; *threon-* (alter. of Gk *erythrón,* neut. of *erythrós* red; see ERYTHRO-) + -INE[2]]

thresh (thresh), *v.t.* **1.** to separate the grain or seeds from (a cereal plant or the like) by some mechanical means, as by beating with a flail or by the action of a threshing machine. **2.** to beat as if with a flail. —*v.i.* **3.** to thresh wheat, grain, etc. **4.** to deliver blows as if with a flail. **5. thresh out** or **over.** See **thrash** (def. 8). —*n.* **6.** the act of threshing. Also, **thrash.** [bef. 900; ME *threschen, thresshen,* OE *threscan;* c. G *dreschen,* Goth *thriskan;* akin to D *dorsen,* ON *thriskja*]

thresh·er (thresh′ər), *n.* **1.** a person or thing that threshes. **2.** Also, **thrasher.** Also called **thresh′er shark′.** a large shark of the genus *Alopias,* esp. *A. vulpinus,* which threshes the water with its long tail to drive together the small fish on which it feeds. [1350–1400; ME *thressher.* See THRESH, -ER[1]]

thresh′ing machine′, *Agric.* a machine for removing grains and seeds from straw and chaff. [1765–75]

thresh·old (thresh′ōld, thresh′hōld), *n.* **1.** the sill of a doorway. **2.** the entrance to a house or building. **3.** any place or point of entering or beginning: *the threshold of a new career.* **4.** Also called **limen.** *Psychol., Physiol.* the point at which a stimulus is of sufficient intensity to begin to produce an effect: *the threshold of consciousness; a low threshold of pain.* [bef. 900; ME *thresshold,* OE *threscold, threscwald;* c. ON *threskǫldr,* dial. Sw *träskvald;* akin to THRESH in old sense "trample, tread"; *-old, -wald* unexplained]

threw (thrōō), *v.* a pt. of **throw.**

thrice (thrīs), *adv.* **1.** three times, as in succession; on three occasions or in three ways. **2.** in threefold quantity or degree. **3.** very; extremely. [1150–1200; ME *thries,* equiv. to obs. *thrie* thrice (OE *thrīga*) + *-s* -S[1]]

thrift (thrift), *n.* **1.** economical management; economy; frugality. **2.** Also called **thrift′ institu′tion.** *Banking.* a savings and loan association, savings bank, or credit union. **3.** Also called **sea pink.** any alpine and maritime plant belonging to the genus *Armeria,* of the leadwort family, having pink or white flowers, esp. *A. maritima,* noted for its vigorous growth. **4.** any of various allied plants. **5.** vigorous growth, as of a plant. **6.** *Obs.* prosperity. [1200–50; ME < ON: well being, prosperity; cf. THRIVE]

thrift·less (thrift′lis), *adj.* **1.** without thrift; improvident; wasteful. **2.** *Archaic.* useless or pointless. [1350–1400; ME: unsuccessful. See THRIFT, -LESS] —**thrift′·less·ly,** *adv.* —**thrift′less·ness,** *n.*

thrift·shop (thrift′shop′), *n.* a retail store that sells secondhand goods at reduced prices. [1940–45; THRIFT + SHOP]

thrift·y (thrif′tē), *adj.,* **thrift·i·er, thrift·i·est.** **1.** practicing thrift or economical management; frugal: *a thrifty shopper.* **2.** thriving, prosperous, or successful. **3.** thriving physically; growing vigorously. [1325–75; ME; see THRIFT, -Y[1]] —**thrift′i·ly,** *adv.* —**thrift′i·ness,** *n.*
—**Syn. 1.** sparing, saving. See **economical.**

thrill (thril), *v.t.* **1.** to affect with a sudden wave of keen emotion or excitement, as to produce a tremor or tingling sensation through the body. **2.** to utter or send forth tremulously, as a melody. —*v.i.* **3.** to affect one with a wave of emotion or excitement. **4.** to be stirred by a tremor or tingling sensation of emotion or excitement: *He thrilled at the thought of home.* **5.** to cause a prickling or tingling sensation; throb. **6.** to move tremulously; vibrate; quiver. —*n.* **7.** a sudden wave of keen emotion or excitement, sometimes manifested as a tremor or tingling sensation passing through the body. **8.** something that produces or is capable of producing such a sensation: *a story full of thrills.* **9.** a thrilling experience: *It was a thrill to see Paris again.* **10.** a vibration or quivering. **11.** *Pathol.* an abnormal tremor or vibration, as in the respiratory or vascular system. [1250–1300; ME *thrillen* orig., to penetrate, metathetic var. of *thirlen* to THIRL]

thrill•er (thril′ər), *n.* **1.** a person or thing that thrills. **2.** an exciting, suspenseful play or story, esp. a mystery story. [1885–90; 1920–25 for def. 2; THRILL + -ER[1]]

thrill•ing (thril′ing), *adj.* **1.** producing sudden, strong, and deep emotion or excitement. **2.** producing a tremor, as by chilling. **3.** vibrating; trembling; quivering. [1520–30; THRILL + -ING[2]] —**thrill′ing•ly,** *adv.*

thrip•pence (thrip′əns), *n.* threepence.

thrips (thrips), *n., pl.* **thrips.** any of several minute insects of the order Thysanoptera, that have long, narrow wings fringed with hairs and that infest and feed on a wide variety of weeds and crop plants. [1650–60; < NL < Gk *thríps* (sing.) woodworm]

thrive (thrīv), *v.i.,* **thrived** or **throve, thrived** or **thriv•en** (thriv′ən), **thriv•ing. 1.** to prosper; be fortunate or successful. **2.** to grow or develop vigorously; flourish: *The children thrived in the country.* [1150–1200; ME *thriven* < ON *thrīfast* to thrive, reflexive of *thrīfa* to grasp] —**thriv′er,** *n.* —**thriv′ing•ly,** *adv.*
—**Syn. 1.** advance. See **succeed.**

thro (thrōō), *prep. Archaic.* through. Also, **thro′.**

throat (thrōt), *n. Anat., Zool.* **1.** the passage from the mouth to the stomach or to the lungs, including the pharynx, esophagus, larynx, and trachea. **2.** some analogous or similar narrowed part or passage. **3.** the front of the neck below the chin and above the collarbone. **4.** the narrow opening between a fireplace and its flue or smoke chamber, often closed by a damper. **5.** *Naut., Mach.* swallow[1] (def. 13). **6.** *Naut.* **a.** Also called **nock.** the forward upper corner of a quadrilateral fore-and-aft sail. See diag. under **sail. b.** jaw[1] (def. 5). **7.** the forward edge of the opening in the vamp of a shoe. **8.** *Auto.* barrel (def. 14). **9. cut one's own throat,** to bring about one's own ruin: *He cut his own throat by being nasty to the boss.* **10. jump down someone's throat,** *Informal.* to disagree with, criticize, or scold overhastily: *Wait and let me finish before you jump down my throat.* **11. lump in one's throat,** a tight or uncomfortable feeling in the throat, as a reaction to an emotion: *The sight of the infant brought a lump to her throat.* **12. ram** or **force (something) down someone's throat,** *Informal.* to force someone to agree to or accept (something). **13. stick in one's throat,** to be difficult of expression; cause to hesitate: *The words of sympathy stuck in her throat.* —*v.t.* **14.** to make a throat in; provide with a throat. **15.** to utter or express from or as from the throat; utter throatily. [bef. 900; ME *throte,* OE *throte, throta, throtu;* akin to OHG *drozza* throat, ON *throti* swelling. See THROTTLE]

throat•ed (thrō′tid), *adj.* having a throat of a specified kind (usually used in combination): *a yellow-throated warbler.* [1520–30; THROAT + -ED[3]]

throat•latch (thrōt′lach′), *n.* a strap that passes under a horse's throat and helps to hold a bridle or halter in place. See illus. under **harness.** [1785–95; THROAT + LATCH]

throat′ mi′crophone, a microphone worn around the throat and actuated by vibrations of the larynx, used when background noise would obscure the sound of speech, as in an airplane cockpit. [1955–60]

throat′ seiz′ing. See **cuckold's knot.** [1865–70]

throat′ sweet′bread, sweetbread (def. 2).

throat•y (thrō′tē), *adj.,* **throat•i•er, throat•i•est.** produced or modified in the throat, as certain sounds; guttural, husky, or hoarse. [1635–45; THROAT + -Y[1]] —**throat′i•ly,** *adv.* —**throat′i•ness,** *n.*

throb (throb), *v.,* **throbbed, throb•bing,** *n.* —*v.i.* **1.** to beat with increased force or rapidity, as the heart under the influence of emotion or excitement; palpitate. **2.** to feel or exhibit emotion: *He throbbed at the happy thought.* **3.** to pulsate; vibrate: *The cello throbbed.* —*n.* **4.** the act of throbbing. **5.** a violent beat or pulsation, as of the heart. **6.** any pulsation or vibration: *the throb of engines.* [1325–75; ME **throbben,* implied in prp. *throbbant* throbbing < ?] —**throb′ber,** *n.* —**throb′bing•ly,** *adv.*
—**Syn. 3.** See **pulsate.**

throe (thrō), *n.* **1.** a violent spasm or pang; paroxysm. **2.** a sharp attack of emotion. **3. throes, a.** any violent convulsion or struggle: *the throes of battle.* **b.** the agony of death. **c.** the pains of childbirth. [1150–1200; ME *throwe,* alter. of *thrawe* (-o- from OE *thrōwian* to suffer, be in pain), OE *thrawu;* c. ON *thrā* (in *līkthrā* leprosy)]
—**Syn. 3a.** upheaval, tumult, chaos, turmoil.

throm•bec•to•my (throm bek′tə mē), *n., pl.* **-mies.** surgical removal of a blood clot from a blood vessel. [‡1960–65; THROMB(US) + -ECTOMY]

throm•bin (throm′bin), *n. Biochem.* an enzyme of the blood plasma that catalyzes the conversion of fibrinogen to fibrin, the last step of the blood clotting process. [1895–1900; THROMB(US) + -IN[2]]

thrombo-, a combining form with the meanings "blood clot," "coagulation," "thrombin," used in the formation of compound words: *thrombocyte.* Also, *esp. before a vowel,* **thromb-.** [< Gk, comb. form of *thrómbos* clot, lump]

throm•boc•la•sis (throm bok′lə sis), *n. Med.* thrombolysis. [‡1960–65; THROMBO- + -CLASIS] —**throm•bo•clas•tic** (throm′bə klas′tik), *adj.*

throm•bo•cyte (throm′bə sīt′), *n. Anat.* **1.** platelet. **2.** one of the minute, nucleate cells that aid coagulation in the blood of those vertebrates that do not have blood platelets. [1905–10; THROMBO- + -CYTE] —**throm•bo•cyt•ic** (throm′bə sit′ik), *adj.*

throm•bo•cy•to•pe•ni•a (throm′bō sī′tə pē′nē ə), *n.* an abnormal decrease in the number of blood platelets. [1920–25; THROMBOCYTE + -O- + -PENIA]

throm•bo•em•bo•lism (throm′bō em′bə liz′əm), *n. Pathol.* the blockage of a blood vessel by a thrombus carried through the bloodstream from its site of formation. [1905–10; THROMBO- + EMBOLISM] —**throm•bo•em•bol•ic** (throm′bō em bol′ik), *adj.*

throm•bo•gen (throm′bə jən, -jen′), *n. Biochem.* prothrombin. [1895–1900; THROMBO- + -GEN]

throm•bol•y•sis (throm bol′ə sis), *n. Med.* the dissolving or breaking up of a thrombus. Also called **thromboclasis.** [‡1960–65; THROMBO- + -LYSIS] —**throm•bo•lyt•ic** (throm′bə lit′ik), *adj.*

throm•bo•phle•bi•tis (throm′bō fli bī′tis), *n. Pathol.* the presence of a thrombus in a vein accompanied by inflammation of the vessel wall. Cf. **phlebothrombosis.** [1895–1900; < NL; see THROMBO-, PHLEBITIS]

throm•bo•plas•tic (throm′bə plas′tik), *adj. Biochem.* causing or accelerating blood-clot formation. [1910–15; THROMBO- + -PLASTIC] —**throm′bo•plas′ti•cal•ly,** *adv.*

throm•bo•plas•tin (throm′bə plas′tin), *n.* **1.** *Biochem.* a lipoprotein in the blood that converts prothrombin to thrombin. **2.** *Pharm.* a commercial form of this substance, obtained from the brains of cattle, used chiefly as a local hemostatic and as a laboratory reagent in blood prothrombin tests. Also called **throm•bo•ki•nase** (throm′bō kī′nās, -kin′ās). [1910–15; THROMBO- + -PLAST + -IN[2]]

throm•bo•sis (throm bō′sis), *n. Pathol.* intravascular coagulation of the blood in any part of the circulatory system, as in the heart, arteries, veins, or capillaries. [1700–10; < NL < Gk *thrómbōsis.* See THROMB-, -OSIS] —**throm•bot•ic** (throm bot′ik), *adj.*

throm•box•ane (throm bok′sān), *n. Biochem.* a compound, $C_{20}H_{32}O_5$, formed in blood platelets, that constricts blood vessels and promotes clotting. [1935–40; THROMB- + OX- + -ANE]

throm•bus (throm′bəs), *n., pl.* **-bi** (-bī). *Pathol.* a fibrinous clot that forms in and obstructs a blood vessel, or that forms in one of the chambers of the heart. [1685–95; < NL < Gk *thrómbos* clot, lump]

throne (thrōn), *n., v.,* **throned, thron•ing.** —*n.* **1.** the chair or seat occupied by a sovereign, bishop, or other exalted personage on ceremonial occasions, usually raised on a dais and covered with a canopy. **2.** the office or dignity of a sovereign: *He came to the throne by succession.* **3.** the occupant of a throne; sovereign. **4.** sovereign power or authority: *to address one's pleas to the throne.* **5.** an episcopal office or authority: *the diocesan throne.* **6.** See **mourner's bench. 7. thrones,** an order of angels. Cf. **angel** (def. 1). **8.** *Facetious.* a toilet. —*v.t., v.i.* **9.** to sit on or as on a throne. [1175–1225; ME < L *thronus* < Gk *thrónos* high seat; r. ME *trone* < OF < L, as above] —**throne′less,** *adj.*

throne′ room′, 1. a chamber, usually containing a throne, used by a sovereign for audiences. **2.** the location of actual power or authority, as in a particular government or business organization. [1860–65]

throng (thrông, throng), *n.* **1.** a multitude of people crowded or assembled together; crowd. **2.** a great number of things crowded or considered together: *a throng of memories.* **3.** *Chiefly Scot.* pressure, as of work. —*v.i.* **4.** to assemble, collect, or go in large numbers; crowd. —*v.t.* **5.** to crowd or press upon; jostle. **6.** to fill or occupy with or as with a crowd: *He thronged the picture with stars.* **7.** to bring or drive together into or as into a crowd, heap, or collection. **8.** to fill by crowding or pressing into: *They thronged the small room.* —*adj.* *Scot. and North Eng.* **9.** filled with people or objects; crowded. **10.** (of time) filled with things to do; busy. [bef. 1000; (n.) ME; OE *gethrang;* c. D *drang,* G *Drang* pressure, ON *throng* throng; (adj. and v.) ME; akin to the n.; cf. obs. *thring* to press]
—**Syn. 1.** horde, host; assemblage. See **crowd.**[1]

thro•nos (thrō′nos), *n., pl.* **-noi** (-noi). an ancient Greek chair, usually highly ornamented, having a high seat and back and rectangular turned or carved legs ending in animal feet. [1960–65; < Gk *thrónos;* see THRONE]

thros•tle (thros′əl), *n.* **1.** *Brit., Chiefly Literary.* the song thrush. **2.** *Obs.* a machine for spinning wool, cotton, etc., in which the twisting and winding are simultaneous and continuous. [bef. 900; ME, OE; c. D *drossel,* G *Drossel;* akin to ON *thrǫstr,* L *turdus* thrush]

throt•tle (throt′l), *n., v.,* **-tled, -tling.** —*n.* **1.** Also called **throttle lever.** a lever, pedal, handle, etc., for controlling or manipulating a throttle valve. **2.** See **throttle valve. 3.** the throat, gullet, or windpipe, as of a horse. **4. at full throttle,** at maximum speed. —*v.t.* **5.** to stop the breath of by compressing the throat; strangle. **6.** to choke or suffocate in any way. **7.** to compress by fastening something tightly around. **8.** to silence or check as if by choking: *His message was throttled by censorship.* **9.** *Mach.* **a.** to obstruct or check the flow of (a fluid), as to control the speed of an engine. **b.** to reduce the pressure of (a fluid) by passing it from a smaller area to a larger one. [1350–1400; (v.) ME *throtelen,* freq. of *throten* to cut the throat of (someone), strangle, deriv. of THROAT; (n.) prob. dim. of ME *throte* THROAT; cf. G *Drossel*] —**throt′tler,** *n.*

throt•tle•a•ble (throt′l ə bəl), *adj. Rocketry.* capable of having the thrust varied. [1955–60; THROTTLE + -ABLE]

throt′tle-bod•y injec′tion, (throt′l bod′ē), *Auto.* a fuel-injection system in which an injector **(throt′tle-body injec′tor)** delivers fuel to a central location within the intake manifold of the engine. *Abbr.:* TBI

Throt•tle•bot•tom (throt′l bot′əm), *n.* (*sometimes l.c.*) a harmless incompetent in public office. [after Alexander *Throttlebottom,* character in *Of Thee I Sing* (1932), musical comedy by George S. Kaufman and Morris Ryskind]

throt•tle•hold (throt′l hōld′), *n.* a stifling suppression: *The new regime kept a throttlehold on academic freedom.* [1930–35; THROTTLE + (STRANGLE)HOLD]

throt′tle lev′er, throttle (def. 1). [1860–65]

throt′tle valve′, a valve for throttling the working fluid of an engine, refrigerator, etc. [1805–15]

through (thrōō), *prep.* **1.** in at one end, side, or surface and out at the other: *to pass through a tunnel; We drove through Denver without stopping. Sun came through the window.* **2.** past; beyond: *to go through a stop sign without stopping.* **3.** from one to the other of; between or among the individual members or parts of: *to swing through the trees; This book has passed through many hands.* **4.** over the surface of, by way of, or within the limits or medium of: *to travel through a country; to fly through the air.* **5.** during the whole period of; throughout: *They worked through the night.* **6.** having reached the end of; done with: *to be through one's work.* **7.** to and including: *from 1900 through 1950.* **8.** by the means or instrumentality of; by the way or agency of: *It was through him they found out.* **9.** by reason of or in consequence of: *to run away through fear.* **10.** in at the first step of a process, treatment, or method of handling, passing through subsequent steps or stages in order, and finished, accepted, or out of the last step or stage: *The body of a car passes through 147 stages on the production line. The new tax bill finally got through Congress.* —*adv.* **11.** in at one end, side, or surface and out at the other: *to push a needle through; just passing through.* **12.** all the way; along the whole distance: *This train goes through to Boston.* **13.** throughout: *soaking wet through.* **14.** from the beginning to the end: *to read a letter through.* **15.** to the end: *to carry a matter through.* **16.** to a favorable or successful conclusion: *He barely managed to pull through.* **17. through and through, a.** through the whole extent of; thoroughly: *cold through and through.* **b.** from beginning to end; in all respects: *an aristocrat through and through.* —*adj.* **18.** having completed an action, process, etc.; finished: *Please be still until I'm through. When will you be through with school?* **19.** at the end of all relations or dealings: *My sister insists she's through with selfish friends.* **20.** passing or extending from one end, side, or surface to the other. **21.** traveling or moving to a destination without changing of trains, planes, etc.: *a through flight.* **22.** (of a road, route, way, course, etc., or of a ticket, routing order, etc.) admitting continuous or direct passage; having no interruption, obstruction, or hindrance: *a through highway; through ticket.* **23.** (of a bridge truss) having a deck or decks within the depth of the structure. Cf. **deck** (def. 21). **24.** of no further use or value; washed-up: *Critics say he's through as a writer.* [bef. 900; ME (prep. and adv.), metathetic var. of *thourgh,* OE *thurh,* c. G *durch;* akin to OE *therh,* Goth *thairh* through, OHG *derh* perforated, OE *thyrel* full of holes (adj.), hole (n.). See THIRL]
—**Syn. 8.** See **by.**

through′ bass′ (bās). See **figured bass.**

through-com•posed (thrōō′kəm pōzd′), *adj.* having different music for each verse: *a through-composed song.* Cf. **strophic** (def. 2).

through•ly (thrōō′lē), *adv. Archaic.* thoroughly. [1400–50; late ME; see THROUGH, -LY]

through-oth•er (thrōō′uth′ər), *adj. Chiefly Scot.* confused. Also, **through-ith•er** (thrōō′ith′ər). [1590–1600]

through•out (thrōō out′), *prep.* **1.** in or to every part of; everywhere in: *They searched throughout the house.* **2.** from the beginning to the end of: *He was bored throughout the play.* —*adv.* **3.** in every part: *rotten throughout.* **4.** at every moment or point: *following the text closely throughout.* [bef. 1000; ME *throw out,* OE *thurh ūt* through and out the other side (of). See THROUGH, OUT]

through•put (thrōō′po͝ot′), *n.* the quantity or amount of raw material processed within a given time, esp. the work done by an electronic computer in a given period of time. Also, **thruput.** [1920–25; from phrase *put through,* modeled on *output*]

through′ stone′, perpend[1]. [1795–1805]

through′ street′, a street along which the traffic has the right of way over vehicles entering or crossing at intersections. Cf. **stop street.** [1925–30]

through′-the-lens′ me′ter (thrōō′thə lenz′), *Photog.* a light meter employing a sensor cell located behind the taking lens. Also called **TTL meter.**

Through′ the Look′ing-Glass, a story for children (1871) by Lewis Carroll: the sequel to *Alice's Adventures in Wonderland.*

through•way (thrōō′wā′), *n.* thruway.

throve (thrōv), *v.* a pt. of **thrive.**

throw (thrō), *v.,* **threw, thrown, throw•ing,** *n.* —*v.t.* **1.** to propel or cast in any way, esp. to project or propel from the hand by a sudden forward motion or straightening of the arm and wrist: *to throw a ball.* **2.** to hurl or project (a missile), as a gun does. **3.** to project or cast (light, a shadow, etc.). **4.** to project (the voice). **5.** to make it appear that one's voice is coming from a place different from its source, as in ventriloquism. **6.** to direct or send forth (words, a glance, etc.). **7.** to put or cause to go or come into some place, position, condition,

CONCISE PRONUNCIATION KEY: *act, cāpe, dâre, pärt; set, ēqual; if, īce; ox, ōver, ôrder, oil, bo͝ok, bo͞ot, out; up, ûrge; child; sing; shoe; thin, that;* zh as in *treasure.* ə = *a* as in *alone, e* as in *system, i* as in *easily, o* as in *gallop, u* as in *circus;* ᵊ as in *fire* (fīᵊr), *hour* (ouᵊr). l and n can serve as syllabic consonants, as in *cradle* (krād′l), and *button* (but′n). See the full key inside the front cover.

etc., as if by hurling: *to throw someone into prison; to throw a bridge across a river; to throw troops into action.* **8.** to put on, off, or away hastily: *to throw a shawl over one's shoulders.* **9.** *Mach.* **a.** to move (a lever or the like) in order to activate, turn on, disconnect, etc., an apparatus or mechanism: *to throw the switch.* **b.** to connect, engage, disconnect, or disengage by such a procedure: *to throw the current.* **10.** to shape on a potter's wheel: *to throw a vase.* **11.** to bring to bear or invest: *Throw all your energy into your work. The FBI threw every available agent into the case.* **12.** to deliver a blow or punch: *He threw a hard left jab to his opponent's chin.* **13.** to cause to fall to the ground, esp. to hurl to the ground, as an opponent in wrestling. **14.** *Cards.* to play (a card). **15.** to lose (a game, race, or other contest) intentionally, as for a bribe. **16.** to cast (dice). **17.** to make (a cast) at dice: *She threw two sixes.* **18.** (of an animal, as a horse) to cause (someone) to fall off; unseat: *The horse threw his rider twice.* **19.** to give or host: *They threw a lavish party celebrating his 80th birthday.* **20.** (of domestic animals) to bring forth (young). **21.** *Textiles.* to twist (filaments) without attenuation in the production of yarn or thread. **22.** *Informal.* to overcome with astonishment or confusion; amaze, disconcert, or confuse: *It was her falsetto voice on top of it all that really threw me.* **23.** to turn on a lathe.
—*v.i.* **24.** to cast, fling, or hurl a missile or the like. **25. throw away, a.** to dispose of; discard. **b.** to employ wastefully; squander. **c.** to fail to use; miss (a chance, opportunity, etc.): *He threw away a college education and a professional career.* **26. throw back, a.** to retard the development or advancement of: *His illness threw him back a year at school.* **b.** to force into dependence upon or necessary use of. **c.** to return to; hark back. **d.** to revert to a type found in one's ancestry; manifest atavism: *Her red hair and blue eyes throw back to her great-grandmother.* **27. throw cold water on.** See **cold** (def. 20). **28. throw down the gauntlet** or **glove.** See **gauntlet**[1] (def. 5). **29. throw in,** *Informal.* **a.** to add as a bonus or gratuity: *They throw in breakfast with the room.* **b.** to bring into (a discussion, plan, etc.) as an addition; interject: *The president threw in an amusing anecdote to relieve the tension.* **c.** *Cards.* to abandon (a hand). **30. throw in the sponge.** See **sponge** (def. 11). **31. throw in the towel.** See **towel** (def. 2). **32. throw off, a.** to free oneself of; cast aside: *to throw off the wet poncho; to throw off the yoke of slavery.* **b.** to escape from or delay, as a pursuer. **c.** to give off; discharge. **d.** to perform or produce with ease: *The entertainer threw off a few songs and jokes to begin the show.* **e.** to confuse; fluster: *Thrown off by jeers, she forgot her lines.* **f.** *Australian Slang.* to criticize or ridicule (usually fol. by *at*). **33. throw oneself at (someone)** or **at (someone's head),** to strive to attract the interest or attention of, esp. in order to win the love or admiration of: *Don't expect me to throw myself at you.* **34. throw oneself into,** to engage in with energy or enthusiasm: *She threw herself into learning the new routines.* **35. throw oneself on** or **upon (someone),** to commit oneself to another's mercy, generosity, support, etc.; trust in: *The members of his wife's family have all thrown themselves on him.* **36. throw out, a.** to cast away; remove; discard. **b.** to bring up for consideration; propose: *The committee threw out a few suggestions.* **c.** to put out of mind; reject: *We can throw out that scheme.* **d.** *Baseball.* to cause to be out by throwing the ball to a fielder, esp. an infielder, in time to prevent a batter or runner from reaching base safely: *The shortstop backhanded the ball and threw the batter out at first.* **e.** to eject from a place, esp. forcibly: *He started making a disturbance so the bartenders threw him out.* **f.** to expel, as from membership in a club. **37. throw out the baby with the bathwater.** See **bathwater** (def. 2). **38. throw over,** to forsake; abandon: *She threw over her first husband for another man.* **39. throw the bull.** See **bull**[3] (def. 2). **40. throw together, a.** to make in a hurried and haphazard manner. **b.** to cause to associate: *Many nationalities have been thrown together in the American melting pot.* **41. throw up, a.** to give up; relinquish. **b.** to build hastily. **c.** to vomit. **d.** to point out, as an error; criticize. **e.** (of a hawk) to fly suddenly upward.
—*n.* **42.** an act or instance of throwing or casting; cast; fling. **43.** the distance to which anything is or may be thrown: *a stone's throw.* **44.** *Informal.* a venture or chance: *It was his last throw.* **45.** *Mach.* **a.** the distance between the center of a crankshaft and the center of the crankpins, equal to one half of the piston stroke. **b.** the distance between the center of a crankshaft and the center of an eccentric. **c.** the movement of a reciprocating part in one direction. **46.** (in a motion-picture theater) the distance between the projector and the screen. **47.** (in an auditorium or the like) the distance between a loudspeaker and the audience. **48.** the length of a beam of light: *a spotlight with a throw of 500 feet.* **49.** a scarf, boa, shawl, or the like. **50.** *Theat.* **a.** the distance to which a spotlight can be projected. **b.** the area illuminated by a spotlight. **51.** a light blanket, as for use when reclining on a sofa; afghan. **52.** a cast of dice. **53.** the number thrown with a pair of dice. **54.** *Wrestling.* the act, method, or an instance of throwing an opponent. **55.** *Geol., Mining.* the amount of vertical displacement produced by a fault. **56. a throw,** *Informal.* each: *He ordered four suits at $300 a throw.* [bef. 1000; ME *throwen, thrawen* (v.), OE *thrāwan* to twist, turn; c. D *draaien,* G *drehen* to turn, spin, twirl, whirl; akin to L *terere,* Gk *teírein* to rub away]
—Syn. 1. fling, launch, send. THROW, CAST, PITCH, TOSS imply projecting something through the air. THROW is the general word, often used with an adverb that indicates direction, destination, etc.: *to throw a rope to someone, the paper away.* CAST is a formal word for THROW, archaic except as used in certain idiomatic expressions (*to cast a net, black looks; cast down;* the compound *broadcast,* etc.): *to cast off a boat.* PITCH implies throwing with some force and definite aim: *to pitch a baseball.* To TOSS is to throw lightly, as with an underhand or sidewise motion, or to move irregularly up and down or back and forth: *to toss a bone to a dog.*

CONCISE ETYMOLOGY KEY: <, descended or borrowed from; >, whence; b., blend of, blended; c., cognate with; cf., compare; deriv., derivative; equiv., equivalent; imit., imitative; obl., oblique; r., replacing; s., stem; sp., spelling, spelled; resp., respelling, respelled; trans., translation; ?, origin unknown; *, unattested; ‡, probably earlier than. See the full key inside the front cover.

throw•a•way (thrō′ə wā′), *adj.* **1.** made or intended to be discarded after use or quick examination: *a throwaway container; a throwaway brochure.* **2.** delivered or expressed casually or extemporaneously: *a funny throwaway line that brings applause.* —*n.* **3.** something that is made or intended to be discarded. **4.** a handbill, advertising circular, pamphlet, etc., intended to be discarded after reading. **5.** Also called **pushout.** *Informal.* a youth who is unwanted or rejected by his or her family, the school system, or society in general. [1900–05; adj., n. use of v. phrase *throw away*]

throw•back (thrō′bak′), *n.* **1.** an act of throwing back. **2.** a setback or check. **3.** the reversion to an ancestral or earlier type or character; atavism. **4.** an example of this. [1855–60; 1915–20 for def. 3; n. use of v. phrase *throw back*]

throwed (thrōd), *v. Nonstandard.* a pt. and pp. of **throw.**

throw•er (thrō′ər), *n.* **1.** a person or thing that throws. **2.** flinger (def. 2). [1400–50; late ME; see THROW, -ER[1]]

throw′ing stick′, 1. a short, straight or curved stick, flat or cylindrical in form, often having a hand grip, and used generally in preliterate societies as a hunting weapon to throw at birds and small game. **2.** *Australian.* a boomerang. [1760–70]

thrown (thrōn), *v.* a pp. of **throw.**

thrown′ silk′, raw silk that has been reeled and twisted into yarn. Also called, *Brit.,* **net silk.** [1680–90]

throw′ pil′low, a small pillow placed on a chair, couch, etc., primarily for decoration. [1955–60]

throw′ rug′. See **scatter rug.** [1925–30]

throw•ster (thrō′stər), *n.* a person who throws silk or synthetic filaments. [1425–75; late ME *throwestre.* See THROW, -STER]

throw′ weight′, the lifting power, or payload maximum, of a ballistic missile exclusive of the weight of the rocket itself, and including the weight of the warhead or warheads and of guidance and penetration systems; ballistic delivery power: *larger Soviet missiles with a throw weight of up to 20 megatons.* Also, **throw′weight′.** [1965–70]

thru (thro͞o), *prep., adv., adj.* an informal, simplified spelling of **through.**

thrum[1] (thrum), *v.,* **thrummed, thrum•ming,** *n.* —*v.i.* **1.** to play on a stringed instrument, as a guitar, by plucking the strings, esp. in an idle, monotonous, or unskillful manner; strum. **2.** to sound when thrummed on, as a guitar or similar stringed instrument. **3.** to drum or tap idly with the fingers. —*v.t.* **4.** to play (a stringed instrument, or a melody on it) by plucking the strings, esp. in an idle, monotonous, or unskillful manner; strum. **5.** to drum or tap idly on. **6.** to recite or tell in a monotonous way. —*n.* **7.** an act or sound of thrumming; dull, monotonous sound. [1545–55; imit.] —**thrum′mer,** *n.*

thrum[2] (thrum), *n., v.,* **thrummed, thrum•ming.** —*n.* **1.** one of the ends of the warp threads in a loom, left unwoven and remaining attached to the loom when the web is cut off. **2. thrums,** the row or fringe of such threads. **3.** any short piece of waste thread or yarn; tuft, tassel, or fringe of threads, as at the edge of a piece of cloth. **4.** Often, **thrums.** *Naut.* short bits of rope yarn used for making mats. —*v.t.* **5.** *Naut.* to insert short pieces of rope yarn through (canvas) and thus give it a rough surface, as for wrapping about a part to prevent chafing. **6.** to furnish or cover with thrums, ends of thread, or tufts. [bef. 1000; ME *throm* end-piece, OE *-thrum,* in *tungethrum* ligament of the tongue, c. OHG *drum* end-piece; akin to ON *thrǫmr* brim, edge, L *terminus,* Gk *térma* end]

thrum•my (thrum′ē), *adj.,* **-mi•er, -mi•est.** of or abounding in thrums; shaggy or tufted. [1590–1600; THRUM[2] + -Y[1]]

thrump (thrump), *n.* a thumping, rumbling sound, usually repetitive: *the thrump of artillery echoing through the valley.* [1870–75; imit.]

thrup•pence (thrup′əns), *n.* threepence.

thru•put (thro͞o′po͝ot′), *n.* throughput.

thrush[1] (thrush), *n.* **1.** any of numerous, medium-sized songbirds of the family Turdinae, usually dull brown and often speckled below, and including many outstanding singers. **2.** any of various superficially similar birds, as the water thrushes. **3.** *Slang.* a female professional singer, esp. of popular songs. [bef. 900; ME *thrusche,* OE *thrysce;* c. OHG *drōsca*] —**thrush′like′,** *adj.*

wood thrush, *Hylocichla mustelina,* length 8 in. (20 cm)

thrush[2] (thrush), *n.* **1.** *Pathol.* a disease, esp. in children, characterized by whitish spots and ulcers on the membranes of the mouth, fauces, etc., caused by a parasitic fungus, *Candida albicans.* **2.** *Vet. Pathol.* (in horses) a diseased condition of the frog of the foot. [1655–65; akin to Dan *tröske,* Sw *torsk*]

thrust (thrust), *v.,* **thrust, thrust•ing,** *n.* —*v.t.* **1.** to push forcibly; shove; put or drive with force: *He thrust his way through the crowd. She thrust a dagger into his back.* **2.** to put boldly forth or impose acceptance of: *to thrust oneself into a conversation between others; to thrust a dollar into the waiter's hand.* **3.** to extend; present: *He thrust his fist in front of my face.* **4.** *Archaic.* to stab or pierce, as with a sword: *She thrust his back with a dagger.* —*v.i.* **5.** to push against something. **6.** to push or force one's way, as against obstacles or through a crowd. **7.** to make a thrust, lunge, or stab at something. —*n.* **8.** an act or instance of thrusting; a forcible push or shove; lunge or stab. **9.** a lunge or stab, as with a sword. **10.** *Mech.* a linear reactive force exerted by a propeller, propulsive gases, etc., to propel a ship, aircraft, etc. **11.** *Geol.* a compressive strain in the crust of the earth that, in its most characteristic development, produces reverse or thrust faults. **12.** the main point, purpose, or essence: *The thrust of his speech was an urgent appeal for votes.* **13.** *Mach.* a pushing force or pressure exerted by a thing or a part against a contiguous one. **14.** *Archit.* the downward and outward force exerted by an arch on each side. **15.** an organized military attack; assault; offensive. [1125–75; ME *thrusten, thrysten* (v.) < ON *thrȳsta* to thrust, force, press]

thrust′ augmenta′tion, *Rocketry.* an increase in the thrust of a jet or rocket engine, as by afterburning or reheating.

thrust′ bear′ing, *Mach.* a bearing designed to absorb thrusts parallel to the axis of revolution. [1860–65]

thrust•er (thrus′tər), *n.* **1.** a person or thing that thrusts. **2.** *Fox Hunting.* a rider who keeps in the front of the field. **3.** *Aerospace.* a small rocket attached to a spacecraft and used to control its attitude or translational motion. [1590–1600; THRUST + -ER[1]]

thrust′ fault′, *Geol.* a low-angle reverse fault produced in rocks subjected to thrust. [1900–05]

thrust′ stage′, a stage that extends beyond the proscenium arch and is usually surrounded on three sides by seats.

thru•way (thro͞o′wā′), *n.* a limited-access toll highway providing a means of direct transportation between distant areas for high-speed automobile traffic. Also, **throughway.** [1940–45; THRU + WAY[1]]

thrym•sa (thrim′zə, -sə), *n.* a coin of Anglo-Saxon England. [bef. 1000; borrowed by 17th-century antiquarians < OE, alter. of *trymesa* (by influence of *thrīe* three), gen. pl. of *trymes* < LL *tremis* a coin, equiv. to L *trē(s)* THREE + *-mis,* as in *semis* SEMIS]

Thu•cyd•i•des (tho͞o sid′i dēz′), *n.* c460–c400 B.C., Greek historian.

thud (thud), *n., v.,* **thud•ded, thud•ding.** —*n.* **1.** a dull sound, as of a heavy blow or fall. **2.** a blow causing such a sound. —*v.i.* **3.** to strike or fall with a dull sound of heavy impact. [1505–15; imit.; cf. ME *thudden,* OE *thyddan* to strike, press] —**thud′ding•ly,** *adv.*

thug (thug), *n.* **1.** a cruel or vicious ruffian, robber, or murderer. **2.** (*sometimes cap.*) one of a former group of professional robbers and murderers in India who strangled their victims. [1800–10; < Hindi *ṭhag* lit., rogue, cheat] —**thug•ger•y** (thug′ə rē), *n.* —**thug′gish,** *adj.*

thug•gee (thug′ē, thu gē′), *n.* (*sometimes cap.*) (in India) robbery and strangulation committed by thugs. [1830–40; < Hindi *ṭhagī*]

thu•ja (tho͞o′jə), *n.* **1.** any tree of the genus *Thuja,* comprising the arborvitaes. **2.** the wood of the sandarac tree. Also, **thuya.** [1750–60; < NL, ML *thuia,* < MGk *thuia,* for Gk *thýa* kind of African tree]

Thu•le (tho͞o′lē *for 1, 2;* to͞o′lē *for 3*), *n.* **1.** the ancient Greek and Latin name for an island or region variously identified as one of the Shetland Islands, Iceland, or Norway: supposed to be the most northerly region of the world. **2.** See **ultima Thule. 3.** a settlement in NW Greenland: site of U.S. air base. 749.

Thu•le (to͞o′lē), *adj.* of or pertaining to an Eskimo culture flourishing from A.D. 500–1400, and extending throughout the Arctic from Greenland to Alaska. [named after THULE, Greenland]

thu•li•a (tho͞o′lē ə), *n. Chem.* a dense, greenish-white powder, TmO_3, that on gentle heating exhibits a reddish incandescence: used in the manufacture of thulium metal. Also called **thu′lium ox′ide.** [1885–90; THULI(UM) + -A[4]]

thu•li•um (tho͞o′lē əm), *n. Chem.* a rare-earth metallic element found in the minerals euxenite, gadolinite, etc. *Symbol:* Tm; *at. wt.:* 168.934; *at. no.:* 69; *sp. gr.:* 9.32. [1875–80; < NL; see THULE, -IUM]

thumb (thum), *n.* **1.** the short, thick, inner digit of the human hand, next to the forefinger. **2.** the corresponding digit in other animals; pollex. **3.** the part of a glove or mitten for containing this digit. **4.** *Archit.* an ovolo or echinus molding. **5. all thumbs,** awkward; clumsy; bungling: *The visitor almost knocked over a vase and seemed to be all thumbs.* **6. thumbs down,** a gesture or expression of dissent or disapproval: *We turned thumbs down to that suggestion.* **7. thumbs up,** a gesture or expression of assent or approval. **8. under one's thumb,** under the power or influence of; subordinate to. Also, **under the thumb of.** —*v.t.* **9.** to soil or wear with the thumbs in handling, as the pages of a book. **10.** to glance through (the pages of a book, leaflet, etc.) quickly. **11.** to play (a guitar or other instrument) with or as with the thumbs. **12.** (of a hitchhiker) to solicit or get (a ride) by pointing the thumb in the desired direction of travel. **13. thumb one's nose, a.** to put one's thumb to one's nose and extend the fingers as a crudely defiant or contemptuous gesture. **b.** to express defiance or contempt; dismiss or reject contemptuously. [bef. 900; ME; OE *thūma*; c. D *duim*, OS, OHG *dūmo* (G *Daumen*), ON *thumall*; akin to L *tumēre* to swell (TUMOR)] —**thumb′less,** *adj.* —**thumb′like′,** *adj.*

thumb·er (thum′ər), *n. Informal.* a hitchhiker. [1930–35; THUMB + -ER[1]]

thumb′ glass′, a drinking glass having external indentations to allow it to be firmly grasped.

thumb·hole (thum′hōl′), *n.* a hole into which a thumb can be inserted, as to provide a grip. [1855–60; THUMB + HOLE]

thumb′ in′dex, a series of labeled notches cut along the fore edge of a book, to indicate the divisions or sections. [1900–05]

thumb-in·dex (thum′in′deks), *v.t.* to provide (a book) with a thumb index.

thumb·kin (thum′kin), *n.* thumbscrew (def. 2). Also, **thumb·i·kin** (thum′i kin), **thumb′i·kins.** [1675–85; THUMB + -KIN]

thumb·nail (thum′nāl′), *n.* **1.** the nail of the thumb. **2.** anything quite small or brief, as a small drawing or short essay. **3.** *Print.* a small, rough dummy. **4.** Also called **porkchop.** *Journ., Print.* a half-column portrait in a newspaper. —*adj.* **5.** quite small or brief; concise: *a thumbnail description of Corsica.* —*v.t.* **6.** to make a thumbnail sketch or description of. [1595–1605; THUMB + NAIL]

thumb·nut (thum′nut′), *n.* See **wing nut.** [1785–95; THUMB + NUT]

thumb′ pian′o, any of various African boxlike musical instruments, such as the kalimba or mbira, having tuned strips of metal or wood that vibrate when played with the thumbs. [1940–45]

thumb·piece (thum′pēs′), *n.* a lever over the hinge on the lid of a tankard, pressed by the thumb to raise the lid. Also called **billet.** [1750–60; THUMB + PIECE]

thumb·print (thum′print′), *n.* a mark or impression of the ventral surface of the last joint of the thumb. [1895–1900; THUMB + PRINT]

thumb·screw (thum′skrōō′), *n.* **1.** a screw, the head of which is so constructed that it may be turned easily with the thumb and a finger. **2.** Often, **thumbscrews.** an old instrument of torture by which one or both thumbs were compressed. [1705–15; THUMB + SCREW]

thumbs-down (thumz′doun′), *n. Informal.* an act or instance of dissent, disapproval, etc. [1885–90]

thumb·stall (thum′stôl′), *n.* a protective sheath of rubber, leather, or the like for the thumb. [1580–90; THUMB + STALL[1]]

thumb·suck·er (thum′suk′ər), *n.* a person who habitually sucks a thumb. —**thumb′-suck′ing,** *n.*

thumbs-up (thumz′up′), *n. Informal.* an act, instance, or gesture of assent, approval, or the like. [1920–25]

thumb·tack (thum′tak′), *n.* **1.** a tack with a large, flat head, designed to be thrust into a board or other fairly soft object or surface by the pressure of the thumb. —*v.t.* **2.** to attach or tack by means of a thumbtack. [1880–85, *Amer.*; THUMB + TACK[1]]

thump (thump), *n.* **1.** a blow with something thick and heavy, producing a dull sound; a heavy knock. **2.** the sound made by or as if by such a blow. —*v.t.* **3.** to strike or beat with something thick and heavy, so as to produce a dull sound; pound. **4.** (of an object) to strike against (something) heavily and noisily. **5.** *Informal.* to thrash severely. —*v.i.* **6.** to strike, beat, or fall heavily, with a dull sound. **7.** to walk with heavy steps; pound. **8.** to palpitate or beat violently, as the heart. [1530–40; imit.] —**thump′er,** *n.*

thump·ing (thum′ping), *adj.* **1.** of, like, or pertaining to a thump. **2.** strikingly great, immense, exceptional, or impressive; resounding: *a thumping victory at the polls.* [1570–80; THUMP + -ING[2]] —**thump′ing·ly,** *adv.*

Thun (tōōn), *n.* **1.** a city in central Switzerland, on the Aar River, near the Lake of Thun. 36,765. **2. Lake of.** German, **Thuner See.** a lake in central Switzerland, formed by a widening in the course of the Aar River. 10 mi. (16 km) long.

thun·ber·gi·a (thun bûr′jē ə), *n.* any of various plants, vines, or shrubs belonging to the genus *Thunbergia*, of the acanthus family, native to Africa and southern Asia, having variously colored flowers and often cultivated as ornamentals in warm regions. [1835–45; < NL, named after Carl P. *Thunberg* (1743–1822), Swedish botanist; see -IA]

thun·der (thun′dər), *n.* **1.** a loud, explosive, resounding noise produced by the explosive expansion of air heated by a lightning discharge. **2.** any loud, resounding noise: *the thunder of applause.* **3.** a threatening or startling utterance, denunciation, or the like. **4. steal someone's thunder, a.** to use for one's own purposes and without the knowledge or permission of the originator the inventions or ideas of another. **b.** to ruin or detract from the effect of a performance, remark, etc., by anticipating it. —*v.i.* **5.** to give forth thunder (often used impersonally with *it* as the subject): *It thundered last night.* **6.** to make a loud, resounding noise like thunder: *The artillery thundered in the hills.* **7.** to utter loud or vehement denunciations, threats, or the like. **8.** to speak in a very loud tone. **9.** to move or go with a loud noise or violent action: *The train thundered through the village.* —*v.t.* **10.** to strike, drive, inflict, give forth, etc., with loud noise or violent action. [bef. 900; (n.) ME *thonder, thunder*, OE *thunor*; c. D *donder*, G *Donner*; ON *thōrr* Thor, lit., thunder; (v.) ME *thondren*, OE *thunrian*, deriv. of the v.; akin to L *tonāre* to thunder] —**thun′der·er,** *n.* —**thun′der·less,** *adj.*

thun·der·a·tion (thun′də rā′shən), *interj.* an exclamation of surprise or petulance. [1830–40, *Amer.*; THUNDER + -ATION]

Thun′der Bay′, a port in W Ontario, in S Canada, on Lake Superior: created in 1970 by the merger of twin cities (**Fort William** and **Port Arthur**) and two adjoining townships. 108,411. Also called **Lakehead.**

thun·der·bird (thun′dər bûrd′), *n.* (in the mythology of some North American Indians) a huge, eaglelike bird capable of producing thunder, lightning, and rain. [1820–30; THUNDER + BIRD]

thun·der·bolt (thun′dər bōlt′), *n.* **1.** a flash of lightning with the accompanying thunder. **2.** an imaginary bolt or dart conceived as the material destructive agent cast to earth in a flash of lightning: *the thunderbolts of Jove.* **3.** something very destructive, terrible, severe, sudden, or startling. **4.** a person who acts with fury or with sudden and irresistible force. [1400–50; late ME *thondre bolte.* See THUNDER, BOLT[1]]

thun·der·clap (thun′dər klap′), *n.* **1.** a crash of thunder. **2.** something resembling a thunderclap, as in loudness or unexpectedness. [1350–1400; ME *thonder clappe.* See THUNDER, CLAP[1]]

thun·der·cloud (thun′dər kloud′), *n.* cumulonimbus. Also, **thun′der·clouds′.** [1690–1700; THUNDER + CLOUD]

thun′der egg′, *Geol.* a globular concretion of opal, agate, or chalcedony weathered out of tuff or basalt. Cf. **geode.** [1940–45]

thun·der·head (thun′dər hed′), *n. Meteorol.* **1.** incus (def. 2). **2.** cumulonimbus. **3.** the upper portion of a cumulus cloud characterized by dense, sharply defined, cauliflowerlike upper parts and sometimes by great verticality. [1850–55, *Amer.*; THUNDER + HEAD]

thun·der·ing (thun′dər ing), *adj.* **1.** of, pertaining to, or accompanied by thunder. **2.** producing a noise or effect like thunder. **3.** very great; extraordinary: *a thundering amount of work.* —*n.* **4.** thunder. [bef. 1100; ME *thundring*, OE *thunring* thunder. See THUNDER, -ING[2], -ING[1]] —**thun′der·ing·ly,** *adv.*

thun′der mug′, *Older Slang.* a chamber pot. [1885–90]

thun·der·ous (thun′dər əs, -drəs), *adj.* producing thunder or a loud noise like thunder: *thunderous applause.* Also, **thundery.** [1575–85; THUNDER + -OUS] —**thun′der·ous·ly,** *adv.*

thun·der·peal (thun′dər pēl′), *n.* a crash of thunder; thunderclap. [1795–1805; THUNDER + PEAL]

thun·der·show·er (thun′dər shou′ər), *n.* a shower accompanied by thunder and lightning. [1690–1700; THUNDER + SHOWER]

thun·der·squall (thun′dər skwôl′), *n.* a combined squall and thunderstorm. [THUNDER + SQUALL[1]]

thun·der·stick (thun′dər stik′), *n.* bull-roarer. [1960–65; THUNDER + STICK[1]]

thun·der·storm (thun′dər stôrm′), *n.* a transient storm of lightning and thunder, usually with rain and gusty winds, sometimes with hail or snow, produced by cumulonimbus clouds. Also called **electrical storm.** [1645–55; THUNDER + STORM]

thun·der·strike (thun′dər strīk′), *v.t.* **-struck** (-struk′), **-struck** or **-strick·en** (-strik′ən), **-strik·ing.** **1.** *Archaic.* to strike with a thunderbolt. **2.** to astonish; dumfound. [1605–15; prob. back formation from earlier *thunderstricken* (adj.); see THUNDER, STRIKE]

thun·der·stroke (thun′dər strōk′), *n.* a stroke of lightning accompanied by thunder. [1580–90; THUNDER + STROKE[1]]

thun·der·struck (thun′dər struk′), *adj.* **1.** overcome with consternation; confounded; astounded: *He was thunderstruck by the news of his promotion.* **2.** *Archaic.* struck by a thunderbolt. Also, **thun·der·strick·en** (thun′dər strik′ən). [1605–15; THUNDER + STRUCK]
—**Syn. 1.** dumbfounded, flabbergasted, overcome.

thun·der·y (thun′də rē), *adj.* thunderous. [1590–1600; THUNDER + -Y[1]]

Thü·nen (tōō′nən), *n.* **Jo·hann Hein·rich von** (yō′hän hīn′rīkh fən), 1783–1850, German economic theorist.

Thu·ner See (tōō′nər zā′), German name of Lake of Thun.

thunk[1] (thungk), *n.* **1.** an abrupt, dull sound: *the thunk of a shutting window.* —*v.i.* **2.** to make such a sound: *The window thunked shut.* [1945–50; b. THUD and CLUNK]

thunk[2] (thungk), *v. Nonstandard.* a pt. and pp. of **think**[1].

Thur., Thursday.

Thur·ber (thûr′bər), *n.* **James (Gro·ver)** (grō′vər), 1894–1961, U.S. writer, caricaturist, and illustrator.

Thur·gau (tōōr′gou), *n.* a canton in NE Switzerland. 184,500; 388 sq. mi. (1005 sq. km). *Cap.:* Frauenfeld.

thu·ri·ble (thŏŏr′ə bəl), *n.* a censer. [1400–50; late ME *turrible, thoryble* < L *t(h)ūribulum* censer, equiv. to *t(h)ūr-* (s. of *t(h)ūs*) incense + *-i-* -I- + *-bulum* instrumental suffix]

thu·ri·fer (thŏŏr′ə fər), *n.* a person who carries the thurible in religious ceremonies. [1850–55; < NL, n. use of L *t(h)ūrifer* incense-bearing, equiv. to *t(h)ūr-* (s. of *t(h)ūs*) incense + *-i-* -I- + *-fer* bearing; see -FER]

Thu·rin·ger (thŏŏr′in jər, tir′-), *n.* a mildly seasoned cervelat, either fresh or smoked. Also, **Thü·ring·er** (thŏŏr′in jər; *Ger.* tʏ′ring ər). [1920–25; < G, short for *Thüringerwurst* Thuringian sausage]

Thu·rin·gi·a (thŏŏ rin′jē ə, -jə), *n.* a state in central Germany. 2,500,000; 5985 sq. mi. (15,500 sq. km). *Cap.:* Erfurt. German, **Thü·ring·en** (tʏ′ring ən). —**Thu·rin′gi·an,** *adj., n.*

Thurin′gian For′est, a forested mountain region in central Germany: a resort area. German, **Thü·ring·er Wald** (tʏ′ring ər vält′).

thurl (thûrl), *n.* the hip joint of cattle. [orig. uncert.]

Thur·low (thûr′lō), *n.* **Edward, 1st Baron,** 1731–1806, British statesman: Lord Chancellor 1778–92.

thurm (thûrm), *v.t.* to carve (a piece of wood, as a post or table leg) across the grain so as to produce an effect of turning. [1895–1900; perh. metathetic var. of THRUM[2]]

Thurs., Thursday.

Thurs·day (thûrz′dā, -dē), *n.* the fifth day of the week, following Wednesday. *Abbr.:* Th., Thur., Thurs. [bef. 950; ME; OE *Thursdæg* < ODan *Thūrsdagr* lit., Thor's day; r. OE *Thunres dæg*; c. D *donderdag*, G *Donnerstag* (all repr. Gmc trans. of LL *diēs Jovis*). See THOR, THUNDER, DAY]

Thurs′day Is′land, an island in Torres Strait between NE Australia and New Guinea; part of Queensland: pearl fishing. 2283; 1½ sq. mi. (4 sq. km).

Thurs·days (thûrz′dāz, -dēz), *adv.* on Thursdays; every Thursday. [THURSDAY + -S[1]]

Thur·ston (thûr′stən), *n.* a male given name: from a Scandinavian word meaning "Thor's stone."

thus (*th*us), *adv.* **1.** in the way just indicated; in this way: *Stated thus, the problem seems trivial.* **2.** in such or the following manner; so: *Thus it came to pass.* **3.** accordingly; consequently: *It is late, and thus you must go.* **4.** to this extent or degree: *thus far.* **5.** as an example; for instance. [bef. 900; ME, OE; c. D *dus*]
—**Usage.** See **thusly.**

thus·ly (*th*us′lē), *adv.* thus. [1860–65, *Amer.*; THUS + -LY]
—**Usage.** Some speakers and writers regard THUSLY as a pointless synonym for THUS, and they avoid it or use it only for humorous effect.

Thus′ Spake′ Zarathus′tra, (German, *Also sprach Zarathustra*), a philosophical work in poetic form (1883) by Friedrich Nietzsche.

Thut·mo·se I (thōōt mō′sə, -mōs′), *n.* fl. c1500 B.C., Egyptian ruler. Also, **Thotmes I, Thothmes I, Thut·mo·sis I** (thōōt mō′sis).

Thutmose II, fl. c1495 B.C., Egyptian ruler, son of Thutmose I, half brother of Thutmose III. Also, **Thotmes II, Thothmes II, Thutmosis II.**

Thutmose III, fl. c1475 B.C., Egyptian ruler: conqueror of the Middle East. Also, **Thotmes III, Thothmes III, Thutmosis III.**

thu·ya (thōō′yə), *n.* thuja.

thwack (thwak), *v.t.* **1.** to strike or beat vigorously with something flat; whack. —*n.* **2.** a sharp blow with something flat. [1520–30; imit.] —**thwack′er,** *n.*

thwart (thwôrt), *v.t.* **1.** to oppose successfully; prevent from accomplishing a purpose. **2.** to frustrate or baffle (a plan, purpose, etc.). **3.** *Archaic.* **a.** to cross. **b.** to extend across. —*n.* **4.** a seat across a boat, esp. one used by a rower. **5.** a transverse member spreading the gunwales of a canoe or the like. —*adj.* **6.** passing or lying crosswise or across; cross; transverse. **7.** perverse; obstinate. **8.** adverse; unfavorable. —*prep., adv.* **9.** across; athwart. [1200–50; ME *thwert* (adv.) < ON *thvert* across, neut. of *thverr* transverse; c. OE *thweorh* crooked, cross, Goth *thwairhs* cross, angry] —**thwart′ed·ly,** *adv.* —**thwart′er,** *n.*
—**Syn. 1.** hinder, obstruct. THWART, FRUSTRATE, BAFFLE imply preventing one, more or less completely, from accomplishing a purpose. THWART and FRUSTRATE apply to purposes, actions, plans, etc., BAFFLE, to the psychological state of the person thwarted. THWART suggests stopping one by opposing, blocking, or in some way running counter to one's efforts. FRUSTRATE implies rendering all attempts or efforts useless or ineffectual, so that nothing ever comes of them. BAFFLE suggests causing defeat by confusing, puzzling, or perplexing, so that a situation seems too hard a problem to understand or solve.

Thwing (twing), *n.* **Charles Franklin,** 1853–1937, U.S. educator and Congregational clergyman.

thy (*th*ī), *pron.* the possessive case of *thou* (used as an attributive adjective before a noun beginning with a consonant sound): *thy table.* Cf. **thine.** [1125–75; ME; var. of THINE]

Thy·a·ti·ra (thī′ə tī′rə), *n.* ancient name of **Akhisar.**

Thy·es·tes (thī es′tēz), *n. Class. Myth.* the brother of Atreus who unknowingly ate the flesh of his own sons when served to him by Atreus. —**Thy·es·te·an** (thī es′tē ən, thī′e stē′ən), **Thy·es′ti·an,** *adj.*

thy·la·cine (thī′lə sīn′, -sin), *n.* a wolflike marsupial, *Thylacinus cynocephalus,* of Tasmania, tan-colored with black stripes across the back: probably extinct. Also called **Tasmanian wolf.** [1830–40; < NL *Thylacinus* genus name, equiv. to *thylac-* (< Gk *thýlakos* pouch) + *-īnus* -INE[1]]

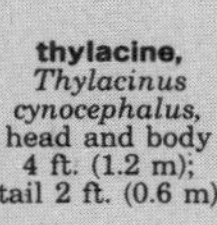

thylacine, *Thylacinus cynocephalus,* head and body 4 ft. (1.2 m); tail 2 ft. (0.6 m)

thy·la·koid (thī′lə koid′), *n. Cell Biol.* a flattened sac or vesicle lined with a pigmented membrane that is the site of photosynthesis, in plants and algae occurring in interconnected stacks constituting a granum of the chloroplast, and in other photosynthesizing organisms occurring either singly or as part of the cell membrane or other structure. [1965–70; < G *Thylakoid* < Gk *thylakoeidḗs* resembling a bag, equiv. to *thýlak(os)* sack + *-oeidēs* -OID]

thyme (tīm; *spelling pron.* thīm), *n.* any of numerous plants belonging to the genus *Thymus,* of the mint family, including the common garden herb *T. vulgaris,* a low subshrub having narrow, aromatic leaves used for seasoning. [1350–1400; ME < L *thymum* < Gk *thýmon*]

thy·mec·to·my (thī mek′tə mē), *n., pl.* **-mies.** surgical removal of the thymus gland. [1900–05; THYM(US) + -ECTOMY]

-thymia, a combining form used in the formation of compound words that denote mental disorders, as specified by the initial element: *alexithymia; cyclothymia; dysthymia.* [< Gk, equiv. to *thȳm(ós)* soul, spirit, mind + *-ia* -IA]

thym·ic[1] (tī′mik; *spelling pron.* thī′mik), *adj.* pertaining to or derived from thyme. [1865–70; THYME + -IC]

thym·ic[2] (thī′mik), *adj.* of or pertaining to the thymus. [1650–60; THYM(US) + -IC]

thy·mi·dine (thī′mi dēn′), *n. Biochem.* a nucleoside, $C_{10}H_{14}N_2O_5$, containing thymine and deoxyribose, that is a constituent of DNA. [b. THYMINE and -IDE]

thy·mine (thī′mēn, -min), *n. Biochem.* a pyrimidine base, $C_5H_6N_2O_2$, that is one of the principal components of DNA, in which it is paired with adenine. *Symbol:* T [1890–95; THYM(IC)[2] + -INE[2]]

thy·mo·cyte (thī′mə sīt′), *n. Immunol.* a cell that develops in the thymus and is the precursor of T cells. [1920–25; THYM(US) + -O- + -CYTE]

thy·mol (thī′mōl, -môl), *n. Chem., Pharm.* a colorless, crystalline, slightly water-soluble solid, $C_{10}H_{14}O$, having a pungent, aromatic taste and odor, obtained from the oil distilled from thyme or prepared synthetically: used chiefly in perfumery, embalming, preserving biological specimens, and in medicine as a fungicide and antiseptic. Also called **thyme′ cam′phor, thym′ic ac′id** (tī′mik). [1855–60; THYME + -OL[2]]

thy·mo·sin (thī′mə sin), *n. Biochem.* a hormone, produced by the thymus gland, that promotes the development of T cells from stem cells. [1966; THYM(US) + -IN[2]]

thy·mus (thī′məs), *n., pl.* **-mus·es, -mi** (-mī). *Anat.* a ductless, butterfly-shaped gland lying at the base of the neck, formed mostly of lymphatic tissue and aiding in the production of T cells of the immune system: after puberty, the lymphatic tissue gradually degenerates. Also called **thy′mus gland′.** [1685–95; < NL < Gk *thýmos* warty excrescence, thymus]

thym·y (tī′mē; *spelling pron.* thī′mē), *adj.,* **thym·i·er, thym·i·est.** of, pertaining to, resembling, or characteristic of thyme: *a thymy fragrance.* [1720–30; THYME + -Y[1]]

Thy·o·ne (thī′ō nē′, thī′ə-), *n. Class. Myth.* Semele, as named by her son Dionysus when he took her from the underworld to Olympus.

thy·ra·tron (thī′rə tron′), *n. Electronics.* a gas-filled, hot-cathode tube in which one or more control electrodes initiate, but do not limit and cannot interrupt, the flow of electrons. [1925–30; < Gk *thýra* DOOR + -TRON]

thy·ris·tor (thī ris′tər), *n. Electronics.* a semiconductor device having two stable states, used as an electronic switch. [1965–70; THYR(ATRON) + (TRANS)ISTOR]

thyro-, a combining form representing **thyroid** in the formation of compound words: *thyrotropin.* Also, *esp. before a vowel,* **thyr-.**

thy·roid (thī′roid), *adj.* **1.** of or pertaining to the thyroid gland. **2.** of or pertaining to the largest cartilage of the larynx, forming the projection known in humans as the Adam's apple. —*n.* **3.** See **thyroid gland. 4.** the thyroid cartilage. See diag. under **larynx. 5.** an artery, vein, etc., in the thyroid region. **6.** *Med.* a preparation made from the thyroid glands of certain animals, used in treating hypothyroid conditions. [1685–95; var. of *thyreoid* < Gk *thyreoeidḗs* shield-shaped, equiv. to *thyre(ós)* oblong shield (lit., doorlike object, equiv. to *thýr(a)* DOOR + *-eos* adj. suffix) + *-oeidēs* -OID] —**thy·roi′dal,** *adj.* —**thy′roid·less,** *adj.*

thy·roid·ec·to·my (thī′roi dek′tə mē), *n., pl.* **-mies.** *Surg.* excision of all or a part of the thyroid gland. [1885–90; THYROID + -ECTOMY]

CONCISE ETYMOLOGY KEY: <, descended or borrowed from; >, whence; b., blend of, blended; c., cognate with; cf., compare; deriv., derivative; equiv., equivalent; imit., imitative; obl., oblique; r., replacing; s., stem; sp., spelling, spelled; resp., respelling, respelled; trans., translation; ?, origin unknown; *, unattested; ‡, probably earlier than. See the full key inside the front cover.

thy′roid gland′, *Anat.* a two-lobed endocrine gland, located at the base of the neck that secretes two hormones that regulate the rates of metabolism, growth, and development. Cf. **thyroxine, triiodothyronine.** [1685–95]

thy·roid·i·tis (thī′roi dī′tis), *n. Pathol.* inflammation of the thyroid gland. [1880–85; THYROID + -ITIS]

thy′roid-stim·u·lat·ing hor′mone (thī′roid stim′yə lā′ting). *Biochem.* thyrotropin. *Abbr.:* TSH [1955–60]

thy·ro·sis (thī rō′sis), *n.* any condition resulting from abnormal functioning of the thyroid gland. [THYR(OID) + -OSIS]

thy·ro·tome (thī′rə tōm′), *n. Surg.* an instrument for cutting the thyroid cartilage. [THYRO- + -TOME]

thy·rot·o·my (thī rot′ə mē), *n., pl.* **-mies.** *Surg.* incision or splitting of the thyroid cartilage; laryngotomy. Cf. **thyroidectomy.** [1875–80; THYRO- + -TOMY]

thy·ro·tox·ic (thī′rō tok′sik), *adj. Pathol.* of or pertaining to a condition caused by excessive thyroid hormone in the system, usually resulting from overactivity of the thyroid gland. [1900–05; THYRO- + TOXIC] —**thy′ro·tox·ic′i·ty** (thī′rō tok sis′i tē), *n.*

thy·ro·tox·i·co·sis (thī′rō tok′si kō′sis), *n. Pathol.* See **Graves' disease.** [1915–20; THYRO- + TOXICOSIS]

thy·ro·troph·ic (thī′rə trof′ik, -trō′fik), *adj.* capable of stimulating the thyroid gland. Also, **thy·ro·trop·ic** (thī′rə trop′ik, -trō′pik). [1920–25; THYRO- + -TROPHIC]

thy·ro·tro·pin (thī′rə trō′pin, thī ro′trə-), *n. Biochem.* an anterior pituitary hormone that regulates the activity of the thyroid gland. Also, **thy·ro·tro·phin** (thī′rə trō′fin, thī ro′trə-). Also called **thyroid-stimulating hormone.** [1935–40; THYRO- + -TROPE + -IN[2]]

thy·ro·tro′pin-re·leas·ing hor′mone, (thī′rə trō′pin ri lē′sing, thī ro′trə-), *Biochem.* a small peptide hormone, produced by the hypothalamus, that controls the release of thyrotropin by the pituitary. Also called **thy·ro·tro′pin-re·leas·ing fac′tor.** *Abbr.:* TRH [1965–70]

thy·rox·ine (thī rok′sēn, -sin), *n.* **1.** *Biochem.* the thyroid gland hormone that regulates the metabolic rate of the body. **2.** *Pharm.* a commercial form of this compound, obtained from the thyroid glands of animals or synthesized, used in the treatment of hypothyroidism. *Symbol.:* T_4 Also, **thy·rox·in** (thī rok′sin). [1915–20; THYR- + OX- + IN(DOL)E (orig. thought to be a chemical component)]

thyrse (thûrs), *n. Bot.* a compact branching inflorescence, as of the lilac, in which the main axis is indeterminate and the lateral axes are determinate. Also, **thyrsus.** [1595–1605; < F < L *thyrsus* THYRSUS]

thyr·soid (thûr′soid), *adj. Bot.* having somewhat the form of a thyrsus. Also, **thyr·soi′dal.** [1820–30; < Gk *thyrsoeidḗs* thyrsuslike. See THYRSUS, -OID]

thyr·sus (thûr′səs), *n., pl.* **-si** (-sī). **1.** *Bot.* a thyrse. **2.** *Gk. Antiq.* a staff tipped with a pine cone and sometimes twined with ivy and vine branches, borne by Dionysus and his votaries. [1585–95; < L < Gk *thýrsos* Bacchic staff, stem of plant]

thy·sa·nop·ter·an (thī′sə nop′tər ən, this′ə-), *adj.* **1.** Also, **thy′sa·nop′ter·ous.** belonging or pertaining to the insect order Thysanoptera, comprising the thrips. —*n.* **2.** Also, **thysanopteron.** a thysanopteran insect; a thrips. [1890–95; < NL *Thysanopter(a)* order name (< Gk *thýsan(os)* tassel, fringe + *-o-* -O- + *-ptera,* neut. pl. of *-pteros* -winged; see -PTEROUS) + -AN]

thy·sa·nop·ter·on (thī′sə nop′tə ron′, this′ə-), *n., pl.* **-ter·a** (-tər ə). thysanopteran.

thy·sa·nu·ran (thī′sə no͝or′ən, -nyo͝or′-, this′ə-), *adj.* **1.** Also, **thy′sa·nu′rous.** belonging or pertaining to the order Thysanura, comprising the bristletails. —*n.* **2.** a thysanuran insect; bristletail. [1820–30; < NL *Thysanur(a)* (< Gk *thýsan(os)* tassel + *-oura,* neut. pl. of *-ouros* -tailed, adj. deriv. of *ourá* tail) + -AN]

thy·self (t͟hī self′), *pron.* **1.** an emphatic appositive to *thou* or *thee.* **2.** a substitute for reflexive *thee.* [bef. 900; ME *thi self* (see THY, SELF (n.)); r. OE *thē self* (see THEE, SELF (adj.))]

Thys·sen (tis′ən), *n.* **Fritz** (frits), 1873–1951, German industrialist.

THz, terahertz.

ti[1] (tē), *n., pl.* **tis.** *Music.* **1.** the syllable for the seventh tone of a diatonic scale. **2.** (in the fixed system of solmization) the tone B. Also, **te.** Cf. **sol-fa** (def. 1). [1835–45; substituted for *si* to avoid confusion with the sharp of *sol.* See GAMUT]

ti[2] (tē), *n., pl.* **tis.** a widely cultivated tropical plant, *Cordyline terminalis,* of the agave family, having narrow, leathery, often variegated leaves and yellowish, white, or reddish flowers. [1830–40; < Polynesian]

Ti, *Symbol, Chem.* titanium.

TIA, See **transient ischemic attack.**

Ti·a·hua·na·co (tē′ə wə nä′kō), *adj.* of or pertaining to a pre-Incan culture existing c300 B.C.–A.D. c900, chiefly in Peru and Bolivia, characterized by the use of megalithic masonry carved with geometric and animal designs, stone statues, polychrome pottery, and bronze artifacts. Also, **Ti·a·hua·na·cu** (tē′ə wə nä′ko͞o). —**Ti′a·hua·na′can,** *n.*

Ti·a Jua·na (tē′ə wä′nə), Tijuana.

Tia·mat (tyä′mät), *n.* an Akkadian goddess, the consort of Apsu and mother of the gods.

Tian′an′men′ Square′ (tyän′än′men′), a large plaza in central Beijing, China: noted esp. as the site of major student demonstrations in 1989 suppressed by the government. Also, **Tienanmen Square.**

Tian·jin (tyän′jin′), *n. Pinyin.* a port in E Hebei province, in NE China. 6,280,000. Also, **Tientsin.**

Tian Shan (tyän′ shän′). See **Tien Shan.**

ti·ar·a (tē ar′ə, -är′ə, -âr′ə), *n.* **1.** a jeweled, ornamental coronet worn by women. **2.** *Rom. Cath. Ch.* a headpiece consisting of three coronets on top of which is an orb and a cross, worn by the pope, or carried before him during certain nonliturgical functions. **3.** the position, authority, and dignity of the pope. **4.** a high headdress, or turban, worn by the ancient Persians and others. [1545–55; < L: headdress < Gk *tiára* kind of turban] —**ti·ar′aed,** *adj.* —**ti·ar′a·like′,** *adj.*

Tib·bett (tib′it), *n.* **Lawrence (Mer·vil)** (mûr′vil), 1896–1960, U.S. baritone.

Ti·ber (tī′bər), *n.* a river in central Italy, flowing through Rome into the Mediterranean. 244 mi. (395 km) long. Italian, **Tevere.**

Ti·be·ri·an (tī bēr′ē ən), *adj.* **1.** of or pertaining to the emperor Tiberius. **2.** of or pertaining to the Sea of Tiberias. [TIBERI(US) or TIBERI(AS) + -AN; cf. L *Tiberiānus*]

Ti·be·ri·as (tī bēr′ē əs), *n.* **Lake.** See **Galilee, Sea of.**

Ti·be·ri·us (tī bēr′ē əs), *n.* (*Tiberius Claudius Nero Caesar*) 42 B.C.–A.D. 37, Roman emperor 14–37.

Ti·bet (ti bet′), *n.* an administrative division of China, N of the Himalayas: prior to 1950 a theocracy under the Dalai Lama; the highest country in the world, average elevation ab. 16,000 ft. (4877 m). 1,250,000; 471,660 sq. mi. (1,221,599 sq. km). *Cap.:* Lhasa. Also, **Thibet.** Also called **Sitsang, Xizang.** Official name, **Tibet′ Auton′omous Re′gion.**

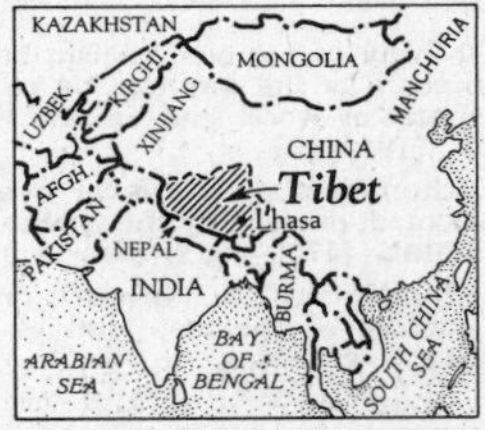

Ti·bet·an (ti bet′n), *adj.* **1.** of or pertaining to Tibet, its inhabitants, or their language. —*n.* **2.** a member of the native Mongolian race of Tibet. **3.** the Sino-Tibetan language of Tibet, esp. in its standard literary form. Also, **Thibetan.** [1740–50; TIBET + -AN]

Tibet′an an′telope, chiru.

Tibet′an span′iel, one of a breed of small alert dogs originally developed in Tibet, with a double coat of any color, well-feathered, pendent ears, and a plumed tail curled over the back. [1925–30]

Tibet′an ter′rier, one of a breed of medium-sized dogs having a long, fine coat, in solid white, cream, gray, black, or parti-colored, with hair falling over the eyes and forming a beard on the lower jaw, and a curled tail, bred originally by lamas in Tibetan monasteries. [1900–05]

Ti·bet·o-Bur·man (ti bet′ō bûr′mən), *n.* a subfamily of Sino-Tibetan languages, including esp. Tibetan and Burmese. [TIBET + -O- + BURM(A) + -AN]

tib·i·a (tib′ē ə), *n., pl.* **tib·i·ae** (tib′ē ē′), **tib·i·as. 1.** *Anat.* the inner of the two bones of the leg, that extend from the knee to the ankle and articulate with the femur and the talus; shinbone. See diag. under **skeleton. 2.** *Zool.* **a.** a corresponding bone in a horse or other hoofed quadruped, extending from the stifle to the hock. **b.** (in insects) the fourth segment of the leg, between the femur and tarsus. See diag. under **coxa.** [1685–95; < L *tībia* lit., reed pipe] —**tib′i·al,** *adj.*

tib·i·o·tar·sus (tib′ē ō tär′səs), *n., pl.* **-si** (-sī). *Ornith.* the main bone of the leg of a bird, between the femur and tarsometatarsus, formed by the fusion of several tarsal bones with the tibia. [1880–85; TIBI(A) + -O- + TARSUS] —**tib′i·o·tar′sal,** *adj.*

Ti·bul·lus (ti bul′əs), *n.* **Al·bi·us** (al′bē əs), c54–c19 B.C., Roman poet.

Ti·bur (tī′bər), *n.* ancient name of **Tivoli.**

tic (tik), *n.* **1.** *Pathol.* **a.** a sudden, spasmodic, painless, involuntary muscular contraction, as of the face. **b.** See **tic douloureux. 2.** a persistent or recurrent behavioral trait; personal quirk: *her distinctive verbal tics.* [1790–1800; < F (of expressive orig.)]

-tic, a suffix, equivalent in meaning to **-ic,** occurring in adjectives of Greek origin (*analytic*), used esp. in the formation of adjectives from nouns with stems in *-sis: hematotic; neurotic.* [< Gk *-tikos,* extracted from adjs. derived with *-ikos* -IC from agent nouns ending in *-tēs;* cf. HIERATIC]

ti·cal (ti käl′, -kôl′, tē′kəl), *n., pl.* **-cals, -cal. 1.** a former silver coin and monetary unit of Siam, equal to 100 satang: replaced in 1928 by the baht. **2.** baht. [1655–65; < Thai < Pg < Malay *tikal*]

tic dou·lou·reux (tik′ do͞o′lə ro͞o′; *Fr.* tēk do͞o lo͞o rœ′), *Pathol.* paroxysmal darting pain and muscular twitching in the face, evoked by rubbing certain points of the face. Also called **facial neuralgia, trifacial neural-**

gia, trigeminal neuralgia. [1790–1800; < F: lit., painful tic]

Ti·ci·no (ti chē′nō; *It.* tē chē′nô), *n.* a canton in S Switzerland. 279,100; 1086 sq. mi. (2813 sq. km). *Cap.:* Bellinzona. French and German, **Tessin.**

tick[1] (tik), *n.* **1.** a slight, sharp, recurring click, tap, or beat, as of a clock. **2.** *Chiefly Brit. Informal.* a moment or instant. **3.** a small dot, mark, check, or electronic signal, as used to mark off an item on a list, serve as a reminder, or call attention to something. **4.** *Manège.* a jumping fault consisting of a light touch of a fence with one or more feet. **5.** a small contrasting spot of color on the coat of a mammal or the feathers of a bird. —*v.i.* **6.** to emit or produce a tick, like that of a clock. **7.** to pass as with ticks of a clock: *The hours ticked by.* —*v.t.* **8.** to sound or announce by a tick or ticks: *The clock ticked the minutes.* **9.** to mark with a tick or ticks; check (usually fol. by *off*); *to tick off the items on the memo.* **10. tick off,** *Slang.* **a.** to make angry: *His mistreatment of the animals really ticked me off.* **b.** *Chiefly Brit.* to scold severely: *The manager will tick you off if you make another mistake.* **11. what makes one tick,** the motive or explanation of one's behavior: *The biographer failed to show what made Herbert Hoover tick.* [1400–50; late ME *tek* little touch; akin to D *tik* a touch, pat, Norw *tikka* to touch or shove slightly. See TICKLE]

tick[2] (tik), *n.* **1.** any of numerous bloodsucking arachnids of the order Acarina, including the families Ixodidae and Argasidae, somewhat larger than the related mites and having a barbed proboscis for attachment to the skin of warm-blooded vertebrates: some ticks are vectors of disease. **2.** See **sheeptick.** [bef. 900; ME *teke, tyke,* OE *ticia* (perh. sp. error for *tiica* (i.e. *tica*) or *ticca*); akin to LG *tieke,* G *Zecke*]

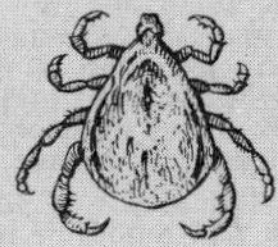
dog tick, *Dermacentor variabilis,* length 1/4 in. (0.6 cm)

tick[3] (tik), *n.* **1.** the cloth case of a mattress, pillow, etc., containing hair, feathers, or the like. **2.** ticking. Also called **bedtick.** [1425–75; late ME *tikke, teke, tyke* (c. D *tijk,* G *Zieche*) << L *tēca, thēca* < Gk *thḗkē* case]

tick[4] (tik), *n. Chiefly Brit. Informal.* **1.** a score or account. **2. on tick,** on credit or trust: *We bought our telly on tick.* [1635–45; short for TICKET]

tick′ bird′, any of various birds that feed on ticks, as an oxpecker. [1860–65]

tick-borne (tik′bôrn′, -bōrn′), *adj.* carried or transmitted by ticks: *tick-borne disease.* [1935–40]

ticked (tikt), *adj. Slang.* angry; miffed. [1935–40; TICK[1] + -ED[2]]

Tick·ell (tik′əl), *n.* **Thomas,** 1686–1740, English poet and translator.

tick·er (tik′ər), *n.* **1.** a telegraphic receiving instrument that automatically prints stock prices, market reports, etc., on a paper tape. **2.** a person or thing that ticks. **3.** *Slang.* a watch. **4.** *Slang.* the heart. [1820–30; 1880–85 for def. 4; TICK[1] + -ER[1]]

tick′er tape′, the ribbon of paper on which a ticker prints quotations or news. Also called **tape.** [1900–05, *Amer.*]

tick′er-tape parade′ (tik′ər tāp′), a parade honoring a visiting dignitary, hero, or the like in which ticker tapes, confetti, shredded newspapers, etc., are showered into the streets from buildings along the parade route.

tick·et (tik′it), *n.* **1.** a slip, usually of paper or cardboard, serving as evidence that the holder has paid a fare or admission or is entitled to some service, right, or the like: *a railroad ticket; a theater ticket.* **2.** a summons issued for a traffic or parking violation. **3.** a written or printed slip of paper, cardboard, etc., affixed to something to indicate its nature, price, or the like; label or tag. **4.** a slate of candidates nominated by a particular party or faction and running together in an election. **5.** the license of a ship's officer or of an aviation pilot. **6.** *Banking.* a preliminary recording of transactions prior to their entry in more permanent books of account. **7.** *Informal.* the proper or advisable thing: *That's the ticket! Warm milk and toast is just the ticket for you.* **8.** *Archaic.* a placard. **9.** *Obs.* a short note, notice, or memorandum. **10. have tickets on oneself,** *Australian Slang.* to be conceited. —*v.t.* **11.** to attach a ticket to; distinguish by means of a ticket; label. **12.** to furnish with a ticket, as on the railroad. **13.** to serve with a summons for a traffic or parking violation. **14.** to attach such a summons to: *to ticket illegally parked cars.* [1520–30; 1925–30 for def. 4; earlier *tiket* < MF *etiquet* memorandum. See ETIQUETTE] —**tick′et·less,** *adj.*

tick′et a′gency, an agency dealing in the sale of tickets, esp. theater tickets. [1930–35]

tick′et a′gent, a person who sells tickets, as for theater seats, train accommodations, etc. [1860–65, *Amer.*]

tick′et of′fice, an office or booth at which tickets are sold, as for a play, a film, or travel accommodations. [1660–70]

tick′et of leave′, *pl.* **tickets of leave.** *Brit.* (formerly) a permit allowing a convict to leave prison, under certain restrictions, and go to work before having served a full term, somewhat similar to a certificate of parole. Also, **tick′et-of-leave′.** [1725–35]

tick′et scalp′er, an unauthorized ticket speculator who buys tickets to a performance or sports event and resells them at inflated prices. [1875–80]

tick·et·y-boo (tik′i tē bo͞o′), *adj. Chiefly Brit. Informal.* fine; OK. [1935–40; perh. expressive alter. of the phrase *that's the ticket*]

tick′ fe′ver, any fever transmitted by ticks, as Rocky Mountain spotted fever, which attacks humans, or Texas fever, which is confined to some animals, as cattle. [1895–1900]

tick·ing (tik′ing), *n.* **1.** a strong cotton fabric, usually twilled, used esp. in making cloth ticks. **2.** a similar cloth in satin weave or Jacquard, used esp. for mattress covers. [1635–45; TICK[3] + -ING[1]]

tick·le (tik′əl), *v.,* **-led, -ling,** *n.* —*v.t.* **1.** to touch or stroke lightly with the fingers, a feather, etc., so as to excite a tingling or itching sensation in; titillate. **2.** to poke some sensitive part of the body so as to excite spasmodic laughter. **3.** to excite agreeably; gratify: *to tickle someone's vanity.* **4.** to excite amusement in: *The clown's antics really tickled the kids.* **5.** to get, move, etc., by or as by tickling: *She tickled him into saying yes.* —*v.i.* **6.** to be affected with a tingling or itching sensation, as from light touches or strokes: *I tickle all over.* **7.** to produce such a sensation. **8. tickled pink,** *Informal.* greatly pleased: *She was tickled pink that someone had remembered her birthday.* —*n.* **9.** an act or instance of tickling. **10.** a tickling sensation. [1300–50; ME *tikelen,* freq. of TICK[1] (in obs. sense) to touch lightly] —**Syn. 4.** amuse, please, delight, enchant.

tick·ler (tik′lər), *n.* **1.** a person or thing that tickles. **2.** See **tickler file. 3.** *Accounting.* a single-entry account arranged according to the due dates of obligations. **4.** *Electronics, Radio.* See **tickler coil.** [1670–80; TICKLE + -ER[1]]

tick′ler coil′, *Electronics, Radio.* the coil by which the plate circuit of a vacuum tube is inductively coupled with the grid circuit in the process of regeneration. [1920–25]

tick′ler file′, a file consisting of memoranda, notices, electronic signals, or the like that serves to remind the user of matters that must be attended to. [1795–1805, *Amer.*]

tick·lish (tik′lish), *adj.* **1.** sensitive to tickling. **2.** requiring careful or delicate handling or action; difficult or risky; dicey: *a ticklish situation.* **3.** extremely sensitive; touchy: *He is ticklish about being interrupted.* **4.** unstable or easily upset, as a boat; unsteady. [1575–85; TICKLE + -ISH[1]] —**tick′lish·ly,** *adv.* —**tick′lish·ness,** *n.*

tick·ly (tik′lē), *adj.,* **-li·er, -li·est.** ticklish. [1520–30; TICKLE + -Y[1]]

Tick·nor (tik′nər, -nôr), *n.* **George,** 1791–1871, U.S. literary historian and educator.

tick·seed (tik′sēd′), *n.* **1.** any of various plants having seeds resembling ticks, as a coreopsis or the bugseed. **2.** See **tick trefoil.** [1555–65; TICK[2] + SEED]

tick·tack (tik′tak′), *n.* **1.** a repetitive sound, as of ticking, tapping, knocking, or clicking: *the ticktack of high heels in the corridor.* **2.** a device for making a tapping sound, as against a window or door in playing a practical joke. —*v.i.* **3.** to make a repeated ticking or tapping sound: *Sleet ticktacked against the window panes.* Also, **tictac.** [1540–50; imit. See TICK[1]]

tick-tack-toe (tik′tak tō′), *n.* **1.** a simple game in which one player marks down only X's and another only O's, each alternating in filling in any of the nine compartments of a figure formed by two vertical lines crossed by two horizontal lines, the winner being the first to fill in three marks in any horizontal, vertical, or diagonal row. **2.** a children's game consisting of trying, with the eyes shut, to bring a pencil down upon one of a set of circled numbers, as on a slate, the number touched being counted as a score. Also, **tick-tack-too** (tik′tak-to͞o′), **tic-tac-toe, tit-tat-toe.** [1865–70; imit. of sound, as of bringing a pencil down on slate; see TICKTACK]

tick·tock (tik′tok′), *n.* **1.** an alternating ticking sound, as that made by a clock. —*v.i.* **2.** to emit or produce a ticking sound, like that of a clock. Also, **tictoc.** [1840–50; imit.]

tick′ tre′foil, any of numerous plants belonging to the genus *Desmodium,* of the legume family, having trifoliolate leaves and jointed pods with hooked hairs by which they adhere to objects. [1855–60, *Amer.*]

tic·ky-tack·y (tik′ē tak′ē), *Informal.* —*adj.* **1.** shoddy and unimaginatively designed; flimsy and dull: *a row of new, ticky-tacky bungalows.* **2.** tacky[2]. —*n.* **3.** ticky-tacky material or something made of it, esp. housing. Also, **tick′y-tack′.** [1960–65; gradational compound based on TACKY[2]]

Ti·co (tē′kō; *Sp.* tē′kô), *n., pl.* **-cos** (-kōz; *Sp.* -kôs), *adj. Slang.* (in Central America) —*n.* **1.** a native or inhabitant of Costa Rica. —*adj.* **2.** of, pertaining to, or characteristic of Costa Rica or its inhabitants: *an exhibition of Tico art.* [< AmerSp *tico,* said to be from Costa Ricans' predilection for diminutives formed with the suffix *-itico*]

Ti·con·der·o·ga (tī′kon də rō′gə), *n.* a village in NE New York, on Lake Champlain: site of French fort captured by the English 1759 and by Americans under Ethan Allen 1775. 2938.

tic·tac (tik′tak′), *n., v.i.,* **-tacked, -tack·ing.** ticktack.

tic-tac-toe (tik′tak tō′), *n.* tick-tack-toe.

tic·toc (tik′tok′), *n., v.i.,* **-tocked, -tock·ing.** ticktock.

t.i.d., (in prescriptions) three times a day. [< L *ter in diē*]

tid·al (tīd′l), *adj.* **1.** of, pertaining to, characterized by, or subject to tides: *a tidal current.* **2.** dependent on the state of the tide as to time of departure: *a tidal steamer.* [1800–10; TIDE[1] + -AL[1]] —**tid′al·ly,** *adv.*

tid′al ba′sin, an artificial body of water open to a river, stream, etc., subject to tidal action. [1855–60]

tid′al bench′mark, a benchmark used as a reference for tidal observations.

tid′al bore′, bore[3].

tid′al da′tum, (in a hydrographic survey) a curved surface representing one phase of a tide, usually mean low water, taken as a datum level.

tid′al flat′, tideland that is flat or nearly flat and often muddy or marshy.

tid′al light′, a light placed at the entrance of a harbor to indicate the depth of the water and the direction of tidal flow.

tid′al pool′, a pool of water remaining on a reef, shore platform, or beach after the tide has receded. Also called **tide pool, tidepool.**

tid′al wave′, 1. (not in technical use) a large, destructive ocean wave, produced by a seaquake, hurricane, or strong wind. Cf. **tsunami. 2.** either of the two great wavelike swellings of the ocean surface that move around the earth on opposite sides and give rise to tide, caused by the attraction of the moon and sun. **3.** any widespread or powerful movement, opinion, or tendency: *a tidal wave of public indignation.* [1820–30]

tid·bit (tid′bit′), *n.* **1.** a delicate bit or morsel of food. **2.** a choice or pleasing bit of anything, as news or gossip. Also, *esp. Brit.,* **titbit.** [1630–40; TIDE[1] (in sense "feast day") + BIT[2]]

tid·dly (tid′lē), *adj. Chiefly Brit. Slang.* slightly drunk; tipsy. [1885–90; orig. uncert.]

tid·dly·winks (tid′lē wingks′), *n.* (*used with a singular v.*) a game played on a flat surface, in which players attempt to snap small plastic disks into a cup by pressing the edges of the disks with larger ones. Also, **tid·dle·dy·winks** (tid′l dē wingks′). [1835–45; pl. of *tiddlywink* (*tiddly* tiny + dial. *wink,* var. of WINCH), referring to the counter used to snap the pieces into place; see -S[3]]

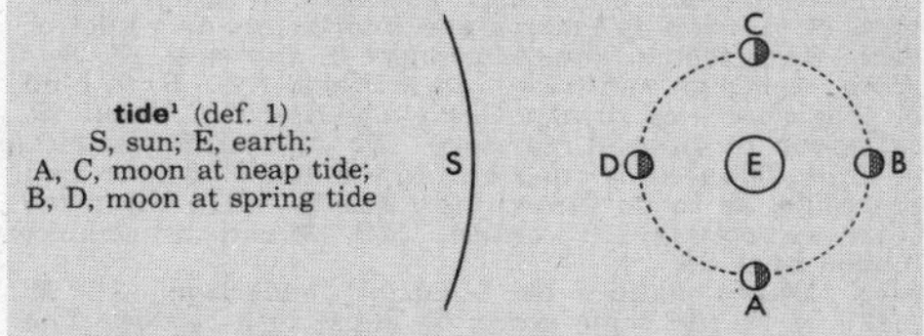

tide[1] (def. 1) S, sun; E, earth; A, C, moon at neap tide; B, D, moon at spring tide

tide[1] (tīd), *n., v.,* **tid·ed, tid·ing.** —*n.* **1.** the periodic rise and fall of the waters of the ocean and its inlets, produced by the attraction of the moon and sun, and occurring about every 12 hours. **2.** the inflow, outflow, or current of water at any given place resulting from the waves of tides. **3.** See **flood tide. 4.** a stream or current. **5.** anything that alternately rises and falls, increases and decreases, etc.: *the tide of the seasons.* **6.** current, tendency, or drift, as of events or ideas: *the tide of international events.* **7.** any extreme or critical period or condition: *The tide of her illness is at its height.* **8.** a season or period in the course of the year, day, etc. (now used chiefly in combination): *wintertide; eventide.* **9.** *Eccles.* a period of time that includes and follows an anniversary, festival, etc. **10.** *Archaic.* a suitable time or occasion. **11.** *Obs.* an extent of time. **12. turn the tide,** to reverse the course of events, esp. from one extreme to another: *The Battle of Saratoga turned the tide of the American Revolution.* —*v.i.* **13.** to flow as the tide; flow to and fro. **14.** to float or drift with the tide. —*v.t.* **15.** to carry, as the tide does. **16. tide over, a.** to assist in getting over a period of difficulty or distress. **b.** to surmount (a difficulty, obstacle, etc.); survive. [bef. 900; ME (n.); OE *tīd* time, hour; c. D *tijd,* G *Zeit,* ON *tīth;* akin to TIME] —**tide′ful,** *adj.* —**tide′less,** *adj.* —**tide′less·ness,** *n.* —**tide′like′,** *adj.*

tide[2] (tīd), *v.i.,* **tid·ed, tid·ing.** *Archaic.* to happen or befall. [bef. 1000; ME *tiden,* OE *tīdan.* See BETIDE]

tide-bound (tīd′bound′), *adj. Naut.* (of a vessel) grounded or otherwise confined at low tide. [1905–10]

tide′ gage′, a gauge for measuring the level of the tide: usually equipped with a marigraph. Also, **tide′ gauge′.** [1830–40]

tide′ gate′, 1. a gate through which water flows when the tide is in one direction and that closes automatically when the tide is in the opposite direction. **2.** a restricted passage, as a strait, through which the tide flows swiftly. [1745–55]

tide·head (tīd′hed′), *n.* the inland limit of the tide. [TIDE[1] + HEAD]

tide·land (tīd′land′), *n.* **1.** land alternately exposed and covered by the ordinary ebb and flow of the tide. **2.** Often, **tidelands.** submerged offshore land within the territorial waters of a state or nation. [1795–1805; TIDE[1] + LAND]

tide′ lock′, a lock at the entrance to a tidal basin. [1885–90]

tide•mark (tīd′märk′), *n.* **1.** the point that something or someone has reached, receded below, or risen above: *He has reached the tidemark of his prosperity.* **2.** a mark left by the highest or lowest point of a tide. **3.** a mark made to indicate the highest or lowest point of a tide. [1790–1800; TIDE[1] + MARK[1]]

tide′ mill′, a mill operated by the tidal movement of water. [1630–40]

tide′ pool′. See **tidal pool.** Also **tide′pool′.**

tide•rip (tīd′rip′), *n.* a rip caused by conflicting tidal currents or by a tidal current crossing a rough bottom. [1820–30; TIDE[1] + RIP[2]]

tide′ ta′ble, a table listing the predicted times and heights of the tides for specific dates and places. [1585–95]

tide•wa•ter (tīd′wô′tər, -wot′ər), *n.* **1.** water affected by the flow and ebb of the tide. **2.** the water covering tideland at flood tide. **3.** seacoast. [1765–75; TIDE[1] + WATER]

tide•way (tīd′wā′), *n.* a channel in which a tidal current runs. Also, **tide′ way′.** [1620–30; TIDE[1] + WAY[1]]

ti•dings (tī′dingz), *n.* (*sometimes used with a singular v.*) news, information, or intelligence: *sad tidings.* [bef. 1100; ME; OE *tīdung;* c. D *tijding,* G *Zeitung* news; akin to ON *tīthindi.* See TIDE[2], -ING[1]]

ti•dy (tī′dē), *adj.,* **-di•er, -di•est,** *v.,* **-died, -dy•ing,** *n., pl.* **-dies.** —*adj.* **1.** neat, orderly, or trim, as in appearance or dress: *a tidy room; a tidy person.* **2.** clearly organized and systematic: *a tidy mind; a tidy way of working.* **3.** tolerably good; acceptable: *They worked out a tidy arrangement agreeable to all.* **4.** fairly large; considerable: *a tidy sum.* —*v.t., v.i.* **5.** to make tidy or neat (often fol. by *up*). —*n.* **6.** any of various articles for keeping things tidy, as a box having small drawers and compartments. **7.** an antimacassar. [1200–50; ME *tidi, tidy* seasonable, hence good; c. D *tijdig.* See TIDE[1], -Y[1]] —**ti′di•ly,** *adv.* —**ti′di•ness,** *n.*
—**Ant. 1.** messy, sloppy.

ti•dy•tips (tī′dē tips′), *n., pl.* **-tips.** (*used with a singular or plural v.*) a composite plant, *Layia platyglossa,* of California, having flower heads with bright yellow, white-tipped rays. [1885–90, *Amer.;* TIDY + TIP[1] + -S[3]]

tie (tī), *v.,* **tied, ty•ing,** *n.* —*v.t.* **1.** to bind, fasten, or attach with a cord, string, or the like, drawn together and knotted: *to tie a tin can on a dog's tail.* **2.** to draw together the parts of with a knotted string or the like: *to tie a bundle tight.* **3.** to fasten by tightening and knotting the string or strings of: *to tie one's shoes.* **4.** to draw or fasten together into a knot, as a cord: *to tie one's shoelace.* **5.** to form by looping and interlacing, as a knot or bow. **6.** to fasten, join, or connect in any way. **7.** *Angling.* to design and make (an artificial fly). **8.** to bind or join closely or firmly: *Great affection tied them.* **9.** *Informal.* to unite in marriage. **10.** to confine, restrict, or limit: *The weather tied him to the house.* **11.** to bind or oblige, as to do something. **12.** to make the same score as; equal in a contest. **13.** *Music.* to connect (notes) by a tie.
—*v.i.* **14.** to make a tie, bond, or connection. **15.** to make or be the same score; be equal in a contest: *The teams tied for first place in the league.* **16. tie down,** to limit one's activities; confine; curtail: *He finds that a desk job ties him down.* **17. tie in, a.** to connect or be connected; be consistent: *His story ties in with the facts.* **b.** *Survey.* to establish the position of (a point not part of a survey control). **c.** to make a tie-in, esp. in advertising or a sale: *The paperback book is tied in with the movie of the same title.* **18. tie off,** to tie a cord or suture around (a vein, blood vessel, or the like) so as to stop the flow within. **19. tie one on,** *Slang.* to get drunk: *Charlie sure tied one on last night!* **20. tie the knot.** See **knot**[1] (def. 13). **21. tie up, a.** to fasten securely by tying. **b.** to wrap; bind. **c.** to hinder; impede. **d.** to bring to a stop; make inactive. **e.** to invest or place (money) in such a way as to render unavailable for other uses. **f.** to place (property) under such conditions or restrictions as to prevent sale or alienation. **g.** to moor a ship. **h.** to engage or occupy completely: *I can't see you now, I'm all tied up.*
—*n.* **22.** that with which anything is tied. **23.** a cord, string, or the like, used for tying, fastening, binding, or wrapping something. **24.** a necktie. **25.** a low shoe fastened with a lace. **26.** a knot, esp. an ornamental one; bow. **27.** anything that fastens, secures, or unites. **28.** a bond or connection, as of affection, kinship, mutual interest, or between two or more people, groups, nations, or the like: *family ties; the ties between Britain and the U.S.* **29.** a state of equality in the result of a contest, as in points scored, votes obtained, etc., among competitors: *The game ended in a tie.* **30.** a match or contest in which this occurs. **31.** any of various structural members, as beams or rods, for keeping two objects, as rafters or the haunches of an arch, from spreading or separating. **32.** *Music.* a curved line connecting two notes on the same line or space to indicate that the sound is to be sustained for their joint value, not repeated. **33.** Also called, *esp. Brit.,* **sleeper.** *Railroads.* any of a number of closely spaced transverse beams, usually of wood, for holding the rails forming a track at the proper distance from each other and for transmitting train loads to the ballast and roadbed. **34.** bride[2] (def. 1). **35.** *Survey.* a measurement made to determine the position of a survey station with respect to a reference mark or other isolated point. [bef. 900; (n.) ME *te(i)gh* cord, rope, OE *tēagh, tēgh,* c. ON *taug* rope; (v.) ME *tien,* OE *tīgan,* deriv. of the n.; cf. ON *teygja* to draw. See TUG, TOW[1]]
—**Syn. 6.** unite, link, knit, yoke, lock. **11.** obligate, constrain. **23.** rope, band, ligature. **24.** cravat. **28.** See **bond.** —**Ant. 1.** loose, loosen.

CONCISE ETYMOLOGY KEY: <, descended or borrowed from; >, whence; b., blend of, blended; c., cognate with; cf., compare; deriv., derivative; equiv., equivalent; imit., imitative; obl., oblique; r., replacing; s., stem; sp., spelling, spelled; resp., respelling, respelled; trans., translation; ?, origin unknown; *, unattested; ‡, probably earlier than. See the full key inside the front cover.

T, **ties** (def. 32)

tie-and-dye (tī′ən dī′), *n.* See **tie dyeing.** [1925–30]

tie•back (tī′bak′), *n.* **1.** a strip or loop of material, heavy braid, or the like, used for holding a curtain back to one side. **2.** a curtain having such a device. [1875–80; n. use of v. phrase *tie back*]

tie′ bar′, a bar-shaped tie clasp.

tie′ beam′, a horizontal timber or the like for connecting two structural members to keep them from spreading apart, as a beam connecting the feet of two principal rafters in a roof truss. See diags. under **king post, queen post.** [1815–25]

tie•break•er (tī′brā′kər), *n.* a system for breaking a tie score at the end of regulation play by establishing a winner through special additional play, usually of a fairly short duration, as in tennis and soccer. [1960–65; TIE + BREAKER[1]]

Tieck (tēk), *n.* **Lud•wig** (lo͞ot′viкн, lo͞od′-), 1773–1853, German writer.

tie′ clasp′, an ornamental metal clasp for securing the two ends of a necktie to a shirt front. Also called **tie′ clip′.**

tied′ house′, *Brit.* **1.** a public house or tavern owned by or under contract to a brewery whose brands of beer, ale, etc., it sells exclusively. **2.** Also called **tied′ cot′tage.** a house owned by an employer and rented to an employee. [1885–90]

tie-down (tī′doun′), *n.* **1.** a device for tying something down. **2.** the act of tying something down. [n. use of v. phrase *tie down*]

tie-dye (tī′dī′), *v.,* **dyed, -dye•ing,** *n.* —*v.t.* **1.** to dye (fabric) by tie-dyeing. —*n.* **2.** tie-dyeing. **3.** *Informal.* a fabric or garment dyed by tie-dyeing. [1935–40]

tie-dye•ing (tī′dī′ing), *n.* a process of hand-dyeing fabric, in which sections of the fabric are tightly bound, as with thread, to resist the dye solution, thereby producing a variegated pattern. Also called **tie-and-dye, tie-dye.** [1900–05; TIE-DYE + -ING[1]]

tie-in (tī′in′), *adj.* **1.** pertaining to or designating a sale in which the buyer in order to get the item desired must also purchase one or more other, usually undesired, items. **2.** of or pertaining to two or more products advertised, marketed, or sold together. —*n.* **3.** an arrangement or campaign whereby related products are promoted, marketed, or sold together: *a book and movie tie-in.* **4.** a tie-in sale or advertisement. **5.** an item in a tie-in sale or advertisement. **6.** any direct or indirect link, relationship, or connection: *There is a tie-in between smoking and cancer.* [1920–25; adj., n. use of v. phrase *tie in*]

tie′ line′, *Telecommunications.* **1.** a line that connects two or more extensions in a PBX telephone system. **2.** a private telephone channel, leased from a telephone company, that connects two or more PBX systems.

tie•mann•ite (tē′mə nīt′), *n.* a mineral, mercuric selenide, HgSe, occurring in the form of a compact mass of gray crystals. [< G *Tiemannit* (1855), after W. *Tiemann,* German scientist who found it; see -ITE[1]]

Tien′an′men′ Square′ (tyen′än′men′). See **Tiananmen Square.**

Tien Shan (tyen′ shän′), a mountain range in central Asia, in China and the Soviet Union. Highest peak, Tengri Khan, ab. 23,950 ft. (7300 m). Also, **Tian Shan.**

Tien•tsin (tin′tsin′; *Chin.* tyen′jin′), *n. Older Spelling.* Tianjin.

tie′-off rail′ (tī′ôf′, -of′). See **trim rail.**

tie•pin (tī′pin′), *n.* a straight pin, usually with an ornamented head and a small metal sheath for its point, for holding together the ends of a necktie or to pin them to a shirt front. Also called **scarfpin.** [1770–80; TIE + PIN]

tie′ plate′, *Railroads.* a plate set between the base of a rail and a crosstie to distribute the rail load over a greater area of the tie and thus reduce wear and damage to it. [1870–75]

tie′ plug′, *Railroads.* a wooden plug driven into the hole left in a tie when a spike has been withdrawn.

Tie•po•lo (tē ep′ə lō′; *It.* tye′pô lô), *n.* **Gio•van•ni Bat•ti•sta** (jō vä′nē bə tē′stə; *It.* jô vän′nē bät tē′stä), 1696–1770, and his son, **Giovanni Do•me•ni•co** (də men′i kō′; *It.* dô me′nē kô), 1727–1804, Italian painters.

tier[1] (tēr), *n.* **1.** one of a series of rows or ranks rising one behind or above another, as of seats in an amphitheater, boxes in a theater, guns in a man-of-war, or oars in an ancient galley. **2.** one of a number of galleries, as in a theater. **3.** a layer; level; stratum: *The wedding cake had six tiers. All three tiers of the firm's management now report to one director.* **4.** *Australian.* a mountain range. —*v.t.* **5.** to arrange in tiers. —*v.i.* **6.** to rise in tiers. [1560–70; earlier also *tire, tyre, teare* < MF, OF *tire, tiere* order, row, rank < Gmc; cf. OE, OS *tīr,* OHG *zēri* glory, adornment]

ti•er[2] (tī′ər), *n.* **1.** a person or thing that ties. **2.** *Naut.* a short rope or band for securing a furled sail. **3.** *New Eng.* a child's apron or pinafore. [1625–35; TIE + -ER[1]]

tierce (tērs), *n.* **1.** an old measure of capacity equivalent to one third of a pipe, or 42 wine gallons. **2.** a cask or vessel holding this quantity. **3.** Also, **terce.** *Eccles.* the third of the seven canonical hours, or the service for it, originally fixed for the third hour of the day (or 9 A.M.). **4.** *Fencing.* the third of eight defensive positions. **5.** *Piquet.* a sequence of three cards of the same suit, as an ace, king, and queen (**tierce′ ma′jor**), or a king, queen, and jack (**tierce′ mi′nor**). **6.** *Obs.* a third or third part. [1325–75; ME < MF, fem. of *tiers* < L *tertius* THIRD]

tierced (tērst), *adj. Heraldry.* (of an escutcheon) divided vertically or horizontally into three equal parts. [1795–1805; TIERCE + -ED[3]; cf. F *tiercé*]

tier•cel (tēr′səl), *n. Falconry.* tercel.

tier•ce•ron (tēr′sər ən), *n.* (in a ribbed vault) a diagonal rib, other than an ogive, springing from a point of support. See illus. under **vault**[1]. [1835–45; < F, equiv. to *tierce* TIERCE + *-eron* n. suffix]

tiered (tērd), *adj.* being or arranged in tiers or layers (usually used in combination): *a two-tiered box of chocolates.* [1800–10; TIER[1] + -ED[3]]

tie′ rod′, **1.** an iron or steel rod serving as a structural tie, esp. one keeping the lower ends of a roof truss, arch, etc., from spreading. **2.** *Auto.* a rod that serves as part of the linkage in the steering system. [1830–40]

Tier•ra del Fue•go (tē er′ə del fwā′gō; *Sp.* tyeʀ′ʀä thel fwe′gô), a group of islands at the S tip of South America, separated from the mainland by the Strait of Magellan: jointly owned by Argentina and Chile; boundary disputed. 27,476 sq. mi. (71,165 sq. km).

tiers é•tat (tyeʀ zā tA′), *French.* See **third estate.**

tier′ ta′ble, a stand having a number of round shelves, one on top of the other.

tie′ tack′, a pin having an ornamental head, pinned through the ends of a necktie to hold it against a shirt. Also, **tie′ tac′.** [1950–55]

tie-up (tī′up′), *n.* **1.** a temporary stoppage or slowing of business, traffic, telephone service, etc., as due to a strike, storm, or accident. **2.** the act or state of tying up or the state of being tied up. **3.** an involvement, connection, or entanglement: *the tie-up between the two companies; his tie-up with the crime syndicate.* **4.** a mooring place; place where a boat may be tied up. **5.** a cow barn with stalls. **6.** a stall allotted to each cow in such a barn. [1705–15; n. use of v. phrase *tie up*]

tiff (tif), *n.* **1.** a slight or petty quarrel. **2.** a slight fit of annoyance, bad mood, or the like. —*v.i.* **3.** to have a petty quarrel. **4.** to be in a tiff. [1720–30; orig. uncert.]
—**Syn. 1.** spat, scrap, misunderstanding, difference.

tif•fa•ny (tif′ə nē), *n., pl.* **-nies.** a sheer, mesh fabric constructed in plain weave, originally made of silk but now often made of cotton or synthetic fibers. [1250–1300; 1595–1605 for current sense; perh. punning use of the earlier word, ME: feast of the Epiphany < OF *tiphanie* Epiphany < LL *theophania.* See THEOPHANY]

Tif•fa•ny (tif′ə nē), *n.* **1. Charles Lewis,** 1812–1902, U.S. jeweler. **2.** his son **Louis Com•fort** (kum′fərt), 1848–1933, U.S. painter and decorator, esp. of glass. **3.** a female given name.

Tif′fany glass′. See **Favrile glass.** [named after L. C. TIFFANY]

Tif′fany set′ting, *Jewelry.* a setting, as in a ring, in which the stone is held with prongs. [named after C. L. TIFFANY]

tif•fin (tif′in), *Brit. Informal.* —*n.* **1.** lunch. —*v.i.* **2.** to eat lunch. —*v.t.* **3.** to provide lunch for; serve lunch to. [1775–85; var. of **tiffing,* equiv. to *tiff* (obs.) to sip, drink + -ING[1]]

Tif•fin (tif′in), *n.* a city in N Ohio. 19,549.

Tif•lis (tif′lis; *Russ.* tyi flyēs′), *n.* former name of **Tbilisi.**

Tif•ton (tif′tən), *n.* a town in central Georgia. 13,749.

Ti•gard (tī′gərd), *n.* a city in NW Oregon, near Portland. 14,286.

ti•ger (tī′gər), *n., pl.* **-gers,** (*esp. collectively for 1, 2, 5*) **-ger. 1.** a large, carnivorous, tawny-colored and black-striped feline, *Panthera tigris,* of Asia, ranging in several races from India and the Malay Peninsula to Siberia: the entire species is endangered, with some races thought to be extinct. **2.** the cougar, jaguar, thylacine, or other animal resembling the tiger. **3.** a person resembling a tiger in fierceness, courage, etc. **4.** an additional cheer (often the word *tiger*) at the end of a round of cheering. **5.** any of several strong, voracious fishes, as a sand shark. **6.** any of numerous animals with stripes similar to a tiger's. [bef. 1000; ME *tigre,* OE *tīgras* (pl.) < L *tigris, tigris* < Gk *tigris*] —**ti′ger•like′,** *adj.*

tiger, *Panthera tigris,* head and body 6 ft. (1.8 m); tail 3 ft. (0.9 m)

ti′ger bee′tle, any of numerous active, usually brightly colored beetles, of the family Cicindelidae, that prey on other insects. [1820–30]

ti′ger cat′, **1.** any of several felines, as the ocelot or margay, that resemble the tiger in coloration or ferocity but are smaller. **2.** a spotted marsupial cat, *Dasyurus (Dasyurops) maculatus.* **3.** a domestic cat having a striped coat resembling that of a tiger. [1690–1700]

ti•ger•eye (tī′gər ī′), *n.* tiger's-eye.

ti•ger•fish (tī′gər fish′), *n., pl.* (*esp. collectively*) **-fish,** (*esp. referring to two or more kinds or species*) **-fish•es.** a large, voracious, freshwater game fish, *Hydrocyenus goliath,* of African rivers. [1890–95; TIGER + FISH]

ti·ger·ish (tī′gər ish), *adj.* **1.** tigerlike, as in strength, fierceness, courage, or coloration. **2.** fiercely cruel; bloodthirsty; relentless. Also, **tigrish.** [1565–75; TIGER + -ISH[1]] **—ti′ger·ish·ly,** *adv.* **—ti′ger·ish·ness,** *n.*

ti′ger lil′y, 1. a lily, *Lilium lancifolium* (or *tigrinum*), having dull-orange flowers spotted with black and small bulbs or bulbils in the axils of the leaves. **2.** any lily, esp. *L. pardalinum*, of similar coloration. [1815–25]

ti′ger liz′ard, either of two lacertid lizards, *Nucras intertexta* and *N. tessellata*, of southern Africa, having a gray or brown body marked with black spots and bars.

ti′ger mosqui′to, a large Asian mosquito, *Aedes albopictus*, introduced into the southern U.S., that is a vector of dengue and other infectious diseases. [1825–35]

ti′ger moth′, any of numerous moths of the family Arctiidae, many of which have conspicuously striped or spotted wings. [1810–20]

ti′ger sal′amander, a salamander, *Ambystoma tigrinum*, common in North America, having a dark body marked with yellowish spots or bars. See illus. under **salamander.** [1905–10, *Amer.*]

ti·ger's-eye (tī′gərz ī′), *n.* **1.** a golden-brown chatoyant stone used for ornament, formed by the alteration of crocidolite, and consisting essentially of quartz colored by iron oxide. **2.** a glass coating or glaze giving the covered object the appearance of this stone. Also, **tigereye.** [1890–95]

ti′ger shark′, a large shark, *Galeocerdo cuvieri*, inhabiting warm seas, noted for its voracious habits. [1775–85]

ti′ger snake′, either of two highly venomous snakes, *Notechis scutatus* and *N. ater*, of Australia and Tasmania, that grow to a length of 5 ft. (1.5 m). [1870–75]

ti′ger swal′lowtail, a yellow swallowtail butterfly, *Papilio glaucus*, of eastern North America, having the forewings striped with black. See illus. under **swallowtail.** [1885–90]

tight (tīt), *adj.* **-er, -est,** *adv.*, **-er, -est.** **—***adj.* **1.** firmly or closely fixed in place; not easily moved; secure: *a tight knot.* **2.** drawn or stretched so as to be tense; taut. **3.** affording little or no extra room; fitting closely, esp. too closely: *a tight collar.* **4.** difficult to deal with or manage: *to be in a tight situation.* **5.** of such close or compacted texture, or fitted together so closely, as to be impervious to water, air, steam, etc.: *a good, tight roof.* **6.** concise; terse: *a tight style of writing.* **7.** firm; rigid: *his tight control of the company.* **8.** carefully arranged or organized and full; affording little leeway; compact: *a tight schedule.* **9.** nearly even; close: *a tight race.* **10.** *Informal.* **a.** close, as friends; familiar or intimate. **b.** united: *The strikers are tight in their refusal to accept the proposed contract.* **11.** parsimonious; stingy. **12.** *Slang.* drunk; tipsy. **13.** characterized by scarcity or eager demand; costly; limited; restricted: *a tight job market; tight money.* **14.** *Journalism.* (of a newspaper) having more news available than is required for or utilizable in a particular issue. **15.** *Baseball.* inside (def. 20). **16.** *Scot. and North Eng.* competent or skillful. **17.** tidy. **18.** neatly or well built or made. **—***adv.* **19.** in a tight manner; closely; firmly; securely; tensely: *Shut the door tight. The shirt fit tight across the shoulders.* **20.** soundly or deeply: *to sleep tight.* **21. sit tight,** to take no action. [1400–50; late ME, sandhi var. of ME *thight* dense, solid, tight < ON *thēttr* (c. OE *-thiht* firm, solid, D, G *dicht* tight, close, dense)] **—tight′ly,** *adv.* **—tight′ness,** *n.*
—Syn. 11. close, niggardly, mean, grasping, frugal, sparing.

tight-assed (tīt′ast′), *adj. Slang (vulgar).* rigidly self-controlled, inhibited, or conservative in attitude. [1965–70]

tight·en (tīt′n), *v.t., v.i.* to make or become tight or tighter. [1720–30; TIGHT + -EN[1]] **—tight′en·er,** *n.*
—Syn. secure, anchor, fasten.

tight′ end′, *Football.* an offensive player positioned at one extremity of the line directly beside a tackle, used as both a blocker and a pass receiver. Cf. **split end.** [1960–65, *Amer.*]

tight-fist·ed (tīt′fis′tid), *adj.* parsimonious; stingy; tight. [1835–45]

tight·fit·ting (tīt′fit′ing), *adj.* (of a garment) fitting closely to the contours of the body: *tightfitting pants.* [1840–50; TIGHT + FIT[1] + -ING[2]]

tight-knit (tīt′nit′), *adj.* well-organized and integrated.

tight-lipped (tīt′lipt′), *adj.* **1.** speaking very little; taciturn; close-mouthed. **2.** having the lips drawn tight. [1875–80]

tight-mouthed (tīt′mouthd′, -moutht′), *adj.* tight-lipped. [1925–30]

tight·rope (tīt′rōp′), *n., v.,* **-roped, -rop·ing.** **—***n.* **1.** a rope or wire cable, stretched tight, on which acrobats perform feats of balancing. **—***v.i.* **2.** to walk, move, or proceed on or as on a tightrope: *He tightroped through enemy territory.* **—***v.t.* **3.** to make (one's way, course, etc.) on or as on a tightrope. [1795–1805; TIGHT + ROPE]

tights (tīts), *n.* (*used with a plural v.*) **1.** a skin-tight, one-piece garment for the lower part of the body and the legs, now often made of stretch fabric, originally worn by dancers, acrobats, gymnasts, etc., and later made for general wear for adults and children. **2.** a leotard with legs and, sometimes, feet. [1825–35; n. use of TIGHT; see -S[3]]

tight′ shot′, *Cinematog.* a shot in which the camera appears to be very close to the subject, as in an extreme closeup.

tight·wad (tīt′wod′), *n. Informal.* a close-fisted or stingy person. [1895–1900, *Amer.*; TIGHT + WAD[1]]

tight·wire (tīt′wīʳr′), *n.* tightrope (def. 1). [1925–30; TIGHT + WIRE]

Tig·lath-pi·le·ser I (tig′lath pi lē′zər, -pī-), died 1102? B.C., king of Assyria c1115–1102?.

Tiglath-pileser III, died 727 B.C., king of Assyria 745–727.

tig·lic (tig′lik), *adj. Chem.* of or derived from tiglic acid. Also, **tig·lin·ic** (ti glin′ik). [1870–75; < NL *tigl(ium)* croton-oil plant (said to be < Gk *til(os)* watery excrement + NL *-ium* -IUM) + -IC]

tig′lic ac′id, *Chem.* a slightly water-soluble, poisonous compound, $C_5H_8O_2$, derived from croton oil and occurring as a thick, syrupy liquid or in colorless crystals. [1870–75]

ti·glon (tī′glən), *n.* the offspring of a male tiger and a female lion. Also, **ti·gon** (tī′gən). Cf. **liger.** [1940–45; TIG(ER) + L(I)ON]

Ti·gré (tē grā′), *n.* **1.** a Semitic language spoken in northern Ethiopia. **2.** a member of a nomadic, Tigrinya-speaking people of northern Ethiopia. **3.** a member of an agricultural, Tigré-speaking people of northern Ethiopia.

ti·gress (tī′gris), *n.* **1.** a female tiger. **2.** a woman resembling a tiger, as in fierceness or courage. [1605–15; earlier *tigresse* < F; see TIGER, -ESS]

Ti·grin·ya (ti grēn′yə), *n.* a Semitic language spoken in northern Ethiopia.

Ti·gris (tī′gris), *n.* a river in SW Asia, flowing SE from SE Turkey through Iraq, joining the Euphrates to form the Shatt-al-Arab. 1150 mi. (1850 km) long.

ti·grish (tī′grish), *adj.* tigerish.

Ti·hua (*Chin.* dē′hwä′), *n. Wade-Giles.* Dihua. Also, *Older Spelling,* **Ti′hwa′.**

Ti·jua·na (tē′ə wä′nə; *Sp.* tē hwä′nä), *n.* a city in NW Mexico, on the Mexico-U.S. border. 335,100. Also, **Tia Juana.**

Ti′jua′na tax′i, *CB Slang.* any vehicle, esp. a police car, with flashing lights and bright markings.

Ti·kal (tē käl′), *n.* an ancient Mayan city occupied c200 B.C. to A.D. 900, an important center of Mayan civilization, situated in Petén in the jungles of northern Guatemala and the site of significant archaeological discoveries in the late 1950's and early 1960's.

tike (tīk), *n.* tyke.

ti·ki (tē′kē), *n.* **1.** (*cap.*) (in Polynesian mythology) the first man on earth. **2.** (in Polynesian cultures) a carved image, as of a god or ancestor, sometimes worn as a pendant around the neck. [1875–80; < Maori and Marquesan]

til (til, tēl), *n.* the sesame plant. Also, **teel.** [1830–40; < Hindi]

'til (til), *prep., conj.* till; until. [aph. var. of UNTIL]
—Usage. See **till[1].**

til·ak (til′ək), *n., pl.* **-ak, -aks.** a distinctive spot of colored powder or paste worn on the forehead by Hindu men and women as a religious symbol. [< Skt *tilaka*]

ti·la·pi·a (tə lä′pē ə, -lā′-), *n.* any freshwater cichlid of the genus *Tilapia*, of African waters: an important food fish. [< NL (1849); ulterior orig. uncert.]

Til·burg (til′bûrg; *Du.* til′bœrkh), *n.* a city in the S Netherlands. 153,117.

til·bur·y (til′ber′ē, -bə rē), *n., pl.* **-ries.** a light two-wheeled carriage without a top. [1790–1800; named after its inventor, a 19th-century English coach-builder]

til·de (til′də), *n.* **1.** a diacritic (˜) placed over an *n*, as in Spanish *mañana*, to indicate a palatal nasal sound or over a vowel, as in Portuguese *são*, to indicate nasalization. **2.** See **swung dash. 3.** *Math.* a symbol (~) indicating equivalency or similarity between two values. **4.** *Logic.* a similar symbol indicating negation. [1860–65; < Sp < L *titulus* superscription. See TITLE]

Til·den (til′dən), *n.* **1. Samuel Jones,** 1814–86, U.S. statesman. **2. William Ta·tem, Jr.** (tā′təm), 1893–1953, U.S. tennis player.

Til·dy (til′dē), *n.* **Zol·tán** (zôl′tän), 1889–1961, Hungarian statesman: premier 1945–46; president 1946–48.

tile (tīl), *n., v.,* **tiled, til·ing.** **—***n.* **1.** a thin slab or bent piece of baked clay, sometimes painted or glazed, used for various purposes, as to form one of the units of a roof covering, floor, or revetment. **2.** any of various similar slabs or pieces, as of linoleum, stone, rubber, or metal. **3.** tiles collectively. **4.** a pottery tube or pipe used for draining land. **5.** Also called **hollow tile.** any of various hollow or cellular units of burnt clay or other materials, as gypsum or cinder concrete, for building walls, partitions, floors, and roofs, or for fireproofing steelwork or the like. **6.** *Informal.* a stiff hat or high silk hat. **—***v.t.* **7.** to cover with or as with tiles. [bef. 900; ME; OE *tigele* (c. G *Ziegel*) < L *tēgula*] **—tile′like′,** *adj.*

tiled (tīld), *adj.* **1.** covered or furnished with tiles. **2.** barred to outsiders, as nonmembers of a lodge. [1400–50; late ME; see TILE, -ED[3]]

tile′ field′, a system of unconnected drain tiles distributing septic tank effluent over an absorption area or providing drainage in wet areas. [1880–85, in sense "ground where tiles are made"]

tile·fish (tīl′fish′), *n., pl.* (*esp. collectively*) **-fish,** (*esp. referring to two or more kinds or species*) **-fish·es. 1.** a large, brilliantly colored food fish, *Lopholatilus chamaeleonticeps*, of deep waters of the Atlantic Ocean. **2.** any of several related fishes of the family Branchiostegidae. [1880–85, *Amer.*; TILE + FISH]

til·er (tī′lər), *n.* **1.** a person who lays tiles. **2.** Also, **tyler.** the doorkeeper of a Masonic lodge. [1250–1300; ME; see TILE, -ER[1]]

til·er·y (tī′lə rē), *n., pl.* **-er·ies.** a factory or kiln for making tiles. [1840–50; TILE + -ERY]

til·i·a·ceous (til′ē ā′shəs), *adj.* belonging to the Tiliaceae, the linden family of plants. Cf. **linden family.** [1890–95; < NL *Tiliace(ae)* (*Tili(a)* a genus (L: linden tree) + *-aceae* -ACEAE) + -OUS]

til·ing (tī′ling), *n.* **1.** the operation of covering with tiles. **2.** tiles collectively. **3.** a tiled surface. **4.** *Math.* a two-dimensional pattern resembling a tiled surface. [1400–50; late ME *tylynge.* See TILE, -ING[1]]

till[1] (til), *prep.* **1.** up to the time of; until: *to fight till death.* **2.** before (used in negative constructions): *He did not come till today.* **3.** near or at a specified time: *till evening.* **4.** *Chiefly Midland, Southern, and Western U.S.* before; to: *It's ten till four on my watch.* **5.** *Scot. and North Eng.* **a.** to. **b.** unto. **—***conj.* **6.** to the time that or when; until. **7.** before (used in negative constructions). [bef. 900; ME; OE (north) *til* < ON *til* to, akin to OE *till* station, G *Ziel* goal. See TILL[2]]
—Usage. TILL[1] and UNTIL are both old in the language and are interchangeable as both prepositions and conjunctions: *It rained till (or until) nearly midnight. The savannah remained brown and lifeless until (or till) the rains began.* TILL is not a shortened form of UNTIL and is not spelled 'TILL. 'TIL is usually considered a spelling error, though widely used in advertising: *Open 'til ten.*

till[2] (til), *v.t.* **1.** to labor, as by plowing or harrowing, upon (land) for the raising of crops; cultivate. **2.** to plow. **—***v.i.* **3.** to cultivate the soil. [bef. 900; ME *tilen*, OE *tilian* to strive after, get, till; c. D *telen* to breed, cultivate, G *zielen* to aim at]

till[3] (til), *n.* **1.** a drawer, box, or the like, as in a shop or bank, in which money is kept. **2.** a drawer, tray, or the like, as in a cabinet or chest, for keeping valuables. **3.** an arrangement of drawers or pigeonholes, as on a desk top. [1425–75; late ME *tylle*, n. use of *tylle* to draw, OE *-tyllan* (in *fortyllan* to seduce); akin to L *dolus* trick, Gk *dólos* bait (for fish), any cunning contrivance, treachery]

till[4] (til), *n.* **1.** *Geol.* glacial drift consisting of an unassorted mixture of clay, sand, gravel, and boulders. **2.** a stiff clay. [1665–75; orig. uncert.]

till·a·ble (til′ə bəl), *adj.* able to be tilled; arable. [1565–75; TILL[2] + -ABLE]

till·age (til′ij), *n.* **1.** the operation, practice, or art of tilling land. **2.** tilled land. [1480–90; TILL[2] + -AGE]

til·land·si·a (ti land′zē ə), *n.* any of numerous, chiefly epiphytic bromeliads of the genus *Tillandsia*, including Spanish moss and many species cultivated as ornamentals. [< NL (Linnaeus), after Elias *Tillands*, 17th-century Finno-Swedish botanist; see -IA]

till·er[1] (til′ər), *n.* **1.** a person who tills; farmer. **2.** a person or thing that tills; cultivator. [1200–50; ME *tiliere.* See TILL[2], -ER[1]]

til·ler[2] (til′ər), *n. Naut.* a bar or lever fitted to the head of a rudder, for turning the rudder in steering. [1375–1425; late ME < AF *teiler* weaver's beam; OF *teilier* < ML *tēlārium*, equiv. to L *tēl(a)* warp + *-ārium* -ARY] **—till′er·less,** *adj.*

til·ler[3] (til′ər), *n.* **1.** a plant shoot that springs from the root or bottom of the original stalk. **2.** a sapling. **—***v.i.* **3.** (of a plant) to put forth new shoots from the root or around the bottom of the original stalk. [bef. 1000; OE *telgor* twig, shoot (not recorded in ME); akin to *telge* rod, ON *tjalga* branch, *telgja* to cut]

til·ler·man (til′ər mən), *n., pl.* **-men.** a person who steers a boat or has charge of a tiller. [1930–35; TILLER[2] + -MAN]

Till Eu·len·spie·gel (til′ oi′lən shpē′gəl), a legendary German peasant of the 14th century whose practical jokes yielded many stories. Also, **Tyll Eulenspiegel, Tyl Eulenspiegel.**

Til·lich (til′ik; *Ger.* til′ikh), *n.* **Paul Jo·han·nes** (pôl yō han′is; *Ger.* poul yō hä′nəs), 1886–1965, U.S. philosopher and theologian, born in Germany.

till·ite (til′īt), *n.* a rock composed of consolidated till. [1915–20; TILL[4] + -ITE[1]]

till′ mon′ey, *Banking.* money set aside for use by a teller, as distinguished from money kept in the vault. [1890–95]

Til·lot·son (til′ət sən), *n.* **John,** 1630–94, English clergyman: archbishop of Canterbury 1691–94.

Til·ly (til′ē), *n.* **1. Count Jo·han Tser·claes von** (yō′hän tseʀ kläs′ fən), 1559–1632, German general in the Thirty Years' War. **2.** Also, **Til′lie.** a female given name, form of **Matilda.**

Til·sit (til′zit, -sit), *n.* **1.** former name of **Sovetsk. 2.** a semihard, light yellow cheese made from whole milk, similar in flavor to mild Limburger.

tilt[1] (tilt), *v.t.* **1.** to cause to lean, incline, slope, or slant. **2.** to rush at or charge, as in a joust. **3.** to hold poised for attack, as a lance. **4.** to move (a camera) up or down on its vertical axis for photographing or televising a moving character, object, or the like. **—***v.i.* **5.** to move into or assume a sloping position or direction. **6.** to strike, thrust, or charge with a lance or the like (usually fol. by *at*). **7.** to engage in a joust, tournament, or similar contest. **8.** (of a camera) to move on its vertical axis: *The camera tilts downward for an overhead shot.* **9.** to incline in opinion, feeling, etc.; lean: *She's tilting toward the other candidate this year.* **10. tilt at windmills,** to contend against imaginary opponents or injustices. Also, **fight with windmills.** **—***n.* **11.** an act or instance of tilting. **12.** the state of being tilted; a sloping position. **13.** a slope. **14.** a joust or any other contest. **15.** a dispute; controversy. **16.** a thrust of a weapon, as at a tilt or joust. **17.** (in aerial photography) the angle formed by the direction of aim of a camera and a perpendicular to the surface of the earth. **18. (at) full tilt.** See **full tilt.** [1300–50; ME *tylten* to upset, tumble < Scand; cf. dial. Norw *tylta* to tiptoe, *tylten* unsteady; akin to OE *tealt* unsteady, *tealtian* to totter, amble, MD *touteren* to sway] **—tilt′a·ble,** *adj.* **—tilt′er,** *n.*

tilt[2] (tilt), *n.* **1.** a cover of coarse cloth, canvas, etc., as for a wagon. **2.** an awning. **—***v.t.* **3.** to furnish with a tilt. [1400–50; late ME, var. of *tild,* OE *teld;* c. G *Zelt* tent, ON *tjald* tent, curtain]

tilt′ board′, **1.** a rectangular board mounted on a fulcrum, for use by acrobats and gymnasts to gain momentum in feats of tumbling. **2.** a similar board, used in exercising, on which the body rests on an inclined plane, with the legs on a higher level than the head and arms. **3.** *New Eng.* See **tilting board.** Also, **tilt′board′.** **—Regional Variation. 3.** See **seesaw.**

tilth (tilth), *n.* **1.** the act or operation of tilling land; tillage. **2.** the state of being tilled or under cultivation. **3.** the physical condition of soil in relation to plant growth. **4.** land that is tilled or cultivated. [bef. 1000; ME, OE. See TILL[2], -TH[1]]

tilt′ ham′mer, a drop hammer used in forging, consisting of a heavy head at one end of a pivoted lever. [1740–50]

tilt′ing board′, *New Eng.* a seesaw. Also, **tilt board, tilt′er·ing board′** (til′tər ing). **—Regional Variation.** See **seesaw.**

tilt′ing chest′, a medieval chest decorated with a representation of a tournament.

tilt·me·ter (tilt′mē′tər), *n. Geol.* an instrument used to measure slight changes in the inclination of the earth's surface, usually in connection with volcanology and earthquake seismology. [1930–35; TILT[1] + -METER]

tilt′-top ta′ble (tilt′top′), a pedestal table having a top that can be tilted vertically.

tilt-up (tilt′up′), *adj. Building Trades.* of or pertaining to a method of casting concrete walls on site in a horizontal position or preassembling wooden wall and partition frames, then tilting them up into their final position: *tilt-up construction.* [1840–50; adj. use of v. phrase *tilt up*]

tilt·yard (tilt′yärd′), *n.* a courtyard or other area for tilting. [1520–30; TILT[1] + YARD[2]]

Tim (tim), *n.* a male given name, form of **Timothy.**

Tim., *Bible.* Timothy.

ti·ma·rau (tē′mə rou′), *n.* tamarau.

Tim·a·ru (tim′ə ro͞o′), *n.* a seaport on the E coast of South Island, in S New Zealand. 29,958.

tim·bal (tim′bəl), *n.* **1.** a kettledrum. **2.** *Entomol.* a vibrating membrane in certain insects, as the cicada. Also, **tymbal.** [1670–80; < F, MF *timbale,* alter. (by assoc. with *cymbale* CYMBAL) of *tamballe,* itself alter. (by assoc. with *tambour* drum, TAMBOUR) of Sp *atabal* < Ar *al ṭabl* the drum]

tim·bale (tim′bəl; *for 1, 2 also Fr.* taN bal′; *Sp.* tēm bä′le *for 3*), *n., pl.* **-bales** (-bəlz; *Fr.* -bal′). **1.** Also, **tim′bale case′.** a small shell made of batter, fried usually in a timbale iron. **2.** a preparation, usually richly sauced, of minced meat, fish, or vegetables served in a timbale or other crust. **3. timbales.** Also called **tim·ba·les cre·o·les** (*Sp.* tēm bä′les kre ô′les). two conjoined Afro-Cuban drums similar to bongos but wider in diameter and played with drumsticks instead of the hands. [1815–25; < F: lit., kettledrum. See TIMBAL]

tim′bale i′ron, a metal mold made in any of several shapes and usually provided with a long handle, for deep-frying timbales. [1890–95]

tim·ber (tim′bər), *n.* **1.** the wood of growing trees suitable for structural uses. **2.** growing trees themselves. **3.** wooded land. **4.** wood, esp. when suitable or adapted for various building purposes. **5.** a single piece of wood forming part of a structure or the like: *A timber fell from the roof.* **6.** *Naut.* (in a ship's frame) one of the curved pieces of wood that spring upward and outward from the keel; rib. **7.** personal character or quality: *He's being talked up as presidential timber.* **8.** *Sports.* a wooden hurdle, as a gate or fence, over which a horse must jump in equestrian sports. *—v.t.* **9.** to furnish with timber. **10.** to support with timber. *—v.i.* **11.** to fell timber, esp. as an occupation. *—interj.* **12.** a lumberjack's call to warn those in the vicinity that a cut tree is about to fall to the ground. [bef. 900; ME, OE: orig., house, building material; c. G *Zimmer* room, ON *timbr* timber; akin to Goth *timrjan,* Gk *démein* to build. See DOME] **—tim′ber·less,** *adj.* **—tim′ber·y,** *adj.*

tim·ber·beast (tim′bər bēst′), *n. Slang.* a logger. [1915–20; TIMBER + BEAST]

tim′ber bee′tle. See **bark beetle.** [1835–45]

tim′ber cruis′er, cruiser (def. 6). [1890–95, *Amer.*]

tim·ber·doo·dle (tim′bər do͞od′l, tim′bər do͞od′l), *n. Informal.* the American woodcock, *Philohela minor.* [1870–75, *Amer.*; TIMBER + DOODLE[1]]

tim·bered (tim′bərd), *adj.* **1.** made of or furnished with timber. **2.** covered with growing trees; wooded: *timbered acres.* [1375–1425; late ME *timbred.* See TIMBER, -ED[3]]

tim·ber·head (tim′bər hed′), *n. Naut.* **1.** the top end of a timber, rising above the deck and serving for belaying ropes. **2.** a bollard resembling this in position and use. [1785–95; TIMBER + HEAD]

tim′ber hitch′, a knot or hitch on a spar or the like, made by taking a turn on the object, wrapping the end around the standing part of the rope, then several times around itself. [1805–15]

tim·ber-hitch (tim′bər hich′), *v.t.* to fasten by means of a timber hitch. [1880–85]

tim·ber·ing (tim′bər ing), *n.* **1.** building material of wood. **2.** timberwork. [1125–75; ME *timbrung.* See TIMBER, -ING[1]]

tim·ber·jack (tim′bər jak′), *n.* a person whose occupation is logging; logger. [1915–20; TIMBER + JACK[1]]

CONCISE ETYMOLOGY KEY: <, descended or borrowed from; >, whence; b., blend of, blended; c., cognate with; cf., compare; deriv., derivative; equiv., equivalent; imit., imitative; obl., oblique; r., replacing; s., stem; sp., spelling, spelled; resp., respelling, respelled; trans., translation; ?, origin unknown; *, unattested; ‡, probably earlier than. See the full key inside the front cover.

tim·ber·land (tim′bər land′), *n.* land covered with timber-producing forests. [1645–55, *Amer.*; TIMBER + -LAND]

tim·ber·line (tim′bər līn′), *n.* **1.** the altitude above sea level at which timber ceases to grow. **2.** the arctic or antarctic limit of tree growth. Also called **tree line.** [1865–70, *Amer.*; TIMBER + LINE[1]]

tim·ber·man (tim′bər mən), *n., pl.* **-men.** a person who prepares, erects, and maintains mine timbers. [1400–50; late ME; see TIMBER, MAN[1]]

tim′ber mill′, a sawmill producing timbers, as for building purposes. [1905–10]

tim′ber rat′tlesnake, a rattlesnake, *Crotalus horridus horridus,* of the eastern U.S., usually having the body marked with dark crossbands. Also called **banded rattlesnake.** See illus. under **rattlesnake.** [1890–95]

tim′ber right′, ownership of standing timber with no rights to the land.

tim′ber wolf′, the gray wolf, *Canis lupus,* sometimes designated as the subspecies *C. lupus occidentalis:* formerly common in northern North America but now greatly reduced in number and rare in the conterminous U.S. [1875–80]

tim·ber·work (tim′bər wûrk′), *n.* structural work formed of timbers. [1350–1400; ME *timberwerk.* See TIMBER, WORK]

tim·bre (tam′bər, tim′-; *Fr.* taN′brᵊ), *n.* **1.** *Acoustics, Phonet.* the characteristic quality of a sound, independent of pitch and loudness, from which its source or manner of production can be inferred. Timbre depends on the relative strengths of the components of different frequencies, which are determined by resonance. **2.** *Music.* the characteristic quality of sound produced by a particular instrument or voice; tone color. [1325–75; ME *tymbre* < F: sound (orig. of bell), MF: bell, timbrel, drum, OF: drum < MGk *timbanon,* var. of Gk *týmpanon* drum]

tim·brel (tim′brəl), *n.* a tambourine or similar instrument. [1490–1500; earlier *timbre* drum (see TIMBRE) + *-el* dim. suffix] **—tim′breled, tim′brelled,** *adj.* **—tim′brel·ist,** *n.*

Tim·buk·tu (tim′buk to͞o′, tim buk′to͞o), *n.* **1.** a town in central Mali, W Africa, near the Niger River. 19,500. French, **Tombouctou. 2.** any faraway place.

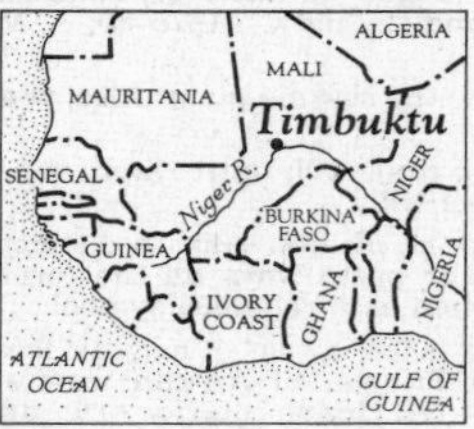

time (tīm), *n., adj., v.,* **timed, tim·ing.** *—n.* **1.** the system of those sequential relations that any event has to any other, as past, present, or future; indefinite and continuous duration regarded as that in which events succeed one another. **2.** duration regarded as belonging to the present life as distinct from the life to come or from eternity; finite duration. **3.** (*sometimes cap.*) a system or method of measuring or reckoning the passage of time: *mean time; apparent time; Greenwich Time.* **4.** a limited period or interval, as between two successive events: *a long time.* **5.** a particular period considered as distinct from other periods: *Youth is the best time of life.* **6.** Often, **times. a.** a period in the history of the world, or contemporary with the life or activities of a notable person: *prehistoric times; in Lincoln's time.* **b.** the period or era now or previously present: *a sign of the times; How times have changed!* **c.** a period considered with reference to its events or prevailing conditions, tendencies, ideas, etc.: *hard times; a time of war.* **7.** a prescribed or allotted period, as of one's life, for payment of a debt, etc. **8.** the end of a prescribed or allotted period, as of one's life or a pregnancy: *His time had come, but there was no one left to mourn over him. When her time came, her husband accompanied her to the delivery room.* **9.** a period with reference to personal experience of a specified kind: *to have a good time; a hot time in the old town tonight.* **10.** a period of work of an employee, or the pay for it; working hours or days or an hourly or daily pay rate. **11.** *Informal.* a term of enforced duty or imprisonment: *to serve time in the army; do time in prison.* **12.** the period necessary for or occupied by something: *The time of the baseball game was two hours and two minutes. The bus takes too much time, so I'll take a plane.* **13.** leisure time; sufficient or spare time: *to have time for a vacation; I have no time to stop now.* **14.** a particular or definite point in time, as indicated by a clock: *What time is it?* **15.** a particular part of a year, day, etc.; season or period: *It's time for lunch.* **16.** an appointed, fit, due, or proper instant or period: *a time for sowing; the time when the sun crosses the meridian; There is a time for everything.* **17.** the particular point in time when an event is scheduled to take place: *train time; curtain time.* **18.** an indefinite, frequently prolonged period or duration in the future: *Time will tell if what we have done here today was right.* **19.** the right occasion or opportunity: *to watch one's time.* **20.** each occasion of a recurring action or event: *to do a thing five times; It's the pitcher's time at bat.* **21. times,** used as a multiplicative word in phrasal combinations expressing how many instances of a quantity or factor are taken together: *Two goes into six three times; five times faster.* **22.** *Drama.* one of the three unities. Cf. **unity** (def. 8). **23.** *Pros.* a unit or a group of units in the measurement of meter. **24.** *Music.* **a.** tempo; relative rapidity of movement. **b.** the metrical duration of a note or rest. **c.** proper or characteristic tempo. **d.** the general movement of a particular kind of musical composition with reference to its rhythm, metrical structure, and tempo. **e.** the movement of a dance or the like to music so arranged: *waltz time.* **25.** *Mil.* rate of marching, calculated on the number of paces taken per minute: *double time; quick time.* **26.** *Manège.* each completed action or movement of the horse. **27. against time,** in an effort to finish something within a limited period: *We worked against time to get out the newspaper.* **28. ahead of time,** before the time due; early: *The building was completed ahead of time.* **29. at one time, a.** once; in a former time: *At one time they owned a restaurant.* **b.** at the same time; at once: *They all tried to talk at one time.* **30. at the same time,** nevertheless; yet: *I'd like to try it, but at the same time I'm a little afraid.* **31. at times,** at intervals; occasionally: *At times the city becomes intolerable.* **32. beat someone's time,** *Slang.* to compete for or win a person being dated or courted by another; prevail over a rival: *He accused me, his own brother, of trying to beat his time.* **33. behind the times,** old-fashioned; dated: *These attitudes are behind the times.* **34. for the time being,** temporarily; for the present: *Let's forget about it for the time being.* **35. from time to time,** on occasion; occasionally; at intervals: *She comes to see us from time to time.* **36. gain time,** to postpone in order to make preparations or gain an advantage; delay the outcome of: *He hoped to gain time by putting off signing the papers for a few days more.* **37. in good time, a.** at the right time; on time; punctually. **b.** in advance of the right time; early: *We arrived at the appointed spot in good time.* **38. in no time,** in a very brief time; almost at once: *Working together, they cleaned the entire house in no time.* **39. in time, a.** early enough: *to come in time for dinner.* **b.** in the future; eventually: *In time he'll see what is right.* **c.** in the correct rhythm or tempo: *There would always be at least one child who couldn't play in time with the music.* **40. keep time, a.** to record time, as a watch or clock does. **b.** to mark or observe the tempo. **c.** to perform rhythmic movements in unison. **41. kill time,** to occupy oneself with some activity to make time pass quickly: *While I was waiting, I killed time counting the cars on the freight trains.* **42. make time, a.** to move quickly, esp. in an attempt to recover lost time. **b.** to travel at a particular speed. **43. make time with,** *Slang.* to pursue or take as a sexual partner. **44. many a time,** again and again; frequently: *Many a time they didn't have enough to eat and went to bed hungry.* **45. mark time, a.** to suspend progress temporarily, as to await developments; fail to advance. **b.** *Mil.* to move the feet alternately as in marching, but without advancing. **46. on one's own time,** during one's free time; without payment: *He worked out more efficient production methods on his own time.* **47. on time, a.** at the specified time; punctually. **b.** to be paid for within a designated period of time, as in installments: *Many people are never out of debt because they buy everything on time.* **48. out of time,** not in the proper rhythm: *His singing was out of time with the music.* **49. pass the time of day,** to converse briefly with or greet someone: *The women would stop in the market to pass the time of day.* **50. take one's time,** to be slow or leisurely; dawdle: *Speed was important here, but he just took his time.* **51. time after time,** again and again; repeatedly; often: *I've told him time after time not to slam the door.* **52. time and time again,** repeatedly; often: *Time and time again I warned her to stop smoking.* Also, **time and again. 53. time of life,** (one's) age: *At your time of life you must be careful not to overdo things.* **54. time of one's life,** *Informal.* an extremely enjoyable experience: *They had the time of their lives on their trip to Europe.*
—adj. **55.** of, pertaining to, or showing the passage of time. **56.** (of an explosive device) containing a clock so that it will detonate at the desired moment: *a time bomb.* **57.** *Com.* payable at a stated period of time after presentment: *time drafts or notes.* **58.** of or pertaining to purchases on the installment plan, or with payment postponed.
—v.t. **59.** to measure or record the speed, duration, or rate of: *to time a race.* **60.** to fix the duration of: *The proctor timed the test at 15 minutes.* **61.** to fix the interval between (actions, events, etc.): *They timed their strokes at six per minute.* **62.** to regulate (a train, clock, etc.) as to time. **63.** to appoint or choose the moment or occasion for; schedule: *He timed the attack perfectly.* *—v.i.* **64.** to keep time; sound or move in unison. [bef. 900; (n.) ME; OE *tīma;* c. ON *tími;* (v.) ME *timen* to arrange a time, deriv. of the n.; akin to TIDE[1]]
—Syn. 4. term, spell, span. **6.** epoch, era.

time′ and a half′, a rate of pay for overtime work equal to one and one half times the regular hourly wage. [1885–90]

time′ and mo′tion stud′y, the systematic investigation and analysis of the motions and the time required to perform a specific operation or task with a view to seeking more efficient methods of production as well as setting time standards. Also called **time study, motion study.**

time′ bill′, a bill of exchange payable at a specified date. [1825–35, *Amer.*]

time-bind·ing (tīm′bīn′ding), *n.* the distinctively human attribute of preserving memories and records of experiences for the use of subsequent generations.

time′ bomb′, **1.** a bomb constructed so as to explode at a certain time. **2.** a situation, condition, etc., resembling such a bomb in having disastrous consequences in the future. [1890–95]

time′ cap′sule, a receptacle containing documents or objects typical of the current period, placed in the earth or in a cornerstone for discovery in the future. [1935–40]

time·card (tīm′kärd′), *n.* a card for recording the time at which an employee arrives at and departs from a job. [1870–75, *Amer.*; TIME + CARD[1]]

time′ chart′, a chart indicating the standard times of certain parts of the world corresponding to a given time at a specific place. [1820–30]

time′ clock′, a clock with an attachment that may be

manually activated to stamp or otherwise record the exact time on a card or tape, used to keep a record of the time of something, as of the arrival and departure of employees. [1885–90, *Amer.*]

time′ con′stant, *Elect.* the time required for a changing quantity in a circuit, as voltage or current, to rise or fall approximately 0.632 of the difference between its old and new value after an impulse has been applied that induces such a change: equal in seconds to the inductance of the circuit in henries divided by its resistance in ohms. [1890–95]

time-con·sum·ing (tīm′kən so͞o′ming), *adj.* (of an action) requiring or wasting much time. [1930–35]

time′ cop′y, *Journalism.* written material set in type and held for future use. Cf. **filler** (def. 5).

time′ depos′it, *Banking.* a deposit that can be withdrawn by the depositor only after giving advance notice or after an agreed period of time has elapsed. [1850–55, *Amer.*]

time′ dilata′tion, *Physics.* (in relativity) the apparent loss of time of a moving clock as observed by a stationary observer. Also, **time′ dila′tion.** [1955–60]

time′ dis′count, a discount allowed for payment of an invoice or bill before it falls due.

time′ draft′, a draft payable within a specified number of days after it is presented. [1860–65, *Amer.*]

timed-re·lease (tīmd′ri lēs′), *adj. Pharm.* sustained-release. Also, **time-release.** [1975–80]

time′ expo′sure, *Photog.* a long exposure in which the shutter is opened and closed by hand or by a mechanism other than the automatic mechanism of the shutter. [1890–95] —**time′-ex·po′sure,** *adj.*

time′ frame′, a period of time during which something has taken or will take place: *We're talking about a time frame of five minutes for the President's visit.* [1960–65]

time-hon·ored (tīm′on′ərd), *adj.* revered or respected because of antiquity and long continuance: *a time-honored custom.* Also, *esp. Brit.,* **time′-hon′oured.** [1585–95]

time′ immemo′rial, 1. Also called **time out of mind.** time in the distant past beyond memory or record: *Those carvings have been there from time immemorial.* **2.** *Law.* time beyond legal memory, fixed by statute in England as prior to the beginning of the reign of Richard I (1189). [1595–1605]

time·keep·er (tīm′kē′pər), *n.* **1.** a person or thing that keeps time. **2.** an official appointed to time, regulate, and record the duration of a sports contest or its component parts, as to give the official time of a race, assure that a round of boxing is ended exactly on time, or announce to football, basketball, hockey, etc., teams the amount of time left to play. **3.** a timepiece: *This watch is a good timekeeper.* **4.** a person employed to keep account of the hours of work done by others. **5.** a person who beats time in music. [1680–90; TIME + KEEPER] —**time′keep′ing,** *n.*

time′ kill′er, 1. a person with free time to spend. **2.** an activity that helps the time to go by agreeably or tolerably; pastime. [1745–55]

time-lag (tīm′lag′), *n.* the period of time between two closely related events, phenomena, etc., as between stimulus and response or between cause and effect: *a time-lag between the declaration of war and full war production.* [1890–95]

time′ lamp′, an oil lamp of the 17th and 18th centuries, burning at a fixed rate and having a reservoir graduated in units of time.

time-lapse (tīm′laps′), *adj.* done by means of time-lapse photography: *a time-lapse study of the blooming of a flower.* [1925–30]

time′-lapse photog′raphy, the photographing on motion-picture film of a slow and continuous process, as the growth of a plant, at regular intervals, esp. by exposing a single frame at a time, for projection at a higher speed.

time·less (tīm′lis), *adj.* **1.** without beginning or end; eternal; everlasting. **2.** referring or restricted to no particular time: *the timeless beauty of great music.* [1550–60; TIME + -LESS] —**time′less·ly,** *adv.* —**time′less·ness,** *n.*
—**Syn. 2.** enduring, lasting, abiding, permanent.

time′ lim′it, a period of time within which an action or procedure must be done or completed. [1875–80]

time′ loan′, a loan repayable at a specified date. Cf. **call loan.** [1905–10]

time′ lock′, a lock, as for the door of a bank vault, equipped with a mechanism that makes it impossible to operate the lock within certain hours. [1865–70]

time·ly (tīm′lē), *adj.,* **-li·er, -li·est,** *adv.* —*adj.* **1.** occurring at a suitable time; seasonable; opportune; well-timed: *a timely warning.* **2.** *Archaic.* early. —*adv.* **3.** seasonably; opportunely. **4.** *Archaic.* early or soon. [bef. 1000; ME *tim(e)liche,* OE *tīmlīce* (adv.). See TIME, -LY] —**time′li·ness,** *n.*
—**Syn. 1.** See **opportune.**

time′ machine′, a theoretical apparatus that would convey one to the past or future. [1890–95]

time′ mon′ey, funds loaned or available to be loaned for repayment within a designated period of time, usually in installments. [1910–15]

time′ note′, a note payable within a specified number of days after it is presented. [1905–10]

ti·me·o Da·na·os et do·na fe·ren·tes (tim′e ō′ dä′nä ōs′ et dō′nä fe ʀen′tes; *Eng.* tim′ē ō′ dan′ā ōs′ et dō′nə fə ren′tēz), *Latin.* I fear the Greeks even when they bear gifts (I fear treacherous persons even when they appear to be friendly). Vergil's *Aeneid:* I, 2:49.

time′ of day′, 1. a definite time as shown by a timepiece; the hour: *Can you tell me the time of day?* **2.** *Informal.* a minimum of attention: *He wouldn't even give her the time of day.* **3.** the current time; the present: *The younger generation in this time of day encounters problems quite different from those of past generations.* [1590–1600]

time·ous (tī′məs), *adj. Chiefly Scot.* timely. [1425–75; TIME + -OUS; r. late ME (Scots) *tymys* (see -ISH[1])]

time-out (tīm′out′), *n., pl.* **-outs. 1.** a brief suspension of activity; intermission or break. **2.** *Sports.* a short interruption in a regular period of play during which a referee or other official stops the clock so that the players may rest, deliberate, make substitutions, etc. Also, **time′out′.** [1870–75]

time′ out of mind′. See **time immemorial** (def. 1). [1470–80]

time·piece (tīm′pēs′), *n.* **1.** an apparatus for measuring and recording the progress of time; chronometer. **2.** a clock or a watch. [1755–65; TIME + PIECE]

time·pleas·er (tīm′plē′zər), *n. Obs.* a timeserver. [1595–1605; TIME + PLEASER]

tim·er (tī′mər), *n.* **1.** a person or thing that times. **2.** a person who measures or records time. **3.** a device for indicating or measuring elapsed time, as a stopwatch. **4.** a device for controlling machinery, appliances, or the like, in a specified way at a predetermined time: *Please put the roast in the oven and set the timer to cook it for two hours.* **5.** (in an internal-combustion engine) a set of points actuated by a cam, which causes the spark for igniting the charge at the instant required. [1490–1500; TIME + -ER[1]]

time-re·lease (tīm′ri lēs′), *adj.* timed-release.

time′ rever′sal, *Physics.* the mathematical operation of reversing the direction of time. *Symbol:* T [1920–25]

times (tīmz), *prep.* multiplied by: *Two times four is eight.* [1350–1400; ME; see TIME (def. 21)]

time·sav·ing (tīm′sā′ving), *adj.* (of methods, devices, etc.) reducing the time spent or required to do something. [1860–65; TIME + SAVING] —**time′sav′er,** *n.*

time′ se′ries, a set of observations, results, or other data obtained over a period of time, usually at regular intervals: *Monthly sales figures, quarterly inventory data, and daily bank balances are all time series.* [1890–95]

time·serv·er (tīm′sûr′vər), *n.* a person who shapes his or her conduct to conform to the opinions of the time or of persons in power, esp. for selfish ends. [1565–75; TIME + SERVER] —**time′serv′ing,** *adj., n.* —**time′·serv′ing·ness,** *n.*

time·share (tīm′shâr′), *v.,* **-shared, -shar·ing,** *n.* —*v.t.* **1.** to use or occupy by time-sharing. —*n.* **2.** time-sharing (def. 2). —**time′-shar′er,** *n.*

time-shar·ing (tīm′shâr′ing), *n.* **1.** *Computers.* a system or service in which a number of users at different terminals simultaneously use a single computer for different purposes. **2.** Also, **time-share.** a plan in which persons share ownership or rental costs of a vacation home, esp. a condominium, entitling each participant to use the residence for a specified time each year. [1960–65]

time′ sheet′, a sheet or card recording the hours worked by an employee, made esp. for payroll purposes. [1890–95]

time′ sig′nal, a signal sent electrically or by radio to indicate a precise moment of time as a means of checking or regulating timepieces. [1875–80]

time′ sig′nature, *Music.* a numerical or other indication at the beginning of a piece showing the meter. [1870–75]

time·span (tīm′span′), *n.* a span of time; time frame. [1930–35; TIME + SPAN[1]]

times′ sign′. See **multiplication sign.** [1945–50]

Times′ Square′, a wide intersection extending from 43rd to 47th Streets in central Manhattan, New York City, where Broadway and Seventh Avenue intersect.

time′ stamp′, a device for stamping the date and time of day that letters, packages, etc., are received or mailed. [1890–95]

time′ stud′y. See **time and motion study.** [1925–30]

time·ta·ble (tīm′tā′bəl), *n.* **1.** a schedule showing the times at which railroad trains, airplanes, etc., arrive and depart. **2.** any schedule or plan designating the times at or within which certain things occur or are scheduled to occur: *a timetable of coming musical events; a timetable of space research.* **3.** *Brit.* **a.** a university or college catalog listing all classes taught during a school semester, along with the time that each class is held, the instructor's name, etc. **b.** a student's class schedule or course of study during a school semester. [1830–40; TIME + TABLE]

time-test·ed (tīm′tes′tid), *adj.* having proved valid, workable, or useful over a long span of time: *a time-tested theory.* [1940–45]

time′ warp′, a hypothetical eccentricity in the progress of time that would allow movement back and forth between eras or that would permit the passage of time to be suspended. [1950–55]

time·work (tīm′wûrk′), *n.* work done and paid for by the hour or day. Cf. **piecework.** [1820–30; TIME + WORK] —**time′work′er,** *n.*

time·worn (tīm′wôrn′, -wōrn′), *adj.* **1.** worn or impaired by time. **2.** showing the effects of age or antiquity; antiquated: *timeworn farming methods.* **3.** commonplace; trite; hackneyed: *a timeworn excuse.* [1720–30; TIME + WORN]

time′ zone′, one of the 24 regions or divisions of the globe approximately coinciding with meridians at successive hours from the observatory at Greenwich, England. [1880–85]

tim·id (tim′id), *adj.,* **-er, -est. 1.** lacking in self-assurance, courage, or bravery; easily alarmed; timorous; shy. **2.** characterized by or indicating fear: *a timid approach to a problem.* [1540–50; < L *timidus* fearful, equiv. to *tim(ēre)* to fear + *-idus* -ID[4]] —**ti·mid′i·ty, tim′id·ness,** *n.* —**tim′id·ly,** *adv.*
—**Syn. 1.** fearful, fainthearted. See **cowardly.**

tim·ing (tī′ming), *n.* **1.** *Theat.* **a.** a synchronizing of the various parts of a production for theatrical effect. **b.** the result or effect thus achieved. **c.** (in acting) the act of adjusting one's tempo of speaking and moving for dramatic effect. **2.** *Sports.* the control of the speed of a stroke, blow, etc., in order that it may reach its maximum at the proper moment. **3.** the selecting of the best time or speed for doing something in order to achieve the desired or maximum result: *I went to ask for a raise, but my timing was bad, since the boss had indigestion.* **4.** an act or instance of observing and recording the elapsed time of an act, contest, process, etc. [1200–50; 1590–1600 for def. 4; ME: hap, occurrence; see TIME, -ING[1]]

tim′ing belt′, an endless belt bearing teeth for engaging sprockets on two mechanisms requiring precise synchronization.

tim′ing chain′, a chain for driving the camshaft of an internal-combustion engine from the crankshaft.

Ti·mi·şoa·ra (tē′mē shwä′ʀä), *n.* a city in W Rumania. 281,320. Hungarian, **Temesvár.**

Tim·mins (tim′inz), *n.* a city in E Ontario, in S Canada: gold-mining center. 46,114.

Ti·moch·a·ris (ti mok′ər is), *n.* a crater in the second

CONCISE PRONUNCIATION KEY: *act, cāpe, dâre, pärt; set, ēqual; if, ice; ox, ōver, ôrder, oil, bo͝ok, bo͞ot, out; up, ûrge; child; sing; shoe; thin, that;* zh as in *treasure.* ə = *a* as in *alone, e* as in *system, i* as in *easily, o* as in *gallop, u* as in *circus;* ᵊ as in *fire* (fīᵊr), *hour* (ouᵊr). l and n can serve as syllabic consonants, as in *cradle* (krād′l), and *button* (but′n). See the full key inside the front cover.

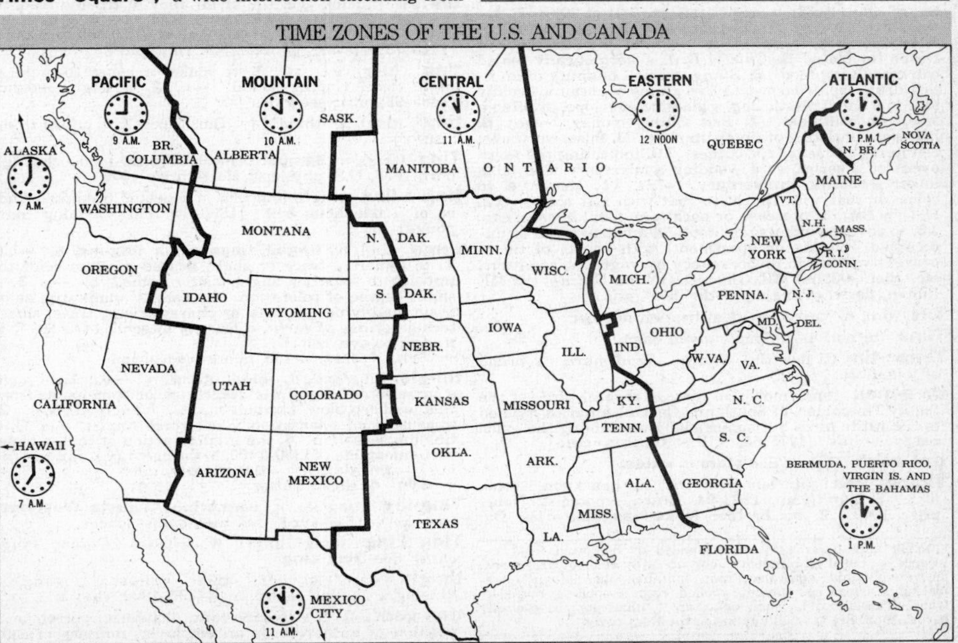

quadrant of the face of the moon: about 25 mi. (40 km) in diameter.

ti•moc•ra•cy (tī mok′rə sē), *n., pl.* **-cies. 1.** a form of government in which love of honor is the dominant motive of the rulers. **2.** a form of government in which a certain amount of property is requisite as a qualification for office. [1580–90; earlier *timocratie* (< F) < Gk *tīmokratía,* equiv. to *tīmo-* (comb. form of *tīmḗ* honor, worth) + *-kratia* -CRACY] —**ti•mo•crat•ic** (tī′mə krat′ik), **ti′mo•crat′i•cal,** *adj.*

tim′o•lol mal′eate (tim′ə lôl′, -lol′), *Pharm.* a beta blocker, $C_{13}H_{24}N_4O_3S \cdot C_4H_4O_4$, used in the treatment of angina, hypertension, and glaucoma. [orig. uncert.; perh. T(H)I- + M(ETHYL) + -OL[1] + -OL[1]]

Ti•mon (tī′mən), *n.* c320–c230 B.C., Greek philosopher.

Ti•mor (tē′môr, tē môr′), *n.* an island in the S part of Indonesia: largest and easternmost of the Lesser Sunda Islands; E half formerly belonged to Portugal. 13,095 sq. mi. (33,913 sq. km).

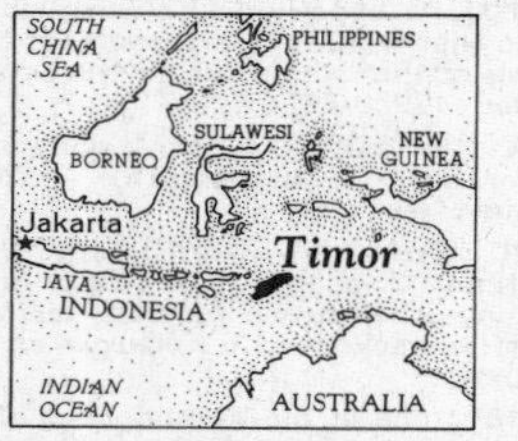

Ti•mo•rese (tē′mô rēz′, -rēs′), *adj., n., pl.* **-rese.** —*adj.* **1.** of or pertaining to Timor. —*n.* **2.** a native or inhabitant of Timor. [TIMOR + -ESE]

tim•or•ous (tim′ər əs), *adj.* **1.** full of fear; fearful: *The noise made them timorous.* **2.** subject to fear; timid. **3.** characterized by or indicating fear: *a timorous whisper.* [1400–50; late ME < ML *timōrōsus* (L *timōr-* (s. of *timor*) fear + *-ōsus* -OUS)] —**tim′or•ous•ly,** *adv.* —**tim′or•ous•ness,** *n.*
—**Syn. 1.** See **cowardly.**

Ti′mor Sea′, an arm of the Indian Ocean, between Timor and NW Australia.

Ti•mo•shen•ko (tim′ə sheng′kō; *Russ.* tyi mu shen′kə), *n.* **Se•mion Kon•stan•ti•no•vich** (syi myôn′ ken stun tyē′nə vyich), 1895–1970, Russian general.

tim•o•thy (tim′ə thē), *n., pl.* **-thies.** a coarse grass, *Phleum pratense,* having cylindrical spikes, used as fodder. Also, **tim′othy grass′.** [1730–40; named after *Timothy* Hanson, American farmer who cultivated it in the early 18th century]

Tim•o•thy (tim′ə thē), *n.* **1.** a disciple and companion of the apostle Paul, to whom Paul is supposed to have addressed two Epistles. **2.** either of these Epistles, I Timothy or II Timothy. *Abbr.:* I Tim., II Tim. **3.** a male given name.

Ti•mour (ti mo͝or′), *n.* Tamerlane. Also, **Ti•mur′.**

tim•pa•ni (tim′pə nē), *n.* (*used with a singular or plural v.*) a set of kettledrums, esp. as used in an orchestra or band. Also, **tympani.** [< It, pl. of *timpano* kettledrum < L *tympanum* < Gk *týmpanon*] —**tim′pa•nist,** *n.*

Tim•rod (tim′rod), *n.* **Henry,** 1828–67, U.S. poet.

ti•mu•cu (ti mo͞o′kə, tim′yə kyo͞o′), *n.* a needlefish, *Strongylura timucu,* inhabiting warm waters of the western Atlantic. [orig. uncert.]

tin (tin), *n., adj., v.,* **tinned, tin•ning.** —*n.* **1.** *Chem.* a low-melting, malleable, ductile metallic element nearly approaching silver in color and luster: used in plating and in making alloys, tinfoil, and soft solders. *Symbol:* Sn; *at. wt.:* 118.69; *at. no.:* 50; *sp. gr.:* 7.31 at 20°C. **2.** See **tin plate. 3.** any shallow pan, esp. one used in baking. **4.** any pot, box, can, or other container or vessel made of tin or tin plate. **5.** *Chiefly Brit.* a hermetically sealed can containing food. **6.** *Slang.* a small quantity of an illicit drug, esp. from two to five grams of cocaine: usually sold in a small plastic bag, a glassine envelope, or often a small tin container. **7.** *Brit. Slang.* money. —*adj.* **8.** made or consisting of tin or tin plate. **9.** false; worthless; counterfeit: *a set of tin values.* **10.** indicating the tenth event of a series, as a wedding anniversary. See table under **wedding anniversary.** —*v.t.* **11.** *Metall.* **a.** to cover or coat with tin. **b.** to coat with soft solder. **12.** *Chiefly Brit.* to preserve or pack (esp. food) in cans; can. **13.** to cover (windows and doors in an abandoned or unoccupied building or apartment) with sheets of tin to prevent vandalism or occupancy by vagrants, squatters, etc. [bef. 900; (n.) ME, OE; c. D, ON *tin,* G *Zinn;* (v.) ME *tinnen,* deriv. of the n.] —**tin′like′,** *adj.*

TIN (tin), *n.* taxpayer identification number.

Ti•na (tē′nə), *n.* a female given name.

Ti•nac•tin (ti nak′tin), *Pharm., Trademark.* a brand of tolnaftate.

tin•a•mou (tin′ə mo͞o′), *n.* any of several birds of the family Tinamidae, of South and Central America, related to the ratite birds but superficially resembling the gallinaceous birds. [1775–85; < F < Carib *tinamu*]

tin′ ash′, *Chem.* See **stannic oxide.**

Tin•ber•gen (tin′bûr gən; *Du.* tin′beʀ′кнən, -кнə), *n.* **1. Jan** (yän), 1903–94, Dutch economist: Nobel prize 1969. **2.** his brother **Ni•ko•laas** (nik′ə ləs; *Du.* nē′kō läs′), born 1907, British ethologist, born in the Netherlands: Nobel prize for medicine 1973.

tin•cal (ting′käl, -kôl), *n.* a former name for crude native borax. [1625–35; < Malay *tingkal*]

tin′ can′, 1. can[2] (def. 1). **2.** *U.S. Navy Slang.* a destroyer. [1760–70, *Amer.*]

tin′ chlo′ride, *Chem.* See **stannic chloride.**

tinct (tingkt), *v.t.* **1.** to tinge or tint, as with color. **2.** *Obs.* to imbue. —*adj.* **3.** tinged; colored; flavored. —*n.* **4.** tint; tinge; coloring. [1425–75 for earlier alchemical sense; 1585–95 for def. 1; 1595–1605 for def. 4; late ME < L *tinctus,* ptp. of *tingere* to dye, color, tinge]

tinct., tincture.

tinc•to•ri•al (tingk tôr′ē əl, -tōr′-), *adj.* pertaining to coloring or dyeing. [1645–55; < L *tinctōri(us)* of or related to dipping, dyeing (see TINCT, -TORY[1]) + -AL[1]] —**tinc•to′ri•al•ly,** *adv.*

tinc•ture (tingk′chər), *n., v.,* **-tured, -tur•ing.** —*n.* **1.** *Pharm.* a solution of alcohol or of alcohol and water, containing animal, vegetable, or chemical drugs. **2.** a slight infusion, as of some element or quality: *A tincture of education had softened his rude manners.* **3.** a trace; a smack or smattering; tinge: *a tincture of irony.* **4.** *Heraldry.* any of the colors, metals, or furs used for the fields, charges, etc., of an escutcheon or achievement of arms. **5.** a dye or pigment. —*v.t.* **6.** to impart a tint or color to; tinge. **7.** to imbue or infuse with something. [1350–1400; ME: dye < L *tinctūra* dyeing. See TINCT, -URE]

Tin•dal (tin′dl), *n.* **1. Matthew,** c1655–1733, English deist. **2.** Also, **Tin′dale, William.** See **Tyndale, William.**

tin•der (tin′dər), *n.* **1.** a highly flammable material or preparation formerly used for catching the spark from a flint and steel struck together for fire or light. **2.** any dry substance that readily takes fire from a spark. [bef. 900; ME; OE *tynder;* akin to G *Zunder,* ON *tundr,* OE *-tendan* (as in *ātendan* to set on fire), Goth *tundnan* to catch fire, G *-zünden* in *entzünden* to kindle]

tin•der•box (tin′dər boks′), *n.* **1.** a box for holding tinder, usually fitted with a flint and steel. **2.** a person or thing that is highly excitable, explosive, inflammable, etc.; a potential source of widespread violence: *Berlin was the tinderbox of Europe.* [1520–30; TINDER + BOX[1]]

tin•der•y (tin′də rē), *adj.* resembling tinder; highly inflammable or inflammatory. [1745–55; TINDER + -Y[1]]

tin′ di•fluor′ide (dī flo͝or′īd, -flôr′-, -flōr′-). See **stannous fluoride.** Also called **tin′ fluor′ide.**

tine (tīn), *n.* a sharp, projecting point or prong, as of a fork. Also, *esp. Brit.,* **tyne.** [bef. 900; late ME *tyne,* ME *tind,* OE; c. OHG *zint,* ON *tindr*] —**tined,** *adj.*

tin•e•a (tin′ē ə), *n. Pathol.* any of several skin diseases caused by fungi; ringworm. [1350–1400; ME < ML; L: larva of a moth or beetle that devours books, clothes, etc.] —**tin′e•al,** *adj.*

tin′ea bar′bae (bär′bē), *Pathol.* See **barber's itch.** [< NL: tinea of the beard]

tin′ea cru′ris (kro͝or′is), *Pathol.* See **jock itch.** [1920–25; < NL: tinea of the leg]

tin′ ear′, 1. an insensitivity to melodic, rhythmic, and harmonic variety in music. **2.** an insensitivity to subtlety or appropriateness in verbal expression: *a tin ear for clear, precise prose.* **3.** See **cauliflower ear.** [1915–20]

tin•e•id (tin′ē id), *n.* **1.** a moth of the family Tineidae, comprising the clothes moths. —*adj.* **2.** belonging or pertaining to the family Tineidae. [< NL *Tineidae.* See TINEA, -ID[2]]

tine′ test′, a screening test for tuberculosis in which an instrument having four sharp prongs dipped in tuberculin antigen is pressed into the skin of the forearm.

tin′ fish′, *Slang.* a torpedo. [1915–20]

tin•foil (tin′foil′), *n.* tin, or an alloy of tin and lead, in the form of a thin sheet, much used as a wrapping for drugs, foods, tobacco, etc. Also called, *Brit.,* **silver paper.** [1425–75; late ME *tynfoile.* See TIN, FOIL[2]]

ting[1] (ting), *v.i., v.t.* **1.** to make or cause to make a high, clear, ringing sound. —*n.* **2.** a tinging sound. [1485–95; imit.; see TANG[2]]

ting[2] (ting), *n.* thing[2]. [< Dan, Norw, Sw; c. Icel *thing* THING[2]]

Ting (ting), *n.* **Samuel C(hao) C(hung)** (chou cho͝ong), born 1936, U.S. physicist: Nobel prize 1976.

ting-a-ling (ting′ə ling′), *n.* a repeated tinkling sound, as of a telephone bell. [1860–65; imit. rhyming compound]

tinge (tinj), *v.,* **tinged, tinge•ing** or **ting•ing,** *n.* —*v.t.* **1.** to impart a trace or slight degree of some color to; tint. **2.** to impart a slight taste or smell to. —*n.* **3.** a slight degree of coloration. **4.** a slight admixture, as of some qualifying property or characteristic; trace; smattering: *a tinge of garlic; a tinge of anger.* [1470–80; < L *tingere* to dye, color]
—**Syn. 4.** hint, shade, nuance, suspicion.

tin•gle (ting′gəl), *v.,* **-gled, -gling,** *n.* —*v.i.* **1.** to have a sensation of slight prickles, stings, or tremors, as from cold, a sharp blow, excitement, etc.: *I tingle all over.* **2.** to cause such a sensation: *The scratch tingles.* —*n.* **3.** a tingling sensation. **4.** the tingling action of cold, a blow, excitement, etc. [1350–1400; ME *tinglen* (v.), var. of TINKLE] —**tin′gler,** *n.* —**tin′gling•ly,** *adv.*
—**Syn. 4.** thrill, flutter.

Ting•ley (ting′lē), *n.* **Katherine Augusta West•cott** (wes′kət), 1847–1929, U.S. theosophist leader.

Ting Ling (ding′ ling′), *Wade-Giles.* (*Chiang Ping-chih*) See **Ding Ling.**

tin•gly (ting′glē), *adj.,* **-gli•er, -gli•est.** tingling or causing a tingling sensation. [1895–1900; TINGLE + -Y[1]]

tin′ god′, 1. a self-important, dictatorial person in a position of authority, as an employer, military officer, critic, or teacher. **2.** a person who considers himself or herself infallible and tries to impose judgments, beliefs, standards of behavior, etc., on subordinates.

tin′ hat′, *Slang.* a steel helmet worn by soldiers. [1915–20]

tin•horn (tin′hôrn′), *Slang.* —*n.* **1.** someone, esp. a gambler, who pretends to be important but actually has little money, influence, or skill. —*adj.* **2.** cheap and insignificant; small-time: *a tinhorn racket.* [1880–85, *Amer.;* TIN + HORN]

Tin•i•a (tin′ē ə), *n.* the chief god of the Etruscans, with powers similar to those of Zeus.

tin•ker (ting′kər), *n.* **1.** a mender of pots, kettles, pans, etc., usually an itinerant. **2.** an unskillful or clumsy worker; bungler. **3.** a person skilled in various minor kinds of mechanical work; jack-of-all-trades. **4.** an act or instance of tinkering: *Let me have a tinker at that motor.* **5.** *Scot., Irish Eng.* **a.** a gypsy. **b.** any itinerant worker. **c.** a wanderer. **d.** a beggar. **6.** See **chub mackerel.** —*v.i.* **7.** to busy oneself with a thing without useful results: *Stop tinkering with that clock and take it to the repair shop.* **8.** to work unskillfully or clumsily at anything. **9.** to do the work of a tinker. —*v.t.* **10.** to mend as a tinker. **11.** to repair in an unskillful, clumsy, or makeshift way. [1225–75; ME *tinkere* (n.), syncopated var. of *tinekere* worker in tin] —**tin′ker•er,** *n.*

tin′ker's cuss′, *Brit.* See **tinker's damn** (def. 1).

tin′ker's dam′, 1. See **tinker's damn. 2.** (in plumbing) a barrier for retaining molten solder within a certain area until it has cooled. [1875–80]

tin′ker's damn′, 1. the least value or merit; nothing or anything at all: *It's not worth a tinker's damn.* **2. care** or **give a tinker's damn,** to have or feel little or no concern; be unaffected or unmoved: *I don't care a tinker's damn for their opinions.* Also, **tinker's dam.** [1830–40; from tinkers' alleged habit of cursing frequently (hence weakening the force of a curse)]

tin′ker's weed′. See **horse gentian.**

Tin•ker•toy (ting′kər toi′), *Trademark.* a brand of children's building toy.

tin•kle (ting′kəl), *v.,* **-kled, -kling,** *n.* —*v.i.* **1.** to give forth or make a succession of short, light, ringing sounds, as a small bell. **2.** to run one's fingers lightly over a keyboard instrument or to play such an instrument simply or badly. **3.** *Baby Talk.* to urinate. —*v.t.* **4.** to cause to tinkle or jingle: *The goat tinkled its bell every time it raised its head. Who's tinkling the piano?* **5.** to make known, call attention to, attract, or summon by tinkling. —*n.* **6.** a tinkling sound or tune. **7.** an act or instance of tinkling. **8.** *Informal.* a telephone call: *Give me a tinkle before you leave for Europe.* [1350–1400; ME *tynclen,* freq. of *tinken* to clink; imit.]

tin•kly (ting′klē), *adj.,* **-kli•er, -kli•est.** tinkling or producing a tinkling sound. [1890–95; TINKLE + -Y[1]]

Tin′ley Park′ (tin′lē), a town in NE Illinois. 26,171.

tin′ liz′zie, *Older Slang.* a small, cheap automobile in run-down condition, esp. a Model T Ford. [1910–15]

tin•man (tin′mən), *n., pl.* **-men.** a tinsmith. [1605–15; TIN + -MAN]

tinned (tind), *adj.* **1.** coated or plated with tin. **2.** *Chiefly Brit.* preserved or packed in a can; canned. [1350–1400; ME; see TIN, -ED[2], -ED[3]]

tin•ner (tin′ər), *n.* **1.** a tinsmith. [1505–15; TIN + -ER[1]]

tin•ner•y (tin′ə rē), *n., pl.* **-ner•ies.** tinworks. [1760–70; TIN + -ERY]

Tin•nev′el•ly sen′na (ti nev′ə lē, tin′ə vel′ē). See under **senna** (def. 2). [after *Tinnevelly* (Tirunelveli), town and district in Tamil Nadu state, India]

tin•ni•ent (tin′ē ənt), *adj.* having a ringing or clinking sound. [1660–70; < L *tinnient-* (s. of *tinniēns*), prp. of *tinnīre* to ring; prob. of imit. orig.]

tin•ning (tin′ing), *n.* **1.** the act or technique of coating with tin. **2.** the act or technique of coating with soft solder. **3.** *Chiefly Brit.* the process, technique, or business of preserving or packing foodstuffs in tins; canning. [1400–50; late ME; see TIN, -ING[1]]

tin•ni•tus (ti nī′təs, tin′i-), *n. Pathol.* a ringing or similar sensation of sound in the ears. [1685–95; < L *tinnītus* a tinkling, equiv. to *tinnī(re)* to tinkle + *-tus* suffix of v. action]

tin•ny (tin′ē), *adj.,* **-ni•er, -ni•est. 1.** of or like tin. **2.** containing tin. **3.** lacking in timbre or resonance; sounding thin or twangy: *a tinny piano.* **4.** not strong or durable; flimsy; shoddy. **5.** having the taste of tin. [1545–55; TIN + -Y[1]] —**tin′ni•ly,** *adv.* —**tin′ni•ness,** *n.*

tin-pan (tin′pan′), *adj.* harsh, tinny, or clanging; noisy. Also, **tin′-pan′ny.** [1840–50, *Amer.*]

Tin′ Pan′ Al′ley, 1. the district of a city, esp. New York City, where most of the popular music is published. **2.** the composers or publishers of popular music as a group.

tin-pan•ning (tin′pan′ing), *n. Dial.* shivaree (def. 1).

tin′ pants′, heavy waterproof trousers, usually of paraffin-soaked canvas, worn by loggers and fishermen.

tin′ par′achute, an employment agreement guaranteeing a worker compensation, esp. in the form of bonuses and benefits, in the event of dismissal as a result of a merger or takeover. [1985–90]

tin′ pest′, the powdering of tin exposed to low temperatures, caused by allotropic transformation.

tin′ plate′, thin iron or steel sheet coated with tin. Also, **tin′plate′.** Also called **tin.** [1670–80]

tin-plate (tin′plāt′), *v.t.,* **-plat•ed, -plat•ing.** to coat (iron or steel sheet) with tin. [1885–90] —**tin′-plat′er,** *n.*

tin-pot (tin′pot′), *adj.* inferior; paltry; shoddy. [1765–75; from the believed inferior quality of a tin pot]

tin′ pyri′tes, *Mineral.* stannite. [1790–1800]

tin•sel (tin′səl), *n., adj., v.,* **-seled, -sel•ing** or (*esp. Brit.*) **-selled, -sel•ling.** —*n.* **1.** a glittering metallic substance, as copper or brass, in thin sheets, used in

CONCISE ETYMOLOGY KEY: <, descended or borrowed from; >, whence; b., blend of, blended; c., cognate with; cf., compare; deriv., derivative; equiv., equivalent; imit., imitative; obl., oblique; r., replacing; s., stem; sp., spelling, spelled; resp., respelling, respelled; trans., translation; ?, origin unknown; *, unattested; ‡, probably earlier than. See the full key inside the front cover.

pieces, strips, threads, etc., to produce a sparkling effect cheaply. **2.** a metallic yarn, usually wrapped around a core yarn of silk, rayon, or cotton, for weaving brocade or lamé. **3.** anything showy or attractive with little or no real worth; showy pretense: *The actress was tired of the fantasy and tinsel of her life.* **4.** *Obs.* a fabric, formerly in use, of silk or wool interwoven with threads of gold, silver, or, later, copper. —*adj.* **5.** consisting of or containing tinsel. **6.** showy; gaudy; tawdry. —*v.t.* **7.** to adorn with tinsel. **8.** to adorn with anything glittering. **9.** to make showy or gaudy. [1495–1505; by aphesis < MF *estincelle* (OF *estincele*) a spark, flash < VL **stincilla*, metathetic var. of L *scintilla* SCINTILLA; first used attributively in phrases *tinsel satin, tinsel cloth*] —**tin′sel·like′,** *adj.*

tin·sel·ly (tin′sə lē), *adj.* **1.** decorated with or abounding in tinsel. **2.** cheap and gaudy. [1805–15; TINSEL + -Y[1]]

tin·sel·ry (tin′səl rē), *n.* cheap and pretentious display. [1820–30; TINSEL + -RY]

Tin·sel·town (tin′səl toun′), *n. Informal.* Hollywood, California, as a center of the movie industry.

tin·smith (tin′smith′), *n.* a person who makes or repairs tinware or items of other light metals. [1805–15; TIN + SMITH]

tin′ sol′dier, a miniature toy soldier of cast metal, usually of lead.

tin′ spir′it, Often, **tin spirits.** any of a group of solutions containing tin salts, used in dyeing. [1875–80]

tin·stone (tin′stōn′), *n. Mineral.* cassiterite. [1595–1605; TIN + STONE]

tint (tint), *n.* **1.** a color or a variety of a color; hue. **2.** a color diluted with white; a color of less than maximum purity, chroma, or saturation. **3.** a delicate or pale color. **4.** any of various commercial dyes for the hair. **5.** *Engraving.* a uniform shading, as that produced by a series of fine parallel lines. **6.** Also called **tint′ block′.** *Print.* a faintly or lightly colored background upon which an illustration or the like is to be printed. —*v.t.* **7.** to apply a tint or tints to; color slightly or delicately; tinge. [1710–20; var. of TINCT]

tin·tack (tin′tak′), *n. Brit.* a short nail made of tin-plated iron. [1830–40; TIN + TACK[1]]

Tin·tag′el Head′, (tin taj′əl), a cape in SW England, on the W coast of Cornwall.

tint·er[1] (tin′tər), *n.* a person who specializes in applying tints or dyes. [1815–25; TINT + -ER[1]]

tin·ter[2] (tin′tər), *n. Western New Eng.* seesaw. Also, **teenter.** [orig. uncert.]
—**Regional Variation.** See **seesaw.**

tin′ tetrachlo′ride, *Chem.* See **stannic chloride.**

tin·tin·nab·u·lar (tin′ti nab′yə lər), *adj.* of or pertaining to bells or bell ringing. Also, **tin·tin·nab·u·lar·y** (tin′ti nab′yə ler′ē), **tin′tin·nab′u·lous.** [1760–70; < L *tintinnābul(um)* bell (*tintinnā(re)* to ring + *-bulum* instrumental suffix) + -AR[1]]

tin·tin·nab·u·la·tion (tin′ti nab′yə lā′shən), *n.* the ringing or sound of bells. [1825–35, *Amer.*; < L *tintinnābul(um)* bell (see TINTINNABULAR) + -ATION]

tint·less (tint′lis), *adj.* without tint or tints; colorless. [1780–90; TINT + -LESS] —**tint′less·ness,** *n.*

tint·om·e·ter (tin tom′i tər), *n.* a precision instrument for comparing tints or colors with those used as arbitrary standards. [1885–90; TINT + -O- + -METER] —**tint·o·met·ric** (tin′tə me′trik), *adj.* —**tint·om′e·try,** *n.*

Tin·to·ret·to (tin′tə ret′ō; *It.* tēn′tô ret′tô), *n.* **Il** (ēl), (*Jacopo Robusti*), 1518–94, Venetian painter.

tin·type (tin′tīp′), *n.* **1.** *Photog.* ferrotype (def. 2). **2.** **not on your tintype,** *Slang.* absolutely not: *Ask her again? Not on your tintype!* [1860–65, *Amer.*; TIN + -TYPE]

tin·ware (tin′wâr′), *n.* articles made of tin plate. [1750–60; TIN + WARE[1]]

tin-white (tin′hwīt′, -wīt′), *adj.* white, as the color of tin; bluish-white. [1790–1800; TIN + WHITE]

tin·work (tin′wûrk′), *n.* **1.** something made of tin. **2.** such things collectively. [1490–1500; TIN + WORK]

tin·works (tin′wûrks′), *n., pl.* **-works.** (*used with a singular or plural v.*) an establishment for the mining or processing of tin or for the making of tinware. [1425–75; late ME; see TIN, WORKS]

ti·ny (tī′nē), *adj.,* **-ni·er, -ni·est.** very small; minute; wee. [1590–1600; late ME *tine* very small (< ?) + -Y[1]] —**ti′ni·ly,** *adv.* —**ti′ni·ness,** *n.*
—**Syn.** little, diminutive, teeny.

-tion, a suffix occurring in words of Latin origin, used to form abstract nouns from verbs or stems not identical with verbs, whether as expressing action (*revolution; commendation*), or a state (*contrition; starvation*), or associated meanings (*relation; temptation*). Also, **-ation, -cion, -ion, -sion, -xion.** [< L *-tiōn-* (s. of *-tiō*), equiv. to *-t(us)* ptp. suffix + *-iōn-* -ION]

-tious, a suffix originally occurring in adjectives borrowed from Latin (*fictitious*); on this model, used with stems of other origin (*bumptious*). Also, **-ious, -ous.** [< L *-tiōsus*, equiv. to *-t(us)* ptp. suffix + *-iōsus* -IOUS]

tip[1] (tip), *n., v.,* **tipped, tip·ping.** —*n.* **1.** a slender or pointed end or extremity, esp. of anything long or tapered: *the tips of the fingers.* **2.** the top, summit, or apex: *the tip of the mountain.* **3.** a small piece or part, as of metal or leather, forming or covering the extremity of something: *a cane with a rubber tip.* **4.** Also called **tip-in, tip-on.** an insert, as an illustration, map, or errata slip, pasted to a page of a book, magazine, etc., usually along the binding margin. **5.** a small, delicate tool made of fine hair cemented between two cards, for applying gold leaf. —*v.t.* **6.** to furnish with a tip. **7.** to serve as or form the tip of. **8.** to mark or adorn the tip of. **9.** to remove the tip or stem of (berries or certain fruits or vegetables). **10.** to frost the ends of (hair strands): *I'm having my hair cut and tipped tomorrow.* **11. tip in,** *Bookbinding.* to paste the inner margin of (a map, illustration, or other plate) into a signature before gathering. [1175–1225; ME; cf. D, LG, Dan *tip*, Sw *tipp*, G *zipf-* in *Zipfel* tip] —**tip′less,** *adj.*

tip[2] (tip), *v.,* **tipped, tip·ping,** *n.* —*v.t.* **1.** to cause to assume a slanting or sloping position; incline; tilt. **2.** to overturn, upset, or overthrow (often fol. by *over*). **3.** to remove or lift (one's hat or cap) in salutation. **4.** *Brit.* to dispose of by dumping: *The dustmen tipped the rubbish on the municipal dump.* —*v.i.* **5.** to assume a slanting or sloping position; incline. **6.** to tilt up at one end and down at the other; slant. **7.** to be overturned or upset: *The car tipped into the ditch.* **8.** to tumble or topple (usually fol. by *over*): *The lamp on the table tipped over.* **9. tip one's hand,** to reveal one's plans, true feelings, etc., often unintentionally. —*n.* **10.** the act of tipping. **11.** the state of being tipped. **12.** *Brit.* **a.** a dump for refuse, as that from a mine. **b.** *Informal.* an untidy place, esp. a room: *They must have packed and left in a rush, because the place is an absolute tip.* [1300–50; earlier *tipen*, ME *typen* to upset, overturn] —**tip′pa·ble,** *adj.*

tip[3] (tip), *n., v.,* **tipped, tip·ping.** —*n.* **1.** a small present of money given directly to someone for performing a service or menial task; gratuity: *He gave the waiter a dollar as a tip.* **2.** a piece of private or secret information, as for use in betting, speculating, or writing a news story: *a tip from a bookie.* **3.** a useful hint or idea; a basic, practical fact: *tips on painting.* —*v.t.* **4.** to give a gratuity to. —*v.i.* **5.** to give a gratuity: *She tipped lavishly.* **6. tip off,** *Informal.* **a.** to supply with private or secret information; inform. **b.** to warn of impending danger or trouble; caution beforehand: *The moonshiners had been tipped off that they were about to be raided.* [1600–10; perh. special use of TIP[4]] —**tip′less,** *adj.* —**tip′pa·ble,** *adj.*
—**Syn. 3.** suggestion, pointer.

tip[4] (tip), *n., v.,* **tipped, tip·ping.** —*n.* **1.** a light, smart blow; tap. **2.** *Baseball.* a batted ball that glances off the bat. Cf. **foul tip.** —*v.t.* **3.** to strike or hit with a light, smart blow; tap. **4.** *Baseball.* to strike (the ball) with a glancing blow. [1425–75; late ME (n.); perh. < LG; cf. G *tippen* to tap < LG]

tip·burn (tip′bûrn′), *n. Plant Pathol.* a disease of lettuce, potatoes, and other plants, characterized by browning of the tips and edges of the leaves, resulting from any of several environmental factors, as excessive heat and humidity. [TIP[1] + BURN[1]]

tip·cart (tip′kärt′), *n.* a cart with a body that can be tipped or tilted to empty it of its contents. [1875–80; TIP[2] + CART]

tip·cat (tip′kat′), *n.* **1.** a game in which a short piece of wood, tapered at both ends, is struck lightly at one end with a bat, causing the wood to spring into the air so that it can be batted for a distance. **2.** Also called **pussy.** the tapered piece of wood used in this game. [1670–80; TIP[4] + CAT[1]]

ti·pi (tē′pē), *n., pl.* **-pis.** tepee.

tip-in[1] (tip′in′), *n. Basketball.* tap-in.

tip-in[2] (tip′in′), *n.* tip[1] (def. 4).

tip-off (tip′ôf′, -of′), *n. Informal.* **1.** the act of tipping off. **2.** a hint or warning: *They got a tip-off on the raid.* [1910–15; n. use of v. phrase *tip off*]

tip·off (tip′ôf′, -of′), *n. Basketball.* a jump ball that begins each period. [1910–15; TIP[4] + (KICK)OFF]

tip-on (tip′on′, -ôn′), *n.* tip[1] (def. 4).

Tip·pe·ca·noe (tip′ē kə nōō′), *n.* a river in N Indiana, flowing SW to the Wabash: battle 1811. 200 mi. (320 km) long.

tip·pee (ti pē′), *n.* a person who receives a tip, as of money or information. [1895–1900; TIPP(ER) + -EE]

tip·per (tip′ər), *n.* a person or thing that tips: *The waiters liked him for being a big tipper.* [1810–20; TIP[3] + -ER[1]]

Tip·per·ar·y (tip′ə râr′ē), *n.* **1.** a county in Munster province, in the S Republic of Ireland. 135,204; 1643 sq. mi. (4255 sq. km). *Co. seat:* Clonmel. **2.** a town in this county. 4592.

tip·pet (tip′it), *n.* **1.** a scarf, usually of fur or wool, for covering the neck, or the neck and shoulders, and usually having ends hanging down in front. Cf. **stole[2]** (def. 2). **2.** *Eccles.* a band of silk or the like worn around the neck with the ends pendent in front. Cf. **stole[2]** (def. 1). **3.** a long, narrow, pendent part of a hood, sleeve, etc. **4.** *Angling.* **a.** a short length of gut, nylon, or the like, for tying an artificial fly to the leader. **b.** a branch of the shaft of a bird feather, serving as the tail of an artificial fly. [1250–1300; ME; see TIP[1], -ET]

Tip·pett (tip′it), *n.* **Sir Michael (Kemp),** born 1905, British composer.

tip·ple[1] (tip′əl), *v.,* **-pled, -pling,** *n.* —*v.i.* **1.** to drink intoxicating liquor, esp. habitually or to some excess. —*v.t.* **2.** to drink (intoxicating liquor), esp. repeatedly, in small quantities. —*n.* **3.** intoxicating liquor. [1490–1500; back formation from ME *tipeler* tapster, equiv. to *tipel-* TAP[2] (c. D *tepel* teat) + *-er* -ER[1]; cf. TIPSY]

tip·ple[2] (tip′əl), *n.* **1.** a device that tilts or overturns a freight car to dump its contents. **2.** a place where loaded cars are emptied by tipping. **3.** *Mining.* a structure where coal is cleaned and loaded in railroad cars or trucks. [1875–80, *Amer.*; n. use of dial. *tipple* to tumble, freq. of TIP[2]; see -LE]

tip·pler[1] (tip′lər), *n.* a person who tipples intoxicating liquor. [1350–1400; ME; see TIPPLE[1], -ER[1]]

tip·pler[2] (tip′lər), *n.* a person who works at a tipple, esp. at a mine. [1825–35; TIPPLE[2] + -ER[1]]

tip·py (tip′ē), *adj.,* **-pi·er, -pi·est.** (of an object) liable to tip over. [1885–90; TIP[2] + -Y[1]]

tip·py·toe (tip′ē tō′), *n., v.i.,* **-toed, -toe·ing,** *adj., adv. Informal.* tiptoe. Also, **tip′py-toe′.** [1935–40; by alter.]

tip′ sheet′, a publication containing the latest information, tips on betting or investing, and predictions for a particular business, stock-market conditions, horse racing results, etc.

tip·staff (tip′staf′, -stäf′), *n., pl.* **-staves** (-stāvz′), **-staffs.** **1.** an attendant or crier in a court of law. **2.** a staff tipped with metal, formerly carried as a badge of office, as by a constable. **3.** any official who carried such a staff. [1535–45; shortened form of earlier *tipped staff;* see TIP[1], -ED[3], STAFF[1]]

tip·ster (tip′stər), *n.* a person who makes a business of furnishing tips, as for betting or speculation. [1860–65; TIP[3] + -STER]

tip·sy (tip′sē), *adj.,* **-si·er, -si·est.** **1.** slightly intoxicated or drunk. **2.** characterized by or due to intoxication: *a tipsy lurch.* **3.** tipping, unsteady, or tilted, as if from intoxication. [1570–80; TIP[2] or obs. *tip* strong drink (perh. back formation from TIPPLE[1]) + -SY. Cf. obs. *bumpsy* in same sense] —**tip′si·ly,** *adv.* —**tip′si·ness,** *n.*

tip·toe (tip′tō′), *n., v.,* **-toed, -toe·ing,** *adj., adv.* —*n.* **1.** the tip or end of a toe. **2. on tiptoe, a.** on the tips of one's toes. **b.** expectant; eager: *With Christmas coming, the children were on tiptoe.* **c.** stealthily; cautiously: *The concert had already begun, so he entered the back of the hall on tiptoe.* —*v.i.* **3.** to move or go on tiptoe, as with caution or stealth: *She tiptoed out of the room.* —*adj.* **4.** characterized by standing or walking on tiptoe. **5.** straining upward. **6.** eagerly expectant. **7.** cautious; stealthy. —*adv.* **8.** eagerly or cautiously; on tiptoe. [1350–1400; ME *tiptoon* (pl. n.). See TIP[1], TOE]

tip·top (*n.* tip′top′; *adj.* tip′top′, -top′; *adv.* tip′top′), *n.* **1.** the extreme top or summit. **2.** *Informal.* the highest point or degree: *the very tiptop of physical condition.* **3.** *Chiefly Brit. Informal.* the highest social class. —*adj.* **4.** situated at the very top. **5.** *Informal.* of the highest quality; excellent: *a tiptop meal.* —*adv.* **6.** in a tiptop manner; very well: *It's shaping up tiptop.* [1695–1705; gradational compound; see TIP[1], TOP[1]]

ti·pu (tē′pōō), *n.* a South American tree, *Tipuana tipu*, having pinnate leaves and showy, golden-yellow flowers, cultivated in warm climates as an ornamental. [< NL, perh. < Pg; further orig. undetermined]

tip′-up ta′ble (tip′up′), a pedestal table having a top folding downward in two leaves. [*tip-up*, adj. use of v. phrase *tip up*]

Ti·pu Sa·hib (tip′ōō sä′ib, -ēb), 1750–99, sultan of Mysore 1782–99.

ti·rade (tī′rād, ti rād′), *n.* **1.** a prolonged outburst of bitter, outspoken denunciation: *a tirade against smoking.* **2.** a long, vehement speech: *a tirade in the Senate.* **3.** a passage dealing with a single theme or idea, as in poetry: *the stately tirades of Corneille.* [1795–1805; < F: lit., a stretch, (continuous) pulling < It *tirata*, n. use of fem. of *tirato*, ptp. of *tirare* to draw, pull, fire (a shot), of obscure orig.]
—**Syn. 2.** harangue, diatribe.

ti·rage (tē RAzh′), *n., pl.* ***-rages*** (-RAzh′). *French.* **1.** the withdrawing of wine from a barrel, as for testing or tasting. **2.** a drawing, as in a lottery.

Ti·ran (ti rän′), *n.* **1. Strait of,** a navigable waterway between the N Red Sea and the Gulf of Aqaba. **2.** an island in this strait, belonging to Saudi Arabia.

Ti·ra·në (ti rä′nə; *Albanian.* tē Rä′nə), *n.* a city in and the capital of Albania, in the central part. 192,300. Italian, **Ti·ra·na** (tē Rä′nä).

Ti·ra·spol (ti ras′pəl; *Russ.* tyi Rä′spəl), *n.* a city in E Moldavia (Moldova), NW of Odessa. 158,000.

tire[1] (tīər), *v.,* **tired, tir·ing,** *n.* —*v.t.* **1.** to reduce or exhaust the strength of, as by exertion; make weary; fatigue: *The long walk tired him.* **2.** to exhaust the interest, patience, etc., of; make weary; bore: *Your stories tire me.* —*v.i.* **3.** to have the strength reduced or exhausted, as by labor or exertion; become fatigued; be sleepy. **4.** to have one's appreciation, interest, patience, etc., exhausted; become or be weary; become bored (usually fol. by *of*): *He soon tired of playing billiards.* —*n.* **5.** *Brit. Dial.* fatigue. [bef. 900; late ME (Scots) *tyren* (v.), OE *tȳrian*, var. of *tēorian* to weary, be wearied]
—**Syn. 2.** exasperate, irk.

tire[2] (tīər), *n., v.,* **tired, tir·ing.** —*n.* **1.** a ring or band of rubber, either solid or hollow and inflated, or of metal, placed over the rim of a wheel to provide traction, resistance to wear, or other desirable properties. **2.** a metal band attached to the outside of the felloes and forming the tread of a wagon wheel. —*v.t.* **3.** to furnish with tires. Also, *Brit.,* **tyre.** [1475–85; special use of TIRE[3]]

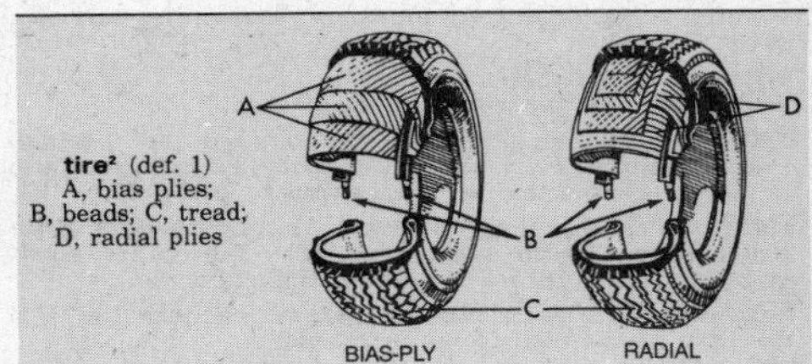

tire[2] (def. 1)
A, bias plies;
B, beads; C, tread;
D, radial plies

tire[3] (tīər), *v.,* **tired, tir·ing,** *n.* —*v.t.* **1.** *Archaic.* to dress (the head or hair), esp. with a headdress. **2.** *Obs.* to attire or array. —*n.* **3.** *Archaic.* a headdress. **4.** *Obs.* attire or dress. [1300–50; ME; aph. var. of ATTIRE]

tire′ chain′, a chain fitting over the tire of a car, truck, or other vehicle, to increase traction and prevent

CONCISE PRONUNCIATION KEY: *act, cāpe, dâre, pärt; set, ēqual; if, īce; ox, ōver, ôrder, oil, bŏŏk, bōōt, out; up, ûrge; child; sing; shoe; thin, that;* zh as in *treasure.* ə = *a* as in *alone, e* as in *system, i* as in *easily, o* as in *gallop, u* as in *circus;* ə as in *fire* (fīər), *hour* (ouər). l and n can serve as syllabic consonants, as in *cradle* (krād′l), and *button* (but′n). See the full key inside the front cover.

skidding on roads covered with ice or snow. Also called **skid chain.**

tired[1] (tīᵊrd), *adj.* **1.** exhausted, as by exertion; fatigued or sleepy: *a tired runner.* **2.** weary or bored (usually fol. by *of*): *tired of the same food every day.* **3.** hackneyed; stale, as a joke, phrase, or sermon. **4.** *Informal.* impatient or disgusted: *You make me tired.* [1350–1400; ME *tyred.* See TIRE[1], -ED[2]]
—Syn. 1. enervated. TIRED, EXHAUSTED, FATIGUED, WEARIED, WEARY suggest a condition in which a large part of one's energy and vitality has been consumed. One who is TIRED has used up a considerable part of his or her bodily or mental resources: *to feel tired at the end of the day.* One who is EXHAUSTED is completely drained of energy and vitality, usually because of arduous or long-sustained effort: *exhausted after a hard run.* One who is FATIGUED has consumed energy to a point where rest and sleep are demanded: *feeling rather pleasantly fatigued.* One who is WEARIED has been under protracted exertion or strain that has gradually worn out his or her strength: *wearied by a long vigil.* WEARY suggests a more permanent condition than wearied: *weary of struggling against misfortunes.* **—Ant. 1.** rested; energetic.

tired[2] (tīᵊrd), *adj.* having a tire or tires. [1890–95; TIRE[2] + -ED[3]]

tire′ i′ron, a short length of steel with one end flattened to form a blade, used as a crowbar for removing tires from wheel rims. [1850–55]

tire·less (tīᵊr′lis), *adj.* untiring; indefatigable: *a tireless worker.* [1585–95; TIRE[1] + -LESS] **—tire′less·ly,** *adv.* **—tire′less·ness,** *n.*
—Syn. unwearied, industrious, hardworking, unfaltering.

Ti·re·si·as (tī rē′sē əs), *n. Class. Myth.* a blind prophet, usually said to have been blinded because he saw Athena bathing, and then to have been awarded the gift of prophecy as a consolation for his blindness. Also, **Teiresias.**

tire·some (tīᵊr′səm), *adj.* **1.** causing or liable to cause a person to tire; wearisome: *a tiresome job.* **2.** annoying or vexatious. [1490–1500; TIRE[1] + -SOME[1]] **—tire′·some·ly,** *adv.* **—tire′some·ness,** *n.*
—Syn. 1. dull, fatiguing, humdrum. **—Ant. 2.** interesting.

tire·wom·an (tīᵊr′wo͝om′ən), *n., pl.* **-wom·en.** *Archaic.* a lady's maid. [1605–15; TIRE[3] + -WOMAN]

Ti·rich Mir (tē′rich mēr′), a mountain in N Pakistan, on the border of Afghanistan: highest peak of the Hindu Kush Mountains. 25,230 ft. (7690 m).

tir′ing room′, *Archaic.* a dressing room, esp. in a theater. [1615–25; aph. var. of *attiring room*]

tirl (tûrl), *Scot.* **—n. 1.** a wheel, cam, or any revolving mechanism or piece of machinery. **2.** an allotted time for action that comes in rotation to each member of a group; turn. **—v.t. 3.** to rotate; turn; twirl. **—v.i. 4.** to make a rattling noise by spinning or revolving. [1480–90; metathetic var. of TRILL[1]]

ti·ro (tī′rō), *n., pl.* **-ros.** tyro.

Ti·rol (ti rōl′, tī-, tī′rōl; *Ger.* tē rōl′), *n.* Tyrol.

Ti·ro·le·an (ti rō′lē ən, tī-), *adj., n.* Tyrolean.

Tir·o·lese (tir′ə lēz′, -lēs′, tī′rə-), *adj., n., pl.* **-lese.** Tyrolese.

Ti·ros (tī′rōs), *n. U.S. Aerospace.* one of a series of satellites for transmitting television pictures of the earth's cloud cover. [*t*(*elevision*) *i*(*nfra*)*r*(*ed*) *o*(*bservational*) *s*(*atellite*)]

Tir·pitz (tir′pits), *n.* **Al·fred von** (äl′frät fən), 1849–1930, German admiral and statesman.

tir·ri·vee (tûr′ə vē′), *n. Scot.* a tantrum. [1805–15; orig. uncert.]

Tir·so de Mo·li·na (tēr′sô the mô lē′nä), (*Gabriel Téllez*) 1571?–1648, Spanish dramatist.

Tir·than·ka·ra (tir tung′kər ə), *n. Jainism.* one of 24 persons who have attained personal immortality through enlightenment. [< Skt *tīrthaṅkara* lit., passage-making]

Tir·u·chi·ra·pal·li (tir′o͝o chi rop′ə lē), *n.* a city in central Tamil Nadu, in S India, on the Cauvery River. 306,247. Also, **Tir′uch·chi·rap′pal·li.** Formerly, **Trichinopoly.**

Ti·ru·nel·ve·li (tēr′o͝o nel′və lē), *n.* a city in S Tamil Nadu, in S India. 108,498.

Tir·yns (tir′inz), *n.* an ancient city in Greece, in Peloponnesus: destroyed in 486 B.C. by the Argives; excavated ruins include Cyclopean walls forming part of a great fortress.

'tis (tiz), a contraction of *it is.*
—Usage. See **contraction.**

ti·sane (ti zan′, -zän′; *Fr.* tē zan′), *n., pl.* **-sanes** (-zanz′, -zänz′; *Fr.* -zan′). **1.** (*italics*) *French.* aromatic or herb-flavored tea. **2.** *Obs.* a ptisan. [1930–35; < F]

Tisch·en·dorf (tish′ən dôrf′), *n.* **Lo·be·gott Frie·drich Kon·stan·tin von** (lō′bə gôt′ frē′drikh kôn′-stän tēn′ fən), 1815–74, German Biblical critic.

Ti·se·li·us (tē sā′lē o͝os′), *n.* **Ar·ne** (är′nə), 1902–71, Swedish biochemist: Nobel prize 1948.

Tish·ah b'Av (*Seph. Heb.* tē shä′ bə äv′; *Ashk. Heb.* tish′ə bôv′), a Jewish fast day observed on the ninth day of the month of Av in memory of the destruction in Jerusalem of the First and Second Temples. Also, **Tish·ah′ b'Ab′.** Also called **Ninth of Av.** [< Heb *tishʿāh bəʾābh*]

Tish·ri (tish′rē, -rā), *n.* the first month of the Jewish calendar. Cf. **Jewish calendar.** [< Heb *tishrī*]

CONCISE ETYMOLOGY KEY: <, descended or borrowed from; >, whence; b., blend of, blended; c., cognate with; cf., compare; deriv., derivative; equiv., equivalent; imit., imitative; obl., oblique; r., replacing; s., stem; sp., spelling, spelled; resp., respelling, respelled; trans., translation; ?, origin unknown; *, unattested; ‡, probably earlier than. See the full key inside the front cover.

Ti·siph·o·ne (ti sif′ə nē′), *n. Class. Myth.* one of the Furies.

Ti·so (tē′sō), *n.* **Jo·sef** (yô′sef), 1887–1947, Slovak Roman Catholic clergyman and politician.

Tis·quan·tum (ti skwon′təm), *n.* Squanto.

Tis·sot (tē sō′), *n.* **James Jo·seph Jacques** (zhäm zhô zef′ zhäk, zhämz), 1836–1902, French painter.

tis·sue (tish′o͞o *or, esp. Brit.,* tis′yo͞o), *n., v.,* **-sued, -su·ing.** **—n. 1.** *Biol.* an aggregate of similar cells and cell products forming a definite kind of structural material with a specific function, in a multicellular organism. **2.** See **tissue paper. 3.** any of several kinds of soft gauzy papers used for various purposes: *cleansing tissue; toilet tissue.* **4.** an interwoven or interconnected series or mass: *a tissue of falsehoods.* **5.** a piece of thin writing paper on which carbon copies are made. **6.** a woven fabric, esp. one of light or gauzy texture, originally woven with gold or silver: *a blouse of a delicate tissue.* **—v.t. 7.** to remove (a cosmetic or cream) with a facial tissue (often fol. by *off*): *Tissue all cosmetics off the face before going to bed.* **8.** to weave, esp. with threads of gold and silver. [1325–75; ME *tissew,* var. of *tissu* < MF, OF, n. use of ptp. of *tistre* to weave < L *texere*] **—tis′su·al,** *adj.* **—tis′su·ey,** *adj.*

tis′sue cul′ture, 1. the technique of cultivating living tissue in a prepared medium outside the body. **2.** the tissue so cultivated. [1920–25]

tis′sue pa′per, a very thin, almost transparent paper used for wrapping delicate articles, covering illustrations in books, copying letters, etc. [1770–80]

tis′sue plasmin′ogen ac′tivator, *Biochem.* **1.** an anticlotting enzyme, naturally occurring in small amounts in the blood. **2.** *Pharm.* the same enzyme, produced in large amounts by genetic engineering techniques for use in dissolving blood clots. *Abbr.:* TPA

tis′sue typ′ing, identification of specific genetically linked antigens in tissue in order to minimize antigenic differences between donor and recipient tissue in organ transplantation. Also called **tis′sue match′ing.** [1960–65]

tis·win (tiz wēn′), *n.* a fermented beverage made by the Apache Indians. Also, **tizwin.** [1875–80, *Amer.;* < Apache < MexSp *tesgüino,* perh. ult. < Nahuatl *tecuīni* for a pot to flare up, for one's heart to pound]

Ti·sza (*Hung.* ti′so), *n.* a river in S central Europe, flowing from the Carpathian Mountains through E Hungary and NE Yugoslavia into the Danube N of Belgrade. 800 mi. (1290 km) long. German, **Theiss.**

tit[1] (tit), *n.* **1.** a titmouse. **2.** any of various other small birds. **3.** *Archaic.* a girl or young woman; hussy. **4.** *Archaic.* a small or poor horse; nag. [1540–50; repr. ME *tite-* (in *titemose* TITMOUSE); c. Norw *tite* titmouse; akin to ON *tittr* tack, pin. See TIT[2]]

tit[2] (tit), *n.* **1.** a teat. **2.** *Slang* (*vulgar*). a breast. [bef. 1100; ME *titte,* OE *titt;* c. MLG, MD *titte,* G *Zitze,* Norw *titta;* akin to TIT[1]]

tit[3] (tit), *n.* See **tit for tat.** [perh. var. of TIP[4]]

Tit., Titus.

tit., title.

Ti·tan (tīt′n), *n.* **1.** *Class. Myth.* **a.** any of the sons of Uranus and Gaea, including Coeus, Crius, Cronus, Hyperion, Iapetus, and Oceanus. **b.** Also, **Ti′tan·ess.** any of the sisters of these, including Mnemosyne, Phoebe, Rhea, Tethys, Themis, and Thia. **c.** any of the offspring of the children of Uranus and Gaea. **2. the Titan,** Helios. **3.** *Astron.* one of the moons of Saturn. **4.** (*usually l.c.*) a person or thing of enormous size, strength, power, influence, etc.: *a titan of industry.* **5.** *Mil.* a two-stage, liquid-fueled U.S. intercontinental ballistic missile in service since the late 1950's and designed for launch from underground silos. **—adj. 6.** (*l.c.*) titanic[2] (def. 2). [1400–50; late ME: the sun, Helios < L *Tītān* < Gk *Tītā́n*]

ti·tan·ate (tīt′n āt′), *n. Chem.* a salt of titanic acid. [1830–40; TITAN(IC ACID) + -ATE[2]]

Ti·tan·esque (tīt′n esk′), *adj.* Titanlike; Titanic. [1880–85; < F; see TITAN, -ESQUE]

ti·ta·ni·a (tī tā′nē ə), *n.* synthetic rutile, TiO_2, used as a gem. [1920–25; < NL; see TITANIUM, -A[4]]

Ti·ta·ni·a (ti tā′nē ə, tī-), *n.* **1.** (in Shakespeare's *Midsummer Night's Dream*) the wife of Oberon and the queen of fairyland. **2.** *Astron.* one of the moons of Uranus.

ti·tan·ic[1] (tī tan′ik, ti-), *adj. Chem.* of or containing titanium, esp. in the tetravalent state. [1820–30; TITA-N(IUM) + -IC]

ti·tan·ic[2] (tī tan′ik), *adj.* **1.** (*cap.*) of, pertaining to, or characteristic of the Titans. **2.** Also, **titan.** of enormous size, strength, power, etc.; gigantic. [1650–60; < Gk *Tītānikós.* See TITAN, -IC] **—ti·tan′i·cal·ly,** *adv.*

Ti·tan·ic (tī tan′ik), *n.* a British luxury liner that sank after colliding with an iceberg in the North Atlantic on its maiden voyage in April, 1912, with a loss of 1517 lives.

ti·tan′ic ac′id (tī tan′ik, ti-), *Chem.* any of various acids derived from titanium dioxide, esp. H_2TiO_3 or $Ti(OH)_4$. [1820–30]

ti·tan·if·er·ous (tīt′n if′ər əs), *adj.* containing or yielding titanium. [1820–30; TITANI(UM) + -FEROUS]

Ti·tan·ism (tīt′n iz′əm), *n.* (*sometimes l.c.*) revolt against tradition, convention, and established order. [1865–70; TITAN + -ISM]

ti·tan·ite (tīt′n īt′), *n. Mineral.* sphene. [1790–1800; < G *Titanit.* See TITANIUM, -ITE[1]]

ti·ta·ni·um (tī tā′nē əm), *n. Chem.* a dark-gray or silvery, lustrous, very hard, light, corrosion-resistant, metallic element, occurring combined in various minerals: used in metallurgy to remove oxygen and nitrogen from steel and to toughen it. *Symbol:* Ti; *at. wt.:* 47.90; *at. no.:* 22; *sp. gr.:* 4.5 at 20°C. [< NL (1795); see TITAN, -IUM]

tita′nium diox′ide, *Chem.* a white, water-insoluble powder, TiO_2, used chiefly in white pigments, plastics, ceramics, and for delustering synthetic fibers. Also called **tita′nium ox′ide, ti·tan′ic ox′ide** (tī tan′ik, ti-). [1920–25]

tita′nium white′, a pigment used in painting, consisting chiefly of titanium dioxide and noted for its brilliant white color, covering power, and permanence. [1920–25]

ti·tan·o·saur (tī tan′ə sôr′, tīt′n ə-), *n.* any amphibious plant-eating dinosaur of the genus *Titanosaurus,* from the Cretaceous Period, having a long, thin neck and a long, whiplike tail. [1890–95; < NL *Titanosaurus.* See TITAN, -O-, -SAUR]

ti·tan·o·there (tī tan′ə thēr′, tīt′n ə-), *n.* any member of the extinct mammalian family Brontotheriidae, large, horned relatives of the horse common in North America and Eurasia from the Eocene to the Oligocene epochs. [< NL *Titanotherium* genus name, equiv. to Gk *Tītā́n* TITAN + -o- -O- + *thēríon* -THERE]

ti·tan·ous (tī tan′əs, ti-), *adj. Chem.* containing trivalent titanium. [1865–70; TITAN(IUM) + -OUS]

tit·bit (tit′bit′), *n. Chiefly Brit.* tidbit.

ti·ter (tī′tər, tē′-), *n. Chem., Med.* **1.** the strength of a solution as determined by titration with a standard substance. **2.** the concentration of a substance in a given sample as determined by titration. Also, *esp. Brit.,* **titre.** [1830–40; < F *titre* title, qualification, fineness of alloyed gold or silver < L *titulus* TITLE]

tit·fer (tit′fər), *n. Chiefly Brit. Slang.* hat. [1895–1900; rhyming slang, shortening of *tit for tat*]

tit′ for tat′, with an equivalent given in retaliation, as a blow for a blow, repartee, etc.: *He answered their insults tit for tat.* [1550–60; perh. var. of earlier *tip for tap*]

tith·a·ble (tī′thə bəl), *adj.* subject to the payment of tithes. [1400–50; late ME *tythable.* See TITHE, -ABLE]

tithe (tīth), *n., v.,* **tithed, tith·ing.** **—n. 1.** Sometimes, **tithes.** the tenth part of agricultural produce or personal income set apart as an offering to God or for works of mercy, or the same amount regarded as an obligation or tax for the support of the church, priesthood, or the like. **2.** any tax, levy, or the like, esp. of one-tenth. **3.** a tenth part or any indefinitely small part of anything. **—v.t. 4.** to give or pay a tithe or tenth of (produce, money, etc.). **5.** to give or pay tithes on (crops, income, etc.). **6.** to exact a tithe from (a person, community, parish, etc.). **7.** to levy a tithe on (crops, income, etc.). **—v.i. 8.** to give or pay a tithe. Also, *Brit.,* **tythe.** [bef. 900; (n.) ME *ti*(*ghe*)*the,* OE *teogotha* TENTH; (v.) ME *tithen,* OE *teogothian* to take the tenth of, deriv. of the n.] **—tithe′less,** *adj.*

tith·er (tī′thər), *n.* **1.** a person who gives or pays tithes, as to a church. **2.** a person who advocates payment of tithes. **3.** a person who collects tithes. [1350–1400; ME; see TITHE, -ER[1]]

tith·ing (tī′thing), *n.* **1.** a tithe. **2.** a giving or an exacting of tithes. **3.** a grouping of men, originally 10 in number, for legal and security purposes in the Anglo-Saxon and Norman system of frankpledge. **4.** a rural division in England, originally regarded as one tenth of a hundred, descended from this system. [bef. 950; ME; OE *tigething.* See TITHE, -ING[1]]

ti·tho·ni·a (ti thō′nē ə, -thōn′yə), *n.* any of several tall composite plants of the genus *Tithonia,* native to Mexico and Central America, having yellow or orange-red ray flowers. Also called **Mexican sunflower.** [1935–40; < NL, equiv. to L *Tīthōn*(*us*) husband of Aurora + *-ia* -IA]

ti·ti[1] (tē tē′), *n., pl.* **-tis.** any of various small reddish or grayish monkeys of the genus *Callicebus,* of South America. [1820–30, *Amer.;* < AmerSp]

ti·ti[2] (tē′tē, tī′tī), *n., pl.* **-tis.** a shrub or small tree of the southern U.S., *Cliftonia monophylla* **(black titi),** having glossy leaves and elongated clusters of fragrant white flowers. [1820–30; orig. uncert.]

Ti·tian (tish′ən), *n.* **1.** (*Tiziano Vecellio*) c1477–1576, Italian painter. **2.** (*l.c.*) a reddish-brown or golden-brown color: *hair of titian.* **—adj. 3.** (*l.c.*) having titian color: *titian hair.* **—Ti′tian·esque′,** *adj.*

Ti·ti·ca·ca (tit′i kä′kə; *Sp.* tē′tē kä′kä), *n.* **Lake,** a lake on the boundary between S Peru and W Bolivia, in the Andes: the largest lake in the region; the highest large lake in the world. 3200 sq. mi. (8290 sq. km); 12,508 ft. (3812 m) above sea level.

tit·il·late (tit′l āt′), *v.t.,* **-lat·ed, -lat·ing. 1.** to excite or arouse agreeably: *to titillate the fancy.* **2.** to tickle; excite a tingling or itching sensation in, as by touching or stroking lightly. [1610–20; < L *titillātus,* ptp. of *titillāre* to tickle; see -ATE[1]] **—tit′il·lat′ing·ly,** *adv.* **—tit′·il·la′tion,** *n.* **—tit′il·la′tive,** *adj.*
—Syn. 1. rouse, tempt, tease.

Ti′tius-Bo′de law′ (tish′əs bō′də), *Astron.* See **Bode's law.**

tit·i·vate[1] (tit′ə vāt′), *v.,* **-vat·ed, -vat·ing. —v.t. 1.** to make smart or spruce: *She titivated her old dress with a* *new belt.* —*v.i.* **2.** to make oneself smart or spruce. Also, **tittivate.** [1795–1805; earlier *tidivate* (TIDY + (ELE)VATE; i.e., tidy up)] —**tit′i·va′tion,** *n.* —**tit′i·va′·tor,** *n.*

tit·i·vate[2] (tit′ə vāt′), *v.t.,* **-vat·ed, -vat·ing.** titillate. [1910–15; by erroneous assoc.]

tit·lark (tit′lärk′), *n.* any of several small, larklike birds, esp. a pipit. [1660–70; TIT[1] + LARK[1]]

ti·tle (tīt′l), *n., adj., v.,* **-tled, -tling.** —*n.* **1.** the distinguishing name of a book, poem, picture, piece of music, or the like. **2.** a descriptive heading or caption, as of a chapter, section, or other part of a book. **3.** See **title page. 4.** a descriptive or distinctive appellation, esp. one belonging to a person by right of rank, office, attainment, etc.: *the title of Lord Mayor.* **5.** *Sports.* the championship: *He won the title three years in a row.* **6.** an established or recognized right to something. **7.** a ground or basis for a claim. **8.** anything that provides a ground or basis for a claim. **9.** *Law.* **a.** legal right to the possession of property, esp. real property. **b.** the ground or evidence of such right. **c.** the instrument constituting evidence of such right. **d.** a unity combining all of the requisites to complete legal ownership. **e.** a division of a statute, lawbook, etc., esp. one larger than an article or section. **f.** (in pleading) the designation of one's basis for judicial relief; the cause of action sued upon, as a contract or tort. **10.** *Eccles.* **a.** a fixed sphere of work and source of income, required as a condition of ordination. **b.** any of certain Roman Catholic churches in Rome, the nominal incumbents of which are cardinals. **11.** Usually, **titles.** *Motion Pictures, Television.* **a.** a subtitle in the viewer's own language: *an Italian movie with English titles.* **b.** any written matter inserted into the film or program, esp. the list of actors, technicians, writers, etc., contributing to it; credits. —*adj.* **12.** of or pertaining to a title: *the title story in a collection.* **13.** that decides a title: *a title bout.* —*v.t.* **14.** to furnish with a title; designate by an appellation; entitle. [bef. 950; ME, var. of *titel,* OE *titul* < L *titulus* superscription, title] —**Syn. 4.** designation, denomination. See **name. 14.** denominate, term, call, style.

Title IX, a clause in the 1972 Education Act stating that no one shall because of sex be denied the benefits of any educational program of activity that receives direct federal aid.

ti′tle cat′alog, *Library Science.* a catalog whose entries are listed by title only. [1930–35]

ti′tled (tīt′ld), *adj.* having a title, esp. of nobility: *the titled families of Europe.* [1740–50; TITLE + -ED[3]]

ti′tle deed′, a deed or document containing or constituting evidence of ownership. [1760–70]

ti′tle en′try, *Library Science.* a catalog entry of a book, document, etc., by title, usually arranged alphabetically by the first word other than an article.

ti·tle·hold·er (tīt′l hōl′dər), *n.* **1.** a person who holds a title. **2.** *Sports.* a person who holds a championship; present champion. [1900–05; TITLE + HOLDER]

ti′tle insur′ance, insurance protecting the owner or mortgagee of real estate from lawsuits or claims arising from a defective title.

ti′tle lin′ing, *Print.* a system for aligning type in which the baseline is established close to the edge of the body, used esp. for titles set in capitals that have no descenders. Cf. **art lining, standard lining.**

ti′tle page′, the page at the beginning of a volume that indicates the title, author's or editor's name, and the publication information, usually the publisher and the place and date of publication. [1605–15]

ti′tle role′, (in a play, opera, etc.) the role or character from which the title is derived: *She sang the title role in* Carmen. [1885–90]

ti·tle·ship (tīt′l ship′), *n.* lawful claim to title, esp. of property. [TITLE + -SHIP]

ti·tlist (tīt′list, -l ist), *n. Sports.* a titleholder; champion. [1935–40; TITLE + -IST]

tit·mouse (tit′mous′), *n., pl.* **-mice** (-mīs′). any of numerous, widely distributed, small songbirds of the family Paridae, esp. of the genus *Parus,* having soft, thick plumage and a short, stout, conical bill. Cf. **tufted titmouse.** [1275–1325; ME *tit(e)mose* (see TIT[1]); *mose,* OE *māse* titmouse; c. G *Meise* titmouse, ON *meis-* in *meisingr* kind of bird; modern *mouse* by folk etym.]

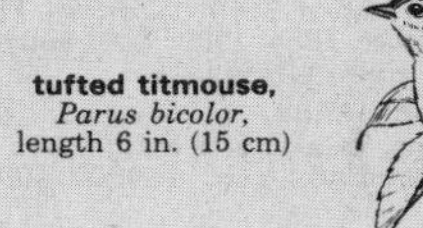

tufted titmouse, *Parus bicolor,* length 6 in. (15 cm)

Ti·to (tē′tō), *n.* **1. Marshal** (*Josip Broz*), 1891–1980, president of Yugoslavia 1953–80. **2.** a male given name.

Ti·to·grad (tē′tō grad′, -gräd′), *n.* former name (1945–92) of **Podgorica.**

Ti·to·ism (tē′tō iz′əm), *n.* a form of communism associated with Tito, characterized by the assertion by a satellite state of its national interests in opposition to Soviet rule. [TITO + -ISM] —**Ti′to·ist,** *adj., n.*

Ti·tov (tē′tôf, -tof; *Russ.* tyi tôf′), *n.* **Herman** or **Gherman Ste·pa·no·vich** (gûr′mən stə pä′nə vich; *Russ.* gyer′mən styi pä′nə vyich), born 1935, Soviet cosmonaut.

ti·trant (tī′trənt), *n. Chem.* the reagent added in a titration. [1935–40; TIT(R)E + -ANT]

ti·trate (tī′trāt), *v.t., v.i.,* **-trat·ed, -trat·ing.** *Chem.* to ascertain the quantity of a given constituent by adding a liquid reagent of known strength and measuring the volume necessary to convert the constituent to another form. [1860–65; TIT(R)E + -ATE[1]] —**ti′tra·ta·ble, ti·tra·ble** (tī′trə bəl), *adj.* —**ti·tra′tion,** *n.*

ti·tre (tī′tər, tē′-), *n. Chiefly Brit.* titer.

ti·tri·met·ric (tī′trə me′trik), *adj. Chem.* using or obtained by titration. [TITR(ATION) or TIT(R)E + -I- + -METRIC] —**ti′tri·met′ri·cal·ly,** *adv.*

tits′ and ass′, *Slang (vulgar).* the presentation of women in titillating costumes or postures, esp. as a feature of an entertainment, as a musical revue. [1970–75]

tit-tat-toe (tit′tat tō′), *n.* tick-tack-toe.

tit·ter (tit′ər), *v.i.* **1.** to laugh in a restrained, self-conscious, or affected way, as from nervousness or in ill-suppressed amusement. —*n.* **2.** a tittering laugh. [1610–20; perh. < Scand; cf. ON *tittra* to quiver, Sw (dial.) *tittra* to giggle] —**tit′ter·er,** *n.* —**tit′ter·ing·ly,** *adv.* —**Syn. 1.** snicker, snigger, giggle.

tit·tie (tit′ē), *n. Scot. Informal.* titty[1].

tit·ti·vate (tit′ə vāt′), *v.t., v.i.,* **-vat·ed, -vat·ing.** titivate[1]. —**tit′ti·va′tion,** *n.* —**tit′ti·va′tor,** *n.*

tit·tle (tit′l), *n.* **1.** a dot or other small mark in writing or printing, used as a diacritic, punctuation, etc. **2.** a very small part or quantity; a particle, jot, or whit: *He said he didn't care a tittle.* [bef. 900; ME *titel,* OE *titul* < ML *titulus* mark over letter or word. See TITLE]

tit·tle-tat·tle (tit′l tat′l), *n., v.,* **-tled, -tling.** —*n.* **1.** gossip or foolish chatter. —*v.i.* **2.** to gossip or chatter. [1520–30; gradational compound based on *tittle* to whisper, gossip] —**tit′tle-tat′tler,** *n.*

tit·tup (tit′əp), *n., v.,* **-tuped, -tup·ing** or (*esp. Brit.*) **-tupped, -tup·ping.** *Chiefly Brit.* —*n.* **1.** an exaggerated prancing, bouncing movement or manner of moving. —*v.i.* **2.** to move, esp. to walk, in an exaggerated prancing or bouncing way, as a spirited horse. [1695–1705; dial. *tit* a jerk, twitch (ME *titte*) + (GALL)OP] —**tit′tup·py,** *adj.*

tit·ty[1] (tit′ē), *n., pl.* **-ties.** *Scot. Informal.* sister. Also, **tittie.** [1715–25; perh. orig. form of SISTER in children's speech]

tit·ty[2] (tit′ē), *n., pl.* **-ties.** *Slang (usually vulgar).* a breast or teat. [1740–50; TIT[2] + -Y[2]]

tit·u·ba·tion (tich′o͝o bā′shən), *n. Pathol.* a disturbance of body equilibrium in standing or walking, resulting in an uncertain gait and trembling, esp. resulting from diseases of the cerebellum. [1635–45; < L *titubātiōn-* (s. of *titubātiō*) a staggering, equiv. to *titubāt(us),* ptp. of *titubāre* to stagger + *-iōn-* -ION] —**tit·u·bant** (tich′o͝o bənt), *adj.*

tit·u·lar (tich′ə lər, tit′yə-), *adj.* **1.** existing or being such in title only; nominal; having the title but none of the associated duties, powers, etc.: *the titular head of the company.* **2.** from whom or which a title or name is taken: *His titular Saint is Michael.* **3.** of, pertaining to, or of the nature of a title. **4.** having a title, esp. of rank. **5.** designating any of the Roman Catholic churches in Rome whose nominal incumbents are cardinals. —*n.* **6.** a person who bears a title. **7.** a person from whom or thing from which a title or name is taken. **8.** *Eccles.* a person entitled to a benefice but not required to perform its duties. [1585–95; < L *titul(us)* TITLE + -AR[1]] —**tit·u·lar·i·ty** (tich′ə lar′i tē, tit′yə-), *n.* —**tit′u·lar·ly,** *adv.*

tit·u·lar·y (tich′ə ler′ē, tit′yə-), *adj., n., pl.* **-lar·ies.** titular. [1595–1605; < L *titul(us)* TITLE + -ARY]

Ti·tus (tī′təs), *n.* **1.** a disciple and companion of the apostle Paul, to whom Paul is supposed to have addressed an Epistle. **2.** this New Testament Epistle. *Abbr.:* Tit. **3.** (*Flavius Sabinus Vespasianus*) A.D. 40?–81, Roman emperor 79–81. **4.** Tatius. **5.** a male given name.

Ti·tus·ville (tī′təs vil′), *n.* **1.** a town in central Florida. 31,910. **2.** a town in NW Pennsylvania: first oil well in U.S. drilled 1859. 6884.

ti·ty·ra (ti tī′rə), *n.* any of several songbirds of the genus *Tityra,* of the American tropics, having gray, black, and white plumage and large swollen bills, and variously classified with the flycatchers or the cotingas. [< NL, perh. < L *Tityrus* name of a shepherd; see -A[2]]

Ti·u (tē′o͞o), *n.* an English god of the sky and of war, the equivalent of Tyr in Scandinavian mythology. [var. of OE *Tīw* god of war. See TUESDAY]

Tiv (tiv), *n., pl.* **Tivs,** (*esp. collectively*) **Tiv. 1.** a member of an African people living N and S of the lower Benue River in E Nigeria. **2.** the Benue-Congo language of the Tiv.

Tiv·er·ton (tiv′ər tn), *n.* a town in SE Rhode Island. 13,256.

Tiv·o·li (tiv′ə lē; *for 1 also It.* tē′vô lē), *n.* **1.** a town in central Italy, E of Rome: ruins of Roman villas. 41,733. Ancient, **Tibur. 2.** a park and entertainment center in Copenhagen, Denmark.

Ti·wa (tē′wə), *n., pl.* **-was,** (*esp. collectively*) **-wa** for 1. *n.* **1.** a member of a cluster of pueblo-dwelling North American Indian peoples of New Mexico. **2.** the Tanoan language of the Tiwa.

tiz·win (tiz wēn′), *n.* tiswin.

tiz·zy (tiz′ē), *n., pl.* **-zies. 1.** *Slang.* **a.** a dither. **b.** a nervous, excited, or distracted state. **2.** *Brit. Obs.* a sixpence. [1795–1805; orig. uncert.]

Tji·re·bon (chir′ə bôn′), *n.* Cirebon.

tk., **1.** tank. **2.** truck.

TKO, *Boxing.* See **technical knockout.** Also, **T.K.O.**

tkt., ticket.

TL, 1. See **target language. 2.** See **trade last. 3.** truckload.

Tl, *Symbol, Chem.* thallium.

TL., (in Turkey) lira; liras.

T/L, time loan.

T.L., 1. Also, **t.l.** See **trade last. 2.** trade list.

Tla·loc (tlä lōk′), *n.* the Aztec god of rain. [< MexSp *Tláloc* < Nahuatl *Tlāloc,* equiv. to *tlāl(li)* earth, land + *oc* lies, is stretched out]

Tlal·pan (tläl pän′), *n.* a city in S Mexico: near site of Cuicuilco mound. 115,528.

Tlax·ca·la (tläs kä′lä), *n.* a state in SE central Mexico. 498,000; 1554 sq. mi. (4025 sq. km). *Cap.:* Tlaxcala.

TLC, tender loving care. Also, **T.L.C., t.l.c.**

Tlem·cen (tlem sen′), *n.* a city in NW Algeria. 500,000. Also, **Tlem·sen′.**

Tlin·git (tling′git), *n., pl.* **-gits,** (*esp. collectively*) **-git. 1.** a member of any of a number of American Indian peoples of the coastal regions of southern Alaska and northern British Columbia. **2.** the language of the Tlingit, a Na-Dene language.

Tlin·kit (tling′kit), *n., pl.* **-kits,** (*esp. collectively*) **-kit.** Tlingit.

t.l.o., *Insurance.* total loss only.

TLR, *Photog.* See **twin-lens reflex camera.**

T lymphocyte, *Immunol.* See **T cell.**

TM, 1. trademark. **2.** See **transcendental meditation.**

Tm, *Symbol, Chem.* thulium.

t.m., true mean.

T-man (tē′man′), *n., pl.* **T-men.** a special investigator of the Department of the Treasury. [1935–40]

T-maze (tē′māz′), *n. Psychol.* a pathway shaped like the letter *T* through which an animal runs during learning experiments.

tme·sis (tə mē′sis), *n.* the interpolation of one or more words between the parts of a compound word, as *be thou ware* for *beware.* [1580–90; < LL *tmēsis* < Gk *tmēsis* a cutting, equiv. to *tmē-* (var. s. of *témnein* to cut) + *-sis* -SIS]

TMI, See **Three Mile Island.**

TMJ, temporomandibular joint.

TMJ syndrome. See **temporomandibular joint syndrome.**

TML, *Chem.* tetramethyllead.

TMO, telegraph money order.

TMV, tobacco mosaic virus.

TN, Tennessee (approved esp. for use with zip code).

Tn, *Symbol, Chem.* thoron.

tn., 1. ton. **2.** town. **3.** train.

TNB, *Chem.* trinitrobenzene, esp. the 1,3,5- isomer.

TNF, See **tumor necrosis factor.**

tng., training.

T-note (tē′nōt′), *n. Informal.* Treasury note.

tnpk., turnpike.

TNT, *Chem.* a yellow, crystalline, water-insoluble, flammable solid, $C_7H_5N_3O_6$, derived from toluene by nitration, a high explosive unaffected by ordinary friction or shock: used chiefly in military and other explosive devices, and as an intermediate in the preparation of dyestuffs and photographic chemicals. Also, **T.N.T.** Also called **trinitrotoluene, trinitrotoluol, methyltrinitrobenzene, trotyl.** [1910–15]

T number, *Photog.* one of a series of calibrations of lens openings according to the intensity of the light actually transmitted by the lens. *Symbol:* T

to (to͞o; *unstressed* to͝o, tə), *prep.* **1.** (used for expressing motion or direction toward a point, person, place, or thing approached and reached, as opposed to *from*): *They came to the house.* **2.** (used for expressing direction or motion or direction toward something) in the direction of; toward: *from north to south.* **3.** (used for expressing limit of movement or extension): *He grew to six feet.* **4.** (used for expressing contact or contiguity) on; against; beside; upon: *a right uppercut to the jaw; Apply varnish to the surface.* **5.** (used for expressing a point of limit in time) before; until: *to this day; It is ten minutes to six. We work from nine to five.* **6.** (used for expressing aim, purpose, or intention): *going to the rescue.* **7.** (used for expressing destination or appointed end): *sentenced to jail.* **8.** (used for expressing agency, result, or consequence): *to my dismay; The flowers opened to the sun.* **9.** (used for expressing a resulting state or condition): *He tore it to pieces.* **10.** (used for expressing the object of inclination or desire): *They drank to her health.* **11.** (used for expressing the object of a right or claim): *claimants to an estate.* **12.** (used for expressing limit in degree, condition, or amount): *wet to the skin; goods amounting to $1000; Tomorrow's high will be 75 to 80°.* **13.** (used for expressing addition or accompaniment) with: *He added insult to injury. They danced to the music. Where is the top to this box?* **14.** (used for expressing attachment or adherence): *She held to her opinion.* **15.** (used for expressing comparison or opposition): *inferior to last year's crop; The score is eight to seven.* **16.** (used for expressing agreement or accordance) according to; by: *a position to one's liking; to the best of my knowledge.* **17.** (used for expressing reference, reaction, or relation). *What will he say to this?* **18.** (used for expressing a relative position): *parallel to the roof.* **19.** (used for expressing a proportion of number or quantity) in; making up: *12 to the dozen; 20 miles to the gallon.* **20.** (used for indicating the indirect object of a verb, for connecting a verb with its complement, or for indicating or limiting the application of an adjective, noun, or pronoun): *Give it to me. I refer to your work.* **21.** (used as the ordinary sign or accompaniment of the infinitive, as in expressing motion, direction, or purpose, in ordinary uses with a substantive object.) **22.** *Math.* raised to the power indicated: *Three to the fourth is 81* ($3^4 = 81$). —*adv.* **23.** toward a point, person, place, or thing, implied or understood. **24.** toward a contact point or closed position: *Pull the door to.* **25.** toward a matter, action, or work: *We turned to with a will.* **26.** into a state of consciousness; out of unconsciousness: *after he came to.* **27. to and fro.** See **fro** (def. 2). [bef. 900; ME, OE *tō;* c. D *te, toe,* G *zu*]

T.O., telegraph office. Also, **TO**

t.o., **1.** turnover. **2.** turn over.

toad (tōd), *n.* **1.** any of various tailless amphibians that are close relatives of the frogs in the order Anura and that typically have dry, warty skin and are terrestrial or semiterrestrial in habit. Cf. **frog**[1] (def. 1). **2.** Also called **true toad.** a toad of the widespread and chiefly terrestrial family Bufonidae, having relatively short hind legs used in hopping and often having at the shoulders swellings containing glands that, along with the skin, secrete an irritating fluid in defense. Cf. **frog**[1] (def. 2). **3.** any of various toadlike animals, as certain lizards. **4.** a person or thing as an object of disgust or aversion. [bef. 1000; ME *tode,* OE *tāde, tādi(g)e*] —**toad′ish, toad′like′,** *adj.* —**toad′ish·ness,** *n.* —**toad′less,** *adj.*

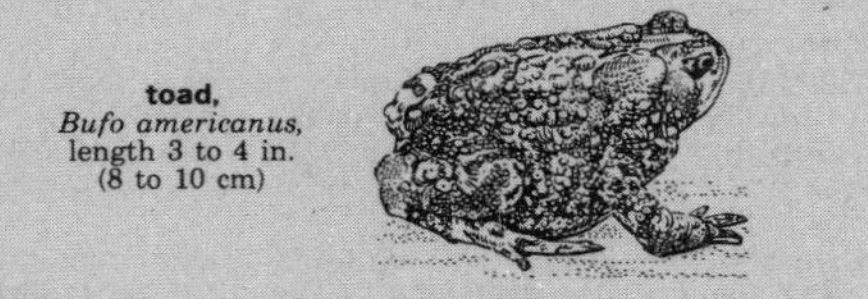

toad, *Bufo americanus,* length 3 to 4 in. (8 to 10 cm)

toad′ bug′, any of several small broad aquatic insect-eating hemipterous insects of the family Gelastocoridae, having toadlike characteristics. [1900–05]

toad·eat·er (tōd′ē′tər), *n.* a toady. [1565–75; TOAD + EATER]

toad·fish (tōd′fish′), *n., pl.* (*esp. collectively*) **-fish,** (*esp. referring to two or more kinds or species*) **-fish·es. 1.** any of several thick-headed, wide-mouthed fishes of the family Batrachoididae, as *Opsanus tau* **(oyster toadfish),** ranging along the Atlantic coast of the U.S. **2.** puffer (def. 2). [1605–15; TOAD + FISH]

toad·flax (tōd′flaks′), *n.* **1.** a common European plant, *Linaria vulgaris,* of the figwort family, having narrow leaves and showy yellow-and-orange flowers, naturalized as a weed in the U.S. **2.** any plant of the same genus. [1570–80; TOAD + FLAX]

toad-in-the-hole (tōd′in *th*ə hōl′), *n. Brit. Cookery.* a dish consisting of beef or pork sausages baked in a coating of batter. [1780–90]

toad·shade (tōd′shād′), *n.* a plant, *Trillium sessile,* of the lily family, native to the southeastern U.S., having broad, mottled leaves and a solitary purplish or greenish flower. [TOAD + SHADE]

toad·stone (tōd′stōn′), *n.* any of various stones or stonelike objects, formerly supposed to have been formed in the head or body of a toad, worn as jewels or amulets. [1550–60; TOAD + STONE]

toad·stool (tōd′sto͞ol′), *n.* **1.** any of various mushrooms having a stalk with an umbrellalike cap, esp. the agarics. **2.** a poisonous mushroom, as distinguished from an edible one. **3.** any of various other fleshy fungi, as the puffballs and coral fungi. [1350–1400; ME *tadstol.* See TOAD, STOOL]

toad·y (tō′dē), *n., pl.* **toad·ies,** *v.,* **toad·ied, toad·y·ing.** —*n.* **1.** an obsequious flatterer; sycophant. —*v.t.* **2.** to be the toady to. —*v.i.* **3.** to be a toady. [1680–90; TOAD + -Y[2]] —**toad′y·ish,** *adj.* —**toad′y·ism,** *n.*
—**Syn. 1.** fawner, yes man, parasite, apple polisher.

to-and-fro (to͞o′ən frō′), *adj., n., pl.* **-fros.** —*adj.* **1.** back-and-forth: *to-and-fro motion.* —*n.* **2.** a continuous or regular movement backward and forward; an alternating movement, flux, flow, etc.: *the to-and-fro of the surf.* [1820–30; adj. and n. use of adv. phrase *to and fro,* ME; see FRO (def. 2)]

toast[1] (tōst), *n.* **1.** sliced bread that has been browned by dry heat. —*v.t.* **2.** to brown, as bread or cheese, by exposure to heat. **3.** to heat or warm thoroughly at a fire: *She toasted her feet at the fireplace.* —*v.i.* **4.** to become toasted. [1350–1400; (v.) ME *to(o)sten* < MF *toster* < VL **tostāre,* deriv. of L *tostus* (< **torstos*), ptp. of *torrēre* to parch, roast, from a base **tors-,* akin to Goth *thaursus,* ON *thurr* dry; (n.) late ME *to(o)ste,* deriv. of the v.; see TORRID, THIRST]

toast[2] (tōst), *n.* **1.** a salutation or a few words of congratulation, good wishes, appreciation, remembrance, etc., uttered immediately before drinking to a person, event, etc. **2.** a person, event, sentiment, or the like, in honor of whom another or others raise their glasses in salutation and then drink. **3.** an act or instance of thus drinking: *They drank a toast to the queen.* **4.** a call on another or others to drink to some person or thing. **5.** a person who is celebrated as with the spirited homage of a toast: *She was the toast of five continents.* —*v.t.* **6.** to drink to the health of or in honor of; propose a toast to or in honor of. **7.** to propose as a toast. —*v.i.* **8.** to propose or drink a toast. [1690–1700; fig. use of TOAST[1] (n.); the name of a lady so honored was said to give flavor to the drink comparable to that given by spiced toast]

toast·er[1] (tō′stər), *n.* **1.** an instrument or appliance for toasting bread, muffins, etc. **2.** a person who toasts something. [1575–85; TOAST[1] + -ER[1]]

toast·er[2] (tō′stər), *n.* a person who proposes or joins in a toast to someone or something. [1695–1705; TOAST[2] + -ER[1]]

toast′er ov′en, an electrical appliance that functions as both an oven and a toaster and is small enough to fit on a kitchen counter or table. Also, **toast′er-ov′en.** [1975–80]

toast′ing fork′, a long-handled fork used for cooking or toasting frankfurters, marshmallows, bread, etc., usually over an open fire. [1830–40]

toast·mas·ter (tōst′mas′tər, -mä′stər), *n.* **1.** a person who presides at a dinner and introduces the after-dinner speakers. **2.** a person who proposes or announces toasts. [1740–50; TOAST[2] + MASTER]

toast·mis·tress (tōst′mis′trəs), *n.* a woman who presides at a dinner, introduces the after-dinner speakers, and often proposes toasts. [1920–25; TOAST[2] + MISTRESS]
—**Usage.** See **-ess.**

toast·y (tō′stē), *adj.,* **toast·i·er, toast·i·est. 1.** comfortably or cozily warm. **2.** characteristic of or resembling toast: *toasty aromas.* [1890–95; TOAST[1] + -Y[1]] —**toast′i·ness,** *n.*

tob (tōb), *n.* tobe.

Tob., Tobit.

to·bac·co (tə bak′ō), *n., pl.* **-cos, -coes. 1.** any of several plants belonging to the genus *Nicotiana,* of the nightshade family, esp. one of those species, as *N. tabacum,* whose leaves are prepared for smoking or chewing or as snuff. **2.** the prepared leaves, as used in cigarettes, cigars, and pipes. **3.** any product or products made from such leaves. **4.** any of various similar plants of other genera. [1525–35; < Sp *tabaco,* perh. < Arawak: a pipe for smoking the plant, or roll of leaves smoked, or the plant] —**to·bac′co·less,** *adj.*

tobac′co a′phid. See **green peach aphid.**

tobac′co bee′tle. See **cigarette beetle.** [1890–95, *Amer.*]

tobac′co bud′worm, the larva of a noctuid moth, *Heliothis virescens,* that damages the buds and young leaves of tobacco. [1915–20]

tobac′co heart′, *Pathol.* a functional disorder of the heart, characterized by a rapid and often irregular pulse, caused by excessive use of tobacco. [1880–85]

tobac′co horn′worm, the larva of a hawk moth, *Manduca sexta,* having a hornlike structure at its posterior end and feeding on the leaves of tobacco and other plants of the nightshade family. Also called **tobac′co worm′.** [1730–40]

tobac′co mosa′ic, *Plant Pathol.* a disease of the nightshade family of plants, particularly tobacco and tomato, caused by the tobacco mosaic virus and characterized by mottled leaves and yellowed, necrotic plants. [1935–40]

tobac′co mosa′ic vi′rus, a retrovirus causing mosaic disease in members of the nightshade family. *Abbr.:* TMV [1935–40]

to·bac·co·nist (tə bak′ə nist), *n.* a dealer in tobacco, esp. the owner of a store that sells pipe tobaccos, cigarettes, and cigars. [1590–1600; TOBACCO + intrusive *-n-* + -IST]

To·ba·go (tə bā′gō), *n.* an island in the SE West Indies, off the NE coast of Venezuela: formerly a British colony in the Federation of the West Indies; now part of the independent republic of Trinidad and Tobago. 39,280; 116 sq. mi. (300 sq. km). —**To·ba·go·ni·an** (tō′bə gō′nē ən, -gōn′yən), *n.*

To·ba·ta (tō bä′tə; *Japn.* tô bä′tä), *n.* See under **Kitakyushu.**

to-be (tə bē′), *adj.* future; soon to be the thing specified (usually used in combination): *bride-to-be.* [1590–1600]

tobe (tōb), *n.* the principal outer garment in some parts of north and central Africa, consisting of a length of cloth that is sewn into a long loose skirt or is draped around the body and fastened over one shoulder. Also, **tob, thaub.** [1825–35; < dial. Ar *tōb,* variant of Ar *thawb* garment]

To·bey (tō′bē), *n.* **Mark,** 1890–1976, U.S. painter.

To·bi·as (tə bī′əs), *n.* **1.** the son of Tobit. **2.** *Douay Bible.* Tobit. **3.** a male given name.

to·bi·ra (tə bī′rə), *n.* a shrub, *Pittosporum tobira,* of China and Japan, having leathery leaves, fragrant, greenish-white flower clusters, densely hairy fruit, and lemon-scented foliage. [< NL < Japn *tobira, tobera;* cf. Korean *ton(-namu),* Chin *(hǎi)tóng* tobira]

To·bit (tō′bit), *n.* **1.** a book of the Apocrypha. **2.** a devout Jew whose story is recorded in this book.

to·bog·gan (tə bog′ən), *n.* **1.** a long, narrow, flat-bottomed sled made of a thin board curved upward and backward at the front, often with low handrails on the sides, used esp. in the sport of coasting over snow or ice. —*v.i.* **2.** to use, or coast on, a toboggan. **3.** to fall rapidly, as prices or one's fortune. [1820–30; < Maliseet-Passamaquoddy *tʰápākən,* Micmac *topağan* (equiv. to Proto-Algonquian **weta·pye·* to drag a cord + **-kan-* instrument for)] —**to·bog′gan·er, to·bog′gan·ist,** *n.*

To·bol (tu bôl′), *n.* a river rising in Kazakhstan, flowing NE through the Russian Federation in Asia to the Irtysh River. 800 mi. (1290 km) long.

To·bolsk (tu bôlsk′), *n.* a town in the W Russian Federation in Asia, on the Irtysh River at its confluence with the Tobol. 65,000.

to·bra·my·cin (tō′brə mī′sin), *n. Pharm.* a highly toxic aminoglycoside antibiotic, $C_{18}H_{37}N_5O_9$, derived from *Streptomyces tenebarius,* used in the treatment of serious infections due to susceptible Gram-positive and Gram-negative organisms. [1970–75; perh. *(Strep)to-(myces) (tene)bra(rias)* + -MYCIN]

to·by (tō′bē), *n., pl.* **-bies. 1.** Also, **Toby, To′by jug′.** a mug in the form of a stout old man wearing a three-cornered hat. **2.** *Older Slang.* a long, slender, cheap cigar. [1830–40; generic use of proper name, short for *Tobias*]

toby (18th century)

To·by (tō′bē), *n., pl.* **-bies** for 3. **1.** a male given name, form of **Tobias. 2.** a female given name. **3.** toby (def. 1).

To·can·tins (tô′kän tēɴs′), *n.* a river in E Brazil, flowing N to the Pará River. 1700 mi. (2735 km) long.

toc·ca·ta (tə kä′tə; *It.* tôk kä′tä), *n. pl.* **-tas, -te** (-tē; *It.* -te). *Music.* a composition in the style of an improvisation, for the piano, organ, or other keyboard instrument, intended to exhibit the player's technique. [1715–25; < It: lit., touched, ptp. fem. of *toccare* to TOUCH]

Toch (tôкʜ), *n.* **Ernst** (ernst), 1887–1964, Austrian composer.

To·char·i·an (tō kâr′ē ən, -kär′-), *n.* **1.** a member of a central Asian people of high culture, who were assimilated with other peoples about the 11th century A.D. **2.** the language of the Tocharians, an extinct Indo-European language, having an eastern dialect **(Tocharian A)** and a western dialect **(Tocharian B),** records of which date from A.D. c600–c1000. —*adj.* **3.** of or pertaining to the Tocharians or their language. Also, **Tokharian.** [1925–30; < Gk *Tóchar(oi)* a Central Asian people (thought to have been the language's speakers when its remains were first discovered) + -IAN]

toch·er (toкʜ′ər), *Scot. and North Eng.* —*n.* **1.** a dowry; marriage settlement given to the groom by the bride or her family. —*v.t.* **2.** to provide with a dowry. [1490–1500; < ScotGael *tochradh;* cf. MIr *tochra* payment made to the bride or bride's father by the groom]

toch·is (tôкʜ′is, to͝oкʜ′əs), *n.* tokus.

to·co·dy·na·mom·e·ter (tō′kō dī′nə mom′i tər, tok′ō-), *n.* tokodynamometer.

to·col·o·gy (tō kol′ə jē), *n.* obstetrics. Also, **tokology.** [1820–30; < Gk *tóko(s)* child, childbirth + -LOGY]

to·com·e·ter (tō kom′i tər), *n.* tokodynamometer. [by shortening]

to·coph·er·ol (tō kof′ə rōl′, -rol′), *n. Biochem.* one of several alcohols that constitute the dietary factor known as vitamin E, occurring in wheat-germ oil, lettuce or spinach leaves, egg yolk, etc. Cf. **vitamin E.** [1935–40; < Gk *tóko(s)* child, childbirth + *phér(ein)* to carry, BEAR[1] + -OL[1]]

To·co·pil·la (tô′kô pē′yä), *n.* a seaport in N Chile. 23,140.

Tocque·ville (tōk′vil, tok′-; *Fr.* tôk vēl′), *n.* **A·lex·is Charles Hen·ri Mau·rice Clé·rel de** (A lek sē′ sʜARl′ äɴ Rē′ mô Rēs′ klā Rel′ də), 1805–59, French statesman and author.

toc·sin (tok′sin), *n.* **1.** a signal, esp. of alarm, sounded on a bell or bells. **2.** a bell used to sound an alarm. [1580–90; < MF < Pr *tocasenh* lit., (it) strikes (the) bell, equiv. to *toca,* 3d sing. pres. of *tocar* to strike, TOUCH + *senh* bell, SIGN]

tod[1] (tod), *n.* **1.** an English unit of weight, chiefly for wool, commonly equal to 28 pounds (12.7 kilograms) but varying locally. **2.** a load. **3.** a bushy mass, esp. of ivy. [1375–1425; late ME *todde;* akin to Fris (East dial.) *todde* small load, ON *toddi* piece, slice]

tod[2] (tod), *n. Scot. and North Eng.* **1.** a fox. **2.** a crafty, foxy person. [1125–75; ME (north) < ?]

to·day (tə dā′), *n.* **1.** this present day: *Today is beautiful.* **2.** this present time or age: *the world of today.* —*adv.* **3.** on this present day: *I will do it today.* **4.** at the present time; in these days: *Today you seldom see horses.* —*adj.* **5.** *Informal.* of the present era; up-to-date: *the today look in clothing styles.* [bef. 900; ME; OE *tō dæg.* See TO, DAY]

Todd (tod), *n.* **1. Alexander Ro·ber·tus** (rō bûr′təs) (*Baron of Trumpington*), born 1907, Scottish chemist: Nobel prize 1957. **2. David,** 1855–1939, U.S. astronomer and teacher. **3.** a male given name.

tod·dle (tod′l), *v.,* **-dled, -dling,** *n.* —*v.i.* **1.** to move with short, unsteady steps, as a young child. —*n.* **2.** the act of toddling. **3.** an unsteady gait. [1490–1500; TO(T-TER) + (WA)DDLE]

tod·dler (tod′lər), *n.* a person who toddles, esp. a young child learning to walk. [1785–95; TODDLE + -ER[1]]

tod·dler·hood (tod′lər ho͝od′), *n.* the state or time of being a toddler; early childhood. [TODDLER + -HOOD]

tod·dy (tod′ē), *n., pl.* **-dies. 1.** a drink made of alcoholic liquor and hot water, sweetened and sometimes spiced with cloves. **2.** the drawn sap, esp. when fermented, of any of several toddy palms, used as a drink. [1600–10; < Hindi *tāḍī*]

tod′dy palm′, any of several tropical Asian palms, as *Caryota urens* or *Borassus flabellifer,* yielding toddy. [1895–1900]

tod′dy ta′ble, a small stand of the 18th century, used for holding drinks.

to-do (tə do͞o′), *n., pl.* **-dos.** *Informal.* bustle; fuss: *They made a great to-do over the dinner.* [bef. 900; ME, OE; n. use of infinitive phrase; see TO, DO[1], ADO]
—**Syn.** See **ado.**

Todt (tōt), *n.* **Fritz** (frits), 1891–1942, German military engineer.

CONCISE ETYMOLOGY KEY: <, descended or borrowed from; >, whence; b., blend of, blended; c., cognate with; cf., compare; deriv., derivative; equiv., equivalent; imit., imitative; obl., oblique; r., replacing; s., stem; sp., spelling, spelled; resp., respelling, respelled; trans., translation; ?, origin unknown; *, unattested; ‡, probably earlier than. See the full key inside the front cover.

to•dy (tō′dē), *n., pl.* **-dies.** any of several small West Indian birds of the family Todidae, related to the motmots and kingfishers, having brightly colored green and red plumage. [appar. < F *todier,* based on NL *Todus* a genus, L: a kind of small bird]

toe (tō), *n., v.,* **toed, toe•ing.** —*n.* **1.** one of the terminal digits of the human foot. **2.** an analogous part in certain animals. **3.** the forepart of the foot or hoof of a horse or the like. **4.** the forepart of anything worn on the foot, as of a shoe or stocking. **5.** a part resembling a toe in shape or position. **6.** *Railroads.* the end of a frog in front of the point and in the direction of the switch. **7.** *Mach.* **a.** a journal or part placed vertically in a bearing, as the lower end of a vertical shaft. **b.** a curved partial cam lifting the flat surface of a follower and letting it drop; wiper. **8.** *Golf.* the outer end of the head of a club. **9. on one's toes,** energetic; alert; ready: *The spirited competition kept them on their toes.* **10. step** or **tread on (someone's) toes,** to offend (a person); encroach on the territory or sphere of responsibility of (another): *The new employee stepped on a lot of toes when he suggested reorganizing the office.* —*v.t.* **11.** to furnish with a toe or toes. **12.** to touch or reach with the toes: *The pitcher toed the mound, wound up, and threw a fastball.* **13.** to kick with the toe. **14.** *Golf.* to strike (the ball) with the toe of the club. **15.** *Carpentry.* **a.** to drive (a nail) obliquely. **b.** to toenail. —*v.i.* **16.** to stand, walk, etc., with the toes in a specified position: *to toe in.* **17.** to tap with the toe, as in dancing. **18. toe the line.** See **line**[1] (def. 70). [bef. 900; ME; OE *tā;* c. D *teen,* G *Zehe,* ON *tā*] —**toe′less,** *adj.* —**toe′like′,** *adj.*

toe•a (toi′ə), *n., pl.* **toe•a, toe•as.** a bronze coin and monetary unit of Papua New Guinea, the 100th part of a kina.

toe′ box′, a piece of stiffened material, as leather, placed between the lining and the toecap of a shoe. [1925–30]

toe•cap (tō′kap′), *n.* a piece of leather or other material covering the toe of a shoe. Also called **toepiece.** [1790–1800; TOE + CAP[1]]

toe′ clip′, a device attached to a bicycle pedal that grips the front part of the rider's shoe to keep the foot from slipping off the pedal. [1890–95]

toe′ crack′, a sand crack on the front of the hoof of a horse. [1900–05]

toed (tōd), *adj.* **1.** having a toe: *a toed clog; toed stockings.* **2.** having a toe of a specific kind or number (usually used in combination): *three-toed sloth.* **3.** *Carpentry.* **a.** (of a nail) driven obliquely. **b.** toenailed. [1605–15; TOE + -ED[3]]

toe′ dance′, a dance performed on the tips of the toes. [1930–35]

toe-dance (tō′dans′, -däns′), *v.i.,* **-danced, -danc•ing.** to perform a toe dance. [v. use of n. phrase TOE DANCE] —**toe′ danc′er.**

TOEFL (tō′fəl), *n.* Test of English as a Foreign Language.

toe•hold (tō′hōld), *n.* **1.** a small ledge or niche just large enough to support the toes, as in climbing. **2.** any slight or initial support, influence, advantage, progress, or the like: *His knowledge of Latin gave him a toehold for learning French.* **3.** a batten nailed to a sloping roof as a support for workers. **4.** *Wrestling.* a hold in which an opponent's foot is twisted. Also, **toe′-hold′.** [1875–80; TOE + HOLD[1]]

toe-in (tō′in′), *n.* the slight forward convergence given to the front wheels of an automobile to improve steering qualities. [1925–30]

toe′ loop′, *Skating.* a jump in which the skater takes off from the back outer edge of one skate, makes one full rotation in the air, and lands on the back outer edge of the same skate. Also called **toe′ loop′ jump′, tap loop jump.** [1960–65]

toe•nail (tō′nāl′), *n.* **1.** a nail of a toe. **2.** *Carpentry.* a nail driven obliquely. **3.** *Print. Slang.* a parenthesis. —*v.t.* **4.** *Carpentry.* to secure with oblique nailing. [1835–45; TOE + NAIL]

toe-out (tō′out′), *n.* the slight forward divergence that the front wheels of an automobile undergo during forward motion, esp. in turns. [1925–30]

toe′ pick′, one of the sharp teeth in the front part of a figure-skating blade.

toe•piece (tō′pēs′), *n.* toecap. [1875–80; TOE + PIECE]

toe•shoe (tō′sho͞o′), *n. Ballet.* a dance slipper fitted with a thick, reinforced toe to enable the ballet dancer to toe-dance. [TOE + SHOE]

toe-to-toe (tō′tə tō′), *adj.* **1.** being in direct confrontation or opposition. —*adv.* **2.** in a position or attitude of direct confrontation: *slugging it out toe-to-toe.* [1925–30]

toe•y (tō′ē), *adj. Australian Informal.* touchy or restive; apprehensive; fractious. [1920–25; orig. in reference to a racehorse; perh. TOE + -Y[1]]

TOFC, trailer-on-flatcar.

toff (tof), *n. Brit. Informal.* a stylishly dressed, fashionable person, esp. one who is or wants to be considered a member of the upper class. [1850–55; perh. var. of TUFT]

tof•fee (tô′fē, tof′ē), *n.* taffy. Also, **tof′fy.**

tof•fee-nosed (tô′fē nōzd′, tof′ē-), *adj. Brit. Slang.* stuck-up; conceited; pretentious: *a toffee-nosed butler; a toffee-nosed shop.* [1920–25]

toft (tôft, toft), *n. Brit. Dial.* **1.** the site of a house and outbuildings. **2.** a house site and its adjoining arable land. [bef. 1050; ME, late OE < ?]

to•fu (tō′fo͞o), *n.* a soft, bland, white cheeselike food, high in protein content, made from curdled soybean milk: used originally in Oriental cookery but now in a wide variety of soups and other dishes. Also called **bean curd.** [1875–80; < Japn *tōfu* < MChin, equiv. to Chin *dòufu* (*dòu* bean + *fǔ* turn sour, ferment)]

tog (tog), *n., v.,* **togged, tog•ging.** —*n.* **1.** a coat. **2.** Usually, **togs.** clothes. —*v.t.* **3.** to dress (often fol. by *out* or *up*). [1775–85; appar. short for earlier cant *togeman(s), togman* cloak, coat, equiv. to *toge* (late ME < L *toga* TOGA) + *-man(s)* obs. cant suffix < ?]

to•ga (tō′gə), *n., pl.* **-gas, -gae** (-jē, -gē). **1.** (in ancient Rome) the loose outer garment worn by citizens in public. **2.** a robe of office, a professorial gown, or some other distinctive garment. [1590–1600; < L; akin to TEGMEN] —**to•gaed** (tō′gəd), *adj.*

toga (def. 1)

to•gate (tō′gāt), *adj.* dressed in a toga. [< L *togātus.* See TOGA, -ATE[1]]

to•gat•ed (tō′gā tid), *adj.* **1.** characteristic of peace; peaceful: *the togated rule of Rome.* **2.** clad in a toga. [1625–35; < L *togāt(us)* clad in a toga (see TOGATE) + -ED[2]]

to•ga vi•ri•lis (tō′gə vi rī′lis, -rē′-; *Lat.* tô′gä wi rē′-lis), *pl.* **to•gae vi•ri•les** (tō′jē vi rī′lēz, -rē′-; *Lat.* tô′gī wi rē′les). the white toga assumed by boys in ancient Rome at the end of their 14th year. [1590–1600; < L *toga virīlis;* see TOGA, VIRILE]

to•geth•er (tə geth′ər), *adv.* **1.** into or in one gathering, company, mass, place, or body: *to call the people together.* **2.** into or in union, proximity, contact, or collision, as two or more things: *to sew things together.* **3.** into or in relationship, association, business, or agreement, etc., as two or more persons: *to bring strangers together.* **4.** taken or considered collectively or conjointly: *This one cost more than all the others together.* **5.** (of a single thing) into or in a condition of unity, compactness, or coherence: *to squeeze a thing together; The argument does not hold together well.* **6.** at the same time; simultaneously: *You cannot have both together.* **7.** without intermission or interruption; continuously; uninterruptedly: *for days together.* **8.** in cooperation; with united action; conjointly: *to undertake a task together.* **9.** with mutual action; mutually; reciprocally: *to confer together; to multiply two numbers together.* —*adj.* **10.** *Slang.* mentally and emotionally stable and well organized: *a together person.* [bef. 900; late ME, var. of earlier *togedere, togadere,* OE *tōgædere;* c. OFris *togadera.* See TO, GATHER]
—**Usage.** See **altogether.**

to•geth•er•ness (tə geth′ər nis), *n.* **1.** warm fellowship, as among members of a family. **2.** the quality, state, or condition of being together. [1650–60; TOGETHER + -NESS]

tog•ger•y (tog′ə rē), *n., pl.* **-ger•ies** for 2. **1.** *Informal.* clothes; garments; togs. **2.** *Chiefly Brit.* a clothing shop. [1805–15; TOG + -ERY]

tog•gle (tog′əl), *n., v.,* **-gled, -gling.** —*n.* **1.** a pin, bolt, or rod placed transversely through a chain, an eye or loop in a rope, etc., as to bind it temporarily to another chain or rope similarly treated. **2.** a toggle joint, or a device having one. **3.** an ornamental, rod-shaped button for inserting into a large buttonhole, loop, or frog, used esp. on sports clothes. **4.** *Theat.* **a.** Also called **tog′gle rail′.** a wooden batten across the width of a flat, for strengthening the frame. **b.** Also called **tog′gle i′ron.** a metal device for fastening a toggle rail to a frame. —*v.t.* **5.** to furnish with a toggle. **6.** to bind or fasten with a toggle. **7.** *Informal.* to turn, twist, or manipulate a toggle switch; dial or turn the switch of (an appliance): *He toggled the TV between the baseball game and the news.* [1760–70; perh. var. of TACKLE] —**tog′gler,** *n.*

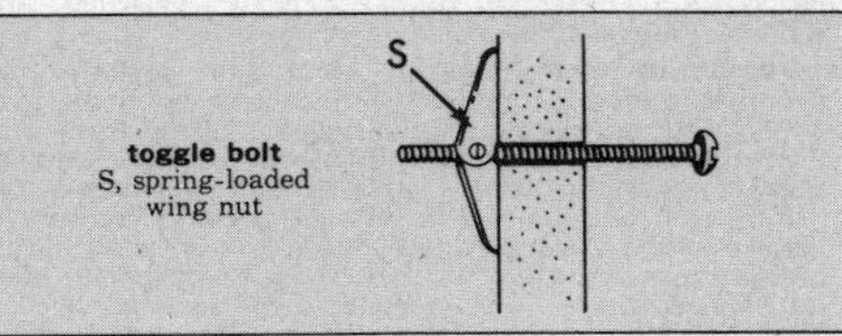

toggle bolt
S, spring-loaded wing nut

tog′gle bolt′, an anchor bolt having two hinged wings, ordinarily held open by a spring, for engaging the rough sides of a hole drilled in masonry or the inner surface of a hollow wall. [1785–95]

tog′gle joint′, *Mach.* any of various devices consisting basically of a rod that can be inserted into an object and then manipulated so that the inserted part spreads, becomes offset, or turns at a right angle to the exterior part, allowing it to be used as a support, handle, linkage, lever, etc. [1840–50]

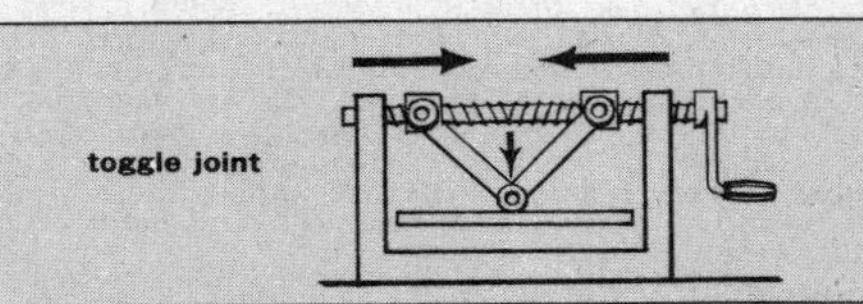
toggle joint

tog′gle switch′, *Elect.* a switch in which a projecting knob or arm, moving through a small arc, causes the contacts to open or close an electric circuit suddenly, as commonly used in most homes. [1920–25]

To•gliat•ti (tô lyät′tē), *n.* **Pal•mi•ro** (päl mē′rô), 1893–1964, Italian Communist party leader.

To•go (tô′gō), *n.* **1. Hei•ha•chi•ro** (hā′hä chē′rô), **Marquis** 1847–1934, Japanese admiral. **2. Shi•ge•no•ri** (shē′ge nô′rē), 1882–1950, Japanese political leader and diplomat.

To•go (tō′gō), *n.* **Republic of,** an independent country in W Africa: formerly a French mandate 1922–46 and trusteeship 1946–60 in E Togoland. 2,197,900; 21,830 sq. mi. (56,540 sq. km). *Cap.:* Lomé.

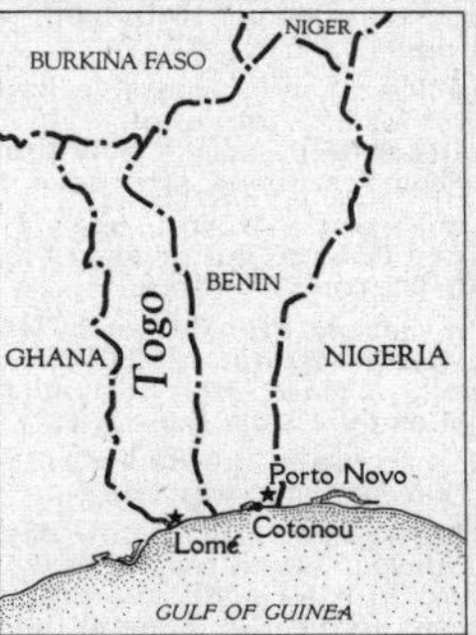

To•go•land (tō′gō land′), *n.* a former German protectorate in W Africa, on the Gulf of Guinea: E part is now the Republic of Togo; W part, a British mandate 1922–46 and trusteeship 1946–57, is now part of Ghana. —**To′go•land′er,** *n.*

To•go•lese (tō′gə lēz′, -lēs′, -gō-), *n., pl.* **-lese,** *adj.* —*n.* **1.** a native or inhabitant of the Republic of Togo. —*adj.* **2.** of, pertaining to, or characteristic of the Togolese or the Republic of Togo. [TOGO + *-lese,* as in *Congolese*]

togue (tōg), *n., pl.* **togues,** (*esp. collectively*) **togue.** *Canadian.* See **lake trout.** [1830–40; < CanF < Eastern Algonquian, perh. shortening of Micmac *atoywa·su* trout]

to•he•ro•a (tō′ə rō′ə), *n., pl.* **-ro•as, -ro•a.** a large marine clam, *Amphidesma ventricosum,* of waters near New Zealand. [1870–75; < Maori]

to•hu•bo•hu (tō′ho͞o bō′ho͞o), *n.* chaos; disorder; confusion. [1605–15; < Heb *tōhū wā-bhōhū*]

toil[1] (toil), *n.* **1.** hard and continuous work; exhausting labor or effort. **2.** a laborious task. **3.** *Archaic.* battle; strife; struggle. —*v.i.* **4.** to engage in hard and continuous work; labor arduously: *to toil in the fields.* **5.** to move or travel with difficulty, weariness, or pain. —*v.t.* **6.** to accomplish or produce by toil. [1250–1300; ME *toile* (n.), *toilen* (v.) < AF *toil* contention, *toiler* to contend < L *tudiculāre* to stir up, beat, v. deriv. of *tudicula* machine for crushing olives, equiv. to *tudi-* (s. of *tundere* to beat) + *-cula* -CULE[2]] —**toil′er,** *n.*
—**Syn. 1.** exertion, travail, pains. See **work. 4.** strive, moil. —**Ant. 1.** indolence, sloth.

toil[2] (toil), *n.* **1.** Usually, **toils.** a net or series of nets in which game known to be in the area is trapped or into which game outside of the area is driven. **2.** Usually, **toils.** trap; snare: *to be caught in the toils of a gigantic criminal conspiracy.* **3.** *Archaic.* any snare or trap for wild beasts. [1520–30; < F *toile* < L *tēla* web]

toile (twäl), *n.* any of various transparent linens and cottons. [1555–65; < F: linen cloth, canvas. See TOIL[2]]

toile de Jouy (*Fr.* twᴀl də zhwē′), a cotton or linen fabric characterized by monochromatic prints on a light background. Also called **Jouy print.** [1915–20; < F: lit., cloth of *Jouy*(-en-Josas), France]

toi•let (toi′lit), *n.* **1.** a bathroom fixture consisting of a bowl, usually with a detachable, hinged seat and lid, and a device for flushing with water, used for defecation and urination. **2.** a lavatory. **3.** a bathroom. **4.** See **toilet bowl. 5.** a dressing room, esp. one containing a bath. **6.** the act or process of dressing or grooming oneself, including bathing and arranging the hair: *to make one's toilet; busy at her toilet.* **7.** See **toilet set. 8.** the dress or costume of a person; any particular costume: *toilet of white silk.* **9.** *Surg.* the cleansing of a part after childbirth or a wound after an operation. **10.** *Archaic.* See **dressing table.** Also, **toilette** (for defs. 6, 8). [1530–40; < F *toilette* small cloth, doily, dressing table, equiv. to *toile* TOIL[2] + *-ette* -ET]

toi′let bowl′, the ceramic bowl of a toilet.

toi′let pa′per, a soft, lightweight, sanitized paper used in bathrooms for personal cleanliness. Also called **toi′let tis′sue, bathroom tissue.** [1880–85]

toi′let pow′der, a fine powder sprinkled or rubbed over the skin, esp. after bathing. [1890–95]

toi•let•ry (toi′li trē), *n., pl.* **-ries.** any article or preparation used in cleaning or grooming oneself, as soap or deodorant. [1825–35; TOILET + -RY]

toi′let seat′, a detachable, ringlike seat of wood or plastic hinged to the top of a toilet bowl.

toi′let set′, a set of articles used in grooming, as a mirror, brush, and comb. [1855–60]

toi′let soap′, a mild and usually perfumed soap for washing the hands and face and for bathing. [1830–40]

toi•lette (twä let′, toi-; *Fr.* twa let′), *n., pl.* **-lettes** (-lets′; *Fr.* -let′). toilet (defs. 6, 8).

toi•let-train (toi′lit trān′), *v.t.* to train (a young child) to use a toilet for bowel and bladder movements.

toi′let train′ing, the training of a very young child to control and regulate bowel and bladder movements and use the toilet. [1920–25]

toi′let wa′ter, a scented liquid used as a light perfume; cologne. [1850–55]

toil•ful (toil′fəl), *adj.* characterized by or involving toil; laborious; toilsome. [1590–1600; TOIL[1] + -FUL] —**toil′ful•ly,** *adv.*

toil•some (toil′səm), *adj.* characterized by or involving toil; laborious or fatiguing. [1575–85; TOIL[1] + -SOME[1]] —**toil′some•ly,** *adv.* —**toil′some•ness,** *n.*
—**Syn.** wearisome, arduous, strenuous, tiring.

toil•worn (toil′wôrn′, -wōrn′), *adj.* **1.** worn by toil: *toilworn hands.* **2.** worn out or aged by toil: *a toilworn farmer.* [1745–55; TOIL[1] + WORN]

toise (toiz), *n.* an old French unit of length equivalent to 6.395 feet (1.949 meters). [1590–1600; < MF < VL **tēsa,* (fem. sing.), L *tēnsa* (*bracchia*) outstretched (arms), neut. pl. taken as fem. sing. See TENSE[1]]

To•jo (tō′jō), *n.* **Hi•de•ki** (hē′de kē′), 1884–1948, Japanese general: executed for war crimes.

to•ka•mak (tō′kə mak′, tok′ə-), *n. Physics.* a type of experimental nuclear fusion reactor in which a plasma of atoms circulates in a toroidal tube and is confined to a narrow beam by an electromagnetic field. [1960–65; < Russ *tokamák,* acronym from *toroidál'naya kámera s aksiál'nym magnítnym pólem* toroidal chamber with an axial magnetic field]

to•kay (tō kā′), *n.* a gecko, *Gekko gecko,* of the Malay Archipelago and southeastern Asia: sometimes kept as a pet. [1745–55; < dial. Malay *tokeʔ* < Javanese *təʔkəʔ* (sp. *tekek*)]

tokay, *Gekko gecko,* length to 14 in. (36 cm)

To•kay (tō kā′), *n.* **1.** an aromatic wine made from Furmint grapes grown in the district surrounding Tokay, a town in NE Hungary. **2.** *Hort.* **a.** a large, red variety of grape, grown for table use. **b.** the vine bearing this fruit, grown in California. **3.** a sweet, strong white wine made in California.

toke[1] (tōk), *n., v.,* **toked, tok•ing.** *Slang.* —*n.* **1.** a tip or gratuity given by a gambler to a dealer or other employee at a casino. —*v.i.* **2.** to provide a toke. —*v.t.* **3.** to give a toke to. [1970–75; orig. uncert.]

toke[2] (tōk), *n., v.,* **toked, tok•ing.** *Slang.* —*n.* **1.** a puff of a marijuana cigarette. —*v.t.* **2.** to light up or puff (a marijuana cigarette). —*v.i.* **3.** to puff a marijuana cigarette (often fol. by *up*). [1950–55, *Amer.*; orig. uncert.]

to•ken (tō′kən), *n.* **1.** something serving to represent or indicate some fact, event, feeling, etc.; sign: *Black is a token of mourning.* **2.** a characteristic indication or mark of something; evidence or proof: *Malnutrition is a token of poverty.* **3.** a memento; souvenir; keepsake: *The seashell was a token of their trip.* **4.** something used to indicate authenticity, authority, etc.; emblem; badge: *Judicial robes are a token of office.* **5.** Also called **to′ken coin′.** a stamped piece of metal, issued as a limited medium of exchange, as for bus fares, at a nominal value much greater than its commodity value. **6.** anything of only nominal value similarly used, as paper currency. **7.** an item, idea, person, etc., representing a group; a part as representing the whole; sample; indication. **8.** *Logic, Ling.* a particular instance of a word, symbol, expression, sentence, or the like: *A printed page might have twenty tokens of the single type-word "and."* Cf. **type** (def. 8). **9. by the same token, a.** in proof of which. **b.** moreover; furthermore: *She has a talent as a painter, and by the same token has a sharp eye for detail.* **10. in token of,** as a sign of; in evidence of: *a ring in token of his love.* —*v.t.* **11.** to be a token of; signify; symbolize. —*adj.* **12.** serving as a token: *a token gift; a token male on an all-female staff.* **13.** slight; perfunctory; minimal: *token resistance.* [bef. 900; ME; OE *tāc(e)n*; c. G *Zeichen,* ON *teikn* sign, mark. See TEACH]
—**Syn. 12.** symbolic.

to′ken econ′omy, *Psychiatry.* a method of encouraging desirable behavior, esp. in a hospital setting, by offering rewards of token money that can be exchanged for special food, access to television, and other bonuses. [1965–70]

to•ken•ism (tō′kə niz′əm), *n.* **1.** the practice or policy of making no more than a token effort or gesture, as in offering opportunities to minorities equal to those of the majority. **2.** any legislation, admissions policy, hiring practice, etc., that demonstrates only minimal compliance with rules, laws, or public pressure: *Admitting one woman to the men's club was merely tokenism.* [1960–65; TOKEN + -ISM] —**to′ken•is′tic,** *adj.*

CONCISE ETYMOLOGY KEY: <, descended or borrowed from; >, whence; b., blend of, blended; c., cognate with; cf., compare; deriv., derivative; equiv., equivalent; imit., imitative; obl., oblique; r., replacing; s., stem; sp., spelling, spelled; resp., respelling, respelled; trans., translation; ?, origin unknown; *, unattested; ‡, probably earlier than. See the full key inside the front cover.

to′ken pay′ment, a small payment binding an agreement or acknowledging a debt.

To•khar•i•an (tō kâr′ē ən, -kär′-), *n.* Tocharian.

To•klas (tō′kləs), *n.* **Alice B.,** 1877–1967, U.S. author in France: friend and companion of Gertrude Stein.

to•ko•dy•na•mom•e•ter (tō′kō dī′nə mom′i tər), *n.* a pressure gauge strapped to the mother's abdomen during labor to measure uterine contractions. Also, **tocodynamometer.** Also called **tocometer.** [< Gk *tók*(*os*) childbirth + -O- + DYNAMOMETER]

to•kol•o•gy (tō kol′ə jē), *n.* tocology.

to•ko•no•ma (tō′kə nō′mə), *n.* (in Japanese architecture) a shallow alcove for the display of kakemonos or flower arrangements. [1895–1900; < Japn, equiv. to *toko* (raised) floor + *-no* grammatical particle + *ma* room]

Tok Pis•in (tôk′ pis′in), Neo-Melanesian.

To•ku•ga•wa (tô′kŏŏ gä′wä), *n.* **1.** a member of a powerful family in Japan that ruled as shoguns, 1603–1867. **2.** a period of Japanese history under the rule of Tokugawa shoguns, characterized by a samurai ruling class, urbanization, and the growth of a merchant class.

tok•us (tô′KHəs, tŏŏKH′əs), *n. Slang.* the buttocks. Also, **tochis, tuchis.** [1910–15, *Amer.*; < Yiddish *tokhes* < Heb *taḥath* under]

To•ku•shi•ma (tô′kŏŏ shē′mä), *n.* a seaport on NE Shikoku, in SW Japan. 249,343.

To•ky•o (tō′kē ō′; *Japn.* tô′kyô), *n.* a seaport in and the capital of Japan, on Tokyo Bay: one of the world's largest cities; destructive earthquake and fire 1923; signing of the Japanese surrender document aboard the U.S.S. *Missouri,* September 2, 1945. 11,468,516. Also, **To′ki•o′.** Formerly, **Edo, Yeddo, Yedo.** —**To′ky•o•ite′,** *n.*

To′kyo Bay′, an inlet of the Pacific, in SE Honshu Island of Japan. 30 mi. (48 km) long; 20 mi. (32 km) wide.

to•la (tō′lä), *n.* a unit of weight in India: the government tola is 180 ser and equals 180 grains (11.7 grams), the weight of a silver rupee. [1605–15; < Hindi *tolā* << Skt *tolaka*]

to•lan (tō′lan), *n. Chem.* a crystalline, water-insoluble, solid, unsaturated compound, $C_{14}H_{10}$, used chiefly in organic synthesis. Also called **diphenylacetylene.** [var. of *tolane.* See TOLUENE, -ANE]

To•land (tō′lənd), *n.* **Gregg,** 1904–48, U.S. cinematographer.

tol•booth (tōl′bōōth′, -bōōth′), *n., pl.* **-booths** (-bōōthz′, -bōōths′). *Chiefly Scot.* **1.** a town jail. **2.** a town hall or guild hall, esp. a place where tolls are paid. Also **tollbooth.** [1300–50; ME; see TOLLBOOTH]

tol•bu•ta•mide (tol byōō′tə mīd′), *n. Pharm.* a white crystalline substance, $C_{12}H_{18}N_2O_3S$, used to augment insulin secretion in the treatment of diabetes mellitus. [1955–60; TOL(U) + BUT(YL) + AMIDE]

told (tōld), *v.* **1.** pt. and pp. of **tell. 2. all told,** counting everyone or everything; in all: *There were 50 guests all told.*

tole[1] (tōl), *n.* enameled or lacquered metalware, usually with gilt decoration, often used, esp. in the 18th century, for trays, lampshades, etc. Also, **tôle.** [1925–30; < F *tôle* sheet of iron, plate, dial. var. of *table* TABLE]

tole[2] (tōl), *v.t.,* **toled, tol•ing.** toll[2] (defs. 5, 6).

To•le•do (tə lē′dō; *for 1, 3, 4, also Sp.* tô le′thô), *n., pl.* **-dos** (-dōz; *Sp.* -thôs) for 4. **1. Fran•cis•co de** (fRän-sēs′kô the), c1515–84?, Spanish administrator: viceroy of Peru 1569–81. **2.** a port in NW Ohio, on Lake Erie. 354,635. **3.** a city in central Spain, on the Tagus River: the capital of Spain under the Romans. 44,382. **4.** a sword or sword blade of finely tempered steel, as formerly made in Toledo, Spain.

tol•er•a•ble (tol′ər ə bəl), *adj.* **1.** capable of being tolerated; endurable: *His arrogance is no longer tolerable.* **2.** fairly good; not bad. **3.** *Informal.* in fair health. [1375–1425; late ME < L *tolerābilis,* equiv. to *tolerā(re)* to endure + *-bilis* -BLE] —**tol′er•a•ble•ness, tol′er•a•bil′i•ty,** *n.* —**tol′er•a•bly,** *adv.*
—**Syn. 1.** bearable, supportable. **2.** passable, middling, indifferent, so-so.

tol•er•ance (tol′ər əns), *n.* **1.** a fair, objective, and permissive attitude toward those whose opinions, practices, race, religion, nationality, etc., differ from one's own; freedom from bigotry. **2.** a fair, objective, and permissive attitude toward opinions and practices that differ from one's own. **3.** interest in and concern for ideas, opinions, practices, etc., foreign to one's own; a liberal, undogmatic viewpoint. **4.** the act or capacity of enduring; endurance: *My tolerance of noise is limited.* **5.** *Med., Immunol.* **a.** the power of enduring or resisting the action of a drug, poison, etc.: *a tolerance to antibiotics.* **b.** the lack of or low levels of immune response to transplanted tissue or other foreign substance that is normally immunogenic. **6.** *Mach.* **a.** the permissible range of variation in a dimension of an object. Cf. **allowance** (def. 8). **b.** the permissible variation of an object or objects in some characteristic such as hardness, weight, or quantity. **7.** Also called **allowance.** *Coining.* a permissible deviation in the fineness and weight of coin, owing to the difficulty of securing exact conformity to the standard prescribed by law. [1375–1425; late ME < L *tolerantia.* See TOLERANT, -ANCE]
—**Syn. 1, 2.** patience, sufferance, forbearance; liberality, impartiality, open-mindedness. TOLERANCE, TOLERATION agree in allowing the right of something that one does not approve. TOLERANCE suggests a liberal spirit toward the views and actions of others: *tolerance toward religious minorities.* TOLERATION implies the allowance or sufferance of conduct with which one is not in accord: *toleration of graft.*

tol•er•ant (tol′ər ənt), *adj.* **1.** inclined or disposed to tolerate; showing tolerance; forbearing: *tolerant of errors.* **2.** favoring toleration: *a tolerant church.* **3.** *Med., Immunol.* **a.** able to endure or resist the action of a drug, poison, etc. **b.** lacking or exhibiting low levels of immune response to a normally immunogenic substance. [1770–80; < L *tolerant-* (s. of *tolerāns*), prp. of *tolerāre* to bear. See TOLERATE, -ANT] —**tol′er•ant•ly,** *adv.*

tol•er•ate (tol′ə rāt′), *v.t.,* **-at•ed, -at•ing. 1.** to allow the existence, presence, practice, or act of without prohibition or hindrance; permit. **2.** to endure without repugnance; put up with: *I can tolerate laziness, but not incompetence.* **3.** *Med.* to endure or resist the action of (a drug, poison, etc.). **4.** *Obs.* to experience, undergo, or sustain, as pain or hardship. [1525–35; < L *tolerātus,* ptp. of *tolerāre* to bear (akin to THOLE[2]); see -ATE[1]] —**tol′er•a′tive,** *adj.* —**tol′er•a′tor,** *n.*
—**Syn. 2.** support, accept.

tol•er•a•tion (tol′ə rā′shən), *n.* **1.** an act or instance of tolerating, esp. of what is not actually approved; forbearance: *to show toleration toward the protesters.* **2.** permission by law or government of the exercise of religions other than an established religion; noninterference in matters of private faith and worship. [1510–20; < L *tolerātiōn-* (s. of *tolerātiō*). See TOLERATE, -ION] —**tol′er•a′tion•ism,** *n.* —**tol′er•a′tion•ist,** *n.*
—**Syn. 1.** See **tolerance.**

Tolera′tion Act′, *Eng. Hist.* See **Act of Toleration.**

tole•ware (tōl′wâr′), *n.* articles made of tole. [TOLE[1] + WARE[1]]

tol•i•dine (tol′i dēn′, -din), *n. Chem.* any of several isomeric derivatives of biphenyl containing two methyl and two amino groups, esp. the ortho isomer that is used as a reagent and in the preparation of dyes. [1895–1900; TOL(UENE) + -ID[3] + -INE[2]]

To•li•ma (tô lē′mä), *n.* a volcano in W Colombia, in the Andes. 18,438 ft. (5620 m).

Tol•kien (tōl′kēn, tol′-), *n.* **J(ohn) R(onald) R(eu•el)** (rōō′əl), 1892–1973, English novelist, philologist, and teacher, born in South Africa.

toll[1] (tōl), *n.* **1.** a payment or fee exacted by the state, the local authorities, etc., for some right or privilege, as for passage along a road or over a bridge. **2.** the extent of loss, damage, suffering, etc., resulting from some action or calamity: *The toll was 300 persons dead or missing.* **3.** a tax, duty, or tribute, as for services or use of facilities. **4.** a payment made for a long-distance telephone call. **5.** (formerly, in England) the right to take such payment. **6.** a compensation for services, as for transportation or transmission. **7.** grain retained by a miller in payment for grinding. —*v.t.* **8.** to collect (something) as toll. **9.** to impose a tax or toll on (a person). —*v.i.* **10.** to collect toll; levy toll. [bef. 1000; (n.) ME, OE *toll* (c. D *tol,* G *Zoll,* ON *tollr*), assimilated var. of OE *toln* < LL *tolōneum,* for *telōnēum* < Gk *telōneîon* tollhouse, akin to *telṓnēs* tax collector, *télos* tax; (v.) ME *tollen,* deriv. of the n.]
—**Syn. 3.** tariff, levy, impost, exaction.

toll[2] (tōl), *v.t.* **1.** to cause (a large bell) to sound with single strokes slowly and regularly repeated, as for summoning a congregation to church, or esp. for announcing a death. **2.** to sound or strike (a knell, the hour, etc.) by such strokes: *In the distance Big Ben tolled five.* **3.** to announce by this means; ring a knell for (a dying or dead person). **4.** to summon or dismiss by tolling. **5.** to lure or decoy (game) by arousing curiosity. **6.** to allure; entice: *He tolls us on with fine promises.* —*v.i.* **7.** to sound with single strokes slowly and regularly repeated, as a bell. —*n.* **8.** the act of tolling a bell. **9.** one of the strokes made in tolling a bell. **10.** the sound made. Also, **tole** (for defs. 5, 6). [1175–1225; ME *tollen* to entice, lure, pull, hence prob. to make (a bell) ring by pulling a rope; akin to OE *-tyllan,* in *fortyllan* to attract, allure]

toll[3] (tōl), *v.t. Law.* to suspend or interrupt (as a statute of limitations). [1425–75; late ME *tollen* to remove, legally annul < AF *tolre, tol(l)er* < L *tollere* to remove, take away]

toll•age (tō′lij), *n.* **1.** toll; tax. **2.** exaction or payment of toll. [1485–95; TOLL[1] + -AGE]

toll′ bar′, a barrier, esp. a gate, across a road or bridge, where toll is collected. [1805–15]

toll•booth (tōl′bōōth′, -bōōth′), *n., pl.* **-booths** (-bōōthz′, -bōōths′). **1.** a booth, as at a bridge or the entrance to a toll road, where a toll is collected. **2.** *Chiefly Scot.* tolbooth. [1300–50; ME *tolbothe.* See TOLL[1], BOOTH]

toll′ bridge′, a bridge at which a toll is charged. [1765–75]

toll′ call′, any telephone call involving a higher base rate than that fixed for a local message. [1925–30]

toll′ collec′tor, a person or device collecting or registering tolls. [1815–25]

toll•er[1] (tō′lər), *n.* **1.** a person or thing that tolls. **2.** Also called **tolling dog.** a small dog trained to entice ducks into shooting range or a trap. **3.** a person who tolls a bell. **4.** a bell used for tolling; a tolling bell. [1400–50; ME: one who lures. See TOLL[2], -ER[1]]

toll•er[2] (tō′lər), *n.* a toll collector. [bef. 1000; ME; OE *tollere.* See TOLL[1], -ER[1]]

Tol•ler (tôl′lər, tol′ər; *Ger.* tô′lər), *n.* **Ernst** (ûrnst; *Ger.* ernst), 1893–1939, German dramatist.

toll-free (tōl′frē′), *adj.* **1.** made, used, provided, etc., without tolls or a charge: *a toll-free highway; a toll-free phone number.* —*adv.* **2.** free of charge: *to call toll-free.* [1965–70]

toll•gate (tōl′gāt′), *n.* a gate where toll is collected. [1765–75; TOLL[1] + GATE]

toll•gath•er•er (tōl′gath′ər ər), *n.* a person who collects tolls, taxes, or other imposts. [1350–1400; ME *tol gaderer.* See TOLL[1], GATHERER]

toll•house (tōl′hous′), *n., pl.* **-hous•es** (-hou′ziz). a house or booth at a tollgate, occupied by a tollkeeper. [1400–50; late ME *tolhowse.* See TOLL[1], HOUSE]

toll′house cook′ie, a crisp cookie containing bits of chocolate and sometimes chopped nuts. [1970–75]

toll′ing dog′, toller[1] (def. 2). [1865–70]

toll•keep•er (tōl′kē′pər), *n.* the collector at a tollgate. [1815–25; TOLL[1] + KEEPER]

toll′ line′, a telephone line for long-distance calls.

toll•man (tōl′mən), *n., pl.* **-men.** a tollkeeper. [1735–45; TOLL[1] + -MAN]

toll′ road′, a road or highway on which a toll is exacted. [1815–25]

toll′ thor′ough, *Brit.* a payment exacted by a municipal government for the right to use a highway, bridge, or the like; toll. [1660–70]

toll′ trav′erse, *Brit.* a payment made for the right to cross privately owned property.

Tol′lund man′ (tō′lənd), the perfectly preserved remains of an Iron Age man, hanged and thrown into a bog at Tollund, in Jutland, Denmark: discovered in 1950.

toll•way (tōl′wā′), *n.* toll road. [1945–50; TOLL[1] + WAY[1]]

tol•ly (tol′ē), *n., pl.* **-lies.** *Brit. Slang.* candle (def. 1). [1850–55; alter. of TALLOW]

tol•naf•tate (tôl naf′tāt, tol-), *n. Pharm.* an antifungal substance, $C_{19}H_{17}NOS$, used topically in the treatment of certain superficial fungal skin infections, as athlete's foot. [TOL(UYL) + *naft-*, resp. of NAPHTH- + -ATE[2]]

Tol•stoy (tōl′stoi, tol′-; *Russ.* tul stoi′), *n.* **Leo** or **Lev Ni•ko•la•e•vich** (lev nik′ə lī′ə vich′; *Russ.* lyef′ nyi ku-lä′yi vyich), **Count,** 1828–1910, Russian novelist and social critic. Also, **Tol′stoi.** —**Tol′stoy•an, Tol′stoi•an,** *adj., n.* —**Tol′stoy•ism,** *n.* —**Tol′stoy•ist,** *n.*

Tol•tec (tōl′tek, tol′-), *n., pl.* **-tecs,** *(esp. collectively)* **-tec,** *adj.* —*n.* **1.** a member of an Indian people living in central Mexico before the advent of the Aztecs and traditionally credited with laying the foundation of Aztec culture. —*adj.* **2.** Also, **Tol•tec′an.** of or pertaining to the Toltecs. [< MexSp *tolteca* < Nahuatl *tōltēcah,* pl. of *tōltēcatl* person from *Tōllān* TULA]

to•lu (tô lōō′, tə-), *n.* **1.** Also called **tolu′ bal′sam, balsam of tolu, tolu resin.** a fragrant, yellowish-brown balsam or resin obtained from a South American leguminous tree, *Myroxylon balsamum,* and used in medicine as a stomachic and expectorant, and in perfumery. **2.** the tree itself. [1665–75; after *Tolú* (now Santiago de Tolú) in Colombia, where balsam is obtained]

tol•u•ate (tol′yōō āt′), *n. Chem.* a salt or ester of any of the four isomeric toluic acids. [1855–60; TOLU(IC ACID) + -ATE[2]]

To•lu•ca (tô lōō′kä), *n.* **1.** a city in and the capital of Mexico state, in S central Mexico. 141,726. **2.** an extinct volcano in central Mexico, in Mexico state. 15,026 ft. (4580 m).

tol•u•ene (tol′yōō ēn′), *n. Chem.* a colorless, water-insoluble, flammable liquid, C_7H_8, having a benzenelike odor, obtained chiefly from coal tar and petroleum: used as a solvent in the manufacture of benzoic acid, benzaldehyde, TNT, and other organic compounds. Also called **methylbenzene, phenylmethane.** [1870–75; TOLU + -ENE]

tol′uene trichlo′ride, *Chem.* benzotrichloride.

tol′uene trifluor′ide, *Chem.* benzotrifluoride.

to•lu•ic (tə lōō′ik, tol′yōō ik), *adj. Chem.* of or derived from toluic acid. [1855–60; TOLU(ENE) + -IC]

tolu′ic ac′id, *Chem.* any of four isomeric acids having the formula $CH_3C_6H_4COOH$: derivatives of toluene.

to•lu•i•dine (tə lōō′i dēn′, -din), *n. Chem.* any of three isomeric amines having the formula C_7H_9N, derived from toluene: used in the dye and drug industries. Cf. **metatoluidine, orthotoluidine, paratoluidine.** [1840–50; TOLU(ENE) + -ID[3] + -INE[2]]

tol•u•ol (tol′yōō ōl′, -ôl′), *n. Chem.* **1.** toluene. **2.** the commercial form of toluene. [1835–45; TOLU + -OL[2]]

tolu′ res′in, tolu.

To•lyat•ti (tôl yä′tē; *Russ.* tu lyät′tyi), *n.* a city in the SW Russian Federation in Europe, on the Volga River. 630,000. Formerly, **Stavropol.**

tol•yl (tol′il), *adj. Chem.* containing a tolyl group; cresyl. [1865–70; TOL(UENE) + -YL]

tol′yl group′, *Chem.* any of three univalent, isomeric groups having the formula C_7H_7-, derived from toluene. Also called **tol′yl rad′ical.**

tom (tom), *n.* **1.** the male of various animals, as the turkey. **2.** a tomcat. [1755–65; generic use of TOM]

Tom (tom), *n., v.,* **Tommed, Tom•ming.** —*n.* **1.** See **Uncle Tom. 2.** a male given name, form of **Thomas.** —*v.i.* **3.** *(often l.c.)* to act like an Uncle Tom.

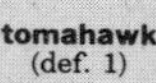
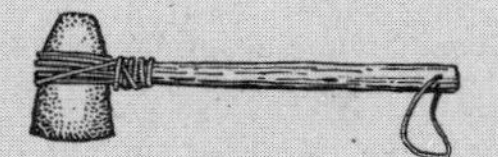

tomahawk (def. 1)

tom•a•hawk (tom′ə hôk′), *n.* **1.** a light ax used by the North American Indians as a weapon and tool. **2.** any of various similar weapons or implements. **3.** (in Australia) a stone hatchet used by the Aborigines. —*v.t.* **4.** to attack, wound, or kill with or as if with a tomahawk. [1605–15; < Virginia Algonquian (E sp.) *tamahaac* hatchet (equiv. to Proto-Algonquian *temah- to cut (it) off + *-a·kan- instrument for)] —**tom′a•hawk′er,** *n.*

tom•al•ley (tom′al′ē), *n., pl.* **-leys.** *Cookery.* the liver of a lobster. [1660–70; earlier *taumali* < Carib]

to•man (tə män′), *n.* a coin of Iran, equal to 10 rials. [1560–70; < Pers *tōmān, tūmān* < Turkic *tümen* ten thousand]

Tom′ and Jer′ry, a hot drink made of rum and water or milk, beaten eggs, spices, and sugar. [1820–30; named after the principal characters in *Life in London* (1821) by Pierce Egan (d. 1849), English writer]

to•ma•til•lo (tō′mə tē′ō, -tēl′yō), *n., pl.* **-loes, -los.** a plant, *Physalis ixocarpa,* of the nightshade family, native to Mexico, having yellow flowers with five blackish spots in the throat and bluish, sticky berries in a purple-veined calyx. Also called **Mexican ground cherry.** [1910–15; < Sp, dim. of *tomate* TOMATO]

to•ma•to (tə mā′tō, -mä′-), *n., pl.* **-toes. 1.** any of several plants belonging to the genus *Lycopersicon,* of the nightshade family, native to Mexico and Central and South America, esp. the widely cultivated species *L. lycopersicum,* bearing a mildly acid, pulpy, usually red fruit eaten raw or cooked as a vegetable. **2.** the fruit itself. **3.** *Older Slang (sometimes offensive).* a girl or woman. [1595–1605; 1915–20 for def. 3; earlier *tomate* < Sp < Nahuatl *tomatl*]

toma′to as′pic, aspic[1] (def. 2).

toma′to egg′plant. See **scarlet eggplant.**

toma′to fruit′worm (frōōt′wûrm′). See **corn earworm.** [1890–95]

toma′to horn′worm, the larva of a hawk moth, *Manduca quinquemaculata,* having a black, hornlike structure at the rear, that feeds on the leaves of tomato, potato, and other plants of the nightshade family. Also called **potato worm.** [1920–25]

toma′to psyl′lid. See **potato psyllid.**

tomb (tōōm), *n.* **1.** an excavation in earth or rock for the burial of a corpse; grave. **2.** a mausoleum, burial chamber, or the like. **3.** a monument for housing or commemorating a dead person. **4.** any sepulchral structure. —*v.t.* **5.** to place in or as if in a tomb; entomb; bury. [1225–75; ME *tumbe* < AF; OF *tombe* < LL *tumba* < Gk *týmbos* burial mound; akin to L *tumēre* to swell. See TUMOR, TUMULUS] —**tomb′al,** *adj.* —**tomb′less,** *adj.* —**tomb′like′,** *adj.*

tom•bac (tom′bak), *n.* an alloy, used to imitate gold, containing from 70 to 92 percent copper with zinc and sometimes tin and other materials forming the remainder. Also, **tambac.** [1595–1605; < D *tombak* < Pg *tambaca* < Malay *tembaga* copper < Indo-Aryan (cf. Hindi *tāmbiyā* copper or brass vessel, Skt *tāmraka* copper]

Tom•bal•ba•ye (tôm′bäl bä′ye), *n.* **Fran•çois** (*Fr.* fräN swa′), 1918–75, African statesman: president of the Republic of Chad 1960–75.

Tom•baugh (tom′bô), *n.* **Clyde William,** born 1906, U.S. astronomer: discovered the planet Pluto 1930.

tom•bé (tom bā′; *Fr.* tôN bā′), *n., pl.* **-bés** (-bāz′; *Fr.* -bā′). *Ballet.* a step in which a dancer falls from one leg to the other, landing with all the weight on the foot that has just moved, while flexing the knee. [< F: fallen, ptp. of *tomber* to fall]

Tom•big•bee (tom big′bē), *n.* a river flowing S through NE Mississippi and SW Alabama to the Mobile River. 525 mi. (845 km) long.

Tomb′ of the Unknowns′. See under **Unknown Soldier.**

tom•bo•la (tom′bə lə), *n. Brit.* house (def. 19). [1875–80; < It, deriv. of *tombolare* to tumble, itself deriv. of *tombare* to fall]

tom•bo•lo (tom′bə lō′), *n., pl.* **-los.** a sand bar connecting an island to the mainland or to another island. [1899; < It < L *tumulus* mound. See TUMULUS]

Tom•bouc•tou (tôN bōōk tōō′), *n.* Timbuktu.

tom•boy (tom′boi′), *n.* an energetic, sometimes boisterous girl whose behavior and pursuits, esp. in games and sports, are considered more typical of boys than of girls. [1545–55; TOM + BOY] —**tom′boy′ish,** *adj.* —**tom′boy′ish•ly,** *adv.* —**tom′boy′ish•ness,** *n.*

tomb•stone (tōōm′stōn′), *n.* a stone marker, usually inscribed, on a tomb or grave. [1555–65; TOMB + STONE]

tomb′stone ad′, a boxed advertisement without artwork or illustrations, esp. one announcing an issue of a stock or bond.

tom•cat (tom′kat′), *n., v.,* **-cat•ted, -cat•ting.** —*n.* **1.** a male cat. **2.** *Slang.* a woman-chaser. —*v.i.* **3.** *Slang.* (of a man) to pursue women in order to make sexual conquests (often fol. by *around*): *He tomcatted around before settling down.* [1750–60; TOM + CAT[1]]

tom•cod (tom′kod′), *n., pl.* *(esp. collectively)* **-cod,** *(esp. referring to two or more kinds or species)* **-cods. 1.** either of two small cods, *Microgadus tomcod,* of the Atlantic Ocean, or *M. proximus,* of the Pacific Ocean. **2.** any of various similar fishes. Also called **tommycod.** [1715–25; TOM (THUMB) + COD[1]]

Tom′ Col′lins, a tall drink containing gin, lemon or lime juice, and carbonated water, sweetened and served with ice. [said to have been named after its inventor]

Tom′, Dick′, and Har′ry, the ordinary person; people generally; everyone: *They invited every Tom, Dick, and Harry to the party.* [1805–15]

tome (tōm), *n.* **1.** a book, esp. a very heavy, large, or learned book. **2.** a volume forming a part of a larger work. [1510–20; < F < L *tomus* < Gk *tómos* slice, piece, roll of paper, book, akin to *témnein* to cut]

-tome, a combining form with the meanings "cutting instrument" (*microtome; osteotome*), "segment, somite" (*sclerotome*), used in the formation of compound words. Cf. **tomo-, -tomous, -tomy.** [comb. form repr. Gk *tomē* a cutting; *tómos* a cut, slice; *-tomon* (neut.), *-tomos* (masc.) -cutting (adj.)]

to•men•tose (tə men′tōs, tō′mən tōs′), *adj. Bot., Entomol.* closely covered with down or matted hair. [1690–1700; < NL *tōmentōsus.* See TOMENTUM, -OSE[1]]

to•men•tum (tə men′təm), *n., pl.* **-ta** (-tə). *Bot., Entomol.* pubescence consisting of longish, soft, entangled hairs pressed close to the surface. [1690–1700; < NL *tōmentum,* L: stuffing (of wool, hair, etc.) for cushions]

tom•fool (tom′fōōl′), *n.* **1.** a grossly foolish or stupid person; a silly fool. —*adj.* **2.** being or characteristic of a tomfool. [1325–75; ME *Thome fole* Tom the fool] —**tom′fool′ish,** *adj.* —**tom′fool′ish•ness,** *n.*

tom•fool•er•y (tom′fōō′lə rē), *n., pl.* **-er•ies. 1.** foolish or silly behavior; tomfoolishness. **2.** a silly act, matter, or thing. [1805–15; TOMFOOL + -ERY] —**Syn. 1.** foolishness, silliness, horseplay, monkeyshines.

Tom•ism (tom′iz əm), *n.* See **Uncle Tomism.**

to•mi•um (tō′mē əm), *n., pl.* **-mi•a** (-mē ə). the cutting edge of a bird's bill. [1825–35; < NL, equiv. to Gk *tóm(os)* a cutting (see TOME) + NL *-ium* -IUM] —**to′mi•al,** *adj.*

Tom′ Jones′, a novel (1749) by Henry Fielding.

Tom•lin•son (tom′lin sən), *n.* **Henry Major,** 1873–1958, English journalist and novelist.

Tom•ma•si•ni (tom′ə sē′nē; *It.* tôm′mä zē′nē), *n.* **Vi•cen•zo** (vē chen′dzô), 1880–1950, Italian composer.

tom•my (tom′ē), *n., pl.* **-mies.** *Brit.* **1.** *(sometimes cap.)* See **Tommy Atkins. 2.** *Slang.* bread, esp. brown bread, or rations, as formerly distributed to troops and workers. [1775–85; by shortening]

Tom•my (tom′ē), *n.* **1.** a male given name, form of **Thomas. 2.** Also, **Tom′mie, Tom′mye.** a female given name, form of **Thomasina.**

Tom′my At′kins, *pl.* **Tommy Atkins.** *Brit.* **1.** any private of the British army. **2.** one of the rank and file of any organization or group.

tom•my•axe (tom′e aks′), *Australia and New Zealand.* a tomahawk. [1895–1900; prob. by false analysis as *tommy-hawk*]

tom•my•cod (tom′ē kod′), *n.* tomcod. [1875–80; TOMMY (see TOMCOD) + COD[1]]

Tom′my gun′, 1. See **Thompson submachine gun. 2.** any submachine gun. [1920–25; by shortening]

tom•my•rot (tom′ē rot′), *n.* nonsense; utter foolishness. [1880–85; *tommy* simpleton (see TOMFOOL) + ROT] —**Syn.** bosh, rot, rubbish, balderdash.

tom•my•to (tom′ē tō′), *n. Chiefly Tennessee and Georgia.* a cherry tomato. [appar. dial. form of TOMATO]

tomo-, a combining form meaning "a cut, section," used in the formation of compound words: *tomography.* [comb. form repr. Gk *tómos* a cut, section; cf. -TOME]

Tom o'Bed•lam (tom′ ə bed′ləm), *pl.* **-lams.** a roving beggar afflicted with or feigning madness. [1595–1605]

to•mo•gram (tō′mə gram′), *n. Med.* the visual record produced by tomography. [1935–40; TOMO- + -GRAM[1]]

to•mo•graph (tō′mə graf′, -gräf′), *n.* a machine for making an x-ray of a selected plane of the body. [TOMO- + -GRAPH] —**to•mo•graph•ic** (tō′mə graf′ik), *adj.* —**to′mo•graph′i•cal•ly,** *adv.* —**to•mog•ra•phy** (tə mog′rə fē), *n.*

To•mo•na•ga (tô′mô nä′gä), *n.* **Shin•i•chi•ro** (shē′nē-chē rô′), 1906–79, Japanese physicist: Nobel prize 1965.

to•mor•row (tə môr′ō, -mor′ō), *n.* **1.** the day following today: *Tomorrow is supposed to be sunny.* **2.** a future period or time: *the stars of tomorrow.* —*adv.* **3.** on the morrow; on the day following today: *Come tomorrow at this same time.* **4.** at some future time: *We shall rest easy tomorrow if we work for peace today.* [1225–75; ME *to mor(o)we, to morghe* (see TO, MORROW), var. of *to mor(o)wen, to morghen* (see MORN)]

-tomous, a combining form meaning "cut, divided," used in the formation of compound words: *dichotomous.* [< Gk *-tomos.* See -TOME, -OUS]

tom•pi•on (tom′pē ən), *n.* tampion.

Tomp•kins (tomp′kinz), *n.* **Daniel D.,** 1774–1825, U.S. politician and jurist: vice president of the U.S. 1817–25.

Tom′ Saw′yer, *(The Adventures of Tom Sawyer)* a novel (1876) by Mark Twain.

Tomsk (tomsk; *Russ.* tômsk), *n.* a city in the central Russian Federation in Asia, E of the Ob River. 502,000.

tom•tate (tom′tāt), *n.* a grunt, *Haemulon aurolineatum,* inhabiting waters off the West Indies and Florida. [1890–95, *Amer.*; orig. uncert.]

Tom′ Thumb′, 1. a diminutive hero of folk tales. **2.** an extremely small person; dwarf. **3. General,** nickname of Charles Sherwood Stratton.

tom•tit (tom′tit′), *n. Brit. Dial.* **1.** a titmouse. **2.** any of various other small birds, as the wren. [1700–10; TOM (THUMB) + TIT[1]]

tom-tom (tom′tom′), *n.* **1.** a drum of American Indian or Asian origin, commonly played with the hands. **2.** a dully repetitious drumbeat or similar sound. Also, **tam-tam.** [1685–95; < Hindi *ṭamṭam*]

-tomy, a combining form meaning "cutting, incision" of an organ, "excision" of an object, as specified by the initial element (*appendectomy; lithotomy*); also occurring in abstract nouns corresponding to adjectives ending in **-tomous** (*dichotomy*). Cf. **-tome, tomo-, -tomous.** [repr. Gk *-tomia;* see -TOME, -Y[3]]

ton[1] (tun), *n.* **1.** a unit of weight, equivalent to 2000 pounds (0.907 metric ton) avoirdupois **(short ton)** in the U.S. and 2240 pounds (1.016 metric tons) avoirdupois **(long ton)** in Great Britain. **2.** Also called **freight ton.** a unit of volume for freight that weighs one ton, varying with the type of freight measured, as 40 cubic feet of oak timber or 20 bushels of wheat. **3.** See **metric ton. 4.** See **displacement ton. 5.** a unit of volume used in transportation by sea, commonly equal to 40 cubic feet (1.13 cu. m) **(shipping ton** or **measurement ton). 6.** a

CONCISE PRONUNCIATION KEY: act, cāpe, dâre, pärt; set, ēqual; *if,* īce; ox, ōver, ôrder, oil, bŏŏk, bōōt, out; up, ûrge; child; sing; shoe; thin, that; zh as in *treasure.* ə = *a* as in *alone, e* as in *system, i* as in *easily, o* as in *gallop, u* as in *circus;* ə as in *fire* (fīər), *hour* (ouər). l and n can serve as syllabic consonants, as in *cradle* (krād′l), and *button* (but′n). See the full key inside the front cover.

unit of internal capacity of ships, equal to 100 cubic feet (2.83 cu. m) **(register ton). 7.** Often, **tons.** *Informal.* a great quantity; a lot: *a ton of jokes; tons of wedding presents.* **8.** *Brit. Informal.* a speed of 100 miles per hour. [1350–1400; ME; var. of TUN]

ton[2] (*Fr.* tôN), *n., pl.* **tons** (*Fr.* tôN). **1.** high fashion; stylishness. **2.** the current fashion, style, or vogue. [1755–65; < F < L *tonus* TONE] **—ton·ish, ton·nish** (ton′ish), *adj.* **—ton′ish·ly, ton′nish·ly,** *adv.* **—ton′·ish·ness, ton′nish·ness,** *n.*

-ton, a suffix formerly used to form nouns from adjectives: *simpleton; singleton.* [var. of dial. *tone* ONE (see TOTHER)]

ton·al (tōn′l), *adj. Music.* pertaining to or having tonality. [1770–80; < ML *tonālis.* See TONE, -AL[1]] **—ton′·al·ly,** *adv.*

ton·al·ist (tōn′l ist), *n.* a person who works with or uses tonality, esp. one who uses traditional tonality rather than atonality in composing music. [1900–05; TONAL + -IST]

to·nal·i·ty (tō nal′i tē), *n., pl.* **-ties. 1.** *Music.* **a.** the sum of relations, melodic and harmonic, existing between the tones of a scale or musical system. **b.** a particular scale or system of tones; a key. **2.** (in painting, graphics, etc.) the system of tones or tints, or the color scheme, of a picture. **3.** the quality of tones. [1830–40; TONAL + -ITY] **—to·nal′i·tive,** *adj.*

to-name (to͞o′nām′), *n. Chiefly Scot.* **1.** a nickname, esp. one to distinguish a person from others of the same name. **2.** a surname. [bef. 950; ME; OE *tōnama.* See TO, NAME]

Ton·a·wan·da (ton′ə won′də), *n.* a city in NW New York, near Buffalo. 18,693.

ton·do (ton′dō; *It.* tôn′dô), *n., pl.* **-di** (-dē). a round painting or relief. [1885–90; < It: plate, circle, round painting, deriv. of the adj.: round, by aphesis for *rotondo,* < L *rotundus;* see ROTUND]

tone (tōn), *n., v.,* **toned, ton·ing.** **—*n.* 1.** any sound considered with reference to its quality, pitch, strength, source, etc.: *shrill tones.* **2.** quality or character of sound. **3.** vocal sound; the sound made by vibrating muscular bands in the larynx. **4.** a particular quality, way of sounding, modulation, or intonation of the voice as expressive of some meaning, feeling, spirit, etc.: *a tone of command.* **5.** an accent peculiar to a person, people, locality, etc., or a characteristic mode of sounding words in speech. **6.** stress of voice on a syllable of a word. **7.** *Ling.* a musical pitch or movement in pitch serving to distinguish two words otherwise composed of the same sounds, as in Chinese. **8.** *Music.* **a.** a musical sound of definite pitch, consisting of several relatively simple constituents called partial tones, the lowest of which is called the fundamental tone and the others harmonics or overtones. **b.** an interval equivalent to two semitones; a whole tone; a whole step. **c.** any of the nine melodies or tunes to which Gregorian plainsong psalms are sung. **9.** a quality of color with reference to the degree of absorption or reflection of light; a tint or shade; value. **10.** that distinctive quality by which colors differ from one another in addition to their differences indicated by chroma, tint, shade; a slight modification of a given color; hue: *green with a yellowish tone.* **11.** *Art.* the prevailing effect of harmony of color and values. **12.** *Physiol.* **a.** the normal state of tension or responsiveness of the organs or tissues of the body. **b.** that state of the body or of an organ in which all its functions are performed with healthy vigor. **c.** normal sensitivity to stimulation. **13.** a normal healthy mental condition. **14.** a particular mental state or disposition; spirit, character, or tenor. **15.** a particular style or manner, as of writing or speech; mood: *the macabre tone of Poe's stories.* **16.** prevailing character or style, as of manners, morals, or philosophical outlook: *the liberal tone of the 1960's.* **17.** style, distinction, or elegance. **—*v.t.* 18.** to sound with a particular tone. **19.** to give the proper tone to (a musical instrument). **20.** to modify the tone or general coloring of. **21.** to give the desired tone to (a painting, drawing, etc.). **22.** *Photog.* to change the color of (a print), esp. by chemical means. **23.** to render as specified in tone or coloring. **24.** to modify the tone or character of. **25.** to give or restore physical or mental tone to. **—*v.i.* 26.** to take on a particular tone; assume color or tint. **27. tone down, a.** to become or cause to become softened or moderated: *The newspaper toned down its attack.* **b.** *Painting.* to make (a color) less intense in hue; subdue. **28. tone up, a.** to give a higher or stronger tone to. **b.** to gain or cause to gain in tone or strength: *toning up little-used muscles.* **29. tone with** or **in with,** to harmonize in tone or coloring; blend: *The painting tones with the room.* [1275–1325; ME (n.) < L *tonus* < Gk *tónos* strain, tone, mode, lit., a stretching, akin to *teínein* to stretch] **—tone′less,** *adj.* **—tone′·less·ly,** *adv.* **—tone′less·ness,** *n.*
—Syn. 1. See **sound**[1]. **15.** spirit, quality, temper.

tone′ arm′, the free-swinging bracket of a phonograph containing the pickup. Also, **tone′arm′.** Also called **pickup arm.** [1910–15]

tone′ clus′ter, *Music.* a group of adjacent notes played on a keyboard instrument typically with the fist, forearm, or elbow, similar groupings also occurring in orchestral music.

tone′ col′or, *Music.* tone quality; timbre. [1880–85]

tone′ control′, a manual control used to adjust the relative responses of an amplifier to high, low, and intermediate audio frequencies.

tone-deaf (tōn′def′), *adj.* unable to distinguish differences in pitch in musical sounds when producing or hearing them. [1890–95] **—tone′ deaf′ness.**

CONCISE ETYMOLOGY KEY: <, descended or borrowed from; >, whence; b., blend of, blended; c., cognate with; cf., compare; deriv., derivative; equiv., equivalent; imit., imitative; obl., oblique; r., replacing; s., stem; sp., spelling, spelled; resp., respelling, respelled; trans., translation; ?, origin unknown; *, unattested; ‡, probably earlier than. See the full key inside the front cover.

tone′ di′aling, a system of calling telephone numbers wherein tones of differing pitch corresponding to the digits in the number called are electronically generated by manipulating pushbuttons (contrasted with *pulse dialing*). **—tone′-di′al·ing,** *adj.*

tone′ lan′guage, a language, as Swedish, Chinese, Yoruba, or Serbo-Croatian, in which words that are otherwise phonologically identical are distinguished by having different pitches or pitch contour. [1905–10]

ton·eme (tō′nēm), *n.* a phoneme consisting of a contrastive feature of tone in a tone language: *Swedish has two tonemes.* [1920–25; TONE + -EME]

tone′ paint′ing, musical description, by harmonic, melodic, or rhythmic means, of the words of a text or the story elements in program music. [1900–05]

tone′ po′em, *Music.* an instrumental composition intended to portray a particular story, scene, mood, etc. Cf. **program music, symphonic poem.** [1900–05]

ton·er (tō′nər), *n.* **1.** a person or thing that tones. **2.** a highly concentrated organic pigment containing little or no inert matter. **3.** a powder, either dry or dispersed in an organic liquid, used in xerography to produce the final image. **4.** Also called **chemical toner.** *Photog., Motion Pictures.* a chemical solution used to change the color of and, in some cases, help preserve black-and-white prints and motion-picture film by altering or replacing the silver image. **5.** a worker for a paint manufacturer who tests the color and quality of paint. **6.** a cosmetic preparation, usually a liquid, used to restore firmness to the skin. [1885–90; TONE + -ER[1]]

tone′ row′, *Music.* a series of tones in which no tone is duplicated, and in which the tones generally recur in fixed sequence, with variations in rhythm and pitch, throughout a composition. Also called **note row, twelve-tone row.** [1940–45]

to·net·ics (tō net′iks), *n.* (*used with a singular v.*) the phonetic study of tone in language. [1920–25; TONE + (PHON)ETICS] **—to·net′ic,** *adj.* **—to·net′i·cal·ly,** *adv.* **—to·ne·ti·cian** (tō′ni tish′ən), *n.*

to·nette (tō net′), *n.* a small end-blown flute of simple construction and narrow range. [1935–40; TONE + -ETTE]

tone-up (tōn′up′), *n.* an exercise for toning up one's body. [n. use of the v. phrase *tone up*]

ton-force (tun′fôrs′, -fōrs′), *n.* two thousand pound-force. *Abbr.:* tonf

tong[1] (tông, tong), *n.* **1.** tongs. **—*v.t.* 2.** to lift, seize, gather, hold, or handle with tongs, as logs or oysters. **—*v.i.* 3.** to use, or work with, tongs. [bef. 900; 1865–70, for def. 2; ME *tong(e)* (sing.), *tongen, tonges* (pl.), OE; c. D *tang,* G *Zange* pair of tongs or pincers; akin to Gk *dáknein* to bite] **—tong′er,** *n.*

tong[2] (tông, tong), *n.* **1.** (in China) an association, society, or political party. **2.** (among Chinese living in the U.S.) a fraternal or secret society, often associated with criminal activities. [1880–85, *Amer.;* < dial. Chin (Guangdong) *tòhng,* akin to Chin *táng* meeting hall]

ton·ga (tong′gə), *n.* a light, two-wheeled, horse-drawn vehicle used in India. [1870–75; < Hindi *tāṅgā*]

Ton·ga (tong′gə), *n.* a Polynesian kingdom consisting of three groups of islands in the S Pacific, NE of New Zealand: a former British protectorate. 100,105; ab. 270 sq. mi. (700 sq. km). *Cap.:* Nukualofa. Also called **Ton′ga Is′lands, Friendly Islands.**

Ton·ga (tong′gə), *n.* Tsonga.

Ton·gan (tong′gən), *n.* **1.** a native or inhabitant of Tonga. **2.** a Polynesian language, the language of the Tongans. **—*adj.* 3.** of or pertaining to Tonga, its people, or their language. [1890–95; TONG(A) + -AN]

Tong·hua (tông′hwä′), *n. Pinyin.* a city in SE Jilin province, in NE China. 275,000. Also, **T'unghua, Tunghwa.**

Tong·king (tong′king′), *n.* Tonkin.

tong·man (tông′mən, tong′-), *n., pl.* **-men.** a member of a Chinese tong. [1880–85, *Amer.;* TONG[2] + MAN[1]]

tongs (tôngz, tongz), *n.* (*usually used with a plural v.*) any of various implements consisting of two arms hinged, pivoted, or otherwise fastened together, for seizing, holding, or lifting something (usually used with *pair of*). [see TONG[1]]

Tong·shan (*Chin.* tông′shän′), *n. Pinyin.* former name of **Xuzhou.** Also, **Tungshan.**

tongue (tung), *n., v.* **tongued, tongu·ing.** **—*n.* 1.** *Anat.* the usually movable organ in the floor of the mouth in humans and most vertebrates, functioning in eating, in tasting, and, in humans, in speaking. See diag. under **mouth. 2.** *Zool.* an analogous organ in invertebrate animals. **3.** the tongue of an animal, as an ox, beef, or sheep, used for food, often prepared by smoking or pickling. **4.** the human tongue as the organ of speech: *No tongue must ever tell the secret.* **5.** the faculty or power of speech: *a sight no tongue can describe.* **6.** speech or talk, esp. mere glib or empty talk. **7.** manner or character of speech: *a flattering tongue.* **8.** the language of a particular people, region, or nation: *the Hebrew tongue.* **9.** a dialect. **10.** (in the Bible) a people or nation distinguished by its language. **11. tongues,** speech, often incomprehensible, typically uttered during moments of religious ecstasy. Cf. **speaking in tongues, glossolalia. 12.** an object that resembles an animal's tongue in shape, position, or function. **13.** a strip of leather or other material under the lacing or fastening of a shoe. **14.** a piece of metal suspended inside a bell that strikes against the side producing a sound; clapper. **15.** a vibrating reed or similar structure in a musical instrument, as in a clarinet, or in part of a musical instrument, as in an organ reed pipe. **16.** the pole extending from a carriage or other vehicle between the animals drawing it. **17.** a projecting strip along the center of the edge or end of a board, for fitting into a groove in another board. **18.** a narrow strip of land extending into a body of water; cape. **19.** a section of ice projecting outward from the submerged part of an iceberg. **20.** *Mach.* a long, narrow projection on a machine. **21.** that part of a railroad switch that is shifted to direct the wheels of a locomotive or car to one or the other track of a railroad. **22.** the pin of a buckle, brooch, etc. **23. find one's tongue,** to regain one's powers of speech; recover one's poise: *She wanted to say something, but couldn't find her tongue.* **24. give tongue, a.** *Fox Hunting.* (of a hound) to bay while following a scent. **b.** to utter one's thoughts; speak: *He wouldn't give tongue to his suspicions.* **25. hold one's tongue,** to refrain from or cease speaking; keep silent. **26. lose one's tongue,** to lose the power of speech, esp. temporarily. **27. on the tip of one's** (or **the**) **tongue, a.** on the verge of being uttered. **b.** unable to be recalled; barely escaping one's memory: *The answer was on the tip of my tongue, but I couldn't think of it.* **28. slip of the tongue,** a mistake in speaking, as an inadvertent remark. **29. (with) tongue in cheek,** ironically or mockingly; insincerely. **—*v.t.* 30.** to articulate (tones played on a clarinet, trumpet, etc.) by strokes of the tongue. **31.** *Carpentry.* **a.** to cut a tongue on (a board). **b.** to join or fit together by a tongue-and-groove joint. **32.** to touch with the tongue. **33.** to articulate or pronounce. **34.** *Archaic.* **a.** to reproach or scold. **b.** to speak or utter. **—*v.i.* 35.** to tongue tones played on a clarinet, trumpet, etc. **36.** to talk, esp. idly or foolishly; chatter; prate. **37.** to project like a tongue. [bef. 900; (n.) ME *tunge,* OE; c. D *tong,* G *Zunge,* ON *tunga,* Goth *tuggo;* akin to L *lingua* (OL *dingua*); (v.) ME *tungen* to scold, deriv. of the n.] **—tongue′less,** *adj.* **—tongue′·like′,** *adj.*

tongue′-and-groove′ joint′ (tung′ən gro͞ov′), *Carpentry.* a joint between two boards in which a raised area on the edge of one board fits into a corresponding groove in the edge of the other to produce a flush surface. [1875–80]

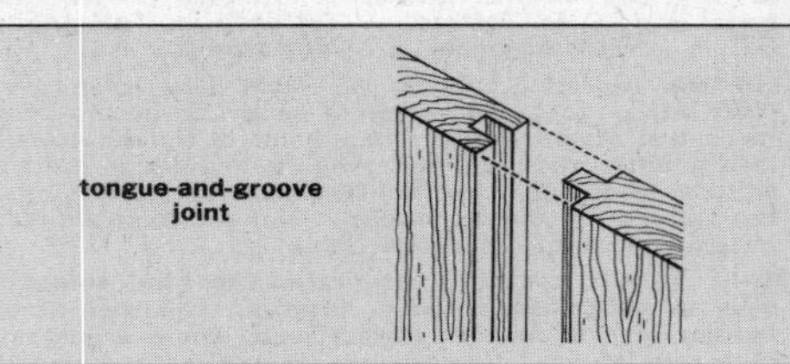

tongue′ cov′er, a loose-leaf binding having a flap of the cover concealing the binding posts.

tongue′ depres′sor, a broad, thin piece of wood used by doctors to hold down the patient's tongue during an examination of the mouth and throat. Also called **tongue′ blade′.** [1870–75]

tongue·fish (tung′fish′), *n., pl.* (*esp. collectively*) **-fish,** (*esp. referring to two or more kinds or species*) **-fish·es.** any of several flatfishes of the family Cynoglossidae, having the tail tapered to a point. [1645–55; TONGUE + FISH]

tongue′ graft′. See **whip graft.** [1700–10]

tongue-lash (tung′lash′), *v.t., v.i.* to scold severely. [1880–85] **—tongue′-lash′ing,** *n.*

tongue′ sole′, tonguefish.

tongue-tie (tung′tī′), *n., v.,* **-tied, -ty·ing.** **—*n.* 1.** impeded motion of the tongue caused esp. by shortness of the frenum, which binds it to the floor of the mouth. **—*v.t.* 2.** to make tongue-tied. [1545–55; back formation from TONGUE-TIED]

tongue-tied (tung′tīd′), *adj.* **1.** unable to speak, as from shyness, embarrassment, or surprise. **2.** affected with tongue-tie. [1520–30; TONGUE + TIED]

tongue′ twist′er, a word or sequence of words difficult to pronounce, esp. rapidly, because of alliteration or a slight variation of consonant sounds, as "She sells seashells by the seashore." [1895–1900]

tongue′ worm′. Also called **pentastomid.** any wormlike invertebrate of the phylum Pentastomida (or subphylum of Arthropoda), having two pairs of hooks at the sides of the mouth: all are parasitic, some in the respiratory tracts of mammals. [1635–45]

tongu·ing (tung′ing), *n. Music.* the manipulation of the tongue in playing a wind instrument to interrupt the tone and produce a staccato effect. [1805–15; TONGUE + -ING[1]]

tongu′ing-and-groov′ing plane′ (tung′ing ən gro͞o′ving), *Carpentry.* a plane for cutting the edges of boards into tongues and grooves. [1890–95]

Tong·zhou (*Chin.* tông′jō′), *n. Pinyin.* former name of **Nantong.** Also, **Tungchow.**

To·ni (tō′nē), *n.* a female given name, form of **Antoinette** or **Antonia.**

-tonia, a combining form with the meaning "muscle tension, nerve tension," as specified by the initial element (*hypertonia*); used also in the formation of words that denote more generally a personality type or personality disorder (*catatonia; somatotonia*). [see TONE, -IA]

ton·ic (ton′ik), *n.* **1.** a medicine that invigorates or strengthens: *a tonic of sulphur and molasses.* **2.** anything invigorating physically, mentally, or morally: *His cheerful greeting was a real tonic.* **3.** See **quinine water. 4.** *Music.* the first degree of the scale; the keynote. **5.** *Chiefly Eastern New Eng.* soda pop. **6.** *Phonet.* a tonic syllable or accent. **—*adj.* 7.** pertaining to, maintaining, increasing, or restoring the tone or health of the body or an organ, as a medicine. **8.** invigorating physically, mentally, or morally. **9.** *Physiol., Pathol.* **a.** pertaining to tension, as of the muscles. **b.** marked by continued muscular tension: *a tonic spasm.* **10.** using differences in tone or pitch to distinguish between words that are otherwise phonemically identical: *a tonic language.* **11.** pertaining to tone or accent in speech. **12.** *Phonet.* (of a syllable) bearing the principal stress or accent, usually accompanied by a change in pitch. **13.** *Music.* **a.** of or pertaining to a tone or tones. **b.** pertaining to or founded on the keynote, or first tone, of a musi-

cal scale: *a tonic chord.* [1640–50; < Gk *tonikós* pertaining to stretching or tones. See TONE, -IC] **—ton′i·cal·ly,** *adv.*
—Syn. 2. stimulant, restorative, bracer, pickup.
—Regional Variation. 5. See **soda pop.**

-tonic, a combining form occurring in adjectives that correspond to nouns ending in **-tonia:** *catatonic.* [see TONIC]

ton′ic ac′cent, prominence given to a syllable in speaking, usually due to a change, esp. a rise, in pitch. [1865–70]

to·nic·i·ty (tō nis′i tē), *n.* **1.** tonic quality or condition. **2.** the state of bodily tone. **3.** *Physiol.* the normal elastic tension of living muscles, arteries, etc., by which the tone of the system is maintained. [1815–25; TONIC + -ITY]

ton′ic sol-fa′, a system of singing characterized by emphasis upon tonality or key relationship, in which tones are indicated by the initial letters of the syllables of the *sol-fa* system rather than by conventional staff notation. [1850–55]

ton′ic spasm′, *Med.* See under **spasm** (def. 1). [1825–35]

ton′ic wa′ter. See **quinine water.**

to·night (tə nīt′), *n.* **1.** this present or coming night; the night of this present day. *—adv.* **2.** on this present night; on the night of this present day. **3.** *Obs.* during last night. [bef. 1000; ME *to night,* OE *tō niht.* See TO, NIGHT]

tonk (tongk), *n.* a form of rummy for two or more players with deuces wild. [1920–25; cf. Brit., Australian *tonk* (informal) to strike, beat, defeat]

ton′ka bean′ (tong′kə), **1.** the fragrant, black almond-shaped seed of a tall tree belonging to the genus *Dipteryx* (or *Coumarouna*), of the legume family, esp. *D. odorata,* of tropical South America, used in perfumes, as a source of coumarin, and as a substitute for vanilla. **2.** the tree itself. [1790–1800; *tonka* prob. < Tupi *tõka*]

Ton·kin (ton′kin′, tong′-), *n.* **1.** a former state in N French Indochina, now part of Vietnam. **2. Gulf of,** an arm of the South China Sea, W of Hainan. 300 mi. (485 km) long. Also, **Tongking, Ton·king** (ton′king′, tong′-).

Ton·le Sap (ton′lā säp′), a lake in W Cambodia, draining into the Mekong River.

ton·let (tun′lit), *n. Armor.* a skirt of plates. Also called **lamboy.** [< F *tonnelet* keg, MF, prob. dim. of *tonel* cask (see TUNNEL) from its resemblance to staves]

ton-mile (tun′mīl′), *n.* a unit of freight transportation measurement equivalent to a ton of freight transported one mile. [1900–05] **—ton′-mile′age,** *n.*

tonn., tonnage.

ton·nage (tun′ij), *n.* **1.** the capacity of a merchant vessel, expressed either in units of weight, as deadweight tons, or of volume, as gross tons. **2.** ships collectively considered with reference to their carrying capacity or together with their cargoes. **3.** a duty on ships or boats at so much per ton of cargo or freight, or according to the capacity in tons. Also, **tunnage.** [1375–1425; late ME: duty < OF. See TON[1], -AGE]

ton′nage deck′, *Naut.* **1.** the upper deck in a vessel with only two decks. **2.** the second deck above the inner bottom in a vessel with more than two decks. [1885–90]

tonne (tun), *n.* See **metric ton.** [1900–05; < F; see TON[1]]

ton·neau (tu nō′), *n., pl.* **-neaus, -neaux** (-nōz′). **1.** a rear part or compartment of an automobile body, containing seats for passengers. **2.** a complete automobile body having such a rear part. **3.** a waterproof cover, generally of canvas or vinyl, that can be fastened over the cockpit of a roadster or convertible to protect the interior. [1900–05; < F: lit., cask; OF *tonel.* See TUNNEL]

ton·ner (tun′ər), *n.* something having a specified weight in tons (used in combination): *The sailboat was a twelve-tonner.* [1850–55; in parasynthetic compounds formed from TON[1] and a quantifier; see -ER[1]]

Tön·nies (tœ′nēs), *n.* **Fer·di·nand** (fer′dē nänt′), 1855–1936, German sociologist.

tono-, a combining form with the meanings "stretching," "tension," "tone," used in the formation of compound words: *tonometer.* [< Gk *tón(os)* (see TONE) + -o-]

to·nom·e·ter (tō nom′i tər), *n.* **1.** an instrument for measuring the frequencies of tones, as a tuning fork or a graduated set of tuning forks. **2.** any of various physiological instruments for measuring intraocular pressure or blood pressure. **3.** *Physical Chem.* an instrument for measuring vapor pressure. [1715–25; TONO- + -METER] **—ton·o·met·ric** (ton′ə me′trik, tō′nə-), *adj.* **—to·nom′e·try,** *n.*

ton·o·plast (ton′ə plast′, tō′nə-), *n. Bot.* a membrane separating a vacuole from the surrounding cytoplasm in a plant cell. [1885–90; TONO- + -PLAST]

ton·sil (ton′səl), *n. Anat.* a prominent oval mass of lymphoid tissue on each side of the throat. [1595–1605; < L *tōnsillae* (pl.) the tonsils] **—ton′sil·lar, ton′sil·ar, ton·sil·lar·y** (ton′sə ler′ē), *adj.*

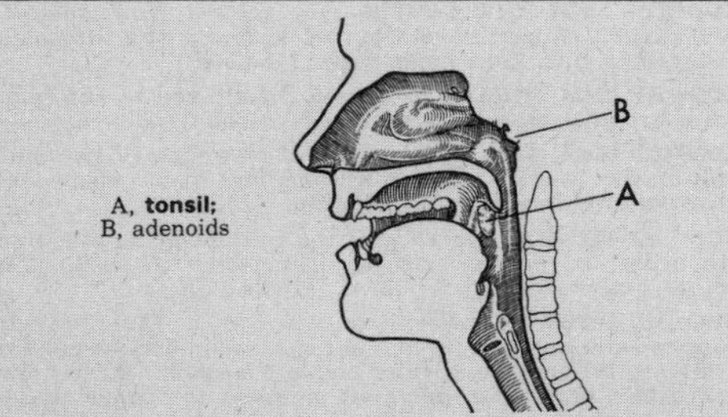

A, **tonsil;**
B, adenoids

ton·sil·lec·to·my (ton′sə lek′tə mē), *n., pl.* **-mies.** *Surg.* the operation of excising or removing one or both tonsils. [1900–05; < L *tōnsill(ae)* tonsils + -ECTOMY]

ton·sil·li·tis (ton′sə lī′tis), *n. Pathol.* inflammation of a tonsil or the tonsils. [1795–1805; < L *tōnsill(ae)* tonsils + -ITIS] **—ton·sil·lit·ic** (ton′sə lit′ik), *adj.*

ton·sil·lot·o·my (ton′sə lot′ə mē), *n., pl.* **-mies.** *Surg.* incision or excision of a portion of a tonsil. [1895–1900; < L *tōnsill(ae)* tonsils + -O- + -TOMY]

ton·so·ri·al (ton sôr′ē əl, -sōr′-), *adj.* of or pertaining to a barber or barbering: *the tonsorial shop.* [1805–15; < L *tōnsōri(us)* of shaving (*tond(ēre)* to shave + *-tōrius* -TORY[1], with *dt* > *s*) + -AL[1]]

ton·sure (ton′shər), *n., v.,* **-sured, -sur·ing.** *—n.* **1.** the act of cutting the hair or shaving the head. **2.** the shaving of the head or of some part of it as a religious practice or rite, esp. in preparation for entering the priesthood or a monastic order. **3.** the part of a cleric's head, usually the crown, left bare by shaving the hair. **4.** the state of being shorn. *—v.t.* **5.** to confer the ecclesiastical tonsure upon. **6.** to subject to tonsure. [1350–1400; ME < L *tōnsūra* a shearing, equiv. to *tōns(us)* (ptp. of *tondēre* to shear, clip, shave) + *-ūra* -URE]

ton·tine (ton′tēn, ton tēn′), *n.* **1.** an annuity scheme in which subscribers share a common fund with the benefit of survivorship, the survivors' shares being increased as the subscribers die, until the whole goes to the last survivor. **2.** the annuity shared. **3.** the share of each subscriber. **4.** the number of subscribers. **5.** any of various forms of life insurance in which the chief beneficiaries are those whose policies are in force at the end of a specified period **(ton′tine pe′riod).** [1755–65; < F; named after Lorenzo *Tonti,* Neapolitan banker who started the scheme in France about 1653. See -INE[1]]

to·nus (tō′nəs), *n. Physiol.* a normal state of continuous slight tension in muscle tissue that facilitates its response to stimulation. [1875–80; < NL, special use of L *tonus* < Gk *tónos* TONE]

ton·y (tō′nē), *adj.,* **ton·i·er, ton·i·est.** *Informal.* high-toned; stylish: *a tony nightclub.* [1875–80, *Amer.*; TONE + -Y[1]]

To·ny (tō′nē), *n., pl.* **-nys.** one of a group of awards made annually by the American Theatre Wing, a professional school for the performing arts, for achievements in theatrical production and performance. [after the nickname of Antoinette Perry]

To·ny (tō′nē), *n.* **1.** a male given name, form of **Anthony. 2.** a female given name, form of **Antoinette** or **Antonia.**

too (to͞o), *adv.* **1.** in addition; also; furthermore; moreover: *young, clever, and rich too.* **2.** to an excessive extent or degree; beyond what is desirable, fitting, or right: *too sick to travel.* **3.** more, as specified, than should be: *too near the fire.* **4.** (used as an affirmative to contradict a negative statement): *I am too!* **5.** extremely; very: *She wasn't too pleased with his behavior.* **6. only too.** See **only** (def. 5). [bef. 900; ME *to,* OE, stressed var. of TO (adv.); sp. *too* since the 16th century]

too·dle-oo (to͞od′l o͞o′), *interj. Informal.* good-bye; so long. [1905–10; perh. *toodle* (var. of dial. *tootle* to TODDLE) + *-oo* interjection]

Too·el·e (to͞o el′ə), *n.* a town in NW Utah. 14,335.

took (to͝ok), *v.* **1.** pt. of **take. 2.** *Nonstandard.* a pp. of **take.**

Tooke (to͝ok), *n.* **(John) Horne** (hôrn), 1736–1812, English politician and philologist.

tool (to͞ol), *n.* **1.** an implement, esp. one held in the hand, as a hammer, saw, or file, for performing or facilitating mechanical operations. **2.** any instrument of manual operation. **3.** the cutting or machining part of a lathe, planer, drill, or similar machine. **4.** the machine itself; a machine tool. **5.** anything used as a means of accomplishing a task or purpose: *Education is a tool for success.* **6.** a person manipulated by another for the latter's own ends; cat's-paw. **7.** the design or ornament impressed upon the cover of a book. **8.** *Underworld Slang.* **a.** a pistol or gun. **b.** a pickpocket. **9.** *Slang (vulgar).* penis. *—v.t.* **10.** to work or shape with a tool. **11.** to work decoratively with a hand tool. **12.** to ornament (the cover of a book) with a bookbinder's tool. **13.** to drive (a vehicle): *He tooled the car along the treacherous path.* **14.** to equip with tools or machinery. *—v.i.* **15.** to work with a tool. **16.** to drive or ride in a vehicle: *tooling along the freeway.* **17. tool up,** to install machinery designed for performing a particular job: *manufacturers tooling up for production.* [bef. 900; ME (n.); OE *tōl;* c. ON *tōl* tools; akin to TAW[2]] **—tool′er,** *n.* **—tool′less,** *adj.*
—Syn. 1. TOOL, IMPLEMENT, INSTRUMENT, UTENSIL refer to contrivances for doing work. A TOOL is a contrivance held in and worked by the hand, for assisting the work of (especially) mechanics or laborers: *a carpenter's tools.* An IMPLEMENT is any tool or contrivance designed or used for a particular purpose: *agricultural implements.* An INSTRUMENT is anything used in doing a certain work or producing a certain result, especially such as requires delicacy, accuracy, or precision: *surgical or musical instruments.* A UTENSIL is especially an article for domestic use: *kitchen utensils.* When used figuratively of human agency, TOOL is generally used in a contemptuous sense; INSTRUMENT, in a neutral or good sense: *a tool of unscrupulous men; an instrument of Providence.*

tool·box (to͞ol′boks′), *n.* **1.** a box or case in which tools are kept. **2.** an attached mechanism, as on planing machines or lathes, that carries the cutting tools. [1835–45; TOOL + BOX[1]]

tool′ engineer′ing, the branch of engineering having to do with planning the tooling and processes required for manufacturing certain products, with the design and manufacture of the tools, dies, and jigs required, and with the control of the production processes. **—tool′ engineer′.**

tool·head (to͞ol′hed′), *n. Mach.* a toolholder that is attached to a machine tool and can be adjusted to orient the tool in various positions. [TOOL + HEAD]

tool·hold·er (to͞ol′hōl′dər), *n.* a device for holding a tool or tools. [1875–80; TOOL + HOLDER]

tool·house (to͞ol′hous′), *n., pl.* **-hous·es** (-hou′ziz). toolshed. [1810–20; TOOL + HOUSE]

tool·ing (to͞o′ling), *n.* **1.** work done with a tool or tools; tooled ornamentation, as on wood, stone, or leather. **2.** *Mach.* **a.** a number of tools, as in a particular factory. **b.** the planning and arrangement of tools for a particular manufacturing process. [1665–75; TOOL + -ING[1]]

tool·mak·er (to͞ol′mā′kər), *n.* a machinist skilled in the building and reconditioning of tools, jigs, and related devices used in a machine shop. [1835–45; TOOL + MAKER] **—tool′mak′ing,** *n.*

tool′ post′, an upright for holding a lathe tool.

tool·room (to͞ol′ro͞om′, -ro͝om′), *n.* a room, as in a machine shop, in which tools are stored, repaired, produced, etc. [1875–80; TOOL + ROOM]

tool·shed (to͞ol′shed′), *n.* a small building where tools are stored, often in the backyard of a house. Also called **toolhouse.** [1830–40; TOOL + SHED[1]]

tool′ steel′, any of various high-carbon steels capable of being hardened and tempered to meet special requirements for machining, etc.

tool′ sub′ject, *Educ.* a subject that, when mastered, equips students with a skill useful in studying other subjects: *Grammar is a tool subject for English composition.*

toom (to͞om), *Scot. and North Eng.* *—adj.* **1.** empty; vacant. *—v.t.* **2.** to empty or drain (a vessel), esp. by drinking the contents. [bef. 900; ME *tome* (adj.), OE *tōm;* c. ON *tōmr*]

Toombs (to͞omz), *n.* **Robert,** 1810–85, U.S. lawyer, orator, and Confederate statesman and army officer.

Too·mer (to͞o′mər), *n.* **Jean,** 1894–1967, U.S. writer.

toon[1] (to͞on), *n.* **1.** an Asian tree, *Cedrela toona,* of the mahogany family, yielding an aromatic red wood resembling but softer than mahogany, used for furniture, carving, etc. **2.** the wood itself. [1800–10; < Hindi *tūn* < Skt *tunna*]

toon[2] (to͞on), *n.* (*sometimes cap.*) a character in an animated cartoon. [1980–85; shortening of CARTOON]

Too′ner·ville trol′ley (to͞o′nər vil′), a dilapidated, outmoded trolley line or railway. [after the train in the comic strip *Toonerville Trolley* by U.S. cartoonist Fontaine T. Fox (1884–1964)]

toot[1] (to͞ot), *v.i.* **1.** (of a horn or whistle) to give forth its characteristic sound. **2.** to make a sound resembling that of a horn, whistle, or the like. **3.** to sound or blow a horn, whistle, or wind instrument. *—v.t.* **4.** to cause (a horn, whistle, or wind instrument) to sound. **5.** to sound (notes, music, etc.) on a horn or the like. *—n.* **6.** an act or sound of tooting. **7.** *Slang.* cocaine. [1500–10; akin to LG, G *tuten,* D *toeten,* Sw *tuta* in same sense; orig. imit.] **—toot′er,** *n.*

toot[2] (to͞ot), *n. Informal.* a period or instance of drunken revelry; binge; spree. [1670–80; orig. uncert.]

toot[3] (to͝ot), *n. Australian Informal.* lavatory; toilet. [1945–50; perh. jocular alter. of TOILET]

toot[4] (to͝ot), *n. Chiefly Pennsylvania German Area.* a paper bag. [< PaG *dutt;* cf. G *Tüte* < LG *tüte* something horn-shaped, paper rolled into the shape of a horn (cf. TOOT[1])]

tooth (to͞oth), *n., pl.* **teeth,** *v.,* **toothed** (to͞otht, to͞othd), **tooth·ing** (to͞o′thing, -thing). *—n.* **1.** (in most vertebrates) one of the hard bodies or processes usually attached in a row to each jaw, serving for the prehension and mastication of food, as weapons of attack or defense, etc., and in mammals typically composed chiefly of dentin surrounding a sensitive pulp and covered on the crown with enamel. See illus. on next page. **2.** (in invertebrates) any of various similar or analogous processes occurring in the mouth or alimentary canal, or on a shell. **3.** any projection resembling or suggesting a tooth. **4.** one of the projections of a comb, rake, saw, etc. **5.** *Mach.* **a.** any of the uniform projections on a gear or rack by which it drives, or is driven by, a gear, rack, or worm. **b.** any of the uniform projections on a sprocket by which it drives or is driven by a chain. **6.** *Bot.* **a.** any small, toothlike marginal lobe. **b.** one of the toothlike divisions of the peristome of mosses. **7.** a sharp, distressing, or destructive attribute or agency. **8.** taste, relish, or liking. **9.** a surface, as on a grinding wheel or sharpening stone, slightly roughened so as to increase friction with another part. **10.** a rough surface created on a paper made for charcoal drawing, watercolor, or the like, or on canvas for oil painting. **11. by the skin of one's teeth,** barely: *He got away by the skin of his teeth.* **12. cast** or **throw in someone's teeth,** to reproach someone for (an action): *History will ever throw this blunder in his teeth.* **13. cut one's teeth on,** to do at the beginning of one's education, career, etc., or in one's youth: *The hunter boasted of having cut his teeth on tigers.* **14. in the teeth of, a.** so as to face or confront; straight into or against: *in the teeth of the wind.* **b.** in defiance of; in opposition to: *She maintained her stand in the teeth of public opinion.* **15. long in the tooth,** old; elderly. **16. put teeth in** or **into,** to establish or increase the effectiveness of: *to put teeth into the law.* **17. set one's teeth,** to become resolute; prepare for difficulty: *He set his teeth and separated the combatants.* **18. set** or **put one's teeth on edge, a.** to induce an unpleasant sensation. **b.** to repel; irritate: *The noise of the machines sets my teeth on edge.* **19. show one's teeth,** to become hostile or threatening; exhibit anger:

Usually friendly, she suddenly began to show her teeth. **20. to the teeth,** entirely; fully: *armed to the teeth; dressed to the teeth in furs.* —*v.t.* **21.** to furnish with teeth. **22.** to cut teeth upon. —*v.i.* **23.** to interlock, as cogwheels. [bef. 900; ME; OE *tōth;* c. D *tand,* G *Zahn,* ON *tǫnn;* akin to Goth *tunthus,* L *dēns,* Gk *odoús* (Ionic *odṓn*), Skt *dánta*] —**tooth′like′,** *adj.*
—**Syn. 8.** fondness, partiality, predilection.

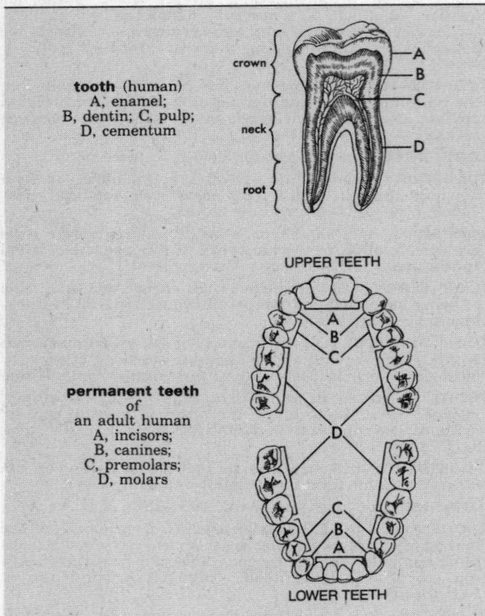

tooth (human) A, enamel; B, dentin; C, pulp; D, cementum

permanent teeth of an adult human A, incisors; B, canines; C, premolars; D, molars

tooth•ache (to͞oth′āk′), *n.* a pain in or about a tooth. [bef. 1050; ME *tothache,* OE *tōthæce, tōthece.* See TOOTH, ACHE] —**tooth′ach′y,** *adj.*

tooth′ache tree′. See **prickly ash** (def. 1). [1720–30, *Amer.*]

tooth′ and nail′, with all one's resources or energy; fiercely: *We fought tooth and nail but lost.* [1525–35]

tooth′ ax′, an ax for dressing stone, having two serrated edges.

tooth•brush (to͞oth′brush′), *n.* a small brush with a long handle, for cleaning the teeth. [1645–55; TOOTH + BRUSH[1]]

tooth•brush•ing (to͞oth′brush′ing), *n.* the act or method of cleaning the teeth with a toothbrush. [1915–20; TOOTHBRUSH + -ING[1]]

tooth′ chis′el, *Masonry.* a stonecutter's chisel having a toothed edge.

tooth′ decay′. See **dental caries.**

toothed′ whale′, any whale of the suborder Odontoceti, having conical teeth in one or both jaws and feeding on fish, squid, etc. Cf. **whalebone whale.** [1835–45]

tooth′ fair′y, a fairy credited with leaving a child money or a small gift in exchange for a baby tooth that has fallen out and been placed under the child's pillow at night.

tooth′ fun′gus, any of various mushrooms of the family Hydnaceae (and, in some classifications, allied families), having on the underside of the cap numerous conical spines rather than gills or pores.

tooth•less (to͞oth′lis), *adj.* **1.** lacking teeth. **2.** without a serrated edge, as a saw. **3.** lacking in force or sharpness; dull; ineffectual: *a toothless argument.* [1350–1400; ME; see TOOTH, -LESS] —**tooth′less•ly,** *adv.* —**tooth′less•ness,** *n.*

tooth•paste (to͞oth′pāst′), *n.* a dentifrice in the form of paste. [1825–35, *Amer.;* TOOTH + PASTE]

tooth•pick (to͞oth′pik′), *n.* a small pointed piece of wood, plastic, etc., for removing substances, esp. food particles, from between the teeth. [1480–90; TOOTH + PICK[2]]

tooth′ pow′der, a dentifrice in the form of a powder. [1535–45]

tooth′ rash′, *Pathol.* strophulus.

tooth′ shell′, **1.** any marine mollusk of the class Scaphopoda, having a curved, tapering shell that is open at both ends. **2.** the shell itself. Also called **tusk shell.** [1705–15]

tooth•some (to͞oth′səm), *adj.* **1.** pleasing to the taste; palatable: *a toothsome dish.* **2.** pleasing or desirable, as fame or power. **3.** voluptuous; sexually alluring: *a toothsome blonde.* [1545–55; TOOTH + -SOME[1]] —**tooth′some•ly,** *adv.* —**tooth′some•ness,** *n.*

tooth•wort (to͞oth′wûrt′, -wôrt′), *n.* **1.** a European plant, *Lathraea squamaria,* of the broomrape family, having a rootstock covered with toothlike scales. **2.** Also called **pepperroot.** any of several plants belonging to the genus *Dentaria,* of the mustard family, having toothlike projections upon the creeping rootstock. [1590–1600; TOOTH + WORT[2]]

CONCISE ETYMOLOGY KEY: <, descended or borrowed from; >, whence; b., blend of, blended; c., cognate with; cf., compare; deriv., derivative; equiv., equivalent; imit., imitative; obl., oblique; r., replacing; s., stem; sp., spelling, spelled; resp., respelling, respelled; trans., translation; ?, origin unknown; *, unattested; ‡, probably earlier than. See the full key inside the front cover.

tooth•y (to͞o′thē, -thē), *adj.,* **tooth•i•er, tooth•i•est. 1.** having or displaying conspicuous teeth: *a toothy smile.* **2.** savory; appetizing; toothsome. **3.** possessing a rough surface: *toothy paper.* **4.** *Archaic.* sharp or caustic: *toothy commentary.* [1520–30; TOOTH + -Y[1]] —**tooth′i•ly,** *adv.* —**tooth′i•ness,** *n.*

too•tle (to͞ot′l), *v.,* **-tled, -tling,** *n.* —*v.i.* **1.** to toot gently or repeatedly on a flute or the like. **2.** to move or proceed in a leisurely way. —*n.* **3.** the sound made by tooting on a flute or the like. [1810–20; TOOT[1] + -LE] —**too′tler,** *n.*

too-too (to͞o′to͞o′), *Informal.* —*adj.* **1.** excessively and tastelessly affected: *The movie was simply too-too.* —*adv.* **2.** in an excessively and tastelessly affected manner. [1890–95; orig. adj. use of adv. phrase *too too*]

toots (to͝ots), *n. Slang.* an affectionate or familiar term of address; honey; baby (sometimes offensive when used to strangers, casual acquaintances, subordinates, etc., esp. by a male to a female). [1940–45; TOOT(SIE) + -S[4]]

toot•sie[1] (to͝ot′sē), *n. Slang.* **1.** a sweetheart; darling. **2.** a prostitute. [1900–05; of uncert. orig.]

toot•sie[2] (to͝ot′sē), *n. Slang.* tootsy.

toot•sy (to͝ot′sē), *n., pl.* **-sies.** *Slang.* a foot. [1850–55; appar. expressive var. of FOOTSY]

toot•sy-woot•sy (to͝ot′sē wo͝ot′sē), *n., pl.* **toot•sy-woot•sies.** *Slang.* tootsie[1]. [1895–1900; redupl. of TOOTSY]

Too•woom•ba (tə wo͝om′bə), *n.* a city in SE Queensland, in E Australia. 63,401.

top[1] (top), *n., adj., v.,* **topped, top•ping.** —*n.* **1.** the highest or loftiest point or part of anything; apex; summit. **2.** the uppermost or upper part, surface, etc., of anything. **3.** the higher end of anything on a slope. **4.** *Brit.* **a.** a part considered as higher: *the top of the street.* **b.** high gear of an automobile. **5. tops, a.** the part of a plant that grows above ground, esp. of an edible root. **b.** one of the tender tips of the branches or shoots of plants. **6.** the part of anything that is first or foremost; beginning: *Let's go over it from the top again.* **7.** the highest or leading place, position, rank, etc.: *at the top of the class.* **8.** the highest point, pitch, or degree: *to talk at the top of one's voice.* **9.** a person or thing that occupies the highest or leading position. **10.** the best or choicest part: *the top of all creation.* **11.** a covering or lid, as of a container or vehicle. **12.** the head. **13.** any of various outer garments for the upper body, as a blouse, shirt, or sweater: *a sale on cotton tops and shorts.* **14.** *Naut.* a platform surrounding the head of a lower mast on a ship, and serving as a foothold, a means of extending the upper rigging, etc. **15.** *Chem.* the part of a mixture under distillation that volatilizes first. **16.** *Bridge.* **a.** the best card of a suit in a player's hand. **b.** (in duplicate bridge) the best score on a hand. **17.** *Sports.* **a.** a stroke that hits the ball above its center. **b.** the forward spin given to the ball by such a stroke. **18.** *Baseball.* **a.** the first half of an inning. **b.** the first three batters in the batting order. **19.** *Textiles.* **a.** a cluster of textile fibers, esp. tow, put on a distaff. **b.** a strand of the long wool fibers in sliver form, separated from noil by combing and wound into a large ball. **c.** a similar strand of rayon. **20.** *Jewelry.* crown (def. 27). **21. blow one's top,** *Informal.* **a.** to become enraged; lose one's temper. **b.** to go mad; become insane: *He must have blown his top to make such a fool of himself.* **22. off the top of one's head,** *Informal.* See **head** (def. 56). **23. on top,** successful; victorious; dominant: *to stay on top.* **24. on top of, a.** over or upon. **b.** in addition to; over and above. **c.** close upon; following upon: *Gale winds came on top of the floods.* **d.** in complete control: *on top of the problem.* **25. on top of the world, a.** successful. **b.** elated: *The success made her feel on top of the world.* **26. over the top, a.** *Mil.* over the top of the parapet before a trench, as in issuing to charge against the enemy. **b.** surpassing a goal, quota, or limit. **27. the tops,** *Informal.* the most outstanding person or thing in ability, favor, etc.: *As a friend, she's the tops.*
—*adj.* **28.** pertaining to, situated at, or forming the top; highest; uppermost; upper: *the top shelf.* **29.** highest in degree; greatest: *to pay top prices.* **30.** foremost, chief, or principal: *to win top honors in a competition.*
—*v.t.* **31.** to furnish with a top; put a top on. **32.** to be at or constitute the top of. **33.** to reach the top of. **34.** to rise above: *The sun had topped the horizon.* **35.** to exceed in height, amount, number, etc. **36.** to surpass, excel, or outdo: *That tops everything.* **37.** *Theat.* (in spoken dialogue) to reply in a voice of greater volume or higher pitch: *King Henry must top the crowd noises in his St. Crispin's Day speech.* **38.** to surmount with something specified: *to top a sundae with whipped cream.* **39.** to remove the top of; crop; prune: *to top a tall tree.* **40.** to get or leap over the top of (a fence, barrier, etc.). **41.** *Chem.* to distill off only the most volatile part of (a mixture). **42.** *Sports.* **a.** to strike (the ball) above its center, giving it a forward spin. **b.** to make (a stroke) by hitting the ball in this manner. **43.** to top-dress (land). **44.** *Obs.* to have coitus with (a woman).
—*v.i.* **45.** to rise aloft. **46. top off,** to climax or complete, esp. in an exceptional manner; finish: *They topped off the evening with a ferryboat ride at midnight.* **47. top out, a.** to finish the top of (a structure). **b.** to reach the highest level. [bef. 1000; ME, OE; c. D *top,* G *Zopf,* ON *toppr* top]
—**Syn. 1.** zenith, acme, peak, pinnacle, vertex. **39.** lop. —**Ant. 1.** bottom.

top[2] (top), *n.* **1.** a toy, often inversely conical, with a point on which it is made to spin. **2. sleep like a top,** to sleep soundly: *After a day of hiking and swimming we slept like tops.* [bef. 1100; ME, OE; c. Fris, dial. D *top*]

top-, var. of **topo-** before a vowel: *toponym.*

to•paz (tō′paz), *n.* **1.** a mineral, a fluosilicate of aluminum, usually occurring in prismatic orthorhombic crystals of various colors, and used as a gem. **2.** citrine (def. 2). **3.** either of two South American hummingbirds, *Topaza pella* or *T. pyra,* having chiefly red and crimson plumage and a yellowish-green throat with a topaz sheen. [1225–75; < L *topazus* < Gk *tópazos;* r. ME *topace* < OF < L, as above] —**to•paz•ine** (tō′pə zēn′, -zin), *adj.*

to′paz quartz′, citrine (def. 2).

top′ banan′a, *Slang.* **1.** a leading comedian in musical comedy, burlesque, vaudeville, etc.: *For many years he was top banana on the circuit.* **2.** the chief person in a group or undertaking. [1950–55]

top′ bill′ing, *Theat.* the first or most prominent position in a list of actors or entertainers, as on a marquee or screen. [1940–45]

top′ boot′, a high boot, esp. one having a cuff of a different material, color, etc., from the rest of the boot. [1760–70]

top′ brass′, *Informal.* brass (def. 5). [1935–40, *Amer.*]

top•cas•tle (top′kas′əl, -kä′səl), *n.* a large fighting top used in medieval ships. [1300–50; ME *top-castel.* See TOP[1], CASTLE]

top•coat (top′kōt′), *n.* **1.** a lightweight overcoat. **2.** the coat of paint applied last to a surface. —*v.t.* **3.** to apply the topcoat to (a surface). [1810–20; TOP[1] + COAT]

top′ dog′, **1.** a person, group, or nation that has acquired a position of highest authority. **2.** the winner of a competition or rivalry; champion: *He was determined to be top dog at the swimming meet.* **3.** *Animal Behav.* the alpha male or alpha female in a dominance hierarchy. [1885–1900] —**top′-dog′,** *adj.*

top′ dol′lar, *Informal.* the maximum amount being or likely to be paid: *to pay top dollar for the jewelry.*

top-down (top′doun′), *adj. Computers.* See under **structured programming.** [1960–65]

top′ drawer′, the highest level in rank, excellence, or importance: *a musician strictly out of the top drawer.* [1900–05] —**top′-drawer′,** *adj.*

top-dress (top′dres′), *v.t.,* **-dressed** or **-drest, -dress•ing.** to manure (land) on the surface. [1725–35; TOP[1] + DRESS]

top′ dress′ing, **1.** a dressing of manure on the surface of land. **2.** the action of one who top-dresses. **3.** a top layer of gravel, crushed rock, etc., on a roadway. [1755–65] —**top′ dress′er.**

tope[1] (tōp), *v.,* **toped, top•ing.** —*v.i.* **1.** to drink alcoholic liquor habitually and to excess. —*v.t.* **2.** to drink (liquor) habitually and to excess. [1645–55; var. of obs. *top* to drink, in phrase *top off* (on the model of *tip off* to drink (a full helping) at a draught), special use of *top* to tilt. See TOPPLE]

tope[2] (tōp), *n.* **1.** a small shark, *Galeorhinus galeus,* inhabiting waters along the European coast. **2.** any of various related sharks of small to medium size. [1680–90; akin to *toper* dogfish (Norfolk dial.)]

tope[3] (tōp), *n.* (in Buddhist countries) a dome-shaped monument, usually for religious relics. [1805–15; < Hindi *top*]

tope[3] (East Indian)

to•pec•to•my (tə pek′tə mē), *n., pl.* **-mies.** *Surg.* excision of part of the cerebral cortex for the relief of unmanageable pain or esp. as a treatment for certain mental disorders. [TOP- + -ECTOMY]

to•pee (tō pē′, tō′pē), *n.* (in India) a lightweight helmet or sun hat made from the pith of the sola plant. Also, **topi.** [1825–35; < Hindi *ṭopī* hat]

To•pe•ka (tə pē′kə), *n.* a city in and the capital of Kansas, in the NE part, on the Kansas River. 115,266.

To•pe•li•us (to͞o pā′lē əs), *n.* **Za•ka•ri•as** (sä′kä Rē′äs), 1818–98, Finnish poet and novelist.

top•er (tō′pər), *n.* a hard drinker or chronic drunkard. [1665–75; TOPE[1] + -ER[1]]

top′ flight′, the highest or most outstanding level, as in achievement or development: *students in the top flight of their class.* —**top′flight′, top′-flight′,** *adj.* —**top′flight′er, top′-flight′er,** *n.*

Top 40, **1.** (*sometimes l.c.*) the 40 most popular or best-selling recordings, songs, etc., within a stated time period. **2.** pertaining to, designating, or being the Top 40. Also, **Top′ For′ty, top′ for′ty.**

top•full (top′fo͝ol′), *adj.* full to the utmost; brimful. [1545–55; TOP[1] + FULL[1]]

top•gal′lant fore′castle, (top′gal′ənt; *Naut.* tə gal′ənt), *Naut.* a partial weather deck on top of a forecastle superstructure; forecastle deck. [1830–40]

topgal′lant mast′, *Naut.* a mast fixed to the head of a topmast on a square-rigged vessel. [1505–15]

topgal′lant sail′, *Naut.* a sail or either of two sails set on the yard or yards of a topgallant mast. Also called **topgallant.** See diag. under **ship.** [1580–90]

top′ graft′ing, *Hort.* grafting in the top, as of a tree, in order to replace existing branches with those of a more desired variety or form. [1895–1900]

top•ham•per (top′ham′pər), *n. Naut.* **1.** the light upper sails and their gear and spars, sometimes used to refer to all spars and gear above the deck. **2.** any unnecessary weight, either aloft or about the upper decks. Also, **top′-ham′per.** [1785–95; TOP[1] + HAMPER[1]]

top′ hat′, a tall, cylindrical hat with a stiff brim usually slightly curved on the sides, worn by men esp. on formal occasions. Cf. **beaver**[1] (def. 4), **opera hat, silk hat.** [1800–10]

top-hat (top′hat′), *adj.* of or pertaining to polite or fashionable society. [1890–95; adj. use of TOP HAT]

top-heav·y (top′hev′ē), *adj.* **1.** having the top disproportionately heavy; liable to fall from too great weight above. **2.** relatively much heavier or larger above the center or waist than below: *a top-heavy wrestler.* **3.** *Finance.* **a.** having a financial structure overburdened with securities that have priority in the payment of dividends. **b.** overcapitalized. [1525–35; TOP[1] + HEAVY] —**top′-heav′i·ly,** *adv.* —**top′-heav′i·ness,** *n.*

To·phet (tō′fit, -fet), *n. Bible.* **1.** a place in the valley of Hinnom, near Jerusalem, where, contrary to the law, children were offered as sacrifices, esp. to Moloch. It was later used as a dumping ground for refuse. **2.** the place of punishment for the wicked after death; hell. **3.** some place, condition, etc., likened to hell. Also, **To·pheth** (tō′fit, -fet). [1350–1400; ME << Heb *tōpheth* a place-name]

top-hole (top′hōl′), *adj. Brit. Slang.* first-rate. [1895–1900; TOP[1] + HOLE]

to·phus (tō′fəs), *n., pl.* **-phi** (-fī). *Pathol.* a calcareous concretion formed in the soft tissue about a joint, in the pinna of the ear, etc., esp. in gout; a gouty deposit. [1545–55; < L *tōphus, tōfus* TUFA] —**to·pha·ceous** (tə fā′shəs), *adj.*

to·pi[1] (tō pē′, tō′pē), *n., pl.* **-pis.** topee.

to·pi[2] (tō′pē), *n., pl.* **-pis.** an antelope, *Damaliscus lunatus,* of east-central Africa, having bluish-black and yellow markings. [1905–10; said to be < Swahili]

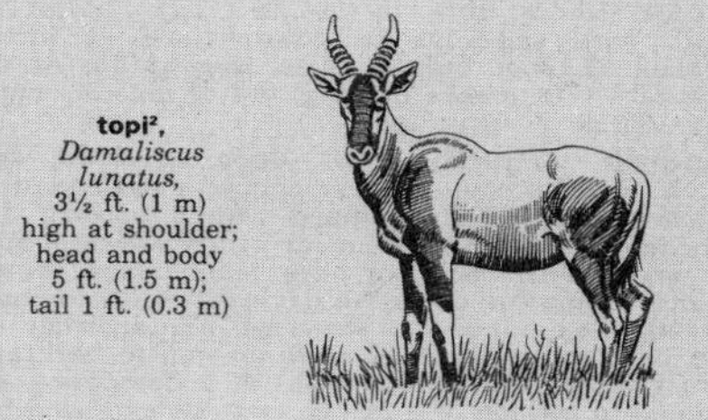
topi[2], *Damaliscus lunatus,* 3½ ft. (1 m) high at shoulder; head and body 5 ft. (1.5 m); tail 1 ft. (0.3 m)

to·pi·ar·y (tō′pē er′ē), *adj., n., pl.* **-ar·ies.** *Hort.* —*adj.* **1.** (of a plant) clipped or trimmed into fantastic shapes. **2.** of or pertaining to such trimming. —*n.* **3.** topiary work; the topiary art. **4.** a garden containing such work. [1585–95; < L *topiārius* pertaining to landscape-gardening or to ornamental gardens, equiv. to *topi(a)* (pl.) artificial landscape (< Gk *tópia* (sing. *topion*), dim. of *tópos* place) + *-ārius* -ARY]

top·ic (top′ik), *n.* **1.** a subject of conversation or discussion: *to provide a topic for discussion.* **2.** the subject or theme of a discourse or of one of its parts. **3.** *Rhet., Logic.* a general field of considerations from which arguments can be drawn. **4.** Also called **theme.** *Ling.* the part of a sentence that announces the item about which the rest of the sentence communicates information, often signaled by initial position in the sentence or by a grammatical marker. Cf. **comment** (def. 6). [1560–70; < L *topica* (pl.) < Gk (*tà*) *topiká* name of work by Aristotle (lit., (things) pertaining to commonplaces), equiv. to *tó-p(os)* commonplace + *-ika,* neut. pl. of *-ikos* -IC; see TOPO-]
—**Syn. 2.** thesis, subject matter. See **subject.**

top·i·cal (top′i kəl), *adj.* **1.** pertaining to or dealing with matters of current or local interest: *a topical reference.* **2.** pertaining to the subject of a discourse, composition, or the like. **3.** of a place; local. **4.** *Med.* of, pertaining to, or applied externally to a particular part of the body; local: *a topical anesthetic.* —*n.* **5.** *Philately.* any of a collection of different stamps treating the same subject. [1580–90; < Gk *topik(ós)* local, pertaining to commonplaces (see TOPO-, -IC) + -AL[1]] —**top′i·cal·ly,** *adv.*

top·i·cal·i·ty (top′i kal′i tē), *n., pl.* **-ties** for 2. **1.** the state or quality of being topical. **2.** a detail or matter of current or local interest. [1900–05; TOPICAL + -ITY]

top·i·cal·ize (top′i kə līz′), *v.t.,* **-ized, -iz·ing.** *Ling.* to introduce as, convert into, or mark as the topic of a sentence. Also, *esp. Brit.,* **top′i·cal·ise′.** [1965–70; TOPICAL + -IZE] —**top′i·cal·i·za′tion,** *n.*

top′ic sen′tence, a sentence that expresses the essential idea of a paragraph or larger section, usually appearing at the beginning. Also, **top′ical sen′tence.** [1915–20]

top·kha·na (tōp′kä nə), *n. Anglo-Indian.* a building where artillery, ammunition, etc., are made, repaired, and stored. [1660–70; < Hindi, Urdu *topkhānā* < Turk *top* cannon + Pers *khānah* house]

top′ kick′, *Mil. Slang.* a first sergeant. [1925–30]

top·knot (top′not′), *n.* **1.** a tuft of hair growing on the top of the head. **2.** hair fashioned into a knob or ball on top of the head. **3.** a tuft or crest of feathers on the head of a bird. **4.** a knot or bow of ribbon worn on the top of the head. [1680–90; TOP[1] + KNOT[1]]

top·less (top′lis), *adj.* **1.** lacking a top: *a topless bathing suit.* **2.** nude above the waist or hips: *topless dancers.* **3.** featuring entertainers, waitresses, etc., who are nude above the waist or hips: *a topless bar.* **4.** extremely high: *a topless mountain.* **5.** *Obs.* without a peer. [1580–90; TOP[1] + -LESS] —**top′less·ness,** *n.*

top-lev·el (top′lev′əl), *adj.* at a high level: *a top-level conference.*

top·line (top′līn′), *adj.* **1.** so important as to be named at or near the top of a newspaper item, advertisement, or the like: *a topline actress; topline news.* **2.** of the highest reputation, importance, etc.: *a topline business firm.* [1925–30; TOP[1] + LINE[1]] —**top′lin′er,** *n.*

top′ load′er, a machine or appliance, as a washing machine, loaded and unloaded through an opening in the top (distinguished from *front loader*). Also **top′-load′er.** [1965–70]

top·loft·y (top′lôf′tē, -lof′-), *adj.* condescending; haughty. Also, **top′loft′i·cal.** [1815–25; TOP[1] + LOFTY] —**top′loft′i·ly,** *adv.* —**top′loft′i·ness,** *n.*

top·man (top′mən), *n., pl.* **-men.** *Naut.* a person stationed for duty in a top. [1505–15; TOP[1] + -MAN]

top·mast (top′mast′, -mäst′; *Naut.* top′məst), *n. Naut.* the mast next above a lower mast, usually formed as a separate spar from the lower mast and used to support the yards or rigging of a topsail or topsails. [1475–85; TOP[1] + MAST[1]]

top·maul (top′môl′), *n.* a heavy hammer with a steel or wooden head, used in shipbuilding. [TOP[1] + MAUL]

top·min·now (top′min′ō), *n., pl.* (*esp. collectively*) **-now,** (*esp. referring to two or more kinds or species*) **-nows.** any of several small, surface-swimming fishes of the egg-laying family Cyprinodontidae and the live-bearing family Poeciliidae, some of which are used in mosquito control. [1880–85, *Amer.*; TOP[1] + MINNOW]

top·most (top′mōst′ *or, esp. Brit.,* -məst), *adj.* highest; uppermost. [1690–1700; TOP[1] + -MOST]

top·neck (top′nek′), *n.* the quahog clam, *Venus mercenaria,* when larger than a cherrystone but still immature. [of undetermined orig.]

top·notch (top′noch′), *adj.* first-rate: *a topnotch job.* Also, **top′-notch′.** [1820–30; TOP[1] + NOTCH]
—**Syn.** outstanding, notable, superior.

topo-, a combining form meaning "place," "local," used in the formation of compound words: *topography; topology.* Also, *esp. before a vowel,* **top-.** [comb. form of Gk *tópos* place, commonplace]

top-off (top′ôf′, -of′), *n. Australian Slang.* a person who informs on another, often as if by accident or as a joke. [1940–45; n. use of v. phrase *top off* to inform (on someone)]

top-of-the-line (top′əv thə līn′), *adj.* being the best and usually the most expensive of its kind: *The company previewed its top-of-the-line carpeting.*

topog., **1.** topographical. **2.** topography.

to·pog·ra·pher (tə pog′rə fər), *n.* **1.** a specialist in topography. **2.** a person who describes the surface features of a place or region. [1595–1605; < Gk *topográ-ph(os)* topographer (see TOPO-, -GRAPH) + -ER[1]]

top′ograph′ic map′, a map showing topographic features, usually by means of contour lines. Cf. **contour map.**

to·pog·ra·phy (tə pog′rə fē), *n., pl.* **-phies.** **1.** the detailed mapping or charting of the features of a relatively small area, district, or locality. **2.** the detailed description, esp. by means of surveying, of particular localities, as cities, towns, or estates. **3.** the relief features or surface configuration of an area. **4.** the features, relations, or configuration of a structural entity. **5.** a schema of a structural entity, as of the mind, a field of study, or society, reflecting a division into distinct areas having a specific relation or a specific position relative to one another. [1400–50; late ME *topographye* < LL *topographia* < Gk *topographía.* See TOPO-, -GRAPHY] —**top·o·graph·ic** (top′ə graf′ik), **top′o·graph′i·cal,** *adj.* —**top′o·graph′i·cal·ly,** *adv.*

topolog′ical equiv′alence, *Math.* the property of two topological spaces such that there is a homeomorphism from one to the other.

top′olog′ical group′, *Math.* a set that is a group and a topological space and for which the group operation and the map of an element to its inverse are continuous functions. [1945–50]

topolog′ical invar′iant, *Math.* a property of a topological space that is a property of every space related to the given space by a homeomorphism.

topolog′ical space′, *Math.* a set with a collection of subsets or open sets satisfying the properties that the union of open sets is an open set, the intersection of two open sets is an open set, and the given set and the empty set are open sets. [1945–50]

topolog′ical transforma′tion, *Math.* homeomorphism (def. 2). [1945–50]

to·pol·o·gy (tə pol′ə jē), *n., pl.* **-gies** for 3. *Math.* **1.** the study of those properties of geometric forms that remain invariant under certain transformations, as bending or stretching. **2.** Also called **point set topology.** the study of limits in sets considered as collections of points. **3.** a collection of open sets making a given set a topological space. [1650–60; TOPO- + -LOGY] —**top·o·log·ic** (top′ə loj′ik), **top′o·log′i·cal,** *adj.* —**top′o·log′i·cal·ly,** *adv.* —**to·pol′o·gist,** *n.*

top·o·nym (top′ə nim), *n.* **1.** a place name. **2.** a name derived from the name of a place. [1890–95; TOP- + -ONYM, or by back formation from TOPONOMY]

to·pon·y·my (tə pon′ə mē), *n.* **1.** the study of toponyms. **2.** *Anat.* the nomenclature of the regions of the body. [1875–80; TOP- + *-onomy,* on the model of HOMONYMY, SYNONYMY; see -ONYM, -Y[3]] —**top·o·nym·ic** (top′ə nim′ik), **top′o·nym′i·cal,** *adj.*

top·o·type (top′ə tīp′), *n. Biol.* a specimen from the locality at which the type was first collected. [1890–95; TOPO- + -TYPE] —**top·o·typ·ic** (top′ə tip′ik), **top′o·typ′i·cal,** *adj.*

top·per (top′ər), *n.* **1.** a person or thing that tops. **2.** a woman's loose, usually lightweight topcoat, esp. one that is knee-length or shorter. **3.** *Informal.* See **top hat.** **4.** capper (def. 2). **5.** *Brit. Slang.* an excellent or well-liked person or thing. [1665–75; TOP[1] + -ER[1]]

top·pie (top′ē), *n.* topknot (def. 3). [1895–1900; TOP-(KNOT) + -IE]

top·ping (top′ing), *n.* **1.** the act of a person or thing that tops. **2.** a distinct part forming a top to something. **3.** something put on a thing at the top to complete it, as a sauce or garnish placed on food. **4. toppings,** the parts removed in topping or cropping plants, as branches. —*adj.* **5.** rising above something else; overtopping. **6.** very high in rank, degree, etc. **7.** *Chiefly Brit. Informal.* excellent; wonderful. [1300–50; ME: top part; see TOP[1], -ING[1], -ING[2]]

top′ping lift′, *Naut.* a line for raising and supporting a spar, as a yard or boom. Also called **lift.** [1735–45]

top·ple (top′əl), *v.,* **-pled, -pling.** —*v.i.* **1.** to fall forward, as from having too heavy a top; pitch; tumble down. **2.** to lean over or jut, as if threatening to fall. —*v.t.* **3.** to cause to topple. **4.** to overthrow, as from a position of authority: *to topple the king.* [1535–45; earlier *top* to tilt, topple (see TOPE[1]) + -LE]
—**Syn. 4.** defeat, vanquish, overcome, overpower.

top′ quark′, *Physics.* a heavy quark having electric charge ⅔ times the elementary charge. Also called **t quark, truth quark.** [1975–80]

top·rail (top′rāl′), *n.* the uppermost rail of the back of a chair or the like; a crest rail. [1670–80; TOP[1] + RAIL[1]]

top′ round′, a cut of beef taken from inside the round, which is below the rump and above the upper leg. Cf. **bottom round.** [1900–05]

tops (tops), *adj.* **1.** ranked among the highest, as in ability, performance, comprehensiveness, or quality: *His work is tops. That car is tops.* —*n.* **2. the tops.** See **top**[1] (def. 27). [1930–35; pl. of TOP[1]]

top·sail (top′sāl′; *Naut.* top′səl), *n. Naut.* a sail, or either of a pair of sails, set immediately above the lowermost sail of a mast and supported by a topmast. See diag. under **ship.** [1350–1400; ME *topseil.* See TOP[1], SAIL]

top′sail schoon′er, a sailing vessel fore-and-aft rigged on all of two or more masts with square sails above the foresail, and often with a square sail before the foresail. Cf. **main-topsail schooner.** [1865–70]

top-se·cret (top′sē′krit), *adj.* (of information, a document, etc.) **1.** bearing the classification *top-secret,* the highest level of classified information. **2.** limited to persons authorized to use anything so classified. Cf. **classification** (def. 5). [1940–45; TOP[1] + SECRET]

top′ ser′geant, *Mil. Slang.* a first sergeant. [1915–20]

top·side (top′sīd′), *n.* **1.** the upper side. **2.** Usually, **topsides.** *Naut.* the outer surface of a hull above the water. **3.** the most authoritative position or level. **4.** *Chiefly Brit.* a cut of beef similar to a U.S. rump roast. Cf. **silverside** (def. 1). **5.** *Brit.* the top or outer side of a round of beef; beef from the outer thigh of a butchered cow. —*adj.* **6.** of, pertaining to, or located on the topside. **7.** of the most authoritative rank. —*adv.* **8.** Also, **top′sides′.** up on the deck: *He left the engine room and went topside.* **9.** to, toward, or at the topside. [1670–80; TOP[1] + SIDE[1]]

Top-Sid·er (top′sī′dər), *Trademark.* a brand of casual shoe with a nonskid sole, designed esp. for wear on boats.

top′ slic′ing, *Mining.* mining of thick orebodies in a series of stopes from top to bottom, the roof being caved with its timbers as each stope is exhausted.

top·smelt (top′smelt′), *n., pl.* **-smelts,** (*esp. collectively*) **-smelt.** a silversides, *Atherinops affinis,* of waters along the Pacific coast of North America: valued as a food fish. Also called **baysmelt.** [TOP[1] + SMELT[2]]

top·soil (top′soil′), *n.* **1.** the fertile, upper part of the soil. —*v.t.* **2.** to cover (land) with topsoil. [1860–65; TOP[1] + SOIL[1]]

top·spin (top′spin′), *n.* a spinning motion imparted to a ball that causes it to rotate forward. [1900–05; TOP[1] + SPIN]

top·stitch (top′stich′), *v.t.* **1.** to sew a line of stitches on the face side of (a garment or the like) alongside a seam. —*n.* **2.** a line of such stitches. [1945–50; TOP[1] + STITCH]

top·sy-tur·vy (top′sē tûr′vē), *adv., adj., n., pl.* **-vies.** —*adv.* **1.** with the top where the bottom should be; upside down. **2.** in or into a reversed condition or order. **3.** in or into a state of confusion or disorder. —*adj.* **4.** turned upside down; inverted; reversed: *a topsy-turvy reflection.* **5.** confused or disorderly: *a topsy-turvy classroom.* —*n.* **6.** inversion of the natural order. **7.** a state of confusion or disorder. [1520–30; perh. var. of *top syd turvye* topside down (with loss of *d* before *t*); *turvy,* var. of *tervy,* equiv. to obs. *terve* to turn over (c. OHG *zerben*) + -Y[1]] —**top′sy-tur′vi·ly,** *adv.* —**top′sy-tur′vi·ness,** *n.*

top·sy-tur·vy·dom (top′sē tûr′vē dəm), *n.* a state of affairs or a region in which everything is topsy-turvy. [1875–80; TOPSY-TURVY + -DOM]

top′ ten′, **1.** the ten most popular songs, records, movies, etc., during a specific period. **2.** the ten best or highest ranked persons, places, or items in a group or category. **3.** Also, **top′-ten′.** pertaining to, constituting, or being among the top ten: *a top ten resort.* Also, **top 10, top-10.**

top′ tim′ber, *Naut.* a timber forming the upper, straighter portion of a frame in a wooden hull. [1620–30]

top′ yeast′, yeast that rises to the surface as froth during fermentation. Also called **surface yeast.**

toque (tōk), *n.* **1.** a brimless and close-fitting hat for women, in any of several shapes. **2.** a velvet hat with a narrow, sometimes turned-up brim, a full crown, and usually a plume, worn by men and women esp. in 16th-century France. **3.** tuque. [1495–1505; < F; r. earlier *toock, towk* (< Pg *touca* coif), *tock, tocque* (< It *tocca* cap), *toke* (< Sp *toca* headdress); ulterior orig. obscure]

toque (def. 2)

tor (tôr), *n.* a rocky pinnacle; a peak of a bare or rocky mountain or hill. [bef. 900; ME; OE *torr* < Celtic; cf. Ir *tor* rocky height, Welsh *twr* heap, pile]

-tor, a suffix found in loanwords from Latin, forming personal agent nouns from verbs and, less commonly, from nouns: *dictator; genitor; janitor; orator; victor.* [< L *-tor* (s. *-tōr-*), c. Gk *-tōr* (s. *-tor-*), Skt *-tar-*]

To·rah (tōr′ə, tôr′ə; *Seph. Heb.* tō rä′; *Ashk. Heb.* tō′rə, toi′rə), *n.* (*sometimes l.c.*) **1.** the Pentateuch, being the first of the three Jewish divisions of the Old Testament. Cf. ***Tanach.*** **2.** a parchment scroll on which the Pentateuch is written, used in synagogue services. **3.** the entire body of Jewish religious literature, law, and teaching as contained chiefly in the Old Testament and the Talmud. **4.** law or instruction. Also, **To′ra.** [< Heb *tōrāh* instruction, law]

to·ran (tôr′ən, tōr′-), *n.* (in Indian Buddhist and Hindu architecture) a gateway having two or three lintels between two posts. Also, **to·ra·na** (tôr′ə nə, tōr′-). [1885–90; < Hindi < Skt *torana*]

tor·ban·ite (tôr′bə nīt′), *n. Petrol.* a dark-brown oil shale containing a large amount of carbonaceous matter. [1855–60; named after *Torbane* (Hill), in Linlithgowshire, Scotland; see -ITE[1]]

Tor·bay (tôr′bā′, -bā′), *n.* a borough in S Devonshire, in SW England: seaside resort. 109,800.

tor·bern·ite (tôr′bər nīt′), *n.* a mineral, hydrated copper uranium phosphate, $CuU_2P_2O_{12}\cdot 12H_2O$, occurring in square tabular crystals of a bright-green color: a minor ore of uranium; copper uranite. Also called **chalcolite.** [1850–55; named after *Torbern* Bergman (1735–84), Swedish chemist; see -ITE[1]]

torc (tôrk), *n.* torque (def. 4).

torch[1] (tôrch), *n.* **1.** a light to be carried in the hand, consisting of some combustible substance, as resinous wood, or of twisted flax or the like soaked with tallow or other flammable substance, ignited at the upper end. **2.** something considered as a source of illumination, enlightenment, guidance, etc.: *the torch of learning.* **3.** any of various lamplike devices that produce a hot flame and are used for soldering, burning off paint, etc. **4.** *Slang.* an arsonist. **5.** *Chiefly Brit.* flashlight (def. 1). **6.** **carry the** or **a torch for,** *Slang.* to be in love with, esp. to suffer from unrequited love for: *He still carries a torch for his ex-wife.* —*v.i.* **7.** to burn or flare up like a torch. —*v.t.* **8.** to subject to the flame or light of a torch, as in order to burn, sear, solder, or illuminate. **9.** *Slang.* to set fire to maliciously, esp. in order to collect insurance. [1250–1300; ME *torche* (n.) < OF < VL **torca* something twisted. See TORQUE] —**torch′a·ble,** *adj.* —**torch′less,** *adj.* —**torch′like′,** *adj.*

torch[2] (tôrch), *v.t.* to point (the joints between roofing slates) with a mixture of lime and hair. [1840–50; < F *torcher* to plaster with a mixture of clay and chopped straw, deriv. of *torche* a twist of straw. See TORCH[1]]

torch·bear·er (tôrch′bâr′ər), *n.* **1.** a person who carries a torch. **2.** a leader in a movement, campaign, etc.: *a torchbearer of democracy.* [1530–40; TORCH[1] + BEARER]

tor·chère (tôr shâr′), *n.* **1.** a tall stand for a candelabrum. **2.** torchiere. [1905–10; < F, equiv. to *torche* TORCH[1] + *-ère,* var. of *-ière,* fem. of *-ier* -IER[2]]

tor·chiere (tôr chēr′), *n.* a floor lamp for indirect lighting, having its source of light within a reflecting bowl that directs the light upward. Also, **torchère, torchier′.** [var. of TORCHÈRE]

torch·light (tôrch′līt′), *n.* the light of a torch or torches. [1375–1425; late ME; see TORCH[1], LIGHT[1]]

torch′ lil′y, tritoma. [1880–85]

tor′chon lace′ (tôr′shon; *Fr.* tôr shôn′), **1.** a bobbin-made linen or cotton lace with loosely twisted threads in simple, open patterns. **2.** a machine-made imitation of this. [1875–80; *torchon* < F: duster, dishcloth, lit., something to wipe with, equiv. to *torch(er)* to wipe (see TORCH[2]) + *-on* n. suffix]

torch′ sing′er, a singer, esp. a woman, who specializes in singing torch songs. [1930–35]

torch′ song′, a popular song concerned with unhappiness or failure in love. [1925–30]

torch·wood (tôrch′wo͝od′), *n.* **1.** any of various resinous woods suitable for making torches, as the wood of the tree *Amyris balsamifera,* of the rue family, native to Florida and the West Indies. **2.** any of the trees yielding these woods. [1595–1605; TORCH[1] + WOOD[1]]

torch·y (tôr′chē), *adj.,* **torch·i·er, torch·i·est.** of, pertaining to, or characteristic of a torch song or a torch singer. [1620–30, in sense "full of torches"; 1940–45 for this sense; TORCH[1] + -Y[1]]

CONCISE ETYMOLOGY KEY: <, descended or borrowed from; >, whence; b., blend of, blended; c., cognate with; cf., compare; deriv., derivative; equiv., equivalent; imit., imitative; obl., oblique; r., replacing; s., stem; sp., spelling, spelled; resp., respelling, respelled; trans., translation; ?, origin unknown; *, unattested; ‡, probably earlier than. See the full key inside the front cover.

Tor·de·si·llas (tôr′the sē′lyäs), *n.* a town in NW Spain, SW of Valladolid: treaty (1494) defining the colonial spheres of Spain and Portugal. 6604.

tore[1] (tôr, tōr), *v.* **1.** pt. of **tear**[2]. **2.** *Nonstandard.* a pp. of **tear**[2].

tore[2] (tôr, tōr), *n.* a torus. [< F < L *torus*]

tor·e·a·dor (tôr′ē ə dôr′; *Sp.* tô′re ä thôr′), *n.* a bullfighter; torero. [1610–20; < Sp, equiv. to *torea(r)* to bait a bull (deriv. of *toro* bull < L *taurus*) + *-dor* -TOR]

Tor′eador Fres′co, The, a mural (c1500 B.C.) from Minoan Crete.

tor′eador pants′, women's close-fitting slacks that extend to or slightly above the calf, styled after the pants traditionally worn by Spanish bullfighters.

To·rel·li (tô rel′ē; *It.* tô rel′lē), *n.* **Giu·sep·pe** (jo͞o-zep′pe), 1650?–1708, Italian composer and violinist.

to·re·ni·a (tə rē′nē ə, -rēn′yə), *n.* any of several plants belonging to the genus *Torenia,* of the figwort family, native to Africa and Asia, having two-lipped, usually blue or purple flowers. Also called **wishbone flower.** [< NL (Linnaeus), after Olof *Torén* (1718–53), chaplain to the Swedish East India Company; see -IA]

to·re·ro (tə râr′ō; *Sp.* tô re′rô), *n., pl.* **-re·ros** (-râr′ōz; *Sp.* -re′rôs). a bullfighter, esp. a matador. [1720–30; < Sp, equiv. to *tor(o)* bull (< L *taurus*) + *-ero* < L *-ārius* -ARY]

to·reu·tic (tə ro͞o′tik), *adj.* of or pertaining to toreutics or the objects produced by this technique. [1830–40; < Gk *toreutikós,* equiv. to *toreú(ein)* to bore, chase, emboss (v. deriv. of *toreús* graving tool) + *-tikos* -TIC]

to·reu·tics (tə ro͞o′tiks), *n.* (*used with a singular v.*) the art or technique of decorating metal or other material, esp. by embossing or chasing. [1655–65; see TOREUTIC, -ICS]

to·ri (tôr′ī, tōr′ī), *n.* pl. of **torus.**

tor·ic (tôr′ik, tor′-), *adj.* **1.** noting or pertaining to a lens with a surface forming a portion of a torus, used for eyeglasses and contact lenses that correct astigmatism. **2.** a toric contact lens. [1895–1900; TOR(US) + -IC]

to·ri·i (tôr′ē ē′, tōr′-), *n., pl.* **to·ri·i.** (in Japan) a form of decorative gateway or portal, consisting of two upright wooden posts connected at the top by two horizontal crosspieces, commonly found at the entrance to Shinto temples. [1720–30; < Japn, equiv. to *tori* bird + *(w)i* perch]

torii

To·ri·no (tô rē′nô), *n.* Turin.

tor·ment (*v.* tôr ment′, tôr′ment; *n.* tôr′ment), *v.t.* **1.** to afflict with great bodily or mental suffering; pain: *to be tormented with violent headaches.* **2.** to worry or annoy excessively: *to torment one with questions.* **3.** to throw into commotion; stir up; disturb. —*n.* **4.** a state of great bodily or mental suffering; agony; misery. **5.** something that causes great bodily or mental pain or suffering. **6.** a source of much trouble, worry, or annoyance. **7.** an instrument of torture, as the rack or the thumbscrew. **8.** the infliction of torture by means of such an instrument or the torture so inflicted. [1250–1300; (n.) ME < OF < L *tormentum* rope, catapult, torture < **torkʷ-ment-* (see TORQUE, -MENT); (v.) ME *tormenten* < OF *tormenter,* deriv. of *torment* (cf. LL *tormentāre*)] —**tor·ment′ed·ly,** *adv.* —**tor·ment′ing·ly,** *adv.* —**tor·ment′ing·ness,** *n.*

—**Syn. 1.** harry, hector, vex, distress, agonize. TORMENT, RACK, TORTURE suggest causing great physical or mental pain, suffering, or harassment. To TORMENT is to afflict or harass as by incessant repetition of vexations or annoyances: *to be tormented by doubts.* To RACK is to affect with such pain as that suffered by one stretched on a rack; to concentrate with painful effort: *to rack one's brains.* To TORTURE is to afflict with acute and more or less protracted suffering: *to torture one by keeping one in suspense.* **2.** plague, pester, tease, provoke, needle, trouble, fret. **4.** torture, distress, anguish. —**Ant. 1.** please.

tor·men·til (tôr′men til), *n.* a low European plant, *Potentilla erecta,* of the rose family, having small, bright-yellow flowers, and a strongly astringent root used in medicine and in tanning and dyeing. [1350–1400; ME *tormentille* < ML *tormentilla,* equiv. to L *torment(um)* TORMENT + *-illa* dim. suffix]

tor·men·tor (tôr men′tər, tôr′men-), *n.* **1.** a person or thing that torments. **2.** *Theat.* a curtain or framed structure behind the proscenium at both sides of the stage, for screening the wings from the audience. Cf. **teaser** (def. 2). Also, **tor·ment′er.** [1250–1300; ME *tormento(u)r* < AF; OF *tormenteor.* See TORMENT, -OR[2]]

torn (tôrn, tōrn), *v.* pp. of **tear**[2].

tor·na·do (tôr nā′dō), *n., pl.* **-does, -dos. 1.** a localized, violently destructive windstorm occurring over land, esp. in the Middle West, and characterized by a long, funnel-shaped cloud extending toward the ground and made visible by condensation and debris. Cf. **waterspout** (def. 3). **2.** a violent squall or whirlwind of small extent, as one of those occurring during the summer on the west coast of Africa. **3.** a violent outburst, as of emotion or activity. **4.** (*cap.*) *Mil.* a supersonic, two-seat, multipurpose military aircraft produced jointly by West Germany, Britain, and Italy and capable of flying in darkness and bad weather. [1550–60; appar. by metathesis < Sp *tronada* thunderstorm, n. use of fem. of *tronado,* ptp. of *tronar* < L *tonāre* to thunder; r. 16th-century *ternado,* with unexplained *e*] —**tor·nad·ic** (tôr-nad′ik, -nā′dik), *adj.* —**tor·na′do·like′,** *adj.*

torna′do belt′, the part of the U.S. in which tornadoes occur most frequently, roughly the area within a 500-mi. (805-km) radius of southern Missouri. [1895–1900]

torna′do cloud′. See **funnel cloud.**

tor·nar·i·a (tôr nâr′ē ə), *n., pl.* **-nar·i·as, -nar·i·ae** (-nâr′ē ē′). the ciliated, free-swimming larva of certain hemichordates. [1885–90; < NL, equiv. to L *torn(us)* lathe (< Gk *tórnos*) + *-āria* -ARIA]

Torn′gat Moun′tains (tôrn′gat), a mountain range in N Labrador, Newfoundland, in E Canada, running N to S along the Atlantic coast.

tor·nil·lo (tôr nil′ō, -nē′ō; *Sp.* tôr nē′lyô, -nē′yô), *n., pl.* **-nil·los** (-nil′ōz, -nē′ōz; *Sp.* -nē′lyôs, -nē′yôs). See **screw bean.** [1835–45, *Amer.*; < Sp: screw, clamp, equiv. to *torn(o)* lathe, gyration (< L *tornus* lathe < Gk *tórnos*) + *-illo* dim. suffix (< L *-illum*)]

to·ro (tô′rô), *n., pl.* ***-ros*** (-rôs). *Spanish.* a bull.

to·roid (tôr′oid, tōr′-), *n. Geom.* **1.** a surface generated by the revolution of any closed plane curve or contour about an axis lying in its plane. **2.** the solid enclosed by such a surface. [1895–1900; TOR(US) + -OID]

to·roi·dal (tô roid′l, tō-, tôr′oi dl, tōr′-), *adj. Geom.* of or pertaining to a torus. [1885–90; TOROID + -AL[1]] —**to·roi′dal·ly,** *adv.*

To·ron·to (tə ron′tō), *n.* a city in and the capital of Ontario, in SE Canada, on Lake Ontario. 633,318. —**To·ron·to·ni·an** (tôr′ən tō′nē ən, tor′-, tə ron-), *adj., n.*

to·rose (tôr′ōs, tōr′-, tô rōs′, tō-), *adj.* **1.** *Bot.* cylindrical, with swellings or constrictions at intervals; knobbed. **2.** *Zool.* bulging. Also, **to·rous** (tôr′əs, tōr′-). [1750–60; < L *torōsus* bulging, full of muscle, equiv. to *tor(us)* bulge + *-ōsus* -OSE[1]]

tor·pe·do (tôr pē′dō), *n., pl.* **-does,** *v.,* **-doed, -do·ing.** —*n.* **1.** a self-propelled, cigar-shaped missile containing explosives and often equipped with a homing device, launched from a submarine or other warship, for destroying surface vessels or other submarines. **2.** any of various submarine explosive devices for destroying hostile ships, as a mine. **3.** a cartridge of gunpowder, dynamite, or the like, exploded in an oil well to facilitate the extraction of oil from the well. **4.** a detonating device fastened to the top of a rail so as to be exploded by the pressure of a locomotive or car, thus giving an audible signal to members of a train crew. **5.** any of various other explosive devices, as a firework that consists of an explosive wrapped up with gravel in a piece of tissue paper and that detonates when thrown forcibly on the ground or against a hard surface. **6.** Also called **torpe′do fish′.** an electric ray, esp. *Torpedo nobiliana,* of the Atlantic Ocean. **7.** an electric catfish, *Malapterurus electricus,* inhabiting waters of tropical central Africa and the Nile valley. **8.** *Informal.* a hero sandwich. **9.** *Slang.* a gangster hired as a murderer. —*v.t.* **10.** to attack, hit, damage, or destroy with torpedoes. **11.** to explode a torpedo in (an oil well) to facilitate the extraction of oil. **12.** to undermine, ruin, or destroy: *He torpedoed our plans.* —*v.i.* **13.** to attack, damage, or sink a ship with torpedoes. [1510–20; < L *torpēdō* numbness, torpidity, electric ray, equiv. to *torpē(re)* to be stiff (see TORPID[1]) + *-dō* n. suffix] —**tor·pe′do·like′,** *adj.*
—**Regional Variation. 8.** See **hero sandwich.**

torpe′do boat′, a small, fast, highly maneuverable boat used for torpedoing enemy shipping. [1800–10, *Amer.*]

tor·pe′do-boat destroy′er (tôr pē′dō bōt′), a vessel somewhat larger than the ordinary torpedo boat, designed for destroying torpedo boats or as a more powerful form of torpedo boat. [1890–95]

tor·pe·do·man (tôr pē′dō man′, -mən), *n., pl.* **-men** (-men′, -mən). a petty officer or warrant officer responsible for the maintenance, use, and repair of underwater weapons and equipment. [1880–85, *Amer.*; TORPEDO + MAN[1]]

torpe′do tube′, a tube through which a self-propelled torpedo is launched, usually by the explosion of a charge of powder. [1895–1900]

Torp·ex (tôr′peks), *n.* (*sometimes l.c.*) a high explosive made of TNT, cyclonite, and aluminum powder and used esp. in torpedoes, mines, and depth bombs. [1945–50; TORP(EDO) + EX(PLOSIVE)]

tor·pid[1] (tôr′pid), *adj.* **1.** inactive or sluggish. **2.** slow; dull; apathetic; lethargic. **3.** dormant, as a hibernating or estivating animal. [1605–15; < L *torpidus* numb, equiv. to *torp(ēre)* to be stiff or numb + *-idus* -ID[4]] —**tor·pid′i·ty, tor′pid·ness,** *n.* —**tor′pid·ly,** *adv.*
—**Syn. 2.** indolent. **3.** See **inactive.** —**Ant. 1.** energetic.

tor·pid[2] (tôr′pid), *n.* an eight-oared, clinker-built boat used for races at Oxford University during the Lenten term. [1830–40; special use of TORPID[1]]

tor·por (tôr′pər), *n.* **1.** sluggish inactivity or inertia. **2.** lethargic indifference; apathy. **3.** a state of suspended physical powers and activities. **4.** dormancy, as of a hibernating animal. [1600–10; < L: numbness, equiv. to *torp(ēre)* to be stiff or numb + *-or* -OR[1]]
—**Syn. 2.** stolidity, listlessness, lethargy. **4.** sleepiness, slumber, drowsiness.

tor·por·if·ic (tôr′pə rif′ik), *adj.* causing torpor. [1760–70; TORPOR + -I- + -FIC]

tor·quate (tôr′kwit, -kwāt), *adj. Zool.* ringed about the neck, as with feathers or a color; collared. [1655–65; < L *torquātus* adorned with a necklace, equiv. to *torqu(ēs)* twisted neck-chain + *-ātus* -ATE[1]]

Tor·quay (tôr kē′), *n.* formerly a borough in SW England: incorporated 1968 with Torbay.

torque (tôrk), *n., v.,* **torqued, torqu·ing.** —*n.* **1.** *Mech.* something that produces or tends to produce torsion or rotation; the moment of a force or system of forces tending to cause rotation. **2.** *Mach.* the measured ability of a rotating element, as of a gear or shaft, to overcome turning resistance. **3.** *Optics.* the rotational effect on plane-polarized light passing through certain liquids or crystals. **4.** Also, **torc.** a collar, necklace, or similar ornament consisting of a twisted narrow band, usually of precious metal, worn esp. by the ancient Gauls and Britons. —*v.t.* **5.** *Mach.* to apply torque to (a nut, bolt, etc.). **6.** to cause to rotate or twist. —*v.i.* **7.** to rotate or twist. [1825–35; < L *torquēre* to twist; (def. 4) < F *torque* < L *torques* TORQUES (*torc* perh. < Ir << L)]

torque′ convert′er, *Mach.* a fluid coupling in which three or more rotors are used, one of which can be checked so that output torque is augmented and output speed diminished. [1925–30]

Tor·que·ma·da (tôr′kə mä′də; *Sp.* tôʀ′ke mä′ᵺä), *n.* **To·más de** (tô mäs′ ᵺe), 1420–98, Spanish inquisitor general.

tor·ques (tôr′kwēz), *n. Zool.* a ringlike band or formation about the neck, as of feathers, hair, or integument of distinctive color or appearance; a collar. [1560–70; < L *torquēs* twisted necklace or collar, equiv. to *torqu(ēre)* to twist (akin to Gk *trépein* to turn) + *-ēs* fem. deverbative n. suffix]

torque′ wrench′, a wrench having a dial or other indicator showing the amount of torque being applied. [1945–50]

torr (tôr), *n.* a unit of pressure, being the pressure necessary to support a column of mercury one millimeter high at 0°C and standard gravity, equal to 1333.2 microbars. [1945–50; named after E. TORRICELLI]

Tor·ral·ba (tô räl′bə; *Sp.* tôʀ räl′vä), *n.* the site of a Lower Paleolithic hunting and butchering station east of Madrid, in the province of Soria, Spain, characterized by butchered elephant remains, stone hand axes, cleavers, and scrapers, and rare pieces of worked wood.

Tor·rance (tôr′əns, tor′-), *n.* a city in SW California, SW of Los Angeles. 131,497.

Tor·re del Gre·co (tôʀ′ʀe del gre′kô), a city in SW Italy, near Naples. 98,939.

tor·re·fy (tôr′ə fī′, tor′-), *v.t.,* **-fied, -fy·ing. 1.** to subject to fire or intense heat; parch, roast, or scorch. **2.** *Pharm.* to dry or parch (drugs) with heat. **3.** to roast, as metallic ores. Also, **torrify.** [1595–1605; < L *torrefacere* to make dry or hot, equiv. to *torre-,* s. of *torrēre* to dry up, parch, scorch + *facere* -FY; see TORRID] —**tor·re·fac·tion** (tôr′ə fak′shən, tor′-), *n.*

Tor·re·mo·li·nos (tôʀ′ʀe mô lē′nôs), *n.* a seaport in S Spain, on the Mediterranean, SW of Málaga: resort. 7980.

Tor·rence (tôr′əns, tor′-), *n.* **(Frederic) Ridge·ly** (rij′lē), 1875–1950, U.S. poet, playwright, and editor.

Tor·rens (tôr′ənz, tor′-), *n.* **Lake,** a salt lake in Australia, in E South Australia. 130 mi. (210 km) long; 2400 sq. mi. (6220 sq. km); 25 ft. (8 m) below sea level.

Tor′rens sys′tem, (in Australia, England, Canada, certain states of the U.S., etc.) a system of registration of land titles in which the titles are settled consequent to establishment and validation by a legal proceeding, designed chiefly to make title insurance unnecessary and to facilitate transfers. [named after Sir Robert *Torrens* (1814–84), British administrator in Australia]

tor·rent (tôr′ənt, tor′-), *n.* **1.** a stream of water flowing with great rapidity and violence. **2.** a rushing, violent, or abundant and unceasing stream of anything: *a torrent of lava.* **3.** a violent downpour of rain. **4.** a violent, tumultuous, or overwhelming flow: *a torrent of abuse.* —*adj.* **5.** torrential. [1595–1605; < L *torrent-* (s. of *torrēns*) seething, lit., burning, prp. of *torrēre* to burn, parch; see TORRID, -ENT]
—**Syn. 4.** outburst, deluge, flood, spate.

tor·ren·tial (tô ren′shəl, tō-, tə-), *adj.* **1.** pertaining to or having the nature of a torrent. **2.** resembling a torrent in rapidity or violence. **3.** falling in torrents: *torrential rains.* **4.** produced by the action of a torrent. **5.** violent, vehement, or impassioned. **6.** overwhelming; extraordinarily copious. [1840–50; TORRENT + -IAL] —**tor·ren′tial·ly,** *adv.*

Tor·re·ón (tôʀ′ʀe ôn′), *n.* a city in N Mexico. 257,000.

Tor·res Bo·det (tôʀ′ʀes bô ᵺet′), **Jai·me** (hī′me), 1902–74, Mexican poet, statesman, and diplomat.

Tor′res Strait′ (tôr′iz, tor′-), a strait between NE Australia and S New Guinea. 80 mi. (130 km) wide.

Tor·rey (tôr′ē, tor′ē), *n.* **John,** 1796–1873, U.S. botanist and chemist.

Tor′rey pine′ (tôr′ē, tor′ē), a rare pine tree, *Pinus torreyana,* having a rounded crown of branches, growing in a limited area on the southern coast of California. [1885–90, *Amer.*; after J. TORREY]

Tor·ri·cel·li (tôr′i chel′ē; *It.* tôʀ′ʀē chel′lē), *n.* **E·van·ge·lis·ta** (e vän′je lē′stä), 1608–47, Italian physicist. —**Tor′ri·cel′li·an,** *adj.*

Tor′ricel′li's law′, *Physics.* the law that states that the speed of flow of a liquid from an orifice is equal to the speed that it would attain if falling freely a distance equal to the height of the free surface of the liquid above the orifice. [after E. TORRICELLI, who discovered the law]

tor·rid (tôr′id, tor′-), *adj.* **1.** subject to parching or burning heat, esp. of the sun, as a geographical area: *the torrid sands of the Sahara.* **2.** oppressively hot, parching, or burning, as climate, weather, or air. **3.** ardent; passionate: *a torrid love story.* [1580–90; < L *torridus* dried up, parched, equiv. to *torr(ēre)* to parch, burn (see TORRENT, THIRST) + *-idus* -ID⁴] —**tor·rid′i·ty, tor′rid·ness,** *n.* —**tor′rid·ly,** *adv.*
—**Syn. 1.** tropical. **2.** scorching, fiery. —**Ant. 1.** arctic. **2.** frigid. **3.** cool.

Tor′rid Zone′, the part of the earth's surface between the tropics of Cancer and Capricorn. See diag. under **zone.**

tor·ri·fy (tôr′ə fī′, tor′-), *v.t.,* **-fied, -fy·ing.** torrefy.

Tor·ri·jos Her·re·ra (tôʀ ʀē′hôs eʀ ʀe′ʀä), **O·mar** (ô mäʀ′), 1929–81, Panamanian military and political leader: chief of state 1972–78.

Tor·ring·ton (tôr′ing tən, tor′-), *n.* a city in NW Connecticut. 30,987.

tor·sade (tôr säd′, -säd′), *n.* **1.** a twisted cord. **2.** any ornamental twist, as of velvet. [1880–85; < F: twisted fringe, equiv. to *tors* twisted (see TORSE) + *-ade* -ADE¹]

torse (tôrs), *n. Heraldry.* a wreath of twisted silks of two alternating tinctures, usually a metal and a color, depicted supporting a crest or coronet, often upon a helmet. See diag. under **coat of arms.** [1565–75; < MF: wreath, n. use of fem. of *tors* twisted < LL *torsus* (ptp.), for L *tortus,* ptp. of *torquēre* to twist]

tor·sel (tôr′səl), *n. Building Trades.* a beam or slab of wood, stone, iron, etc., laid on a masonry wall to receive and distribute the weight from one end of a beam. [alter. of TASSEL]

tor·si (tôr′sē), *n.* a pl. of **torso.**

tor·si·bil·i·ty (tôr′sə bil′i tē), *n.* resistance to torsion. [1860–65; < LL *tors(us)* (see TORSE) + -IBILITY]

tor·sion (tôr′shən), *n.* **1.** the act of twisting. **2.** the state of being twisted. **3.** *Mech.* **a.** the twisting of a body by two equal and opposite torques. **b.** the internal torque so produced. **4.** *Math.* **a.** the degree of departure of a curve from a plane. **b.** a number measuring this. [1375–1425; 1535–45 for def. 1; late ME *torcion* wringing one's bowels < OF *torsion* < LL *torsiōn-* (s. of *torsiō*) torment, equiv. to *tors(us)* twisted (see TORSE) + *-iōn-* -ION] —**tor′sion·al,** *adj.* —**tor′sion·al·ly,** *adv.*

tor′sion bal′ance, an instrument for measuring small forces, as electric attraction or repulsion, by determining the amount of torsion or twisting they cause in a slender wire or filament. [1820–30]

tor′sion bar′, a metal bar having elasticity when subjected to torsion: used as a spring in various machines and in automobile suspensions. [1945–50]

tor′sion-free group′ (tôr′shən frē′), *Math.* a group in which every element other than the identity has infinite order.

tor′sion group′, *Math.* a group in which every element has finite order.

tor′sion mod′ulus, *Physics.* See **shear modulus.**

tor′sion pen′dulum, *Horol.* a pendulum the weight of which is rotated alternately in opposite directions through a horizontal plane by the torsion of the suspending rod or spring: used for clocks intended to run a long time between windings. [1880–85]

torsk (tôrsk), *n., pl.* **torsks,** (*esp. collectively*) **torsk. 1.** a cod. **2.** cusk (def. 1). [1700–10; < Norw; ON *thorskr,* akin to *thurr* dry. See THIRST]

tor·so (tôr′sō), *n., pl.* **-sos, -si** (-sē). **1.** the trunk of the human body. **2.** a sculptured form representing the trunk of a nude female or male figure. **3.** something mutilated or incomplete. [1715–25; < It: stalk, trunk of statue < L *thyrsus* < Gk *thýrsos* wand, stem]

tor′so mur′der, a murder in which the body of the victim is dismembered at the torso.

tort (tôrt), *n. Law.* a wrongful act, not including a breach of contract or trust, that results in injury to another's person, property, reputation, or the like, and for which the injured party is entitled to compensation. [1350–1400; ME: injury, wrong < OF < ML *tortum* wrong, injustice, n. use of neut. of L *tortus* twisted, crooked, dubious, ptp. of *torquēre* to twist, wring]

torte (tôrt; *Ger.* tôʀ′tə), *n., pl.* **tortes** (tôrts), *Ger.* **tor·ten** (tôʀ′tn). a rich cake, esp. one containing little or no flour, usually made with eggs and ground nuts or bread crumbs. [1955–60; < G < It *torta* < LL (Vulgate) *tōrta* (*panis*) round loaf (of bread), prob. fem. of L *tortus* twisted (see TORT), with VL lengthening of *o* (cf. F *tourte*)]

tor·tel·li·ni (tôr′tl ē′nē; *It.* tôʀ′tel lē′nē), *n.pl. Italian Cookery.* small rounds of pasta, filled, as with a meat or cheese stuffing, and then shaped into rings and boiled: often served in broth or with a sauce. [1905–10; < It, pl. of *tortellino,* dim. of *tortello* stuffed pastry, dim. (with gender change) of *torta* cake; see TORTE]

tort·fea·sor (tôrt′fē′zər, -zôr, -fē′-), *n. Law.* a person who commits a tort. Also, **tort′-fea′sor.** [1650–60; < AF *tortfesor* wrongdoer (F *tortfaiseur*). See TORT, FEASANCE, -OR²]

tor·ti·col·lis (tôr′ti kol′is), *n. Pathol.* a condition in which the neck is twisted and the head inclined to one side, caused by spasmodic contraction of the muscles of the neck. Also called **wryneck.** [1805–15; < NL, equiv. to L *tort(us)* twisted (see TORT) + *-i-* -I- + *coll(um)* neck + *-is* n. suffix]

tor·tile (tôr′til), *adj.* twisted; coiled. [1650–60; < L *tortilis,* equiv. to *tort(us)* twisted (see TORT) + *-ilis* -ILE]

tor·til·la (tôr tē′ə; *Sp.* tôʀ tē′yä), *n., pl.* **-til·las** (-tē′əz; *Sp.* -tē′yäs). *Mexican Cookery.* a thin, round, unleavened bread prepared from cornmeal or sometimes wheat flour, baked on a flat plate of iron, earthenware, or the like. [1690–1700; < Sp, equiv. to *tort(a)* cake (see TORTE) + *-illa* dim. suffix < L *-ella*]

Tortil′la Flat′, a novel (1935) by John Steinbeck.

tor·til·lon (tôr′tē on′, -ōn′; *Fr.* tôʀ tē yôɴ′), *n., pl.* **-til·lons** (-tē onz′, -ōnz′; *Fr.* -tē yôɴ′). a stump made of paper twisted to a point, used in drawing. [1890–95; < F: lit., something twisted < *tortill(er)* to twist (see TORT) + *-on* n. suffix]

tor·tious (tôr′shəs), *adj. Law.* of the nature of or pertaining to a tort. [1350–1400; ME *torcious* < AF, equiv. to *torci(on)* TORSION + *-ous* -OUS; meaning influenced by TORT] —**tor′tious·ly,** *adv.*

tor·toise (tôr′təs), *n.* **1.** a turtle, esp. a terrestrial turtle. **2.** a very slow person or thing. **3.** testudo (def. 1). [1350–1400; var. of earlier (15th-century) *tortuse, tortose, tortuce,* ME *tortuca* < ML *tortūca,* for LL *tartarūcha* (fem. adj.) of Tartarus (< Gk *tartaroûcha*), the tortoise being regarded as an infernal animal; ML form influenced by L *tortus* crooked, twisted (see TORT)]

tor′toise bee′tle, any of several turtle-shaped leaf beetles, as *Chelymorpha cassidea* **(argus tortoise beetle** or **milkweed tortoise beetle),** which resembles the ladybird beetle and feeds primarily on bindweed and milkweed. [1705–15]

tor′toise brooch′, a domed, oval brooch worn in pairs by Viking women.

tor·toise-core (tôr′təs kôr′, -kōr′), *n. Archaeol.* a late Lower and Middle Paleolithic stone core characteristic of the Levalloisian tradition of toolmaking, having a rounded top and flattish bottom and prepared in advance to permit the removal of a single ellipsoid flake with one blow from a stone hammer. [1915–20]

tor′toise plant′, elephant's-foot. [1865–70]

tor·toise·shell (tôr′təs shel′), *n.* Also, **tor′toise shell′. 1.** a horny substance of a mottled brown and yellow coloration, composing the laminae that cover the inner body plates of the carapace of a hawksbill turtle, used for making combs and ornamental articles, inlaying, etc. **2.** any synthetic substance made to look like natural tortoise shell. **3.** Also, **tor′toiseshell but′·terfly.** any of several nymphalid butterflies of the genus *Nymphalis,* as *N. californica,* having variegated markings of red, yellow, or orange on the wings. —*adj.* Also, **tor′toise-shell′. 4.** mottled or variegated like tortoiseshell, esp. with yellow and brown and sometimes other colors. **5.** made of tortoiseshell. [1595–1605; TORTOISE + SHELL]

tor′toise·shell cat′. See **calico cat.**

tor′toiseshell tur′tle. See **hawksbill turtle.** [1885–90]

Tor·to·la (tôr tō′lə), *n.* the principal island of the British Virgin Islands, in the NE West Indies. 9730; 21 sq. mi. (54 sq. km).

tor·to·ni (tôr tō′nē), *n.* **1.** ice cream made with eggs and heavy cream, often containing chopped cherries or topped with minced almonds or crumbled macaroons. **2.** See **biscuit tortoni.** [1940–45; said to be after an Italian café owner in Paris in the 18th century]

tor·tri·cid (tôr′trə sid), *n.* **1.** Also called **tor·trix** (tôr′triks). any of numerous moths of the family Tortricidae, comprising the leaf rollers, having broad, squarish, slightly fringed wings. —*adj.* **2.** belonging or pertaining to the family Tortricidae. [< NL *Tortricidae* (1829), equiv. to *Tortric-,* s. of *Tortrix* a genus (L *tor(quēre)* to twist, wind, wrap + *-trix* -TRIX) + *-idae* -ID²]

Tor·tu·ga (tôr to͞o′gə), *n.* an island off the N coast of and belonging to Haiti: formerly a pirate stronghold. 23 mi. (37 km) long; 70 sq. mi. (180 sq. km). French, **La Tortue.**

tor·tu·os·i·ty (tôr′cho͞o os′i tē), *n., pl.* **-ties. 1.** the state of being tortuous; twisted form or course; crookedness. **2.** a twist, bend, or crook. **3.** a twisting or crooked part, passage, or thing. [1595–1605; < LL *tortuōsitās.* See TORTUOUS, -ITY]

tor·tu·ous (tôr′cho͞o əs), *adj.* **1.** full of twists, turns, or bends; twisting, winding, or crooked: *a tortuous path.* **2.** not direct or straightforward, as in procedure or speech; intricate; circuitous: *tortuous negotiations lasting for months.* **3.** deceitfully indirect or morally crooked, as proceedings, methods, or policy; devious. [1350–1400; ME < L *tortuōsus,* equiv. to *tortu(s)* a twisting (*tor(quēre)* to twist, bend + *-tus* suffix of v. action) + *-ōsus* -OUS] —**tor′tu·ous·ly,** *adv.* —**tor′tu·ous·ness,** *n.*
—**Syn. 1.** bent, sinuous, serpentine. **2.** evasive, roundabout, indirect.
—**Usage.** See **torturous.**

tor·ture (tôr′chər), *n., v.,* **-tured, -tur·ing.** —*n.* **1.** the act of inflicting excruciating pain, as punishment or revenge, as a means of getting a confession or information, or for sheer cruelty. **2.** a method of inflicting such pain. **3.** Often, **tortures.** the pain or suffering caused or undergone. **4.** extreme anguish of body or mind; agony. **5.** a cause of severe pain or anguish. —*v.t.* **6.** to subject to torture. **7.** to afflict with severe pain of body or mind: *My back is torturing me.* **8.** to force or extort by torture: *We'll torture the truth from his lips!* **9.** to twist, force, or bring into some unnatural position or form: *trees tortured by storms.* **10.** to distort or pervert (language, meaning, etc.). [1530–40; < LL *tortūra* a twisting, torment, torture. See TORT, -URE] —**tor′tur·a·ble,** *adj.* —**tor′tured·ly,** *adv.* —**tor′tur·er,** *n.* —**tor′ture·some,** *adj.* —**tor′tur·ing·ly,** *adv.*
—**Syn. 6.** See **torment.**

tor·tur·ous (tôr′chər əs), *adj.* pertaining to, involving, or causing torture or suffering. [1490–1500; < AF; OF *tortureus.* See TORTURE, -OUS] —**tor′tur·ous·ly,** *adv.*
—**Usage.** TORTUROUS refers specifically to what involves or causes pain or suffering: *prisoners working in the torturous heat; torturous memories of past injustice.* Some speakers and writers use TORTUROUS for TORTUOUS, especially in the senses "twisting, winding" and "convoluted": *a torturous road; torturous descriptions.* Others, however, keep the two adjectives (and their corresponding adverbs) separate in all senses: *a tortuous* (twisting) *road; tortuous* (convoluted) *descriptions; torturous* (painful) *treatments.*

tor·u·la (tôr′yə lə, -ə lə, tôr′-), *n.* a highly nutritious yeast produced commercially on a sugar recovered from the manufacture of wood products or from processed fruit. Also called **tor′ula yeast′.** [< NL *Torula* (1796) a fungus genus, equiv. to L *tor(us)* TORUS + *-ula* -ULE]

tor·u·lo·sis (tôr′yə lō′sis, tôr′ə-, tor′-), *n. Pathol.* cryptococcosis. [< NL *Torul(a)* (see TORULA) + -OSIS]

CONCISE PRONUNCIATION KEY: *act, cāpe, dâre, pärt; set, ēqual; if, īce; ox, ōver, ôrder, oil, bo͝ok, bo͞ot, out; up, ûrge; child; sing; shoe; thin, that;* zh as in *treasure.* ə = *a* as in *alone, e* as in *system, i* as in *easily, o* as in *gallop, u* as in *circus;* ᵊ as in *fire* (fīᵊr), *hour* (ouᵊr). l and n can serve as syllabic consonants, as in *cradle* (krād′l), and *button* (but′n). See the full key inside the front cover.

To·ruń (tô′ro͝on′yᵊ), *n.* a city in N Poland, on the Vistula. 149,000. German, **Thorn.**

to·rus (tôr′əs, tōr′-), *n., pl.* **to·ri** (tôr′ī, tōr′ī). **1.** *Archit.* a large convex molding, more or less semicircular in profile, commonly forming the lowest molding of the base of a column, directly above the plinth, sometimes occurring as one of a pair separated by a scotia and fillets. See illus. at **molding. 2.** *Geom.* **a.** a doughnut-shaped surface generated by the revolution of a conic, esp. a circle, about an exterior line lying in its plane. **b.** the solid enclosed by such a surface. **3.** *Bot.* **a.** the receptacle of a flower. **b.** a thickening of the wall membrane in the bordered pits occurring in the tracheid cells of the wood of many conifers. **4.** *Anat.* a rounded ridge; a protuberant part. [1555–65; < L: lit., strand, thong, raised ridge]

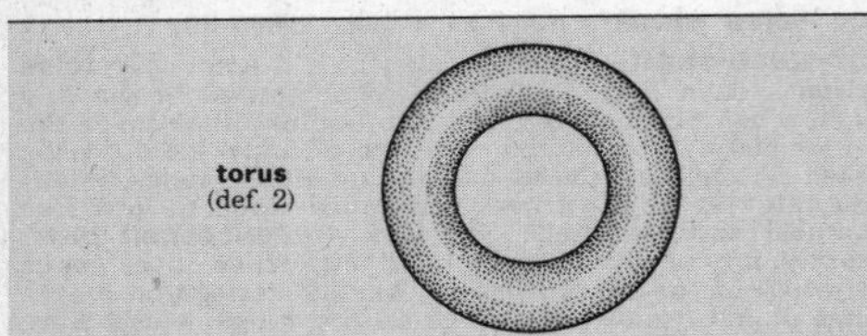
torus (def. 2)

To·ry (tôr′ē, tōr′ē), *n., pl.* **-ries,** for 1–5, *adj.* —*n.* **1.** a member of the Conservative Party in Great Britain or Canada. **2.** a member of a political party in Great Britain from the late 17th century to about 1832 that favored royal authority over Parliament and the preservation of the existing social and political order: succeeded by the Conservative party. **3.** (*often l.c.*) an advocate of conservative principles; one opposed to reform or radicalism. **4.** a person who supported the British cause in the American Revolution; a loyalist. **5.** (in the 17th century) a dispossessed Irishman who resorted to banditry, esp. after the invasion of Oliver Cromwell and suppression of the royalist cause (1649–52). **6.** a male or female given name. —*adj.* **7.** of, belonging to, or characteristic of the Tories. **8.** being a Tory. **9.** (*sometimes l.c.*) opposed to reform or radicalism; conservative. [1640–50; < Ir **tóraighe* outlaw, bandit, deriv. of *tóir* chase, pursuit]

-tory¹, a suffix occurring in loanwords from Latin, orig. adjectival derivatives of agent nouns ending in **-tor** (*predatory*); also forming adjectival derivatives directly from verbs (*obligatory; transitory*). [< L *-tōrius,* equiv. to *-tōr-* -TOR + *-ius* adj. suffix]

-tory², a suffix occurring in loanwords from Latin, usually derivatives from agent nouns ending in **-tor** or directly from verbs, denoting a place or object appropriate for the activity of the verb: *dormitory; repository.* [< L *-tōrium,* n. use of neut. of *-tōrius* -TORY¹]

To·ry·ish (tôr′ē ish, tōr′-), *adj.* of, pertaining to, or resembling a Tory. [1675–85; TORY + -ISH]

To·ry·ism (tôr′ē iz′əm, tōr′-), *n.* **1.** the act or fact of being a Tory. **2.** the principles, beliefs, and practices of Tories. [TORY + -ISM]

Tos·ca (tos′kə; *It.* tôs′kä), *n.* an opera (1900) by Giacomo Puccini.

Tos·ca·na (tôs kä′nä), *n.* Italian name of **Tuscany.**

Tos·ca·ni·ni (tos′kə nē′nē; *It.* tôs′kä nē′nē), *n.* **Ar·tu·ro** (är to͝or′ō; *It.* är to͞o′rô), 1867–1957, Italian orchestra conductor, in the U.S. after 1928.

tosh¹ (tosh), *n. Chiefly Brit. Informal.* nonsense; bosh. [1890–95; perh. b. TRASH + BOSH¹]

tosh² (tosh), *Scot.* —*v.t.* **1.** to make neat or tidy. —*adj.* **2.** neat; tidy. [1770–80; orig. uncert.] —**tosh′ly,** *adv.*

toss (tôs, tos), *v.,* **tossed** or (*Literary*) **tost; toss·ing;** *n.* —*v.t.* **1.** to throw, pitch, or fling, esp. to throw lightly or carelessly: *to toss a piece of paper into the wastebasket.* **2.** to throw or send from one to another, as in play: *to toss a ball.* **3.** to throw or pitch with irregular or careless motions; fling or jerk about: *The ship was tossed by waves.* **4.** to agitate, disturb, or disquiet. **5.** to throw, raise, or jerk upward suddenly: *She tossed her head disdainfully.* **6.** to speak or express in a sudden offhand manner; interject: *He tossed jokes into their serious discussion.* **7.** to throw (a coin) into the air in order to decide something by the side turned up when it falls (sometimes fol. by *up*). **8.** to toss a coin with (someone). **9.** to stir or mix (a salad) lightly until the ingredients are coated with the dressing. —*v.i.* **10.** to pitch, rock, sway, or move irregularly, as a ship on a rough sea or a flag or plumes in the breeze. **11.** to fling or jerk oneself or move restlessly about, esp. on a bed or couch: *to toss in one's sleep.* **12.** to throw something. **13.** to throw a coin into the air in order to decide something by the way it falls (sometimes fol. by *up*). **14.** to go with a fling of the body: *to toss out of a room in a fit of anger.* **15. toss off, a.** to accomplish quickly or easily. **b.** to consume rapidly, esp. to drink something up in one swallow: *He tossed off a cocktail before dinner.* **c.** *Brit. Slang.* to masturbate. **16. toss one's cookies,** *Slang.* See **cookie** (def. 6). **17. toss up,** *Informal.* to vomit. —*n.* **18.** an act or instance of tossing. **19.** a pitching about or up and down. **20.** a throw or pitch. **21.** tossup (def. 1). **22.** the distance to which something is or may be thrown. **23.** a sudden fling or jerk of the body, esp. a quick upward or backward movement of the head. [1595–1605; orig. uncert.] —**toss′er,** *n.* —**toss′ing·ly,** *adv.*
—**Syn. 1.** See **throw.**

tossed′ sal′ad, a salad consisting of one or more greens, tomatoes, etc., tossed with a dressing.

CONCISE ETYMOLOGY KEY: <, descended or borrowed from; >, whence; b., blend of, blended; c., cognate with; cf., compare; deriv., derivative; equiv., equivalent; imit., imitative; obl., oblique; r., replacing; s., stem; sp., spelling, spelled; resp., respelling, respelled; trans., translation; ?, origin unknown; *, unattested; ‡, probably earlier than. See the full key inside the front cover.

toss·pot (tôs′pot′, tos′-), *n.* a tippler; drunkard. [1560–70; TOSS + POT]

toss·up (tôs′up′, tos′-), *n.* **1.** the tossing of a coin to decide something by its fall. **2.** an even choice or chance: *It's a tossup whether they'll come or not.* [1740–50; n. use of v. phrase *toss up*]

tost (tôst, tost), *v. Literary.* a pt. and pp. of **toss.**

tos·ta·da (tō stä′də; *Sp.* tôs tä′thä), *n., pl.* **-das** (-dəz; *Sp.* -thäs). *Mexican Cookery.* a tortilla fried until crisp and usually topped with a variety of ingredients, as shredded meat or chicken, refried beans, lettuce, tomatoes, and cheese. Also **tos·ta·do** (tō stä′dō). [1935–40; < MexSp, n. use of ptp. of Sp *tostar* to TOAST¹]

tot¹ (tot), *n.* **1.** a small child. **2.** *Chiefly Brit.* a small portion of a beverage, esp. a dram of liquor. **3.** a small quantity of anything. [1680–90; perh. short for TOTTERER]

tot² (tot), *v.,* **tot·ted, tot·ting,** *n.* —*v.t., v.i.* **1.** to add; total (often fol. by *up*). —*n.* **2.** a total. **3.** the act of adding. **4.** *Brit. Informal.* a column of numbers to be added. [1745–55; < L: so much, so many]

tot. total.

to·tal (tōt′l), *adj., n., v.,* **-taled, -tal·ing** or (*esp. Brit.*) **-talled, -tal·ling.** —*adj.* **1.** constituting or comprising the whole; entire; whole: *the total expenditure.* **2.** of or pertaining to the whole of something: *the total effect of a play.* **3.** complete in extent or degree; absolute; unqualified; utter: *a total failure.* **4.** involving all aspects, elements, participants, resources, etc.; unqualified; all-out: *total war.* —*n.* **5.** the total amount; sum; aggregate: *a total of $200.* **6.** the whole; an entirety: *the impressive total of Mozart's achievement.* —*v.t.* **7.** to bring to a total; add up. **8.** to reach a total of; amount to. **9.** *Slang.* to wreck or demolish completely: *He totaled his new car in the accident.* —*v.i.* **10.** to amount (often fol. by *to*). [1350–1400; ME (adj.) < ML *tōtālis,* equiv. to L *tōt(us)* entire + *-ālis* -AL¹]
—**Syn. 1.** complete. **5, 6.** gross, totality. **6.** See **whole.**

to′tal bas′es (bā′siz), *Baseball.* the number of bases reached by a batter as a result of base hits.

to′tal communica′tion, (*sometimes caps.*) **1.** the theory or practice of incorporating all means of communication, including speech, speechreading, auditory training, sign language, and writing, in the education of deaf or hearing-impaired children. **2.** simultaneous communication by spoken language and sign language.

to′tal deprav′ity, the Calvinist doctrine that humankind's entire nature, including its reason, is corrupt or sinful as a result of the Fall and that people are therefore completely dependent on God for regeneration. [1785–95]

to′tal eclipse′, an eclipse in which the surface of the eclipsed body is completely obscured. Cf. **annular eclipse.** [1665–75]

to′tal heat′, *Thermodynam.* enthalpy.

to′tal im′pulse, *Rocketry.* a measure of the maximum momentum that a given reaction engine and fuel supply can impart to a vehicle.

to′tal inter′nal reflec′tion, *Optics.* See **total reflection.**

to·tal·ism (tōt′l iz′əm), *n.* totalitarianism. [1940–45; TOTAL + -ISM]

to·tal·is·tic (tōt′l is′tik), *adj.* totalitarian. [1930–35; TOTAL + -ISTIC]

to·tal·i·tar·i·an (tō tal′i târ′ē ən), *adj.* **1.** of or pertaining to a centralized government that does not tolerate parties of differing opinion and that exercises dictatorial control over many aspects of life. **2.** exercising control over the freedom, will, or thought of others; authoritarian; autocratic. —*n.* **3.** an adherent of totalitarianism. [1925–30; TOTALIT(Y) + -ARIAN]

to·tal·i·tar·i·an·ism (tō tal′i târ′ē ə niz′əm), *n.* **1.** the practices and principles of a totalitarian regime. **2.** absolute control by the state or a governing branch of a highly centralized institution. **3.** the character or quality of an autocratic or authoritarian individual, group, or government: *the totalitarianism of the father.* [1920–25; TOTALITARIAN + -ISM] —**to·tal′i·tar′i·an·ist,** *n.*

to·tal·i·tar·i·an·ize (tō tal′i târ′ē ə nīz′), *v.t.,* **-ized, -iz·ing.** to make totalitarian. Also, *esp. Brit.,* **to·tal′i·tar′i·an·ise′.** [1930–35; TOTALITARIAN + -IZE]

to·tal·i·ty (tō tal′i tē), *n., pl.* **-ties. 1.** something that is total or constitutes a total; the total amount; a whole. **2.** the state of being total; entirety. **3.** *Astron.* total obscuration in an eclipse. [1590–1600; TOTAL + -ITY]

to·tal·i·za·tor (tōt′l ə zā′tər), *n.* **1.** an apparatus for registering and indicating the total of operations, measurements, etc. **2.** a pari-mutuel machine. [1875–80; TOTALIZE + -ATOR]

to·tal·ize (tōt′l īz′), *v.t.,* **-ized, -iz·ing.** to make total; combine into a total. Also, *esp. Brit.,* **to′tal·ise′.** [1810–20; TOTAL + -IZE] —**to′tal·i·za′tion,** *n.*

to·tal·iz·er (tōt′l ī′zər), *n.* **1.** a person or thing that totals. **2.** a totalizator. **3.** a machine for adding and subtracting. [1885–90; TOTALIZE + -ER¹]

to·tal·ly (tōt′l ē), *adv.* wholly; entirely; completely. [1500–10; TOTAL + -LY]

to′tally or′dered set′, *Math.* a set in which a relation, as "less than or equal to," holds for all pairs of elements of the set. Also called **chain, linearly ordered set, simply ordered set.** Cf. **partially ordered set, well-ordered set.**

to′tal paren′teral nutri′tion, *Med.* intravenous administration of a solution of essential nutrients to patients unable to ingest food, esp. in cases of severe gastrointestinal or malabsorption disorders or prolonged coma. *Abbr.:* TPN Also called **hyperalimentation.**

to′tal quan′tum num′ber, *Physics.* See **principal quantum number.**

to′tal re′call, the ability to remember with complete, detailed accuracy. [1925–30]

to′tal reflec′tion, *Optics.* the effect that occurs when light meets the interface between the medium in which it is traveling and a medium of smaller refractive index at an angle of incidence greater than the critical angle, all light being reflected back to the first medium. Also called **total internal reflection.**

tote¹ (tōt), *v.,* **tot·ed, tot·ing,** *n.* —*v.t.* **1.** to carry, as on one's back or in one's arms: *to tote a bundle.* **2.** to carry on one's person: *to tote a gun.* **3.** to transport or convey, as on a vehicle or boat. —*n.* **4.** the act or course of toting. **5.** something that is toted. **6.** See **tote bag.** [1670–80, *Amer.*; orig. uncert.] —**tot′a·ble, tote′a·ble,** *adj.* —**tot′er,** *n.*

tote² (tōt), *v.t.,* **tot·ed, tot·ing.** *Informal.* to add up; total. [1885–90; prob. v. use of *tote,* shortening of TOTAL]

tote³ (tōt), *n. Informal.* a totalizator. [1890–95; by shortening]

tote′ bag′, an open handbag or shopping bag used esp. for carrying packages or small items. Also called **tote.** [1895–1900, *Amer.*]

tote′ board′, *Informal.* a totalizator. [1945–50]

tote′ box′, a box for holding and carrying tools, machine parts, etc.

to·tem (tō′təm), *n.* **1.** a natural object or an animate being, as an animal or bird, assumed as the emblem of a clan, family, or group. **2.** an object or natural phenomenon with which a family or sib considers itself closely related. **3.** a representation of such an object serving as the distinctive mark of the clan or group. **4.** anything serving as a distinctive, often venerated, emblem or symbol. [1750–60, *Amer.*; < Ojibwa *ninto·te·m* my totem, *oto·te·man* his totem (prob. orig. my clan-village-mate, deriv. of s. *o·te·* dwell in or as a village; cf. *o·te·na* village)] —**to·tem·ic** (tō tem′ik), *adj.* —**to·tem′i·cal·ly,** *adv.*

to·tem·ism (tō′tə miz′əm), *n.* **1.** the practice of having totems. **2.** the system of tribal division according to totems. [1785–95, *Amer.*; TOTEM + -ISM] —**to′tem·is′·tic,** *adj.*

to·tem·ist (tō′tə mist), *n.* a member of a clan, family, or group distinguished by a totem. [1880–85; TOTEM + -IST]

to·tem·ite (tō′tə mīt′), *n.* totemist. [1900–05; TOTEM + -ITE¹]

to′tem pole′, **1.** a pole or post carved and painted with totemic figures, erected by Indians of the northwest coast of North America, esp. in front of their houses. **2.** a hierarchical system: *the bureaucratic totem pole.* [1875–80]

tote′ road′, an unpaved road for carrying supplies, as to a camp or clearing. [1855–60]

To′ the Light′house, a novel (1927) by Virginia Woolf.

toth·er (tuth′ər), *adj., pron. Older Use.* that other; the other. Also, **t'oth′er.** [1175–1225; ME *the tother* for *thet other,* var. of *that other* the other; see THAT, OTHER]

toti-, a combining form meaning "entire," "entirely," used in the formation of compound words: *totipalmation.* [comb. form repr. L *tōtus*]

to·ti·dem ver·bis (tô′ti dem′ weʀ′bēs; *Eng.* tot′i-dem′ vûr′bis), *Latin.* with just so many words; in these words.

tot·ing (tō′ting), *n. Southern U.S.* **1.** the practice of taking home food from an employer by a person engaged in domestic service. **2.** the food so taken. [1855–60, *Amer.*; TOTE¹ + -ING¹]

to·ti·pal·mate (tō′tə pal′māt, -mit, -päl′-, -pä′māt), *adj. Ornith.* having all four toes fully webbed. [1870–75; TOTI- + PALMATE]

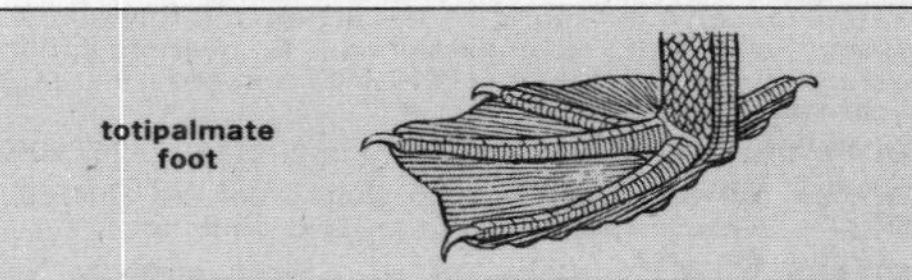
totipalmate foot

to·ti·pal·ma·tion (tō′tə pal mā′shən, -päl-, -pä mā′-), *n.* totipalmate condition or formation. [1880–85; TOTI- + PALMATION]

to·tip·o·tent (tō tip′ə tənt), *adj. Biol.* (of a cell or part) having the potential for developing in various specialized ways in response to external or internal stimuli. [1895–1900; TOTI- + POTENT] —**to·tip′o·ten·cy,** *n.*

to·tis vi·ri·bus (tō′tis wē′ʀi bo͝os′; *Eng.* tō′tis vir′ə-bəs), *Latin.* with all one's might.

Tol·le·ben (tôt′le ben, tot leb′ən; *Russ.* tut lye′byin), *n.* **Franz E·du·ard I·va·no·vich** (fränts′ e do͞o ärt′ ē vä′nə vyich), **Count,** 1818–84, Russian military engineer and general.

to·to cae·lo (tō′tō kī′lō; *Eng.* tō′tō sē′lō), *Latin.* by the entire extent of the heavens; diametrically.

To·to·wa (tō′tə wə), *n.* a borough in N New Jersey. 11,448.

Tot·ten·ham (tot′n əm, tot′nəm), *n.* a former borough, now part of Haringey, in SE England, N of London.

Tot′ten trust′ (tot′n), *Law.* a trust created by opening a savings account in which the depositor is trustee for another, such trust being revocable at any time during the depositor's lifetime.

tot·ter (tot′ər), *v.i.* **1.** to walk or go with faltering steps, as if from extreme weakness. **2.** to sway or rock on the base or ground, as if about to fall: *The tower*

seemed to totter in the wind. The government was tottering. **3.** to shake or tremble: *a load that tottered.* —*n.* **4.** the act of tottering; an unsteady movement or gait. [1150–1200; ME *toteren* to swing < ?] —**tot′ter·er,** *n.*
—**Syn. 1.** See **stagger. 2.** waver. **3.** oscillate, quiver.

tot·ter·ing (tot′ər ing), *adj.* **1.** walking unsteadily or shakily. **2.** lacking security or stability; threatening to collapse; precarious: *a tottering empire.* [TOTTER + -ING²] —**tot′ter·ing·ly,** *adv.*

tot·ter·y (tot′ə rē), *adj.* tottering; shaky. [1745–55; TOTTER + -Y¹]

tou·can (to͞o′kan, -kän, to͞o kän′), *n.* **1.** any of several usually brightly colored, fruit-eating birds of the family Ramphastidae, of tropical America, having a very large bill. **2.** (*cap.*) *Astron.* the constellation Tucana. [1550–60; < F < Pg *tucano* < Tupi *tucan* (imit. of its cry)]

red-billed toucan, *Ramphastos monilis,* length 22 in. (56 cm)

tou·can·et (to͞o′kə net′, to͞o′kə net′), *n.* any of several small South and Central American toucans, esp. of the genus *Aulacorhynchus.* [1815–25; TOUCAN + -ET]

touch (tuch), *v.t.* **1.** to put the hand, finger, etc., on or into contact with (something) to feel it: *He touched the iron cautiously.* **2.** to come into contact with and perceive (something), as the hand or the like does. **3.** to bring (the hand, finger, etc., or something held) into contact with something: *She touched a match to the papers.* **4.** to give a slight tap or pat to with the hand, finger, etc.; strike or hit gently or lightly. **5.** to come into or be in contact with. **6.** *Geom.* (of a line or surface) to be tangent to. **7.** to be adjacent to or border on. **8.** to come up to; reach; attain. **9.** to attain equality with; compare with (usually used with a negative): *a style that cannot touch that of Shakespeare.* **10.** to mark by strokes of the brush, pencil, or the like. **11.** to mark or relieve slightly, as with color: *a gray dress touched with blue.* **12.** to stop at (a place), as a ship: *The ship touched shore several times during the cruise.* **13.** to treat or affect in some way by contact. **14.** to affect as if by contact; tinge; imbue. **15.** to affect with some feeling or emotion, esp. tenderness, pity, gratitude, etc.: *Their sufferings touched his heart.* **16.** to handle, use, or have to do with in any way (usually used with a negative): *She can't touch the money until she's 21.* **17.** to eat or drink; consume; taste (usually used with a negative): *He won't touch another drink.* **18.** to lay hands on, often in a violent manner: *Don't you touch this child!* **19.** to deal with or treat in speech or writing. **20.** to refer or allude to. **21.** to pertain or relate to: *a critic in all matters touching the kitchen.* **22.** to be a matter of importance to; make a difference to; affect: *This grave decision touches all of us.* **23.** *Metall.* to stamp (metal) as being of standard purity. **24.** *Slang.* to apply to for money, or succeed in getting money from: *He touched me for five dollars.* **25.** *Slang.* to steal from. **26.** *Archaic.* **a.** to strike the strings, keys, etc., of (a musical instrument) so as to cause it to sound. **b.** to play or perform (an air, notes, etc.) on a musical instrument.
—*v.i.* **27.** to place the hand, finger, etc., on or in contact with something. **28.** to come into or be in contact. **29.** to make a stop or a short call at a place, as a ship or those on board (usually fol. by *at*). **30. touch base with.** See **base**¹ (def. 29). **31. touch down,** (of an airplane) to come into contact with the ground; land. **32. touch off, a.** to represent or characterize precisely. **b.** to cause to ignite or explode. **c.** to give rise to; initiate: *This incident will touch off another crisis.* **33. touch on** or **upon, a.** to mention a subject briefly or casually: *In his lecture he touched on the major aspects of the controversy.* **b.** to come close to; approach. **c.** to relate or pertain to. **34. touch up, a.** to make minor changes or improvements in the appearance of. **b.** to modify or improve (a painting, photograph, etc.) by adding small strokes or making slight changes. **c.** to rouse by or as if by striking: *This should touch up your memory.*
—*n.* **35.** the act or state of touching; state or fact of being touched. **36.** that sense by which anything material is perceived by means of physical contact. **37.** the quality of something touched that imparts a sensation: *an object with a slimy touch.* **38.** a coming into or being in contact. **39.** mental or moral perception, sensitivity, or understanding: *He has a marvelous touch in dealing with people.* **40.** ability, skill, or dexterity; knack: *to lose one's touch.* **41.** *Fencing.* the contact of the point of a foil or épée or the point or edge of the blade of a saber with a specified portion of the opponent's body, counting one point for the scorer. **42.** close communication, agreement, sympathy, or the like: *to be out of touch with reality; Let's keep in touch.* **43.** a slight stroke or blow. **44.** a slight attack, as of illness or disease: *a touch of rheumatism.* **45.** a slight added action or effort in doing or completing any piece of work: *to provide the finishing touches.* **46.** manner of execution in artistic work. **47.** the act or manner of touching or fingering a keyboard instrument. **48.** the mode of action of the keys of an instrument, as of a piano or typewriter. **49.** *Change Ringing.* a partial series of changes on a peal of bells. **50.** a stroke or dash, as with a brush, pencil, or pen. **51.** a detail in any artistic work. **52.** a slight amount of some quality, attribute, etc.: *a touch of sarcasm in his voice.* **53.** a slight quantity or degree: *a touch of salt.* **54.** a distinguishing characteristic or trait: *the touch of the master.* **55.** quality or kind in general. **56.** an act of testing something. **57.** something that serves as a test; touchstone. **58.** *Slang.* **a.** the act of approaching someone for money as a gift or a loan. **b.** the obtaining of money in this manner. **c.** the money obtained. **d.** a person considered from the standpoint of the relative ease with which he or she will lend money: *I can always hit him for ten—he's an easy touch.* **59.** *Slang.* theft. **60.** *Metall.* **a.** an official mark put upon precious metal after testing to indicate its purity. **b.** a die, stamp, or the like for impressing such a mark. **c.** an identifying mark impressed on pewter by its maker. **61.** *Soccer.* the area outside the touchlines. **62.** *Rugby.* either of the touchlines or the area outside of the touchlines. **63. put the touch on,** *Informal.* to try to borrow money from: *Willie put the touch on me for another ten last night.* [1250–1300; (v.) ME *to(u)chen* < OF *tochier* < VL **toccāre* to knock, strike, touch, of expressive orig.; (n.) partly continuing ME *touche* state or act of touching < OF, deriv. of *tochier,* partly deriv. of the v.] —**touch′a·ble,** *adj.* —**touch′a·ble·ness, touch′a·bil′i·ty,** *n.* —**touch′er,** *n.* —**touch′less,** *adj.*
—**Syn. 1.** handle, feel. **13.** impress. **15.** move, strike, stir, melt, soften. **21.** concern, regard, affect. **43.** pat, tap. **53.** hint, trace, suggestion.

touch′ and go′, 1. a precarious or delicate state of affairs: *It was touch and go there for a while during the operation.* **2.** quick action or movement: *the touch and go of city traffic.* [1645–55]

touch-and-go (tuch′ən gō′), *adj.* **1.** risky; precarious: *a touch-and-go descent down the mountain.* **2.** hasty, sketchy, or desultory. [1805–15]

touch·back (tuch′bak′), *n. Football.* a play in which the ball is downed after having been kicked into the end zone by the opposing team or having been recovered or intercepted there, or in which it has been kicked beyond the end zone. Cf. **safety** (def. 6a). [1885–90; TOUCH + BACK²]

touch·down (tuch′doun′), *n.* **1.** *Football.* an act or instance of scoring six points by being in possession of the ball on or behind the opponent's goal line. **2.** *Rugby.* the act of a player who touches the ball on or to the ground inside his own in-goal. **3.** the act or the moment of landing: *the aircraft's touchdown.* [1860–65; TOUCH + DOWN¹]

tou·ché (to͞o shā′), *interj.* **1.** *Fencing.* (an expression used to indicate a hit or touch.) **2.** (an expression used for acknowledging a telling remark or rejoinder.) [1920–25; < F: lit., touched]

touched (tucht), *adj.* **1.** moved; stirred: *They were very touched by your generosity.* **2.** slightly crazy; unbalanced: *touched in the head.* [1350–1400; ME; see TOUCH, -ED²]

touch′ foot′ball, an informal variety of football in which the touching, usually with both hands, of a ball-carrier by a member of the opposing team results in a down. [1930–35]

touch·hole (tuch′hōl′), *n.* the vent in the breech of an early firearm or cannon through which the charge was ignited. See diag. under **flintlock.** [1495–1505; TOUCH + HOLE]

touch·ing (tuch′ing), *adj.* **1.** affecting; moving; pathetic: *a touching scene of farewell.* **2.** that touches. —*prep.* **3.** in reference or relation to; concerning; about: *He wrote touching future plans.* [1250–1300; TOUCH + -ING²] —**touch′ing·ly,** *adv.* —**touch′ing·ness,** *n.*
—**Syn. 1.** stirring; poignant; piteous. **2.** tangent.

touch-in-goal (tuch′in gōl′), *n. Rugby.* the area at each end of the field outside of a touch-in-goal line.

touch′-in-goal′ line′, *Rugby.* either of the two touchlines at each end of the field between the goal line and the dead-ball line.

touch·line (tuch′līn′), *n. Rugby, Soccer.* any of the outer lines bordering the playing field. [1545–55; TOUCH + LINE¹]

touch·mark (tuch′märk′), *n.* touch (def. 60a, c). [1690–1700; TOUCH + MARK¹]

touch-me-not (tuch′mē not′), *n.* any of several plants belonging to the genus *Impatiens,* of the balsam family, esp. *I. noli-tangere,* bearing pods that, when ripe, burst on being touched, scattering the seeds. Cf. **jewelweed.** [1590–1600]

touch′ pa′per, paper saturated with potassium nitrate to make it burn slowly, used for igniting explosives and fireworks. [1740–50]

touch′ plate′, a pewter plate belonging to a guild of pewterers and bearing samples of the touchmarks of all pewterers belonging to the guild. [1500–10]

touch·screen (tuch′skrēn′), *n. Computers.* a touch-sensitive display screen: touching different portions of the screen with a finger will cause the computer to take actions determined by a program. Also, **touch′ screen′.** [1970–75; TOUCH + SCREEN]

touch·stone (tuch′stōn′), *n.* **1.** a test or criterion for the qualities of a thing. **2.** a black siliceous stone formerly used to test the purity of gold and silver by the color of the streak produced on it by rubbing it with either metal. [1475–85; TOUCH + STONE]
—**Syn. 1.** standard, measure, model, pattern.

touch′ sys′tem, a system of typing in which each finger is assigned to one or more keys, thereby enabling a person to type without looking at the keyboard. Cf. **hunt and peck.** [1915–20]

touch-tack·le (tuch′tak′əl), *n.* See **touch football.**

touch-tone (tuch′tōn′), *adj.* **1.** of or pertaining to a tone-dialing system or a push-button phone operating on tone dialing. —*n.* **2.** (*sometimes cap.*) a tone-dialing system. **3.** a telephone utilizing this system. Also, **touch′-tone′.** [1955–60, *Amer.*]

touch-type (tuch′tīp′), *v.i.,* **-typed, -typ·ing.** to type by means of the touch system. [1940–45, *Amer.*] —**touch′-typ′ist,** *n.*

touch-up (tuch′up′), *n.* an act or instance of touching up: *Her makeup needed a touch-up.* [1880–85; n. use of v. phrase *touch up*]

touch·wood (tuch′wo͝od′), *n.* **1.** wood converted into an easily ignitible substance by the action of certain fungi, and used as tinder; punk. **2.** *Mycol.* amadou. [1570–80; TOUCH + WOOD¹]

touch·y (tuch′ē), *adj.,* **touch·i·er, touch·i·est. 1.** apt to take offense on slight provocation; irritable: *He is very touchy when he's sick.* **2.** requiring caution, tactfulness, or expert handling; precarious; risky: *a touchy subject; a touchy situation.* **3.** sensitive to touch. **4.** easily ignited, as tinder. [1595–1605; var. of TECHY, by assoc. with TOUCH] —**touch′i·ly,** *adv.* —**touch′i·ness,** *n.*
—**Syn. 1.** testy, irascible, edgy, snappish, cranky. See **irritable.**

touch·y-feel·y (tuch′ē fē′lē), *adj. Informal.* emphasizing or marked by emotional openness and enthusiastic physicality: *a touchy-feely encounter group.*

Toug·gourt (to͞o go͝ort′), *n.* a city in NE Algeria. 26,486.

tough (tuf), *adj.,* **-er, -est,** *adv., n., v.* —*adj.* **1.** strong and durable; not easily broken or cut. **2.** not brittle or tender. **3.** difficult to masticate, as food: *a tough steak.* **4.** of viscous consistency, as liquid or semiliquid matter: *tough molasses.* **5.** capable of great endurance; sturdy; hardy: *tough troops.* **6.** not easily influenced, as a person; unyielding; stubborn: *a tough man to work for.* **7.** hardened; incorrigible: *a tough criminal.* **8.** difficult to perform, accomplish, or deal with; hard, trying, or troublesome: *a tough problem.* **9.** hard to bear or endure (often used ironically): *tough luck.* **10.** vigorous; severe; violent: *a tough struggle.* **11.** vicious; rough; rowdyish: *a tough character; a tough neighborhood.* **12.** practical, realistic, and lacking in sentimentality; tough-minded. **13.** *Slang.* remarkably excellent; first-rate; great. **14. hang tough,** *Slang.* See **hang** (def. 50). —*adv.* **15.** in a tough manner. —*n.* **16.** a ruffian; rowdy. —*v.t.* **17. tough it out,** *Informal.* to endure or resist hardship or adversity. [bef. 900; ME (adj.); OE *tōh;* cf. D *taai,* G *zäh(e)*] —**tough′ly,** *adv.* —**tough′ness,** *n.*
—**Syn. 1.** firm, hard. **5.** durable. **6.** inflexible.

tough·en (tuf′ən), *v.t., v.i.* to make or become tough or tougher. [1575–85; TOUGH + -EN¹] —**tough′en·er,** *n.*
—**Syn.** harden, firm, strengthen, stiffen.

tough·ie (tuf′ē), *n. Informal.* **1.** a tough person, esp. one who is belligerent. **2.** a difficult problem or situation: *That math test was a real toughie!* **3.** a harsh or blunt book, movie, etc. Also, **toughy.** [TOUGH + -IE]

tough·ish (tuf′ish), *adj.* somewhat tough. [1770–80; TOUGH + -ISH¹]

tough′ love′, a mixture of toughness and warmth used in a relationship, esp. with an adolescent. [1977; after *Toughlove,* a network of support groups]

tough-mind·ed (tuf′mīn′did), *adj.* **1.** characterized by a practical, unsentimental attitude or point of view. **2.** strong-willed; vigorous; not easily swayed. [1905–10] —**tough′-mind′ed·ly,** *adv.* —**tough′-mind′ed·ness,** *n.*

tough′ pitch′, *Metall.* the state of refined copper when it is soft, malleable, and flexible. [1880–85]

tough·y (tuf′ē), *n., pl.* **tough·ies.** toughie.

tou·jours per·drix (to͞o zho͞or per drē′), *French.* too much of a good thing. [lit., always partridge]

Toul (to͞ol), *n.* a fortress town in NE France, on the Moselle: siege 1870. 16,832.

Tou·lon (to͞o lôN′), *n.* a seaport in SE France: naval base. 185,050.

Tou·louse (to͞o lo͞oz′), *n.* a city in and the capital of Haute-Garonne, in S France, on the Garonne River. 383,176.

Tou·louse-Lau·trec (to͞o lo͞os′lō trek′, -lə-; *Fr.* to͞o lo͞oz lō trek′), *n.* **Hen·ri Ma·rie Ray·mond de** (äN rē′ ma rē′ re môN′ də), 1864–1901, French painter and lithographer.

tou·pee (to͞o pā′), *n.* **1.** a man's wig. **2.** a patch of false hair for covering a bald spot. **3.** (formerly) a curl or an artificial lock of hair on the top of the head, esp. as a crowning feature of a periwig. [1720–30; var. of *toupet* < F, equiv. to OF *to(u)p* tuft (< Gmc; see TOP¹) + *-et* -ET]

tour (to͝or), *n.* **1.** a traveling around from place to place. **2.** a long journey including the visiting of a number of places in sequence, esp. with an organized group led by a guide. **3.** a brief trip through a place, as a building or a site, in order to view or inspect it: *The visiting prime minister was given a tour of the chemical plant.* **4.** a journey from town to town to fulfill engagements, as by a theatrical company or an entertainer: *to go on tour; a European concert tour.* **5.** a period of duty at one place or in one job. —*v.i.* **6.** to travel from place to place. **7.** to travel from town to town fulfilling engagements. —*v.t.* **8.** to travel through (a place). **9.** to send or take (a theatrical company, its production, etc.) from town to town. **10.** to guide (someone) on a tour: *He toured us through the chateaus of the Loire Valley.* [1250–1300; ME (n.) < MF < L *tornus* < Gk *tórnos* tool for making a circle. See TURN]
—**Syn. 2.** trip, expedition. **6, 8.** visit.

tou·ra·co (to͝or′ə kō′), *n., pl.* **-cos.** any of several large, brightly colored birds of the family Musophagidae, of Africa, having a helmetlike crest. Also, **turaco.** [< F *touraco* or D *toerako;* ulterior orig. obscure]

Tou·raine (to͞o ren′; *Fr.* to͞o ren′), *n.* a former province in W France. *Cap.:* Tours.

Tou·rane (to͞o rän′), *n.* former name of **Danang.**

tour·bil·lion (to͝or bil′yən), *n.* **1.** a whirlwind or something resembling a whirlwind. **2.** a firework that rises spirally. **3.** *Horol.* a frame for the escapement of a time-

CONCISE PRONUNCIATION KEY: act, cāpe, dâre, pärt; set, ēqual; if, īce; ox, ōver, ôrder, oil, bo͝ok, bo͞ot, out; up, ûrge; child; sing; shoe; thin, *th*at; zh as in *treasure.* ə = *a* as in *alone, e* as in *system, i* as in *easily, o* as in *gallop, u* as in *circus;* ᵊ as in *fire* (fīᵊr), *hour* (ouᵊr). l and n can serve as syllabic consonants, as in *cradle* (krād′l), and *button* (but′n). See the full key inside the front cover.

piece, esp. a watch, geared to the going train in such a way as to rotate the escapement about once a minute in order to minimize positional error. Cf. **karrusel.** [1470–80; earlier *turbilloun* < MF *to(u)rbillon* < VL **turbiliōnem*, dissimilated var. of **turbiniōnem*, acc. of **turbiniō* whirlwind. See TURBINE, -ION]

Tour·coing (to͝or kwaN′), *n.* a city in N France, near the Belgian border. 102,543.

tour de force (to͝or′ də fôrs′, -fōrs′; *Fr.* to͞or də fôrs′), *pl.* **tours de force** (to͝orz′ də fôrs′, -fōrs′; *Fr.* to͞or də fôrs′). **1.** an exceptional achievement by an artist, author, or the like, that is unlikely to be equaled by that person or anyone else; stroke of genius: *Herman Melville's* Moby Dick *was a tour de force.* **2.** a particularly adroit maneuver or technique in handling a difficult situation: *The way the president got his bill through the Senate was a tour de force.* **3.** a feat requiring unusual strength, skill, or ingenuity. [1795–1805; < F: feat of strength or skill]

Tour-de-France (to͝or′də frans′, -fräns′; *Fr.* to͞or də fräNs′), *n.* a bicycle touring race, held over a period of 21 days: it covers about 2500 mi. (4000 km) in France, Belgium, Italy, Germany, Spain, and Switzerland. [< F: tour of France]

tour d'ho·ri·zon (to͞or dô rē zôN′), *French.* a general survey; overview.

Tou·ré (*Fr.* to͞o rā′), *n.* **Sé·kou** (sā′ko͞o), 1922–84, Guinean political leader: prime minister 1958–72; president 1958–84.

tou·relle (to͝o rel′), *n.* a turret. [1300–50; ME < OF; see TOWER, -ELLE]

tour en l'air (*Fr.* to͞or äN ler′), *pl.* **tours en l'air** (*Fr.* to͞or zäN ler′). *Ballet.* a turn executed in the air. [< F: turn in the air]

Tourette's′ syn′drome (to͝o rets′), *Pathol.* a neurological disorder characterized by recurrent involuntary movements, including multiple neck jerks and sometimes vocal tics, as grunts, barks, or words, esp. obscenities. Also, **Tourette′ syn′drome.** Also called **Tourette's′ disease′.** [after Georges Gilles de la *Tourette* (1857–1904), French neurologist, who described it in 1885]

tour′ing car′, **1.** an open automobile designed for five or more passengers. **2.** a modern two-door coupe. Cf. **GT.** [1900–05]

tour·ism (to͝or′iz əm), *n.* **1.** the activity or practice of touring, esp. for pleasure. **2.** the business or industry of providing information, accommodations, transportation, and other services to tourists. **3.** the promotion of tourist travel, esp. for commercial purposes. [1805–15; TOUR + -ISM]

tour·ist (to͝or′ist), *n.* **1.** a person who is traveling, esp. for pleasure. **2.** See **tourist class.** —*adv.* **3.** in tourist-class accommodations, or by tourist-class conveyance: *to travel tourist.* [1770–80; TOUR + -IST]

tour·is·ta (to͝o rē′stə), *n.* traveler's diarrhea, esp. as experienced by some visitors to Latin America. Also, **turista.** [1955–60; appar. jocular use of Sp *turista* TOURIST]

tour′ist car′, a railroad sleeping car, usually having seats that can be converted into berths. [1890–95, *Amer.*]

tour′ist class′, the least costly class of accommodations on regularly scheduled ships and airplanes. Cf. **third class** (def. 2). [1930–35] —**tour′ist-class′,** *adj., adv.*

tour′ist court′, motel. [1915–20]

tour′ist home′, a private home with rooms for rent, usually for one night, to tourists, travelers, etc.

tour·is·tic (to͝o ris′tik), *adj.* of, pertaining to, or typical of tourists or tourism: *She embarked on her itinerary with high touristic fervor.* Also, **tour·is′ti·cal.** [1840–50; TOURIST + -IC] —**tour·is′ti·cal·ly,** *adv.*

tour·is·try (to͝or′ə strē), *n.* **1.** tourists collectively: *the yearly invasion of American touristry.* **2.** the fact or practice of touring. [1875–80; TOURIST + -RY]

tour′ist trap′, a place, as a restaurant, shop, or hotel, that exploits tourists by overcharging.

tour·ist·y (to͝or′i stē), *adj.* **1.** pertaining to or characteristic of tourists: *a touristy attitude.* **2.** appealing to or frequented by tourists: *a touristy restaurant near the Eiffel Tower.* [1905–10; TOURIST + -Y[1]]

tour je·té (*Fr.* to͞or zhə tā′), *pl.* **tours je·tés** (*Fr.* to͞or zhə tā′). *Ballet.* a movement in which the dancer leaps from one foot, makes a half turn in the air, and lands on the other foot. [< F: lit., flung turn]

tour·ma·line (to͝or′mə lin, -lēn′), *n.* any of a group of silicate minerals of complex composition, containing boron, aluminum, etc., usually black but having various colored, transparent varieties used as gems. Also, **tour·ma·lin** (to͝or′mə lin), **turmaline.** [1750–60; earlier *tourmalin* < G *Turmalin*, ult. < Sinhalese *tōramalliya* carnelian; see -IN[2]] —**tour·ma·lin·ic** (to͝or′mə lin′ik), *adj.*

Tour·nai (to͝or nā′; *Fr.* to͞or ne′), *n.* a city in W Belgium, on the Scheldt River. 33,164. Also, **Tour·nay′.**

tour·na·ment (to͝or′nə mənt, tûr′-), *n.* **1.** a trial of skill in some game, in which competitors play a series of contests: *a chess tournament.* **2.** a meeting for contests in a variety of sports, as between teams of different nations. **3.** *Hist.* **a.** a contest or martial sport in which two opposing parties of mounted and armored combatants fought for a prize, with blunted weapons and in accordance with certain rules. **b.** a meeting at an appointed time and place for the performance of knightly exercises and sports. [1175–1225; ME *tornement* < OF *torneiement*, equiv. to *torne(ier)* to TOURNEY + *-ment* -MENT]

CONCISE ETYMOLOGY KEY: <, descended or borrowed from; >, whence; b., blend of, blended; c., cognate with; cf., compare; deriv., derivative; equiv., equivalent; imit., imitative; obl., oblique; r., replacing; s., stem; sp., spelling, spelled; resp., respelling, respelled; trans., translation; ?, origin unknown; *, unattested; ‡, probably earlier than. See the full key inside the front cover.

tour·ne·dos (to͝or′ni dō′, to͝or′ni dō′; *Fr.* to͞or nə dō′), *n., pl.* **-dos** (-dōz′, -dōz′; *Fr.* -dō′). small slices of fillet of beef, round and thick, served with a variety of sauces and garnished. [1920–25; < F, equiv. to *tourne(r)* to TURN + *dos* (< L *dorsum* back)]

Tour·neur (tûr′nər), *n.* **Cyril,** 1575?–1626, English dramatist.

tour·ney (to͝or′nē, tûr′-), *n., pl.* **-neys,** *v.,* **-neyed, -ney·ing.** —*n.* **1.** a tournament. —*v.i.* **2.** to contend or engage in a tournament. [1300–50; (v.) ME *tourneyen* < OF *torneier* < VL **tornidiāre* to wheel, keep turning; (n.) ME *tourneie* < OF *tornei*, deriv. of *torneier.* See TURN]

tour·ni·quet (tûr′ni kit, to͝or′-), *n.* **1.** *Med., Surg.* any device for arresting bleeding by forcibly compressing a blood vessel, as a bandage tightened by twisting. **2.** a device for pulling the parts of a wooden piece of furniture together, consisting of a pair of twisted cords passed around the parts. [1685–95; < F, deriv. of *tourner* to TURN]

tour·nois (to͝or nwä′; *Fr.* to͞or nwa′), *adj.* (of coins) minted in Tours, France: *livre tournois.* [1400–50; < F, MF *tournois* of Tours < ML *Turōnēnsis*, equiv. to *Turōn(ēs)* TOURS + *-ēnsis* -ENSIS; r. late ME *Tourneys* < AF]

tour′ of du′ty, tour (def. 5). [1865–70]

Tours (to͝or; *Fr.* to͞or), *n.* a city in and the capital of Indre-et-Loire, in W France, on the Loire River: Charles Martel defeated the Saracens near here A.D. 732. 145,441.

tour·tière (to͝or tyâr′), *n.* a Canadian, esp. French Canadian, pastry-covered pie containing minced pork or other chopped meat and various chopped vegetables. Also, **tour·tiere′.** [1950–55; < CanF; F: plate for tarts, equiv. to *tourte* tart (see TORTE) + *-ière*, fem. of *-ier* -IER[2]; see BOUTONNIERE]

touse (touz; *Scot.* to͞oz, to͞os), *v.,* **toused, tous·ing,** *n. Chiefly Brit. Dial.* —*v.t.* **1.** to handle roughly; dishevel. —*v.i.* **2.** to struggle; tussle. —*n.* **3.** a commotion; rumpus. [1250–1300; ME *-t(o)usen*, in *betusen*, *fortusen* to handle roughly (simple verb first recorded in the early 16th century); c. OFris *tūsen* to rend, G *zausen* to tousle]

tou·sle (tou′zəl), *v.,* **-sled, -sling,** *n.* —*v.t.* **1.** to disorder or dishevel: *The wind tousled our hair.* **2.** to handle roughly. —*n.* **3.** a disheveled or rumpled mass, esp. of hair. **4.** a disordered, disheveled, or tangled condition. Also, **touzle.** [1400–50; late ME *touselen* (v.); c. LG *tūseln.* See TOUSE, -LE]

tou·sled (tou′zəld), *adj.* disordered or disheveled: *tousled hair; tousled clothes.* [1840–50; TOUSLE + -ED[2]] —**Syn.** messy, tangled, untidy, rumpled.

tous-les-mois (to͞o′lə mwä′), *n.* a large-grained farinaceous food resembling arrowroot, obtained from a South American canna, *Canna edulis*, and used in baby food. [1830–40; < F: all the months, said to be by folk etym. from Antillean Creole *toloman*, of uncert. orig.]

Tous·saint L'Ou·ver·ture (*Fr.* to͞o saN′ lo͞o ver-tyr′), (*Francis Dominique Toussaint*) 1743–1803, Haitian military and political leader.

tout (tout), *Informal.* —*v.i.* **1.** to solicit business, employment, votes, or the like, importunately. **2.** *Horse Racing.* to act as a tout. —*v.t.* **3.** to solicit support for importunately. **4.** to describe or advertise boastfully; publicize or promote; praise extravagantly: *a highly touted nightclub.* **5.** *Horse Racing.* **a.** to provide information on (a horse) running in a particular race, esp. for a fee. **b.** to spy on (a horse in training) in order to gain information for the purpose of betting. **6.** to watch; spy on. —*n.* **7.** a person who solicits business, employment, support, or the like, importunately. **8.** *Horse Racing.* **a.** a person who gives information on a horse, esp. for a fee. **b.** *Chiefly Brit.* a person who spies on a horse in training for the purpose of betting. **9.** *Brit.* a ticket scalper. [1350–1400; ME *tuten* to look out, peer; prob. akin to OE *tōtian* to peep out]

tout à fait (to͞o ta fe′), *French.* entirely.

tout à vous (to͞o ta vo͞o′), *French.* sincerely yours.

tout com·pren·dre, c'est tout par·don·ner (to͞o kôN präN′drᵊ, se to͞o par dô nā′), *French.* to understand all is to forgive all.

tout de suite (to͞ot swēt′), *French.* at once; immediately.

tout en·sem·ble (to͞o täN säN′blᵊ), *French.* **1.** all together. **2.** the assemblage of parts or details, as in a work of art, considered as forming a whole; the ensemble.

tout·er (tou′tər), *n. Informal.* a tout. [1745–55; TOUT + -ER[1]]

tout le monde (to͞olᵊ môNd′), *French.* the whole world; everyone; everybody.

tou·zle (tou′zəl), *v.t.,* **-zled, -zling,** *n.* tousle.

to·va·rishch (tu vä′ryishch; *Eng.* tō vär′ish), *n. Russian.* comrade (used as a term of address in the Soviet Union). Also, **to·va′rich, to·va′rish, to·va′risch.**

To·vey (tō′vē), *n.* **Sir Donald Francis,** 1875–1940, English music scholar.

tow[1] (tō), *v.t.* **1.** to pull or haul (a car, barge, trailer, etc.) by a rope, chain, or other device: *The car was towed to the service station.* —*n.* **2.** an act or instance of towing. **3.** something being towed. **4.** something, as a boat or truck, that tows. **5.** a rope, chain, metal bar, or other device for towing: *The trailer is secured to the car by a metal tow.* **6.** See **ski tow.** **7.** **in tow, a.** in the state of being towed. **b.** under one's guidance; in one's charge. **c.** as a follower, admirer, or companion: *a professor who always had a graduate student in tow.* **8.** **under tow,** in the condition of being towed; in tow. [bef. 1000; ME *towen* (v.), OE *togian* to pull by force, drag; c. MHG *zogen* to draw, tug, drag. See TUG] —**tow′a·ble,** *adj.* —**tow′a·bil′i·ty,** *n.*
—**Syn.** **1.** trail, draw, tug.

tow[2] (tō), *n.* **1.** the fiber of flax, hemp, or jute prepared for spinning by scutching. **2.** the shorter, less desirable flax fibers separated from line fibers in hackling. **3.** synthetic filaments prior to spinning. —*adj.* **4.** made of tow. [1300–50; ME; OE *tōw-* (in *tōwlic* pertaining to thread, *tōwhūs* spinning house); akin to ON *tō* wool]

tow[3] (tō), *n. Scot.* a rope. [1425–75; late ME (Scots); OE *toh-* (in *tohlīne* towline); c. ON *tog* towline. See TOW[1]]

TOW (tō), *n.* a U.S. Army antitank missile, steered to its target by two thin wires connected to a computerized launcher, which is mounted on a vehicle or helicopter. [*t(ube-launched,) o(ptically-guided,) w(ire-tracked missile)*]

tow·age (tō′ij), *n.* **1.** the act of towing. **2.** the state of being towed. **3.** the price or charge for towing. [1555–65; TOW[1] + -AGE]

to·ward (*prep.* tôrd, tōrd, tə wôrd′, twôrd, twōrd; *adj.* tôrd, tōrd), *prep.* Also, **to·wards′.** **1.** in the direction of: *to walk toward the river.* **2.** with a view to obtaining or having; for: *They're saving money toward a new house.* **3.** in the area or vicinity of; near: *Our cabin is toward the top of the hill.* **4.** turned to; facing: *Her back was toward me.* **5.** shortly before; close to: *toward midnight.* **6.** as a help or contribution to: *to give money toward a person's expenses.* **7.** with respect to; as regards: *his attitude toward women.* —*adj.* **8.** about to come soon; imminent. **9.** going on; in progress; afoot: *There is work toward.* **10.** propitious; favorable. **11.** *Obs.* **a.** promising or apt, as a student. **b.** compliant; docile. [bef. 900; ME; OE *tōweard.* See TO, -WARD] —**to·ward′ness,** *n.*

to·ward·ly (tôrd′lē, tōrd′-), *adj. Archaic.* **1.** apt to learn; promising. **2.** docile; tractable. **3.** propitious; seasonable. [1475–85; TOWARD + -LY] —**to·ward′li·ness,** *n.*

tow·a·way (tō′ə wā′), *n.* **1.** an act or instance of towing away a vehicle that has been illegally parked. **2.** the vehicle towed away. —*adj.* **3.** designated as an area illegal for parking and from which parked cars will be towed away: *a towaway zone.* [1955–60; n., adj. use of v. phrase *tow away*]

tow′ bar′, a metal bar for attaching a vehicle to a load to be towed. Also, **tow′bar′.** [1955–60]

tow·boat (tō′bōt′), *n.* **1.** a diesel-powered or steam-powered boat used esp. on inland waterways to push groups of barges lashed to it in front or on one side or both. **2.** tugboat. [1805–15; TOW[1] + BOAT]

tow′ bug′. See **cigarette beetle.**

tow′ car′, wrecker (def. 3). [1890–95, *Amer.*]

tow·el (tou′əl, toul), *n., v.,* **-eled, -el·ing** or (*esp. Brit.*) **-elled, -el·ling.** —*n.* **1.** an absorbent cloth or paper for wiping and drying something wet, as one for the hands, face, or body after washing or bathing. **2.** **throw in the towel,** *Informal.* to concede defeat; give up; yield: *He vowed he would never throw in the towel.* —*v.t.* **3.** to wipe or dry with a towel. [1250–1300; ME (n.) < OF *toaille* cloth for washing or wiping < WGmc **thwahliō* (> OHG *dwahilla*, akin to *dwahal* bath); c. Goth *thwahl, thwēal* washing]

tow·el·ette (tou′ə let′, tou′let′), *n.* a small paper towel, usually premoistened in a sealed package. [1900–05; TOWEL + -ETTE]

tow·el·ing (tou′ə ling, tou′ling), *n.* a narrow fabric of cotton or linen, in plain, twill, or huck weave, used for hand towels or dishtowels. Also, *esp. Brit.,* **tow′el·ling.** [1575–85; TOWEL + -ING[1]]

tow′el rack′, a rack consisting of one or more bars on which towels or washcloths are hung. [1875–80]

tow·er[1] (tou′ər), *n.* **1.** a building or structure high in proportion to its lateral dimensions, either isolated or forming part of a building. **2.** such a structure used as or intended for a stronghold, fortress, prison, etc. **3.** any of various fully enclosed fireproof housings for vertical communications, as staircases, between the stories of a building. **4.** any structure, contrivance, or object that resembles or suggests a tower. **5.** a tall, movable structure used in ancient and medieval warfare in storming a fortified place. **6.** *Aviation.* See **control tower.** **7.** **tower of strength,** a person who can be relied on for support, aid, or comfort, esp. in times of difficulty. —*v.i.* **8.** to rise or extend far upward, as a tower; reach or stand high: *The skyscraper towers above the city.* **9.** to rise above or surpass others: *She towers above the other students.* **10.** *Falconry.* (of a hawk) to rise straight into the air; to ring up. [bef. 900; (n.) ME *tour*, earlier *tur, tor* < OF < L *turris* < Gk *týrris*, var. of *týrsis* tower; ME *tor* perh. in some cases continuing OE *torr* < L *turris*, as above; (v.) late ME *touren*, deriv. of the n.] —**tow′er·less,** *adj.* —**tow′er·like′,** *adj.*

tow·er[2] (tō′ər), *n.* a person or thing that tows. [1485–95; TOW[1] + -ER[1]]

tow′er block′ (tou′ər), *Chiefly Brit.* a high-rise building. [1965–70]

tow′er bolt′ (tou′ər). See **barrel bolt.** [1920–25]

Tow′er Ham′lets (tou′ər), a borough of Greater London, England. 150,000.

tow·er·ing (tou′ər ing), *adj.* **1.** very high or tall; lofty: *a towering oak.* **2.** surpassing others; very great: *a towering figure in American poetry.* **3.** rising to an extreme degree of violence or intensity: *a towering rage.* **4.** beyond the proper or usual limits; inordinate; excessive: *towering pride; towering ambitions.* [1400–50; late ME; see TOWER[1], -ING[2]] —**tow′er·ing·ly,** *adv.*
—**Syn.** **1.** elevated. See **high.** —**Ant.** **1.** short.

tow·er·man (tou′ər mən), *n., pl.* **-men.** **1.** *Railroads.* a person who works in a switch tower and, by means of a signal box, directs the movement of trains. **2.** *Aviation.* an air-traffic controller. [1890–95, *Amer.*; TOWER[1] + -MAN]

tow·er-mill (tou′ər mil′), *n.* a windmill of which only the cap rotates to face the sails into the wind. [TOWER[1] + MILL[1]]

Tow′er of Ba′bel (tou′ər). See under **Babel** (def. 1).

Tow′er of Lon′don (tou′ər), a historic fortress in

London, England: originally a royal palace, later a prison, now an arsenal and museum.

tow′er of si′lence (tou′ər), a circular stone platform, typically 30 ft. (9.1 m) in height, on which the Parsees of India leave their dead to be devoured by vultures. Also called **dakhma.**

tow′er wag′on (tou′ər), a trailer carrying an extensible ladder for use in firefighting, photography, repairing overhead wires, trimming trees, etc. Cf. **cherry picker** (def. 2). [1910–15]

tow•er•y (tou′ə rē), *adj.* **1.** having towers: *a towery city.* **2.** very tall; lofty: *towery oaks.* [1605–15; TOWER[1] + -Y[1]]

tow•head (tō′hed′), *n.* **1.** a head of very light blond, almost white hair. **2.** a person with such hair. **3.** a sand bar in a river, esp. a sand bar with a stand of cottonwood trees. [1820–30, *Amer.*; TOW[2] + HEAD] —**tow′-head′ed,** *adj.*

tow•hee (tou′hē, tō′hē, tō′ē), *n.* any of several long-tailed North American finches of the genera *Pipilo* and *Chlorura.* [1720–30, *Amer.*; imit.]

tow•ie (tō′ē), *n.* a form of contract bridge for three players in which the players bid for the dummy hand after six of its cards have been turned up. [1930–35; of undetermined orig.]

tow•line (tō′līn′), *n.* a line, hawser, or the like, by which anything is or may be towed. [1710–20; TOW[1] + LINE[1]; cf. OE *tohline* (see TOW[3])]

tow•mond (tō′mənd), *n. Scot.* twelvemonth. Also, **tow•mont** (tō′mənt). [1425–75; late ME (Scots) *towlmonyth* < ON *tōlfmānathr* twelvemonth]

town (toun), *n.* **1.** a thickly populated area, usually smaller than a city and larger than a village, having fixed boundaries and certain local powers of government. **2.** a densely populated area of considerable size, as a city or borough. **3.** (esp. in New England) a municipal corporation with less elaborate organization and powers than a city. **4.** (in most U.S. states except those of New England) a township. **5.** any urban area, as contrasted with its surrounding countryside. **6.** the inhabitants of a town; townspeople; citizenry. **7.** the particular town or city in mind or referred to: *living on the outskirts of town; to be out of town.* **8.** a nearby or neighboring city; the chief town or city in a district: *I am staying at a friend's apartment in town.* **9.** the main business or shopping area in a town or city; downtown. **10.** *Brit.* **a.** a village or hamlet in which a periodic market or fair is held. **b.** any village or hamlet. **11.** *Scot.* **a** farmstead. **12. go to town,** *Informal.* **a.** to be successful. **b.** to do well, efficiently, or speedily: *The engineers really went to town on those plans.* **c.** to lose restraint or inhibition; overindulge. **13. on the town,** *a. Informal.* in quest of entertainment in a city's nightclubs, bars, etc.; out to have a good time: *a bunch of college kids out on the town.* **b.** supported by the public charity of the state or community; on relief. **14. paint the town.** See **paint** (def. 16). —*adj.* **15.** of, pertaining to, characteristic of, or belonging to a town: *town laws; town government; town constable.* [bef. 900; ME *toun, tun,* OE *tūn* walled or fenced place, courtyard, farmstead, village; c. ON *tūn* homefield, G *Zaun* fence, OIr *dún* fort] —**town′less,** *adj.*
—**Syn. 1.** See **community.**

Town (toun), *n.* **Ith•i•el** (ith′ē əl), 1784–1844, U.S. architect.

town′ car′, an automobile having an enclosed rear seat separated by a glass partition from the open driver's seat. [1915–20]

town′ clerk′, a town official who keeps records and issues licenses. [1300–50; ME]

town′ cri′er, (formerly) a person employed by a town to make public announcements or proclamations, usually by shouting in the streets. [1595–1605]

town•er (tou′nər), *n.* a person who lives in a town or city. [TOWN + -ER[1]]

Townes (tounz), *n.* **Charles Hard,** born 1915, U.S. physicist and educator: Nobel prize for physics 1964.

town′ hall′, a hall or building belonging to a town, used for the transaction of the town's business and often also as a place of public assembly. [1475–85]

town•home (toun′hōm′), *n.* See **town house** (def. 3). [1975–80; TOWN + HOME]

town′ house′, **1.** a house in the city, esp. as distinguished from a house in the country owned by the same person. **2.** a luxurious house in a large city, occupied entirely by one family. **3.** one of a row of houses joined by common sidewalls. Also, **town′house′.** [1520–30]

town•ie (tou′nē), *n. Informal.* a resident of a town, esp. a nonstudent resident of a college town. Also, **town′ee, towny.** [1820–30; TOWN + -IE]

town•ish (tou′nish), *adj.* **1.** of or pertaining to qualities or features typical of or befitting a town or city. **2.** (of a person) characterized by the attitudes, opinions, manners, etc., of town or city living. [1375–1425; late ME *townysche.* See TOWN, -ISH[1]] —**town′ish•ly,** *adv.* —**town′ish•ness,** *n.*

town•let (toun′lit), *n.* a small town. [1545–55; TOWN + -LET]

town′ man′ager, an official appointed to direct the administration of a town government. [1920–25]

town′ meet′ing, **1.** a general meeting of the inhabitants of a town. **2.** (esp. in New England) a legislative assembly of the qualified voters of a town. [1630–40]

town′ plan′ning. See **city planning.** [1900–05] —**town′ plan′ner.**

town•scape (toun′skāp′), *n.* **1.** a scene or view, either pictorial or natural, of a town or city. **2.** the planning and building of structures in a town or city, with special concern for aesthetically pleasing results. [1875–80; TOWN + -SCAPE]

Town′send av′alanche (toun′zənd), *Physics.* avalanche (def. 3). [named after J. S. E. *Townsend* (1868–1957), Irish physicist]

Town′send plan′, a pension plan, proposed in the U.S. in 1934 but never passed by Congress, that would have awarded $200 monthly to persons over 60 who were no longer gainfully employed, provided that such allowance was spent in the U.S. within 30 days. [after Francis E. *Townsend* (1867–1960), U.S. reformer, its proposer]

Town′send's sol′itaire, a brownish, slender-billed songbird, *Myadestes townsendi,* of western North America. [1885–90, *Amer.*; named after John Kirk *Townsend* (1809–51), U.S. ornithologist]

towns•folk (tounz′fōk′), *n.pl.* townspeople. [1730–40; TOWN + 's[1] + FOLK]

Town′shend Acts′ (toun′zənd), *Amer. Hist.* acts of the British Parliament in 1767, esp. the act that placed duties on tea, paper, lead, paint, etc., imported into the American colonies. [named after Charles *Townshend* (1725–67), English statesman, their sponsor]

town•ship (toun′ship), *n.* **1.** a unit of local government, usually a subdivision of a county, found in most midwestern and northeastern states of the U.S. and in most Canadian provinces. **2.** (in U.S. surveys of public land) a region or district approximately 6 miles square (93.2 sq. km), containing 36 sections. **3.** *Eng. Hist.* **a.** one of the local divisions or districts of a large parish, each containing a village or small town, usually with a church of its own. **b.** the manor, parish, etc., itself. **c.** its inhabitants. **4.** (in Australia) **a.** a small town or settlement serving as the business center of a rural area. **b.** the business center of a town or suburb. **5.** (in South Africa) a segregated residential settlement for blacks, located outside a city or town. [bef. 900; ME *tounship* community, OE *tūnscipe* village community. See TOWN, -SHIP]

town′ship line′, *Survey.* one of two parallel lines running east and west that define the north and south borders of a township. Cf. **range line, township** (def. 2). [1805–15, *Amer.*]

towns•man (tounz′mən), *n., pl.* **-men. 1.** a native or inhabitant of a town. **2.** a native or inhabitant of one's own or the same town. **3.** (in New England) a selectman. [bef. 1000; ME; OE *tūnesman* fellow member of a township. See TOWN, 's[1], MAN[1]]
—**Usage.** See **-man.**

towns•peo•ple (tounz′pē′pəl), *n.pl.* **1.** the inhabitants or citizenry of a town. **2.** people who were raised in a town or city. Also called **townsfolk.** [1640–50; TOWN + 's[1] + PEOPLE]

Towns•ville (tounz′vil), *n.* a seaport on the E coast of Queensland, in E Australia. 86,112.

towns•wom•an (tounz′wo͝om′ən), *n., pl.* **-wom•en. 1.** a female native or inhabitant of a town. **2.** a female native or inhabitant of one's own or the same town. [1675–85; TOWN + 's[1] + WOMAN]
—**Usage.** See **-woman.**

town talk (toun′ tôk′ *for 1;* toun′ tôk′ *for 2*), **1.** the usual talk, gossip, or rumors, as in a village or town. **2.** the subject of gossip, rumor, or the like: *They've been the town talk ever since their elopement.* [1535–45]

town•wear (toun′wâr′), *n.* tailored, usually conservative clothing appropriate for business or other activities in a town or city. [TOWN + WEAR]

town•y (tou′nē), *n., pl.* **town•ies.** townie.

tow•path (tō′path′, -päth′), *n., pl.* **-paths** (-paṯhz′, -päṯhz′, -paths′, -päths′). a path along the bank of a canal or river, for use in towing boats. [1780–90, *Amer.*; TOW[1] + PATH]

tow•rope (tō′rōp′), *n.* a rope or hawser used in towing boats. [1735–45; TOW[1] + ROPE]

tow•sack (tō′sak′), *n. South Midland and Southern U.S.* gunnysack. [1925–30, *Amer.*; appar. TOW[1] + SACK[1]]
—**Regional Variation.** See **gunnysack.**

tow•ser (tou′zər), *n.* **1.** a big dog. **2.** *Informal.* a big, hearty person, esp. one who is very energetic: *He is a towser for rough outdoor work.* [1670–80; TOUSE + -ER[1]]

Tow•son (tou′sən), *n.* a town in central Maryland, near Baltimore. 51,083.

tow′ truck′, wrecker (def. 3). [1940–45]

tow•y (tō′ē), *adj.* of the nature of or resembling the fiber tow. [1595–1605; TOW[2] + -Y[1]]

tox-, var. of **toxo-** before a vowel: *toxemia.*

tox., toxicology.

tox•al•bu•min (tok′sal byo͞o′mən), *n. Biochem.* any poisonous protein occurring in certain bacterial cultures, plants, or snake venoms. [1885–90; TOX- + ALBUMIN]

tox•a•phene (tok′sə fēn′), *n. Chem.* an amber, waxy, water-insoluble solid, whose principal constituent is chlorinated camphene, used as an insecticide and as a rodenticide. [1945–50; TOX- + (C)A(M)PHENE]

tox•e•mi•a (tok sē′mē ə), *n. Pathol.* **1.** blood poisoning resulting from the presence of toxins, as bacterial toxins, in the blood. **2.** See **toxemia of pregnancy.** Also, **tox•ae′mi•a.** [1855–60; TOX- + -EMIA]

toxe′mia of preg′nancy, *Pathol.* an abnormal condition of pregnancy characterized by hypertension, fluid retention, edema, and the presence of protein in the urine. Cf. **eclampsia, preeclampsia.**

tox•e•mic (tok sē′mik, -sem′ik), *adj. Pathol.* **1.** pertaining to or of the nature of toxemia. **2.** affected with toxemia. Also, **tox•ae′mic.** [1875–80; TOXEM(IA) + -IC]

tox•ic (tok′sik), *adj.* **1.** of, pertaining to, affected with, or caused by a toxin or poison: *a toxic condition.* **2.** acting as or having the effect of a poison; poisonous: *a toxic drug.* —*n.* **3.** a toxic chemical or other substance. [1655–65; < LL *toxicus* poisonous, adj. deriv. of L *toxicum* poison < Gk *toxikón* (orig. short for *toxikòn phármakon* lit., bow poison, i.e., poison used on arrows), equiv. to *tóx(on)* bow + *-ikon,* neut. of *-ikos* -IC] —**tox′i•cal•ly,** *adv.*

tox•i•cant (tok′si kənt), *adj.* **1.** poisonous; toxic. —*n.* **2.** a poison. [1880–85; < ML *toxicant-* (s. of *toxicāns*), prp. of *toxicāre* to poison. See TOXIC, -ANT]

tox•i•ca•tion (tok′si kā′shən), *n.* poisoning. [1815–25; < ML *toxicātiōn-* (s. of *toxicātiō*), equiv. to *toxicāt(us)* (ptp. of *toxicāre* to poison; see TOXIC, -ATE[1]) + *-iōn-* -ION]

tox•ic•i•ty (tok sis′i tē), *n., pl.* **-ties.** the quality, relative degree, or specific degree of being toxic or poisonous: *to determine the toxicity of arsenic.* [1880–85; TOXIC + -ITY]

toxico-, a combining form representing **toxic** in compound words: *toxicology.* Cf. **toxo-.**

tox•i•co•gen•ic (tok′si kō jen′ik), *adj. Pathol.* generating or producing toxic products or poisons. [1895–1900; TOXICO- + -GENIC]

toxicol., toxicology.

tox•i•col•o•gy (tok′si kol′ə jē), *n.* the science dealing with the effects, antidotes, detection, etc., of poisons. [1790–1800; TOXICO- + -LOGY] —**tox•i•co•log•i•cal** (tok′si kə loj′i kəl), **tox′i•co•log′ic,** *adj.* —**tox′i•co•log′i•cal•ly,** *adv.* —**tox′i•col′o•gist,** *n.*

tox•i•co•sis (tok′si kō′sis), *n. Pathol.* an abnormal condition produced by the action of a poison. [1855–60; TOXIC + -OSIS]

tox′ic psycho′sis, a psychosis resulting from the toxic effect of chemicals, drugs, or certain intrinsic metabolic states.

tox′ic shock′ syn′drome, *Pathol.* a rapidly developing, sometimes fatal infection characterized by sudden onset of fever, gastrointestinal upsets, a sunburnlike rash, and a drop in blood pressure: caused by a *Staphylococcus aureus* toxin and occurring esp. in menstruating women using high-absorbency tampons. *Abbr.:* TSS [1975–80]

tox•i•gen•ic (tok′si jen′ik), *adj.* (esp. of microorganisms) producing toxins. [1920–25; TOXI(CO)- + -GENIC]

tox•in (tok′sin), *n.* any poison produced by an organism, characterized by antigenicity in certain animals and high molecular weight, and including the bacterial toxins that are the causative agents of tetanus, diphtheria, etc., and such plant and animal toxins as ricin and snake venom. Cf. **antitoxin, endotoxin, exotoxin, phytotoxin, venom.** [1885–90; TOX(IC) + -IN[2]]
—**Syn.** See **poison.**

tox•in-an•ti•tox•in (tok′sin an′ti tok′sin, -an′tē-, -an′ti tok′sin, -an′tē-), *n. Immunol.* a mixture of toxin and antitoxin, formerly used to induce active immunity against certain diseases, esp. diphtheria. [1900–05]

tox•i•pho•bi•a (tok′sə fō′bē ə), *n. Psychiatry.* an abnormal fear of being poisoned. [1875–80; TOXI(CO)- + -PHOBIA]

toxo-, var. of **toxico-:** *toxoplasmosis.* Also, *esp. before a vowel,* **tox-.**

tox•oid (tok′soid), *n.* a toxin rendered nontoxic by treatment with chemical agents or by physical means and used for administration into the body in order to produce specific immunity by stimulating the production of antibodies. Also called **anatoxin.** [1890–95; TOX(IN) + -OID]

tox•oph•i•lite (tok sof′ə līt′), *n.* a devotee of archery; archer. [1785–95; *Toxophil(us)* bow-lover (coined by Roger Ascham in his 1545 book so entitled < Gk *tóxo(n)* bow + *-philos* -PHILE) + -ITE[1]] —**tox•oph•i•lit•ic** (tok-sof′ə lit′ik), *adj.* —**tox•oph′i•ly,** *n.*

tox•o•plas•ma (tok′sə plaz′mə), *n., pl.* **-ma•ta** (-mə tə), **-mas.** any protist of the genus *Toxoplasma,* esp. *T. gondii,* the causative agent of toxoplasmosis. [< NL *Toxoplasma* (1909); see TOXO-, PLASMA] —**tox′o•plas′mic,** *adj.*

tox•o•plas•mo•sis (tok′sō plaz mō′sis), *n. Pathol.* infection with the parasite *Toxoplasma gondii,* transmitted to humans by consumption of insufficiently cooked meat containing the parasite or by contact with contaminated cats or their feces: the illness produced is usually mild, but in pregnant women may damage the fetus. [1925–30; < NL *Toxoplasm(a)* (see TOXOPLASMA) + -OSIS]

toy (toi), *n.* **1.** an object, often a small representation of something familiar, as an animal or person, for children or others to play with; plaything. **2.** a thing or matter of little or no value or importance; a trifle. **3.** something that serves for or as if for diversion, rather than for serious pratical use. **4.** a small article of little value but prized as a souvenir or for some other special reason; trinket; knickknack; bauble. **5.** something diminutive, esp. in comparison with like objects. **6.** an animal of a breed or variety noted for smallness of size: *The winning terrier at the dog show was a toy.* **7.** a close-fitting cap of linen or wool, with flaps coming down to the shoulders, formerly worn by women in Scotland. **8.** a simple, light piece of music, esp. of 16th or 17th century England, written for the virginal. **9.** *Obs.* **a.** amorous dallying. **b.** a playful or amusing act; diversion; pastime. —*adj.* **10.** made or designed for use as a toy: *a toy gun.* **11.** of or resembling a toy, esp. diminutive in size. —*v.i.* **12.** to amuse oneself; play. **13.** to act idly; or with indifference; trifle: *to toy with one's food.* **14.** to dally amorously; flirt. [1275–1325; ME *toye* dalliance; of obscure orig.] —**toy′er,** *n.* —**toy′less,** *adj.* —**toy′like′,** *adj.*

To•ya•ma (tō′yä mä′), *n.* a city on W Honshu, in central Japan. 305,054.

toy′ dog′, one of any of several breeds of very small dogs, as the Yorkshire terrier, English toy spaniel, Shih Tzu, and Pomeranian. [1800–10]

CONCISE PRONUNCIATION KEY: *act, cāpe, dâre, pärt; set, ēqual; if, ice; ox, ōver, ôrder, oil, bo͝ok, bo͞ot, out; up, ûrge; child; sing; shoe; thin, that;* zh as in *treasure.* ə = *a* as in *alone, e* as in *system, i* as in *easily, o* as in *gallop, u* as in *circus;* ᵊ as in *fire* (fīᵊr), *hour* (ouᵊr). l and n can serve as syllabic consonants, as in *cradle* (krād′l), and *button* (but′n). See the full key inside the front cover.

toy·mak·er (toi′mā′kər), *n.* **1.** a person who makes toys. **2.** a company that manufactures toys. [1955–60; TOY + MAKER]

Toyn·bee (toin′bē), *n.* **Arnold J(oseph),** 1889–1975, English historian.

To·yo·ha·ra (*Japn.* tô′yô hä′RÄ), *n.* former name of **Yuzhno-Sakhalinsk.**

To·yo·ha·shi (tô′yô hä′shē), *n.* a seaport on S Honshu, in central Japan. 304,274.

to·yon (toi′on, -ōn), an evergreen, rosaceous shrub or small tree, *Heteromeles arbutifolia* (or *Photinia arbutifolia*), of California and northern Mexico, having clusters of small, white flowers and bright red berries. Also called **Christmas berry.** [1840–50, *Amer.*; var. of *tollon* < MexSp *tollón*]

To·yo·na·ka (tô′yô nä′kä), *n.* a city on S Honshu, in Japan, N of Osaka. 403,185.

To·yo·ta (tô′yô tä′; *Eng.* tô yō′tə), *n.* a city on S Honshu, in Japan. 281,609.

toy·shop (toi′shop′), *n.* an establishment where toys are sold and sometimes also manufactured. [1790–1800; TOY + SHOP]

tp., **1.** township. **2.** troop.

t.p., **1.** title page. **2.** *Survey.* turning point.

TPA, See **tissue plasminogen activator.**

tpd, tons per day.

tph, tons per hour.

tpi, **1.** teeth per inch. **2.** turns per inch.

tpk., turnpike.

tpm, tons per minute.

TPN, total parenteral nutrition.

TPR, *Med.* temperature, pulse, respiration: used esp. in recording a patient's vital signs on a medical chart.

t quark, *Physics.* See **top quark.**

tr., **1.** tare. **2.** tincture. **3.** trace. **4.** train. **5.** transaction. **6.** transitive. **7.** translated. **8.** translation. **9.** translator. **10.** transpose. **11.** transposition. **12.** treasurer. **13.** *Music.* trill. **14.** troop. **15.** trust. **16.** trustee.

T.R., **1.** in the time of the king. [< L *tempore rēgis*] **2.** See **Roosevelt, Theodore.** **3.** tons registered. **4.** trust receipt.

TRA, Thoroughbred Racing Association.

tra·be·at·ed (trā′bē ā′tid), *adj. Archit.* **1.** constructed with a beam or on the principle of a beam, as an entablature or flat ceiling. **2.** denoting a form of architecture or system of construction employing beams or lintels exclusively. Also, **tra·be·ate** (trā′bē it, -āt′). [1835–45; *trabeat(ion)* structure with beams (< L *trabē(s)* beam + -ATION) + -ED[2]] **—tra′be·a′tion,** *n.*

tra·bec·u·la (trə bek′yə lə), *n., pl.* **-lae** (-lē′). **1.** *Anat., Bot.* a structural part resembling a small beam or crossbar. **2.** *Bot.* one of the projections from the cell wall that extends across the cavity of the ducts of certain plants, or the plate of cells across the cavity of the sporangium of a moss. [1815–25; < NL *trabēcula,* L: little beam, equiv. to *trabē(s)* beam + *-cula* -CULE[1]] **—tra·bec′u·lar, tra·bec·u·late** (trə bek′yə lit, -lāt′), *adj.*

Trab·zon (*Turkish.* tRäb zôn′), *n.* official name of **Trebizond.**

trace[1] (trās), *n., v.,* **traced, trac·ing.** **—***n.* **1.** a surviving mark, sign, or evidence of the former existence, influence, or action of some agent or event; vestige: *traces of an advanced civilization among the ruins.* **2.** a barely discernible indication or evidence of some quantity, quality, characteristic, expression, etc.: *a trace of anger in his tone.* **3.** an extremely small amount of some chemical component: *a trace of copper in its composition.* **4.** **traces,** the series of footprints left by an animal. **5.** the track left by the passage of a person, animal, or object: *the trace of her skates on the ice.* **6.** *Meteorol.* precipitation of less than 0.005 in. (0.127 mm). **7.** a trail or path, esp. through wild or open territory, made by the passage of people, animals, or vehicles. **8.** engram. **9.** a tracing, drawing, or sketch of something. **10.** a lightly drawn line, as the record drawn by a self-registering instrument. **11.** *Math.* **a.** the intersection of two planes, or of a plane and a surface. **b.** the sum of the elements along the principal diagonal of a square matrix. **c.** the geometric locus of an equation. **12.** the visible line or lines produced on the screen of a cathode-ray tube by the deflection of the electron beam. **13.** *Ling.* (in generative grammar) a construct that is phonologically empty but serves to mark the place in the surface structure of a sentence from which a noun phrase has been moved by a transformational operation. **14.** *Obs.* a footprint. **—***v.t.* **15.** to follow the footprints, track, or traces of. **16.** to follow, make out, or determine the course or line of, esp. by going backward from the latest evidence, nearest existence, etc.: *to trace one's ancestry to the Pilgrims.* **17.** to follow (footprints, evidence, the history or course of something, etc.). **18.** to follow the course, development, or history of: *to trace a political movement.* **19.** to ascertain by investigation; find out; discover: *The police were unable to trace his whereabouts.* **20.** to draw (a line, outline, figure, etc.). **21.** to make a plan, diagram, or map of. **22.** to copy (a drawing, plan, etc.) by following the lines of the original on a superimposed transparent sheet. **23.** to mark or ornament with lines, figures, etc. **24.** to make an impression or imprinting of (a design, pattern, etc.). **25.** (of a self-registering instrument) to print in a curved, broken, or wavy-lined manner. **26.** to put down in writing. **—***v.i.* **27.** to go back in history, ancestry, or origin; date back in time: *Her family traces back to Paul Revere.* **28.** to follow a course, trail, etc.; make one's way. **29.** (of a self-registering instrument) to print a record in a curved, broken, or wavy-lined manner. [1250–1300; late ME *tracen,* ME: to make one's way, proceed < MF *tracier* < VL **tractiāre,* deriv. of L *tractus,* ptp. of *trahere* to draw, drag; (n.) ME: orig., way, course, line of footprints < OF, deriv. of *tracier*]

—Syn. **1.** TRACE, VESTIGE agree in denoting marks or signs of something, usually of the past. TRACE, the broader term, denotes any mark or slight indication of something past or present: *a trace of ammonia in water.* VESTIGE is more limited and refers to some slight, though actual, remains of something that no longer exists: *vestiges of one's former wealth.* **2.** hint, suggestion, taste, touch. **5.** spoor, trail, record. **15.** trail. **—Ant.** **3.** abundance, plethora.

trace[2] (trās), *n.* **1.** either of the two straps, ropes, or chains by which a carriage, wagon, or the like is drawn by a harnessed horse or other draft animal. See illus. under **harness.** **2.** a piece in a machine, as a bar, transferring the movement of one part to another part, being hinged to each. **3.** **kick over the traces,** to throw off restraint; become independent or defiant: *He kicked over the traces and ran off to join the navy.* [1300–50; ME *trais* < MF, pl. of *trait* strap for harness, action of drawing < L *tractus* a drawing, dragging; see TRACT[1]]

trace·a·ble (trā′sə bəl), *adj.* **1.** capable of being traced. **2.** attributable or ascribable (usually fol. by *to*): *a victory traceable to good coaching.* [1740–50; TRACE[1] + -ABLE] **—trace′a·bil′i·ty, trace′a·ble·ness,** *n.* **—trace′a·bly,** *adv.*

trace′ el′ement, *Biochem.* any element that is required in minute quantities for physiological functioning. Also called **trace mineral.** [1935–40]

trace′ fos′sil, a fossilized track, trail, burrow, boring, or other structure in sedimentary rock that records the presence or behavior of the organism that made it.

trace·less (trās′lis), *adj.* having or leaving no trace: *a traceless crime.* [1645–55; TRACE[1] + -LESS] **—trace′less·ly,** *adv.*

trac·er (trā′sər), *n.* **1.** a person or thing that traces. **2.** a person whose business or work is the tracing of missing property, parcels, persons, etc. **3.** an inquiry sent from point to point to trace a missing shipment, parcel, or the like, as in a transportation system. **4.** any of various devices for tracing drawings, plans, etc. **5.** Also called **trac′er ammuni′tion.** ammunition containing a chemical substance that causes a projectile to trail smoke or fire so as to make its path visible and indicate a target to other firers, esp. at night. **6.** the chemical substance contained in such ammunition. **7.** a substance, esp. a radioactive one, traced through a biological, chemical, or physical system in order to study the system. [1535–45; TRACE[1] + -ER[1]]

trac′er bul′let, a bullet containing a tracer. [1915–20]

trac·er·ied (trā′sə rēd), *adj.* ornamented or decorated with tracery. [1835–45; TRACERY + -ED[3]]

trac·er·y (trā′sə rē), *n., pl.* **-er·ies.** **1.** ornamental work consisting of ramified ribs, bars, or the like, as in the upper part of a Gothic window; in panels, screens, etc. **2.** any delicate, interlacing work of lines, threads, etc., as in carving or embroidery; network. [1425–75; late ME; see TRACE[1], -ERY]

window tracery

tra·che·a (trā′kē ə *or, esp. Brit.,* trə kē′ə), *n., pl.* **tra·che·ae** (trā′kē ē′ *or, esp. Brit.,* trə kē′ē), **tra·che·as.** **1.** *Anat., Zool.* the tube in humans and other air-breathing vertebrates extending from the larynx to the bronchi, serving as the principal passage for conveying air to and from the lungs; the windpipe. See diag. under **lung.** **2.** (in insects and other arthropods) one of the air-conveying tubes of the respiratory system. **3.** *Bot.* vessel (def. 5). [1350–1400; ME *trache* < ML *trāchēa,* for LL *trāchia* < Gk *trācheîa,* short for *artēría trācheîa* rough artery, i.e., windpipe]

tra·che·al (trā′kē əl *or, esp. Brit.,* trə kē′əl), *adj.* **1.** *Anat., Zool.* pertaining to or connected with the trachea or tracheae. **2.** *Bot.* of the nature of or composed of tracheae or vessels. [1700–10; TRACHE(A) + -AL[1]]

tra·che·ate (trā′kē āt′, -it *or, esp. Brit.,* trə kē′it), *adj.* **1.** (of an arthropod) having tracheae. **—***n.* **2.** a tracheate arthropod. [1875–80; < NL *Tracheata* name of the class, n. use of neut. pl. of *tracheātus* having tracheae. See TRACHEA, -ATE[1]]

tra·che·a·tion (trā′kē ā′shən), *n.* the arrangement of tracheae in insects and other arthropods. [TRACHE(A) + -ATION]

tra·che·id (trā′kē id), *n. Bot.* an elongated, tapering xylem cell having lignified, pitted, intact walls, adapted for conduction and support. Cf. **vessel** (def. 5). [1870–75; TRACHE(A) + -ID[3]] **—tra·che·i·dal** (trə kē′i dl, trā′kē-id′l), *adj.*

tra·che·i·tis (trā′kē ī′tis), *n. Pathol.* inflammation of the trachea. [1835–45; TRACHE(A) + -ITIS]

tra·che·li·um (trə kē′lē əm), *n., pl.* **-li·a** (-lē ə). (in classical architecture) any member between the hypotrachelium and the capital of a column. [< NL < Gk *trá-chēl(os)* neck + L *-ium* -IUM]

tracheo-, a combining form representing **trachea** in compound words: *tracheotomy.*

tra·che·o·bron·chi·al (trā′kē ō brong′kē əl), *adj. Anat.* of, pertaining to, or affecting the trachea and bronchi. [1895–1900; TRACHEO- + BRONCHIAL]

tra·che·ole (trā′kē ōl′), *n. Entomol.* any of the smallest branches of an insect trachea. [1900–05; TRACHE(A) + -OLE[1]]

tra·che·o·phyte (trā′kē ə fīt′), *n.* any plant of the former division Tracheophyta, comprising all the vascular plants. [1935–40; < NL *Tracheophyta* name of the division. See TRACHEO-, -PHYTE]

tra·che·os·co·py (trā′kē os′kə pē), *n. Med.* examination of the interior of the trachea, as with a laryngoscope. [1875–80; TRACHEO- + -SCOPY] **—tra·che·o·scop·ic** (trā′kē ə skop′ik), *adj.* **—tra′che·os′co·pist,** *n.*

tra·che·os·to·my (trā′kē os′tə mē), *n., pl.* **-mies.** *Surg.* **1.** the construction of an artificial opening through the neck into the trachea, usually for the relief of difficulty in breathing. **2.** the opening so constructed. [1920–25; TRACHEO- + -STOMY]

tra·che·ot·o·my (trā′kē ot′ə mē), *n., pl.* **-mies.** *Surg.* the operation of cutting into the trachea. [1720–30; TRACHEO- + -TOMY] **—tra′che·ot′o·mist,** *n.*

Tra·chin·i·ae (trə kin′ē ē′), *n.* a tragedy (c430 B.C.) by Sophocles.

tra·chle (trä′KHəl), *n., v.,* **-chled, -chling.** *Scot.* **—***n.* **1.** an exhausting effort, esp. walking or working. **2.** an exhausted or bedraggled person. **—***v.t.* **3.** to fatigue; tire; wear out. **4.** to bedraggle. Also, **trauchle.** [1540–50; < D dial. *tragelen* to walk laboriously; cf. D *traag* sluggish]

tra·cho·ma (trə kō′mə), *n. Ophthalm.* a chronic, contagious infection of the conjunctiva and cornea, characterized by the formation of granulations and scarring and caused by the bacterium *Chlamydia trachomatis.* [1685–95; < Gk *trāchōma* roughness, equiv. to *trāch(ýs)* rough + *-ōma* -OMA] **—tra·chom·a·tous** (trə kom′ə-təs, -kō′mə-), *adj.*

trachy-, a combining form meaning "rough," used in the formation of compound words: *trachycarpous.* [comb. form repr. Gk *trāchýs*]

tra·chy·ba·salt (trā′kē bə sôlt′, -bas′ôlt, -bā′sôlt, trak′ē-), *n.* a fine-grained volcanic rock containing sanidine and calcic plagioclase. [1885–90; TRACHY- + BASALT]

tra·chy·car·pous (trā′kē kär′pəs, trak′ē-), *adj. Bot.* having rough-skinned fruit. [1855–60; TRACHY- + -CARPOUS]

tra·chy·sper·mous (trā′kē spûr′məs, trak′ē-), *adj. Bot.* having seeds with a rough coat. [1890–95; TRACHY- + -SPERMOUS]

tra·chyte (trā′kīt, trak′īt), *n.* a fine-grained volcanic rock consisting essentially of alkali feldspar and one or more subordinate minerals, as hornblende or mica: the extrusive equivalent of syenite. [1815–25; < F < Gk *trāchýtēs* roughness, equiv. to *trāchý(s)* rough + *-tēs* n. suffix] **—tra·chyt·ic** (trə kit′ik), **trach·y·toid** (trak′i-toid′, trā′ki-), *adj.*

trac·ing (trā′sing), *n.* **1.** the act of a person or thing that traces. **2.** something that is produced by tracing. **3.** a copy of a drawing, map, plan, etc., made by tracing on a transparent sheet placed over the original. **4.** the record made by a self-registering instrument. [1350–1400; ME; see TRACE[1], -ING[1]]

trac′ing pa′per, a thin, transparent paper for making tracings. [1815–25]

trac′ing tape′, (on a building site) one of several lines stretched between batter boards to outline the foundations.

track (trak), *n.* **1.** a structure consisting of a pair of parallel lines of rails with their crossties, on which a railroad train, trolley, or the like runs. **2.** a wheel rut. **3.** evidence, as a mark or a series of marks, that something has passed. **4.** Usually, **tracks.** footprints or other marks left by an animal, person, or vehicle: *a lion's tracks; car tracks.* **5.** a path made or beaten by or as if by the feet of people or animals; trail: *to follow the track of a murderer.* **6.** a line of travel or motion: *the track of a bird.* **7.** a course or route followed. **8.** a course of action, conduct, or procedure: *on the right track to solve the problem.* **9.** a path or course made or laid out for some particular purpose. **10.** a series or sequence of events or ideas. **11.** something associated with making a track, as the wheel span of a vehicle or the tread of a tire. **12.** a caterpillar tread. **13.** *Sports.* **a.** a course laid out for running or racing. **b.** the group of sports performed on such a course, as running or hurdling, as distinguished from field events. **c.** both track and field events as a whole. **14.** *Recording.* **a.** a band of recorded sound laid along the length of a magnetic tape. **b.** band[2] (def. 6). **c.** an individual song or segment of a recording: *a title track.* **d.** a discrete, separate recording that is combined with other parts of a musical recording to produce the final aural version: *a special rhythm track added to the basic track.* **15.** *Auto.* the distance between the centers of the treads of either the front or rear wheels of a vehicle. **16.** *Computers.* a data-recording path on a storage medium, as a magnetic disk, tape, or drum, that is accessible to a read-write head in a given position as the medium moves past. **17.** **tracks,** *Slang.* needle marks on the arm, leg, or body of a drug user caused by habitual injections. **18.** sound track. **19.** a metal strip or rail along which something, as lighting or a curtain, can be mounted or moved. **20.** *Educ.* a study program or level of curriculum to which a student is assigned on the basis of aptitude or need; academic course or path. **21.** **in one's tracks,** *Informal.* in the spot in which one is or is standing at the moment: *He stopped dead in his tracks, listening for the sound to be repeated.* **22.** **keep track,** to be aware; keep informed: *Have you been keeping track of the time?* **23.** **lose track,** to fail to keep informed; neglect to keep a record: *He soon lost track of how much money he had spent.* **24.** **make**

tracks, *Informal.* to go or depart in a hurry: *to make tracks for the store before closing time.* **25. off the track,** departing from the objective or the subject at hand; astray: *He can't tell a story without getting off the track.* **26. on the track of,** in search or pursuit of; close upon: *They are on the track of a solution to the problem.* **27. on the wrong** or **right side of the tracks,** from a poor or wealthy part of a community or of society: *born on the wrong side of the tracks.* —*v.t.* **28.** to follow or pursue the track, traces, or footprints of. **29.** to follow (a track, course, etc.). **30.** to make one's way through; traverse. **31.** to leave footprints on (often fol. by *up* or *on*): *to track the floor with muddy shoes.* **32.** to make a trail of footprints with (dirt, snow, or the like): *The dog tracked mud all over the living room rug.* **33.** to observe or monitor the course or path of (an aircraft, rocket, satellite, star, etc.), as by radar or radio signals. **34.** to observe or follow the course of progress of; keep track of. **35.** to furnish with a track or tracks, as for railroad trains. **36.** *Railroads.* to have (a certain distance) between wheels, runners, rails, etc. —*v.i.* **37.** to follow or pursue a track or trail. **38.** to run in the same track, as the wheels of a vehicle. **39.** to be in alignment, as one gearwheel with another. **40.** to have a specified span between wheels or runners: *The car's wheels track about five feet.* **41.** *Motion Pictures, Television.* dolly (def. 12). **42.** *Recording.* to follow the undulations in the grooves of a phonograph record. **43. track down,** to pursue until caught or captured; follow: *to track down a killer.* [1425–75; late ME *trak* (n.) < MF *trac,* perh. < ON *trathk* trodden spot; cf. Norw *trakke* to trample; akin to TREAD] —**track′a·ble,** *adj.* —**track′a·bil′i·ty,** *n.* —**track′er,** *n.*
—**Syn. 3.** trace, record, spoor. **28.** stalk, hunt.

track·age (trak′ij), *n.* **1.** the whole quantity of track owned by a railroad. **2.** the right of one railroad company to use the tracks of another. **3.** the money paid for this right. [1875–80, *Amer.;* TRACK + -AGE]

track′ and field′, a sport performed indoors or outdoors and made up of several events, as running, pole-vaulting, shot-putting, and broad-jumping.

track-and-field (trak′ən fēld′), *adj.* of, pertaining to, or participating in the sports of running, pole-vaulting, broad-jumping, etc.: *a track-and-field athlete.* [1930–35]

track·ball (trak′bôl′), *n.* a computer input device for controlling the pointer on a display screen by rotating a ball set inside a case. [1975–80]

track′ brake′, a mechanism that slows or stops a vehicle by pressing against the track rather than the wheels. [1900–05]

track′ geom′etry car′, a railroad car equipped with instruments for providing a continuous printed record of the cross level, gauge, alignment, warp, curvature, and bank of a track.

track·ing (trak′ing), *n.* See **track system.**

Track′ing and Da′ta Re′lay Sat′ellite, *U.S. Aerospace.* one of a series of geostationary satellites that relay communications between a space shuttle and mission control. *Abbr.:* TDRS

track′ing shot′, *Motion Pictures, Television.* See **dolly shot.** Also called **trucking shot.** [1940–45]

track′ing sta′tion, a facility equipped with instrumentation for following the flight path of, communicating with, and collecting data from a rocket or spacecraft. [1960–65]

track′ing sys′tem, *Educ.* See **track system.** [1925–30]

track·lay·er (trak′lā′ər), *n.* See **section hand.** [1860–65, *Amer.;* TRACK + LAYER]

track·less (trak′lis), *adj.* **1.** without a track, as a snow-covered meadow. **2.** not making or leaving a track: *The rain rendered the route trackless.* **3.** not on tracks: *a trackless vehicle.* [1650–60; TRACK + -LESS] —**track′less·ly,** *adv.* —**track′less·ness,** *n.*

track′less trol′ley. See **trolley bus.** [1910–15, *Amer.*]

track′ light′ing, lighting for a room or other area in which individual spotlight fixtures are attached along a narrow, wall- or ceiling-mounted metal track through which current is conducted, permitting flexible positioning of the lights. [1970–75] —**track′ light′.**

track·man (trak′mən), *n., pl.* **-men. 1.** a person who assists in inspecting, installing, or maintaining railroad tracks. **2.** a trackwalker. [1870–75, *Amer.;* TRACK + -MAN]
—**Usage.** See **-man.**

track′ meet′, a series of athletic contests such as running and jumping, usually including most track-and-field events. [1900–05, *Amer.*]

track′ rec′ord, a record of achievements or performance: *an executive with a good track record.* [1950–55]

track′ shoe′, 1. a light, heelless, usually leather shoe having either steel spikes for use outdoors on a cinder or dirt track, or a rubber sole for use indoors on a board floor. **2.** the part of a track-brake mechanism that slows or stops a vehicle. [1905–10]

track′ shot′. See **dolly shot.**

track·side (trak′sīd′), *adj.* located next to a railroad track. [1885–90; TRACK + SIDE[1]]

track′ spike′, a chisel-pointed spike used to secure the rails of a railroad track to wooden ties. See illus. under **spike.**

track′ suit′, a sweat suit, usually with a long-sleeved jacket and long pants, worn by athletes, esp. runners, before and after actual competition or during workouts. [1950–55]

track′ sys′tem, *Educ.* a system whereby students are separated into different groups or classes according to test scores or relative scholastic ability, as to assure that gifted students are not inhibited by slower learners. Also, **tracking system.** Also called **tracking, ability grouping.** [1955–60]

track′-train′ dynam′ics (trak′trān′), the interaction between the track and a moving train.

track·walk·er (trak′wô′kər), *n.* a person employed to walk over and inspect a certain section of railroad track at intervals. [1870–75, *Amer.;* TRACK + WALKER]

track·way (trak′wā′), *n.* **1.** railway (def. 3). **2.** a path or roadway; track. [1810–20; TRACK + WAY[1]]

tract[1] (trakt), *n.* **1.** an expanse or area of land, water, etc.; region; stretch. **2.** *Anat.* **a.** a definite region or area of the body, esp. a group, series, or system of related parts or organs: *the digestive tract.* **b.** a bundle of nerve fibers having a common origin and destination. **3.** a stretch or period of time; interval; lapse. **4.** *Rom. Cath. Ch.* an anthem consisting of verses of Scripture, sung after the gradual in the Mass from Septuagesima until the day before Easter and on certain other occasions, taking the place of the alleluias and the verse that ordinarily accompany the gradual. **5.** *Ornith.* a pteryla. [1350–1400; (in senses referring to extent of space) < L *tractus* stretch (of space or time), a drawing out, equiv. to *trac-,* var. s. of *trahere* to draw + *-tus* suffix of v. action; (def. 4) < ML *tractus,* appar. identical with the above, though literal sense unexplained]
—**Syn. 1.** district, territory.

tract[2] (trakt), *n.* a brief treatise or pamphlet for general distribution, usually on a religious or political topic. [1400–50; late ME *tracte,* appar. shortening of ML *tractātus* TRACTATE] —**Syn.** essay, homily, disquisition.

trac·ta·ble (trak′tə bəl), *adj.* **1.** easily managed or controlled; docile; yielding: *a tractable child; a tractable disposition.* **2.** easily worked, shaped, or otherwise handled; malleable. [1495–1505; < L *tractābilis,* equiv. to *tractā(re)* to handle, deal with (freq. of *trahere* to draw) + *-bilis* -BLE] —**trac′ta·bil′i·ty, trac′ta·ble·ness,** *n.* —**trac′ta·bly,** *adv.* —**Syn. 1.** manageable, willing, governable.

Trac·tar·i·an (trak târ′ē ən), *n.* **1.** one of the supporters of Tractarianism; a supporter of the Oxford movement. —*adj.* **2.** of or pertaining to Tractarianism or Tractarians. [1815–25; TRACT[2] + -ARIAN]

Trac·tar·i·an·ism (trak târ′ē ə niz′əm), *n.* the religious opinions and principles of the Oxford movement, esp. in its early phase, given in a series of 90 papers called *Tracts for the Times,* published at Oxford, England, 1833–41. [1830–40; TRACTARIAN + -ISM]

trac·tate (trak′tāt), *n.* a treatise; essay. [1425–75; late ME < ML *tractātus,* L: handling, treatment, equiv. to *tractā(re)* to handle, treat (freq. of *trahere* to draw) + *-tus* suffix of v. action]

tract′ house′, a house forming part of a real-estate development, usually having a plan and appearance common to some or all of the houses in the development.

trac·tile (trak′til, -tīl), *adj.* **1.** capable of being drawn out in length; ductile. **2.** capable of being drawn. [1620–30; < L *tract(us)* (see TRACTION) + -ILE] —**trac·til·i·ty** (trak til′i tē), *n.*

trac·tion (trak′shən), *n.* **1.** the adhesive friction of a body on some surface, as a wheel on a rail or a tire on a road. **2.** the action of drawing a body, vehicle, train, or the like, along a surface, as a road, track, railroad, or waterway. **3.** *Med.* the deliberate and prolonged pulling of a muscle, organ, or the like, as by weights, to correct dislocation, relieve pressure, etc. **4.** transportation by means of railroads. **5.** the act of drawing or pulling. **6.** the state of being drawn. **7.** attracting power or influence; attraction. [1605–15; < ML *tractiōn-* (s. of *tractiō*) act of drawing, equiv. to *tract(us),* ptp. of *trahere* to draw + *-iōn-* -ION] —**trac′tion·al,** *adj.*

trac′tion en′gine, a locomotive operating on surfaces other than tracks and pulling heavy loads, as fallen logs.

trac·tive (trak′tiv), *adj.* having or exerting traction; drawing. [1605–15; < L *tract(us)* (see TRACTION) + -IVE]

trac′tive ef′fort, the force exerted by a locomotive or other powered vehicle on its driving wheels.

trac·tor (trak′tər), *n.* **1.** a powerful motor-driven vehicle with large, heavy treads, used for pulling farm machinery, other vehicles, etc. **2.** Also called **truck tractor.** a short truck with a driver's cab but no body, designed for hauling a trailer or semitrailer. **3.** something used for drawing or pulling. **4.** *Aeron.* **a.** a propeller mounted at the front of an airplane, thus exerting a pull. **b.** Also called **trac′tor air′plane.** an airplane with a propeller so mounted. [1855–60; < L *trac-,* var. s. of *trahere* to draw, pull + *-tor* -TOR]

tractor (def. 1)

tractor (def. 2)

trac′tor feed′, *Computers.* a mechanism for aligning and transporting paper for a printer by means of pins that catch in perforations along the edges of the paper.

trac′tor pull′, a contest in which tractors compete to pull the heaviest load. [1985–90]

trac·tor-trail·er (trak′tər trā′lər), *n.* a combination trucking unit consisting of a tractor hooked up to a full trailer or a semitrailer. Also called **semitrailer, semitruck.** Cf. **rig**[1] (def. 10).

trac·trix (trak′triks), *n., pl.* **trac·tri·ces** (trak trī′sēz, trak′trə sēz′). *Geom.* a curve whose tangents are all of equal length; the involute of a catenary. [< NL, equiv. to L *trac-,* var. s. of *trahere* to pull + *-trix* -TRIX]

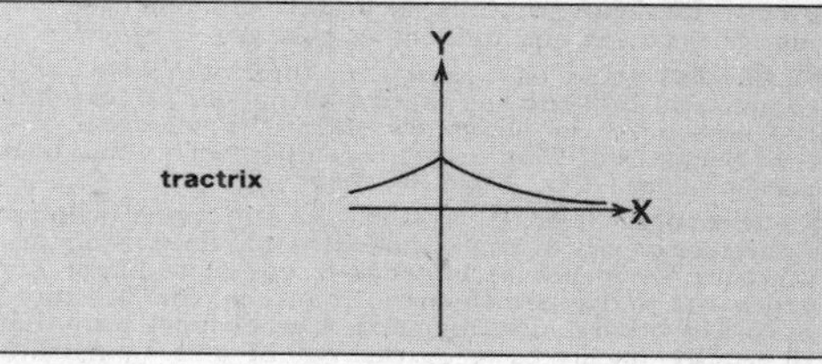

tract′ soci′ety, a society that publishes and distributes religious pamphlets. [1750–60, *Amer.*]

Tra·cy (trā′sē), *n.* **1. Spencer,** 1900–67, U.S. film actor. **2.** a city in central California. 18,428. **3.** a town in S Quebec, in E Canada, on the St. Lawrence. 12,843. **4.** a male or female given name.

trade (trād), *n., v.,* **trad·ed, trad·ing,** *adj.* —*n.* **1.** the act or process of buying, selling, or exchanging commodities, at either wholesale or retail, within a country or between countries: *domestic trade; foreign trade.* **2.** a purchase or sale; business deal or transaction. **3.** an exchange of items, usually without payment of money. **4.** any occupation pursued as a business or livelihood. **5.** some line of skilled manual or mechanical work; craft: *the trade of a carpenter; printer's trade.* **6.** people engaged in a particular line of business: *a lecture of interest only to the trade.* **7.** market: *an increase in the tourist trade.* **8.** a field of business activity: *a magazine for the furniture trade.* **9.** the customers of a business establishment. **10.** *Informal.* See **trade paper. 11. trades.** See **trade wind** (def. 1). —*v.t.* **12.** to buy and sell; barter; traffic in. **13.** to exchange: *to trade seats.* —*v.i.* **14.** to carry on trade. **15.** to traffic (usually fol. by *in*): *a tyrant who trades in human lives.* **16.** to make an exchange. **17.** to make one's purchases; shop; buy. **18. trade down,** to exchange a more valuable or desirable item for a less valuable or desirable one. **19. trade in,** to give (a used article) as payment to be credited toward a purchase: *We trade in our car every three years.* **20. trade off,** to exchange something for or with another. **21. trade on** or **upon,** to turn to one's advantage, esp. selfishly or unfairly; exploit: *to trade on the weaknesses of others.* **22. trade up,** to exchange a less valuable or desirable item for a more valuable or desirable one. —*adj.* **23.** of or pertaining to trade or commerce. **24.** used by, serving, or intended for a particular trade: *trade journal.* **25.** Also, **trades.** of, composed of, or serving the members of a trade: *a trade club.* [1300–50; 1540–50 for def. 4; ME: course, path, track < MLG, MD (OS *trada*), c. OHG *trata;* akin to TREAD] —**trad′a·ble, trade′a·ble,** *adj.* —**trade′less,** *adj.*
—**Syn. 1.** business, barter, dealing. TRADE, COMMERCE, TRAFFIC refer to the exchanging of commodities for other commodities or money. TRADE is the general word: *a brisk trade between the nations.* COMMERCE applies to trade on a large scale and over an extensive area: *international commerce.* TRAFFIC may refer to a particular kind of trade; but it usually suggests the travel, transportation, and activity associated with or incident to trade: *the opium traffic; heavy traffic on the railroads.* **3.** swap. **4.** vocation, métier, employment, living, craft. See **occupation. 12.** TRADE, BARGAIN, BARTER, SELL refer to exchange or transfer of ownership for some kind of material consideration. TRADE conveys the general idea, but often means to exchange articles of more or less even value: *to trade with Argentina.* BARGAIN suggests a somewhat extended period of coming to terms: *to bargain about the price of a horse.* BARTER applies esp. to exchanging goods, wares, labor, etc., with no transfer of money for the transaction: *to barter wheat for machinery.* SELL implies transferring ownership, usually for a sum of money: *to sell a car.*

trade′ accept′ance, a bill of exchange drawn by the seller of goods on the buyer, and accepted by the buyer for payment at a future date. [1915–20]

trade′ associa′tion, an association of people or companies in a particular business or trade, organized to promote their common interests. [1925–30]

trade′ bal′ance. See **balance of trade.** [1925–30]

trade′ bar′rier, any regulation or policy that restricts international trade, esp. tariffs, quotas, etc.

trade′ book′, a book designed for the general public and available through an ordinary book dealer, as distinguished from a limited-edition book, textbook, mass market paperback, etc. [1940–45]

trade′ coun′cil, a central council composed of local trade unions. Also, **trades council.**

trade′ dis′count, a discount, as from the list price of goods, granted by a manufacturer or wholesaler to a retailer. [1900–05]

trade′ dol′lar, a silver coin of the U.S., containing

CONCISE PRONUNCIATION KEY: act, cāpe, dâre, pärt; set, ēqual; if, īce; ox, ōver, ôrder, oil, bo͝ok, bo͞ot, out; up, ûrge; child; sing; shoe; thin, *that;* zh as in *treasure.* ə = *a* as in *alone, e* as in *system, i* as in *easily, o* as in *gallop, u* as in *circus;* ᵊ as in *fire* (fīᵊr), *hour* (ouᵊr). l and n can serve as syllabic consonants, as in *cradle* (krād′l), and *button* (but′n). See the full key inside the front cover.

slightly more silver than the standard dollar, issued from 1873 to 1885 for trade with the Orient. [1870–75, *Amer.*]

trade′ edi′tion, an edition of a book for distribution through general bookstores. [1840–50]

trade′ guild′, a medieval guild composed of tradesmen. [1870–75]

trade-in (trād′in′), *n.* **1.** goods given in whole or, usually, part payment of a purchase: *We used our old car as a trade-in for the new one.* **2.** a business transaction involving a trade-in. *—adj.* **3.** of or pertaining to the valuation of goods used in a trade-in: *trade-in price.* **4.** of or pertaining to such a business transaction: *trade-in terms.* [1920–25; n., adj. use of v. phrase *trade in*]

trade′ lan′guage, a lingua franca, esp. one used primarily for trade and conducting business. [1955–65]

trade-last (trād′last′, -läst′), *n. Informal Older Use.* a compliment that one has heard and that one offers to tell the person so complimented under the condition that that person will first report a compliment made about oneself. *Abbr.:* T.L. [1890–95, *Amer.*]

trade•mark (trād′märk′), *n.* **1.** any name, symbol, figure, letter, word, or mark adopted and used by a manufacturer or merchant in order to designate his or her goods and to distinguish them from those manufactured or sold by others. A trademark is a proprietary term that is usually registered with the Patent and Trademark Office to assure its exclusive use by its owner. **2.** a distinctive mark or feature particularly characteristic of or identified with a person or thing. *—v.t.* **3.** to stamp or otherwise place a trademark designation upon. **4.** to register the trademark of. [1565–75; TRADE + MARK[1]]

trade′ name′, **1.** the name used by a manufacturer, merchant, service company, farming business, etc., to identify itself individually as a business. **2.** a word or phrase used in a trade to designate a business, service, or a particular class of goods, but that is not technically a trademark, either because it is not susceptible of exclusive appropriation as a trademark or because it is not affixed to goods sold in the market. **3.** the name by which an article or substance is known to the trade. [1860–65]

trade-name (trād′nām′), *v.t.,* **-named, -nam•ing.** to designate with or register under a trade name. [1860–65]

trade-off (trād′ôf′, -of′), *n.* the exchange of one thing for another of more or less equal value, esp. to effect a compromise. Also, **trade′off′.** [1960–65; n. use of v. phrase *trade off*]

trade′ pa′per, a newspaper publishing news of a specific profession or business.

trade′ pa′perback, a softbound book that is usually larger and more expensive than a mass market paperback and is sold primarily in bookstores as a trade book. Also called **quality paperback.**

trad•er (trā′dər), *n.* **1.** a person who trades; a merchant or businessperson. **2.** a ship used in trade, esp. foreign trade. **3.** a member of a stock exchange trading privately and not on behalf of customers. [1575–85; TRADE + -ER[1]] **—trad′er•ship′,** *n.*

trade′ rat′. See **pack rat** (def. 1). [1910–15]

trade′ route′, any route usually taken by merchant ships, caravans, etc. [1875–80]

trade′ school′, a high school giving instruction chiefly in the skilled trades. [1885–90]

trades′ coun′cil. See **trade council.**

trade′ se′cret, a secret process, technique, method, etc., used to advantage in a trade, business, profession, etc. [1900–05]

trade′ show′, show (def. 24). [1925–30]

trades•man (trādz′mən), *n., pl.* **-men. 1.** a person engaged in trade. **2.** a worker skilled in a particular craft; artisan; craftsman. **3.** *Chiefly Brit.* a shopkeeper. [1590–1600; TRADE + 's[1] + -MAN]
—Usage. See **-man.**

trades•peo•ple (trādz′pē′pəl), *n.pl.* **1.** those persons who are engaged in trade; tradesmen. **2.** *Chiefly Brit.* **a.** tradesmen. **b.** shopkeepers collectively. Also, **trades•folk** (trādz′fōk′). [1720–30; TRADE + 's[1] + PEOPLE]

trades•wom•an (trādz′wŏŏm′ən), *n., pl.* **-wom•en.** a woman engaged in trade. [1700–10; TRADE + 's[1] + -WOMAN]
—Usage. See **-woman.**

trade′ un′ion, **1.** a labor union of craftspeople or workers in related crafts, as distinguished from general workers or a union including all workers in an industry. **2.** See **labor union.** [1825–35] **—trade′-un′ion,** *adj.*

trade′ un′ionism, **1.** the system, methods, or practice of trade or labor unions. **2.** trade unions collectively. Also, **trade′-un′ion•ism, trades′-un′ion•ism.** [1870–75]

trade′ un′ionist, **1.** a member of a trade union. **2.** a person who favors or advocates trade unionism. Also, **trade′-un′ion•ist, trades′-un′ion•ist.** [1830–40]

trade′ wind′ (wind), **1.** Also **trade′ winds′.** Also called **trades.** any of the nearly constant easterly winds that dominate most of the tropics and subtropics throughout the world, blowing mainly from the northeast in the Northern Hemisphere, and from the southeast in the Southern Hemisphere. **2.** any wind that blows in one regular course, or continually in the same direction. [1625–35]

trad′ing card′, one of a set of small cards, as one depicting professional athletes, either sold separately or included as a premium with packages of bubblegum or the like, collected and traded, esp. by children.

CONCISE ETYMOLOGY KEY: <, descended or borrowed from; >, whence; b., blend of, blended; c., cognate with; cf., compare; deriv., derivative; equiv., equivalent; imit., imitative; obl., oblique; r., replacing; s., stem; sp., spelling, spelled; resp., respelling, respelled; trans., translation; ?, origin unknown; *, unattested; ‡, probably earlier than. See the full key inside the front cover.

trad′ing post′, **1.** a store established in an unsettled or thinly settled region by a trader or trading company to obtain furs and local products in exchange for supplies, clothing, other goods, or for cash. **2.** post[2] (def. 5). [1790–1800, *Amer.*]

trad′ing stamp′, a stamp with a certain value given as a premium by a retailer to a customer, specified quantities of these stamps being exchangeable for various articles. [1895–1900, *Amer.*]

tra•di•tion (trə dish′ən), *n.* **1.** the handing down of statements, beliefs, legends, customs, information, etc., from generation to generation, esp. by word of mouth or by practice: *a story that has come down to us by popular tradition.* **2.** something that is handed down: *the traditions of the Eskimos.* **3.** a long-established or inherited way of thinking or acting: *The rebellious students wanted to break with tradition.* **4.** a continuing pattern of culture beliefs or practices. **5.** a customary or characteristic method or manner: *The winner took a victory lap in the usual track tradition.* **6.** *Theol.* **a.** (among Jews) body of laws and doctrines, or any one of them, held to have been received from Moses and originally handed down orally from generation to generation. **b.** (among Christians) a body of teachings, or any one of them, held to have been delivered by Christ and His apostles but not originally committed to writing. **c.** (among Muslims) a hadith. **7.** *Law.* an act of handing over something to another, esp. in a formal legal manner; delivery; transfer. [1350–1400; ME *tradicion* < OF < L *trāditiōn-* (s. of *trāditiō*) a handing over or down, transfer, equiv. to *trādit(us),* ptp. of *trādere* to give over, impart, surrender, betray (*trā-,* var. of *trāns-* TRANS- + *-ditus,* comb. form of *datus* given; see DATE[1]) + *-iōn-* -ION] **—tra•di′tion•less,** *adj.*
—Syn. 2. custom, practice, habit, convention, usage.

tra•di•tion•al (trə dish′ə nl), *adj.* **1.** of or pertaining to tradition. **2.** handed down by tradition. **3.** in accordance with tradition. **4.** of, pertaining to, or characteristic of the older styles of jazz, esp. New Orleans style, Chicago style, Kansas City style, and Dixieland. Cf. **mainstream** (def. 4). Also, **tra•di•tion•ar•y** (trə dish′ə ner′ē) (for defs. 1–3). [1585–95; < ML *trāditiōnālis.* See TRADITION, -AL[1]] **—tra•di′tion•al′i•ty,** *n.* **—tra•di′tion•al•ly,** *adv.*
—Syn. 1, 2. conventional, customary, established.

tra•di•tion•al•ism (trə dish′ə nl iz′əm), *n.* **1.** adherence to tradition as authority, esp. in matters of religion. **2.** a system of philosophy according to which all knowledge of religious truth is derived from divine revelation and received by traditional instruction. [1855–60; TRADITIONAL + -ISM] **—tra•di′tion•al•ist,** *n., adj.* **—tra•di′•tion•al•is′tic,** *adj.*

tra•di•tion•al•ize (trə dish′ə nl īz′), *v.t.,* **-ized, -iz•ing.** to make traditional: *to traditionalize family reunions.* Also, *esp. Brit.,* **tra•di′tion•al•ise′.** [1880–85; TRADITIONAL + -IZE]

tradi′tional log′ic, formal logic based on syllogistic formulas, esp. as developed by Aristotle.

tra•di•tion•ist (trə dish′ə nist), *n.* **1.** a traditionalist. **2.** a person who records, transmits, or is versed in traditions. [1660–70; TRADITION + -IST]

trad•i•tive (trad′i tiv), *adj.* traditional. [1605–15; TRADIT(ION) + -IVE]

trad•i•tor (trad′i tər), *n., pl.* **trad•i•to•res** (trad′i tôr′ēz, -tōr′-). an early Christian who betrayed other Christians at the time of the Roman persecutions. [1325–75; ME < L *trāditor* traitor, equiv. to *trādi-,* var. s. of *trādere* (see TRADITION) + *-tor* -TOR]

tra•duce (trə dōōs′, -dyōōs′), *v.t.,* **-duced, -duc•ing.** to speak maliciously and falsely of; slander; defame: *to traduce someone's character.* [1525–35; < L *trādūcere,* var. of *trānsdūcere* to transfer, display, expose, equiv. to *trāns-* TRANS- + *dūcere* to lead] **—tra•duce′ment,** *n.* **—tra•duc′er,** *n.* **—tra•duc′ing•ly,** *adv.*
—Syn. vilify, decry, disparage. **—Ant.** praise.

tra•du•cian•ism (trə dōō′shə niz′əm, -dyōō′-), *n. Theol.* the doctrine that the human soul is propagated along with the body. Cf. **creationism** (def. 3). [1840–50; < LL *trādūciānus* transmitter (*trāduci-,* s. of *trādux* lineage (L: vine led across for propagation, deriv. of *trādūcere* to lead across; see TRADUCE) + *-ānus* -AN) + -ISM] **—tra•du′cian•ist, tra•du′cian,** *n., adj.* **—tra•du′cian•is′tic,** *adj.*

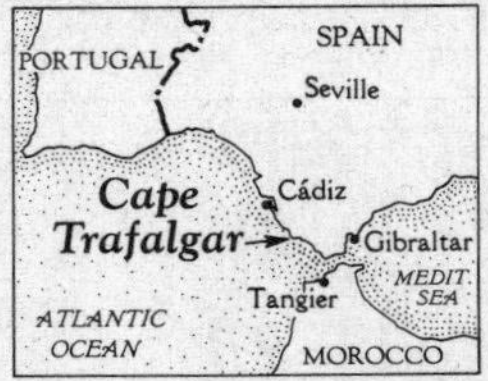

Tra•fal•gar (trə fal′gər; *Sp.* trä′fäl gär′), *n.* **Cape,** a cape on the SW coast of Spain, W of Gibraltar: British naval victory over the French and Spanish fleets 1805.

traf•fic (traf′ik), *n., v.,* **-ficked, -fick•ing.** *—n.* **1.** the movement of vehicles, ships, persons, etc., in an area, along a street, through an air lane, over a water route, etc.: *the heavy traffic on Main Street.* **2.** the vehicles, persons, etc., moving in an area, along a street, etc. **3.** the transportation of goods for the purpose of trade, by sea, land, or air: *ships of traffic.* **4.** trade; buying and selling; commercial dealings. **5.** trade between different countries or places; commerce. **6.** the business done by a railroad or other carrier in the transportation of freight or passengers. **7.** the aggregate of freight, passengers, telephone or telegraph messages, etc., handled, esp. in a given period. **8.** communication, dealings, or contact between persons or groups: *traffic between the Democrats and the Republicans.* **9.** mutual exchange or communication: *traffic in ideas.* **10.** trade in some specific commodity or service, often of an illegal nature: *the vast traffic in narcotics.* *—v.i.* **11.** to carry on traffic, trade, or commercial dealings. **12.** to trade or deal in a specific commodity or service, often of an illegal nature (usually fol. by *in*): *to traffic in opium.* [1495–1505; earlier *traffyk* < MF *trafique* (n.), *trafiquer* (v.) < It *traffico* (n.), *trafficare* (v.), of disputed orig.] **—traf′fick•er,** *n.* **—traf′fic•less,** *adj.*
—Syn. 4. See **trade.**

traf•fic•a•bil•i•ty (traf′i kə bil′i tē), *n.* **1.** the condition of soil or terrain with regard to its being traveled over, as by people, vehicles, or machinery. **2.** the skill of maneuvering over a terrain. [1895–1900; TRAFFICABLE + -ITY]

traf•fic•a•ble (traf′i kə bəl), *adj.* **1.** that can be traveled upon: *a trafficable road.* **2.** suitable for marketing, commercial dealings, etc. [1595–1605; TRAFFIC + -ABLE]

traf•fi•ca•tor (traf′i kā′tər), *n. Brit.* a directional signal on a vehicle for indicating which way it is going to turn. [TRAFFIC + (INDIC)ATOR]

traf′fic cir′cle, a circular arrangement constructed at the intersection of two or more roads in order to facilitate the passage of vehicles from one road to another. Also called **rotary;** *Brit.,* **roundabout.** [1945–50]

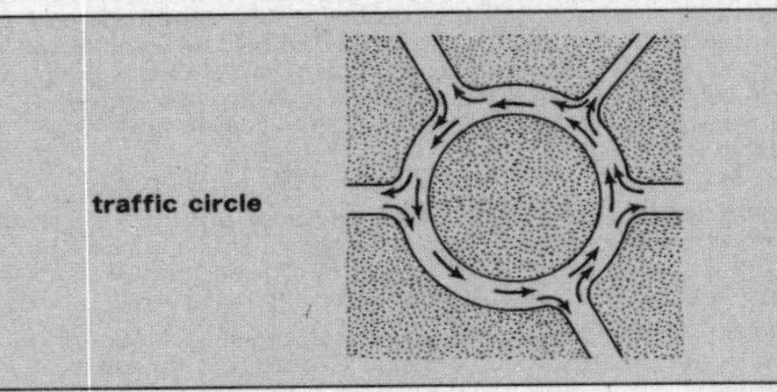

traf′fic cop′, *Informal.* a police officer who directs the flow of traffic, usually at an intersection. [1910–15, *Amer.*]

traf′fic court′, a court that passes on alleged violations of traffic laws. [1925–30]

traf′fic engineer′ing, a branch of civil engineering concerned with the design and construction of streets and roads that will best facilitate traffic movement. [1930–35] **—traf′fic engineer′.**

traf′fic is′land, a raised or marked-off area between lanes of a roadway, used by pedestrians to get out of the flow of traffic, as a place for traffic signals, for separating lanes, etc. [1935–40]

traf′fic jam′, jam[1] (def. 16). **—traf′fic-jammed′,** *adj.*

traf′fic light′, a set of electrically operated signal lights used to direct or control traffic at intersections. Also called **stoplight, traf′fic sig′nal, traf′fic control′ sig′nal.** [1925–30]

traf′fic man′ager, **1.** a person who supervises the transportation of goods for an employer. **2.** a person in a transportation company who schedules space, for freight or passengers. **3.** (in business management) an office employee, esp. an executive, responsible for routing items of business within a company for appropriate action by various departments. [1860–65]

traf′fic pat′tern, **1.** *Aeron.* a system of courses about an airfield that aircraft are assigned to fly when taking off, landing, or preparing to land. **2.** any systematic movement of people or vehicles: *The kitchen was designed to accommodate the family's traffic pattern.*

trag•a•canth (trag′ə kanth′, traj′-), *n.* a gummy substance derived from various low, spiny, Asian shrubs belonging to the genus *Astragalus,* of the legume family, esp. *A. gummifer:* used to impart firmness to pills and lozenges, stiffen calicoes, etc. Also called **gum tragacanth.** [1565–75; < L *tragacantha* goat's thorn < Gk *tragákantha,* equiv. to *trág(os)* goat + *ákantha* thorn. Cf. TRAGEDY, ACANTHO-]

tra•ge•di•an (trə jē′dē ən), *n.* **1.** an actor especially noted for performing tragic roles. **2.** a writer of tragedy. [1325–75; TRAGEDY + -AN; r. ME *tragedien* < MF]

tra•ge•di•enne (trə jē′dē en′), *n.* an actress especially noted for performing tragic roles. [1850–55; < F, fem. of *tragédien* TRAGEDIAN]
—Usage. See **-enne.**

trag•e•dize (traj′i dīz′), *v.t.,* **-dized, -diz•ing.** to make tragic; imbue with the aspects of tragedy: *a story tragedized by calamity and loss of hope.* Also, *esp. Brit.,* **trag′e•dise′.** [1585–95; TRAGED(Y) + -IZE]

trag•e•dy (traj′i dē), *n., pl.* **-dies. 1.** a dramatic composition, often in verse, dealing with a serious or somber theme, typically that of a great person destined through a flaw of character or conflict with some overpowering force, as fate or society, to downfall or destruction. **2.** the branch of the drama that is concerned with this form of composition. **3.** the art and theory of writing and producing tragedies. **4.** any literary composition, as a novel, dealing with a somber theme carried to a tragic conclusion. **5.** the tragic element of drama, of literature generally, or of life. **6.** a lamentable, dreadful, or fatal event or affair; calamity; disaster: *the tragedy of war.* [1325–75; ME *tragedie* < ML *tragēdia,* L *tragoedia* < Gk *tragōidía,* equiv. to *trág(os)* goat + *ōidḗ* song (see ODE) + *-ia* -Y[3]; reason for name variously explained]

trag•ic (traj′ik), *adj.* **1.** characteristic or suggestive of tragedy: *tragic solemnity.* **2.** extremely mournful, melancholy, or pathetic: *a tragic plight.* **3.** dreadful, calamitous, disastrous, or fatal: *a tragic event.* **4.** of, pertaining to, characterized by, or of the nature of tragedy: *the tragic drama.* **5.** acting in or writing tragedy: *a tragic actor; a tragic poet.* **6. the tragic,** the element or quality of tragedy in literature, art, drama, etc.: *lives that had never known anything but the tragic.* Also, **trag′i•cal.** [1535–45; < L *tragicus* < Gk *tragikós* of tragedy,

equiv. to *trág(os)* goat + *-ikos* -IC] **—trag′i·cal·ly,** *adv.* **—trag′i·cal·ness,** *n.*
—Syn. 2. distressing, pitiful. **—Ant. 1–3.** comic.

trag′ic flaw′, *Literature.* the character defect that causes the downfall of the protagonist of a tragedy; hamartia. [1950–55]

trag′ic i′rony, dramatic irony in tragic drama. [1825–35]

trag·i·com·e·dy (traj′i kom′i dē), *n., pl.* **-dies. 1.** a dramatic or other literary composition combining elements of both tragedy and comedy. **2.** an incident, or series of incidents, of mixed tragic and comic character. [1570–80; < LL *tragicōmoedia,* syncopated var. of L *tragicocōmoedia.* See TRAGIC, -O-, COMEDY] **—trag·i·com·ic** (traj′i kom′ik), **trag′i·com′i·cal,** *adj.* **—trag′i·com′i·cal·ly,** *adv.*

tra·gi·on (trā′jē on′), *n., pl.* **-gi·a** (-jē ə), **-gi·ons.** *Cephalom.* a point in the depth of the notch just above the tragus of the ear. [1560–70; TRAG(US) + -ION]

trag·o·pan (trag′ə pan′), *n.* any of several Asian pheasants of the genus *Tragopan,* having two fleshy, erectile horns on the head and wattles on the throat. [1615–25; < NL, special use of L *tragopān* fabulous Ethiopian bird < Gk *trágopān,* equiv. to *trágo(s)* goat + *Pān* PAN]

tra·gus (trā′gəs), *n., pl.* **-gi** (-jī). *Anat.* a fleshy prominence at the front of the external opening of the ear. See diag. under **ear.** [1685–95; < LL < Gk *trágos* hairy part of ear, lit., he-goat]

Tra·herne (trə hûrn′), *n.* **Thomas,** 1637?–74, English writer.

traik (trāk), *v.i. Scot.* **1.** to become ill or lose one's good health. **2.** to stroll, wander, or stray. [1500–10; orig. uncert.]

trail (trāl), *v.t.* **1.** to drag or let drag along the ground or other surface; draw or drag along behind. **2.** to bring or have floating after itself or oneself: *a racing car trailing clouds of dust.* **3.** to follow the track, trail, or scent of; track. **4.** to follow along behind (another), as in a race. **5.** to mark out, as a track. **6.** to tread down or make a path through (grass or the like). **7.** to draw out, as speech; protract. **8.** *Ceram.* to pour (slip) on a biscuit so as to produce a pattern. **—*v.i.*** **9.** to be drawn or dragged along the ground or some other surface, as when hanging from something moving: *Her long bridal gown trailed across the floor.* **10.** to hang down loosely from something. **11.** to stream from or float after something moving, as dust, smoke, and sparks do. **12.** to follow as if drawn along. **13.** to fish by trailing a line from a moving boat; troll. **14.** to go slowly, lazily, or wearily along. **15.** to pass or extend in a straggling line. **16.** to change gradually or wander from a course, so as to become weak, ineffectual, etc. (usually fol. by *off* or *away*): *Her voice trailed off into silence.* **17.** to arrive or be last: *He finally trailed in at 10 o'clock.* **18.** to be losing in a contest: *The home team was trailing 20 to 15.* **19.** to creep or crawl, as a serpent. **20.** to follow a track or scent, as of game. **21.** (of a plant) to extend itself in growth along the ground rather than taking root or clinging by tendrils, etc. **22. trail arms,** *Mil.* **a.** to hold a rifle in the right hand at an oblique angle, with the muzzle forward and the butt a few inches off the ground. **b.** a command to trail arms. **—*n.*** **23.** a path or track made across a wild region, over rough country, or the like, by the passage of people or animals. **24.** the track, scent, or the like, left by an animal, person, or thing, esp. as followed by a hunter, hound, or other pursuer. **25.** something that is trailed or that trails behind, as the train of a skirt or robe. **26.** a stream of dust, smoke, light, people, vehicles, etc., behind something moving. **27.** *Artillery.* the part of a gun carriage that rests on the ground when the piece is unlimbered. **28.** *Archit.* a running vine, leaf, or tendril ornament, as in a Gothic molding. [1275–1325; ME *trailen* to draw or drag in the rear; cf. OE *træglian* to tear off; c. MD *traghelen* to drag; akin to Latvian *dragât* to tear off, drag] **—trail′ing·ly,** *adv.* **—trail′less,** *adj.*
—Syn. 3. trace, hunt. **16.** diminish, shrink, dwindle. **23.** See **path. 24.** spoor.

trail·a·ble (trā′lə bəl), *adj.* **1.** capable of being trailed. **2.** suitable for transport by trailer. [1975–80; TRAIL + -ABLE]

trail′ bike′, a small motorcycle designed and built with special tires and suspension for riding on unpaved roads and over rough terrain. Also called **dirt bike.** [1965–70]

trail·blaze (trāl′blāz′), *v.,* **-blazed, -blaz·ing.** **—*v.t.*** **1.** to blaze a trail through (a forest, wilderness, or the like) for others to follow. **2.** to be a pioneer in (a particular subject, technique, etc.). **—*v.i.*** **3.** to work or serve as a trailblazer. [back formation from TRAILBLAZER]

trail·blaz·er (trāl′blā′zər), *n.* **1.** a person who blazes a trail for others to follow through unsettled country or wilderness; pathfinder. **2.** a pioneer in any field of endeavor: *a trailblazer in science.* Also called **trail·break·er** (trāl′brā′kər). [1905–10; TRAIL + BLAZE[2] + -ER[1]]

trail·board (trāl′bôrd′, -bōrd′), *n. Naut.* an ornamented board extending on each side of the bow of a vessel from a figurehead or the like to abaft the hawse. [1695–1705; TRAIL + BOARD]

trail′ boss′, (in Western U.S.) a person responsible for driving a herd of cattle. [1885–90, *Amer.*]

trail·er (trā′lər), *n.* **1.** a large van or wagon drawn by an automobile, truck, or tractor, used esp. in hauling freight by road. Cf. **full trailer, semitrailer. 2.** Also called **travel trailer.** a vehicle attached to an automobile and used as a mobile home or place of business, usually equipped with furniture, kitchen facilities, bathroom, etc. Cf. **tent trailer. 3.** a person or thing that trails. **4.** a trailing plant. **5.** a short promotional film composed of clips showing highlights of a movie due for release in the near future. **6.** blank film at the end of a reel or strip of film, for winding off the film in a motion-picture camera or projector. Cf. **leader** (def. 6). **7.** *Ceram.* a can with a spout, used in slip trailing. [1580–90; TRAIL + -ER[1]]

trail′er camp′, an area where house trailers may be parked, usually having running water, electrical outlets, etc. Also called **trail′er court′, trail′er park′.** [1920–25, *Amer.*]

trail′er car′, *Railroads.* **1.** a second flatcar used for transporting an object or objects of excessive weight or length. **2.** a passenger car, not self-propelled, included in a train of self-propelled cars. [1885–90, *Amer.*]

trail′er truck′. See **truck trailer.**

trail·head (trāl′hed′), *n.* the point where a trail starts. [1945–50; TRAIL + HEAD]

trail′ herd′, a herd of cattle driven along a trail, esp. from their home range to market.

trail′ing arbu′tus, Also called **arbutus, mayflower.** a creeping eastern North American plant, *Epigaea repens,* of the heath family, having leathery, oval leaves and terminal clusters of fragrant pink or white flowers. [1775–85]

trail′ing edge′, *Aeron.* the rear edge of a propeller blade or airfoil. [1905–10]

trail′ing fuch′sia, a shrub, *Fuchsia procumbens,* of the evening primrose family, native to New Zealand, having long-stalked leaves and drooping, orange-and-purple flowers, used in hanging baskets.

trail′ing phlox′, a prostrate plant, *Phlox nivalis,* of the southeastern U.S., having pink or white flowers.

trail′ man′, a cowboy on horseback who helps in driving a cattle herd. [1880–85, *Amer.*]

trail·man (trāl′mən), *n., pl.* **-men.** trailsman. [TRAIL + MAN[1]]

trail′ mix′, gorp.

trail′ rope′, a guide rope on an aerostat. [1840–50, *Amer.*]

trails·man (trālz′mən), *n., pl.* **-men.** a person who follows a trail. Also, **trailman.** [1855–60; TRAIL + 'S[1] + -MAN]

train (trān), *n.* **1.** *Railroads.* a self-propelled, connected group of rolling stock. **2.** a line or procession of persons, vehicles, animals, etc., traveling together. **3.** *Mil.* an aggregation of vehicles, animals, and personnel accompanying an army to carry supplies, baggage, ammunition, etc. **4.** a series or row of objects or parts. **5.** *Mach.* a connected set of three or more rotating elements, usually gears, through which force is transmitted, or motion or torque changed. **6.** order, esp. proper order: *Matters were in good train.* **7.** something that is drawn along; a trailing part. **8.** an elongated part of a skirt or robe trailing behind on the ground. **9.** a trail or stream of something from a moving object. **10.** a line or succession of persons or things following one after the other. **11.** a body of followers or attendants; retinue. **12.** a series of proceedings, events, ideas, etc. **13.** the series of results or circumstances following or proceeding from an event, action, etc.; aftermath: *Disease came in the train of war.* **14.** a succession of connected ideas; a course of reasoning: *to lose one's train of thought.* **15.** *Astron.* **a.** the trace of light created by a meteor falling through the earth's atmosphere. **b.** the tail of a comet. **16.** a line of combustible material, as gunpowder, for leading fire to an explosive charge. **17.** *Physics.* a succession of wave fronts, oscillations, or the like. **—*v.t.*** **18.** to develop or form the habits, thoughts, or behavior of (a child or other person) by discipline and instruction: *to train an unruly boy.* **19.** to make proficient by instruction and practice, as in some art, profession, or work: *to train soldiers.* **20.** to make (a person) fit by proper exercise, diet, practice, etc., as for an athletic performance. **21.** to discipline and instruct (an animal), as in the performance of tasks or tricks. **22.** to treat or manipulate so as to bring into some desired form, position, direction, etc.: *to train one's hair to stay down.* **23.** *Hort.* to bring (a plant, branch, etc.) into a particular shape or position, by bending, pruning, or the like. **24.** to bring to bear on some object; point, aim, or direct, as a firearm, camera, telescope, or eye. **25.** to entice; allure. **—*v.i.*** **26.** to give the discipline and instruction, drill, practice, etc., designed to impart proficiency or efficiency. **27.** to undergo discipline and instruction, drill, etc. **28.** to get oneself into condition for an athletic performance through exercise, diet, practice, etc. **29.** to travel or go by train: *to train to New York.* [1350–1400; (v.) late ME *traynyn* to pull or drag in the rear < MF *trainer,* OF *tra(h)iner* < VL **trāgināre,* deriv. of **tragina* something dragged or drawn (cf. ML *tragina* carriage), deriv. of **tragere* to pull, for L *trahere;* (n.) ME *train, traine* < OF *tra(h)in* (masc.) series of people, animals, or things, *tra(h)ine* (fem.) something dragged behind, both deriv. of *tra(h)iner*] **—train′less,** *adj.*
—Syn. 3. convoy. **6.** array, arrangement. **10.** file, column. **18, 19.** See **teach. 19.** exercise, drill, practice, school.

train·a·ble (trā′nə bəl), *adj.* **1.** capable of being trained. **2.** *Educ.* of or pertaining to moderately retarded individuals who may achieve some self-sufficiency, as in personal care. [1540–50; TRAIN + -ABLE] **—train′a·bil′i·ty,** *n.*

train·band (trān′band′), *n. Eng. Hist.* a company of trained militia organized in London and elsewhere in the 16th, 17th, and 18th centuries. [1620–30; TRAIN(ED) + BAND[1]]

trained′ nurse′. See **graduate nurse.** [1885–90]

train·ee (trā nē′), *n.* **1.** a person being trained, esp. in a vocation; apprentice. **2.** an enlisted person undergoing military training. [1840–50; TRAIN + -EE]

train·ee·ship (trā nē′ship), *n.* **1.** the state or position of being a trainee. **2.** a period of service as a trainee. **3.** a grant enabling a person to serve as a trainee. [1960–65; TRAINEE + -SHIP]

train·er (trā′nər), *n.* **1.** a person or thing that trains. **2.** a staff member on an athletic team who gives first aid and therapy to injured players. **3.** a person who trains athletes; coach. **4.** a person who trains racehorses or other animals for contests, shows, or performances. **5.** an airplane or a simulated aircraft used in training aircrew members, esp. pilots. [1590–1600; TRAIN + -ER[1]]

train·ing (trā′ning), *n.* **1.** the education, instruction, or discipline of a person or thing that is being trained: *He's in training for the Olympics.* **2.** the status or condition of a person who has been trained: *athletes in top training.* **—*adj.*** **3.** of, pertaining to, or used in or for training: *a training manual.* **4.** intended for use during an introductory, learning, or transitional period: *a training cup for weaning a baby; a training bra.* [1400–50; late ME (n.); see TRAIN, -ING[1], -ING[2]]
—Syn. 1. See **education.**

train′ing aid′, a mechanical contrivance used to supplement other forms and methods of training: *Motion pictures and slides were used as training aids.*

train′ing col′lege, *Brit.* a school providing training for a special field or profession. [1820–30]

train′ing pants′, briefs or shorts of cotton with added thickness, worn by a young child during toilet training.

train′ing school′, **1.** a school that provides training in some art, profession, or vocation. **2.** an institution for the care of juvenile delinquents. [1820–30]

train′ing ship′, a ship equipped for training novices in seamanship, as for naval service. [1855–60]

train′ing ta′ble, a table in a dining hall, as at a college, where athletes are provided with special meals to aid their conditioning. [1890–95]

train′ing wall′, an artificial embankment or wall for directing the course of a stream. [1880–85]

train′ing wheels′, a pair of small wheels attached one on each side of the rear wheel of a bicycle for stability while one is learning to ride.

train·line (trān′līn′), *n.* a pipe or hose distributing compressed air through a train for operation of the brakes. Also called **train·pipe** (trān′pīp′). [TRAIN + LINE[1]]

train·load (trān′lōd′), *n. Railroads.* **1.** the cargo or passenger capacity of a train. **2.** a specified minimum number of loaded cars or tons of cargo necessary to secure a special rate **(train′load rate′).** [1880–85; TRAIN + LOAD]

train·man (trān′mən), *n., pl.* **-men.** a member of the crew that operates a railroad train, usually an assistant to the conductor, such as a brakeman or flagman. [1635–45, in sense "member of a trainband"; 1875–80 for current sense; TRAIN + -MAN]

train·mas·ter (trān′mas′tər, -mä′stər), *n.* a person who has charge of operations over one portion of a railroad. [1855–60, *Amer.*; TRAIN + MASTER]

train′ oil′, oil obtained from the blubber of whales or from seals, walruses, or other marine animals. [1545–55; earlier *trane* < D *traan* train oil, tear; c. G *Träne* tear]

train·shed (trān′shed′), *n.* (in a railroad station) a shelter completely covering railroad tracks and their adjoining platforms. [1890–95, *Amer.*; TRAIN + SHED[1]]

train·sick (trān′sik′), *adj.* ill with train sickness. [1905–10; TRAIN + SICK[1]]

train′ sick′ness, nausea and dizziness, sometimes accompanied by vomiting, resulting from the motion of the train in which one is traveling. Cf. **motion sickness.** [1905–10]

traipse (trāps), *v.,* **traipsed, traips·ing,** *n. Informal.* **—*v.i.*** **1.** to walk or go aimlessly or idly or without finding or reaching one's goal: *We traipsed all over town looking for a copy of the book.* **—*v.t.*** **2.** to walk over; tramp: *to traipse the fields.* **—*n.*** **3.** a tiring walk. Also, **trapes.** [1585–95; earlier *trapse,* unexplained var. of *trape,* obscurely akin to TRAMP]

trait (trāt; *Brit. also* trā), *n.* **1.** a distinguishing characteristic or quality, esp. of one's personal nature: *bad traits of character.* **2.** a pen or pencil stroke. **3.** a stroke, touch, or strain, as of some quality: *a trait of pathos; a trait of ready wit.* [1470–80; < MF: lit., something drawn < L *tractus.* See TRACT[1]]
—Syn. 1. peculiarity, mark, attribute, property.

trai·tor (trā′tər), *n.* **1.** a person who betrays another, a cause, or any trust. **2.** a person who commits treason by betraying his or her country. [1175–1225; ME < OF < L *trāditōr-,* s. of *trāditor* betrayer. See TRADITOR] **—trai′tor·ship′,** *n.*

trai·tor·ous (trā′tər əs), *adj.* **1.** having the character of a traitor; treacherous; perfidious. **2.** characteristic of a traitor. **3.** of the nature of treason; treasonable: *a traitorous act.* [1350–1400; ME *treterous, traytrous* < OF *traitreus;* see TRAITOR, -OUS] **—trai′tor·ous·ly,** *adv.* **—trai′tor·ous·ness,** *n.*
—Syn. 1–3. disloyal, treasonous, faithless.

trai·tress (trā′tris), *n.* a woman who is a traitor. Also, **trai·tor·ess** (trā′tər is). [1400–50; late ME *traitresse* < OF; see TRAITOR, -ESS]

Tra·jan (trā′jən), *n.* (*Marcus Ulpius Nerva Trajanus*) A.D. 53?–117, Roman emperor 98–117.

tra·ject (trə jekt′), *v.t. Archaic.* to transport, transmit, or transpose. [1545–55; < L *trājectus* (ptp. of *trāicere* to cast, throw over or across), equiv. to *trā-* (var. of *trāns-* TRANS-) + *-jec-* (comb. form of *jacere* to throw) + *-tus* ptp. suffix] **—tra·jec′tion,** *n.*

tra·jec·to·ry (trə jek′tə rē), *n., pl.* **-ries. 1.** the curve described by a projectile, rocket, or the like in its flight. **2.** *Geom.* a curve or surface that cuts all the curves or surfaces of a given system at a constant angle. [1660–70; < NL *trājectōria,* n. use of fem. of ML *trājectōrius* cast-

CONCISE PRONUNCIATION KEY: *act, cāpe, dâre, pärt; set, ēqual; if, īce; ox, ōver, ôrder, oil, bŏŏk, bōōt, out; up, ûrge; child; sing; shoe; thin, that;* zh as in *treasure.* ə = *a* as in *alone, e* as in *system, i* as in *easily, o* as in *gallop, u* as in *circus;* ə as in *fire* (fīər), *hour* (ouər). l and n can serve as syllabic consonants, as in *cradle* (krād′l), and *button* (but′n). See the full key inside the front cover.

ing over. See TRAJECT, -TORY[1]] —**tra·jec·tile** (trə jek′til, -tīl), *adj.* —**tra·jec·tion** (trə jek′shən), *n.*

tra-la (trä lä′), *n.* nonsense syllables sung as a refrain, expressing gaiety. Also, **tra′-la-la′.** [1815–25]

Tra·lee (trə lē′), *n.* a city in and the county seat of Kerry, in the SW Republic of Ireland. 16,491.

tram[1] (tram), *n., v.,* **trammed, tram·ming.** —*n.* **1.** *Brit.* a streetcar. **2.** a tramway; tramroad. **3.** Also called **tram·car** (tram′kär′). a truck or car on rails for carrying loads in a mine. **4.** the vehicle or cage of an overhead carrier. —*v.t., v.i.* **5.** to convey or travel by tram. [1490–1500 for an earlier sense; 1820–30 for def. 2; orig. shafts of a barrow or cart, rails for carts (in mines); perh. < MD *trame* beam] —**tram′less,** *adj.*

tram[2] (tram), *n., v.,* **trammed, tram·ming.** —*n.* **1.** trammel (def. 3). —*v.t.* **2.** *Mach.* to adjust (something) correctly. [1880–85; short for TRAMMEL]

tram[3] (tram), *n.* silk that has been slightly or loosely twisted, used weftwise in weaving silk fabrics. Cf. **organzine.** [1300–50 for an earlier sense; 1670–80 for current sense; ME *tram(m)e* machination, contrivance < OF *traime* weft, cunning contrivance < L *trāma* warp]

tra·ma (trā′mə), *n. Mycol.* a specialized hyphal tissue constituting the internal structure of mushroom gills, pore tubes, or spines. [1855–60; < L *trāma* warp (in weaving)] —**tra′mal,** *adj.*

tram·line (tram′līn′), *n. Brit.* **1.** a streetcar system. **2.** a streetcar route or track. Also, **tramway.** [1885–90; TRAM[1] + LINE[1]]

tram·mel (tram′əl), *n., v.,* **-meled, -mel·ing** or (*esp. Brit.*) **-melled, -mel·ling.** —*n.* **1.** Usually, **trammels.** a hindrance or impediment to free action; restraint: *the trammels of custom.* **2.** an instrument for drawing ellipses. **3.** Also called **tram.** a device used to align or adjust parts of a machine. **4.** See **trammel net. 5.** a fowling net. **6.** a contrivance hung in a fireplace to support pots or kettles over the fire. **7.** a fetter or shackle, esp. one used in training a horse to amble. —*v.t.* **8.** to involve or hold in trammels; restrain. **9.** to catch or entangle in or as in a net. [1325–75; ME *tramayle* < MF *tramail,* var. of *tremail* three-mesh net < LL *trēmaculum,* equiv. to L *trē(s)* THREE + *macula* mesh] —**tram′·mel·er;** *esp. Brit.,* **tram′mel·ler,** *n.*
—**Syn. 1.** drag, hobble, curb, inhibition. **8.** hinder, impede, obstruct, encumber.

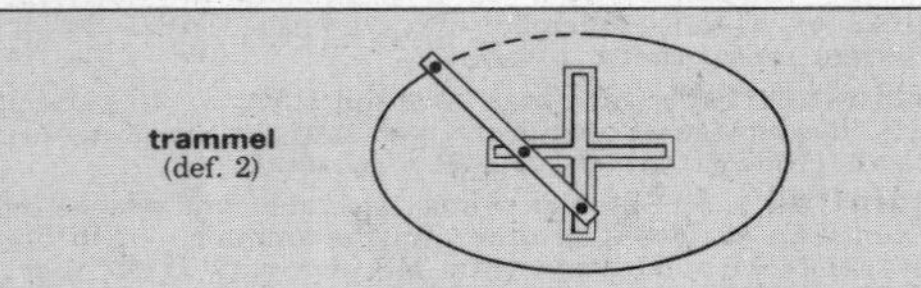
trammel (def. 2)

tram′mel net′, a three-layered fishing net, the middle layer of which is fine-meshed, the others coarse-meshed, so that fish attempting to pass through the net will become entangled in one or more of the meshes. [1510–20]

tra·mon·ta·na (trä′mən tä′nə, -tan′ə; *It.* trä′môn-tä′nä), *n., pl.* **-nas,** *It.* **-ne** (-ne). **1.** a cold wind from the north or northeast that blows in the western Mediterranean. **2.** any north wind issuing from a mountainous region. [1605–15; < It, n. use of fem. of *tramontano* TRAMONTANE]

tra·mon·tane (trə mon′tān, tram′ən tān′), *adj.* Also, **transmontane. 1.** being or situated beyond the mountains. **2.** beyond the Alps as viewed from Italy; transalpine. **3.** of, pertaining to, or coming from the other side of the mountains. **4.** foreign; barbarous. —*n.* **5.** a person who lives beyond the mountains: formerly applied by the Italians to the peoples beyond the Alps, and by the latter to the Italians. **6.** a foreigner; outlander; barbarian. **7.** a violent, polar wind from the northwest that blows in southern France. [1300–50 for an earlier sense; 1585–95 for def. 5; ME *tramountayne* pole star < It *tramontano* < L *trānsmontānus* beyond the mountains. See TRANS-, MOUNT[2], -AN]

tramp (tramp), *v.i.* **1.** to tread or walk with a firm, heavy, resounding step. **2.** to tread heavily or trample (usually fol. by *on* or *upon*): *to tramp on a person's toes.* **3.** to walk steadily; march; trudge. **4.** to go on a walking excursion or expedition; hike. **5.** to go about as a vagabond or tramp. **6.** to make a voyage on a tramp steamer. —*v.t.* **7.** to tramp or walk heavily or steadily through or over. **8.** to traverse on foot: *to tramp the streets.* **9.** to tread or trample underfoot: *to tramp grapes.* **10.** to travel over as a tramp. **11.** to run (a ship) as a tramp steamer. —*n.* **12.** the act of tramping. **13.** a firm, heavy, resounding tread. **14.** the sound made by such a tread. **15.** a long, steady walk; trudge. **16.** a walking excursion or expedition; hike. **17.** a person who travels on foot from place to place, esp. a vagabond living on occasional jobs or gifts of money or food. **18.** a sexually promiscuous woman; prostitute. **19.** a freight vessel that does not run regularly between fixed ports, but takes a cargo wherever shippers desire. Cf. **cargo liner. 20.** a piece of iron affixed to the sole of a shoe. [1350–1400; ME *trampen* to stamp; c. LG *trampen;* akin to Goth *ana-trimpan* to press hard upon. See TRAIPSE, TRAMPLE] —**tramp′er,** *n.* —**tramp′ish,** *adj.* —**tramp′ish·ly,** *adv.* —**tramp′ish·ness,** *n.*
—**Syn. 17.** vagrant, bum, hobo.

CONCISE ETYMOLOGY KEY: <, descended or borrowed from; >, whence; b., blend of, blended; c., cognate with; cf., compare; deriv., derivative; equiv., equivalent; imit., imitative; obl., oblique; r., replacing; s., stem; sp., spelling, spelled; resp., respelling, respelled; trans., translation; ?, origin unknown; *, unattested; ‡, probably earlier than. See the full key inside the front cover.

tramp′ art′, folk art of the 19th and 20th centuries utilizing recycled found materials, as cedar or mahogany cigar boxes, shaped into containers, lamps, picture frames, or other objects by a technique involving the gluing or nailing together of successive thin layers of wood that are then whittled into intricate geometric designs to produce a protruding multifaceted surface. —**tramp′ art′ist.**

tramp·ing (tram′ping), *n.* hiking, esp. on trails having huts at regular intervals for hikers to use overnight. [1810–20; TRAMP + -ING[1]]

tram·ple (tram′pəl), *v.,* **-pled, -pling,** *n.* —*v.i.* **1.** to tread or step heavily and noisily; stamp. **2.** to tread heavily, roughly, or crushingly (usually fol. by *on, upon,* or *over*): *to trample on a flower bed.* **3.** to act in a harsh, domineering, or cruel manner, as if treading roughly (usually fol. by *on, upon,* or *over*): *to trample on another's feelings.* —*v.t.* **4.** to tread heavily, roughly, or carelessly on or over; tread underfoot. **5.** to domineer harshly over; crush: *to trample law and order.* **6.** to put out or extinguish by trampling (usually fol. by *out*): *to trample out a fire.* —*n.* **7.** the act of trampling. **8.** the sound of trampling. [1350–1400; ME *tramplen* to stamp (c. G *trampeln*); see TRAMP, -LE] —**tram′pler,** *n.*

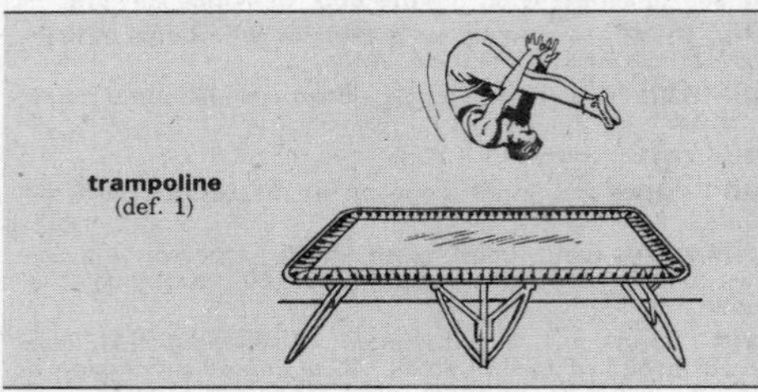
trampoline (def. 1)

tram·po·line (tram′pə lēn′, tram′pə lēn′, -lin), *n.* **1.** a sheet, usually of canvas, attached by resilient cords or springs to a horizontal frame several feet above the floor, used by acrobats and gymnasts as a springboard in tumbling. **2.** *Naut.* a fabric deck stretched on the braces connecting the hulls of a catamaran or trimaran, resembling a gymnastic trampoline. [1790–1800; var. of *trampolin* < It *trampolino* springboard, equiv. to *trampol(i)* stilts (< Gmc; see TRAMPLE) + *-ino* -INE[1]] —**tram′po·lin′er, tram′po·lin′ist,** *n.*

tramp′ steam′er, tramp (def. 19). [1885–90]

tram·road (tram′rōd′), *n.* (in a mine) a small railroad for trams. [1785–95; TRAM[1] + ROAD]

tram·way (tram′wā′), *n.* **1.** a crude railroad of wooden rails or of wooden rails capped with metal treads. **2.** *Brit.* tramline. **3.** *Mining.* a track, usually elevated, or roadway for mine haulage. **4.** Also called **aerial railway, aerial tramway, cable tramway, ropeway.** a system for hauling passengers and freight in vehicles suspended from a cable or cables supported by a series of towers, hangers, or the like: used over canyons, between mountain peaks, etc. [1815–25; TRAM[1] + WAY[1]]

trance[1] (trans, träns), *n., v.,* **tranced, tranc·ing.** —*n.* **1.** a half-conscious state, seemingly between sleeping and waking, in which ability to function voluntarily may be suspended. **2.** a dazed or bewildered condition. **3.** a state of complete mental absorption or deep musing. **4.** an unconscious, cataleptic, or hypnotic condition. **5.** *Spiritualism.* a temporary state in which a medium, with suspension of personal consciousness, is controlled by an intelligence from without and used as a means of communication, as from the dead. —*v.t.* **6.** to put in a trance; stupefy. **7.** to entrance; enrapture. [1300–50; ME *traunce* state of extreme dread, swoon, dazed state < MF *transe* lit., passage (from life to death), deriv. of *transir* to go across, pass over < L *trānsīre,* equiv. to *trāns-* TRANS- + *īre* to go] —**tranced·ly** (transt′lē, tran′sid lē), *adv.* —**trance′like′,** *adj.*

trance[2] (träns), *n., v.,* **tranced, tranc·ing.** *Scot.* —*n.* **1.** a passageway, as a hallway, alley, or the like. —*v.i.* **2.** to move or walk rapidly or briskly. Also, **transe.** [1325–75; ME (v.); orig. uncert.]

tran·chet (trän shā′; *Fr.* träN she′), *n., pl.* **-chets** (-shāz′; *Fr.* -she′). *Archaeol.* a stone implement with a horizontal, chisellike cutting edge, found at Mesolithic and Neolithic sites in macrolithic form, used as an adz, and in microlithic form, often mounted as the cutting head of an arrow. Cf. **macrolith, microlith.** [< F, equiv. to *tranch(er)* to cut (see TRENCH) + *-et* -ET]

tranfd., transferred.

tran·gam (trang′gəm), *n. Archaic.* an odd gadget; gewgaw; trinket. [1650–60; orig. uncert.]

trank[1] (trangk), *n. Slang.* a tranquilizer. [by shortening and resp.]

trank[2] (trangk), *n.* **1.** the piece of leather from which one glove is cut. **2.** the cut or shaped trank, not including thumb, gussets, and fourchettes. [1860–65; orig. uncert.]

tran·quil (trang′kwil), *adj.* **1.** free from commotion or tumult; peaceful; quiet; calm: *a tranquil country place.* **2.** free from or unaffected by disturbing emotions; unagitated; serene; placid: *a tranquil life.* [1595–1605; earlier *tranquill* < L *tranquillus* quiet, calm, still] —**tran′·quil·ly,** *adv.* —**tran′quil·ness,** *n.*
—**Syn. 1.** See **peaceful.** —**Ant. 1.** agitated.

tran·quil·ize (trang′kwə līz′), *v.t., v.i.,* **-ized, -iz·ing.** to make or become tranquil. Also, **tran′quil·lize′;** *esp. Brit.,* **tran′quil·lise′.** [1615–25; TRANQUIL + -IZE] —**tran′quil·i·za′tion,** *n.*

tran·quil·iz·er (trang′kwə lī′zər), *n.* **1.** a person or thing that tranquilizes. **2.** a drug that has a sedative or calming effect without inducing sleep. **3.** See **antianxiety drug. 4.** antipsychotic (def. 2). Also, **tran′quil·liz′·er.** [1790–1800; TRANQUILIZE + -ER[1]]

tran·quil·li·ty (trang kwil′i tē), *n.* quality or state of being tranquil; calmness; peacefulness; quiet; serenity. Also, **tran·quil′i·ty.** [1325–75; ME *tranquillite* < L *tranquillitās.* See TRANQUIL, -ITY]

trans-, **1.** a prefix occurring in loanwords from Latin (*transcend; transfix*); on this model, used with the meanings "across," "beyond," "through," "changing thoroughly," "transverse," in combination with elements of any origin: *transisthmian; trans-Siberian; transempirical; transvalue.* **2.** *Chem.* a prefix denoting a geometric isomer having a pair of identical atoms or groups on the opposite sides of two atoms linked by a double bond. Cf. **cis-** (def. 2). **3.** *Astron.* a prefix denoting something farther from the sun (than a given planet): *trans-Martian; trans-Neptunian.* [< L, comb. form of *trāns* (adv. and prep.) across, beyond, through]
—**Note.** The lists at the bottom of this and following pages provide the spelling, syllabification, and stress for words whose meanings may be easily inferred by combining the meanings of TRANS- and an attached base word, or base word plus a suffix. Appropriate parts of speech are also shown. Words prefixed by TRANS- that have special meanings or uses are entered in their proper alphabetical places in the main vocabulary or as derived forms run on at the end of a main vocabulary entry.

trans., **1.** transaction; transactions. **2.** transfer. **3.** transferred. **4.** transformer. **5.** transit. **6.** transitive. **7.** translated. **8.** translation. **9.** translator. **10.** transparent. **11.** transportation. **12.** transpose. **13.** transverse.

trans·act (tran sakt′, -zakt′), *v.t.* **1.** to carry on or conduct (business, negotiations, activities, etc.) to a conclusion or settlement. —*v.i.* **2.** to carry on or conduct business, negotiations, etc.: *He was ordered to transact only with the highest authorities.* [1575–85; < L *trānsāctus* (ptp. of *trānsigere* to carry out, accomplish), equiv. to *trāns-* TRANS- + *ag(ere)* to drive, lead + *-tus* ptp. suffix] —**trans·ac′tor,** *n.*
—**Syn. 1.** enact, conclude, settle, manage, negotiate. See **perform.**

trans·ac·ti·nide (trans ak′tə nīd′, tranz-), *adj. Chem.* noting or pertaining to elements having higher atomic weights than those of the actinide series. [1965–70; TRANS- + ACTINIDE]

trans·ac·tion (tran sak′shən, -zak′-), *n.* **1.** the act of transacting or the fact of being transacted. **2.** an instance or process of transacting something. **3.** something that is transacted, esp. a business agreement. **4.** *Psychol.* an interaction of an individual with one or more other persons, esp. as influenced by their assumed relational roles of parent, child, or adult. **5. transactions,** the published records of the proceedings, as papers read, addresses delivered, or discussions, at the meetings of a learned society or the like. [1425–75; late ME < L *trānsāctiōn-* (s. of *trānsāctiō*) completion, transaction. See TRANSACT, -ION] —**trans·ac′tion·al,** *adj.* —**trans·ac′tion·al·ly,** *adv.*
—**Syn. 2.** deal, bargain, enterprise, venture, affair.

transac′tional anal′ysis, *Psychol.* a form of individual or group psychotherapy focusing on social interactions, psychological games, and analysis of relationships as persons shift among the roles of parent, child, and adult. *Abbr.:* TA [1960–65]

Trans′ Alai′ (trans, tranz), a mountain range in central Asia, between Kirghizia (Kyrgyzstan) and Tadzhikistan (Tajikistan). Highest peak, Lenin Peak.

Trans′-A·las′ka Pipe′line (trans′ə las′kə, tranz′-, trans′-, tranz′-), a pipeline system opened in 1977 that transports oil 800 mi. (1300 km) across Alaska, from Prudhoe Bay on the North Slope S to Valdez harbor.

trans·al·pine (trans al′pīn, -pin, tranz-), *adj.* **1.** situated beyond the Alps, esp. toward the north as viewed from Italy. **2.** passing or extending across or through the Alps: *a transalpine railway.* **3.** of, pertaining to, or characteristic of peoples or lands beyond the Alps. —*n.* **4.** a native or inhabitant of a country beyond the Alps. [1580–90; < L *trānsalpīnus* across the Alps, equiv. to *trāns-* TRANS- + *Alp(ēs)* the Alps + *-īnus* -INE[1]]

Transal′pine Gaul′. See under **Gaul** (def. 1).

trans·am·i·nase (trans am′ə nās′, -nāz′, tranz-), *n. Biochem.* any of a class of enzymes, occurring in most plant and animal tissue, that cause transamination. [1940–45; TRANSAMIN(ATION) + -ASE]

trans·am·i·na·tion (trans am′ə nā′shən, tranz-), *n. Biochem., Chem.* the transfer of an amino group from one compound to another. [1940–45; TRANS- + AMIN(O) + -ATION]

trans·an·nu·lar (trans an′yə lər, tranz-), *adj. Chem.* of or pertaining to tautomerism in cyclic compounds that is characterized by the migration of an atom or group from one position in the ring to another. [TRANS- + ANNULAR]

trans·arc·tic (trans ärk′tik, tranz-), *adj.* across or beyond the arctic. [TRANS- + ARCTIC]

trans·at·lan·tic (trans′ət lan′tik, tranz′-), *adj.* **1.** crossing or reaching across the Atlantic: *a transatlantic liner.* **2.** situated beyond the Atlantic. [1770–80; TRANS- + ATLANTIC] —**trans′at·lan′ti·cal·ly,** *adv.*

trans·ax·le (trans ak′səl, tranz-), *n.* a unit combining

trans′-A·dri·at′ic, *adj.*
trans-Af′ri·can, *adj.*
trans-Al·ge′ri·an, *adj.*
trans′-Al·le·ghe′ni·an, *adj.*
trans′-A·mer′i·can, *adj.*
trans′-An·de′an, *adj.*
trans-An′dine, *adj.*
trans′-Ant·arc′tic, *adj.*
trans-Ap′en·nine′, *adj.*
trans′a·quat′ic, *adj.*
trans′-A·ra′bi·an, *adj.*
trans′-A·si·at′ic, *adj.*
trans·au′di·ent, *adj.*
trans′-Aus·tral′ian, *adj.*
trans-Aus′tri·an, *adj.*
trans-Bal′kan, *adj.*
trans-Bal′tic, *adj.*
trans·bay′, *adj.*
trans·bor′der, *adj.*
trans·bound′a·ry, *adj.*
trans′-Ca·na′di·an, *adj.*
trans′-Car·pa′thi·an, *adj.*
trans-Cas′pi·an, *adj.*
trans·change′, *v.t.,* **-changed, -chang·ing.**

the transmission and differential of a motor vehicle and connected directly to the axles of the driving wheels. [1955–60; TRANS(MISSION) + AXLE]

trans•ca•lent (trans kā′lənt), *adj.* permitting the passage of heat. [1825–35; TRANS- + L *calent-* (s. of *calēns*), prp. of *calēre* to be hot; see -ENT] —**trans•ca•len•cy** (trans kā′lən sē), *n.*

Trans•cau•ca•sia (trans′kô kā′zhə, -shə), *n.* a region in SE Europe, S of the Caucasus Mountains, between the Black and Caspian seas: constituted a republic 1922–36 (**Transcauca′sian So′cialist Fed′erated So′viet Repub′lic**); area now includes the republics of Armenia, Azerbaijan, and Georgia. —**Trans•cau•ca•sian** (trans′kô kā′zhən, -shən, -kazh′ən, -kash′-), *adj., n.*

trans•ceiv•er (tran sē′vər), *n. Radio.* a transmitter and receiver combined in one unit. [1935–40; TRANS(MITTER) + (RE)CEIVER]

tran•scend (tran send′), *v.t.* **1.** to rise above or go beyond; overpass; exceed: *to transcend the limits of thought; kindness transcends courtesy.* **2.** to outdo or exceed in excellence, elevation, extent, degree, etc.; surpass; excel. **3.** *Theol.* (of the Deity) to be above and independent of (the universe, time, etc.). —*v.i.* **4.** to be transcendent or superior; excel: *His competitiveness made him want to transcend.* [1300–50; ME < L *trānscendere* to surmount, equiv to *trāns-* TRANS- + *-scendere,* comb. form of *scandere* to climb] —**tran•scend′•ing•ly,** *adv.*
—**Syn. 2.** outstrip.

tran•scend•ence (tran sen′dəns), *n.* the quality or state of being transcendent. Also, **tran•scend′en•cy.** [1595–1605; < ML *trānscendentia.* See TRANSCENDENT, -ENCE]

tran•scend•ent (tran sen′dənt), *adj.* **1.** going beyond ordinary limits; surpassing; exceeding. **2.** superior or supreme. **3.** *Theol.* (of the Deity) transcending the universe, time, etc. Cf. **immanent** (def. 3). **4.** *Philos.* **a.** *Scholasticism.* above all possible modes of the infinite. **b.** *Kantianism.* transcending experience; not realizable in human experience. Cf. **transcendental** (defs. 5a, c). **c.** (in modern realism) referred to, but beyond, direct apprehension; outside consciousness. —*n. Math.* **5.** a transcendental function. [1575–85; < L *trānscendent-* (s. of *trānscendēns*), prp. of *trānscendere.* See TRANSCEND, -ENT] —**tran•scend′ent•ly,** *adv.* —**tran•scend′ent•ness,** *n.*

tran•scen•den•tal (tran′sen den′tl, -sən-), *adj.* **1.** transcendent, surpassing, or superior. **2.** being beyond ordinary or common experience, thought, or belief; supernatural. **3.** abstract or metaphysical. **4.** idealistic, lofty, or extravagant. **5.** *Philos.* **a.** beyond the contingent and accidental in human experience, but not beyond all human knowledge. Cf. **transcendent** (def. 4b). **b.** pertaining to certain theories, etc., explaining what is objective as the contribution of the mind. **c.** *Kantianism.* of, pertaining to, based upon, or concerned with a priori elements in experience, which condition human knowledge. Cf. **transcendent** (def. 4b). —*n.* **6.** *Math.* See **transcendental number. 7. transcendentals,** *Scholasticism.* categories that have universal application, as being, one, true, good. [1615–25; < ML *trānscendentālis.* See TRANSCENDENT, -AL[1]] —**tran′scen•den•tal′i•ty,** *n.* —**tran′scen•den′tal•ly,** *adv.*

transcenden′tal aesthet′ic, (in Kantian epistemology) the study of space and time as the a priori forms of perception.

transcenden′tal analyt′ic, *Kantianism.* (in transcendental logic) the study of the means by which the mind categorizes data from the sensory manifold.

transcenden′tal dialec′tic, *Kantianism.* (in transcendental logic) the study of the fallacious attribution of objective reality to the perceptions by the mind of external objects. Cf. **dialectic** (def. 8).

tran′scenden′tal e′go, (in Kantian epistemology) that part of the self that is the subject and never the object.

transcenden′tal equa′tion, *Math.* an equation that involves transcendental functions.

tran′scenden′tal func′tion, *Math.* a function that is not an algebraic function. [1875–80]

tran•scen•den•tal•ism (tran′sen den′tl iz′əm, -sən-), *n.* **1.** transcendental character, thought, or language. **2.** Also called **transcenden′tal philos′ophy.** any philosophy based upon the doctrine that the principles of reality are to be discovered by the study of the processes of thought, or a philosophy emphasizing the intuitive and spiritual above the empirical: in the U.S., associated with Emerson. [1795–1805; < G *Transcendentalismus.* See TRANSCENDENTAL, -ISM] —**tran′scen•den′tal•ist,** *n., adj.*

tran•scen•den•tal•ize (tran′sen den′tl īz′, -sən-), *v.t.,* **-ized, -iz•ing. 1.** to cause to become transcendent. **2.** to cause to become transcendental; idealize. Also, *esp. Brit.,* **tran′scen•den′tal•ise′.** [1840–50; TRANSCENDENTAL + -IZE] —**tran′scen•den′tal•i•za′tion,** *n.*

tran′scenden′tal log′ic, (in Kantian epistemology) the study of the mind with reference to its perceptions of external objects and to the objective truth of such perceptions. Cf. **transcendental analytic, transcendental dialectic.** [1790–1800]

transcenden′tal medita′tion, a technique, based on ancient Hindu writings, by which one seeks to achieve a relaxed state through regular periods of meditation during which a mantra is repeated. *Abbr.:* TM [1965–70]

tran′scenden′tal num′ber, *Math.* a number that is not a root of any algebraic equation having integral coefficients, as π or *e.* Also called **transcendental.**

transcenden′tal u′nity of appercep′tion, (in Kantian epistemology) the meaningful organization, within the consciousness, of individual objects of perception.

tran•scen•sion (tran sen′shən), *n.* transcendence. [1605–15; < ML, LL *trānscēnsiōn-,* s. of *trānscēnsiō* lit., a passing over. See TRANSCEND, -SION]

trans•con•duct•ance (trans′kən duk′təns), *n. Electronics.* **1.** the ratio of a small change in anode current of an electron tube at a certain level of output to the corresponding small change of control-electrode voltage, usually expressed in mhos or micromhos. **2.** (loosely) the amplification factor of a tube divided by its anode resistance. [TRANS- + CONDUCTANCE]

trans•con•ti•nen•tal (trans′kon tn en′tl), *adj.* **1.** passing or extending across a continent: *a transcontinental railroad.* **2.** on the other, or far, side of a continent. [1850–55, *Amer.*; TRANS- + CONTINENTAL] —**trans′con•ti•nen′tal•ly,** *adv.*

tran•scribe (tran skrīb′), *v.t.,* **-scribed, -scrib•ing. 1.** to make a written copy, esp. a typewritten copy, of (dictated material, notes taken during a lecture, or other spoken material). **2.** to make an exact copy of (a document, text, etc.). **3.** to write out in another language or alphabet; translate or transliterate: *to transcribe Chinese into English characters.* **4.** *Phonet.* to represent (speech sounds) in written phonetic or phonemic symbols. **5.** *Radio.* to make a recording of (a program, announcement, etc.) for broadcasting. **6.** *Music.* to arrange (a composition) for a medium other than that for which it was originally written. **7.** *Genetics.* to effect genetic transcription of (a DNA molecule template). [1545–55; < L *trānscrībere* to copy off, equiv. to *trāns-* TRANS- + *scrībere* to write. See SCRIBE] —**tran•scrib′er,** *n.*

tran•script (tran′skript), *n.* **1.** a written, typewritten, or printed copy; something transcribed or made by transcribing. **2.** an exact copy or reproduction, esp. one having an official status. **3.** an official report supplied by a school on the record of an individual student, listing subjects studied, grades received, etc. **4.** a form of something as rendered from one alphabet or language into another. [1250–1300; ME < L *trānscrīptum* thing copied (n. use of neut. of ptp. of *trānscrībere* see TRANSCRIBE); r. ME *transcrit* < OF < L, as above; see SCRIPT]

tran•scrip•tase (tran skrip′tās, -tāz), *n. Biochem.* See **RNA polymerase.** [1963; TRANSCRIPT(ION) + -ASE]

tran•scrip•tion (tran skrip′shən), *n.* **1.** the act or process of transcribing. **2.** something transcribed. **3.** a transcript; copy. **4.** *Music.* **a.** the arrangement of a composition for a medium other than that for which it was originally written. **b.** a composition so arranged. **5.** *Radio and Television.* a recording made esp. for broadcasting. **6.** *Genetics.* the process by which genetic information on a strand of DNA is used to synthesize a strand of complementary RNA. [1590–1600; < L *trānscrīptiōn-* (s. of *trānscrīptiō*). See TRANSCRIPT, -ION] —**tran•scrip′•tion•al,** *adj.* —**tran•scrip′tion•al•ly,** *adv.* —**tran•scrip′tion•ist,** *n.* —**tran•scrip•tive** (tran skrip′tiv), *adj.* —**tran•scrip′tive•ly,** *adv.*

trans•crys•tal•line (trans kris′tl in, -in′), *adj. Crystall.* situated within or passing through the crystals of a substance. Cf. **intercrystalline.** [TRANS- + CRYSTALLINE]

trans•cul•tu•ra•tion (trans kul′chə rā′shən), *n.* acculturation. [1940–45; TRANS- + CULTURE + -ATION]

trans•cur•rent (trans kûr′ənt, -kur′-), *adj.* running or extending across or transversely. [1600–10; < L *trānscurrent-* (s. of *trānscurrēns*), prp. of *trānscurrere* to run across. See TRANS-, CURRENT]

trans•cu•ta•ne•ous (trans′kyo͞o tā′nē əs), *adj.* by way of or through the skin. Also, **trans′cu•ta′ne•al, transdermal.** [1940–45; TRANS- + CUTANEOUS]

trans•der•mal (trans dûr′məl, tranz-), *adj.* **1.** Also, **trans•der′mic.** transcutaneous. **2.** *Pharm.* (of a medication) applied to the skin, usually as part of an adhesive patch, for absorption into the bloodstream. [TRANS- + DERMAL]

trans•di•a•lect (trans dī′ə lekt′, tranz-), *v.t.* to translate (speech, writing, etc.) into a different dialect. [1690–1700; TRANS- + DIALECT]

trans•duce (trans do͞os′, -dyo͞os′, tranz-), *v.t.,* **-duced, -duc•ing. 1.** to convert (energy) from one form into another. **2.** *Genetics.* to cause transduction in (a cell). [1945–50; back formation from TRANSDUCER or TRANSDUCTION]

trans•duc•er (trans do͞o′sər, -dyo͞o′-, tranz-), *n.* a device that receives a signal in the form of one type of energy and converts it to a signal in another form: *A microphone is a transducer that converts acoustic energy into electrical impulses.* [1920–25; < L *trānsdūc*(*ere*) to transfer (see TRADUCE) + -ER[1]]

trans•duc•tion (trans duk′shən, tranz-), *n. Genetics.* the transfer of genetic material from one cell to another by means of a virus. [1952; TRANS- + *-duction,* as in INDUCTION, PRODUCTION, etc.] —**trans•duc•tant** (trans duk′tənt, tranz-), *n.* —**trans•duc′tion•al,** *adj.*

transe (träns), *n., v.i.,* **transed, trans•ing.** *Scot.* trance[2].

tran•sect (tran sekt′), *v.t.* to cut across; dissect transversely. [1625–35; TRAN(S)- + L *sectus,* ptp. of *secāre* to cut, sever (see SECTION)] —**tran•sec′tion,** *n.*

trans•el•e•ment (trans el′ə mənt, tranz-), *v.t.* to change the elements of; transmute. [1560–70; < ML *trānselementāre,* equiv. to L *trāns-* TRANS- + *element(um)* ELEMENT + *-āre* inf. suffix]

trans•el•e•ment•ate (trans el′ə mən tāt′, tranz-), *v.t.,* **-at•ed, -at•ing.** transelement. [1570–80; < ML *trānselementātus,* ptp. of *trānselementāre.* See TRANSELEMENT, -ATE[1]] —**trans•el′e•men•ta′tion,** *n.*

trans•em•pir•i•cal (trans′em pir′i kəl, tranz′-), *adj.* beyond the range of experiential knowledge. [1905–10; TRANS- + EMPIRICAL]

tran•sen•na (tran sen′ə), *n., pl.* **-sen•nae** (-sen′ē). (in early Christian architecture) an openwork screen of stone or metal enclosing a shrine. [< L *trā(n)senna* net trap for birds]

tran•sept (tran′sept), *n. Archit.* **1.** any major transverse part of the body of a church, usually crossing the nave, at right angles, at the entrance to the choir. **2.** an arm of this, on either side of the central aisle of a church. [1530–40; < AL *trānseptum.* See TRANS-, SEPTUM] —**tran•sep′tal,** *adj.* —**tran•sep′tal•ly,** *adv.*

trans•es•ter•i•fi•ca•tion (trans′e ster′ə fi kā′shən, tranz′-), *n. Chem.* a reaction between an ester of one alcohol and a second alcohol to form an ester of the second alcohol and an alcohol from the original ester, as that of methyl acetate and ethyl alcohol to form ethyl acetate and methyl alcohol; interesterification. [TRANS- + ESTERIFICATION]

trans•e•unt (tran′sē ənt), *adj. Philos.* (of a mental act) producing an effect outside of the mind. Also, **transient.** Cf. **immanent** (def. 2). [1615–25; < L *trānseunt-,* oblique s. of *trānsiēns* passing beyond; see TRANSIENT]

transf., 1. transfer. **2.** transferred. **3.** transformer.

transfd., transferred.

trans•fect (trans fekt′), *v.t. Microbiol.* to cause transfection in (a cell). [1964; TRANS- + (IN)FECT]

trans•fec•tion (trans fek′shən), *n. Biotech.* the insertion into a cell of a bacterial plasmid that contains a foreign virus or genetic material. [1964; TRANS- + (IN)FECTION]

trans•fer (*v.* trans fûr′, trans′fər; *n., adj.* trans′fər), *v.,* **-ferred, -fer•ring,** *n., adj.* —*v.t.* **1.** to convey or remove from one place, person, etc., to another: *He transferred the package from one hand to the other.* **2.** to cause to pass from one person to another, as thought, qualities, or power; transmit. **3.** *Law.* to make over the possession or control of: *to transfer a title to land.* **4.** to imprint, impress, or otherwise convey (a drawing, design, pattern, etc.) from one surface to another. —*v.i.* **5.** to remove oneself from one place to another: *to transfer from the New York office to London.* **6.** to withdraw from one school, college, or the like, and enter another: *I transferred from Rutgers to Tulane.* **7.** to be moved from one place to another: *to transfer to overseas duty.* **8.** to change by means of a transfer from one bus, train, or the like, to another. —*n.* **9.** a means or system of transferring. **10.** an act of transferring. **11.** the fact of being transferred. **12.** a point or place for transferring. **13.** a ticket entitling a passenger to continue a journey on another bus, train, or the like. **14.** a drawing, design, pattern, or the like, that is or may be transferred from one surface to another, usually by direct contact. **15.** a person who changes or is changed from one college, military unit, business department, etc., to another. **16.** *Law.* a conveyance, by sale, gift, or otherwise, of real or personal property, to another. **17.** *Finance.* the act of having the ownership of a stock or registered bond transferred. **18.** Also called **transfer of training.** *Psychol.* the positive or negative influence of prior learning on subsequent learning. Cf. **generalization** (def. 4). **19.** Also called **language transfer.** *Ling.* the application of native-language rules in attempted performance in a second language, in some cases resulting in deviations from target-language norms and in other cases facilitating second-language acquisition. —*adj.* **20.** of, pertaining to, or involving transfer payments. [1350–1400; ME *transferren* (v.) < L *trānsferre,* equiv. to *trāns-* TRANS- + *ferre* to BEAR[1], carry] —**trans•fer′a•ble, trans•fer′•ra•ble,** *adj.* —**trans•fer′a•bil′i•ty,** *n.* —**trans•fer′•rer,** *n.*

trans′fer a′gent, a person, bank, or trust company officially designated to act for a corporation in executing and recording the transfers of its stock from one legal owner to another.

trans•fer•al (trans fûr′əl), *n.* transference; transfer. Also, **transferral.** [1860–65; TRANSFER + -AL[2]]

trans•fer•ase (trans′fə rās′, -rāz′), *n. Biochem.* any of the class of enzymes, as the transaminases that catalyze the transfer of an organic group from one compound to another. [1945–50; TRANSFER + -ASE]

trans′fer com′pany, a company that transports people or luggage for a relatively short distance, as between terminals of two railroad lines. [1875–80, *Amer.*]

trans•fer•ee (trans′fə rē′), *n.* **1.** a person who is

CONCISE PRONUNCIATION KEY: act, cāpe, dâre, pärt; set, ēqual; if, īce; ox, ōver, ôrder, oil, bo͝ok, bo͞ot, out; up, ûrge; child; sing; shoe; thin, that; zh as in *treasure.* ə = *a* as in *alone, e* as in *system, i* as in *easily, o* as in *gallop, u* as in *circus;* ᵊ as in *fire* (fīᵊr), *hour* (ouᵊr). l and n can serve as syllabic consonants, as in *cradle* (krād′l), and *button* (but′n). See the full key inside the front cover.

trans•chang′er, *n.*
trans•chan′nel, *adj.*
trans•col′or, *adj.*
trans′col•or•a′tion, *n.*
trans•col′our, *adj.*
trans′col•our•a′tion, *n.*
trans•con′dy•lar, *adj.*
trans•con′dy•loid′, *adj.*
trans-Con′go, *adj.*
trans′-Cor•dil•le′ran, *adj.*
trans′cor•po′re•al, *adj.*
trans•cul′tur•al, *adj.;* **-ly,** *adv.*
trans•cur′sive, *adj.;* **-ly,** *adv.*
trans′cur•va′tion, *n.*
trans′-Dan•u′bi•an, *adj.*
trans′de•nom′i•na′tion•al, *adj.*
trans•des′ert, *adj.*
trans′di•a•phrag•mat′ic, *adj.*
trans′di•ur′nal, *adj.*
trans′-E•gyp′tian, *adj.*
trans•el′e•ment, *n.*
trans′el•e•men′tal, *adj.*
trans′el•e•men′ta•ry, *adj.*
trans′e•qua•to′ri•al, *adj.;* **-ly,** *adv.*

transferred or removed, as from one place to another. **2.** *Law.* a person to whom a transfer is made, as of property. [1730–40; TRANSFER + -EE]

trans·fer·ence (trans fûr′əns, trans′fər əns), *n.* **1.** the act or process of transferring. **2.** the fact of being transferred. **3.** *Psychoanal.* **a.** the shift of emotions, esp. those experienced in childhood, from one person or object to another, esp. the transfer of feelings about a parent to an analyst. **b.** displacement (def. 7). [1675–85; < NL *trānsferentia.* See TRANSFER, -ENCE]

transfer′ence num′ber, *Physical Chem.* that fraction of the total electric current that anions and cations carry in passing through an electrolytic solution. Also called **transport number.** [1895–1900]

trans·fer·en·tial (trans′fə ren′shəl), *adj.* of, pertaining to, or involving transference. [1885–90; < NL *trānsferenti(a)* TRANSFERENCE + -AL[1]]

trans′fer fac′tor, *Immunol.* a lymphocyte product that, when extracted from T cells of an individual with immunity to a particular antigen, can confer that immunity when administered to another individual of the same species. [1955–60]

trans′fer mold′ing, a method of molding thermosetting plastic in which the plastic enters a closed mold from an adjoining chamber in which it has been softened. [1935–40]

trans′fer of train′ing, *Psychol.* transfer (def. 19).

trans·fer·or (trans fûr′ər), *n. Law.* a person who makes a transfer, as of property. [1870–75; TRANSFER + -OR[2]]

trans′fer or′bit, the flight path of a space vehicle moving from a nearly circular orbit to one with different parameters.

trans′fer pay′ment, **1.** any payment made by a government for a purpose other than that of purchasing goods or services, as for welfare benefits. **2.** any money received that is neither a payment for goods or services nor investment income. [1940–45]

trans·fer·ral (trans fûr′əl), *n.* transferal.

trans·fer·rin (trans fer′in), *n. Biochem.* a plasma glycoprotein that transports dietary iron to the liver, spleen, and bone marrow. [1947; TRANS- + L *ferr(um)* iron + -IN[2]]

transfer RNA, *Genetics.* a small RNA molecule, consisting of a strand of nucleotides folded into a clover-leaf shape, that picks up an unattached amino acid within the cell cytoplasm and conveys it to the ribosome for protein synthesis. *Abbr.:* tRNA [1960–65]

trans′fer sta′tion, a place where residential garbage and commercial wastes are compressed, baled, and loaded on vehicles for moving to disposal sites, as for landfill.

trans·fig·u·ra·tion (trans′fig yə rā′shən, trans fig′-), *n.* **1.** the act of transfiguring. **2.** the state of being transfigured. **3.** (*cap.*) the supernatural and glorified change in the appearance of Jesus on the mountain. Matt. 17:1–9. **4.** (*cap.*) the church festival commemorating this, observed on August 6. [1325–75; ME *Transfiguracion* < L *trānsfigūrātiōn-* (s. of *trānsfigūrātiō*) change of shape. See TRANSFIGURE, -ATION]

trans·fig·ure (trans fig′yər *or, esp. Brit.,* -fig′ər), *v.t.,* **-ured, -ur·ing.** **1.** to change in outward form or appearance; transform. **2.** to change so as to glorify or exalt. [1250–1300; ME *transfiguren* < L *trānsfigūrāre* to change in shape. See TRANS-, FIGURE] —**trans·fig′ure·ment,** *n.*
—**Syn. 1.** transmute, renew.

trans·fi·nite (trans fī′nīt), *adj.* **1.** going beyond or surpassing the finite. —*n.* **2.** See **transfinite number.** [1900–05; TRANS- + FINITE]

transfi′nite num′ber, *Math.* an infinite cardinal or ordinal number. [1900–05]

trans·fix (trans fiks′), *v.t.,* **-fixed** or **fixt, fix·ing. 1.** to make or hold motionless with amazement, awe, terror, etc. **2.** to pierce through with or as if with a pointed weapon; impale. **3.** to hold or fasten with or on something that pierces. [1580–90; < L *trānsfixus* (ptp. of *trānsfigere* to pierce through), equiv. to *trāns-* TRANS- + *fig(ere)* to pierce + *-sus,* var. of *-tus* ptp. suffix] —**trans·fix·ion** (trans fik′shən), *n.*
—**Syn. 1.** fascinate, spellbind, engross, captivate.

trans·form (*v.* trans fôrm′; *n.* trans′fôrm), *v.t.* **1.** to change in form, appearance, or structure; metamorphose. **2.** to change in condition, nature, or character; convert. **3.** to change into another substance; transmute. **4.** *Elect.* **a.** to increase or decrease (the voltage and current characteristics of an alternating-current circuit), as by means of a transformer. **b.** to decrease (the voltage and current characteristics of a direct-current circuit), as by means of a transformer. **5.** *Math.* to change the form of (a figure, expression, etc.) without in general changing the value. **6.** *Physics.* to change into another form of energy. —*v.i.* **7.** to undergo a change in form, appearance, or character; become transformed. —*n.* **8.** *Math.* **a.** a mathematical quantity obtained from a given quantity by an algebraic, geometric, or functional transformation. **b.** the transformation itself. **9.** the result of a transformation. **10.** a transformation. **11.** *Logic.* transformation (def. 5). **12.** *Ling.* a structure derived by a transformation. [1300–50; ME *transformen* < L *trānsfōrmāre* to change in shape. See TRANS-, FORM] —**trans·form′a·ble,** *adj.* —**trans·form′a·tive,** *adj.*
—**Syn. 1.** transfigure. TRANSFORM, CONVERT mean to change one thing into another. TRANSFORM suggests changing from one form, appearance, structure, or type to another: *to transform soybeans into oil and meal by pressure.* CONVERT suggests so changing the characteristics as to change the use or purpose: *to convert a barn into a house.*

trans·for·ma·tion (trans′fər mā′shən), *n.* **1.** the act or process of transforming. **2.** the state of being transformed. **3.** change in form, appearance, nature, or character. **4.** *Theat.* a seemingly miraculous change in the appearance of scenery or actors in view of the audience. **5.** *Logic.* Also called **transform.** one of a set of algebraic formulas used to express the relations between elements, sets, etc., that form parts of a given system. **6.** *Math.* **a.** the act, process, or result of transforming or mapping. **b.** function (def. 4a). **7.** *Ling.* **a.** See **transformational rule. b.** the process by which deep structures are converted into surface structures using transformational rules. **8.** *Genetics.* the transfer of genetic material from one cell to another resulting in a genetic change in the recipient cell. **9.** a wig or hairpiece for a woman. [1400–50; late ME < LL *trānsfōrmātiōn-* (s. of *trānsfōrmātiō*) change of shape. See TRANS-, FORMATION] —**trans′for·ma′tion·al,** *adj.*

trans·for·ma′tion·al-gen′er·a·tive gram′mar (trans′fər mā′shə nl jen′ər ə tiv, -ə rā′tiv), a grammar that combines the principles of generative grammar and transformational grammar. [1975–80]

transforma′tional gram′mar, a system of grammatical analysis, esp. a form of generative grammar, that posits the existence of deep structure and surface structure, using a set of transformational rules to derive surface structure forms from deep structure; a grammar that uses transformations to express the relations between equivalent structures. [1960–65]

trans·for·ma·tion·al·ist (trans′fər mā′shə nl ist), *n.* a person who follows or promotes the theories of transformational grammar. [1960–65; TRANSFORMATIONAL (GRAMMAR) + -IST] —**trans′for·ma′tion·al·ism,** *n.*

transforma′tional rule′, *Ling.* a rule of transformational grammar that relates two phrase markers in the course of a derivation from the deep to the surface syntactic representation of a sentence, as by reordering, inserting, or deleting elements; a rule that converts deep structures into surface structures.

trans·for·ma·tion·ist (trans′fər mā′shə nist), *n.* transformist. [1885–90; TRANSFORMATION + -IST]

transforma′tion point′, *Metall.* a temperature at which the transformation of one microconstituent to another begins or ends during heating or cooling. Also called **transforma′tion tem′perature.**

transforma′tion range′, *Metall.* the temperature range within which austenite forms when a ferrous metal is heated, or within which it disappears when the metal is cooled.

trans·form·er (trans fôr′mər), *n.* **1.** a person or thing that transforms. **2.** *Elect.* an electric device consisting essentially of two or more windings wound on the same core, which by electromagnetic induction transforms electric energy from one set of one or more circuits to another set of one or more circuits such that the frequency of the energy remains unchanged while the voltage and current usually change. [1595–1605; TRANSFORM + -ER[1]]

trans′form fault′, *Geol.* a strike-slip fault that offsets a mid-ocean ridge in opposing directions on either side of an axis of seafloor spreading. Cf. **fracture zone.**

trans·form·ism (trans fôr′miz əm), *n. Biol.* **1.** the doctrine of gradual transformation of one species into another by descent with modification through many generations. **2.** such transformation itself. **3.** any doctrine or instance of evolution. [1875–80; TRANSFORM + -ISM, modeled on F *transformisme*]

trans·form·ist (trans fôr′mist), *n.* an adherent of transformism. [1790–1800; TRANSFORM + -IST, modeled on F *transformiste*] —**trans′form·is′tic,** *adj.*

trans·fuse (trans fyo͞oz′), *v.t.,* **-fused, -fus·ing. 1.** to transfer or pass from one to another; transmit; instill: *to transfuse a love of literature to one's students.* **2.** to diffuse into or through; permeate; infuse. **3.** *Med.* **a.** to transfer (blood) into the veins or arteries of a person or animal. **b.** to inject, as a saline solution, into a blood vessel. **4.** *Archaic.* to pour from one container into another. [1375–1425; late ME *transfusen* < L *trānsfūsus,* ptp. of *trānsfundere* to transfer by pouring. See TRANS-, FUSE[2]] —**trans·fus′er,** *n.* —**trans·fus′i·ble, trans·fus′a·ble,** *adj.* —**trans·fu·sive** (trans fyo͞o′siv, -ziv), *adj.*

trans·fu·sion (trans fyo͞o′zhən), *n.* **1.** the act or process of transfusing. **2.** *Med.* the direct transferring of blood, plasma, or the like into a blood vessel. [1570–80; < L *trānsfūsiōn-* (s. of *trānsfūsiō*) decanting, intermingling, equiv. to *trānsfūs(us)* (see TRANSFUSE) + *-iōn-* -ION]

trans·gen·ic (trans jen′ik, tranz-), *adj.* of, pertaining to, or containing a gene or genes transferred from another species: *transgenic mice.* [1980–85]

trans·gress (trans gres′, tranz-), —*v.i.* **1.** to violate a law, command, moral code, etc.; offend; sin. —*v.t.* **2.** to pass over or go beyond (a limit, boundary, etc.): *to transgress bounds of prudence.* **3.** to go beyond the limits imposed by (a law, command, etc.); violate; infringe: *to transgress the will of God.* [1520–30; < L *trānsgressus* (ptp. of *trānsgredī* to step across), equiv. to *trāns-* TRANS- + *-gred-* (comb. form of *gradī* to step; see GRADE) + *-tus* ptp. suffix, with *dt* > *ss*] —**trans·gres′sive,** *adj.* —**trans·gres′sive·ly,** *adv.* —**trans·gres′sor,** *n.*
—**Syn. 1.** err, trespass. **3.** contravene, disobey.

trans·gres·sion (trans gresh′ən, tranz-), *n.* an act of transgressing; violation of a law, command, etc.; sin. [1400–50; late ME < L *trānsgressiōn-* (s. of *trānsgressiō*) a stepping across. See TRANSGRESS, -ION]
—**Syn.** See **breach.**

tran·ship (tran ship′), *v.t., v.i.,* **-shipped, -ship·ping.** transship. —**tran·ship′ment,** *n.* —**tran·ship′per,** *n.*

trans·hu·mance (trans hyo͞o′məns *or, often,* yo͞o′-, tranz-), *n.* the seasonal migration of livestock, and the people who tend them, between lowlands and adjacent mountains. [1900–05; < F, equiv. to *transhum(er)* to shift ground (modeled on Sp *trashumar;* see TRANS-, HUMUS) + *-ance* -ANCE] —**trans·hu′mant,** *adj.*

tran·sience (tran′shəns, -zhəns, -zē əns), *n.* transient state or quality. Also, **tran′sien·cy.** [1735–45; TRANSI(ENT) + -ENCE]

tran·sient (tran′shənt, -zhənt, -zē ənt), *adj.* **1.** not lasting, enduring, or permanent; transitory. **2.** lasting only a short time; existing briefly; temporary: *transient authority.* **3.** staying only a short time: *the transient guests at a hotel.* **4.** *Philos.* transeunt. —*n.* **5.** a person or thing that is transient, esp. a temporary guest, boarder, laborer, or the like. **6.** *Math.* **a.** a function that tends to zero as the independent variable tends to infinity. **b.** a solution, esp. of a differential equation, having this property. **7.** *Physics.* **a.** a nonperiodic signal of short duration. **b.** a decaying signal, wave, or oscillation. **8.** *Elect.* a sudden pulse of voltage or current. [1590–1600; < L *trānsi(ēns)* (nom. sing.), prp. of *trānsīre* to pass by, lit., go across + -ENT; see TRANSEUNT] —**tran′sient·ly,** *adv.* —**tran′sient·ness,** *n.*
—**Syn. 2.** fleeting, flitting, flying, fugitive, evanescent. See **temporary.** —**Ant. 2.** permanent.

tran′sient ische′mic attack′, *Pathol.* a brief vascular spasm in which a partially blocked artery impedes blood flow to the brain, resulting in symptoms such as impaired vision, dizziness, numbness, or unconsciousness. *Abbr.:* TIA

tran′sient modula′tion, *Music.* a modulation of a temporary nature. Also called **passing modulation.**

tran·sig·ni·fi·ca·tion (tran sig′nə fi kā′shən), *n. Theol.* (in the Eucharist) a change in the significance of the bread and wine to symbolize the body and blood of Christ. Cf. **transubstantiation.** [1965–70; TRAN(S)- + SIGNIFICATION]

tran·sil·i·ent (tran sil′ē ənt, -sil′yənt), *adj.* leaping or passing from one thing or state to another. [1805–15; < L *trānsilient-* (s. of *trānsiliēns*), prp. of *trānsilīre* to leap across, equiv. to *trāns-* TRANS- + *-sili-* (comb. form of *salīre* to leap) + *-ent-* -ENT] —**tran·sil′i·ence,** *n.*

trans·il·lu·mi·nate (trans′i lo͞o′mə nāt′, tranz′-), *v.t.,* **-nat·ed, -nat·ing. 1.** to cause light to pass through. **2.** *Med.* to throw a strong light through (an organ or part) as a means of diagnosis. [1885–90; TRANS- + ILLUMINATE] —**trans′il·lu′mi·na′tion,** *n.* —**trans′il·lu′mi·na′tor,** *n.*

tran·sis·tor (tran zis′tər), *n.* **1.** *Electronics.* a semiconductor device that amplifies, oscillates, or switches the flow of current between two terminals by varying the current or voltage between one of the terminals and a third: although much smaller in size than a vacuum tube, it performs similar functions without requiring current to heat a cathode. **2.** *Informal.* a transistorized radio. —*adj.* **3.** *Informal.* transistorized: *a transistor radio.* [1945–50; TRANS(FER) + (RES)ISTOR]

tran·sis·tor·ize (tran zis′tə rīz′), *v.t.,* **-ized, -iz·ing.** *Electronics.* to equip with or convert to a circuit employing transistors. Also, *esp. Brit.,* **tran·sis′tor·ise′.** [1950–55; TRANSISTOR + -IZE]

tran·sit (tran′sit, -zit), *n., v.,* **-sit·ed, -sit·ing.** —*n.* **1.** the act or fact of passing across or through; passage from one place to another. **2.** conveyance or transportation from one place to another, as of persons or goods, esp., local public transportation: *city transit.* Cf. **mass transit. 3.** a transition or change. **4.** *Astron.* **a.** the passage of a heavenly body across the meridian of a given location or through the field of a telescope. **b.** the passage of Mercury or Venus across the disk of the sun, or of a satellite or its shadow across the face of its primary. **c.** See **meridian circle. 5.** *Astrol.* the passage of a planet in aspect to another planet or a specific point in a horoscope. **6.** *Survey.* **a.** Also called **transit instrument.** an instrument, as a theodolite, having a telescope that can be transited, used for measuring horizontal and sometimes vertical angles. **b.** a repeating transit theodolite. **7.** (*cap.*) *U.S. Aerospace.* one of a series of satellites for providing positional data to ships and aircraft. —*v.t.* **8.** to pass across or through. **9.** *Survey.* to turn (the telescope of a transit) in a vertical plane in order to reverse direction; plunge. **10.** *Astron.* to cross (a meridian, celestial body, etc.). —*v.i.* **11.** to pass over or through something; make a transit. **12.** *Astron.* to make a transit across a meridian, celestial body, etc. [1400–50; late ME (n. and v.) < L *trānsitus* a going across, passage, equiv. to *trānsi-,* var. s. of *trānsīre* to cross (*trāns-* TRANS- + *-īre* to go) + *-tus* suffix of v. action]

tran·sit·a·ble (tran′si tə bəl, -zi-), *adj.* capable of being crossed or passed over. [1835–45; TRANSIT + -ABLE]

tran′sit cir′cle, *Astron.* See **meridian circle.** [1835–45]

tran′sit in′strument, **1.** *Astron.* See **meridian circle. 2.** *Survey.* transit (def. 6a). [1805–15]

tran·si·tion (tran zish′ən, -sish′-), *n.* **1.** movement, passage, or change from one position, state, stage, subject, concept, etc., to another; change: *the transition from adolescence to adulthood.* **2.** *Music.* **a.** a passing from one key to another; modulation. **b.** a brief modulation; a modulation used in passing. **c.** a sudden, unprepared

CONCISE ETYMOLOGY KEY: <, descended or borrowed from; >, whence; b., blend of, blended; c., cognate with; cf., compare; deriv., derivative; equiv., equivalent; imit., imitative; obl., oblique; r., replacing; s., stem; sp., spelling, spelled; resp., respelling, respelled; trans., translation; ?, origin unknown; *, unattested; ‡, probably earlier than. See the full key inside the front cover.

trans′es·sen′ti·ate′, *v.t.,* **-at·ed, -at·ing.**
trans′-Eu·phra′tes, *adj.*
trans′ex·pe′ri·en′tial, *adj.*
trans·fash′ion, *n.*
trans·fea′ture, *v.t.,* **-tured, -tur·ing.**
trans′fil·tra′tion, *n.*
trans·flu′ent, *adj.*
trans·flu′vi·al, *adj.*
trans·flux′, *n.*
trans·fron′tal, *adj.;* **-ly,** *adv.*
trans′fron·tier′, *adj.*
trans′-Ger·man′ic, *adj.*
trans-Gram′pi·an, *adj.*
trans′-Him·a·lay′an, *adj.*
trans′-His·pan′ic, *adj.*
trans·hu′man, *adj.*
trans′-I·be′ri·an, *adj.*
trans·il′i·ac′, *adj.*
trans-In′di·an, *adj.*
trans′in·di·vid′u·al, *adj.*
trans-In′dus, *adj.*
trans·in′su·lar, *adj.*
trans′-I·ra′ni·an, *adj.*
trans′-I·raq′, *adj.*

modulation. **3.** a passage from one scene to another by sound effects, music, etc., as in a television program, theatrical production, or the like. —*v.i.* **4.** to make a transition: *He had difficulty transitioning from enlisted man to officer.* [1545–55; < L *trānsitiōn-* (s. of *trānsitiō*) a going across, equiv. to *trānsit(us)* (ptp. of *transīre* to cross; cf. TRANSIT) + *-iōn-* -ION] —**tran·si′tion·al, tran·si·tion·a·ry** (tran zish′ə ner′ē, -sish′-), *adj.* —**tran·si′·tion·al·ly,** *adv.*
—**Syn. 1.** changeover, passing, conversion.

transi′tion ar′ea, *Ling.* (in dialect geography) an area whose dialect has been influenced by the dialect of one or more neighboring focal areas. Cf. **focal area, relic area.** Also called **graded area.**

transi′tion el′ement, *Chem.* any element in any of the series of elements with atomic numbers 21–29, 39–47, 57–79, and 89–107, that in a given inner orbital has less than a full quota of electrons. Also called **transi′tion met′al.** [1920–25]

transi′tion probabil′ity, *Math.* the probability of going from a given state to the next state in a Markov process.

transi′tion tem′perature, *Physics.* a temperature at which a substance undergoes some abrupt change in its properties, as when it passes from the normal to the superconducting state. Also called **transi′tion point′.**

tran·si·tive (tran′si tiv, -zi-), *adj.* **1.** *Gram.* having the nature of a transitive verb. **2.** characterized by or involving transition; transitional; intermediate. **3.** passing over to or affecting something else; transeunt. **4.** *Math.* noting a relation in which one element in relation to a second element and the second in relation to a third element implies the first element is in relation to the third element, as the relation "less than or equal to." —*n.* **5.** *Gram.* See **transitive verb.** [1550–60; < LL *trānsitīvus,* equiv. to L *trānsit(us)* (see TRANSITION) + *-īvus* -IVE] —**tran′si·tive·ly,** *adv.* —**tran′si·tive·ness, tran′si·tiv′i·ty,** *n.*

tran′sitive verb′, *Gram.* a verb accompanied by a direct object and from which a passive can be formed, as *deny, rectify, elect.* [1580–90]

tran·sit·man (tran′sit mən, -zit-), *n., pl.* **-men.** *Survey.* a person who makes observations with a transit. [TRANSIT + -MAN]

tran′sit num′ber, an identifying number assigned by a banking organization to a bank and printed on its checks.

tran·si·to·ry (tran′si tôr′ē, -tōr′ē, -zi-), *adj.* **1.** not lasting, enduring, permanent, or eternal. **2.** lasting only a short time; brief; short-lived; temporary. [1325–75; ME *transitorie* < LL *trānsitōrius* fleeting (see TRANSIT, -TORY[1]); r. ME *transitoire* < MF < LL, as above] —**tran·si·to·ri·ly** (tran′si tôr′ə lē, -tōr′-, tran′si tôr′-, -tōr′-, -zi-), *adv.* —**tran′si·to′ri·ness,** *n.*
—**Syn. 2.** See **temporary.** —**Ant. 2.** permanent.

tran′sit shed′, a building located on or near a pier (**piershed**) or wharf (**wharf shed**) used for short-term storage of cargo in transit.

tran′sit theod′olite, a theodolite having a telescope that can be transited. [1860–65]

Trans·jor·dan (trans jôr′dn, tranz-), *n.* an area east of the Jordan River, in SW Asia: a British mandate (1921–23); an emirate (1923–49); now the major part of the kingdom of Jordan. Also, **Trans-Jor′dan.**

Trans·kei (trans kā′, -kī′), *n.* a self-governing Bantu territory of South Africa on the Indian Ocean: granted independence in 1976 by South Africa, but not recognized by any other country as an independent state. 1,900,000; 16,910 sq. mi. (43,798 sq. km). *Cap.:* Umtata. —**Trans·kei′an,** *adj., n.*

transl., **1.** translated. **2.** translation. **3.** translator.

trans·late (trans lāt′, tranz-, trans′lāt, tranz′-), *v.,* **-lat·ed, -lat·ing.** —*v.t.* **1.** to turn from one language into another or from a foreign language into one's own: *to translate Spanish.* **2.** to change the form, condition, nature, etc., of; transform; convert: *to translate wishes into deeds.* **3.** to explain in terms that can be more easily understood; interpret. **4.** to bear, carry, or move from one place, position, etc., to another; transfer. **5.** *Mech.* to cause (a body) to move without rotation or angular displacement; subject to translation. **6.** *Computers.* to convert (a program, data, code, etc.) from one form to another: *to translate a FORTRAN program into assembly language.* **7.** *Telegraphy.* to retransmit or forward (a message), as by a relay. **8.** *Eccles.* **a.** to move (a bishop) from one see to another. **b.** to move (a see) from one place to another. **c.** to move (relics) from one place to another. **9.** to convey or remove to heaven without natural death. **10.** *Math.* to perform a translation on (a set, function, etc.). **11.** to express the value of (a currency) in a foreign currency by applying the exchange rate. **12.** to exalt in spiritual or emotional ecstasy; enrapture. —*v.i.* **13.** to provide or make a translation; act as translator. **14.** to admit of translation: *The Greek expression does not translate easily into English.* [1250–1300; ME *translaten* < L *trānslātus* (ptp. of *trānsferre* to transfer), equiv. to *trāns-* TRANS- + *-lātus* (suppletive ptp. of *ferre* to BEAR[1]), earlier **tlātus,* equiv. to **tlā-* bear (akin to THOLE[2]) + *-tus* ptp. suffix] —**trans·lat′a·ble,** *adj.* —**trans·lat′a·bil′i·ty, trans·lat′a·ble·ness,** *n.*

trans·lat·er (trans lā′tər, tranz-, trans′lā tər, tranz′-), *n.* translator (def. 1).

trans·la·tion (trans lā′shən, tranz-), *n.* **1.** the rendering of something into another language or into one's own from another language. **2.** a version of such a rendering: *a new translation of Plato.* **3.** change or conversion to another form, appearance, etc.; transformation: *a swift translation of thought into action.* **4.** the act or process of translating. **5.** the state of being translated. **6.** *Mech.* motion in which all particles of a body move with the same velocity along parallel paths. **7.** *Telegraphy.* the retransmitting or forwarding of a message, as by relay. **8.** *Math.* **a.** a function obtained from a given function by adding the same constant to each value of the variable of the given function and moving the graph of the function a constant distance to the right or left. **b.** a transformation in which every point of a geometric figure is moved the same distance in the same direction. **9.** *Genetics.* the process by which a messenger RNA molecule specifies the linear sequence of amino acids on a ribosome for protein synthesis. Cf. **genetic code.** [1300–50; < L *trānslātiōn-* (s. of *trānslātiō*) a transferring, equiv. to *trānslāt(us)* (see TRANSLATE) + *-iōn-* -ION; r. ME *translacioun* < AF < L, as above] —**trans·la′tion·al,** *adj.* —**trans·la′tion·al·ly,** *adv.*
—**Syn. 2.** TRANSLATION, PARAPHRASE, VERSION refer to a rewording of something. A TRANSLATION is a rendering of the same ideas in a different language from the original: *a translation from Greek into English.* A PARAPHRASE is a free rendering of the sense of a passage in other words, usually in the same language: *a paraphrase of a poem.* A VERSION is a translation, esp. of the Bible, or else an account of something illustrating a particular point of view: *the Douay Version.*

transla′tion of ax′es (ak′sēz), *Math.* the process of replacing the axes in a Cartesian coordinate system with a new set of axes, parallel to the first, used to write equations of curves not centered about the origin.

trans·la·tive (trans lā′tiv, tranz-, trans′lā-, tranz′-), *adj.* **1.** of or pertaining to the transfer of something from one person, position, or place to another. **2.** of translation; serving to translate. **3.** *Gram.* noting a case, as in Finnish, whose distinctive function is to indicate a change from one state into another. —*n.* **4.** the translative case. [1580–90; < L *trānslātīvus,* equiv. to *trānslāt(us)* (see TRANSLATE) + *-īvus* -IVE]

trans·la·tor (trans lā′tər, tranz-, trans′lā tər, tranz′-), *n.* **1.** Also, **translater.** a person who translates. **2.** *Television.* a relay station that receives programming on one frequency and rebroadcasts it at another frequency for improved local reception. [1350–1400; ME *translatour* (< MF) < LL *trānslātor* (L: one who transfers a thing); see TRANSLATE, -TOR]

trans·lit·er·ate (trans lit′ə rāt′, tranz-), *v.t.,* **-at·ed, -at·ing.** to change (letters, words, etc.) into corresponding characters of another alphabet or language: *to transliterate the Greek* X *as* ch. [1860–65; TRANS- + L *liter(a)* LETTER[1] + -ATE[1]] —**trans·lit′er·a′tion,** *n.* —**trans·lit′·er·a′tor,** *n.*

trans·lo·cate (trans lō′kāt, tranz-), *v.t.,* **-cat·ed, -cat·ing.** to move or transfer from one place to another; cause to change location; displace; dislocate. [1825–35; TRANS- + LOCATE]

trans·lo·ca·tion (trans′lō kā′shən, tranz′-), *n.* **1.** a change of location. **2.** *Genetics.* a chromosomal rearrangement in which a segment of genetic material from one chromosome becomes heritably linked to another chromosome. **3.** *Bot.* the conduction of soluble food material from one part of a plant to another. [1615–25; TRANS- + LOCATION]

trans·lu·cent (trans lo͞o′sənt, tranz-), *adj.* **1.** permitting light to pass through but diffusing it so that persons, objects, etc., on the opposite side are not clearly visible: *Frosted window glass is translucent but not transparent.* **2.** easily understandable; lucid: *a translucent explication.* **3.** clear; transparent: *translucent seawater.* [1590–1600; < L *trānslūcent-* (s. of *trānslūcēns*), prp. of *trānslūcēre* to shine through. See TRANS-, LUCENT] —**trans·lu′·cence, trans·lu′cen·cy,** *n.* —**trans·lu′cent·ly,** *adv.*
—**Syn. 1.** See **transparent.** —**Ant. 1.** opaque.

trans·lu·cid (trans lo͞o′sid, tranz-), *adj.* translucent. [1620–30; < L *trānslūcidus* clear, transparent. See TRANS-, LUCID]

trans·lu·ci·dus (trans lo͞o′si dəs, tranz-), *adj. Meteorol.* (of a cloud) sufficiently transparent as not to obscure the sun, moon, or higher clouds. [< NL; see TRANSLUCID]

trans·lu·nar (trans′lo͞o′nər, tranz′-; trans lo͞o′nər, tranz-), *adj.* **1.** translunary. **2.** *Aerospace, Astron.* of or pertaining to the region of space extending beyond the moon's orbit. [1925–30; TRANS- + LUNAR]

trans·lu·nar·y (trans′lo͞o ner′ē, tranz′-; trans lo͞o′nə rē, tranz-), *adj.* **1.** situated beyond or above the moon; superlunary. **2.** celestial, rather than earthly. **3.** ideal; visionary. Also, **translunar.** [1620–30; TRANS- + *lunary* < F *lun(aire)* or L *lun(āris)* LUNAR + -ARY]

trans·ma·rine (trans′mə rēn′, tranz′-), *adj.* **1.** being on or coming from the opposite side of the sea or ocean. **2.** being or crossing over the sea or ocean. [1575–85; < L *trānsmarīnus.* See TRANS-, MARINE]

trans·mem·brane (trans mem′brān, tranz-), *adj. Biol.* occurring across a membrane, as an electric potential or the transport of ions or gases. [1940–45; TRANS- + MEMBRANE]

trans·meth·yl·a·tion (trans′meth ə lā′shən, tranz′-), *n. Chem.* the transfer of a methyl group from one compound to another. [TRANS- + METHYLATION]

trans·mi·grant (trans mī′grənt, tranz-), *n.* **1.** a person or thing that transmigrates. **2.** a person passing through a country or place on the way to another place in which he or she intends to settle. —*adj.* **3.** passing from one place or state to another. [1665–75; < L *trānsmigrant-* (s. of *trānsmigrāns*), prp. of *trānsmigrāre* to depart, migrate. See TRANS-, MIGRANT]

trans·mi·grate (trans mī′grāt, tranz-), *v.,* **-grat·ed, -grat·ing.** —*v.i.* **1.** to move or pass from one place to another. **2.** to migrate from one country to another in order to settle there. **3.** (of the soul) to be reborn after death in another body. —*v.t.* **4.** to cause to transmigrate, as a soul; transfer. [1400–50; late ME < L *trānsmigrātus* (ptp. of *trānsmigrāre* to depart, migrate). See TRANS-, MIGRATE] —**trans·mi′gra·tor,** *n.* —**trans·mi·gra·to·ry** (trans mī′grə tôr′ē, -tōr′ē, tranz-), **trans·mi′·gra·tive,** *adj.*

trans·mi·gra·tion (trans′mī grā′shən, tranz′-), *n.* **1.** the act of transmigrating. **2.** the passage of a soul after death into another body; metempsychosis. Cf. **reincarnation.** [1250–1300; ME *transmigracion* < LL *trānsmigrātiōn-* (s. of *trānsmigrātiō*) removal. See TRANS-, MIGRATION]

trans·mis·si·ble (trans mis′ə bəl, tranz-), *adj.* capable of being transmitted. [1635–45; < L *trānsmiss(us)* (see TRANSMISSION) + -IBLE] —**trans·mis′si·bil′i·ty,** *n.*

trans·mis·sion (trans mish′ən, tranz-), *n.* **1.** the act or process of transmitting. **2.** the fact of being transmitted. **3.** something that is transmitted. **4.** *Mach.* **a.** transference of force between machines or mechanisms, often with changes of torque and speed. **b.** a compact, enclosed unit of gears or the like for this purpose, as in an automobile. **5.** *Radio and Television.* the broadcasting of electromagnetic waves from one location to another, as from a transmitter to a receiver. **6.** *Physics.* transmittance. [1605–15; < L *trānsmissiōn-* (s. of *trānsmissiō*) a sending across, equiv. to *trānsmiss(us)* (ptp. of *trānsmittere* to send across) + *-iōn-* -ION. See TRANS-, MISSION] —**trans·mis·sive** (trans mis′iv, tranz-), *adj.* —**trans·mis′sive·ly,** *adv.* —**trans·mis′sive·ness,** *n.*
—**Syn. 1, 2.** transfer, passage, passing, conveyance.

transmis′sion line′, *Elect.* a system of conductors, as coaxial cable, a wave guide, or a pair of parallel wires, used to transmit signals. [1905–10]

transmis′sion stop′ sys′tem. See **T-stop system.**

trans-Mis·sis·sip·pi (trans′mis ə sip′ē, tranz′-), *adj.* across or beyond the Mississippi River. —**trans′-Mis·sis·sip′i·an,** *adj., n.*

trans·mis·siv·i·ty (trans′mi siv′i tē, tranz′-), *n. Physics.* a measure of the ability of a material or medium to transmit electromagnetic energy, as light. Cf. **transmittance.** [1910–15; TRANSMISS(ION) + -IVE + -ITY]

trans·mis·som·e·ter (trans′mə som′i tər, tranz′-), *n. Meteorol.* an instrument for measuring visibility or the transmission of light in the atmosphere. Also called **hazemeter, transmit′tance me′ter.** [1930–35; TRANSMISS(ION) + -O- + -METER]

trans·mit (trans mit′, tranz-), *v.,* **-mit·ted, -mit·ting.** —*v.t.* **1.** to send or forward, as to a recipient or destination; dispatch; convey. **2.** to communicate, as information or news. **3.** to pass or spread (disease, infection, etc.) to another. **4.** to pass on (a genetic characteristic) from parent to offspring: *The mother transmitted her red hair to her daughter.* **5.** *Physics.* **a.** to cause (light, heat, sound, etc.) to pass through a medium. **b.** to convey or pass along (an impulse, force, motion, etc.). **c.** to permit (light, heat, etc.) to pass through: *Glass transmits light.* **6.** *Radio and Television.* to emit (electromagnetic waves). —*v.i.* **7.** to send a signal by wire, radio, or television waves. **8.** to pass on a right or obligation to heirs or descendants. [1350–1400; ME *transmitten* < L *trānsmittere* to send across, equiv. to *trāns-* TRANS- + *mittere* to send] —**trans·mit′ta·ble, trans·mit′ti·ble,** *adj.*
—**Syn. 1.** transfer, remit. **2.** bear. See **carry.**

trans·mit·tal (trans mit′l, tranz-), *n.* transmission. [1715–25; TRANSMIT + -AL[2]]

trans·mit·tance (trans mit′ns, tranz-), *n. Physics.* the ratio of the radiant flux transmitted through and emerging from a body to the total flux incident on it: equivalent to one minus the absorptance. Also called **transmission.** [1850–55; TRANSMIT + -ANCE]

trans·mit·ter (trans mit′ər, tranz-), *n.* **1.** a person or thing that transmits. **2.** Also called **transmit′ting set′.** *Radio.* a device for sending electromagnetic waves; the part of a broadcasting apparatus that generates and modulates the radiofrequency current and conveys it to the antenna. **3.** the part of a telephonic or telegraphic apparatus that converts sound waves or mechanical movements into corresponding electric waves or impulses. **4.** *Biochem.* neurotransmitter. [1720–30; TRANSMIT + -ER[1]]

trans·mog·ri·fy (trans mog′rə fī′, tranz-), *v.t.,* **-fied, -fy·ing.** to change in appearance or form, esp. strangely or grotesquely; transform. [1650–60; earlier also *transmigrify, transmography;* appar. a pseudo-Latinism with TRANS-, -IFY] —**trans·mog′ri·fi·ca′tion,** *n.*

CONCISE PRONUNCIATION KEY: act, cāpe, dâre, pärt; set, ēqual; *if,* īce; ox, ōver, ôrder, oil, bo͝ok, bo͞ot, out; up, ûrge; child; sing; shoe; thin, *that;* zh as in *treasure.* ə = *a* as in *alone, e* as in *system, i* as in *easily, o* as in *gallop, u* as in *circus;* ° as in *fire* (fī°r), *hour* (ou°r). l and n can serve as syllabic consonants, as in *cradle* (krād′l), and *button* (but′n). See the full key inside the front cover.

trans·isth′mi·an, *adj.*
trans-Jo′vi·an, *adj.*
trans′-Li·be′ri·an, *adj.*
trans-Lib′y·an, *adj.*
trans·light′, *n.*
trans·make′, *v.t.,* **-made, -mak·ing.**
trans′-Man·chu′ri·an, *adj.*
trans·mar′gi·nal, *adj.;* **-ly,** *adv.*
trans-Mar′tian, *adj.*
trans′ma·te′ri·al, *adj.*
trans′-Med·i·ter·ra′ne·an, *adj.*
trans·men′tal, *adj.;* **-ly,** *adv.*
trans′me·rid′i·o·nal, *adj.;* **-ly,** *adv.*
trans·mold′, *v.t.*
trans′-Mon·go′li·an, *adj.*
trans·mould′, *v.t.*
trans′mun·dane′, *adj.*
trans·mus′cle, *n.*
trans·mu′tu·al, *adj.;* **-ly,** *adv.*
trans·nat′ur·al, *adj.;* **-ly,** *adv.*
trans′-Nep·tu′ni·an, *adj.*
trans-Ni′ger, *adj.*
trans·nor′mal, *adj.;* **-ly,** *adv.*
trans·oc′u·lar, *adj.*
trans·or′bi·tal, *adj.*

trans·mon·tane (trans mon′tān, tranz-, trans′mon tān′, tranz′-), *adj.* tramontane. [1720–30; < L *trānsmontānus*; see TRANS-, MOUNT[2], -AN]

trans·mun·dane (trans′mun dān′, tranz′-; trans mun′dān, tranz-), *adj.* reaching beyond or existing outside the physical or visible world. [1770–80; TRANS- + MUNDANE]

trans·mu·ta·tion (trans′myo͞o tā′shən, tranz′-), *n.* **1.** the act or process of transmuting. **2.** the fact or state of being transmuted. **3.** change into another nature, substance, form, or condition. **4.** *Biol.* the transformation of one species into another. Cf. **transformism. 5.** *Physics.* any process in which a nuclide is transformed into a different nuclide, usually one of a different element. **6.** *Alchemy.* the supposed conversion of base metals into metals of greater value, esp. into gold or silver. [1350–1400; ME *transmutacio(u)n* (< OF *transmutation*) < L *trānsmūtātiōn-* (s. of *trānsmūtātiō*) a changing, shifting, equiv. to *trānsmūtāt(us)* (ptp. of *trānsmūtāre* to change) + *-iōn-* -ION. See TRANSMUTE, -ATION] **—trans′mu·ta′tion·al, trans·mut·a·tive** (trans myo͞o′tə tiv, tranz-), *adj.* **—trans′mu·ta′tion·ist,** *n.*

trans·mute (trans myo͞ot′, tranz-), *v.t., v.i.,* **-mut·ed, -mut·ing.** to change from one nature, substance, form, or condition into another; transform. [1400–50; late ME < L *trānsmūtāre* to shift, equiv. to *trāns-* TRANS- + *mūtāre* to change.] **—trans·mut′a·ble,** *adj.* **—trans·mut′a·bil′i·ty, trans·mut′a·ble·ness,** *n.* **—trans·mut′a·bly,** *adv.* **—trans·mut′er,** *n.*
—Syn. metamorphose, convert, alter.

trans·na·tion·al (trans nash′ə nl, tranz-), *adj.* **1.** going beyond national boundaries or interests: *a transnational economy.* **2.** comprising persons, sponsors, etc., of different nationalities: *a transnational company.* **—***n.* **3.** a company, organization, etc., representing two or more nationalities. [1920–25; TRANS- + NATIONAL] **—trans·na′tion·al·ism,** *n.* **—trans·na′tion·al·ly,** *adv.*

trans·o·ce·an·ic (trans′ō shē an′ik, tranz′-), *adj.* **1.** extending across or traversing the ocean: *a transoceanic cable.* **2.** situated or living beyond the ocean: *transoceanic peoples.* [1820–30; TRANS- + OCEANIC]

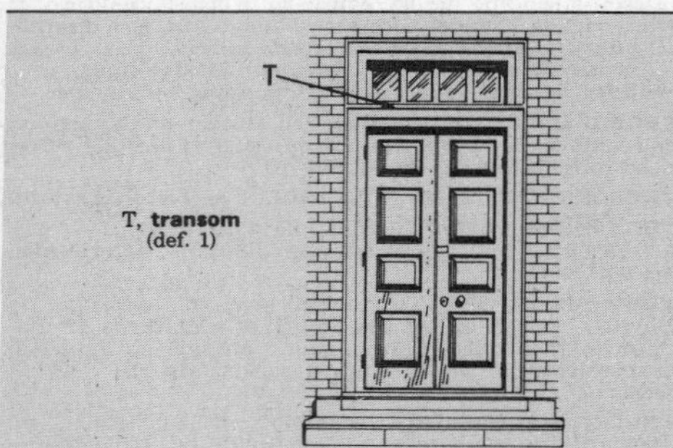

T, transom (def. 1)

tran·som (tran′səm), *n.* **1.** a crosspiece separating a door or the like from a window or fanlight above it. **2.** Also called **tran′som light′, transom window.** a window above such a crosspiece. **3.** a crossbar of wood or stone, dividing a window horizontally. **4.** a window so divided. **5.** *Naut.* **a.** a flat termination to a stern, above the water line. **b.** framework running athwartships in way of the sternpost of a steel or iron vessel, used as a support for the frames of the counter. **6.** *Artillery.* a metal piece connecting the sidepieces of the tail or the cheeks of a gun carriage. [1325–75; late ME *traunsum, traunsom,* ME *transyn,* prob. alter. (by assoc. with TRANS-) of *traversayn* < OF *traversin* crosspiece, deriv. of *travers* breadth; see TRAVERSE] **—tran′somed,** *adj.*

T, transom (def. 5a)

tran′som win′dow, 1. a window divided by a transom. **2.** transom (def. 2). [1680–90]

tran·son·ic (tran son′ik), *adj. Chiefly Aeron.* close to the speed of propagation of sound; moving at 700–780 mph (1127–1255 km/h) at sea level. Also, **transsonic.** [1940–45; TRANS- + SONIC]

transon′ic bar′rier. See **sound barrier.**

transp., 1. transparent. **2.** transportation.

trans·pa·cif·ic (trans′pə sif′ik), *adj.* **1.** passing or extending across the Pacific. **2.** beyond or on the other side of the Pacific. [1890–95; TRANS- + PACIFIC]

trans·pa·dane (trans′pə dān′, trans pā′dān), *adj.* on the farther side, esp. the northern side of the Po River. [1610–20; < L *trānspadānus* beyond the Po, equiv. to *trāns-* TRANS- + *Pad(us)* Po + *-ānus* -ANE]

trans·par·en·cy (trans pâr′ən sē, -par′-), *n., pl.* **-cies. 1.** Also, **trans·par′ence.** the quality or state of being transparent. **2.** something transparent, esp. a picture, design, or the like on glass or some translucent substance, made visible by light shining through from behind. **3.** *Photog.* **a.** the proportion of the light that is passed through the emulsion on an area of a photographic image. **b.** a photographic print on a clear base for viewing by transmitted light. [1585–95; < ML *trānsparentia.* See TRANSPARENT, -ENCY]

trans·par·ent (trans pâr′ənt, -par′-), *adj.* **1.** having the property of transmitting rays of light through its substance so that bodies situated beyond or behind can be distinctly seen. **2.** admitting the passage of light through interstices. **3.** so sheer as to permit light to pass through; diaphanous. **4.** easily seen through, recognized, or detected: *transparent excuses.* **5.** manifest; obvious: *a story with a transparent plot.* **6.** open; frank; candid: *the man's transparent earnestness.* **7.** *Computers.* (of a process or software) operating in such a way as to not be perceived by users. **8.** *Obs.* shining through, as light. [1375–1425; late ME < ML *trānspārent-* (s. of *trānspārēns*) showing through (prp. of *trānspārēre*), equiv. to L *trāns-* TRANS- + *pārent-* (s. of *pārēns*), prp. of *pārēre* to appear; see APPARENT] **—trans·par′ent·ly,** *adv.* **—trans·par′ent·ness,** *n.*
—Syn. 1. clear, pellucid, limpid, crystalline. TRANSPARENT, TRANSLUCENT agree in describing material that light rays can pass through. That which is TRANSPARENT allows objects to be seen clearly through it: *Clear water is transparent.* That which is TRANSLUCENT allows light to pass through, diffusing it, however, so that objects beyond are not distinctly seen: *Ground glass is translucent.* **—Ant. 1.** opaque. **6.** secretive.

trans·pep·ti·da·tion (trans pep′ti dā′shən), *n. Biochem.* the process of transferring an amino acid or group of amino acids from one compound to another. [TRANS- + PEPTIDE + -ATION]

trans·per·son·al (trans pûr′sə nl), *adj.* extending beyond or transcending the personal. [1905–10; TRANS- + PERSONAL] **—trans·per′son·al·ly,** *adv.*

transper′sonal psychol′ogy, a branch of psychology or psychotherapy that recognizes altered states of consciousness and transcendent experiences as a means to understand the human mind and treat psychological disorders. [1970–75]

tran·spic·u·ous (tran spik′yo͞o əs), *adj.* transparent. [1630–40; < NL *trānspicuus,* equiv. to *trāns-* TRANS- + *(per)spicuus* transparent; see PERSPICUOUS] **—tran·spic′u·ous·ly,** *adv.*

trans·pierce (trans pērs′), *v.t.,* **-pierced, -pierc·ing.** to pierce through; penetrate; pass through. [1585–95; TRANS- + PIERCE; cf. F *transpercer*]

tran·spi·ra·tion (tran′spə rā′shən), *n.* **1.** an action or instance of transpiring. **2.** *Bot.* the passage of water through a plant from the roots through the vascular system to the atmosphere. [1545–55; TRANS- + L *spīrātiōn-,* s. of *spīrātiō* breathing (*spīrāt(us),* ptp. of *spīrāre* to breathe + *-iōn-* -ION); perh. directly < F or NL]

tran·spire (tran spīᵊr′), *v.,* **-spired, -spir·ing.** **—***v.i.* **1.** to occur; happen; take place. **2.** to emit or give off waste matter, watery vapor, etc., through the surface, as of the body or of leaves. **3.** to escape, as moisture or odor, through or as if through pores. **4.** to be revealed or become known. **—***v.t.* **5.** to emit or give off (waste matter, watery vapor, an odor, etc.) through the surface, as of the body or of leaves. [1590–1600; < MF *transpirer* < ML *trānspīrāre,* equiv. to L *trāns-* TRANS- + *spīrāre* to breathe] **—tran·spir′a·ble,** *adj.* **—tran·spir·a·to·ry** (tran spīr′ə tôr′ē, -tōr′ē), *adj.*
—Usage. 1. From its earlier literal sense "to escape as vapor" TRANSPIRE came to mean "to escape from concealment, become known" in the 18th century. Somewhat later, it developed the meaning "to occur, happen," a sentence such as *He was not aware of what had transpired yesterday* being taken to mean *He was not aware of what had happened yesterday.* In spite of two centuries of use in all varieties of speech and writing, this now common meaning is still objected to by some on the grounds that it arose from a misapprehension of the word's true meaning.

trans·pla·cen·tal (trans′plə sen′tl), *adj.* across or passing through the placenta. [1925–30; TRANS- + PLACENTAL]

trans·plan·e·tar·y (trans plan′i ter′ē), *adj.* farther from the sun than a given planet. [TRANS- + PLANETARY]

trans·plant (*v.* trans plant′, -plänt′; *n.* trans′plant′, -plänt′), *v.t.* **1.** to remove (a plant) from one place and plant it in another. **2.** *Surg.* to transfer (an organ, tissue, etc.) from one part of the body to another or from one person or animal to another. **3.** to move from one place to another. **4.** to bring (a family, colony, etc.) from one country, region, etc., to another for settlement; relocate. **—***v.i.* **5.** to undergo or accept transplanting: *to transplant easily.* **—***n.* **6.** the act or process of transplanting. **7.** a plant, organ, person, etc., that has been transplanted. [1400–50; late ME < LL *trānsplantāre,* equiv. to L *trāns-* TRANS- + *plantāre* to PLANT] **—trans·plant′a·ble,** *adj.* **—trans′plan·ta′tion,** *n.* **—trans·plant′er,** *n.*

transplanta′tion an′tigen, *Immunol.* a histocompatibility antigen identified by its effect on the rejection of transplanted cells or tissues.

trans·plant·ee (trans′plan tē′), *n.* a person who is undergoing or has undergone an organ transplant. [TRANSPLANT + -EE]

tran·spon·der (tran spon′dər), *n.* a radio, radar, or sonar transceiver that automatically transmits a signal upon reception of a designated incoming signal. Also, **tran·spon′dor.** [1940–45; TRANS(MITTER) + (RES)PONDER]

trans·po·ni·ble (trans pō′nə bəl), *adj.* capable of being transposed. [1890–95; < L *trānspōn(ere)* to transfer, remove (*trāns-* TRANS- + *pōnere* to place) + -IBLE] **—trans·po′ni·bil′i·ty,** *n.*

trans·pon·tine (trans pon′tin, -tīn), *adj.* **1.** across or beyond a bridge. **2.** on the southern side of the Thames in London. [1835–45; TRANS- + L *pont-* (s. of *pōns*) bridge + -INE[1]]

trans·port (*v.* trans pôrt′, -pōrt′; *n.* trans′pôrt, -pōrt), *v.t.* **1.** to carry, move, or convey from one place to another. **2.** to carry away by strong emotion; enrapture. **3.** to send into banishment, esp. to a penal colony. **—***n.* **4.** the act of transporting or conveying; conveyance. **5.** a means of transporting or conveying, as a truck or bus. **6.** a ship or plane employed for transporting soldiers, military stores, etc. **7.** an airplane carrying freight or passengers as part of a transportation system. **8.** a system of public travel. **9.** transportation (def. 6). **10.** strong emotion; ecstatic joy, bliss, etc. **11.** a convict sent into banishment, esp. to a penal colony: *The country had been colonized largely by transports.* **12.** *Recording.* Also called **tape transport.** a mechanism that moves magnetic tape past the head in a tape deck or tape recorder. [1325–75; ME *transporten* (v.) < L *trānsportāre* to carry across. See TRANS-, PORT[5]] **—trans·port′a·ble,** *adj.* **—trans·port′a·bil′i·ty,** *n.* **—trans·port′ive,** *adj.*
—Syn. 1. See **carry. 10.** rapture. See **ecstasy.**

trans·por·ta·tion (trans′pər tā′shən), *n.* **1.** the act of transporting. **2.** the state of being transported. **3.** the means of transport or conveyance. **4.** the business of conveying people, goods, etc. **5.** price of travel or transport by public conveyance; fare. **6.** tickets or permits for transport or travel. **7.** banishment, as of a criminal to a penal colony; deportation. **8.** (*cap.*) Also called **Transporta′tion Depart′ment.** *Informal.* the Department of Transportation. [1530–40; TRANSPORT + -ATION]

trans·port·ed (trans pôr′tid, -pōr′-), *adj.* **1.** emotionally moved; ecstatic: *transported by the music* **2.** taken or carried from one place to another. [1590–1600; TRANSPORT + -ED[2]] **—trans·port′ed·ly,** *adv.*

trans·port·er (trans pôr′tər, -pōr′-, trans′pôr′tər, -pōr′-), *n.* a person or thing that transports, esp. a very large truck for large or heavy loads, as missiles or automobiles. [1525–35; TRANPORT + -ER[1]]

transport′er bridge′, a bridge for carrying passengers and vehicles by means of a platform suspended from a trolley. Also called **ferry bridge.** [1900–05]

trans′port num′ber, *Physical Chem.* See **transference number.**

trans·pos·al (trans pō′zəl), *n.* transposition. [1685–95; TRANSPOSE + -AL[2]]

trans·pose (*v.* trans pōz′; *n.* trans′pōz), *v.,* **-posed, -pos·ing,** *n.* **—***v.t.* **1.** to change the relative position, order, or sequence of; cause to change places; interchange: *to transpose the third and fourth letters of a word.* **2.** to transfer or transport. **3.** *Algebra.* to bring (a term) from one side of an equation to the other, with corresponding change of sign. **4.** *Math.* (of a matrix) to interchange rows and columns. **5.** *Music.* to reproduce in a different key, by raising or lowering in pitch. **6.** to transform; transmute. **—***v.i.* **7.** to perform a piece of music in a key other than the one in which it is written: *to transpose at sight.* **—***n.* **8.** *Math.* a matrix formed from a given matrix by transposing. [1350–1400; ME *transposen* to transmute < MF *transposer.* See TRANS-, POSE[1]] **—trans·pos′a·ble,** *adj.* **—trans·pos′a·bil′i·ty,** *n.* **—trans·pos′er,** *n.*
—Syn. 1, 5. rearrange. **3.** invert.

trans′posed con′jugate, *Math.* adjoint (def. 2).

transpos′ing in′strument, a musical instrument played at a pitch different from that indicated in the score. [1880–85]

trans·po·si·tion (trans′pə zish′ən), *n.* **1.** an act of transposing. **2.** the state of being transposed. **3.** a transposed form of something. **4.** *Genetics.* the movement of a gene or set of genes from one DNA site to another. **5.** *Photog.* the process of reversing the tonality of an image, as from negative to positive. **6.** *Math.* a permutation of a set of elements that interchanges two elements and leaves the remaining elements in their original positions. [1530–40; < ML *trānspositiōn-* (s. of *trānspositiō*). See TRANS-, POSITION] **—trans′po·si′tion·al, trans·pos·i·tive** (trans poz′i tiv), *adj.*

transposi′tion ci′pher, *Cryptography.* a cipher that rearranges the letters of the plain text in a different sequence. Cf. **substitution cipher.** [1935–40]

trans·po·son (trans pō′zon), *Genetics.* a segment of DNA that is capable of inserting copies of itself into other DNA sites within the same cell. [1974; TRANSPOS(ITION) + -ON[1]]

trans·ra·cial (trans rā′shəl, tranz-), *adj.* involving or between two or more races: *transracial adoptions.* [1970–75; TRANS- + RACIAL] **—trans·ra′cial·ly,** *adv.*

trans·rec·ti·fi·ca·tion (trans rek′tə fi kā′shən, tranz-), *n. Elect., Electronics.* rectification occurring in one circuit as a result of the application of an alternating voltage to another circuit. [TRANS- + RECTIFICATION]

trans·rec·ti·fi·er (trans rek′tə fī′ər, tranz-), *n. Electronics.* a device, usually a vacuum tube, that provides transrectification. [TRANS- + RECTIFIER]

trans·sex·u·al (trans sek′sho͞o əl), *n.* **1.** a person having a strong desire to assume the physical character-

CONCISE ETYMOLOGY KEY: <, descended or borrowed from; >, whence; b., blend of, blended; c., cognate with; cf., compare; deriv., derivative; equiv., equivalent; imit., imitative; obl., oblique; r., replacing; s., stem; sp., spelling, spelled; resp., respelling, respelled; trans., translation; ?, origin unknown; *, unattested; ‡, probably earlier than. See the full key inside the front cover.

trans′o·var′i·an, *adj.*
trans·pal′mar, *adj.*
trans′-Pan·a·ma′ni·an, *adj.*
trans′-Par·a·guay′an, *adj.*
trans′pa·ri′e·tal, *adj.*
trans·par′ish, *adj.*
trans·pas′sion·al, *adj.*
trans·pa′tron·ize′, *v.t.,* **-ized, -iz·ing.**
trans·pen′e·tra·ble, *adj.*
trans′pen·e·tra′tion, *n.*
trans′pen·in′su·lar, *adj.*
trans′per·i·to·ne′al, *adj.;* **-ly,** *adv.*
trans-Per′sian, *adj.*
trans·phys′i·cal, *adj.;* **-ly,** *adv.*
trans·pleu′ral, *adj.;* **-ly,** *adv.*
trans·po′lar, *adj.*
trans·pour′, *v.t.*
trans·proc′ess, *n.*
trans·pul′mo·nar′y, *adj.*
trans′-Pyr·e·ne′an, *adj.*
trans·ra′tion·al, *adj.;* **-ly,** *adv.*
trans·re′al, *adj.*
trans-Rhen′ish, *adj.*
trans·riv′er·ine′, *adj.*
trans′-Sa·har′a, *adj.*

istics and gender role of the opposite sex. **2.** a person who has undergone hormone treatment and surgery to attain the physical characteristics of the opposite sex. —*adj.* **3.** of, pertaining to, or characteristic of transsexuals. [1955–60; TRANS- + SEXUAL, orig. in *transsexualism* (coined in 1953)] —**trans·sex′u·al·ism, trans·sex′u·al′i·ty,** *n.*

trans·ship (trans ship′), *v.,* **-shipped, -ship·ping.** —*v.t.* **1.** to transfer from one ship, truck, freight car, or other conveyance to another. —*v.i.* **2.** to change from one ship or other conveyance to another. Also, **tranship.** [1785–95; TRANS- + SHIP] —**trans·ship′ment,** *n.*

Trans′-Si·be′ri·an Rail′road (trans′sī bēr′ē ən, trans′-), a railroad traversing Siberia, from Chelyabinsk in the Ural Mountains to Vladivostok: constructed by the Russian government 1891–1916. over 4000 mi. (6440 km) long.

trans·son·ic (trans son′ik), *adj.* transonic.

tran·sub·stan·ti·ate (tran′səb stan′shē āt′), *v.t.,* **-at·ed, -at·ing. 1.** to change from one substance into another; transmute. **2.** *Theol.* to change (the bread and wine) into the body and blood of Christ in the Eucharist. [1400–50; v. use of late ME *transsubstanciate* (adj.) transubstantiated < ML *trānssubstantiātus,* ptp. of *trānssubstantiāre.* See TRANS-, SUBSTANCE, -ATE[1]] —**tran′·sub·stan′tial,** *adj.* —**tran′sub·stan′tial·ly,** *adv.*

tran·sub·stan·ti·a·tion (tran′səb stan′shē ā′shən), *n.* **1.** the changing of one substance into another. **2.** *Theol.* the changing of the elements of the bread and wine, when they are consecrated in the Eucharist, into the body and blood of Christ (a doctrine of the Roman Catholic Church). Cf. **transignification.** [1350–1400; ME *transubstanciacioun* < ML *trānssubstantiātiōn-* (s. of *trānssubstantiātiō*). See TRANSUBSTANTIATE, -ION]

tran·su·da·tion (tran′so͞o dā′shən), *n.* **1.** the act or process of transuding. **2.** a substance that has transuded. Also, **tran′su·date′.** [1605–15; < NL *trānsūdātiōn-* (s. of *trānsūdātiō*). See TRANSUDE, -ATE[1], -ION] —**tran·su·da·tive** (tran so͞o′də tiv), **tran·su·da·to·ry** (tran so͞o′də tôr′ē, -tōr′ē), *adj.*

tran·sude (tran so͞od′), *v.i.,* **-sud·ed, -sud·ing.** to pass or ooze through pores or interstices, as a fluid. [1655–65; < NL *trānsūdāre,* equiv. to L *trāns-* TRANS- + *sūdāre* to SWEAT]

trans′u·ran′ic el′e·ment (trans′yo͝o ran′ik, tranz′-, trans′-, tranz′-), *Chem., Physics.* any element having an atomic number greater than 92, the atomic number of uranium. All such elements are radioactive and can be synthesized by bombarding a heavy element with a light particle or element. Also, **trans·u·ra′ni·um el′ement** (trans′yo͝o rā′nē əm, tranz′-). [1930–35; TRANS- + URAN(IUM) + -IC]

Trans·vaal (trans väl′, tranz-), *n.* a province in the NE Republic of South Africa. 8,717,530; 110,450 sq. mi. (286,066 sq. km). *Cap.:* Pretoria. Formerly, **South African Republic.** —**Trans·vaal′er,** *n.* —**Trans·vaal′i·an,** *adj.*

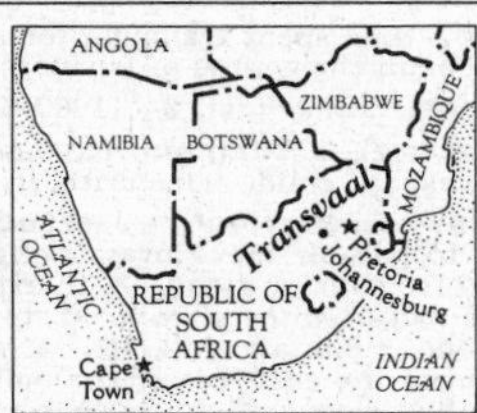

Trans′vaal dai′sy, a composite plant, *Gerbera jamesonii,* native to southern Africa, having showy, many-rayed, variously colored flower heads. [1900–05]

Trans′vaal jade′, a green grossularite, used as a gem: not a true jade. Also called **garnet jade, South African jade.**

trans·val·ue (trans val′yo͞o, tranz-), *v.t.,* **-ued, -u·ing.** to reestimate the value of, esp. on a basis differing from accepted standards; reappraise; reevaluate. [1905–10; TRANS- + VALUE] —**trans′val·u·a′tion,** *n.*

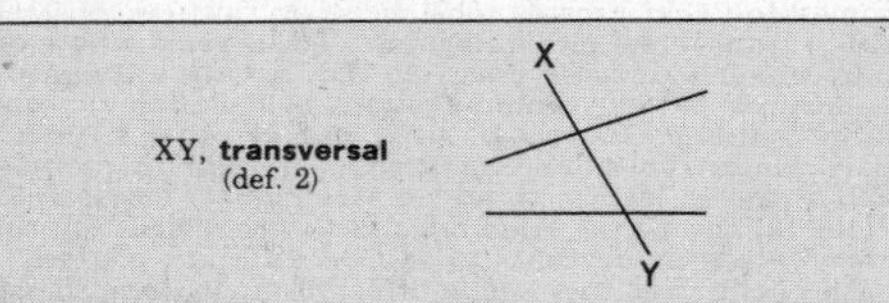

XY, **transversal** (def. 2)

trans·ver·sal (trans vûr′səl, tranz-), *adj.* **1.** transverse. —*n.* **2.** *Geom.* a line intersecting two or more lines. [1400–50; late ME (adj.) < ML *trānsversālis.* See TRANSVERSE, -AL[1]] —**trans·ver′sal·ly,** *adv.*

trans·verse (trans vûrs′, tranz-; trans′vûrs, tranz′-), *adj.* **1.** lying or extending across or in a cross direction; cross. **2.** (of a flute) having a mouth hole in the side of the tube, near its end, across which the player's breath is directed. Cf. **end-blown. 3.** (of an automotive engine) mounted with the crankshaft oriented sideways. —*n.* **4.** something that is transverse. **5.** *Naut.* See **web frame. 6.** *Geom.* See **transverse axis. 7.** a city road that cuts through a park or other area of light traffic; shortcut. [1610–20; < L *trānsversus* going or lying across, athwart. See TRAVERSE] —**trans·verse′ly,** *adv.*

trans′verse ax′is, *Geom.* **1.** the axis of a hyperbola that passes through the two foci. **2.** the segment of such an axis included between the vertices of the hyperbola. Also called **transverse.** See diag. under **hyperbola.** [1695–1705]

trans′verse co′lon (kō′lən), *Anat.* the middle portion of the colon, lying across the upper abdominal cavity between the ascending colon on the right and the descending colon on the left. See diag. under **intestine.** [1855–60]

transverse′ magnifica′tion, *Optics.* See **lateral magnification.**

transverse′ presenta′tion, *Obstet.* presentation in which the fetus is turned with its long axis across the mouth of the uterus, at right angles to the axis of the birth canal. Also called **crossbirth.**

trans′verse proc′ess, a process that projects from the sides of a vertebra. See diag. under **vertebra.** [1690–1700]

trans′verse sec′tion. See **cross section** (def.1).

transverse′ vibra′tions, *Physics.* periodic disturbances for which the particle oscillations of the medium are perpendicular to the direction of propagation.

trans′verse wave′, *Physics.* a wave in which the direction of displacement is perpendicular to the direction of propagation, as a surface wave of water. Cf. **longitudinal wave.** [1920–25]

trans·ves·tite (trans ves′tīt, tranz-), *n.* a person, esp. a male, who assumes the dress and manner usually associated with the opposite sex. [1925–30; < G *Transvestit;* see TRANSVESTISM, -ITE[1]]

trans·ves·tism (trans ves′tiz əm, tranz-), *n.* the practice, esp. of men, of wearing clothing usually associated with the opposite sex for psychological gratification. Also, **trans·ves·ti·tism** (trans ves′ti tiz′əm, tranz-). [1925–30; < G *Transvestismus* < L *trāns-* TRANS- + *vest(ire)* to clothe + G *-ismus* -ISM] —**trans·ves′tic,** *adj.*

Tran·syl·va·nia (tran′sil vān′yə, -vā′nē ə), *n.* a region and former province in central Rumania: formerly part of Hungary. 24,027 sq. mi. (62,230 sq. km). —**Tran′·syl·va′nian,** *adj., n.*

Tran′sylva′nian Alps′, a mountain range in S Rumania, forming a SW extension of the Carpathian Mountains. Highest peak, Mt. Negoiul, 8345 ft. (2544 m).

trant·er (tran′tər), *n. Brit. Dial.* a peddler, hawker, or carrier using a horse and cart. [1350–1400; alter. of late ME *traventer* < ML *travetārius,* perh. for L *trānsvect-(us),* ptp. of *trānsvehere* to carry across + *-ārius* -ARY]

trap[1] (trap), *n., v.,* **trapped, trap·ping.** —*n.* **1.** a contrivance used for catching game or other animals, as a mechanical device that springs shut suddenly. **2.** any device, stratagem, trick, or the like for catching a person unawares. **3.** any of various devices for removing undesirable substances from a moving fluid, vapor, etc., as water from steam or cinders from coal gas. **4.** Also called **air trap.** an arrangement in a pipe, as a double curve or a U-shaped section, in which liquid remains and forms a seal for preventing the passage or escape of air or of gases through the pipe from behind or below. **5. traps,** the percussion instruments of a jazz or dance band. **6.** *Trapshooting, Skeet.* a device for hurling clay pigeons into the air. **7.** the piece of wood, shaped somewhat like a shoe hollowed at the heel, and moving on a pivot, used in playing the game of trapball. **8.** the game of trapball. **9.** See **trap door. 10.** *Sports.* an act or instance of trapping a ball. **11.** Also called **mousetrap, trap play.** *Football.* a play in which a defensive player, usually a guard or tackle, is allowed by the team on offense to cross the line of scrimmage into the backfield and is then blocked out from the side, thereby letting the ball-carrier run through the opening in the line. **12.** *Slang.* mouth: *Keep your trap shut.* **13.** *Chiefly Brit.* a carriage, esp. a light, two-wheeled one. —*v.t.* **14.** to catch in a trap; ensnare: *to trap foxes.* **15.** to catch by stratagem, artifice, or trickery. **16.** to furnish or set with traps. **17.** to provide (a drain or the like) with a trap. **18.** to stop and hold by a trap, as air in a pipe. **19.** *Sports.* to catch (a ball) as it rises after having just hit the ground. **20.** *Football.* to execute a trap against (a defensive player). —*v.i.* **21.** to set traps for game: *He was busy trapping.* **22.** to engage in the business of trapping animals for their furs. **23.** *Trapshooting, Skeet.* to work the trap. [bef. 1000; ME *trappe* (n.), *trappen* (v.), OE *træppe* (n.), c. MD *trappe* (D *trap*) trap, step, staircase; akin to OE *treppan* to tread, G *Treppe* staircase] —**trap′like′,** *adj.*

—**Syn. 1, 2.** TRAP, PITFALL, SNARE apply to literal or figurative contrivances for deceiving and catching animals or people. Literally, a TRAP is a mechanical contrivance for catching animals, the main feature usually being a spring: *a trap baited with cheese for mice.* Figuratively, TRAP suggests the scheme of one person to take another by surprise and thereby gain an advantage: *a trap for the unwary.* A PITFALL is (usually) a concealed pit arranged for the capture of large animals or of people who may fall into it; figuratively, it is any concealed danger, error, or source of disaster: *to avoid the pitfalls of life.* A SNARE is a device for entangling birds, rabbits, etc., with intent to capture; figuratively, it implies enticement and inveiglement: *the temptress' snare.*

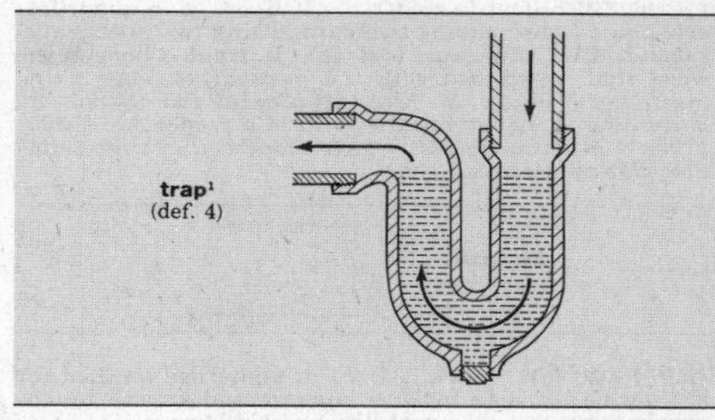
trap[1] (def. 4)

trap[2] (trap), *n., v.,* **trapped, trap·ping.** —*n.* **1. traps,** *Informal.* personal belongings; baggage. —*v.t.* **2.** to furnish with or as with trappings; caparison. [1300–50; ME *trappe* (n.), *trappen* (v.) < ?]

trap[3] (trap), *n. Geol.* any of various fine-grained, dark-colored igneous rocks having a more or less columnar structure, esp. some form of basalt. Also called **traprock.** [1785–95; < Sw *trapp,* var. of *trappa* stair (so named from the stepped appearance of their outcrops) < MLG *trappe.* See TRAP[1]]

trap[4] (trap), *n. Scot.* a ladder or ladderlike device used to reach a loft, attic, etc. [1750–60; < D: stepladder; see TRAP[1]]

Tra·pa·ni (trä′pä nē), *n.* a seaport in NW Sicily. 70,035.

trap·ball (trap′bôl′), *n.* **1.** an old game in which a ball placed on the hollowed end of a trap is thrown into the air by striking the other end of the trap with a bat and then driven to a distance with the bat. **2.** the ball used in this game. [1650–60; TRAP[1] + BALL[1]]

trap′ car′, a railroad car used at a terminal for collecting and distributing freight.

trap′ cut′, *Jewelry.* See **step cut.** [1850–55]

trap·door (trap′dôr′, -dōr′), *n.* **1.** a door flush with the surface of a floor, ceiling, or roof. **2.** the opening that it covers. —*adj.* **3.** of, pertaining to, or like a trapdoor. [1325–75; ME *trappe dore.* See TRAP[1], DOOR]

trapdoor′ func′tion, *Math.* a function defined from data by means of a mathematical procedure in such a way that it is easy to obtain the function when the data are known, but when the procedure and data are not known it becomes very difficult to determine the original data: used in cryptography, where the data are the characters of the plain text, or message, and the trapdoor function is the cryptogram. [1975–80; by analogy with a trapdoor in a floor, through which it is easier to fall than to reemerge after a fall]

trap′-door spi′der, any of several burrowing spiders, of the family Ctenizidae, that construct a tubular nest with a hinged lid. [1820–30]

trapes (trāps), *v.i., v.t., n.* traipse.

tra·peze (tra pēz′ *or, esp. Brit.,* trə-), *n.* **1.** an apparatus, used in gymnastics and acrobatics, consisting of a short horizontal bar attached to the ends of two suspended ropes. **2.** (on a small sailboat) a device by which a crew member can be suspended almost completely outboard while hiking. [1860–65; < F, special use of *trapèze* TRAPEZIUM]

trapeze′ art′ist, a person who performs, esp. professionally, on a trapeze. Also called **tra·pez′ist.**

tra·pe·zi·form (trə pē′zə fôrm′), *adj.* formed like a trapezium. [1770–80; TRAPEZI(UM) + -FORM]

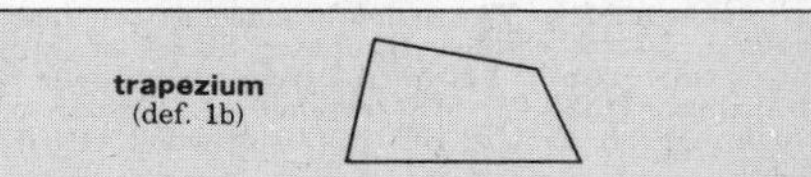
trapezium (def. 1b)

tra·pe·zi·um (trə pē′zē əm), *n., pl.* **-zi·ums, -zi·a** (-zē ə). **1.** *Geom.* **a.** (in Euclidean geometry) any rectilinear quadrilateral plane figure not a parallelogram. **b.** a quadrilateral plane figure of which no two sides are parallel. **c.** *Brit.* trapezoid (def. 1a). **2.** *Anat.* a bone in the wrist that articulates with the metacarpal bone of the thumb. [1545–55; < NL < Gk *trapézion* kind of quadrilateral, lit., small table, equiv. to *trápez(a)* table (shortening of **tetrapeza* object having four feet, equiv. to *tetra-* four + *péza* foot, akin to *poús, podós;* see TETRA-, FOOT) + *-ion* dim. suffix] —**tra·pe′zi·al,** *adj.*

tra·pe·zi·us (trə pē′zē əs), *n., pl.* **-us·es.** *Anat.* a broad, flat muscle on each side of the upper and back part of the neck, shoulders, and back, the action of which raises, or rotates, or draws back the shoulders, and pulls

CONCISE PRONUNCIATION KEY: act, cāpe, dâre, pärt; set, ēqual; if, īce; ox, ōver, ôrder, oil, bo͝ok, bo͞ot, out; up, ûrge; child; sing; shoe; thin, *th*at; zh as in treasure. ə = *a* as in *alone, e* as in *system, i* as in *easily, o* as in *gallop, u* as in *circus;* ᵊ as in fire (fīᵊr), hour (ouᵊr). l and n can serve as syllabic consonants, as in *cradle* (krād′l), and *button* (but′n). See the full key inside the front cover.

trans′-Sa·har′an, *adj.*
trans′-Sa·tur′ni·an, *adj.*
trans·sea′son·al, *adj.*
trans′seg·men′tal, *adj.;* **-ly,** *adv.*
trans·sen′su·al, *adj.;* **-ly,** *adv.*
trans·sep′tal, *adj.*
trans′se·pul′chral, *adj.*
trans-Sev′ern, *adj.*
trans·shape′, *v.t.,* **-shaped, -shap·ing.**
trans·shift′, *v.*
trans′-Si·be′ri·an, *adj.*
trans·sol′id, *adj.*
trans·stel′lar, *adj.*
trans-Styg′i·an, *adj.*
trans′tha·lam′ic, *adj.*
trans′tho·rac′ic, *adj.*
trans-Ti′ber, *adj.*
trans′-Ti·be′ri·an, *adj.*
trans·tra′che·al, *adj.*
trans′-U′ral, *adj.*
trans′-U·ra′li·an, *adj.*
trans′u·re′thral, *adj.*
trans·u′ter·ine, *adj.*
trans-Vol′ga, *adj.*

the head backward or to one side. [1685–95; < NL, short for *trapezius musculus* trapeziform muscle]

tra·pe·zo·he·dron (trə pē′zə hē′drən, trap′ə-), *n., pl.* **-drons, -dra** (-drə). **1.** *Crystall.* a crystal form having all faces trapeziums. **2.** *Geom.* a trapezoid trisoctahedron. [1810–20; TRAPEZ(OID) + -O + -HEDRON] **—tra·pe′zo·he′dral,** *adj.*

trap·e·zoid (trap′ə zoid′), *n.* **1.** *Geom.* **a.** a quadrilateral plane figure having two parallel and two nonparallel sides. **b.** *Brit.* trapezium (def. 1b). **2.** *Anat.* a bone in the wrist that articulates with the metacarpal bone of the forefinger. **—*adj.*** **3.** Also, **trap′e·zoi′dal.** *Geom.* of, pertaining to, or having the form of a trapezoid. [1695–1705; < NL *trapezoīdēs* < LGk *trapezoeidḗs* trapeziumlike. See TRAPEZIUM, -OID]

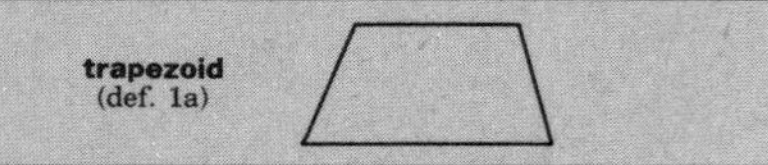

trapezoid (def. 1a)

trap′ezoi′dal rule′, *Math.* a numerical method for evaluating the area between a curve and an axis by approximating the area with the areas of trapezoids.

Trappe, La (*Fr.* lA trap′). See **La Trappe.**

trap·per (trap′ər), *n.* **1.** a person or thing that traps. **2.** a person whose business is the trapping of animals for their furs. [1615–25; TRAP[1] + -ER[1]]

trap·pings (trap′ingz), *n.* (*used with a plural v.*) **1.** articles of equipment or dress, esp. of an ornamental character. **2.** conventional adornment; characteristic signs: *trappings of democracy.* **3.** Sometimes, **trapping.** an ornamental covering for a horse; caparison. [1350–1400; ME; see TRAP[2], -ING[1], -S[3]]
—Syn. 1. costume, raiment, attire, apparel.

Trap·pist (trap′ist), *n.* **1.** *Rom. Cath. Ch.* a member of a branch of the Cistercian order, observing the austere reformed rule established at La Trappe in 1664. **—*adj.*** **2.** of or pertaining to the Trappists. [1805–15; < F *trappiste,* based on the name of the monastery. See LA TRAPPE, -IST]

Trap′pist cheese′, a semisoft, mild, yellow cheese from whole milk, made by Trappist monks. Also called **Gethsemane cheese.**

trap′ play′, *Football.* trap[1] (def. 11).

trap·py (trap′ē), *adj.,* **-pi·er, -pi·est. 1.** difficult or tricky: *trappy terrain.* **2.** catching one unawares: *trappy pitfalls.* **3.** (of horses) moving with the legs lifted high in a short and rapid manner. [1870–75, *Amer.*; TRAP[1] + -Y[1]] **—trap′pi·ness,** *n.*

trap·rock (trap′rok′), *n.* trap[3]. [1805–15; TRAP[3] + ROCK[1]]

trap·shoot·ing (trap′sho͞o′ting), *n.* the sport of shooting at clay pigeons hurled into the air from a trap. Cf. **skeet**[1]. [1870–75; TRAP[1] + SHOOTING] **—trap′·shoot′er,** *n.*

trap′ shot′, *Sports.* See **half volley.** [1890–95]

tra·pun·to (trə po͝on′tō), *n., pl.* **-tos.** quilting having an embossed design produced by outlining the pattern with single stitches and then padding it with yarn or cotton. [1920–25; < It: embroidery, n. use of the adj.: embroidered, lit., pricked through (ptp. of *trapungere*), equiv. to *tra-* (< L *trā-,* var. of *trāns-* TRANS-) + *-punto* < L *pūnctus,* equiv. to *pung-* (s. of *pungere* to prick) + *-tus* ptp. suffix; see PUNCTURE]

Tras·en·tine (traz′ən tēn′), *n. Pharm., Trademark.* a brand of adiphenine.

trash (trash), *n.* **1.** anything worthless, useless, or discarded; rubbish. **2.** foolish or pointless ideas, talk, or writing; nonsense. **3.** a worthless or disreputable person. **4.** such persons collectively. **5.** literary or artistic material of poor or inferior quality. **6.** broken or torn bits, as twigs, splinters, rags, or the like. **7.** something that is broken or lopped off from anything in preparing it for use. **8.** the refuse of sugar cane after the juice has been expressed. **—*v.t.*** **9.** *Slang.* to destroy, damage, or vandalize, as in anger or protest: *The slovenly renters had trashed the house.* **10.** to condemn, dismiss, or criticize as worthless: *The article trashed several recent best-sellers.* **11.** to remove the outer leaves of (a growing sugar cane plant). **12.** to free from superfluous twigs or branches. [1325–75; ME *trasches* (pl.), appar. c. Norw *trask* rubbish; akin to OE *trus* brushwood, ON *tros* rubbish]
—Syn. 5. drivel, rot, hogwash, nonsense.

trash′ can′, a container for the disposal of dry waste matter. Cf. **garbage can.**

trashed (trasht), *adj. Slang.* intoxicated; drunk. [1925–30, for an earlier sense; TRASH + -ED[2]]

trash·er (trash′ər), *n. Informal.* a person who trashes something, esp. in anger or protest. [1900–05; TRASH + -ER[1]]

trash′ fish′, a fish traditionally sold only for animal feed or manufactured products. [1940–45]

trash·man (trash′man′, -mən), *n., pl.* **-men** (-men′, -mən). a person who collects trash for removal in a truck. [1950–55; TRASH + MAN[1]]
—Usage. See **-man.**

trash′ rack′, a grating for retaining floating objects from water entering a penstock. See diag. under **dam**[1]. [1910–15]

trash·y (trash′ē), *adj.,* **trash·i·er, trash·i·est. 1.** of the nature of trash; inferior in quality; rubbishy; useless or worthless. **2.** (of a field) strewn with trash, esp. the withered vegetation from an earlier crop. [1610–20; TRASH + -Y[1]] **—trash′i·ly,** *adv.* **—trash′i·ness,** *n.*

CONCISE ETYMOLOGY KEY: <, descended or borrowed from; >, whence; b., blend of, blended; c., cognate with; cf., compare; deriv., derivative; equiv., equivalent; imit., imitative; obl., oblique; r., replacing; s., stem; sp., spelling, spelled; resp., respelling, respelled; trans., translation; ?, origin unknown; *, unattested; ‡, probably earlier than. See the full key inside the front cover.

Tra·si·me·no (trä′zē me′nô), *n.* a lake in central Italy, in Umbria near Perugia: Romans defeated by Hannibal 217 B.C. ab. 50 sq. mi. (130 sq. km). Also called **Lake of Perugia.** Latin, **Tras·i·me·nus** (tras′ə mē′nəs).

trat·to·ri·a (trä′tə rē′ə), *n.* a usually inexpensive or informal restaurant or cafe specializing in Italian dishes. [1825–35; < It: public eating place, restaurant, equiv. to *trattor(e)* restaurateur (*tratt(are)* to TREAT + *-ore* -OR[2], as trans. of F *traiteur*) + *-iu* -IA]

Trau·bel (trou′bəl), *n.* **Helen,** 1903–72, U.S. soprano.

trau·chle (trä′KHəl), *n., v.t.,* **-chled, -chling.** *Scot.* trachle.

trau·ma (trou′mə, trô′-), *n., pl.* **-mas, -ma·ta** (-mə tə). **1.** *Pathol.* **a.** a body wound or shock produced by sudden physical injury, as from violence or accident. **b.** the condition produced by this; traumatism. **2.** *Psychiatry.* **a.** an experience that produces psychological injury or pain. **b.** the psychological injury so caused. [1685–95; < Gk *traûma* wound]

trau′ma cen′ter, a hospital or medical center equipped to treat victims of trauma.

trau′ma kit′, a medical kit containing supplies useful for controlling bleeding and injuries in emergencies.

trau·mat·ic (trə mat′ik, trô-, trou-), *adj.* **1.** of, pertaining to, or produced by a trauma or wound. **2.** adapted to the cure of wounds. **3.** psychologically painful. [1650–60; < LL *traumaticus* < Gk *traumatikós* pertaining to wounds, equiv. to *traumat-* (s. of *traûma* TRAUMA) + *-ikos* -IC] **—trau·mat′i·cal·ly,** *adv.*

trau·ma·tism (trou′mə tiz′əm, trô′-), *n. Pathol.* **1.** any abnormal condition produced by a trauma. **2.** the trauma or wound itself. [1855–60; < LGk *traumatismós* a wounding. See TRAUMATIC, -ISM]

trau·ma·tize (trou′mə tīz′, trô′-), *v.t.,* **-tized, -tiz·ing. 1.** *Pathol.* to injure (tissues) by force or by thermal, chemical, etc., agents. **2.** *Psychiatry.* to cause a trauma in (the mind): *to be traumatized by a childhood experience.* Also, *esp. Brit.,* **trau′ma·tise′.** [1900–05; < Gk *traumatízein* to wound. See TRAUMATIC, -IZE] **—trau′·ma·ti·za′tion,** *n.*

trau·ma·tol·o·gy (trou′mə tol′ə jē, trô′-), *n.* a branch of surgery dealing with major wounds caused by accidents or violence. [1895–1900; < Gk *traumat-,* s. of *traûma* wound (see TRAUMA) + -O- + -LOGY] **—trau′·ma·tol′o·gist,** *n.*

trav., 1. traveler. **2.** travels.

tra·vail (trə vāl′, trav′āl), *n.* **1.** painfully difficult or burdensome work; toil. **2.** pain, anguish or suffering resulting from mental or physical hardship. **3.** the pain of childbirth. **—*v.i.*** **4.** to suffer the pangs of childbirth; be in labor. **5.** to toil or exert oneself. [1200–50; (v.) ME *travaillen* < OF *travaillier* to torment < VL **trepaliāre* to torture, deriv. of LL *trepālium* torture chamber, lit., instrument of torture made with three stakes (see TRI-, PALE[2]); (n.) ME < OF: suffering, deriv. of *travailler*]
—Syn. 1. labor, moil. **2.** torment, agony.

Trav·an·core (trav′ən kôr′, -kōr′), *n.* a former state in SW India: merged 1949 with Cochin to form a new state (**Trav′ancore and Co′chin**); reorganized 1956 to form the larger part of Kerala state. Cf. **Cochin.**

trave[1] (trāv), *n. Archit.* **1.** a crossbeam. **2.** a section or bay formed by crossbeams. [1350–1400; ME < MF *trave* < L *trabem,* acc. of *trabs* beam, timber]

trave[2] (trāv), *n.* a device to inhibit a wild or untrained horse or one being shod. [1350–1400; ME; orig. uncert.; cf. later *travail* in same sense < MF; see TRAVOIS]

trav·el (trav′əl), *v.,* **-eled, -el·ing** or (*esp. Brit.*) **-elled, -el·ling,** *n., adj.* **—*v.i.*** **1.** to go from one place to another, as by car, train, plane, or ship; take a trip; journey: *to travel for pleasure.* **2.** to move or go from one place or point to another. **3.** to proceed or advance in any way. **4.** to go from place to place as a representative of a business firm. **5.** to associate or consort: *He travels in a wealthy crowd.* **6.** *Informal.* to move with speed. **7.** to pass, or be transmitted, as light or sound. **8.** *Basketball.* walk (def. 9). **9.** to move in a fixed course, as a piece of mechanism. **—*v.t.*** **10.** to travel, journey, or pass through or over, as a country or road. **11.** to journey or traverse (a specified distance): *We traveled a hundred miles.* **12.** to cause to journey; ship: *to travel logs downriver.* **—*n.*** **13.** the act of traveling; journeying, esp. to distant places: *to travel to other planets.* **14. travels, a.** journeys; wanderings: *to set out on one's travels.* **b.** journeys as the subject of a written account or literary work: *a book of travels.* **c.** such an account or work. **15.** the coming and going of persons or conveyances along a way of passage; traffic: *an increase in travel on state roads.* **16.** *Mach.* **a.** the complete movement of a moving part, esp. a reciprocating part, in one direction, or the distance traversed; stroke. **b.** length of stroke. **17.** movement or passage in general: *to reduce the travel of food from kitchen to table.* **—*adj.*** **18.** used or designed for use while traveling: *a travel alarm clock.* [1325–75; ME (north and Scots), orig. the same word as TRAVAIL (by shift "to toil, labor" > "to make a laborious journey")] **—trav′el·a·ble,** *adj.*

trav′el a′gency, a business that accommodates travelers, as by securing tickets, arranging for reservations, and giving information. Also called **trav′el bu′reau.**

trav′el a′gent, 1. a person who owns, operates, or works for a travel agency. **2.** a travel agency. [1925–30]

trav·eled (trav′əld), *adj.* **1.** having traveled, esp. to distant places; experienced in travel. **2.** used by travelers: *a heavily traveled road.* Also, *esp. Brit.,* **travelled.** [1375–1425; late ME; see TRAVEL, -ED[2]]

trav·el·er (trav′ə lər, trav′lər), *n.* **1.** a person or thing that travels. **2.** a person who travels or has traveled in distant places or foreign lands. **3.** See **traveling salesman. 4.** part of a mechanism constructed to move in a fixed course. **5.** *Textiles.* (in ring spinning) a small metal device that moves rapidly around the ring and guides the yarn onto the revolving bobbin. **6.** *Naut.* **a.** a metal ring or thimble fitted to move freely on a rope, spar, or rod. **b.** Also called **horse.** the rope, spar, or rod itself. **7.** Also, **trav′eler cur′tain.** *Theat.* a transverse curtain opened by being drawn from both sides of the proscenium. **8.** (*often cap.*) *Chiefly Brit.* a member of any of a number of traditionally itinerant peoples of the British Isles and other English-speaking areas, including, in addition to people of Gypsy origin, autochthonous groups such as the speakers of Shelta. Also, *esp. Brit.,* **traveller.** [1325–75; ME *travaillour.* See TRAVEL, -ER[1]]

trav′eler's check′, a check issued in any of various denominations by a bank, travel agency, etc., that is signed by the purchaser upon purchase and again, in the presence of the payee, when cashing the check or using it to pay for goods or services. [1905–10]

trav′elers' diarrhe′a, persistent and often severe diarrhea experienced by a traveler whose digestive system is unaccustomed to the bacteria in local food and water.

trav·el·er's-joy (trav′ə lərz joi′, trav′lərz-), *n.* a woody vine, *Clematis vitalba,* of the buttercup family, native to Europe and northern Africa, having long-plumed fruit and slightly fragrant, white flowers. Also called **old-man's-beard, withywind.** [1590–1600]

trav·el·er's-tree (trav′ə lərz trē′, trav′lərz-), *n.* a bananalike tree, *Ravenala madagascariensis,* of Madagascar, having large leaves, the petioles of which contain a clear, watery sap. [1855–60]

trav′eling bag′, a small bag, as a valise or suitcase, usually made of leather, having an oblong shape, and used chiefly to hold clothes. [1830–40]

trav′eling block′, (in a hoisting tackle) the block hooked to and moving with the load.

trav′eling sales′man, a representative of a business firm who travels in an assigned territory soliciting orders for a company's products or services. [1875–80, *Amer.*]

trav′eling sales′man prob′lem, any mathematical problem that involves determination of the shortest path through several points. [1950–55; from the idea that a traveling salesman would face such a problem in making rounds within a territory]

trav′eling-wave′ tube′ (trav′ə ling wāv′, trav′-ling-), *Electronics.* an electron tube used in microwave communications systems, having an electron beam directed coaxially through a wire helix to produce amplification.

trav·elled (trav′əld), *adj. Chiefly Brit.* traveled.

trav·el·ler (trav′ə lər, trav′lər), *n. Chiefly Brit.* traveler.

trav·e·logue (trav′ə lôg′, -log′), *n.* a lecture, slide show, or motion picture describing travels. Also, **trav′e·log′.** [1900–05, *Amer.*; b. TRAVEL and MONOLOGUE]

trav′el shot′, *Motion Pictures, Television.* a camera shot taken from a mobile platform, dolly, or the like, that keeps within range of a moving subject.

trav′el time′, time spent traveling for a job, as from home to work or in the course of business. [1885–90]

trav′el trail′er, trailer (def. 2). [1960–65]

Trav·ers (trav′ərz), *n.* **P(amela) L.,** born 1906, Australian writer, esp. of children's stories, in England.

trav·erse (trav′ərs, trə vûrs′), *v.,* **-ersed, -ers·ing,** *n., adj.* **—*v.t.*** **1.** to pass or move over, along, or through. **2.** to go to and fro over or along. **3.** to extend across or over: *A bridge traverses the stream.* **4.** to go up, down, or across (a rope, mountain, hill, etc.) at an angle: *The climbers traversed the east face of the mountain.* **5.** to ski across (a hill or slope). **6.** to cause to move laterally. **7.** to look over, examine, or consider carefully; review; survey. **8.** to go counter to; obstruct; thwart. **9.** to contradict or deny. **10.** *Law.* **a.** (in the law of pleading) to deny formally (an allegation of fact set forth in a previous pleading). **b.** to join issue upon. **11.** to turn and point (a gun) in any direction.
—*v.i.* **12.** to pass along or go across something; cross: *a point in the river where we could traverse.* **13.** to ski across a hill or slope on a diagonal. **14.** to turn laterally, as a gun. **15.** *Fencing.* to glide the blade toward the hilt of the contestant's foil while applying pressure to the blade.
—*n.* **16.** the act of passing across, over, or through. **17.** something that crosses, obstructs, or thwarts; obstacle. **18.** a transversal or similar line. **19.** a place where one may traverse or cross; crossing. **20.** *Archit.* a transverse gallery or loft of communication in a church or other large building. **21.** a bar, strip, rod, or other structural part placed or extending across; crosspiece; crossbar. **22.** a railing, lattice, or screen serving as a barrier. **23.** *Naut.* **a.** the zigzag track of a vessel compelled by contrary winds or currents to sail on different courses. **b.** each of the runs in a single direction made in such sailing. **24.** *Fort.* **a.** a defensive barrier, parapet, or the like, placed transversely. **b.** a defensive barrier thrown across the terreplein or the covered way of a fortification to protect it from enfilade fire. **25.** *Gunnery.* the horizontal turning of a gun so as to make it point in any required direction. **26.** *Mach.* **a.** the motion of a lathe tool or grinding wheel along a piece of work. **b.** a part moving along a piece of work in this way, as the carriage of a lathe. **27.** *Survey.* a series of intersecting surveyed lines whose lengths and angles of intersection, measured at instrument stations, are recorded graphically on a map and in numerical form in data tables. Cf. **closed traverse. 28.** *Law.* a formal denial of some matter of fact alleged by the other side.
—*adj.* **29.** lying, extending, or passing across; transverse. [1250–1300; (v.) ME *traversen* < MF *traverser* to cross < LL *trānsversāre,* deriv. of L *trānsversus* (see TRANS-, VERSUS); (n.) ME *travers(e)* < MF *traverse* (< L *trānsversa* something lying across, fem. of *trānsversus*) and *travers* (< L *trānsversum* passage across, neut. of *trānsversus*)] **—tra·vers′a·ble,** *adj.* **—tra·vers′al,** *n.* **—tra·vers′er,** *n.*
—Syn. 1. cross. **9.** gainsay, dispute, challenge.

Trav′erse Cit′y (trav′ərs), a city in NW Michigan. 15,516.

trav′erse ju′ry. See **petty jury.** [1815–25]

trav′erse rod′, a horizontal rod upon which drapes slide to open or close when pulled by cords.

trav•er•tine (trav′ər tēn′, -tin), *n.* a form of limestone deposited by springs, esp. hot springs, used in Italy for building. Also, **trav•er•tin** (trav′ər tin). [1545–55; < It *travertino,* equiv. to *tra-* across (< L *trāns-* TRANS-) + (*ti*)*vertino* < L *Tiburtīnus,* equiv. to *Tiburt-* (s. of *Tībur*) the territory of Tibur (see TIVOLI) + *-īnus* -INE[1]]

trav•es•ty (trav′ə stē), *n., pl.* **-ties,** *v.,* **-tied, -ty•ing.** —*n.* **1.** a literary or artistic burlesque of a serious work or subject, characterized by grotesque or ludicrous incongruity of style, treatment, or subject matter. **2.** a literary or artistic composition so inferior in quality as to be merely a grotesque imitation of its model. **3.** any grotesque or debased likeness or imitation: *a travesty of justice.* —*v.t.* **4.** to make a travesty on; turn (a serious work or subject) to ridicule by burlesquing. **5.** to imitate grotesquely or absurdly. [1655–65; < F *travesti,* ptp. of *travestir* to disguise < It *travestire,* equiv. to *tra-* (< L *trāns-* TRANS-) + *vestire* to clothe < L *vestire;* see VEST] —**Syn. 1.** See **burlesque. 3.** mockery, perversion, sham, distortion.

Trav•is (trav′is), *n.* **1. William Barret,** 1809–36, U.S. soldier: commander during the battle of the Alamo. **2.** a male given name.

tra•vois (trə voi′), *n., pl.* **-vois** (-voiz′). a transport device, formerly used by the Plains Indians, consisting of two poles joined by a frame and drawn by an animal. [1840–50; *Amer.;* pseudo-F sp. of earlier *travoy* < North American F; cf. CanF *travail* shaft of a cart to which the horse is hitched, F: frame in which unruly horses are held while they are shod (prob. < LL *trepālium;* see TRAVAIL)]

trawl (trôl), *n.* **1.** Also called **trawl′ net′.** a strong fishing net for dragging along the sea bottom. **2.** Also called **trawl′ line′.** a buoyed line used in sea fishing, having numerous short lines with baited hooks attached at intervals. —*v.i.* **3.** to fish with a net that drags along the sea bottom to catch the fish living there. **4.** to fish with a trawl line. **5.** to troll. —*v.t.* **6.** to catch with a trawl net or a trawl line. **7.** to drag (a trawl net). **8.** to troll. [1475–85; < MD *tragel* (n.), *tragelen* (v.); c. TRAIL] —**trawl′a•ble,** *adj.* —**trawl′a•bil′i•ty,** *n.*

trawl•er (trô′lər), *n.* **1.** a person who trawls. **2.** any of various types of vessels used in fishing with a trawl net. [1590–1600; TRAWL + -ER[1]]

tray[1] (trā), *n.* **1.** a flat, shallow container or receptacle made of wood, metal, etc., usually with slightly raised edges, used for carrying, holding, or displaying articles of food, glass, china, etc. **2.** a removable receptacle of this shape in a cabinet, box, trunk, or the like, sometimes forming a drawer. **3.** a tray and its contents: *to order a breakfast tray from room service.* [bef. 1050; ME; OE *trēg, trīg;* c. OSw *trö* corn measure; akin to TREE]

tray[2] (trā), *n. Australian Slang.* a coin worth threepence. Also called **tray′ bit′.** [1895–1900; cf. earlier argot *trey, tray* three, a set of three, prob. ult. < It *tre* (< L *trēs* THREE); cf. TREY]

tray′ ag′riculture, hydroponics.

tray′ ta′ble, a folding stand for supporting a tray.

tra•zo•done (trā′zə dōn′), *n. Pharm.* a white crystalline powder, $C_{19}H_{22}ClN_5O$, used in the treatment of major depression disorders. [TR(I)- + AZO- + (PYRI)D(INE) + -ONE]

treach•er•ous (trech′ər əs), *adj.* **1.** characterized by faithlessness or readiness to betray trust; traitorous. **2.** deceptive, untrustworthy, or unreliable. **3.** unstable or insecure, as footing. **4.** dangerous; hazardous: *a treacherous climb.* [1300–50; ME *trecherous* < AF, equiv. to *trecher* deceiver (*trech*(*ier*) to deceive + *-er* -ER[2]) + *-ous* -OUS. Cf. F *tricheur* trickster] —**treach′er•ous•ly,** *adv.* —**treach′er•ous•ness,** *n.*
—**Syn. 1.** unfaithful, faithless, treasonous. **2.** deceitful. —**Ant. 1.** loyal. **2.** reliable.

treach•er•y (trech′ə rē), *n., pl.* **-er•ies. 1.** violation of faith; betrayal of trust; treason. **2.** an act of perfidy, faithlessness, or treason. [1175–1225; ME *trecherie* < MF, OF, equiv. to *trech*(*ier*) to deceive + *-erie* -ERY] —**Syn. 1.** See **disloyalty.** —**Ant. 1.** loyalty.

trea•cle (trē′kəl), *n.* **1.** contrived or unrestrained sentimentality: *a movie plot of the most shameless treacle.* **2.** *Brit.* **a.** molasses, esp. that which is drained from the vats used in sugar refining. **b.** Also called **golden syrup.** a mild mixture of molasses, corn syrup, etc., used in cooking or as a table syrup. **3.** *Pharm. Obs.* any of various medicinal compounds, formerly used as antidotes for poison. [1275–1325; ME, var. of *triacle* antidote < MF, OF < L *thēriaca* < Gk *thēriakḗ,* n. use of fem. of *thēriakós* concerning wild beasts, equiv. to *thērí*(*on*) wild beast (*thḗr* wild beast + *-ion* dim. suffix) + *-akos* -AC] —**trea•cly** (trē′klē), *adj.*

tread (tred), *v.,* **trod, trod•den** or **trod, tread•ing,** *n.* —*v.i.* **1.** to set down the foot or feet in walking; step; walk. **2.** to step, walk, or trample so as to press, crush, or injure something (usually fol. by *on* or *upon*): *to tread on a person's foot.* **3.** (of a male bird) to copulate. —*v.t.* **4.** to step or walk on, about, in, or along. **5.** to trample or crush underfoot. **6.** to form by the action of walking or trampling: *to tread a path.* **7.** to treat with disdainful harshness or cruelty; crush; oppress. **8.** to perform by walking or dancing: *to tread a measure.* **9.** (of a male bird) to copulate with (a female bird). **10. tread on someone's toes** or **corns,** to offend or irritate someone. **11. tread the boards,** to act on the stage, esp. professionally: *He recalled the days when he had trod the boards.* **12. tread water, a.** *Swimming.* to maintain the body erect in the water with the head above the surface usually by a pumping up-and-down movement of the legs and sometimes the arms. **b.** *Slang.* to make efforts that maintain but do not further one's status, progress, or performance: *He's just treading water here until he can find another job.* —*n.* **13.** the action of treading, stepping, or walking. **14.** the sound of footsteps. **15.** manner of treading or walking. **16.** a single step as in walking. **17.** any of various things or parts on which a person or thing treads, stands, or moves. **18.** the part of the under surface of the foot or of a shoe that touches the ground. **19.** the horizontal upper surface of a step in a stair, on which the foot is placed. **20.** the part of a wheel, tire, or runner that bears on the road, rail, etc. See diag. under **tire**[2]. **21.** the pattern raised on or cut into the face of a rubber tire. **22.** See **caterpillar tread. 23.** *Railroads.* that part of a rail in contact with the treads of wheels. [bef. 900; (v.) ME *treden,* OE *tredan;* c. OFris *treda,* OS *tredan,* D *treden,* G *treten;* akin to ON *trotha,* Goth *trudan;* (n.) ME *tred* footprint, deriv. of the v.] —**tread′er,** *n.*

trea•dle (tred′l), *n., v.,* **-dled, -dling.** —*n.* **1.** a lever or the like worked by continual action of the foot to impart motion to a machine. **2.** a platform, as on a bus or trolleycar, for opening an exit door. —*v.i.* **3.** to work a treadle. [bef. 1000; ME *tredel* stairstep, OE. See TREAD, -LE] —**tread•ler** (tred′lər), *n.*

trea′dle loom′. See **floor loom.**

tread•mill (tred′mil′), *n.* **1.** an apparatus for producing rotary motion by the weight of people or animals, treading on a succession of moving steps or a belt that forms a kind of continuous path, as around the periphery of a pair of horizontal cylinders. **2.** any monotonous, wearisome routine in which there is little or no satisfactory progress. [1815–25; TREAD + MILL[1]]

treas., 1. treasurer. **2.** treasury. Also, **Treas.**

trea•son (trē′zən), *n.* **1.** the offense of acting to overthrow one's government or to harm or kill its sovereign. **2.** a violation of allegiance to one's sovereign or to one's state. **3.** the betrayal of a trust or confidence; breach of faith; treachery. [1175–1225; ME *tre*(*i*)*so*(*u*)*n* < AF; OF *traïson* < L *trāditiōn-* (s. of *trāditiō*) a handing over, betrayal. See TRADITION]
—**Syn. 1.** TREASON, SEDITION mean disloyalty or treachery to one's country or its government. TREASON is any attempt to overthrow the government or impair the well-being of a state to which one owes allegiance; the crime of giving aid or comfort to the enemies of one's government. SEDITION is any act, writing, speech, etc., directed unlawfully against state authority, the government, or constitution, or calculated to bring it into contempt or to incite others to hostility, ill will or disaffection; it does not amount to treason and therefore is not a capital offense. **2.** See **disloyalty.**

trea•son•a•ble (trē′zə nə bəl), *adj.* **1.** of the nature of treason. **2.** involving treason; traitorous. [1325–75; ME *tresonabill.* See TREASON, ABLE] —**trea′son•a•bly,** *adv.*

trea•son•ous (trē′zə nəs), *adj.* treasonable. [1585–95; TREASON + -OUS] —**trea′son•ous•ly,** *adv.*

treasr., treasurer.

treas•ure (trezh′ər), *n., v.,* **-ured, -ur•ing.** —*n.* **1.** wealth or riches stored or accumulated, esp. in the form of precious metals, money, jewels, or plate. **2.** wealth, rich materials, or valuable things. **3.** any thing or person greatly valued or highly prized: *This book was his chief treasure.* —*v.t.* **4.** to retain carefully or keep in store, as in the mind. **5.** to regard or treat as precious; cherish. **6.** to put away for security or future use, as money. [1125–75; (n.) ME *tresor* < OF < L *thēsaurus* storehouse, hoard (see THESAURUS); (v.) ME, deriv. of the n.] —**treas′ur•a•ble,** *adj.* —**treas′ure•less,** *adj.*
—**Syn. 1, 6.** hoard. **5.** value, esteem.

treas′ure house′, 1. a building, room, or chamber used as a storage place for valuables; treasury. **2.** a place or source where things of value or worth may be found: *Books are the treasure house of ideas.* Also, **treas′ure-house′.** [1425–75; late ME]

treas′ure hunt′, a game in which each person or team attempts to be first in finding something that has been hidden, using written directions or clues.

Treas′ure Is′land, 1. (*italics*) a novel (1883) by R. L. Stevenson. **2.** an artificial island in San Francisco Bay, in W California; naval base.

treas•ur•er (trezh′ər ər), *n.* **1.** a person in charge of treasure or a treasury. **2.** an officer of a government, corporation, association, or the like, in charge of the receipt, care, and disbursement of money. [1250–1300; ME *tresorer* < AF < LL *thēsaurārius.* See TREASURE, -ER[2]] —**treas′ur•er•ship′,** *n.*

Treas′urer of the Unit′ed States′, the official in the Department of the Treasury charged with the responsibility of issuing and redeeming paper currency as well as for the receipt, safekeeping, and disbursement of the federal government's money.

Treas′ure State′, Montana (used as a nickname).

treas•ure-trove (trezh′ər trōv′), *n.* **1.** anything of the nature of treasure or a treasury that one finds: *Mother's attic was a treasure-trove of memorabilia.* **2.** *Law.* any money, bullion, or the like, of unknown ownership, found hidden in the earth or any other place: in the absence of statutory provisions to the contrary it may be kept by the finder. [1300–50; ME < AF *tresor trové* found treasure. See TREASURE, TROVER]

treas•ur•y (trezh′ə rē), *n., pl.* **-ur•ies. 1.** a place where the funds of the government, of a corporation, or the like are deposited, kept, and disbursed. **2.** funds or revenue of a government, public or private corporation, etc. **3.** (*cap.*) the department of government that has control over the collection, management, and disbursement of the public revenue. **4.** a building, room, chest, or other place for the preservation of treasure or valuable objects. **5.** a collection or supply of excellent or highly prized writings, works of art, etc.: *a treasury of American poetry.* **6. Treasuries,** *Informal.* Treasury bills, bonds, and notes. [1250–1300; ME *tresorie* < OF. See TREASURE, -Y[3]]

Treas′ury bill′, an obligation of the U.S. government represented by promissory notes in denominations ranging from $1000 to $1,000,000, with a maturity of about 90 days but bearing no interest, and sold periodically at a discount on the market. Also, **treas′ury bill′.** [1790–1800]

Treas′ury bond′, any of various interest-bearing bonds issued by the U.S. Treasury Department, usually maturing over a long period of time. Also, **treas′ury bond′.** [1855–60]

Treas′ury certif′icate, an obligation of the U.S. government represented by certificates in denominations ranging from $1000 to $1,000,000, maturing in one year or less with interest periodically payable by the redemption of coupons. Also, **treas′ury certif′icate.** [1785–95]

Treas′ury note′, a note or bill issued by the U.S. Department of the Treasury, receivable as legal tender for all debts except as otherwise expressly provided. Also, **treas′ury note′.** [1750–60]

treas′ury of mer′its, *Rom. Cath. Ch.* the superabundant store of merits and satisfactions, comprising those of Christ, the Virgin Mary, and the saints. Also called **treas′ury of the Church′.** [1920–25]

treas′ury stock′, outstanding shares of stock reacquired and held by the issuing corporation. [1900–05, *Amer.*]

treat (trēt), *v.t.* **1.** to act or behave toward (a person) in some specified way: *to treat someone with respect.* **2.** to consider or regard in a specified way, and deal with accordingly: *to treat a matter as unimportant.* **3.** to deal with (a disease, patient, etc.) in order to relieve or cure. **4.** to deal with in speech or writing; discuss. **5.** to deal with, develop, or represent artistically, esp. in some specified manner or style: *to treat a theme realistically.* **6.** to subject to some agent or action in order to bring about a particular result: *to treat a substance with an acid.* **7.** to entertain; give hospitality to: *He treats diplomats in the lavish surroundings of his country estate.* **8.** to provide food, entertainment, gifts, etc., at one's own expense: *Let me treat you to dinner.* —*v.i.* **9.** to deal with a subject in speech or writing; discourse: *a work that treats of the caste system in India.* **10.** to give, or bear the expense of, a treat: *Is it my turn to treat?* **11.** to carry on negotiations with a view to a settlement; discuss terms of settlement; negotiate. —*n.* **12.** entertainment, food, drink, etc., given by way of compliment or as an expression of friendly regard. **13.** anything that affords particular pleasure or enjoyment. **14.** the act of treating. **15.** one's turn to treat. [1250–1300; ME *treten* (v.) < OF *tretier, traitier* < L *tractāre* to drag, handle, treat, freq. of *trahere* to drag. See TRACT[1]] —**treat′•er,** *n.*

treat•a•ble (trē′tə bəl), *adj.* able to be treated, esp. medically: *Some diseases are treatable but not curable.* [TREAT + -ABLE] —**treat′a•bil′i•ty,** *n.*

trea•tise (trē′tis), *n.* a formal and systematic exposition in writing of the principles of a subject, generally longer and more detailed than an essay. [1300–50; ME *tretis* < AF *tretiz,* akin to OF *traitier* to TREAT]

treat•ment (trēt′mənt), *n.* **1.** an act or manner of treating. **2.** action or behavior toward a person, animal, etc. **3.** management in the application of medicines, surgery, etc. **4.** literary or artistic handling, esp. with reference to style. **5.** subjection to some agent or action. **6.** *Motion Pictures, Television.* a preliminary outline of a film or teleplay laying out the key scenes, characters, and locales. [1550–60; TREAT + -MENT]
—**Syn. 1.** handling, management, conduct, approach.

trea•ty (trē′tē), *n., pl.* **-ties. 1.** a formal agreement between two or more states in reference to peace, alliance, commerce, or other international relations. **2.** the formal document embodying such an international agreement. **3.** any agreement or compact. [1350–1400; ME *trete* < AF < L *tractātus* TRACTATE]

trea′ty port′, *Hist.* any of the ports in China, Japan, or Korea through which trade with foreign countries was permitted by special treaty. [1880–85]

Treb•bia (treb′byä), *n.* a river in N Italy, flowing N into the Po at Piacenza: Romans defeated by Hannibal near here 218 B.C. 70 mi. (113 km) long.

Treb•i•zond (treb′ə zond′), *n.* **1.** a medieval empire in NE Asia Minor 1204–1461. **2.** Official name, **Trabzon.** a seaport in NE Turkey, on the Black Sea: an ancient Greek colony; capital of the medieval empire of Trebizond. 80,795.

tre•ble (treb′əl), *adj., n., v.,* **-bled, -bling.** —*adj.* **1.** threefold; triple. **2.** *Music.* **a.** of or pertaining to the highest part in harmonized music; soprano. **b.** of the highest pitch or range, as a voice part, voice, singer, or instrument. **c.** high in pitch; shrill. —*n.* **3.** *Music.* **a.** the treble or soprano part. **b.** a treble voice, singer, or instrument. **4.** a high or shrill voice or sound. **5.** the highest-pitched peal of a bell. —*v.t., v.i.* **6.** to make or become three times as much or as many; triple. [1275–1325; (adj. and n.) ME < MF < L *triplus* TRIPLE; (v.) ME *treblen,* deriv. of the adj.] —**tre•bly** (treb′lē), *adv.*

tre′ble clef′, *Music.* a sign that locates the G above middle C, placed on the second line of the staff, counting up; G clef. See illus. under **clef.** Also called **violin clef.** [1795–1805]

tre′ble staff′, *Music.* a staff, bearing a treble clef. [1900–05]

Tre•blin•ka (tre bleng′kä; *Eng.* trə bling′kə), *n.* a Nazi concentration camp in Poland, near Warsaw.

treb•u•chet (treb′yo͝o shet′, treb′yo͝o shet′), *n.* a medieval engine of war with a sling for hurling missiles. Also, **tre•buck•et** (trē′buk′it, treb′yo͝o ket′). [1300–50; ME < MF, equiv. to *trebuch*(*er*) to overturn, fall (*tre*(*s*) across, over (< L *trāns-* TRANS-) + *buc* trunk of body < Gmc; cf. OE *būc* belly) + *-et* -ET]

tre•cen•to (trā chen′tō; *It.* tre chen′tô), *n.* (*often cap.*) the 14th century, with reference to Italy, and esp. to its art or literature. [1835–45; < It, short for *mille trecento* 1300, hence repr. the years 1300–99, dates beginning with these numbers] —**tre·cen′tist,** *n.*

tre cor·de (trā kôr′dā; *It.* tʀe kôʀ′de), with the soft pedal released (a musical direction in piano playing). Cf. **una corda.** [< It: lit., three strings]

tre·de·cil·lion (trē′di sil′yən), *n., pl.* **-lions,** (*as after a numeral*) **-lion,** *adj.* —*n.* **1.** a cardinal number represented in the U.S. by 1 followed by 42 zeros, and in Great Britain by 1 followed by 78 zeros. —*adj.* **2.** amounting to one tredecillion in number. [1930–35; < L *trē(s)* THREE + DECILLION] —**tre′de·cil′lionth,** *adj., n.*

tree (trē), *n., v.,* **treed, tree·ing.** —*n.* **1.** a plant having a permanently woody main stem or trunk, ordinarily growing to a considerable height, and usually developing branches at some distance from the ground. **2.** any of various shrubs, bushes, and plants, as the banana, resembling a tree in form and size. **3.** something resembling a tree in shape, as a clothes tree or a crosstree. **4.** *Math., Ling.* See **tree diagram. 5.** See **family tree. 6.** a pole, post, beam, bar, handle, or the like, as one forming part of some structure. **7.** a shoetree or boot tree. **8.** a saddletree. **9.** a treelike group of crystals, as one forming in an electrolytic cell. **10.** a gallows or gibbet. **11.** the cross on which Christ was crucified. **12.** *Computers.* a data structure organized like a tree whose nodes store data elements and whose branches represent pointers to other nodes in the tree. **13.** See **Christmas tree. 14. up a tree,** *Informal.* in a difficult or embarrassing situation; at a loss; stumped. —*v.t.* **15.** to drive into or up a tree, as a pursued animal or person. **16.** *Informal.* to put into a difficult position. **17.** to stretch or shape on a tree, as a boot. **18.** to furnish (a structure) with a tree. [bef. 900; ME; OE *trēo(w)*; c. OFris, ON *trē*, OS *treo*, Goth *triu*; akin to Gk *drŷs* oak, Skt, Avestan *dru* wood] —**tree′like′,** *adj.*

Tree (trē), *n.* **Sir Herbert Beer·bohm** (bēr′bōm), (*Herbert Beerbohm*), 1853–1917, English actor and theater manager; brother of Max Beerbohm.

tree′ as′ter, any of various composite shrubs or trees of the genus *Olearia*, native chiefly to Australia and New Zealand, having large, often leathery leaves and daisylike flower heads.

tree′ crab′. See **coconut crab.**

tree′ creep′er. See under **creeper** (def. 6).

tree′ crick′et. See under **cricket**[1] (def. 1). [1855–60, *Amer.*]

treed (trēd), *adj.* **1.** planted with trees; wooded: *a treed hillside.* **2.** driven up a tree: *a treed animal.* **3.** fitted with trees: *treed boots.* [1855–60; TREE + -ED[3]]

tree′ di′agram, *Math., Ling.* a diagram in which lines branch out from a central point or stem without forming any closed loops. Also called **tree.** Cf. **phrase structure tree.** [1960–65]

tree′ ear′, a thin, stemless, rubbery, edible fungus, *Auricularia auricula*, that grows on trees. Also called **wood ear.**

tree′ farm′, a tree-covered area managed as a business enterprise under a plan of reforestation that makes continuous production of timber possible. [1940–45]

tree′ fern′, any of various ferns, mostly tropical and chiefly of the family Cyatheaceae, that attain the size of trees, sending up a straight trunklike stem with foliage at the summit. [1840–50]

tree·fish (trē′fish′), *n., pl.* **-fish·es,** (*esp. collectively*) **-fish.** a rockfish, *Sebastes serriceps*, of waters off southern California, marked with black bands. [1880–85, *Amer.*; TREE + FISH]

tree′-form frame′ (trē′fôrm′), a rigid frame having a pair of inclined girders branching from each column, as to form principals of a roof.

tree′ frog′, any of various arboreal frogs, esp. of the family Hylidae, usually having adhesive disks at the tip of each toe. [1730–40]

tree′ heath′, the brier, *Erica arborea.* [1770–80]

tree·hop·per (trē′hop′ər), *n.* any of numerous homopterous jumping insects of the family Membracidae, that have an enlarged prothorax and feed on the juices of plants, often injuring the plants. [1830–40; TREE + HOPPER]

tree′ house′, a small house, esp. one for children to play in, built or placed up in the branches of a tree.

tree-hug·ger (trē′hug′ər), *n.* an environmentalist, esp. one concerned with preserving forests. [1985–90] —**tree′-hug′ging,** *adj.*

tree′ hy′rax, an arboreal hyrax of the genus *Dendrohyrax*, of central and southern Africa.

tree′ kangaroo′, any arboreal kangaroo of the genus *Dendrolagus*, of Queensland, Australia, and New Guinea.

tree′ lawn′, a strip of grass-covered ground between sidewalk and curb, often planted with shade trees.

tree′ line′, timberline.

tree·lined (trē′līnd′), *adj.* having a line of trees: *a treelined road.* [TREE + LINE[1] + -ED[2]]

tree′ lu′pine, a shrubby, Californian tree, *Lupinus arboreus*, of the legume family, having hairy, finger-shaped leaflets and fragrant, sulphur-yellow flowers. [1880–85]

tre·en (trē′ən), *adj.* **1.** made entirely of wood. —*n.* **2.** treenware. [bef. 1000; ME (adj.); OE *trēowen.* See TREE, -EN[2]]

tree·nail (trē′nāl′, tren′l, trun′l), *n.* a wooden pin that swells when moist, used for fastening together timbers, as those of ships. Also, **trenail, trunnel.** [1250–1300; ME *trenayl.* See TREE, NAIL]

tre·en·ware (trē′ən wâr′), *n.* household utensils, dishes, etc., made entirely of wood. [TREEN + WARE[1]]

tree′ of heav′en, an Asiatic tree, *Ailanthus altissima*, having large oblong leaves and rank-smelling flowers, often planted as a shade tree. Also called **stinkweed.** [1835–45]

tree′ of Jes′se, a pictorial or sculpted image representing the family tree of Christ. Also called **Jesse tree.**

tree′ of knowl′edge of good′ and e′vil, the tree in the Garden of Eden bearing the forbidden fruit that was tasted by Adam and Eve. Gen. 2:17; 3:6–24. Also called **tree′ of knowl′edge.** [1525–35]

tree′ of life′, 1. a tree in the Garden of Eden that yielded food giving everlasting life. Gen 2:9; 3:22. **2.** a tree in the heavenly Jerusalem with leaves for the healing of the nations. Rev. 22:2. **3.** See **arbor vitae.** [1350–1400; ME]

tree′ of sad′ness. See **night jasmine** (def. 1).

tree′ pe′ony, a shrubby plant, *Paeonia suffruticosa*, of China, having rose-red or white flowers nearly 12 in. (30.5 cm) wide. [1835–45]

Tree′ Plant′ers State′, Nebraska (used as a nickname).

tree′ pop′py, a Californian shrub, *Dendromecon rigida*, of the poppy family, having leathery evergreen leaves and showy, usually yellow flowers. Also called **bush poppy.** [1865–70, *Amer.*]

tree′ post′. See **king post** (def. 1).

tree′ ring′. See **annual ring.** [1915–20]

tree′ shrew′, any of several insectivorous, arboreal mammals of the family Tupaiidae, of southern Asia and adjacent islands, resembling a squirrel and having a long snout. [1890–95]

tree′ snail′, any tree- or bush-living gastropod of the family Bulimulidae, inhabiting tropical and temperate regions and characterized by brightly colored shells with distinct central whorls.

tree′ spar′row, 1. a Eurasian bird, *Passer montanus*, related to but smaller than the house sparrow. **2.** a North American finch, *Spizella arborea*, common in winter in the northern U.S. [1760–70]

tree′ squir′rel, any squirrel of the genus *Sciurus*, with a long, bushy tail, familiar in parks and wooded areas throughout temperate regions. [1870–75]

tree′ sur′gery, the repair of damaged trees, as by the removal of diseased parts, filling of cavities, and prevention of further decay, and by strengthening branches with braces. [1915–20] —**tree′-sur′geon,** *n.*

tree′ swal′low, a bluish-green and white swallow, *Iridoprocne bicolor*, of North America, that nests in tree cavities. [1890–95, *Amer.*]

tree′ swift′, any of several birds of the family Hemiprocnidae, of southeast Asia and the East Indies, related to the true swifts but differing in having erectile crests and the habit of perching in trees. Also, **tree′-swift′.** Also called **crested swift.**

tree′ toad′. See **tree frog.** [1770–80, *Amer.*]

tree′ tobac′co, a treelike South American plant, *Nicotiana glauca*, of the nightshade family, having blue-green foliage, heart-shaped leaves, and white, greenish-yellow, or purple flowers, the corolla yellow, grown as an ornamental. [1890–95]

tree′ toma′to, tamarillo.

tree·top (trē′top′), *n.* the top or uppermost branches of a tree. [1520–30; TREE + TOP[1]]

tree′ yuc′ca. See **Joshua tree.** [1955–60]

tref (trāf), *adj. Judaism.* unfit to be eaten or used, according to religious laws; not kosher. Also, **terefah.** [< Yiddish *treyf* < Heb *ṭərēphāh* torn flesh, lit., something torn]

tref·lé (tref lā′), *adj. Heraldry.* botonée. [1715–25; < F, deriv. of *trefle* TREFOIL]

tre·foil (trē′foil, tref′oil), *n.* **1.** any of numerous plants belonging to the genus *Trifolium*, of the legume family, having usually digitate leaves of three leaflets and reddish, purple, yellow, or white flower heads, comprising the common clovers. **2.** any of various similar plants. **3.** *Archit.* an ornament composed of three lobes, divided by cusps, radiating from a common center. **4.** such an ornamental figure used by the Girl Scouts as its official emblem. —*adj.* **5.** of, pertaining to, or shaped like a trefoil. [1350–1400; ME < AF *trifoil* < L *trifolium* triple leaf, the three-leaved plant, clover, equiv. to *tri-* TRI- + *folium* leaf]

trefoils (def. 3)

tre′foil arch′, *Archit.* an arch with cusplike intrados.

tre′foil knot′, a knot having the form of a trefoil.

tre·ha·la (tri hä′lə), *n.* an edible, sugary substance secreted by certain Asiatic beetles of the genus *Larinus*, forming their pupal covering. [1860–65; < NL < Turk *tigala* < Pers *tighāl*]

tre·ha·lose (trē′hə lōs′, tri hä′lōs), *n. Chem.* a white, crystalline disaccharide, $C_{12}H_{22}O_{11}$, occurring in yeast, certain fungi, etc., and used to identify certain bacteria. [1860–65; TREHAL(A) + -OSE[2]]

treil·lage (trā′lij; *Fr.* tʀe yazh′), *n.* latticework; a lattice or trellis. [1690–1700; < F, equiv. to *treille* vine-arbor, trellis (< L *trichila*; cf. ML *trelia*) + *-age* -AGE]

Trein·ta y Tres (tʀān′tä ē tʀes′), a city in E Uruguay. 25,000.

Treitsch·ke (tʀīch′kə), *n.* **Hein·rich von** (hīn′ʀiKH fən), 1834–96, German historian.

trek (trek), *v.,* **trekked, trek·king,** *n.* —*v.i.* **1.** to travel or migrate, esp. slowly or with difficulty. **2.** *South Africa.* to travel by ox wagon. —*v.t.* **3.** *South Africa.* (of a draft animal) to draw (a vehicle or load). —*n.* **4.** a journey or trip, esp. one involving difficulty or hardship. **5.** *South Africa.* a migration or expedition, as by ox wagon. **6.** *South Africa.* a stage of a journey, esp. by ox wagon, between one stopping place and the next. [1815–25; < Afrik < D *trek* (n.), *trekken* (v.) to draw (a vehicle or load), migrate]

Tre·law·ney (tri lô′nē), *n.* **Edward John,** 1792-1881, English adventurer and author.

trel·lis (trel′is), *n.* **1.** a frame or structure of latticework; lattice. **2.** a framework of this kind used as a support for growing vines or plants. **3.** a summerhouse, gazebo, arch, etc., made chiefly or completely of latticework. **4.** *Heraldry.* a charge of bendlets overlying bendlets sinister, the whole being cloué at the crossings. —*v.t.* **5.** to furnish with a trellis. **6.** to enclose in a trellis. **7.** to train or support on a trellis. **8.** to form into or like a trellis. [1350–1400; ME *trelis* < MF (n.) < LL *trilīcius* (for L *trilix*) woven with three threads, equiv. to L *tri-* TRI- + *lici(um)* thread + *-us* adj. suffix]

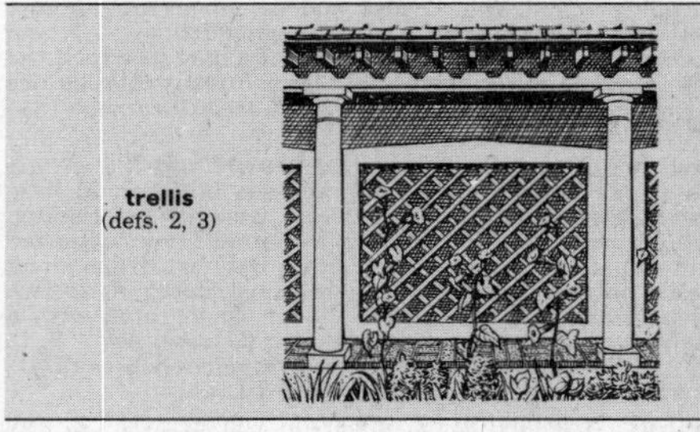
trellis (defs. 2, 3)

trel·lised (trel′ist), *adj. Armor.* noting armor having diagonally crisscrossed strips of leather enframing metal plates, the whole being sewn to a flexible backing. [1425–75; late ME; see TRELLIS, -ED[3]]

trel·lis·work (trel′is wûrk′), *n.* latticework. [1705–15; TRELLIS + WORK]

Trem·a·to·da (trem′ə tō′də, trē′mə-), *n.* the class comprising the trematodes. [< NL; see TREMATODE]

trem·a·tode (trem′ə tōd′, trē′mə-), *n.* any parasitic platyhelminth or flatworm of the class Trematoda, having one or more external suckers; fluke. [1830–40; < NL *Trematoda* class name < Gk *trēmatṓdēs* having holes, equiv. to *trēmat-* (s. of *trēma*) hole + *-ōdēs* -ODE[1]]

trem·ble (trem′bəl), *v.,* **-bled, -bling,** *n.* —*v.i.* **1.** to shake involuntarily with quick, short movements, as from fear, excitement, weakness, or cold; quake; quiver. **2.** to be troubled with fear or apprehension. **3.** (of things) to be affected with vibratory motion. **4.** to be tremulous, as light or sound: *His voice trembled.* —*n.* **5.** the act of trembling. **6.** a state or fit of trembling. **7. trembles,** (*used with a singular v.*) **a.** *Pathol.* See **milk sickness. b.** *Vet. Pathol.* a toxic condition of cattle and sheep caused by the eating of white snakeroot and characterized by muscular tremors. [1275–1325; ME *trem(b)len* (v.) < OF *trembler* < VL **tremulāre*, deriv. of L *tremulus* TREMULOUS] —**trem′bling·ly,** *adv.*
—**Syn. 1.** shudder. See **shake. 3.** oscillate.

trem·bler (trem′blər), *n.* **1.** a person or thing that trembles. **2.** an oscine bird, *Cinclocerthia ruficauda*, of the Lesser Antilles, related to the thrashers, noted for its habit of trembling violently. **3.** Also, **trem′blor.** *Informal.* a temblor. [1545–55; TREMBLE + -ER[1]]

trem·bly (trem′blē), *adj.* **-bli·er, -bli·est.** quivering; tremulous; shaking. [1840–50; TREMBLE + -Y[1]]

tre·men·dous (tri men′dəs), *adj.* **1.** extraordinarily great in size, amount, or intensity: *a tremendous ocean liner; tremendous talent.* **2.** extraordinary in excellence: *a tremendous movie.* **3.** dreadful or awful, as in character or effect; exciting fear; frightening; terrifying. [1625–35; < L *tremendus* dreadful, to be shaken by, equiv. to *trem(ere)* to shake, quake + *-endus* ger. suffix] —**tre·men′dous·ly,** *adv.* —**tre·men′dous·ness,** *n.*
—**Syn. 1.** See **huge.**

trém·ie (trem′ē; *Fr.* tʀā mē′), *n., pl.* **trém·ies** (trem′ēz; *Fr.* tʀā mē′). a funnellike device lowered into water to deposit concrete. [1900–05; < F: hopper < L *trimodia* three-peck measure, equiv. to *tri-* TRI- + *mod(ius)* measure of grain + *-ia* -IA]

tre·mis·sis (tri mis′is), *n., pl.* **-mis·ses** (-mis′ēz). **1.** Also called **triens.** a gold coin of the Eastern Roman Empire, the third part of a solidus, first issued in the 3rd century A.D. **2.** a Merovingian gold coin imitating this. [1700–10; < LL *trēmissis*, equiv. to L *trē(s)* THREE + *-missis* as in *sēmissis*, LL form of L *sēmis* SEMIS (falsely analyzed as *sē-* + *-missis*)]

trem·o·lant (trem′ə lənt), *adj.* **1.** having a tremulous or vibrating tone, as certain pipes of an organ. —*n.* **2.** an organ pipe producing a tremolant tone. [1850–55; < G < It *tremolante* TREMULANT]

trem·o·lite (trem′ə līt′), *n. Mineral.* a white or grayish variety of amphibole, $Ca_2Mg_5Si_8O_{22}(OH)_2$, usually occurring in bladed crystals. [1790–1800; named after *Tremola*, valley in Switzerland; see -ITE[1]] —**trem·o·lit·ic** (trem′ə lit′ik), *adj.*

trem·o·lo (trem′ə lō′), *n., pl.* **-los.** *Music.* **1.** a tremu-

CONCISE ETYMOLOGY KEY: <, descended or borrowed from; >, whence; b., blend of, blended; c., cognate with; cf., compare; deriv., derivative; equiv., equivalent; imit., imitative; obl., oblique; r., replacing; s., stem; sp., spelling, spelled; resp., respelling, respelled; trans., translation; ?, origin unknown; *, unattested; ‡, probably earlier than. See the full key inside the front cover.

lous or vibrating effect produced on certain instruments and in the human voice, as to express emotion. **2.** a mechanical device in an organ by which such an effect is produced. [1715–25; < It: trembling < L *tremulus* TREMULOUS]

trem·or (trem′ər, trē′mər), *n.* **1.** involuntary shaking of the body or limbs, as from disease, fear, weakness, or excitement; a fit of trembling. **2.** any tremulous or vibratory movement; vibration: *tremors following an earthquake.* **3.** a trembling or quivering effect, as of light. **4.** a quavering sound, as of the voice. [1325–75; ME < L: a trembling, equiv. to *trem(ere)* to tremble + *-or* -OR¹] —**trem′or·ous,** *adj.*
—**Syn. 1.** shudder, shiver, quiver. **3.** oscillation.

trem·u·lant (trem′yə lənt), *adj.* trembling; tremulous. [1830–40; < ML *tremulant-* (s. of *tremulāns*) prp. of *tremulāre* to TREMBLE; see -ANT]

trem·u·lous (trem′yə ləs), *adj.* **1.** (of persons, the body, etc.) characterized by trembling, as from fear, nervousness, or weakness. **2.** timid; timorous; fearful. **3.** (of things) vibratory, shaking, or quivering. **4.** (of writing) done with a trembling hand. [1605–15; < L *tremulus,* equiv. to *trem(ere)* to tremble + *-ulus* adj. suffix] —**trem′u·lous·ly,** *adv.* —**trem′u·lous·ness,** *n.*
—**Syn. 1.** faltering, hesitant, wavering. **2.** afraid.

tre·nail (trē′nāl′, tren′l, trun′l), *n.* treenail.

trench (trench), *n.* **1.** *Fort.* a long, narrow excavation in the ground, the earth from which is thrown up in front to serve as a shelter from enemy fire or attack. **2. trenches,** a system of such excavations, with their embankments, etc. **3.** a deep furrow, ditch, or cut. **4.** *Oceanog.* a long, steep-sided, narrow depression in the ocean floor. —*v.t.* **5.** to surround or fortify with trenches; entrench. **6.** to cut a trench in. **7.** to set or place in a trench. **8.** to form (a furrow, ditch, etc.) by cutting into or through something. **9.** to make a cut in; cut into; carve. —*v.i.* **10.** to dig a trench. **11. trench on** or **upon, a.** to encroach or infringe on. **b.** to come close to; verge on: *His remarks were trenching on poor taste.* [1350–1400; ME *trenche* path made by cutting < OF: act of cutting, a cut, deriv. of *trenchier* to cut < VL **trincāre,* for L *truncāre* to lop; see TRUNCATE]

Trench (trench), *n.* **Richard Chen·e·vix** (shen′ə vē), 1807–86, English clergyman and scholar, born in Ireland.

trench·ant (tren′chənt), *adj.* **1.** incisive or keen, as language or a person; caustic; cutting: *trenchant wit.* **2.** vigorous; effective; energetic: *a trenchant policy of political reform.* **3.** clearly or sharply defined; clear-cut; distinct. [1275–1325; ME *tranchaunt* < AF; OF *trenchant,* prp. of *trenchier* to cut. See TRENCH, -ANT] —**trench′an·cy,** *n.* —**trench′ant·ly,** *adv.*
—**Syn. 1.** sharp, biting, acute.

Tren·chard (tren′chärd, -chərd), *n.* **Hugh Montague, 1st Viscount,** 1873–1956, British Royal Air Force marshal.

trench′ coat′, a waterproof overcoat styled along military lines, belted, with straps on the shoulders and lower sleeves. [1915–20]

trench·er (tren′chər), *n.* **1.** a person or thing that digs trenches. **2.** ditchdigger (def. 3). **3.** a rectangular or circular flat piece of wood on which meat, or other food, is served or carved. **4.** such a piece of wood and the food on it. **5.** *Archaic.* food; the pleasures of good eating. [1275–1325; ME *trenchour* something to cut with or on < AF; MF *trencheoir.* See TRENCH, -ORY²]

trench·er·man (tren′chər mən), *n., pl.* **-men. 1.** a person who has a hearty appetite. **2.** *Archaic.* a hanger-on; parasite. [1580–90; TRENCHER + -MAN]

trench′ fe′ver, *Pathol.* a recurrent fever, often suffered by soldiers in trenches in World War I, caused by a rickettsia transmitted by the body louse. [1910–15]

trench′ foot′, *Pathol.* injury of the skin, blood vessels, and nerves of the feet due to prolonged exposure to cold and wet, common among soldiers serving in trenches. [1910–15]

trench′ knife′, a short knife for stabbing, sometimes equipped with brass knuckles as a guard, used in modern warfare in hand-to-hand combat. [1915–20]

trench′ mor′tar, a portable, muzzle-loaded mortar, usually having a smooth bore, fired at high angles of elevation to reach concealed enemy targets. [1915–20]

trench′ mouth′. See **Vincent's angina.** [1915–20; so called from its high incidence among soldiers in the trenches]

trench′ war′fare, combat in which each side occupies a system of protective trenches. [1915–20]

trend (trend), *n.* **1.** the general course or prevailing tendency; drift: *trends in the teaching of foreign languages; the trend of events.* **2.** style; vogue: *the new trend in women's apparel.* **3.** the general direction followed by a road, river, coastline, or the like. —*v.i.* **4.** to have a general tendency, as events, conditions, etc. **5.** to tend to take a particular direction; extend in some direction indicated. **6.** to veer or turn off in a specified direction, as a river, mountain range, etc.: *The river trends toward the southeast.* [bef. 1000; ME *trenden* to turn, roll, OE *trendan;* akin to OE *trinde* ball, D *trent* circumference, Sw *trind* round. See TRINDLE, TRUNDLE]
—**Syn. 1.** See **tendency. 5.** stretch, run, incline.

trend·line (trend′līn′), *n.* an upward or downward line on a chart indicating movements of average prices, as of stocks, over a period of time. Also, **trend′ line′.** [1910–15 for more general sense; TREND + LINE¹]

trend·set·ter (trend′set′ər), *n.* a person or thing that establishes a new trend or fashion. [1960–65; from the v. phrase *set a trend;* see -ER¹]

trend·set·ting (trend′set′ing), *adj.* establishing or influencing a new trend or fashion. [1955–60; from the v. phrase *set a trend;* see -ING²]

trend·y (tren′dē), *adj.,* **trend·i·er, trend·i·est,** *n., pl.* **trend·ies.** —*adj.* **1.** of, in, or pertaining to the latest trend or style. **2.** following the latest trends or fashions; up-to-date or chic: *the trendy young generation.* **3.** appealing to faddish taste: *a trendy hotel.* —*n.* **4.** a trendy person, place, object, or idea. [1960–65; TREND + -Y¹] —**trend′i·ly,** *adv.* —**trend′i·ness,** *n.*

Treng·ga·nu (treng gä′no͞o), *n.* a state in Malaysia, on the E central Malay Peninsula. 405,368; 5050 sq. mi. (13,080 sq. km). *Cap.:* Kuala Trengganu. Also, **Terengganu.**

Trent (trent), *n.* **1.** Italian, **Trento.** Ancient, **Tridentum.** a city in N Italy, on the Adige River. 98,006. **2. Council of,** the ecumenical council of the Roman Catholic Church that met at Trent intermittently from 1545 to 1563, and defined church doctrine and condemned the Reformation. **3.** a river in central England, flowing NE from Staffordshire to the Humber. 170 mi. (275 km) long.

tren·tal (tren′tl), *n. Rom. Cath. Ch.* a series of 30 Requiems celebrated one each day for 30 consecutive days. [1300–50; ME < ML *trentāle,* equiv. to VL **trent(a)* (for L *trīgintā* thirty) + L *-āle* -AL². Cf. OF *trentel*]

trente et qua·rante (tränt′ ā kə ränt′; *Fr.* tʀäɴ tā ka ʀäɴt′). See **rouge et noir.** [1665–75; < F]

Tren·ti·no-Al·to A·di·ge (tʀen tē′nô äl′tô ä′dē je), a region in NE Italy. 870,238; 5256 sq. mi. (13.615 sq. km).

Tren·to (tʀen′tô), *n.* Italian name of **Trent.**

Tren·ton (tren′tn), *n.* **1.** a city in and the capital of New Jersey, in the W part, on the Delaware River: Washington defeated Hessian troops here 1776. 92,124. **2.** a city in SE Michigan, S of Detroit. 22,762. **3.** a town in SE Ontario, in S Canada. 15,085. —**Tren·to·ni·an** (tren tō′nē ən), *n.*

tre·pan¹ (tri pan′), *n., v.,* **-panned, -pan·ning.** —*n.* **1.** a tool for cutting shallow holes by removing a core. **2.** *Surg.* an obsolete form of the trephine resembling a carpenter's bit and brace. —*v.t.* **3.** *Mach.* to cut circular disks from (plate stock) using a rotating cutter. **4.** *Surg.* to operate upon with a trepan; trephine. [1350–1400; (n.) ME *trepane* < MF *trepan* crown saw < ML *trepanum* < Gk *trýpanon* borer, akin to *trýpa* hole, *trypân* to bore; (v) late ME *trepanen,* deriv. of the n.] —**trep·a·na·tion** (trep′ə nā′shən), *n.* —**tre·pan′ner,** *n.*

tre·pan² (tri pan′), *n., v.,* **-panned, -pan·ning.** *Archaic.* —*n.* **1.** a person who ensnares or entraps others. **2.** a stratagem; a trap. —*v.t.* **3.** to ensnare or entrap. **4.** to entice. **5.** to cheat or swindle. [1635–45; earlier *trapan,* equiv. to TRAP¹ + *-an* < ?] —**trep·a·na·tion** (trep′ə nā′shən), *n.* —**tre·pan′ner,** *n.*

tre·pang (tri pang′), *n.* any of various holothurians or sea cucumbers, as *Holothuria edulis,* used as food in China. [1775–85; < Malay *təripaŋ* (sp. *teripang*) < an unidentified source]

tre·phine (tri fīn′, -fēn′), *n., v.,* **-phined, -phin·ing.** *Surg.* —*n.* **1.** a small circular saw with a center pin mounted on a strong hollow metal shaft to which is attached a transverse handle: used in surgery to remove circular disks of bone from the skull. —*v.t.* **2.** to operate upon with a trephine. [1620–30; sp. var. of *trefine,* orig. *trafine,* b. *trapan* (var. of TREPAN¹) and L phrase *trēs fīnēs* three ends (the inventor's explanation)] —**treph·i·na·tion** (tref′ə nā′shən), *n.*

trep·id (trep′id), *adj.* fearful or apprehensive, esp. trembling from fear. [1640–50; < L *trepidus*]

trep·i·dant (trep′i dənt), *adj.* trepid. [1890–95; < L *trepidant-,* s. of *trepidāns,* prp. of *trepidāre;* see TREPIDATION, -ANT]

trep·i·da·tion (trep′i dā′shən), *n.* **1.** tremulous fear, alarm, or agitation; perturbation. **2.** trembling or quivering movement; tremor. [1595–1605; < L *trepidātiōn-* (s. of *trepidātiō*), equiv. to *trepidāt(us)* (ptp. of *trepidāre* to hurry, alarm; see TREPID, -ATE¹) + *-iōn-* -ION]

trep·o·ne·ma (trep′ə nē′mə), *n., pl.* **-mas, -ma·ta** (-mə tə). any of several anaerobic spirochetes of the genus *Treponema,* certain species of which are parasitic in and pathogenic for humans and warm-blooded animals. [1905–10; < NL: genus name < Gk *trép(ein)* to turn + *-o-* -O- + *nêma* thread] —**trep·o·nem·a·tous** (trep′ə nem′ə təs, -nē′mə-), **trep′o·ne′mal,** *adj.*

trep·o·ne·ma·to·sis (trep′ə nē′mə tō′sis), *n. Pathol.* an infection caused by an organism of the genus *Treponema,* as syphilis, pinta, bejel, or yaws. [1940–45; < NL *Treponemat-* (s. of *Treponema;* see TREPONEMA) + -OSIS]

trep·o·ne·mi·a·sis (trep′ə nə mī′ə sis), *n. Pathol.* infection with treponema; syphilis. [TREPONEM(A) + -IASIS]

tres·pass (tres′pəs, -pas), *n.* **1.** *Law.* **a.** an unlawful act causing injury to the person, property, or rights of another, committed with force or violence, actual or implied. **b.** a wrongful entry upon the lands of another. **c.** the action to recover damages for such an injury. **2.** an encroachment or intrusion. **3.** an offense, sin, or wrong. —*v.i.* **4.** *Law.* to commit a trespass. **5.** to encroach on a person's privacy, time, etc.; infringe (usually fol. by *on* or *upon*). **6.** to commit a transgression or offense; transgress; offend; sin. [1250–1300; (n.) ME *trespas* transgression, offense < OF, deriv. of *trespasser,* equiv. to *tres-* (< L *trāns-* TRANS-) + *passer* to PASS; (v.) ME *trespassen,* deriv. of the n.] —**tres′pass·er,** *n.*
—**Syn. 4, 5.** TRESPASS, ENCROACH, INFRINGE, INTRUDE imply overstepping boundaries and assuming possession of others' property or crowding onto the right of others. To TRESPASS is to pass unlawfully within the boundaries of another's property: *Hunters trespass on a farmer's fields.* To ENCROACH is to creep, gradually and often stealthily, upon territory, rights, or privileges, so that a footing is imperceptibly established: *The sea slowly encroached upon the land.* To INFRINGE is to break in upon or invade rights, customs, or the like, by violating or disregarding them: *to infringe upon a patent.* To INTRUDE is to thrust oneself into the presence of a person or into places or circumstances where one is not welcome: *to intrude into a private conversation.*

tress (tres), *n.* **1.** Usually, **tresses.** long locks or curls of hair. **2.** a plait or braid of hair. [1250–1300; ME *tresse* < MF: plait or braid of hair < ?]

tressed (trest), *adj.* **1.** (of the hair) arranged or formed into tresses; braided; plaited. **2.** having tresses (usually used in combination): *auburn-tressed; golden-tressed.* [1300–50; ME; see TRESS, -ED³]

tres·sure (tresh′ər), *n.* **1.** *Heraldry.* a narrower diminutive of the orle, usually ornamented with fleurs-de-lis at the edges and often doubled. **2.** *Numis.* an ornamental border enclosing the type on a coin or medal. [1275–1325; late ME < MF, equiv. to *tress(er)* to braid, plait (deriv. of *tresse* TRESS) + *-ure* -URE; r. ME *tressour* < MF *tresseor, tressoir*] —**tres′sured,** *adj.*

tress·y (tres′ē), *adj.,* **tress·i·er, tress·i·est.** *Archaic.* resembling or having tresses. [1605–15; TRESS + -Y¹]

tres·tine (tres′tīn), *n.* See **royal antler.** Also, **treztine.** [perh. < L *trēs* THREE + TINE]

tres·tle (tres′əl), *n.* **1.** a frame typically composed of a horizontal bar or beam rigidly joined or fitted at each end to the top of a transverse A-frame, used as a barrier, a transverse support for planking, etc.; horse. **2.** *Civ. Engin.* **a.** one of a number of bents, having sloping sides of framework or piling, for supporting the deck or stringers of a bridge. **b.** a bridge made of these. [1300–50; ME *trestel* < MF, by dissimilation from OF *trestre* << L *trānstrum* crossbeam]

trestle
(def. 2b)

tres′tle ta′ble, 1. a table having transverse slabs or rigid frames for supports, and usually strengthened by a long stretcher. **2.** a table composed of a movable top supported by trestles. [1890–95]

tres·tle·tree (tres′əl trē′), *n. Naut.* either of a pair of timbers or metal shapes lying along the tops of the hounds or cheeks of a mast to support crosstrees or a top. [1615–25; TRESTLE + TREE]

tres·tle·work (tres′əl wûrk′), *n.* a structural system composed of trestles. [1840–50; TRESTLE + WORK]

tret (tret), *n.* (formerly) an allowance for waste, after deduction for tare. [1490–1500; < AF, var. of *trait* act of drawing; see TRAIT]

Tre·ta Yu·ga (trā′tə yo͝og′ə), *Hinduism.* the second Yuga, not as good as the Satya Yuga but better than the Dvapara Yuga. [< Skt *tretāyuga;* cf. YUGA]

tre·tin·o·in (trə tin′ō in), *n.* a drug chemically related to vitamin A, used as a topical ointment to treat skin disorders, esp. acne. [1960–65; T(RI) + *retino-* (< Gk *rhētínē* resin) + -IN¹]

tre·val·ly (trə val′ē), *n., pl.* **-lies.** any of several popular Australian food fish of the genus *Caranx,* esp. *Caranx georgianus.* [orig. uncert.]

Tre·vel·yan (tri vel′yən, -vil′-), *n.* **1. George Macaulay,** 1876–1962, English historian. **2.** his father, **Sir George Otto,** 1838–1928, English biographer, historian, and statesman.

Treves (trēvz), *n.* Trier. French, **Trèves** (tʀev).

Tre·vi·so (tʀe vē′zô), *n.* a city in NE Italy. 90,632.

Trev·i·thick (trev′ə thik), *n.* **Richard,** 1771–1833, English engineer.

Trev·or (trev′ər), *n.* a male given name.

Trev·or-Ro·per (trev′ər rō′pər) *n.* **Hugh (Red·wald)** (red′wôld), born 1914, British historian.

trews (tro͞oz), *n.* (*used with a plural v.*) close-fitting tartan trousers, worn esp. by certain Scottish regiments. [1560–70; < Ir and ScotGael *triubhas* < OF *trebus* breeches]

trey (trā), *n.* a playing card or a die having three pips. [1350–1400; ME < MF *trei(s)* < L *trēs* THREE]

trez·tine (trez′tīn), *n.* See **royal antler.**

TRF, thyrotropin-releasing factor.

trf, 1. transfer. **2.** tuned radio frequency.

TRH, thyrotropin-releasing hormone.

tri-, a combining form meaning "three," used in the formation of compound words: *triacid; triatomic.* [ME < L, comb. form repr. L *trēs, tria,* Gk *treîs, tría* THREE]

tri·a·ble (trī′ə bəl), subject or liable to judicial trial. [1400–50; late ME < AF. See TRY, -ABLE]

tri·ac (trī′ak), *n. Electronics.* a type of thyristor designed for electronic control of the current supplied to a circuit, used esp. in dimmers for lighting systems. [1960–65; TRI(ODE) + A.C. alternating current]

tri·ac·e·tate (trī as′i tāt′), *n. Chem.* an acetate containing three acetate groups. [1855–60; TRI- + ACETATE]

triac′etate fi′ber, a textile fiber made of cellulose triacetate.

tri·ac·id (trī as′id), *adj. Chem.* **1.** capable of combining with three molecules of a monobasic acid: *a triacid base.* **2.** noting acid salts containing three replaceable hydrogen atoms. [1885–90; TRI- + ACID]

tri·a·con·ta·nol (trī′ə kon′tə nôl′, -nol′), *n. Biochem.* a long-chain alcohol, $CH_3(CH_2)_{28}CH_2OH$, occurring in plant waxes and beeswax, that is a plant growth regula-

CONCISE PRONUNCIATION KEY: *act, cāpe, dâre, pärt; set, ēqual; if, īce; ox, ōver, ôrder, oil, bo͝ok, bo͞ot, out; up, ûrge; child; sing; shoe; thin, that;* zh as in *treasure.* ə = *a* as in *alone, e* as in *system, i* as in *easily, o* as in *gallop, u* as in *circus;* ᵊ as in *fire* (fīᵊr), *hour* (ouᵊr). l and n can serve as syllabic consonants, as in *cradle* (krād′l), and *button* (but′n). See the full key inside the front cover.

tor. Also called **melissyl alcohol.** [*1-(hydroxy)triacontane* chemical name + -OL[1]]

tri•ad (trī′ad, -əd), *n.* **1.** a group of three, esp. of three closely related persons or things. **2.** *Chem.* **a.** an element, atom, or group having a valence of three. Cf. **monad** (def. 2), **dyad** (def. 3). **b.** a group of three closely related compounds or elements, as isomers or halides. **3.** *Music.* a chord of three tones, esp. one consisting of a given tone with its major or minor third and its perfect, augmented, or diminished fifth. **4.** (*cap.*) *Mil.* the three categories of strategic-nuclear-weapons delivery systems: bombers, land-based missiles, and missile-firing submarines. [1540–50; < L *triad-* (s. of *trias*) < Gk *triás* See TRI-, -AD[1]] —**tri•ad′ic,** *adj.* —**tri′ad•ism,** *n.*

tri•a•del•phous (trī′ə del′fəs), *adj. Bot.* (of stamens) united by the filaments into three sets or bundles. [1820–30; TRI- + -ADELPHOUS]

tri•age (trē äzh′), *n., adj., v.,* **-aged, ag•ing.** —*n.* **1.** the process of sorting victims, as of a battle or disaster, to determine medical priority in order to increase the number of survivors. **2.** the determination of priorities for action in an emergency. —*adj.* **3.** of, pertaining to, or performing the task of triage: *a triage officer.* —*v.t.* **4.** to act on or in by triage: *to triage a crisis.* [1925–30; < F: sorting, equiv. to *tri(er)* to sort (see TRY) + *-age* -AGE]

tri•al (trī′əl, trīl), *n.* **1.** *Law.* **a.** the examination before a judicial tribunal of the facts put in issue in a cause, often including issues of law as well as those of fact. **b.** the determination of a person's guilt or innocence by due process of law. **2.** the act of trying, testing, or putting to the proof. **3.** test; proof. **4.** an attempt or effort to do something. **5.** a tentative or experimental action in order to ascertain results; experiment. **6.** the state or position of a person or thing being tried or tested; probation. **7.** subjection to suffering or grievous experiences; a distressed or painful state: *comfort in the hour of trial.* **8.** an affliction or trouble. **9.** a trying, distressing, or annoying thing or person. **10.** *Ceram.* a piece of ceramic material used to try the heat of a kiln and the progress of the firing of its contents. **11. on trial, a.** undergoing examination before a judicial tribunal. **b.** undergoing a probationary or trial period. —*adj.* **12.** of, pertaining to, or employed in a trial. **13.** done or made by way of trial, proof, or experiment. **14.** used in testing, experiments, etc. **15.** acting or serving as a sample, experimental specimen, etc.: *a trial offer.* [1520–30; TRY + -AL[2]]

—**Syn. 2, 3, 5.** examination. TRIAL, EXPERIMENT, TEST imply an attempt to find out something or to find out about something. TRIAL is the general word for a trying of anything: *articles sent for ten days' free trial.* EXPERIMENT is a trial conducted to prove or illustrate the truth or validity of something, or an attempt to discover something new: *an experiment in organic chemistry.* TEST is a more specific word, referring to a trial under approved and fixed conditions, or a final and decisive trial as a conclusion of past experiments: *a test of a new type of airplane.* **4.** endeavor, essay, struggle. **7.** grief, tribulation, distress, sorrow, trouble, hardship. See **affliction.**

Trial, The, (German, *Der Prozess*), a novel (1925) by Franz Kafka.

tri′al and er′ror, experimentation or investigation in which various methods or means are tried and faulty ones eliminated in order to find the correct solution or to achieve the desired result or effect. [1800–10] —**tri′•al-and-er′ror,** *adj.*

tri′al bal′ance, *Bookkeeping.* a statement of all the open debit and credit items, made preliminary to balancing a double-entry ledger. [1830–40]

tri′al balloon′, a statement, program, or the like issued publicly as a means of determining reactions in advance: *The speech was a trial balloon for a new law.* [1930–35]

tri′al court′, the court in which a controversy is first adjudicated (distinguished from *appellate division*). [1885–90]

tri′al dock′et, docket (def. 1).

tri′al exam′iner, *Law.* a person appointed to hold hearings and report findings and recommendations to an administrative or quasi-judicial agency or tribunal. [1945–50]

tri′al horse′, *Informal.* an opponent who performs against a superior foe in a workout or exhibition. [1900–05]

tri′al ju′ry. See **petty jury.** [1885–90]

tri′al law′yer, a lawyer who specializes in appearing before trial courts. [1910–15]

tri′al mar′riage, an arrangement by which a couple live together for a period of time to see if they are compatible for marriage. Cf. **companionate marriage.** [1920–25]

tri•a•logue (trī′ə lôg′, -log′), *n.* a discussion or conversation in which three persons or groups participate. [1525–35; TRI- + (DI)ALOGUE, mistaken as a formation with DI-[1]]

tri′al run′, a preliminary performance or test of something, as of the operation of a ship or the effectiveness of a play. [1900–05]

tri•am•cin•o•lone (trī′am sin′ə lōn′), *n. Pharm.* a synthetic glucocorticoid drug, $C_{21}H_{27}FO_6$, used in the symptomatic treatment of inflammation. [1955–60; *triamcin-* (of unexplained derivation) + (PREDNIS)OLONE]

Tri•an•da (trē än′də; *Gk.* trē än′dä), *n.* a town on the Greek island of Rhodes, in the Aegean Sea: built on the site of ancient Ialysus. Also, **Trianta.**

tri•an•gle (trī′ang′gəl), *n.* **1.** a closed plane figure having three sides and three angles. **2.** a flat triangular piece, usually of plastic, with straight edges, used in connection with a T square for drawing perpendicular lines, geometric figures, etc. **3.** any three-cornered or three-sided figure, object, or piece: *a triangle of land.* **4.** a musical percussion instrument that consists of a steel triangle, open at one corner, that is struck with a steel rod. **5.** a group of three; triad. **6.** a situation involving three persons, esp. one in which two of them are in love with the third. **7.** (*cap.*) *Astron.* the constellation Triangulum. [1350–1400; ME < L *triangulum,* n. use of neut. of *triangulus* three-cornered. See TRI-, ANGLE[1]] —**tri′an′gled,** *adj.*

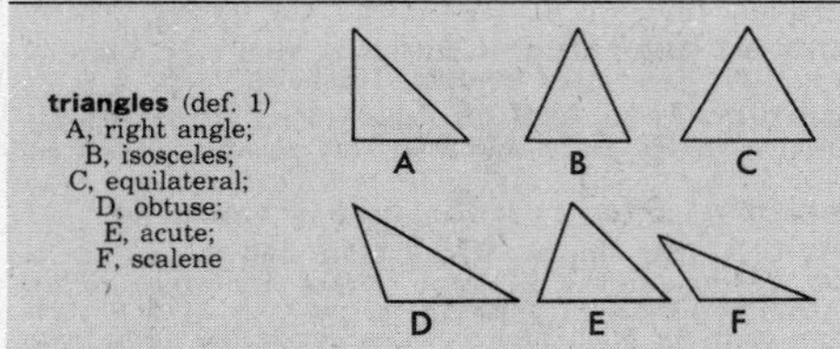

triangles (def. 1)
A, right angle;
B, isosceles;
C, equilateral;
D, obtuse;
E, acute;
F, scalene

tri′angle inequal′ity, *Math.* **1.** the theorem that the absolute value of the sum of two quantities is less than or equal to the sum of the absolute values of the quantities. **2.** the related theorem that the magnitude of the sum of two vectors is less than or equal to the sum of the magnitudes of the vectors. **3.** (for metric spaces) the related theorem that the distance between two points does not exceed the sum of their distances from any third point. [1960–65]

tri•an•gu•lar (trī ang′gyə lər), *adj.* **1.** pertaining to or having the form of a triangle; three-cornered. **2.** having a triangle as base or cross section: *a triangular prism.* **3.** comprising three parts or elements; triple. **4.** pertaining to or involving a group of three, as three persons, parties, or things. [1535–45; < L *triangulāris,* equiv. to *triangul(um)* TRIANGLE + *-āris* -AR[1]] —**tri•an•gu•lar•i•ty** (trī ang′gyə lar′i tē), *n.* —**tri•an′gu•lar•ly,** *adv.*

trian′gular ma′trix, *Math.* a square matrix in which either all the entries above the principal diagonal, or all the entries below the principal diagonal, are zero.

trian′gular trade′, *Amer. Hist.* a pattern of colonial commerce in which slaves were bought on the African Gold Coast with New England rum and then traded in the West Indies for sugar or molasses, which was brought back to New England to be manufactured into rum.

tri•an•gu•late (*adj.* trī ang′gyə lit, -lāt′; *v.* trī ang′gyə lāt′), *adj., v.,* **-lat•ed, -lat•ing.** —*adj.* **1.** composed of or marked with triangles. —*v.t.* **2.** to make triangular. **3.** to divide into triangles. **4.** to survey (an area) by triangulation. [1600–10; < ML *triangulātus,* ptp. of *triangulāre* to make triangles. See TRIANGLE, -ATE[1]] —**tri•an′gu•la′tor,** *n.*

tri•an•gu•la•tion (trī ang′gyə lā′shən), *n. Survey., Navig.* **1.** a technique for establishing the distance between any two points, or the relative position of two or more points, by using such points as vertices of a triangle or series of triangles, such that each triangle has a side of known or measurable length (**base** or **base line**) that permits the size of the angles of the triangle and the length of its other two sides to be established by observations taken either upon or from the two ends of the base line. **2.** the triangles thus formed and measured. [1810–20; < ML *triangulātiōn-* (s. of *triangulātiō*) the making of triangles. See TRIANGULATE, -ION]

triangulation (def. 1)
A, B, points known;
C, point visible from both A and B, the position of which is plotted by measuring angles A and B

C
A
B

Tri•an•gu•lum (trī ang′gyə ləm), *n., gen.* **-li** (-lī′). *Astron.* the Triangle, a northern constellation between Pisces and Perseus. [1545–55; < NL]

Tri•an•gu•lum Aus•tra•le (trī ang′gyə ləm ô strā′lē), *gen.* **Tri•an•gu•li Aus•tra•lis** (trī ang′gyə lī′ ô strā′lis). *Astron.* the Southern Triangle, a southern constellation between Pavo and Circinus. [< NL]

tri•an•nu•al (trī an′yo͞o əl), *adj.* **1.** done, occurring, issued, etc., three times a year. **2.** triennial. —*n.* **3.** a triannual publication, contest, etc. **4.** triennial. [1630–40; TRI- + ANNUAL] —**tri•an′nu•al•ly,** *adv.*

Tri•an•ta (*Gk.* trē än′dä), *n.* Trianda.

tri•ap•si•dal (trī ap′si dl), *adj. Archit.* having three apses. [1870–75; TRI- + APSIDAL]

tri•ar•chy (trī′är kē), *n., pl.* **-chies. 1.** government by three persons. **2.** a set of three joint rulers; a triumvirate. **3.** a country divided into three governments. **4.** a group of three countries or districts, each under its own ruler. [1595–1605; < Gk *triarchía* triumvirate. See TRI-, -ARCHY]

tri•ar•yl (trī ar′il), *adj. Chem.* containing three aryl groups. [TRI- + ARYL]

tri•ar•yl•meth′ane dye′ (trī ar′il meth′ān), *Chem.* any of the class of dyes containing three aryl groups attached to a central carbon atom: used chiefly for dyeing cotton, wool, and silk. [TRIARYL + METHANE]

Tri•as•sic (trī as′ik), *Geol.* —*adj.* **1.** noting or pertaining to a period of the Mesozoic Era, occurring from 230 to 190 million years ago and characterized by the advent of dinosaurs and coniferous forests. See table under **geologic time.** —*n.* **2.** Also, **Tri•as** (trī′əs) the Triassic Period or System. [1835–45; *Trias* the three-part series of strata characterizing the period (< G < Gk *triás;* see TRIAD) + -IC]

tri•ath•lete (trī ath′lēt), *n.* a competitor in a triathlon. [1980–85; b. TRIATHLON and ATHLETE]

tri•ath•lon (trī ath′lən), *n.* **1.** an athletic contest comprising three consecutive events, usually swimming, bicycling, and distance running. **2.** a women's track-and-field competition comprising the 100-meter dash, high jump, and shot put. **3.** *Brit.* a competition comprising fly-casting, horseback-riding, and trapshooting events. [1970–75; TRI- + (DEC)ATHLON]

tri•at′ic stay′ (trī at′ik), *Naut.* a backstay for the head of a fore-and-aft-rigged topmast, running down to the head of the lower mast next aft. [1835–45; perh. TRI- + -ATE[1] + -IC]

tri•a•tom•ic (trī′ə tom′ik), *adj. Chem.* **1.** having three atoms in a molecule. **2.** having three replaceable hydrogen atoms. **3.** having three replaceable hydroxyl groups. [1860–65; TRI- + ATOMIC] —**tri′a•tom′i•cal•ly,** *adv.*

tri•ax•i•al (trī ak′sē əl), *adj.* having three axes. [1885–90; TRI- + AXIAL] —**tri•ax′i•al′i•ty,** *n.*

tri•a•zine (trī′ə zēn′, -zin, trī az′ēn, -in), *n. Chem.* **1.** any of a group of three compounds containing three nitrogen and three carbon atoms arranged in a six-membered ring and having the formula $C_3H_3N_3$. **2.** any of a number of their derivatives. [1890–95; TRI- + AZINE]

tri•a•zo•ic (trī′ə zō′ik), *adj. Chem.* hydrazoic. [TRI- + AZOIC[2]]

tri•a•zole (trī′ə zōl′, trī az′ōl), *n. Chem.* **1.** any of a group of four compounds containing three nitrogen and two carbon atoms arranged in a five-membered ring and having the formula $C_2H_3N_3$. **2.** any of a number of their derivatives. [1885–90; TRI- + AZOLE] —**tri•a•zol•ic** (trī′ə zol′ik), *adj.*

trib., tributary.

trib•ade (trib′əd), *n.* lesbian. [1595–1605; < F < L *tribad-* (s. of *tribas*) < Gk *tribás,* equiv. to *trib-,* var. s. of *trī́b(ein)* to rub + *-as* (s. *-ad-*) -ADE[2]] —**tri•bad•ic** (tri bad′ik), *adj.*

trib•a•dism (trib′ə diz′əm), *n.* lesbianism. [1810–20; TRIBADE + -ISM]

trib•al (trī′bəl), *adj.* of, pertaining to, or characteristic of a tribe: *tribal customs.* [1625–35; TRIBE + -AL[1]] —**trib′al•ly,** *adv.*

trib•al•ism (trī′bə liz′əm), *n.* **1.** the customs and beliefs of tribal life and society. **2.** strong loyalty to one's own tribe, party, or group. [1885–90; TRIBAL + -ISM] —**trib′al•ist,** *n.* —**tri′bal•is′tic,** *adj.*

tri•ba•sic (trī bā′sik), *adj. Chem.* **1.** (of an acid) having three atoms of hydrogen replaceable by basic atoms or groups. **2.** containing three atoms or groups, each having a valence of one, as tribasic sodium phosphate, Na_3PO_4. [1830–40; TRI- + BASIC] —**tri•ba•sic•i•ty** (trī′bā sis′i tē), *n.*

triba′sic so′dium phos′phate. See **sodium phosphate** (def. 3).

tribe (trīb), *n.* **1.** any aggregate of people united by ties of descent from a common ancestor, community of customs and traditions, adherence to the same leaders, etc. **2.** a local division of an aboriginal people. **3.** a division of some other people. **4.** a class or type of animals, plants, articles, or the like. **5.** *Animal Husb.* a group of animals, esp. cattle, descended through the female line from a common female ancestor. **6.** *Biol.* **a.** a category in the classification of organisms usually between a subfamily and a genus or sometimes between a suborder and a family. **b.** any group of plants or animals. **7.** a company, group, or number of persons. **8.** a class or set of persons, esp. one with strong common traits or interests. **9.** a large family. **10.** *Rom. Hist.* **a.** any one of three divisions of the people representing the Latin, Sabine, and Etruscan settlements. **b.** any of the later political divisions of the people. **11.** *Gk. Hist.* a phyle. [1200–50; ME < L *tribus* tribe, orig., each of the three divisions of the Roman people; often taken as deriv. of *trēs* THREE, though formation unclear]

tribe•let (trīb′lit), *n.* a tribe having few members, esp. one that is a component of a larger tribal organization. [1850–55; TRIBE + -LET]

tribes•man (trībz′mən), *n., pl.* **-men.** a member of a tribe. [1790–1800; TRIBE + 's[1] + -MAN]

tribes•peo•ple (trībz′pē′pəl), *n.pl.* the members of a tribe. [1885–90; TRIBE + 's[1] + PEOPLE]

tribo-, a combining form meaning "friction," used in the formation of compound words: *triboelectricity.* [comb. form repr. Gk *trī́bein* to rub; see -o-]

tri•bo•e•lec•tric•i•ty (trī′bō i lek tris′i tē, -ē′lek-, trib′ō-), *n. Elect.* electricity generated by friction. [1915–20; TRIBO- + ELECTRICITY] —**tri•bo•e•lec•tric** (trī′bō i lek′trik, trib′ō-), *adj.*

tri•bol•o•gy (trī bol′ə jē, tri-), *n.* the study of the effects of friction on moving machine parts and of methods, as lubrication, of obviating them. [1965–70; TRIBO- + -LOGY] —**tri•bol′o•gist,** *n.*

tri•bo•lu•mi•nes•cence (trī′bō lo͞o′mə nes′əns, trib′ō-), *n. Physics.* luminescence produced by friction, usually within a crystalline substance. [1885–90; TRIBO- + LUMINESCENCE] —**tri′bo•lu′mi•nes′cent,** *adj.*

tri•brach (trī′brak, trib′rak), *n. Pros.* a foot of three short syllables. [< L *tribrachys* < Gk *tríbrachys,* equiv. to *tri-* TRI- + *brachýs* short; see BRACHY-] —**tri•brach′•ic,** *adj.* —**tri•brach′i•al,** *adj.*

tri•bro•mide (trī brō′mīd), *n. Chem.* a bromide containing three atoms of bromine. [TRI- + BROMIDE]

tri•bro•mo•ac•et•al•de•hyde (trī brō′mō as′i tal′də hīd′), *n. Pharm.* bromal. [TRI- + BROMO- + ACETALDEHYDE]

CONCISE ETYMOLOGY KEY: <, descended or borrowed from; >, whence; b., blend of, blended; c., cognate with; cf., compare; deriv., derivative; equiv., equivalent; imit., imitative; obl., oblique; r., replacing; s., stem; sp., spelling, spelled; resp., respelling, respelled; trans., translation; ?, origin unknown; *, unattested; ‡, probably earlier than. See the full key inside the front cover.

tri·bro·mo·eth·a·nol (trī brō′mō eth′ə nôl′, -nol′), *n. Pharm.* a white, crystalline powder, $C_2H_3Br_3O$, used as a basal anesthetic. [TRI- + BROMO- + ETHANOL]

trib·u·la·tion (trib′yə lā′shən), *n.* **1.** grievous trouble; severe trial or suffering. **2.** an instance of this; an affliction, trouble, etc. [1175–1225; ME < L *tribulātiōn-* (s. of *tribulātiō*) distress, trouble, equiv. to *tribulāt(us)* (ptp. of *tribulāre* to press, squeeze, deriv. of *tribulum* threshing sledge, equiv. to *tri-*, var. s. of *terere* to rub, crush + *-bulum* n. suffix of instrument) + *-iōn-* -ION]
—Syn. 1. affliction, hardship, distress, adversity.

tri·bu·nal (trī byōōn′l, tri-), *n.* **1.** a court of justice. **2.** a place or seat of judgment. **3.** Also called **tribune.** a raised platform for the seats of magistrates, as in an ancient Roman basilica. [1520–30; < L *tribūnal, tribūnāle* judgment seat, equiv. to *tribūn(us)* TRIBUNE[1] + *-āl(e)* -AL[2]]

trib·u·nate (trib′yə nit, -nāt′, tri byōō′nit, -nāt), *n.* **1.** the office of tribune. **2.** a body of tribunes. [1540–50; < L *tribūnātus* the office of a tribune. See TRIBUNE[1], -ATE[3]]

trib·une[1] (trib′yōōn, tri byōōn′), *n.* **1.** a person who upholds or defends the rights of the people. **2.** *Rom. Hist.* **a.** any of various administrative officers, esp. one of 10 officers elected to protect the interests and rights of the plebeians from the patricians. **b.** any of the six officers of a legion who rotated in commanding the legion during the year. [1325–75; ME < L *tribūnus,* deriv. of *tribus* TRIBE] **—trib′une·ship′,** *n.* **—trib·u·ni·tial, trib·u·ni·cial** (trib′yə nish′əl), *adj.*

trib·une[2] (trib′yōōn, tri byōōn′), *n.* **1.** a raised platform for a speaker; a dais, rostrum, or pulpit. **2.** a raised part, or gallery, with seats, as in a church. **3.** (in a Christian basilica) the bishop's throne, occupying a recess or apse. **4.** the apse itself. **5.** tribunal (def. 3). [1635–45; < ML *tribūna;* r. L *tribūnāle* TRIBUNAL]

trib·u·tar·y (trib′yə ter′ē), *n., pl.* **-tar·ies,** *adj.* **—***n.* **1.** a stream that flows to a larger stream or other body of water. **2.** a person or nation that pays tribute in acknowledgment of subjugation or the like. **—***adj.* **3.** (of a stream) flowing into a larger stream or other body of water. **4.** furnishing subsidiary aid; contributory. **5.** paying or required to pay tribute. **6.** paid as tribute. **7.** subject; subordinate: *a tributary nation.* [1325–75; ME (adj. and n.) < L *tribūtārius* of tribute, one who pays tribute. See TRIBUTE, -ARY] **—trib′u·tar′i·ly,** *adv.*

trib·ute (trib′yōōt), *n.* **1.** a gift, testimonial, compliment, or the like, given as due or in acknowledgment of gratitude or esteem. **2.** a stated sum or other valuable consideration paid by one sovereign or state to another in acknowledgment of subjugation or as the price of peace, security, protection, or the like. **3.** a rent, tax, or the like, as that paid by a subject to a sovereign. **4.** any exacted or enforced payment or contribution. **5.** obligation or liability to make such payment. [1300–50; ME *tribut* < L *tribūtum* a levied payment, n. use of neut. of ptp. of *tribuere* to assign, allot, deriv. of *tribus* TRIBE]
—Syn. 1. recognition, commendation, eulogy. **4.** levy, toll, impost, duty.

tri·cal′ci·um sil′icate (trī kal′sē əm), *Chem.* a component of cement, Ca_3SiO_5, also used in food to prevent caking. [TRI- + CALCIUM]

tri·car·box·yl·ic (trī kär′bok sil′ik), *adj. Chem.* pertaining to a molecule that contains three carboxyl groups. [1915–20; TRI- + CARBOXYLIC]

tri′carboxyl′ic ac′id cy′cle, *Biochem.* See **Krebs cycle.** [1940–45]

tri·car·pel·lar·y (trī kär′pə ler′ē), *adj. Bot.* having three carpels. [1870–75; TRI- + CARPELLARY]

trice[1] (trīs), *n.* a very short time; an instant: *in a trice.* [1400–50; late ME *tryse;* prob. special use of *trise a pull, tug, deriv. of *trisen,* to pull; see TRICE[2]]

trice[2] (trīs), *v.t.,* **triced, tric·ing.** *Naut.* **1.** to pull or haul with a rope. **2.** to haul up and fasten with a rope (usually fol. by *up*). [1350–1400; ME *trisen* < MD *trisen* to hoist, deriv. of *trīse* pulley]

-trice, var. of **-trix.** [< F or It *-trice* < L *-trīcem,* acc. of *-trīx* -TRIX]

tri·cen·ten·ni·al (trī′sen ten′ē əl), *adj.* **1.** pertaining to 300 years or a period of 300 years. **2.** marking the completion of such a period: *a tricentennial celebration.* **—***n.* **3.** a 300th anniversary or its celebration. Also, **tercentenary, tercentennial.** [1880–85; TRI- + CENTENNIAL]

tri·ceps (trī′seps), *n., pl.* **-ceps·es** (-sep siz), **-ceps.** *Anat.* a muscle having three heads or points of origin, esp. the muscle on the back of the arm, the action of which straightens the elbow. [1570–80; < L: three-headed, equiv. to *tri-* TRI- + *-ceps,* s. *-cipit-* -headed, deriv. of *caput* head]

triceratops, *Triceratops elatus,* 8 ft. (2.4 m) high at shoulder; length 20 ft. (6 m); horns 3¼ ft. (1 m); skull 8 ft. (2.4 m)

tri·cer·a·tops (trī ser′ə tops′), *n.* any of various dinosaurs of the genus *Triceratops,* of the late Cretaceous Period, having a bony crest on the neck, a long horn over each eye, and a shorter horn on the nose. [1890–95; < NL < Gk *trikérat(os)* three-horned (see TRI-, CERAT-), + *ōps* face, EYE]

trich-, var. of **tricho-** before a vowel: *trichuriasis.*

-trich, a combining form meaning "one having hair" of the kind or number specified by the initial element; often used to name a single member of a taxonomic group ending in **-tricha:** *heterotrich; hypotrich.* [< Gk *-trichos* haired, adj. deriv. of *thríx* (s. *trich-*) hair]

-tricha, a combining form meaning "ones having hair" of the kind or number specified by the initial element, used in taxonomic names, esp. in taxa of ciliated protozoans: *Chonotricha; Spirotricha.* [< NL < Gk, neut. pl. of *-trichos* (see -TRICH)]

tri·chi·a·sis (tri kī′ə sis), *n. Pathol.* a condition in which the eyelashes grow inwardly. [1655–65; < LL < Gk *trichíāsis.* See TRICH-, -IASIS]

tri·chi·na (tri kī′nə), *n., pl.* **-nae** (-nē). a nematode, *Trichinella spiralis,* the adults of which live in the intestine and produce larvae that encyst in the muscle tissue, esp. in pigs, rats, and humans. [1825–35; < NL < Gk *trichína,* n. use of fem. of *tríchinos* of hair. See TRICH-, -INE[1]]

trich·i·nize (trik′ə nīz′), *v.t.,* **-nized, -niz·ing.** *Pathol.* to infect with trichinae. Also, *esp. Brit.,* **trich′i·nise′.** [1860–65; TRICHIN(A) + -IZE] **—trich′i·ni·za′tion,** *n.*

Trich·i·nop·o·ly (trik′ə nop′ə lē), *n.* former name of **Tiruchirapalli.**

trich·i·no·sis (trik′ə nō′sis), *n. Pathol.* a disease resulting from infestation with *Trichinella spiralis,* occurring in humans, caused by ingestion of infested, undercooked pork, and characterized by fever, muscle weakness, and diarrhea. Also, **trich·i·ni·a·sis** (trik′ə nī′ə sis). [1865–70; TRICHIN(A) + -OSIS]

trich·i·nous (trik′ə nəs), *adj. Pathol.* **1.** pertaining to or of the nature of trichinosis. **2.** infected with trichinae. [1855–60; TRICHIN(A) + -OUS]

trich·i·on (trik′ē on′), *n., pl.* **trich·i·a** (trik′ē ə), **trich·i·ons.** *Physical Anthropol.* the point of intersection of the normal hairline and the middle line of the forehead. [< Gk *trichíon,* dim. of *thríx* hair (see TRICHO-)]

trich·ite (trik′īt), *n. Petrog.* any of various minute, hairlike mineral bodies occurring in certain vitreous igneous rocks, esp. obsidian. [1865–70; < Gk *trich-,* s. of *thríx* hair + -ITE[1]] **—tri·chit·ic** (tri kit′ik), *adj.*

tri·chlor·fon (trī klôr′fon, -klōr′-), *n. Chem., Pharm.* metrifonate. [1955–60; *trichlor(o)-* (see TRI-, CHLORO-) + *(phos)phon(ic acid)* (see PHOSPH-, -ONIC), components of the chemical name, resp. as *-fon*]

tri·chlo·ride (trī klôr′īd, -id, -klōr′-), *n. Chem.* a chloride having three atoms of chlorine, as ferric chloride, $FeCl_3$. [1860–65; TRI- + CHLORIDE]

tri·chlo·ro·ac·e·tal·de·hyde (trī klôr′ō as′i tal′də hīd′, -klōr′-), *n. Chem.* chloral (def. 1). Also called **tri·chlo′roace′tic ac′id al′dehyde.** [TRI- + CHLORO-[2] + ACETALDEHYDE]

tri·chlo′ro·a·ce′tic ac′id (trī klôr′ō ə sē′tik, -set′ik, -klōr′-, -klôr′-, -klōr′-), *Chem.* a toxic, deliquescent, and colorless crystalline compound, $C_2HCl_3O_2$, soluble in water, alcohol, and ether: used in the synthesis of pharmaceuticals, herbicides, and other chemicals, and as a reagent for the detection of albumin. *Abbr.:* TCA [1880–85; TRI- + CHLORO-[2] + ACETIC ACID]

tri·chlo·ro·eth·yl·ene (trī klôr′ō eth′ə lēn′, -klōr′-), *n. Chem.* a colorless, poisonous liquid, C_2HCl_3, used chiefly as a degreasing agent for metals and as a solvent, esp. in dry cleaning, for fats, oils, and waxes. *Abbr.:* TCE [1915–20; TRI- + CHLORO-[2] + ETHYLENE]

tri·chlo·ro·fluor·o·meth·ane (trī klôr′ō flŏŏr′ō meth′ān, -flôr′-; trī klôr′ō flŏŏr′ō meth′ān, -flōr′-), *n. Chem.* chlorotrifluoromethane. [TRI- + CHLORO- + FLUORO- + METHANE]

tri·chlo·ro·meth·ane (trī klôr′ō meth′ān, -klōr′-), *n. Chem.* chloroform (def. 1). [1910–15; TRI- + CHLORO-[2] + METHANE]

tri·chlo·ro·meth·yl chlo·ro·form·ate (trī klôr′ō meth′əl klôr′ə fôr′mit, -māt; trī klôr′ō meth′əl klōr′ə fôr′mit, -māt), *Chem.* diphosgene. [TRI- + CHLORO-[2] + METHYL]

tri·chlo·ro·ni·tro·meth·ane (trī klôr′ō nī′trō meth′ān, -klōr′-), *n. Chem.* chloropicrin. [TRI- + CHLORO-[2] + NITROMETHANE]

tri·chlo′ro·phe·nox·y·a·ce′tic ac′id (trī klôr′ō fə nok′sē ə sē′tik, -set′ik, -klôr′-, -klōr′-, -klōr′-), *Chem.* a light-tan, water-insoluble solid, $C_8H_5Cl_3O_3$, used chiefly for killing weeds. Also called **2,4,5-T.** [TRI- + CHLORO-[2] + PHEN- + OXY-[2] + ACETIC ACID]

tricho-, a combining form meaning "hair," used in the formation of compound words: *trichocyst.* Also, *esp. before a vowel,* **trich-.** [< Gk *tricho-,* comb. form of *thríx* (gen. *trichós*)]

trich·o·cyst (trik′ə sist′), *n. Zool.* an organ of offense and defense embedded in the outer cytoplasm of certain protozoans, consisting of a small elongated sac containing a fine, hairlike filament capable of being ejected. [1850–55; TRICHO- + CYST] **—trich′o·cyst′ic,** *adj.*

trich·o·gram·ma (trik′ə gram′ə), *n.* any minute wasp of the genus *Trichogramma,* comprising a beneficial group of chalcidflies that parasitize the eggs of a variety of insect pests. [< NL; see TRICHO-, -GRAM[1]]

trich·o·gyne (trik′ə jīn′, -jin), *n. Bot., Mycol.* a hairlike prolongation of a carpogonium, serving as a receptive organ for the spermatium. [1870–75; TRICHO- + -GYNE] **—trich·o·gyn·i·al** (trik′ə jin′ē əl), **trich′o·gyn′ic,** *adj.*

trich·oid (trik′oid), *adj.* resembling hair; hairlike. [1850–55; TRICH- + -OID]

tri·chol·o·gy (tri kol′ə jē), *n.* the science dealing with the study of the hair and its diseases. [1855–60; TRICHO- + -LOGY] **—tri·chol′o·gist,** *n.*

trich·ome (trik′ōm, trī′kōm), *n.* **1.** *Bot.* an outgrowth from the epidermis of plants, as a hair. **2.** a microorganism composed of many filamentous cells arranged in strands or chains. [1870–75; < Gk *tríchōma* growth of hair. See TRICH-, -OMA] **—tri·chom·ic** (tri kom′ik, -kō′mik), *adj.*

trich·o·mon·ad (trik′ə mon′ad, -mō′nad), *n.* any flagellate protozoan of the genus *Trichomonas,* parasitic in humans or animals. [1860–65; < NL *Trichomonad-* (s. of *Trichomonas*) genus name. See TRICHO-, MONAD] **—trich·o·mon·a·dal** (trik′ə mon′ə dl, -mō′nə-), **trich·o·mon·al** (trik′ə mon′l, -mōn′l, tri kom′ə nl), *adj.*

trich·o·mo·ni·a·sis (trik′ə mə nī′ə sis), *n. Pathol.* **1.** a sexually transmitted disease typically asymptomatic in men and resulting in vaginitis with a copious, frothy discharge and itching in women, caused by a trichomonad *Trichomonas vaginalis.* **2.** any of various other diseases caused by a trichomonad. [1915–20; TRICHOMON(AD) + -IASIS]

trich·o·not·id (trik′ə not′id), *n.* **1.** any fish of the family Trichonotidae, comprising the sand divers. **—***adj.* **2.** belonging or pertaining to the family Trichonotidae. [< NL *Trichonotidae* name of the family, equiv. to *Trichonot(us)* a species (< Gk *tricho-* TRICHO- + *-nōtos* -backed, deriv. of *nôton* back, spine) + *-idae* -ID[2]]

trich·o·nymph (trik′ə nimf′), *n.* a flagellated protozoan of the genus *Trichonympha* that lives in the intestine of wood-eating termites, transforming the cellulose in the wood into soluble carbohydrates that can be utilized by the insect. [< NL; see TRICHO-, NYMPH]

tri·chop·ter·an (tri kop′tər ən), *adj.* **1.** trichopterous. **—***n.* **2.** Also, **trichopteron.** a trichopterous insect; caddisfly. [1835–45; < NL *Trichopter(a)* (see TRICHOPTEROUS) + -AN]

tri·chop·ter·on (tri kop′tə ron′), *n., pl.* **-ter·a** (-tər ə). trichopteran.

tri·chop·ter·ous (tri kop′tər əs), *adj.* belonging or pertaining to the insect order Trichoptera, comprising the caddisflies. [1810–20; < NL *Trichopter(a)* (< Gk *tricho-* TRICHO- + *-ptera,* neut. pl. of *-pteros* -winged; see -PTEROUS) + -OUS]

tri·cho·sis (tri kō′sis), *n. Pathol.* any disease of the hair. [1685–95; TRICH- + -OSIS]

tri·cho·the·cene (trī′kə thē′sin), *n.* any of a group of toxins derived from various imperfect fungi, as of the genera *Fusarium* and *Trichothecium.* [1970–75; < NL *Trichothec(ium)* genus name (see TRICHO-, THECIUM) + -ENE]

trich·o·til·lo·ma·ni·a (trik′ə til′ə mā′nē ə), *n. Psychiatry.* a compulsion to pull out one's hair. [1900–05; TRICHO- + Gk *tíll(ein)* to pluck, pull out + *-o-* + -MANIA]

tri·chot·o·my (tri kot′ə mē), *n., pl.* **-mies.** **1.** division into three parts, classes, categories, etc. **2.** an instance of such a division, as in thought, structure, or object. **3.** the three-part division of human beings into body, spirit, and soul. [1600–10; < NL *trichotomia* < Gk *trích(a)* in three parts + NL *-tomia* -TOMY] **—trich·o·tom·ic** (trik′ə tom′ik), **tri·chot′o·mous,** *adj.* **—tri·chot′o·mous·ly,** *adv.*

trichot′omy prop′erty, *Math.* the property that for natural numbers *a* and *b,* either *a* is less than *b, a* equals *b,* or *a* is greater than *b.* Also called **law of trichotomy, trichot′omy law′, trichot′omy prin′ciple.**

tri·chro·ic (trī krō′ik), *adj. Crystall.* manifesting trichroism. [1880–85; TRI- + -CHROIC]

tri·chro·ism (trī′krō iz′əm), *n. Crystall.* pleochroism of a biaxial crystal such that it exhibits three different colors when viewed from three different directions under transmitted light. [1840–50; TRICHRO(IC) + -ISM]

tri·chro·mat·ic (trī′krō mat′ik, -krə-), *adj.* **1.** pertaining to the use or combination of three colors, as in printing or in color photography. **2.** pertaining to, characterized by, or involving three colors. **3.** *Ophthalm.* of, pertaining to, or exhibiting normal color vision. Also, **tri·chro·mic** (trī krō′mik). [1890–95; TRI- + CHROMATIC]

tri·chro·ma·tism (trī krō′mə tiz′əm), *n.* **1.** the quality or condition of being trichromatic. **2.** the use or combination of three colors, as in printing or photography. **3.** *Ophthalm.* normal color vision. Cf. **monochromatism** (def. 2), **dichromatism** (def. 2). [1885–90; TRICHROMAT(IC) + -ISM]

trich·u·ri·a·sis (trik′ə rī′ə sis), *n. Pathol.* intestinal infestation with the roundworm *Trichuris trichiura,* producing nausea, abdominal discomfort, and diarrhea, common in tropical areas with poor sanitation. [1920–25; < NL *Trichur(is)* genus name (*trich-* TRICH- + Gk *our(á)* tail + *-is* adj. ending) + -IASIS]

tri·cit·y (trī′sit′ē, -sit′ē), *adj.* **1.** of or pertaining to a metropolitan area consisting of three separate but interdependent cities: *an instance of tri-city cooperation.* **—***n.* **2.** any one of three such cities.

trick (trik), *n.* **1.** a crafty or underhanded device, maneuver, stratagem, or the like, intended to deceive or cheat; artifice; ruse; wile. **2.** an optical illusion: *It must have been some visual trick caused by the flickering candlelight.* **3.** a roguish or mischievous act; practical joke; prank: *She likes to play tricks on her friends.* **4.** a mean, foolish, or childish action. **5.** a clever or ingenious device or expedient; adroit technique: *the tricks of the trade.* **6.** the art or knack of doing something skillfully: *You seem to have mastered the trick of making others laugh.* **7.** a clever or dexterous feat intended to entertain, amuse, etc.: *He taught his dog some amazing tricks.* **8.** a feat of magic or legerdemain: *card tricks.* **9.** a behavioral peculiarity; trait; habit; mannerism. **10.** a period of duty or turn; stint; tour of duty: *I relieved the pilot after he had completed his trick at the wheel.* **11.** *Cards.* **a.** the group or set of cards played and won in one round. **b.** a point or scoring unit. **c.** a card that is a potential winner. Cf. **honor trick.** **12.** *Informal.* a child or young girl: *a pretty little trick.* **13.** *Slang.* **a.** a prostitute's customer. **b.** a sexual act between a prostitute and a customer. **14.** *Heraldry.* **a.** a preliminary sketch of a coat of arms. **b.** See **engraver's trick.** **15. do** or **turn the trick,** to achieve the desired effect or result: *Another turn of the pliers should do the trick.* **16. turn**

a trick, *Slang.* (of a prostitute) to engage in a sexual act with a customer. —*adj.* **17.** of, pertaining to, characterized by, or involving tricks: *trick shooting.* **18.** designed or used for tricks: *a trick chair.* **19.** (of a joint) inclined to stiffen or weaken suddenly and unexpectedly: *a trick shoulder.* —*v.t.* **20.** to deceive by trickery. **21.** *Heraldry.* to indicate the tinctures of (a coat of arms) with engraver's tricks. **22.** to cheat or swindle (usually fol. by *out of*): *to trick someone out of an inheritance.* **23.** to beguile by trickery (usually fol. by *into*). —*v.i.* **24.** to practice trickery or deception; cheat. **25.** to play tricks; trifle (usually fol. by *with*). **26.** *Slang.* to engage in sexual acts for hire. **27. trick out,** *Informal.* to embellish or adorn with or as if with ornaments or other attention-getting devices. [1375–1425; late ME *trik* (n.) < ONF *trique* deceit, deriv. of *trikier* to deceive < VL **triccāre,* for L *trīcārī* to play tricks] —**trick′er,** *n.* —**trick′ing·ly,** *adv.*

—**Syn. 1.** deception. TRICK, ARTIFICE, RUSE, STRATAGEM, WILE are terms for crafty or cunning devices that are intended to deceive. TRICK, the general term, refers usually to an underhanded act designed to cheat someone, but it sometimes refers merely to a pleasurable deceiving of the senses: *to win by a trick.* Like TRICK, but to a greater degree, ARTIFICE emphasizes the cleverness, ingenuity, or cunning with which the proceeding is devised: *an artifice of diabolical ingenuity.* RUSE and STRATAGEM emphasize the purpose for which the trick is designed; RUSE is the more general term of the two, and STRATAGEM sometimes implies a more elaborate procedure or a military application: *He gained entrance by a ruse. His stratagem gave them command of the hill.* WILE emphasizes the disarming effect of the trick upon those who are deceived: *His wiles charmed them into trusting him.* **20.** See **cheat.**

trick′ end′ing, an ending of a story or play, etc., that employs a surprise element or character to resolve the plot.

trick·er·y (trik′ə rē), *n., pl.* **-er·ies. 1.** the use or practice of tricks or stratagems to deceive; artifice; deception. **2.** a trick used to deceive. [1790–1800; TRICK + -ERY]

—**Syn. 1.** See **deceit.**

trick·ish (trik′ish), *adj.* tricky. [1695–1705; TRICK + -ISH[1]] —**trick′ish·ly,** *adv.* —**trick′ish·ness,** *n.*

trick′ knee′, a condition of the knee in which the joint suddenly stiffens or abandons its support.

trick·le (trik′əl), *v.,* **-led, -ling,** *n.* —*v.i.* **1.** to flow or fall by drops, or in a small, gentle stream: *Tears trickled down her cheeks.* **2.** to come, go, or pass bit by bit, slowly, or irregularly: *The guests trickled out of the room.* —*v.t.* **3.** to cause to trickle. —*n.* **4.** a trickling flow or stream. **5.** a small, slow, or irregular quantity of anything coming, going, or proceeding: *a trickle of visitors throughout the day.* [1325–75; ME *triklen, trekelen* (v.), appar. sandhi var. of *strikle,* perh. equiv. to STRIKE (in obs. sense "flow") + -LE] —**trick′ling·ly,** *adv.*

—**Syn. 4.** dribble, seepage, drip.

trick′le charge′, *Elect.* a continuous, slow charge supplied to a storage battery to keep it in a fully charged state. [1955–60]

trick·le-down (trik′əl doun′), *adj.* of, pertaining to, or based on the trickle-down theory: *the trickle-down benefits to the local community.* [1950–55; adj. use of v. phrase *trickle down*]

trick′le-down the′ory, an economic theory that monetary benefits directed esp. by the government to big business will in turn pass down to and profit smaller businesses and the general public. [1950–55]

trick′le irriga′tion. See **drip irrigation.** [1970–75]

trick′ or treat′, a children's Halloween custom, in which they call on neighbors, using this phrase, and threaten to play a trick if a treat is not given. [1940–45]

trick-or-treat (trik′ər trēt′), *v.i.* to become involved or take part in trick or treat. [1940–45] —**trick′-or-treat′er,** *n.*

trick·some (trik′səm), *adj.* **1.** tricksy (def. 1). **2.** tricky (def. 1). [1640–50; TRICK + -SOME[1]]

trick·ster (trik′stər), *n.* **1.** a deceiver; cheat; fraud. **2.** a person who plays tricks. **3.** a supernatural figure appearing in various guises and typically engaging in mischievous activities, important in the folklore and mythology of many primitive peoples and usually conceived as a culture hero. [1705–15; TRICK + -STER] —**trick′ster·ing,** *n.*

trick·sy (trik′sē), *adj.,* **-si·er, -si·est. 1.** Also, **tricksome.** given to tricks; mischievous; playful; prankish. **2.** difficult to handle or deal with. **3.** *Archaic.* tricky; crafty; wily. **4.** *Archaic.* fashionably trim; spruce; smart. [1545–55; TRICK + -S[3] + -Y[1]; cf. -SY] —**trick′si·ly,** *adv.* —**trick′si·ness,** *n.*

trick-track (trik′trak′), *n.* a variety of backgammon. Also, **trictrac.** [1645–55; < F *trictrac;* so called in imitation of the clicking sound made in moving the pieces]

trick·y (trik′ē), *adj.,* **trick·i·er, trick·i·est. 1.** given to or characterized by deceitful tricks; crafty; wily. **2.** skilled in clever tricks or dodges. **3.** deceptive, uncertain, or difficult to deal with or handle. [1780–90; TRICK + -Y[1]] —**trick′i·ly,** *adv.* —**trick′i·ness,** *n.*

—**Syn. 1.** artful, sly, shrewd. **2.** skillful, adroit. **3.** doubtful, unpredictable, unreliable, perilous.

tri·clad (trī′klad), *n.* a planarian. [1885–90; < NL *Tricladida* name of the order of flatworms including planarians. See TRI-, CLAD-, -IDA]

tri·clin·ic (trī klin′ik), *adj. Crystall.* noting or pertaining to a system of crystallization in which the three axes are unequal and intersect at oblique angles. Cf. **crystal system.** [1850–55; TRI- + Gk *klīn(ein)* to LEAN[1], slope + -IC]

tri·clin·i·um (trī klin′ē əm), *n., pl.* **-clin·i·a** (-klin′ē ə). *Rom. Hist.* **1.** a couch extending along three sides of a table, for reclining on at meals. **2.** a dining room, esp. one containing such a couch. [1640–50; < L *trīclīnium* < Gk *triklīnion,* dim. of *tríklīnos* having three couches (adj.), dining room so furnished (n.), equiv. to *tri-* TRI- + *klīn(ē)* couch (see CLINIC) + *-ion* dim. suffix]

tric·o·lette (trik′ə let′), *n.* a knitted fabric made of silk or synthetic yarn, used in the manufacture of wearing apparel. [1915–20; TRICO(T) + (FLANNE)LETTE]

tri·col·or (trī′kul′ər; *esp. Brit.* trik′ə lər), *adj.* **1.** Also, **tri′col′ored;** *esp. Brit.,* **tri′col′oured.** having three colors. —*n.* **2.** a flag having three colors. **3.** the national flag of France, adopted during the French Revolution, consisting of vertical bands of blue, white, and red. Also, *esp. Brit.,* **tri′col′our.** [1780–90; < LL *tricolor,* equiv. to *tri-* TRI- + *-color* colored; see COLOR]

tri′color cam′era, a camera for taking color photographs in which three separation negatives are exposed simultaneously by splitting the light from the subject with prisms and mirrors, and exposing through appropriate filters.

tri′colored her′on, an American heron, *Hydranassa tricolor,* that is dark bluish-gray above and white below with seasonally red neck stripes in the male. Also called **Louisiana heron.**

tri·corn (trī′kôrn), *adj.* **1.** having three horns or hornlike projections; three-cornered. —*n.* **2.** Also, **tri′·corne.** a hat with the brim turned up on three sides. [1750–60; < L *tricornis* having three horns, equiv. to *tri-* TRI- + *corn(ū)* HORN + *-is* adj. suffix]

tri·cor·nered (trī′kôr′nərd), *adj.* having three corners; tricorn. [1810–20; TRI- + CORNERED]

tri·cos·tate (trī kos′tāt, -kô′stāt), *adj. Bot., Zool.* having three ribs, costae, or raised lines. [1860–65; TRI- + COSTATE]

tri·cot (trē′kō), *n.* **1.** a warp-knit fabric of various natural or synthetic fibers, as wool, silk, or nylon, having fine vertical ribs on the face and horizontal ribs on the back, used esp. for making garments. **2.** a kind of worsted cloth. [1870–75; < F: knitting, knitted fabric, sweater, deriv. of *tricoter* to knit << Gmc; akin to G *stricken* to knit]

tric·o·tine (trik′ə tēn′, trē′kə-), *n.* See **cavalry twill.** [1895–1900; < F, equiv. to *tricot* TRICOT + *-ine* -INE[1]]

tri·cot·y·le·don·ous (trī kot′l ēd′n əs, trī′kot-), *adj. Bot.* having three cotyledons. [1820–30; TRI- + COTYLEDON + -OUS]

tri·cre·sol (trī krē′sôl, -sol), *n. Chem.* a mixture of the three isomeric cresols. [TRI- + CRESOL]

tri·crot·ic (trī krot′ik), *adj. Physiol.* **1.** having three arterial beats for one heartbeat, as certain pulses. **2.** pertaining to such a pulse. [1875–80; < Gk *tríkrot(os)* with triple beat (*tri-* TRI- + *krótos* beat) + -IC] —**tri·cro·tism** (trī′krə tiz′əm, trik′rə-), *n.*

tric·trac (trik′trak′), *n.* tricktrack.

tri·cus·pid (trī kus′pid), *adj.* **1.** Also, **tri·cus′pi·dal.** having three cusps or points, as a tooth. Cf. **bicuspid. 2.** *Anat.* of, pertaining to, or affecting the tricuspid valve. —*n.* **3.** *Anat.* a tricuspid part, as a tooth. [1660–70; < L *tricuspid-* (s. of *tricuspis*) having three points. See TRI-, CUSPID]

tri·cus·pi·date (trī kus′pi dāt′), *adj. Anat.* having three cusps or flaps. [1745–55; TRICUSPID + -ATE[1]]

tricus′pid valve′, *Anat.* the valve, consisting of three triangular flaps of tissue between the right auricle and ventricle of the heart, that keeps blood from flowing back into the auricle. Cf. **mitral valve.** [1660–70]

tri′cy·an′ic ac′id (trī′sī an′ik, trī′-). See **cyanuric acid.** [TRI- + CYANIC ACID]

tri·cy·cle (trī′si kəl, -sik′əl), *n.* **1.** a vehicle, esp. one for children, having one large front wheel and two small rear wheels, propelled by foot pedals. **2.** a velocipede with three wheels propelled by pedals or hand levers. **3.** a three-wheeled motorcycle. [1820–30; < F; see TRI-, CYCLE]

tri·cy·clic (trī sī′klik, -sik′lik), *adj.* **1.** pertaining to or embodying three cycles. —*n.* **2.** Also called **tricy′clic antidepres′sant.** *Pharm.* any of a group of pharmacologically active substances, as imipramine, that share a common three-ring structure, used to treat depression and cocaine abuse. [1890–95; TRI- + CYCLIC]

trid., (in prescriptions) three days. [< L *trīduum*]

Tri·dac·na (trī dak′nə), *n.* a genus of giant clams inhabiting reefs in the South Pacific, attaining a diameter of 4 ft. (1.2 m) or more, and weighing over 500 lb. (227 kg). [1770–80; < NL, n. use of fem. of L *tridacnus* requiring three bites < Gk *trídaknos,* equiv. to *tri-* TRI- + *dákn(ein)* to bite + *-os* adj. suffix]

tri·dac·tyl (trī dak′til), *adj. Zool.* having three fingers or toes, as certain reptiles. [1805–15; TRI- + -DACTYL]

tri′darn cup′board (trī′därn), a Welsh cupboard of the late 17th and 18th centuries, with an open, canopied upper section for display. [*tridarn* < Welsh, equiv. to *tri* THREE + *darn* piece]

tri·dent (trīd′nt), *n.* **1.** a three-pronged instrument or weapon. **2.** *Rom. Hist.* a three-pronged spear used by a retiarius in gladiatorial combats. **3.** *Class. Myth.* the three-pronged spear forming a characteristic attribute of the sea god Poseidon, or Neptune. **4.** a fish spear having three prongs. **5.** (*cap.*) *Mil.* a 34-ft (10-m) submarine-launched U.S. ballistic missile with eight to ten warheads and a range of 6500 mi. (10,459 km). —*adj.* **6.** Also, **tri·den·tal** (trī den′tl). having three prongs or tines. [1580–90; < L *trident-* (s. of *tridēns*) having three teeth. See TRI-, DENT[2]]

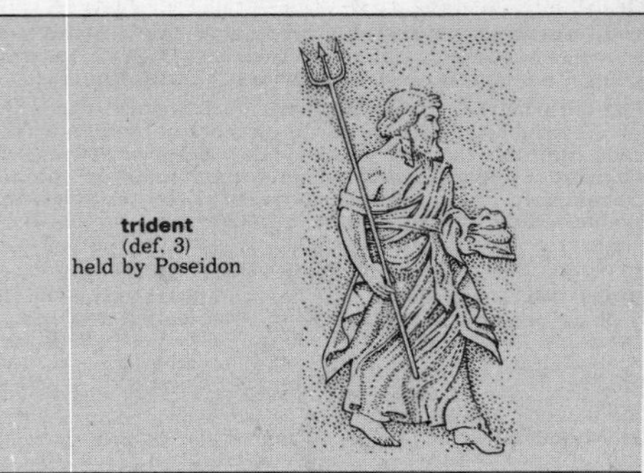

trident (def. 3) held by Poseidon

tri·den·tate (trī den′tāt), *adj.* having three teeth or toothlike parts or processes. [1745–55; TRIDENT + -ATE[1]]

Tri·den·tine (trī den′tin, -tīn, -tēn), *adj.* **1.** of or pertaining to the city of Trent. **2.** of or pertaining to the Council of Trent. **3.** conforming to the decrees and doctrines of the Council of Trent. [1555–65; < ML *Tridentīnus,* adj. use of L *Tridentīnus* area of the Rhaetian Alps around Tridentum; see -INE[1]]

Tri·den·tum (trī den′təm), *n.* ancient name of Trent, Italy.

tri·di·men·sion·al (trī′di men′shə nl, -dī-), *adj.* having three dimensions. [1870–75; TRI- + DIMENSIONAL] —**tri′di·men′sion·al′i·ty,** *n.* —**tri′di·men′sion·al·ly,** *adv.*

trid·u·um (trij′o͞o əm, trid′yo͞o-), *n. Rom. Cath. Ch.* a series of special religious observances over a three-day period, in preparation for a great feast. [1880–85; < L *trīduum* period of three days, equiv. to *trī-* TRI- + *-duum* < **diwom,* akin to *diēs* day (long *i* perh. after *postrīdiē* on the following day)]

trid·y·mite (trid′ə mīt′), *n. Mineral.* a polymorph of quartz occurring in the form of small crystals, commonly twinned, in siliceous volcanic rocks. [1865–70; < G *Tridymit,* equiv. to *tridym-* (Gk *trídym(os)* triple, equiv. to *tri-* TRI- + *(dí)dymos* DIDYMOUS) + *-it* -ITE[1]]

tri·e·cious (trī ē′shəs), *adj. Bot.* trioecious. —**tri·e′·cious·ly,** *adv.*

tried (trīd), *v.* **1.** pt. and pp. of **try.** —*adj.* **2.** tested and proved good, dependable, or trustworthy. **3.** subjected to hardship, worry, trouble, or the like.

tried-and-true (trīd′n tro͞o′), *adj.* tested and found to be reliable or workable. [1930–35]

tri·ene (trī′ēn), *n. Chem.* any compound containing three double bonds. [1925–30; TRI- + -ENE]

tri·en·ni·al (trī en′ē əl), *adj.* **1.** occurring every three years. **2.** lasting three years. —*n.* **3.** a third anniversary. **4.** something that appears or occurs every three years. **5.** a period of three years; triennium. [1555–65; TRIENNI(UM) + -AL[1]] —**tri·en′ni·al·ly,** *adv.*

tri·en·ni·um (trī en′ē əm), *n., pl.* **-en·ni·ums, -en·ni·a** (-en′ē ə). a period of three years. [1840–50; < L: period of three years, equiv. to *trienn(is)* pertaining to three years (*tri-* TRI- + *-enn-,* comb. form of *annus* year + *-is* adj. suffix) + *-ium* -IUM]

tri·ens (trī′enz), *n., pl.* **tri·en·tes** (trī en′tēz). **1.** a copper coin of ancient Rome, issued during the Republic, a third part of an as. **2.** tremissis (def. 1). [1595–1605; < L *triēns* third part]

tri·er (trī′ər), *n.* a person or thing that tries or tests; tester. [1300–50; ME *triour.* See TRY, -ER[1]]

Trier (trēr), *n.* a city in W Germany, on the Moselle River: extensive Roman ruins; cathedral. 93,472. Also called **Treves.** French, **Trèves.**

tri·er·arch (trī′ə rärk′), *n. Gk. Hist.* **1.** the commander of a trireme. **2.** (in Athens) a citizen who, singly, or jointly with other citizens, was required to fit out a trireme for the public service. [1650–60; < Gk *triḗrarchos,* equiv. to *triḗr(ēs)* trireme + *archós* commander. See TRI-, -ARCH]

tri·er·ar·chy (trī′ə rär′kē), *n., pl.* **-chies.** *Gk. Hist.* **1.** the office of a trierarch. **2.** trierarchs collectively. **3.** (in Athens) the duty of fitting out or furnishing triremes for the public service. [1830–40; < Gk *triērarchía.* See TRIERARCH, -Y[3]]

tries (trīz), *n.* **1.** pl. of **try.** —*v.* **2.** 3rd pers. sing. pres. ind. of **try:** *She tries to be at the head of her class.*

Tri·este (trē est′; *It.* trē es′te), *n.* **1.** a seaport in NE Italy, on the Gulf of Trieste. 237,191. **2. Free Territory of,** an area bordering the N Adriatic: originally a part of Italy; designated a free territory by the UN 1947; N zone, including the city of Trieste, 86 sq. mi. (223 sq. km) administered by the U.S. and Great Britain from 1947 until it was turned over to Italy in 1954; S zone 199 sq. mi. (515 sq. km) incorporated into Yugoslavia; now part of Slovenia. **3. Gulf of,** an inlet at the N end of the Adriatic, in NE Italy. 20 mi. (32 km) wide.

tri·eth·yl (trī eth′əl), *adj. Chem.* containing three ethyl groups. [1855–60; TRI- + ETHYL]

tri·eth·yl·a·mine (trī eth′əl ə mēn′, -eth′əl ə mēn′, -am′in), *n. Chem.* a colorless, flammable liquid, $C_6H_{15}N$, used chiefly as a solvent in chemical synthesis. [1840–50; TRI- + ETHYL + AMINE]

trieth′yl orthofor′mate, *Chem.* a colorless liquid, $C_7H_{16}O_3$, used chiefly in organic synthesis. Also called **aethon.**

tri·fa·cial (trī fā′shəl), *adj.* trigeminal. [1830–40; TRI- + FACIAL]

trifa′cial neural′gia, *Pathol.* See **tic douloureux.** [1895–1900]

tri·fect·a (trī′fek′tə), *n.* **1.** a type of bet, esp. on horse races, in which the bettor must select the first three

CONCISE ETYMOLOGY KEY: <, descended or borrowed from; >, whence; b., blend of, blended; c., cognate with; cf., compare; deriv., derivative; equiv., equivalent; imit., imitative; obl., oblique; r., replacing; s., stem; sp., spelling, spelled; resp., respelling, respelled; trans., translation; ?, origin unknown; *, unattested; ‡, probably earlier than. See the full key inside the front cover.

finishers in exact order. **2.** a race in which such bets are made. Cf. **superfecta.** Also called **triple.** [1970–75; TRI- + (PER)FECTA]

tri·fid (trī′fid), *adj.* cleft into three parts or lobes. [1745–55; < L *trifidus* split in three. See TRI-, -FID]

tri′fid foot′, *Furniture.* a pad foot having the form of three connected lobes. Also called **drake foot.**

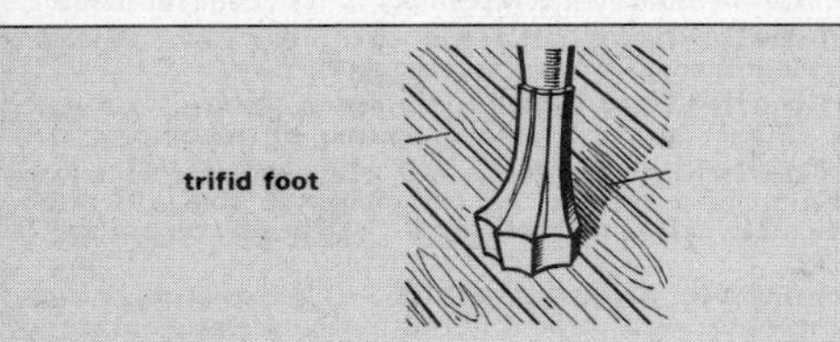
trifid foot

tri·fle (trī′fəl), *n., v.,* **-fled, -fling.** —*n.* **1.** an article or thing of very little value. **2.** a matter, affair, or circumstance of trivial importance or significance. **3.** a small, inconsiderable, or trifling sum of money. **4.** a small quantity or amount of anything; a little: *She's still a trifle angry.* **5.** a literary, musical, or artistic work of a light or trivial character having no great or lasting merit; bagatelle. **6.** a kind of pewter of medium hardness. **7. trifles,** articles made of this. **8.** *English Cookery.* a dessert usually consisting of custard and cake soaked in wine or liqueur, and jam, fruit, or the like. —*v.i.* **9.** to deal lightly or without due seriousness or respect: *Don't trifle with me!* **10.** to play or toy by handling or fingering: *He sat trifling with a pen.* **11.** to act or talk in an idle or frivolous way. **12.** to pass time idly or frivolously; waste time; idle. —*v.t.* **13.** to pass or spend (time) idly or frivolously (usually fol. by *away*). [1175–1225; (n.) ME *tru(f)fle* idle talk, deceit < OF, var. of *truf(f)e* mockery, deceit; (v.) ME *treoflen* to mock < OF *trufler* to make sport of] —**tri′fler,** *n.*
—**Syn. 1.** bauble, toy. **13.** fritter.

tri·fling (trī′fling), *adj.* **1.** of very little importance; trivial; insignificant: *a trifling matter.* **2.** of small value, cost, or amount: *a trifling sum.* **3.** frivolous; shallow; light: *trifling conversation.* **4.** mean; worthless. —*n.* **5.** idle or frivolous conduct, talk, etc. **6.** foolish delay or waste of time. [1350–1400; ME; see TRIFLE, -ING[2], -ING[1]] —**tri′fling·ly,** *adv.* —**tri′fling·ness,** *n.*
—**Syn. 1.** unimportant, slight, inconsequential. See **petty. 2.** negligible, piddling. —**Ant. 1.** important.

tri·flu·o·per·a·zine (trī flo͞o′ə per′ə zēn′), *n. Pharm.* a compound, $C_{21}H_{24}F_3N_3S$, used as an antipsychotic. [1955–60; TRI- + FLUO- + (PI)PERAZINE]

tri·fluor·ide (trī flo͝or′īd, -flôr′-, -flōr′-), *n. Chem.* a fluoride containing three atoms of fluorine. [1840–50; TRI- + FLUORIDE]

tri·fluor·o·chlo·ro·meth·ane (trī flo͝or′ō klôr′ō-meth′ān, -flôr′-; trī flo͝or′ō klōr′ō meth′ān, -flōr′-), *n. Chem.* chlorotrifluoromethane. [TRI- + FLUORO- + CHLORO-[2] + METHANE]

tri·flu·ra·lin (trī flo͝or′ə lin), *n. Chem.* a selective herbicide, $C_{13}H_{16}F_3N_3O_4$, used to control weeds. [1960–65; prob. *triflu(o)r(omethyl)a(ni)lin(e),* a chemical component; see TRI-, FLUORO-, METHYL, ANILINE]

tri·fo·cal (trī fō′kəl, trī′fō′-), *adj.* **1.** *Optics.* having three foci. **2.** (of an eyeglass lens) having three portions, one for near, one for intermediate, and one for far vision. —*n.* **3. trifocals,** eyeglasses with trifocal lenses. [1945–50; TRI- + FOCAL]

tri·fold (trī′fōld′), *adj.* **1.** triple; threefold. **2.** having three parts: *a trifold screen.* [1570–80; TRI- + -FOLD]

tri·fo·li·ate (trī fō′lē it, -āt′), *adj.* **1.** having three leaflets, lobes, or foils; trefoil. **2.** *Bot.* trifoliolate. Also, **tri·fo′li·at′ed.** [1690–1700; TRI- + FOLIATE]

trifo′liate or′ange, a spiny, Chinese orange tree, *Poncirus trifoliata,* used as a stock in grafting and for hedges.

tri·fo·li·o·late (trī fō′lē ə lāt′), *adj. Bot.* **1.** having three leaflets, as a compound leaf. **2.** having leaves with three leaflets, as a plant. [1820–30; TRI- + FOLIOLATE]

triforium

tri·fo·ri·um (trī fôr′ē əm, -fōr′-), *n., pl.* **-fo·ri·a** (-fôr′ē ə, -fōr′-). *Archit.* (in a church) the wall at the side of the nave, choir, or transept, corresponding to the space between the vaulting or ceiling and the roof of an aisle, often having a blind arcade or an opening in a gallery. [1695–1705; < AL, special use of ML *triforium* kind of gallery, lit., something with three openings, equiv. to L *tri-* TRI- + *for(is)* opening, DOOR + *-ium* -IUM] —**tri·fo′ri·al,** *adj.*

tri·form (trī′fôrm′), *adj.* **1.** formed of three parts; in three divisions. **2.** existing or appearing in three different forms. **3.** combining three different forms. Also, **tri′formed′.** [1400–50; < L *triformis.* See TRI-, -FORM]

tri·func·tion·al (trī fungk′shə nl), *adj. Chem.* pertaining to molecules that can react at three sites. [1925–30; TRI- + FUNCTIONAL]

tri·fur·cate (trī fûr′kāt, trī′fər kāt′; *adj. also* trī-fûr′kit, trī′fər-), *v.,* **-cat·ed, -cat·ing,** *adj.* —*v.i.* **1.** to divide into three forks or branches. —*adj.* **2.** Also, **tri·fur′cat·ed.** divided into three forks or branches. [1650–60; see TRI-, FURCATE] —**tri′fur·ca′tion,** *n.*

trig[1] (trig), *n. Informal.* trigonometry. [by shortening]

trig[2] (trig), *adj., v.,* **trigged, trig·ging.** —*adj. Chiefly Brit.* **1.** neat, trim, smart, or spruce. **2.** in good physical condition; sound; well. —*v.t.* **3.** *Chiefly Brit. Dial.* to make trim, smart, etc. (often fol. by *up* or *out*). [1150–1200 for earlier sense; 1505–15 for def. 1; ME *trigg* true, trusty < ON *tryggr* loyal, safe; c. Goth *triggws* true, faithful. See TRUE] —**trig′ness,** *n.*
—**Syn. 1.** tidy, orderly.

trig[3] (trig), *v.,* **trigged, trig·ging,** *n.* —*v.t. Dial.* **1.** to support or prop, as with a wedge. **2.** to act as a check on (the moving of wheels, vehicles, etc.). —*n.* **3.** a wedge or block used to prevent a wheel, cask, or the like, from rolling. [1585–95; < ON *tryggja* to make fast, secure]

trig., **1.** trigonometric. **2.** trigonometrical. **3.** trigonometry.

tri·ga (trē′gə, trī′-), *n., pl.* **-gae** (-gī, -jē, -gē). *Class. Antiq.* a two-wheeled chariot drawn by a team of three horses. Cf. **biga, quadriga.** [< LL *triga,* contr. of L *trijuga,* equiv. to *tri-* TRI- + *juga,* fem. deriv. of *jugum* YOKE[1]]

trig·a·mous (trig′ə məs), *adj.* **1.** of or pertaining to trigamy or a trigamist. **2.** *Bot.* having staminate, pistillate, and hermaphrodite flowers in the same flower head. [1835–45; < Gk *trígamos* thrice married. See TRI-, -GAMOUS]

trig·a·my (trig′ə mē), *n.* **1.** the state of having three wives or three husbands at one time. **2.** the state of having been lawfully married to three wives or three husbands at different times. [1605–15; < LL *trigamia* < Gk *trigamía,* equiv. to *trígam(os)* thrice-married + *-ia* -Y[3]. See TRI-, -GAMY] —**trig′a·mist,** *n.*

tri·gem·i·nal (trī jem′ə nl), *Anat.* —*adj.* **1.** of or pertaining to the trigeminal nerve. —*n.* **2.** Also called **trigem′inal nerve′.** either one of the fifth pair of cranial nerves, consisting of motor fibers that innervate the muscles of mastication, and of sensory fibers that conduct impulses from the head and face to the brain. [1820–30; < NL *trigemin(us)* (L: triple, equiv. to *tri-* TRI- + *geminus* twin, double) + -AL[1]]

trigem′inal neural′gia, *Pathol.* See **tic douloureux.** [1870–75]

Tri·gère (tri zhâr′, -jâr′; *Fr.* trē zher′), *n.* **Pauline,** born 1912, U.S. fashion designer, born in France.

trig′ func′tion, *Math.* See **trigonometric function.**

trig·ger (trig′ər), *n.* **1.** a small projecting tongue in a firearm that, when pressed by the finger, actuates the mechanism that discharges the weapon. **2.** a device, as a lever, the pulling or pressing of which releases a detent or spring. **3.** anything, as an act or event, that serves as a stimulus and initiates or precipitates a reaction or series of reactions. **4.** *Slang.* triggerman. **5. quick on the trigger,** *Informal.* quick to act or respond; impetuous; alert. —*v.t.* **6.** to initiate or precipitate (a chain of events, scientific reaction, psychological process, etc.): *Their small protest triggered a mass demonstration.* **7.** to fire or explode (a gun, missile, etc.) by pulling a trigger or releasing a triggering device: *He accidentally triggered his rifle.* —*v.i.* **8.** to release a trigger. **9.** to become active; activate. [1615–25; earlier *tricker* < D *trekker,* equiv. to *trekk(en)* to pull + *-er* -ER[1]]

trig′ger fin′ger, 1. any finger, usually the forefinger, that presses the trigger of a gun. **2.** either forefinger, depending on which hand is dominant. **3.** *Pathol.* difficulty in straightening or bending a ring finger, caused by inflammation and thickening of its tendon. [1820–30]

trig·ger·fish (trig′ər fish′), *n., pl.* (*esp. collectively*) **-fish,** (*esp. referring to two or more kinds or species*) **-fish·es.** any of various compressed, deep-bodied fishes of the genus *Balistes* and allied genera, chiefly inhabiting tropical seas, having an anterior dorsal fin with three stout spines: some are edible while others are poisonous. [1880–85; TRIGGER + FISH]

trig·ger-hap·py (trig′ər hap′ē), *adj. Informal.* **1.** ready to fire a gun at the least provocation, regardless of the situation or probable consequences: *a trigger-happy hunter.* **2.** heedless and foolhardy in matters of great importance and recklessly advocating action that can result in war: *Some called him a trigger-happy candidate.* **3.** eager to point out the mistakes or shortcomings of others; aggressively or wantonly critical: *He's a trigger-happy editor with a nervous blue pencil.* [1940–45]

trig·ger·man (trig′ər mən, -man′), *n., pl.* **-men** (-mən, -men′). *Informal.* **1.** a gangster who specializes in gunning people down. **2.** a bodyguard, esp. of a gangster. Also called **trigger.** [1920–25; TRIGGER + MAN[1]]

trig′ger mech′anism, a physiological or psychological process caused by a stimulus and resulting in a usually severe reaction.

tri·glyc·er·ide (trī glis′ə rīd′, -ər id), *n., Biochem., Chem.* an ester obtained from glycerol by the esterification of three hydroxyl groups with fatty acids, naturally occurring in animal and vegetable tissues: an important energy source forming much of the fat stored by the body. Cf. **glyceride.** [1855–60; TRI- + GLYCERIDE]

tri·glyph (trī′glif′), *n. Archit.* a structural member of a Doric frieze, separating two consecutive metopes, and consisting typically of a rectangular block with two vertical grooves or glyphs, and two chamfers or half grooves at the sides, together counting as a third glyph, and leaving three flat vertical bands on the face of the block. See diag. under **column.** [1555–65; < L *triglyphus* < Gk *tríglyphos* thrice-grooved, equiv. to *tri-* TRI- + *glyph(ḗ)* GLYPH + *-os* adj. suffix] —**tri′glyphed′,** *adj.* —**tri·glyph′ic, tri·glyph′i·cal,** *adj.*

tri·go (trē′gō; *Sp.* trē′gô), *n., pl.* **-gos** (-gōz; *Sp.* -gôs). wheat; field of wheat. [< Sp < L *triticum* wheat, equiv. to *trīt(us)* ground, rubbed to pieces (ptp. of *terere* to rub, grind) + *-icum* -IC]

tri·gon (trī′gon), *n.* **1.** a triangle. **2.** an ancient Greek stringed instrument with a triangular shape. **3.** *Astrol. Archaic.* **a.** trine. **b.** triplicity. [1555–65; < L *trigōnum* triangle < Gk *trígōnon,* n. use of neut. of *trígōnos* three-angled. See TRI-, -GON]

trigon., **1.** trigonometric. **2.** trigonometrical. **3.** trigonometry.

trig·o·nal (trig′ə nl), *adj.* **1.** of, pertaining to, or shaped like a triangle; having three angles; triangular. **2.** *Crystall.* having threefold symmetry. [1560–70; TRIGON + -AL[1]] —**trig′o·nal·ly,** *adv.*

trig′onal trisoctahe′dron, a trisoctahedron whose faces are triangles. [1890–95]

tri·gone (trī′gōn), *n.* **1.** Also, **trigonum.** *Anat.* **a.** a triangular part or area. **b.** the area on the floor of the urinary bladder between the opening of the urethra in front and the two ureters at the sides. **2.** *Bot.* a thickened area where three or more plant cells come together. [1825–35; < F < L *trigōnum* triangle; see TRIGON]

trig′onomet′ric equa′tion, *Math.* an equation involving trigonometric functions of unknown angles, as $\cos B = \frac{1}{2}$.

trig′onomet′ric func′tion, *Math.* **1.** Also called **circular function.** a function of an angle, as sine or cosine, expressed as the ratio of the sides of a right triangle. **2.** any function involving only trigonometric functions and constants. **3.** the generalization of these to functions of real or complex numbers. Also called **trig function** (for defs. 1, 2). [1905–10]

trig′onomet′ric se′ries, *Math.* an infinite series involving sines and cosines of increasing integral multiples of a variable.

trig·o·nom·e·try (trig′ə nom′i trē), *n.* the branch of mathematics that deals with the relations between the sides and angles of plane or spherical triangles, and the calculations based on them. [1605–15; < NL *trigōnometria;* see TRIGON, -O-, -METRY] —**trig·o·no·met·ric** (trig′ə nə me′trik), **trig′o·no·met′ri·cal,** *adj.* —**trig′o·no·met′ri·cal·ly,** *adv.*

trig·o·nous (trig′ə nəs), *adj.* having three angles or corners, as a stem or seed; triangular. [1750–60; < L *trigōnus* triangular < Gk *trígōnos.* See TRI-, -GON, -OUS]

tri·go·num (trī gō′nəm), *n., pl.* **-na** (-nə). *Anat.* trigone. [1720–30; < L *trigōnum* triangle. See TRIGON]

tri·gram (trī′gram), *n.* a sequence of three adjacent letters or symbols. [1600–10; TRI- + -GRAM[1]]

tri·graph (trī′graf, -gräf), *n.* a group of three letters representing a single speech sound, as *eau* in *beau.* [1830–40; TRI- + -GRAPH] —**tri·graph·ic** (trī graf′ik), *adj.*

tri·he·dral (trī hē′drəl), *adj. Geom.* **1.** having, or formed by, three planes meeting in a point: *a trihedral angle.* —*n.* **2.** a trihedron. [1780–90; TRI- + -HEDRAL]

tri·he·dron (trī hē′drən), *n., pl.* **-drons, -dra** (-drə). *Geom.* the figure determined by three planes meeting in a point. Also, **trihedral.** [1820–30; TRI- + -HEDRON]

tri·hy·drate (trī hī′drāt), *n. Chem.* a hydrate that contains three molecules of water, as potassium pyrophosphate, $K_4P_2O_7{\cdot}3H_2O$. [1850–55; TRI- + HYDRATE] —**tri·hy′drat·ed,** *adj.*

tri·hy·dric (trī hī′drik), *adj. Chem.* (esp. of alcohols and phenols) trihydroxy. [1865–70; TRI- + -HYDRIC]

tri·hy·drox·y (trī′hī drok′sē), *adj. Chem.* containing three hydroxyl groups. [1900–05; TRI- + *hydroxy,* independent use of HYDROXY-]

tri·i·o·do·meth·ane (trī′ī ō′dō meth′ān, -ī od′ō-), *n. Chem.* iodoform. [TRI- + IODO- + METHANE]

tri·i·o·do·thy·ro·nine (trī′ī ō′dō thī′rə nēn′, -ī od′-ō-), *n.* **1.** *Biochem.* a thyroid hormone, $C_{15}H_{12}I_3NO_4$, similar to thyroxine but several times more potent. **2.** *Pharm.* a preparation of this hormone, used in treating hypothyroidism. *Abbr.:* T_3 [1950–55; TRI- + IODO- + *thyronine* (perh. deriv., with -ONE, of THYROXINE)]

tri·jet (trī′jet′), *n.* an airplane powered by three jet engines. [1965–70; TRI- + JET[1]]

tri·ju·gate (trī′jo͝o gāt′, trī jo͞o′git, -gāt), *adj. Bot.* having three pairs of leaflets. Also, **tri·ju·gous** (trī′jo͝o-gəs, trī jo͞o′-). [1875–80; TRI- + JUGATE]

trike (trīk), *n. Informal.* tricycle. [by shortening and alter.; see BIKE[1]]

Tri·ko·ra (tri kôr′ä), *n.* a mountain in central Irian Jaya, in Indonesia, in the Jajawijaja Range. 15,584 ft. (4750 m). Formerly, **Mount Wilhelmina.**

Tril·a·fon (tril′ə fon′), *Pharm., Trademark.* a brand of perphenazine.

tri·lat·er·al (trī lat′ər əl), *adj.* having three sides. [1650–60; < L *trilater(us)* three-sided + -AL[1]. See TRI-, LATERAL] —**tri·lat′er·al′i·ty,** *n.* —**tri·lat′er·al·ly,** *adv.*

tri·lat·er·a·tion (trī lat′ə rā′shən), *n. Survey.* a method of determining the relative positions of three or more points by treating these points as vertices of a triangle or triangles of which the angles and sides can be measured. [TRILATER(AL) + -ATION]

CONCISE PRONUNCIATION KEY: act, cāpe, dâre, pärt; set, ēqual; if, īce; ox, ōver, ôrder, oil, bo͝ok, bo͞ot, out; up, ûrge; child; sing; shoe; thin, *th*at; zh as in *treasure.* ə = *a* as in *alone, e* as in *system, i* as in *easily, o* as in *gallop, u* as in *circus;* ᵊ as in *fire* (fīᵊr), *hour* (ouᵊr). l and n can serve as syllabic consonants, as in *cradle* (krād′l), and *button* (but′n). See the full key inside the front cover.

tril·by (tril′bē), *n., pl.* **-bies.** *Chiefly Brit.* a hat of soft felt with an indented crown. Also called **tril′by hat′.** [1895–1900; short for *Trilby hat,* after the hat worn by a character in an illustration for the novel *Trilby* (1894) by George du Maurier]

tri·lem·ma (trī lem′ə), *n.* **1.** a situation, analogous to a dilemma, in which there are three almost equally undesirable alternatives: *His trilemma consisted in not knowing whether to acknowledge receipt, deny it, or simply leave.* **2.** *Logic.* a form of argument in which three choices are presented, each of which is indicated to have consequences that may be unfavorable. [1665–75; TRI- + (DI)LEMMA]

tri·lin·e·ar (trī lin′ē ər), *adj.* of, pertaining to, or bounded by three lines. [1705–15; TRI- + LINEAR]

tri·lin·gual (trī ling′gwəl *or, Can.,* -ling′gyo͞o əl), *adj.* using, speaking, or involving three languages. [1825–35; < L *trilingu(is)* triple-tongued + -AL¹. See TRI-, LINGUAL] **—tri·lin′gual·ism,** *n.* **—tri·lin′gual·ly,** *adv.*

tri·lit·er·al (trī lit′ər əl), *adj.* **1.** using or consisting of three letters. **2.** (of Semitic roots) consisting of three consonants. **—***n.* **3.** a triliteral word or root. [1745–55; TRI- + LITERAL]

tri·lit·er·al·ism (trī lit′ər ə liz′əm), *n.* the characteristic presence of triliteral roots in a language, as in the Semitic languages. [1835–45; TRILITERAL + -ISM]

tri·lith·on (trī lith′on, trī′lə thon′), *n.* a prehistoric structure consisting of two upright stones supporting a horizontal stone. Also, **tri·lith** (trī′lith). [1730–40; < Gk *trílithon,* neut. of *trílithos* having three stones. See TRI-, -LITH]

trill¹ (tril), *v.t.* **1.** to sing or play with a vibratory or quavering effect. **2.** *Phonet.* to produce (a sound) with a trill. **3.** (of birds, insects, etc.) to sing or utter in a succession of rapidly alternating sounds. **—***v.i.* **4.** to resound vibrantly, or with a rapid succession of sounds, as the voice, song, or laughter. **5.** to utter or make a sound or succession of sounds resembling such singing, as a bird, frog, grasshopper, or person laughing. **6.** to execute a shake or trill with the voice or on a musical instrument. **7.** *Phonet.* to execute a trill, esp. with the tongue, as while singing, talking, or whistling. **—***n.* **8.** the act or sound of trilling. **9.** *Music.* a rapid alternation of two adjacent tones; a shake. **10.** a similar sound, or succession of sounds, uttered or made by a bird, an insect, a person laughing, etc. **11.** *Phonet.* **a.** a sequence of repetitive, rapid, vibratory movements produced in any free articulator or membrane by a rush of air expelled from the lungs and often causing a corresponding sequence of contacts between the vibrating articulator and another organ or surface. **b.** a speech sound produced by such a trill. [1635–45; < It *trillo* quaver or warble in singing << Gmc; cf. D *trillen* to vibrate, late ME *trillen* to shake or rock (something)]

trill¹ (def. 9)

trill² (tril), *Archaic., v.i.* **1.** to flow in a thin stream; trickle. **—***v.t.* **2.** to cause to flow in a thin stream. [1300–50; ME *trillen* to make (something) turn, to roll, flow (said of tears, water) < ODan *trillæ* to roll (said, e.g., of tears and of a wheelbarrow); cf. Norw *trille,* Sw *trilla.* See TRILL¹]

Tril·ling (tril′ing), *n.* **Lionel,** 1905–75, U.S. critic and author.

tril·lion (tril′yən), *n., pl.* **-lions,** (*as after a numeral*) **-lion,** *adj.* **—***n.* **1.** a cardinal number represented in the U.S. by 1 followed by 12 zeros, and in Great Britain by 1 followed by 18 zeros. **—***adj.* **2.** amounting to one trillion in number. [1680–90; < F, equiv. to *tr(i)-* TRI- + *(m)illion* MILLION] **—tril′lionth,** *n., adj.*

tril·li·um (tril′ē əm), *n.* any of several plants belonging to the genus *Trillium,* of the lily family, having a whorl of three leaves from the center of which rises a solitary, three-petalled flower. [< NL (Linnaeus), appar. alter. of Sw *trilling* triplet, alluding to the foliation]

tri·lo·bate (trī lō′bāt, trī′lə bāt′), *adj.* having three lobes. Also, **tri·lo′bat·ed.** [1765–75; TRI- + LOBATE]

trilobate leaf

tri·lobed (trī′lōbd′), *adj.* trilobate. [1820–30; TRI- + LOBED]

tri·lo·bite (trī′lə bīt′), *n.* any marine arthropod of the extinct class Trilobita, from the Paleozoic Era, having a flattened, oval body varying in length from 1 in. (2.5 cm) or less to 2 ft. (61 cm). [1825–35; < NL *Trilobites,* equiv. to Gk *trílob(os)* three-lobed (see TRI-, LOBE) + *-ītes* -ITE¹] **—tri·lo·bit·ic** (trī′lə bit′ik), *adj.*

CONCISE ETYMOLOGY KEY: <, descended or borrowed from; >, whence; b., blend of, blended; c., cognate with; cf., compare; deriv., derivative; equiv., equivalent; imit., imitative; obl., oblique; r., replacing; s., stem; sp., spelling, spelled; resp., respelling, respelled; trans., translation; ?, origin unknown; *, unattested; ‡, probably earlier than. See the full key inside the front cover.

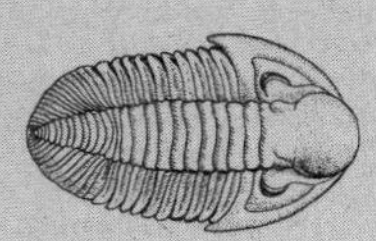
trilobite, *Griffithides bufo,* length 1¼ in. (3.2 cm)

tri·loc·u·lar (trī lok′yə lər), *adj. Bot., Zool.* having three loculi, chambers, or cells. [1745–55; TRI- + LOCULAR]

tril·o·gy (tril′ə jē), *n., pl.* **-gies.** **1.** a series or group of three plays, novels, operas, etc., that, although individually complete, are closely related in theme, sequence, or the like. **2.** (in ancient Greek drama) a series of three complete and usually related tragedies performed at the festival of Dionysus and forming a tetralogy with the satyr play. **3.** a group of three related things. [1655–65; < Gk *trilogía.* See TRI-, -LOGY]

trim (trim), *v.,* **trimmed, trim·ming,** *n., adj.,* **trim·mer, trim·mest,** *adv.* **—***v.t.* **1.** to put into a neat or orderly condition by clipping, paring, pruning, etc.: *to trim a hedge.* **2.** to remove (something superfluous or dispensable) by or as if by cutting (often fol. by *off*): *to trim off loose threads from a ragged edge.* **3.** to cut down, as to required size or shape: *trim a budget; trim a piece of wood.* **4.** *Aeron.* to level off (an airship or airplane) in flight. **5.** *Naut.* **a.** to distribute the load of (a ship) so that it sits well in the water. **b.** to stow or arrange, as cargo. **c.** to adjust (the sails or yards) with reference to the direction of the wind and the course of the ship. **6.** to decorate or adorn with ornaments or embellishments: *to trim a dress with fur.* **7.** to arrange goods in (a store window, showcase, etc.) as a display. **8.** to prepare or adjust (a lamp, fire, etc.) for proper burning. **9.** *Informal.* **a.** to rebuke or reprove. **b.** to beat or thrash. **c.** to defeat. **10.** to dress or array (often fol. by *up*). **—***v.i.* **11.** *Naut.* **a.** to assume a particular position or trim in the water, as a vessel. **b.** to adjust the sails or yards with reference to the direction of the wind and the course of the ship. **12.** to pursue a neutral or cautious policy between parties. **13.** to accommodate one's views to the prevailing opinion for reasons of expediency. **14. trim one's sails.** See **sail** (def. 11). **—***n.* **15.** the condition, order, or fitness of a person or thing for action, work, use, etc. **16.** *Naut.* **a.** the set of a ship in the water, esp. the most advantageous one. **b.** the condition of a ship with reference to its fitness for sailing. **c.** the adjustment of sails, rigging, etc., with reference to wind direction and the course of the ship. **d.** the condition of a submarine as regards buoyancy. **17.** a person's dress, adornment, or appearance. **18.** material used for decoration or embellishment; decorative trimming. **19.** decoration of a store window for the display of merchandise; window dressing. **20.** a trimming by cutting, clipping, or the like. **21.** a haircut that restores the previous cut to neatness without changing the hair style. **22.** something that is cut off or eliminated. **23.** *Aeron.* the attitude of an airplane with respect to all three axes, at which balance occurs in forward flight under no controls. **24.** *Building Trades.* finished woodwork or the like used to decorate or border openings or wall surfaces, as cornices, baseboards, or moldings. **25.** *Auto.* **a.** the upholstery, knobs, handles, and other equipment inside a motor car. **b.** ornamentation on the exterior of an automobile, esp. in metal or a contrasting color. **—***adj.* **26.** pleasingly neat or smart in appearance: *trim lawns.* **27.** in good condition or order. **28.** (of a person) in excellent physical condition: *Swimming is a good way to keep trim.* **29.** slim; lean. **30.** *Obs.* good, excellent, or fine. **—***adv.* **31.** trimly. [bef. 900; prob. continuing OE *trymman, trymian* to strengthen, prepare (not recorded in ME), deriv. of *trum* strong, active; akin to Ir *dron* strong, Gk *drȳmós* coppice, L *dūrus* hard. See TREE] **—trim′ly,** *adv.* **—trim′ness,** *n.*
—Syn. 1. shear, shave, cut, lop. **6.** deck, bedeck, ornament, embellish, garnish. **18.** adornment, garnish. **26.** compact, trig, spruce.

tri·ma·ran (trī′mə ran′), *n.* a vessel similar to a catamaran but having three separate hulls. [1950–55; TRI- + (CATA)MARAN]

trim′ die′, *Metalworking.* a die for trimming flash from a casting, forging, or stamping. Also, **trimming die.**

trime (trīm), *n.* a former silver three-cent coin of the U.S., issued from 1851 to 1873. [perh. TRI- + (DI)ME]

tri·mer (trī′mər), *n. Chem.* **1.** a molecule composed of three identical, simpler molecules. **2.** a polymer derived from three identical monomers. Cf. **oligomer.** [1925–30; < Gk *trimerḗs* having three parts. See TRI-, -MER] **—tri·mer·ic** (trī mer′ik), *adj.*

trim·er·ous (trim′ər əs), *adj.* **1.** *Bot.* (of flowers) having members in each whorl in groups of three. **2.** *Entomol.* having three segments or parts. [1820–30; < NL *trimerus,* equiv. to *trimer-* (see TRIMER) + *-us* -OUS]

tri·mes·ter (trī mes′tər, trī′mes-), *n.* **1.** a term or period of three months. **2.** one of the three approximately equal terms into which the year is divided by some colleges, schools, etc. [1815–25; < F *trimestre* < L *trimē(n)stris* of three months, equiv. to *tri-* TRI- + *-mē(n)stris* (see SEMESTER)] **—tri·mes·tral** (trī mes′trəl), **tri·mes′tri·al,** *adj.*

tri·me·tal·lic (trī′mə tal′ik), *adj.* **1.** of three metals. **2.** *Engraving.* (of an offset plate) consisting of a face layer of chromium, stainless steel, or chemically prepared aluminum over a layer of copper with a strengthening backup layer of steel or other metal. [1885–90; TRI- + METALLIC]

trim·e·ter (trim′i tər), *Pros.* **—***n.* **1.** a verse of three measures or feet. **—***adj.* **2.** consisting of three measures or feet. **3.** *Class. Pros.* composed of six feet or three dipodies. [1560–70; < L *trimetrus* having three measures < Gk *trímetros.* See TRI-, METER²]

tri·meth·a·di·one (trī meth′ə dī′ōn), *n. Pharm.* a synthetic, white, crystalline powder, $C_6H_9NO_3$, used as an anticonvulsant to control petit mal epileptic seizures. [*trimeth(yl)* + *(ox)a(zolidine)dione,* components of its chemical name]

tri·meth·o·prim (trī meth′ə prim), *n. Pharm.* a synthetic crystalline compound, $C_{14}H_{18}N_4O_3$, usually combined with a sulfonamide as an antibiotic preparation in the treatment of urinary tract infections and pneumocystis pneumonia. [1960–65; *trimetho(xyphenyl)* + *p(y)rim(idinediamine),* components of its chemical name]

tri·meth·yl·ene (trī meth′ə lēn′), *n. Chem., Biochem.* cyclopropane. [TRI- + METHYLENE]

tri·meth·yl·gly·cine (trī meth′əl glī′sēn, -glī sēn′), *n. Chem.* betaine. [TRI- + METHYL + GLYCINE]

tri·met·ric (trī me′trik), *adj.* **1.** pertaining to or consisting of a trimeter or trimeters. **2.** *Crystall.* orthorhombic. Also, **tri·met′ri·cal.** [1830–40; TRIMET(E)R + -IC]

trimet′ric projec′tion, *Geom.* a three-dimensional projection with three different linear scales at arbitrary angles.

tri·met·ro·gon (trī me′trə gon′), *adj.* of or pertaining to a system of aerial photography using three cameras, one pointed directly downward and the others at 60° to it. [1940–45; TRI- + Gk *métro(n)* measure + -GON]

trim·mer¹ (trim′ər), *n.* **1.** a person or thing that trims. **2.** a tool or machine for trimming, clipping, paring, or pruning. **3.** a machine for trimming lumber. **4.** *Building Trades.* **a.** a joist or rafter supporting one of the ends of a header at the edge of a wellhole. **b.** a wall tile or floor tile for finishing an edge or angle. **5.** an apparatus for stowing, arranging, or shifting cargo, coal, or the like. **6.** a person who has no firm position, opinion, or policy, esp. in politics. **7.** a person who is committed to no particular political party, adapting to one side or another as expediency may dictate. [1510–20; TRIM + -ER¹]

trim·mer² (trim′ər), *adj.* comparative of **trim.**

trim′mer arch′, *Building Trades.* an arch, usually of brick and in the form of half of a segmental arch, between a chimney and a header in a floor structure to support a hearth. [1825–35]

trim·ming (trim′ing), *n.* **1.** anything used or serving to decorate or complete: *the trimmings of a Christmas tree.* **2.** Usually, **trimmings.** an accompaniment or garnish to a main dish: *roast turkey with all the trimmings.* **3. trimmings,** pieces cut off in trimming, clipping, paring, or pruning. **4.** the act of a person or thing that trims. **5.** *Informal.* a beating or thrashing. **6.** *Informal.* a defeat: *Our team took quite a trimming.* [1510–20; TRIM + -ING¹]

trim′ming die′, *Metalworking.* See **trim die.**

trim′ming tab′, *Aeron.* See **trim tab.**

tri·mod·al (trī mōd′l), *adj. Statistics.* (of a distribution) having three modes. [TRI- + MODAL] **—tri′mo·dal′i·ty,** *n.*

tri·mo·lec·u·lar (trī′mə lek′yə lər), *adj. Chem.* pertaining to or having three molecules. [TRI- + MOLECULAR]

tri·month·ly (trī munth′lē), *adj.* occurring, taking place, done, or acted upon every three months. [1855–60; TRI- + MONTHLY]

tri·morph (trī′môrf), *n. Crystall.* **1.** a substance existing in three structurally distinct forms; a trimorphous substance. **2.** any of the three forms. [1905–10; < Gk *trímorphos* having three forms. See TRI-, -MORPH]

tri·mor·phism (trī môr′fiz əm), *n.* **1.** *Zool.* the occurrence of three forms distinct in structure, coloration, etc., among animals of the same species. **2.** *Bot.* the occurrence of three different forms of flowers, leaves, etc., on the same plant or on distinct plants of the same species. **3.** *Crystall.* the property of some substances of crystallizing in three structurally distinct forms. **4.** the property or condition of occurring in three distinct forms. [1855–60; < Gk *trímorph(os)* of three forms (see TRI-, -MORPH) + -ISM] **—tri·mor′phic, tri·mor′phous,** *adj.*

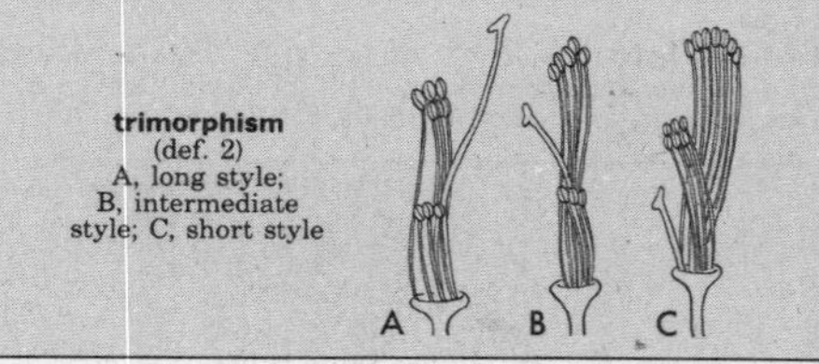

trimorphism (def. 2) A, long style; B, intermediate style; C, short style

tri·mo·tor (trī′mō′tər), *n.* an airplane or other vehicle that has three motors. [1920–25; TRI- + MOTOR] **—tri·mo′tored,** *adj.*

trim′ rail′, *Theat.* the lower row of pins or cleats on a pin rail, used for tying off or fastening lines after lowering scenery into position. Also called **tie-off rail.**

trim′ size′, the final size of a product after its unnecessary parts have been cut off or removed: *The trim size of the book in 6½ inches by 9 inches.* [1925–30]

trim′ tab′, *Aeron.* an independently controlled tab set in the trailing edge of a control surface, as an elevator, aileron, or rudder, to hold it in a position suitable for stabilizing the aircraft in a flight attitude. Also, **trimming tab.**

Tri·mur·ti (tri mo͝or′tē), *n.* (in later Hinduism) a trinity consisting of Brahma the Creator, Vishnu the Preserver, and Shiva the Destroyer. [1800–10; < Skt *trimūrti,* equiv. to *tri* THREE + *mūrti* shape]

Tri·na·cri·a (tri nā′krē ə, -nak′rē ə, trī-), *n.* an ancient name of **Sicily.** **—Tri·na′cri·an,** *adj.*

tri·nal (trīn′l), *adj.* threefold; triple; trine. [1555–65; < LL *trīnālis.* See TRINE, -AL¹]

tri·na·ry (trī′nə rē), *adj.* consisting of three parts, or proceeding by three; ternary. [1425–75; late ME *trynary* < LL *trīnārius* of three kinds, equiv. to L *trīn(ī)* by threes (alter. of *ternī* (deriv. of *ter* thrice; see TER-) on the model of *bīnī* by twos; see BINARY) + *-ārius* -ARY]

tri•na•tion (trī nā′shən), *n.* celebration of Mass three times on the same day by the same priest. [< NL *trīnāt(us)* (ptp. of *trīnāre* to triple, perh. deriv. of L *trīnī* by threes) + -ION]

Trin•co•ma•lee (tring′kō mə lē′), *n.* a seaport in E Sri Lanka. 39,000. Also, **Trin′co•ma•li′.**

trin•dle (trin′dl, trin′l), *n., v.,* **-dled, -dling.** **1.** *Brit. Dial.* a wheel, esp. of a wheelbarrow. —*v.t., v.i.* **2.** *Dial.* to roll; trundle. [bef. 1000; ME *trindel,* OE *tryndel* circle, ring; akin to LG *tründeln* to roll. See TREND]

trine (trīn), *adj.* **1.** threefold; triple. **2.** *Astrol.* of or pertaining to the trigon aspect of two planets distant from each other 120°, or the third part of the zodiac. —*n.* **3.** a set or group of three; triad. **4.** (*cap.*) the Trinity. **5.** *Astrol.* a trine aspect of two planets, indicative of ease and accomplishment. [1350–1400; ME: threefold (< OF *trin(e)*) < L *trīnus,* sing. of *trīnī* by threes (see TRINARY)]

trine′ immer′sion, a form of baptism in which the candidate is immersed three times, once for each person of the Trinity. [1630–40]

trin•gle (tring′gəl), *n.* a narrow, straight molding, as a fillet. [1690–1700; < F: curtain rod, rod, alter. of MF *tingle;* cf. MD *tingel* lathe]

Trin•i•dad (trin′i dad′; *for 2 also Sp.* trē′nē thäth′), *n.* **1.** an island in the SE West Indies, off the NE coast of Venezuela: formerly a British colony in the Federation of the West Indies; now part of the republic of Trinidad and Tobago. 945,210; 1864 sq. mi. (4828 sq. km). **2.** a city in central Bolivia. 72,000. —**Trin•i•da•di•an** (trin′i dā′dē ən, -dad′ē-), *adj., n.*

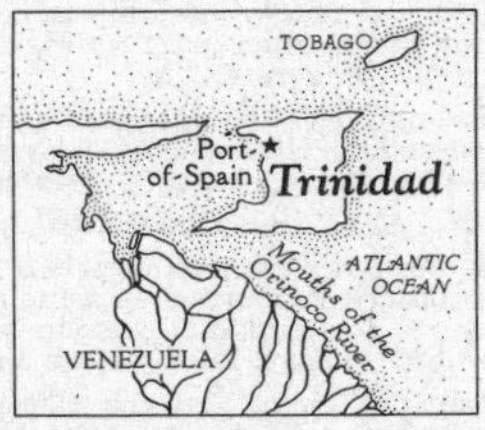

Trin′idad and Toba′go, an independent republic in the West Indies, comprising the islands of Trinidad and Tobago: member of the Commonwealth of Nations. 1,073,800; 1980 sq. mi. (5128 sq. km). *Cap.:* Port-of-Spain. —**Trin′i•da′di•an and To′ba•go′ni•an.**

Trin•i•tar•i•an (trin′i târ′ē ən), *adj.* **1.** believing in or adhering to the doctrine of the Trinity. **2.** pertaining to Trinitarians, or believers in the doctrine of the Trinity. **3.** belonging or pertaining to the religious order of Trinitarians. **4.** of or pertaining to the Trinity. **5.** (*l.c.*) forming a trinity; threefold; triple. —*n.* **6.** a person who believes in the doctrine of the Trinity. **7.** a member of the "Order of the Holy Trinity," a religious order founded in 1198 to redeem Christian captives of the Muslims. [1555–65; < NL *trīnitāri(us)* of the Trinity (see TRINITY, -ARY) + -AN]

Trin•i•tar•i•an•ism (trin′i târ′ē ə niz′əm), *n.* the belief in, or doctrine of, the Trinity. [TRINITARIAN + -ISM]

trinitro-, *Chem.* a combination of **tri-** and **nitro-:** *trinitrotoluene.*

tri•ni•tro•ben•zene (trī nī′trō ben′zēn, -ben zēn′), *n. Chem.* any of three yellow crystalline compounds having the formula $C_6H_3N_3O_6$, capable of more explosive power and requiring more impact than TNT. Also called **TNB** [TRINITRO- + BENZENE]

tri•ni•tro•cre•sol (trī nī′trō krē′sōl), *n. Chem.* a yellow, crystalline compound, $C_7H_5N_3O_7$, used in high explosives. [TRINITRO- + CRESOL]

tri•ni•tro•glyc•er•in (trī nī′trō glis′ər in), *n. Chem.* nitroglycerin. [1860–65; TRINITRO- + GLYCERIN]

tri•ni•tro•phe•nol (trī nī′trō fē′nôl, -nol), *Chem.* See **picric acid.** [TRINITRO- + PHENOL]

tri•ni•tro•phen•yl•meth•yl•ni•tra•mine (trī nī′trō-fen′l meth′əl nī′trə mēn′, -nī tram′in, -fēn′-), *n. Chem.* tetryl. [TRINITRO- + PHENYL + METHYL + NITRAMINE]

tri•ni•tro•tol•u•ene (trī nī′trō tol′yōō ēn′), *n. Chem.* See **TNT.** Also, **tri•ni•tro•tol•u•ol** (trī nī′trō tol′yōō ōl′). [1895–1900; TRINITRO- + TOLUENE]

Trin•i•ty (trin′i tē), *n., pl.* **-ties** for 2, 4. **1.** Also called **Blessed Trinity, Holy Trinity.** the union of three persons (Father, Son, and Holy Ghost) in one Godhead, or the threefold personality of the one Divine Being. **2.** a representation of this in art. **3.** See **Trinity Sunday. 4.** (*l.c.*) a group of three; triad. **5.** (*l.c.*) the state of being threefold or triple. [1175–1225; ME *Trinite* < OF < LL *trīnitās* triad, trio, the Trinity, equiv. to *trīn(us)* threefold (see TRINE) + *-itās* -ITY]

Trin′ity Sun′day, the Sunday after Pentecost, observed as a festival in honor of the Trinity. [1400–50; late ME]

Trin•i•ty•tide (trin′i tē tīd′), *n.* the period between Trinity Sunday and Advent. [1505–15; TRINITY + TIDE[1]]

trin•ket (tring′kit), *n.* **1.** a small ornament, piece of jewelry, etc., usually of little value. **2.** anything of trivial value. —*v.i.* **3.** to deal secretly or surreptitiously. [1525–35; orig. uncert.]

trin•ket•er (tring′ki tər), *n.* a person who deals secretly or surreptitiously. [1645–55; TRINKET + -ER[1]]

trin•ket•ry (tring′ki trē), *n.* trinkets collectively. [1800–10; TRINKET + -RY]

trin•oc•u•lar (trī nok′yə lər), *adj. Micros.* of or pertaining to a binocular microscope equipped with a third lens system for photographic recording. [1955–60; TRI- + (BI)NOCULAR]

tri•nod•al (trī nōd′l), *adj. Bot.* having three nodes or joints. [1650–60; < L *trinōd(is)* having three knots (*tri-* TRI- + *nōd(us)* NODE + *-is* adj. suffix) + -AL[1]]

tri•no•mi•al (trī nō′mē əl), *adj.* **1.** *Algebra.* consisting of or pertaining to three terms. **2.** *Biol.* **a.** pertaining to a scientific name comprising three terms, as of genus, species, and subspecies or variety. **b.** characterized by the use of such names. —*n.* **3.** *Algebra.* an expression that is a sum or difference of three terms, as $3x + 2y + z$ or $3x^3 + 2x^2 + x$. **4.** *Biol.* a trinomial name, as *Rosa gallica pumila.* [1665–75; TRI- + (BI)NOMIAL] —**tri•no′•mi•al•ly,** *adv.*

tri•nu•cle•o•tide (trī nōō′klē ə tīd′, -nyōō′-), *n. Genetics.* three linked nucleotides; triplet. [1915–20; TRI- + NUCLEOTIDE]

tri•o (trē′ō), *n., pl.* **tri•os. 1.** a musical composition for three voices or instruments. **2.** a company of three singers or players. **3.** any group of three persons or things. **4.** a subordinate division of a minuet, scherzo, march, etc., usually in a contrasted key and style (perhaps originally written for three instruments or in three parts). [1715–25; < It, equiv. to *tri-* TRI- + *(du)o* TWO]

tri•ode (trī′ōd), *n. Electronics.* a vacuum tube containing three elements, usually anode, cathode, and control grid. [1920–25; TRI- + (ELECTR)ODE]

tri•oe•cious (trī ē′shəs), *adj. Bot.* of or pertaining to a species having male, female, and hermaphrodite flowers on different plants. Also, **triecious.** [1855–60; < NL *Trioeci(a)* former order name (Gk *tri-* TRI- + *oikía,* pl. of *oíkion* house, equiv. to *oîk(os)* house + *-ion* dim. suffix) + -OUS] —**tri•oe′cious•ly,** *adv.*

tri•ol (trī′ôl, -ol), *n. Chem.* a compound having three hydroxyl groups. [1935–40; TRI- + -OL[1]]

tri•o•le•in (trī ō′lē in), *n. Chem.* olein (def. 1). [1850–55; TRI- + OLEIN]

tri•o•let (trē′ə lā′, trī′ə lit), *n.* a short poem of fixed form, having a rhyme scheme of *ab, aa, abab,* and having the first line repeated as the fourth and seventh lines, and the second line repeated as the eighth. [1645–55; < F: lit., little trio]

tri•ose (trī′ōs), *n.* a monosaccharide that has three atoms of carbon. [1890–95; TRI- + -OSE[2]]

tri•ox•ide (trī ok′sīd, -sid), *n. Chem.* an oxide containing three oxygen atoms, as As_2O_3. [1865–70; TRI- + OXIDE]

trip[1] (trip), *n., v.,* **tripped, trip•ping.** —*n.* **1.** a journey or voyage: *to win a trip to Paris.* **2.** a journey, voyage, or run made by a boat, train, bus, or the like, between two points: *It's a short trip from Baltimore to Philadelphia.* **3.** See **round trip** (defs. 1, 2). **4.** a single journey or course of travel taken as part of one's duty, work, etc.: *his daily trip to the bank.* **5.** a stumble; misstep. **6.** a sudden impeding or catching of a person's foot so as to throw the person down, esp. in wrestling. **7.** a slip, mistake, error, or blunder. **8.** an error or lapse in conduct or etiquette. **9.** a light, nimble step or movement of the feet. **10.** *Mach.* **a.** a projecting object mounted on a moving part for striking a control lever to stop, reverse, or otherwise control the actions of some machine, as a milling machine or printing press. **b.** a sudden release or start. **11.** a catch of fish taken by a fishing vessel in a single voyage. **12.** *Slang.* **a.** an instance or period of being under the influence of a hallucinogenic drug, esp. LSD. **b.** the euphoria, illusions, etc., experienced during such a period. **c.** any stimulating or exciting experience: *The class reunion was a real trip.* **d.** any intense interest or preoccupation: *She's been on a nostalgia trip all week.* **e.** a period of time, experience, or lifestyle: *Those early years in college were a bad trip.* **13. lay a trip on,** *Slang.* to inflict one's preoccupations or obsessions on (another person): *Mother's been trying to lay a guilt trip on me about leaving home.* —*v.i.* **14.** to stumble: *to trip over a child's toy.* **15.** to make a slip, error, or mistake, as in conversation or conduct. **16.** to step lightly or nimbly; skip; dance. **17.** to go with a light, quick step or tread: *She tripped gaily across the room.* **18.** to make a journey or excursion. **19.** to tip or tilt. **20.** *Horol.* (of a tooth on an escape wheel) to slide past the face of the pallet by which it is supposed to be locked and strike the pallet in such a way as to move the balance or pendulum improperly. **21.** *Slang.* to be under the influence of a hallucinogenic drug, esp. LSD (often fol. by *out*): *He tripped out on peyote.* —*v.t.* **22.** to cause to stumble (often fol. by *up*): *The rug tripped him up.* **23.** to cause to fail; hinder, obstruct, or overthrow. **24.** to cause to make a slip or error (often fol. by *up*): *to trip up a witness by skillful questioning.* **25.** to catch in a slip or error. **26.** to tip or tilt. **27.** *Naut.* **a.** to break out (an anchor) by turning over or lifting from the bottom by a line (**tripping line**) attached to the anchor's crown. **b.** to tip or turn (a yard) from a horizontal to a vertical position. **c.** to lift (an upper mast) before lowering. **28.** to operate, start, or set free (a mechanism, weight, etc.) by suddenly releasing a catch, clutch, or the like. **29.** *Mach.* to release or operate suddenly (a catch, clutch, etc.). **30.** wedge (def. 17). **31.** to tread or dance lightly upon (the ground, floor, etc.). **32.** *Archaic.* to perform with a light or tripping step, as a dance. **33. trip the light fantastic,** *Facetious.* to go dancing. [1350–1400; 1960–65 for def. 12; ME *trippen* to step lightly < OF *trip(p)er* < MD; cf. early D *trippen,* D *trippelen* (freq. with *-el*), akin to OE *treppan* to tread]

—**Syn. 1.** excursion, tour, jaunt, junket. TRIP, EXPEDITION, JOURNEY, PILGRIMAGE, VOYAGE are terms for a course of travel made to a particular place, usually for some specific purpose. TRIP is the general word, indicating going any distance and returning, by walking or any means of locomotion, for either business or pleasure, and in either a hurried or a leisurely manner: *a trip to Europe; a vacation trip; a bus trip.* An EXPEDITION, made often by an organized company, is designed to accomplish a specific purpose: *an archaeological expedition.* JOURNEY indicates a trip of considerable length, wholly or mainly by land, for business or pleasure or other reasons, and is now applied to travel that is more leisurely or more fatiguing than a trip; a return is not necessarily indicated: *the long journey to Tibet.* A PILGRIMAGE is made as to a shrine, from motives of piety or veneration: *a pilgrimage to Lourdes.* A VOYAGE is travel by water or air, usually for a long distance and for business or pleasure; if by water, leisure is indicated: *a voyage around the world.* **7.** lapse, oversight. **15.** bungle, blunder, err.

trip[2] (trip), *n. Brit. Dial.* a group of animals, as sheep, goats, or fowl; flock. [1275–1325; ME; appar. special use of TRIP[1] in the sense of a group moving together, hence gang, flock]

tri•pal•mi•tin (trī pal′mi tin, -päl′-, -pä′mi-), *n. Chem.* palmitin. [1850–55; TRI- + PALMITIN]

tri•part•ed (trī pär′tid), *adj.* divided into three parts. Also, **tri′part′.** [1375–1425; late ME: alter. of TRIPARTITE; see -ED[2]]

tri•par•tite (trī pär′tīt), *adj.* **1.** divided into or consisting of three parts: *the tripartite occupation of West Germany.* **2.** involving, participated in, or made by three parties: *a tripartite treaty signed by Argentina, Brazil, and Chile.* **3.** *Bot.* divided into three parts. [1375–1425; late ME < L *tripartītus* divided into three parts, equiv. to *tri-* TRI- + *partītus,* ptp. of *partīre* to divide. See PART, -ITE[2]]

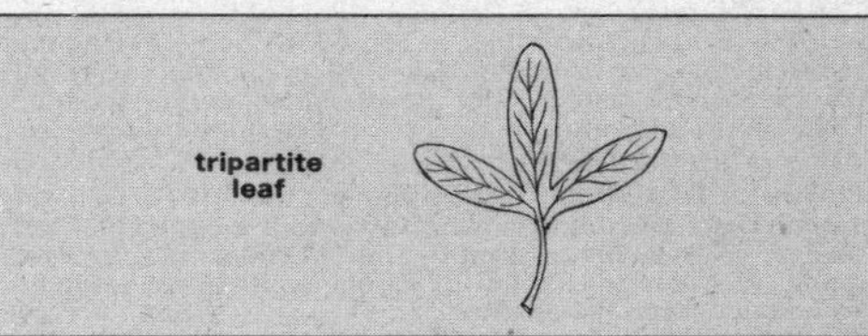

tripar′tite and fret′ty, *Heraldry.* (of a cross) having the limbs divided into three longitudinal strips each, intermingled in the manner of those in a cross parted and fretty.

tri•par•ti•tion (trī′pär tish′ən, -pər-), *n.* division into three parts. [1645–55; TRI- + PARTITION]

tripe (trīp), *n.* **1.** the first and second divisions of the stomach of a ruminant, esp. oxen, sheep, or goats, used as food. Cf. **honeycomb tripe, plain tripe. 2.** *Slang.* something, esp. speech or writing, that is false or worthless; rubbish. [1250–1300; 1885–90 for def. 2; ME < OF < ?]

tri•ped•al (trī′ped′l, trip′i dl), *adj.* having three feet. [1615–25; < L *tripedālis.* See TRI-, PEDAL]

tripe-de-roche (trēp′də rôsh′, -rōsh′), *n.* See **rock tripe.** [1800–10; < F: rock tripe]

tri•pel•en•na•mine (trī′pe len′ə mēn′, -min), *n. Pharm.* a white, crystalline, antihistamine, $C_{16}H_{21}N_3$, used for the treatment of allergic disorders. [TRI- + P(YRIDINE) + E(THY)LENE + (DI)AMINE]

tri•per•son•al (trī pûr′sə nl), *adj.* (*sometimes cap.*) consisting of or existing in three persons, as the Godhead. [1635–45; TRI- + PERSONAL]

tri•per•son•al•i•ty (trī′pûr sə nal′i tē), *n.* (*sometimes cap.*) the state or condition of being tripersonal; existence in three persons, as the Godhead. [1665–75; TRIPERSONAL + -ITY]

tri•pet•al•ous (trī pet′l əs), *adj. Bot.* having three petals. [1680–90; TRI- + PETALOUS]

trip•ham•mer (trip′ham′ər), *n.* **1.** *Mach.* a heavy hammer raised and then let fall by means of some tripping device, as a cam. —*adj.* **2.** of, resembling, or characteristic of the repetitive and forceful pounding of a triphammer: *He was subjected to triphammer interrogation by the police detectives.* Also, **trip′ ham′mer.** [1775–85, *Amer.;* TRIP[1] + HAMMER]

tri•pha•sic (trī fā′zik), *adj.* **1.** having or existing in three phases. —*n.* **2.** a combination drug given in three phases and eliciting three physiological effects. [1900–05; TRI- + PHASE + -IC]

tri•phen•yl•meth•ane (trī fen′l meth′ān, -fēn′-), *n. Chem.* a colorless, crystalline, solid compound containing three benzene rings, $C_{19}H_{16}$, from which many dyes are derived. [1880–85; TRI- + PHENYL + METHANE]

triphen′ylmeth′ane dye′, *Chem.* any of a great number of dyes, as gentian violet, fuchsin, and rosaniline, produced from triphenylmethane by replacement of the ring hydrogen atoms with hydroxy, amino, sulfo, or other atoms or groups. [1930–35]

tri•phib•i•an (trī fib′ē ən), *Mil.* —*adj.* **1.** skilled in combat equally on land, sea, and in the air. **2.** (of an aircraft) equipped to take off from land, water, snow, or ice. **3.** triphibious. —*n.* **4.** a person who is triphibian. **5.** a triphibian airplane. [1940–45; TRI- + (AM)PHIBIAN]

tri•phib•i•ous (trī fib′ē əs), *adj.* employing or involving land, naval, and air forces in a combined operation. Also, **triphibian.** [1940–45; TRI- + (AM)PHIBIOUS]

tri•phos•phate (trī fos′fāt), *n. Chem.* a salt derived from triphosphoric acid. [1820–30; TRI- + PHOSPHATE]

tri′phos•phor′ic ac′id (trī′fos fôr′ik, -for′-, trī′-), *Chem.* the hypothetical acid $H_5P_3O_{10}$, known chiefly by its salts. [TRI- + PHOSPHORIC ACID]

triph•thong (trif′thông, -thong, trip′-), *n.* **1.** *Phonet.* a monosyllabic speech-sound sequence perceived as being made up of three differing vowel qualities, as the pronunciation of *our,* esp. in r-dropping dialects. **2.** (not in technical use) a trigraph. [1590–1600; < NL *triphthongus* < MGk *tríphthongos* with three vowels,

CONCISE PRONUNCIATION KEY: act, cāpe, dâre, pärt; set, ēqual; if, īce; ox, ōver, ôrder, oil, bŏŏk, bōōt, out; up, ûrge; child; sing; shoe; thin, *th*at; zh as in *treasure.* ə = a as in *alone,* e as in *system,* i as in *easily,* o as in *gallop,* u as in *circus;* ə as in *fire* (fīər), *hour* (ouər). l and n can serve as syllabic consonants, as in *cradle* (krād′l), and *button* (but′n). See the full key inside the front cover.

equiv. to *tri-* TRI- + *phthóngos* voice, sound] —**triph·thong·al** (trif thông′gəl, -thong′-, trip-), *adj.*

triph·y·lite (trif′ə līt′), *n.* a mineral, a rare phosphate of lithium, iron, and manganese, usually occurring in masses of a bluish or greenish color. Also called **triph·y·line** (trif′ə lēn′, -lin). [1830–40; TRI- + Gk *phŷl(ē)* tribe, PHYLE + -ITE[1]; r. *triphyline* < G *Triphylin*]

tri·phyl·lous (trī fil′əs), *adj. Bot.* having three leaves. [1750–60; TRI- + -PHYLLOUS]

tri·pin·nate (trī pin′āt), *adj. Bot.* bipinnate, as a leaf, with the divisions also pinnate. Also, **tri·pin′nat·ed.** [1750–60; TRI- + PINNATE] —**tri·pin′nate·ly,** *adv.*

Tri·pit·a·ka (tri pit′ə kə), *n. Buddhism.* See **Pali Canon.** [< Skt, equiv. to *tri-* TRI- + *piṭaka* basket]

tri·plane (trī′plān′), an airplane with three supporting wings, one above another: a design used mainly in the early history of the airplane. [1905–10; TRI- + PLANE[1]]

tri·ple (trip′əl), *adj., n., v.,* **-pled, -pling.** —*adj.* **1.** threefold; consisting of three parts: *a triple knot.* **2.** of three kinds; threefold in character or relationship. **3.** three times as great. **4.** *Internat. Law.* tripartite. —*n.* **5.** an amount, number, etc., three times as great as another. **6.** a group, set, or series of three; triad. **7.** Also called **three-base hit.** *Baseball.* a base hit that enables a batter to reach third base safely. **8.** *Bowling.* three strikes in succession. **9.** trifecta. —*v.t.* **10.** to make triple. **11.** *Baseball.* to cause to come into home plate by a triple: *to triple a runner home; to triple a run in.* —*v.i.* **12.** to become triple. **13.** *Baseball.* to make a triple. [1325–75; ME (n. and v.) < L *triplus* (adj.), equiv. to *tri-* TRI- + *(du)plus* DUPLE]

Tri′ple Alli′ance, 1. the alliance (1882–1915) of Germany, Austria-Hungary, and Italy. **2.** a league (1717) of France, Great Britain, and the Netherlands against Spain. **3.** a league (1668) of England, Sweden, and the Netherlands against France.

tri′ple bo′gey, *Golf.* a score of three strokes over par on a hole.

tri′ple bond′, *Chem.* a chemical linkage consisting of three covalent bonds between two atoms of a molecule, represented in chemical formulas by three lines or six dots, as CH≡CH or CH⋮⋮CH.

tri′ple coun′terpoint, *Music.* invertible counterpoint involving three transposable voices. [1865–70]

tri′ple cream′, a fresh, soft cheese of France, containing at least 72 percent fat, made from cow's milk enriched with cream. Also, **tri′ple crème′.**

tri·ple-deck·er (trip′əl dek′ər), *n.* three-decker (defs. 3, 4). [1945–50]

tri·ple-dig·it (trip′əl dij′it), *adj.* being in the hundreds or in a figure or amount from 100 through 999: *triple-digit budget figures.* [1975–80]

tri·ple-dou·ble (trip′əl dub′əl), *n.* a score in a basketball game of at least ten points, ten rebounds, and ten assists by a single player.

tri′ple dress′er, *Furniture.* a dresser having three drawers across for most of its height.

Tri′ple Entente′, 1. an informal understanding among Great Britain, France, and Russia based on a Franco-Russian military alliance (1894), an Anglo-French entente (1904), and an Anglo-Russian entente (1907). It was considered a counterbalance to the Triple Alliance but was terminated when the Bolsheviks came into control in Russia in 1917. **2.** the member nations of this entente.

tri·ple-ex·pan·sion (trip′əl ik span′shən), *adj.* noting a power source, esp. a steam engine, using the same fluid at three successive stages of expansion to do work in three or more cylinders.

tri′ple fugue′, *Music.* **1.** a fugue with a subject and two countersubjects developed simultaneously. **2.** a fugue with three subjects that are developed at first successively and finally together. [1875–80]

tri·ple-head·er (trip′əl hed′ər), *n. Sports.* a set of three games, as of basketball, each game being played in the same arena on the same day and often between different pairs of teams. [1945–50]

tri′ple in′tegral, *Math.* an integral in which the integrand involves a function of three variables and which requires three applications of the integration process to evaluate. Cf. **double integral.**

tri′ple jump′, *Track and Field.* a jumping event for distance in which a participant leaps on one foot from a takeoff point, lands on the same foot, steps forward on the other foot, leaps, and lands on both feet. Also called **hop, step, and jump.** [1960–65]

tri′ple meas′ure, *Music.* See **triple time.**

tri·ple-nerved (trip′əl nûrvd′), *adj. Bot.* noting a leaf in which two prominent nerves emerge from the middle nerve a little above its base. [1805–15]

tri′ple play′, *Baseball.* a play in which three putouts are made. [1865–70, *Amer.*]

tri′ple point′, *Physics.* the particular temperature and pressure at which the solid, liquid, and gaseous phases of a given substance are all at equilibrium with one another. [1870–75]

tri′ple rhyme′. See under **feminine rhyme.**

tri′ple rhythm′, *Pros.* a rhythmic pattern created by a succession of trisyllabic feet. [1720–30]

tri′ple sca′lar prod′uct, *Math.* See **scalar triple product.**

tri′ple sec′, a type of curaçao liqueur.

tri·ple-space (trip′əl spās′), *v.t., v.i.,* **-spaced, -spac·ing.** to type (text, copy, etc.) so as to have two blank lines after each typed line. [1935–40]

tri′ple superphos′phate, superphosphate (def. 2).

tri·plet (trip′lit), *n.* **1.** one of three children or offspring born at the same birth. **2. triplets,** three offspring born at one birth. **3.** any group or combination of three. **4.** *Pros.* three successive verses or lines, esp. when rhyming and of the same length; a stanza of three lines. **5.** Also called **tercet.** *Music.* a group of three notes to be performed in the time of two ordinary notes of the same kind. **6.** an assembled imitation gem with three parts, the center one giving the color, the top and bottom, sometimes genuine, supplying the wearing qualities. **7.** *Genetics.* a sequence of three nucleotides; a codon in messenger RNA and an anticodon in transfer RNA. **8.** *Optics.* a compound lens in which three lenses are combined. **9. triplets,** (in some card games) three cards of the same denomination. [TRIPLE + -ET]

tri·ple·tail (trip′əl tāl′), *n.* **1.** a large food fish, *Lobotes surinamensis,* inhabiting the warmer waters of the Atlantic Ocean and the Mediterranean Sea, having the lobes of its dorsal and anal fins extending backward and, with the caudal fin, suggesting a three-lobed tail. **2.** any similar fishes of the genus *Lobotes,* of the Pacific and Indian oceans. [1795–1805; TRIPLE + TAIL[1]]

tri′ple threat′, 1. an expert in three different fields or in three different skills in the same field. **2.** *Football.* a back who is proficient at running, passing, and punting: *The triple threat is a rare find for coaches.*

tri′ple time′, *Music.* time or rhythm characterized by three beats to the measure with an accent on the first beat. Also called **triple measure, triplex.** [1655–65]

tri·ple·ton (trip′əl tən), *n.* (esp. in bridge) a set of three cards of the same suit in a hand as dealt. [TRIPLE + -TON. See DOUBLETON, SINGLETON]

tri·ple-tongue (trip′əl tung′), *v.i.,* **-tongued, -tongu·ing.** *Music.* to interrupt the wind flow by moving the tongue as if pronouncing *t* and *t* and *k* successively, esp. in playing rapid passages or staccato notes on a brass instrument. Cf. **double-tongue.** [1900–05]

tri′ple voile′, a lightweight, sheer voile of silk or synthetic fibers constructed in plain or novelty weaves. Cf. **ninon.**

tri′ple witch′ing hour′, the last hour of trading on the New York Stock Exchange on the four Fridays each year when stock options, stock index futures, and options on such futures simultaneously expire: regarded as a time of extreme volatility in trading. [1985–90]

tri·plex (trip′leks, trī′pleks), *adj.* **1.** threefold; triple. —*n.* **2.** something triple. **3.** *Music.* See **triple time. 4.** an apartment having three floors. **5.** a multiplex of three theaters or movie houses. [1595–1605; < L *triplex* (s. *triplic-*) threefold, equiv. to *tri-* TRI- + *-plex* -PLEX]

trip·li·cate (*n., adj.* trip′li kit, -kāt′; *v.* trip′li kāt′), *n., v.,* **-cat·ed, -cat·ing,** *adj.* —*n.* **1.** one of three identical items, esp. copies of typewritten material. **2. in triplicate, a.** in three identical copies: *This letter should be done in triplicate.* **b.** threefold: *That goes for me, too, in triplicate.* —*v.t.* **3.** to make threefold; triple. **4.** to make in triplicate. —*adj.* **5.** produced in or consisting of three copies or parts; threefold; triple: *triplicate contracts.* [1400–50; late ME (adj.) < L *triplicātus* (ptp. of *triplicāre* to triple), equiv. to *triplic-* (s. of *triplex*) TRIPLEX + *-ātus* -ATE[1]] —**trip′li·ca′tion,** *n.*

tri·plic·i·ty (tri plis′i tē), *n., pl.* **-ties. 1.** the quality or state of being triple; threefold character or condition. **2.** a group or combination of three; triad. **3.** *Astrol.* the division of the signs of the zodiac into four groups of three signs each, the fire signs, the earth signs, the air signs, and the water signs, with each sign separated from others within the group by 120 degrees of the ecliptic. Cf. **element** (def. 12). [1350–1400; ME *triplicite* < LL *triplicitās* threefold state. See TRIPLEX, -ITY]

trip′ line′, 1. (in lumbering) a line for freeing a dog hook from a log at a distance. **2.** haulback. [1900–05]

trip·lite (trip′līt), *n.* a dark-brown, massive mineral, fluorophosphate of iron and manganese. [1840–50; < G *Triplit.* See TRIPLE, -ITE[1]]

trip·lo·blas·tic (trip′lō blas′tik), *adj. Zool.* having three primary germ layers, as the embryos of vertebrates. [1885–90; < Gk *tripló(os)* threefold + *blastikós* budding. See TRI-, -FOLD, -BLAST, -IC]

trip·loid (trip′loid), *Biol.* —*adj.* **1.** having a chromosome number that is three times the basic or haploid number. —*n.* **2.** a triploid cell or organism. [1910–15; TRI- + -PLOID] —**trip′loi·dy,** *n.*

trip·ly (trip′lē), *adv.* **1.** to a triple number, measure, or degree. **2.** in a triple manner; threefold. [1650–60; TRIPLE + -LY]

trip·me·ter (trip′mē′tər), *n. Auto.* a type of odometer that can be set back to zero so that the distance of a particular trip can be measured. [TRIP[1] + -METER]

tri·pod (trī′pod), *n.* **1.** a stool, table, pedestal, etc., with three legs. **2.** a three-legged stand or support, as for a camera or telescope. **3.** the oracular seat of the priestess of Apollo at Delphi. [1595–1605; < L *tripod-* (s. of *tripūs*) < Gk *tripod-* (s. of *trípous*) orig., three-footed. See TRI-, -POD]

trip·o·dal (trip′ə dl, trī′pod l), *adj.* **1.** pertaining to or having the form of a tripod. **2.** having three feet or legs. [1635–45; TRIPOD + -AL[1]]

tri·pod·ic (trī pod′ik), *adj.* having or using three feet or legs. [1890–95; TRIPOD + -IC]

trip·o·dy (trip′ə dē), *n., pl.* **-dies.** *Pros.* a measure of three feet. [1880–85; < Gk *tripodía.* See TRI-, -POD, -Y[3]]

Trip·o·li (trip′ə lē), *n.* **1.** Also, **Trip·o·li·ta·ni·a** (trip′ə li tā′nē ə, -tān′yə; *It.* trē′pô lē tä′nyä). one of the former Barbary States of N Africa: later a province of Turkey; now a part of Libya. **2.** a seaport in and the capital of Libya, in the NW part. 551,477. **3.** a seaport in N Lebanon, on the Mediterranean. 175,000. **4.** (*l.c.*) any of several siliceous substances, as rottenstone, used in polishing. —**Tri·pol·i·tan** (tri pol′i tn), *n., adj.*

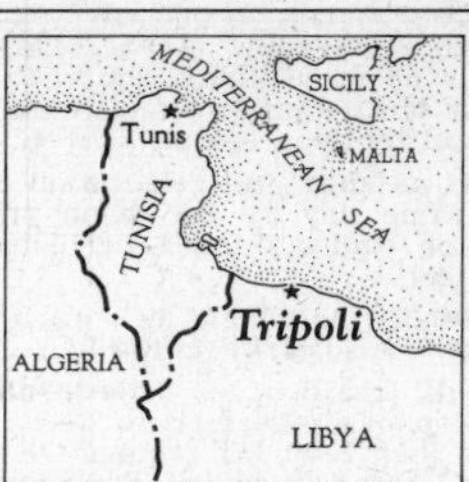

Tripol′itan War′, a war (1801–05) that Tripoli declared on the United States because of American refusal to pay tribute for the safe passage of shipping in Barbary Coastal waters. Cf. **Barbary Coast Wars.**

tri·pos (trī′pos), *n., pl.* **-pos·es.** (at Cambridge University, England) any of various final honors examinations. [1580–90; pseudo-Hellenization of L *tripūs* TRIPOD]

tri·po·tas′si·um phos′phate (trī′pə tas′ē əm), *Chem.* See under **potassium phosphate.** Also called **tripotas′sium orthophos′phate.** [TRI- + POTASSIUM]

trip·pant (trip′ənt), *adj. Heraldry.* (of a deer or the like) represented in the act of walking: *a stag trippant.* [1650–60; alter. of TRIPPING; see -ANT]

trip·per (trip′ər), *n.* **1.** a person or thing that trips. **2.** *Mach.* **a.** a tripping mechanism; a trip. **b.** an apparatus causing a signal or other operating device to be tripped or actuated. **3.** *Brit. Informal.* a person who goes on a pleasure trip or excursion; excursionist. **4.** *Slang.* a person who is under the influence of a hallucinogenic drug, esp. LSD. [1350–1400; ME; see TRIP[1], -ER[1]]

trip·pet (trip′it), *n. Mach.* a projection, cam, or the like, for striking some other part at regular intervals. [1300–50; ME *trypet.* See TRIP[1], -ET]

trip·ping (trip′ing), *adj.* **1.** light and quick, as a step or pace. **2.** proceeding with a light, easy movement or rhythm. [1555–65; TRIP[1] + -ING[2]] —**trip′ping·ly,** *adv.*

trip′ping line′, *Naut.* See under **trip**[1] (def. 27a).

trip·tane (trip′tān), *n. Chem.* a colorless liquid, C_7H_{17}, having high antiknock properties as a fuel: used chiefly as an admixture to airplane gasolines. [1940–45; *tri(methyl) b(u)tane* (with *p* for *b* before *t*).]

trip·ter·al (trip′tər əl), *adj.* (of a classical building) having a triple pteron. [< Gk *trípter(os)* having three wings (see TRIPTEROUS) + -AL[1]]

trip·ter·ous (trip′tər əs), *adj. Bot.* three-winged; having three wings or winglike expansions. [1865–70; < Gk *tripteros;* see TRI-, -PTEROUS]

Trip·tol·e·mus (trip tol′ə məs), *n. Class. Myth.* a favorite of Demeter and the inventor of the plow and patron of agriculture, connected with the Eleusinian mysteries. Also, **Trip·tol′e·mos.**

trip·tych (trip′tik), *n.* **1.** *Fine Arts.* a set of three panels or compartments side by side, bearing pictures, carvings, or the like. **2.** a hinged, three-leaved tablet, written on, in ancient times, with a stylus. [1725–35; < Gk *tríptychos* of three plates, equiv. to *tri-* TRI- + *ptych-* (s. of *ptýx*) plate + *-os* adj. suffix]

Trip·u·ra (trip′ər ə), *n.* a state in E India. 1,760,000; 4033 sq. mi. (10,445 sq. km). *Cap.:* Agartala.

trip·wire (trip′wīᵊr′), *n.* **1.** a wire used to set off concealed explosives, as one stretched across a footpath to be struck and activated by the foot of an enemy soldier. **2.** a wire that activates a trap, camera, or other device when stepped on, tripped on, or otherwise disturbed. [TRIP[1] + WIRE]

tri·que·tra (trī kwē′trə, -kwe′-), *n.* a geometrical figure having three points, esp. one formed of three intersecting ellipses: *The triquetra was often used in ancient art to symbolize a triune deity.* [1580–90; < NL, n. use of fem. of L *triquetrus* TRIQUETROUS] —**tri·quet·ric** (trī kwe′trik), *adj.*

tri·que·trous (trī kwē′trəs, -kwe′-), *adj.* **1.** three-sided; triangular. **2.** having a triangular cross section. [1650–60; < L *triquetrus* triangular, equiv. to *tri-* TRI- + *-quetrus* cornered]

tri·ra·di·ate (trī rā′dē it, -āt′), *adj.* having three rays or raylike processes. Also, **tri·ra′di·at′ed.** [1840–50; TRI- + RADIATE (adj.)] —**tri·ra′di·ate·ly,** *adv.*

tri·ra·di·us (trī rā′dē əs), *n., pl.* **-di·i** (-dē ī′), **-di·us·es.** *Physical Anthropol.* a Y-shaped group of ridges on the palm of the hand at the base of each finger. [TRI- + RADIUS]

Tri·rat·na (trē rut′nə), *n.* (*used with a plural v.*) *Buddhism.* the three components of Buddhism, which are the Buddha, or teacher, the dharma, or teaching, and the Sangha, or priesthood. [< Skt: three jewels, equiv. to *tri* THREE + *ratna* jewel]

tri·reme (trī′rēm), *n. Class. Hist.* a galley with three rows or tiers of oars on each side, one above another, used chiefly as a warship. [1595–1605; < L *trirēmis* having three banks of oars, equiv. to *tri-* TRI- + *rēm(us)* oar + *-is* adj. suffix]

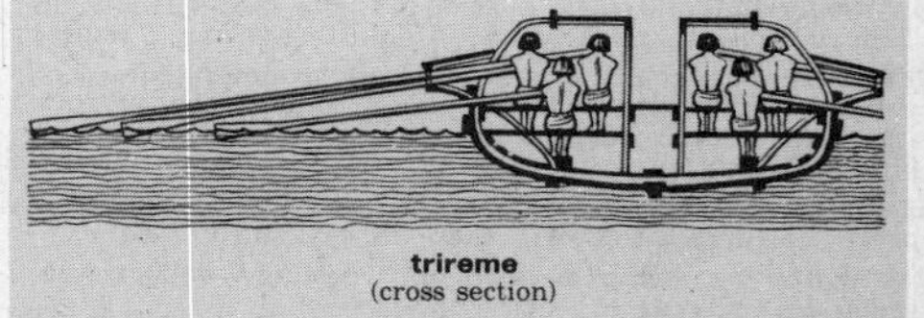

trireme
(cross section)

CONCISE ETYMOLOGY KEY: <, descended or borrowed from; >, whence; b., blend of, blended; c., cognate with; cf., compare; deriv., derivative; equiv., equivalent; imit., imitative; obl., oblique; r., replacing; s., stem; sp., spelling, spelled; resp., respelling, respelled; trans., translation; ?, origin unknown; *, unattested; ‡, probably earlier than. See the full key inside the front cover.

tri·sac·cha·ride (trī sak′ə rīd′, -ər id), *n. Chem.* a carbohydrate composed of three monosaccharide units, and hydrolyzable to a monosaccharide or a mixture of monosaccharides. [1895–1900; TRI- + SACCHARIDE]

tri·sect (trī sekt′, trī′sekt), *v.t.* to divide into three parts, esp. into three equal parts. [1685–95; TRI- + *-sect* < L *sectus,* ptp. of *secāre* to cut, sever; see SECTION] **—tri·sec′tion,** *n.* **—tri·sec′tor,** *n.*

tri·sep·al·ous (trī sep′ə ləs), *adj. Bot.* having three sepals. [1820–30; TRI- + SEPALOUS]

tri·sep·tate (trī sep′tāt), *adj. Bot., Zool.* having three septa. [1870–75; TRI- + SEPTATE]

tri·se·ri·al (trī sēr′ē əl), *adj.* **1.** arranged in three series or rows. **2.** *Bot.* having only three verticils. [1855–60; TRI- + SERIAL]

tri·shaw (trī′shô′), *n.* pedicab. [1944–50; TRI- + (RICK)SHAW]

tris·kai·dek·a·pho·bi·a (tris′kī dek′ə fō′bē ə, tris′-kə-), *n.* fear or a phobia concerning the number 13. [1910–15; < Gk *triskaídeka* thirteen + -PHOBIA] **—tris′·kai·dek′a·pho′bic,** *adj.*

tris·kel·i·on (tri skel′ē on′, -ən, trī-), *n., pl.* **tris·kel·i·a** (tri skel′ē ə, trī-). a symbolic figure consisting of three legs, arms, or branches radiating from a common center, as the device of Sicily and the Isle of Man. Also, **tris·kele** (tris′kēl, trī′skēl). [1855–60; < Gk *triskel(és)* three-legged (*tri-* TRI- + *skél(os)* leg + *-ēs* adj. suffix) + *-ion* dim. suffix]

triskelion

Tris·me·gis·tus (triz′mə jis′təs, tris′-), *n.* See **Hermes Trismegistus.**

tris·mus (triz′məs, tris′-), *n., pl.* **-mus·es.** *Pathol.* **1.** a spasm of the jaw muscles that makes it difficult to open the mouth. **2.** lockjaw. [1685–95; < NL < Gk *trismós* a grinding] **—tris′mic,** *adj.*

tris·oc·ta·he·dron (tris ok′tə hē′drən), *n., pl.* **-drons, -dra** (-drə). a solid bounded by 24 identical faces in groups of three, each group corresponding to one face of an octahedron. [1840–50; < Gk *trís* thrice + OCTOHEDRON] **—tris·oc′ta·he′dral,** *adj.*

tri·so·di·um (trī sō′dē əm), *adj. Chem.* pertaining to molecules containing three sodium atoms. [TRI- + SODIUM]

triso′dium phos′phate, *Chem.* See **sodium phosphate** (def. 3). [1920–25]

tri·some (trī′sōm), *n. Genetics.* a trisomic individual. [TRI- + -SOME[3]]

tri·so·mic (trī sō′mik), *adj. Genetics.* having one chromosome in addition to the usual diploid number. [TRISOME + -IC]

tri·so·my (trī′sō mē), *n. Pathol.* an abnormality characterized by the presence of an additional chromosome to the normal diploid number. [1925–30; TRI- + -SOME[3] + -Y[3]]

trisomy 21. See **Down syndrome.**

tri·spast (trī′spast), *n.* an ancient hoist or hauling device having three blocks. [1700–10; < L *trispastos* having a triple pulley < Gk *tríspastos,* equiv. to *tri-* TRI- + *spas-,* s. of *spân* to draw, pull + *-tos* verbid suffix]

tri·sper·mous (trī spûr′məs), *adj. Bot.* having three seeds. [1750–60; TRI- + -SPERMOUS]

Tris·tan (tris′tən, -tan; *Ger.* tris′tän), *n.* a male given name, form of **Tristram.** Also, **Tris·tam** (tris′təm, -tam).

Tris·tan da Cu·nha (tris′tən də ko͞o′nə, ko͞on′yə), a group of four volcanic islands in the S Atlantic, belonging to St. Helena. 40 sq. mi. (104 sq. km).

Tris·tan und I·sol·de (tris′tən ənd i sōld′, i sōl′də, -tan; *Ger.* tris′tän o͝ont ē zôl′də), a music drama (composed, 1857–59; première, 1865) by Richard Wagner.

tri·state (trī′stāt′), *adj.* **1.** pertaining to a territory made up of three adjoining states: *a tristate league.* **2.** pertaining to the three adjoining parts of such states: *the tristate region of Missouri, Kansas, and Nebraska.* Also, **tri′-state′.** [TRI- + STATE]

triste (trēst), *adj. French.* sad; sorrowful; melancholy.

tri·ste·za (tri stā′zə), *n. Plant Pathol.* a disease of certain citrus trees, characterized by yellowed leaves, wilting, and root destruction, caused by a virus. [1900–05; < AmerSp: lit., sadness < L *tristitia*]

trist·ful (trist′fəl), *adj.* full of sadness; sorrowful. [1485–95; obs. *trist* sad, gloomy (< OF *triste* < L *tristis*) + -FUL] **—trist′ful·ly,** *adv.* **—trist′ful·ness,** *n.*

tris·tich (tris′tik), *n. Pros.* a strophe, stanza, or poem consisting of three lines. [1805–15; TRI- + STICH[1]] **—tris·tich′ic,** *adj.*

tris·tich·ous (tris′ti kəs), *adj.* **1.** arranged in three rows. **2.** *Bot.* arranged in or characterized by three vertical rows. [1855–60; < Gk *trístichos* of three rows or verses. See TRI-, -STICHOUS]

Tris·tram (tris′trəm), *n.* **1.** one of the knights of the Round Table, whose love for Iseult, wife of King Mark, is the subject of many romances. **2.** a male given name.

Tris·tram Shan′dy (shan′dē), a novel (1759–67) by Laurence Sterne.

tri·sty·lous (trī stī′ləs), *adj. Bot.* having three styles. [1890–95; TRI- + -STYLE[1] + -OUS] **—tri′sty·ly,** *n.*

tri·sub·sti·tut·ed (trī sub′sti to͞o′tid, -tyo͞o′-), *adj. Chem.* pertaining to a molecule containing three substituents. [1895–1900; TRI- + SUBSTITUTE + -ED[2]]

tri·sul·fide (trī sul′fīd, -fid), *n. Chem.* a sulfide containing three sulfur atoms. [1865–70; TRI- + SULFIDE]

tri·syl·la·ble (trī′sil′ə bəl, trī sil′-, tri-), *n.* a word of three syllables, as *pendulum.* [1580–90; TRI- + SYLLABLE, modeled on Gk *trisýllabos* having three syllables] **—tri·syl·lab·ic** (trī′si lab′ik, tris′i-), **tri′syl·lab′i·cal,** *adj.* **—tri′syl·lab′i·cal·ly,** *adv.* **—tri·syl′lab·ism,** *n.*

trit., triturate.

tri·tag·o·nist (tri tag′ə nist), *n.* (in ancient Greece) the third member of an acting troupe, which always consisted of three actors. Cf. **protagonist** (def. 4), **deuteragonist.** [1885–90; < Gk *tritagōnistés,* equiv. to *trít(os)* THIRD + *agōnistés* actor, competitor, agent deriv. of *agōnízesthai* to contend, struggle, compete for the acting prize]

trit·an·o·pi·a (trīt′n ō′pē ə), *n. Ophthalm.* a defect of vision in which the retina fails to respond to blue and yellow. [< NL, equiv. to *trit-* (< Gk *trítos* THIRD) + *an-* AN-[1] + *-opia* -OPIA] **—trit·an·op·ic** (trīt′n op′ik), *adj.*

trite (trīt), *adj.,* **trit·er, trit·est. 1.** lacking in freshness or effectiveness because of constant use or excessive repetition; hackneyed; stale: *the trite phrases in his letter.* **2.** characterized by hackneyed expressions, ideas, etc.: *The commencement address was trite and endlessly long.* **3.** *Archaic.* rubbed or worn by use. [1540–50; < L *trītus* worn, common, equiv. to *trī-* (var. s. of *terere* to rub, wear down) + *-tus* ptp. suffix] **—trite′ly,** *adv.* **—trite′ness,** *n.*

—Syn. 1. ordinary. See **commonplace. —Ant. 1.** original.

tri·the·ism (trī′thē iz′əm), *n. Theol.* belief in three Gods, esp. in the doctrine that the three persons of the Trinity (Father, Son, and Holy Ghost) are three distinct Gods, each an independent center of consciousness and determination. [1670–80; TRI- + THEISM] **—tri′the·ist,** *n., adj.* **—tri′the·is′tic, tri′the·is′ti·cal,** *adj.*

tri·thing (trī′thing), *n.* riding[2]. [1250–1300; ME, var. of *thrithing* < Scand; see RIDING[2]]

trit·i·ca·le (trit′i kā′lē), *n.* a hybrid produced by crossing wheat, *Triticum aestivum,* and rye, *Secale cereale.* [1935–40; < NL *Triti(cum)* wheat + *(Se)cale* rye]

trit·i·um (trit′ē əm, trish′-, trish′əm), *n. Chem.* an isotope of hydrogen having an atomic weight of three. [1930–35; < NL < Gk *trít(os)* THIRD (*tri-* TRI- + *-tos* adj. suffix) + NL *-ium* -IUM]

trit·o·ma (trit′ə mə), *n.* any of various plants belonging to the genus *Kniphofia,* of the lily family, native to Africa, esp. *K. uvaria,* having long, dense clusters of tubular red or yellow flowers. Also called **poker plant, red-hot poker, torch lily.** [1880–85; < NL *Tritoma* alternate genus name < Gk *trítom(os)* thrice-cut (*tri-* TRI- + *-tomos* -TOMOUS) + NL *-a* -A[2]]

tri·ton (trī′ton), *n. Physics.* a positively-charged particle consisting of a proton and two neutrons, equivalent to the nucleus of an atom of tritium. Cf. **deuteron.** [1930–35; < Gk *tríton,* neut. of *trítos* THIRD, equiv. to *tri-* TRI- + *-ton* neut. adj. suffix; cf. -ON[1]]

Tri·ton (trīt′n), *n.* **1.** *Class. Myth.* a son of Poseidon and Amphitrite, represented as having the head and trunk of a man and the tail of a fish, and as using a conch-shell trumpet. **2.** *Astron.* a moon of Neptune. **3.** (*l.c.*) any of various marine gastropods of the family Cymatiidae, having a large, spiral, often beautifully colored shell. **4.** (*l.c.*) the shell of a triton. **—Tri·ton·ic** (trī ton′ik), *adj.*

tri·tone (trī′tōn′), *n. Music.* an interval consisting of three whole tones; an augmented fourth. [1600–10; < ML *tritonus* < Gk *trítonos* having three tones. See TRI-, TONE]

Tri·to·nis (trī tō′nis), *n.* (in ancient geography) a mythical lake near the Mediterranean coast of Libya.

trit·u·ra·ble (trich′ər ə bəl), *adj.* capable of being triturated. [1640–50; TRITUR(ATE) + -ABLE]

trit·u·rate (*v.* trich′ə rāt′; *n.* trich′ər it), *v.,* **-rat·ed, -rat·ing,** *n.* **—***v.t.* **1.** to reduce to fine particles or powder by rubbing, grinding, bruising, or the like; pulverize. **—***n.* **2.** a triturated substance. **3.** *Pharm.* trituration (def. 3). [1615–25; < LL *trītūrātus* (ptp. of *trītūrāre* to thresh), equiv. to L *trītūr(a)* a threshing (*trīt(us)* rubbed, crushed (see TRITE) + *-ūra* -URE) + *-ātus* -ATE[1]] **—trit′·u·ra′tor,** *n.*

trit·u·ra·tion (trich′ə rā′shən), *n.* **1.** the act of triturating. **2.** the state of being triturated. **3.** *Pharm.* **a.** a mixture of a medicinal substance with sugar of milk, triturated to an impalpable powder. **b.** any triturated substance. [1640–50; < LL *trītūrātiōn-* (s. of *trītūrātiō*), equiv. to *trītūrāt(us)* threshed (see TRITURATE) + *-ion* -ION]

tri·umph (trī′əmf, -umf), *n.* **1.** the act, fact, or condition of being victorious or triumphant; victory; conquest. **2.** a significant success or noteworthy achievement; instance or occasion of victory. **3.** exultation resulting from victory; joy over success. **4.** *Rom. Hist.* the ceremonial entrance into Rome of a victorious commander with his army, spoils of war, and captives, authorized by the senate in honor of an important military or naval victory. Cf. **ovation** (def. 2). **5.** a public pageant, spectacle, or the like. **—***v.i.* **6.** to gain a victory; be victorious; win. **7.** to gain mastery; prevail: *to triumph over fear.* **8.** to be successful; achieve success. **9.** to exult over victory; rejoice over success. **10.** to be elated or glad; rejoice proudly; glory. **11.** to celebrate a triumph, as a victorious Roman commander. **—***v.t.* **12.** to conquer; triumph over. [bef. 900; ME *triumphe* (n.), OE *triumpha* < L *triump(h)us,* perh. < Etruscan < Gk *thríambos* hymn to Dionysus] **—tri′umph·er,** *n.*

—Syn. 1. success. See **victory. 3.** jubilation, celebration. **6.** succeed. **—Ant. 1.** defeat, loss.

tri·um·phal (trī um′fəl), *adj.* **1.** of, pertaining to, celebrating, or commemorating a triumph or victory: *a triumphal banquet; a triumphal ode.* **2.** triumphant (def. 2). [1400–50; late ME < L *triumphālis.* See TRIUMPH, -AL[1]]

trium′phal arch′, 1. a monumental archway, often erected in permanent materials as a commemorative structure, straddling the line of march of a victorious army during a triumphal procession. **2.** an architectural motif resembling in its composition an ancient Roman triumphal arch, having one high central archway flanked by side elements composed of lower arches, compartments, bas-reliefs, etc., the whole usually adorned by a huge order. [1540–50]

tri·um·phal·ism (trī um′fə liz′əm), *n.* **1.** triumphant spirit or character. **2.** the attitude or practices of a church that seeks a position of power and dominance in the world. Cf. **servant church.** [1960–65; TRIUMPHAL + -ISM]

tri·um·phant (trī um′fənt), *adj.* **1.** having achieved victory or success; victorious; successful. **2.** exulting over victory; rejoicing over success; exultant. **3.** *Archaic.* triumphal (def. 1). **4.** *Obs.* splendid; magnificent. [1485–95; < L *triumphant-,* s. of *triumphāns,* prp. of *triumphāre* to triumph. See TRIUMPH, -ANT] **—tri·um′·phant·ly,** *adv.*

tri·um·vir (trī um′vər), *n., pl.* **-virs, -vi·ri** (-və rī′). **1.** *Rom. Hist.* one of three officers or magistrates mutually exercising the same public function. **2.** one of three persons associated in any office or position of authority. [1570–80; < L: lit., one man of three, back formation from *trium virōrum* of three men] **—tri·um′vi·ral,** *adj.*

tri·um·vi·rate (trī um′vər it, -və rāt′), *n.* **1.** *Rom. Hist.* the office or magistracy of a triumvir. **2.** a government of three officers or magistrates functioning jointly. **3.** a coalition of three magistrates or rulers for joint administration. **4.** any association of three in office or authority. **5.** any group or set of three. [1575–85; < L *triumvirātus.* See TRIUMVIR, -ATE[3]]

tri·une (trī′yo͞on), *adj.* **1.** three in one; constituting a trinity in unity, as the Godhead. **—***n.* **2.** (*cap.*) the Trinity. [1595–1605; TRI- + *-une* < L *ūnus* one]

tri·u·ni·tar·i·an (trī yo͞o′ni târ′ē ən), *n.* Trinitarian. [1810–20; TRIUNE + *-itarian* as in UNITARIAN]

tri·u·ni·ty (trī yo͞o′ni tē), *n., pl.* **-ties.** Trinity (defs. 4, 5). [1615–25; TRIUNE + -ITY]

tri·va·lent (trī vā′lənt, triv′ə lənt), *adj.* **1.** *Chem.* having a valence of three. **2.** *Immunol.* having three binding sites, as certain antigens. [1865–70; TRI- + VALENT] **—tri·va′lence, tri·va′len·cy,** *n.*

tri·valve (trī′valv′), *adj.* **1.** having three valves, as a shell. **—***n.* **2.** a trivalve shell. [1675–85; TRI- + VALVE]

Tri·van·drum (tri van′drəm), *n.* a city in and the capital of Kerala state, in S India: Vishnu pilgrimage center. 409,761.

triv·et[1] (triv′it), *n.* **1.** a small metal plate with short legs, esp. one put under a hot platter or dish to protect a table. **2.** a three-footed or three-legged stand or support, esp. one of iron placed over a fire to support cooking vessels or the like. [1375–1425; late ME *trevet,* OE *trefet,* appar. b. OE *thrifēte* three-footed and L *triped-,* s. of *tripēs* three-footed (with VL *-e-* for L *-i-*)]

triv·et[2] (triv′it), *n.* a special knife for cutting pile loops, as of velvet or carpets. Also, **triv′ette.** [orig. uncert.]

triv·i·a (triv′ē ə), *n.pl.* matters or things that are very unimportant, inconsequential, or nonessential; trifles; trivialities. [1900–05; pseudo-L *trivia* (neut. pl.), taken as the base of TRIVIAL]

Triv·i·a (triv′ē ə), *n.* (in Roman religion) Hecate: so called because she was the goddess of the crossroads. [< L, fem. of *trivius* (adj.), deriv. of *trivium* place where three roads meet, equiv. to *tri-* TRI- + *-vium,* deriv. of *via* way, road]

triv·i·al (triv′ē əl), *adj.* **1.** of very little importance or value; insignificant: *Don't bother me with trivial matters.* **2.** commonplace; ordinary. **3.** *Biol.* (of names of organisms) specific, as distinguished from generic. **4.** *Math.* **a.** noting a solution of an equation in which the value of every variable of the equation is equal to zero. **b.** (of a theorem, proof, or the like) simple, transparent, or immediately evident. **5.** *Chem.* (of names of chemical compounds) derived from the natural source, or of historic origin, and not according to the systematic nomenclature: *Picric acid is the trivial name of 2,4,6-trinitrophenol.* [1400–50; late ME < L *triviālis* belonging to the crossroads or street corner, hence commonplace, equiv. to *tri-* TRI- + *vi(a)* road + *-ālis* -AL[1]] **—triv′i·al·ly,** *adv.*

—Syn. 1. unimportant, nugatory, slight, immaterial, inconsequential, frivolous, trifling. See **petty. —Ant. 1.** important.

triv·i·al·ism (triv′ē ə liz′əm), *n.* **1.** trivial character. **2.** something trivial. [1820–30; TRIVIAL + -ISM]

triv·i·al·i·ty (triv′ē al′i tē), *n., pl.* **-ties. 1.** something trivial; a trivial matter, affair, remark, etc.: *cocktail conversation marked by trivialities.* **2.** Also, **triv·i·al·ness** (triv′ē əl nis). trivial quality or character. [1590–1600; TRIVIAL + -ITY]

triv·i·al·ize (triv′ē ə līz′), *v.t.,* **-ized, -iz·ing.** to make trivial; cause to appear unimportant, trifling, etc. Also, *esp. Brit.,* **triv′i·al·ise′.** [1840–50; TRIVIAL + -IZE] **—triv′i·al·i·za′tion,** *n.*

triv·i·um (triv′ē əm), *n.* (during the Middle Ages) the lower division of the seven liberal arts, comprising grammar, rhetoric, and logic. Cf. **quadrivium.** [1795–1805; < ML, special use of L *trivium* public place, lit., place where three roads meet. See TRIVIAL]

tri·week·ly (trī wēk′lē), *adv., adj., n., pl.* **-lies. —***adv.*

CONCISE PRONUNCIATION KEY: act, cāpe, dâre, pärt; set, ēqual; *if,* īce; ox, ōver, ôrder, oil, bo͝ok, bo͞ot, out; up, ûrge; child; sing; shoe; thin, *th*at; zh as in *treasure.* ə = *a* as in *alone,* e as in *system,* i as in *easily,* o as in *gallop,* u as in *circus;* ə as in *fire* (fīər), *hour* (ouər). l and n can serve as syllabic consonants, as in *cradle* (krād′l), and *button* (but′n). See the full key inside the front cover.

1. every three weeks. 2. three times a week. —*adj.* 3. occurring or appearing every three weeks. 4. occurring or appearing three times a week. —*n.* 5. a triweekly publication. [1825–35; TRI- + WEEKLY]

-trix, a suffix occurring in loanwords from Latin, where it formed feminine nouns or adjectives corresponding to agent nouns ending in **-tor** (*Bellatrix*). On this model, **-trix** is used in English to form feminine nouns (*aviatrix; executrix*) and geometrical terms denoting straight lines (*directrix*). Also, **-trice.** [< L *-trix*, s. *-tric-*]
—**Usage.** A suffix borrowed directly from Latin, -TRIX has been used since the 15th century on feminine agent nouns that correspond to a masculine (in Latin) or generic (in English) agent noun ending in *-tor: aviator, aviatrix; legislator, legislatrix; orator, oratrix.* Most nouns in -TRIX have dropped from general use, so that terms like *aviatrix, benefactrix, legislatrix, oratrix,* and *proprietrix* occur rarely or not at all in present-day English. The forms in *-tor* are applied to both men and women: *Her sister is the proprietor of a new restaurant.* When relevant, sex is specified with the generic term: *Amelia Earhart was a pioneer woman aviator.* Legal documents still use *administratrix, executrix, inheritrix,* and the like, but these forms too are giving way to the *-tor* forms. See also **-enne, -ess, -ette.**

Trix·ie (trik′sē), *n.* a female given name, form of **Beatrix.**

TRM, trademark.

tRNA, See **transfer RNA.**

TRO, *Law.* temporary restraining order.

Tro·ad (trō′ad), *n.* **The,** a region in NW Asia Minor surrounding ancient Troy. Also called **Tro·as** (trō′as).

tro·bar clus (trō bär′ klo͞os′), a complex and obscure style of writing adopted by some 12th-century Provençal poets. [< Pr: lit., closed composition]

Tro′bri·and Is′lands (trō′brē änd′, -and′, -ənd), a group of islands north of the eastern end of New Guinea: part of Papua New Guinea. 170 sq. mi. (440 sq. km).

tro·car (trō′kär), *n. Surg.* a sharp-pointed instrument enclosed in a cannula, used for withdrawing fluid from a cavity, as the abdominal cavity. [1700–10; earlier *trocart* < F, lit., three-sided, equiv. to *tro-* (var. of *trois* three) + *cart*, var. of *carre* side < L *quadra* something square]

troch., (in prescriptions) troche.

tro·cha·ic (trō kā′ik), *Pros.* —*adj.* 1. pertaining to the trochee. 2. consisting of or employing a trochee or trochees. —*n.* 3. a trochee. 4. Usually, **trochaics.** a verse or poem written in trochees. [1580–90; < L *trochaicus* < Gk *trochaïkós*, equiv. to *trocha(îos)* TROCHEE + *-ikos* -IC] —**tro·cha′i·cal·ly,** *adv.*

tro·chal (trō′kəl), *adj. Zool.* resembling a wheel. [1835–45; < Gk *troch(ós)* wheel + -AL[1]]

tro·chan·ter (trō kan′tər), *n.* 1. *Anat.* either of two knobs at the top of the femur, the greater on the outside and the lesser on the inside, serving for the attachment of muscles between the thigh and pelvis. 2. *Zool.* any similar prominence on the femur in many other vertebrates. 3. *Entomol.* (in an insect) the usually small second segment of the leg, between the coxa and femur. See diag. under **coxa.** [1605–15; < NL < Gk *trochantḗr* ball on which the hip bone turns in its socket] —**tro·chan·ter·ic** (trō′kən ter′ik), **tro·chan′ter·al,** *adj.*

tro·che (trō′kē), *n. Pharm.* a small tablet or lozenge, usually a circular one, made of medicinal substance worked into a paste with sugar and mucilage or the like, and dried. [1590–1600; back formation from *troches,* earlier *tro(s)chies,* late ME *trocis* (taken as pl.) < MF *trocisse* < L *trochiscus* < Gk *trochískos*, equiv. to *troch(ós)* wheel (akin to *tréchein* to run) + *-iskos* dim. suffix]

tro·chee (trō′kē), *n. Pros.* a foot of two syllables, a long followed by a short in quantitative meter, or a stressed followed by an unstressed in accentual meter. [1580–90; < L *trochaeus* < Gk (*poùs*), *trochaîos* running (foot), equiv. to *troch-* (var. s. of *tréchein* to run) + *-aios* adj. suffix]

troch·el·minth (trok′əl minth), *n.* any invertebrate of the phylum Trochelminthes (now usually broken up into several phyla), comprising the rotifers, gastrotrichs, and several other forms. [< NL *Trochelminthes* phylum name, equiv. to Gk *troch(ós)* wheel + *helminth-* HELMINTH + *-es* pl. n. suffix]

troch·i·lus (trok′ə ləs), *n., pl.* **-li** (-lī′). *Archit.* scotia. [1555–65; < Gk *tróchilos;* see TROCHLEA]

troch·le·a (trok′lē ə), *n., pl.* **-le·ae** (-lē ē′), **-le·as.** *Anat.* a pulleylike structure or arrangement of parts. [1685–95; < L: pulley block or sheave < Gk *trochiléa, trochil(e)ía;* akin to *tróchilos* sheave, runner, akin to *tréchein* to run]

troch·le·ar (trok′lē ər), *adj.* 1. *Anat.* of, pertaining to, or connected with a trochlea. 2. *Physiol., Anat.* pulleylike. 3. *Bot.* circular and contracted in the middle so as to resemble a pulley. —*n.* 4. See **trochlear nerve.** [1675–85; TROCHLE(A) + -AR[1]]

troch′lear nerve′, *Anat.* either one of the fourth pair of cranial nerves, consisting of motor fibers that innervate the superior oblique muscle of the upper part of the eyeball. [1885–90]

tro·choid (trō′koid), *n.* 1. *Geom.* a curve traced by a point on a radius or an extension of the radius of a circle that rolls, without slipping, on a curve, another circle, or a straight line. Equation: $x = a\theta - b \sin \theta$, $y = a - b \cos \theta$. —*adj.* 2. rotating on an axis, as a wheel. [1695–1705; < Gk *trochoeidḗs* round like a wheel. See TROCHE, -OID] —**tro·choi′dal,** *adj.* —**tro·choi′dal·ly,** *adv.*

CONCISE ETYMOLOGY KEY: <, descended or borrowed from; >, whence; b., blend of, blended; c., cognate with; cf., compare; deriv., derivative; equiv., equivalent; imit., imitative; obl., oblique; r., replacing; s., stem; sp., spelling, spelled; resp., respelling, respelled; trans., translation; ?, origin unknown; *, unattested; ‡, probably earlier than. See the full key inside the front cover.

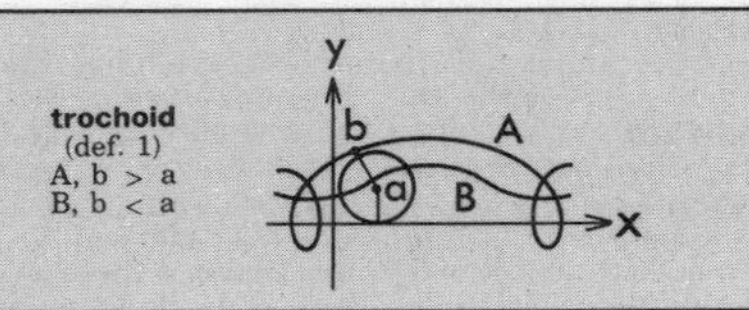

trochoid (def. 1) A, b > a B, b < a

troch·o·phore (trok′ə fôr′, -fōr′), *n. Zool.* a ciliate, free-swimming larva common to several groups of invertebrates, as many mollusks and rotifers. [1890–95; < Gk *trochó(s)* wheel + -PHORE]

trod (trod), *v.* a pt. and pp. of **tread.**

trod·den (trod′n), *v.* a pp. of **tread.**

Troe·zen (trē′zən), *n.* (in ancient geography) a town in E Peloponnesus near the coast of the Saronic Gulf, regarded in mythology as the birthplace of Theseus.

trof·fer (trof′ər, trô′fər), *n.* a trough-shaped reflector holding one or more fluorescent lamps. [1940–45; *troff* (var. of TROUGH) + -ER[1]]

trog·lo·bi·ont (trog′lə bī′ont), *n.* any creature having a cave-dwelling mode of life. Also called **trog·lo·bite** (trog′lə bīt′). [1920–25; < Gk *trōglo-* (see TROGLODYTE) + *biont-*, s. of *biṓn*, prp. of *bioûn* to live]

trog·lo·dyte (trog′lə dīt′), *n.* 1. a prehistoric cave dweller. 2. a person of degraded, primitive, or brutal character. 3. a person living in seclusion. 4. a person unacquainted with affairs of the world. 5. an animal living underground. [1545–55; < L *trōglodyta* < Gk *trōglodýtēs* one who creeps into holes, cave dweller, equiv. to *trōglo-* (comb. form of *trṓglē* a gnawed hole; cf. TROGON) + *dý(ein)* to creep into + *-tēs* agent suffix] —**trog·lo·dyt·ic** (trog′lə dit′ik), **trog′lo·dyt′i·cal,** *adj.* —**trog·lo·dyt·ism** (trog′lə dī tiz′əm), *n.*

tro·gon (trō′gon), *n.* any of several brilliantly colored birds of the family Trogonidae, esp. of the genus *Trogon,* of tropical and subtropical regions of the New World. [1785–95; < NL < Gk *trṓgōn*, prp. of *trṓgein* to gnaw] —**tro·gon·oid** (trō′gə noid′), *adj.*

Troi·a (troi′ə), *n.* See **Troy Game, The.**

troi·ka (troi′kə), *n.* 1. a Russian carriage, wagon, or sleigh drawn by a team of three horses abreast. 2. a team of three horses driven abreast. 3. any group of three persons, nations, etc., acting equally in unison to exert influence, control, or the like. [1835–45; < Russ *tróĭka* threesome, troika, deriv. of *tróe* three (collective), akin to *tri* THREE]

troika (def. 1)

tro·i·lite (trō′ə līt′, troi′līt), *n.* a mineral, iron sulfide, FeS, occurring in meteorites. [1865–70; named after D. *Troili,* 18th-century Italian savant who described a meteorite containing it. See -ITE[1]]

Troi·lus (troi′ləs, trō′ə-), *n. Class. and Med. Legend.* a warrior son of Priam, mentioned by Homer and Vergil and later represented as the lover of Cressida.

Troi′lus and Cres′sida, a satiric comedy (1598–1602?) by Shakespeare.

troi′lus but′terfly. See **spicebush swallowtail.** [< NL, the butterfly's specific epithet, appar. after TROILUS]

trois (TRWä), *n. French.* the number 3.

Trois-Ri·vières (TRWä Rē vyeR′), *n.* French name of **Three Rivers.**

Trois-Ri·vières-Ouest (TRWä Rē vyeR west′), *n.* French name of **West Three Rivers.**

Tro·jan (trō′jən), *adj.* 1. of or pertaining to ancient Troy or its inhabitants. —*n.* 2. a native or inhabitant of Troy. 3. a person who shows pluck, determination, or energy: *to work like a Trojan.* [bef. 900; ME; OE *Trōiān* < L *Trōjānus*, equiv. to *Trōj(a)* TROY + *-ānus* -AN]

Tro′jan group′, *Astron.* a group of asteroids oscillating about either of two points, equidistant from the sun and Jupiter, that forms an equilateral triangle with the sun and Jupiter.

Tro′jan horse′, 1. *Class. Myth.* a gigantic hollow wooden horse, left by the Greeks upon their pretended abandonment of the siege of Troy. The Trojans took it into Troy and Greek soldiers concealed in the horse opened the gates to the Greek army at night and conquered the city. 2. a person or thing intended to undermine or destroy from within. 3. a nonreplicating computer program planted illegally in another program to do damage locally when the software is activated.

Tro′jan War′, *Class. Myth.* a ten-year war waged by the confederated Greeks under Agamemnon against the Trojans to avenge the abduction of Helen, wife of Menelaus, by Paris, son of the Trojan king Priam, and ending in the plundering and burning of Troy.

Tro′jan Wom′en, The, a tragedy (415 B.C.) by Euripides.

troke (trōk), *n., v.,* **troked, trok·ing.** *Scot.* —*n.* 1. truck[2] (defs. 4–7). —*v.t., v.i.* 2. truck[2]. —**trok′er,** *n.*

troll[1] (trōl), *v.t.* 1. to sing or utter in a full, rolling voice. 2. to sing in the manner of a round or catch. 3. to fish for or in with a moving line, working the line up or down with a rod, as in fishing for pike, or trailing the line behind a slow-moving boat. 4. to move (the line or bait) in doing this. 5. to cause to turn round and round; roll. 6. *Obs.* to hand around, as a bowl of liquor at table. —*v.i.* 7. to sing with a full, rolling voice. 8. to be uttered or sounded in such tones. 9. to fish by trolling. 10. to roll; turn round and round. 11. to move nimbly, as the tongue in speaking. —*n.* 12. a song whose parts are sung in succession; a round. 13. the act of trolling. 14. a lure used in trolling. 15. the fishing line containing the lure and hook for use in trolling. [1350–1400; ME *trollen* to roll, stroll < MF *troller* to run here and there < MHG *trollen* walk or run with short steps] —**troll′er,** *n.*

troll[2] (trōl), *n.* 1. (in Scandinavian folklore) any of a race of supernatural beings, sometimes conceived as giants and sometimes as dwarfs, inhabiting caves or subterranean dwellings. 2. *Slang.* a person who lives or sleeps in a park or under a viaduct or bridge, as a bag lady or derelict. [1610–20; < ON *troll* demon]

trol·ley (trol′ē), *n., pl.* **-leys,** *v.,* **-leyed, -ley·ing.** —*n.* 1. a trolley car. 2. a pulley or truck traveling on an overhead track and serving to support and move a suspended object. 3. a grooved metallic wheel or pulley carried on the end of a pole **(trol′ley pole′)** by an electric car or locomotive, and held in contact with an overhead conductor, usually a suspended wire **(trol′ley wire′),** from which it collects the current for the propulsion of the car or locomotive. 4. any of various devices for collecting current for such a purpose, as a pantograph, or a bowlike structure **(bow trolley)** sliding along an overhead wire, or a device **(underground trolley)** for taking current from the underground wire or conductor used by some electric railways. 5. a small truck or car operated on a track, as in a mine or factory. 6. a serving cart, as one used to serve desserts. 7. *Chiefly Brit.* any of various low carts or vehicles, as a railway handcar or costermonger's cart. 8. **off one's trolley,** *Slang.* **a.** in a confused mental state. **b.** insane. —*v.t., v.i.* 9. to convey or go by trolley. Also, **trolly.** [1815–25; orig. dial.; appar. akin to TROLL[1]]

trol′ley bus′, a passenger bus operating on tires and having an electric motor that draws power from overhead wires. Also called **trackless trolley, trol′ley coach′.** [1910–15]

trol′ley car′, a streetcar propelled electrically by current taken by means of a trolley from a conducting wire strung overhead or running beneath a slot between the tracks. [1885–90]

trol′ley line′, 1. the route of a trolley car or trolley bus. 2. a public or private transportation system using trolley cars or trolley buses. [1890–95, *Amer.*]

trol·lop (trol′əp), *n.* 1. an immoral or promiscuous woman, esp. a prostitute. 2. an untidy or slovenly woman; slattern. [1605–15; earlier *trollops;* perh. akin to TROLL[1]] —**trol′lop·y,** *adj.*

Trol·lope (trol′əp), *n.* **Anthony,** 1815–82, English novelist. —**Trol·lop·i·an, Trol·lop·e·an** (trə lop′ē ən, -lō′pē-, trol′ə pē′-), *adj., n.*

trol·ly (trol′ē), *n., pl.* **-lies,** *v.t., v.i.,* **-lied, -ly·ing.** trolley.

trom·ba ma·ri·na (trom′bə mə rē′nə; *It.* tRôm′bä mä Rē′nä), *pl.* **trom·be ma·ri·ne** (trom′bā mə rē′nā; *It.* tRôm′be mä Rē′ne). See **trumpet marine.** [< It: lit., marine trumpet (literal sense unclear); cf. TROMBONE]

Trombe′ wall′ (tromb, trôNb), a glass-fronted exterior masonry wall that absorbs solar heat for radiation into a building. [1975–80; after Frenchman Félix *Trombe,* one of its developers]

trom·bic·u·li·a·sis (trom bik′yə lī′ə sis), *n. Vet. Pathol.* the condition of being infested with chiggers. Also, **trom·bi·di·o·sis** (trom′bi dī ō′sis). [1910–15; < NL *Trombi(dium)* genus name + -CULE[1] + -IASIS]

trom·bone (trom bōn′, trom′bōn), *n.* a musical wind instrument consisting of a cylindrical metal tube expanding into a bell and bent twice in a U shape, usually equipped with a slide **(slide trombone).** [1715–25; < It, equiv. to *tromb(a)* trumpet (< Pr < Gmc; cf. OHG *trumpa, trumba* horn, trumpet) + *-one* aug. suffix] —**trom·bon·ist** (trom bō′nist, trom′bō-), *n.*

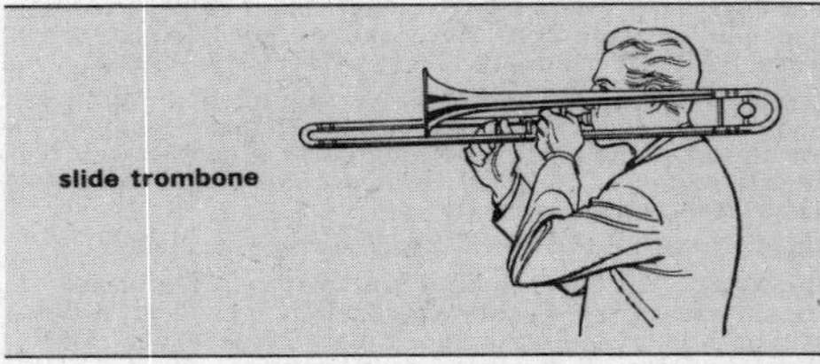
slide trombone

trom·mel (trom′əl), *n.* a rotary, cylindrical or conical screen for sorting ore, coal, gravel, etc., according to size. [1875–80, *Amer.;* < G *Trommel* drum]

tromp (tromp), *v.t. Informal.* 1. to tramp or trample. 2. to defeat soundly; trounce. [1880–85; gradational var. of TRAMP, perh. with vowel of STOMP]

Tromp (tRômp), *n.* **Cor·ne·lis** (kôR nä′lis), 1629–91, and his father, **Maar·ten Har·perts·zoon** (mär′tən här′pərt sōn′), 1597–1653, Dutch admirals.

trompe (tromp), *n. Metall.* a device formerly used for inducing a blast of air upon the hearth of a forge by means of a current of falling water. [1820–30; < F]

trompe l'oeil (*Fr.* tRôNp lœʹyᵊ; *Eng.* trômp′ lā′, loi′), 1. visual deception, esp. in paintings, in which objects are rendered in extremely fine detail emphasizing the illusion of tactile and spatial qualities. 2. a painting, mural, or panel of wallpaper designed to create such an effect. [1895–1900; < F: lit., (it) fools the eye]

Troms·ö (trom′sō; *Nor.* trŏŏms′œ), *n.* a seaport in N Norway. 43,819.

-tron, a combining form extracted from **electron,** used with nouns or combining forms, principally in the names of electron tubes (*ignitron; klystron; magnetron*) and of devices for accelerating subatomic particles (*cosmotron; cyclotron*); also, more generally, in the names of any kind of chamber or apparatus used in experiments (*biotron*). [by initial shortening of ELECTRON, with perh. accidental allusion to the Gk instrumental suffix *-tron,* as in *árotron* plough]

tro·na (trō′nə), *n.* a monoclinic mineral, grayish or yellowish hydrous sodium carbonate and bicarbonate, $Na_2CO_3 \cdot NaHCO_3 \cdot 2H_2O$, occurring in dried or partly evaporated lake basins. [1790–1800; < Sp < dial. Ar *ṭrōn,* aph. var. of *naṭrūn* NATRON]

Trond·heim (tron′hām; *Swed.* trôn′hām), *n.* a seaport in central Norway, on Trondheim Fiord. 134,889. Formerly, **Nidaros, Trond·hjem** (tron′yem; *Swed.* trôn′yem).

Trond′heim Fiord′, an inlet of the North Sea, extending into N Norway. 80 mi. (129 km) long.

trond·hjem·ite (tron′ye mīt′), *n. Petrol.* a coarse-grained igneous rock composed of quartz, plagioclase feldspar, and a small amount of biotite. [*Trondhjem* (now TRONDHEIM) + -ITE[1]]

trone (trōn), *n. Scot. and North Eng.* a large pair of scales, a spring balance, or other weighing device located in a town or marketplace to weigh goods and merchandise. [1400–50; late ME (Scots) < AF << L *trūtina* < Gk *trytánē* balance, scales]

troop (trōōp), *n.* **1.** an assemblage of persons or things; company; band. **2.** a great number or multitude: *A whole troop of children swarmed through the museum.* **3.** *Mil.* an armored cavalry or cavalry unit consisting of two or more platoons and a headquarters group. **4. troops,** a body of soldiers, police, etc.: *Mounted troops quelled the riot.* **5.** a unit of Boy Scouts or Girl Scouts usually having a maximum of 32 members under the guidance of an adult leader. **6.** a herd, flock, or swarm. **7.** *Archaic.* a band or troupe of actors. —*v.i.* **8.** to gather in a company; flock together. **9.** to come, go, or pass in great numbers; throng. **10.** to walk, as if in a march; go: *to troop down to breakfast.* **11.** to walk, march, or pass in rank or order: *The students trooped into the auditorium.* **12.** to associate or consort (usually fol. by *with*). —*v.t.* **13.** *Brit. Mil.* to carry (the flag or colors) in a ceremonial way before troops. **14.** *Obs.* to assemble or form into a troop or troops. [1535–45; < F *troupe,* OF *trope,* prob. back formation from *tropel* herd, flock (F *troupeau*), equiv. to *trop-* (< Gmc; see THORP) + *-el* << L *-ellus* dim. suffix]
—**Syn. 1.** body, group, crowd. See **company. 2.** crowd, herd, flock, swarm, throng. **7.** TROOP, TROUPE both mean a band, company, or group. TROOP has various meanings as indicated in the definitions above. With the spelling TROUPE the word has the specialized meaning of a company of actors, singers, acrobats, or other performers. **8.** collect. **9.** swarm.

troop′ car′rier, 1. a transport airplane used for carrying troops and their equipment. **2.** an armored vehicle, often amphibious and mounted with light weapons, for transporting infantry troops and equipment. [1920–25]

troop·er (trōō′pər), *n.* **1.** a horse-cavalry soldier. **2.** a mounted police officer; a police officer on horseback. **3.** See **state trooper. 4.** a cavalry horse. **5.** *Chiefly Brit.* a troopship. **6. like a trooper,** with great energy, enthusiasm, or display: *He swears like a trooper.* [1630–40; TROOP + -ER[1]]

troop·ship (trōōp′ship′), *n.* a ship for the conveyance of military troops; transport. [1860–65; TROOP + SHIP]

troost·ite (trōō′stīt), *n.* a microconstituent of hardened and tempered steel, consisting of a very fine aggregate of ferrite and cementite. [1900–05; named after L. J. *Troost* (d. 1911), French chemist; see -ITE[1]] —**troost·it·ic** (trōō stit′ik), *adj.*

trop (trō), *adv. French.* too; too much or too many.

trop-, var. of **tropo-** before a vowel: *tropism.*

trop., 1. tropic. **2.** tropical.

tro·pae·o·lin (trō pē′ə lin), *n. Chem.* any of a number of orange or yellow azo dyes of complex molecular structure. Also, **tropeolin.** [1875–80; < NL *Tropaeol(um)* nasturtium, genus of plants yielding the dyes (equiv. to L *tropae(um)* TROPHY + *-olum,* neut. of *-olus* -OLE[1]) + -IN[2]]

tropaeolin D, *Chem.* See **methyl orange.**

tro·pae·um (trō pē′əm), *n., pl.* **-pae·a** (-pē′ə). a monument erected in ancient Greece or, esp., Rome to commemorate a military or naval victory. Also, **trophaeum.** [1540–50; < L; see TROPHY]

tro·pai·on (trō pī′on), *n., pl.* **-pai·a** (-pī′ə). a tropaeum, esp. in Greece. [< Gk *trópaion;* see TROPHY]

trope (trōp), *n.* **1.** *Rhet.* **a.** any literary or rhetorical device, as metaphor, metonymy, synecdoche, and irony, that consists in the use of words in other than their literal sense. **b.** an instance of this. Cf. **figure of speech. 2.** a phrase, sentence, or verse formerly interpolated in a liturgical text to amplify or embellish. **3.** (in the philosophy of Santayana) the principle of organization according to which matter moves to form an object during the various stages of its existence. [1525–35; < L *tropus* figure in rhetoric < Gk *trópos* turn, turning, turn or figure of speech, akin to *trépein* to turn]

-trope, a combining form meaning "one turned toward" that specified by the initial element (*heliotrope*); also occurring in concrete nouns that correspond to abstract nouns ending in **-tropy** or **-tropism:** *allotrope.* [< Gk *-tropos;* see TROPE, TROPO-]

tro·pe·o·lin (trō pē′ə lin), *n. Chem.* tropaeolin.

tropeolin D, *Chem.* See **methyl orange.**

troph-, var. of **tropho-** before a vowel: *trophallaxis.*

-troph, a combining form used in the formation of nouns with the general sense "nutrient matter" (*embryotroph*), "an organism with given nutritional requirements" (*heterotroph*); also forming concrete nouns corresponding to abstract nouns ending in **-trophy** or adjectives ending in **-trophic.**

tro·phae·um (trō fē′əm), *n., pl.* **-phae·a** (-fē′ə). tropaeum.

troph·al·lax·is (trof′ə lak′sis, trō′fə-), *n., pl.* **-lax·es** (-lak′sēz). (among social insects) the exchange of nutriments or other secretions between members of a colony. [1915–20; TROPH- + Gk *állaxis* exchange, equiv. to *allak-* (verbid s. of *allássein* to change; see ALLO-) + *-sis* -SIS] —**troph·al·lac·tic** (trof′ə lak′tik, trō′fə-), *adj.*

tro·phi (trō′fī), *n.pl. Entomol.* the mouthparts of an insect, including the labrum, mandibles, maxillae, labium, and hypopharynx. [1820–30; < NL *trophī* < Gk *trophoí,* pl. of *trophós* feeder, nurse, akin to *tréphein* to nourish]

troph·ic (trof′ik, trō′fik), *adj.* of or pertaining to nutrition; concerned in nutritive processes. [1870–75; < Gk *trophikós* pertaining to food. See TROPHO-, -IC] —**troph′i·cal·ly,** *adv.*

-trophic, a combining form with the meanings "having nutritional habits or requirements" of the kind specified by the initial element (*autotrophic*), "affecting the activity of, maintaining" that specified (*gonadotrophic*) (in this sense often interchangeable with **-tropic**); also forming adjectives corresponding to nouns ending in **-troph** or **-trophy** (*hypertrophic*). [see TROPHIC]

tro·phied (trō′fēd), *adj.* adorned with trophies. [1615–25; TROPHY + -ED[3]]

tropho-, a combining form meaning "nourishment," used in the formation of compound words: *trophosome.* Also, *esp. before a vowel,* **troph-.** [comb. form of Gk *trophḗ* nourishment, food; akin to *tréphein* to feed, nourish]

troph·o·blast (trof′ə blast′, trō′fə-), *n. Embryol.* the layer of extraembryonic ectoderm that chiefly nourishes the embryo or develops into fetal membranes with nutritive functions. [1885–90; TROPHO- + -BLAST] —**troph′o·blas′tic,** *adj.*

troph·o·some (trof′ə sōm′, trō′fə-), *n. Zool.* **1.** an organ in deep-sea tube worms that is colonized by bacteria supplying the host worm with food and energy. **2.** a similar organ in other marine worms. [1865–70; TROPHO- + -SOME[3]]

troph·o·zo·ite (trof′ə zō′īt, trō′fə-), *n. Zool.* a protozoan in the metabolically active growth stage. [1905–10; TROPHO- + -ZO(ON) + -ITE[1]]

tro·phy (trō′fē), *n., pl.* **-phies. 1.** anything taken in war, hunting, competition, etc., esp. when preserved as a memento; spoil, prize, or award. **2.** anything serving as a token or evidence of victory, valor, skill, etc. **3.** a carving, painting, or other representation of objects associated with or symbolic of victory or achievement. **4.** any memento or memorial. **5.** a memorial erected by certain ancient peoples, esp. the Greeks and Romans, in commemoration of a victory in war and consisting of arms or other spoils taken from the enemy and hung upon a tree, pillar, or the like. [1505–15; earlier *trophe* < F *trophée* < L *trop(h)aeum* < Gk *trópaion,* n. use of neut. of *trópaios,* Attic var. of *tropaîos* of turning or putting to flight, equiv. to *trop(ḗ)* a turning (akin to *trépein* to turn) + *-aios* adj. suffix. See TROPE] —**tro′phy·less,** *adj.*

-trophy, a combining form used in the formation of nouns with the general senses "nourishment, feeding" (*mycotrophy*), "growth" (*hypertrophy*); also forming abstract nouns corresponding to adjectives ending in **-trophic.** [< Gk *-trophia* nutrition, equiv. to *troph(ḗ)* food + *-ia* -Y[3]]

tro′phy room′, a room in which a person or group keeps and displays trophies, as for bowling or golf.

tro′phy wife′, the young, often second, wife of a rich middle-aged man. [1985–90, *Amer.*]

trop·ic (trop′ik), *n.* **1.** *Geog.* **a.** either of two corresponding parallels of latitude on the terrestrial globe, one **(tropic of Cancer)** about 23½° N, and the other **(tropic of Capricorn)** about 23½° S of the equator, being the boundaries of the Torrid Zone. See diag. under **zone. b. the tropics,** the regions lying between and near these parallels of latitude; the Torrid Zone and neighboring regions. **2.** *Astron.* either of two circles on the celestial sphere, one lying in the same plane as the tropic of Cancer, the other in the same plane as the tropic of Capricorn. —*adj.* **3.** of, pertaining to, characteristic of, or occurring in the tropics; tropical: *romance under the tropic skies of Old Mexico.* [1350–1400; ME < L *tropicus* < Gk *tropikós* pertaining to a turn, equiv. to *tróp(os)* turn + *-ikos* -IC]

-tropic, a combining form with the meanings "turned toward, with an orientation toward" that specified by the initial element (*geotropic*), "having an affinity for, affecting" what is specified (*lipotropic; neurotropic; psychotropic*), "affecting the activity of, maintaining" a specified organ (*gonadotropic*). Cf. **-trophic.** [see TROPIC]

trop·i·cal (trop′i kəl *for 1–4, 6;* trō′pi kəl *for 5*), *adj.* **1.** pertaining to, characteristic of, occurring in, or inhabiting the tropics, esp. the humid tropics: *tropical flowers.* **2.** very hot and humid: *a tropical climate.* **3.** designed for use in the tropics or in very hot weather (often used in combination): *tropical-weight woolens.* **4.** of or pertaining to either or both of the astronomical tropics. **5.** pertaining to, characterized by, or of the nature of a trope or tropes; metaphorical. —*n.* **6. tropicals,** lightweight clothing, suitable for warm, esp. summer weather. [1520–30; TROPIC + -AL[1]] —**trop′i·cal′i·ty,** *n.* —**trop′i·cal·ly,** *adv.*

trop′ical aquar′ium, an aquarium designed for the maintenance and breeding of tropical fish and kept at a suitably warm temperature. [1945–50]

trop′ical cy′clone, a cyclone that originates over a tropical ocean area and can develop into the destructive storm known in the U.S. as a hurricane, in the western Pacific region as a typhoon, and elsewhere by other names. Cf. **extratropical cyclone, hurricane** (def. 1), **willy-willy.** [1915–20]

trop′ical disturb′ance, *Meteorol.* a very weak, or incipient, tropical cyclone.

trop′ical fish′, any of numerous small, usually brightly colored fishes, indigenous to the tropics, and often kept and bred in home aquariums. [1930–35]

trop·i·cal·ize (trop′i kə līz′), *v.t.,* **-ized, -iz·ing. 1.** to make tropical, as in character or appearance. **2.** to adapt or make suitable for use in tropical regions, esp. in regard to protection against the destructive effects of moisture and fungi. Also, *esp. Brit.,* **trop′i·cal·ise′.** [1880–85; TROPICAL + -IZE] —**trop′i·cal·i·za′tion,** *n.*

trop′ical med′icine, the branch of medicine dealing with the study and treatment of diseases occurring in the tropics.

trop′ical storm′, *Meteorol.* a tropical cyclone of less than hurricane force. [1940–45]

trop′ical year′, year (def. 4b). [1585–95]

trop′ic bird′, any of several web-footed seabirds of the family Phaethontidae, chiefly of tropical seas, having white plumage with black markings and a pair of greatly elongated central tail feathers. Also, **trop′ic·bird′.** Also called **boatswain bird.** [1675–85]

trop′ic of Can′cer. See under **tropic** (def. 1a).

trop′ic of Cap′ricorn. See under **tropic** (def. 1a).

tro·pine (trō′pēn, -pin), *n. Chem.* a white, crystalline, hygroscopic, water-soluble, poisonous alkaloid, $C_8H_{15}NO$, obtained chiefly by the hydrolysis of atropine or hyoscyamine. [1880–85; aph. var. of ATROPINE]

tro·pism (trō′piz əm), *n. Biol.* an orientation of an organism to an external stimulus, as light, esp. by growth rather than by movement. [1895–1900; independent use of -TROPISM] —**tro·pis·mat·ic** (trō′piz mat′ik), *adj.* —**tro·pis·tic** (trō pis′tik), *adj.*

-tropism, var. of **-tropy.** [see -TROPY, -ISM]

tropo-, a combining form meaning "turn," "reaction, response," "change," "troposphere," used in the formation of compound words: *tropophilous.* Also, *esp. before a vowel,* **trop-.** Cf. **-trope, -tropism, -tropy, -tropic, -tropous.** [comb. form repr. Gk *trópos* turn, *tropḗ* a turning]

tro·pol·o·gy (trō pol′ə jē), *n., pl.* **-gies** for 2. **1.** the use of figurative language in speech or writing. **2.** a treatise on figures of speech or tropes. **3.** the use of a Scriptural text so as to give it a moral interpretation or significance apart from its direct meaning. [1510–20; < LL *tropologia* < Gk *tropología.* See TROPE, -O-, -LOGY] —**trop·o·log·ic** (trop′ə loj′ik, trō′pə-), **trop′o·log′i·cal,** *adj.* —**trop′o·log′i·cal·ly,** *adv.*

tro·po·nin (trō′pə nin, trop′ə-), *n. Biochem.* a protein of muscle tissue that binds calcium ions and is involved in contraction. [1965–70; *tropo(myosin)* (see TROPO-, MYOSIN) + *-n-* (of uncert. orig.) + -IN[2]]

trop·o·pause (trop′ə pôz′, trō′pə-), *n. Meteorol.* the boundary, or transitional layer, between the troposphere and the stratosphere. [1915–20; TROPO- + PAUSE]

tro·poph·i·lous (trō pof′ə ləs), *adj. Ecol.* adapted to a climate characterized by marked environmental changes. [1895–1900; TROPO- + -PHILOUS]

trop·o·phyte (trop′ə fīt′, trō′pə-), *n.* a tropophilous plant, as a broad-leaved tree. [1895–1900; TROPO- + -PHYTE] —**trop·o·phyt·ic** (trop′ə fit′ik, trō′pə-), *adj.*

trop·o·sphere (trop′ə sfēr′, trō′pə-), *n. Meteorol.* the lowest layer of the atmosphere, 6 mi. (10 km) high in some areas and as much as 12 mi. (20 km) high in others, within which there is a steady drop in temperature with increasing altitude and within which nearly all cloud formations occur and weather conditions manifest themselves. [1905–10; TROPO- + SPHERE] —**trop·o·spher·ic** (trop′ə sfer′ik, -sfēr′-, trō′pə-), *adj.*

trop′ospher′ic scat′ter, *Telecommunications.* transmission of radio frequency signals that have been scattered from irregularities in the troposphere to locations hundreds of kilometers distant. [1950–55]

trop·o·tax·is (trop′ə tak′sis, trō′pə-), *n. Zool.* straight movement by an organism toward or away from a source of stimulation as a result of comparing information received by paired sensory receptors on both sides of the body. Cf. **klinotaxis.** [1930–35; TROPO- + -TAXIS]

-tropous, a combining form meaning "turned, curved" in the direction specified by the initial element: *anatropous.* [< Gk *-tropos* pertaining to a turn]

trop·po[1] (trop′ō; *It.* trôp′pô), *adv. Music.* too much; excessively. [< It; OIt dial.: much, very, prob. < OPr *trop* orig., herd, flock; see TROOP]

trop·po[2] (trop′ō), *adj. Australian Slang.* mentally disturbed. [1940–45; TROP(IC) + -O, orig. in reference to the supposed psychological effects of life in tropical climates, esp. military service]

-tropy, a combining form occurring in abstract nouns that correspond to adjectives ending in **-tropic** or **-tropous:** *neurotropy.* Also, **-tropism.** [< Gk *-tropia.* See -TROPE, -Y[3]]

Tros·sachs (tros′əks), *n.* a valley in central Scotland, in Perth county, near Loch Katrine.

trot[1] (trot), *v.,* **trot·ted, trot·ting,** *n.* —*v.i.* **1.** (of a horse) to go at a gait between a walk and a run, in which the legs move in diagonal pairs, but not quite simultaneously, so that when the movement is slow one foot at least is always on the ground, and when fast all four feet are momentarily off the ground at once. **2.** to go at a

CONCISE PRONUNCIATION KEY: *act, cāpe, dâre, pärt; set, ēqual; if, īce; ox, ōver, ôrder, oil, bŏŏk, bōōt, out; up, ûrge; child; sing; shoe; thin,* that; *zh as in treasure.* ə = *a as in alone, e as in system, i as in easily, o as in gallop, u as in circus;* ᵊ *as in fire* (fīᵊr), *hour* (ouᵊr). l and n can serve as syllabic consonants, as in *cradle* (krād′l), and *button* (but′n). See the full key inside the front cover.

quick, steady pace; move briskly; bustle; hurry. —*v.t.* **3.** to cause to trot. **4.** to ride (a horse) at a trot. **5.** to lead at a trot. **6.** to travel over by trotting: *to spend the day trotting the country byways.* **7.** to execute by trotting. **8. trot out,** *Informal.* **a.** to bring forward for inspection. **b.** to bring to the attention of; introduce; submit: *He trots out his old jokes at every party.* —*n.* **9.** the gait of a horse, dog, or other quadruped, when trotting. **10.** the sound made by an animal when trotting. **11.** the jogging gait of a human being, between a walk and a run. **12.** *Harness Racing.* a race for trotters. **13.** brisk, continuous movement or activity: *I've been on the trot all afternoon.* **14.** *Disparaging.* an old woman. **15.** *Slang.* a literal translation used illicitly in doing schoolwork; crib; pony. **16. the trots,** *Informal.* diarrhea. **17.** *Informal.* a toddling child. [1250–1300; (v.) ME *trotten* < MF *troter* < Gmc; akin to OHG *trottōn* to tread, whence MHG *trotten* to run; (n.) ME < MF, deriv. of *troter*]

trot[2] (trot), *n.* **1.** a trotline. **2.** a short line with hooks, attached to the trotline. [1880–85; short for TROTLINE]

troth (trôth, trōth), *n.* **1.** faithfulness, fidelity, or loyalty: *by my troth.* **2.** truth or verity: *in troth.* **3.** one's word or promise, esp. in engaging oneself to marry. [1125–75; ME *trowthe, trouthe,* var. of *treuthe,* OE *trēowth.* See TRUTH] —**troth′less,** *adj.*

troth•plight (trôth′plīt′, trōth′-), *Archaic.* —*n.* **1.** engagement to be married; betrothal. —*v.t.* **2.** to betroth. —*adj.* **3.** betrothed. [1300–50; ME *trouth plight* having plighted troth, betrothed; see TROTH, PLIGHT[2]]

trot•line (trot′līn′), *n.* a strong fishing line strung across a stream, or deep into a river, having individual hooks attached by smaller lines at intervals. [1825–35; perh. TROT[1] + LINE[1]]

Trot•sky (trot′skē; *Russ.* trôt′skyə), *n.* **Leon** (*Lev,* or *Leib, Davidovich Bronstein*), 1879–1940, Russian revolutionary and writer: minister of war 1918–25. Also, **Trot′ski.**

Trot•sky•ism (trot′skē iz′əm), *n.* the form of Communism advocated by Leon Trotsky, based on an immediate, worldwide revolution by the proletariat. [1920–25; TROTSKY + -ISM]

Trot′skyist Interna′tional. See **Fourth International.**

Trot•sky•ite (trot′skē īt′), *n.* **1.** a supporter of Trotsky or Trotskyism. —*adj.* **2.** of or pertaining to Trotsky or Trotskyism. Also, **Trot′sky•ist.** [L. TROTSKY + -ITE[1]]

trot•ter (trot′ər), *n.* **1.** an animal that trots, esp. a horse bred and trained for harness racing. **2.** a person who moves about briskly and constantly. **3.** the foot of an animal, esp. of a sheep or pig, used as food. [1325–75; ME; see TROT[1], -ER[1]]

trot′ting race′, a horse race using trotters. [1830–40]

trot•ty (trot′ē), *adj.* resembling a trot. [1890–95; TROT[1] + -Y[1]]

tro•tyl (trō′til, -tēl), *n. Chem.* See **TNT.** [1915–20; (TRINI)TROT(OLUENE) + -YL]

trou•ba•dour (tro͞o′bə dôr′, -dōr′, -do͝or′), *n.* **1.** one of a class of medieval lyric poets who flourished principally in southern France from the 11th to 13th centuries, and wrote songs and poems of a complex metrical form in langue d'oc, chiefly on themes of courtly love. Cf. **trouvère. 2.** any wandering singer or minstrel. [1720–30; < F < Pr *trobador,* equiv. to *trob(ar)* to find, compose (see TROVER) + *-ador* < L *-ātor* -ATOR]

Trou•betz•koy (tro͞o′bit skoi′; *Russ.* tro͞o byits koi′), *n.* **N(i•ko•lai) S(er•ge•ie•vich)** (nyi ku lī′ syir gye′yivyich). See **Trubetzkoy, N(ikolai) S(ergeievich).**

trou•ble (trub′əl), *v.,* **-bled, -bling,** *n.* —*v.t.* **1.** to disturb the mental calm and contentment of; worry; distress; agitate. **2.** to put to inconvenience, exertion, pains, or the like: *May I trouble you to shut the door?* **3.** to cause bodily pain, discomfort, or disorder to; afflict: *to be troubled by arthritis.* **4.** to annoy, vex, or bother: *Don't trouble her with petty complaints now.* **5.** to disturb, agitate, or stir up so as to make turbid, as water or wine: *A heavy gale troubled the ocean waters.* —*v.i.* **6.** to put oneself to inconvenience, extra effort, or the like. **7.** to be distressed or agitated mentally; worry: *She always troubled over her son's solitariness.* —*n.* **8.** difficulty, annoyance, or harassment: *It would be no trouble at all to advise you.* **9.** unfortunate or distressing position, circumstance, or occurrence; misfortune: *Financial trouble may threaten security.* **10.** civil disorder, disturbance, or conflict: *political trouble in the new republic; labor troubles.* **11.** a physical disorder, disease, ailment, etc.; ill health: *heart trouble; stomach trouble.* **12.** mental or emotional disturbance or distress; worry: *Trouble and woe were her lot in life.* **13.** an instance of this: *some secret trouble weighing on his mind; a mother who shares all her children's troubles.* **14.** effort, exertion, or pains in doing something; inconvenience endured in accomplishing some action, deed, etc.: *The results were worth the trouble it took.* **15.** an objectionable feature; problem; drawback: *The trouble with your proposal is that it would be too costly to implement.* **16.** something or someone that is a cause or source of disturbance, distress, annoyance, etc. **17.** a personal habit or trait that is a disadvantage or a cause of mental distress: *His greatest trouble is oversensitivity.* **18. the Troubles, a.** the violence and civil war in Ireland, 1920–22. **b.** the conflict between Protestants and Catholics in Northern Ireland, beginning in 1969. **19. in trouble,** *Informal.* pregnant out of wedlock (used as a euphemism). [1175–1225; (v.) ME *troublen* < OF *troubler* < VL **turbulare,* deriv. of **turbulus* turbid, back formation from L *turbulentus* TURBULENT; (n.) ME < MF, deriv. of *troubler*] —**trou′bled•ly,** *adv.* —**trou′bled•ness,** *n.* —**trou′bler,** *n.* —**trou′bling•ly,** *adv.*

—**Syn. 1.** concern, upset, confuse. **4.** pester, plague, fret, torment, hector, harass, badger. **12.** concern, grief, agitation, care, suffering. **14.** See **care. 15.** trial, tribulation, affliction, misfortune. —**Ant. 1.** mollify; delight.

trou′bled wa′ters, a confused or chaotic state of affairs: *The situation was terrible, but like many politicians he was attracted by troubled waters.* [1575–85]

trou•ble•mak•er (trub′əl mā′kər), *n.* a person who causes difficulties, distress, worry, etc., for others, esp. one who does so habitually as a matter of malice. [1910–15; TROUBLE + MAKER] —**trou′ble•mak′ing,** *n.*

—**Syn.** instigator, fomenter, inciter, rabble-rouser.

trou′ble man′, troubleshooter (def. 2). [1885–90, *Amer.*]

trou•ble•proof (trub′əl pro͞of′), *adj.* not easily disturbed, disabled, injured, or put out of working order. [TROUBLE + -PROOF]

trou•ble•shoot (trub′əl sho͞ot′), *v.,* **-shoot•ed** or **-shot, -shoot•ing.** —*v.i.* **1.** to act or be employed as a troubleshooter: *She troubleshoots for a large industrial firm.* —*v.t.* **2.** to deal with in the capacity of a troubleshooter. Also, **trou′ble-shoot′.** [1930–35; back formation from TROUBLESHOOTER]

trou•ble•shoot•er (trub′əl sho͞o′tər), *n.* **1.** a person with special skill in resolving disputes, impasses, etc., as in business, national, or international affairs: *a diplomatic troubleshooter in the Middle East.* **2.** an expert in discovering and eliminating the cause of trouble in mechanical equipment, power lines, etc. Also, **trou′ble-shoot′er.** [1900–05; TROUBLE + SHOOTER]

trou•ble•some (trub′əl səm), *adj.* **1.** causing trouble, annoyance, or difficulty; vexatious: *a troublesome situation; a troublesome person.* **2.** laborious; difficult. **3.** *Archaic.* full of distress or affliction. [1540–50; TROUBLE + -SOME[1]] —**trou′ble•some•ly,** *adv.* —**trou′ble•some•ness,** *n.*

—**Syn. 1.** perplexing, galling, harassing. **2.** arduous, hard, burdensome. —**Ant. 2.** easy.

trou′ble spot′, an area in which trouble exists or is expected to develop: *There are several diplomatic trouble spots in Central America.*

trou•blous (trub′ləs), *adj.* **1.** characterized by trouble; unsettled: *troublous times.* **2.** turbulent; stormy: *a troublous sea.* **3.** causing annoyance; troublesome. **4.** causing disturbance; restless: *a troublous preacher.* [1400–50; late ME *troub(e)lous,* equiv. to *trouble* turbid (< MF < VL **turbulus;* see TROUBLE) + -OUS] —**trou′blous•ly,** *adv.* —**trou′blous•ness,** *n.*

trou-de-loup (tro͞od′l o͞o′), *n., pl.* **trous-de-loup** (tro͞od′l o͞o′). *Mil.* a conical or pyramidal pit with a pointed stake fixed vertically in the center, rows of which are dug in front of a fortification to hinder an enemy's approach, formerly used chiefly against cavalry. [1780–90; < F: lit., wolf hole]

trough (trôf, trof *or, sometimes,* trôth, troth), *n.* **1.** a long, narrow, open receptacle, usually boxlike in shape, used chiefly to hold water or food for animals. **2.** any of several similarly shaped receptacles used for various commercial or household purposes. **3.** a channel or conduit for conveying water, as a gutter under the eaves of a building for carrying away rain water. **4.** any long depression or hollow, as between two ridges or waves. **5.** *Oceanog.* a long, wide, and deep depression in the ocean floor having gently sloping sides, wider and shallower than a trench. Cf. **trench** (def. 4). **6.** *Meteorol.* an elongated area of relatively low pressure. **7.** the lowest point, esp. in an economic cycle. [bef. 900; ME; OE *trōh;* c. D, G, ON *trog*] —**trough′like′,** *adj.*

trough′ roof′. See **M roof.** [1900–05, *Amer.*]

trounce (trouns), *v.t.,* **trounced, trounc•ing. 1.** to beat severely; thrash. **2.** to punish. **3.** to defeat decisively. [1545–55; orig. uncert.] —**trounc′er,** *n.*

troupe (tro͞op), *n., v.,* **trouped, troup•ing.** *Theat.* —*n.* **1.** a company, band, or group of singers, actors, or other performers, esp. one that travels about. —*v.i.* **2.** to travel as a member of a theatrical company; barnstorm. [1815–25, *Amer.;* < F: TROOP]

—**Syn. 1.** See **troop.**

troup•er (tro͞o′pər), *n.* **1.** an actor, esp. a member of a touring company. **2.** a veteran actor. **3.** a loyal, dependable worker or participant in an undertaking: *He's a real trouper, even when the going is rough.* [1885–90, *Amer.;* TROUPE + -ER[1]]

troup•i•al (tro͞o′pē əl), *n.* any of several American birds of the family Icteridae, esp. one with brilliantly colored plumage, as *Icterus icterus,* of South America. [1815–25; < F *troupiale* (so called from its gregariousness). See TROOP, -IAL]

trou•ser (trou′zər), *adj.* **1.** of or pertaining to trousers or a trouser: *trouser cuffs; a trouser seam.* —*n.* **2.** a leg of a pair of trousers. [1600–10; back formation from TROUSERS]

trou•sers (trou′zərz), *n.* (*used with a plural v.*) **1.** Sometimes, **trouser.** Also called **pants.** a usually loose-fitting outer garment for the lower part of the body, having individual leg portions that reach typically to the ankle but sometimes to any of various other points from the upper leg down. Cf. **Bermuda shorts, breeches, knickers** (def. 1), **short** (def. 37a), **slacks. 2.** pantalets. [1585–95; *trouse* (var. of TREWS) + (DRAW)ERS] —**trou′ser•less,** *adj.*

trou′ser suit′, *Brit.* pantsuit. [1935–40]

trous•seau (tro͞o′sō, tro͞o sō′), *n., pl.* **-seaux** (-sōz, -sōz′), **-seaus.** an outfit of clothing, household linen, etc., for a bride. [1175–1225; < F; MF *troussel,* equiv. to *trousse* parcel, bundle (of straw, etc.), n. deriv. of *tro(u)sser* to fasten (see TRUSS) + *-el* dim. suffix (see -ELLE)]

trout (trout), *n., pl.* (*esp. collectively*) **trout,** (*esp. referring to two or more kinds or species*) **trouts. 1.** any of several game fishes of the genus *Salmo,* related to the salmon. Cf. **brown trout, cutthroat trout, rainbow trout. 2.** any of various game fishes of the salmon family of the genus *Salvelinus.* Cf. **brook trout** (def. 1), **char**[2], **Dolly Varden** (def. 4), **lake trout. 3.** any of several unrelated fishes, as a bass, *Micropterus salmoides,* a drum of the genus *Cynoscion,* or a greenling of the genus *Hexagrammos.* [bef. 1050; ME *trou(h)te,* OE *truht* < L *tructa* < Gk *trṓktēs* gnawer, a sea fish, equiv. to *trṓg(ein)* to gnaw + *-tēs* agent n. suffix] —**trout′less,** *adj.* —**trout′like′,** *adj.*

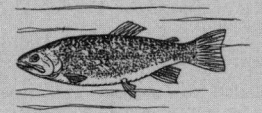

brook trout, *Salvelinus fontinalis,* length 1½ ft. (0.5 m)

trout′ lil′y. See **dogtooth violet** (def. 1).

trout•perch (trout′pûrch′), *n., pl.* **-perch•es,** (*esp. collectively*) **-perch.** a North American freshwater fish, *Percopsis omiscomaycas,* exhibiting characteristics of both trouts and perches. [1810–20, *Amer.;* TROUT + PERCH[2]]

trou•vère (tro͞o vâr′; *Fr.* tro͞o ver′), *n., pl.* **-vères** (-vârz′; *Fr.* -ver′). one of a class of medieval poets who flourished in northern France during the 12th and 13th centuries, wrote in langue d'oïl, and composed chiefly the *chansons de geste* and works on the themes of courtly love. Also, **trouveur.** Cf. **troubador** (def. 1). [1785–95; < F; OF *troveor,* equiv. to *trov(er)* to find, compose (see TROVER) + *-eor* < L *-ātor* -ATOR]

trou•veur (tro͞o vûr′; *Fr.* tro͞o vœr′), *n., pl.* **-veurs** (-vûrz′; *Fr.* -vœr′). trouvère.

Trou•ville (tro͞o vēl′), *n.* a seaport in NW France, on the English Channel: resort. 6577. Also called **Trouville-sur-Mer** (tro͞o vēl syr mer′).

Tro•va•to•re, Il (il trō′və tôr′ē; *It.* ēl trô′vä tô′re), an opera (1853) by Giuseppe Verdi.

trove (trōv), *n.* **1.** a collection of objects. **2.** treasure-trove (def. 2). [1885–90; short for TREASURE-TROVE]

tro•ver (trō′vər), *n. Law.* an action for the recovery of the value of personal property wrongfully converted by another to his or her own use. [1585–95; < MF, OF: to find, prob. < VL **tropāre* to compose, invent, deriv. of L *tropus* TROPE; cf. CONTRIVE]

trow (trō), *v.i., v.t. Archaic.* to believe, think, or suppose. [bef. 900; ME *trowen,* OE *trēow(i)an* to believe, deriv. of *trēow* belief; akin to ON *trūa,* G *trauen,* Goth *trauan* to trust, believe. See TRUST, TRUE]

trow•el (trou′əl), *n., v.,* **-eled, -el•ing** or (*esp. Brit.*) **-elled, -el•ling.** —*n.* **1.** any of various tools having a flat blade with a handle, used for depositing and working mortar, plaster, etc. **2.** a similar tool with a curved, scooplike blade, used in gardening for taking up plants, turning up earth, etc. —*v.t.* **3.** to apply, shape, smooth, or dig with or as if with a trowel. [1300–50; ME < OF *truelle* < LL *truella,* equiv. to L *tru(a)* ladle + *-ella* -ELLE] —**trow′el•er;** *esp. Brit.,* **trow′el•ler,** *n.*

troy (troi), *adj.* expressed or computed in troy weight. [1350–1400; ME *troye,* after TROYES, France, where it was standard]

Troy (troi), *n.* **1.** Latin, **Ilium.** Greek, **Ilion.** an ancient ruined city in NW Asia Minor: the seventh of nine settlements on the site is commonly identified as the Troy of the *Iliad.* **2.** a city in SE Michigan, near Detroit. 67,107. **3.** a city in E New York, on the Hudson River. 56,638. **4.** a city in W Ohio. 19,086. **5.** a city in S Alabama. 12,587. **6.** a male given name.

Troyes (trwä), *n.* a city in and the capital of Aube, in NE France, on the Seine: truce treaty in Hundred Year's War. 75,500.

Troy′ Game′, The, a solemn ritual performed at irregular intervals by the ancient Romans to signalize their alleged descent from the Trojans: notable for the interweaving labyrinthine maneuvers executed by youths on horseback. Also called **Troia.**

Tro•yon (trwa yôn′), *n.* **Con•stant** (kôn stän′), 1813–65, French painter.

troy′ weight′, a system of weights in use for precious metals and gems (formerly also for bread, grain, etc.): 24 grains = 1 pennyweight (1.555 grams); 20 pennyweights = 1 ounce (31.103 grams); 12 ounces = 1 pound (0.373 kilogram). The grain, ounce, and pound are the same as in apothecaries' weight, the grain alone being the same as in avoirdupois weight. The troy pound is no longer a standard weight in Great Britain. [1425–75; late ME]

Trp, *Biochem.* tryptophan.

trp, *Mil.* troop.

tru•an•cy (tro͞o′ən sē), *n., pl.* **-cies. 1.** the act or state of being truant. **2.** an instance of being truant: *His parents were questioned about his many truancies.* Also, **truantry.** [1775–85; TRU(ANT) + -ANCY]

tru•ant (tro͞o′ənt), *n.* **1.** a student who stays away from school without permission. **2.** a person who shirks or neglects his or her duty. —*adj.* **3.** absent from school without permission. **4.** neglectful of duty or responsibil-

CONCISE ETYMOLOGY KEY: <, descended or borrowed from; >, whence; b., blend of, blended; c., cognate with; cf., compare; deriv., derivative; equiv., equivalent; imit., imitative; obl., oblique; r., replacing; s., stem; sp., spelling, spelled; resp., respelling, respelled; trans., translation; ?, origin unknown; *, unattested; ‡, probably earlier than. See the full key inside the front cover.

ity; idle. **5.** of, pertaining to, or characteristic of a truant. —*v.i.* **6.** to be truant. [1250–1300; ME < OF: vagrant, beggar < Celtic; cf. Welsh *truan* wretched, wretch] —**tru′ant·ly,** *adv.*
—**Syn. 2.** idler, shirker, layabout, loafer, malingerer.

tru′ant of′ficer, a public-school official who investigates unauthorized absences from school. Also called **attendance officer.** [1870–75, *Amer.*]

tru·ant·ry (tro͞o′ən trē), *n., pl.* **-ries.** truancy. [1400–50; late ME; see TRUANT, -RY]

Tru·betz·koy (tro͞o′bit skoi′; *Russ.* tro͞o byits koi′), *n.* **N(i·ko·lai) S(er·ge·ie·vich)** (nyi ku lī′ syir gye′yi-vyich), 1890–1938, Russian linguist in Austria. Also, **Tru′bets·koi′, Troubetzkoy.**

truce (tro͞os), *n.* **1.** a suspension of hostilities for a specified period of time by mutual agreement of the warring parties; cease-fire; armistice. **2.** an agreement or treaty establishing this. **3.** a temporary respite, as from trouble or pain. [1175–1225; ME *trewes,* pl. of *trewe,* OE *trēow* belief, pledge, treaty. See TROW] —**truce′less,** *adj.*
—**Syn. 3.** lull, pause, rest, stay.

Tru′cial Coast′ (tro͞o′shəl). See under **United Arab Emirates.** [*trucial,* equiv. to TRUCE + -IAL, referring to a maritime truce created in 1853 between Britain and certain Omani sheiks]

Tru′cial O·man′ (ō män′), a former name of **United Arab Emirates.** Also called **Tru′cial Sheik′doms, Tru′cial States′.**

truck[1] (truk), *n.* **1.** any of various forms of vehicle for carrying goods and materials, usually consisting of a single self-propelled unit but also often composed of a trailer vehicle hauled by a tractor unit. **2.** any of various wheeled frames used for transporting heavy objects. **3.** Also called **hand truck.** a barrowlike frame with low wheels, a ledge at the bottom, and handles at the top, used to move heavy luggage, packages, cartons, etc. **4.** a low, rectangular frame on which heavy boxes, crates, trunks, etc., are moved; a dolly. **5.** a tiered framework on casters. **6.** a group of two or more pairs of wheels in one frame, for supporting one end of a railroad car, locomotive, etc. **7.** *Motion Pictures.* a dolly on which a camera is mounted. **8.** *Brit.* a freight car having no top. **9.** a small wooden wheel, cylinder, or roller, as on certain old-style gun carriages. **10.** *Naut.* a circular or square piece of wood fixed on the head of a mast or the top of a flagstaff, usually containing small holes for signal halyards. —*v.t.* **11.** to transport by truck. **12.** to put on a truck. **13.** dolly (def. 11). —*v.i.* **14.** to convey articles or goods on a truck. **15.** to drive a truck. **16.** dolly (def. 12). —*adj.* **17.** of, pertaining to, or for a truck or trucks: *a truck drive; truck tires.* [1605–15; back formation from *truckle* wheel. See TRUCKLE[2]] —**truck′a·ble,** *adj.*

truck[2] (truk), *n.* **1.** vegetables raised for the market. **2.** miscellaneous articles of little worth; odds and ends. **3.** *Informal.* trash or rubbish: *That's a lot of truck.* **4.** *Informal.* dealings: *I'll have no truck with him.* **5.** barter. **6.** a bargain or deal. **7.** the payment of wages in goods instead of money. **8.** See **truck system.** —*v.t.* **9.** to exchange; trade; barter. —*v.i.* **10.** to exchange commodities; barter. **11.** to traffic; have dealings. [1175–1225; ME *trukien* to exchange < OF *troquer* to exchange]

truck[3] (truk), *n.* **1.** a shuffling jitterbug step. —*v.i.* **2.** to dance with such steps. **3.** *Slang.* to walk or stroll, esp. in a jaunty manner: *trucking down the avenue on a Sunday afternoon.* [1935–40; special use of TRUCK[1]]

truck·age (truk′ij), *n.* **1.** conveyance by a truck or trucks. **2.** the charge for this. [1820–30; TRUCK[1] + -AGE]

truck′ bol′ster, *Railroads.* the upper transverse member of a car truck that holds the truck center plate and receives the car's weight. Cf. **body bolster.** [1890–95]

truck′ camp′er, a type of camper designed to be mounted on a pickup truck. Cf. **camper truck.**

truck′ cen′ter plate′. See under **center plate.**

truck′ crop′, a vegetable crop raised on a truck farm. [1890–95, *Amer.*]

truck·driv·er (truk′drī′vər), *n.* a person who drives a truck. [1890–95; TRUCK[1] + DRIVER]

Truck·ee (truk′ē), *n.* a river in E California and W Nevada, rising in Lake Tahoe and flowing E and NE for about 125 mi. (201 km).

truck·er[1] (truk′ər), *n.* **1.** a person who drives a truck; truckdriver. **2.** a person whose business is trucking goods. [1875–80; TRUCK[1] + -ER[1]]

truck·er[2] (truk′ər), *n.* a truck farmer. [1530–40; TRUCK[2] + -ER[1]]

truck′ farm′, a farm for the growing of vegetables for the market. Also called **truck′ gar′den;** *esp. Brit.,* **market garden.** [1865–70, *Amer.*] —**truck′ farm′er.** —**truck′ farm′ing.**

truck·ing[1] (truk′ing), *n.* the art or business of conveying articles or goods on trucks. [1800–10; TRUCK[1] + -ING[1]]

truck·ing[2] (truk′ing), *n.* **1.** the growing of vegetables for the market. **2.** commercial bartering. [1585–95; TRUCK[2] + -ING[1]]

truck′ing shot′, *Motion Pictures, Television.* See **dolly shot.**

truck′ job′ber, a jobber or wholesaler who makes calls carrying goods on a truck, thereby being able to take and deliver orders on the same call. Also called **wagon jobber.**

truck·le[1] (truk′əl), *v.i.,* **-led, -ling.** to submit or yield obsequiously or tamely (usually fol. by *to*): *Don't truckle to unreasonable demands.* [1605–15; special use of obs. *truckle* to sleep on a truckle bed. See TRUCKLE[2]] —**truck′ler,** *n.* —**truck′ling·ly,** *adv.*
—**Syn.** grovel, bow, concede, kowtow.

truck·le[2] (truk′əl), *n.* **1.** See **truckle bed. 2.** a pulley. [1375–1425; late ME *trocle* sheave, roller < AF < L *trochlea* pulley. See TROCHLEA]

truck′le bed′, a low bed moving on casters, usually pushed under another bed when not in use. Also called **trundle bed.** [1425–75; late ME]

truck·line (truk′līn′), *n.* a transportation line utilizing trucks. [1920–25; TRUCK[1] + LINE[1]]

truck·load (truk′lōd′), *n.* **1.** the amount that a truck can carry. **2.** the minimum weight legally required for making shipments at a rate (**truck′load rate′**) below that charged for shipments under this minimum. [1860–65; TRUCK[1] + LOAD]

truck·man (truk′mən), *n., pl.* **-men. 1.** a truckdriver. **2.** a person who is in the business of trucking goods, produce, etc. [1780–90, *Amer.;* TRUCK[1] + -MAN]

truck′ stop′, a gas station, usually at the side of a major highway, where truck drivers stop for fuel, and often including a restaurant, sleeping and showering rooms, a store selling basic items, etc. [1960–65]

truck′ sys′tem, the system of paying wages in goods instead of money. Also called **truck.** [1820–30]

truck′ trac′tor, tractor (def. 2).

truck′ trail′er, *Auto.* a trailer designed to be drawn by a truck tractor or other motor truck. Also called **trailer truck.**

truc·u·lent (truk′yə lənt, tro͞o′kyə-), *adj.* **1.** fierce; cruel; savagely brutal. **2.** brutally harsh; vitriolic; scathing: *his truculent criticism of her work.* **3.** aggressively hostile; belligerent. [1530–40; < L *truculentus,* equiv. to *truc-,* s. of *trux* savage, pitiless + *-ulentus* -ULENT] —**truc′u·lence, truc′u·len·cy,** *n.* —**truc′u·lent·ly,** *adv.*
—**Syn. 1.** See **fierce.** —**Ant. 1.** amiable, gentle.

Tru·deau (tro͞o dō′), *n.* **Pi·erre Elliott** (pē âr′), born 1919, Canadian political leader: prime minister 1968–79 and 1980–84.

trudge (truj), *v.,* **trudged, trudg·ing,** *n.* —*v.i.* **1.** to walk, esp. laboriously or wearily: *to trudge up a long flight of steps.* —*v.t.* **2.** to walk laboriously or wearily along or over: *He trudged the deserted road for hours.* —*n.* **3.** a laborious or tiring walk; tramp. [1540–50; perh. b. TREAD and DRUDGE] —**trudg′er,** *n.*
—**Syn. 1.** tramp. See **pace**[1].

trudg·en (truj′ən), *n. Swimming.* a stroke in which a double overarm motion and a scissors kick are used. Also called **trudg′en stroke′.** [1890–95; named after John *Trudgen* (1852–1902), British swimmer]

Tru·dy (tro͞o′dē), *n.* a female given name, form of **Gertrude.**

true (tro͞o), *adj.,* **tru·er, tru·est,** *n., adv., v.,* **trued, tru·ing** or **true·ing.** —*adj.* **1.** being in accordance with the actual state or conditions; conforming to reality or fact; not false: *a true story.* **2.** real; genuine; authentic: *true gold; true feelings.* **3.** sincere; not deceitful: *a true interest in someone's welfare.* **4.** firm in allegiance; loyal; faithful; steadfast: *a true friend.* **5.** being or reflecting the essential or genuine character of something: *the true meaning of his statement.* **6.** conforming to or consistent with a standard, pattern, or the like: *a true copy.* **7.** exact; precise; accurate; correct: *a true balance.* **8.** of the right kind; such as it should be; proper: *to arrange things in their true order.* **9.** properly so called; rightly answering to a description: *true statesmanship.* **10.** legitimate or rightful: *the true heir.* **11.** reliable, unfailing, or sure: *a true sign.* **12.** exactly or accurately shaped, formed, fitted, or placed, as a surface, instrument, or part of a mechanism. **13.** honest; honorable; upright. **14.** *Biol.* conforming to the type, norm, or standard of structure of a particular group; typical: *The lion is a true cat.* **15.** *Animal Husb.* purebred. **16.** *Navig.* (of a bearing, course, etc.) determined in relation to true north. **17.** *Archaic.* truthful. —*n.* **18.** exact or accurate formation, position, or adjustment: *to be out of true.* **19. the true,** something that is true; truth. —*adv.* **20.** in a true manner; truly; truthfully. **21.** exactly or accurately. **22.** in conformity with the ancestral type: *to breed true.* **23. come true,** to have the expected or hoped-for result; become a reality: *She couldn't believe that her dream would ever come true.* —*v.t.* **24.** to make true; shape, adjust, place, etc., exactly or accurately: *to true the wheels of a bicycle after striking a pothole.* **25.** (esp. in carpentry) to make even, symmetrical, level, etc. (often fol. by *up*): *to true up the sides of a door.* [bef. 900; ME *trewe* (adj. and adv.), OE *trēowe* (adj.) loyal, trusty, honest (see TROW, TRUCE); akin to D *trouw,* G *treu,* ON *tryggr,* Goth *triggws*] —**true′ness,** *n.*
—**Syn. 1.** factual, veracious. See **real**[1]. **3.** honest. **4.** trustworthy; staunch, constant, steady, unwavering. **7.** faithful.

true′ anom′aly, *Astron.* the anomaly of a planet; its angular distance from perihelion or aphelion.

true′ bacte′ria, eubacteria.

true′ believ′er, 1. a person who has been thoroughly convinced of something. **2.** a fanatic, esp. a religious or political one.

true′ bill′, a bill of indictment endorsed by a grand jury as being sufficiently supported by evidence to justify a hearing of the case. Cf. **no bill.** [1760–70]

true′ blue′, 1. a nonfading blue dye or pigment. **2.** a person who is true-blue. **3.** (in the 17th century) the color adopted by the Covenanters in contradistinction to the royal red. [1665–75]

true-blue (tro͞o′blo͞o′), *adj.* unwaveringly loyal or faithful; staunch; unchangingly true. [1665–75]

true·born (tro͞o′bôrn′), *adj.* genuinely or authentically so because of birth: *a trueborn son of Ireland; a trueborn Parisian.* [1585–95; TRUE + BORN]

true·bred (tro͞o′bred′), *adj.* **1.** marked by qualities of good breeding and education; well-bred. **2.** thoroughbred or purebred: *a truebred Lippizaner.* [1590–1600; TRUE + BRED]

true′ bug′, bug[1] (def. 1). [1890–95]

true′ course′, *Navig.* a course whose bearing is given relative to the geographical meridian. Cf. **compass course, magnetic course.**

true′-false′ test′ (tro͞o′fôls′), *Educ.* a test requiring one to mark statements as true or false. [1920–25]

true′ fly′, fly[2] (def. 1).

true′ fres′co, fresco (def. 1).

true′ frog′, frog (def. 2).

true′ fruit′. See **simple fruit.**

true·heart·ed (tro͞o′här′tid), *adj.* **1.** faithful; loyal. **2.** honest; sincere. Also, **true′-heart′ed.** [1425–75; late ME *true hartyd;* see TRUE, HEART, -ED[3]] —**true′heart′ed·ness,** *n.*

true′ lev′el, an imaginary surface everywhere perpendicular to the plumb line, or line of gravity.

true-life (tro͞o′līf′), *adj.* similar to everyday life; realistic: *true-life episodes.* [1925–30]

true·love (tro͞o′luv′), *n.* a sweetheart; a truly loving or loved person. [1350–1400; ME *trewe love.* See TRUE, LOVE]

true′love knot′, a complicated ornamental knot, esp. a double knot having two interlacing bows, regarded as an emblem of true love or interwoven affections. Also called **true′ lov′er's knot′, true′-lov′er's knot′.** [1485–95]

true′ north′, *Navig., Survey.* the direction of the north pole from a given point.

true·pen·ny (tro͞o′pen′ē), *n., pl.* **-nies.** a trusty, honest fellow. [1580–90; TRUE + PENNY]

true′ rhyme′. See **full rhyme.** [1965–70]

true′ rib′, *Anat.* one member of the first seven pairs of ribs that are attached in humans to the sternum by costal cartilages. [1735–45]

true′ seal′. See **earless seal.**

true′ time′, apparent solar time; the time as shown by a sundial.

true′ toad′, toad (def. 2).

true′ vo′cal cords′, *Anat.* the lower pair of vocal cords, the edges of which can be made to tense and relax by the passage of air from the lungs, thus producing vocal sound. Also called **vocal folds.** Cf. **false vocal cord, vocal cords.**

Truf·faut (tro͞o fō′; *Fr.* try fō′), *n.* **Fran·çois** (fran-swä′; *Fr.* fräN swa′), 1932–84, French film director.

truffe (tryf), *n. French.* **1.** truffle. **2.** *Slang.* peasant; boor.

truf·fle (truf′əl, tro͞o′fəl), *n.* **1.** any of several subterranean, edible, ascomycetous fungi of the genus *Tuber.* **2.** any of various similar fungi of other genera. **3.** a candy made of soft chocolate, shaped into a ball and dusted with cocoa, or sometimes a three-layered cube of light and dark chocolate. [1585–95; < D *truffel(e)* < MF *truffle, truffe* < OPr *trufa* < LL *tūfera,* **tūfer,* prob. < an Osco-Umbrian cognate of L *tūber* TUBER[1]] —**truf′fled,** *adj.*

trug (trug, tro͝og), *n. Brit.* **1.** a shallow basket for carrying flowers, vegetables, etc., made from strips of wood. **2.** a shallow wooden milk pan. **3.** a wooden tray for holding mortar. [1570–80; orig. uncert.]

tru·ism (tro͞o′iz əm), *n.* a self-evident, obvious truth. [1700–10; TRUE + -ISM] —**tru·is′tic, tru·is′ti·cal,** *adj.*
—**Syn.** cliché, platitude.

Tru·ji·llo (tro͞o hē′ō; *Sp.* tro͞o hē′yō), *n.* **1. Ra·fa·el Le·o·ni·das** (raf′ā el′ lē on′i dəs; *Sp.* rä′fä el′ le′ō-ne′thäs), (*Rafael Leonidas Trujillo Molina*), 1891–1961, Dominican general and politician: president 1930–38, 1942–52. **2.** a seaport in NW Peru. 240,322.

Tru·ji·llo Al·to (tro͞o hē′ō äl′tō; *Sp.* tro͞o hē′yô äl′tô), a city in NE Puerto Rico, SE of San Juan. 41,141.

Truk′ Is′lands (truk, tro͝ok), a group of the Caroline Islands, in the N Pacific: part of the Federated States of Micronesia; an important Japanese naval base in World War II. 35,220; 50 sq. mi. (130 sq. km). Also called **Truk.**

T-rule (tē′ro͞ol′), *n. Ling.* See **transformational rule.**

trull (trul), *n.* a prostitute; strumpet. [1510–20; of uncert. orig.; cf. TROLLOP, G *Trulle* loose woman]

trul·lo (tro͞o′lō), *n., pl.* **-li** (-lē). a dwelling of the Apulia region of Italy, roofed with conical constructions of corbeled dry masonry. [1905–10 < It < Apulian dial. *truḍḍu* < MGk, LGk *trŷllos* cupola, ult. < L *trulla* ladle, scoop (cf. TROWEL), prob. by intermediary sense "cup, goblet"; cf. similar development of CUPOLA]

tru·ly (tro͞o′lē), *adv.* **1.** in accordance with fact or truth; truthfully. **2.** exactly; accurately; correctly. **3.** rightly; properly; duly. **4.** legitimately; by right. **5.** really; genuinely; authentically. **6.** indeed; verily. **7.** sincerely: *yours truly.* **8.** *Archaic.* faithfully; loyally. [bef. 1000; ME *treuli,* OE *trēowlice.* See TRUE, -LY]

Tru·man (tro͞o′mən), *n.* **1. Harry S,** 1884–1972, 33rd president of the U.S. 1945–53. **2.** a male given name.

Tru′man Doc′trine, the policy of President Truman, as advocated in his address to Congress on March 12, 1947, to provide military and economic aid to Greece and Turkey and, by extension, to any country threatened by Communism or any totalitarian ideology.

Trum·bull (trum′bəl), *n.* **1. John,** 1756–1843, U.S. painter (son of Jonathan Trumbull). **2. Jonathan,** 1710–85, U.S. statesman. **3.** a town in SW Connecticut. 32,989.

tru·meau (tro͞o mō′; *Fr.* try mō′), *n., pl.* **-meaux** (-mōz′; *Fr.* -mō′). **1.** a mirror having a painted or

CONCISE PRONUNCIATION KEY: act, cāpe, dâre, pärt; set, ēqual; if, īce; ox, ōver, ôrder, oil, bo͝ok, bo͞ot, out; up, ûrge; child; sing; shoe; thin, that; zh as in treasure. ə = a as in *alone,* e as in *system,* i as in *easily,* o as in *gallop,* u as in *circus;* ᵊ as in *fire* (fīᵊr), *hour* (ouᵊr). l and n can serve as syllabic consonants, as in *cradle* (krād′l), and *button* (but′n). See the full key inside the front cover.

carved panel above or below the glass in the same frame. **2.** *Archit.* a column supporting a tympanum of a doorway at its center. See illus. under **tympanum.** [< F]

trump[1] (trump), *n.* **1.** *Cards.* **a.** any playing card of a suit that for the time outranks the other suits, such a card being able to take any card of another suit. **b.** Often, **trumps.** (*used with a singular v.*) the suit itself. **2.** *Informal.* a fine person; brick. —*v.t.* **3.** *Cards.* to take with a trump. **4.** to excel; surpass; outdo. —*v.i.* **5.** *Cards.* **a.** to play a trump. **b.** to take a trick with a trump. **6. trump up,** to devise deceitfully or dishonestly, as an accusation; fabricate: *Try as they might, they were unable to trump up a convincing case against him.* [1520–30; unexplained var. of TRIUMPH] —**trump′less,** *adj.*

trump[2] (trump), *Literary.* —*n.* **1.** a trumpet. **2.** its sound. —*v.i.* **3.** to blow a trumpet. [1250–1300; (n.) ME *trompe* < OF < OHG *trumpa,* var. of *trumba* trumpet; (v.) ME *trompen* < OF *tromper,* deriv. of *trompe*]

trump card (trump′ kärd′ *for 1;* trump′ kärd′ *for 2*). **1.** *Cards.* trump[1] (def. 1a). **2.** *Informal.* something that gives one person or group the advantage over another: *The surprise witness was his trump card.* [1815–25]

trumped-up (trumpt′up′), *adj.* spuriously devised; fraudulent; fabricated: *He was arrested on some trumped-up charge.* [1720–30; special use of TRUMP[1]; see -ED[2]]

Trum·pel·dor (trum′pəl dôr′), *n.* **Joseph,** 1880–1920, Zionist leader, born in Russia.

trump·er·y (trum′pə rē), *n., pl.* **-ries,** *adj.* —*n.* **1.** something without use or value; rubbish; trash; worthless stuff. **2.** nonsense; twaddle: *His usual conversation is pure trumpery.* **3.** *Archaic.* worthless finery. —*adj.* **4.** of little or no value; trifling, worthless; rubbishy; trashy. [1425–75; late ME *trompery* deceit < MF *tromperie,* equiv. to *tromp(er)* to deceive + *-erie* -ERY]

trumpet (def. 1a)

trum·pet (trum′pit), *n.* **1.** *Music.* **a.** any of a family of brass wind instruments with a powerful, penetrating tone, consisting of a tube commonly curved once or twice around on itself and having a cup-shaped mouthpiece at one end and a flaring bell at the other. **b.** an organ stop having a tone resembling that of a trumpet. **c.** a trumpeter. **2.** something used as or resembling a trumpet, esp. in sound. **3.** a sound like that of a trumpet. **4.** the loud shrill cry of an animal, esp. an elephant. **5.** See **ear trumpet. 6. trumpets,** any of several pitcher plants of the southeastern U.S. —*v.i.* **7.** to blow a trumpet. **8.** to emit a loud, trumpetlike cry, as an elephant. —*v.t.* **9.** to sound on a trumpet. **10.** to utter with a sound like that of a trumpet. **11.** to proclaim loudly or widely. [1300–50; ME *trumpette, trompette* < F, equiv. to *trompe* TRUMP[2] + *-ette* -ET] —**trum′pet·less,** *adj.* —**trum′·pet·like′,** *adj.*

trum′pet creep′er, any climbing plant belonging to the genus *Campsis,* of the bignonia family, esp. *C. radicans,* of the southern U.S., having elliptic leaves and large, red, trumpet-shaped flowers. [1825–35, *Amer.*]

trum·pet·er (trum′pi tər), *n.* **1.** a person who plays a trumpet; trumpet player. **2.** a person who proclaims or announces something with a trumpet. **3.** a soldier, usually in a mounted unit, whose duty is to sound the required trumpet calls. **4.** a person who proclaims, commends, or extols something loudly or widely; eulogizer. **5.** any of several large South American birds of the family Psophiidae, esp. *Psophia crepitans,* related to the cranes and rails, having a loud, harsh, prolonged cry. **6.** See **trumpeter swan. 7.** one of a breed of domestic pigeons. [1490–1500; TRUMPET + -ER[1]]

trum′peter swan′, a large, pure-white, wild swan, *Cygnus buccinator,* of North America, having a sonorous cry: once near extinction, the species is now recovering. [1700–10]

trum·pet·fish (trum′pit fish′), *n., pl.* (*esp. collectively*) **-fish,** (*esp. referring to two or more kinds or species*) **-fish·es.** any of several fishes of the family Aulostomidae, having a long, tubular snout, as the slender, brown-flecked *Aulostomus maculatus,* inhabiting waters on both sides of the tropical Atlantic Ocean, having the habit of orienting vertically in the water and capturing its prey from that position. [1660–70; TRUMPET + FISH]

trum′pet flow′er, **1.** any of various plants with pendent flowers shaped like a trumpet. **2.** See **trumpet creeper. 3.** See **trumpet honeysuckle. 4.** the flower of any of these plants. [1720–30, *Amer.*]

trum′pet hon′eysuckle, an American honeysuckle, *Lonicera sempervirens,* having spikes of large, tubular flowers, deep-red outside and yellow within. Also called **coral honeysuckle.** [1725–35, *Amer.*]

trum·pet-leaf (trum′pit lēf′), *n., pl.* **-leaves.** trumpets. [1860–65, *Amer.*]

trum′pet leg′, *Furniture.* a turned leg that flares upward and outward from a narrow lower end.

CONCISE ETYMOLOGY KEY: <, descended or borrowed from; >, whence; b., blend of, blended; c., cognate with; cf., compare; deriv., derivative; equiv., equivalent; imit., imitative; obl., oblique; r., replacing; s., stem; sp., spelling, spelled; resp., respelling, respelled; trans., translation; ?, origin unknown; *, unattested; ‡, probably earlier than. See the full key inside the front cover.

trumpet legs

trum′pet marine′, an obsolete musical instrument having a long, wooden, pyramid-shaped body, characteristically with one string that is touched with the finger to produce harmonics and is bowed between the touching finger and the upper end. Also called **nun's fiddle, tromba marina, trumscheit.** [1665–75]

trum·pet·ry (trum′pi trē), *n.* **1.** the manner of playing the trumpet: *The character of modern trumpetry has changed.* **2.** the sound, esp. the blaring sound, of trumpets. **3.** trumpets collectively. [1855–60; TRUMPET + -RY]

trum·pets (trum′pits), *n., pl.* **-pets.** a showy pitcher plant, *Sarracenia flava,* of the southeastern U.S., having prominently veined, crimson-throated, yellow-green leaves and yellow flowers from 2 to 4 in. (5.1 to 10.2 cm) wide. Also called **trumpet-leaf, yellow pitcher plant.** [pl. of TRUMPET]

trum·pet-tree (trum′pit trē′), *n.* a tropical American tree, *Cecropia peltata,* of the mulberry family, having hollow, jointed stems and branches used in making certain wind instruments. Also called **trum·pet·wood** (trum′pit wŏŏd′). [1750–60]

trum′pet vine′. See **trumpet creeper.** [1700–10, *Amer.*]

trum·scheit (trŏŏm′shit), *n.* See **trumpet marine.** [< G *Trummscheit,* equiv. to *Trumm-* (OHG *trumba* trumpet; see TRUMP[2]) + *Scheit* piece of wood, board]

trun·cate (trung′kāt), *v.,* **-cat·ed, -cat·ing,** *adj.* —*v.t.* **1.** to shorten by cutting off a part; cut short: *Truncate detailed explanations.* **2.** *Math., Computers.* to shorten (a number) by dropping a digit or digits: *The numbers 1.4142 and 1.4987 can both be truncated to 1.4.* —*adj.* **3.** truncated. **4.** *Biol.* **a.** square or broad at the end, as if cut off transversely. **b.** lacking the apex, as certain spiral shells. [1480–90; < L *truncātus* (ptp. of *truncāre* to lop), equiv. to *trunc(us)* TRUNK + *-ātus* -ATE[1]] —**trun′cate·ly,** *adv.*

—**Syn. 1.** abridge, trim, curtail, abbreviate.

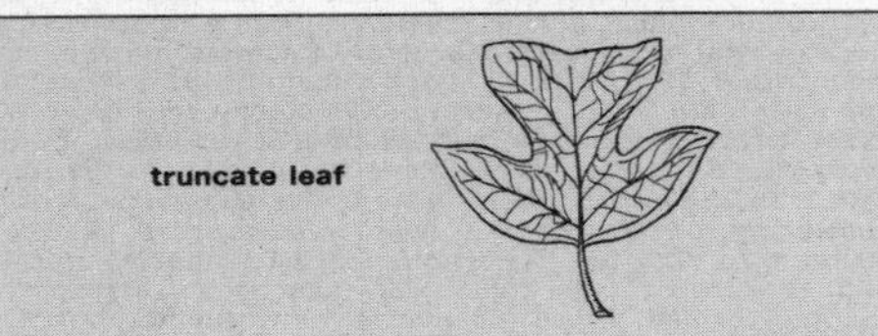
truncate leaf

trun·cat·ed (trung′kā tid), *adj.* **1.** shortened by or as if by having a part cut off; cut short: *an unnecessarily truncated essay.* **2.** (of a geometric figure or solid) having the apex, vertex, or end cut off by a plane: *a truncated cone or pyramid.* **3.** *Crystall.* (of a crystal) having corners, angles, or edges cut off or replaced by a single plane. **4.** *Biol.* truncate (def. 4). **5.** *Pros.* (of a line of verse) lacking at the beginning or end one or more unstressed syllables needed to fill out the metrical pattern. [1480–90; TRUNCATE + -ED[2]]

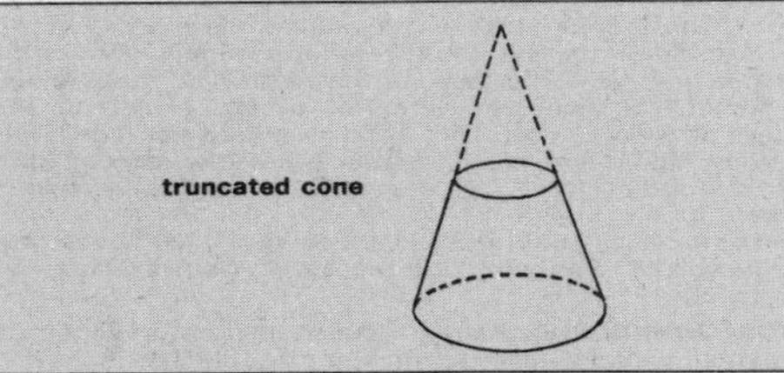
truncated cone

trun·ca·tion (trung kā′shən), *n.* **1.** the act or process of truncating. **2.** the quality or state of being truncated. **3.** *Pros.* the omission of one or more unaccented syllables at the beginning or the end of a line of verse. **4.** *Banking.* a system of electronic check recording under which canceled checks are not returned to customers by the bank. [1570–80; < LL *truncātiōn-* (s. of *truncātiō*), equiv. to L *truncātus* (see TRUNCATE) + *-iōn-* -ION]

trun·cheon (trun′chən), *n.* **1.** the club carried by a police officer; billy. **2.** a staff representing an office or authority; baton. **3.** the shattered shaft of a spear. **4.** *Obs.* cudgel; bludgeon. —*v.t.* **5.** *Archaic.* to beat with a club. [1300–50; ME *tronchon* fragment < MF < VL **trunciōn-*, s. of **trunciō* lit., a lopping. See TRUNK, -ION]

trun·dle (trun′dl), *v.,* **-dled, -dling,** *n.* —*v.t.* **1.** to cause (a circular object) to roll along; roll. **2.** to convey or move in a wagon, cart, or other wheeled vehicle; wheel: *The farmer trundled his produce to market in a rickety wagon.* **3.** *Archaic.* to cause to rotate; twirl; spin. —*v.i.* **4.** to roll along. **5.** to move or run on a wheel or wheels. **6.** to travel in a wheeled vehicle: *He got into his car and trundled downtown.* **7.** to move or walk with a rolling gait. —*n.* **8.** a small wheel, roller, or the like. **9.** a lantern wheel. **10.** each of the bars of a lantern wheel. **11.** a truck or carriage on low wheels. [1555–65; var. of TRINDLE] —**trun′dler,** *n.*

trun′dle bed′. See **truckle bed.** [1535–45]

trun·dle·tail (trun′dl tāl′), *n. Archaic.* a dog with a curly tail. [1480–90; TRUNDLE + TAIL[1]]

trunk (trungk), *n.* **1.** the main stem of a tree, as distinct from the branches and roots. **2.** a large, sturdy box or chest for holding or transporting clothes, personal effects, or other articles. **3.** a large compartment, usually in the rear of an automobile, in which luggage, a spare tire, and other articles may be kept. **4.** the body of a person or an animal excluding the head and limbs; torso. **5.** *Ichthyol.* the part of a fish between the head and the anus. **6.** *Archit.* **a.** the shaft of a column. **b.** the dado or die of a pedestal. **7.** the main channel, artery, or line in a river, railroad, highway, canal, or other tributary system. **8.** *Telephony, Telegraphy.* **a.** a telephone line or channel between two central offices or switching devices that is used in providing telephone connections between subscribers generally. **b.** a telegraph line or channel between two main or central offices. **9.** *Anat.* the main body of an artery, nerve, or the like, as distinct from its branches. **10. trunks, a.** brief shorts, loose-fitting or tight, worn by men chiefly for boxing, swimming, and track. **b.** *Obs.* See **trunk hose. 11.** the long, flexible, cylindrical nasal appendage of the elephant. **12.** *Naut.* **a.** a large enclosed passage through the decks or bulkheads of a vessel, for cooling, ventilation, or the like. **b.** any of various watertight casings in a vessel, as the vertical one above the slot for a centerboard in the bottom of a boat. **13.** a conduit; shaft; chute. —*adj.* **14.** of, pertaining to, or noting a main channel or line, as of a railroad or river. [1400–50; late ME *trunke* < L *truncus* stem, trunk, stump, n. use of *truncus* lopped] —**trunk′less,** *adj.*

trunk cabin

trunk′ cab′in, a cabin of a yacht that presents a long, low profile with a relatively unbroken line fore and aft. Cf. **doghouse** (def. 2). [1885–90, *Amer.*]

trunk′ call′, *Chiefly Brit.* a long-distance phone call. [1905–10]

trunk′ en′gine, **1.** an engine having a trunk piston or pistons. **2.** a double-acting steam engine having a connecting rod passing through a trunk to the piston. [1860–65]

trunk·fish (trungk′fish′), *n., pl.* (*esp. collectively*) **-fish,** (*esp. referring to two or more kinds or species*) **-fish·es.** any plectognath fish of the family Ostraciontidae, of warm seas, having a boxlike body encased in bony, polygonal plates. Also called **boxfish.** [1795–1805; TRUNK + FISH]

trunk·ful (trungk′fŏŏl), *n., pl.* **-fuls. 1.** the amount that a trunk will hold. **2.** *Informal.* a full or abundant supply: *a trunkful of hopes.* [1700–10; TRUNK + -FUL] —**Usage.** See **-ful.**

trunk′ hose′, full, baglike breeches covering the body from the waist to the middle of the thigh or lower, sometimes having the stockings attached in one piece, worn by men in the 16th and 17th centuries. [1615–25]

trunk′ line′, **1.** a major long-distance transportation line. **2.** trunk (def. 8). [1850–55]

trunk′ pis′ton, *Mach.* a piston with a long skirt to take the side thrust, as in an automobile engine.

trun·nel (trun′l), *n.* treenail. [var. of TREENAIL, perh. by association with TRUNDLE]

trun·nion (trun′yən), *n.* **1.** either of the two cylindrical projections on a cannon, one on each side for supporting the cannon on its carriage. **2.** any of various similar supports for machinery. [1615–25; < F *trognon* trunk, stump, core (of fruit)] —**trun′nioned,** *adj.*

Tru·ro (trŏŏr′ō), *n.* a town in central Nova Scotia, in SE Canada. 12,552.

truss (trus), *v.t.* **1.** to tie, bind, or fasten. **2.** to make fast with skewers, thread, or the like, as the wings or legs of a fowl in preparation for cooking. **3.** to furnish or support with a truss or trusses. **4.** to tie or secure (the body) closely or tightly; bind (often fol. by *up*). **5.** *Falconry.* (of a hawk, falcon, etc.) to grasp (prey) firmly. —*n.* **6.** *Civ. Engin., Building Trades.* **a.** any of various structural frames based on the geometric rigidity of the triangle and composed of straight members subject only to longitudinal compression, tension, or both: functions as a beam or cantilever to support bridges, roofs, etc. Cf. **complete** (def. 8), **incomplete** (def. 3), **redundant** (def. 5c). **b.** any of various structural frames constructed on principles other than the geometric rigidity of the triangle or deriving stability from other factors, as the rigidity of joints, the abutment of masonry, or the stiffness of beams. **7.** *Med.* an apparatus consisting of a pad usually supported by a belt for maintaining a hernia in a reduced state. **8.** *Hort.* a compact terminal cluster or head of flowers growing upon one stalk. **9.** *Naut.* a device for supporting a standing yard, having a pivot permitting the yard to swing horizontally when braced. **10.** a collection of things tied together or packed in a receptacle; bundle; pack. **11.** *Chiefly Brit.* a bundle of hay or straw, esp. one containing about 56 lb. (25.4 kg) of old hay, 60 lb. (27.2 kg) of new hay, or 36 lb. (16.3 kg) of straw.

[1175–1225; (v.) ME *trussen* < OF *tr(o)usser,* var. of *torser,* prob. < VL **torsāre,* deriv. of **torsus,* for L *tortus* ptp. of *torquere* to twist, wind, wrap; (n.) ME: bundle < OF *trousse, torse,* deriv. of *torser*] **—truss′er,** *n.*

truss′ bridge′, a bridge in which the loads are supported by trusses. [1830–40, *Amer.*]

trussed (trust), *adj. Heraldry.* close (def. 59). [1400–50; late ME; see TRUSS, -ED[2]]

truss′ hoop′, a hoop placed around the staves of a barrel to secure them in place. Also, **truss′-hoop′.** [1645–55]

truss·ing (trus′ing), *n.* **1.** the members that form a truss. **2.** a structure consisting of trusses. **3.** trusses collectively. [1300–50; ME *trossinge;* see TRUSS, -ING[1]]

truss′ rod′, *Building Trades.* **1.** a tie rod in a truss. **2.** a diagonal iron or steel reinforcement in a wooden beam. **3.** any iron or steel rod serving as a tension member. [1870–75]

trust (trust), *n.* **1.** reliance on the integrity, strength, ability, surety, etc., of a person or thing; confidence. **2.** confident expectation of something; hope. **3.** confidence in the certainty of future payment for property or goods received; credit: *to sell merchandise on trust.* **4.** a person on whom or thing on which one relies: *God is my trust.* **5.** the condition of one to whom something has been entrusted. **6.** the obligation or responsibility imposed on a person in whom confidence or authority is placed: *a position of trust.* **7.** charge, custody, or care: *to leave valuables in someone's trust.* **8.** something committed or entrusted to one's care for use or safekeeping, as an office, duty, or the like; responsibility; charge. **9.** *Law.* **a.** a fiduciary relationship in which one person (the trustee) holds the title to property (the trust estate or trust property) for the benefit of another (the beneficiary). **b.** the property or funds so held. **10.** *Com.* **a.** an illegal combination of industrial or commercial companies in which the stock of the constituent companies is controlled by a central board of trustees, thus making it possible to manage the companies so as to minimize production costs, control prices, eliminate competition, etc. **b.** any large industrial or commercial corporation or combination having a monopolistic or semimonopolistic control over the production of some commodity or service. **11.** *Archaic.* reliability. **12. in trust,** in the position of being left in the care or guardianship of another: *She left money to her uncle to keep in trust for her children.* —*adj.* **13.** *Law.* of or pertaining to trusts or a trust. —*v.i.* **14.** to rely upon or place confidence in someone or something (usually fol. by *in* or *to*): *to trust in another's honesty; trusting to luck.* **15.** to have confidence; hope: *Things work out if one only trusts.* **16.** to sell merchandise on credit. —*v.t.* **17.** to have trust or confidence in; rely or depend on. **18.** to believe. **19.** to expect confidently; hope (usually fol. by a clause or infinitive as object): *trusting the job would soon be finished; trusting to find oil on the land.* **20.** to commit or consign with trust or confidence. **21.** to permit to remain or go somewhere or to do something without fear of consequences: *He does not trust his children out of his sight.* **22.** to invest with a trust; entrust with something. **23.** to give credit to (a person) for goods, services, etc., supplied: *Will you trust us till payday?* **24. trust to,** to rely on; trust: *Never trust to luck!* [1175–1225; (n.) ME < ON *traust* trust (c. G *Trost* comfort); (v.) ME *trusten* < ON *treysta,* deriv. of *traust*] **—trust′a·ble,** *adj.* **—trust′a·bil′i·ty,** *n.* **—trust′er,** *n.*
—Syn. 1. certainty, belief, faith. TRUST, ASSURANCE, CONFIDENCE imply a feeling of security. TRUST implies instinctive unquestioning belief in and reliance upon something: *to have trust in one's parents.* CONFIDENCE implies conscious trust because of good reasons, definite evidence, or past experience: *to have confidence in the outcome of events.* ASSURANCE implies absolute confidence and certainty: *to feel an assurance of victory.* **8.** commitment, commission. **18.** credit. **20.** entrust.

trust′ account′, **1.** an account of property established with a trust company by a grantor, for distribution during or after the grantor's lifetime. **2.** Also called **trustee′ account′.** *Banking* a savings account over which the depositor, while living, has sole control as trustee, and which upon the death of the depositor becomes payable to the beneficiary.

trust·bust·er (trust′bus′tər), *n.* a federal official who seeks to dissolve business trusts, esp. through vigorous application of antitrust regulations. [1900–05, *Amer.*; TRUST + BUSTER]

trust′ com′pany, a company or corporation organized to exercise the functions of a trustee, but usually engaging also in other banking and financial activities. [1825–35, *Amer.*]

trust′ deed′, a written instrument legally conveying property to a trustee, such as a bank, often for the purpose of securing a mortgage or promissory note. Also called **deed of trust.** [1745–55]

trust·ee (tru stē′), *n., v.* **-eed, -ee·ing.** *Law.* —*n.* **1.** a person, usually one of a body of persons, appointed to administer the affairs of a company, institution, etc. **2.** a person who holds the title to property for the benefit of another. **3.** (in New England) a garnishee. **4.** a trusty. —*v.t.* **5.** to place in the hands of a trustee or trustees. **6.** (in New England) to garnish. [1640–50; TRUST + -EE]

trustee′ in bank′ruptcy, *Law.* a person appointed by a court to administer the property of a bankrupt.

trustee′ proc′ess, *Law.* (in New England) garnishment (def. 1). [1800–10, *Amer.*]

trust·ee·ship (tru stē′ship), *n.* **1.** *Law.* the office or function of a trustee. **2.** the administrative control of a territory granted to a country by a body (**Trustee′ship Coun′cil**) of the United Nations. **3.** See **trust territory.** [1720–30; TRUSTEE + -SHIP]

trust·ful (trust′fəl), *adj.* full of trust; free of distrust, suspicion, or the like; confiding: *a trustful friend.* [1570–80; TRUST + -FUL] **—trust′ful·ly,** *adv.* **—trust′ful·ness,** *n.*

trust′ fund′, **1.** money, securities, property, etc., held in trust. **2.** a government fund used and administered separately from other funds and used for a specified purpose: *a highway trust fund.* [1860–65]

trust·i·fi·ca·tion (trus′tə fi kā′shən), *n.* the practice or process of forming a monopolistic system or trusts: *the trustification of the oil business.* [1900–05; TRUST + -IFICATION]

trust·ing (trus′ting), *adj.* inclined to trust; confiding; trustful: *a trusting child.* [1400–50; late ME; see TRUST, -ING[2]] **—trust′ing·ly,** *adv.* **—trust′ing·ness,** *n.*
—Syn. unsuspicious, innocent, naive, unwary.

trust′ in′ter vi′vos, *Law.* See **living trust.**

trust·less (trust′lis), *adj.* **1.** not worthy of trust; faithless; unreliable; false: *He was trustless when money was involved.* **2.** distrustful; suspicious: *a doorman trustless of all strangers.* [1520–30; TRUST + -LESS] **—trust′less·ly,** *adv.* **—trust′less·ness,** *n.*

trus·tor (trus′tər, tru stôr′), *n. Law.* a person who creates a trust. [1530–40; TRUST + -OR[2]]

trust′ ter′ritory, a territory under the administrative control of a country designated by the United Nations.

trust·wor·thy (trust′wûr′thē), *adj.* deserving of trust or confidence; dependable; reliable: *The treasurer was not entirely trustworthy.* [1800–10; TRUST + WORTHY] **—trust′wor′thi·ly,** *adv.* **—trust′wor′thi·ness,** *n.*
—Syn. true, accurate, honest, faithful. See **reliable.**

trust·y (trus′tē), *adj.,* **trust·i·er, trust·i·est,** *n., pl.* **trust·ies.** —*adj.* **1.** able to be trusted or relied on; trustworthy; reliable. **2.** *Archaic.* trustful. —*n.* **3.** a person or thing that is trusted. **4.** a well-behaved and trustworthy convict to whom special privileges are granted. [1175–1225; ME; see TRUST, -Y[1]] **—trust′i·ly,** *adv.* **—trust′i·ness,** *n.*

truth (tro͞oth), *n., pl.* **truths** (tro͞othz, tro͞oths). **1.** the true or actual state of a matter: *He tried to find out the truth.* **2.** conformity with fact or reality; verity: *the truth of a statement.* **3.** a verified or indisputable fact, proposition, principle, or the like: *mathematical truths.* **4.** the state or character of being true. **5.** actuality or actual existence. **6.** an obvious or accepted fact; truism; platitude. **7.** honesty; integrity; truthfulness. **8.** (*often cap.*) ideal or fundamental reality apart from and transcending perceived experience: *the basic truths of life.* **9.** agreement with a standard or original. **10.** accuracy, as of position or adjustment. **11.** *Archaic.* fidelity or constancy. **12. in truth,** in reality; in fact; actually: *In truth, moral decay hastened the decline of the Roman Empire.* [bef. 900; ME *treuthe,* OE *trēowth* (c. ON *tryggth* faith). See TRUE, -TH[1]] **—truth′less,** *adj.* **—truth′less·ness,** *n.*
—Syn. 1. fact. **2.** veracity. **7.** sincerity, candor, frankness. **10.** precision, exactness. **—Ant. 1.** falsehood. **2, 4, 7.** falsity.

Truth (tro͞oth), *n.* **So·journ·er** (sō′jûr nər, sō jûr′nər), (*Isabella Van Wagener*), 1797?–1883, U.S. abolitionist, orator, and women's-rights advocate, born a slave.

truth′ claim′, *Pragmatism.* a hypothesis not yet verified by experience.

truth·ful (tro͞oth′fəl), *adj.* **1.** telling the truth, esp. habitually: *a truthful person.* **2.** conforming to truth: *a truthful statement.* **3.** corresponding with reality: *a truthful portrait.* [1590–1600; TRUTH + -FUL] **—truth′·ful·ly,** *adv.* **—truth′ful·ness,** *n.*
—Syn. 1. honest, trustworthy; candid, frank.

truth-func·tion (tro͞oth′fungk′shən), *n. Logic.* a statement so constructed from other statements that its truth-value depends on the truth-values of the other statements rather than on their meanings. **—truth′-func′tion·al,** *adj.* **—truth′-func′tion·al·ly,** *adv.*

truth′ or con′sequences, a game in which each contestant is asked a question and upon failure to answer or give a correct answer receives a penalty imposed by the leader or the group.

truth′ quark′, *Physics.* See **top quark.**

truth′ se′rum, a drug, as the barbiturate thiopental, that induces in the subject a desire to talk or a state of heightened suggestibility, used in psychotherapy and in interrogation to discover repressed or consciously withheld information. Also, **truth′ drug′.** Cf. **narcoanalysis.** [1920–25]

truth′ ta′ble, *Logic, Math., Computers.* a table that gives the truth-values of a compound sentence formed from component sentences by means of logical connectives, as AND, NOT, or OR, for every possible combination of truth-values of the component sentences. [1935–40]

truth-val·ue (tro͞oth′val′yo͞o), *n. Logic.* the truth or falsehood of a proposition: *The truth-value of "2 + 2 = 5" is falsehood.* [1915–20]

try (trī), *v.,* **tried, try·ing,** *n., pl.* **tries.** —*v.t.* **1.** to attempt to do or accomplish: *Try it before you say it's simple.* **2.** to test the effect or result of (often fol. by *out*): *to try a new method; to try a recipe out.* **3.** to endeavor to evaluate by experiment or experience: *to try a new field; to try a new book.* **4.** to test the quality, value, fitness, accuracy, etc., of: *Will you try a spoonful of this and tell me what you think of it?* **5.** *Law.* to examine and determine judicially, as a cause; determine judicially the guilt or innocence of (a person). **6.** to put to a severe test; subject to strain, as of endurance, patience, affliction, or trouble; tax: *to try one's patience.* **7.** to attempt to open (a door, window, etc.) in order to find out whether it is locked: *Try all the doors before leaving.* **8.** to melt down (fat, blubber, etc.) to obtain the oil; render (usually fol. by *out*). **9.** *Archaic.* **a.** to determine the truth or right of (a quarrel or question) by test or battle (sometimes fol. by *out*). **b.** to find to be right by test or experience. —*v.i.* **10.** to make an attempt or effort; strive: *Try to complete the examination.* **11.** *Naut.* to lie to in heavy weather under just sufficient sail to head into the wind. **12. try it, that,** etc., **on,** *Chiefly Brit. Informal.* **a.** to put on airs: *She's been trying it on ever since the inheritance came through.* **b.** to be forward or presumptuous, esp. with a member of the opposite sex: *She avoided him after he'd tried it on with her.* **13. try on,** to put on an article of clothing in order to judge its appearance and fit: *You can't really tell how it will look until you try it on.* **14. try out,** to use experimentally; test: *to try out a new car.* **15. try out for,** to compete for (a position, membership, etc.): *Over a hundred boys came to try out for the football team.* —*n.* **16.** an attempt or effort: *to have a try at something.* **17.** *Rugby.* a score of three points earned by advancing the ball to or beyond the opponents' goal line. **18. give it the old college try,** *Informal.* to make a sincere effort: *I gave it the old college try and finally found an apartment.* [1250–1300; ME *trien* to try (a legal case) < AF *trier,* OF: to sift, cull, of uncert. orig.]
—Syn. 1, 10. TRY, ATTEMPT, ENDEAVOR, STRIVE all mean to put forth an effort toward a specific end. TRY is the most often used and most general term: *to try to decipher a message; to try hard to succeed.* ATTEMPT, often interchangeable with TRY, sometimes suggests the possibility of failure and is often used in reference to more serious or important matters: *to attempt to formulate a new theory of motion.* ENDEAVOR emphasizes serious and continued exertion of effort, sometimes aimed at dutiful or socially appropriate behavior: *to endeavor to fulfill one's obligations.* STRIVE, stresses persistent, vigorous, even strenuous effort, often in the face of obstacles: *to strive to overcome a handicap.*
—Usage. 10. TRY followed by *and* instead of *to* has been in standard use since the 17th century: *The Justice Department has decided to try and regulate jury-selection practices.* The construction occurs only with the base form TRY, not with *tries* or *tried* or *trying.* Although some believe that *try and* is less formal than *try to,* both patterns occur in all types of speech and writing.

try·ing (trī′ing), *adj.* extremely annoying, difficult, or the like; straining one's patience and goodwill to the limit: *a trying day; a trying experience.* [1570–80 for general sense; 1710–20 for current sense; TRY + -ING[2]] **—try′ing·ly,** *adv.* **—try′ing·ness,** *n.*
—Syn. irritating, irksome, bothersome, vexing.

try·ma (trī′mə), *n., pl.* **-ma·ta** (-mə tə). *Bot.* a nut having an outer shell that becomes tough and dry and eventually splits open, as in the walnut and hickory. [1855–60; < NL < Gk *trȳma* hole, equiv. to *trȳ(ein)* to rub down, wear away + *-ma* n. suffix marking result]

try·out (trī′out′), *n.* **1.** a trial or test to ascertain fitness for some purpose. **2.** *Theat.* performances of a play in preparation for an official opening, often taking place away from a major theatrical center. [1900–05, *Amer.*; n. use of v. phrase *try out*]

tryp·a·fla·vine (trip′ə flā′vin, -vēn, trī′pə-), *n. Chem.* See **acriflavine hydrochloride.** [< Gk *trȳpa* hole + FLAVINE]

tryp′afla′vine neu′tral, *Chem.* acriflavine.

try·pan·o·so·ma (tri pan′ə sō′mə, trip′ə nə-), *n., pl.* **-ma·ta** (-mə tə). trypanosome.

try·pan·o·some (tri pan′ə sōm′, trip′ə nə-), *n.* any minute, flagellate protozoan of the genus *Trypanosoma,* parasitic in the blood or tissues of humans and other vertebrates, usually transmitted by insects, often causing serious diseases, as African sleeping sickness in humans, and many diseases in domestic animals. [1900–05; < Gk *trȳpano-* (comb. form of *trȳpanon* borer) + -SOME[3]] **—try·pan′o·so′mal, try·pan·o·som·ic** (tri pan′ə som′ik, trip′ə nə-), *adj.*

try·pan·o·so·mi·a·sis (tri pan′ə sō mī′ə sis, trip′ə-nə-), *n. Pathol.* any infection caused by a trypanosome. [1900–05; TRYPANOSOME + -IASIS]

tryp·ars·am·ide (tri pär′sə mīd′, -mid), *n. Pharm.* a white, crystalline powder, $C_8H_{10}O_4N_2AsNa \cdot \frac{1}{2}H_2O$, used chiefly in treating African sleeping sickness. [1900–05; formerly a trademark]

try-pot (trī′pot′), *n.* See under **tryworks.** [1830–40]

tryp·sin (trip′sin), *n. Biochem.* a proteolytic enzyme of the pancreatic juice, capable of converting proteins into peptone. [1875–80; irreg. < Gk *trîps(is)* friction (*trī́b(ein)* to rub + *-sis* -SIS) + -IN[2]; so called because first obtained by rubbing the pancreas] **—tryp·tic** (trip′tik), *adj.*

tryp·sin·o·gen (trip sin′ə jən, -jen′), *n. Biochem.* a precursor of trypsin that is secreted by the pancreas and is activated to trypsin in the small intestine. [1885–90; TRYPSIN + -O- + -GEN]

tryp·to·phan (trip′tə fan′), *n. Biochem.* an essential amino acid, $(C_8H_6N)CH_2CH(NH_2)COOH$, colorless, crystalline, and aromatic, released from proteins by tryptic digestion and a precursor of serotonin. *Abbr.:* Trp; *Symbol:* W Also, **tryp·to·phane** (trip′tə fān′). [1900–05; *trypto-* (irreg. comb. form repr. Gk *triptós* rubbed) + -PHAN(E)]

try·sail (trī′sāl′; *Naut.* trī′səl), *n. Naut.* a triangular or quadrilateral sail having its luff hooped or otherwise bent to a mast, used for lying to or keeping a vessel headed into the wind; spencer. [1760–70; TRY + SAIL]

try′sail mast′, *Naut.* a small auxiliary mast fastened just abaft the mainmast or foremast of a sailing vessel. [1760–70]

try′ square′, a device for testing the squareness of carpentry work or the like, or for laying out right angles, consisting of a pair of straightedges fixed at right angles to one another. [1875–80]

tryst (trist, trīst), *n.* **1.** an appointment to meet at a certain time and place, esp. one made somewhat secretly by lovers. **2.** an appointed meeting. **3.** an appointed place of meeting. —*v.t.* **4.** *Chiefly Scot.* to make an appointment or arrange a meeting with. —*v.i.* **5.** *Chiefly*

Scot. to make an appointment or agreement. [1325–75; ME *triste* set hunting-station < OF < Gmc; cf. Goth *trausti* agreement, arrangement, akin to ME *trist* confidence (OE **tryst*). See TROW, TRUST] —**tryst′er,** *n.* —**Syn. 1, 2.** assignation. **1–3.** rendezvous.

tryst′ing place′, a place for a meeting, esp. a secret meeting of lovers; rendezvous. [1625–35]

try•works (trī′wûrks′), *n.pl.* (in whaling) a furnace in which a kettle (**try-pot**) is placed for rendering blubber. [1785–95; TRY + WORKS]

TS, 1. tool shed. **2.** top secret. **3.** Also, **t.s.** *Slang* (*vulgar*). tough shit. **4.** *Informal.* transsexual. Also, **T.S.**

tsa•di (tsä′dē), *n.* sadhe.

Tsa•ko•ni•an (tsə kō′nē ən), *n.* a modern Greek dialect spoken on the east coast of the Peloponnesus, descended from the Laconian dialect of ancient Sparta.

Tsa•na (tsä′nä, -nə), *n.* **Lake.** See **Tana, Lake.**

Ts'ao Hsüeh-ch'in (tsou′ shyĕ′chin′), (*Ts'ao Chan*) c1717–63, Chinese novelist: author of *The Dream of the Red Chamber.*

Ts'ao Yü (*Chin.* tsou′ yʏ′), *Wade-Giles.* (*Wan Chia-pao*). See **Cao Yu.**

tsar (zär, tsär), *n.* czar.

Tsa′ra•ta•na′na Massif′ (tsär′ə tä nä′nə, tsär′-), a mountain range in N Madagascar. Highest peak, 9436 ft. (2876 m).

tsar•dom (zär′dəm, tsär′-), *n.* czardom.

tsar•e•vitch (zär′ə vich, tsär′-), *n.* czarevitch.

tsa•rev•na (zä rev′nə, tsä-), *n.* czarevna.

tsa•ri•na (zä rē′nə, tsä-), *n.* czarina.

tsar•ism (zär′iz əm, tsär′-), *n.* czarism.

tsar•ist (zär′ist, tsär′-), *adj., n.* czarist.

tsar•is•tic (zä ris′tik, tsä-), *adj.* czarist.

Tsa•ri•tsyn (tsə rēt′sin; *Russ.* tsu ʀyē′tsin), *n.* a former name of **Volgograd.**

tsa•rit•za (zä rit′sə, tsä-), *n.* czaritza.

tsats•ke (tsäts′kə), *n. Slang.* tchotchke.

tsa•vo•rite (tsä′və rīt′, sä′-), *n.* a green variety of grossularite, found in Kenya in 1975 and used as a gem. [named after *Tsavo* National Park, Kenya, near where it was found; see -ITE¹ (-*r*- unexplained)]

Tschai•kov•sky (chī kôf′skē, -kof′-; *Russ.* chyē kôf′skyə), *n.* **Peter Il•yich** (il′yich). See **Tchaikovsky, Peter Ilyich.** Also, **Tschai•kow′sky, Chaikovski.**

tscher•no•sem (cher′nə zem′; *Russ.* chyiʀ nu zyôm′), *n.* chernozem. Also, **tscher′no•zem′, tsher′no•sem′.**

Tse•li•no•grad (tsə lin′ə gräd′; *Russ.* tsi lyi nu gʀät′), *n.* a city in N central Kazakhstan, in Asia. 276,000. Formerly, **Akmolinsk.**

Tseng Kuo-fan (dzung′ gwô′fän′), 1811–72, Chinese general and statesman.

tset′se fly′ (tset′sē, tet′-, tsē′tsē, tē′-), any of several bloodsucking African flies of the genus *Glossina,* that act as a vector of sleeping sickness and other trypanosome infections of humans and domestic animals. Also, **tzetze fly.** Also called **tset′se, tzetze, glossina.** [1860–65; < Tswana *tsètsè* fly]

tsetse fly, *Glossina morsitans,* length ¼ in. (0.6 cm)

T.Sgt., technical sergeant.

TSH, thyroid-stimulating hormone. Cf. **thyrotropin.**

Tshi (chwē, chē), *n.* Twi.

Tshi•lu•ba (chi lo͞o′bə), *n.* Luba (def. 2).

T-shirt (tē′shûrt′), *n.* a lightweight, usually knitted, pullover shirt, close-fitting and with a round neckline and short sleeves, worn as an undershirt or outer garment. Also, **tee-shirt.** Also called **T, tee.** [1940–45; named from its shape]

Tshom•be (chom′bā), *n.* **Mo•ise Ka•pen•da** (mō ēs′ kə pen′də), 1919–69, African political leader in the Republic of the Congo (now Zaire): prime minister 1964–65.

tsi, tons per square inch.

tsim•mes (tsim′is), *n.* tzimmes.

Tsim•shi•an (chim′shē ən, tsim′-), *n., pl.* **-ans,** (*esp. collectively*) **-an. 1.** a member of an American Indian people of the coastal region of British Columbia. **2.** the Penutian language of the Tsimshian.

Tsin (*Chin.* jin), *n.* Chin (def. 1).

Tsi•nan (*Chin.* jē′nän′), *n. Older Spelling.* Jinan.

Tsing Hai (*Chin.* ching′ hī′). See **Qing Hai.**

Tsing•hai (*Chin.* ching′hī′), *n. Older Spelling.* Qinghai.

Tsing•tao (tsing′tou′; *Chin.* ching′dou′), *n. Older Spelling.* a seaport in E Shandong province, in E China. Municipal district, 1,300,000. Cf. **Jiaozhou.**

Tsing•yuan (*Chin.* ching′yʏän′), *n. Older Spelling.* Qingyuan.

Tsin•kiang (*Chin.* jin′gyäng′), *n. Older Spelling.* former name of **Quanzhou.**

CONCISE ETYMOLOGY KEY: <, descended or borrowed from; >, whence; b., blend of, blended; c., cognate with; cf., compare; deriv., derivative; equiv., equivalent; imit., imitative; obl., oblique; r., replacing; s., stem; sp., spelling, spelled; resp., respelling, respelled; trans., translation; ?, origin unknown; *, unattested; ‡, probably earlier than. See the full key inside the front cover.

Tsin•ling Shan (chin′ling′ shän′), a mountain range in central China: highest peak over 12,000 ft. (3660 m).

Tsiol•kov•sky (tsyôl kôf′skē, -kof′-; *Russ.* tsul kôf′skyē), *n.* **Kon•stan•tin E•du•ar•do•vich** (kon′stən tēn ed wär′də vich; *Russ.* kən stun tyēn′ e do͞o är′də-vyich), 1857–1935, Russian inventor and rocket expert.

Tsi•ra•na•na (tsē rä′nä nä), *n.* **Phil•i•bert** (fil′ə bərt), 1910–78, president of the Malagasy Republic (now Madagascar) 1959–72.

Tsi•tsi•har (tsē′tsē′här′; *Chin.* chē′chē′häʀ′), *n. Older Spelling.* Qiqihar. Also, **Chichihar, Chichihaerh, Tsi′tsi′haerh′.**

tsk (*pronounced as an alveolar click; spelling pron.* tisk), *interj.* **1.** (used, often in quick repetition, as an exclamation of contempt, disdain, impatience, etc.) **2.** for shame! —*n.* **3.** an exclamation of "tsk." —*v.i.* **4.** to utter the exclamation "tsk." Also, **tsk′tsk′.**

Tskhin•va•li (skin′və lē, tskin′-; *Russ.* tskʜyēn′vəlyi), *n.* a city in and the capital of the South Ossetian Autonomous Region, NW of Tbilisi. 34,000.

Tson•ga (tsong′gə), *n.* a Bantu language spoken in Mozambique, Zambia, and South Africa. Also, **Thonga, Tonga.**

tsour•is (tso͝or′is, tsûr′-), *n. Slang.* tsuris.

TSP, *Chem.* See **sodium phosphate** (def. 3).

tsp., 1. teaspoon. **2.** teaspoonful.

T square on drawing board

T square, a T-shaped ruler, used primarily in mechanical drawing, having a short crosspiece that slides along the edge of the drawing board as a guide to the perpendicular longer section in making parallel lines, right angles, etc., and as a support for triangles. [1775–85]

TSR, *n., pl.* **TSRs, TSR's.** a computer program with any of several ancillary functions, usu. held resident in RAM for instant activation while one is using another program. [*t*(*erminate and*) *s*(*tay*) *r*(*esident*)]

TSS, toxic shock syndrome.

T-stop (tē′stop′), *n. Photog.* a camera lens aperture setting calibrated to a T number. [1955–60]

T-stop system, *Photog.* a system of stops calibrated by T numbers. Also called **transmission stop system.**

T-strap (tē′strap′), *n.* **1.** a strap on the upper of a shoe that extends backward from the vamp and joins with a strap that crosses the upper part of the instep, forming a T. **2.** a shoe having such a strap.

tsu•na•mi (tso͝o nä′mē), *n.* an unusually large sea wave produced by a seaquake or undersea volcanic eruption. Also called **seismic sea wave.** [1905–10; < Japn, equiv. to *tsu* harbor (earlier *tu*) + *nami* wave] —**tsu•na•mic** (tso͝o nä′mik, -nam′ik), *adj.*

T suppressor cell, *Immunol.* See **suppressor T cell.**

tsur•is (tso͝or′is, tsûr′-), *n. Slang.* trouble; woe. Also, **tsouris.** [1970–75; < Yiddish *tsures, tsores,* pl. of *tsure, tsore* < Heb *ṣarā,* pl. *ṣarōth* troubles]

Tsu•shi•ma (tso͞o′shē mä′), *n.* two adjacent Japanese islands between Korea and Kyushu: Russian fleet defeated by Japanese fleet 1905. 58,672; 271 sq. mi. (702 sq. km).

Tsu′shima Cur′rent, a warm ocean current flowing northward along the west coast of Japan.

Tsu′shima Strait′, a channel between the Tsushima islands and Kyushu island, connecting the Sea of Japan and the East China Sea: sometimes considered part of the Korea Strait, ab. 60 mi. (97 km) long; 40 mi. (64 km) wide.

tsu′tsu•ga•mu′shi disease′ (tso͞o′tsə gə mo͞o′shē, tso͞o′-), *Pathol.* See **scrub typhus.** [< Japn *tsutsugamushi* typhus mite, equiv. to *tsutsuga* hindrance, ailment (earlier *tutu*(*n*)*ga,* deriv. of *tutumi* to hinder, with *ka* place) + *mushi* vermin]

Tswa•na (tswä′nə, swä′-), *n., pl.* **-nas,** (*esp. collectively*) **-na. 1.** a member of a numerous people of Botswana and neighboring parts of South Africa. **2.** the language of the Tswana, a Bantu language.

TT, Trust Territories (approved esp. for use with zip code).

TTL meter, *Photog.* See **through-the-lens meter.**

TTS, Teletypesetter.

TTY, teletypewriter.

Tu, *Chem.* (formerly) thulium.

Tu., Tuesday.

T.U., 1. toxic unit. **2.** Trade Union. **3.** Training Unit.

t.u., trade union.

Tu•a•mo′tu Archipel′ago (to͞o′ə mō′to͞o), a group of French islands in the S Pacific. 6664; 332 sq. mi. (860 sq. km). Also called **Low Archipelago, Paumotu Archipelago.**

Tua•reg (twä′reg), *n.* **1.** a Berber or Hamitic-speaking member of the Muslim nomads of the Sahara. **2.** the language of the Tuaregs, a Berber language of the Afroasiatic family. [< dial. Ar *Ṭawāriq*]

tu•a•ta•ra (to͞o′ə tär′ə), *n.* a large, primarily nocturnal, lizardlike reptile, *Sphenodon punctatum,* of islands near the coast of New Zealand: the only surviving rhynchocephalian. Also, **tu•a•te•ra** (to͞o′ə târ′ə). Also called **sphenodon.** [1810–20; < Maori, equiv. to *tua* dorsal + *tara* spine]

tuatara, *Sphenodon punctatum,* length to 2½ ft. (0.8 m)

Tu•a•tha Dé Da•nann (to͞o′ə hə dā dä′nən), *Irish Legend.* a race of gods or demigods who defeated the Fomorians and ruled Ireland during a golden age. Also, **Tu′atha dé Da′naan, Tu′atha Dé′.**

tub (tub), *n., v.,* **tubbed, tub•bing.** —*n.* **1.** a bathtub. **2.** a broad, round, open, wooden container, usually made of staves held together by hoops and fitted around a flat bottom. **3.** any of various containers resembling or suggesting a tub: *a tub for washing clothes.* **4.** the amount a tub will hold. **5.** *Informal.* a short and fat person. **6.** *Naut.* an old, slow, or clumsy vessel. **7.** *Brit. Informal.* a bath in a bathtub. **8.** *Mining.* an ore car; tram. **9.** *Mil. Slang.* a two-seat aircraft, esp. a trainer. —*v.t.* **10.** to place or keep in a tub. **11.** *Brit. Informal.* to bathe in a bathtub. —*v.i.* **12.** *Brit. Informal.* to bathe oneself in a bathtub. **13.** *Informal.* to undergo washing, esp. without damage, as a fabric: *This cotton print tubs well.* [ME *tubbe* (n.) < MD *tobbe;* c. MLG *tubbe, tobbe*] —**tub′ba•ble,** *adj.* —**tub′ber,** *n.* —**tub′like′,** *adj.*

tu•ba (to͞o′bə, tyo͞o′-), *n., pl.* **-bas** for 1a, b, 2; **-bae** (-bē) for 1c. **1.** *Music.* **a.** a valved, brass wind instrument having a low range. **b.** an organ reed stop of large scale with tones of exceptional power. **c.** an ancient Roman trumpet. **2.** *Meteorol.* See **funnel cloud.** [< L: trumpet]

tuba (def. 1a)

tu•bal (to͞o′bəl, tyo͞o′-), *adj. Anat.* pertaining to a tube, as a Fallopian tube. [1725–35; TUBE + -AL¹]

Tu•bal-cain (to͞o′bəl kān′, tyo͞o′-), *n.* the son of Lamech and Zillah: the progenitor of metalworkers. Gen. 4:22. Also, **Tu′bal-cain′.**

tub′al liga′tion, a method of permanent sterilization for women, involving the surgical sealing of the fallopian tubes to prevent the ovum from passing from the ovary to the uterus. [1945–50]

tu•bate (to͞o′bāt, tyo͞o′-), *adj.* having or forming a tube or tubes; tubular. [1865–70; TUBE + -ATE¹]

tub•by (tub′ē), *adj.,* **-bi•er, -bi•est. 1.** short and fat: *a tubby child.* **2.** having a dull, thumping sound; lacking resonance. [1800–10; TUB + -Y¹] —**tub′bi•ness,** *n.*

tub′ chair′, *English Furniture.* an easy chair having a semicircular back and, with the wings or arms, forming a single upholstered piece. [1830–40]

tube (to͞ob, tyo͞ob), *n., v.,* **tubed, tub•ing.** —*n.* **1.** a hollow, usually cylindrical body of metal, glass, rubber, or other material, used esp. for conveying or containing liquids or gases. **2.** a small, collapsible, cylinder of metal or plastic sealed at one end and having a capped opening at the other from which paint, toothpaste, or some other semifluid substance may be squeezed. **3.** *Anat., Zool.* any hollow, cylindrical vessel or organ: *the bronchial tubes.* **4.** *Bot.* **a.** any hollow, elongated body or part. **b.** the united lower portion of a gamopetalous corolla or a gamosepalous calyx. **5.** See **inner tube. 6.** *Electronics.* See **electron tube. 7.** *Informal.* **a.** television. **b.** a television set. **8.** See **mailing tube. 9.** the tubular tunnel in which an underground railroad runs. **10.** the railroad itself. **11.** *Surfing Slang.* the curled hollow formed on the underside of a cresting wave. **12.** *Brit.* subway (def. 1). **13.** *Australian Slang.* a can of beer. **14.** *Older Slang.* a telescope. **15. down the tube** or **tubes,** *Informal.* into a ruined, wasted, or abandoned state or condition. —*v.t.* **16.** to furnish with a tube or tubes. **17.** to convey or enclose in a tube. **18.** to make tubular. [< L *tubus* pipe] —**tube′less,** *adj.* —**tube′like′,** *adj.*

tu•bec•to•my (to͞o bek′tə mē, tyo͞o-), *n., pl.* **-mies.** *Surg.* salpingectomy. [1920–25; TUBE + -ECTOMY]

tube′ foot′, one of numerous small, tubular processes on the ventral body surface of most echinoderms, used for locomotion and grasping. [1885–90]

tube′less tire′, a rubber balloon tire made as a single piece without an inner tube. [1945–50, *Amer.*]

tube•nose (to͞ob′nōz′, tyo͞ob′-), *n.* tubesnout. [TUBE + NOSE]

tube-nosed (to͞ob′nōzd′, tyo͞ob-), *adj.* **1.** having a long, tubelike beak or snout. **2.** (of a petrel or similar bird) having extended tubelike nostrils.

tube′ pan′, a circular cake pan having a hollow cone-shaped centerpiece: used for baking ring-shaped cakes.

tu•ber¹ (to͞o′bər, tyo͞o′-), *n.* **1.** *Bot.* a fleshy, usually oblong or rounded thickening or outgrowth, as the potato, of a subterranean stem or shoot, bearing minute scalelike leaves with buds or eyes in their axils from which new plants may arise. **2.** *Anat.* a rounded swelling or protuberance; a tuberosity; a tubercle. [1660–70;

< L *tūber* bump, swelling. Cf. TRUFFLE] **—tu′ber·less,** *adj.* **—tu′ber·oid′,** *adj.*

tub·er[2] (to͞o′bər, tyo͞o′-), *n.* **1.** a person or thing that forms, installs, or operates with tubes. **2.** Also called **inner-tuber.** a person who participates in the sport of tubing. [1920–25; TUBE + -ER[1]]

tube′ rail′way, *Brit.* subway (def. 1). [1895–1900]

tu·ber·cle (to͞o′bər kəl, tyo͞o′-), *n.* **1.** a small rounded projection or excrescence, as on a bone or on the surface of the body. **2.** *Pathol.* **a.** a small, firm, rounded nodule or swelling. **b.** such a swelling as the characteristic lesion of tuberculosis. **3.** *Bot.* a tuberlike swelling or nodule. [1570–80; < L *tūberculum.* See TUBER[1], -CLE[1]]

tu′bercle bacil′lus, the bacterium, *Mycobacterium tuberculosis,* causing tuberculosis. [1895–1900]

tu·ber·cu·lar (to͝o bûr′kyə lər, tyo͝o-), *adj.* **1.** pertaining to tuberculosis; tuberculous. **2.** of, pertaining to, or of the nature of a tubercle or tubercles. **3.** characterized by or having tubercles. **—***n.* **4.** a tuberculous person. [1790–1800; < L *tūbercul(um)* TUBERCLE + -AR[1]] **—tu·ber′cu·lar·ly,** *adv.*

tu·ber·cu·late (to͝o bûr′kyə lit, -lāt′, tyo͝o-), *adj.* **1.** Also, **tu·ber′cu·lat′ed, tuberculose.** having tubercles. **2.** tubercular. [1775–85; < NL *tūberculātus,* equiv. to *tūbercul(um)* TUBERCLE + *-ātus* -ATE[1]] **—tu·ber′cu·la′tion,** *n.*

tu·ber·cu·lin (to͝o bûr′kyə lin, tyo͝o-), *n. Med.* a sterile liquid prepared from cultures of the tubercle bacillus, used in the diagnosis and, formerly, in the treatment of tuberculosis. [1890–95; < L *tūbercul(um)* TUBERCLE + -IN[2]]

tu·ber·cu·lin·ize (to͝o bûr′kyə lə nīz′, tyo͝o-), *v.,* **-ized, -iz·ing.** **—***v.t.* **1.** to inoculate with tuberculin. **2.** to cause to form tubercles. **—***v.i.* **3.** to form tubercles. Also, *esp. Brit.,* **tu·ber′cu·lin·ise′.** [1890–95; TUBERCULIN + -IZE] **—tu·ber′cu·lin·i·za′tion, tu·ber′cu·li·na′tion,** *n.*

tuber′culin test′, a test for tuberculosis in which a hypersensitive reaction to a given quantity of tuberculin indicates a past or present infection. [1900–05]

tu·ber·cu·loid (to͝o bûr′kyə loid′, tyo͝o-), *adj.* **1.** resembling a tubercle. **2.** resembling tuberculosis. [1890–95; < L *tūbercul(um)* TUBERCLE OR TUBERCUL(OSIS) + -OID]

tu·ber·cu·lose (to͝o bûr′kyə lōs′, tyo͝o-), *adj.* tuberculate. [1745–55; < NL *tūberculōsus;* see TUBERCLE, -OSE[1]]

tu·ber·cu·lo·sis (to͝o bûr′kyə lō′sis, tyo͝o-), *n. Pathol.* **1.** an infectious disease that may affect almost any tissue of the body, esp. the lungs, caused by the organism *Mycobacterium tuberculosis,* and characterized by tubercles. **2.** this disease when affecting the lungs; pulmonary phthisis; consumption. **3.** any disease caused by a mycobacterium. Also called **TB** (for defs. 1, 2). [1855–60; < NL *tūberculōsis;* see TUBERCLE, -OSIS]

tu·ber·cu·lous (to͝o bûr′kyə ləs, tyo͝o-), *adj.* **1.** tubercular. **2.** affected with tuberculosis: *a hospital for tuberculous people.* [1740–50; < L *tūbercul(um)* TUBERCLE + -OUS] **—tu·ber′cu·lous·ly,** *adv.*

tu·ber·cu·lum (to͝o bûr′kyə ləm, tyo͝o-), *n., pl.* **-la** (-lə). a tubercle. [1685–95; < NL, L]

tu′ber fern′, a tropical, erect fern, *Nephrolepis cordifolia,* having sharply toothed and numerously segmented fronds.

tube·rose[1] (to͞ob′rōz′, tyo͞ob′-, to͞o′bə rōz′, tyo͞o′-), *n.* a bulbous plant, *Polianthes tuberosa,* of the agave family, cultivated for its spike of fragrant, creamy-white, lily-like flowers. [1655–65; < NL *tuberosa,* the specific epithet, fem. of L *tūberōsus* TUBEROSE[2]]

tu·ber·ose[2] (to͞o′bə rōs′, tyo͞o′-), *adj.* tuberous. [1695–1705; < L *tūberōsus* knobby. See TUBER[1], -OSE[1]]

tu·ber·os·i·ty (to͞o′bə ros′i tē, tyo͞o′-), *n., pl.* **-ties.** a rough projection or protuberance of a bone, as for the attachment of a muscle. [1535–45; < ML *tūberōsitās.* See TUBEROSE[2], -ITY]

tu·ber·ous (to͞o′bər əs, tyo͞o′-), *adj.* **1.** characterized by the presence of rounded or wartlike prominences or tubers. **2.** of the nature of such a prominence. **3.** *Bot.* bearing tubers. **4.** having the nature of or resembling a tuber. Also, **tuberose.** [1640–50; < L *tūberōsus* knobby. See TUBER[1], -OUS]

tu′berous root′, a true root so thickened as to resemble a tuber, but bearing no buds or eyes. See illus. under **root**[1]. [1660–70] **—tu′ber·ous-root′ed,** *adj.*

tube·snout (to͞ob′snout′, tyo͞ob′-), *n.* a slender, marine fish, *Aulorhynchus flavidus,* inhabiting coastal waters from southern California to Alaska, having a long, tubelike snout. Also called **tubenose.** [TUBE + SNOUT]

tube′ sock′, a casual sock that is not shaped at the heel. [1975–80]

tube′ top′, a woman's strapless top, usually of elasticized fabric that fits snugly on the body.

tube·worm (to͞ob′wûrm′, tyo͞ob′-), *n. Zool.* any of various marine worms that produce and inhabit a tube, some being adapted to a hydrothermal vent environment. Also, **tube′ worm′.** [1925–30; TUBE + WORM]

tubi-, a combining form representing **tube** in compound words: *tubiform.* [< L *tub(us)* TUBE + -I-]

tu·bi·fex (to͞o′bə feks′, tyo͞o′-), *n., pl.* **-fex·es,** (*esp. collectively*) **-fex.** any common, bottom-dwelling worm of the genus *Tubifex,* often used as food for aquarium fish. Also called **red worm.** [< NL (1816); see TUBI-, -FEX]

tu·bi·flo·rous (to͞o′bə flôr′əs, -flōr′-, tyo͞o′-), *adj. Bot.* tubuliflorous.

tu·bi·form (to͞o′bə fôrm′, tyo͞o′-), *adj.* shaped like a tube. [1735–45; TUBI- + -FORM]

tub·ing (to͞o′bing, tyo͞o′-), *n.* **1.** material in the form of a tube: *glass tubing.* **2.** tubes collectively. **3.** a piece of tube: *two feet of copper tubing.* **4.** Also called **inner-tubing.** the sport or recreation of floating down a river or stream on an inner tube. [1835–45; TUBE + -ING[1]]

Tu Bi·she·vat (to͞o′ bi shə vät′, -shvät′), *Judaism.* the 15th day of the month of Shevat, observed as a new year for trees by planting trees and by eating fruits. Also, **Tu Bi·she·bat** (to͞o′ bi shə bät′, -shbät′). Also called **Hamishah Asar Bishevat.** [< Heb *ṭū bishbhāṭ* equiv. to *ṭū* fifteen + *bi* of + *shəbhāṭ* SHEVAT]

tub·man (tub′mən), *n., pl.* **-men.** *Old Eng. Law.* a barrister in the Court of Exchequer who had precedence in motions over every other barrister except the postman. Cf. **postman**[2]. [1635–45; TUB + -MAN]

Tub·man (tub′mən), *n.* **1. Harriet** (*Araminta*), 1820?–1913, U.S. abolitionist: escaped slave and leader of the Underground Railroad; served as a Union scout during Civil War. **2. William Va·can·a·rat Shadrach** (və kan′ə rat′), 1895–1971, president of Liberia 1944–71.

tu·bo·cu·ra·rine (to͞o′bō kyo͝o rär′ēn, -in, tyo͞o′-), *n. Pharm.* the principal active alkaloid of curare, $C_{38}H_{44}Cl_2N_2O$, used as a muscle relaxant, esp. as an adjunct to anesthesia. [1895–1900; < G *Tubocurarin,* equiv. to *Tubocurar(e)* (see TUBE, -O-, CURARE) + *-in* -IN[2]]

tu·boid (to͞o′boid, tyo͞o′-), *adj.* having or approximating a tubular form. [TUBE + -OID]

tub-thump·er (tub′thum′pər), *n.* a vociferous supporter or promoter, as of a cause. [1655–65] **—tub′-thump′ing,** *n., adj.*

tu·bu·lar (to͞o′byə lər, tyo͞o′-), *adj.* **1.** having the form or shape of a tube; tubiform. **2.** of or pertaining to a tube or tubes. **3.** characterized by or consisting of tubes. [1665–75; < NL *tubulāris;* see TUBULE, -AR[1]] **—tu′bu·lar′i·ty,** *n.* **—tu′bu·lar·ly,** *adv.*

tu′bular skate′, a type of ice skate consisting of a steel blade set into an aluminum tube and connected to the shoe by tubular supports, used for both hockey and racing skates. Cf. **hockey skate, racing skate.**

tu·bu·late (*adj.* to͞o′byə lit, -lāt′, tyo͞o′-; *v.* to͞o′byə-lāt′, tyo͞o′-), *adj., v.,* **-lat·ed, -lat·ing.** **—***adj.* **1.** Also, **tu′bu·lat′ed.** shaped like or having a tube. **—***v.t.* **2.** to form into or furnish with a tube. [1745–55; < L *tubulātus;* see TUBULE, -ATE[1]] **—tu′bu·la′tion,** *n.* **—tu′bu·la′tor,** *n.*

tu·bule (to͞o′byo͞ol, tyo͞o′-), *n.* **1.** a small tube; a minute tubular structure. **2.** See **convoluted tubule.** [1670–80; < L *tubulus,* equiv. to *tub(us)* pipe + *-ulus* -ULE]

tu·bu·li·flo·rous (to͞o′byə lə flôr′əs, -flōr′-, tyo͞o′-), *adj. Bot.* having the corolla tubular in all the perfect flowers of a head, as certain composite plants. Also, **tubiflorous.** [1890–95; TUBULE + -I- + -FLOROUS]

tu·bu·lin (to͞o′byə lin, tyo͞o′-), *n. Biochem.* either of two globular proteins that form the structural subunits of microtubules. [1965–70; TUBULE + -IN[2]]

tu·bu·lous (to͞o′byə ləs, tyo͞o′-), *adj.* **1.** containing or consisting of tubes. **2.** having the form of a tube; tubular. **3.** *Bot.* having tubular flowers. [1655–65; < NL *tubulōsus.* See TUBULE, -OUS] **—tu′bu·lous·ly,** *adv.*

tu·bu·lure (to͞o′byə lər, tyo͞o′-), *n.* a short tubular opening, as in a glass jar or at the top of a retort. [1790–1800; < F; see TUBULE, -URE]

tu·bu·phone (to͞o′byə fōn′, tyo͞o′-), *n.* an instrument resembling a glockenspiel but with metal tubes instead of bars. [< L *tubu(s)* TUBE + -PHONE]

Tu·can·a (to͞o kan′ə, -kä′nə, -kā′-, tyo͞o-), *n., gen.* **-can·ae** (-kan′ē, -kä′nē, -kā′-). *Astron.* the Toucan, a southern constellation between Octans and Phoenix. [< NL: TOUCAN]

tuch·is (to͝oKH′əs, tô′KHəs), *n. Slang.* tokus.

Tuch·man (tuk′mən), *n.* **Barbara (Wert·heim)** (wûrt′hīm), born 1912, U.S. historian and writer.

tu·chun (do͞o′jyn′), *n. Chinese Hist.* **1.** the title of a military governor of a province during the period 1916–28. **2.** a war lord. [1915–20; < Chin (Wade-Giles) *tu*[1] *chün*[1], (pinyin) *dūjūn* lit., oversee troops]

tuck[1] (tuk), *v.t.* **1.** to put into a small, close, or concealing place: *Tuck the money into your wallet.* **2.** to thrust in the loose end or edge of (a garment, covering, etc.) so as to hold closely in place (usually fol. by *in, up, under,* etc.): *Tuck in your blouse. Tuck the edge of the sheet under the mattress.* **3.** to cover snugly in or as if in this manner: *She tucked the children into bed.* **4.** to pull up into a fold or folds; draw up into a folded arrangement (usually fol. by *in, up,* etc.): *to tuck up one's skirts; to tuck one's knees under one's chin.* **5.** *Needlework.* to sew tucks in. **6.** to pass (a strand) above or below another one. **7.** *Informal.* to eat or drink (usually fol. by *in, away,* etc.): *He tucked away a big meal.* **—***v.i.* **8.** to draw together; contract; pucker. **9.** *Needlework.* to make tucks. **10.** to fit securely or snugly: *a bed that tucks into the corner.* **11. tuck into,** to eat with gusto: *We tucked into a roast beef dinner.* **—***n.* **12.** something tucked or folded in. **13.** *Sewing.* a fold, or one of a series of folds, made by doubling cloth upon itself and stitching parallel with the edge of the fold, used for decoration or for shortening or fitting a garment. **14.** *Diving, Gymnastics.* a body position in which the head is lowered and the thighs held against the chest with the knees bent and the arms locked around the shins. Cf. **layout** (def. 10), **pike**[7]. **15.** *Skiing.* a crouch in which the ski poles are held close to the chest, extending back under the arms and parallel to the ground, as to maximize speed downhill. **16.** *Informal.* a plastic surgery operation: *a tummy tuck.* **17.** *Naut.* the part of a vessel where the after ends of the outside planking or plating unite at the sternpost. **18.** (in tying knots) the operation of passing one strand above or below another. **19.** *Brit. Slang.* food. [bef. 900; ME *t(o)uken* to stretch (cloth), torment, OE *tūcian* to torment; akin to MLG *tucken* to tug, G *zucken* to jerk. See TOW[1]]

tuck[2] (tuk), *n. Informal.* tuxedo. [by shortening and resp.]

tuck[3] (tuk), *n. Archaic.* a rapier or estoc. [1500–10; earlier *tocke,* appar. sandhi var. of obs. *stock* sword < It *stocco* < G *Stock* stick; c. STOCK]

tuck[4] (tuk), *n. Chiefly Scot.* a drumbeat or the sound of one beat on a drum. [1300–50; ME *tukken* to beat, sound (said of a drum) < MF (north) *toker* to strike, touch. See TOUCH]

tuck·a·hoe (tuk′ə hō′), *n.* **1.** Also called **Indian bread.** the edible, underground sclerotium of the fungus *Poria cocos,* found on the roots of trees in the southern United States. **2.** See **arrow arum. 3.** (*usually cap.*) a Virginian, esp. one inhabiting the lowland E of the Blue Ridge. [1605–15, *Amer.;* earlier applied to various roots and underground fungi < Virginia Algonquian (E sp.) *tockwhogh, tockawhoughe, taccaho* arrow arum root (used for bread), deriv. of Proto-Algonquian **takwah-* to pound (it) fine, reduce (it) to flour; cf. Shawnee *takhwa* bread]

tuck′a·way ta′ble (tuk′ə wā′), a table having a support folding into one plane and a tilting or drop-leaf top. [TUCK[1] + AWAY]

tuck·er[1] (tuk′ər), *n.* **1.** a person or thing that tucks. **2.** a piece of linen, muslin, or the like, worn by women about the neck and shoulders. **3.** chemisette. **4.** a sewing machine attachment for making tucks. **5.** *Australian.* food. [1225–75; ME *tokere.* See TUCK[1], -ER[1]]

tuck·er[2] (tuk′ər), *v.t. Informal.* to weary; tire; exhaust (often fol. by *out*): *The game tuckered him out.* [1825–35, *Amer.;* TUCK[1] + -ER[6]]

Tuck·er (tuk′ər), *n.* **1. Richard,** 1915–75, U.S. operatic tenor. **2. Sophie** (*Sophie Abruza*), 1884–1966, U.S. singer and entertainer, born in Russia.

tuck·er-bag (tuk′ər bag′), *n. Australian.* a bag used to carry food. [1900–05]

tuck·er-box (tuk′ər boks′), *n. Australian.* a box used to store or carry food. [1900–05]

tuck·et (tuk′it), *n.* a trumpet fanfare. [1585–95; TUCK[4] + -ET]

tuck-point (tuk′point′), *v.t.* to finish (masonry) with tuck pointing. [1880–85]

tuck′ point′ing, *Masonry.* pointing that has an ornamental fillet of putty, lime, or chalk projecting from the mortar joint. Also called **tuck′ and pat′ point′ing.** [1880–85] **—tuck′-point′er,** *n.*

tuck-shop (tuk′shop′), *n. Brit.* a shop where pastry, candy, or the like is sold. [1855–60]

tu·co-tu·co (to͞o′kō to͞o′kō), *n., pl.* **-cos.** any of several burrowing rodents of the genus *Ctenomys,* of South America, resembling the pocket gopher. [1825–35; < AmerSp *tucotuco,* imit. of its cry]

Tuc·son (to͞o′son, to͞o son′), *n.* a city in S Arizona: health resort. 330,537.

Tu·cu·mán (to͞o′ko͞o män′), *n.* a city in NW Argentina. 496,914.

-tude, a suffix appearing in abstract nouns (generally formed from Latin adjectives or participles) of Latin origin (*latitude; altitude*); on this model, used in the formation of new nouns: *platitude.* [< L *-tūdō* (> F *-tude*)]

Tu·dor (to͞o′dər, tyo͞o′-), *n.* **1. Antony,** 1909–87, English choreographer and dancer. **2. Mary.** See **Mary I. 3.** a member of the royal family that ruled in England from 1485 to 1603. **—***adj.* **4.** pertaining or belonging to the English royal house of Tudor. **5.** of, pertaining to, or characteristic of the periods of the reigns of the Tudor sovereigns: *Tudor architecture.*

Tu′dor arch′, a four-centered arch, the inner pair of curves having a radius much greater than that of the outer pair. See illus. under **arch.** [1805–15]

tu·e·bor (to͞o ā′bôr; *Eng.* to͞o ē′bôr, tyo͞o-), *v. Latin.* I will defend: motto on the coat of arms of Michigan.

Tues., Tuesday. Also, **Tue.**

Tues·day (to͞oz′dā, -dē, tyo͞oz′-), *n.* the third day of the week, following Monday. [bef. 1050; ME *tewesday,* OE *tiwesdæg* (c. OHG *ziestac,* ON *tysdagr*), orig. phrase *Tīwes daeg* Tiu's day, translating L *diēs Mārtis* day of Mars. See TIU, 'S[1], DAY]
—Pronunciation. See **new.**

Tues·days (to͞oz′dāz, -dēz, tyo͞oz′-), *adv.* every Tuesday; on Tuesdays: *Tuesdays I work at home.* [TUESDAY + -S[1]]

tu·fa (to͞o′fə, tyo͞o′-), *n. Geol.* **1.** Also called **calcareous tufa, calc-tufa, calc-tuff.** a porous limestone formed from calcium carbonate deposited by springs or the like. Cf. **travertine. 2.** (not in technical use) tuff[2]. [1760–70; < It *tufo* < L *tōfus*] **—tu·fa·ceous** (to͞o fā′shəs, tyo͞o-), *adj.*

tuff[1] (tuf), *adj. Slang.* tough (def. 13).

tuff[2] (tuf), *n. Geol.* a fragmental rock consisting of the smaller kinds of volcanic detritus, as ash or cinder, usually more or less stratified. Also called **volcanic tuff.** [1560–70; < F *tuf* < It *tufo.* See TUFA] **—tuff·a·ceous** (tu fā′shəs), *adj.*

tuft (tuft), *n.* **1.** a bunch or cluster of small, usually soft and flexible parts, as feathers or hairs, attached or fixed closely together at the base and loose at the upper ends. **2.** a cluster of short, fluffy threads, used to decorate cloth, as for a bedspread, robe, bath mat, or window curtain. **3.** a cluster of cut threads, used as a decorative finish attached to the tying or holding threads of mattresses, quilts, upholstery, etc. **4.** a covered or finished button designed for similar use. **5.** a cluster of short-stalked flowers, leaves, etc., growing from a common point. **6.** a small clump of bushes, trees, etc. **7.** a gold tassel on the cap formerly worn at English universities by titled undergraduates. **8.** a titled undergraduate at an English university. —*v.t.* **9.** to furnish or decorate with a tuft or tufts. **10.** to arrange in a tuft or tufts. **11.** *Upholstery.* to draw together (a cushion or the like) by passing a thread through at regular intervals, the depressions thus produced being usually ornamented with tufts or buttons. —*v.i.* **12.** to form into or grow in a tuft or tufts. [1350–1400; ME, var. of *toft(e)* < MF *tofe, toffe* < ?; E parasitic *t* as in GRAFT[1]] —**tuft′er,** *n.*

tuft•ed (tuf′tid), *adj.* **1.** furnished or decorated with tufts. **2.** formed into or growing in a tuft or tufts. [1600–10; TUFT + -ED[3]]

tuft′ed duck′, an Old World wild duck, *Aythya fuligula,* having a tufted head and black and white plumage. [1760–70]

tuft′ed tit′mouse, a gray titmouse, *Parus bicolor,* of the eastern and midwestern U.S., having a crested head. See illus. under **titmouse.** [1825–35, *Amer.*]

tuft•ing (tuf′ting), *n.* **1.** the act or process of making tufts. **2.** tufts collectively, esp. as decoration. [1545–55; TUFT + -ING[1]]

tuft•y (tuf′tē), *adj.,* **tuft•i•er, tuft•i•est. 1.** abounding in tufts. **2.** covered or adorned with tufts. **3.** growing in or forming tufts. [1605–15; TUFT + -Y[1]] —**tuft′i•ly,** *adv.* —**tuft′i•ness,** *n.*

Tu Fu (do͞o′ fo͞o′), A.D. 712–770, Chinese poet.

tug (tug), *v.,* **tugged, tug•ging,** *n.* —*v.t.* **1.** to pull at with force, vigor, or effort. **2.** to move by pulling forcibly; drag; haul. **3.** to tow (a vessel) by means of a tugboat. —*v.i.* **4.** to pull with force or effort: *to tug at a stuck drawer.* **5.** to strive hard; labor; toil. —*n.* **6.** an act or instance of tugging; pull; haul. **7.** a strenuous contest between opposing forces, groups, or persons; struggle: *the tug of young minds in a seminar.* **8.** tugboat. **9.** that by which something is tugged, as a rope or chain. **10.** (on a harness) **a.** trace[2] (def. 1). **b.** any of various supporting or pulling parts. [1175–1225; ME *toggen* to play-wrestle, contend; akin to OE *togian* to TOW[1]] —**tug′ger,** *n.* —**tug′less,** *adj.*
—**Syn. 1.** yank, jerk, wrench.

tug•boat (tug′bōt′), *n.* a small, powerful boat for towing or pushing ships, barges, etc. Also called **towboat, tug.** [1820–30, *Amer.*; TUG + BOAT]

tug′ of war′, 1. an athletic contest between two teams at opposite ends of a rope, each team trying to drag the other over a line. **2.** a hard-fought, critical struggle for supremacy. [1670–80 for def. 2; 1875–80 for def. 1]

tu•grik (to͞o′grik), *n.* an aluminum-bronze or cupronickel coin and monetary unit of the Mongolian People's Republic, equal to 100 mongo. Also, **tu′ghrik, tukhrik.** [< mod. Mongolian *tögrög, tögrig* lit., circle, disk]

tu•i (to͞o′ē), *n.* a black New Zealand honey eater, *Prosthemadera novaeseelandiae,* having a patch of white feathers on each side of the throat, sometimes tamed as a pet. Also called **parson bird.** [1825–35; < Maori *tūī*]

Tuil•er•ies (twē′lə rēz; *Fr.* twēl[ə] RĒ′), *n.* a former royal palace in Paris: begun by Catherine de Médicis in 1564; burned by supporters of the Commune in 1871. The gardens that formed part of the palace grounds remain as a public park **(Tui′leries Gar′dens).**

tuille (twēl), *n.* a tasset. [1350–1400; ME *toile* < MF *tuille,* var. of *teuille* < L *tēgula* TILE]

Tu•i•nal (to͞o′i nôl′), *Pharm., Trademark.* a brand name for a combination of amobarbital and secobarbital used as a prompt and sustained sedative and hypnotic.

tu•i•tion (to͞o ish′ən, tyo͞o-), *n.* **1.** the charge or fee for instruction, as at a private school or a college or university: *The college will raise its tuition again next year.* **2.** teaching or instruction, as of pupils: *a school offering private tuition in languages.* **3.** *Archaic.* guardianship or custody. [1250–1300; ME *tuicion* a looking after, guarding < L *tuitiōn-* (s. of *tuitiō*), equiv. to *tuit(us)* (ptp. of *tuērī* to watch; cf. TUTELAGE) + *-iōn-* -ION] —**tu•i′tion•al, tu•i•tion•ar•y** (to͞o ish′ə ner′ē, tyo͞o-), *adj.* —**tu•i′tion•less,** *adj.*

tu•khrik (to͞o′grik), *n.* tugrik.

Tu•la (to͞o′lə), *n.* **1.** a city in the W Russian Federation in Europe, S of Moscow. 540,000. **2.** a city in SW Hidalgo, in central Mexico, NW of Mexico City: site of ruins believed to be of the ancient Toltec city of Tula, fl. A.D. c1000–1200. 10,720.

tu•la•di (to͞o′lə dē), *n., pl.* (*esp. collectively*) **-di,** (*esp. referring to two or more kinds or species*) **-dis.** *Canadian.* See **lake trout.** [1840–50; < CanF *touladi,* perh. of Algonquian orig.]

Tu•lar•e (to͞o lâr′ē, to͞o lâr′), *n.* a city in central California. 22,475.

tu•la•re•mi•a (to͞o′lə rē′mē ə), *n. Pathol., Vet. Pathol.* a plaguelike disease of rabbits, squirrels, etc., caused by a bacterium, *Francisella tularensis,* transmitted to humans by insects or ticks or by the handling of infected animals and causing fever, muscle pain, and symptoms associated with the point of entry into the body. Also, **tu′la•rae′mi•a.** Also called **deer fly fever, rabbit fever.** [1920–25, *Amer.*; *Tulare,* California county where first found + -EMIA] —**tu′la•re′mic, tu′la•rae′mic,** *adj.*

tu•le (to͞o′lē; *Sp.* to͞o′le), *n., pl.* **-les** (-lēz; *Sp.* -les). either of two large bulrushes, *Scirpus lacustris* or *S. acutus,* found in California and adjacent regions in inundated lands and marshes. [1830–40, *Amer.*; < MexSp < Nahuatl *tōlin*]

Tu•lé•ar (*Fr.* ty lā AR′), *n.* a city on SW Madagascar. 39,000.

CONCISE ETYMOLOGY KEY: <, descended or borrowed from; >, whence; b., blend of, blended; c., cognate with; cf., compare; deriv., derivative; equiv., equivalent; imit., imitative; obl., oblique; r., replacing; s., stem; sp., spelling, spelled; resp., respelling, respelled; trans., translation; ?, origin unknown; *, unattested; ‡, probably earlier than. See the full key inside the front cover.

tu′le fog′, dense ground fog that occurs in low-lying areas of the Central Valley of California.

tu′le perch′. See under **perch**[2] (def. 3).

tu•lip (to͞o′lip, tyo͞o′-), *n.* **1.** any of various plants belonging to the genus *Tulipa,* of the lily family, cultivated in many varieties, and having lance-shaped leaves and large, showy, usually erect, cup-shaped or bell-shaped flowers in a variety of colors. **2.** a flower or bulb of such a plant. [1570–80; earlier *tulipa* < NL, appar. back formation from It *tulipano* (taken as adj.) < Turk *tülbent* turban (from a fancied likeness); see TURBAN] —**tu′lip•like′,** *adj.*

tu′lip chair′, an armchair designed by Eero Saarinen in 1956, having a contoured seat of molded plastic supported by a slender, stemlike pedestal of plastic-covered cast metal that terminates in a large, flat, round foot. Also called **tu′lip ped′estal chair′.**

tu•lip•o•ma•ni•a (to͞o′lə pə mā′nē ə, -mān′yə), *n.* (in 17th-century Holland) a widespread obsession with tulips, esp. of highly prized varieties, as those of a streaked, variegated, or unusual color. [1700–10; TULIP + -O- + -MANIA]

tu′lip tree′, a tall tree, *Liriodendron tulipifera,* of the magnolia family, native to the eastern U.S., having large, cup-shaped, green and orange flowers: the state tree of Indiana, Kentucky, and Tennessee. Also called **tu′lip pop′lar, yellow poplar.** [1695–1705, *Amer.*]

tu•lip•wood (to͞o′lip wo͝od′, tyo͞o′-), *n.* **1.** the wood of the tulip tree. **2.** any of various striped or variegated woods of other trees. **3.** any of these trees. [1835–45; TULIP + WOOD[1]]

Tul•la•ho•ma (tul′ə hō′mə), *n.* a city in S Tennessee: summer resort. 15,800.

tulle (to͞ol; *Fr.* tʏl), *n.* a thin, fine, machine-made net of acetate, nylon, rayon, or silk. [1810–20; < F, after TULLE, France, where first made]

Tulle (to͞ol; *Fr.* tʏl), *n.* a city in and the capital of Corrèze, in S central France. 21,634.

tul•li•bee (tul′ə bē′), *n.* a commercially important deep-bodied Canadian whitefish, *Coregonus artedi tullibee.* [1780–90; earlier *telibee* < CanF *toulibi* < early Ojibwa dial. **oto·lipi·* (cf. Ojibwa (E sp.) *o-doon-ne-be, odonabee,* Menominee *otu·nepih*)]

Tul•li•us (tul′ē əs), *n.* **Servius.** See **Servius Tullius.**

Tul•ly (tul′ē), *n.* See **Cicero, Marcus Tullius.**

Tul•sa (tul′sə), *n.* a city in NE Oklahoma: center of a rich oil-producing region. 360,919. —**Tul′san,** *n.*

Tu•lu (to͞o′lo͞o), *n.* a Dravidian language spoken in Karnataka in southern India.

Tu•luá (to͞ol wä′), *n.* a city in W Colombia. 84,386.

tul•war (tul′wär, tul wär′), *n.* any of several Indian sabers. [1825–35; < Hindi *talwār, tarwār* < Skt *taravāri*]

tum (tum), *v.t.,* **tummed, tum•ming.** to tease (wool) in the preliminary carding operation, or to open out the fibers prior to carding. [1605–15; orig. uncert.]

Tu•ma•co (to͞o mä′kô), *n.* a seaport in SW Colombia. 80,279.

Tum•bes (to͞om′bes), *n.* a seaport in NW Peru. 34,600.

tum•ble (tum′bəl), *v.,* **-bled, -bling,** *n.* —*v.i.* **1.** to fall helplessly down, end over end, as by losing one's footing, support, or equilibrium; plunge headlong: *to tumble down the stairs.* **2.** to roll end over end, as in falling: *The stones tumbled down the hill.* **3.** to fall or decline rapidly; drop: *Prices on the stock market tumbled today.* **4.** to perform gymnastic feats of skill and agility, as leaps or somersaults. **5.** to fall suddenly from a position of power or authority; suffer overthrow: *As one dictator tumbles, another is rising to take his place.* **6.** to fall in ruins, as from age or decay; collapse; topple: *The walls of the old mansion tumbled down upon the intruders.* **7.** to roll about by turning one way and another; pitch about; toss. **8.** to stumble or fall (usually fol. by *over*): *to tumble over a sled.* **9.** to go, come, get, etc., in a hasty and confused way: *The people tumbled out of the theater. He tumbled hurriedly into his clothes.* **10.** *Informal.* to understand or become aware of some fact or circumstance (often fol. by *to*): *He finally tumbled to what they were doing.* **11.** *Rocketry.* (of a missile) to rotate without control end over end. —*v.t.* **12.** to cause to fall or roll end over end; throw over or down. **13.** to throw or toss about; cause disarray, as in handling or searching. **14.** to put in a disordered or rumpled condition. **15.** to throw, cast, put, send, etc., in a precipitate, hasty, or rough manner. **16.** to cause to fall from a position of authority or power; overthrow; topple: *They tumbled him from his throne.* **17.** to cause to fall or collapse in ruins: *The wreckers tumbled the walls of the building.* **18.** to subject to the action of a tumbling box. —*n.* **19.** an act of tumbling or falling. **20.** a gymnastic or acrobatic feat. **21.** an accidental fall; spill. **22.** a drop in value, as of stocks. **23.** a fall from a position of power or authority: *The great director took a tumble when he was replaced by a newcomer.* **24.** a response indicating interest, affection, etc.: *She wouldn't give me a tumble.* **25.** tumbled condition; disorder or confusion. **26.** a confused heap: *a tumble of papers, ashes, pens, and keys on the desk.* **27.** *Chiefly New Eng.* a haycock. **28. take a tumble to,** *Australian Slang.* to come to understand. [1250–1300; ME *tum(b)len* to dance in acrobatic style (c. D *tuimelen,* LG *tummeln*), freq. of ME *tomben,* OE *tumbian,* (c. ON *tumba,* akin to OHG *tūmōn* to reel (perh. < OLG); cf. F *tomber* to fall < Gmc); see -LE]

tum•ble•bug (tum′bəl bug′), *n.* any of several dung beetles that roll balls of dung in which they deposit their eggs and in which the young develop. [1795–1805, *Amer.*; TUMBLE + BUG[1]]

tum′ble cart′, a horse-drawn cart having two solid wheels. Also called **tum′ble car′.** [1885–90]

tum•ble-down (tum′bəl doun′), *adj.* dilapidated; ruined; rundown: *He lived in a tumble-down shack.* [1810–20]

tum•ble-dry (tum′bəl drī′), *v.t.* **-dried, -dry•ing.** to dry (washing) in a clothes drier in which articles are rotated vertically through heated air. [1965–70]

tum′ble home′, 1. *Naut.* an inward and upward slope of the middle body of a vessel. **2.** Also, **tum′ble•home′.** a similar shape for the body of an automobile. [1825–35]

tum•bler (tum′blər), *n.* **1.** a person who performs leaps, somersaults, and other bodily feats. **2.** (in a lock) any locking or checking part that, when lifted or released by the action of a key or the like, allows the bolt to move. **3.** a stemless drinking glass having a flat, often thick bottom. **4.** (in a gunlock) a leverlike piece that by the action of a spring forces the hammer forward when released by the trigger. **5.** *Mach.* **a.** a part moving a gear into place in a selective transmission. **b.** a single cog or cam on a rotating shaft, transmitting motion to a part with which it engages. **6.** a tumbling box or barrel. **7.** a person who operates a tumbling box or barrel. **8.** one of a breed of dogs resembling a small greyhound, used formerly in hunting rabbits. **9.** Also called **roller.** one of a breed of domestic pigeons noted for the habit of tumbling backward in flight. **10.** a toy, usually representing a fat, squatting figure, that is weighted and rounded at the bottom so as to rock when touched. **11.** a tumbrel or tumble cart. [1300–50; ME: acrobat; see TUMBLE, -ER[1]. Cf. LG *tümeler* drinking-cup, kind of pigeon]

tum′bler gear′, *Mach.* a transmission having gears actuated by a tumbler.

tum•ble•weed (tum′bəl wēd′), *n.* any of various plants, as *Amaranthus albus, A. graecizans,* or the Russian thistle, *Salsola kali,* whose branching upper parts become detached from the roots and are driven about by the wind. [1885–90, *Amer.*; TUMBLE + WEED[1]]

tum•bling (tum′bling), *n.* the act, practice, or art of performing acrobatic tumbles, usually on a mat or the ground. [1375–1425; late ME *tomblyng.* See TUMBLE, -ING[1]]

tum′bling bar′rel, a rotating drum for subjecting materials or small manufactured objects, loosely placed inside, to a tumbling action, as to mix materials or to polish objects by friction with one another or with an abrasive. [1885–90]

tum′bling box′, a box, pivoted at two corners, used in the manner of a tumbling barrel. Also called **rumble.** [1875–80]

tum•brel (tum′brəl), *n.* **1.** one of the carts used during the French Revolution to convey victims to the guillotine. **2.** a farmer's cart, esp. one for hauling manure, that can be tilted to discharge its load. **3.** *Obs.* a two-wheeled covered cart accompanying artillery for carrying tools, ammunition, etc. Also, **tum′bril.** [1275–1325; ME *tumberell* ducking stool < ML *tumberellus* < OF *tumberel* dump-cart, equiv. to *tombe(r)* to fall (see TUMBLE) + *-rel* -REL]

tu•me•fa•ci•ent (to͞o′mə fā′shənt, tyo͞o′-), *adj.* tumefying; causing to swell. [1880–85; < L *tumefacient-,* s. of *tumefaciēns* (prp. of *tumefacere* to cause to swell). See TUMEFY, -FACIENT]

tu•me•fac•tion (to͞o′mə fak′shən, tyo͞o′-), *n.* an act of making or becoming swollen or tumid. [1590–1600; < F < L *tumefactiōn-* (s. of *tumefactiō* a causing to swell), equiv. to *tumefact(us)* (ptp. of *tumefacere;* see TUMEFY) + *-iōn-* -ION]

tu•me•fy (to͞o′mə fī′, tyo͞o′-), *v.t., v.i.,* **-fied, -fy•ing.** to make or become swollen or tumid. [1590–1600; back formation from *tumefied,* Anglicization of L *tumefactus* (ptp. of *tumefacere* to cause to swell), equiv. to *tume(re)* to swell + *-factus* made, done; see FACT, -FY]

Tu•men (tʏ′mœn′), *n. Pinyin, Wade-Giles.* a river in E Asia, flowing NE along the China-North Korea border and then SE along the border between China and Russia to the Sea of Japan. ab. 325 mi. (525 km) long. Also called, *Wade-Giles,* **Tu′men′ Chiang′** (jyäng); *Pinyin,* **Tu′men′ Jiang′** (jyäng).

tu•mesce (to͞o mes′, tyo͞o-) *v.t., v.i.,* **-mesced, -mesc•ing.** to make or become tumescent. [1970–75; back formation from TUMESCENT]

tu•mes•cent (to͞o mes′ənt, tyo͞o-), *adj.* **1.** swelling; slightly tumid. **2.** exhibiting or affected with many ideas or emotions; teeming. **3.** pompous and pretentious, esp. in the use of language; bombastic. [1880–85; < L *tumēscent-* (s. of *tumēscēns,* prp. of *tumēscere* to begin to swell), equiv. to *tum(ēre)* to swell + *-ēscent-* -ESCENT] —**tu•mes′cence,** *n.*

tu•mid (to͞o′mid, tyo͞o′-), *adj.* **1.** swollen, or affected with swelling, as a part of the body. **2.** pompous or inflated, as language; turgid; bombastic. **3.** seeming to swell; bulging. [1535–45; < L *tumidus* swollen, equiv. to *tum(ēre)* to swell + *-idus* -ID[4]] —**tu•mid′i•ty, tu′mid•ness,** *n.* —**tu′mid•ly,** *adv.*
—**Syn. 1.** distended, turgid. **2.** flatulent. —**Ant. 1.** deflated.

tumm•ler (to͞om′lər), *n.* **1.** a male entertainer, as formerly employed by resorts in the Catskill Mountains, who combined the duties of a comedian, activities director, and master of ceremonies to keep the guests amused throughout the day. **2.** any lively, prankish, or mischievous man. [1930–35; < Yiddish *tumler* one who makes a racket, stir, equiv. to *tuml(en)* to make a racket + *-er* -ER[1]; cf. MHG *getümel* noise; see TUMBLE]

tum•my (tum′ē), *n., pl.* **-mies.** *Informal.* stomach: *The baby had a pain in his tummy.* [1865–70; nursery alter. of STOMACH]

tum′my tuck′, *Informal.* plastic surgery of the abdomen involving removal of excess fatty tissue and excess skin; abdominoplasty.

tu•mor (to͞o′mər, tyo͞o′-), *n.* **1.** a swollen part; swelling; protuberance. **2.** an uncontrolled, abnormal, circumscribed growth of cells in any animal or plant tissue; neoplasm. **3.** *Archaic.* **a.** inflated pride; haughtiness. **b.** pompous language; bombast. Also, *esp. Brit.,* **tu′mour.** [1535–45; < L: a swelling, swollen state, equiv. to *tu-*

m(ēre) to swell + *-or* -OR[1]] —**tu′mor·like′,** *adj.* —**tu′·mor·ous, tu′mor·al,** *adj.*

tu·mor·i·gen·e·sis (to͞o′mər i jen′ə sis, tyo͞o′-), *n.* the production or development of tumors. [1945–50; TUMOR + -I- + -GENESIS]

tu·mor·i·gen·ic (to͞o′mər i jen′ik, tyo͞o′-), *adj.* (of cells or a substance) capable of producing tumors. [1940–45; TUMOR + -I- + -GENIC] —**tu·mor·i·ge·nic·i·ty** (to͞o′mər i jə nis′i tē, tyo͞o′-), *n.*

tu′mor necro′sis fac′tor, a protein, produced in humans and other animals, that is destructive to cells showing abnormally rapid growth: identical with cachectin. *Abbr.:* TNF

tump (tump), *n. Brit. Dial.* **1.** a small mound, hill, or rise of ground. **2.** a clump of grass, shrubs, or trees, esp. rising from a swamp or bog. **3.** a heap or stack, as a haystack. [1580–90; of obscure orig.]

tump·line (tump′līn′), *n.* a strap or sling passed around the chest or forehead to help support a pack carried on a person's back. [1790–1800; *tump* (earlier *mattump, metomp* < Southern New England Algonquian < proto-Eastern Algonquian **mat-* empty root appearing in names of manufactured objects + **-a·pəy* string) + LINE[1]]

tu·mu·lar (to͞o′myə lər, tyo͞o′-), *adj.* of, pertaining to, resembling, or characterized by a tumulus or tumuli. [1820–30; < L *tumul(us)* TUMULUS + -AR[1]]

tu·mu·lous (to͞o′myə ləs, tyo͞o′-), *adj.* having mounds; full of mounds; tumular. Also, **tu·mu·lose** (to͞o′myə lōs′, tyo͞o′-). [1820–30; < L *tumulōsus,* equiv. to *tumul(us)* TUMULUS + *-ōsus* -OUS]

tu·mult (to͞o′məlt, tyo͞o′-), *n.* **1.** violent and noisy commotion or disturbance of a crowd or mob; uproar: *The tumult reached its height during the premier's speech.* **2.** a general outbreak, riot, uprising, or other disorder: *The tumult moved toward the embassy.* **3.** highly distressing agitation of mind or feeling; turbulent mental or emotional disturbance: *His placid facade failed to conceal the tumult of his mind.* [1375–1425; late ME *tumult(e)* < L *tumultus* an uproar, akin to *tumēre* to swell]
—**Syn. 1.** disorder, turbulence. See **ado. 2.** revolt, revolution, mutiny. **3.** excitement, perturbation.

tu·mul·tu·ar·y (to͞o mul′cho͞o er′ē, tyo͞o-), *adj.* **1.** tumultuous; turbulent. **2.** confused; disorderly; haphazard: *tumultuary habits of studying.* [1580–90; < L *tumultuārius* pertaining to bustle or hurry, equiv. to *tumultu(s)* TUMULT + *-ārius* -ARY[1]]

tu·mul·tu·ous (to͞o mul′cho͞o əs, tyo͞o-), *adj.* **1.** full of tumult or riotousness; marked by disturbance and uproar: *a tumultuous celebration.* **2.** raising a great clatter and commotion; disorderly or noisy: *a tumultuous crowd of students.* **3.** highly agitated, as the mind or emotions; distraught; turbulent. [1540–50; < L *tumultuōsus,* equiv. to *tumultu(s)* TUMULT + *-ōsus* -OUS] —**tu·mul′tu·ous·ly,** *adv.* —**tu·mul′tu·ous·ness,** *n.*
—**Syn. 1.** uproarious, turbulent, violent. **2.** boisterous. **3.** unquiet. —**Ant. 1–3** calm, quiet.

tu·mu·lus (to͞o′myə ləs, tyo͞o′-), *n., pl.* **-lus·es, -li** (-lī′). **1.** *Archaeol.* an artificial mound, esp. over a grave; barrow. **2.** *Geol.* a domelike swelling or mound formed in congealed lava. [1680–90; < L: mound, swelling, equiv. to *tum(ēre)* to swell + *-ulus* -ULE]

tun (tun), *n., v.,* **tunned, tun·ning.** —*n.* **1.** a large cask for holding liquids, esp. wine, ale, or beer. **2.** a measure of liquid capacity, usually equivalent to 252 wine gallons. —*v.t.* **3.** to put into or store in a tun or tuns. [bef. 900; (n.) ME *tunne,* OE; c. D *ton,* G *Tonne* (< LG), ON *tunna;* (v.) late ME, deriv. of the n.]

Tun., Tunisia.

tu·na[1] (to͞o′nə, tyo͞o′-), *n., pl. (esp. collectively)* **-na,** *(esp. referring to two or more kinds or species)* **-nas. 1.** any of several large food and game fishes of the family Scombridae, inhabiting temperate and tropical seas. Cf. **albacore, bluefin tuna, yellowfin tuna. 2.** any of various related fishes. **3.** Also called **tu′na fish′.** the flesh of the tuna, used as food. [1880–85, *Amer.;* < AmerSp, var. of Sp *atún* < Ar *al* the + *tūn* < Gk *thýnnos* TUNNY]

bluefin tuna, *Thunnus thynnus,* length to 14 ft. (4.3 m)

tu·na[2] (to͞o′nə, tyo͞o′-), *n.* **1.** any of various prickly pears, esp. either of two erect, treelike species, *Opuntia tuna* or *O. ficus-indica,* of Mexico, bearing a sweet, edible fruit. **2.** the fruit of these plants. [1545–55; < Sp < Taino]

tun·a·ble (to͞o′nə bəl, tyo͞o′-), *adj.* **1.** capable of being tuned. **2.** *Archaic.* harmonious; tuneful; melodious. [1490–1500; TUNE + -ABLE] —**tun′a·bil′i·ty, tun′a·ble·ness,** *n.* —**tun′a·bly,** *adv.*

Tun′bridge ware′ (tun′brij′), decorative wooden ware, including tables, trays, boxes, and ornamental objects, produced esp. in the late 17th and 18th centuries in Tunbridge Wells, England, with mosaiclike marquetry sawed from square-sectioned wooden rods of different natural colors. [1765–75]

Tun′bridge Wells′, a city in SW Kent, in SE England: mineral springs; resort. 95,200.

tun·dish (tun′dish′), *n. Metall.* **1.** (in a vacuum induction furnace) a trough through which molten metal flows under vacuum to a mold chamber. **2.** Also called **pouring box, pouring basket, pouring basin.** a refractory-lined vessel having holes for distributing metal being teemed into ingot molds. [1350–1400; ME; see TUN, DISH]

tun·dra (tun′drə, to͞on′-), *n.* one of the vast, nearly level, treeless plains of the arctic regions of Europe, Asia, and North America. [1835–45; < Russ *túndra* < Lappish; cf. Kola Lappish *tūndar* flat elevated area]

tun′dra swan′, a swan, *Cygnus columbianus,* nesting in tundra regions of both the New and Old Worlds, having a black bill with a yellow spot at the base. Cf. **whistling swan, Bewick's swan.**

tune (to͞on, tyo͞on), *n., v.,* **tuned, tun·ing.** —*n.* **1.** a succession of musical sounds forming an air or melody, with or without the harmony accompanying it. **2.** a musical setting of a hymn, poem, psalm, etc., usually in four-part harmony. **3.** the state of being in the proper pitch: *to be in tune.* **4.** agreement in pitch; unison; harmony. **5.** proper adjustment, as of radio instruments or circuits with respect to frequency. **6.** harmonious relationship; accord; agreement. **7.** *Archaic.* frame of mind; mood. **8.** *Obs.* a tone or sound. **9. call the tune,** to decide matters of policy; control: *He was technically running the business, but his father still called the tune.* **10. change one's tune,** to reverse one's views; change one's mind: *She changed her tune about children when she married and had her own.* **11. sing a different tune,** to be forced to change one's ways, attitude, behavior, etc.: *He will sing a different tune when he has to earn his own money.* **12. to the tune of,** *Informal.* in or about the amount of: *In order to expand, they will need capital to the tune of six million dollars.*
—*v.t.* **13.** to adjust (a musical instrument) to a correct or given standard of pitch (often fol. by *up*). **14.** to adapt (the voice, song, etc.) to a particular tone, to the expression of a particular feeling, or the like. **15.** to bring (someone or something) into harmony. **16.** to adjust (a motor, mechanism, or the like) for proper functioning. **17.** *Radio and Television.* **a.** to adjust (a circuit, frequency, or the like) so as to bring it into resonance with another circuit, a given frequency, or the like. **b.** to adjust (a receiving apparatus) so as to make it compatible in frequency with a transmitting apparatus whose signals are to be received. **c.** to adjust (a receiving apparatus) so as to receive the signals of a particular transmitting station. **18.** to put into or cause to be in a receptive condition, mood, etc.; bring into harmony or agreement. **19.** *Archaic.* **a.** to utter, sound, or express musically. **b.** to play upon (a lyre).
—*v.i.* **20.** to put a musical instrument in tune (often fol. by *up*). **21.** to give forth a musical sound. **22.** to be in harmony or accord; become responsive. **23. tune in,** to adjust a radio or television set so as to receive (signals, a particular station, etc.). **24. tune out, a.** to adjust a radio or television set so as to stop or avoid receiving (a station or channel). **b.** *Slang.* to stop paying attention to a person, situation, etc. **25. tune up, a.** to cause a group of musical instruments to be brought to the same pitch. **b.** to begin to sing. **c.** to bring into proper operating order, as a motor: *Before starting on our trip we should have the car tuned up.* [1350–1400; ME (n.); unexplained var. of TONE]
—**Syn. 18.** harmonize, balance. **21.** chime.

tune·ful (to͞on′fəl, tyo͞on′-), *adj.* **1.** full of melody; melodious: *tuneful compositions.* **2.** producing musical sounds or melody. [1585–95; TUNE + -FUL] —**tune′ful·ly,** *adv.* —**tune′ful·ness,** *n.*
—**Syn. 1.** musical, harmonious, dulcet, sweet. —**Ant. 1.** discordant.

tune·less (to͞on′lis, tyo͞on′-), *adj.* **1.** unmelodious; unmusical. **2.** making or giving no music; silent: *In the corner stood a tuneless old piano.* [1585–95; TUNE + -LESS] —**tune′less·ly,** *adv.*

tun·er (to͞o′nər, tyo͞o′-), *n.* **1.** a person or thing that tunes. **2.** the portion of a radio or television receiver that captures the broadcast signal and feeds it to other circuits in the set for further processing. [1570–80; 1905–10 for def. 2; TUNE + -ER[1]]

tune·smith (to͞on′smith′, tyo͞on′-), *n. Informal.* a person who composes popular music or songs. [1925–30; TUNE + SMITH]

tune-up (to͞on′up′, tyo͞on′-), *n.* **1.** an adjustment, as of a motor, to improve working order or condition: *The car needs a tune-up badly.* **2.** *Informal.* a preparatory activity or warm-up, as before a contest or game: *The track meet served as a tune-up for the Olympics.* [1945–50; n. use of v. phrase *tune up*]

Tung·chow (*Chin.* to͝ong′jō′), *n. Older Spelling.* Tongzhou.

Tung·hwa (*Chin.* to͝ong′hwä′), *n. Older Spelling.* Tonghua. Also, *Wade-Giles,* **T'ung′hua′.**

tun·go (tung′gō), *n., pl.* **-gos.** *n. Australian.* rat-kangaroo. [of obscure orig.]

tung′ oil′ (tung), a yellow drying oil derived from the seeds of a tung tree, *Aleurites fordii,* used in varnishes, linoleum, etc. [1880–85; *tung* < Chin *tóng* tung tree]

tung′-oil tree′ (tung′oil′). See **tung tree.**

Tung·shan (*Chin.* to͝ong′shän′), *n. Wade-Giles.* Tongshan.

tung·state (tung′stāt), *n. Chem.* a salt of any tungstic acid. Also called **wolframate.** [1790–1800; TUNGST(IC ACID) + -ATE[2]]

tung·sten (tung′stən), *n. Chem.* a rare, metallic element having a bright-gray color, a metallic luster, and a high melting point, 3410° C, and found in wolframite, tungstite, and other minerals: used in alloys of high-speed cutting tools, electric-lamp filaments, etc. *Symbol:* W; *at. wt.:* 183.85; *at. no.:* 74; *sp. gr.:* 19.3. Also called **wolfram.** [1760–70; < Sw, equiv. to *tung* heavy + *sten* stone] —**tung·sten·ic** (tung sten′ik), *adj.*

tung′sten lamp′, an incandescent electric lamp in which the filament is made of tungsten. [1905–10]

tung′sten rat′ing, a film-speed rating that indicates the relative sensitivity of a particular film stock to light from incandescent lamps with tungsten filaments. Also called **tung′sten speed′.**

tung′sten steel′, an alloy steel containing tungsten. [1860–65]

tung′sten triox′ide, *Chem.* a heavy, canary-yellow, water-insoluble powder, WO_3, used in the manufacture of tungstates. Also called **tung′sten ox′ide, tung′stic ac′id hydrox′ide, tung′stic anhy′dride.**

tung·stic (tung′stik), *adj. Chem.* of or containing tungsten, esp. in the pentavalent or hexavalent state. [1790–1800; TUNGST(EN) + -IC]

tung′stic ac′id, *Chem.* **1.** a hydrate of tungsten trioxide, $H_2WO_4 \cdot H_2O$, used in the manufacture of tungsten-lamp filaments. **2.** any of a group of acids derived from tungsten by the addition of acid to a soluble tungstate or to a mixture of a tungstate and a silicate, phosphate, etc. [1790–1800]

tung·stite (tung′stīt), *n.* a yellow or yellowish-green mineral, tungsten trioxide, WO_3, usually occurring in a pulverulent form. [1865–70; TUNGST(EN) + -ITE[1]]

Tung·ting (do͝ong′ting′), *n.* a lake in S China, in Hunan province. 1450 sq. mi. (3755 sq. km).

tung′ tree′, any of several trees belonging to the genus *Aleurites,* of the spurge family, esp. *A. fordii,* of China, bearing seeds that yield tung oil. Also called **tung-oil tree.** [1890–95; see TUNG OIL]

Tun·gus (to͝ong go͞oz′), *n., pl.* **-gus·es,** *(esp. collectively)* **-gus. 1.** Evenki. **2.** any member of a Tungusic-speaking people. [1620–30; << Russ *tungús,* prob. < Tatar, a formation with the Turkic suffix **-guz,* used in ethnic names; identity of 1st element obscure]

Tun·gus·ic (to͝ong go͞o′zik), *n.* **1.** a family of languages spoken or formerly spoken in Manchuria and central and SE Siberia, including Manchu, Evenki, Even, and languages of the Amur River region, as Nanay. —*adj.* **2.** of or pertaining to Tungusic or its speakers. [1865–70; TUNGUS + -IC]

Tun·gu·ska (to͝ong go͞o′skə; *Russ.* to͞on go͞o′skə), *n.* any of three tributaries of the Yenisei River in the central Russian Federation in Asia: includes the Lower Tunguska 2000 mi. (3220 km) long; the Upper Tunguska or the lower course of the Angara; and the Stony Tunguska ab. 975 mi. (1570 km) long.

Tun·guz (to͝ong go͞oz′), *n., pl.* **-guz·es,** *(esp. collectively)* **-guz.** Tungus.

tu·nic (to͞o′nik, tyo͞o′-), *n.* **1.** *Chiefly Brit.* a coat worn as part of a military or other uniform. **2.** a gownlike outer garment, with or without sleeves and sometimes belted, worn by the ancient Greeks and Romans. **3.** a woman's upper garment, either loose or close-fitting and extending over the skirt to the hips or below. **4.** a garment with a short skirt, worn by women for sports. **5.** *Eccles.* a tunicle. **6.** *Anat., Zool.* any covering or investing membrane or part, as of an organ. **7.** *Bot.* an integument, as that covering a seed. [bef. 900; (< F *tunique*) < L *tunica;* perh. also continuing OE *tunece, tunica* < L]

tu·ni·ca (to͞o′ni kə, tyo͞o′-), *n., pl.* **-cae** (-sē′). *Anat., Zool., Bot.* a tunic. [< NL, special use of L *tunica* tunic]

tu·ni·cate (to͞o′ni kit, -kāt′, tyo͞o′-), *n.* **1.** *Zool.* any sessile marine chordate of the subphylum Tunicata (Urochordata), having a saclike body enclosed in a thick membrane or tunic and two openings or siphons for the ingress and egress of water. —*adj.* Also, **tu′ni·cat′ed. 2.** (esp. of the Tunicata) having a tunic or covering. **3.** of or pertaining to the tunicates. **4.** *Bot.* having or consisting of a series of concentric layers, as a bulb. [1615–25; < L *tunicātus* wearing a tunic. See TUNIC, -ATE[1]]

tu′nic flow′er. See **coat flower.**

tu·ni·cle (to͞o′ni kəl, tyo͞o′-), *n. Eccles.* a vestment worn over the alb by subdeacons, as at the celebration of the Mass, and by bishops. [1350–1400; ME < L *tunicula,* equiv. to *tunic(a)* tunic + *-ula* -ULE]

tun′ing fork′, a steel instrument consisting of a stem with two prongs, producing a musical tone of definite, constant pitch when struck, and serving as a standard for tuning musical instruments, making acoustical experiments, and the like. [1765–75]

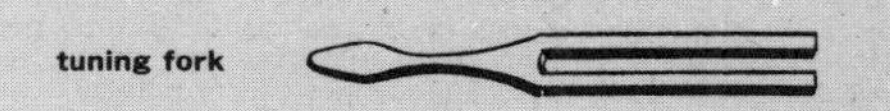
tuning fork

tun′ing pipe′. See **pitch pipe.** [1925–30]

Tu·nis (to͞o′nis, tyo͞o′-), *n.* **1.** a city in and the capital of Tunisia, in the NE part. 944,000. **2.** one of the former Barbary States in N Africa, once notorious for its pirates: constitutes modern Tunisia.

Tu·ni·sia (to͞o nē′zhə, -shə, -nizh′ə, -nish′ə, tyo͞o-), *n.* a republic in N Africa, on the Mediterranean: a French protectorate until 1956. 6,000,000. 48,330 sq. mi. (125,175 sq. km). *Cap.:* Tunis. —**Tu·ni′sian,** *adj., n.*

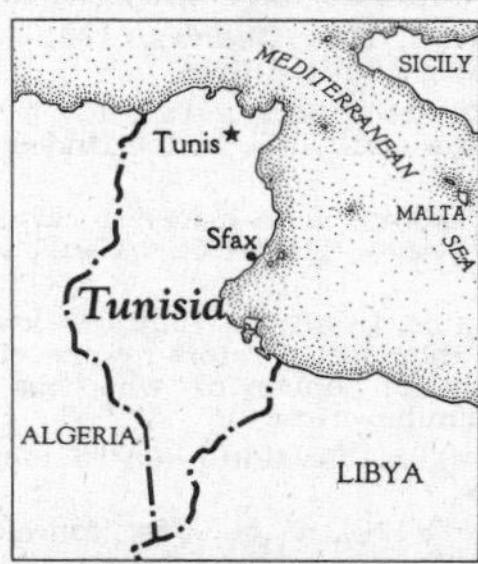

CONCISE PRONUNCIATION KEY: act, cāpe, dâre, pärt; set, ēqual; if, īce; ox, ōver, ôrder, oil, bo͝ok, bo͞ot, out; up, ûrge; child; sing; shoe; thin, *th*at; zh as in *treasure.* ə = *a* as in *alone, e* as in *system, i* as in *easily, o* as in *gallop, u* as in *circus;* ° as in *fire* (fī°r), *hour* (ou°r). l and n can serve as syllabic consonants, as in *cradle* (krād′l), and *button* (but′n). See the full key inside the front cover.

T-u·nit (tē′yōō′nit), *n.* a minimal unit constituting a complete sentence, consisting of one independent clause and any dependent clauses connected to it: used as a measure of the structural complexity of sentences. [1960–65; *t*(*erminable*) *unit*]

Tun·ja (tōōng′hä), *n.* a city in central Colombia. 55,600.

tun·ka (tung′kə), *n.* See **wax gourd.** [< Chin (Wade-Giles) *tung*[1]*kua*[1], (pinyin) *dōngguā* lit., winter melon]

Tun·ker (tung′kər), *n.* Dunker.

tun·nage (tun′ij), *n.* tonnage.

tun·nel (tun′l), *n., v.,* **-neled, -nel·ing** or (*esp. Brit.*) **-nelled, -nel·ling.** —*n.* **1.** an underground passage. **2.** a passageway, as for trains or automobiles, through or under an obstruction, as a city, mountain, river, harbor, or the like. **3.** an approximately horizontal gallery or corridor in a mine. **4.** the burrow of an animal. **5.** *Dial.* a funnel. —*v.t.* **6.** to construct a passageway through or under: *to tunnel a mountain.* **7.** to make or excavate (a tunnel or underground passage): *to tunnel a passage under a river.* **8.** to move or proceed by or as if by boring a tunnel: *The river tunneled its way through the mountain.* **9.** to pierce or hollow out, as with tunnels. —*v.i.* **10.** to make a tunnel or tunnels: *to tunnel through the Alps.* [1400–50; late ME *tonel* (n.) < MF *tonele, tonnelle* funnel-shaped net, fem. of *tonnel* cask, dim. of *tonne* TUN; see -ELLE] —**tun′nel·er;** *esp. Brit.,* **tun′nel·ler,** *n.* —**tun′nel·like′,** *adj.*

tun′nel disease′, *Pathol.* **1.** aeroembolism (def. 2). **2.** hookworm (def. 2). [1885–90]

tun′nel effect′, *Physics.* a quantum-mechanical process by which a particle can pass through a potential energy barrier that is higher than the energy of the particle: first postulated to explain the escape of alpha particles from atomic nuclei. Also called **tun′nel·ing.** [1930–35]

tun′nel of love′, a ride in an amusement park consisting of a dark, narrow, covered passageway through which small cars or boats are mechanically conveyed, usually frequented by couples. [1955–60]

tun′nel vault′. See **barrel vault.**

tun′nel vi′sion, **1.** a drastically narrowed field of vision, as in looking through a tube, symptomatic of retinitis pigmentosa. **2.** an extremely narrow or prejudiced outlook; narrow-mindedness. [1940–45] —**tun′nel-vi′sioned,** *adj.*

Tun·ney (tun′ē), *n.* **James Joseph** (*"Gene"*), 1898–1978, U.S. boxer: world heavyweight champion 1926–28.

tun·ny (tun′ē), *n., pl.* (*esp. collectively*) **-ny,** (*esp. referring to two or more kinds or species*) **-nies.** *Chiefly Brit.* tuna[1]. [1520–30; by apocope < ML *tunnīna* false tunny, n. use of fem. of *tunnīnus* like a tunny, equiv. to *tunn*(*us*) tunny (var. of L *thynnus* < Gk *thýnnos*) + *-inus* -INE[1]]

Tuo·ne·la (twô′ne lə), *n. Finnish Myth.* the afterworld, an island on which the sun and moon never shine. Also called **Manala.**

tup (tup), *n., v.,* **tupped, tup·ping.** —*n.* **1.** *Chiefly Brit.* a male sheep; ram. **2.** the head of a falling hammerlike mechanism, as of a steam hammer or pile driver. —*v.t.* **3.** *Chiefly Brit.* (of a ram) to copulate with (a ewe). —*v.i.* **4.** *Chiefly Brit.* (of a ewe) to copulate. [1300–50; ME *tope, tupe* ram, of obscure orig.]

tu·pe·lo (tōō′pə lō′, tyōō′-), *n., pl.* **-los. 1.** any of several trees of the genus *Nyssa,* having ovate leaves, clusters of minute flowers, and purple, berrylike fruit, esp. *N. aquatica,* of swampy regions of the eastern, southern, and midwestern U.S. **2.** the soft, light wood of these trees. [1720–30, *Amer.*; perh. < Creek **topilwa* lit., swamp tree (equiv. to *íto* tree + *opílwa* swamp)]

Tu·pe·lo (tōō′pə lō′, tyōō′-), *n.* a city in NE Mississippi. 23,905.

Tu·pi (tōō pē′, tōō′pē), *n., pl.* **-pis,** (*esp. collectively*) **-pi** for 1. **1.** a member of any of several related Indian peoples living in the valleys of various Brazilian rivers, esp. the Amazon. **2.** the language spoken in northern Brazil by the Tupi Indians. Also, **Tu·pí′.** —**Tu·pi′an,** *adj.*

Tu·pi-Gua·ra·ni (tōō pē′gwär′ə nē′, tōō′pē-), *n.* a family of Indian languages including Tupi, Guarani, lingua geral, and many others of central South America. —**Tu·pi-Gua·ra·ni·an** (tōō pē′gwär′ə nē′ən, tōō′pē-), *adj., n.*

Tu·po·lev (tōō pō′ləf; *Russ.* tōō′pə lyif), *n.* **An·drei Ni·ko·la·ye·vich** (un dʀyā′ nyi ku lä′yi vyich), 1888–1972, Russian engineer and aircraft designer.

tup·pence (tup′əns), *n. Brit.* twopence. [1505–15; earlier *tuppens,* reduction of TWOPENCE]

tup·pen·ny (tup′ə nē), *adj.* twopenny (defs. 1–3).

Tup·per (tup′ər), *n.* **Sir Charles,** 1821–1915, Canadian statesman: prime minister 1896.

Tu·pun·ga·to (tōō′pōōng gä′tô), *n.* a mountain between Argentina and Chile, in the Andes. ab. 22,310 ft. (6800 m).

tuque (tōōk, tyōōk), *n.* a heavy stocking cap worn in Canada. Also, **toque.** [1870–75; < CanF, var. of F *toque* TOQUE]

tu quo·que (tōō kwō′kwe; *Eng.* tōō kwō′kwē, -kwā, tyōō), *Latin.* thou too: a retort by one charged with a crime accusing an opponent who has brought the charges of a similar crime.

Tu·ra (tōō′rä), *n.* **Co·si·mo** (kô′zē mô), c1430–98?, Italian painter.

tu·ra·co (tōōr′ə kō′), *n., pl.* **-cos.** touraco.

CONCISE ETYMOLOGY KEY: <, descended or borrowed from; >, whence; b., blend of, blended; c., cognate with; cf., compare; deriv., derivative; equiv., equivalent; imit., imitative; obl., oblique; r., replacing; s., stem; sp., spelling, spelled; resp., respelling, respelled; trans., translation; ?, origin unknown; *, unattested; ‡, probably earlier than. See the full key inside the front cover.

Tu·ra·ni·an (tōō rā′nē ən, tyōō-), *adj.* **1.** belonging or pertaining to a group of Asian peoples or languages comprising nearly all of those that are neither Indo-European nor Semitic. **2.** Ural-Altaic. —*n.* **3.** a member of any of the peoples speaking a Turanian, esp. a Ural-Altaic, language. **4.** a member of any of the Ural-Altaic peoples. [1770–80; < Pers *Tūrān* Turkestan + -IAN]

tur·ban (tûr′bən), *n.* **1.** a man's headdress worn chiefly by Muslims in southern Asia, consisting of a long cloth of silk, linen, cotton, etc., wound either about a cap or directly around the head. **2.** any headdress resembling this. **3.** any of various off-the-face hats for women that are close-fitting, of a soft fabric, and brimless, or that have a narrow, sometimes draped, brim. [1555–65; earlier *torbant,* var. of *tulbant* < Turk *tülbent* < Pers *dulband*] —**tur′baned,** *adj.* —**tur′ban·less,** *adj.* —**tur′ban·like′,** *adj.*

turban (def. 1)

tur′ban squash′, a turban-shaped variety of winter squash, *Cucurbita maxima turbaniformis.* [1905–10, *Amer.*]

tur·ba·ry (tûr′bə rē), *n., pl.* **-ries. 1.** land, or a piece of land, where turf or peat may be dug or cut. **2.** *Law.* the right to cut turf or peat on a common land or on another person's land. [1275–1325; ME *turbarye* < ML *turbāria,* equiv. to *turb*(*a*) TURF + *-āria* -ARY[1]]

tur·bel·lar·i·an (tûr′bə lâr′ē ən), *adj.* **1.** belonging to the Turbellaria, a class of platyhelminths or flatworms, mostly aquatic and having cilia on the body surface. —*n.* **2.** a turbellarian platyhelminth. [1875–80; < NL *Turbellari*(*a*) (L *turbell*(*ae*) a stir, row (pl. dim. of *turba* turmoil) + *-āria,* neut. pl. of *-ārius* -ARY) + -AN]

tur·bid (tûr′bid), *adj.* **1.** not clear or transparent because of stirred-up sediment or the like; clouded; opaque; obscured: *the turbid waters near the waterfall.* **2.** thick or dense, as smoke or clouds. **3.** confused; muddled; disturbed. [1620–30; < L *turbidus* disturbed, equiv. to *turb*(*āre*) to disturb (deriv. of *turba* turmoil) + *-idus* -ID[4]] —**tur·bid′i·ty, tur′bid·ness,** *n.* —**tur′bid·ly,** *adv.*
—**Syn. 1.** murky, cloudy, roiled, muddy.

tur·bi·dim·e·ter (tûr′bi dim′i tər), *n.* a device for measuring the turbidity of water or other liquids. [1910–15; TURBID + -I- + -METER] —**tur′bi·dim′e·try,** *n.* —**tur·bi·di·met·ric** (tûr′bi də me′trik), *adj.* —**tur′bi·di·met′ri·cal·ly,** *adv.*

tur·bi·dite (tûr′bi dīt′), *n. Geol.* a sedimentary deposit laid down by a turbidity current. [1955–60; TURBID + -ITE[1]]

turbid′ity cur′rent, *Geol.* a turbid, dense current of sediments in suspension moving along the slope and bottom of a lake or ocean. Also called **density current.**

tur·bi·nal (tûr′bə nl), *adj.* **1.** turbinate. —*n.* **2.** *Anat.* a turbinate bone. [1575–85; < L *turbin-* (s. of *turbō* a whirlwind, top; see TURBINE) + -AL[1]]

tur·bi·nate (tûr′bə nit, -nāt′), *adj.* Also, **tur′bi·nat′ed. 1.** having the shape of an inverted cone; scroll-like; whorled; spiraled. **2.** *Anat.* of or pertaining to certain scroll-like, spongy bones of the nasal passages in humans and other vertebrates. **3.** inversely conical. —*n.* **4.** a turbinate shell. **5.** Also called **nasal concha.** *Anat.* a turbinate bone. [1655–65; < L *turbinātus* shaped like a top, equiv. to *turbin-* (s. of *turbō* a top; see TURBINE) + *-ātus* -ATE[1]] —**tur′bi·na′tion,** *n.*

tur·bine (tûr′bin, -bīn), *n.* any of various machines having a rotor, usually with vanes or blades, driven by the pressure, momentum, or reactive thrust of a moving fluid, as steam, water, hot gases, or air, either occurring in the form of free jets or as a fluid passing through and entirely filling a housing around the rotor. Cf. **impulse turbine, reaction turbine.** [1815–25; < F < L *turbin-,* s. of *turbō* something that spins, e.g., top, spindle, whirlwind; akin to TURBID]

tur′bine ven′tilator, a ventilator, usually mounted on the roof of a building, deck of a ship, etc., having at its head a globular, vaned rotor that is rotated by the wind, conveying air through a duct to and from a chamber below.

tur·bit (tûr′bit), *n.* one of a breed of domestic pigeons having a stout, roundish body, a short head and beak, and a ruffled breast and neck. [1680–90; var. of TURBOT; appar. because, like the fish, the bird is toplike in outline]

tur·bo (tûr′bō), *n., pl.* **-bos. 1.** turbine. **2.** *Informal.* turbocharger. **3.** an automobile powered by an internal-combustion engine equipped with a turbocharger. [1655–65, in sense "tornado"; 1900–05 for def. 1; in part < L *turbō* top, whirlwind, in part by shortening of TURBOCHARGED OR TURBOCHARGER]

turbo-, a combining form representing **turbine** in compound words: *turbojet.* [TURB(INE) + -O-]

tur·bo·charge (tûr′bō chärj′), *v.t.,* **-charged, -charg·ing.** to equip (an internal-combustion engine) with a turbocharger. [TURBO- + (SUPER)CHARGE]

tur·bo·charg·er (tûr′bō chär′jər), *n.* a supercharger that is driven by a turbine turned by exhaust gases from the engine. Also called **turbo.** [1930–35; TURBO- + (SUPER)CHARGER]

tur·bo-e·lec·tric (tûr′bō i lek′trik), *adj.* noting, pertaining to, or utilizing machinery that includes a generator driven by a turbine: *turbo-electric engine; turbo-electric propulsion.* [1900–05]

tur·bo·fan (tûr′bō fan′), *n.* a jet engine having a large impeller that takes in air, part of which is used in combustion of fuel, the remainder being mixed with the products of combustion to form a low-velocity exhaust jet. Also called **tur′bofan en′gine.** [1940–45; TURBO- + FAN[1]]

tur·bo·jet (tûr′bō jet′), *n.* **1.** See **turbojet engine. 2.** an airplane equipped with one or more turbojet engines. [1940–45; TURBO- + JET[1]]

tur′bojet en′gine, a jet-propulsion engine in which air from the atmosphere is compressed for combustion by a turbine-driven compressor. [1940–45]

tur·bo·prop (tûr′bō prop′), *n.* **1.** See **turbo-propeller engine. 2.** an airplane equipped with one or more turbo-propeller engines. [1940–45; TURBO- + PROP[3]]

tur′bo-pro·pel·ler en′gine (tûr′bō prə pel′ər), *Aeron.* a jet engine with a turbine-driven propeller that produces the principal thrust, augmented by the thrust of the jet exhaust. Also called **propjet engine, tur′boprop en′gine.** [1945–50]

tur·bo·pump (tûr′bō pump′), *n.* a turbine-driven pump, as one used to feed propellant to a rocket engine. [1900–05; TURBO- + PUMP[1]]

tur·bo-ram′jet en′gine (tûr′bō ram′jet′), a combination engine that can be operated as a turbojet or ramjet engine. [1945–50]

tur·bo·shaft (tûr′bō shaft′, -shäft′), *n. Aeron.* a gas turbine used to deliver shaft power, as to a helicopter rotor. Also called **tur′boshaft en′gine.** [1955–60; TURBO- + SHAFT]

tur·bo·su·per·charg·er (tûr′bō sōō′pər chär′jər), *n.* (formerly) a turbocharger. [1930–35; TURBO- + SUPERCHARGER]

tur·bot (tûr′bət), *n., pl.* (*esp. collectively*) **-bot,** (*esp. referring to two or more kinds or species*) **-bots. 1.** a European flatfish, *Psetta maxima,* having a diamond-shaped body: valued as a food fish. **2.** any of several other flatfishes. **3.** a triggerfish. [1250–1300; ME *turbut* < AF; OF *tourbot* < ML *turb*(*ō*) turbot (L: top; appar. applied to the fish because of its outline; see TURBINE, TURBIT) + OF *-ot* n. suffix]

tur·bo·train (tûr′bō trān′), *n.* a train powered by a gas-turbine locomotive. [1965–70; TURBO- + TRAIN]

tur·bu·lence (tûr′byə ləns), *n.* **1.** the quality or state of being turbulent; violent disorder or commotion. **2.** *Hydraulics.* the haphazard secondary motion caused by eddies within a moving fluid. **3.** *Meteorol.* irregular motion of the atmosphere, as that indicated by gusts and lulls in the wind. Also, **tur′bu·len·cy.** [1590–1600; < LL *turbulentia.* See TURBULENT, -ENCE]

tur·bu·lent (tûr′byə lənt), *adj.* **1.** being in a state of agitation or tumult; disturbed: *turbulent feelings or emotions.* **2.** characterized by, or showing disturbance, disorder, etc.: *the turbulent years.* **3.** given to acts of violence and aggression: *the turbulent young soldiers.* [1530–40; < L *turbulentus* restless, equiv. to *turb*(*a*) turmoil + *-ulentus* -ULENT] —**tur′bu·lent·ly,** *adv.*
—**Syn. 1.** agitated, tumultuous, violent, tempestuous, disordered.

tur′bulent flow′, *Hydraul.* the flow of a fluid past an object such that the velocity at any fixed point in the fluid varies irregularly. Cf. **streamline flow.** [1920–25]

Turco-, a combining form representing **Turkish** or **Turkic** in compound words. Also, **Turko-.**

Tur·co·man (tûr′kə mən), *n., pl.* **-mans. 1.** Turkoman. **2.** Turkmen.

Tur·co·phile (tûr′kə fīl′), *n.* **1.** a person who favors or admires Turkey, Turkish customs, or Turks. —*adj.* **2.** tending to favor Turkey or Turkish customs. Also, **Tur·co·phil** (tûr′kə fil), **Turkophile, Turkophil.** [1875–80; TURCO- + -PHILE]

Tur·co·phobe (tûr′kə fōb′), *n.* a person who has a morbid fear of Turks. Also, **Turkophobe.** [1895–1900; TURCO- + -PHOBE] —**Tur′co·pho′bi·a,** *n.*

turd (tûrd), *n. Slang* (*vulgar*). **1.** a piece of excrement. **2.** a mean, contemptible person. [bef. 1000; ME; OE *tord*]

tur·dine (tûr′dīn, -din), *adj.* belonging or pertaining to the family Turdidae, comprising the true thrushes. [1885–90; < NL *Turdinae* subfamily name, equiv. to *Turd*(*us*) genus name (L: thrush) + *-inae* -INAE; see -INE[1]]

Tu·reck (tōōr′ek, tyōōr′-), *n.* **Ros·a·lyn** (roz′ə lin), born 1914, U.S. pianist.

tu·reen (tōō rēn′, tyōō-), *n.* a large, deep, covered dish for serving soup, stew, or other foods. [1700–10; earlier *terrene* < F *terrine* earthenware dish, MF, fem. of *terrin* of the earth, earthen < VL **terrinus,* equiv. to L *terr*(*a*) earth + *-inus* -INE[1]]

Tu·renne (tōō ren′; *Fr.* tʏ ʀen′), *n.* **Hen·ri de la Tour d'Au·vergne de** (äɴ ʀē′ də lᴀ tōōʀ′ dō veʀn′yᵊ də), 1611–75, French general and marshal.

turf (tûrf), *n., pl.* **turfs,** (*esp. Brit.*) **turves;** *v.* —*n.* **1.** a layer of matted earth formed by grass and plant roots. **2.** peat, esp. as material for fuel. **3.** a block or piece of peat dug for fuel. **4.** *Slang.* **a.** the neighborhood over which a street gang asserts its authority. **b.** a familiar area, as of residence or expertise: *Denver is her turf. When you talk literature you're getting into my turf.* **5.** *Chiefly Brit.* a piece cut or torn from the surface of grassland; sod. **6. the turf, a.** the track over which horse races are run. **b.** the practice or sport of racing horses. —*v.t.* **7.** to cover with turf or sod. **8.** *Brit. Slang.* to remove from a desirable office or position; expel; kick out: *He was turfed from leadership of the group.* [bef. 900; 1930–35 for def. 5; ME, OE, c. D *turf,* G *Torf* (< LG), ON *torf,* akin to Skt *darbha* tuft of grass. See TURBARY] —**turf′less,** *adj.* —**turf′like′,** *adj.*

turf•man (tûrf′mən), *n., pl.* **-men.** a person who is extremely devoted to horse racing. [1810–20; TURF + -MAN]

turf•ski (tûrf′skē′), *n., pl.* **-skis.** a short ski with rollers on the bottom used in turfskiing. [1965–70; TURF + SKI]

turf•ski•ing (tûrf′skē′ing), *n.* the sport of skiing down grass slopes on skis outfitted with rollers. Also called **grass skiing.** [TURF + SKIING]

turf•y (tûr′fē), *adj.*, **turf•i•er, turf•i•est. 1.** covered with or consisting of grassy turf. **2.** resembling turf; turflike. **3.** of the nature of or abounding in peat. **4.** of, pertaining to, or characteristic of horse racing. [1545–55; TURF + -Y[1]] —**turf′i•ness,** *n.*

Tur•ge•nev (tûr gen′yəf, -gān′-; *Russ.* to͝or gye′nyif), *n.* **I•van Ser•ge•e•vich** (ē vän′ syir gye′yi vyich), 1818–83, Russian novelist. Also, **Tur•ge′niev.**

tur•ges•cent (tûr jes′ənt), *adj.* becoming swollen; swelling. [1720–30; < L *turgēscent-* (s. of *turgēscēns*), prp. of *turgēscere* to begin to swell] —**tur•ges′cence, tur•ges′cen•cy,** *n.*

tur•gid (tûr′jid), *adj.* **1.** swollen; distended; tumid. **2.** inflated, overblown, or pompous; bombastic: *turgid language.* [1660–70; < L *turgidus,* equiv. to *turg(ēre)* to swell + *-idus* -ID[4]] —**tur•gid′i•ty, tur′gid•ness,** *n.* —**tur′gid•ly,** *adv.*

tur•gor (tûr′gər), *n.* **1.** *Plant Physiol.* the normal distention or rigidity of plant cells, resulting from the pressure exerted by the cell contents on the cell walls. **2.** the state of being swollen or distended. [1875–80; < LL, equiv. to L *turg(ēre)* to swell + *-or* -OR[1]]

Tur•got (tyr gō′), *n.* **Anne Ro•bert Jacques** (an′ rô ber′ zhäk′), 1727–81, French statesman, financier, and economist.

Tu•rin (to͝or′in, tyo͝or′-, to͞o rin′, tyo͞o-), *n.* a city in NW Italy, on the Po: capital of the Kingdom of Italy 1860–65. 1,188,689. Italian, **Torino.**

Tu′ring machine′ (to͝or′ing, tyo͝or′-), *Math.* a hypothetical device with a set of logical rules of computation: the concept is used in mathematical studies of the computability of numbers and in the mathematical theories of automata and computers. [after Alan M. *Turing* (1912–54), English mathematician, who described such a machine in 1936]

tu•ri•on (to͝or′ē on′, tyo͝or′-), *n. Bot.* a small shoot, as of asparagus or certain aquatic plants, from which a new plant can develop. [< L *turiōn-* (s. of *turiō*) young shoot]

tu•ris•ta (to͞o rē′stə), *n.* tourista.

tu•ri•ya (tə rē′yə), *n. Yoga.* the fourth state of consciousness, beyond thought, love, and will, and beyond the awareness of variety, duality, and unity. Also, **turya.** [< Skt *turīya*]

Turk (tûrk), *n.* **1.** a native or inhabitant of Turkey. **2.** (formerly) a native or inhabitant of the Ottoman Empire. **3.** a Muslim, esp. a subject of the Sultan of Turkey. **4.** a member of any of the peoples speaking Turkic languages. **5.** one of a breed of Turkish horses closely related to the Arabian horse. **6.** any Turkish horse. **7.** See **Young Turk. 8.** *Archaic.* a cruel, brutal, and domineering man. [1300–50; ME << Turkish *Türk*; cf. ML *Turcus,* MGk *Toûrkos,* MF *turc,* It *turco,* Pers *turk*]

Turk., 1. Turkey. **2.** Also, **Turk** Turkish.

Tur•ka•na (to͝or kä′nə), *n., pl.* **-nas,** (*esp. collectively*) **-na** for 1. **1.** a member of a seminomadic people of northwestern Kenya and bordering areas of Uganda. **2.** the Nilotic language of the Turkana. **3. Lake.** Formerly, **Rudolf.** a lake in E Africa, in NE Kenya. 185 mi. (298 km) long; 3500 sq. mi. (9100 sq. km).

Tur•ke•stan (tûr′kə stan′, -stän′), *n.* a vast region in W and central Asia, E of the Caspian Sea: includes territory in the S central part of Xinjiang province in China **(Eastern Turkestan** or **Chinese Turkestan),** a strip of N Afghanistan, and the area **(Russian Turkestan)** comprising the republics of Kazakhstan, Kirghizia (Kyrgyzstan), Tadzhikistan (Tajikistan), Turkmenistan, and Uzbekistan. Also, **Turkistan.** —**Tur′ke•stan′i•an,** *adj., n.*

tur•key (tûr′kē), *n., pl.* **-keys,** (*esp. collectively*) **-key. 1.** a large, gallinaceous bird of the family Meleagrididae, esp. *Meleagris gallopavo,* of America, that typically has green, reddish-brown, and yellowish-brown plumage of a metallic luster and that is domesticated in most parts of the world. See illus. in next column. **2.** the flesh of this bird, used as food. **3.** See **ocellated turkey. 4.** *Slang.* **a.** a person or thing of little appeal; dud; loser. **b.** a naive, stupid, or inept person. **c.** a poor and unsuccessful theatrical production; flop. **5.** *Bowling.* three strikes in succession. **6. talk turkey,** *Informal.* to talk frankly; mean business. [1545–55; short for *Turkey cock* and *Turkey hen* cock and hen of Turkey, first applied to guinea fowl, later confused with the American bird]

Tur•key (tûr′kē), *n.* a republic in W Asia and SE Europe. 40,000,000; 296,184 sq. mi. (767,120 sq. km). (286,928 sq. mi. (743,145 sq. km) in Asia; 9257 sq. mi. (23,975 sq. km) in Europe). *Cap.:* Ankara. Cf. **Ottoman Empire.**

tur′key buz′zard. See **turkey vulture.** [1665–75, *Amer.*]

tur′key cock′, 1. the male of the turkey. **2.** a strutting, pompous, conceited person. [1535–45]

tur′key oak′, any of several oaks, as *Quercus cerris,* of Eurasia, or *Q. laevis* and *Q. incana,* of the southern U.S., that grow on dry, sandy barrens. [1700–10, *Amer.*]

Tur′key red′, 1. a bright red produced in fabrics by madder, alizarin, or synthetic dyes. **2.** cotton cloth of this color. **3.** See **Adrianople red.** [1780–90]

tur′key shoot′, 1. a marksmanship contest, usually at a festive gathering, in which rifles are fired at moving targets, originally live turkeys. **2. a.** something easily accomplished; piece of cake. **b.** an easy destruction of enemy troops, esp. of flying aircraft. [1835–45, *Amer.*]

tur′key trot′, a round dance, danced by couples, properly to ragtime, the step being a springy walk with little or no bending of the knees, and accompanied by a swinging motion of the body with shoulder movements up and down. [1830–40, *Amer.*]

tur•key-trot (tûr′kē trot′), *v.i.*, **-trot•ted, -trot•ting.** to dance the turkey trot.

tur′key vul′ture, a blackish-brown vulture, *Cathartes aura,* from the southern U.S. to South America, having a bare, wrinkled, red head and neck. Also called **turkey buzzard.** See illus. under **vulture.** [1815–25, *Amer.*]

Tur•ki (tûr′kē, to͝or′-), *n.* **1.** the Turkic languages of central Asia, taken collectively. —*adj.* **2.** of or pertaining to Turki or to the peoples speaking these languages. [< Pers, equiv. to *Turk* TURK + *-ī* suffix of appurtenance]

Tur•kic (tûr′kik), *n.* **1.** a family of closely related languages of southwest, central, and northern Asia and eastern Europe, including Turkish, Azerbaijani, Turkmen, Uzbek, Kirghiz, and Yakut. —*adj.* **2.** of or pertaining to Turkic or Turkic-speaking peoples. Also called **Turko-Tatar.** [1855–60; TURK + -IC]

Turk•ish (tûr′kish), *adj.* **1.** of, pertaining to, characteristic of, or derived from Turkey or the Turks. **2.** of or pertaining to the language of Turkey. **3.** (loosely) Turkic. —*n.* **4.** the Turkic language of Turkey. *Abbr.:* Turk **5.** (loosely) Turkic. [1835–45; TURK + -ISH[1]] —**Turk′ish•ly,** *adv.* —**Turk′ish•ness,** *n.*

Turk′ish bath′, a bath in which the bather, after copious perspiration in a steam room, showers and has a rubdown. [1635–45]

Turk′ish cof′fee, a strong, usually sweetened coffee, made by boiling the pulverized coffee beans. [1915–20]

Turk′ish cres′cent, crescent (def. 6).

Turk′ish delight′, a candy made of fruit juice and gelatin, cubed and dusted with sugar. Also called **Turk′ish paste′.** [1865–70]

Turk′ish Em′pire. See **Ottoman Empire.**

Turk′ish knot′. See **Ghiordes knot.**

Turk′ish pound′, the Turkish lira.

Turk′ish rug′, any of a large variety of handwoven rugs produced in Turkey, characterized by coarse, heavy yarn and a long, uneven pile. Also called **Turk′ish car′pet.** [1900–05]

Turk′ish tobac′co, a strongly aromatic tobacco, grown chiefly in Turkey and Greece, used in cigarettes.

Turk′ish tow′el, a thick cotton towel with a long nap usually composed of uncut loops. Also, **turk′ish tow′el.**

Turk•ism (tûr′kiz əm), *n.* the culture, beliefs, principles, practices, etc., of the Turks. [1585–95; TURK + -ISM]

Tur•ki•stan (tûr′kə stan′, -stän′), *n.* Turkestan.

Turk•man (tûrk′mən), *n., pl.* **-men.** a native or inhabitant of Turkmenistan. [1475–85; alter. of TURKOMAN] —**Turk•me•ni•an** (tûrk mē′nē ən), *adj.*

Turk•men (tûrk′men, -mən), *n.* the language of the Turkman people, a Turkic language spoken mostly east of the Caspian Sea in Turkmenistan but also in parts of European Russia, Iran, and the Caucasus. Also, **Turkoman, Turcoman.** [< Turk *Türkmen*]

turkey (def. 1), *Meleagris gallopavo,* length to 4 ft. (1.2 m)

Turk•me•ni•stan (tûrk′me nə stan′, -stän′), *n.* a republic in central Asia, bordering the Caspian Sea, Iran, and Afghanistan. 3,534,000; 188,417 sq. mi. (488,000 sq. km). *Cap.:* Ashkhabad. Also called **Turkomen.** Formerly, **Turk′men So′viet So′cialist Repub′lic.**

Turko-, var. of **Turco-.**

Tur•ko•man (tûr′kə mən), *n., pl.* **-mans. 1.** a member of a Turkish people consisting of a group of tribes that inhabit the region near the Aral Sea and parts of Iran and Afghanistan. **2.** Turkmen. Also, **Turcoman.** [< ML *Turcomannus* < Pers *turkmān* TURKMEN]

Tur′koman rug′, any of a number of handwoven rugs produced by the Turkomans and characterized by coarse warp and filling yarn, a short, even pile made with the Sehna knot, and a variety of geometric, marine, and serpentine designs. Also called **Tur′koman car′pet.**

Tur•ko•men (tûr′kə men′, -mən), *n.* Turkmenistan.

Tur•ko•phile (tûr′kə fīl′), *n., adj.* Turcophile. Also, **Tur•ko•phil** (tûr′kə fil).

Tur•ko•phobe (tûr′kə fōb′), *n.* Turcophobe. —**Tur′ko•pho′bi•a,** *n.*

Tur•ko-Ta•tar (tûr′kō tä′tər), *n., adj.* Turkic.

Turks′ and Cai′cos Is′lands (tûrks; kī′kōs, kā′-), two groups of islands in the SE Bahamas: British crown colonies. 5675; ab. 166 sq. mi. (430 sq. km). *Cap.:* Grand Turk.

Turk′s′-cap lil′y (tûrks′kap′), either of two lilies, *Lilium martagon* or *L. superbum,* having nodding flowers with the perianth segments rolled backward. Also called **Martagon lily.** [1785–95]

Turk′s-head (tûrks′hed′), *n.* a turbanlike knot of small cords, made around a rope, spar, etc. [1715–25]

Turk′s′-head cac′tus, a cactus, *Melocactus communis,* of Jamaica, having needlelike spines and a cylindrical body with a tawny-red, fezlike terminal part bearing red flowers. Also called **Turk′s′-cap cac′tus.**

Tur•ku (to͝or′ko͞o), *n.* a seaport in SW Finland. 163,400. Swedish, **Åbo.**

turle′ knot′ (tûrl), *Angling.* a special kind of knot for tying a leader, esp. of gut, to an eyed hook or fly. [after W. G. *Turle,* 19th-century English angler]

Tur•lock (tûr′lok′), *n.* a town in central California. 26,291.

tur•ma•line (to͝or′mə lin; -lēn′, tûr′-), *n.* tourmaline.

tur•mer•ic (tûr′mər ik), *n.* **1.** the aromatic rhizome of an Asian plant, *Curcuma domestica* (or *C. longa*), of the ginger family. **2.** a powder prepared from it, used as a condiment, as in curry powder, or as a yellow dye, a medicine, etc. **3.** the plant itself. **4.** any of various similar substances or plants. [1530–40; earlier *tarmaret* < ML *terra merita* merited earth, unexplained name for curcuma]

tur′meric pa′per, paper treated with turmeric: used to indicate the presence of alkalis, which turn it brown, or of boric acid, which turns it reddish-brown. [1800–10]

tur•moil (tûr′moil), *n.* **1.** a state of great commotion, confusion, or disturbance; tumult; agitation; disquiet: *mental turmoil caused by difficult decisions.* **2.** *Obs.* harassing labor. [1505–15; orig. as v.: to agitate; etym. uncert.; perh. TUR(N) + MOIL]
—**Syn. 1.** turbulence, disorder, uproar. See **agitation.**
—**Ant. 1.** order, quiet.

turn (tûrn), *v.t.* **1.** to cause to move around on an axis or about a center; rotate: *to turn a wheel.* **2.** to cause to move around or partly around, as for the purpose of opening, closing, or tightening: *to turn a key; to turn the cap of a jar.* **3.** to reverse the position or placement of: *to turn a page; to turn an egg; to turn a person around.* **4.** to bring the lower layers of (sod, soil, etc.) to the surface, as in plowing. **5.** to change the position of, by or as if by rotating; move into a different position: *to turn the handle one notch.* **6.** to change or alter the course of; divert; deflect: *He turned the blow with his arm.* **7.** to change the focus or tendency of: *She skillfully turned the conversation away from so unpleasant a subject.* **8.** to reverse the progress of; cause to retreat: *The police turned the advancing rioters by firing over their heads.* **9.** to change or alter the nature, character, or appearance of: *Worry turned his hair gray.* **10.** to change or convert (usually fol. by *into* or *to*): *to turn water into ice; to turn tears into laughter.* **11.** to render or make by some change: *Fear turned him cowardly and craven.* **12.** to change the color of (leaves). **13.** to cause to become sour, to ferment, or the like: *Warm weather turns milk.* **14.** to cause (the stomach) to reject food, liquid, etc.; affect with nausea. **15.** to change from one language or form of expression to another; translate. **16.** to

put or apply to some use or purpose: *He turned his mind to practical matters.* 17. to go or pass around or to the other side of: *to turn a street corner.* 18. to get beyond or pass (a certain age, time, amount, etc.): *His son just turned four.* 19. to direct, aim, or set toward, away from, or in a specified direction: *to turn the car toward the center of town; to turn one's back to the audience.* 20. to direct (the eyes, face, etc.) another way; avert. 21. to shape (a piece of metal, wood, etc.) into rounded form with a cutting tool while rotating the piece on a lathe. 22. to bring into a rounded or curved form in any way. 23. to shape artistically or gracefully, esp. in rounded form. 24. to form or express gracefully: *to turn a phrase well.* 25. to direct (thought, attention, desire, etc.) toward or away from something. 26. to cause to go; send; drive: *to turn a person from one's door.* 27. to revolve in the mind; ponder (often fol. by over): *He turned the idea over a couple of times before acting on it.* 28. to persuade (a person) to change or reorder the course of his or her life. 29. to cause to be prejudiced against: *to turn a son against his father.* 30. to maintain a steady flow or circulation of (money or articles of commerce). 31. to earn or gain: *He turned a huge profit on the sale.* 32. to reverse or remake (a garment, shirt collar, etc.) so that the inner side becomes the outer. 33. to pour from one container into another by inverting. 34. to curve, bend, or twist. 35. to twist out of position or sprain; wrench: *He turned his ankle.* 36. to bend back or blunt (the edge of a blade). 37. to perform (a gymnastic feat) by rotating or revolving: *to turn a somersault.* 38. to disturb the mental balance of; distract; derange. 39. to disorder or upset the placement or condition of: *He turned the room upside down.* 40. *Obs.* a. to convert. b. to pervert.
—*v.i.* 41. to move around on an axis or about a center; rotate. 42. to move partly around through the arc of a circle, as a door on a hinge. 43. to hinge or depend (usually fol. by *on* or *upon*): *The question turns on this point.* 44. to direct or set one's course toward, away from, or in a particular direction. 45. to direct the face or gaze toward or away from someone or something. 46. to direct one's thought, attention, desire, etc., toward or away from someone or something. 47. to give or apply one's interest, attention, effort, etc., to something; pursue: *He turned to the study and practice of medicine.* 48. to change or reverse a course so as to go in a different or the opposite direction: *to turn to the right.* 49. to change position so as to face in a different or the opposite direction. 50. to change or reverse position or posture as by a rotary motion. 51. to shift the body about as if on an axis: *to turn on one's side while sleeping.* 52. to assume a curved form; bend. 53. to become blunted or dulled by bending, as the cutting edge of a knife or saw. 54. to be affected with nausea, as the stomach. 55. to be affected with giddiness or dizziness; have a sensation of whirling or reeling. 56. to adopt religion, a manner of life, etc., esp. as differing from a previous position or attitude: *He turned to Christianity in his old age.* 57. to change or transfer one's loyalties; defect: *He turned from the Democrats and joined the Republicans.* 58. to change an attitude or policy: *to turn in favor of someone; to turn against a person.* 59. to change or alter, as in nature, character, or appearance. 60. to become sour, rancid, fermented, or the like, as milk or butter. 61. to change color: *The leaves began to turn in October.* 62. to change so as to be; become: *a lawyer turned poet; to turn pale.* 63. to become mentally unbalanced or distracted. 64. to put about or tack, as a ship. 65. *Journalism.* (of copy) to run either from the bottom of the last column on one page to the top of the first column on the following page or from one column on a page to the expected place in the next column on the page (opposed to *jump*). 66. **turn back,** a. to retrace one's footsteps; turn around to return. b. to cause to go no further or to return, as by not welcoming; send away. c. to fold (a blanket, sheet of paper, etc.) on itself: *Turn back the page to keep the place.* 67. **turn down,** a. to turn over; fold down. b. to lower in intensity; lessen. c. to refuse or reject (a person, request, etc.): *The Marine Corps turned him down.* 68. **turn in,** a. to hand in; submit: *to turn in a resignation.* b. to inform on or deliver up: *She promptly turned him in to the police.* c. to turn from one path or course into another; veer. d. *Informal.* to go to bed; retire: *I never turn in before eleven o'clock.* 69. **turn into,** a. to drive a vehicle or to walk into (a street, store, etc.): *We turned into the dead-end street. He turned into the saloon at the corner.* b. to be changed, transformed, or converted into: *He has turned into a very pleasant fellow. The caterpillar turned into a butterfly.* 70. **turn off,** a. to stop the flow of (water, gas, etc.), as by closing a faucet or valve. b. to extinguish (a light). c. to divert; deflect. d. to diverge or branch off, as a side road from a main road. e. to drive a vehicle or walk onto (a side road) from a main road: *You turn off at 96th Street. Turn off the highway on the dirt road.* f. *Slang.* to stop listening: *You could see him turn off as the speaker droned on.* g. *Slang.* to disaffect, alienate, or disgust. h. *Chiefly Brit.* to discharge an employee. 71. **turn on,** a. to cause (water, gas, etc.) to flow, as by opening a valve. b. to switch on (a light). c. to put into operation; activate. d. to start suddenly to affect or show: *She turned on the charm and won him over.* e. *Slang.* to induce (a person) to start taking a narcotic drug. f. *Slang.* to take a narcotic drug. g. *Slang.* to arouse or excite the interest of; engage: *the first lecture that really turned me on.* h. *Slang.* to arouse sexually. i. Also, **turn upon.** to become suddenly hostile to: *The dog turned on its owner.* 72. **turn one's hand to.** See **hand** (def. 74). 73. **turn out,** a. to extinguish (a light). b. to produce as the result of labor: *She turned out four tapestries a year.* c. to drive out; dismiss; discharge: *a premier turned out of office.* d. to fit out; dress; equip. e. to result; issue. f. to come to be; become ultimately. g. to be found or known; prove. h. to be present at; appear. i. *Informal.* to get out of bed. j. *Naut.* to order (a seaman or seamen) from quarters for duty. k. to cause to turn outward, as the toes. 74. **turn over,** a. to move or be moved from one side to another. b. to put in reverse position; invert. c. to consider; meditate; ponder. d. to transfer; give. e. to start (an engine): *He turned over the car motor.* f. (of an engine) to start: *The motor turned over without any trouble.* g. *Com.* to purchase and then sell (goods or commodities). h. *Com.* to do business or sell goods to the amount of (a specified sum). i. *Com.* to invest or recover (capital) in some transaction or in the course of business. 75. **turn the tables.** See **table** (def. 19). 76. **turn the tide.** See **tide**[1] (def. 12). 77. **turn to,** a. to apply to for aid; appeal to: *When he was starting out as an artist he turned to his friends for loans.* b. to begin to attend to or work at something: *After the storm we turned to and cleaned up the debris.* c. to change to: *The ice turned to water.* 78. **turn up,** a. to fold (material, a hem, cuffs, etc.) up or over in order to alter a garment. b. to bring to the surface by digging: *to turn up a shovelful of earth.* c. to uncover; find. d. to intensify or increase. e. to happen; occur: *Let's wait and see what turns up.* f. to appear; arrive: *She turned up at the last moment.* g. to be recovered: *I'm sure your watch will turn up eventually.* h. to come to notice; be seen.
—*n.* 79. a movement of partial or total rotation: *a slight turn of the handle.* 80. an act of changing or reversing position or posture, as by a rotary movement: *a turn of the head.* 81. a time or opportunity for action which comes in due rotation or order to each of a number of persons, animals, etc.: *It's my turn to pay the bill.* 82. an act of changing or reversing the course or direction: *to make a turn to the right.* 83. a place or point at which such a change occurs. 84. a place where a road, river, or the like turns; bend: *About a mile ahead, you'll come to a turn in the road.* 85. a single revolution, as of a wheel. 86. an act of turning so as to face or go in a different direction. 87. direction, drift, or trend: *The conversation took an interesting turn.* 88. any change, as in nature, character, condition, affairs, circumstances, etc.; alteration; modification: *a turn for the better.* 89. the point or time of change. 90. the time during which a worker or a set of workers is at work in alternation with others. 91. that which is done by each of a number of persons acting in rotation or succession. 92. rounded or curved form. 93. the shape or mold in which something is formed or cast. 94. a passing or twisting of one thing around another, as of a rope around a mast. 95. the state of or a manner of being twisted. 96. a single circular or convoluted shape, as of a coiled or wound rope. 97. a small latch operated by a turning knob or lever. 98. style, as of expression or language. 99. a distinctive form or style imparted: *a happy turn of expression.* 100. a short walk, ride, or the like out and back, esp. by different routes: *Let's go for a turn in the park.* 101. a natural inclination, bent, tendency, or aptitude: *one's turn of mind.* 102. a spell or period of work; shift. 103. a spell or bout of action or activity, esp. in wrestling. 104. an attack of illness or the like. 105. an act of service or disservice: *He once did her a good turn. She repaid it with a bad turn.* 106. requirement, exigency, or need: *This will serve your turn.* 107. treatment or rendering, esp. with reference to the form or content of a work of literature, art, etc.; twist: *He gave the story a new turn.* 108. *Informal.* a nervous shock, as from fright or astonishment: *It certainly gave me quite a turn to see him.* 109. *Stock Exchange.* a complete securities transaction that includes both a purchase and sale. 110. *Music.* a melodic embellishment or grace, commonly consisting of a principal tone with two auxiliary tones, one above and the other below it. 111. *Chiefly Brit.* an individual stage performance, esp. in a vaudeville theater or music hall. 112. *Mil.* a drill movement by which a formation changes fronts. 113. a contest or round; a bout, as in wrestling. 114. **at every turn,** in every case or instance; constantly: *We met with kindness at every turn.* 115. **by turns,** one after another; in rotation or succession; alternately: *They did their shopping and cleaning by turns.* 116. **hand's turn,** a period or piece of work: *It won't be necessary for you to do a hand's turn yourself, but rather to supervise.* 117. **in turn,** in due order of succession: *Each generation in turn must grapple with the same basic problems.* 118. **on the turn,** on the verge or in the process of turning; changing: *She said she hoped to be alive to see the century on the turn.* 119. **out of turn,** a. not in the correct succession; out of proper order. b. at an unsuitable time; imprudently; indiscreetly: *He spoke out of turn and destroyed the cordial atmosphere of the meeting.* 120. **take turns,** to succeed one another in order; rotate; alternate: *They took turns walking the dog.* 121. **to a turn,** to just the proper degree; to perfection: *The steak was done to a turn.* 122. **turn and turn about** or **turn about,** by turns: *They fought the fire, turn and turn about, until daybreak.* [bef. 1000; (v.) ME *turnen,* partly continuing OE *turnian, tyrnan* < L *tornāre* to turn in a lathe, round off (deriv. of *tornus* lathe < Gk *tórnos* tool for making circles), partly < OF *torner, t(o)urner* < L, as above; (n.) ME, partly deriv. of the v., partly < AF **torn, t(o)urn;* OF *tor, t(o)ur* < L *tornus,* as above] —**turn′a·ble,** *adj.*
—**Syn.** 9. metamorphose, transmute, transform. 23, 24. fashion, mold. 41. TURN, REVOLVE, ROTATE, SPIN indicate moving in a more or less rotary, circular fashion. TURN is the general and popular word for motion on an axis or around a center, but it is used also of motion that is less than a complete circle: *A gate turns on its hinges.* REVOLVE refers esp. to movement in an orbit around a center, but is sometimes exchangeable with ROTATE, which refers only to the motion of a body around its own center or axis: *The moon revolves about the earth. The earth rotates on its axis.* To SPIN is to rotate very rapidly: *A top spins.* 79. spin, gyration, revolution. 88. deviation, bend, twist, vicissitude, variation. 101. talent, proclivity. TURN, CAST, TWIST are colloquial in use and imply a bent, inclination, or habit. TURN means a tendency or inclination for something: *a turn for art.* CAST means an established habit of thought, manner, or style: *a melancholy cast.* TWIST means a bias: *a strange twist of thought.*

turn·a·bout (tûrn′ə bout′), *n.* 1. the act of turning in a different or opposite direction. 2. a change of opinion, loyalty, etc. 3. a reciprocal action; act of doing to someone exactly as that person has done to oneself or another: *Turnabout is fair play.* 4. a person who changes things; a radical. 5. *Chiefly Brit.* merry-go-round. [1590–1600; n. use of v. phrase *turn about*]

turn′-and-bank′ in′dicator (tûrn′ən bangk′), *Aeron.* See **bank-and-turn indicator.**

turn′-and-slip′ in′dicator (tûrn′ən slip′). See **bank-and-turn indicator.** [1950–55]

turn·a·round (tûrn′ə round′), *n.* 1. the total time consumed in the round trip of a ship, aircraft, vehicle, etc. 2. turnabout. 3. change of allegiance, opinion, mood, policy, etc. 4. a place or area having sufficient room for a vehicle to turn around. 5. the time required between receiving and finishing or processing work or materials. 6. *Com.* a. a reversal, as in business sales, esp. from loss to profit. b. the time between the making of an investment and receiving a return. 7. *Aviation.* the elapsed time between an aircraft's arrival at an airfield terminal and its departure. [1925–30; n. use of v. phrase *turn around*]

turn·buck·le (tûrn′buk′əl), *n.* a link or sleeve with a swivel at one end and an internal screw thread at the other, or with an internal screw thread at each end, used as a means of uniting or coupling, and of tightening, two parts, as the ends of two rods. [1695–1705; TURN + BUCKLE]

turn′ but′ton, button (def. 9). [1840–50]

turn·coat (tûrn′kōt′), *n.* a person who changes to the opposite party or faction, reverses principles, etc.; renegade. [1550–60; TURN + COAT]

turn·down (tûrn′doun′), *adj.* 1. that is or may be turned down; folded or doubled down: *a turndown collar.* —*n.* 2. an act or instance of being refused or rejected: *He got turndowns from all the better colleges.* [1830–40; from v. phrase *turn down*]

turned′ com′ma, *Brit.* See **quotation mark.** Also called **inverted comma.**

turned-on (tûrnd′on′, -ôn′), *adj. Slang.* 1. lively and chic; switched-on. 2. full of or characterized by excitement. 3. under the influence of a narcotic or hallucinogen, as marijuana. 4. sexually aroused. [1965–70]

turn·er[1] (tûr′nər), *n.* 1. a person or thing that turns or is employed in turning. 2. a person who fashions or shapes objects on a lathe. [1350–1400; ME; see TURN, -ER[1]]

turn·er[2] (tûr′nər, to͝or′-), *n.* a member of a turnverein; tumbler or gymnast. [1850–55; < G *Turner* gymnast, deriv. of *turnen* to exercise < F *tourner* to TURN; see -ER[1]]

Tur·ner (tûr′nər), *n.* 1. **Frederick Jackson,** 1861–1932, U.S. historian. 2. **Joseph Mal·lord William,** (mal′ərd), 1775–1851, English painter. 3. **Nat,** 1800–31, American black slave leader: led uprising of slaves in Southampton County, Virginia, 1831.

Tur′ner's syn′drome, *Pathol.* an abnormal congenital condition resulting from a defect on or absence of the second sex chromosome, characterized by retarded growth of the gonads. [named after Henry Hubert *Turner* (1892–1970), U.S endocrinologist, who described it in 1938]

turn·er·y (tûr′nə rē), *n., pl.* **-er·ies.** 1. the process or art of forming or shaping objects on a lathe. 2. objects or articles fashioned on a lathe collectively. 3. a workshop where such work is done. [1635–45; TURNER[1] + -Y[3]]

turn′ in′dicator, *Aeron.* a flight instrument that indicates the angular rate of turn of an aircraft about its vertical axis. Cf. **bank-and-turn indicator.** [1915–20]

turn·ing (tûr′ning), *n.* 1. the act of a person or thing that turns. 2. an act of reversing position. 3. the place or point at which anything bends or changes direction. 4. the forming of objects on a lathe. 5. an object, as a spindle, turned on a lathe. 6. an act of shaping or forming something: *the skillful turning of verses.* [1200–50; ME; see TURN, -ING[1]]

turn′ing chis′el, a chisel used for shaping work on a lathe. [1875–80]

turn′ing piece′, a wooden pattern for an arch built without centering. [1815–25]

turn′ing point′, 1. a point at which a decisive change takes place; critical point; crisis. 2. a point at which something changes direction, esp. a high or low point on a graph. 3. *Survey.* a point temporarily located and marked in order to establish the elevation or position of a surveying instrument at a new station. [1850–55]

tur·nip (tûr′nip), *n.* 1. the thick, fleshy, edible root of either of two plants of the mustard family, the white-fleshed *Brassica rapa rapifera* or the yellow-fleshed rutabaga. 2. the plant itself. 3. the root of this plant used as a vegetable. [1525–35; earlier *turnep(e),* equiv. to TURN (with reference to its neatly rounded shape) + *nepe* NEEP] —**tur′nip·like′,** *adj.*

tur′nip broc′coli. See **broccoli rabe.**

tur′nip cab′bage, kohlrabi. [1755–65]

tur′nip-root·ed cel′ery (tûr′nip ro͞o′tid, -ro͝ot′id), celeriac. [1895–1900]

turn·key (tûrn′kē′), *n., pl.* **-keys,** *adj.* —*n.* 1. a person who has charge of the keys of a prison; jailer. —*adj.* 2. Also, **turn′-key′.** of, pertaining to, or resulting from an arrangement under which a private contractor designs and constructs a project, building, etc., for sale when completely ready for occupancy or operation: *turn-*

CONCISE ETYMOLOGY KEY: <, descended or borrowed from; >, whence; b., blend of, blended; c., cognate with; cf., compare; deriv., derivative; equiv., equivalent; imit., imitative; obl., oblique; r., replacing; s., stem; sp., spelling, spelled; resp., respelling, respelled; trans., translation; ?, origin unknown; *, unattested; ‡, probably earlier than. See the full key inside the front cover.

key housing, turnkey contract. **3.** fully equipped; ready to go into operation: *a turnkey business.* [1645–55; TURN + KEY[1]]

turn′key sys′tem, *Computers.* a computer system purchased from hardware and software vendors, customized and put in working order by a firm that then sells the completed system to the client that ordered it. [1965–70]

turn•off (tûrn′ôf′, -of′), *n.* **1.** a small road that branches off from a larger one, esp. a ramp or exit leading off a major highway: *He took the wrong turnoff and it took him some 15 minutes to get back on the turnpike.* **2.** a place at which one diverges from or changes a former course. **3.** an act of turning off. **4.** the finished product of a certain manufacturing process, as weaving. **5.** the quantity of fattened livestock distributed to market. **6.** *Slang.* something or someone that makes one unsympathetic or antagonistic. [1680–90; n. use of v. phrase *turn off*]

Turn′ of the Screw′, The, a short novel (1898) by Henry James.

turn•on (tûrn′on′, -ôn′), *n. Slang.* something that arouses one's interest or excitement. [1960–65, in sense "activation"; 1965–70, *Amer.* for current sense; n. use of v. phrase *turn on*]

turn•out (tûrn′out′), *n.* **1.** the gathering of persons who come to an exhibition, party, spectacle, or the like: *They had a large turnout at the meeting.* **2.** quantity of production; output. **3.** an act of turning out. **4.** the manner or style in which a person or thing is equipped, dressed, etc. **5.** equipment; outfit. **6.** a short side track, space, spur, etc., that enables trains, automobiles, etc., to pass one another or park. **7.** *Ballet.* the turning out of the legs from the hips, with the feet back to back or heel to heel. **8.** *Railroads.* a track structure composed of a switch, a frog, and closure rails, permitting a train to leave a given track for a branching or parallel track. Cf. **crossover** (def. 6). [1680–90; n. use of v. phrase *turn out*]

turn•o•ver (tûrn′ō′vər), *n.* **1.** an act or result of turning over; upset. **2.** change or movement of people, as tenants or customers, in, out, or through a place: *The restaurant did a lively business and had a rapid turnover.* **3.** the aggregate of worker replacements in a given period in a given business or industry. **4.** the ratio of the labor turnover to the average number of employees in a given period. **5.** the total amount of business done in a given time. **6.** the rate at which items are sold, esp. with reference to the depletion of stock and replacement of inventory: *Things are slow now, but they expect an increased turnover next month.* **7.** the number of times that capital is invested and reinvested in a line of merchandise during a specified period of time. **8.** the turning over of the capital or stock of goods involved in a particular transaction or course of business. **9.** the rate of processing or the amount of material that has undergone a particular process in a given period of time, as in manufacturing. **10.** a change from one position, opinion, etc., to another, often to one that is opposed to that previously held. **11.** a reorganization of a political organization, business, etc., esp. one involving a change or shift of personnel. **12.** a baked or deep-fried pastry with a sweet or savory filling in which half the dough is turned over the filling and the edges sealed to form a semicircle or triangle. **13.** *Basketball, Football.* the loss of possession of the ball to the opponents, through misplays or infractions of the rules. —*adj.* **14.** that is or may be turned over. **15.** having a part that turns over, as a collar. [1605–15; n. use of v. phrase *turn over*]

turn•pike (tûrn′pīk′), *n.* **1.** a high-speed highway, esp. one maintained by tolls. **2.** (formerly) a barrier set across such a highway to stop passage until a toll has been paid; tollgate. [1375–1425; late ME *turnepike* road barrier (in def. 1, short for *turnpike road*). See TURN, PIKE[2]]

turn′ sig′nal, any of four signal lights on the front left, front right, rear left, and rear right of an automotive vehicle that, when actuated by the driver, flash in pairs on the side toward which a turn is to be made. Also, **turn′-sig′nal.** Also called **directional signal.**

turn•sole (tûrn′sōl′), *n.* **1.** any of several plants regarded as turning with the movement of the sun. **2.** heliotrope (def. 2). **3.** a European plant, *Chrozophora tinctoria,* of the spurge family, yielding a purple dye. **4.** the purple dye prepared from this plant; litmus. [1325–75; ME *turnesole* < MF *tournesol* the dye < It *tornasole* the plant, lit., (it) turns (toward the) sun, on the model of Gk *hēliotrópion* HELIOTROPE]

turn•spit (tûrn′spit′), *n.* **1.** a spit that rotates or can be rotated. **2.** a mechanically or manually operated device for turning a spit on which meat is roasted. **3.** a person who turns a spit. **4.** a small dog having a long body and short legs, used formerly to work a treadmill that turned a spit. [1570–80; TURN + SPIT[2]]

turn•stile (tûrn′stīl′), *n.* **1.** a structure of four horizontally revolving arms pivoted atop a post and set in a gateway or opening in a fence to allow the controlled passage of people. **2.** a similar device set up in an entrance to bar passage until a charge is paid, to record the number of persons passing through, etc. [1635–45; TURN + STILE[1]]

turn•stone (tûrn′stōn′), *n.* **1.** any shorebird of the genus *Arenaria,* characterized by the habit of turning over stones in search of food. **2.** *Brit.* See **ruddy turnstone.** [1665–75; TURN + STONE]

turn•ta•ble (tûrn′tā′bəl), *n.* **1.** the rotating disk that spins the record on a phonograph. **2.** *Railroads.* a rotating, track-bearing platform pivoted in the center, used for turning locomotives and cars around. **3.** a rotating stand used in sculpture, metalwork, and ceramics. [1825–35; TURN + TABLE]

turn•up (tûrn′up′), *n.* **1.** something that is turned up or that turns up. **2.** upturn (def. 6). **3.** *Brit.* a cuff on a pair of trousers. **4.** *Chiefly Brit.* fight; row; disturbance. —*adj.* **5.** that is or may be turned up. [1605–15; n. use of v. phrase *turn up*]

turn•ver•ein (tûrn′və rīn′, to͝orn′-; *Ger.* to͝orn′fer-īn′), *n.* an athletic club, esp. of gymnasts. [1850–55, *Amer.*; < G: gymnastic club, equiv. to *turn(en)* to practice gymnastics (see TURNER[2]) + *Verein* union]

tur•pen•tine (tûr′pən tīn′), *n., v.,* **-tined, -tin•ing.** —*n.* **1.** any of various oleoresins derived from coniferous trees, esp. the longleaf pine, *Pinus palustris,* and yielding a volatile oil and a resin when distilled. **2.** Also called **Chian turpentine.** an oleoresin exuded by the terebinth, *Pistacia terebinthus.* **3.** See **oil of turpentine.** —*v.t.* **4.** to treat with turpentine; apply turpentine to. **5.** to gather or take crude turpentine from (trees). [1275–1325; late ME, alter. of ME *ter(e)bentyn(e)* < ML *ter(e)bentina,* for L *terebinthina,* n. use of fem. of *terebinthinus* of the turpentine tree, equiv. to *terebinth(us)* turpentine tree (< Gk *terébinthos*) + *-īnus* -INE[1]] —**tur•pen•tin•ic** (tûr′pən tin′ik), **tur•pen•tin•ous** (tûr′pən-tin′əs, -tī′nəs), **tur•pen•tin•y** (tûr′pən tī′nē), *adj.*

tur•peth (tûr′pith), *n.* **1.** the root of an East Indian plant, *Merremia* (or *Operculina*) *turpethum,* of the morning glory family, formerly used as a purgative. **2.** the plant itself. [1350–1400; < ML *turpethum* < Ar *turbid* < Pers; akin to Skt *tripuṭā*; r. ME *turbit(h)(e)* < OF *turbit(h)* < Ar *turbid,* as above]

Tur•pin (tûr′pin), *n.* **1. Ben,** 1874–1940, U.S. silent-film comedian. **2. Richard** (*Dick*), 1706–39, English highwayman.

tur•pi•tude (tûr′pi to͞od′, -tyo͞od′), *n.* **1.** vile, shameful, or base character; depravity. **2.** a vile or depraved act. [1480–90; < L *turpitūdō,* equiv. to *turpi(s)* base, vile + *-tūdō* -TUDE]
—**Syn. 1.** wickedness, vice, vileness, wrongdoing.

tur•quoise (tûr′koiz, -kwoiz), *n.* **1.** Also, **tur′quois.** an opaque mineral, a basic hydrous copper aluminum phosphate often containing a small amount of iron, sky-blue or greenish-blue in color, cut cabochon as a gem. Cf. **bone turquoise. 2.** Also called **tur′quoise blue′.** a greenish blue or bluish green. [1350–1400; < F: Turkish (stone), equiv. to *Turc* TURK + *-oise,* fem. of *-ois* -ESE; r. ME *turkeis* < MF]

tur′quoise green′, a light bluish green. [1885–90]

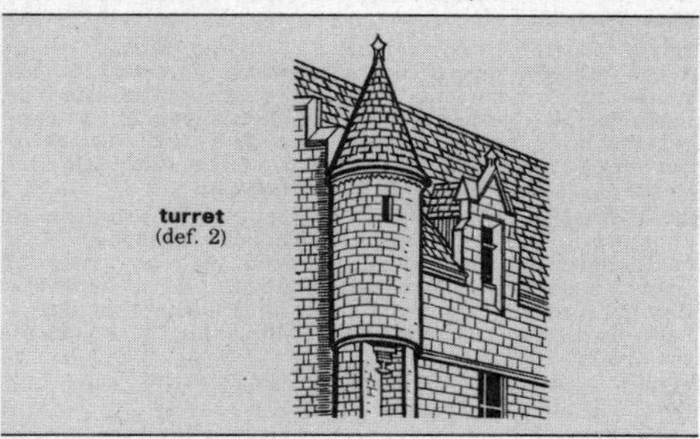
turret (def. 2)

tur•ret (tûr′it, tur′-), *n.* **1.** a small tower, usually one forming part of a larger structure. **2.** a small tower at an angle of a building, as of a castle or fortress, frequently beginning some distance above the ground. **3.** Also called **tur•ret•head** (tûr′it hed′, tur′-). a pivoted attachment on a lathe or the like for holding a number of tools, each of which can be presented to the work in rapid succession by a simple rotating movement. **4.** *Mil.* a domelike, sometimes heavily armored structure, usually revolving horizontally, within which guns are mounted, as on a fortification, ship, or aircraft. **5.** *Fort.* a tall structure, usually moved on wheels, formerly employed in breaching or scaling a fortified place, a wall, or the like. [1300–50; ME *turet* < MF *turete,* equiv. to *tur* TOWER + *-ete* -ET] —**tur′ret•less,** *adj.*

tur•ret•ed (tûr′i tid, tur′-), *adj.* **1.** furnished with a turret or turrets. **2.** having a turretlike part or parts. **3.** *Zool.* having whorls in the form of a long or towering spiral, as certain shells. [1540–50; TURRET + -ED[3]]

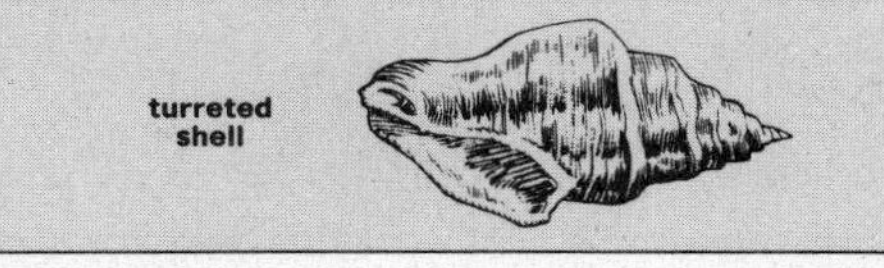
turreted shell

tur′ret lathe′, a lathe fitted with a turret. [1870–75]

tur•ri•cal (tûr′i kəl), *adj.* of, pertaining to, or resembling a turret. [< L *turr(is)* TOWER + -ICAL]

tur•ric•u•late (tə rik′yə lit, -lāt′), *adj.* furnished with or resembling a turret or turrets. Also, **tur•ric′u•lat′ed.** [1835–45; < L *turricula* little tower (see TOWER, -CULE[1]) + -ATE[1]]

Tur•sha (tûr′shə), *n.* an ancient people of the Mediterranean region, variously identified with the Lydians, Etruscans, or Trojans.

tur•tle[1] (tûr′tl), *n., pl.* **-tles,** (*esp. collectively*) **-tle,** *v.,* **-tled, -tling.** —*n.* **1.** any reptile of the order Testudines, comprising aquatic and terrestrial species having the trunk enclosed in a shell consisting of a dorsal carapace and a ventral plastron. **2.** (not used technically) an aquatic turtle as distinguished from a terrestrial one. Cf. **tortoise** (def. 1). **3. turn turtle, a.** *Naut.* to capsize or turn over completely in foundering. **b.** to overturn; upset: *Several of the cars turned turtle in the course of the race.* —*v.i.* **4.** to catch turtles, esp. as a business. [1625–35; alter. (influenced by TURTLE[2]) of F *tortue* < ML *tortūca* TORTOISE] —**tur′tler,** *n.*

box turtle, *Terrapene carolina,* length 6 in. (15 cm)

tur•tle[2] (tûr′tl), *n. Archaic.* a turtledove. [bef. 1000; ME, OE < L *turtur* (imit.)]

tur•tle•back (tûr′tl bak′), *n.* **1.** *Archaeol.* tortoise-core. **2.** *Furniture.* an oval or elliptical boss. [1880–85; TURTLE[1] + BACK[1]]

tur•tle•dove (tûr′tl duv′), *n.* **1.** any of several small to medium-sized Old World doves of the genus *Streptopelia,* esp. *S. turtur,* of Europe, having a long, graduated tail: noted for its soft, cooing call. **2.** See **mourning dove. 3.** a sweetheart or beloved mate. [1250–1300; ME *turtildove,* equiv. to *turtil* TURTLE[2] + *dove* DOVE[1]]

tur•tle•head (tûr′tl hed′), *n.* any of several North American plants belonging to the genus *Chelone,* of the figwort family, having opposite, serrated leaves and spikes of purple or white, two-lipped flowers. [1855–60, *Amer.*; TURTLE[1] + HEAD, so called from the appearance of its flower]

tur•tle•neck (tûr′tl nek′), *n.* **1.** a high, close-fitting collar, often rolled or turned down, appearing esp. on pullover sweaters. **2.** a sweater with such a collar. [1905–10; TURTLE[1] + NECK]

turt•let (tûrt′lit), *n.* a young or small turtle. [1825–35; TURTLE[1] + -ET]

turves (tûrvz), *n. Chiefly Brit.* pl. of **turf.**

tur•ya (tûr′yə), *n. Yoga.* turiya.

Tus•ca•loo•sa (tus′kə lo͞o′sə), *n.* a city in W Alabama. 75,143.

Tus•can (tus′kən), *adj.* **1.** of, pertaining to, or characteristic of Tuscany, its people, or their dialect. **2.** *Archit.* noting or pertaining to one of the five classical orders: developed in Rome, it is basically a simplified Roman Doric, with unfluted columns and with no decoration other than moldings. See illus. under **order.** Cf. **composite** (def. 3), **Corinthian** (def. 2), **Doric** (def. 3), **Ionic** (def. 1). —*n.* **3.** the standard literary form of the Italian language. **4.** any Italian dialect of Tuscany. **5.** a native of Tuscany. [1350–1400; ME < L *Tuscānus* Etruscan, equiv. to *Tusc(ī)* the Etruscans + *-ānus* -AN]

Tus•ca•ny (tus′kə nē), *n.* a region in W central Italy: formerly a grand duchy. 3,578,814; 8879 sq. mi. (22,995 sq. km). Italian, **Toscana.**

Tus•ca•ro•ra (tus′kə rôr′ə, -rōr′ə), *n., pl.* **-ras,** (*esp. collectively*) **-ra. 1.** a member of an Indian people living originally in North Carolina and later, after their admission into the Iroquois confederacy, in New York. **2.** an Iroquoian language, the language of the Tuscarora people.

tusch•e (to͝osh; *Ger.* to͝osh′ə), *n.* a greaselike liquid used in lithography as a medium receptive to lithographic ink, and in etching and silkscreen as a resist. [1905–10; < G *Tusche,* n. deriv. of *tuschen* to lay on color or ink < F *toucher* to TOUCH]

Tus•cu•lum (tus′kyə ləm), *n.* an ancient city of Latium, SE of Rome: Roman villas, esp. that of Cicero. —**Tus′cu•lan,** *adj.*

tush[1] (tush), *interj.* **1.** (used as an exclamation of impatience, disdain, contempt, etc.) —*n.* **2.** an exclamation of "tush!" [1400–50; late ME]

tush[2] (tush), *n.* **1.** one of the four canine teeth of the horse. **2.** *Chiefly Midland and Southern U.S.* a tusk. [bef. 900; ME; OE *tusc.* See TUSK] —**tushed,** *adj.*

tush[3] (to͝osh), *n. Slang.* tushie. [see TUSHIE]

tush•ie (to͝osh′ē), *n. Slang.* the buttocks. Also, **tushy.** [1960–65, *Amer.*; appar. alter. of Yiddish *tokhes* TOKUS, with *-sh-* substituted for *-kh-*; see -Y[2]]

tush•y (to͝osh′ē), *n., pl.* **tush•ies.** tushie.

Tu•si (to͞o′sē), *n., pl.* **-sis,** (*esp. collectively*) **-si.** Tutsi.

tusk (tusk), *n.* **1.** (in certain animals) a tooth developed to great length, usually one of a pair, as in the elephant, walrus, and wild boar, but singly in the narwhal. See illus. on next page. **2.** a long, pointed, or protruding tooth. **3.** a projection resembling the tusk of an animal. **4.** Also called **gain.** *Carpentry.* a diagonally cut shoulder at the end of a timber for strengthening a tenon. —*v.t.* **5.** to dig up or tear off with the tusks. **6.** to gore with a

CONCISE PRONUNCIATION KEY: act, cāpe, dâre, pärt; set, ēqual; if, īce; ox, ōver, ôrder, oil, bo͝ok, bo͞ot, out; up, ûrge; child; sing; shoe; thin, *th*at; zh as in *treasure.* ə = *a* as in *alone, e* as in *system, i* as in *easily, o* as in *gallop, u* as in *circus;* ᵊ as in *fire* (fīᵊr), *hour* (ouᵊr). l and n can serve as syllabic consonants, as in *cradle* (krād′l), and *button* (but′n). See the full key inside the front cover.

tusk. —*v.i.* **7.** to dig up or thrust at the ground with the tusks. [bef. 900; ME, metathetic var. of *tux*, OE, var. of *tusc* TUSH[2]; c. OFris *tusk;* akin to TOOTH] —**tusk′less,** *adj.* —**tusk′like′,** *adj.*

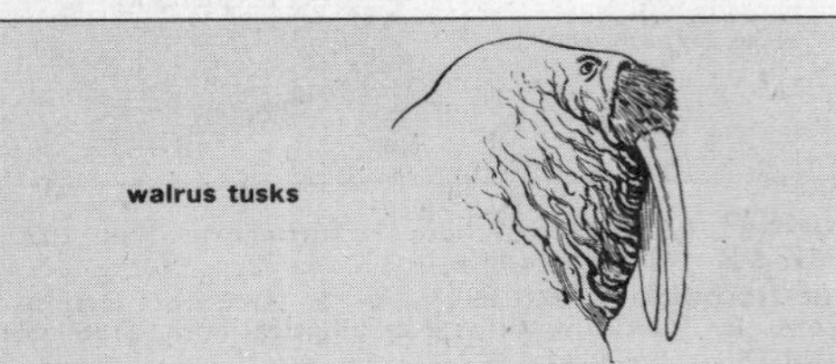
walrus tusks

Tus•ke•gee (tus kē′gē), *n.* a city in E Alabama: location of Tuskegee Institute. 12,716.

tusk•er (tus′kər), *n.* an animal with tusks, as an elephant or a wild boar. [1855–60; TUSK + -ER[1]]

tusk′ shell′. See **tooth shell.** [1860–65, *Amer.*]

tus•sah (tus′ə), *n.* **1.** a tan silk from India. Cf. **Shantung** (def. 3). **2.** the silkworm of an oriental moth of the genus *Antheraea*, as *A. mylitta*, that produces this silk. Also, **tus′seh, tus•ser** (tus′ər), **tussor, tussore, tussur.** Also called **wild silk.** [1580–90; earlier *tusser* < Hindi *tasar* shuttle < Skt *tasara, trasara* kind of silkworm]

tus•sal (tus′əl), *adj. Pathol.* pertaining to tussis. [1885–90; < L *tuss(is)* cough + -AL[1]]

Tus•saud (tōō sō′, tə-; *Fr.* ty sō′), *n.* **Marie Gros•holtz** (grōs′hōlts), (*"Madame Tussaud"*), 1760–1850, Swiss wax modeler in France and England: wax museum founder.

Tus•si (tōō′sē), *n., pl.* **-sis,** (*esp. collectively*) **-si.** Tutsi.

tus•sic•u•la•tion (tə sik′yə lā′shən) *n.* a hacking cough. [1885–90; < L *tussi(s)* cough + -CULE[1] + -ATION]

tus•sis (tus′is), *n. Pathol.* a cough. [< L: a cough]

tus•sive (tus′iv), *adj. Pathol.* of or pertaining to a cough. [1855–60; < L *tuss(is)* cough + -IVE]

tus•sle (tus′əl), *v.,* **-sled, -sling,** *n.* —*v.i.* **1.** to struggle or fight roughly or vigorously; wrestle; scuffle. —*n.* **2.** a rough physical contest or struggle; scuffle. **3.** any vigorous or determined struggle, conflict, etc.: *I had quite a tussle with that chemistry exam.* [1425–75; late ME (north and Scots) *tusillen*, deriv. (see -LE) of *tusen* to TOUSE]

tus•sock (tus′ək), *n.* a tuft or clump of growing grass or the like. [1540–50; appar. akin to MHG *zūsach* thicket, deriv. of *zūse* lock (of hair), brushwood. See -OCK] —**tus′socked,** *adj.*

tus′sock cat′erpillar, the larva of a tussock moth.

tus′sock grass′, any of various grasses that grow in tuftlike clumps. [1835–45]

tus′sock moth′, any of several moths of the family Lymantriidae, the larvae of which have characteristic tufts of hair on the body and feed on the leaves of various deciduous trees. [1820–30]

tus•sock•y (tus′ə kē), *adj.* **1.** abounding in tussocks. **2.** forming tussocks. [1655–65; TUSSOCK + -Y[1]]

tus•sor (tus′ər), *n.* tussah.

tus•sore (tus′ôr, -ōr), *n.* tussah.

tus•sur (tus′ər), *n.* tussah.

Tus•tin (tus′tin), *n.* a city in SW California. 32,073.

tut (*pronounced as an alveolar click; spelling pron.* tut), *interj., n., v.,* **tut•ted, tut•ting.** —*interj.* **1.** (used as an exclamation of contempt, disdain, impatience, etc.) **2.** for shame! —*n.* **3.** an exclamation of "tut." —*v.i.* **4.** to utter the exclamation "tut." Also, **tut-tut.** [1520–30]

Tut•ankh•a•men (tōōt′äng kä′mən), *n.* 14th century B.C., a king of Egypt of the 18th dynasty. Also, **Tut′•ankh•a′mon, Tut′ankh•a′mun, Tut•enkh•a•mon** (tōōt′eng kä′mən).

tu•tee (tōō tē′, tyōō-), *n.* a person who is being tutored; the pupil of a tutor. [1925–30; TUT(OR) + -EE]

tu•te•lage (tōōt′l ij, tyōōt′-), *n.* **1.** the act of guarding, protecting, or guiding; office or function of a guardian; guardianship. **2.** instruction; teaching; guidance: *His knowledge of Spanish increased under private tutelage.* **3.** the state of being under a guardian or a tutor. [1595–1605; < L *tūtēl(a)* guardianship (deriv. of *tuērī* to watch; see TUITION) + -AGE]
—**Syn. 2.** direction, supervision, tutoring, coaching.

tu•te•lar•y (tōōt′l er′ē, tyōōt′-), *adj., n., pl.* **-lar•ies.** —*adj.* **1.** having the position of guardian or protector of a person, place, or thing: *tutelary saint.* **2.** of or pertaining to a guardian or guardianship. —*n.* **3.** a person who has tutelary powers, as a saint, deity, or guardian. Also, **tu•te•lar** (tōōt′l ər, tyōōt′-). [1605–15; < L *tūtēlārius* guardian; see TUTELAGE, -ARY]

tu•te•nag (tōōt′n ag′, tyōōt′-), *n.* a nickel silver containing about 45 percent copper, with varying proportions of nickel and zinc and often smaller amounts of other metals. [1615–25; < Marathi *tuttināg,* allegedly derived from Skt *tuttha-* sulfate of copper + *nāga* tin, lead]

tu•tor (tōō′tər, tyōō′-), *n.* **1.** a person employed to instruct another in some branch or branches of learning, esp. a private instructor. **2.** a teacher of academic rank lower than instructor in some American universities and colleges. **3.** a teacher without institutional connection who assists students in preparing for examinations. **4.** (esp. at Oxford and Cambridge) a university officer, usually a fellow, responsible for teaching and supervising a number of undergraduates. **5.** the guardian of a boy or girl below the age of puberty or majority. —*v.t.* **6.** to act as a tutor to; teach or instruct, esp. privately. **7.** to have the guardianship, instruction, or care of. **8.** to instruct underhandedly; coach: *to tutor a witness before he testifies.* **9.** *Archaic.* **a.** to train, school, or discipline. **b.** to admonish or reprove. —*v.i.* **10.** to act as a tutor or private instructor. **11.** to study privately with a tutor. [1350–1400; ME < L *tūtor* protector, equiv. to *tū-* (var. s. of *tuērī* to guard; see TUTELAGE) + *-tor* -TOR] —**tu′tor•less,** *adj.* —**tu′tor•ship′,** *n.*
—**Syn. 6.** See **teach.**

tu•tor•age (tōō′tər ij, tyōō′-), *n.* **1.** the office, authority, or care of a tutor. **2.** the charge for instruction by a tutor. [1610–20; TUTOR + -AGE]

tu•tor•ess (tōō′tər is, tyōō′-), *n.* a woman who is a tutor. [1605–15; TUTOR + -ESS]
—**Usage.** See **-ess.**

tu•to•ri•al (tōō tôr′ē əl, -tōr′-, tyōō-), *adj.* **1.** pertaining to or exercised by a tutor: *tutorial functions or authority.* —*n.* **2.** a class in which a tutor gives intensive instruction in some subject to an individual student or a small group of students. **3.** *Computers.* **a.** programmed instruction provided to a user at a computer terminal, often concerning the use of a particular software package and built into that package. **b.** a manual explaining how to use a particular software package or computer system. [1735–45; < L *tūtōri(us)* of a guardian + -AL[1]]

tuto′rial sys′tem, a system of education, esp. in some colleges, in which instruction is given personally by tutors, who also act as general advisers of a small group of students in their charge. [1855–60]

tu•toy•er (tōō′twä yā′; *Fr.* ty twa yā′), *v.t.,* **-toy•ered** or **-toy•ed** (-twä yād′), **-toy•er•ing** (-twä yā′ing). to address (someone), esp. in French, using the familiar forms of the pronoun "you" rather than the more formal forms; address familiarly. [1690–1700; < F, to address as *tu* and *toi* (the familiar sing. forms for "you" in French)]

Tut•si (tōōt′sē), *n., pl.* **-sis,** (*esp. collectively*) **-si.** a member of a very tall, slender, cattle-raising people of Rwanda and Burundi. Also, **Tusi, Tussi.** Also called **Watusi, Watutsi.**

tut•ti (tōō′tē; *It.* tōōt′tē), *adj., n., pl.* **-tis.** *Music.* —*adj.* **1.** all; all the voices or instruments together. **2.** intended for or performed by all (or most of) the voices or instruments together, as a passage or movement in concert music (opposed to *solo*). —*n.* **3.** a tutti passage or movement. **4.** the tonal product or effect of a tutti performance. [1715–25; < It, pl. of *tutto* all]

tut•ti-frut•ti (tōō′tē frōō′tē), *n.* **1.** a preserve of chopped mixed fruits, often with brandy syrup. **2.** a confection, esp. ice cream, flavored with a variety of fruits, usually candied and minced. **3.** a synthetic flavoring combining the flavors of a variety of fruits: *tutti-frutti chewing gum.* [1875–80, *Amer.*; < It: lit., all the fruits]

tut•to (tōō′tō; *It.* tōōt′tô), *adj. Music.* all; entire. [< It: all, whole < L *tōtus*]

tut-tut (*pronounced as two alveolar clicks; spelling pron.* tut′tut′), *interj., n., v.i.,* **-tut•ted, -tut•ting.** tut. [1585–95]

tut•ty (tut′ē), *n.* an impure oxide of zinc obtained from the flues of smelting furnaces, or a similar substance occurring as a native mineral, used chiefly as a polishing powder. [1350–1400; ME *tutie* < MF < ML *tūtia* < Ar *tūtiyā* oxide of zinc < Pers < Skt *tutthaṁ* blue vitriol]

tu•tu (tōō′tōō; *Fr.* ty ty′), *n., pl.* **-tus** (-tōōz; *Fr.* -ty′). a short, full skirt, usually made of several layers of tarlatan or tulle, worn by ballerinas. [1925–30; < F]

tutu

Tu•tu (tōō′tōō), *n.* **Desmond (Mpi•lo)** (əm pē′lō), born 1931, South African Anglican clergyman and civil-rights activist: Nobel peace prize 1984; archbishop of Cape Town since 1986.

Tu•tu•i•la (tōō′tōō ē′lə), *n.* the largest of the islands of American Samoa: excellent harbor at Pago Pago. 27,000; 53 sq. mi. (137 sq. km). —**Tu′tu•i′lan,** *adj., n.*

Tu•va (tōō′və), *n., pl.* **-vas,** (*esp. collectively*) **-va** for 1. **1.** a member of a people living in the Tuva Autonomous Republic and adjacent areas. **2.** the Turkic language of the Tuva people. Also, **Tu•vin•i•an** (tōō vin′ē ən).

Tu′va Auton′omous Re•pub′lic, an autonomous republic in the Russian Federation in Asia: formerly an independent republic in Mongolia. 309,000; 65,810 sq. mi. (170,500 sq. km). *Cap.:* Kyzyl. Also, **Tuvin′ian Auton′•omous Repub′lic.** Formerly, **Tannu Tuva People's Republic, Tannu Tuva.**

Tu•va•lu (tōō′və lōō′, tōō vä′lōō), *n.* a parliamentary state consisting of a group of islands in the central Pacific, S of the equator: a former British colony; gained independence 1978. 7000; 10 sq. mi. (26 sq. km). *Cap.:* Funafuti. Formerly, **Ellice Islands, Lagoon Islands.** —**Tu′va•lu′an,** *adj., n.*

tu-whit tu-whoo (tōō hwit′ tōō hwōō′; tōō wit′ tōō-wōō′), (imitation of the cry of an owl). [1580–90]

tux (tuks), *n. Informal.* tuxedo. Also, **tuck.** [1920–25; by shortening]

tux•e•do (tuk sē′dō), *n., pl.* **-dos. 1.** Also called **dinner jacket.** a man's jacket for semiformal evening dress, traditionally of black or dark-blue color and characteristically having satin or grosgrain facing on the lapels. **2.** the complete semiformal outfit, including this jacket, dark trousers, often with silk stripes down the sides, a bow tie, and usually a cummerbund. [1890–95, *Amer.;* short for *Tuxedo coat*, after country club at Tuxedo Park, N.Y.] —**tux•e′doed,** *adj.*

tuxe′do so′fa, an overstuffed sofa with upholstered arms, either straight or curving slightly outward, at the same height as the back. Also called **tuxe′do couch′.**

Tux•tla Gu•tiér•rez (tōōs′tlä gōō tyer′res), *n.* a city in and the capital of Chiapas, in SE Mexico. 69,326. Also called **Tux′tla.**

tu•yère (twē yâr′, tōō-, twēr; *Fr.* ty yer′), *n., pl.* **tu•yères** (twē yârz′, tōō-, twērz; *Fr.* ty yer′). *Metall.* an opening through which the blast of air enters a blast furnace, cupola, forge, or the like, to facilitate combustion. Also, **tu•yer** (twē yâr′, tōō-, twēr). See diag. under **blast furnace.** [1665–75; < F, deriv. of *tuyau* pipe < Gmc]

Tuz (tōōz), *n.* a saltwater lake, above sea level, in W central Turkey. ab. 625 sq. mi. (1620 sq. km).

TV, 1. Also, **tv** television. **2.** *Slang.* transvestite.

TVA, 1. tax on value added: a sales tax imposed by member nations of the Common Market on imports from the U.S. and other countries. **2.** *U.S. Govt.* Tennessee Valley Authority: a three-member board, created in 1933, charged with developing the Tennessee River and its tributaries to promote their use for inexpensive electric power, irrigation, flood control, navigation, etc. Since 1933 many projects have been constructed, including numerous dams.

TV dinner, a quick-frozen meal, typically consisting of meat, potato, and a vegetable, packaged in a tray for heating before serving. [1950–55]

Tver (tvâr; *Russ.* tvyer), *n.* a city in the W Russian Federation in Europe, NW of Moscow, on the Volga. 447,000. Formerly (1934–90), **Kalinin.**

TVP, *Trademark.* a brand of textured soy protein having various commercial uses as a meat substitute or extender.

TV print, *Motion Pictures, Television.* a release print with a color balance and contrast range suitable for television broadcasting.

TV table. See **snack table.**

twa (twä, twô), *n., adj. Scot.* two.

Twa (twä), *n., pl.* **Twas,** (*esp. collectively*) **Twa.** a member of a Pygmy people of Burundi, Rwanda, and Zaire. Also called **Batwa.**

twad•dle (twod′l), *n., v.,* **-dled, -dling.** —*n.* **1.** trivial, feeble, silly, or tedious talk or writing. —*v.i.* **2.** to talk in a trivial, feeble, silly, or tedious manner; prate. —*v.t.* **3.** to utter as twaddle. [1540–50; var. of *twattle,* b. TWIDDLE and TATTLE] —**twad′dler,** *n.* —**twad′dly,** *adj.*
—**Syn. 1.** drivel, nonsense, prattle, rubbish.

twain (twān), *adj., n.* two. [ME *twayn* orig., nom. and acc. masc., OE *twēgen* (cf. TWO); c. obs. G *zween*]

Twain (twān), *n.* **Mark,** pen name of Samuel Langhorne Clemens.

twang (twang), *v.i.* **1.** to give out a sharp, vibrating sound, as the string of a musical instrument when plucked. **2.** to produce such a sound by plucking a stringed musical instrument. **3.** to have or produce a sharp, nasal tone, as the human voice. —*v.t.* **4.** to cause to make a sharp, vibrating sound, as a string of a musical instrument. **5.** to produce (music) by plucking the strings of a musical instrument. **6.** to pluck the strings of (a musical instrument): *to twang a guitar.* **7.** to speak with a sharp, nasal tone. **8.** to pull the string of (an archer's bow). **9.** to let fly (an arrow). —*n.* **10.** the sharp, ringing sound produced by plucking or suddenly releasing a tense string. **11.** a sound resembling this. **12.** an act of plucking or picking: *He gave his guitar strings a twang.* **13.** a sharp, nasal tone, as of the human voice. [1535–45; imit.]

twan•gle (twang′gəl), *n., v.t., v.i.,* **-gled, -gling.** twang. [1805–15; TWANG + -LE]

twang•y (twang′ē), *adj.* **1.** having the sharp, vibrating tone of a plucked string. **2.** having a nasal voice quality. [1885–90; TWANG + -Y[1]] —**twang′i•ness,** *n.*

'twas (twuz, twoz; *unstressed* twəz), contraction of *it was.*
—**Usage.** See **contraction.**

twat (twät), *n. Slang (vulgar).* vulva. [1650–60; perh. orig. dial. var. of *thwat, *thwot, presumed mod. E outcome of OE *thwāt, akin to ON *thveit* cut, slit, forest clearing (> E dial. (N England) *thwaite* forest clearing)]

tway•blade (twā′blād′), *n.* any of various orchids, esp. of the genera *Listera* and *Liparis*, characterized by two nearly opposite broad leaves. [1570–80; dial. *tway* (apocopated form of OE *twēgen* TWAIN) + BLADE]

tweak (twēk), *v.t.* **1.** to pinch and pull with a jerk and twist: *to tweak someone's ear; to tweak someone's nose.* **2.** to pull or pinch the nose of, esp. gently: *He tweaked the baby on greeting.* —*n.* **3.** an act or instance of tweaking; a sharp, twisting pull or jerk. [1595–1605; akin to TWITCH]

twee (twē), *adj. Chiefly Brit.* affectedly dainty or quaint: *twee writing about furry little creatures.* [1900–05; appar. reduced from *tweet* (perh. via pron. *twi?*), mimicking child's pron. of SWEET]

tweed (twēd), *n.* **1.** a coarse wool cloth in a variety of weaves and colors, either hand-spun and handwoven in Scotland or reproduced, often by machine, elsewhere. **2.**

CONCISE ETYMOLOGY KEY: <, descended or borrowed from; >, whence; b., blend of, blended; c., cognate with; cf., compare; deriv., derivative; equiv., equivalent; imit., imitative; obl., oblique; r., replacing; s., stem; sp., spelling, spelled; resp., respelling, respelled; trans., translation; ?, origin unknown; *, unattested; ‡, probably earlier than. See the full key inside the front cover.

tweeds, garments made of this cloth. **3.** a paper having a rough surface, used esp. for certain photographic prints. [1835–45; appar. back formation from Scots *tweedling* twilling (now obs.) < ?]

Tweed (twēd), *n.* **1. William Mar•cy** (mär′sē) ("*Boss Tweed*"), 1823–78, U.S. politician. **2.** a river flowing E from S Scotland along part of the NE boundary of England into the North Sea. 97 mi. (156 km) long. **3.** a male given name.

Tweed•dale (twēd′dāl′), *n.* Peebles.

twee•dle (twēd′l), *v.,* **-dled, -dling.** —*v.i.* **1.** to produce high-pitched, modulated sounds, as a singer, bird, or musical instrument. **2.** to perform lightly upon a musical instrument. —*v.t.* **3.** to lure by or as by music: *The Pied Piper tweedled the children into following him.* [1675–85; imit.]

Twee•dle•dum and Twee•dle•dee (twēd′l dum′ ən twēd′l dē′), two persons or things nominally different but practically the same; a nearly identical pair. [1715–25; humorous coinage, appar. first applied as nicknames to Giovanni Bononcini and Handel, with reference to their musical rivalry; see TWEEDLE]

Tweeds•muir (twēdz′myŏŏr), *n.* **Baron.** See **Buchan, John.**

tweed•y (twē′dē), *adj.,* **tweed•i•er, tweed•i•est. 1.** made of or resembling tweed, as in texture, appearance, or the like. **2.** wearing or favoring tweeds, esp. as a mark of a casual, sporty, or intellectual way of life, as at college or in the country: *a tweedy sportswoman.* **3.** accustomed to, preferring, or characterized by the wearing of tweeds, as in genteel country life or academia. [1910–15; TWEED + -Y[1]] —**tweed′i•ness,** *n.*

'tween (twēn), *prep.* **1.** contraction of *between.* —*n.* **2.** Also, **tween, tweeny.** a youngster between 10 and 12 years of age, considered too old to be a child and too young to be a teenager. [1250–1300; ME *twene,* aph. var. of *atwene* (see A-[1]) or *betwene* BETWEEN]

'tween′ deck′, *Naut.* any space between two continuous decks in the hull of a vessel, as between a shelter deck and a freeboard deck. [1810–20]

tween•y (twē′nē), *n., pl.* **tween•ies. 1.** 'tween (def. 2). **2.** *Brit. Informal.* an auxiliary maid. [1885–90; (BE)TWEEN + -Y[2]]

tweet (twēt), *n.* **1.** a weak chirping sound, as of a young or small bird. —*v.i.* **2.** to make such a sound. [1835–45; imit.]

tweet•er (twē′tər), *n.* a small loudspeaker designed for the reproduction of high-frequency sounds. [1935–40; TWEET + -ER[1]]

tweeze (twēz), *v.t.,* **tweezed, tweez•ing.** to pluck, as with tweezers. [1940–45; back formation from TWEEZERS]

tweez•er (twē′zər), *n.* tweezers.

tweez•ers (twē′zərz), *n.* (*used with a singular or plural v.*) small pincers or nippers for plucking out hairs, extracting splinters, picking up small objects, etc. [1645–55; pl. of *tweezer,* equiv. to obs. *tweeze* case of surgical instruments (aph. form of earlier *etweese* < F *étuis,* pl. of *étui,* n. deriv. of OF *étuier* to keep < L *stŭdiāre* to care for) + -ER[1]]

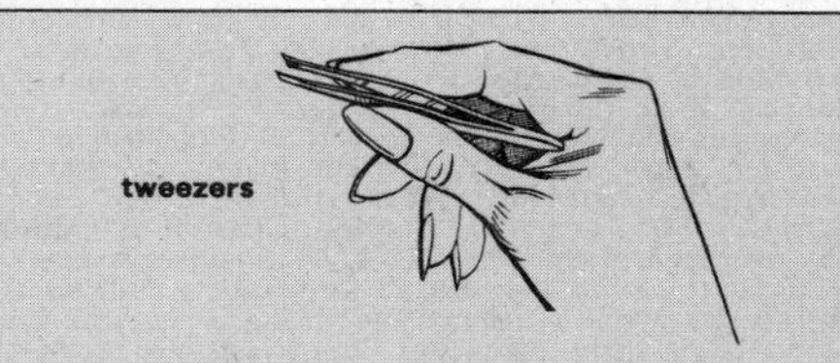

tweezers

twelfth (twelfth), *adj.* **1.** next after the eleventh; being the ordinal number for 12. **2.** being one of 12 equal parts. —*n.* **3.** a twelfth part, esp. of one (1/12). **4.** the twelfth member of a series. [bef. 900; ME *twelfthe, twelfte,* OE *twelfta,* equiv. to *twelf* TWELVE + *-ta* -TH[2]]

Twelfth′ Amend′ment, an amendment to the U.S. Constitution, ratified in 1804, providing for election of the president and vice president by the electoral college: should there be no majority vote for one person, the House of Representatives (one vote per state) chooses the president and the Senate the vice president.

Twelfth′ Day′, the 12th day after Christmas, January 6, on which the festival of the Epiphany is celebrated: formerly observed as the last day of the Christmas festivities. [bef. 900; ME; OE]

Twelfth′ Night′, 1. the evening before Twelfth Day, formerly observed with various festivities. **2.** the evening of Twelfth Day itself. **3.** (*italics*) a comedy (1602) by Shakespeare. [bef. 900; ME; OE]

Twelfth•tide (twelfth′tīd′), *n.* the season of Twelfth Night and Twelfth Day. [1520–30; TWELFTH (DAY or NIGHT) + TIDE[1]]

twelve (twelv), *n.* **1.** a cardinal number, 10 plus 2. **2.** a symbol for this number, as 12 or XII. **3.** a set of this many persons or things. **4. the Twelve,** the 12 apostles chosen by Christ. —*adj.* **5.** amounting to 12 in number. [bef. 900; ME *twelve,* inflected form of *twelf,* OE *twelfe* lit., (ten and) two leave, i.e., two left over; c. OFris *twelef, twelf,* OHG *zwelif,* ON *tōlf,* Goth *twalif;* cf. Lith *dvýlika;* see TWO, LEAVE[1], ELEVEN]

twelve•fold (*adj.* twelv′fōld′; *adv.* twelv′fōld′), *adj.* **1.** having twelve sections, aspects, divisions, kinds, etc. **2.** being twelve times more, larger, greater, etc., as a given quantity size, intensity, or the like. —*adv.* **3.** twelve times in amount or degree. [1550–60; OE *twelffeald.* See TWELVE, -FOLD]

twelve-inch (twelv′inch′), a phonograph record twelve inches in diameter, esp. one with two or more remixes of the same song. Cf. **seven-inch.**

twelve′-mile lim′it (twelv′mīl′), the offshore boundary of a state, extending 12 miles (19 km) at sea. Cf. **three-mile limit.**

twelve•mo (twelv′mō), *n., pl.* **-mos,** *adj.* duodecimo. [1810–20; TWELVE + -MO]

twelve•month (twelv′munth′), *n. Chiefly Brit.* a year. [bef. 1050; ME *twelfmoneth.* See TWELVE, MONTH] —**twelve′month′ly,** *adv.*

twelve′ pa′triarchs. See under **patriarch** (def. 5).

Twelv•er (twel′vər), *n. Islam.* Imamite. [1585–95; TWELVE + -ER[1]; i.e., follower of the twelve Imams or prophets]

Twelve′ Step′, *adj.* of or based on a program for recovery from addiction originating with Alcoholics Anonymous and providing 12 progressive levels toward attainment. Also, **12-step.** [1985–90] —**12-stepper,** *n.*

twelve′-string guitar′ (twelv′string′), an acoustic guitar having twelve strings instead of six, with each pair tuned an octave apart, and more difficult to play than the standard guitar.

twelve-tone (twelv′tōn′), *adj. Music.* **1.** based on or incorporating the twelve-tone technique. **2.** using or advocating the twelve-tone technique. [1935–40]

twelve′-tone row′ (rō). See **tone row.** Also, **twelve-note row** (twelv′nōt rō′). [1940–45]

twelve′-tone technique′, *Music.* a modern system of tone relationships in which the 12 tones of an octave are not centered around any one tone, but are unified by a selected order of tones for a given composition. Also called **serialism, serial technique.**

twen•ti•eth (twen′tē ith, twun′-), *adj.* **1.** next after the nineteenth; being the ordinal number for 20. **2.** being one of 20 equal parts. —*n.* **3.** a twentieth part, esp. of one (1/20). **4.** the twentieth member of a series. [bef. 900; ME *twentithe,* OE *twentigotha.* See TWENTY, -ETH[2]]

Twen′tieth Amend′ment, an amendment to the U.S. Constitution, ratified in 1933, that abolished the December to March session of those Congressmen defeated for reelection in November. Also called **Lame Duck Amendment.**

twen•ty (twen′tē, twun′-), *n., pl.* **-ties,** *adj.* —*n.* **1.** a cardinal number, 10 times 2. **2.** a symbol for this number, as 20 or XX. **3.** a set of this many persons or things. **4.** *Informal.* a twenty-dollar bill: *Can you give me two tens for a twenty?* **5. twenties,** the numbers, years, degrees, or the like, from 20 through 29, as in referring to numbered streets, indicating the years of a lifetime or of a century, or referring to degrees of temperature. —*adj.* **6.** amounting to 20 in number. [bef. 900; ME; OE *twēntig;* c. OFris *tw(e)intich,* OHG *zweinzug* (G *zwanzig*), Goth *twai tigjus* two tens]

twen•ty-eight (twen′tē āt′, twun′-), *n.* **1.** a cardinal number, 20 plus 8. **2.** a symbol for this number, as 28 or XXVIII. **3.** a set of this many persons or things. —*adj.* **4.** amounting to 28 in number.

twen•ty-eighth (twen′tē ātth′, -āth′, twun′-), *adj.* **1.** next after the twenty-seventh; being the ordinal number for 28. **2.** being one of 28 equal parts. —*n.* **3.** a twenty-eighth part, esp. of one (1/28). **4.** the twenty-eighth member of a series.

twen•ty-fifth (twen′tē fifth′, twun′-), *adj.* **1.** next after the twenty-fourth; being the ordinal number for 25. **2.** being one of 25 equal parts. —*n.* **3.** a twenty-fifth part, esp. of one (1/25). **4.** the twenty-fifth member of a series.

Twen′ty-fifth′ Amend′ment, an amendment to the U.S. Constitution, ratified in 1967, establishing the succession to the presidency in the event of the president's death, resignation, or incapacity.

twen•ty-first (twen′tē fûrst′, twun′-), *adj.* **1.** next after the twentieth; being the ordinal number for 21. **2.** being one of 21 equal parts. —*n.* **3.** a twenty-first part, esp. of one (1/21). **4.** the twenty-first member of a series.

Twen′ty-first′ Amend′ment, an amendment to the U.S. Constitution, ratified in 1933, providing for the repeal of the Eighteenth Amendment, which had outlawed the manufacture, sale, and transportation of alcoholic beverages.

twen•ty-five (twen′tē fīv′, twun′-), *n.* **1.** a cardinal number, 20 plus 5. **2.** a symbol for this number, as 25 or XXV. **3.** a set of this many persons or things. —*adj.* **4.** amounting to 25 in number.

twen•ty-fold (*adj.* twen′tē fōld′, twun′-; *adv.* twen′tē fōld′, twun′-), *adj.* **1.** having twenty sections, aspects, divisions, kinds, etc. **2.** being twenty times as large, great, many, etc. —*adv.* **3.** twenty times in amount or degree. [1600–10; TWENTY + -FOLD]

twen•ty-four (twen′tē fôr′, -fōr′, twun′-), *n.* **1.** a cardinal number, 20 plus 4. **2.** a symbol for this number, as 24 or XXIV. **3.** a set of this many persons or things. —*adj.* **4.** amounting to 24 in number.

twen•ty-four•mo (twen′tē fôr′mō, -fōr′-, twun′-), *n., pl.* **-mos,** *adj.* —*n.* **1.** a book size of about 3⅝ × 5⅛ in. (9 × 13 cm), determined by printing on sheets folded to form 24 leaves or 48 pages. **2.** a book of this size. *Symbol:* 24mo, 24° —*adj.* **3.** in twenty-fourmo. Also called **vigesimoquarto.** [1835–45; TWENTY-FOUR + -MO]

twen•ty-fourth (twen′tē fôrth′, -fōrth′, twun′-), *adj.* **1.** next after the twenty-third; being the ordinal number for 24. **2.** being one of 24 equal parts. —*n.* **3.** a twenty-fourth part, esp. of one (1/24). **4.** the twenty-fourth member of a series.

Twen′ty-fourth′ Amend′ment, an amendment to the U.S. Constitution, ratified in 1964, forbidding the use of the poll tax as a requirement for voting in national or U.S. Congressional elections.

twen•ty•mo (twen′tē mō′, twun′-), *n., pl.* **-mos,** *adj.* —*n.* **1.** a book size of about 3 × 5 in. (8 × 12 cm), determined by printing on sheets folded to form 20 leaves or 40 pages. **2.** a book of this size. *Symbol:* 20mo, 20° —*adj.* **3.** in twentymo. Also called **vigesimo.** [1835–45; TWENTY + -MO]

twen•ty-nine (twen′tē nīn′, twun′-), *n.* **1.** a cardinal number, 20 plus 9. **2.** a symbol for this number, as 29 or XXIX. **3.** a set of this many persons or things. —*adj.* **4.** amounting to 29 in number.

twen•ty-ninth (twen′tē nīnth′, twun′-), *adj.* **1.** next after the twenty-eighth; being the ordinal number for 29. **2.** being one of 29 equal parts. —*n.* **3.** a twenty-ninth part, esp. of one (1/29). **4.** the twenty-ninth member of a series.

twen•ty-one (twen′tē wun′, twun′-), *n.* **1.** a cardinal number, 20 plus 1. **2.** a symbol for this number, as 21 or XXI. **3.** a set of this many persons or things. **4.** Also, **21.** Also called **blackjack.** a gambling game at cards, in which the object is to obtain from the dealer cards whose values add up to, or close to, 21 but which do not exceed it. —*adj.* **5.** amounting to 21 in number.

twen′ty ques′tions, an oral game in which one player selects a word or object whose identity the other players attempt to guess by asking up to twenty questions that can be answered with a yes or a no.

twen•ty-sec•ond (twen′tē sek′ənd, twun′-), *adj.* **1.** next after the twenty-first; being the ordinal number for 22. **2.** being one of 22 equal parts. —*n.* **3.** a twenty-second part, esp. of one (1/22). **4.** the twenty-second member of a series.

Twenty-sec′ond Amend′ment, an amendment to the U.S. Constitution, ratified in 1951, limiting presidential terms to two for any one person, or to one elected term if the person has completed more than two years of another's term.

twen•ty-sev•en (twen′tē sev′ən, twun′-), *n.* **1.** a cardinal number, 20 plus 7. **2.** a symbol for this number, as 27 or XXVII. **3.** a set of this many persons or things. —*adj.* **4.** amounting to 27 in number.

twen•ty-sev•enth (twen′tē sev′ənth, twun′-), *adj.* **1.** next after the twenty-sixth; being the ordinal number for 27. **2.** being one of 27 equal parts. —*n.* **3.** a twenty-seventh part, esp. of one (1/27). **4.** the twenty-seventh member of a series.

twen•ty-six (twen′tē siks′, twun′-), *n.* **1.** a cardinal number, 20 plus 6. **2.** a symbol for this number, as 26 or XXVI. **3.** a set of this many persons or things. —*adj.* **4.** amounting to 26 in number.

twen•ty-sixth (twen′tē siksth′, twun′-), *adj.* **1.** next after the twenty-fifth; being the ordinal number for 26. **2.** being one of 26 equal parts. —*n.* **3.** a twenty-sixth part, esp. of one (1/26). **4.** the twenty-sixth member of a series.

Twen′ty-sixth′ Amend′ment, an amendment to the U.S. Constitution, ratified in 1971, lowering the voting age to 18.

twen•ty-third (twen′tē thûrd′, twun′-), *adj.* **1.** next after the twenty-second; being the ordinal number for 23. **2.** being one of 23 equal parts. —*n.* **3.** a twenty-third part, esp. of one (1/23). **4.** the twenty-third member of a series.

Twen′ty-third′ Amend′ment, an amendment to the U.S. Constitution, ratified in 1961, allowing District of Columbia residents to vote in presidential elections.

Twen′ty Thou′sand Leagues′ Un′der the Sea′, a novel (1870) by Jules Verne.

twen•ty-three (twen′tē thrē′, twun′-), *n.* **1.** a cardinal number, 20 plus 3. **2.** a symbol for this number, as 23 or XXIII. **3.** a set of this many persons or things. —*adj.* **4.** amounting to 23 in number.

twen•ty-twen•ty (twen′tē twen′tē, twun′tē twun′tē), *adj.* **1.** *Ophthalm.* having normal visual acuity. **2.** keenly or acutely perceptive: *an opinion based on twenty-twenty hindsight.* Also, **20-20.** [1935–40]

twen•ty-two (twen′tē tōō′, twun′-), *n.* **1.** a cardinal number, 20 plus 2. **2.** a symbol for this number, as 22 or XXII. **3.** a set of this many persons or things. **4.** See **.22.** —*adj.* **5.** amounting to 22 in number.

.22 (twen′tē tōō′, twun′-), *n., pl.* **.22s, .22's. 1.** a rifle or pistol using a cartridge .22 inch in diameter and of varying length. **2.** the cartridge itself. Also, **twenty-two.**

'twere (twûr; *unstressed* twər), contraction of *it were.* —**Usage.** See **contraction.**

twerp (twûrp), *n. Slang.* an insignificant or despicable fellow.Also, **twirp.** [1920–25; orig. uncert.]

Twi (chwē, chē, twē), *n.* a Kwa language spoken in Ghana that is mutually intelligible with Fanti. Also, **Tshi.**

twi-, a combining form meaning "two," "twice": *twibill.* [ME, OE; c. G *zwie-* (OHG *zwi-*), L *bi-,* Gk *di-.* See TWO]

twi•bill (twī′bil′), *n.* **1.** a mattock with one arm like that of an adz and the other like that of an ax. **2.** *Archaic.* a double-bladed battle-ax. [bef. 1000; ME, OE. See TWI-, BILL[3]]

twice (twīs), *adv.* **1.** two times, as in succession: *Write twice a week.* **2.** on two occasions; in two instances: *I phoned him twice.* **3.** in twofold quantity or degree; in double the amount or degree: *twice as much.* [bef. 1150; ME *twies,* equiv. to *twie* twice (OE *twige,* c. OFris *twia,* OS *tuuio;* see TWI-) + *-s* -S[1]]

twice-born (twīs′bôrn′), *adj.* **1.** *Hinduism.* of or pertaining to members of the Indian castes of Brahmins, Kshatriyas, and Vaisyas, who undergo a spiritual rebirth and initiation in adolescence. **2.** having undergone reincarnation. **3.** born-again (def. 1). **4.** denoting any moral or religious experience that brings about a major reorientation of a person's character or personality. [1400–50, 1785–95 for def. 1; late ME: an epithet of Bacchus]

twice-laid (twīs′lād′), *adj.* **1.** made from strands of

CONCISE PRONUNCIATION KEY: act, cāpe, dâre, pärt; set, ēqual; if, īce; ox, ōver, ôrder, oil, bŏŏk, bōōt, out; up, ûrge; child; sing; shoe; thin, *th*at; zh as in *treasure.* ə = *a* as in *alone, e* as in *system, i* as in *easily, o* as in *gallop, u* as in *circus;* ᵊ as in *fire* (fīᵊr), *hour* (ouᵊr). l and n can serve as syllabic consonants, as in *cradle* (krād′l), and *button* (but′n). See the full key inside the front cover.

used rope. **2.** made from makeshift or used material. [1585–95]

twic·er (twī′sər), *n.* **1.** *Slang.* a two-time loser. **2.** *Australian.* **a.** a deceiver. **b.** a crook. [1670–80; TWICE + -ER[1]]

twice-told (twīs′tōld′), *adj.* having been told before; related two times. [1400–50; late ME]

Twick·en·ham (twik′ə nəm), *n.* a former borough, now part of Richmond upon Thames, in SE England.

twid·dle (twid′l), *v.*, **-dled, -dling,** *n.* —*v.t.* **1.** to turn about or play with lightly or idly, esp. with the fingers; twirl. —*v.i.* **2.** to play or trifle idly with something; fiddle. **3.** to turn about lightly; twirl. **4. twiddle one's thumbs,** to do nothing; be idle: *Business was slack, and the salespeople were twiddling their thumbs.* —*n.* **5.** the act of twiddling; turn; twirl. [1530–40; perh. b. TWITCH and FIDDLE] —**twid′dler,** *n.*

twig[1] (twig), *n.* **1.** a slender shoot of a tree or other plant. **2.** a small offshoot from a branch or stem. **3.** a small, dry, woody piece fallen from a branch: *a fire of twigs.* **4.** *Anat.* one of the minute branches of a blood vessel or nerve. [bef. 950; ME; OE *twig, twigge,* orig. (something) divided in two; akin to OHG *zwig* (G *Zweig*), D *twijg;* cf. Skt *dvikás* double] —**twig′less,** *adj.* —**twig′like′,** *adj.*

twig[2] (twig), *v.*, **twigged, twig·ging.** *Brit.* —*v.t.* **1.** to look at; observe: *Now, twig the man climbing there, will you?* **2.** to see; perceive: *Do you twig the difference in colors?* **3.** to understand. —*v.i.* **4.** to understand. [1755–65; < Ir *tuigim* I understand, with E *w* reflecting the offglide before *i* of the velarized Ir *t* typical of southern Ireland; cf. DIG[2]]

twig[3] (twig), *n. Brit.* style; fashion. [1805–15; orig. uncert.]

twig′ blight′, *Plant Pathol.* blight affecting the twigs of a plant. [1885–90, *Amer.*]

twig′ bor′er, any of several beetles, beetle larvae, or moth larvae that bore into the twigs of plants.

twig′ gir′dler. See under **girdler** (def. 2). [1890–95, *Amer.*]

twig·gy (twig′ē), *adj.*, **-gi·er, -gi·est.** **1.** of, pertaining to, or resembling twigs. **2.** full of twigs. [1555–65; TWIG[1] + -Y[1]]

twi·light (twī′līt′), *n.* **1.** the soft, diffused light from the sky when the sun is below the horizon, either from daybreak to sunrise or, more commonly, from sunset to nightfall. **2.** the period in the morning or, more commonly, in the evening during which this light prevails. **3.** a terminal period, esp. after full development, success, etc.: *the twilight of his life.* **4.** a state of uncertainty, vagueness, or gloom. —*adj.* **5.** of, pertaining to, or resembling twilight; dim; obscure: *in the twilight hours.* **6.** appearing or flying at twilight; crepuscular. [1375–1425; late ME; see TWI-, LIGHT[1]] —**twi′light′y,** *adj.*

twi′light glow′. See under **airglow.** [1810–20]

Twi′light of the Gods′, *German Myth.* Götterdämmerung. Cf. **Ragnarok.**

twi′light sleep′, *Med.* a state of semiconsciousness, usually produced by hypodermic injections of scopolamine and morphine, used chiefly to effect relatively painless childbirth. [1910–15]

twi′light zone′, **1.** the lowest level of the ocean that light can reach. **2.** an ill-defined area between two distinct conditions, categories, etc., usually comprising certain features of both; an indefinite boundary: *a twilight zone between fantasy and reality.* [1905–10]

twi·lit (twī′lit′), *adj.* lighted by or as by twilight: *a twilit cathedral.* [1865–70; TWI(LIGHT) + LIT[1]]

twill (twil), *n.* **1.** a fabric constructed in twill weave. **2.** a garment, as a suit or trousers, of this fabric. **3.** See **twill weave.** —*v.t.* **4.** to weave in the manner of a twill. **5.** to weave in twill construction. [1300–50; north and Scots var. of *twilly* (n.), ME *twyle,* OE *twilī(c),* half trans., half adoption of L *bilīc-* (s. of *bilix*) having double thread. See TWI-]

'twill (twil), a contraction of *it will.* —**Usage.** See **contraction.**

twill′ weave′, one of the basic weave structures in which the filling threads are woven over and under two or more warp yarns, producing a characteristic diagonal pattern. Also called **twill.** Cf. **plain weave, satin weave.**

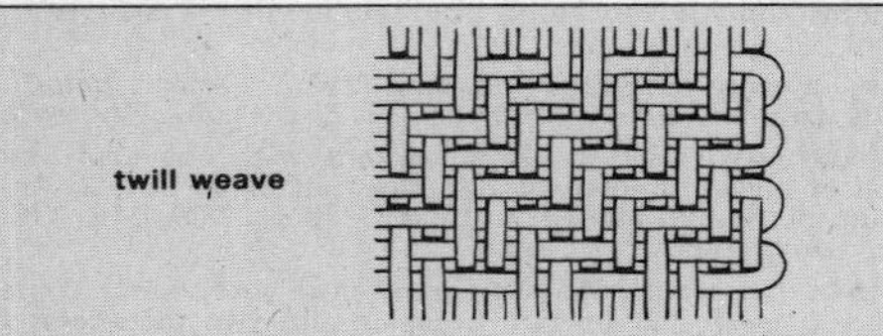
twill weave

T.W.I.M.C., to whom it may concern.

twin[1] (twin), *n.*, *adj.*, *v.*, **twinned, twin·ning.** —*n.* **1.** either of two children or animals brought forth at a birth. **2.** either of two persons or things closely related to or closely resembling each other. **3.** See **twin bed.** **4.** Also called **twin room.** a type of hotel accommodation with twin beds, for occupancy by two persons. Cf. **double** (def. 13). **5.** Also called **hemitrope.** *Crystall.* a compound crystal consisting of two or more parts or crystals definitely oriented each to the other; macle. **6. Twins,** *Astron., Astrol.* the constellation or sign of Gemini. —*adj.* **7.** being a twin or twins: *twin sisters.* **8.** being two persons or things closely related to or closely resembling each other. **9.** being one of a pair; identical: *a twin bracelet; a twin peak.* **10.** consisting of two similar parts or elements joined or connected: *a twin vase.* **11.** *Bot., Zool.* occurring in pairs; didymous. **12.** *Crystall.* of the nature of a twin; hemitrope. **13.** twofold or double. —*v.t.* **14.** to bring together in close relationship; pair; couple. **15.** to furnish a counterpart to or a replica of; match. **16.** *Informal.* to divide or convert into two, parts, similar items, etc.: *The old movie palace will be twinned, making two smaller theaters.* **17.** *Informal.* to link or combine with: *The new grocery store is twinned with a restaurant.* **18.** *Crystall.* to form into a twin. **19.** *Obs.* to give birth to as twins. —*v.i.* **20.** to give birth to twins. **21.** to be paired or coupled. [bef. 900; ME; OE *twinn* (adj.), *getwinn* (n. and adj.); akin to OFris *twine,* ON *tvinnr* double, Goth *twaihnai*[1]]

twin[2] (twin), *v.t.*, *v.i.*, **twinned, twin·ning.** *Scot.* twine[2].

twin′ bed′, a twin-size bed, esp. one of a matching pair in a bedroom; single bed. [1915–20, *Amer.*]

twin·ber·ry (twin′ber′ē, -bə rē), *n.*, *pl.* **-ries.** **1.** the partridgeberry, *Mitchella repens.* **2.** a North American honeysuckle shrub, *Lonicera involucrata,* having involucrate flowers of various colors. [1815–25, *Amer.* TWIN[1] + BERRY]

twin′ bill′, *Sports.* a doubleheader, as in baseball. [1945–50]

twin·born (twin′bôrn′), *adj.* born at the same birth. [1590–1600; TWIN[1] + BORN]

Twin′ Cit′ies, the cities of St. Paul and Minneapolis.

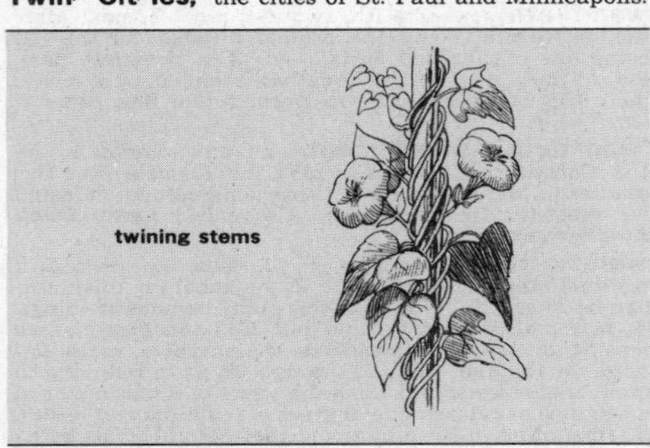
twining stems

twine[1] (twīn), *n.*, *v.*, **twined, twin·ing.** —*n.* **1.** a strong thread or string composed of two or more strands twisted together. **2.** an act of twining, twisting, or interweaving. **3.** a coiled or twisted object or part; convolution. **4.** a twist or turn in anything. **5.** a knot or tangle. —*v.t.* **6.** to twist together; intertwine; interweave. **7.** to form by or as by twisting together: *to twine a wreath.* **8.** to twist (one strand, thread, or the like) with another; interlace. **9.** to insert with a twisting or winding motion (usually fol. by *in* or *into*): *He twined his fingers in his hair.* **10.** to clasp or enfold (something) around something else; place by or as if by winding (usually fol. by *about, around,* etc.): *She twined her arms about the sculpture and carried it away.* **11.** to cause (a person, object, etc.) to be encircled with something else; wreathe; wrap: *They twined the arch with flowers.* —*v.i.* **12.** to wind about something; twist itself in spirals (usually fol. by *about, around,* etc.): *Strangling vines twined about the tree.* **13.** to wind in a sinuous or meandering course. [bef. 900; ME *twine* (n.), *twinen* (v.), OE *twin* (n.) lit., a double or twisted thread; c. D *twijn;* akin to G *Zwirn,* ON *tvinni* thread, twine; see TWI-] —**twine′a·ble,** *adj.* —**twin′er,** *n.*

twine[2] (twīn), *v.t.*, *v.i.*, **twined, twin·ing.** *Scot.* to separate; part. Also, **twin.** [1175–1225; like late ME *twinen,* var. of earlier *twinnen,* deriv. of *twin* TWIN[1]]

twin-en·gine (twin′en′jən), *adj.* having two engines of equal power as prime movers: *a twin-engine airplane.* [1930–35]

Twin′ Falls′, **1.** a city in S Idaho. 26,209. **2.** a waterfall near there, on the Snake River. ab. 180 ft. (55 m) high.

twin·flow·er (twin′flou′ər), *n.* either of two slender, creeping, evergreen, caprifoliaceous plants, *Linnaea borealis,* of Europe, or *L. americana,* of North America, having pink or purplish nodding flowers borne in pairs on threadlike stalks. [1810–20, *Amer.;* TWIN[1] + FLOWER]

twinge (twinj), *n.*, *v.*, **twinged, twing·ing.** —*n.* **1.** a sudden, sharp pain: *On damp days, he's often bothered by a twinge of rheumatism.* **2.** a mental or emotional pang: *a twinge of guilt; twinges of sorrow.* —*v.t.* **3.** to affect (the body or mind) with a sudden, sharp pain or pang. **4.** to pinch; tweak; twitch. —*v.i.* **5.** to have or feel a sudden, sharp pain. [bef. 1000; ME *twengen* to pinch, OE *twengan*] —**Syn. 1.** spasm, cramp, pang, stab.

twi-night (twī′nīt′), *adj. Baseball.* pertaining to or noting a doubleheader in which the first game begins late in the afternoon and the second in the evening under lights. [1945–50; TWI(LIGHT) + NIGHT]

twi-night·er (twī′nī′tər), *n. Baseball.* a twi-night doubleheader. [TWI-NIGHT + -ER[1]]

Twi·ning (twī′ning), *n.* **Nathan Farragut,** 1897–1982, U.S. Air Force general: chairman of the Joint Chiefs of Staff 1957–60.

twin·jet (twin′jet′), *n.* an airplane powered by two jet engines. [1945–50; TWIN[1] + JET[1]]

twink (twingk), *v.i.*, *v.t.*, *n.* **1.** wink. **2.** twinkle. [1350–1400; ME *twinken;* c. G *zwinken* to wink; akin to TWINKLE]

twin′ kill′ing, *Baseball Slang.* See **double play.**

twin·kle (twing′kəl), *v.*, **-kled, -kling,** *n.* —*v.i.* **1.** to shine with a flickering gleam of light, as a star or distant light. **2.** to sparkle in the light: *The diamond on her finger twinkled in the firelight.* **3.** (of the eyes) to be bright with amusement, pleasure, etc. **4.** to move flutteringly and quickly, as flashes of light; flit. **5.** *Archaic.* to wink; blink. —*v.t.* **6.** to emit (light) in intermittent gleams or flashes. **7.** *Archaic.* to wink (the eyes or eyelids). —*n.* **8.** a flickering or intermittent brightness or light. **9.** a scintillating brightness in the eyes; sparkle. **10.** the time required for a wink; twinkling. **11.** *Archaic.* a wink. [bef. 900; ME *twinklen* (v.), OE *twinclian;* see TWINK, -LE] —**twin′kler,** *n.*

twin·kling (twing′kling), *n.* **1.** an act of shining with intermittent gleams of light. **2.** the time required for a wink; an instant. **3.** *Archaic.* winking; a wink. [1250–1300; ME; see TWINKLE, -ING[1]]

twin′-lens cam′era (twin′lenz′), *Photog.* a camera having two separately mounted lenses coordinated to eliminate parallax errors or for making stereoscopic photographs. Cf. **twin-lens reflex camera.**

twin′-lens re′flex cam′era. See under **reflex camera.** Also called **twin′-lens re′flex.** *Abbr.:* TLR

twinned (twind), *adj.* **1.** born two at one birth. **2.** closely or intimately associated, joined, or united; coupled; paired. [1600–10; TWIN[1] + -ED[2]]

twin·ning (twin′ing), *n.* **1.** the bearing of two children at one birth. **2.** the coupling of two persons or things; union. **3.** *Crystall.* the union of crystals to form a twin. [1565–75; TWIN[1] + -ING[1]]

twin′ room′, twin[1] (def. 4).

twin-screw (twin′skrōō′), *adj. Naut.* (of a vessel) having two screw propellers, which usually revolve in opposite directions. [1860–65]

twin-size (twin′sīz′), *adj.* **1.** (of a bed) approximately 39 in. (99 cm) wide and between 75 and 76 in. (191 and 193 cm) long; single. **2.** pertaining to or made for a twin-size bed: *twin-size sheets.* Cf. **full-size, king-size, queen-size.** Also, **twin′-sized′.** [1925–30]

twirl (twûrl), *v.t.* **1.** to cause to rotate rapidly; spin; revolve; whirl. **2.** to twiddle: *to twirl my thumbs.* **3.** to wind idly, as about something. —*v.i.* **4.** to rotate rapidly; whirl. **5.** to turn quickly so as to face or point in another direction. —*n.* **6.** an act or instance of twirling; spin; whirl. **7.** something convoluted or having a spiral shape; coil; curl; convolution. [1590–1600; TW(IST) + (WH)IRL]

twirl·er (twûr′lər), *n.* **1.** a person or thing that twirls. **2.** *Baseball.* a pitcher. [1800–10; TWIRL + -ER[1]]

twirp (twûrp), *n.* twerp.

twist (twist), *v.t.* **1.** to combine, as two or more strands or threads, by winding together; intertwine. **2.** to form by or as if by winding strands together: *Several fibers were used to twist the rope.* **3.** to entwine (one thing) with another; interlace (something) with something else; interweave; plait. **4.** to wind or coil (something) about something else; encircle; entwine; wreathe. **5.** to alter in shape, as by turning the ends in opposite directions, so that parts previously in the same straight line and plane are located in a spiral curve: *The sculptor twisted the form into an arabesque. He twisted his body around to look behind him.* **6.** to turn sharply or wrench out of place; sprain: *He twisted his ankle.* **7.** to pull, tear, or break off by turning forcibly: *He twisted the arm off the puppet.* **8.** to distort (the features) by tensing or contracting the facial muscles; contort: *She twisted her face in a wry smile.* **9.** to distort the meaning or form of; pervert: *He twisted my comment about to suit his own purpose.* **10.** to cause to become mentally or emotionally distorted; warp: *The loss of his business twisted his whole outlook on life.* **11.** to form into a coil, knot, or the like by winding, rolling, etc.: *to twist the hair into a knot.* **12.** to bend tortuously. **13.** to cause to move with a rotary motion, as a ball pitched in a curve. **14.** to turn (something) from one direction to another, as by rotating or revolving: *I twisted my chair to face the window.* **15.** to combine or associate intimately. —*v.i.* **16.** to be or become intertwined. **17.** to wind or twine about something. **18.** to writhe or squirm. **19.** to take a spiral form or course; wind, curve, or bend. **20.** to turn or rotate, as on an axis; revolve, as about something; spin. **21.** to turn so as to face in another direction. **22.** to turn, coil, or bend into a spiral shape. **23.** to change shape under forcible turning or twisting. **24.** to move with a progressive rotary motion, as a ball pitched in a curve. **25.** to dance the twist. **26. twist one's arm,** *Informal.* to coerce: *I didn't want to go, but he twisted my arm.* —*n.* **27.** a deviation in direction; curve; bend; turn. **28.** the action of turning or rotating on an axis; rotary motion; spin. **29.** anything formed by or as if by twisting or twining parts together. **30.** the act or process of twining strands together, as in thread, yarn, or rope. **31.** a twisting awry or askew. **32.** distortion or perversion, as of meaning or form. **33.** a peculiar attitude or bias; eccentric turn or bent of mind; eccentricity. **34.** spiral disposition, arrangement, or form. **35.** spiral movement or course. **36.** an irregular bend; crook; kink. **37.** a sudden, unanticipated change of course, as of events. **38.** a treatment, method, idea, version, etc., esp. one differing from that which preceded: *The screenwriters gave the old plot a new twist.* **39.** the changing of the shape of anything by or as by turning the ends in opposite directions. **40.** the stress causing this alteration; torque. **41.** the resulting state. **42.** a twisting or torsional action, force, or stress; torsion. **43.** a strong, twisted silk thread, heavier than ordinary sewing silk, for working buttonholes and for other purposes. **44.** the direction of twisting in weaving yarn; S twist or Z twist. **45.** a loaf or roll of dough twisted and baked. **46.** a strip of citrus peel that has been twisted and placed in a drink to add flavor. **47.** a kind of tobacco manufactured in the form of a rope or thick cord. **48.** a dance performed by couples and characterized by strongly rhythmic turns and twists of the arms, legs, and torso. **49.** the degree of spiral formed by the grooves in a rifled firearm or cannon. **50.** *Gymnastics, Diving.* a full rota-

tion of the body about the vertical axis. **51.** a wrench. [1300–50; ME *twisten* to divide, deriv. of *twist* divided object, rope (cf. OE *-twist* in *candel-twist* pair of snuffers); c. D *twisten* to quarrel, G *Zwist* a quarrel. See TWI-] —**twist′a·ble,** *adj.* —**twist′a·bil′i·ty,** *n.* —**twist′ed·ly,** *adv.* —**twist′ing·ly,** *adv.*
—**Syn. 7.** wrench, wrest, yank. **33.** See **turn.**

twist′ drill′, *Mach.* a drill with one or more deep helical grooves in the body. [1870–75]

twist′ed stom′ach worm′. See **stomach worm.** [1955–60]

twist·er (twis′tər), *n.* **1.** a person or thing that twists. **2.** *Informal.* a whirlwind or tornado. **3.** *Chiefly Brit. Informal.* a deceitful, unscrupulous person. [1475–85; 1895–1900 for def. 2; TWIST + -ER[1]]

twist·ing (twis′ting), *n.* the practice of an insurance agent of tricking the holder of a life insurance policy into letting it lapse so that the insured will replace it with one of a company represented by the agent. [1905–10; TWIST + -ING[1]]

twist′ tie′, a short wire, usually enveloped in paper or plastic, used to tie closed a bag, wrapper, etc.

twist·y (twis′tē), *adj.,* **twist·i·er, twist·i·est.** (esp. of a road) twisting or winding: *a twisty little path through the woods.* [1855–60; TWIST + -Y[1]]

twit[1] (twit), *v.,* **twit·ted, twit·ting,** *n.* —*v.t.* **1.** to taunt, tease, ridicule, etc., with reference to anything embarrassing; gibe at. **2.** to reproach or upbraid. —*n.* **3.** an act of twitting. **4.** a derisive reproach; taunt; gibe. [1520–30; aph. var. of obs. *atwite,* ME *atwiten,* OE *ætwītan* to taunt, equiv. to *æt-* AT[1] + *wītan* to blame]

twit[2] (twit), *n.* a weak or thin place in yarn caused by uneven spinning. [1810–20; orig. uncert.]

twit[3] (twit), *n. Informal.* an insignificant or bothersome person. [1920–25; perh. orig. n. deriv. of TWIT[1], i.e., "one who twits others," but altered in sense by assoc. with expressive words with *tw-* (TWADDLE, TWAT, TWERP, etc.) and by rhyme with NITWIT]

twit[4] (twit), *n.* an excited state; dither: *to be in a twit about company coming.* [prob. shortened from TWITTER]

twitch (twich), *v.t.* **1.** to tug or pull at with a quick, short movement; pluck: *She twitched him by the sleeve.* **2.** to jerk rapidly: *The rider twitched the reins a couple of times.* **3.** to move (a part of the body) with a sudden, jerking motion. **4.** to pinch or pull at sharply and painfully; give a smarting pinch to; nip. —*v.i.* **5.** to move spasmodically or convulsively; jerk; jump. **6.** to give a sharp, sudden pull; tug; pluck (usually fol. by *at*): *He constantly twitched at his collar.* **7.** to ache or hurt with a sharp, shooting pain; twinge: *That back tooth twitches a bit.* —*n.* **8.** a quick, jerky movement of the body or of some part of it. **9.** involuntary, spasmodic movement of a muscle; tic: *He gets a twitch in his left eye when he's nervous.* **10.** a short, sudden pull or tug; jerk. **11.** a bodily or mental twinge, as of pain, conscience, etc.; pang. **12.** a loop or noose placed over the muzzle of a horse and tightened by twisting a stick or handle to which it is attached, used as a restraining device during a painful operation. [1125–75; ME *twicchen* (v.); akin to OE *twiccian* to pluck; c. G *zwicken* to pinch] —**twitch′er,** *n.* —**twitch′ing·ly,** *adv.*

twitch′ grass′. See **couch grass.** [1680–90; alter. of *quitch grass*]

twitch′ing trail′, *Canadian* (*chiefly New Brunswick*). a logging road sufficiently developed to allow the hauling of logs along it by horse or tractor.

twitch·y (twich′ē), *adj.,* **twitch·i·er, twitch·i·est. 1.** twitching or tending to twitch. **2.** nervous; jumpy: *All that pressure at the office has made him twitchy.* [1740–50; TWITCH + -Y[1]] —**twitch′i·ness,** *n.*

twite (twīt), *n.* a small finch, *Carduelis flavirostris,* of northern Europe, having streaked brown plumage and, in the male, a pink breast. [1555–65; imit.]

twit·ter (twit′ər), *v.i.* **1.** to utter a succession of small, tremulous sounds, as a bird. **2.** to talk lightly and rapidly, esp. of trivial matters; chatter. **3.** to titter; giggle. **4.** to tremble with excitement or the like; be in a flutter. —*v.t.* **5.** to express or utter by twittering. —*n.* **6.** an act of twittering. **7.** a twittering sound. **8.** a state of tremulous excitement. [1325–75; ME *twiteren* (v.); akin to G *zwitschern*] —**twit′ter·er,** *n.* —**twit′ter·ing·ly,** *adv.*
—**Syn. 8.** flutter, tizzy, fluster.

twit·ter·y (twit′ə rē), *adj.* **1.** given to or characterized by twittering. **2.** tremulous; shaky. [1880–85; TWITTER + -Y[1]]

′twixt (twikst), *prep.* contraction of *betwixt.*

two (to͞o), *n.* **1.** a cardinal number, 1 plus 1. **2.** a symbol for this number, as 2 or II. **3.** a set of this many persons or things. **4.** a playing card, die face, or half of a domino face with two pips. **5. in two,** into two separate parts, as halves: *A bolt of lightning split the tree in two.* **6. put two and two together,** to draw a correct conclusion from the given circumstances; infer: *It didn't require a great mind to put two and two together.* —*adj.* **7.** amounting to two in number. [bef. 900; ME; OE *twā* (fem. and neut.; cf. TWAIN); c. G *zwei;* cf. L *duo,* Gk *dýo*]

two-a-cat (to͞o′ə kat′), *n.* See **two old cat.**

two-bag·ger (to͞o′bag′ər), *n. Baseball. Informal.* See **two-base hit.** [1870–75, *Amer.;* *two bag(s)* + -ER[1]]

two′-base hit′ (to͞o′bās′), *Baseball.* a base hit that enables a batter to reach second base safely. Also called **double.** [1870–75, *Amer.*]

two-beat (to͞o′bēt′), *adj.* having four beats to the measure with the second and fourth beats accented: *two-beat jazz.*

two-bit (to͞o′bit′), *adj. Slang.* **1.** costing twenty-five cents. **2.** inferior or unimportant; small-time: *a two-bit actor.* [1795–1805, *Amer.*]

two′ bits′, *Slang.* twenty-five cents. [1720–30, *Amer.*]

two′-bod′y prob′lem (to͞o′bod′ē), *Astron., Mech.* the problem of calculating the motions of two bodies in space moving solely under the influence of their mutual gravitational attraction. Cf. **three-body problem.**

two-by-four (to͞o′bi fôr′, -fōr′, -bə-), *adj.* **1.** two units thick and four units wide, esp. in inches. **2.** *Informal.* lacking adequate space; cramped: *a small, two-by-four room.* **3.** *Informal.* unimportant; insignificant: *Theirs was a petty, two-by-four operation.* —*n.* **4.** a timber measuring 2 by 4 in. (5 × 10 cm) in cross section, when untrimmed: equivalent to 1⅝ by 3⅝ in. (4½ × 9 cm) when trimmed. [1880–85, *Amer.*]

two′ cents′, **1.** something of insignificant value; a paltry amount: *We wouldn't give two cents for their chances of success.* **2. two cents worth,** an opinion, usually unsolicited and unwelcome: *Who asked you to add your two cents worth?* [1840–50]

two-col·or (to͞o′kul′ər), *adj.* **1.** having or using two colors. **2.** noting or pertaining to a photomechanical process similar to the three-color process, but using only two primary or secondary colors. [1640–50]

two-cy·cle (to͞o′sī′kəl), *adj.* noting or pertaining to an internal-combustion engine in which two strokes are required to complete a cycle (**two-stroke cycle**), one to admit and compress air or an air-fuel mixture and one to ignite fuel, do work, and scavenge the cylinder. Cf. **four-cycle.** [1900–05]

two-di·men·sion·al (to͞o′di men′shə nl, -dī-), *adj.* **1.** having the dimensions of height and width only: *a two-dimensional surface.* **2.** (of a work of art) having its elements organized in terms of a flat surface, esp. emphasizing the vertical and horizontal character of the picture plane: *the two-dimensional structure of a painting.* **3.** (in a literary work) shallow, unconvincing, or superficial in execution: *a novel having two-dimensional characters.* [1895–1900] —**two′-di·men′sion·al′i·ty,** *n.* —**two′-di·men′sion·al·ly,** *adv.*

two-edged (to͞o′ejd′), *adj.* **1.** having two edges, as a sword. **2.** cutting or effective both ways. [1520–30]

two-faced (to͞o′fāst′), *adj.* **1.** having two faces. **2.** deceitful or hypocritical. Cf. **Janus-faced.** [1610–20] —**two-fac·ed·ly** (to͞o′fā′sid lē, -fāst′lē), *adv.* —**two′-fac′ed·ness,** *n.*
—**Syn. 2.** treacherous, devious, dishonest, false.

two′-fam·i·ly house′ (to͞o′fam′ə lē, -fam′lē), a house designed for occupation by two families in contiguous apartments, as on separate floors.

two·fer (to͞o′fər), *n. Informal.* **1.** a card or ticket entitling the holder to purchase two tickets to a theatrical performance at a reduced price. **2.** a coupon or offer entitling a person to purchase two items or services for approximately the price of one. **3.** a person who belongs to two minority groups and can satisfy two quotas or appeal to two political constituencies, esp. a black woman, who can be counted twice in a position she holds, as fulfilling a racial and a sexual quota. [1885–90; from the phrase *two for* (*the price of one, a nickel,* etc.), with final (ər) humorously taken as -ER[1]; cf. GOFER]

two-fist·ed (to͞o′fis′tid), *adj.* **1.** ready for or inclined to physical combat. **2.** strong and vigorous. [1765–75, *Amer.;* TWO + FIST[1] + -ED[3]]

two-fold (to͞o′fōld′), *n. Theat.* a unit of stage scenery consisting of two flats hinged together.

two·fold (*adj.* to͞o′fōld′; *adv.* to͞o′fōld′), *adj.* **1.** having two elements or parts. **2.** twice as great or as much; double. —*adv.* **3.** in twofold measure; doubly. [1125–75; ME; see TWO, -FOLD] —**two′fold′ness,** *n.*

two′fold pur′chase, *Mach., Mech.* a purchase using a double standing block and a double running block so as to give a mechanical advantage of four or five, neglecting friction, depending on whether the hauling is on the standing block or the running block.

2,4-D (to͞o′fôr′dē′, fōr′-). See **dichlorophenoxyacetic acid.**

2,4,5-T (to͞o′fôr′fīv′tē′, fōr′). See **trichlorophenoxyacetic acid.**

Two′ Gen′tlemen of Vero′na, The, a comedy (1594–95) by Shakespeare.

two-hand·ed (to͞o′han′did), *adj.* **1.** having two hands. **2.** using both hands equally well; ambidextrous. **3.** involving or requiring the use of both hands: *a two-handed sword; a two-handed backhand.* **4.** requiring the hands of two persons to operate: *a two-handed saw.* **5.** engaged in by two persons: *a two-handed game.* [1400–50; late ME] —**two′-hand′ed·ly,** *adv.* —**two′-hand′ed·ness,** *n.*

two·leg·ged (to͞o′leg′id, -legd′), *adj.* having two legs. [1555–65; TWO + LEG + -ED[3]]

two-mast·er (to͞o′mas′tər, -mä′stər), *n. Naut.* a vessel rigged with two masts. [1895–1900; *two mast(s)* + -ER[1]] —**two′-mast′ed,** *adj.*

two′-min·ute warn′ing (to͞o′min′it), *Football.* a time-out called by an official to notify both teams that two minutes remain in a half.

two′-name pa′per (to͞o′nām′), *Banking.* commercial paper having more than one obligor, usually a maker and endorser, both of whom are fully liable.

2-naph·thol (to͞o′naf′thôl, -thol, -nap′-), *n. Chem.* beta-naphthol. See under **naphthol.**

two old cat (to͞o′ ə kat′), *Games.* one old cat played with two batters. Also, **two′ o′ cat′, two-a-cat.** [1840–50, *Amer.*]

two′ pair′, *Poker.* a set of two cards of the same denomination together with another matched set of different denomination from the first.

two′-part time′ (to͞o′pärt′), *Music.* See **duple time.**

two′-par·ty sys′tem (to͞o′pär′tē), *Govt.* a political system consisting chiefly of two major parties, more or less equal in strength. [1900–05]

two·pence (tup′əns), *n., pl.* **-pence, -pen·ces** for 2–4. **1.** (*used with a singular or plural v.*) *Brit.* a sum of two pennies. **2.** a bronze coin of the United Kingdom equal to two pennies: issued after decimalization in 1971. **3.** a former copper coin of Great Britain, equal to two pennies, issued under George III. **4.** a former silver coin of England, equal to two pennies: issued only as maundy money after 1662. **5.** a trifle. Also, **tuppence.** [1400–50; late ME *two pens;* see TWO, PENCE]

two·pen·ny (tup′ə nē, to͞o′pen′ē), *adj.* **1.** of the amount or value of twopence. **2.** costing twopence. **3.** of very little value; trifling; worthless. Also, **tuppenny.** [1525–35; TWO + PENNY]

two-phase (to͞o′fāz′), *adj. Elect.* diphase. [1895–1900]

two-piece (to͞o′pēs′), *adj.* **1.** having or consisting of two parts or pieces, esp. two matching pieces of a clothing ensemble: *a two-piece bathing suit.* —*n.* **2.** Also, **two′-piec′er.** a two-piece garment. [1905–10]

two-ply (to͞o′plī′), *adj.* consisting of two thicknesses, layers, strands, or the like. [1840–50]

two′-point perspec′tive (to͞o′point′). See under **linear perspective.**

Two′ Riv′ers, a city in E Wisconsin. 13,354.

Twor·kov (twôr′kof), *n.* **Jack,** 1900–82, U.S. painter, born in Poland.

two-seat·er (to͞o′sē′tər), *n.* a vehicle accommodating two persons. [1890–95; *two seat(s)* + -ER[1]]

two-shot (to͞o′shot′), *n. Motion Pictures, Television.* a camera shot, as a close-up, of two persons.

Two′ Sic′ilies, a former kingdom in Sicily and S Italy that existed intermittently from 1130 to 1861.

two-sid·ed (to͞o′sī′did), *adj.* **1.** having two sides; bilateral. **2.** having two aspects or characters. [1860–65; TWO + SIDE[1] + -ED[3]] —**two′-sid′ed·ness,** *n.*

2,6-di·chlo·ro·ben·zon·i·trile (to͞o′siks′dī klôr′ə-ben zon′i tril, -klōr′-), *n.* dichlobenil. [DI-[1] + CHLORO-[2] + BENZO- + NITRILE]

two·some (to͞o′səm), *adj.* **1.** consisting of two; twofold. **2.** performed or played by two persons. —*n.* **3.** two together or in company; couple; duo. **4.** *Golf.* a match between two persons. [1325–75; ME (north); see TWO, -SOME[2]]

two-spot (to͞o′spot′), *n.* **1.** a playing card or the upward face of a die that bears two pips, or a domino one half of which bears two pips. **2.** *Informal.* a two-dollar bill. [1880–85, *Amer.*]

two′-spot·ted spi′der mite′ (to͞o′spot′id), a widespread web-spinning mite, *Tetranychus urticae,* that is a pest of fruit trees and houseplants. [1945–50]

two-star (to͞o′stär′), *adj.* of or being a major general, as indicated by two stars on an insignia.

two-step (to͞o′step′), *n., v.,* **-stepped, -step·ping.** —*n.* **1.** a ballroom dance in duple meter, marked by sliding steps. **2.** a piece of music for, or in the rhythm of, this dance. —*v.i.* **3.** to dance the two-step. [1890–95]

two′-stroke cy′cle (to͞o′strōk′). See under **two-cycle.**

two-suit·er (to͞o′so͞o′tər), *n.* **1.** a suitcase designed to hold two suits and additional smaller items. **2.** *Bridge.* a hand having at least five cards in each of two suits. [1920–25 for def. 2; 1955–60, *Amer.* for def. 1; *two suit(s)* + -ER[1]]

two′-thirds rule′ (to͞o′thûrdz′), a former rule in the Democratic party, effective 1832–1936, requiring a vote of at least two thirds of its national convention delegates to nominate a presidential and vice-presidential candidate.

two-tier (to͞o′tēr′), *adj.* **1.** consisting of two tiers, floors, levels, or the like: *a two-tier wedding cake.* **2.** consisting of two separate price structures, sets of regulations, etc.: *a two-tier fare system for subways and buses.* Also, **two′-tiered′.** [1970–75]

two-time (to͞o′tīm′), *v.t.,* **-timed, -tim·ing.** *Informal.* **1.** to be unfaithful to (a lover or spouse). **2.** to double-cross. [1925–30] —**two′-tim′er,** *n.*

two′-time los′er, *Slang.* **1.** a person who has been sentenced to prison twice, esp. for a major crime in a state where a third sentence is mandatory life imprisonment. **2.** a person who has failed at the same endeavor twice. [1930–35]

two′-toed ant′eater (to͞o′tōd′). See **silky anteater.**

two′-toed sloth′, either of two sloths of the genus *Choloepus,* having two claws on the forelimbs and three on the hind limbs, including *C. didactylus* and *C. hoffmanni.* Also called **unau.** See illus. under **sloth.** [1765–75]

two-tone (to͞o′tōn′), *adj.* having two colors or two shades of the same color: *a two-tone automobile.* Also, **two′-toned′.** [1925–30]

two-track (to͞o′trak′), *Dressage.* —*n.* **1.** an oblique movement of a horse in which the forehand and hindquarters move on two distinct parallel tracks and the body is maintained uniformly in the direction of the movement. —*v.i.* **2.** (of a horse) to execute a two-track. —*v.t.* **3.** to cause (a horse) to two-track.

′twould (two͝od), contraction of *it would.*
—**Usage.** See **contraction.**

two-up (to͞o′up′), *n.* a game in which two players bet that two tossed coins will land either with matching or nonmatching sides facing up. [1930–35, *Amer.*]

two-way (to͞o′wā′), *adj.* **1.** providing for or allowing movement in opposite directions, or both to and from a place: *two-way traffic.* **2.** allowing or entailing communication or exchange between two persons, groups, countries, etc. **3.** involving two parties or participants, as a relationship or agreement; two-sided: *a two-way race for the nomination.* **4.** entailing responsibilities, obliga-

CONCISE PRONUNCIATION KEY: act, cāpe, dâre, pärt; set, ēqual; *if,* ice; ox, ōver, ôrder, oil, bo͝ok, bo͞ot, out; up, ûrge; child; sing; shoe; thin, *that;* zh as in *treasure.* ə = *a* as in *alone, e* as in *system, i* as in *easily, o* as in *gallop, u* as in *circus;* ᵊ as in *fire* (fīᵊr), *hour* (ouᵊr). l and n can serve as syllabic consonants, as in *cradle* (krād′l), and *button* (but′n). See the full key inside the front cover.

tions, etc., on both such parties. **5.** capable of both receiving and sending signals: *a two-way radio.* **6.** capable of being used in two ways. [1565–75]

two-wheel•er (to͞o′hwē′lər, -wē′-), *n.* a vehicle, esp. a bicycle, having two wheels: *The boy changed his tricycle for a two-wheeler.* [1860–65]

two′-word verb′ (to͞o′wûrd′), *Gram.* a phrasal verb.

twp., township.

TWU, Transport Workers Union of America.

TWX, (*often* twiks), a teletypewriter exchange service operating in the United States and Canada for the exchange of printed messages. [*t*(*eletype*)*w*(*riter*) (*e*)*x*-(*change service*)]

TX, Texas (approved esp. for use with zip code).

-ty[1], a suffix of numerals denoting multiples of ten: *twenty; thirty.* [ME; OE *-tig;* c. OFris *-tich,* G *-zig,* ON *-tigr,* Goth *-tigjus*]

-ty[2], a suffix occurring in nouns of Latin origin, denoting quality, state, etc.: *unity; enmity.* [ME *-te*(*e*) < OF *-te*(*t*) < L *-tātem,* acc. of *-tās*]

Ty., Territory.

Ty•burn (tī′bərn), *n.* a former place of public execution in London, England.

Ty•che (tī′kē), *n.* the ancient Greek goddess of fortune. [< Gk *týchē* luck, fortune]

Ty•cho (tī′kō), *n.* a prominent crater in the third quadrant of the face of the moon, about 56 miles (90 km) in diameter.

Ty•chon′ic sys′tem (tī kon′ik), *Astron.* a model for planetary motion devised by Tycho Brahe in which the earth is stationary and at the center of the planetary system, the sun and moon revolve around the earth, and the other planets revolve around the sun. [1670–80; *Tychon-* (s. of *Tycho* (BRAHE), Latinized form of Dan *Tyge*) + -IC]

ty•coon (tī ko͞on′), *n.* **1.** a businessperson of great wealth and power; magnate. **2.** (*often cap.*) a title used with reference to the shogun of Japan. [1855–60; < Japn *taikun* < MChin, equiv. to Chin *dà* great + *jūn* prince]

Ty•de•us (tī′dē əs, -dyo͞os, tid′ē əs), *n. Class. Myth.* the father of Diomedes: one of the Seven Against Thebes.

ty•ee (tī′ē), *n.* See **chinook salmon.** Also called **ty′ee salm′on.** [1790–1800, *Amer.*; < Chinook Jargon: chief, boss (< Nootka *ta·yi·* elder brother, senior); as a name for the fish perh. analogous with KING SALMON]

ty•ing (tī′ing), *v.* present participle of **tie.**

tyke[1] (tīk), *n.* **1.** a child, esp. a small boy. **2.** any small child. **3.** a cur; mongrel. **4.** *Chiefly Scot.* a low, contemptible fellow; boor. Also, **tike.** [1350–1400; ME < ON *tīk* bitch]

tyke[2] (tīk), *n. Australia and New Zealand Informal.* a Roman Catholic. Also, **tike.** [1940–45; cf. Ulster E *Taig* contemptuous term for a Roman Catholic Irishman, archaic E *teague* derogatory name for an Irishman < Ir *Tadhg* a common personal name]

Ty•le•nol (tī′lə nôl′, -nol′), *Pharm., Trademark.* a brand of acetaminophen.

tyl•er (tī′lər), *n.* tiler (def. 2).

Ty•ler (tī′lər), *n.* **1. John,** 1790–1862, 10th president of the U.S. 1841–45. **2. Moses Coit** (koit), 1835–1900, U.S. historian and educator. **3. Wat** (wot) or **Walter,** died 1381, English rebel: leader of the peasants' revolt of 1381. **4.** a city in E Texas. 70,508. **5.** a male given name.

Tyll Eu•len•spie•gel (til′ oi′lən shpē′gəl). See **Till Eulenspiegel.** Also, **Tyl′ Eu′lenspiegel.**

ty•lo•sis (tī lō′sis), *n., pl.* **-ses** (-sēz). *Bot.* a bubblelike formation in the cavity of tracheids or vessels in the wood of trees, consisting of protoplasm intruded from adjacent parenchyma cells. [1875–80; < Gk *týlōsis* act of making callous, equiv. to *tylō-,* var. s. of *tyloûn* to make callous, hard, deriv. of *týlos* callus, lump, knob + *-sis* -SIS]

tym•bal (tim′bəl), *n.* timbal.

tym•pan (tim′pən), *n.* **1.** *Print.* a padlike device interposed between the platen or its equivalent and the sheet to be printed, in order to soften and equalize the pressure. **2.** tympanum (defs. 2, 4). [bef. 900; ME: drum, OE < L *tympanum* TYMPANUM]

tym•pa•ni (tim′pə nē), *n. pl.* (*often used with a singular v.*) timpani.

tym•pan•ic (tim pan′ik), *adj.* pertaining or belonging to a tympanum. [1800–10; TYMPAN(UM) + -IC]

tympan′ic bone′, *Anat., Zool.* (in mammals) a bone of the skull, supporting the tympanic membrane and enclosing part of the tympanum or middle ear. [1840–50]

tympan′ic mem′brane, *Anat., Zool.* eardrum. See diag. under **ear.** [1855–60]

tym•pa•nist (tim′pə nist), *n.* a person who plays the drums, esp. the kettledrums, in an orchestra. [1605–15; < L *tympanista* < Gk *tympanistés,* equiv. to *tympan*(*ízein*) to beat a drum + *-istēs* -IST]

tym•pa•ni•tes (tim′pə nī′tēz), *n. Pathol.* distention of the abdominal wall, as in peritonitis, caused by the accumulation of gas or air in the intestine or peritoneal cavity. [1350–1400; ME < LL *tympanītēs* < Gk *tympanítēs,* deriv. of *týmpanon* drum (see TYMPANUM)] —**tym•pa•nit•ic** (tim′pə nit′ik), *adj.*

CONCISE ETYMOLOGY KEY: <, descended or borrowed from; >, whence; b., blend of, blended; c., cognate with; cf., compare; deriv., derivative; equiv., equivalent; imit., imitative; obl., oblique; r., replacing; s., stem; sp., spelling, spelled; resp., respelling, respelled; trans., translation; ?, origin unknown; *, unattested; ‡, probably earlier than. See the full key inside the front cover.

tym•pa•ni•tis (tim′pə nī′tis), *n. Pathol.* inflammation of the middle ear; otitis media. [1790–1800; TYMPAN(UM) + -ITIS]

tym•pa•no•plas•ty (tim′pə nə plas′tē), *n. Surg.* reconstruction of the eardrum and the bones of the middle ear. [1950–55; TYMPAN(UM) + -O- + -PLASTY]

tym•pa•num (tim′pə nəm), *n., pl.* **-nums, -na** (-nə). **1.** *Anat., Zool.* **a.** See **middle ear. b.** See **tympanic membrane. 2.** *Archit.* **a.** the recessed, usually triangular space enclosed between the horizontal and sloping cornices of a pediment, often decorated with sculpture. **b.** a similar space between an arch and the horizontal head of a door or window below. **3.** *Elect.* the diaphragm of a telephone. **4.** a drum or similar instrument. **5.** the stretched membrane forming a drumhead. [1610–20; < L < Gk *týmpanon* drum, akin to *týptein* to beat, strike]

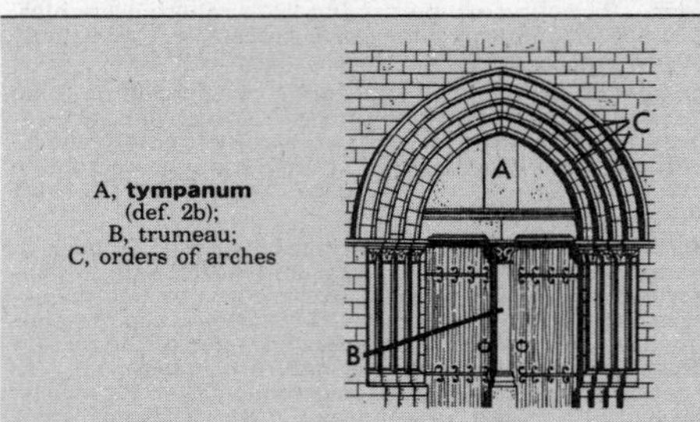

A, **tympanum** (def. 2b); B, trumeau; C, orders of arches

tym•pa•ny (tim′pə nē), *n.* **1.** *Pathol.* tympanites. **2.** *Archaic.* inflated or pretentious style; bombast; turgidity. [1520–30; < ML *tympanias* < Gk *tympaniās* tympanites]

Tyn•dale (tin′dl), *n.* **William,** c1492–1536, English religious reformer, translator of the Bible into English, and martyr. Also, **Tindal, Tindale.**

Tyn•dall (tin′dl), *n.* **John,** 1820–93, English physicist.

Tyn′dall beam′, *Physical Chem.* the visible path of light produced by the scattering action (**Tyn′dall effect′**) of the particles in a colloidal solution on a beam of light passed through it. [named after J. TYNDALL]

Tyn•dar•e•us (tin dâr′ē əs), *n. Class. Myth.* the husband of Leda and father of Clytemnestra and Castor.

tyne (tīn), *n. Chiefly Brit.* tine.

Tyne (tīn), *n.* a river in NE England, in Northumberland, flowing E into the North Sea. ab. 30 mi. (48 km) long.

Tyne′ and Wear′ (wēr), a metropolitan county in N England. 1,192,600.

Tyne•mouth (tīn′məth, tin′-), *n.* a seaport in Tyne and Wear, in NE England, at the mouth of the Tyne River. 68,861.

Tyn•wald (tin′wəld), *n.* the legislature of the Isle of Man, consisting of the lieutenant governor, the council, and the House of Keys. [< ON *thingvollr.* See THING[2]]

typ., **1.** typographer. **2.** typographic. **3.** typographical. **4.** typography.

typ•al (tī′pəl), *adj.* **1.** of, pertaining to, or constituting a type. **2.** serving as a type; representative; typical. [1850–55; TYPE + -AL[1]]

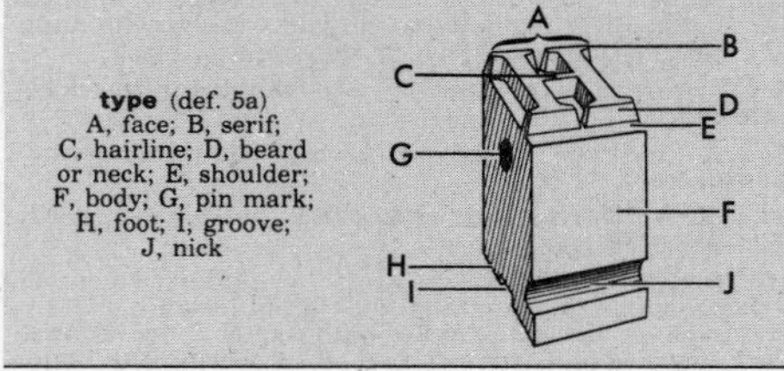

type (def. 5a) A, face; B, serif; C, hairline; D, beard or neck; E, shoulder; F, body; G, pin mark; H, foot; I, groove; J, nick

type (tīp), *n., v.,* **typed, typ•ing.** —*n.* **1.** a number of things or persons sharing a particular characteristic, or set of characteristics, that causes them to be regarded as a group, more or less precisely defined or designated; class; category: *a criminal of the most vicious type.* **2.** a thing or person regarded as a member of a class or category; kind; sort (usually fol. by *of*): *This is some type of mushroom.* **3.** *Informal.* a person, regarded as reflecting or typifying a certain line of work, environment, etc.: *a couple of civil service types.* **4.** a thing or person that represents perfectly or in the best way a class or category; model: *the very type of a headmaster.* **5.** *Print.* **a.** a rectangular piece or block, now usually of metal, having on its upper surface a letter or character in relief. **b.** such pieces or blocks collectively. **c.** a similar piece in a typewriter or the like. **d.** such pieces collectively. **e.** a printed character or printed characters: *a headline in large type.* **f.** face (defs. 19b, c). **6.** *Biol.* **a.** a genus or species that most nearly exemplifies the essential characteristics of a higher group. **b.** the one or more specimens on which the description and naming of a species is based. **7.** *Agric.* **a.** the inherited features of an animal or breed that are favorable for any given purpose: *dairy type.* **b.** a strain, breed, or variety of animal, or a single animal, belonging to a specific kind. **8.** *Logic, Ling.* Also called **type-word.** the general form of a word, expression, symbol, or the like in contrast to its particular instances: *The type "and" in "red and white and blue" has two separate tokens.* Cf. **token** (def. 8). **9.** the pattern or model from which something is made. **10.** an image or figure produced by impressing or stamping, as the principal figure or device on either side of a coin or medal. **11.** a distinctive or characteristic mark or sign. **12.** a symbol of something in the future, as an Old Testament event serving as a prefiguration of a New Testament event. **13.** *Med.* See **blood group.** —*v.t.* **14.** to write on a typewriter; typewrite or keyboard. **15.** to reproduce in type or in print. **16.** *Med.* to ascertain the type of (a blood or tissue sample). **17.** to typecast. **18.** to be a type or symbol of; typify; symbolize; represent. **19.** to represent prophetically; foreshadow; prefigure. —*v.i.* **20.** to typewrite. [1425–75; late ME: symbol, figure (< MF) < L *typus* bas-relief, ground plan < Gk *týpos* blow, impression]
—**Syn. 1.** sort, classification, form, stamp. **2.** sample, example.
—**Usage. 2.** When preceded by a modifier, TYPE meaning "kind, sort" is sometimes used without a following *of: This type furnace uses very little current.* In writing, a hyphen is often placed between TYPE and the preceding word or words: *a magnetic-type holder; a New England-type corn pudding.* This construction is frequently criticized by usage guides; it is most typical of journalistic writing and advertising and occurs rarely in formal speech or writing. In almost all cases the construction can be rendered fully standard either by restoring *of* after TYPE, with no hyphen (*this type of furnace; a New England type of corn pudding*) or by omitting TYPE altogether (*a magnetic holder*).

-type, a suffix representing **type** (*prototype*), esp. in names of photographic processes: *ferrotype.* Cf. **typo-.**

Type A, *Psychol.* **1.** of or pertaining to a pattern of behavior characterized by competitiveness, a sense of urgency, impatience, perfectionism, and assertiveness, and possibly associated with an increased risk of heart disease. **2.** of or pertaining to a person who exhibits Type A behavior.

Type B, *Psychol.* **1.** of or pertaining to a pattern of behavior characterized by an unhurried, patient, tolerant manner, an ability to relax easily, and amiability, and possibly associated with a decreased risk of heart disease. **2.** of or pertaining to a person who exhibits Type B behavior.

type•bar (tīp′bär′), *n.* (on a typewriter or some computer printers) one of a series of thin metal bars containing type and actuated by the keyboard or computer signal. [1885–90; TYPE + BAR[1]]

type-cast (tīp′kast′, -käst′), *v.,* **-cast, -cast•ing,** *adj. Print.* —*v.t., v.i.* **1.** to cast (type). —*adj.* **2.** (of text to be printed) having the type already cast. [1875–80] —**type′-cast′er,** *n.*

type•cast (tīp′kast′, -käst′), *v.t.,* **-cast, -cast•ing.** *Theat.* **1.** to cast (a performer) in a role that requires characteristics of physique, manner, personality, etc., similar to those possessed by the performer. **2.** to cast (a performer) repeatedly in a kind of role closely patterned after that of the actor's previous successes. **3.** to stereotype: *He realizes now he's been typecast as an executive errand boy.* [1930–35; TYPE + CAST]

Type I diabetes, diabetes (def. 3)

Type II diabetes, diabetes (def. 4)

Type I error, the error made in the statistical testing of a hypothesis by rejecting the null hypothesis when it is actually true. [1960–65]

Type II error, the error made in the statistical testing of a hypothesis by accepting the null hypothesis when it is actually false.

type•face (tīp′fās′), *n.* face (defs. 19b, c). See chart on next page. [1900–05; TYPE + FACE]

type′ found′er, a person engaged in the making of metallic types for printers. [1790–1800] —**type′ found′ing.** —**type′found′ry.**

type′ ge′nus, *Biol.* the genus that is formally held to be typical of the family or other higher group to which it belongs. [1830–40]

type-high (tīp′hī′), *adj. Print.* of a height equal to the distance from the foot to the face of a type: 0.918 in. (23.3 mm). [1895–1900]

type•hold•er (tīp′hōl′dər), *n. Print.* a small device for holding a few lines of type, used in stamping titles on book covers, or the like. Also called **pallet.** [TYPE + HOLDER]

type′ local′ity, **1.** *Biol.* the locality in which a type specimen was collected. **2.** *Geol.* the place at which a type section is located.

type′ met′al, an alloy for making printing types, consisting chiefly of lead and antimony, and sometimes small quantities of tin, copper, etc. [1790–1800]

type-out (tīp′out′), *n.* **1.** the act of typing or printing a text. **2.** the matter so typed or printed, esp. by a printer linked to a computer; printout. Also, **type′out′.** [n. use of the v. phrase *type out*]

type•script (tīp′skript′), *n.* **1.** a typewritten copy of a literary composition, document, or the like, esp. as prepared for a printer. **2.** typewritten matter, as distinguished from handwritten or printed matter. [1890–95, *Amer.*; TYPE + SCRIPT (on the model of *manuscript*)]

type′ sec′tion, *Geol.* the sequence of strata referred to in establishing a stratigraphic unit, as a member or formation.

type•set (tīp′set′), *v.t.,* **-set, -set•ting,** *adj.* —*v.t.* **1.** to set (textual matter) in type. —*adj.* **2.** (of written, textual matter) set in type. [1865–70; back formation from TYPESETTER]

type•set•ter (tīp′set′ər), *n.* **1.** a person who sets or composes type; compositor. **2.** a typesetting machine. [1825–35; TYPE + SETTER]

type•set•ting (tīp′set′ing), *n.* **1.** the process or action of setting type. —*adj.* **2.** used or intended for setting type. [1855–60; TYPE + SETTING]

type-site (tīp′sīt′), *n. Archaeol.* the place where artifacts characteristic of a particular culture or cultural

TYPEFACES IN COMMON USE

TEXT FACES

Baskerville

ABCDEFGHIJKLMNOPQRSTUVWXYZ abcdefghijklmnopqrstuvwxyz 1234567890

ABCDEFGHIJKLMNOPQRSTUVWXYZ abcdefghijklmnopqrstuvwxyz 1234567890

Bembo

ABCDEFGHIJKLMNOPQRSTUVWXYZ abcdefghijklmnopqrstuvwxyz 1234567890

ABCDEFGHIJKLMNOPQRSTUVWXYZ abcdefghijklmnopqrstuvwxyz 1234567890

Bodoni

ABCDEFGHIJKLMNOPQRSTUVWXYZ abcdefghijklmnopqrstuvwxyz 1234567890

ABCDEFGHIJKLMNOPQRSTUVWXYZ abcdefghijklmnopqrstuvwxyz 1234567890

Caledonia

ABCDEFGHIJKLMNOPQRSTUVWXYZ abcdefghijklmnopqrstuvwxyz 1234567890

ABCDEFGHIJKLMNOPQRSTUVWXYZ abcdefghijklmnopqrstuvwxyz 1234567890

Century Schoolbook

ABCDEFGHIJKLMNOPQRSTUVWXYZ abcdefghijklmnopqrstuvwxyz 1234567890

ABCDEFGHIJKLMNOPQRSTUVWXYZ abcdefghijklmnopqrstuvwxyz 1234567890

DeVinne

ABCDEFGHIJKLMNOPQRSTUVWXYZ abcdefghijklmnopqrstuvwxyz 1234567890

ABCDEFGHIJKLMNOPQRSTUVWXYZ abcdefghijklmnopqrstuvwxyz 1234567890

Electra

ABCDEFGHIJKLMNOPQRSTUVWXYZ abcdefghijklmnopqrstuvwxyz 1234567890

ABCDEFGHIJKLMNOPQRSTUVWXYZ abcdefghijklmnopqrstuvwxyz 1234567890

Garamond

ABCDEFGHIJKLMNOPQRSTUVWXYZ abcdefghijklmnopqrstuvwxyz 1234567890

ABCDEFGHIJKLMNOPQRSTUVWXYZ abcdefghijklmnopqrstuvwxyz 1234567890

Janson

ABCDEFGHIJKLMNOPQRSTUVWXYZ abcdefghijklmnopqrstuvwxyz 1234567890

ABCDEFGHIJKLMNOPQRSTUVWXYZ abcdefghijklmnopqrstuvwxyz 1234567890

Melior

ABCDEFGHIJKLMNOPQRSTUVWXYZ abcdefghijklmnopqrstuvwxyz 1234567890

ABCDEFGHIJKLMNOPQRSTUVWXYZ abcdefghijklmnopqrstuvwxyz 1234567890

Optima

ABCDEFGHIJKLMNOPQRSTUVWXYZ abcdefghijklmnopqrstuvwxyz 1234567890

ABCDEFGHIJKLMNOPQRSTUVWXYZ abcdefghijklmnopqrstuvwxyz 1234567890

Plantin

ABCDEFGHIJKLMNOPQRSTUVWXYZ abcdefghijklmnopqrstuvwxyz 1234567890

ABCDEFGHIJKLMNOPQRSTUVWXYZ abcdefghijklmnopqrstuvwxyz 1234567890

Times Roman

ABCDEFGHIJKLMNOPQRSTUVWXYZ abcdefghijklmnopqrstuvwxyz 1234567890

ABCDEFGHIJKLMNOPQRSTUVWXYZ abcdefghijklmnopqrstuvwxyz 1234567890

DISPLAY FACES

Avant Garde

ABCDEFGHIJKLMNOPQRSTUVWXYZ abcdefghijklmnopqrstuvwxyz 1234567890

ABCDEFGHIJKLMNOPQRSTUVWXYZ abcdefghijklmnopqrstuvwxyz 1234567890

Friz Quadrata

ABCDEFGHIJKLMNOPQRSTUVWXYZ abcdefghijklmnopqrstuvwxyz 1234567890

Futura

ABCDEFGHIJKLMNOPQRSTUVWXYZ abcdefghijklmnopqrstuvwxyz 1234567890

ABCDEFGHIJKLMNOPQRSTUVWXYZ abcdefghijklmnopqrstuvwxyz 1234567890

Helvetica Heavy

ABCDEFGHIJKLMNOPQRSTUVWXYZ abcdefghijklmnopqrstuvwxyz 1234567890

ABCDEFGHIJKLMNOPQRSTUVWXYZ abcdefghijklmnopqrstuvwxyz 1234567890

Italia

ABCDEFGHIJKLMNOPQRSTUVWXYZ abcdefghijklmnopqrstuvwxyz 1234567890

ITC Franklin Gothic

ABCDEFGHIJKLMNOPQRSTUVWXYZ abcdefghijklmnopqrstuvwxyz 1234567890

ABCDEFGHIJKLMNOPQRSTUVWXYZ abcdefghijklmnopqrstuvwxyz 1234567890

Palatino

ABCDEFGHIJKLMNOPQRSTUVWXYZ abcdefghijklmnopqrstuvwxyz 1234567890

ABCDEFGHIJKLMNOPQRSTUVWXYZ abcdefghijklmnopqrstuvwxyz 1234567890

Serif Gothic

ABCDEFGHIJKLMNOPQRSTUVWXYZ abcdefghijklmnopqrstuvwxyz 1234567890

Stymie

ABCDEFGHIJKLMNOPQRSTUVWXYZ abcdefghijklmnopqrstuvwxyz 1234567890

ABCDEFGHIJKLMNOPQRSTUVWXYZ abcdefghijklmnopqrstuvwxyz 1234567890

stage have first been found *in situ,* customarily adopted as the name of that culture or stage. [1930–35; TYPE + SITE]

type′ spe′cies, *Biol.* the species of a genus that is regarded as the best example of the generic characters of the genus; the species from which a genus was originally named. [1830–40]

type′ spec′imen, *Biol.* an individual organism from which the description of a species has been prepared. [1890–95]

type·word (tīp′wûrd′), *n. Logic., Ling.* type (def. 8).

type·write (tīp′rīt′), *v.t., v.i.,* **-wrote, -writ·ten, -writ·ing.** to write by means of a typewriter; type. [1885–90; back formation from TYPEWRITER]

type·writ·er (tīp′rī′tər), *n.* **1.** a machine for writing mechanically in letters and characters like those produced by printers' types. See illus. under **keyboard. 2.** *Print.* a type style that gives the appearance of typewritten copy. **3.** *Older Use.* a typist. [1865–70, *Amer.*; TYPE + WRITER]

type·writ·ing (tīp′rī′ting), *n.* **1.** the act or skill of using a typewriter. **2.** printed work done on a typewriter. [1865–70; TYPEWRIT(ER) + -ING[1]]

typ·ey (tī′pē), *adj.,* **typ·i·er, typ·i·est.** typy.

typh·li·tis (tif lī′tis), *n. Pathol.* inflammation of the cecum. [1855–60; < Gk *typhl(ós)* blind (for sense cf. CECUM) + -ITIS] **—typh·lit·ic** (tif lit′ik), *adj.*

typh·lol·o·gy (tif lol′ə jē), *n.* the study of the causes and treatment of blindness. [1870–75; < Gk *typhló(s)* blind + -LOGY]

typh·lo·sis (tif lō′sis), *n. Pathol.* blindness. [< Gk *typhl(ós)* blind + -OSIS disease]

typh·lo·sole (tif′lə sōl′), *n. Zool.* (in annelids and many bivalve mollusks) an infolding along the inner wall of the intestine. [1855–60; < Gk *typhlo-* (comb. form of *typhlós* blind) + *-sole* (appar. irreg. shortening of Gk *sōlḗn* pipe, channel)]

ty·pho·gen·ic (tī′fə jen′ik), *adj. Pathol.* producing typhus or typhoid fever. [1895–1900; TYPH(US) or TYPH(OID) + -O- + -GENIC]

ty·phoid (tī′foid), *Pathol.* **—***n.* **1.** Also called **ty′phoid fe′ver.** an infectious, often fatal, febrile disease, usually of the summer months, characterized by intestinal inflammation and ulceration, caused by the typhoid bacillus, which is usually introduced with food or drink. **—***adj.* **2.** resembling typhus; typhous. **3.** typhoidal. [1790–1800; TYPH(US) + -OID]

ty·phoi·dal (tī foid′l), *adj. Pathol.* of, pertaining to, or resembling typhoid. [1880–85; TYPHOID + -AL[1]]

ty′phoid bacil′lus, the bacterium *Salmonella typhosa,* causing typhoid fever. [1895–1900]

ty·phoi·din (tī foi′din), *n. Med.* a culture of dead typhoid bacilli used by cutaneous inoculation to detect the presence of a typhoid infection. [TYPHOID + -IN[1]]

Ty′phoid Mar′y, a carrier or transmitter of anything undesirable, harmful, or catastrophic. [after *Mary* Mallon (d. 1938), Irish-born cook in the U.S., who was found to be a typhoid carrier]

ty·phon (tī′fon), *n. Naut.* a signal horn operated by compressed air or steam. [appar. after *Typhon,* mythical monster associated with tempests]

ty·phoon (tī fo͞on′), *n.* **1.** a tropical cyclone or hurricane of the western Pacific area and the China seas. **2.** a violent storm or tempest of India. **3.** (*cap.*) *Mil.* **a.** a single-engine British ground attack aircraft of World War II. **b.** NATO's name for a class of nuclear-powered Soviet ballistic missile submarine carrying 20 multiwarhead missiles. [1580–90; < dial. Chin, akin to Chin *dà fēng* great wind, altered by association with Gk *tŷphōn* violent wind] **—ty·phon·ic** (tī fon′ik), *adj.*

ty·phus (tī′fəs), *n. Pathol.* an acute, infectious disease caused by several species of *Rickettsia,* transmitted by lice and fleas, and characterized by acute prostration, headache, and a peculiar eruption of reddish spots on the body. Also called **ty′phus fe′ver.** [1635–45; < NL < Gk *tŷphos* vapor] **—ty′phous,** *adj.*

typ·i·cal (tip′i kəl), *adj.* **1.** of the nature of or serving as a type or representative specimen. **2.** conforming to a particular type. **3.** *Biol.* exemplifying most nearly the essential characteristics of a higher group in natural history, and forming the type: *the typical genus of a family.* **4.** characteristic or distinctive: *He has the mannerisms typical of his class.* **5.** pertaining to, of the nature of, or serving as a type or emblem; symbolic. Also, **typ′ic.** [1605–15; < ML *typicālis,* equiv. to LL *typic(us)* (< Gk *typikós,* equiv. to *týp(os)* TYPE + *-ikos* -IC) + L *-ālis* -AL[1]] **—typ′i·cal·ly,** *adv.* **—typ′i·cal·ness, typ′i·cal′i·ty,** *n.*
—Syn. 1. normal, average, stock, usual.

ty·pi·con (tip′i kon′), *n. Eastern Ch.* the instructions for the orders of the services during the ecclesiastical year, contained in a manual. [< MGk *typikón,* n. use of neut. of *typikós* according to rule, regular, Gk: conforming to type, TYPICAL]

typ·i·fy (tip′ə fī′), *v.t.,* **-fied, -fy·ing. 1.** to serve as a typical example of; exemplify. **2.** to serve as a symbol or emblem of; symbolize; prefigure. **3.** to represent by a type or symbol. [1625–35; < L *typ(us)* TYPE + -IFY] **—typ′i·fi·ca′tion,** *n.* **—typ′i·fi′er,** *n.*

typ′ing el′ement, a spherelike device, usually of molded metal, having on its surface raised letters, numerals, and other characters. When actuated by a typewriter keyboard or computer command, the device revolves quickly, striking an inked ribbon and impressing the character on paper.

typ·ist (tī′pist), *n.* a person who operates a typewriter. [1835–45 for earlier sense "typesetter"; 1880–85 for current sense; TYPE + -IST]

ty·po (tī′pō), *n., pl.* **-pos.** *Informal.* See **typographical error.** [1890–95; shortened form; see -O]

typo-, a combining form representing **type** in compound words: *typography, typology.* Cf. **-type.**

typo., 1. typographer. **2.** typographic. **3.** typographical. **4.** typography.

typog., 1. typographer. **2.** typographic. **3.** typographical. **4.** typography.

ty·pog·ra·pher (tī pog′rə fər), *n.* a person skilled or engaged in typography. [1635–45; TYPOGRAPH(Y) + -ER[1]]

ty·po·graph·ic (tī′pə graf′ik), *adj.* of or pertaining to typography. Also, **ty′po·graph′i·cal.** [1770–80; < NL *typographicus,* equiv. to ML *typograph(ia)* TYPOGRAPHY + *-icus* -IC] **—ty′po·graph′i·cal·ly,** *adv.*

typograph′ical er′ror, an error in printed or typewritten matter resulting from striking the improper key of a keyboard, from mechanical failure, or the like.

ty·pog·ra·phy (tī pog′rə fē), *n.* **1.** the art or process of printing with type. **2.** the work of setting and arranging types and of printing from them. **3.** the general character or appearance of printed matter. [1635–45; < NL *typographia,* equiv. to Gk *týpo(s)* TYPE + *graphia* -GRAPHY]

ty·pol·o·gy (tī pol′ə jē), *n.* **1.** the doctrine or study of types or prefigurative symbols, esp. in scriptural literature. **2.** a systematic classification or study of types. **3.** symbolism. **4.** *Ling.* the study and classification of languages according to structural features, esp. patterns of phonology, morphology, and syntax, without reference to their histories. [1835–45; TYPO- + -LOGY] **—ty·po·log·i·cal** (tī′pə loj′i kəl), **ty′po·log′ic,** *adj.* **—ty′po·log′i·cal·ly,** *adv.* **—ty·pol′o·gist,** *n.*

ty·poth·e·tae (tī poth′i tē′, tī′pə thē′tē), *n.pl.* printers, esp. master printers: used in the names of associations. [< NL, equiv. to Gk *týpo(s)* TYPE + *-thetae,* Latinized pl. of Gk *thétēs* one who places; see THETIC]

typp (tip), *n. Textiles.* a number representing the aggregate of thousands of yards of yarn weighing one pound. [*t(housand) y(ards) p(er) p(ound)*]

typw., 1. typewriter. **2.** typewritten.

typ·y (tī′pē), *adj.,* **typ·i·er, typ·i·est.** (of a domestic animal) embodying the ideal characteristics of its variety or breed. Also, **typey.** [1930–35; TYPE + -Y[1]]

Tyr (tēr, tyr), *n. Scand. Myth.* the god of strife. [< ON *Týr* (pl. *tívar* gods); see TIU]

Tyr, *Biochem.* tyrosine.

ty·ra·mine (tī′rə mēn′), *n. Biochem.* an amine, $C_8H_{11}NO$, abundant in ripe cheese as a breakdown product of tyrosine by removal of the carboxyl group (COOH).

ty·ran·ni·cal (ti ran′i kəl, tī-), *adj.* **1.** of or characteristic of a tyrant. **2.** unjustly cruel, harsh, or severe; arbitrary or oppressive; despotic: *a tyrannical ruler.* Also, **ty·ran′nic.** [1530–40; < L *tyrannic(us)* (< Gk *tyrannikós,* equiv. to *týrann(os)* TYRANT + *-ikos* -IC) + -AL[1]] **—ty·ran′ni·cal·ly,** *adv.* **—ty·ran′ni·cal·ness,** *n.*
—Syn. 2. dictatorial; imperious, domineering.

ty·ran·ni·cide (ti ran′ə sīd′, tī-), *n.* **1.** the act of killing a tyrant. **2.** a person who kills a tyrant. [1640–50; < L *tyrannicīdium* (def. 1), *tyrannicīda* (def. 2). See TYRANT, -I-, -CIDE] **—ty·ran′ni·cid′al,** *adj.*

tyr·an·nize (tir′ə nīz′), *v.,* **-nized, -niz·ing.** **—***v.i.* **1.** to exercise absolute power or control, esp. cruelly or oppressively (often fol. by *over*). **2.** to govern despotically, cruelly, or oppressively. **3.** to govern or reign as a tyrant. **—***v.t.* **4.** to rule or govern tyrannically; treat oppressively. Also, *esp. Brit.,* **tyr′an·nise′.** [1485–95; < F *tyranniser* < LL *tyrannizāre,* equiv. to *tyrann(us)* TYRANT + *-izāre* -IZE] **—tyr′an·niz′er,** *n.* **—tyr′an·niz′ing·ly,** *adv.*

ty·ran·no·saur (ti ran′ə sôr′, tī-), *n.* a large, carnivorous dinosaur, *Tyrannosaurus rex,* from the Late Cretaceous Epoch of North America, that walked erect on its hind feet. See illus. under **dinosaur.** [< NL *Tyrannosaurus* (1905), equiv. to Gk *tyranno-* (comb. form repr. *týrannos* TYRANT) + *saûros* -SAUR]

tyr·an·nous (tir′ə nəs), *adj.* tyrannical. [1485–95; < L *tyrann(us)* TYRANT + -OUS] **—tyr′an·nous·ly,** *adv.* **—tyr′an·nous·ness,** *n.*

ty·ran·nu·let (ti ran′yə lit), *n.* any of numerous flycatchers of tropical America belonging to several genera and having in common chiefly their small size. [< NL *Tyrannul(us)* genus name (see TYRANT, -ULE) + -ET]

tyr·an·ny (tir′ə nē), *n., pl.* **-nies. 1.** arbitrary or unrestrained exercise of power; despotic abuse of authority. **2.** the government or rule of a tyrant or absolute ruler. **3.** a state ruled by a tyrant or absolute ruler. **4.** oppressive or unjustly severe government on the part of any ruler. **5.** undue severity or harshness. **6.** a tyrannical act or proceeding. [1325–75; ME *tyrannie* < OF < ML *tyrannia,* equiv. to L *tyrann(us)* TYRANT + *-ia* -Y[3]]
—Syn. 1. despotism, absolutism, dictatorship.

ty·rant (tī′rənt), *n.* **1.** a sovereign or other ruler who uses power oppressively or unjustly. **2.** any person in a position of authority who exercises power oppressively or despotically. **3.** a tyrannical or compulsory influence. **4.** an absolute ruler, esp. one in ancient Greece or Sicily. [1250–1300; ME *tirant* < OF < L *tyrannus* < Gk *týrannos*]
—Syn. 1. despot, autocrat, dictator.

ty′rant fly′catcher, flycatcher (def. 2). [1775–85]

tyre (tīᵊr), *n., v.t.,* **tyred, tyr·ing.** *Brit.* tire[2].

Tyre (tīᵊr), *n.* an ancient seaport of Phoenicia: one of the great cities of antiquity, famous for its navigators and traders; site of modern Sur.

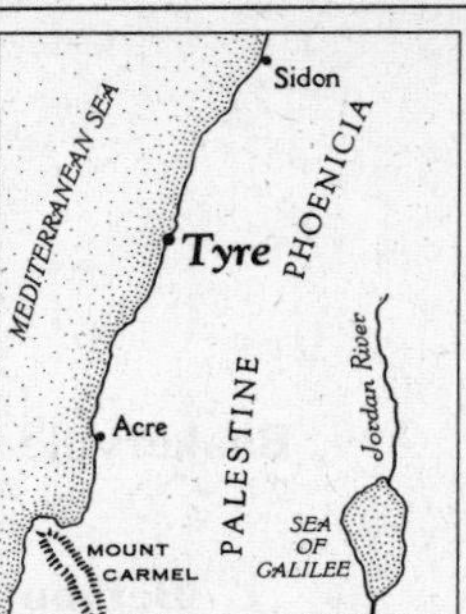

Ty·ree (tī rē′), *n.* **Mount,** a mountain in Antarctica, near Ronne Ice Shelf. ab. 16,290 ft. (4965 m).

Tyr·i·an (tir′ē ən), *adj.* **1.** of or pertaining to ancient Tyre or its people. **2.** of the color of Tyrian purple. [1505–15; < L *Tyri(us)* (< Gk *Týrios,* deriv. of *Týros* TYRE) + -AN]

Tyr′ian pur′ple, 1. Also called **Tyr′ian dye′.** a highly prized crimson or purple dye of classical antiquity, originally obtained at great expense from a certain shellfish: later shown to be an indigo derivative and synthetically produced, and now replaced by other synthetic dyes. **2.** a vivid, purplish red. [1575–85]

ty·ro (tī′rō), *n., pl.* **-ros.** a beginner in learning anything; novice. Also, **tiro.** [1605–15; < L *tīrō* recruit] **—ty·ron·ic** (tī ron′ik), *adj.*
—Syn. neophyte, learner.

Ty·rol (ti rōl′, tī-, tī′rōl; *Ger.* tē ʀōl′), *n.* **1.** an alpine region in W Austria and N Italy: a former Austrian crown land. **2.** a province in W Austria. 586,139; 4883 sq. mi. (12,645 sq. km). *Cap.:* Innsbruck. Also, **Tirol.**

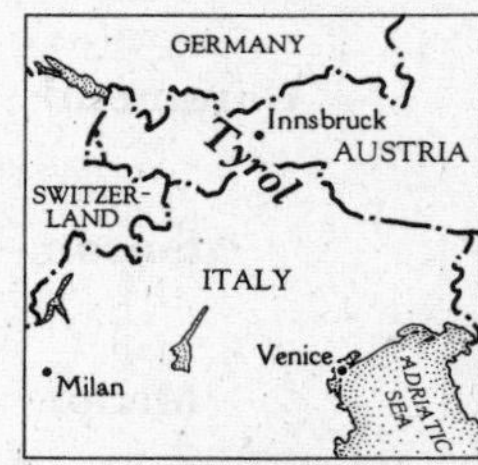

Ty·ro·le·an (ti rō′lē ən, tī-), *adj.* **1.** of, pertaining to, or characteristic of the Tyrol or its inhabitants. **2.** designating or typifying the peasant dress of the Tyrol, esp. a man's soft-brimmed, usually green felt hat with a peaked crown and a feather or brush ornament on the hatband. **—***n.* **3.** a native or inhabitant of the Tyrol. Also, **Tirolean, Tyrolese, Tirolese.** [1800–10; TYROL + *-ean* (var. of -IAN)]

Tyr·o·lese (tir′ə lēz′, -lēs′, tī′rə-), *adj., n., pl.* **-lese.** Tyrolean. Also, **Tirolese.** [1800–10; TYROL + -ESE]

Ty·ro·li·enne (ti rō′lē en′, tī-; *Fr.* tē ʀô lyen′), *n., pl.* **-li·ennes** (-lē enz′; *Fr.* -lyen′). **1.** a dance of the Tyrolean peasants. **2.** a song or melody, characteristically a yodel, suitable for such a dance. [1885–90; < F, fem. of *tyrolien* pertaining to the TYROL]

Ty·rone (ti rōn′ *or, for 2,* tī′rōn), *n.* **1.** a former administrative county in W Northern Ireland: replaced by several new districts 1973. **2.** a male given name.

ty·ro·si·nase (tī′rō si nās′, -nāz′, tir′ō-), *n. Biochem.* an oxidizing enzyme, occurring in plant and animal tissues, that catalyzes the aerobic oxidation of tyrosine into melanin and other pigments. [1895–1900; TYROSINE + -ASE]

ty·ro·sine (tī′rə sēn′, -sin, tir′ə-), *n. Biochem.* a crystalline amino acid, $HOC_6H_4CH_2CH(NH_2)COOH$, abundant in ripe cheese, that acts as a precursor of norepinephrine and dopamine. *Abbr.:* Tyr; *Symbol:* Y [1855–60; < Gk *tȳrós* cheese + -INE[2]]

ty·ro·si·ne·mi·a (tī′rō si nē′mē ə, tir′ō-), *n. Pathol.* an inherited disorder of tyrosine metabolism that can lead to liver and kidney disease and mental retardation unless controlled by a special diet. [1960–65; TYROSINE + -EMIA]

ty·ro·sin·o·sis (tī′rō si nō′sis, tir′ō-), *n. Pathol.* a condition characterized by abnormally large amounts of tyrosine in the urine, caused by faulty metabolism. [1930–35; TYROSINE + -OSIS]

Tyrr (tēr, tyr), *n.* Tyr.

Tyr·rhe′ni·an Sea′ (ti rē′nē ən), a part of the Mediterranean, bounded by W Italy, Corsica, Sardinia, and Sicily.

Tyr·rhe·us (tī′rē əs, ti′ryo͞os), *n. Rom. Legend.* a shepherd. The killing of his tame stag by Ascanius was a cause of the war between Aeneas' Trojans and the people of Latium. Also, **Tyr·rhus** (ti′rəs).

Tyr·tae·us (tûr tē′əs), *n.* fl. 7th century B.C., Greek poet.

Tyr·whitt-Wil·son (tir′it wil′sən), *n.* **Gerald Hugh, 14th Baron Ber·ners** (bûr′nərz), 1883–1950, English composer, painter, and author.

tythe (tīth), *n., v.t., v.i.,* **tythed, tyth·ing.** *Brit.* tithe.

Tyu·men (tyo͞o men′; *Russ.* tyo͞o myen′), *n.* a city in the SW Russian Federation in Asia. 456,000.

CONCISE ETYMOLOGY KEY: <, descended or borrowed from; >, whence; b., blend of, blended; c., cognate with; cf., compare; deriv., derivative; equiv., equivalent; imit., imitative; obl., oblique; r., replacing; s., stem; sp., spelling, spelled; resp., respelling, respelled; trans., translation; ?, origin unknown; *, unattested; ‡, probably earlier than. See the full key inside the front cover.

Ty·zine (tī′zēn), *Pharm., Trademark.* a brand of tetrahydrozoline.

tzad·dik (*Seph.* tsä dēk′; *Ashk., Eng.* tsä′dik), *n., pl.* ***tzad·di·kim*** (*Seph.* tsä dē kēm′; *Ashk., Eng.* tsä dē′kim, -dik′im). *Hebrew.* zaddik.

tzar (zär, tsär), *n.* czar.

tzar·dom (zär′dəm, tsär′-), *n.* czardom.

tzar·e·vich (zär′ə vich, tsär′-), *n.* czarevitch.

tza·rev·na (zä rev′nə, tsä-), *n.* czarevna.

tza·ri·na (zä rē′nə, tsä-), *n.* czarina.

tzar·ism (zär′iz əm, tsär′-), *n.* czarism.

tzar·ist (zär′ist, tsär′-), *adj., n.* czarist.

tzar·is·tic (zä ris′tik, tsä-), *adj.* czarist.

tza·rit·za (zä rit′sə, tsä-), *n.* czaritza.

tze·da·kah (*Seph.* tsə dä kä′; *Ashk.* tsə dô′kə), *n. Hebrew.* charity or the giving of charity. Also, ***zedakah.***

Tze·kung (*Chin.* dzu′gŏŏng′), *n. Older Spelling.* Zigong.

Tze·po (*Chin.* dzu′bô′), *n. Older Spelling.* Zibo.

tzet′ze fly′ (tset′sē, tet′-, tsē′tsē, tē′-). See **tsetse fly.** Also called **tzet′ze.**

Tzi·gane (tsi gän′), *adj.* **1.** (*often l.c.*) of, consisting of, or pertaining to Gypsies: *Tzigane music.* —*n.* **2.** a Gypsy, esp. a Hungarian one. [1880–85; < F *tzigane,* prob. < Hungarian *cigány,* akin to G *Zigeuner,* Rumanian *ţigan,* Serbo-Croatian *cìganin,* Bulg *tsíganin,* all ult. < MGk *(a)tsínganos,* earlier *athínganos* member of a heretical sect of Phrygia, perh. lit., "untouchable, inviolable" (Gk *a-* A-[6] + *-thinganos,* deriv. of *thingánein* to touch)]

Tzi·ga·ny (tsi gä′nē), *adj., n., pl.* **-nies.** Tzigane.

tzim·mes (tsim′is), *n.* **1.** Also, **tsimmes.** *Jewish Cookery.* any of various sweetened combinations of vegetables, fruit, and sometimes meat, prepared as a casserole or stew. **2.** fuss; uproar; hullabaloo: *He made such a tzimmes over that mistake!* [1890–95; < Yiddish *tsimes,* akin to dial. G (Swabia) *zimmes, zimbes* compote, stew, Swiss G *zimis* lunch; compound (orig. prep. phrase) with MHG *z, ze* unstressed var. of *zuo* (G *zu*) at, TO + MHG, OHG *imbiz, imbiz* snack, light meal (G *Imbiss*), n. deriv. of OHG *enbīzan* to take nourishment; see IN-[1], BITE]

tzi·tzith (*Seph. Heb.* tsē tsēt′; *Ashk. Heb., Eng.* tsit′sis), *n.* (*used with a singular or plural v.*) *Judaism.* zizith. Also, **tzi·tzit′, tzi·tzis′.**

Tzom Ge·dal·iah (tsôm′ gə däl′yə), a Jewish fast day observed on the third day of the month of Tishri in memory of the treacherous murder of Gedaliah, Jewish governor of Judah appointed by King Nebuchadnezzar of Babylonia. Also called **Fast of Gedaliah.**

Tz'u Hsi (tsōō′ shē′), 1835–1908, empress dowager of China: regent 1862–73, 1875–89, 1898–1908. Also, **Tzu′ Hsi′.**

Tzu·kung (*Chin.* dzu′gŏŏng′), *n. Wade-Giles.* Zigong.

Tzu·po (*Chin.* dzu′bô′), *n. Wade-Giles.* Zibo.

CONCISE PRONUNCIATION KEY: *act, cāpe, dâre, pärt; set, ēqual; if, ice; ox, ōver, ôrder, oil, bŏŏk, bōōt, out; up, ûrge; child; sing; shoe; thin, that;* zh as in *treasure.* ə = *a* as in *alone, e* as in *system, i* as in *easily, o* as in *gallop, u* as in *circus;* ᵊ as in *fire* (fīᵊr), *hour* (ouᵊr). l and n can serve as syllabic consonants, as in *cradle* (krād′l), and *button* (but′n). See the full key inside the front cover.

DEVELOPMENT OF MAJUSCULE								
NORTH SEMITIC	GREEK		ETR	LATIN		MODERN		
						GOTHIC	ITALIC	ROMAN
Y	Ч	Y	Y	V	V	𝔘	*U*	U

DEVELOPMENT OF MINUSCULE					
ROMAN CURSIVE	ROMAN UNCIAL	CAROL. MIN.	MODERN		
			GOTHIC	ITALIC	ROMAN
u	u	u	𝔲	*u*	u

The twenty-first letter of the English alphabet developed as a transformation of North Semitic *waw* into Greek *upsilon* (υ). (See **F, W.**) In Etruscan, the *u*-sound was signified by V, and Classical Latin monumental writing later used the V for both U and V. U and V were used interchangeably for both sounds in the early Middle Ages, with U appearing in the monumental writing and V in the manuscripts. Their separation did not crystallize until after the Middle Ages.

U, u (yo͞o), *n., pl.* **U's** or **Us, u's** or **us.** **1.** the 21st letter of the English alphabet, a vowel. **2.** any spoken sound represented by the letter *U* or *u*, as in *music, rule, curious, put,* or *jug.* **3.** something having the shape of a U. **4.** a written or printed representation of the letter *U* or *u.* **5.** a device, as a printer's type, for reproducing the letter *U* or *u.*

U (yo͞o), *pronoun. Pron. Spelling.* you: *Shoes Fixed While U Wait.*

U (yo͞o), *adj. Informal.* characteristic of or appropriate to the upper class, esp. of Great Britain. [*u(pper class)*]

U (o͞o), *n.* a Burmese title of respect applicable to a man: used before the proper name.

U, *Symbol.* **1.** the 21st in order or in a series, or, when *I* is omitted, the 20th. **2.** *Chem.* uranium. **3.** *Biochem.* uracil. **4.** *Thermodynam.* See **internal energy. 5.** *Brit.* a designation for motion pictures determined as being acceptable for viewing by all age groups. Cf. **A** (def. 11), **X** (def. 9).

U., **1.** uncle. **2.** and. [< G *und*] **3.** uniform. **4.** union. **5.** unit. **6.** united. **7.** university. **8.** unsatisfactory. **9.** upper.

u., **1.** and. [< G *und*] **2.** uniform. **3.** unit. **4.** unsatisfactory. **5.** upper.

U-235, *Chem.* See **uranium 235.** Also, **U 235.**

U-238, *Chem.* See **uranium 238.** Also, **U 238.**

U-239, *Chem.* See **uranium 239.** Also, **U 239.**

U.A.E., See **United Arab Emirates.** Also, **UAE**

ua·ka·ri (wä kär′ē), *n., pl.* **-ris.** any of several medium-sized, tree-dwelling Amazon basin monkeys of the genus *Cacajao*, the only New World monkeys having a short tail: all are now rare. [1860–65; < Tupi and Guarani *uakari*]

UAM, underwater-to-air missile.

u·a ma·u ke e·a o ka a·i·na i ka po·no (o͞o′ä mä′o͝o kā ä′ä ō kä ä′ē nä′ ē kä pō′nō), *Hawaiian.* the life of the land is maintained by righteousness: motto of Hawaii.

u. & l.c., *Print.* upper and lower case.

U.A.R., See **United Arab Republic.**

UAW, United Automobile Workers (full name: International Union of United Automobile, Aerospace, and Agricultural Implement Workers of America). Also, **U.A.W.**

U.B., United Brethren.

U·ban·gi (yo͞o bang′gē, o͞o bäng′-), *n.* **1.** French, **Oubangi.** a river in W central Africa, forming part of the boundary between Zaire and the Central African Republic, flowing W and S into the Congo (Zaire) River. 700 mi. (1125 km) long. **2.** a woman of the Sara tribe in the Central African Republic whose lips are pierced and stretched around flat wooden disks.

U·ban·gi-Sha·ri (yo͞o bang′gē shär′ē, o͞o bäng′-), *n.* former name of the **Central African Republic.** French, **Oubangi-Chari.**

U·be (o͞o′bē; *Japn.* o͝o be′), *n.* a seaport on SW Honshu, in SW Japan. 168,960.

U·be·ra·ba (o͞o′bi rä′bä), *n.* a city in E Brazil. 199,000.

U·ber·lân·dia (o͞o′bir län′dyä), *n.* a city in E Brazil. 241,000.

Ü·ber·mensch (y′bər mensh′), *n., pl.* **-mensch·en** (-men′shən). *German.* superman (def. 2).

u·bi·e·ty (yo͞o bī′i tē), *n.* the property of having a definite location at any given time; state of existing and being localized in space. [1665–75; < L *ubi* where? + *-ety*, var. (after *-i-*) of -ITY]

u·bi·que (o͝o bē′kwe; *Eng.* yo͞o bī′kwē, -bē′kwā), *adv. Latin.* everywhere.

U·biq·ui·tar·i·an (yo͞o bik′wi târ′ē ən), *Theol.* —*adj.* **1.** of or pertaining to the doctrine, esp. as advocated by Luther, that the body of Christ is omnipresent and therefore exists in the Eucharistic bread. —*n.* **2.** Also, **U·bi·quar·i·an** (yo͞o′bi kwâr′ē ən), **U·bi·quist** (yo͞o′bi-kwist). a person who advocates this doctrine. [1630–40; < NL *ubiquit(ārius)* being everywhere at once (see UBIQUITY, -ARY) + -ARIAN] —**U·biq′ui·tar′i·an·ism,** *n.*

u·biq·ui·tin (yo͞o bik′wi tin), *n.* a small protein, present in all eukaryotic cells, that participates in the destruction of defective proteins and in the synthesis of new proteins. [1985–90; UBIQUIT(OUS) + -IN[1]]

u·biq·ui·tous (yo͞o bik′wi təs), *adj.* existing or being everywhere, esp. at the same time; omnipresent: *ubiquitous fog; ubiquitous little ants.* Also, **u·biq·ui·tar·y** (yo͞o-bik′wi ter′ē). [1830–40; UBIQUIT(Y) + -OUS] —**u·biq′ui·tous·ly,** *adv.* —**u·biq′ui·tous·ness,** *n.*
—**Syn.** See **omnipresent.**

u·biq·ui·ty (yo͞o bik′wi tē), *n.* **1.** the state or capacity of being everywhere, esp. at the same time; omnipresence: *the ubiquity of magical beliefs.* **2.** (*cap.*) *Theol.* the omnipresence of God or Christ. [1570–80; < NL *ubiquitās*, equiv. to L *ubīqu(e)* everywhere + *-itās* -ITY]

u·bi sunt (o͞o′bē so͝ont′), a poetic motif emphasizing the transitory nature of youth, life, and beauty, found esp. in medieval Latin poems. [1910–15; < ML *Ubi sunt (quī ante nōs fuērunt?)* Where are (those who were before us?)]

u·bi su·pra (o͞o′bē so͞o′prä; *Eng.* yo͞o′bī so͞o′prə, -bē), *Latin.* See **u.s.** (def. 1).

U-boat (yo͞o′bōt′), *n.* a German submarine. [1910–15; < G *U-Boot*, short for *Unterseeboot* lit., undersea boat]

U bolt, a bar of iron bent into the shape of a U, fitted with a screw thread and nut at each end. [1880–85]

U.C., **1.** Upper Canada. **2.** under construction. **3.** undercover.

u.c., **1.** *Music.* una corda. **2.** *Print.* upper case.

U·ca·ya·li (o͞o′kä yä′lē), *n.* a river in W South America, flowing N from E Peru and joining the Marañón to form the Amazon. 1200 mi. (1930 km) long.

Uc·cel·lo (o͞o chel′ō; *It.* o͞ot chel′lô), *n.* **Pa·o·lo** (pä′ô-lô), (*Paolo di Dono*), 1397–1475, Italian painter.

UCR, See **Uniform Crime Report.**

U.C.V., United Confederate Veterans.

U/D, under deed.

UDAG (yo͞o′dag), *n.* a U.S. government program providing federal funds to local governments or private investors for urban redevelopment projects. [*U(rban) D(evelopment) A(ction) G(rant)*]

U·dai·pur (o͞o dī′po͝or, o͞o′dī po͝or′), *n.* **1.** a city in S Rajasthan, in NW India. 162,934. **2.** Also called **Mewar.** a former state in NW India: merged into Rajasthan state 1948.

U·dall (yo͞o′dôl *or, for 1,* yo͞od′l), *n.* **1.** Also called **Uvedale. Nicholas,** 1505–56, English translator and playwright, esp. of comedy. **2. Stewart Lee,** born 1920, U.S. politician: Secretary of the Interior 1961–69.

U.D.C., United Daughters of the Confederacy.

ud·der (ud′ər), *n.* a mamma or mammary gland, esp. when baggy and with more than one teat, as in cows. [bef. 1000; ME *uddre*, OE *ūder*; c. G *Euter*, L *ūber*, Gk *oûthar*, Skt *ū́dhar*]

U·di·ne (o͞o′dē ne), *n.* a city in NE Italy. 103,504.

Ud·murt (o͝od mo͞ort′; *Russ.* o͞od mo͞ort′), *n., pl.* **-murts,** (*esp. collectively*) **-murt** for 1. **1.** a member of a Uralic people living in the Udmurt Autonomous Republic and adjacent areas of the Kama River basin. **2.** the Permic language of the Udmurt. Also called **Votyak.** [< Russ *udmurt* < Udmurt: a self-designation (*ud-* (cf. VOTYAK) + *murt* man, human being)]

Ud′murt Auton′omous Repub′lic, an autonomous republic in the Russian Federation in Europe. 1,609,000; 16,250 sq. mi. (42,088 sq. km). *Cap.:* Izhevsk.

u·do (o͞o′dō), *n., pl.* **u·dos.** a plant, *Aralia cordata*, of the ginseng family, cultivated, esp. in Japan and China, for its edible shoots. [< Japn]

U·don Tha·ni (o͞o′dôn′ tä′nē′), a city in NE Thailand. 36,088.

Ue·le (wā′lə), *n.* a river in central Africa flowing W from NE Zaire to the Ubangi River. 700 mi. (1125 km) long.

U·fa (o͞o fä′), *n.* a city in and the capital of the Bashkir Autonomous Republic, in the Russian Federation in Europe. 1,083,000.

U.F.C., United Free Church (of Scotland).

UFO (yo͞o′ef′ō′ *or, sometimes,* yo͞o′fō), *n., pl.* **UFO's, UFOs.** any unexplained moving object observed in the sky, esp. one assumed by some observers to be of extraterrestrial origin. Also called **unidentified flying object.** Cf. **flying saucer.** [1950–55; *u(nidentified) f(lying) o(bject)*]

u·fol·o·gy (yo͞o fol′ə jē), *n.* the study of unidentified flying objects. [1955–60; UFO + -LOGY] —**u·fo·log·i·cal** (yo͞o′fə loj′i kəl), *adj.* —**u·fol′o·gist,** *n.*

UFT, United Federation of Teachers.

UFW, United Farm Workers of America.

U·gan·da (yo͞o gan′də, o͞o gän′dä), *n.* an independent state in E Africa, between NE Zaire and Kenya: member of the Commonwealth of Nations; formerly a British protectorate. 12,700,000; 93,981 sq. mi. (243,410 sq. km). *Cap.:* Kampala. —**U·gan′dan,** *adj., n.*

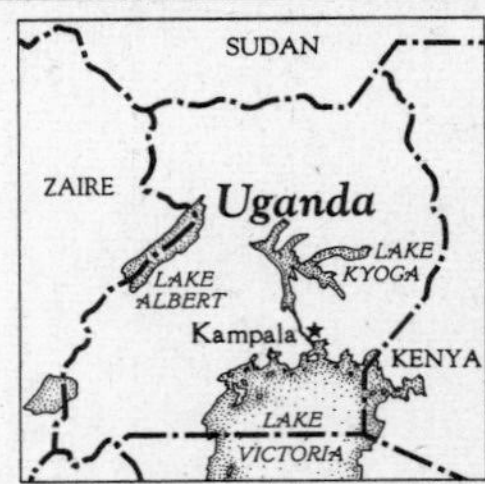

U·ga·rit (o͞o′gə rēt′, yo͞o′-), *n.* an ancient city in Syria, on the site of modern Ras Shamra: fl. 2nd millennium B.C.; excavations have yielded tablets written in cuneiform and hieroglyphic script that reveal information on Canaanite mythology.

U·ga·rit·ic (o͞o′gə rit′ik, yo͞o′-), *adj.* **1.** of or pertaining to Ugarit, its people, or their language. —*n.* **2.** Also, **U·ga·ri·tian** (o͞o′gə rish′ən, yo͞o′-). the Semitic language of the Ugaritic people, related to Hebrew and Phoenician and written in a cuneiform alphabet having 30 characters. [1935–40; UGARIT + -IC]

ugh (o͝okh, ukh, u, o͝o; *spelling pron.* ug), *interj.* **1.** (used as an exclamation expressing disgust, aversion, horror, or the like). —*n.* **2.** the sound of a cough, grunt, or the like.

Ug·li (ug′lē), *Trademark.* a large, sweet variety of tangelo, of Jamaican origin, having rough, wrinkled, yellowish skin.

ug·li·fy (ug′lə fī′), *v.t.,* **-fied, -fy·ing.** to make ugly. [1570–80; UGLY + -FY] —**ug′li·fi·ca′tion,** *n.* —**ug′li·fi′er,** *n.*

CONCISE ETYMOLOGY KEY: <, descended or borrowed from; >, whence; b., blend of, blended; c., cognate with; cf., compare; deriv., derivative; equiv., equivalent; imit., imitative; obl., oblique; r., replacing; s., stem; sp., spelling, spelled; resp., respelling, respelled; trans., translation; ?, origin unknown; *, unattested; ‡, probably earlier than. See the full key inside the front cover.

ug•ly (ug′lē), *adj.*, **-li•er, -li•est.** **1.** very unattractive or unpleasant to look at; offensive to the sense of beauty; displeasing in appearance. **2.** disagreeable; unpleasant; objectionable: *ugly tricks; ugly discords.* **3.** morally revolting: *ugly crime.* **4.** threatening trouble or danger: *ugly symptoms.* **5.** mean; hostile; quarrelsome: *an ugly mood; an ugly frame of mind.* **6.** (esp. of natural phenomena) unpleasant or dangerous: *ugly weather; an ugly sea.* [1200–50; ME *ugly, uglike* < ON *ugligr* fearful, dreadful, equiv. to *ugg(r)* fear + *-ligr* -LY] —**ug′li•ly,** *adv.* —**ug′li•ness,** *n.*
—**Syn. 1.** ill-favored, hard-featured, uncomely, unsightly, unlovely, homely. **3.** base, heinous, vile, monstrous, corrupt. **4.** disadvantageous, ominous. **5.** surly, spiteful. **6.** stormy, tempestuous. —**Ant. 1.** beautiful.

ug′ly cus′tomer, a hostile or dangerous person. [1805–15]

ug′ly duck′ling, an unattractive or unpromising child who becomes a beautiful or much-admired adult. [1880–85; after the bird in the story of the same name by Hans Christian Andersen]

U•gri•an (o͞o′grē ən, yo͞o′-), *adj.* **1.** denoting or pertaining to an ethnological group including the Magyars and related peoples of western Siberia. —*n.* **2.** a member of any of the Ugrian peoples. **3.** Ugric.

U•gric (o͞o′grik, yo͞o′-), *n.* **1.** a branch of the Uralic family of languages, consisting of Hungarian and two languages, Khanty and Mansi, spoken in western Siberia. —*adj.* **2.** Ugrian. [UGR(IAN) + -IC]

ug•some (ug′səm), *adj. Scot. and North Eng.* horrid; loathsome. [1350–1400; ME, equiv. to *ugg(en)* to fear, cause loathing (< ON *ugga* to fear, dread; cf. UGLY) + *-some* -SOME¹] —**ug′some•ness,** *n.*

uh (u, un), *interj.* **1.** (used to indicate hesitation, doubt, or a pause). **2.** huh. [1595–1605]

Uh•de (o͞o′də), *n.* **Fritz Karl Her•mann von** (frits kärl her′män fən), 1848–1911, German painter.

UHF, See **ultrahigh frequency.** Also, **uhf**

uh-huh (u hu′, un hun′), *interj.* (used to indicate agreement, confirmation, attentiveness, or general satisfaction).

uh•lan (o͞o′län, yo͞o′lən), *n.* **1.** one of a group of lancers in a light-cavalry unit, first appearing in Europe in the Polish army. **2.** one of such a group as later developed into heavy cavalry in western European armies, esp. in Germany. Also, **ulan.** [1745–55; < G < Pol *ulan* << Turk *oğlan* boy, lad]

Uh•land (o͞o′länt′), *n.* **Jo•hann Lud•wig** (yō′hän lo͞ot′-vikh, lo͞od′-), 1787–1862, German poet and writer.

uh-oh (u′ō′), *interj.* (used to indicate concern or chagrin at a mildly unfortunate event).

UHT, ultrahigh temperature.

uh-uh (un′un′, un′un′, un′un′), *interj.* (used to indicate disagreement, disapproval, or dissatisfaction).

u•hu•ru (o͞o ho͞o′ro͞o; *Eng.* o͞o ho͝or′o͞o), *n. Swahili.* freedom; independence.

UI, unemployment insurance.

u.i., ut infra.

Ui•gur (wē′go͝or), *n.* **1.** a member of a Turkish people dominant in Mongolia and eastern Turkestan from the 8th to 12th centuries A.D., and now living mainly in western China. **2.** the Turkic language of the Uigurs. —*adj.* **3.** of, pertaining to, or characteristic of the Uigurs. Also, **Ui′ghur.** —**Ui•gu•ri•an, Ui•ghu•ri•an** (wē go͝or′ē ən), **Ui•gu′ric, Ui•ghu′ric,** *adj.*

u•in•ta•ite (yo͞o in′tə īt′), *n.* an extremely pure asphalt particularly valuable for the manufacture of paints and varnishes. Also, **u•in′tah•ite′.** Also called **gilsonite.** [1885–90; named after the UINTA MOUNTAINS; see -ITE¹]

U•in′ta Moun′tains (yo͞o in′tə), a mountain range in NE Utah, part of the Rocky Mountains. Highest peak, Kings Peak, 13,498 ft. (4115 m).

u•in•ta•there (yo͞o in′tə thēr′), *n.* any hoofed North American mammal of the extinct genus *Dinoceras,* of the Eocene Epoch, having a massive body and three pairs of horns. [< NL *Uintatherium* (1872) a related genus, equiv. to *Uinta* Co., SW Wyoming, where fossils of the animal were found + Gk *thēríon* -THERE]

Uis•liu (o͝osh′lyo͞o), *n.* Uisnech.

Uis•nech (o͝osh′nəkh), *n. Irish Legend.* the father of Naoise. Also called **Uisliu.**

UIT, unit investment trust.

uit•land•er (īt′lan′dər, oit′-; *Du.* œit′län′dər), *n.* (*often cap.*) a foreigner, esp. a British settler in the Boer republics prior to the formation of the Union of South Africa. [1890–95; < Afrik < obs. D, equiv. to *uit* OUT + *land* LAND + *-er* -ER¹]

Ui•tzi•lo•poch•tli (wē′tsē lō pōch′tlē), *n.* Huitzilopochtli.

U•ji•ji (o͞o jē′jē), *n.* See under **Kigoma-Ujiji.**

Uj•jain (o͞o′jīn), *n.* a city in W Madhya Pradesh, in W central India: one of the seven holy cities of India. 203,278. Also, **U′jain.**

Uj•pest (o͞oy′pesht), *n.* a suburb of Budapest, in N Hungary. 1,940,212. German, **Neupest.**

U•jung Pan•dang (o͞o jo͝ong′ pän däng′), a seaport on SW Sulawesi (Celebes), in central Indonesia. 709,038. Formerly, **Macassar, Makassar, Makasar.**

U.K., United Kingdom.

u•kase (yo͞o kās′, -kāz′, yo͞o′kās, -kāz), *n.* **1.** (in czarist Russia) an edict or order of the czar having the force of law. **2.** any order or proclamation by an absolute or arbitrary authority. [1720–30; < F < Russ *ukáz,* ORuss *ukazŭ,* n. deriv. of *ukazati* to show, indicate, assign, command, equiv. to *u-* prefix + *kazati* to show, order] —**Syn. 2.** edict, directive, ruling, decree, fiat.

uke (yo͞ok), *n. Informal.* ukulele. [by shortening]

U•ki•ah (yo͞o kī′ə), *n.* a town in NW California. 12,035.

u•ki•yo-e (yo͞o kē′ō ā′; *Japn.* o͞o kē′yô e′), *n.* a genre style of painting and printmaking developed in Japan from the 17th to the 19th centuries and marked by the depiction of the leisure activities of ordinary people. [1895–1900; < Japn, equiv. to *uki-yo* transitory world (*uki* float + *yo* world) + *(w)e* picture (perh. < MChin; cf. Chin *huà*)]

Ukr., Ukraine.

U•kra•i•na (*Russ.* o͞o kru yē′nə), *n.* Ukraine.

U•kraine (yo͞o krān′, -krīn′, yo͞o′krān), *n.* a republic in SE Europe: rich agricultural and industrial region. 51,704,000; 233,090 sq. mi. (603,700 sq. km). *Cap.:* Kiev. Russian, **Ukraina.** Formerly, **Ukrain′ian So′viet So′cialist Repub′lic.**

U•krain•i•an (yo͞o krā′nē ən, -krī′-), *adj.* **1.** of or pertaining to Ukraine, its people, or their language. —*n.* **2.** a native or inhabitant of Ukraine. **3.** a Slavic language spoken in Ukraine, closely related to Russian. [1810–20; UKRAINE + -IAN]

u•ku•le•le (yo͞o′kə lā′lē; *Hawaiian.* o͞o′ko͞o lā′lā), *n.* a small, guitarlike musical instrument associated chiefly with Hawaiian music. Also, **u′ke•le′le.** [1895–1900, *Amer.*; < Hawaiian *'ukulele* leaping flea (*'uku* flea + *lele* to jump, leap), a nickname given to British army officer Edward Purvis (who popularized the instrument at the court of King Kalakaua), in reference to his lively playing style]

UL, Underwriters' Laboratories (used esp. on labels for electrical appliances approved by this nonprofit safety-testing organization).

'u•la•ma' (o͞o′lə mä′), *n.pl. Islam.* the doctors of Muslim religion and law. Also, **ulema.** [1680–90; < Ar *'ulamā'* learned men]

u•lan (o͞o′län, yo͞o′lən), *n.* uhlan.

U•lan Ba•tor (o͞o′län bä′tôr), a city in and the capital of the Mongolian People's Republic, in E central Asia: former holy city of Mongols. 418,000. Chinese, **Kulun.** Formerly, **Urga.**

U•la•no•va (o͞o lä′nə və), *n.* **Ga•li•na (Ser•ge•yev•na)** (gə lē′nə sûr gā′əv nə; *Russ.* gu lye′nə syir gye′yivnə), born 1910, Soviet ballerina.

U•lan U•de (o͞o län′ o͞o de′), a city in and the capital of the Buryat Autonomous Republic, in the SE Russian Federation in Asia, on the Selenga River. 353,000. Formerly, **Verkhneudinsk.**

Ul•bricht (o͝ol′brikht), *n.* **Wal•ter** (väl′tər), 1893–1973, German Communist leader: chairman of the East German Council of State 1960–73.

ULCC, a supertanker with a deadweight capacity of over 250,000 tons. Cf. **supertanker, VLCC.** [*u(ltra) l(arge) c(rude) c(arrier)*]

ul•cer (ul′sər), *n.* **1.** *Pathol.* a sore on the skin or a mucous membrane, accompanied by the disintegration of tissue, the formation of pus, etc. **2.** See **peptic ulcer. 3.** any chronically corrupting or disrupting condition, element, etc. [1350–1400; ME < L *ulcer-* (s. of *ulcus*); akin to Gk *hélkos*]

ul•cer•ate (ul′sə rāt′), *v.,* **-at•ed, -at•ing.** —*v.i.* **1.** to form an ulcer; become ulcerous: *His skin ulcerated after exposure to radioactive material.* —*v.t.* **2.** to cause an ulcer on or in: *Continued worry ulcerated his stomach.* [1375–1425; late ME < L *ulcerātus* (ptp. of *ulcerāre* to make sore), equiv. to *ulcer-* (see ULCER) + *-ātus* -ATE¹] —**ul′cer•a′tion,** *n.*

ul•cer•a•tive (ul′sə rā′tiv, -sər ə tiv), *adj.* **1.** causing ulceration. **2.** of the nature of or characterized by ulceration. [1565–75; < ML *ulcerātīvus,* equiv. to L *ulcerāt(us)* (see ULCERATE) + *-īvus* -IVE]

ul′cerative coli′tis, *Pathol.* chronic ulceration in the large intestine, characterized by painful abdominal cramps and profuse diarrhea containing pus, blood, and mucus.

ul•cer•o•gen•ic (ul′sə rō jen′ik), *adj. Pathol.* producing or inducing the formation of an ulcer. [1945–50; ULCER + -O- + -GENIC]

ul•cer•ous (ul′sər əs), *adj.* **1.** of the nature of an ulcer; characterized by the formation of ulcers. **2.** affected with an ulcer or ulcers. [1570–80; < L *ulcerōsus* full of sores, ulcerous, equiv. to *ulcer-* a sore, ULCER + *-ōsus* -OUS] —**ul′cer•ous•ly,** *adv.* —**ul′cer•ous•ness,** *n.*

u•le (o͞o′lā), *n.* **1.** caucho. **2.** a tree that produces caucho. [1840–50; < MexSp *(h)ule* < Nahuatl *ōlli* caoutchouc]

-ule, a suffix occurring in loanwords from Latin, originally diminutive nouns (*capsule; globule; nodule*) or noun derivatives of verbs (*ligule*). [< F < L *-ulus, -ula, -ulum* dim. formative with nouns of the 1st and 2d declensions << *-el-* (cf. -CLE¹, -ELLE, -OLE¹); the deverbal suffix *-ulus,* etc. (cf. CINGULUM, TUMULUS) is of distinct orig.]

u•le•ma (o͞o′lə mä′), *n.pl. Islam.* 'ulama'.

-ulent, a suffix occurring in adjectives borrowed from Latin, with the meaning "having in quantity, full of" that specified by the initial element: *corpulent; fraudulent; opulent; purulent.* Also, **-lent.** [< L *-ulentus*]

u•lex•ite (yo͞o lek′sīt), *n.* a mineral, hydrous sodium and calcium borate, $NaCaB_5O_9 \cdot 8H_2O$, occurring in arid regions in the form of white acicular crystals: a major source of borax. [1865–70; named after George L. *Ulex,* German chemist; see -ITE¹]

Ul•fi•las (ul′fi ləs), *n.* A.D. c311–c382, Christian bishop to the Goths: translated Bible into the Gothic language. Also, **Ul•fi•la** (ul′fi lə), **Wulfila.**

Ul•has•na•gar (o͞ol′häs nug′ər), *n.* a city in W Maharashtra, in W central India, NE of Bombay. 168,462.

u•lig•i•nous (yo͞o lij′ə nəs), *adj. Bot.* growing in swamps or muddy places. Also, **u•lig•i•nose** (yo͞o lij′ə-nōs′). [1570–80; < L *ūlīginōsus* full of moisture, wet, equiv. to *ūlīgin-* (s. of *ūlīgō*) moisture + *-ōsus* -OUS]

ul•lage (ul′ij), *n.* **1.** the amount by which the contents fall short of filling a container, as a cask or bottle. **2.** the quantity of wine, liquor, or the like, remaining in a container that has lost part of its contents by evaporation, leakage, or use. **3.** *Rocketry.* the volume of a loaded tank of liquid propellant in excess of the volume of the propellant; the space provided for thermal expansion of the propellant and the accumulation of gases evolved from it. [1400–50; late ME < AF *ulliage;* OF *ouillage, (h)eullage* wine needed to fill a cask, equiv. to *(a)ouill(er)* to fill (a cask) (deriv. of *ouil* eye, hole < L *oculus*) + *-age* -AGE] —**ul′laged,** *adj.*

Ulm (o͝olm), *n.* a city in E Baden-Württemberg, in S Germany, on the Danube. 103,600.

ul•ma•ceous (ul mā′shəs), *adj.* belonging to the Ulmaceae, the elm family of plants. Cf. **elm family.** [1840–50; < NL *Ulmace(ae)* family name (*Ulm(us)* a genus (L: ELM) + *-aceae* -ACEAE) + -OUS]

ul•na (ul′nə), *n., pl.* **-nae** (-nē), **-nas. 1.** *Anat.* the bone of the forearm on the side opposite to the thumb. Cf. **radius** (def. 7). See diag. under **skeleton. 2.** a corresponding bone in other vertebrates. [1835–45; < L: elbow; akin to Gk *ōlénē,* OE *eln* ELL²] —**ul′nar,** *adj.*

ulno-, a combining form of **ulna:** *ulnoradial.*

u•lot•ri•chous (yo͞o lo′tri kəs), *adj.* belonging to a group of people having woolly or crisply curly hair. [1855–60; < NL *Ulotrich(i)* (pl.) formerly a name for a division of mankind (< Gk *oulótrichos* (sing.) curly-haired, equiv. to *oûlo(s)* thick, fleecy + *-trichos* -haired, deriv. of *thríx* hair + -OUS]

-ulous, a suffix occurring in adjectives borrowed from Latin, with the meaning "inclined to do, habitually engaging in" the action specified by the initial element: *bibulous; credulous; garrulous; tremulous.* [< L *-ulus, -ula, -ulum;* see -ULE, -OUS]

ul•pan (o͞ol′pän, o͞ol pän′), *n., pl.* **ul•pa•nim** (o͞ol′pä-nēm′). an institute or school for intensive study of Hebrew, esp. by immigrants to Israel. [1945–50; < Mod Heb: lit., instruction < Aram *ūlpān*]

Ul•pi•an (ul′pē ən), *n.* (*Domitius Ulpianus*) died A.D. 228?, Roman jurist.

Ul•san (o͞ol′sän′), *n.* a city in SE South Korea. 157,088.

Ul•ster (ul′stər), *n.* **1.** a former province in Ireland, now comprising Northern Ireland and a part of the Republic of Ireland. **2.** a province in N Republic of Ireland. 229,720; 3123 sq. mi. (8090 sq. km). **3.** *Informal.* See **Northern Ireland. 4.** (*l.c.*) a long, loose, heavy overcoat, originally of Irish frieze, now also of any of various other woolen cloths. —**Ul•ster•ite** (ul′stə rīt′).

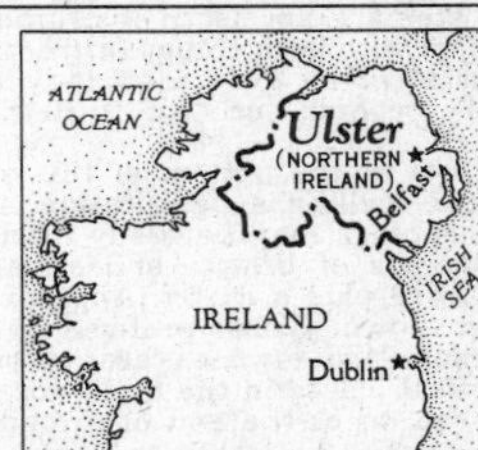

Ul•ster•man (ul′stər mən), *n., pl.* **-men.** a native or inhabitant of Ulster. [1835–45; ULSTER + MAN¹]

ult., **1.** ultimate. **2.** ultimately. **3.** ultimo.

ul•te•ri•or (ul tēr′ē ər), *adj.* **1.** being beyond what is seen or avowed; intentionally kept concealed: *ulterior motives.* **2.** coming at a subsequent time or stage; future; further: *ulterior action.* **3.** lying beyond or outside of some specified or understood boundary; more remote: *a suggestion ulterior to the purposes of the present dis-*

cussion. [1640–50; < L: farther, akin to *ultrā* on the far side; cf. ULTRA-] **—ul·te′ri·or·ly,** *adv.*
—Syn. 1. hidden, covert, undisclosed, undivulged.

ul·ti·ma (ul′tə mə), *n.* the last syllable of a word. [1860–65; < L, fem. of *ultimus,* superl. corresponding to *ulterior* ULTERIOR]

ul·ti·ma·cy (ul′tə mə sē), *n., pl.* **-cies. 1.** the state or quality of being ultimate. **2.** a basic or fundamental quality: *to question the ultimacies of one's religious beliefs.* [1835–45; ULTIM(ATE) + -ACY]

ul·ti·ma ra·ti·o re·gum (ŏŏl′ti mä′ rä′tē ō′ rā′-gŏŏm; *Eng.* ul′tə mə rā′shē ō′ rē′gəm), *Latin.* the final argument of kings (a resort to arms): motto engraved on the cannon of Louis XIV.

ul·ti·mate (ul′tə mit), *adj.* **1.** last; furthest or farthest; ending a process or series: *the ultimate point in a journey; the ultimate style in hats.* **2.** maximum; decisive; conclusive: *the ultimate authority; the ultimate weapon.* **3.** highest; not subsidiary: *ultimate goal in life.* **4.** basic; fundamental; representing a limit beyond which further progress, as in investigation or analysis, is impossible: *the ultimate particle; ultimate principles.* **5.** final; total: *the ultimate consequences; the ultimate cost of a project.* **6.** not to be improved upon or surpassed; greatest; unsurpassed: *the ultimate vacation spot; the ultimate stupidity.* **—***n.* **7.** the final point; final result. **8.** a fundamental fact or principle. **9.** the best, greatest, or most extreme of its kind. [1645–55; < LL *ultimātus* (ptp. of *ultimāre* to come to an end), equiv. to L *ultim(us)* last, most distant (see ULTIMA) + *-ātus* -ATE[1]] **—ul′ti·mate·ly,** *adv.* **—ul′ti·mate·ness,** *n.*
—Syn. 1. extreme, remotest, uttermost. **2.** supreme. **5.** See **last**[1]. **—Ant. 5.** first.

ul′timate constit′uent, *Grammar.* an element of a construction that cannot be further divided into grammatical constituents: the morphemes of an utterance are usually considered to be its ultimate constituents. Cf. **immediate constituent.**

ul′timate strength′, *Engin.* the quantity of the utmost tensile, compressive, or shearing stress that a given unit area of a certain material is expected to bear without failing. Also called **ul′timate stress′.**

ul·ti·ma Thu·le (ul′tə mə thōō′lē; *Lat.* ŏŏl′ti mä′ tōō′le), **1.** (*italics*) *Latin.* the highest degree attainable. **2.** the farthest point; the limit of any journey. **3.** the point believed by the ancients to be farthest north. Also called **Thule.** [1655–65; lit., farthest Thule]

ul·ti·ma·tum (ul′tə mā′təm, -mä′-), *n., pl.* **-tums, -ta** (-tə). **1.** a final, uncompromising demand or set of terms issued by a party to a dispute, the rejection of which may lead to a severance of relations or to the use of force. **2.** a final proposal or statement of conditions. [1725–35; < NL, n. use of neut. of LL *ultimātus.* See ULTIMATE]

ul·ti·mo (ul′tə mō′), *adv.* in or of the month preceding the current one: *on the 12th ultimo. Abbr.:* ult., ulto. Cf. **instant** (def. 11), **proximo.** [1575–85; < L *ultimō* (*mēnse* or *diē*) in the last (month) or on the last (day)]

ul·ti·mo·gen·i·ture (ul′tə mō jen′i chər, -chŏŏr′), *n.* postremogeniture. [1880–85; < L *ultim(us)* (see ULTIMA) + (PRIM)OGENITURE] **—ul·ti·mo·gen·i·tar·y** (ul′tə mō-jen′i ter′ē), *adj.*

ul·ti·sol (ul′tə sôl′, -sol′), *n.* a weathered, red and yellow acidic soil of warm, humid areas that is agriculturally productive when treated with lime and organic fertilizers. [1965–70; ULTI(MATE) + -SOL]

ulto., ultimo.

ul·tra (ul′trə), *adj.* **1.** going beyond what is usual or ordinary; excessive; extreme. **—***n.* **2.** an extremist, as in politics, religion, fashion, etc. **3.** (*cap.*) *Mil.* the British code name for intelligence gathered by decrypting German wireless communications enciphered on the Enigma machine during World War II. [independent use of ULTRA-, or shortening of words prefixed with it]

ultra-, a prefix occurring originally in loanwords from Latin, with the basic meaning "on the far side of, beyond." In relation to the base to which it is prefixed, **ultra-** has the senses "located beyond, on the far side of" (*ultramontane; ultraviolet*), "carrying to the furthest degree possible, on the fringe of" (*ultraleft; ultramodern*), "extremely" (*ultralight*); nouns to which it is added denote, in general, objects, properties, phenomena, etc., that surpass customary norms, or instruments designed to produce or deal with such things (*ultramicroscope; ultrasound; ultrastructure*). [< L *ultrā* (adv. and prep.) on the far side (of), beyond, deriv. of **ult(e)r-* located beyond]
—Note. The lists at the bottom of this and following pages provide the spelling, syllabification, and stress for words whose meanings may be easily inferred by combining the meanings of ULTRA- and an attached base word, or base word plus a suffix. Appropriate parts of speech are also shown. Words prefixed by ULTRA- that have special meanings or uses are entered in their proper alphabetical places in the main vocabulary or as derived forms run on at the end of a main vocabulary entry.

ul·tra·ba·sic (ul′trə bā′sik), *adj.* (of rocks) containing iron and magnesium, with little or no silica. Also, **ultramafic.** [1890–95; ULTRA- + BASIC]

ul·tra·cen·tri·fuge (ul′trə sen′trə fyōōj′), *n., v.,* **-fuged, -fug·ing.** *Physical Chem.* **—***n.* **1.** a high-speed centrifuge for subjecting sols or solutions to forces many times that of gravity and producing concentration differences depending on the weight of the micelle or molecule. **—***v.t.* **2.** to subject to the action of an ultracentrifuge. [1925–30; ULTRA- + CENTRIFUGE] **—ul·tra·cen·trif·u·gal** (ul′trə sen trif′yə gəl, -ə gəl), *adj.* **—ul′tra·cen·trif′u·gal·ly,** *adv.*

ul·tra·clean (ul′trə klēn′), *adj.* extremely clean, esp. free of germs: *an ultraclean laboratory.* [1965–70; ULTRA- + CLEAN]

ul·tra·con·serv·a·tive (ul′trə kən sûr′və tiv), *adj.* **1.** extremely conservative, esp. in politics. **—***n.* **2.** an ultraconservative person or group. [ULTRA- + CONSERVATIVE] **—ul′tra·con·serv′a·tism,** *n.*

ul·tra·crit·i·cal (ul′trə krit′i kəl), *adj.* hypercritical. [ULTRA- + CRITICAL] **—ul′tra·crit′i·cal·ly,** *adv.*

ul·tra·di·an (ul trā′dē ən), *adj.* of or pertaining to a biorhythm having a period of less than 24 hours. [1960–65; ULTRA- + L *di(ēs)* day + -AN]

ul·tra·fast (ul′trə fast′, -fäst′), *adj.* extremely fast: *ultrafast computers.* [ULTRA- + FAST[1]]

ul·tra·fiche (ul′trə fēsh′), *n.* a form of microfiche with the images greatly reduced in size, generally by a factor of 100 or more. [1965–70; ULTRA- + (MICRO)FICHE]

ul·tra·fil·ter (ul′trə fil′tər), *n.* **1.** *Physical Chem.* a filter for purifying sols, having a membrane with pores sufficiently small to prevent the passage of the suspended particles. **2.** *Math.* a filter in a topological space, having the property that no other filter exists in the space having among its subsets all the subsets in the given filter. **—***v.t.* **3.** *Physical Chem.* to purify by means of an ultrafilter. [ULTRA- + FILTER] **—ul·tra·fil·tra·tion** (ul′trə fil trā′shən), *n.*

ul·tra·fil·trate (ul′trə fil′trāt), *n. Physical Chem.* a liquid that has been passed through an ultrafilter. [ULTRAFILT(E)R + -ATE[1]]

ul·tra·high (ul′trə hī′), *adj.* extremely high: *ultrahigh skyscrapers of 100 stories.* [1945–50; ULTRA- + HIGH]

ul′trahigh fre′quency, *Radio.* any frequency between 300 and 3000 megahertz. *Abbr.:* UHF, uhf [1935–40] **—ul′tra·high′-fre′quen·cy,** *adj.*

ul·tra·ism (ul′trə iz′əm), *n.* **1.** extremism. **2.** an extremist point of view or act. [1815–25; ULTRA- + -ISM] **—ul′tra·ist,** *n., adj.* **—ul′tra·is′tic,** *adj.*

ul′tralarge′ crude′ car′rier, *Naut.* See **ULCC.** [1980–85; ULTRA- + LARGE]

ul·tra·left (ul′trə left′), *adj.* **1.** of or belonging to the extreme political Left; extremely liberal or radical. **—***n.* **2. the ultraleft,** the aggregate of ultraleft persons or groups. [1950–55; ULTRA- + LEFT[1]]

ul·tra·left·ist (ul′trə lef′tist), *adj.* **1.** ultraleft. **—***n.* **2.** a supporter or advocate of ultraleft causes, goals, etc. [1970–75; ULTRALEFT + -IST] **—ul′tra·left′ism,** *n.*

ul·tra·lib·er·al (ul′trə lib′ər əl, -lib′rəl), *adj.* **1.** extremely liberal, esp. in politics. **—***n.* **2.** an ultraliberal person or group. [1815–25; ULTRA- + LIBERAL] **—ul′tra·lib′er·al·ism,** *n.*

ul·tra·light (*adj.* ul′trə līt′, ul′trə līt′; *n.* ul′trə līt′), *adj.* **1.** extremely lightweight in comparison with others of its kind: *a car with an ultralight engine.* **—***n.* **2.** something that is ultralight. **3.** a small, light, inexpensive single-seat airplane that is essentially a motorized hang glider. [1970–75; ULTRA- + LIGHT[2]]

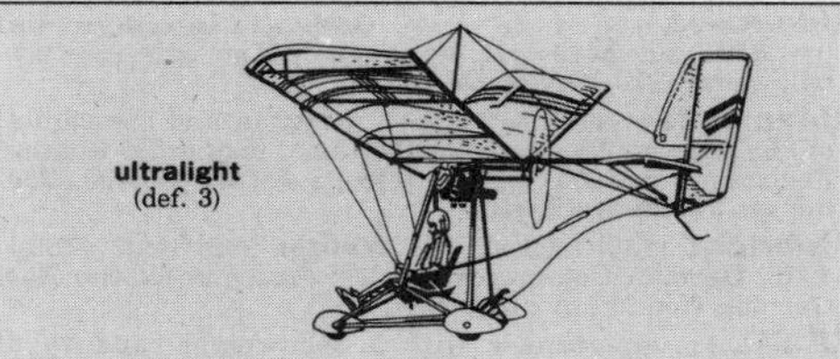
ultralight (def. 3)

ul·tra·maf·ic (ul′trə maf′ik), *adj. Geol.* ultrabasic. [1940–45; ULTRA- + MAFIC]

ul·tra·mar·a·thon (ul′trə mar′ə thon′, -thən), *n.* any footrace of 50 or more miles. [1975–80; ULTRA- + MARATHON]

ul·tra·ma·rine (ul′trə mə rēn′), *adj.* **1.** of the color ultramarine. **2.** beyond the sea. **—***n.* **3.** a blue pigment consisting of powdered lapis lazuli. **4.** a similar artificial blue pigment. **5.** any of various other pigments. **6.** a deep-blue color. [1590–1600; < ML *ultrāmarīnus,* equiv. to L *ultrā* ULTRA- + *marīnus* MARINE]

ul·tra·met·a·mor·phism (ul′trə met′ə môr′fiz əm), *n. Geol.* metamorphism during which the temperature of a rock exceeds its melting point. [ULTRA- + METAMORPHISM] **—ul′tra·met′a·mor′phic,** *adj.*

ul·tra·mi·cro·bal·ance (ul′trə mī′krə bal′əns), *n. Chem.* a balance for weighing precisely, to a hundredth of a microgram or less, minute quantities of material. [ULTRA- + MICROBALANCE]

ul·tra·mi·cro·chem·is·try (ul′trə mī′krō kem′ə-strē), *n.* the branch of microchemistry dealing with minute quantities of material weighing one microgram or less. [ULTRA- + MICROCHEMISTRY] **—ul′tra·mi′cro·chem′ist,** *n.* **—ul·tra·mi·cro·chem·i·cal** (ul′trə mī′-krō kem′i kəl), *adj.*

ul·tra·mi·cro·fiche (ul′trə mī′krə fēsh′), *n.* ultrafiche. [1965–70; ULTRA- + MICROFICHE]

ul·tra·mi·crom·e·ter (ul′trə mī krom′i tər), *n.* a micrometer calibrated to a very fine scale and capable of measuring extremely small magnitudes. [1925–30; ULTRA- + MICROMETER]

ul·tra·mi·cro·scope (ul′trə mī′krə skōp′), *n.* an instrument that uses scattering phenomena to detect the position of objects too small to be seen by an ordinary microscope. [1905–10; ULTRA- + MICROSCOPE] **—ul·tra·mi·cro·scop·ic** (ul′trə mī′krə skop′ik), **ul′tra·mi′cro·scop′i·cal,** *adj.*

ul·tra·mi·cros·co·py (ul′trə mī kros′kə pē, -mī′krə-skō′pē), *n.* the use of the ultramicroscope. [ULTRA- + MICROSCOPY]

ul·tra·mi·cro·tome (ul′trə mī′krə tōm′), *n. Histol.* a microtome capable of producing very fine slices of tissue or cellular specimens for electron microscopic examination. [1945–50; ULTRA- + MICROTOME]

ul·tra·min·i·a·ture (ul′trə min′ē ə chər, -chŏŏr′, -min′ə chər), *adj.* subminiature. [1940–45; ULTRA- + MINIATURE]

ul·tra·min·i·a·tur·ize (ul′trə min′ē ə chə rīz′, -min′-ə chə-), *v.t.,* **-ized, -iz·ing.** to reduce to an ultraminiature size or scale. Also, *esp. Brit.,* **ul′tra·min′i·a·tur·ise′.** [1940–45; ULTRA- + MINIATURE + -IZE] **—ul′tra·min′i·a·tur·i·za′tion,** *n.*

ul·tra·mod·ern (ul′trə mod′ərn), *adj.* very advanced in ideas, design, or techniques. [1835–45; ULTRA- + MODERN] **—ul′tra·mod′ern·ism,** *n.* **—ul′tra·mod′ern·ist,** *n.*

ul·tra·mon·tane (ul′trə mon tān′, -mon′tān), *adj.* **1.** beyond the mountains. **2.** of or pertaining to the area south of the Alps, esp. Italy. **3.** *Rom. Cath. Ch.* **a.** of, pertaining to, or advocating ultramontanism. **b.** of, pertaining to, or supporting the belief that the pope is the spiritual head of the Church in all countries. **4.** (formerly) north of the Alps; tramontane. **—***n.* **5.** a person who lives beyond the mountains. **6.** a person living south of the Alps. **7.** *Rom. Cath. Ch.* a person who supports ultramontanism. **8.** (formerly) a person living to the north of the Alps. [1585–95; < ML *ultrāmontānus,* equiv. to L *ultrā* ULTRA- + *montānus* MONTANE]

ul·tra·mon·ta·nism (ul′trə mon′tn iz′əm), *n.* (*sometimes cap.*) the policy of the party in the Roman Catholic Church that favors increasing and enhancing the power and authority of the pope. Cf. **Gallicanism.** [1820–30; < F *ultramontanisme,* equiv. to *ultramontain* ULTRAMONTANE + *-isme* -ISM] **—ul′tra·mon′ta·nist,** *n.*

ul·tra·mun·dane (ul′trə mun dān′, -mun′dān), *adj.* **1.** outside or beyond the earth or the orbits of the planets. **2.** outside the sphere of physical existence. [1540–50; < L *ultrāmundānus,* equiv. to L *ultrā* ULTRA- + *mundānus* MUNDANE]

ul·tra·na·tion·al·ism (ul′trə nash′ə nl iz′əm), *n.* extreme devotion to or advocacy of the interests of a nation, esp. regardless of the effect on any other nations. [ULTRA- + NATIONALISM] **—ul′tra·na′tion·al,** *adj.*

ul·tra·na·tion·al·ist (ul′trə nash′ə nl ist), *n.* **1.** an advocate of ultranationalism. **—***adj.* **2.** Also, **ul′tra·na′tion·al·is′tic.** of or pertaining to ultranationalism or ultranationalists. [1925–30; ULTRA- + NATIONALIST] **—ul′tra·na′tion·al·is′ti·cal·ly,** *adv.*

ul·tra·net (ul′trə net′), *n. Math.* a net in a topological space that is residually in every set or its complement in the space. [ULTRA- + NET[1]]

ul·tra·pure (ul′trə pyŏŏr′), *adj.* extremely pure, esp. without impurities: *ultrapure silicon for semiconductors.* [1960–65; ULTRA- + PURE] **—ul′tra·pure′ly,** *adv.* **—ul′tra·pu′ri·ty,** *n.*

ul·tra·red (ul′trə red′), *n.* (not in technical use) infrared. [1865–70; ULTRA- + RED[1]]

ul·tra·right (ul′trə rīt′), *adj.* **1.** of or belonging to the extreme political Right; extremely conservative or reactionary. **—***n.* **2. the ultraright,** the aggregate of ultraright persons or groups. [ULTRA- + RIGHT]

ul·tra·right·ist (ul′trə rī′tist), *adj.* **1.** ultraright. **—***n.* **2.** a supporter or advocate of ultraright causes, goals, or the like. [1970–75; ULTRA- + RIGHTIST] **—ul′tra·right′ism,** *n.*

ul·tra·short (ul′trə shôrt′), *adj.* **1.** extremely short. **2.** (of a wavelength) smaller than 10 meters. [1925–30; ULTRA- + SHORT]

ul·tra·son·ic (ul′trə son′ik), *adj.* of, pertaining to, or utilizing ultrasound. [1925–30; ULTRA- + SONIC] **—ul′tra·son′i·cal·ly,** *adv.*

ul·tra·son·ics (ul′trə son′iks), *n.* (*used with a singular v.*) the branch of science that deals with the effects of sound waves above human perception. [1930–35; see ULTRASONIC, -ICS]

ul·tra·so·nog·ra·phy (ul′trə sə nog′rə fē, -sō-), *n.* a diagnostic imaging technique utilizing reflected high-frequency sound waves to delineate, measure, or examine internal body structures or organs. [1950–55; ULTRA- + SONO- + -GRAPHY]

ul·tra·sound (ul′trə sound′), *n.* **1.** *Physics.* sound with a frequency greater than 20,000 Hz, approximately

CONCISE ETYMOLOGY KEY: <, descended or borrowed from; >, whence; b., blend of, blended; c., cognate with; cf., compare; deriv., derivative; equiv., equivalent; imit., imitative; obl., oblique; r., replacing; s., stem; sp., spelling, spelled; resp., respelling, respelled; trans., translation; ?, origin unknown; *, unattested; ‡, probably earlier than. See the full key inside the front cover.

ul′tra·a·bys′mal, *adj.*
ul′tra·care′ful, *adj.;* **-ly,** *adv.*
ul′tra·cas′u·al, *adj.;* **-ly,** *adv.* **-ness,** *n.*
ul′tra·cau′tious, *adj.;* **-ly,** *adv.;* **-ness,** *n.*
ul′tra·chic′, *adj.*
ul′tra·civ′i·lized′, *adj.*
ul′tra·com·mer′cial, *adj.*
ul′tra·com·pact′, *adj.*
ul′tra·com′pe·tent, *adj.*
ul′tra·con′fi·dent, *adj.*
ul′tra·con·tem′po·rar′y, *adj., n., pl.* **-rar·ies.**
ul′tra·con·ven′ient *adj.;* **-ly,** *adv.*
ul′tra·cool′, *adj.*
ul′tra·dense′, *adj.*
ul′tra·dis′tant, *adj.*
ul′tra·dry′, *adj.*
ul′tra·en′er·get′ic, *adj.*
ul′tra·ex·clu′sive, *adj.;* **-ly,** *adv.;* **-ness,** *n.*
ul′tra·fa·mil′iar, *adj.*
ul′tra·fash′ion·a·ble, *adj.;* **-bly,** *adv.*
ul′tra·fas·tid′i·ous, *adj.;* **-ly,** *adv.;* **-ness,** *n.*
ul′tra·fem′i·nine, *adj.*
ul′tra·fine′, *adj.*
ul′tra·glam′or·ous, *adj.*
ul′tra·haz′ard·ous, *adj.*
ul′tra·heav′y, *adj.*
ul′tra·hot′, *adj.*
ul′tra·hu′man, *adj.*
ul′tra·large′, *adj.*
ul′tra·light′weight′, *adj.*
ul′tra·low′, *adj.*
ul′tra·mas′cu·line, *adj.*
ul′tra·mil′i·tant, *adj.*
ul′tra·or′tho·dox′, *adj.*
ul′tra·par′a·dox′i·cal, *adj.;* **-ly,** *adv.*
ul′tra·pas′teur·ized′, *adj.*
ul′tra·pa′tri·ot′ic, *adj.;* **-ly,** *adv.*
ul′tra·pow′er·ful, *adj.*
ul′tra·prac′ti·cal, *adj.*

the upper limit of human hearing. 2. *Med.* the application of ultrasonic waves to therapy or diagnostics, as in deep-heat treatment of a joint or imaging of internal structures. Cf. **ultrasonography.** [1920–25; ULTRA- + SOUND[1]]

ul·tra·struc·ture (ul′trə struk′chər), *n. Cell Biol.* the structures of a cell that are revealed by electron microscopy. Also called **fine structure.** [1935–40; ULTRA- + STRUCTURE] —**ul′tra·struc′tur·al,** *adj.*

Ul·tra·suede (ul′trə swād′), *Trademark.* a brand of washable, synthetic, suedelike fabric.

ul·tra·thin (ul′trə thin′), *adj.* extremely thin: *an ultrathin wristwatch.* [1945–50; ULTRA- + THIN]

ul·tra·trop·i·cal (ul′trə trop′i kəl), *adj.* 1. outside the tropics. 2. hotter than the average or usual tropical climate. [1850–55; ULTRA- + TROPICAL]

ul·tra·vi·o·let (ul′trə vī′ə lit), *adj.* 1. beyond the violet in the spectrum, corresponding to light having wavelengths shorter than 4000 angstrom units. 2. pertaining to, producing, or utilizing light having such wavelengths: *an ultraviolet lamp.* Cf. **infrared.** —*n.* 3. ultraviolet radiation. [1870–75; ULTRA- + VIOLET]

ultravi′olet fil′ter, *Photog.* a filter used on a lens to absorb ultraviolet radiation that may impart an undesirable blue cast to a photograph. Also called **UV filter.**

ul·tra vi·res (ul′trə vī′rēz), *Law.* beyond the legal power or authority of a corporation, corporate officer, etc. (opposed to *intra vires*). [1785–95; < L *ultrā vīrēs* lit., beyond strength]

ul·tra·vi·rus (ul′trə vī′rəs), *n., pl.* **-rus·es.** See **filterable virus.** [ULTRA- + VIRUS]

u·lu (o͞o′lo͞o), *n.* a knife with a broad, nearly semicircular blade joined to a short haft at a right angle to the unsharpened side: a traditional tool of Eskimo women. [< Inuit]

U·lú·a (o͞o lo͞o′ä), *n.* a river in NW Honduras, flowing NE to the Caribbean Sea. ab. 200 mi. (320 km) long.

ul·u·lant (ul′yə lənt, yo͞ol′-), *adj.* howling; ululating. [1865–70; < L *ululant-* (s. of *ululāns*), prp. of *ululāre.* See ULULATE, -ANT]

ul·u·late (ul′yə lāt′, yo͞ol′-), *v.i.,* **-lat·ed, -lat·ing.** 1. to howl, as a dog or a wolf; hoot, as an owl. 2. to utter howling sounds, as in shrill, wordless lamentation; wail. 3. to lament loudly and shrilly. [1615–25; < L *ululātus,* ptp. of *ululāre* to howl, shriek, of imit. orig.; see -ATE[1]] —**ul′u·la′tion,** *n.*

Ul·ya·novsk (o͞ol yä′nôfsk, -nofsk; *Russ.* o͞o lyä′nəfsk), *n.* a city in the W Russian Federation, on the Volga River: birthplace of Lenin. 625,000. Formerly, **Simbirsk.**

U·lys·ses (yo͞o lis′ēz; *also Brit.* yo͞o′lə sēz′), *n.* 1. Latin name for **Odysseus.** 2. (*italics*) a psychological novel (1922) by James Joyce. 3. a male given name.

um (um, UN, əm, ən), *interj.* (used as an expression of doubt, hesitation, deliberation, interest, etc.)

U·may·yad (o͞o mī′ad), *n.* Omayyad.

um·bel (um′bəl), *n. Bot.* an inflorescence in which a number of flower stalks or pedicels, nearly equal in length, spread from a common center. See illus. under **inflorescence.** [1590–1600; < L *umbella* a sunshade, parasol, deriv. of *umbra* shadow, shade; for formation see CASTELLUM]

um·bel·late (um′bə lit, -lāt′, um bel′it), *adj.* having or forming an umbel or umbels. [1750–60; < NL *umbellātus,* equiv. to L *umbell(a)* (see UMBEL) + *-ātus* -ATE[1]] —**um′bel·lar, um′bel·lat′ed,** *adj.* —**um′bel·late·ly,** *adv.*

um·bel·let (um′bə lit), *n.* an umbellule. [1785–95; < L *umbell(a)* (see UMBEL) + -ET]

um·bel·lif·er·ous (um′bə lif′ər əs), *adj.* 1. bearing an umbel or umbels. 2. belonging to the Umbelliferae, the parsley family of plants. Cf. **parsley family.** [1655–65; < NL *umbellifer* (*umbelli-,* comb. form of L *umbella* (see UMBEL) + *-fer* -FER) + -OUS]

um·bel·lule (um′bəl yo͞ol′, um bel′yo͞ol), *n.* one of the secondary umbels in a compound umbel. [1785–95; < NL *umbellula,* equiv. to L *umbell(a)* (see UMBEL) + *-ula* -ULE] —**um·bel·lu·late** (um bel′yə lit, -lāt′), *adj.*

um·ber (um′bər), *n.* 1. an earth consisting chiefly of a hydrated oxide of iron and some oxide of manganese, used in its natural state as a brown pigment **(raw umber)** or, after heating, as a reddish-brown pigment **(burnt umber).** 2. the color of such a pigment; dark dusky brown or dark reddish brown. 3. *Ichthyol.* the European grayling, *Thymallus thymallus.* 4. *North Eng. Dial.* shade; shadow. —*adj.* 5. of the color umber. —*v.t.* 6. to color with or as if with umber. [1250–1300; ME *umbre, umber* shade, shadow < OF *umbre* < L *umbra;* in sense "earth" < F *terre d'ombre* or It *terra di ombra*]

Um·ber·to (*It.* o͞om beR′tô), *n.* See **Humbert I.**

um·bil·i·cal (um bil′i kəl), *adj.* 1. of, pertaining to, or characteristic of an umbilicus or umbilical cord. 2. joined together by or as if by an umbilical cord; heavily dependent in a close relationship. 3. adjacent to or located near the navel; central to the abdomen: *the umbilical region.* 4. serving as or containing a conduit through which power is transferred, esp. to a unit that will be or is designed to be ultimately self-sufficient or independent: *an umbilical cable for launching a rocket; an umbilical plug for starting jet engines.* —*n.* 5. See **umbilical cord.** [1535–45; < ML *umbilicālis,* equiv. to L *umbilīc(us)* (see UMBILICUS) + *-ālis* -AL[1]] —**um·bil′i·cal·ly,** *adv.*

umbil′ical cord′, 1. *Anat.* a cord or funicle connecting the embryo or fetus with the placenta of the mother and transporting nourishment from the mother and wastes from the fetus. 2. any electrical, fuel, or other cable or connection for servicing, operating, or testing equipment, as in a rocket or missile, that is disconnected from the equipment at completion. 3. *Aerospace Slang.* a strong lifeline by which an astronaut on a spacewalk is connected to the vehicle and supplied with air, a communication system, etc. [1745–55; 1965–70 for def. 2]

umbil′ical her′nia, *Pathol.* a hernia of the umbilicus.

um·bil·i·cate (um bil′i kit, -kāt′), *adj.* 1. having the form of an umbilicus or navel. 2. having an umbilicus. Also, **um·bil′i·cat′ed.** [1690–1700; < L *umbilicātus,* equiv. to *umbilīc(us)* (see UMBILICUS) + *-ātus* -ATE[1]]

um·bil·i·ca·tion (um bil′i kā′shən), *n.* 1. a central navellike depression. 2. an umbilicate condition or formation. [1870–75; UMBILIC(US) + -ATION]

um·bil·i·cus (um bil′i kəs, um′bə lī′kəs), *n., pl.* **-bil·i·ci** (-bil′ə sī′, -bə lī′sī). 1. *Anat.* the depression in the center of the surface of the abdomen indicating the point of attachment of the umbilical cord to the embryo; navel. 2. *Bot., Zool.* a navellike formation, as the hilum of a seed. [1605–15; < L *umbilīcus* navel, middle, center; see NAVEL]

um·bil·i·form (um bil′ə fôrm′), *adj.* having the form of an umbilicus. [UMBILI(CUS) + -FORM]

um′ble pie′ (um′bəl). See **humble pie** (def. 1). [1655–65]

um·bles (um′bəlz), *n.pl.* numbles. [1400–50; late ME]

um·bo (um′bō), *n., pl.* **um·bo·nes** (um bō′nēz), **um·bos.** 1. a boss on a shield, as one at the center of a circular shield. 2. any similar boss or protuberance. 3. *Zool.* the beak of a bivalve shell; the protuberance of each valve above the hinge. 4. *Anat.* the depressed area on the outer surface of the tympanic membrane. 5. a blunt or rounded protuberance arising from a surface, as on a pine cone scale. [1715–25; < L *umbō* boss (of a shield), knob, projecting part; akin to *umbilīcus* (see UMBILICUS)]

um·bo·nal (um′bə nl), *adj.* 1. having the shape or appearance of an umbo; bosslike: *an umbonal structure.* 2. of, pertaining to, or near the umbo: *the umbonal region.* Also, **um·bon·ic** (um bon′ik). [1850–55; < L *umbōn-* (s. of *umbō;* see UMBO) + -AL[1]]

um·bo·nate (um′bə nit, -nāt′), *adj.* 1. having an umbo or projecting boss. 2. shaped like an umbo; having a rounded convex form: *an umbonate fungus.* [1820–30; < L *umbōn-* (s. of *umbō;* see UMBO) + -ATE[1]]

um·bra (um′brə), *n., pl.* **-bras, -brae** (-brē). 1. shade; shadow. 2. the invariable or characteristic accompaniment or companion of a person or thing. 3. *Astron.* **a.** the complete or perfect shadow of an opaque body, as a planet, where the direct light from the source of illumination is completely cut off. Cf. **penumbra** (def. 1a). **b.** the dark central portion of a sunspot. Cf. **penumbra** (def. 1b). 4. a phantom or shadowy apparition, as of someone or something not physically present; ghost; spectral image. [1590–1600; < L: shade, shadow] —**um′bral,** *adj.*

um·brage (um′brij), *n.* 1. offense; annoyance; displeasure: *to feel umbrage at a social snub; to give umbrage to someone; to take umbrage at someone's rudeness.* 2. the slightest indication or vaguest feeling of suspicion, doubt, hostility, or the like. 3. leaves that afford shade, as the foliage of trees. 4. shade or shadows, as cast by trees. 5. a shadowy appearance or semblance of something. [1400–50; late ME < OF; see UMBRA, -AGE] —**Syn.** 1. pique, grudge, resentment.

um·bra·geous (um brā′jəs), *adj.* 1. creating or providing shade; shady: *an umbrageous tree.* 2. apt to take offense. [1580–90; UMBRAGE + -OUS] —**um·bra′geous·ly,** *adv.* —**um·bra′geous·ness,** *n.*

um·brel·la (um brel′ə), *n.* 1. a light, small, portable, usually circular cover for protection from rain or sun, consisting of a fabric held on a collapsible frame of thin ribs radiating from the top of a carrying stick or handle. 2. the saucer- or bowl-shaped, gelatinous body of a jellyfish; bell. 3. something that covers or protects from above, as military aircraft safeguarding surface forces: *an air umbrella.* 4. any general kind of protection: *a price umbrella.* 5. something, as an organization or policy, that covers or encompasses a number of groups or elements. —*adj.* 6. shaped like or intended to perform the function of an umbrella. 7. having the quality or function of covering or applying simultaneously to a number of similar items, elements, or groups: *an umbrella organization; umbrella coverage in an insurance policy.* [1600–10; 1965–70 for def. 7; < It *ombrella,* earlier var. of *ombrello* < LL *umbrella,* alter. (with influence of L *umbra* shade) of L *umbella* sunshade. See UMBEL] —**um·brel′la·less,** *adj.* —**um·brel′la·like′,** *adj.*

umbrel′la bird′, any of several large trogons of the genus *Cephalopterus,* of Central and South America, as *C. ornatus,* having an umbrellalike crest above the head. Also, **um·brel′la·bird′.** [1840–50]

umbrel′la palm′, an Australian feather palm, *Hedyscepe canterburyana,* characterized by the umbrellalike manner of growth of its leaves. [1790–1800]

umbrel′la pine′, 1. a Japanese evergreen tree, *Sciadopitys verticillata,* having linear leaves growing in umbrellalike whorls, cultivated as an ornamental. 2. See **stone pine** (def. 1). Also called **parasol pine.** [1870–75]

umbrel′la plant′, 1. an African plant, *Cyperus alternifolius,* of the sedge family, that has several stems growing directly upward from a mass of roots and an umbrella-shaped cluster of leaves at the top of each stem. 2. *North Midland U.S.* the May apple plant. 3. Also called **wild buckwheat.** any of various plants belonging to the genus *Eriogonum,* of the buckwheat family, native to the western U.S. and Mexico, having rounded heads or umbels of white, yellow, or red flowers. [1870–75]

umbrel′la skirt′, a full skirt with many gores that flare gradually from the waist to the hem.

umbrel′la step′, (in the game of giant steps) a step executed by extending one foot forward and whirling on the heel. Cf. **baby step.**

umbrel′la tent′, a small tent with a metal frame consisting of ribs that radiate from a single supporting pole. [1890–95]

umbrel′la tree′, 1. an American magnolia, *Magnolia tripetala,* having large leaves in umbrellalike clusters. 2. any of various other trees resembling an umbrella. [1730–40, *Amer.*]

um·brette (um bret′), *n.* hammerhead (def. 3). [1880–85; < NL *umbretta* < F *ombrette* shade, shadow. See UMBRA, -ETTE]

Um·bri·a (um′brē ə; *It.* o͞om′brē ä), *n.* 1. an ancient district in central and N Italy. 2. a region in central Italy. 799,721; 3270 sq. mi. (8470 sq. km).

Um·bri·an (um′brē ən), *adj.* 1. of or pertaining to Umbria, its inhabitants, or their language. —*n.* 2. a native or inhabitant of Umbria. 3. the extinct Italic language of the ancient Umbrians. [1595–1605; UMBRI(A) + -AN]

Um·bri·el (um′brē el′), *n. Astron.* a moon of the planet Uranus.

um·brif·er·ous (um brif′ər əs), *adj.* casting or making shade. [1610–20; < L *umbrifer* shade-bringing, shady (*umbri-,* comb. form of *umbra* shade + *-fer* -FER) + -OUS] —**um·brif′er·ous·ly,** *adv.*

Um·bun·du (əm bo͝on′do͞o), *n.* Mbundu (def. 2).

U·me (ʏ′mə), *n.* a river in N Sweden, flowing SE from the W border to the Gulf of Bothnia. ab. 285 mi. (460 km) long.

U·me·å (ʏ′mə ô′), *n.* a city in NE Sweden, on the Gulf of Bothnia. 81,088.

u·mi·ak (o͞o′mē ak′), *n.* an open Eskimo boat that consists of a wooden frame covered with skins and provided with several thwarts: used for transport of goods and passengers. [1760–70; < Inuit *umiaq* women's boat]

um·laut (o͝om′lout), *Ling.* —*n.* 1. a mark (¨) used as a diacritic over a vowel, as *ä, ö, ü,* to indicate a vowel sound different from that of the letter without the diacritic, esp. as so used in German. Cf. **dieresis.** 2. (in Germanic languages) assimilation in which a vowel is influenced by a following vowel or semivowel; apophony. —*v.t.* 3. to modify by umlaut. 4. to write an umlaut over. [1835–45; < G, equiv. to *um-* about (i.e., changed) + *Laut* sound]

um·mah (um′ə), *n. Islam.* the Islamic community. Also, **um′ma.** [1880–85; < Ar: lit., nation]

ump (ump), *n., v.t., v.i., Slang.* umpire. [shortened form]

umph (əm, əmf; *spelling pron.* umf), *interj., v.i., v.t.* humph.

um·pir·age (um′pīər ij, -pər ij), *n.* 1. the office or authority of an umpire. 2. the decision of an umpire; arbitrament. [1480–90; UMPIRE + -AGE]

um·pire (um′pīər), *n., v.,* **-pired, -pir·ing.** —*n.* 1. a person selected to rule on the plays in a game. 2. one selected to settle disputes about the application of settled rules or usages; a person agreed on by disputing parties to arbitrate their differences. —*v.t.* 3. to act as umpire in (a game). 4. to decide or settle (a controversy, dispute, or the like) as umpire; arbitrate. —*v.i.* 5. to act as umpire. [1350–1400; ME *umpere,* var. of *noumpere* (*a noumpere* taken as *an oumpere;* cf. ADDER, APRON) < OF *nomper, nonper* arbiter, i.e., one not equal. See NON-, PEER[1]] —**Syn.** 1. referee, arbiter, arbitrator. 2. See **judge.**

ump·teen (ump′tēn′), *adj. Informal.* innumerable;

CONCISE PRONUNCIATION KEY: act, cāpe, dâre, pärt; set, ēqual; if, īce; ox, ōver, ôrder, oil, bo͝ok, bo͞ot, out; up, ûrge; child; sing; shoe; thin, *th*at; zh as in *treasure.* ə = *a* as in *alone, e* as in *system, i* as in *easily, o* as in *gallop, u* as in *circus;* ə as in *fire* (fīər), *hour* (ouər). l and n can serve as syllabic consonants, as in *cradle* (krād′l), and *button* (but′n). See the full key inside the front cover.

ul′tra·pre·cise′, *adj.*
ul′tra·pre·ci′sion, *n.*
ul′tra·pro·gres′sive, *adj., n.;* **-ly,** *adv.;* **-ness,** *n.*
ul′tra·pure′, *adj.;* **-ly,** *adv.*
ul′tra·rad′i·cal, *adj., n.;* **-ly,** *adv.*
ul′tra·rap′id, *adj.;* **-ly,** *adv.*
ul′tra·rare′, *adj.;* **-ly,** *adv.*
ul′tra·rar′e·fied′, *adj.*
ul′tra·ra′tion·al, *adj.;* **-ly,** *adv.*
ul′tra·re′al·ism, *n.*
ul′tra·re′al·ist, *n.*
ul′tra·re′al·is′tic, *adj.*
ul′tra·re·fined′, *adj.*
ul′tra·rel′a·tiv·is′tic, *adj.*
ul′tra·re·li′a·ble, *adj.;* **-ly,** *adv.*
ul′tra·re·li′gious, *adj.;* **-ly** *adv.;* **-ness,** *n.*
ul′tra·re·spect′a·ble, *adj.;* **-bly,** *adv.;* **-ble·ness,** *n.*
ul′tra·rev′o·lu′tion·ar′y, *adj., n., pl.* **-ar·ies.**
ul′tra·rich′, *adj., n.*
ul′tra·ro·man′tic, *adj.*
ul′tra·roy′al·ist, *n., adj.*
ul′tra·safe′, *adj.*
ul′tra·se′cret, *adj.;* **-ly,** *adv.*
ul′tra·seg′re·ga′tion·ist, *n., adj.*
ul′tra·sen′si·tive, *adj.;* **-ly,** *adv.*
ul′tra·se′ri·ous, *adj.;* **-ly,** *adv.;* **-ness,** *n.*
ul′tra·sharp′, *adj.*
ul′tra·sim′ple, *adj.*
ul′tra·slick′, *adj.*
ul′tra·slow′, *adj.;* **-ly,** *adv.*
ul′tra·small′, *adj.*
ul′tra·smart′, *adj.*
ul′tra·soft′, *adj.;* **-ly,** *adv.;* **-ness,** *n.*
ul′tra·so·phis′ti·cat′ed, *adj.;* **-ly,** *adv.*
ul′tra·vi′o·lent, *adj.;* **-ly,** *adv.*
ul′tra·vir′ile, *adj.*
ul′tra·vi·ril′i·ty, *n.*
ul′tra·wide′, *adj.*

many. Also, **ump·steen** (ump′stēn′), **um′teen′.** [1915–20; *ump(ty),* fanciful designation for an indeterminate number (with *-ty* as in *twenty,* etc.) + -TEEN]

ump·teenth (ump′tēnth′), *adj. Informal.* of an indefinitely large number in succession: *He was the umpteenth person to arrive.* Also, **um·teenth** (um′tēnth′). [1915–20; UMPTEEN + -TH[2]]

ump·ty-umpth (ump′tē umpth′), *adj.* umpteenth. Also, **ump·ty-ump** (ump′tē ump′).

'um·rah (um′rə), *n. Islam.* the pilgrimage, consisting of rituals performed at various shrines, made by a Muslim upon entering Mecca: often part of the hajj. Also, **'um′ra.** Also called **lesser pilgrimage.** [< Ar: lit., visit]

UMT, universal military training.

Um·ta·li (o͝om tä′lē), *n.* former name of **Mutare.**

Um·ta·ta (o͝om tä′tə), *n.* a city in and the capital of Transkei, SE Africa. 24,805.

UMW, United Mine Workers. Also, **U.M.W.**

un (ən), *pron. Dial.* one: *young uns; He's a bad un.* Also, **'un.**

UN, See **United Nations** (def. 1). Also, **U.N.**

un-[1], a prefix meaning "not," freely used as an English formative, giving negative or opposite force in adjectives and their derivative adverbs and nouns (*unfair; unfairly; unfairness; unfelt; unseen; unfitting; unformed; unheard-of; un-get-at-able*), and less freely used in certain other nouns (*unrest; unemployment*). [ME *un-, on-,* OE; c. D *on-,* Goth, G *un-,* ON *ū-, ō-;* akin to L *in-,* Gk *an-, a-.* See A-[6], AN-[1], IN-[3]]
—**Syn.** See **in-**[3].
—**Note.** The lists at the bottom of this and following pages provide the spelling, syllabification, and stress for words whose meanings may be easily inferred by combining the meanings of UN-[1] or UN-[2] and an attached base word, or base word plus a suffix. Appropriate parts of speech are also shown. Words formed with these prefixes that have special meanings or uses are entered in their proper alphabetical places in the main vocabulary or as derived forms run on at the end of a main vocabulary entry.

un-[2], a prefix freely used in English to form verbs expressing a reversal of some action or state, or removal, deprivation, release, etc. (*unbend; uncork; unfasten;* etc.), or to intensify the force of a verb already having such a meaning (*unloose*). [ME, OE *un-, on-;* c. Goth *and-,* D *ont-,* G *ent-;* akin to L *ante,* Gk *anti;* cf. ANTE-, ANTI-]
—**Note.** See **un-**[1].

U·na (o͞o′nə, yo͞o′-), *n.* a female given name: from a Latin word meaning "one."

un·a·bat·ed (un′ə bā′tid), *adj.* with undiminished force, power, or vigor. [1605–15; UN-[1] + ABATED] —**un′·a·bat′ed·ly,** *adv.*

un·a·ble (un ā′bəl), *adj.* lacking the necessary power, competence, etc., to accomplish some specified act: *He was unable to swim.* [1350–1400; ME; see UN-[1], ABLE]
—**Syn.** See **incapable.**

un·a·bridged (un′ə brijd′), *adj.* **1.** not abridged or shortened, as a book. —*n.* **2.** a dictionary that has not been reduced in size by omission of terms or definitions; the most comprehensive edition of a given dictionary. [1590–1600; UN-[1] + ABRIDGED]
—**Syn. 1.** entire, complete, uncut, uncondensed.

un·ac·cent·ed (un ak′sen tid, un′ak sen′-), *adj.* not accented; unstressed. [1590–1600; UN-[1] + ACCENT + -ED[2]]

un·ac·com·mo·dat·ed (un′ə kom′ə dā′tid), *adj.* **1.** not accommodated; not adapted. **2.** not having accommodations. **3.** not furnished with something wanted or needed; not given satisfaction: *customers left unaccommodated at the counter.* [1595–1605; UN-[1] + ACCOMMODATED]

un·ac·com·pa·nied (un′ə kum′pə nēd), *adj.* **1.** not accompanied; alone: *The shipment arrived unaccompanied by an invoice.* **2.** *Music.* without an accompaniment: *a sonata for unaccompanied violin.* [1535–45; UN-[1] + ACCOMPANIED]
—**Syn. 1.** solitary, lone, unattended.

un·ac·com·plished (un′ə kom′plisht), *adj.* **1.** not accomplished; incomplete or not carried out: *Many tasks remain unaccomplished.* **2.** without accomplishments; inexpert: *an unaccomplished musician.* [1515–25; UN-[1] + ACCOMPLISHED]

un·ac·count·a·ble (un′ə koun′tə bəl), *adj.* **1.** impossible to account for; unexplained; inexplicable: *The boat has an unaccountable tendency to yaw.* **2.** exempt from being called to account; not answerable: *As a subordinate, he is unaccountable for errors in policy.* [1635–45; UN-[1] + ACCOUNTABLE] —**un′ac·count′a·ble·ness, un′ac·count′a·bil′i·ty,** *n.* —**un′ac·count′a·bly,** *adv.*
—**Syn. 1.** incomprehensible, inscrutable, mysterious, unintelligible. **2.** unanswerable, irresponsible.

un·ac·count·ed-for (un′ə koun′tid fôr′), *adj.* not accounted for; not understood; unexplained: *an explosion resulting from some unaccounted-for mechanical failure.* [1790–1800; formed on the v. phrase *account for;* see UN-[1], -ED[2]]

un·ac·cus·tomed (un′ə kus′təmd), *adj.* **1.** not accustomed or habituated: *to be unaccustomed to hardships.* **2.** unusual; unfamiliar: *A brief after-dinner speech is an unaccustomed pleasure.* [1520–30; UN-[1] + ACCUSTOMED] —**un′ac·cus′tomed·ness,** *n.*
—**Syn. 2.** uncommon, extraordinary, curious, peculiar, unexpected.

u·na cor·da (o͞o′nə kôr′də; *It.* o͞o′nä kôʀ′dä), with the soft pedal depressed (a musical direction in piano playing). [1840–50; < It: lit., one string, since depressing the soft pedal shifts the hammers so as to strike only two (orig. one) of the strings provided for each note]

u′na cor′da ped′al. See **soft pedal** (def. 1).

un·a·dul·ter·at·ed (un′ə dul′tə rā′tid), *adj.* **1.** not diluted or made impure by adulterating; pure: *unadulterated maple syrup.* **2.** utter; absolute: *unadulterated nonsense.* [1710–20; UN-[1] + ADULTERATE + -ED[2]] —**un′·a·dul′ter′at′ed·ly,** *adv.*

un·ad·vised (un′əd vīzd′), *adj.* **1.** without advice or counsel; uninformed: *a defendant unadvised of her legal rights.* **2.** imprudent; rash; ill-advised: *He purchased a business with unadvised haste.* [1300–50; ME *onavised.* See UN-[1], ADVISED] —**un·ad·vis·ed·ly** (un′əd vī′zid lē), *adv.* —**un′ad·vis′ed·ness,** *n.*

un·aes·thet·ic (un′es thet′ik *or, esp. Brit.,* -ēs-), *adj.* offensive to the aesthetic sense; lacking in beauty or sensory appeal; unpleasant, as an object, design, arrangement, etc.: *an unaesthetic combination of colors.* Also, **unesthetic, un′aes·thet′i·cal.** [1825–35; UN-[1] + AESTHETIC] —**un′aes·thet′i·cal·ly,** *adv.*

un·af·fect·ed[1] (un′ə fek′tid), *adj.* **1.** free from affectation; sincere; genuine: *The man showed unaffected grief at the death of his former opponent.* **2.** unpretentious, as a personality or literary style. [1580–90; UN-[1] + AFFECTED[2]] —**un′af·fect′ed·ly,** *adv.* —**un′af·fect′·ed·ness,** *n.*
—**Syn. 1.** plain, natural, simple, honest, real, unfeigned, artless; naive, guileless.

un·af·fect·ed[2] (un′ə fek′tid), *adj.* not affected, acted upon, or influenced; unchanged; unaltered: *The laboratory clock remained accurate, unaffected by the explosion.* [1580–90; UN-[1] + AFFECTED[1]]
—**Syn.** unmoved, untouched, unimpressed, unstirred.

U·na·lach·ti·go (o͞o′nə läch′ti gō′), *n., pl.* **-gos,** (*esp. collectively*) **-go** for 1. **1.** a member of a North American Indian people, one of the Delaware group. **2.** the Eastern Algonquian language of the Unalachtigo, originally spoken in the middle Delaware Valley.

U·na·las·ka (o͞o′nə las′kə, un′ə las′-), *n.* an island off the coast of SW Alaska, one of the Aleutian Islands. ab. 75 mi. (120 km) long.

un·al·ien·a·ble (un āl′yə nə bəl, -ā′lē ə-), *adj.* inalienable. [UN-[1] + ALIENABLE]

un·al·ter·a·ble (un ôl′tər ə bəl), *adj.* not capable of being altered, changed, or modified. Also, **inalterable.** [1610–15; UN-[1] + ALTERABLE] —**un·al′ter·a·ble·ness, un·al′ter·a·bil′i·ty,** *n.* —**un·al′ter·a·bly,** *adv.*

un·al·tered (un ôl′tərd), *adj.* **1.** not altered, changed, or modified: *We approved the unaltered designs.* **2.** (of an animal) not neutered. [1545–55; UN-[1] + ALTER + -ED[2]]

un·am·biv·a·lent (un′am biv′ə lənt), *adj.* not ambivalent; definite; certain. [1940–45; UN-[1] + AMBIVALENT]

un-A·mer·i·can (un′ə mer′i kən), *adj.* not American; not characteristic of or proper to the U.S.; foreign or opposed to the characters, values, standards, goals, etc., of the U.S. [1810–20, *Amer.*] —**un′-A·mer′i·can·ism,** *n.*

U·na·mi (o͞o nä′mē, yo͞o nam′ē), *n., pl.* **-mis,** (*esp. collectively*) **-mi** for 1. **1.** a member of a North American Indian people, one of the Delaware group. **2.** the East-

CONCISE ETYMOLOGY KEY: <, descended or borrowed from; >, whence; b., blend of, blended; c., cognate with; cf., compare; deriv., derivative; equiv., equivalent; imit., imitative; obl., oblique; r., replacing; s., stem; sp., spelling, spelled; resp., respelling, respelled; trans., translation; ?, origin unknown; *, unattested; ‡, probably earlier than. See the full key inside the front cover.

un′a·ban′doned, *adj.*
un′a·ban′don·ing, *adj.*
un′a·based′, *adj.*
un′a·bash′a·ble, *adj.*
un′a·bashed′, *adj.*
un′a·bash′ed·ly, *adv.*
un′a·bas′ing, *adj.*
un′a·bat′a·ble, *adj.*
un′a·bat′ing, *adj.;* **-ly,** *adv.*
un′ab·bre′vi·at′ed, *adj.*
un′ab′di·cat′ed, *adj.*
un′ab′di·cat′ing, *adj.*
un′ab·di′ca′tive, *adj.*
un′ab·duct′ed, *adj.*
un′a·bet′ted, *adj.*
un′a·bet′ting, *adj.*
un′ab·horred′, *adj.*
un′ab·hor′rent·ly, *adv.*
un′a·bid′ing, *adj.;* **-ly,** *adv.;* **-ness,** *n.*
un·ab′ject, *adj.;* **-ly,** *adv.;* **-ness,** *n.*
un′ab·jec′tive, *adj.*
un′ab·jur′a·to′ry, *adj.*
un′ab·jured′, *adj.*
un′ab·la′tive, *adj.*
un·ab′ne·gat′ed, *adj.*
un·ab′ne·gat′ing, *adj.*
un′a·bol′ish·a·ble, *adj.*
un′a·bol′ished, *adj.*
un′a·bort′ed, *adj.*
un′a·bor′tive, *adj.;* **-ly,** *adv.;* **-ness,** *n.*
un′a·brad′ed, *adj.*
un′a·bra′sive, *adj.;* **-ly,** *adv.*
un·ab′ro·ga·ble, *adj.*
un·ab′ro·gat′ed, *adj.*
un·ab′ro·ga′tive, *adj.*
un′ab·rupt′ly, *adv.*
un·ab′scessed, *adj.*
un′ab·solved′, *adj.*
un′ab·sorb′a·ble, *adj.*
un′ab·sorbed′, *adj.*
un′ab·sorb′ent, *adj.*
un′ab·sorb′ing, *adj.;* **-ly,** *adv.*
un′ab·sorp′tive, *adj.;* **-ness,** *n.*
un′ab·ste′mi·ous, *adj.;* **-ly,** *adv.;* **-ness,** *n.*
un′ab·sten′tious, *adj.*
un′ab·stract′ed, *adj.;* **-ly,** *adv.;* **-ness,** *n.*
un′ab·strac′tive, *adj.;* **-ly,** *adv.*
un′a·bus′a·ble, *adj.*
un′a·bused′, *adj.*
un′a·bu′sive, *adj.;* **-ly,** *adv.;* **-ness,** *n.*
un′a·but′ting, *adj.*
un′ac·a·dem′ic, *adj.*
un′ac·a·dem′i·cal, *adj.;* **-ly,** *adv.*
un′ac·ced′ing, *adj.*
un′ac·cel′er·at′ed, *adj.*
un′ac·cel′er·a′tive, *adj.*
un′ac·cen′tu·at′ed, *adj.*
un′ac·cept′a·bil′i·ty, *n.*
un′ac·cept′a·ble, *adj.;* **-ble·ness,** *n.;* **-bly,** *adv.*
un′ac·cept′ance, *n.*
un′ac·cept′ant, *adj.*
un′ac·cept′ed, *adj.*
un′ac·ces′si·bil′i·ty, *n.*
un′ac·ces′si·ble, *adj.;* **-bly,** *adv.*
un′ac·ces′sion·al, *adj.*
un′ac·ci·den′tal, *adj.;* **-ly,** *adv.*
un′ac·claimed′, *adj.*
un′ac′cli·mat′ed, *adj.*
un′ac·cli′ma·tized′, *adj.*
un′ac·cliv′i·tous, *adj.;* **-ly,** *adv.*
un′ac·com′mo·da·ble, *adj.*
un′ac·com′mo·dat′ing, *adj.;* **-ly,** *adv.*
un′ac·com′plish·a·ble, *adj.*
un′ac·cord′a·ble, *adj.*
un′ac·cord′ant, *adj.*
un′ac·cord′ed, *adj.*
un′ac·cost′a·ble, *adj.*
un′ac·cost′ed, *adj.*
un′ac·count′ed, *adj.*
un′ac·cou′tered, *adj.*
un′ac·cred′it·ed, *adj.*
un′ac·crued′, *adj.*
un′ac·cul′tur·at′ed, *adj.*
un′ac·cu′mu·la·ble, *adj.*
un′ac·cu′mu·lat′ed, *adj.*
un′ac·cu′mu·la′tive, *adj.;* **-ly,** *adv.;* **-ness,** *n.*
un·ac′cu·rate, *adj.;* **-ly,** *adv.;* **-ness,** *n.*
un′ac·cus′a·ble, *adj.*
un′ac·cused′, *adj.*
un′ac·cus′ing, *adj.;* **-ly,** *adv.*
un′ac·cus′tom, *v.t.*
un′a·cer′bic, *adj.*
un′a·cer′bi·cal·ly, *adv.*
un′a·ce′tic, *adj.*
un′a·chiev′a·ble, *adj.*
un′a·chieved′, *adj.*
un·ach′ing, *adj.;* **-ly,** *adv.*
un′a·cid′ic, *adj.*
un′a·cid′u·lat′ed, *adj.*
un′ac·knowl′edged, *adj.*
un′ac·knowl′edg·ing, *adj.*
un′a·cous′tic, *adj.*
un′a·cous′ti·cal, *adj.;* **-ly,** *adv.*
un′ac·quaint′ed, *adj.*
un′ac·qui·es′cent, *adj.;* **-ly,** *adv.*
un′ac·quir′a·ble, *adj.*
un′ac·quired′, *adj.*
un′ac·quis′i·tive, *adj.;* **-ly,** *adv.;* **-ness,** *n.*
un′ac·quit′ted, *adj.*
un′ac·ri·mo′ni·ous, *adj.;* **-ly,** *adv.;* **-ness,** *n.*
un·act′a·ble, *adj.*
un·act′ed, *adj.*
un·act′ing, *adj.*
un′ac·tin′ic, *adj.*
un·ac′tion·a·ble, *adj.*
un·ac′ti·vat′ed, *adj.*
un·ac′tu·at′ed, *adj.*
un′a·cu′mi·nous, *adj.*
un·ad′a·mant, *adj.*
un′a·dapt′a·ble, *adj.;* **-ness,** *n.*
un′a·dapt′ed, *adj.*
un′a·dap′tive, *adj.;* **-ly,** *adv.;* **-ness,** *n.*
un·add′a·ble, *adj.*
un·add′ed, *adj.*
un·add′i·ble, *adj.*
un′ad·dict′ed, *adj.*
un·ad′dled, *adj.*
un′ad·dressed′, *adj.*
un′ad·duce′a·ble, *adj.*
un′ad·duced′, *adj.*
un′ad·duc′i·ble, *adj.*
un′a·dept′, *adj.;* **-ly,** *adv.;* **-ness,** *n.*
un′ad·her′ing, *adj.*
un′ad·he′sive, *adj.;* **-ly,** *adv.;* **-ness,** *n.*
un′ad·ja′cent, *adj.;* **-ly,** *adv.*
un′ad·joined′, *adj.*
un′ad·join′ing, *adj.*
un′ad·journed′, *adj.*
un′ad·judged′, *adj.*
un′ad·ju′di·cat′ed, *adj.*
un′ad·junc′tive, *adj.;* **-ly,** *adv.*
un′ad·just′a·ble, *adj.;* **-bly,** *adv.*
un′ad·just′ed, *adj.*
un′ad·min′is·tered, *adj.*
un′ad·min′is·tra·ble, *adj.*
un′ad·min′is·tra′tive, *adj.;* **-ly,** *adv.*
un·ad′mi·ra·ble, *adj.;* **-ble·ness,** *n.;* **-bly,** *adv.*
un′ad·mired′, *adj.*
un′ad·mir′ing, *adj.;* **-ly,** *adv.*
un′ad·mis′si·ble, *adj.;* **-ble·ness,** *n.;* **-bly,** *adv.*
un′ad·mis′sive, *adj.*
un′ad·mit′ted, *adj.;* **-ly,** *adv.*
un′ad·mon′ished, *adj.*
un′ad·mon′i·to′ry, *adj.*
un′a·dopt′a·ble, *adj.*
un′a·dopt′ed, *adj.*
un′a·dop′tion·al, *adj.*
un′a·dop′tive, *adj.;* **-ly,** *adv.*
un′a·dor′a·ble, *adj.;* **-ble·ness,** *n.;* **-bly,** *adv.*
un′a·dored′, *adj.*
un′a·dor′ing, *adj.;* **-ly,** *adv.*
un′a·dorn′a·ble, *adj.*
un′a·dorned′, *adj.*
un′a·dorn′ment, *n.*
un′a·droit′, *adj.;* **-ly,** *adv.;* **-ness,** *n.*
un·ad′u·lat′ing, *adj.*
un·ad′u·la·to′ry, *adj.*
un′a·dult′, *adj.*
un′a·dul′ter·ate, *adj.*
un′a·dul′ter·ous, *adj.;* **-ly,** *adv.*
un′ad·vanc′ing, *adj.*
un′ad·van′taged, *adj.*
un′ad·van·ta′geous, *adj.;* **-ly,** *adv.;* **-ness,** *n.*
un′ad·ven′tur·ing, *adj.*
un′ad·ven′tur·ous, *adj.;* **-ly,** *adv.;* **-ness,** *n.*
un′ad·verse′, *adj.;* **-ly,** *adv.;* **-ness,** *n.*
un·ad′ver·tised′, *adj.*
un′ad·vis′a·ble, *adj.;* **-ble·ness,** *n.;* **-bly,** *adv.*
un·ad′vo·cat′ed, *adj.*
un·aer′at·ed, *adj.*
un·af′fa·ble, *adj.;* **-ble·ness,** *n.;* **-bly,** *adv.*
un′af·fect′ing, *adj.*
un′af·fec′tion·ate, *adj.;* **-ly,** *adv.*
un′af·fil′i·at′ed, *adj.*
un′af·firmed′, *adj.*
un′af·fixed′, *adj.*
un′af·flict′ed, *adj.;* **-ly,** *adv.;* **-ness,** *n.*
un′af·flict′ing, *adj.*
un·af′flu·ent, *adj.*
un′af·ford′a·bil′i·ty, *n.*
un′af·ford′a·ble, *adj.*
un′af·ford′ed, *adj.*
un′af·fright′ed, *adj.;* **-ly,** *adv.*
un′af·front′ed, *adj.*
un′a·fraid′, *adj.*
un·aged′, *adj.*
un′ag·glom′er·a′tive, *adj.*
un·ag′gra·vat′ed, *adj.*
un·ag′gra·vat′ing, *adj.*
un·ag′gre·gat′ed, *adj.*
un′ag·gres′sive, *adj.;* **-ly,** *adv.;* **-ness,** *n.*
un·ag′ile, *adj.;* **-ly,** *adv.*
un·ag′ing, *adj.*
un·ag′i·tat′ed, *adj.;* **-ly,** *adv.*
un′a·grar′i·an, *adj.*
un′a·greed′, *adj.*
un·ag′ri·cul′tur·al, *adj.;* **-ly,** *adv.*
un·aid′a·ble, *adj.*
un·aid′ed, *adj.;* **-ly,** *adv.*
un·aid′ing, *adj.*
un·aimed′, *adj.*
un·aim′ing, *adj.*
un·air′a·ble, *adj.*
un·aired′, *adj.*
un·air′i·ly, *adv.*
un·air′wor′thy, *adj.*
un·aisled′, *adj.*
un′a·lac′ri·tous, *adj.*
un′a·larmed′, *adj.*
un′a·larm′ing, *adj.;* **-ly,** *adv.*
un·al′co·hol·ized′, *adj.*
un·al′der·man·ly, *adj.*
un′a·lert′ed, *adj.*
un·al′ge·bra′i·cal, *adj.*
un·al′ien·at′ed, *adj.*
un·al′ien·at′ing, *adj.*
un′a·lign′a·ble, *adj.*
un′a·ligned′, *adj.*
un′a·like′, *adj., adv.*
un·al′i·men′ta·ry, *adj.*
un·al′i·men′ta·tive, *adj.*
un′al·lay′a·ble, *adj.;* **-bly,** *adv.*
un′al·layed′, *adj.*
un′al·leged′, *adj.*
un′al·leg′ed·ly, *adv.*
un′al·le·gor′i·cal, *adj.;* **-ly,** *adv.*
un·al′le·go·rized′, *adj.*
un′al·ler′gic, *adj.*
un′al·le′vi·at′ed, *adj.;* **-ly,** *adv.*
un′al·le′vi·at′ing, *adj.;* **-ly,** *adv.*
un′al·le′vi·a′tive, *adj.*

ern Algonquian language of the Unami, originally spoken in the middle and lower Delaware Valley.

U·na·mu·no (o͞o′nə mo͞o′nō; *Sp.* o͞o′nä mo͞o′nô), *n.* **Miguel de** (mē gel′ de), 1864–1936, Spanish philosopher, poet, novelist, and essayist.

un·a·neled (un′ə nēld′), *adj. Archaic.* not having received extreme unction. [1595–1605; UN-[1] + ANELED]

u·na·nim·i·ty (yo͞o′nə nim′i tē), *n.* the state or quality of being unanimous; a consensus or undivided opinion: *The unanimity of the delegates was obvious on the first ballot.* [1400–50; late ME *unanimite* < MF < L *ūnanimitās*, equiv. to *ūnanim(us)* UNANIMOUS + *-itās* -ITY]
—**Syn.** harmony, unity, unison, concert. —**Ant.** disagreement.

u·nan·i·mous (yo͞o nan′ə məs), *adj.* **1.** of one mind; in complete agreement; agreed. **2.** characterized by or showing complete agreement: *a unanimous vote.* [1615–25; < L *ūnanim(us)* (*ūn(us)* one + *animus* mind, heart, feeling) + -OUS] —**u·nan′i·mous·ly,** *adv.* —**u·nan′i·mous·ness,** *n.*

un·an·swer·a·ble (un an′sər ə bəl, -än′-), *adj.* **1.** not capable of being answered; not having a known or discoverable answer: *an unanswerable question.* **2.** not open to dispute or rebuttal; irrefutable; conclusive: *an unanswerable proof.* [1605–15; UN-[1] + ANSWERABLE] —**un·an′swer·a·ble·ness,** *n.* —**un·an′swer·a·bly,** *adv.*

un·ap·peal·a·ble (un′ə pē′lə bəl), *adj.* **1.** not appealable to a higher court, as a cause. **2.** incapable of being appealed from, as a judgment. [1625–35; UN-[1] + APPEALABLE] —**un′ap·peal′a·ble·ness,** *n.* —**un′ap·peal′a·bly,** *adv.*

un·ap·proach·a·ble (un′ə prō′chə bəl), *adj.* **1.** not capable of being approached; remote; unreachable: *an unapproachable spot; an unapproachable person.* **2.** impossible to equal or rival: *unapproachable mastery of her art.* [1575–85; UN-[1] + APPROACHABLE] —**un′ap·proach′a·bil′i·ty, un′ap·proach′a·ble·ness,** *n.* —**un′ap·proach′a·bly,** *adv.*
—**Syn. 1.** inaccessible, aloof, distant, austere, cold.

un·ap·pro·pri·at·ed (un′ə prō′prē ā′tid), *adj.* **1.** not set apart or voted for some purpose or use, as money, revenues, etc. **2.** not taken into possession by any person: *A portion of the land remained unappropriated.* [1750–60; UN-[1] + APPROPRIATED]

un·apt (un apt′), *adj.* **1.** not appropriate; unfit; unsuitable: *an unapt answer.* **2.** not prone, likely, or disposed: *She is unapt to waste what she has accumulated with such effort.* **3.** deficient in aptitude or capacity; slow; dull: *an unapt student.* [1325–75; ME; see UN-[1], APT] —**un·apt′ly,** *adv.* —**un·apt′ness,** *n.*

un·ar·gued (un är′gyo͞od), *adj.* **1.** undisputed; not subject to argument or discussion: *an unargued right.* **2.** undebated; unopposed by argument; admitted: *an unargued objection.* [1610–20; UN-[1] + ARGUED]

un·arm (un ärm′), *v.t.* to deprive or relieve of arms; disarm. [1300–50; ME *unarmen.* See UN-[2], ARM[2]]

un·armed (un ärmd′), *adj.* **1.** without weapons or armor. **2.** not having claws, thorns, scales, etc., as animals or plants. **3.** (of an artillery shell) not armed. [1250–1300; ME; see UN-[1], ARMED]

u·na·ry (yo͞o′nə rē), *adj. Math.* pertaining to a function whose domain is a given set and whose range is contained in that set. [1570–80; < L *ūn(us)* one + -ARY, on the model of BINARY]

u′nary opera′tion, an operation in a mathematical system by which one element is used to yield a single result, as squaring or taking the square root. Cf. **binary operation, ternary operation.** [1930–35]

un·a·shamed (un′ə shāmd′), *adj.* **1.** not ashamed; not restrained by embarrassment or consciousness of moral guilt: *a liar unashamed even after public disgrace.* **2.** open; unconcealed; unabashed: *to eat with unashamed gusto.* [1590–1600; UN-[1] + ASHAMED] —**un·a·sham·ed·ly** (un′ə shā′mid lē), *adv.* —**un′a·sham′ed·ness,** *n.*

un·asked (un askt′, -äskt′), *adj.* **1.** not asked: *an unasked question.* **2.** not asked for: *unasked advice.* **3.** uninvited. [1225–75; ME; see UN-[1], ASK, -ED[2]]
—**Syn. 2.** unsolicited, unsought, unrequested.

un·as·sail·a·ble (un′ə sā′lə bəl), *adj.* **1.** not open to attack or assault, as by military force or argument: *unassailable fortifications; unassailable logic.* **2.** not subject to denial or dispute: *Shakespeare's genius gives his works an unassailable position in world literature.* [1590–1600; UN-[1] + ASSAILABLE] —**un′as·sail′a·ble·ness,** *n.* —**un′as·sail′a·bly,** *adv.*

un·as·sum·ing (un′ə so͞o′ming), *adj.* modest; unpretentious. [1720–30; UN-[1] + ASSUMING] —**un′as·sum′ing·ly,** *adv.* —**un′as·sum′ing·ness,** *n.*

un·at·tached (un′ə tacht′), *adj.* **1.** not attached. **2.** not connected or associated with any particular body, group, organization, or the like; independent. **3.** not engaged or married. [1490–1500; UN-[1] + ATTACHED]

un·at·tend·ed (un′ə ten′did), *adj.* **1.** without attendance; lacking an audience, spectators, etc.: *an unattended meeting.* **2.** not accompanied; not associated with, as a concomitant effect or result: *a flash of lightning unattended by thunder.* **3.** not cared for or ministered to: *unattended patients; an unattended injury.* **4.** not taken in charge; not watched over: *an unattended switchboard.* **5.** not accompanied, as by an attendant or companion; alone: *The queen was unattended.* **6.** unheeded; not listened to; disregarded: *unattended warning signals.* **7.** not tended to; not done or carried out, as a task (usually fol. by *to*): *He left his studies unattended to.* [1595–1605; UN-[1] + ATTEND + -ED[2]]

u·nau (yo͞o nô′, o͞o nou′), *n.* See **two-toed sloth.** [1765–75; < F < Tupian; akin to Tupi *unáu*]

un·a·vail·ing (un′ə vā′ling), *adj.* ineffectual; futile. [1660–70; UN-[1] + AVAIL + -ING[2]] —**un′a·vail′ing·ly,** *adv.*

un·a·void·a·ble (un′ə voi′də bəl), *adj.* unable to be avoided; inevitable: *an unavoidable delay.* [1570–80; UN-[1] + AVOIDABLE] —**un′a·void′a·bil′i·ty, un′a·void′a·ble·ness,** *n.* —**un′a·void′a·bly,** *adv.*
—**Syn.** inescapable, unpreventable, fated, sure, certain.

un·a·ware (un′ə wâr′), *adj.* **1.** not aware or conscious; unconscious: *to be unaware of any change.* —*adv.* **2.** unawares. [1585–95; UN-[1] + AWARE; cf. ME *unywar* (see Y-)] —**un′a·ware′ly,** *adv.* —**un′a·ware′ness,** *n.*
—**Syn. 1.** unsuspecting, ignorant, unknowing.

un·a·wares (un′ə wârz′), *adv.* **1.** while not aware or conscious of a thing oneself; unknowingly or inadvertently. **2.** without warning; by surprise; suddenly; unexpectedly: *to come upon someone unawares.* [1525–35; UNAWARE + -S[1]]

un·backed (un bakt′), *adj.* **1.** without backing or support. **2.** not supported by bets: *an unbacked challenger.* **3.** not endorsed: *an unbacked product.* **4.** never having been mounted by a rider, as a horse. [1585–95; UN-[1] + BACKED]

un·bal·ance (un bal′əns), *v.*, **-anced, -anc·ing,** *n.* —*v.t.* **1.** to throw or put out of balance. **2.** to disorder or derange, as the mind. —*n.* **3.** unbalanced condition. [1580–90; UN-[2] + BALANCE] —**un·bal′ance·a·ble,** *adj.*

un·bal·anced (un bal′ənst), *adj.* **1.** not balanced or not properly balanced. **2.** lacking steadiness and soundness of judgment. **3.** mentally disordered; deranged. **4.** (of an account) not adjusted; not brought to an equality of debits and credits. **5.** *Football.* of or pertaining to an offensive line formation having more than three linemen on one side of the center. Cf. **balanced** (def. 2). [1640–50; UN-[1] + BALANCED]
—**Syn. 3.** disturbed, unsound, irrational.

un·bal·last·ed (un bal′ə stid), *adj.* **1.** not fitted with or carrying ballast. **2.** not properly steadied or regulated. [1635–45; UN-[1] + BALLASTED]

un·bar (un bär′), *v.t.*, **-barred, -bar·ring.** to remove a bar or bars from; open; unlock; unbolt: *to unbar a door.* [1300–50; ME *unbarren.* See UN-[2], BAR[1]]

un·barbed (un bärbd′), *adj.* barbless. [1555–65; UN-[1] + BARB[1] + -ED[3]]

un·barred (un bärd′), *adj.* **1.** not provided or fastened with a bar or bars: *an unbarred door.* **2.** not marked with stripes or bands. [1540–50; UN-[1] + BARRED]

un·bat·ed (un bā′tid), *adj.* **1.** not abated; undiminished; unlessened. **2.** *Archaic.* not blunted, as a lance or fencer's foil. [1590–1600; UN-[1] + BATE[1] + -ED[2]]

un·bear·a·ble (un bâr′ə bəl), *adj.* not bearable; unendurable; intolerable. [1400–50; late ME; see UN-[1], BEARABLE] —**un·bear′a·ble·ness,** *n.* —**un·bear′a·bly,** *adv.*

un·beat·a·ble (un bē′tə bəl), *adj.* **1.** incapable of being beaten; impossible to defeat: *an unbeatable football team.* **2.** of surpassingly good quality; excellent: *an unbeatable combination of brains and talent.* [1895–1900; UN- + BEATABLE] —**un·beat′a·bly,** *adv.*

un·beat·en (un bēt′n), *adj.* **1.** not struck, pounded, or

CONCISE PRONUNCIATION KEY: act, cāpe, dâre, pärt; set, ēqual; *if,* īce; ox, ōver, ôrder, oil, bo͝ok, bo͞ot, out; up, ûrge; child; sing; shoe; thin, *th*at; zh as in *treasure.* ə = *a* as in *alone, e* as in *system, i* as in *easily, o* as in *gallop, u* as in *circus;* ᵊ as in *fire* (fīᵊr), *hour* (ouᵊr). l and n can serve as syllabic consonants, as in *cradle* (krād′l), and *button* (but′n). See the full key inside the front cover.

un′al·lied′, *adj.*
un′al·lit′er·at′ed, *adj.*
un′al·lit′er·a·tive, *adj.*
un·al′lo·cat′ed, *adj.*
un′al·lot′ted, *adj.*
un′al·low′a·ble, *adj.*
un′al·lowed′, *adj.*
un′al·loyed′, *adj.*
un′al·lured′, *adj.*
un′al·lur′ing, *adj.*; **-ly,** *adv.*
un′al·lu′sive, *adj.*; **-ly,** *adv.*; **-ness,** *n.*
un′al·pha·bet′ic, *adj.*
un′al·pha·bet′i·cal, *adj.*; **-ly,** *adv.*
un·al′pha·bet·ized′, *adj.*
un·al′ter·ing, *adj.*
un·al′ter·nat′ed, *adj.*
un·al′ter·nat′ing, *adj.*
un′a·mal′ga·ma·ble, *adj.*
un′a·mal′ga·mat′ed, *adj.*
un′a·mal′ga·mat′ing, *adj.*
un′a·mal′ga·ma′tive, *adj.*
un′a·massed′, *adj.*
un·am′a·tive, *adj.*; **-ly,** *adv.*
un′a·mazed′, *adj.*
un′a·maz′ed·ly, *adv.*
un′a·maz′ed·ness, *n.*
un·am′bi·ent, *adj.*; **-ly,** *adv.*
un′am·big′u·ous, *adj.*; **-ly,** *adv.*; **-ness,** *n.*
un′am·bi′tious, *adj.*; **-ly,** *adv.*; **-ness,** *n.*
un·am′bu·lant, *adj.*
un′a·mel′io·ra·ble, *adj.*
un′a·mel′io·rat′ed, *adj.*
un′a·mel′io·ra′tive, *adj.*
un′a·me′na·ble, *adj.*; **-bly,** *adv.*
un′a·mend′a·ble, *adj.*
un′a·mend′ed, *adj.*
un′a·mend′ing, *adj.*
un′a·merce′a·ble, *adj.*
un′a·merced′, *adj.*
un·a′mi·a·ble, *adj.*; **-ble·ness,** *n.*; **-bly,** *adv.*
un·am′i·ca·bil′i·ty, *n.*
un·am′i·ca·ble, *adj.*; **-ble·ness,** *n.*; **-bly,** *adv.*
un′am·mo′ni·at′ed, *adj.*
un·am′o·rous, *adj.*; **-ly,** *adv.*; **-ness,** *n.*
un·am′or·tized′, *adj.*
un·am′pli·fi′a·ble, *adj.*
un·am′pli·fied′, *adj.*
un·am′pu·tat′ed, *adj.*
un·am′pu·ta′tive, *adj.*
un′a·mus′a·ble, *adj.*; **-bly,** *adv.*
un′a·mused′, *adj.*
un′a·mus′ing, *adj.*; **-ly,** *adv.*; **-ness,** *n.*
un′a·nach′ro·nis′tic, *adj.*
un′a·nach′ro·nis′ti·cal, *adj.*; **-ly,** *adv.*
un′a·nach′ro·nous, *adj.*; **-ly,** *adv.*
un′a·nae′mic, *adj.*
un′an·a·log′i·cal, *adj.*; **-ly,** *adv.*
un′a·nal′o·gized′, *adj.*
un′a·nal′o·gous, *adj.*; **-ly,** *adv.*; **-ness,** *n.*
un′an·a·lyt′ic, *adj.*
un′an·a·lyt′i·cal, *adj.*; **-ly,** *adv.*
un·an′a·lyz′a·ble, *adj.*; **-bly,** *adv.*
un·an′a·lyzed′, *adj.*
un·an′a·lyz′ing, *adj.*
un′an·ar′chic, *adj.*
un′an·ar·chis′tic, *adj.*
un′a·nat′o·miz′a·ble, *adj.*
un′a·nat′o·mized′, *adj.*
un·an′chored, *adj.*
un′an·ec·do′tal, *adj.*; **-ly,** *adv.*
un′a·ne′mic, *adj.*
un·an′gered, *adj.*
un·an′gri·ly, *adv.*
un·an′gry, *adj.*
un·an′guished, *adj.*
un·an′gu·lar, *adj.*; **-ly,** *adv.*; **-ness,** *n.*
un·an′i·mat′ed, *adj.*; **-ly,** *adv.*
un·an′i·mat′ing, *adj.*; **-ly,** *adv.*
un′an·nealed′, *adj.*
un′an·nex′a·ble, *adj.*
un′an·nexed′, *adj.*
un′an·ni′hi·la·ble, *adj.*
un′an·ni′hi·lat′ed, *adj.*
un′an·ni′hi·la′tive, *adj.*
un′an·ni′hi·la·to′ry, *adj.*
un·an′no·tat′ed, *adj.*
un′an·nounced′, *adj.*
un′an·noyed′, *adj.*
un′an·noy′ing, *adj.*; **-ly,** *adv.*
un′an·nul′la·ble, *adj.*
un′an·nulled′, *adj.*
un′an·nun′ci·a·ble, *adj.*
un′an·nun′ci·a′tive, *adj.*
un′a·noint′ed, *adj.*
un·an′swered, *adj.*
un·an′swer·ing, *adj.*
un·an·tag′o·niz′a·ble, *adj.*
un·an·tag′o·nized′, *adj.*
un·an·tag′o·niz′ing, *adj.*; **-ly,** *adv.*
un′an·thol′o·gized′, *adj.*
un′an·tic′i·pat′ed, *adj.*
un′an·tic′i·pat′ing, *adj.*; **-ly,** *adv.*
un′an·tic′i·pa′tive, *adj.*
un·an′ti·quat′ed, *adj.*
un·ant′lered, *adj.*
un·anx′ious, *adj.*; **-ly,** *adv.*; **-ness,** *n.*
un′a·pha′sic, *adj.*
un′a·pol′o·get′ic, *adj.*
un′a·pol′o·get′i·cal·ly, *adv.*
un′a·pol′o·giz′ing, *n.*
un′a·pos′ta·tized′, *adj.*
un′a·pos′tro·phized′, *adj.*
un′ap·palled′, *adj.*
un′ap·pall′ing, *adj.*; **-ly,** *adv.*
un′ap·par′eled, *adj.*
un′ap·par′ent, *adj.*; **-ly,** *adv.*; **-ness,** *n.*
un′ap·pealed′, *adj.*
un′ap·peal′ing, *adj.*; **-ly,** *adv.*
un′ap·peas′a·ble, *adj.*; **-bly,** *adv.*
un′ap·peased′, *adj.*
un′ap·peas′ing, *adj.*; **-ly,** *adv.*
un′ap·pend′aged, *adj.*
un′ap·pend′ed, *adj.*
un′ap·per·ceived′, *adj.*
un′ap·per·cep′tive, *adj.*
un·ap′pe·tiz′ing, *adj.*; **-ly,** *adv.*
un′ap·plaud′a·ble, *adj.*
un′ap·plaud′ed, *adj.*
un′ap·plaud′ing, *adj.*
un′ap·plau′sive, *adj.*
un′ap·pli′a·ble, *adj.*; **-bly,** *adv.*
un·ap′pli·ca·bil′i·ty, *n.*
un·ap′pli·ca·ble, *adj.*; **-ble·ness,** *n.*; **-bly,** *adv.*
un·ap′pli·ca′tive, *adj.*
un′ap·plied′, *adj.*
un′ap·pli·quéd′, *adj.*
un′ap·point′a·ble, *adj.*
un′ap·point′ed, *adj.*
un′ap·por′tioned, *adj.*
un′ap·pos′a·ble, *adj.*
un·ap′po·site, *adj.*; **-ly,** *adv.*; **-ness,** *n.*
un′ap·praised′, *adj.*
un′ap·pre′ci·a·ble, *adj.*; **-bly,** *adv.*
un′ap·pre′ci·at′ed, *adj.*
un′ap·pre′ci·at′ing, *adj.*
un′ap·pre′ci·a′tion, *n.*
un′ap·pre′cia·tive, *adj.*; **-ly,** *adv.*; **-ness,** *n.*
un′ap·pre·hend′a·ble, *adj.*; **-bly,** *adv.*
un′ap·pre·hend′ed, *adj.*
un′ap·pre·hend′ing, *adj.*
un′ap·pre·hen′si·ble, *adj.*
un′ap·pre·hen′sive, *adj.*; **-ly,** *adv.*; **-ness,** *n.*
un′ap·pren′ticed, *adj.*
un′ap·prised′, *adj.*
un′ap·proached′, *adj.*
un′ap·proach′ing, *adj.*
un′ap·pro′pri·a·ble, *adj.*
un′ap·prov′a·ble, *adj.*; **-bly,** *adv.*
un′ap·proved′, *adj.*
un′ap·prov′ing, *adj.*; **-ly,** *adv.*
un′a·proned′, *adj.*
un·ar′bi·trar′i·ly, *adv.*
un·ar′bi·trar′y, *adj.*
un·ar′bi·trat′ed, *adj.*
un·ar′bi·tra′tive, *adj.*
un·ar′bored, *adj.*
un·arched′, *adj.*
un·arch′ing, *adj.*
un·ar′chi·tect′ed, *adj.*
un′ar·chi·tec′tur·al, *adj.*; **-ly,** *adv.*
un·arch′ly, *adv.*
un·ar′du·ous, *adj.*; **-ly,** *adv.*; **-ness,** *n.*
un·ar′gu·a·ble, *adj.*; **-bly,** *adv.*
un′ar·gu·men′ta·tive, *adj.*; **-ly,** *adv.*; **-ness,** *n.*
un′a·ris′to·crat′ic, *adj.*
un′a·ris′to·crat′i·cal·ly, *adv.*
un′ar·ith·met′i·cal, *adj.*; **-ly,** *adv.*
un·ar′mored, *adj.*
un′ar·mo′ri·al, *adj.*
un′ar·o·mat′ic, *adj.*
un′ar·o·mat′i·cal·ly, *adv.*
un′a·rous′a·ble, *adj.*
un′a·roused′, *adj.*
un′a·rous′ing, *adj.*
un′ar·raign′a·ble, *adj.*
un′ar·raigned′, *adj.*
un′ar·ranged′, *adj.*
un′ar·rayed′, *adj.*
un′ar·rest′a·ble, *adj.*
un′ar·rest′ed, *adj.*
un′ar·rest′ing, *adj.*
un′ar·res′tive, *adj.*
un′ar·rived′, *adj.*
un′ar·riv′ing, *adj.*
un·ar′ro·gant, *adj.*; **-ly,** *adv.*
un·ar′ro·gat′ed, *adj.*
un·ar′ro·gat′ing, *adj.*
un·art′ful, *adj.*; **-ly,** *adv.*; **-ness,** *n.*
un·ar′ti·cled, *adj.*
un′ar·tic′u·late, *adj.*; **-ly,** *adv.*
un′ar·tic′u·lat′ed, *adj.*
un′ar·tic′u·la′tive, *adj.*
un′ar·tic′u·la·to′ry, *adj.*
un′ar·ti·fi′cial, *adj.*; **-ly,** *adv.*
un′ar·tis′tic, *adj.*
un′ar·tis′ti·cal·ly, *adv.*
un′as·cend′a·ble, *adj.*
un′as·cend′ant, *adj.*
un′as·cend′ed, *adj.*
un′as·cend′ent, *adj.*
un′as·cer·tain′a·ble, *adj.*; **-bly,** *adv.*
un′as·cer·tained′, *adj.*
un′as·cet′ic, *adj.*
un′as·cet′i·cal·ly, *adv.*
un′as·cribed′, *adj.*
un·ask′a·ble, *adj.*
un·ask′ing, *adj.*; **-ly,** *adv.*
un′as·persed′, *adj.*
un′as·per′sive, *adj.*
un·as′phalt·ed, *adj.*
un·as′pi·rat′ed, *adj.*
un′as·pir′ing, *adj.*; **-ly,** *adv.*
un′as·sailed′, *adj.*
un′as·sail′ing, *adj.*
un′as·sas′si·nat′ed, *adj.*
un′as·sault′a·ble, *adj.*
un′as·sault′ed, *adj.*
un′as·sayed′, *adj.*
un′as·say′ing, *adj.*
un′as·sem′bled, *adj.*
un′as·sent′ing, *adj.*
un′as·sen′tive, *adj.*
un′as·sert′ed, *adj.*
un′as·ser′tive, *adj.*; **-ly,** *adv.*; **-ness,** *n.*
un′as·sess′a·ble, *adj.*
un′as·sessed′, *adj.*
un′as·sib′i·lat′ed, *adj.*

whipped: *unbeaten eggs.* **2.** not defeated or never defeated. **3.** untrodden: *unbeaten paths.* [1225–75; ME *unbeten;* see UN-[1], BEATEN]

un•be•com•ing (un′bi kum′ing), *adj.* detracting from one's appearance, character, or reputation; unattractive or unseemly: *an unbecoming hat; unbecoming language.* [1590–1600; UN-[1] + BECOMING] —**un′be•com′ing•ly,** *adv.* —**un′be•com′ing•ness,** *n.*
—**Syn.** unapt, unsuitable, unfit. See **improper.**

un•be•got•ten (un′bi got′n), *adj.* **1.** not yet begotten; as yet unborn: *decisions that will affect our unbegotten children.* **2.** without a beginning; eternal. [1525–35; UN-[1] + BEGOTTEN]

un•be•known (un′bi nōn′), *adj.* unknown; unperceived; without one's knowledge (usually fol. by *to*). Also, **un•be•knownst** (un′bi nōnst′). [1630–40; UN-[1] + *beknown* (late ME *beknowe,* ptp. of *beknowen*); see BE-, KNOWN]

un•be•lief (un′bi lēf′), *n.* the state or quality of not believing; incredulity or skepticism, esp. in matters of doctrine or religious faith. [1125–75; ME *unbelefe;* see UN-[1], BELIEF]

un•be•liev•a•ble (un′bi lē′və bəl), *adj.* **1.** too dubious or improbable to be believed: *an unbelievable excuse.* **2.** so remarkable as to strain credulity; extraordinary: *the unbelievable fury of the storm; an unbelievable athlete.* [1540–50; UN-[1] + BELIEVABLE] —**un′be•liev′a•bly,** *adv.*

un•be•liev•er (un′bi lē′vər), *n.* **1.** a person who does not believe. **2.** a person who does not accept any, or some particular, religious belief. [1520–30; UN-[1] + BELIEVER]

un•be•liev•ing (un′bi lē′ving), *adj.* **1.** not believing; skeptical. **2.** not accepting any, or some particular, religious belief. [1350–1400; ME; see UN-[1], BELIEVING] —**un′be•liev′ing•ly,** *adv.* —**un′be•liev′ing•ness,** *n.*
—**Syn. 1.** doubting, questioning, incredulous.

un•belt (un belt′), *v.t.* **1.** to remove the belt from. **2.** to remove by undoing a supporting belt: *to unbelt a sword.* [1475–85; UN-[2] + BELT]

un•bend (un bend′), *v.,* **-bent** or (*Archaic*) **-bend•ed, -bend•ing.** —*v.t.* **1.** to straighten from a bent form or position. **2.** to release from the strain of formality, intense effort, etc.; relax: *to unbend one's mind.* **3.** to release from tension, as a bow. **4.** *Naut.* **a.** to loose or untie, as a sail or rope. **b.** to unfasten from spars or stays, as sails. —*v.i.* **5.** to relax the strictness of formality or ceremony; act in an easy, genial manner: *Imagine him unbending!* **6.** to become unbent; straighten. [1200–50; ME; see UN-[2], BEND[1]] —**un•bend′a•ble,** *adj.*

un•bend•ing (un ben′ding), *adj.* **1.** not bending or curving; inflexible; rigid. **2.** refusing to yield or compromise; resolute. **3.** austere or formal; aloof. [1545–55; UN-[1] + BENDING] —**un•bend′ing•ly,** *adv.* —**un•bend′ing•ness,** *n.*

un•bent (un bent′), *v.* **1.** pt. and pp. of **unbend.** —*adj.* **2.** not bent; unbowed. **3.** not having yielded or submitted. [1475–85; (in defs. 2 and 3) UN-[1] + BENT[1]]

un•bi•ased (un bī′əst), *adj.* not biased or prejudiced; fair; impartial. Also, *esp. Brit.,* **un•bi′assed.** [1600–10; UN-[1] + BIASED] —**un•bi′ased•ly,** *adv.*
—**Syn.** fair, equitable, tolerant, neutral.

un•bib•li•cal (un bib′li kəl), *adj.* not in accord with or sanctioned by biblical teaching. [1820–30; UN-[1] + BIBLICAL]

un•bid•den (un bid′n), *adj.* **1.** not ordered or commanded; spontaneous. **2.** not asked or summoned; uninvited. Also, **un•bid′.** [bef. 1050; ME *unbiden,* OE *unbēden.* See UN-[1], BIDDEN]

un•bind (un bīnd′), *v.t.,* **-bound, -bind•ing.** **1.** to release from bonds or restraint, as a prisoner; free. **2.** to unfasten or loose, as a bond or tie. [bef. 950; ME *unbinden,* OE *unbindan;* c. G *entbinden.* See UN-[2], BIND]

un•bit•ted (un bit′id), *adj.* **1.** not bitted or bridled. **2.** uncontrolled. [1580–90; UN-[1] + BITTED]

un•blenched (un blencht′), *adj. Archaic.* undaunted. [1625–35; UN-[1] + BLENCH[1] + -ED[2]]

un•blessed (un blest′), *adj.* **1.** excluded from or lacking a blessing. **2.** not sanctified or hallowed. **3.** wicked; evil. **4.** unhappy; wretched. Also, **un•blest′.** [1275–1325; ME; see UN-[1], BLESSED] —**un•bless•ed•ness** (un bles′id nis), *n.*

un•blind•ed (un blīn′did), *adj.* **1.** not physically blinded. **2.** without illusions: *an unblinded view of reality.* [1605–15; UN-[1] + BLIND + -ED[2]]

un•blink•ing (un bling′king), *adj.* **1.** not blinking. **2.** without displaying response, as surprise, confusion, or chagrin: *an unblinking reaction to the charges.* **3.** not varying or wavering; fearless; forthright: *unblinking devotion.* [1905–10; UN-[1] + BLINKING] —**un•blink′ing•ly,** *adv.*

un•block (un blok′), *v.t.* **1.** to remove a block or obstruction from: *to unblock a channel; to unblock a person's credit.* **2.** *Bridge.* to play (a suit) so that the last card of the suit in one hand can provide access to the hand of the partnership having the longer holding in the suit. [1605–15; UN-[2] + BLOCK]

un•blood•ed (un blud′id), *adj.* **1.** not having a good pedigree: *an unblooded horse.* **2.** unbloodied. [1585–95; UN-[1] + BLOODED]

un•blood•ied (un blud′ēd), *adj.* not stained or smeared with blood: *an unbloodied dagger at the scene of the crime.* [1585–95; UN-[1] + BLOODIED]

un•blush•ing (un blush′ing), *adj.* **1.** showing no shame or remorse; shameless: *an unblushing confession.* **2.** not blushing. [1585–95; UN-[1] + BLUSHING] —**un•blush′ing•ly,** *adv.* —**un•blush′ing•ness,** *n.*

un•bod•ied (un bod′ēd), *adj.* **1.** incorporeal; disembodied. **2.** lacking a form; formless; shapeless. [1505–15; UN-[1] + BODIED]

un•bolt (un bōlt′), *v.t.* **1.** to open (a door, window, etc.) by or as if by removing a bolt; unlock; unfasten. **2.** to release, as by the removal of threaded bolts: *He unscrewed the nuts and unbolted the inspection cover.* —*v.i.* **3.** to become unbolted or unfastened. [1425–75; late ME; see UN-[2] + BOLT[1]]

un•bolt•ed[1] (un bōl′tid), *adj.* not fastened or secured, as with a bolt or bolts. [1570–80; UN-[1] + BOLT[1] + -ED[2]]

un•bolt•ed[2] (un bōl′tid), *adj.* not sifted, as grain. [1560–70; UN-[1] + BOLT[2] + -ED[2]]

un•boned (un bōnd′), *adj.* **1.** lacking bones. **2.** not having the bones removed: *an unboned chicken.* [1640–50; UN-[1] + BONED]

un•bon•net (un bon′it), *v.i.* **1.** to uncover the head, as in respect. —*v.t.* **2.** to remove the bonnet from. [1800–10; UN-[2] + BONNET]

un•bon•net•ed (un bon′i tid), *adj.* bareheaded. [1595–1605; UN-[1] + BONNET + -ED[2]]

un•born (un bôrn′), *adj.* **1.** not yet born; yet to come; future: *unborn generations.* **2.** not yet delivered; still existing in the mother's womb: *an unborn baby.* **3.** existing without birth or beginning. [bef. 900; ME; OE *unboren.* See UN-[1], BORN]

un•bos•om (un bŏŏz′əm, -bōō′zəm), *v.t.* **1.** to disclose (a confidence, secret, etc.). —*v.i.* **2.** to disclose one's thoughts, feelings, or the like, esp. in confidence. **3. unbosom oneself,** to disclose one's thoughts, feelings, etc., to another person; confide one's private affairs: *He unbosomed himself to a complete stranger.* [1580–90; UN-[2] + BOSOM (v.)] —**un•bos′om•er,** *n.*

un•bound (un bound′), *v.* **1.** pt. and pp. of **unbind.** —*adj.* **2.** not bound, as a book. **3.** free; not attached, as by a chemical bond: *unbound electrons.* [bef. 900; (adj.) ME *unbounde, unbunden,* OE *unbunden;* see UN-[1], BOUND[1]]

un•bound•ed (un boun′did), *adj.* **1.** having no limits, borders, or bounds. **2.** unrestrained; uncontrolled: *unbounded enthusiasm.* [1590–1600; UN-[1] + BOUND[3] + -ED[3]] —**un•bound′ed•ly,** *adv.* —**un•bound′ed•ness,** *n.*
—**Syn. 1.** limitless, immense, vast, infinite, immeasurable. **2.** unconfined, immoderate.

un•bowed (un boud′), *adj.* **1.** not bowed or bent. **2.** not yielding or submitting, as to defeat; not subjugated: *Even when their country was occupied, the people of Norway remained unbowed.* [1325–75; ME; see UN-[1] + BOWED]

un•brace (un brās′), *v.t.,* **-braced, -brac•ing.** **1.** to remove the braces of. **2.** to free from tension; relax. **3.** to weaken. [1350–1400; ME *unbracen* to free of clothing or armor. See UN-[2], BRACE]

un•braid (un brād′), *v.t.* to separate (anything braided, as hair) into the several strands. [1820–30; UN-[2] + BRAID]

un•brand•ed (un bran′did), *adj.* **1.** not branded or marked to show ownership: *an unbranded calf.* **2.** *Com.* carrying no brand or trademark of a manufacturer: *unbranded canned foods.* [1635–45; UN- + BRAND + -ED[2], -ED[3]]

CONCISE ETYMOLOGY KEY: <, descended or borrowed from; >, whence; b., blend of, blended; c., cognate with; cf., compare; deriv., derivative; equiv., equivalent; imit., imitative; obl., oblique; r., replacing; s., stem; sp., spelling, spelled; resp., respelling, respelled; trans., translation; ?, origin unknown; *, unattested; ‡, probably earlier than. See the full key inside the front cover.

un′as•sid′u•ous, *adj.;* **-ly,** *adv.;* **-ness,** *n.*
un′as•sign′a•ble, *adj.;* **-bly,** *adv.*
un′as•signed′, *adj.*
un′as•sim′i•la•ble, *adj.*
un′as•sim′i•lat′ed, *adj.*
un′as•sim′i•lat′ing, *adj.*
un′as•sim′i•la′tive, *adj.*
un′as•sist′ant, *adj.*
un′as•sist′ed, *adj.*
un′as•sist′ing, *adj.*
un′as•so′ci•a•ble, *adj.;* **-bly,** *adv.*
un′as•so′ci•at′ed, *adj.*
un′as•so′ci•a′tive, *adj.;* **-ly,** *adv.*
un′as•sort′ed, *adj.*
un′as•suage′a•ble, *adj.*
un′as•suaged′, *adj.*
un′as•suag′ing, *adj.*
un′as•sua′sive, *adj.*
un′as•sum′a•ble, *adj.*
un′as•sumed′, *adj.*
un′as•sured′, *adj.*
un′as•sur′ed•ly, *adv.*
un′as•sur′ed•ness, *n.*
un′as•sur′ing, *adj.*
un′asth•mat′ic, *adj.*
un′as•ton′ished, *adj.*
un′ath•let′ic, *adj.*
un′ath•let′i•cal•ly, *adv.*
un′at•mos•pher′ic, *adj.*
un′a•toned′, *adj.*
un′a•ton′ing, *adj.*
un•at′ro•phied, *adj.*
un′at•tach′a•ble, *adj.*
un′at•tack′a•ble, *adj.*
un′at•tacked′, *adj.*
un′at•tain′a•bil′i•ty, *n.*
un′at•tain′a•ble, *adj.;* **-ble•ness,** *n.;* **-bly,** *adv.*
un′at•tained′, *adj.*
un′at•tain′ing, *adj.*
un′at•taint′ed, *adj.*
un′at•tem′pered, *adj.*
un′at•tempt′a•ble, *adj.*
un′at•tempt′ed, *adj.*
un′at•tempt′ing, *adj.*
un′at•tend′ance, *n.*
un′at•tend′ant, *adj.*
un′at•ten′tive, *adj.;* **-ly,** *adv.;* **-ness,** *n.*
un′at•ten′u•at′ed, *adj.;* **-ly,** *adv.*
un′at•test′ed, *adj.*
un′at•tired′, *adj.*
un′at•tract′a•ble, *adj.*
un′at•tract′ed, *adj.*
un′at•tract′ing, *adj.*
un′at•trac′tive, *adj.;* **-ly,** *adv.;* **-ness,** *n.*
un′at•trib′ut•a•ble, *adj.;* **-bly,** *adv.*
un′at•trib′ut•ed, *adj.*
un′at•trib′u•tive, *adj.;* **-ly,** *adv.;* **-ness,** *n.*
un′at•tuned′, *adj.*
un′auc′tioned, *adj.*
un′au•da′cious, *adj.;* **-ly,** *adv.;* **-ness,** *n.*
un•au′dit•ed, *adj.*
un′au•di′tioned, *adj.*
un′aug•ment′a•ble, *adj.*
un′aug•ment′a•tive, *adj.*
un′aug•ment′ed, *adj.*
un′aus•pi′cious, *adj.;* **-ly,** *adv.*
un′aus•tere′, *adj.;* **-ly,** *adv.*
un′-Aus•tral′ian, *adj.*
un-Aus′tri•an, *adj.*
un′au•then′tic, *adj.*
un′au•then′ti•cal, *adj.;* **-ly,** *adv.;* **-ness,** *n.*
un′au•then′ti•cat′ed, *adj.*
un′au•then•tic′i•ty, *n.*
un′au•thor′i•ta′tive, *adj.;* **-ly,** *adv.;* **-ness,** *n.*
un•au′thor•ized′, *adj.*
un′au•tis′tic, *adj.*
un•au′to•graphed′, *adj.*
un′au•to•mat′ed, *adj.*
un′au•to•mat′ic, *adj.*
un′au•to•mat′i•cal•ly, *adv.*
un′au•tum′nal, *adj.*
un′a•vail′a•bil′i•ty, *n.*
un′a•vail′a•ble, *adj.;* **-ble•ness,** *n.;* **-bly,** *adv.*
un′a•vailed′, *adj.*
un′a•venge′a•ble, *adj.*
un′a•venged′, *adj.*
un′a•veng′ing, *adj.;* **-ly,** *adv.*
un•av′er•aged, *adj.*
un′a•verred′, *adj.*
un′a•vert′ed, *adj.*
un•av′id, *adj.;* **-ly,** *adv.;* **-ness,** *n.*
un′a•void′ing, *adj.*
un′a•vouched′, *adj.*
un′a•vow′a•ble, *adj.;* **-ble•ness,** *n.;* **-bly,** *adv.*
un′a•vowed′, *adj.*
un′a•wake′, *adj.*
un′a•wake′a•ble, *adj.*
un′a•waked′, *adj.*
un′a•wak′en•ing, *adj.*
un′a•wak′ing, *adj.*
un′a•ward′a•ble, *adj.*
un′a•ward′ed, *adj.*
un•awed′, *adj.*
un•aw′ful, *adj.;* **-ness,** *n.*
un•awk′ward, *adj.;* **-ly,** *adv.;* **-ness,** *n.*
un•awned′, *adj.*
un•axed′, *adj.*
un′ax•i•o•mat′ic, *adj.*
un′ax•i•o•mat′i•cal•ly, *adv.*
un•ax′ised, *adj.*
un•ax′led, *adj.*
un•back′ward, *adj.*
un′bac•te′ri•al, *adj.*
un•badged′, *adj.*
un•badg′ered, *adj.*
un•badg′er•ing, *adj.*
un•baf′fled, *adj.*
un•baf′fling, *adj.;* **-ly,** *adv.*
un•bagged′, *adj.*
un•bail′a•ble, *adj.*
un•bailed′, *adj.*
un•bait′, *v.t.*
un•baked′, *adj.*
un•bal′co•nied, *adj.*
un•bale′, *v.t.,* **-baled, -bal•ing.**
un•balked′, *adj.*
un•balk′ing, *adj.;* **-ly,** *adv.*
un•bal′lot•ed, *adj.*
un•band′age, *v.t.,* **-aged, -ag•ing.**
un•band′ed, *adj.*
un•ban′gled, *adj.*
un•ban′ished, *adj.*
un•bank′a•ble, *adj.;* **-ble•ness,** *n.;* **-bly,** *adv.*
un•banked′, *adj.*
un•banned′, *adj.*
un•ban′nered, *adj.*
un•ban′ter•ing, *adj.;* **-ly,** *adv.*
un•bap′tized, *adj.*
un•bar′ba•rize′, *v.t.,* **-rized, -riz•ing.**
un•bar′ba•rous, *adj.;* **-ly,** *adv.;* **-ness,** *n.*
un•bar′bered, *adj.*
un•bar′gained, *adj.*
un•bark′ing, *adj.*
un•bar′ra•ble, *adj.*
un•bar′reled, *adj.*
un•bar′relled, *adj.*
un•bar′ren, *adj.;* **-ly,** *adv.;* **-ness,** *n.*
un•bar′ri•cade′, *v.t.,* **-cad•ed, -cad•ing.**
un•bar′tered, *adj.*
un•bar′ter•ing, *adj.*
un•base′, *adj.*
un•based′, *adj.*
un•bash′ful, *adj.;* **-ly,** *adv.;* **-ness,** *n.*
un•bas′ket•like′, *adj.*
un•bas′tard•ized′, *adj.*
un•bast′ed, *adj.*
un′bas•ti•na′doed, *adj.*
un•bathed′, *adj.*
un•bat′ing, *adj.*
un•bat′ted, *adj.*
un•bat′ter•a•ble, *adj.*
un•bat′tered, *adj.*
un•bat′tling, *adj.*
un•beached′, *adj.*
un•bea′coned, *adj.*
un•bead′ed, *adj.*
un•beamed′, *adj.*
un•beam′ing, *adj.*
un•beard′, *v.t.*
un•beard′ed, *adj.*
un•bear′ing, *adj.*
un•beaued′, *adj.*
un•beau′te•ous, *adj.;* **-ly,** *adv.;* **-ness,** *n.*
un•beau′ti•fied′, *adj.*
un•beau′ti•ful, *adj.;* **-ly,** *adv.*
un•beck′oned, *adj.*
un′be•cloud′ed, *adj.*
un′be•dab′bled, *adj.*
un′be•daubed′, *adj.*
un′be•decked′, *adj.*
un′be•dimmed′, *adj.*
un′be•di′zened, *adj.*
un′be•drag′gled, *adj.*
un′be•fit′ting, *adj.*
un′be•friend′ed, *adj.*
un•beg′gar•ly, *adj.*
un•begged′, *adj.*
un′be•grudged′, *adj.*
un′be•guiled′, *adj.*
un′be•guil′ing, *adj.*
un′be•hav′ing, *adj.*
un′be•head′ed, *adj.*
un′be•held′, *adj.*
un′be•hold′a•ble, *adj.*
un′be•hold′en, *adj.*
un′be•lied′, *adj.*
un•bel′li•cose′, *adj.*
un′bel•lig′er•ent, *adj.;* **-ly,** *adv.*
un′be•long′ing, *adj.*
un′be•loved′, *adj.*
un•belt′ed, *adj.*
un′be•moaned′, *adj.*
un′be•mused′, *adj.*
un•bench′, *v.t.*
un•ben′e•ficed, *adj.*
un′be•nef′i•cent, *adj.;* **-ly,** *adv.*
un′ben•e•fi′cial, *adj.;* **-ly,** *adv.;* **-ness,** *n.*
un•ben′e•fit•ed, *adj.*
un•ben′e•fit•ing, *adj.*
un′be•nev′o•lence, *n.*
un′be•nev′o•lent, *adj.;* **-ly,** *adv.*
un′be•nign′, *adj.;* **-ly,** *adv.*
un′be•nig′nant, *adj.;* **-ly,** *adv.*
un′be•nig′ni•ty, *n., pl.* **-ties.**
un′be•numbed′, *adj.*
un′be•queath′a•ble, *adj.*
un′be•queathed′, *adj.*
un′be•reaved′, *adj.*
un′be•rouged′, *adj.*
un•berth′, *v.t.*
un′be•seech′ing, *adj.;* **-ly,** *adv.*
un′be•seem′ing, *adj.*
un′be•set′, *adj.*
un′be•sieged′, *adj.*
un′be•smeared′, *adj.*
un′be•smirched′, *adj.*
un′be•smut′ted, *adj.*
un′be•sought′, *adj.*
un′be•spo′ken, *adj.*
un′be•sprin′kled, *adj.*
un′be•stowed′, *adj.*
un•bet′, *adj.*
un′be•trayed′, *adj.*
un′be•tray′ing, *adj.*
un′be•trothed′, *adj.*
un•bet′tered, *adj.*
un•bev′eled, *adj.*
un•bev′elled, *adj.*
un′be•wailed′, *adj.*
un′be•wail′ing, *adj.*
un′be•wil′dered, *adj.;* **-ly,** *adv.*
un′be•wil′der•ing, *adj.;* **-ly,** *adv.*
un′be•witched′, *adj.*
un′be•witch′ing, *adj.;* **-ly,** *adv.*
un′be•wrayed′, *adj.*
un•bib′u•lous, *adj.;* **-ly,** *adv.;* **-ness,** *n.*

un•breathed (un brēthd′), *adj.* **1.** not breathed: *unbreathed air.* **2.** not disclosed; uncommunicated, as a secret. [1580–90; UN-[1] + BREATHED]

un•bred (un bred′), *adj.* **1.** not taught or trained. **2.** not bred or mated, as a stock animal; not yet bred: *An unbred cow gives no milk.* [1590–1600; UN-[1] + BRED]

un•bri•dle (un brīd′l), *v.t.,* **-dled, -dling. 1.** to remove the bridle from (a horse, mule, etc.). **2.** to free from restraint. [1350–1400; ME *unbridlen.* See UN-[2], BRIDLE (v.)]

un•bri•dled (un brīd′ld), *adj.* **1.** not controlled or restrained: *unbridled enthusiasm.* **2.** not fitted with a bridle. [1325–75; ME *unbrydled.* See UN-[1], BRIDLED]

un•broke (un brōk′), *adj. Obs.* unbroken.

un•bro•ken (un brō′kən), *adj.* **1.** not broken; whole; intact. **2.** uninterrupted; continuous. **3.** not tamed, as a horse. **4.** undisturbed; unimpaired. [1250–1300; ME; see UN-[1], BROKEN] **—un•bro′ken•ly,** *adv.* **—un•bro′ken•ness,** *n.*
—Syn. 1. complete, entire.

un•buck•le (un buk′əl), *v.,* **-led, -ling.** **—***v.i.* **1.** to unfasten the buckle or buckles of. **—***v.i.* **2.** to undo a buckle. [1350–1400; ME *unboclen.* See UN-[2], BUCKLE]

un•budge•a•ble (un buj′ə bəl), *adj.* incapable of being budged or changed; inflexible: *an unbudgeable opinion.* [1925–30; UN-[1] + BUDGE[1] + -ABLE] **—un•budge′a•bil′i•ty, un•budge′a•ble•ness,** *n.* **—un•budge′a•bly,** *adv.*

un•build (un bild′), *v.t.,* **-built, -build•ing.** to demolish (something built); raze. [1600–10; UN-[2] + BUILD]

un•bun•dle (un bun′dl), *v.,* **-dled, -dling. —***v.t.* **1.** to separate the charges for (related products or services usually offered as a package): *to unbundle computer hardware and software.* **2.** to separate (charges for related products or services): *to unbundle charges for telephone service.* **—***v.i.* **3.** to set separate charges for related products or services. [1600–10 for literal sense; 1965–70 for def. 1; UN-[2] + BUNDLE]

un•bun•dled (un bun′dld), *adj.* (of related products or services) sold separately rather than as a package: *unbundled financial services.* [1965–70; UNBUNDLE + -ED[2]]

un•bur•den (un bûr′dn), *v.t.* **1.** to free from a burden. **2.** to relieve (one's mind, conscience, etc.) by revealing or confessing something. **3.** to cast off or get rid of, as a burden or something burdensome; disclose; reveal: *He unburdened the worries that plagued him.* [1530–40; UN-[2] + BURDEN[1]]
—Syn. 3. confide.

un•but•ton (un but′n), *v.t.* **1.** to free (buttons) from buttonholes; unfasten or undo. **2.** to unfasten by or as if by unbuttoning: *to unbutton a jacket.* **3.** to disclose (one's feelings, thoughts, etc.) after deliberate or prolonged silence. **—***v.i.* **4.** to unfasten a button or one's buttons. [1275–1325; ME *unbotenen.* See UN-[2], BUTTON]

un•but•toned (un but′nd), *adj.* **1.** not buttoned. **2.** *Informal.* free open, or informal; unrestrained: *unbuttoned humor.* [1575–85; UNBUTTON + -ED[2] or UN-[1] + BUTTONED]

UNC, United Nations Command. Also, **U.N.C.**

un•cage (un kāj′), *v.t.,* **-caged, -cag•ing.** to set free from or as if from a cage; free from confinement or restraint. [1610–20; UN-[2] + CAGE]

un•caged (un kājd′), *adj.* **1.** not confined in a cage. **2.** free or set free from confinement or restraint: *the uncaged spirit of a freethinker.* [1725–35; UN-[1] + CAGE + -ED[2] for def. 1; UNCAGE + -ED[2] for def. 2]

un•called-for (un kôld′fôr′), *adj.* **1.** not called for; not required; superfluous; unwanted. **2.** unwarranted; unjustified; improper: *an uncalled-for criticism.* [1600–10]

un•can•ny (un kan′ē), *adj.* **1.** having or seeming to have a supernatural or inexplicable basis; beyond the ordinary or normal; extraordinary: *uncanny accuracy; an uncanny knack of foreseeing trouble.* **2.** mysterious; arousing superstitious fear or dread; uncomfortably strange: *Uncanny sounds filled the house.* [1590–1600; UN-[1] + CANNY] **—un•can′ni•ly,** *adv.* **—un•can′ni•ness,** *n.*
—Syn. 2. preternatural, odd. See **weird. —Ant. 2.** ordinary, natural.

un•ca•non•i•cal (un′kə non′i kəl), *adj.* **1.** not in accordance with canons or rules. **2.** not belonging to the canon of Scripture. [1625–35; UN-[1] + CANONICAL] **—un′ca•non′i•cal•ly,** *adv.*

un•cap (un kap′), *v.,* **-capped, -cap•ping. —***v.t.* **1.** to remove a cap or cover from (a bottle, container, etc.). **2.** to free from limits or restrictions: *The union is demanding that cost-of-living allowances be uncapped.* **3.** to remove a cap or hat from (the head of a person). **—***v.i.* **4.** to remove the cap or hat from the head, as in respect. [1560–70; UN-[2] + CAP[1]]

un•ca•pa•ble (un kā′pə bəl), *adj.* incapable. [1580–90; UN-[1] + CAPABLE]

un•cared-for (un kârd′fôr′), *adj.* **1.** untended; neglected; unkempt: *The garden had an uncared-for look.* **2.** not cared for; not liked or favored: *uncared-for reminders of youth.* [1590–1600]

Un•cas (ung′kəs), *n.* (*"the Circler"*) 1588?–1683?, Mohegan leader.

un•case (un kās′), *v.t.,* **-cased, -cas•ing. 1.** to remove from a case; remove the case from. **2.** to remove the cover from; put on view. **3.** to make known; reveal. [1560–70; UN-[2] + CASE[2]]

un•caused (un kôzd′), *adj.* not resulting from some antecedent cause. [1620–30; UN-[1] + CAUSED]

un•ceas•ing (un sē′sing), *adj.* not ceasing or stopping; continuous: *an unceasing flow of criticism.* [1350–1400; ME *uncesyng;* see UN-[1], CEASE, -ING[2]] **—un•ceas′ing•ly,** *adv.* **—un•ceas′ing•ness,** *n.*

un•cer•e•mo•ni•ous (un′ser ə mō′nē əs), *adj.* **1.** discourteously abrupt; hasty; rude: *He made an unceremonious departure in the middle of my speech.* **2.** without ceremony or formalities; informal. [1590–1600; UN-[1] + CEREMONIOUS] **—un′cer•e•mo′ni•ous•ly,** *adv.* **—un′cer•e•mo′ni•ous•ness,** *n.*

un•cer•tain (un sûr′tn), *adj.* **1.** not definitely ascertainable or fixed, as in time of occurrence, number, dimensions, or quality. **2.** not confident, assured, or free from hesitancy: *an uncertain smile.* **3.** not clearly or precisely determined; indefinite; unknown: *a manuscript of uncertain origin.* **4.** vague; indistinct; not perfectly apprehended: *an abstruse novel with uncertain themes.* **5.** subject to change; variable; capricious; unstable: *a person of uncertain opinions.* **6.** ambiguous; unreliable; undependable: *Her loyalties are uncertain.* **7.** dependent on chance or unpredictable factors; doubtful; of unforeseeable outcome or effect. **8.** unsteady or flickering, as light; of changing intensity or quality. [1250–1300; ME; see UN-[1], CERTAIN] **—un•cer′tain•ly,** *adv.* **—un•cer′tain•ness,** *n.*
—Syn. 1. unsure, unpredictable. UNCERTAIN, INSECURE, PRECARIOUS imply a lack of predictability. That which is UNCERTAIN is doubtful or problematical; it often involves danger through an inability to predict or to place confidence in the unknown: *The time of his arrival is uncertain.* That which is INSECURE is not firm, stable, reliable, or safe, and hence is likely to give way, fail, or be overcome: *an insecure foundation, footing, protection.* PRECARIOUS suggests great susceptibility to failure, or exposure to imminent danger: *a precarious means of existence.* **3.** unsettled, undetermined. **8.** irregular.

un•cer•tain•ty (un sûr′tn tē), *n., pl.* **-ties** for 2. **1.** the state of being uncertain; doubt; hesitancy: *His uncertainty gave impetus to his inquiry.* **2.** an instance of uncertainty, doubt, etc. **3.** unpredictability; indeterminacy; indefiniteness. [1350–1400; ME *uncerteynte;* see UN-[1], CERTAINTY]
—Syn. 1. hesitation, irresolution, indecision, ambivalence.

uncer′tainty prin′ciple, *Physics.* the principle of quantum mechanics, formulated by Heisenberg, that the accurate measurement of one of two related, observable quantities, as position and momentum or energy and time, produces uncertainties in the measurement of the other, such that the product of the uncertainties of both quantities is equal to or greater than $h/2\pi$, where h equals Planck's constant. Also called **indeterminacy principle, Heisenberg uncertainty principle.** [1930–35]

uncertif′icated share′. See **book share.**

un•chain (un chān′), *v.t.* to free from or as if from chains; set free. [1575–85; UN-[2] + CHAIN] **—un•chain′a•ble,** *adj.*

un•chanc•y (un chan′sē, -chän′-), *adj. Chiefly Scot.* **1.** unlucky. **2.** dangerous. [1525–35; UN-[1] + CHANCY]

CONCISE PRONUNCIATION KEY: *act, cāpe, dâre, pärt; set, ēqual; if, īce; ox, ōver, ôrder, oil, bŏŏk, bōōt, out; up, ûrge; child; sing; shoe; thin, that;* zh as in *treasure.* ə = *a* as in *alone, e* as in *system, i* as in *easily, o* as in *gallop, u* as in *circus;* ᵊ as in *fire* (fīᵊr), *hour* (ouᵊr). l and n can serve as syllabic consonants, as in *cradle* (krād′l), and *button* (but′n). See the full key inside the front cover.

un•bick′ered, *adj.*
un•bick′er•ing, *adj.*
un•bid′da•ble, *adj.*
un•big′a•mous, *adj.;* **-ly,** *adv.*
un•big′ot•ed, *adj.*
un•bil′ious, *adj.;* **-ly,** *adv.;* **-ness,** *n.*
un•bill′a•ble, *adj.*
un•billed′, *adj.*
un•bil′let•ed, *adj.*
un•binned′, *adj.*
un′bi•o•graph′i•cal, *adj.;* **-ly,** *adv.*
un′bi•o•log′i•cal, *adj.;* **-ly,** *adv.*
un•bird′like′, *adj.*
un•bit′, *v.t.,* **-bit•ted, -bit•ting.**
un•bit′, *adj.*
un•bit′ing, *adj.*
un•bit′ten, *adj.*
un•bit′ter, *adj.*
un•blacked′, *adj.*
un•black′ened, *adj.*
un•blade′, *v.t.,* **-blad•ed, -blad•ing.**
un•blam′a•ble, *adj.;* **-ble•ness,** *n.;* **-bly,** *adv.*
un•blamed′, *adj.*
un•blam′ing, *adj.*
un•blanched′, *adj.*
un•blan′ket•ed, *adj.*
un•blas′phemed, *adj.*
un•blast′ed, *adj.*
un•bla′zoned, *adj.*
un•bleached′, *adj.*
un•bleach′ing, *adj.*
un•bled′, *adj.*
un•bleed′ing, *adj.*
un•blem′ish•a•ble, *adj.*
un•blem′ished, *adj.*
un•blem′ish•ing, *adj.*
un•blench′ing, *adj.;* **-ly,** *adv.*
un•blend′a•ble, *adj.*
un•blend′ed, *adj.*
un•blent′, *adj.*
un•blight′ed, *adj.;* **-ly,** *adv.;* **-ness,** *n.*
un•blind′fold′ed, *adj.*
un•blind′ing, *adj.*
un•blink′ered, *adj.*
un•bliss′ful, *adj.;* **-ly,** *adv.;* **-ness,** *n.*
un•blis′tered, *adj.*
un•bloat′ed, *adj.*
un′block•ad′ed, *adj.*
un•blocked′, *adj.*
un•blood′i•ly, *adv.*
un•blood′i•ness, *n.*
un•blood′y, *adj.*
un•bloomed′, *adj.*
un•blos′somed, *adj.*
un•blos′som•ing, *adj.*
un•blot′ted, *adj.*
un•bloused′, *adj.*
un•blown′, *adj.*
un•blued′, *adj.*
un•bluff′a•ble, *adj.*
un•bluffed′, *adj.*
un•bluff′ing, *adj.*
un•blun′der•ing, *adj.*
un•blunt′ed, *adj.*
un•blurred′, *adj.*
un•blus′ter•ous, *adj.;* **-ly,** *adv.*
un•board′ed, *adj.*
un•boast′ed, *adj.*
un•boast′ful, *adj.;* **-ly,** *adv.;* **-ness,** *n.*
un•boast′ing, *adj.*
un•bobbed′, *adj.*
un•bod′ing, *adj.*
un•bog′gy, *adj.*
un•boiled′, *adj.*
un•bois′ter•ous, *adj.;* **-ly,** *adv.;* **-ness,** *n.*
un•bold′, *adj.;* **-ly,** *adv.;* **-ness,** *n.*
un•bol′ster, *v.t.*
un•bol′stered, *adj.*
un′bom•bard′ed, *adj.*
un′bom•bas′tic, *adj.*
un′bom•bas′ti•cal•ly, *adv.*
un•bombed′, *adj.*
un•bond′a•ble, *adj.*
un•bond′ed, *adj.*
un•booked′, *adj.*
un•book′ish, *adj.;* **-ly,** *adv.;* **-ness,** *n.*
un•boot′ed, *adj.*
un•bor′dered, *adj.*
un•bored′, *adj.*
un•bor′ing, *adj.*
un•borne′, *adj.*
un•bor′rowed, *adj.*
un•bor′row•ing, *adj.*
un•bossed′, *adj.*
un′bo•tan′i•cal, *adj.*
un•both′ered, *adj.*
un•both′er•ing, *adj.*
un•bot′tle, *v.t.,* **-tled, -tling.**
un•bot′tom, *v.t.*
un•bought′, *adj.*
un•boun′te•ous, *adj.;* **-ly,** *adv.;* **-ness,** *n.*
un•boun′ti•ful, *adj.;* **-ly,** *adv.;* **-ness,** *n.*
un•bowd′ler•ized′, *adj.*
un•bow′ing, *adj.*
un•bowled′, *adj.*
un•box′, *v.t.*
un•boy′ish, *adj.;* **-ly,** *adv.;* **-ness,** *n.*
un•brace′let•ed, *adj.*
un•brack′et•ed, *adj.*
un•brag′ging, *adj.*
un′-Brah•min′i•cal, *adj.*
un•brailed′, *adj.*
un•branched′, *adj.*
un•branch′ing, *adj.*
un•bran′died, *adj.*
un•brave′, *adj.;* **-ly,** *adv.;* **-ness,** *n.*
un•braved′, *adj.*
un•brawl′ing, *adj.*
un•brawn′y, *adj.*
un•bra′zen, *adj.;* **-ly,** *adv.;* **-ness,** *n.*
un•breach′a•ble, *adj.;* **-ble•ness,** *n.;* **-bly,** *adv.*
un•breached′, *adj.*
un•bread′ed, *adj.*
un•break′a•ble, *adj.;* **-ble•ness,** *n.;* **-bly,** *adv.*
un•break′ing, *adj.*
un•breath′a•ble, *adj.*
un•breath′ing, *adj.*
un•breeched′, *adj.*
un•breez′y, *adj.*
un•brewed′, *adj.*
un•brib′a•ble, *adj.;* **-bly,** *adv.*
un•bribed′, *adj.*
un•brib′ing, *adj.*
un•bricked′, *adj.*
un•bridge′a•ble, *adj.*
un•bridged′, *adj.*
un•brief′, *adj.;* **-ly,** *adv.;* **-ness,** *n.*
un•briefed′, *adj.*
un•bright′, *adj.;* **-ly,** *adv.;* **-ness,** *n.*
un•bright′ened, *adj.*
un•bril′liant, *adj.;* **-ly,** *adv.;* **-ness,** *n.*
un•brim′ming, *adj.*
un•brined′, *adj.*
un•bris′tled, *adj.*
un•brit′tle, *adj.;* **-ness,** *n.*
un•broached′, *adj.*
un•broad′cast′ed, *adj.*
un•broad′ened, *adj.*
un′bro•cad′ed, *adj.*
un•broiled′, *adj.*
un•bronzed′, *adj.*
un•brooch′, *v.t.*
un•brood′ed, *adj.*
un•brood′ing, *adj.*
un•broth′ered, *adj.*
un•broth′er•li•ness, *n.*
un•broth′er•ly, *adj., adv.*
un•brought′, *adj.*
un•browned′, *adj.*
un•brows′ing, *adj.*
un•bruised′, *adj.*
un•brush′a•ble, *adj.*
un•brushed′, *adj.*
un•bru′tal•ize′, *v.t.,* **-ized, -iz•ing.**
un•brut′ize, *v.t.,* **-ized, -iz•ing.**
un•bud′, *v.t.,* **-bud•ded, -bud•ding.**
un•budged′, *adj.*
un•budg′et•ed, *adj.*
un•budg′ing, *adj.*
un•buffed′, *adj.*
un•buff′ered, *adj.*
un•buf′fet•ed, *adj.*
un•bugged′, *adj.*
un•build′a•ble, *adj.*
un•bulk′y, *adj.*
un•bul′lied, *adj.*
un•bul′ly•ing, *adj.*
un•bumped′, *adj.*
un•bump′tious, *adj.;* **-ly,** *adv.;* **-ness,** *n.*
un•bunched′, *adj.*
un•bun′gling, *adj.*
un•buoy′ant, *adj.;* **-ly,** *adv.*
un•buoyed′, *adj.*
un•bur′den•some, *adj.*
un′bu•reau•crat′ic, *adj.*
un′bu•reau•crat′i•cal•ly, *adv.*
un•bur′glar•ized′, *adj.*
un•bur′ied, *adj.*
un′bur•lesqued′, *adj.*
un•bur′ly, *adj.*
un•burn′a•ble, *adj.*
un•burned′, *adj.*
un•burn′ing, *adj.*
un•bur′nished, *adj.*
un•burnt′, *adj.*
un•bur′rowed, *adj.*
un•burst′, *adj.*
un•burst′a•ble, *adj.*
un•bus′i•ly, *adv.*
un•busi′ness•like′, *adj.*
un•bus′kined, *adj.*
un•bus′tling, *adj.*
un•bus′y, *adj.*
un•butch′ered, *adj.*
un•but′tered, *adj.*
un•but′tressed, *adj.*
un•buy′a•ble, *adj.*
un•buy′ing, *adj.*
un•by′lined′, *adj.*
un•cab′ined, *adj.*
un•ca′bled, *adj.*
un′ca•coph′o•nous, *adj.*
un•ca′denced, *adj.*
un′ca•jol′ing, *adj.*
un•cake′, *v.t.,* **-caked, -cak•ing.**
un′ca•lam′i•tous, *adj.;* **-ly,** *adv.*
un′cal•car′e•ous, *adj.*
un•cal′ci•fied′, *adj.*
un•cal′cined, *adj.*
un•cal′cu•la•ble, *adj.;* **-bly,** *adv.*
un•cal′cu•lat′ed, *adj.*
un•cal′cu•lat′ing, *adj.;* **-ly,** *adv.*
un•cal′cu•la′tive, *adj.*
un•cal′en•dared, *adj.*
un•cal′i•brat′ed, *adj.*
un•calk′, *v.t.*
un•calked′, *adj.*
un•called′, *adj.*
un•cal′lous, *adj.;* **-ly,** *adv.;* **-ness,** *n.*
un•cal′lused, *adj.*
un•calm′, *adj.;* **-ly,** *adv.;* **-ness,** *n.*
un•cal′ma•tive, *adj.*
un′cal•o•rif′ic, *adj.*
un′ca•lum′ni•ous, *adj.;* **-ly,** *adv.*
un•cam′bered, *adj.*
un•cam′ou•flaged′, *adj.*
un′cam•paign′ing, *adj.*
un•camped′, *adj.*
un•cam′phor•at′ed, *adj.*
un′ca•nal′ized, *adj.*
un•can′cel•a•ble, *adj.*
un•can′celed, *adj.*
un•can′cel•la•ble, *adj.*
un•can′celled, *adj.*
un•can′cer•ous, *adj.*

un·charge (un chärj′), *v.t.*, **-charged, -charg·ing.** *Obs.* to acquit. [1275–1325; ME *unchargen;* see UN-[2], CHARGE]

un·charged (un chärjd′), *adj.* not charged, esp. with electricity; electrically neutral: *an uncharged battery; an uncharged particle.* [1425–75; late ME: unburdened, uncalled; see UN-[1], CHARGED]

un·char·i·ta·ble (un char′i tə bəl), *adj.* deficient in charity; unkind; harsh; unforgiving; censorious; merciless: *an uncharitable attitude; an uncharitable neighbor.* [1425–75; late ME; see UN-[1], CHARITABLE] —**un·char′i·ta·ble·ness,** *n.* —**un·char′i·ta·bly,** *adv.*

un·chart·ed (un chär′tid), *adj.* not shown or located on a map; unexplored; unknown, as a place or region: *the uncharted depths of space.* [1840–50; UN-[1] + CHART + -ED[2]]

un·char·tered (un chär′tərd), *adj.* **1.** without a charter. **2.** without regulation; lawless. [1795–1805; UN-[1] + CHARTER + -ED[2]]

un·chaste (un chāst′), *adj.* **1.** not chaste; not virtuous; not pure: *an unchaste woman.* **2.** characterized by sexual suggestiveness, transgression, or excess; lascivious; bawdy: *an unchaste exhibition.* [1350–1400; ME; see UN-[1], CHASTE] —**un·chaste′ly,** *adv.* —**un·chaste′·ness, un·chas·ti·ty** (un chas′ti tē), *n.*

un·chic (un shēk′), *adj.* not chic; inelegant; passé. [1955–60; UN-[1] + CHIC]

un·choke (un chōk′), *v.t.*, **-choked, -chok·ing.** to free of obstruction or congestion. [1580–90; UN-[2] + CHOKE]

un·chris·tian (un kris′chən), *adj.* **1.** not conforming to Christian teaching or principles: *unchristian selfishness.* **2.** not Christian. **3.** *Informal.* unsuitable for Christians; uncivilized; objectionable: *She declared she would not pay such an unchristian amount of money for a hotel room.* [1545–55; UN-[1] + CHRISTIAN] —**un·chris′tian·ly,** *adv.*

un·church (un chûrch′), *v.t.* **1.** to expel (a person) from a church; excommunicate. **2.** to deprive of the character and rights of a church. [1610–20; UN-[2] + CHURCH]

un·churched (un chûrcht′), *adj.* not being a member of a church; not attending any church. [1675–85; UN-[1] + CHURCH + -ED[2]]

un·ci·a (un′shē ə), *n., pl.* **-ci·ae** (-shē ē′). **1.** a bronze coin of ancient Rome, the 12th part of an as. **2.** (in prescriptions) an ounce of weight or volume. [1685–95; < L: a twelfth part, akin to *ūnus* one; cf. INCH[1]]

un·ci·al (un′shē əl, -shəl), *adj.* **1.** designating, written in, or pertaining to a form of majuscule writing having a curved or rounded shape and used chiefly in Greek and Latin manuscripts from about the 3rd to the 9th century A.D. —*n.* **2.** an uncial letter. **3.** uncial writing. **4.** a manuscript written in uncials. [1640–50; < LL *unciālēs* (*litterae*) (Jerome) uncial (letters), pl. of L *unciālis* weighing one twelfth of a libra (see UNCIA, -AL[1]); literal sense is unclear] —**un′ci·al·ly,** *adv.*

CONCISE ETYMOLOGY KEY: <, descended or borrowed from; >, whence; b., blend of, blended; c., cognate with; cf., compare; deriv., derivative; equiv., equivalent; imit., imitative; obl., oblique; r., replacing; s., stem; sp., spelling, spelled; resp., respelling, respelled; trans., translation; ?, origin unknown; *, unattested; ‡, probably earlier than. See the full key inside the front cover.

uncials (Latin) (8th century)

un·ci·form (un′sə fôrm′), *adj.* hook-shaped. [1725–35; < NL *unciformis,* equiv. to L *unc(us)* a hook, barb (c. Gk *ónkos*) + *-i-* -I- + *-formis* -FORM]

un·ci·na·ri·a·sis (un′sə nə rī′ə sis), *n. Pathol.* hookworm (def. 2). [1900–05; < NL *Uncinar(ia)* name of the genus (L *uncīn(us)* (see UNCINATE) + *-āria* -ARIA) + *-iasis* -IASIS]

un·ci·nate (un′sə nit, -nāt′), *adj. Biol.* hooked; bent at the end like a hook. [1750–60; < L *uncināt(us)* furnished with hooks, equiv. to *uncīnus* hook (*unc(us)* hook + *-īnus* -INE[1]) + *-ātus* -ATE[1]]

uncinate thorns

un′cinate proc′ess, *Ornith.* a curved, bony process on certain ribs of birds that projects backward and overlaps the succeeding rib, serving to strengthen the thorax. [1880–85]

UNCIO, United Nations Conference on International Organization.

un·cir·cum·cised (un sûr′kəm sīzd′), *adj.* **1.** not circumcised. **2.** not Jewish; gentile. **3.** heathen; unregenerate. [1350–1400; ME; see UN-[1], CIRCUMCISED]

un·cir·cum·ci·sion (un′sûr kəm sizh′ən), *n.* **1.** the state or condition of being uncircumcised. **2.** people who are not circumcised; gentiles. Rom. 2:26. [1520–30; UN-[1] + CIRCUMCISION]

un·civ·il (un siv′əl), *adj.* **1.** without good manners; unmannerly; rude; impolite; discourteous. **2.** uncivilized. [1545–55; UN-[1] + CIVIL] —**un·ci·vil·i·ty** (un′sə vil′i tē), **un·civ′il·ness,** *n.* —**un·civ′il·ly,** *adv.*

—**Syn. 1.** disrespectful, uncouth, boorish.

un·civ·i·lized (un siv′ə līzd′), *adj.* not civilized or cultured; barbarous. [1600–10; UN-[1] + CIVILIZED] —**un·civ·i·liz·ed·ly** (un siv′ə lī′zid lē, -līzd′-), *adv.* —**un·civ′i·liz′ed·ness,** *n.*

un·clad (un klad′), *v.* **1.** a pt. and pp. of **unclothe.** —*adj.* **2.** naked; nude; undressed. [1375–1425; late ME; see UN-[1], CLAD]

un·clamp (un klamp′), *v.t.* to undo the clamps of: *to unclamp one's ski boots.* [1800–10; UN-[2] + CLAMP]

un·clasp (un klasp′, -kläsp′), *v.t.* **1.** to undo the clasp or clasps of; unfasten. **2.** to release from the grasp: *to unclasp a sword handle.* —*v.i.* **3.** to become unclasped, as the hands or arms. **4.** to release or relax the grasp. [1520–30; UN-[2] + CLASP]

un·clas·si·cal (un klas′i kəl), *adj.* **1.** not classical; contrary to classical precepts. **2.** *Physics.* (formerly) nonclassical (def. 2). [1715–25; UN-[1] + CLASSICAL] —**un·clas′si·cal·ly,** *adv.*

un·clas·si·fied (un klas′ə fīd′), *adj.* **1.** not assigned to a class or category; not arranged according to characteristics: *Reported instances fall into two main types, with a few unclassified anomalies.* **2.** (of data, documents, etc.) not belonging to a category that is restricted for reasons of security; not secret: *unclassified plans; unclassified information.* [1860–65; UN-[1] + CLASSIFIED]

un·class·y (un klas′ē), *adj. Slang.* not classy; lacking in good taste or sense; crude: *Always being late for appointments is unclassy.* [UN-[1] + CLASSY]

un·cle (ung′kəl), *n.* **1.** a brother of one's father or mother. **2.** an aunt's husband. **3.** a familiar title or term of address for any elderly man. **4.** *Slang.* a pawnbroker. **5.** (*cap.*) *Informal.* Uncle Sam. **6.** a word formerly used in communications to represent the letter *U.* **7. say** or **cry uncle,** *Informal.* to concede defeat: *They ganged up on him in the schoolyard and made him say uncle.* [1250–1300; ME < AF *uncle,* OF *oncle* < L *avunculus* mother's brother, equiv. to *av(us)* mother's father + *-unculus* suffix extracted from dims. of n-stems (see HOMUNCULUS)] —**un′cle·less,** *adj.* —**un′cle·ship′,** *n.*

un·clean (un klēn′), *adj.*, **-er, -est. 1.** not clean; dirty. **2.** morally impure; evil; vile: *unclean thoughts.* **3.** *Chiefly Biblical.* having a physical or moral blemish so as to make impure according to the laws, esp. the dietary or ceremonial laws: *an unclean animal; unclean persons.* [bef. 900; ME *unclene,* OE *unclǣne.* See UN-[1], CLEAN] —**un·clean′ness,** *n.*

—**Syn. 1.** soiled, filthy. **2.** base, unchaste, sinful, corrupt, polluted.

un·clean·ly[1] (un klēn′lē), *adv.* in an unclean manner. [bef. 950; OE *unclǣnlīce* (not recorded in ME). See UN-[1], CLEANLY]

un·clean·ly[2] (un klen′lē), *adj.*, **-li·er, -li·est.** unclean. [bef. 1000; ME *onclenlich,* OE *unclǣnlic.* See UNCLEAN, -LY] —**un·clean′li·ness,** *n.*

un·clench (un klench′), *v.t., v.i.* to open or become opened from a clenched state. Also, **un·clinch** (un-klinch′). [1300–50; ME *unclenchen.* See UN-[2], CLENCH]

Un′cle Re′mus (rē′məs), a character in several books by Joel Chandler Harris: a former plantation slave who tells animal tales to a little boy.

Un′cle Sam′, a personification of the government or people of the U.S.: represented as a tall, lean man with white chin whiskers, wearing a blue tailcoat, red-and-white-striped trousers, and a top hat with a band of stars. [1805–15, *Amer.*; extension of the initials U.S.]

Un′cle Tom′, *Disparaging and Offensive.* a black man considered by other blacks to be subservient to or to curry favor with whites. Cf. **Aunt Jemima.** [1920–25,

un·can′did, *adj.;* **-ly,** *adv.;* **-ness,** *n.*
un·can′died, *adj.*
un·can′dled, *adj.*
un·caned′, *adj.*
un·can′kered, *adj.*
un·canned′, *adj.*
un′can·on·i·za′tion, *n.*
un·can′on·ize′, *v.t.,* **-ized, -iz·ing.**
un·can′o·pied, *adj.*
un·can′toned, *adj.*
un·can′vassed, *adj.*
un′ca·pa′cious, *adj.;* **-ly,** *adv.;* **-ness,** *n.*
un′ca·par′i·soned, *adj.*
un·caped′, *adj.*
un·ca′per·ing, *adj.*
un′cap·i·tal·is′tic, *adj.*
un·cap′i·tal·ized′, *adj.*
un′ca·pit′u·lat′ed, *adj.*
un′ca·pit′u·lat′ing, *adj.*
un′ca·pri′cious, *adj.;* **-ly,** *adv.;* **-ness,** *n.*
un·cap′siz·a·ble, *adj.*
un·cap′sized, *adj.*
un·cap′suled, *adj.*
un·cap′tained, *adj.*
un·cap′tioned, *adj.*
un·cap′tious, *adj.;* **-ly,** *adv.;* **-ness,** *n.*
un·cap′ti·vat′ed, *adj.*
un·cap′ti·vat′ing, *adj.*
un·cap′ti·va′tive, *adj.*
un·cap′tur·a·ble, *adj.*
un·cap′tured, *adj.*
un·car′a·mel·ized′, *adj.*
un·car′bon·at′ed, *adj.*
un·car′bon·ized′, *adj.*
un·car′bu·ret′ed, *adj.*
un·car′bu·ret′ted, *adj.*
un·card′ed, *adj.*
un·car′di·nal·ly, *adv.*
un′ca·ressed′, *adj.*
un′ca·ress′ing, *adj.;* **-ly,** *adv.*
un·car′i·ca·tured, *adj.*
un·car′ing, *adj.*
un′car·niv′o·rous, *adj.;* **-ly,** *adv.;* **-ness,** *n.*
un·car′oled, *adj.*
un·car′olled, *adj.*
un′ca·rous′ing, *adj.*
un·car′pen·tered, *adj.*
un·car′pet·ed, *adj.*
un·car′ried, *adj.*
un·cart′ed, *adj.*
un·car′toned, *adj.*
un′car·tooned′, *adj.*
un·carved′, *adj.*
un′cas·cad′ed, *adj.*
un′cas·cad′ing, *adj.*
un·case′mat′ed, *adj.*
un·cashed′, *adj.*
un·cask′, *v.t.*
un·casked′, *adj.*
un·cas′ket·ed, *adj.*
un·cast′, *adj.*
un·cas′ti·gat′ed, *adj.*
un·cas′ti·ga′tive, *adj.*
un·cas′tled, *adj.*
un·cas′trat·ed, *adj.*
un·cas′u·al, *adj.;* **-ly,** *adv.;* **-ness,** *n.*
un·cat′a·loged′, *adj.*
un·cat′a·logued′, *adj.*
un′cat·a·stroph′ic, *adj.*
un′cat·a·stroph′i·cal·ly, *adv.*
un·catch′a·ble, *adj.*
un·cat′e·chized′, *adj.*
un′cat·e·gor′i·cal, *adj.;* **-ly,** *adv.;* **-ness,** *n.*
un·cat′e·go·riz′a·ble, *adj.*
un·cat′e·go·rized′, *adj.*
un·cat′e·nat′ed, *adj.*
un·ca′tered, *adj.*
un·ca′ter·ing, *adj.*
un′ca·thar′tic, *adj.*
un·cath′o·lic, *adj.*
un′cath·o·lic′i·ty, *n.*
un′ca·thol′i·cize′, *v.t.,* **-cized, -ciz·ing.**
un·caught′, *adj.*
un·caus′a·ble, *adj.*
un·caus′al, *adj.*
un·caus′a·tive, *adj.;* **-ly,** *adv.;* **-ness,** *n.*
un·caus′tic, *adj.*
un·caus′ti·cal·ly, *adv.*
un·cau′ter·ized′, *adj.*
un·cau′tioned, *adj.*
un·cau′tious, *adj.;* **-ly,** *adv.;* **-ness,** *n.*
un′cav·a·lier′, *adj.;* **-ly,** *adv.*
un·cav′ern·ous, *adj.;* **-ly,** *adv.*
un·cav′il·ing, *adj.*
un·cav′il·ling, *adj.*
un·cav′i·tied, *adj.*
un·ceased′, *adj.*
un·ced′ed, *adj.*
un·ceil′inged, *adj.*
un·cel′e·brat′ed, *adj.*
un·cel′e·brat′ing, *adj.*
un′ce·les′tial, *adj.*
un·cel′i·bate, *adj.*
un·cen′sor·a·ble, *adj.*
un·cen′sored, *adj.*
un′cen·so′ri·ous, *adj.;* **-ly,** *adv.;* **-ness,** *n.*
un·cen′sur·a·ble, *adj.*
un·cen′sured, *adj.*
un·cen′sur·ing, *adj.*
un·cen′tered, *adj.*
un·cen′tral, *adj.;* **-ly,** *adv.*
un·cen′tral·ized′, *adj.*
un·cen′tric, *adj.*
un·cen′tri·cal, *adj.*
un′cen·trip′e·tal, *adj.*
un′ce·phal′ic, *adj.*
un·ce′rat·ed, *adj.*
un·cer′e·bric, *adj.*
un′cer·e·mo′ni·al, *adj.;* **-ly,** *adv.*
un′ce·rif′er·ous, *adj.*
un·cer′ti·fi′a·ble, *adj.;* **-bly,** *adv.*
un′cer·tif′i·cat′ed, *adj.*
un·cer′ti·fied′, *adj.*
un·cer′ti·fy′ing, *adj.*
un·cer′ti·tude′, *n.*
un·chafed′, *adj.*
un·chaffed′, *adj.*
un·chaff′ing, *adj.*
un′cha·grined′, *adj.*
un·chained′, *adj.*
un·chair′, *v.t.*
un·chalked′, *adj.*
un·chalk′y, *adj.*
un·chal′lenge·a·ble, *adj.;* **-bly,** *adv.*
un·chal′lenged, *adj.*
un·chal′leng·ing, *adj.*
un·cham′bered, *adj.*
un·cham′fered, *adj.*
un·cham′pi·oned, *adj.*
un·chance′a·ble, *adj.*
un·chanced′, *adj.*
un′change·a·bil′i·ty, *n.*
un·change′a·ble, *adj., n.;* **-bly,** *adv.*
un·changed′, *adj.*
un·change′ful, *adj.;* **-ly,** *adv.;* **-ness,** *n.*
un·chang′ing, *adj.;* **-ly,** *adv.;* **-ness,** *n.*
un·chan′neled, *adj.*
un·chan′nel·ized′, *adj.*
un·chan′nelled, *adj.*
un·chant′ed, *adj.*
un′cha·ot′ic, *adj.*
un′cha·ot′i·cal·ly, *adv.*
un·chap′er·oned′, *adj.*
un·chap′let·ed, *adj.*
un·chapped′, *adj.*
un·chap′ter, *v.t.*
un·chap′tered, *adj.*
un·char′ac·tered, *adj.*
un′char·ac·ter·is′tic, *adj.*
un′char·ac·ter·is′ti·cal·ly, *adv.*
un·char′ac·ter·ized′, *adj.*
un·charge′a·ble, *adj.*
un·char′i·ly, *adv.*
un·char′i·ot, *v.t.*
un′char·is·mat′ic, *adj.*
un·charm′a·ble, *adj.*
un·charmed′, *adj.*
un·charm′ing, *adj.*
un·charred′, *adj.*
un·char′y, *adj.*
un·chased′, *adj.*
un·chas′tened, *adj.*
un′chas·tis′a·ble, *adj.*
un·chas′tised, *adj.*
un·chas′tis·ing, *adj.*
un·chat′ter·ing, *adj.*
un·chauf′feured, *adj.*
un′chau·vin·is′tic, *adj.*
un·cheap′ened, *adj.*
un·cheap′ly, *adv.*
un·cheat′ed, *adj.*
un·cheat′ing, *adj.*
un·check′a·ble, *adj.*
un·checked′, *adj.*
un·check′ered, *adj.*
un·check′mat′ed, *adj.*
un·cheer′a·ble, *adj.*
un·cheered′, *adj.*
un·cheer′ful, *adj.;* **-ly,** *adv.;* **-ness,** *n.*
un·cheer′i·ly, *adv.*
un·cheer′i·ness, *n.*
un·cheer′ing, *adj.*
un·cheer′y, *adj.*
un·chem′i·cal, *adj.;* **-ly,** *adv.*
un·cher′ished, *adj.*
un·cher′ish·ing, *adj.*
un·chest′ed, *adj.*
un·chev′roned, *adj.*
un·chew′a·ble, *adj.*
un·chewed′, *adj.*
un·chid′, *adj.*
un·chid′den, *adj.*
un·chid′ed, *adj.*
un·chid′ing, *adj.;* **-ly,** *adv.*
un·child′ish, *adj.;* **-ly,** *adv.;* **-ness,** *n.*
un·child′like′, *adj.*
un·chilled′, *adj.*
un·chim′ing, *adj.*
un·chinked′, *adj.*
un·chip′pa·ble, *adj.*
un·chipped′, *adj.*
un·chip′ping, *adj.*
un·chis′eled, *adj.*
un·chis′elled, *adj.*
un·chiv′al·ric, *adj.*
un·chiv′al·rous, *adj.;* **-ly,** *adv.;* **-ness,** *n.*
un·chiv′al·ry, *n.*
un·chlo′ri·dized′, *adj.*
un·chlo′ri·nat′ed, *adj.*
un·choke′a·ble, *adj.*
un·choked′, *adj.*
un·chol′er·ic, *adj.*
un·choos′a·ble, *adj.*
un·chopped′, *adj.*
un·cho′re·o·graphed′, *adj.*
un·cho′sen, *adj.*
un·chris′tened, *adj.*
un·chris′tian·ize′, *v.t.,* **-ized, -iz·ing.**
un·Christ′mas·like′, *adj.*
un′chro·mat′ic, *adj.*
un·chromed′, *adj.*
un·chron′ic, *adj.*
un·chron′i·cal·ly, *adv.*
un·chron′i·cled, *adj.*
un′chron·o·log′i·cal, *adj.;* **-ly,** *adv.*
un·church′ly, *adj.*
un·churl′ish, *adj.;* **-ly,** *adv.;* **-ness,** *n.*
un·churn′, *v.t.*
un·churned′, *adj.*
un·cil′i·at′ed, *adj.*
un·cinch′, *v.t.*
un·cinc′tured, *adj.*
un′cin·e·mat′ic, *adj.*
un·cir′cled, *adj.*
un′cir·cu′i·tous, *adj.;* **-ly,** *adv.;* **-ness,** *n.*

Amer.; so called after the leading character in *Uncle Tom's Cabin*] —**Un′cle Tom′ish.**

Un′cle Tom′ism, a policy of relationship between whites and blacks involving a benevolent but patronizing attitude on the part of the whites and a willingly submissive attitude on the part of the blacks. Also called **Tomism.** [1935–40, *Amer.*; UNCLE TOM + -ISM]

Un′cle Tom′s′ Cab′in, an antislavery novel (1852) by Harriet Beecher Stowe.

Un′cle Van′ya (vän′yə), a play (1897) by Anton Chekhov.

un·cloak (un klōk′), *v.t.* **1.** to remove the cloak from. **2.** to reveal; expose: *His motives were uncloaked at last.* —*v.i.* **3.** to take off the cloak or the outer garments generally. [1590–1600; UN-[2] + CLOAK]

un·clog (un klog′, -klôg′), *v.,* **-clogged, -clog·ging.** —*v.t.* **1.** to free of an obstruction or impediment: *to unclog a drain; to unclog rush-hour traffic.* —*v.i.* **2.** to become unclogged: *I can't wash the dishes until the drain unclogs.* [1600–10; UN-[2] + CLOG] —**un·clog′ger,** *n.*

un·close (un klōz′), *v.t., v.i.,* **-closed, -clos·ing.** to bring or come out of a closed state; open. [1300–50; ME *unclosen.* See UN-[2], CLOSE]

un·closed (un klōzd′), *adj.* **1.** not closed: *an unclosed door.* **2.** not brought to a conclusion or settlement; unfinished. [1350–1400; ME; see UN-[1], CLOSED]

un·clothe (un klōth′), *v.t.,* **-clothed** or **-clad** (-klad′), **-cloth·ing.** **1.** to strip of clothes. **2.** to remove a covering from; lay bare; uncover. [1250–1300; ME *unclothen.* See UN-[2], CLOTHE]

un·club·ba·ble (un klub′ə bəl), *adj. Brit.* not acceptable as a person with whom one can enjoy good fellowship; socially unappealing. [1755–65; UN-[1] + CLUBBABLE]

un·co (ung′kō), *adj., adv., n., pl.* **-cos.** *Scot. and North Eng.* —*adj.* **1.** remarkable; extraordinary. **2.** unusual; strange. **3.** uncanny. —*adv.* **4.** remarkably; extremely. —*n.* **5.** something extraordinary or unusual; a novelty. **6. uncos,** news. **7.** *Obs.* a stranger. [1375–1425; late ME; var. of UNCOUTH]

un·cod·ed (un kō′did), *adj.* **1.** not coded; not in code: *an uncoded message.* **2.** being or pertaining to mail with no zip code or an incorrect one; unzipped. [1915–20; UN-[1] + CODED]

un·cof·fined (un kô′find, -kof′ind), *adj.* not put into a coffin: *an uncoffined corpse.* [1640–50; UN-[1] + COFFIN + -ED[3]]

un·coil (un koil′), *v.t., v.i.* to unwind from a coiled position. [1705–15; UN-[2] + COIL[1]]

un·col·lat·er·al·ized (un′kə lat′ər ə līzd′), *adj.* lacking or needing no collateral: *uncollateralized loans.* [UN-[1] + COLLATERAL + -IZE + -ED[2]]

un·col·lect·i·ble (un′kə lek′tə bəl), *adj.* **1.** that cannot be collected: *an uncollectible debt.* —*n.* **2.** something, as a financial obligation, that cannot be collected: *an increase in the company's uncollectibles.* Also, **un′col·lect′a·ble.** [UN-[1] + COLLECT[1] + -IBLE]

un·com·fort·a·ble (un kumf′tə bəl, -kum′fər tə bəl), *adj.* **1.** causing discomfort or distress; painful; irritating. **2.** in a state of discomfort; uneasy; conscious of stress or strain. [1585–95; UN-[1] + COMFORTABLE] —**un·com′fort·a·ble·ness,** *n.* —**un·com′fort·a·bly,** *adv.*
—**Syn. 2.** awkward, nervous, discomfited, strained.

un·com·mer·cial (un′kə mûr′shəl), *adj.* **1.** not engaged in or involved with commerce or trade. **2.** not in accordance with commercial principles or practices. **3.** not producing or likely to produce a profit: *an artistic but uncommercial film.* [1760–70; UN-[1] + COMMERCIAL]

un·com·mit·ted (un′kə mit′id), *adj.* not committed, esp. not pledged or bound to a specific cause, candidate, or course of action: *uncommitted delegates; uncommitted reserves.* [1350–1400; ME; see UN-[1], COMMITTED]

un·com·mon (un kom′ən), *adj.,* **-er, -est.** **1.** not common; unusual; rare: *an uncommon word.* **2.** unusual in amount or degree; above the ordinary: *an uncommon amount of mail.* **3.** exceptional; remarkable. [1540–50; UN-[1] + COMMON] —**un·com′mon·ness,** *n.*
—**Syn. 1.** scarce, infrequent; odd, singular, strange, peculiar, queer. **2.** extraordinary. **3.** outstanding.

un·com·mon·ly (un kom′ən lē), *adv.* **1.** in an uncommon or unusual manner or degree. **2.** exceptionally; outstandingly. **3.** rarely; infrequently. [1740–50; UNCOMMON + -LY]

un·com·mu·ni·ca·ble (un′kə myōō′ni kə bəl), *adj.* incommunicable. [1350–1400; ME; see UN-[1], COMMUNICABLE] —**un′com·mu′ni·ca·bly,** *adv.*

un·com·mu·ni·ca·tive (un′kə myōō′ni kə tiv, -kā′tiv), *adj.* not inclined to talk or disclose information; reserved; taciturn. [1685–95; UN-[1] + COMMUNICATIVE] —**un′com·mu′ni·ca·tive·ly,** *adv.* —**un′com·mu′ni·ca·tive·ness,** *n.*
—**Syn.** reticent, withdrawn, retiring, shy.

un·com·pro·mis·ing (un kom′prə mī′zing), *adj.* **1.** not admitting of compromise or adjustment of differences; making no concessions; inaccessible to flexible bargaining; unyielding: *an uncompromising attitude.* **2.** without reservation or exception; undeviating; absolute, as believing in or adhering to a principle, position, or the like: *an uncompromising abolitionist.* [1820–30; UN-[1] + COMPROMISING] —**un·com′pro·mis′ing·ly,** *adv.* —**un·com′pro·mis′ing·ness,** *n.*
—**Syn. 1.** rigid, obstinate. **2.** firm, steadfast.

un·con·ceiv·a·ble (un′kən sē′və bəl), *adj. Archaic.* inconceivable. [1605–15; UN-[1] + CONCEIVABLE] —**un′con·ceiv′a·ble·ness,** *n.* —**un′con·ceiv′a·bly,** *adv.*

un·con·cern (un′kən sûrn′), *n.* **1.** absence of feeling or concern; indifference. **2.** freedom from anxiety. [1660–70; UN-[1] + CONCERN]
—**Syn. 1.** nonchalance, insouciance. See **indifference.**

un·con·cerned (un′kən sûrnd′), *adj.* **1.** not involved or interested; disinterested. **2.** not caring; unworried; free from solicitude or anxiety. [1625–35; UN-[1] + CONCERNED] —**un·con·cern·ed·ly** (un′kən sûr′nid lē), *adv.* —**un′con·cern′ed·ness,** *n.*
—**Syn. 2.** untroubled, unperturbed, composed, carefree.

un·con·di·tion·al (un′kən dish′ə nl), *adj.* **1.** not limited by conditions; absolute: *an unconditional promise.* **2.** *Math.* absolute (def. 12). [1660–70; UN-[1] + CONDITIONAL] —**un′con·di′tion·al·ly,** *adv.* —**un′con·di′tion·al·ness, un′con·di′tion·al′i·ty,** *n.*
—**Syn. 1.** complete, unqualified, categorical.

uncondi′tional conver′gence, *Math.* **1.** the property of a convergent infinite series that remains convergent when the terms are arranged in any order. **2.** See **absolute convergence.**

un·con·di·tioned (un′kən dish′ənd), *adj.* **1.** not subject to conditions; absolute. **2.** *Psychol.* not proceeding from or dependent on a conditioning of the individual; natural; innate: *unconditioned behavior.* Cf. **conditioned** (def. 3). [1625–35; UN-[1] + CONDITIONED] —**un′con·di′tioned·ness,** *n.*

un·con·form·a·ble (un′kən fôr′mə bəl), *adj.* **1.** not conformable; not conforming. **2.** *Geol.* indicating discontinuity of any type in a stratigraphic sequence. [1585–95; UN-[1] + CONFORMABLE] —**un′con·form′a·bil′i·ty,** *n.* —**un′con·form′a·bly,** *adv.*

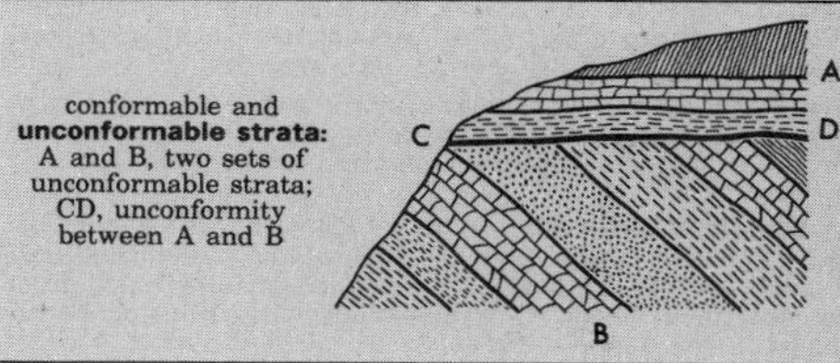

conformable and **unconformable strata:** A and B, two sets of unconformable strata; CD, unconformity between A and B

un·con·form·i·ty (un′kən fôr′mi tē), *n., pl.* **-ties.** **1.** lack of conformity; incongruity; inconsistency. **2.** *Geol.* **a.** a discontinuity in rock sequence indicating interruption of sedimentation, commonly accompanied by erosion of rocks below the break. **b.** the interface between such strata. See illus. under **unconformable.** [1590–1600; UN-[1] + CONFORMITY]

un·con·nect·ed (un′kə nek′tid), *adj.* **1.** not connected; not joined together or attached: *an unconnected wire.* **2.** lacking coherence: *an unconnected account of the accident.* [1730–40; UN-[1] + CONNECTED] —**un′con·nect′ed·ly,** *adv.* —**un′con·nect′ed·ness,** *n.*

un·con·scion·a·ble (un kon′shə nə bəl), *adj.* **1.** not guided by conscience; unscrupulous. **2.** not in accordance with what is just or reasonable: *unconscionable behavior.* **3.** excessive; extortionate: *an unconscionable profit.* [1555–65; UN-[1] + CONSCIONABLE] —**un·con′scion·a·ble·ness,** *n.* —**un·con′scion·a·bly,** *adv.*

CONCISE PRONUNCIATION KEY: act, cāpe, dâre, pärt; set, ēqual; *if,* īce; ox, ōver, ôrder, oil, bŏŏk, bōōt, out; up, ûrge; child; sing; shoe; thin, *th*at; zh as in *treasure.* ə = *a* as in *alone, e* as in *system, i* as in *easily, o* as in *gallop, u* as in *circus;* ^{ə} as in *fire* (fī^{ə}r), *hour* (ou^{ə}r). l and n can serve as syllabic consonants, as in *cradle* (krād′l), and *button* (but′n). See the full key inside the front cover.

un·cir′cu·lar, *adj.;* **-ly,** *adv.*
un·cir′cu·lar·ized′, *adj.*
un·cir′cu·lat′ed, *adj.*
un·cir′cu·lat′ing, *adj.*
un·cir′cu·la′tive, *adj.*
un′cir·cum·loc′u·to′ry, *adj.*
un′cir·cum·scrib′a·ble, *adj.*
un·cir′cum·scribed′, *adj.*
un·cir′cum·spect′, *adj.;* **-ly,** *adv.;* **-ness,** *n.*
un′cir·cum·spec′tive, *adj.*
un′cir·cum·stan′tial, *adj.;* **-ly,** *adv.*
un′cir·cum·vent′ed, *adj.*
un·cit′a·ble, *adj.*
un·cite′a·ble, *adj.*
un·cit′ed, *adj.*
un·cit′ied, *adj.*
un·cit′i·zen·like′, *adj.*
un·cit′i·zen·ly, *adj.*
un·civ′ic, *adj.*
un·civ′i·liz′a·ble, *adj.*
un·civ′i·lize′, *v.t.,* **-lized, -liz·ing.**
un·claimed′, *adj.*
un·claim′ing, *adj.*
un·clam′or·ous, *adj.;* **-ly,** *adv.;* **-ness,** *n.*
un·clamped′, *adj.*
un′clan·des′tine·ly, *adv.*
un·clan′nish, *adj.;* **-ly,** *adv.;* **-ness,** *n.*
un·clar′i·fied′, *adj.*
un·clar′i·fy′ing, *adj.*
un·clar′i·ty, *n.*
un·clash′ing, *adj.*
un·class′a·ble, *adj.*
un·classed′, *adj.*
un·clas′si·fi′a·ble, *adj.;* **-ble·ness,** *n.;* **-bly,** *adv.*
un·clas′si·fy′ing, *adj.*
un·clawed′, *adj.*
un·clayed′, *adj.*
un·clean′a·ble, *adj.*
un·cleaned′, *adj.*
un·cleans′a·ble, *adj.*
un·cleansed′, *adj.*
un·clear′, *adj.;* **-ly,** *adv.*
un·clear′a·ble, *adj.*
un·cleared′, *adj.*
un·clear′ing, *adj.*
un·cleav′a·ble, *adj.*
un·cleft′, *adj.*
un·cler′i·cal, *adj.;* **-ly,** *adv.*
un·clerk′ly, *adj.*
un·clev′er, *adj.;* **-ly,** *adv.;* **-ness,** *n.*
un′cli·mac′tic, *adj.*
un·cli′maxed, *adj.*
un·climb′a·ble, *adj.*
un·climbed′, *adj.*
un·climb′ing, *adj.*
un·cling′ing, *adj.*
un·clin′i·cal, *adj.*
un·clip′, *v.t.,* **-clipped, -clip·ping.**
un·clip′per, *n.*
un·clois′tered, *adj.*
un·clois′tral, *adj.*
un·clos′a·ble, *adj.*
un·clos′et·ed, *adj.*
un·clot′ted, *adj.*
un·cloud′ed, *adj.*
un·cloud′y, *adj.*
un·clo′ven, *adj.*
un·cloyed′, *adj.*
un·cloy′ing, *adj.*
un·clus′tered, *adj.*
un·clus′ter·ing, *adj.*
un·clutch′a·ble, *adj.*
un·clutched′, *adj.*
un·clut′ter, *v.t.*
un·clut′tered, *adj.*
un·coach′a·ble, *adj.*
un·coached′, *adj.*
un′co·ag′u·la·ble, *adj.*
un′co·ag′u·lat′ed, *adj.*
un′co·ag′u·lat′ing, *adj.*
un′co·ag′u·la′tive, *adj.*
un′co·a·les′cent, *adj.*
un·coarse′, *adj.;* **-ly,** *adv.;* **-ness,** *n.*
un·coat′ed, *adj.*
un·coax′a·ble, *adj.*
un′co·ax′al, *adj.*
un·coaxed′, *adj.*
un′co·ax′i·al, *adj.*
un·coax′ing, *adj.*
un·cob′bled, *adj.*
un·cock′, *v.t.*
un·cocked′, *adj.*
un·cod′dled, *adj.*
un·cod′i·fied′, *adj.*
un′co·erced′, *adj.*
un·cof′fin, *v.t.*
un·co′gent, *adj.;* **-ly,** *adv.*
un·cogged′, *adj.*
un·cog′ni·za·ble, *adj.*
un·cog′ni·zant, *adj.*
un·cog′nized, *adj.*
un′cog·nos′ci·bil′i·ty, *n.*
un′cog·nos′ci·ble, *adj.*
un′co·he′sive, *adj.;* **-ly,** *adv.;* **-ness,** *n.*
un·coifed′, *adj.*
un·coiled′, *adj.*
un′co·in·cid′ed, *adj.*
un′co·in′ci·dent, *adj.;* **-ly,** *adv.*
un′co·in′ci·den′tal, *adj.;* **-ly,** *adv.*
un′co·in·cid′ing, *adj.*
un·coined′, *adj.*
un·coked′, *adj.*
un′col·lab′o·ra′tive, *adj.;* **-ly,** *adv.*
un′col·laps′a·ble, *adj.*
un′col·lapsed′, *adj.*
un′col·laps′i·ble, *adj.*
un·col′lar, *v.t.*
un·col′lat·ed, *adj.*
un′col·lect′ed, *adj.*
un′col·lec′tive, *adj.;* **-ly,** *adv.*
un′col·le′giate, *adj.*
un′col·lo′qui·al, *adj.;* **-ly,** *adv.*
un′col·lu′sive, *adj.*
un′co·lo′ni·al, *adj.*
un·col′o·nize′, *v.t.,* **-nized, -niz·ing.**
un·col′or·a·ble, *adj.;* **-bly,** *adv.*
un·col′ored, *adj.;* **-ly,** *adv.;* **-ness,** *n.*
un·col′or·ful, *adj.*
un·comb′a·ble, *adj.*
un′com·bat′a·ble, *adj.*
un′com·bat′ant, *adj.*
un′com·bat′ed, *adj.*
un′com·bat′ive, *adj.*
un·combed′, *adj.*
un′com·bin′a·ble, *adj.;* **-bly,** *adv.*
un·com′bi·na′tion·al, *adj.*
un′com·bi′na·tive, *adj.*
un′com·bined′, *adj.*
un′com·bin′ing, *adj.*
un′com·bus′ti·ble, *adj.*
un′com·bus′tive, *adj.*
un·come′ly, *adj.*
un·com′fort·ed, *adj.*
un·com′fort·ing, *adj.*
un·com′ic, *adj.*
un·com′i·cal, *adj.;* **-ly,** *adv.*
un′com·mand′ed, *adj.*
un′com·mand′er·like′, *adj.*
un′com·mem′o·rat′ed, *adj.*
un′com·mem′o·ra′tive, *adj.;* **-ly,** *adv.*
un′com·menced′, *adj.*
un′com·mend′a·ble, *adj.;* **-bly,** *adv.*
un′com·mend′ed, *adj.*
un′com·mend′a·to′ry, *adj.*
un′com·men′su·rate, *adj.;* **-ly,** *adv.*
un·com′ment·ed, *adj.*
un·com′ment·ing, *adj.*
un′com·mer′cial·ized′, *adj.*
un′com·min′gled, *adj.*
un′com·min′ut·ed, *adj.*
un′com·mis′er·at′ed, *adj.*
un′com·mis′er·at′ing, *adj.*
un′com·mis′er·a′tive, *adj.;* **-ly,** *adv.*
un′com·mis′sioned, *adj.*
un′com·mit′, *v.,* **-mit·ted, -mit·ting.**
un′com·mit′ting, *adj.*
un′com·mo′di·ous, *adj.*
un·com′mon·place′, *adj.*
un′com·mu′nal, *adj.*
un′com·mu′ni·cat′ing, *adj.*
un′com·mut′a·ble, *adj.*
un′com·mu′ta·tive, *adj.;* **-ly,** *adv.;* **-ness,** *n.*
un′com·mut′ed, *adj.*
un′com·pact′ed, *adj.*
un′com·pan′ion·a·ble, *adj.*
un′com·pan′ioned, *adj.*
un·com′pa·ra·ble *adj.;* **-ble·ness,** *n.;* **-bly,** *adv.*
un′com·pared′, *adj.*
un′com·pass·a·ble, *adj.*
un′com·pas′sion, *n.*
un′com·pas′sion·ate, *adj.;* **-ly,** *adv.;* **-ness,** *n.*
un′com·pas′sioned, *adj.*
un′com·pel′la·ble, *adj.*
un′com·pelled′, *adj.*
un′com·pel′ling, *adj.*
un′com·pen′di·ous, *adj.*
un·com′pen·sat′ed, *adj.*
un·com′pen·sat′ing, *adj.*
un′com·pen′sa·tive, *adj.*
un′com·pen′sa·to′ry, *adj.*
un·com′pe·tent, *adj.;* **-ly,** *adv.*
un′com·pet′i·tive, *adj.;* **-ly,** *adv.;* **-ness,** *n.*
un′com·piled′, *adj.*
un′com·pla′cent, *adj.;* **-ly,** *adv.*
un′com·plained′, *adj.*
un′com·plain′ing, *adj.;* **-ly,** *adv.*
un′com·plai′sance, *n.*
un′com·plai′sant, *adj.;* **-ly,** *adv.*
un·com′ple·men′tal, *adj.;* **-ly,** *adv.*
un·com′ple·men′ta·ry, *adj.*
un·com′ple·ment′ed, *adj.*
un′com·plet′a·ble, *adj.*
un′com·plete′, *adj.;* **-ly,** *adv.;* **-ness,** *n.*
un′com·plet′ed, *adj.*
un′com·plex′, *adj.;* **-ly,** *adv.;* **-ness,** *n.*
un′com·pli′a·ble, *adj.;* **-ble·ness,** *n.;* **-bly,** *adv.*
un′com·pli′ant, *adj.;* **-ly,** *adv.*
un·com′pli·cate′, *v.t.,* **-cat·ed, -cat·ing.**
un·com′pli·cat′ed, *adj.*
un·com′pli·men′ta·ry, *adj.*
un·com′pli·ment′ed, *adj.*
un·com′pli·ment′ing, *adj.*
un′com·ply′ing, *adj.*
un′com·port′a·ble, *adj.*
un′com·pos′a·ble, *adj.*
un′com·posed′, *adj.*
un′com·pound′a·ble, *adj.*
un′com·pound′ed, *adj.*
un′com·pound′ing, *adj.*
un·com′pre·hend′ed, *adj.*
un·com′pre·hend′ing, *adj.;* **-ly,** *adv.*
un·com′pre·hen′si·ble, *adj.;* **-ble·ness,** *n.;* **-bly,** *adv.*
un·com′pre·hen′sion, *n.*
un·com′pre·hen′sive, *adj.;* **-ly,** *adv.;* **-ness,** *n.*
un′com·pressed′, *adj.*
un′com·press′i·ble, *adj.*
un′com·pro′mis·a·ble, *adj.*
un·com′pro·mised′, *adj.*
un′com·pul′sive, *adj.;* **-ly,** *adv.*
un′com·pul′so·ry, *adj.*
un′com·put′a·ble, *adj.;* **-ble·ness,** *n.;* **-bly,** *adv.*
un′com·put′ed, *adj.*
un′com·put′er·ized′, *adj.*
un′con·cat′e·nat′ed, *adj.*
un′con·cat′e·nat′ing, *adj.*
un′con·cealed′, *adj.*
un′con·ceal′ing, *adj.;* **-ly,** *adv.*
un′con·ced′ed, *adj.*

—**Syn.** 3. extreme, immoderate, unwarranted, inordinate.

un•con•scious (un kon′shəs), *adj.* **1.** not conscious; without awareness, sensation, or cognition. **2.** temporarily devoid of consciousness. **3.** not perceived at the level of awareness; occurring below the level of conscious thought: *an unconscious impulse.* **4.** not consciously realized, planned, or done; without conscious volition or intent: *an unconscious social slight.* **5.** not endowed with mental faculties: *the unconscious stones.* —*n.* **6.** **the unconscious,** *Psychoanal.* the part of the mind containing psychic material that is only rarely accessible to awareness but that has a pronounced influence on behavior. [1705–15; 1915–20 for def. 6; UN-[1] + CONSCIOUS] —**un•con′scious•ly,** *adv.* —**un•con′scious•ness,** *n.*

un•con•sti•tu•tion•al (un′kon sti to͞o′shə nl, -tyo͞o′-), *adj.* not constitutional; unauthorized by or inconsistent with the constitution, as of a country. [1735–45; UN-[1] + CONSTITUTIONAL] —**un′con•sti•tu′tion•al•ism,** *n.* —**un′con•sti•tu′tion•al′i•ty,** *n.* —**un′con•sti•tu′tion•al•ly,** *adv.*

un•con•straint (un′kən strānt′), *n.* lack of constraint: *Their home has a feeling of unconstraint and warm hospitableness.* [1705–15; UN-[1] + CONSTRAINT]

un•con•struct•ed (un′kən struk′tid), *adj.* (of clothing) made with little or no padding, interfacing, or lining, so as to fit loosely or softly on the body. [1965–70; UN-[1] + CONSTRUCT + -ED[2]]

un•con•trol•la•ble (un′kən trō′lə bəl), *adj.* **1.** incapable of being controlled or restrained: *uncontrollable anger.* —*n.* **2.** something, as an obligation, that cannot be controlled, reduced, or dispensed with: *the uncontrollables in the new federal budget.* [1570–80; UN-[1] + CONTROL + -ABLE] —**un′con•trol′la•bly,** *adv.*

un•con•ven•tion•al (un′kən ven′shə nl), *adj.* not conventional; not bound by or conforming to convention, rule, or precedent; free from conventionality: *an unconventional artist; an unconventional use of material.* [1830–40; UN-[1] + CONVENTIONAL] —**un′con•ven′tion•al•ist,** *n.* —**un′con•ven′tion•al•ly,** *adv.*
—**Syn.** eccentric, individualistic, idiosyncratic, atypical.

un•con•ven•tion•al•i•ty (un′kən ven′shə nal′i tē), *n., pl.* **-ties** for 2. **1.** disregard for convention; the state or quality of being inconsistent with customs, rules, etc.; originality. **2.** something unconventional, as an act. [1850–55; UN-[1] + CONVENTIONALITY]

un′conven′tional war′fare, warfare that is conducted within enemy lines through guerrilla tactics or subversion, usually supported at least in part by external forces.

un•cool (un ko͞ol′), *adj. Slang.* **1.** not self-assured or relaxed: *He felt very uncool, making a speech to strangers.* **2.** not sophisticated or worldly-wise. [1955–60; UN-[1] + COOL (def. 14)]

un•cork (un kôrk′), *v.t.* **1.** to draw the cork from. **2.** *Informal.* to release or unveil; unleash: *to uncork one's pent-up emotions.* [1720–30; UN-[2] + CORK]

un•cor•rect (un′kə rekt′), *v.t. Navig.* **1.** to convert (a true course) into a magnetic course. **2.** to convert (a magnetic course) into a compass course. [1495–1505; UN-[2] + CORRECT]

un•count•a•ble (un koun′tə bəl), *adj.* **1.** not countable; incapable of having the total precisely ascertained: *uncountable colonies of bacteria; uncountable kindnesses and small favors.* **2.** indefinitely large in number; infinite: *the uncountable days of eternity.* [1350–1400; ME; see UN-[1], COUNTABLE]

un•count•ed (un koun′tid), *adj.* **1.** not counted. **2.** innumerable: *Uncounted generations of tiny creatures built the coral atolls.* [1490–1500; UN-[1] + COUNT[1] + -ED[2]]

un•cou•ple (un kup′əl), *v.,* **-pled, -pling.** —*v.t.* **1.** to release the coupling or link between; disconnect; let go: *to uncouple railroad cars.* —*v.i.* **2.** to become unfastened; let go: *The glider uncoupled from the tow plane.* [1300–50; ME *unco(u)plen;* see UN-[2], COUPLE]

un•cour•te•ous (un kûr′tē əs), *adj.* impolite; discourteous. [1275–1325; ME *uncurteis.* See UN-[1], COURTEOUS] —**un•cour′te•ous•ly,** *adv.* —**un•cour′te•ous•ness,** *n.*

un•court•ly (un kôrt′lē, -kōrt′-), *adj.* **1.** not courtly; rude. **2.** not conforming to the customs or usage of a royal court: *an uncourtly lack of respect for hereditary rank.* [1590–1600; UN-[1] + COURTLY] —**un•court′li•ness,** *n.*

un•couth (un ko͞oth′), *adj.* **1.** awkward, clumsy, or unmannerly: *uncouth behavior; an uncouth relative who embarrasses the family.* **2.** strange and ungraceful in appearance or form. **3.** unusual or strange. [bef. 900; ME; OE *uncūth* (see UN-[1], COUTH[2]); c. D *onkond*] —**un•couth′ly,** *adv.* —**un•couth′ness,** *n.*
—**Syn.** **1.** discourteous, rude, uncivil. See **boorish. 3.** odd, unfamiliar. —**Ant. 1.** courteous.

un•cov•e•nant•ed (un kuv′ə nən tid), *adj.* **1.** not agreed to or promised by covenant. **2.** not having joined in a covenant. [1640–50; UN-[1] + COVENANT + -ED[3]]

un•cov•er (un kuv′ər), *v.t.* **1.** to lay bare; disclose; reveal. **2.** to remove the cover or covering from. **3.** to remove a hat from (the head). —*v.i.* **4.** to remove a cover or covering. **5.** to take off one's hat or other head covering as a gesture of respect. [1250–1300; ME *uncoveren.* See UN-[2], COVER]

un•cov•ered (un kuv′ərd), *adj.* **1.** having no cover or covering. **2.** having the head bare. **3.** not protected by collateral or other security, as a loan. **4.** not protected by insurance: *Workers want their uncovered spouses to join the health plan.* [1350–1400; ME *uncovert.* See UN-[1], COVER, -ED[2]]

un•crit•i•cal (un krit′i kəl), *adj.* **1.** not inclined or able to judge, esp. by the application of comparative standards: *an uncritical reader.* **2.** undiscriminating; not applying or not guided by the standards of analysis: *an uncritical estimate; their uncritical acceptance of traditional values.* [1650–60; UN-[1] + CRITICAL] —**un•crit′i•cal•ly,** *adv.*
—**Syn. 2.** shallow, superficial, casual.

un•cross (un krôs′, -kros′), *v.t.* to change from a crossed position, as the legs. [1590–1600; UN-[2] + CROSS]

un•crossed (un krôst′, -krost′), *adj.* **1.** not crossed. **2.** not marked with a line across: *to leave one's t's uncrossed.* [1550–60; UN-[1] + CROSSED]

un•crown (un kroun′), *v.t.* **1.** to deprive or divest of a crown. **2.** to reduce from dignity or preeminence. [1250–1300; ME *uncrounen.* See UN-[2], CROWN]

un•crowned (un kround′), *adj.* **1.** not crowned; not having yet assumed the crown. **2.** having royal rank or power without occupying the royal office. [1350–1400; ME *uncrouned.* See UN-[1], CROWNED]

unc•tion (ungk′shən), *n.* **1.** an act of anointing, esp. as a medical treatment or religious rite. **2.** an unguent or ointment; salve. **3.** something soothing or comforting. **4.** an excessive, affected, sometimes cloying earnestness or fervor in manner, esp. in speaking. **5.** *Relig.* **a.** the oil used in religious rites, as in anointing the sick or dying. **b.** the shedding of a divine or spiritual influence upon a person. **c.** the influence shed. **d.** See **extreme unction. 6.** the manifestation of spiritual or religious inspiration. [1350–1400; ME *unctioun* < L *ūnctiōn-* (s. of *ūnctiō*) anointing, besmearing, equiv. to *ūnct(us)* (ptp. of *ung(u)ere* to smear, anoint) + *-iōn-* -ION] —**unc′tion•less,** *adj.*

unc•tu•ar•i•um (ungk′cho͞o âr′ē əm), *n., pl.* **-ar•i•a** (-âr′ē ə). alipterion. [appar. erroneously for L *ūnctōrium,* influenced by UNCTUOUS, -ARIUM]

unc•tu•ous (ungk′cho͞o əs), *adj.* **1.** characterized by excessive piousness or moralistic fervor, esp. in an affected manner; excessively smooth, suave, or smug. **2.** of the nature of or characteristic of an unguent or ointment; oily; greasy. **3.** having an oily or soapy feel, as certain minerals. [1350–1400; ME < ML *ūnctuōsus,* equiv. to L *ūnctu(s)* act of anointing (*ung(uere)* to smear, anoint + *-tus* suffix of v. action) + *-ōsus* -OUS] —**unc′tu•ous•ly,** *adv.* —**unc′tu•ous•ness, unc•tu•os•i•ty** (ungk′cho͞o os′i tē), *n.*

un•cul•ture (un kul′chər), *n.* the lack or absence of culture: *Much modern fiction is a product of unculture.* [1615–25; UN-[1] + CULTURE] —**un•cul′tured,** *adj.*

un•curl (un kûrl′), *v.t., v.i.* to straighten or become straightened out from a curl or curled position. [1580–90; UN-[2] + CURL]

un•cus (ung′kəs), *n., pl.* **un•ci** (un′sī). *Anat.* any hook-shaped or curved part of a body process, esp. the hippocampal gyrus in the temporal lobe of the brain. [1820–30; < NL, L: lit., hook]

un•cut (un kut′), *adj.* **1.** not cut. **2.** not shortened or condensed; unabridged: *an uncut version of the play.* **3.** in the original form; neither reduced in size nor given shape, as a diamond. **4.** not diluted or mixed with other substances: *uncut heroin.* **5.** *Bookbinding.* untrimmed

CONCISE ETYMOLOGY KEY: <, descended or borrowed from; >, whence; b., blend of, blended; c., cognate with; cf., compare; deriv., derivative; equiv., equivalent; imit., imitative; obl., oblique; r., replacing; s., stem; sp., spelling, spelled; resp., respelling, respelled; trans., translation; ?, origin unknown; *, unattested; ‡, probably earlier than. See the full key inside the front cover.

un′con•ced′ing, *adj.*
un′con•ceit′ed, *adj.;* **-ly,** *adv.*
un′con•ceived′, *adj.*
un•con′cen•trat′ed, *adj.;* **-ly,** *adv.*
un•con′cen•tra′tive, *adj.*
un′con•cen′tric, *adj.*
un′con•cen′tri•cal•ly, *adv.*
un′con•cep′tu•al, *adj.;* **-ly,** *adv.*
un′con•cert′a•ble, *adj.*
un′con•cert′ed, *adj.;* **-ly,** *adv.*
un′con•cil′i•a•ble, *adj.*
un′con•cil′i•at′ed, *adj.*
un′con•cil′i•at′ing, *adj.*
un′con•cil′i•a′tive, *adj.*
un′con•cil′i•a•to′ry, *adj.*
un′con•clud′a•ble, *adj.*
un′con•clud′ed, *adj.*
un′con•cord′ant, *adj.;* **-ly,** *adv.*
un′con•crete′, *adj.;* **-ly,** *adv.*
un′con•cret′ed, *adj.*
un′con•curred′, *adj.*
un′con•cur′rent, *adj.;* **-ly,** *adv.*
un′con•cur′ring, *adj.*
un′con•dem′na•ble, *adj.*
un′con•demned′, *adj.*
un′con•demn′ing, *adj.;* **-ly,** *adv.*
un′con•den′sa•ble, *adj.;* **-ble•ness,** *n.;* **-bly,** *adv.*
un•con′den•sa′tion•al, *adj.*
un′con•densed′, *adj.*
un′con•dens′ing, *adj.*
un′con•de•scend′ing, *adj.;* **-ly,** *adv.*
un′con•di′tion, *v.t.*
un•con′do•la•to′ry, *adj.*
un′con•doled′, *adj.*
un′con•dol′ing, *adj.*
un′con•doned′, *adj.*
un′con•don′ing, *adj.*
un′con•duc′ing, *adj.*
un′con•du′cive, *adj.;* **-ly,** *adv.;* **-ness,** *n.*
un′con•duct′ed, *adj.*
un′con•duct′i•ble, *adj.*
un′con•duc′tive, *adj.*
un′con•fect′ed, *adj.*
un′con•fed′er•at′ed, *adj.*
un′con•ferred′, *adj.*
un′con•fessed′, *adj.*
un′con•fess′ing, *adj.*
un′con•fid′ed, *adj.*
un•con′fi•dent, *adj.;* **-ly,** *adv.*
un′con•fid′ing, *adj.*
un′con•fin′a•ble, *adj.*
un′con•fined′, *adj.*
un′con•fin′ing, *adj.*
un′con•firm′, *v.t.*
un′con•firm′a•bil′i•ty, *n.*
un′con•firm′a•tive, *adj.*
un′con•firm′a•to′ry, *adj.*
un′con•firmed′, *adj.*
un′con•fis′ca•ble, *adj.*
un•con′fis•cat′ed, *adj.*
un′con•fis′ca•to′ry, *adj.*
un′con•flict′ing, *adj.;* **-ly,** *adv.*
un′con•flic′tive, *adj.*
un′con•formed′, *adj.*
un′con•form′ing, *adj.*
un′con•found′, *v.t.*
un′con•found′ed•ly, *adv.*
un′con•found′ing, *adj.;* **-ly,** *adv.*
un′con•front′a•ble, *adj.*
un′con•front′ed, *adj.*
un′con•fus′a•ble, *adj.;* **-bly,** *adv.*
un′con•fused′, *adj.*
un′con•fus′ed•ly, *adv.*
un′con•fus′ing, *adj.*
un′con•fut′a•ble, *adj.*
un′con•fut′a•tive, *adj.*
un′con•fut′ed, *adj.*
un′con•fut′ing, *adj.*
un′con•geal′, *v.i.*
un′con•geal′a•ble, *adj.*
un′con•gen′ial, *adj.;* **-ly,** *adv.*
un′con•ge′ni•al′i•ty, *n.*
un′con•gest′ed, *adj.*
un′con•ges′tive, *adj.*
un′con•glom′er•at′ed, *adj.*
un′con•glu′ti•nat′ed, *adj.*
un′con•glu′ti•na′tive, *adj.*
un′con•grat′u•lat′ed, *adj.*
un′con•grat′u•lat′ing, *adj.*
un′con•grat′u•la•to′ry, *adj.*
un•con′gre•gat′ed, *adj.*
un′con•gre•ga′tion•al, *adj.*
un•con′gre•ga′tive, *adj.*
un′con•gres′sion•al, *adj.*
un•con′gru•ous, *adj.;* **-ly,** *adv.;* **-ness,** *n.*
un•con′i•cal, *adj.*
un′con•jec′tur•a•ble, *adj.*
un′con•jec′tur•al, *adj.*
un′con•jec′tured, *adj.*
un′con•joined′, *adj.*
un•con′ju•gal, *adj.*
un•con′ju•gat′ed, *adj.*
un′con•junc′tive, *adj.*
un•con′jured, *adj.*
un•conned′, *adj.*
un′con•nived′, *adj.*
un′con•niv′ing, *adj.*
un•con′no•ta′tive, *adj.*
un•con′quer•a•ble, *adj.;* **-bly,** *adv.*
un•con′quered, *adj.*
un•con′sci•en′tious, *adj.;* **-ly,** *adv.;* **-ness,** *n.*
un•con′se•crat′ed, *adj.*
un•con′se•cra′tion, *n.*
un•con′se•cra′tive, *adj.*
un′con•sec′u•tive, *adj.;* **-ly,** *adv.*
un•con′sen•ta′ne•ous, *adj.;* **-ly,** *adv.;* **-ness,** *n.*
un′con•sen′tient, *adj.*
un′con•sent′ing, *adj.*
un′con•serv′a•ble, *adj.*
un′con•serv′a•tive, *adj.;* **-ly,** *adv.;* **-ness,** *n.*
un′con•served′, *adj.*
un′con•serv′ing, *adj.*
un′con•sid′er•a•ble, *adj.;* **-bly,** *adv.*
un′con•sid′ered, *adj.*
un′con•sid′er•ing, *adj.*
un′con•sign′a•ble, *adj.*
un′con•signed′, *adj.*
un′con•so′ci•at′ed, *adj.*
un′con•sol′a•bil′i•ty, *n.*
un′con•sol′a•ble, *adj.;* **-bly,** *adv.*
un′con•sol′a•to′ry, *adj.*
un′con•soled′, *adj.*
un′con•sol′i•dat′ed, *adj.*
un′con•sol′i•dat′ing, *adj.*
un′con•sol′i•da′tion, *n.*
un′con•sol′ing, *adj.;* **-ly,** *adv.*
un•con′so•nant, *adj.*
un′con•spired′, *adj.*
un′con•spir′ing, *adj.;* **-ly,** *adv.*
un•con′stant, *adj.;* **-ly,** *adv.*
un•con′stel•lat′ed, *adj.*
un•con′ster•nat′ed, *adj.*
un•con′sti•pat′ed, *adj.*
un•con′sti•tut′ed, *adj.*
un′con•strain′a•ble, *adj.*
un′con•strained′, *adj.*
un′con•strain′ing, *adj.*
un′con•strict′ed, *adj.*
un′con•stric′tive, *adj.*
un•con′stru•a•ble, *adj.*
un′con•struc′tive, *adj.;* **-ly,** *adv.*
un′con•strued′, *adj.*
un′con•sult′a•ble, *adj.*
un′con•sult′a•tive, *adj.*
un′con•sul′ta•to′ry, *adj.*
un′con•sult′ed, *adj.*
un′con•sult′ing, *adj.*
un′con•sum′a•ble, *adj.*
un′con•sumed′, *adj.*
un′con•sum′ing, *adj.*
un′con•sum′mate, *adj.;* **-ly,** *adv.*
un•con′sum•mat′ed, *adj.*
un•con′sum•ma′tive, *adj.*
un′con•sump′tive, *adj.;* **-ly,** *adv.*
un′con•tact′ed, *adj.*
un′con•ta′gious, *adj.;* **-ly,** *adv.*
un′con•tain′a•ble, *adj.*
un′con•tained′, *adj.*
un′con•tam′i•na•ble, *adj.*
un′con•tam′i•nat′ed, *adj.*
un′con•tam′i•na′tive, *adj.*
un′con•temned′, *adj.*
un′con•temn′ing, *adj.;* **-ly,** *adv.*
un′con•tem′pla•ble, *adj.*
un•con′tem•plat′ed, *adj.*
un•con′tem•pla′tive, *adj.;* **-ly,** *adv.;* **-ness,** *n.*
un′con•tem′po•ra′ne•ous, *adj.;* **-ly,** *adv.;* **-ness,** *n.*
un′con•tem′po•rar′y, *adj.*
un′con•tempt′i•bil′i•ty, *n.*
un′con•tempt′i•ble, *adj.;* **-ble•ness,** *n.;* **-bly,** *adv.*
un′con•temp′tu•ous, *adj.;* **-ly,** *adv.;* **-ness,** *n.*
un′con•tend′ed, *adj.*
un′con•tend′ing, *adj.*
un′con•ten′tious, *adj.;* **-ly,** *adv.;* **-ness,** *n.*
un′con•test′a•bil′i•ty, *n.*
un′con•test′a•ble, *adj.;* **-bly,** *adv.*
un′con•test′ant, *n.*
un′con•test′ed, *adj.;* **-ly,** *adv.*
un′con•tig′u•ous, *adj.;* **-ly,** *adv.;* **-ness,** *n.*
un•con′ti•nence, *n.*
un•con′ti•nent, *adj.;* **-ly,** *adv.*
un′con•tin′gent, *adj.;* **-ly,** *adv.*
un′con•tin′u•al, *adj.;* **-ly,** *adv.*
un′con•tin′ued, *adj.*
un′con•tin′u•ous, *adj.;* **-ly,** *adv.*
un′con•tort′ed, *adj.;* **-ly,** *adv.*
un′con•tor′tioned, *adj.*
un′con•tor′tive, *adj.*
un•con′toured, *adj.*
un′con•tract′ed, *adj.*
un′con•trac′tile, *adj.*
un′con•tra•dict′a•ble, *adj.;* **-bly,** *adv.*
un′con•tra•dict′ed, *adj.;* **-ly,** *adv.*
un′con•tra•dic′tious, *adj.*
un′con•tra•dic′tive, *adj.*
un′con•tra•dic′to•ry, *adj.*
un′con•trast′a•ble, *adj.;* **-bly,** *adv.*
un′con•trast′ed, *adj.*
un′con•trast′ing, *adj.*
un′con•tras′tive, *adj.;* **-ly,** *adv.*
un′con•trib′ut•ed, *adj.*
un′con•trib′ut•ing, *adj.*
un′con•trib′u•tive, *adj.;* **-ly,** *adv.;* **-ness,** *n.*
un′con•trib′u•to′ry, *adj.*
un′con•trite′, *adj.*
un′con•trived′, *adj.*
un′con•triv′ing, *adj.*
un′con•trolled′, *adj.*
un′con•trol′ling, *adj.*
un′con•tro•ver′sial, *adj.;* **-ly,** *adv.*
un•con′tro•vert′ed, *adj.;* **-ly,** *adv.*
un′con•tro•vert′i•ble, *adj.;* **-bly,** *adv.*
un′con•tu•ma′cious, *adj.;* **-ly,** *adv.;* **-ness,** *n.*
un′con•ven′a•ble, *adj.*
un′con•vened′, *adj.*
un′con•ven′ing, *adj.*
un′con•ven′tion, *n.*
un′con•verged′, *adj.*
un′con•ver′gent, *adj.*
un′con•verg′ing, *adj.*
un′con•vers′a•ble, *adj.*
un•con′ver•sant, *adj.*
un′con•ver•sa′tion•al, *adj.*
un′con•vert′ed, *adj.*
un′con•vert′i•bil′i•ty, *n.*
un′con•vert′i•ble, *adj.;* **-ble•ness,** *n.;* **-bly,** *adv.*
un′con•vict′ed, *adj.*
un′con•vict′ing, *adj.*
un′con•vic′tive, *adj.*
un′con•vinced′, *adj.*
un′con•vin′ci•ble, *adj.*

(def. 2). **6.** *Slang.* not circumcised. [1400–50; late ME *unkyt.* See UN-[1], CUT]

un·damped (un dampt′), *adj.* **1.** not damped or dampened; undiminished, as in energy, vigor, etc.: *undamped spirits.* **2.** *Physics.* (of an oscillation) having constant or increasing amplitude. [1735–45; UN-[1] + DAMP + -ED[2]]

un·daunt·ed (un dôn′tid, -dän′-), *adj.* **1.** undismayed; not discouraged; not forced to abandon purpose or effort: *undaunted by failure.* **2.** undiminished in courage or valor; not giving way to fear; intrepid: *Although outnumbered, he was undaunted.* [1375–1425; late ME; see UN-[1], DAUNT, -ED[2]] **—un·daunt′ed·ly,** *adv.* **—un·daunt′ed·ness,** *n.*

un·dec·a·gon (un dek′ə gon′), *n.* a polygon having 11 angles and 11 sides. [1720–30; < L *un-,* as in *undecim* eleven (*ūn*(*us*) one + *-decim,* comb. form of *decem* TEN) + DECAGON]

un·de·ceive (un′di sēv′), *v.t.,* **-ceived, -ceiv·ing.** to free from deception, fallacy, or mistake. [1590–1600; UN-[2] + DECEIVE] **—un′de·ceiv′a·ble,** *adj.* **—un′de·ceiv′er,** *n.*

un·de·cid·ed (un′di sī′did), *adj.* **1.** not decided or determined. **2.** not having one's mind firmly made up. **—*n.* 3.** a person who is undecided: *Are you still among the undecideds?* [1530–40; UN-[1] + DECIDED] **—un′de·cid′ed·ly,** *adv.* **—un′de·cid′ed·ness,** *n.*
—Syn. 2. indecisive, fluctuating, wavering, vacillating; irresolute.

un·de·cil·lion (un′di sil′yən), *n., pl.* **-lions,** (*as after a numeral*) **-lion,** *adj.* **—*n.* 1.** a cardinal number represented in the U.S. by 1 followed by 36 zeros, and in Great Britain by 1 followed by 66 zeros. **—*adj.* 2.** amounting to one undecillion in number. [1930–35; < L *undec*(*im*) eleven (*ūn*(*us*) one + *-decim,* comb. form of *decem* TEN) + *-illion,* as in *million*] **—un′de·cil′lionth,** *adj., n.*

un′dec·y·len′ic ac′id (un′des ə len′ik, un′-), *Chem.* a light-colored liquid with a fruity odor, $C_{11}H_{21}O_2$, soluble in alcohol and ether: used in perfumes, flavors, plastics, and medicine. [1905–10; *undec*(*a*)- eleven (as in UNDECAGON) + -YL + -ENE + -IC]

un·de·fined (un′di fīnd′), *adj.* **1.** without fixed limits; indefinite in form, extent, or application: *undefined authority; undefined feelings of sadness.* **2.** not given meaning or significance, as by a definition; not defined or explained: *an undefined term.* [1605–15; UN-[1] + DEFINED] **—un·de·fin·ed·ly** (un′di fī′nid lē, -fīnd′-), *adv.* **—un′de·fin′ed·ness,** *n.*

un·de·mon·stra·tive (un′də mon′strə tiv), *adj.* not given to open exhibition or expression of emotion, esp. of affection. [1840–50; UN-[1] + DEMONSTRATIVE] **—un′de·mon′stra·tive·ly,** *adv.* **—un′de·mon′stra·tive·ness,** *n.*
—Syn. reserved, shy; unresponsive, impassive.

un·de·ni·a·ble (un′di nī′ə bəl), *adj.* **1.** incapable of being denied or disputed: *undeniable evidence of arson.* **2.** not open to refusal: *an undeniable call for help.* **3.** unquestioned as to quality, merit, etc.; indisputably good: *undeniable artistic talent.* [1540–50; UN-[1] + DENIABLE] **—un′de·ni′a·ble·ness,** *n.* **—un′de·ni′a·bly,** *adv.*
—Syn. 1. incontrovertible, incontestable, unquestionable; obvious, evident, clear, certain, sure.

un·de·nom·i·na·tion·al (un′di nom′ə nā′shə nl), *adj.* free from religious sects or denominationalism; not limited or belonging to any particular religious group or groups. [1870–75; UN-[1] + DENOMINATIONAL] **—un′de·nom′i·na′tion·al·ly,** *adv.*

un·der (un′dər), *prep.* **1.** beneath and covered by: *under a table; under a tree.* **2.** below the surface of: *under water; under the skin.* **3.** at a point or position lower or further down than: *He was hit just under his eye.* **4.** in the position or state of bearing, supporting, sustaining, enduring, etc.: *to sink under a heavy load.* **5.** beneath the heading or within the category of: *Classify the books under "Fiction" and "General."* **6.** as designated, indicated, or represented by: *to register under a new name.* **7.** below in degree, amount, etc.; less than: *purchased under cost.* **8.** below in rank; of less dignity, importance, or the like: *A corporal is under a sergeant.* **9.** subject to the authority, direction, or supervision of: *a bureau functioning under the prime minister.* **10.** subject to the instruction or advice of: *to study the violin under Heifetz.* **11.** subject to the influence, condition, force, etc., of: *under these circumstances; born under the sign of Taurus.* **12.** protected, controlled, or watched by: *under guard.* **13.** authorized, warranted, or attested by: *under one's hand or seal.* **14.** in accordance with: *under the provisions of the law.* **15.** during the rule, administration, or government of: *new laws passed under President Reagan.* **16.** in the state or process of: *under repair; a matter under consideration.* **17.** *Naut.* powered by the means indicated: *under sail; under steam.* **18. under wraps.** See **wrap** (def. 16). **—*adv.* 19.** below or beneath something: *Go over the fence, not under.* **20.** beneath the surface. **21.** in a lower place. **22.** in a lower degree, amount, etc.: *selling blouses for $25 and under.* **23.** in a subordinate position or condition. **24.** in or into subjection or submission. **25. go under, a.** to give in; succumb; yield: *She tried desperately to fight off her drowsiness, but felt herself going under.* **b.** to fail in business: *After 20 years on the same corner they finally went under.* **—*adj.* 26.** beneath or on the underside: *the under threads of the embroidery.* **27.** lower in position. **28.** lower in degree, amount, etc. **29.** lower in rank or condition. **30.** subject to the control, effect, etc., as of a person, drug, or force: *The hypnotist had her subject under at once. The patient was under as soon as he breathed the anesthetic.* [bef. 900; ME, OE; c. D *onder,* G *unter,* ON *undir,* L *inferus* located below]
—Syn. 2. See **below.**

under-, a prefixal use of **under,** as to indicate place or situation below or beneath (*underbrush; undertow*); lower in grade or dignity (*undersheriff; understudy*); of lesser degree, extent, or amount (*undersized*); or insufficiency (*underfeed*). [ME; OE]
—Note. The lists at the bottom of this and following pages provide the spelling, syllabification, and stress for words whose meanings may be easily inferred by combining the meanings of UNDER- and an attached base word, or base word plus a suffix. Appropriate parts of speech are also shown. Words prefixed by UNDER- that have special meanings or uses are entered in their alphabetical places in the main vocabulary entry.

un·der·a·chieve (un′dər ə chēv′), *v.i.,* **-achieved, -a·chiev·ing. 1.** to perform, esp. academically, below the potential indicated by tests of one's mental ability or aptitude. **2.** to perform below expectations or achieve less than expected, esp. by others. [1950–55; UNDER- + ACHIEVE] **—un′der·a·chieve′ment,** *n.*

un·der·a·chiev·er (un′dər ə chē′vər), *n.* **1.** a student who performs less well in school than would be expected on the basis of abilities indicated by intelligence and aptitude tests, etc. **2.** a person or thing that performs below expectations. [1945–50; UNDER- + ACHIEVER]

un·der·act (un′dər akt′), *v.t., v.i.* to underplay. [1615–25; UNDER- + ACT] **—un′der·ac′tor,** *n.*

un·der·ac·tive (un′dər ak′tiv), *adj.* insufficiently active: *an underactive thyroid gland.* [1955–60; UNDER- + ACTIVE] **—un′der·ac·tiv′i·ty, un′der·ac′tive·ness,** *n.*

un·der·age[1] (un′dər āj′), *adj.* lacking the required age, esp. that of legal maturity. [1585–95; UNDER- + AGE]

un·der·age[2] (un′dər ij), *n.* shortage; deficiency in amount. [1605–15; UNDER- + -AGE]

un·der·arm (un′dər ärm′), *adj.* **1.** of, situated, or for use under the arm or in the armpit: *an underarm deodorant.* **2.** underhand: *an underarm pitch in softball.* **—*n.* 3.** armpit. **—*adv.* 4.** underhand. [1810–20; UNDER- + ARM[1]]

un·der·armed (un′dər ärmd′), *adj.* not having sufficient weapons. [UNDER- + ARMED]

un·der·bear·er (un′dər bâr′ər), *n. Nova Scotia.* a pallbearer. [1690–1700; UNDER- + BEARER]

un·der·bel·ly (un′dər bel′ē), *n., pl.* **-lies. 1.** the lower abdomen; posterior ventral area, as of an animal's body. **2.** the lower surface of an object; underside: *the underbelly of an airplane.* **3.** a vulnerable area; weak point: *an attack on the soft underbelly of Europe.* **4.** a dark, seamy, often hidden area or side: *a police officer continually exposed to the underbelly of society.* [1600–10; UNDER- + BELLY]

un·der·bid (un′dər bid′), *v.t.,* **-bid, -bid·ding. 1.** to bid less than (another bid) or less than the bid of (another bidder), esp. in seeking a contract to be awarded to the lowest bid or bidder; make an offer at a lower price than. **2.** *Cards.* to bid less than the value or worth of (a contract or hand). **—*v.i.* 3.** to bid lower than another or too low for the value of something. [1585–95; UNDER- + BID] **—un′der·bid′der,** *n.*

un·der·bite (un′dər bīt′), *n. Dentistry.* occlusion in

CONCISE PRONUNCIATION KEY: act, cāpe, dâre, pärt; set, ēqual; if, īce; ox, ōver, ôrder, oil, bŏŏk, bōōt, out; up, ûrge; child; sing; shoe; thin, that; zh as in *treasure.* ə = *a* as in *alone,* *e* as in *system,* *i* as in *easily,* *o* as in *gallop,* *u* as in *circus;* ^{ə} as in *fire* (fī^{ə}r), *hour* (ou^{ə}r). l and n can serve as syllabic consonants, as in *cradle* (krād′l), and *button* (but′n). See the full key inside the front cover.

un′der·ac·com′mo·dat′ed, *adj.*
un′der·ad·just′ment, *n.*
un′der·a′gen·cy, *n., pl.* **-cies.**
un′der·a′gent, *n.*
un′der·ag′i·ta′tion, *n.*
un′der·aim′, *n.*
un′der·aim′, *v.*
un′der·al′der·man, *n., pl.* **-men.**
un′der·av′er·age, *adj.*
un′der·bail′iff, *n.*
un′der·bake′, *v.t.,* **-baked, -bak·ing.**
un′der·bal′ance, *v.t.,* **-anced, -anc·ing.**
un′der·bal′last, *v.t.*
un′der·bank′, *v.*
un′der·bea′dle, *n.*
un′der·beak′, *n.*
un′der·beam′, *n.*
un′der·beat′, *n.*
un′der·beat′en, *adj.*
un′der·bev′el·ing, *n.*
un′der·bev′el·ling, *n.*
un′der·bil′low, *v.i.*
un′der·bish′op, *n.*
un′der·bish′op·ric, *n.*
un′der·boil′, *v.*
un′der·boom′, *v.*
un′der·bot′tom, *n.*
un′der·bough′, *n.*
un′der·box′, *n.*
un′der·brace′, *n.*
un′der·brace′, *v.t.,* **-braced, -brac·ing.**
un′der·branch′, *n.*
un′der·brew′, *v.t.*
un′der·bridge′, *v.t.,* **-bridged, -bridg·ing.**
un′der·bridge′, *n.*
un′der·brig′a·dier′, *n.*
un′der·bud′, *n.*
un′der·bud′, *v.,* **-bud·ded, -bud·ding.**
un′der·build′, *v.,* **-built, -build·ing.**
un′der·build′er, *n.*
un′der·build′ing, *n.*
un′der·bur′sar, *n.*
un′der·but′ler, *n.*
un′der·can′vass, *v.*
un′der·cap′, *n.*
un′der·cap′tain, *n.*
un′der·car′ry, *v.t.,* **-ried, -ry·ing.**
un′der·carve′, *v.t.,* **-carved, -carv·ing.**
un′der·case′, *n.*
un′der·cas′ing, *n.*
un′der·cause′, *n.*
un′der·ceil′ing, *n.*
un′der·cham′ber, *n.*
un′der·cham′ber·lain, *n.*
un′der·chan′cel·lor, *n.*
un′der·chan′cel·lor·ship′, *n.*
un′der·chant′er, *n.*
un′der·chap′, *n.*
un′der·chief′, *n.*
un′der·chin′, *n.*
un′der·chord′, *n.*
un′der·cir′cle, *v.t.,* **-cled, -cling.**
un′der·cir′cle, *n.*
un′der·cit′i·zen, *n.*
un′der·cit′i·zen·ry, *n., pl.* **-ries.**
un′der·clad′, *adj.*
un′der·clad′ding, *n.*
un′der·clerk′, *n.*
un′der·clerk′ship, *n.*
un′der·cloak′, *n.*
un′der·cloth′, *n.*
un′der·clothed′, *adj.*
un′der·clutch′, *v.t.*
un′der·clutch′, *n.*
un′der·coach′man, *n., pl.* **-men.**
un′der·col·lat′er·al·ized′, *adj.*
un′der·col·lec′tor, *n.*
un′der·col′or, *n.*

un′con·vinc′ing, *adj.;* **-ly,** *adv.*
un·con·vo·lute′, *adj.;* **-ly,** *adv.*
un·con′vo·lut′ed, *adj.*
un·con′voyed, *adj.*
un′con·vulsed′, *adj.*
un′con·vul′sive, *adj.;* **-ly,** *adv.;* **-ness,** *n.*
un·cook′a·ble, *adj.*
un·cooked′, *adj.*
un·cooled′, *adj.*
un·coop′, *v.t.*
un′co·op′er·at′ing, *adj.*
un′co·op′er·a·tive, *adj.;* **-ly,** *adv.;* **-ness,** *n.*
un·coop′ered, *adj.*
un′co·or′di·nate, *adj.;* **-ly,** *adv.;* **-ness,** *n.*
un′co·or′di·nat′ed, *adj.*
un·cop′i·a·ble, *adj.*
un·cop′ied, *adj.*
un·co′pi·ous, *adj.*
un·cop′y·right′ed, *adj.*
un′co·quet′tish, *adj.;* **-ly,** *adv.;* **-ness,** *n.*
un·cor′dial, *adj.;* **-ly,** *adv.;* **-ness,** *n.*
un′cor·dial′i·ty, *n.*
un·core′, *v.t.,* **-cored, -cor·ing.**
un·corned′, *adj.*
un·cor′nered, *adj.*
un·cor′o·net′ed, *adj.*
un·cor′pu·lent, *adj.;* **-ly,** *adv.*
un′cor·rect′a·ble, *adj.;* **-bly,** *adv.*
un′cor·rect′ed, *adj.*
un′cor·rec′tive, *adj.*
un·cor′re·lat′ed, *adj.;* **-ly,** *adv.*
un′cor·rel′a·tive, *adj.;* **-ly,** *adv.;* **-ness,** *n.*
un′cor·rel′a·tiv′i·ty, *n.*
un′cor·re·spond′ing, *adj.;* **-ly,** *adv.*
un·cor′ri·dored, *adj.*
un′cor·rob′o·rant, *adj.*
un′cor·rob′o·rat′ed, *adj.*
un′cor·rob′o·ra′tive, *adj.;* **-ly,** *adv.*
un′cor·rob′o·ra·to′ry, *adj.*
un′cor·rod′ed, *adj.*
un·cor′ru·gat′ed, *adj.*
un′cor·rupt′, *adj.;* **-ly,** *adv.;* **-ness,** *n.*
un′cor·rupt′ed, *adj.;* **-ly,** *adv.;* **-ness,** *n.*
un′cor·rupt′i·ble, *adj.;* **-ble·ness,** *n.;* **-bly,** *adv.*
un′cor·rupt′ing, *adj.*
un′cor·rup′tive, *adj.*
un·cor′set·ed, *adj.*
un′cos·mo·pol′i·tan, *adj.*
un·cos′set·ed, *adj.*
un·cost′ly, *adj.*
un·cos′tumed, *adj.*
un·cot′toned, *adj.*
un·coun′seled, *adj.*
un·coun′selled, *adj.*
un·coun′te·nanced, *adj.*
un′coun·ter·act′ed, *adj.*
un′coun·ter·bal′anced, *adj.*
un·coun′ter·feit′ed, *adj.*
un′coun·ter·mand′a·ble, *adj.*
un′coun·ter·mand′ed, *adj.*
un′coun·ter·vailed′, *adj.*
un·coun′tri·fied′, *adj.*
un′cou·ra′geous, *adj.;* **-ly,** *adv.;* **-ness,** *n.*
un·court′ed, *adj.*
un·cour′te·sy, *n., pl.* **-sies.**
un·cour′ti·er·like′, *adj.*
un·court′ing, *adj.*
un·cov′et·ed, *adj.*
un·cov′et·ing, *adj.*
un·cov′et·ous, *adj.;* **-ly,** *adv.;* **-ness,** *n.*
un·cowed′, *adj.*
un·coy′, *adj.;* **-ly,** *adv.;* **-ness,** *n.*
un·cracked′, *adj.*
un·cra′dled, *adj.*
un·craft′i·ly, *adv.*
un·craft′i·ness, *n.*
un·craft′y, *adj.*
un·crag′gy, *adj.*
un·cramp′, *v.t.*
un·cramped′, *adj.*
un·cranked′, *adj.*
un·cran′nied, *adj.*
un·crate′, *v.t.,* **-crat·ed, -crat·ing.**
un·crat′ed, *adj.*
un·cra·vat′ted, *adj.*
un·cra′ven, *adj.*
un·crav′ing, *adj.;* **-ly,** *adv.*
un·creased′, *adj.*
un′cre·at′a·ble, *adj.*
un′cre·at′ed, *adj.*
un′cre·a′tive, *adj.;* **-ly,** *adv.;* **-ness,** *n.*
un′cre·a·tiv′i·ty, *n.*
un·crea′ture·ly, *adj.*
un′cre·den′tialed, *adj.*
un·cred′it·a·ble, *adj.;* **-ble·ness,** *n.;* **-bly,** *adv.*
un·cred′it·ed, *adj.*
un·cred′u·lous, *adj.;* **-ly,** *adv.;* **-ness,** *n.*
un·creep′ing, *adj.*
un·cre′mat·ed, *adj.*
un·cre′o·sot′ed, *adj.*
un·crest′ed, *adj.*
un′cre·vassed′, *adj.*
un·crib′, *v.t.,* **-cribbed, -crib·bing.**
un·cried′, *adj.*
un·crim′i·nal, *adj.;* **-ly,** *adv.*
un·crip′pled, *adj.*
un·crit′i·ciz′a·ble, *adj.;* **-bly,** *adv.*
un·crit′i·cized′, *adj.*
un·crit′i·ciz′ing, *adj.;* **-ly,** *adv.*
un·crook′ed, *adj.;* **-ly,** *adv.*
un·cropped′, *adj.*
un·cross′a·ble, *adj.*
un′cross-ex·am′ined, *adj.*
un·crowd′ed, *adj.*
un·cru′ci·fied′, *adj.*
un·crude′, *adj.;* **-ly,** *adv.;* **-ness,** *n.*
un·cru′di·ty, *n., pl.* **-ties.**
un·cru′el, *adj.;* **-ly,** *adv.;* **-ness,** *n.*
un·crum′bled, *adj.*
un·crum′bly, *adj.*
un·crum′pled, *adj.*
un·crum′pling, *adj.*
un·crush′a·ble, *adj.*
un·crushed′, *adj.*
un·crust′ed, *adj.*
un·cry′ing, *adj.*
un·crys′taled, *adj.*
un·crys′talled, *adj.*
un·crys′tal·line, *adj.*
un·crys′tal·liz′a·ble, *adj.*
un·crys′tal·lized′, *adj.*
un·cu′bic, *adj.*
un·cu′bi·cal, *adj.;* **-ly,** *adv.;* **-ness,** *n.*
un·cudg′eled, *adj.*
un·cudg′elled, *adj.*
un·cuffed′, *adj.*
un·culled′, *adj.*
un·cul′pa·ble, *adj.*
un·cul′ti·va·ble, *adj.*
un·cul′ti·vat′a·ble, *adj.*
un·cul′ti·vat′ed, *adj.*
un′cul·ti·va′tion, *n.*
un·cul′tur·a·ble, *adj.*
un·cum′bered, *adj.*
un·cum′brous, *adj.;* **-ly,** *adv.;* **-ness,** *n.*
un·cu′mu·la·tive, *adj.*
un·cupped′, *adj.*
un·cur′a·ble, *adj.;* **-ble·ness,** *n.;* **-bly,** *adv.*
un·curb′, *v.t.*
un·curb′a·ble, *adj.*

which the lower incisor teeth overlap the upper. [1975–80; UNDER- + BITE]

un•der•bod•ice (un′dər bod′is), *n.* a bodice worn under an outer bodice. [1890–95; UNDER- + BODICE]

un•der•bod•y (un′dər bod′ē), *n., pl.* **-bod•ies. 1.** the bottom or underneath part, as of a mechanism or animal: *the underbody of a tank.* **2.** *Naut.* the portion of a hull that is normally underwater. [1615–25; UNDER- + BODY]

un•der•boss (un′dər bôs′, -bos′), *n.* a lesser or minor boss, often the second in command, as in an underworld hierarchy. [1970–75; UNDER- + BOSS[1]]

un•der•bred (un′dər bred′), *adj.* **1.** having inferior breeding or manners; vulgar. **2.** not of pure breed, as a horse. [1640–50; UNDER- + BRED] **—un•der•breed•ing** (un′dər brē′ding), *n.*

un•der•brush (un′dər brush′), *n.* shrubs, saplings, low vines, etc., growing under the large trees in a wood or forest. Also, **un•der•bush** (un′dər bo͝osh′). [1765–75, *Amer.*; UNDER- + BRUSH[2]]

un•der•budg•et•ed (un′dər buj′i tid), *adj.* furnished with an insufficient budget; not having sufficient funds made available. [1960–65; UNDER- + BUDGET + -ED[2]]

un•der•buy (un′dər bī′), *v.,* **-bought, -buy•ing.** **—***v.t.* **1.** to buy more cheaply than (another). **2.** to buy at less than the actual value. **—***v.i.* **3.** to buy an insufficient quantity, as of supplies or stock in trade. [1605–15; UNDER- + BUY]

un•der•cap•i•tal•ize (un′dər kap′i tl īz′), *v.t.,* **-ized, -iz•ing.** to provide an insufficient amount of capital for (a business enterprise). Also, *esp. Brit.,* **un′der•cap′i•tal•ise′.** [UNDER- + CAPITALIZE] **—un′der•cap′i•tal•i•za′tion,** *n.*

un•der•car•riage (un′dər kar′ij), *n.* **1.** the supporting framework underneath a vehicle, as an automobile or trailer; the structure to which the wheels, tracks, or the like are attached or fitted. **2.** the portions of an aircraft that are below the body. [1785–95; UNDER- + CARRIAGE]

un•der•cast (un′dər kast′, -käst′), *n.* **1.** *Mining.* a crossing of two passages, as airways, dug at the same level so that one descends to pass beneath the other without any opening into it. Cf. **overcast** (def. 9). **2.** *Meteorol.* an overcast layer of clouds viewed from above. [1880–85; UNDER- + CAST]

un•der•cel•lar (un′dər sel′ər), *n.* a cellar beneath another cellar; subbasement. [1870–75; UNDER- + CELLAR]

un•der•charge (*v.* un′dər chärj′; *n.* un′dər chärj′), *v.,* **-charged, -charg•ing,** *n.* **—***v.t.* **1.** to charge (a purchaser) less than the proper or fair price. **2.** to charge (a stated amount) less than the proper price: *They undercharged several dollars for storing the goods.* **3.** to put an insufficient charge or load into. **—***v.i.* **4.** to charge too little. **—***n.* **5.** a charge or price less than is proper or customary. **6.** an insufficient charge or load. [1625–35; UNDER- + CHARGE]

CONCISE ETYMOLOGY KEY: <, descended or borrowed from; >, whence; b., blend of, blended; c., cognate with; cf., compare; deriv., derivative; equiv., equivalent; imit., imitative; obl., oblique; r., replacing; s., stem; sp., spelling, spelled; resp., respelling, respelled; trans., translation; ?, origin unknown; *, unattested; ‡, probably earlier than. See the full key inside the front cover.

un•der•class (un′dər klas′, -kläs′), *n.* a social stratum consisting of impoverished persons with very low social status. [1915–20; UNDER- + CLASS]
—Usage. See **collective noun.**

un•der•class•man (un′dər klas′mən, -kläs′-), *n., pl.* **-men.** a freshman or sophomore in a secondary school or college. [1870–75, *Amer.*; UNDER- + CLASS + -MAN]

un•der•clothes (un′dər klōz′, -klōthz′), *n.* (*used with a plural v.*) **1.** clothes worn under outer clothes. **2.** underwear. Also called **un•der•cloth•ing** (un′dər klō′thing). [1825–35; UNDER- + CLOTHES]

un•der•coat (un′dər kōt′), *n.* **1.** a coat or jacket worn under another. **2.** *Zool.* a growth of short fur or hair lying beneath a longer growth. **3.** an undercoating. **4.** a coat of paint or the like applied under the finishing coat. **5.** a paint, sealer, or the like specially prepared for use underneath a finishing coat. **—***v.t.* **6.** to apply an undercoating to. [1640–50; UNDER- + COAT]

un•der•coat•ing (un′dər kō′ting), *n.* a protective seal applied to the underside of an automobile to reduce corrosion and vibration. [1920–25; UNDERCOAT + -ING[1]]

un•der•com•pen•sate (un′dər kom′pən sāt′), *v.t.,* **-sat•ed, -sat•ing.** to compensate or pay less than is fair, customary, or expected. [UNDER- + COMPENSATE] **—un′der•com′pen•sa′tion,** *n.*

un•der•cool (un′dər ko͞ol′), *v.t.* **1.** *Chem.* **a.** to cool less than necessary for a given process or purpose. **b.** to supercool. **2.** *Metall.* to cool (molten metal) without forming crystals to a temperature below that at which crystallization normally takes place: *Metal must be absolutely still to be undercooled.* [1900–05; UNDER- + COOL]

un•der•count (*v.* un′dər kount′; *n.* un′dər kount′), *v.t.* **1.** to count less than the full number or amount of: *The mayor claimed the census had undercounted the city's population.* **—***n.* **2.** a count or total that is less than the actual number or amount. [1950–55; UNDER- + COUNT[1]]

un•der•cov•er (un′dər kuv′ər, un′dər kuv′-), *adj.* **1.** working or done out of public sight; secret: *an undercover investigation.* **2.** engaged in spying or securing confidential information: *an undercover agent.* [1850–55; UNDER- + COVER]
—Syn. 1. concealed, covert, clandestine, hidden.

un•der•croft (un′dər krôft′, -kroft′), *n.* a vault or chamber under the ground, esp. in a church. [1350–1400; ME; see UNDER, CROFT]

un•der•cur•rent (un′dər kûr′ənt, -kur′-), *n.* **1.** a tendency underlying or at variance with the obvious or superficial significance of words, actions, etc.: *Even in his friendliest remarks, one could sense an undercurrent of hostility.* **2.** a current, as of air or water, that flows below the upper currents or surface. [1675–85; UNDER- + CURRENT]

un•der•cut (*v.* un′dər kut′, un′dər kut′; *n., adj.,* un′dər kut′), *v.,* **-cut, -cut•ting,** *n., adj.* **—***v.t.* **1.** to cut under or beneath. **2.** to cut away material from so as to leave a portion overhanging, as in carving or sculpture. **3.** to offer goods or services at a lower price or rate than (a competing price or rate) or than that of (a competitor). **4.** to weaken or destroy the impact or effectiveness of; undermine. **5.** *Golf.* to hit (the ball) so as to cause a backspin. **6.** *Tennis.* to slice (the ball) using an underhand motion. **7.** to cut (a sound recording) with grooves too shallow or with insufficient lateral motion of the stylus. **8.** *Forestry.* to cut a notch in (a tree) in order to control the direction in which the tree is to fall. **—***v.i.* **9.** to undercut material, a competitor, a ball, etc. **—***n.* **10.** a cut or a cutting away underneath. **11.** a notch cut in a tree to determine the direction in which the tree is to fall and to prevent splitting. **12.** *Golf.* a backspin. **13.** *Tennis.* a slice or cut made with an underhand motion. **14.** *Chiefly Brit.* a tenderloin of beef including the fillet. **15.** *Dentistry.* a tooth cavity prepared with a wide base for anchoring a filling securely. **—***adj.* **16.** having or resulting from an undercut. [1350–1400; ME *undercutten* to cut down; see UNDER-, CUT]

un•der•cut•ter (un′dər kut′ər), *n.* *Railroads.* a track-maintenance machine that cleans the ballast section to any predetermined depth. [1890–95; UNDERCUT + -ER[1]]

un•der•de•vel•op (un′dər di vel′əp), *v.t.* to develop (something) short of the required amount: *to underdevelop film.* [UNDER- + DEVELOP] **—un′der•de•vel′op•ment,** *n.*

un•der•de•vel•oped (un′dər di vel′əpt), *adj.* **1.** improperly or insufficiently developed. **2.** *Photog.* (of a negative) less developed than is normal, so as to produce a relatively dark positive lacking in contrast. **3.** developing (def. 2). [1890–95; UNDER- + DEVELOP + -ED[2]]

un•der•do (un′dər do͞o′), *v.i., v.t.,* **-did, -done, -do•ing.** to do less or in a lesser fashion than is usual or requisite. [1605–15; UNDER- + DO[1]]

un•der•dog (un′dər dôg′, -dog′), *n.* **1.** a person who is expected to lose in a contest or conflict. **2.** a victim of social or political injustice: *The underdogs were beginning to organize their protests.* [1875–80, *Amer.*; UNDER- + DOG[1]]

un•der•done (un′dər dun′), *adj.* **1.** (of food) not thoroughly cooked; not cooked enough. **2.** *Chiefly Brit.* (of meat) rare. [1675–85; UNDER- + DONE]

un•der•draft (un′dər draft′, -dräft′), *n.* *Metalworking.* a tendency of a rolled piece to curve downward after passing through a stand, occurring when the upper roll is faster than the lower. Cf. **overdraft** (def. 7). [UNDER- + DRAFT]

un•der•drain (*n.* un′dər drān′; *v.* un′dər drān′), *n.* **1.** a drain placed beneath the surface of cultivated fields, streets, etc. **—***v.t.* **2.** to equip or supply with an underdrain or underdrains. [1795–1805; UNDER- + DRAIN]

un•der•drain•age (un′dər drā′nij), *n.* drainage of agricultural lands and removal of excess water and of alkali by drains buried beneath the surface. [1800–10; UNDER- + DRAINAGE]

un•der•draw (un′dər drô′), *v.t.,* **-drew, -drawn,**

---

un′der•col′ored, *adj.*
un′der•com•mand′er, *n.*
un′der•com′ment, *n.*
un′der•com′ment, *v.*
un′der•con•cerned′, *adj.*
un′der•con′scious•ness, *n.*
un′der•con′sta•ble, *n.*
un′der•con•sume′, *v.t.,* **-sumed, -sum•ing.**
un′der•con•sump′tion, *n.*
un′der•cook′, *n., v.t.*
un′der•coop′er, *n.*
un′der•cor•rect′, *v.t.*
un′der•coun′te•nance, *n.*
un′der•course′, *v.,* **-coursed, -cours•ing,** *n.*
un′der•cour′ti•er, *n.*
un′der•crawl′, *v.i.*
un′der•crest′, *n.*
un′der•cri′er, *n.*
un′der•crust′, *n.*
un′der•crypt′, *n.*
un′der•cup′, *n.*
un′der•curl′, *n.*
un′der•curl′, *v.*
un′der•curve′, *n.*
un′der•curve′, *v.i.,* **-curved, -curv•ing.**
un′der•dea′con, *n.*
un′der•deal′ing, *n.*
un′der•de•greed′, *adj.*
un′der•de•pre′ci•ate′, *v.t.,* **-at•ed, -at•ing.**
un′der•de•pre′ci•a′tion, *n.*
un′der•de•sign′, *v.t.*
un′der•dev′il, *n.*
un′der•di′ag•nose′, *v.t.,* **-nosed, -nos•ing.**
un′der•di′a•logue′, *n.*
un′der•dig′, *v.,* **-dug, -dig•ging.**
un′der•dish′, *n.*
un′der•dis•tinc′tion, *n.*
un′der•dis•trib′u•tor, *n.*
un′der•dive′, *n.*
un′der•dive′, *v.i.,* **-dived** or **-dove, -dived, -div•ing.**
un′der•doc′tor, *n.*
un′der•dose′, *n.*
un′der•dose′, *v.t.,* **-dosed, -dos•ing.**
un′der•dot′, *n.*
un′der•dot′, *v.t.,* **-dot•ted, -dot•ting.**
un′der•down′, *n.*
un′der•draught′, *n.*
un′der•drum′ming, *n.*
un′der•dry′, *v.t.,* **-dried, -dry•ing.**
un′der•eat′, *v.i.,* **-ate, -eat•en, -eat•ing.**
un′der•edge′, *n.*
un′der•ed′u•cat′ed, *adj.*
un′der•en•grav′er, *n.*
un′der•en•rolled′, *adj.*
un′der•ex′er•cise′, *v.i.,* **-cised, -cis•ing.**
un′der•eye′, *n., v.t.,* **-eyed, -ey•ing** or **-eye•ing.**
un′der•face′, *n.*
un′der•face′, *v.t.,* **-faced, -fac•ing.**
un′der•fac′tion, *n.*
un′der•fac′tor, *n.*
un′der•fac′ul•ty, *n., pl.* **-ties.**
un′der•fal′con•er, *n.*
un′der•farm′er, *n.*
un′der•feath′er•ing, *n.*
un′der•fea′ture, *n.*
un′der•feel′ing, *n.*
un′der•fiend′, *n.*
un′der•fi•nance′, *v.t.,* **-nanced, -nanc•ing.**
un′der•fit′ting, *n.*
un′der•flame′, *n.*
un′der•flood′, *v.*

---

un•curbed′, *adj.*
un•curd′, *v.t.*
un•cur′dled, *adj.*
un•cur′dling, *adj.*
un•cured′, *adj.*
un•cu′ri•ous, *adj.;* **-ly,** *adv.*
un•cur′rent, *adj.;* **-ly,** *adv.*
un•cur′ried, *adj.*
un•cursed′, *adj.*
un•curs′ing, *adj.*
un′cur•tail′a•ble, *adj.;* **-bly,** *adv.*
un′cur•tailed′, *adj.*
un′cur•tained, *adj.*
un•curved′, *adj.*
un•curv′ing, *adj.*
un•cush′ioned, *adj.*
un•cusped′, *adj.*
un•cus′tom•ar′i•ly, *adv.*
un•cus′tom•ar′y, *adj.*
un•cut′ta•ble, *adj.*
un•cyn′i•cal, *adj.;* **-ly,** *adv.*
un•dab′bled, *adj.*
un•dag′gled, *adj.*
un•dain′ti•ly, *adv.*
un•dain′ti•ness, *n.*
un•dain′ty, *adj.*
un•dal′ly•ing, *adj.*
un•dam′, *v.t.,* **-dammed, -dam•ming.**
un•dam′age•a•ble, *adj.*
un•dam′aged, *adj.*
un•dam′ag•ing, *adj.*
un•dam′asked, *adj.*
un•dam′ni•fied′, *adj.*
un•damp′ened, *adj.*
un•dance′a•ble, *adj.*
un•danc′ing, *adj.*
un•dan′dled, *adj.*
un•dan′gered, *adj.*
un•dan′ger•ous, *adj.;* **-ly,** *adv.*
un•dap′per, *adj.*
un•dap′pled, *adj.*
un•dared′, *adj.*
un•dar′ing, *adj.*
un•dark′en, *v.t.*
un•darned′, *adj.*
un•dat′a•ble, *adj.*
un•date′a•ble, *adj.*
un•dat′ed, *adj.*
un•daubed′, *adj.*
un•daugh′ter•ly, *adj.*
un•daunt′ing, *adj.*
un•dawned′, *adj.*
un•dawn′ing, *adj.*
un•dazed′, *adj.*
un•daz′ing, *adj.*
un•daz′zled, *adj.*
un•daz′zling, *adj.*
un•dead′ened, *adj.*
un•dead′locked′, *adj.*
un•deaf′, *adj.*
un•deal′a•ble, *adj.*
un•dealt′, *adj.*
un′de•based′, *adj.*
un′de•bat′a•ble, *adj.*
un′de•bat′ed, *adj.*
un′de•bat′ing, *adj.*
un′de•bauched′, *adj.*
un′de•bil′i•tat′ed, *adj.*
un′de•bil′i•tat′ing, *adj.*
un′de•bil′i•ta′tive, *adj.*
un•deb′it•ed, *adj.*
un′dec′a•dent, *adj.;* **-ly,** *adv.*
un′de•cay′a•ble, *adj.*
un′de•cayed′, *adj.*
un′de•cay′ing, *adj.*
un′de•ceased′, *adj.*
un′de•ceit′ful, *adj.*
un′de•cep′tive, *adj.;* **-ly,** *adv.;* **-ness,** *n.*
un′de•cid′a•ble, *adj.*
un′de•ci′pher•a•ble, *adj.;* **-bly,** *adv.*
un′de•ci′phered, *adj.*
un•decked′, *adj.*
un′de•claimed′, *adj.*
un′de•claim′ing, *adj.*
un′de•clam′a•to′ry, *adj.*
un′de•clar′a•ble, *adj.*
un′de•clar′a•tive, *adj.*
un′de•clared′, *adj.*
un′de•clin′a•ble, *adj.*
un′de•clined′, *adj.*
un′de•clin′ing, *adj.*
un′de•coct′ed, *adj.*
un′de•com•pos′a•ble, *adj.*
un′de•com•posed′, *adj.*
un′de•com•pound′ed, *adj.*
un•dec′o•rate′, *v.t.* **-rat•ed, -rat•ing.**
un•dec′o•rat′ed, *adj.*
un•dec′o•ra•tive, *adj.*
un•dec′o•rous, *adj.;* **-ly,** *adv.;* **-ness,** *n.*
un′de•cor′ti•cat′ed, *adj.*
un′de•creased′, *adj.*
un′de•creas′ing, *adj.;* **-ly,** *adv.*
un′de•creed′, *adj.*
un′de•crep′it, *adj.*
un′de•cre′tive, *adj.*
un•dec′re•to′ry, *adj.*
un′de•cried′, *adj.*
un•ded′i•cat′ed, *adj.*
un′de•duced′, *adj.*
un′de•duc′i•ble, *adj.*
un′de•duct′ed, *adj.*
un′de•duct′i•ble, *adj.*
un′de•duc′tive, *adj.;* **-ly,** *adv.*
un•deed′ed, *adj.*
un•deep′, *adj.;* **-ly,** *adv.*
un•deep′ened, *adj.*
un′de•face′a•ble, *adj.*
un′de•faced′, *adj.*
un′de•fal′cat•ed, *adj.*
un′de•fam′a•to′ry, *adj.*
un′de•famed′, *adj.*
un′de•fam′ing, *adj.*
un′de•fault′ed, *adj.*
un′de•fault′ing, *adj.*
un′de•feat′a•ble, *adj.;* **-ble•ness,** *n.;* **-bly,** *adv.*
un′de•feat′ed, *adj.;* **-ly,** *adv;* **-ness,** *n.*
un′de•fec′tive, *adj.;* **-ly,** *adv.;* **-ness,** *n.*
un′de•fend′a•ble, *adj.;* **-ble•ness,** *n.;* **-bly,** *adv.*
un′de•fend′ant, *adj.*
un′de•fend′ed, *adj.*
un′de•fend′ing, *adj.*
un′de•fensed′, *adj.*
un′de•fen′si•ble, *adj.;* **-ble•ness,** *n.;* **-bly,** *adv.*
un′de•fen′sive, *adj.;* **-ly,** *adv.;* **-ness,** *n.*
un′def•er•en′tial, *adj.;* **-ly,** *adv.*
un′de•fer′ra•ble, *adj.;* **-bly,** *adv.*
un′de•ferred′, *adj.*
un′de•fi′a•ble, *adj.;* **-bly,** *adv.*
un′de•fi′ant, *adj.;* **-ly,** *adv.*
un′de•fi′cient, *adj.;* **-ly,** *adv.*
un′de•fied′, *adj.*
un′de•filed′, *adj.*
un′de•fin′a•ble, *adj.*
un•def′i•nite, *adj.;* **-ly,** *adv.;* **-ness,** *n.*
un′de•fin′i•tive, *adj.;* **-ly,** *adv.;* **-ness,** *n.*
un′de•flect′ed, *adj.*
un′de•flec′tive, *adj.*
un′de•fo′li•at′ed, *adj.*
un′de•form′a•ble, *adj.*
un′de•formed′, *adj.*
un′de•fraud′ed, *adj.*
un′de•frayed′, *adj.*
un•deft′, *adj.*
un′de•gen′er•a•cy, *n.*
un′de•gen′er•ate, *adj.*
un′de•gen′er•at′ed, *adj.*
un′de•gen′er•at′ing, *adj.*
un′de•gen′er•a•tive, *adj.*
un′de•grad′ed, *adj.*
un′de•grad′ing, *adj.*
un′de•greed′, *adj.*
un•de′i•fied′, *adj.*

-draw·ing. to line the underside of (a structure, as a floor) with plasterwork, boarding, or the like. [1790–1800; UNDER- + DRAW]

un·der·draw·ers (un′dər drôrz′), *n.* (*used with a plural v.*) an undergarment for the lower part of the body, typically covering at least part of the legs. Cf. **drawer** (def. 2). [1825–35; UNDER- + DRAWERS]

un·der·dress (*v.* un′dər dres′; *n.* un′dər dres′), *v.*, **-dressed** or **-drest, -dress·ing,** *n.* —*v.i.* **1.** to clothe oneself less completely or formally than is usual or fitting for the circumstances. —*n.* **2.** garments worn beneath others; underclothes. **3.** a slip, petticoat, or other underskirt, esp. one designed to be seen when worn, as beneath a redingote. [1775–85; UNDER- + DRESS]

un·der·ed·u·cate (un′dər ej′o͞o kāt′), *v.t.*, **-cat·ed, -cat·ing.** to educate too little or poorly. [UNDER- + EDUCATE] —**un′der·ed′u·ca′tion,** *n.*

un·der·em·pha·sis (un′dər em′fə sis), *n.* inadequate emphasis. [1960–65; UNDER- + EMPHASIS]

un·der·em·pha·size (un′dər em′fə sīz′), *v.t.*, **-sized, -siz·ing.** to give less than sufficient emphasis to; minimize. Also, *esp. Brit.*, **un′der·em′pha·sise′.** [1965–70; UNDER- + EMPHASIZE]

un·der·em·ployed (un′dər em ploid′), *adj.* **1.** employed at a job that does not fully use one's skills or abilities. **2.** employed only part-time when one is available for full-time work. **3.** not utilized fully. —*n.* **4.** underemployed workers collectively. [1905–10; UNDER- + EMPLOY + -ED²] —**un′der·em·ploy′ment,** *n.*

un·der·en·dowed (un′dər en doud′), *adj.* **1.** (of a school, hospital, or other institution) lacking sufficient income from an endowment. **2.** lacking certain desirable traits, faculties, or the like: *Nobody ever accused him of being underendowed with ambition.* [UNDER- + ENDOW + -ED²]

un·der·es·ti·mate (*v.* un′dər es′tə māt′; *n.* un′dər-es′tə mit, -māt′), *v.*, **-mat·ed, -mat·ing,** *n.* —*v.t.* **1.** to estimate at too low a value, rate, or the like. —*v.i.* **2.** to make an estimate lower than that which would be correct. —*n.* **3.** an estimate that is too low. [1805–15; UNDER- + ESTIMATE] —**un′der·es′ti·ma′tion,** *n.*
—**Syn. 1.** undervalue, underrate, misjudge, miscalculate.

un·der·ex·pose (un′dər ik spōz′), *v.t.*, **-posed, -pos·ing.** to expose either to insufficient light or to sufficient light for too short a period, as in photography. [1885–90; UNDER- + EXPOSE]

un·der·ex·po·sure (un′dər ik spō′zhər), *n.* **1.** inadequate exposure, as of photographic film. **2.** a photographic negative or print that is imperfect because of insufficient exposure. [1870–75; UNDER- + EXPOSURE]

un·der·feed (un′dər fēd′ *for 1;* un′dər fēd′ *for 2*), *v.t.*, **-fed, -feed·ing.** **1.** to feed insufficiently. **2.** to feed with fuel from beneath. [1650–60; UNDER- + FEED]

un·der·fired (un′dər fī°rd′), *adj.* supplied with fuel or heat from beneath. [1885–90; UNDER- + FIRE + -ED²]

un·der·foot (un′dər fo͝ot′), *adv.* **1.** under the foot or feet; on the ground; underneath or below: *The climb was difficult because there were so many rocks underfoot.* **2.** so as to form an obstruction, as in walking; in the way: *the ends of her sash falling constantly underfoot.* —*adj.* **3.** lying under the foot or feet; in a position to be trodden upon. [1150–1200; ME *underfot* (adv.). See UNDER-, FOOT]

un·der·frame (un′dər frām′), *n.* the lower frame on which a vehicular structure rests: *the underframe of a bus.* [1850–55; UNDER- + FRAME]

un·der·fur (un′dər fûr′), *n.* the fine, soft, thick, hairy coat under the longer and coarser outer hair in certain animals, as seals, otters, and beavers. Also called **underwool.** [1875–80; UNDER- + FUR]

un·der·gar·ment (un′dər gär′mənt), *n.* an article of underwear. [1520–30; UNDER- + GARMENT]

un·der·gird (un′dər gûrd′), *v.t.*, **-gird·ed** or **-girt, -gird·ing.** **1.** to strengthen; secure, as by passing a rope or chain under and around: *to undergird a top-heavy load.* **2.** to give fundamental support; provide with a sound or secure basis: *ethics undergirded by faith.* [1520–30; UNDER- + GIRD]

un·der·glaze (un′dər glāz′), *Ceram.* —*adj.* **1.** (of a color or decoration) applied to a piece before the piece is glazed. —*n.* **2.** color or decoration applied to a piece before it is glazed. [1875–80; UNDER- + GLAZE]

un·der·go (un′dər gō′), *v.t.*, **-went, -gone, -go·ing.** **1.** to be subjected to; experience; pass through: *to undergo surgery.* **2.** to endure; sustain; suffer: *to undergo sustained deprivation.* [bef. 1000; ME *undergon,* OE *undergān.* See UNDER-, GO¹] —**un′der·go′er,** *n.*
—**Syn. 1.** See **experience. 2.** bear, tolerate. —**Ant. 1.** avoid.

un·der·grad (un′dər grad′), *n. Informal.* an undergraduate. [by shortening]

un·der·grad·u·ate (un′dər graj′o͞o it, -āt′), *n.* **1.** a student in a university or college who has not received a first, esp. a bachelor's, degree. —*adj.* **2.** having the standing of an undergraduate. **3.** of, for, pertaining to, or characteristic of undergraduates. [1620–30; UNDER- + GRADUATE] —**un′der·grad′u·ate·ship′,** *n.*

un·der·ground (*adv.*, un′dər ground′; *adj.*, *n.*, *v.* un′dər ground′), *adv.* **1.** beneath the surface of the ground: *traveling underground by subway.* **2.** in concealment or secrecy; not openly: *subversion carried on underground.* —*adj.* **3.** existing, situated, operating, or taking place beneath the surface of the ground. **4.** used, or for use, underground. **5.** hidden or secret; not open: *underground political activities.* **6.** published or produced by political or social radicals or nonconformists: *an underground newspaper.* **7.** avant-garde; experimental: *an underground movie.* **8.** critical of or attacking the established society or system: *underground opinion.* **9.** of or for nonconformists; unusual: *an underground vegetarian restaurant.* —*n.* **10.** the place or region beneath the surface of the ground. **11.** an underground space or passage. **12.** a secret organization fighting the established government or occupation forces: *He fought in the French underground during the Nazi occupation of France.* **13.** (*often cap.*) a movement or group existing outside the establishment and usually reflecting unorthodox, avant-garde, or radical views. **14.** *Chiefly Brit.* a subway system. —*v.t.* **15.** to place beneath the surface of the ground: *to underground utility lines.* [1565–75; UNDER- + GROUND¹]

un′derground mov′ie, a movie produced independently on a low budget and often using experimental techniques and avant-garde themes. [1965–70]

un′derground rail′road, **1.** Also called **un′derground rail′way.** a railroad running through a continuous tunnel, as under city streets; subway. **2.** (*often caps.*) *U.S. Hist.* (before the abolition of slavery) a system for helping fugitive slaves to escape into Canada or other places of safety. [1825–35]

un′derground trol′ley. See under **trolley** (def. 4).

un·der·grown (un′dər grōn′, un′dər grōn′), *adj.* **1.** not grown to normal size or height: *sickly and undergrown cattle.* **2.** having an undergrowth: *an undergrown thicket tangled with creeping vines.* [1350–1400; ME; see UNDER-, GROWN]

un·der·growth (un′dər grōth′), *n.* **1.** low-lying vegetation or small trees growing beneath larger trees; underbrush. **2.** the condition of being undergrown or undersized. **3.** short, fine hair underlying longer, outer wool or fur. [1590–1600; UNDER- + GROWTH]

un·der·hand (un′dər hand′), *adj.* **1.** not open and aboveboard; secret and crafty or dishonorable: *an underhand deal with the chief of police.* **2.** executed with the hand below the level of the shoulder and the palm turned upward and forward: *an underhand delivery of a ball.* —*adv.* **3.** with the hand below the level of the shoulder and the palm turned upward and forward: *to bowl underhand.* **4.** secretly; stealthily; slyly. [bef. 900; 1530–40 for def. 1; ME *under hande* (adv.) under rule, OE *underhand.* See UNDER-, HAND]
—**Syn. 1.** stealthy, sly, clandestine, surreptitious.

un·der·hand·ed (un′dər han′did), *adj.* **1.** underhand. **2.** short-handed: *By the time of the Navy game, Army usually finds itself underhanded.* [1800–10; UNDER- + HANDED] —**un′der·hand′ed·ly,** *adv.* —**un′der·hand′·ed·ness,** *n.*

un·der·housed (un′dər houzd′), *adj.* **1.** (of persons) having inadequate or poor housing. **2.** (of a community or area) not having enough dwellings. [UNDER- + HOUSE + -ED²]

un·der·hung (un′dər hung′), *adj.* **1.** *Anat.* **a.** (of the lower jaw) projecting beyond the upper jaw. **b.** having the lower jaw so projecting. **2.** resting on a track beneath instead of being overhung, as a sliding door. [1675–85; UNDER- + HUNG]

un·der·in·sur·ance (un′dər in sho͝or′əns, -shûr′-), *n.* insurance purchased against damage or loss of property

CONCISE PRONUNCIATION KEY: *act, cāpe, dâre, pärt; set, ēqual; if, īce; ox, ōver, ôrder, oil, bo͝ok, bo͞ot, out; up, ûrge; child; sing; shoe; thin, that;* zh as in *treasure.* ə = *a* as in *alone, e* as in *system, i* as in *easily, o* as in *gallop, u* as in *circus;* ° as in *fire* (fī°r), *hour* (ou°r). l and n can serve as syllabic consonants, as in *cradle* (krād′l), and *button* (but′n). See the full key inside the front cover.

un′der·floor′, *n.*
un′der·floor′ing, *n.*
un′der·flow′, *n.*
un′der·fold′ed, *adj.*
un′der·foot′age, *n.*
un′der·foot′man, *n., pl.* **-men.**
un′der·form′, *n.*
un′der·for′ti·fy′, *v.t.*, **-fied, -fy·ing.**
un′der·frame′work′, *n.*
un′der·fre′quen·cy, *n., pl.* **-cies.**
un′der·fringe′, *n.*
un′der·frock′, *n.*
un′der·fund′, *v.t.*
un′der·fund′ed, *adj.*
un′der·fund′ing, *n.*
un′der·fur′nish, *v.t.*
un′der·game′keep′er, *n.*
un′der·gaol′er, *n.*
un′der·garb′, *n.*
un′der·gar′den·er, *n.*
un′der·gar′nish, *v.t.*
un′der·gen′er·al, *n.*
un′der·gen′tle·man, *n., pl.* **-men.**
un′der·girth′, *n.*
un′der·gloom′, *n.*
un′der·glow′, *n.*
un′der·gnaw′, *v.t.*
un′der·god′, *n.*
un′der·gov′ern·ess, *n.*
un′der·gov′ern·ment, *n.*
un′der·gov′er·nor, *n.*
un′der·grain′ing, *n.*
un′der·grass′, *n.*
un′der·groan′, *n.*
un′der·growl′, *n.*
un′der·guard′, *n.*
un′der·guard′i·an, *n.*
un′der·gun′ner, *n.*
un′der·hab′it, *n.*
un′der·ham′mer, *n.*
un′der·hang′, *v.*, **-hung, -hang·ing.**
un′der·hang′man, *n., pl.* **-men.**
un′der·hatch′, *v.t.*
un′der·heat′, *v.t.*
un′der·heav′en, *n.*
un′der·help′, *n.*
un′der·hill′, *n.*
un′der·his′to·ry, *n., pl.* **-ries.**
un′der·horse′, *v.t.*, **-horsed, -hors·ing.**
un′der·horse′man, *n., pl.* **-men.**
un′der·house′maid′, *n.*
un′der·hum′, *n.*
un′der·in·flat′ed, *adj.*
un′der·in′stru·ment, *n.*
un′der·in·vest′, *v.i.*
un′der·in·vest′ed, *adj.*
un′der·is′sue, *n.*
un′der·jack′et, *n.*
un′der·jail′er, *n.*
un′der·jan′i·tor, *n.*
un′der·jaw′, *n.*
un′der·job′bing, *n.*
un′der·join′, *v.t.*
un′der·joint′, *n.*
un′der·judge′, *v.t.*, **-judged, -judg·ing.**
un′der·judge′, *n.*
un′der·jun′gle, *n.*
un′der·keep′er, *n.*
un′der·king′, *n.*
un′der·king′dom, *n.*
un′der·la′bor·er, *n.*
un′der·land′, *n.*
un′der·lash′, *n.*
un′der·laun′dress, *n.*
un′der·law′yer, *n.*
un′der·leath′er, *n.*
un′der·leg′ate, *n.*
un′der·les·see′, *n.*
un′der·lev′el, *adj.*
un′der·lid′, *n.*
un′der·lieu·ten′ant, *n.*
un′der·life′, *n.*

un′de·is′ti·cal, *adj.*
un′de·ject′ed, *adj.*; **-ly,** *adv.*; **-ness,** *n.*
un′de·lay′a·ble, *adj.*
un′de·layed′, *adj.*
un′de·lay′ing, *adj.*; **-ly,** *adv.*
un′de·lec′ta·ble, *adj.*; **-bly,** *adv.*
un·del′e·gat′ed, *adj.*
un′de·let′ed, *adj.*
un′del·e·te′ri·ous, *adj.*; **-ly,** *adv.*; **-ness,** *n.*
un′de·lib′er·ate, *adj.*; **-ly,** *adv.*; **-ness,** *n.*
un′de·lib′er·at′ing, *adj.*; **-ly,** *adv.*
un′de·lib′er·a·tive, *adj.*; **-ly,** *adv.*; **-ness,** *n.*
un′de·li′cious, *adj.*; **-ly,** *adv.*
un′de·light′ed, *adj.*; **-ly,** *adv.*
un′de·light′ful, *adj.*; **-ly,** *adv.*
un′de·light′ing, *adj.*
un′de·lin′e·a·ble, *adj.*
un′de·lin′e·at′ed, *adj.*
un′de·lin′e·a·tive, *adj.*
un′de·lin′quent, *adj.*; **-ly,** *adv.*
un′de·lir′i·ous, *adj.*; **-ly,** *adv.*
un′de·liv′er·a·ble, *adj.*
un′de·liv′ered, *adj.*
un′de·lud′ed, *adj.*; **-ly,** *adv.*
un′de·lud′ing, *adj.*
un·del′uged, *adj.*
un′de·lu′sive, *adj.*; **-ly,** *adv.*; **-ness,** *n.*
un′de·lu′so·ry, *adj.*
un·delved′, *adj.*
un′de·mand′ed, *adj.*
un′de·mand′ing, *adj.*
un′de·mised′, *adj.*
un′dem·o·crat′ic, *adj.*
un′dem·o·crat′i·cal·ly, *adv.*
un′de·moc′ra·ti·za′tion, *n.*
un′de·moc′ra·tize′, *v.t.*, **-tized, -tiz·ing.**
un′de·mol′ish·a·ble, *adj.*
un′de·mol′ished, *adj.*
un′de·mon′stra·ble, *adj.*; **-ble·ness,** *n.*; **-bly,** *adv.*
un·dem′on·strat′ed, *adj.*
un′dem·on·stra′tion·al, *adj.*
un′de·mure′, *adj.*; **-ly,** *adv.*; **-ness,** *n.*
un′de·mur′ring, *adj.*
un′de·nied′, *adj.*
un·den′i·zened, *adj.*
un·de·nom′i·nat′ed, *adj.*
un′de·not′a·ble, *adj.*
un·de′no·ta·tive, *adj.*; **-ly,** *adv.*
un′de·not′ed, *adj.*
un′de·nounced′, *adj.*
un·dent′ed, *adj.*
un′de·nud′ed, *adj.*
un′de·nun′ci·at′ed, *adj.*
un′de·nun′ci·a·to′ry, *adj.*
un′de·part′ed, *adj.*
un′de·part′ing, *adj.*
un′de·pend′a·bil′i·ty, *n.*
un′de·pend′a·ble, *adj.*; **-ble·ness,** *n.*; **-bly,** *adv.*
un′de·pend′ent, *adj.*
un′de·pict′ed, *adj.*
un′de·plet′ed, *adj.*
un′de·plored′, *adj.*
un′de·port′ed, *adj.*
un′de·pos′a·ble, *adj.*
un′de·posed′, *adj.*
un′de·pos′it·ed, *adj.*
un′de·praved′, *adj.*
un·dep′re·cat′ed, *adj.*
un·dep′re·cat′ing, *adj.*; **-ly,** *adv.*
un·dep′re·ca′tive, *adj.*; **-ly,** *adv.*
un′de·pre′ci·a·ble, *adj.*
un′de·pre′ci·at′ed, *adj.*
un′de·pre′ci·a·tive, *adj.*
un′de·pre′ci·a·to′ry, *adj.*
un′de·pressed′, *adj.*
un′de·press′i·ble, *adj.*
un′de·press′ing, *adj.*
un′de·pres′sive, *adj.*; **-ly,** *adv.*; **-ness,** *n.*
un′de·prived′, *adj.*
un′de·put′ed, *adj.*
un·dep′u·tized, *adj.*
un′de·ranged′, *adj.*
un′de·rid′ed, *adj.*
un′de·ris′i·ble, *adj.*
un′de·ri′sive, *adj.*; **-ly,** *adv.*; **-ness,** *n.*
un′de·ri′so·ry, *adj.*
un′de·riv′a·ble, *adj.*
un′de·riv′a·tive, *adj.*; **-ly,** *adv.*
un·der′o·gat′ing, *adj.*
un′de·rog′a·tive, *adj.*; **-ly,** *adv.*
un′de·scend′a·ble, *adj.*
un′de·scend′ed, *adj.*
un′de·scend′ent, *adj.*
un′de·scend′i·ble, *adj.*
un′de·scend′ing, *adj.*
un′de·scrib′a·ble, *adj.*; **-ble·ness,** *n.*; **-bly,** *adv.*
un′de·scribed′, *adj.*
un′de·scried′, *adj.*
un′de·scrip′tive, *adj.*; **-ly,** *adv.*; **-ness,** *n.*
un′de·scry′ing, *adj.*
un·des′e·crat′ed, *adj.*
un′de·sert′ed, *adj.*
un′de·served′, *adj.*
un′de·serv′ed·ly, *adv.*
un′de·serv′ing, *adj.*; **-ly,** *adv.*; **-ness,** *n.*
un·des′ic·cat′ed, *adj.*
un·des′ig·nat′ed, *adj.*
un·des′ig·na′tive, *adj.*
un′de·sired′, *adj.*
un′de·sir′ing, *adj.*
un′de·sir′ous, *adj.*; **-ly,** *adv.*
un′de·sist′ing, *adj.*
un′de·spaired′, *adj.*
un′de·spair′ing, *adj.*; **-ly,** *adv.*
un′des·patched′, *adj.*
un′de·spised′, *adj.*
un′de·spis′ing, *adj.*
un′de·spoiled′, *adj.*
un′de·spond′ent, *adj.*; **-ly,** *adv.*
un′de·spond′ing, *adj.*; **-ly,** *adv.*
un′des·pot′ic, *adj.*
un′des·pot′i·cal·ly, *adv.*
un·des′tined, *adj.*
un·des′ti·tute′, *adj.*
un′de·stroyed′, *adj.*
un′de·struct′i·ble, *adj.*; **-ble·ness,** *n.*; **-bly,** *adv.*
un′de·struc′tive, *adj.*; **-ly,** *adv.*; **-ness,** *n.*
un′de·tach′a·ble, *adj.*
un′de·tached′, *adj.*
un′de·tailed′, *adj.*
un′de·tain′a·ble, *adj.*
un′de·tained′, *adj.*
un′de·tect′a·ble, *adj.*; **-bly,** *adv.*
un′de·tect′ed, *adj.*
un′de·tect′i·ble, *adj.*
un′de·te′ri·o·rat′ed, *adj.*
un′de·te′ri·o·rat′ing, *adj.*
un′de·te′ri·o·ra′tive, *adj.*
un′de·ter′mi·na·ble, *adj.*; **-ble·ness,** *n.*; **-bly,** *adv.*
un′de·ter′mined, *adj.*
un′de·ter′min·ing, *adj.*
un′de·ter′ra·bil′i·ty, *n.*
un′de·ter′ra·ble, *adj.*; **-bly,** *adv.*
un′de·terred′, *adj.*
un′de·ter′ring, *adj.*
un′de·test′a·bil′i·ty, *n.*
un′de·test′a·ble, *adj.*; **-ble·ness,** *n.*; **-bly,** *adv.*
un′de·test′ed, *adj.*
un′de·test′ing, *adj.*
un′de·throned′, *adj.*
un·det′o·nat′ed, *adj.*
un′de·tract′ing, *adj.*; **-ly,** *adv.*
un′de·trac′tive, *adj.*; **-ly,** *adv.*
un′de·trac′to·ry, *adj.*
un′det·ri·men′tal, *adj.*; **-ly,** *adv.*
un·dev′as·tat′ed, *adj.*

in an amount less than its true value, sometimes bought intentionally by the insured with full knowledge of the risk. [UNDER- + INSURANCE]

un·der·in·sure (un′dər in shŏŏr′, -shûr′), *v.t.*, **-sured, -sur·ing.** to insure for an amount less than the true or replacement value: *It's risky to underinsure your home.* [UNDER- + INSURE] **—un′der·in·sured′,** *adj.*

un·de·rived (un′di rīvd′), *adj.* not derived; fundamental, as an axiom or postulate; immediate. [1620–30; UN-[1] + DERIVED]

un·der·laid (un′dər lād′), *adj.* **1.** placed or laid underneath, as a foundation or substratum. **2.** having an underneath layer (often fol. by *with*): *a lace tablecloth underlaid with damask; courtesy underlaid with reserve.* —*v.* **3.** pt. and pp. of **underlay.** [bef. 1100; late OE *under lede* (not recorded in ME); see UNDER-, LAID]

un·der·lap (un′dər lap′), *v.t.*, **-lapped, -lap·ping.** to extend partly under. [1865–70; UNDER- + LAP[2]]

un·der·lay (*v.* un′dər lā′; *n.* un′dər lā′), *v.*, **-laid, -lay·ing,** *n.* —*v.t.* **1.** to lay under or beneath. **2.** to provide with something laid underneath; raise or support with something laid underneath: *The manufacturer underlays the chrome finish with a zinc coating.* **3.** to extend across the bottom of. —*n.* **4.** something underlaid. **5.** *Print.* a piece or pieces of paper put under type or cuts to bring them to the proper height for printing. [bef. 900; ME *underleyen,* OE *underlecgan;* see UNDER-, LAY[1]]

un·der·lay·er (un′dər lā′ər), *n.* a layer lying beneath another; substratum. [1895–1900; UNDER- + LAYER]

un·der·lay·ment (un′dər lā′mənt), *n.* material laid between a subfloor and a finish floor of linoleum, asphalt tile, etc. [1945–50; UNDERLAY + -MENT]

un·der·let (un′dər let′), *v.t.*, **-let, -let·ting.** **1.** to let below the true value. **2.** to sublet. [1670–80; UNDER- + LET[1]]

un·der·lie (un′dər lī′), *v.t.* **-lay, -lain, -ly·ing.** **1.** to lie under or beneath; be situated under. **2.** to be at the basis of; form the foundation of. **3.** *Gram.* to function as the root morpheme or original or basic form of (a derived form): *The form "boy" underlies "boyish."* **4.** *Finance.* to be primary to another right or security. [bef. 900; ME *underlyen* (v.), OE *underlicgan.* See UNDER-, LIE[2]]

un·der·line (*v.* un′dər līn′, un′dər līn′; *n.* un′dər līn′), *v.*, **-lined, -lin·ing,** *n.* —*v.t.* **1.** to mark with a line or lines underneath; underscore. **2.** to indicate the importance of; emphasize, as by stressing or italicizing. —*n.* **3.** *Print.* a caption under an illustration. **4.** a line drawn under something; an underscore. [1715–25; UNDER- + LINE[1]] **—un·der·lin·e·a·tion** (un′dər lin′ē ā′shən), *n.* **—un′der·lin′er,** *n.*

CONCISE ETYMOLOGY KEY: <, descended or borrowed from; >, whence; b., blend of, blended; c., cognate with; cf., compare; deriv., derivative; equiv., equivalent; imit., imitative; obl., oblique; r., replacing; s., stem; sp., spelling, spelled; resp., respelling, respelled; trans., translation; ?, origin unknown; *, unattested; ‡, probably earlier than. See the full key inside the front cover.

un·der·ling (un′dər ling), *n.* a subordinate, esp. one of slight importance. [1125–75; ME. See UNDER-, -LING[1]] **—Syn.** menial, flunky, lackey, hireling.

un·der·lit (un′dər lit′), *adj.* lacking adequate light. [UNDER- + LIT[1]]

un·der·ly·ing (un′dər lī′ing), *adj.* **1.** lying or situated beneath, as a substratum. **2.** fundamental; basic: *the underlying cause of their discontent.* **3.** implicit; discoverable only by close scrutiny or analysis: *an underlying seriousness in his witticisms.* **4.** (of a claim, mortgage, etc.) taking precedence; anterior; prior. **5.** *Ling.* belonging to an earlier stage in the transformational derivation of a sentence or other structure; belonging to the deep structure. [1605–15; UNDERLIE + -ING[2]]

un·der·manned (un′dər mand′), *adj.* lacking a normal or sufficient work force, complement of troops, or the like; understaffed; short-handed. [1865–70; UNDER- + MANNED]

un·der·mine (un′dər mīn′ *or, esp. for 1, 2, 4,* un′dər-mīn′), *v.t.*, **-mined, -min·ing.** **1.** to injure or destroy by insidious activity or imperceptible stages, sometimes tending toward a sudden dramatic effect. **2.** to attack by indirect, secret, or underhand means; attempt to subvert by stealth. **3.** to make an excavation under; dig or tunnel beneath, as a military stronghold. **4.** to weaken or cause to collapse by removing underlying support, as by digging away or eroding the foundation. [1300–50; ME *underminen.* See UNDER-, MINE[2]] **—un′der·min′er,** *n.* **—un′der·min′ing·ly,** *adv.*

un·der·most (un′dər mōst′), *adj., adv.* lowest, as in position, status, or the like. [1545–55; UNDER- + -MOST]

un·der·neath (un′dər nēth′, -nēth′), *prep.* **1.** below the surface or level of; directly or vertically beneath; at or on the bottom of. **2.** under the control of; in a lower position in a hierarchy of authority: *Underneath the department heads are the junior executives.* **3.** hidden, disguised, or misrepresented, as by a false appearance or pretense: *Underneath his bluster is a timid nature.* —*adv.* **4.** below; at a lower level or position; on the underside. —*adj.* **5.** lower; situated below or under. —*n.* **6.** the bottom; underside; lowest part. [bef. 900; ME *undernethe,* OE *underneothan.* See UNDER, BENEATH]

un·der·nour·ished (un′dər nûr′isht, -nur′-), *adj.* **1.** not nourished with sufficient or proper food to maintain or promote health or normal growth. **2.** not given essential elements for proper development: *emotionally undernourished.* [1925–30; UNDER- + NOURISH + -ED[2]] **—un′der·nour′ish·ment,** *n.*

un·der·nu·tri·tion (un′dər nōō trish′ən, -nyōō-), *n.* nutritional deficiency resulting from lack of food or from the inability of the body to convert or absorb it. [1895–1900; UNDER- + NUTRITION]

un·der·paint·ing (un′dər pān′ting), *n.* the first coat of paint, esp. the initial painting on a canvas in which the major areas, tones, colors, and forms are indicated in mass. [1865–70; UNDER- + PAINTING]

un·der·pants (un′dər pants′), *n.* (*used with a plural v.*) drawers or shorts worn under outer clothing, usually next to the skin. [1920–25; UNDER- + PANTS]

un·der·part (un′dər pärt′), *n.* **1.** the lower part or side: *The underpart of the plane's fuselage scraped the treetops.* **2.** an auxiliary or secondary part or role. [1655–65; UNDER- + PART]

un·der·pass (un′dər pas′, -päs′), *n.* a passage running underneath, esp. a passage for pedestrians or vehicles, or both, crossing under a railroad, road, etc. [1900–05; UNDER- + PASS]

un·der·pay (un′dər pā′), *v.t.*, **-paid, -pay·ing.** to pay less than is deserved or usual. [1840–50; UNDER- + PAY[1]] **—un·der·pay·ment** (un′dər pā′mənt, un′dər pā′-), *n.*

un·der·per·form (un′dər pər fôrm′), *v.t., v.i.* to perform less well than (another of its kind, a general average, etc.) or less well than expected: *Surprisingly, the stock has underperformed the market indexes all year. Several of our best players consistently underperform.* [UNDER- + PERFORM] **—un′der·per·for′mance,** *n.*

un·der·pin (un′dər pin′), *v.t.*, **-pinned, -pin·ning.** **1.** to prop up or support from below; strengthen, as by reinforcing a foundation. **2.** to replace or strengthen the foundation of (a building or the like). **3.** to furnish a foundation for; corroborate: *The author's conclusions are underpinned by references to experimental findings.* [1515–25; UNDER- + PIN]

un·der·pin·ning (un′dər pin′ing), *n.* **1.** a system of supports beneath a wall or the like. **2.** Often, **underpinnings.** a foundation or basis: *to uncover the emotional underpinnings of an illness.* **3. underpinnings,** *Informal.* **a.** underwear, esp. women's underwear. **b.** the legs. [1480–90; UNDER + PIN + -ING[1]]

un′der·pitch vault′ (un′dər pich′), a construction having a central vault intersected by vaults of lower pitch. Also called **Welsh vault.** See illus. under **vault.** [UNDER- + PITCH[1]]

un·der·play (un′dər plā′, un′dər plā′), *v.t.* **1.** to act (a part) sketchily. **2.** to act subtly and restrainedly. **3.** to understate or de-emphasize; downplay: *The ambassador underplayed his role in the peace negotiations.* —*v.i.* **4.** to leave out of one's acting all subtlety and enriching detail. **5.** to achieve an effect in acting with a minimum of emphasis. [1725–35; UNDER- + PLAY]

un·der·plot (un′dər plot′), *n.* a plot subordinate to another plot, as in a novel. [1660–70; UNDER- + PLOT]

un·der·pop·u·lat·ed (un′dər pop′yə lā′tid), *adj.* having a population lower than is normal or desirable. [1880–85; UNDER- + POPULATE + -ED[2]] **—un′der·pop′u·la′tion,** *n.*

un·der·praise (un′dər prāz′), *v.t.*, **-praised, -prais·ing.** to praise to a lesser degree or extent than the circumstances warrant. [1690–1700; UNDER- + PRAISE]

un·der·price (un′dər prīs′), *v.t.*, **-priced, -pric·ing.** **1.** to price (goods or merchandise) lower than the standard price or fair value. **2.** to undercut (a competitor) by underselling or setting prices below actual cost. [1750–60; UNDER- + PRICE]

un·der·priv·i·leged (un′dər priv′ə lijd, -priv′lijd),

un′der·lift′, *n.*
un′der·light′, *n.*
un′der·lik′ing, *n.*
un′der·limbed′, *adj.*
un′der·lim′it, *n.*
un′der·lim′it, *v.t.*
un′der·line′man, *n., pl.* **-men.**
un′der·lin′en, *n.*
un′der·lip′, *n.*
un′der·load′, *v.t.*
un′der·lock′, *n.*
un′der·lodg′ing, *n.*
un′der·loft′, *n.*
un′der·made′, *adj.*
un′der·maid′, *n.*
un′der·main·tain′, *v.t.*
un′der·main·tained′, *adj.*
un′der·mak′er, *n.*
un′der·man′, *v.t.*, **-manned, -man·ning.**
un′der·man′age, *v.t.*, **-aged, -ag·ing.**
un′der·man′aged, *adj.*
un′der·man′ag·er, *n.*
un′der·mark′, *n.*
un′der·mark′, *v.t.*
un′der·mar′ket, *v.t.*
un′der·mar′shal, *n.*
un′der·mast′ed, *adj.*
un′der·mas′ter, *n.*
un′der·mate′, *n.*
un′der·mean′ing, *n.*
un′der·meas′ure, *v.t.*, **-ured, -ur·ing,** *n.*
un′der·me′di·a′tor, *n.*
un′der·mel′o·dy, *n., pl.* **-dies.**
un′der·men′tioned, *adj.*
un′der·mill′er, *n.*
un′der·min′er·al·i·za′tion, *n.*
un′der·min′is·ter, *n.*
un′der·min′is·try, *n., pl.* **-tries.**
un′der·mist′, *n.*
un′der·moat′ed, *adj.*
un′der·mor′al, *adj.*
un′der·mo′tion, *n.*
un′der·mount′, *n.*
un′der·moun′tain, *n.*
un′der·mu′sic, *n.*
un′der·mus′lin, *n.*
un′der·name′, *n.*
un′der·named′, *adj.*
un′der·note′, *n.*
un′der·not′ed, *adj.*
un′der·nurse′, *n.*
un′der·oc′cu·pied′, *adj.*
un′der·of′fi·cer, *n.*
un′der·of·fi′cial, *adj.*
un′der·o·pin′ion, *n.*
un′der·or′gan·i·za′tion, *n.*
un′der·ox′i·dize′, *v.t.*, **-dized, -diz·ing.**
un′der·pack′ing, *n.*
un′der·pain′, *n.*
un′der·par·tic′i·pa′tion, *n.*
un′der·part′ner, *n.*
un′der·peep′, *v.i.*
un′der·peer′, *v.i.*
un′der·pen′, *n.*
un′der·peo′pled, *adj.*
un′der·pet′ti·coat′, *n.*
un′der·pet′ti·coat′ed, *adj.*
un′der·pier′, *n.*
un′der·pi·las′ter, *n.*
un′der·pile′, *n.*
un′der·pitched′, *adj.*
un′der·plain′, *adj.*
un′der·plan′, *n.*
un′der·plan′, *v.t.*, **-planned, -plan·ning.**
un′der·plant′, *v.t.*
un′der·plate′, *n.*
un′der·ply′, *n., pl.* **-plies.**
un′der·point′, *n.*
un′der·point′, *v.i.*

un·dev′as·tat′ing, *adj.;* **-ly,** *adv.*
un′de·vel′op·a·ble, *adj.*
un′de·vel′op·ing, *adj.*
un′de·vel′op·ment, *n.*
un′de·vel′op·men′tal, *adj.;* **-ly,** *adv.*
un·de′vi·a·ble, *adj.*
un·de′vi·at′ed, *adj.*
un·de′vi·at′ing, *adj.;* **-ly,** *adv.*
un·dev′il·ish, *adj.*
un·de′vi·ous, *adj.;* **-ly,** *adv.;* **-ness,** *n.*
un′de·vis′a·ble, *adj.*
un′de·vised′, *adj.*
un′de·vot′ed, *adj.*
un′de·vo′tion·al, *adj.*
un′de·voured′, *adj.*
un′de·vout′, *adj.;* **-ly,** *adv.;* **-ness,** *n.*
un·dewed′, *adj.*
un·dew′i·ly, *adv.*
un·dew′i·ness, *n.*
un·dew′y, *adj.*
un·dex′ter·ous, *adj.;* **-ly,** *adv.;* **-ness,** *n.*
un·dex′trous, *adj.;* **-ly,** *adv.;* **-ness,** *n.*
un′di·a·bet′ic, *adj.*
un′di·ag·nos′a·ble, *adj.*
un·di′ag·nosed′, *adj.*
un·di′a·gramed′, *adj.*
un′di·a·gram·mat′ic, *adj.*
un′di·a·gram·mat′i·cal, *adj.;* **-ly,** *adv.*
un·di′a·grammed′, *adj.*
un′di·a·lec′ti·cal, *adj.*
un·di′aled, *adj.*
un·di′alled, *adj.*
un·di′a·lyzed′, *adj.*
un′di·a·met′ric, *adj.*
un′di·a·met′ri·cal, *adj.;* **-ly,** *adv.*
un·dia′pered, *adj.*
un′di·aph′a·nous, *adj.;* **-ly,** *adv.;* **-ness,** *n.*
un′di·a·ton′ic, *adj.*
un′di·a·ton′i·cal·ly, *adv.*
un′di·chot′o·mous, *adj.;* **-ly,** *adv.*
un·dic′tat·ed, *adj.*
un′dic·ta·to′ri·al, *adj.;* **-ly,** *adv.*
un′di·dac′tic, *adj.*
un·dif′fer·ent, *adj.;* **-ly,** *adv.*
un′dif·fer·en′ti·a·ble, *adj.;* **-bly,** *adv.*
un′dif·fer·en′ti·at′ed, *adj.*
un·dif′fer·ing, *adj.*
un·dif′fi·cult′, *adj.;* **-ly,** *adv.*
un·dif′fi·dent, *adj.;* **-ly,** *adv.*
un′dif·fract′ed, *adj.*
un′dif·frac′tive, *adj.;* **-ly,** *adv.;* **-ness,** *n.*
un′dif·fused′, *adj.*
un′dif·fus′i·ble, *adj.*
un′dif·fu′sive, *adj.;* **-ly,** *adv.;* **-ness,** *n.*
un′di·gest′ed, *adj.*
un′di·gest′ing, *adj.*
un·dig′i·tat′ed, *adj.*
un·dig′ni·fied′, *adj.;* **-ly,** *adv.*
un′di·gres′sive, *adj.;* **-ly,** *adv.;* **-ness,** *n.*
un·diked′, *adj.*
un′di·lap′i·dat′ed, *adj.*
un′di·lat′a·ble, *adj.*
un′di·lat′ed, *adj.*
un′di·lat′ing, *adj.*
un′di·la′tive, *adj.*
un·dil′a·to′ri·ly, *adv.*
un·dil′a·to′ry, *adj.*
un·dil′i·gent, *adj.;* **-ly,** *adv.*
un′di·lute′, *adj.*
un′di·lut′ed, *adj.*
un′di·lut′ing, *adj.*
un′di·lu′vi·al, *adj.*
un′di·lu′vi·an, *adj.*
un·dim′, *adj.;* **-ly,** *adv.*
un′di·men′sioned, *adj.*
un·dim′er·ous, *adj.*
un′di·mid′i·at′ed, *adj.*
un′di·min′ish·a·ble, *adj.;* **-ble·ness,** *n.;* **-bly,** *adv.*
un′di·min′ished, *adj.*
un′di·min′ish·ing, *adj.*
un·dimmed′, *adj.*
un·dim′pled, *adj.*
un′di·plo′maed, *adj.*
un′dip·lo·mat′ic, *adj.*
un′dip·lo·mat′i·cal·ly, *adv.*
un·dipped′, *adj.*
un′di·rec′tion·al, *adj.*
un′dis·a′bled, *adj.*
un′dis·a·gree′a·ble, *adj.*
un′dis·ap·pear′ing, *adj.*
un′dis·ap·point′a·ble, *adj.*
un′dis·ap·point′ed, *adj.*
un′dis·ap·point′ing, *adj.*
un′dis·armed′, *adj.*
un′dis·as′trous, *adj.;* **-ly,** *adv.*
un′dis·band′ed, *adj.*
un′dis·barred′, *adj.*
un′dis·bursed′, *adj.*
un′dis·card′a·ble, *adj.*
un′dis·card′ed, *adj.*
un′dis·cern′a·ble, *adj.;* **-bly,** *adv.*
un′dis·cerned′, *adj.*
un′dis·cern′i·ble, *adj.;* **-bly,** *adv.*
un′dis·cern′ing, *adj.;* **-ly,** *adv.*
un′dis·charge′a·ble, *adj.*
un′dis·charged′, *adj.*
un·dis′ci·plin′a·ble, *adj.*
un·dis′ci·plined, *adj.*
un′dis·claimed′, *adj.*
un′dis·closed′, *adj.*
un′dis·col′ored, *adj.*
un′dis·com′fit·ed, *adj.*
un′dis·com·posed′, *adj.*
un′dis·con·cert′ed, *adj.*
un′dis·con·nect′ed, *adj.;* **-ly,** *adv.*
un′dis·con·tin′ued, *adj.*
un′dis·cord′ant, *adj.;* **-ly,** *adv.*
un′dis·cord′ing, *adj.*
un′dis·count′a·ble, *adj.*
un·dis′count·ed, *adj.*
un′dis·cour′age·a·ble, *adj.*
un′dis·cour′aged, *adj.*
un′dis·cour′ag·ing, *adj.;* **-ly,** *adv.*
un′dis·cov′er·a·ble, *adj.*
un′dis·cov′ered, *adj.*
un′dis·cred′it·a·ble, *adj.*
un′dis·cred′it·ed, *adj.*
un′dis·crim′i·nat′ed, *adj.*
un′dis·crim′i·nat′ing, *adj.;* **-ly,** *adv.*
un′dis·crim′i·na·to′ry, *adj.*
un′dis·cuss′a·ble, *adj.*
un′dis·cussed′, *adj.*
un′dis·cuss′i·ble, *adj.*
un′dis·dain′ing, *adj.*
un′dis·eased′, *adj.*
un′dis·es·tab′lished, *adj.*
un′dis·fig′ured, *adj.*
un′dis·fran′chised, *adj.*
un′dis·gorged′, *adj.*
un′dis·graced′, *adj.*
un′dis·guis′a·ble, *adj.*
un′dis·guised′, *adj.*
un′dis·guis′ed·ly, *adv.*
un′dis·gust′ed, *adj.*
un′dis·heart′ened, *adj.*
un′di·shev′eled, *adj.*
un′dis·hon′ored, *adj.*
un′dis·il·lu′sioned, *adj.*
un′dis·in·fect′ed, *adj.*
un′dis·in·her′it·a·ble, *adj.*
un′dis·in·her′it·ed, *adj.*
un′dis·joined′, *adj.*
un′dis·joint′ed, *adj.*
un·dis′lo·cat′ed, *adj.*
un′dis·lodged′, *adj.*
un′dis·man′tled, *adj.*
un′dis·may′a·ble, *adj.*
un′dis·mayed′, *adj.*

adj. denied the enjoyment of the normal privileges or rights of a society because of low economic and social status. [1920–25; UNDER- + PRIVILEGED] **—Syn.** disadvantaged, deprived.

un•der•pro•duce (un′dər prə do͞os′, -dyo͞os′), *v.i., v.t.,* **-duced, -duc•ing.** to produce less or in a lesser manner or degree than is normal or required. [1965–70; UNDER- + PRODUCE] **—un′der•pro•duc′er,** *n.*

un•der•pro•duc•tion (un′dər prə duk′shən), *n.* production that is less than normal or than is required by the demand. [1885–90; UNDER- + PRODUCTION] **—un•der•pro•duc•tiv•i•ty** (un′dər prō′duk tiv′i tē, -prod′-ək-), *n.* **—un′der•pro•duc′tive,** *adj.*

un•der•proof (un′dər pro͞of′), *adj.* containing a smaller proportion of alcohol than proof spirit. [1855–60; UNDER- + PROOF]

un•der•prop (un′dər prop′), *v.t.,* **-propped, -prop•ping.** to prop underneath; support; uphold. [1505–15; UNDER- + PROP[1]] **—un′der•prop′per,** *n.*

un•der•quote (un′dər kwōt′), *v.t.,* **-quot•ed, -quot•ing. 1.** to offer (stocks, merchandise, etc.) at a price lower than the market price or some other quoted price; offer at a price reduced by (a specified amount). **2.** to quote a price lower than that of (a specified competitor). [1890–95; UNDER- + QUOTE]

un•der•rate (un′dər rāt′), *v.t.,* **-rat•ed, -rat•ing.** to rate or evaluate too low; underestimate. [1615–25; UNDER- + RATE[1]]

un•der•re•act (un′dər rē akt′), *v.i.* to react with less than the expected or appropriate emotion. [1965–70; UNDER- + REACT] **—un′der•re•ac′tion,** *n.*

un•der•re•port (un′dər ri pôrt′, -pōrt′), *v.t., v.i.* to report as less or fewer than is correct: *to underreport the enemy's strength.* [1945–50; UNDER- + REPORT]

un•der•ripe (un′dər rīp′), *adj.* not completely ripe, as fruit. [1700–10; UNDER- + RIPE]

un•der•run (un′dər run′), *v.,* **-ran, -run, -run•ning,** *n.* —*v.t.* **1.** to run, pass, or go under. **2.** *Naut.* to pass beneath (a stretched rope, net, etc.) in a boat or the like for the purpose of inspection or repairs. —*n.* **3.** something that runs or passes underneath, as a current. **4.** an instance of costing or spending less than estimated. **5.** a production run of a manufactured or printed item below the quantity ordered. [1540–50; UNDER- + RUN]

un•der•sat•u•rat•ed (un′dər sach′ə rā′tid), *adj.* *Chem.* unsaturated (def. 2). [1820–30; UNDER- + SATURATED] **—un′der•sat′u•ra′tion,** *n.*

un•der•score (*v.* un′dər skôr′, -skōr′, un′dər skôr′, -skōr′; *n.* un′dər skôr′, -skōr′), *v.,* **-scored, -scor•ing,** *n.* —*v.t.* **1.** to mark with a line or lines underneath; underline, as for emphasis. **2.** to stress; emphasize: *The recent tragedy underscores the danger of disregarding safety rules.* —*n.* **3.** a line drawn beneath something written or printed. **4.** music for a film soundtrack; background for a film or stage production. [1765–75; UNDER- + SCORE]

un•der•sea (un′dər sē′), *adj.* **1.** located, carried on, or used under the surface of the sea: *undersea life.* —*adv.* **2.** underseas. [1605–15; UNDER- + SEA]

un•der•seas (un′dər sēz′), *adv.* beneath the surface of the sea. [1675–85; UNDERSEA + -S[1]]

un•der•sec•re•tar•i•at (un′dər sek′ri târ′ē it, un′-dər sek′ri ter′-), *n.* a department or section of a ministry of which an under secretary is in charge. [1945–50; UNDER- + SECRETARIAT]

un′der sec′retary, (*often caps.*) an official who is subordinate to a principal secretary, as in the U.S. cabinet: *Under Secretary of the Treasury.* Also, **un′der•sec′•re•tar•y.** [1680–90]

un•der•sell (un′dər sel′), *v.t.,* **-sold, -sell•ing. 1.** to sell more cheaply than. **2.** to advertise with restraint; understate the merits of (something): *By underselling his product, he let his hearers convince themselves of its importance.* **3.** to sell for less than the actual value. [1615–25; UNDER- + SELL] **—un′der•sell′er,** *n.*

un•der•serv•ant (un′dər sûr′vənt), *n.* a servant of inferior or subordinate rank. [1540–50; UNDER- + SERVANT]

un•der•set (un′dər set′), *n.* a current of water below the surface and flowing in a direction contrary to the water on the surface. [1500–10; UNDER- + SET] **—Syn.** See **undertow.**

un•der•sexed (un′dər sekst′), *adj.* having a weaker sexual drive than is considered usual or normal. [1930–35; UNDER- + SEXED]

un•der•sher•iff (un′dər sher′if), *n.* a sheriff's deputy, esp. one on whom the sheriff's duties devolve when the office is vacant. [1400–50; late ME; see UNDER-, SHERIFF]

un•der•shirt (un′dər shûrt′), *n.* a collarless, usually pullover undergarment for the torso, usually of cotton and either sleeveless and low-cut or with sleeves, worn chiefly by men and children. [1640–50; UNDER- + SHIRT]

un•der•shoot (un′dər sho͞ot′, un′dər sho͞ot′), *v.,* **-shot, -shoot•ing.** —*v.t.* **1.** to shoot or launch a projectile that strikes under or short of (a target). **2.** *Aeron.* (of an aircraft or pilot) to land before reaching (a landing strip) because of a too rapid loss of altitude. —*v.i.* **3.** to shoot or launch a projectile so as to strike under or short of a target. [1655–65; UNDER- + SHOOT]

un•der•shorts (un′dər shôrts′), *n.* (*used with a plural v.*) short underpants for men and boys. [1945–50; UNDER- + SHORTS]

un•der•shot (un′dər shot′; *for 3 also* un′dər shot′), *adj.* **1.** having the front teeth of the lower jaw projecting in front of the upper teeth, as a bulldog. **2.** driven by water passing beneath: *an undershot vertical water wheel.* —*v.* **3.** pt. and pp. of **undershoot.** [1600–10; UNDER- + SHOT[2]]

un•der•shrub (un′dər shrub′), *n.* a low shrub. [1590–1600; UNDER- + SHRUB[1]]

un•der•side (un′dər sīd′), *n.* an under or lower side. [1670–80; UNDER- + SIDE[1]]

un•der•sign (un′dər sīn′, un′dər sīn′), *v.t.* to sign one's name under or at the end of (a letter or document); affix one's signature to. [1570–80; UNDER- + SIGN]

un•der•signed (*adj.* un′dər sīnd′, un′dər sīnd′; *n.* un′dər sīnd′), *adj.* **1.** being the one or ones whose signature appears at the end of a letter or document: *All of the undersigned persons are bound by the contract.* **2.** signed at the bottom or end of, as a writing: *The undersigned names guarantee the good faith of the statement.* —*n.* **3. the undersigned,** the person or persons signing a letter or document. [1635–45; UNDER- + SIGN + -ED[2]]

un•der•size (un′dər sīz′), *adj.* **1.** undersized. **2.** (of screened minerals) passing through a sieve of given mesh. [1785–95; UNDER- + SIZE[1]]

un•der•sized (un′dər sīzd′), *adj.* smaller than the usual or normal size. [1650–60; UNDER- + SIZE[1] + -ED[3]]

un•der•skirt (un′dər skûrt′), *n.* a skirt, as a petticoat, worn under another skirt or a dress. [1860–65; UNDER- + SKIRT]

un•der•sleeve (un′dər slēv′), *n.* a separate sleeve worn under the sleeve of a dress and visible through it or extending beyond it. [1540–50; UNDER- + SLEEVE]

un•der•slung (un′dər slung′), *adj.* **1.** suspended from an upper support, as the chassis of a vehicle from the axles. **2.** supported from above; placed or suspended below the source of support: *Conestoga wagons with underslung bundles and kettles.* **3.** more massive at the bottom than the top; squat: *The high wings and large fuselage give the plane an underslung look.* [1900–05; UNDER- + SLUNG]

un•der•soil (un′dər soil′), *n.* subsoil. [1700–10; UNDER- + SOIL[1]]

un•der•sparred (un′dər spärd′), *adj.* *Naut.* having spars too small to carry the necessary sail. [1835–45; UNDER- + SPAR[1] + -ED[3]]

un•der•spin (un′dər spin′), *n.* backspin. [1900–05; UNDER- + SPIN]

un•der•staffed (un′dər staft′, -stäft′), *adj.* having an insufficient number of personnel: *The hospital is understaffed.* [1890–95; UNDER- + STAFF[1] + -ED[3]]

un•der•stand (un′dər stand′), *v.,* **-stood, -stand•ing.** —*v.t.* **1.** to perceive the meaning of; grasp the idea of; comprehend: *to understand Spanish; I didn't understand your question.* **2.** to be thoroughly familiar with; apprehend clearly the character, nature, or subtleties of: *to understand a trade.* **3.** to assign a meaning to; interpret: *He understood her suggestion as a complaint.* **4.** to grasp the significance, implications, or importance of: *He does not understand responsibility.* **5.** to regard as firmly communicated; take as agreed or settled: *I understand that you will repay this loan in 30 days.* **6.** to learn or hear: *I understand that you are going out of*

CONCISE PRONUNCIATION KEY: act, cāpe, dâre, pärt; set, ēqual; if, īce; ox, ōver, ôrder, oil, bo͝ok, bo͞ot, out; up, ûrge; child; sing; shoe; thin, *th*at; zh as in *treasure.* ə = *a* as in *alone, e* as in *system, i* as in *easily, o* as in *gallop, u* as in *circus;* ᵊ as in *fire* (fīᵊr), *hour* (ouᵊr). l and n can serve as syllabic consonants, as in *cradle* (krād′l), and *button* (but′n). See the full key inside the front cover.

un′der•pop′u•late′, *v.t.,* **-lat•ed, -lat•ing.**
un•der•porch′, *n.*
un′der•por′ter, *n.*
un′der•pos•ses′sor, *n.*
un′der•pot′, *n.*
un′der•pow′ered, *adj.*
un′der•pre′fect, *n.*
un′der•pren′tice, *n.*
un′der•press′er, *n.*
un′der•pres′sure, *n.*
un′der•priest′, *n.*
un′der•prin′ci•pal, *n.*
un′der•pri′or, *n.*
un′der•prize′, *v.t.,* **-prized, -priz•ing.**
un′der•pro•fi′cient, *adj.*
un′der•prompt′er, *n.*
un′der•pro•por′tioned, *adj.*
un′der•prop′o•si′tion, *n.*
un′der•pros′pect, *n.*
un′der•qual′i•fied′, *adj.*
un′der•queen′, *n.*
un′der•rang′er, *n.*
un′der•read′er, *n.*
un′der•re′al•ize′, *v.t.,* **-ized, -iz•ing.**
un′der•realm′, *n.*
un′der•re•ceiv′er, *n.*
un′der•reck′on, *v.t.*
un′der•rec′om•pense′, *v.t.,* **-pensed, -pens•ing,** *n.*
un′der•re′gion, *n.*
un′der•reg′is•tra′tion, *n.*
un′der•rep′re•sent′, *v.t.*
un′der•rep′re•sen•ta′tion, *n.*
un′der•re•search′, *v.t.*
un′der•re•spect′ed, *adj.*
un′der•rid′dle, *n.*
un′der•rigged′, *adj.*
un′der•ring′, *n.*
un′der•ring′, *v.t.,* **-rang, -rung, -ring•ing.**
un′der•rip′ened, *adj.*
un′der•roar′er, *n.*
un′der•roast′, *v.t.*
un′der•robe′, *n.*
un′der•rogue′, *n.*
un′der•roll′er, *n.*
un′der•roof′, *n.*
un′der•room′, *n.*
un′der•root′ed, *adj.*
un′der•row′er, *n.*
un′der•rule′, *n.*
un′der•rule′, *v.,* **-ruled, -rul•ing.**
un′der•rul′er, *n.*
un′der•sac′ris•tan, *n.*
un′der•sat′is•fac′tion, *n.*
un′der•sav′ior, *n.*
un′der•saw′, *n.*
un′der•saw′, *v.t.*
un′der•saw′yer, *n.*
un′der•scale′, *v.t.,* **-scaled, -scal•ing.**
un′der•scaled′, *adj.*
un′der•scheme′, *n.*
un′der•school′, *n.*
un′der•scoop′, *n.*
un′der•scoop′, *v.t.*
un′der•scribe′, *n.*
un′der•script′, *n.*
un′der•scru′pu•lous, *adj.;* **-ly,** *adv.*
un′der•seam′, *n.*
un′der•search′, *n.*
un′der•seat′ed, *adj.*
un′der•sec′re•tar′y•ship′, *n.*
un′der•sect′, *n.*
un′der•see′, *v.i.,* **-saw, -seen, -see•ing.**
un′der•seed′ed, *adj.*
un′der•se′quence, *n.*
un′der•served′, *adj.*
un′der•serv′ice, *n.*
un′der•sex′ton, *n.*
un′der•sheath′ing, *n.*

un′dis•missed′, *adj.*
un′dis•or′dered, *adj.*
un′dis•or′der•ly, *adj.*
un′dis•or′gan•ized′, *adj.*
un′dis•par′aged, *adj.*
un′dis•pas′sion•ate, *adj.;* **-ly,** *adv.*
un′dis•patch′a•ble, *adj.*
un′dis•patched′, *adj.*
un′dis•patch′ing, *adj.*
un′dis•pel′la•ble, *adj.*
un′dis•pelled′, *adj.*
un′dis•pen′sa•ble, *adj.*
un′dis•pensed′, *adj.*
un′dis•persed′, *adj.*
un′dis•pers′ing, *adj.*
un′dis•place′a•ble, *adj.*
un′dis•placed′, *adj.*
un′dis•play′a•ble, *adj.*
un′dis•played′, *adj.*
un′dis•play′ing, *adj.*
un′dis•prov′a•ble, *adj.*
un′dis•proved′, *adj.*
un′dis•put′a•ble, *adj.*
un′dis•pu•ta′tious, *adj.;* **-ly,** *adv.;* **-ness,** *n.*
un′dis•put′ed, *adj.;* **-ly,** *adv.*
un′dis•put′ing, *adj.*
un′dis•qual′i•fi′a•ble, *adj.*
un′dis•qual′i•fied′, *adj.*
un′dis•qui′et•ed, *adj.*
un′dis•rupt′ed, *adj.*
un′dis•sect′ed, *adj.*
un′dis•sem′bled, *adj.*
un′dis•sem′bling, *adj.;* **-ly,** *adv.*
un′dis•sem′i•nat′ed, *adj.*
un′dis•sent′ing, *adj.*
un′dis•sev′ered, *adj.*
un•dis′si•pat′ed, *adj.*
un′dis•sol′u•ble, *adj.*
un•dis′so•lute′, *adj.*
un′dis•solv′a•ble, *adj.*
un′dis•solved′, *adj.*
un′dis•solv′ing, *adj.*
un•dis′so•nant, *adj.;* **-ly,** *adv.*
un′dis•suad′a•ble, *adj.*
un•dis′tant, *adj.;* **-ly,** *adv.*
un′dis•taste′ful, *adj.*
un′dis•tem′pered, *adj.*
un′dis•tend′, *v.t.*
un′dis•tilled′, *adj.*
un′dis•tin′guish•a•ble, *adj.*
un′dis•tin′guish•ing, *adj.;* **-ly,** *adv.*
un′dis•tort′ed, *adj.;* **-ly,** *adv.*
un′dis•tort′ing, *adj.*
un′dis•tract′ed, *adj.;* **-ly,** *adv.;* **-ness,** *n.*
un′dis•tract′ing, *adj.;* **-ly,** *adv.*
un′dis•trained′, *adj.*
un′dis•traught′, *adj.*
un′dis•tressed′, *adj.*
un′dis•trib′ut•ed, *adj.*
un′dis•trust′ful, *adj.;* **-ly,** *adv.;* **-ness,** *n.*
un′dis•turb′a•ble, *adj.*
un′dis•turbed′, *adj.*
un′dis•turb′ing, *adj.;* **-ly,** *adv.*
un′dith•y•ram′bic, *adj.*
un′di•u•ret′ic, *adj.*
un′di•ur′nal, *adj.;* **-ly,** *adv.*
un′di•ver′gent, *adj.;* **-ly,** *adv.*
un′di•verg′ing, *adj.*
un′di•verse′, *adj.;* **-ly,** *adv.;* **-ness,** *n.*
un′di•ver′si•fied′, *adj.*
un′di•ver′si•fy′ing, *n.*
un′di•vert′ed, *adj.*
un′di•vert′i•ble, *adj.*
un′di•ver′tive, *adj.*
un′di•vest′ed, *adj.*
un′di•vid′a•ble, *adj.*
un′di•vid′ed, *adj.*
un′di•vid′ing, *adj.*
un′di•vin′a•ble, *adj.*
un′di•vined′, *adj.*
un′di•vin′ing, *adj.*
un′di•vis′i•ble, *adj.*
un′di•vi′sive, *adj.;* **-ly,** *adv.;* **-ness,** *n.*
un′di•vorce′a•ble, *adj.*
un′di•vorced′, *adj.*
un′di•vulge′a•ble, *adj.*
un′di•vulged′, *adj.*
un′di•vulg′ing, *adj.*
un•docked′, *adj.*
un•dock′et•ed, *adj.*
un•doc′tored, *adj.*
un′doc′tri•naire′, *adj.*
un•doc′tri•nal, *adj.;* **-ly,** *adv.*
un•doc′trined, *adj.*
un•doc′u•men′ta•ry, *adj.*
un•dodged′, *adj.*
un′dog•mat′ic, *adj.*
un′dog•mat′i•cal, *adj.;* **-ly,** *adv.*
un•dol′or•ous, *adj.;* **-ly,** *adv.;* **-ness,** *n.*
un•domed′, *adj.*
un′do•mes′tic, *adj.*
un′do•mes′ti•ca•ble, *adj.*
un′do•mes′ti•cal•ly, *adv.*
un′do•mes′ti•cat′ed, *adj.*
un•dom′i•ciled′, *adj.*
un•dom′i•nat′ed, *adj.*
un•dom′i•na′tive, *adj.*
un′dom•i•neer′ing, *adj.*
un′do•min′i•cal, *adj.*
un•do′nat•ed, *adj.*
un•doped′, *adj.*
un•dot′ing, *adj.*
un•dot′ted, *adj.*
un•doubt′a•ble, *adj.*
un•doubt′ful, *adj.;* **-ly,** *adv.;* **-ness,** *n.*
un•doubt′ing, *adj.*
un•douched′, *adj.*
un•dough′ty, *adj.*
un•dow′eled, *adj.*
un•dow′elled, *adj.*
un•dow′ered, *adj.*
un•downed′, *adj.*
un′draft•a•bil′i•ty, *n.*
un•draft′a•ble, *adj.*
un•draft′ed, *adj.*
un′dra•gooned′, *adj.*
un•drain′a•ble, *adj.*
un•drained′, *adj.*
un′dra•mat′ic, *adj.*
un′dra•mat′i•cal, *adj.*
un•dram′a•tiz′a•ble, *adj.*
un•dram′a•tized′, *adj.*
un•dra′per•ied, *adj.*
un•draw′a•ble, *adj.*
un•dread′ed, *adj.*
un•dread′ing, *adj.*
un•dreamed′, *adj.*
un•dream′ing, *adj.*
un•dream′like′, *adj.*
un•dreamt′, *adj.*
un•dredged′, *adj.*
un•drenched′, *adj.*
un•dried′, *adj.*
un•drift′ing, *adj.*
un•drill′a•ble, *adj.*
un•drilled′, *adj.*
un•drink′a•ble, *adj.*
un•drink′ing, *adj.*
un•driv′a•ble, *adj.*
un•driv′en, *adj.*
un•droop′ing, *adj.*
un•dropped′, *adj.*
un•drop′si•cal, *adj.*
un•dross′y, *adj.*
un•drowned′, *adj.*
un•drubbed′, *adj.*
un•drugged′, *adj.*
un•drunk′, *adj.*
un•drunk′en, *adj.*
un•dry′, *adj.*
un•dry′a•ble, *adj.*
un•dry′ing, *adj.*
un′du•al•is′tic, *adj.*
un′du•al•is′ti•cal•ly, *adv.*
un•dubbed′, *adj.*

town. **7.** to accept as true; believe: *I understand that you are trying to be truthful, but you are wrong.* **8.** to construe in a particular way: *You are to understand the phrase literally.* **9.** to supply mentally (something that is not expressed). —*v.i.* **10.** to perceive what is meant; grasp the information conveyed: *She told them about it in simple words, hoping they would understand.* **11.** to accept tolerantly or sympathetically: *If you can't do it, I'll understand.* **12.** to have knowledge or background, as on a particular subject: *He understands about boats.* **13.** to have a systematic interpretation or rationale, as in a field or area of knowledge: *He can repeat every rule in the book, but he just doesn't understand.* [bef. 900; ME *understanden, understonden,* OE *understondan;* c. D *onderstaan.* See UNDER-, STAND]
—Syn. 1. See **know**[1].

un·der·stand·a·ble (un′dər stan′də bəl), *adj.* capable of being understood; comprehensible. [1350–1400; ME: orig., capable of understanding; see UNDERSTAND, -ABLE] **—un′der·stand′a·bil′i·ty,** *n.* **—un′der·stand′·a·bly,** *adv.*

un·der·stand·ing (un′dər stan′ding), *n.* **1.** mental process of a person who comprehends; comprehension; personal interpretation: *My understanding of the word does not agree with yours.* **2.** intellectual faculties; intelligence; mind: *a quick understanding.* **3.** superior power of discernment; enlightened intelligence: *With her keen understanding she should have become a leader.* **4.** knowledge of or familiarity with a particular thing; skill in dealing with or handling something: *an understanding of accounting practice.* **5.** a state of cooperative or mutually tolerant relations between people: *To him, understanding and goodwill were the supreme virtues.* **6.** a mutual agreement, esp. of a private, unannounced, or tacit kind: *They had an understanding about who would do the dishes.* **7.** an agreement regulating joint activity or settling differences, often informal or preliminary in character: *After hours of negotiation, no understanding on a new contract was reached.* **8.** *Philos.* **a.** the power of abstract thought; logical power. **b.** *Kantianism.* the mental faculty resolving the sensory manifold into the transcendental unity of apperception. —*adj.* **9.** characterized by understanding; prompted by, based on, or demonstrating comprehension, intelligence, discernment, empathy, or the like: *an understanding attitude.* [bef. 1050; ME *understanding,* late OE *understandyncge* (n.). See UNDERSTAND, -ING[1], -ING[2]] **—un′der·stand′ing·ly,** *adv.*

un·der·state (un′dər stāt′), *v.t.,* **-stat·ed, -stat·ing.** to state or represent less strongly or strikingly than the facts would bear out; set forth in restrained, moderate, or weak terms: *The casualty lists understate the extent of the disaster.* [1815–25; UNDER- + STATE] **—un·der·state·ment** (un′dər stāt′mənt, un′dər stāt′-) *n.*

CONCISE ETYMOLOGY KEY: <, descended or borrowed from; >, whence; b., blend of, blended; c., cognate with; cf., compare; deriv., derivative; equiv., equivalent; imit., imitative; obl., oblique; r., replacing; s., stem; sp., spelling, spelled; resp., respelling, respelled; trans., translation; ?, origin unknown; *, unattested; ‡, probably earlier than. See the full key inside the front cover.

un·der·stat·ed (un′dər stā′tid), *adj.* restrained in design, presentation, etc.; low-key: *the understated elegance of the house.* [1935–40; UNDERSTATE + -ED[2]] **—un′der·stat′ed·ness,** *n.*

un·der·steer (*n.* un′dər stēr′; *v.* un′dər stēr′), *n.* **1.** a handling characteristic of an automotive vehicle that causes it to turn less sharply than the driver intends because the front wheels slide to the outside of the turn before the rear wheels lose traction. —*v.i.* **2.** (of an automotive vehicle) to undergo understeer, esp. excessively. Cf. **oversteer.** [1935–40; UNDER- + STEER[1]]

un·der·stock (*v.* un′dər stok′; *n.* un′dər stok′), *v.t.* **1.** to provide an insufficient quantity, as of merchandise, supplies, or livestock. —*n.* **2.** *Hort.* (in grafting) the rooted plant that receives the scion. [1755–65; UNDER- + STOCK]

un·der·stood (un′dər sto͝od′), *v.* **1.** pt. and pp. of **understand.** —*adj.* **2.** agreed upon; known in advance; assented to: *It is the understood policy of this establishment to limit credit.* **3.** implied but not stated; left unexpressed: *The understood meaning of a danger sign is "Do not approach."*

un·der·sto·ry (un′dər stôr′ē, -stōr′ē), *n.* the shrubs and plants growing beneath the main canopy of a forest. [1900–05; UNDER- + STORY[2]]

un·der·strap·per (un′dər strap′ər), *n.* an underling. [1695–1705; UNDER- + STRAPPER]

un·der·stra·tum (un′dər strā′təm, -strat′əm), *n., pl.* **-stra·ta** (-strā′tə, -strat′ə), **-stra·tums.** a substratum. [1725–35; UNDER- + STRATUM]

un·der·strength (un′dər strengkth′, -strength′, -strenth′), *adj.* **1.** having insufficient organizational strength; lacking in personnel: *an understrength army.* **2.** insufficient in power or efficacy. [1920–25; UNDER- + STRENGTH]

un·der·struc·ture (un′dər struk′chər), *n.* **1.** a structure serving as a support; a base or foundation: *The building has a strong understructure.* **2.** any thing, condition, etc., establishing support; a basis: *an argument that rests on a sound understructure of knowledge.* [UNDER- + STRUCTURE]

un·der·stud·y (un′dər stud′ē), *v.,* **-stud·ied, -stud·y·ing,** *n., pl.* **-stud·ies.** —*v.t.* **1.** to learn (a role) in order to replace the regular actor or actress when necessary. **2.** to act as understudy to (an actor or actress): *to understudy the lead.* —*v.i.* **3.** to act or work as an understudy. —*n.* **4.** a performer who learns the role of another in order to serve as a replacement if necessary. [1870–75; UNDER- + STUDY]

un·der·sur·face (un′dər sûr′fis), *n.* **1.** underside; bottom surface. —*adj.* **2.** submerged; under the surface, as of water, earth, etc.: *the undersurface speed of a submarine.* [1725–35; UNDER- + SURFACE]

un·der·take (un′dər tāk′), *v.,* **-took, -tak·en, -tak·ing.** —*v.t.* **1.** to take upon oneself, as a task, performance, etc.; attempt: *She undertook the job of answering all the mail.* **2.** to promise, agree, or obligate oneself (fol. by an infinitive): *The married couple undertook to love, honor, and cherish each other.* **3.** to warrant or guarantee (fol. by a clause): *The sponsors undertake that their candidate meets all the requirements.* **4.** to take in charge; assume the duty of attending to: *The lawyer undertook a new case.* —*v.i.* **5.** *Archaic.* to engage oneself by promise; give a guarantee, or become surety. [1150–1200; ME *undertaken;* see UNDER-, TAKE]

un·der·tak·er (un′dər tā′kər *for 1;* un′dər tā′kər *for 2*), *n.* **1.** See **funeral director. 2.** a person who undertakes something. [1350–1400; ME; see UNDERTAKE, -ER[1]]

un·der·tak·ing (un′dər tā′king, un′dər tā′- *for 1–3;* un′dər tā′king *for 4*), *n.* **1.** the act of a person who undertakes any task or responsibility. **2.** a task, enterprise, etc., undertaken. **3.** a promise; pledge; guarantee. **4.** the business of an undertaker or funeral director. [1325–75; ME; see UNDER, TAKING]
—Syn. 2. project, endeavor, job, effort, venture.

un·der·ten·ant (un′dər ten′ənt), *n.* a subtenant. [1540–50; UNDER- + TENANT] **—un′der·ten′an·cy,** *n.*

un·der-the-count·er (un′dər t͟hə koun′tər), *adj.* **1.** (of merchandise) sold clandestinely. **2.** illegal; unauthorized: *under-the-counter payments.* [1945–50]

un·der-the-ta·ble (un′dər t͟hə tā′bəl), *adj.* transacted in secret or in an underhanded manner. [1945–50]

un·der·things (un′dər thingz′), *n.pl.* women's underclothes. [1840–50; UNDER- + THINGS]

un·der·throat·ing (un′dər thrō′ting), *n.* (on a cornice) a cove extended outward and downward to form a drip. [UNDER- + THROAT + -ING[1]]

un·der·thrust (un′dər thrust′), *n. Geol.* a thrust fault in which the footwall moved and the hanging wall did not (opposed to *overthrust*). [1890–95; UNDER- + THRUST]

un·der·tint (un′dər tint′), *n.* a subdued tint. [1880–85; UNDER- + TINT]

un·der·tone (un′dər tōn′), *n.* **1.** a low or subdued tone: *to speak in undertones.* **2.** an unobtrusive or background sound: *an undertone of static from the receiver.* **3.** an underlying quality or element; undercurrent: *There was an undertone of regret in his refusal.* **4.** a subdued color; a color modified by an underlying color. [1800–10; UNDER- + TONE]

un·der·took (un′dər to͝ok′), *v.* pt. of **undertake.**

un·der·tow (un′dər tō′), *n.* **1.** the seaward, subsurface flow or draft of water from waves breaking on a beach. **2.** any strong current below the surface of a body of water, moving in a direction different from that of the surface current. [1810–20; UNDER- + TOW[1]]
—Syn. 2. UNDERTOW, UNDERSET, RIPTIDE are terms for a usually strong undercurrent in the ocean, contrary to the direction of surface water. UNDERTOW and another nautical term, UNDERSET (a set or current contrary to the general set of the water, or contrary to the wind), came into notice early in the 19th century. The former is still in general use along the Atlantic coast; the latter now less well known. RIP, in use in the U.S. by the late 18th century, properly means a violently disturbed place in a body of water, usually by the meeting of opposing tides. Of recent years, in the form RIPTIDE, it has also been

un′der·shep′herd, *n.*
un′der·shield′, *n.*
un′der·shine′, *n.*
un′der·shine′, *v.,* **-shone** or **-shined, -shin·ing.**
un′der·shire′, *n.*
un′der·shoe′, *n.*
un′der·shore′, *n.*
un′der·shore′, *v.t.,* **-shored, -shor·ing.**
un′der·short′en, *v.t.*
un′der·sight′, *n.*
un′der·sight′ed, *adj.*
un′der·sig′nal·man, *n., pl.* **-men.**
un′der·sill′, *n.*
un′der·skilled′, *adj.*
un′der·skin′, *n.*
un′der·sleep′, *v.i.,* **-slept, -sleep·ing.**
un′der·slept′, *adj.*
un′der·slip′, *n.*
un′der·sluice′, *n.*
un′der·so·ci′e·ty, *n., pl.* **-ties.**
un′der·sole′, *n.*
un′der·sor′cer·er, *n.*
un′der·sort′, *v.t.*
un′der·soul′, *n.*
un′der·sound′, *n.*
un′der·sov′er·eign, *n.*
un′der·sow′, *n.*
un′der·span′, *n.*
un′der·spar′, *n.*
un′der·spe′cies, *n., pl.* **-cies.**
un′der·spec′i·fied′, *adj.*
un′der·spec′i·fy′, *v.t.,* **-fied, -fy·ing.**
un′der·spend′, *v.,* **-spent, -spend·ing.**
un′der·spin′ner, *n.*
un′der·splice′, *v.t.,* **-spliced, -splic·ing.**
un′der·spread′, *v.t.,* **-spread, -spread·ing.**
un′der·spring′, *n.*
un′der·spring′, *v.i.,* **-sprang** or **-sprung, -sprung, -spring·ing.**
un′der·sprout′, *n.*
un′der·sprout′, *v.i.*
un′der·staff′, *n.*
un′der·stage′, *n.*
un′der·stain′, *n.*
un′der·stain′, *v.t.*
un′der·stamp′, *n.*
un′der·stamp′, *v.t.*
un′der·stay′, *n.*
un′der·stay′, *v.i.*
un′der·stem′, *n.*
un′der·step′, *n.*
un′der·stew′ard, *n.*
un′der·stew′ard·ship′, *n.*
un′der·stim′u·lus, *n., pl.* **-li.**
un′der·strain′, *n.*
un′der·strap′, *n.*
un′der·strap′, *v.t.,* **-strapped, -strap·ping.**
un′der·stream′, *n.*
un′der·stress′, *n.*
un′der·stress′, *v.t.*
un′der·strew′, *v.t.,* **-strewed, -strewn** or **-strewed, -strew·ing.**
un′der·strife′, *n.*
un′der·strike′, *v.t.,* **-struck, -struck** or **-strick·en, -strik·ing.**
un′der·stuff′, *v.t.*
un′der·stuff′ing, *n.*
un′der·suit′, *n.*
un′der·suit′, *v.t.*
un′der·sup·ply′, *n., pl.* **-plies.**
un′der·sup·ply′, *v.t.,* **-plied, -ply·ing.**
un′der·sup·port′, *n.*
un′der·swain′, *n.*
un′der·swamp′, *n.*
un′der·sward′, *n.*
un′der·swear′er, *n.*

un·du′bi·ous, *adj.;* **-ly,** *adv.;* **-ness,** *n.*
un·du′bi·ta′tive, *adj.;* **-ly,** *adv.*
un·du′cal, *adj.*
un·duc′tile, *adj.*
un·dug′, *adj.*
un·dulled′, *adj.*
un·dumped′, *adj.*
un·dup′a·ble, *adj.*
un·duped′, *adj.*
un·du′pli·cat′ed, *adj.*
un·du′pli·ca′tive, *adj.*
un·du′ra·bil′i·ty, *n.*
un·du′ra·ble, *adj.;* **-ble·ness,** *n.;* **-bly,** *adv.*
un·dust′ed, *adj.*
un·dust′y, *adj.*
un·du′te·ous, *adj.;* **-ly,** *adv.;* **-ness,** *n.*
un·du′ti·a·ble, *adj.*
un·du′ti·ful, *adj.;* **-ly,** *adv.*
un·dwarfed′, *adj.*
un·dwell′a·ble, *adj.*
un·dwin′dling, *adj.*
un·dy′a·ble, *adj.*
un·dyed′, *adj.*
un′dy·nam′ic, *adj.*
un′dy·nam′i·cal·ly, *adv.*
un·dy′na·mit′ed, *adj.*
un·ea′ger, *adj.;* **-ly,** *adv.;* **-ness,** *n.*
un·ear′marked′, *adj.*
un·ear′nest, *adj.;* **-ly,** *adv.;* **-ness,** *n.*
un·east′ern, *adj.*
un·eat′a·ble, *adj.*
un·eat′en, *adj.*
un·eat′ing, *adj.*
un·eaved′, *adj.*
un·ebbed′, *adj.*
un·ebb′ing, *adj.*
un′e·bul′lient, *adj.*
un′ec·cen′tric, *adj.*
un′ec·cen′tri·cal·ly, *adv.*
un′ec·cle′si·as′tic, *adj.*
un′ec·cle′si·as′ti·cal·ly, *adv.*
un·ech′oed, *adj.*
un′e·cho′ic, *adj.*
un·ech′o·ing, *adj.*
un′ec·lec′tic, *adj.*
un′ec·lec′ti·cal·ly, *adv.*
un′e·clipsed′, *adj.*
un′e·clips′ing, *adj.*
un′e·clip′tic, *adj.*
un′e·clip′ti·cal, *adj.;* **-ly,** *adv.*
un′ec·o·log′i·cal, *adj.;* **-ly,** *adv.*
un′ec·o·nom′ic, *adj.*
un′ec·o·nom′i·cal, *adj.;* **-ly,** *adv.*
un′e·con′o·miz′ing, *adj.*
un′ec·stat′ic, *adj.*
un′ec·stat′i·cal·ly, *adv.*
un′e·da′cious, *adj.;* **-ly,** *adv.*
un·ed′died, *adj.*
un·ed′dy·ing, *adj.*
un·edge′, *v.t.,* **-edged, -edg·ing.**
un·ed′i·ble, *adj.*
un·ed·i·fi′cial, *adj.*
un·ed′i·fied′, *adj.*
un·ed′i·fy′ing, *adj.*
un·ed′it·a·ble, *adj.*
un·ed′it·ed, *adj.*
un′ed·u·ca·bil′i·ty, *n.*
un·ed′u·ca·ble, *adj.*
un·ed′u·ca′tive, *adj.*
un′e·duced′, *adj.*
un′ef·face′a·ble, *adj.*
un′ef·faced′, *adj.*
un′ef·fect′ed, *adj.*
un′ef·fect′i·ble, *adj.*
un′ef·fec′tive, *adj.;* **-ly,** *adv.;* **-ness,** *n.*
un′ef·fec′tu·at′ed, *adj.*
un′ef·fem′i·nate, *adj.;* **-ly,** *adv.*
un′ef·fer·ves′cent, *adj.;* **-ly,** *adv.*
un′ef·fete′, *adj.;* **-ness,** *n.*
un′ef·fi·ca′cious, *adj.;* **-ly,** *adv.*
un′ef·fi′cient, *adj.*
un′ef·ful′gent, *adj.;* **-ly,** *adv.*
un′ef·fused′, *adj.*
un′ef·fus′ing, *adj.*
un′ef·fu′sive, *adj.;* **-ly,** *adv.;* **-ness,** *n.*
un′e·go·is′ti·cal, *adj.;* **-ly,** *adv.*
un′e·go·tis′ti·cal, *adj.;* **-ly,** *adv.*
un′e·gre′gious, *adj.;* **-ly,** *adv.;* **-ness,** *n.*
un′e·jac′u·lat′ed, *adj.*
un′e·ject′ed, *adj.*
un′e·jec′tive, *adj.*
un′e·lab′o·rate, *adj.;* **-ly,** *adv.;* **-ness,** *n.*
un′e·lab′o·rat′ed, *adj.*
un′e·lapsed′, *adj.*
un′e·las′tic, *adj.*
un′e·las′ti·cal·ly, *adv.*
un′e·las·tic′i·ty, *n.*
un′e·lat′ed, *adj.*
un′e·lat′ing, *adj.*
un·eld′er·ly, *adj.*
un′e·lect′a·ble, *adj.*
un′e·lect′ed, *adj.*
un′e·lec′tive, *adj.*
un′e·lec′tric, *adj.*
un′e·lec′tri·cal, *adj.;* **-ly,** *adv.*
un′e·lec′tri·fied′, *adj.*
un′e·lec′tri·fy′ing, *adj.*
un′e·lec·tron′ic, *adj.*
un′el·ee·mos′y·nar′y, *adj.*
un·el′e·gant, *adj.;* **-ly,** *adv.*
un′el·e·men′tal, *adj.;* **-ly,** *adv.*
un′el·e·men′ta·ry, *adj.*
un·el′e·vat′ed, *adj.*
un′e·lic′it·a·ble, *adj.*
un′e·lic′it·ed, *adj.*
un′e·lid′ed, *adj.*
un′e·lid′i·ble, *adj.*
un′e·lim′i·nat′ed, *adj.*
un′el·lip′ti·cal, *adj.*
un′e·lon′gat·ed, *adj.*
un′e·loped′, *adj.*
un′e·lop′ing, *adj.*
un·el′o·quent, *adj.;* **-ly,** *adv.*
un′e·lu′ci·dat′ed, *adj.*
un′e·lu′ci·dat′ing, *adj.*
un′e·lu′ci·da′tive, *adj.*
un′e·lud′a·ble, *adj.*
un′e·lud′ed, *adj.*
un′e·lu′sive, *adj.;* **-ly,** *adv.;* **-ness,** *n.*
un′e·lu′so·ry, *adj.*
un′e·ma′ci·at′ed, *adj.*
un·em′a·na′tive, *adj.*
un′e·man′ci·pat′ed, *adj.*
un′e·man′ci·pa′tive, *adj.*
un′e·mas′cu·lat′ed, *adj.*
un′e·mas′cu·la′tive, *adj.*
un′e·mas′cu·la·to′ry, *adj.*
un′em·balmed′, *adj.*
un′em·banked′, *adj.*
un′em·bar′ras·sa·ble, *adj.*
un′em·bar′rassed, *adj.*
un′em·bat′tled, *adj.*
un′em·bayed′, *adj.*
un′em·bel′lished, *adj.*
un′em·bez′zled, *adj.*
un′em·bit′tered, *adj.*
un′em·bla′zoned, *adj.*
un′em·bossed′, *adj.*
un′em·bow′eled, *adj.*
un′em·bow′elled, *adj.*
un′em·bow′ered, *adj.*
un′em·brace′a·ble, *adj.*
un′em·braced′, *adj.*
un′em·broi′dered, *adj.*
un′em·broiled′, *adj.*
un·em′bry·o·nal, *adj.*
un·em′bry·on′ic, *adj.*
un′e·mend′a·ble, *adj.*
un′e·mend′ed, *adj.*
un′e·merged′, *adj.*
un′e·mer′gent, *adj.*
un′e·merg′ing, *adj.*
un·em′i·grant, *adj.*
un·em′i·grat′ing, *adj.*

used, esp. on the Pacific coast, to mean much the same as UNDERTOW, dangerous to bathers where heavy surf prevails.

un·der·trick (un′dər trik′), n. *Bridge.* a trick that a declarer failed to win in relation to the number of tricks necessary to make the contract. Cf. **overtrick.** [1900–05; UNDER- + TRICK]

un·der·trump (un′dər trump′, un′dər trump′), v.t., v.i. *Cards.* to trump with a lower trump than has already been played. [1860–65; UNDER- + TRUMP[1]]

un·der·used (un′dər yōōzd′), adj. not completely or sufficiently used: *underused talents.* [1905–10; UNDER- + USE + -ED[2]]

un·der·u·ti·lize (un′dər yōōt′l īz′), v.t., **-lized, -liz·ing.** to fail to utilize fully: *to underutilize natural resources.* Also, *esp. Brit.,* **un′der·u′ti·lise′.** [1950–55; UNDER- + UTILIZE] —**un′der·u′ti·li·za′tion,** n.

un·der·val·ue (un′dər val′yōō), v.t., **-ued, -u·ing.** **1.** to value below the real worth; put too low a value on. **2.** to diminish in value; make of less value. **3.** to have insufficient regard or esteem for; hold too low an opinion of. [1590–1600; UNDER- + VALUE] —**un′der·val′u·a′tion,** n.
—**Syn. 1.** underrate, underestimate, depreciate.

un·der·vest (un′dər vest′), n. *Brit.* an undershirt. [1805–15; UNDER- + VEST]

un·der·waist (un′dər wāst′), n. **1.** a blouse worn under another. **2.** such a blouse to which other undergarments are pinned or buttoned, worn by infants and small children. [1855–60, *Amer.*; UNDER- + WAIST]

un·der·wa·ter (un′dər wô′tər, -wot′ər), adj. **1.** existing or occurring under water. **2.** designed to be used under water. **3.** located below a ship's waterline. —*adv.* **4.** beneath the water: *to travel underwater.* —*n.* **5.** the water beneath the surface: *cold currents in the underwater.* **6. underwaters,** the depths, as of a sea, lake, etc. [1620–30; UNDER- + WATER]

underwa′ter archaeol′ogy. See **marine archaeology.**

un′der way′, 1. Also, **underway.** (of a ship) no longer in port, at anchor, etc.; moving. **2.** no longer at rest, stationary, etc.; in motion; traveling: *We'll put our bags in the car and be under way.* **3.** proceeding; in progress: *Plans are under way to sell the company.*

un·der·way (un′dər wā′ *for 1;* un′dər wā′ *for* 2), adj. **1.** occurring while under way: *the underway activities on a cruise ship.* **2.** See **under way** (def. 1). [1735–45; adj. use of the prep. phrase *under way;* see WAY[1]]

un·der·wear (un′dər wâr′), n. clothing worn next to the skin under outer clothes. Also called **underclothes, underclothing.** [1870–75; UNDER- + WEAR]

un·der·weight (*adj.* un′dər wāt′; *n.* un′dər wāt′), *adj.* **1.** weighing less than is usual, required, or proper. —*n.* **2.** deficiency in weight below a standard or requirement. [1590–1600; UNDER- + WEIGHT]

un·der·went (un′dər went′), v. pt. of **undergo.**

un·der·whelm (un′dər hwelm′, -welm′), v.t. *Informal.* to fail to interest or astonish: *After all the ballyhoo, most critics were underwhelmed by the movie.* [1945–50; UNDER- + (OVER)WHELM]

un·der·wing (un′dər wing′), n. **1.** one of the hind wings of an insect. **2.** any of several noctuid moths of the genus *Catocala,* characterized by red-, yellow-, or orange-banded hind wings. [1525–35; UNDER- + WING]

un·der·wire (un′dər wīᵊr′), n. **1.** a wire sewn into the underside of each cup of a brassiere, used for support and shape. **2.** a brassiere with such wires. [UNDER- + WIRE]

un·der·with·hold (un′dər with hōld′, -with-), v., **-held, -hold·ing.** —v.t. **1.** to withhold too little. **2.** to deduct (withholding tax) less than the necessary amount. —v.i. **3.** to withhold oneself too little. **4.** to deduct less withholding tax than necessary. [UNDER- + WITHHOLD]

un·der·wood (un′dər wŏŏd′), n. **1.** woody shrubs or small trees growing among taller trees. **2.** a clump or stretch of such growth. [1275–1325; ME *underwode.* See UNDER-, WOOD[1]] —**un′der·wood′ed,** *adj.*

un·der·wool (un′dər wŏŏl′), n. underfur. [1905–10 in sense "underwear"; 1935–40 for current sense; UNDER- + WOOL]

un·der·work (un′dər wûrk′), v., **-worked, -work·ing.** —v.t. **1.** to do less work on than is necessary or required: *to underwork an idea.* **2.** to employ inadequately: *He underworks his mind and overworks his feet.* —v.i. **3.** to do less work than is normal or proper: *He is fat because he underworks and overeats.* [1495–1505; UNDER- + WORK] —**un′der·work′er,** n.

un·der·world (un′dər wûrld′), n. **1.** the criminal element of human society. **2.** the imagined abode of departed souls or spirits; Hades. **3.** a region below the surface, as of the earth or a body of water. **4.** the opposite side of the earth; the antipodes. **5.** *Archaic.* the earth. [1600–10; UNDER- + WORLD]

un·der·write (un′dər rīt′, un′dər rīt′), v., **-wrote, -writ·ten, -writ·ing.** —v.t. **1.** to write under or at the foot of, esp. under other written matter. **2.** to sign one's name, as to a document. **3.** to show agreement with or to support by or as if by signing one's name to, as a statement or decision. **4.** to bind oneself to contribute a sum of money to (an undertaking): *Wealthy music lovers underwrote the experimental concerts.* **5.** to guarantee the sale of (a security issue to be offered to the public for subscription). **6.** *Insurance.* **a.** to write one's name at the end of (a policy), thereby becoming liable in case of certain losses specified in the policy. **b.** to insure. **c.** to assume liability to the extent of (a specified sum) by way of insurance. **d.** to select or rate (risks) for insurance. —v.i. **7.** to underwrite something. **8.** to carry on the business of an underwriter. [1400–50; late ME, trans. of L *subscribere* to write underneath, sign, SUBSCRIBE]

un·der·writ·er (un′dər rī′tər), n. **1.** a person or company that underwrites policies of insurance or carries on insurance as a business. **2.** a person or company that underwrites shares or bonds. **3.** a person or organization that finances something; backer: *the underwriters of the ballet company.* [1610–20; UNDERWRITE + -ER[1]]

un·der·writ·ten (un′dər rit′n, un′dər rit′-), v. pp. of **underwrite.**

un·der·wrote (un′dər rōt′, un′dər rōt′), v. pt. of **underwrite.**

un·de·signed (un′di zīnd′), adj. not planned beforehand; unpremeditated; unintentional. [1645–55; UN-[1] + DESIGNED] —**un·de·sign·ed·ly** (un′di zī′nid lē), *adv.*

un·de·sign·ing (un′di zī′ning), adj. not characterized by underhand schemes or selfish motives; without an ulterior design. [1665–75; UN-[1] + DESIGNING]

un·de·sir·a·ble (un′di zīᵊr′ə bəl), adj. **1.** not desirable or attractive; objectionable: *undesirable qualities.* —n. **2.** a person or thing considered undesirable: *a collection of malcontents and undesirables.* [1660–70; UN-[1] + DESIRABLE] —**un′de·sir′a·bil′i·ty, un′de·sir′a·ble·ness,** n. —**un′de·sir′a·bly,** adv.

un′desir′able dis′charge, *U.S. Mil.* **1.** a discharge under other than honorable conditions of a person from military service by administrative action. **2.** a certificate of such a discharge.

un·de·vel·oped (un′di vel′əpt), adj. not developed. [1730–40; UN-[1] + DEVELOP + -ED[2]]

un·did (un did′), v. pt. of **undo.**

un·dies (un′dēz), n.pl. women's or children's underwear. [1895–1900; UND(ERWEAR) + -IE + -S[3]]

un·di·gest·i·ble (un′di jes′tə bəl, -dī-), adj. indigestible. [1605–15; UN-[1] + DIGESTIBLE]

un·dine (un dēn′, un′dēn), n. any of a group of female water spirits described by Paracelsus. [< NL *undina* (1658; coined by Paracelsus), equiv. to L *und(a)* wave, water + *-ina* -INE[1]]
—**Syn.** See **sylph.**

un·di·rect·ed (un′di rek′tid, -dī-), adj. **1.** not directed; not guided: *He wasted his time on undirected activity.* **2.** bearing no address, as a letter. [1590–1600; UN-[1] + DIRECTED]

un·dis·posed (un′di spōzd′), adj. **1.** not disposed of. **2.** not favorably inclined; not prepared; unwilling: *They are both disinclined to work and undisposed to starve.* [1350–1400; ME; see UN-[1], DISPOSED]

un·dis·so·ci·at·ed (un′di sō′shē ā′tid, -sē ā′-), adj. *Chem.* not dissociated, esp. into ions or into simpler molecules. [1905–10; UN-[1] + DISSOCIATED]

un·dis·tin·guished (un′di sting′gwisht), adj. **1.** having no distinguishing marks or features. **2.** without any claim to distinction: *an undistinguished performance.* **3.** unnoticed; inconspicuous: *He was an undistinguished part of the crowd.* **4.** not separated or divided, as by sets or categories. [1585–95; UN-[1] + DISTINGUISHED]

CONCISE PRONUNCIATION KEY: act, cāpe, dâre, pärt; set, ēqual; if, īce; ox, ōver, ôrder, oil, bŏŏk, bōōt, out; up, ûrge; child; sing; shoe; thin, *th*at; zh as in *treasure.* ə = *a* as in *alone, e* as in *system, i* as in *easily, o* as in *gallop, u* as in *circus;* ᵊ as in *fire* (fīᵊr), *hour* (ouᵊr). l and n can serve as syllabic consonants, as in *cradle* (krād′l), and *button* (but′n). See the full key inside the front cover.

un′der·sweep′, v.t., -swept, -sweep·ing.
un′der·swell′, v.i., -swelled, -swelled or -swol·len, -swell·ing.
un′der·swell′, n.
un′der·talk′, n.
un′der·tap′ster, n.
un′der·taxed′, adj.
un′der·teach′, v., -taught, -teach·ing.
un′der·teach′er, n.
un′der·teamed′, adj.
un′der·tell′er, n.
un′der·ten′ure, n.
un′der·ter·res′tri·al, adj.
un′der·test′, v.t.
un′der·thane′, n.
un′der·thaw′, v.
un′der·thief′, n., pl. -thieves.
un′der·thought′, n.
un′der·tide′, n.
un′der·tie′, n.
un′der·tie′, v.t., -tied, -ty·ing.
un′der·ti′tle, n.
un′der·trade′, v., -trad·ed, -trad·ing.
un′der·trad′er, n.
un′der·train′, v.t.
un′der·trained′, adj.
un′der·treas′ur·er, n.
un′der·tribe′, n.
un′der·truck′, n.
un′der·truss′, v.t.
un′der·tub′, n.
un′der·tune′, n.
un′der·tune′, v.t., -tuned, -tun·ing.
un′der·tu′nic, n.
un′der·tu′tor, n.
un′der·twig′, n.
un′der·ty′rant, n.
un′der·use′, v.t., -used, -us·ing, n.
un′der·ush′er, n.
un′der·u′ti·lized′, adj.
un′der·valve′, n.
un′der·vas′sal, n.
un′der·vault′ed, adj.
un′der·vault′ing, n.
un′der·veg′e·ta′tion, n.
un′der·ven′ti·late′, v.t., -lat·ed, -lat·ing.
un′der·ven′ti·lat′ed, adj.
un′der·ven′ti·la′tion, n.
un′der·verse′, n.
un′der·vic′ar, n.
un′der·view′er, n.
un′der·vil′lain, n.
un′der·vi′tal·ized′, adj.
un′der·voice′, n.
un′der·wage′, n.
un′der·waist′coat′, n.
un′der·war′den, n.
un′der·wash′, v.
un′der·watch′er, n.
un′der·wave′, n.
un′der·wav′ing, n.
un′der·weft′, n.
un′der·wheel′, n.
un′der·wind′, n.
un′der·wind′, v.t., -wound, -wind·ing.
un′der·witch′, n.
un′der·work′man, n., pl. -men.
un′der·wrap′, n.
un′der·wrap′, v.t., -wrapped, -wrap·ping.
un′der·wrought′, adj.
un′der·yield′, n.
un′der·yield′, v.i.
un′der·yoke′, n.
un′der·zeal′, n.
un′der·zeal′ot, n.
un′der·zeal′ous, adj.; -ly, adv.; -ness, n.

un·em′i·nent, adj.; -ly, adv.
un′e·mis′sive, adj.
un′e·mit′ted, adj.
un′e·mit′ting, adj.
un′e·mo′tion·al, adj.; -ly, adv.
un′e·mo′tioned, adj.
un′e·mo′tive, adj.; -ly, adv.; -ness, n.
un′em·pan′eled, adj.
un′em·pan′elled, adj.
un′em′pha·sized′, adj.
un′em′pha·siz′ing, adj.
un′em·phat′ic, adj.
un′em·phat′i·cal·ly, adv.
un′em·pir′i·cal, adj.; -ly, adv.
un′em·poi′soned, adj.
un′em·pow′ered, adj.
un·emp′tied, adj.
un·emp′ty, adj.
un·em′u·la′tive, adj.
un·em′u·lous, adj.
un′e·mul′si·fied′, adj.
un′en·act′ed, adj.
un′e·nam′eled, adj.
un′e·nam′elled, adj.
un′en·am′ored, adj.
un′en·camped′, adj.
un′en·chant′ed, adj.
un′en·ci′phered, adj.
un′en·cir′cled, adj.
un′en·closed′, adj.
un′en·com′passed, adj.
un′en·coun′ter·a·ble, adj.
un′en·coun′tered, adj.
un′en·cour′aged, adj.
un′en·cour′ag·ing, adj.
un′en·croached′, adj.
un′en·croach′ing, adj.
un′en·cum′bered, adj.
un′en·cum′ber·ing, adj.
un′en·cyst′ed, adj.
un·end′a·ble, adj.
un′en·dan′gered, adj.
un′en·deared′, adj.
un′en·dear′ing, adj.; -ly, adv.
un·end′ed, adj.
un′en·dem′ic, adj.
un·end′ing, adj.; -ly, adv.
un′en·dors′a·ble, adj.
un′en·dorsed′, adj.
un′en·dowed′, adj.
un′en·dow′ing, adj.
un′en·dued′, adj.
un′en·dur′a·bil′i·ty, adj.
un′en·dur′a·ble, adj.; -ble·ness, n.; -bly, adv.
un′en·dured′, adj.
un′en·dur′ing, adj.; -ly, adv.
un′en·er·get′ic, adj.
un′en·er·get′i·cal·ly, adv.
un·en′er·gized′, adj.
un′en·er′vat′ed, adj.
un′en·fee′bled, adj.
un′en·fi′lad′ed, adj.
un′en·force′a·bil′i·ty, n.
un′en·force′a·ble, adj.
un′en·forced′, adj.
un′en·forc′ed·ly, adv.
un′en·fran′chised, adj.
un′en·gaged′, adj.
un′en·gag′ing, adj.
un′en·gen′dered, adj.
un′en·gi·neered′, adj.
un′en·graved′, adj.
un′en·grossed′, adj.
un′en·gross′ing, adj.
un′en·hanced′, adj.
un′en·ig·mat′ic, adj.
un′en·ig·mat′i·cal, adj.; -ly, adv.
un′en·joined′, adj.
un′en·joy′a·ble, adj.; -ble·ness, n.; -bly, adv.
un′en·joyed′, adj.
un′en·joy′ing, adj.; -ly, adv.
un′en·larged′, adj.
un′en·larg′ing, adj.
un′en·light′ened, adj.
un′en·light′en·ing, adj.
un′en·list′ed, adj.
un′en·liv′ened, adj.
un′en·liv′en·ing, adj.
un′en·no′bled, adj.
un′en·no′bling, adj.
un′e·nounced′, adj.
un′en·quired′, adj.
un′en·quir′ing, adj.
un′en·rap′tured, adj.
un′en·rich′a·ble, adj.
un′en·riched′, adj.
un′en·rich′ing, adj.
un′en·rolled′, adj.
un′en·shrined′, adj.
un′en·slaved′, adj.
un′en·snared′, adj.
un′en·sured′, adj.
un′en·tailed′, adj.
un′en·tan′gle·a·ble, adj.
un′en·tan′gled, adj.
un′en·tan′gling, adj.
un·en′ter·a·ble, adj.
un·en′tered, adj.
un·en′ter·pris′ing, adj.; -ly, adv.
un′en·ter·tain′a·ble, adj.
un′en·ter·tained′, adj.
un′en·ter·tain′ing, adj.; -ly, adv.
un′en·thralled′, adj.
un′en·thrall′ing, adj.
un′en·thused′, adj.
un′en·thu′si·asm, n.
un′en·thu′si·as′tic, adj.
un′en·thu′si·as′ti·cal·ly, adv.
un′en·tice′a·ble, adj.
un′en·ticed′, adj.
un′en·tic′ing, adj.
un·en·ti′tled, adj.
un′en·tombed′, adj.
un′en·to·mo·log′i·cal, adj.
un′en·tranced′, adj.
un′en·trapped′, adj.
un′en·treat′a·ble, adj.
un′en·treat′ed, adj.
un′en·treat′ing, adj.
un′en·trenched′, adj.
un′en·twined′, adj.
un′e·nu′mer·at′ed, adj.
un′e·nu′mer·a′tive, adj.
un′e·nun′ci·a·ble, adj.
un′e·nun′ci·at′ed, adj.
un′e·nun′ci·a′tive, adj.
un′en·vel′oped, adj.
un′en·ven′omed, adj.
un′en·vi′a·bil′i·ty, n.
un·en′vi·a·ble, adj.; -bly, adv.
un·en′vied, adj.
un·en′vi·ous, adj.; -ly, adv.
un′en·vi′roned, adj.
un·en′vy·ing, adj.; -ly, adv.
un·ep′au·let′ed, adj.
un·ep′au·let′ted, adj.
un′e·phem′er·al, adj.; -ly, adv.
un·ep′ic, adj.
un′ep·i·cu·re′an, adj.
un′ep·i·gram·mat′ic, adj.
un′ep·i·gram·mat′i·cal·ly, adv.
un·ep′i·logued′, adj.
un′e·pis′to·lar′y, adj.
un·ep′i·taphed′, adj.
un′ep·i·the′li·al, adj.
un′e·pit′o·mized′, adj.
un·ep′och·al, adj.
un′eq·ua·bil′i·ty, n.
un·eq′ua·ble, adj.; -ble·ness, n.; -bly, adv.
un·e′qual·ize′, v.t., -ized, -iz·ing.
un′e·quat′ed, adj.
un′e·qua·to′ri·al, adj.
un′e·ques′tri·an, adj.
un′e·qui·an′gu·lar, adj.
un′e·qui·lat′er·al, adj.; -ly, adv.
un′e·quil′i·brat′ed, adj.
un·e′quine, adj.

—**Syn. 1.** ordinary, common, unexceptional, unremarkable.

un′distrib′uted mid′dle, *Logic.* a middle term of a syllogism that does not refer to its entire class in the major premise or minor premise, with the result that the syllogism is not valid. [1820–30]

un′divid′ed prof′its, earnings that have neither been distributed as dividends to stockholders nor transferred to the earned surplus account.

un•do (un do͞o′), *v.t.,* **-did, -done, -do•ing. 1.** to reverse the doing of; cause to be as if never done: *Murder once done can never be undone.* **2.** to do away with; erase; efface: *to undo the havoc done by the storm.* **3.** to bring to ruin or disaster; destroy: *In the end his lies undid him.* **4.** to unfasten by releasing: *to undo a gate; to undo a button.* **5.** to untie or loose (a knot, rope, etc.). **6.** to open (a package, wrapping, etc.). **7.** *Archaic.* to explain; interpret. [bef. 900; ME; OE *undōn;* c. D *ontdoen.* See UN-², DO¹] —**un•do′a•ble,** *adj.*

un•dock (un dok′), *Aerospace.* —*v.t.* **1.** to uncouple (two spacecraft modules or a spacecraft and space station). —*v.i.* **2.** (of a spacecraft module or spacecraft) to uncouple. [1920–25; UN-² + DOCK¹]

un•doc•u•ment•ed (un dok′yə men′tid), *adj.* **1.** lacking documentation or authentication. **2.** lacking proper immigration or working papers. [1880–85; UN-¹ + DOCUMENTED]

un•do•ing (un do͞o′ing), *n.* **1.** the reversing of what has been done; annulling. **2.** a bringing to destruction, ruin, or disaster. **3.** a cause of destruction or ruin. **4.** the act of unfastening or loosing. **5.** *Psychiatry.* an unconscious defense mechanism through which an attempt is made to reverse a psychologically unacceptable act by doing its opposite, usually repetitiously, in order to relieve anxiety. [1300–50; ME; see UNDO, -ING¹]
—**Syn. 1.** reversal, negation, thwarting.

un•done¹ (un dun′), *adj.* not done; not accomplished or completed. [1250–1300; ME *un-dun.* See UN-¹, DONE]

un•done² (un dun′), *v.* **1.** pp. of **undo.** —*adj.* **2.** brought to destruction or ruin. **3.** unfastened.

un•dou•ble (un dub′əl), *v.t.,* **-bled, -bling.** to unfold; render single. [1590–1600; UN-² + DOUBLE]

un•doubt•ed (un dou′tid), *adj.* not called in question; accepted as beyond doubt; undisputed. [1425–75; late ME; see UN-¹, DOUBT, -ED²] —**un•doubt′ed•ly,** *adv.*

un•drape (un drāp′), *v.t.,* **-draped, -drap•ing.** to strip of drapery; uncover. [1865–70; UN-² + DRAPE]

un•draw (un drô′), *v.,* **-drew, -drawn, -draw•ing.** —*v.t.* **1.** to draw open or aside: *to undraw a curtain.* —*v.i.* **2.** to be drawn open or aside. [1350–1400; ME *undrawen* to withdraw; see UN-², DRAW]

un•dress (un dres′), *v.,* **-dressed** or **-drest, -dress•ing,** *n., adj.* —*v.t.* **1.** to take the clothes off (a person); disrobe. **2.** to remove the dressing from (a wound, sore, etc.). **3.** to strip or divest of or as if of a covering; expose: *to undress a pretense.* —*v.i.* **4.** to take off one's clothes. —*n.* **5.** dress of a style designed to be worn on other than highly formal or ceremonial occasions; informal dress, as opposed to full dress. **6.** dress of a style not designed to be worn in public; dishabille; negligee: *She couldn't receive guests in such a state of undress.* **7.** the condition of being unclothed; nakedness. —*adj.* **8.** of or pertaining to clothing of a style less formal than full dress: *undress uniform.* **9.** characterized by informality of dress, manners, or the like: *an undress dinner party.* [1590–1600; UN-² + DRESS]

un•dressed (un drest′), *adj.* **1.** wearing few or no clothes. **2.** wearing informal clothing or clothing not meant to be worn in public. **3.** not dressed; not specially prepared: *undressed poultry; an undressed salad.* **4.** (of leather) having a napped finish on the flesh side. [1400–50; late ME; see UN-¹, DRESS, -ED²]

undress′ u′niform, *Mil., Navy.* a uniform worn on other than formal occasions. [1820–30]

Und•set (o͝on′set), *n.* **Sig•rid** (sig′rid; *Norw.* si′grı), 1882–1949, Norwegian novelist: Nobel prize 1928.

und so wei•ter (o͝ont zō vī′tər), *German.* and so forth; et cetera. *Abbr.:* usw, u.s.w.

un•due (un do͞o′, -dyo͞o′), *adj.* **1.** unwarranted; excessive: *undue haste.* **2.** inappropriate; unjustifiable; improper: *undue influence.* **3.** not owed or currently payable. [1350–1400; ME *undewe.* See UN-¹, DUE]

un•du•lant (un′jə lənt, un′dyə-, -də-), *adj.* undulating; wavelike in motion or pattern: *an undulant edge.* [1820–30; UNDUL(ATE) + -ANT] —**un′du•lance,** *n.*

un′dulant fe′ver, *Pathol.* brucellosis. [1895–1900]

un•du•late (*v.* un′jə lāt′, un′dyə-, -də-; *adj.* un′jə lit, -lāt′, un′dyə-, -də-), *v.,* **-lat•ed, -lat•ing,** *adj.* —*v.i.* **1.** to move with a sinuous or wavelike motion; display a smooth rising-and-falling or side-to-side alternation of movement: *The flag undulates in the breeze.* **2.** to have a wavy form or surface; bend with successive curves in alternate directions. **3.** (of a sound) to rise and fall in pitch: *the wail of a siren undulating in the distance.* —*v.t.* **4.** to cause to move in waves. **5.** to give a wavy form to. —*adj.* **6.** Also, **un′du•lat′ed.** having a wavelike or rippled form, surface, edge, etc.; wavy. [1650–60; < L *undulātus* waved, equiv. to *und(a)* wave + *-ul(a)* -ULE + *-ātus* -ATE¹] —**un′du•la′tor,** *n.*

un•du•la•tion (un′jə lā′shən, un′dyə-, -də-), *n.* **1.** an act of undulating; a wavelike motion. **2.** a wavy form or outline. **3.** one of a series of wavelike bends, curves, or elevations. **4.** *Physics.* **a.** a wave. **b.** the motion of waves. [1640–50; UNDUL(ATE) + -ATION]

un•du•la•to•ry (un′jə lə tôr′ē, -tōr′ē, un′dyə-, -də-), *adj.* **1.** Also, **un′du•lar.** moving in undulations. **2.** having the form or appearance of waves. Also, **un•du•la•tive** (un′jə lā′tiv, un′dyə-, -də-). [1720–30; UNDULATE + -ORY¹]

un′dulatory the′ory, *Physics.* See **wave theory** (def. 1). [1795–1805]

un•du•la•tus (un′do͞o lā′təs, -dyo͞o-), *n. Meteorol.* See **billow cloud.** [< NL, L *undulātus.* See UNDULATE]

un•du•ly (un do͞o′lē, -dyo͞o′-), *adv.* **1.** excessively: *unduly worried.* **2.** in an inappropriate, unjustifiable, or improper manner: *unduly critical.* [1350–1400; ME *undewely.* See UNDUE, -LY]

un•dy•ing (un dī′ing), *adj.* deathless; unending. [1250–1300; ME; see UN-¹, DYING] —**un•dy′ing•ly,** *adv.*
—**Syn.** unceasing, immortal, perpetual, enduring.

un•earned (un ûrnd′), *adj.* **1.** not received in exchange for labor or services; not gained by lawful work or employment. **2.** not earned; unmerited; undeserved: *unearned promotion.* **3.** not yet earned: *Lenders are not permitted to take borrowers' unearned wages as collateral.* [1150–1200; ME; see UN-¹, EARN¹, -ED²]

un′earned in′come, income received from property, as interest, dividends, or the like. Cf. **earned income.**

un′earned in′crement, the increase in the value of property, esp. land, due to natural causes, as growth of population, rather than to any labor or expenditure by the owner. [1870–75]

un′earned run′, *Baseball.* a run scored as the result of defensive errors. Cf. **earned run.**

un•earth (un ûrth′), *v.t.* **1.** to dig or get out of the earth; dig up. **2.** to uncover or bring to light by search, inquiry, etc.: *The lawyer unearthed new evidence.* [1400–50; late ME *unerthen.* See UN-², EARTH]

un•earth•ly (un ûrth′lē), *adj.* **1.** seeming not to belong to this earth or world: *unearthly beauty.* **2.** supernatural; ghostly; unnaturally strange; weird: *an unearthly scream.* **3.** out of the ordinary; unreasonable or absurd: *to get up at an unearthly hour.* [1605–15; UN-¹ + EARTHLY] —**un•earth′li•ness,** *n.*
—**Syn. 2.** preternatural, spectral. See **weird.**

un•eas•y (un ē′zē), *adj.,* **-eas•i•er, -eas•i•est. 1.** not easy in body or mind; uncomfortable; restless; disturbed; perturbed. **2.** not easy in manner; constrained; awkward. **3.** not conducive to ease; causing bodily discomfort. [1250–1300; ME *unesy.* See UN-¹, EASY] —**un•ease′,** *n.* —**un•eas′i•ly,** *adv.* —**un•eas′i•ness,** *n.*

un•ed•u•cat•ed (un ej′o͝o kā′tid, -ed′yo͝o-), *adj.* not educated. [1580–90; UN-¹ + EDUCATED]
—**Syn.** untutored, unschooled, untaught, uninstructed, unenlightened, uninformed, uncultivated. See **ignorant.**

UNEF, United Nations Emergency Force.

un•em•ploy•a•ble (un′em ploi′ə bəl), *adj.* **1.** unsuitable for employment; unable to find or keep a job. —*n.* **2.** an unemployable individual. [1885–90; UN-¹ + EMPLOYABLE] —**un′em•ploy′a•bil′i•ty,** *n.*

un•em•ployed (un′em ploid′), *adj.* **1.** not employed; without a job; out of work: *an unemployed secretary.* **2.** not currently in use: *unemployed productive capacity.* **3.** not productively used: *unemployed capital.* —*n.* **4.** (*used with a plural v.*) people who do not have jobs (usu-

CONCISE ETYMOLOGY KEY: <, descended or borrowed from; >, whence; b., blend of, blended; c., cognate with; cf., compare; deriv., derivative; equiv., equivalent; imit., imitative; obl., oblique; r., replacing; s., stem; sp., spelling, spelled; resp., respelling, respelled; trans., translation; ?, origin unknown; *, unattested; ‡, probably earlier than. See the full key inside the front cover.

un′e•quipped′, *adj.*
un′e•quiv′a•lent, *adj.;* **-ly,** *adv.*
un′e•quiv′o•cat′ing, *adj.*
un′e•rad′i•ca•ble, *adj.*
un′e•rad′i•cat′ed, *adj.*
un′e•rad′i•ca′tive, *adj.*
un′e•ras′a•ble, *adj.*
un′e•rased′, *adj.*
un′e•ras′ing, *adj.*
un′e•rect′, *adj.*
un′e•rect′ed, *adj.*
un′er•mined, *adj.*
un′e•rod′a•ble, *adj.*
un′e•rod′ed, *adj.*
un′e•rod′i•ble, *adj.*
un′e•rod′ent, *adj.*
un′e•rod′ing, *adj.*
un′e•ro′sive, *adj.*
un′e•rot′ic, *adj.*
un•er′rant, *adj.;* **-ly,** *adv.*
un′er•rat′ic, *adj.*
un•er′u•dite′, *adj.*
un′e•rupt′ed, *adj.*
un′e•rup′tive, *adj.*
un′es•cal′loped, *adj.*
un′es•cap′a•ble, *adj.;* **-bly,** *adv.*
un′es•caped′, *adj.*
un′es•cheat′a•ble, *adj.*
un′es•cheat′ed, *adj.*
un′es•chewed′, *adj.*
un′es•cort′ed, *adj.*
un•es•cutch′eoned, *adj.*
un′es•o•ter′ic, *adj.*
un′es•pied′, *adj.*
un′es•pous′a•ble, *adj.*
un′es•poused′, *adj.*
un′es•sayed′, *adj.*
un′es•tab′lish•a•ble, *adj.*
un′es•teemed′, *adj.*
un•es′ti•ma•ble, *adj.*
un•es′ti•mat′ed, *adj.*
un′es•topped′, *adj.*
un′es•tranged′, *adj.*
un•etched′, *adj.*
un′e•ter′nized, *adj.*
un′e•the′re•al, *adj.;* **-ly,** *adv.;* **-ness,** *n.*
un•eth′i•cal, *adj.;* **-ly,** *adv.*
un′eth•no•log′ic, *adj.*
un′eth•no•log′i•cal, *adj.;* **-ly,** *adv.*
un•eth′yl•at′ed, *adj.*
un′et•y•mo•log′ic, *adj.*
un′et•y•mo•log′i•cal, *adj.;* **-ly,** *adv.*
un′-Eu•cha•ris′tic, *adj.*
un′-Eu•cha•ris′ti•cal, *adj.;* **-ly,** *adv.*
un′eu•gen′ic, *adj.*
un′eu•gen′i•cal, *adj.;* **-ly,** *adv.*
un•eu′lo•gized′, *adj.*
un′eu•phe•mis′tic, *adj.*
un′eu•phe•mis′ti•cal, *adj.;* **-ly,** *adv.*
un′eu•phon′ic, *adj.*
un′eu•pho′ni•ous, *adj.;* **-ly,** *adv.;* **-ness,** *n.*
un′-Eu•ro•pe′an, *adj.*
un′e•vac′u•at′ed, *adj.*
un′e•vad′a•ble, *adj.*
un′e•vad′ed, *adj.*
un′e•vad′i•ble, *adj.*
un′e•vad′ing, *adj.*
un′e•val′u•at′ed, *adj.*
un′ev•a•nes′cent, *adj.;* **-ly,** *adv.*
un′e•van•gel′ic, *adj.*
un′e•van•gel′i•cal, *adj.;* **-ly,** *adv.*
un′e•van′ge•lized′, *adj.*
un′e•vap′o•rat′ed, *adj.*
un′e•vap′o•ra′tive, *adj.*
un′e•va′sive, *adj.;* **-ly,** *adv.;* **-ness,** *n.*
un′e•ver′si•ble, *adj.*
un′e•vert′ed, *adj.*
un′e•vict′ed, *adj.*
un•ev′i•denced, *adj.*
un′ev•i•den′tial, *adj.*
un•e′vil, *adj.;* **-ly,** *adv.*
un′e•vinced′, *adj.*
un′e•vin′ci•ble, *adj.*
un′e•vis′cer•at′ed, *adj.*
un•ev′o•ca•ble, *adj.*
un′e•voc′a•tive, *adj.*
un′e•voked′, *adj.*
un′ev•o•lu′tion•al, *adj.*
un′ev•o•lu′tion•ar′y, *adj.*
un′e•volved′, *adj.*
un′ex•ac′er•bat′ed, *adj.*
un′ex•ac′er•bat′ing, *adj.*
un′ex•act′ed, *adj.*
un′ex•act′ing, *adj.*
un′ex•ag′ger•at′ed, *adj.*
un′ex•ag′ger•at′ing, *adj.*
un′ex•ag′ger•a′tive, *adj.*
un′ex•ag′ger•a•to′ry, *adj.*
un′ex•alt′ed, *adj.*
un′ex•alt′ing, *adj.*
un′ex•am′in•a•ble, *adj.*
un′ex•am′ined, *adj.*
un′ex•am′in•ing, *adj.*
un′ex•as′per•at′ed, *adj.*
un′ex•as′per•at′ing, *adj.*
un•ex′ca•vat′ed, *adj.*
un′ex•ceed′a•ble, *adj.*
un′ex•ceed′ed, *adj.*
un′ex•celled′, *adj.*
un′ex•cel′ling, *adj.*
un•ex′cel•lent, *adj.;* **-ly,** *adv.*
un′ex•cept′a•ble, *adj.*
un′ex•cept′ed, *adj.*
un′ex•cept′ing, *adj.*
un′ex•cep′tive, *adj.*
un′ex•cerpt′ed, *adj.*
un′ex•ces′sive, *adj.;* **-ly,** *adv.*
un′ex•change′a•bil′i•ty, *n.*
un′ex•change′a•ble, *adj.;* **-ness,** *n.*
un′ex•changed′, *adj.*
un′ex•cised′, *adj.*
un′ex•cit′a•bil′i•ty, *n.*
un′ex•cit′a•ble, *adj.;* **-ly,** *adv.*
un′ex•cit′ed, *adj.*
un′ex•cit′ing, *adj.*
un′ex•claim′ing, *adj.*
un′ex•clud′a•ble, *adj.*
un′ex•clud′ed, *adj.*
un′ex•clud′ing, *adj.*
un′ex•clu′sive, *adj.;* **-ly,** *adv.;* **-ness,** *n.*
un′ex•cog′i•ta•ble, *adj.*
un′ex•cog′i•tat′ed, *adj.*
un′ex•cog′i•ta′tive, *adj.*
un′ex•com•mu′ni•cat′ed, *adj.*
un′ex•co′ri•at′ed, *adj.*
un′ex•cres′cent, *adj.;* **-ly,** *adv.*
un′ex•cret′ed, *adj.*
un′ex•cru′ci•at′ing, *adj.*
un′ex•cul′pa•ble, *adj.*
un•ex′cul•pat′ed, *adj.*
un′ex•cur′sive, *adj.;* **-ly,** *adv.*
un′ex•cus′a•ble, *adj.;* **-bly,** *adv.*
un′ex•cused′, *adj.*
un′ex•cus′ed•ly, *adv.*
un′ex•cus′ing, *adj.*
un•ex′e•crat′ed, *adj.*
un•ex′e•cut′a•ble, *adj.*
un•ex′e•cut′ed, *adj.*
un•ex′e•cut′ing, *adj.*
un′ex•ec′u•to′ri•al, *adj.*
un′ex•em′pla•ry, *adj.*
un′ex•empt′, *adj.*
un′ex•empt′ed, *adj.*
un′ex•empt′i•ble, *adj.*
un′ex•empt′ing, *adj.*
un•ex′er•cis′a•ble, *adj.*
un•ex′er•cised′, *adj.*
un′ex•ert′ed, *adj.*
un′ex•haled′, *adj.*
un′ex•haust′ed, *adj.;* **-ly,** *adv.*
un′ex•haus′tive, *adj.;* **-ly,** *adv.*
un′ex•hib′it•a•ble, *adj.*
un′ex•hib′it•ed, *adj.*
un′ex•hil′a•rat′ed, *adj.*
un′ex•hil′a•rat′ing, *adj.*
un′ex•hil′a•ra′tive, *adj.*
un′ex•hor′ta•tive, *adj.*
un′ex•hort′ed, *adj.*
un′ex•humed′, *adj.*
un•ex′i•gent, *adj.;* **-ly,** *adv.*
un•ex′i•gi•ble, *adj.*
un′ex•iled′, *adj.*
un′ex•ist′ent, *adj.*
un′ex•is•ten′tial, *adj.;* **-ly,** *adv.*
un′ex•ist′ing, *adj.*
un′ex•on′er•at′ed, *adj.*
un′ex•on′er•a′tive, *adj.*
un′ex•or′bi•tant, *adj.;* **-ly,** *adv.*
un•ex′or•cised′, *adj.*
un′ex•ot′ic, *adj.*
un′ex•ot′i•cal•ly, *adv.*
un′ex•pand′a•ble, *adj.*
un′ex•pand′ed, *adj.*
un′ex•pand′ing, *adj.*
un′ex•pan′si•ble, *adj.*
un′ex•pan′sive, *adj.;* **-ly,** *adv.;* **-ness,** *n.*
un′ex•pect′a•bil′i•ty, *n.*
un′ex•pect′a•ble, *adj.;* **-bly,** *adv.*
un′ex•pect′ant, *adj.;* **-ly,** *adv.*
un′ex•pect′ing, *adj.;* **-ly,** *adv.*
un′ex•pec′to•rat′ed, *adj.*
un′ex•pe′di•ent, *adj.;* **-ly,** *adv.*
un′ex•pe•dit′a•ble, *adj.*
un•ex′pe•dit′ed, *adj.*
un′ex•pe•di′tious, *adj.;* **-ly,** *adv.;* **-ness,** *n.*
un′ex•pel′la•ble, *adj.*
un′ex•pelled′, *adj.*
un′ex•pend′ed, *adj.*
un′ex•pe′ri•enced, *adj.*
un′ex•pe′ri•en′tial, *adj.;* **-ly,** *adv.*
un′ex•per′i•men′tal, *adj.;* **-ly,** *adv.*
un′ex•per′i•ment′ed, *adj.*
un′ex•pert′, *adj.*
un•ex′pi•a•ble, *adj.*
un•ex′pi•at′ed, *adj.*
un′ex•pired′, *adj.*
un′ex•pir′ing, *adj.*
un′ex•plain′a•ble, *adj.;* **-bly,** *adv.*
un′ex•plained′, *adj.*
un′ex•plain′ed•ly, *adv.*
un′ex•plain′ing, *adj.*
un′ex•plan′a•to′ry, *adj.*
un•ex′pli•cat′ed, *adj.*
un•ex′pli•ca′tive, *adj.*
un′ex•plic′it, *adj.;* **-ly,** *adv.*
un′ex•plod′a•ble, *adj.*
un′ex•plod′ed, *adj.*
un′ex•ploit′a•ble, *adj.*
un′ex•ploit′a•tive, *adj.*
un′ex•ploit′ed, *adj.*
un′ex•ploit′ive, *adj.*
un′ex•plor′a•ble, *adj.*
un′ex•plor′a•tive, *adj.*
un′ex•plor′a•to′ry, *adj.*
un′ex•plored′, *adj.*
un′ex•plo′sive, *adj.;* **-ly,** *adv.;* **-ness,** *n.*
un′ex•po′ni•ble, *adj.*
un′ex•port′a•ble, *adj.*
un′ex•port′ed, *adj.*
un′ex•port′ing, *adj.*
un′ex•pos′a•ble, *adj.*
un′ex•posed′, *adj.*
un′ex•pos′tu•lat′ing, *adj.*
un′ex•pound′a•ble, *adj.*
un′ex•pound′ed, *adj.*
un′ex•press′i•ble, *adj.*
un′ex•press′ly, *adv.*
un′ex•pro′pri•a•ble, *adj.*
un′ex•pro′pri•at′ed, *adj.*
un′ex•punged′, *adj.*
un•ex′pur•gat′ed, *adj.*
un′ex•tend′a•ble, *adj.*
un′ex•tend′ed, *adj.;* **-ly,** *adv.*
un′ex•tend′i•ble, *adj.*
un′ex•ten′si•ble, *adj.*
un′ex•ten′u•at′ed, *adj.*
un′ex•ten′u•at′ing, *adj.*
un′ex•ter′mi•na•ble, *adj.*
un′ex•ter′mi•nat′ed, *adj.*
un′ex•tinct′, *adj.*
un′ex•tin′guish•a•ble, *adj.*
un′ex•tin′guished, *adj.*
un•ex′tir•pat′ed, *adj.*

ally prec. by *the*): *programs to help the unemployed.* [1590–1600; UN-[1] + EMPLOY + -ED[2]]
—**Syn. 1.** unoccupied, idle, at liberty, jobless.

un•em•ploy•ment (un′em ploi′mənt), *n.* **1.** the state of being unemployed, esp. involuntarily: *Automation poses a threat of unemployment for many unskilled workers.* **2.** the number of persons who are unemployed. **3.** *Informal.* See **unemployment benefit.** [1885–90; UN-[1] + EMPLOYMENT]

unemploy′ment ben′efit, an allowance of money paid, usually weekly, to an unemployed worker by a state or federal agency or by the worker's labor union or former employer during all or part of the period of unemployment. Also called **unemploy′ment compensa′tion.** [1925–30]

unemploy′ment insur′ance, a government program that provides a limited number of payments to eligible workers who are involuntarily unemployed. [1920–25]

un-Eng•lish (un ing′glish), *adj.* **1.** not English; not characteristic of the English. **2.** not conforming to standard, accepted, or native English language usage.

un•e•qual (un ē′kwəl), *adj.* **1.** not equal; not of the same quantity, quality, value, rank, ability, etc.: *People are unequal in their capacities.* **2.** not adequate, as in amount, power, ability, etc. (usually fol. by *to*): *strength unequal to the task.* **3.** not evenly proportioned or balanced; not having the parts alike or symmetrical: *an unequal leaf.* **4.** uneven or variable in character, quality, etc. **5.** *Obs.* inequitable; unfair; unjust. —*n.* **6. unequals,** persons or things not equal to each other: *a contest between obvious unequals.* [1525–35; UN-[1] + EQUAL] —**un•e′qual•ly,** *adv.* —**un•e′qual•ness,** *n.*

un•e•qualed (un ē′kwəld), *adj.* not equaled or surpassed; matchless: *an unequaled record of victories.* Also, *esp. Brit.,* **un•e′qualled.** [1615–25; UN-[1] + EQUALED]
—**Syn.** peerless, unrivaled, inimitable, incomparable.

un•eq•ui•ta•ble (un ek′wi tə bəl), *adj.* inequitable. [UN-[1] + EQUITABLE]

un•e•quiv•o•cal (un′i kwiv′ə kəl), *adj.* **1.** not equivocal; unambiguous; clear; having only one possible meaning or interpretation: *an unequivocal indication of assent; unequivocal proof.* **2.** absolute; unqualified; not subject to conditions or exceptions: *The cosigner of a note gives unequivocal assurance that it will be paid when due.* [1745–55; UN-[1] + EQUIVOCAL] —**un′e•quiv′o•cal•ly,** *adv.* —**un′e•quiv′o•cal•ness,** *n.*
—**Syn. 1.** certain, direct, obvious, unmistakable.

un•err•ing (un ûr′ing, -er′-), *adj.* **1.** not erring; not going astray or missing the mark: *The captain set an unerring course for home.* **2.** undeviatingly accurate throughout; not containing any error or flaw: *She gave an unerring recital of the day's events.* **3.** invariably precise or correct: *unerring taste.* [1615–25; UN-[1] + ERRING] —**un•err′ing•ly,** *adv.* —**un•err′ing•ness,** *n.*

UNESCO (yo͞o nes′kō), *n.* an agency of the United Nations charged with instituting and administering programs for cooperative, coordinated action by member states in education, science, and the arts. [*U*(*nited*) *N*(*ations*) *E*(*ducational*), *S*(*cientific, and*) *C*(*ultural*) *O*(*rganization*)]

un•es•sen•tial (un′ə sen′shəl), *adj.* **1.** not of prime importance; not indispensable. —*n.* **2.** an unessential thing; nonessential. [1650–60; UN-[1] + ESSENTIAL] —**un′es•sen′tial•ly,** *adv.*
—**Syn. 1.** unnecessary, dispensable, unimportant.

un•es•tab•lished (un′i stab′lisht), *adj.* **1.** not established. **2.** *Brit.* (of a worker or job) temporary, part-time, or having a special or unique routine. [1640–50; UN-[1] + ESTABLISHED]

un•es•thet•ic (un′es thet′ik), *adj.* unaesthetic.

un•e•ven (un ē′vən), *adj.* **1.** not level or flat; rough; rugged: *The wheels bumped and jolted over the uneven surface.* **2.** irregular; varying; not uniform: *The book is uneven in quality.* **3.** not equitable or fair; one-sided: *an uneven contest.* **4.** not equally balanced; not symmetrical or parallel. **5.** (of a number) odd; not divisible into two equal integers: *The numerals 3, 5, and 7 are uneven.* [bef. 900; ME; OE *unefen;* c. G *uneben.* See UN-[1], EVEN[1]] —**un•e′ven•ly,** *adv.* —**un•e′ven•ness,** *n.*
—**Syn. 3.** unfair, unequal, lopsided.

une′ven par′allel bars′, *Gymnastics.* **1.** an apparatus consisting of two parallel wooden bars, fixed at specific different heights from the floor on upright supports, on which women compete by performing various spinning moves and acrobatic swings. **2.** a competitive event on such an apparatus.

un•e•vent•ful (un′i vent′fəl), *adj.* not eventful; lacking in important or striking occurrences: *an uneventful day at the office.* [1790–1800; UN-[1] + EVENTFUL] —**un′e•vent′ful•ly,** *adv.* —**un′e•vent′ful•ness,** *n.*
—**Syn.** quiet, routine, ordinary, usual.

un•ex•am•pled (un′ig zam′pəld, -zäm′-), *adj.* unprecedented; unparalleled; unlike anything previously known: *unexampled kindness; unexampled depravity.* [1600–10; UN-[1] + EXAMPLE + -ED[2]]

un•ex•cep•tion•a•ble (un′ik sep′shə nə bəl), *adj.* not offering any basis for exception or objection; beyond criticism: *an unexceptionable record of achievement.* [1655–65; UN-[1] + EXCEPTIONABLE] —**un′ex•cep′tion•a•ble•ness,** *n.* —**un′ex•cep′tion•a•bly,** *adv.*

un•ex•cep•tion•al (un′ik sep′shə nl), *adj.* **1.** not exceptional; not unusual or extraordinary. **2.** admitting of no exception to the general rule. **3.** unexceptionable. [1765–75; UN-[1] + EXCEPTIONAL] —**un′ex•cep′tion•al•ly,** *adv.*

un•ex•pect•ed (un′ik spek′tid), *adj.* not expected; unforeseen; surprising: *an unexpected pleasure; an unexpected development.* [1580–90; UN-[1] + EXPECT + -ED[2]] —**un′ex•pect′ed•ly,** *adv.* —**un′ex•pect′ed•ness,** *n.*
—**Syn.** unanticipated. See **sudden.**

un•ex•pend•a•ble (un′ik spen′də bəl), *adj.* **1.** essential; absolutely required: *unexpendable resources vital to our security.* **2.** not capable of being expended; inexhaustible: *an unexpendable source of energy.* **3.** not available for expenditure: *The principal of the trust fund is unexpendable.* [UN-[1] + EXPENDABLE]

un•ex•pressed (un′ik sprest′), *adj.* **1.** not expressed; not indicated or communicated, as in words, intimations, or the like: *an unexpressed desire.* **2.** tacit; understood without explicit statement: *an unexpressed agreement.* [1555–65; UN-[1] + EXPRESS + -ED[2]]

un•ex•pres•sive (un′ik spres′iv), *adj.* **1.** not expressive; lacking in expression of meaning, feeling, etc.: *a bland and unexpressive person.* **2.** *Obs.* inexpressible. [1590–1600; UN-[1] + EXPRESSIVE] —**un′ex•pres′sive•ly,** *adv.* —**un′ex•pres′sive•ness,** *n.*

un•faced (un fāst′), *adj. Crystall.* without crystal faces. [1930–35; UN-[1] + FACED]

un•fact (un fakt′), *n. Informal.* a fabrication that is disseminated as fact. [1885–90; UN-[1] + FACT]

un•fail•ing (un fā′ling), *adj.* **1.** not failing; not giving way; not falling short of expectation; completely dependable: *an unfailing friend.* **2.** inexhaustible; endless: *unfailing resources; unfailing good humor.* [1350–1400; ME; see UN-[1], FAILING] —**un•fail′ing•ly,** *adv.* —**un•fail′ing•ness,** *n.*

un•fair (un fâr′), *adj.* **1.** not fair; not conforming to approved standards, as of justice, honesty, or ethics: *an unfair law; an unfair wage policy.* **2.** disproportionate; undue; beyond what is proper or fitting: *an unfair share.* [bef. 900; 1705–15 for def. 1; ME: uncomely, ugly; OE *unfæger;* c. ON *ūfagr.* See UN-[1], FAIR[1]] —**un•fair′ly,** *adv.* —**un•fair′ness,** *n.*

unfair′ competi′tion, 1. acts done by a seller to confuse or deceive the public with intent to acquire a larger portion of the market, as by cutting prices below cost, misleading advertising, selling a spurious product under a false identity, etc. **2.** the use of any such methods.

un′fair prac′tice, 1. See **unfair competition. 2.** any practice in business involving the general public or competing parties that is prohibited by statute and regulated by an appropriate government agency.

un•faith•ful (un fāth′fəl), *adj.* **1.** not faithful; false to duty, obligation, or promises; faithless; disloyal. **2.** not sexually faithful to a spouse or lover. **3.** not accurate or complete; inexact: *an unfaithful translation.* **4.** *Obs.* unbelieving; infidel. [1350–1400; ME *unfeithful.* See UN-[1], FAITHFUL] —**un•faith′ful•ly,** *adv.* —**un•faith′ful•ness,** *n.*
—**Syn. 1.** untrustworthy, deceitful, treacherous, recreant. **3.** imprecise, untrue.

un•fa•mil•iar (un′fə mil′yər), *adj.* **1.** not familiar; not acquainted with or conversant about: *to be unfamiliar with a subject.* **2.** different; unaccustomed; unusual; strange: *an unfamiliar treat.* [1585–95; UN-[1] + FAMILIAR] —**un•fa•mil•i•ar•i•ty** (un′fə mil′ē ar′i tē), *n.* —**un′fa•mil′iar•ly,** *adv.*
—**Syn. 2.** curious, novel, new.

un•fas•ten (un fas′ən, -fä′sən), *v.t.* **1.** to release from

CONCISE PRONUNCIATION KEY: act, cāpe, dâre, pärt; set, ēqual; if, īce; ox, ōver, ôrder, oil, bo͝ok, bo͞ot, out; up, ûrge; child; sing; shoe; thin, *th*at; zh as in *treasure.* ə = a as in *alone,* e as in *system,* i as in *easily,* o as in *gallop,* u as in *circus;* ′ as in *fire* (fī′r), *hour* (ou′r). l and n can serve as syllabic consonants, as in *cradle* (krād′l), and *button* (but′n). See the full key inside the front cover.

un′ex•tolled′, *adj.*
un′ex•tort′a•ble, *adj.*
un′ex•tort′ed, *adj.*
un′ex•tract′a•ble, *adj.*
un′ex•tract′ed, *adj.*
un•ex′tra•dit′ed, *adj.*
un′ex•tra′ne•ous, *adj.;* **-ly,** *adv.*
un′ex•traor′di•nar′y, *adj.*
un′ex•trav′a•gant, *adj.;* **-ly,** *adv.*
un′ex•trav′a•sat′ed, *adj.*
un′ex•treme′, *adj.*
un•ex′tri•ca•ble, *adj.*
un•ex′tri•cat′ed, *adj.*
un′ex•trin′sic, *adj.*
un′ex•trud′ed, *adj.*
un′ex•u′ber•ant, *adj.;* **-ly,** *adv.*
un′ex•u′da•tive, *adj.*
un′ex•ud′ed, *adj.*
un′ex•ult′ant, *adj.;* **-ly,** *adv.*
un•eye′a•ble, *adj.*
un•fa′bled, *adj.*
un•fa′bling, *adj.*
un•fab′ri•cat′ed, *adj.*
un•fab′u•lous, *adj.;* **-ly,** *adv.*
un′fa•çad′ed, *adj.*
un•face′a•ble, *adj.*
un•fac′et•ed, *adj.*
un′fa•ce′tious, *adj.;* **-ly,** *adv.;* **-ness,** *n.*
un•fac′ile, *adj.;* **-ly,** *adv.*
un′fa•cil′i•tat′ed, *adj.*
un•fac′tion•al, *adj.*
un•fac′tious, *adj.;* **-ly,** *adv.*
un•fac′tor•a•ble, *adj.*
un•fac′tored, *adj.*
un•fac′tu•al, *adj.;* **-ly,** *adv.*
un•fad′a•ble, *adj.*
un•fad′ed, *adj.*
un•fad′ing, *adj.*
un•fagged′, *adj.*
un•fag′ot•ed, *adj.*
un•failed′, *adj.*
un•faint′ing, *adj.*
un•faint′ly, *adv.*
un•fak′a•ble, *adv.*
un•faked′, *adj.*
un′fal•la′cious, *adj.;* **-ly,** *adv.*
un•fall′en, *adj.*
un•fall′ing, *adj.*
un•fal′lowed, *adj.*
un•fal′si•fi′a•ble, *adj.*
un•fal′si•fied′, *adj.*
un•fal′ter•ing, *adj.;* **-ly,** *adv.*
un′fa•mil′iar•ized′, *adj.*
un•fa′mous, *adj.*
un′fa•nat′i•cal, *adj.;* **-ly,** *adv.*
un•fan′cied, *adj.*
un•fan′ci•ful, *adj.*
un•fan′cy, *adj.*
un•fanged′, *adj.*
un•fanned′, *adj.*
un′fan•tas′tic, *adj.*
un′fan•tas′ti•cal•ly, *adv.*
un•far′, *adj., adv.*
un•farced′, *adj.*
un•far′ci•cal, *adj.*
un•farm′a•ble, *adj.*
un•farmed′, *adj.*
un•farm′ing, *adj.*
un•fas′ci•ate′, *adj.*
un•fas′ci•at′ed, *adj.*
un•fas′ci•nat′ed, *adj.*
un•fas′ci•nat′ing, *adj.*
un•fash′ion•a•ble, *adj.;* **-bly,** *adv.*
un•fash′ioned, *adj.*
un•fas′ten•a•ble, *adj.*
un•fas′ten•er, *n.*
un•fas•tid′i•ous, *adj.;* **-ly,** *adv.;* **-ness,** *n.*
un•fast′ing, *adj.*
un′fa•tal•is′tic, *adj.*
un′fa•tal•is′ti•cal•ly, *adv.*
un•fat′ed, *adj.*
un•fa′ther•ly, *adj.*
un′fath•om•a•bil′i•ty, *n.*
un•fath′om•a•ble, *adj.;* **-ness,** *n.*
un•fath′omed, *adj.*
un•fat′i•ga•ble, *adj.*
un′fa•tigued′, *adj.*
un′fa•ti′guing, *adj.*
un•fat′ted, *adj.*
un•fat′ty, *adj.*
un′fa•tu′i•tous, *adj.;* **-ly,** *adv.*
un•fau′cet•ed, *adj.*
un•fault′y, *adj.*
un•fa′vored, *adj.*
un•fa′vor•ing, *adj.*
un•fa′vor•ite, *adj.*
un•fawn′ing, *adj.*
un•fe′al•ty, *n., pl.* **-ties.**
un•feared′, *adj.*
un•fear′ful, *adj.;* **-ly,** *adv.;* **-ness,** *n.*
un•fear′ing, *adj.*
un′fea•si•bil′i•ty, *n.*
un•fea′si•ble, *adj.;* **-ble•ness,** *n.;* **-bly,** *adv.*
un•feast′ed, *adj.*
un•feath′ered, *adj.*
un•fea′tured, *adj.*
un•fe′brile, *adj.*
un•fe′cund, *adj.*
un•fe′cun•dat′ed, *adj.*
un•fed′, *adj.*
un•fed′er•at′ed, *adj.*
un•fed′er•a′tive, *adj.;* **-ly,** *adv.*
un•fee′ble, *adj.;* **-ble•ness,** *n.;* **-bly,** *adv.*
un•feed′a•ble, *adj.*
un•feed′ing, *adj.*
un•feign′a•ble, *adj.*
un•feign′ing, *adj.;* **-ly,** *adv.*
un′fe•lic′i•tat′ed, *adj.*
un′fe•lic′i•tat′ing, *adj.*
un′fe•lic′i•tous, *adj.;* **-ly,** *adv.;* **-ness,** *n.*
un•fe′line, *adj.*
un•fell′a•ble, *adj.*
un•felled′, *adj.*
un′fe•lo′ni•ous, *adj.;* **-ly,** *adv.*
un•felt′, *adj.*
un•felt′ed, *adj.*
un•fe′male, *adj.*
un•fem′i•nine, *adj.;* **-ly,** *adv.*
un•fem′i•nist, *n.*
un•fem′i•nize′, *v.t.,* **-nized, -niz•ing.**
un•fence′, *v.t.,* **-fenced, -fenc•ing.**
un•fend′ed, *adj.*
un•fend′ered, *adj.*
un′fe•nes′tral, *adj.*
un′fe•nes′trat•ed, *adj.*
un•feoffed′, *adj.*
un′fer•ment′a•ble, *adj.*
un′fer•ment′a•tive, *adj.*
un′fer•ment′ed, *adj.*
un′fer•ment′ing, *adj.*
un′fe•ro′cious, *adj.;* **-ly,** *adv.*
un•fer′ret•ed, *adj.*
un•fer′ret•ing, *adj.*
un•fer′ried, *adj.*
un•fer′tile, *adj.*
un′fer•til′i•ty, *n.*
un•fer′ti•liz′a•ble, *adj.*
un•fer′ti•lized′, *adj.*
un•fer′ti•liz′ing, *adj.*
un•fer′vent, *adj.;* **-ly,** *adv.*
un•fer′vid, *adj.;* **-ly,** *adv.*
un•fes′tered, *adj.*
un•fes′ter•ing, *adj.*
un•fes′tive, *adj.;* **-ly,** *adv.*
un′fes•tooned′, *adj.*
un•fetched′, *adj.*
un•fetch′ing, *adj.*
un•fet′ed, *adj.*
un•feu′dal, *adj.;* **-ly,** *adv.*
un•feu′dal•ize′, *v.t.,* **-ized, -iz•ing.**
un•fe′vered, *adj.*
un•fe′ver•ish, *adj.*
un•fib′bing, *adj.*
un•fi′bered, *adj.*
un•fibrous, *adj.;* **-ly,** *adv.*
un•fick′le, *adj.*
un′fic•ti′tious, *adj.;* **-ly,** *adv.*
un′fi•del′i•ty, *n., pl.* **-ties.**
un•fidg′et•ing, *adj.*
un′fi•du′cial, *adj.*
un•field′ed, *adj.*
un•fierce′, *adj.;* **-ly,** *adj.*
un•fier′y, *adj.*
un•fight′a•ble, *adj.*
un•fight′ing, *adj.*
un•fig′ur•a•ble, *adj.*
un•fig′ur•a•tive, *adj.;* **-ly,** *adv.;* **-ness,** *n.*
un′fil•a•men′tous, *adj.*
un•filched′, *adj.*
un•file′, *v.t.,* **-filed, -fil•ing.**
un•filled′, *adj.*
un•fill′ing, *adj.*
un•filmed′, *adj.*
un•fil′ter•a•ble, *adj.*
un•fil′tered, *adj.*
un•fil′ter•ing, *adj.*
un•fil′trat•ed, *adj.*
un•fim′bri•at′ed, *adj.*
un•fi′na•ble, *adj.*
un′fi′na•lized′, *adj.*
un′fi•nanced′, *adj.*
un′fi•nan′ci•ble, *adj.*
un•fine′, *adj.*
un•fine′a•ble, *adj.*
un•fined′, *adj.*
un•fin′i•cal, *adj.*
un•fin′ish•a•ble, *adj.*
un•fi′nite, *adj.*
un•fired′, *adj.*
un•fir′ing, *adj.*
un•firm′, *adj.;* **-ly,** *adv.;* **-ness,** *n.*
un•fis′cal, *adj.;* **-ly,** *adv.*
un•fish′a•ble, *adj.*
un•fished′, *adj.*
un•fis′sile, *adj.*
un•fis′tu•lous, *adj.*
un•fit′ta•ble, *adj.*
un•fit′ted, *adj.*
un•fit′ting, *adj.;* **-ly,** *adv.*
un•fix′a•ble, *adj.*
un•fix′at•ed, *adj.*
un•fix′a•tive, *adj.*
un•fix′i•ty, *n.*
un•flagged′, *adj.*
un•flag′ging, *adj.;* **-ly,** *adv.*
un′fla•gi′tious, *adj.*
un•fla′grant, *adj.;* **-ly,** *adv.*
un•flaked′, *adj.*
un•flak′ing, *adj.*
un•flak′y, *adj.*
un′flam•boy′ant, *adj.;* **-ly,** *adv.*
un•flam′ing, *adj.*
un•flanged′, *adj.*
un•flank′, *v.t.*
un•flap′ping, *adj.*
un•flared′, *adj.*
un•flar′ing, *adj.*
un•flash′ing, *adj.*
un•flash′y, *adj.*
un•flat′, *adj.*
un•flat′ted, *adj.*
un•flat′tened, *adj.*
un•flat′ter•a•ble, *adj.*
un•flat′tered, *adj.*
un•flat′ter•ing, *adj.;* **-ly,** *adv.*
un•flaunt′ed, *adj.*
un•flaunt′ing, *adj.;* **-ly,** *adv.*
un•fla′vored, *adj.*
un•fla′vor•ous, *adj.*
un•flawed′, *adj.*
un•flayed′, *adj.*
un•flecked′, *adj.*
un•fleeced′, *adj.*
un•flee′ing, *adj.*
un•fleet′ing, *adj.*
un•fleshed′, *adj.*
un•fletched′, *adj.*
un•flexed′, *adj.*
un′flex•i•bil′i•ty, *n.*
un•flex′i•ble, *adj.;* **-bly,** *adv.*
un•flick′er•ing, *adj.;* **-ly,** *adv.*
un•flight′y, *adj.*
un•flip′pant, *adj.;* **-ly,** *adv.*
un′flir•ta′tious, *adj.;* **-ly,** *adv.;* **-ness,** *n.*
un•flitched′, *adj.*

or as from fastenings; detach. **2.** to undo or open (something fastened). —*v.i.* **3.** to become unfastened. [1175–1225; ME *unfastnen.* See UN-[2], FASTEN]

un·fa·thered (un fä′thərd), *adj.* **1.** having no father; fatherless. **2.** of illegitimate or unknown paternity; bastard. **3.** not ascribable to a particular author or source: *unfathered tales.* [1590–1600; UN-[1] + FATHER + -ED[3]]

un·fa·vor·a·ble (un fā′vər ə bəl), *adj.* **1.** not favorable; contrary; adverse: *an unfavorable wind.* **2.** not propitious: *an unfavorable omen.* **3.** unfortunate; undesirable; disadvantageous: *an unfavorable development.* [1540–50; ME; see UN-[1], FAVORABLE] —**un·fa′vor·a·ble·ness,** *n.* —**un·fa′vor·a·bly,** *adv.*

un·fazed (un fāzd′), *adj.* not dismayed or disconcerted; undaunted: *He was unfazed by his previous failures.* [UN-[1] + FAZE + -ED[2]]

Unfed′erated Ma′lay States′, a former group of five states in the Malay Peninsula, under indirect British control and forming a part of the former Federation of Malaya: now part of the federation of Malaysia. 24,347 sq. mi. (63,059 sq. km).

un·feel·ing (un fē′ling), *adj.* **1.** not feeling; devoid of feeling; insensible or insensate. **2.** unsympathetic; callous: *an intelligent but unfeeling man.* [bef. 1000; ME; OE *unfelende.* See UN-[1], FEEL, -ING[2]] —**un·feel′ing·ly,** *adv.* —**un·feel′ing·ness,** *n.*
—**Syn. 1.** numb. **2.** hardhearted. See **hard.** —**Ant. 2.** sympathetic.

un·feigned (un fānd′), *adj.* not feigned; sincere; genuine. [1325–75; ME *unfeynid.* See UN-[1], FEIGN, -ED[2]] —**un·feign·ed·ly** (un fā′nid lē), *adv.* —**un·feign′ed·ness,** *n.*

un·fet·ter (un fet′ər), *v.t.* **1.** to release from fetters. **2.** to free from restraint; liberate. [1325–75; ME *unfeteren.* See UN-[2], FETTER]

un·fil·i·al (un fil′ē əl), *adj.* not befitting a son or daughter; violating the customary obligation of a child to a parent. [1605–15; UN-[1] + FILIAL] —**un·fil′i·al·ly,** *adv.*

un·find·a·ble (un fīn′də bəl), *adj.* not capable of being found: *an unfindable treasure.* [1785–95; UN-[1] + FINDABLE]

un·fin·ished (un fin′isht), *adj.* **1.** not finished; incomplete or unaccomplished. **2.** lacking some special finish or surface treatment, as polish, paint, etc. **3.** (of cloth) not sheared following the looming process. **4.** (of worsted) given a slight nap. [1530–40; UN-[1] + FINISHED] —**un·fin′ished·ness,** *n.*

un·fit (un fit′), *adj.* **1.** not fit; not adapted or suited; unsuitable: *He was unfit for his office.* **2.** unqualified or incompetent. **3.** not physically fit or in due condition. **4.** *Biol.* pertaining to an organism or population that is not adapted to prevailing conditions or is not producing offspring in sufficient numbers to maintain its contribution to the gene pool of the next generation. —*v.t.* **5.** to render unfit or unsuitable; disqualify. [1535–45; UN-[1] + FIT[1]] —**un·fit′ness,** *n.*
—**Syn. 1.** inappropriate, unapt. **2.** incapable.

un·fix (un fiks′), *v.t.,* **-fixed** or **-fixt, -fix·ing. 1.** to render no longer fixed; unfasten; detach; loosen; free. **2.** to unsettle, as the mind, traditions, or habits. [1590–1600; UN-[2] + FIX] —**un·fix·ed·ness** (un fik′sid nis, -fikst′nis), *n.*

un·flap·pa·ble (un flap′ə bəl), *adj.* not easily upset or confused, esp. in a crisis; imperturbable. [1950–55; UN-[1] + FLAP + -ABLE] —**un·flap′pa·bil′i·ty,** *n.* —**un·flap′pa·bly,** *adv.*

un·fledged (un flejd′), *adj.* **1.** not fledged; without sufficient feathers for flight, as a young bird. **2.** immature; callow. [1595–1605; UN-[1] + FLEDGED]

un·flesh·ly (un flesh′lē), *adj.* not fleshly; not carnal or corporeal; spiritual. [1850–55; UN-[1] + FLESHLY] —**un·flesh′li·ness,** *n.*

un·flinch·ing (un flin′ching), *adj.* not flinching; unshrinking: *unflinching courage.* [1720–30; UN-[1] + FLINCH[1] + -ING[2]] —**un·flinch′ing·ly,** *adv.*
—**Syn.** steady, constant, steadfast, unfaltering.

un·fo·cused (un fō′kəst), *adj.* **1.** not brought into focus; lacking proper focus: *an unfocused camera.* **2.** lacking a clear purpose or direction: *an unfocused meeting.* Also, *esp. Brit.,* **un·fo′cussed.** [1885–90; UN-[1] + FOCUSED]

un·fold (un fōld′), *v.t.* **1.** to bring out of a folded state; spread or open out: *Unfold your arms.* **2.** to spread out or lay open to view. **3.** to reveal or display. **4.** to reveal or disclose in words, esp. by careful or systematic exposition; set forth; explain. —*v.i.* **5.** to become unfolded; open. **6.** to develop. **7.** to become clear, apparent, or known: *The protagonist's character unfolds as the story reaches its climax.* [bef. 900; ME *unfolden,* OE *unfealdan;* c. G *entfalten.* See UN-[2], FOLD[1]] —**un·fold′a·ble,** *adj.* —**un·fold′er,** *n.* —**un·fold′ment,** *n.*

un·for·get·ta·ble (un′fər get′ə bəl), *adj.* impossible to forget; indelibly impressed on the memory: *scenes of unforgettable beauty.* [1800–10; UN-[1] + FORGETTABLE] —**un′for·get′ta·ble·ness,** *n.* —**un·for·get′ta·bly,** *adv.*

un·for·giv·ing (un′fər giv′ing), *adj.* **1.** not disposed to forgive or show mercy; unrelenting. **2.** not allowing for mistakes, carelessness, or weakness: *the unforgiving nature of aviation.* [1705–15; UN-[1] + FORGIVING] —**un′for·giv′ing·ness,** *n.*

un·for·mat·ted (un fôr′mat id), *adj. Computers.* pertaining to a disk that has not been electronically prepared to receive files or other text; blank: *You cannot save files on an unformatted disk.* [UN-[1] + FORMATTED]

un·formed (un fôrmd′), *adj.* **1.** not definitely shaped; shapeless or formless. **2.** undeveloped; crude. **3.** not formed; not created. [1275–1325; ME *unfourmed.* See UN-[1], FORM, -ED[2]]

un·for·tu·nate (un fôr′chə nit), *adj.* **1.** suffering from bad luck: *an unfortunate person.* **2.** unfavorable or inauspicious: *an unfortunate beginning.* **3.** regrettable or deplorable: *an unfortunate remark.* **4.** marked by or inviting misfortune: *an unfortunate development.* **5.** lamentable; sad: *the unfortunate death of her parents.* —*n.* **6.** an unfortunate person. [1520–30; UN-[1] + FORTUNATE] —**un·for′tu·nate·ly,** *adv.* —**un·for′tu·nate·ness,** *n.*
—**Syn. 1.** unsuccessful, hapless.

un·found·ed (un foun′did), *adj.* **1.** without foundation; not based on fact, realistic considerations, or the like: *unfounded suspicions.* **2.** not established; not founded: *the prophet of a religion as yet unfounded.* [1640–50; UN-[1] + FOUND[2] + -ED[2]] —**un·found′ed·ly,** *adv.* —**un·found′ed·ness,** *n.*
—**Syn. 1.** groundless, idle, false, unjustified, unsubstantiated.

un·freeze (un frēz′), *v.,* **-froze, -fro·zen, -freez·ing.** —*v.t.* **1.** to cause to thaw; melt. **2.** to remove or relax controls or restrictions on (funds, prices, rents, etc.). —*v.i.* **3.** to become unfrozen; thaw. [1575–85; UN-[2] + FREEZE]

un·fre·quent·ed (un frē′kwən tid, -fri kwen′-), *adj.* not habitually visited, traveled, or occupied: *an unfrequented side street.* [1580–90; UN-[1] + FREQUENTED]

un·friend·ed (un fren′did), *adj.* without friends; not befriended. [1505–15; UN-[1] + FRIEND + -ED[3]]

un·friend·ly (un frend′lē), *adj.,* **-li·er, -li·est,** *adv.* —*adj.* **1.** not amicable; not friendly or kindly in disposition; unsympathetic; aloof: *an unfriendly coldness of manner.* **2.** hostile; antagonistic: *an unfriendly act of aggression.* **3.** unfavorable; inhospitable or inimical, as an environment: *an unfriendly climate for new ideas.* —*adv.* **4.** in an unfriendly manner. [bef. 900; ME (adj.); OE *unfreondliche* (adv.). See UN-[1], FRIENDLY] —**un·friend′li·ness,** *n.*

un·frock (un frok′), *v.t.* **1.** to deprive (a monk, priest, minister, etc.) of ecclesiastical rank, authority, and function; depose. **2.** to divest or strip of a frock. Also, **defrock.** [1635–45; UN-[2] + FROCK]

un·froze (un frōz′), *v.* pt. of **unfreeze.**

un·fruit·ful (un fro͞ot′fəl), *adj.* **1.** not providing satisfaction; unprofitable: *unfruitful efforts.* **2.** not producing offspring; sterile: *an unfruitful marriage.* **3.** not yielding good crops; infertile: *unfruitful acres.* **4.** not bearing fruit; fruitless; barren: *an unfruitful tree.* [1350–1400; ME; see UN-[1], FRUITFUL] —**un·fruit′ful·ly,** *adv.* —**un·fruit′ful·ness,** *n.*
—**Syn. 1.** fruitless, unproductive, vain, unrewarding.

un·fund·ed (un fun′did), *adj.* **1.** not provided with a fund or money; not financed. **2.** *Finance.* floating (def. 5b). [1765–75; UN-[1] + FUNDED]

un·furl (un fûrl′), *v.t.* **1.** to spread or shake out from a furled state, as a sail or a flag; unfold. —*v.i.* **2.** to become unfurled. [1635–45; UN-[2] + FURL] —**un·furl′a·ble,** *adj.*

ung., (in prescriptions) ointment. [< L *unguentum*]

un·gain·ly (un gān′lē), *adj.,* **-li·er, li·est,** *adv.* —*adj.*

CONCISE ETYMOLOGY KEY: <, descended or borrowed from; >, whence; b., blend of, blended; c., cognate with; cf., compare; deriv., derivative; equiv., equivalent; imit., imitative; obl., oblique; r., replacing; s., stem; sp., spelling, spelled; resp., respelling, respelled; trans., translation; ?, origin unknown; *, unattested; ‡, probably earlier than. See the full key inside the front cover.

---

un·float′a·ble, *adj.*
un·float′ing, *adj.*
un·flog′ga·ble, *adj.*
un·flogged′, *adj.*
un·flood′ed, *adj.*
un·floor′, *v.t.*
un·flor′id, *adj.*
un·floss′y, *adj.*
un·flounced′, *adj.*
un·floun′der·ing, *adj.*
un·floured′, *adj.*
un·flour′ish·ing, *adj.*
un·flout′ed, *adj.*
un·flow′ered, *adj.*
un·flow′er·ing, *adj.*
un·flow′er·y, *adj.*
un·flow′ing, *adj.*
un·flown′, *adj.*
un·fluc′tu·ant, *adj.*
un·fluc′tu·at′ing, *adj.*
un·flu′ent, *adj.;* **-ly,** *adv.*
un·fluffed′, *adj.*
un·fluff′y, *adj.*
un·flu′id, *adj.*
un·fluked′, *adj.*
un·flunked′, *adj.*
un′fluo·res′cent, *adj.*
un·fluor′i·nat′ed, *adj.*
un·flur′ried, *adj.*
un·flushed′, *adj.*
un·flus′tered, *adj.*
un·flut′ed, *adj.*
un·flut′ter·a·ble, *adj.*
un·flut′tered, *adj.*
un·flut′ter·ing, *adj.*
un·flu′vi·al, *adj.*
un·fly′a·ble, *adj.*
un·fly′ing, *adj.*
un·foaled′, *adj.*
un·foamed′, *adj.*
un·foam′ing, *adj.*
un·fo′cus·ing, *adj.*
un·fo′cus·sing, *adj.*
un·fogged′, *adj.*
un·fog′ging, *adj.*
un·fog′gy, *adj.*
un·foil′a·ble, *adj.*
un·foiled′, *adj.*
un·foist′ed, *adj.*
un·fo′li·aged, *adj.*
un·fo′li·at′ed, *adj.*
un·fol′low·a·ble, *adj.*
un·fol′lowed, *adj.*
un′fo·ment′ed, *adj.*
un·fond′, *adj.;* **-ly,** *adv.;* **-ness,** *n.*
un·fon′dled, *adj.*
un·fool′a·ble, *adj.*
un·fooled′, *adj.*
un·fool′ing, *adj.*
un·fool′ish, *adj.;* **-ly,** *adv.;* **-ness,** *n.*
un·for′aged, *adj.*
un′for·bear′ing, *adj.*
un′for·bid′den, *adj.*
un′for·bid′ding, *adj.*
un·force′a·ble, *adj.*
un·forced′, *adj.*
un·forc′ed·ly, *adv.*
un·force′ful, *adj.;* **-ly,** *adv.*
un·for′ci·ble, *adj.;* **-ble·ness,** *n.;* **-bly,** *adv.*
un·forc′ing, *adj.*
un·ford′a·ble, *adj.*
un·ford′ed, *adj.*
un′fore·bod′ed, *adj.*
un′fore·bod′ing, *adj.*
un·fore′cast, *adj.*
un·fore′cast′ed, *adj.*
un′fore·gone′, *adj.*
un·for′eign, *adj.*
un′fore·know′a·ble, *adj.*
un′fore·known′, *adj.*
un′fo·ren′sic, *adj.*
un′fo·ren′si·cal·ly, *adv.*
un′fore·see′a·ble, *adj.;* **-ble·ness,** *n.;* **-bly,** *adv.*
un′fore·see′ing, *adj.*
un′fore·seen′, *adj.*
un′fore·short′ened, *adj.*
un′fore·stall′a·ble, *adj.*
un′fore·stalled′, *adj.*
un·for′est·ed, *adj.*
un′fore·tell′a·ble, *adj.*
un′fore·told′, *adj.*
un′fore·warned′, *adj.*
un·for′feit·a·ble, *adj.*
un·for′feit·ed, *adj.*
un·for′feit·ing, *adj.*
un′for·ge·a·bil′i·ty, *n.*
un·forge′a·ble, *adj.*
un·forged′, *adj.*
un′for·get′ful, *adj.;* **-ly,** *adv.;* **-ness,** *n.*
un′for·get′ting, *adj.*
un′for·giv′a·ble, *adj.;* **-ble·ness,** *n.;* **-bly,** *adv.*
un′for·giv′en, *adj.*
un′for·gone′, *adj.*
un′for·got′ten, *adj.*
un·fork′, *v.t.*
un·forked′, *adj.*
un′for·lorn′, *adj.*
un′for·mal·is′tic, *adj.*
un·for′mal·ized′, *adj.*
un·form′a·tive, *adj.*
un·for′mi·da·ble, *adj.;* **-ble·ness,** *n.;* **-bly,** *adv.*
un·for′mu·lat′ed, *adj.*
un′for·mu·lis′tic, *adj.*
un′for·sak′en, *adj.*
un′for·sak′ing, *adj.*
un′for·sworn′, *adj.*
un′forth·com′ing, *adj.*
un·forth′right′, *adj.*
un·for′ti·fi′a·ble, *adj.*
un·for′ti·fied′, *adj.*
un′for·tu′i·tous, *adj.;* **-ly,** *adv.;* **-ness,** *n.*
un·for′ward, *adj.;* **-ly,** *adv.*
un·for′ward·ed, *adj.*
un′fos·sil·if′er·ous, *adj.*
un·fos′sil·ized′, *adj.*
un·fos′tered, *adj.*
un·fos′ter·ing, *adj.*
un·fought′, *adj.*
un·foul′, *adj.;* **-ly,** *adv.*
un·fouled′, *adj.*
un·found′, *adj.*
un·foun′dered, *adj.*
un·foun′der·ing, *adj.*
un·foun′tained, *adj.*
un·foxed′, *adj.*
un·fox′y, *adj.*
un·frac′tious, *adj.;* **-ly,** *adv.;* **-ness,** *n.*
un·frac′tured, *adj.*
un·frag′ile, *adj.*
un·frag′ment·ed, *adj.*
un·fra′grant, *adj.;* **-ly,** *adv.*
un·frail′, *adj.*
un·fram′a·ble, *adj.;* **-ble·ness,** *n.;* **-bly,** *adv.*
un·frame′a·ble, *adj.;* **-ble·ness,** *n.;* **-bly,** *adv.*
un·framed′, *adj.*
un·fran′chised, *adj.*
un·frank′, *adj.;* **-ly,** *adv.;* **-ness,** *n.*
un′fra·ter′nal, *adj.;* **-ly,** *adv.*
un·frat′er·nized′, *adj.*
un·frat′er·niz′ing, *adj.*
un·fraud′u·lent, *adj.;* **-ly,** *adv.*
un·fraught′, *adj.*
un·frayed′, *adj.*
un·fraz′zled, *adj.*
un·freak′ish, *adj.;* **-ly,** *adv.;* **-ness,** *n.*
un·freck′led, *adj.*
un·free′, *v.t.,* **-freed, -free·ing,** *adj.;* **-ly,** *adv.*
un·free′dom, *n.*
un·freez′a·ble, *adj.*
un·freight′ed, *adj.*
un-French′, *adj.*
un·fren′zied, *adj.*
un·fre′quent, *adj.;* **-ly,** *adv.*
un′fre·quent′a·ble, *adj.*
un′fre·quen′ta·tive, *adj.*
un·fret′ful, *adj.;* **-ly,** *adv.*
un·fret′ted, *adj.*
un·fret′ting, *adj.*
un·fret′ty, *adj.*
un·fri′a·ble, *adj.;* **-ble·ness,** *n.*
un·fric′a·tive, *adj.*
un·fric′tion·al, *adj.;* **-ly,** *adv.*
un·fric′tioned, *adj.*
un·fried′, *adj.*
un·fright′ed, *adj.*
un·fright′ened, *adj.*
un·fright′en·ing, *adj.*
un·fright′ful, *adj.*
un·frig′id, *adj.;* **-ly,** *adv.;* **-ness,** *n.*
un′fri·gid′i·ty, *n.*
un·frill′, *v.t.*
un·frill′y, *adj.*
un·fringe′, *v.t.,* **-fringed, -fring·ing.**
un·frisk′ing, *adj.*
un·frisk′y, *adj.*
un·frit′tered, *adj.*
un·friv′o·lous, *adj.;* **-ly,** *adv.;* **-ness,** *n.*
un·friz′zled, *adj.*
un·friz′zly, *adj.*
un·friz′zy, *adj.*
un·front′ed, *adj.*
un·frost′, *v.t.*
un·frost′ed, *adj.*
un·frost′y, *adj.*
un·frothed′, *adj.*
un·froth′ing, *adj.*
un·frounced′, *adj.*
un·fro′ward, *adj.;* **-ly,** *adv.*
un·frown′ing, *adj.*
un·fro′zen, *adj.*
un·fruc′ti·fied′, *adj.*
un·fruc′tu·ous, *adj.*
un·fru′gal, *adj.;* **-ly,** *adv.;* **-ness,** *n.*
un′fru·gal′i·ty, *n.*
un·fruit′y, *adj.*
un·frus′trat·a·ble, *adj.*
un·frus′trat·ed, *adj.*
un·fud′dled, *adj.*
un·fudged′, *adj.*
un·fu′eled, *adj.*
un·fu′elled, *adj.*
un·fu′gal, *adj.;* **-ly,** *adv.*
un·fu′gi·tive, *adj.;* **-ly,** *adv.*
un′ful·fill′a·ble, *adj.*
un′ful·filled′, *adj.*
un′ful·fill′ing, *adj.*
un·ful′gent, *adj.;* **-ly,** *adv.*
un·full′, *adj.*
un·ful′ly, *adv.*
un·ful′mi·nant, *adj.*
un·ful′mi·nat′ed, *adj.*
un·ful′mi·nat′ing, *adj.*
un·ful′some, *adj.*
un·fum′bled, *adj.*
un·fum′bling, *adj.*
un·fu′mi·gat′ed, *adj.*
un·fum′ing, *adj.*
un·func′tion·al, *adj.;* **-ly,** *adv.*
un·func′tion·ing, *adj.*
un·fund′a·ble, *adj.*
un′fun·da·men′tal, *adj.;* **-ly,** *adv.*
un′fu·ne′re·al, *adj.;* **-ly,** *adv.*
un·fun′gi·ble, *adj.*
un·fun′ni·ly, *adv.*
un·fun′ni·ness, *n.*
un·fun′ny, *adj.*
un′fur·be·lowed′, *adj.*
un·fur′bished, *adj.*
un·fur′cate, *adj.*
un·fur′nished, *adj.*
un·fur′ni·tured, *adj.*
un·furred′, *adj.*
un·fur′rowed, *adj.*
un·fused′, *adj.*
un′fu·si·bil′i·ty, *n.*
un·fu′si·ble, *adj.;* **-ness,** *n.*
un·fussed′, *adj.*
un·fuss′i·ly, *adv.*
un·fuss′i·ness, *n.*

1. not graceful; awkward; unwieldy; clumsy: *an ungainly child; an ungainly prose style.* —*adv.* **2.** in an awkward manner. [1150–1200; (adv.) ME *ungeinliche,* equiv. to *un-* UN-[1] + later ME *geyn* straight, well-disposed, handy (< ON *gegn* straight, direct; cf. ON *ūgegn* unreasonable) + *-liche* -LY; (adj.) UN-[1] + obs. *gainly* proper, becoming, gracious, ME *gaynlych* (*geyn* as above + *-lych* -LY); cf. GAINLY, AGAIN] —**un·gain′li·ness,** *n.*

Un·ga·va (ung gä′və, -gā′-), *n.* a region in NE Canada, comprising the larger part of the peninsula of Labrador: incorporated into Quebec province 1912.

Unga′va Bay′, an inlet of the Hudson Strait in NE Quebec province, in E Canada, between Ungava Peninsula and N Labrador.

Unga′va Penin′sula, a peninsula in NW Ungava region, in N Quebec, in E Canada.

un·gen·er·ous (un jen′ər əs), *adj.* **1.** stingy; niggardly; miserly: *an ungenerous portion; an ungenerous employer.* **2.** uncharitable; petty: *an ungenerous critic; an ungenerous impulse.* [1635–45; UN-[1] + GENEROUS] —**un·gen·er·os·i·ty** (un′jen ə ros′i tē), *n.* —**un·gen′er·ous·ly,** *adv.*

un·gird (un gûrd′), *v.t.,* **-gird·ed** or **-girt, -gird·ing. 1.** to loosen or remove a girdle or belt from. **2.** to loosen or remove by unfastening a belt: *to ungird a sword.* [bef. 900; ME *ungirden,* OE *ungyrdan;* see UN-[2], GIRD; c. G *entgürten*]

un·girt (un gûrt′), *adj.* **1.** having a girdle loosened or removed. **2.** slack; relaxed; not taut or pulled together: *ungirt thinking.* [1250–1300; ME *ungyrt.* See UN-[1], GIRT[1]]

un·glue (un glōō′), *v.t.,* **-glued, -glu·ing. 1.** to separate or detach by or as if by overcoming an adhesive agent: *to unglue a sticker from a wall.* **2.** *Slang.* **a.** to confuse or upset: *He was unglued by his opponent's superb defense.* **b.** to cause to fail or lose effectiveness. [1540–50; UN-[2] + GLUE]

un·glued (un glōōd′), *adj.* **1.** separated or detached; not glued. **2. come unglued,** *Slang.* **a.** to become upset, disorganized, or confused; lose emotional control: *to come unglued in an emergency.* **b.** to disintegrate or collapse; fall apart; break down: *The negotiators tried to keep the fragile peace agreement from coming unglued.* [1685–95; (def. 1) UN-[1] + GLUED; (def. 2) UNGLUE + -ED[2]]

un·god·ly (un god′lē), *adj.,* **-li·er, -li·est. 1.** not accepting God or a particular religious doctrine; irreligious; atheistic: *an ungodly era.* **2.** sinful; wicked; impious; not conforming to religious tenets or canons: *an ungodly life.* **3.** outrageous; shocking; dreadful; insufferable: *an ungodly roar; an ungodly hour to drop in.* [1520–30; UN-[1] + GODLY] —**un·god′li·ness,** *n.*
—**Syn. 2.** profane, evil, corrupt, blasphemous.

un·got·ten (un got′n), *adj.* **1.** not obtained or gained. **2.** *Obs.* not begotten. Also, **un·got′.** [1400–50; late ME; see UN-[1], GOTTEN]

un·gov·ern·a·ble (un guv′ər nə bəl), *adj.* impossible to govern, rule, or restrain; uncontrollable. [1665–75; UN-[1] + GOVERNABLE] —**un·gov′ern·a·bil′i·ty, un·gov′·ern·a·ble·ness,** *n.* —**un·gov′ern·a·bly,** *adv.*

un·grace·ful (un grās′fəl), *adj.* lacking charm or elegance; awkward. [1660–70; UN-[1] + GRACEFUL] —**un·grace′ful·ly,** *adv.* —**un·grace′ful·ness,** *n.*

un·gra·cious (un grā′shəs), *adj.* **1.** discourteous; ill-mannered: *ungracious behavior.* **2.** unpleasant; disagreeable; unrewarding: *an ungracious task.* **3.** ungraceful; unpleasing. [1175–1225; ME; see UN-[1], GRACIOUS] —**un·gra′cious·ly,** *adv.* —**un·gra′cious·ness,** *n.*

un·gram·mat·i·cal (un′grə mat′i kəl), *adj.* grammatically incorrect or awkward; not conforming to the rules or principles of grammar or accepted usage: *an ungrammatical sentence.* [1645–55; UN-[1] + GRAMMATICAL] —**un′gram·mat′i·cal·ly,** *adv.*

un·grate·ful (un grāt′fəl), *adj.* **1.** unappreciative; not displaying gratitude; not giving due return or recompense for benefits conferred: *ungrateful heirs.* **2.** unpleasant; distasteful; repellent: *an ungrateful task.* [1545–55; UN-[1] + GRATEFUL] —**un·grate′ful·ly,** *adv.* —**un·grate′ful·ness,** *n.*

un·grudg·ing (un gruj′ing), *adj.* not begrudging; not stinting; wholehearted: *an ungrudging supporter of charities.* [1760–70; UN-[1] + GRUDGING] —**un·grudg′·ing·ly,** *adv.*

ungt., (in prescriptions) ointment. [< L *unguentum*]

un·gual (ung′gwəl), *adj.* of, pertaining to, bearing, or shaped like a nail, claw, or hoof. [1825–35; < L *ungu(is)* a nail, claw, hoof (akin to Gk *ónyx*) + -AL[1]]

un·guard·ed (un gär′did), *adj.* **1.** not guarded; unprotected; undefended. **2.** open; frank; guileless: *an unguarded manner.* **3.** exposed to attack or capture by the opponent without recourse by the player, as a card, chess piece, etc.: *an unguarded queen of clubs; an unguarded pawn.* **4.** not cautious or discreet; careless: *In an unguarded moment he had told her about his affair.* **5.** without a safeguard, as a cover, barrier, or shield, for protection: *an unguarded buzz saw.* [1585–95; UN-[1] + GUARDED] —**un·guard′ed·ly,** *adv.* —**un·guard′ed·ness,** *n.*
—**Syn. 1.** defenseless. **4.** indiscreet.

un·guent (ung′gwənt), *n.* an ointment or salve, usually liquid or semiliquid, for application to wounds, sores, etc. [1400–50; late ME < L *unguentum,* alter. (prob. by assoc. with the suffixes *-men, -mentum*) of *unguen* fat, grease, deriv. of *unguere* to smear, anoint] —**un·guen·tar·y** (ung′gwən ter′ē), *adj.*

un·guen·tum (ung gwen′təm), *n., pl.* **-ta** (-tə). (in prescriptions) ointment. [< L]

un·guic·u·late (ung gwik′yə lit, -lāt′), *adj.* Also, **un·guic′u·lat′ed. 1.** bearing or resembling a nail or claw. **2.** *Zool.* belonging or pertaining to the former superorder Unguiculata, comprising mammals having nails or claws, as distinguished from hoofs. **3.** *Bot.* having a clawlike base, as certain petals. —*n.* **4.** an unguiculate animal. [1795–1805; < NL *unguiculātus,* equiv. to L *unguicul(us)* fingernail (*ungu(is)* (see UNGUIS) + *-i-* -I- + *-culus* -CULE[1]) + *-ātus* -ATE[1]]

un·gui·nous (ung′gwi nəs), *adj.* resembling, containing, or consisting of fat or oil; greasy; oily. [1595–1605; < L *unguinōsus,* equiv. to *unguin-* (s. of *unguen*) ointment + *-ōsus* -OUS]

un·guis (ung′gwis), *n., pl.* **-gues** (-gwēz). **1.** a nail, claw, or hoof. **2.** *Bot.* the clawlike base of certain petals. [1685–95; < L *unguis* a nail, claw, hoof; akin to Gk *ónyx*]

un·gu·la (ung′gyə lə), *n., pl.* **-lae** (-lē′). *Bot.* an unguis. [1350–1400; ME < L *ungula* a claw, hoof, talon, dim. of *unguis* UNGUIS]

un·gu·lar (ung′gyə lər), *adj.* pertaining to or of the nature of an ungula; ungual. [UNGUL(A) + -AR[1]]

un·gu·late (ung′gyə lit, -lāt′), *adj.* **1.** having hoofs. **2.** belonging or pertaining to the Ungulata, a former order of all hoofed mammals, now divided into the odd-toed perissodactyls and even-toed artiodactyls. **3.** hooflike. —*n.* **4.** a hoofed mammal. [1795–1805; < LL *ungulātus* having claws or hoofs. See UNGULA, -ATE[1]]

Unh, *Symbol, Chem., Physics.* unnilhexium.

un·hair (un hâr′), *v.t.* **1.** to remove the hair from, as a hide in preparation for tanning. **2.** to remove the guard hairs from, as for a pelt or animal skin to be made into a garment. —*v.i.* **3.** to become hairless: *After soaking, the hides unhair easily.* [1350–1400; ME *unheeren.* See UN-[2], HAIR] —**un·hair′er,** *n.*

un·hal·low (un hal′ō), *v.t.* to desecrate; profane. [1525–35; UN-[2] + HALLOW[1]]

un·hal·lowed (un hal′ōd), *adj.* **1.** not hallowed or consecrated; not regarded as holy or sacred: *unhallowed ground.* **2.** impious; unholy. **3.** wicked or sinful: *unhallowed practices.* [bef. 1000; ME *unhalewed,* OE *unhālghod, ungehālghod;* see UN-[1], HALLOWED]

un·hand (un hand′), *v.t.* to take the hand or hands from; release from a grasp; let go: *Unhand me, you wretched coward!* [1595–1605; UN-[2] + HAND]

un·han·dled (un han′dld), *adj.* **1.** not handled; not touched. **2.** (of animals) untamed; unbroken; untrained. [1550–60; UN-[1] + HANDLED]

un·hand·some (un han′səm), *adj.* **1.** lacking good looks; not attractive in physical appearance; plain or ugly. **2.** ungracious; discourteous; unseemly: *an unhandsome exchange of epithets.* **3.** ungenerous; illiberal: *an unhandsome reward.* [1520–30; UN-[1] + HANDSOME] —**un·hand′some·ly,** *adv.* —**un·hand′some·ness,** *n.*

un·hand·y (un han′dē), *adj.,* **-hand·i·er, -hand·i·est. 1.** not skillful in manual work: *He's unhandy when it comes to fixing things around the house.* **2.** inconveniently placed or arranged. **3.** difficult to handle or use, as tools or objects. [1655–65; UN-[1] + HANDY] —**un·hand′i·ly,** *adv.* —**un·hand′i·ness,** *n.*
—**Syn. 1.** clumsy, awkward, inept, bumbling.

CONCISE PRONUNCIATION KEY: *act, cāpe, dâre, pärt; set, ēqual; if, īce; ox, ōver, ôrder, oil, bŏŏk, bōōt, out; up, ûrge; child; sing; shoe; thin, that;* zh as in *treasure.* ə = *a* as in *alone, e* as in *system, i* as in *easily, o* as in *gallop, u* as in *circus;* ° as in *fire* (fī°r), *hour* (ou°r). l and n can serve as syllabic consonants, as in *cradle* (krād′l), and *button* (but′n). See the full key inside the front cover.

un·fuss′ing, *adj.*
un·fuss′y, *adj.*
un·fu′tile, *adj.*
un′fu·tur·is′tic, *adj.*
un·ga′bled, *adj.*
un·gag′, *v.t.,* **-gagged, -gag·ging.**
un·gain′a·ble, *adj.*
un·gained′, *adj.*
un·gain′ful, *adj.;* **-ly,** *adv.*
un·gain′ing, *adj.*
un·gain′said′, *adj.*
un·gait′ed, *adj.*
un·gal′lant, *adj.;* **-ly,** *adv.*
un·galled′, *adj.*
un·gal′ler·ied, *adj.*
un·gall′ing, *adj.*
un·gal′lop·ing, *adj.*
un·gal′va·nized′, *adj.*
un·gam′bled, *adj.*
un·gam′bling, *adj.*
un·gam′boled, *adj.*
un·gam′bol·ing, *adj.*
un·gam′bolled, *adj.*
un·gam′bol·ling, *adj.*
un·game′like′, *adj.*
un·gam′y, *adj.*
un·ganged′, *adj.*
un·gan′grened, *adj.*
un·gan′gre·nous, *adj.*
un·gap′ing, *adj.*
un′ga·raged′, *adj.*
un·garbed′, *adj.*
un·gar′bled, *adj.*
un·gar′dened, *adj.*
un·gar′land, *v.t.*
un·gar′ment·ed, *adj.*
un·gar′nered, *adj.*
un·gar′nished, *adj.*
un·gar′ri·soned, *adj.*
un·gar′ru·lous, *adj.;* **-ly,** *adv.;* **-ness,** *n.*
un·gar′ter, *v.t.*
un·gashed′, *adj.*
un·gassed′, *adj.*
un·gat′ed, *adj.*
un·gath′ered, *adj.*
un·gaud′i·ly, *adv.*
un·gaud′i·ness, *n.*
un·gaud′y, *adj.*
un·gauged′, *adj.*
un·gaunt′let·ed, *adj.*
un′ga·zet′ted, *adj.*
un·gaz′ing, *adj.*
un·geared′, *adj.*
un′ge·lat′i·nized′, *adj.*
un′ge·lat′i·nous, *adj.;* **-ly,** *adv.;* **-ness,** *n.*
un·geld′ed, *adj.*
un·gen′er·a·ble, *adj.*
un·gen′er·al·ized′, *adj.*
un·gen′er·al·iz′ing, *adj.*
un·gen′er·at′ed, *adj.*
un·gen′er·at′ing, *adj.*
un·gen′er·a·tive, *adj.*
un′ge·ner′ic, *adj.*
un′ge·ner′i·cal, *adj.;* **-ly,** *adv.*
un·gen′ial, *adj.;* **-ly,** *adv.;* **-ness,** *n.*
un·gen′i·tive, *adj.*
un′gen·teel′, *adj.*
un·gen′tile, *adj.*
un′gen·til′i·ty, *n.*
un·gen′tle, *adj.;* **-tle·ness,** *n.;* **-tly,** *adv.*
un·gen′tle·man·like′, *adj.*
un·gen′tle·man·ly, *adj.*
un·gen′u·ine, *adj.;* **-ly,** *adv.;* **-ness,** *n.*
un′ge·o·det′ic, *adj.*
un′ge·o·det′i·cal·ly, *adv.*
un′ge·o·graph′ic, *adj.*
un′ge·o·graph′i·cal, *adj.;* **-ly,** *adv.*
un′ge·o·log′i·cal, *adj.;* **-ly,** *adv.*
un′ge·o·met′ric, *adj.*
un′ge·o·met′ri·cal, *adj.;* **-ly,** *adv.*
un-Ger′man, *adj.*
un·ger·mane′, *adj.*
un·ger′mi·nant, *adj.*
un·ger′mi·nat′ed, *adj.*
un·ger′mi·nat′ing, *adj.*
un·ger′mi·na′tive, *adj.*
un′ges·tic′u·lar, *adj.*
un′ges·tic′u·lat′ing, *adj.*
un′ges·tic′u·la′tive, *adj.*
un′ges·tic′u·la·to′ry, *adj.*
un·ges′tur·al, *adj.*
un·ges′tur·ing, *adj.*
un·ghost′like′, *adj.*
un·ghost′ly, *adj.*
un·gid′dy, *adj.*
un·gift′ed, *adj.*
un·gild′ed, *adj.*
un·gilled′, *adj.*
un·gilt′, *adj.*
un·gim′mick·y, *adj.*
un·ginned′, *adj.*
un·gir′dle, *v.t.,* **-dled, -dling.**
un·girl′ish, *adj.;* **-ly,** *adv.;* **-ness,** *n.*
un·girthed′, *adj.*
un·give′a·ble, *adj.*
un·giv′en, *adj.*
un·giv′ing, *adj.*
un·gla′cial, *adj.;* **-ly,** *adv.*
un·gla′ci·at′ed, *adj.*
un·glad′, *adj.;* **-ly,** *adv.*
un·glad′den, *v.t.*
un·glam′or·ized′, *adj.*
un·glam′or·ous, *adj.;* **-ly,** *adv.;* **-ness,** *n.*
un·glam′our·ized′, *adj.*
un·glam′our·ous, *adj.;* **-ly,** *adv.;* **-ness,** *n.*
un·glan′du·lar, *adj.*
un·glar′ing, *adj.*
un·glassed′, *adj.*
un·glass′y, *adj.*
un·glazed′, *adj.*
un·gleam′ing, *adj.*
un·gleaned′, *adj.*
un·glee′ful, *adj.;* **-ly,** *adv.*
un·glib′, *adj.;* **-ly,** *adv.*
un·glid′ing, *adj.*
un·glimpsed′, *adj.*
un·glis′ten·ing, *adj.*
un·glit′ter·ing, *adj.*
un·glit′ter·y, *adj.*
un·gloat′ing, *adj.*
un·glob′u·lar, *adj.;* **-ly,** *adv.*
un·gloom′, *v.t.*
un·gloom′i·ly, *adv.*
un·gloom′y, *adj.*
un·glo′ri·fied′, *adj.*
un·glo′ri·fy′ing, *adj.*
un·glo′ri·ous, *adj.;* **-ly,** *adv.*
un·glos′sa·ried, *adj.*
un·glossed′, *adj.*
un·gloss′y, *adj.*
un·gloved′, *adj.*
un·glow′er·ing, *adj.;* **-ly,** *adv.*
un·glow′ing, *adj.*
un·glozed′, *adj.*
un′glu·ti·nos′i·ty, *n.*
un·glu′ti·nous, *adj.;* **-ly,** *adv.;* **-ness,** *n.*
un·glut′ted, *adj.*
un·glut′ton·ous, *adj.*
un·gnarled′, *adj.*
un·gnawed′, *adj.*
un·gnawn′, *adj.*
un·gnos′tic, *adj.*
un·goad′ed, *adj.*
un·god′like′, *adj.*
un·gog′gled, *adj.*
un·goi′tered, *adj.*
un·gold′en, *adj.*
un·good′ly, *adj., adv.*
un·gored′, *adj.*
un·gorged′, *adj.*
un·gos′sip·ing, *adj.*
un·gos′sip·y, *adj.*
un·goth′ic, *adj.*
un·gouged′, *adj.*
un·gout′y, *adj.*
un·gov′erned, *adj.*
un·gov′ern·ing, *adj.*
un′gov·ern·men′tal, *adj.;* **-ly,** *adv.*
un·gowned′, *adj.*
un·grab′bing, *adj.*
un·graced′, *adj.*
un·gra′dat·ed, *adj.*
un·gra′dat·ing, *adj.*
un·grad′ed, *adj.*
un·grad′u·al, *adj.;* **-ly,** *adv.*
un·grad′u·at′ed, *adj.*
un·grad′u·at′ing, *adj.*
un·graft′ed, *adj.*
un·grain′a·ble, *adj.*
un·grained′, *adj.*
un·grand′, *adj.*
un·grant′a·ble, *adj.*
un·gran′u·lar, *adj.*
un·gran′u·lat′ed, *adj.*
un·graph′a·ble, *adj.*
un·graph′ic, *adj.*
un·graph′i·cal, *adj.;* **-ly,** *adv.*
un·graph′i·tized′, *adj.*
un·grap′pled, *adj.*
un·grap′pling, *adj.*
un·grasp′a·ble, *adj.*
un·grasped′, *adj.*
un·grasp′ing, *adj.*
un·grassed′, *adj.*
un·grass′y, *adj.*
un·grat′ed, *adj.*
un·grat′i·fi′a·ble, *adj.*
un·grat′i·fied′, *adj.*
un·grat′i·fy′ing, *adj.*
un·grat′ing, *adj.*
un·grat′i·tude′, *n.*
un′gra·tu′i·tous, *adj.;* **-ly,** *adv.;* **-ness,** *n.*
un·graved′, *adj.*
un·grav′eled, *adj.*
un·grav′elled, *adj.*
un·grav′el·ly, *adj.*
un·grave′ly, *adv.*
un·grav′en, *adj.*
un·grav′i·tat′ing, *adj.*
un′grav·i·ta′tion·al, *adj.*
un·grav′i·ta′tive, *adj.*
un·grayed′, *adj.*
un·grazed′, *adj.*
un·greased′, *adj.*
un·greas′y, *adj.*
un·greed′y, *adj.*
un·greened′, *adj.*
un·greet′ed, *adj.*
un′gre·gar′i·ous, *adj.;* **-ly,** *adv.;* **-ness,** *n.*
un·greyed′, *adj.*
un·grieved′, *adj.*
un·griev′ing, *adj.*
un·grilled′, *adj.*
un·grimed′, *adj.*
un·grind′a·ble, *adj.*
un·grip′, *v.,* **-gripped, -grip·ping.**
un·grit′ty, *adj.*
un·griz′zled, *adj.*
un·groan′ing, *adj.*
un·groined′, *adj.*
un·groomed′, *adj.*
un·grooved′, *adj.*
un·gross′, *adj.*
un′gro·tesque′, *adj.*
un·ground′, *adj.*
un·ground′a·ble, *adj.*
un·ground′ed, *adj.*
un·group′a·ble, *adj.*
un·grouped′, *adj.*
un·grout′ed, *adj.*
un·grov′el·ing, *adj.*
un·grov′el·ling, *adj.*
un·grow′ing, *adj.*
un·growl′ing, *adj.*
un·grown′, *adj.*
un·grudged′, *adj.*
un·grue′some, *adj.*
un·gruff′, *adj.*
un·grum′bling, *adj.*
un·grump′y, *adj.*
un′guar·an·teed′, *adj.*
un·guard′a·ble, *adj.*
un·guer′doned, *adj.*
un·guess′a·ble, *adj.*

un·hap·py (un hap′ē), *adj.,* **-pi·er, -pi·est.** **1.** sad; miserable; wretched: *Why is she so unhappy?* **2.** unfortunate; unlucky: *an unhappy incident.* **3.** unfavorable; inauspicious: *an unhappy omen.* **4.** infelicitous; unsuitable: *an unhappy choice of words.* **5.** *Archaic.* causing trouble; reprehensible; troublesome. [1250–1300; ME: causing misfortune, objectionable; see UN-[1], HAPPY] **—un·hap′pi·ly,** *adv.* **—un·hap′pi·ness,** *n.*
—Syn. 1. sorrowful, downcast, cheerless, distressed. **2.** hapless. **3.** unpropitious. **4.** inappropriate, inapt.

un·har·ness (un här′nis), *v.t.* **1.** to strip of harness; detach the harness from (a horse, mule, etc.). **2.** to divest of armor, as a knight or warhorse. [1400–50; ME *onharnesen.* See UN-[2], HARNESS]

un·hasp (un hasp′), *v.t.* to loosen the hasp of. [1300–50; ME *unhaspen.* See UN-[2], HASP]

UNHCR, United Nations High Commissioner for Refugees.

un·health·ful (un helth′fəl), *adj.* not conducive to good health; unwholesome: *unhealthful food.* [1570–80; UN-[1] + HEALTHFUL] **—un·health′ful·ness,** *n.*

un·health·y (un hel′thē), *adj.,* **-health·i·er, -health·i·est.** **1.** not in a state of good or normal health; in an unsound, weak, or morbid condition. **2.** symptomatic of or resulting from bad health: *an unhealthy pallor.* **3.** not conducive to good health; unhealthful: *Night air was formerly considered unhealthy.* **4.** morally bad, harmful, or contaminating: *unhealthy examples for the young.* **5.** dangerous; risky: *Asking questions in this neighborhood can be unhealthy.* [1585–95; UN-[1] + HEALTHY] **—un·health′i·ly,** *adv.* **—un·health′i·ness,** *n.*
—Syn. 1. sickly. **3.** unhygienic, deleterious.

un·heard (un hûrd′), *adj.* **1.** not heard; not perceived by the ear. **2.** not given a hearing or audience. **3.** *Archaic.* unheard-of. [1250–1300; ME *unherd.* See UN-[1], HEARD]

un·heard-of (un hûrd′uv′, -ov′, -əv), *adj.* **1.** that was never heard of; unknown: *an unheard-of artist.* **2.** such as was never known before; unprecedented: *an unheard-of salary.* **3.** shocking or outrageous: *unheard-of conduct.* [1585–95]

un·her·ald·ed (un her′əl did), *adj.* **1.** appearing without fanfare, publicity, or advance acclaim: *The young pianist proved to be an unheralded genius.* **2.** appearing without warning or prior announcement; unexpected. [1835–45; UN-[1] + HERALDED]

un·hes·i·tat·ing (un hez′i tā′ting), *adj.* **1.** without hesitation; not delayed by uncertainty: *an unhesitating decision.* **2.** unwavering; unfaltering; steady: *an unhesitating adherence to duty.* [1745–55; UN-[1] + HESITATING] **—un·hes′i·tat′ing·ly,** *adv.*

un·hinge (un hinj′), *v.t.,* **-hinged, -hing·ing.** **1.** to remove (a door or the like) from hinges. **2.** to open wide by or as if by removing supporting hinges: *to unhinge one's jaws.* **3.** to upset; unbalance; disorient; throw into confusion or turmoil: *to unhinge the mind.* **4.** to dislocate or disrupt the normal operation of; unsettle: *to unhinge plans.* **5.** to detach or separate from something. **6.** to cause to waver or vacillate: *to unhinge supporters of conservative policies.* [1605–15; UN-[2] + HINGE] **—un·hinge′ment,** *n.*

un·hinged (un hinjd′), *adj.* **1.** having no hinge or hinges, or with the hinges removed: *an unhinged gate.* **2.** unsettled, disordered, or distraught: *He became unhinged when his friend died.* [1710–20; (def. 1) UN-[1] + HINGED; (def. 2) UNHINGE + -ED[2]]

un·hip (un hip′), *adj. Slang.* ill-informed about or unsympathetic to current fads or trends. [1935–40; UN-[1] + HIP[4]]

un·hitch (un hich′), *v.t.* **1.** to free from attachment; unfasten: *to unhitch a locomotive from a train.* —*v.i.* **2.** to become uncoupled or unfastened. [1615–25; UN-[2] + HITCH]

un·ho·ly (un hō′lē), *adj.,* **-li·er, -li·est.** **1.** not holy; not sacred or hallowed. **2.** impious; sinful; wicked. **3.** *Informal.* dreadful; ungodly: *They got us out of bed at the unholy hour of three in the morning.* [bef. 1000; ME; OE *unhālig* (c. D *onheilig,* ON *ūheilagr*). See UN-[1], HOLY] **—un·ho′li·ness,** *n.*

un·hood (un ho͝od′), *v.t.* **1.** to divest of a hood or covering. **2.** to remove from (a hawk) the hood used to blind it. [1565–75; UN-[2] + HOOD[1]]

un·hook (un ho͝ok′), *v.t.* **1.** to detach by or as if by releasing a hook: *to unhook a tractor from a trailer.* **2.** to unfasten or open by undoing a hook or hooks: *to unhook a door; to unhook a corset.* —*v.i.* **3.** to become unhooked. [1605–15; UN-[2] + HOOK[1]]

un·hoped (un hōpt′), *adj. Archaic.* not expected or anticipated; unhoped-for. [1325–75; ME; see UN-[1], HOPE, -ED[2]]

un·hoped-for (un hōpt′fôr′), *adj.* unexpected; unanticipated: *an unhoped-for piece of good luck.* [1590–1600; from the phrase *hope for;* see UN-[1], -ED[2]]

un·horse (un hôrs′), *v.t.,* **-horsed, -hors·ing.** **1.** to cause to fall from a horse, as in battle; dislodge from the saddle: *Sir Gawain unhorsed the strange knight.* **2.** to defeat; overcome; dislodge, as from a position or office: *His vigorous campaign unhorsed his adversary.* [1350–1400; ME *unhorsen.* See UN-[2], HORSE]

un·house (un houz′), *v.t.,* **-housed, -hous·ing.** to drive from a house or habitation; deprive of shelter. [1325–75; ME *unhousen.* See UN-[2], HOUSE]

un·hou·seled (un hou′zəld), *adj. Archaic.* not having received the Eucharist. [1525–35; UN-[1] + HOUSEL + -ED[2]]

un·hur·ried (un hûr′ēd, -hur′-), *adj.* not hurried; leisurely; deliberate: *an unhurried day; an unhurried decision.* [1760–70; UN-[1] + HURRIED] **—un·hur′ried·ly,** *adv.* **—un·hur′ried·ness,** *n.*

un·husk (un husk′), *v.t.* to free from or as if from a husk. [1590–1600; UN-[2] + HUSK]

u·ni (yo͞o′nē), *n. Australian Informal.* university. [1895–1900; by shortening]

uni-, a combining form occurring in loanwords from Latin (*universe*), used, with the meaning "one," in the formation of compound words (*unicycle*). [< L *ūni-* comb. form of *ūnus* one; see -I-]

u·ni·al·gal (yo͞o′nē al′gəl), *adj.* of, pertaining to, or derived from a single algal cell. [1914; UNI- + ALGAL]

U·ni·ate (yo͞o′nē it, -āt′), *n.* a member of an Eastern church that is in union with the Roman Catholic Church, acknowledges the Roman pope as supreme in matters of faith, but maintains its own liturgy, discipline, and rite. Also, **U·ni·at** (yo͞o′nē at′). [1825–35; < Ukrainian *uni(y)át,* equiv. to *úni(ya)* the Union of Brest-Litovsk (1596), an acceptance of papal supremacy by some Orthodox clerics in Poland (< Pol *uni(j)a* < L *ūniō* UNION) + *-(y)at* << L *-ātus* -ATE[1]] **—U′ni·at·ism,** *n.*

u·ni·ax·i·al (yo͞o′nē ak′sē əl), *adj.* **1.** having one axis. **2.** *Crystall.* (of a crystal) having one direction in which double refraction does not occur. **3.** *Bot.* (of a plant) having a primary stem that does not branch and that terminates in a flower. [1820–30; UNI- + AXIAL] **—u′ni·ax′i·al·ly,** *adv.*

u·ni·cam·er·al (yo͞o′ni kam′ər əl), *adj.* consisting of a single chamber, as a legislative assembly. [1850–55; UNI- + L *camer(a)* CHAMBER + -AL[1]] **—u′ni·cam′er·al·ism,** *n.* **—u′ni·cam′er·al·ly,** *adv.*

UNICEF (yo͞o′nə sef′), *n.* United Nations Children's Fund: an agency, created by the United Nations General Assembly in 1946, concerned with improving the health and nutrition of children and mothers throughout the world; Nobel Peace Prize 1965. [*U(nited) N(ations) I(nternational) C(hildren's) E(mergency) F(und)* (an earlier official name)]

u·ni·cel·lu·lar (yo͞o′nə sel′yə lər), *adj.* having or consisting of a single cell. [1855–60; UNI- + CELLULAR] **—u′ni·cel′lu·lar′i·ty,** *n.*

u·ni·cel·lu·late (yo͞o′nə sel′yə lit, -lāt′), *n.* **1.** a unicellular organism. **2.** a single-celled protist. [< NL *Unicellulata* subkingdom name; see UNI-, CELLULE, -ATA[1]]

u·ni·col·or (yo͞o′ni kul′ər, yo͞o′ni kul′-), *adj.* having only one color. Also, **u′ni·col′ored;** *esp. Brit.,* **u′ni·col′our, u′ni·col′oured.** [1775–85; UNI- + COLOR]

u·ni·corn (yo͞o′ni kôrn′), *n.* **1.** a mythical creature resembling a horse, with a single horn in the center of its forehead: often symbolic of chastity or purity. See illus. on next page. **2.** a heraldic representation of this animal, in the form of a horse with a lion's tail and with a long, straight, and spirally twisted horn. **3.** (*cap.*) *Astron.* the constellation Monoceros. **4.** an animal mentioned in the Bible, Deut. 33:17: now believed by some to be a description of a wild ox or rhinoceros. **5.** a former

CONCISE ETYMOLOGY KEY: <, descended or borrowed from; >, whence; b., blend of, blended; c., cognate with; cf., compare; deriv., derivative; equiv., equivalent; imit., imitative; obl., oblique; r., replacing; s., stem; sp., spelling, spelled; resp., respelling, respelled; trans., translation; ?, origin unknown; *, unattested; ‡, probably earlier than. See the full key inside the front cover.

un·guessed′, *adj.*
un·guid′a·ble, *adj.*
un·guid′ed, *adj.;* **-ly,** *adv.*
un·guile′ful, *adj.*
un·guil′lo·tined′, *adj.*
un·gummed′, *adj.*
un·gush′ing, *adj.*
un·gus′ta·to′ry, *adj.*
un·gut′ted, *adj.*
un·gut′tur·al, *adj.;* **-ly,** *adv.;* **-ness,** *n.*
un·guyed′, *adj.*
un·guz′zled, *adj.*
un′gym·nas′tic, *adj.*
un·gy′rat·ing, *adj.*
un·gyved′, *adj.*
un·hab′it·a·ble, *adj.;* **-ble·ness,** *n.;* **-bly,** *adv.*
un·hab′it·ed, *adj.*
un′ha·bit′u·al, *adj.;* **-ly,** *adv.*
un′ha·bit′u·at′ed, *adj.*
un·hacked′, *adj.*
un·hack′led, *adj.*
un·hack′neyed, *adj.*
un·haft′, *v.t.*
un·hag′gled, *adj.*
un·hag′gling, *adj.*
un·hail′a·ble, *adj.*
un·hailed′, *adj.*
un·hair′i·ness, *n.*
un·hair′y, *adj.*
un·hale′, *adj.*
un′hal·lu′ci·nat′ed, *adj.*
un′hal·lu′ci·nat′ing, *adj.*
un′hal·lu′ci·na·to′ry, *adj.*
un·ha′loed, *adj.*
un·halt′ed, *adj.*
un·hal′tered, *adj.*
un·hal′ter·ing, *adj.*
un·halt′ing, *adj.;* **-ly,** *adv.*
un·halved′, *adj.*
un·ham′mered, *adj.*
un·ham′pered, *adj.*
un·ham′per·ing, *adj.*
un·hand·cuff′, *v.t.*
un·hand′i·capped′, *adj.*
un·hand′seled, *adj.*
un·hand′selled, *adj.*
un·hanged′, *adj.*
un·hang′ing, *adj.*
un·hanked′, *adj.*
un′ha·rangued′, *adj.*
un·ha·rassed′, *adj.*
un·har′bored, *adj.*
un·hard′en, *v.t.*
un·hard′en·a·ble, *adj.*
un·hard′ened, *adj.*
un·harked′, *adj.*
un·harm′a·ble, *adj.*
un·harmed′, *adj.*
un·harm′ful, *adj.;* **-ly,** *adv.*
un·harm′ing, *adj.*
un′har·mon′ic, *adj.*
un′har·mon′i·cal·ly, *adv.*
un′har·mo′ni·ous, *adj.;* **-ly,** *adv.*
un·har′mo·nize′, *v.t.,* **-nized, -niz·ing.**
un·harped′, *adj.*
un·harp′ing, *adj.*
un·har′ried, *adj.*
un·har′rowed, *adj.*
un·harsh′, *adj.;* **-ly,** *adv.*
un·har′vest·ed, *adj.*
un·hashed′, *adj.*
un·has′sled, *adj.*
un·hast′ed, *adj.*
un·has′tened, *adj.*
un·hast′i·ly, *adv.*
un·hast′ing, *adj.*
un·hast′y, *adj.*
un′hatch·a·bil′i·ty, *n.*
un·hatch′a·ble, *adj.*
un·hatched′, *adj.*
un·hat′ed, *adj.*
un·hate′ful, *adj.*
un·hat′ing, *adj.;* **-ly,** *adv.*
un·hauled′, *adj.*
un·haunt′ed, *adj.*
un·hawked′, *adj.*
un·hayed′, *adj.*
un·haz′ard·ed, *adj.*
un·haz′ard·ing, *adj.*
un·haz′ard·ous, *adj.;* **-ly,** *adv.*
un·hazed′, *adj.*
un·ha′zi·ly, *adv.*
un·ha′zi·ness, *n.*
un·ha′zy, *adj.*
un·head′ed, *adj.*
un·head′y, *adj.*
un·heal′a·ble, *adj.*
un·healed′, *adj.*
un·heal′ing, *adj.*
un·heaped′, *adj.*
un·hear′a·ble, *adj.*
un·hear′ing, *adj.*
un·heart′i·ly, *adv.*
un·heart′y, *adj.*
un·heat′a·ble, *adj.*
un·heat′ed, *adj.*
un·hea′then, *adj.*
un·heaved′, *adj.*
un·heav′en·ly, *adj.*
un·heav′i·ly, *adv.*
un·heav′i·ness, *n.*
un·heav′y, *adj.*
un·hec′tic, *adj.*
un·hec′ti·cal·ly, *adv.*
un·hec′tored, *adj.*
un·hedge′, *v.t.,* **-hedged, -hedg·ing.**
un·hedged′, *adj.*
un′he·do·nis′tic, *adj.*
un′he·do·nis′ti·cal·ly, *adv.*
un·heed′ed, *adj.;* **-ly,** *adv.*
un·heed′ful, *adj.;* **-ly,** *adv.;* **-ness,** *n.*
un·heed′ing, *adj.;* **-ly,** *adv.*
un·heeled′, *adj.*
un·heft′ed, *adj.*
un·height′ened, *adj.*
un·held′, *adj.*
un·hel′met·ed, *adj.*
un·help′a·ble, *adj.*
un·helped′, *adj.*
un·help′ful, *adj.;* **-ly,** *adv.*
un·help′ing, *adj.*
un·helved′, *adj.*
un·hemmed′, *adj.*
un′he·ral′dic, *adj.*
un′her·ba′ceous, *adj.*
un·herd′ed, *adj.*
un·her′it·a·ble, *adj.*
un′her·met′ic, *adj.*
un′her·mit′ic, *adj.*
un′her·mit′i·cal, *adj.;* **-ly,** *adv.*
un′he′ro, *n., pl.* **-roes.**
un′he·ro′ic, *adj.;* **-ness,** *n.*
un′he·ro′i·cal, *adj.;* **-ly,** *adv.;* **-ness,** *n.*
un·he′ro·like′, *adj.*
un·hes′i·tant, *adj.;* **-ly,** *adv.*
un·hes′i·ta′tive, *adj.;* **-ly,** *adv.*
un′heu·ris′tic, *adj.*
un′heu·ris′ti·cal·ly, *adv.*
un·hew′a·ble, *adj.*
un·hewed′, *adj.*
un·hewn′, *adj.*
un·hid′, *adj.*
un·hid′den, *adj.*
un·hid′e·ous, *adj.;* **-ly,** *adv.;* **-ness,** *n.*
un′hi·er·at′ic, *adj.*
un′hi·er·at′i·cal, *adj.;* **-ly,** *adv.*
un′hi·lar′i·ous, *adj.;* **-ly,** *adv.;* **-ness,** *n.*
un·hill′y, *adj.*
un·hin′der·a·ble, *adj.;* **-bly,** *adv.*
un·hin′dered, *adj.*
un·hin′der·ing, *adj.;* **-ly,** *adv.*
un·hint′ed, *adj.*
un·hipped′, *adj.*
un·hir′a·ble, *adj.*
un·hire′a·ble, *adj.*
un·hired′, *adj.*
un·hissed′, *adj.*
un′his·tor′ic, *adj.*
un′his·tor′i·cal, *adj.;* **-ly,** *adv.*
un·his′to·ried, *adj.*
un·his′to·ry, *n., pl.* **-ries.**
un′his·tri·on′ic, *adj.*
un·hit′, *adj.*
un·hit′ta·ble, *adj.*
un·hoard′ed, *adj.*
un·hoard′ing, *adj.*
un·hoar′y, *adj.*
un·hoaxed′, *adj.*
un·hob′bled, *adj.*
un·hob′bling, *adj.*
un·hocked′, *adj.*
un·hoed′, *adj.*
un·hogged′, *adj.*
un·hoist′ed, *adj.*
un·hol′low, *adj.*
un·hol′lowed, *adj.*
un·home′li·ness, *n.*
un·home′ly, *adj.*
un′hom·i·cid′al, *adj.*
un′hom·i·let′ic, *adj.*
un′hom·i·let′i·cal, *adj.;* **-ly,** *adv.*
un′ho·mo·ge′ne·ous, *adj.;* **-ly,** *adv.;* **-ness,** *n.*
un′ho·mog′e·nized′, *adj.*
un′ho·mo·log′ic, *adj.*
un′ho·mo·log′i·cal, *adj.;* **-ly,** *adv.*
un′ho·mol′o·gized′, *adj.*
un′ho·mol′o·gous, *adj.*
un·honed′, *adj.*
un·hon′eyed, *adj.*
un·hon′ied, *adj.*
un·hon′ored, *adj.*
un·hood′winked′, *adj.*
un·hoofed′, *adj.*
un·hooped′, *adj.*
un·hoot′ed, *adj.*
un·hope′ful, *adj.;* **-ly,** *adv.*
un·hop′ing, *adj.;* **-ly,** *adv.*
un′ho·ri′zoned, *adj.*
un′hor·i·zon′tal, *adj.;* **-ly,** *adv.*
un·horned′, *adj.*
un′hor·o·scop′ic, *adj.*
un·hor′ri·fied′, *adj.*
un·hor′ta·tive, *adj.;* **-ly,** *adv.*
un·hosed′, *adj.*
un·hos′pi·tal·ized′, *adj.*
un·hos′tile, *adj.;* **-ly,** *adv.*
un·hot′, *adj.*
un·hound′ed, *adj.*
un·house′wife′ly, *adj.*
un′hu·bris′tic, *adj.*
un·hud′dle, *v.t.,* **-dled, -dling.**
un·hued′, *adj.*
un·hugged′, *adj.*
un·hull′, *v.t.*
un·hu′man, *adj.;* **-ly,** *adv.;* **-ness,** *n.*
un′hu·mane′, *adj.;* **-ly,** *adv.;* **-ness,** *n.*
un′hu·man·is′tic, *adj.*
un′hu·man′i·tar′i·an, *adj.*
un·hu′man·ize′, *v.t.,* **-ized, -iz·ing.**
un·hum′ble, *adj.;* **-ble·ness,** *n.;* **-bly,** *adv.*
un·hum′bled, *adj.*
un·hu′mid, *adj.*
un′hu·mid′i·fied′, *adj.*
un′hu·mid′i·fy′ing, *adj.*
un′hu·mil′i·at′ed, *adj.*
un′hu·mil′i·at′ing, *adj.;* **-ly,** *adv.*
un·hu′mored, *adj.*
un·hu′mor·ous, *adj.;* **-ly,** *adv.*
un·hung′, *adj.*
un·hunt′a·ble, *adj.*
un·hunt′ed, *adj.*
un·hur′dled, *adj.*
un·hurled′, *adj.*
un·hur′ry·ing, *adj.;* **-ly,** *adv.*
un·hurt′, *adj.*
un·hurt′ful, *adj.;* **-ly,** *adv.*
un·hurt′ing, *adj.*
un·hus′band·ed, *adj.*
un·hush′a·ble, *adj.*
un·hush′ing, *adj.*
un·husk′a·ble, *adj.*
un·husked′, *adj.*
un·hus′tled, *adj.*
un·hus′tling, *adj.*
un·hutched′, *adj.*
un′huz·zahed′, *adj.*

gold coin of Scotland, first issued by James III in 1486, having an obverse bearing the figure of a unicorn. [1175–1225; ME *unicorne* (< OF) < L *ūnicornis* one-horned, equiv. to *uni-* UNI- + *corn(ū)* HORN + *-is* adj. suffix]

unicorn (def. 1)

u′nicorn plant′, a North American plant, *Proboscidea (Martynia) louisianica,* having creamy-white to red flowers blotched with purple, and a woody capsule with a long, curved beak. [1790–1800]

u•ni•cos•tate (yo͞o′ni kos′tāt, -kô′stāt), *adj.* **1.** having only one costa, rib, or ridge. **2.** *Bot.* (of a leaf) having only one primary or prominent rib, the midrib. [1840–50; UNI- + COSTATE]

u•ni•cus•pid (yo͞o′ni kus′pid), *adj.* having but one cusp. [UNI- + CUSPID]

u•ni•cy•cle (yo͞o′nə sī′kəl), *n., v.,* **-cled, -cling.** —*n.* **1.** a vehicle with one wheel, esp. a pedal-driven device kept upright and steered by body balance, commonly used by acrobats and other performers. —*v.i.* **2.** to ride a unicycle. [1865–70, *Amer.*; UNI- + CYCLE] —**u′ni•cy′clist,** *n.*

uniden′tified fly′ing ob′ject. See **UFO.**

u•ni•di•men•sion•al (yo͞o′ni di men′shə nl, -dī-), *adj.* one-dimensional. [1880–85; UNI- + DIMENSIONAL]

u•ni•di•rec•tion•al (yo͞o′ni di rek′shə nl, -dī-), *adj.* operating or moving in one direction only; not changing direction: *a unidirectional flow.* [1880–85; UNI- + DIRECTIONAL]

u•ni•face (yo͞o′nə fās′), *n. Numis.* a coin or medal having a blank reverse. [1875–80; UNI- + FACE]

u•ni•fac•to•ri•al (yo͞o′nə fak tôr′ē əl, -tōr′-), *adj. Genetics.* **1.** of or pertaining to a single gene. **2.** of a phenotypic character controlled by a single gene. [1930–35; UNI- + FACTOR + -IAL]

u•ni•fi•a•ble (yo͞o′nə fī′ə bəl), *adj.* capable of being unified. [UNIFY + -ABLE]

u•nif•ic (yo͞o nif′ik), *adj.* unifying; uniting: *the unific influence of a common language.* [1780–90; UNI- + -FIC]

u•ni•fi•ca•tion (yo͞o′nə fi kā′shən), *n.* **1.** the process of unifying or uniting; union: *the unification of the 13 original colonies.* **2.** the state or condition of being unified: *The unification of the manufacturing and distribution functions under one executive has advantages.* [1850–55; UNI(FY) + -FICATION]
—**Syn. 1, 2.** consolidation, merger, coalition.

U′nifica′tion Church′, a religious sect that combines elements of Protestantism and Buddhism, founded by the Rev. Sun Myung Moon in 1954: many of its members live in communes sponsored by the sect.

u′nified field′ the′ory, *Physics.* **1.** See **electroweak theory. 2.** any field theory, esp. Einstein's, that attempts to combine the gravitational and electromagnetic fields in a single mathematical framework, thus extending the general theory of relativity.

u•ni•fi•lar (yo͞o′nə fī′lər), *adj.* having or involving only one thread, wire, or the like. [1855–60; UNI- + FILAR]

u•ni•flag•el•late (yo͞o′nə flaj′ə lit, -lāt′), *adj.* having only one flagellum. [1880–85; UNI- + FLAGELLATE]

u•ni•flor•ous (yo͞o′nə flôr′əs, -flōr′-), *adj. Bot.* having only one flower. [1750–60; UNI- + -FLOROUS]

u′ni•flow en′gine (yo͞o′nə flō′), a double-acting steam engine exhausting from the middle of each cylinder at each stroke so that the motion of the steam from admission to exhaust is continuous in one direction. [UNI- + FLOW]

u•ni•fo•li•ate (yo͞o′nə fō′lē it, -āt′), *adj.* **1.** having only one leaf. **2.** unifoliolate. [1840–50; UNI- + FOLIATE]

unifoliolate leaf

u•ni•fo•li•o•late (yo͞o′nə fō′lē ə lāt′), *adj. Bot.* **1.** compound in structure yet having only one leaflet, as the orange. **2.** bearing such leaves. [1865–70; UNI- + FOLIOLATE]

u•ni•form (yo͞o′nə fôrm′), *adj.* **1.** identical or consistent, as from example to example, place to place, or moment to moment: *uniform spelling; a uniform building code.* **2.** without variations in detail: *uniform output; a uniform surface.* **3.** constant; unvarying; undeviating: *uniform kindness; uniform velocity.* **4.** constituting part of a uniform: *to be issued uniform shoes.* **5.** *Math.* occurring in a manner independent of some variable, parameter, function, etc.: *a uniform bound.* —*n.* **6.** an identifying outfit or style of dress worn by the members of a given profession, organization, or rank. **7.** a word used in communications to represent the letter *U.* —*v.t.* **8.** to make uniform or standard. **9.** to clothe in or furnish with a uniform. [1530–40; < L *ūnifōrmis* (adj.), equiv. to *ūni-* UNI- + *-fōrmis* -FORM] —**u′ni•form′ly,** *adv.* —**u′ni•form′ness,** *n.*

U′niform Code′ of Mil′itary Jus′tice, the body of laws and legal procedures of the armed forces: replaced the Articles of War in 1951.

U′niform Crime′ Report′, an annual report issued by the FBI that presents data on selected categories of crimes reported to the police. *Abbr.:* UCR

u•ni•formed (yo͞o′nə fôrmd′), *adj.* wearing a uniform. [1805–15; UNIFORM + -ED[3]]

u•ni•form•i•tar•i•an (yo͞o′nə fôr′mi târ′ē ən), *adj.* **1.** supporting, conforming to, or derived from a theory or doctrine about uniformity, esp. on the subject of geology. **2.** *Geol.* of or pertaining to the thesis that processes that operated in the remote geological past are not different from those observed now. —*n.* **3.** a person who accepts or supports a uniformitarian theory. [1830–40; UNIFORMIT(Y) + -ARIAN] —**u′ni•form′i•tar′i•an•ism,** *n.*

u•ni•form•i•ty (yo͞o′nə fôr′mi tē), *n., pl.* **-ties. 1.** the state or quality of being uniform; overall sameness, homogeneity, or regularity: *uniformity of style.* **2.** something uniform. [1400–50; late ME *uniformite* < MF *uniformite* < LL *ūnifōrmitās,* equiv. to L *ūnifōrm(is)* UNIFORM + *-itās* -ITY]

Uniform′ity Act′, *Eng. Hist.* See **Act of Uniformity.**

u•ni•form•ize (yo͞o′nə fôr mīz′), *v.t.,* **-ized, -iz•ing.** to bring into uniformity. Also, *esp. Brit.,* **u′ni•form•ise′.** [1865–70; < F *uniformiser.* See UNIFORM, -IZE] —**u′ni•form′i•za′tion,** *n.*

u•ni•fy (yo͞o′nə fī′), *v.t., v.i.,* **-fied, -fy•ing.** to make or become a single unit; unite: *to unify conflicting theories; to unify a country.* [1495–1505; < LL *ūnificāre,* equiv. to L *ūni-* UNI- + *-ficāre* -FY] —**u′ni•fi′er,** *n.*
—**Syn.** combine, merge, fuse, coalesce.

u•nij•u•gate (yo͞o nij′ə gāt′, yo͞o′ni jo͞o′git, -gāt), *adj. Bot.* (of a pinnate leaf) having only a single pair of leaflets. [1840–50; < L *ūnijug(us)* having one yoke (equiv. to *ūni-* UNI- + *jug(um)* YOKE[1] + *-us* adj. suffix) + -ATE[1]]

unijugate leaf

u•ni•lat•er•al (yo͞o′nə lat′ər əl), *adj.* **1.** relating to, occurring on, or involving one side only: *unilateral development; a unilateral approach.* **2.** undertaken or done by or on behalf of one side, party, or faction only; not

CONCISE PRONUNCIATION KEY: act, cāpe, dâre, pärt; set, ēqual; if, īce; ox, ōver, ôrder, oil, bo͝ok, bo͞ot, out; up, ûrge; child; sing; shoe; thin, *th*at; zh as in *treasure.* ə = a as in *alone,* e as in *system,* i as in *easily,* o as in *gallop,* u as in *circus;* ᵊ as in *fire* (fīᵊr), *hour* (ouᵊr). l and n can serve as syllabic consonants, as in *cradle* (krād′l), and *button* (but′n). See the full key inside the front cover.

un′hy′drat•ed, *adj.*
un′hy•drau′lic, *adj.*
un′hy′dro•lyzed′, *adj.*
un′hy•gi•en′ic, *adj.*
un′hy•gi•en′i•cal•ly, *adv.*
un′hy•gro•met′ric, *adj.*
un′hy•me•ne′al, *adj.*
un•hymned′, *adj.*
un•hy′phen•a•ble, *adj.*
un•hy′phen•at′ed, *adj.*
un•hy′phened, *adj.*
un′hyp•not′ic, *adj.*
un′hyp•not′i•cal•ly, *adv.*
un•hyp′no•tiz′a•ble, *adj.*
un•hyp′no•tize′, *v.t.,* **-tized, -tiz•ing.**
un′hyp•o•crit′i•cal, *adj.;* **-ly,** *adv.*
un′hy•poth′e•cat′ed, *adj.*
un′hy•po•thet′i•cal, *adj.;* **-ly,** *adv.*
un′hys•ter′i•cal, *adj.;* **-ly,** *adv.*
un′i•am′bic, *adj.*
un•ice′, *v.t.,* **-iced, -ic•ing.**
un•iced′, *adj.*
un′i•con′o•clas′tic, *adj.*
un′i•con′o•clas′ti•cal•ly, *adv.*
un′i•de′al, *adj.*
un′i•de′al•is′tic, *adj.*
un′i•de′al•is′ti•cal•ly, *adv.*
un′i•de′al•ized′, *adj.*
un•i′de•at′ed, *adj.*
un•i′de•at′ing, *adj.*
un′i•de•a′tion•al, *adj.*
un′i•den′ti•cal, *adj.;* **-ly,** *adv.*
un′i•den′ti•fi′a•ble, *adj.;* **-bly,** *adv.*
un′i•den′ti•fied′, *adj.*
un′i•den′ti•fy′ing, *adj.*
un′id•e•o•graph′ic, *adj.*
un′id•e•o•graph′i•cal, *adj.;* **-ly,** *adv.*
un′id•e•o•log′i•cal, *adj.*
un′id•i•o•mat′ic, *adj.*
un′id•i•o•mat′i•cal•ly, *adv.*
un•i′dle, *adj.*
un•i′dling, *adj.*
un•i′dly, *adv.*
un′i•dol′a•trous, *adj.*
un•i′dol•ized′, *adj.*
un′i•dyl′lic, *adj.*
un′ig•nit′a•ble, *adj.*
un′ig•nit′ed, *adj.*
un′ig•nit′ing, *adj.*
un′ig•no•min′i•ous, *adj.;* **-ly,** *adv.;* **-ness,** *n.*
un′ig•nor′a•ble, *adj.;* **-bly,** *adv.*
un•ig′no•rant, *adj.;* **-ly,** *adv.*
un′ig•nored′, *adj.*
un′ig•nor′ing, *adj.*
un′il•lumed′, *adj.*
un′il•lu′mi•nant, *adj.*
un′il•lu′mi•nat′ed, *adj.*
un′il•lu′mi•nat′ing, *adj.*
un′il•lu′mi•na′tive, *adj.*
un′il•lu′sive, *adj.*
un′il•lu′so•ry, *adj.*
un•il′lus•trat′ed, *adj.*
un′il•lus′tra•tive, *adj.*
un′il•lus′tri•ous, *adj.;* **-ly,** *adv.;* **-ness,** *n.*
un•im′aged, *adj.*
un′im•ag′i•na•ble, *adj.;* **-ble•ness,** *n.;* **-bly,** *adv.*
un′im•ag′i•nar′y, *adj.*
un′im•ag′i•na•tive, *adj.;* **-ly,** *adv.*
un′im•ag′ined, *adj.*
un′im•bibed′, *adj.*
un′im•bib′ing, *adj.*
un′im•bued′, *adj.*
un•im′i•ta•ble, *adj.*
un•im′i•tat′ed, *adj.*
un•im′i•tat′ing, *adj.*
un•im′i•ta′tive, *adj.*
un′im•mac′u•late, *adj.;* **-ly,** *adv.;* **-ness,** *n.*
un•im′ma•nent, *adj.;* **-ly,** *adv.*
un′im•me′di•ate, *adj.;* **-ly,** *adv.;* **-ness,** *n.*
un′im•merged′, *adj.*
un′im•mersed′, *adj.*
un•im′mi•grat′ing, *adj.*
un•im′mi•nent, *adj.*
un•im′mo•lat′ed, *adj.*
un•im′mu•nized′, *adj.*
un′im•mured′, *adj.*
un′im•pact′ed, *adj.*
un′im•pair′a•ble, *adj.*
un′im•paired′, *adj.*
un′im•pan′eled, *adj.*
un′im•pan′elled, *adj.*
un′im•part′ed, *adj.*
un′im•par′tial, *adj.;* **-ly,** *adv.*
un′im•part′i•ble, *adj.*
un′im•pas′sion•ate, *adj.;* **-ly,** *adv.*
un′im•pas′sioned, *adj.*
un′im•pas′sioned•ly, *adv.*
un•im•pa′tient, *adj.;* **-ly,** *adv.*
un′im•pawned′, *adj.*
un′im•peached′, *adj.*
un′im•pearled′, *adj.*
un′im•ped′ed, *adj.*
un′im•ped′ing, *adj.;* **-ly,** *adv.*
un′im•pelled′, *adj.*
un′im•per′a•tive, *adj.;* **-ly,** *adv.*
un′im•pe′ri•al, *adj.;* **-ly,** *adv.*
un′im•pe′ri•al•is′tic, *adj.*
un′im•pe′ri•ous, *adj.;* **-ly,** *adv.*
un′im•per′ti•nent, *adj.;* **-ly,** *adv.*
un′im•ping′ing, *adj.*
un′im•plant′ed, *adj.*
un•im′pli•cat′ed, *adj.*
un′im•plic′it•ly, *adv.*
un′im•plied′, *adj.*
un′im•plor′a•ble, *adj.*
un′im•plored′, *adj.*
un′im•por′tance, *n.*
un′im•por′tant, *adj.;* **-ly,** *adv.*
un′im•port′ed, *adj.*
un′im•port′ing, *adj.*
un′im•por′tu•nate, *adj.;* **-ly,** *adv.;* **-ness,** *n.*
un′im•por•tuned′, *adj.*
un′im•posed′, *adj.*
un′im•pound′ed, *adj.*
un′im•pov′er•ished, *adj.*
un•im′pre•cat′ed, *adj.*
un′im•preg′nat•ed, *adj.*
un′im•pressed′, *adj.*
un′im•press′i•bil′i•ty, *n.*
un′im•press′i•ble, *adj.*
un′im•pres′sion•a•ble, *adj.*
un′im•pres′sive, *adj.;* **-ly,** *adv.*
un′im•print′ed, *adj.*
un′im•pris′on•a•ble, *adj.*
un′im•pris′oned, *adj.*
un′im•pro′pri•at′ed, *adj.*
un•im′pro•vised′, *adj.*
un′im•pugn′a•ble, *adj.*
un′im•pugned′, *adj.*
un′im•pul′sive, *adj.;* **-ly,** *adv.*
un′im•put′a•ble, *adj.*
un′im•put′ed, *adj.*
un′in•au′gu•rat′ed, *adj.*
un′in•car′cer•at′ed, *adj.*
un′in•car′nate, *adj.*
un′in•car′nat•ed, *adj.*
un′in•censed′, *adj.*
un′in•cep′tive, *adj.;* **-ly,** *adv.*
un′in•ces′tu•ous, *adj.;* **-ly,** *adv.*
un′in•cho′a•tive, *adj.*
un′in•ci•den′tal, *adj.;* **-ly,** *adv.*
un′in•cin′er•at′ed, *adj.*
un′in•cised′, *adj.*
un′in•ci′sive, *adj.;* **-ly,** *adv.;* **-ness,** *n.*
un′in•cit′ed, *adj.*
un′in•clin′a•ble, *adj.*
un′in•clined′, *adj.*
un′in•clin′ing, *adj.*
un′in•closed′, *adj.*
un′in•clud′a•ble, *adj.*
un′in•clud′ed, *adj.*
un′in•clud′i•ble, *adj.*
un′in•clu′sive, *adj.*
un′in•con•ven′ienced, *adj.*
un′in•creas′a•ble, *adj.*
un′in•creased′, *adj.*
un′in•creas′ing, *adj.*
un′in•crim′i•nat′ed, *adj.*
un′in•crim′i•nat′ing, *adj.*
un•in′cu•bat′ed, *adj.*
un′in•cum′bered, *adj.*
un′in•dem′ni•fied′, *adj.*
un′in•den′tured, *adj.*
un•in′dexed, *adj.*
un•in′di•cat′ed, *adj.*
un′in•dic′a•tive, *adj.;* **-ly,** *adv.*
un′in•dict′a•ble, *adj.*
un′in•dict′ed, *adj.*
un′in•dig′e•nous, *adj.;* **-ly,** *adv.*
un′in•dig′nant, *adj.*
un′in•di•vid′u•al•ized′, *adj.*
un′in•di•vid′u•at′ed, *adj.*
un′in•doc′tri•nat′ed, *adj.*
un′in•dorsed′, *adj.*
un′in•duced′, *adj.*
un′in•duc′i•ble, *adj.*
un′in•duct′ed, *adj.*
un′in•duc′tive, *adj.*
un′in•dulged′, *adj.*
un′in•dul′gent, *adj.;* **-ly,** *adv.*
un′in•dulg′ing, *adj.*
un•in′du•rate, *adj.*
un•in′du•ra′tive, *adj.*
un′in•dus′tri•al, *adj.*
un′in•dus′tri•al•ized′, *adj.*
un′in•dus′tri•ous, *adj.;* **-ly,** *adv.*
un′in•e′bri•at′ed, *adj.*
un′in•e′bri•at′ing, *adj.*
un′in•ert′, *adj.;* **-ly,** *adv.*
un′in•fat′u•at′ed, *adj.*
un′in•fect′a•ble, *adj.*
un′in•fect′ed, *adj.*
un′in•fec′tious, *adj.;* **-ly,** *adv.;* **-ness,** *n.*
un′in•fec′tive, *adj.*
un′in•fer′a•ble, *adj.;* **-bly,** *adv.*
un′in•fer•en′tial, *adj.;* **-ly,** *adv.*
un′in•ferred′, *adj.*
un′in•fer′ri•ble, *adj.;* **-bly,** *adv.*
un′in•fest′ed, *adj.*
un′in•fil′trat•ed, *adj.*
un•in′fi•nite, *adj.;* **-ly,** *adv.;* **-ness,** *n.*
un′in•fixed′, *adj.*
un′in•flamed′, *adj.*
un′in•flam′ma•bil′i•ty, *n.*
un′in•flam′ma•ble, *adj.*
un′in•flat′ed, *adj.*
un′in•flect′ed, *adj.*
un′in•flec′tive, *adj.*
un′in•flict′ed, *adj.*
un•in′flu•enced, *adj.*
un•in′flu•enc•ing, *adj.*
un′in•flu•en′tial, *adj.;* **-ly,** *adv.*
un′in•fold′ed, *adj.*
un′in•form′a•tive, *adj.;* **-ly,** *adv.*
un′in•formed′, *adj.*
un′in•form′ing, *adj.*
un′in•fract′ed, *adj.*
un′in•fringed′, *adj.*
un′in•fu′ri•at′ed, *adj.*
un′in•fused′, *adj.*
un′in•fus′ing, *adj.*
un′in•fu′sive, *adj.*
un′in•gest′ed, *adj.*
un′in•ges′tive, *adj.*
un′in•graft′ed, *adj.*
un′in•grained′, *adj.*
un′in•gra′ti•at′ing, *adj.*
un′in•hab′it•a•bil′i•ty, *n.*
un′in•hab′it•a•ble, *adj.*
un′in•hab′it•ed, *adj.*
un′in•hal′a•ble, *adj.*
un′in•haled′, *adj.*
un′in•her′ent, *adj.;* **-ly,** *adv.*
un′in•her′it•a•bil′i•ty, *n.*
un′in•her′it•a•ble, *adj.*
un′in•her′it•ed, *adj.*
un′in•hib′it•ing, *adj.*
un′in•humed′, *adj.*
un′in•im′i•cal, *adj.;* **-ly,** *adv.*
un′in•iq′ui•tous, *adj.;* **-ly,** *adv.;* **-ness,** *n.*
un′in•i′tialed, *adj.*
un′in•i′tialled, *adj.*
un′in•i′ti•ate, *adj.*

mutual: *a unilateral decision; unilateral disarmament.* **3.** having only one side or surface; without a reverse side or inside, as a Möbius strip. **4.** *Law.* **a.** pertaining to a contract that can be formed only when the party to whom an offer is made renders the performance for which the offeror bargains. **b.** pertaining to a contract in which obligation rests on only one party, as a binding promise to make a gift. **5.** *Bot.* having all the parts disposed on one side of an axis, as an inflorescence. **6.** through forebears of one sex only, as through either the mother's or father's line. Cf. **bilateral** (def. 5). **7.** *Phonet.* (of an *l*-sound) characterized by passage of air on only one side of the tongue. [1795–1805; < NL *ūnilaterālis.* See UNI-, LATERAL] **—u′ni·lat′er·al′i·ty,** *n.* **—u′ni·lat′er·al·ly,** *adv.*

u·ni·lat·er·al·ism (yo͞o′nə lat′ər ə liz′əm), *n.* the advocacy or pursuit of a unilateral policy, esp. in disarmament. [1925–30; UNILATERAL + -ISM] **—u′ni·lat′er·al·ist,** *n., adj.*

u·ni·lin·e·al (yo͞o′nə lin′ē əl), *adj.* unilateral (def. 6). [1950–55; UNI- + LINEAL]

u·ni·lin·e·ar (yo͞o′nə lin′ē ər), *adj.* developing or evolving in a steady, consistent, and undeviating way. [1925–30; UNI- + LINEAR]

u·ni·lin·gual (yo͞o′nə ling′gwəl *or, Can.,* -ling′gyo͞o əl), *adj.* using only one language: *a unilingual book.* [1865–70; UNI- + LINGUAL] **—u′ni·lin′gual·ism,** *n.*

un·il·lu·sioned (un′i lo͞o′zhənd), *adj.* having or manifesting no illusions; free from illusions: *to be unillusioned about one's chances for success.* [1925–30; UN-[1] + ILLUSION + -ED[3]]

u·ni·lobed (yo͞o′nə lōbd′), *adj.* having or consisting of a single lobe, esp. of the maxilla of an insect. [1850–55; UNI- + LOBED]

u·ni·loc·u·lar (yo͞o′nə lok′yə lər), *adj. Biol.* having or consisting of only one loculus, chamber, or cell. [1745–55; UNI- + LOCULAR]

u·ni·mod·al (yo͞o′nə mōd′l), *adj. Statistics.* (of a distribution) having a single mode. [1920–25; UNI- + MODAL]

u·ni·mod·u·lar (yo͞o′nə moj′ə lər), *adj. Math.* (of a matrix) having its determinant equal to 1. [1865–70; UNI- + MODULAR]

un·im·peach·a·ble (un′im pē′chə bəl), *adj.* above suspicion; impossible to discredit; impeccable: *unimpeachable motives.* [1775–85; UN-[1] + IMPEACHABLE] **—un′im·peach′a·bil′i·ty, un′im·peach′a·ble·ness,** *n.* **—un′im·peach′a·bly,** *adv.*

un·im·pos·ing (un′im pō′zing), *adj.* not imposing; unimpressive: *an unimposing spectacle; a man of unimposing stature.* [1730–40; UN-[1] + IMPOSING]

CONCISE ETYMOLOGY KEY: <, descended or borrowed from; >, whence; b., blend of, blended; c., cognate with; cf., compare; deriv., derivative; equiv., equivalent; imit., imitative; obl., oblique; r., replacing; s., stem; sp., spelling, spelled; resp., respelling, respelled; trans., translation; ?, origin unknown; *, unattested; ‡, probably earlier than. See the full key inside the front cover.

un·im·proved (un′im pro͞ovd′), *adj.* **1.** not developed to full potential, as resources or the mind. **2.** not showing improvement, as one's health, appearance, etc. **3.** (of land) not fitted for a profitable use, as by clearing, cultivation, addition of facilities for dwelling or business purposes, or the like. **4.** not used to advantage; neglected: *an unimproved opportunity.* **5.** (of animal or plant species) not made more useful or attractive by selective breeding or cultivation. **6.** not enhanced; not increased: *Our chance of success is unimproved.* [1655–65; UN-[1] + IMPROVED]

un·in·cor·po·rat·ed (un′in kôr′pə rā′tid), *adj.* **1.** not chartered as a corporation; lacking the powers and immunities of a corporate enterprise: *an unincorporated business.* **2.** not chartered as a self-governing village or city; lacking the tax, police, and other powers conferred by the state on incorporated towns: *an unincorporated hamlet.* **3.** not combined into a single body or unit; not made part of; not included: *Many unincorporated research notes are appended to the text of the book.* [1705–15; UN-[1] + INCORPORATED]

un·in·hib·it·ed (un′in hib′i tid), *adj.* **1.** not inhibited or restricted: *uninhibited freedom to act.* **2.** not restrained by social convention or usage; unconstrained: *an uninhibited discussion of the causes of divorce.* [1905–10; UN-[1] + INHIBIT + -ED[2]] **—un′in·hib′it·ed·ly,** *adv.* **—un′in·hib′it·ed·ness,** *n.*

un·in·spired (un′in spīərd′), *adj.* not inspired; not creative or spirited: *an uninspired performance; an uninspired teacher.* [1680–90; UN-[1] + INSPIRED]

un·in·struct·ed (un′in struk′tid), *adj.* **1.** not instructed; uninformed; uneducated. **2.** (of a person acting in a representative capacity) not furnished with orders on how to proceed or vote; uncommitted: *uninstructed convention delegates.* [1590–1600; UN-[1] + INSTRUCT + -ED[2]] **—un′in·struct′ed·ly,** *adv.*

un·in·tel·li·gent (un′in tel′i jənt), *adj.* **1.** deficient in intelligence; dull; stupid. **2.** not endowed with intelligence. [1600–10; UN-[1] + INTELLIGENT] **—un′in·tel′li·gence,** *n.* **—un′in·tel′li·gent·ly,** *adv.*

un·in·tel·li·gi·ble (un′in tel′i jə bəl), *adj.* not intelligible; not capable of being understood. [1610–20; UN-[1] + INTELLIGIBLE] **—un′in·tel′li·gi·bil′i·ty, un′in·tel′li·gi·ble·ness,** *n.* **—un′in·tel′li·gi·bly,** *adv.*
—Syn. incomprehensible, baffling, undecipherable.

un·in·ten·tion·al (un′in ten′shə nl), *adj.* not intentional or deliberate: *an unintentional omission from the list.* [1775–85; UN-[1] + INTENTIONAL] **—un′in·ten′tion·al·ly,** *adv.*
—Syn. accidental, unplanned, inadvertent.

un·in·ter·est·ed (un in′tər ə stid, -trə stid, -tə res′tid), *adj.* **1.** having or showing no feeling of interest; indifferent. **2.** not personally concerned in something. [1640–50; UN-[1] + INTERESTED] **—un·in′ter·est·ed·ly,** *adv.* **—un·in′ter·est·ed·ness,** *n.*
—Syn. 2. unconcerned.
—Usage. See **disinterested.**

u·ni·nu·cle·ate (yo͞o′nə no͞o′klē it, -āt′, -nyo͞o′-), *adj. Biol.* (of a cell) having one nucleus. [1880–85; UNI- + NUCLEATE]

un·in·vit·ing (un′in vī′ting), *adj.* not inviting; unpleasant: *a region with an uninviting climate.* [1680–90; UN-[1] + INVITING] **—un′in·vit′ing·ly,** *adv.* **—un′in·vit′ing·ness,** *n.*
—Syn. unappealing, unattractive, disagreeable.

u·ni·oc·u·lar (yo͞o′nē ok′yə lər), *adj.* monocular. [1820–30; UNI- + OCULAR]

union (def. 10a) A ∪ B

un·ion (yo͞on′yən), *n.* **1.** the act of uniting two or more things. **2.** the state of being united. **3.** something formed by uniting two or more things; combination. **4.** a number of persons, states, etc., joined or associated together for some common purpose: *student union; credit union.* **5.** a group of states or nations united into one political body, as that of the American colonies at the time of the Revolution, that of England and Scotland in 1707, or that of Great Britain and Ireland in 1801. **6.** **the Union.** the United States: *The Union defeated the Confederacy in 1865.* **7.** a device emblematic of union, used in a flag or ensign, sometimes occupying the upper corner next to the staff or occupying the entire field. **8.** the act of uniting or an instance of being united in marriage or sexual intercourse: *an ideal union; an illicit union.* **9.** an organization of workers; a labor union. **10.** *Math.* **a.** Also called **join, logical sum, sum.** the set consisting of elements each of which is in at least one of two or more given sets. *Symbol:* ∪ **b.** the least upper bound of two elements in a lattice. **11.** the process or result of merging or integration of disjoined, severed, or fractured elements, as the healing of a wound or broken bone, the growing together of the parts in a plant graft, the fusion of pieces in a welding process, or the like. **12.** the junction or location at which the merging process has taken place. **13.** any of various contrivances for connecting parts of machinery or the like. **14.** *Textiles.* **a.** a fabric of two kinds of yarn. **b.** a yarn of two or more fibers. [1400–50; late ME < MF < LL *ūniōn-* (s. of *ūniō*), equiv. to L *ūn(us)* one + *-iōn-* -ION]
—Syn. 1. UNION, UNITY agree in referring to a oneness, either created by putting together, or by being undivided. A UNION is a state of being united, a combination, as the result of joining two or more things into one: *to promote the union between two families; the Union of England and Scotland.* UNITY is the state or inherent quality of being one, single, individual, and indivisible (often as a consequence of union): *to find unity in diversity; to give unity to a work of art.* **5.** See **alliance. 8.** wedlock; liaison. **—Ant. 1, 2.** separation, division.

Un·ion (yo͞on′yən), *n.* **1.** a township in NE New Jersey. 50,184. **2.** a city in NW South Carolina. 10,523.

un′ion bust′er, 1. any of a group of persons hired by a company to disperse picketers, end a strike or job action, etc., esp. by violence or intimidation. **2.** any person or group that tries to destroy or weaken a union, as

un′in·i′ti·at′ed, *adj.*
un′in·i′ti·a·tive, *adj.*
un′in·ject′a·ble, *adj.*
un′in·ject′ed, *adj.*
un·in′jured, *adj.*
un′in·jur′ing, *adj.*
un′in·ju′ri·ous, *adj.;* **-ly,** *adv.;* **-ness,** *n.*
un·inked′, *adj.*
un′in·laid′, *adj.*
un′in·nate′, *adj.;* **-ly,** *adv.;* **-ness,** *n.*
un·in′no·cent, *adj.;* **-ly,** *adv.*
un′in·noc′u·ous, *adj.;* **-ly,** *adv.;* **-ness,** *n.*
un·in′no·vat′ing, *adj.*
un·in′no·va′tive, *adj.*
un′in·oc′u·la·ble, *adj.*
un′in·oc′u·lat′ed, *adj.*
un′in·oc′u·la′tive, *adj.*
un′in·quired′, *adj.*
un′in·quir′ing, *adj.*
un′in·quis′i·tive, *adj.;* **-ly,** *adv.;* **-ness,** *n.*
un′in·quis′i·to′ri·al, *adj.;* **-ly,** *adv.*
un′in·scribed′, *adj.*
un′in·sert′ed, *adj.*
un′in·sid′i·ous, *adj.;* **-ly,** *adv.;* **-ness,** *n.*
un′in·sin′u·at′ed, *adj.*
un′in·sin′u·at′ing, *adj.*
un′in·sin′u·a′tive, *adj.*
un′in·sist′ent, *adj.;* **-ly,** *adv.*
un·in′so·lat′ed, *adj.*
un·in′so·lat′ing, *adj.*
un′in·spect′ed, *adj.*
un′in·spir′a·ble, *adj.*
un′in·spir′ing, *adj.;* **-ly,** *adv.*
un′in·spir′it·ed, *adj.*
un′in·spis′sat·ed, *adj.*
un′in·stalled′, *adj.*
un·in′stanced, *adj.*
un′in·stat′ed, *adj.*
un·in′sti·gat′ed, *adj.*
un·in′sti·ga′tive, *adj.*
un′in·stilled′, *adj.*
un′in·stinc′tive, *adj.;* **-ly,** *adv.;* **-ness,** *n.*
un·in′sti·tut′ed, *adj.*
un·in′sti·tu′tion·al, *adj.;* **-ly,** *adv.*
un·in′sti·tu′tive, *adj.;* **-ly,** *adv.*
un′in·struct′i·ble, *adj.*
un′in·struct′ing, *adj.*
un′in·struc′tive, *adj.;* **-ly,** *adv.*
un′in·stru·men′tal, *adj.;* **-ly,** *adv.*
un·in′su·lar, *adj.*
un·in′su·lat′ed, *adj.*
un′in·sult′a·ble, *adj.*
un′in·sult′ed, *adj.*
un′in·sult′ing, *adj.*
un′in·sur′a·bil′i·ty, *n.*
un′in·sur′a·ble, *adj.*
un′in·sured′, *adj.*
un·in′te·gra·ble, *adj.*
un·in′te·gral, *adj.;* **-ly,** *adv.*
un·in′te·grat′ed, *adj.*
un·in′te·gra′tive, *adj.*
un′in·tel·lec′tive, *adj.*
un′in·tel·lec′tu·al, *adj.;* **-ly,** *adv.*
un′in·tel·lec′tu·al′i·ty, *n.*
un′in·tend′ed, *adj.;* **-ly,** *adv.*
un′in·ten′si·fied, *adj.*
un′in·ten′sive, *adj.;* **-ly,** *adv.*
un′in·tent′, *adj.;* **-ly,** *adv.*
un′in·ter′ca·lat′ed, *adj.*
un′in·ter·cept′ed, *adj.*
un′in·ter·cept′ing, *adj.*
un′in·ter·change′a·ble, *adj.*
un′in·ter·dict′ed, *adj.*
un·in′ter·est·ing, *adj.;* **-ly,** *adv.*
un′in·ter·ject′ed, *adj.*
un′in·ter·laced′, *adj.*
un′in·ter·leaved′, *adj.*
un′in·ter·lined′, *adj.*
un′in·ter·linked′, *adj.*
un′in·ter·locked′, *adj.*
un′in·ter·me′di·ate, *adj.;* **-ly,** *adv.;* **-ness,** *n.*
un′in·ter·min′gled, *adj.*
un′in·ter·mis′sive, *adj.*
un′in·ter·mit′ted, *adj.*
un′in·ter·mit′tent, *adj.;* **-ly,** *adv.*
un′in·ter·mit′ting, *adj.*
un′in·ter′nal·ized′, *adj.*
un′in·ter·na′tion·al, *adj.*
un′in·ter·plead′ed, *adj.*
un′in·ter′po·lat′ed, *adj.*
un′in·ter′po·la′tive, *adj.*
un′in·ter·posed′, *adj.*
un′in·ter·pos′ing, *adj.*
un′in·ter′pret·a·ble, *adj.*
un′in·ter′pre·ta′tive, *adj.*
un′in·ter′pret·ed, *adj.*
un′in·ter′pre·tive, *adj.;* **-ly,** *adv.*
un′in·terred′, *adj.*
un′in·ter′ro·ga·ble, *adj.*
un′in·ter′ro·gat′ed, *adj.*
un′in·ter·rog′a·tive, *adj.;* **-ly,** *adv.*
un′in·ter·rog′a·to′ry, *adj.*
un′in·ter·rupt′ed, *adj.;* **-ly,** *adv.;* **-ness,** *n.*
un′in·ter·rupt′i·ble, *adj.*
un′in·ter·rupt′ing, *adj.*
un′in·ter·rup′tive, *adj.*
un′in·ter·sect′ed, *adj.*
un′in·ter·sect′ing, *adj.*
un′in·ter·spersed′, *adj.*
un′in·ter·ven′ing, *adj.*
un·in′ter·viewed′, *adj.*
un′in·ter·volved′, *adj.*
un′in·ter·wo′ven, *adj.*
un′in·thralled′, *adj.*
un·in′ti·mate, *adj.;* **-ly,** *adv.*
un·in′ti·mat′ed, *adj.*
un′in·tim′i·dat′a·ble, *adj.*
un′in·tim′i·dat′ed, *adj.*
un′in·tim′i·dat′ing, *adj.*
un′in·toned′, *adj.*
un′in·tox′i·cat′ed, *adj.*
un′in·tox′i·cat′ing, *adj.*
un′in·trenched′, *adj.*
un·in′tri·cate, *adj.;* **-ly,** *adv.;* **-ness,** *n.*
un′in·trigued′, *adj.*
un′in·tri′guing, *adj.*
un′in·tro·duced′, *adj.*
un′in·tro·duc′i·ble, *adj.*
un′in·tro·duc′tive, *adj.*
un′in·tro·duc′to·ry, *adj.*
un′in·tro·mis′sive, *adj.*
un′in·tro·mit′ted, *adj.*
un′in·tro·spec′tive, *adj.;* **-ly,** *adv.*
un′in·tro·ver′sive, *adj.*
un′in·tro·vert′ed, *adj.*
un′in·trud′ed, *adj.*
un′in·trud′ing, *adj.;* **-ly,** *adv.*
un′in·tru′sive, *adj.;* **-ly,** *adv.*
un′in·tu′it·a·ble, *adj.*
un′in·tu·i′tion·al, *adj.*
un′in·tu′i·tive, *adj.;* **-ly,** *adv.*
un·in′un·dat′ed, *adj.*
un′in·ured′, *adj.*
un′in·urned′, *adj.*
un′in·vad′a·ble, *adj.*
un′in·vad′ed, *adj.*
un′in·vag′i·nat′ed, *adj.*
un′in·va′sive, *adj.*
un′in·vec′tive, *adj.*
un′in·veigh′ing, *adj.*
un′in·vei′gled, *adj.*
un′in·vent′ed, *adj.*
un′in·ven′tive, *adj.;* **-ly,** *adv.*
un′in·vert′ed, *adj.*
un′in·vert′i·ble, *adj.*
un′in·vest′a·ble, *adj.*
un′in·vest′ed, *adj.*
un′in·ves′ti·ga·ble, *adj.*
un′in·ves′ti·gat′ed, *adj.*
un′in·ves′ti·gat′ing, *adj.*
un′in·ves′ti·ga′tive, *adj.*
un′in·ves′ti·ga·to′ry, *adj.*
un′in·vid′i·ous, *adj.;* **-ly,** *adv.*
un′in·vig′or·at′ed, *adj.*
un′in·vig′or·at′ing, *adj.*
un′in·vig′or·a′tive, *adj.;* **-ly,** *adv.*
un′in·vin′ci·ble, *adj.;* **-ble·ness,** *n.;* **-bly,** *adv.*
un′in·vit′ed, *adj.*
un′in·vo′ca·ble, *adj.*
un′in·voc′a·tive, *adj.*
un·in′voiced, *adj.*
un′in·voked′, *adj.*
un·in′vo·lut′ed, *adj.*
un′in·volved′, *adj.*
un′in·wo′ven, *adj.*
un·i′o·dized′, *adj.*
un·i′o·nized′, *adj.*
un′i·ras′ci·bil′i·ty, *n.*
un′i·ras′ci·ble, *adj.*
un′i·ren′ic, *adj.*
un′ir·i·des′cent, *adj.;* **-ly,** *adv.*
un·i′roned, *adj.*
un′i·ron′i·cal, *adj.;* **-ly,** *adv.*
un′ir·ra′di·at′ed, *adj.*
un′ir·ra′di·a′tive, *adj.*
un·ir′ri·ga·ble, *adj.*
un·ir′ri·gat′ed, *adj.*
un·ir′ri·ta·ble, *adj.;* **-bly,** *adv.*
un·ir′ri·tant, *adj.*
un·ir′ri·tat′ed, *adj.*
un·ir′ri·tat′ing, *adj.*
un·ir′ri·ta′tive, *adj.*
un′ir·rupt′ed, *adj.*
un′ir·rup′tive, *adj.*
un·i′so·late′, *v.t.,* **-lat·ed, -lat·ing.**
un′i·so·la′tion·ist, *adj.*
un·i′so·la′tive, *adj.*
un′i·so·mer′ic, *adj.*
un′i·so·met′ri·cal, *adj.*
un′i·so·mor′phic, *adj.*
un′i·so·trop′ic, *adj.*
un′i·sot′ro·pous, *adj.*
un·is′su·a·ble, *adj.*
un·is′su·ant, *adj.*
un·is′sued, *adj.*
un′i·tal′i·cized′, *adj.*
un·i′tem·ized′, *adj.*
un·it′er·at′ed, *adj.*
un·it′er·a′tive, *adj.*
un′i·tin′er·ant, *adj.*
un·jack′et·ed, *adj.*
un·jad′ed, *adj.*
un·jag′ged, *adj.*
un·jailed′, *adj.*
un·jam′, *v.t.,* **-jammed, -jam·ming.**
un·jam′ma·ble, *adj.*
un′ja·panned′, *adj.*
un·jarred′, *adj.*
un·jar′ring, *adj.*
un·jaun′ty, *adj.*
un·jeal′ous, *adj.;* **-ly,** *adv.*
un·jeered′, *adj.*
un·jeer′ing, *adj.*
un·jelled′, *adj.*
un·jel′lied, *adj.*
un·jeop′ard·ized′, *adj.*
un·jest′ing, *adj.;* **-ly,** *adv.*
un′-Jes·u·it′ic, *adj.*
un′-Jes·u·it′i·cal, *adj.;* **-ly,** *adv.*
un·jew′eled, *adj.*
un·jew′elled, *adj.*
un·jilt′ed, *adj.*
un′jo·cose′, *adj.;* **-ly,** *adv.;* **-ness,** *n.*
un·joc′und, *adj.*
un·jogged′, *adj.*
un·jog′ging, *adj.*
un·join′, *v.*
un·join′a·ble, *adj.*
un·joint′ed, *adj.*
un·join′tured, *adj.*
un·jok′ing, *adj.;* **-ly,** *adv.*
un·jol′ly, *adj.*
un·jolt′ed, *adj.*
un·jos′tled, *adj.*
un′jour·nal·is′tic, *adj.*
un·jour′nal·ized′, *adj.*
un·jo′vi·al, *adj.;* **-ly,** *adv.*
un·joyed′, *adj.*
un·joy′ful, *adj.;* **-ly,** *adv.*
un·joy′ous, *adj.;* **-ly,** *adv.*

through prosecution or intimidation: *The district attorney has a reputation as a union buster.* **—un′ion-bust′ing,** *adj., n.*

un′ion card′, a card identifying one as a member of a particular labor union. [1870–75, *Amer.*]

un′ion cat′alog, a catalog containing bibliographic records that indicate locations of materials in more than one library or in several units of one library. Also called **repertory catalog.** [1905–10, *Amer.*]

un′ion church′, a congregation or denomination formed by the combination of two or more churches. [1840–50, *Amer.*]

Un′ion Cit′y, 1. a city in NE New Jersey. 55,593. **2.** a town in W California. 39,406. **3.** a town in NW Tennessee. 10,436.

Un•ion•dale (yōōn′yən dāl′), *n.* a town on W Long Island, in SE New York. 20,016.

Un′ion Day′, a legal holiday in the Republic of South Africa commemorating the founding of the country on May 31, 1910.

un•ion•ism (yōōn′yə niz′əm), *n.* **1.** the principle of union, esp. trade unionism. **2.** attachment to a union. **3.** (*cap.*) loyalty to the federal union of the United States of America, esp. at the time of the Civil War. [1835–45; UNION + -ISM]

un•ion•ist (yōōn′yə nist), *n.* **1.** a person whose activities or beliefs are characterized by unionism. **2.** a member of a trade union. **3.** (*cap.*) a supporter of the federal union of the United States of America, esp. during the Civil War. **4.** *Brit. Politics.* (formerly) an upholder of the legislative union of Great Britain and Northern Ireland. [1790–1800; UNION + -IST] **—un′ion•is′tic,** *adj.*

un•ion•ize (yōōn′yə nīz′), *v.,* **-ized, -iz•ing.** *—v.t.* **1.** to form into a union. **2.** to organize into a labor union; bring into or incorporate in a labor union. **3.** to subject to the rules of a labor union. *—v.i.* **4.** to form a union. **5.** to join in a labor union. Also, *esp. Brit.,* **un′ion•ise′.** [1835–45; UNION + -IZE] **—un′ion•i•za′tion,** *n.* **—un′ion•iz′er,** *n.*

un′ion jack′, 1. a jack consisting of the union of a national flag or ensign, as the U.S. jack, which has the white stars and blue field of the union of the U.S. national flag. **2.** (*often cap.*) the British national flag. **3.** any flag the design of which is a union. [1665–75]

un′ion la′bel, a tag or stamped imprint on a product indicating that it has been made by union labor.

un′ion lan′guage, a form of a language, used in literature and for official and educational purposes, that combines vocabulary and grammatical features from a number of related dialects, thus representing a compromise between them.

un′ion list′, a list of materials, as in a designated format or on a designated subject, that are available in a group of libraries: *a union list of serials or microforms.*

un•ion-made (yōōn′yən mād′), *adj.* produced by workers belonging to a labor union.

Un′ion of Bur′ma, former official name of **Burma.**

Un′ion of South′ Af′rica, former name for **South Africa, Republic of.**

Un′ion of So′viet So′cialist Repub′lics, a former federal union of 15 constituent republics, in E Europe and W and N Asia, comprising the larger part of the former Russian Empire: dissolved in December 1991. 8,650,069 sq. mi. (22,402,200 sq. km). *Cap.:* Moscow. Also called **Russia, Soviet Union.** See map above. *Abbr.:* U.S.S.R., USSR

un′ion scale′, scale³ (def. 6). [1975–80]

un′ion shop′, 1. a shop, business establishment, or part thereof, in which terms and conditions of employment for all employees are fixed by agreement between the employer and a labor union. **2.** a shop, business, etc., in which membership in a union is made a condition of employment, but in which the employer may hire nonunion workers provided that they become members after a stated period, usually 30 days. Cf. **nonunion shop.** [1900–05]

un′ion suit′, a close-fitting, knitted undergarment combining shirt and drawers in one piece and often having a drop seat. [1890–95]

Un•ion•town (yōōn′yən toun′), *n.* a city in SW Pennsylvania. 14,510.

u•ni•pa•ren•tal (yōō′nə pə ren′tl), *adj. Biol.* having one parent, as an organism produced by parthenogen-

CONCISE PRONUNCIATION KEY: *act, cāpe, dâre, pärt; set, ēqual; if, īce; ox, ōver, ôrder, oil, bŏŏk, bōōt, out; up, ûrge; child; sing; shoe; thin, that;* zh as in *treasure.* ə = *a* as in *alone, e* as in *system, i* as in *easily, o* as in *gallop, u* as in *circus;* ° as in *fire* (fī°r), *hour* (ou°r). l and n can serve as syllabic consonants, as in *cradle* (krād′l), and *button* (but′n). See the full key inside the front cover.

un•ju′bi•lant, *adj.;* **-ly,** *adv.*
un•judge′a•ble, *adj.*
un•judged′, *adj.*
un•judge′like′, *adj.*
un•judg′ing, *adj.*
un′judg•men′tal, *adj.*
un•ju′di•ca•ble, *adj.*
un•ju′di•ca′tive, *adj.*
un′ju•di′ci•a•ble, *adj.*
un′ju•di′cial, *adj.;* **-ly,** *adv.*
un•jug′gled, *adj.*
un•juic′i•ly, *adv.*
un•juic′y, *adj.*
un•jum′bled, *adj.*
un•jump′a•ble, *adj.*
un′ju•rid′ic, *adj.*
un′ju•rid′i•cal, *adj.;* **-ly,** *adv.*
un•jus′ti•fi′a•ble, *adj.;* **-ble•ness,** *n.;* **-bly,** *adv.*
un•jus′ti•fied′, *adj.*
un•ju′ve•nile, *adj.;* **-ly,** *adv.;* **-ness,** *n.*
un•keeled′, *adj.*
un•kept′, *adj.*
un•keyed′, *adj.*
un•kid′naped, *adj.*
un•kid′napped, *adj.*
un•killed′, *adj.*
un•kill′ing, *adj.*
un•kilned′, *adj.*
un•kind′heart′ed, *adj.*
un•kin′dled, *adj.*
un•kin′dling, *adj.*
un•kinged′, *adj.*
un•king′like′, *adj.*
un•king′ly, *adj., adv.*
un•kink′, *v.*
un•kissed′, *adj.*
un•knead′ed, *adj.*
un•kneel′ing, *adj.*
un•knelled′, *adj.*
un•knight′ed, *adj.*
un•knocked′, *adj.*
un•knock′ing, *adj.*
un•knot′ty, *adj.*
un•knowl′edge•a•ble, *adj.*
un•ko′sher, *adj.*
un•la′beled, *adj.*
un•la′belled, *adj.*
un•la′bi•al•ize′, *v.t.,* **-ized, -iz•ing.**
un•la′bi•ate′, *adj.*
un•la′bored, *adj.*
un•la′bor•ing, *adj.*
un′la•bo′ri•ous, *adj.;* **-ly,** *adv.;* **-ness,** *n.*
un•lac′er•at′ed, *adj.*
un•lac′er•at′ing, *adj.*
un•lack′eyed, *adj.*
un′la•con′ic, *adj.*
un•lac′quered, *adj.*
un•lad′en, *adj.*
un•la′dled, *adj.*
un•la′dy•like′, *adj.*
un•lag′ging, *adj.*
un•lame′, *adj.*
un•lamed′, *adj.*
un•lam′en•ta•ble, *adj.*
un′la•ment′ed, *adj.*
un•lam′i•nat′ed, *adj.*
un′lam•pooned′, *adj.*
un•lanced′, *adj.*
un•land′ed, *adj.*
un•land′marked′, *adj.*
un•lan′guid, *adj.;* **-ly,** *adv.;* **-ness,** *n.*
un•lan′guish•ing, *adj.*
un•lan′terned, *adj.*
un•lapped′, *adj.*
un•lapsed′, *adj.*
un•laps′ing, *adj.*
un•lar′ce•nous, *adj.;* **-ly,** *adv.*
un•lard′ed, *adj.*
un•large′, *adj.*
un•las′soed, *adj.*
un•last′ing, *adj.*
un•lath′ered, *adj.*
un•Lat′in•ized′, *adj.*
un•lat′ticed, *adj.*
un•laud′a•ble, *adj.;* **-ble•ness,** *n.;* **-bly,** *adv.*
un•laud′a•tive, *adj.*
un•laud′a•to′ry, *adj.*
un•laud′ed, *adj.*
un•laugh′ing, *adj.*
un•launched′, *adj.*
un•laun′dered, *adj.*
un•lau′reled, *adj.*
un•lau′relled, *adj.*
un•laved′, *adj.*
un•lav′ing, *adj.*
un•lav′ish, *adj.*
un•lav′ished, *adj.*
un•law′yer•like′, *adj.*
un•law′yer•ly, *adj.*
un•lay′a•ble, *adj.*
un•leached′, *adj.*
un•leaf′, *v.t.*
un•leaf′like′, *adj.*
un•leak′a•ble, *adj.*
un•leak′y, *adj.*
un•lean′, *adj.*
un•learn′ing, *adj.*
un•leas′a•ble, *adj.*
un•leased′, *adj.*
un•leath′ered, *adj.*
un•leaved′, *adj.*
un•leav′en•a•ble, *adj.*
un•lech′er•ous, *adj.;* **-ly,** *adv.;* **-ness,** *n.*
un•lec′tured, *adj.*
un•led′, *adj.*
un•ledged′, *adj.*
un•left′, *adj.*
un•le′gal, *adj.;* **-ly,** *adv.;* **-ness,** *n.*
un•le′gal•ized′, *adj.*
un•leg′i•ble, *adj.*
un•leg′is•lat′ed, *adj.*
un•leg′is•la′tive, *adj.;* **-ly,** *adv.*
un•lei′sured, *adj.*
un•lei′sure•ly, *adj.*
un•length′ened, *adj.*
un•le′ni•ent, *adj.;* **-ly,** *adv.*
un•lensed′, *adj.*
un•lent′, *adj.*
un•less′ened, *adj.*
un•let′, *adj.*
un•le′thal, *adj.;* **-ly,** *adv.*
un′le•thar′gic, *adj.*
un′le•thar′gi•cal, *adj.;* **-ly,** *adv.*
un•lev′el, *adj.;* **-ly,** *adv.;* **-ness,** *n.*
un•lev′eled, *adj.*
un•lev′elled, *adj.*
un•lev′er•aged, *adj.*
un•lev′i•a•ble, *adj.*
un•lev′ied, *adj.*
un•lev′i•gat′ed, *adj.*
un′lex•i•co•graph′i•cal, *adj.;* **-ly,** *adv.*
un•li′a•ble, *adj.*
un•li′beled, *adj.*
un•li′belled, *adj.*
un•li′bel•lous, *adj.;* **-ly,** *adv.*
un•li′bel•ous, *adj.;* **-ly,** *adv.*
un•lib′er•al, *adj.;* **-ly,** *adv.*
un•lib′er•al•ized′, *adj.*
un•lib′er•at′ed, *adj.*
un′li•bid′i•nous, *adj.;* **-ly,** *adv.*
un′li•cen′ti•at′ed, *adj.*
un′li•cen′tious, *adj.;* **-ly,** *adv.;* **-ness,** *n.*
un•li′chened, *adj.*
un•lid′ded, *adj.*
un•life′like′, *adj.*
un•lift′a•ble, *adj.*
un•lift′ed, *adj.*
un•lift′ing, *adj.*
un•lig′a•tured, *adj.*
un•light′, *adj.*
un•light′ed, *adj.*
un•light′ened, *adj.*
un•lig′ni•fied′, *adj.*
un•lik′a•ble, *adj.;* **-ble•ness,** *n.;* **-bly,** *adv.*
un•like′a•ble, *adj.;* **-ble•ness,** *n.;* **-bly,** *adv.*
un•liked′, *adj.*
un•lik′ened, *adj.*
un•limed′, *adj.*
un•limned′, *adj.*
un•limp′, *adj.*
un•lin′e•al, *adj.*
un•lined′, *adj.*
un•lin′ger•ing, *adj.*
un•li′on•ized′, *adj.*
un•liq′ue•fi′a•ble, *adj.*
un•liq′ue•fied′, *adj.*
un′li•ques′cent, *adj.*
un•liq′uid, *adj.*
un•liq′ui•dat′ed, *adj.*
un•liq′ui•dat′ing, *adj.*
un•lisp′ing, *adj.*
un•lis′ten•a•ble, *adj.*
un•lis′ten•ing, *adj.*
un•lit′, *adj.*
un•lit′er•al, *adj.;* **-ly,** *adv.*
un•lit′er•al•ized′, *adj.*
un•lit′er•ar′y, *adj.*
un•lit′er•ate, *adj.*
un′lith•o•graph′ic, *adj.*
un•lit′i•gat′ed, *adj.*
un•lit′i•gat′ing, *adj.*
un•li•ti′gious, *adj.;* **-ly,** *adv.;* **-ness,** *n.*
un•lit′tered, *adj.*
un•liv′a•ble, *adj.;* **-ble•ness,** *n.*
un•live′a•ble, *adj.;* **-ble•ness,** *n.*
un•lived′-in′, *adj.*
un•live′li•ness, *n.*
un•live′ly, *adj., adv.*
un•liv′er•ied, *adj.*
un•liv′ing, *adj.*
un•loaf′ing, *adj.*
un•loaned′, *adj.*
un•loan′ing, *adj.*
un•loath′, *adj.;* **-ly,** *adv.*
un•loathed′, *adj.*
un•loath′ful, *adj.*
un•loath′some, *adj.*
un•lob′bied, *adj.*
un•lob′by•ing, *adj.*
un•lobed′, *adj.*
un•lo′cal, *adj.;* **-ly,** *adv.*
un•lo′cal•iz′a•ble, *adj.*
un•lo′cal•ize′, *v.t.,* **-ized, -iz•ing.**
un•lo′cat•ed, *adj.*
un•loc′a•tive, *adj.*
un′lo•co•mo′tive, *adj.*
un•lodged′, *adj.*
un•loft′y, *adj.*
un•logged′, *adj.*
un•log′i•cal, *adj.;* **-ly,** *adv.*
un′lo•gis′tic, *adj.*
un′lo•gis′ti•cal, *adj.*
un•lone′ly, *adj.*
un•longed′-for′, *adj.*
un•loop′, *v.t.*
un•loot′ed, *adj.*
un•lopped′, *adj.*
un′lo•qua′cious, *adj.;* **-ly,** *adv.*
un′los•a•bil′i•ty, *n.*
un•los′a•ble, *adj.*
un•lost′, *adj.*
un•lot′ted, *adj.*
un•loud′ly, *adj.*
un•loung′ing, *adj.*
un•lov′a•ble, *adj.;* **-ble•ness,** *n.;* **-bly,** *adv.*
un•love′a•ble, *adj.;* **-ble•ness,** *n.;* **-bly,** *adv.*
un•loved′, *adj.*
un•lov′ing, *adj.*
un•low′ered, *adj.*
un•low′ly, *adj.*
un•loy′al, *adj.;* **-ly,** *adv.*
un•loy′al•ty, *n., pl.* **-ties.**
un•lu′bri•cant, *adj.*
un•lu′bri•cat′ed, *adj.*
un•lu′bri•cat′ing, *adj.*
un•lu′bri•ca′tive, *adj.*
un′lu•bri′cious, *adj.*
un•lu′cent, *adj.*
un•lu′cid, *adj.;* **-ly,** *adv.;* **-ness,** *n.*
un•lu′cra•tive, *adj.*
un•lu′di•crous, *adj.;* **-ly,** *adv.;* **-ness,** *n.*
un•luffed′, *adj.*
un•lugged′, *adj.*

esis. [1895–1900; UNI- + PARENTAL] —**u′ni·pa·ren′tal·ly,** *adv.*

u·nip·a·rous (yo͞o nip′ər əs), *adj.* **1.** *Zool.* producing only one egg or offspring at a time. **2.** *Bot.* (of a cyme) producing only one axis at each branching. [1640–50; < NL *ūniparus.* See UNI-, -PAROUS]

u·ni·per·son·al (yo͞o′nə pûr′sə nl), *adj.* **1.** consisting of or existing as one person only. **2.** *Gram.* (of a verb) used in only one person, esp. the third person singular; impersonal. [1800–10; UNI- + PERSONAL]

u·ni·pet·al·ous (yo͞o′nə pet′l əs), *adj. Bot.* having only one petal. [1840–50; UNI- + PETALOUS]

u·ni·pla·nar (yo͞o′nə plā′nər), *adj.* confined to a single plane or two-dimensional continuum: *uniplanar motion.* [1865–70; UNI- + PLANAR]

u·ni·pod (yo͞o′nə pod′), *n.* something that is formed with a single leg or foot, as a one-legged support for a camera. [UNI- + -POD]

u·ni·po·lar (yo͞o′nə pō′lər), *adj.* **1.** Also, **homopolar.** *Physics.* having or pertaining to a single magnetic or electric pole. **2.** *Anat.* of or pertaining to a nerve cell in spinal and cranial ganglia in which the incoming and outgoing processes fuse outside the cell body. [1805–15; UNI- + POLAR] —**u·ni·po·lar·i·ty** (yo͞o′nə pō lar′i tē, -pə-), *n.*

u·nip·o·tent (yo͞o nip′ə tənt), *adj. Biol.* (of cells) capable of developing into only one type of cell or tissue. [UNI- + POTENT]

u·ni·po·ten·tial (yo͞o′nə pə ten′shəl), *adj.* **1.** *Elect., Electronics.* having uniform electric potential throughout, as a hot cathode **(u′nipoten′tial cath′ode)** indirectly heated by a separate heater circuit so that there is no lateral change of voltage across the cathode due to resistance to a heating current. **2.** *Biol.* unipotent. [UNI- + POTENTIAL]

u·nique (yo͞o nēk′), *adj.* **1.** existing as the only one or as the sole example; single; solitary in type or characteristics: *a unique copy of an ancient manuscript.* **2.** having no like or equal; unparalleled; incomparable: *Bach was unique in his handling of counterpoint.* **3.** limited in occurrence to a given class, situation, or area: *a species unique to Australia.* **4.** limited to a single outcome or result; without alternative possibilities: *Certain types of problems have unique solutions.* **5.** not typical; unusual: *She has a very unique smile.* —*n.* **6.** the embodiment of unique characteristics; the only specimen of a given kind: *The unique is also the improbable.* [1595–1605; < F < L *ūnicus,* equiv. to *ūn(us)* one + *-icus* -IC] —**u·nique′ly,** *adv.* —**u·nique′ness,** *n.*

—**Usage.** Many authors of usage guides, editors, teachers, and others feel strongly that such "absolute" words as *complete, equal, perfect,* and especially UNIQUE cannot be compared because of their "meaning": a word that denotes an absolute condition cannot be described as denoting more or less than that absolute condition. However, all such words have undergone semantic development and are used in a number of senses, some of which can be compared by words like *more, very, most, absolutely, somewhat,* and *totally* and some of which cannot.

The earliest meanings of UNIQUE when it entered English around the beginning of the 17th century were "single, sole" and "having no equal." By the mid-19th century UNIQUE had developed a wider meaning, "not typical, unusual," and it is in this wider sense that it is compared: *The foliage on the late-blooming plants is more unique than that on the earlier varieties.* The comparison of so-called absolutes in senses that are not absolute is standard in all varieties of speech and writing. See also **a**[1], **complete, perfect.**

u·ni·ra·mous (yo͞o′nə rā′məs), *adj. Biol.* having one branch. [UNI- + RAMOUS]

u·ni·sep·tate (yo͞o′nə sep′tāt), *adj. Biol.* having only one septum or partition, as a silicle. [1865–70; UNI- + SEPTATE]

u·ni·sex (yo͞o′nə seks′), *adj.* **1.** of, designed, or suitable for both sexes; not distinguishing between male and female; undifferentiated as to sex: *unisex clothes.* —*n.* **2.** the state or quality of being unisex. **3.** unisex styles or fashions. [1965–70; UNI- + SEX]

u·ni·sex·u·al (yo͞o′nə sek′sho͞o əl), *adj.* **1.** of or pertaining to one sex only. **2.** having only male or female organs in one individual, as an animal or a flower. **3.** unisex. [1795–1805; UNI- + SEXUAL] —**u′ni·sex′u·al′i·ty,** *n.* —**u′ni·sex′u·al·ly,** *adv.*

u·ni·size (yo͞o′nə sīz′), *adj.* made to fit all sizes, types, weights, etc., within the ordinary range: *unisize swimming trunks.* [1985–90]

u·ni·son (yo͞o′nə sən, -zən), *n.* **1.** coincidence in pitch of two or more musical tones, voices, etc. **2.** the musical interval of a perfect prime. **3.** the performance of musical parts at the same pitch or at the octave. **4.** a sounding together in octaves, esp. of male and female voices or of higher and lower instruments of the same class. **5.** a process in which all elements behave in the same way at the same time; simultaneous or synchronous parallel action: *to march in unison.* **6. in unison,** in perfect accord; corresponding exactly: *My feelings on the subject are in unison with yours.* [1565–75; < ML *ūnisonus* of a single sound, equiv. to L *ūni-* UNI- + *sonus* sound]

u·nis·o·nous (yo͞o nis′ə nəs), *adj.* being in unison. Also, **u·nis′o·nal, u·nis′o·nant.** [1775–85; < ML *ūnison(us)* (see UNISON) + -OUS]

u·ni·spi·ral (yo͞o′nə spī′rəl), *adj.* having one spiral. [UNI- + SPIRAL]

u·nit (yo͞o′nit), *n.* **1.** a single thing or person. **2.** any group of things or persons regarded as an entity: *They formed a cohesive unit.* **3.** one of the individuals or groups that together constitute a whole; one of the parts or elements into which a whole may be divided or analyzed. **4.** one of a number of things, organizations, etc., identical or equivalent in function or form: *a rental unit; a unit of rolling stock.* **5.** any magnitude regarded as an independent whole; a single, indivisible entity. **6.** Also called **dimension.** any specified amount of a quantity, as of length, volume, force, momentum, or time, by comparison with which any other quantity of the same kind is measured or estimated. **7.** the least positive integer; one. **8.** Also called **unit's place. a.** (in a mixed number) the position of the first digit to the left of the decimal point. **b.** (in a whole number) the position of the first digit from the right of the decimal point. **9.** a machine, part, or system of machines having a specified purpose; apparatus: *a heating unit.* **10.** *Educ.* a division of instruction centering on a single theme. **11.** *Mil.* an organized body of soldiers, varying in size and constituting a subdivision of a larger body. **12.** *Med.* **a.** the measured amount of a substance necessary to cause a certain effect; a clinical quantity used when a substance cannot be readily isolated in pure form and its activity determined directly. **b.** the amount necessary to cause a specific effect upon a specific animal or upon animal tissues. **13.** *Math.* **a.** an identity element. **b.** an element in a group, ring, etc., that possesses an inverse. [1570; coined by John Dee as a trans. of Gk *mónas* (previously rendered as *unity*); perh. influenced by *digit*]

Unit., Unitarian.

u·nit·age (yo͞o′ni tij), *n.* specification of the amount making up a unit in a system of measurement. [1635–45 in sense "act of uniting"; UNIT + -AGE]

u·ni·tard (yo͞o′ni tärd′), *n.* a one-piece leotard with full-length stockings; bodysuit. [UNI- + (LEO)TARD]

u·ni·tar·i·an (yo͞o′ni târ′ē ən), *n.* **1.** a person who maintains that God is one being, rejecting the doctrine of the Trinity. **2.** (*cap.*) a member of a liberal religious denomination founded upon the doctrine that God is one being, and giving each congregation complete control over its affairs. Cf. **Unitarian Universalism. 3.** an advocate of unity or centralization, as in government. —*adj.* **4.** (*cap.*) pertaining to the Unitarians or their doctrines; accepting Unitarianism; belonging to the Unitarians. **5.** unitary. [1680–90; < NL *ūnitāri(us)* (L *ūnit(ās)* UNITY + *-ārius* -ARY) + -AN]

U·ni·tar·i·an·ism (yo͞o′ni târ′ē ə niz′əm), *n.* **1.** the beliefs, principles, and practices of Unitarians. Cf. **Unitarian Universalism. 2.** (*l.c.*) any system advocating unity or centralization, as in government. [UNITARIAN + -ISM]

Unitar′ian Univer′salism, a North American liberal religious denomination in the Judeo-Christian heritage, formed in 1961 by the merger of the Unitarians, organized in 1825, and the Universalists, organized in 1793.

u·ni·tar·y (yo͞o′ni ter′ē), *adj.* **1.** of or pertaining to a unit or units. **2.** of, pertaining to, characterized by, or aiming toward unity: *the unitary principles of nationalism.* **3.** of the nature of a unit; having the indivisible character of a unit; whole. **4.** serving as a unit, as of measurement or estimation. **5.** of or pertaining to the use of units: *A unitary method was applied.* **6.** *Govt.* of or pertaining to a system of government in which the executive, legislative, and judicial powers of each state in a body of states are vested in a central authority. [1810–20; UNIT, UNIT(Y) + -ARY] —**u′ni·tar′i·ness,** *n.*

u′nit card′, *Library Science.* a main entry catalog card, duplicates of which are used for added entries. Cf. **added entry, main entry.**

u′nit cell′, *Crystall.* the simplest unit of a regular lattice. [1935–40]

u′nit char′acter, *Genetics.* a characteristic, usually controlled by a single gene, that is transmitted as a unit in heredity. [1905–10]

u′nit cir′cle, *Math.* a circle whose radius has a length of one unit. [1950–55]

u′nit cost′, the cost of a specified unit of a product or service.

u·nite[1] (yo͞o nīt′), *v.,* **u·nit·ed, u·nit·ing.** —*v.t.* **1.** to join, combine, or incorporate so as to form a single whole or unit. **2.** to cause to adhere: *to unite two pieces of wood with glue.* **3.** to cause to be in a state of mutual sympathy, or to have a common opinion or attitude. **4.** to have or exhibit in union or combination: *a person who unites generosity and forgiveness.* **5.** to join in marriage. —*v.i.* **6.** to become joined together or combined so as to form a single whole. **7.** to act in concert or agreement. **8.** to share a common opinion, attitude, etc. **9.** to be joined by or as if by adhesion. [1400–50; late ME *uniten*

CONCISE ETYMOLOGY KEY: <, descended or borrowed from; >, whence; b., blend of, blended; c., cognate with; cf., compare; deriv., derivative; equiv., equivalent; imit., imitative; obl., oblique; r., replacing; s., stem; sp., spelling, spelled; resp., respelling, respelled; trans., translation; ?, origin unknown; *, unattested; ‡, probably earlier than. See the full key inside the front cover.

un′lu·gu′bri·ous, *adj.;* **-ly,** *adv.;* **-ness,** *n.*
un·lum′ber·ing, *adj.*
un′lu·mi·nes′cent, *adj.*
un′lu·mi·nif′er·ous, *adj.*
un·lu′mi·nous, *adj.;* **-ly,** *adv.;* **-ness,** *n.*
un·lumped′, *adj.*
un·lump′y, *adj.*
un·lu′nar, *adj.*
un·lu′nate, *adj.*
un·lu′nat·ed, *adj.*
un·lured′, *adj.*
un·lurk′ing, *adj.*
un·lush′, *adj.*
un·lus′tered, *adj.*
un·lust′ful, *adj.;* **-ly,** *adv.*
un·lust′ing, *adj.*
un·lus′trous, *adj.;* **-ly,** *adv.*
un·lust′y, *adj.*
un·lux′at·ed, *adj.*
un′lux·u′ri·ant, *adj.;* **-ly,** *adv.*
un′lux·u′ri·at′ing, *adj.*
un′lux·u′ri·ous, *adj.;* **-ly,** *adv.*
un·ly′ing, *adj.*
un·lyr′ic, *adj.*
un·lyr′i·cal, *adj.;* **-ly,** *adv.;* **-ness,** *n.*
un′mac·ad′am·ized′, *adj.*
un·mac′er·at′ed, *adj.*
un′ma·chin′a·ble, *adj.*
un·mach′i·nat′ed, *adj.*
un·mach′i·nat′ing, *adj.*
un′ma·chine′a·ble, *adj.*
un′ma·chined′, *adj.*
un·ma′cho, *adj.*
un·mad′, *adj.*
un·mad′ded, *adj.*
un·mad′dened, *adj.*
un·mag′i·cal, *adj.;* **-ly,** *adv.*
un·mag′is·te′ri·al, *adj.*
un′mag·nan′i·mous, *adj.;* **-ly,** *adv.;* **-ness,** *n.*
un′mag·net′ic, *adj.*
un′mag·net′i·cal, *adj.*
un·mag′net·ized′, *adj.*
un·mag′ni·fied′, *adj.*
un·mag′ni·fy′ing, *adj.*
un·maid′en·like′, *adj.*
un·maid′en·li·ness, *n.*
un·maid′en·ly, *adj.*
un·mail′a·ble, *adj.*
un·mailed′, *adj.*
un·maim′a·ble, *adj.*
un·maimed′, *adj.*
un′main·tain′a·ble, *adj.*
un′main·tained′, *adj.*
un′ma·jes′tic, *adj.*
un′ma·jes′ti·cal·ly, *adv.*
un′ma·lar′i·al, *adj.*
un′mal·e·dic′tive, *adj.*
un′mal·e·dic′to·ry, *adj.*
un′ma·lev′o·lent, *adj.;* **-ly,** *adv.*
un′ma·li′cious, *adj.;* **-ly,** *adv.*
un′ma·lig′nant, *adj.;* **-ly,** *adv.*
un′ma·ligned′, *adj.*
un′mal·le·a·bil′i·ty, *n.*
un·mal′le·a·ble, *adj.*
un·malt′a·ble, *adj.*
un·malt′ed, *adj.*
un′mam·ma′li·an, *adj.*
un·man′a·cled, *adj.*
un·man′age·a·ble, *adj.;* **-ble·ness,** *n.;* **-bly,** *adv.*
un·man′aged, *adj.*
un·man′dat·ed, *adj.*
un·man′da·to′ry, *adj.*
un·maned′, *adj.*
un′ma·neu′vered, *adj.*
un·man′ful, *adj.;* **-ly,** *adv.;* **-ness,** *n.*
un·man′gled, *adj.*
un′ma·ni′a·cal, *adj.;* **-ly,** *adv.*
un·man′i·cured′, *adj.*
un·man′i·fest′, *adj.*
un·man·i·fes′ta·tive, *adj.*
un·man′i·fest′ed, *adj.*
un′ma·nip′u·la·ble, *adj.*
un′ma·nip′u·lat′a·ble, *adj.*
un′ma·nip′u·lat′ed, *adj.*
un′ma·nip′u·la′tive, *adj.*
un′ma·nip′u·la·to′ry, *adj.*
un·man′nish, *adj.;* **-ly,** *adv.;* **-ness,** *n.*
un·man′tled, *adj.*
un·man′u·al, *adj.;* **-ly,** *adv.*
un′man·u·fac′tur·a·ble, *adj.*
un′man·u·fac′tured, *adj.*
un′man·u·mit′ted, *adj.*
un′ma·nur′a·ble, *adj.*
un·map′pa·ble, *adj.*
un·mapped′, *adj.*
un·mar′bel·ize′, *v.t.,* **-ized, -iz·ing.**
un·mar′bled, *adj.*
un·mar′ble·ize′, *v.t.,* **-ized, -iz·ing.**
un·march′ing, *adj.*
un·mar′gin·al, *adj.;* **-ly,** *adv.*
un·mar′gin·at′ed, *adj.*
un′ma·rine′, *adj.*
un·mar′i·time′, *adj.*
un·mark′a·ble, *adj.*
un·mar′ket·a·ble, *adj.*
un·mar′ket·ed, *adj.*
un·marled′, *adj.*
un·marred′, *adj.*
un·mar′riage·a·ble, *adj.*
un·mar′ried, *adj., n.*
un·mar′ring, *adj.*
un·mar′ry·ing, *adj.*
un·mar′shaled, *adj.*
un·mar′shalled, *adj.*
un·mar′tial, *adj.*
un·mar′tyred, *adj.*
un·mar′vel·ous, *adj.;* **-ly,** *adv.;* **-ness,** *n.*
un·mar′vel·ous, *adj.;* **-ly,** *adv.;* **-ness,** *n.*
un·mas′cu·line, *adj.;* **-ly,** *adv.*
un·mashed′, *adj.*
un·masked′, *adj.*
un·mask′ing, *adj.*
un·mas′sa·cred, *adj.*
un·massed′, *adj.*
un·mast′, *v.t.*
un·mas′ter·a·ble, *adj.*
un·mas′tered, *adj.*
un·mas′ter·ful, *adj.;* **-ly,** *adv.*
un·mas′ti·cat′ed, *adj.*
un·mas′ti·ca·to′ry, *adj.*
un·match′a·ble, *adj.*
un·matched′, *adj.*
un·match′ing, *adj.*
un·mate′, *v.t.,* **-mat·ed, -mat·ing.**
un′ma·te′ri·al, *adj.;* **-ly,** *adv.*
un′ma·te′ri·al·is′tic, *adj.*
un′ma·te′ri·al·is′ti·cal·ly, *adv.*
un′ma·te′ri·al·ized′, *adj.*
un′ma·ter′nal, *adj.;* **-ly,** *adv.*
un′math·e·mat′i·cal, *adj.;* **-ly,** *adv.*
un·mat′ing, *adj.*
un′ma·tric′u·lat′ed, *adj.*
un′mat·ri·mo′ni·al, *adj.;* **-ly,** *adv.*
un·mat′ted, *adj.*
un′ma·tur′a·tive, *adj.*
un′ma·ture′, *adj.;* **-ly,** *adv.*
un′ma·tured′, *adj.*
un′ma·tur′ing, *adj.*
un·maud′lin, *adj.;* **-ly,** *adv.*
un·mauled′, *adj.*
un′me·an′der·ing, *adj.;* **-ly,** *adv.*
un·meant′, *adj.*
un′me·chan′i·cal, *adj.;* **-ly,** *adv.*
un′mech·a·nis′tic, *adj.*
un·mech′a·nized′, *adj.*
un·med′aled, *adj.*
un·med′alled, *adj.*
un·med′dled, *adj.*
un·med′dle·some, *adj.*
un·med′dling, *adj.;* **-ly,** *adv.*
un′me·di·ae′val, *adj.*
un·me′di·at′ed, *adj.*
un·me′di·at′ing, *adj.*
un·me′di·a′tive, *adj.*
un·med′i·ca·ble, *adj.*
un·med′i·cal, *adj.;* **-ly,** *adv.*
un·med′i·cat′ed, *adj.*
un·med′i·ca′tive, *adj.*
un′me·dic′i·nal, *adj.;* **-ly,** *adv.*
un′me·di·e′val, *adj.*
un·med′i·tat′ed, *adj.*
un·med′i·tat′ing, *adj.*
un·med′i·ta′tive, *adj.;* **-ly,** *adv.*
un′mel·an·chol′ic, *adj.*
un′mel·an·chol′i·cal·ly, *adv.*
un·mel′an·chol′y, *adj.*
un·mel′io·rat′ed, *adj.*
un′mel·lif′lu·ent, *adj.;* **-ly,** *adv.*
un′mel·lif′lu·ous, *adj.;* **-ly,** *adv.*
un·mel′low, *adj.*
un·mel′lowed, *adj.*
un′me·lod′ic, *adj.*
un′me·lod′i·cal·ly, *adv.*
un′me·lo′di·ous, *adj.;* **-ly,** *adv.;* **-ness,** *n.*
un·mel′o·dized′, *adj.*
un′mel·o·dra·mat′ic, *adj.*
un′mel·o·dra·mat′i·cal·ly, *adv.*
un·melt′a·ble, *adj.*
un·melt′ed, *adj.*
un·melt′ing, *adj.*
un·mem′o·ra·ble, *adj.*
un′me·mo′ri·al·ized′, *adj.*
un·mem′o·ried, *adj.*
un·men′aced, *adj.*
un·men′ac·ing, *adj.*
un·mend′a·ble, *adj.*
un′men·da′cious, *adj.;* **-ly,** *adv.*
un·mend′ed, *adj.*
un·me′ni·al, *adj.;* **-ly,** *adv.*
un·men′stru·at′ing, *adj.*
un·men′sur·a·ble, *adj.*
un·men′tal, *adj.;* **-ly,** *adv.*
un·men′tho·lat′ed, *adj.*
un·men′tioned, *adj.*
un·mer′can·tile′, *adj.*
un′mer·ce·nar′i·ly, *adv.*
un·mer′ce·nar′i·ness, *n.*
un·mer′ce·nar′y, *adj.*
un·mer′cer·ized′, *adj.*
un·mer′chan·dised′, *adj.*
un·mer′chant·a·ble, *adj.*
un·mer′chant·ly, *adj., adv.*
un′mer·cur′i·al, *adj.;* **-ly,** *adv.;* **-ness,** *n.*
un′mer·e·tri′cious, *adj.;* **-ly,** *adv.;* **-ness,** *n.*
un·merge′, *v.t.,* **-merged, -merg·ing.**
un′me·rid′i·o·nal, *adj.;* **-ly,** *adv.*
un·me′ringued′, *adj.*
un·mer′it·ed, *adj.;* **-ly,** *adv.*
un′mer·i·to′ri·ous, *adj.;* **-ly,** *adv.;* **-ness,** *n.*
un·mer′ri·ly, *adv.*
un·mer′ry, *adj.*

< L *ūnītus,* ptp. of *ūnīre* to join together, unite, equiv. to *ūn*(*us*) one + *-ītus* -ITE[1]] —**u·nit′a·ble, u·nite′a·ble,** *adj.* —**u·nit′er,** *n.*
—**Syn. 1, 2.** conjoin, couple, link, yoke, amalgamate, consolidate, weld, fuse, blend, merge. See **join.**

u·nite[2] (yo͞o′nīt, yo͞o nīt′), *n.* a former gold coin of England, equal to 20 shillings, issued under James I and Charles I. [1595–1605; n. use of earlier ptp. of UNITE[1], referring to union of England and Scotland]

u·nit·ed (yo͞o nī′tid), *adj.* **1.** made into or caused to act as a single entity: *a united front.* **2.** formed or produced by the uniting of things or persons: *a united effort.* **3.** agreed; in harmony. [1545–55; UNITE[1] + -ED[2]] —**u·nit′·ed·ly,** *adv.* —**u·nit′ed·ness,** *n.*

Unit′ed Ar′ab Emir′ates, an independent federation in E Arabia, formed in 1971, now comprising seven emirates on the S coast (formerly, **Pirate Coast** or **Trucial Coast**) of the Persian Gulf, formerly under British protection: Abu Dhabi, Dubai, Sharjah, Ajman, Umm al-Qaiwain, Ras al-Khaimah (joined 1972), and Fujairah. 1,130,000; ab. 32,300 sq. mi. (83,657 sq. km). *Cap.:* Abu Dhabi. *Abbr.:* U.A.E. Formerly, **Trucial Oman, Trucial Sheikdoms, Trucial States.**

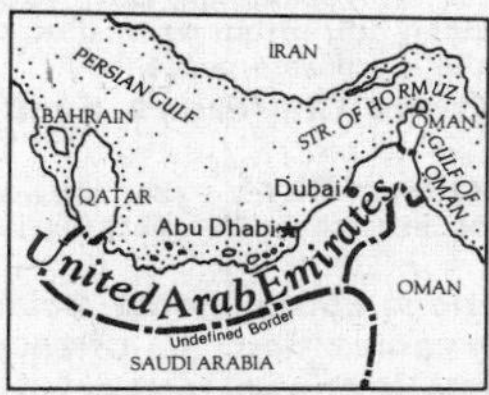

Unit′ed Ar′ab Repub′lic, a name given the union of Egypt and Syria from 1958 to 1961; after that, the official name of Egypt alone until 1971. *Abbr.:* U.A.R. Cf. **Egypt.**

Unit′ed Ar′ab States′, a former (1958–61) federation of the United Arab Republic (Egypt and Syria) and Yemen.

Unit′ed Breth′ren, a Protestant denomination, of Wesleyan beliefs and practices, founded in 1800.

Unit′ed Church′ of Christ′, an American Protestant denomination formed in 1957 by a union of the Evangelical and Reformed churches and the Congregational Christian churches.

Unit′ed Commu′nity Funds′ and Coun′cils of Amer′ica, a former name (1965–70) of the United Way of America. See under **United Way.**

unit′ed front′, 1. a coalition formed to oppose a force that menaces the interests of all the members: *They presented a united front against the enemy.* **2.** See **popular front.**

Unit′ed King′dom, a kingdom in NW Europe, con-

CONCISE PRONUNCIATION KEY: act, cāpe, dâre, pärt; set, ēqual; *if,* ice; ox, ōver, ôrder, oil, bo͝ok, bo͞ot, out; up, ûrge; child; sing; shoe; thin, *th*at; zh as in *treasure.* ə = *a* as in *alone, e* as in *system, i* as in *easily, o* as in *gallop, u* as in *circus;* ə as in *fire* (fīər), *hour* (ouər). l and n can serve as syllabic consonants, as in *cradle* (krād′l), and *button* (but′n). See the full key inside the front cover.

un·mesh′, *v.t.*
un′mes·mer′ic, *adj.*
un′mes·mer′i·cal·ly, *adv.*
un·mes′mer·ized′, *adj.*
un·met′, *adj.*
un′me·tab′o·lized′, *adj.*
un·met′aled, *adj.*
un·met′al·ized′, *adj.*
un·met′alled, *adj.*
un′me·tal′lic, *adj.*
un′me·tal′li·cal·ly, *adv.*
un·met′al·lur′gic, *adj.*
un′met·al·lur′gi·cal, *adj.;* **-ly,** *adv.*
un′met·a·mor′phic, *adj.*
un′met·a·mor′phosed, *adj.*
un′met·a·phys′ic, *adj.*
un′met·a·phys′i·cal, *adj.;* **-ly,** *adv.*
un·met′ed, *adj.*
un′me·te·or·o·log′ic, *adj.*
un′me·te·or·o·log′i·cal, *adj.;* **-ly,** *adv.*
un·me′tered, *adj.*
un′me·thod′ic, *adj.*
un′me·thod′i·cal, *adj.;* **-ly,** *adv.;* **-ness,** *n.*
un·meth′od·ized′, *adj.*
un·meth′od·iz′ing, *adj.*
un·meth′yl·at′ed, *adj.*
un′me·tic′u·lous, *adj.;* **-ly,** *adv.;* **-ness,** *n.*
un·met′ric, *adj.*
un·met′ri·cal, *adj.;* **-ly,** *adv.*
un·met′ri·fied′, *adj.*
un′met·ro·pol′i·tan, *adj.*
un′mi·as′mal, *adj.*
un′mi·as·mat′ic, *adj.*
un′mi·as·mat′i·cal, *adj.*
un′mi·as′mic, *adj.*
un′mi·ca′ceous, *adj.*
un′mi·cro′bi·al, *adj.*
un′mi·cro′bic, *adj.*
un′mi·cro·scop′ic, *adj.*
un′mi·cro·scop′i·cal·ly, *adv.*
un·mi′grant, *adj.*
un·mi′grat·ing, *adj.*
un·mi′gra·tive, *adj.*
un·mi′gra·to·ry, *adj.*
un·miked′, *adj.*
un·mil′dewed′, *adj.*
un·mil′i·tant, *adj.;* **-ly,** *adv.*
un′mil·i·tar′i·ly, *adv.*
un′mil·i·ta·ris′tic, *adj.*
un′mil·i·ta·ris′ti·cal·ly, *adv.*
un·mil′i·ta·rized′, *adj.*
un·mil′i·tar′y, *adj.*
un·milked′, *adj.*
un·milled′, *adj.*
un·milt′ed, *adj.*
un·mim′e·o·graphed′, *adj.*
un′mi·met′ic, *adj.*
un′mi·met′i·cal·ly, *adv.*
un·mim′icked, *adj.*
un·min′a·ble, *adj.*
un·minced′, *adj.*
un·minc′ing, *adj.*
un·mind′ing, *adj.*
un·mined′, *adj.*
un·min′er·al·ized′, *adj.*
un·min′gled, *adj.*
un·min′i·mized′, *adj.*
un·min′i·miz′ing, *adj.*
un·min′is·tered, *adj.*
un′min·is·te′ri·al, *adj.;* **-ly,** *adv.*
un·min′is·trant, *adj.*
un·min′is·tra′tive, *adj.*
un·mint′ed, *adj.*
un·min′ut·ed, *adj.*
un·mir′a·cled, *adj.*
un′mi·rac′u·lous, *adj.;* **-ly,** *adv.*
un·mired′, *adj.*
un·mir′rored, *adj.*
un·mirth′ful, *adj.;* **-ly,** *adv.*
un·mir′y, *adj.*
un′mis·an·throp′ic, *adj.*
un′mis·an·throp′i·cal, *adj.;* **-ly,** *adv.*
un·mis′chie·vous, *adj.;* **-ly,** *adv.*
un·mis′ci·ble, *adj.*
un·mi′ser·ly, *adj.*
un·mis·giv′ing, *adj.;* **-ly,** *adv.*
un·mis·guid′ed, *adj.;* **-ly,** *adv.*
un′mis·in·ter′pret·a·ble, *adj.*
un·mis·led′, *adj.*
un·miss′a·ble, *adj.*
un·missed′, *adj.*
un′mis·tak′en, *adj.*
un′mis·tak′ing, *adj.;* **-ly,** *adv.*
un′mis·trust′ed, *adj.*
un′mis·trust′ful, *adj.;* **-ly,** *adv.*
un′mis·trust′ing, *adj.*
un′mis·un·der·stand′a·ble, *adj.*
un′mis·un·der·stood′, *adj.*
un·mit′i·ga·ble, *adj.*
un·mit′i·ga′tive, *adj.*
un·mit′tened, *adj.*
un·mix′, *v.t.*
un·mix′a·ble, *adj.*
un·moaned′, *adj.*
un·moan′ing, *adj.*
un·moat′ed, *adj.*
un·mobbed′, *adj.*
un·mo′bile, *adj.*
un·mo′bi·lized′, *adj.*
un·mocked′, *adj.*
un·mock′ing, *adj.;* **-ly,** *adv.*
un·mod′eled, *adj.*
un·mod′elled, *adj.*
un·mod′er·at′ed, *adj.*
un·mod′er·at′ing, *adj.*
un·mod′ern, *adj.*
un′mo·der′ni·ty, *n., pl.* **-ties.**
un·mod′ern·ized′, *adj.*
un·mod′est, *adj.;* **-ly,** *adv.*
un·mod′i·fi′a·ble, *adj.*
un·mod′i·fi·ca′tive, *adj.*
un·mod′i·fied′, *adj.*
un·mod′ish, *adj.;* **-ly,** *adv.*
un·mod′u·lat′ed, *adj.*
un·mod′u·la′tive, *adj.*
un·moiled′, *adj.*
un·mois′ten, *v.t.*
un·mold′ered, *adj.*
un·mold′er·ing, *adj.*
un·mold′y, *adj.*
un′mo·lest′ed, *adj.*
un′mo·lest′ing, *adj.*
un·mol′li·fi′a·ble, *adj.*
un·mol′li·fied′, *adj.*
un·mol′li·fy′ing, *adj.*
un·mol′ten, *adj.*
un′mo·men′tous, *adj.;* **-ly,** *adv.;* **-ness,** *n.*
un′mo·nar′chic, *adj.*
un′mo·nar′chi·cal, *adj.;* **-ly,** *adv.*
un′mo·nas′tic, *adj.*
un′mo·nas′ti·cal·ly, *adv.*
un·mon′e·tar′y, *adj.*
un′mo·nis′tic, *adj.*
un·mon′i·tor·a·ble, *adj.*
un·mon′i·tored, *adj.*
un·mon′o·grammed′, *adj.*
un′mo·nop′o·lized′, *adj.*
un′mo·nop′o·liz′ing, *adj.*
un′mo·not′o·nous, *adj.;* **-ly,** *adv.*
un′mon·u·men′tal, *adj.*
un′mon′u·ment′ed, *adj.*
un·mood′y, *adj.*
un·moot′ed, *adj.*
un·mopped′, *adj.*
un′mor·al·is′tic, *adj.*
un·mor′al·iz′ing, *adj.*
un·mor′bid, *adj.;* **-ly,** *adv.;* **-ness,** *n.*
un·mor′dant, *adj.;* **-ly,** *adv.*
un·mor′i·bund′, *adj.;* **-ly,** *adv.*
un·mo·rose′, *adj.;* **-ly,** *adv.;* **-ness,** *n.*
un′mor·pho·log′i·cal, *adj.;* **-ly,** *adv.*
un·mor′tal, *adj.*
un·mor′tared, *adj.*
un·mort′gage, *v.t.,* **-gaged, -gag·ing.**
un·mort′gage·a·ble, *adj.*
un·mor′ti·fied′, *adj.*
un·mossed′, *adj.*
un·moss′y, *adj.*
un·moth′-eat′en, *adj.*
un·moth′ered, *adj.*
un·moth′er·ly, *adj.*
un·mo′tile, *adj.*
un·mo′tion·a·ble, *adj.*
un·mo′tioned, *adj.*
un·mo′tion·ing, *adj.*
un·mo′ti·vat′ed, *adj.*
un·mo′ti·vat′ing, *adj.*
un·mo′tored, *adj.*
un·mo′tor·ized′, *adj.*
un·mot′tled, *adj.*
un·mound′ed, *adj.*
un·mount′a·ble, *adj.*
un·moun′tain·ous, *adj.*
un·mount′ed, *adj.*
un·mount′ing, *adj.*
un·mourned′, *adj.*
un·mourn′ful, *adj.;* **-ly,** *adv.*
un·mourn′ing, *adj.*
un·mouth′a·ble, *adj.*
un·mouthed′, *adj.*
un·mov′a·ble, *adj.*
un·move′a·ble, *adj.*
un·moved′, *adj.*
un·mowed′, *adj.*
un·mown′, *adj.*
un·mu′ci·laged, *adj.*
un·mud′ded, *adj.*
un·mud′died, *adj.*
un·mud′dled, *adj.*
un·mud′dy, *adj.*
un·mulct′ed, *adj.*
un·mul′ish, *adj.*
un·mulled′, *adj.*
un·mul′lioned, *adj.*
un·mul′ti·pli′a·ble, *adj.*
un′mul·ti·plic′a·ble, *adj.*
un·mul′ti·pli·ca′tive, *adj.*
un·mul′ti·plied′, *adj.*
un·mul′ti·ply′ing, *adj.*
un·mum′bled, *adj.*
un·mum′bling, *adj.*
un·mum′mied, *adj.*
un·mum′mi·fied′, *adj.*
un·mum′mi·fy′ing, *adj.*
un·munched′, *adj.*
un′mun·dane′, *adj.;* **-ly,** *adv.*
un·mun′di·fied′, *adj.*
un′mu·nic′i·pal·ized′, *adj.*
un′mu·nif′i·cent, *adj.;* **-ly,** *adv.*
un′mu·ni′tioned, *adj.*
un·mur′mured, *adj.*
un·mur′mur·ing, *adj.;* **-ly,** *adv.*
un·mur′mur·ous, *adj.;* **-ly,** *adv.*
un·mus′cled, *adj.*
un·mus′cu·lar, *adj.;* **-ly,** *adv.*
un′mu·si·cal′i·ty, *n.*
un′mu·si′cian·ly, *adj.*

sisting of Great Britain and Northern Ireland: formerly comprising Great Britain and Ireland 1801–1922. 55,900,000; 94,242 sq. mi. (244,100 sq. km). *Cap.:* London. *Abbr.:* U.K. Official name, **Unit′ed King′dom of Great′ Brit′ain and North′ern Ire′land.**

Unit′ed Meth′odist Church′, 1. the largest denomination of the Methodist church in the U.S., formed in 1939 from the merger of the Methodist Episcopal Church, the Methodist Episcopal Church, South, and the Methodist Protestant Church, with the addition in 1968 of the Evangelical United Brethren. 2. a British Methodist church formed in 1907 by a union of three Methodist churches and united in 1932 with the Wesleyan Methodist Church and the Primitive Methodist Church to form the Methodist Church in Great Britain.

Unit′ed Na′tions, 1. an international organization, with headquarters in New York City, formed to promote international peace, security, and cooperation under the terms of the charter signed by 51 founding countries in San Francisco in 1945. *Abbr.:* UN Cf. **General Assembly, Security Council.** 2. the nations that signed the joint declaration in Washington, D.C., January 2, 1942, pledging to employ full resources against the Axis powers, not to make a separate peace, etc.

Unit′ed Na′tions Chil′dren's Fund′. See **UNICEF.**

Unit′ed Na′tions Day′, the anniversary of the United Nations on October 24, marking its founding in 1945.

Unit′ed Na′tions Educa′tional, Scientif′ic, and Cul′tural Organiza′tion. See **UNESCO.**

Unit′ed Na′tions Organiza′tion, the United Nations. *Abbr.:* UNO, U.N.O.

Unit′ed Presbyte′rian, 1. a member of the United Presbyterian Church of North America, founded in Pittsburgh in 1858 by a union of two Presbyterian groups. 2. a member of the United Presbyterian Church in the U.S.A., founded in Pittsburgh in 1958 by combining the United Presbyterian Church of North America with another Presbyterian body.

Unit′ed Press′ Interna′tional, a business organization of newspapers in the U.S., together with representatives abroad, for the reporting and interchange of news. *Abbr.:* UPI, U.P.I.

Unit′ed Prov′inces, 1. former name of **Uttar Pradesh.** 2. *Hist.* the seven northern provinces in the Low Countries that declared their independence from Spain in 1581 and laid the foundation for the establishment of the Netherlands.

Unit′ed Prov′inces of A′gra and Oudh′, former official name of **Uttar Pradesh.**

CONCISE ETYMOLOGY KEY: <, descended or borrowed from; >, whence; b., blend of, blended; c., cognate with; cf., compare; deriv., derivative; equiv., equivalent; imit., imitative; obl., oblique; r., replacing; s., stem; sp., spelling, spelled; resp., respelling, respelled; trans., translation; ?, origin unknown; *, unattested; ‡, probably earlier than. See the full key inside the front cover.

MEMBER NATIONS OF THE UNITED NATIONS

Afghanistan (1946)
Albania (1955)
Algeria (1962)
Angola (1976)
Antigua and Barbuda (1981)
Argentina*
Armenia (1992)
Australia*
Austria (1955)
Azerbaijan (1992)
Bahamas (1973)
Bahrain (1971)
Bangladesh (1974)
Barbados (1966)
Belgium*
Belize (1981)
Benin (1960)
Bhutan (1971)
Bolivia*
Bosnia and Herzegovina (1992)
Botswana (1966)
Brazil*
Brunei (1984)
Bulgaria (1955)
Burkina Faso (1960)
Burma (Myanmar) (1948)
Burundi (1962)
Byelorussia (Belarus)*
Cambodia (1955)
Cameroon (1960)
Canada*
Cape Verde (1975)
Central African Republic (1960)
Chad (1960)
Chile*
China*[1]
Colombia*
Comoros (1975)
Congo (1960)
Costa Rica*
Croatia (1992)
Cuba*
Cyprus (1960)
Czech Republic (1993)
Denmark*
Djibouti (1977)
Dominica (1978)
Dominican Republic*
Ecuador*
Egypt*
El Salvador*
Equatorial Guinea (1968)
Estonia (1991)
Ethiopia*
Fiji (1970)
Finland (1955)
France*
Gabon (1960)
Gambia (1965)
Georgia (1992)
Germany (1973)
Ghana (1957)
Greece*
Grenada (1974)
Guatemala*
Guinea (1958)
Guinea-Bissau (1974)
Guyana (1966)
Haiti*
Honduras*
Hungary (1955)
Iceland (1946)
India*
Indonesia (1950)
Iran*
Iraq*
Ireland (1955)
Israel (1949)
Italy (1955)
Ivory Coast (1960)
Jamaica (1962)
Japan (1956)
Jordan (1955)
Kazakhstan (1992)
Kenya (1963)
Kirghizia (1992)
Kuwait (1963)
Laos (1955)
Latvia (1991)
Lebanon*
Lesotho (1966)
Liberia*
Libya (1955)
Liechtenstein (1990)
Lithuania (1991)
Luxembourg*
Madagascar (1960)
Malawi (1964)
Malaysia (1957)
Maldives (1965)
Mali (1960)
Malta (1964)
Marshall Islands (1991)
Mauritania (1961)
Mauritius (1968)
Mexico*
Micronesia (1991)
Moldavia (1992)
Mongolia (1961)
Morocco (1956)
Mozambique (1975)
Namibia (1990)
Nepal (1955)
Netherlands*
New Zealand*
Nicaragua*
Niger (1960)
Nigeria (1960)
North Korea (1991)
Norway*
Oman (1971)
Pakistan (1947)
Panama*
Papua New Guinea (1975)
Paraguay*
Peru*
Philippines*
Poland*
Portugal (1955)
Qatar (1971)
Rumania (1955)
Russian Federation*
Rwanda (1962)
St. Kitts-Nevis (1983)
St. Lucia (1979)
St. Vincent and the Grenadines (1980)
San Marino (1990)
São Tomé and Príncipe (1975)
Saudi Arabia*
Senegal (1960)
Seychelles (1976)
Sierra Leone (1961)
Singapore (1965)
Slovakia (1993)
Slovenia (1992)
Solomon Islands (1978)
Somalia (1960)
South Africa*
South Korea (1991)
Spain (1955)
Sri Lanka (1955)
Sudan (1956)
Suriname (1975)
Swaziland (1968)
Sweden (1946)
Syria*
Tadzhikistan (1992)
Tanzania (1961)
Thailand (1946)
Togo (1960)
Trinidad and Tobago (1962)
Tunisia (1956)
Turkey*
Turkmenistan (1992)
Uganda (1962)
Ukraine*
United Arab Emirates (1971)
United Kingdom*
United States*
Uruguay (1945)
Uzbekistan (1992)
Vanuatu (1981)
Venezuela*
Vietnam (1977)
Western Samoa (1976)
Yemen (1947)
Yugoslavia*
Zaire (1960)
Zambia (1964)
Zimbabwe (1980)

*Indicates charter member in 1945. (Year in parentheses shows date of admission.)
[1]The People's Republic of China replaced the Republic of China in 1971.

un·mus′ing, *adj.*
un·musked′, *adj.*
un·mus′ter·a·ble, *adj.*
un·mus′tered, *adj.*
un·mu′ta·ble, *adj.*
un·mu′tant, *adj.*
un·mu′tat·ed, *adj.*
un′mu·ta′tion·al, *adj.*
un·mu′ta·tive, *adj.*
un·mut′ed, *adj.*
un·mu′ti·lat′ed, *adj.*
un·mu′ti·la′tive, *adj.*
un·mu′ti·nous, *adj.;* **-ly,** *adv.;* **-ness,** *n.*
un·mut′tered, *adj.*
un·mut′ter·ing, *adj.;* **-ly,** *adv.*
un·mu′tu·al, *adj.;* **-ly,** *adv.*
un·mu′tu·al·ized′, *adj.*
un′my·op′ic, *adj.*
un′mys·te′ri·ous, *adj.;* **-ly,** *adv.;* **-ness,** *n.*
un·mys′tic, *adj.*
un·mys′ti·cal, *adj.;* **-ly,** *adv.;* **-ness,** *n.*
un·mys′ti·cize′, *v.t.,* **-cized, -ciz·ing.**
un·mys′ti·fied′, *adj.*
un·myth′i·cal, *adj.;* **-ly,** *adv.*
un′myth·o·log′i·cal, *adj.;* **-ly,** *adv.*
un·na′cre·ous, *adj.*
un·nagged′, *adj.*
un·nag′ging, *adj.;* **-ly,** *adv.*
un′na·ive′, *adj.;* **-ly,** *adv.*
un·na′ked, *adj.*
un·nam′a·ble, *adj.*
un·name′a·ble, *adj.*
un·napped′, *adj.*
un′nar·cis·sis′tic, *adj.*
un′nar·cot′ic, *adj.*
un·nar′rat·a·ble, *adj.*
un·nar′rat·ed, *adj.*
un·nar′ra·tive, *adj.*
un·nar′row, *adj.;* **-ly,** *adv.*
un·nar′rowed, *adj.*
un·nar′row-mind′ed, *adj.;* **-ly,** *adv.;* **-ness,** *n.*
un·na′sal, *adj.;* **-ly,** *adv.*
un·nas′cent, *adj.*
un·na′tion·al, *adj.;* **-ly,** *adv.*
un′na·tion·al·is′tic, *adj.*
un′na·tion·al·is′ti·cal·ly, *adv.*
un·na′tion·al·ized′, *adj.*
un·na′tive, *adj.*
un′nat·u·ral·is′tic, *adj.*
un·nau′se·at′ed, *adj.*
un·nau′se·at′ing, *adj.*
un·nau′ti·cal, *adj.*
un′nav·i·ga·bil′i·ty, *n.*
un·nav′i·ga·ble, *adj.;* **-ble·ness,** *n.;* **-bly,** *adv.*
un·nav′i·gat′ed, *adj.*
un·neat′, *adj.;* **-ly,** *adv.;* **-ness,** *n.*
un′ne·ces′si·tat′ed, *adj.*
un′ne·ces′si·tat′ing, *adj.*
un′ne·ces′si·tous, *adj.;* **-ly,** *adv.;* **-ness,** *n.*
un·need′ed, *adj.*
un·need′ful, *adj.;* **-ly,** *adv.*
un·need′y, *adj.*
un′ne·far′i·ous, *adj.;* **-ly,** *adv.;* **-ness,** *n.*
un′ne·gat′ed, *adj.*
un′ne·glect′ed, *adj.*
un′ne·glect′ful, *adj.;* **-ly,** *adv.*
un·neg′li·gent, *adj.*
un′ne·go′ti·a·ble, *adj.*
un′ne·go′ti·at′ed, *adj.*
un·Ne′gro, *adj.*
un·neigh′bor·li·ness, *n.*
un·neigh′bor·ly, *adj.*
un′ne·phrit′ic, *adj.*
un·nerv′ous, *adj.;* **-ly,** *adv.;* **-ness,** *n.*
un·nes′tled, *adj.*
un·net′ted, *adj.*
un·net′tled, *adj.*
un·neu′ral, *adj.*
un′neu·ral′gic, *adj.*
un′neu·rot′ic, *adj.*
un′neu·rot′i·cal·ly, *adv.*
un·neu′tral, *adj.;* **-ly,** *adv.*
un′neu·tral′i·ty, *n.*
un·neu′tral·ize′, *v.t.,* **-ized, -iz·ing.**
un·new′, *adj.;* **-ness,** *n.*
un·news′wor′thy, *adj.*
un·nibbed′, *adj.*
un·nib′bled, *adj.*
un·nice′, *adj.;* **-ly,** *adv.;* **-ness,** *n.*
un·niched′, *adj.*
un·nicked′, *adj.*
un·nick′named′, *adj.*
un·nig′gard, *adj.;* **-ly,** *adv.*
un·nigh′, *adj.*
un′ni·hil·is′tic, *adj.*
un·nim′ble, *adj.;* **-ble·ness,** *n.;* **-bly,** *adv.*
un·nipped′, *adj.*
un′noc·tur′nal, *adj.;* **-ly,** *adv.*
un·nod′ding, *adj.*
un·noised′, *adj.*
un·nois′i·ly, *adv.*
un·nois′y, *adj.*
un′no·mad′ic, *adj.*
un·nom′i·na′tive, *adj.*
un·nor′mal, *adj.;* **-ly,** *adv.;* **-ness,** *n.*
un·nor′mal·ized′, *adj.*
un·nor′mal·iz′ing, *adj.*
un·nor′ma·tive, *adj.*
un·north′ern, *adj.*
un·nosed′, *adj.*
un·not′a·ble, *adj.*
un′no·ta′tion·al, *adj.*
un·notched′, *adj.*
un·not′ed, *adj.*
un·note′wor′thy, *adj.*
un·no′tice·a·ble, *adj.;* **-ble·ness,** *n.;* **-bly,** *adv.*
un·no′ticed, *adj.*
un·no′tic·ing, *adj.*
un·no′ti·fied′, *adj.*
un·not′ing, *adj.*
un·no′tion·al, *adj.;* **-ly,** *adv.*
un·no′tioned, *adj.*
un·nour′ish·a·ble, *adj.*
un·nour′ished, *adj.*
un·nour′ish·ing, *adj.*
un·nov′el, *adj.*
un·nu′anced, *adj.*
un·nu′cle·at′ed, *adj.*
un·nul′li·fied′, *adj.*
un·numbed′, *adj.*
un·nu′mer·at′ed, *adj.*
un′nu·mer′i·cal, *adj.*
un·nu′mer·ous, *adj.;* **-ly,** *adv.;* **-ness,** *n.*
un·nur′tured, *adj.*
un′nu·tri′tious, *adj.;* **-ly,** *adv.*
un·nu′tri·tive, *adj.*
un·nymph′al, *adj.*
un·nymph′like′, *adj.*
un·oared′, *adj.*
un·ob′du·rate, *adj.;* **-ly,** *adv.;* **-ness,** *n.*
un′o·bese′, *adj.;* **-ly,** *adv.;* **-ness,** *n.*
un′o·beyed′, *adj.*
un′o·bey′ing, *adj.*
un·ob′fus·cat′ed, *adj.*
un′ob·ject′ed, *adj.*
un′ob·jec′tion·a·ble, *adj.*
un′ob·jec′tive, *adj.;* **-ly,** *adv.*
un·ob′li·gat′ed, *adj.*
un·ob′li·ga′tive, *adj.*
un′o·blig′a·to′ry, *adj.*
un′o·bliged′, *adj.*
un′o·blig′ing, *adj.*
un′ob·lit′er·at′ed, *adj.*
un′ob·liv′i·ous, *adj.;* **-ly,** *adv.;* **-ness,** *n.*
un′ob·nox′i·ous, *adj.;* **-ly,** *adv.*
un′ob·scene′, *adj.;* **-ly,** *adv.;* **-ness,** *n.*
un′ob·scure′, *adj.;* **-ly,** *adv.;* **-ness,** *n.*
un′ob·scured′, *adj.*
un′ob·se′qui·ous, *adj.;* **-ly,** *adv.;* **-ness,** *n.*
un′ob·serv′a·ble, *adj.*
un′ob·serv′ant, *adj.;* **-ly,** *adv.*
un′ob·served′, *adj.*
un′ob·serv′ing, *adj.*
un′ob·sessed′, *adj.*
un′ob·so·lete′, *adj.*
un·ob′sti·nate, *adj.;* **-ly,** *adv.*
un′ob·struct′ed, *adj.*
un′ob·struc′tive, *adj.*
un·ob′stru·ent, *adj.;* **-ly,** *adv.*
un′ob·tain′a·ble, *adj.*
un′ob·tained′, *adj.*
un′ob·trud′ed, *adj.*
un′ob·trud′ing, *adj.*
un′ob·vert′ed, *adj.*
un·ob′vi·a·ble, *adj.*
un·ob′vi·at′ed, *adj.*
un·ob′vi·ous, *adj.;* **-ly,** *adv.;* **-ness,** *n.*
un′oc·ca′sion·al, *adj.;* **-ly,** *adv.*
un′oc·ci·den′tal, *adj.;* **-ly,** *adv.*
un′oc·clud′ed, *adj.*
un·oc′cu·pan·cy, *n.*
un′oc·cur′ring, *adj.*
un·oc′u·lar, *adj.*
un·o′di·ous, *adj.;* **-ly,** *adv.;* **-ness,** *n.*
un·o′dored, *adj.*
un′o·dor·if′er·ous, *adj.;* **-ly,** *adv.;* **-ness,** *n.*
un′of·fend′a·ble, *adj.*
un′of·fend′ed, *adj.*
un′of·fend′ing, *adj.*
un′of·fen′sive, *adj.;* **-ly,** *adv.;* **-ness,** *n.*
un·of′fered, *adj.*
un′of·fi′cial, *adj.;* **-ly,** *adv.*
un′of·fi′ci·at′ed, *adj.*
un′of·fi′ci·at′ing, *adj.*
un′of·fi′cious, *adj.;* **-ly,** *adv.;* **-ness,** *n.*
un·oiled′, *adj.*
un·oil′ing, *adj.*
un·oil′y, *adj.*
un·om′i·nous, *adj.;* **-ly,** *adv.;* **-ness,** *n.*
un′o·mit′ted, *adj.*
un′om·nip′o·tent, *adj.;* **-ly,** *adv.*
un′om·nis′cient, *adj.;* **-ly,** *adv.*
un·on′er·ous, *adj.;* **-ly,** *adv.;* **-ness,** *n.*
un·o′pen·a·ble, *adj.*
un·o′pened, *adj.*
un·o′pen·ing, *adj.*
un·op′er·at′a·ble, *adj.*
un·op′er·at′ed, *adj.*
un′op·er·at′ic, *adj.*
un′op·er·at′i·cal·ly, *adv.*
un·op′er·at′ing, *adj.*
un·op′er·a·tive, *adj.*

Unit′ed States′, a republic in the N Western Hemisphere comprising 48 conterminous states, the District of Columbia, and Alaska in North America, and Hawaii in the N Pacific. 226,545,805; conterminous United States, 3,022,387 sq. mi. (7,827,982 sq. km); with Alaska and Hawaii, 3,615,122 sq. mi. (9,363,166 sq. km). *Cap.:* Washington, D.C. *Abbr.:* U.S., US Also called **United States of America, America.**

Unit′ed States′ Air′ Force′, the permanent or regular military air force of the United States, established in 1947 as a separate service under the authority of the Department of Defense: a branch of the U.S. Army before 1947. *Abbr.:* USAF

Unit′ed States′ Ar′my, the permanent or regular military land force of the United States, under the authority of the Department of Defense since 1947. *Abbr.:* USA

Unit′ed States′ Cus′toms Serv′ice, *U.S. Govt.* the division of the Department of the Treasury that collects customs and enforces laws dealing with smuggling.

Unit′ed States′ Employ′ment Serv′ice, *U.S. Govt.* the division of the Department of Labor that supervises and coordinates the activities of state employment agencies. *Abbr.:* USES

Unit′ed States′ Informa′tion A′gency, *U.S. Govt.* an independent agency, created in 1953 and known from 1978 to 1982 as the International Communication Agency, that administers the government's overseas information and cultural programs. *Abbr.:* USIA

Unit′ed States′ Interna′tional Devel′opment Coopera′tion A′gency, *U.S. Govt.* an independent agency, created in 1979, that administers government programs for economic relations with developing countries.

Unit′ed States′ Interna′tional Trade′ Commis′sion, *U.S. Govt.* a federal agency, created in 1916, that conducts research, makes reports, and resolves problems in international trade and tariffs.

Unit′ed States′ Marine′ Corps′. See **Marine Corps.** *Abbr.:* USMC

Unit′ed States′ Na′val Acad′emy, an institution founded in 1845 at Annapolis, Maryland, for the training of U.S. naval officers.

Unit′ed States′ Na′vy, the permanent or regular naval force of the United States, under the authority of the Department of Defense since 1947. *Abbr.:* USN

Unit′ed States′ of Amer′ica. See **United States.** *Abbr.:* U.S.A., USA

Unit′ed States′ of Brazil′, former official name of **Brazil.**

Unit′ed States′ of Indone′sia, former official name of the Republic of Indonesia.

Unit′ed States′ Post′al Serv′ice, an independent federal agency created in 1971 to replace the Post Office Department as the division of the federal government responsible for postal services. *Abbr.:* USPS

Unit′ed Way′, **1.** a nationwide civic organization

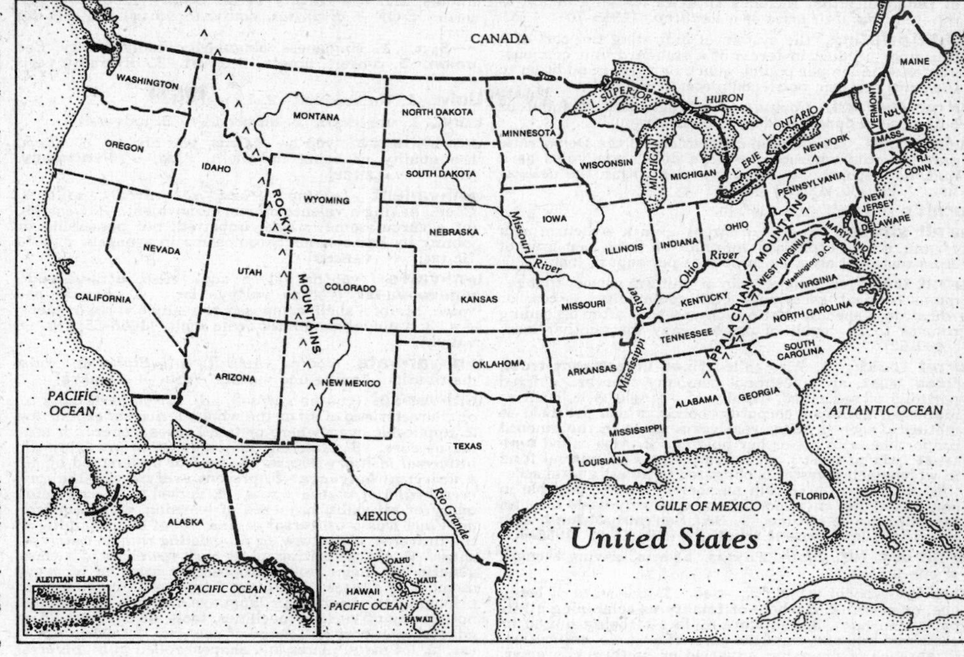

(**Unit′ed Way′ of Amer′ica**) or any of its affiliated local groups that raise funds through individual contributions and allocate them to benefit civic and charitable programs and organizations, as the YMCA and Red Cross. Formerly, **Community Chests and Councils of America, United Community Funds and Councils of America. 2.** a similar and related organization (**Unit′ed Way′ of Can′ada**) in Canada.

u′nit el′ement, *Math.* identity (def. 9b).

u′nit fac′tor, *Biol.* a gene; a sequence of nucleotides that functions as the hereditary unit for a single character.

u′nit invest′ment trust′. See **unit trust** (defs. 1, 2).

u·ni·tive (yo͞o′ni tiv), *adj.* **1.** capable of causing unity or serving to unite. **2.** marked by or involving union. [1520–30; < LL *ūnitīvus* uniting, equiv. to L *ūnit(us)* (see UNITE) + *-īvus* -IVE] **—u′ni·tive·ly,** *adv.* **—u′ni·tive·ness,** *n.*

u·nit·ize (yo͞o′ni tīz′), *v.t.,* **-ized, -iz·ing. 1.** to form or combine into one unit, as by welding parts together: *a car with a unitized body.* **2.** to divide or separate into units. Also, *esp. Brit.,* **u′nit·ise′.** [1840–50; UNIT + -IZE] **—u′nit·i·za′tion,** *n.* **—u′nit·iz′er,** *n.*

u′nit magnet′ic pole′, *Physics.* the unit of magnetic pole strength equal to the strength of a magnetic pole that repels a similar pole with a force of one dyne, the two poles being placed in a vacuum and separated by a distance of one centimeter. [1885–90]

u′nit price′, **1.** rate[1] (def. 3). **2.** a price for a service

CONCISE PRONUNCIATION KEY: *act, cāpe, dâre, pärt; set, ēqual; if, ice; ox, ōver, ôrder, oil, bo͝ok, bo͞ot, out; up, ûrge; child; sing; shoe; thin, that; zh as in treasure.* ə = *a* as in *alone, e* as in *system, i* as in *easily, o* as in *gallop, u* as in *circus;* ᵊ as in *fire* (fīᵊr), *hour* (ouᵊr). l and n can serve as syllabic consonants, as in *cradle* (krād′l), and *button* (but′n). See the full key inside the front cover.

un′o·pi·at′ic, *adj.*
un′o·pined′, *adj.*
un′o·pin′ion·at′ed, *adj.*
un′o·pin′ioned, *adj.*
un′op·por·tune′, *adj.;* **-ly,** *adv.;* **-ness,** *n.*
un′op·por·tun·is′tic, *adj.*
un′op·pos′a·ble, *adj.*
un′op·posed′, *adj.*
un′op·pos′ing, *adj.*
un′op·po·si′tion·al, *adj.*
un′op·pressed′, *adj.*
un′op·press′i·ble, *adj.*
un′op·pres′sive, *adj.;* **-ly,** *adv.;* **-ness,** *n.*
un′op·pro′bri·ous, *adj.;* **-ly,** *adv.;* **-ness,** *n.*
un′op·pugned′, *adj.*
un·opt′ed, *adj.*
un′op·ti·mis′tic, *adj.*
un′op·ti·mis′ti·cal, *adj.;* **-ly,** *adv.*
un·op′tion·al, *adj.;* **-ly,** *adv.*
un·op′u·lence, *n.*
un·op′u·lent, *adj.;* **-ly,** *adv.*
un·o′ral, *adj.;* **-ly,** *adv.*
un′o·ra′tion·al, *adj.*
un′o·ra·tor′i·cal, *adj.;* **-ly,** *adv.*
un·orbed′, *adj.*
un·or′bi·tal, *adj.;* **-ly,** *adv.*
un·or′ches·trat′ed, *adj.*
un′or·dain′a·ble, *adj.*
un′or·dained′, *adj.*
un·or′der·a·ble, *adj.*
un·or′dered, *adj.*
un·or′der·ly, *adj.*
un·or′di·nal, *adj.*
un·or′di·nar′y, *adj.*
un′or·gan′ic, *adj.*
un′or·gan′i·cal·ly, *adv.*
un·or′gan·iz′a·ble, *adj.*
un′o·ri·en′tal, *adj.;* **-ly,** *adv.*
un′o·rig′i·nal, *adj.;* **-ly,** *adv.*
un′o·rig′i·nal′i·ty, *n.*
un′or·na·men′tal, *adj.;* **-ly,** *adv.*
un·or′na·ment′ed, *adj.*
un′or·nate′, *adj.;* **-ly,** *adv.;* **-ness,** *n.*
un′or·ni·tho·log′i·cal, *adj.*
un·or′phaned, *adj.*
un·or′tho·dox, *adj.;* **-ly,** *adv.*
un·or′tho·dox′y, *n., pl.* **-dox·ies.**
un′or·tho·graph′i·cal, *adj.;* **-ly,** *adv.*
un·os′cil·lat′ing, *adj.*
un·os′cu·lat′ed, *adj.*
un′os·mot′ic, *adj.*
un·os′si·fied′, *adj.*
un·os′si·fy′ing, *adj.*
un′os·ten′si·ble, *adj.;* **-bly,** *adv.*
un′os·ten′sive, *adj.;* **-ly,** *adv.*
un′os·ten·ta′tious, *adj.;* **-ly,** *adv.*
un·oust′ed, *adj.*
un·out′lawed′, *adj.*
un·out′raged, *adj.*
un′out·spo′ken, *adj.*
un′out·worn′, *adj.*
un′o·ver·come′, *adj.*
un′o·ver·drawn′, *adj.*
un′o·ver·flow′ing, *adj.*
un′o·ver·hauled′, *adj.*
un′o·ver·looked′, *adj.*
un′o·ver·paid′, *adj.*
un′o·ver·pow′ered, *adj.*
un′o·ver·ruled′, *adj.*
un′o·vert′, *adj.*
un′o·ver·tak′en, *adj.*
un′o·ver·thrown′, *adj.*
un′o·ver·whelmed′, *adj.*
un·ow′ing, *adj.*
un·owned′, *adj.*
un·ox′i·dat′ed, *adj.*
un·ox′i·da′tive, *adj.*
un·ox′i·diz′a·ble, *adj.*
un·ox′i·dized′, *adj.*
un·ox′y·gen·at′ed, *adj.*
un·ox′y·gen·ized′, *adj.*
un·paced′, *adj.*
un·pac′i·fi′a·ble, *adj.*
un′pa·cif′ic, *adj.*
un·pac′i·fied′, *adj.*
un·pac′i·fist, *adj.*
un′pac·i·fis′tic, *adj.*
un·pack′aged, *adj.*
un·pad′ded, *adj.*
un·pad′locked′, *adj.*
un·pa′gan, *adj.*
un·pa′gan·ize′, *v.t.,* **-ized, -iz·ing.**
un·pag′i·nal, *adj.*
un·pag′i·nat′ed, *adj.*
un·paid′, *adj.*
un·pained′, *adj.*
un·pain′ful, *adj.;* **-ly,** *adv.*
un·pain′ing, *adj.*
un·paint′ed, *adj.*
un·paired′, *adj.*
un·pal′a·tal, *adj.;* **-ly,** *adv.*
un′pa·la′tial, *adj.*
un·pale′, *adj.*
un·paled′, *adj.*
un·pal′i·sad′ed, *adj.*
un·pal′i·sa′doed, *adj.*
un·palled′, *adj.*
un·pal′li·at′ed, *adj.*
un·pal′li·a′tive, *adj.*
un·pal′pa·ble, *adj.;* **-bly,** *adv.*
un·pal′pi·tat′ing, *adj.*
un·pal′sied, *adj.*
un·pal′try, *adj.*
un·pam′pered, *adj.*
un·pan′e·gy·rized′, *adj.*
un·pan′eled, *adj.*
un·pan′elled, *adj.*
un·pan′ick·y, *adj.*
un·pan′niered, *adj.*
un·pan′o·plied, *adj.*
un′pan·the·is′tic, *adj.*
un′pan·the·is′ti·cal, *adj.;* **-ly,** *adv.*
un·pant′ing, *adj.*
un·pa′pal, *adj.*
un·pa′pered, *adj.*
un′pa·rad′ed, *adj.*
un′par·a·dox′al, *adj.*
un′par·a·dox′i·cal, *adj.;* **-ly,** *adv.*
un·par′a·graphed′, *adj.*
un·par′al·lel′, *adj.*
un·par′a·lyzed′, *adj.*
un·par′a·phrased′, *adj.*
un′par·a·sit′ic, *adj.*
un′par·a·sit′i·cal, *adj.;* **-ly,** *adv.*
un·par′a·si·tized′, *adj.*
un·par′celed, *adj.*
un·par′cel·ing, *adj.*
un·par′celled, *adj.*
un·par′cel·ling, *adj.*
un·parched′, *adj.*
un·parch′ing, *adj.*
un·par′don·a·ble, *adj.;* **-bly,** *adv.*
un·par′doned, *adj.*
un·par′don·ing, *adj.*
un·pared′, *adj.*
un′pa·ren′tal, *adj.;* **-ly,** *adv.*
un′pa·ren′the·sized′, *adj.*
un′par·en·thet′ic, *adj.*
un′par·en·thet′i·cal, *adj.;* **-ly,** *adv.*
un·par′get·ed, *adj.*
un·parked′, *adj.*
un·park′ing, *adj.*
un′par·lia·ment′ed, *adj.*
un′pa·ro′chi·al, *adj.;* **-ly,** *adv.*
un·par′o·died, *adj.*
un′pa·rol′a·ble, *adj.*
un′pa·roled′, *adj.*
un·par′ried, *adj.*
un·par′ry·ing, *adj.*
un·parsed′, *adj.*
un′par·si·mo′ni·ous, *adj.;* **-ly,** *adv.*
un·par′tak′en, *adj.*
un·par·tak′ing, *adj.*
un·part′ed, *adj.*
un·par′ti·ble, *adj.*
un′par·tic′i·pant, *adj.*
un′par·tic′i·pat′ed, *adj.*
un′par·tic′i·pat′ing, *adj.*
un′par·tic′i·pa′tive, *adj.*
un′par·tic′u·lar, *adj.*
un′par·tic′u·lar·ized′, *adj.*
un′par·tic′u·lar·iz′ing, *adj.*
un·par′ti·san, *adj.*
un·par′ti·tioned, *adj.*
un·par′ti·tive, *adj.*
un·par′ti·zan, *adj.*
un·pass′a·ble, *adj.*
un·passed′, *adj.*
un·pass′ing, *adj.*
un·pas′sion·ate, *adj.;* **-ly,** *adv.;* **-ness,** *n.*
un·pas′sioned, *adj.*
un·pas′sive, *adj.;* **-ly,** *adv.*
un·paste′, *v.t.,* **-past·ed, -past·ing.**
un·pas′teur·ized′, *adj.*
un·pas′to·ral, *adj.;* **-ly,** *adv.*
un·pas′tured, *adj.*
un·patched′, *adj.*
un·pat′ent, *adj.*
un·pat′ent·a·bil′i·ty, *n.*
un·pat′ent·a·ble, *adj.*
un·pat′ent·ed, *adj.*
un′pa·ter′nal, *adj.;* **-ly,** *adv.*
un′pa·thet′ic, *adj.*
un′pa·thet′i·cal·ly, *adv.*
un′path·o·log′i·cal, *adj.;* **-ly,** *adv.*
un·pa′tient, *adj.;* **-ly,** *adv.*
un·pat′i·nat′ed, *adj.*
un′pa·tri·ar′chal, *adj.;* **-ly,** *adv.*
un′pa·tri′cian, *adj.*
un′pa·tri·ot′ic, *adj.*
un′pa·tri·ot′i·cal·ly, *adv.*
un′pa·tris′tic, *adj.*
un′pa·tris′ti·cal, *adj.;* **-ly,** *adv.*
un′pa·trolled′, *adj.*
un·pa′tron·iz′a·ble, *adj.*
un·pa′tron·iz′ing, *adj.;* **-ly,** *adv.*
un·pat′ted, *adj.*
un·pat′terned, *adj.*
un·pat′tern·ized′, *adj.*
un·paus′ing, *adj.*
un·paved′, *adj.*
un′pa·vil′ioned, *adj.*
un·pawed′, *adj.*
un·pawned′, *adj.*
un·pay′a·ble, *adj.;* **-bly,** *adv.*
un·pay′ing, *adj.*
un·peace′a·ble, *adj.;* **-bly,** *adv.*
un·peace′ful, *adj.;* **-ly,** *adv.*
un·peaked′, *adj.*
un·pealed′, *adj.*
un·pearled′, *adj.*
un·peb′bled, *adj.*
un·pecked′, *adj.*
un·pec′u·lat′ing, *adj.*
un′pe·cu′liar, *adj.;* **-ly,** *adv.*
un·ped′a·gog′ic, *adj.*
un·ped′a·gog′i·cal·ly, *adv.*
un′pe·dan′tic, *adj.*
un′pe·dan′ti·cal, *adj.*
un·ped′dled, *adj.*
un·ped′es·tal, *v.t.,* **-taled, -tal·ing** or (*esp. Brit.*) **-talled, -tal·ling.**
un·ped′i·greed′, *adj.*
un·peel′a·ble, *adj.*
un·peeled′, *adj.*
un·peel′ing, *adj.*
un·pee′vish, *adj.;* **-ly,** *adv.;* **-ness,** *n.*
un′pe·jo′ra·tive, *adj.;* **-ly,** *adv.*
un·pelt′ed, *adj.*
un·pe′nal, *adj.;* **-ly,** *adv.*
un·pe′nal·ized′, *adj.*
un·pen′anced, *adj.*
un·pen′ciled, *adj.*
un·pen′cilled, *adj.*
un·pend′ant, *adj.*
un·pend′ent, *adj.*
un·pend′ing, *adj.*
un·pen′du·lous, *adj.;* **-ly,** *adv.;* **-ness,** *n.*

or commodity that includes all extra costs incidental to the item: *the unit price of a wedding.* [1965–70]

u′nit pric′ing, the system of indicating the cost of a consumer product in terms of a standard unit of measure, as so much per pound, quart, or yard, in addition to the price per can, bottle, or piece. [1965–70]

u′nit rec′ord, *Computers.* a single unit of input or output, as a punch card or line of printout.

u′nit rule′, (in national conventions of the Democratic party) a rule whereby a state's delegation votes as a unit, not recognizing minority votes within the delegation. [1880–85, *Amer.*]

u′nit's place′, unit (def. 8).

u′nit stress′, *Engin.* a stress upon a structure at a certain place, expressed in units of force per unit of cross-sectional area, as in pounds per square inch.

u′nit train′, a freight train of uniform consist that remains coupled, carrying a bulk commodity, as coal or wheat, to a specific destination and that after unloading returns to the point of origin ready for another load. [1960–65]

u′nit trust′, **1.** Also called **fixed investment trust, fixed trust.** an investment company that has a fixed portfolio of securities, usually of a single type, such as municipal bonds or corporate bonds, which are held to maturity: each investor receives a share in the amount proportionate to his or her holding. **2.** Also called **u·ni·trust** (yo͞o′ni trust′). an inflexible type of mutual fund in which each investor is obligated to invest a total specified amount in a certain number of shares, payable in equal amounts on a monthly or quarterly basis over an extended period of time. **3.** *Brit.* See **mutual fund.** Also called **unit investment trust** (for defs. 1, 2). [1935–40]

u′nit vec′tor, *Math., Physics.* a vector having a length of one unit.

u·ni·ty (yo͞o′ni tē), *n., pl.* **-ties. 1.** the state of being one; oneness. **2.** a whole or totality as combining all its parts into one. **3.** the state or fact of being united or combined into one, as of the parts of a whole; unification. **4.** absence of diversity; unvaried or uniform character. **5.** oneness of mind, feeling, etc., as among a number of persons; concord, harmony, or agreement. **6.** *Math.* **a.** the number one; a quantity regarded as one. **b.** identity (def. 9). **7.** (in literature and art) a relation of all the parts or elements of a work constituting a harmonious whole and producing a single general effect. **8.** one of the three principles of dramatic structure **(the three unities)** derived from Aristotelian aesthetics and formalized in the neoclassic canon in which a play is required to represent action as taking place in one day **(u′nity of time′),** as occurring within one place **(u′nity of place′),** and as having a single plot with a beginning, middle, and end **(u′nity of ac′tion).** [1250–1300; ME *unite* < OF < L *ūnitās,* equiv. to *ūn(us)* one + *-itās* -ITY]
—Syn. 1. singleness, singularity, individuality. See **union. 5.** concert, unison. **—Ant. 1.** diversity, variety.

CONCISE ETYMOLOGY KEY: <, descended or borrowed from; >, whence; b., blend of, blended; c., cognate with; cf., compare; deriv., derivative; equiv., equivalent; imit., imitative; obl., oblique; r., replacing; s., stem; sp., spelling, spelled; resp., respelling, respelled; trans., translation; ?, origin unknown; *, unattested; ‡, probably earlier than. See the full key inside the front cover.

Univ., 1. Universalist. **2.** University.

univ., 1. universal. **2.** universally. **3.** university.

u·ni·va·lence (yo͞o′nə vā′ləns, yo͞o niv′ə-), *n. Chem.* the quality of being univalent. Also, **u′ni·va′len·cy.** [UNI- + VALENCE]

u·ni·va·lent (yo͞o′nə vā′lənt, yo͞o niv′ə-), *adj.* **1.** *Chem.* having a valence of one; monovalent. **2.** *Genetics.* (of a chromosome) single; unpaired; not possessing or joining its homologous chromosome in synapsis. [1865–70; UNI- + -VALENT]

u·ni·valve (yo͞o′nə valv′), *adj.* Also, **u′ni·valved′, u·ni·val·vu·lar** (yo͞o′nə val′vyə lər). **1.** having one valve. **2.** (of a shell) composed of a single valve or piece. —*n.* **3.** a univalve mollusk or its shell. [1655–65; UNI- + VALVE]

u·ni·var·i·ate (yo͞o′nə vâr′ē it), *adj. Statistics.* (of a distribution) having one variate. [UNI- + VARIATE]

u·ni·ver·sal (yo͞o′nə vûr′səl), *adj.* **1.** of, pertaining to, or characteristic of all or the whole: *universal experience.* **2.** applicable everywhere or in all cases; general: *a universal cure.* **3.** affecting, concerning, or involving all: *universal military service.* **4.** used or understood by all: *a universal language.* **5.** present everywhere: *the universal calm of southern seas.* **6.** versed in or embracing many or all skills, branches of learning, etc.: *Leonardo da Vinci was a universal genius.* **7.** of or pertaining to the universe, all nature, or all existing things: *universal cause.* **8.** characterizing all or most members of a class; generic. **9.** *Logic.* (of a proposition) asserted of every member of a class. **10.** *Ling.* found in all languages or belonging to the human language faculty. **11.** *Mach.* noting any of various machines, tools, or devices widely adaptable in position, range of use, etc. **12.** *Metalworking.* **a.** (of metal plates and shapes) rolled in a universal mill. **b.** (of a rolling mill or rolling method) having or employing vertical edging rolls. —*n.* **13.** something that may be applied throughout the universe to many things, usually thought of as an entity that can be in many places at the same time. **14.** a trait, characteristic, or property, as distinguished from a particular individual or event, that can be possessed in common, as the care of a mother for her young. **15.** *Logic.* a universal proposition. **16.** *Philos.* **a.** a general term or concept or the generic nature that such a term signifies; a Platonic idea or Aristotelian form. **b.** an entity that remains unchanged in character in a series of changes or changing relations. **c.** *Hegelianism.* See **concrete universal. 17.** See **language universal. 18.** *Mach.* See **universal joint.** [1325–75; ME *universel* (adj.) < MF < L *ūniversālis.* See UNIVERSE, -AL[1]] **—u′ni·ver′sal·ness,** *n.*
—Syn. 5. See **general.**

univer′sal affirm′ative, *Logic.* a proposition of the form "All S is P." *Symbol:* A, a

u′niver′sal chuck′, a chuck, as on a lathe headstock, having three stepped jaws moving simultaneously for precise centering of a workpiece of any of a wide range of sizes. [1815–25]

U′niver′sal Cit′y, a city in S central Texas. 10,720.

u′niver′sal class′, *Logic.* (in the theory of classes) the class that includes all other classes and is composed of all individuals composing these classes.

u′niver′sal cou′pling, *Mach.* See **universal joint.**

u′niver′sal do′nor, a person with blood of group O. [1920–25]

u′niver′sal gas′ con′stant, *Physics.* a constant, 8.314 joules per degree Kelvin, equal to the product of the pressure and the volume of one gram molecule of an ideal gas divided by the absolute temperature. *Symbol:* R Also called **gas constant.** Cf. **Boltzmann constant.**

u′niver′sal gram′mar, *Ling.* **1.** a grammar that attempts to establish the properties and constraints common to all possible human languages. **2.** an innate system of principles underlying the human language faculty.

u·ni·ver·sal·ism (yo͞o′nə vûr′sə liz′əm), *n.* **1.** universal character; universality. **2.** a universal range of knowledge, interests, or activities. **3.** (*cap.*) the doctrine that emphasizes the universal fatherhood of God and the final salvation of all souls. Cf. **apocatastasis** (def. 2). [1795–1805; UNIVERSAL + -ISM]

u·ni·ver·sal·ist (yo͞o′nə vûr′sə list), *n.* **1.** a person characterized by universalism, as in knowledge, interests, or activities. **2.** (*cap.*) a member of a liberal religious denomination advocating Universalism. Cf. **Unitarian Universalism.** —*adj.* **3.** (*cap.*) Also, **U′ni·ver′sal·is′tic.** of or pertaining to Universalism or Universalists. [1620–30; UNIVERSAL + -IST]

u·ni·ver·sal·i·ty (yo͞o′nə vər sal′i tē), *n., pl.* **-ties. 1.** the character or state of being universal; existence or prevalence everywhere. **2.** relation, extension, or applicability to all. **3.** universal character or range of knowledge, interests, etc. [1325–75; ME *universalite* < LL *ūniversālitās.* See UNIVERSAL, -ITY]

u·ni·ver·sal·ize (yo͞o′nə vûr′sə līz′), *v.t.,* **-ized, -iz·ing.** to make universal. Also, *esp. Brit.,* **u′ni·ver′sal·ise′.** [1635–45; UNIVERSAL + -IZE] **—u′ni·ver′sal·i·za′tion,** *n.* **—u′ni·ver′sal·iz′er,** *n.*

u′niver′sal joint′, *Mach.* a coupling between rotating shafts set at an angle to one another, allowing for rotation in three planes. Also called **universal, universal coupling.** [1670–80]

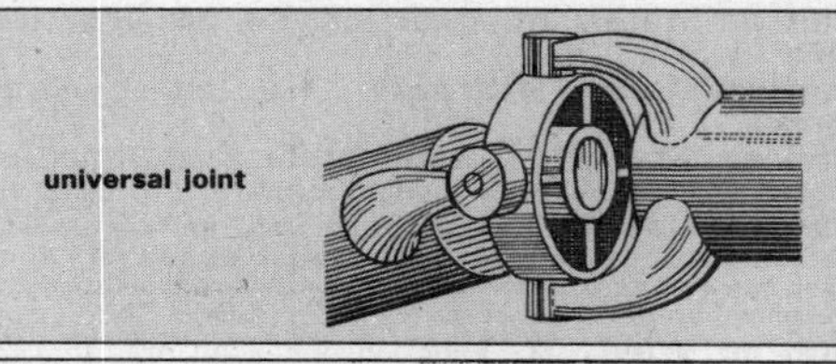
universal joint

un·pen′e·tra·ble, *adj.;* **-bly,** *adv.*
un·pen′e·trant, *adj.*
un·pen′e·trat′ed, *adj.*
un·pen′e·trat′ing, *adj.;* **-ly,** *adv.*
un·pen′e·tra′tive, *adj.;* **-ly,** *adv.*
un·pen′i·tent, *adj.;* **-ly,** *adv.*
un′pen·i·ten′tial, *adj.;* **-ly,** *adv.*
un·pen′nied, *adj.*
un·pen′noned, *adj.*
un·pen′sion·a·ble, *adj.*
un·pen′sioned, *adj.*
un·pen′sion·ing, *adj.*
un·pent′, *adj.*
un′pe·nu′ri·ous, *adj.;* **-ly,** *adv.;* **-ness,** *n.*
un·pep′pered, *adj.*
un·pep′per·y, *adj.*
un′per·ceiv′a·ble, *adj.;* **-bly,** *adv.*
un′per·ceived′, *adj.*
un′per·ceiv′ing, *adj.*
un′per·cep′ti·ble, *adj.;* **-ble·ness,** *n.;* **-bly,** *adv.*
un′per·cep′tion·al, *adj.*
un′per·cep′tive, *adj.;* **-ly,** *adv.*
un′per·cep′tu·al, *adj.;* **-ly,** *adv.*
un·perched′, *adj.*
un′per·cip′i·ent, *adj.*
un·per′co·lat′ed, *adj.*
un′per·cussed′, *adj.*
un′per·cus′sive, *adj.*
un′per·dur′a·ble, *adj.;* **-bly,** *adv.*
un′per·emp′to·ri·ly, *adv.*
un′per·emp′to·ri·ness, *n.*
un′per·emp′to·ry, *adj.*
un·per′fect, *adj.*
un′per·fect′ed, *adj.*
un′per·fect′i·ble, *adj.*
un′per·fec′tive, *adj.;* **-ly,** *adv.;* **-ness,** *n.*
un′per·fid′i·ous, *adj.;* **-ly,** *adv.;* **-ness,** *n.*
un·per′for·a·ble, *adj.*
un·per′fo·rat′ed, *adj.*
un·per′fo·rat′ing, *adj.*
un·per′fo·ra′tive, *adj.*
un′per·form′a·ble, *adj.*
un′per·formed′, *adj.*
un′per·form′ing, *adj.*
un′per·fumed′, *adj.*
un·per′il·ous, *adj.;* **-ly,** *adv.*
un′pe·ri·od′ic, *adj.*
un′pe·ri·od′i·cal, *adj.;* **-ly,** *adv.*
un′pe·riph′er·al, *adj.;* **-ly,** *adv.*
un′per·i·phras′tic, *adj.*
un′per·i·phras′ti·cal·ly, *adv.*
un·per′ish·a·ble, *adj.*
un·per′ished, *adj.*
un·per′ish·ing, *adj.*
un·per′jured, *adj.*
un·per′jur·ing, *adj.*
un·per′ma·nent, *adj.;* **-ly,** *adv.*
un·per′me·a·ble, *adj.*
un·per′me·ant, *adj.*
un·per′me·at′ed, *adj.*
un·per′me·at′ing, *adj.*
un·per′me·a′tive, *adj.*
un′per·mis′si·ble, *adj.;* **-bly,** *adv.*
un′per·mis′sive, *adj.*
un′per·mit′ted, *adj.*
un′per·mit′ting, *adj.*
un′per·ni′cious, *adj.;* **-ly,** *adv.*
un′per·pen·dic′u·lar, *adj.;* **-ly,** *adv.*
un·per′pe·trat′ed, *adj.*
un′per·pet′u·a·ble, *adj.*
un′per·pet′u·at′ed, *adj.*
un′per·pet′u·at′ing, *adj.*
un′per·plexed′, *adj.*
un′per·plex′ing, *adj.*
un·per′se·cut′ed, *adj.*
un·per′se·cut′ing, *adj.*
un·per′se·cu′tive, *adj.*
un′per·sist′ing, *adj.*
un·per′son·a·ble, *adj.*
un·per′son·al, *adj.;* **-ly,** *adv.*
un·per′son·al·ized′, *adj.*
un·per′son·al·iz′ing, *adj.*
un′per·son′i·fied′, *adj.*
un′per·son′i·fy′ing, *adj.*
un′per·spic′u·ous, *adj.;* **-ly,** *adv.;* **-ness,** *n.*
un′per·spired′, *adj.*
un′per·spir′ing, *adj.*
un′per·suad′a·ble, *adj.;* **-bly,** *adv.*
un′per·suad′ed, *adj.*
un′per·sua′si·ble, *adj.*
un′per·sua′sive, *adj.;* **-ly,** *adv.;* **-ness,** *n.*
un′per·tain′ing, *adj.*
un·per′ti·nent, *adj.;* **-ly,** *adv.*
un′per·turb′a·ble, *adj.*
un′per·turbed′, *adj.*
un′per·turb′ing, *adj.*
un′pe·ruked′, *adj.*
un′pe·rus′a·ble, *adj.*
un′pe·rused′, *adj.*
un′per·vad′ed, *adj.*
un′per·vad′ing, *adj.*
un′per·va′sive, *adj.;* **-ly,** *adv.;* **-ness,** *n.*
un′per·verse′, *adj.;* **-ly,** *adv.*
un′per·ver′sive, *adj.*
un′per·vert′ed, *adj.;* **-ly,** *adv.*
un·per′vi·ous, *adj.;* **-ly,** *adv.;* **-ness,** *n.*
un·pes′si·mis′tic, *adj.*
un·pes′si·mis′ti·cal·ly, *adv.*
un·pes′tered, *adj.*
un·pes′ter·ous, *adj.*
un·pes′ti·lent, *adj.;* **-ly,** *adv.*
un′pes·ti·len′tial, *adj.*
un·pet′aled, *adj.*
un·pet′alled, *adj.*
un′pe·ti′tioned, *adj.*
un·pet′ri·fied′, *adj.*
un·pet′ri·fy′ing, *adj.*
un·pet′ted, *adj.*
un·pet′ti·coat′ed, *adj.*
un·pet′u·lant, *adj.;* **-ly,** *adv.*
un·phased′, *adj.*
un′phe·nom′e·nal, *adj.;* **-ly,** *adv.*
un′phil·an·throp′ic, *adj.*
un′phil·an·throp′i·cal·ly, *adv.*
un′phil·o·log′ic, *adj.*
un′phil·o·log′i·cal, *adj.*
un′phil·o·soph′ic, *adj.*
un′phil·o·soph′i·cal, *adj.;* **-ly,** *adv.*
un′phleg·mat′ic, *adj.*
un′phleg·mat′i·cal, *adj.;* **-ly,** *adv.*
un′pho·net′ic, *adj.*
un′pho·net′i·cal, *adj.;* **-ly,** *adv.*
un·phos′pha·tized′, *adj.*
un′pho·to·graph′a·ble, *adj.*
un·pho′to·graphed′, *adj.*
un·phrased′, *adj.*
un·phys′i·cal, *adj.;* **-ly,** *adv.*
un′phys·i·o·log′i·cal, *adj.;* **-ly,** *adv.*
un′pic·a·resque′, *adj.*
un·pick′a·ble, *adj.*
un·picked′, *adj.*
un·pick′et·ed, *adj.*
un·pick′led, *adj.*
un′pic·to′ri·al, *adj.;* **-ly,** *adv.*
un′pic·to′ri·al·ize′, *v.t.,* **-ized, -iz·ing.**
un·pic′tured, *adj.*
un′pic·tur·esque′, *adj.;* **-ly,** *adv.;* **-ness,** *n.*
un·pieced′, *adj.*
un·pierce′a·ble, *adj.*
un·pierced′, *adj.*
un·pierc′ing, *adj.*
un·pi′e·ty, *n., pl.* **-ties.**
un·pig′ment·ed, *adj.*
un·pil′fered, *adj.*
un·pil′laged, *adj.*
un·pil′lared, *adj.*
un·pil′lo·ried, *adj.*
un·pil′lowed, *adj.*
un·pi′lot·ed, *adj.*
un·pim′pled, *adj.*
un·pinched′, *adj.*
un·pin′ioned, *adj.*
un′pi·o·neer′ing, *adj.*
un·pi′ous, *adj.;* **-ly,** *adv.*
un·piped′, *adj.*
un·piqued′, *adj.*
un·pi′rat·ed, *adj.*
un′pi·rat′i·cal, *adj.;* **-ly,** *adv.*
un·pitched′, *adj.*
un·pit′e·ous, *adj.;* **-ly,** *adv.*
un·pit′i·a·ble, *adj.;* **-bly,** *adv.*
un·pit′ied, *adj.*
un·pit′i·ful, *adj.;* **-ly,** *adv.;* **-ness,** *n.*
un·pit′ted, *adj.*
un·pit′y·ing, *adj.*
un·pla′cat·ed, *adj.*
un·pla′ca·to′ry, *adj.*
un·placed′, *adj.*
un·plac′id, *adj.;* **-ly,** *adv.;* **-ness,** *n.*
un·pla′gia·rized′, *adj.*
un·plagued′, *adj.*
un·plan′, *v.t.,* **-planned, -plan·ning.**
un·planed′, *adj.*
un·plan′ished, *adj.*
un·planked′, *adj.*
un·plant′a·ble, *adj.*
un·plant′ed, *adj.*
un·plashed′, *adj.*
un·plas′ter, *v.t.*
un·plas′tic, *adj.*
un·plas′ti·cized′, *adj.*
un·plat′ed, *adj.*
un′plat·i·tu′di·nous, *adj.;* **-ly,** *adv.;* **-ness,** *n.*
un·plat′ted, *adj.*
un·plau′si·ble, *adj.;* **-ble·ness,** *n.;* **-bly,** *adv.*
un·play′a·ble, *adj.*
un·played′, *adj.*
un·play′ful, *adj.;* **-ly,** *adv.*
un·play′ing, *adj.*
un·pleached′, *adj.*
un·plead′a·ble, *adj.*
un·plead′ed, *adj.*
un·plead′ing, *adj.*
un·pleas′a·ble, *adj.*
un·pleased′, *adj.*
un·pleas′ing, *adj.*
un·pleas′ur·a·ble, *adj.*
un·pleat′ed, *adj.*
un′ple·be′ian, *adj.*
un·pledged′, *adj.*
un·plen′ished, *adj.*
un·plen′te·ous, *adj.;* **-ly,** *adv.*
un·plen′ti·ful, *adj.;* **-ly,** *adv.*
un·pli′a·ble, *adj.;* **-ble·ness,** *n.;* **-bly,** *adv.*
un·pli′an·cy, *n.*
un·pli′ant, *adj.;* **-ly,** *adv.;* **-ness,** *n.*
un·plied′, *adj.*
un·plight′ed, *adj.*
un·plod′ding, *adj.*
un·plot′ted, *adj.*
un·plot′ting, *adj.*
un·ploughed′, *adj.*
un·plow′a·ble, *adj.*
un·plowed′, *adj.*
un·plucked′, *adj.*
un·plumb′, *adj.*
un·plumed′, *adj.*
un·plum′met·ed, *adj.*
un·plun′dered, *adj.*
un·plun′der·ous, *adj.;* **-ly,** *adv.*
un·plunged′, *adj.*
un′plu·ral·is′tic, *adj.*
un·plu′ral·ized′, *adj.*
un′plu·to·crat′ic, *adj.*
un′plu·to·crat′i·cal, *adj.*
un′pneu·mat′ic, *adj.*
un′pneu·mat′i·cal·ly, *adv.*
un·poached′, *adj.*
un·pock′et, *v.t.*
un·pod′ded, *adj.*
un′po·et′ic, *adj.*
un′po·et′i·cal, *adj.;* **-ly,** *adv.*
un′po·et′i·cized′, *adj.*
un·po′et·ized′, *adj.*

u′niver′sal lan′guage, **1.** an auxiliary language that is used and understood everywhere. **2.** any kind of expression that is used and understood everywhere: *Music is a universal language.*

u′niver′sal life′ insur′ance, a type of insurance in which the payments of the insured are placed in an investment fund, earnings from which pay the premium on term life insurance while any remainder continues to increase the policy's value. Also called **u′niver′sal-life′ insur′ance.** —**u′ni·ver′sal-life′,** *adj.*

u·ni·ver·sal·ly (yo͞o′nə vûr′sə lē), *adv.* in a universal manner; in every instance or place; without exception. [1350–1400; ME; see UNIVERSAL, -LY]

univer′sal mil′itary train′ing, a program for maintaining a nation's pool of trained military personnel, requiring all qualified citizens to serve for a period of active and reserve duty. *Abbr.:* UMT

u′niver′sal mill′, *Metalworking.* a rolling mill having both horizontal and vertical rolls.

u′niver′sal mo′tor, a series-wound motor, of one-half horsepower or less, using alternating or direct current. [1920–25]

u′niver′sal neg′ative, *Logic.* a proposition of the form "No S is P." *Symbol:* E, e

U′niver′sal Post′al Un′ion, an international organization, formed in Bern, Switzerland (1875), that administers and regulates international postal service. *Abbr.:* UPU Formerly, **General Postal Union.**

U′niver′sal Prod′uct Code′, a bar code that indicates price, product classification, etc., and can be read electronically, as at checkout counters in supermarkets. *Abbr.:* UPC Cf. **bar code.** [1970–75]

u′niver′sal quan′tifier, *Logic.* a quantifier indicating that the sentential function within its scope is true for all values of any variable included in the quantifier. Cf. **existential quantifier.**

u′niver′sal stage′, a small theodolite mounted on the stage of a polarizing microscope and used in the petrographic analysis of rocks.

u′niver′sal suf′frage, suffrage for all persons over a certain age, usually 18 or 21, who in other respects satisfy the requirements established by law. [1700–10]

univer′sal time′, (*often caps.*) See **Greenwich Time.** *Abbr.:* UT [1885–90]

univer′sal time′ coor′dinated, Greenwich Time that is adjusted to minimize its divergence from international atomic time. *Abbr.:* UTC

u·ni·verse (yo͞o′nə vûrs′), *n.* **1.** the totality of known or supposed objects and phenomena throughout space; the cosmos; macrocosm. **2.** the whole world, esp. with reference to humanity: *a truth known throughout the universe.* **3.** a world or sphere in which something exists or prevails: *his private universe.* **4.** Also called **u′niverse of dis′course.** *Logic.* the aggregate of all the objects, attributes, and relations assumed or implied in a given discussion. **5.** Also called **u′niver′sal set′.** *Math.* the set of all elements under discussion for a given problem. **6.** *Statistics.* the entire population under study. [1325–75; ME < OF *univers* < L *ūniversum,* n. use of neut. of *ūniversus* entire, all, lit., turned into one, equiv. to *ūni-* UNI- + *versus* (ptp. of *vertere* to turn)]

u·ni·ver·si·ty (yo͞o′nə vûr′si tē), *n., pl.* **-ties.** an institution of learning of the highest level, having a college of liberal arts and a program of graduate studies together with several professional schools, as of theology, law, medicine, and engineering, and authorized to confer both undergraduate and graduate degrees. Continental European universities usually have only graduate or professional schools. [1250–1300; ME *universite* < OF < ML *ūniversitās,* LL: guild, corporation, L: totality, equiv. to *ūnivers(us)* (see UNIVERSE) + *-itās* -ITY] —**u·ni·ver·si·tar·i·an** (yo͞o′nə vûr′si târ′ē ən), *n., adj.*

Univer′sity Cit′y, a city in E Missouri, near St. Louis. 42,738.

univer′sity exten′sion, a system by which an institution provides educational programs, as evening classes, for students otherwise unable to attend. Cf. **extension courses.**

Univer′sity Heights′, a city in NE Ohio, near Cleveland. 15,401.

Univer′sity Park′, a city in N Texas. 22,254.

univer′sity profes′sor, a professor entitled to teach courses in more than one field or discipline at a university. [1905–10]

Univer′sity Wits′, a name given to an Elizabethan group of university-trained playwrights and pamphleteers, among them Robert Greene, John Lyly, Thomas Nash, and George Peele.

u·niv·o·cal (yo͞o niv′ə kəl, yo͞o′nə vō′-), *adj.* having only one meaning; unambiguous. [1535–45; < LL *ūnivōc(us)* (*ūni-* UNI- + *-vōcus,* adj. deriv. of *vōx,* s. *vōc-,* VOICE) + -AL[1]] —**u·niv′o·cal·ly,** *adv.*

un·jaun·diced (un jôn′dist, -jän′-), *adj.* devoid of distorted or prejudiced views. [1765–75; UN-[1] + JAUNDICED]

un·joint (un joint′), *v.t.* to sever or dislocate a joint of; disjoint. [1350–1400; ME; see UN-[2], JOINT]

un·just (un just′), *adj.* **1.** not just; lacking in justice or fairness: *unjust criticism; an unjust ruler.* **2.** *Archaic.* unfaithful or dishonest. [1350–1400; ME; see UN-[1], JUST[1]] —**un·just′ly,** *adv.* —**un·just′ness,** *n.*
—**Syn. 1.** inequitable, partial, unfair, prejudiced, biased; undeserved, unmerited, unjustifiable.

Un·ke·los (ung′kə los′), *n.* Onkelos.

un·kempt (un kempt′), *adj.* **1.** not combed: *unkempt hair.* **2.** uncared-for or neglected; disheveled; messy: *unkempt clothes; an unkempt lawn.* **3.** unpolished; rough; crude. [1590–1600; var. of *unkembed;* see UN-[1], KEMPT] —**un·kempt′ly,** *adv.* —**un·kempt′ness,** *n.*

un·kenned (un kend′; *Scot.* un kent′), *adj. Chiefly Scot.* unknown. [1250–1300; ME; see UN-[1], KEN, -ED[2]]

un·ken·nel (un ken′l), *v.,* **-neled, -nel·ing** or (*esp. Brit.*) **-nelled, -nel·ling.** —*v.t.* **1.** to drive (a fox or other animal) from a den or lair. **2.** to release from or as if from a kennel: *to unkennel hounds before a hunt; to unkennel a gang of cutthroats.* **3.** to make known; disclose or uncover. —*v.i.* **4.** to come out of a kennel, den, lair, or the like. [1570–80; UN-[2] + KENNEL[1]]

un·kind (un kīnd′), *adj.,* **-er, -est.** lacking in kindness or mercy; severe. [1200–50; ME; see UN-[1], KIND[1]] —**un·kind′ness,** *n.*

un·kind·ly (un kīnd′lē), *adj.,* **-li·er, -li·est. 1.** not kindly; unkind; ill-natured. **2.** inclement or bleak, as weather or climate. **3.** unfavorable for crops: *unkindly soil.* —*adv.* **4.** in an unkind manner. [1175–1225; ME; see UN-[1], KINDLY] —**un·kind′li·ness,** *n.*

un·knight·ly (un nīt′lē), *adj.* **1.** unworthy of a knight. **2.** not like a knight. —*adv.* **3.** in a manner unworthy of a knight. [1375–1425; late ME (adj.); see UN-[1], KNIGHTLY]

un·knit (un nit′), *v.,* **-knit·ted** or **-knit, -knit·ting.** —*v.t.* **1.** to untie or unfasten (a knot, tangle, etc.); unravel (something knitted); undo. **2.** to weaken, undo, or destroy. **3.** to smooth out (something wrinkled). —*v.i.* **4.** to become undone. [bef. 1000; ME *unknytten,* OE *uncnyttan.* See UN-[2], KNIT] —**un·knit′ta·ble,** *adj.*

un·knot (un not′), *v.t.,* **-knot·ted, -knot·ting.** to untie by or as if by undoing a knot: *to unknot a tie.* [1590–1600; UN-[2] + KNOT[1]]

un·know·a·ble (un nō′ə bəl), *adj.* **1.** not knowable; incapable of being known or understood. —*n.* **2.** something that is unknowable. **3. the Unknowable,** the postulated reality lying behind all phenomena but not cognizable by any of the processes by which the mind cognizes phenomenal objects. [1325–75; ME; see UN-[1], KNOWABLE]

un·know·ing (un nō′ing), *adj.* ignorant or unaware: *unknowing aid to the enemy.* [1250–1300; ME; see UN-[1], KNOWING] —**un·know′ing·ly,** *adv.*

un·known (un nōn′), *adj.* **1.** not known; not within the range of one's knowledge, experience, or understanding; strange; unfamiliar. **2.** not discovered, explored, identified, or ascertained: *the unknown parts of Antarctica.* **3.** not widely known; not famous; obscure: *an unknown writer.* —*n.* **4.** a thing, influence, area, factor, or person that is unknown: *the many unknowns in modern medicine; The director cast an unknown in the leading role.* **5.** *Math.* a symbol representing an unknown quantity: in algebra, analysis, etc., frequently represented by a letter from the last part of the alphabet, as *x, y,* or *z.* [1250–1300; ME *unknow(e)n.* See UN-[1], KNOWN]

Un′known Sol′dier, an unidentified soldier killed in battle and buried with honors, the tomb serving as a memorial to all the unidentified dead of a nation's armed forces. The tomb of the American Unknown Soldier, commemorating a serviceman killed in World War I, was

CONCISE PRONUNCIATION KEY: *act, cāpe, dâre, pärt; set, ēqual; if, ice; ox, ōver, ôrder, oil, bo͝ok, bo͞ot, out; up, ûrge; child; sing; shoe; thin, that;* zh as in *treasure.* ə = *a* as in *alone, e* as in *system, i* as in *easily, o* as in *gallop, u* as in *circus;* ° as in *fire* (fī°r), *hour* (ou°r). l and n can serve as syllabic consonants, as in *cradle* (krād′l), and *button* (but′n). See the full key inside the front cover.

un·poign′ant, *adj.;* **-ly,** *adv.*
un·point′ed, *adj.*
un·point′ing, *adj.*
un·poised′, *adj.*
un·poi′son·a·ble, *adj.*
un·poi′soned, *adj.*
un·poi′son·ous, *adj.;* **-ly,** *adv.*
un·po′lar·ized′, *adj.*
un·poled′, *adj.*
un′po·lem′ic, *adj.*
un′po·lem′i·cal, *adj.;* **-ly,** *adv.*
un′po·liced′, *adj.*
un·pol′ish·a·ble, *adj.*
un·pol′ished, *adj.*
un′po·lit′i·cal, *adj.;* **-ly,** *adv.*
un·pol′lard·ed, *adj.*
un·pol′lened, *adj.*
un′pol·lut′ed, *adj.*
un′pol·lut′ing, *adj.*
un·po·lym′er·ized′, *adj.*
un·pomp′ous, *adj.;* **-ly,** *adv.;* **-ness,** *n.*
un·pon′der·a·ble, *adj.*
un·pon′dered, *adj.*
un·pon′der·ous, *adj.;* **-ly,** *adv.;* **-ness,** *n.*
un′pon·tif′i·cal, *adj.;* **-ly,** *adv.*
un·pooled′, *adj.*
un·pop′u·lar·ized′, *adj.*
un·pop′u·lat′ed, *adj.*
un·pop′u·lous, *adj.;* **-ly,** *adv.;* **-ness,** *n.*
un·por′ce·lain·ized′, *adj.*
un′por·no·graph′ic, *adj.*
un·po′rous, *adj.;* **-ness,** *n.*
un·port′a·ble, *adj.*
un′por·tend′ed, *adj.*
un′por·ten′tous, *adj.;* **-ly,** *adv.;* **-ness,** *n.*
un·por′ti·coed′, *adj.*
un·por′tion·a·ble, *adj.*
un·por′tioned, *adj.*
un·port′ly, *adj.*
un′por·tray′a·ble, *adj.*
un′por·trayed′, *adj.*
un·posh′, *adj.*
un·pos′ing, *adj.*
un·pos′i·tive, *adj.;* **-ly,** *adv.;* **-ness,** *n.*
un′pos·i·tiv·is′tic, *adj.*
un′pos·sess′a·ble, *adj.*
un′pos·sessed′, *adj.*
un′pos·sess′ing, *adj.*
un′pos·ses′sive, *adj.;* **-ly,** *adv.;* **-ness,** *n.*
un·post′ed, *adj.*
un·post′ered, *adj.*
un·post′marked′, *adj.*
un′post·pon′a·ble, *adj.*
un′post·poned′, *adj.*
un·pos′tu·lat′ed, *adj.*
un·pot′, *v.t.,* **-pot·ted, -pot·ting.**
un·po′ta·ble, *adj.*
un·po′tent, *adj.;* **-ly,** *adv.*
un·pot′ted, *adj.*
un·pouched′, *adj.*
un·poul′ticed, *adj.*
un·pounced′, *adj.*
un·pound′ed, *adj.*
un·pour′a·ble, *adj.*
un·poured′, *adj.*
un·pout′ing, *adj.;* **-ly,** *adv.*
un·pow′dered, *adj.*
un·pow′er·ful, *adj.*
un′prag·mat′ic, *adj.*
un′prag·mat′i·cal, *adj.;* **-ly,** *adv.*
un·prais′a·ble, *adj.*
un·praised′, *adj.*
un·praise′ful, *adj.*
un·praise′wor′thy, *adj.*
un·prais′ing, *adj.*
un·pranked′, *adj.*
un·prat′ing, *adj.*
un·prayer′ful, *adj.;* **-ly,** *adv.;* **-ness,** *n.*
un·pray′ing, *adj.*
un·preached′, *adj.*
un·preach′ing, *adj.*
un′pre·car′i·ous, *adj.;* **-ly,** *adv.;* **-ness,** *n.*
un′pre·cau′tioned, *adj.*
un′pre·ced′ed, *adj.*
un′prec·e·den′tial, *adj.*
un′pre·cep′tive, *adj.;* **-ly,** *adv.*
un·pre′cious, *adj.;* **-ly,** *adv.;* **-ness,** *n.*
un·prec′i·piced, *adj.*
un′pre·cip′i·tant, *adj.;* **-ly,** *adv.*
un′pre·cip′i·tate, *adj.;* **-ly,** *adv.;* **-ness,** *n.*
un′pre·cip′i·tat′ed, *adj.*
un′pre·cip′i·ta′tive, *adj.;* **-ly,** *adv.*
un′pre·cip′i·tous, *adj.;* **-ly,** *adv.;* **-ness,** *n.*
un′pre·cise′, *adj.;* **-ly,** *adv.;* **-ness,** *n.*
un′pre·ci′sive, *adj.*
un′pre·clud′a·ble, *adj.*
un′pre·clud′ed, *adj.*
un′pre·clu′sive, *adj.;* **-ly,** *adv.*
un′pre·co′cious, *adj.;* **-ly,** *adv.;* **-ness,** *n.*
un′pre·da′ceous, *adj.;* **-ly,** *adv.;* **-ness,** *n.*
un′pre·da′cious, *adj.;* **-ly,** *adv.;* **-ness,** *n.*
un·pred′a·to′ry, *adj.*
un′pre·des′tined, *adj.*
un′pre·dic′a·ble, *adj.;* **-ble·ness,** *n.;* **-bly,** *adv.*
un·pred′i·cat′ed, *adj.*
un·pred′i·ca′tive, *adj.;* **-ly,** *adv.*
un′pre·dict′ed, *adj.*
un′pre·dict′ing, *adj.*
un′pre·dic′tive, *adj.;* **-ly,** *adv.*
un′pre·dis·posed′, *adj.*
un′pre·dis·pos′ing, *adj.*
un′pre·empt′ed, *adj.*
un·preened′, *adj.*
un′pre·fab′ri·cat′ed, *adj.*
un·pref′aced, *adj.*
un·pref′er·a·ble, *adj.;* **-ble·ness,** *n.;* **-bly,** *adv.*
un′pre·ferred′, *adj.*
un′pre·fig′ured, *adj.*
un′pre·fix′al, *adj.;* **-ly,** *adv.*
un′pre·fixed′, *adj.*
un·preg′nant, *adj.*
un′prej·u·di′cial, *adj.;* **-ly,** *adv.*
un′pre·lat′ic, *adj.*
un′prel·ud′ed, *adj.*
un′pre·ma·ture′, *adj.;* **-ly,** *adv.;* **-ness,** *n.*
un′pre·med′i·tat′ed, *adj.*
un′pre·mon′ished, *adj.*
un′pre·oc′cu·pied′, *adj.*
un′pre·or·dained′, *adj.*
un′pre·pared′, *adj.*
un′pre·par′ed·ly, *adv.*
un′pre·par′ed·ness, *n.*
un′pre·par′ing, *adj.*
un′pre·pon′der·at′ed, *adj.*
un′pre·pon′der·at′ing, *adj.*
un′pre·pos·sess′ing, *adj.;* **-ly,** *adv.*
un′pre·pos′ter·ous, *adj.;* **-ly,** *adv.;* **-ness,** *n.*
un·pres′aged, *adj.*
un·pres′ag·ing, *adj.*
un·pre′scient, *adj.;* **-ly,** *adv.*
un′pre·scind′ed, *adj.*
un′pre·scribed′, *adj.*
un′pre·sent′a·ble, *adj.;* **-ble·ness,** *n.;* **-bly,** *adv.*
un′pre·sent′a·tive, *adj.*
un′pre·sent′ed, *adj.*
un′pre·serv′a·ble, *adj.*
un′pre·served′, *adj.*
un′pres·i·den′tial, *adj.;* **-ly,** *adv.*
un′pre·sid′ing, *adj.*
un·pressed′, *adj.*
un·pres′sured, *adj.*
un·pres′sur·ized′, *adj.*
un′pre·sum′a·ble, *adj.;* **-bly,** *adv.*
un′pre·sumed′, *adj.*
un′pre·sum′ing, *adj.*
un′pre·sump′tive, *adj.;* **-ly,** *adv.*
un′pre·sump′tu·ous, *adj.;* **-ly,** *adv.;* **-ness,** *n.*
un′pre·tend′ed, *adj.*
un′pre·ter·mit′ted, *adj.*
un′pre·ter·nat′u·ral, *adj.;* **-ly,** *adv.*
un·pret′ti·fied′, *adj.*
un·pret′ti·ly, *adv.*
un·pret′ti·ness, *n.*
un·pret′ty, *adj.*
un′pre·vail′ing, *adj.*
un·prev′a·lent, *adj.;* **-ly,** *adv.*
un′pre·var′i·cat′ing, *adj.*
un′pre·vent′a·ble, *adj.*
un′pre·vent′a·tive, *adj.*
un′pre·vent′ed, *adj.*
un′pre·vent′i·ble, *adj.*
un′pre·ven′tive, *adj.;* **-ly,** *adv.;* **-ness,** *n.*
un′pre·viewed′, *adj.*
un·prey′ing, *adj.*
un·pricked′, *adj.*
un·prick′led, *adj.*
un·prick′ly, *adj.*
un·pride′ful, *adj.;* **-ly,** *adv.*
un·priest′like′, *adj., adv.*
un·priest′ly, *adj.*
un·prig′gish, *adj.*
un·prim′, *adj.;* **-ly,** *adv.;* **-ness,** *n.*
un·primed′, *adj.*
un·prim′i·tive, *adj.;* **-ly,** *adv.;* **-ness,** *n.*
un′prim·i·tiv·is′tic, *adj.*
un·primmed′, *adj.*
un·prince′ly, *adj.*
un·print′ed, *adj.*
un′pris·mat′ic, *adj.*
un′pris·mat′i·cal, *adj.;* **-ly,** *adv.*
un·pris′on·a·ble, *adj.*
un·pri′vate, *adj.;* **-ly,** *adv.;* **-ness,** *n.*
un·priv′i·leged, *adj.*
un·prized′, *adj.*
un′pro·bat·ed, *adj.*
un′pro·ba′tion·al, *adj.*
un′pro·ba′tion·ar′y, *adj.*
un′pro′ba·tive, *adj.*
un·probed′, *adj.*
un′prob·lem·at′ic, *adj.*
un′prob·lem·at′i·cal, *adj.;* **-ly,** *adv.*
un·proc′essed, *adj.*
un′pro·ces′sion·al, *adj.*
un′pro·claimed′, *adj.*
un′pro·cras′ti·nat′ed, *adj.*
un·pro′cre·ant, *adj.*
un·pro′cre·at′ed, *adj.*
un·proc′tored, *adj.*
un′pro·cur′a·ble, *adj.*
un′pro·cured′, *adj.*
un·prod′ded, *adj.*
un′pro·di′gious, *adj.;* **-ly,** *adv.;* **-ness,** *n.*
un′pro·duced′, *adj.*
un′pro·duc′i·ble, *adj.*
un′pro·duc′tive, *adj.;* **-ly,** *adv.;* **-ness,** *n.*
un′pro·duc·tiv′i·ty, *n.*
un′pro·fan′a·ble, *adj.*
un′pro·fane′, *adj.;* **-ly,** *adv.;* **-ness,** *n.*
un′pro·faned′, *adj.*
un′pro·fessed′, *adj.*
un′pro·fess′ing, *adj.*
un′pro·fes·so′ri·al, *adj.;* **-ly,** *adv.*
un·prof′fered, *adj.*
un·prof′it·ed, *adj.*
un·prof′it·eer′ing, *adj.*
un·prof′it·ing, *adj.*
un′pro·found′, *adj.;* **-ly,** *adv.*
un′pro·fuse′, *adj.;* **-ly,** *adv.;* **-ness,** *n.*
un′prog·nos′ti·cat′ed, *adj.*
un′prog·nos′ti·ca′tive, *adj.*
un·pro′gram·ma·ble, *adj.*
un′pro·gram·mat′ic, *adj.*
un·pro′grammed, *adj.*
un′pro·gressed′, *adj.*

established in the Arlington National Cemetery in Virginia in 1921. In 1958, the remains of personnel of World War II and the Korean War were buried alongside the tomb (now called the **Tomb of the Unknowns**). In 1984, a serviceman of the Vietnam War was interred next to the others. Also called, *Brit.,* **Un′known War′rior.** [1920–25]

un•lace (un lās′), *v.t.,* **-laced, -lac•ing. 1.** to loosen or undo the lacing or laces of (a pair of shoes, a corset, etc.). **2.** to loosen or remove the garments of (a person) by or as if by undoing laces. [1300–50; ME *unlacen.* See UN-[2], LACE]

un•lade (un lād′), *v.,* **-lad•ed, -lad•ing.** —*v.t.* **1.** to take the lading, load, or cargo from; unload. **2.** to discharge (a load or cargo). —*v.i.* **3.** to discharge a load or cargo. [1350–1400; ME *unladen.* See UN-[2], LADE]

un•laid (un lād′), *adj.* **1.** not laid or placed: *The table is still unlaid.* **2.** (of dead bodies) not laid out; not prepared for burial. **3.** not laid to rest, as a spirit. **4.** untwisted, as a rope. [1425–75; late ME *unleyd.* See UN-[1], LAID]

un•lash (un lash′), *v.t.* to loosen, unfasten, or detach, as something lashed or tied fast. [1740–50; UN-[2] + LASH[2]]

un•latch (un lach′), *v.t.* **1.** to unfasten (a door, window shutter, etc.) by lifting the latch. —*v.i.* **2.** to become unlatched. [1635–45; UN-[2] + LATCH]

un•law•ful (un lô′fəl), *adj.* **1.** not lawful; contrary to law; illegal. **2.** born out of wedlock; illegitimate. [1250–1300; ME *unlaweful.* See UN-[1], LAWFUL] —**un•law′ful•ly,** *adv.* —**un•law′ful•ness,** *n.*
—**Syn. 1.** illicit. See **illegal. 2.** bastard, natural.

un•lax (un laks′), *v.t., v.i. Slang.* to relax; rest.

un•lay (un lā′), *v.t.,* **-laid, -lay•ing. 1.** to separate (a strand) from a rope. **2.** to untwist (a rope) in order to separate its strands. [1720–30; UN-[2] + LAY[1]]

un•lead•ed (un led′id), *adj.* **1.** (of gasoline) containing no tetraethyllead; lead-free. **2.** *Print.* not separated or spaced with leads, as lines of type or printed matter. —*n.* **3.** an unleaded product, esp. gasoline that contains no tetraethyllead. [1605–15; UN-[1] + LEAD[2] + -ED[3]]

un•learn (un lûrn′), *v.t.* **1.** to forget or lose knowledge of. **2.** to discard or put aside certain knowledge as being false or binding: *to unlearn preconceptions.* —*v.i.* **3.** to lose or discard knowledge. [1400–50; late ME *unlernen.* See UN-[2], LEARN]

un•learn•ed (un lûr′nid *for 1, 2, 5;* un lûrnd′ *for 3, 4*), *adj.* **1.** not learned; not scholarly or erudite. **2.** uneducated; untaught; unschooled; ignorant. **3.** not acquired by instruction, study, etc. **4.** known without being learned. **5.** of or pertaining to uneducated persons. [1350–1400; ME *unlerned.* See UN-[1], LEARNED] —**un•learn′ed•ly,** *adv.*

CONCISE ETYMOLOGY KEY: <, descended or borrowed from; >, whence; b., blend of, blended; c., cognate with; cf., compare; deriv., derivative; equiv., equivalent; imit., imitative; obl., oblique; r., replacing; s., stem; sp., spelling, spelled; resp., respelling, respelled; trans., translation; ?, origin unknown; *, unattested; ‡, probably earlier than. See the full key inside the front cover.

un•leash (un lēsh′), *v.t.* **1.** to release from or as if from a leash; set loose to pursue or run at will. **2.** to abandon control of: *to unleash his fury.* [1665–75; UN-[2] + LEASH]

un•leav•ened (un lev′ənd), *adj.* (of bread, cake, cookies, etc.) containing no leaven or leavening agent. [1520–30; UN-[1] + LEAVEN + -ED[3]]

un•less (un les′, ən-), *conj.* **1.** except under the circumstances that: *I'll be there at nine, unless the train is late.* —*prep.* **2.** except; but; save: *Nothing will come of it, unless disaster.* [1400–50; late ME prepositional phrase *on less* (also *o less(e),* earlier *upon less*) on a lesser footing or condition (than); first used as a prep. and conj. in the early 16th century; see ON, LESS]

un•les•soned (un les′ənd), *adj.* not educated or trained. [1540–50; UN-[1] + LESSON + -ED[3]]

un•let•tered (un let′ərd), *adj.* **1.** not educated; uneducated; untutored; ignorant. **2.** not literate; illiterate. **3.** not marked with letters, as a tombstone. [1300–50; ME; see UN-[1], LETTERED]
—**Syn. 1.** See **ignorant.**

un•li•censed (un lī′sənst), *adj.* **1.** having no license. **2.** done or undertaken without license or permission; unauthorized. **3.** unrestrained; unbridled. [1600–10; UN-[1] + LICENSED]

un•licked (un likt′), *adj.* **1.** not licked. **2.** *Archaic.* **a.** not brought into final or proper shape; unfinished. **b.** unpolished or crude. [1585–95; UN-[1] + LICK + -ED[2]]

un•like (un līk′), *adj.* **1.** different, dissimilar, or unequal; not alike: *They contributed unlike sums to charity.* —*prep.* **2.** dissimilar to; different from: *She is unlike my sister in many ways.* **3.** not typical or characteristic of: *It is unlike her to enjoy herself so much.* —*n.* **4.** a person or thing differing from another or others. [1150–1200; ME *unlik.* See UN-[1], LIKE[1]] —**un•like′ness,** *n.*

un•like•li•hood (un līk′lē ho͝od′), *n.* the state of being unlikely; improbability. [1475–85; UNLIKELY + -HOOD]

un•like•ly (un līk′lē), *adj.,* **-li•er, -li•est,** *adv.* —*adj.* **1.** not likely to be or occur; improbable; marked by doubt. **2.** holding little prospect of success; unpromising; likely to fail: *He is an unlikely candidate for reelection.* **3.** not ingratiating; objectionable. —*adv.* **4.** in an unlikely way. [1325–75; ME *unlikli.* See UN-[1], LIKELY] —**un•like′li•ness,** *n.*

un•lim•ber[1] (un lim′bər), *adj.* **1.** not limber; inflexible; stiff. —*v.i., v.t.* **2.** limber[1]. [(def. 1) UN-[1] + LIMBER[1]; (def. 2) UN-[2] + LIMBER[1]]

un•lim•ber[2] (un lim′bər), *v.t.* **1.** to detach (a gun) from its limber or prime mover. **2.** to make ready for use or action. —*v.i.* **3.** to prepare for action. —*n.* **4.** the act of changing a gun from traveling to firing position. [1795–1805; UN-[2] + LIMBER[2]]

un•lim•it•ed (un lim′i tid), *adj.* **1.** not limited; unrestricted; unconfined: *unlimited trade.* **2.** boundless; infinite; vast: *the unlimited skies.* **3.** without any qualification or exception; unconditional. [1400–50; late ME; see UN-[1], LIMITED] —**un•lim′it•ed•ly,** *adv.*
—**Syn. 1.** unconstrained, unrestrained, unfettered.

un•link (un lingk′), *v.t.* **1.** to separate the links of (a chain, linked bracelet, watchband, etc.); unfasten. **2.** to detach or separate by or as if by undoing one or more connecting links: *to unlink hands.* —*v.i.* **3.** to become detached. [1590–1600; UN-[2] + LINK[1]]

un•list•ed (un lis′tid), *adj.* **1.** not listed; not entered in a list or directory: *an unlisted telephone number.* **2.** (of a security) not admitted to trading privileges on an exchange. [1635–45; UN-[1] + LIST[1] + -ED[2]]

un•lis•ten•a•ble (un lis′ə nə bəl, -lis′nə-), *adj.* that cannot be listened to agreeably or comfortably. [UN-[1] + LISTENABLE]

un•live (un liv′), *v.t.,* **-lived, -liv•ing.** to undo or reverse (past life, experiences, etc.): *to unlive his crimes by making retribution.* [1585–95; UN-[2] + LIVE[1]]

un•load (un lōd′), *v.t.* **1.** to take the load from; remove the cargo or freight from: *to unload a truck; to unload a cart.* **2.** to remove or discharge (a load, group of people, etc.): *to unload passengers.* **3.** to remove the charge from (a firearm). **4.** to relieve of anything burdensome, oppressive, etc.: *He unloaded his responsibilities.* **5.** to get rid of (goods, shares of stock, etc.) by sale in large quantities. —*v.i.* **6.** to unload something. **7.** *Informal.* to relieve one's stress by talking, confessing, or the like. [1515–25; UN-[2] + LOAD] —**un•load′er,** *n.*

un•loan•a•ble (un lō′nə bəl), *adj.* that cannot or may not be loaned. [UN-[1] + LOANABLE]

un•lock (un lok′), *v.t.* **1.** to undo the lock of (a door, chest, etc.), esp. with a key. **2.** to open or release by or as if by undoing a lock. **3.** to open (anything firmly closed or joined): *to unlock the jaws.* **4.** to lay open; disclose: *to unlock the secrets of one's heart.* —*v.i.* **5.** to become unlocked. [1350–1400; ME *unloken;* see UN-[2], LOCK[1]] —**un•lock′a•ble,** *adj.*

un•looked (un lo͝okt′), *adj.* not examined, investigated, or heeded (usually fol. by *into, on,* or *at*): *a crime that remains unlooked into.* [1250–1300 for earlier sense; 1555–65 for current sense; ME: neglected; see UN-[1], LOOK, -ED[2]]

un•looked-for (un lo͝okt′fôr′), *adj.* not expected, anticipated, or foreseen: *They were confronted with an unlooked-for situation.* [1525–35; from phrase *look for;* see UN-[1], -ED[2]]

un•loose (un lo͞os′), *v.t.,* **-loosed, -loos•ing. 1.** to loosen or relax (the grasp, hold, fingers, etc.). **2.** to let loose or set free; free from restraint. **3.** to undo or untie (a fastening, knot, etc.); unfasten. [1325–75; ME *unloosen;* see UN-[2], LOOSE]

un•loos•en (un lo͞o′sən), *v.t.* to unloose; loosen. [1400–50; late ME *unlosnen;* see UN-[2], LOOSEN]

un•love•ly (un luv′lē), *adj.* **1.** not lovely; without beauty or charm. **2.** harsh or repellent in character; unpleasant; disagreeable; objectionable. [1350–1400; ME; see UN-[1], LOVELY] —**un•love′li•ness,** *n.*

un•luck•y (un luk′ē), *adj.,* **-luck•i•er, -luck•i•est. 1.**

un′pro•gres′sive, *adj.;* **-ly,** *adv.;* **-ness,** *n.*
un′pro•hib′it•ed, *adj.*
un′pro•hib′i•tive, *adj.;* **-ly,** *adv.*
un′pro•ject′ed, *adj.*
un′pro•ject′ing, *adj.*
un′pro•jec′tive, *adj.*
un′pro•lif′er•ous, *adj.*
un′pro•lif′ic, *adj.;* **-ness,** *n.*
un′pro•lif′i•cal•ly, *adv.*
un′pro•lix′, *adj.*
un•pro′logued, *adj.*
un′pro•long′a•ble, *adj.*
un′pro•longed′, *adj.*
un′pro•mis′cu•ous, *adj.;* **-ly,** *adv.;* **-ness,** *n.*
un•prom′ised, *adj.*
un′pro•mot′a•ble, *adj.*
un′pro•mot′ed, *adj.*
un′pro•mo′tion•al, *adj.*
un′pro•mo′tive, *adj.*
un•prompt′, *adj.;* **-ly,** *adv.;* **-ness,** *n.*
un•prompt′ed, *adj.*
un•prom′ul•gat′ed, *adj.*
un′pro•nounce′a•ble, *adj.*
un′pro•nounced′, *adj.*
un′pro•nounc′ing, *adj.*
un•proofed′, *adj.*
un•proof′read′, *adj.*
un•prop′a•ga•ble, *adj.*
un•prop′a•gan•dis′tic, *adj.*
un•prop′a•gat′ed, *adj.*
un•prop′a•ga′tive, *adj.*
un′pro•pelled′, *adj.*
un′pro•pel′lent, *adj.*
un•prop′er, *adj.;* **-ly,** *adv.*
un•prop′er•tied, *adj.*
un•proph′e•sied′, *adj.*
un′pro•phet′ic, *adj.*
un′pro•phet′i•cal, *adj.;* **-ly,** *adv.*
un′pro•pi′ti•a•ble, *adj.*
un′pro•pi′ti•at′ed, *adj.*
un′pro•pi′ti•at′ing, *adj.*
un′pro•pi′ti•a′tive, *adj.*
un′pro•pi′ti•a•to′ry, *adj.*
un′pro•pi′tious, *adj.;* **-ly,** *adv.;* **-ness,** *n.*
un′pro•por′tion•a•ble, *adj.;* **-bly,** *adv.*
un′pro•por′tion•al, *adj.;* **-ly,** *adv.*
un′pro•por′tion•ate, *adj.;* **-ly,** *adv.*
un′pro•por′tioned, *adj.*
un′pro•pos′a•ble, *adj.*
un′pro•posed′, *adj.*
un′pro•pos′ing, *adj.*
un′pro•pound′ed, *adj.*
un•propped′, *adj.*
un′pro•rogued′, *adj.*
un′pro•sa′ic, *adj.;* **-ness,** *n.*
un′pro•sa′i•cal, *adj.;* **-ly,** *adv.*
un′pro•scrib′a•ble, *adj.*
un′pro•scribed′, *adj.*
un′pro•scrip′tive, *adj.;* **-ly,** *adv.*
un•pros′pered, *adj.*
un•pros′per•ing, *adj.*
un•pros′per•ous, *adj.;* **-ly,** *adv.;* **-ness,** *n.*
un•pros′ti•tut′ed, *adj.*
un•pros′trat•ed, *adj.*
un′pro•tect′a•ble, *adj.*
un′pro•tect′ed, *adj.*
un′pro•tect′ing, *adj.*
un′pro•tec′tive, *adj.;* **-ly,** *adv.*
un•prot′es•tant, *adj.*
un′pro•test′ed, *adj.*
un′pro•test′ing, *adj.;* **-ly,** *adv.*
un′pro•tract′ed, *adj.*
un′pro•trac′tive, *adj.*
un′pro•trud′ed, *adj.*
un′pro•trud′ent, *adj.*
un′pro•trud′ing, *adj.*
un′pro•tru′si•ble, *adj.*
un′pro•tru′sive, *adj.;* **-ly,** *adv.*
un′pro•tu′ber•ant, *adj.;* **-ly,** *adv.*
un•proud′, *adj.;* **-ly,** *adv.*
un•prov′a•ble, *adj.*
un•proved′, *adj.*
un•prov′en, *adj.*
un′pro•ver′bi•al, *adj.;* **-ly,** *adv.*
un′pro•vid′a•ble, *adj.*
un′pro•vid′ed, *adj.*
un•prov′i•dent, *adj.;* **-ly,** *adv.*
un•prov′i•den′tial, *adj.;* **-ly,** *adv.*
un′pro•vin′cial, *adj.;* **-ly,** *adv.*
un•prov′ing, *adj.*
un′pro•vi′sion•al, *adj.*
un′pro•vi′sioned, *adj.*
un′pro•voc′a•tive, *adj.;* **-ly,** *adv.;* **-ness,** *n.*
un′pro•voked′, *adj.*
un′pro•vok′ing, *adj.;* **-ly,** *adv.*
un•prowl′ing, *adj.*
un•pru′dent, *adj.;* **-ly,** *adv.*
un′pru•den′tial, *adj.;* **-ly,** *adv.*
un•prun′a•ble, *adj.*
un•pruned′, *adj.*
un•pry′ing, *adj.*
un•psy′chic, *adj.*
un•psy′chi•cal•ly, *adv.*
un′psy•cho•log′i•cal, *adj.;* **-ly,** *adv.*
un′psy•cho•path′ic, *adj.*
un′psy•chot′ic, *adj.*
un•pub′lic, *adj.;* **-ly,** *adv.*
un•pub′li•cized′, *adj.*
un•pub′lish•a•ble, *adj.*
un•pub′lished, *adj.*
un•puck′ered, *adj.*
un•pud′dled, *adj.*
un•puffed′, *adj.*
un•puff′ing, *adj.*
un′pu•gil•is′tic, *adj.*
un′pug•na′cious, *adj.;* **-ly,** *adv.;* **-ness,** *n.*
un•pul′leyed, *adj.*
un•pulped′, *adj.*
un•pul′sat•ing, *adj.*
un•pul′sa•tive, *adj.*
un•puls′ing, *adj.*
un•pul′ver•a•ble, *adj.*
un•pul′ver•ized′, *adj.*
un•pul′vi•nate′, *adj.*
un•pul′vi•nat′ed, *adj.*
un•pum′meled, *adj.*
un•pum′melled, *adj.*
un•pump′a•ble, *adj.*
un•pumped′, *adj.*
un•punc′tate, *adj.*
un•punc′tat•ed, *adj.*
un′punc•til′i•ous, *adj.;* **-ly,** *adv.;* **-ness,** *n.*
un•punc′tu•al, *adj.;* **-ly,** *adv.;* **-ness,** *n.*
un′punc•tu•al′i•ty, *n.*
un•punc′tu•at′ed, *adj.*
un•punc′tu•at′ing, *adj.*
un•punc′tured, *adj.*
un•pun′ish•a•ble, *adj.*
un•pun′ished, *adj.*
un•pun′ish•ing, *adj.;* **-ly,** *adv.*
un•pu′ni•tive, *adj.*
un•pur′chas•a•ble, *adj.*
un•pur′chased, *adj.*
un•pure′, *adj.;* **-ly,** *adv.;* **-ness,** *n.*
un•pur′ga•tive, *adj.;* **-ly,** *adv.*
un•purge′a•ble, *adj.*
un•purged′, *adj.*
un•pu′ri•fied′, *adj.*
un•pu′ri•fy′ing, *adj.*
un′pu•ris′tic, *adj.*
un•pu′ri•tan, *adj.*
un′pu•ri•tan′ic, *adj.*
un′pu•ri•tan′i•cal, *adj.;* **-ly,** *adv.*
un•purled′, *adj.*
un′pur•loined′, *adj.*
un′pur•port′ed, *adj.*
un•pur′posed, *adj.*
un•pur′pose•ly, *adv.*
un•pur′pos•ing, *adj.*
un•pur′pos•ive, *adj.*
un′pur•su′a•ble, *adj.*
un′pur•su′ant, *adj.*
un′pur•sued′, *adj.*
un′pur•su′ing, *adj.*
un•pushed′, *adj.*
un•pu′ta•tive, *adj.;* **-ly,** *adv.*
un•pu′tre•fi′a•ble, *adj.*
un•pu′tre•fied′, *adj.*
un•pu′trid, *adj.;* **-ly,** *adv.;* **-ness,** *n.*
un′pu•trid′i•ty, *n.*
un•put′tied, *adj.*
un•puz′zle, *v.t.,* **-zled, -zling.**
un•quad′ded, *adj.*
un•quaffed′, *adj.*
un•quail′ing, *adj.*
un•quak′ing, *adj.*
un•qual′i•fy′ing, *adj.;* **-ly,** *adv.*
un•quan′ti•fi′a•ble, *adj.*
un•quan′ti•fied′, *adj.*
un•quan′ti•ta′tive, *adj.*
un•quar′an•tined′, *adj.*
un•quar′rel•ing, *adj.*
un•quar′rel•ling, *adj.*
un•quar′rel•some, *adj.*
un•quar′ried, *adj.*
un•quar′tered, *adj.*
un•quashed′, *adj.*
un•qua′ver•ing, *adj.*
un•quayed′, *adj.*
un•queen′ly, *adj.*
un•quell′a•ble, *adj.*
un•quelled′, *adj.*
un•quench′a•ble, *adj.*
un•quenched′, *adj.*
un•que′ried, *adj.*
un•quer′u•lous, *adj.;* **-ly,** *adv.;* **-ness,** *n.*
un•quest′ed, *adj.*
un•ques′tion•ing, *adj.*
un•quib′bling, *adj.*
un•quick′, *adj.;* **-ly,** *adv.;* **-ness,** *n.*
un•quick′ened, *adj.*
un•qui′et•a•ble, *adj.*
un•qui′et•ed, *adj.*
un•qui′et•ing, *adj.*
un•quilt′ed, *adj.*
un•quit′ted, *adj.*
un•quiv′ered, *adj.*
un•quiv′er•ing, *adj.*
un′quix•ot′ic, *adj.*
un′quix•ot′i•cal, *adj.;* **-ly,** *adv.*
un•quiz′za•ble, *adj.*
un•quizzed′, *adj.*
un•quiz′zi•cal, *adj.;* **-ly,** *adv.*
un•quot′a•ble, *adj.*
un•quot′ed, *adj.*
un•rab′bet•ed, *adj.*
un′rab•bin′ic, *adj.*
un′rab•bin′i•cal, *adj.*
un•rack′, *v.t.*
un•ra′di•ant, *adj.*
un•ra′di•at′ed, *adj.*
un•ra′di•a′tive, *adj.*
un•rad′i•cal, *adj.;* **-ly,** *adv.*
un′ra•di•o•ac′tive, *adj.*
un•raf′fled, *adj.*
un•raf′tered, *adj.*
un•raid′ed, *adj.*
un•railed′, *adj.*
un•rail′road′ed, *adj.*
un•rail′wayed′, *adj.*
un•rain′y, *adj.*
un•rais′a•ble, *adj.*
un•raise′a•ble, *adj.*
un•raised′, *adj.*
un•raked′, *adj.*
un•rak′ing, *adj.*
un•ral′lied, *adj.*
un•ral′ly•ing, *adj.*
un•ram′bling, *adj.*
un•ram′i•fied′, *adj.*
un•rammed′, *adj.*
un•ramped′, *adj.*
un•ranched′, *adj.*
un•ran′cid, *adj.*
un•ran′cored, *adj.*
un•ran′cor•ous, *adj.*
un•rang′ing, *adj.*
un•ranked′, *adj.*
un•ran′kled, *adj.*
un•ran′sacked, *adj.*
un•ran′som•a•ble, *adj.*
un•ran′somed, *adj.*

(of a person) not lucky; lacking good fortune; ill-fated. **2.** (of an event or circumstance) inauspicious or characterized by misfortune; ominous. [1520–30; UN-[1] + LUCKY] —**un•luck′i•ly,** *adv.* —**un•luck′i•ness,** *n.*
—**Syn.** hapless, unsuccessful, unfortunate, ill-omened.

un•made (un mād′), *adj.* **1.** not made. **2.** *Falconry.* unmanned (def. 2). [1200–50; ME; see UN-[1], MADE]

un•make (un māk′), *v.t.,* **-made, -mak•ing. 1.** to cause to be as if never made; reduce to the original elements or condition; undo; destroy. **2.** to depose from office or authority; demote in rank. **3.** to change the essential point of (a book, play, etc.). **4.** to alter the opinion of (one's mind). **5.** to change or alter the character of. [1350–1400; ME *unmaken.* See UN-[2], MAKE]

un•man (un man′), *v.t.,* **-manned, -man•ning. 1.** to deprive of courage or fortitude; break down the manly spirit of: *Constant conflict finally unmanned him.* **2.** to deprive of virility; emasculate; castrate. [1590–1600; UN-[2] + MAN[1]]

un•man•ly (un man′lē), *adj.,* **-li•er, -li•est. 1.** not manly; not characteristic of or befitting a man; weak, timid, or cowardly. **2.** effeminate. [1350–1400; ME; see UN-[1], MANLY] —**un•man′li•ness,** *n.*

un•manned (un mand′), *adj.* **1.** without the physical presence of people in control: *an unmanned spacecraft.* **2.** *Falconry.* (of a captured hawk) untrained for hunting with a master; unmade. [1535–45; UN-[1] + MANNED]

un•man•nered (un man′ərd), *adj.* **1.** lacking good manners; rude or ill-bred. **2.** without affectation or insincerity; ingenuous: *He is a refreshingly unmannered person.* [1400–50; late ME; see UN-[1], MANNERED]

un•man•ner•ly (un man′ər lē), *adj.* **1.** not mannerly; impolite; discourteous; coarse. —*adv.* **2.** with ill manners. [1300–50; ME; see UN-[1], MANNERLY] —**un•man′ner•li•ness,** *n.*
—**Syn. 1.** ill-bred, uncouth, loutish.

un•marked (un märkt′), *adj.* **1.** not marked. **2.** *Ling.* **a.** characterized by the absence of a distinctive phonological feature, as (p), which, in contrast to (b), lacks the distinctive feature of voicing. **b.** characterized by the absence of a grammatical marker, as the singular in English in contrast to the plural, which is typically marked by an -s ending. **c.** neutral with regard to an element of meaning specified by a semantically related item. **d.** occurring more typically than an alternative form. Cf. **marked** (def. 4). [1400–50; late ME; see UN-[1], MARKED]

un•mask (un mask′, -mäsk′), *v.t.* **1.** to strip a mask or disguise from. **2.** to reveal the true character of; disclose; expose. **3.** *Mil.* to reveal the presence of (guns) by firing. —*v.i.* **4.** to put off one's mask; appear in true nature. [1580–90; UN-[2] + MASK] —**un•mask′er,** *n.*

un•mean•ing (un mē′ning), *adj.* **1.** not meaning anything; devoid of intelligence, sense, or significance, as words or actions; pointless; empty. **2.** expressionless, vacant, or unintelligent, as the face; insipid. [1695–1705; UN-[1] + MEANING] —**un•mean′ing•ly,** *adv.*

un•mean•ing•ful (un mē′ning fəl), *adj.* not meaningful; without significance. [UN-[1] + MEANINGFUL] —**un•mean′ing•ful•ly,** *adv.*

un•meas•ured (un mezh′ərd), *adj.* **1.** of undetermined or indefinitely great extent or amount; unlimited; measureless: *the unmeasured heavens.* **2.** unrestrained; intemperate: *unmeasured rage.* **3.** *Pros.* not metrical. [1350–1400; ME *unmesured.* See UN-[1], MEASURED] —**un•meas′ur•a•ble,** *adj.* —**un•meas′ur•a•bly,** *adv.* —**un•meas′ured•ly,** *adv.*
—**Syn. 1.** immense, vast. **2.** unstinting, lavish.

un•meet (un mēt′), *adj.* not meet; not fitting, suitable, or proper; not becoming or seemly. [bef. 900; ME *unmete,* OE *unmǣte.* See UN-[1], MEET[2]]

un•men•tion•a•ble (un men′shə nə bəl), *adj.* **1.** not mentionable; inappropriate, unfit, or improper for mention, as in polite conversation; unspeakable. —*n.* **2.** something that is not to be mentioned: *That subject was classed among the unmentionables.* **3. unmentionables, a.** undergarments. **b.** (formerly) trousers or breeches. [1820–30; UN-[1] + MENTIONABLE] —**un•men′tion•a•ble•ness,** *n.*

un•mer•ci•ful (un mûr′si fəl), *adj.* **1.** merciless; relentless; severe; cruel; pitiless. **2.** unsparingly great, extreme, or excessive, as amounts: *to talk for an unmerciful length of time.* [1475–85; UN-[1] + MERCIFUL] —**un•mer′ci•ful•ly,** *adv.* —**un•mer′ci•ful•ness,** *n.*

un•mer•it•a•ble (un mer′i tə bəl), *adj.* not worthy or deserving of merit. [1585–95; UN-[1] + MERIT + -ABLE] —**un•mer′it•a•bil′i•ty,** *n.*

un•mer•it•ing (un mer′i ting), *adj.* not meriting; unearned; undeserving. [1585–95; UN-[1] + MERIT + -ING[2]]

un•mew (un myōō′), *v.t.* to set free (something mewed up); release, as from confinement. [1810–20; UN-[2] + MEW[3]]

un•mind•ful (un mīnd′fəl), *adj.* not mindful; unaware; heedless; forgetful; careless; neglectful: *unmindful of obligations.* [1350–1400; ME *unmyndeful.* See UN-[1], MINDFUL] —**un•mind′ful•ly,** *adv.* —**un•mind′ful•ness,** *n.*
—**Syn.** inattentive, negligent, unobservant.

un•mis•tak•a•ble (un′mi stā′kə bəl), *adj.* not mistakable; clear; obvious. [1660–70; UN-[1] + MISTAKABLE] —**un′mis•tak′a•ble•ness,** *n.* —**un′mis•tak′a•bly,** *adv.*

un•mi•ter (un mī′tər), *v.t.* to deprive of a miter; depose from the rank of a bishop. Also, *esp. Brit.,* **unmitre.** [1590–1600; UN-[2] + MITER]

un•mit•i•gat•ed (un mit′i gā′tid), *adj.* **1.** not mitigated; not softened or lessened: *unmitigated suffering.* **2.** unqualified or absolute: *an unmitigated bore.* [1590–1600; UN-[1] + MITIGATED] —**un•mit′i•gat′ed•ly,** *adv.*
—**Syn. 1.** unrelieved, unabated, unbroken, persistent.

un•mi•tre (un mī′tər), *v.t.,* **-tred, -tring.** *Chiefly Brit.* unmiter.

un•mixed (un mikst′), *adj.* not mixed; pure: *unmixed joy.* Also, **un•mixt′.** [1520–30; UN-[1] + MIXED] —**un•mix•ed•ly** (un mik′sid lē, -mikst′lē), *adv.*

un•mold (un mōld′), *v.t.* **1.** to take out of a mold: *to unmold a gelatin dessert.* **2.** to destroy the mold or shape of. Also, *esp. Brit.,* **un•mould′.** [1605–15; UN-[2] + MOLD[1]]

un•moor (un mŏŏr′), *v.t.* **1.** to loose (a vessel) from moorings or anchorage. **2.** to bring to the state of riding with a single anchor after being moored by two or more. —*v.i.* **3.** (of a vessel) to become unmoored. [1490–1500; ME *unmooren.* See UN-[2], MOOR[2]]

un•mor•al (un môr′əl, -mor′-), *adj.* neither moral nor immoral; amoral; nonmoral: *Nature is unmoral.* [1835–45; UN-[1] + MORAL] —**un•mo•ral•i•ty** (un′mə ral′i tē, -mô-), *n.* —**un•mor′al•ly,** *adv.*
—**Syn.** See **immoral.**

un•mor•tise (un môr′tis), *v.t.,* **-tised, -tis•ing.** to unfasten or separate (something mortised). [UN-[2] + MORTISE]

un′moved mov′er, *Aristotelianism.* See **prime mover** (def. 3).

un•mov•ing (un mōō′ving), *adj.* **1.** not moving; still; motionless. **2.** not stirring the emotions. [1375–1425; late ME; see UN-[1], MOVING]

un•muf•fle (un muf′əl), *v.,* **-fled, -fling.** —*v.t.* **1.** to strip of or free from something that muffles. —*v.i.* **2.** to throw off something that muffles. [1605–15; UN-[2] + MUFFLE[1]]

un•mu•si•cal (un myōō′zi kəl), *adj.* **1.** not musical; deficient in melody, harmony, rhythm, or tone. **2.** acoustically and aesthetically harsh on the ear; strident; dissonant; cacophonous. **3.** not fond of or skilled in music. [1600–10; UN-[1] + MUSICAL] —**un•mu′si•cal•ly,** *adv.* —**un•mu′si•cal•ness,** *n.*

un•muz•zle (un muz′əl), *v.t.,* **-zled, zling. 1.** to remove a muzzle from (a dog, cat, etc.). **2.** to free from restraint, as speech or expression. [1590–1600; UN-[2] + MUZZLE]

un•my•e•li•nat•ed (un mī′ə lə nā′tid), *adj. Anat.* pertaining to nerve fibers that are not covered with a myelin sheath. [1915–20; UN-[1] + MYELINATED]

un•nail (un nāl′), *v.t.* to take out the nails from. [1425–75; late ME *unnaillen;* see UN-[2], NAIL]

un•named (un nāmd′), *adj.* **1.** without a name; nameless. **2.** not indicated or mentioned by name; unidentified: *an unnamed lover.* [1500–10; UN-[1] + NAMED]

un•nat•u•ral (un nach′ər əl, -nach′rəl), *adj.* **1.** contrary to the laws or course of nature. **2.** at variance with the character or nature of a person, animal, or plant. **3.** at variance with what is normal or to be expected: *the unnatural atmosphere of the place.* **4.** lacking human qualities or sympathies; monstrous; inhuman: *an obsessive and unnatural hatred.* **5.** not genuine or spontaneous; artificial or contrived: *a stiff, unnatural manner.* **6.** *Obs.* lacking a valid or natural claim; illegitimate. [1375–1425; late ME; see UN-[1], NATURAL] —**un•nat′u•ral•ly,** *adv.* —**un•nat′u•ral•ness,** *n.*
—**Syn. 3.** irregular, aberrant. **4.** heartless, brutal.

CONCISE PRONUNCIATION KEY: act, cāpe, dâre, pärt; set, ēqual; *if,* ice; ox, ōver, ôrder, oil, bŏŏk, bōōt, out; up, ûrge; child; sing; shoe; thin, that; zh as in *treasure.* ə = a as in *alone,* e as in *system,* i as in *easily,* o as in *gallop,* u as in *circus;* ᵊ as in *fire* (fīᵊr), *hour* (ouᵊr). l and n can serve as syllabic consonants, as in *cradle* (krād′l), and *button* (but′n). See the full key inside the front cover.

un•rant′ing, *adj.*
un′ra•pa′cious, *adj.;* **-ly,** *adv.;* **-ness,** *n.*
un•raped′, *adj.*
un•rap′tured, *adj.*
un•rap′tur•ous, *adj.;* **-ly,** *adv.;* **-ness,** *n.*
un•rar′e•fied′, *adj.*
un•rash′, *adj.;* **-ly,** *adv.;* **-ness,** *n.*
un•rasped′, *adj.*
un•rasp′ing, *adj.*
un•rasp′y, *adj.*
un•rat′a•ble, *adj.*
un•rat′ed, *adj.*
un•rat′i•fied′, *adj.*
un•ra′tion•a•ble, *adj.*
un•ra′tion•al, *adj.;* **-ly,** *adv.*
un•ra′tion•al•ized′, *adj.*
un•ra′tion•al•iz′ing, *adj.*
un•ra′tioned, *adj.*
un•rav′aged, *adj.*
un•rav′ing, *adj.*
un•rav′ished, *adj.*
un•rayed′, *adj.*
un•razed′, *adj.*
un•ra′zored, *adj.*
un•reach′a•ble, *adj.*
un•reached′, *adj.*
un′re•ac′tion•ar′y, *adj.*
un′re•ac′tive, *adj.*
un•re′al•ism, *n.*
un•re•al•is′tic, *adj.*
un′re•al•is′ti•cal•ly, *adv.*
un•re′al•ize′, *v.t.,* **-ized, -iz•ing.**
un•realmed′, *adj.*
un•reaped′, *adj.*
un•reared′, *adj.*
un•rea′soned, *adj.*
un′re•as•sur′ing, *adj.;* **-ly,** *adv.*
un•reav′ing, *adj.*
un•re′bat•ed, *adj.*
un′re•bel′lious, *adj.;* **-ly,** *adv.;* **-ness,** *n.*
un′re•buff′a•ble, *adj.*
un′re•buffed′, *adj.*
un′re•built′, *adj.*
un′re•buk′a•ble, *adj.*
un′re•buked′, *adj.*
un′re•but′ta•ble, *adj.*
un′re•but′ted, *adj.*
un′re•cal′ci•trant, *adj.*
un′re•call′a•ble, *adj.*
un′re•called′, *adj.*
un′re•cant′ed, *adj.*
un′re•cant′ing, *adj.*
un′re•cap′tured, *adj.*
un′re•ced′ing, *adj.*
un′re•ceipt′ed, *adj.*
un′re•ceiv′a•ble, *adj.*
un′re•ceiv′ing, *adj.*
un′re•cep′tive, *adj.;* **-ly,** *adv.;* **-ness,** *n.*
un′re•cep•tiv′i•ty, *n.*
un′re•ces′sive, *adj.;* **-ly,** *adv.*
un′re•charge′a•ble, *adj.*
un′re•cip′i•ent, *adj.*
un′re•cip′ro•cal, *adj.;* **-ly,** *adv.*
un′re•cip′ro•cat′ed, *adj.*
un′re•cip′ro•cat′ing, *adj.*
un•rec′i•ta′tive, *adj.*
un′re•cit′ed, *adj.*
un•reck′on, *v.t.*
un•reck′on•a•ble, *adj.*
un•reck′oned, *adj.*
un′re•claim′a•ble, *adj.*
un′re•claimed′, *adj.*
un′re•claim′ing, *adj.*
un′re•clined′, *adj.*
un′re•clin′ing, *adj.*
un′re•cluse′, *adj.*
un′re•clu′sive, *adj.*
un′re•cog′ni•to′ry, *adj.*
un•rec′og•niz′a•ble, *adj.;* **-bly,** *adv.*
un•rec′og•nized′, *adj.*
un•rec′og•niz′ing, *adj.*
un′rec•ol•lect′ed, *adj.*
un′rec•ol•lec′tive, *adj.*
un′rec•om•mend′a•ble, *adj.*
un′rec•om•mend′ed, *adj.*
un′rec•om•pens′a•ble, *adj.*
un•rec′om•pensed′, *adj.*
un′rec•on•cil′a•ble, *adj.;* **-ble•ness,** *n.;* **-bly,** *adv.*
un•rec′on•ciled′, *adj.*
un•rec′on•cil′ing, *adj.*
un′rec•on•dite′, *adj.*
un′re•con•noi′tered, *adj.*
un′re•con•sid′ered, *adj.*
un′re•cord′a•ble, *adj.*
un′re•count′a•ble, *adj.*
un′re•count′ed, *adj.*
un′re•coup′a•ble, *adj.*
un′re•cov′er•a•ble, *adj.*
un′re•cov′ered, *adj.*
un•rec′re•ant, *adj.*
un′rec•re•a′tion•al, *adj.*
un′re•crim′i•na′tive, *adj.*
un′re•cruit′a•ble, *adj.*
un′re•cruit′ed, *adj.*
un′rec•tan′gu•lar, *adj.;* **-ly,** *adv.*
un•rec′ti•fi′a•ble, *adj.*
un•rec′ti•fied′, *adj.*
un′re•cum′bent, *adj.;* **-ly,** *adv.*
un′re•cu′per•at′ed, *adj.*
un′re•cu′per•a•tive, *adj.;* **-ness,** *n.*
un′re•cu′per•a•to′ry, *adj.*
un′re•cur′rent, *adj.;* **-ly,** *adv.*
un′re•cur′ring, *adj.*
un•rec′u•sant, *adj.*
un′re•cy′cled, *adj.*
un′re•dact′ed, *adj.*
un′re•deem′a•ble, *adj.;* **-bly,** *adv.*
un′re•deemed′, *adj.*
un′re•deem′ing, *adj.*
un′re•demp′tive, *adj.*
un′re•dress′a•ble, *adj.*
un′re•dressed′, *adj.*
un′re•duced′, *adj.*
un′re•duc′i•ble, *adj.;* **-bly,** *adv.*
un•reefed′, *adj.*
un•ref′er•enced, *adj.*
un′re•ferred′, *adj.*
un′re•filled′, *adj.*
un′re•fin′ing, *adj.*
un′re•fit′ted, *adj.*
un′re•form′a•ble, *adj.*
un′re•form′a•tive, *adj.*
un′re•formed′, *adj.*
un′re•form′ing, *adj.*
un′re•fract′ed, *adj.*
un′re•fract′ing, *adj.*
un′re•frac′tive, *adj.;* **-ly,** *adv.;* **-ness,** *n.*
un′re•frac′to•ry, *adj.*
un′re•frain′a•ble, *adj.*
un′re•frained′, *adj.*
un′re•frain′ing, *adj.*
un′re•fran′gi•ble, *adj.*
un′re•freshed′, *adj.*
un′re•fresh′ing, *adj.;* **-ly,** *adv.*
un′re•frig′er•at′ed, *adj.*
un′re•fueled′, *adj.*
un′re•ful′gent, *adj.;* **-ly,** *adv.*
un′re•fund′a•ble, *adj.*
un′re•fund′ed, *adj.*
un′re•fund′ing, *adj.*
un′re•fus′a•ble, *adj.*
un′re•fused′, *adj.*
un′re•fus′ing, *adj.*
un′re•fut′a•ble, *adj.;* **-bly,** *adv.*
un′re•fut′ed, *adj.*
un′re•fut′ing, *adj.*
un′re•gain′a•ble, *adj.*
un′re•gained′, *adj.*
un•re′gal, *adj.;* **-ly,** *adv.*
un′re•galed′, *adj.*
un′re•gard′a•ble, *adj.*
un′re•gard′ant, *adj.*
un′re•gard′ed, *adj.;* **-ly,** *adv.*
un′re•gard′ful, *adj.*
un′re•gen′er•a•ble, *adj.*
un′re•gen′er•at′ing, *adj.*
un′re•gen′er•a•tive, *adj.*
un•reg′i•men′tal, *adj.;* **-ly,** *adv.*
un•reg′i•ment′ed, *adj.*
un•reg′is•tra•ble, *adj.*
un•reg′is•tered, *adj.*
un′re•gres′sive, *adj.;* **-ly,** *adv.;* **-ness,** *n.*
un′re•gret′ful, *adj.;* **-ly,** *adv.;* **-ness,** *n.*
un′re•gret′ta•ble, *adj.;* **-bly,** *adv.*
un′re•gret′ted, *adj.*
un′re•gret′ting, *adj.*
un•reg′u•la•ble, *adj.*
un•reg′u•lar•ized′, *adj.*
un•reg′u•lat′ed, *adj.*
un•reg′u•la′tive, *adj.*
un•reg′u•la•to′ry, *adj.*
un′re•gur′gi•tat′ed, *adj.*
un′re•ha•bil′i•tat′ed, *adj.*
un′re•hears′a•ble, *adj.*
un′re•hearsed′, *adj.*
un′re•hears′ing, *adj.*
un•reign′ing, *adj.*
un′re•im•burs′a•ble, *adj.*
un′re•im•bursed′, *adj.*
un•reined′, *adj.*
un′re•in•forced′, *adj.*
un′re•in•stat′ed, *adj.*
un′re•it′er•a•ble, *adj.*
un′re•it′er•at′ed, *adj.*
un′re•it′er•at′ing, *adj.*
un′re•it′er•a′tive, *adj.*
un′re•ject′a•ble, *adj.*
un′re•ject′ed, *adj.*
un′re•jec′tive, *adj.*
un′re•joiced′, *adj.*
un′re•joic′ing, *adj.*
un′re•ju′ve•nat′ed, *adj.*
un′re•ju′ve•nat′ing, *adj.*
un′re•laps′ing, *adj.*
un′re•lat′ed, *adj.*
un′re•lat′ing, *adj.*
un′re•la′tion•al, *adj.*
un•rel′a•tive, *adj.;* **-ly,** *adv.*
un′rel•a•tiv•is′tic, *adj.*
un′re•lax′a•ble, *adj.*
un′re•laxed′, *adj.*
un′re•lax′ing, *adj.*
un′re•layed′, *adj.*
un′re•leas′a•ble, *adj.*
un′re•leased′, *adj.*
un′re•leas′i•ble, *adj.*
un′re•leas′ing, *adj.*
un•rel′e•ga•ble, *adj.*
un•rel′e•gat′ed, *adj.*
un′re•lent′ed, *adj.*
un•rel′e•vant, *adj.;* **-ly,** *adv.*
un′re•li′ant, *adj.*
un′re•liev′a•ble, *adj.*
un′re•lieved′, *adj.*
un′re•liev′ed•ly, *adv.*
un′re•liev′ing, *adj.*
un′re•li′gioned, *adj.*
un′re•lin′quish•a•ble, *adj.*
un′re•lin′quished, *adj.*
un′re•lin′quish•ing, *adj.*
un•rel′ish•a•ble, *adj.*
un•rel′ished, *adj.*
un•rel′ish•ing, *adj.*
un′re•luc′tant, *adj.;* **-ly,** *adv.*
un′re•main′ing, *adj.*
un′re•mand′ed, *adj.*
un′re•mark′a•ble, *adj.;* **-bly,** *adv.*
un′re•marked′, *adj.*
un′re•mar′ried, *adj.*
un′re•me′di•a•ble, *adj.*
un•rem′e•died, *adj.*
un′re•mem′bered, *adj.*
un′re•mem′ber•ing, *adj.*
un′re•mind′ed, *adj.*
un•rem′i•nis′cent, *adj.;* **-ly,** *adv.*
un′re•mis′si•ble, *adj.*
un′re•mis′sive, *adj.*
un′re•mit′ta•ble, *adj.*
un′re•mon′strant, *adj.*
un′re•mon′strat•ed, *adj.*
un′re•mon′strat•ing, *adj.*
un′re•mon′stra•tive, *adj.*
un′re•morse′ful, *adj.;* **-ly,** *adv.;* **-ness,** *n.*
un′re•mote′, *adj.;* **-ly,** *adv.;* **-ness,** *n.*

un·nec·es·sar·y (un nes′ə ser′ē), *adj., n., pl.* **-sar·ies.** —*adj.* **1.** not necessary or essential; needless; unessential. —*n.* **2. unnecessaries,** things that are not necessary or essential. [1540–50; UN-[1] + NECESSARY] —**un·nec·es·sar·i·ly** (un nes′ə sâr′ə lē, -nes′ə ser′-), *adv.* —**un·nec′es·sar′i·ness,** *n.*

un·nerve (un nûrv′), *v.t.,* **-nerved, -nerv·ing.** to deprive of courage, strength, determination, or confidence; upset: *Fear unnerved him.* [1595–1605; UN-[2] + NERVE]

un·nil·hex·i·um (yo͞o′nil hek′sē əm), *n. Chem., Physics.* provisional name for the transuranic element with atomic number 106. *Symbol:* Unh Also called **element 106.** [1975–80; < L *ūn(us)* ONE + *nil* nothing + Gk *héx* SIX + NL *-ium* -IUM]

un·nil·pen·ti·um (yo͞o′nil pen′tē əm), *n. Chem., Physics.* provisional name for the transuranic element with atomic number 105. *Symbol:* Unp Also called **element 105, hahnium.** [1975–80; < L *ūn(us)* ONE + *nil* nothing + Gk *pént(e)* FIVE + NL *-ium* -IUM]

un·nil·qua·di·um (yo͞o′nil kwod′ē əm), *n. Chem., Physics.* provisional name for the transuranic element with atomic number 104. *Symbol:* Unq Also called **element 104, rutherfordium.** [1975–80; < L *ūn(us)* ONE + *nīl* nothing + QUAD(RI)- + NL *-ium* -IUM]

un·nil·sep·ti·um (yo͞o′nil sep′tē əm), *n. Chem., Physics.* provisional name for the transuranic element with atomic number 107. *Symbol:* Uns Also called **element 107.** [< L *ūn(us)* ONE + *nīl* nothing + *sept(em)* SEVEN + NL *-ium* -IUM]

un·num·bered (un num′bərd), *adj.* **1.** having no number or numbers as identification: *unnumbered pages.* **2.** countless; innumerable: *the unnumbered grains of sand.* **3.** uncounted. [1325–75; ME *unnoumbred.* See UN-[1], NUMBERED]

UNO, United Nations Organization. Also, **U.N.O.**

un·ob·tru·sive (un′əb tro͞o′siv), *adj.* not obtrusive; inconspicuous, unassertive, or reticent. [1735–45; UN-[1] + OBTRUSIVE] —**un′ob·tru′sive·ly,** *adv.* —**un′ob·tru′sive·ness,** *n.*

un·oc·cu·pied (un ok′yə pīd′), *adj.* **1.** without occupants; empty; vacant. **2.** not held or controlled by invading forces: *unoccupied nations.* **3.** not busy or active; idle; not gainfully employed: *an unoccupied person.* **4.** without inhabitants; deserted. [1350–1400; ME; see UN-[1], OCCUPIED]

un·or·gan·ized (un ôr′gə nīzd′), *adj.* **1.** not organized; without organic structure. **2.** not formed into an organized or systematized whole: *an unorganized essay.* **3.** without definite boundaries: *unorganized territory.* **4.** not thinking or acting methodically. **5.** not belonging to or represented by a labor union: *unorganized workers.* [1680–90; UN-[1] + ORGANIZED]
—**Syn. 2.** casual, unsystematic, random, haphazard.

CONCISE ETYMOLOGY KEY: <, descended or borrowed from; >, whence; b., blend of, blended; c., cognate with; cf., compare; deriv., derivative; equiv., equivalent; imit., imitative; obl., oblique; r., replacing; s., stem; sp., spelling, spelled; resp., respelling, respelled; trans., translation; ?, origin unknown; *, unattested; ‡, probably earlier than. See the full key inside the front cover.

unor′ganized fer′ment, ferment (def. 2).

Unp, *Symbol, Chem., Physics.* unnilpentium.

un·pack (un pak′), *v.t.* **1.** to undo or remove the contents from (a box, trunk, etc.). **2.** to remove (something) from a container, suitcase, etc. **3.** to unburden, as the mind; reveal. **4.** to decipher or discern (the meaning of symbols, statements, etc.): *Each statement could be unpacked in the general theory.* **5.** to remove a pack or load from (a horse, vehicle, etc.). —*v.i.* **6.** to remove the contents of a container. [1425–75; late ME *unpakken.* See UN-[2], PACK[1]] —**un·pack′er,** *n.*

un·paged (un pājd′), *adj.* (of a publication) having unnumbered pages. [1870–75; UN-[1] + PAGE[1] + -ED[2]]

un·paid-for (un pād′fôr′), *adj.* not paid for. [1425–75; late ME *un-payd for;* see UN-[1], PAID, FOR]

un·pal·at·a·ble (un pal′ə tə bəl), *adj.* **1.** not palatable; unpleasant to the taste. **2.** disagreeable or unacceptable; obnoxious: *unpalatable behavior.* [1675–85; UN-[1] + PALATABLE] —**un·pal′at·a·bil′i·ty,** *n.* —**un·pal′at·a·bly,** *adv.*

un·par·al·leled (un par′ə leld′), *adj.* not paralleled; unequaled or unmatched; peerless; unprecedented: *unparalleled athletic ability.* Also, *esp. Brit.,* **un·par′al·lelled′.** [1585–95; UN-[1] + PARALLEL + -ED[2]]

un·par·lia·men·ta·ry (un′pär lə men′tə rē, -trē), *adj.* not parliamentary; at variance with or contrary to the methods employed by parliamentary bodies. [1620–30; UN-[1] + PARLIAMENTARY]

un·peg (un peg′), *v.t.,* **-pegged, -peg·ging. 1.** to remove the pegs from. **2.** to open, unfasten, or unfix by or as if by removing a peg. **3.** to stop pegging (commodity prices, exchange rates, etc.). [1595–1605; UN-[2] + PEG]

un·pen (un pen′), *v.t.,* **-penned, -pen·ning.** to release from confinement. [1585–95; UN-[2] + PEN[2]]

un·peo·ple (un pē′pəl), *v.t.,* **-pled, -pling.** to deprive of people; depopulate. [1525–35; UN-[2] + PEOPLE]

un·peo·pled (un pē′pəld), *adj.* without people; uninhabited. [1580–90; UN-[1] + PEOPLED]

un·per·son (un′pûr′sən), *n.* **1.** a public figure, esp. in a totalitarian country, who, for political or ideological reasons, is not recognized or mentioned in government publications or records or in the news media. **2.** a person accorded no recognition or consideration by another or by a specific group. [UN-[1] + PERSON; introduced in George Orwell's novel *1984* (1949)]

un·pick (un pik′), *v.t.* to take out the stitches of (sewing, knitting, etc.). [1350–1400 for earlier sense; 1770–80 for current sense; ME *unpiken* to pick (a lock); see UN-[2], PICK[1]]

un·pile (un pīl′), *v.,* **-piled, -pil·ing.** —*v.t.* **1.** to disentangle or remove from a piled condition: *to unpile boxes.* —*v.i.* **2.** to become removed or separated from a piled condition: *The football players unpiled after each play.* [1605–15; UN-[2] + PILE[1]]

un·pin (un pin′), *v.t.,* **-pinned, -pin·ning. 1.** to remove pins from. **2.** to unfasten or loosen by or as if by removing a pin; detach. [1300–50; ME *unpynnen* to unbolt; see UN-[2], PIN]

un·plait (un plāt′, -plat′), *v.t.* to alter from a plaited state; unbraid, as hair. [1325–75; ME *unpleyten;* see UN-[2], PLAIT]

un·pleas·ant (un plez′ənt), *adj.* not pleasant; displeasing; disagreeable; offensive: *an unpleasant taste; an unpleasant situation; an unpleasant manner.* [1525–35; UN-[1] + PLEASANT] —**un·pleas′ant·ly,** *adv.*

un·pleas·ant·ness (un plez′ənt nis), *n.* **1.** the quality or state of being unpleasant. **2.** something that is displeasing or offensive, as an experience, event, or situation: *An unpleasantness made them ill-at-ease.* **3.** an unpleasant feeling or sensation caused by disagreeable or painful stimuli. [1540–50; UNPLEASANT + -NESS]

un·pleas·ant·ry (un plez′ən trē), *n., pl.* **-ries.** an unpleasant word, action, comment, etc.: *comments filled with unpleasantries.* [1820–30; UN-[1] + PLEASANTRY]

un·plug (un plug′), *v.,* **-plugged, -plug·ging.** —*v.t.* **1.** to remove a plug or stopper from. **2.** to free of an obstruction; unclog. **3.** to disconnect (an appliance, a telephone, etc.) by removing a plug: *to unplug a toaster.* **4.** to remove (an electric plug) from an outlet. —*v.i.* **5.** to become unplugged. [1765–75; UN-[2] + PLUG] —**un·plug′ga·ble,** *adj.*

un·plumbed (un plumd′), *adj.* **1.** not plumbed; not tested or measured with a plumb line. **2.** not understood or explored in depth, as an idea, theory, feeling, or experience. [1615–25; UN-[1] + PLUMB + -ED[3]]

un′polished rice′, a partly refined rice, hulled and deprived of its germ but retaining some bran.

un·po·lite (un′pə līt′), *adj.* impolite. [1640–50; UN-[1] + POLITE] —**un′po·lite′ly,** *adv.*

un·pol·i·tic (un pol′i tik), *adj.* impolitic. [1540–50; UN-[1] + POLITIC]

un·polled (un pōld′), *adj.* **1.** not registered, cast, or counted at the polls: *the unpolled vote.* **2.** not consulted or canvassed in a poll: *the unpolled public.* [1640–50; UN-[1] + POLL[1] + -ED[2]]

un·pop·u·lar (un pop′yə lər), *adj.* **1.** not popular; disliked or ignored by the public or by persons generally. **2.** in disfavor with a particular person or group of persons. [1640–50; UN-[1] + POPULAR] —**un′pop·u·lar′i·ty,** *n.* —**un·pop′u·lar·ly,** *adv.*

un·posed (un pōzd′), *adj.* not posed; not done for effect; natural or candid: *her unposed manner; an unposed photograph.* [UN-[1] + POSE[1] + -ED[2]]

un·prac·ti·ca·ble (un prak′ti kə bəl), *adj.* impracticable. [1640–50; UN-[1] + PRACTICABLE] —**un′prac·ti·ca·bil′i·ty, un·prac′ti·ca·ble·ness,** *n.* —**un·prac′ti·ca·bly,** *adv.*

un·prac·ti·cal (un prak′ti kəl), *adj.* not practical; impractical; lacking practical usefulness or wisdom. [1630–40; UN-[1] + PRACTICAL] —**un′prac·ti·cal′i·ty, un·prac′·ti·cal·ness,** *n.* —**un·prac′ti·cal·ly,** *adv.*

un′re·mount′ed, *adj.*
un′re·mov′a·ble, *adj.*; **-ble·ness,** *n.*; **-bly,** *adv.*
un′re·moved′, *adj.*
un′re·mu′ner·at′ed, *adj.*
un′re·mu′ner·a·tive, *adj.*; **-ly,** *adv.*
un·ren′der·a·ble, *adj.*
un·ren′dered, *adj.*
un′re·new′a·ble, *adj.*
un′re·newed′, *adj.*
un′re·nounce′a·ble, *adj.*
un′re·nounced′, *adj.*
un′re·nounc′ing, *adj.*
un·ren′o·vat′ed, *adj.*
un·ren′o·va′tive, *adj.*
un′re·nowned′, *adj.*
un·rent′a·ble, *adj.*
un·rent′ed, *adj.*
un′re·nun′ci·a·ble, *adj.*
un′re·nun′ci·a′tive, *adj.*
un′re·nun′ci·a·to′ry, *adj.*
un′re·or′gan·ized′, *adj.*
un′re·paid′, *adj.*
un′re·pa′tri·at′ed, *adj.*
un′re·pay′a·ble, *adj.*
un′re·peal′a·bil′i·ty, *n.*
un′re·peal′a·ble, *adj.*
un′re·pealed′, *adj.*
un′re·peat′a·ble, *adj.*
un′re·peat′ed, *adj.*
un′re·pel′la·ble, *adj.*
un′re·pelled′, *adj.*
un′re·pel′lent, *adj.*; **-ly,** *adv.*
un′re·pent′ant, *adj.*; **-ly,** *adv.*
un′re·pent′ed, *adj.*
un′re·pent′ing, *adj.*; **-ly,** *adv.*
un′rep·e·ti′tious, *adj.*; **-ly,** *adv.*; **-ness,** *n.*
un′re·pet′i·tive, *adj.*; **-ly,** *adv.*
un′re·pined′, *adj.*
un′re·pin′ing, *adj.*
un′re·place′a·ble, *adj.*
un′re·placed′, *adj.*
un′re·plen′ish·a·ble, *adj.*
un′re·plen′ished, *adj.*
un′re·plete′, *adj.*; **-ness,** *n.*
un′re·plev′in·a·ble, *adj.*
un′re·plev′ined, *adj.*
un′re·plev′is·a·ble, *adj.*
un′re·plied′, *adj.*
un′re·ply′ing, *adj.*
un′re·port′a·ble, *adj.*
un′re·port′ed, *adj.*
un′rep·or·to′ri·al, *adj.*
un′re·pose′, *n.*
un′re·posed′, *adj.*
un′re·pose′ful, *adj.*; **-ly,** *adv.*; **-ness,** *n.*
un′re·pos′ing, *adj.*
un′re·pos·sessed′, *adj.*
un·rep′re·hend′ed, *adj.*
un′rep·re·hen′si·ble, *adj.*; **-ble·ness,** *n.*; **-bly,** *adv.*
un′rep·re·sent′a·ble, *adj.*
un′rep·re·sen·ta′tion·al, *adj.*
un′rep·re·sent′a·tive, *adj.*; **-ly,** *adv.*; **-ness,** *n.*
un′rep·re·sent′ed, *adj.*
un′re·pressed′, *adj.*
un′re·press′i·ble, *adj.*
un′re·pres′sive, *adj.*; **-ly,** *adv.*; **-ness,** *n.*
un′re·priev′a·ble, *adj.*
un′re·prieved′, *adj.*
un·rep′ri·mand′ed, *adj.*
un·rep′ri·mand′ing, *adj.*
un′re·print′ed, *adj.*
un′re·proach′a·ble, *adj.*; **-ble·ness,** *n.*; **-bly,** *adv.*
un′re·proached′, *adj.*
un′re·proach′ful, *adj.*; **-ly,** *adv.*; **-ness,** *n.*
un′re·proach′ing, *adj.*
un·rep′ro·bat′ed, *adj.*
un·rep′ro·ba′tive, *adj.*; **-ly,** *adv.*
un′re·proc′essed, *adj.*
un′re·pro·duc′i·ble, *adj.*
un′re·pro·duc′tive, *adj.*; **-ly,** *adv.*; **-ness,** *n.*
un′re·prov′a·ble, *adj.*
un′re·proved′, *adj.*
un′re·prov′ing, *adj.*
un′re·pub′li·can, *adj.*
un′re·pu′di·a·ble, *adj.*
un′re·pu′di·at′ed, *adj.*
un′re·pu′di·a′tive, *adj.*
un′re·pug′nant, *adj.*; **-ly,** *adv.*
un′re·pulsed′, *adj.*
un′re·puls′ing, *adj.*
un′re·pul′sive, *adj.*; **-ly,** *adv.*; **-ness,** *n.*
un·rep′u·ta·ble, *adj.*
un′re·put′ed, *adj.*
un′re·qual′i·fied′, *adj.*
un′re·quest′ed, *adj.*
un′re·quired′, *adj.*
un·req′ui·site, *adj.*; **-ly,** *adv.*; **-ness,** *n.*
un·req·ui·si′tioned, *adj.*
un′re·quit′a·ble, *adj.*
un′re·quit′al, *n.*
un′re·quit′ing, *adj.*
un′re·scind′ed, *adj.*
un′re·scis′sa·ble, *adj.*
un′re·scis′so·ry, *adj.*
un·res′cu·a·ble, *adj.*
un·res′cued, *adj.*
un′re·searched′, *adj.*
un′re·sect′a·ble, *adj.*
un′re·sem′blant, *adj.*
un′re·sem′bling, *adj.*
un′re·sent′ed, *adj.*
un′re·sent′ful, *adj.*; **-ly,** *adv.*; **-ness,** *n.*
un′re·sent′ing, *adj.*
un·res′i·dent, *adj.*
un′res·i·den′tial, *adj.*
un′re·sid′u·al, *adj.*
un′re·signed′, *adj.*
un′re·sil′ient, *adj.*; **-ly,** *adv.*
un·res′in·ous, *adj.*
un′re·sist′a·ble, *adj.*
un′re·sist′ant, *adj.*
un′re·sist′ed, *adj.*
un′re·sist′i·ble, *adj.*
un′re·sist′ing, *adj.*
un′re·sis′tive, *adj.*
un·res′o·lute′, *adj.*; **-ly,** *adv.*; **-ness,** *n.*
un′re·solv′a·ble, *adj.*
un′re·solved′, *adj.*
un′re·solv′ing, *adj.*
un·res′o·nant, *adj.*; **-ly,** *adv.*
un·res′o·nat′ing, *adj.*
un′re·sound′ed, *adj.*
un′re·source′ful, *adj.*; **-ly,** *adv.*; **-ness,** *n.*
un′re·spect′a·bil′i·ty, *n.*
un′re·spect′a·ble, *adj.*
un′re·spect′ed, *adj.*
un′re·spect′ful, *adj.*; **-ly,** *adv.*; **-ness,** *n.*
un·res′pi·ra·ble, *adj.*
un′re·spired′, *adj.*
un·res′pit·ed, *adj.*
un′re·splend′ent, *adj.*; **-ly,** *adv.*
un′re·spond′ing, *adj.*
un′re·spon′si·ble, *adj.*; **-ble·ness,** *n.*; **-bly,** *adv.*
un′re·spon′sive, *adj.*; **-ly,** *adv.*; **-ness,** *n.*
un·rest′ed, *adj.*
un·rest′ful, *adj.*; **-ly,** *adv.*; **-ness,** *n.*
un·rest′ing, *adj.*
un·res′ti·tu′tive, *adj.*
un′re·stor′a·ble, *adj.*
un′re·stor′a·tive, *adj.*
un′re·stored′, *adj.*
un′re·strain′a·ble, *adj.*
un′re·strict′a·ble, *adj.*
un′re·strict′ed, *adj.*; **-ly,** *adv.*
un′re·stric′tive, *adj.*; **-ly,** *adv.*
un′re·sumed′, *adj.*
un′re·sump′tive, *adj.*
un′res·ur·rect′ed, *adj.*
un′re·sus′ci·ta·ble, *n.*
un′re·sus′ci·tat′ed, *adj.*
un′re·sus′ci·tat′ing, *adj.*
un′re·sus′ci·ta′tive, *adj.*
un′re·tain′a·ble, *adj.*
un′re·tained′, *adj.*
un′re·tain′ing, *adj.*
un′re·tal′i·at′ed, *adj.*
un′re·tal′i·at′ing, *adj.*
un′re·tal′i·a′tive, *adj.*
un′re·tal′i·a·to′ry, *adj.*
un′re·tard′a·ble, *adj.*
un′re·tard′ed, *adj.*
un′re·ten′tive, *adj.*; **-ly,** *adv.*; **-ness,** *n.*
un·ret′i·cent, *adj.*; **-ly,** *adv.*
un·ret′i·nued′, *adj.*
un′re·tired′, *adj.*
un′re·tir′ing, *adj.*
un′re·tort′ed, *adj.*
un′re·touched′, *adj.*
un′re·tract′a·ble, *adj.*
un′re·tract′ed, *adj.*
un′re·trac′tive, *adj.*
un′re·treat′ed, *adj.*
un′re·treat′ing, *adj.*
un′re·trench′a·ble, *adj.*
un′re·trenched′, *adj.*
un′re·trib′u·tive, *adj.*
un′re·trib′u·to′ry, *adj.*
un′re·triev′a·ble, *adj.*
un′re·trieved′, *adj.*
un′ret·ro·ac′tive, *adj.*; **-ly,** *adv.*
un·ret′ro·grad′ed, *adj.*
un·ret′ro·grad′ing, *adj.*
un′ret·ro·gres′sive, *adj.*; **-ly,** *adv.*
un·ret′ted, *adj.*
un′re·turn′a·ble, *adj.*
un′re·turned′, *adj.*
un′re·turn′ing, *adj.*
un′re·veal′a·ble, *adj.*
un′re·vealed′, *adj.*
un′re·veal′ing, *adj.*; **-ly,** *adv.*
un′rev·e·la′tion·al, *adj.*
un·rev′el·ing, *adj.*
un·rev′el·ling, *adj.*
un′re·venged′, *adj.*
un′re·venge′ful, *adj.*; **-ly,** *adv.*; **-ness,** *n.*
un′re·veng′ing, *adj.*
un′re·ver′ber·ant, *adj.*
un′re·ver′ber·at′ed, *adj.*
un′re·ver′ber·at′ing, *adj.*
un′re·ver′ber·a′tive, *adj.*
un′re·vered′, *adj.*
un·rev′er·enced, *adj.*
un·rev′er·ent, *adj.*; **-ly,** *adv.*
un·rev′er·en′tial, *adj.*; **-ly,** *adv.*
un′re·versed′, *adj.*
un′re·vers′i·ble, *adj.*; **-ble·ness,** *n.*; **-bly,** *adv.*
un′re·vert′ed, *adj.*
un′re·vert′i·ble, *adj.*
un′re·vert′ing, *adj.*
un′re·vet′ted, *adj.*
un′re·view′a·ble, *adj.*
un′re·viewed′, *adj.*
un′re·viled′, *adj.*
un′re·vil′ing, *adj.*
un′re·vised′, *adj.*
un′re·viv′a·ble, *adj.*
un′re·vived′, *adj.*
un·rev′o·ca·ble, *adj.*; **-bly,** *adv.*
un′re·vok′a·ble, *adj.*
un′re·voked′, *adj.*
un′re·volt′ed, *adj.*
un′re·volt′ing, *adj.*
un′rev·o·lu′tion·ar′y, *adj.*
un′rev·o·lu′tion·ized′, *adj.*
un′re·volved′, *adj.*
un′re·volv′ing, *adj.*
un′re·ward′a·ble, *adj.*
un′re·ward′ed, *adj.*
un′re·ward′ing, *adj.*
un′re·word′ed, *adj.*
un′rhap·sod′ic, *adj.*
un′rhap·sod′i·cal, *adj.*; **-ly,** *adv.*
un′rhe·tor′i·cal, *adj.*; **-ly,** *adv.*
un′rheu·mat′ic, *adj.*

un·prac·ticed (un prak′tist), *adj.* **1.** not trained or skilled; inexpert: *an unpracticed actor.* **2.** not practiced; not usually or generally used or done; not put into effect. Also, *esp. Brit.,* **un·prac′tised.** [1530–40; UN-[1] + PRACTICED]

un·prec·e·dent·ed (un pres′i den′tid), *adj.* without previous instance; never before known or experienced; unexampled or unparalleled: *an unprecedented event.* [1615–25; UN-[1] + PRECEDENT + -ED[2]] —**un·prec′e·dent′ed·ly,** *adv.* —**un·prec′e·dent′ed·ness,** *n.*
—**Syn.** unique, extraordinary, exceptional, novel.

un·pre·dict·a·ble (un′pri dik′tə bəl), *adj.* **1.** not predictable; not to be foreseen or foretold: *an unpredictable occurrence.* —*n.* **2.** something that is unpredictable: *the unpredictables of life.* [1855–60; UN-[1] + PREDICTABLE] —**un′pre·dict′a·bil′i·ty, un′pre·dict′a·ble·ness,** *n.* —**un′pre·dict′a·bly,** *adv.*
—**Syn. 1.** erratic, fitful, variable, uncertain.

un·prej·u·diced (un prej′ə dist), *adj.* **1.** not prejudiced; without preconception; unbiased; impartial: *the unprejudiced view of the judge.* **2.** *Obs.* not damaged; unimpaired. [1605–15; UN-[1] + PREJUDICED] —**un·prej′u·diced·ly,** *adv.* —**un·prej′u·diced·ness,** *n.*
—**Syn. 1.** See **fair**[1].

un·pre·ten·tious (un′pri ten′shəs), *adj.* not pretentious; modest; without ostentatious display; plain: *his unpretentious demeanor; an unpretentious summer resort.* [1855–60; UN-[1] + PRETENTIOUS] —**un′pre·ten′tious·ly,** *adv.* —**un′pre·ten′tious·ness,** *n.*
—**Syn.** humble, unpretending, plain, open, easy.

un·priced (un prīst′), *adj.* **1.** not priced; having no price shown or set. **2.** beyond price; priceless. [1855–60; UN-[1] + PRICED]

un·prin·ci·pled (un prin′sə pəld), *adj.* **1.** lacking or not based on moral scruples or principles: *an unprincipled person; unprincipled behavior.* **2.** not instructed in the principles of something (usually fol. by *in*). [1625–35; UN-[1] + PRINCIPLED] —**un·prin′ci·pled·ness,** *n.*
—**Syn. 1.** tricky, dishonest. See **unscrupulous.**

un·print·a·ble (un prin′tə bəl), *adj.* improper or unfit for print, esp. because of obscenity or offensiveness. [1855–60; UN-[1] + PRINTABLE] —**un·print′a·ble·ness,** *n.* —**un·print′a·bly,** *adv.*

un·pris·on (un priz′ən), *v.t.* to release from prison. [1350–1400; ME *unprisonen;* see UN-[2], PRISON]

un·priz·a·ble (un prī′zə bəl), *adj.* not worthy to be prized; of little worth. [1595–1605; UN-[1] + PRIZE[2] + -ABLE]

un·pro·fes·sion·al (un′prə fesh′ə nl), *adj.* **1.** not professional; not pertaining to or characteristic of a profession. **2.** at variance with or contrary to professional standards or ethics; not befitting members of a profession, as language, behavior, or conduct. **3.** not belonging to a profession; nonprofessional. **4.** not done with professional competence, as a play staged or an opera performed by amateurs; amateurish. **5.** *Sports.* nonprofessional (def. 2). —*n.* **6.** a person who is not a professional; amateur. [1800–10; UN-[1] + PROFESSIONAL] —**un′pro·fes′sion·al·ly,** *adv.*

un·prof·it·a·ble (un prof′i tə bəl), *adj.* **1.** being without profit; not showing or turning a profit: *a series of unprofitable ventures.* **2.** pointless or futile: *an unprofitable three years in a routine job.* [1275–1325; ME. See UN-[1], PROFITABLE] —**un·prof′it·a·ble·ness, un·prof′it·a·bil′i·ty,** *n.* —**un·prof′it·a·bly,** *adv.*

un·prom·is·ing (un prom′ə sing), *adj.* unlikely to be favorable or successful, as the weather, a situation, or a career. [1625–35; UN-[1] + PROMISING] —**un·prom′is·ing·ly,** *adv.*

unpub′lished work′, *Law.* a literary work that has not been reproduced for sale or publicly distributed.

un·put·down·a·ble (un′pŏŏt dou′nə bəl), *adj. Informal.* (esp. of a book or periodical) so interesting or suspenseful as to compel reading. [from phrase *put down;* see UN-[1], -ABLE]

Unq, *Symbol, Chem., Physics.* unnilquadium.

Un·qua·chog (ung′kwə chog′), *n., pl.* **-chogs,** (*esp. collectively*) **-chog** for 1. **1.** a member of an American Indian people of eastern Long Island, New York. **2.** the Eastern Algonquian language of the Unquachog.

un·qual·i·fied (un kwol′ə fīd′), *adj.* **1.** not qualified; not fit; lacking requisite qualifications: *unqualified for the job.* **2.** not modified, limited, or restricted in any way; without reservations: *unqualified praise.* **3.** absolute; complete; out-and-out: *an unqualified liar.* [1550–60; UN-[1] + QUALIFIED] —**un·qual′i·fi′a·ble,** *adj.* —**un·qual′i·fied′ly,** *adv.* —**un·qual′i·fied′ness,** *n.*
—**Syn. 1.** unfit, incompetent. **2.** unmitigated. **3.** downright, thorough. **2, 3.** See **absolute.**

un·ques·tion·a·ble (un kwes′chə nə bəl), *adj.* **1.** not open to question; beyond doubt or dispute; indisputable; undeniable; certain: *an unquestionable fact.* **2.** above criticism; unexceptionable: *a man of unquestionable principles.* [1590–1600; UN-[1] + QUESTIONABLE] —**un·ques′tion·a·ble·ness,** *n.* —**un·ques′tion·a·bly,** *adv.*

un·ques·tioned (un kwes′chənd), *adj.* **1.** not open to doubt or question; undisputed: *Dante's poetic mastery remains unquestioned.* **2.** not inquired into, investigated, or interrogated: *The eyewitness went unquestioned.* [1595–1605; UN-[1] + QUESTION + -ED[2]]

un·qui·et (un kwī′it), *adj.* **1.** agitated; restless; disordered; turbulent: *unquiet times.* **2.** mentally or emotionally disturbed; vexed or perturbed; uneasy: *He felt unquiet and alone.* —*n.* **3.** a state of agitation, turbulence, disturbance, etc.: *Unquiet spread throughout the land.* [1515–25; UN-[1] + QUIET[1] (defs. 1, 2), QUIET[2] (def. 3)] —**un·qui′et·ly,** *adv.* —**un·qui′et·ness,** *n.*

un·quote (un kwōt′; *contrastively* un′kwōt′), *v.i.,* **-quot·ed, -quot·ing.** to close a quotation (often used with the word *quote,* which notes the opening of the quotation): *The senator said, quote, I am unalterably opposed to this policy, unquote.* [1910–15; UN-[2] + QUOTE]

un·rav·el (un rav′əl), *v.,* **-eled, -el·ing** or (*esp. Brit.*) **-elled, -el·ling.** —*v.t.* **1.** to separate or disentangle the threads of (a woven or knitted fabric, a rope, etc.). **2.** to free from complication or difficulty; make plain or clear; solve: *to unravel a situation; to unravel a mystery.* **3.** *Informal.* to take apart; undo; destroy (a plan, agreement, or arrangement). —*v.i.* **4.** to become unraveled. [1595–1605; UN-[2] + RAVEL] —**un·rav′el·er;** *esp. Brit.,* **un·rav′el·ler,** *n.* —**un·rav′el·ment,** *n.*

un·read (un red′), *adj.* **1.** not read, as a letter or newspaper. **2.** lacking in knowledge gained by reading; having read little or nothing: *She was intelligent but unread.* **3.** having little knowledge of a specific field: *a brilliant chemist unread in biology.* [1425–75; late ME *unred.* See UN-[1], READ[2]]

un·read·a·ble (un rē′də bəl), *adj.* **1.** not readable; undecipherable; scribbled: *His scrawl was almost unreadable.* **2.** not interesting to read; dull; tedious; *an unreadable treatise.* **3.** extraordinarily difficult to read or comprehend; obscure; incomprehensible: *an unreadable dream; an unreadable expression.* [1795–1805; UN-[1] + READABLE] —**un·read′a·bil′i·ty, un·read′a·ble·ness,** *n.* —**un·read′a·bly,** *adv.*

un·read·y (un red′ē), *adj.* **1.** not ready; not made ready: *The new stadium is as yet unready for use.* **2.** not in a state of readiness; unprepared: *emotionally unready for success.* **3.** lacking in presence of mind, as when a quick decision or a sharp answer is required: *Awkward situations often found him unready.* **4.** *Brit. Dial.* not dressed. **5.** not prompt or quick. [1250–1300; ME *unredy.* See UN-[1], READY] —**un·read′i·ness,** *n.*

un·re·al (un rē′əl, -rēl′), *adj.* **1.** not real or actual. **2.** imaginary; fanciful; illusory; delusory; fantastic. **3.** lacking in truth; not genuine; false; artificial: *unreal propaganda serving as news.* [1595–1605; UN-[1] + REAL[1]] —**un·re′al·ly,** *adv.*
—**Syn.** sham, spurious, fictitious, illusive, theoretical, impractical, vague.

un·re·al·i·ty (un′rē al′i tē), *n., pl.* **-ties. 1.** lack of reality; quality of being unreal: *the unreality of dreams.* **2.** something that is unreal, invalid, imaginary, or illusory: *She appeared to be living in a world of unrealities.* **3.** incompetence or impracticality, esp. in everyday matters. [1745–55; UN-[1] + REALITY]

un·re·al·iz·a·ble (un rē′ə lī′zə bəl), *adj.* **1.** incapable of being made actual or real, as an ideal or ambition: *His dream of military glory was unrealizable.* **2.** incapable of being sensed or understood; unthinkable. [1830–40; UN-[1] + REALIZABLE]

un·re·al·ized (un rē′ə līzd′), *adj.* **1.** not made real or actual; not resulting in accomplishment, as a task or aim: *unrealized ambitions.* **2.** not known or suspected: *unrealized talent.* [1765–75; UN-[1] + REALIZED]

un·rea·son (un rē′zən), *n.* **1.** inability or unwillingness to think or act rationally, reasonably, or sensibly; irrationality. **2.** lack of reason or sanity; madness; confusion; disorder; chaos: *a world torn by unreason.* —*v.t.* **3.** to upset or disrupt the reason or sanity of: *The devi-*

CONCISE PRONUNCIATION KEY: act, cāpe, dâre, pärt; set, ēqual; *if,* ice; ox, ōver, ôrder, oil, bŏŏk, bōōt, out; up, ûrge; child; sing; shoe; thin, *th*at; zh as in *treasure.* ə = *a* as in *alone, e* as in *system, i* as in *easily, o* as in *gallop, u* as in *circus;* ə as in *fire* (fīər), *hour* (ouər). l and n can serve as syllabic consonants, as in *cradle* (krād′l), and *button* (but′n). See the full key inside the front cover.

un·rhyme′, *v.t.,* **-rhymed, -rhym·ing.**
un·rhyth′mic, *adj.*
un·rhyth′mi·cal, *adj.;* **-ly,** *adv.*
un·ribbed′, *adj.*
un·rib′boned, *adj.*
un·rid′a·ble, *adj.*
un·rid′den, *adj.*
un·rid′ered, *adj.*
un·ridged′, *adj.*
un·rid′i·culed′, *adj.*
un′ri·dic′u·lous, *adj.;* **-ly,** *adv.;* **-ness,** *n.*
un·rife′, *adj.*
un·rif′fled, *adj.*
un·ri′fled, *adj.*
un·rift′ed, *adj.*
un·right′a·ble, *adj.*
un·right′ed, *adj.*
un·right′ful, *adj.;* **-ly,** *adv.;* **-ness,** *n.*
un·rig′id, *adj.;* **-ly,** *adv.;* **-ness,** *n.*
un·rig′or·ous, *adj.;* **-ly,** *adv.;* **-ness,** *n.*
un·rimed′, *adj.*
un·ring′a·ble, *adj.*
un·ring′ing, *adj.*
un·rinsed′, *adj.*
un·ri′ot·ing, *adj.*
un·ri′ot·ous, *adj.;* **-ly,** *adv.;* **-ness,** *n.*
un·rip′ened, *adj.*
un·rip′en·ing, *adj.*
un·rip′pa·ble, *adj.*
un·rip′pled, *adj.*
un·rip′pling, *adj.;* **-ly,** *adv.*
un·ris′en, *adj.*
un·ris′i·ble, *adj.*
un·ris′ing, *adj.*
un·risk′a·ble, *adj.*
un·risked′, *adj.*
un·risk′y, *adj.*
un·rit′u·al, *adj.;* **-ly,** *adv.*
un′rit·u·al·is′tic, *adj.*
un·ri′val·a·ble, *adj.*
un·ri′val·ing, *adj.*
un·ri′val·ling, *adj.*
un·ri′val·rous, *adj.*
un·rived′, *adj.*
un·riv′en, *adj.*
un·riv′et·ed, *adj.*
un·riv′et·ing, *adj.*
un·road′wor′thy, *adj.*
un·roam′ing, *adj.*
un·roast′ed, *adj.*
un·robbed′, *adj.*
un′ro·bust′, *adj.;* **-ly,** *adv.;* **-ness,** *n.*
un·rocked′, *adj.*
un·rock′y, *adj.*
un·rod′ded, *adj.*
un·roiled′, *adj.*
un·roll′a·ble, *adj.*
un′ro·man′tic, *adj.*
un′ro·man′ti·cal·ly, *adv.*
un′ro·man′ti·cized′, *adj.*
un·roofed′, *adj.*
un·room′y, *adj.*
un·roost′ed, *adj.*
un·roost′ing, *adj.*
un·roped′, *adj.*
un·rosed′, *adj.*
un·ro′ta·ry, *adj.*
un·ro′tat·ed, *adj.*
un·ro′tat·ing, *adj.*
un′ro·ta′tion·al, *adj.*
un·ro′ta·tive, *adj.*
un·ro′ta·to′ry, *adj.*
un·rot′ted, *adj.*
un·rot′ten, *adj.*
un′ro·tund′, *adj.*
un·rouged′, *adj.*
un·rough′ened, *adj.*
un·roused′, *adj.*
un·rous′ing, *adj.*
un·rout′a·ble, *adj.*
un·rout′ed, *adj.*
un′rou·tine′, *adj.;* **-ly,** *adv.*
un·rov′ing, *adj.*
un·row′dy, *adj.*
un·rowed′, *adj.*
un·row′eled, *adj.*
un·row′elled, *adj.*
un·rubbed′, *adj.*
un·ru′bi·fied′, *adj.*
un·ru′bri·cal, *adj.;* **-ly,** *adv.*
un·ru′bri·cat′ed, *adj.*
un·rud′dered, *adj.*
un·rud′dled, *adj.*
un·rude′, *adj.;* **-ly,** *adv.*
un·rued′, *adj.*
un·rue′ful, *adj.;* **-ly,** *adv.;* **-ness,** *n.*
un·ruff′a·ble, *adj.*
un·ruffed′, *adj.*
un′ruf·fla·bil′i·ty, *n.*
un·ruf′fla·ble, *adj.*
un·rug′ged, *adj.*
un·ru′in·a·ble, *adj.*
un·ru′in·ous, *adj.;* **-ly,** *adv.;* **-ness,** *n.*
un·ruled′, *adj.*
un·ru′mi·nant, *adj.*
un·ru′mi·nat′ed, *adj.*
un·ru′mi·nat′ing, *adj.;* **-ly,** *adv.*
un·ru′mi·na′tive, *adj.*
un·rum′maged, *adj.*
un·ru′mored, *adj.*
un·rum′pled, *adj.*
un·run′, *adj.*
un·rung′, *adj.*
un·rup′tur·a·ble, *adj.*
un·rup′tured, *adj.*
un·ru′ral, *adj.;* **-ly,** *adv.*
un·rushed′, *adj.*
un·rush′ing, *adj.*
un·rust′, *v.t.*
un·rus′tic, *adj.*
un·rus′ti·cal·ly, *adv.*
un·rus′ti·cat′ed, *adj.*
un·rus′tling, *adj.*
un·sa′bered, *adj.*
un·sa′bled, *adj.*
un·sab′o·taged′, *adj.*
un·sac′cha·rine, *adj.*
un′sac·er·do′tal, *adj.;* **-ly,** *adv.*
un·sacked′, *adj.*
un′sac·ra·men′tal, *adj.;* **-ly,** *adv.*
un′sac·ra·men·tar′i·an, *adj.*
un·sa′cred, *adj.;* **-ly,** *adv.*
un·sac′ri·fice′a·ble, *adj.*
un·sac′ri·ficed′, *adj.*
un′sac·ri·fi′cial, *adj.;* **-ly,** *adv.*
un·sac′ri·fic′ing, *adj.*
un′sac·ri·le′gious, *adj.;* **-ly,** *adv.;* **-ness,** *n.*
un·sad′, *adj.;* **-ly,** *adv.;* **-ness,** *n.*
un·sad′dened, *adj.*
un′sa·dis′tic, *adj.*
un′sa·dis′ti·cal·ly, *adv.*
un·safe′, *adj.;* **-ly,** *adv.;* **-ness,** *n.*
un·safe′guard′ed, *adj.*
un′sa·ga′cious, *adj.;* **-ly,** *adv.;* **-ness,** *n.*
un·sage′, *adj.;* **-ly,** *adv.;* **-ness,** *n.*
un·sag′ging, *adj.*
un·sail′a·ble, *adj.*
un·sailed′, *adj.*
un·saint′ed, *adj.*
un·saint′ly, *adj.*
un′sal·a·bil′i·ty, *n.*
un·sal′a·ble, *adj.;* **-bly,** *adv.*
un′sa·la′cious, *adj.;* **-ly,** *adv.;* **-ness,** *n.*
un·sal′a·ried, *adj.*
un·sale′a·ble, *adj.;* **-bly,** *adv.*
un·sa′li·ent, *adj.;* **-ly,** *adv.*
un·sa′line, *adj.*
un·sal′i·vat′ed, *adj.*
un·sal′i·vat′ing, *adj.*
un·sal′low, *adj.;* **-ness,** *n.*
un·sal′ly·ing, *adj.*
un·salt′a·ble, *adj.*
un·sal′ta·to′ri·al, *adj.*
un·sal′ta·to′ry, *adj.*
un·salt′ed, *adj.*
un·salt′y, *adj.*
un′sa·lu′bri·ous, *adj.;* **-ly,** *adv.;* **-ness,** *n.*
un·sal′u·tar′y, *adj.*
un′sa·lu′ta·to′ry, *adj.*
un′sa·lut′ed, *adj.*
un′sa·lut′ing, *adj.*
un·sal′vage·a·ble, *adj.;* **-bly,** *adv.*
un·sal′vaged, *adj.*
un·salved′, *adj.*
un·sanc′ti·fied′, *adj.*
un·sanc′ti·fy′ing, *adj.*
un′sanc·ti·mo′ni·ous, *adj.;* **-ly,** *adv.;* **-ness,** *n.*
un·sanc′tion·a·ble, *adj.*
un·sanc′tioned, *adj.*
un·sanc′tion·ing, *adj.*
un·sanc′ti·tude′, *n.*
un·sanc′ti·ty, *n., pl.* **-ties.**
un·san′daled, *adj.*
un·san′dalled, *adj.*
un·sand′ed, *adj.*
un·san′gui·nar′i·ly, *adv.*
un·san′gui·nar′i·ness, *n.*
un·san′gui·nar′y, *adj.*
un·san′guine, *adj.;* **-ly,** *adv.*
un′san·guin′e·ous, *adj.;* **-ly,** *adv.*
un·san′i·tized′, *adj.*
un·san′i·ty, *n.*
un·sa′pi·ent, *adj.;* **-ly,** *adv.*
un′sa·pi·en′tial, *adj.;* **-ly,** *adv.*
un′sa·pon′i·fi′a·ble, *adj.*
un′sa·pon′i·fied′, *adj.*
un·sapped′, *adj.*
un′sar·cas′tic, *adj.*
un′sar·cas′ti·cal, *adj.;* **-ly,** *adv.*
un′sar·don′ic, *adj.*
un′sar·don′i·cal·ly, *adv.*
un′sar·to′ri·al, *adj.;* **-ly,** *adv.*
un·sashed′, *adj.*
un·sat′a·ble, *adj.*
un′sa·tan′ic, *adj.*
un′sa·tan′i·cal, *adj.;* **-ly,** *adv.*
un·satch′eled, *adj.*
un·sat′ed, *adj.*
un′sa·tia·bil′i·ty, *n.*
un·sa′tia·ble, *adj.;* **-ble·ness,** *n.;* **-bly,** *adv.*
un·sa′ti·at′ed, *adj.*
un·sa′ti·at′ing, *adj.*
un·sat′ing, *adj.*
un′sa·tir′ic, *adj.*
un′sa·tir′i·cal, *adj.;* **-ly,** *adv.;* **-ness,** *n.*
un·sat′i·riz′a·ble, *adj.*
un·sat′i·rized′, *adj.*
un·sat′is·fi′a·ble, *adj.*
un·sat′is·lut′ed, *adj.*
un·sat′is·fied′, *adj.*
un·sat′u·ra·ble, *adj.*
un·sauced′, *adj.*
un·sav′a·ble, *adj.*
un·sav′age, *adj.;* **-ly,** *adv.;* **-ness,** *n.*
un·save′a·ble, *adj.*
un·saved′, *adj.*
un·sav′ing, *adj.;* **-ly,** *adv.*
un·sa′vored, *adj.*
un·sawed′, *adj.*
un·sawn′, *adj.*
un·say′a·ble, *adj.*
un·scab′bard, *v.t.*
un·scab′bed, *adj.*
un·scab′rous, *adj.;* **-ly,** *adv.;* **-ness,** *n.*
un·scaf′fold·ed, *adj.*
un·scal′a·ble, *adj.*
un·scald′ed, *adj.*
un·scald′ing, *adj.*
un·scaled′, *adj.*
un·scal′loped, *adj.*
un·scal′y, *adj.*
un·scamped′, *adj.*
un·scan′dal·ized′, *adj.*
un·scan′dal·ous, *adj.;* **-ly,** *adv.*
un·scan′na·ble, *adj.*
un·scanned′, *adj.*
un·scant′y, *adj.*

ous plot soon unreasoned the general. [1250–1300; ME *un-reson.* See UN-[1], REASON]

un·rea·son·a·ble (un rē′zə nə bəl, -rēz′nə-), *adj.* **1.** not reasonable or rational; acting at variance with or contrary to reason; not guided by reason or sound judgment; irrational: *an unreasonable person.* **2.** not in accordance with practical realities, as attitude or behavior; inappropriate: *His Bohemianism was an unreasonable way of life for one so rich.* **3.** excessive, immoderate, or exorbitant; unconscionable: *an unreasonable price; unreasonable demands.* **4.** not having the faculty of reason. [1300–50; ME *unresonabel.* See UN-[1], REASONABLE] **—un·rea′son·a·ble·ness,** *n.* **—un·rea′son·a·bly,** *adv.*
—Syn. 1, 2. senseless, foolish, silly. **2.** preposterous, absurd, stupid, nonsensical. **3.** extravagant.

un·rea·son·ing (un rē′zə ning), *adj.* not reasoning or exercising reason; reasonless; thoughtless; irrational: *an unreasoning fanatic.* [1745–55; UN-[1] + REASONING] **—un·rea′son·ing·ly,** *adv.*

un·re·con·struct·ed (un′rē kən struk′tid), *adj.* **1.** stubbornly maintaining earlier positions, beliefs, etc.; not adjusted to new or current situations: *an unreconstructed conservative.* **2.** *U.S. Hist.* (of Southern states) not accepting the conditions for reinstatement in the Union after the Civil War. [1865–70, *Amer.*; UN-[1] + RECONSTRUCTED]

un·re·con·struc·ti·ble (un′rē kən struk′tə bəl), *adj.* not capable of being reconstructed. [UN-[1] + RECONSTRUCT + -IBLE]

un·re·cord·ed (un′ri kôr′did), *adj.* **1.** not recorded; not reported in an official record. **2.** not noted in historical documents: *an unrecorded event; an unrecorded tradition.* [1575–85; UN-[1] + RECORD + -ED[2]]

un·reel (un rēl′), *v.t.* **1.** to unwind from or as if from a reel: *to unreel some wire; to unreel a tangled skein.* —*v.i.* **2.** to become unreeled. [1560–70; UN-[2] + REEL[1]] **—un·reel′a·ble,** *adj.* **—un·reel′er,** *n.*

un·reeve (un rēv′), *v.*, **-rove** or **-reeved, -reev·ing.** —*v.t.* **1.** *Naut.* to withdraw (a rope) from a block, thimble, etc. —*v.i.* **2.** to unreeve a rope. **3.** (of a rope) to become unreeved. [1590–1600; UN-[2] + REEVE[2]]

un·re·fined (un′ri fīnd′), *adj.* **1.** not refined; not purified, as substances: *unrefined metal.* **2.** coarse or crude; lacking in refinement of taste, feeling, manners, language, etc. [1585–95; UN-[1] + REFINED]
—Syn. 1. unpurified, crude, coarse. **2.** unpolished, uncultured, ill-bred, rude, boorish, vulgar, gross.

un·re·flect·ed (un′ri flek′tid), *adj.* **1.** not reflected on; not given consideration: *unreflected opinions.* **2.** not cast back, as light, heat, or an image: *the unreflected heat of the sun.* [1660–70; UN-[1] + REFLECT + -ED[2]]

CONCISE ETYMOLOGY KEY: <, descended or borrowed from; >, whence; b., blend of, blended; c., cognate with; cf., compare; deriv., derivative; equiv., equivalent; imit., imitative; obl., oblique; r., replacing; s., stem; sp., spelling, spelled; resp., respelling, respelled; trans., translation; ?, origin unknown; *, unattested; ‡, probably earlier than. See the full key inside the front cover.

un·re·flect·ing (un′ri flek′ting), *adj.* not reflecting; unthinking: *an unreflecting, self-satisfied man.* [1655–65; UN-[1] + REFLECT + -ING[2]] **—un′re·flect′ing·ly,** *adv.*

un·re·flec·tive (un′ri flek′tiv), *adj.* not reflective; thoughtless; lacking in due deliberation; heedless; rash: *a sweeping, unreflective pessimism.* [1850–55; UN-[1] + REFLECTIVE] **—un′re·flec′tive·ly,** *adv.*

un·re·gen·er·ate (un′ri jen′ər it), *adj.* Also, **un·re·gen·er·at·ed** (un′ri jen′ə rā′tid). **1.** not regenerate; not renewed in heart and mind or reborn in spirit; unrepentant: *an unregenerate sinner.* **2.** refusing to believe in the existence of God: *an unregenerate atheist; an unregenerate skeptic.* **3.** unconvinced by or unconverted to a particular religion, sect, or movement; unreconstructed. **4.** persisting in the holding of prior convictions; opposing new ideas, causes, etc.; stubborn; obstinate: *an unregenerate reactionary.* **5.** not reformed; wicked; sinful; profligate; dissolute: *an unregenerate way of life.* —*n.* **6.** an unregenerate person. [1605–15; UN-[1] + REGENERATE] **—un·re·gen·er·a·cy** (un′ri jen′ər ə sē), *n.* **—un′re·gen′er·ate·ly,** *adv.*

un·re·lent·ing (un′ri len′ting), *adj.* **1.** not relenting; not yielding or swerving in determination or resolution, as of or from opinions, convictions, ambitions, ideals, etc.; inflexible: *an unrelenting opponent of the Equal Rights Amendment.* **2.** not easing or slackening in severity: *an unrelenting rain.* **3.** maintaining speed, effort, vigor, intensity, rate of advance, etc.: *an unrelenting attack.* [1580–90; UN-[1] + RELENT + -ING[2]] **—un′re·lent′ing·ly,** *adv.* **—un′re·lent′ing·ness,** *n.*
—Syn. 1. relentless, merciless, unmerciful, ruthless, pitiless, cruel, remorseless. **2.** unremitting, implacable, inexorable.

un·re·li·a·ble (un′ri lī′ə bəl), *adj.* not reliable; not to be relied or depended on. [1830–40; UN-[1] + RELIABLE] **—un′re·li′a·bil′i·ty, un′re·li′a·ble·ness,** *n.* **—un′re·li′a·bly,** *adv.*
—Syn. undependable, irresponsible, untrustworthy.

un·re·li·gious (un′ri lij′əs), *adj.* **1.** irreligious. **2.** having no connection with or relation to religion; neither religious nor irreligious; nonreligious: *His thinking, while unreligious, did not oppose religion.* [1350–1400; ME; see UN-[1], RELIGIOUS] **—un′re·li′gious·ly,** *adv.*

un·re·mit·ted (un′ri mit′id), *adj.* **1.** not remitted, as a debt. **2.** unpardoned, as a sin. **3.** steadily maintained; uninterrupted; constant: *He gave the matter his unremitted attention.* [1640–50; UN-[1] + REMITTED]

un·re·mit·ted·ly (un′ri mit′id lē), *adv.* continuously; uninterruptedly; constantly. [1780–90; UNREMITTED + -LY]

un·re·mit·tent (un′ri mit′nt), *adj.* (esp. of a fever) unremitting. [1870–75; UN-[1] + REMITTENT] **—un′re·mit′tence, un′re·mit′ten·cy,** *n.* **—un′re·mit′tent·ly,** *adv.*

un·re·mit·ting (un′ri mit′ing), *adj.* not slackening or abating; incessant: *unremitting noise; unremitting attention.* [1720–30; UN-[1] + REMITTING] **—un′re·mit′ting·ly,** *adv.* **—un′re·mit′ting·ness,** *n.*

un·rent (un rent′), *adj.* not rent; not torn, disturbed, pained, or the like: *unrent garments; unrent silence; unrent feelings.* [1590–1600; UN-[1] + RENT[2]]

un·re·pair (un′ri pâr′), *n.* lack of repair; disrepair; dilapidation: *in a state of unrepair.* [1870–75; UN-[1] + REPAIR[1]] **—un′re·paired′,** *adj.*

un·re·pair·a·ble (un′ri pâr′ə bəl), *adj.* **1.** that cannot be repaired: *Some old clocks are unrepairable.* **2.** that cannot be rectified or remedied; irreparable. [1605–15; UN-[1] + REPAIR[1] + -ABLE]

un·re·quit·ed (un′ri kwī′tid), *adj.* **1.** not returned or reciprocated: *unrequited love.* **2.** not avenged or retaliated: *an unrequited wrong.* **3.** not repaid or satisfied. [1535–45; UN-[1] + REQUITE + -ED[2]]

un·re·serve (un′ri zûrv′), *n.* absence of reserve; frankness; candor. [1745–55; UN-[1] + RESERVE]

un·re·served (un′ri zûrvd′), *adj.* **1.** not restricted; without reservation; full; entire; unqualified: *unreserved approval.* **2.** free from reserve; frank; open: *unreserved behavior.* **3.** not kept or set apart for a particular use or person: *unreserved seats.* [1530–40; UN-[1] + RESERVED] **—un·re·serv·ed·ly** (un′ri zûr′vid lē), *adv.* **—un′re·serv′ed·ness,** *n.*
—Syn. 1. complete, unlimited. **2.** ingenuous, candid, artless, guileless, sincere.

un·rest (un rest′), *n.* **1.** lack of rest; a restless, troubled, or uneasy state; disquiet: *the unrest within himself.* **2.** disturbance or turmoil; agitation: *political unrest.* [1300–50; ME; see UN-[1], REST[1]] **—un·rest′ing,** *adj.*
—Syn. 2. ferment, discord, turbulence.

un·re·strained (un′ri strānd′), *adj.* **1.** not restrained or controlled; uncontrolled or uncontrollable: *the unrestrained birthrate in some countries.* **2.** not constrained; spontaneous: *unrestrained laughter.* [1580–90; UN-[1] + RESTRAINED] **—un·re·strain·ed·ly** (un′ri strā′nid lē), *adv.* **—un′re·strain′ed·ness,** *n.*
—Syn. 1. unchecked, unrepressed, unbridled, excessive.

un·re·straint (un′ri strānt′), *n.* absence of or freedom from restraint. [1795–1805; UN-[1] + RESTRAINT]

un·rid·dle (un rid′l), *v.t.*, **-dled, -dling.** to solve (a riddle, mystery, etc.). [1580–90; UN-[2] + RIDDLE[1]] **—un·rid′dler,** *n.*

un·rig (un rig′), *v.t.*, **-rigged, -rig·ging. 1.** to strip of rigging, as a ship. **2.** to strip of equipment. **3.** *Chiefly Brit. Dial.* to undress. [1570–80; UN-[2] + RIG]

un·right·eous (un rī′chəs), *adj.* **1.** not righteous; not upright or virtuous; wicked; sinful; evil: *an unrighteous king.* **2.** not in accordance with right or justice; unfair or unjust: *an unrighteous law.* [bef. 900; ME *unrightwyse,* OE *unrihtwīs.* See UN-[1], RIGHTEOUS] **—un·right′eous·ly,** *adv.* **—un·right′eous·ness,** *n.*

un·rip (un rip′), *v.t.*, **-ripped, -rip·ping. 1.** to undo by ripping; cut or tear open; rip; take apart or detach. **2.** to make known; disclose; reveal. [1505–15; UN-[2] + RIP[1]]

un·ripe (un rīp′), *adj.* **1.** not ripe; immature; not fully developed: *unripe fruit.* **2.** too early; premature. [bef. 1000; ME *unrype,* OE *unripe.* See UN-[1], RIPE] **—un·ripe′ly,** *adv.* **—un·ripe′ness,** *n.*

un·scarce′, *adj.*; **-ly,** *adv.*; **-ness,** *n.*
un·scared′, *adj.*
un·scarfed′, *adj.*
un·scar′i·fied′, *adj.*
un·scarred′, *adj.*
un·scat′tered, *adj.*
un·scav′enged, *adj.*
un·sce′nic, *adj.*
un·sce′ni·cal·ly, *adv.*
un·scent′ed, *adj.*
un·scep′tered, *adj.*
un·scep′ti·cal, *adj.*; **-ly,** *adv.*
un·sched′uled, *adj.*
un′sche·mat′ic, *adj.*
un′sche·mat′i·cal·ly, *adv.*
un·sche′ma·tized′, *adj.*
un·schemed′, *adj.*
un·schem′ing, *adj.*
un′schis·mat′ic, *adj.*
un′schis·mat′i·cal, *adj.*
un·schiz′oid, *adj.*
un′schiz·o·phren′ic, *adj.*
un·schol′ar·like′, *adj.*
un·schol′ar·ly, *adj.*
un′scho·las′tic, *adj.*
un′scho·las′ti·cal·ly, *adv.*
un·scin′til·lant, *adj.*
un·scin′til·lat′ing, *adj.*
un·scis′sored, *adj.*
un·scoffed′, *adj.*
un·scoff′ing, *adj.*
un·scold′ed, *adj.*
un·scold′ing, *adj.*
un·sconced′, *adj.*
un·scooped′, *adj.*
un·scorched′, *adj.*
un·scorch′ing, *adj.*
un·scored′, *adj.*
un·sco′ri·fied′, *adj.*
un·scor′ing, *adj.*
un·scorned′, *adj.*
un·scorn′ful, *adj.*; **-ly,** *adv.*; **-ness,** *n.*
un·scotched′, *adj.*
un·scoured′, *adj.*
un·scourged′, *adj.*
un·scourg′ing, *adj.*
un·scour′ing, *adj.*
un·scowl′ing, *adj.*; **-ly,** *adv.*
un·scraped′, *adj.*
un·scrap′ing, *adj.*
un·scratch′a·ble, *adj.*
un·scratched′, *adj.*
un·scratch′ing, *adj.*
un·scrawled′, *adj.*
un·scrawl′ing, *adj.*
un·screen′a·ble, *adj.*
un·screened′, *adj.*
un·scrib′al, *adj.*
un·scrib′bled, *adj.*
un·scribed′, *adj.*
un·scrimped′, *adj.*
un·scrip′tur·al, *adj.*; **-ly,** *adv.*
un·scrubbed′, *adj.*
un·scru′pled, *adj.*
un·scru′ta·ble, *adj.*
un·scru′ti·nized′, *adj.*
un·scru′ti·niz′ing, *adj.*; **-ly,** *adv.*
un·sculp′tur·al, *adj.*
un·sculp′tured, *adj.*
un·scummed′, *adj.*
un·searched′, *adj.*
un·search′ing, *adj.*; **-ly,** *adv.*
un·seared′, *adj.*
un·sea′wor′thi·ness, *n.*
un·sea′wor′thy, *adj.*
un′se·ced′ed, *adj.*
un′se·ced′ing, *adj.*
un′se·clud′ed, *adj.*; **-ly,** *adv.*
un′se·clud′ing, *adj.*
un′se·clu′sive, *adj.*; **-ly,** *adv.*; **-ness,** *n.*
un·sec′ond·ed, *adj.*
un′sec·re·tar′i·al, *adj.*
un′se·cret′ed, *adj.*
un′se·cret′ing, *adj.*
un·se′cre·tive, *adj.*; **-ly,** *adv.*; **-ness,** *n.*
un·se′cret·ly, *adv.*
un′sec·tar′i·an, *adj.*
un′sec·tar′i·an·ize′, *v.t.*, **-ized, -iz·ing.**
un·sec′tion·al, *adj.*; **-ly,** *adv.*
un·sec′tion·al·ized′, *adj.*
un·sec′tioned, *adj.*
un·sec′u·lar, *adj.*; **-ly,** *adv.*
un·sec′u·lar·ized′, *adj.*
un′se·cure′, *adj.*; **-ly,** *adv.*; **-ness,** *n.*
un′se·date′, *adj.*; **-ly,** *adv.*; **-ness,** *n.*
un·sed′a·tive, *adj.*
un·sed′en·tar′y, *adj.*
un′sed·i·men·tar′i·ly, *adv.*
un′sed·i·men′ta·ry, *adj.*
un′se·di′tious, *adj.*; **-ly,** *adv.*; **-ness,** *n.*
un′se·duc′i·ble, *adj.*; **-ble·ness,** *n.*; **-bly,** *adv.*
un′se·duc′tive, *adj.*; **-ly,** *adv.*; **-ness,** *n.*
un·sed′u·lous, *adj.*; **-ly,** *adv.*; **-ness,** *n.*
un·see′a·ble, *adj.*
un·seed′ed, *adj.*
un·seed′ing, *adj.*
un·see′ing, *adj.*; **-ly,** *adv.*; **-ness,** *n.*
un·seek′ing, *adj.*
un·seethed′, *adj.*
un·seeth′ing, *adj.*
un′seg·men′tal, *adj.*; **-ly,** *adv.*
un·seg′men·tar′y, *adj.*
un·seg′ment·ed, *adj.*
un·seg′re·ga·ble, *adj.*
un·seg′re·gat′ing, *adj.*
un′seg·re·ga′tion·al, *adj.*
un·seg′re·ga′tive, *adj.*
un′seign·ior′al, *adj.*
un′sei·gno′ri·al, *adj.*
un·seis′mal, *adj.*
un·seis′mic, *adj.*
un·seiz′a·ble, *adj.*
un·seized′, *adj.*
un′se·lect′, *adj.*
un′se·lect′ed, *adj.*
un′se·lec′tive, *adj.*
un′self-cen′tered, *adj.*
un′self-know′ing, *adj.*
un′self-pos·sessed′, *adj.*
un′self-right′eous, *adj.*; **-ly,** *adv.*; **-ness,** *n.*
un′self-sac′ri·fi′cial, *adj.*; **-ly,** *adv.*
un′self-sac′ri·fic′ing, *adj.*
un′self-suf·fi′cien·cy, *n.*
un′self-suf·fi′cient, *adj.*; **-ly,** *adv.*
un′se·nes′cent, *adj.*
un·se′nile, *adj.*
un·sen′sate, *adj.*
un′sen·sa′tion·al, *adj.*; **-ly,** *adv.*
un·sensed′, *adj.*
un′sen·si·bil′i·ty, *n.*, *pl.* **-ties.**
un·sen′si·ble, *adj.*; **-ble·ness,** *n.*; **-bly,** *adv.*
un·sens′ing, *adj.*
un·sen′si·tive, *adj.*; **-ly,** *adv.*; **-ness,** *n.*
un·sen′si·tize′, *v.t.*, **-tized, -tiz·ing.**
un·sen′so·ry, *adj.*
un·sen′su·al, *adj.*; **-ly,** *adv.*
un′sen·su·al·is′tic, *adj.*
un·sen′su·al·ized′, *adj.*
un·sen′su·ous, *adj.*; **-ly,** *adv.*; **-ness,** *n.*
un·sent′, *adj.*
un·sen′tenced, *adj.*
un′sen·ten′tious, *adj.*; **-ly,** *adv.*; **-ness,** *n.*
un·sen′tient, *adj.*; **-ly,** *adv.*
un′sen·ti·men′tal, *adj.*; **-ly,** *adv.*
un′sen·ti·men′tal·ized′, *adj.*
un·sen′ti·neled, *adj.*
un·sen′ti·nelled, *adj.*
un·sep′a·ra·ble, *adj.*; **-ble·ness,** *n.*; **-bly,** *adv.*
un·sep′a·rate, *adj.*; **-ly,** *adv.*; **-ness,** *n.*
un·sep′a·rat′ed, *adj.*
un·sep′a·rat′ing, *adj.*
un·sep′a·ra·tive, *adj.*
un·sep′ul·cher, *v.t.*
un′se·pul′chral, *adj.*; **-ly,** *adv.*
un·sep′ul·tured, *adj.*
un·se′quenced, *adj.*
un·se′quent, *adj.*
un′se·quen′tial, *adj.*; **-ly,** *adv.*
un′se·ques′tered, *adj.*
un′se·raph′ic, *adj.*
un′se·raph′i·cal, *adj.*; **-ly,** *adv.*
un·sere′, *adj.*
un′ser·e·nad′ed, *adj.*
un′se·rene′, *adj.*; **-ly,** *adv.*; **-ness,** *n.*
un·se′ri·al·ized′, *adj.*
un·se′ri·ous, *adj.*; **-ly,** *adv.*; **-ness,** *n.*
un·ser′rate, *adj.*
un·ser′rat·ed, *adj.*
un·ser′ried, *adj.*
un·serv′a·ble, *adj.*
un·served′, *adj.*
un·ser′vice·a·ble, *adj.*; **-ble·ness,** *n.*; **-bly,** *adv.*
un·serv′iced, *adj.*
un·ser′vile, *adj.*; **-ly,** *adv.*
un·serv′ing, *adj.*
un′ses·qui·pe·da′li·an, *adj.*
un·set′ting, *adj.*
un·set′tle·a·ble, *adj.*
un·sev′er·a·ble, *adj.*
un′se·vere′, *adj.*; **-ly,** *adv.*; **-ness,** *n.*
un·sev′ered, *adj.*
un·sex′u·al, *adj.*; **-ly,** *adv.*
un·sex′y, *adj.*
un·shab′bi·ly, *adv.*
un·shab′by, *adj.*
un·shade′, *v.t.*, **-shad·ed, -shad·ing.**
un·shad′i·ly, *adv.*
un·shad′i·ness, *n.*
un·shad′ow·a·ble, *adj.*
un·shad′y, *adj.*
un·shaft′ed, *adj.*
un·shak′a·ble, *adj.*; **-ly,** *adv.*
un·shake′a·ble, *adj.*; **-ly,** *adv.*
un·sha′ken, *adj.*
un·shak′ing, *adj.*
un·sham′a·ble, *adj.*
un·shame′a·ble, *adj.*
un·shamed′, *adj.*
un·shammed′, *adj.*
un·shanked′, *adj.*
un·shap′a·ble, *adj.*
un·shape′a·ble, *adj.*
un·shape′li·ness, *n.*
un·shape′ly, *adj.*
un·shap′ing, *adj.*
un·shar′a·ble, *adj.*
un·share′a·ble, *adj.*
un·shared′, *adj.*
un·shar′ing, *adj.*
un·sharp′, *adj.*; **-ly,** *adv.*; **-ness,** *n.*
un·sharped′, *adj.*
un·sharp′ened, *adj.*
un·sharp′en·ing, *adj.*
un·sharp′ing, *adj.*
un·shat′ter·a·ble, *adj.*
un·shat′tered, *adj.*
un·shav′a·ble, *adj.*
un·shave′a·ble, *adj.*
un·shaved′, *adj.*
un·shav′en, *adj.*
un·sheared′, *adj.*
un·shed′, *adj.*
un·shed′ding, *adj.*
un·sheer′, *adj.*; **-ness,** *n.*
un·sheet′ed, *adj.*
un·sheet′ing, *adj.*
un·shelled′, *adj.*
un·shel′tered, *adj.*
un·shel′ter·ing, *adj.*
un·shelved′, *adj.*
un·shep′herd·ed, *adj.*
un·shep′herd·ing, *adj.*

un·ri·valed (un rī′vəld), *adj.* having no rival or competitor; having no equal; incomparable; supreme: *His work is unrivaled for the beauty of its prose.* Also, *esp. Brit.,* **un·ri′valled.** [1585–95; UN-¹ + RIVALED]

un·robe (un rōb′), *v.t., v.i.,* **-robed, -rob·ing.** to disrobe; undress. [1590–1600; UN-² + ROBE]

un·roll (un rōl′), *v.t.* **1.** to open or spread out (something rolled or coiled): *to unroll a bolt of fabric.* **2.** to lay open; display; reveal. **3.** *Obs.* to strike from a roll or register. —*v.i.* **4.** to become unrolled or spread out: *The scrolls unroll easily.* **5.** to become continuously visible or apparent: *The landscape unrolled before our eyes.* [1375–1425; late ME *unrollen.* See UN-², ROLL]

un·roof (un ro͞of′, -ro͝of′), *v.t.* to take off the roof or covering of. [1590–1600; UN-² + ROOF]

un·root (un ro͞ot′, -ro͝ot′), *v.t.* **1.** to uproot. —*v.i.* **2.** to become unrooted. [1400–50; late ME *unrooten.* See UN-², ROOT¹]

un·round (un round′), *v.t. Phonet.* to articulate (an ordinarily rounded vowel) without rounding the lips; delabialize. Cf. **round¹** (def. 57c), **spread** (def. 14). [1605–15; UN-² + ROUND¹]

un·round·ed (un roun′did), *adj. Phonet.* (of a vowel) pronounced without rounding the lips, as the vowel of *bit.* Cf. **rounded** (def. 2), **spread** (def. 41). [1875–80; UN-¹ + ROUNDED]

un·rove (un rōv′), *Naut.* —*v.t., v.i.* **1.** pt. and pp. of **unreeve.** —*adj.* **2.** withdrawn from a block, thimble, etc.

UNRRA (un′rə), United Nations Relief and Rehabilitation Administration. Also, **U.N.R.R.A.**

un·ruf·fle (un ruf′əl), *v.,* **-fled, -fling.** —*v.t.* **1.** to calm (someone). **2.** to smooth out (something). —*v.i.* **3.** to become calm or smoothed out. [1690–1700; UN-² + RUFFLE]

un·ruf·fled (un ruf′əld), *adj.* **1.** calm; not emotionally upset or agitated; steady; unflustered: *He became all excited, but she remained unruffled.* **2.** not ruffled, as a garment; smooth. [1650–60; UN-¹ + RUFFLE + -ED²] —**un·ruf′fled·ness,** *n.*
—**Syn. 1.** unperturbed, tranquil, serene, imperturbable, cool, composed, peaceful, undisturbed.

un·ru·ly (un ro͞o′lē), *adj.,* **-li·er, -li·est.** not submissive or conforming to rule; ungovernable; turbulent; intractable; refractory; lawless: *an unruly class; an unruly wilderness.* [1350–1400; ME *unruely,* equiv. to *un-* UN-¹ + *ruly, ruely* governable, controllable; see RULE, -Y¹] —**un·ru′li·ness,** *n.*
—**Syn.** disobedient, unmanageable, uncontrollable, stubborn, disorderly, riotous. UNRULY, INTRACTABLE, RECALCITRANT, REFRACTORY describe persons or things that resist management or control. UNRULY suggests persistently disorderly behavior or character in persons or things: *an unruly child, peevish and willful; wild, unruly hair.* INTRACTABLE suggests in persons a determined resistance to all attempts to guide or direct them, in things a refusal to respond to attempts to shape, improve, or modify them: *an intractable social rebel; a seemingly intractable problem in logistics.* RECALCITRANT and REFRACTORY imply not only a lack of submissiveness but also an open, often violent, rebellion against authority or direction. RECALCITRANT, the stronger of the two terms, suggests a stubborn and absolute noncompliance: *a recalcitrant person, openly contemptuous of all authority.* REFRACTORY implies active, mulish disobedience, but leaves open the possibility of eventual compliance: *refractory students, resisting efforts to interest them in their studies.*

UNRWA, United Nations Relief and Works Agency.

Uns, *Symbol, Chem., Physics.* unnilseptium.

un·sad·dle (un sad′l), *v.,* **-dled, -dling.** —*v.t.* **1.** to take the saddle from. **2.** to cause to fall or dismount from a saddle; unhorse. —*v.i.* **3.** to take the saddle from a horse. [1350–1400; ME *unsadelen;* see UN-², SADDLE; cf. D *ontsadelen,* OHG *intsatalôn*]

un·safe·ty (un sāf′tē), *n.* unsafe state or condition; exposure to danger or risk; insecurity. [1590–1600; UN-¹ + SAFETY] —**un·safe′tied,** *adj.*

un·said¹ (un sed′), *v.* pt. and pp. of **unsay.**

un·said² (un sed′), *adj.* not said; thought but not mentioned or discussed; unstated: *It was best left unsaid.* [bef. 1000; ME *unsa(i)d,* OE *unsǣd;* see UN-¹, SAID]

un·san·i·tar·y (un san′i ter′ē), *adj.* not sanitary; unhealthy or unhealthful; tending to harbor or spread disease: *unsanitary living conditions.* Also, **insanitary.** [1870–75; UN-¹ + SANITARY] —**un·san′i·tar′i·ly,** *adv.*

un·sat·is·fac·to·ry (un′sat is fak′tə rē), *adj.* not satisfactory; not satisfying or meeting one's demands; inadequate. [1630–40; UN-¹ + SATISFACTORY] —**un′sat·is·fac′to·ri·ly,** *adv.* —**un′sat·is·fac′to·ri·ness,** *n.*
—**Syn.** disappointing, insufficient.

un·sat·u·rat·ed (un sach′ə rā′tid), *adj.* **1.** not saturated; having the power to dissolve still more of a substance. **2.** *Chem.* (of an organic compound) having a double or triple bond and capable of taking on elements or groups by direct chemical combination without the liberation of other elements or compounds, as ethylene, $CH_2{=}CH_2$; undersaturated. [1750–60; UN-¹ + SATURATED] —**un·sat·u·rate** (un sach′ər it, -ə rāt′), *n.* —**un′sat·u·ra′tion,** *n.*

un·sa·vor·y (un sā′və rē), *adj.* **1.** not savory; tasteless or insipid: *an unsavory meal.* **2.** unpleasant in taste or smell; distasteful. **3.** unappealing or disagreeable, as a pursuit: *Poor teachers can make education unsavory.* **4.** socially or morally objectionable or offensive: *an unsavory past; an unsavory person.* Also, *esp. Brit.,* **un·sa′vour·y.** [1175–1225; ME; see UN-¹, SAVORY¹] —**un·sa′vor·i·ly,** *adv.* —**un·sa′vor·i·ness,** *n.*
—**Syn. 1.** flat, unappetizing.

un·sav·vy (un sav′ē), *adj. Informal.* inexperienced or untrained: *a term used only by unsavvy freshmen.* [UN-¹ + SAVVY]

un·say (un sā′), *v.t.,* **-said, -say·ing.** to withdraw (something said), as if it had never been said; retract. [1425–75; late ME *unsayen.* See UN-², SAY¹]

un·scathed (un skāthd′), *adj.* not scathed; unharmed; uninjured: *She survived the accident unscathed.* [1325–75; ME; see UN-¹, SCATHED]
—**Syn.** unhurt, unscratched, untouched, safe, whole.

un·schooled (un sko͞old′), *adj.* **1.** not schooled, taught, or trained: *Though unschooled, he had a grasp of the subject.* **2.** not acquired or artificial; natural: *an unschooled talent.* [1580–90; UN-¹ + SCHOOL¹ + -ED²]

un·sci·en·tif·ic (un′sī ən tif′ik), *adj.* **1.** not scientific; not employed in science: *an unscientific measuring device.* **2.** not conforming to the principles or methods of science: *an unscientific approach to a problem.* **3.** not demonstrating scientific knowledge or scientific methods: *an unscientific report.* [1765–75; UN-¹ + SCIENTIFIC] —**un′sci·en·tif′i·cal·ly,** *adv.*

un·scram·ble (un skram′bəl), *v.t.,* **-bled, -bling. 1.** to bring out of a scrambled condition; reduce to order or intelligibility. **2.** Also, **descramble.** to make (a scrambled radio or telephonic message) comprehensible by systematically tuning the receiver to the frequencies used in transmission. Cf. **decode** (def. 2). [1915–20; UN-² + SCRAMBLE]

un·scram·bler (un skram′blər), *n.* **1.** a person or thing that unscrambles. **2.** Also, **descrambler.** an electronic device that makes scrambled telecommunications signals intelligible by systematically tuning the receiver to the frequencies used in transmission. Cf. **scrambler** (def. 2). [1950–55; UNSCRAMBLE + -ER¹]

un·screw (un skro͞o′), *v.t.* **1.** to draw or loosen a screw from (a hinge, bracket, etc.). **2.** to unfasten or withdraw by turning, as a screw or lid. **3.** to open (a jar, bottle, etc.) by turning the lid or cover. —*v.i.* **4.** to permit of being unscrewed. [1595–1605; UN-² + SCREW]

un·script·ed (un skrip′tid), *adj.* **1.** not scripted; lacking a script: *an unscripted idea for a movie.* **2.** *Informal.* that has not been planned for or anticipated: *an unscripted interruption of the speech.* [1940–45; UN-¹ + SCRIPT + -ED²]

un·scru·pu·lous (un skro͞o′pyə ləs), *adj.* not scrupulous; unrestrained by scruples; conscienceless; unprincipled. [1795–1805; UN-¹ + SCRUPULOUS] —**un·scru′pu·lous·ly,** *adv.* —**un·scru′pu·lous·ness, un·scru·pu·los·i·ty** (un skro͞o′pyə los′i tē), *n.*
—**Syn.** UNSCRUPULOUS, UNPRINCIPLED refer to lack of moral standards or conscience to guide one's conduct. The UNSCRUPULOUS person is without scruples of conscience, and disregards, or has contempt for, laws of right or justice with which he or she is perfectly well acquainted, and which should restrain his or her actions: *unscrupulous in methods of making money, in taking advantage of the unfortunate.* The UNPRINCIPLED person is without moral principles or ethical standards in his or her conduct or actions: *an unprincipled rogue; unprincipled conduct.*

CONCISE PRONUNCIATION KEY: *act, cāpe, dâre, pärt; set, ēqual; if, īce; ox, ōver, ôrder, oil, bo͝ok, bo͞ot, out; up, ûrge; child; sing; shoe; thin, that;* zh as in *treasure.* ə = *a* as in *alone, e* as in *system, i* as in *easily, o* as in *gallop, u* as in *circus;* ᵊ as in *fire* (fīᵊr), *hour* (ouᵊr). l and n can serve as syllabic consonants, as in *cradle* (krād′l), and *button* (but′n). See the full key inside the front cover.

un·shield′a·ble, *adj.*
un·shield′ed, *adj.*
un·shield′ing, *adj.*
un·shift′ing, *adj.*
un·shift′y, *adj.*
un·shim′mer·ing, *adj.;* **-ly,** *adv.*
un·shined′, *adj.*
un·shin′gled, *adj.*
un·shin′ing, *adj.*
un·shin′y, *adj.*
un·ship′pa·ble, *adj.*
un·shirked′, *adj.*
un·shirk′ing, *adj.*
un·shirred′, *adj.*
un·shirt′ed, *adj.*
un·shiv′ered, *adj.*
un·shiv′er·ing, *adj.*
un′shock·a·bil′i·ty, *n.*
un·shock′a·ble, *adj.*
un·shocked′, *adj.*
un·shock′ing, *adj.*
un·shod′, *adj.*
un·shoed′, *adj.*
un·shoot′a·ble, *adj.*
un·shored′, *adj.*
un·shorn′, *adj.*
un·short′, *adj.*
un·short′en, *adj.*
un·shot′ted, *adj.*
un·shoul′dered, *adj.*
un·shout′ed, *adj.*
un·shout′ing, *adj.*
un·shoved′, *adj.*
un·shov′eled, *adj.*
un·shov′elled, *adj.*
un·show′a·ble, *adj.*
un·showed′, *adj.*
un·show′ered, *adj.*
un·show′er·ing, *adj.*
un·show′i·ly, *adv.*
un·show′i·ness, *n.*
un·shown′, *adj.*
un·show′y, *adj.*
un·shred′ded, *adj.*
un·shrewd′, *adj.;* **-ly,** *adv.;* **-ness,** *n.*
un·shrew′ish, *adj.*
un·shrill′, *adj.*
un·shrined′, *adj.*
un′shrink·a·bil′i·ty, *n.*
un·shrink′a·ble, *adj.*
un·shrink′ing, *adj.;* **-ly,** *adv.*
un·shrived′, *adj.*
un·shriv′eled, *adj.*
un·shriv′elled, *adj.*
un·shriv′en, *adj.*
un·shrug′ging, *adj.*
un·shrunk′, *adj.*
un·shrunk′en, *adj.*
un·shud′der·ing, *adj.*
un·shuf′fled, *adj.*
un·shun′na·ble, *adj.*
un·shunned′, *adj.*
un·shunt′ed, *adj.*
un·shut′, *adj.*
un·shut′tered, *adj.*
un·shy′, *adj.;* **-ly,** *adv.;* **-ness,** *n.*
un·sib′i·lant, *adj.*
un·sic′ca·tive, *adj.*
un·sick′, *adj.;* **-ly,** *adv.*
un·sick′ened, *adj.*
un·sid′ed, *adj.*
un′si·de·re′al, *adj.*
un·sid′ing, *adj.*
un·si′dling, *adj.*
un·sieged′, *adj.*
un·sieved′, *adj.*
un·sift′ed, *adj.*
un·sigh′ing, *adj.*
un·sight′ed, *adj.*
un·sign′a·ble, *adj.*
un·sig′naled, *adj.*
un·sig′nal·ized′, *adj.*
un·sig′nalled, *adj.*
un·sig′na·tured, *adj.*
un·signed′, *adj.*
un·sig′net·ed, *adj.*
un·sig′ni·fi′a·ble, *adj.*
un′sig·nif′i·cant, *adj.;* **-ly,** *adv.*
un′sig·nif′i·ca′tive, *adj.*
un·sig′ni·fied′, *adj.*
un·sig′ni·fy′ing, *adj.*
un·si′lenced, *adj.*
un·si′lent, *adj.;* **-ly,** *adv.*
un′sil·hou·et′ted, *adj.*
un′si·lic′i·fied′, *adj.*
un·sil′ly, *adj.*
un·sil′vered, *adj.*
un·sim′i·lar, *adj.;* **-ly,** *adv.*
un′sim·i·lar′i·ty, *n., pl.* **-ties.**
un·sim′mered, *adj.*
un·sim′mer·ing, *adj.*
un·sim′per·ing, *adj.*
un·sim′ple, *adj.;* **-ple·ness,** *n.;* **-ply,** *adv.*
un·sim′pli·fied′, *adj.*
un·sim′pli·fy′ing, *adj.*
un·sim′u·lar, *adj.*
un·sim′u·lat′ed, *adj.*
un·sim′u·lat′ing, *adj.*
un·sim′u·la′tive, *adj.*
un′si·mul·ta′ne·ous, *adj.;* **-ly,** *adv.;* **-ness,** *n.*
un·sin′ewed, *adj.*
un·sin′ew·ing, *adj.*
un·sin′ew·y, *adj.*
un·sin′ful, *adj.;* **-ly,** *adv.;* **-ness,** *n.*
un·sing′a·ble, *adj.*
un·singed′, *adj.*
un·sin′gle, *adj.*
un·sin′gu·lar, *adj.;* **-ly,** *adv.;* **-ness,** *n.*
un·sin′is·ter, *adj.;* **-ly,** *adv.;* **-ness,** *n.*
un′sink·a·bil′i·ty, *n.*
un·sink′a·ble, *adj.*
un·sink′ing, *adj.*
un·sin′ning, *adj.*
un·sin′u·ate, *adj.;* **-ly,** *adv.*
un·sin′u·at′ed, *adj.*
un·sin′u·ous, *adj.;* **-ly,** *adv.;* **-ness,** *n.*
un·sipped′, *adj.*
un·sis′tered, *adj.*
un·sis′ter·ly, *adj.*
un·sit′u·at′ed, *adj.*
un·siz′a·ble, *adj.*
un·size′a·ble, *adj.*
un·sized′, *adj.*
un·skep′ti·cal, *adj.;* **-ly,** *adv.*
un·sketch′a·ble, *adj.*
un·sketched′, *adj.*
un·skewed′, *adj.*
un·skew′ered, *adj.*
un·skimmed′, *adj.*
un·skinned′, *adj.*
un·skirt′ed, *adj.*
un·slack′, *adj.*
un·slacked′, *adj.*
un·slack′ened, *adj.*
un·slack′en·ing, *adj.*
un·slack′ing, *adj.*
un·slagged′, *adj.*
un·slain′, *adj.*
un·slak′a·ble, *adj.*
un·slake′a·ble, *adj.*
un·slaked′, *adj.*
un·slammed′, *adj.*
un·slan′dered, *adj.*
un·slan′der·ous, *adj.;* **-ly,** *adv.;* **-ness,** *n.*
un·slant′ed, *adj.*
un·slant′ing, *adj.*
un·slapped′, *adj.*
un·slashed′, *adj.*
un·slat′ed, *adj.*
un·slat′ing, *adj.*
un·slat′ted, *adj.*
un·slaugh′tered, *adj.*
un·slay′a·ble, *adj.*
un·sleaved′, *adj.*
un·sleek′, *adj.*
un·sleep′ing, *adj.*
un·sleep′y, *adj.*
un·sleeved′, *adj.*
un·slen′der, *adj.*
un·sliced′, *adj.*
un·slicked′, *adj.*
un·slid′ing, *adj.*
un·slight′ed, *adj.*
un·slim′, *adj.;* **-ly,** *adv.;* **-ness,** *n.*
un·slimmed′, *adj.*
un·slink′ing, *adj.*
un·slipped′, *adj.*
un·slip′pered, *adj.*
un·slip′per·y, *adj.*
un·slip′ping, *adj.*
un·sloped′, *adj.*
un·slop′ing, *adj.*
un·slopped′, *adj.*
un·slot′ted, *adj.*
un·slouched′, *adj.*
un·slouch′ing, *adj.*
un·slouch′y, *adj.*
un·sloughed′, *adj.*
un·slough′ing, *adj.*
un·slow′, *adj.;* **-ly,** *adv.;* **-ness,** *n.*
un·slowed′, *adj.*
un·slug′gish, *adj.;* **-ly,** *adv.;* **-ness,** *n.*
un·sluiced′, *adj.*
un·slum′ber·ing, *adj.*
un·slum′ber·y, *adj.*
un·slum′brous, *adj.*
un·slumped′, *adj.*
un·slump′ing, *adj.*
un·slung′, *adj.*
un·slurred′, *adj.*
un·sly′, *adj.;* **-ly,** *adv.;* **-ness,** *n.*
un·smacked′, *adj.*
un·smart′, *adj.*
un·smart′ing, *adj.*
un·smashed′, *adj.*
un·smeared′, *adj.*
un·smelled′, *adj.*
un·smell′ing, *adj.*
un·smelt′ed, *adj.*
un·smil′ing, *adj.;* **-ly,** *adv.*
un·smirched′, *adj.*
un·smirk′ing, *adj.;* **-ly,** *adv.*
un·smit′ten, *adj.*
un·smocked′, *adj.*
un·smok′a·ble, *adj.*
un·smoke′a·ble, *adj.*
un·smoked′, *adj.*
un·smok′i·ly, *adv.*
un·smok′i·ness, *n.*
un·smok′ing, *adj.*
un·smok′y, *adj.*
un·smol′der·ing, *adj.*
un·smooth′, *adj.;* **-ly,** *adv.;* **-ness,** *n.*
un·smoothed′, *adj.*
un·smooth′ened, *adj.*
un·smoth′er·a·ble, *adj.*
un·smoth′ered, *adj.*
un·smoth′er·ing, *adj.*
un·smoul′der·ing, *adj.;* **-ly,** *adv.*
un·smudge′a·ble, *adj.*
un·smudged′, *adj.*
un·smug′, *adj.;* **-ly,** *adv.;* **-ness,** *n.*
un·smug′gled, *adj.*
un·smutched′, *adj.*
un·smut′ted, *adj.*
un·smut′ty, *adj.*
un·snaf′fled, *adj.*
un·snagged′, *adj.*
un·snak′y, *adj.*
un·snared′, *adj.*
un·snatched′, *adj.*
un·sneak′ing, *adj.*
un·sneak′y, *adj.*
un·sneer′ing, *adj.;* **-ly,** *adv.*
un·snipped′, *adj.*
un·snob′bish, *adj.;* **-ly,** *adv.;* **-ness,** *n.*
un·snor′ing, *adj.*
un·snout′ed, *adj.*
un·snubbed′, *adj.*
un·snuffed′, *adj.*
un·snug′, *adj.;* **-ly,** *adv.;* **-ness,** *n.*
un·soaked′, *adj.*
un·soaped′, *adj.*
un·soar′a·ble, *adj.*
un·soar′ing, *adj.*

un•seal (un sēl′), *v.t.* **1.** to break or remove the seal of; open, as something sealed or firmly closed: *to unseal a letter; to unseal a tomb.* **2.** to free from constraint, as a person's thought, speech, or behavior: *Their friendship unsealed her vivacity.* [1375–1425; late ME *unselen;* see UN-[2], SEAL[1]] —**un•seal′a•ble,** *adj.*

un•sealed (un sēld′), *adj.* **1.** not sealed; not stamped or marked with a seal: *unsealed cargo.* **2.** not shut or closed with or as if with a seal: *an unsealed letter; an unsealed crate.* **3.** not verified, certain, or confirmed: *His fate was still unsealed.* [1350–1400; ME *unseled;* see UN-[1], SEAL[1], -ED[2]]

un•seam (un sēm′), *v.t.* to open the seam or seams of; undo; rip apart: *to unseam a dress.* [1585–95; UN-[2] + SEAM]

un•search•a•ble (un sûr′chə bəl), *adj.* not searchable; not lending itself to research or exploration; not to be understood by searching; hidden; unfathomable; mysterious: *the unsearchable ways of the universe.* [1350–1400; ME *unserchable.* See UN-[1], SEARCHABLE] —**un•search′a•ble•ness,** *n.* —**un•search′a•bly,** *adv.*

un•sea•son•a•ble (un sē′zə nə bəl), *adj.* **1.** not seasonable; being out of season; unseasonal: *unseasonable weather.* **2.** not befitting the occasion; untimely; ill-timed; inopportune; inappropriate: *Their visits were usually unseasonable.* [1400–50; late ME; see UN-[1], SEASONABLE] —**un•sea′son•a•ble•ness,** *n.* —**un•sea′son•a•bly,** *adv.*

un•sea•son•al (un sē′zə nl), *adj.* not characteristic or typical of a particular season; unseasonable: *unseasonal April snows.* [UN-[1] + SEASONAL]

un•sea•soned (un sē′zənd), *adj.* **1.** (of things) not seasoned; not matured, dried, etc., by due seasoning: *unseasoned wood.* **2.** (of persons) not inured to a climate, work, etc.; inexperienced: *an unseasoned crew.* **3.** (of food) not flavored with seasoning: *a tasteless, unseasoned meal.* [1575–85; UN-[1] + SEASON + -ED[2]]

un•seat (un sēt′), *v.t.* **1.** to dislodge from a seat, esp. to throw from a saddle, as a rider; unhorse. **2.** to remove from political office by an elective process, by force, or by legal action: *The corrupt mayor was finally unseated.* [1590–1600; UN-[2] + SEAT]

un•se•cured (un′si kyŏŏrd′), *adj.* **1.** not secured, esp. not insured against loss, as by a bond or pledge: *an unsecured loan.* **2.** not made secure, as a door or lock of hair; unfastened. **3.** not protected against tapping or interception, as a telephone line or radio communication. [1770–80; UN-[1] + SECURED]

un•se•duced (un′si dōōst′, -dyōōst′), *adj.* not seduced, esp. by the lure of personal gain, power, fame, etc.: *He remained unseduced by the graft offered him.* [1555–65; UN-[1] + SEDUCED]

CONCISE ETYMOLOGY KEY: <, descended or borrowed from; >, whence; b., blend of, blended; c., cognate with; cf., compare; deriv., derivative; equiv., equivalent; imit., imitative; obl., oblique; r., replacing; s., stem; sp., spelling, spelled; resp., respelling, respelled; trans., translation; ?, origin unknown; *, unattested; ‡, probably earlier than. See the full key inside the front cover.

un•seem•ly (un sēm′lē), *adj.,* **-li•er, -li•est,** *adv.* —*adj.* **1.** not seemly; not in keeping with established standards of taste or proper form; unbecoming or indecorous in appearance, speech, conduct, etc.: *an unseemly act; unseemly behavior.* **2.** inappropriate for time or place: *an unseemly hour.* —*adv.* **3.** in an unseemly manner. [1250–1300; ME; see UN-[1], SEEMLY] —**un•seem′li•ness,** *n.*
—**Syn. 1.** unbefitting, inappropriate. See **improper.**

un•seen (un sēn′), *adj.* **1.** not seen; unperceived; unobserved; invisible. **2.** recognized or comprehended without prior study, as a written text or musical score. [1150–1200; ME *unsene, unsehene;* see UN-[1], SEEN]

un•seg•re•gat•ed (un seg′ri gā′tid), *adj.* not segregated, esp. not subject to racial division; integrated: *an unsegregated community.* [1905–10; UN-[1] + SEGREGATED]

un•self•con•scious (un′self kon′shəs), *adj.* not self-conscious; without affectation or pretense: *an unselfconscious manner.* [1830–40; UN-[1] + SELF-CONSCIOUS] —**un′self•con′scious•ly,** *adv.* —**un′self•con′scious•ness,** *n.*

un•self•ish (un sel′fish), *adj.* not selfish; disinterested; generous; altruistic. [1690–1700; UN-[1] + SELFISH] —**un•self′ish•ly,** *adv.* —**un•self′ish•ness,** *n.*

un•sell (un sel′), *v.t.,* **-sold, -sell•ing.** to dissuade from a belief in the desirability, value, wisdom, or truth of something: *He tried to unsell the public on its faith in rearmament.* [1925–30; UN-[2] + SELL[1]]

Un•ser (un′sər), *n.* **Albert** (*Al*), born 1939, and his brother **Robert** (*Bobby*), born 1934, U.S. racing-car drivers.

un•set (un set′), *adj.* **1.** not set; not solidified or made firm, as concrete or asphalt. **2.** (of a gemstone) not mounted in a setting. [1350–1400; ME: (of a time) unappointed; see UN-[2], SET]

un•set•tle (un set′l), *v.,* **-tled, -tling.** —*v.t.* **1.** to alter from a settled state; cause to be no longer firmly fixed or established; render unstable; disturb: *Violence unsettled the government.* **2.** to shake or weaken (beliefs, feelings, etc.); cause doubt or uncertainty about: *doubts unsettling his religious convictions.* **3.** to vex or agitate the mind or emotions of; upset; discompose: *The quarrel unsettled her.* —*v.i.* **4.** to become unfixed or disordered. [1535–45; UN-[2] + SETTLE[1]]
—**Syn. 2.** upset, disturb, unbalance, confuse, disconcert.

un•set•tled (un set′ld), *adj.* **1.** not settled; not fixed or stable; without established order; unorganized; disorganized: *an unsettled social order; still unsettled in their new home.* **2.** continuously moving or changing; not situated in one place: *an unsettled life.* **3.** wavering or uncertain, as in opinions or behavior; unstable; erratic: *an unsettled state of mind.* **4.** not populated or settled, as a region: *an unsettled wilderness.* **5.** undetermined, as a point at issue; undecided; doubtful: *After many years the matter was still unsettled.* **6.** not adjusted, closed, or disposed of, as an account, estate, or law case. **7.** liable to change; inconstant; variable: *unsettled weather.* [1585–95; UN-[1] + SETTLE[1] + -ED[2]] —**un•set′tled•ness,** *n.*
—**Syn. 3.** UNSETTLED, UNSTABLE, UNSTEADY imply a lack of fixity, firmness, and dependability. That which is UNSETTLED is not fixed or determined: *unsettled weather; unsettled claims.* That which is UNSTABLE is wavering, changeable; easily moved, shaken, or overthrown: *unstable equilibrium; an unstable decision.* That which is UNSTEADY is infirm or shaky in position or movement: *unsteady on one's feet; unsteady of purpose.* **5.** indeterminate, unsure. **7.** vacillating, fickle, faltering, irresolute. —**Ant. 1, 3.** stable.

un•set•tle•ment (un set′l mənt), *n.* **1.** an act or an instance of unsettling. **2.** the state or quality of being unsettled: *Such strange behavior caused me some unsettlement.* [1640–50; UNSETTLE + -MENT]

un•sew (un sō′), *v.t.,* **-sewed, -sewn** or **-sewed, -sew•ing.** to remove or rip the stitches of (something sewed). [1300–50; ME *unsouwen.* See UN-[2], SEW[1]]

un•sex (un seks′), *v.t.* **1.** to deprive of sexual power; render impotent or frigid; spay or castrate. **2.** to deprive (oneself or another) of the proper or appropriate character and qualities of one's sex, as by unnatural conduct. [1595–1605; UN-[2] + SEX]

un•shack•le (un shak′əl), *v.t.,* **-led, -ling. 1.** to free from shackles; unfetter. **2.** to free from restraint, as conversation. [1605–15; UN-[2] + SHACKLE]

un•shad•owed (un shad′ōd), *adj.* not shadowed; not darkened or obscured by shadow; free from gloom. [1585–95; UN-[1] + SHADOW + -ED[2]]

un•shaped (un shāpt′), *adj.* not shaped or definitely formed. [1565–75; UN-[1] + SHAPED]

un•shap•en (un shā′pən), *adj.* **1.** not shaped or definitely formed; shapeless; formless; indefinite. **2.** not shapely; unpleasing in shape; ill-formed. **3.** misshapen or deformed. [1300–50; ME; OE *unsceapen.* See UN-[1], SHAPE, -EN[3]]

un•sheathe (un shēth′), *v.t.,* **-sheathed, -sheath•ing. 1.** to draw from a sheath, as a sword, knife, or the like. **2.** to bring or put forth from a covering, threateningly or otherwise. [1325–75; ME *unshethen* to dislodge; see UN-[2], SHEATHE]

un•shell (un shel′), *v.t.* to remove or liberate from or as from a shell. [1590–1600; UN-[2] + SHELL]

un•shift (un shift′), *v.i.* to release the shift key, as on a typewriter or the keyboard of a computer terminal. [1965–70; UN-[2] + SHIFT]

un•shift•ed (un shif′tid), *adj.* **1.** (of a keyboard shift key) not pressed or activated. **2.** (of a keyboard key) not requiring the shift key to activate: *The semicolon is an unshifted key.* [UN-[1] + SHIFT + -ED[2]]

un•ship (un ship′), *v.,* **-shipped, -ship•ping.** —*v.t.* **1.** to put or take off from a ship, as persons or goods. **2.** to remove from the place proper for its use, as an oar or tiller. —*v.i.* **3.** to become unloaded or removed. [1400–50; late ME *unshippen;* see UN-[2], SHIP]

un•shipped (un shipt′), *adj.* **1.** not shipped, as goods.

un•so′ber, *adj.;* **-ly,** *adv.;* **-ness,** *n.*
un•so′bered, *adj.*
un•so′ber•ing, *adj.*
un•so′cial, *adj.;* **-ly,** *adv.*
un•so′cial•ism, *n.*
un′so•cial•is′tic, *adj.*
un•so′cial•iz′a•ble, *adj.*
un•so′cial•ized′, *adj.*
un•so′cial•iz′ing, *adj.*
un′so•ci•o•log′i•cal, *adj.;* **-ly,** *adv.*
un•sock′et•ed, *adj.*
un•soft′, *adj.;* **-ly,** *adv.;* **-ness,** *n.*
un•soft′en•ing, *adj.*
un•sog′gy, *adj.*
un•soiled′, *adj.*
un•soil′ing, *adj.*
un•sol′aced, *adj.*
un•sol′ac•ing, *adj.*
un•so′lar, *adj.*
un•sold′, *adj.*
un•sol′dier•like′, *adj.*
un•sole′, *v.t.,* **-soled, -sol•ing.**
un•sol′emn, *adj.;* **-ly,** *adv.;* **-ness,** *n.*
un′so•lem′ni•fied′, *adj.*
un•sol′em•nized′, *adj.*
un′so•lic′it•ed, *adj.*
un′so•lic′i•tous, *adj.;* **-ly,** *adv.;* **-ness,** *n.*
un•sol′id, *adj.;* **-ly,** *adv.;* **-ness,** *n.*
un′sol•i•dar′i•ty, *n.*
un′so•lid′i•fied′, *adj.*
un′so•lid′i•ty, *n.*
un•sol′i•tar′y, *adj.*
un•sol′u•ble, *adj.;* **-ble•ness,** *n.;* **-bly,** *adv.*
un•solv′a•ble, *adj.;* **-ble•ness,** *n.;* **-bly,** *adv.*
un•solved′, *adj.*
un′so•mat′ic, *adj.*
un•som′ber, *adj.;* **-ly,** *adv.;* **-ness,** *n.*
un•som′no•lent, *adj.;* **-ly,** *adv.*
un•so′nant, *adj.*
un′so•nan′tal, *adj.*
un′so•no′rous, *adj.;* **-ly,** *adv.;* **-ness,** *n.*
un•sooth′a•ble, *adj.*
un•soothed′, *adj.*
un•sooth′ing, *adj.;* **-ly,** *adv.*
un•soot′y, *adj.*
un•so•phis′tic, *adj.*
un′so•phis′ti•cal, *adj.;* **-ly,** *adv.*
un′soph•o•mor′ic, *adj.*
un′soph•o•mor′i•cal, *adj.;* **-ly,** *adv.*
un′sop•o•rif′er•ous, *adj.;* **-ly,** *adv.;* **-ness,** *n.*
un′sop•o•rif′ic, *adj.*
un•sor′did, *adj.;* **-ly,** *adv.;* **-ness,** *n.*
un•sore′, *adj.;* **-ly,** *adv.;* **-ness,** *n.*
un•sor′row•ing, *adj.*
un•sor′ry, *adj.*
un•sort′, *v.t.*
un•sort′a•ble, *adj.*
un•sort′ed, *adj.*
un•sought′, *adj.*
un•soul′ful, *adj.;* **-ly,** *adv.;* **-ness,** *n.*
un•soul′ish, *adj.*
un•sound′a•ble, *adj.*
un•sound′ed, *adj.*
un•sound′ing, *adj.*
un•sour′, *adj.;* **-ly,** *adv.;* **-ness,** *n.*
un•soused′, *adj.*
un•sov′er•eign, *adj.*
un•sowed′, *adj.*
un•sown′, *adj.*
un•spaced′, *adj.*
un•spa′cious, *adj.;* **-ly,** *adv.;* **-ness,** *n.*
un•spad′ed, *adj.*
un•span′, *v.t.,* **-spanned, -span•ning.**
un•span′gled, *adj.*
un•spanked′, *adj.*
un•spanned′, *adj.*
un•spared′, *adj.*
un•sparked′, *adj.*
un•spark′ling, *adj.*
un•sparred′, *adj.*
un•sparse′, *adj.;* **-ly,** *adv.;* **-ness,** *n.*
un•spasmed′, *adj.*
un′spas•mod′ic, *adj.*
un′spas•mod′i•cal, *adj.;* **-ly,** *adv.*
un•spa′tial, *adj.;* **-ly,** *adv.*
un•spa′ti•al′i•ty, *n.*
un•spat′tered, *adj.*
un•spawned′, *adj.*
un•spayed′, *adj.*
un•speared′, *adj.*
un•spe′cial•ized′, *adj.*
un•spe′cial•iz′ing, *adj.*
un•spec′i•fi′a•ble, *adj.*
un′spe•cif′ic, *adj.*
un′spe•cif′i•cal•ly, *adv.*
un•spec′i•fied′, *adj.*
un•spec′i•fy′ing, *adj.*
un•spe′cious, *adj.;* **-ly,** *adv.;* **-ness,** *n.*
un•specked′, *adj.*
un•speck′led, *adj.*
un•spec′ta•cled, *adj.*
un′spec•tac′u•lar, *adj.;* **-ly,** *adv.*
un•spec′u•lat′ing, *adj.*
un•spec′u•la′tive, *adj.*
un•spec′u•la•to′ry, *adj.*
un•speed′i•ly, *adv.*
un•speed′i•ness, *n.*
un•speed′y, *adj.*
un•spell′a•ble, *adj.*
un•spelled′, *adj.*
un•spelt′, *adj.*
un•spend′a•ble, *adj.*
un•spend′ing, *adj.*
un•spewed′, *adj.*
un•spher′i•cal, *adj.*
un•spher′ing, *adj.*
un•spiced′, *adj.*
un•spic′i•ly, *adv.*
un•spic′i•ness, *n.*
un•spic′y, *adj.*
un•spied′, *adj.*
un•spilled′, *adj.*
un•spilt′, *adj.*
un•spin′na•ble, *adj.*
un•spin′ning, *adj.*
un•spi′ral, *adj.;* **-ly,** *adv.*
un•spi′raled, *adj.*
un•spi′ralled, *adj.*
un•spired′, *adj.*
un•spir′ing, *adj.*
un•spir′it•ed, *adj.;* **-ly,** *adv.*
un•spir′it•ing, *adj.*
un•spir′i•tu•al, *adj.;* **-ly,** *adv.*
un′spir•i•tu•al′i•ty, *n.*
un•spir′i•tu•al•ized′, *adj.*
un•spir′i•tu•al•iz′ing, *adj.*
un•spir′it•u•ous, *adj.*
un•spit′ed, *adj.*
un•spite′ful, *adj.;* **-ly,** *adv.*
un•spit′ted, *adj.*
un•splashed′, *adj.*
un•splat′tered, *adj.*
un•splayed′, *adj.*
un•spleen′ish, *adj.;* **-ly,** *adv.*
un•splen′did, *adj.;* **-ly,** *adv.;* **-ness,** *n.*
un•splen′dor•ous, *adj.;* **-ly,** *adv.*
un′sple•net′ic, *adj.*
un′sple•net′i•cal•ly, *adv.*
un•spliced′, *adj.*
un•splint′ed, *adj.*
un•splin′tered, *adj.*
un•split′, *adj.*
un•split′ta•ble, *adj.*
un•spoil′a•ble, *adj.*
un•spoiled′, *adj.*
un•spoilt′, *adj.*
un•sponged′, *adj.*
un•spong′y, *adj.*
un•spon′sored, *adj.*
un′spon•ta′ne•ous, *adj.;* **-ly,** *adv.;* **-ness,** *n.*
un•spool′, *v.t.*
un•sport′ed, *adj.*
un•sport′ful, *adj.*
un•sport′ing, *adj.*
un•spor′tive, *adj.;* **-ly,** *adv.;* **-ness,** *n.*
un•sports′man•like′, *adj.*
un•sports′man•ly, *adj.,* *adv.*
un•spot′light′ed, *adj.*
un•spot′ta•ble, *adj.*
un•spoused′, *adj.*
un•spout′ed, *adj.*
un•sprained′, *adj.*
un•spray′a•ble, *adj.*
un•sprayed′, *adj.*
un•spread′, *adj.*
un•spread′a•ble, *adj.*
un•spread′ing, *adj.*
un•spright′ly, *adj.,* *adv.*
un•spring′ing, *adj.*
un•sprin′kled, *adj.*
un•sprin′klered, *adj.*
un•sprout′ed, *adj.*
un•sprout′ing, *adj.*
un•spruced′, *adj.*
un•sprung′, *adj.*
un•spun′, *adj.*
un•spu′ri•ous, *adj.;* **-ly,** *adv.;* **-ness,** *n.*
un•spurned′, *adj.*
un•spurred′, *adj.*
un•sput′ter•ing, *adj.*
un•spy′ing, *adj.*
un•squab′bling, *adj.*
un•squan′dered, *adj.*
un•squar′a•ble, *adj.*
un•squared′, *adj.*
un•squash′a•ble, *adj.*
un•squashed′, *adj.*
un•squeam′ish, *adj.;* **-ly,** *adv.;* **-ness,** *n.*
un•squeez′a•ble, *adj.*
un•squeezed′, *adj.*
un•squelch′a•ble, *adj.*
un•squelched′, *adj.*
un•squint′ing, *adj.*
un•squired′, *adj.*
un•squirm′ing, *adj.*
un•squirt′ed, *adj.*
un•stabbed′, *adj.*
un•sta′bi•lized′, *adj.*
un•sta′bi•liz′ing, *adj.*
un•sta′bled, *adj.*
un•stack′, *adj.,* *v.*
un•stacked′, *adj.*
un•staffed′, *adj.*
un•staged′, *adj.*
un•stag′gered, *adj.*
un•stag′ger•ing, *adj.*
un•stag′i•ly, *adv.*
un•stag′i•ness, *n.*
un•stag′nant, *adj.;* **-ly,** *adv.*
un•stag′nat•ing, *adj.*
un•stag′y, *adj.*
un•staid′, *adj.;* **-ly,** *adv.;* **-ness,** *n.*
un•staked′, *adj.*
un•staled′, *adj.*
un•stale′mat′ed, *adj.*
un•stalled′, *adj.*
un•stam′mer•ing, *adj.;* **-ly,** *adv.*
un•stamped′, *adj.*
un′stam•ped′ed, *adj.*
un•stanch′, *adj.*
un•stanch′a•ble, *adj.*
un•stand′ard, *adj.*
un•stand′ard•iz′a•ble, *adj.*
un•stand′ard•ized′, *adj.*
un•stand′ing, *adj.*
un′stan•za′ic, *adj.*
un•sta′ple, *v.t.,* **-pled, -pling.**
un•sta′pled, *adj.*
un•starched′, *adj.*
un•starred′, *adj.*
un•start′a•ble, *adj.*
un•start′ed, *adj.*
un•start′ing, *adj.*

2. (of a person) having no ship. **3.** out of position or formation, as a boat or ship. [1710–20; UN-[1] + SHIPPED]

un•shroud (un shroud′), *v.t.* to divest of a shroud or something that shrouds or hides: *to unshroud a corpse; to unshroud a mystery.* [1575–85; UN-[2] + SHROUD]

un•sick•er (un sik′ər), *adj. Scot.* unsafe; untrustworthy. [1175–1225; ME *unsiker.* See UN-[1], SICKER[2]] **—un•sick′ered,** *adj.* **—un•sick′er•ly,** *adv.* **—un•sick′er•ness,** *n.*

un•sight (un sīt′), *adj.* without inspection or examination: *to buy a thing unsight, unseen.* [1615–25; appar. UN-[1] + SIGHT, for expected *unsighted*]

un•sight•ly (un sīt′lē), *adj.,* **-li•er, -li•est.** distasteful or unpleasant to look at: *an unsightly wound; unsightly disorder.* [1375–1425; late ME; see UN-[1], SIGHTLY] **—un•sight′li•ness,** *n.*
—Syn. unattractive, ugly, disagreeable. **—Ant.** beautiful.

un•skilled (un skild′), *adj.* **1.** of or pertaining to workers who lack technical training or skill. **2.** not demanding special training or skill: *unskilled occupations.* **3.** exhibiting a marked lack of skill or competence: *an unskilled painting; an unskilled writer.* **4.** not skilled or expert: *He was unskilled in the art of rhetoric.* [1575–85; UN-[1] + SKILLED]

un′skilled la′bor, 1. work that requires practically no training or experience for its adequate or competent performance. **2.** the labor force employed for such work. [1825–35]

un•skill•ful (un skil′fəl), *adj.* not skillful; clumsy or bungling. Also, *esp. Brit.,* **un•skil′ful.** [1350–1400; 1555–65 for current sense; ME *unskylful* unreasonable. See UN-[1], SKILLFUL] **—un•skill′ful•ly,** *adv.* **—un•skill′ful•ness,** *n.*
—Syn. untrained, maladroit, inept.

un•sling (un sling′), *v.t.,* **-slung, -sling•ing. 1.** to remove (something) from being slung: *to unsling a rifle from one's shoulder.* **2.** *Naut.* to take off the slings of; release from slings. [1620–30; UN-[2] + SLING[1]]

un•snap (un snap′), *v.t.,* **-snapped, -snap•ping.** to undo by or as if by opening snap fasteners: *to unsnap a dress.* [1860–65; UN-[2] + SNAP]

un•snarl (un snärl′), *v.t.* to bring out of a snarled condition; disentangle. [1545–55; UN-[2] + SNARL[2]]

un•so•cia•ble (un sō′shə bəl), *adj.* **1.** not sociable; having, showing, or marked by a disinclination to friendly social relations; withdrawn. **2.** lacking or preventing social relationships: *an unsociable boardinghouse.* [1590–1600; UN-[1] + SOCIABLE] **—un′so•cia•bil′i•ty, un•so′cia•ble•ness,** *n.* **—un•so′cia•bly,** *adv.*

un•sol•der (un sod′ər), *v.t.* **1.** to separate (something soldered). **2.** to disunite; sunder: *to unsolder ties of friendship.* [1530–40; UN-[2] + SOLDER]

un•son•sy (un son′sē), *adj. Brit. Dial.* bringing or boding ill luck. [1550–60; UN-[1] + SONSY]

un•so•phis•ti•cat•ed (un′sə fis′ti kā′tid), *adj.* **1.** not sophisticated; simple; artless. **2.** without complexity or refinements: *a relatively unsophisticated mechanism.* **3.** unadulterated; pure; genuine. [1620–30; UN-[1] + SOPHISTICATED] **—un′so•phis′ti•cat′ed•ly,** *adv.* **—un′so•phis′ti•cat′ed•ness, un′so•phis′ti•ca′tion,** *n.*
—Syn. 1. ingenuous, naive, inexperienced.

un•sound (un sound′), *adj.,* **-er, -est. 1.** not sound; unhealthy, diseased, or disordered, as the body or mind. **2.** decayed or impaired, as timber or foods; defective. **3.** not solid or firm, as foundations. **4.** not well-founded or valid; fallacious: *an unsound argument.* **5.** easily broken; light: *unsound slumber.* **6.** not financially strong; unreliable: *an unsound corporation.* [1275–1325; ME; see UN-[1], SOUND[2]] **—un•sound′ly,** *adv.* **—un•sound′ness,** *n.*
—Syn. 1. infirm, sick, ill, unhealthy. **2.** rotten, unwholesome. **4.** false, erroneous, faulty.

un•spar•ing (un spâr′ing), *adj.* **1.** not sparing; liberal or profuse; excessive. **2.** unmerciful; harsh; severe. [1580–90; UN-[1] + SPARING] **—un•spar′ing•ly,** *adv.* **—un•spar′ing•ness,** *n.*
—Syn. 1. generous, lavish, bountiful. **2.** merciless, unrelenting, relentless.

un•speak (un spēk′), *v.t.,* **-spoke, -spo•ken, -speak•ing.** *Obs.* to recant; unsay. [1595–1605; UN-[2] + SPEAK]

un•speak•a•ble (un spē′kə bəl), *adj.* **1.** not speakable; that may not be spoken. **2.** exceeding the power of speech; unutterable; inexpressible; indescribable. **3.** inexpressibly bad or objectionable. [1350–1400; ME *unspekeabill.* See UN-[1], SPEAKABLE] **—un•speak′a•ble•ness,** *n.* **—un•speak′a•bly,** *adv.*
—Syn. 2. ineffable, unimaginable.

un•spent (un spent′), *adj.* **1.** not spent or used, as money. **2.** not used up or consumed: *unspent energy.* [1425–75; late ME; see UN-[1], SPENT]

un•sphere (un sfēr′), *v.t.,* **-sphered, -spher•ing.** to remove from its or one's sphere; displace. [1605–15; UN-[2] + SPHERE]

un•spo•ken (un spō′kən), *adj.* **1.** implied or understood without being spoken or uttered. **2.** not addressed (usually fol. by *to*). **3.** not talking; silent. [1325–75; ME *unspokyn.* See UN-[1], SPOKEN]

un•spot•ted (un spot′id), *adj.* **1.** having no spots or stains; without spots; spotless: *an unspotted breed of dog; unspotted trousers.* **2.** having no moral blemish or stigma: *an unspotted reputation.* [1350–1400; ME; see UN-[1], SPOTTED] **—un•spot′ted•ness,** *n.*

un•sta•ble (un stā′bəl), *adj.* **1.** not stable; not firm or firmly fixed; unsteady. **2.** liable to fall or sway. **3.** unsteadfast; inconstant; wavering: *unstable convictions.* **4.** marked by emotional instability: *an unstable person.* **5.** irregular in movement: *an unstable heartbeat.* **6.** *Chem.* noting compounds that readily decompose or change into other compounds. [1175–1225; ME; see UN-[1], STABLE[2]] **—un•sta′ble•ness,** *n.* **—un•sta′bly,** *adv.*
—Syn. 2. precarious. **2, 3.** See **unsettled. 3.** vacillating.

un•stain•a•ble (un stā′nə bəl), *adj.* **1.** that cannot be spotted or stained, as garments. **2.** that cannot be morally reprehensible: *an unstainable person.* [1575–85; UN-[1] + STAINABLE]

un•stained (un stānd′), *adj.* **1.** not stained or spotted; unsoiled. **2.** without moral blemish. [1545–55; UN-[1] + STAIN + -ED[2]]

un•stalked (un stôkt′), *adj.* without a stalk or stalks. [1870–75; UN-[1] + STALK[1] + -ED[2]]

un•state (un stāt′), *v.t.,* **-stat•ed, -stat•ing. 1.** *Archaic.* to deprive (a person) of office or rank. **2.** *Obs.* to deprive (a nation, government, etc.) of its character or dignity as a state. [1580–90; UN-[2] + STATE]

un•stead•y (un sted′ē), *adj., v.,* **-stead•ied, -stead•y•ing.** *—adj.* **1.** not steady or firm; unstable; shaky: *an unsteady hand.* **2.** fluctuating or wavering: *an unsteady flame; unsteady prices.* **3.** irregular or uneven: *an unsteady development.* *—v.t.* **4.** to make unsteady. [1525–35; UN-[1] + STEADY] **—un•stead′i•ly,** *adv.* **—un•stead′i•ness,** *n.*
—Syn. 1. See **unsettled. 2.** vacillating, flickering.

un•steel (un stēl′), *v.t.* to bring out of a steeled condition; soften. [1740–50; UN-[2] + STEEL]

un•step (un step′), *v.t.,* **-stepped, -step•ping.** to lift from its step, as a mast. [1850–55; UN-[2] + STEP]

un•stick (un stik′), *v.,* **-stuck, -stick•ing.** *—v.t.* **1.** to free, as one thing stuck to another. *—v.i.* **2.** to become unstuck: *Finally, the car's horn unstuck.* [1700–10; UN-[2] + STICK[2]]

un•stop (un stop′), *v.t.,* **-stopped, -stop•ping. 1.** to remove the stopper from: *to unstop a bottle.* **2.** to free from any obstruction; open: *to unstop a sewer.* **3.** to draw out the stops of (an organ). [1350–1400; ME *unstoppen.* See UN-[2], STOP]

un•stop•pa•ble (un stop′ə bəl), *adj.* that cannot be stopped or surpassed; unbeatable: *an unstoppable ball team.* [1830–40; UN-[1] + STOPPABLE] **—un•stop′pa•bly,** *adv.*

un•stop•per (un stop′ər), *v.t.* to unstop. [1830–40; UN-[2] + STOPPER]

un•sto•ried (un stôr′ēd, -stōr′-), *adj.* without a history; not written as history or told as folklore: *an unstoried island.* [1765–75; UN-[1] + STORIED[1]]

un•stow (un stō′), *v.t.* to remove (tools, utensils, equipment, etc.) from stowage, esp. in preparation for use. [1720–30; UN-[2] + STOW[1]]

unstpd., unstamped.

un•strained (un strānd′), *adj.* **1.** not under strain or tension: *an easy, unstrained manner.* **2.** not separated or cleared by straining: *unstrained orange juice.* [1300–50; ME; see UN-[1], STRAIN[1], -ED[2]]

CONCISE PRONUNCIATION KEY: act, cāpe, dâre, pärt; set, ēqual; *if,* ice; ox, ōver, ôrder, oil, bŏŏk, bōōt, out; up, ûrge; child; sing; shoe; thin, *that;* zh as in *treasure.* ə = *a* as in *alone, e* as in *system, i* as in *easily, o* as in *gallop, u* as in *circus;* ᵊ as in *fire* (fīᵊr), *hour* (ouᵊr). l and n can serve as syllabic consonants, as in *cradle* (krād′l), and *button* (but′n). See the full key inside the front cover.

un•star′tled, *adj.*
un•star′tling, *adj.*
un•starved′, *adj.*
un•stat′a•ble, *adj.*
un•state′a•ble, *adj.*
un•stat′ed, *adj.*
un•states′man•like′, *adj.*
un•stat′ic, *adj.*
un•stat′i•cal, *adj.;* **-ly,** *adv.*
un•sta′tion, *v.t.*
un•sta′tion•ar′y, *adj.*
un•sta′tioned, *adj.*
un′sta•tis′tic, *adj.*
un′sta•tis′ti•cal, *adj.;* **-ly,** *adv.*
un•stat′ued, *adj.*
un′stat•u•esque′, *adj.;* **-ly,** *adv.;* **-ness,** *n.*
un•staunch′, *adj.*
un•staunch′a•ble, *adj.*
un•staved′, *adj.*
un•stay′a•ble, *adj.*
un•stayed′, *adj.*
un•stay′ing, *adj.*
un•stead′fast′, *adj.;* **-ly,** *adv.;* **-ness,** *n.*
un•stealth′i•ly, *adv.*
un•stealth′i•ness, *n.*
un•stealth′y, *adj.*
un•steamed′, *adj.*
un•steam′ing, *adj.*
un•steeped′, *adj.*
un•stee′pled, *adj.*
un•steer′a•ble, *adj.*
un•steered′, *adj.*
un•stemmed′, *adj.*
un′sten•to′ri•an, *adj.*
un′sten•to′ri•ous•ly, *adj.*
un•ster′e•o•typed′, *adj.*
un•ster′ile, *adj.*
un•ster′i•lized′, *adj.*
un•stern′, *adj.;* **-ly,** *adv.;* **-ness,** *n.*
un•steth′o•scoped′, *adj.*
un•stewed′, *adj.*
un•stick′y, *adj.*
un•stiff′, *adj.;* **-ly,** *adv.;* **-ness,** *n.*
un•stiff′ened, *adj.*
un•sti′fled, *adj.*
un•sti′fling, *adj.*
un′stig•mat′ic, *adj.*
un•stig′ma•tized′, *adj.*
un•stilled′, *adj.*
un•stilt′ed, *adj.*
un•stim′u•la•ble, *adj.*
un•stim′u•lat′ed, *adj.*
un•stim′u•lat′ing, *adj.;* **-ly,** *adv.*
un•stim′u•la′tive, *adj.*
un•sting′ing, *adj.;* **-ly,** *adv.*
un•stint′ed, *adj.*
un•stint′ing, *adj.;* **-ly,** *adv.*
un•stip′pled, *adj.*
un•stip′u•lat′ed, *adj.*
un•stir′ra•ble, *adj.*
un•stirred′, *adj.*
un•stir′ring, *adj.*
un•stitch′, *v.*
un•stitched′, *adj.*
un•stitch′ing, *adj.*
un•stocked′, *adj.*
un•stock′inged, *adj.*
un•sto′ic, *adj.*
un•sto′i•cal, *adj.;* **-ly,** *adv.*
un•stoked′, *adj.*
un•sto′len, *adj.*
un•ston′a•ble, *adj.*
un•stone′a•ble, *adj.*
un•stoned′, *adj.*
un•ston′i•ly, *adv.*
un•ston′i•ness, *n.*
un•ston′y, *adj.*
un•stooped′, *adj.*
un•stoop′ing, *adj.*
un•stor′a•ble, *adj.*
un•storm′a•ble, *adj.*
un•stormed′, *adj.*
un•storm′i•ly, *adv.*
un•storm′i•ness, *n.*
un•storm′y, *adj.*
un•stout′, *adj.;* **-ly,** *adv.;* **-ness,** *n.*
un•strad′dled, *adj.*
un•strafed′, *adj.*
un•straight′, *adj.;* **-ness,** *n.*
un•straight′ened, *adj.*
un′straight•for′ward, *adj.*
un•strait′ened, *adj.*
un•strand′ed, *adj.*
un•strange′, *adj.;* **-ly,** *adv.;* **-ness,** *n.*
un•stran′gled, *adj.*
un•stran′gu•la•ble, *adj.*
un′stra•te′gic, *adj.*
un′stra•te′gi•cal, *adj.;* **-ly,** *adv.*
un•stray′ing, *adj.*
un•streaked′, *adj.*
un•stream′ing, *adj.*
un•stream′lined′, *adj.*
un•strength′ened, *adj.*
un•strength′en•ing, *adj.*
un•stren′u•ous, *adj.;* **-ly,** *adv.;* **-ness,** *n.*
un•strep′i•tous, *adj.*
un•stress′ful, *adj.*
un•stretch′a•ble, *adj.*
un•stretched′, *adj.*
un•strewed′, *adj.*
un•strewn′, *adj.*
un•stri′at•ed, *adj.*
un•strick′en, *adj.*
un•strict′, *adj.;* **-ly,** *adv.;* **-ness,** *n.*
un•stri′dent, *adj.;* **-ly,** *adv.*
un•strid′u•lat′ing, *adj.*
un•strid′u•lous, *adj.*
un•strik′a•ble, *adj.*
un•strik′ing, *adj.*
un•strin′gent, *adj.;* **-ly,** *adv.*
un•stripped′, *adj.*
un•striv′ing, *adj.*
un•stroked′, *adj.*
un•struc′tur•a•ble, *adj.*
un•struc′tur•al, *adj.;* **-ly,** *adv.*
un•strug′gling, *adj.*
un•stubbed′, *adj.*
un•stub′bled, *adj.*
un•stub′born, *adj.;* **-ly,** *adv.;* **-ness,** *n.*
un•stuc′coed, *adj.*
un•stud′ded, *adj.*
un•stu′di•ous, *adj.;* **-ly,** *adv.;* **-ness,** *n.*
un•stuff′, *v.t.*
un•stuffed′, *adj.*
un•stuff′i•ly, *adv.*
un•stuff′i•ness, *n.*
un•stuff′y, *adj.*
un•stul′ti•fied′, *adj.*
un•stul′ti•fy′ing, *adj.*
un•stum′bling, *adj.*
un•stung′, *adj.*
un•stunned′, *adj.*
un•stunt′ed, *adj.*
un•stu′pe•fied′, *adj.*
un•stu′pid, *adj.;* **-ly,** *adv.;* **-ness,** *n.*
un•stur′di•ly, *adv.*
un•stur′di•ness, *n.*
un•stur′dy, *adj.*
un•stut′tered, *adj.*
un•stut′ter•ing, *adj.*
un•styled′, *adj.*
un•styl′ish, *adj.;* **-ly,** *adv.;* **-ness,** *n.*
un•styl′ized, *adj.*
un′sub•di•vid′ed, *adj.*
un′sub•du′a•ble, *adj.*
un′sub•duct′ed, *adj.*
un′sub•dued′, *adj.*
un•sub′ject, *adj.*
un′sub•ject′ed, *adj.*
un′sub•jec′tive, *adj.;* **-ly,** *adv.*
un•sub′ju•gat′ed, *adj.*
un•sub′li•mat′ed, *adj.*
un′sub•limed′, *adj.*
un′sub•merged′, *adj.*
un′sub•mer′gi•ble, *adj.*
un′sub•merg′ing, *adj.*
un′sub•mer′si•ble, *adj.*
un′sub•mis′sive, *adj.;* **-ly,** *adv.;* **-ness,** *n.*
un′sub•mit′ted, *adj.*
un′sub•mit′ting, *adj.*
un′sub•or′di•nate, *adj.*
un′sub•or′di•nat′ed, *adj.*
un′sub•or′di•na′tive, *adj.*
un′sub•orned′, *adj.*
un′sub•poe′naed, *adj.*
un•sub′ro•gat′ed, *adj.*
un′sub•scribed′, *adj.*
un′sub•scrib′ing, *adj.*
un′sub•ser′vi•ent, *adj.;* **-ly,** *adv.*
un′sub•sid′ed, *adj.*
un′sub•sid′i•ar′y, *adj.*
un′sub•sid′ing, *adj.*
un•sub′si•dized′, *adj.*
un′sub•stan′ti•at′a•ble, *adj.*
un•sub′stan•tive, *adj.*
un•sub′sti•tut′ed, *adj.*
un•sub′sti•tu′tive, *adj.*
un•sub′ti′tled, *adj.*
un•sub′tle, *adj.;* **-tle•ness,** *n.;* **-tly,** *adv.*
un′sub•tract′ed, *adj.*
un′sub•trac′tive, *adj.*
un′sub•ur′ban, *adj.*
un′sub•urbed′, *adj.*
un′sub•ven′tioned, *adj.*
un′sub•ven′tion•ized′, *adj.*
un′sub•ver′sive, *adj.;* **-ly,** *adv.;* **-ness,** *n.*
un′sub•vert′ed, *adj.*
un′suc•ceed′ed, *adj.*
un′suc•ceed′ing, *adj.*
un′suc•ces′sive, *adj.;* **-ly,** *adv.;* **-ness,** *n.*
un′suc•cinct′, *adj.;* **-ly,** *adv.*
un•suc′cor•a•ble, *adj.*
un•suc′cored, *adj.*
un•suc′cu•lent, *adj.;* **-ly,** *adv.*
un′suc•cumb′ing, *adj.*
un•sucked′, *adj.*
un•suck′led, *adj.*
un•sued′, *adj.*
un•suf′fer•a•ble, *adj.;* **-ble•ness,** *n.;* **-bly,** *adv.*
un•suf′fer•ing, *adj.*
un′suf•fic′ing, *adj.*
un•suf′fixed, *adj.*
un•suf′fo•cat′ed, *adj.*
un•suf′fo•ca′tive, *adj.*
un′suf•fused′, *adj.*
un′suf•fu′sive, *adj.*
un•sug′ared, *adj.*
un•sug′ar•y, *adj.*
un′sug•gest′ed, *adj.*
un′sug•gest′i•ble, *adj.*
un′sug•gest′ing, *adj.*
un′sug•ges′tive, *adj.;* **-ly,** *adv.;* **-ness,** *n.*
un′su•i•cid′al, *adj.;* **-ly,** *adv.*
un•suit′ed, *adj.*
un•suit′ing, *adj.*
un•sul′fo•nat′ed, *adj.*
un′sul•fu′re•ous, *adj.;* **-ness,** *n.*
un•sul′fu•rized′, *adj.*
un•sulk′i•ly, *adv.*
un•sulk′i•ness, *n.*
un•sulk′y, *adj.*
un•sul′len, *adj.;* **-ly,** *adv.*
un•sul′li•a•ble, *adj.*
un•sul′lied, *adj.*
un•sul′try, *adj.*
un•sum′ma•ble, *adj.*
un•sum′ma•riz′a•ble, *adj.*
un•sum′ma•rized′, *adj.*
un•sum′mer•y, *adj.*
un•sum′mon•a•ble, *adj.*
un•sum′moned, *adj.*
un•sump′tu•ous, *adj.;* **-ly,** *adv.;* **-ness,** *n.*
un•sun′burned′, *adj.*
un•sun′burnt′, *adj.*
un•sun′dered, *adj.*
un•sunk′, *adj.*
un•sunk′en, *adj.*
un•sun′ny, *adj.*
un′su•per•cil′i•ous, *adj.;* **-ly,** *adv.;* **-ness,** *n.*
un′su•per•fi′cial, *adj.;* **-ly,** *adv.*

un·strap (un strap′), *v.t.,* **-strapped, -strap·ping.** to take off or slacken the strap of. [1820–30; UN-[2] + STRAP]

un·strat·i·fied (un strat′ə fīd′), *adj.* not stratified; not arranged in strata or layers: *unstratified rocks.* [1765–75; UN-[1] + STRATIFIED]

un·stressed (un strest′), *adj.* **1.** without stress or emphasis, as a syllable in a word. **2.** not receiving or subjected to stress, wear, etc.: *the unstressed parts of a car body.* [1880–85; UN-[1] + STRESS + -ED[2]]

un·string (un string′), *v.t.,* **-strung, -string·ing. 1.** to deprive of strings: *to unstring a violin.* **2.** to take from a string: *to unstring beads.* **3.** to loosen the strings of: *to unstring a bow.* **4.** to relax the tension of. **5.** to relax unduly, or weaken (the nerves). **6.** to weaken the nerves of. [1605–15; UN-[2] + STRING]

un·striped (un strīpt′, -strī′pid), *adj.* not striped; nonstriated, as muscular tissue. [1835–45; UN-[1] + STRIPED]

un·struc·tured (un struk′chərd), *adj.* lacking a clearly defined structure or organization: *an unstructured conference; an unstructured school environment.* [1940–45; UN-[1] + STRUCTURED]

un·strung (un strung′), *v.* **1.** pt. and pp. of **unstring.** —*adj.* **2.** having the string or strings loosened or removed, as a bow or harp. **3.** weakened or nervously unhinged, as a person or a person's nerves; unnerved; discomposed: *The incident left him unstrung.*

un·stuck (un stuk′), *adj.* **1.** freed or loosened from being fastened or stuck: *When firmly pushed, the door became unstuck.* **2.** out of order, control, or coherence; undone: *Their well-laid plans came unstuck under pressure.* [UN-[1] + STUCK]

un·stud·ied (un stud′ēd), *adj.* **1.** not studied; not premeditated or labored; natural; unaffected. **2.** not having studied; not possessing knowledge in a specific field; unversed: *He is unstudied in law.* [1350–1400; ME; see UN-[1], STUDIED]

un·sub·stan·tial (un′səb stan′shəl), *adj.* **1.** not substantial; having no foundation in fact; fanciful; insubstantial: *an unsubstantial argument; unsubstantial hopes.* **2.** without material substance: *an unsubstantial ghost.* **3.** lacking material substance; materially paltry: *an unsubstantial dinner of bread and cheese.* **4.** lacking strength or solidity; flimsy: *an unsubstantial wall of cardboard.* [1425–75; late ME; see UN-[1], SUBSTANTIAL] —**un′sub·stan′ti·al′i·ty,** *n.* —**un′sub·stan′tial·ly,** *adv.*

un·sub·stan·ti·at·ed (un′səb stan′shē ā′tid), *adj.* **1.** not substantiated; unproved or unverified: *unsubstantiated allegations.* **2.** being without form or substance. [1765–75; UN-[1] + SUBSTANTIATE + -ED[2]]

CONCISE ETYMOLOGY KEY: <, descended or borrowed from; >, whence; b., blend of, blended; c., cognate with; cf., compare; deriv., derivative; equiv., equivalent; imit., imitative; obl., oblique; r., replacing; s., stem; sp., spelling, spelled; resp., respelling, respelled; trans., translation; ?, origin unknown; *, unattested; ‡, probably earlier than. See the full key inside the front cover.

un·suc·cess (un′sək ses′), *n.* lack of success; failure. [1580–90; UN-[1] + SUCCESS]

un·suc·cess·ful (un′sək ses′fəl), *adj.* not achieving or not attended with success: *an unsuccessful person; an unsuccessful venture.* [1610–20; UN-[1] + SUCCESSFUL] —**un′suc·cess′ful·ly,** *adv.* —**un′suc·cess′ful·ness,** *n.* —**Syn.** hapless, unfortunate, foiled, baffled.

un·suit·a·ble (un sōō′tə bəl), *adj.* not suitable; inappropriate; unfitting; unbecoming. [1580–90; UN-[1] + SUITABLE] —**un′suit·a·bil′i·ty, un·suit′a·ble·ness,** *n.* —**un·suit′a·bly,** *adv.*

un·sung (un sung′), *adj.* **1.** not sung; not uttered or rendered by singing. **2.** not celebrated in song or verse; not praised or acclaimed: *the unsung heroes of the war.* [1375–1425 for def. 1; 1660–70 for def 2; late ME; see UN-[1], SUNG]

un·sus·pect·ed (un′sə spek′tid), *adj.* **1.** not regarded or considered with suspicion: *unsuspected in the crime.* **2.** not imagined to exist: *a person of unsuspected talents.* [1520–30; UN-[1] + SUSPECT + -ED[2]] —**un′sus·pect′ed·ly,** *adv.* —**un′sus·pect′ed·ness,** *n.*

un·sus·tain·a·ble (un′sə stā′nə bəl), *adj.* not sustainable; not to be supported, maintained, upheld, or corroborated. [1670–80; UN-[1] + SUSTAINABLE] —**un′sus·tain′a·bly,** *adv.*

un·swathe (un swoth′, -swāth′), *v.t.,* **-swathed, -swath·ing.** to free from something that swathes: *to unswath the child of her bandages.* [1350–1400; ME *unswaden;* see UN-[2], SWATHE[1]] —**un·swathe′a·ble,** *adj.*

un·swear (un swâr′), *v.t., v.i.,* **-swore, -sworn, -swear·ing.** to retract (something sworn or sworn to); recant by a subsequent oath; abjure. [1585–95; UN-[2] + SWEAR]

un·tack (un tak′), *v.t.* **1.** to unfasten (something tacked). **2.** to loose or detach by removing a tack or tacks. [1635–45; UN-[2] + TACK[1]]

un·tan·gle (un tang′gəl), *v.t.,* **-gled, -gling. 1.** to bring out of a tangled state; disentangle; unsnarl. **2.** to straighten out or clear up (anything confused or perplexing). [1540–50; UN-[2] + TANGLE]

un·taught (un tôt′), *v.* **1.** pt. and pp. of **unteach.** —*adj.* **2.** not taught; not acquired by teaching; natural: *untaught gentleness.* **3.** not instructed or educated; naive; ignorant. [(defs. 2, 3) UN-[1] + TAUGHT]

un·teach (un tēch′), *v.t.,* **-taught, -teach·ing. 1.** to cause to be forgotten or disbelieved, as by contrary teaching. **2.** to cause to forget or disbelieve something previously taught. [1525–35; UN-[2] + TEACH]

un·ten·a·ble (un ten′ə bəl), *adj.* **1.** incapable of being defended, as an argument, thesis, etc.; indefensible. **2.** not fit to be occupied, as an apartment, house, etc. [1640–50; UN-[1] + TENABLE] —**un′ten·a·bil′i·ty, un·ten′a·ble·ness,** *n.* —**Syn. 1.** baseless, groundless, unsound, weak, questionable.

un·ten·ured (un ten′yərd), *adj.* **1.** unheld, as property or a position. **2.** lacking tenure, as a college instructor. **3.** not offering or leading to tenure, as some college teaching positions. [UN-[1] + TENURED]

Un·ter·mey·er (un′tər mī′ər), *n.* **Louis,** 1885–1977, U.S. poet, critic, and editor.

Un·ter·wal·den (*Ger.* ōōn′tər väl′dən), *n.* a canton in central Switzerland: divided into demicantons. Cf. **Obwalden, Nidwalden.**

un·teth·er (un teth′ər), *v.t.* to release from a tether: *to untether a horse.* [1765–75; UN-[2] + TETHER]

un·thank·ful (un thangk′fəl), *adj.* **1.** not thankful; ungrateful. **2.** not repaid with thanks; thankless: *an unthankful task.* [1350–1400; ME; see UN-[1], THANKFUL] —**un·thank′ful·ly,** *adv.* —**un·thank′ful·ness,** *n.*

un·thatch (un thach′), *v.t.* to remove or throw off the thatch from: *to unthatch a roof.* [1690–1700; UN-[2] + THATCH]

un·think (un thingk′), *v.,* **-thought, -think·ing.** —*v.i.* **1.** to end one's thought or reverse the process of thought. —*v.t.* **2.** to dispel from the mind: *Unthink your thoughts.* [1590–1600; UN-[2] + THINK[1]]

un·think·a·ble (un thing′kə bəl), *adj.* **1.** inconceivable; unimaginable: *the unthinkable size of the universe.* **2.** not to be considered; out of the question: *Such a suggestion is unthinkable.* —*n.* **3.** something that cannot be conceived or imagined, as something too unusual, vague, or disagreeable: *Today's unthinkables are tomorrow's realities.* [1400–50; late ME; see UN-[1], THINKABLE] —**un′think·a·bil′i·ty, un·think′a·ble·ness,** *n.* —**un·think′a·bly,** *adv.*

un·think·ing (un thing′king), *adj.* **1.** thoughtless; heedless; inconsiderate: *an unthinking, tactless person.* **2.** indicating lack of thought or reflection: *a dull, unthinking expression on his face.* **3.** not endowed with the faculty of thought: *unthinking matter.* **4.** not exercising thought; not given to reflection: *This book will not profit an unthinking person.* **5.** not thinking; unmindful: *chores done in an unthinking manner.* [1670–80; UN-[1] + THINKING] —**un·think′ing·ly,** *adv.* —**un·think′ing·ness,** *n.*

un·thought[1] (un thôt′), *v.* **1.** pt. and pp. of **unthink.** —*adj.* **2.** not thought; not framed in a thought or thoughts: *an unthought advantage.* **3.** not expected; not anticipated (often fol. by *of*): *an unthought-of place to find the key.* [1530–40; (defs. 2, 3) UN-[1] + THOUGHT[2]]

un·thought[2] (un thôt′), *n.* an absence of thought. [1865–70; UN-[1] + THOUGHT[1]]

un·thread (un thred′), *v.t.* **1.** to draw out or take out the thread from: *to unthread a sewing machine.* **2.** to thread one's way through or out of, as a densely wooded forest. **3.** to disentangle; separate out of a raveled or confused condition: *to unthread a mystery.* [1585–95; UN-[2] + THREAD]

un·throne (un thrōn′), *v.t.,* **-throned, -thron·ing.** to dethrone or remove as if by dethroning. [1605–15; UN-[2] + THRONE]

un·ti·dy (un tī′dē), *adj.,* **-di·er, -di·est,** *v.,* **-died, -dy·ing.** —*adj.* **1.** not tidy or neat; slovenly; disordered: *an untidy room; an untidy person.* **2.** not well-organized or carried out: *an untidy plan.* —*v.t.* **3.** to mess up; disorder; disarrange: *The guests untidied the room.* [1175–

un′su·per′flu·ous, *adj.;* **-ly,** *adv.;* **-ness,** *n.*
un′su·pe′ri·or, *adj.;* **-ly,** *adv.*
un′su·per′la·tive, *adj.;* **-ly,** *adv.;* **-ness,** *n.*
un·su′per·nat′u·ral, *adj.;* **-ly,** *adv.;* **-ness,** *n.*
un·su′per·scribed′, *adj.*
un′su·per·sed′ed, *adj.*
un′su·per·sed′ing, *adj.*
un′su·per·sti′tious, *adj.;* **-ly,** *adv.;* **-ness,** *n.*
un·su′per·vised′, *adj.*
un·su′per·vi′so·ry, *adj.*
un′su·pine′, *adj.*
un′sup·plant′a·ble, *adj.*
un′sup·plant′ed, *adj.*
un·sup′ple, *adj.;* **-ple·ness,** *n.;* **-ply,** *adv.*
un·sup′ple·men′tal, *adj.*
un·sup′ple·men′ta·ry, *adj.*
un·sup′ple·ment′ed, *adj.*
un·sup′pli′a·ble, *adj.*
un·sup′pli·ant, *adj.*
un·sup′pli·cat′ed, *adj.*
un·sup′pli·cat′ing, *adj.;* **-ly,** *adv.*
un′sup·plied′, *adj.*
un′sup·port′a·ble, *adj.;* **-ble·ness,** *n.;* **-bly,** *adv.*
un′sup·port′ed, *adj.;* **-ly,** *adv.*
un′sup·port′ing, *adj.*
un′sup·port′ive, *adj.*
un′sup·pos′a·ble, *adj.*
un′sup·posed′, *adj.*
un′sup·po·si′tion·al, *adj.*
un′sup·pos′i·tive, *adj.*
un′sup·pressed′, *adj.*
un′sup·press′i·ble, *adj.*
un′sup·pres′sive, *adj.*
un·sup′pu·rat′ed, *adj.*
un·sup′pu·ra′tive, *adj.*
un′sur·charged′, *adj.*
un·sure′, *adj.;* **-ly,** *adv.;* **-ness,** *n.*
un·sur′faced, *adj.*
un·sur′feit·ed, *adj.*
un·sur′feit·ing, *adj.*
un·sur′gi·cal, *adj.;* **-ly,** *adv.*
un·surg′ing, *adj.*
un·sur′li·ly, *adv.*
un·sur′li·ness, *n.*
un·sur′ly, *adj.*
un′sur·mised′, *adj.*
un′sur·mis′ing, *adj.*
un′sur·mount′a·ble, *adj.*
un′sur·mount′ed, *adj.*
un·sur′named, *adj.*
un′sur·pass′a·ble, *adj.*
un′sur·passed′, *adj.*
un·sur′pliced, *adj.*
un′sur·prised′, *adj.*
un′sur·pris′ing, *adj.;* **-ly,** *adv.*
un′sur·re′al·is′tic, *adj.*
un′sur·re′al·is′ti·cal·ly, *adv.*
un′sur·ren′dered, *adj.*
un′sur·ren′der·ing, *adj.*
un′sur·round′ed, *adj.*
un′sur·vey′a·ble, *adj.*
un′sur·veyed′, *adj.*
un′sur·viv′a·ble, *adj.*
un′sur·vived′, *adj.*
un′sur·viv′ing, *adj.*
un′sus·cep′ti·bil′i·ty, *n.*
un′sus·cep′ti·ble, *adj.;* **-ble·ness,** *n.;* **-bly,** *adv.*
un′sus·cep′tive, *adj.*
un′sus·pect′ful, *adj.;* **-ly,** *adv.;* **-ness,** *n.*
un′sus·pect′ing, *adj.;* **-ly,** *adv.*
un′sus·pend′ed, *adj.*
un′sus·pend′i·ble, *adj.*
un′sus·pi′cious, *adj.;* **-ly,** *adv.;* **-ness,** *n.*
un′sus·tained′, *adj.*
un′sus·tain′ing, *adj.*
un·su′tured, *adj.*
un·swabbed′, *adj.*
un·swad′dled, *adj.*
un·swad′dling, *adj.*
un·swag′ger·ing, *adj.;* **-ly,** *adv.*
un·swal′low·a·ble, *adj.*
un·swal′lowed, *adj.*
un·swamp′y, *adj.*
un·swapped′, *adj.*
un·swarm′ing, *adj.*
un·sway′a·ble, *adj.*
un·swayed′, *adj.*
un·sway′ing, *adj.*
un·sweat′ed, *adj.*
un·sweat′ing, *adj.*
un·sweep′a·ble, *adj.*
un·sweet′ened, *adj.*
un·swelled′, *adj.*
un·swell′ing, *adj.*
un·swel′tered, *adj.*
un·swel′ter·ing, *adj.*
un·swept′, *adj.*
un·swerv′a·ble, *adj.*
un·swerved′, *adj.*
un·swerv′ing, *adj.;* **-ly,** *adv.;* **-ness,** *n.*
un·swilled′, *adj.*
un·swin′gled, *adj.*
un·switch′a·ble, *adj.*
un·switched′, *adj.*
un·swiv′el, *v.t.,* **-eled, -el·ing** or (*esp. Brit.*) **-elled, -el·ling.**
un·swol′len, *adj.*
un·swoon′ing, *adj.*
un·swung′, *adj.*
un′syl·lab′i·cat′ed, *adj.*
un′syl·lab′i·fied, *adj.*
un·syl′la·bled, *adj.*
un′syl·lo·gis′tic, *adj.*
un′syl·lo·gis′ti·cal, *adj.;* **-ly,** *adv.*
un′sym·bol′ic, *adj.*
un′sym·bol′i·cal, *adj.;* **-ly,** *adv.*
un·sym′bol·ized′, *adj.*
un′sym·met′ri·cal, *adj.;* **-ly,** *adv.*
un·sym′me·trized′, *adj.*
un′sym·pa·thet′ic, *adj.*
un′sym·pa·thet′i·cal·ly, *adv.*
un·sym′pa·thized′, *adj.*
un·sym′pa·thiz′ing, *adj.;* **-ly,** *adv.*
un′sym·pho′ni·ous, *adj.;* **-ly,** *adv.*
un′symp·to·mat′ic, *adj.*
un′symp·to·mat′i·cal, *adj.;* **-ly,** *adv.*
un·syn′chro·nized′, *adj.*
un·syn′chro·nous, *adj.;* **-ly,** *adv.;* **-ness,** *n.*
un·syn′co·pat′ed, *adj.*
un·syn′di·cat′ed, *adj.*
un′syn·on′y·mous, *adj.;* **-ly,** *adv.*
un′syn·tac′tic, *adj.*
un′syn·tac′ti·cal, *adj.;* **-ly,** *adv.*
un·syn′the·sized′, *adj.*
un′syn·thet′ic, *adj.*
un′syn·thet′i·cal·ly, *adv.*
un·syr′inged, *adj.*
un′sys·tem·at′ic, *adj.*
un′sys·tem·at′i·cal, *adj.;* **-ly,** *adv.*
un·sys′tem·a·tized′, *adj.*
un·sys′tem·a·tiz′ing, *adj.*
un·tab′er·nac′led, *adj.*
un·ta′bled, *adj.*
un·tab′u·la·ble, *adj.*
un·tab′u·lat′ed, *adj.*
un·tac′i·turn′, *adj.;* **-ly,** *adv.*
un·tack′ling, *adj.*
un·tact′ful, *adj.;* **-ly,** *adv.*
un·tac′ti·cal, *adj.;* **-ly,** *adv.*
un·tac′tile, *adj.*
un·tac′tu·al, *adj.;* **-ly,** *adv.*
un·tagged′, *adj.*
un·tailed′, *adj.*
un·tai′lored, *adj.*
un·taint′a·ble, *adj.*
un·taint′ed, *adj.*
un·taint′ing, *adj.*
un·tak′a·ble, *adj.*
un·take′a·ble, *adj.*
un·tak′ing, *adj.*
un·tal′ent·ed, *adj.*
un·talk′a·tive, *adj.*
un·talk′ing, *adj.*
un·tal′lied, *adj.*
un·tal′lowed, *adj.*
un·tal′oned, *adj.*
un·tam′a·ble, *adj.*
un·tame′, *adj.;* **-ly,** *adv.;* **-ness,** *n.*
un·tame′a·ble, *adj.*
un·tamed′, *adj.*
un·tam′per·a·ble, *adj.*
un·tam′pered, *adj.*
un′tan·gen′tal, *adj.;* **-ly,** *adv.*
un′tan·gen′tial, *adj.;* **-ly,** *adv.*
un·tan′gi·ble, *adj.*
un·tanned′, *adj.*
un·tan′ta·lized′, *adj.*
un·tan′ta·liz′ing, *adj.*
un·taped′, *adj.*
un·ta′pered, *adj.*
un·ta′per·ing, *adj.*
un·tap′es·tried, *adj.*
un·tap′pa·ble, *adj.*
un·tapped′, *adj.*
un·tar′get·a·ble, *adj.*
un·tar′get·ed, *adj.*
un·tar′nish·a·ble, *adj.*
un·tar′nished, *adj.*
un·tar′nish·ing, *adj.*
un·tarred′, *adj.*
un·tar′ried, *adj.*
un·tar′ry·ing, *adj.*
un·tar′tar·ized′, *adj.*
un·tasked′, *adj.*
un·tas′seled, *adj.*
un·tas′selled, *adj.*
un·tast′a·ble, *adj.*
un·taste′a·ble, *adj.*
un·tast′ed, *adj.*
un·taste′ful, *adj.;* **-ly,** *adv.;* **-ness,** *n.*
un·tast′ing, *adj.*
un·tast′i·ly, *adv.*
un·tast′y, *adj.*
un·tat′tered, *adj.*
un′tat·tooed′, *adj.*
un·taunt′ed, *adj.*
un·taunt′ing, *adj.;* **-ly,** *adv.*
un·taut′, *adj.;* **-ly,** *adv.;* **-ness,** *n.*
un′tau·to·log′i·cal, *adj.;* **-ly,** *adv.*
un·taw′dry, *adj.*
un·tawed′, *adj.*
un·tax′, *v.t.*
un·tax′a·ble, *adj.*
un·tax′ied, *adj.*
un·tax′ing, *adj.*
un·teach′a·ble, *adj.*
un·teamed′, *adj.*
un·tear′a·ble, *adj.*
un·teased′, *adj.*
un·tea′seled, *adj.*
un·tea′selled, *adj.*
un·tech′ni·cal, *adj.;* **-ly,** *adv.*
un·ted′ded, *adj.*
un·te′di·ous, *adj.;* **-ly,** *adv.*
un·teem′ing, *adj.*
un·tel′e·graphed′, *adj.*
un·tel′e·vised′, *adj.*
un·tel′ic, *adj.*
un·tell′a·ble, *adj.*
un·tell′ing, *adj.*
un·tem′per·a·ble, *adj.*
un′tem·per·a·men′tal, *adj.;* **-ly,** *adv.*
un·tem′per·ate, *adj.;* **-ly,** *adv.;* **-ness,** *n.*
un·tem′pered, *adj.*
un·tem′per·ing, *adj.*
un′tem·pes′tu·ous, *adj.;* **-ly,** *adv.;* **-ness,** *n.*
un·tem′pled, *adj.*
un·tem′po·ral, *adj.;* **-ly,** *adv.*
un·tem′po·rar′y, *adj.*
un·tempt′a·ble, *adj.*
un·tempt′ed, *adj.*
un·tempt′ing, *adj.;* **-ly,** *adv.*
un′te·na′cious, *adj.;* **-ly,** *adv.;* **-ness,** *n.*

1225; ME; see UN-[1], TIDY] —**un·ti′di·ly,** *adv.* —**un·ti′·di·ness,** *n.*

un·tie (un tī′), *v.,* **-tied, -ty·ing.** —*v.t.* **1.** to loose or unfasten (anything tied); let or set loose by undoing a knot. **2.** to undo the string or cords of. **3.** to undo, as a cord or a knot; unknot. **4.** to free from restraint. **5.** to resolve, as perplexities. —*v.i.* **6.** to become untied. [bef. 1000; ME *untyen,* OE *untīegan.* See UN-[2], TIE]

un·til (un til′), *conj.* **1.** up to the time that or when; till: *He read until his guests arrived.* **2.** before (usually used in negative constructions): *They did not come until the meeting was half over.* —*prep.* **3.** onward to or till (a specified time or occurrence): *She worked until 6 P.M.* **4.** before (usually used in negative constructions): *He did not go until night.* **5.** *Scot. and North Eng.* to; unto. [1150–1200; ME *untill,* equiv. to *un-* (< ON *unz* up to, as far as) + *till* TILL[1]]
—**Usage.** See **till**[1].

un·time·ly (un tīm′lē), *adj.,* **-li·er, -li·est,** *adv.* —*adj.* **1.** not timely; not occurring at a suitable time or season; ill-timed or inopportune: *An untimely downpour stopped the game.* **2.** happening too soon or too early; premature: *his untimely demise.* —*adv.* **3.** prematurely. **4.** unseasonably. [1150–1200; ME *untimliche.* See UN-[1], TIMELY] —**un·time′li·ness,** *n.*
—**Syn. 1.** unseasonable, inappropriate, inconvenient, unsuitable.

un·time·ous (un tī′məs), *adj. Scot.* untimely. [1490–1500; UN-[1] + TIMEOUS]

un·tinged (un tinjd′), *adj.* **1.** not colored, as by paint or the sun. **2.** not biased or affected: *a report untinged by sentimentality.* [1655–65; UN-[1] + TINGED]

un·ti·tled (un tīt′ld), *adj.* **1.** without a title: *an untitled gentleman; an untitled book.* **2.** having no right or claim. [1580–90; UN-[1] + TITLED]

un·to (un′to͞o; *unstressed* un′tə), *prep.* **1.** to (in its various uses, except as the accompaniment of the infinitive). **2.** until; till. [1250–1300; ME, equiv. to *un(till)* UNTIL + *to* TO]

un·to·geth·er (un′to͞o geth′ər), *adj. Slang.* disorganized; confused; chaotic: *Right after the divorce was a very untogether time for me.* [1965–70; UN-[1] + TOGETHER]

un·told (un tōld′), *adj.* **1.** not told; not related; not revealed: *untold thoughts.* **2.** not numbered or enumerated; uncounted: *She used untold sheets of paper in writing the book.* **3.** inexpressible; incalculable: *untold suffering.* [bef. 1000; ME; OE *unteald.* See UN-[1], TOLD]

un·touch·a·bil·i·ty (un′tuch ə bil′i tē), *n. Hinduism.* the quality or condition of being an untouchable, ascribed in the Vedic tradition to persons of low caste or to persons excluded from the caste system. [1920–25; UNTOUCH(ABLE) + -ABILITY]

un·touch·a·ble (un tuch′ə bəl), *adj.* **1.** that may not be touched; of a nature such that it cannot be touched; not palpable; intangible. **2.** too distant to be touched. **3.** vile or loathsome to the touch. **4.** beyond criticism, control, or suspicion: *Modern writers consider no subject untouchable.* —*n.* **5.** *Hinduism.* a member of a lower caste in India whose touch is believed to defile a high-caste Hindu; Harijan. **6.** a person who is beyond reproach as to honesty, diligence, etc. **7.** a person disregarded or shunned by society or a particular group; social outcast: *political untouchables.* **8.** a person or thing considered inviolable or beyond criticism: *such untouchables as Social Security in the federal budget.* [1560–70; UN-[1] + TOUCHABLE] —**un·touch′a·bly,** *adv.*

un·touched (un tucht′), *adj.* **1.** not touched or handled, as material. **2.** not explored or visited: *untouched lands.* **3.** not eaten or drunk. **4.** remaining in a pristine state; unchanged: *an untouched innocent; an untouched world.* **5.** not injured or hurt; undamaged: *untouched by the exploding bombs.* **6.** not affected or altered: *She was untouched by the life around her.* **7.** emotionally unmoved; indifferent: *She was left untouched by the music.* **8.** not mentioned or described, as in conversation or a book: *an untouched subject.* [1350–1400; ME; see UN-[1], TOUCH, -ED[2]] —**un·touched′ness,** *n.*

un·tour·ist·y (un to͝or′i stē), *adj. Informal.* **1.** not typical of a tourist: *They're the most untouristy couple you ever met.* **2.** not conforming to the usual tours or itineraries: *This time we want to see the untouristy Europe.* [UN-[1] + TOURISTY]

un·to·ward (un tôrd′, -tōrd′), *adj.* **1.** unfavorable or unfortunate: *Untoward circumstances forced him into bankruptcy.* **2.** improper: *untoward social behavior.* **3.** *Archaic.* froward; perverse. [1520–30; UN-[1] + TOWARD] —**un·to·ward′ly,** *adv.* —**un·to·ward′ness,** *n.*

un·tracked (un trakt′), *adj.* **1.** that is not or cannot be tracked or traced: *untracked marauders of the jungle.* **2.** *Informal.* achieving a superior level of performance after a slow start: *The team suddenly got untracked and began to score.* [1595–1605; (def. 1) UN-[1] + TRACK + -ED[2]; (def. 2) UN-[2] + TRACK + -ED[2]]

un·trav·eled (un trav′əld), *adj.* **1.** not having traveled, esp. to distant places; not having gained experience by travel. **2.** not traveled through or over; not frequented by travelers: *an untraveled country lane.* Also, *esp. Brit.,* **un·trav′elled.** [1575–85; UN-[1] + TRAVELED]

un·tread (un tred′), *v.t.,* **-trod, -trod·den** or **-trod, -tread·ing.** to go back through in the same steps. [1585–95; UN-[2] + TREAD]

un·tried (un trīd′), *adj.* **1.** not tried; not attempted, proved, or tested. **2.** not yet tried at law. [1520–30; UN-[1] + TRIED]

un·trimmed (un trimd′), *adj.* **1.** not trimmed. **2.** Also, **uncut.** *Bookbinding.* (of gathered sections of a book) having the bolts untrimmed by a guillotine or plow. [1525–35; UN-[1] + TRIMMED] —**un·trimmed′·ness,** *n.*

un·trod (un trod′), *adj.* not trod; not traversed: *the untrod wastes of Antarctica.* Also, **un·trod′den.** [1585–95; UN-[1] + TROD]

un·true (un tro͞o′), *adj.,* **-tru·er, -tru·est.** **1.** not true, as to a person or a cause, to fact, or to a standard. **2.** unfaithful; false. **3.** incorrect or inaccurate. [bef. 1050; ME *untrewe,* OE *un(ge)trēowe;* see UN-[1], TRUE] —**un·true′ness,** *n.*
—**Syn. 1.** groundless, unfounded, erroneous.

un·truss (un trus′), *v.t., v.i. Archaic.* to loose from or as if from a truss. [1350–1400; ME; see UN-[2], TRUSS]

un·truth (un tro͞oth′), *n., pl.* **-truths** (-tro͞oth͟z′, -tro͞oths′). **1.** the state or character of being untrue. **2.** want of veracity; divergence from truth. **3.** something untrue; a falsehood or lie. **4.** *Archaic.* unfaithfulness; disloyalty. [bef. 900; ME; OE *untrēowth.* See UN-[1], TRUTH]
—**Syn. 3.** fiction, story, tale, fabrication, invention. See **falsehood.**

un·truth·ful (un tro͞oth′fəl), *adj.* not truthful; wanting in veracity; diverging from or contrary to the truth; not corresponding with fact or reality. [1325–75; ME; see UN-[1], TRUTHFUL] —**un·truth′ful·ly,** *adv.* —**un·truth′·ful·ness,** *n.*

un·tuck (un tuk′), *v.t.* to release from or bring out of a tucked condition: *She untucked her legs.* [1605–15; UN-[2] + TUCK[1]]

un·tune (un to͞on′, -tyo͞on′), *v.t.,* **-tuned, -tun·ing.** **1.** to render or cause to become out of tune: *Changes in weather can untune a violin.* **2.** to discompose; upset, as the mind or emotions. [1590–1600; UN-[2] + TUNE]

un·tu·tored (un to͞o′tərd, -tyo͞o′-), *adj.* **1.** not tutored; untaught; uninstructed. **2.** naive, ignorant, or unsophisticated. [1585–95; UN-[1] + TUTOR + -ED[2]]

un·twine (un twīn′), *v.t., v.i.,* **-twined, -twin·ing.** to bring or come out of a twined condition. [1300–50; ME *untwinen;* see UN-[2], TWINE[1]] —**un·twine′a·ble,** *adj.*

un·twist (un twist′), *v.t., v.i.* to bring or come out of a twisted condition. [1530–40; UN-[2] + TWIST]

un·twist·ed (un twis′tid), *adj.* not twisted. [1565–75; UN-[1] + TWIST + -ED[2]]

U Nu (o͞o′ no͞o′). See **Nu, U.**

un·used (un yo͞ozd′ *for 1, 2;* un yo͞ost′ *for 3*), *adj.* **1.** not used; not put to use: *an unused room.* **2.** never having been used: *an unused postage stamp.* **3.** not accustomed: *unused to cold winters.* [1250–1300; ME; see UN-[1], USED]

un·u·su·al (un yo͞o′zho͞o əl, -yo͞ozh′wəl), *adj.* not usual, common, or ordinary; uncommon in amount or degree; exceptional: *an unusual sound; an unusual hobby; an unusual response.* [1575–85; UN-[1] + USUAL] —**un·u′su·al·ly,** *adv.* —**un·u′su·al·ness,** *n.*
—**Syn.** extraordinary, remarkable; rare, strange, singular, curious, queer, odd.

un·u·su·al·i·ty (un yo͞o′zho͞o al′i tē), *n., pl.* **ties.** **1.** unusualness; the state or condition of being unusual. **2.** something that is unusual: *to make room in one's life for the unusualities.* [1790–1800; UNUSUAL + -ITY]

un·ut·ter·a·ble (un ut′ər ə bəl), *adj.* **1.** not communi-

CONCISE PRONUNCIATION KEY: act, cāpe, dâre, pärt; set, ēqual; *if,* ice; ox, ōver, ôrder, oil, bo͝ok, bo͞ot, out; up, ûrge; child; sing; shoe; thin, t͟hat; zh as in *treasure.* ə = *a* as in *alone, e* as in *system, i* as in *easily, o* as in *gallop, u* as in *circus;* ᵊ as in *fire* (fīᵊr), *hour* (ouᵊr). l and n can serve as syllabic consonants, as in *cradle* (krād′l), and *button* (but′n). See the full key inside the front cover.

un′te·nac′i·ty, *n.*
un·ten′ant·a·ble, *adj.*
un·ten′ant·ed, *adj.*
un·tend′ed, *adj.*
un·ten′dered, *adj.*
un·ten′der·ized′, *adj.*
un·ten′der·ly, *adv.*
un·ten′e·brous, *adj.*
un·tense′, *adj.;* **-ly,** *adv.;* **-ness,** *n.;* *v.,* **-tensed, -tens·ing.**
un′ten·si·bil′i·ty, *n.*
un·ten′si·ble, *adj.;* **-bly,** *adv.*
un·ten′sile, *adj.*
un·tens′ing, *adj.*
un·ten′ta·cled, *adj.*
un·ten′tered, *adj.*
un·ten′u·ous, *adj.;* **-ly,** *adv.;* **-ness,** *n.*
un·ter′mi·nat′ed, *adj.*
un·ter′mi·nat′ing, *adj.*
un′ter·mi·na′tion·al, *adj.*
un·ter′mi·na′tive, *adj.*
un·ter′raced, *adj.*
un′ter·res′tri·al, *adj.*
un·ter′ri·ble, *adj.*
un′ter·rif′ic, *adj.*
un′ter·rif′i·cal·ly, *adv.*
un·ter′ri·fied′, *adj.*
un·ter′ri·fy′ing, *adj.*
un·ter′ror·ized′, *adj.*
un·terse′, *adj.;* **-ly,** *adv.;* **-ness,** *n.*
un·tes′sel·lat′ed, *adj.*
un·test′a·ble, *adj.*
un′tes·ta·men′tal, *adj.*
un′tes·ta·men′ta·ry, *adj.*
un·test′ed, *adj.*
un·tes′ti·fy′ing, *adj.*
un·teth′ered, *adj.*
un·teth′er·ing, *adj.*
un·tex′tu·al, *adj.;* **-ly,** *adv.*
un·tex′tur·al, *adj.*
un·thanked′, *adj.*
un·thank′ing, *adj.*
un·thawed′, *adj.*
un·thaw′ing, *adj.*
un′the·at′ric, *adj.*
un′the·at′ri·cal, *adj.;* **-ly,** *adv.*
un′the·is′tic, *adj.*
un′the·is′ti·cal, *adj.;* **-ly,** *adv.*
un′the·mat′ic, *adj.*
un′the·mat′i·cal·ly, *adv.*
un′the·o·log′ic, *adj.*
un′the·o·log′i·cal, *adj.;* **-ly,** *adv.*
un′the·o·ret′ic, *adj.*
un′the·o·ret′i·cal, *adj.;* **-ly,** *adv.*
un′ther·a·peu′tic, *adj.*
un′ther·a·peu′ti·cal, *adj.;* **-ly,** *adv.*
un·thick′, *adj.;* **-ly,** *adv.;* **-ness,** *n.*
un·thick′en, *v.t.*
un·thiev′ish, *adj.;* **-ly,** *adv.;* **-ness,** *n.*
un·thinned′, *adj.*
un·thin′ning, *adj.*
un·thirst′ing, *adj.*
un·thirst′y, *adj.*
un·thorn′, *v.t.*
un·thorn′y, *adj.*
un·thor′ough, *adj.;* **-ly,** *adv.;* **-ness,** *n.*
un·thought′ful, *adj.;* **-ly,** *adv.;* **-ness,** *n.*
un·thralled′, *adj.*
un·thrashed′, *adj.*
un·thread′a·ble, *adj.*
un·thread′ed, *adj.*
un·threat′en·ing, *adj.;* **-ly,** *adv.*
un·threshed′, *adj.*
un·thrift′i·ly, *adv.*
un·thrift′i·ness, *n.*
un·thrift′y, *adj.*
un·thrilled′, *adj.*
un·thrill′ing, *adj.*
un·thriv′ing, *adj.*
un·throat′i·ly, *adv.*
un·throat′y, *adj.*
un·throb′bing, *adj.*
un·thronged′, *adj.*
un·throt′tled, *adj.*
un·throw′a·ble, *adj.*
un·thrown′, *adj.*
un·thrust′, *adj.*
un·thumped′, *adj.*
un·thun′der·ing, *adj.*
un·thwacked′, *adj.*
un·thwart′a·ble, *adj.*
un·thwart′ed, *adj.*
un·thwart′ing, *adj.*
un·tick′et·ed, *adj.*
un·tick′led, *adj.*
un·tid′al, *adj.*
un·tiered′, *adj.*
un·tight′en, *v.t.*
un·tiled′, *adj.*
un·till′a·ble, *adj.*
un·tilled′, *adj.*
un·till′ing, *adj.*
un·tilt′, *v.t.*
un·tim′bered, *adj.*
un·timed′, *adj.*
un·tim′id, *adj.;* **-ly,** *adv.;* **-ness,** *n.*
un·tim′or·ous, *adj.;* **-ly,** *adv.;* **-ness,** *n.*
un·tinc′tured, *adj.*
un·tin′dered, *adj.*
un·tin′kered, *adj.*
un·tinned′, *adj.*
un·tin′seled, *adj.*
un·tin′selled, *adj.*
un·tint′ed, *adj.*
un·tip′pa·ble, *adj.*
un·tip′pled, *adj.*
un·tired′, *adj.;* **-ly,** *adv.*
un·tir′ing, *adj.;* **-ly,** *adv.*
un·tis′sued, *adj.*
un·tith′a·ble, *adj.*
un·tithed′, *adj.*
un·tit′il·lat′ed, *adj.*
un·tit′il·lat′ing, *adj.*
un·tit′ter·ing, *adj.*
un·tit′u·lar, *adj.;* **-ly,** *adv.*
un·toad′y·ing, *adj.*
un·toast′ed, *adj.*
un·to′gaed, *adj.*
un·toil′ing, *adj.*
un·tol′er·a·ble, *adj.;* **-ble·ness,** *n.;* **-bly,** *adv.*
un·tol′er·at′ed, *adj.*
un·tol′er·at′ing, *adj.*
un·tol′er·a′tive, *adj.*
un·tolled′, *adj.*
un·tombed′, *adj.*
un·toned′, *adj.*
un·tongued′, *adj.*
un·ton′sured, *adj.*
un·tooled′, *adj.*
un′top·o·graph′i·cal, *adj.;* **-ly,** *adv.*
un·top′pa·ble, *adj.*
un·topped′, *adj.*
un·top′ping, *adj.*
un·top′pled, *adj.*
un′tor·ment′ed, *adj.*
un′tor·ment′ing, *adj.;* **-ly,** *adv.*
un·torn′, *adj.*
un′tor·pe′doed, *adj.*
un·tor′pid, *adj.;* **-ly,** *adv.*
un′tor·por·if′ic, *adj.*
un·tor′rid, *adj.;* **-ly,** *adv.;* **-ness,** *n.*
un′tor·rid′i·ty, *n.*
un·tor′tious, *adj.;* **-ly,** *adv.*
un·tor′tu·ous, *adj.;* **-ly,** *adv.;* **-ness,** *n.*
un·tor′tured, *adj.*
un·tossed′, *adj.*
un·to′taled, *adj.*
un·to′talled, *adj.*
un·tot′ted, *adj.*
un·tot′ter·ing, *adj.*
un·touch′ing, *adj.*
un·tough′, *adj.;* **-ly,** *adv.;* **-ness,** *n.*
un·toured′, *adj.*
un·tox′ic, *adj.*
un·tox′i·cal·ly, *adv.*
un·trace′a·ble, *adj.*
un·traced′, *adj.*
un·trac′er·ied, *adj.*
un·track′a·ble, *adj.*
un′trac·ta·bil′i·ty, *n.*
un·trac′ta·ble, *adj.;* **-ble·ness,** *n.;* **-bly,** *adv.*
un·trad′a·ble, *adj.*
un·trade′a·ble, *adj.*
un·trad′ed, *adj.*
un·trad′ing, *adj.*
un′tra·di′tion·al, *adj.;* **-ly,** *adv.*
un′tra·duced′, *adj.*
un·traf′ficked, *adj.*
un·trag′ic, *adj.*
un·trag′i·cal, *adj.;* **-ly,** *adv.;* **-ness,** *n.*
un·trailed′, *adj.*
un·trail′ing, *adj.*
un·trail′er·a·ble, *adj.*
un·trail′ered, *adj.*
un·train′a·ble, *adj.*
un·trained′, *adj.*
un·trai′tor·ous, *adj.;* **-ly,** *adv.;* **-ness,** *n.*
un·trammed′, *adj.*
un·tram′meled, *adj.*
un·tram′melled, *adj.*
un·tramped′, *adj.*
un·tram′pled, *adj.*
un·tran′quil, *adj.;* **-ly,** *adv.;* **-ness,** *n.*
un·tran′quil·ize′, *v.t.,* **-ized, -iz·ing.**
un′trans·act′ed, *adj.*
un′tran·scend′ed, *adj.*
un′tran·scend′ent, *adj.*
un′tran·scen·den′tal, *adj.;* **-ly,** *adv.*
un′tran·scrib′a·ble, *adj.*
un′tran·scribed′, *adj.*
un′trans·fer′a·ble, *adj.*
un′trans·ferred′, *adj.*
un′trans·fer′ring, *adj.*
un′trans·fig′ured, *adj.*
un′trans·fixed′, *adj.*
un′trans·form′a·ble, *adj.*
un′trans·form′a·tive, *adj.*
un′trans·formed′, *adj.*
un′trans·form′ing, *adj.*
un′trans·fused′, *adj.*
un′trans·fus′i·ble, *adj.*
un′trans·gressed′, *adj.*
un·tran′sient, *adj.;* **-ly,** *adv.;* **-ness,** *n.*
un′tran·si′tion·al, *adj.;* **-ly,** *adv.*
un·tran′si·tive, *adj.;* **-ly,** *adv.;* **-ness,** *n.*
un·tran′si·to′ri·ly, *adv.*
un·tran′si·to′ri·ness, *n.*
un·tran′si·to′ry, *adj.*
un′trans·lat′a·bil′i·ty, *n.*
un′trans·lat′a·ble, *adj.*
un′trans·lat′ed, *adj.*
un′trans·mi′grat′ed, *adj.*
un′trans·mis′si·ble, *adj.*
un′trans·mis′sive, *adj.*
un′trans·mit′ted, *adj.*
un′trans·mut′a·bil′i·ty, *n.*
un′trans·mut′a·ble, *adj.;* **-ble·ness,** *n.;* **-bly,** *adv.*
un′trans·mut′ed, *adj.*
un′trans·par′ent, *adj.;* **-ly,** *adv.;* **-ness,** *n.*
un′tran·spired′, *adj.*
un′tran·spir′ing, *adj.*
un′trans·plant′ed, *adj.*
un′trans·port′a·ble, *adj.*
un′trans·port′ed, *adj.*
un′trans·posed′, *adj.*
un′tran·sub·stan′ti·at′ed, *adj.*
un·trap′, *v.t.,* **-trapped, -trap·ping.**
un·trapped′, *adj.*
un·trashed′, *adj.*
un′trau·mat′ic, *adj.*
un·trau′ma·tized′, *adj.*
un·trav′el·ing, *adj.*
un·trav′el·ling, *adj.*
un′tra·vers′a·ble, *adj.*
un·trav′ersed, *adj.*
un·trav′es·tied, *adj.*

cable by utterance; unspeakable; beyond expression: *unutterable joy.* **2.** not utterable; not pronounceable: *an unutterable foreign word.* [1580–90; UN-[1] + UTTERABLE] **—un·ut′ter·a·bly,** *adv.*

un·var·nished (un vär′nisht), *adj.* **1.** plain; clear; straightforward; without vagueness or subterfuge; frank: *the unvarnished truth.* **2.** unfinished, as floors or furniture; not coated with or as if with varnish. [1595–1605; UN-[1] + VARNISH + -ED[3], -ED[2]] **—Syn. 1.** bare, naked, candid, direct.

un·veil (un vāl′), *v.t.* **1.** to remove a veil or other covering from; display; reveal: *The woman unveiled herself.* **2.** to reveal or disclose by or as if by removing a veil or covering: *to unveil a monument; to unveil a secret; to unveil a truth.* —*v.i.* **3.** to become revealed by or as if by removing a veil. [1590–1600; UN-[2] + VEIL] **—Syn. 2.** divulge, bare, broadcast, expose.

un·veiled (un văld′), *adj.* **1.** not hidden by a veil or other covering; bare. **2.** revealed to public knowledge or scrutiny; made evident or manifest: *the unveiled purpose of their wicked plan.* [1600–10; (def. 1) UN-[1] + VEILED; (def. 2) UNVEIL + -ED[2]]

un·veil·ing (un vā′ling), *n.* **1.** a ceremony in which a statue or monument is presented or displayed for the first time by removing its covering. **2.** an act or instance of presenting, displaying, or revealing, esp. for the first time: *the unveiling of a new play.* [1760–70; UNVEIL + -ING[1]]

un·vo·cal (un vō′kəl), *adj.* **1.** not outspoken; reserved; not eloquent in speech; inarticulate. **2.** not mellifluous, as the speaking voice. **3.** not melodious; unmusical: *unvocal attempts at writing art songs.* [1765–75; UN-[1] + VOCAL]

un·voice (un vois′), *v.t., v.i.* **-voiced, -voic·ing.** *Phonet.* devoice. [1630–40; UN-[2] + VOICE]

un·voiced (un voist′), *adj.* **1.** not voiced; not uttered: *unvoiced complaints.* **2.** *Phonet.* voiceless; without voice; surd: *unvoiced consonants.* [1855–60; UN-[1] + VOICED]

un·warped (un wôrpt′), *adj.* **1.** not warped, as a phonograph record or flooring. **2.** impartial; undistorted, as a point of view, judgment, or analysis. [1735–45; UN-[1] + WARP + -ED[2]]

CONCISE ETYMOLOGY KEY: <, descended or borrowed from; >, whence; b., blend of, blended; c., cognate with; cf., compare; deriv., derivative; equiv., equivalent; imit., imitative; obl., oblique; r., replacing; s., stem; sp., spelling, spelled; resp., respelling, respelled; trans., translation; ?, origin unknown; *, unattested; ‡, probably earlier than. See the full key inside the front cover.

un·war·y (un wâr′ē), *adj.,* **-war·i·er, -war·i·est.** not wary; not cautious or watchful, as against danger or misfortune. [1570–80; UN-[1] + WARY] **—un·war′i·ly,** *adv.* **—un·war′i·ness,** *n.* **—Syn.** incautious, indiscreet, rash, heedless. **—Ant.** careful, cautious.

un·washed (un wosht′, -wôsht′), *adj.* **1.** not cleaned or purified by or as if by washing: *unwashed dishes; the unwashed soul of a sinner.* **2.** pertaining to or characteristic of the common people; untutored, unsophisticated, or ignorant; plebeian: *the power of the unwashed electorate.* —*n.* **3.** (*used with a plural v.*) an ignorant or lower-class group; rabble (usually prec. by *the*): *The author claimed that the unwashed would not understand his books.* [1350–1400; ME; see UN-[1], WASHED]

un·wea·ried (un wēr′ēd), *adj.* **1.** not wearied; not fatigued. **2.** indefatigable. [1200–50; ME; see UN-[1], WEARY, -ED[3]] **—un·wea′ried·ly,** *adv.* **—un·wea′ried·ness,** *n.*

un·weave (un wēv′), *v.t.,* **-wove, -wo·ven, -weav·ing.** to undo, take apart, or separate (something woven); unravel. [1535–45; UN-[2] + WEAVE]

un·weighed (un wād′), *adj.* **1.** not weighed, as for poundage. **2.** not carefully thought about, as statements or opinions. [1475–85; UN-[1] + WEIGH[1] + -ED[2]]

un·weight (un wāt′), *v.i.* *Skiing.* to lessen downward force and friction between the skis and the snow by a quick upward or downward shifting of the body or by using bumps in the terrain. [1935–40; UN-[2] + WEIGHT]

un·weight·ed (un wā′tid), *adj.* **1.** not burdened or encumbered with a heavy load or with mental or emotional matters, problems, etc. **2.** not considered important or significant, as one's opinions or sources: *an unweighted point of view.* [1880–85; UN-[1] + WEIGHTED]

un·well (un wel′), *adj.* **1.** not well; ailing; ill. **2.** *Older Use.* menstruating. [1400–50; late ME; see UN-[1], WELL[1]] **—un·well′ness,** *n.*

un·wept (un wept′), *adj.* **1.** not wept for; unmourned: *an unwept loss.* **2.** not wept or shed, as tears. [1585–95; UN-[1] + WEPT]

un·whole·some (un hōl′səm), *adj.* **1.** not wholesome; unhealthful; deleterious to health or physical or moral well-being: *unwholesome food; unwholesome activities.* **2.** not sound in health; unhealthy, esp. in appearance; suggestive of disease: *an unwholesome pallor.* [1150–1200; ME; see UN-[1], WHOLESOME] **—un·whole′some·ly,** *adv.* **—un·whole′some·ness,** *n.* **—Syn. 1.** insalubrious, noxious, pernicious.

un·wield·y (un wēl′dē), *adj.,* **-wield·i·er, -wield·i·est.** not wieldy; wielded with difficulty; not readily handled or managed in use or action, as from size, shape, or weight; awkward; ungainly. Also, **un·wield′ly.** [1350–1400; ME *unweldy.* See UN-[1], WIELDY] **—un·wield′i·ly,** *adv.* **—un·wield′i·ness,** *n.* **—Syn.** bulky, unmanageable, clumsy.

un·willed (un wild′), *adj.* not willed; involuntary; unintentional: *an unwilled accident.* [1530–40; UN-[1] + WILLED]

un·will·ing (un wil′ing), *adj.* **1.** not willing; reluctant; loath; averse: *an unwilling partner in the crime.* **2.** opposed; offering resistance; stubborn or obstinate; refractory: *an unwilling captive.* [bef. 900; OE *unwillende* (not recorded in ME); see UN-[1], WILLING] **—un·will′ing·ly,** *adv.* **—un·will′ing·ness,** *n.*

un·winc·ing (un win′sing), *adj.* that does not wince; unflinching; fearless. [1795–1805; UN-[1] + WINCING]

un·wind (un wīnd′), *v.,* **-wound, -wind·ing.** —*v.t.* **1.** to undo or loosen from or as if from a coiled condition: *to unwind a rolled bandage; to unwind a coiled rope.* **2.** to reduce the tension of; relax: *to unwind a person with a drink.* **3.** to disentangle or disengage; untwist: *to unwind one's legs from around the stool.* —*v.i.* **4.** to become unwound. **5.** to become relieved of tension; relax: *After work we can have a drink and unwind.* [1275–1325; ME *onwinden;* see UN-[2], WIND[2]] **—un·wind′a·ble,** *adj.* **—un·wind′er,** *n.*

un·wired (un wīərd′), *adj.* not wired, esp. not connected by power lines, cables, or wires to receive electricity or cable television. [UN-[1] + WIRED]

un·wis·dom (un wiz′dəm), *n.* lack of wisdom; folly; rashness; recklessness: *an act of unwisdom.* [bef. 900; ME; OE *unwīsdōm.* See UN-[1], WISDOM]

un·wise (un wīz′), *adj.,* **-wis·er, -wis·est.** not wise; foolish; imprudent; lacking in good sense or judgment: *an unwise choice; an unwise man.* [bef. 900; ME; OE *unwīs.* See UN-[1], WISE[1]] **—un·wise′ly,** *adv.* **—un·wise′ness,** *n.*

un·wish (un wish′), *v.t.* **1.** to cease to wish for. **2.** *Obs.* to wish away. [1585–95; UN-[2] + WISH]

un·wished (un wisht′), *adj.* unwished-for. [1575–85; UN-[1] + WISH + -ED[2]]

un·wished-for (un wisht′fôr′), *adj.* undesired; unwelcome: *an unwished-for occurrence.* [1610–20]

un·wit (un wit′), *v.t.,* **-wit·ted, -wit·ting.** *Obs.* to render devoid of wit; derange. [1595–1605; UN-[2] + WIT[1]]

un·wit·nessed (un wit′nist), *adj.* **1.** lacking the signature of a witness: *an unwitnessed legal document.* **2.** not perceived by the senses; not noticed or observed: *unwitnessed everyday occurrences.* [1375–1425; late ME; see UN-[1], WITNESS, -ED[2]]

un·treach′er·ous, *adj.;* **-ly,** *adv.;* **-ness,** *n.*
un·tread′a·ble, *adj.*
un·trea′son·a·ble, *adj.*
un·treas′ur·a·ble, *adj.*
un·treas′ured, *adj.*
un·treat′a·ble, *adj.*
un·treat′ed, *adj.*
un·treed′, *adj.*
un·trekked′, *adj.*
un·trel′lised, *adj.*
un·trem′bling, *adj.;* **-ly,** *adv.*
un·tre·men′dous, *adj.;* **-ly,** *adv.;* **-ness,** *n.*
un·trem′o·lant, *adj.*
un·trem′u·lant, *adj.*
un·trem′u·lent, *adj.*
un·trem′u·lous, *adj.;* **-ly,** *adv.;* **-ness,** *n.*
un·trenched′, *adj.*
un·trend′y, *adj.*
un′tre·panned′, *adj.*
un·tres′passed, *adj.*
un·tres′pass·ing, *adj.*
un·tressed′, *adj.*
un·tri′a·ble, *adj.;* **-ness,** *n.*
un·trib′al, *adj.;* **-ly,** *adv.*
un·trib′u·tar′i·ly, *adv.*
un·trib′u·tar′y, *adj.*
un·triced′, *adj.*
un·trick′a·ble, *adj.*
un·tricked′, *adj.*
un·tri′fling, *adj.;* **-ly,** *adv.*
un·trig′, *adj.*
un·trig′gered, *adj.*
un′trig·o·no·met′ric, *adj.*
un′trig·o·no·met′ri·cal, *adj.;* **-ly,** *adv.*
un·trim′ma·ble, *adj.*
un′trin·i·tar′i·an, *adj.*
un·tripped′, *adj.*
un·trip′ping, *adj.*
un·trite′, *adj.;* **-ly,** *adv.;* **-ness,** *n.*
un·trit′u·rat′ed, *adj.*
un′tri·um′phant, *adj.;* **-ly,** *adv.*
un·triv′i·al, *adj.;* **-ly,** *adv.*
un′tro·cha′ic, *adj.*
un·trolled′, *adj.*
un·tro′phied, *adj.*
un·trop′ic, *adj.*
un·trop′i·cal, *adj.;* **-ly,** *adv.*
un·trot′ted, *adj.*
un·trou′bled, *adj.*
un·trou′ble·some, *adj.*
un·trounced′, *adj.*
un·tru′ant, *adj.*
un·truck′led, *adj.*
un·truck′ling, *adj.*
un·trumped′, *adj.*
un·trum′pet·ed, *adj.*
un·trump′ing, *adj.*
un·trun′dled, *adj.*
un·trust′a·ble, *adj.*
un·trust′ed, *adj.*
un·trust′ful, *adj.;* **-ly,** *adv.*
un·trust′ing, *adj.*
un·trust′wor′thi·ly, *adv.;* **-ness,** *n.*
un·trust′wor′thy, *adj.*
un·try′ing, *adj.*
un·tubbed′, *adj.*
un′tu·ber′cu·lar, *adj.*
un′tu·ber′cu·lous, *adj.*
un·tucked′, *adj.*
un·tuft′ed, *adj.*
un·tugged′, *adj.*
un·tum′bled, *adj.*
un·tu′me·fied′, *adj.*
un·tu′mid, *adj.;* **-ly,** *adv.;* **-ness,** *n.*
un′tu·mid′i·ty, *n.*
un′tu·mul′tu·ous, *adj.;* **-ly,** *adv.;* **-ness,** *n.*
un·tun′a·ble, *adj.;* **-ble·ness,** *n.;* **-bly,** *adv.*
un·tune′a·ble, *adj.;* **-ble·ness,** *n.;* **-bly,** *adv.*
un·tuned′, *adj.*
un·tune′ful, *adj.;* **-ly,** *adv.*
un·tun′neled, *adj.*
un·tun′nelled, *adj.*
un·tur′baned, *adj.*
un·tur′bid, *adj.;* **-ly,** *adv.*
un·tur′bu·lent, *adj.;* **-ly,** *adv.*
un·turfed′, *adj.*
un·tur′gid, *adj.;* **-ly,** *adv.*
un·turn′a·ble, *adj.*
un·turned′, *adj.*
un·turn′ing, *adj.*
un·tur′pen·tined′, *adj.*
un·tur′ret·ed, *adj.*
un·tusked′, *adj.*
un·tu′te·lar, *adj.*
un·tu′te·lar′y, *adj.*
un·twilled′, *adj.*
un·twin′kled, *adj.*
un·twin′kling, *adj.*
un·twinned′, *adj.*
un·twirled′, *adj.*
un·twirl′ing, *adj.*
un·twist′a·ble, *adj.*
un·twitched′, *adj.*
un·twitch′ing, *adj.*
un·typed′, *adj.*
un·typ′i·cal, *adj.;* **-ly,** *adv.*
un′ty·ran′nic, *adj.*
un′ty·ran′ni·cal, *adj.;* **-ly,** *adv.*
un·tyr′an·nized′, *adj.*
un·ty′rant-like′, *adj.*
un′u·biq′ui·tous, *adj.;* **-ly,** *adv.;* **-ness,** *n.*
un·ul′cer·at′ed, *adj.*
un·ul′cer·a′tive, *adj.*
un·ul′cer·ous, *adj.;* **-ly,** *adv.;* **-ness,** *n.*
un·um′pired, *adj.*
un′un·der·stand′a·ble, *adj.*
un·u′ni·fi′a·ble, *adj.*
un·u′ni·fied′, *adj.*
un·u′ni·formed′, *adj.*
un·un′ion·ized′, *adj.*
un′u·nique′, *adj.;* **-ly,** *adv.;* **-ness,** *n.*
un′u·nit′a·ble, *adj.*
un′u·nit′ed, *adj.*
un′u·nit′ing, *adj.*
un′up·braid′ed, *adj.*
un′up·braid′ing, *adj.;* **-ly,** *adv.*
un′up·hol′stered, *adj.*
un′up·set′, *adj.*
un′up·set′ta·ble, *adj.*
un·ur′ban, *adj.*
un′ur·bane′, *adj.;* **-ly,** *adv.*
un·ur′ban·ized′, *adj.*
un·urged′, *adj.*
un·ur′gent, *adj.;* **-ly,** *adv.*
un·urg′ing, *adj.*
un·us′a·ble, *adj.;* **-ble·ness,** *n.;* **-bly,** *adv.*
un·use′a·ble, *adj.;* **-ble·ness,** *n.;* **-bly,** *adv.*
un·use′ful, *adj.;* **-ly,** *adv.;* **-ness,** *n.*
un·ush′ered, *adj.*
un′u·su′ri·ous, *adj.;* **-ly,** *adv.;* **-ness,** *n.*
un′u·surped′, *adj.*
un′u·surp′ing, *adj.*
un′u·til′i·tar′i·an, *adj.*
un·u′ti·liz′a·ble, *adj.*
un·u′ti·lized′, *adj.*
un·ut′tered, *adj.*
un′ux·o′ri·ous, *adj.;* **-ly,** *adv.;* **-ness,** *n.*
un·va′cant, *adj.;* **-ly,** *adv.*
un·va′cat·ed, *adj.*
un·vac′ci·nat′ed, *adj.*
un·vac′il·lat′ing, *adj.*
un·vac′u·ous, *adj.;* **-ly,** *adv.;* **-ness,** *n.*
un·va′grant, *adj.;* **-ly,** *adv.;* **-ness,** *n.*
un·vague′, *adj.;* **-ly,** *adv.;* **-ness,** *n.*
un·vain′, *adj.;* **-ly,** *adv.;* **-ness,** *n.*
un·val′et·ed, *adj.*
un·val′iant, *adj.;* **-ly,** *adv.;* **-ness,** *n.*
un·val′i·dat′ed, *adj.*
un·val′i·dat′ing, *adj.*
un·val′or·ous, *adj.;* **-ly,** *adv.;* **-ness,** *n.*
un·val′u·a·ble, *adj.;* **-bly,** *adv.*
un·val′ued, *adj.*
un·vamped′, *adj.*
un·van′ish·ing, *adj.*
un·van′quish·a·ble, *adj.*
un·van′quished, *adj.*
un·van′quish·ing, *adj.*
un·va′por·ized′, *adj.*
un′va·por·os′i·ty, *n.*
un·va′por·ous, *adj.;* **-ly,** *adv.;* **-ness,** *n.*
un·var′i·a·ble, *adj.;* **-ble·ness,** *n.;* **-bly,** *adv.*
un·var′i·ant, *adj.*
un·var′ied, *adj.*
un·var′i·e·gat′ed, *adj.*
un·var′y·ing, *adj.;* **-ly,** *adv.*
un·vas′cu·lar, *adj.;* **-ly,** *adv.*
un·vas′cu·lous, *adj.*
un·vat′ted, *adj.*
un·vault′ed, *adj.*
un·vault′ing, *adj.;* **-ly,** *adv.*
un·veer′ing, *adj.*
un·ve′he·ment, *adj.;* **-ly,** *adv.*
un·veined′, *adj.*
un·vel′vet·y, *adj.*
un·ve′nal, *adj.*
un·vend′a·ble, *adj.*
un·vend′ed, *adj.*
un·vend′i·ble, *adj.*
un′ve·neered′, *adj.*
un′ven·er·a·bil′i·ty, *n.*
un·ven′er·a·ble, *adj.;* **-ble·ness,** *n.;* **-bly,** *adv.*
un·ven′er·at′ed, *adj.*
un·ven′er·a′tive, *adj.*
un′ve·ne′re·al, *adj.*
un·venge′ful, *adj.*
un·ve′ni·al, *adj.;* **-ly,** *adv.;* **-ness,** *n.*
un·ve·ni·al′i·ty, *n.*
un·ven′omed, *adj.*
un·ven′om·ous, *adj.;* **-ly,** *adv.;* **-ness,** *n.*
un·vent′a·ble, *adj.*
un·vent′ed, *adj.*
un·ven′ti·lat′ed, *adj.*
un·ven′tured, *adj.*
un·ven′ture·some, *adj.*
un·ven′tur·ous, *adj.;* **-ly,** *adv.;* **-ness,** *n.*
un′ve·ra′cious, *adj.;* **-ly,** *adv.;* **-ness,** *n.*
un·ver′bal, *adj.;* **-ly,** *adv.*
un·ver′bal·ized′, *adj.*
un′ver·bose′, *adj.;* **-ly,** *adv.;* **-ness,** *n.*
un·ver′dant, *adj.;* **-ly,** *adv.*
un·ver′dured, *adj.*
un·ver′dur·ous, *adj.;* **-ness,** *n.*
un′ve·rid′ic, *adj.*
un′ve·rid′i·cal, *adj.;* **-ly,** *adv.*
un′ver·i·fi′a·bil′i·ty, *n.*
un·ver′i·fi′able, *adj.*
un·ver′i·fi·ca′tive, *adj.*
un·ver′i·fied′, *adj.*
un·ver′i·ta·ble, *adj.;* **-ble·ness,** *n.;* **-bly,** *adv.*
un′ver·mic′u·lat′ed, *adj.*
un·ver′min·ous, *adj.;* **-ly,** *adv.;* **-ness,** *n.*
un·ver′sa·tile, *adj.;* **-ly,** *adv.;* **-ness,** *n.*
un′ver·sa·til′i·ty, *n.*
un·versed′, *adj.*
un·ver′si·fied′, *adj.*
un·ver′te·brate′, *adj.*
un·ver′ti·cal, *adj.;* **-ly,** *adv.*
un′ver·tig′i·nous, *adj.;* **-ly,** *adv.;* **-ness,** *n.*
un′ve·sic′u·lat′ed, *adj.*
un·ves′seled, *adj.*
un·vest′ed, *adj.*
un·ve′toed, *adj.*
un′vex·a′tious, *adj.;* **-ly,** *adv.;* **-ness,** *n.*
un·vexed′, *adj.*
un·vi′a·ble, *adj.*
un·vi′brant, *adj.;* **-ly,** *adv.*
un·vi′brat·ed, *adj.*
un·vi′brat·ing, *adj.*
un′vi·bra′tion·al, *adj.*
un′vi·car′i·ous, *adj.;* **-ly,** *adv.;* **-ness,** *n.*
un·vi′cious, *adj.;* **-ly,** *adv.;* **-ness,** *n.*
un·vic′tim·ized′, *adj.*
un′-Vic·to′ri·an, *adj.*
un′vic·to′ri·ous, *adj.*
un·vic′tualed, *adj.*
un·vic′tualled, *adj.*
un·view′a·ble, *adj.*
un·viewed′, *adj.*
un·vig′i·lant, *adj.;* **-ly,** *adv.*
un·vig′or·ous, *adj.;* **-ly,** *adv.;* **-ness,** *n.*
un·vil′i·fied′, *adj.*
un·vil′lain·ous, *adj.;* **-ly,** *adv.*
un·vin′di·ca·ble, *adj.*
un·vin′di·cat′ed, *adj.*
un′vin·dic′tive, *adj.;* **-ly,** *adv.;* **-ness,** *n.*
un·vi′nous, *adj.*
un·vin′taged, *adj.*

un•wit•ting (un wit′ing), *adj.* **1.** inadvertent; unintentional; accidental: *His insult, though unwitting, pained her.* **2.** not knowing; unaware; ignorant; oblivious; unconscious: *an unwitting person.* [bef. 900; ME; OE *unwittende;* see UN-[1], WIT[2], -ING[2]] —**un•wit′ting•ly,** *adv.* —**un•wit′ting•ness,** *n.*

un•wit•ty (un wit′ē), *adj.* not clever or intelligent; silly; nonsensical. [bef. 1000; ME; OE *unwittig.* See UN-[1], WITTY]

un•wont•ed (un wôn′tid, -wōn′-, -wun′-), *adj.* **1.** not customary or usual; rare: *unwonted kindness.* **2.** *Archaic.* unaccustomed or unused. [1545–55; UN-[1] + WONTED] —**un•wont′ed•ly,** *adv.* —**un•wont′ed•ness,** *n.*

un•world•ly (un wûrld′lē), *adj.* **1.** not worldly; not seeking material advantage; spiritually minded. **2.** naive; unsophisticated; provincial. **3.** not terrestrial; unearthly. [1700–10; UN-[1] + WORLDLY] —**un•world′li•ness,** *n.*

un•wor•thy (un wûr′thē), *adj.*, **-thi•er, -thi•est,** *n., pl.* **-thies.** —*adj.* **1.** not worthy; lacking worth or excellence. **2.** beneath the dignity (usually fol. by *of*): *behavior unworthy of a king.* **3.** of a kind not worthy (often fol. by *of*). **4.** not of adequate merit or character. **5.** not commendable or creditable. **6.** not deserving. —*n.* **7.** an unworthy person. [1200–50; ME; see UN-[1], WORTHY] —**un•wor′thi•ly,** *adv.* —**un•wor′thi•ness,** *n.*
—**Syn. 3, 4.** unseemly, unfit, unsuitable, ignoble.
—**Ant. 1.** deserving, admirable, commendable.

un•wound (un wound′), *v.* pt. and pp. of **unwind.**

un•wrap (un rap′), *v.*, **-wrapped, -wrap•ping.** —*v.t.* **1.** to remove or open the wrapping of. **2.** to open (something wrapped): *Sheila unwrapped the Christmas presents quickly.* —*v.i.* **3.** to become unwrapped. [1200–50; ME *unwrappen;* see UN-[2], WRAP]

un•wreathe (un rēth′), *v.t.*, **-wreathed, -wreath•ing.** to bring out of a wreathed condition; untwist; untwine. [1585–95; UN-[2] + WREATHE]

un•wrin•kle (un ring′kəl), *v.t.*, **-kled, -kling.** to smooth the wrinkles from. [1605–15; UN-[2] + WRINKLE[1]]

un•writ•ten (un rit′n), *adj.* **1.** not actually formulated or expressed; customary; traditional. **2.** not written; not put in writing or print; oral: *an unwritten agreement.* **3.** containing no writing; blank. [1325–75; ME *unwriten;* see UN-[1], WRITTEN]
—**Syn. 1.** implicit, understood, tacit, inferred. —**Ant. 1.** specified, stipulated, designated.

unwrit′ten constitu′tion, a constitution, as in Great Britain, not codified as a document but defined by custom and precedent as embodied in statutes and judicial decisions. [1885–90]

unwrit′ten law′, 1. a law that rests for its authority on custom, judicial decision, etc., as distinguished from law originating in written command, statute, or decree. **2. the unwritten law,** the supposed principle of the right of the individual to avenge wrongs against personal or family honor, esp. in cases involving relations between the sexes: sometimes urged in justification of persons guilty of criminal acts of vengeance. [1635–45]

un•yoke (un yōk′), *v.*, **-yoked, -yok•ing.** —*v.t.* **1.** to free from or as if from a yoke. **2.** to part or disjoin, as by removing a yoke. —*v.i. Obs.* **3.** to remove a yoke. **4.** to cease work. [bef. 1000; ME *unyoken,* OE *ungeocian.* See UN-[2], YOKE[1]]

un•zip (un zip′), *v.*, **-zipped, -zip•ping.** —*v.t.* **1.** to open the zipper of. —*v.i.* **2.** to become unzipped. [1935–40; UN-[2] + ZIP[2]]

un•zipped[1] (un zipt′), *adj.* **1.** (esp. of a garment) not zipped or zipped up; with the zipper unfastened. **2.** *Slang.* **a.** crazy; demented. **b.** overwrought; hysterical. [UNZIP + -ED[2] or UN-[1] + *zipped*]

un•zipped[2] (un zipt′), *adj. Informal.* uncoded (def. 2). [UN-[1] + ZIP[4] + -ED[2]]

U. of S. Afr., Union of South Africa.

up (up), *adv., prep., adj., n., v.,* **upped, up•ping.** —*adv.* **1.** to, toward, or in a more elevated position: *to climb up to the top of a ladder.* **2.** to or in an erect position: *to stand up.* **3.** out of bed: *to get up.* **4.** above the horizon: *The moon came up.* **5.** to or at any point that is considered higher. **6.** to or at a source, origin, center, or the like: *to follow a stream up to its source.* **7.** to or at a higher point or degree, as of rank, size, value, pitch, loudness, brightness, maturity, or speed: *to move up in a firm; to pump up a tire; to turn a lantern up; Prices are going up. Speak up! Hurry up!* **8.** ahead; in a leading position in a competition: *He managed to get up on his opponent by three points.* **9.** in continuing contact, esp. as reflecting continuing awareness, knowledge, etc.: *to keep up with the latest developments in mathematics.* **10.** into or in activity, operation, etc.: *to set up vibrations.* **11.** into a state of emotional agitation or distress: *His insults left her all roiled up.* **12.** into existence, visible form, etc.: *His sample was worked up in the studio.* **13.** into view, prominence, or consideration: *The lost papers have turned up.* **14.** into or in a place of safekeeping, storage, retirement, etc.: *to lay up riches; to put up preserves.* **15.** into or in a state of union, contraction, etc.: *to add up a column of figures; to fold up.* **16.** to the required or final point: *to pay up one's debts; burned up.* **17.** to a state of completion; to an end: *She finished it all up.* **18.** to a halt: *The riders reined up and dismounted.* **19.** *Baseball.* being the player or team batting; at bat. **20.** (used as a function word for additional emphasis, sometimes prec. by *it*): *Go wake your father up. What plugged it up? We laughed it up.* **21.** ahead of an opponent or opponents in points, games, etc.: *The golfer was two strokes up on his nearest competitor.* **22.** each; apiece: *The score was seven up in the final quarter.* **23.** (of machines or equipment, as computers) working; in working order or in operation. **24.** *Informal.* without the addition of ice; straight up: *Bring me a martini, up.* **25.** *Naut.* toward the wind: *Put the helm up.* **26. all up with,** at or approaching the end of; with defeat or ruin imminent for: *He realized it was all up with him when the search party began to close in.* **27. go up in one's lines.** See **line**[1] (def. 58). **28. up against,** faced or confronted with: *They were up against formidable obstacles.* **29. up against it,** in a difficult situation, esp. in financial straits: *There was no one to help him when he was up against it.* **30. up and around,** recovered from an illness; able to leave one's bed. Also, **up and about. 31. up and down, a.** back and forth; backward and forward: *He paced up and down.* **b.** from top to bottom or head to toe: *She looked me up and down before replying.* **32. up for,** considered as eligible or as a possibility for (something): *The child is up for adoption. Three actresses are up for the role.* **33. up to, a.** as far as or approaching (a certain part, degree, point, etc.): *She went wading up to her knees. I am up to the eighth lesson.* **b.** in full realization or attainment of: *He worked up to president of the company.* **c.** as many as; to the limit of: *The car will seat up to five persons.* **d.** having adequate powers or ability for; capable of; equal to: *He didn't think I was up to the job.* **e.** the duty or responsibility of; incumbent upon: *It's up to you to break the news to him.* **f.** engaged in; contriving; doing: *What have you been up to lately?*
—*prep.* **34.** to, toward, or at an elevated place on or in: *They went up the stairs. The cat is up the tree.* **35.** to, toward, or at a high or higher station, condition, or rank on or in: *He is well up the social ladder.* **36.** at or to a farther point or higher place on or in: *She is up the street. I'm going up the street.* **37.** toward the source, origin, etc., of: *up the stream.* **38.** toward a particular direction or in the interior of, as a region or territory: *The explorers were up north.* **39.** in a course or direction that is contrary to that of: *to row up the current.* **40. up your ass,** *Slang (vulgar).* See **shove** (def. 6). Also, **up yours.**

CONCISE PRONUNCIATION KEY: act, cāpe, dâre, pärt; set, ēqual; *if,* ice; ox, ōver, ôrder, oil, bŏŏk, bōōt, out; up, ûrge; child; sing; shoe; thin, *th*at; zh as in *treasure.* ə = a as in *alone,* e as in *system,* i as in *easily,* o as in *gallop,* u as in *circus;* ᵊ as in *fire* (fīᵊr), *hour* (ouᵊr). l and n can serve as syllabic consonants, as in *cradle* (krād′l), and *button* (but′n). See the full key inside the front cover.

un•vi•o•la•ble, *adj.;* **-ble•ness,** *n.;* **-bly,** *adv.*
un•vi′o•lat′ed, *adj.*
un•vi′o•la′tive, *adj.*
un•vi′o•lent, *adj.;* **-ly,** *adv.*
un•vir′gin, *adj.*
un•vir′gin•al, *adj.*
un•vir′gin•like′, *adj.*
un•vir′ile, *adj.*
un•vir′tu•ous, *adj.;* **-ly,** *adv.;* **-ness,** *n.*
un•vir′u•lent, *adj.;* **-ly,** *adv.*
un•vis′cer•al, *adj.*
un•vis′i•ble, *adj.;* **-ble•ness,** *n.;* **-bly,** *adv.*
un•vi′sion•ar′y, *adj.*
un•vi′sioned, *adj.*
un•vis′it•a•ble, *adj.*
un•vis′it•ed, *adj.*
un•vis′it•ing, *adj.*
un•vi′sored, *adj.*
un•vis′taed, *adj.*
un•vis′u•al, *adj.;* **-ly,** *adv.*
un•vis′u•al•ized′, *adj.*
un•vi′tal, *adj.;* **-ly,** *adv.;* **-ness,** *n.*
un•vi′tal•ized′, *adj.*
un•vi′tal•iz′ing, *adj.*
un•vi′ti•a•ble, *adj.*
un•vi′ti•at′ed, *adj.*
un•vi′ti•at′ing, *adj.*
un′vi•tre•os′i•ty, *n.*
un•vit′re•ous, *adj.;* **-ly,** *adv.;* **-ness,** *n.*
un′vi•tres′cent, *adj.*
un•vit′ri•fi′a•ble, *adj.*
un•vit′ri•fied′, *adj.*
un•vit′ri•ol•ized′, *adj.*
un•vi•tu′per•at′ed, *adj.*
un′vi•tu′per•a′tive, *adj.;* **-ly,** *adv.;* **-ness,** *n.*
un′vi•va′cious, *adj.;* **-ly,** *adv.;* **-ness,** *n.*
un•viv′id, *adj.;* **-ly,** *adv.;* **-ness,** *n.*
un•viv′i•fied′, *adj.*
un•viz′ard•ed, *adj.*
un•vi′zored, *adj.*
un•vo′ca•ble, *adj.*
un•vo′cal•ized′, *adj.*
un′vo•cif′er•ous, *adj.;* **-ly,** *adv.;* **-ness,** *n.*
un•void′, *adj.;* **-ness,** *n.*
un•void′a•ble, *adj.*
un•void′ed, *adj.*
un•vol′a•tile, *adj.*
un•vol′a•til•ized′, *adj.*
un′vol•can′ic, *adj.*
un′vol•can′i•cal•ly, *adv.*
un′vo•li′tion•al, *adj.*
un•vol′i•tive, *adj.*
un•vol′u•ble, *adj.;* **-ble•ness,** *n.;* **-bly,** *adv.*
un′vo•lu′mi•nous, *adj.;* **-ly,** *adv.;* **-ness,** *n.*
un•vol′un•tar′i•ly, *adv.*
un•vol′un•tar′y, *adj.*
un′vol•un•teer′ing, *adj.*
un′vo•lup′tu•ous, *adj.;* **-ly,** *adv.;* **-ness,** *n.*
un•vom′it•ed, *adj.*
un′vo•ra′cious, *adj.;* **-ly,** *adv.;* **-ness,** *n.*
un•vot′ed, *adj.*
un•vot′ing, *adj.*
un•vouched′, *adj.*
un′vouch•safed′, *adj.*
un•vowed′, *adj.*
un•voy′ag•ing, *adj.*
un•vul′can•ized′, *adj.*
un•vul′gar, *adj.;* **-ly,** *adv.;* **-ness,** *n.*
un•vul′gar•ize′, *v.t.,* **-ized, -iz•ing.**
un•vul′ner•a•ble, *adj.*
un•vul′tur•ine′, *adj.*
un•vul′tur•ous, *adj.*
un•vy′ing, *adj.*
un•wad′a•ble, *adj.*
un•wad′ded, *adj.*
un•wad′dling, *adj.*
un•wade′a•ble, *adj.*
un•wad′ed, *adj.*
un•wad′ing, *adj.*
un•waft′ed, *adj.*
un•wa′gered, *adj.*
un•wagged′, *adj.*
un•wailed′, *adj.*
un•wail′ing, *adj.*
un•wain′scot•ed, *adj.*
un•wain′scot•ted, *adj.*
un•waived′, *adj.*
un•waked′, *adj.*
un•wake′ful, *adj.;* **-ly,** *adv.;* **-ness,** *n.*
un•wak′ened, *adj.*
un•wak′en•ing, *adj.*
un•wak′ing, *adj.*
un•walked′, *adj.*
un•wall′, *v.t.*
un•wan′der•ing, *adj.;* **-ly,** *adv.*
un•waned′, *adj.*
un•wan′ing, *adj.*
un•want′ed, *adj.*
un•want′ed•ly, *adj.*
un•want′ed•ness, *n.*
un•wan′ton, *adj.*
un•war′bled, *adj.*
un•war′like′, *adj.*
un•warm′a•ble, *adj.*
un•warmed′, *adj.*
un•warm′ing, *adj.*
un•warned′, *adj.*
un•warp′a•ble, *adj.*
un•warp′ing, *adj.*
un•war′rant•a•ble, *adj.;* **-bly,** *adv.;* **-ness,** *n.*
un•war′rant•ed, *adj.;* **-ly,** *adv.*
un•wash′a•ble, *adj.*
un•wast′a•ble, *adj.*
un•wast′ed, *adj.*
un•waste′ful, *adj.;* **-ly,** *adv.;* **-ness,** *n.*
un•watch′a•ble, *adj.*
un•watched′, *adj.*
un•watch′ful, *adj.;* **-ly,** *adv.;* **-ness,** *n.*
un•watch′ing, *adj.*
un•wa′tered, *adj.*
un•wa′ter•marked′, *adj.*
un•wa′ter•y, *adj.*
un•wat′tled, *adj.*
un•waved′, *adj.*
un•wa′ver•a•ble, *adj.*
un•wa′vered, *adj.*
un•wa′ver•ing, *adj.;* **-ly,** *adv.*
un•wav′ing, *adj.*
un•waxed′, *adj.*
un•way′ward, *adj.*
un•weak′ened, *adj.*
un•weak′en•ing, *adj.*
un•wealth′y, *adj.*
un•weaned′, *adj.*
un•weap′oned, *adj.*
un•wear′a•ble, *adj.*
un•wear′ing, *adj.*
un•wea′ri•some, *adj.*
un•wea′ry, *adj.*
un•wea′ry•ing, *adj.*
un•weath′ered, *adj.*
un•webbed′, *adj.*
un•wed′, *adj.*
un•wed′ded, *adj.*
un•wedge′, *v.t.,* **-wedged, -wedg•ing.**
un•weed′ed, *adj.*
un•weened′, *adj.*
un•weep′ing, *adj.*
un•weigh′a•ble, *adj.*
un•weigh′ing, *adj.*
un•weight′y, *adj.*
un•wel′come, *adj.*
un•wel′comed, *adj.*
un•wel′com•ing, *adj.*
un•weld′a•ble, *adj.*
un•weld′ed, *adj.*
un•welt′ed, *adj.*
un•west′ern, *adj.*
un•west′ern•ized′, *adj.*
un•wet′, *adj.*
un•wet′ted, *adj.*
un•whee′dled, *adj.*
un•wheel′, *v.t.*
un•whelped′, *adj.*
un•whet′ted, *adj.*
un•whim′per•ing, *adj.;* **-ly,** *adv.*
un•whim′si•cal, *adj.;* **-ly,** *adv.;* **-ness,** *n.*
un•whin′ing, *adj.;* **-ly,** *adv.*
un•whipped′, *adj.*
un•whipt′, *adj.*
un•whirled′, *adj.*
un•whisked′, *adj.*
un•whisk′ered, *adj.*
un•whis′per•a•ble, *adj.*
un•whis′pered, *adj.*
un•whis′per•ing, *adj.*
un•whis′tled, *adj.*
un•white′, *adj.*
un•whit′ed, *adj.*
un•whit′ened, *adj.*
un•white′washed′, *adj.*
un•wick′ed, *adj.;* **-ly,** *adv.*
un•wid′ened, *adj.*
un•wid′owed, *adj.*
un•wield′a•ble, *adj.*
un•wife′like′, *adj.*
un•wife′ly, *adj.*
un•wig′, *v.t.,* **-wigged, -wig•ging.**
un•wild′, *adj.;* **-ly,** *adv.;* **-ness,** *n.*
un•wil′ful, *adj.;* **-ly,** *adv.;* **-ness,** *n.*
un•will′a•ble, *adj.*
un•will′ful, *adj.;* **-ly,** *adv.;* **-ness,** *n.*
un•wilt′ed, *adj.*
un•wilt′ing, *adj.*
un•wil′y, *adj.*
un•wind′ed, *adj.*
un•win′dowed, *adj.*
un•wind′y, *adj.*
un•winged′, *adj.*
un•wink′ing, *adj.*
un•win′na•ble, *adj.*
un•win′ning, *adj.*
un•win′nowed, *adj.*
un•win′some, *adj.*
un•win′try, *adj.*
un•wiped′, *adj.*
un•wir′a•ble, *adj.*
un•wish′ful, *adj.;* **-ly,** *adv.;* **-ness,** *n.*
un•wist′ful, *adj.;* **-ly,** *adv.;* **-ness,** *n.*
un′with•draw′a•ble, *adj.*
un′with•draw′ing, *adj.*
un′with•drawn′, *adj.*
un•with′er•a•ble, *adj.*
un•with′ered, *adj.*
un•with′er•ing, *adj.*
un′with•held′, *adj.*
un′with•hold′ing, *adj.*
un′with•stand′ing, *adj.*
un′with•stood′, *adj.*
un•woe′ful, *adj.;* **-ly,** *adv.;* **-ness,** *n.*
un•wom′an•ish, *adj.*
un•wom′an•like′, *adj.*
un•wom′an•ly, *adj.,* *adv.*
un•womb′, *v.t.*
un•won′, *adj.*
un•won′der•ful, *adj.;* **-ly,** *adv.*
un•won′der•ing, *adj.*
un•wood′ed, *adj.*
un•wooed′, *adj.*
un•word′a•ble, *adj.;* **-bly,** *adv.*
un•work′a•bil′i•ty, *n.*
un•work′a•ble, *adj., n.*
un•worked′, *adj.*
un•work′ing, *adj.*
un•work′man•like′, *adj.*
un•work′man•ly, *adj.*
un•worm′-eat′en, *adj.*
un•worm′i•ness, *n.*
un•worm′y, *adj.*
un•worn′, *adj.*
un•wor′ried, *adj.*
un•wor′shiped, *adj.*
un•wor′ship•ing, *adj.*
un•wor′shipped, *adj.*
un•wor′ship•ping, *adj.*
un•wound′ed, *adj.*
un•wo′ven, *adj.*
un•wran′gling, *adj.*
un•wrath′ful, *adj.;* **-ly,** *adv.;* **-ness,** *n.*
un•wrecked′, *adj.*
un•wrenched′, *adj.*
un•wrest′ed, *adj.*
un•wrest′ing, *adj.*
un•wres′tled, *adj.*
un•wretch′ed, *adj.*
un•wrig′gled, *adj.*
un•wrin′kle•a•ble, *adj.*
un•writ′a•ble, *adj.*
un•writ′ing, *adj.*
un•wronged′, *adj.*
un•wrong′ful, *adj.;* **-ly,** *adv.;* **-ness,** *n.*
un•wrought′, *adj.*
un•wrung′, *adj.*
un•yachts′man•like′, *adj.*
un•yearned′, *adj.*
un•yearn′ing, *adj.*
un•yield′ed, *adj.*
un•yield′ing, *adj.;* **-ly,** *adv.;* **-ness,** *n.*
un•youth′ful, *adj.;* **-ly,** *adv.;* **-ness,** *n.*
un•zeal′ous, *adj.;* **-ly,** *adv.*
un•zone′, *v.t.,* **-zoned, -zon•ing.**

—*adj.* **41.** moving in or related to a direction that is up or is regarded as up: *the up elevator; the up train traveling north; the up platform of a railroad station.* **42.** informed; familiar; aware (usually fol. by *on* or *in*): *She is always up on current events.* **43.** concluded; ended; finished; terminated: *The game is up. Your hour is up.* **44.** going on or happening; taking place; occurring: *What's up over there?* **45.** having a high position or station: *He is up in society.* **46.** in an erect, vertical, or raised position: *The gate at the railroad crossing is up. The tent is up.* **47.** above the earth or ground: *The corn is up and ready to be harvested.* **48.** in the air; aloft: *The meteorological balloons are up. The airplanes are up for their reconnaissance flights.* **49.** (of heavenly bodies) risen above the horizon: *The sun is up.* **50.** awake or out of bed: *to be up with insomnia.* **51.** mounted on horseback: *He knows which jockeys are up in every race.* **52.** (of water in natural bodies) high with relation to the banks or shore: *The tide is up.* **53.** built; constructed: *The new museum is up and open to the public.* **54.** facing upward: *He is resting and his face is up.* **55.** See **sunnyside up. 56.** (of roads, highways, etc.) having the surface broken or removed (usually used in combination): *a torn-up road.* **57.** in revolt, mutiny, or rebellious agitation: *Many territories were up and preparing to send troops against the government.* **58.** in a state of agitation: *Beware of him when his temper is up.* **59.** *Informal.* cheerful or optimistic; high-spirited; happy; exuberant; upbeat. **60.** *Informal.* productive, favorable, or profitable: *a string of up months for the company.* **61.** afoot or amiss: *Her nervous manner told me that something was up.* **62.** in a state of enthusiastic or confident readiness (usually fol. by *for*): *The team was definitely up for the game.* **63.** bound; on the way: *She was on a ship up for Australia.* **64.** resolved in an unfavorable or undesired way: *They knew that their game was up.* **65.** higher than formerly in cost, amount, degree, etc.: *The price of meat was up.* **66.** (of age) advanced (usually fol. by *in*): *He is rather spry for a man so up in years.* **67.** active: *The captain wished to set sail as soon as the wind was up.* **68.** in a legal proceeding as defendant: *He is up for murder.* **69.** in operation or ready for use: *The theater's lights are up.* **70.** (of points or other standards used to determine the winner in a competition) ahead; in advance: *He won the game with two points up over his opponent.* **71.** considered or under consideration: *a candidate up for reelection; a bill that is up before Congress.* **72.** wagered; bet: *He won all the money up in the game.* **73.** living or located inland or on elevated ground: *They live in a village two miles up from the coast.* **74.** (used with a preceding numeral to indicate that a score is tied in a competition): *It was 10 up at the end of the first half.* **75.** ahead of an opponent or opponents: *They scored three times in a row to go two up.* **76. straight up.** See **straight** (def. 38). **77. up and doing,** *Informal.* actively engaged; alert; busy: *During her convalescence she longed to be up and doing.*
—*n.* **78.** an upward movement; ascent. **79.** a rise of fortune, mood, etc. **80.** a time of good fortune, prosperity, or happiness: *He has had more ups than downs in his career.* **81.** an upbound means of public transportation, as a train or bus. **82.** *Informal.* a feeling or state of happiness, exuberance, or elation. **83.** *Slang.* upper (def. 10). **84.** a person or thing that is in a favorable position of wealth, fortune, etc.: *People who were ups in the business world suffered losses in the economic depression.* **85.** an upward slope; elevation. **86.** an upward course or rise, as in price or value: *The landlord promised his tenants there would be no further ups in the rent this year.* **87.** *Slang.* upper[2]. **88. on the up and up,** *Informal.* frank; honest; sincere: *He seems to be on the up and up.* Also, **on the up-and-up.**
—*v.t.* **89.** to put or take up. **90.** to make larger; step up: *to up output.* **91.** to raise; go better than (a preceding wager): *to up the ante.*
—*v.i.* **92.** *Informal.* to start up; begin something abruptly (usually fol. by *and* and another verb): *Then he upped and ran away from home.* **93.** (often used imperatively or hortatively) to rise up: *Up, men, and fight until all the enemy are defeated!* [bef. 900; ME *up(pe)* (adv.), OE *up(p)* to a higher position, *uppe* in a higher position; c. OFris *up,* OS *up,* MD *up, op,* ON *upp;* akin to OHG *ūf* (> G *auf*), Goth *iup*]

up-, a combining form of **up:** *upland; upshot; upheaval.* [ME; OE]

U.P. See **Upper Peninsula.**

up., **1.** underproof (alcohol). **2.** upper.

up•a•long (up′ə lông′, -long′), *adj., adv. Newfoundland.* of or on the Canadian mainland, exclusive of Labrador. [1545–55; cf. Brit. dial. (SW England) *upalong* along in a particular direction, in the larger community; see UP, ALONG]

up•an•chor (up′ang′kər, up′ang′-), *v.i.* to weigh anchor. [1895–1900]

up-and-com•ing (up′ən kum′ing), *adj.* likely to succeed; bright and industrious: *an up-and-coming young executive.* [1840–50, *Amer.*] **—up′-and-com′er,** *n.*

up-and-down (up′ən doun′), *adj.* **1.** moving alternately up and down: *the up-and-down swing of levers; an up-and-down tune.* **2.** having an uneven surface: *up-and-down countryside.* **3.** changeable: *up-and-down luck.* **4.** perpendicular or nearly so: *a straight up-and-down hillside.* [1610–20] **—up′-and-down′ness,** *n.*

U•pan•i•shad (o͞o pan′i shad′, o͞o pä′ni shäd′), *n. Hinduism.* any of a class of speculative prose treatises composed between the 8th and 6th centuries B.C. and first written A.D. c1300: they represent a philosophical development beyond the Vedas, having as their principal message the unity of Brahman and Atman. [< Skt *upaniṣad,* equiv. to *upa* near + *ni-* down + *-ṣad,* sandhi variant of *sad-* SIT[1]] **—U•pan′i•shad′ic,** *adj.*

u•pas (yo͞o′pəs), *n.* **1.** the poisonous milky sap of a large tree, *Antiaris toxicaria,* of the mulberry family, native to tropical Asia, Africa, and the Philippine Islands, used for arrow poison. **2.** the tree itself. [1775–85; < Javanese: poison, esp. dart poison]

u•pa•ya (o͞o pä′yə), *n. Buddhism.* any device, as a koan, used for purposes of instruction. [< Skt *upāya* means]

up•bear (up bâr′), *v.t.,* **-bore, -borne, -bear•ing.** to bear up; raise aloft; sustain or support. [1250–1300; ME *upberen.* See UP-, BEAR[1]] **—up•bear′er,** *n.*

up•beat (up′bēt′), *n. Music.* **1.** an unaccented beat, esp. immediately preceding a downbeat. **2.** the upward stroke with which a conductor indicates such a beat. —*adj.* **3.** optimistic; happy; cheerful: *television dramas with predictably upbeat endings.* [1865–70; 1950–55 for def. 3; UP- + BEAT]

up•bound (up′bound′), *adj.* traveling or affording passage toward the north or in a direction regarded as up: *an upbound freighter; the upbound lane of a highway.* [1880–85; UP- + BOUND[4]]

up-bow (up′bō′), *n.* (in bowing on a stringed instrument) a stroke toward the heel of the bow: indicated in scores by the symbol V (opposed to *down-bow*). [1885–90]

up•braid (up brād′), *v.t.* **1.** to find fault with or reproach severely; censure: *The military tribunal upbraided the soldier for his cowardice.* **2.** (of things) to bring reproach on; serve as a reproach to. —*v.i.* **3.** *Archaic.* to utter reproaches. [bef. 1000; ME; OE *upbrēdan* to adduce as a fault. See UP-, BRAID] **—up•braid′er,** *n.*
—Syn. 1. reprove, blame. See **reprimand.**

up•braid•ing (up brā′ding), *n.* **1.** the act or words of a person who upbraids; severe reproof or censure: *an upbraiding from one's superiors.* —*adj.* **2.** severely reproachful or reproving; censorious: *upbraiding remarks.* [1175–1225; ME; see UPBRAID, -ING[1], -ING[2]] **—up•braid′•ing•ly,** *adv.*

up•bring•ing (up′bring′ing), *n.* the care and training of young children or a particular type of such care and training: *His religious upbringing fitted him to be a missionary.* [1475–85; UP- + BRINGING]

up•build (up bild′), *v.t.,* **-built, -build•ing.** to build up, as with the result of establishing, increasing, enlarging, or fortifying. [1505–15; UP- + BUILD] **—up•build′er,** *n.*

up•burst (up′bûrst′), *n.* a burst upward. [1835–45; UP- + BURST]

UPC, See **Universal Product Code.**

up•card (up′kärd′), *n.* **1.** *Stud Poker.* a card properly dealt face up. Cf. **hole card. 2.** *Cards.* the first card turned up from the stock after the deal. [1935–40; UP- + CARD[1]]

up•cast (up′kast′, -käst′), *n., adj., v.,* **-cast, -cast•ing.** —*n.* **1.** an act of casting upward. **2.** the state of being cast upward. **3.** something that is cast or thrown up, as soil or earth in digging. **4.** a shaft or passage up which air passes, as from a mine (opposed to *downcast*). —*adj.* **5.** cast up; directed or thrown upward: *The child looked at her father with upcast eyes.* —*v.t.* **6.** to cast up or upward. [1300–50; ME *upcasten* (v.). See UP-, CAST]

up•charge (up′chärj′), *n.* an additional charge: *How much is the upcharge for white sidewall tires?* [UP- + CHARGE]

up•chuck (up′chuk′), *v.i., v.t. Informal.* to vomit. [1920–25; UP- + CHUCK[1]]

up•com•ing (up′kum′ing), *adj.* coming up; about to take place, appear, or be presented: *the upcoming spring fashions.* [1300–50; ME; see UP-, COMING]
—Syn. impending, prospective, imminent, looming.

up•coun•try (*adj., n.* up′kun′trē; *adv.* up kun′trē), *adj. Chiefly Southern U.S.* **1.** of, relating to, residing in, or situated in the interior of a region or country; inland. **2.** *Disparaging.* unsophisticated. —*n.* **3.** the interior of a region or country. —*adv.* **4.** toward, into, or in the interior of a country: *The explorers trekked upcountry.* [1680–90; UP- + COUNTRY]

up•crop•ping (up′krop′ing), *n.* an act of cropping up; appearance; growth: *an upcropping of corn.* [1895–1900; UP- + CROPPING, after v. phrase *crop up*]

up•date (*v.* up dāt′, up′dāt′; *n.* up′dāt′), *v.,* **-dat•ed, -dat•ing,** *n.* —*v.t.* **1.** to bring (a book, figures, or the like) up to date, as by adding new information or making corrections: *to update a science textbook.* **2.** *Computers.* to incorporate new or more accurate information in (a database, program, procedure, etc.). **3.** to bring (a person, organization, etc.) up to date on a particular subject: *The magazine article will update you on the international situation.* —*n.* **4.** an act or instance of updating: *to make an update in a financial ledger.* **5.** information or data used in updating. **6.** an updated version, model, or the like. [1940–45; UP- + DATE[1]] **—up•dat′a•ble,** *adj.* **—up•dat′er,** *n.*

Up•dike (up′dīk′), *n.* **John,** born 1932, U.S. novelist and short-story writer.

up•do (up′do͞o′), *n., pl.* **-dos.** an upswept hairdo. [UP(SWEPT) + (HAIR)DO]

up•draft (up′draft′, -dräft′), *n.* the movement upward of air or other gas. [1400–50; late ME; see UP-, DRAFT]

up•drift (up′drift′), *n.* a slow, upward movement: *an updrift in housing starts and home mortgages.* [UP- + DRIFT]

up•end (up end′), *v.t.* **1.** to set on end, as a barrel or ship. **2.** to affect drastically or radically, as tastes, opinions, reputations, or systems. **3.** to defeat in competition, as in boxing or business. —*v.i.* **4.** to become upended. **5.** to place the body back-end up, as a dabbling duck. [1815–25; UP- + END[1]]

up•fold (up fōld′), *v.t.* to fold up or together: *Some morning-glories upfold their flowers by noon.* [1300–50; ME *upfolden.* See UP-, FOLD[1]]

up-front (up′frunt′), *Informal.* —*adj.* Also, **up′•front′. 1.** invested or paid in advance or as beginning capital: *an up-front fee of five percent and an additional five percent when the job is done.* **2.** honest; candid; straightforward: *He's very up-front about discussing his past.* **3.** conspicuous or prominent: *The company has an up-front position in its industry.* **4.** located in the front or forward section: *to request up-front seats on a plane.* —*adv.* Also, **up′ front′. 5.** as an initial investment, beginning capital, or an advance payment: *They'll need a half-million dollars up-front before opening the business.* **6.** before other payments, deductions, or returning a profit: *Estimated operating expenses will be deducted up-front.* [1965–70]

up•gath•er (up gath′ər), *v.t.* to gather up or together: *to upgather information.* [1580–90; UP- + GATHER]

up•grade (*n.* up′grād′; *adj., adv.* up′grād′; *v.* up-grād′, up′grād′), *n., adj., adv., v.,* **-grad•ed, -grad•ing.** —*n.* **1.** an incline going up in the direction of movement. **2.** an increase or improvement: *an upgrade in the year's profit forecast.* **3.** a new version, improved model, etc.: *The company is offering an upgrade of its sports sedan.* **4.** an increase or improvement in one's service, accommodations, privileges, or the like: *If the ship isn't full we'll receive an upgrade to a deluxe stateroom.* **5.** something, as a piece of equipment, that serves to improve or enhance: *a full range of upgrades available for your computer.* —*adj.* **6.** uphill; of, pertaining to, on, or along an upgrade. —*adv.* **7.** up a slope. —*v.t.* **8.** to promote to a higher grade or rank: *He has been upgraded to senior vice president.* **9.** to improve or enhance the quality or value of: *to upgrade property by landscaping it.* —*v.i.* **10.** to improve the quality, value, effectiveness, or performance of something: *Buy this basic computer and upgrade whenever you're ready.* [1870–75, *Amer.*; UP- + GRADE] **—up•grad′a•ble, up•grade′a•ble,** *adj.* **—up•grad′a•bil′i•ty, up•grade′a•bil′i•ty,** *n.* **—up′•grad′er,** *n.*

up•growth (up′grōth′), *n.* **1.** the process of growing up; development: *the upgrowth of nuclear science.* **2.** something that grows or has grown in an upward direction: *Part of the pituitary gland is an upgrowth of the roof of the mouth.* [1835–45; UP- + GROWTH]

up•heav•al (up hē′vəl), *n.* **1.** strong or violent change or disturbance, as in a society: *the upheaval of war.* **2.** an act of upheaving, esp. of a part of the earth's crust. **3.** the state of being upheaved. **4.** *Geol.* an upward warping of a part of the earth's crust, forcing certain areas into a relatively higher position than before. [1830–40; UPHEAVE + -AL[2]]
—Syn. 1. disruption, disorder, turmoil.

up•heave (up hēv′), *v.,* **-heaved** or **-hove, -heav•ing.** —*v.t.* **1.** to heave or lift up; raise up or aloft. **2.** to force or throw up violently or with much power, as an erupting volcano. **3.** to cause a major disturbance or disorder in: *The revolution upheaved the government, causing its leaders to flee the country.* —*v.i.* **4.** to rise upward, esp. extensively or powerfully. [1250–1300; ME *upheven.* See UP-, HEAVE] **—up•heav′er,** *n.*

up•held (up held′), *v.* pt. and pp. of **uphold.**

up•hill (*adv., adj.* up′hil′; *n.* up′hil′), *adv.* **1.** up or as if up the slope of a hill or other incline; upward: *The soldiers marched uphill. Water does not run uphill without assistance.* —*adj.* **2.** going or tending upward on or as if on a hill: *an uphill road.* **3.** at a high place or point: *an uphill village.* **4.** laboriously fatiguing or difficult: *an uphill struggle to become wealthy.* —*n.* **5.** a rising terrain; ascent. [1540–50; UP- + HILL]
—Syn. 4. arduous, hard, strenuous, taxing, grueling.

up•hold (up hōld′), *v.t.,* **-held, -hold•ing. 1.** to support or defend, as against opposition or criticism: *He fought the duel to uphold his family's honor.* **2.** to keep up or keep from sinking; support: *Stout columns upheld the building's heavy roof. Her faith upheld her in that time of sadness.* **3.** to lift upward; raise: *The pilgrims upheld their eyes and thanked heaven for their safe journey.* **4.** *Brit.* **a.** to upholster. **b.** to maintain in good condition; take care of. [1175–1225; ME *up holden.* See UP-, HOLD] **—up•hold′er,** *n.*
—Syn. 1. See **support.**

up•hol•ster (up hōl′stər, ə pōl′-), *v.t.* **1.** to provide (chairs, sofas, etc.) with coverings, cushions, stuffing, springs, etc. **2.** to furnish (an interior) with hangings, curtains, carpets, or the like. [1850–55, *Amer.*; back formation from UPHOLSTERER]

up•hol•ster•er (up hōl′stər ər, ə pōl′-), *n.* a person whose business it is to upholster furniture and, sometimes, to furnish and put in place hangings, curtains, carpets, etc. [1605–15; earlier *upholster* in same sense (see UPHOLD, -STER) + -ER[1]]

up•hol•ster•y (up hōl′stə rē, -strē, ə pōl′-), *n., pl.* **-ster•ies. 1.** the materials used to cushion and cover furniture. **2.** the business of an upholsterer. [1640–50; UPHOLSTER(ER) + -Y[3]]

UPI, See **United Press International.** Also, **U.P.I.**

Up•ing•ton (up′ing tən), *n.* a city in the N Cape of Good Hope province, in the N Republic of South Africa. 28,000.

Up•john (up′jon′), *n.* **Richard,** 1802–78, and his son, **Richard Mi•chell** (mi shel′), 1828–1903, U.S. architects, born in England.

up•keep (up′kēp′), *n.* **1.** the process or activity of providing an establishment, machine, person, etc., with necessary or proper maintenance, repairs, support, or the like: *The machine's faulty operation shows that no one has attended to its upkeep.* **2.** the total sum of the costs or expenses for this. [1880–85; UP- + KEEP]

up•land (up′lənd, -land′), *n.* **1.** land elevated above other land. **2.** the higher ground of a region or district; an elevated region. **3.** land or an area of land lying above the level where water flows or where flooding occurs. —*adj.* **4.** of or pertaining to uplands or elevated regions. [1560–70; UP- + LAND] **—up′land•er,** *n.*

CONCISE ETYMOLOGY KEY: <, descended or borrowed from; >, whence; b., blend of, blended; c., cognate with; cf., compare; deriv., derivative; equiv., equivalent; imit., imitative; obl., oblique; r., replacing; s., stem; sp., spelling, spelled; resp., respelling, respelled; trans., translation; ?, origin unknown; *, unattested; ‡, probably earlier than. See the full key inside the front cover.

Up·land (up′lənd), *n.* a city in S California. 47,647.

up′land cot′ton, a plant, *Gossypium hirsutum,* of warm regions of the New World, that is the chief commercial cotton crop in the U.S. Also called **American cotton.** [1810–20, *Amer.*]

up′land sand′piper, a large, field-inhabiting sandpiper, *Bartramia longicauda,* of eastern North America, resembling a plover: now protected and increasing in numbers. Also called **up′land plov′er, Bartramian sandpiper.** [1825–35, *Amer.*]

up·lift (*v.* up lift′; *n.* up′lift′), *v.t.* **1.** to lift up; raise; elevate. **2.** to improve socially, culturally, morally, or the like: *to uplift downtrodden and deprived peoples.* **3.** to exalt emotionally or spiritually. —*v.i.* **4.** to become uplifted. —*n.* **5.** an act of lifting up or raising; elevation. **6.** the process or work of improving, as socially, intellectually, or morally. **7.** emotional or spiritual exaltation. **8.** a brassiere. **9.** *Geol.* an upheaval. [1300–50; ME *upliften.* See UP-, LIFT] —**up·lift′ment,** *n.*
—**Syn. 7.** enrichment, betterment, enhancement.

up·lift·ed (up lif′tid), *adj.* **1.** improved, as in mood or spirit. **2.** raised or elevated, as a beam. [1250–1300; ME: orig., ptp. of UPLIFT]

up·lift·er (up lif′tər), *n.* **1.** a person or thing that uplifts. **2.** a person engaged in or devoted to social or moral uplift. [1575–85; UPLIFT + -ER[1]]

up·lift·ing (up lif′ting), *adj.* inspirational; offering or providing hope, encouragement, salvation, etc.: *an uplifting sermon.* [1810–20; UPLIFT + -ING[2]]

up·light (up′lit′), *n.* a lamp, often a light bulb set in a cylinder or other container, placed on the floor so that a beam of light is directed upward. [1980–85; UP- + LIGHT[1]]

up·link (up′lingk′), *n.* **1.** a transmission path for transmitting data or other signals from an earth station to a communications satellite or an airborne platform. —*adj.* **2.** of or pertaining to such transmission. Cf. **downlink.** [1965–70; UP- + LINK[1]]

up·load (up′lōd′), *v.t. Computers.* to transfer (software, data, character sets, etc.) from a smaller to a larger computer. [UP- + LOAD]

up·man·ship (up′mən ship′), *n.* one-upmanship. Also, **ups·man·ship** (ups′mən ship′). [1960–65; shortening of ONE-UPMANSHIP]

up·mar·ket (up′mär′kit), *adj.* **1.** appealing or catering to high-income consumers; of high quality; not easily affordable or accessible: *upmarket fashions.* —*adv.* **2.** in an upmarket way. [1970–75; UP- + MARKET]

up·most (up′mōst′ *or, esp. Brit.,* -məst), *adj.* uppermost. [1550–60; UP- + -MOST]

U·po·lu (o͞o pō′lo͞o), *n.* an island in Western Samoa, in the S Pacific: the home of Robert Louis Stevenson for the last five years of his life. 108,000; 430 sq. mi. (1113 sq. km). *Cap.:* Apia.

up·on (ə pon′, ə pôn′), *prep.* **1.** up and on; upward so as to get or be on: *He climbed upon his horse and rode off.* **2.** in an elevated position on: *There is a television antenna upon every house in the neighborhood.* **3.** in or into complete or approximate contact with, as an attacker or an important or pressing occasion: *The enemy was upon us and our soldiers had little time to escape. The Christmas holiday will soon be upon us and we have hardly begun to buy gifts. The time to take action is upon us.* **4.** immediately or very soon after: *She went into mourning upon her husband's death.* **5.** on the occasion of: *She was joyful upon seeing her child take his first steps.* **6.** on (in any of various senses, used as an equivalent of *on* with no added idea of ascent or elevation, and preferred in certain cases only for euphonic or metrical reasons): *He swore upon his honor as a gentleman.* [1150–1200; ME; see UP (adv.), ON (prep.)]

up-or-out (up′ər out′), *adj.* of or pertaining to a system or policy of employment in which one is either promoted or discharged: *the pressures of an up-or-out promotion system.*

up·per[1] (up′ər), *adj.* **1.** higher, as in place, position, pitch, or in a scale: *the upper stories of a house; the upper register of a singer's voice.* **2.** superior, as in rank, dignity, or station. **3.** (of places) at a higher level, more northerly, or farther from the sea: *the upper slopes of a mountain; upper New York State.* **4.** (*often cap.*) *Stratig.* denoting a later division of a period, system, or the like: *the Upper Devonian.* —*n.* **5.** the part of a shoe or boot above the sole, comprising the quarter, vamp, counter, and lining. **6.** an upper berth. **7.** a gaiter made of cloth. Cf. **gaiter** (def. 1). **8.** Usually, **uppers, a.** an upper dental plate. **b.** an upper tooth. **9.** *Informal.* the higher of two bunks or berths. **10. on one's uppers,** *Informal.* reduced to poverty; without sufficient means: *They are on their uppers but manage to hide the fact from their friends.* [1300–50; ME; see UP (adj.), -ER[4]]

up·per[2] (up′ər), *n. Slang.* **1.** a stimulant drug, esp. an amphetamine. **2.** a pleasant or elating experience, person, or situation. [1965–70, *Amer.*; UP + -ER[1]]

up′per air′, *Meteorol.* the atmosphere above the lower portion of the troposphere. Cf. **upper atmosphere.** [1875–80]

Up′per Ar′lington, a city in central Ohio, near Columbus. 35,648.

up′per arm′, the part of the arm between the shoulder and the elbow. [1875–80]

up′per at′mosphere, *Meteorol.* the portion of the atmosphere above the troposphere. Cf. **upper air.** [1890–95]

Up′per Aus′tria, a province in N Austria. 1,270,426; 4631 sq. mi. (11,995 sq. km). *Cap.:* Linz.

up′per bound′, *Math.* an element greater than or equal to all the elements in a given set: 3 and 4 are upper bounds of the set consisting of 1, 2, and 3. Cf. **bound**[3] (def. 4), **greatest lower bound, least upper bound, lower bound.**

Up′per Can′ada, a former British province in Canada 1791–1840: now the S part of Ontario province.

Up′per Cana′dian, *Canadian* (*chiefly the Maritime Provinces*). **1.** a native or inhabitant of Ontario. **2.** of or pertaining to Ontario.

Up′per Carbonif′erous, *Geol.* Pennsylvanian (defs. 2, 4).

up′per case′, *Print.* See under **case**[2] (def. 8). [1675–85]

up·per·case (up′ər kās′), *adj., v.,* **-cased, -cas·ing,** *n.* —*adj.* **1.** (of an alphabetical character) capital. **2.** *Print.* pertaining to or belonging in the upper case. —*v.t.* **3.** to print or write with an uppercase letter. —*n.* **4.** a capital letter. Cf. **lowercase.** [1730–40; UPPER[1] + CASE[2]]

up′per cham′ber. See **upper house.**

Up′per Chinook′, a Chinookan language of the Columbia River valley from the Deschutes River to the estuary.

up′per class′, a class of people above the middle class, having the highest social rank or standing based on wealth, family connections, and the like. [1830–40] —**up′per-class′,** *adj.*

up·per·class·man (up′ər klas′mən, -kläs′-), *n., pl.* **-men.** a junior or senior in a secondary school or college. [1870–75, *Amer.*; UPPER[1] + CLASS + -MAN]

up′per crust′, **1.** the topmost layer of crust, as of a pie. **2.** *Informal.* the highest social class. [1425–75; 1830–35 for def. 2; late ME] —**up′per-crust′,** *adj.*

up·per·cut (up′ər kut′), *n., v.,* **-cut, -cut·ting.** —*n.* **1.** a swinging blow directed upward, as to an adversary's chin. **2.** *Bridge.* a play of a higher trump than necessary knowing it can be overtrumped by an opponent but that if overtrumped, one or more trump winners in the hand of one's partner will be established. —*v.t.* **3.** to strike (an opponent) with an uppercut. —*v.i.* **4.** to deliver an uppercut. **5.** *Bridge.* to make an uppercut. [1840–50; UPPER[1] + CUT]

Up′per Dar′by, a town in SE Pennsylvania, near Philadelphia. 84,054.

up′per deck′, *Naut.* the uppermost continuous deck that is capable of being made watertight; freeboard deck. [1585–95]

Up′per E′gypt. See under **Egypt.**

up′per hand′, the dominating or controlling position; advantage: *to have the upper hand in the fight.* [1475–85]

up′per house′, one of two branches of a legislature generally smaller and less representative than the lower branch, as the Senate of the U.S. Congress. [1525–35]

Up′per Klam′ath Lake′. See under **Klamath Lakes.**

Up′per Mich′igan. See **Upper Peninsula.**

up·per·most (up′ər mōst′ *or, esp. Brit.,* -məst), *adj.* Also, **upmost. 1.** highest in place, order, rank, power, etc.: *the uppermost peaks of the mountain; the uppermost class of society.* **2.** topmost; predominant: *a subject of uppermost concern.* —*adv.* **3.** in or into the uppermost place, rank, or predominance: *The blossoms grow uppermost on the stems of these flowers; the thoughts that came uppermost to her mind.* [1475–85; UPPER[1] + -MOST]

Up′per Palat′inate. See under **Palatinate** (def. 1).

Up′per Paleolith′ic. See under **Paleolithic.**

up′per par′tial tone′, *Music.* overtone (def. 1). [1875–80]

Up′per Penin′sula, the peninsula between lakes Superior and Michigan constituting the N part of Michigan. *Abbr.:* U.P. Also called **Upper Michigan, Northern Michigan.**

up′per school′, a scholastic division, esp. in a private school, including the terminal secondary grades. [1620–30]

Up′per Sile′sia, a highly industrialized region divided between Germany and Poland after World War I.

Up′per Tungu′ska, the lower course of the Angara River. Cf. **Angara.**

Up′per Vol′ta, former name of **Burkina Faso.** —**Up′per Vol′tan,** *adj., n.*

up·phase (up′fāz′), *n.* a period when the economy is strong and business profits are high or increasing.

up·pish (up′ish), *adj. Informal.* arrogant; condescending; uppity. [1670–80; UP + -ISH[1]] —**up′pish·ly,** *adv.* —**up′pish·ness,** *n.*

up·pi·ty (up′i tē), *adj. Informal.* **1.** affecting an attitude of inflated self-esteem; haughty; snobbish. **2.** rebelliously self-assertive; not inclined to be tractable or deferential. [1875–80, *Amer.*; prob. UP + *-ity,* extended form of -Y[1]; cf. PERNICKETY] —**up′pi·ty·ness,** *n.*

Upp·sa·la (up′sä lə, -sə-; *Swed.* o͝op′sä′lä), *n.* a city in SE Sweden. 146,192. Also, **Upsala.**

up′ quark′, *Physics.* the quark having electric charge ⅔ times the elementary charge and strangeness and charm equal to 0. Also called **u quark.** [1975–80]

up·raise (up rāz′), *v.t.,* **-raised, -rais·ing. 1.** to raise up; lift or elevate. **2.** to raise from a depressed or dejected humor; cheer. [1250–1300; ME *upreisen.* See UP-, RAISE] —**up·rais′er,** *n.*

up·rate (up rāt′), *v.t.,* **-rat·ed, -rat·ing.** to raise in rate, power, size, classification, etc.; upgrade: *to uprate a rocket engine.* [1965–70; UP- + RATE[1]]

up·rear (up rēr′), *v.t.* **1.** to raise up; lift: *The horse upreared its head and whinnied.* **2.** to build; erect: *to uprear a monument in stone.* **3.** to elevate the dignity of; exalt: *God upreared Abraham by making him the father of many nations.* **4.** to bring up; rear: *to uprear children in a good environment.* —*v.i.* **5.** to rise. [1250–1300; ME *upreren.* See UP-, REAR[2]]

up·right (up′rīt′, up rīt′), *adj.* **1.** erect or vertical, as in position or posture. **2.** raised or directed vertically or upward. **3.** adhering to rectitude; righteous, honest, or just: *an upright person.* **4.** being in accord with what is right: *upright dealings.* —*n.* **5.** the state of being upright or vertical. **6.** something standing erect or vertical, as a piece of timber. **7.** an upright piano. **8.** Usually, **uprights.** *Chiefly Football.* the goalposts. —*adv.* **9.** in an upright position or direction; vertically. —*v.t.* **10.** to make upright. [bef. 900; ME, OE *upriht* (c. G *aufrecht*). See UP, RIGHT] —**up′right′ly,** *adv.* —**up′right′ness,** *n.*
—**Syn. 1.** plumb. UPRIGHT, ERECT, VERTICAL, PERPENDICULAR imply that something is in the posture of being straight upward, not leaning. That which is UPRIGHT is in a position corresponding to that of a person standing up: *a decaying tree no longer standing upright; an upright piano.* ERECT emphasizes the straightness of position or posture: *proud and erect; A flagpole stands erect.* VERTICAL suggests upward direction, esp. along the shortest line from the earth to a level above it: *the vertical edge of a door; ornamented by vertical lines.* PERPENDICULAR, a term frequently interchangeable with VERTICAL, is used esp. in mathematics: *the perpendicular side of a right triangle; to erect a perpendicular line from the base of a figure.* **3.** honorable. **6.** pole, prop, pier, pile, column.
—**Ant. 1.** leaning, horizontal.

up′right pian′o, a piano with an upright rectangular body and with its strings running vertically. Cf. **spinet** (def. 1).

up·rise (*v.* up rīz′; *n.* up′rīz′), *v.,* **-rose, -ris·en, -ris·ing,** *n.* —*v.i.* **1.** to rise up; get up, as from a lying or sitting posture. **2.** to rise into view: *As we approached the city, the spires of tall buildings uprose as if to greet us.* **3.** to rise in revolt. **4.** to come into existence or prominence: *Many calamities uprose to plague the people during the war.* **5.** to move upward; mount up; ascend. **6.** to come above the horizon. **7.** to slope upward: *The land uprises from the river to the hills.* **8.** to swell or grow, as a sound: *A blare of trumpets uprose to salute the king.* —*n.* **9.** an act of rising up. [1250–1300; ME *uprisen.* See UP-, RISE] —**up·ris′er,** *n.*

up·ris·ing (up′rī′zing, up rī′zing), *n.* **1.** an insurrection or revolt. **2.** an act of rising up. **3.** an ascent or acclivity. [1200–50; ME; see UP-, RISING]
—**Syn. 1.** rebellion.

up·riv·er (up′riv′ər), *adv., adj.* in the direction of or nearer the source of a river: *It's hard to paddle a canoe upriver; an upriver settlement of tribes.* [1830–40, *Amer.*; UP- + RIVER[1]]

up·roar (up′rôr′, -rōr′), *n.* **1.** a state of violent and noisy disturbance, as of a multitude; turmoil. **2.** an instance of this. [1520–30; < D *oproer* revolt, tumult, trans. of G *Aufruhr*; sense and sp. influenced by ROAR]
—**Syn. 1.** tumult, turbulence, commotion, hubbub, furor. See **disorder. 2.** clamor.

up·roar·i·ous (up rôr′ē əs, -rōr′-), *adj.* **1.** characterized by or in a state of uproar; tumultuous. **2.** making an uproar; confused and noisy, as an assembly, person, etc. **3.** very funny, as a person or situation. **4.** very loud, as sounds or utterances. **5.** expressed by or producing uproar. [1810–20; UPROAR + -IOUS] —**up·roar′i·ous·ly,** *adv.* —**up·roar′i·ous·ness,** *n.*
—**Syn. 1.** raging, stormy, riotous, turbulent.

up·root (up ro͞ot′, -ro͝ot′), *v.t.* **1.** to pull out by or as if by the roots: *The hurricane uprooted many trees and telephone poles.* **2.** to remove violently or tear away from a native place or environment: *The industrial revolution uprooted large segments of the rural population.* **3.** to destroy or eradicate as if by pulling out roots: *The conquerors uprooted many of the native traditions.* **4.** to displace, as from a home or country; tear away, as from customs or a way of life: *to uproot a people.* —*v.i.* **5.** to become uprooted. [1610–20; UP- + ROOT[2]] —**up·root′ed·ness,** *n.* —**up·root′er,** *n.*
—**Syn. 3.** extirpate, banish, eliminate, remove.

up·rose (up rōz′), *v.* pt. of **uprise.**

up·rouse (up rouz′), *v.t.,* **-roused, -rous·ing.** to rouse up; arouse; awake. [1805–15; UP- + ROUSE[1]]

up·rush (up′rush′), *n.* **1.** an upward rush, as of water or air. **2.** an abrupt increase: *an uprush of business during the noon hour.* [1870–75; UP- + RUSH[1]]

UPS, *Trademark.* United Parcel Service.

up·sa·dai·sy (up′sə dā′zē), *interj.* upsy-daisy.

Up·sa·la (up′sä lə, -sə-; *Swed.* o͝op′sä′lä), *n.* Uppsala.

ups′ and downs′, rises and falls of fortune; good and bad times: *Every business has its ups and downs.* [1650–60]

up·scale (*adj.* up′skāl′; *v.* up skāl′; *n.* up′skāl′), *adj., v.,* **-scaled, -scal·ing,** *n. Informal.* —*adj.* **1.** located at, moving toward, or of or for the upper end of a social or economic scale: *The boutique caters to upscale young career people.* **2.** luxurious, costly, or elegant. —*v.t.* **3.** to improve the quality, value, or rating of: *a five-year plan to upscale the neighborhood.* —*n.* **4.** (*used with a plural v.*) elegant, elite, privileged persons collectively (usually prec. by *the*): *shops that only the upscale can afford to patronize.* [1970–75, *Amer.*; UP- + SCALE[3]]

up·set (*v., adj.* up set′; *n.* up′set′), *v.,* **-set, -set·ting,** *n., adj.* —*v.t.* **1.** to overturn: *to upset a pitcher of milk.* **2.** to disturb mentally or emotionally; perturb: *The incident upset her.* **3.** to disturb or derange completely; put out of order; throw into disorder: *to upset a system; to upset a mechanism; to upset an apartment.* **4.** to disturb physically: *It upset his stomach.* **5.** to defeat or overthrow an opponent that is considered more formidable, as in war, politics, or sports. **6.** *Metalworking.* to thicken the end of (a piece of heated metal) by hammering on the end against the length of the piece. —*v.i.* **7.**

CONCISE PRONUNCIATION KEY: act, cāpe, dâre, pärt; set, ēqual; *if,* ice; ox, ōver, ôrder, oil, bo͝ok, bo͞ot, out; up, ûrge; child; sing; shoe; thin, *that;* zh as in *treasure.* ə = *a* as in *alone, e* as in *system, i* as in *easily, o* as in *gallop, u* as in *circus;* ᵊ as in *fire* (fīᵊr), *hour* (ouᵊr). l and n can serve as syllabic consonants, as in *cradle* (krād′l), and *button* (but′n). See the full key inside the front cover.

to become upset or overturned. —*n.* **8.** an upsetting or instance of being upset; overturn; overthrow. **9.** the defeat of a person, team, etc., that is considered more formidable. **10.** a nervous, irritable state of mind. **11.** a disordered or confused arrangement. **12.** *Metalworking.* **a.** a tool used for upsetting. **b.** something that is upset, as a bar end. —*adj.* **13.** overturned: *an upset milk pail.* **14.** disordered; disorganized: *The house is upset.* **15.** distressed; disturbed: *She had an upset stomach. He is emotionally upset.* **16.** *Archaic.* raised up. [1300–50; ME: raised up; see UP-, SET] —**up·set′ta·ble,** *adj.* —**up·set′ter,** *n.* —**up·set′ting·ly,** *adv.*
—**Syn. 1.** UPSET, CAPSIZE, OVERTURN imply a change from an upright or other stable position to a prostrate one. UPSET is a familiar word, applied to simple, everyday actions: *to upset a table, a glass of water.* CAPSIZE is applied especially to the upsetting of a boat or other vessel: *to capsize a canoe.* OVERTURN usually suggests violence in upsetting something supposedly stable: *The earthquake overturned houses.* All three are used figuratively, also: *to upset the stock market; to capsize a plan; to overturn a government.* **2.** unnerve, disconcert, fluster. **5.** depose, displace. **10.** perturbation, disturbance. **11.** mess. **15.** disconcerted, agitated, perturbed, annoyed. —**Ant. 2, 3.** steady.

up′set price′, the lowest price at which a person is permitted to bid for something being sold at auction. [1805–15]

up·set·ting (up set′ing), *adj.* tending to disturb or upset: *an upsetting experience.* [1870–75; UPSET + -ING²]

upset′ting lev′er, *Naval Archit.* the horizontal distance between the center of gravity, acting downward, and the center of buoyancy, acting upward, when they are so placed as to form a couple **(upset′ting cou′ple)** tending to capsize the boat.

upset′ting mo′ment, *Naval Archit.* the moment of an upsetting couple. Also called **capsizing moment.**

up·shift (up′shift′), *v.i.* **1.** to shift an automotive transmission or vehicle into a higher gear. —*v.t.* **2.** to shift (an automotive transmission or vehicle) into a higher gear. —*n.* **3.** an act or instance of upshifting. [1950–55; UP- + SHIFT]

up·shot (up′shot′), *n.* **1.** the final issue, the conclusion, or the result: *The upshot of the disagreement was a new bylaw.* **2.** the gist, as of an argument or thesis. [1525–35; UP- + SHOT¹]
—**Syn. 1.** consequence, outgrowth, aftereffect.

up·side (up′sīd′), *n.* **1.** the upper side or part. **2.** that part of a chart or graph that shows a higher level, esp. in price. **3.** an upward trend, as in stock prices. **4. get upsides with,** *Brit.* to get even with. —*adj.* **5.** going higher, esp. in price or worth: *This stock has a nice upside potential.* [1605–15; UP- + SIDE¹]

up′side down′, 1. with the upper part undermost. **2.** in or into complete disorder; topsy-turvy: *The burglars turned the house upside down.* [1300–50; re-formation (see UPSIDE) of ME *upsedoun,* earlier *up so doun* (see UP, SO¹, DOWN¹; sense of *so* obscure)] —**up′side-down′,** *adj.* —**up′side-down′ness,** *n.*

up′side-down′ cake′, a cake that is baked on a layer of fruit, then turned before serving so that the fruit is on top. [1920–25, *Amer.*]

up·si·lon (yo͞op′sə lon′, -lən, up′-; *esp. Brit.* yo͞op sī′lən), *n.* **1.** the 20th letter of the Greek alphabet (Υ, υ). **2.** the vowel sound represented by this letter. **3.** Also called **up′silon par′ticle,** *Physics.* any of a family of heavy, short-lived, neutral mesons that are composed of a bottom quark and its antiquark. *Symbol:* Υ, υ [1615–25; < LGk *ŷ psilón* lit., simple *u* (to distinguish it from the digraph *oi,* pronounced the same in LGk)]

up·spin (up′spin′), *n.* a sudden, upward, spiraling movement, trend, etc.: *another upspin in construction costs.* [UP- + SPIN]

up·spring (*v.* up spring′, *n.* up′spring′), *v.,* **-sprang** or **-sprung, -sprung, -spring·ing,** *n.* —*v.i.* **1.** to spring up. **2.** to come into being or existence; arise: *Prosperity began to upspring after the war.* —*n. Archaic.* **3.** growth or development. **4.** a coming into existence; origin. [bef. 1000; (v.) ME *upspringen,* OE *upspringan;* (n.) ME; OE *upspringe.* See UP-, SPRING]

up·stage (up′stāj′), *adv., adj., v.,* **-staged, -stag·ing,** *n.* —*adv.* **1.** on or toward the back of the stage. —*adj.* **2.** of, pertaining to, or located at the back of the stage. **3.** haughtily aloof; supercilious. —*v.t.* **4.** to overshadow (another performer) by moving upstage and forcing the performer to turn away from the audience. **5.** to outdo professionally, socially, etc. **6.** to behave snobbishly toward. —*n.* **7.** the rear half of the stage. **8.** any stage position to the rear of another. [1905–10; UP- + STAGE]

up·stairs (up′stârz′), *adv., adj., n., pl.* **-stairs.** —*adv.* **1.** up the stairs; to or on an upper floor. **2.** *Informal.* in the mind: *to be a little weak upstairs.* **3.** to or at a higher level of authority: *You may have to take the matter upstairs.* **4.** *Mil. Slang.* at or to a higher level in the air. **5. kick upstairs,** to promote (a person) to a higher position, usually having less authority, in order to be rid of him or her. —*adj.* **6.** Also, **up′stair′.** of, pertaining to, or situated on an upper floor: *an upstairs window; an upstairs apartment.* —*n.* **7.** (*usually used with a singular v.*) an upper story or stories; the part of a building or house that is above the ground floor: *The upstairs of this house is entirely rented.* **8.** a higher command or level of authority: *We can't take action till we have approval from upstairs.* [1590–1600; UP- + STAIRS]

up·stand·ing (up stan′ding), *adj.* **1.** upright; honorable; straightforward. **2.** of a fine, vigorous type. **3.** erect; erect and tall. [bef. 1000; ME; OE *upstandende;* see UP-, STAND, -ING²] —**up·stand′ing·ness,** *n.*

CONCISE ETYMOLOGY KEY: <, descended or borrowed from; >, whence; b., blend of, blended; c., cognate with; cf., compare; deriv., derivative; equiv., equivalent; imit., imitative; obl., oblique; r., replacing; s., stem; sp., spelling, spelled; resp., respelling, respelled; trans., translation; ?, origin unknown; *, unattested; ‡, probably earlier than. See the full key inside the front cover.

up·start (*n., adj.* up′stärt′; *v.* up stärt′), *n.* **1.** a person who has risen suddenly from a humble position to wealth, power, or a position of consequence. **2.** a presumptuous and objectionable person who has so risen; parvenu. —*adj.* **3.** being, resembling, or characteristic of an upstart. —*v.i.* **4.** to spring into existence or into view. **5.** to start up; spring up, as to one's feet. —*v.t.* **6.** to cause to start up. [1275–1325; ME (v.); see UP-, START] —**up′start′ness,** *n.*

up·state (up′stāt′), *n.* **1.** the part of a state that is farther north or farther from the chief city, esp. the northerly part of New York State. —*adj.* **2.** of or coming from such an area. **3.** located in or characteristic of this part. —*adv.* **4.** in, to, or into the upstate area. [1900–05, *Amer.;* UP- + STATE] —**up′stat′er,** *n.*

up·stream (up′strēm′), *adv.* **1.** toward or in the higher part of a stream; against the current. —*adj.* **2.** directed upstream; situated upstream: *an upstream journey; an upstream hideout.* **3.** *Com.* of or pertaining to the early stages in the operations of a business or industry, as exploration and production in the oil business (opposed to *downstream*). **4.** against or opposite to the direction of transcription, translation, or synthesis of a DNA, RNA, or protein molecule. [1675–85; UP- + STREAM]

up·stretched (up strecht′), *adj.* stretched upward, as the arms. [1555–65; UP- + STRETCH + -ED²]

up·stroke (up′strōk′), *n.* an upward stroke, esp. of a pen or pencil, or of a piston in a vertical cylinder. [1820–30; UP- + STROKE¹]

up·surge (*v.* up sûrj′; *n.* up′sûrj′), *v.,* **-surged, -surg·ing,** *n.* —*v.i.* **1.** to surge up; increase; rise: *Water upsurged. Crime upsurged.* —*n.* **2.** the act of surging up; a large or rapid increase: *an upsurge in sales.* [1915–20; UP- + SURGE]

up·sweep (*v.* up swēp′; *n.* up′swēp′), *v.,* **-swept, -sweep·ing,** *n.* —*v.t.* **1.** to sweep upward. —*v.i.* **2.** to be arranged in an upsweep. —*n.* **3.** a sweeping upward, as an increase in elevation or a steep slope. **4.** a hairdo produced by having the hair combed or brushed upward to the top of the head; an upswept hairdo. **5.** a strongly pronounced rise in activity, as in business. **6.** a curved shape of the lower jaw of some animals. [1885–90; UP- + SWEEP]

up·swell (up swel′), *v.i., v.t.,* **-swelled, -swelled** or **-swol·len, -swell·ing.** to swell up. [1350–1400; ME; see UP-, SWELL]

up·swept (up′swept′), *adj.* **1.** curved or sloped upward: *upswept automobile fenders.* **2.** combed or brushed upward to the top of the head. [1785–95; ptp. of UPSWEEP]

up·swing (*n.* up′swing′; *v.* up swing′), *n., v.,* **-swung, -swing·ing.** —*n.* **1.** an upward swing or swinging movement, as of a pendulum. **2.** a marked increase or improvement: *an upswing in stock prices.* —*v.i.* **3.** to make or undergo an upswing. [1920–25; UP- + SWING¹]

up·sy-dai·sy (up′sē dā′zē), *interj.* (used, as for reassurance, at the moment of lifting a baby up.) Also, **upsadaisy.** [1860–65; cf. earlier *up-a-daisy,* dial. *up-a-day,* perh. UP + (LACK)ADAY, (*lack*)*adaisy; -sy* perh. to be identified with -SY]

up·take (up′tāk′), *n.* **1.** apprehension; understanding or comprehension; mental grasp: *quick on the uptake.* **2.** an act or instance of taking up; a lifting: *the uptake of fertilizer by machines.* **3.** Also called **take-up.** *Mach.* a pipe or passage leading upward from below, as for conducting smoke or a current of air. **4.** *Physiol.* absorption. [1810–20; UP- + TAKE; cf. *take-up*]

up·tear (up târ′), *v.t.,* **-tore, -torn, -tear·ing.** to wrench or tear out by or as if by the roots or foundations; destroy. [1585–95; UP- + TEAR²]

up-tem·po (up′tem′pō), *n., pl.* **-pos, -pi** (-pē). a bouncy, fast tempo in music. [1945–50]

up·throw (*n.* up′thrō′; *v.* up thrō′), *n., v.,* **-threw, -thrown, -throw·ing.** —*n.* **1.** an upheaval, as of the earth's surface. **2.** *Geol.* an upward displacement of rock on one side of a fault. —*v.t.* **3.** to throw or cast up or upward. [1590–1600; UP- + THROW]

up·thrust (up′thrust′), *n.* **1.** a thrust in an upward direction. **2.** a sudden and forceful upward movement, as of a nation's economy or the stock market: *Market observers are hoping the upthrust can be sustained.* **3.** *Geol.* an upheaval. —*v.i.* **4.** to thrust upward: *Frost caused the ground to upthrust.* [1840–50; UP- + THRUST]

up·tick (up′tik′), *n.* **1.** a rise or improvement in business activity, in mood, etc. **2.** *Stock Exchange.* **a.** a selling price that is higher than the last price. **b.** a slight upward trend in price. Cf. **downtick.** [1950–55; UP- + TICK¹]

up·tight (up′tīt′), *adj. Slang.* **1.** tense, nervous, or jittery. **2.** annoyed or angry. **3.** stiffly conventional in manner or attitudes. [1960–65, *Amer.;* UP (perh. as intensifier) + TIGHT] —**up·tight′ness,** *n.*

up·tilt (up tilt′), *v.t.* to tilt up. [1900–05; UP- + TILT¹]

up·time (up′tīm′), *n.* **1.** the time during which a machine or piece of equipment, as a computer, is operating or can be operated. **2.** the time during which an employee is actually working. Cf. **downtime.** [1955–60; UP (in sense "operating") + TIME]

up-to-date (up′tə dāt′), *adj.* **1.** (of persons, buildings, etc.) keeping up with the times, as in outlook, information, ideas, appearance, or style. **2.** in accordance with the latest or newest ideas, standards, techniques, styles, etc.; modern. **3.** extending to the present time; current; including the latest information or facts: *an up-to-date report.* [1865–70] —**up′-to-date′ly,** *adv.* —**up′-to-date′ness,** *n.*

Up·ton (up′tən), *n.* a male given name: from an Old English word meaning "upper town."

up·torn (up tôrn′, -tōrn′), *v.* pp. of **uptear.**

up-to-the-min·ute (up′tə thə min′it), *adj.* extending to the present moment, as information, facts, or style: *an up-to-the-minute news report.* [1910–15]

up·town (*adv., n.* up′toun′; *adj.* up′toun′), *adv.* **1.** to, toward, or in the upper part of a town or city: *He rode uptown on the bus.* —*adj.* **2.** moving toward, situated in, or pertaining to the upper part of a town: *Take the uptown bus.* **3.** of, for, or characteristic of affluent people; elegant, stylish, or luxurious: *uptown fashions; uptown tastes.* —*n.* **4.** the uptown section of a town or city: *Uptown is less crowded.* [1830–40; UP- + TOWN] —**up′town′er,** *n.*

up·trade (up trād′), *v.t.,* **-trad·ed, -trad·ing.** to trade (a piece of equipment, car, etc.) for something similar but of greater value or quality: *to uptrade one's stereo components.* [UP- + TRADE]

up·trend (up′trend′), *n.* a tendency upward or toward growth, esp. in economic development. [1940–45; UP- + TREND]

up·turn (*v.* up tûrn′, up′tûrn′; *n.* up′tûrn′), *v.t.* **1.** to turn up or over: *The farmer upturned clumps of sod with his spade.* **2.** to cause disorder; upheave: *The storm upturned the town.* **3.** to direct or turn upward: *She upturned her face toward heaven and prayed.* —*v.i.* **4.** to turn up or upward: *Her eyes upturned to see his face.* —*n.* **5.** chaos or extreme disorder, as in society; an upheaval. **6.** an upward turn, or a changing and rising movement, as in prices or business. [1300–50; ME: to overturn; see UP-, TURN]

up·turned (up tûrnd′, up′tûrnd′), *adj.* **1.** turned or directed upward: *upturned eyes.* **2.** turned over; upside down: *an upturned canoe.* **3.** having a turned-up end: *an upturned nose.* [1585–95; UP- + TURN + -ED²]

UPU, See **Universal Postal Union.**

up·val·ue (up′val′yo͞o), *v.t.,* **-ued, -u·ing.** **1.** to raise the value of: *to upvalue inventories.* **2.** to increase the exchange value of (a currency). [1965–70; UP- + VALUE] —**up′val·u·a′tion,** *n.*

U.P.W.A., United Packinghouse Workers of America.

up·ward (up′wərd), *adv.* Also, **up′wards.** **1.** toward a higher place or position: *The birds flew upward.* **2.** toward a higher or more distinguished condition, rank, level, etc.: *His employer wishes to move him upward in the company.* **3.** to a greater degree; more: *fourscore and upward.* **4.** toward a large city, the source or origin of a stream, or the interior of a country or region: *They followed the Thames River upward from the North Sea to London.* **5.** in the upper parts; above. **6. upwards of,** more than; above: *My vacation cost me upwards of a thousand dollars.* —*adj.* **7.** moving or tending upward; directed at or situated in a higher place or position. [bef. 900; ME; OE *upweard* (c. D *opwaart*). See UP-, -WARD] —**up′ward·ly,** *adv.* —**up′ward·ness,** *n.*

up′ward mobil′ity. See under **vertical mobility** (def. 1). [1945–50] —**up′wardly mo′bile.**

up·warp (up′wôrp′), *n.* a geologic structure, usually of relatively large dimensions, whose flanks slope gradually away from the center. Also called **dome.** [1915–20; UP- + WARP]

up·well (up wel′), *v.i.* to well up, as water from a spring. [1880–85; UP- + WELL²]

up·well·ing (up wel′ing), *n.* **1.** an act or instance of welling up: *an upwelling of public support; an upwelling of emotion in his voice.* **2.** *Oceanog.* the process by which warm, less-dense surface water is drawn away from along a shore by offshore currents and replaced by cold, denser water brought up from the subsurface. [1850–55; UPWELL + -ING¹]

up·whirl (up hwûrl′, -wûrl′), *v.t.* **1.** to cause (something) to whirl upward. —*v.i.* **2.** to be whirled upward. [1835–45; UP- + WHIRL]

up·wind (*adv., adj.* up′wind′; *n.* up′wind′), *adv.* **1.** toward or against the wind or the direction from which it is blowing: *The hunters stalked upwind.* —*adj.* **2.** moving or situated toward or in the direction from which the wind is blowing: *an upwind leap; the upwind portions of the aircraft.* —*n.* **3.** a wind that blows against one's course or up a slope. [1830–40; UP- + WIND¹]

u quark, *Physics.* See **up quark.** [1975–80]

Ur (ûr, o͝or), *n.* an ancient Sumerian city on the Euphrates, in S Iraq: extensive excavations, esp. of royal tombs.

ur-¹, var. of **uro-¹:** *uranalysis.*

ur-², var. of **uro-²** before a vowel: *urite.*

ur-³, (*sometimes cap.*) a combining form meaning "earliest, original," used in words denoting the primal stage of a historical or cultural entity or phenomenon: *urcivilization; urtext.* [< G *ur-,* MHG, OHG; c. OE *or-*]

u·ra·cil (yo͝or′ə sil), *n. Biochem.* a pyrimidine base, $C_4H_4N_2O_2$, that is one of the fundamental components of RNA, in which it forms base pairs with adenine. *Symbol:* U [1905–10; UR-¹ + AC(ETIC) + -*il,* of uncert. orig.]

u·rae·mi·a (yo͝o rē′mē ə), *n. Pathol.* uremia. —**u·rae′mic,** *adj.*

u·rae·us (yo͝o rē′əs), *n., pl.* **-us·es.** the sacred asp as represented upon the headdress of divinities and royal personages of ancient Egypt, usually directly over the forehead, as an emblem of supreme power. [1825–35; < NL < LGk *ouraîos,* perh. based ult. on Egyptian *y′rt* cobra, altered by assoc. with Gk *ouraîos* of the tail; see URO-²]

U, uraeus

U·ral (yŏŏr′əl), *n.* **1.** a river in the Russian Federation, flowing S from the S Ural Mountains to the Caspian Sea. 1575 mi. (2535 km) long. **2.** a former administrative division comprising a region in the Ural Mountains and its slopes. —*adj.* **3.** of or pertaining to the Ural Mountains or the Ural River.

U·ral-Al·ta·ic (yŏŏr′əl al tā′ik), *adj.* **1.** of or pertaining to the Ural Mountains, on the border between the Russian Federation in Europe and Siberia, and the Altai Mountains, in S Siberia and NW Mongolia, or the country or peoples around them. **2.** of or pertaining to Ural-Altaic. **3.** speaking a Ural-Altaic language. —*n.* **4.** a postulated family of languages comprising Uralic and Altaic.

U·ra·li·an (yŏŏ rā′lē ən, -rāl′yən), *adj.* **1.** of or pertaining to the Ural Mountains or their inhabitants. **2.** Uralic. [1790–1800; URAL + -IAN]

Ura′lian em′erald, demantoid: not a true emerald.

U·ral·ic (yŏŏ ral′ik), *n.* **1.** a family of languages that comprises Finno-Ugric and Samoyed as subfamilies. Hungarian, Finnish, and Estonian belong to Uralic. —*adj.* **2.** Also, **Uralian.** of or pertaining to Uralic. [1860–65; URAL + -IC]

u·ral·ite (yŏŏr′ə līt′), *n. Mineral.* a fibrous, dark-green hornblende formed by the hydrothermal alteration of pyroxene. [1825–35; < G *Uralit,* named after the URAL Mountains, where found; see -ITE[1]] —**u·ral·it·ic** (yŏŏr′ə lit′ik), *adj.*

U′ral Moun′tains, a mountain range in the W Russian Federation, extending N and S from the Arctic Ocean to near the Caspian Sea, forming a natural boundary between Europe and Asia. Highest peak, Mt. Narodnaya, 6214 ft. (1894 m). Also called **U′rals.**

U·ralsk (yŏŏ ralsk′; *Russ.* ōō rälsk′), *n.* a city in W Kazakhstan, on the Ural River. 201,000.

u·ran (yŏŏ ran′), *n.* monitor (def. 13). [< F *ouran, varan* < Ar *waran*]

u·ra·ni·a (yŏŏ rā′nē ə, -rān′yə), *n. Chem.* See **uranium dioxide.** [URANI(UM) + -A[4]]

U·ra·ni·a (yŏŏ rā′nē ə, -rān′yə), *n. Class. Myth.* the Muse of astronomy.

U·ra·ni·an (yŏŏ rā′nē ən, -rān′yən), *adj.* pertaining to the planet Uranus. [1835–45; URAN(US) + -IAN]

u·ran·ic[1] (yŏŏ ran′ik), *adj. Chem.* **1.** of or containing uranium, esp. in the tetravalent state. **2.** containing uranium in a valence state higher than the corresponding uranous compound. [1830–40; URAN(IUM) + -IC]

u·ran·ic[2] (yŏŏ ran′ik), *adj.* of or pertaining to the heavens; astronomical: *uranic principles.* [1855–60; < Gk *ouran(ós)* heaven + -IC]

uran′ic ox′ide, *Chem.* See **uranium dioxide.** [1870–75]

u·ran·i·nite (yŏŏ ran′ə nīt′, -rä′nə-), *n.* a mineral, probably originally uranium dioxide, UO_2, but altered by radioactive decay, and usually containing uranium trioxide, lead, radium, and helium, occurring in several varieties, including pitchblende: the most important ore of uranium. [1875–80; URAN(IUM) + -IN[2] + -ITE[1]]

u·ra·nis·cus (yŏŏr′ə nis′kəs), *n., pl.* **-nis·ci** (-nis′ī). *Archit.* a starlike ornament, as in a coffer of a ceiling. [< Gk *ouranískos* ceiling, equiv. to *ouran(ós)* heaven + *-iskos* dim. suffix]

u·ra·nite (yŏŏr′ə nīt′), *n. Mineral.* any of the uranium phosphates, as autunite or torbernite. [1785–95; < G *Uranit.* See URANIUM, -ITE[1]] —**u·ra·nit·ic** (yŏŏr′ə nit′ik), *adj.*

u′ranite group′, the mineralogical group including uranites and related minerals.

u·ra·ni·um (yŏŏ rā′nē əm), *n. Chem.* a white, lustrous, radioactive, metallic element, occurring in pitchblende, and having compounds that are used in photography and in coloring glass. The 235 isotope is used in atomic and hydrogen bombs and as a fuel in nuclear reactors. *Symbol:* U; *at. wt.:* 238.03; *at. no.:* 92; *sp. gr.:* 19.07. [1790–1800; < NL; see URANUS, -IUM]

uranium 235, *Chem.* the radioactive uranium isotope having a mass number of 235, comprising 0.715 percent of natural uranium. When bombarded with neutrons it undergoes fission with the release of energy. Also called **U-235, U 235, actinouranium.** [1935–40]

uranium 238, *Chem.* the radioactive uranium isotope having a mass number 238, comprising 99.28 percent of natural uranium: used chiefly in nuclear reactors as a source of the fissionable isotope plutonium 239. Also called **U-238, U 238.** [1940–45]

uranium 239, *Chem.* the uranium isotope with a mass number 239. It is artificially produced by the neutron bombardment of uranium 238. Also called **U-239, U 239.**

ura′nium dat′ing, a method of dating archaeological or geological specimens by determining the decay activity of the uranium in a given sample.

ura′nium diox′ide, *Chem.* a black, crystalline compound, UO_2, insoluble in water, used in nuclear fuel rods, in ceramics, and pigments. Also called **urania, uranic oxide, uranium oxide.**

ura′nium hexafluor′ide, *Chem.* a colorless, water-insoluble, crystalline, volatile solid, UF_6, used in its gaseous state in separating uranium 235 from uranium. [1940–45]

ura′nium ox′ide, *Chem.* **1.** any of the compounds of uranium and oxygen, as UO_2, UO_3, U_4O_9, or U_3O_8. **2.** See **uranium dioxide.** Cf. **yellowcake.** [1885–90]

ura′nium se′ries, *Chem.* the radioactive series that starts with uranium 238 and ends with a stable isotope of lead of mass number 206. Also, **u·ra′ni·um-ra′di·um se′ries** (yŏŏ rā′nē əm rā′dē əm).

urano-, a combining form meaning "heavens," used in the formation of compound words: *uranography; uranometry.* [< Gk, comb. form of *ouranós* heavens, heaven]

u·ra·nog·ra·phy (yŏŏr′ə nog′rə fē), *n.* the branch of astronomy concerned with the description and mapping of the heavens, and esp. of the fixed stars. Also called **uranology.** [1640–50; < Gk *ouranographía.* See URANO-, -GRAPHY] —**u′ra·nog′ra·pher, u′ra·nog′ra·phist,** *n.* —**u·ra·no·graph·ic** (yŏŏr′ə nə graf′ik), **u′ra·no·graph′i·cal,** *adj.*

u·ra·nol·o·gy (yŏŏr′ə nol′ə jē), *n., pl.* **-gies.** *Astron.* **1.** uranography. **2.** a treatise on the celestial bodies. [1725–35; URANO- + -LOGY] —**u·ra·no·log·i·cal** (yŏŏr′ənl oj′i kəl), *adj.*

u·ra·nom·e·try (yŏŏr′ə nom′i trē), *n. Astron.* **1.** a chart of the positions of the heavenly bodies on the celestial sphere. **2.** the measurement of the positions of heavenly bodies. [1705–15; < NL *uranometria.* See URANO-, -METRY] —**u·ra·no·met·ri·cal** (yŏŏr′ə nə me′tri kəl), *adj.*

u·ra·nos·co·pid (yŏŏr′ə nos′kə pid), *n.* **1.** any fish of the family Uranoscopidae, comprising the stargazers. —*adj.* **2.** belonging or pertaining to the family Uranoscopidae. [< NL *Uranoscopidae* name of the family, equiv. to *Uranoscop(us)* a genus (L: kind of fish with upturned eyes < Gk *ouranoskópos* lit., observing the heavens; see URANO-, -SCOPE) + *-idae* -IDAE; see -ID[2]]

u·ra·nous (yŏŏr′ə nəs, yŏŏ rā′-), *adj. Chem.* containing trivalent uranium. [1835–45; URAN(IUM) + -OUS]

U·ra·nus (yŏŏr′ə nəs, yŏŏ rā′-), *n.* **1.** *Astron.* the planet seventh in order from the sun, having an equatorial diameter of 32,600 miles (56,460 km), a mean distance from the sun of 1,784 million miles (2,871 million km), a period of revolution of 84.07 years, and 15 moons. See table under **planet. 2.** Also, **Ouranos.** *Class. Myth.* the personification of Heaven and ruler of the world, son and husband of Gaea (Earth) and father of the Titans, who was castrated and dethroned by his youngest son, Cronus, at the instigation of Gaea.

u·ra·nyl (yŏŏr′ə nil), *n. Chem.* the bivalent ion UO_2^{+2}, or the group UO_2, which forms salts with acids. [1840–50; URAN(IUM) + -YL] —**u′ra·nyl′ic,** *adj.*

U·rar·ti·an (ŏŏ rär′tē ən), *adj.* **1.** of or pertaining to Urartu, its people, or their language. —*n.* **2.** a native or inhabitant of Urartu. **3.** the non-Semitic, non-Indo-European language of Urartu, written in a cuneiform syllabic script. [URART(U) + -IAN]

U·rar·tu (ŏŏ rär′tōō), *n.* an ancient kingdom, c1270–750 B.C., in E Turkey, on the shore of Lake Van: often invaded by Assyria.

u·rase (yŏŏr′ās, -āz), *n. Biochem.* urease.

u·rate (yŏŏr′āt), *n. Chem.* a salt of uric acid. [1790–1800; UR(IC ACID) + -ATE[2]] —**u·rat·ic** (yŏŏ rat′ik), *adj.*

U·ra·wa (ŏŏ rä′wä; *Eng.* ŏŏ rä′wə), *n.* a city in E Honshu, in Japan. 358,180.

urb (ûrb), *n. Informal.* an urban area. [1965–70; back formation from SUBURB]

ur·ban (ûr′bən), *adj.* **1.** of, pertaining to, or designating a city or town. **2.** living in a city. **3.** characteristic of or accustomed to cities; citified: *He is an urban type.* [1610–20; < L *urbānus,* equiv. to *urb-* (s. of *urbs*) city + *-ānus* -AN]

Urban I (ûr′bən), **Saint,** pope A.D. 222–230.

Urban II, (*Odo* or *Otho*) c1042–99, French ecclesiastic: pope 1088–99.

Urban III, (*Uberto Crivelli*) Italian ecclesiastic: pope 1185–87.

Urban IV, (*Jacques Pantaléon*) died 1264, French ecclesiastic: pope 1261–64.

Urban V, (*Guillaume de Grimoard*) c1310–70, French ecclesiastic: pope 1362–70.

Urban VI, (*Bartolomeo Prignano*) c1318–89, Italian ecclesiastic: pope 1378–89.

Urban VII, (*Giovanni Battista Castagna*) 1521–90, Italian ecclesiastic: pope 1590.

Urban VIII, (*Maffeo Barberini*) 1568–1644, Italian ecclesiastic: pope 1623–44.

Ur·ban·a (ûr ban′ə), *n.* **1.** a city in E Illinois, adjoining Champaign. 35,978. **2.** a city in W Ohio. 10,762.

Ur·ban·dale (ûr′bən dāl′), *n.* a town in central Iowa. 17,869.

ur′ban dis′trict, a minor administrative division in England, Wales, and Northern Ireland, with local self-government by a district council, but lacking the charter of a borough.

ur·bane (ûr bān′), *adj.* **1.** having the polish and suavity regarded as characteristic of sophisticated social life in major cities: *an urbane manner.* **2.** reflecting elegance, sophistication, etc., esp. in expression: *He maintained an urbane tone in his letters.* [1525–35; (< MF *urbain*) < L *urbānus* (see URBAN; for difference in stress and second syllable cf. HUMAN, HUMANE)] —**ur·bane′ly,** *adv.* —**ur·bane′ness,** *n.*
—**Syn. 1.** suave, cosmopolitan.

ur′ban guerril′la, a member of any underground political group engaged in terrorism or violence in urban areas, esp. during the 1970's. [1965–70]

ur′ban home′steading, homesteading (def. 2). [1970–75; HOMESTEAD + -ING[1]] —**ur′ban home′steader.**

ur·ban·ism (ûr′bə niz′əm), *n.* **1.** the way of life of people who live in a large city. **2.** urbanization. **3.** See **city planning.** [1885–90; URBAN + -ISM, modeled on F *urbanisme*]

ur·ban·ist (ûr′bə nist), *n.* a person who is a specialist in urban planning. [1515–25; URBAN + -IST]

ur·ban·is·tic (ûr′bə nis′tik), *adj.* of or pertaining to urbanism. [URBAN(ISM) + -ISTIC] —**ur′ban·is′ti·cal·ly,** *adv.*

ur·ban·ite (ûr′bə nīt′), *n.* a resident of a city or urban community. [1895–1900; URBAN + -ITE[1]]

ur·ban·i·ty (ûr ban′i tē), *n., pl.* **-ties. 1.** the quality of being urbane; refined courtesy or politeness; suavity: *He was the last word in urbanity.* **2. urbanities,** civilities or amenities. **3.** the quality or state of being urban. [1525–35; < L *urbānitās.* See URBANE, -ITY]

ur·ban·ize (ûr′bə nīz′), *v.t.,* **-ized, -iz·ing.** to make or cause to become urban, as a locality. Also, *esp. Brit.,* **ur′ban·ise′.** [1635–45; URBAN + -IZE] —**ur′ban·i·za′·tion,** *n.*

ur·ban·ol·o·gy (ûr′bə nol′ə jē), *n.* the study of urban problems, esp. as a social science. [1960–65; URBAN + -O- + -LOGY] —**ur′ban·ol′o·gist,** *n.*

ur′ban plan′ning. See **city planning.**

ur′ban renew′al, the rehabilitation of city areas by renovating or replacing dilapidated buildings with new housing, public buildings, parks, roadways, industrial areas, etc., often in accordance with comprehensive plans. Also called **ur′ban redevel′opment.** [1950–55]

ur′ban sociol′ogy, the sociological study of cities and their role in the development of society.

ur′ban sprawl′, the uncontrolled spread of urban development into neighboring regions. [1955–60]

ur·bi·cul·ture (ûr′bi kul′chər), *n.* the way of life characteristic of cities. [1950–55; < L *urb(s)* city + -I- + CULTURE]

ur·bi et or·bi (ŏŏr′bē et ôr′bē), *Latin.* to the city (Rome) and the world: the form of address of papal bulls.

ur·ce·o·late (ûr′sē ə lit, -lāt′), *adj.* shaped like a pitcher; swelling out like the body of a pitcher and contracted at the orifice, as a corolla. [1750–60; < NL *urceolātus,* equiv. to L *urceol(us),* dim. of *urceus* pitcher + *-ātus* -ATE[1]]

ur·chin (ûr′chin), *n.* **1.** a mischievous boy. **2.** any small boy or youngster. **3.** See **sea urchin. 4.** either of two small rollers covered with card clothing used in conjunction with the cylinder in carding. **5.** *Chiefly Brit. Dial.* a hedgehog. **6.** *Obs.* an elf or mischievous sprite. [1300–50; ME *urchun, urchon* hedgehog < ONF *(h)erichon,* OF *heriçun* < VL **hēriciōn-* (s. of **hēriciō*), equiv. to L *ēric(ius)* hedgehog + *-iōn-* -ION]
—**Syn. 1.** rascal, scamp.

urd (ŏŏrd, ûrd), *n.* a plant, *Vigna mungo,* of the legume family, widely cultivated in tropical Asia for its edible seeds and for forage. Also called **gram, black gram.** [< Hindi *urd, urdh, urad, uṛad,* Prakrit *uḍidda-* a pulse]

Urd (ŏŏrd), *n. Scand. Myth.* See under **Norn.** [< ON *Urthr,* c. OE *wyrd* (see WEIRD), deriv. of the Gmc root of ON *vertha* to become, G *werden;* see WORTH[2]]

Ur·du (ŏŏr′dōō, ûr′-; ŏŏr dōō′, ûr-), *n.* one of the official languages of Pakistan, a language derived from Hindustani, used by Muslims, and written with Persian-Arabic letters. [< Urdu, Hindi *urdū,* extracted from Pers *zabān i urdū* lit., language of the camp (ult. < Turkic; see HORDE)]

URE, Undergraduate Record Examination.

-ure, an abstract-noun suffix of action, result, and instrument, occurring in loanwords from French and Latin: *pressure; legislature.* [< F *-ure* < L *-ūra*]

u·re·a (yŏŏ rē′ə, yŏŏr′ē ə), *n.* **1.** *Biochem.* a compound, $CO(NH_2)_2$, occurring in urine and other body fluids as a product of protein metabolism. **2.** *Chem.* a water-soluble powder form of this compound, obtained by the reaction of liquid ammonia and liquid carbon dioxide: used as a fertilizer, animal feed, in the synthesis of plastics, resins, and barbiturates, and in medicine as a diuretic and in the diagnosis of kidney function. Also called **carbamide.** [1800–10; < NL < F *urée;* ult. < Gk *oûron* urine or *oureîn* to urinate; see URO-[1]] —**u·re′al, u·re′ic,** *adj.*

ure′a cy′cle, *Biochem.* a metabolic process by which ammonia derived from amino acids is converted into urea in the liver. Also called **Krebs urea cycle.**

u·re′a-form·al′de·hyde res′in (yŏŏ rē′ə fôr mal′də hīd′, -fər-, yŏŏr′ē ə-), *Chem.* any of a group of resins formed by the interaction of urea and formaldehyde under conditions that include heat and pH control: used chiefly in the manufacture of buttons, baking enamels, and for making fabrics wrinkle-resistant. [1940–45]

u·re·ase (yŏŏr′ē ās′, -āz′), *n. Biochem.* an enzyme that changes urea into ammonium carbonate, occurring in bacteria, fungi, etc. [1895–1900; URE(A) + -ASE]

u·re·din·i·um (yŏŏr′i din′ē əm), *n., pl.* **-din·i·a** (-din′ē ə). *Mycol.* the fruiting body of the rust fungi that bears urediospores. Also, **uredium.** Also called **uredosorus.** [1905–10; < NL < *ūrēdin-* (s. of L *ūrēdō;* see UREDO) + *-ium* -IUM] —**u′re·din′i·al,** *adj.*

u·re·di·o·spore (yŏŏ rē′dē ə spôr′, -spōr′), *n. Mycol.* the spore of the rust fungi that appears between the aeciospore and the teliospore, commonly the summer spore. Also, **u·re·do·spore** (yŏŏ rē′də spôr′, -spōr′). [1870–75; UREDI(UM) + -O- + SPORE]

u·re·di·um (yŏŏ rē′dē əm), *n., pl.* **-di·a** (-dē ə). *Mycol.* uredinium. [< NL; see UREDO, -IUM] —**u·re′di·al,** *adj.*

u·re·do (yŏŏ rē′dō), *n. Pathol.* a skin irritation; hives; urticaria. [1700–10; < L *ūrēdō* blast, blight, burning itch, equiv. to *ūr(ere)* to burn + *-ēdō* n. suffix]

u·re·do·so·rus (yŏŏ rē′də sôr′əs, -sōr′-), *n., pl.* **-so·ri** (-sôr′ī, -sōr′ī). *Mycol.* uredinium. [UREDO + SORUS]

u·re·ide (yŏŏr′ē īd′, -id), *n. Chem.* an acyl urea. [1855–60; URE(A) + -IDE]

u·re·mi·a (yŏŏ rē′mē ə), *n. Pathol.* a condition resulting from the retention in the blood of constituents normally excreted in the urine. Also, **uraemia.** [1855–60; < NL; see UR-[1], -EMIA]

u·re·mic (yŏŏ rē′mik), *adj. Pathol.* **1.** pertaining to uremia. **2.** afflicted with uremia. Also, **uraemic.** [< NL; see UREMIA, -IC]

CONCISE PRONUNCIATION KEY: *act, cāpe, dâre, pärt; set, ēqual; if, īce; ox, ōver, ôrder, oil, bŏŏk, bōōt, out; up, ûrge; child; sing; shoe; thin, that;* zh as in *treasure.* ə = *a* as in *alone, e* as in *system, i* as in *easily, o* as in *gallop, u* as in *circus;* ᵊ as in *fire* (fīᵊr), *hour* (ouᵊr). l and n can serve as syllabic consonants, as in *cradle* (krād′l), and *button* (but′n). See the full key inside the front cover.

u•re•na (yo͝o rē′nə), *n.* any tropical plant or shrub belonging to the genus *Urena,* of the mallow family, having clusters of small, yellow flowers, esp. *U. lobata,* which yields a bast fiber. [< NL, prob. < Malayalam *uriñña* name for various vitaceous or sapindaceous plants]

-uret, a suffix used in chemical terminology, identical in sense with **-ide,** which has now generally replaced it: *carburet* (now *carbide*); *phosphuret* (now *phosphide*). [< NL *-urētum, -ōretum,* of uncert. orig.]

u•re•ter (yo͝o rē′tər), *n. Anat., Zool.* a muscular duct or tube conveying the urine from a kidney to the bladder or cloaca. See diag. under **kidney.** [1570–80; < NL < Gk *ourētḗr,* equiv. to *ourē-* (verbid s. of *oureîn* to URINATE) + *-tēr* n. suffix] —**u•re′ter•al, u•re•ter•ic** (yo͝or′i ter′ik), *adj.*

u•re•ter•o•li•thot•o•my (yo͝o rē′tə rō li thot′ə mē), *n., pl.* **-mies.** *Surg.* incision of a ureter for removal of a calculus. [1890–95; URETER + -O- + LITHOTOMY]

u•re•ter•os•to•my (yo͝o rē′tə ros′tə mē), *n., pl.* **-mies.** *Surg.* **1.** the construction of an artificial opening from the ureter through the abdominal wall or the flanks, permitting the passage of urine. **2.** the opening so constructed. [1900–05; URETER + -O- + -STOMY]

u•re•thane (yo͝or′ə thān′), *n. Chem.* **1.** any derivative of carbamic acid having the formula CH_2NO_2R. **2.** Also called **ethyl carbamate, ethyl urethane.** a white, crystalline, water-soluble powder, $C_3H_7NO_2$: used chiefly as a solvent, in organic synthesis, as a fungicide and pesticide, and formerly in cancer treatment. Also, **u•re•than** (yo͝or′ə than′). [< F *uréthane* (1833); see UREA, ETHANE]

urethr-, var. of **urethro-** before a vowel: *urethrectomy.*

u•re•thra (yo͝o rē′thrə), *n., pl.* **-thrae** (-thrē), **-thras.** *Anat.* the membranous tube that extends from the urinary bladder to the exterior and that in the male conveys semen as well as urine. [1625–35; < LL < Gk *ourḗthra,* equiv. to *ourē-* (see URETER) + *-thra* n. suffix] —**u•re′thral,** *adj.*

u•re•threc•to•my (yo͝or′ə threk′tə mē), *n., pl.* **-mies.** *Surg.* excision or removal of part or all of the urethra. [1890–95; URETHR- + -ECTOMY]

u•re•thri•tis (yo͝or′ə thrī′tis), *n. Pathol.* inflammation of the urethra. [1815–25; < NL; see URETHR-, -ITIS] —**u•re•thrit•ic** (yo͝or′ə thrit′ik), *adj.*

urethro-, a combining form representing **urethra** in compound words: *urethroscope.* Also, *esp. before a vowel,* **urethr-.**

u•re•thro•scope (yo͝o rē′thrə skōp′), *n. Med.* an apparatus for observing the urethra. [1865–70; URETHRO- + -SCOPE] —**u•re•thro•scop•ic** (yo͝o rē′thrə skop′ik), *adj.*

u•re•thros•co•py (yo͝or′ə thros′kə pē), *n. Med.* observation of the urethra by a urethroscope. [1885–90; URETHRO- + -SCOPY]

u•re•thros•to•my (yo͝or′ə thros′tə mē), *n., pl.* **-mies.** *Surg.* **1.** the construction of an artificial opening from the urethra through the perineum, permitting the passage of urine. **2.** the opening so constructed. [1895–1900; URETHRO- + -STOMY]

u•re•throt•o•my (yo͝or′ə throt′ə mē), *n., pl.* **-mies.** *Surg.* an operation to cut a stricture of the urethra. [1840–50; URETHRO- + -TOMY]

u•ret•ic (yo͝o ret′ik), *adj.* of, pertaining to, or occurring in the urine. [1840–50; < LL *ūrēticus* < Gk *ourētikós,* equiv. to *ourē-* (see URETER) + *-tikos* -TIC]

U•re•we (o͞o rä′wä), *adj. Archaeol.* of or pertaining to an early Iron Age pottery tradition of central Africa beginning in the second half of the first millennium B.C. and associated with the spread of ironworking and possibly cattle raising and the Bantu language. [after the type site in Kenya, near the NE shore of Lake Victoria]

U•rey (yo͝or′ē), *n.* **Harold Clay•ton** (klāt′n), 1893–1981, U.S. chemist: Nobel prize 1934.

Ur•fa (o͝or fä′), *n.* a city in SE Turkey, E of the Euphrates River: on the site of ancient Edessa. 132,982.

Ur•ga (o͝or′gä), *n.* former name of **Ulan Bator.**

urge (ûrj), *v.,* **urged, urg•ing,** *n.* —*v.t.* **1.** to push or force along; impel with force or vigor: *to urge the cause along.* **2.** to drive with incitement to speed or effort: *to urge dogs on with shouts.* **3.** to press, push, or hasten (the course, activities, etc.): *to urge one's escape.* **4.** to impel, constrain, or move to some action: *urged by necessity.* **5.** to endeavor to induce or persuade, as by entreaties; entreat or exhort earnestly: *to urge a person to greater caution.* **6.** to press (something) upon the attention: *to urge a claim.* **7.** to insist on, allege, or assert with earnestness: *to urge the need of haste.* **8.** to press by persuasion or recommendation, as for acceptance, performance, or use; recommend or advocate earnestly: *to urge a plan of action.* —*v.i.* **9.** to exert a driving or impelling force; give an impulse to haste or action: *Hunger urges.* **10.** to make entreaties or earnest recommendations. **11.** to press arguments or allegations, as against a person, action, or cause: *The senator urged against the confirmation of the appointment.* —*n.* **12.** an act of urging; impelling action, influence, or force; impulse. **13.** an involuntary, natural, or instinctive impulse: *the sex urge.* [1550–60; < L *urgēre* to press, force, drive, urge] —**urg′ing•ly,** *adv.*
—**Syn. 4.** incite, goad, stimulate, spur. **7.** aver, asseverate. —**Ant. 1–3.** deter. **4, 5.** discourage.

Ur•gel (o͝or hel′), *n.* a town in NE Spain, SSW of Andorra: cathedral. 8007. Also called **Seo de Urgel.**

ur•gen•cy (ûr′jən sē), *n., pl.* **-cies. 1.** urgent character; imperativeness; insistence; importunateness. **2. urgencies,** urgent requirements or needs. [1530–40; < LL *urgentia* pressure; see URGENT, -ENCY]

CONCISE ETYMOLOGY KEY: <, descended or borrowed from; >, whence; b., blend of, blended; c., cognate with; cf., compare; deriv., derivative; equiv., equivalent; imit., imitative; obl., oblique; r., replacing; s., stem; sp., spelling, spelled; resp., respelling, respelled; trans., translation; ?, origin unknown; *, unattested; ‡, probably earlier than. See the full key inside the front cover.

ur•gent (ûr′jənt), *adj.* **1.** compelling or requiring immediate action or attention; imperative; pressing: *an urgent matter.* **2.** insistent or earnest in solicitation; importunate, as a person: *an urgent pleader.* **3.** expressed with insistence, as requests or appeals: *an urgent tone of voice.* [1490–1500; < L *urgent-* (s. of *urgēns*), prp. of *urgēre* to URGE; see -ENT] —**ur′gent•ly,** *adv.*

urg•er (ûr′jər), *n.* **1.** a person or thing that urges. **2.** *Australian Slang.* **a.** a horse-racing tipster; tout. **b.** a person who takes advantage of others; confidence man. [1565–75; URGE + -ER[1]]

ur•gi•cen•ter (ûr′jə sen′tər), *n.* a clinic or facility where a person can get immediate medical help in an emergency or treatment for a minor illness or injury. [1980–85; URG(ENT) + -I- + CENTER]

-urgy, a combining form occurring in loanwords from Greek, where it meant "work" (*dramaturgy*): on this model, used in the formation of compound words (*metallurgy*). [< Gk *-ourgia,* akin to *érgon* to WORK]

Ur•hei•mat (o͝or′hī′mät; *Ger.* o͞or′hī′mät), *n.* the primeval habitation of a people, esp. the prehistoric homeland of the speakers of a protolanguage. [1930–35; < G, equiv. to *ur-* UR- + *Heimat* home, homeland]

U•ri (*Ger.* o͞o′rē; *Eng.* o͝or′ē), *n.* a canton in central Switzerland. 33,400; 415 sq. mi. (1075 sq. km). *Cap.:* Altdorf.

-uria, a combining form with the meanings "presence in the urine" of that specified by the initial element (*albuminuria; pyuria*), "condition of the urinary tract," "tendency to urinate," as specified (*polyuria*). [< Gk *-ouria.* See URO-[1], -IA]

U•ri•ah (yo͝o rī′ə), *n.* **1.** Also, *Douay Bible,* **U•ri•as** (yo͝o rī′əs). Also called **Uri′ah the Hit′tite.** the husband of Bathsheba, and an officer in David's army. II Sam. 11. **2.** a male given name: from a Hebrew word meaning "God is light."

Uri′ah Heep′ (hēp), the hypocritical and villainous clerk in Dickens' *David Copperfield.*

ur•i•al (o͝or′ē əl), *n.* a wild, bearded sheep, *Ovis vignei,* of southern Asia, having a reddish coat. [1885–90; < Punjabi *hureāl*]

u•ric (yo͝or′ik), *adj.* of, pertaining to, contained in, or derived from urine. [1790–1800; UR-[1] + -IC]

uric-, var. of **urico-,** esp. before a vowel.

u′ric ac′id, 1. *Biochem.* a compound, $C_5H_4N_4O_3$, present in mammalian urine in small amounts, and the principal nitrogenous component of the excrement of reptiles and birds, that in the form of its salts occurs in the joints in gout and as the major constituent of kidney stones. **2.** *Chem.* a white, crystalline, odorless, tasteless, very slightly water-soluble powder form of this compound, obtained chiefly from urine or bird excrement or synthesized, used chiefly in organic synthesis. [1790–1800] —**u′ric-ac′id,** *adj.*

u•ric•ac•i•de•mi•a (yo͝or′ik as′i dē′mē ə), *n. Med.* lithemia. [1890–95; URIC ACID + -EMIA]

u•ri•col•y•sis (yo͝or′i kol′ə sis), *n. Biochem.* the decomposition of uric acid. [URIC + -O- + -LYSIS] —**u•ri•co•lyt•ic** (yo͝or′i kō lit′ik), *adj.*

u•ri•dine (yo͝or′i dēn′, -din), *n. Biochem.* a ribonucleoside composed of ribose and uracil.

U•ri•el (yo͝or′ē əl), *n.* one of the archangels. II Esdras 4.

U•rim and Thum•mim (yo͝or′im, o͝or′-; thum′im, to͝om′-), *Judaism.* objects, possibly made of metal or precious stones and inscribed with symbols, worn in the breastplate of the high priest and used, perhaps like lots, to determine God's response to a question answerable by "yes" or "no." Ex. 28:30. [1530–40; partial trans. of Heb *ūrīm wəthummīm*]

u•ri•nal (yo͝or′ə nl), *n.* **1.** a flushable fixture, as in a public lavatory, used by men for urinating. **2.** a building or enclosure containing such fixtures. **3.** a receptacle for urine, as of a bedridden person. [1225–75; ME < OF < LL *ūrīnāle,* neut. of *ūrīnālis* of urine. See URINE, -AL[2]]

u•ri•nal•y•sis (yo͝or′ə nal′ə sis), *n., pl.* **-ses** (-sēz′). *Med.* an examination of the urine to determine the general health of the body and, specifically, kidney function, usually including measurement of pH, tests for protein, glucose, ketones, and blood, and microscopic evaluation of sediment obtained by centrifugation. [1885–90; URINE + (AN)ALYSIS]

u•ri•nar•y (yo͝or′ə ner′ē), *adj., n., pl.* **-nar•ies.** —*adj.* **1.** of or pertaining to urine. **2.** pertaining to the organs secreting and discharging urine. —*n. Archaic.* **3.** urinal. [1570–80; < NL *ūrīnārius.* See URINE, -ARY]

u′rinary blad′der, *Anat., Zool.* a distensible, muscular and membranous sac, in which the urine is retained until it is discharged from the body. Also called **bladder.** [1720–30]

u′rinary cal′culus, *Pathol.* a calcareous concretion in the urinary tract. [1785–95]

u′rinary tract′ infec′tion, infection of any part of the urinary tract, esp. the urethra or bladder, usually caused by a bacterium, *Escherichia coli,* and often precipitated by increased sexual activity, vaginitis, enlargement of the prostate, or stress. *Abbr.:* UTI

u•ri•nate (yo͝or′ə nāt′), *v.i.,* **-nat•ed, -nat•ing.** to pass or discharge urine. [1590–1600; < ML *ūrīnātus,* ptp. of *ūrīnāre,* equiv. to L *ūrīn(a)* URINE + *-ātus* -ATE[1]] —**u′ri•na′tion,** *n.* —**u′ri•na′tive,** *adj.*

u•rine (yo͝or′in), *n.* the liquid-to-semisolid waste matter excreted by the kidneys, in humans being a yellowish, slightly acid, watery fluid. [1275–1325; ME < OF < L *ūrīna*]

u′rine anal′ysis, urinalysis. [1880–85]

u•ri•nif•er•ous (yo͝or′ə nif′ər əs), *adj.* conveying urine. [1735–45; URINE + -I- + -FEROUS]

urinif′erous tu′bule, a urine-bearing tubule in a nephron of a kidney. [1855–65]

urino-, a combining form of **urine:** *urinoscopy.* [< L *ūrīn(a)* URINE + -O-]

u•ri•no•gen•i•tal (yo͝or′ə nō jen′i tl), *adj.* genitourinary. [1830–40; URINO- + GENITAL]

u•ri•nom•e•ter (yo͝or′ə nom′i tər), *n.* a device for assessing the specific gravity of urine; a hydrometer for use on urine specimens. [1835–45; URINO- + -METER]

u•ri•nos•co•py (yo͝or′ə nos′kə pē), *n. Med.* uroscopy. [1830–40; URINO- + -SCOPY]

u•ri•nous (yo͝or′ə nəs), *adj.* of, pertaining to, resembling, or having the odor or qualities of urine. Also, **u•ri•nose** (yo͝or′ə nōs′). [1635–45; < NL *ūrīnōsus.* See URINE, -OUS]

Ur•mi•a (o͝or′mē ə), *n.* **Lake,** a salt lake in NW Iran. ab. 2000 sq. mi. (5180 sq. km). Also called **Lake Urumiyeh.**

urn (ûrn), *n.* **1.** a large or decorative vase, esp. one with an ornamental foot or pedestal. **2.** a vase for holding the ashes of the cremated dead. **3.** a large metal container with a spigot, used for making or serving tea or coffee in quantity. **4.** *Bot.* the spore-bearing part of the capsule of a moss, between lid and seta. [1325–75; ME *urne* < L *urna* earthen vessel for ashes, water, etc., akin to *urceus* pitcher, Gk *hýrchē* jar] —**urn′like′,** *adj.*

urn (def. 1)

Ur-Nam•mu (o͝or′nä′mo͞o), *n.* king of the Sumerian city-state of Ur c2000 B.C.

urn•field (ûrn′fēld′), *n.* a Bronze Age cemetery in which the ashes of the dead were buried in urns. [1885–90; URN + FIELD]

uro-[1], a combining form meaning "urine," used in the formation of compound words: *urology.* Also, *esp. before a vowel,* **ur-.** [< Gk, comb. form of *oûron* urine]

uro-[2], a combining form meaning "tail," used in the formation of compound words: *uropod.* Also, *esp. before a vowel,* **ur-.** [< NL *ūro-,* comb. form repr. Gk *ourá*]

u•ro•chord (yo͝or′ə kôrd′), *n. Zool.* the notochord of an ascidian or tunicate, more conspicuous in the larva than in the adult and confined chiefly to the caudal region. [1875–80; URO-[2] + CHORD[1]] —**u′ro•chor′dal,** *adj.*

u•ro•chor•date (yo͝or′ə kôr′dāt), *Zool.* —*adj.* **1.** having a urochord. —*n.* **2.** a urochordate animal. [1945–50; < NL *Urochordata;* see URO-[2], CHORD[1], -ATA[1]]

u•ro•chrome (yo͝or′ə krōm′), *n. Biochem.* a yellow-colored pigment that gives the color to urine. [1860–65; URO-[1] + CHROME]

Ur′ of the Chal•dees′ (kal dēz′, kal′dēz), the city where Abraham was born, sometimes identified with the Sumerian city of Ur. Gen. 11:28, 31; 15:7; Neh. 9:7.

u•ro•gen•i•tal (yo͝or′ō jen′i tl), *adj.* genitourinary. [1840–50; URO-[1] + GENITAL]

u•rog•e•nous (yo͝o roj′ə nəs), *adj. Physiol.* **1.** secreting or producing urine. **2.** contained in urine. [URO-[1] + -GENOUS]

u•ro•ki•nase (yo͝or′ə kī′nās, -nāz), *n. Biochem., Pharm.* an enzyme, present in the blood and urine of mammals, that activates plasminogen and is used medicinally to dissolve blood clots. [1955–60; URO-[1] + KINASE]

u•ro•lith (yo͝or′ə lith), *n. Pathol.* a urinary calculus. [1895–1900; URO-[1] + -LITH] —**u′ro•lith′ic,** *adj.*

u•ro•li•thi•a•sis (yo͝or′ō li thī′ə sis), *n. Pathol.* a diseased condition marked by the formation of stones in the urinary tract. [1855–60; URO-[1] + LITHIASIS]

u•rol•o•gy (yo͝o rol′ə jē), *n.* the scientific, clinical, and esp. surgical aspects of the study of the urine and the genitourinary tract in health and disease. [1745–55; URO-[1] + -LOGY] —**u•ro•log•ic** (yo͝or′ə loj′ik), **u′ro•log′i•cal,** *adj.* —**u•rol′o•gist,** *n.*

u•ro•mere (yo͝or′ə mēr′), *n.* any segment of the abdomen of an arthropod. [1895–1900; URO-[2] + -MERE] —**u•ro•mer•ic** (yo͝or′ə mer′ik), *adj.*

u•ron′ic ac′id (yo͝o ron′ik), *Biochem.* any of a group of organic acids, as glucuronic acid, derived from oxidation of aldose sugars and occurring in urine. [1920–25; < Gk *oûron* urine (cf. URO-[1]) + -IC]

u•ro•pod (yo͝or′ə pod′), *n.* an abdominal limb of an arthropod, esp. one of those on either side of the telson, as in a lobster. [1885–90; URO-[2] + -POD] —**u•rop•o•dal** (yo͝o rop′ə dl), **u•rop′o•dous,** *adj.*

u•ro•pyg•i•al (yo͝or′ə pij′ē əl), *adj. Ornith.* of or pertaining to the uropygium. [1865–70; UROPYGI(UM) + -AL[1]]

uropyg′ial gland′, *Ornith.* a gland opening on the back at the base of the tail in most birds that secretes an oily fluid used by the bird in preening its feathers. Also called **oil gland, preen gland.** [1865–70]

u•ro•pyg•i•um (yo͝or′ə pij′ē əm), *n. Ornith.* the projecting terminal portion of a bird's body, from which the tail feathers spring. [1805–15; < NL < Gk *ouropýgion,* var. (with *ouro-* URO-[2]) of *orropýgion,* equiv. to *orro-,* comb. form of *órros* sacral bone + *pȳg(ḗ)* rump, buttocks + *-ion* dim. suffix]

u•ros•co•py (yo͝o ros′kə pē), *n. Med.* inspection or analysis of the urine as a means of diagnosis. Also, **urinoscopy.** [1640–50; URO-[1] + -SCOPY] —**u•ro•scop•ic** (yo͝or′ə skop′ik), *adj.* —**u•ros′co•pist,** *n.*

u•ro•style (yo͝or′ə stīl′), *n. Anat.* the fused vertebrae at the posterior end of the spinal column of some fishes and tailless amphibians. [1870–75; URO-[2] + -STYLE[2]]

Ur·quhart (ûr′kərt, -kärt), *n.* **Sir Thomas,** 1611–60, Scottish author and translator.

Ur·sa Ma·jor (ûr′sə mā′jər), *gen.* **Ur·sae Ma·jor·is** (ûr′sē mə jôr′is, -jōr′-). *Astron.* the Great Bear, the most prominent northern constellation, containing the seven stars that form the Big Dipper. [1350–1400; ME]

Ur·sa Mi·nor (ûr′sə mī′nər), *gen.* **Ur·sae Mi·nor·is** (ûr′sē mi nôr′is, -nōr′-). *Astron.* the Little or Lesser Bear, the northernmost constellation, containing the stars that form the Little Dipper, the outermost of which, at the end of the handle, is Polaris. [1590–1600]

ur·sid (ûr′sid), *n.* any plantigrade carnivore of the family Ursidae, comprising the spectacled bear, the black, brown, and sun bears, and various extinct species that also gave rise to the giant panda of the family Ailuropodidae. [< NL *Ursidae*, equiv. to *Urs*(*us*) a genus (L: bear) + *-idae* -ID[2]]

Ur·sids (ûr′sidz), *n.* (*used with a plural v.*) *Astron.* a collection of meteors comprising a meteor shower **(Ur′·sid me′teor show′er)** visible around December 22 and having its apparent origin in the constellation Ursa Major. [URS(A MAJOR) + -ID[1] + -S[3]]

ur·si·form (ûr′sə fôrm′), *adj.* having the form of a bear; bear-shaped: *the ursiform koala.* [1785–95; < L *urs*(*us*) bear + -I- + -FORM]

ur·sine (ûr′sīn, -sin), *adj.* **1.** of or pertaining to a bear or bears. **2.** bearlike. [1540–50; < L *ursīnus*, equiv. to *urs*(*us*) bear + *-īnus* -INE[1]]

ur′sine das′yure. See **Tasmanian devil.** [1835–45]

ur′sine howl′er, the red howling monkey, *Alouatta seniculus,* of northern South America. [1880–85]

Ur·sprä·che (o͝or′shprä′KHə; *Ger.* o͞oR′shprä′KHə), *n.* a hypothetically reconstructed parent language, as Proto-Germanic, the ancestor of the Germanic languages. [< G, equiv. to *ur-* UR-[3] + *Sprache* speech]

Ur·su·la (ûr′sə lə, ûrs′yo͝o-), *n.* **1. Saint,** a legendary British princess who, with 11,000 virgins, is said to have been martyred by the Huns at Cologne. **2.** a female given name: from a Latin word meaning "bear."

Ur·su·line (ûr′sə lin, -līn′, -lēn′, ûrs′yo͝o-), *n.* **1.** *Rom. Cath. Ch.* a member of an order of nuns founded at Brescia, Italy, about 1537, devoted to teaching. —*adj.* **2.** of or pertaining to the Ursulines. [1685–95; Saint URSUL(A) + -INE[1]]

ur·text (ûr′tekst′, o͝or′-), *n.* (*sometimes cap.*) the original form of a text, esp. of a musical composition. [1950–55; UR-[3] + TEXT]

ur·ti·ca·ceous (ûr′ti kā′shəs), *adj.* belonging to the Urticaceae, the nettle family of plants. Cf. **nettle family.** [1830–40; < NL *Urticace*(*ae*) (*Urtic*(*a*) the type genus (L *urtīca* nettle) + *-aceae* -ACEAE) + -OUS]

ur·ti·cant (ûr′ti kənt), *adj.* urticating. [1865–70; < ML *urticant-* (s. of *urticāns*), prp. of *urticāre* to sting. See URTICATE]

ur·ti·car·i·a (ûr′ti kâr′ē ə), *n. Pathol.* a transient condition of the skin, usually caused by an allergic reaction, characterized by pale or reddened irregular, elevated patches and severe itching; hives. [1765–75; < NL, equiv. to L *urtic*(*a*) nettle + *-āria*, fem. of *-ārius* -ARY] —**ur′ti·car′i·al,** *adj.*

ur·ti·cate (ûr′ti kāt′), *v.,* **-cat·ed, -cat·ing.** —*v.t.* **1.** to sting with or as if with nettles. **2.** to whip with or as if with nettles, esp. so as to produce a stinging sensation; flog; lash. —*v.i.* **3.** to sting in the manner of a nettle. [1835–45; < ML *urticātus* (ptp. of *urticāre* to sting), equiv. to L *urtic*(*a*) nettle + *-ātus* -ATE[1]]

ur·ti·ca·tion (ûr′ti kā′shən), *n. Pathol.* the development or eruption of urticaria. [1645–55; < ML *urticātiōn-* (s. of *urticātiō*) a stinging, equiv. to *urticāt*(*us*) (see URTICATE) + *-iōn-* -ION]

Uru., Uruguay.

U·rua·pan (o͞o rwä′pän; *Eng.* o͝or wä′pän), *n.* a city in central Michoacán, in SW Mexico: near Paricutín volcano. 114,979. Also called **Urua′pan del Pro·gre′so** (del prô gre′sô; *Eng.* del prə gres′ō).

U·ru·bam·ba (o͞o′Ro͞o väm′bä; *Eng.* o͝or′ə bäm′bə), *n.* a river rising in SE Peru, flowing NW through the Andes Mountains to central Peru to meet the Apurímac River and form the Ucayali River. 450 mi. (725 km) long.

U·ru·gua·ia·na (o͞o′Ro͞o gwä yä′nä), *n.* a city in SW Brazil, on the Uruguay River. 74,581.

U·ru·guay (yo͝or′ə gwā′, -gwī′; *Sp.* o͞o′Ro͞o gwī′), *n.* **1.** a republic in SE South America. 2,763,964; 72,172 sq. mi. (186,925 sq. km). *Cap.:* Montevideo. **2.** a river in SE South America, flowing from S Brazil along the boundary of E Argentina into the Río de la Plata. 981 mi. (1580 km) long. —**U·ru·guay·an** (yo͝or′ə gwā′ən, -gwī′ən), *adj., n.*

U·ruk (o͞o′ro͝ok), *n.* an ancient Sumerian city in S Iraq, near the Euphrates, important before 2000 B.C.: exclusive archaeological excavations, notably of a ziggurat and of tablets with very early Sumerian script. Biblical name, **Erech.**

U·ru·mi·yeh (*Turk.* o͝o′Ro͞o mē ye′), *n.* **Lake.** See **Urmia, Lake.**

Ü·rüm·qi (Y′RYM′chē′) *n.* a city in and the capital of Xinjiang Uygur region, in NW China. 500,000. Also, **U′rum′chi′, U′rum′tsi′.** Formerly, **Dihua.**

U·run·di (o͝o ro͞on′dē), *n.* former name of **Burundi.** Cf. **Ruanda-Urundi.**

u·rus (yo͝or′əs), *n., pl.* **u·rus·es.** the aurochs. [1595–1605; < L *ūrus* a kind of wild ox (c. Gk *oûros*) < Gmc; cf. OE, OHG *ūr*, ON *ūrr*]

u·ru·shi·ol (o͝o ro͞o′shē ôl′, -ol′), *n.* a toxic, liquid, catechol derivative, the active irritant principle in several species of the plant genus *Rhus,* as in poison ivy. [1910–15; < Japn *urushi* lacquer + -OL]

us (us), *pron.* **1.** the objective case of **we,** used as a direct or indirect object: *They took us to the circus. She asked us the way.* **2.** *Informal.* (used in place of the pronoun *we* in the predicate after the verb *to be*): *It's us!* **3.** *Informal.* (used instead of the pronoun *our* before a gerund): *She graciously forgave us spilling the gravy on the tablecloth.* [bef. 900; ME, OE; c. G, Goth *uns*]
—**Usage. 2, 3.** See **me.**

US, 1. See **United States. 2.** United States highway (used with a number): *US 66.*

U.S., 1. Uncle Sam. **2.** United Service. **3.** See **United States.**

u.s., 1. where mentioned above. [< L *ubi suprā*] **2.** as above: a formula in judicial acts, directing that what precedes be reviewed. [< L *ut suprā*]

USA, 1. United States of America. **2.** United States Army.

U.S.A., 1. Union of South Africa. **2.** United States of America. **3.** United States Army.

U.S.A., a trilogy of novels (1939) by John Dos Passos, consisting of *The 42nd Parallel, 1919,* and *The Big Money.*

us·a·ble (yo͞o′zə bəl), *adj.* **1.** available or convenient for use: *2000 square feet of usable office space.* **2.** capable of being used: *That saw is no longer usable.* Also, **useable.** [1350–1400; ME < MF; see USE, -ABLE] —**us′·a·bil′i·ty, us′a·ble·ness,** *n.* —**us′a·bly,** *adv.*

U.S.A.F., United States Air Force. Also, **USAF**

USAFI, United States Armed Forces Institute.

U.S.A.F.R., United States Air Force Reserve. Also, **USAFR**

us·age (yo͞o′sij, -zij), *n.* **1.** a customary way of doing something; a custom or practice: *the usages of the last 50 years.* **2.** the customary manner in which a language or a form of a language is spoken or written: *English usage; a grammar based on usage rather than on arbitrary notions of correctness.* **3.** a particular instance of this: *a usage borrowed from French.* **4.** any manner of doing or handling something; treatment: *rough usage.* **5.** habitual or customary use; long-continued practice: *immemorial usage.* **6.** an act of using or employing; use. [1250–1300; ME < AF, OF < ML *ūsāticum*, equiv. to L *ūs*(*us*) (see USE) + *-āticum* -AGE]
—**Syn. 1.** tradition, habit, convention.
—**Usage.** The nouns USAGE and USE are related in origin and meaning and to some extent overlap in their use. USAGE usually refers to habitual or customary practices or procedures: *Some usages of the Anglican Church are similar to those of the Roman Catholic Church.* It is also commonly used in reference to language practices: *English usage is divided in the pronunciation of* aunt. USE refers to the act of using or employing (something): *She put her extra money to good use.* Perhaps in the belief that it is the more impressive term, USAGE is sometimes used where USE would be more natural: *Has your usage of a personal computer made the work any easier?*

u·sage·as·ter (yo͞o′sij as′tər), *n.* a self-styled authority on language usage. [USAGE + -ASTER]

us·ance (yo͞o′zəns), *n.* **1.** *Com.* a length of time, exclusive of days of grace and varying in different places, allowed by custom or usage for the payment of foreign bills of exchange. **2.** *Econ.* the income of benefits of every kind derived from the ownership of wealth. **3.** *Archaic.* **a.** use. **b.** custom; habit. **4.** *Obs.* usury. [1350–1400; ME *usaunce* < OF *usance*, prob. < ML *ūsantia*, deriv. of L *ūsant-* (s. of *ūsāns*), prp. of *ūsāre* to USE; see -ANCE]

USAR, United States Army Reserve.

Us·beg (o͝os′beg, us′-, o͝os beg′), *n., pl.* **-begs,** (*esp. collectively*) **-beg.** Uzbek.

Us·bek (o͝os′bek, us′-, o͝os bek′), *n., pl.* **-beks,** (*esp. collectively*) **-bek.** Uzbek.

U.S.C., 1. United States Code. **2.** United States of Colombia. Also, **USC**

U.S.C.A., United States Code Annotated. Also, **USCA**

U.S.C.&G.S., United States Coast and Geodetic Survey.

USCG, United States Coast Guard. Also, **U.S.C.G.**

USCRC, United States Citizens Radio Council.

U.S.C. Supp., *Law.* United States Code Supplement.

USDA, United States Department of Agriculture. Also, **U.S.D.A.**

use (*v.* yo͞oz *or, for pt. form of 9,* yo͞ost; *n.* yo͞os), *v.,* **used, us·ing,** *n.* —*v.t.* **1.** to employ for some purpose; put into service; make use of: *to use a knife.* **2.** to avail oneself of; apply to one's own purposes: *to use the facilities.* **3.** to expend or consume in use: *We have used the money provided.* **4.** to treat or behave toward: *He did not use his employees with much consideration.* **5.** to take unfair advantage of; exploit: *to use people to gain one's own ends.* **6.** to drink, smoke, or ingest habitually: *to use drugs.* **7.** to habituate or accustom. **8.** *Archaic.* to practice habitually or customarily; make a practice of. —*v.i.* **9.** to be accustomed, wont, or customarily found (used with an infinitive expressed or understood, and, except in archaic use, now only in the past): *He used to go every day.* **10.** *Archaic.* to resort, stay, or dwell customarily. **11. use up, a.** to consume entirely. **b.** to exhaust of vigor or usefulness; finish: *By the end of the war he felt used up and sick of life.*
—*n.* **12.** the act of employing, using, or putting into service: *the use of tools.* **13.** the state of being employed or used. **14.** an instance or way of employing or using something: *proper use of the tool; the painter's use of color.* **15.** a way of being employed or used; a purpose for which something is used: *He was of temporary use. The instrument has different uses.* **16.** the power, right, or privilege of employing or using something: *to lose the use of the right eye; to be denied the use of a library card.* **17.** service or advantage in or for being employed or used; utility or usefulness: *of no practical use.* **18.** help; profit; resulting good: *What's the use of pursuing the matter?* **19.** occasion or need, as for something to be employed or used: *Would you have any use for another calendar?* **20.** continued, habitual, or customary employment or practice; custom: *to follow the prevailing use of such occasions.* **21.** *Law.* **a.** the enjoyment of property, as by the employment, occupation, or exercise of it. **b.** the benefit or profit of lands and tenements in the possession of another who simply holds them for the beneficiary. **c.** the equitable ownership of land to which the legal title is in another's name. **22.** *Liturgy.* the distinctive form of ritual or of any liturgical observance used in a particular church, diocese, community, etc. **23.** usual or customary experience. **24. have no use for, a.** to have no occasion or need for: *She appears to have no use for the city.* **b.** to refuse to tolerate; discount: *He had no use for his brother.* **c.** to have a distaste for; dislike: *He has no use for dictators.* **25. make use of,** to use for one's own purposes; employ: *Charitable organizations will make use of your old furniture and clothing.* **26. of no use,** of no advantage or help: *It's of no use to look for that missing earring. It's no use asking her to go.* Also, **no use. 27. put to use,** to apply; employ to advantage: *What a shame that no one has put that old deserted mansion to use!* [1175–1225; (v.) ME *usen* < OF *user* < L *ūsus*, ptp. of *ūtī* to use; (n.) ME < OF < L *ūsus* act of using a thing, application, employment, equiv. to *ūt-*, s. of *ūtī* to use + *-tus* suffix of v. action, with *tt* > *s*]
—**Syn. 1.** USE, UTILIZE mean to make something serve one's purpose. USE is the general word: *to use a telephone; to use a saw and other tools; to use one's eyes; to use eggs in cooking.* (What is USED often has depreciated or been diminished, sometimes completely consumed: *a used automobile; All the butter has been used.*) As applied to persons, USE implies some selfish or sinister purpose: *to use another to advance oneself.* UTILIZE implies practical or profitable use: *to utilize the means at hand, a modern system of lighting.* **3.** exhaust, waste. **7.** familiarize, inure. **13.** employment, utilization, application, exercise. **14.** handling.
—**Usage.** See **usage.**

use·a·ble (yo͞o′zə bəl), *adj.* usable. —**use′a·bil′i·ty, use′a·ble·ness,** *n.* —**use′a·bly,** *adv.*

USECC, United States Employees' Compensation Commission.

used (yo͞ozd *or, for 4,* yo͞ost), *adj.* **1.** previously used or owned; secondhand: *a used car.* **2.** showing wear or being worn out. **3.** employed for a purpose; utilized. **4. used to,** accustomed or habituated to: *I'm not used to cold weather. They weren't used to getting up so early.* [1325–75; ME; see USE, -ED[2]]

use·ful (yo͞os′fəl), *adj.* **1.** being of use or service; serving some purpose; advantageous, helpful, or of good effect: *a useful member of society.* **2.** of practical use, as for doing work; producing material results; supplying common needs: *the useful arts; useful work.* [1585–95; USE + -FUL] —**use′ful·ly,** *adv.* —**use′ful·ness,** *n.*
—**Syn. 1, 2.** profitable, efficacious, beneficial. —**Ant. 1, 2.** useless.

use′ immu′nity (yo͞os), *Law.* a type of immunity guaranteeing that the testimony of the witness will not be used as evidence against him or her in court, although he or she can still be prosecuted on evidence of others. Cf. **immunity bath.** [1970–75]

use·less (yo͞os′lis), *adj.* **1.** of no use; not serving the purpose or any purpose; unavailing or futile: *It is useless to reason with him.* **2.** without useful qualities; of no practical good: *a useless person; a useless gadget.* [1585–95; USE + -LESS] —**use′less·ly,** *adv.* —**use′less·ness,** *n.*
—**Syn. 1.** fruitless, profitless, valueless, worthless, inutile. USELESS, FUTILE, INEFFECTUAL, VAIN refer to that which is unavailing. That is USELESS which is unavailing because of the circumstances of the case or some inherent defect: *It is useless to cry over spilt milk.* FUTILE suggests wasted effort and complete failure to attain a desired end: *All attempts were futile.* That which is INEFFECTUAL weakly applies energy in an ill-advised way and does not produce a desired effect: *an ineffectual effort.* That which is VAIN is fruitless or hopeless even after all possible effort: *It is vain to keep on hoping.* **2.** unserviceable, unusable. —**Ant. 1.** effective.

us·er[1] (yo͞o′zər), *n.* **1.** a person or thing that uses. **2.** one who uses drugs, esp. as an abuser or addict. **3.** *Computers.* a person who uses a computer. [1350–1400; ME *usere*; see USE, -ER[1]]

us·er[2] (o͞o′zər), *n. Law.* the exercise of a right to the enjoyment of property. [n. use of AF *user* to USE]

us·er-friend·ly (yo͞o′zər frend′lē), *adj.* easy to use, operate, understand, etc.: *the most user-friendly personal* *computer now on the market.* [1980–85] —**us′·er-friend′li·ness,** *n.*

us′er group′ (yo͞o′zər), *Computers.* a club in which owners of a specific computer or software program exchange information or services, as purchasing or troubleshooting. Also, **us′er's group′.** [1970–75]

us′er's fee′, a fee charged for the use of something, as one charged by a city government for the use of one of its services, as garbage collection or fire protection. Also, **us′er fee′.**

USES, See **United States Employment Service.** Also, **U.S.E.S.**

use′ tax′ (yo͞os), a state tax imposed on goods purchased outside a state for which state sales tax has not been paid.

U.S.G.A., United States Golf Association. Also, **USGA**

USHA, United States Housing Authority. Also, **U.S.H.A.**

u·shab·ti (yo͞o shab′tē, o͞o-), *n., pl.* **-ti, -tis, -ti·u** (-tē o͞o′). shawabti.

Ush·ant (ush′ənt), *n.* an island off the NW coast of France: naval battles 1778, 1794. 1800; 4½ mi. (7 km) long. French, **Ouessant.**

U-shaped (yo͞o′shāpt′), *adj.* being in the form of a U. [1835–45]

Ush·as (o͝osh′əs, o͝o shäs′), *n.* Dawn, a Vedic deity, daughter of Sky and sister of Night. Also, **Ush·a** (o͝osh′ə, o͝o shä′). [< Skt *uṣas*]

ush·er (ush′ər), *n.* **1.** a person who escorts people to seats in a theater, church, etc. **2.** a person acting as an official doorkeeper, as in a courtroom or legislative chamber. **3.** a male attendant of a bridegroom at a wedding. **4.** an officer whose business it is to introduce strangers or to walk before a person of rank. **5.** *Brit. Archaic.* a subordinate teacher or an assistant in a school. —*v.t.* **6.** to act as an usher to; lead, introduce, or conduct: *She ushered them to their seats.* **7.** to attend or bring at the coming or beginning; precede or herald (usually fol. by *in*): *to usher in the new theater season.* —*v.i.* **8.** to act as an usher: *He ushered at the banquet.* [1350–1400; ME *uscher* doorkeeper < AF *usser,* OF *(h)uissier* doorman, officer of justice < VL **ustiārius,* equiv. to L *ōsti(um)* door + *-ārius* -ARY; see -ER²] —**ush′er·ship′,** *n.*

Ush·er (ush′ər), *n.* **James.** See **Ussher, James.**

ush·er·ette (ush′ə ret′), *n.* a woman who escorts persons to seats in a theater, church, etc. [1925–30; USHER + -ETTE]
—**Usage.** See **-ette.**

Ush·ki (o͞osh′kē), *n.* an archaeological site at Kamchatka, U.S.S.R., revealing a late Pleistocene culture producing bifacial points with affinities to those of western North America.

Us·hua·ia (o͞o swī′ə), *n.* a city in S Argentina, on the S coast of Tierra del Fuego: the southernmost city in the world. 10,998.

USIA, See **United States Information Agency.** Also, **U.S.I.A.**

USIS, United States Information Service. Also, **U.S.I.S.**

USITC, United States International Trade Commission.

Usk (usk), *n.* a river flowing S and SE from SE Wales through SW England into the Severn estuary. 60 mi. (97 km) long.

Üs·küb (ʏs kʏp′), *n.* Turkish name of **Skoplje.** Also, **Üs·küp′.**

Üs·kü·dar (o͞os′kə där′; *Turk.* ʏs′kʏ där′), *n.* a town in NW Turkey, on the Asian shore of the Bosporus: a suburb of Istanbul. 143,938. Formerly, **Scutari.**

U.S.L.T.A., United States Lawn Tennis Association. Also, **USLTA**

USM, **1.** United States Mail. **2.** United States Marines. **3.** United States Mint. Also, **U.S.M.**

U.S.M.A., United States Military Academy. Also, **USMA**

USMC, **1.** United States Marine Corps. **2.** United States Maritime Commission. Also, **U.S.M.C.**

USMS, United States Maritime Service.

USN, United States Navy. Also, **U.S.N.**

USNA, **1.** United States National Army. **2.** United States Naval Academy. Also, **U.S.N.A.**

us·ne·a (us′nē ə), *n.* any pale-green or gray, mosslike lichen of the genus *Usnea,* common on rocks and trees. [1590–1600; < NL, ML < Ar or Pers *ushnah*]

USNG, United States National Guard. Also, **U.S.N.G.**

us′nic ac′id (us′nik), *Pharm.* an antibacterial substance, $C_{18}H_{16}O_7$, derived from lichens of the genus *Usnea.* [1840–50; < NL *Usn(ea)* USNEA + -IC]

USNR, United States Naval Reserve. Also, **U.S.N.R.**

USO, United Service Organizations. Also, **U.S.O.**

U·so·lye (o͞o sô′lyə), *n.* a city in the W RSFSR, in the E central Soviet Union in Europe, on the Volga. 103,000.

U.S.P., United States Pharmacopeia. Also, **U.S. Pharm.**

Us·pa·lla′ta Pass′ (o͞os′pä yä′tə; *Sp.* o͞os′pä yä′tä), a mountain pass in S South America, in the Andes, connecting Mendoza, Argentina, and Santiago, Chile. ab. 12,600 ft. (3840 m) high. Also called **La Cumbre.**

USPHS, United States Public Health Service. Also, **U.S.P.H.S.**

USPO, United States Post Office. Also, **U.S.P.O.**

CONCISE ETYMOLOGY KEY: <, descended or borrowed from; >, whence; b., blend of, blended; c., cognate with; cf., compare; deriv., derivative; equiv., equivalent; imit., imitative; obl., oblique; r., replacing; s., stem; sp., spelling, spelled; resp., respelling, respelled; trans., translation; ?, origin unknown; *, unattested; ‡, probably earlier than. See the full key inside the front cover.

USPS, See **United States Postal Service.** Also, **U.S.P.S.**

us·que·baugh (us′kwi bô′, -bä′), *n.* (in Scotland and Ireland) whiskey. [1575–85; < Ir *uisce beatha* or Scot-Gael *uisge beatha;* see WHISKEY]

USR, United States Reserves. Also, **U.S.R.**

USRC, United States Reserve Corps. Also, **U.S.R.C.**

U.S. RDA, *Nutrition.* United States recommended daily allowance: the daily amount of a protein, vitamin, or mineral that the FDA has established as sufficient to maintain the nutritional health of persons in various age groups and categories, derived from the RDA developed by the Food and Nutrition Board of the National Academy of Sciences and used in the nutritional labeling of food. Cf. **recommended dietary allowance.**

U.S.S., **1.** United States Senate. **2.** United States Service. **3.** United States Ship. **4.** United States Steamer. **5.** United States Steamship. Also, **USS**

U.S.S.B., United States Shipping Board. Also, **USSB**

U.S.S.Ct., United States Supreme Court.

Ussh·er (ush′ər), *n.* **James,** 1581–1656, Irish prelate and scholar. Also, **Usher.**

U.S.S.R., Union of Soviet Socialist Republics. Also, **USSR**

U.S.S.S., United States Steamship. Also, **USSS**

Us·su·ri (o͞o so͞or′ē; *Russ.* o͞o so͞o′ʀyi), *n.* a river in E Asia, forming part of the boundary between E Manchuria and the SE Russian Federation in Asia, flowing N to the Amur River. 500 mi. (805 km) long. Also called **Wusuli Jiang.**

Us·su·riisk (o͞o′so͞o rēsk′; *Russ.* o͞o so͞o ʀyēsk′), *n.* a city in the SE Russian Federation in Asia. 147,000. Formerly, **Voroshilov.**

USTA, United States Trademark Association.

USTC, United States Tariff Commission.

Ust-Ka·me·no·gorsk (o͞ost′kə myi nu gôʀsk′), *n.* a city in E Kazakhstan, on the Irtysh River. 321,000.

USTS, United States Travel Service: part of the Department of Commerce.

Ust Sy·solsk (*Russ.* o͞ost′ si sôlsk′), former name of **Syktyvkar.**

us·tu·late (*adj.* us′chə lit, -lāt′; *v.,* us′chə lāt′), *adj., v.,* **-lat·ed, -lat·ing.** —*adj.* **1.** colored or blackened as if scorched. —*v.t.* **2.** *Obs.* to burn; sear; scorch. [1615–25; < L *ūstulātus* ptp. of *ūstulāre* to scorch, burn, deriv. of *ūrere* to burn; see -ATE¹]

us·tu·la·tion (us′chə lā′shən), *n.* **1.** the act of scorching or burning. **2.** *Pharm.* the roasting or drying of moist substances. [1650–60; < ML *ūstulātiōn-* (s. of *ūstulātiō*) a scorching, equiv. to L *ūstulāt(us)* (see USTULATE) + *-iōn-* -ION]

usu., **1.** usual. **2.** usually.

u·su·al (yo͞o′zho͞o əl, yo͞ozh′wəl), *adj.* **1.** habitual or customary: *her usual skill.* **2.** commonly met with or observed in experience; ordinary: *the usual January weather.* **3.** commonplace; everyday: *He says the usual things.* **4. as usual,** in the customary or usual manner: *As usual, he forgot my birthday.* —*n.* **5.** something that is usual: *He could expect only the usual.* [1350–1400; ME < LL *ūsuālis,* equiv. to L *ūsu-,* s. of *ūsus* use (see USE (n.)) + *-ālis* -AL¹; cf. OF *usuel*] —**u′su·al·ly,** *adv.* —**u′su·al·ness,** *n.*
—**Syn. 1.** accustomed. USUAL, CUSTOMARY, HABITUAL refer to a settled and constant practice. USUAL indicates something that is to be expected by reason of previous experience, which shows it to occur more often than not: *There were the usual crowds at the celebration.* Something that is CUSTOMARY is in accordance with prevailing usage or individual practice: *It is customary to finish up with a bonfire.* That which is HABITUAL has become settled or constant as the result of habit on the part of the individual: *The merchants wore habitual smiles throughout the season.* **2.** general, prevailing, prevalent, familiar, regular. **3.** expected, predictable.

u·su·ca·pi·on (yo͞o′zə kā′pē on′, -sə-), *n. Roman Law.* the acquisition of property through long, undisturbed possession. Also, **u·su·cap·tion** (yo͞o′zə kap′shən, -sə-). [1600–10; < L *ūsūcapiōn-,* s. of *ūsūcapiō,* equiv. to *ūsū,* abl. sing. of *ūsus* (see USE (n.)) + *capiō* a taking (*cap(ere)* to take + *-iō* (s. *-iōn-*) -ION)]

u·su·fruct (yo͞o′zo͞o frukt′, -so͞o-, yo͞oz′yo͞o-, yo͞os′-), *n. Roman and Civil Law.* the right of enjoying all the advantages derivable from the use of something that belongs to another, as far as is compatible with the substance of the thing not being destroyed or injured. [1620–30; < LL *ūsūfrūctus,* equiv. to L *ūsū,* abl. of *ūsus* (see USE (n.)) + *frūctus* (see FRUIT)]

u·su·fruc·tu·ar·y (yo͞o′zo͞o fruk′cho͞o er′ē, -so͞o-, yo͞oz′yo͞o-, yo͞os′-), *adj., n., pl.* **-ar·ies.** *Roman and Civil Law.* —*adj.* **1.** of, pertaining to, or of the nature of usufruct. —*n.* **2.** a person who has a usufruct property. [1610–20; < LL *ūsūfrūctuārius,* equiv. to *ūsūfrūctu(s)* USUFRUCT + *-ārius* -ARY]

U·su·ma·cin·ta (o͞o′so͞o mä sēn′tä), *n.* a river in Central America, flowing NW along the W Guatemala-SE Mexico border, through Mexico, to the Gulf of Campeche. ab. 600 mi. (965 km) long.

U·sum·bu·ra (o͞o′so͞om bo͞or′ə), *n.* former name of **Bujumbura.**

u·su·rer (yo͞o′zhər ər), *n.* **1.** a person who lends money and charges interest, esp. at an exorbitant or unlawful rate; moneylender. **2.** *Obs.* a person who lends money at interest. [1250–1300; ME < AF < ML *ūsūrārius,* equiv. to *ūsūr(ia)* USURY + L *-ārius* -ARY]

u·su·ri·ous (yo͞o zho͞or′ē əs), *adj.* **1.** practicing usury; charging illegal or exorbitant rates of interest for the use of money: *a usurious moneylender.* **2.** constituting or characterized by usury: *usurious rates of interest; a usurious loan.* [1600–10; USURY + -OUS] —**u·su′ri·ous·ly,** *adv.* —**u·su′ri·ous·ness,** *n.*

u·surp (yo͞o sûrp′, -zûrp′), *v.t.* **1.** to seize and hold (a position, office, power, etc.) by force or without legal right: *The pretender tried to usurp the throne.* **2.** to use without authority or right; employ wrongfully: *The magazine usurped copyrighted material.* —*v.i.* **3.** to commit forcible or illegal seizure of an office, power, etc.; encroach. [1275–1325; ME < L *ūsūrpāre* to take possession through use, equiv. to *ūsū* (abl. of *ūsus* USE (n.)) + *-rp-,* reduced form of *-rip-,* comb. form of *rapere* to seize + *-āre* inf. ending] —**u·surp′er,** *n.* —**u·surp′ing·ly,** *adv.*

u·sur·pa·tion (yo͞o′sər pā′shən, -zər-), *n.* **1.** an act of usurping; wrongful or illegal encroachment, infringement, or seizure. **2.** illegal seizure and occupation of a throne. [1350–1400; ME < L *ūsūrpātiōn-* (s. of *ūsūrpātiō,* equiv. to *ūsūrpāt(us)* (ptp. of *ūsūrpāre* to USURP) + *-iōn-* -ION] —**u·sur·pa·tive** (yo͞o sûr′pə tiv, -zûr′-), **u·sur·pa·to·ry** (yo͞o sûr′pə tôr′ē, -tōr′ē, -zûr′-), *adj.*

u·su·ry (yo͞o′zhə rē), *n., pl.* **-ries.** **1.** the lending or practice of lending money at an exorbitant interest. **2.** an exorbitant amount or rate of interest, esp. in excess of the legal rate. **3.** *Obs.* interest paid for the use of money. [1275–1325; ME *usurie* < ML *ūsūria* (cf. L *ūsūra*), equiv. to L *ūs(us)* (see USE) + *-ūr(a)* -URE + *-ia* -Y³]

U.S.V., United States Volunteers. Also, **USV**

USW, ultrashort wave.

usw, *German.* See **und so weiter.** Also, **u.s.w.**

us·ward (us′wərd), *adv. Archaic.* toward us. [1350–1400; ME *to usward.* See US, -WARD]

ut (ut, o͞ot), *n. Music.* the syllable once generally used for the first tone or keynote of a scale and sometimes for the tone C: now commonly superseded by *do.* Cf. **sol-fa.** [1275–1325; ME; see GAMUT]

UT, **1.** Also, **u.t.** universal time. **2.** Utah (approved esp. for use with zip code).

Ut., Utah.

U/T, under trust.

u·ta (yo͞o′tə), *n.* any of several iguanid lizards of the genus *Uta,* of the western U.S. and northern Mexico. [< NL, prob. Latinization of UTE]

U·tah (yo͞o′tô, -tä), *n.* **1.** a state in the W United States. 1,461,037; 84,916 sq. mi. (219,930 sq. km). *Cap.:* Salt Lake City. *Abbr.:* UT (for use with zip code), Ut. **2.** *Mil.* the World War II Allies' code name for the easternmost of the D-Day invasion beaches on France's Normandy coast, assaulted by American troops. —**U·tah·an, U·tahn** (yo͞o′tôn, tän), *adj., n.*

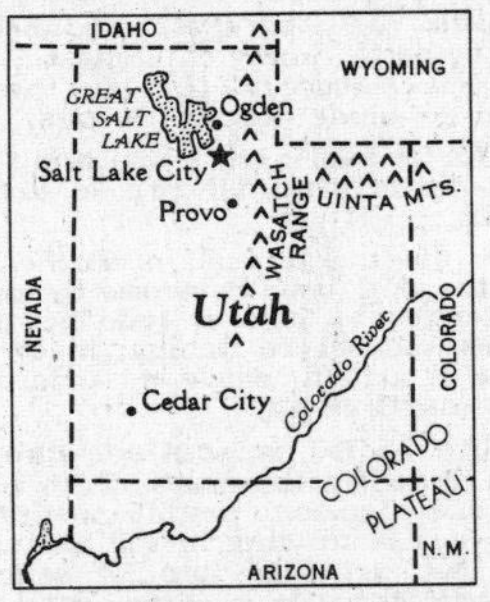

U·ta·ma·ro (o͞o′tä mä′ʀô; *Eng.* o͞o′tə mär′ō), *n.* **Ki·ta·ga·wa** (kē′tä gä′wä), 1753–1806, Japanese painter, draftsman, and designer of prints.

UTC, universal time coordinated.

ut dict., (in prescriptions) as directed. [< L *ut dictum*]

Ute (yo͞ot, yo͞o′tē), *n., pl.* **Utes,** (*esp. collectively*) **Ute.** **1.** a member of an important tribe of the Shoshonean stock of North American Indians, now on reservations in Utah and Colorado. **2.** their language, of the Uto-Aztecan family of languages.

utend., (in prescriptions) to be used. [< L *ūtendum*]

u·ten·sil (yo͞o ten′səl), *n.* **1.** any of the instruments or vessels commonly used in a kitchen, dairy, etc.: *eating utensils; baking utensils.* **2.** any instrument, vessel, or tool serving a useful purpose: *smoking utensils; fishing utensils; farming utensils.* [1325–75; ME (collective sing.): household articles < MF *utensile* < L *ūtensilia,* neut. pl. of *ūtensilis* useful, deriv. of *ūti* to USE]
—**Syn. 2.** See **tool.**

uter-, var. of **utero-** before a vowel: *uteralgia.*

u·ter·al·gia (yo͞o′tə ral′jə), *n. Med.* pain in or near the uterus. [1400–50; UTER- + -ALGIA]

u·ter·ine (yo͞o′tər in, -tə rīn′), *adj.* **1.** of or pertaining to the uterus or womb. **2.** related through having had the same mother. [1400–50; late ME < LL *uterinus* of, pertaining to the uterus. See UTERUS, -INE¹]

utero-, a combining form representing **uterus** in compound words: *uterovaginal.* Also, *esp. before a vowel,* **uter-.**

u·ter·us (yo͞o′tər əs), *n., pl.* **u·ter·i** (yo͞o′tə rī′), **u·ter·us·es.** *Anat., Zool.* the enlarged, muscular, expandable portion of the oviduct in which the fertilized ovum implants and develops or rests during prenatal development; the womb of certain mammals. [1605–15; < L: the womb, matrix; akin to Gk *hystéra* womb, Skt *udara* belly]

Ut·gard (o͞ot′gärd), *n. Scand. Myth.* a home of the Jotuns, outside Midgard and Asgard: probably synonymous with Jotunheim. [< ON *Útgarthar,* equiv. to *út* OUT + *garthar* YARD²; cf. GARTH]

Ut·gard-Lo·ki (o͞ot′gärd lō′kē), *n. Scand. Myth.* a Jotun appearing in the story of Thor's voyage to Utgard: at first disguised under another name **(Skrymir).**

U Thant (o͞o′ thänt′, thônt′). 1909–74, Burmese statesman: secretary-general of the United Nations 1962–71.

U·ther (yo͞o′thər), *n. Arthurian Romance.* king of Britain and father of Arthur. Also called **U′ther Pen·drag′on.**

UTI, urinary tract infection.

U·ti·ca (yo͞o′ti kə), *n.* **1.** an ancient city on the N coast of Africa, NW of Carthage. **2.** a city in central New York, on the Mohawk River. 75,632.

u·tile (yo͞o′til, -tīl), *adj.* useful. [1475–85; < OF < L *ūtilis,* equiv. to *ūt(i)* to use + *-ilis* -ILE]

u·ti·le dul·ci (o͞o′ti le do͞ol′kē; *Eng.* yo͞ot′l ē dul′sī, -sē), *Latin.* the useful with the pleasurable.

U·til·i·care (yo͞o til′i kâr′), *n.* a usually state-funded program that helps elderly persons of low income to pay their utility bills, esp. heating bills in winter. [UTILI(TY) + CARE, as in *Medicare*]

u·til·i·dor (yo͞o til′i dôr′), *n. Canadian.* an above-ground, insulated network of pipes and cables, used to convey water and electricity in communities situated in areas of permafrost. [UTILI(TY) + *-dor,* as in *thermidor*]

u·til·i·tar·i·an (yo͞o til′i târ′ē ən), *adj.* **1.** pertaining to or consisting in utility. **2.** having regard to utility or usefulness rather than beauty, ornamentation, etc. **3.** of, pertaining to, or adhering to the doctrine of utilitarianism. —*n.* **4.** an adherent of utilitarianism. [1775–85; UTILIT(Y) + -ARIAN]
—**Syn. 2.** practical, useful, functional, sensible.

u·til·i·tar·i·an·ism (yo͞o til′i târ′ē ə niz′əm), *n.* the ethical doctrine that virtue is based on utility, and that conduct should be directed toward promoting the greatest happiness of the greatest number of persons. [1820–30; UTILITARIAN + -ISM]

u·til·i·ty (yo͞o til′i tē), *n., pl.* **-ties,** *adj.* —*n.* **1.** the state or quality of being useful; usefulness: *This chemical has no utility as an agricultural fertilizer.* **2.** something useful; a useful thing. **3.** a public service, as a telephone or electric-light system, a streetcar or railroad line, or the like. Cf. **public utility** (def. 1). **4.** Often, **utilities.** a useful or advantageous factor or feature: *the relative utilities of a religious or a secular education.* **5.** *Econ.* the capacity of a commodity or a service to satisfy some human want. **6.** the principle and end of utilitarian ethics; well-being or happiness; that which is conducive to the happiness and well-being of the greatest number. **7.** *Computers.* See **utility program. 8. utilities,** stocks or bonds of public utilities. **9.** a grade of beef immediately below commercial. —*adj.* **10.** (of domestic animals) raised or kept as a potentially profitable product rather than for show or as pets: *utility breeds; utility livestock.* **11.** having or made for a number of useful or practical purposes rather than a single, specialized one: *a utility knife.* **12.** designed chiefly for use or service rather than beauty, high quality, or the like: *a utility vehicle; utility furniture.* [1350–1400; ME *utilite* < OF *utelite* < L *ūtilitās,* equiv. to *ūtil(is)* useful (see UTILE) + *-itās* -ITY]

util′ity man′, 1. a worker expected to serve in any capacity when called on. **2.** an actor of miscellaneous small parts. **3.** *Baseball.* a player who is not a regular and whose value lies in an ability to play several positions. [1850–55]

util′ity pole′, one of a series of large, upright poles used to support telephone wires, electric cables, or the like. Also called **telephone pole.**

util′ity pro′gram, *Computers.* system software used to perform standard operations, as sorting data or copying data from one file to another, for application programs or other system software. Also, **utility.** [1960–65]

util′ity room′, a room, esp. in a house, reserved for the furnace, washing machine, and other appliances.

u·ti·lize (yo͞ot′l īz′), *v.t.,* **-lized, -liz·ing.** to put to use; turn to profitable account: *to utilize a stream to power a mill.* Also, *esp. Brit.,* **u′ti·lise′.** [1800–10; < F *utiliser,* equiv. to *utile* useful (see UTILE) + *-iser* -IZE] —**u′ti·liz′a·ble,** *adj.* —**u′ti·li·za′tion,** *n.* —**u′ti·liz′er,** *n.*
—**Syn.** See **use.**

ut in·fra (o͝ot in′frä; *Eng.* ut in′frə), *Latin.* as (stated or shown) below: used in a book, text, etc.

u·ti pos·si·de·tis (yo͞o′tī pos′i dē′tis), *Internat. Law.* the principle that vests in either of the belligerents at the end of a war all territory actually occupied and controlled by them. [< L *utī possidētis* lit., as you possess, as you hold]

ut·most (ut′mōst′ *or, esp. Brit.,* -məst), *adj.* **1.** of the greatest or highest degree, quantity, or the like; greatest: *of the utmost importance.* **2.** being at the farthest point or extremity; farthest: *the utmost reef of the island.* —*n.* **3.** Also, **uttermost.** the greatest degree or amount: *the utmost that can be said; The hotel provides the utmost in comfort.* **4.** the most or best of one's abilities, powers, etc.: *He did his utmost to finish on time.* **5.** the extreme limit or extent: *His patience was taxed to the utmost.* [bef. 900; ME *utmest,* OE *ūtemest.* See OUT, -MOST]
—**Syn. 1.** maximum, highest, foremost, chief, major.

Ut·na·pish·tim (o͝ot′nə pish′tim), *n.* (in the *Poem of Gilgamesh*) the favorite of the gods, who survived the great flood and became immortal.

U·to-Az·tec·an (yo͞o′tō az′tek ən), *n.* **1.** an American Indian language family, widespread from Idaho to Central America and from the Rocky Mountains to the Pacific: this family includes Hopi, Ute, Shoshone, Comanche, Nahuatl, Papago, Pima, and other languages. —*adj.* **2.** of or pertaining to Uto-Aztecan. [1891; UTE + -O- + AZTECAN]

U·to·pi·a (yo͞o tō′pē ə), *n.* **1.** an imaginary island described in Sir Thomas More's *Utopia* (1516) as enjoying perfection in law, politics, etc. **2.** (*usually l.c.*) an ideal place or state. **3.** (*usually l.c.*) any visionary system of political or social perfection. [< NL (1516) < Gk *ou* not + *tóp(os)* a place + *-ia* -Y[3]]

U·to·pi·an (yo͞o tō′pē ən), *adj.* **1.** of, pertaining to, or resembling Utopia. **2.** (*usually l.c.*) founded upon or involving idealized perfection. **3.** (*usually l.c.*) given to impractical or unrealistic schemes of such perfection. —*n.* **4.** an inhabitant of Utopia. **5.** (*usually l.c.*) an impractical political or social reformer; visionary; idealist. [1545–55; < NL *Utopiānus.* See UTOPIA, -AN]
—**Syn. 3.** visionary, idealistic; impracticable.

u·to·pi·an·ism (yo͞o tō′pē ə niz′əm), *n.* (*sometimes cap.*) the views or habit of mind of a utopian; impracticable schemes of political or social reform. [1655–65; UTOPIAN + -ISM] —**u·to′pi·an·ist,** *n.*

uto′pian so′cialism, (*sometimes cap.*) an economic system based on the premise that if capital voluntarily surrendered its ownership of the means of production to the state or the workers, unemployment and poverty would be abolished. Cf. **socialism.** [1920–25]

Uto′pia Pla·ni′tia (plə nē′shə), *Astron.* a plain in the northern hemisphere of Mars that was the landing site of the Viking II space probe on September 3, 1976.

u·to·pism (yo͞o′tə piz′əm, yo͞o tō′piz-), *n.* (*sometimes cap.*) utopianism. [UTOP(IA) + -ISM] —**u′to·pist,** *n.* —**u′to·pis′tic,** *adj.*

U·tra·quist (yo͞o′trə kwist), *n.* Calixtine. [1830–40; < NL *Utraquista,* equiv. to L *utrāque* (abl. sing. fem. of *uterque* each of two, equiv. to *uter* either + *-que* and) + NL *-ista* -IST] —**U′tra·quism,** *n.*

U·trecht (yo͞o′trekt; *Du.* Y′trekHt), *n.* **1.** a province in central Netherlands. 907,729; 511 sq. mi. (1325 sq. km). **2.** a city in and the capital of this province: treaties ending the War of the Spanish Succession signed here 1714. 489,161.

u·tri·cle (yo͞o′tri kəl), *n.* **1.** a small sac or baglike body, as an air-filled cavity in a seaweed. **2.** *Bot.* a thin bladderlike pericarp or seed vessel. **3.** *Anat.* the larger of two sacs in the membranous labyrinth of the internal ear. Cf. **saccule** (def. 1). [1725–35; < L *utriculus,* dim. of *uter* bag; see -CLE[1]]

u·tric·u·lar (yo͞o trik′yə lər), *adj.* **1.** pertaining to or of the nature of a utricle; baglike. **2.** having a utricle or utricles. [1750–60, *Amer.;* < L *utricul(us)* UTRICLE + -AR[1]]

u·tric·u·late (yo͞o trik′yə lit, -lāt′), *adj. Archaic.* having a utricle; utricular; baglike. [1855–60; UTRICUL(AR) + -ATE[1]]

u·tric·u·li·tis (yo͞o trik′yə lī′tis), *n. Pathol.* inflammation of the utricle. [< NL; see UTRICLE, -ITIS]

U·tril·lo (yo͞o tril′ō, o͞o tril′ō; *Fr.* Y trē yō′), *n.* **Maurice** (mô rēs′; *Fr.* mô Rēs′), 1883–1955, French painter (son of Suzanne Valadon).

U·tsu·no·mi·ya (o͝o tso͞o′nô mē′yä), *n.* a city on central Honshu, in central Japan. 377,748.

ut su·pra (*Lat.* o͝ot so͞o′prä; *Eng.* ut so͞o′prə). See **u.s.** (def. 2).

Ut·tar Pra·desh (o͝ot′ər prə däsh′, -desh′), a state in N India: a former province of British India. 97,380,000; 113,409 sq. mi. (293,730 sq. km). *Cap.:* Lucknow. Formerly, **United Provinces.** Former official name, **United Provinces of Agra and Oudh.**

ut·ter[1] (ut′ər), *v.t.* **1.** to give audible expression to; speak or pronounce: *unable to utter her feelings; Words were uttered in my hearing.* **2.** to give forth (cries, notes, etc.) with the voice: *to utter a sigh.* **3.** *Phonet.* to produce (speech sounds, speechlike sounds, syllables, words, etc.) audibly, with or without reference to formal language. **4.** to express (oneself or itself), esp. in words. **5.** to give forth (a sound) otherwise than with the voice: *The engine uttered a shriek.* **6.** to express by written or printed words. **7.** to make publicly known; publish: *to utter a libel.* **8.** to put into circulation, as coins, notes, and esp. counterfeit money or forged checks. **9.** to expel; emit. **10.** *Obs.* to publish, as a book. **11.** *Obs.* to sell. —*v.i.* **12.** to employ the faculty of speech; use the voice to talk, make sounds, etc.: *His piety prevented him from uttering on religion.* **13.** to sustain utterance; undergo speaking: *Those ideas are so dishonest they will not utter.* [1350–1400; ME *outren* (see OUT, -ER[6]); c. G *äussern* to declare] —**ut′ter·a·ble,** *adj.* —**ut′ter·er,** *n.* —**ut′ter·less,** *adj.*

ut·ter[2] (ut′ər), *adj.* **1.** complete; total; absolute: *her utter abandonment to grief.* **2.** unconditional; unqualified: *an utter denial.* [bef. 900; ME; OE *uttra, ūtera* outer. See OUT, -ER[4]] —**ut′ter·ness,** *n.*
—**Syn. 1.** See **absolute.**

ut·ter·ance[1] (ut′ər əns), *n.* **1.** an act of uttering; vocal expression. **2.** manner of speaking; power of speaking: *His very utterance was spellbinding.* **3.** something uttered; a word or words uttered; a cry, animal's call, or the like. **4.** *Ling.* any speech sequence consisting of one or more words and preceded and followed by silence: it may be coextensive with a sentence. **5.** *Obs.* a public sale of goods. [1400–50; late ME; see UTTER[1], -ANCE]

ut·ter·ance[2] (ut′ər əns), *n. Archaic.* the utmost extremity, esp. death. [1350–1400; ME < OF *outrance, oultrance,* equiv. to *oultr(er)* to pass beyond (< L *ultrā* beyond) + *-ance* -ANCE]

ut′ter bar′. See **outer bar.**

ut′ter bar′rister. See **outer barrister.**

ut·ter·ing (ut′ər ing), *n. Law.* the crime of knowingly tendering or showing a forged instrument or counterfeit coin to another with intent to defraud. [1350–1400; ME; see UTTER[1], -ING[1]]

ut·ter·ly (ut′ər lē), *adv.* in an utter manner; completely; absolutely. [1175–1225; ME; see UTTER[2], -LY]
—**Syn.** entirely, fully, wholly, totally.

ut·ter·most (ut′ər mōst′ *or, esp. Brit.,* -məst), *adj.* **1.** most remote or outermost; farthest: *the uttermost stars.* **2.** of the greatest or highest degree, quantity, etc.; greatest: *The country's art has reached uttermost creativity.* —*n.* **3.** utmost. [1300–50; ME; see UTTER[2], -MOST]

U·tu (o͞o′to͞o), *n.* the Sumerian sun god: the counterpart of the Akkadian Shamash.

U·tua·do (o͞o twä′thô), *n.* a city in central Puerto Rico. 11,113.

U-turn (yo͞o′tûrn′), *n.* **1.** a U-shaped turn made by a vehicle so as to head in the opposite direction from its original course. **2.** a reversal of policy, tactics, or the like, resembling such a maneuver. —*v.i.* **3.** to execute a U-turn: *to U-turn into oncoming traffic.* [1925–30]

U.T.W.A., United Textile Workers of America. Also, **UTWA**

UUM, underwater-to-underwater missile.

UV, ultraviolet. Also, **U.V.**

U·val·de (yo͞o val′dē), *n.* a city in SW Texas. 14,178.

U-val·ue (yo͞o′val′yo͞o), *n.* a measure of the flow of heat through an insulating or building material: the lower the U-value, the better the insulating ability. Cf. **R-value.** [1945–50; *U,* symbol for internal energy]

u·va·rov·ite (o͞o vär′ə vīt′, yo͞o-), *n. Mineral.* a variety of garnet colored emerald-green by the presence of chromium. [1825–35; < G, named after Count S. S. *Uvarov* (1785–1855), president of St. Petersburg Academy; see -ITE[1]]

UV Ceti star. See **flare star.** [after the designation for such a star in the constellation Cetus]

u·ve·a (yo͞o′vē ə), *n. Anat.* the vascular tunic of the eye, comprising the iris, choroid coat, and ciliary body. [1515–25; < ML *ūvea,* var. of L *ūva* fruit of the vine, grape] —**u′ve·al, u′ve·ous,** *adj.*

Uve·dale (yo͞od′l, yo͞ov′dāl), *n.* **Nicholas.** See **Udall.**

u·ve·i·tis (yo͞o′vē ī′tis), *n. Pathol.* inflammation of the uvea. [1840–50; < NL; see UVEA, -ITIS] —**u·ve·it·ic** (yo͞o′vē it′ik), *adj.*

UV filter, *Photog.* See **ultraviolet filter.** [1935–40]

u·vu·la (yo͞o′vyə lə), *n., pl.* **-las, -lae** (-lē′). *Anat.* the small, fleshy, conical body projecting downward from the middle of the soft palate. See diag. under **mouth.** [1350–1400; ME < ML *ūvula,* equiv. to L *ūv(a)* grape + *-ula* -ULE]

u·vu·lar (yo͞o′vyə lər), *adj.* **1.** of or pertaining to the uvula. **2.** *Phonet.* articulated with the back of the tongue held close to or touching the uvula, as in the *r*-sound of Parisian French. —*n.* **3.** *Phonet.* a uvular sound. [1700–10; < NL *ūvulāris.* See UVULA, -AR[1]] —**u′vu·lar·ly,** *adv.*

u·vu·lec·to·my (yo͞o′vyə lek′tə mē), *n., pl.* **-mies.** *Surg.* excision of the uvula. [UVUL(A) + -ECTOMY]

u·vu·li·tis (yo͞o′vyə lī′tis), *n. Pathol.* inflammation of the uvula. [1840–50; UVUL(A) + -ITIS]

U/W, under will.

U/w, underwriter. Also, **u/w**

ux., *Chiefly Law.* uxor (used chiefly in the legal abbreviation *et ux.*).

Ux·mal (o͞os mäl′), *n.* an ancient ruined city in SE Mexico, in Yucatán: a center of later Mayan civilization.

ux·or (uk′sôr, -sōr, ug′zôr, -zōr), *n. Latin.* wife (used chiefly in the legal phrase *et uxor*).

ux·o·ri·al (uk sôr′ē əl, -sōr′-, ug zôr′-, -zōr′-), *adj.* of or pertaining to a wife; typical of or befitting a wife. [1790–1800; < L *ūxōri(us)* pertaining to a wife + -AL] —**ux·o′ri·al·ly,** *adv.*

ux·o·ri·cide (uk sôr′ə sīd′, -sōr′-, ug zôr′-, -zōr′-), *n.* **1.** the act of murdering one's wife. **2.** a man who murders his wife. [1855–60; < L *ūxor* wife + -I- + -CIDE] —**ux·o′ri·cid′al,** *adj.*

ux·o·ri·lo·cal (uk sôr′ə lō′kəl, -sōr′-, ug zôr′-, -zōr′-), *adj.* matrilocal. [< L *ūxor* wife + -I- + LOCAL]

ux·o·ri·ous (uk sôr′ē əs, -sōr′-, ug zôr′-, -zōr′-), *adj.* doting upon, foolishly fond of, or affectionately submissive toward one's wife. [1590–1600; < L *ūxōrius,* equiv. to *ūxor* wife + *-ius* -IOUS] —**ux·o′ri·ous·ly,** *adv.* —**ux·o′ri·ous·ness,** *n.*

Uz·beg (o͝oz′beg, uz′-, o͝oz beg′), *n., pl.* **-begs,** (*esp. collectively*) **-beg.** Uzbek.

Uz·bek (o͝oz′bek, uz′-, o͝oz bek′), *n., pl.* **-beks,** (*esp. collectively*) **-bek. 1.** a member of a town-dwelling Turkic people of Turkestan and Uzbekistan. **2.** the Turkic language of the Uzbeks. Also, **Usbeg, Usbek, Uzbeg.**

Uz·bek·i·stan (o͝oz bek′ə stan′, -stän′, uz-), *n.* a republic in S central Asia. 19,906,000; 172,741 sq. mi. (447,400 sq. km). *Cap.:* Tashkent. Formerly, **Uz′bek So′viet So′cialist Repub′lic.**

U·zi (o͞o′zē), *n., pl.* **U·zis.** a compact 9mm submachine gun of Israeli design. [1955–60; after *Uzi*(el Gal), Israeli army officer who designed it]

Uz·zi·ah (ə zī′ə), *n.* the son and successor of Amaziah as king of Judah, reigned 783?–742? B.C. II Kings 15:13, 30–34. Also, **Azariah.**

CONCISE PRONUNCIATION KEY: act, cāpe, dâre, pärt; set, ēqual; *if,* īce; ox, ōver, ôrder, oil, bo͝ok, bo͞ot, out; up, ûrge; child; sing; shoe; thin, *th*at; zh as in *treasure.* ə = *a* as in *alone, e* as in *system, i* as in *easily, o* as in *gallop, u* as in *circus;* ᵊ as in *fire* (fīᵊr), *hour* (ouᵊr). l and n can serve as syllabic consonants, as in *cradle* (krād′l), and *button* (but′n). See the full key inside the front cover.

DEVELOPMENT OF MAJUSCULE							
NORTH SEMITIC	GREEK	ETR.	LATIN		MODERN		
					GOTHIC	ITALIC	ROMAN
SEE LETTER U		V	V	V	𝔙	*V*	V

DEVELOPMENT OF MINUSCULE					
ROMAN CURSIVE	ROMAN UNCIAL	CAROL. MIN.	MODERN		
			GOTHIC	ITALIC	ROMAN
SEE U	v	—	𝔳	*v*	v

The twenty-second letter of the English alphabet originated in Etruscan, where it signified the *u*-sound. The use of V for the *v*-sound dates from the end of the Middle Ages.

V, v (vē), *n., pl.* **V's** or **Vs, v's** or **vs.** **1.** the 22nd letter of the English alphabet, a consonant. **2.** any spoken sound represented by the letter *V* or *v,* as in *victor, flivver,* or *shove.* **3.** something having the form of a V. **4.** a written or printed representation of the letter *V* or *v.* **5.** a device, as a printer's type, for reproducing the letter *V* or *v.*

V, **1.** vagabond. **2.** *Math.* vector. **3.** velocity. **4.** verb. **5.** victory. **6.** *Elect.* volt; volts. **7.** vowel.

V, *Symbol.* **1.** the 22nd in order or in a series, or, when *I* is omitted, the 21st. **2.** (*sometimes l.c.*) the Roman numeral for five. Cf. **Roman numerals.** **3.** *Chem.* vanadium. **4.** *Biochem.* valine. **5.** *Physics.* electric potential. **6.** (esp. during World War II) the symbol of Allied victory.

v, **1.** variable. **2.** velocity. **3.** vicinal. **4.** victory. **5.** *Elect.* volt; volts.

V., **1.** valve. **2.** Venerable. **3.** verb. **4.** verse. **5.** version. **6.** versus. **7.** very. **8.** Vicar. **9.** vice. **10.** see. [< L *vidē*] **11.** Village. **12.** violin. **13.** Virgin. **14.** Viscount. **15.** vision. **16.** visual acuity. **17.** vocative. **18.** volume.

v., **1.** valve. **2.** (in personal names) van. **3.** vector. **4.** vein. **5.** ventral. **6.** verb. **7.** verse. **8.** version. **9.** verso. **10.** versus. **11.** very. **12.** vicar. **13.** vice. **14.** see. [< L *vidē*] **15.** village. **16.** violin. **17.** vision. **18.** vocative. **19.** voice. **20.** volt. **21.** voltage. **22.** volume. **23.** (in personal names) von.

V-1 (vē′wun′), *n., pl.* **V-1's.** a robot bomb developed by the Germans in World War II and launched from bases on the ground, chiefly against England. Also, **V-one.** [< G *V(ergeltungswaffe)* retaliation weapon]

V-2 (vē′to͞o′), *n., pl.* **V-2's.** a liquid-fueled rocket used as a ballistic missile by the Germans, mainly against London, late in World War II. Also, **V-two.**

V-4 (vē′fôr′, -fōr′), *n., pl.* **V-4's.** V-four.

V-6 (vē′siks′), *n., pl.* **V-6's.** V-six.

V-8 (vē′āt′), *n., pl.* **V-8's.** V-eight.

VA, **1.** See **Veterans Administration.** **2.** Virginia (approved esp. for use with zip code). **3.** Also, **va** *Elect.* volt-ampere; volt-amperes.

Va., Virginia.

V.A., **1.** See **Veterans Administration.** **2.** Vicar Apostolic. **3.** Vice-Admiral. **4.** (Order of) Victoria and Albert.

v.a., **1.** verb active. **2.** verbal adjective.

va·ad (*Seph.* vä äd′; *Ashk.* vä′äd), *n., pl.* ***va·a·dim*** (*Seph.* vä ä dēm′; *Ashk.* vä ä′dim). *Hebrew.* a Jewish council offering advice on or having authority over certain community affairs.

Vaal (väl), *n.* a river in S Africa, in the Republic of South Africa, flowing SW from the Transvaal to the Orange River. 700 mi. (1125 km) long.

Vaa·sa (vä′sä), *n.* a seaport in W Finland, on the Gulf of Bothnia. 53,720.

vac (vak), *n. Informal.* See **vacuum cleaner.** [by shortening]

va·can·cy (vā′kən sē), *n., pl.* **-cies.** **1.** the state of being vacant; emptiness. **2.** a vacant, empty, or unoccupied place, as untenanted lodgings or offices: *This building still has no vacancies.* **3.** a gap; opening; breach. **4.** an unoccupied position or office: *a vacancy on the Supreme Court.* **5.** lack of thought or intelligence; vacuity: *a look of utter vacancy.* **6.** *Crystall.* (in a crystal) an imperfection resulting from an unoccupied lattice position. Cf. **interstitial** (def. 3). **7.** *Archaic.* absence of activity; idleness. [1570–80; < ML *vacantia.* See VACANT, -ANCY]

CONCISE ETYMOLOGY KEY: <, descended or borrowed from; >, whence; b., blend of, blended; c., cognate with; cf., compare; deriv., derivative; equiv., equivalent; imit., imitative; obl., oblique; r., replacing; s., stem; sp., spelling, spelled; resp., respelling, respelled; trans., translation; ?, origin unknown; *, unattested; ‡, probably earlier than. See the full key inside the front cover.

va·cant (vā′kənt), *adj.* **1.** having no contents; empty; void: *a vacant niche.* **2.** having no occupant; unoccupied: *no vacant seats on this train.* **3.** not in use: *a vacant room.* **4.** devoid of thought or reflection: *a vacant mind.* **5.** characterized by, showing, or proceeding from lack of thought or intelligence: *a vacant answer; a vacant expression on a face.* **6.** not occupied by an incumbent, official, or the like, as a benefice or office. **7.** free from work, business, activity, etc.: *vacant hours.* **8.** characterized by or proceeding from absence of occupation: *a vacant life.* **9.** devoid or destitute (often fol. by *of*): *He was vacant of human sympathy.* **10.** *Law.* **a.** having no tenant and devoid of furniture, fixtures, etc. (distinguished from *unoccupied*): *a vacant house.* **b.** idle or unutilized; open to any claimant, as land. **c.** without an incumbent; having no heir or claimant; abandoned: *a vacant estate.* [1250–1300; ME < L *vacant-* (s. of *vacāns,* prp. of *vacāre* to be empty); see -ANT] **—va′cant·ly,** *adv.* **—va′cant·ness,** *n.*
—Syn. **1, 2.** See **empty.** **5.** blank, vacuous, inane.

va·cate (vā′kāt *or, esp. Brit.,* və kāt′, vā-), *v.,* **-cat·ed, -cat·ing.** *—v.t.* **1.** to give up possession or occupancy of: *to vacate an apartment.* **2.** to give up or relinquish (an office, position, etc.): *to vacate the presidency of a firm.* **3.** to render inoperative; deprive of validity; void; annul: *to vacate a legal judgment.* **4.** to cause to be empty or unoccupied; make vacant: *to vacate one's mind of worries.* *—v.i.* **5.** to withdraw from occupancy; surrender possession: *We will have to vacate when our lease expires.* **6.** to give up or leave a position, office, etc. **7.** to leave; go away. [1635–45; < L *vacātus* ptp. of *vacāre* to be empty; see -ATE[1]] **—va′cat·a·ble,** *adj.*

va·ca·tion (vā kā′shən, və-), *n.* **1.** a period of suspension of work, study, or other activity, usually used for rest, recreation, or travel; recess or holiday: *Schoolchildren are on vacation now.* **2.** a part of the year, regularly set aside, when normal activities of law courts, legislatures, etc., are suspended. **3.** freedom or release from duty, business, or activity. **4.** an act or instance of vacating. *—v.i.* **5.** to take or have a vacation: *to vacation in the Caribbean.* [1350–1400; < L *vacātiōn-* (s. of *vacātiō* freedom from something; see VACATE, -ION); r. ME *vacacioun* < AF] **—va·ca′tion·er, va·ca′tion·ist,** *n.* **—va·ca′tion·less,** *adj.*

Vaca′tion Bi′ble School′, a religious school conducted by some churches during the summer for students on vacation.

va·ca·tion·land (vā kā′shən land′, və-), *n.* an area having recreational facilities, historic or picturesque sights, etc., that attract vacationists. [VACATION + -LAND]

Vac·a·ville (vak′ə vil′), *n.* a city in central California. 43,367.

vac·ci·nal (vak′sə nl), *adj.* of, pertaining to, or caused by vaccine or vaccination. [1855–60; VACCIN(ATION) + -AL[1]; cf. F *vaccinal*]

vac·ci·nate (vak′sə nāt′), *v.,* **-nat·ed, -nat·ing.** *Med.* *—v.t.* **1.** to inoculate with the vaccine of cowpox so as to render the subject immune to smallpox. **2.** to inoculate with the modified virus of any of various other diseases, as a preventive measure. *—v.i.* **3.** to perform or practice vaccination. [1800–10; back formation from VACCINATION]

vac·ci·na·tion (vak′sə nā′shən), *n. Med.* the act or practice of vaccinating; inoculation with vaccine. [1800–10; VACCINE (adj.) + -ATION]

vac·ci·na·tor (vak′sə nā′tər), *n. Med.* **1.** a person who vaccinates. **2.** an instrument used in vaccination. [1800–10; VACCINATE + -OR[2]]

vac·cine (vak sēn′ *or, esp. Brit.,* vak′sēn, -sin), *n.* **1.** any preparation used as a preventive inoculation to confer immunity against a specific disease, usually employing an innocuous form of the disease agent, as killed or weakened bacteria or viruses, to stimulate antibody production. **2.** the virus of cowpox, used in vaccination, obtained from pox vesicles of a cow or person. **3.** a software program that helps to protect against computer viruses, as by detecting them and warning the user. *—adj.* **4.** of or pertaining to vaccination. **5.** of or pertaining to vaccinia. **6.** of, pertaining to, or derived from cows. [< NL (*variolae*) *vaccīnae* cowpox (in title of E. Jenner's treatise of 1798), equiv. to *vacc(a)* cow + *-īnae,* fem. pl. of *-īnus* -INE[1]]

vac·ci·nee (vak′sə nē′), *n.* a person who receives a vaccination. [1885–90; VACCIN(ATE) + -EE]

vaccine′ point′, *Med.* a thin, pointed, vaccine-coated piece of bone or the like, for use in vaccinating.

vac·cin·i·a (vak sin′ē ə), *n.* **1.** a variant of the cowpox virus that became established in vaccines derived from cowpox-inoculated humans. **2.** *Pathol.* an acute infection caused by inoculation with vaccinia virus as a prophylactic against smallpox, characterized by localized pustular eruptions. [1800–10; < NL; see VACCINE, -IA] **—vac·cin′i·al,** *adj.*

vac·ci·ni·za·tion (vak′sə nə zā′shən), *n. Med.* a vaccination produced by a series of virus inoculations. [1885–90; VACCINE + -IZATION]

Va·chel (vā′chəl), *n.* a male given name: from a Latin word meaning "little cow."

vac·il·lant (vas′ə lənt), *adj.* wavering; hesitant; indecisive; vacillating. [1515–25; < L *vacillant-* (s. of *vacillāns*), prp. of *vacillāre* to VACILLATE; see -ANT]

vac·il·late (vas′ə lāt′), *v.i.,* **-lat·ed, -lat·ing.** **1.** to waver in mind or opinion; be indecisive or irresolute: *His tendency to vacillate makes him a poor leader.* **2.** to sway unsteadily; waver; totter; stagger. **3.** to oscillate or fluctuate. [1590–1600; < L *vacillātus* (ptp. of *vacillāre* to sway to and fro); see -ATE[1]] **—vac′il·la′tor,** *n.*
—Syn. **1.** hesitate. See **waver.** **2.** reel.

vac·il·lat·ing (vas′ə lā′ting), *adj.* **1.** not resolute; wavering; indecisive; hesitating: *an ineffectual, vacillating person.* **2.** oscillating; swaying; fluctuating: *a vacillating indicator.* Also, **vacillant.** [1805–15; VACILLATE + -ING[2]] **—vac′il·lat′ing·ly,** *adv.*
—Syn. **1.** See **fickle.**

vac·il·la·tion (vas′ə lā′shən), *n.* **1.** an act or instance of vacillating. **2.** a state of indecision or irresolution. **3.** unsteady movement; fluctuation. [1350–1400; ME *vacillacion* < L *vacillātiōn-* (s. of *vacillātiō*) a swaying. See VACILLATE, -ION]

vac·il·la·to·ry (vas′ə lə tôr′ē, -tōr′ē), *adj.* marked by or displaying vacillation: *a vacillatory policy of action.* [1725–35; VACILLATE + -ORY[1]]

vac·u·a (vak′yo͞o ə), *n.* a pl. of **vacuum.**

va·cu·i·ty (va kyo͞o′i tē, və-), *n., pl.* **-ties.** **1.** the state of being vacuous or without contents; vacancy; emptiness: *the vacuity of the open sea.* **2.** absence of thought or intelligence; inanity; blankness: *a mind of undeniable vacuity.* **3.** a time or state of dullness, lacking in mental or physical action or productivity: *the vacuity of modern existence.* **4.** an empty space; void: *a vacuity in the earth formed by erosion.* **5.** absence or lack of something specified: *a vacuity of feeling.* **6.** something inane, senseless, or stupid: *conversation full of vacuities.* **7.** a vacuum. [1535–45; < L *vacuitās.* See VACUOUS, -ITY]

vac·u·o·late (vak′yo͞o ə lit, -lāt′, -yə lit, -lāt′), *adj.* having a vacuole or vacuoles. Also, **vac′u·o·lat′ed** [1855–60; VACUOLE + -ATE[1]]

vac·u·o·la·tion (vak′yo͞o ə lā′shən, -yə lā′-), *n.* **1** the formation of vacuoles. **2.** the state of being vacuolate. **3.** a system of vacuoles. [1855–60; VACUOLE + -ATION]

vac·u·ole (vak′yo͞o ōl′), *n. Biol.* **1.** a membrane-bound cavity within a cell, often containing a watery liquid or secretion. See diag. under **cell.** **2.** a minute cavity or vesicle in organic tissue. [1850–55; < F; see VACUUM, -OLE[1]] **—vac·u·o·lar** (vak′yo͞o ō′lər, vak′yo͞o ə-, vak′yə lər), *adj.*

vac·u·ous (vak′yo͞o əs), *adj.* **1.** without contents empty: *the vacuous air.* **2.** lacking in ideas or intelligence: *a vacuous mind.* **3.** expressing or characterized by a lack of ideas or intelligence; inane; stupid: *a vacuous book.* **4.** purposeless; idle: *a vacuous way of life.*

[1645–55; < L *vacuus* empty; see -OUS] **—vac′u·ous·ly,** *adv.* **—vac′u·ous·ness,** *n.*

vac·u·um (vak′yo͞om, -yo͞o əm, -yəm), *n., pl.* **vac·u·ums** for 1, 2, 4–6, **vac·u·a** (vak′yo͞o ə) for 1, 2, 4, 6; *adj.; v.* **—n. 1.** a space entirely devoid of matter. **2.** an enclosed space from which matter, esp. air, has been partially removed so that the matter or gas remaining in the space exerts less pressure than the atmosphere (opposed to *plenum*). **3.** the state or degree of exhaustion in such an enclosed space. **4.** a space not filled or occupied; emptiness; void: *The loss left a vacuum in his heart.* **5.** a vacuum cleaner or sweeper. **6.** *Physics.* a state of lowest energy in a quantum field theory. **—adj. 7.** of, pertaining to, employing, or producing a vacuum. **8.** (of a hollow container) partly exhausted of gas or air. **9.** pertaining to a device or process that makes use of a vacuum to accomplish a desired task. **10.** noting or pertaining to canning or packaging in which air is removed from the container to prevent deterioration of the contents. **—v.t. 11.** to use a vacuum cleaner on; clean with a vacuum cleaner: *to vacuum rugs.* **12.** to treat with any vacuum device, as a vacuum drier. **—v.i. 13.** to use a vacuum cleaner: *to vacuum in the dining room.* [1540–50; < L, neut. of *vacuus* empty]

vac′uum aspira′tion, *Med.* **1.** See under **menstrual extraction. 2.** a method of sampling the contents of the uterus for diagnostic purposes. [1965–70]

vac′uum bot′tle, a bottle or flask having a vacuum liner that prevents the escape of heat from hot contents, usually liquids, or the entrance of heat into cold contents; thermos. [1905–10]

vac′uum clean′er, an electrical appliance for cleaning carpets, floors, etc., by suction. Also called **vac′uum sweep′er.** [1900–05]

vac′uum cof′fee mak′er, a coffee pot with upper and lower glass units, the upper for ground coffee and the lower for water that, when boiled, rises through the filter-stoppered bottom of the upper unit and remains there until drawn back down to the lower unit as brewed coffee by a reduction in pressure caused by the removal of heat.

vac′uum con′crete, concrete from which excess moisture and air are sucked to quicken hardening and increase strength.

vac′uum distilla′tion, *Chem.* a process of distillation employing a vacuum that by lowering the pressure on a liquid allows volatilization at a lower temperature than normal. [1895–1900]

vac′uum gauge′, a device for measuring pressures below atmospheric pressure in the receiver of an air pump, in steam condensers, and the like. [1860–65]

vac·u·um·ize (vak′yo͞o mīz′, -yo͞o ə-, -yə-), *v.t.,* **-ized, -iz·ing. 1.** to create a vacuum in. **2.** vacuum (def. 11). **3.** vacuum-pack. Also, *esp. Brit.,* **vac′u·um·ise′.** [1905–10; VACUUM + -IZE]

vac·u·um-pack (vak′yo͞om pak′, -yo͞o əm-, -yəm-), *v.t.* to pack (food) in a vacuum-packed container.

vac·u·um-packed (vak′yo͞om pakt′, -yo͞o əm-, -yəm-), *adj.* packed and sealed in a container, as a can or jar, with as much air as possible evacuated before sealing, chiefly to preserve freshness. [1925–30]

vac′uum pan′, a vessel equipped with a vacuum pump used for rapid evaporation by boiling a substance at a low temperature under reduced pressure.

vac′uum pump′, a pump or device by which a partial vacuum can be produced. [1855–60]

vac′uum tube′, 1. Also called, *esp. Brit.,* **vac′uum valve′.** an electron tube from which almost all air or gas has been evacuated: formerly used extensively in radio and electronics. **2.** a sealed glass tube with electrodes and a partial vacuum or a highly rarefied gas, used to observe the effects of a discharge of electricity passed through it. [1775–85]

va·de me·cum (vā′dē mē′kəm, vä′-), *pl.* **va·de me·cums. 1.** something a person carries about for frequent or regular use. **2.** a book for ready reference; manual; handbook. [1620–30; < L *vāde mēcum* lit., go with me]

V. Adm., Vice-Admiral.

va·dose (vā′dōs), *adj. Geol.* found or located above the water table: *vadose water; vadose zone.* [1895–1900; < L *vadōsus* shallow, equiv. to *vad(um)* a shoal, ford + *-ōsus* -OSE[1]]

Vads·ö (vät′sœ), *n.* a seaport in NE Norway. 5625.

Va·duz (fä do͞ots′), *n.* a city in and the capital of Liechtenstein, on the upper Rhine. 7500.

vae vic·tis (wī′ wik′tēs; *Eng.* vē′ vik′tis), *Latin.* woe to the vanquished.

Va·fi·o (vä′fē ō′; *Gk.* vä fyô′), *n.* Vaphio.

vag·a·bond (vag′ə bond′), *adj.* **1.** wandering from place to place without any settled home; nomadic: *a vagabond tribe.* **2.** leading an unsettled or carefree life. **3.** disreputable; worthless; shiftless. **4.** of, pertaining to, or characteristic of a vagabond: *vagabond habits.* **5.** having an uncertain or irregular course or direction: *a vagabond voyage.* **—n. 6.** a person, usually without a permanent home, who wanders from place to place; nomad. **7.** an idle wanderer without a permanent home or visible means of support; tramp; vagrant. **8.** a carefree, worthless, or irresponsible person; rogue. [1400–50; late ME *vagabond* (< OF *vagabond*) < LL *vagābundus* wandering, vagrant, equiv. to L *vagā(rī)* to wander + *-bundus* adj. suffix] **—vag′a·bond′ish,** *adj.*
—Syn. 7. hobo, loafer. See **vagrant. 8.** knave, idler.

vag·a·bond·age (vag′ə bon′dij), *n.* **1.** the state or condition of being a vagabond; idle wandering. **2.** vagabonds collectively. Also called **vag′a·bond′ism.** [1805–15; VAGABOND + -AGE]

va·gal (vā′gəl), *adj.* of or pertaining to a vagus nerve. [1850–55; VAG(US) + -AL[1]]

va′gal block′, *Med.* the obstruction of vagus nerve impulses by the administration of drugs, a treatment for reducing acid secretion by the stomach. Cf. **vagotomy.**

va·gar·i·ous (və gâr′ē əs), *adj.* **1.** characterized by vagaries; erratic; capricious: *a vagarious foreign policy.* **2.** roving; wandering: *vagarious artists.* [1790–1800; VAGARY + -OUS] **—va·gar′i·ous·ly,** *adv.*

va·gar·y (və gâr′ē, vā′gə rē), *n., pl.* **-gar·ies. 1.** an unpredictable or erratic action, occurrence, course, or instance: *the vagaries of weather; the vagaries of the economic scene.* **2.** a whimsical, wild, or unusual idea, desire, or action. [1565–75, in sense "wandering journey"; appar. < L *vagārī* to wander]
—Syn. 2. caprice, whim, quirk, crotchet.

vag·ile (vaj′əl *or, esp. Brit.,* -īl), *adj. Biol.* endowed with or having freedom of movement. [1885–90; < L *vag(us)* wandering + -ILE]

va·gil·i·ty (və jil′i tē), *n. Biol.* the ability of an organism to move about freely and migrate. [1935–40; VAGILE + -ITY]

vagin-, var. of **vagino-** before a vowel: *vaginectomy.*

va·gi·na (və jī′nə), *n., pl.* **-nas, -nae** (-nē). **1.** *Anat., Zool.* **a.** the passage leading from the uterus to the vulva in certain female mammals. Cf. **oviduct. b.** a sheathlike part or organ. **2.** *Bot.* the sheath formed by the basal part of certain leaves where they embrace the stem. [1675–85; < NL; L *vāgīna* sheath]

vag·i·nal (vaj′ə nl), *adj.* **1.** *Anat., Zool.* pertaining to or involving the vagina. **2.** pertaining to or resembling a sheath. **—vag′i·nal·ly,** *adv.* [1720–30; VAGIN(A) + -AL[1]]

vag·i·nate (vaj′ə nit, -nāt′), *adj. Bot.* having a vagina or sheath; sheathed. [1840–50; < NL *vāgīnātus.* See VAGINA, -ATE[1]]

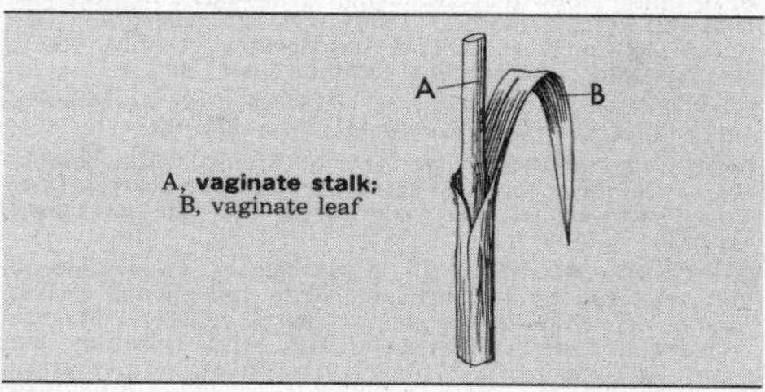

A, **vaginate stalk;**
B, vaginate leaf

vag·i·nec·to·my (vaj′ə nek′tə mē), *n., pl.* **-mies.** *Surg.* excision of part or all of the vagina. [VAGIN(A) + -ECTOMY]

vag·i·nis·mus (vaj′ə niz′məs), *n. Pathol.* a painful spasm of the vagina. [1865–70; < NL; see VAGINA, -ISM]

vag·i·ni·tis (vaj′ə nī′tis), *n. Pathol.* inflammation of the vagina. Also called **colpitis.** [1840–50; VAGIN(A) + -ITIS]

vagino-, a combining form representing **vagina** in compound words: *vaginotomy.* Also, *esp. before a vowel,* **vagin-.**

vag·i·no·my·co·sis (vaj′ə nō mī kō′sis), *n. Pathol.* a fungous infection of the vagina. [VAGINO- + MYCOSIS]

vag·i·not·o·my (vaj′ə not′ə mē), *n., pl.* **-mies.** *Surg.* colpotomy. [VAGINO- + -TOMY]

vago-, a combining form with the meaning "vagus nerve," used in the formation of compound words: *vagotomy.* [see VAGUS, -O-]

va·go·de·pres·sor (vā′gō di pres′ər), *Pharm.* **—adj. 1.** decreasing or mimicking the decrease of the activity of the vagus nerve. **—n. 2.** any such substance. [VAGO- + DEPRESSOR]

va·got·o·my (vā got′ə mē), *n., pl.* **-mies.** the surgical severance of vagus nerve fibers, performed to reduce acid secretion by the stomach. Cf. **vagal block.** [1900–05; VAGO- + -TOMY]

va·go·to·ni·a (vā′gə tō′nē ə), *n. Pathol.* hyperexcitability of the vagus nerve, producing bradycardia, decreased heart output, and faintness. [1910–15; VAGO- + -TONIA] **—va·go·ton·ic** (vā′gə ton′ik), *adj.*

va·go·trop·ic (vā′gə trop′ik, -trō′pik), *adj. Physiol.* affecting the vagus nerve. [VAGO- + -TROPIC]

va·gran·cy (vā′grən sē), *n., pl.* **-cies. 1.** the state or condition of being a vagrant: *an arrest for vagrancy.* **2.** the conduct of a vagrant. **3.** mental wandering; reverie. [1635–45; VAGR(ANT) + -ANCY]

va·grant (vā′grənt), *n.* **1.** a person who wanders about idly and has no permanent home or employment; vagabond; tramp. **2.** *Law.* an idle person without visible means of support, as a tramp or beggar. **3.** a person who wanders from place to place; wanderer; rover. **4.** wandering idly without a permanent home or employment; living in vagabondage: *vagrant beggars.* **5.** of, pertaining to, or characteristic of a vagrant: *the vagrant life.* **—adj. 6.** wandering or roaming from place to place; nomadic. **7.** (of plants) straggling in growth. **8.** not fixed or settled, esp. in course; moving hither and thither: *a vagrant leaf blown by the wind.* [1400–50; late ME *vagaraunt,* appar. prp. of AF **vagrer,* perh. < ME **vagren,* b. *vagen* (< L *vagārī* to wander) and **walcren* (> OF *wa(u)crer*), equiv. to *walc-* (see WALK) + *-r-* freq. suffix + *-en* inf. suffix] **—va′grant·ly,** *adv.* **—va′grant·ness,** *n.*
—Syn. 1. VAGRANT, VAGABOND describe an idle, disreputable person who lacks a fixed abode. VAGRANT suggests a tramp, a person with no settled abode or livelihood, an idle and disorderly person: *picked up by police as a vagrant.* VAGABOND especially emphasizes the idea of worthless living, often by trickery, thieving, or other disreputable means: *Actors were once classed with rogues and vagabonds.*

va·grom (vā′grəm), *adj. Archaic.* vagrant. [1590–1600; var. of VAGRANT]

vague (vāg), *adj.,* **va·guer, va·guest. 1.** not clearly or explicitly stated or expressed: *vague promises.* **2.** indefinite or indistinct in nature or character, as ideas or feelings: *a vague premonition of disaster.* **3.** not clear or distinct to the sight or any other sense; perceptible or recognizable only in an indefinite way: *vague shapes in the dark; vague murmurs behind a door.* **4.** not definitely established, determined, confirmed, or known; uncertain: *a vague rumor; The date of his birth is vague.* **5.** (of persons) not clear or definite in thought, understanding, or expression: *vague about his motives; a vague person.* **6.** (of the eyes, expression, etc.) showing lack of clear perception or understanding: *a vague stare.* [1540–50; (< MF) < L *vagus* wandering] **—vague′ly,** *adv.* **—vague′ness,** *n.*
—Syn. 1. unspecific, imprecise. **3.** obscure, hazy, shadowy.

va·gus (vā′gəs), *n., pl.* **-gi** (-jī, -gī). See **vagus nerve.** [1830–40; < L: wandering]

va′gus nerve′, *pl.* **vagus nerves.** *Anat.* either one of the tenth pair of cranial nerves, consisting of motor fibers that innervate the muscles of the pharynx, larynx, heart, and thoracic and abdominal viscera, and of sensory fibers that conduct impulses from these structures to the brain. [1830–40]

vail[1] (vāl), *v.t.* **1.** to let sink; lower. **2.** *Archaic.* to take off or doff (one's hat), as in respect or submission. [1300–50; ME *valen,* aph. var. of *avalen* (now obs.) < MF *avaler* to move down, v. deriv. of phrase *a val* down (lit., to the valley) (*a* to (< L *ad*) + *val* VALE)]

vail[2] (vāl), *Archaic.* **—v.i., v.t. 1.** to be of use or profit; avail. **—n. 2.** a tip; gratuity. [1250–1300; ME; aph. var. of AVAIL]

vail[3] (vāl), *Obs.* **—n. 1.** a veil. **—v.t. 2.** to veil.

vain (vān), *adj.,* **-er, -est. 1.** excessively proud of or concerned about one's own appearance, qualities, achievements, etc.; conceited: *a vain dandy.* **2.** proceeding from or showing personal vanity: *vain remarks.* **3.** ineffectual or unsuccessful; futile: *a vain effort.* **4.** without real significance, value, or importance; baseless or worthless: *vain pageantry; vain display.* **5.** *Archaic.* senseless or foolish. **6. in vain, a.** without effect or avail; to no purpose: *to apologize in vain.* **b.** in an improper or irreverent manner: *to take God's name in vain.* [1250–1300; ME < OF < L *vānus* empty, vain] **—vain′ly,** *adv.* **—vain′ness,** *n.*
—Syn. 1. egotistical, self-complacent, vainglorious, proud, arrogant, overweening. **3.** fruitless, unavailing. **4.** unimportant, trivial, trifling, nugatory. See **useless.**
—Ant. 1. humble. **3.** useful.

Väi·nä·möi·nen (vī′nə moi′nen; *Fin.* vai′na mœi′-nen), *n. Finnish Legend.* an old magician, the hero of the *Kalevala,* who opposes the magician Joukahainen and the sorceress Louhi.

vain·glo·ri·ous (vān glôr′ē əs, -glōr′-), *adj.* **1.** filled with or given to vainglory: *a vainglorious actor.* **2.** characterized by, showing, or proceeding from vainglory: *a vainglorious estimate of one's ability.* [1470–80; VAINGLORY + -OUS] **—vain·glo′ri·ous·ly,** *adv.* **—vain·glo′ri·ous·ness,** *n.*

vain·glo·ry (vān′glôr′ē, -glōr′ē, vān glôr′ē, -glōr′ē), *n.* **1.** excessive elation or pride over one's own achievements, abilities, etc.; boastful vanity. **2.** empty pomp or show. [1250–1300; ME *vainglorie,* trans. of ML *vāna glōria;* see VAIN, GLORY]
—Syn. 1. See **pride. 2.** ostentation. **—Ant. 1.** humility.

vair (vâr), *n.* **1.** a fur much used for lining and trimming garments in the 13th and 14th centuries, generally assumed to have been that of a variety of squirrel with a gray back and white belly. Cf. **miniver** (def. 1). **2.** *Heraldry.* a fur represented by a pattern of escutcheon- or bell-shaped figures, each outlining the adjacent sides of those beside it so that the figures alternate vertically and horizontally both in position and in tinctures, of which argent and azure are common. [1250–1300; ME < OF < L *varium* something particolored; see VARIOUS]

Vai·she·shi·ka (vī′she shē′kə, vī shā′shi kə), *n. Indian Philos.* a school of thought asserting the existence of a universe formed by a god out of atoms of earth, air, fire, and water, as well as out of space, time, ether, mind, and soul, all conceived as substances coexisting eternally with the god. [< Skt *vaiśeṣika,* deriv. of *viśeṣa* difference, particular property]

Vaish·na·va (vīsh′nə və), *n. Hinduism.* a Bhakti sect devoted to Vishnu. **—Vaish′na·vism,** *n.*

Vais·ya (vīs′yə, vīsh′-), *n.* a member of the Hindu mercantile and professional class, above the Shudras and below the Kshatriyas. Cf. **Brahman** (def. 1). [1785–95; < Skt *vaiśya*]

vai·vode (vī′vōd), *n.* voivode.

vaj·ra (vuj′rə), *n. Hinduism.* (in Vedic mythology) the thunderbolt of Indra. [< Skt]

va·keel (və kēl′), *n. Anglo-Indian.* a native lawyer. Also, **va·kil′.** [1615–25; < Hindi *vakīl* < Ar *wakīl*]

Val (val), *n.* **1.** a male given name, form of **Valentine. 2.** a female given name, form of **Valerie.**

Val (val), *n.* Valenciennes (def. 2).

Val, *Biochem.* valine.

val., 1. valentine. **2.** valuation. **3.** value. **4.** valued.

Va·la (vä′lə), *n. Scand. Myth.* a prophetess.

Va·la·don (VA LA dôN′), *n.* **Su·zanne** (SY ZAN′), 1865–1938, French painter (mother of Maurice Utrillo).

Va·lais (*Fr.* VA le′; *Eng.* va lā′), *n.* a canton in SW Switzerland. 211,600; 2021 sq. mi. (5235 sq. km). *Cap.:* Sion.

val·ance (val′əns, vā′ləns), *n.* **1.** a short curtain or piece of drapery that is hung from the edge of a canopy, from the frame of a bed, etc. **2.** a short ornamental piece of drapery placed across the top of a window.

[1400–50; late ME; perh. after VALENCE, French city noted for cloth-making] —**val′anced,** *adj.*

Val-Bél·air (val′bel âr′; *Fr.* val bā leʀ′), *n.* a town in S Quebec, in E Canada. 10,716.

Val·cour′ Is′land (val ko͝or′), an island in NE New York, in Lake Champlain: battle 1776.

Val·dai′ Hills′ (väl dī′; *Russ.* vul dī′), a region of hills and plateaus in the W Russian Federation in Europe, at the source of the Volga River: highest point, 1140 ft. (347 m).

Val·de·mar I (väl′də mär′). See **Waldemar I.**

Val-de-Marne (val də maʀn′), *n.* a department in N France. 1,215,674; 94 sq. mi. (243 sq. km). *Cap.:* Créteil.

Val·dez (val dēz′), *n.* an ice-free port in S Alaska, at N end of the Gulf of Alaska: S terminus of the Trans-Alaska Pipeline. 3079.

Val·di·via (bäl dē′vyä), *n.* a seaport in S Chile. 92,763.

Val-d'Oise (val dwaz′), *n.* a department in N France. 840,885; 482 sq. mi. (1248 sq. km). *Cap.:* Pontoise.

Val d'Or (*Fr.* val dôʀ′), a city in SW Quebec, in S Canada. 19,915.

Val·dos·ta (val dos′tə), *n.* a city in S Georgia. 37,596.

vale (vāl), *n.* **1.** a valley. **2.** the world, or mortal or earthly life: *this vale of tears.* [1250–1300; ME < OF *val* < L *vallem,* acc. of *vallis, vallēs* valley]

val·e·dic·tion (val′i dik′shən), *n.* **1.** an act of bidding farewell or taking leave. **2.** an utterance, oration, or the like, given in bidding farewell or taking leave; valedictory. [1605–15; < L *valedictiōn-* (s. of *valedictiō*), equiv. to *valedict(us),* ptp. of *valedīcere* (*vale* farewell + *dictus,* ptp. of *dīcere* to say) + *-iōn-* -ION]

Valedic′tion Forbid′ding Mourn′ing, A, a poem (1612) by John Donne.

val·e·dic·to·ri·an (val′i dik tôr′ē ən, -tōr′-), *n.* a student, usually the one ranking highest academically in a school graduating class, who delivers the valedictory at the commencement exercises. [1750–60, *Amer.;* VALEDICTORY + -AN]

val·e·dic·to·ry (val′i dik′tə rē), *adj., n., pl.* **-ries.** —*adj.* **1.** bidding good-bye; saying farewell: *a valedictory speech.* **2.** of or pertaining to an occasion of leave-taking: *a valedictory ceremony.* —*n.* **3.** an address or oration delivered at the commencement exercises of a college or school on behalf of the graduating class. **4.** any farewell address or oration. [1645–55; < L *valedict(us)* (see VALEDICTION) + -ORY[1]]

va·lence (vā′ləns), *n.* **1.** *Chem.* **a.** the quality that determines the number of atoms or groups with which any single atom or group will unite chemically. **b.** the relative combining capacity of an atom or group compared with that of the standard hydrogen atom. The chloride ion, Cl–, with a valence of one, has the capacity to unite with one atom of hydrogen or its equivalent, as in HCl or NaCl. **2.** *Immunol.* the number of determinants per molecule of antigen. **3.** the capacity of one person or thing to react with or affect another in some special way, as by attraction or the facilitation of a function or activity. Also, **valency.** [1865–70; < L *valentia* strength, worth, equiv. to *valent-* (s. of *valēns*), prp. to be strong + *-ia* n. suffix; see -ENCE]

Va·lence (va läɴs′), *n.* a city in and the capital of Drôme, in SE France. 70,307.

va′lence elec′tron, *Chem.* an electron of an atom, located in the outermost shell (**va′lence shell′**) of the atom, that can be transferred to or shared with another atom. [1925–30]

Va·len·ci·a (və len′shē ə, -shə, -sē ə; *Sp.* bä len′syä *or, for 2, 3,* -thyä), *n.* **1. Guil·ler·mo Le·ón** (gē yeʀ′mô le ôn′), 1909–71, Colombian diplomat and statesman: president 1962–66. **2.** a province in E Spain: the region was formerly a Moorish kingdom. 1,767,327; 9085 sq. mi. (23,530 sq. km). **3.** a seaport in E Spain. 700,000. **4.** a city in N Venezuela. 463,418. **5.** a variety of the sweet orange, *Citrus sinensis,* originally from the Mediterranean area and cultivated extensively in Florida and California. **6.** Also, **Va·len·ti·a** (və len′shē ə, -shə). a female given name.

Va·len·ci·ennes (və len′sē enz′; *Fr.* va läɴ syen′), *n.* **1.** a city in N France, SE of Lille. 43,202. **2.** Also called **Valen′ciennes′ lace′, Val, Val lace.** *Textiles.* **a.** a flat bobbin lace of linen, worked in one piece with the same thread forming the ground and the motif. **b.** a cotton imitation of it. [1710–20, for def. 2]

va·len·cy (vā′lən sē), *n., pl.* **-cies.** *Chem.* valence.

Va·lens (vā′lənz), *n.* **Fla·vi·us** (flā′vē əs), A.D. c328–378, emperor of the Eastern Roman Empire 364–378.

-valent, a combining form with the meanings "having a valence" (*quadrivalent*), "having homologous chromosomes" (*univalent*), "having antibodies" (*multivalent*), of the number specified by the initial element. [< L *valent-* (s. of *valēns,* prp. of *valēre* to be strong); see EQUIVALENT]

val·en·tine (val′ən tīn′), *n.* **1.** a card or message, usually amatory or sentimental but sometimes satirical or comical, or a token or gift sent by one person to another on Valentine Day, sometimes anonymously. **2.** a sweetheart chosen or greeted on this day. **3.** a written or other artistic work, message, token, etc., expressing affection for something or someone: *His photographic essay is a valentine to Paris.* [1400–50; late ME, after the feast of Saint VALENTINE]

Val·en·tine (val′ən tīn′), *n.* **1. Saint,** died A.D. c270, Christian martyr at Rome. **2.** Also, **Valentinus.** pope A.D. 827. **3.** a male given name: from a Latin word meaning "strong."

Val′entine Day′, February 14, observed in honor of St. Valentine as a day for the exchange of valentines and other tokens of affection. Also, **Val′entine's Day′.** Also called **Saint Valentine's Day.**

Val·en·tin·i·an I (val′ən tin′ē ən), A.D. 321?–375, emperor of Western Roman Empire 364–375. Also, **Val·en·tin·i·a·nus I** (val′ən tin′ē ā′nəs).

Valentinian II, A.D. c371–392, emperor of the Western Roman Empire 375–392. Also, **Valentinianus II.**

Valentinian III, A.D. 419?–455, emperor of the Western Roman Empire 425–455. Also, **Valentinianus III.**

val·en·tin·ite (val′ən ti nīt′, -tē′nīt), *n.* a mineral, antimony trioxide, Sb_2O_3, formed by the oxidation of various minerals containing antimony and occurring in the form of white orthorhombic crystals. [1855–60; < G *Valentinit,* named after Basil *Valentine,* 15th-century German alchemist; see -ITE[1]]

Val·en·ti·no (val′ən tē′nō), *n.* **Rudolph** (*Rodolpho d'Antonguolla*), 1895–1926, U.S. motion-picture actor, born in Italy.

Val·en·ti·nus (val′ən tī′nəs), *n.* Valentine (def. 2).

Va·le·ra (və lâr′ə, -lēr′ə; *for 1 also Irish* vä lā′ʀä; *for 2 also Sp.* bä le′ʀä), *n.* **1. Ea·mon De** (ā′mən de). See **De Valera.** **2.** a city in W Venezuela. 71,223.

Va·le·ra y Al·ca·lá Ga·lia·no (bä le′ʀä ē äl′kä lä′ gä lyä′nô), **Juan** (hwän), 1824–1905, Spanish novelist, critic, diplomat, and statesman.

va·le·ri·an (və lēr′ē ən), *n.* **1.** any plant of the genus *Valeriana,* as the common valerian *V. officinalis,* having small, fragrant flowers of white, lavender, or pink and a root that is used medicinally. **2.** a drug consisting of or made from the root, formerly used as a nerve sedative and antispasmodic. [1350–1400; ME *valirian* < ML *valeriāna* (herb) of *Valeria* (old Roman province, where plant is said to have been common); see -AN]

Va·le·ri·an (və lēr′ē ən), *n.* (*Publius Licinius Valerianus*), died A.D. c260, Roman emperor 253–60.

va·le·ri·a·na·ceous (və lēr′ē ə nā′shəs), *adj.* belonging to the plant family Valerianaceae. Cf. **valerian family.** [1835–45; < NL *Valerianace(ae)* (see VALERIAN, -ACEAE) + -OUS]

valer′ian fam′ily, the plant family Valerianaceae, characterized by herbaceous plants and shrubs having simple or compound, opposite leaves, clusters of small flowers, and dry, indehiscent fruit, and including corn salad, spikenard (*Nardostachys jatamansi*), and valerian.

va·ler·ic (və ler′ik, -lēr′-), *adj.* pertaining to or derived from valerian. Also, **va·le·ri·an·ic** (və lēr′ē an′ik). [1850–55; VALER(IAN) + -IC]

valer′ic ac′id, *Chem.* any of several isomeric organic acids having the formula $C_5H_{10}O_2$, the common one being a liquid of pungent odor obtained from valerian roots: used chiefly as an intermediate in perfumery. [1855–60]

Val·e·rie (val′ə rē), *n.* a female given name. Also, **Va·le·ri·a** (və lēr′ē ə), **Val′e·ry.**

Va·lé·ry (va lā ʀē′), *n.* **Paul** (pôl), 1871–1945, French poet and philosopher.

val·et (va lā′, val′it, val′ā), *n., v.,* **-et·ed, -et·ing.** —*n.* **1.** a male servant who attends to the personal needs of his employer, as by taking care of clothing or the like; manservant. **2.** a man who is employed for cleaning and pressing, laundering, and similar services for patrons of a hotel, passengers on a ship, etc. **3.** an attendant who parks cars for patrons at a hotel, restaurant, etc. **4.** a stand or rack for holding coats, hats, etc. —*v.t., v.i.* **5.** to serve as a valet. [1560–70; < F; MF *va(s)let* squire, equiv. to *vas-* (< ML *vassus* servant) + *-let* -LET; see VASSAL] —**val′et·less,** *adj.*

va·let de cham·bre (va le də shäɴ′bʀᵊ), *pl.* ***va·lets de cham·bre*** (va le də shäɴ′bʀᵊ). *French.* valet (def. 1).

val·e·tu·di·nar·i·an (val′i to͞od′n âr′ē ən, -tyo͞od′-), *n.* **1.** an invalid. **2.** a person who is excessively concerned about his or her poor health or ailments. —*adj.* **3.** in poor health; sickly; invalid. **4.** excessively concerned about one's poor health or ailments. **5.** of, pertaining to, or characterized by invalidism. [1695–1705; VALETUDINARY + -AN]

val·e·tu·di·nar·i·an·ism (val′i to͞od′n âr′ē ə niz′əm, -tyo͞od′-), *n.* the state, condition, or habits of a valetudinarian. [1830–40; VALETUDINARIAN + -ISM]

val·e·tu·di·nar·y (val′i to͞od′n er′ē, -tyo͞od′-), *n., pl.* **-nar·ies.** valetudinarian. [1575–85; < L *valētūdinārius* sickly, equiv. to *valētūdin-* (s. of *valētūdō*) good or bad state of health (*valē(re)* to be well + *-tūdō* -TUDE) + *-ārius* -ARY]

val·gus (val′gəs), *n., pl.* **-gus·es.** *Pathol.* —*n.* **1.** an abnormally turned position of a part of the bone structure of a human being, esp. of the leg. —*adj.* **2.** of or in such a position; bowlegged, knock-kneed, or the like. [1790–1800; < L: knock-kneed]

Val·hal·la (val hal′ə, väl hä′lə), *n. Scand. Myth.* the hall of Odin into which the souls of heroes slain in battle and others who have died bravely are received. Also, **Val·hall** (val hal′, val′hal), **Walhalla, Walhall.** [1760–70; Latinized form of ON *Valhǫll,* equiv. to *val(r)* the slain in battle, slaughter (c. OE *wæl*) + *hǫll* HALL]

val·ian·cy (val′yən sē), *n.* valiant nature or quality; valor; bravery; courage. Also, **val′iance.** [1565–75; VALI(ANT) + -ANCY]

val·iant (val′yənt), *adj.* **1.** boldly courageous; brave; stout-hearted: *a valiant soldier.* **2.** marked by or showing bravery or valor; heroic: *to make a valiant effort.* **3.** worthy; excellent. [1275–1325; ME *valia(u)nt* < AF; MF *vaillant,* prp. of *valoir* to be of worth < L *valēre;* see -ANT] —**val′iant·ly,** *adv.* —**val′iant·ness,** *n.*
—**Syn. 1.** valorous, dauntless. See **brave.**

val·id (val′id), *adj.* **1.** sound; just; well-founded: *a valid reason.* **2.** producing the desired result; effective: *a valid antidote for gloom.* **3.** having force, weight, or cogency; authoritative. **4.** legally sound, effective, or binding; having legal force: *a valid contract.* **5.** *Logic.* (of an argument) so constructed that if the premises are jointly asserted, the conclusion cannot be denied without contradiction. **6.** *Archaic.* robust; well; healthy. [1565–75; < L *validus* strong, equiv. to *val(ēre)* to be strong + *-idus* -ID[4]] —**val′id·ly,** *adv.* —**val′id·ness,** *n.*
—**Syn. 3.** substantial, cogent. **5.** logical, convincing.

val·i·date (val′i dāt′), *v.t.,* **-dat·ed, -dat·ing.** **1.** to make valid; substantiate; confirm: *Time validated our suspicions.* **2.** to give legal force to; legalize. **3.** to give official sanction, confirmation, or approval to, as elected officials, election procedures, documents, etc.: *to validate a passport.* [1640–50; < ML *validātus* (ptp. of *validāre* to make valid), equiv. to *valid-* (see VALID) + *-ātus* -ATE[1]] —**val′i·da′tion,** *n.* —**val′i·da′tor,** *n.* —**val·i·da·to·ry** (val′i də tôr′ē, -tōr′ē), *adj.*
—**Syn. 1.** authenticate, verify, prove. —**Ant. 1.** disprove.

va·lid·i·ty (və lid′i tē), *n.* **1.** the state or quality of being valid: *to question the validity of the argument.* **2.** legal soundness or force. [1540–50; < LL *validitās,* equiv. to L *valid(us)* VALID + *-itās* -ITY]

Va·lin·da (və lin′də), *n.* a town in SW California. 18,700.

val·ine (val′ēn, -in, vā′lēn, -lin), *n. Biochem.* an essential amino acid, $(CH_3)_2CHCH(NH_2)COOH$, white, crystalline, and water-soluble, present in most plant and animal proteins, required for growth. *Abbr.:* Val; *Symbol:* V [1910–15; VAL(ERIC) + -INE[2]]

val·in·o·my·cin (val′ə nō mī′sin), *n. Pharm.* a cyclic, peptide antibiotic, $C_{54}H_{90}N_6O_{18}$, produced by the bacterium *Streptomyces fulvissimus;* used experimentally to transport potassium across membranes. [< G *Valinomycin* (1955); see VALINE, -O-, -MYCIN]

va·lise (və lēs′ *or, esp. Brit.,* -lēz′), *n.* a small piece of luggage that can be carried by hand, used to hold clothing, toilet articles, etc.; suitcase; traveling bag. [1605–15; < F < It *valigia,* of obscure orig.; cf. ML *valēsium*]

Val·i·um (val′ē əm), *Pharm., Trademark.* a brand of diazepam.

Val·kyr·ie (val kēr′ē, -kī′rē, väl-, val′kə rē), *n. Scand. Myth.* any of the beautiful maidens attendant upon Odin who bring the souls of slain warriors chosen by Odin or Tyr to Valhalla and there wait upon them. Also, **Walkyrie.** [< ON *valkyrja* chooser of the slain (c. OE *wælcyrie* witch), equiv. to *val(r)* the slain in battle, slaughter (c. OE *wæl*) + *kyrja* chooser (c. OE *cyrie*); akin to CHOOSE] —**Val·kyr′i·an,** *adj.*

Val·la (väl′lä), *n.* **Lo·ren·zo** (lô ʀen′dzô), 1407–57, Italian humanist and critic.

Val′ lace′, Valenciennes (def. 2).

Va·lla·do·lid (val′ə də lid′; *Sp.* bä′lyä t͟hô lēt͟h′), *n.* a city in N Spain, NW of Madrid: Columbus died here 1506. 236,341.

val·late (val′āt), *adj.* bordered by a ridge, raised edge, or the like. [1875–80; < LL *vallātus* (ptp. of *vallāre* to surround, border with a wall, rampart), equiv. to *vall(um)* rampart, WALL + *-ātus* -ATE[1]]

val·la·tion (va lā′shən), *n. Fort.* **1.** a rampart or entrenchment. **2.** the process or technique of constructing ramparts. [1655–65; < LL *vallāt(us)* (see VALLATE) + *-iōn-* -ION]

val·lec·u·la (va lek′yə lə), *n., pl.* **-lae** (-lē′). *Biol.* a furrow or depression. [1855–60; < LL, equiv. to *valle(s)* VALLEY + L *-cula* -CULE[1]] —**val·lec′u·lar,** *adj.*

val·lec·u·late (va lek′yə lāt′, -lit), *adj.* having a vallecula or valleculae. [VALLECUL(A) + -ATE[1]]

Val·le d'A·o·sta (väl′le dä ô′stä), a region in NW Italy. 114,162; 1259 sq. mi. (3260 sq. km).

Va·lle de la Pas·cua (bä′ye t͟he lä päs′kwä), a city in N Venezuela. 38,630.

Va·lle·jo (və lā′ō, -hō; *for 1, 2 also Sp.* bä ye′hô), *n.* **1. Cé·sar** (*Sp.* se′säʀ), 1895–1938, Peruvian poet. **2. Ma·ri·a·no Gua·da·lupe** (mär′ē ä′nō gwäd′l o͞op′, -o͞o′pē, mar′-; *Sp.* mä ʀyä′nô gwä′t͟hä lo͞o′pe), 1808–90, military and political leader in California, serving the Mexican government until 1846; elected senator to the first state legislature 1849. **3.** a city in W California, on San Pablo Bay, NE of San Francisco. 80,188.

Va·lle·nar (bä′ye näʀ′), *n.* a city in central Chile. 18,000.

Val′les Mar·i·ner′is (val′əs mar′ə nâr′is), *Astron.* a canyon on Mars, 3100 mi. (5000 km) in length, named after the Mariner spacecraft.

Val·let·ta (və let′ə), *n.* a seaport in and the capital of Malta, on the NE coast. 14,049.

val·ley (val′ē), *n., pl.* **-leys.** **1.** an elongated depression between uplands, hills, or mountains, esp. one following the course of a stream. **2.** an extensive, more or less flat, and relatively low region drained by a great river system. **3.** any depression or hollow resembling a valley. **4.** a low point or interval in any process, representation, or situation. **5.** any place, period, or situation that is filled with fear, gloom, foreboding, or the like: *the valley of despair.* **6.** *Archit.* a depression or angle formed by the meeting of two inclined sides of a roof. **7.** the lower phase of a horizontal wave motion. [1250–1300; ME *valeie, valey* < OF *valee,* equiv. to *val* VALE[1] + *-ee* < L *-āta,* fem. of *-ātus* -ATE[1]] —**val′ley·like′,** *adj.*

Val′ley East′, a town in S Ontario, in S Canada. 20,443.

val′ley fe′ver, *Pathol.* coccidioidomycosis. [1935–40; so called because it is common in the San Joaquin Valley in California]

Val·ley·field (val′ē fēld′), *n.* a city in S Quebec, in E Canada, SW of Montreal, on the St. Lawrence. 29,574.

Val′ley Forge′, a village in SE Pennsylvania: winter quarters of Washington's army 1777–78.

Val′ley of Ten′ Thou′sand Smokes′, a volcanic area in SW Alaska, in Katmai National Monument.

Val′ley of the Kings′, a valley on the west bank of the Nile near the site of Thebes: the necropolis of many of the kings and queens of the 18th and 19th dynasties of ancient Egypt, c1350–c1200 B.C. Also called **Val′ley of the Tombs′.**

CONCISE ETYMOLOGY KEY: <, descended or borrowed from; >, whence; b., blend of, blended; c., cognate with; cf., compare; deriv., derivative; equiv., equivalent; imit., imitative; obl., oblique; r., replacing; s., stem; sp., spelling, spelled; resp., respelling, respelled; trans., translation; ?, origin unknown; *, unattested; ‡, probably earlier than. See the full key inside the front cover.

Val′ley Stream′, a village on W Long Island, in SE New York. 35,769.

val′ley wind′ (wind), a wind that ascends a mountain valley during the day. Cf. **mountain wind.**

Val•lom•bro•sa (väl′lôm brô′zä), *n.* a resort in central Italy, near Florence: famous abbey.

Val•mid (val′mid), *Pharm., Trademark.* a brand of ethinamate.

Val•mi•ki (väl mē′kē), *n.* Hindu poet and reputed author of the Ramayana.

Va•lois (VA LWA′ *for 1, 3;* val′wä *for 2*), *n.* **1.** a member of a ruling family of France that reigned from 1328 to 1589. **2. Dame Ni•nette de** (ni net′). See **de Valois, Dame Ninette. 3.** a county in the Île de France, which became united to the French crown in 1167 and was established as a duchy in 1406.

Va•lo•na (və lō′nə; *It.* vä lô′nä), *n.* Italian name of **Vlorë.**

va•lo•ni•a (və lō′nē ə), *n.* acorn cups of an Old World oak, *Quercus macrolepis* (or *Q. aegilops*), used in tanning, dyeing, and making ink. [1715–25; < It *vallonia* < ModGk *balánia,* pl. of *baláni* acorn]

val•or (val′ər), *n.* boldness or determination in facing great danger, esp. in battle; heroic courage; bravery: *a medal for valor.* Also, *esp. Brit.,* **val′our.** [1350–1400; ME *valo(u)r* < AF; MF *valeur* < LL *valōr-,* s. of *valor* worth, equiv. to L *val(ēre)* to be of worth + *-or* -OR[1]] **—Syn.** intrepidity, spirit. See **courage. —Ant.** cowardice.

val•or•ize (val′ə rīz′), *v.t.,* **-ized, -iz•ing.** to provide for the maintaining of the value or price of (a commercial commodity) by a government's purchasing the commodity at the fixed price or by its making special loans to the producers. Also, *esp. Brit.,* **val′or•ise′.** [1905–10; < LL *valor* worth (see VALOR) + -IZE] **—val′or•i•za′tion,** *n.*

val•or•ous (val′ər əs), *adj.* **1.** having valor; courageous; valiant; brave. **2.** characterized by valor: *valorous deeds.* [1470–80; < ML *valōrōsus* valiant. See VALOR, -OUS] **—val′or•ous•ly,** *adv.* **—val′or•ous•ness,** *n.*

Val•pa•rai•so (val′pə rī′zō, -sō), *n.* **1.** Spanish, **Val•pa•ra•í•so** (bäl′pä Rä ē′sô). a seaport in central Chile. 248,972. **2.** a city in NW Indiana. 22,247.

Val•po•li•cel•la (val′pō li chel′ə; *It.* väl′pô lē chel′lä), *n.* a dry, red table wine from the Veneto region of northern Italy. [1940–45; after *Valpolicella,* an area of alluvium-filled valleys NW of Verona, where the wine is produced]

val•pro′ic ac′id (val prō′ik), *Pharm.* a carboxylic acid, $C_8H_{16}O_2$, used for its antiepileptic properties in the treatment of various seizures including petit mal. [1970–75; VAL(ERIC) + PRO(PYL) + -IC]

Val•sal′va maneu′ver (val sal′və), a forced expiratory effort against a closed glottis that decreases intrathoracic pressure, hampering venous return to the heart, and that can be used to inflate the Eustachian tubes and adjust pressure in the middle ear. [named after Antonio M. *Valsalva* (1666–1723), Italian anatomist who devised the maneuver]

valse (VAls), *n., pl.* ***valses*** (VAls). *French.* waltz.

val•u•a•ble (val′yo͞o ə bəl, -yə bəl), *adj.* **1.** having considerable monetary worth; costing or bringing a high price: *a valuable painting; a valuable crop.* **2.** having qualities worthy of respect, admiration, or esteem: *a valuable friend.* **3.** of considerable use, service, or importance: *valuable information.* —*n.* **4.** Usually, **valuables.** articles of considerable value, as of personal property, esp. those of relatively small size: *They locked their valuables in the hotel safe.* [1580–90; VALUE (v.) + -ABLE] **—val′u•a•ble•ness,** *n.* **—val′u•a•bly,** *adv.*
—Syn. 1, 3. VALUABLE, PRECIOUS refer to that which has pecuniary or other value. VALUABLE applies to whatever has value, but esp. to what has considerable monetary value or special usefulness, rarity, etc.: *a valuable watch.* That which is PRECIOUS has a very high intrinsic value or is very dear for its own sake, associations, or the like: *a precious jewel, friendship.* **—Ant. 1–3.** worthless.

val•u•ate (val′yo͞o āt′), *v.t.,* **-at•ed, -at•ing.** to set a value on; appraise. [1870–75; back formation from VALUATION] **—val′u•a′tor,** *n.*

val•u•a•tion (val′yo͞o ā′shən), *n.* **1.** the act of estimating or setting the value of something; appraisal. **2.** an estimated value or worth. **3.** the awareness or acknowledgment of the quality, nature, excellence, or the like of something: *public valuation of the importance of education.* [1520–30; VALUE + -ATION; cf. MF *valuation*] **—val′u•a′tion•al,** *adj.* **—val′u•a′tion•al•ly,** *adv.*

val•ue (val′yo͞o), *n., v.,* **-ued, -u•ing.** —*n.* **1.** relative worth, merit, or importance: *the value of a college education; the value of a queen in chess.* **2.** monetary or material worth, as in commerce or trade: *This piece of land has greatly increased in value.* **3.** the worth of something in terms of the amount of other things for which it can be exchanged or in terms of some medium of exchange. **4.** equivalent worth or return in money, material, services, etc.: *to give value for value received.* **5.** estimated or assigned worth; valuation: *a painting with a current value of $500,000.* **6.** denomination, as of a monetary issue or a postage stamp. **7.** *Math.* **a.** magnitude; quantity; number represented by a figure, symbol, or the like: *the value of an angle; the value of x; the value of a sum.* **b.** a point in the range of a function; a point in the range corresponding to a given point in the domain of a function: *The value of x^2 at 2 is 4.* **8.** import or meaning; force; significance: *the value of a word.* **9.** liking or affection; favorable regard. **10. values,** *Sociol.* the ideals, customs, institutions, etc., of a society toward which the people of the group have an affective regard. These values may be positive, as cleanliness, freedom, or education, or negative, as cruelty, crime, or blasphemy. **11.** *Ethics.* any object or quality desirable as a means or as an end in itself. **12.** *Fine Arts.* **a.** degree of lightness or darkness in a color. **b.** the relation of light and shade in a painting, drawing, or the like. **13.** *Music.* the relative length or duration of a tone signified by a note. **14. values,** *Mining.* the marketable portions of an orebody. **15.** *Phonet.* **a.** quality. **b.** the phonetic equivalent of a letter, as the sound of *a* in *hat, sang,* etc. —*v.t.* **16.** to calculate or reckon the monetary value of; give a specified material or financial value to; assess; appraise: *to value their assets.* **17.** to consider with respect to worth, excellence, usefulness, or importance. **18.** to regard or esteem highly: *He values her friendship.* [1275–1325; ME < OF, n. use of fem. ptp. (cf. VALUTA) of *valoir* < L *valēre* to be worth]
—Syn. 1. utility. VALUE, WORTH imply intrinsic excellence or desirability. VALUE is that quality of anything which renders it desirable or useful: *the value of sunlight or good books.* WORTH implies esp. spiritual qualities of mind and character, or moral excellence: *Few knew her true worth.* **3.** cost, price. **18.** prize. See **appreciate.**

val•ue-add•ed (val′yo͞o ad′id), *n.* **1.** something, as an item of equipment, that has been added to a product by a marketer or distributor to warrant a markup in the retail price. —*adj.* **2.** of, pertaining to, or supplying value-added: *software supplied by a value-added distributor.* [1930–35]

val′ue-add′ed tax′, an excise tax based on the value added to a product at each stage of production or distribution: value added is arrived at by subtracting from the total value of the product at the end of each production or distibution stage the value of the goods bought at its inception. *Abbr.:* VAT Also called **added-value tax.** [1930–35]

val•ued (val′yo͞od), *adj.* **1.** highly regarded or esteemed: *a valued friend.* **2.** estimated; appraised: *jewels valued at $100,000.* **3.** having value of a specified kind: *a triple-valued offer.* [1595–1605; VALUE + -ED[2]]

val′ue date′, *Banking.* the date on which an entry made on an account becomes effective, used esp. in connection with foreign accounts.

val′ued pol′icy, *Insurance.* a policy in which the company and the policyholder agree to the amount to be paid in the event of total loss of property, regardless of the value of the property. [1755–65]

val′ue judg′ment, an estimate, usually subjective, of the worth, quality, goodness, evil, etc., of something or someone. [1895–1900]

val•ue•less (val′yo͞o lis), *adj.* without worth or value; worthless: *valueless stocks; a valueless promise.* [1555–65; VALUE + -LESS] **—val′ue•less•ness,** *n.*

val•u•er (val′yo͞o ər), *n.* **1.** *Brit.* an appraiser. **2.** a person who values. [VALUE + -ER[1]]

va•lu•ta (və lo͞o′tə), *n.* (in Europe) the value of a currency expressed in terms of its rate of exchange with another currency. [1915–20; < It < VL **valūta,* for L *valita,* fem. ptp. of L *valēre* to be worth]

val•val (val′vəl), *adj.* valvular. [1890–95; VALVE + -AL[1]]

val•var (val′vər), *adj.* valvular. [1890–95; VALVE + -AR[1]]

val•vate (val′vāt), *adj.* **1.** furnished with or opening by a valve or valves. **2.** serving as or resembling a valve. **3.** *Bot.* **a.** opening by valves, as certain capsules and anthers. **b.** meeting without overlapping, as the parts of certain buds. **c.** composed of or characterized by such parts. [1820–30; < L *valvātus* with folding doors. See VALVE, -ATE[1]]

valve (valv), *n., v.,* **valved, valv•ing.** —*n.* **1.** any device for halting or controlling the flow of a liquid, gas, or other material through a passage, pipe, inlet, outlet, etc. **2.** a hinged lid or other movable part that closes or modifies the passage in such a device. **3.** *Anat.* a membranous fold or other structure that controls the flow of a fluid, as one that permits blood to flow in one direction only. **4.** (in musical wind instruments of the trumpet class) a device for changing the length of the air column to alter the pitch of a tone. **5.** *Zool.* **a.** one of the two or more separable pieces composing certain shells. **b.** either half of the silicified shell of a diatom. **6.** *Bot.* **a.** one of the segments into which a capsule dehisces. **b.** a flap or lidlike part of certain anthers. **7.** *Electronics. Chiefly Brit.* See **vacuum tube** (def. 1). **8.** *Archaic.* one of the leaves of a double or folding door. —*v.t.* **9.** to provide with a means of controlling the flow of liquid, gas, etc., by inserting a valve. [1350–1400; ME < L *valvae* leaves of a door] **—valve′less,** *adj.* **—valve′like′,** *adj.*

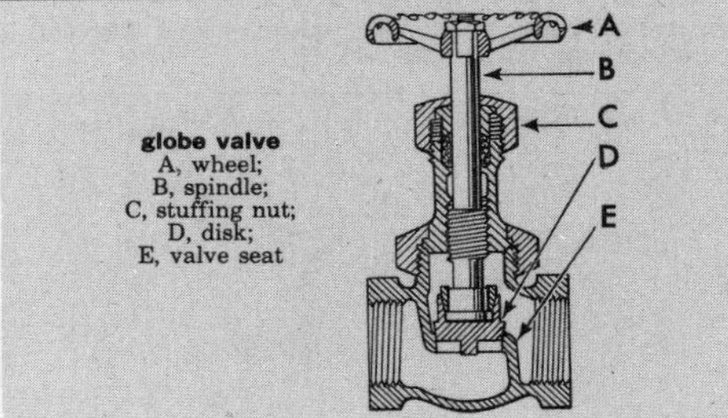

globe valve
A, wheel;
B, spindle;
C, stuffing nut;
D, disk;
E, valve seat

valved (valvd), *adj.* having or furnished with valves: *a valved trumpet.* [1670–80; VALVE + -ED[3]]

valve′ gear′, (in a reciprocating engine) the mechanism for opening and closing the valves at certain points in each stroke. Also called **valve′ train′.**

valve′-in-head′ en′gine (valv′in hed′). See **I-head engine.** [1930–35]

valve•let (valv′lit), *n.* a small valve; valvule. [1785–95; VALVE + -LET]

valve′ lift′er, *Auto., Mach.* (in an internal-combustion engine) a tappet that opens a valve when actuated by a camshaft.

valve′ stem′, stem[1] (def. 14). [1830–40]

valve′ trombone′, a trombone equipped with three or four valves in place of a slide.

val•vu•la (val′vyə lə), *n., pl.* **-lae** (-lē′). *Anat.* **1.** a small valve or valvule. **2.** a cusp of certain valves, as the aortic valve. [1605–15; < NL; L *valv(a)* VALVE + *-ula* -ULE]

val•vu•lar (val′vyə lər), *adj.* **1.** having the form or function of a valve. **2.** operating by a valve or valves. **3.** of or pertaining to a valve or valves, esp. of the heart. Also, **valval, valvar.** [1790–1800; < NL *valvulāris,* equiv. to *valvul(a)* VALVULE + *-āris* -AR[1]]

val′vular insuffi′ciency, *Pathol.* abnormal closure of a heart valve resulting in failure to prevent regurgitation of blood. Also called **val′vular incom′petence.**

val•vule (val′vyo͞ol), *n.* a small valve or a part resembling a valve. [1745–55; < NL *valvula.* See VALVE, -ULE]

val•vu•li•tis (val′vyə lī′tis), *n. Pathol.* inflammation of a valve, esp. a heart valve, often caused by rheumatic fever. [1890–95; VALVULE + -ITIS]

val•vu•lot•o•my (val′vyə lot′ə mē), *n., pl.* **-mies.** *Surg.* the opening, slitting, or fracturing of a heart valve. [VALVULE + -O- + -TOMY]

vam•brace (vam′brās), *n. Armor.* **1.** a piece of plate armor for the forearm; a lower cannon. Cf. **rerebrace.** See diag. under **armor. 2.** plate armor for the arm, usually including upper and lower cannons and a couter. [1300–50; ME *va(u)mbras* < AF *(a)vantbras,* equiv. to *avant-* fore- (see AVAUNT) + *bras* arm (see BRACE)] **—vam′braced,** *adj.*

va•moose (va mo͞os′), *v.,* **-moosed, -moos•ing.** *Slang.* —*v.i.* **1.** to leave hurriedly or quickly; decamp. —*v.t.* **2.** to leave hurriedly or quickly from; decamp from. [1830–40; < Sp *vamos* let us go, impv. 1st pers. pl. of *ir* to go]

va•mose (va mōs′), *v.i., v.t.,* **-mosed, -mos•ing.** *Slang.* vamoose.

vamp[1] (vamp), *n.* **1.** the portion of a shoe or boot upper that covers the instep and toes. **2.** something patched up or pieced together. **3.** *Jazz.* an accompaniment, usually improvised, consisting of a succession of simple chords. —*v.t.* **4.** to furnish with a vamp, esp. to repair (a shoe or boot) with a new vamp. **5.** to patch up; repair. **6.** to give (something) a new appearance by adding a patch or piece. **7.** to concoct or invent (often fol. by *up*): *He vamped up a few ugly rumors to discredit his enemies.* **8.** *Jazz.* to improvise (an accompaniment or the like). —*v.i.* **9.** *Jazz.* to improvise an accompaniment, tune, etc. [1175–1225; ME *vampe* < AF; MF *avant-pie,* equiv. to *avant-* fore- (see AVAUNT) + *pie* foot (F *pied;* see -PED)] **—vamp′er,** *n.* **—vamp′ish,** *adj.*

vamp[2] (vamp), *n.* **1.** a seductive woman who uses her sensuality to exploit men. —*v.t.* **2.** to use feminine charms upon; seduce. —*v.i.* **3.** to act as a vamp. [1905–10; short for VAMPIRE]

vamp•horn (vamp′hôrn′), *n.* a megaphone in use during the 18th and early 19th centuries for public address in church services. [VAMP[1] + HORN; so called from its use in amplifying one voice as an accompaniment in choral singing]

vam•pire (vam′pīər), *n.* **1.** a preternatural being, commonly believed to be a reanimated corpse, that is said to suck the blood of sleeping persons at night. **2.** (in Eastern European folklore) a corpse, animated by an undeparted soul or demon, that periodically leaves the grave and disturbs the living, until it is exhumed and impaled or burned. **3.** a person who preys ruthlessly upon others; extortionist. **4.** a woman who unscrupulously exploits, ruins, or degrades the men she seduces. **5.** an actress noted for her roles as an unscrupulous seductress: *the vampires of the silent movies.* [1725–35; (< F) < G *Vampir* < Serbo-Croatian *vàmpīr,* alter. of earlier *upir* (by confusion with doublets such as *văzdŭh, ŭzdŭh* air (< Slavic *vŭ-*), and with intrusive nasal, as in *dŭbrava, dumbrăva* grove); akin to Czech *upír,* Pol *upiór,* ORuss *upyrĭ, upirĭ,* (Russ *upýr′*) < Slavic **u-pirĭ* or **ǫ-pirĭ,* prob. a deverbal compound with **per-* fly, rush (literal meaning variously interpreted)] **—vam•pir•ic** (vam pir′ik), **vam•pir•ish** (vam′pīər ish), *adj.*

vam′pire bat′, 1. any of several New World tropical bats of the genera *Desmodus, Diphylla,* and *Diaemus,* the size of a small mouse, feeding on small amounts of blood obtained from resting mammals and birds by means of a shallow cut made with specialized incisor teeth. **2.** any of several large South American bats of the genera *Phyllostomus* and *Vampyrus,* erroneously believed to feed on blood. **3.** See **false vampire.** [1780–90]

vam•pir•ism (vam′pīər iz′əm, -pə riz′-), *n.* **1.** belief in the existence of vampires. **2.** the acts or practices of vampires. **3.** unscrupulous exploitation, ruin, or degradation of others. [1785–95; VAMPIRE + -ISM]

vam•plate (vam′plāt′), *n. Armor.* a metal plate mounted on a lance in front of the grip to protect the hand. [1300–50; ME *vaunplate* < AF *vaunt-* fore- (see AVAUNT) + *plate* PLATE[1]]

van[1] (van), *n.* **1.** the foremost or front division of an army, a fleet, or any group leading an advance or in position to lead an advance. **2.** those who are in the forefront of a movement or the like. **3.** the forefront in any movement, course of progress, or the like. [1600–10; short for VANGUARD]

van[2] (van), *n., v.,* **vanned, van•ning.** —*n.* **1.** a covered vehicle, usually a large truck or trailer, used for moving furniture, goods, animals, etc. **2.** a smaller boxlike vehicle that resembles a panel truck, often has double doors both at the rear and along the curb side, and that can be used as a truck, fitted with rows of seats, or equipped with living quarters for traveling and camping. See illus. on next page. **3.** *Brit.* **a.** a railway baggage car. **b.** a covered, boxlike railway car, as one used to carry freight. **c.** a small, horse-drawn wagon or a small truck, as one used by tradespeople to carry light goods. **4.** Also called **van conversion.** a conventional van whose cargo area has been equipped with living facilities, extra windows, and often increased headroom. —*v.t.* **5.** to transport or carry (freight, passengers, etc.) in a van. —*v.i.* **6.** to travel in a van. [1820–30; short for CARAVAN]

van[2] (def. 2)

van[3] (van; *Du.* vän), *prep.* (*often cap.*) from; of (used in Dutch personal names, originally to indicate place of origin). [< D]

van[4] (van), *n.* a wing. [1400–50; late ME, var. of FAN[1]]

Van (van; *for 1, 2 also Turk.* vän), *n.* **1. Lake,** a salt lake in E Turkey. 1454 sq. mi. (3766 sq. km). **2.** a town on this lake. 88,597. **3.** a male given name.

van·a·date (van′ə dāt′), *n. Chem.* a salt or ester of a vanadic acid. Also, **va·na·di·ate** (və nā′dē āt′). [1830–40; VANAD(IC ACID) + -ATE[2]]

va·nad·ic (və nad′ik, -nā′dik), *adj. Chem.* of or containing vanadium, esp. in the trivalent or pentavalent state. [1830–40; VANAD(IUM) + -IC]

vanad′ic ac′id, *Chem.* any of certain acids containing vanadium, esp. one having the formula H_3VO_4. [1830–40]

va·nad·i·nite (və nad′n īt′, -nād′-), *n.* a mineral, $Pb_5(VO_4)_3Cl$, occurring in yellow, brown, or greenish crystals: an ore of lead and vanadium. [1850–55; VANAD(IUM) + -IN[2] + -ITE[1]]

va·na·di·um (və nā′dē əm), *n. Chem.* a rare element occurring in certain minerals and obtained as a light-gray powder with a silvery luster or as a ductile metal: used as an ingredient of steel to toughen it and increase its shock resistance. *Symbol:* V; *at. wt.:* 50.942; *at. no.:* 23; *sp. gr.:* 5.96. [< NL (1830) < Icel *Vanad(ís)* epithet of Freya (*Vana,* gen. of *Vanir* VANIR + *dís* goddess) + NL *-ium* -IUM]

vana′dium pentox′ide, *Chem.* a yellow to red crystalline compound, V_2O_5, slightly soluble in water, used as a catalyst for organic reactions, in glass to absorb ultraviolet radiation, and as a photographic developer. [1880–85]

vana′dium steel′, an alloy steel containing vanadium. [1905–10]

van·a·dous (van′ə dəs), *adj. Chem.* containing divalent or trivalent vanadium. Also, **va·na·di·ous** (və nā′dē əs). [1855–60; VANAD(IUM) + -OUS]

Van Al·len (van al′ən), **James Alfred,** born 1914, U.S. physicist.

Van Al′len belt′, *Physics.* either of two regions of high-energy-charged particles surrounding the earth, the inner region centered at an altitude of 2000 mi. (3200 km) and the outer region at an altitude between 9000 and 12,000 mi. (14,500 and 19,000 km). Also called **Van Al′len radia′tion belt′.** [1955–60; named after J. A. VAN ALLEN]

Van·brugh (van brōō′ *or, esp. Brit.,* van′brə), *n.* **John,** 1664–1726, English dramatist and architect.

Van Bu·ren (van byŏŏr′ən), **1. Martin,** 1782–1862, 8th president of the U.S. 1837–41. **2.** a town in central Arkansas. 12,020. **3.** a male given name.

Vance (vans), *n.* a male given name.

van·co·my·cin (vang′kə mī′sin, van′-), *n. Pharm.* a bactericidal antibiotic, $C_{66}H_{75}ClN_9O_{24}$, produced by *Streptomyces orientalis,* used in the treatment of antibiotic-associated colitis and endocarditis. [1956; *vanco-,* of unexplained orig. + -MYCIN]

van′ conver′sion, van[2] (def. 4).

Van·cou·ver (van kōō′vər), *n.* **1. George,** 1758–98, English explorer. **2.** a large island in SW Canada, off the SW coast of British Columbia. 410,188; 12,408 sq. mi. (32,135 sq. km). **3.** a seaport in SW British Columbia, on the Strait of Georgia opposite SE Vancouver island. 396,563; with suburbs 1,135,774. **4.** a city in SW Washington. 42,834. **5. Mount,** a mountain on the boundary between Alaska and Canada, in the St. Elias Mountains. 15,700 ft. (4785 m).

CONCISE ETYMOLOGY KEY: <, descended or borrowed from; >, whence; b., blend of, blended; c., cognate with; cf., compare; deriv., derivative; equiv., equivalent; imit., imitative; obl., oblique; r., replacing; s., stem; sp., spelling, spelled; resp., respelling, respelled; trans., translation; ?, origin unknown; *, unattested; ‡, probably earlier than. See the full key inside the front cover.

van·da (van′də), *n.* any of several epiphytic orchids of the genus *Vanda,* of tropical regions of the Eastern Hemisphere, having large white, lilac, blue, or greenish flowers. [1795–1805; < NL < Skt *vandā* mistletoe]

van·dal (van′dl), *n.* **1.** (*cap.*) a member of a Germanic people who in the 5th century A.D. ravaged Gaul and Spain, settled in Africa, and in A.D. 455 sacked Rome. **2.** a person who willfully or ignorantly destroys or mars something beautiful or valuable. —*adj.* **3.** (*cap.*) of or pertaining to the Vandals. **4.** imbued with or characterized by vandalism. [1545–55; < LL *Vandalus,* Latinized tribal name]

Van·da·lia (van dāl′yə), *n.* a town in W Ohio. 13,161.

van·dal·ic (van dal′ik), *adj.* **1.** (*cap.*) of, pertaining to, or characteristic of the Vandals. **2.** of or pertaining to vandalism. [1660–70; VANDAL + -IC]

van·dal·ism (van′dl iz′əm), *n.* **1.** deliberately mischievous or malicious destruction or damage of property: *vandalism of public buildings.* **2.** the conduct or spirit characteristic of the Vandals. **3.** willful or ignorant destruction of artistic or literary treasures. **4.** a vandalic act. [1790–1800; VANDAL + -ISM; cf. F *vandalisme*] —**van′dal·is′tic, van′dal·ish,** *adj.*

van·dal·ize (van′dl īz′), *v.t.,* **-ized, -iz·ing.** to destroy or deface by vandalism: *Someone vandalized the museum during the night.* Also, *esp. Brit.,* **van′dal·ise′.** [1790–1800; VANDAL + -IZE]

Van′ de Graaff′ gen′erator (van′ də graf′), *Physics, Elect.* a device for producing high-voltage static electricity. Also called **electrostatic generator.** [1935–40; named after R. J. *Van de Graaff* (1901–66), American physicist]

Van·den·berg (van′dən bûrg′), *n.* **1. Arthur Hendrick,** 1884–1951, U.S. statesman. **2. Hoyt Sanford,** 1899–1954, U.S. general: Chief of Staff of Air Force 1948–53.

Van·der·bilt (van′dər bilt), *n.* **1. Cornelius,** 1794–1877, U.S. financier. **2. Harold Stir·ling** (stûr′ling), 1884–1970, U.S. business executive.

Van der Hum (van′ dər hōōm′; *Du.* vän′ dər hʏm′), a spicy liqueur from South Africa, flavored with tangerine and herbs. [1860–65; allegedly after a Dutch sea captain who favored the drink]

van der Roh·e (van dər rō′ə, fän), **Lud·wig Mies** (lud′wig mēz, mēs). See **Mies van der Rohe, Ludwig.**

van′ der Waals′ equa′tion (van′ dər wälz′, wôlz′; *Du.* vän′ dər väls′), *Thermodynamics.* an equation of state relating the pressure, volume, and absolute temperature of a gas, taking into account the finite size of the molecules and the attractive force between them. Also, **van′ der Waals′ equa′tion.** [named after J. D. *van der Waals* (1837–1923), Dutch scientist]

van′ der Waals′ forc′es, *Physical Chem.* weak, nonspecific forces between molecules. Also, **van′ der Waals′ forc′es.** [1925–30; see VAN DER WAALS' EQUATION]

Van Der Zee (van′ dər zē′), **James,** 1886–1983, U.S. photographer. Also, **Van′ Der·Zee′.**

Van De·van·ter (van′ di van′tər), **Willis,** 1859–1941, U.S. jurist: associate justice of the U.S. Supreme Court 1910–37.

Van Die′men's Land′ (van dē′mənz), former name of **Tasmania.**

Van Dine (van dīn′), **S. S.** See **Wright, Willard Huntington.**

van Dong·en (van dong′ən; *Du.* vän dông′ən, dông′ə), **Kees** (kās), (*Cornelius Theodorus Marie*), 1877–1968, French painter, born in the Netherlands.

Van Do·ren (van dôr′ən, dōr′-), **1. Carl,** 1885–1950, U.S. writer. **2.** his brother, **Mark,** 1894–1972, U.S. writer and critic.

Van Dru·ten (van drōōt′n), **John William,** 1901–57, U.S. playwright, born in England.

Van Dyck (van dīk′; *Flem.* vän dīk′), **Sir Anthony,** 1599–1641, Flemish painter. Also, **Vandyke.**

Van·dyke (van dīk′), *n.* **1. Sir Anthony.** See **Van Dyck, Sir Anthony. 2.** See **Vandyke beard. 3.** See **Vandyke collar. 4.** *Print.* a proof having white lines on a brown ground or vice versa, made from a negative for a plate. Also, **van·dyke′** (for defs. 2, 3).

Vandyke′ beard′, a short, pointed beard. Also called **Vandyke, vandyke.** [1890–95]

Vandyke beard

Vandyke′ brown′, 1. a medium brown color. **2.** any of several dark-brown pigments consisting of iron oxide mixed with lampblack or similar materials. [1840–50]

Vandyke′ col′lar, a wide collar of lace and linen with the edge formed into scallops or deep points. Also, **vandyke′ col′lar.** Also called **Vandyke, vandyke.**

vane (vān), *n.* **1.** See **weather vane. 2.** a blade, plate, sail, etc., in the wheel of a windmill, to be moved by the air. **3.** any of a number of blades or plates attached radially to a rotating drum or cylinder, as in a turbine or pump, that move or are moved by a fluid, as steam, water, hot gases, or air. **4.** a person who is readily changeable or fickle. **5.** *Aerospace.* **a.** any fixed or movable plane surface on the outside of a rocket providing directional control while the rocket is within the atmosphere. **b.** a similar plane surface located in the exhaust jet of a reaction engine, providing directional control while the engine is firing. **6.** *Ornith.* the web of a feather. See illus. under **feather. 7.** *Navig., Survey.* either of two fixed projections for sighting an alidade or the like. **8.** *Archery.* feather (def. 5). [bef. 1100; ME; OE *fana* flag; c. G *Fahne* flag, Goth *fana* segment of cloth; cf. GONFANON] —**vaned,** *adj.* —**vane′less,** *adj.*

Vane (vān), *n.* **Sir Henry** (*Sir Harry Vane*), 1613–62, British statesman and author.

Vä·nern (ven′ərn), *n.* a lake in SW Sweden. 2141 sq. mi. (5545 sq. km). Also, **Vä·ner** (ven′ər), **Vener.**

Va·nes·sa (və nes′ə), *n.* a female given name.

Van Fleet (van flēt′), **James Al·ward** (al′wərd), born 1892, U.S. army general.

vang (vang), *n. Naut.* a rope extending from the peak of a gaff to the ship's rail or to a mast, used to steady the gaff. [1760–70; < D: device for securing something; cf. *vanglijn* bow rope, equiv. to *vang* + *lijn* line]

van′ga shrike′ (vang′gə), any of several birds of the family Vangidae, endemic to Madagascar, some of which resemble shrikes, with great diversity in size, color, and bill shape. [*vanga* < Malagasy]

van Gogh (van gō′, gôkh′; *Du.* vän khôkh′), **Vincent** (vin′sənt; *Du.* vin sent′), 1853–90, Dutch painter.

van·guard (van′gärd′), *n.* **1.** the foremost division or the front part of an army; advance guard; van. **2.** the forefront in any movement, field, activity, or the like. **3.** the leaders of any intellectual or political movement. **4.** (*cap.*) *Rocketry.* a U.S. three-stage, satellite-launching rocket, the first two stages powered by liquid-propellant engines and the third by a solid-propellant engine. [1480–90; earlier *van(d)gard(e)* < MF *avangarde,* var. of *avant-garde;* see AVAUNT, GUARD]

van·guard·ism (van′gär diz′əm), *n.* the beliefs and activities of persons who consider themselves to be leaders in a particular field or school of thought. [VANGUARD + -ISM] —**van′guard·ist,** *n.*

Va·nier (van′yā, van yā′; *for 1, 3 also Fr.* VA nyā′), *n.* **1. Georges P.** (jôrj; *Fr.* zhôrzh), 1888–1967, Canadian soldier and diplomat: governor-general 1959–67. **2.** a city in SE Ontario, in S Canada, near Ottawa, on the Ottawa River. 18,792. **3.** a town in S Quebec, in E Canada: suburb of Quebec. 10,725.

va·nil·la (və nil′ə *or, often,* -nel′ə), *n.* **1.** any tropical, climbing orchid of the genus *Vanilla,* esp. *V. planifolia,* bearing podlike fruit yielding an extract used in flavoring food, in perfumery, etc. **2.** Also called **vanil′la bean′.** the fruit or bean of this orchid. **3.** the extract of this fruit. —*adj.* **4.** containing or flavored with vanilla: *vanilla custard.* **5.** *Informal.* plain-vanilla. [1655–65; < NL < Sp *vainilla* little pod, equiv. to *vain(a)* a sheath (< L *vāgina* sheath) + *-illa* dim. suffix (< LL)]

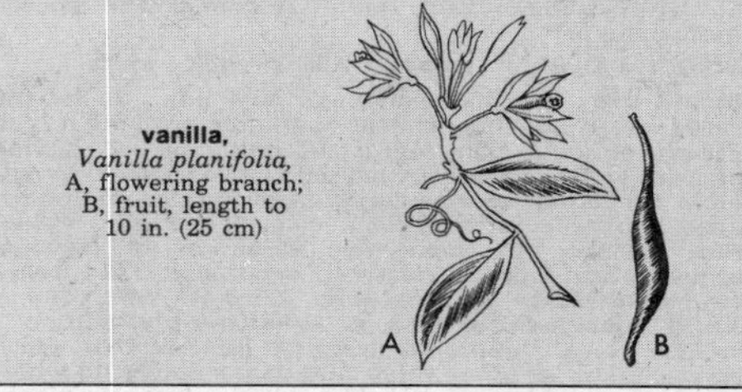

vanilla, *Vanilla planifolia,* A, flowering branch; B, fruit, length to 10 in. (25 cm)

vanil′la plant′, a composite plant, *Trilisa odoratissima* (or *Carphephorus odoratissimus*), of the southeastern U.S., having purplish flower heads and vanilla-scented leaves used to flavor tobacco. Also called **vanil′la leaf′, wild vanilla.** [1745–55]

va·nil·lic (və nil′ik), *adj.* of, derived from, or resembling vanilla or vanillin. [1865–70; VANILL(A) + -IC]

va·nil·lin (və nil′in, van′l-), *n. Chem.* a white, crystalline, water-soluble, alcohol-soluble solid, $C_8H_8O_3$, obtained by extraction from the vanilla bean or prepared synthetically: used chiefly as a flavoring agent and in perfumery. Also, **va·nil·line** (və nil′in, -ēn, van′l in, -ēn′). Also called **vanil′lic al′dehyde.** [1865–70; VANILL(A) + -IN[2]]

Va·nir (vä′nir), *n.* (*often l.c.*) (*used with a plural v.*) *Scand. Myth.* a race of gods, first in conflict with the Aesir, later allied with them. They function as fertility divinities and include Njord, Frey, and Freyja. [< ON, prob. from the same root as *vinr* friend, L *Venus* VENUS, Skt *vánas* desire]

van·ish (van′ish), *v.i.* **1.** to disappear from sight, esp. quickly; become invisible: *The frost vanished when the sun came out.* **2.** to go away, esp. furtively or mysteriously; disappear by quick departure: *The thief vanished in the night.* **3.** to disappear by ceasing to exist; come to an end: *The pain vanished after he took an aspirin.* **4.** *Math.* (of a number, quantity, or function) to become zero. —*v.t.* **5.** to cause to disappear. —*n.* **6.** *Phonet.* the last part of a vowel sound when it differs noticeably in quality from the main sound, as the faint (ē) at the end of the (ā) in the pronunciation of *pain.* [1275–1325; ME *vanisshen, vanissen* < MF *evaniss-,* long s. of *e(s)vanir* << L *ex-* EX- + *vānēscere* to pass away, equiv. to *vān(us)* VAIN + *-ēscere* inchoative suffix] —**van′ish·er,** *n.* —**van′ish·ing·ly,** *adv.* —**van′ish·ment,** *n.*
—**Syn. 1.** evanesce. See **disappear.** —**Ant. 1.** appear.

van′ishing cream′, a cosmetic similar to cold cream but less oily, applied usually to the face and neck as a base, night cream, or moisturizer.

van′ishing point′, 1. a point of disappearance, cessation, or extinction: *His patience had reached the vanishing point.* **2.** (in the study of perspective in art) that point toward which receding parallel lines appear to converge. [1790–1800]

van·i·to·ry (van′i tôr′ē, -tōr′ē), *n., pl.* **-ries.** a combined dressing table and lavatory basin. [1950–55; VANI(TY) + (LAVA)TORY]

van·i·ty (van′i tē), *n., pl.* **-ties,** *adj.* —*n.* **1.** excessive pride in one's appearance, qualities, abilities, achievements, etc.; character or quality of being vain; conceit: *Failure to be elected was a great blow to his vanity.* **2.** an instance or display of this quality or feeling. **3.** something about which one is vain. **4.** lack of real value; hollowness; worthlessness: *the vanity of a selfish life.* **5.** something worthless, trivial, or pointless. **6.** See **vanity case.** **7.** See **dressing table.** **8.** a wide, counterlike shelf containing a wash basin, as in the bathroom of a hotel or residence, often equipped with shelves, drawers, etc., underneath. **9.** a cabinet built below or around a bathroom sink, primarily to hide exposed pipes. **10.** compact[1] (def. 13). —*adj.* **11.** produced as a showcase for one's own talents, esp. as a writer, actor, singer, or composer: *a vanity production.* **12.** of, pertaining to, or issued by a vanity press: *a spate of vanity books.* [1200–50; ME *vanite* < OF < L *vānitās,* equiv. to *vān-* (see VAIN) + *-itās* -ITY] —**van′i·tied,** *adj.*
—**Syn.** **1.** egotism, complacency, vainglory, ostentation. See **pride.** **4.** emptiness, sham, unreality, folly, triviality, futility. —**Ant.** **1.** humility.

van′ity case′, a small luggage bag or case for holding cosmetics or toiletries. Also called **van′ity bag′, van′ity box′.** [1900–05]

Van′ity Fair′, **1.** (in Bunyan's *Pilgrim's Progress*) a fair that goes on perpetually in the town of Vanity and symbolizes worldly ostentation and frivolity. **2.** (*often l.c.*) any place or group, as the world or fashionable society, characterized by or displaying a preoccupation with idle pleasures or ostentation. **3.** (*italics*) a novel (1847–48) by Thackeray.

van′ity plate′, a vehicle license plate bearing a combination of letters or numbers requested by the licensee, as a name or occupation. [1965–70]

van′ity press′, a printing house that specializes in publishing books for which the authors pay all or most of the costs. Also called **van′ity pub′lisher.** [1945–50]

van Ley·den (vän līd′n). See **Lucas van Leyden.**

van′ line′, a transportation company that uses large motor vans for the long-distance moving of household effects.

Van Loon (van lōōn′, lōn′), **Hen·drik Wil·lem** (hen′drik vil′əm), 1882–1944, U.S. author, born in the Netherlands.

van·man (van′man′, -mən), *n., pl.* **-men** (-men′, -mən). a person who works on a van, esp. the driver. [1880–85; VAN[2] + MAN[1]]

van·ner (van′ər), *n.* the owner or driver of a van, esp. one of customized design. [1970–75; VAN[2] + -ER[1]]

Vannes (VAN), *n.* a city in and the capital of Morbihan, in NW France. 43,507.

van·ning (van′ing), *n.* travel by means of a small van or truck that has been fitted out with living accommodations. [VAN[2] + -ING[1]] —**van′ner,** *n.*

Van Paas·sen (vän pä′sən), **Pi·erre** (pē âr′), (*Pieter Anthonie Laurusse*), 1895–1968, U.S. journalist, author, and clergyman; born in the Netherlands.

van′ pool′, a type of car pool utilizing a van that can usually transport 6 to 15 passengers: often provided by a company for its commuting employees for a nominal charge or at cost. [1970–75] —**van′ pool′ing.**

van·quish (vang′kwish, van′-), *v.t.* **1.** to conquer or subdue by superior force, as in battle. **2.** to defeat in any contest or conflict; be victorious over: *to vanquish one's opponent in an argument.* **3.** to overcome or overpower: *He vanquished all his fears.* [1300–50; ME *vencuschen, venquisshen* < OF *vencus* ptp. and *venquis* past tense of *veintre* < L *vincere* to overcome] —**van′quish·a·ble,** *adj.* —**van′quish·er,** *n.* —**van′quish·ment,** *n.*
—**Syn.** **1.** subjugate, suppress, crush, quell.

Van Rens·se·laer (van ren′sə lēr′, ren′sə lər; *for 1 also Du.* vän REN′sə lär′), **1.** **Ki·li·aen** (kē′lē än′), 1595–1644, Dutch merchant: founder of Dutch West India Company 1621; large landowner in America, colonizing along the Hudson River (ancestor of Stephen Van Rensselaer). **2.** **Stephen** ("*the Patroon*"), 1765–1839, U.S. political leader and major general.

Van·sit·tart (van sit′ərt), **Sir Robert Gilbert, 1st Baron Vansittart of Denham,** 1881–1957, British statesman and diplomat.

Van·sit·tart·ism (van sit′ər tiz′əm), *n.* a doctrine holding that the militaristic and aggressive policies of German leaders since the time of the Franco-Prussian war have had the support of the German people and that Germany should undergo a program of demilitarization and corrective education to prevent similar action in the future. [VANSITTART + -ISM]

van·tage (van′tij, vän′-), *n.* **1.** a position, condition, or place affording some advantage or a commanding view. **2.** an advantage or superiority: *the vantage of wisdom that often comes with age.* **3.** *Brit.* advantage (def. 5). [1250–1300; ME < AF, aph. var. of *avantage* ADVANTAGE]

van′tage ground′, a position or place that gives one an advantage, as for action, view, or defense. [1605–15]

van′tage point′, a position or place that affords a wide or advantageous perspective; viewpoint: *to survey a valley from the vantage point of a high hill.* [1860–65]

van't Hoff (vänt hôf′), **Ja·co·bus Hen·dri·cus** (yä-kō′bœs hen drē′kœs), 1852–1911, Dutch chemist: Nobel prize 1901.

Va·nu·a Le·vu (və nōō′ə lev′ōō), an island in the S Pacific, one of the Fiji Islands. 94,000; 2137 sq. mi. (5535 sq. km).

Va·nu·a·tu (vä′nōō ä′tōō), *n.* a republic consisting of a group of 80 islands in the S Pacific, ab. 1000 mi. (1600 km) NE of Australia: formerly under joint British and French administration; gained independence 1980. 113,000; ab. 5700 sq. mi. (14,763 sq. km). *Cap.:* Vila. Formerly, **New Hebrides.** —**Va′nu·a′tu·an,** *adj., n.*

Van Vech·ten (van vek′tən), **Carl,** 1880–1964, U.S. author.

Van Vleck (van vlek′), **John H(as·brouck)** (haz′-brŏŏk), 1899–1980, U.S. physicist: Nobel prize 1977.

van·ward (van′wərd), *adj., adv.* toward or in the van or front. [1810–20; VAN[1] + -WARD]

Van Wert (van wûrt′), a city in NW Ohio. 11,035.

Van Zee·land (vän zā′länt′), **Paul** (poul), 1893–1973, Belgian statesman: premier 1935–37.

Van·zet·ti (van zet′ē; *It.* vän dzet′tē), *n.* **Bar·to·lo·me·o** (bär′tô lô me′ô), 1888–1927, Italian anarchist, in U.S. after 1908. Cf. **Sacco, Nicola.**

Va·phi·o (vä′fē ō′; *Gk.* vä fyô′), *n.* an archaeological site in S Greece, in Peloponnesus. Also, **Vafio.**

vap·id (vap′id), *adj.* **1.** lacking or having lost life, sharpness, or flavor; insipid; flat: *vapid tea.* **2.** without liveliness or spirit; dull or tedious: *a vapid party; vapid conversation.* [1650–60; < L *vapidus;* akin to VAPOR] —**va·pid′i·ty, vap′id·ness,** *n.* —**vap′id·ly,** *adv.*
—**Syn.** **1.** lifeless, flavorless. **2.** spiritless, unanimated, tiresome, prosaic. —**Ant.** **1.** pungent. **2.** stimulating.

va·por (vā′pər), *n.* **1.** a visible exhalation, as fog, mist, steam, smoke, or noxious gas, diffused through or suspended in the air: *the vapors rising from the bogs.* **2.** *Physics.* a gas at a temperature below its critical temperature. **3.** a substance converted into vapor for technical or medicinal uses. **4.** a combination of a vaporized substance and air. **5.** gaseous particles of drugs that can be inhaled as a therapeutic agent. **6.** *Archaic.* **a.** a strange, senseless, or fantastic notion. **b.** something insubstantial or transitory. **7.** **vapors,** *Archaic.* **a.** mental depression or hypochondria. **b.** injurious exhalations formerly supposed to be produced within the body, esp. in the stomach. —*v.t.* **8.** to cause to rise or pass off in, or as if in, vapor; vaporize. **9.** *Archaic.* to affect with vapors; depress. —*v.i.* **10.** to rise or pass off in the form of vapor. **11.** to emit vapor or exhalations. **12.** to talk or act grandiloquently, pompously, or boastfully; bluster. Also, *esp. Brit.,* **vapour.** [1325–75; ME *vapour* < L *vapor* steam] —**va′por·a·ble,** *adj.* —**va′por·a·bil′i·ty,** *n.* —**va′por·er,** *n.* —**va′por·less,** *adj.* —**va′por·like′,** *adj.*

va′por bar′rier, *Building Trades.* a layer of material, as plastic film or foil, used to protect installed insulation by retarding the transmission of moisture from the interior environment. [1940–45]

va·por·es·cence (vā′pə res′əns), *n.* production or formation of vapor. [1835–45; VAPOR + -ESCENCE] —**va′por·es′cent,** *adj.*

va·po·ret·to (vap′ə ret′ō; *It.* vä′pô RET′tô), *n., pl.* **-tos,** *It.* **-ti** (-tē). a motorboat used as a passenger bus along a canal in Venice, Italy. [1945–50; < It, equiv. to *vapor(e)* steamboat + *-etto* -ET]

va·por·if·ic (vā′pə rif′ik), *adj.* **1.** producing vapor; tending to form vapor. **2.** of, pertaining to, or of the nature of vapor; vaporous. [1775–85; VAPOR + -I- + -FIC]

va·por·im·e·ter (vā′pə rim′i tər), *n.* an instrument for measuring vapor pressure or volume. [1875–80; VAPOR + -I- + -METER]

va·por·ing (vā′pər ing), *adj.* **1.** that gives forth vapor. **2.** boastful; bragging. —*n.* **3.** an act or instance of bragging or blustering; boastful talk. [1620–30; VAPOR + -ING[2], -ING[1]] —**va′por·ing·ly,** *adv.*

va·por·ish (vā′pər ish), *adj.* **1.** of the nature of or resembling vapor: *a vaporish chiffon dress.* **2.** abounding in vapor: *vaporish autumn mornings.* **3.** *Archaic.* inclined to or affected by low spirits; depressed. [1635–45; VAPOR + -ISH[1]] —**va′por·ish·ness,** *n.*

va·por·i·za·tion (vā′pər ə zā′shən), *n.* **1.** the act of vaporizing. **2.** the state of being vaporized. **3.** the rapid change of water into steam, esp. in a boiler. **4.** *Med.* a vapor therapy. [1790–1800; VAPOR + -IZATION]

va·por·ize (vā′pə rīz′), *v.,* **-ized, -iz·ing.** —*v.t.* **1.** to cause to change into vapor. —*v.i.* **2.** to become converted into vapor. **3.** to indulge in boastful talk; speak braggingly. Also, *esp. Brit.,* **va′por·ise′.** [1625–35; VAPOR + -IZE] —**va′por·iz′a·ble,** *adj.*

va·por·iz·er (vā′pə rī′zər), *n.* **1.** a person or thing that vaporizes. **2.** a device for turning liquid into vapor, as an atomizer, esp. one that converts a medicinal substance into a vapor that is inhaled for respiratory relief. [1840–50; VAPORIZE + -ER[1]]

va′por lock′, an obstruction to the flow of fuel to a gasoline engine, caused by the formation of bubbles in the gasoline as a result of overheating.

va·por·ous (vā′pər əs), *adj.* **1.** having the form or characteristics of vapor: *a vaporous cloud.* **2.** full of or abounding in vapor; foggy; misty: *a vaporous twilight.* **3.** producing or giving off vapor: *a vaporous bog.* **4.** dimmed or obscured with vapor: *a low valley surrounded by vaporous mountains.* **5.** unsubstantial; diaphanous; airy: *vaporous fabrics; vaporous breezes.* **6.** vaguely formed, fanciful, or unreliable: *vaporous promises.* [1520–30; VAPOR + -OUS] —**va′por·ous·ly,** *adv.* —**va′·por·ous·ness, va·por·os·i·ty** (vā′pə ros′i tē), *n.*

va′por pres′sure, the pressure exerted by the molecules of a vapor, esp. that part of the total pressure exerted by vapor in a mixture of gases, as by water vapor in air. Also called **vapor tension.** [‡1895–1900]

va′por ten′sion, **1.** See **vapor pressure.** **2.** the maximum vapor pressure possible, at a given temperature, in a system composed of a liquid or solid substance in contact with the vapor of that substance. [1860–65]

va′por trail′, contrail. [1940–45]

va·por·ware (vā′pər wâr′), *n.* *Computer Jargon.* a product, esp. software, that is promoted or marketed while it is still in development and that may never be produced. [VAPOR + WARE[1]]

va·por·y (vā′pə rē), *adj.* **1.** vaporous. **2.** vaporish. [1590–1600; VAPOR + -Y[1]]

va·pour (vā′pər), *n., v.t., v.i. Chiefly Brit.* vapor. —**Usage.** See **-or**[1].

va·que·ro (vä kâr′ō; *Sp.* bä ke′Rô), *n., pl.* **-que·ros** (-kâr′ōz; *Sp.* -ke′Rôs). *Southwestern U.S.* a cowboy or herdsman. [1790–1800; < Sp, equiv. to *vac(a)* cow (< L *vacca*) + *-ero* < L *-ārius* -ARY]

Var (VAR), *n.* a department in SE France. 626,093; 2326 sq. mi. (6025 sq. km). *Cap.:* Draguignan.

var., **1.** variable. **2.** variant. **3.** variation. **4.** variety. **5.** variometer. **6.** various.

va·ra (vär′ə; *Sp.* bä′Rä; *Port.* vä′Rə), *n., pl.* **va·ras** (vär′əz; *Sp.* bä′Räs; *Port.* vä′Rəsh). **1.** a unit of length in Spanish- and Portuguese-speaking countries, varying from about 32 in. (81 cm) to about 43 in. (109 cm). **2.** the square vara, used as a unit of area. [1595–1605; < Sp < L *vāra* forked pole, n. use of fem. of *vārus* crooked, bent]

va·rac·tor (və rak′tər), *n.* a semiconductor diode whose capacitance changes to match applied voltage, used to tune circuits by varying the reactance. [1955–60; *var(iable re)actor*]

Va·ra·na·si (və rä′nə sē), *n.* a city in SE Uttar Pradesh, in NE India, on the Ganges River: Hindu holy city. 582,915. Formerly, **Banares, Benares.**

Va·ran·gi·an (və ran′jē ən), *n.* **1.** any of the Northmen who, under Rurik, established a dynasty in Russia in the 9th century. **2.** a member of the bodyguard **(Varan′gian guard′)** of the Byzantine emperors, esp. in the 11th and 12th centuries, made up of Northmen, Anglo-Saxons, and other northern Europeans. —*adj.* **3.** of or pertaining to the Varangians.

Var·dar (vär′där), *n.* a river in S Europe, flowing from NW Macedonia through N Greece into the Gulf of Salonika. 200 mi. (322 km) long.

Var·dha·ma·na (vär′də mä′nə), *n.* *Jainism.* a semilegendary teacher, believed to have died c480 B.C., who reformed older doctrines to establish Jainism in its present form: regarded as the twenty-fourth and latest Tirthankara. Also called **Vardhama′na Mahavi′ra, Mahavira.**

Var·don (vär′dn), *n.* **Harry,** 1870–1937, British golfer.

Va·re·se (vä RE′ze; *Eng.* və rā′zē, -sē), *n.* a city in N Italy, NW of Milan. 90,011.

Va·rèse (və räz′, -rez′, *Fr.* VA REZ′), *n.* **Ed·gard** (ed-GAR′), 1885–1965, U.S. composer, born in France.

Var·gas (vär′gəs), *n.* **Ge·tu·lio Dor·nel·les** (*Port.* zhi-tōō′lyŏŏ dôRR ne′lis), 1883–1954, Brazilian statesman.

Var·gi·nha (vaR zhē′nyä), *n.* a city in E Brazil. 38,473.

var·gue·no (vär gān′yō), *n., pl.* **-nos.** *Sp. Furniture.* a fall-front desk of the 16th, 17th, and early 18th centuries, having the form of a chest upon a small table. [< Sp *bargueño* (work) of *Bargas* (town near Toledo)]

va·ri (vä rē′, vär′ē), *n.* a nocturnal, nesting lemur, *Varecia variegata,* native to Madagascar, having black and white fur and a mane: an endangered species. Also called **ruffed lemur.** [1765–75; < Malagasy *vàrika*]

var·i·a (vâr′ē ə), *n.pl.* miscellaneous items, esp. a miscellany of literary works. [1925–30; < NL, L, neut. pl. of *varius* VARIOUS]

var·i·a·ble (vâr′ē ə bəl), *adj.* **1.** apt or liable to vary or change; changeable: *variable weather; variable moods.* **2.** capable of being varied or changed; alterable: *a variable time limit for completion of a book.* **3.** inconstant; fickle: *a variable lover.* **4.** having much variation or diversity. **5.** *Biol.* deviating from the usual type, as a species or a specific character. **6.** *Astron.* (of a star) changing in brightness. **7.** *Meteorol.* (of wind) tending to change in direction. **8.** *Math.* having the nature or characteristics of a variable. —*n.* **9.** something that may or does vary; a variable feature or factor. **10.** *Math., Computers.* **a.** a quantity or function that may assume any given value or set of values. **b.** a symbol that represents this. **11.** *Logic.* (in the functional calculus) a symbol for an unspecified member of a class of things or statements. Cf. **bound variable, free variable.** **12.** *Astron.* See **variable star.** **13.** *Meteorol.* **a.** a shifting wind, esp. as distinguished from a trade wind. **b.** **variables,** doldrums (def. 2a). [1350–1400; late ME < L *variābilis,* equiv. to *vari(us)* VARIOUS + *-ābilis* -ABLE] —**var′i·a·bil′i·ty, var′i·a·ble·ness,** *n.* —**var′i·a·bly,** *adv.*
—**Syn.** **3.** vacillating, wavering, fluctuating, unsteady, mercurial. —**Ant.** **1, 3.** constant.

var′iable annu′ity, an annuity in which the premiums are invested chiefly in common stocks or other securities, the annuitant receiving payments based on the yield of the investments instead of in fixed amounts.

var′iable con′trast pa′per, *Photog.* printing paper in which the contrast of the image is controlled by the color of the printing light.

var′iable cost′, a cost that varies with a change in the volume of output while remaining uniform on a per-unit basis, as cost of labor (distinguished from *fixed cost*).

var′iable life′ insur′ance, an insurance policy whose annuity payments or payment to the beneficiary are not fixed but depend on the income earned by the investment of the premiums.

var·i·a·ble-pitch (vâr′ē ə bəl pich′), *adj.* *Aeron., Naut.* (of a propeller) controllable-pitch.

var·i·a·ble-rate (vâr′ē ə bəl rāt′), *adj.* providing for

CONCISE PRONUNCIATION KEY: act, cāpe, dâre, pärt; set, ēqual; *if,* ice; ox, ōver, ôrder, oil, bŏŏk, bōōt, out; up, ûrge; child; sing; shoe; thin, *that;* zh as in *treasure.* ə = *a* as in *alone, e* as in *system, i* as in *easily, o* as in *gallop, u* as in *circus;* ᵊ as in *fire* (fīᵊr), *hour* (ouᵊr). l and n can serve as syllabic consonants, as in *cradle* (krād′l), and *button* (but′n). See the full key inside the front cover.

changes in the interest rate, adjusted periodically in accordance with prevailing market conditions: *a variable-rate mortgage.*

var′iable re′gion, *Immunol.* a configuration in the upper branches of the Y of an antibody molecule, unique in each antibody type, that binds with the determinant of a specific antigen.

var′iable star′, *Astron.* a star that varies markedly in brightness from time to time. Also called **variable.** [1780–90]

var′iable time′ fuze′. See **proximity fuze.**

Var′iable Zone′. See **Temperate Zone.**

va•ri•a lec•ti•o (wä′ri ä′ lek′ti ō′; *Eng.* vâr′ē ə lek′shē ō′), *pl.* ***va•ri•ae lec•ti•o•nes*** (wä′ri ī′ lek′ti ō′nes; *Eng.* vâr′ē ē′ lek′shē ō′nēz). *Latin.* a variant reading.

var•i•ance (vâr′ē əns), *n.* **1.** the state, quality, or fact of being variable, divergent, different, or anomalous. **2.** an instance of varying; difference; discrepancy. **3.** Also called **mean square deviation.** *Statistics.* the square of the standard deviation. **4.** *Physics, Chem.* the number of degrees of freedom of a system. **5.** *Law.* **a.** a difference or discrepancy, as between two statements or documents in law that should agree. **b.** a departure from the cause of action originally stated in the complaint. **6.** an official permit to do something normally forbidden by regulations, esp. by building in a way or for a purpose normally forbidden by a zoning law or a building code. **7.** a disagreement, dispute, or quarrel. **8. at variance, a.** (of things) in a state of difference or disagreement. **b.** (of persons) in a state of controversy or dissension: *at variance with one's superiors.* [1300–50; ME < L *variantia,* equiv. to *vari(āre)* to VARY) + *-antia* -ANCE]

var′iance anal′ysis, *Statistics.* See **analysis of variance.**

var•i•ant (vâr′ē ənt), *adj.* **1.** tending to change or alter; exhibiting variety or diversity; varying: *variant shades of color.* **2.** not agreeing or conforming; differing, esp. from something of the same general kind. **3.** not definitive, as a version of part of a text; different; alternative: *a variant reading.* **4.** not universally accepted. —*n.* **5.** a person or thing that varies. **6.** a different spelling, pronunciation, or form of the same word: *"Vehemency" is a variant of "vehemence."* [1325–75; ME < L *variant-,* s. of *variāns,* prp. of *variāre* to VARY; see -ANT]

var•i•ate (vâr′ē it, -āt′), *n.* **1.** *Statistics.* See **random variable. 2.** variant. [1810–20; < L *variātus* ptp. of *variāre* to VARY; see -ATE[1]]

var•i•a•tion (vâr′ē ā′shən), *n.* **1.** the act, process, or accident of varying in condition, character, or degree: *Prices are subject to variation.* **2.** an instance of this: *There is a variation in the quality of fabrics in this shipment.* **3.** amount, rate, extent, or degree of change: *a temperature variation of 40° in a particular climate.* **4.** a different form of something; variant. **5.** *Music.* **a.** the transformation of a melody or theme with changes or elaborations in harmony, rhythm, and melody. **b.** a varied form of a melody or theme, esp. one of a series of such forms developing the capacities of the subject. **6.** *Ballet.* a solo dance, esp. one forming a section of a pas de deux. **7.** *Astron.* any deviation from the mean orbit of a heavenly body, esp. of a planetary or satellite orbit. **8.** Also called **magnetic declination, magnetic variation.** *Navig.* the angle between the geographic and the magnetic meridian at a given point, expressed in plus degrees east or minus degrees west of true north. Cf. **deviation** (def. 4). **9.** *Biol.* a difference or deviation in structure or character from others of the same species or group. [1350–1400; < L *variātiōn-* (s. of *variātiō*), equiv. to *variāt(us)* (see VARIATE) + *-iōn-* -ION; r. ME *variacioun* < AF < L, as above] —**var′i•a′tion•al, var•i•a•tive** (vâr′ē ā′tiv), *adj.* —**var′i•a′tion•al•ly, var′i•a′tive•ly,** *adv.*
—**Syn. 1.** mutation, alteration, modification; deviation, divergence, difference.

var•i•cel•la (var′ə sel′ə), *n. Pathol.* See **chickenpox.** [1765–75; < NL, equiv. to *vari(ola)* VARIOLA + *-cella* dim. suffix] —**var′i•cel′lar,** *adj.*

var•i•cel•late (var′ə sel′it, -āt), *adj.* having small varices, as certain shells. [< NL *varicell(a)* (for L *varicula,* dim. of *varix* varicose vein) + -ATE[1]]

var′icel′la zos′ter vi′rus, a type of herpesvirus that causes chickenpox and shingles. Also called **herpes zoster virus.**

var•i•cel•loid (var′ə sel′oid), *adj.* resembling varicella. [1870–75; VARICELL(A) + -OID]

var•i•ces (vâr′ə sēz′), *n.* pl. of **varix.**

varico-, a combining form meaning "varix," "varicose vein," used in the formation of compound words: *varicocele.* [< L *varic-* (s. of *varix*) + -O-. See VARIX]

var•i•co•cele (var′i kō sēl′), *n. Pathol.* a varicose condition of the spermatic veins of the scrotum. [1730–40; VARICO- + -CELE[1]]

var•i•co•ce•lec•to•my (var′i kō si lek′tə mē), *n., pl.* **-mies.** the surgical removal or ligation of varicose veins in the scrotal sac. [1890–95; VARICOCELE + -ECTOMY]

var•i•col•ored (vâr′i kul′ərd), *adj.* having various colors; variegated; motley: *a varicolored print.* [1655–65; VARI(OUS) + COLORED]

var•i•cose (var′i kōs′), *adj.* **1.** abnormally or unusually enlarged or swollen: *a varicose vein.* **2.** pertaining to or affected with varices, which often affect the superficial portions of the lower limbs. [1720–30; < L *varicōsus* suffering from varicose veins. See VARIX, -OSE[1]]

var•i•co•sis (var′i kō′sis), *n. Pathol.* **1.** the formation of a varix or varices. **2.** varicosity. [< NL; see VARIX, -OSIS]

var•i•cos•i•ty (var′i kos′i tē), *n., pl.* **-ties.** *Pathol.* **1.** the state or condition of being varicose. **2.** varix (def. 1). [1835–45; VARICOSE + -ITY]

var•i•cot•o•my (var′i kot′ə mē), *n., pl.* **-mies.** surgical removal of a varicose vein. [VARICO- + -TOMY]

var•ied (vâr′ēd), *adj.* **1.** characterized by or exhibiting variety; various; diverse; diversified: *varied backgrounds.* **2.** changed; altered: *a varied estimate.* **3.** having several different colors; variegated. [1580–90; VARY + -ED[2]] —**var′ied•ly,** *adv.* —**var′ied•ness,** *n.*

var′ied thrush′, a plump thrush, *Ixoreus naevius,* of western North America, resembling a robin with a dark band across the chest. [1830–40, *Amer.*]

var•i•e•gate (vâr′ē i gāt′, vâr′i gāt′), *v.t.,* **-gat•ed, -gat•ing. 1.** to make varied in appearance, as by adding different colors. **2.** to give variety to; diversify. [1645–55; < LL *variegātus* (ptp. of *variegāre* to make (something) look varied), equiv. to L *vari(us)* VARIOUS + *-eg-* (comb. form of *agere* to do; see AGENT) + *-ātus* -ATE] —**var′i•e•ga′tor,** *n.*

var•i•e•gat•ed (vâr′ē i gā′tid, vâr′i gā′-), *adj.* **1.** varied in appearance or color; marked with patches or spots of different colors. **2.** varied; diversified; diverse. [1655–65; VARIEGATE + -ED[2]]

var•i•e•ga•tion (vâr′ē i gā′shən, vâr′i gā′-), *n.* **1.** an act of variegating. **2.** the state or condition of being variegated; varied coloration. [1640–50; VARIEGATE + -ION]

var•i•er (vâr′ē ər), *n.* a person or thing that varies. [1605–15; VARY + -ER[1]]

va•ri•e•tal (və rī′i tl), *adj.* **1.** of, pertaining to, designating, or characteristic of a variety. **2.** constituting a variety. **3.** (in U.S. winemaking) designating a wine made entirely or chiefly from one variety of grape. —*n.* **4.** a varietal wine named for such a grape (distinguished from *generic*). [1865–70; VARIET(Y) + -AL[1]] —**va•ri′e•tal•ly,** *adv.*

va•ri•e•ty (və rī′i tē), *n., pl.* **-ties,** *adj.* —*n.* **1.** the state of being varied or diversified: *to give variety to a diet.* **2.** difference; discrepancy. **3.** a number of different types of things, esp. ones in the same general category: *a large variety of fruits.* **4.** a kind or sort. **5.** a different form, condition, or phase of something: *varieties of pastry; a variety of economic reforms.* **6.** a category within a species, based on some hereditary difference. **7.** a type of animal or plant produced by artificial selection. **8.** *Philately.* a stamp differing from others of the same issue through an accident other than an error of an artist or printer. Cf. **error** (def. 8), **freak[1]** (def. 5). **9.** Also called **vari′ety show′.** entertainment of mixed character, consisting of a number of individual performances or acts, as of singing, dancing, or skits. Cf. **vaudeville** (def. 1). —*adj.* **10.** of, pertaining to, or characteristic of a variety: *a variety performer.* [1525–35; < L *varietās,* equiv. to *vari(us)* VARIOUS + *-etās,* var. of *-itās* -ITY after a vowel]
—**Syn. 1.** diversity, multiplicity. **3.** assortment, collection, group. **5.** kind, sort, class, species. —**Ant. 1.** sameness.
—**Usage. 3, 5.** As a collective noun, VARIETY, when preceded by *a,* is often treated as a plural: *A variety of inexpensive goods are sold here.* When preceded by *the,* it is usually treated as a singular: *The variety of products is small.* See also **collective noun, number.**

vari′ety meat′, edible meat other than the usual flesh, esp. organs, as tongue and liver. [1945–50]

vari′ety store′, a retail store, as a five-and-ten, carrying a large variety of goods, esp. low-priced articles. [1760–70, *Amer.*]

var•i•form (vâr′ə fôrm′), *adj.* varied in form; having various forms. [1655–65; VARI(OUS) + -FORM] —**var′i•form′ly,** *adv.*

var•i•o•cou•pler (vâr′ē ō kup′lər), *n. Elect.* a transformer having coils with a self-impedance that is essentially constant but a mutual impedance that can be varied by moving one coil with respect to the other. [1920–25; VARI(ABLE) + -O- + COUPLER]

va•ri•o•la (və rī′ə lə), *n. Pathol.* smallpox. [1795–1805; < ML, equiv. to L *vari(us)* speckled (see VARIOUS) + *-ola* -OLE[1]]

var•i•o•late (vâr′ē ə lāt′, -lit), *adj. Pathol.* resembling smallpox, as a lesion. [1785–95; VARIOL(A) + -ATE[1]]

var•i•ole (vâr′ē ōl′), *n.* **1.** a shallow pit or depression like the mark left by a smallpox pustule; foveola. **2.** a light-colored spherule, common in some igneous rocks, that gives a pockmarked appearance to weathered rock surfaces. [1820–30; < F: VARIOLA]

var•i•o•lit•ic (vâr′ē ə lit′ik), *adj.* **1.** *Petrog.* containing or resembling varioles, esp. in texture. **2.** spotted; speckled. [1860–65; *variolite* rock containing varioles (see VARIOLE, -ITE[1]) + -IC]

var•i•o•loid (vâr′ē ə loid′), *adj.* **1.** resembling smallpox. **2.** of or pertaining to a mild case of smallpox. —*n.* **3.** a mild smallpox, esp. as occurring in persons who were vaccinated or previously had the disease. [1815–25; VARIOL(A) + -OID]

va•ri•o•lous (və rī′ə ləs), *adj.* **1.** of or pertaining to smallpox. **2.** affected with smallpox. **3.** having pits like those left by smallpox. Also, **va•ri′o•lar.** [1660–70; VARIOL(A) + -OUS]

var•i•om•e•ter (vâr′ē om′i tər), *n.* **1.** *Elect.* an instrument for measuring inductance, consisting essentially of an inductor with two or more coils whose relative position may be changed to vary the inductance. **2.** an instrument for indicating a change in a component of a magnetic field vector, esp. one related to the earth's magnetic field. **3.** *Aeron.* an instrument that indicates the rate of climb or descent. [1895–1900; *vari-* (see VARIOUS) + -O- + -METER]

var•i•o•rum (vâr′ē ôr′əm, -ōr′-), *adj.* **1.** containing different versions of the text by various editors: *a variorum edition of Shakespeare.* **2.** containing many notes and commentaries by a number of scholars or critics: *a variorum text of Cicero.* —*n.* **3.** a variorum edition or text. [1720–30; short for L *ēditiō cum notīs variōrum* edition with the notes of various persons]

var•i•ous (vâr′ē əs), *adj.* **1.** of different kinds, as two or more things; differing one from another: *Various experiments have not proved his theory.* **2.** marked by or exhibiting variety or diversity: *houses of various designs.* **3.** presenting or having many different qualities or aspects: *a woman of various talent.* **4.** having a variety of colors; varicolored. **5.** different from each other; dissimilar. **6.** variant. **7.** numerous; many: *living at various hotels.* **8.** individual (in a group, class, kind, etc.); separate: *permission from various officials in Washington.* —*pron.* **9.** *Informal.* several, many, or numerous ones: *I spoke with various of them.* [1545–55; < L *varius* speckled, variegated, hence manifold, diverse; see -OUS] —**var′i•ous•ly,** *adv.* —**var′i•ous•ness,** *n.*
—**Syn. 1.** VARIOUS, DIFFERENT, DISTINCT, DIVERSE describe things that are not identical or alike. VARIOUS stresses the multiplicity of sorts or instances of a thing or a class of things: *various sorts of seaweed; busy with various duties.* DIFFERENT emphasizes separateness and dissimilarity: *two different* (or *differing*) *versions of the same story.* DISTINCT implies a uniqueness that is clear and unmistakable: *plans similar in objective but distinct in method.* DIVERSE usually suggests a disparity capable of leading to conflict or disagreement: *diverse views on how the area should be zoned.* **2.** sundry. **3.** diversified, variegated, varied. —**Ant. 1.** identical, same, uniform, similar.

var•is•cite (var′ə sīt′), *n.* a secondary mineral, hydrated phosphate of aluminum, $Al(PO_4)\cdot 2H_2O$, occurring mainly as massive, bluish-green nodules: sometimes used as a gem. [< G *Variscit,* named after *Variscia* Latinized German district name; see -ITE[1]]

var•i•sized (vâr′ə sīzd′), *adj.* of several or various sizes: *varisized patterns on a fabric.* [1940–45; VARI(OUS) + SIZED]

var•is•tor (va ris′tər, və-), *n. Elect.* a resistor whose resistance automatically varies in proportion to the voltage of the current through it. [1940–45; VAR(IABLE) + (RES)ISTOR]

var•i•type (vâr′i tīp′), *v.,* **-typed, -typ•ing.** —*v.i.* **1.** to operate a Varityper. —*v.t.* **2.** to set (type) on a Varityper. [back formation from VARITYPER] —**var′i•typ′•ist,** *n.*

Var•i•typ•er (vâr′i tī′pər), *Trademark.* a brand of typewriterlike machine with interchangeable typefaces, for composing justified matter.

var•ix (vâr′iks), *n., pl.* **var•i•ces** (vâr′ə sēz′). **1.** Also called **varicosity.** *Pathol.* a permanent abnormal dilation and lengthening of a vein, usually accompanied by some tortuosity; a varicose vein. **2.** *Zool.* a ridgelike mark or scar on the surface of a shell at a former position of the lip of the aperture. [1350–1400; ME < L: varicose vein]

var•let (vär′lit), *n. Archaic.* **1.** a knavish person; rascal. **2. a.** an attendant or servant. **b.** a page who serves a knight. [1425–75; late ME < MF; var. of VALET]

var•let•ry (vär′li trē), *n. Archaic.* **1.** varlets collectively. **2.** the mob or rabble. [1600–10; VARLET + -RY]

Var′ley loop′ (vär′lē), *Elect.* a device containing a Wheatstone bridge, for comparing resistances and for locating faults in circuits. [named after C. F. *Varley* (1828–83), English electrical engineer]

var•mint (vär′mənt), *n.* **1.** *Chiefly Southern and South Midland U.S.* **a.** vermin. **b.** an objectionable or undesirable animal, usually predatory, as a coyote or bobcat. **2.** a despicable, obnoxious, or annoying person. Also, **var′ment.** [1530–40; var. of VERMIN (with regular outcome of ME *ĕr* before consonant (cf. ARGAL[3], PARSON) and parasitic *t*)]

var•na (vär′nə, vur′-), *n. Hinduism.* class (def. 13). [< Skt *varna* lit., cover, color, hence sort, class]

Var•na (vär′nə), *n.* a seaport in NE Bulgaria, on the Black Sea. 186,591. Formerly, **Stalin.**

var•nish (vär′nish), *n.* **1.** a preparation consisting of resinous matter, as copal or lac, dissolved in an oil **(oil varnish)** or in alcohol **(spirit varnish)** or other volatile liquid. When applied to the surface of wood, metal, etc., it dries and leaves a hard, more or less glossy, usually transparent coating. **2.** the sap of certain trees, used for the same purpose **(natural varnish). 3.** any of various other preparations similarly used, as one having India rubber, pyroxylin, or asphalt as its chief constituent. **4.** a coating or surface of varnish. **5.** something resembling or suggesting a coat of varnish; gloss. **6.** superficial polish or external show, esp. to conceal some defect or inadequacy: *The play has a varnish of witty dialogue.* **7.** *Brit.* nail polish. —*v.t.* **8.** to apply varnish to; coat or cover with varnish. **9.** to give a glossy appearance to. **10.** to give an improved appearance to; adorn. **11.** to give a superficially pleasing appearance to, esp. in order to deceive: *to varnish the truth.* [1300–50; ME *varnisch* < MF *vernis, verniz* < ML *vernicium* sandarac < MGk *bernī́kē,* syncopated var. of Gk *Berenī́kē,* city in Cyrenaica] —**var′nish•er,** *n.* —**var′nish•y,** *adj.*
—**Syn. 11.** gild, disguise.

var′nishing day′, vernissage (def. 1). [1815–25]

var′nish tree′, 1. any of various trees yielding sap or other substances used for varnish, as *Rhus verniciflua,* of Japan. **2.** an Asian tree, *Koelreuteria paniculata,* of the soapberry family, having showy clusters of yellow flowers from 12 to 18 in. (30 to 46 cm) long, and papery, brilliantly colored pods with black seeds, grown as an ornamental. [1750–60, *Amer.*]

va•room (və rōōm′, -rŏŏm′), *n., v.* vroom.

Var•ro (var′ō), *n.* **Marcus Te•ren•ti•us** (tə ren′shē əs, -shəs), c116–27? B.C., Roman scholar and author.

var•si•ty (vär′si tē), *n., pl.* **-ties,** *adj.* —*n.* **1.** any first-string team, esp. in sports, that represents a school, college, university, or the like: *He is on the varsity in*

CONCISE ETYMOLOGY KEY: <, descended or borrowed from; >, whence; b., blend of, blended; c., cognate with; cf., compare; deriv., derivative; equiv., equivalent; imit., imitative; obl., oblique; r., replacing; s., stem; sp., spelling, spelled; resp., respelling, respelled; trans., translation; ?, origin unknown; *, unattested; ‡, probably earlier than. See the full key inside the front cover.

tennis and in debating. **2.** *Chiefly Brit. Informal.* university. —*adj.* **3.** of or pertaining to a university or school team, activity, or competition: *a varsity debater.* [1840–50; cf. *versity* university, in 17th century; pron. prob. preserves historical outcome of ME *ĕr,* as in VARMINT]

Var·so·vi·an (vär sō′vē ən), *n.* **1.** a native or inhabitant of Warsaw. —*adj.* **2.** of or pertaining to Warsaw or its inhabitants. [1900–05; *Varsovi(a)* Latinization of Pol *Warszawa* WARSAW + -AN, perh. on the model of F *varsovien*]

Var·u·na (vûr′o͝o nə, vär′ə-), *n. Hinduism.* the Vedic god of natural and moral law, probably a sky god originally: thought to correspond to the Zoroastrian god Ahura Mazda.

var·us (vâr′əs), *n. Pathol.* abnormal angulation of a bone or joint, with the angle pointing away from the midline. [1790–1800; < L *vārus* crooked, bent]

varve (värv), *n. Geol.* (in lake sediments) an annual deposit usually consisting of two layers, one of fine materials and the other of coarse. [1920–25; < Sw *varv* a round, (complete) turn]

var·y (vâr′ē), *v.,* **var·ied, var·y·ing.** —*v.t.* **1.** to change or alter, as in form, appearance, character, or substance: *to vary one's methods.* **2.** to cause to be different from something else: *The orchestra varied last night's program with one new selection.* **3.** to avoid or relieve from uniformity or monotony; diversify: *to vary one's diet.* **4.** *Music.* to alter (a melody or theme) by modification or embellishments without changing its identity. —*v.i.* **5.** to show diversity; be different: *The age at which children are ready to read varies.* **6.** to undergo change in appearance, form, substance, character, etc.: *The landscape begins to vary as one drives south.* **7.** to change periodically or in succession; differ or alternate: *Demand for certain products varies with the season.* **8.** to diverge; depart; deviate (usually fol. by *from*): *to vary from the norm.* **9.** *Math.* to be subject to change. **10.** *Biol.* to exhibit variation. [1300–50; ME *varien* < L *variāre,* equiv. to *vari(us)* (see VARIOUS) + *-āre* inf. suffix] —**var′i·er,** *n.* —**var′y·ing·ly,** *adv.*
—**Syn. 1.** modify, mutate.

var′ying hare′. See **snowshoe hare.** [1775–85]

vas (vas), *n., pl.* **va·sa** (vā′sə). *Anat., Zool., Bot.* a vessel or duct. [1645–55; < L *vās* vessel]

vas-, var. of **vaso-** before a vowel: *vasectomy.*

va·sa mur·rhi·na (vā′sə mə rī′nə, -rē′-), an American art glass, consisting of colored glass dusted with flakes or grains of metal and flashed with clear glass. [< NL: lit., murrhine vessel]

va·sa·na (vä′sə nə), *n. Yoga.* any subconscious force that affects character. [< Skt *vāsanā*]

Va·sa·ri (və zär′ē, -sär′ē; *It.* vä zä′rē), *n.* **Gior·gio** (jôr′jō), 1511–74, Italian painter, architect, and art historian.

Vas·co da Ga·ma (vas′kō də gam′ə, gä′mə; *Port.* väsh′ko͞o də gä′mə). See **Gama, Vasco da.**

vas·cu·lar (vas′kyə lər), *adj. Biol.* pertaining to, composed of, or provided with vessels or ducts that convey fluids, as blood, lymph, or sap. Also, **vas·cu·lose** (vas′kyə lōs′), **vas·cu·lous** (vas′kyə ləs). [1665–75; < NL *vāsculāris.* See VASCULUM, -AR[1]] —**vas·cu·lar·i·ty** (vas′kyə lar′i tē), *n.* —**vas′cu·lar·ly,** *adv.*

vas′cular bun′dle, *Bot.* a longitudinal arrangement of strands of xylem and phloem, and sometimes cambium, that forms the fluid-conducting channels of vascular tissue in the rhizomes, stems, and leaf veins of vascular plants, the arrangement varying with the type of plant. [1880–85]

vas·cu·lar·ize (vas′kyə lə rīz′), *v.,* **-ized, -iz·ing.** —*v.i. Biol.* **1.** (of a tissue or embryo) to develop or extend blood vessels or other fluid-bearing vessels or ducts; become vascular. —*v.t. Biol., Surg.* **2.** to supply (an organ or tissue) with blood vessels. Also, *esp. Brit.,* **vas′·cu·lar·ise′.** [1890–95; VASCULAR + -IZE] —**vas′cu·lar·i·za′tion,** *n.*

vas·cu·lar·ized (vas′kyə lə rīzd′), *adj.* **1.** rendered vascular by the formation of new blood vessels. **2.** vascular. [1955–60; VASCULARIZE + -ED[2]]

vas′cular plant′, a plant having a vascular system. [1860–65]

vas′cular ray′, *Bot.* a radiate band of parenchyma in the secondary xylem extending into the secondary phloem of the stems of certain vascular plants, formed by the cambium and serving for the storage of food and the conduction of nutriments. [1665–75]

vas′cular tis′sue, *Bot.* plant tissue consisting of ducts or vessels, that, in the higher plants, forms the system **(vas′cular sys′tem)** by which sap is conveyed through the plant. [1805–15]

vas·cu·lum (vas′kyə ləm), *n., pl.* **-la** (-lə), **-lums.** a kind of case or box used by botanists for carrying specimens as they are collected. [1825–35; < L *vāsculum* little vessel. See VAS, -CULE[1]]

vas de·fe·rens (vas′ def′ə renz′, -ər ənz), *pl.* **va·sa de·fe·ren·ti·a** (vā′sə def′ə ren′shē ə, -shə). *Anat., Zool.* the duct that transports the sperm from the epididymis to the penis. [1880–85; < NL *vās dēferēns* lit., vessel for carrying off. See VAS, DEFERENT[2]]

vase (vās, vāz, väz), *n.* a vessel, as of glass, porcelain, earthenware, or metal, usually higher than it is wide, used chiefly to hold cut flowers or for decoration. [1555–65; < F < L *vās* vessel] —**vase′like′,** *adj.*

vas·ec·to·my (va sek′tə mē), *n., pl.* **-mies.** *Surg.* excision of the vas deferens, or of a portion of it: performed to effect sterility in men. [1895–1900; VAS (DEFERENS) + -ECTOMY]

vas ef·fer·ens (vas′ ef′ə renz′, -ər ənz), *pl.* **va·sa ef·fer·en·ti·a** (vā′sə ef′ə ren′shē ə, -shə), *Anat.* any of a number of short ducts that carry sperm from the testis to the epididymus. [1855–60; < NL: lit., vessel for carrying out. See VAS, EFFERENT]

Vas·e·line (vas′ə lēn′, vas′ə lēn′), *Trademark.* a brand of petrolatum.

Vash·ti (vash′tē, -tī), *n.* the queen of Ahasuerus who was banished for refusing to appear before the king's guests. Esther 1:9–22.

va·si·form (vā′zə fôrm′, vas′ə-), *adj.* **1.** having the form of a duct or tube. **2.** having the shape of a vase. [1825–35; < L *vās* vessel + -I- + -FORM]

vaso-, a combining form meaning "vessel," used in the formation of compound words: *vasoconstrictor.* Also, *esp. before a vowel,* **vas-.** [< L *vās* vessel + -o-]

vas·o·ac·tive (vas′ō ak′tiv, vā′zō-), *adj. Physiol., Pharm.* of or pertaining to a substance, drug, or event that changes the diameter of a blood vessel. [1920–25; VASO- + ACTIVE]

vas·o·con·stric·tion (vas′ō kən strik′shən, vā′zō-), *n. Physiol.* constriction of the blood vessels, as by the action of a nerve. [1895–1900; VASO- + CONSTRICTION]

vas·o·con·stric·tive (vas′ō kən strik′tiv, vā′zō-), *adj. Physiol.* causing vasoconstriction. [1885–90; VASO- + CONSTRICTIVE]

vas·o·con·stric·tor (vas′ō kən strik′tər, vā′zō-), *n. Physiol., Pharm.* a nerve or drug that causes vasoconstriction. [1875–80; VASO- + CONSTRICTOR]

vas·o·de·pres·sor (vas′ō di pres′ər, vā′zō-), *adj., n. Physiol., Pharm.* vasodilator. [VASO- + DEPRESSOR]

vas·o·dil·a·ta·tion (vas′ō dil′ə tā′shən, -dī′lə-, vā′zō-), *n. Physiol.* dilatation of the blood vessels, as by the action of a nerve. Also, **vas·o·di·la·tion** (vas′ō dī lā′shən, -di-, vā′zō-). [1895–1900; VASO- + DILATATION]

vas·o·di·la·tor (vas′ō dī lā′tər, -di-, -dī′lā-, vā′zō-), *n. Physiol., Pharm.* a nerve or drug that causes vasodilatation. [1880–85; VASO- + DILATOR]

vas·o·in·hib·i·tor (vas′ō in hib′i tər, vā′zō-), *n. Physiol., Pharm.* an agent, as a drug, that inhibits the action of the vasomotor nerves. [VASO- + INHIBITOR] —**vas·o·in·hib·i·to·ry** (vas′ō in hib′i tôr′ē, -tōr′ē, vā′zō-), *adj.*

vas·o·li·ga·tion (vas′ō lī gā′shən, vā′zō-), *n. Surg.* ligation of the vas deferens. Also, **vasoligature.** [VASO- + LIGATION]

vas·o·lig·a·ture (vas′ō lig′ə chər, -cho͝or′, vā′zō-), *n. Surg.* vasoligation. [VASO- + LIGATURE]

vas·o·mo·tion (vas′ō mō′shən, vā′zō-), *n. Physiol.* the change in diameter of a blood vessel. [VASO- + MOTION]

vas·o·mo·tor (vas′ō mō′tər, vā′zō-), *adj. Physiol.* regulating the diameter of blood vessels, as certain nerves. [1860–65; VASO- + MOTOR]

vas·o·pres·sin (vas′ō pres′in), *n.* **1.** *Biochem.* a peptide hormone, synthesized in the hypothalamus and released by the posterior pituitary gland, that stimulates capillary muscles and reduces the flow of urine and increases its concentration. **2.** *Pharm.* a synthetic preparation of this hormone, used as an antidiuretic in the treatment of diabetes insipidus. Also called **antidiuretic hormone, ADH.** [1928; orig. trademark]

vas·o·pres·sor (vas′ō pres′ər, vā′zō-), *n. Biochem., Pharm.* a hormone, as epinephrine, or other agent that raises the blood pressure by causing contraction of the arteriole muscles, narrowing the arteriole passage. [1925–30; VASO- + PRESSOR]

vas·o·spasm (vas′ō spaz′əm, vā′zō-), *n.* sudden constriction of an artery, leading to a decrease in its diameter and in the amount of blood it can deliver. [1900–05; VASO- + SPASM]

vas·o·stim·u·lant (vas′ō stim′yə lənt, vā′zō-), *adj.* **1.** stimulating the action of the vasomotor nerves. —*n.* **2.** a vasostimulant agent, as a drug. [VASO- + STIMULANT]

vas·ot·o·my (va sot′ə mē), *n., pl.* **-mies.** *Surg.* incision or opening of the vas deferens. [VASO- + -TOMY]

vas·o·ton·ic (vas′ō ton′ik, vā′zō-), *adj. Physiol.* pertaining to or regulating the tone of the blood vessels. [VASO- + TONIC]

vas·o·va·sos·to·my (vas′ō va sos′tə mē, vā′zō-), *n., pl.* **-mies.** the reversal of a vasectomy, performed by surgical reconnection of the severed ends of the vas deferens. [VASO- + VASO- + -STOMY]

Vas·sa (vas′ə), *n.* **Gustavus** (*Olaudah Equiano*), c1745–1801?, African slave, sold in the West Indies, and, after gaining freedom, abolitionist and writer in England.

vas·sal (vas′əl), *n.* **1.** (in the feudal system) a person granted the use of land, in return for rendering homage, fealty, and usually military service or its equivalent to a lord or other superior; feudal tenant. **2.** a person holding some similar relation to a superior; a subject, subordinate, follower, or retainer. **3.** a servant or slave. —*adj.* **4.** of, pertaining to, or characteristic of a vassal. **5.** having the status or position of a vassal. [1300–50; ME < MF < ML *vassallus,* equiv. to *vass(us)* servant (< Celtic; cf. Welsh *gwas* young man, Ir *foss* servant) + *-allus* n. suffix] —**vas′sal·less,** *adj.*

vas·sal·age (vas′ə lij), *n.* **1.** the state or condition of a vassal. **2.** homage or service required of a vassal. **3.** a territory held by a vassal. **4.** vassals collectively. **5.** dependence, subjection, or servitude. [1275–1325; ME < MF; see VASSAL, -AGE]

vas·sal·ic (va sal′ik), *adj.* of, pertaining to, or resembling a vassal or vassalage. [1895–1900; VASSAL + -IC]

Vas·sar (vas′ər), *n.* **Matthew,** 1792–1868, U.S. merchant, philanthropist, and supporter of education for women; born in England: founder of Vassar College.

vast (vast, väst), *adj.,* **-er, -est,** *n.* —*adj.* **1.** of very great area or extent; immense: *the vast reaches of outer space.* **2.** of very great size or proportions; huge; enormous: *vast piles of rubble left in the wake of the war.* **3.** very great in number, quantity, amount, etc.: *vast sums of money.* **4.** very great in degree, intensity, etc.: *an artisan of vast skill.* —*n.* **5.** *Literary.* an immense or boundless expanse or space. [1565–75; < L *vastus* empty, immense] —**vast′ly,** *adv.* —**vast′ness,** *n.*
—**Syn. 1.** measureless, boundless, gigantic, colossal, stupendous. —**Ant. 1.** small.

Väs·ter·ås (ves′tər ôs′), *n.* a city in central Sweden. 117,487.

Vas·thi (vas′thī), *n. Douay Bible.* Vashti.

vas·ti·tude (vas′ti to͞od′, -tyo͞od′, vä′sti-), *n.* **1.** vastness; immensity: *the vastitude of his love for all humankind.* **2.** a vast expanse or space: *the ocean vastitude.* [1535–45; < L *vastitūdō.* See VAST, -I-, -TUDE]

vas·ti·ty (vas′ti tē, vä′sti-), *n.* **1.** immensity; vastness. **2.** *Archaic.* wasteness; desolation. [1535–45; < MF *vastite* < L *vastitās;* see VAST, -ITY]

vas·tus (vas′təs), *n., pl.* **-ti** (-tī). *Anat.* any of several muscles in the front part of the thigh constituting part of the quadriceps muscle, the action of which assists in extending the leg. [< L: VAST]

vast·y (vas′tē, vä′stē), *adj.,* **vast·i·er, vast·i·est.** vast; immense. [1590–1600; VAST + -Y[1]]

vat (vat), *n., v.,* **vat·ted, vat·ting.** —*n.* **1.** a large container, as a tub or tank, used for storing or holding liquids: *a wine vat.* **2.** *Chem.* **a.** a preparation containing an insoluble dye converted by reduction into a soluble leuco base. **b.** a vessel containing such a preparation. —*v.t.* **3.** to put into or treat in a vat. [bef. 1100; ME (south); OE *fæt* vessel; c. ON *fat* vessel, G *Fass* keg]

VAT, See **value-added tax.**

Vat., Vatican.

vat′ dye′, *Chem.* any of the class of insoluble dyes impregnated into textile fibers by reduction into soluble leuco bases that regenerate the insoluble dye on oxidation. [1900–05]

vat·ic (vat′ik), *adj.* of, pertaining to, or characteristic of a prophet. Also, **vat′i·cal.** [1595–1605; < L *vāt(ēs)* seer + -IC]

Vat·i·can (vat′i kən), *n.* **1.** Also called **Vat′ican Pal′·ace.** the chief residence of the popes in Vatican City, now also including a library, archives, art museum, apartments, and administrative offices. **2.** the authority and government of the pope (distinguished from the *Quirinal*). [1545–55; < L *Vāticānus* (*mōns*) Vatican (hill)]

Vatican II. See **Second Vatican Council.**

Vat′ican Cit′y, an independent state within the city of Rome, on the right bank of the Tiber. Established in 1929, it is ruled by the pope and includes St. Peter's Church and the Vatican, 1000; 109 acres (44 hectares). Italian, **Città del Vaticano.**

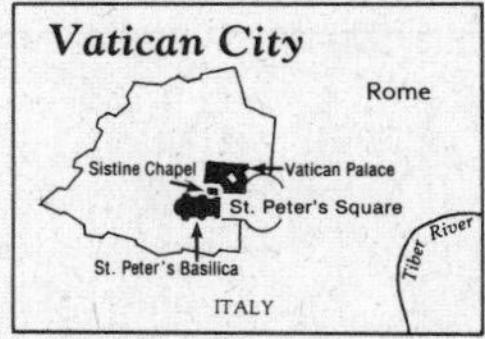

Vat′ican Coun′cil, the ecumenical council, convoked in Rome, 1869–70, by Pope Pius IX, that declared the dogma of papal infallibility.

Vat·i·can·ism (vat′i kə niz′əm), *n. Usually Disparaging.* the doctrine of the absolute supremacy of the pope. [1870–75; VATICAN + -ISM] —**Vat′i·can·ist,** *n.*

Vat′ican Swin′dle, The. See ***Lafcadio's Adventures.***

vat·i·cide (vat′ə sīd′), *n.* **1.** a person who murders a prophet. **2.** the act of killing a prophet. [1720–30; < L *vāti-* (s. of *vātēs* seer) + -CIDE]

va·tic·i·nal (və tis′ə nl), *adj.* of, pertaining to, or characterized by prophecy; prophetic. [1580–90; < L *vāticin(us)* prophetic (*vāticin(ārī)* to prophesy + *-us* adj. suffix) + -AL[1]; see VATICINATE]

va·tic·i·nate (və tis′ə nāt′), *v.t., v.i.,* **-nat·ed, -nat·ing.** to prophesy. [1615–25; < L *vāticinātus* (ptp. of *vāticinārī* to prophesy), equiv. to *vāti-* (s. of *vātēs* seer) + *-cin-* (comb. form of *canere* to sing, prophesy) + *-ātus* -ATE[1]] —**va·tic′i·na′tor,** *n.*

va·tic·i·na·tion (və tis′ə nā′shən, vat′ə sə-), *n.* **1.** an act of prophesying. **2.** a prophesy. [1595–1605; < L *vāticinātiōn-* (s. of *vāticinātiō*). See VATICINATE, -ION]

vat·man (vat′mən), *n., pl.* **-men.** *Papermaking.* the worker who shakes the pulp onto the wire. [1830–40; VAT + MAN[1]]

Vat·tel (*Ger.* fät′l), *n.* **Em·me·rich** (*Ger.* em′ə rikh), 1714–67, Swiss jurist and diplomat.

Vät·ter (vet′tər), *n.* a lake in S Sweden. 80 mi. (130 km) long; 733 sq. mi. (1900 sq. km). Also, **Vät·tern** (vet′tərn), **Vetter.**

vat·ting (vat′ing), *n.* the stage of winemaking during which the expressed juice of grapes has been placed in vats and left to ferment. [1835–45; VAT + -ING[1]]

va·tu (vä′to͞o), *n.* a nickel-brass coin and monetary unit of Vanuatu.

Vau·ban (vō bäN′), *n.* **Sé·bas·tien le Pres·tre de** (sā bas tyan′ lə pre′trᵊ də), 1633–1707, French military engineer and marshal.

CONCISE PRONUNCIATION KEY: act, cāpe, dâre, pärt; set, ēqual; *if,* īce; ox, ōver, ôrder, oil, bo͝ok, bo͞ot, out; up, ûrge; child; sing; shoe; thin, that; zh as in *treasure.* ə = *a* as in *alone, e* as in *system, i* as in *easily, o* as in *gallop, u* as in *circus;* ᵊ as in *fire* (fīᵊr), *hour* (ouᵊr). l and n can serve as syllabic consonants, as in *cradle* (krād′l), and *button* (but′n). See the full key inside the front cover.

Vau·cluse (vō klyz′), *n.* a department in SE France. 390,446; 1382 sq. mi. (3580 sq. km). *Cap.:* Avignon.

Vaud (vō), *n.* a canton in W Switzerland. 521,600; 1239 sq. mi. (3210 sq. km). *Cap.:* Lausanne. German, **Waadt.**

vaude·ville (vôd′vil, vōd′-, vô′də-), *n.* **1.** theatrical entertainment consisting of a number of individual performances, acts, or mixed numbers, as by comedians, singers, dancers, acrobats, and magicians. Cf. **variety** (def. 9). **2.** a theatrical piece of light or amusing character, interspersed with songs and dances. **3.** a satirical cabaret song. [1730–40; < F, shortened alter. of MF *chanson du vau de Vire* song of the VALE[1] of *Vire,* a valley of Calvados, France, noted for satirical folksongs]

vaude·vil·lian (vôd vil′yən, vōd-, vô′də-), *n.* **1.** Also, **vaude′vil·list.** a person who writes for or performs in vaudeville. —*adj.* **2.** of, pertaining to, or characteristic of vaudeville. [1925–30; VAUDEVILLE + -IAN]

Vau·dois (vō dwä′), *n., pl.* **-dois** for 1. **1.** a native or inhabitant of Vaud. **2.** the dialect of French spoken in Vaud. [< F; MF *Vaudeis.* See VAUD, -ESE]

Vau·dois (vō dwä′), *n.* (*used with a singular v.*) Waldenses.

Vaughan (vôn), *n.* **1. Henry,** 1622–95, English poet and mystic. **2. Sarah (Lois),** 1924–90, U.S. jazz singer. **3.** a town in SW Ontario, in S Canada, near Toronto. 29,674. **4.** a male given name: from a Welsh word meaning "small."

Vaughan Wil·liams (vôn wil′yəmz), **Ralph,** 1872–1958, English composer.

Vaughn (vôn), *n.* a male or female given name.

vault[1] (vôlt), *n.* **1.** an arched structure, usually made of stones, concrete, or bricks, forming a ceiling or roof over a hall, room, sewer, or other wholly or partially enclosed construction. **2.** an arched structure resembling a vault. **3.** a space, chamber, or passage enclosed by a vault or vaultlike structure, esp. one located underground. **4.** an underground chamber, as a cellar or a division of a cellar. **5.** a room or compartment, often built of or lined with steel, reserved for the storage and safekeeping of valuables, esp. such a place in a bank. **6.** a strong metal cabinet, usually fireproof and burglarproof, for the storage and safekeeping of valuables, important papers, etc. **7.** a burial chamber. **8.** *Anat.* an arched roof of a cavity. **9.** something likened to an arched roof: *the vault of heaven.* —*v.t.* **10.** to construct or cover with a vault. **11.** to make in the form of a vault; arch. **12.** to extend or stretch over in the manner of an arch; overarch: *An arbor vaulted the path.* **13.** to store in a vault. —*v.i.* **14.** to curve or bend in the form of a vault. [1300–50; (n.) alter. of ME *voute* < OF *vou(l)te, volte* < VL **volvita,* for L *volūta,* n. use of fem. ptp. of L *volvere* to turn (see REVOLVE); (v.) alter. of ME *vouten* < OF *vou(l)ter, volter,* deriv. of *vou(l)te, volte*] —**vault′like′,** *adj.*

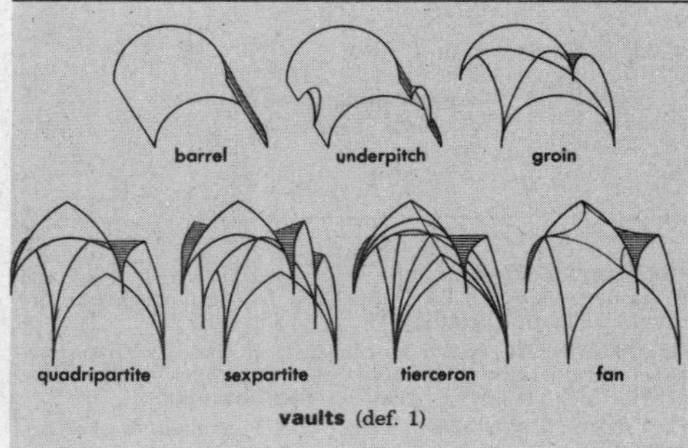

vaults (def. 1)

vault[2] (vôlt), *v.i.* **1.** to leap or spring, as to or from a position or over something: *He vaulted over the tennis net.* **2.** to leap with the hands supported by something, as by a horizontal pole. **3.** *Gymnastics.* to leap over a vaulting or pommel horse, using the hands for pushing off. **4.** to arrive at or achieve something as if by a spring or leap: *to vault into prominence.* —*v.t.* **5.** to leap over: *to vault a fence.* **6.** to cause to leap over or surpass others: *Advertising has vaulted the new perfume into first place.* —*n.* **7.** the act of vaulting. **8.** a leap of a horse; curvet. **9.** *Gymnastics.* a running jump over a vaulting or pommel horse, usually finishing with an acrobatic dismount. [1530–40; < F *volte* a turn and *volter* to turn, respectively < It *volta* (n.) and *voltare* (v.); see VOLT[2]] —**vault′er,** *n.*
—**Syn. 1.** See **jump.**

vault·ed (vôl′tid), *adj.* **1.** constructed or covered with a vault, as a building or chamber. **2.** provided with a vault. **3.** resembling a vault: *the vaulted sky.* [1525–35; VAULT[1] + -ED[2]]

vault·ing[1] (vôl′ting), *n.* **1.** the act or process of constructing vaults. **2.** the structure forming a vault. **3.** a vault, vaulted ceiling, etc., or such structures collectively. [1505–15; VAULT[1] + -ING[1]]

vault·ing[2] (vôl′ting), *adj.* **1.** leaping up or over. **2.** used in vaulting: *a vaulting pole.* **3.** excessive in ambition or presumption; overweening; high-flown: *vaulting ambition; vaulting pride.* [1525–35; VAULT[2] + -ING[2]]

vault′ing horse′, *Gymnastics.* a padded, somewhat cylindrical floor-supported apparatus, braced horizontally at an adjustable height, used for hand support and pushing off in vaulting. Also called **long horse.** Cf. **pommel horse.** [1870–75]

CONCISE ETYMOLOGY KEY: <, descended or borrowed from; >, whence; b., blend of, blended; c., cognate with; cf., compare; deriv., derivative; equiv., equivalent; imit., imitative; obl., oblique; r., replacing; s., stem; sp., spelling, spelled; resp., respelling, respelled; trans., translation; ?, origin unknown; *, unattested; ‡, probably earlier than. See the full key inside the front cover.

vault′ light′, a windowlike structure set in a pavement or the like to illuminate areas beneath, consisting of thick glass blocks set in a metal frame. Also called **pavement light.**

vault·y (vôl′tē), *adj.* having the appearance or characteristics of a vault; arching: *the vaulty rows of elm trees.* [1535–45; VAULT[1] + -Y[1]]

vaunt (vônt, vänt), *v.t.* **1.** to speak vaingloriously of; boast of: *to vaunt one's achievements.* —*v.i.* **2.** to speak boastfully; brag. —*n.* **3.** a boastful action or utterance. [1350–1400; ME *vaunten* < MF *vanter* to boast < LL *vānitāre,* freq. of **vānāre,* deriv. of L *vānus* VAIN. See VANITY] —**vaunt′er,** *n.* —**vaunt′ing·ly,** *adv.*

vaunt-cour·i·er (vônt′kûr′ē ər, -ko͝or′-, vänt′-), *n. Archaic.* a person who goes in advance, as a herald. [1550–60; < F *avant-courrier* forerunner, herald. See AVAUNT, COURIER]

vaunt·ed (vôn′tid, vän′-), *adj.* praised boastfully or excessively: *the vaunted beauties of Paris.* [1625–35; VAUNT + -ED[2]]

vaunt·ful (vônt′fəl, vänt′-), *adj. Archaic.* boastful. [1580–90; VAUNT + -FUL]

vaunt·ing (vôn′ting, vän′-), *adj.* **1.** having a boastfully proud disposition: *a vaunting dictator.* **2.** marked by boastful pride. [1580–90; VAUNT + -ING[2]]

vaunt·y (vôn′tē, vän′-), *adj. Scot.* boastful; vain. [1715–25; VAUNT + -Y[1]]

Vau·que·lin (vōkᵉ laN′), *n.* **Louis Ni·co·las** (lwē nē kô lä′), 1763–1829, French chemist: discoverer of chromium and beryllium.

v. aux., auxiliary verb.

vav (väv, vôv), *n.* **1.** the sixth letter of the Hebrew alphabet. **2.** any of the sounds represented by this letter. [< Heb *wāw* lit., hook]

vav·a·sor (vav′ə sôr′, -sōr′), *n.* (in the feudal system) a vassal ranking just below a baron. Also, **vav·a·sour** (vav′ə so͝or′). [1300–50; ME *vavasour* < OF, perh. contr. of ML *vassus vassōrum* vassal of vassals; see VASSAL]

vav·a·so·ry (vav′ə sôr′ē, -sōr′ē), *n., pl.* **-ries. 1.** the tenure of a fee held by a vavasor. **2.** lands held by a vavasor. [1605–15; < ML *vavasoria* < MF *vavassourie.* See VAVASOR, -Y[3]]

va·ward (vä′wôrd′, vou′ôrd), *n. Archaic.* vanguard. [1325–75; ME, var. of *va(u)mwarde, vantward,* aphetic for *avantward* < AF *avantwarde,* equiv. to *avant* (see AVAUNT) + *warde* < OE *weard* WARD]

vb., **1.** verb. **2.** verbal.

V block, a block having a precise V-shaped groove for checking the roundness or concentricity of a machine part or the like, or for holding cylindrical pieces of work.

VC, **1.** venture capital. **2.** Vietcong. **3.** See **vital capacity.**

V.C., **1.** venture capital. **2.** Veterinary Corps. **3.** Vice-Chairman. **4.** Vice-Chancellor. **5.** Vice-Consul. **6.** See **Victoria Cross. 7.** Vietcong.

VCR, See **videocassette recorder.**

VD, venereal disease. Also, **V.D.**

v.d., various dates.

V-Day (vē′dā′), *n.* a day of final military victory. Cf. **V-E Day, V-J Day.** [1940–45; short for *Victory Day*]

V.D.M., Minister of the Word of God. [< L *Verbī Dei Minister*]

VDT, *Computers.* **1.** video display terminal. **2.** *Chiefly Brit.* visual display terminal.

VDU, *Computers.* visual display unit.

Ve (ve), *n. Scand. Myth.* a brother of Odin.

've, contraction of *have: I've got it. We've been there.* —**Usage.** See **contraction.**

Ve·a·dar (vē′ə där′, -ä där′, vā′-, vē′ə där′, -ä där′), *n.* an intercalary month of the Jewish calendar. Also called **Adar Sheni.** Cf. **Jewish calendar.** [< Heb *wə* and + *ădhār* ADAR]

veal (vēl), *n.* **1.** Also, **veal·er** (vē′lər). a calf raised for its meat, usually a milk-fed animal less than three months old. **2.** the flesh of the calf as used for food. [1350–1400; ME *ve(e)l* < AF *vel* (OF *veel, veal*) < L *vitellus,* dim. of *vitulus* calf]

veal·y (vē′lē), *adj.* **1.** resembling veal. **2.** *Informal.* young or immature: *a vealy youth.* [1760–70; VEAL + -Y[1]]

Veb·len (veb′lən), *n.* **1. Oswald,** 1880–1960, U.S. mathematician. **2. Thor·stein** (thôr′stin, -stən), 1857–1929, U.S. economist and sociologist.

Veb·le·ni·an (ve blē′nē ən), *n.* **1.** Also called **Veb·len·ite** (veb′lə nit′). a person who adheres to the economic or sociological theories of Thorstein Veblen. —*adj.* **2.** of, pertaining to, or suggesting the theories of Thorstein Veblen. [VEBLEN + -IAN]

Veb·len·ism (veb′lə niz′əm), *n.* the economic or social theories originated by Thorstein Veblen. [VEBLEN + -ISM]

vec·tion (vek′shən), *n. Med.* the transference of a disease from one person to another. [1600–10; < L *vectiōn-* (s. of *vectiō* a carrying). See VECTOR, -TION]

vec·tor (vek′tər), *n.* **1.** *Math.* **a.** a quantity possessing both magnitude and direction, represented by an arrow the direction of which indicates the direction of the quantity and the length of which is proportional to the magnitude. Cf. **scalar** (def. 4). **b.** such a quantity with the additional requirement that such quantities obey the parallelogram law of addition. **c.** such a quantity with the additional requirement that such quantities are to transform in a particular way under changes of the coordinate system. **d.** any generalization of the above quantities. **2.** the direction or course followed by an airplane, missile, or the like. **3.** *Biol.* **a.** an insect or other organism that transmits a pathogenic fungus, virus, bacterium, etc. **b.** any agent that acts as a carrier or transporter, as a virus or plasmid that conveys a genetically engineered DNA segment into a host cell. **4.** *Computers.* an array of data ordered such that individual items can be located with a single index or subscript. —*v.t.* **5.** *Aeron.* to guide (an aircraft) in flight by issuing appropriate headings. **6.** *Aerospace.* to change direction of (the thrust of a jet or rocket engine) in order to steer the craft. [1695–1705; < L: one that conveys, equiv. to *vec-,* var. s. of *vehere* to carry + *-tor* -TOR] —**vec·to·ri·al** (vek tôr′ē əl, -tōr′-), *adj.* —**vec·to′ri·al·ly,** *adv.*

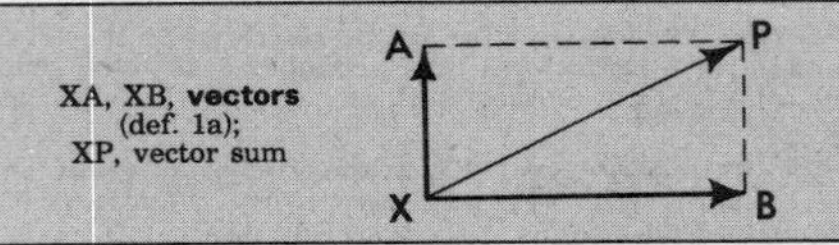

vec′tor addi′tion, *Math.* the process of finding one vector that is equivalent to the result of the successive application of two or more given vectors.

vec′tor anal′ysis, the branch of calculus that deals with vectors and processes involving vectors.

vec·tor·car·di·o·gram (vek′tər kär′dē ə gram′), *n.* the graphic record produced by vectorcardiography. [VECTOR + CARDIOGRAM]

vec·tor·car·di·og·ra·phy (vek′tər kär′dē og′rə fē), *n.* a method of determining the direction and magnitude of the electrical forces of the heart. [VECTOR + CARDIOGRAPHY] —**vec·tor·car·di·o·graph·ic** (vek′tər-kär′dē ə graf′ik), *adj.*

vec′tor field′, *Math., Physics.* a region, domain, set, etc., with a vector assigned at each point; vector function.

vec′tor func′tion, *Math.* a function that assigns a vector to each point in a given set.

vec′tor graph′ics, a method of electronically coding graphic images so that they are represented in lines rather than fixed bit maps, allowing an image, as on a computer display screen, to be rotated or proportionally scaled.

vec′tor prod′uct. See **cross product.** [1875–80]

vec′tor space′, *Math.* an additive group in which addition is commutative and with which is associated a field of scalars, as the field of real numbers, such that the product of a scalar and an element of the group or a vector is defined, the product of two scalars times a vector is associative, one times a vector is the vector, and two distributive laws hold. Also called **linear space.**

vec′tor sum′, *Math.* the vector obtained by applying vector addition to two or more given vectors. [1900–05]

vec·ture (vek′chər), *n.* a token used to pay transportation fares. [1615–25; perh. by back formation from VECTURIST]

vec·tur·ist (vek′chə rist), *n.* a person who collects transportation tokens as a hobby. [< L *vectūr(a)* transport, money paid for transport, fare (*vect(us)* ptp. of *vehere* to convey + *-ūra* -URE) + -IST]

Ve·da (vā′də, vē′-), *n. Hinduism.* **1.** Sometimes, **Vedas.** the entire body of Hindu sacred writings, chief among which are four books, the Rig-Veda, the Sama-Veda, the Atharva-Veda, and the Yajur-Veda. **2.** Also called **Samhita.** each of these four books. **3. Vedas,** these four books, along with the Brahmanas and Upanishads. [< Skt] —**Ve·da·ic** (vi dā′ik), *adj.* —**Ve·da·ism** (vā′də iz′əm, vē′-), *n.*

Ve·dan·ta (vi dän′tə, -dan′-), *n.* the chief Hindu philosophy, dealing mainly with the Upanishadic doctrine of the identity of Brahman and Atman, that reached its highest development A.D. c800 through the philosopher Shankara. Cf. **Advaita, dvaita** (def. 2). [< Skt, equiv. to *veda* VEDA + *anta* end] —**Ve·dan′tic,** *adj.* —**Ve·dan′tism,** *n.* —**Ve·dan′tist,** *n.*

V-E Day, May 8, 1945, the day of victory in Europe for the Allies in World War II.

Ved·da (ved′ə), *n.* a Sri Lankan aborigine. Also, **Ved′dah.**

Ved·doid (ved′oid), *n.* **1.** a member of an ancient race of southern and southeastern Asia and northern Australia, characterized by dark brown skin, slim build, and wavy hair. —*adj.* **2.** of or pertaining to Veddoids. [1945–50; VEDD(A) + -OID]

ve·dette (vi det′), *n.* (formerly) **1.** Also called **vedette′ boat′.** a small naval launch used for scouting. **2.** a mounted sentry in advance of the outposts of an army. Also, **vidette.** [1680–90; < F < It *vedetta* outlook where a sentinel is posted, alter. of earlier *veletta* (of debated orig.) by assoc. with *vedere* to see; see -ETTE]

Ve·dic (vā′dik, vē′-), *adj.* **1.** of or pertaining to the Veda or Vedas. **2.** of or pertaining to the Aryans who settled in India c1500 B.C., or to their literature or religion. —*n.* **3.** Also called **Ve′dic San′skrit.** the language of the Veda, closely related to classical Sanskrit. [1855–60; VED(A) + -IC]

vee (vē), *adj.* **1.** shaped like the letter *V: a vee neckline.* —*n.* **2.** anything shaped like or suggesting a V. [1880–85; sp. of the letter name]

Veeck (vek), *n.* **William Louis, Jr.,** 1914–86, U.S. baseball team owner and promoter.

vee·jay (vē′jā′), *n. Informal.* See **video jockey.** [VEE (repr. VIDEO) + (DEE)JAY]

vee·na (vē′nə), *n.* vina.

veep (vēp), *n. Informal.* a vice president. Also called **vee·pee** (vē′pē′). [1945–50, *Amer.*; from V.P.]

veer[1] (vēr), *v.i.* **1.** to change direction or turn about or aside; shift, turn, or change from one course, position, inclination, etc., to another: *The speaker kept veering from his main topic. The car veered off the road.* **2.** (of the wind) **a.** to change direction clockwise (opposed to *back*). **b.** *Naut.* to shift to a direction more nearly astern (op-

posed to *haul*). —*v.t.* **3.** to alter the direction or course of; turn. **4.** *Naut.* to turn (a vessel) away from the wind; wear. —*n.* **5.** a change of direction, position, course, etc.: *a sudden veer in a different direction.* [1575–85; < MF *virer* to turn] —**veer′ing·ly,** *adv.*
—**Syn. 1.** deviate, swerve, diverge.

veer[2] (vēr), *v.t. Naut.* to slacken or let out: *to veer chain.* [1425–75; late ME *vere* < MD *vieren* to let out]

veer·y (vēr′ē), *n., pl.* **veer·ies.** a thrush, *Catharus fuscescens,* common in the eastern and northern U.S., noted for its song. Also called **Wilson's thrush.** [1830–40, *Amer.*; perh. VEER[1] + -Y[2]]

veg (vej), *n., pl.* **veg.** *Chiefly Brit. Informal.* a vegetable. [1940–45; by shortening]

Ve·ga (vē′gə, vā′-), *n. Astron.* a star of the first magnitude in the constellation Lyra. [1630–40; < ML < Ar *(al-nasr-al-) wāqiʿ* (the) falling (eagle), orig. designating the three stars Alpha, Epsilon and Zeta Lyrae]

Ve·ga (vā′gə; *Sp.* be′gä), *n.* **1. Lo·pe de** (lô′pe t͟he), *(Lope Félix de Vega Carpio),* 1562–1635, Spanish dramatist and poet. **2.** See **Garcilaso de la Vega.**

Ve·ga Al·ta (vā′gə äl′tə; *Sp.* be′gä äl′tä), a city in N Puerto Rico. 10,582.

Ve·ga Ba·ja (vā′gə bä′hə; *Sp.* be′gä vä′hä), a city in N Puerto Rico. 18,233.

veg·an (vej′ən; *esp. Brit.* vē′gən), *n.* a vegetarian who omits all animal products from the diet. [1940–45; VEG(ETARI)AN] —**veg′an·ism,** *n.*

Veg·e·mite (vej′ə mīt′), *Trademark.* an Australian vegetable extract used as a flavoring or spread.

veg·e·ta·ble (vej′tə bəl, vej′i tə-), *n.* **1.** any plant whose fruit, seeds, roots, tubers, bulbs, stems, leaves, or flower parts are used as food, as the tomato, bean, beet, potato, onion, asparagus, spinach, or cauliflower. **2.** the edible part of such a plant, as the tuber of the potato. **3.** any member of the vegetable kingdom; plant. **4.** *Informal.* a person who is so severely impaired mentally or physically as to be largely incapable of conscious responses or activity. **5.** a dull, spiritless, and uninteresting person. —*adj.* **6.** of, consisting of, or made from edible vegetables: *a vegetable diet.* **7.** of, pertaining to, or characteristic of plants: *the vegetable kingdom.* **8.** derived from plants: *vegetable fiber; vegetable oils.* **9.** consisting of, comprising, or containing the substance or remains of plants: *vegetable matter; a vegetable organism.* **10.** of the nature of or resembling a plant: *the vegetable forms of Art Nouveau ornament.* **11.** inactive; inert; dull; uneventful: *a vegetable existence.* [1350–1400; ME (adj.) < LL *vegetābilis* able to live and grow, equiv. to *vegetā(re)* to quicken (see VEGETATE) + *-bilis* -BLE]

veg′etable but′ter, any of various fixed vegetable fats resembling butter in consistency, as cocoa butter. [1830–40]

veg′etable cel′lar, a usually underground storage room where fresh vegetables can be stored at normally cool temperatures for later use. [1885–90]

veg′etable gold′, saffron (def. 1).

veg′etable i′vory, ivory (def. 9). [1835–45]

veg′etable king′dom. See **plant kingdom.**

veg′etable mar′row, any of various summer squashes, as the cocozelle and zucchini. [1810–20]

veg′etable oil′, any of a large group of oils that are esters of fatty acids and glycerol, obtained from the leaves, fruit, or seeds of plants. [1895–1900]

veg′etable oys′ter, salsify. [1810–20, *Amer.*]

veg′etable pear′, chayote.

veg′etable silk′, a fine, glossy fiber, similar to silk cotton, from the seeds of a spiny Brazilian tree, *Chorisia speciosa.* [1850–55]

veg′etable sponge′, loofah (def. 2).

veg′etable tal′low, any of several tallowlike substances of vegetable origin, used in making candles, soap, etc., and as lubricants. [1840–50]

veg′etable tan′ning, the act or process of tanning hide by the infusion of plant extract.

veg′etable wax′, a wax, or a substance resembling wax, obtained from various plants, as the wax palm. [1805–15]

veg′etable wool′. See under **wool** (def. 5). [1880–85]

veg·e·ta·bly (vej′tə blē, vej′i tə-), *adv.* like or in the manner of a vegetable. [1645–55; VEGETABLE + -LY]

veg·e·tal (vej′i tl), *adj.* **1.** of, pertaining to, or of the nature of plants or vegetables. **2.** vegetative (def. 5). [1350–1400; ME < L *veget(āre)* to quicken (see VEGETATE) + *-al* -AL[1]]

veg′etal pole′, *Embryol.* the relatively inactive part of an ovum opposite the animal pole, containing much yolk and little cytoplasm. Cf. **animal pole.** [1895–1900]

veg·e·tar·i·an (vej′i târ′ē ən), *n.* **1.** a person who does not eat or does not believe in eating meat, fish, fowl, or, in some cases, any food derived from animals, as eggs or cheese, but subsists on vegetables, fruits, nuts, grain, etc. —*adj.* **2.** of or pertaining to vegetarianism or vegetarians. **3.** devoted to or advocating this practice. **4.** consisting solely of vegetables: *vegetarian vegetable soup.* Cf. **lacto-ovo-vegetarian, lactovegetarian, vegan.** [1835–45; VEGET(ABLE) + -ARIAN]

veg·e·tar·i·an·ism (vej′i târ′ē ə niz′əm), *n.* the beliefs or practices of a vegetarian. [1850–55; VEGETARIAN + -ISM]

veg·e·tate (vej′i tāt′), *v.i.,* **-tat·ed, -tat·ing. 1.** to grow in, or as in, the manner of a plant. **2.** to be passive or unthinking; to do nothing: *to lie on the beach and vegetate.* **3.** *Pathol.* to grow, or increase by growth, as an excrescence. [1595–1605; < L *vegetātus* (ptp. of *vegetāre* to quicken, enliven), equiv. to *veget(us)* lively (orig. ptp. of *vegēre* to give vigor) + *-ātus* -ATE[1]]

veg·e·ta·tion (vej′i tā′shən), *n.* **1.** all the plants or plant life of a place, taken as a whole: *the vegetation of the Nile valley.* **2.** the act or process of vegetating. **3.** a dull existence; life devoid of mental or social activity. **4.** *Pathol.* a morbid growth, or excrescence. [1555–65; < ML *vegetātiōn-* (s. of *vegetātiō*), equiv. to *vegetāt-* (see VEGETATE) + *-iōn-* -ION] —**veg′e·ta′tion·al,** *adj.* —**veg′e·ta′tion·less,** *adj.*
—**Syn. 3.** inactivity, idleness, sloth, lethargy.

veg·e·ta·tive (vej′i tā′tiv), *adj.* **1.** growing or developing as or like plants; vegetating. **2.** of, pertaining to, or concerned with vegetation or vegetable growth. **3.** of or pertaining to the plant kingdom. **4.** noting the parts of a plant not specialized for reproduction. **5.** (of reproduction) asexual. **6.** denoting or pertaining to those bodily functions that are performed unconsciously or involuntarily. **7.** having the power to produce or support growth in plants: *vegetative mold.* **8.** characterized by a lack of activity; inactive; passive: *a vegetative state.* Also, **veg·e·tive** (vej′i tiv). [1350–1400; ME *vegetatyf* < ML *vegetātīvus.* See VEGETATE, -IVE] —**veg′e·ta′tive·ly,** *adv.* —**veg′e·ta′tive·ness,** *n.*

veg·gie (vej′ē), *n. Informal.* **1.** a vegetable. **2.** a vegetarian. Also, **veg′ie.** [1965–70; by shortening; see -IE]

ve·he·mence (vē′ə məns), *n.* **1.** the quality of being vehement; ardor; fervor. **2.** vigorous impetuosity; fury: *the vehemence of his attack.* Also, **ve′he·men·cy.** [1520–30; < L *vehementia;* see VEHEMENT, -ENCE]
—**Syn. 1.** eagerness, verve, zeal, enthusiasm, fervency. **2.** passion. —**Ant. 1, 2.** apathy.

ve·he·ment (vē′ə mənt), *adj.* **1.** zealous; ardent; impassioned: *a vehement defense; vehement enthusiasm.* **2.** characterized by rancor or anger; violent: *vehement hostility.* **3.** strongly emotional; intense or passionate: *vehement desire.* **4.** marked by great energy or exertion; strenuous: *vehement clapping.* [1475–85; < L *vehement-,* s. of *vehemēns, vēmēns* violent, forceful (of uncert. derivation)] —**ve′he·ment·ly,** *adv.*
—**Syn. 1.** earnest, fervent, fervid. **2.** burning, fiery.
—**Ant. 1, 2.** dispassionate.

ve·hi·cle (vē′i kəl *or, sometimes,* vē′hi-), *n.* **1.** any means in or by which someone travels or something is carried or conveyed; a means of conveyance or transport: *a motor vehicle; space vehicles.* **2.** a conveyance moving on wheels, runners, tracks, or the like, as a cart, sled, automobile, or tractor. **3.** a means of transmission or passage: *Air is the vehicle of sound.* **4.** a carrier, as of infection. **5.** a medium of communication, expression, or display: *The novel is a fitting vehicle for his talents. Language is the vehicle of thought.* **6.** *Theat., Motion Pictures.* a play, screenplay, or the like, having a role suited to the talents of and often written for a specific performer. **7.** a means of accomplishing a purpose: *College is a vehicle for success.* **8.** *Rhet.* the thing or idea to which the subject of a metaphor is compared, as "rose" in "she is a rose." Cf. **tenor** (def. 3). **9.** *Pharm.* a substance, usually fluid, possessing little or no medicinal action, used as a medium for active remedies. **10.** *Painting.* a liquid, as oil, in which a pigment is mixed before being applied to a surface. [1605–15; < L *vehiculum,* equiv. to *veh(ere)* to convey + *-i-* -I- + *-culum* -CLE[2]]
—**Pronunciation.** Because the primary stress in *vehicle* is on the first syllable, the (h) in the second syllable tends to disappear: (vē′i kəl). A pronunciation with primary stress on the second syllable and a fully pronounced (h) is usually considered nonstandard: (vē hik′əl). In the adjective *vehicular,* where the primary stress is normally on the second syllable, the (h) is always pronounced.

ve·hic·u·lar (vē hik′yə lər), *adj.* **1.** of, pertaining to, or for vehicles: *a vehicular tunnel.* **2.** serving as a vehicle. **3.** caused by a vehicle; attributed or attributable to vehicles: *vehicular homicide.* **4.** carried on or transported by means of a vehicle: *vehicular recording units.* [1610–20; < LL *vehiculāris.* See VEHICLE, -AR[1]]

V-eight (vē′āt′), *adj.* **1.** noting an internal-combustion engine having two opposed banks of four cylinders, each inclined so that the axes of the cylinders form a V-shaped angle as seen from the end of the engine. —*n.* **2.** such an engine. Also, **V-8.** [1945–50]

Ve·ii (vē′yī, vā′yē), *n.* an ancient city in central Italy, in Etruria, near Rome: Etruscan city destroyed by the Romans 396 B.C.

veil (vāl), *n.* **1.** a piece of opaque or transparent material worn over the face for concealment, for protection from the elements, or to enhance the appearance. **2.** a piece of material worn so as to fall over the head and shoulders on each side of the face, forming a part of the headdress of a nun. **3.** the life of a nun, esp. a cloistered life. **4.** something that covers, separates, screens, or conceals: *a veil of smoke.* **5.** a mask, disguise, or pretense: *to find fault under a veil of humor.* **6.** *Bot., Anat., Zool.* a velum. **7.** *Mycol.* a membrane that covers the immature mushroom of many fungi and breaks apart as the mushroom expands, leaving distinctive remnants on the cap, stalk, or stalk base. **8.** *Scot. and North Eng.* a caul. **9. take the veil,** to become a nun. —*v.t.* **10.** to cover or conceal with or as with a veil: *She veiled her face. A heavy fog veiled the shoreline.* **11.** to hide the real nature of; mask; disguise: *to veil one's intentions.* —*v.i.* **12.** to don or wear a veil. [1175–1225; (n.) ME *veile* < AF < L *vēla,* neut. pl. (taken in VL as fem. sing.) of *vēlum* covering; (v.) ME *veilen* < AF *veiler,* deriv. of *veile*] —**veil′less,** *adj.* —**veil′like′,** *adj.*

veiled (vāld), *adj.* **1.** having a veil: *a veiled hat.* **2.** covered or concealed by, or as if by, a veil: *a veiled woman.* **3.** not openly or directly expressed; masked; disguised; hidden; obscure: *a veiled threat.* **4.** lacking clarity or distinctness: *veiled sounds; a veiled image.* [1585–95; VEIL + -ED[3]] —**veil·ed·ly** (vā′lid lē), *adv.*

veil·ing (vā′ling), *n.* **1.** an act of covering with or as if with a veil. **2.** a veil. **3.** a thin net for veils. [1350–1400; ME; see VEIL, -ING[1]]

veil·leuse (ve yœz′), *n., pl.* **veil·leuses** (ve yœz′). *Fr. Furniture.* a sofa having a low and a high end, with a back that slopes from one end to the other. [< F: lit., watcher (opposed to sleeper), equiv. to *veill(er)* to watch (< L *vigilāre;* see VIGIL) + *-euse* -EUSE]

veil′tail gold′fish (vāl′tāl′), an artificially bred, indoor variety of goldfish, usually golden or calico and of a spheroid shape, having a fully divided, drooping tail fin exceeding the body in length. Also called **veil′tail′.** Cf. **fantail goldfish.** See illus. under **goldfish.**

vein (vān), *n.* **1.** one of the system of branching vessels or tubes conveying blood from various parts of the body to the heart. **2.** (loosely) any blood vessel. **3.** one of the riblike thickenings that form the framework of the wing of an insect. **4.** one of the strands or bundles of vascular tissue forming the principal framework of a leaf. **5.** any body or stratum of ore, coal, etc., clearly separated or defined: *a rich vein of coal.* **6.** a body or mass of igneous rock, deposited mineral, or the like occupying a crevice or fissure in rock; lode. **7.** a natural channel or watercourse beneath the surface of the earth. **8.** the water running through such a channel. **9.** a streak or marking, as of a different shade or color, running through marble, wood, etc. **10.** a condition, mood, or temper: *a vein of pessimism.* **11.** a tendency, quality, or strain traceable in character, conduct, writing, etc.; manner or style: *to write in a poetic vein.* —*v.t.* **12.** to furnish with veins. **13.** to mark with lines or streaks suggesting veins. **14.** to extend over or through in the manner of veins: *Broad new highways vein the countryside.* [1250–1300; ME *veine* < OF < L *vēna* vein of the body, channel, ore deposit] —**vein′al,** *adj.* —**vein′less,** *adj.* —**vein′like′,** *adj.*
—**Syn. 11.** tone, streak, touch, hint, thread.

vein·ing (vā′ning), *n.* **1.** the act or process of forming veins or an arrangement or marking resembling veins. **2.** a vein or a pattern of veins or markings suggesting veins. [1680–90; VEIN + -ING[1]]

vein·let (vān′lit), *n.* a small vein. [1825–35; VEIN + -LET]

vein·ule (vān′yo͞ol), *n.* venule. Also, **vein·u·let** (vān′yə lit). [VEIN + -ULE]

vein·y (vā′nē), *adj.,* **vein·i·er, vein·i·est.** full of veins; prominently veined: *a veiny hand.* [1585–95; VEIN + -Y[1]]

Ve·io·vis (vē yō′vis, vā-), *n. Rom. Religion.* a god of the dead, sometimes believed to be of Etruscan origin.

vel., vellum.

ve·la (vē′lə), *n.* pl. of **velum.**

Ve·la (vē′lə, vā′-), *n., gen.* **Ve·lo·rum** (vē lôr′əm, -lōr′-, vā-) for 1. *Astron.* **1.** the Sail, a southern constellation: one of the subordinate constellations into which Argo is divided. **2.** *U.S. Aerospace.* one of a series of reconnaissance satellites designed to detect nuclear explosions. [< L, pl. of *vēlum* sail]

ve·la·men (və lā′min), *n., pl.* **-lam·i·na** (-lam′ə nə). **1.** *Anat.* a membranous covering; velum. **2.** *Bot.* the thick, spongy integument or epidermis covering the aerial roots of epiphytic orchids. [1880–85; < L *vēlāmen,* equiv. to *vēlā(re)* to cover + *-men* n. suffix of result]

ve·lar (vē′lər), *adj.* **1.** of or pertaining to a velum, esp. the soft palate. **2.** *Phonet.* articulated with the back of the tongue held close to or touching the soft palate. —*n.* **3.** *Phonet.* a velar sound. [1720–30; < L *vēlāris.* See VELUM, -AR[1]]

ve·lar′ic air′stream (vi lâr′ik, -lar′-), *Phonet.* a current of mouth air produced by the action of the tongue, operant in forming click sounds. [VELAR + -IC]

ve·lar·i·um (və lâr′ē əm), *n., pl.* **-lar·i·a** (-lâr′ē ə). *Rom. Antiq.* an awning drawn over a theater or amphitheater as a protection from rain or the sun. [1825–35; < L *vēlārium* (a word known only from a passage in Juvenal; the intended sense may be "curtain" rather than "awning"); see VELUM, -ARY]

ve·lar·ize (vē′lə rīz′), *v.t.,* **-ized, -iz·ing.** *Phonet.* to pronounce with velar articulation. Also, *esp. Brit.,* **ve′·lar·ise′.** [1930–35; VELAR + -IZE] —**ve′lar·i·za′tion,** *n.*

ve·lar·ized (vē′lə rīzd′), *adj. Phonet.* pronounced with velar coarticulation. [VELARIZE + -ED[2]]

Ve·las·co I·bar·ra (be läs′kô ē vär′rä), **Jo·sé Ma·rí·a** (hô se′ mä rē′ä), 1893–1979, Ecuadorean political leader: president 1934–35, 1944–47, 1952–56, 1960–61, 1968–72.

ve·late (*adj.* vē′lit, -lāt; *v.* vē′lāt), *adj., v.,* **-lat·ed, -lat·ing.** —*adj.* **1.** *Biol.* having a velum. —*v.t.* **2.** *Phonet.* to velarize. [1855–60; < NL *vēlātus.* See VELUM, -ATE[1]]

ve·la·tion (vē lā′shən), *n. Phonet.* pronunciation with velar articulation. [1890–95; VELATE + -ION]

Ve·láz·quez (və läs′kās, -kəs; *Sp.* be läth′keth), *n.* **Die·go Ro·drí·guez de Sil·va y** (dye′gô rô t͟hrē′geth t͟he sēl′vä ē), 1599–1660, Spanish painter. Also, **Ve·lás′quez.**

Vel·cro (vel′krō), *Trademark.* a brand of fastening tape consisting of opposing pieces of fabric, one with a dense arrangement of tiny nylon hooks and the other with a dense nylon pile, that interlock when pressed together, used as a closure on garments, luggage, etc., in place of buttons, zippers, and the like.

veld (velt, felt), *n.* the open country, bearing grass, bushes, or shrubs, or thinly forested, characteristic of parts of southern Africa. Also, **veldt.** [1795–1805; < Afrik < D: FIELD]

ve·lel·la (və lel′ə), *n.* a floating colony of hydrozoans of the genus *Velella,* having a vertical crest that is used as a sail. [1825–35; < NL, equiv. to L *vēl(um)* sail + *-ella* -ELLA] —**ve·lel′li·dous,** *adj.*

ve·lic (vē′lik), *adj. Phonet.* pertaining to the operation of the velum in relation to the passageway into the nasal cavity: *velic closure.* [VEL(UM) + -IC]

ve·li·ger (vē′li jər), *n.* a larval stage of certain mollusks, intermediate between the trochophore and the adult form. [1875–80; < NL; see VELUM, -I-, -GEROUS]

Ve·li·ki·ye Lu·ki (və lē′kē yə lo͞o′kē; *Russ.* vyi lyē′-

kyi yə lo͞o′kyi), a city in the NW RSFSR, in the NW Soviet Union in Europe, NW of Moscow. 102,000.

vel·i·ta·tion (vel′i tā′shən), *n.* a minor dispute or contest. [1600–10; < L *vēlitātiōn-* (s. of *vēlitātiō*), equiv. to *vēlitāt(us)* (ptp. of *vēlitārī* to skirmish, deriv. of *vēles* (s. *vēlit-*) foot soldier; see -ATE[1]) + *-iōn-* -ION]

vel·le·i·ty (və lē′i tē), *n., pl.* **-ties.** **1.** volition in its weakest form. **2.** a mere wish, unaccompanied by an effort to obtain it. [1610–20; < NL *velleitās*, equiv. to L *velle* to be willing + *-itās* -ITY]

vel·li·cate (vel′i kāt′), *v.,* **-cat·ed, -cat·ing.** —*v.t.* **1.** to pluck; twitch. **2.** to nip, pinch, or the like. **3.** to cause to twitch. —*v.i.* **4.** to move with spasmodic convulsions; twitch. [1595–1605; < L *vellicātus*, ptp. of *vellicāre*, freq. of *vellere* to pull, twitch; see -ATE[1]] —**vel′li·ca′tion,** *n.* —**vel′li·ca′tive,** *adj.*

vel·lum (vel′əm), *n.* **1.** calfskin, lambskin, kidskin, etc., treated for use as a writing surface. **2.** a manuscript or the like on vellum. **3.** a texture of paper or cloth resembling vellum. —*adj.* **4.** made of or resembling vellum. **5.** bound in vellum. [1400–50; late ME *velum, velim* < MF *ve(e)lin* of a calf. See VEAL, -IN[1]]

Vel·ma (vel′mə), *n.* a female given name, form of **Wilhelmina.**

ve·lo·ce (*It.* ve lô′che), *adj.* played at a fast tempo (used as a musical direction). [1815–25; < It < L *vēlōcem*, acc. of *vēlōx* quick]

ve·lo·cim·e·ter (vē′lō sim′ə tər, vel′ō-), *n.* any of various instruments for measuring velocity, as of a wave in water or of sound in air. [1842; VELOCI(TY) + -METER]

ve·loc·i·pede (və los′ə pēd′), *n.* **1.** a vehicle, usually having two or three wheels, that is propelled by the rider. **2.** an early kind of bicycle or tricycle. **3.** a light, three-wheeled, pedal-driven vehicle for railway inspection, used for carrying one person on a railroad track. [1810–20; < F *vélocipède* bicycle, equiv. to *véloci-* (< L, s. of *vēlōx* quick) + *-pède* -PED] —**ve·loc′i·ped′ist,** *n.*

ve·loc·i·ty (və los′i tē), *n., pl.* **-ties.** **1.** rapidity of motion or operation; swiftness; speed: *a high wind velocity.* **2.** *Mech.* the time rate of change of position of a body in a specified direction. **3.** the rate of speed with which something happens; rapidity of action or reaction. [1540–50; < L *vēlōcitās* speed. See VELOCIPEDE, -TY[2]]
—**Syn. 1.** See **speed.**

veloc′ity mi′crophone, a microphone in which the output varies according to the instantaneous velocity of the air molecules in the incident sound waves.

veloc′ity of mon′ey, *Econ.* the frequency with which a single unit of currency or the total money supply turns over within the economy in a given year. Also called **veloc′ity of circula′tion.**

ve·lo·drome (vē′lə drōm′, vel′ə-), *n.* a sports arena equipped with a banked track for cycling. [1890–95; < F *vélodrome*, equiv. to *vélo*, shortened form of *vélocipède* VELOCIPEDE + *-drome* -DROME]

ve·lour (və lo͝or′), *n.* **1.** a velvetlike fabric of rayon, wool, or any of several other natural or synthetic fibers, used for outerwear and upholstery. **2.** a velvety fur felt, as of beaver, for hats. Also, **ve·lours** (və lo͝or′; *Fr.* və lo͞oʀ′). [1700–10; earlier *velours* < F, MF; OF *velous* < OPr *velos* velvet < L *villōsus* hairy. See VILLUS, -OSE[1]]

ve·lou·té (və lo͞o tā′), *n.* a smooth white sauce made with meat, poultry, or fish stock. Also called **velouté′ sauce′.** [< F: lit., velvety, velvetiness, MF *velluté*, equiv. to *vellut-* (< Pr *velut* VELVET) + *-é* -ATE[1]]

Ve·lox (vē′loks), *Trademark.* a brand of photographic print that has been screened for reproduction as a line cut.

Vel·sen (vel′sən), *n.* a seaport in W Netherlands. 60,470.

vel·thei·mi·a (vel thē′mē ə), *n.* any of several bulbous plants of the genus *Veltheimia*, esp. *V. viridifolia*, native to southern Africa, having glossy, strap-shaped leaves and a long cluster of tubular pinkish flowers. [< NL (1769), after August Ferdinand, Graf von *Veltheim* (1741–1801), German patron of botany; see -IA]

ve·lum (vē′ləm), *n., pl.* **-la** (-lə), for 1, 2, **-lum** for 3. **1.** *Biol.* any of various veillike or curtainlike membranous partitions. **2.** *Anat.* the soft palate. See under **palate** (def. 1). **3.** *Meteorol.* a thin cloud, large in horizontal area, that is draped over or penetrated by cumuliform clouds. [1765–75; < L *vēlum* sail, covering]

ve·lure (və lo͝or′), *n., v.,* **-lured, -lur·ing.** —*n.* **1.** velvet or a substance resembling it. **2.** a hatter's pad of velvet, plush, or the like for smoothing or dressing silk hats. —*v.t.* **3.** to smooth or dress (a hat) with a velure. [1580–90; by alter. < MF *velour* VELOUR; see -URE]

ve·lu·ti·nous (və lo͞ot′n əs), *adj.* having a soft, velvety surface, as certain plants. [1820–30; < NL *velūtinus* lit., velvety. See VELVET, -INE[1], -OUS]

vel·vet (vel′vit), *n.* **1.** a fabric of silk, nylon, acetate, rayon, etc., sometimes having a cotton backing, with a thick, soft pile formed of loops of the warp thread either cut at the outer end or left uncut. **2.** something likened to the fabric velvet, as in softness or texture: *the velvet of her touch; the velvet of the lawn.* **3.** the soft, deciduous covering of a growing antler. **4.** *Informal.* a very pleasant, luxurious, desirable situation. **5.** *Informal.* **a.** money gained through gambling; winnings. **b.** clear gain or profit, esp. when more than anticipated. —*adj.* **6.** Also, **vel′vet·ed.** made of velvet or covered with velvet. **7.** Also, **vel′vet·like′.** resembling or suggesting velvet; smooth; soft; velvety: *a velvet night; a cat's velvet fur.* [1275–1325; ME *velvet, veluet, veluwet* < OF *veluotte*, equiv. to *velu* (< ML *vil(l)ūtus*; L *vill(us)* shaggy nap (cf. VILLUS) + LL *-ūtus* for L *-ātus* -ATE[1]) + *-otte* n. suffix]

CONCISE ETYMOLOGY KEY: <, descended or borrowed from; >, whence; b., blend of, blended; c., cognate with; cf., compare; deriv., derivative; equiv., equivalent; imit., imitative; obl., oblique; r., replacing; s., stem; sp., spelling, spelled; resp., respelling, respelled; trans., translation; ?, origin unknown; *, unattested; ‡, probably earlier than. See the full key inside the front cover.

vel′vet ant′, any of several fuzzy, often brightly colored wasps of the family Mutillidae, the wingless, antlike female of which inflicts a severe sting. [1740–50, *Amer.*]

vel′vet bean′, a vine, *Mucuna deeringiana*, of the legume family, having long clusters of purplish flowers and densely hairy pods, grown in warm regions for forage or as an ornamental. [1895–1900, *Amer.*]

vel′vet bent′. See **brown bent.**

vel′vet car′pet, a carpet or rug of pile weave resembling Wilton.

vel·vet·een (vel′vi tēn′), *n.* **1.** a cotton pile fabric with short pile. **2. velveteens,** trousers of this fabric. —*adj.* **3.** made of velveteen: *a velveteen jumper.* [1770–80; VELVET + *-een*, var. of -INE[1]]

vel′vet glove′, an outwardly gentle or friendly manner used to disguise one's firm or ruthless determination.

vel·vet·leaf (vel′vit lēf′), *n., pl.* **-leafs, -leaves.** See **Indian mallow.** [1700–10; VELVET + LEAF]

vel′vet plant′, **1.** a composite plant, *Gynura aurantiaca*, native to the Old World tropics, having leaves and stems covered with dense, velvety, purple hairs and often cultivated as a houseplant. Cf. **purple passion. 2.** the common mullein, *Verbascum thapsus.*

vel·vet·y (vel′vi tē), *adj.* **1.** suggestive of or resembling velvet; smooth; soft: *velvety rose petals; a velvety voice; a velvety cream sauce.* **2.** (of liquor) smooth-tasting; mild; mellow: *a velvety Scotch.* [1745–55; VELVET + -Y[1]] —**vel′vet·i·ness,** *n.*

Ven., **1.** Venerable. **2.** Venice.

ve·na (vē′nə), *n., pl.* **-nae** (-nē). *Anat.* a vein. [1350–1400; ME < L *vēna* VEIN]

ve·na ca·va (vē′nə kā′və), *pl.* **ve·nae ca·vae** (vē′nē kā′vē). *Anat.* either of two large veins discharging blood into the right atrium of the heart, one **(superior vena cava** or **precava)** conveying blood from the head, chest, and upper extremities and the other **(inferior vena cava** or **postcava)** conveying blood from all parts below the diaphragm. See diag. under **heart.** [1590–1600; < L *vēna cava* hollow vein]

ve·na con·trac·ta (vē′nə kən trak′tə), *pl.* **ve·nae con·trac·tae** (vē′nē kən trak′tē). *Hydraul.* any of the locations in a jet of fluid emerging from an orifice where the cross section of the jet is at a minimum, esp. the location of minimum cross section nearest the orifice. [< NL: contracted vein]

ve·nal (vēn′l), *adj.* **1.** willing to sell one's influence, esp. in return for a bribe; open to bribery; mercenary: *a venal judge.* **2.** able to be purchased, as by a bribe: *venal acquittals.* **3.** associated with or characterized by bribery: *a venal administration; venal agreements.* [1645–55; < L *vēnālis*, equiv. to *vēn(um)* (acc.) for sale (cf. VEND) + *-ālis* -AL[1]] —**ve′nal·ly,** *adv.*
—**Syn. 1.** bribable, corruptible. See **corrupt.** —**Ant. 1.** incorruptible.

ve·nal·i·ty (vē nal′i tē, və-), *n.* the condition or quality of being venal; openness to bribery or corruption. [1605–15; < LL *vēnālitas*. See VENAL, -ITY]

ve·nat·ic (vē nat′ik), *adj.* of or pertaining to hunting. Also, **ve·nat′i·cal.** [1650–60; < L *vēnāticus*, equiv. to *vēnāt(us)* (ptp. of *vēnārī* to hunt) + *-icus* -IC] —**ve·nat′i·cal·ly,** *adv.*

ve·na·tion (vē nā′shən, və-), *n.* **1.** the arrangement of veins, as in a leaf or in the wing of an insect. **2.** these veins collectively. [1640–50; < L *vēn(a)* VEIN + -ATION] —**ve·na′tion·al,** *adj.*

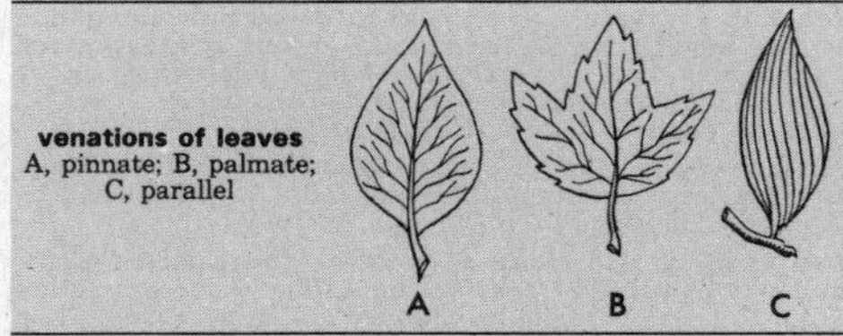

venations of leaves
A, pinnate; B, palmate; C, parallel

vend (vend), *v.t.* **1.** to sell as one's business or occupation, esp. by peddling: *to vend flowers at a sidewalk stand.* **2.** to give utterance to (opinions, ideas, etc.); publish. —*v.i.* **3.** to engage in the sale of merchandise. **4.** to be disposed of by sale. [1610–20; < L *vendere* to sell, contr. of *vēnum* (or *vēnō*) *dare* to offer for sale; see VENAL] —**vend′a·ble,** *adj.*

Ven·da (ven′də), *n.* a self-governing Bantu territory of South Africa in the NE part: granted independence in 1979 by South Africa, but not recognized by any other country as an independent state. 513,890; 2510 sq. mi. (6500 sq. km). *Cap.:* Thohoyandou.

ven·dace (ven′dis, -dās), *n., pl.* **-dac·es,** (*esp. collectively*) **-dace.** a whitefish, *Coregonus vandesius*, inhabiting lakes in Scotland and England. [1690–1700; orig. Scots, appar. < F *vandoise*, OF *vendoise* any of various cyprinid fish (< Gallo-Rom **vindisia*, prob. deriv. of Celtic **wind-* white, bright; cf. OIr *find*, Welsh *gwyn*); perh. conflated with a local Scots word (cf. the var. *gevenaces*)]

Ven·de·an (ven dē′ən, vän dā′-), *adj.* **1.** of or pertaining to the Vendée or its inhabitants. —*n.* **2.** a native or inhabitant of the Vendée, esp. one who participated in the royalist revolt in 1793. [1790–1800; VENDÉE + -AN]

vend·ee (ven dē′), *n. Chiefly Law.* the person to whom a thing is sold. [1540–50; VEND + -EE]

Ven·dée (vän dā′), *n.* a department in W France, on the Atlantic: royalist revolt 1793–95. 450,641; 2709 sq. mi. (7015 sq. km). *Cap.:* La Roche-sur-Yon.

Ven·dé·miaire (vän dā myeʀ′), *n.* (in the French Revolutionary calendar) the first month of the year, extending from September 22 to October 21. [< F, equiv. to *vendémi-* (< L *vindēmia* vintage) + *-aire* -ARY]

vend·er (ven′dər), *n.* vendor. [1590–1600; VEND + -ER[1]]

ven·det·ta (ven det′ə), *n.* **1.** a private feud in which the members of the family of a murdered person seek to avenge the murder by killing the slayer or one of the slayer's relatives, esp. such vengeance as once practiced in Corsica and parts of Italy. **2.** any prolonged and bitter feud, rivalry, contention, or the like: *a political vendetta.* [1850–55; < It < L *vindicta* vengeance; see VINDICTIVE] —**ven·det′tist,** *n.*

ven·deuse (väɴ dœz′), *n., pl.* **-deuses** (-dœz′). *French.* a female shop assistant; shopgirl.

vend·i·ble (ven′də bəl), *adj.* **1.** capable of being vended; salable: *vendible commodities.* **2.** *Obs.* mercenary; venal. —*n.* **3.** Usually, **vendibles.** vendible articles. [1350–1400; ME < L *vendibilis*. See VEND, -IBLE] —**vend′i·bil′i·ty, vend′i·ble·ness,** *n.* —**vend′i·bly,** *adv.*

Ven·di·dad (ven dē′däd), *n. Zoroastrianism.* a book of formulas to be used against demons. Also called **Videvdat.**

vend′ing machine′, a coin-operated machine for selling small articles, beverages, etc. [1905–10]

ven·di·tion (ven dish′ən), *n.* the act of vending; sale. [1535–45; < L *venditiōn-* (s. of *venditiō*), equiv. to *vendit(us)* (ptp. of *vendere* to VEND; see -ITE[2]) + *-iōn-* -ION]

Ven·dôme (väɴ dōm′), *n.* **Louis Jo·seph de** (lwē zhô zef′ də), 1654–1712, French general and marshal.

ven·dor (ven′dər; *esp. contrastively* ven dôr′), *n.* **1.** a person or agency that sells. **2.** See **vending machine.** Also, **vender.** [1585–95; < AF *vendo(u)r* < L *venditor.* See VEND, -OR[2]]

ven·due (ven do͞o′, -dyo͞o′), *n.* a public auction. [1680–90; < D *vendu* < MF *vendue* sale, n. use of fem. of *vendu*, ptp. of *vendre* to sell; see VEND]

ve·neer (və nēr′), *n.* **1.** a thin layer of wood or other material for facing or inlaying wood. **2.** any of the thin layers of wood glued together to form plywood. **3.** *Building Trades.* a facing of a certain material applied to a different one or to a type of construction not ordinarily associated with it, as a facing of brick applied to a frame house. **4.** a superficially valuable or pleasing appearance: *a cruel person with a veneer of kindliness.* —*v.t.* **5.** to overlay or face (wood) with thin sheets of some material, as a fine wood, ivory, or tortoise shell. **6.** to face or cover (an object) with any material that is more desirable as a surface material than the basic material of the object; revet. **7.** to cement (layers of wood veneer) to form plywood. **8.** to give a superficially valuable or pleasing appearance to. [1695–1705; earlier *fineering, faneering* < G *Fourni(e)rung, Furni(e)rung*, equiv. to *furni(e)ren* to FURNISH (< F *fournir*) + *-ung* -ING[1]] —**ve·neer′er,** *n.*
—**Syn. 4.** façade, front, show, mask, guise.

ve·neer·ing (və nēr′ing), *n.* **1.** the process, act, or craft of applying veneers. **2.** material applied as a veneer. **3.** the surface formed by the application of veneers. **4.** a superficial covering, display, or appearance: *a veneering of civilization.* [1700–10; VENEER + -ING[1]]

veneer′ patch′, a patch made in one of the veneers of a sheet of plywood before layup. Cf. **panel patch.**

ve·nene (və nēn′, ven′ēn), *n. Biochem.* venin. [1655–65; VEN(OM) + -ENE]

ven·e·nose (ven′ə nōs′), *adj.* venomous; poisonous. Also, **ven·e·nous** (ven′ə nəs). [1665–75; < LL *venēnōsus*, equiv. to L *venēn(um)* drug, VENOM + *-ōsus* -OSE[1]]

ven·e·punc·ture (ven′ə pungk′chər, vē′nə-), *n. Med.* venipuncture. [1920–25; *vene-* (see VENESECTION) + PUNCTURE]

Ve·ner (ven′ər), *n.* Vänern.

Ve·ner·a (və nâr′ə; *Russ.* vyi nye′ʀə), *n.* one of a series of Soviet space probes that obtained scientific information about the atmosphere of Venus. [1961; < Russ *Venéra* VENUS (< L *Vener-*, s. of *Venus*)]

ven·er·a·ble (ven′ər ə bəl), *adj.* **1.** commanding respect because of great age or impressive dignity; worthy of veneration or reverence, as because of high office or noble character: *a venerable member of Congress.* **2.** a title for someone proclaimed by the Roman Catholic Church to have attained the first degree of sanctity or of an Anglican archdeacon. **3.** (of places, buildings, etc.) hallowed by religious, historic, or other lofty associations: *the venerable halls of the abbey.* **4.** impressive or interesting because of age, antique appearance, etc.: *a venerable oak tree.* **5.** extremely old or obsolete; ancient: *a venerable automobile.* —*n.* **6.** a venerable person. [1400–50; late ME < L *venerābilis*, equiv. to *venerā(rī)* to VENERATE + *-bilis* -BLE] —**ven′er·a·bil′i·ty, ven′er·a·ble·ness,** *n.* —**ven′er·a·bly,** *adv.*

ven·er·ate (ven′ə rāt′), *v.t.,* **-at·ed, -at·ing.** to regard or treat with reverence; revere. [1615–25; < L *venerātus*, ptp. of *venerārī* to solicit the goodwill of (a god), worship, revere, v. deriv. of *vener-*, s. of *venus*, presumably in its original sense "desire"; see VENUS)] —**ven′er·a′tor,** *n.*

ven·er·a·tion (ven′ə rā′shən), *n.* **1.** the act of venerating. **2.** the state of being venerated. **3.** the feeling of a person who venerates; a feeling of awe, respect, etc.; reverence: *They were filled with veneration for their priests.* **4.** an expression of this feeling: *A memorial was erected in veneration of the dead of both world wars.* [1400–50; late ME < L *venerātiōn-* (s. of *venerātiō*), equiv. to *venerāt(us)* (see VENERATE) + *-iōn-* -ION] —**ven′er·a′tion·al, ven′er·a′tive,** *adj.* —**ven′er·a′tive·ly,** *adv.* —**ven′er·a′tive·ness,** *n.*
—**Syn. 3.** See **respect.** —**Ant. 3.** disrespect.

ve·ne·re·al (və nēr′ē əl), *adj.* **1.** arising from, connected with, or transmitted through sexual intercourse, as an infection. **2.** pertaining to conditions so arising. **3.** infected with or suffering from a sexually transmitted disease: *a venereal patient.* **4.** adapted to the cure of such disease: *a venereal remedy.* **5.** of or pertaining to sexual desire or intercourse. **6.** serving or tending to excite sexual desire; aphrodisiac. [1400–50; late ME < L *venere(us)* of sexual love (*vener-*, s. of *venus* sexual charm (see VENUS) + *-eus* adj. suffix) + -AL[1]]

vene′real disease′, *Pathol.* See **sexually transmitted disease.** *Abbr.:* VD [1650–60]

vene′real wart′, *Pathol.* a soft warty nodule of viral origin that occurs on the mucosal surfaces of the genitalia or around the anus, often in a cluster; condyloma acuminatum.

ve•ne•re•ol•o•gy (və nēr′ē ol′ə jē), *n.* the branch of medicine dealing with the study and treatment of venereal, or sexually transmitted, disease. Also, **ven•er•ol•o•gy** (ven′ə rol′ə jē). [1895–1900; < L *venere(us)* VENEREAL + -O- + -LOGY] **—ve•ne′re•ol′o•gist,** *n.*

ven•er•er (ven′ər ər), *n. Archaic.* a huntsman. [1835–45; VENER(Y)[2] + -ER[1]]

ven•er•y[1] (ven′ə rē), *n. Archaic.* the gratification of sexual desire. [1490–1500; < L *vener-* (s. of *venus;* see VENUS) + -Y[3]; cf. L *venera* amours]

ven•er•y[2] (ven′ə rē), *n. Archaic.* the practice or sport of hunting; the chase. [1275–1325; ME *venerie* hunting < MF, equiv. to *ven(er)* to hunt << L *vēnārī* + *-erie* -ERY]

ven•e•sec•tion (ven′ə sek′shən, vē′nə-), *n. Surg.* phlebotomy. Also, **venisection.** [1655–65; < NL or ML *vēnae sectiō* cutting of a vein; see VEIN, SECTION]

Ven•e•ti (ven′i tī′), *n.pl.* **1.** an ancient people of NE Italy absorbed by Rome after the Second Punic War. **2.** an ancient Celtic people of Brittany, conquered by Julius Caesar, 56 B.C. Also, **Ven•e•tes** (ven′i tēz′). [< L]

Ve•ne•ti•a (və nē′shē ə, -shə), *n.* **1.** an ancient district in NE Italy: later a Roman province bounded by the Alps, the Po River, and the Adriatic Sea. **2.** Venezia (def. 1). **3.** a female given name.

Ve•ne•tian (və nē′shən), *adj.* **1.** of or pertaining to Venice or its inhabitants. **2.** pertaining to or designating a style of painting developed in Venice principally during the 15th and 16th centuries, characterized chiefly by rich, often warm colors and the illusion of deep space. **3.** in or in imitation of the style typical of Venice: *Venetian architecture.* —*n.* **4.** a native or inhabitant of Venice. **5.** (*l.c.*) See **venetian blind. 6. venetians,** a tape or braid for supporting the slats of a venetian blind. **7.** Also called **Vene′tian cloth′.** *Textiles.* **a.** a wool or worsted fabric made in satin or twill weave and sometimes napped, used in the manufacture of lightweight coats, suits, skirts, and dresses. **b.** a cotton fabric constructed in satin or twill weave, used chiefly for linings. [1400–50; < ML *Venetiānus,* equiv. to *Veneti(a)* Venice + L *-ānus* -AN; r. ME *Venicien* < MF]

Vene′tian ball′, a small glass ball containing colorful objects or pieces, used chiefly as a paperweight. [1850–55]

vene′tian blind′, a blind, as for a window, having overlapping horizontal slats that may be opened or closed, esp. one in which the slats may be raised and drawn together above the window by pulling a cord. [1760–70] **—ve•ne′tianed,** *adj.*

Vene′tian blue′, a strong blue similar to cobalt blue. Also, **vene′tian blue′.** [1830–40]

Vene′tian den′til, *Archit.* (on an archivolt or molding) one of a series of small rectangular blocks having chamfers at alternate edges. [1895–1900]

Vene′tian door′, a doorway having a form similar to that of a Palladian window. [1725–35]

Vene′tian glass′, ornamental glassware of the type made at Venice, esp. that from the island of Murano. [1835–45]

Vene′tian red′, **1.** a red pigment, originally prepared from a natural oxide of iron, now usually made by calcining a mixture of lime and ferrous sulfate. **2.** a dark shade of orangish red. [1745–55]

Vene′tian school′, any of various groups of artists identified with Venice throughout the history of Italian art but most notably the painters of the 18th century, as Giovanni Battista Tiepolo, Francesco Guardi, and Antonio Canaletto. [1740–50]

Vene′tian su′mac. See **smoke tree** (def. 2). [1745–55]

Vene′tian win′dow. See **Palladian window.** [1770–80]

Ve•net•ic (və net′ik), *n.* an Indo-European language of NE Italy, possibly belonging to the Italic branch, known from inscriptions from the 4th to 2nd centuries B.C. [1875–80; < L *Veneticus,* equiv. to *Venet(ī)* the Veneti + *-icus* -IC]

Venez., Venezuela.

Ve•ne•zia (ve ne′tsyä), *n.* **1.** Also, **Venetia.** Also called **Ve•ne•to** (ve′ne tô). a region in NE Italy. 4,305,393; 7095 sq. mi. (18,375 sq. km). **2.** Italian name of **Venice.**

Ve•ne•zia Giu•lia (ve ne′tsyä jo͞o′lyä), a former region of NE Italy, at the N end of the Adriatic: now mainly in Croatia and Slovenia. The larger part, including the area surrounding the Free Territory of Trieste, was ceded to Yugoslavia 1947; the part remaining in Italy merged with Udine to form Friuli-Venezia Giulia.

Ve•ne•zia Tri•den•ti•na (ve ne′tsyä trē′den tē′nä), a former department in N Italy, now forming the greater part of the region of Trentino-Alto Adige.

Ven•e•zue•la (ven′ə zwā′lə, -zwē′-; *Sp.* be′ne swe′lä), *n.* a republic in N South America. 12,300,000; 352,143 sq. mi. (912,050 sq. km). *Cap.:* Caracas. **—Ven′e•zue′•lan,** *adj., n.*

venge (venj), *v.t.,* **venged, veng•ing.** *Archaic.* to avenge. [1250–1300; ME *vengen* < OF *veng(i)er* < L *vindicāre;* see VINDICATE]

venge•ance (ven′jəns), *n.* **1.** infliction of injury, harm, humiliation, or the like, on a person by another who has been harmed by that person; violent revenge: *But have you the right to vengeance?* **2.** an act or opportunity of inflicting such trouble: *to take one's vengeance.* **3.** the desire for revenge: *a man full of vengeance.* **4.** *Obs.* hurt; injury. **5.** *Obs.* curse; imprecation. **6. with a vengeance, a.** with force or violence. **b.** greatly; extremely. **c.** to an unreasonable, excessive, or surprising degree: *He attacked the job with a vengeance.* [1250–1300; ME < OF, equiv. to *vengi(er)* to avenge (see VENGE) + *-ance* -ANCE]
—Syn. 1. requital, retaliation. See **revenge. —Ant. 1.** forgiveness.

venge•ful (venj′fəl), *adj.* **1.** desiring or seeking vengeance; vindictive: *a vengeful attitude.* **2.** characterized by or showing a vindictive spirit: *vengeful intentions.* **3.** serving to inflict vengeance: *a vengeful killing.* [1580–90; shortened form of REVENGEFUL] **—venge′ful•ly,** *adv.* **—venge′ful•ness,** *n.*
—Syn. 1. revengeful, spiteful.

V-en•gine (vē′en′jən), *n.* an internal-combustion engine having two opposed banks of cylinders inclined so that they form a V-shaped angle. [1920–25]

ve•ni•al (vē′nē əl, vēn′yəl), *adj.* **1.** able to be forgiven or pardoned; not seriously wrong, as a sin (opposed to *mortal*). **2.** excusable; trifling; minor: *a venial error; a venial offense.* [1250–1300; ME < ML *veniālis,* equiv. to L *veni(a)* grace, favor, indulgence (akin to *venus;* see VENERATE, VENUS) + *-ālis* -AL[1]] **—ve′ni•al′i•ty, ve′ni•al•ness,** *n.* **—ve′ni•al•ly,** *adv.*
—Syn. 2. slight, pardonable, forgivable.

ve′nial sin′, *Rom. Cath. Ch.* a transgression against the law of God that does not deprive the soul of divine grace either because it is a minor offense or because it was committed without full understanding of its seriousness or without full consent of the will. Cf. **mortal sin.** [1350–1400; ME]

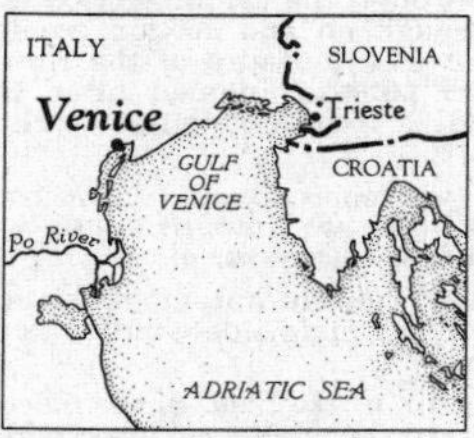

Ven•ice (ven′is), *n.* **1.** Italian, **Venezia.** a seaport in NE Italy, built on numerous small islands in the **Lagoon of Venice.** 361,722. **2. Gulf of,** the N arm of the Adriatic Sea. **3.** a town in SW Florida. 12,153.

ven•in (ven′in, vē′nin), *n. Biochem.* any of several poisonous substances occurring in snake venom. Also, **venene, ven•ine** (ven′ēn). [VEN(OM) + -IN[2]]

ven•i•punc•ture (ven′ə pungk′chər, vē′nə-), *n. Med.* the puncture of a vein for surgical or therapeutic purposes or for collecting blood specimens for analysis. Also, **venepuncture.** [1900–05; var. of VENEPUNCTURE with -I-]

ve•ni•re fa•ci•as (və nī′rē fā′shē as′, -nēr′ē), *Law.* **1.** a writ directing the appropriate official to summon a jury. **2.** the entire jury panel from which a trial jury is selected. [1400–50; late ME < L *venire faciās* lit., make come]

ve•ni•re•man (vi nī′rē mən, -nēr′ē-), *n., pl.* **-men.** *Law.* a person summoned under a venire facias. [1770–80, *Amer.; venire* (see VENIRE FACIAS) + MAN[1]]

ven•i•sec•tion (ven′ə sek′shən, vē′nə-), *n. Surg.* phlebotomy. Also, **venesection.** [VEN(A) + -I- + SECTION]

ven•i•son (ven′ə sən, -zən), *n.* the flesh of a deer or similar animal as used for food. [1250–1300; ME *venison* < OF *veneison, venaison* < L *vēnātiōn* (s. of *vēnātiō* hunting), equiv. to *vēnāt(us)* (see VENATIC) + *-iōn-* -ION]

Ve•ni•te (vi nī′tē, ve nē′tā), *n.* **1.** the 95th Psalm (94th in the Vulgate and Douay), used as a canticle at matins or morning prayers. **2.** a musical setting of this psalm. [1175–1225; ME < L: come ye; so called from the first word of Vulgate text]

ve•ni, vi•di, vi•ci (wā′nē wē′dē wē′kē; *Eng.* vē′nī vī′dī vī′sī, ven′ē vē′dē vē′chē, -sē), *Latin.* I came, I saw, I conquered.

Ve•ni•ze•los (ve′nē ze′lôs), *n.* **E•leu•the•rios** (e′lefthe′Ryôs), 1864–1936, prime minister of Greece 1910–15, 1917–20, 1928–33.

Ven•lo (ven′lō), *n.* a city in SE Netherlands. 62,543. Also, **Ven•loo** (ven′lō).

Venn′ di′agram (ven), *Math., Symbolic Logic.* a diagram that uses circles to represent sets and their relationships. [1940–45; named after John *Venn* (1834–1923), English logician]

veno-, a combining form with the meaning "vein," used in the formation of compound words: *venostasis.* [< L *vēn(a)* VEIN + -O-]

ve•no•gram (vē′nə gram′), *n.* an x-ray of the veins produced by venography. Also called **phlebogram.** [VENO- + -GRAM[1]]

ve•nog•ra•phy (vē nog′rə fē), *n.* x-ray examination of a vein or veins following injection of a radiopaque substance. Also called **phlebography.** [1925–30; VENO- + -GRAPHY]

ve•nol•o•gy (vē nol′ə jē), *n.* phlebology. [VENO- + -LOGY]

ven•om (ven′əm), *n.* **1.** the poisonous fluid that some animals, as certain snakes and spiders, secrete and introduce into the bodies of their victims by biting, stinging, etc. **2.** something resembling or suggesting poison in its effect; spite; malice: *the venom of jealousy.* **3.** *Archaic.* poison in general. —*v.t.* **4.** *Archaic.* to make venomous; envenom. [1175–1225; var. of ME *venim* < AF; OF *venim, venin* < VL **venimen,* for L *venēnum* magical herb or potion, poison < **wenes-nom,* equiv. to **wenes-* desire (see VENERATE, VENUS) + **-nom* n. suffix] **—ven′om•less,** *adj.*
—Syn. 1. See **poison. 2.** malignity, acrimony, bitterness, acerbity, gall, spleen, hate.

ven•om•ous (ven′ə məs), *adj.* **1.** (of an animal) having a gland or glands for secreting venom; able to inflict a poisoned bite, sting, or wound: *a venomous snake.* **2.** full of or containing venom; poisonous: *a venomous wound; a venomous potion.* **3.** spiteful; malignant: *a venomous attack; a venomous tongue.* [1250–1300; ME *venim(o)us* < AF *venimus* (OF *venimeux*). See VENOM, -OUS] **—ven′om•ous•ly,** *adv.* **—ven′om•ous•ness, ven′om•ness,** *n.*
—Syn. 3. malicious, hostile, rancorous, ill-disposed.

ve•nose (vē′nōs), *adj.* **1.** having many or prominent veins. **2.** venous. [1655–65; < L *vēnōsus,* equiv. to *vēn(a)* VEIN + *-ōsus* -OSE[1]]

ve•nos•i•ty (vi nos′i tē), *n. Physiol.* the state or quality of being venous. [1850–55; VENOSE + -ITY]

ve•no•sta•sis (vē′nō stā′sis), *n.* retardation or stoppage of blood flow through a vein. [VENO- + STASIS]

ve•nous (vē′nəs), *adj.* **1.** of, pertaining to, or of the nature of a vein. **2.** having, characterized by, or composed of veins. **3.** pertaining to the blood in the pulmonary artery, right side of the heart, and most veins, that has become deoxygenated and charged with carbon dioxide during its passage through the body and that in humans is normally dark red. [1620–30; var. of VENOSE; see -OUS] **—ve′nous•ly,** *adv.* **—ve′nous•ness,** *n.*

vent[1] (vent), *n.* **1.** an opening, as in a wall, serving as an outlet for air, smoke, fumes, or the like. **2.** an opening at the earth's surface from which volcanic material, as lava, steam, or gas, is emitted. **3.** *Zool.* the anal or excretory opening of animals, esp. of those below mammals, as birds and reptiles. **4.** the small opening at the breech of a gun by which fire is communicated to the charge. **5.** a means of exit or escape; an outlet, as from confinement. **6.** expression; utterance; release: *to give vent to one's emotions.* **7.** *Obs.* the act or fact of venting; emission or discharge. —*v.t.* **8.** to give free play or expression to (an emotion, passion, etc.): *to vent rage.* **9.** to give public utterance to: *to vent one's opinions.* **10.** to relieve by giving expression to something: *He vented his disappointment by criticizing his successor.* **11.** to release or discharge (liquid, smoke, etc.). **12.** to furnish or provide with a vent or vents. —*v.i.* **13.** to be relieved of pressure or discharged by means of a vent. **14.** (of an otter or other animal) to rise to the surface of the water to breathe. [1350–1400; (v.) ME *venten* to furnish (a vessel) with a vent, by aphesis < OF *esventer* (*es-* EX- + *-venter,* v. deriv. of *vent* < L *ventus* WIND[1]), in later use deriv. of the E n.; (n.) partly < F *vent* (< L *ventus*), partly by aphesis < F *évent* (OF *esvent,* deriv. of *esventer*), partly deriv. of the E v.] **—vent′less,** *adj.*

vent[2] (vent), *n.* a slit in the back or side of a coat, jacket, or other garment, at the bottom part of a seam. [1400–50; late ME *vente;* r. ME *fente* < MF, deriv. of *fendre* to slit < L *findere* to split]

CONCISE PRONUNCIATION KEY: act, cāpe, dâre, pärt; set, ēqual; if, ice; ox, ōver, ôrder, oil, bo͝ok, bo͞ot, out; up, ûrge; child; sing; shoe; thin, *th*at; zh as in *treasure.* ə = *a* as in *alone, e* as in *system, i* as in *easily, o* as in *gallop, u* as in *circus;* ᵊ as in *fire* (fīᵊr), *hour* (ouᵊr). l and n can serve as syllabic consonants, as in *cradle* (krād′l), and *button* (but′n). See the full key inside the front cover.

vent·age (ven′tij), *n.* a small hole or vent, as one of the fingerholes of a flute. [1595–1605; VENT[1] + -AGE]

ven·tail (ven′tāl), *n.* **1.** the pivoted middle element of a face defense of a close helmet. See diag. under **close helmet. 2.** a flap of mail attached to a coif and fastened across the lower part of the face during combat. Also, **aventail.** [1300–50; ME < MF *ventaille,* equiv. to *vent* (< L *ventus* WIND[1]) + *-aille* -AL[2]]

Ven·tan′a Cave′ (ven tan′ə), a Paleo-Indian archaeological site near Tucson, Arizona.

ven·ter (ven′tər), *n.* **1.** *Anat., Zool.* **a.** the abdomen or belly. **b.** a bellylike cavity or concavity. **c.** a bellylike protuberance. **2.** *Law.* the womb, or a wife or mother, as a source of offspring. [1535–45; < L *venter* belly, womb]

ven·ti·fact (ven′tə fakt′), *n. Geol.* a pebble or cobble that has been faceted, grooved, and polished by the erosive action of wind-driven sand. [1910–15; < L *venti-* (comb. form of *ventus* WIND[1]) + *factum* something made (see FACT); perh. modeled on ARTIFACT]

ven·ti·late (ven′tl āt′), *v.t.,* **-lat·ed, -lat·ing. 1.** to provide (a room, mine, etc.) with fresh air in place of air that has been used or contaminated. **2.** *Med.* **a.** to oxygenate (blood) by exposure to air in the lungs or gills. **b.** to assist the breathing of (a person), as with a respirator. **3.** (of air or wind) to circulate through or blow on, so as to cool or freshen the air of: *Cool breezes ventilated the house.* **4.** to expose to the action of air or wind: *to ventilate floor timbers.* **5.** to submit (a question, problem, etc.) to open, full examination and discussion. **6.** to give utterance or expression to (an opinion, complaint, etc.). **7.** to furnish with a vent or opening, as for the escape of air or gas. —*v.i.* **8.** to give utterance or expression to one's emotions, opinions, complaints, etc. [1400–50; late ME *ventilatten* to blow (something) away < L *ventilātus* (ptp. of *ventilāre* to fan), equiv. to *vent(us)* WIND[1] + *-il-* v. suffix (var. of *-ul-,* orig. after derivs. of nouns ending in *-ulus* -ULE; cf. SPECULATE) + *-ātus* -ATE[1]] —**ven′ti·la·ble,** *adj.*
—**Syn. 5.** broadcast, publicize, circulate, report.

ven·ti·la·tion (ven′tl ā′shən), *n.* **1.** the act of ventilating. **2.** the state of being ventilated. **3.** facilities or equipment for providing ventilation. [1425–75; late ME *ventilacioun* < L *ventilātiōn-* (s. of *ventilātiō*), equiv. to *ventilāt(us)* (see VENTILATE) + *-iōn-* -ION] —**ven·ti·la·to·ry** (ven′tl ə tôr′ē, -tōr′ē), *adj.*

ven·ti·la·tion·ist (ven′tl ā′shə nist), *adj.* **1.** of, pertaining to, or advocating the ventilation of emotions: *a ventilationist approach to dealing with anger.* —*n.* **2.** an advocate or practitioner of emotional ventilation. [VENTILATION + -IST]

ven·ti·la·tive (ven′tl ā′tiv), *adj.* **1.** promoting or producing ventilation. **2.** of or pertaining to ventilation. [1785–95; VENTILATE + -IVE]

ven·ti·la·tor (ven′tl ā′tər), *n.* **1.** a person or thing that ventilates. **2.** a contrivance or opening for replacing foul or stagnant air with fresh air. **3.** *Med.* a respirator. [1735–45; VENTILATE + -OR[2]]

Vent′nor Cit′y (vent′nər), a town in SE New Jersey. 11,704.

ven·tose (ven′tōs), *adj. Archaic.* given to empty talk; windy; flatulent. [1715–25; < L *ventōsus* windy, equiv. to *vent(us)* WIND[1] + *-ōsus* -OSE[1]] —**ven·tos·i·ty** (ven tos′i tē), *n.*

Ven·tôse (väN tōz′), *n.* (in the French Revolutionary calendar) the sixth month of the year, extending from February 19 to March 20. [< F < L *ventōsus;* see VENTOSE]

vent′ pipe′, *Plumbing.* a pipe above a waste pipe or soil pipe that allows gas to escape from the system. [1855–60]

ventr-, var. of **ventro-** before a vowel.

ven·trad (ven′trad), *adv. Anat., Zool.* toward the ventral side; ventrally. [1840–50; VENTR- + -AD[3]]

ven·tral (ven′trəl), *adj.* **1.** of or pertaining to the venter or belly; abdominal. **2.** *Anat., Zool.* situated on or toward the lower, abdominal plane of the body; equivalent to the front, or anterior, in humans. **3.** *Bot., Mycol.* of or designating the lower or inner surface of a structure. Cf. **dorsal.** [1730–40; < L *ventrālis,* equiv. to *vent(e)r* VENTER + *-ālis* -AL[1]] —**ven′tral·ly,** *adv.*

ven′tral fin′. See **pelvic fin.** [1745–55]

ven′tral root′. See under **nerve root.** [1920–25]

ventri-, var. of **ventro-.** Also, **ventr-.**

ven·tri·cle (ven′tri kəl), *n.* **1.** *Zool.* any of various hollow organs or parts in an animal body. **2.** *Anat.* **a.** either of the two lower chambers on each side of the heart that receive blood from the atria and in turn force it into the arteries. See diag. under **heart. b.** one of a series of connecting cavities of the brain. [1350–1400; ME < L *ventriculus* belly, ventricle. See VENTER, -I-, -CLE[1]]

ven·tri·cose (ven′tri kōs′), *adj.* **1.** swollen, esp. on one side or unequally; protuberant. **2.** having a large abdomen. [1750–60; < NL *ventricōsus.* See VENTER, -IC, -OSE[1]] —**ven·tri·cos·i·ty** (ven′tri kos′i tē), *n.*

ven·tric·u·lar (ven trik′yə lər), *adj.* **1.** of, pertaining to, or of the nature of a ventricle. **2.** of or pertaining to a belly or to something resembling one. [1815–25; < L *ventricul(us)* (see VENTRICLE) + -AR[1]]

ventric′ular fibrilla′tion, *Pathol.* a cardiac arrhythmia characterized by rapid, chaotic electrical impulses to the ventricles, incomplete ventricular contractions, and resultant loss of pulse and blood pressure.

ventric′ular tachycar′dia, *Pathol.* a cardiac arrhythmia in which the muscles of the ventricles contract irregularly in a rapid, uncoordinated manner, impairing the normal pumping of blood.

ven·tric·u·lus (ven trik′yə ləs), *n., pl.* **-li** (-lī′). *Zool.* **1.** the part of the food tract in which digestion takes place, esp. the lower cavity of a compound stomach in insects. **2.** gizzard (def. 1). [1685–95; < L; see VENTRICLE]

ven·tri·lo·qui·al (ven′trə lō′kwē əl), *adj.* of, pertaining to, or using ventriloquism. Also, **ven·tril·o·qual** (ven tril′ə kwəl). [1830–40; VENTRILOQUY + -AL[1]] —**ven′tri·lo′qui·al·ly,** *adv.*

ven·tril·o·quism (ven tril′ə kwiz′əm), *n.* the art or practice of speaking, with little or no lip movement, in such a manner that the voice does not appear to come from the speaker but from another source, as from a wooden dummy. Also called **ven·tril·o·quy** (ven tril′ə-kwē). [1790–1800; *ventriloqu(y)* (< ML *ventriloquium,* equiv. to LL *ventriloqu(us)* a ventriloquist (*ventri-* VENTRI- + *-loquus,* deriv. of *loquī* to speak) + *-ium* -IUM) + -ISM]

ven·tril·o·quist (ven tril′ə kwist), *n.* a person who performs or is skilled in ventriloquism. [1650–60; VENTRILOQU(Y) + -IST] —**ven·tril′o·quis′tic,** *adj.*

ven·tril·o·quize (ven tril′ə kwīz′), *v.i., v.t.,* **-quized, -quiz·ing.** to speak or sound in the manner of a ventriloquist. Also, *esp. Brit.,* **ven·tril′o·quise′.** [1835–45; VENTRILOQU(Y) + -IZE]

Ven·tris (ven′tris), *n.* **Michael George Francis,** 1922–56, English architect and linguist.

ventro-, a combining form meaning "abdomen," used in the formation of compound words: *ventrodorsal.* Also, **ventr-, ventri-.** [comb. form of NL *venter* VENTER; see -O-]

ven·tro·dor·sal (ven′trō dôr′səl), *adj. Anat., Zool.* pertaining to the ventral and dorsal aspects of the body; extending from the ventral to the dorsal side. [1890–95; VENTRO- + DORSAL[1]]

ven·tro·lat·er·al (ven′trō lat′ər əl), *adj. Anat., Zool.* of, pertaining to, or affecting the front and side. [1825–35; VENTRO- + LATERAL] —**ven′tro·lat′er·al·ly,** *adv.*

ven·ture (ven′chər), *n., v.,* **-tured, -tur·ing,** *adj.* —*n.* **1.** an undertaking involving uncertainty as to the outcome, esp. a risky or dangerous one: *a mountain-climbing venture.* **2.** a business enterprise or speculation in which something is risked in the hope of profit; a commercial or other speculation. **3.** the money, ship, cargo, merchandise, or the like, on which risk is taken in a business enterprise or speculation. **4.** *Obs.* hazard or risk. **5. at a venture,** according to chance; at random: *A successor was chosen at a venture.* —*v.t.* **6.** to expose to hazard; risk: *to venture one's fortune; to venture one's life.* **7.** to take the risk of; brave the dangers of: *to venture a voyage into space.* **8.** to undertake to express, as when opposition or resistance appears likely to follow; be bold enough; dare: *I venture to say that you are behaving foolishly.* **9.** to take the risk of sending. —*v.i.* **10.** to make or embark upon a venture; dare to go: *He ventured deep into the jungle.* **11.** to take a risk; dare; presume: *to venture on an ambitious program of reform.* **12.** to invest venture capital. —*adj.* **13.** of or pertaining to an investment or investments in new businesses: *a venture fund.* [1400–50; late ME, aph. var. of *aventure* ADVENTURE] —**ven′tur·er,** *n.*
—**Syn. 6.** endanger, imperil, jeopardize. **11.** See **dare.**

ven′ture cap′ital, funds invested or available for investment in a new or unproven business enterprise. Also called **risk capital.** [1940–45] —**ven′ture cap′italism.** —**ven′ture cap′italist.**

ven·ture·some (ven′chər səm), *adj.* **1.** having or showing a disposition to undertake risky or dangerous activities; daring: *a venturesome investor; a venturesome explorer.* **2.** attended with risk; hazardous: *Auto racing is a venturesome sport.* [1655–65; VENTURE + -SOME[1]] —**ven′ture·some·ly,** *adv.* —**ven′ture·some·ness,** *n.*
—**Syn. 1.** enterprising; rash. **2.** risky, perilous, unsafe. —**Ant. 1.** cautious.

ven·tu′ri tube′ (ven to͝or′ē), a device for measuring the flow of a fluid, consisting of a tube with a short, narrow center section and widened, tapered ends, so that a fluid flowing through the center section at a higher velocity than through an end section creates a pressure differential that is a measure of the flow of the fluid. Also, **Ven·tu′ri tube′.** [named after G. B. Venturi (1746–1822), Italian physicist whose work led to its invention]

ven·tur·ous (ven′chər əs), *adj.* venturesome. [1555–65; VENTURE + -OUS; see ADVENTUROUS] —**ven′tur·ous·ly,** *adv.* —**ven′tur·ous·ness,** *n.*

vent′ win′dow, (on an automobile) a small, pivoting window fitted into a main side window to provide draft-free ventilation.

ven·ue (ven′yo͞o), *n.* **1.** *Law.* **a.** the place of a crime or cause of action. **b.** the county or place where the jury is gathered and the cause tried. **c.** the designation, in the pleading, of the jurisdiction where a trial will be held. **d.** the statement naming the place and person before whom an affidavit was sworn. **2.** the scene or locale of any action or event. **3.** the position taken by a person engaged in argument or debate; ground. [1300–50; ME *venue* an attack < MF: lit., a coming, OF, fem. ptp. of *venir* to come < VL **venūta,* for L *venta,* equiv. to *ven(īre)* to COME + *-ta* fem. ptp. suffix]

ven·ule (ven′yo͞ol), *n.* **1.** a small vein. **2.** one of the branches of a vein in the wing of an insect. Also, **vein·ule, veinulet.** [1840–50; < L *vēnula* little vein. See VEIN, -ULE] —**ven′u·lar,** *adj.*

ven·u·lose (ven′yə lōs′), *adj.* having venules. Also, **ven·u·lous** (ven′yə ləs). [1855–60; VENULE + -OSE[1]]

Ve·nus (vē′nəs), *n., pl.* **-us·es** for 2. **1.** an ancient Italian goddess of gardens and spring, identified by the Romans with Aphrodite as the goddess of love and beauty. **2.** an exceptionally beautiful woman. **3.** (*sometimes l.c.*) *Archaeol.* a statuette of a female figure, usually carved of ivory and typically having exaggerated breasts, belly, or buttocks, often found in Upper Paleolithic cultures from Siberia to France. **4.** *Astron.* the planet second in order from the sun, having an equatorial diameter of 7521 miles (12,104 km), a mean distance from the sun of 67.2 million miles (108.2 million km), a period of revolution of 224.68 days, and no moons. It is the most brilliant planet in the solar system. See table under **planet. 5.** *Chem. Obs.* copper. [< L *Venus,* s. *Vener-* orig. a neut. common n. meaning "physical desire, sexual appetite," hence "qualities exciting desire, seductiveness, charm," "a goddess personifying sexual attractiveness"; c. Skt *vanaḥ* desire, akin to WISH; cf. VENERATE, VENOM]

Ve′nus and Adon′is, a narrative poem (1593) by Shakespeare.

Ve·nus·berg (vē′nəs bûrg′; *Ger.* vā′no͝os beʀk′), *n.* a mountain in central Germany in the caverns of which, according to medieval legend, Venus held court.

Ve′nus de Mi′lo (də mē′lō, mī′-), a Greek statue of Venus in marble, c200 B.C., found in 1820 on Melos and now in the Louvre, Paris. Also, **Ve′nus of Me′los.** Also called **Aphrodite of Melos.**

Ve′nus fig′ure, Venus (def. 3). Also called **Ve′nus figurine′, Venus statuette.**

Ve′nus hair′stone (hâr′stōn′), a variety of rutilated quartz, used as a gemstone. Cf. **sagenite.** [1880–85; HAIR + STONE]

Ve·nu·si·an (və no͞o′shən, -shē ən, -sē ən, -nyo͞o′-), *adj.* **1.** of or pertaining to the planet Venus. —*n.* **2.** a supposed being inhabiting or coming from Venus. [1895–1900; VENUS + -IAN]

Ve′nus of Wil′lendorf. See under **Willendorf.**

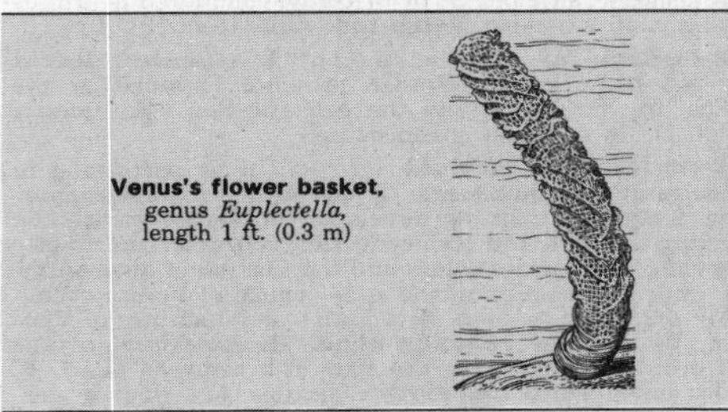

Venus's flower basket, genus *Euplectella,* length 1 ft. (0.3 m)

Ve′nus's flow′er bas′ket, a glass sponge of the genus *Euplectella,* inhabiting deep waters off the Philippines and Japan, having a cylindrical skeleton formed of an intricate latticework of siliceous spicules. [1870–75]

Ve·nus's-fly·trap (vē′nə siz flī′trap′), *n.* a carnivorous plant, *Dionaea muscipula,* native to bogs of North and South Carolina, having roundish leaves with two lobes that close like a trap when certain delicate hairs on them are irritated, as by a fly: the range is now reduced, though the plants are still locally abundant. Also called **Ve′nus fly′trap.** [1760–70, *Amer.*]

Venus's-flytrap, *Dionaea muscipula,* height about 1 ft. (0.3 m)

Ve′nus's gir′dle, an iridescent blue-and-green comb jelly, *Cestum veneris,* having a ribbon-shaped, gelatinous body. [1865–70]

Ve·nus's-hair (vē′nə siz hâr′), *n.* a delicate maidenhair fern, *Adiantum capillus-veneris.* [1540–50]

Ve′nus statuette′. Venus (def. 3).

ver., 1. verse; verses. **2.** version.

ver·a (ver′ə, var′ə), *adj., adv. Scot.* very.

Ve·ra (vēr′ə), *n.* a female given name: from a Russian word meaning "faith."

ve·ra·cious (və rā′shəs), *adj.* **1.** habitually speaking the truth; truthful; honest: *a veracious witness.* **2.** characterized by truthfulness; true, accurate, or honest in content: *a veracious statement; a veracious account.* [1670–80; VERACI(TY) + -OUS] —**ve·ra′cious·ly,** *adv.* —**ve·ra′cious·ness,** *n.*
—**Ant. 1, 2.** mendacious.

ve·rac·i·ty (və ras′i tē), *n., pl.* **-ties** for 4. **1.** habitual observance of truth in speech or statement; truthfulness: *He was not noted for his veracity.* **2.** conformity to truth or fact; accuracy: *to question the veracity of his account.* **3.** correctness or accuracy, as of the senses or of a scientific instrument. **4.** something veracious; a truth. [1615–25; < ML *vērācitās,* equiv. to L *vērāc-* (s. of *vērāx*) true + *-itās* -ITY]
—**Syn. 1.** honesty, integrity, credibility.

Ve·ra·cruz (ver′ə kro͞oz′; *Sp.* be′rä kro͞os′), *n.* **1.** a state in E Mexico, on the Gulf of Mexico. 4,917,000; 27,759 sq. mi. (71,895 sq. km). *Cap.:* Jalapa. **2.** a seaport in this state: the chief port of Mexico. 289,000. Formerly, **Ve′ra Cruz′.**

ve·ran·da (və ran′də), *n.* **1.** Also **ve·ran′dah.** *Chiefly South Midland and Southern U.S.* a large, open porch, usually roofed and partly enclosed, as by a railing, often extending across the front and sides of a house; gallery. **2.** piazza. [1705–15; < Hindi *baraṇḍā, barāmdā* < Pers *bar āmadah* coming out (unless the Hindi word is < Pg *varanda,* Sp *baranda* railing, balustrade; cf. BAR[1])]

ve•ran•daed (və ran′dəd), *adj.* having a veranda: *a verandaed house.* [1810–20; VERANDA + -ED[3]]

ve•ra•pam•il (vĕr′ə pam′əl, ver′-), *n. Pharm.* a white crystalline powder, $C_{27}H_{38}N_2O_4$, used as a calcium blocker in the treatment of angina and certain arrhythmias. [1965–70; perh. by rearrangement of letters from *valeronitrile* and *aminopropyl,* two of its chemical components]

ve•rat•ri•dine (və ra′tri dēn′, -din), *n. Chem.* a yellowish-white, amorphous, water-soluble, poisonous alkaloid, $C_{36}H_{51}NO_{11}$, occurring with veratrine in the seeds of the sabadilla. [1905–10; < L *vērātr(um)* hellebore + -ID[3] + -INE[2]]

ver•a•trine (ver′ə trēn′, -trin), *n. Chem.* a white or grayish-white, slightly water-soluble, poisonous mixture of alkaloids obtained by extraction from the seeds of the sabadilla: formerly used in medicine as a counterirritant in the treatment of rheumatism and neuralgia. Also, **ve•ra•tri•a** (və rā′trē ə, -ra′-). [1815–25; < F < L *vērātr(um)* hellebore + F *-ine* -INE[2]]

verb (vûrb), *n.* any member of a class of words that are formally distinguished in many languages, as in English by taking the past ending in *-ed,* that function as the main elements of predicates, that typically express action, state, or a relation between two things, and that (when inflected) may be inflected for tense, aspect, voice, mood, and to show agreement with their subject or object. [1350–1400; ME *verbe* < L *verbum* WORD] **—verb′less,** *adj.*

ver•bal (vûr′bəl), *adj.* **1.** of or pertaining to words: *verbal ability.* **2.** consisting of or in the form of words: *verbal imagery.* **3.** expressed in spoken words; oral rather than written: *verbal communication; verbal agreement.* **4.** consisting of or expressed in words (as opposed to actions): *a verbal protest.* **5.** pertaining to or concerned with words only (as opposed to ideas, facts, or realities): *a purely verbal distinction between two concepts.* **6.** corresponding word for word; verbatim: *a verbal translation.* **7.** using words: *verbal facility.* **8.** based on the use of words (as opposed to other activity): *a verbal score in a test; verbal IQ.* **9.** *Gram.* **a.** of, pertaining to, or derived from a verb. **b.** used in a sentence as or like a verb, as participles and infinitives. **—***n.* **10.** *Gram.* a word, particularly a noun or adjective, derived from a verb. [1485–95; < L *verbālis,* equiv. to *verb(um)* word (see VERB) + *-ālis* -AL[1]] **—ver′bal•ly,** *adv.*
—Syn. 3. spoken.
—Usage. 3, 4. VERBAL has had the meaning "spoken" since the late 16th century and is thus synonymous with *oral: He wrote a memorandum to confirm the verbal agreement.* Slightly earlier, VERBAL had developed the meaning "expressed in words, whether spoken or written (as opposed to actions)": *Verbal support is no help without money and supplies.* Although some say that the use of VERBAL to mean "spoken" produces ambiguity, it rarely does so. VERBAL is used in this sense in all varieties of speech and writing and is fully standard. The context usually makes the meaning clear: *No documents are necessary; a verbal agreement* (or contract or order) *will suffice. Oral* can be used instead of VERBAL if the context demands: *My lawyer insists on a written contract because oral agreements are too difficult to enforce.*

ver′bal ad′jective, *Gram.* an adjective derived from a verb, as, in English, *smiling* in *smiling eyes,* or, in Greek, *batós* "going," "moving," derived from *baínen* "to go," "to move." [1810–20]

ver′bal auxil′iary, an auxiliary verb, esp. when considered as a member of a separate class of words used with verbs rather than as a special subclass of verbs. [1955–60]

ver•bal•ism (vûr′bə liz′əm), *n.* **1.** a verbal expression, as a word or phrase. **2.** the way in which something is worded; choice of words; phrasing. **3.** a phrase or sentence having little or no meaning. **4.** a use of words considered as predominating over or obscuring ideas or reality; verbiage. [1780–90; VERBAL + -ISM]

ver•bal•ist (vûr′bə list), *n.* **1.** a person skilled in the use of words. **2.** a person who is more concerned with words than with ideas or reality. [1600–10; VERBAL + -IST] **—ver′bal•is′tic,** *adj.*

ver•bal•i•ty (vər bal′i tē), *n., pl.* **-ties** for 2. **1.** wordiness; verbal diffuseness: *a speech full of tedious verbality.* **2.** a verbal expression of an idea or thought. **3.** the quality or character of a verb. [1635–45; VERBAL + -ITY]

ver•bal•ize (vûr′bə līz′), *v.,* **-ized, -iz•ing.** **—***v.t.* **1.** to express in words: *He couldn't verbalize his feelings.* **2.** *Gram.* to convert into a verb: *to verbalize "butter" into "to butter."* **—***v.i.* **3.** to use many words; be verbose. **4.** to express something verbally. Also, *esp. Brit.,* **ver′bal•ise′.** [1600–10; VERBAL + -IZE; cf. F *verbaliser*] **—ver′•bal•i•za′tion,** *n.* **—ver′bal•iz′er,** *n.*

ver′bal noun′, *Gram.* a noun derived from a verb, esp. by a process applicable to most or all verbs, as, in English, the *-ing* form of *Eating is fun* or of *Smoking is forbidden.* [1700–10]

ver•ba•tim (vər bā′tim), *adv.* **1.** in exactly the same words; word for word: *to repeat something verbatim.* **—***adj.* **2.** corresponding word for word to the original source or text: *a verbatim record of the proceedings.* **3.** skilled at recording or noting down speeches, proceedings, etc., with word-for-word accuracy: *a verbatim stenographer.* [1475–85; < ML *verbātim,* equiv. to *verb(um)* word + *-ātim* adv. suffix]

ver•ba•tim et li•te•ra•tim (weʀ bä′tim et lē′te rä′tim; *Eng.* vər bā′tim et lit′ə rā′tim), *Latin.* word for word and letter for letter; in exactly the same words. Also, **ver•ba•tim ac li•te•ra•tim** (weʀ bä′tim äk lē′te-ʀä′tim; *Eng.* vər bā′tim ak lit′ə rā′tim).

ver•be•na (vər bē′nə), *n.* **1.** any of various plants of the genus *Verbena,* esp. any of several hybrid species cultivated for their showy flower clusters. Cf. **verbena family. 2.** any of various other plants, as the lemon verbena or sand verbena. [1560–70; < ML *verbēna,* L: leafy twig; see VERVAIN]

ver•be•na•ceous (vûr′bə nā′shəs), *adj.* belonging to the plant family Verbenaceae. Cf. **verbena family.** [1880–85; < NL *Verbenace(ae)* (see VERBENA, -ACEAE) + -OUS]

verbe′na fam′ily, the plant family Verbenaceae, characterized by herbaceous plants, shrubs, and trees having opposite or whorled leaves, clusters of irregular, sometimes fragrant flowers, and fleshy or dry fruit, and including the beautyberry, lantana, teak, verbena, and vervain. Also called **vervain family.**

ver•bi•age (vûr′bē ij), *n.* **1.** overabundance or superfluity of words, as in writing or speech; wordiness; verbosity. **2.** manner or style of expressing something in words; wording: *a manual of official verbiage.* [1715–25; < F, equiv. to MF *verbi(er)* to gabble + *-age* -AGE]

ver•bi•cide (vûr′bə sīd′), *n.* **1.** the willful distortion or depreciation of the original meaning of a word. **2.** a person who willfully distorts the meaning of a word. [1855–60; < L *verb(um)* word + -I- + -CIDE]

ver•bid (vûr′bid), *n. Gram.* a nonfinite verb form; a verbal; an infinitive, participle, or gerund. [1910–15; VERB + -ID[2]]

ver•bi•fy (vûr′bə fī′), *v.t.,* **-fied, -fy•ing.** to change into or employ as a verb, as a noun. [1805–15; VERB + -IFY] **—ver′bi•fi•ca′tion,** *n.*

ver•big•er•a•tion (vər bij′ə rā′shən), *Pathol.* the constant or obsessive repetition of meaningless words or phrases. [1890–95; < L *verbiger(āre)* to chat, converse (*verb(um)* word + *-i-* -I- + *-gerāre* durative deriv. of *gerere* to carry on, transact) + -ATION]

ver•bose (vər bōs′), *adj.* characterized by the use of many or too many words; wordy: *a verbose report.* [1665–75; < L *verbōsus,* equiv. to *verb(um)* WORD + *-ōsus* -OSE[1]] **—ver•bose′ly,** *adv.* **—ver•bose′ness,** *n.*
—Syn. prolix; tedious, inflated, turgid; voluble, talkative, loquacious. See **bombastic. —Ant.** laconic.

ver•bos•i•ty (vər bos′i tē), *n.* the state or quality of being verbose; superfluity of words; wordiness: *His speeches were always marred by verbosity.* [1535–45; < LL *verbōsitās.* See VERBOSE, -ITY]
—Syn. prolixity, redundancy, turgidity. **—Ant.** terseness, pithiness.

ver•bo•ten (vər bōt′n; *Ger.* feʀ bōt′n), *adj.* forbidden, as by law; prohibited. [1910–15; < G: ptp. of *verbieten* to FORBID]

verb′ phrase′, *Gram.* **1.** a group of words including a verb and its complements, objects, or other modifiers that functions syntactically as a verb. In English a verb phrase combines with a noun or noun phrase acting as subject to form a simple sentence. **2.** a phrase consisting of a main verb and any auxiliaries but not including modifiers, objects, or complements.

ver•bum sap (vûr′bəm sap′), a word to the wise is sufficient; no more need be said. Also, **verb. sap.** (vûrb′ sap′), **ver•bum sat** (vûr′bəm sat′). [1640–50; short for L *verbum sapientī sat est*]

Ver•cel•li (ver chel′ē, ver-; *It.* veʀ chel′lē), *n.* a city in NW Italy, W of Milan. 55,161.

Vercel′li Book′, a codex of Old English poems and sermons found in the chapter house at Vercelli.

Ver•cin•get•o•rix (vûr′sin jet′ə riks, -get′-), *n.* died 45? B.C., Gallic chieftain conquered by Caesar.

Ver•dan•di (ver′dän dē), *n. Scand. Myth.* See under **Norn.** [< ON *verthandi,* prp. of *vertha* to become; see URD]

ver•dant (vûr′dnt), *adj.* **1.** green with vegetation; covered with growing plants or grass: *a verdant oasis.* **2.** of the color green: *a verdant lawn.* **3.** inexperienced; unsophisticated: *verdant college freshmen.* [1575–85; VERD(URE) + -ANT] **—ver′dan•cy,** *n.* **—ver′dant•ly,** *adv.*
—Syn. 1. lush, grassy.

verd′ antique′ (vûrd), **1.** a green, mottled or impure serpentine, sold as a marble and much used for decorative purposes. **2.** any of various similar green stones. Also, **verde′ antique′.** [1735–45; < F < It *verde antico* lit., antique green. See VERDURE, ANTIQUE]

Verde (vûrd), *n.* **Cape,** a cape in Senegal, near Dakar: the westernmost point of Africa.

ver•der•er (vûr′dər ər), *n.* an English judicial officer in the royal forests having charge esp. of the vert, or trees and undergrowth. Also, **ver′de•ror.** [1535–45; < AF *verderer,* OF *verd(i)er* < L *viridārius,* equiv. to *viri-d(is)* green + *-ārius* -ARY (see -ER[2]); doubling of *-er* in AF perh. by falsely taking *verder* as a form of *verdure* VERDURE] **—ver′der•er•ship′,** *n.*

Ver•di (vâr′dē; *It.* veʀ′dē), *n.* **Giu•sep•pe** (jo͞o zep′pe), 1813–1901, Italian composer.

ver•dict (vûr′dikt), *n.* **1.** *Law.* the finding or answer of a jury given to the court concerning a matter submitted to their judgment. **2.** a judgment; decision: *the verdict of the critics.* [1250–1300; ME < ML *vērdictum,* var. of *vērēdictum* lit., something said truly; r. ME *verdit* < AF < L *vērum dictum* true word]

ver•di•gris (vûr′di grēs′, -gris), *n.* a green or bluish patina formed on copper, brass, or bronze surfaces exposed to the atmosphere for long periods of time, consisting principally of basic copper sulfate. Also called **aerugo.** [1250–1300; < MF *vert de gris;* r. ME *vertegrez* < AF *vert de Grece,* OF *vere grez* green of Greece] **—ver′•di•gris′y,** *adj.*

ver•din (vûr′dn), *n.* a small, yellow-headed, titmouse-like bird, *Auriparus flaviceps,* of arid regions of the southwestern U.S. and Mexico, which builds a compact, spherical nest of thorny twigs. [1880–85, *Amer.;* < F: a green passerine bird of Southeast Asia (*Chloropsis* sp.), deriv. of *vert* green (see VERT)]

ver•di•ter (vûr′di tər), *n.* either of two pigments, consisting usually of carbonate of copper prepared by grinding either azurite **(blue verditer)** or malachite **(green verditer).** [1495–1505; < MF *verd de terre* (F *vert de terre*) green of earth]

Ver•dun (ver dun′, vûr-; *Fr.* veʀ dœɴ′), *n.* **1.** a fortress city in NE France, on the Meuse River. A German offensive was stopped here in 1916 in the bloodiest fighting of World War I. 26,927. **2.** a city in S Quebec, in SE Canada. 68,013.

ver•dure (vûr′jər), *n.* **1.** greenness, esp. of fresh, flourishing vegetation. **2.** green vegetation, esp. grass or herbage. **3.** freshness in general; flourishing condition; vigor. [1250–1300; ME < MF, equiv. to *verd* green (see VERT) + *-ure* -URE] **—ver′dured,** *adj.* **—ver′•dure•less,** *adj.*

ver•dur•ous (vûr′jər əs), *adj.* **1.** rich in verdure; freshly green; verdant. **2.** covered with verdure, as places. **3.** consisting of verdure. **4.** of, pertaining to, or characteristic of verdure. [1595–1605; VERDURE + -OUS] **—ver′dur•ous•ness,** *n.*

ver•e•cund (ver′i kund′), *adj. Archaic.* bashful; modest. [1540–50; < L *verēcundus,* equiv. to *verē(rī)* to fear + *-cundus* adj. suffix]

Ve•ree•ni•ging (fə rā′nə ᴋʜəng), *n.* a city in the S Transvaal, in NE Republic of South Africa, S of Johannesburg. 196,357.

Ver•ein (feʀ īn′; *Eng.* və rīn′), *n., pl.* ***-ein•e*** (-ī′nə), *Eng.* **-eins.** *German.* a union, association, or society.

Ve•re•shcha•gin (ver′ə shä′gin; *Russ.* vyi ʀyi-shchä′gyin), *n.* **Va•si•li Va•si•lie•vich** (vu syĕ′lyē vu-syĕ′lyi vyich), 1842–1904, Russian painter.

verge[1] (vûrj), *n., v.,* **verged, verg•ing.** **—***n.* **1.** the edge, rim, or margin of something: *the verge of a desert; to operate on the verge of fraud.* **2.** the limit or point beyond which something begins or occurs; brink: *on the verge of a nervous breakdown.* **3.** a limiting belt, strip, or border of something. **4.** *Brit.* a narrow strip of turf bordering on a pathway, sidewalk, roadway, etc. **5.** a decorative border, as on or around an object, structural part, etc. **6.** limited room or scope for something: *an action within the verge of one's abilities.* **7.** an area or district subject to a particular jurisdiction. **8.** *Hist.* an area or district in England embracing the royal palace, being the jurisdiction of the Marshalsea Court. **9.** the part of a sloping roof that projects beyond the gable wall. **10.** *Archit.* the shaft of a column or colonette. **11.** a rod, wand, or staff, esp. one carried as an emblem of authority or of the office of a bishop, dean, or the like. **12.** *Horol.* a palletlike lever formerly used in inexpensive pendulum clocks. **13.** *Obs.* a stick or wand held in the hand of a person swearing fealty to a feudal lord on being admitted as a tenant. **—***v.i.* **14.** to be on the edge or margin; border: *Our property verges on theirs.* **15.** to come close to or be in transition to some state, quality, etc. (usually fol. by *on*): *a statesman who verged on greatness; a situation that verged on disaster.* **—***v.t.* **16.** to serve as the verge or boundary of: *a high hedge verging the yard.* [1350–1400; late ME: shaft, column, rod (hence boundary or jurisdiction symbolized by a steward's rod), ME: penis < MF: rod < L *virga*]
—Syn. 1. brim, lip, brink.

verge[2] (vûrj), *v.i.,* **verged, verg•ing. 1.** to incline; tend (usually fol. by *to* or *toward*): *The economy verges toward inflation.* **2.** to slope or sink. [1600–10; < L *vergere* to turn, bend, be inclined]

verge•board (vûrj′bôrd′, -bōrd′), *n.* bargeboard. [1825–35; VERGE[1] + BOARD]

ver•gence (vûr′jəns), *n. Ophthalm.* the turning motion of the eyeballs toward or away from each other. Cf. **convergence** (def. 4), **divergence** (def. 3). [1900–05; VERGE[2] + -ENCE]

verg•er (vûr′jər), *n.* **1.** *Chiefly Brit.* a church official who serves as sacristan, caretaker, usher, and general attendant. **2.** *Brit.* an official who carries the verge or other symbol of office before a bishop, dean, or other dignitary. [1425–75; late ME; see VERGE[1], -ER[1]]

Ver•gil (vûr′jil), *n.* **1.** (*Publius Vergilius Maro*), 70–19 B.C., Roman poet: author of *The Aeneid.* **2.** a male given name. Also, **Virgil.**

Ver•gil•i•an (vər jil′ē ən, -jil′yən), *adj.* pertaining to or characteristic of the poet Vergil. Also, **Virgilian.** [1505–15; < L *Vergiliānus;* see -AN]

ver•glas (ver glä′), *n., pl.* **-glases** (-glä′, -gläz′). glaze (def. 17). [1800–10; < F; OF *verre-glaz* lit., glass-ice, equiv. to *verre* glass (< L *vitrum*) + *glaz* ice (< LL *glacia;* see GLACIAL)]

ve•rid•i•an (və rid′ē ən), *n.* viridian.

ve•rid•i•cal (və rid′i kəl), *adj.* **1.** truthful; veracious. **2.** corresponding to facts; not illusory; real; actual; genuine. Also, **ve•rid′ic.** [1645–55; < L *vēridicus* (*vēr(us)* true + *-i-* -I- + *-dicus* speaking) + -AL[1]] **—ve•rid′i•cal′i•ty,** *n.* **—ve•rid′i•cal•ly,** *adv.*

ver•i•est (ver′ē ist), *adj.* **1.** utmost; most complete: *the veriest stupidity.* **2.** superlative of **very.** [VERY + -EST]

verifiabil′ity prin′ciple, *Logical Positivism.* the doctrine that if a nonanalytic statement is to be cognitively meaningful it must be empirically verifiable. [1965–70]

ver•i•fi•ca•tion (ver′ə fi kā′shən), *n.* **1.** the act of verifying. **2.** the state of being verified. **3.** evidence that establishes or confirms the accuracy or truth of something: *We could find no verification for his fantastic claims.* **4.** a formal assertion of the truth of something, as by oath or affidavit. **5.** the process of research, examination, etc., required to prove or establish authenticity or validity. **6.** *Law.* a short confirmatory affidavit at the end of a pleading or petition. [1515–25; < ML *vērificātiōn-* (s. of *vērificātiō*), equiv. to *vērificāt(us)* (ptp.

of *vērificāre;* see VERIFY, -ATE[1]) + *-iōn-* -ION] —**ver′i·fi·ca′tive, ver′i·fi·ca′to·ry,** *adj.*

ver·i·fied (ver′ə fīd′), *adj.* confirmed as to accuracy or truth by acceptable evidence, action, etc. [1585–95; VERIFY + -ED[2]]

ver·i·fy (ver′ə fī′), *v.t.,* **-fied, -fy·ing. 1.** to prove the truth of, as by evidence or testimony; confirm; substantiate: *Events verified his prediction.* **2.** to ascertain the truth or correctness of, as by examination, research, or comparison: *to verify a spelling.* **3.** to act as ultimate proof or evidence of; serve to confirm. **4.** *Law.* **a.** to prove or confirm (an allegation). **b.** to state to be true, esp. in legal use, formally or upon oath. [1275–1325; ME *verifien* < MF *verifier* < ML *vērificāre,* equiv. to *vēri-,* comb. form of *vērus* true + *-ficāre* -FY] —**ver′i·fi′a·bil′i·ty, ver′i·fi′a·ble·ness,** *n.* —**ver′i·fi′a·ble,** *adj.* —**ver′i·fi′er,** *n.*
—**Syn. 2.** authenticate, validate.

ver·i·ly (ver′ə lē), *adv.* in truth; really; indeed. [1250–1300; ME; see VERY, -LY]

ver·i·sim·i·lar (ver′ə sim′ə lər), *adj.* having the appearance of truth; likely; probable: *a verisimilar tale.* [1675–85; < L *vērisimil(is)* (*vērī,* gen. sing. of *vērum* truth, + *similis* like) + -AR[1]] —**ver′i·sim′i·lar·ly,** *adv.*

ver·i·si·mil·i·tude (ver′ə si mil′i to͞od′, -tyo͞od′), *n.* **1.** the appearance or semblance of truth; likelihood; probability: *The play lacked verisimilitude.* **2.** something, as an assertion, having merely the appearance of truth. [1595–1605; < L *vērisimilitūdō,* equiv. to *vērī* (gen. sing. of *vērum* truth) + *similitūdō* SIMILITUDE]

ver·ism (vēr′iz əm, ver′-), *n.* the theory that rigid representation of truth and reality is essential to art and literature, and therefore the ugly and vulgar must be included. [1890–95; < L *vēr(um)* truth + -ISM; cf. VERISMO] —**ver′ist,** *n., adj.* —**ve·ris′tic,** *adj.*

ve·ris·mo (və riz′mō; *It.* ve rēz′mô), *n.* the use of everyday life and actions in artistic works: introduced into opera in the early 1900's in reaction to contemporary conventions, which were seen as artificial and untruthful. [1905–10; < It: realism, equiv. to *ver(o)* true (< L *vērus*) + *-ismo* -ISM]

Ve·rís·si·mo (və rē′si mo͞o), *n.* **É·ri·co Lo·pes** (e′ʀi-ko͞o lô′pəs), born 1905, Brazilian novelist.

ver·i·ta·ble (ver′i tə bəl), *adj.* **1.** being truly or very much so: *a veritable triumph.* **2.** *Obs.* true, as a statement or tale. [1425–75; late ME < AF, MF. See VERITY, -ABLE] —**ver′i·ta·ble·ness,** *n.* —**ver′i·ta·bly,** *adv.*
—**Syn. 1.** real, genuine; utter. See **authentic.**

ve·ri·tas (wä′ʀi täs′; *Eng.* ver′i tas′, -täs′), *n. Latin.* truth.

vé·ri·té (vā ʀē tā′), *n. French.* **1.** truth; truthfulness. **2.** See **cinéma vérité.**

ver·i·ty (ver′i tē), *n., pl.* **-ties** for 2. **1.** the state or quality of being true; accordance with fact or reality: *to question the verity of a statement.* **2.** something that is true, as a principle, belief, idea, or statement: *the eternal verities.* [1325–75; ME < L *vēritās,* equiv. to *vēr(us)* true + *-itās* -ITY]

ver·juice (vûr′jo͞os′), *n.* **1.** an acid liquor made from the sour juice of crab apples, unripe grapes, etc., formerly much used for culinary and other purposes. **2.** sourness, as of temper or expression. —*adj.* Also, **ver′·juiced′. 3.** of or pertaining to verjuice. **4.** sour in temper, expression, etc. [1275–1325; ME *verjuis* < MF *vertjus,* equiv. to *vert* green (< L *viridis*) + *jus* JUICE]

Ver·khne·u·dinsk (vûʀkн′nə o͞o′dinsk; *Russ.* vyiʀ-кнnyi o͞o′dyinsk), *n.* former name of **Ulan Ude.**

Ver·laine (veʀ len′), *n.* **Paul** (pôl), 1844–96, French poet.

Ver·meer (vər mēr′; *Du.* vəʀ mâʀ′), *n.* **Jan** (yän), (*Jan van der Meer van Delft*), 1632–75, Dutch painter.

ver·meil (vûr′mil, -māl *or, esp. for 2,* vər mā′), *n.* **1.** vermilion red. **2.** metal, as silver or bronze, that has been gilded. —*adj.* **3.** of the color vermilion. [1350–1400; ME < MF < LL *vermiculus* kermes (insect and dye), L: larva, grub; see VERMICULE]

vermi-, a combining form meaning "worm," used in the formation of compound words: *vermifuge.* [comb. form of L *vermis* WORM]

ver·mi·an (vûr′mē ən), *adj.* **1.** resembling or of the nature of a worm. **2.** of or pertaining to worms. [1875–80; < L *vermi(s)* WORM + -AN]

ver·mi·cel·li (vûr′mi chel′ē, -sel′ē), *n.* a kind of pasta in the form of long, slender, solid threads, resembling spaghetti but thinner. Cf. **macaroni** (def. 1). [1660–70; < It, pl. of *vermicello,* dim. of *verme* worm < L *vermis*]

ver·mi·cide (vûr′mə sīd′), *n.* a substance or agent used to kill worms, esp. a drug used to kill parasitic intestinal worms. [1840–50; VERMI- + -CIDE] —**ver′mi·cid′al,** *adj.*

ver·mic·u·lar (vər mik′yə lər), *adj.* **1.** of, pertaining to, or done by worms. **2.** consisting of or characterized by sinuous or wavy outlines or markings resembling the form or tracks of a worm. [1645–55; < ML *vermiculāris,* equiv. to L *vermicul(us)* VERMICULE + *-āris* -AR[1]] —**ver·mic′u·lar·ly,** *adv.*

ver·mic·u·late (*v.* vər mik′yə lāt′; *adj.* vər mik′yə lit, -lāt′), *v.,* **-lat·ed, -lat·ing,** *adj.* —*v.t.* **1.** to work or ornament with wavy lines or markings resembling the form or tracks of a worm. —*adj.* Also, **ver·mic·u·lat·ed** (vər mik′yə lā′tid). **2.** worm-eaten, or appearing as if worm-eaten. **3.** vermicular. **4.** sinuous; tortuous; intricate: *vermiculate thought processes.* [1595–1605; < L *vermiculātus* (ptp. of *vermiculārī* to be worm-eaten). See VERMICULE, -ATE[1]] —**ver·mic′u·la′tion,** *n.*

CONCISE ETYMOLOGY KEY: <, descended or borrowed from; >, whence; b., blend of, blended; c., cognate with; cf., compare; deriv., derivative; equiv., equivalent; imit., imitative; obl., oblique; r., replacing; s., stem; sp., spelling, spelled; resp., respelling, respelled; trans., translation; ?, origin unknown; *, unattested; ‡, probably earlier than. See the full key inside the front cover.

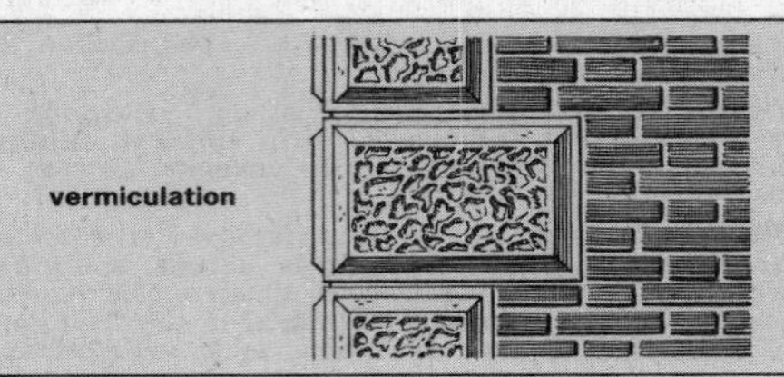
vermiculation

ver·mi·cule (vûr′mi kyo͞ol′), *n. Zool.* a small, wormlike structure. [1705–15; < L *vermiculus* larva, maggot. See VERMI-, -CULE[1]]

ver·mic·u·lite (vər mik′yə līt′), *n.* any of a group of platy minerals, hydrous silicates of aluminum, magnesium, and iron, that expand markedly on being heated: used in the expanded state for heat insulation and as a plant growth medium. [1815–25, *Amer.;* VERMICUL(AR) + -ITE[1]]

ver·mi·cul·ture (vûr′mi kul′chər), *n.* the raising and production of earthworms and their by-products. [VERMI- + CULTURE]

ver·mi·form (vûr′mə fôrm′), *adj.* resembling a worm in shape; long and slender. [1720–30; < ML *vermiformis.* See VERMI-, -FORM]

ver′miform appen′dix, *Anat., Zool.* a narrow, blind tube protruding from the cecum, having no known useful function, in humans being 3 to 4 in. (8 to 10 cm) long and situated in the lower right-hand part of the abdomen. See diag. under **intestine.** Also called **appendix.** [1770–80]

ver′miform proc′ess, 1. See **vermiform appendix. 2.** the vermis. [1830–40]

ver·mi·fuge (vûr′mə fyo͞oj′), *adj.* **1.** serving to expel worms or other animal parasites from the intestines, as a medicine. —*n.* **2.** a vermifuge medicine or agent. [1690–1700; VERMI- + -FUGE]

ver·mil·ion (vər mil′yən), *n.* **1.** a brilliant scarlet red. **2.** a bright-red, water-insoluble pigment consisting of mercuric sulfide, once obtained from cinnabar, now usually produced by the reaction of mercury and sulfur. —*adj.* **3.** of the color vermilion. —*v.t.* **4.** to color with or as if with vermilion. [1250–1300; ME *vermilioun, vermillon* < AF, OF *verm(e)illon,* equiv. to *vermeil* VERMEIL + *-on* n. suffix]

Ver·mil·ion (vər mil′yən), *n.* a town in N Ohio. 11,012.

vermil′ion rock′fish, a scarlet-red rockfish, *Sebastes miniatus,* inhabiting waters along the Pacific coast of North America, important as a food fish. Also called **rasher.**

ver·min (vûr′min), *n., pl.* **ver·min. 1.** noxious, objectionable, or disgusting animals collectively, esp. those of small size that appear commonly and are difficult to control, as flies, lice, bedbugs, cockroaches, mice, and rats. **2.** an objectionable or obnoxious person, or such persons collectively. **3.** animals that prey upon game, as coyotes or weasels. [1300–50; ME *vermyne* < AF, MF *vermin, vermine* < VL **verminum,* **vermina,* based on L *vermin-;* see VERMINATE]

ver·mi·nate (vûr′mə nāt′), *v.i.,* **-nat·ed, -nat·ing. 1.** to become infested with vermin, esp. parasitic vermin. **2.** *Archaic.* to breed or infest with vermin. [1685–95; < L *verminātus,* ptp. of *vermināre* to be infested with maggots, to have racking pains, equiv. to *vermin(a)* racking pain + *-ātus* -ATE[1]; dual sense of *vermināre* by assoc. with *vermis* worm, maggot, *vermin-* being taken, perh. erroneously, as an extended s. of this word] —**ver′mi·na′tion,** *n.*

ver·min·ous (vûr′mə nəs), *adj.* **1.** of the nature of or resembling vermin. **2.** of, pertaining to, or caused by vermin: *verminous diseases.* **3.** infested with vermin, esp. parasitic vermin: *verminous shacks.* [1610–20; < L *verminōsus* infested with maggots; see VERMINATE, -OUS] —**ver′min·ous·ly,** *adv.* —**ver′min·ous·ness,** *n.*

ver·mis (vûr′mis), *n., pl.* **-mes** (-mēz). *Anat.* the median lobe or division of the cerebellum. See diag. under **brain.** [1885–90; < NL; L: WORM; so called from its shape]

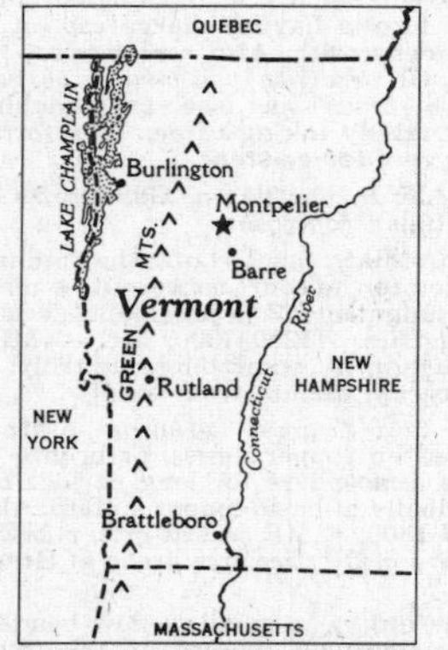

Ver·mont (vər mont′), *n.* a state of the NE United States: a part of New England. 511,456; 9609 sq. mi. (24,885 sq. km). *Cap.:* Montpelier. *Abbr.:* VT (for use with zip code), Vt.

Ver·mont·er (vər mon′tər), *n.* a native or inhabitant of Vermont. [1770–80, *Amer.;* VERMONT + -ER[1]]

ver·mouth (vər mo͞oth′), *n.* an aromatized white wine in which herbs, roots, barks, bitters, and other flavorings have been steeped. [1800–10; < F (now *vermout*) < G *Wermuth* (now *Wermut*) absinthe, WORMWOOD]

vermouth′ cassis′, a mixed drink made with dry vermouth, crème de cassis, soda or mineral water, and cracked ice. [< F; see VERMOUTH, CRÈME DE CASSIS]

Vern (vûrn), *n.* a male given name, form of **Vernon.**

Ver·na (vûr′nə), *n.* a female given name.

ver·nac·u·lar (vər nak′yə lər, və nak′-), *adj.* **1.** (of language) native or indigenous (opposed to *literary* or *learned*). **2.** expressed or written in the native language of a place, as literary works: *a vernacular poem.* **3.** using such a language: *a vernacular speaker.* **4.** of or pertaining to such a language. **5.** using plain, everyday, ordinary language. **6.** of, pertaining to, or characteristic of architectural vernacular. **7.** noting or pertaining to the common name for a plant or animal. **8.** *Obs.* (of a disease) endemic. —*n.* **9.** the native speech or language of a place. **10.** the language or vocabulary peculiar to a class or profession. **11.** a vernacular word or expression. **12.** the plain variety of language in everyday use by ordinary people. **13.** the common name of an animal or plant as distinguished from its Latin scientific name. **14.** a style of architecture exemplifying the commonest techniques, decorative features, and materials of a particular historical period, region, or group of people. **15.** any medium or mode of expression that reflects popular taste or indigenous styles. [1595–1605; < L *vernācul(us)* household, domestic, native (appar. adj. use of *vernāculus,* dim. of *verna* slave born in the master's household, though derivation unclear) + -AR[1]] —**ver·nac′u·lar·ly,** *adv.*
—**Syn. 9, 10.** See **language.**

ver·nac·u·lar·ism (vər nak′yə lə riz′əm, və nak′-), *n.* **1.** a vernacular word or expression. **2.** the use of the vernacular. [1840–50; VERNACULAR + -ISM]

ver·nac·u·lar·ize (vər nak′yə lə rīz′, və nak′-), *v.t.,* **-ized, -iz·ing.** to translate into the natural speech peculiar to a people. Also, *esp. Brit.,* **ver·nac′u·lar·ise′.** [1815–25; VERNACULAR + -IZE] —**ver·nac′u·lar·i·za′·tion,** *n.*

ver·nal (vûr′nl), *adj.* **1.** of or pertaining to spring: *vernal sunshine.* **2.** appearing or occurring in spring: *vernal migratory movements.* **3.** appropriate to or suggesting spring; springlike: *vernal greenery.* **4.** belonging to or characteristic of youth: *vernal longings.* [1525–35; < L *vernālis,* equiv. to *vern(us)* of spring (*vēr* spring + *-nus* adj. suffix) + *-ālis* -AL[1]] —**ver′nal·ly,** *adv.*
—**Syn. 4.** youthful, fresh, new.

ver′nal e′quinox, 1. See under **equinox** (def. 1). **2.** Also called **ver′nal point′.** the position of the sun at the time of the vernal equinox. [1525–35]

ver·nal·ize (vûr′nl īz′), *v.t.,* **-ized, -iz·ing.** to shorten the growth period of (a plant) by chilling or other special treatment of it, its seeds, or its bulbs. Also, *esp. Brit.,* **ver′nal·ise′.** [1820–30; VERNAL + -IZE] —**ver′nal·i·za′tion,** *n.*

ver·na·tion (vər nā′shən), *n. Bot.* the arrangement of the foliage leaves within the bud. [1785–95; < NL *vernātiōn-* (s. of *vernātiō*), equiv. to L *vernāt(us)* (ptp. of *vernāre* to be verdant; see VERNAL, -ATE[1]) + *-iōn-* -ION]

Verne (vûrn; *Fr.* veʀn), *n.* **1. Jules** (jo͞olz; *Fr.* zhyl), 1828–1905, French novelist. **2.** a male given name, form of **Vernon.**

Ver·ner (vûr′nər, vâr′-; *Dan.* veʀ′nəʀ), *n.* **1. Karl A·dolph** (kärl ä′dolf), 1846–96, Danish linguist. **2.** a male given name, form of **Warner.**

Ver′ner's law′, *Ling.* the statement by K. Verner of a regularity behind some apparent exceptions in the Germanic languages to Grimm's law, namely, that Proto-Germanic voiceless fricatives became voiced when between voiced sounds if the immediately preceding vowel was not accented in Proto-Indo-European. [1890–95]

Ver·net (veʀ ne′), *n.* **1. Claude Jo·seph** (klōd zhô-zef′), 1714–89, French painter. **2.** his grandson **(É·mile Jean) Hor·ace** (ā mēl′ zhäN ô ʀas′), 1789–1863, French painter.

Verneuil′ proc′ess (vûr noi′; *Fr.* veʀ nœ′yᵊ), a process for making synthetic rubies, sapphires, spinels, etc., by the fusion at high temperatures of powdered compounds. Also called **flame-fusion process.** [named after A.V.L. *Verneuil,* 19th-century French mineralogist]

ver·ni·cle (vûr′ni kəl), *n.* (*sometimes cap.*) veronica[1]. [1325–75; ME < OF < ML *vernicula,* var. (after L dims. in *-cula* CULE[1]) of *veronica* VERONICA[1]]

ver·ni·er (vûr′nē ər), *n.* **1.** Also, **ver′nier scale′.** a small, movable, graduated scale running parallel to the fixed graduated scale of a sextant, theodolite, barometer, etc., and used for measuring a fractional part of one of the divisions of the fixed scale. See illus. under **sextant. 2.** *Mach.* an auxiliary device for giving a piece of apparatus a higher adjustment accuracy. —*adj.* **3.** equipped with a vernier: *a vernier barometer.* [1760–70; named after P. VERNIER]

Ver·nier (vûr′nē ər; *Fr.* veʀ nyā′), *n.* **Pierre** (pyeʀ), 1580–1637, French mathematician and inventor.

ver′nier cal′iper, a caliper formed of two pieces sliding across one another, one having a graduated scale and the other a vernier. Also called **ver′nier microm′eter.** [1875–80]

vernier caliper

ver′nier com′pass, *Survey.* a compass on a transit (**ver′nier tran′sit**) having a vernier for adjusting magnetic bearings to read as true bearings.

ver′nier en′gine, *Rocketry.* a small, low-thrust rocket engine for correcting the heading and velocity of a long-range ballistic missile.

ver•nis mar•tin (ver nē′ mär tan′; *Fr.* ver nē mar-tan′), a finish for furniture, invented in France in the 18th century in imitation of Chinese lacquer. Also, **vernis′ Martin′.** [1875–80; < F: lit., Martin varnish, named after the brothers *Martin,* 18th-century French craftsmen]

ver•nis•sage (ver′nə säzh′; *Fr.* ver nē sazh′), *n., pl.* **-sages** (-sä′zhiz; *Fr.* -sazh′). **1.** Also called **varnishing day.** the day before the opening of an art exhibition traditionally reserved for the artist to varnish the paintings. **2.** a reception at a gallery for an artist whose show is about to open to the public. [1910–15; < F: lit., a varnishing, touching up (of paintings). See VARNISH, -AGE]

ver•nix ca•se•o•sa (vûr′niks kā′sē ō′sə), *Med.* the fatty matter, consisting chiefly of dead epidermal cells and sebaceous secretions, covering the skin of a fetus and newborn. [< NL: cheeselike varnish]

Ver•no•le•ninsk (vûr′nl ə ninsk′; *Russ.* vyir nə lyi-nyĕnsk′), *n.* former name of **Nikolayev.**

Ver•non (vûr′nən), *n.* **1. Edward** ("*Old Grog*"), 1684–1757, British admiral. **2.** a town in N Connecticut. 27,974. **3.** a city in S British Columbia, in SW Canada. 19,987. **4.** a city in N Texas. 12,695. **5.** a male given name: from a Latin word meaning "springlike."

Ver•ny (vyer′nē), *n.* former name of **Alma-Ata.**

Ve′ro Beach′ (vēr′ō), a town in central Florida. 16,176.

Ve•ro•na (və rō′nə; *for 1 also It.* ve rô′nä), *n.* **1.** a city in N Italy, on the Adige River. 271,451. **2.** a town in NE New Jersey. 14,166.

Ve•ro•nese (ver′ə nēz′, -nēs′), *adj., n., pl.* **-nese.** —*adj.* **1.** of or pertaining to the city or town of Verona. —*n.* **2.** a native or inhabitant of Verona. [1750–60; VERON(A) + -ESE]

Ve•ro•ne•se (ver′ə nā′zē; *It.* ve′rô ne′ze), *n.* **Pa•o•lo** (pä′ô lô), (*Paolo Cagliari*), 1528–88, Venetian painter.

ve•ron•i•ca[1] (və ron′i kə), *n.* (*sometimes cap.*) **1.** the image of the face of Christ, said to have been impressed on the handkerchief or veil that St. Veronica gave to Him to wipe His face on the way to Calvary. **2.** the handkerchief or veil itself. **3.** Also called **sudarium.** any handkerchief, veil, or cloth bearing a representation of the face of Christ. Also called **vernicle.** [1690–1700; < ML *veronica,* alleged to be an alter. of *vēra iconica* true image (see VERY, ICON), subsequently also taken as the name of the woman who gave Christ the cloth]

ve•ron•i•ca[2] (və ron′i kə), *n.* any of numerous plants belonging to the genus *Veronica,* of the figwort family, having opposite leaves and clusters of small flowers, as the speedwell. [1520–30; < NL or ML, perh. after VERONICA[1] or St. *Veronica* (but cf. MGk *berenikion* plant name, equiv. to *Bereník(ē)* proper name + *-ion* dim. suffix)]

ve•ron•i•ca[3] (və ron′i kə), *n.* (in bullfighting) a pass in which the matador keeps his feet and legs absolutely still while slowly swinging the open cape away from the charging bull. [1925–30; < Sp *verónica* prob. lit., VERONICA[1]]

Ve•ron•i•ca (və ron′i kə), *n.* a female given name. Also, **Ve•ron′i•ka.**

Ver•ra•za•no (ver′ə zä′nō; *It.* ver′rä tsä′nô), *n.* **Gio•van•ni da** (jô vän′nē dä), c1480–1527?, Italian navigator and explorer. Also, **Ver•raz•za•no** (ver′rät tsä′nô), **Ver•ra•za•ni** (ver′rä tsä′nē).

Ver•ra•za′no-Nar′rows Bridge′ (ver′ə zä′nō-nar′ōz, -əd zä′-), a suspension bridge connecting Brooklyn and Staten Island in New York City. 4260-ft. (1298-m) center span, the longest in North America.

ver•ri•ère (ver′ē âr′; *Fr.* ve ryer′), *n., pl.* **ver•ri•ères** (ver′ē ârz′; *Fr.* ve ryer′). a French bowl similar to a monteith in form and use. [< F: glass stand, frame]

Ver•roc•chio (və rō′kē ō′; *It.* ver rôk′kyô), *n.* **An•dre•a del** (än dre′ä del), 1435–88, Italian goldsmith, sculptor, and painter.

ver•ru•ca (və rōō′kə, ve-), *n., pl.* **-cae** (-sē). **1.** *Med.* a wart. **2.** *Zool.* a small, flattish, wartlike prominence. [1555–65; < L *verrūca*]

verru′ca vul•ga′ris (vul gâr′əs), the common wart. [1900–05; < NL *verrūca vulgāris,* L]

ver•ru•cose (ver′ə kōs′, və rōō′kōs), *adj.* studded with wartlike protuberances or elevations. [1580–90; VERRUC(A) + -OSE[1]] —**ver•ru•cos•i•ty** (ver′ə kos′i tē), **ver′ru•cose′ness,** *n.*

ver•ru•cous (ver′ə kəs, və rōō′-), *adj.* of, pertaining to, marked by, or like a wart or warts. [1650–60; var. of VERRUCOSE; see -OUS]

vers., *Trig.* See **versed sine.**

Ver•sailles (ver sī′, vər- *or, Fr.* ver sä′yᵊ), *n.* a city in and the capital of Yvelines, in N France, ab. 12 mi. (19 km) SW of Paris: palace of the French kings; peace treaty between the Allies and Germany 1919. 97,133.

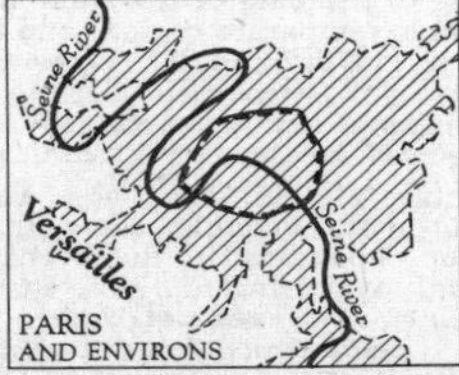

ver•sal (vûr′səl), *adj. Archaic.* universal or whole. [1585–95; shortening of UNIVERSAL; cf. VARSITY]

ver•sant (vûr′sənt), *n.* **1.** a slope of a mountain or mountain chain. **2.** the general slope of a country or region. [1850–55; < F, n. use of prp. of *verser* to turn < L *versāre,* freq. of *vertere* to turn; see VERSE, -ANT]

ver•sa•tile (vûr′sə tl *or, esp. Brit.,* -tīl′), *adj.* **1.** capable of or adapted for turning easily from one to another of various tasks, fields of endeavor, etc.: *a versatile writer.* **2.** having or capable of many uses: *a versatile tool.* **3.** *Bot.* attached at or near the middle so as to swing freely, as an anther. **4.** *Zool.* turning either forward or backward: *a versatile toe.* **5.** variable or changeable, as in feeling, purpose, or policy: *versatile moods.* [1595–1605; < L *versātilis* revolving, many-sided, equiv. to *versāt(us)* (ptp. of *versāre,* freq. of *vertere* to turn; see VERSE, -ATE[1]) + *-ilis* -ILE] —**ver′sa•tile•ly,** *adv.* —**ver′sa•til′i•ty, ver′sa•tile•ness,** *n.*
—**Syn. 1, 2.** adaptable, all-around. **2.** handy.

versatile (def. 3) A, versatile anthers

vers de so•cié•té (ver də sô syā tā′; *Eng.* ver′ də sō′sē i tā′), *French.* humorous light verse dealing with fashions and foibles of the time.

verse (vûrs), *n., adj., v.,* **versed, vers•ing.** —*n.* **1.** (not in technical use) a stanza. **2.** a succession of metrical feet written, printed, or orally composed as one line; one of the lines of a poem. **3.** a particular type of metrical line: *a hexameter verse.* **4.** a poem, or piece of poetry. **5.** metrical composition; poetry, esp. as involving metrical form. **6.** metrical writing distinguished from poetry because of its inferior quality: *a writer of verse, not poetry.* **7.** a particular type of metrical composition: *elegiac verse.* **8.** the collective poetry of an author, period, nation, etc.: *Miltonian verse; American verse.* **9.** one of the short conventional divisions of a chapter of the Bible. **10.** *Music.* **a.** that part of a song following the introduction and preceding the chorus. **b.** a part of a song designed to be sung by a solo voice. **11.** *Rare.* a line of prose, esp. a sentence, or part of a sentence, written as one line. **12.** *Rare.* a subdivision in any literary work. —*adj.* **13.** of, pertaining to, or written in verse: *a verse play.* —*v.i.* **14.** versify. —*v.t.* **15.** to express in verse. [bef. 900; ME *vers(e), fers* line of poetry, section of a psalm, OE *fers* < L *versus* a row, line (of poetry), lit., a turning, equiv. to *vert(ere)* to turn (ptp. *versus*) + *-tus* suffix of v. action, with *dt* > *s*; akin to -WARD, WORTH[2]]
—**Syn. 1.** VERSE, STANZA, STROPHE, STAVE are terms for a metrical grouping in poetic composition. VERSE is often mistakenly used for STANZA, but is properly only a single metrical line. A STANZA is a succession of lines (verses) commonly bound together by a rhyme scheme, and usually forming one of a series of similar groups that constitute a poem: *The four-line stanza is the one most frequently used in English.* STROPHE (originally the section of a Greek choral ode sung while the chorus was moving from right to left) is in English poetry practically equivalent to "section"; a STROPHE may be unrhymed or without strict form, but may be a stanza: *Strophes are divisions of odes.* STAVE is a word (now seldom used) that means a stanza set to music or intended to be sung: *a stave of a hymn; a stave of a drinking song.* **4, 5, 6.** See **poetry.**

versed (vûrst), *adj.* experienced; practiced; skilled; learned (usually fol. by *in*): *She was well versed in Greek and Latin.* [1600–10; < L *versātus* busied, engaged (see VERSATILE), with -ED[2] for L *-ātus*]

versed′ co′sine. See **coversed sine.**

versed′ sine′, *Trig.* one minus the cosine of a given angle or arc. *Abbr.:* vers. Also called **versine, versin.** [1590–1600]

vers•et (vûr′sit), *n.* **1.** *Pros.* a brief verse, esp. from Scripture. **2.** *Music.* a brief piece for pipe organ, formerly used as part of the music for the Catholic Mass. **3.** *Archaic.* versicle. [1175–1225; ME < OF. See VERSE, -ET]

ver•si•cle (vûr′si kəl), *n.* **1.** a little verse. **2.** *Eccles.* a short verse, usually from the Psalms, said or sung by the officiant, after which the congregation recites a response. Cf. **response** (def. 3a). [1350–1400; ME < L *versiculus.* See VERSE, -I-, -CLE[1]]

ver•si•col•or (vûr′si kul′ər), *adj.* **1.** changeable in color: *versicolor skies.* **2.** of various colors; parti-colored: *a versicolor flower arrangement.* Also, *esp. Brit.,* **ver′si•col′our.** [1620–30; < L, equiv. to *vers(us)* ptp. of *vertere* to turn (see VERSE) + *-i-* -I- + *color* COLOR]

ver•sic•u•lar (vər sik′yə lər), *adj.* of or consisting of verses. [1805–15; < L *versicul(us)* VERSICLE + -AR[1]]

ver•sie•ra (vers yâr′ə, vûrs-), *n. Geom.* See **witch of Agnesi.** [< It: witch, fem. of OIt *aversiere* < OF, OPr *aversier* devil < L *adversārius* ADVERSARY]

ver•si•fi•ca•tion (vûr′sə fi kā′shən), *n.* **1.** the act of versifying. **2.** verse form; metrical structure. **3.** a metrical version of something. **4.** the art or practice of composing verses. [1595–1605; < L *versificātiōn-* (s. of *versificātiō*), equiv. to *versificāt(us)* (ptp. of *versificāre* to VERSIFY; see -ATE[1]) + *-iōn-* -ION]

ver•si•fy (vûr′sə fī′), *v.,* **-fied, -fy•ing.** —*v.t.* **1.** to relate, describe, or treat (something) in verse. **2.** to convert (prose or other writing) into metrical form. —*v.i.* **3.** to compose verses. [1350–1400; ME *versifien* < OF *versifier* < L *versificāre.* See VERSE, -IFY] —**ver′si•fi′er,** *n.*

ver•sine (vûr′sīn), *n. Trig.* See **versed sine.** Also, **ver′sin.**

ver•sion (vûr′zhən, -shən), *n.* **1.** a particular account of some matter, as from one person or source, contrasted with some other account: *two different versions of the accident.* **2.** a particular form or variant of something: *a modern version of an antique.* **3.** a translation. **4.** (*often cap.*) a translation of the Bible or a part of it. **5.** *Med.* the act of turning a child in the uterus so as to bring it into a more favorable position for delivery. **6.** *Pathol.* an abnormal direction of the axis of the uterus or other organ. [1575–85; < L *versiōn-* (s. of *versiō*) a turning, equiv. to *vers(us)* (ptp. of *vertere* to turn; see VERSE) + *-iōn-* -ION] —**ver′sion•al,** *adj.*
—**Syn. 1.** story, impression. **3.** See **translation.**

vers li•bre (ver′ lē′brə; *Fr.* ver lē′brᵊ). See **free verse.** [1915–20; < F]

vers-li•brist (vâr lē′brist), *n.* a person who writes free verse. [1915–20; see VERS-LIBRISTE]

vers-li•briste (vâr′lē brēst′; *Fr.* ver lē brēst′), *n., pl.* **-li•bristes** (-lē brēsts′; *Fr.* -lē brēst′). vers-librist. [< F; see VERS LIBRE, -IST]

ver•so (vûr′sō), *n., pl.* **-sos.** *Print.* a left-hand page of an open book or manuscript (opposed to *recto*). [1830–40; short for L *in versō foliō* on the turned leaf]

verst (vûrst, verst), *n.* a Russian measure of distance equivalent to 3500 feet or 0.6629 mile or 1.067 kilometers. Also, **verste, werste.** [1545–55; < F *verste* or G *Werst* < Russ *verstá;* ORuss *vĭrsta* age, agemate, pair, measure of length, c. Czech *vrstva,* Pol *warstwa* layer, Serbo-Croatian *vŕsta* sort, kind, OCS *vrĭsta* age, time of life < Slavic **vĭrsta* lit., turn, bend, akin to **vert-* turn (v. base), L *vertere* to turn (see CONVERT, VERSE)]

ver•sus (vûr′səs, -səz), *prep.* **1.** against (used esp. to indicate an action brought by one party against another in a court of law, or to denote competing teams or players in a sports contest): *Smith versus Jones; Army versus Navy.* **2.** as compared to or as one of two choices; in contrast with: *traveling by plane versus traveling by train. Abbr.:* v., vs. [1400–50; late ME < L: towards, i.e., turned so as to face (something), opposite, over against, orig. ptp. of *vertere* to turn; see VERSE]

vert (vûrt), *n.* **1.** *Eng. Forest Law.* **a.** vegetation bearing green leaves in a forest and capable of serving as a cover for deer. **b.** the right to cut such vegetation. **2.** *Heraldry.* the tincture, or color, green. —*adj.* **3.** *Heraldry.* of the tincture green: *a lion vert.* [1400–50; late ME *verte* < AF, MF *vert, verd* < L *viridis* green, equiv. to *vir(ēre)* to be green + *-idis,* appar. irreg. for *-idus* -ID[4]]

vert., vertical.

vertebr-, a combining form of **vertebra:** *vertebral.*

ver•te•bra (vûr′tə brə), *n., pl.* **-brae** (-brē′, -brā′), **-bras.** *Anat., Zool.* any of the bones or segments composing the spinal column, consisting typically of a cylindrical body and an arch with various processes, and forming a foramen, or opening, through which the spinal cord passes. [1570–80; < L: (spinal) joint, equiv. to *verte(re)* to turn (see VERSE) + *-bra* n. suffix]

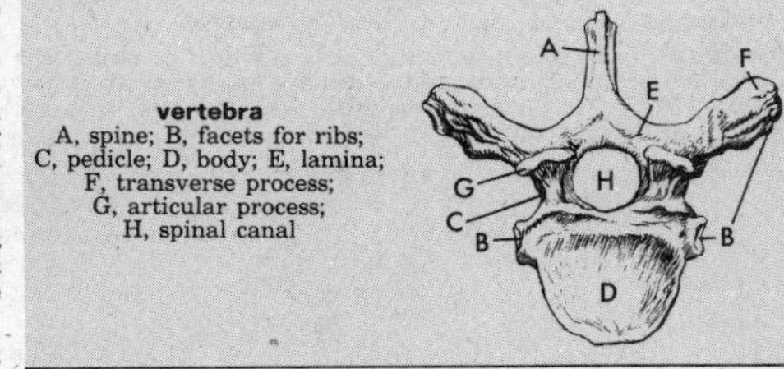

vertebra A, spine; B, facets for ribs; C, pedicle; D, body; E, lamina; F, transverse process; G, articular process; H, spinal canal

ver•te•bral (vûr′tə brəl), *adj.* **1.** of or pertaining to a vertebra or the vertebrae; spinal. **2.** resembling a vertebra. **3.** composed of or having vertebrae. [1675–85; VERTEBR(A) + -AL[1]] —**ver′te•bral•ly,** *adv.*

ver′tebral canal′. See **spinal canal.** [1825–35]

ver′tebral col′umn. See **spinal column.** [1815–25]

Ver•te•bra•ta (vûr′tə brā′tə, -brä′-), *n.* the subphylum comprising the vertebrate animals. [1820–30; < NL, neut. pl. of L *vertebrātus* VERTEBRATE]

ver•te•brate (vûr′tə brit, -brāt′), *adj.* **1.** having vertebrae; having a backbone or spinal column. **2.** belonging or pertaining to the Vertebrata (or Craniata), a subphylum of chordate animals, comprising those having a brain enclosed in a skull or cranium and a segmented spinal column; a major taxonomic group that includes mammals, birds, reptiles, amphibians, and fishes. —*n.* **3.** a vertebrate animal. [1820–30; < L *vertebrātus* jointed. See VERTEBRA, -ATE[1]]

ver•te•brat•ed (vûr′tə brā′tid), *adj.* **1.** having vertebrae; vertebral; vertebrate. **2.** composed of or having segments resembling vertebrae. [1820–30; VERTEBRATE + -ED[2]]

ver•te•bra•tion (vûr′tə brā′shən), *n.* vertebrate formation. [1880–85; VERTEBRATE + -ION]

ver•te•bra•tus (vûr′tə brā′təs), *adj. Meteorol.* (of a cloud) having elements arranged in a riblike pattern. [< NL; see VERTEBRATE]

ver•tex (vûr′teks), *n., pl.* **-tex•es, -ti•ces** (-tə sēz′). **1.**

CONCISE PRONUNCIATION KEY: act, cāpe, dâre, pärt; set, ēqual; if, īce; ox, ōver, ôrder, oil, bŏŏk, bōōt, out; up, ûrge; child; sing; shoe; thin, *th*at; zh as in *treasure.* ə = *a* as in *alone, e* as in *system, i* as in *easily, o* as in *gallop, u* as in *circus;* ᵊ as in *fire* (fīᵊr), *hour* (ouᵊr). l and n can serve as syllabic consonants, as in *cradle* (krād′l), and *button* (but′n). See the full key inside the front cover.

the highest point of something; apex; summit; top: *the vertex of a mountain.* **2.** *Anat., Zool.* the crown or top of the head. **3.** *Craniom.* the highest point on the midsaggital plane of the skull or head viewed from the left side when the skull or head is in the Frankfurt horizontal. **4.** *Astron.* a point in the celestial sphere toward which or from which the common motion of a group of stars is directed. **5.** *Geom.* **a.** the point farthest from the base: *the vertex of a cone or of a pyramid.* **b.** a point in a geometrical solid common to three or more sides. **c.** the intersection of two sides of a plane figure. [1560–70; < L: a whirl, top (of the head), equiv. to *vert(ere)* to turn + *-ex* (s. *-ic-*) n. suffix]

ver·ti·cal (vûr′ti kəl), *adj.* **1.** being in a position or direction perpendicular to the plane of the horizon; upright; plumb. **2.** of, pertaining to, or situated at the vertex. **3.** of or pertaining to the cranial vertex. **4.** *Bot.* **a.** (of a leaf) having the blade in a perpendicular plane, so that neither of the surfaces can be called upper or lower. **b.** being in the same direction as the axis; lengthwise. **5.** of, constituting, or resulting in vertical combination. **6.** of or pertaining to a product or service from initial planning to sale. **7.** of, pertaining to, or noting a stratified society, nation, etc. —*n.* **8.** something vertical, as a line or plane. **9.** a vertical or upright position. **10.** a vertical structural member in a truss. [1550–60; < L *verticālis,* equiv. to *vertic-* (s. of *vertex*) VERTEX + *-ālis* -AL[1]] —**ver′ti·cal′i·ty, ver′ti·cal·ness, ver′ti·cal·ism,** *n.* —**ver′ti·cal·ly,** *adv.*
—**Syn. 1.** See **upright.** —**Ant. 1.** horizontal.

ver′tical an′gle, *Geom.* one of two opposite and equal angles formed by the intersection of two lines. [1565–75]

ver′tical cir′cle, *Astron.* a great circle on the celestial sphere passing through the zenith. [1550–60]

ver′tical combina′tion, the integration within one company of individual businesses working separately in related phases of the production and sale of a product. Also called **ver′tical integra′tion.**

ver′tical divest′iture, the disposal of some or all the subsidiaries that make up a company's vertical combination through voluntary sale or legal compulsion. [1970–75]

ver′tical envel′opment, *Mil.* envelopment of an enemy accomplished by parachuting and landing airborne troops at the rear of the enemy's position.

ver′tical file′, 1. a collection of pamphlets, pictures, clippings, or other materials stored upright, as in a filing cabinet or cabinets. **2.** a cabinet for such storage. [1905–10]

ver′tical lift′ bridge′. See **lift bridge.** Also, **ver′ti·cal-lift′ bridge′.**

ver′tical mobil′ity, *Sociol.* **1.** movement from one social level to a higher one **(upward mobility)** or a lower one **(downward mobility),** as by changing jobs or marrying. **2.** cultural diffusion from one social level to another, as the adoption by one economic class of the fashions current or formerly current in a higher class. Cf. **horizontal mobility.**

ver′tical sta′bilizer, *Aeron.* the fixed vertical surface of an aircraft empennage, to which the rudder is hinged. Also called **fin, ver′tical fin′.**

ver′tical un′ion. See **industrial union.** [1930–35]

ver·ti·ces (vûr′tə sēz′), *n.* a pl. of **vertex.**

ver·ti·cil (vûr′tə sil), *n. Bot., Zool.* a whorl or circle, as of leaves or hairs, arranged around a point on an axis. [1695–1705; < L *verticillus* spindle whorl, equiv. to *vertic-* (s. of *vertex*) VERTEX + *-illus* dim. suffix]

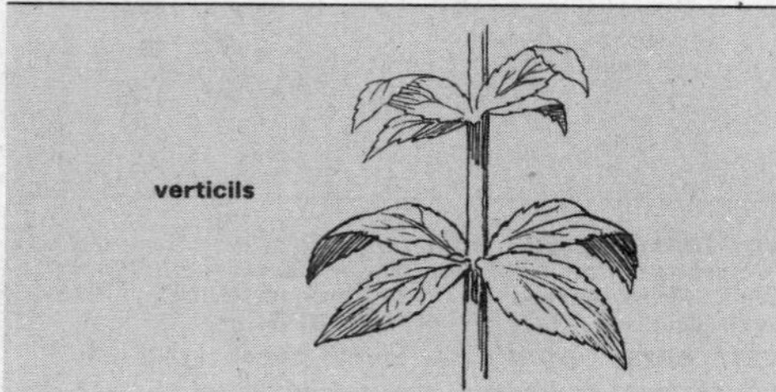
verticils

ver·ti·cil·las·ter (vûr′tə si las′tər), *n. Bot.* an inflorescence in which the flowers are arranged in a seeming whorl, consisting in fact of a pair of opposite axillary, usually sessile, cymes, as in many mints. [1825–35; < L *verticill(us)* VERTICIL + -ASTER[1]] —**ver·ti·cil·las·trate** (vûr′tə si las′trāt, -trit), *adj.*

ver·tic·il·late (vər tis′ə lit, -lāt′, vûr′tə sil′āt, -it), *adj. Biol.* **1.** disposed in or forming verticils or whorls, as flowers or hairs. **2.** having flowers, hairs, etc., so arranged or disposed. Also, **ver·tic′il·lat′ed.** [1660–70; < L *verticill(us)* VERTICIL + -ATE[1]] —**ver·tic′il·late·ly,** *adv.* —**ver·tic′il·la′tion,** *n.*

ver·ti·cil′li·um wilt′ (vûr′tə sil′ē əm), *Plant Pathol.* a disease affecting many temperate-climate plants in hot weather, caused by soil-inhabiting fungi of the genus *Verticillium* and characterized by wilt, dulling or yellowing of leaf color, and withering near the base. [1940–45; < NL *Verticillium* a fungus genus; see VERTICIL, -IUM]

ver·tig·i·nous (vər tij′ə nəs), *adj.* **1.** whirling; spinning; rotary: *vertiginous currents of air.* **2.** affected with vertigo; dizzy. **3.** liable or threatening to cause vertigo: *a vertiginous climb.* **4.** apt to change quickly; unstable: *a vertiginous economy.* [1600–10; < L *vertīginōsus* dizzy, equiv. to *vertīgin-* (s. of *vertīgō*) VERTIGO + *-ōsus* -OUS] —**ver·tig′i·nous·ly,** *adv.* —**ver·tig′i·nous·ness,** *n.*

ver·ti·go (vûr′ti gō′), *n., pl.* **ver·ti·goes, ver·tig·i·nes** (vər tij′ə nēz′). *Pathol.* a dizzying sensation of tilting within stable surroundings or of being in tilting or spinning surroundings. [1520–30; < L *vertīgō* a turning or whirling round, equiv. to *vert(ere)* to turn (see VERSE) + *-īgō* n. suffix]

ver·ti·sol (vûr′tə sôl′, -sol′), *n.* a clay-rich soil in which deep cracks form during the dry season. Cf. **black land.** [1955–60; VERTI(CAL) + -SOL]

ver·tu (vər to͞o′, vûr′to͞o), *n.* virtu.

Ver·u·la·mi·an (ver′yo͞o lā′mē ən), *adj.* of or pertaining to Francis Bacon, Baron Verulam. [1665–75; *Verulam* + -IAN]

Ver·u·la·mi·um (ver′yo͞o lā′mē əm), *n.* ancient name of **St. Albans.**

ver·vain (vûr′vān), *n.* any plant belonging to the genus *Verbena,* of the verbena family, having elongated or flattened spikes of stalkless flowers. [1350–1400; ME *vervaine* < AF, MF *verveine* < L *verbēna* leafy twig, holy bough carried by priests]

ver′vain fam′ily. See **verbena family.**

verve (vûrv), *n.* **1.** enthusiasm or vigor, as in literary or artistic work; spirit: *Her latest novel lacks verve.* **2.** vivaciousness; liveliness; animation: *I like a teacher with plenty of verve.* **3.** *Archaic.* talent. [1690–1700; < F: enthusiasm, whim, chatter, appar. < L *verba* words, talk, pl. (taken in VL as fem. sing.) of *verbum* word; see VERB]

ver·velle (vûr vel′), *n. Armor.* any of a number of staples riveted along the base of a basinet to hold an aventail. [appar. < MF *vervelle,* OF *verviele* hinge, ring on a hawk's leash < VL **vertibellum,* dim. of LL *vertibulum,* re-formation of L *vertebra* joint, VERTEBRA]

ver·vet (vûr′vit), *n.* an African monkey, *Cercopithecus aethiops pygerythrus,* allied to the green monkey and the grivet, but distinguished by a rusty patch at the root of the tail. [1880–85; < F, equiv. to *ver(t)* green (see VERT) + *(gri)vet* GRIVET]

Ver·woerd (fər vo͞ort′), *n.* **Hen·drik Frensch** (hen′drik frens), 1901–66, South African political leader, born in the Netherlands: prime minister 1958–66.

ver·y (ver′ē), *adv., adj.,* (*Obs.*) **ver·i·er, ver·i·est.** —*adv.* **1.** in a high degree; extremely; exceedingly: *A giant is very tall.* **2.** (used as an intensive emphasizing superlatives or stressing identity or oppositeness): *the very best thing; in the very same place as before.* —*adj.* **3.** precise; particular: *That is the very item we want.* **4.** mere: *The very thought of it is distressing.* **5.** sheer; utter: *He wept from the very joy of knowing he was safe.* **6.** actual: *He was caught in the very act of stealing.* **7.** being such in the true or fullest sense of the term; extreme: *the very heart of the matter.* **8.** true; genuine; worthy of being called such: *the very God; a very fool.* **9.** rightful or legitimate. [1200–50; ME < AF; OF *verai* (F *vrai*) < VL **vērācus,* for L *vērāx* truthful, equiv. to *vē-r(us)* true (c. OE *wǣr,* G *wahr* true, correct) + *-āx* adj. suffix]
—**Syn. 5.** pure, simple, plain.
—**Usage.** Past participles that have become established as adjectives can, like most English adjectives, be modified by the adverb VERY: *a very driven person; We were very concerned for your safety.* VERY does not modify past participles that are clearly verbal; for example, *The lid was very sealed* is not an idiomatic construction, while *The lid was very tightly sealed* is. Sometimes confusion arises over whether a given past participle is adjectival and thus able to be modified by VERY without an intervening adverb. However, there is rarely any objection to the use of this intervening adverb, no matter how the past participle is functioning. Such use often occurs in edited writing: *We were very much relieved to find the children asleep. They were very greatly excited by the news. I feel very badly cheated.*

ver′y high′ fre′quency, any frequency between 30 and 300 megahertz. *Abbr.:* VHF

Very′ Large′ Array′, *Astron.* a set of 27 radio telescopes arranged in a Y-shaped pattern, each arm of which is approximately 13 mi. (21 km) long, and located near Socorro, N.M.; computer-processed data from the set provide high-resolution images of distant astronomical objects. *Abbr.:* VLA

ver′y large′ crude′ car′rier. See **VLCC** [1980–85]

ver′y large′ scale′ integra′tion, *Electronics.* See **VLSI.**

Ver′y lights′ (ver′ē), a variety of colored signal flares, fired from a special pistol **(Ver′y pis′tol).** [1910–15; after E. W. *Very* (1847–1907), U.S. inventor]

ver′y long′ base′line interferom′etry, *Radio Astron.* an interferometry technique that enhances angular resolution in the observation of radio signals from distant celestial objects, as quasars, by combining signals from several radio telescopes around the earth or such signals with those from an earth-orbiting satellite. *Abbr.:* VLBI

ver′y low′ fre′quency, any frequency between 3 and 30 kilohertz. *Abbr.:* VLF [1940–45]

Ver′y Rev′erend, the official form of address for officers of the clergy or religious orders below the rank of bishop, abbot, or abbess.

Ve·sa·li·us (vi sā′lē əs, -sāl′yəs), *n.* **An·dre·as** (än′drē äs′), 1514–64, Flemish anatomist.

Ve·sey (vē′zē), *n.* **Denmark,** 1767–1822, black freedman, born probably on St. Thomas, Danish West Indies: hanged as alleged leader of a slave insurrection, in Charleston, S.C.

ve·si·ca (və sī′kə, -sē′-, ves′i kə), *n., pl.* **-cae** (-sē, -sē′, -kē, -kē′). **1.** *Anat.* a bladder. **2.** See **vesica piscis.** [1675–85; < L *vēsīca*]

ves·i·cal (ves′i kəl), *adj.* **1.** of or pertaining to a vesica or bladder, esp. the urinary bladder. **2.** resembling a bladder, as in shape or form; elliptical. [1790–1800; < ML *vēsīcālis,* equiv. to L *vēsīc(a)* bladder + *-ālis* -AL[1]]

ves·i·cant (ves′i kənt), *adj.* **1.** producing a blister or blisters, as a medicinal substance; vesicating. —*n.* **2.** a vesicant agent or substance. **3.** (in chemical warfare) a chemical agent that causes burns and destruction of tissue both internally and externally. [1655–65; < NL *vēsīcant-* (s. of *vēsīcāns*), prp. of *vēsīcāre* to VESICATE; see -ANT]

ve·si·ca pis·cis (və sī′kə pī′sis, pis′is; və sē′kə pis′kis, ves′i kə), *Fine Arts.* an elliptical figure in pointed form, usually one made by the intersection of two arcs and used, esp. in early Christian art, as an emblem of Christ. [1800–10; < NL *vēsīca piscis* lit., bladder of a fish]

vesica piscis

ves·i·cate (ves′i kāt′), *v.t.,* **-cat·ed, -cat·ing.** to raise vesicles or blisters on; blister. [1650–60; < NL *vēsīcātus* (ptp. of *vēsīcāre* to blister), equiv. to *vēsīc(a)* (see VESICA) + *-ātus* -ATE[1]] —**ves′i·ca′tion,** *n.*

ves·i·ca·to·ry (ves′i kə tôr′ē, -tōr′ē, və sik′ə-), *adj., n., pl.* **-ries.** vesicant. [1595–1605; < NL *vēsīcātōrius.* See VESICATE, -TORY[1]]

ves·i·cle (ves′i kəl), *n.* **1.** a small sac or cyst. **2.** *Biol.* a small bladderlike cavity, esp. one filled with fluid. **3.** *Pathol.* a circumscribed elevation of the epidermis containing serous fluid; blister. **4.** *Geol.* a small, usually spherical cavity in a rock or mineral, formed by expansion of a gas or vapor before the enclosing body solidified. [1570–80; < L *vēsīcula* little bladder. See VESICA, -ULE]

ve·sic·u·lar (və sik′yə lər), *adj.* **1.** of or pertaining to a vesicle or vesicles. **2.** having the form of a vesicle. **3.** characterized by or consisting of vesicles. [1705–15; < NL *vēsīculāris,* equiv. to L *vēsīcul(a)* VESICLE + *-āris* -AR[1]] —**ve·sic′u·lar·ly,** *adv.*

vesic′ular exanthe′ma, *Vet. Pathol.* an infectious viral disease of swine, characterized by blisters on the snout, mucous membranes, and feet.

vesic′ular stomati′tis, *Vet. Pathol.* a disease of horses, swine, and cattle, similar in its symptoms to foot-and-mouth disease, and characterized by blisters on the lips, snout, and oral mucous membranes. [1900–05]

ve·sic·u·late (*adj.* və sik′yə lit, -lāt′; *v.* və sik′yə-lāt′), *adj., v.,* **-lat·ed, -lat·ing.** —*adj.* **1.** characterized by or covered with vesicles. **2.** of the nature of a vesicle. —*v.t., v.i.* **3.** to make or become vesicular. [1820–30; < NL *vēsīculātus,* equiv. to L *vēsīcul(a)* VESICLE + *-ātus* -ATE[1]] —**ve·sic′u·la′tion,** *n.*

Ves·pa·sian (ve spā′zhən, -zhē ən), *n.* (*Titus Flavius Sabinus Vespasianus*), A.D. 9–79, Roman emperor 70–79.

ves·per (ves′pər), *n.* **1.** (*cap.*) the evening star, esp. Venus; Hesper. **2.** Also called **ves′per bell′.** a bell rung at evening. **3. vespers,** (*sometimes cap.*) *Eccles.* **a.** a religious service in the late afternoon or the evening. **b.** the sixth of the seven canonical hours, or the service for it, occurring in the late afternoon or the evening. **c.** *Rom. Cath. Ch.* a part of the office to be said in the evening by those in major orders, frequently made a public ceremony in the afternoons or evenings of Sundays and holy days. **d.** evensong. **4.** *Archaic.* evening. —*adj.* **5.** of, pertaining to, appearing in, or proper to the evening. **6.** of or pertaining to vespers. [1350–1400; ME, partly < L: evening, evening star; partly < OF *vespres* evening service < ML *vesperās,* acc. pl. of L *vespera,* fem. var. of *vesper;* c. Gk *hésperos;* akin to WEST]

ves·per·al (ves′pər əl), *n. Eccles.* **1.** the part of an antiphonary containing the chants for vespers. **2.** a cloth used between offices to cover the altar cloth. [1615–25; < LL *vesperālis.* See VESPER, -AL[1]]

ves′per mouse′. See **white-footed mouse.** [1855–60, *Amer.*]

ves′per spar′row, a common finch, *Pooecetes gramineus,* of fields and pastures in North America, noted for its evening song. Also called **grass finch.** [1860–65, *Amer.*]

ves·per·tide (ves′pər tīd′), *n.* the period of vespers; evening. [1800–10; VESPER + TIDE[1]]

ves·per·til·i·o·nine (ves′pər til′ē ə nin′, -nin), *adj.* of or pertaining to the bats of the subfamily Vespertilioninae, common in temperate regions and including most familiar species. [1870–75; < NL *Vespertilionae,* equiv. to *Vespertilion-,* s. of *Vespertilio* a genus (L *vespertiliō* bat, deriv. of *vesper* evening; see VESPER) + *-inae* -INAE] —**ves·per·til·i·o·nid** (ves′pər til′ē ə nid), *n., adj.*

ves·per·tine (ves′pər tin, -tīn′), *adj.* **1.** of, pertaining to, or occurring in the evening: *vespertine stillness.* **2.** *Bot.* opening or expanding in the evening, as certain flowers. **3.** *Zool.* appearing or flying in the early evening; crepuscular. Also, **ves·per·ti·nal** (ves′pər tīn′l). [1495–1505; < L *vespertīnus,* equiv. to *vesper* VESPER + *-tīnus* adj. suffix]

CONCISE ETYMOLOGY KEY: <, descended or borrowed from; >, whence; b., blend of, blended; c., cognate with; cf., compare; deriv., derivative; equiv., equivalent; imit., imitative; obl., oblique; r., replacing; s., stem; sp., spelling, spelled; resp., respelling, respelled; trans., translation; ?, origin unknown; *, unattested; ‡, probably earlier than. See the full key inside the front cover.

ves•pi•ar•y (ves′pē er′ē), *n., pl.* **-ar•ies.** a nest of social wasps. [1810–20; < L *vesp(a)* WASP + (AP)IARY]

ves•pid (ves′pid), *n.* **1.** any of numerous, mostly colonial, nest-building wasps of the family Vespidae, as the yellow jackets, hornets, and mason wasps. —*adj.* **2.** belonging or pertaining to the family Vespidae. [1895–1900; < NL *Vespidae*, equiv. to *Vesp(a)* a genus (L: WASP) + *-idae* -ID[2]]

ves•pine (ves′pīn, -pin), *adj.* **1.** of or pertaining to wasps. **2.** resembling a wasp. [1835–45; < L *vesp(a)* WASP + -INE[1]]

Ves•puc•ci (ve spo͞o′chē, -spyo͞o′-; *It.* ves po͞ot′chē), *n.* **A•me•ri•go** (ə mer′i gō′; *It.* ä′me Rē′gô), (*Americus Vespucius*), 1451–1512, Italian merchant, adventurer, and explorer after whom America was named.

ves•sel (ves′əl), *n.* **1.** a craft for traveling on water, now usually one larger than an ordinary rowboat; a ship or boat. **2.** an airship. **3.** a hollow or concave utensil, as a cup, bowl, pitcher, or vase, used for holding liquids or other contents. **4.** *Anat., Zool.* a tube or duct, as an artery or vein, containing or conveying blood or some other body fluid. **5.** *Bot.* a duct formed in the xylem, composed of connected cells that have lost their intervening partitions, that conducts water and mineral nutrients. Cf. **tracheid. 6.** a person regarded as a holder or receiver of something, esp. something nonmaterial: *a vessel of grace; a vessel of wrath.* [1250–1300; ME < AF, OF *vessel, va(i)ssel* < L *vāscellum*, equiv. to *vās* (see VASE) + *-cellum* dim. suffix] —**ves′seled;** *esp. Brit.,* **ves′selled,** *adj.*

vest (vest), *n.* **1.** a close-fitting, waist-length, sleeveless garment that buttons down the front, designed to be worn under a jacket. **2.** a part or trimming simulating the front of such a garment; vestee. Cf. **dickey**[1] (def. 1). **3.** a waist-length garment worn for protective purposes: *a bulletproof vest.* **4.** a sleeveless, waist- or hip-length garment made of various materials, with a front opening usually secured by buttons, a zipper, or the like, worn over a shirt, blouse, dress, or other article for style or warmth: *a sweater vest; a down vest.* **5.** *Brit.* an undervest or undershirt. **6.** a long garment resembling a cassock, worn by men in the time of Charles II. **7.** *Archaic.* **a.** dress; apparel. **b.** an outer garment, robe, or gown. **c.** an ecclesiastical vestment. **8. play it close to the vest,** *Informal.* to avoid taking unnecessary risks. —*v.t.* **9.** to clothe; dress; robe. **10.** to dress in ecclesiastical vestments: *to vest a bishop.* **11.** to cover or drape (an altar). **12.** to place or settle (something, esp. property, rights, powers, etc.) in the possession or control of someone (usually fol. by *in*): *to vest authority in a new official.* **13.** to invest or endow (a person, group, committee, etc.) with something, as powers, functions, or rights: *to vest the board with power to increase production; to vest an employee with full benefits in the pension plan.* —*v.i.* **14.** to put on vestments. **15.** to become vested in a person, as a right. **16.** to devolve upon a person as possessor; pass into possession or ownership. [1375–1425; (n.) late ME < It *veste* robe, dress < L *vestis* garment; (v.) late ME < MF *vestir* < L *vestīre* to clothe, deriv. of *vestis;* akin to WEAR] —**vest′less,** *adj.* —**vest′like′,** *adj.*

Ves•ta (ves′tə), *n.* **1.** the ancient Roman goddess of the hearth, worshiped in a temple containing an altar on which a sacred fire was kept burning by the vestal virgins: identified with the Greek Hestia. **2.** *Astron.* the third largest and one of the four brightest asteroids. **3.** (*l.c.*) *Brit.* a short friction match with a wood or wax shank. **4.** a female given name. [1350–1400; ME < L]

ves•tal (ves′tl), *adj.* **1.** of or pertaining to the goddess Vesta. **2.** of, pertaining to, or characteristic of a vestal virgin; chaste; pure. —*n.* **3.** See **vestal virgin. 4.** a chaste unmarried woman; virgin. **5.** a nun. [1400–50; late ME (adj.) < L *vestālis.* See VESTA, -AL[1]]

ves′tal vir′gin, (in ancient Rome) one of four, later six, virgins consecrated to Vesta and to the tending of the sacred fire on her altar. [1400–50; late ME]

Ves•ta′vi•a Hills′ (ve stā′vē ə), a city in central Alabama, near Birmingham. 15,733.

vest•ed (ves′tid), *adj.* **1.** held completely, permanently, and inalienably: *vested rights.* **2.** protected or established by law, commitment, tradition, ownership, etc.: *vested contributions to a fund.* **3.** clothed or robed, esp. in ecclesiastical vestments: *a vested priest.* **4.** having a vest; sold with a vest: *a vested suit.* [1665–75; VEST + -ED[2]]

vest′ed in′terest, 1. a special interest in an existing system, arrangement, or institution for particular personal reasons. **2.** a permanent right given to an employee under a pension plan. **3. vested interests,** the persons, groups, etc., who benefit the most from existing business or financial systems. [1810–20]

vest•ee (ve stē′), *n.* **1.** a decorative front piece worn under a woman's jacket or blouse so as to be visible at the neckline. **2.** vest (def. 2). Cf. **dickey**[1] (def. 1). [1905–10; VEST (n.) + *-ee*, sp. var. of -Y[2]]

Ves′ter•å•len Is′lands (ves′tə rô′lən), a group of islands, belonging to Norway, in the Norwegian Sea, NE of the Lofoten Islands: rich fishing grounds.

ves•ti•ar•y (ves′tē er′ē), *adj.* of or pertaining to garments or vestments. [1615–25; < ML *vestiārius*, equiv. to *vesti(s)* (see VEST) + *-ārius* -ARY]

ves•tib•u•lar (ve stib′yə lər), *adj.* of, pertaining to, or resembling a vestibule. [1830–40; VESTIBULE + -AR[1]]

vestib′ular nerve′, *Anat.* the part of the auditory nerve in the inner ear that carries sensory information related to body equilibrium. [1870–75]

ves•ti•bule (ves′tə byo͞ol′), *n., v.,* **-buled, -bul•ing.** —*n.* **1.** a passage, hall, or antechamber between the outer door and the interior parts of a house or building. **2.** *Railroads.* an enclosed space at the end of a passenger car, serving as a sheltered entrance to the car from another car or from outside the train. **3.** *Anat., Zool.* any of various cavities or hollows regarded as forming an approach or entrance to another cavity or space, as that of the internal ear. See diag. under **ear.** —*v.t.* **4.** to provide with a vestibule. [1615–25; < L *vestibulum* forecourt, entrance]

ves′tibule school′, a school in an industrial establishment where new employees are given specific training in the jobs they are to perform. [1915–20]

ves•tige (ves′tij), *n.* **1.** a mark, trace, or visible evidence of something that is no longer present or in existence: *A few columns were the last vestiges of a Greek temple.* **2.** a surviving evidence or remainder of some condition, practice, etc.: *These superstitions are vestiges of an ancient religion.* **3.** a very slight trace or amount of something: *Not a vestige remains of the former elegance of the house.* **4.** *Biol.* a degenerate or imperfectly developed organ or structure that has little or no utility, but that in an earlier stage of the individual or in preceding evolutionary forms of the organism performed a useful function. **5.** *Archaic.* a footprint; track. [1535–45; < MF < L *vestigium* footprint]
—**Syn. 1.** token. See **trace. 3.** hint, suggestion.

ves•tig•i•al (ve stij′ē əl, -stij′əl), *adj.* of, pertaining to, or of the nature of a vestige: *a vestigial tail.* [1880–85; < L *vestigi(um)* VESTIGE + -AL[1]] —**ves•tig′i•al•ly,** *adv.*

ves•tig•i•um (ve stij′ē əm), *n., pl.* **ves•tig•i•a** (ve stij′ē ə). *Anat.* a vestigial structure of any kind; vestige. [1630–40; < L *vestigium* footprint, trace]

vest•ing (ves′ting), *n.* **1.** cloth that is usually of medium or heavy weight and has figures or ridges, as piqué, jacquard, dobby silk, or Bedford cord, originally used for decorative vests and now also for a variety of other garments. **2.** the granting to an eligible employee of the right to specified pension benefits, regardless of discontinued employment status, usually after a fixed period of employment. [1805–15; VEST (n.) + -ING[1]]

Vest•man•na•ey•jar (vest′mä nə ā′yär), *n.* **1.** a group of 14 small Icelandic islands off the S coast of Iceland. **2.** the main town of these islands. 4618.

vest•ment (vest′mənt), *n.* **1.** a garment, esp. an outer garment. **2. vestments,** *Chiefly Literary.* attire; clothing. **3.** an official or ceremonial robe. **4.** *Eccles.* **a.** one of the garments worn by the clergy and their assistants, choristers, etc., during divine service and on other occasions. **b.** one of the garments worn by the celebrant, deacon, and subdeacon during the celebration of the Eucharist. **5.** something that clothes or covers like a garment: *a mountaintop with a vestment of clouds.* [1250–1300; syncopated var. of ME *vestiment* < ML *vestimentum* priestly robe, L: garment, equiv. to *vestī(re)* to dress (see VEST) + *-mentum* -MENT] —**vest•men•tal** (vest men′tl), *adj.* —**vest′ment•ed,** *adj.*

vest-pock•et (vest′pok′it), *adj.* **1.** designed to be carried in the pocket of the vest, in a purse, or in a similarly small space; miniature: *a vest-pocket dictionary.* **2.** very small: *a vest-pocket version of Versailles.* [1910–15]

vest′-pocket park′. See **pocket park.** [1965–70]

ves•try (ves′trē), *n., pl.* **-tries. 1.** a room in or a building attached to a church, in which the vestments, and sometimes liturgical objects, are kept; sacristy. **2.** (in some churches) a room in or a building attached to a church, used as a chapel, for prayer meetings, for the Sunday school, etc. **3.** *Episc. Ch.* a committee elected by members of a congregation to serve with the churchwardens in managing the temporal affairs of the church. **4.** *Ch. of Eng.* a meeting attended by all the parishioners or by a committee of parishioners during which the official business of the church is discussed. [1350–1400; ME *vestrie, vestrye.* See VEST (v.), -ERY] —**ves′tral,** *adj.*

ves•try•man (ves′trē mən), *n., pl.* **-men.** a member of a church vestry. [1605–15; VESTRY + MAN[1]]

ves•ture (ves′chər), *n., v.,* **-tured, -tur•ing.** —*n.* **1.** *Law.* **a.** everything growing on and covering the land, with the exception of trees. **b.** any such covering, as grass or wheat. **2.** *Archaic.* **a.** clothing; garments. **b.** something that covers like a garment; covering. —*v.t.* **3.** *Archaic.* to clothe or cover. [1300–50; ME < AF; OF *vesteure* < VL **vestītūra*, equiv. to L *vestīt(us)*, ptp. of *vestīre* (see VEST) + *-ūra* -URE] —**ves′tur•al,** *adj.*

Ve•su•vi•an (və so͞o′vē ən), *adj.* **1.** of, pertaining to, or resembling Mount Vesuvius; volcanic. —*n.* **2.** (*l.c.*) a type of match formerly used for lighting cigars; fusee. [1665–75; VESUVI(US) + -AN]

ve•su•vi•an•ite (və so͞o′vē ə nīt′), *n.* a mineral, chiefly a hydrous silicate of calcium and aluminum, commonly in tetragonal crystals and usually of a brown to green color; idocrase. [1885–90; VESUVIAN + -ITE[1]]

vesu′vianite jade′, a green variety of vesuvianite, used as a gem: not a true jade. Also, **vesu′vian jade′.** Also called **californite.**

Ve•su•vi•us (və so͞o′vē əs), *n.* **Mount,** an active volcano in SW Italy, near Naples. Its eruption destroyed the ancient cities of Pompeii and Herculaneum A.D. 79. ab. 3900 ft. (1190 m).

vet[1] (vet), *n., v.,* **vet•ted, vet•ting.** *Informal.* —*n.* **1.** veterinarian. —*v.t.* **2.** to examine or treat in one's capacity as a veterinarian or as a doctor. **3.** to appraise, verify, or check for accuracy, authenticity, validity, etc.: *An expert vetted the manuscript before publication.* —*v.i.* **4.** to work as a veterinarian. [1860–65; short for VETERINARIAN]

vet[2] (vet), *n., adj. Informal.* veteran. [1865–70, *Amer.;* shortened form]

vet., 1. veteran. **2.** veterinarian. **3.** veterinary.

vetch (vech), *n.* **1.** any of several mostly climbing plants belonging to the genus *Vicia*, of the legume family, having pinnate leaves ending in tendrils and bearing pealike flowers, esp. *V. sativa* **(spring vetch),** cultivated for forage and soil improvement. **2.** any of various allied plants, as *Lathyrus sativus*, of Europe, cultivated for their edible seeds and for forage. **3.** the beanlike seed or fruit of any such plant. [1325–75; ME *ve(c)che* < AF; OF *vecce* (F *vesce*) < L *vicia*] —**vetch′like′,** *adj.*

vetch•ling (vech′ling), *n.* any of several slender, climbing plants belonging to the genus *Lathyrus*, of the legume family, similar to the vetch but having a winged or angular stem, as *L. palustris*, of North America. [1570–80; VETCH + -LING[1]]

veter., veterinary.

vet•er•an (vet′ər ən, ve′trən), *n.* **1.** a person who has had long service or experience in an occupation, office, or the like: *a veteran of the police force; a veteran of many sports competitions.* **2.** a person who has served in a military force, esp. one who has fought in a war: *a Vietnam veteran.* —*adj.* **3.** (of soldiers) having had service or experience in warfare: *veteran troops.* **4.** experienced through long service or practice; having served for a long period: *a veteran member of Congress.* **5.** of, pertaining to, or characteristic of veterans. [1495–1505; < L *veterānus* mature, experienced, equiv. to *veter-* (s. of *vetus*) old + *-ānus* -AN]

Vet′erans Administra′tion, the federal agency charged with administering benefits provided by law for veterans of the armed forces. *Abbr.:* VA, V.A.

Vet′erans Day′, November 11, a legal holiday in the U.S. in commemoration of the end of World Wars I and II and in honor of veterans of the armed services. Formerly, **Armistice Day.** [‡1950–55, *Amer.*]

Vet′erans of For′eign Wars′ of the Unit′ed States′. See **V.F.W.**

vet•er•i•nar•i•an (vet′ər ə nâr′ē ən, ve′trə-), *n.* a person who practices veterinary medicine or surgery. [1640–50; < L *veterīnāri(us)* VETERINARY + -AN]

vet•er•i•nar•y (vet′ər ə ner′ē, ve′trə-), *n., pl.* **-nar•ies,** *adj.* —*n.* **1.** a veterinarian. —*adj.* **2.** of or pertaining to the medical and surgical treatment of animals, esp. domesticated animals. [1780–90; < L *veterīnārius*, equiv. to *veterīn(ae)* beasts of burden (n. use of fem. pl. of *veterīnus* pertaining to such beasts, equiv. to *veter-*, s. of *vetus* old, i.e., grown, able to take a load + *-īnus* -INE[1]) + *-ārius* -ARY]

vet′erinary med′icine, the branch of medicine dealing with the study, prevention, and treatment of diseases in animals, esp. domesticated animals. [1780–90]

vet′erinary sur′geon, 1. *Chiefly Brit.* a veterinarian. **2.** a veterinarian who practices surgery. [1795–1805]

vet•i•ver (vet′ə vər), *n.* **1.** the long, fibrous, aromatic roots of an East Indian grass, *Vetiveria zizanioides*, used for making hangings and screens and yielding an oil used in perfumery. **2.** Also called **khus-khus.** the grass itself. [1840–50; < Tamil *veṭṭivēr*]

vet. med., veterinary medicine.

ve•to (vē′tō), *n., pl.* **-toes,** *v.,* **-toed, -to•ing.** —*n.* **1.** the power or right vested in one branch of a government to cancel or postpone the decisions, enactments, etc., of another branch, esp. the right of a president, governor, or other chief executive to reject bills passed by the legislature. **2.** the exercise of this right. **3.** Also called **ve′to mes′sage.** a document exercising such right and setting forth the reasons for such action. **4.** a nonconcurring vote by which one of the five permanent members of the UN Security Council can overrule the actions or decisions of the meeting on matters other than procedural. **5.** an emphatic prohibition of any sort. **6.** See **pocket veto.** —*v.t.* **7.** to reject (a proposed bill or enactment) by exercising a veto. **8.** to prohibit emphatically. Also called **ve′to pow′er** (for defs. 1, 4). [1620–30; < L *vetō* I forbid] —**ve′to•er,** *n.*

vet. sci., veterinary science.

Vet•ter (vet′ər), *n.* Vätter.

vex (veks), *v.t.* **1.** to irritate; annoy; provoke: *His noisy neighbors often vexed him.* **2.** to torment; trouble; distress; plague; worry: *Lack of money vexes many.* **3.** to discuss or debate (a subject, question, etc.) with vigor or at great length: *to vex a question endlessly without agreeing.* **4.** to disturb by motion; stir up; toss about. **5.** to afflict with physical pain. [1375–1425; late ME *vexen* < OF *vexer* < L *vexāre* to shake, jolt, harass, annoy, freq. of *vehere* to carry, convey] —**vex′er,** *n.* —**vex′•ing•ly,** *adv.*
—**Syn. 1.** anger, irk, fret, nettle. **2.** hector, harry, harass. —**Ant. 1.** delight.

vex•a•tion (vek sā′shən), *n.* **1.** the act of vexing. **2.** the state of being vexed; irritation; annoyance: *vexation at missing the bus.* **3.** something that vexes; a cause of annoyance; nuisance: *Rush-hour traffic is a daily vexation.* [1350–1400; ME *vexacioun* < L *vexātiōn-* (s. of *vexātiō*), equiv. to *vexāt(us)* (ptp. of *vexāre* to VEX; see -ATE[1]) + *-iōn-* -ION]

vex•a•tious (vek sā′shəs), *adj.* **1.** causing vexation; troublesome; annoying: *a vexatious situation.* **2.** *Law.* (of legal actions) instituted without sufficient grounds and serving only to cause annoyance to the defendant. **3.** disorderly; confused; troubled. [1525–35; VEXATI(ON) + -OUS] —**vex•a′tious•ly,** *adv.* —**vex•a′tious•ness,** *n.*
—**Syn. 1.** disturbing, provoking, irritating. —**Ant. 1.** delightful.

vexed (vekst), *adj.* **1.** irritated; annoyed: *vexed at the slow salesclerks.* **2.** much discussed or disputed: *a vexed question.* **3.** tossed about, as waves. [1400–50; late ME; see VEX, -ED[2]] —**vex•ed•ly** (vek′sid lē), *adv.* —**vex′ed•ness,** *n.*

vex•il•lar•y (vek′sə ler′ē), *n., pl.* **-lar•ies,** *adj.* —*n.* **1.** (in ancient Rome) one of a class of veteran soldiers who served under a special banner. —*adj.* **2.** of or pertaining to flags. **3.** of or pertaining to a vexillum. [1585–95; < L *vexillārius* standard-bearer. See VEXILLUM, -ARY]

vex•il•late (vek′sə lit, -lāt′, vek sil′it), *adj.* having a vexillum or vexilla. [VEXILL(UM) + -ATE[1]]

CONCISE PRONUNCIATION KEY: act, cāpe, dâre, pärt; set, ēqual; *if,* ice; ox, ōver, ôrder, oil, bo͝ok, bo͞ot, out; up, ûrge; child; sing; shoe; thin, *that;* zh as in *treasure.* ə = *a* as in *alone, e* as in *system, i* as in *easily, o* as in *gallop, u* as in *circus;* ᵊ as in *fire* (fīᵊr), *hour* (ouᵊr). l and n can serve as syllabic consonants, as in *cradle* (krād′l), and *button* (but′n). See the full key inside the front cover.

vex•il•log•ra•pher (vek′sə log′rə fər), *n.* a person who designs or makes flags. [< L *vexill(um)* flag, VEXILLUM + -O- + -GRAPHER]

vex•il•lol•o•gy (vek′sə lol′ə jē), *n.* the study of flags. [1955–60; < L *vexill(um)* flag, VEXILLUM + -O- + -LOGY] —**vex•il•log•ic**(vek sil′ə loj′ik), **vex•il′lo•log′i•cal,** *adj.* —**vex•il•lol′o•gist,** *n.*

vex•il•lum (vek sil′əm), *n., pl.* **vex•il•la** (vek sil′ə). **1.** a military standard or flag carried by ancient Roman troops. **2.** a group of men serving under such a standard. **3.** video frequency. **4.** Also, **vex•il** (vek′sil). *Bot.* the large upper petal of a papilionaceous flower. See diag. under **papilionaceous. 5.** *Ornith. Rare.* the web or vane of a feather. [1720–30; < L: standard, flag, dim. from the base of *vēlum* sail (see VEIL)]

VF, 1. *Bot.* a designation applied to various plant varieties, indicating resistance to verticillium wilt and fusarium wilt. **2.** video frequency. **3.** visual field. **4.** voice frequency.

VFD, volunteer fire department.

V-four (vē′fôr′, -fōr′), *n.* *Auto.* a four-cylinder V-engine. Also, **V-4.**

VFR, visual flight rules.

V.F.W., Veterans of Foreign Wars of the United States: a society composed of veterans of the U.S. armed forces who have served overseas during wartime. Also, **VFW**

VG, very good.

V.G., Vicar-General.

v.g., for example. [< L *verbi gratiā*]

VHF, See **very high frequency.** Also, **vhf, V.H.F.**

VHS, *Trademark.* a format for recording and playing VCR tape, incompatible with other formats. Cf. **Beta** (def. 7).

VI, Virgin Islands (approved esp. for use with zip code).

Vi, *Symbol, Chem.* virginium.

V.I., 1. Vancouver Island. **2.** Virgin Islands.

v.i., 1. intransitive verb. **2.** see below. [< L *vidē infrā*]

vi•a (vī′ə, vē′ə), *prep.* **1.** by a route that touches or passes through; by way of: *to fly to Japan via the North Pole.* **2.** by the agency or instrumentality of: *a solution via an inquiry.* —*n.* **3.** *Archit.* a space between two mutules. [1770–80; < L *viā*, abl. of *via* way]

vi•a•ble (vī′ə bəl), *adj.* **1.** capable of living. **2.** *Physiol.* **a.** physically fitted to live. **b.** (of a fetus) having reached such a stage of development as to be capable of living, under normal conditions, outside the uterus. **3.** *Bot.* able to live and grow. **4.** vivid; real; stimulating, as to the intellect, imagination, or senses: *a period of history that few teachers can make viable for students.* **5.** practicable; workable: *a viable alternative.* **6.** having the ability to grow, expand, develop, etc.: *a new and viable country.* [1820–30; < F, equiv. to *vie* life (< L *vīta*) + *-able* -ABLE] —**vi′a•bil′i•ty,** *n.* —**vi′a•bly,** *adv.*
—Syn. 5. practical, feasible, usable, adaptable.

vi′a do•lo•ro′sa (dol′ə rō′sə, dō′lə-), **1.** (*caps.*) Christ's route to Golgotha. **2.** a trying, painful, or sorrowful course or series of experiences. [< L *via dolōrōsa* lit., sorrowful road]

vi•a•duct (vī′ə dukt′), *n.* a bridge for carrying a road, railroad, etc., over a valley or the like, consisting of a number of short spans. [1810–20; < L *via* way + (AQUE)DUCT]

vi•al (vī′əl, vīl), *n., v.,* **-aled, -al•ing** or (*esp. Brit.*) **-alled, -al•ling.** —*n.* **1.** Also, **phial.** a small container, as of glass, for holding liquids: *a vial of rare perfume; a vial of medicine.* **2. pour out vials of wrath,** to wreak vengeance or express anger: *In her preface she pours out vials of wrath on her detractors.* —*v.t.* **3.** to put into or keep in a vial. [1300–50; ME *viole*, var. of *fiole* PHIAL]

vi•a me•di•a (vī′ə mē′dē ə, mā′-, vē′ə; *Lat.* wē′ä me′dē ä), a middle way; a mean between two extremes. [1835–45; < L]

vi•and (vī′ənd), *n.* **1.** an article of food. **2. viands,** articles or dishes of food, now usually of a choice or delicate kind. [1350–1400; ME *viaunde* < MF *viande* < VL **vivanda*, for L *vivenda* things to be lived on, neut. pl. ger. of *vivere* to live]

vi′ ap′ple (vē). See **Otaheite apple.** [*vi* < Tahitian]

vi•at•i•cum (vī at′i kəm, vē-), *n., pl.* **-ca** (-kə), **-cums. 1.** *Eccles.* the Eucharist or Communion as given to a person dying or in danger of death. **2.** (among the ancient Romans) a provision or allowance for traveling, originally of transportation and supplies, later of money, made to officials on public missions. **3.** money or necessities for any journey. [1555–65; < L *viāticum*, neut. of *viāticus*, equiv. to *viāt(us)* (ptp. of *viāre* to travel; see VIA, -ATE[1]) + *-icus* -IC; cf. VOYAGE]

vi•a•tor (vī ā′tôr, -tər), *n., pl.* **vi•a•to•res** (vī′ə tôr′ēz, -tōr′-). a wayfarer; traveler. [1495–1505; < L *viātor* equiv. to *viā(re)* to travel (deriv. of *via* way) + *-tor* -TOR]

vibe (vīb), *n.* **1.** *Informal.* vibration (def. 4). **2.** Often, **vibes.** *Slang.* vibration (def. 6). [1965–70, *Amer.*; by shortening]

vibes (vībz), *n.pl. Informal.* vibraharp. [1965–70; by shortening] —**vib′ist,** *n.*

Vi•borg (vē′bôr y[ə]), *n.* Swedish name of **Vyborg.**

vi•brac•u•lum (vī brak′yə ləm), *n., pl.* **-la** (-lə). any of the modified polyps on the surface of certain bryozoan colonies, having a long, whiplike appendage that clears away debris. [1850–55; < NL, equiv. to L *vibrā(re)* to shake + *-culum* -CULE[2]] —**vi•brac′u•lar,** *adj.* —**vi•brac′u•loid′,** *adj.*

CONCISE ETYMOLOGY KEY: <, descended or borrowed from; >, whence; b., blend of, blended; c., cognate with; cf., compare; deriv., derivative; equiv., equivalent; imit., imitative; obl., oblique; r., replacing; s., stem; sp., spelling, spelled; resp., respelling, respelled; trans., translation; ?, origin unknown; *, unattested; ‡, probably earlier than. See the full key inside the front cover.

vibracula

vi•bra•harp (vī′brə härp′), *n.* a musical percussion instrument that resembles a marimba and is played with mallets, but that has metal instead of wooden bars and has a set of electrically powered resonators for sustaining the tone or creating a vibrato. Also called **vibraphone.** [1925–30; < L *vibrā(re)* to shake + HARP] —**vi′bra•harp′ist,** *n.*

Vi•bram (vī′brəm), *Trademark.* a brand of lightweight, rubberlike material used for the soles of shoes and boots.

vi•brant (vī′brənt), *adj.* **1.** moving to and fro rapidly; vibrating. **2.** vibrating so as to produce sound, as a string. **3.** (of sounds) characterized by perceptible vibration; resonant; resounding. **4.** pulsating with vigor and energy: *the vibrant life of a large city.* **5.** vigorous; energetic; vital: *a vibrant personality.* **6.** exciting; stimulating; lively: *vibrant colors; a vibrant performance.* **7.** *Phonet.* made with tonal vibration of the vocal cords; voiced. —*n.* **8.** *Phonet.* a vibrant sound. [1540–50; < L *vibrant-* (s. of *vibrāns*), prp. of *vibrāre* to shake, move to and fro; see -ANT] —**vi′bran•cy, vi′brance,** *n.* —**vi′brant•ly,** *adv.*

vi•bra•phone (vī′brə fōn′), *n.* vibraharp. [1925–30; < L *vibrā(re)* to shake + -PHONE] —**vi•bra•phon•ist** (vī′brə fō′nist, vī brof′ə-), *n.*

vi•brate (vī′brāt), *v.,* **-brat•ed, -brat•ing.** —*v.i.* **1.** to move rhythmically and steadily to and fro, as a pendulum; oscillate. **2.** to move to and fro or up and down quickly and repeatedly; quiver; tremble. **3.** (of sounds) to produce or have a quivering or vibratory effect; resound. **4.** to thrill, as in emotional response. **5.** to move between alternatives or extremes; fluctuate; vacillate. —*v.t.* **6.** to cause to move rhythmically and steadily to and fro, swing, or oscillate. **7.** to cause to move to and fro or up and down quickly and repeatedly; cause to quiver or tremble. **8.** to give forth or emit by, or as by, vibration. **9.** to measure or indicate by vibration or oscillation: *a pendulum vibrating seconds.* [1610–20; < L *vibrātus* (ptp. of *vibrāre* to move to and fro); see -ATE[1]] —**vi′brat•ing•ly,** *adv.*
—Syn. 2. See **shake. 3.** echo.

vi•bra•tile (vī′brə til, -tīl′), *adj.* **1.** capable of vibrating or of being vibrated. **2.** having a vibratory motion. **3.** of, pertaining to, or of the nature of vibration. [1820–30; VIBRATE + -ILE] —**vi•bra•til•i•ty** (vī′brə til′i tē), *n.*

vi•bra•tion (vī brā′shən), *n.* **1.** the act of vibrating. **2.** the state of being vibrated. **3.** *Physics.* **a.** the oscillating, reciprocating, or other periodic motion of a rigid or elastic body or medium forced from a position or state of equilibrium. **b.** the analogous motion of the particles of a mass of air or the like, whose state of equilibrium has been disturbed, as in transmitting sound. **4.** an instance of vibratory motion; oscillation; quiver; tremor. **5.** a supernatural emanation, bearing good or ill, that is sensed by or revealed to those attuned to the occult. **6.** Often, **vibrations.** *Informal.* a general emotional feeling one has from another person or a place, situation, etc.: *I usually get good vibrations from him.* [1645–55; 1965–70 for def. 6; < L *vibrātiōn-* (s. of *vibrātiō*). See VIBRATE, -ION] —**vi•bra′tion•al,** *adj.* —**vi•bra′tion•less,** *adj.*

vibra′tional quan′tum num′ber, *Physics.* any one of the quantum numbers describing the energy levels associated with the vibrational motion of molecules.

vi•bra•to (vi brä′tō, vī-), *n., pl.* **-tos.** *Music.* a pulsating effect, produced in singing by the rapid reiteration of emphasis on a tone, and on bowed instruments by a rapid change of pitch corresponding to the vocal tremolo. [1860–65; < It < L *vibrātus* (ptp.); see VIBRATE]

vi•bra•tor (vī′brā tər), *n.* **1.** a person or thing that vibrates. **2.** any of various machines or devices causing a vibratory motion or action. **3.** a small appliance of variable shape, made to oscillate very rapidly and used in vibratory massage. **4.** *Elect.* **a.** a device in which, by continually repeated impulses, a steady current is changed into an oscillating current. **b.** a device for producing electric oscillations. [1860–65; VIBRATE + -OR[2]]

vi•bra•to•ry (vī′brə tôr′ē, -tōr′ē), *adj.* **1.** capable of or producing vibration. **2.** vibrating. **3.** of the nature of or consisting in vibration. **4.** of or pertaining to vibration. Also, **vi•bra•tive** (vī′brə tiv, -brā-) [1720–30; VIBRATE + -ORY[1]]

vib•ri•o (vib′rē ō′), *n., pl.* **-ri•os.** *Bacteriol.* any of several comma- or S-shaped bacteria of the genus *Vibrio*, certain species of which are pathogenic for humans and other animals. [< NL (1854), equiv. to L *vibr(āre)* to shake + *-iō* n. suffix] —**vib•ri•oid** (vib′rē oid′), *adj.*

vib•ri•on•ic (vib′rē on′ik), *adj.* of or pertaining to an infection by a bacterium of the genus *Vibrio.* [1870–75; < NL *Vibrion-* (s. of *Vibrio*) VIBRIO + -IC]

vib•ri•o•sis (vib′rē ō′sis), *n.* *Vet. Pathol.* a venereal disease of cattle and sheep, caused by the organism *Vibrio fetus*, characterized by delayed female fertility and by spontaneous abortion. [1945–50; < NL; see VIBRIO, -OSIS]

vi•bris•sa (vī bris′ə), *n., pl.* **-bris•sae** (-bris′ē). **1.** one of the stiff, bristly hairs growing about the mouth of certain animals, as a whisker of a cat. **2.** one of the long, slender, bristlelike feathers growing along the side of the mouth in many birds. [1685–95; < ML, deriv. of L *vibrāre* to shake] —**vi•bris′sal,** *adj.*

vibro-, a combining form meaning "vibration," used in the formation of compound words: *vibrometer.* [< L *vibr(āre)* to shake, move to and fro + -O-]

vi•bro•graph (vī′brə graf′, -gräf′), *n.* a device for recording mechanical vibrations. [1870–75; VIBRO- + -GRAPH]

vi•brom•e•ter (vī brom′i tər), *n.* a vibrograph that measures the amplitude of vibrations. [1885–90; VIBRO- + -METER]

vi•bur•num (vī bûr′nəm), *n.* **1.** any of numerous shrubs or trees belonging to the genus *Viburnum*, of the honeysuckle family, certain species of which, as the cranberry bush, *V. opulus*, or snowball, are cultivated for ornament. **2.** the dried bark of various species of *Viburnum*, used in medicine. [1725–35; < L *viburnum* wayfaring tree]

Vic (vik), *n.* a male given name, form of **Victor.**

Vic., 1. Vicar. **2.** Vicarage. **3.** Victoria.

vic., vicinity.

vic•ar (vik′ər), *n.* **1.** *Ch. of Eng.* **a.** a person acting as priest of a parish in place of the rector, or as representative of a religious community to which tithes belong. **b.** the priest of a parish the tithes of which are impropriated and who receives only the smaller tithes or a salary. **2.** *Prot. Episc. Ch.* **a.** a member of the clergy whose sole or chief charge is a chapel dependent on the church of a parish. **b.** a bishop's assistant in charge of a church or mission. **3.** *Rom. Cath. Ch.* an ecclesiastic representing the pope or a bishop. **4.** a person who acts in place of another; substitute. **5.** a person who is authorized to perform the functions of another; deputy: *God's vicar on earth.* [1250–1300; ME < AF *vicare*; OF *vicaire* < L *vicārius* a substitute, n. use of adj.; see VICARIOUS] —**vic′ar•ship′,** *n.*

vic•ar•age (vik′ər ij), *n.* **1.** the residence of a vicar. **2.** the benefice of a vicar. **3.** the office or duties of a vicar. [1375–1425; late ME; see VICAR, -AGE]

vic′ar apostol′ic, *pl.* **vicars apostolic. 1.** *Rom. Cath. Ch.* a titular bishop serving either in a district where no episcopal see has been established, or in one where the succession of bishops has been interrupted. **2.** *Eccles. Hist.* an archbishop, bishop, or other ecclesiastic to whom the pope delegated a portion of his jurisdiction. [1760–70]

vic•ar•ate (vik′ər it, -ə rāt′), *n.* vicariate. [1880–85; VICAR + -ATE[3]]

vic′ar capit′ular, *pl.* **vicars capitular.** *Rom. Cath. Ch.* a cleric chosen by a cathedral chapter to manage a bishopric during a vacancy. [1840–50]

vic′ar cho′ral, *pl.* **vicars choral.** *Anglican Ch.* a member of the clergy or a layperson in a cathedral who sings certain parts of the service. [1520–30]

vic′ar fo•rane′ (fô rān′, fō-), *pl.* **vicars forane.** *Rom. Cath. Ch.* dean[1] (def. 2b). [1885–90; *forane* < ML *forāneus* living away; cf. FOREIGN]

vic•ar-gen•er•al (vik′ər jen′ər əl), *n., pl.* **vic•ars-gen•er•al. 1.** *Rom. Cath. Ch.* a priest deputized by a bishop to assist him in the administration of a diocese. **2.** *Ch. of Eng.* an ecclesiastical officer, usually a layperson, who assists a bishop or an archbishop in the discharge of his judicial or administrative duties. [1350–1400; ME] —**vic′ar-gen′er•al•ship′,** *n.*

vi•car•i•al (vī kâr′ē əl, vi-), *adj.* **1.** of or pertaining to a vicar. **2.** acting as or holding the office of a vicar. **3.** delegated or vicarious: *vicarial powers.* [1610–20; < L *vicāri(us)* VICAR + -AL[1]]

vi•car•i•ate (vī kâr′ē it, -āt′, vi-), *n.* **1.** the office or authority of a vicar. **2.** the district presided over by a vicar. Also, **vicarate.** [1600–10; < ML *vicāriātus*, equiv. to L *vicāri(us)* VICAR + *-ātus* -ATE[3]]

vicar′iate apostol′ic, *pl.* **vicariates apostolic.** *Rom. Cath. Ch.* a district under the jurisdiction of a vicar apostolic.

vi•car•i•ous (vī kâr′ē əs, vi-), *adj.* **1.** performed, exercised, received, or suffered in place of another: *vicarious punishment.* **2.** taking the place of another person or thing; acting or serving as a substitute. **3.** felt or enjoyed through imagined participation in the experience of others: *a vicarious thrill.* **4.** *Physiol.* noting or pertaining to a situation in which one organ performs part of the functions normally performed by another. [1630–40; < L *vicārius* substituting, equiv. to *vic(is)* (gen.) interchange, alternation (see VICE[3]), + *-ārius* -ARY; see -OUS] —**vi•car′i•ous•ly,** *adv.* —**vi•car′i•ous•ness, vi•car′i•ism,** *n.*

vic•ar•ly (vik′ər lē), *adj.* of, pertaining to, suggesting, or resembling a vicar: *vicarly duties; a vicarly manner.* [1590–1600; VICAR + -LY]

Vic′ar of Christ′, *Rom. Cath. Ch.* the pope, with reference to his claim to stand in the place of Jesus Christ and possess His authority in the church. Also, **Vic′ar of Je′sus Christ′.** [1475–85]

Vic′ar of Wake′field, The, a novel (1766) by Goldsmith.

vice[1] (vīs), *n.* **1.** an immoral or evil habit or practice. **2.** immoral conduct; depraved or degrading behavior: *a life of vice.* **3.** sexual immorality, esp. prostitution. **4.** a particular form of depravity. **5.** a fault, defect, or shortcoming: *a minor vice in his literary style.* **6.** a physical defect, flaw, or infirmity: *a constitutional vice.* **7.** a bad habit, as in a horse. **8.** (*cap.*) a character in the English morality plays, a personification of general vice or of a particular vice, serving as the buffoon. [1250–1300; ME < AF, OF < L *vitium* a fault, defect, vice]
—Syn. 1. See **fault. 2.** depravity, sin, iniquity, wickedness, corruption. **5.** blemish. **—Ant. 1, 2.** virtue.

vice[2] (vīs), *n., v.t.,* **viced, vic•ing.** vise.

vi•ce[3] (vī′sē, -sə, vīs), *prep.* instead of; in the place of. [1760–70; < L: instead of, abl. of *vicis* (gen.; not attested in nom.) interchange, alternation]

vice-, a combining form meaning "deputy," used in the formation of compound words, usually titles of officials who serve in the absence of the official denoted by the base word: *viceroy; vice-chancellor.* [ME << L *vice* VICE[3]]

vice-ad•mi•ral (vīs′ad′mər əl), *n.* a naval officer next in rank below an admiral. [1510–20] **—vice′-ad′mi·ral·ty,** *n.*

vice-chair·man (vīs′châr′mən), *n., pl.* **-men.** a member of a committee, board, group, etc., designated as immediately subordinate to a chairman and serving as such in the latter's absence; a person who acts for and assists a chairman. [1855–60]

vice-chan·cel·lor (vīs′chan′sə lər, -chän′-), *n.* **1.** a substitute, deputy, or subordinate chancellor. **2.** a chancery judge acting in place of a chancellor. **3.** the chief administrator of certain British universities. Cf. **chancellor** (def. 7). [1400–50; late ME] **—vice′-chan′cel·lor·ship′,** *n.*

vice-con·sul (vīs′kon′səl), *n.* a consular officer of a grade below that of consul. Also, **vice′ con′sul.** [1550–60] **—vice′-con′su·lar,** *adj.* **—vice′-con′su·late,** *n.* **—vice′-con′sul·ship′,** *n.*

vice·ge·ral (vīs jēr′əl), *adj.* of or pertaining to a vicegerent or a vicegerent's position. [VICEGER(ENT) + -AL[1]]

vice·ge·ren·cy (vīs jēr′ən sē), *n., pl.* **-cies. 1.** the position, government, or office of a vicegerent. **2.** the territory or district under a vicegerent. [1590–1600; VICEGER(ENT) + -ENCY]

vice·ge·rent (vīs jēr′ənt), *n.* **1.** an officer appointed as deputy by and to a sovereign or supreme chief. **2.** a deputy in general. *—adj.* **3.** exercising delegated powers. **4.** characterized by delegation of powers. [1530–40; < NL *vicegerent-* (s. of *vicegerēns* managing instead of), equiv. to L *vice* (see VICE[3]) + *gerent-* (s. of *gerēns,* prp. of *gerere* to carry on, conduct); see -ENT]

vice·less (vīs′lis), *adj.* free from vices. [1550–60; VICE[1] + -LESS]

vic·e·nar·y (vis′ə ner′ē), *adj.* of, pertaining to, or consisting of twenty. [1595–1605; < L *vicēnārius,* equiv. to *vicēn(ī)* twenty each + *-ārius* -ARY]

vi·cen·ni·al (vī sen′ē əl), *adj.* **1.** of or for 20 years. **2.** occurring every 20 years. [1730–40; < L *vicenni(um)* twenty-year period (*vīc(ēnī)* twenty each + *-enn(us),* comb. form of *annus* year + *-ium* -IUM) + -AL[1]]

Vi·cen·za (vē chen′dzä), *n.* a city in central Venezia, in NE Italy. 118,994.

vice pres., vice president. Also, **Vice Pres.**

vice′ pres′ident, 1. an officer next in rank to a president who serves as president in the president's absence. **2.** an officer next in rank to a president who serves as a deputy to the president or oversees a special division or function. **3.** *(caps.) U.S. Govt.* the officer of this rank who is elected at the same time as the President and who succeeds to the presidency on the resignation, removal, death, or disability of the President. See table under **president.** Also, **vice′-pres′ident.** [1565–75] **—vice′ pres′idency. —vice′-pres′i·den·cy,** *n.* **—vice′-pres·i·den′tial,** *adj.*

vice·re·gal (vīs rē′gəl), *adj.* of or pertaining to a viceroy. [1830–40; VICE- + REGAL] **—vice·re′gal·ly,** *adv.*

vice-re·gent (*n.* vīs′rē′jənt; *adj.* vīs rē′jənt), *n.* **1.** a deputy regent; a person who acts in the place of a ruler, governor, or sovereign. *—adj.* **2.** of, pertaining to, or occupying the position of a vice-regent. [1550–60] **—vice′-re′gen·cy,** *n.*

vice·reine (vīs′rān), *n.* the wife of a viceroy. [1815–25; < F, equiv. to *vice-* VICE- + *reine* queen < L *rēgīna* (*rēg-,* s. of *rēx* king + *-ina* fem. n. suffix)]

vice·roy (vīs′roi), *n.* **1.** a person appointed to rule a country or province as the deputy of the sovereign: *the viceroy of India.* **2.** a brightly marked American butterfly, *Limenitis archippus,* closely mimicking the monarch butterfly in coloration. [1515–25; < MF, equiv. to *vice-* VICE- + *roy* king < L *rēgem,* acc. of *rēx*] **—vice′·roy·ship′,** *n.*

vice·roy·al·ty (vīs roi′əl tē, vīs′roi′-), *n., pl.* **-ties. 1.** the dignity, office, or period of office of a viceroy. **2.** a country or province ruled by a viceroy. [1695–1705; VICE- + ROYALTY, modeled on F *vice-royauté*]

vice′ squad′, a police squad charged with enforcing laws dealing with gambling, prostitution, and other forms of vice.

vi·ce ver·sa (vī′sə vûr′sə, vīs′, vī′sē), in reverse order from that stated; conversely: *She dislikes me, and vice versa.* [1595–1605; < L, equiv. to *vice* VICE[3] + *versā,* abl. sing. fem. of *versus,* ptp. of *vertere* to turn]

Vi·chy (vish′ē; *Fr.* vē shē′), *n.* **1.** a city in central France: provisional capital of unoccupied France 1940–1942; hot springs. 32,251. **2.** *(often l.c.)* See **vichy water.**

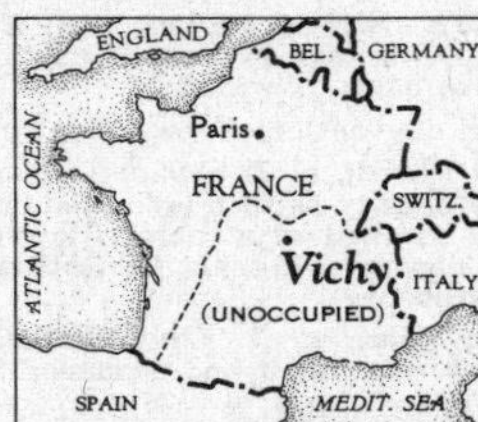

Vi·chy·ite (vish′ē īt′, vē′shē-), *n.* a member or adherent of the government established 1940 at Vichy by Marshal Henri Pétain. [VICHY + -ITE[1]]

vi·chys·soise (vish′ē swäz′, vē′shē swäz′), *n.* a cream soup of potatoes and leeks, usually served chilled and often garnished with chopped chives. [1915–20; < F *(crème) vichyssoise* (cream soup) of VICHY]

vi′chy wa′ter (vish′ē), **1.** a natural mineral water from springs at Vichy, containing sodium bicarbonate, other alkaline salts, etc., used in the treatment of digestive disturbances, gout, etc. **2.** a water of similar composition, either natural or artificial. Also, **Vi′chy wa′·ter.** Also called **vichy, Vichy.** [1855–60]

vic·i·nage (vis′ə nij), *n.* **1.** the region near or about a place; vicinity. **2.** a particular neighborhood or district, or the people belonging to it. **3.** proximity. [1275–1325; < L *vīcīn(us)* near (see VICINITY) + -AGE; r. ME *vesinage* < MF < L, as above]

vic·i·nal (vis′ə nl), *adj.* **1.** of, pertaining to, or belonging to a neighborhood or district. **2.** neighboring; adjacent. **3.** *Crystall.* noting a plane the position of which varies very little from that of a fundamental plane of the form. [1615–25; < L *vīcīnālis,* equiv. to *vīcīn(us)* near + *-ālis* -AL[1]; see VICINITY]

vi·cin·i·ty (vi sin′i tē), *n., pl.* **-ties. 1.** the area or region near or about a place; surrounding district; neighborhood: *There are no stores in the vicinity of our house.* **2.** state or fact of being near; proximity; propinquity: *He was troubled by the vicinity of the nuclear testing area.* [1550–60; < L *vīcīnitās,* equiv. to *vīcīn(us)* near (*vīc(us)* WICK[3], neighborhood + *-īnus* -INE[1]) + *-itās* -ITY]

vi·cious (vish′əs), *adj.* **1.** addicted to or characterized by vice; grossly immoral; depraved; profligate: *a vicious life.* **2.** given or readily disposed to evil: *a vicious criminal.* **3.** reprehensible; blameworthy; wrong: *a vicious deception.* **4.** spiteful; malicious: *vicious gossip; a vicious attack.* **5.** unpleasantly severe: *a vicious headache.* **6.** characterized or marred by faults or defects; faulty; unsound: *vicious reasoning.* **7.** savage; ferocious: *They all feared his vicious temper.* **8.** (of an animal) having bad habits or a cruel or fierce disposition: *a vicious bull.* **9.** *Archaic.* morbid, foul, or noxious. [1300–50; ME (< AF) < L *vitiōsus,* equiv. to *viti(um)* fault, VICE[1] + *-ōsus* -OUS] **—vi′cious·ly,** *adv.* **—vi′cious·ness,** *n.*
—Syn. 1. abandoned, corrupt, iniquitous, sinful. **4.** malevolent. **—Ant. 1.** moral.

vi′cious cir′cle, 1. *Logic.* **a.** (in demonstration) the use of each of two propositions to establish the other. **b.** (in definition) the use of each of two terms to define the other. **2.** a situation in which effort to solve a given problem results in aggravation of the problem or the creation of a worse problem: *a vicious circle where the more I give them, the more they expect.* [1785–95]

vi·cis·si·tude (vi sis′i to͞od′, -tyo͞od′), *n.* **1.** a change or variation occurring in the course of something. **2.** interchange or alternation, as of states or things. **3. vicissitudes,** successive, alternating, or changing phases or conditions, as of life or fortune; ups and downs: *They remained friends through the vicissitudes of 40 years.* **4.** regular change or succession of one state or thing to another. **5.** change; mutation; mutability. [1560–70; < L *vicissitūdō,* equiv. to *viciss(im)* in turn (perh. by syncope < **vice-cessim; vice* in the place of (see VICE[3]) + *cessim* giving way, adv. deriv. of *cēdere* to go, proceed) + *-i-* -I- *-tūdō* -TUDE] **—vi·cis·si·tu·di·nar·y** (vi sis′i to͞od′n er′ē, -tyo͞od′-), **vi·cis′si·tu′di·nous,** *adj.*

Vick (vik), *n.* a male given name, form of **Victor.**

Vick·ers (vik′ərz), *n.* **Jon,** born 1926, Canadian operatic tenor.

Vick′ers num′ber, *Metall.* a numerical expression of the hardness of a metal as determined by a test **(Vick′ers test′)** in which the sample is indented under a known pressure by the point of a diamond and the surface area of the indentation is divided into the amount of pressure applied. [after *Vickers* Armstrong Ltd., British steel firm]

Vicks·burg (viks′bûrg), *n.* a city in W Mississippi, on the Mississippi River: important Civil War siege and Confederate surrender 1863. 25,434.

Vick·y (vik′ē), *n.* a female given name, form of **Victoria.** Also, **Vick′ie.**

Vi·co (vik′ō, vē′kō; *It.* vē′kô), *n.* **Gio·van·ni Bat·tis·ta** (jô vän′nē bät tēs′tä), 1668–1744, Italian philosopher and jurist. **—Vi·co·ni·an** (vi kō′nē ən), *adj.*

vi·comte (vē kônt′), *n., pl.* **-comtes** (-kônt′). a French viscount. [< F: VISCOUNT]

vi·com·tesse (vē kôn tes′), *n., pl.* **-tesses** (-tes′). the wife or widow of a vicomte; a French viscountess. [< F, equiv. to *vicomte* VISCOUNT + *-esse* -ESS]

vi·con·ti·el (vī kon′tē əl), *adj. Early Eng. Law.* pertaining to the sheriff or viscount. [1540–50; < AF *viconitel;* see VISCOUNT, -AL[1]]

Vict., 1. Victoria. **2.** Victorian.

vic·tim (vik′tim), *n.* **1.** a person who suffers from a destructive or injurious action or agency: *a victim of an automobile accident.* **2.** a person who is deceived or cheated, as by his or her own emotions or ignorance, by the dishonesty of others, or by some impersonal agency: *a victim of misplaced confidence; the victim of a swindler; a victim of an optical illusion.* **3.** a person or animal sacrificed or regarded as sacrificed: *war victims.* **4.** a living creature sacrificed in religious rites. [1490–1500; < L *victima* sacrificial animal] **—vic′tim·hood′,** *n.* **—vic′tim·less,** *adj.*

vic·tim·ize (vik′tə mīz′), *v.t.,* **-ized, -iz·ing. 1.** to make a victim of. **2.** to dupe, swindle, or cheat: *to victimize poor widows.* **3.** to slay as or like a sacrificial victim. Also, *esp. Brit.,* **vic′tim·ise′.** [1820–30; VICTIM + -IZE] **—vic′tim·i·za′tion,** *n.* **—vic′tim·iz′er,** *n.*
—Syn. 2. defraud, fool, hoodwink, beguile. See **cheat.**

vic′timless crime′, a legal offense, as prostitution or gambling, to which all participating parties have consented. [1960–65]

Vic·toire (vēk twar′), *n.* a female given name, French form of **Victoria.**

vic·tor (vik′tər), *n.* **1.** a person who has overcome or defeated an adversary; conqueror. **2.** a winner in any struggle or contest. **3.** a word used in communications to represent the letter *V.* [1300–50; ME < L, equiv. to *vic-,* var. s. of *vincere* to conquer + *-tor* -TOR]

Vic·tor (vik′tər), *n.* **1.** an ancient Roman epithet variously applied to Jupiter, Mars, and Hercules. **2.** *Mil.* the NATO name for a class of nuclear-powered Soviet attack submarines. **3.** a male given name.

Victor I, Saint, pope A.D. 189–198.

Victor II, *(Gebhard)* 1018–57, German ecclesiastic: pope 1055–57.

Victor III, *(Dauferius)* 1027–87, Italian ecclesiastic: pope 1086–87.

Vic′tor Char′lie, *Mil. Slang.* a Vietcong or the Vietcong; the VC. [1965–70; communications code for V(IET) C(ONG)]

Victor Em·man·u·el I (i man′yo͞o əl), 1759–1824, king of Sardinia 1802–21.

Victor Emmanuel II, 1820–78, king of Sardinia 1849–78; first king of Italy 1861–78.

Victor Emmanuel III, 1869–1947, king of Italy 1900–46.

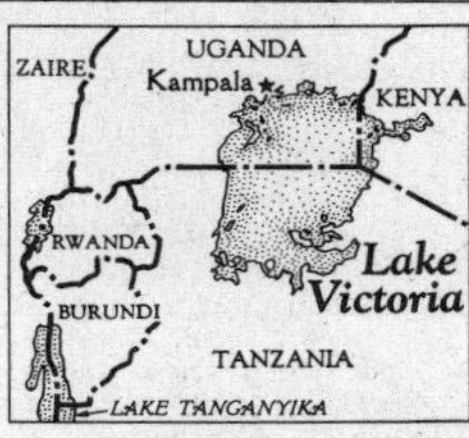

Vic·to·ri·a (vik tôr′ē ə, -tōr′-; *for 3 also Sp.* bēk tô′·ryä), *n.* **1.** the ancient Roman goddess of victory, identified with the Greek goddess Nike. **2.** 1819–1901, queen of Great Britain 1837–1901; empress of India 1876–1901. **3. Gua·da·lupe** (gwäd′l o͞op′, -o͞o′pē; *Sp.* gwä′thä lo͞o′·pe) *(Manuel Félix Fernández),* 1789–1843, Mexican military and political leader: first president of the republic 1824–29. **4.** Also called **Hong Kong, Xianggang.** a seaport in and the capital of the Hong Kong colony, on the N coast of Hong Kong island, facing the seaport of Kowloon. 1,100,000. **5.** a state in SE Australia. 3,832,443; 87,884 sq. mi. (227,620 sq. km). *Cap.:* Melbourne. **6.** a seaport in and the capital of British Columbia, on Vancouver Island, in SW Canada. 62,551. **7.** a city in S Texas. 50,695. **8.** a former name of **Nyanda. 9.** a port in and the capital of the Seychelles. 13,736. **10. Lake.** Also called **Victoria Nyanza.** a lake in E central Africa, in Uganda, Tanzania, and Kenya: second largest freshwater lake in the world; source of the White Nile. 26,828 sq. mi. (69,485 sq. km). **11. Mount,** a mountain on E New Guinea, in SE Papua New Guinea, in the Owen Stanley Range. 13,240 ft. (4036 m). **12.** *(l.c.)* a low, light, four-wheeled carriage with a calash top, a seat for two passengers, and a perch in front for the driver. **13.** *(l.c.)* an open touring car having a folding top that usually covers only the rear seat. **14.** *(l.c.)* any of several large-leaved water lilies of the genus *Victoria.* Cf. **royal water lily. 15.** a female given name.

victoria
(def. 12)

Victo′ria Cross′, a British decoration awarded to soldiers and sailors for acts of conspicuous bravery in the presence of the enemy. *Abbr.:* V.C. [1855–60]

Victo′ria Day′, (in Canada) the first Monday preceding May 25, observed as a national holiday.

Victo′ria Des′ert. See **Great Victoria Desert.**

Victo′ria Falls′, 1. falls of the Zambezi River in S Africa, between Zambia and Zimbabwe, near Livingstone. 420 ft. (130 m) high; more than 1 mi. (1.6 km) wide. **2.** former name of **Iguassú Falls.**

Victo′ria Is′land, an island off the coast of N Canada, in the Arctic Ocean. 80,340 sq. mi. (208,081 sq. km).

Victo′ria Land′, a region in Antarctica, bordering on the Ross Sea, mainly in Ross Dependency.

Vic·to·ri·an (vik tôr′ē ən, -tōr′-), *adj.* **1.** of or pertaining to Queen Victoria or the period of her reign: *Victorian poets.* **2.** having the characteristics usually attributed to the Victorians, esp. prudishness and observance of the conventionalities. **3.** *Archit.* **a.** noting or pertaining to the architecture, furnishings, and decoration of English-speaking countries between c1840 and c1900, characterized by rapid changes of style as a consequence of aesthetic and philosophical controversy, technological innovations, and changes of fashion, by the frequent presence of ostentatious ornament, and by an overall trend from classicism at the start to romanticism and eclecticism at the middle of the period and thence to classicism again, with attempts at stylistic innovation occurring from time to time. **b.** noting or pertaining to the massive, elaborate work characteristic esp. of the period c1855–80, derived mainly from the Baroque and Gothic styles and characterized by the presence of heavy carved ornament, elaborate moldings, etc., by the use of strong and generally dark colors, by the frequent use of dark varnished woodwork, by the emphasis on geometrical form rather than on textural effects, and frequently by

an effect of harshness. —*n.* **4.** a person who lived during the Victorian period. **5.** a house in or imitative of the Victorian style. [1870–75; VICTORI(A) + -AN]
—Syn. 2. prudish, conventional, priggish, straight-laced, smug, prim, narrow.

Victorian sideboard

Vic•to•ri•an•a (vik tôr′ē an′ə, -ä′nə, -tōr′-), *n.pl.* Victorian art objects, furnishings, bric-a-brac, etc. [1945–50; VICTORI(AN) + -ANA]

Victo′rian box′, a tree, *Pittosporum undulatum,* of Australia, having shiny, wavy-margined, oblong leaves and fragrant clusters of yellowish flowers. Also called **banyalla.**

Vic•to•ri•an•ism (vik tôr′ē ə niz′əm, -tōr′-), *n.* **1.** the distinctive character, thought, tendencies, etc., of the Victorian period. **2.** an instance or example of such thought, tendencies, etc. [1900–05; VICTORIAN + -ISM]

Victo′ria Ny•an′za (nī an′zə, nē-, nyän′zä), Victoria (def. 10).

vic•to•ri•ate (vik tôr′ē it, -āt′, -tōr′-), *n.* a silver coin of ancient Rome, first issued in the late 3rd century B.C., having a figure of Victory on the reverse. [1595–1605; < L (*nummus* coin) *victōriātus,* equiv. to *victōri(a)* VICTORY + *-ātus* -ATE[1]]

Vic•to•ri•a•ville (vik tôr′ē ə vil′, -tōr′-), *n.* a town in S Quebec, in E Canada. 21,838.

vic•to•rine (vik′tə rēn′), *n.* a fur tippet with long tabs at the ends. [1840–50; prob. after Queen VICTORIA; see -INE[2]]

Vic•to•rine (vik′tə rēn′), *n.* a canon regular of the Order of St. Victor, founded in Paris, France, in 1110, which was famous for its learning and influence in the Middle Ages, and which became extinct during the French Revolution. [1880–85; < F *Victorin*]

Vic•to•ri•o (vik tôr′ē ō′, -tōr′-), *n.* 1809?–80, leader of the Chiricahua Apache tribe.

vic•to•ri•ous (vik tôr′ē əs, -tōr′-), *adj.* **1.** having achieved a victory; conquering; triumphant: *our victorious army.* **2.** of, pertaining to, or characterized by victory. [1350–1400; ME; see VICTORY, -OUS] **—vic•to′ri•ous•ly,** *adv.* **—vic•to′ri•ous•ness,** *n.*

Vic•tor•ville (vik′tər vil′), *n.* a city in SE California. 14,220.

vic•to•ry (vik′tə rē, vik′trē), *n., pl.* **-ries. 1.** a success or triumph over an enemy in battle or war. **2.** an engagement ending in such triumph: *American victories in the Pacific were won at great cost.* **3.** the ultimate and decisive superiority in any battle or contest: *The new vaccine effected a victory over poliomyelitis.* **4.** a success or superior position achieved against any opponent, opposition, difficulty, etc.: *a moral victory.* **5.** (*cap.*) the ancient Roman goddess Victoria, often represented in statues or on coins as the personification of victory. [1275–1325; ME *victorie* < L *victōria,* equiv. to *victōr-,* s. of *victor* VICTOR + *-ia* -Y[3]] **—vic′to•ry•less,** *adj.*
—Syn. 3. VICTORY, CONQUEST, TRIUMPH refer to a successful outcome of a struggle. VICTORY suggests the decisive defeat of an opponent in a contest of any kind: *victory in battle; a football victory.* CONQUEST implies the taking over of control by the victor, and the obedience of the conquered: *the conquest of Peru.* TRIUMPH implies a particularly outstanding victory: *the triumph of justice.* **—Ant. 1–3.** defeat.

vic′tory gar′den, a vegetable garden, esp. a home garden, cultivated to increase food production during a war or period of shortages. Also, **Vic′tory gar′den.** [1940–45]

Vic′tory Med′al, 1. a round bronze medal awarded to all those who served in the armed forces of the U.S. during World War I. **2.** a similar medal awarded after World War II.

Vic′tory of Sam′othrace. See **Winged Victory.**

Vic′tory ship′, a fast, turbine-powered cargo ship of World War II, having a capacity of about 11,000 deadweight tons. [1940–45, *Amer.*]

vic•tress (vik′tris), *n.* a woman who is victorious. [1595–1605; VICT(O)R + -ESS]
—Usage. See **-ess.**

vic•trix (vik′triks), *n., pl.* **vic•tri•ces** (vik′trə sēz′). victress. [1645–55; < L; see VICTOR, -TRIX]
—Usage. See **-trix.**

Vic•trix (vik′triks), *n.* an ancient Roman epithet variously applied to Venus, Diana, and other goddesses.

Vic•tro•la (vik trō′lə), *Trademark.* a brand of phonograph.

CONCISE ETYMOLOGY KEY: <, descended or borrowed from; >, whence; b., blend of, blended; c., cognate with; cf., compare; deriv., derivative; equiv., equivalent; imit., imitative; obl., oblique; r., replacing; s., stem; sp., spelling, spelled; resp., respelling, respelled; trans., translation; ?, origin unknown; *, unattested; ‡, probably earlier than. See the full key inside the front cover.

vict•ual (vit′l), *n., v.,* **-ualed, -ual•ing** or (*esp. Brit.*) **-ualled, -ual•ling.** —*n.* **1. victuals,** food supplies; provisions. **2.** food or provisions for human beings. —*v.t.* **3.** to supply with victuals. —*v.i.* **4.** to take or obtain victuals. **5.** *Archaic.* to eat or feed. Also, **vittle.** [1275–1325; ME *vitaille* < AF, MF *vitail(l)e,* OF *vituaille* < LL *victuālia* provisions, n. use of neut. pl. of L *victuālis* pertaining to food, equiv. to *victu(s)* nourishment, way of living (*vic-,* var. s. of *vīvere* to live + *-tus* suffix of v. action) + *-ālis* -AL[1]; mod. sp. < L] **—vict′•ual•less,** *adj.*

vict•ual•age (vit′l ij), *n.* food; provisions; victuals. [1615–25; VICTUAL + -AGE]

vict•ual•er (vit′l ər), *n.* **1.** a person who furnishes victuals, esp. a sutler. **2.** a supply ship. **3.** Also called **licensed victualer.** *Brit.* the keeper of an inn or tavern, esp. one licensed to sell liquor. Also, *esp. Brit.,* **vict′ual•ler.** [1350–1400; ME *vitailler* < AF; MF *vitail(l)ier.* See VICTUAL, -ER[2]]

vi•cu•na (vī ko͞o′nə, -kyo͞o′-, vi-, vi ko͞o′nyə), *n.* **1.** a wild South American ruminant, *Vicugna vicugna,* of the Andes, related to the guanaco but smaller, and yielding a soft, delicate wool: an endangered species, now increasing in numbers. **2.** a fabric of this wool or of some substitute, usually twilled and finished with a soft nap. **3.** a garment, esp. an overcoat, of vicuna. Also, **vi•cu′ña.** [1585–95; < Sp *vicuña* < Quechua *wik'uña*]

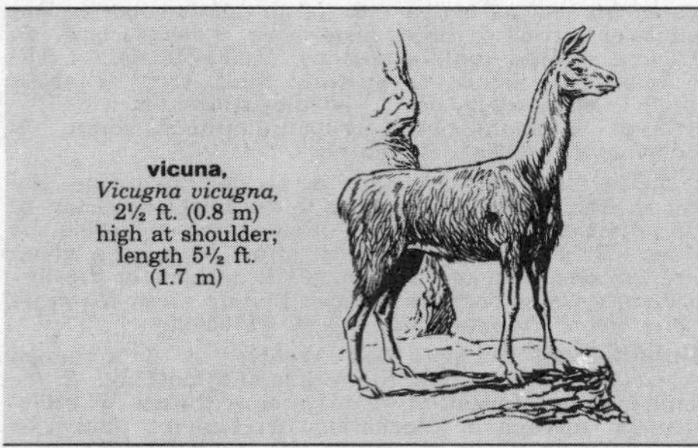
vicuna, *Vicugna vicugna,* 2½ ft. (0.8 m) high at shoulder; length 5½ ft. (1.7 m)

vid., vide.

Vi•da (vē′də, vī′də), *n.* a female given name.

Vi•da Bre•ve, La (*Sp.* lä bē′thä brē′ve), an opera (1905) by Manuel de Falla.

Vi•dal•ia (vi dāl′yə), *n.* a town in central Georgia. 10,393.

Vi•dar (vē′där), *n. Scand. Myth.* a son of Odin, who will survive Ragnarok after killing Fenrir.

vi•dar•a•bine (vī dar′ə bīn′), *n. Pharm.* an antiviral substance, $C_{10}H_{15}N_5O_4$, produced by the bacterium *Streptomyces antibioticus* and used in immunosuppressed patients for the treatment of serious infections caused by herpesviruses. Also called **adenosine arabinoside.** [1975–80; VI(RAL) + D- + ARAB(INOSE) + (ADEN)INE]

vi•de (wē′de; *Eng.* vī′dē, vē′-), *v. Latin.* see (used esp. to refer a reader to parts of a text).

vi•de ante (wē′de än′te; *Eng.* vī′dē an′tē, vē′-), *Latin.* see before (used esp. to refer a reader to parts of a text).

vi•de in•fra (wē′de in′frä; *Eng.* vī′dē in′frə, vē′-), *Latin.* see below (used esp. to refer a reader to parts of a text).

vi•de•li•cet (wi dā′li ket′; *Eng.* vi del′ə sit), *adv. Latin.* that is to say; namely (used esp. to introduce examples, details, etc.). *Abbr.:* viz.

vid•e•o (vid′ē ō′), *n.* **1.** *Television.* **a.** the elements of television, as in a program or script, pertaining to the transmission or reception of the image (distinguished from *audio*). **b.** the video part of a television broadcast. **2.** *Informal.* videotape. **3.** *Informal.* television: *She is a star of stage and video.* **4.** a program, movie, or the like, that is available commercially on videocassette. **5.** See **music video.** —*adj.* **6.** of or pertaining to the electronic apparatus for producing the television picture: *video amplifier.* **7.** of or pertaining to television, esp. the visual elements. **8.** of or pertaining to videocassettes, videocassette recorders, music video, etc.: *a video shop.* **9.** pertaining to or employed in the transmission or reception of television pictures. [1930–35; < L *vidē(re)* to see + -O as in AUDIO]

vid′eo art′, an art form involving the creative exploitation of video technology to produce videotapes for viewing on a television screen. [1970–75] **—vid′eo art′ist.**

vid•e•o•cas•sette (vid′ē ō kə set′, -ka-), *n.* a cassette enclosing a length of tape for video recording or reproduction. [1965–70; VIDEO + CASSETTE]

vid′eocassette record′er, an electronic apparatus capable of recording television programs or other signals onto videocassettes and playing them back through a television receiver. Also called **VCR** [1970–75]

vid•e•o•cast (vid′ē ō kast′, -käst′), *v.,* **-cast** or **-cast•ed, -cast•ing,** *n.* —*v.t., v.i.* **1.** to telecast only the video portion of (a program, scene, etc.). —*n.* **2.** a television broadcast of the video only. [VIDEO + (TELE)CAST]

vid•e•o•con•fer•ence (vid′ē ō kon′fər əns, -frəns), *n.* a teleconference conducted via television equipment. [1970–75; VIDEO + CONFERENCE]

vid•e•o•con•fer•enc•ing (vid′ē ō kon′fər ən sing, -frən-), *n.* the holding of videoconferences. [1975–80; VIDEOCONFERENCE + -ING[1]]

vid•e•o•disk (vid′ē ō disk′), *n.* See under **record** (def. 17). Also, **vid′e•o•disc′.** [1965–70; VIDEO + DISK]

vid′eodisk play′er, an electronic device for playing videodisks through a television set.

vid′eo display′ ter′minal, *Computers.* a computer terminal consisting of a screen on which data or graphics can be displayed. *Abbr.:* VDT Also called **visual display terminal;** *esp. Brit.,* **visual display unit.** [1975–80]

vid′eo dra′ma, teledrama.

vid′eo fre′quency, *Television.* **1.** transmission frequency of the television picture. **2.** any of the frequencies present in the output of a television camera, from almost 0 to over 4 megahertz. **3.** any frequency applied to the receiver's picture tube in order to display the picture. [1935–40]

vid′eo game′, 1. any of various games played using a microcomputer with a keyboard and often joysticks to manipulate changes or respond to the action or questions on the screen. **2.** any of various games played using a microchip-controlled device, as an arcade machine or hand-held toy. Also called **electronic game.** [1970–75]

vid•e•o•gen•ic (vid′ē ō jen′ik), *adj.* telegenic. [VIDEO + -GENIC]

vid•e•og•ra•pher (vid′ē og′rə fər), *n.* a person who makes videotapes with a camcorder. [1970–75; VIDEO + (PHOTO)GRAPHER]

vid′eo jock′ey, a person who plays, announces, and comments on videocassette recordings, as on a music video broadcast or at a discotheque.

vid′eo jour′nalism, *Television.* **1.** the techniques, methods, etc., of preparing and broadcasting informational, social, political, and other nonfiction subjects via news and documentary programs. **2.** the news items, programs, etc., that are broadcast. **—vid′eo jour′nalist.**

vid•e•o•phile (vid′ē ə fīl′), *n.* an enthusiast of television, video recording, video equipment, or the like. [VIDEO + -PHILE]

vid•e•o•phone (vid′ē ō fōn′), *n.* a telephone that incorporates both voice and video capabilities. Cf. **Picturephone.** [1950–55; VIDEO + (TELE)PHONE]

vid•e•o•play (vid′ē ō plā′), *n.* teleplay. [VIDEO + PLAY]

vid•e•o•porn (vid′ē ō pôrn′), *n. Informal.* pornographic movies available commercially on videocassettes or, sometimes, shown on subscription television. [VIDEO + PORN]

vid′eo rec′ord. See **music video.** [1960–65]

vid•e•o•re•cord (vid′ē ō ri kôrd′), *v.t.* to record (programs, broadcasts, or the like) on videotape or videodisk. [1960–65]

vid•e•o•re•cord•er (vid′ē ō ri kôr′dər), *n. Television.* an electronic device for recording video signals on magnetic tape or on videodisks. Also, **vid′eo record′er.** Cf. **videocassette recorder.** [1950–55; VIDEO + RECORDER]

vid′eo screen′, *Computers.* screen (def. 6a). Also, **vid′e•o•screen′.**

vid•e•o•tape (vid′ē ō tāp′), *n., v.,* **-taped, -tap•ing.** —*n.* **1.** magnetic tape on which the electronic impulses produced by the video and audio portions of a television program, motion picture, etc., are recorded (distinguished from *audiotape*). —*v.t.* **2.** to record (programs, etc.) on videotape. [VIDEO + TAPE] **—vid′e•o•tap′er,** *n.*

vid′eotape record′er, *Television.* a device for recording television programs on magnetic tape. Also called **VTR** [1950–55]

vid•e•o•tex (vid′ē ō teks′), *n.* an electronic information transmission and retrieval technology enabling interactive communication, for such purposes as data acquisition and dissemination and electronic banking and shopping, between typically large and diverse computer databases and users of home or office display terminals connected to telephone or cable-television lines, or through use of broadcast television signals. Also, **vid•e•o•text, vid•e•o•text** (vid′ē ō tekst′). Cf. **teletext, viewdata.** [1975–80; VIDEO + TEX(T)]

vid′eo vé•ri•té′ (ver′i tā′; *Fr.* vā rē tā′), *Television.* a technique, derived from cinéma vérité, in which people in real life are portrayed as they actually are without rehearsal. [1965–70; see CINÉMA VÉRITÉ]

vi•de post (wē′de pōst′; *Eng.* vī′dē pōst′, vē′-), *Latin.* see after or further (used esp. to refer a reader to parts of a text).

vi•de su•pra (wē′de so͞o′prä; *Eng.* vī′dē so͞o′prə, vē′-), *Latin.* see above (used esp. to refer a reader to parts of a text).

vi•dette (vi det′), *n.* vedette.

vi•de ut su•pra (wē′de o͝ot so͞o′prä; *Eng.* vī′dē ut so͞o′prə, vē′-), *Latin.* see as (stated) above (used esp. to refer a reader to parts of a text).

Vi•dev•dat (vi dāv′dät), *n. Zoroastrianism.* Vendidad.

vid•i•con (vid′i kon′), *n. Television.* a camera tube in which a charge-density pattern is formed on a photoconductive surface scanned by a beam of low-velocity electrons for transmission as signals. Cf. **Saticon.** [1945–50; VID(EO) + ICON(OSCOPE)]

Vi•dor (vē′dôr, -dōr), *n.* **1. King (Wallis),** 1895–1982, U.S. motion-picture director and producer. **2.** a town in SE Texas. 12,117.

vi•du•i•ty (vi do͞o′i tē, -dyo͞o′-), *n.* quality, state, or period of being a widow. [1375–1425; late ME (Scots) *viduite* < L *viduitās,* equiv. to *vidu(a)* WIDOW + *-itās* -ITY]

vid•ya (vid′yä), *n. Hinduism, Buddhism.* transcendental knowledge leading toward Brahman. Cf. **avidya.** [< Skt *vidyā* knowledge]

vie (vī), *v.,* **vied, vy•ing.** —*v.i.* **1.** to strive in competition or rivalry with another; contend for superiority: *Swimmers from many nations were vying for the title.* —*v.t.* **2.** *Archaic.* to put forward in competition or rivalry. **3.** *Obs.* to stake in card playing. [1525–35; by aphesis < MF *envier* to raise the stake (at cards), OF: to

challenge, provoke < L *invītāre* to entertain, INVITE] —**vi′er,** *n.*
—**Syn. 1.** compete, contest, struggle.

Vi•en•na (vē en′ə), *n.* **1.** German, **Wien.** a port in and the capital of Austria, in the NE part, on the Danube. 1,515,666. **2.** a city in NE Virginia. 15,469. **3.** a town in W West Virginia. 11,618.

Vien′na Interna′tional, a socialist organization formed in Vienna in 1921 and merged in 1923 with the Second International to form the Labor and Socialist International. Cf. **international** (def. 6).

Vien′na sau′sage, a small frankfurter, often served as an hors d'oeuvre. Also, **vien′na sau′sage.** [1900–05]

Vienne (vyen), *n.* **1.** a city in SE France, on the Rhone River, S of Lyons: Roman ruins. 28,753. **2.** a department in W France. 357,366; 2720 sq. mi. (7045 sq. km). *Cap.:* Poitiers.

Vi•en•nese (vē′ə nēz′, -nēs′), *adj., n., pl.* **-nese.** —*adj.* **1.** of, pertaining to, or characteristic of Vienna: *a Viennese waltz; a Viennese café.* —*n.* **2.** a native or inhabitant of Vienna. [1830–40; VIENN(A) + -ESE]

Vi′ennese ta′ble, a dessert buffet, as at a reception, featuring a variety of fancy cakes, tarts, mousses, etc.

Vien•tiane (vyen tyän′), *n.* a city in and the capital of Laos, on the Mekong River, in the NW part. 176,637.

Vie•reck (vēr′ek), *n.* **Peter,** born 1916, U.S. poet and historian.

Vi•et (vē et′, vyet), *Informal.* —*n.* **1.** South Vietnam, North Vietnam, or both. —*adj.* **2.** Vietnamese. [1955–60; by shortening]

Vi•et•cong (vē et′kong′, -kông′, vyet′-, vē′it-), *n., pl.* **-cong,** *adj.* (during the Vietnam War) —*n.* **1.** a Communist-led army and guerrilla force in South Vietnam that fought its government and was supported by North Vietnam. **2.** a member or supporter of this force. —*adj.* **3.** of or pertaining to this force or one of its members or supporters. Also, **Vi•et′ Cong′.** [1960–65; < Vietnamese *Việt-cộng*]

Vi•et•minh (vē et′min′, vyet′-, vē′it-), *n.* **1.** a Vietnamese, Communist-led organization whose forces fought against the Japanese and esp. against the French in Indochina: officially in existence 1941–51. **2.** (*used with a plural v.*) the leaders, supporters, and fighters of this organization. —*adj.* **3.** of or pertaining to the Vietminh. Also, **Vi•et′ Minh′.** [< Vietnamese *Việt-Minh,* short for *Việt-Nam Độc-Lập Đồng-Minh* Vietnam Independence League]

Vi•et•nam (vē et′näm′, -nam′, vyet′-, vē′it-), *n.* **1.** Official name, **Socialist Republic of Vietnam.** a country in SE Asia, comprising the former states of Annam, Tonkin, and Cochin-China: formerly part of French Indochina; divided into North Vietnam and South Vietnam during the Vietnam War but now reunified. 49,200,000; 126,104 sq. mi. (326,609 sq. km). *Cap.:* Hanoi. Cf. **North Vietnam, South Vietnam. 2.** See **Vietnam War.** Also, **Vi•et′ Nam′.**

Vi•et•nam•ese (vē et′nä mēz′, -mēs′, -nə-, vyet′-, vē′it-), *n., pl.* **-ese,** *adj.* —*n.* **1.** a native or inhabitant of Vietnam. **2.** Formerly, **Annamese, Annamite.** the language of Vietnam, of uncertain linguistic affiliation. —*adj.* **3.** of or pertaining to Vietnam or its inhabitants. [1945–50; VIETNAM + -ESE]

Vi•et•nam•i•za•tion (vē et′nə mə zā′shən, vyet′-, vē′it-), *n.* a U.S. policy during the Vietnam War of giving the South Vietnamese government responsibility for carrying on the war, so as to allow for the withdrawal of American troops. [1965–70; VIETNAM + -IZATION]

Vi•et•nam•ize (vē et′nə mīz′, vyet′-, vē′it-), *v.t.,* **-ized, -iz•ing.** to place under Vietnamese control or responsibility; subject to Vietnamization. Also, *esp. Brit.,* **Vi•et′nam•ise′.** [1955–60; VIETNAM + -IZE]

Viet′nam War′, a conflict, starting in 1954 and ending in 1975, between South Vietnam (later aided by the U.S., South Korea, Australia, the Philippines, Thailand, and New Zealand) and the Vietcong and North Vietnam. [1960–65]

Vi•ë•tor (fē′ā tôr′), *n.* **Wil•helm** (vil′helm), 1850–1918, German philologist and phonetician.

Vieux•temps (*Fr.* vyœ tän′), *n.* **Hen•ri Fran•çois Jo•seph** (*Fr.* äɴ rē′ fräɴ swä′ zhô zef′), 1820–81, Belgian violinist and composer.

view (vyo͞o), *n.* **1.** an instance of seeing or beholding; visual inspection. **2.** sight; vision. **3.** range of sight or vision: *Several running deer came into the view of the hunters.* **4.** a sight or prospect of a landscape, the sea, etc.: *His apartment affords a view of the park.* **5.** a picture or photograph of something: *The postcard bears a view of Vesuvius.* **6.** a particular manner of looking at something: *From a practical view, the situation presents several problems.* **7.** contemplation or consideration of a matter with reference to action: *a project in view.* **8.** aim, intention, or purpose. **9.** prospect; expectation: *the view for the future.* **10.** a sight afforded of something from a position stated or qualified: *a bird's-eye view.* **11.** a general account or description of a subject. **12.** a conception of a thing; opinion; theory: *His view was not supported by the facts.* **13.** a survey; inspection: *a view of Restoration comedy.* **14. in view, a.** within range of vision. **b.** under consideration. **c.** as an end sought: *She went over the material with the scholarship examination in view.* **15. in view of,** in consideration of; on account of: *In view of the circumstances, it seems best to wait until tomorrow.* **16. on view,** in a place for public inspection; on exhibition: *The latest models of automobiles are now on view.* **17. with a view to, a.** with the aim or intention of. **b.** with the expectation or hope of: *They saved their money with a view to being able to buy a house someday.* —*v.t.* **18.** to see; watch: *to view a movie.* **19.** to look at; survey; inspect: *to view the construction of a road.* **20.** to contemplate mentally; consider: *to view the repercussions of a decision.* **21.** to regard in a particular light or as specified: *She views every minor setback as a disaster.* **22.** *Fox Hunting.* to sight (a fox). [1375–1425; late ME *v(i)ewe* (n.) < AF; MF *veue* sight < VL **vidūta,* n. use of fem. of **vidūtus,* for L *vīsus,* ptp. of *vidēre* to see]
—**Syn. 4.** VIEW, PROSPECT, SCENE, VISTA refer to a landscape or perspective. VIEW is a general word, referring to whatever lies open to sight: *a fine view of the surrounding country.* PROSPECT suggests a sweeping and often distant view, as from a place of vantage: *a beautiful prospect to the south.* SCENE suggests an organic unity in the details such as is to be found in a picture: *a woodland scene.* VISTA suggests a long, narrow view, as along an avenue between rows of trees: *a pleasant vista.* **8.** object, design, end, intent. **12.** belief, judgment, estimation, assessment, impression, valuation. See **opinion. 18.** witness, contemplate, regard.

view•a•ble (vyo͞o′ə bəl), *adj.* **1.** capable of being viewed; visible. **2.** having sufficient interest to warrant being seen; worthy of being viewed: *a viewable movie.* [VIEW + -ABLE]

view′ cam′era, a camera equipped with a lens mount and film holder that can be raised or set at an angle, a bellows that can be additionally extended, and a back that has a ground glass for focusing, used especially for portraits and landscapes.

view•da•ta (vyo͞o′dā′tə, -dat′ə, -dä′tə), *n.* an interactive videotex service provided over a telephone line or television cable. [1970–75; VIEW + DATA]

view•er (vyo͞o′ər), *n.* **1.** a person or thing that views. **2.** a person who watches television, often a devotee of television or of a particular kind of television program: *a weekly show aimed at teenage viewers.* **3.** any of various optical devices to facilitate viewing, esp. one that is small and boxlike with a magnifying lens, and sometimes a light source, in which a photographic transparency may be viewed. **4.** an eyepiece or viewfinder. **5.** an official inspector of property, public works, or the like. [1375–1425; late ME; see VIEW, -ER[1]]

view•er•ship (vyo͞o′ər ship′), *n.* an audience of viewers, esp. of television, either generally or of a particular kind or program: *Viewership is at its peak in the evening hours.* [1950–55; VIEWER + -SHIP]

view•find•er (vyo͞o′fīn′dər), *n. Photog.* finder (def. 2b). [1890–95; VIEW + FINDER]

view′ halloa′, *Fox Hunting.* the shout made by a hunter on seeing a fox break cover. [1755–65]

view•ing (vyo͞o′ing), *n.* **1.** an act, ceremony, or occasion of seeing, watching, or inspecting: *the viewing of a corpse.* **2.** an instance of watching television: *Which channel offers the best viewing?* [1540–50; VIEW + -ING[1]]

view′ing lens′, *Photog.* See under **reflex camera.**

view•less (vyo͞o′lis), *adj.* **1.** giving no view: *a viewless window.* **2.** without an opinion or opinions. **3.** *Obs.* that cannot be seen; invisible. [1595–1605; VIEW + -LESS] —**view′less•ly,** *adv.*

view′ mark′, a mark stamped on antique armor or metalwork to indicate inspection and approval by the guild or by officials at the place of manufacture.

view•point (vyo͞o′point′), *n.* **1.** a place affording a view of something; position of observation: *to sketch a river from the viewpoint of a bluff.* **2.** an attitude of mind, or the circumstances of an individual that conduce to such an attitude: *new marketing techniques seen from the consumer's viewpoint.* [1855–60; alter. of *point of view,* modeled on *standpoint*]
—**Syn. 2.** standpoint, perspective, position, stance, angle.

view•y (vyo͞o′ē), *adj.,* **view•i•er, view•i•est. 1.** having impractical views; speculative; visionary. **2.** eye-catching; showy. [1840–50; VIEW + -Y[1]]

vi•ga (vē′gə), *n.* a rough-hewn beam, usually of fir, used to support the roof in adobe construction. [1835–45; < Sp]

Vi•gée-Le•brun (vē zhā lə brœɴ′), *n.* **(Ma•rie Anne) É•li•sa•beth** (mä rē′ än ā lē zä bet′), 1755–1842, French painter.

vi•gen•ten•ni•al (vī′jen ten′ē əl), *n.* **1.** a 20th anniversary. **2.** a celebration, meeting, reunion, etc., commemorating such an anniversary. [< L *vīgēn(i)* twenty each + (CEN)TENNIAL]

vi•ges•i•mal (vī jes′ə məl), *adj.* **1.** of, pertaining to, or based on twenty. **2.** twentieth. **3.** proceeding by twenties. [1650–60; < L *vīgēsim(us),* var. (with *g* of *vīgintī* twenty) of *vīcēsimus, vīcēnsimus* twentieth + -AL[1]]

vi•ges•i•mo (vī jes′ə mō′), *n., pl.* **-mos,** *adj. Bookbinding.* twentymo. [1860–65; < L *vīgēsimō*]

vi•ges•i•mo-quar•to (vī jes′ə mō kwôr′tō), *n., pl.* **-tos,** *adj. Bookbinding.* twenty-fourmo. [1860–65]

vi•gi•a (vi jē′ə; *Sp.* bē hē′ä), *n., pl.* **-gi•as** (-jē′əz; *Sp.* -hē′äs). a navigational hazard whose existence or position is uncertain. [1865–70; < Sp *vigía* lookout, reef, prob. < Pg *vigia,* n. deriv. of *vigiar* to watch < L *vigilāre;* see VIGILANT]

vig•il (vij′əl), *n.* **1.** wakefulness maintained for any reason during the normal hours for sleeping. **2.** a watch or a period of watchful attention maintained at night or at other times: *The nurse kept her vigil at the bedside of the dying man.* **3.** a period of wakefulness from inability to sleep. **4.** *Eccles.* **a.** a devotional watching, or keeping awake, during the customary hours of sleep. **b.** Sometimes, **vigils.** a nocturnal devotional exercise or service, esp. on the eve before a church festival. **c.** the eve, or day and night, before a church festival, esp. an eve that is a fast. [1200–50; ME *vigil(i)e* < AF < ML *vigilia* eve of a holy day, special use of L *vigilia* watchfulness, equiv. to *vigil* sentry + *-ia* -Y[3]]

vig•i•lance (vij′ə ləns), *n.* **1.** state or quality of being vigilant; watchfulness: *Vigilance is required in the event of treachery.* **2.** *Pathol.* insomnia. [1560–70; alter. (-ANCE for -ANCY) of obs. *vigilancy* < L *vigilantia;* see VIGILANT, -ANCY]
—**Syn. 1.** alertness, attention, heedfulness, concern, care.

vig′ilance commit′tee, 1. an unauthorized committee of citizens organized for the maintenance of order and the summary punishment of crime in the absence of regular or efficient courts. **2.** *Hist.* (in the South) an organization of citizens using extralegal means to control or intimidate blacks and abolitionists and, during the Civil War, to suppress Union loyalists. [1825–35, *Amer.*]

vig•i•lant (vij′ə lənt), *adj.* **1.** keenly watchful to detect danger; wary: *a vigilant sentry.* **2.** ever awake and alert; sleeplessly watchful. [1470–80; < L *vigilant-* (s. of *vigilāns*), prp. of *vigilāre* to be watchful. See VIGIL, -ANT] —**vig′i•lant•ly,** *adv.* —**vig′i•lant•ness,** *n.*
—**Syn. 2.** wide-awake, sleepless. See **alert.** —**Ant. 1.** careless.

vig•i•lan•te (vij′ə lan′tē), *n.* **1.** a member of a vigilance committee. **2.** any person who takes the law into his or her own hands, as by avenging a crime. —*adj.* **3.** done violently and summarily, without recourse to lawful procedures: *vigilante justice.* [1825–35, *Amer.;* < Sp: vigilant] —**vig•i•lan′te•ism, vig•i•lan•tism** (vij′ə lan′tiz əm, vij′ə lən tiz′əm), *n.*

Vi•gil•i•us (vi jil′ē əs), *n.* died A.D. 555, pope 537–555.

vig′il light′, 1. a small candle in a church lighted as a devotional act. **2.** a candle or small light kept burning before a shrine, icon, etc. [1930–35]

vi•gin•til•lion (vī′jin til′yən), *n., pl.* **-lions,** (*as after a numeral*) **-lion,** *adj.* —*n.* **1.** a cardinal number represented in the U.S. by 1 followed by 63 zeros, and in Great Britain by 1 followed by 120 zeros. —*adj.* **2.** amounting to one vigintillion in number. [1900–05; < L *vīgint(ī)* twenty + *-illion,* as in *million*] —**vi′gin•til′lionth,** *adj.*

vigne•ron (vēnyᵊ rôɴ′), *n., pl.* **-rons** (-rôɴ′). *French.* a winemaker.

vi•gnette (vin yet′), *n., v.,* **-gnet•ted, -gnet•ting.** —*n.* **1.** a decorative design or small illustration used on the title page of a book or at the beginning or end of a chapter. **2.** an engraving, drawing, photograph, or the like that is shaded off gradually at the edges so as to leave no definite line at the border. **3.** a decorative design representing branches, leaves, grapes, or the like, as in a manuscript. **4.** any small, pleasing picture or view. **5.** a small, graceful literary sketch. —*v.t.* **6.** *Photog.* to finish (a picture, photograph, etc.) in the manner of a vignette. [1745–55; < F: lit., little vine (see VINE, -ETTE); so called from vinelike decorations in early books] —**vi•gnet′tist,** *n.*

vi•gnet•ter (vin yet′ər), *n.* **1.** *Photog.* a device for blurring the edges of a photographic image so as to fade them into a plain surrounding area. **2.** a vignettist. [1870–75; VIGNETTE + -ER[1]]

Vi•gno•la (vē nyô′lä), *n.* **Gia•co•mo da** (jä′kô mô dä), (*Giacomo Barocchio* or *Barozzi*), 1507–73, Italian architect.

Vi•gny (vē nyē′), *n.* **Al•fred Vic•tor de** (al fred′ vēk tôr′ də), 1797–1863, French poet, novelist, and dramatist.

Vi•go (vē′gō; *for 1 also Fr.* vē gō′; *for 2, 3 also Sp.* bē′gô), *n.* **1. Jean** (zhäɴ), (*Jean Almereyda*), 1905–34, French film director. **2. Bay of,** an inlet of the Atlantic, in NW Spain. 19 mi. (31 km) long. **3.** a seaport on this bay: naval battle 1702. 197,144.

vig•or (vig′ər), *n.* **1.** active strength or force. **2.** healthy physical or mental energy or power; vitality. **3.** energetic activity; energy; intensity: *The economic recovery has given the country a new vigor.* **4.** force of healthy growth in any living matter or organism, as a plant. **5.** active or effective force, esp. legal validity. Also, *esp. Brit.,* **vig′our.** [1300–50; ME *vigo(u)r* < AF; MF *vigeur* < L *vigor* force, energy, equiv. to *vig(ēre)* to be vigorous, thrive + *-or* -OR[1]] —**vig′or•less,** *adj.*
—**Syn. 2.** drive, force, strength.

vig•or•ish (vig′ər ish), *n. Slang.* **1.** a charge paid on a bet, as to a bookie. **2.** interest paid to a moneylender, esp. a usurer. [1910–15, *Amer.;* earlier *viggresh,* perh. < an adaptation in Yiddish slang of Ukrainian *vyhrash* or Russ *výigrysh* winnings, profit]

vi•go•ro•so (vig′ə rō′sō; *It.* vē′gô rô′zô), *adj.* (a musical direction) vigorous or spirited in manner. [1715–25; < It: VIGOROUS]

vig•or•ous (vig′ər əs), *adj.* **1.** full of or characterized by vigor: *a vigorous effort.* **2.** strong; active; robust: *a vigorous youngster.* **3.** energetic; forceful: *vigorous steps; a vigorous personality.* **4.** powerful in action or effect: *vigorous law enforcement.* **5.** growing well, as a plant. [1300–50; ME < OF < ML *vigorōsus.* See VIGOR, -OUS] —**vig′or•ous•ly,** *adv.* —**vig′or•ous•ness,** *n.*
—**Syn. 2.** sturdy, sound, healthy. See **active. 3.** powerful. —**Ant. 1–5.** weak.

vi•gou•reux (vē′gə ro͞o′; *Fr.* vē go͞o rœ′), *n.* a fabric

CONCISE PRONUNCIATION KEY: act, cāpe, dâre, pärt; set, ēqual; if, īce; ox, ōver, ôrder, oil, bo͝ok, bo͞ot, out; up, ûrge; child; sing; shoe; thin, *that;* zh as in *treasure.* ə = *a* as in *alone, e* as in *system, i* as in *easily, o* as in *gallop, u* as in *circus;* ᵊ as in *fire* (fīᵊr), *hour* (ouᵊr). l and n can serve as syllabic consonants, as in *cradle* (krād′l), and *button* (but′n). See the full key inside the front cover.

having a dark and light pattern produced by vigoureux printing. [see VIGOREUX PRINTING]

vigoureux′ print′ing, a printing method in which worsted fibers are printed with the desired color while in sliver form and then processed into yarn, producing a mixed color in the spun yarn and woven fabric. [named after *Vigoureux,* 19th-century French inventor]

Vi·grid (vē′grid), *n. Scand. Myth.* the field on which the last battle between the gods and their enemies is to be fought at the time of Ragnarok. [< ON *Vigrithr,* equiv. to *vīg* battle + *-rīthr,* deriv. of *rītha* to RIDE]

vi·ha·ra (vi här′ə), *n.* **1.** a meeting place of Buddhist monks. **2.** a Buddhist monastery. **3.** (*cap.*) Also called **Brahma Vihara.** one of the four states of mind, namely love, compassion, sympathetic gladness, and equanimity, to be developed by every Buddhist. [1875–80; < Skt *vihāra*]

Vii·pu·ri (vē′po͝o ʀi), *n.* Finnish name of **Vyborg.**

Vi·ja·ya·wa·da (vē′jə yə wä′də), *n.* a city in E Andhra Pradesh, in SE India, on the delta of the Krishna River. 317,258. Also, **Vi·ja·ya·va·da** (vē′jə yə wä′də). Formerly, **Bezwada.**

Vik·i (vik′ē), *n.* a female given name, form of **Victoria.** Also, **Vik′ki.**

Vi·king (vī′king), *n.* (*sometimes l.c.*) **1.** any of the Scandinavian pirates who plundered the coasts of Europe from the 8th to 10th centuries. **2.** a sea-roving bandit; pirate. **3.** a Scandinavian. **4.** *U.S. Aerospace.* one of a series of space probes that obtained scientific information about Mars. [1800–10; < Scand; cf. ON *vikingr;* cf. OE *wīcing* pirate; etym. disputed]

vil., village.

Vi·la (vē′lə), *n.* a seaport in and the capital of Vanuatu. 14,000.

Vi·la No·va de Gai·a (vē′lə nô′və də gī′ə), a city in NW Portugal. 50,805.

vi·la·yet (vē′lä yet′), *n.* a province or main administrative division of Turkey. Also, **eyalet.** [1865–70; < Turk < Ar *wilāyah*]

vile (vīl), *adj.,* **vil·er, vil·est. 1.** wretchedly bad: *a vile humor.* **2.** highly offensive, unpleasant, or objectionable: *vile slander.* **3.** repulsive or disgusting, as to the senses or feelings: *a vile odor.* **4.** morally debased, depraved, or despicable: *vile deeds.* **5.** foul; filthy: *vile language.* **6.** poor; wretched: *vile workmanship.* **7.** of mean or low condition: *a vile beggar.* **8.** menial; lowly: *vile tasks.* **9.** degraded; ignominious: *vile servitude.* **10.** of little value or account; paltry: *a vile recompense.* [1250–1300; ME *vil* < OF < L *vīlis* of little worth, base, cheap] —**vile′ly,** *adv.* —**vile′ness,** *n.*
—**Syn. 1.** See **mean**[2]. **3.** repellent. **4.** vicious, evil, iniquitous. **5.** vulgar, obscene. **9, 10.** contemptible. **10.** trivial, trifling. —**Ant. 1.** good. **4.** elevated.

vil·i·fy (vil′ə fī′), *v.t.,* **-fied, -fy·ing. 1.** to speak ill of; defame; slander. **2.** *Obs.* to make vile. [1400–50; late ME < LL *vīlificāre.* See VILE, -FY] —**vil′i·fi·ca′tion,** *n.* —**vil′i·fi′er,** *n.* —**vil′i·fy′ing·ly,** *adv.*
—**Syn. 1.** depreciate, disparage, calumniate, malign, abuse, asperse, blacken. —**Ant. 1.** commend.

vil·i·pend (vil′ə pend′), *v.t.* **1.** to regard or treat as of little value or account. **2.** to vilify; depreciate. [1425–75; late ME < LL *vīlipendere,* equiv. to L *vīli(s)* cheap (see VILE) + *pendere* to consider (see PENSIVE)] —**vil′i·pend′er,** *n.*

vill (vil), *n.* **1.** a territorial division under the feudal system; township. **2.** village. [1590–1600; < AF; OF *vile, vylle, ville* farm, village; see VILLA]

vil·la (vil′ə), *n.* **1.** a country residence or estate. **2.** any imposing or pretentious residence, esp. one in the country or suburbs maintained as a retreat. **3.** *Brit.* a detached or semidetached dwelling house, usually suburban. [1605–15; (< It) < L *villa* a country house, farm, akin to *vīcus* village, WICK[3]] —**vil′la·like′,** *adj.*

Vil·la (vē′ə; *Sp.* bē′yä), *n.* **Fran·cis·co** (frän sēs′kô), (*Doroteo Arango, "Pancho Villa"*), 1877–1923, Mexican general and revolutionist.

Vi·lla Cis·ne·ros (bē′lyä thēs ne′ʀôs, bē′yä sēs ne′ʀôs), former name of **Dakhla** (def. 2).

vil·la·dom (vil′ə dəm), *n. Brit.* **1.** villas collectively. **2.** suburban life and society; suburbia. [1875–80; VILLA + -DOM]

vil·lage (vil′ij), *n.* **1.** a small community or group of houses in a rural area, larger than a hamlet and usually smaller than a town, and sometimes (as in parts of the U.S.) incorporated as a municipality. **2.** the inhabitants of such a community collectively. **3.** a group of animal dwellings resembling a village: *a gopher village.* —*adj.* **4.** of, pertaining to, or characteristic of a village: *village life.* [1350–1400; ME < MF < L *villāticum,* neut. of *villāticus* VILLATIC. See -AGE] —**vil′lage·less,** *adj.* —**vil′lage·y, vil′lag·y,** *adj.*
—**Syn. 1.** See **community.**

Vil·lage (vil′ij), *n.* **The,** a city in central Oklahoma. 11,049.

vil′lage commu′nity, an early form of community organization in which land belonged to the village, the arable land being allotted to the members or households of the community by more or less permanent arrangements and the waste or excess land remaining undivided.

vil·lag·er (vil′i jər), *n.* an inhabitant of a village. [1560–70; VILLAGE + -ER[1]]

vil·lage·ry (vil′ij rē), *n.* villages. [1580–90; VILLAGE + -RY]

vil·lag·i·za·tion (vil′i jə zā′shən), *n.* the transfer of land to village control. [1965–70; VILLAGE + -IZATION]

CONCISE ETYMOLOGY KEY: <, descended or borrowed from; >, whence; b., blend of, blended; c., cognate with; cf., compare; deriv., derivative; equiv., equivalent; imit., imitative; obl., oblique; r., replacing; s., stem; sp., spelling, spelled; resp., respelling, respelled; trans., translation; ?, origin unknown; *, unattested; ‡, probably earlier than. See the full key inside the front cover.

Vi·lla·her·mo·sa (bē′yä eʀ mô′sä), *n.* a city in and the capital of Tabasco, in E Mexico. 142,384.

vil·lain (vil′ən), *n.* **1.** a cruelly malicious or evil person; scoundrel. **2.** a character in a play, novel, or the like, who constitutes an important evil agency in the plot. **3.** villein. [1275–1325; ME *vilein, vilain* < MF < LL *villānus* a farm servant. See VILLA, -AN]
—**Syn. 1.** knave, rascal, rapscallion, rogue, scamp.

vil·lain·age (vil′ə nij), *n.* villeinage. Also, **vil′lan·age.**

vil·lain·ess (vil′ə nis), *n.* a villainous woman. [1580–90; VILLAIN + -ESS]
—**Usage.** See **-ess.**

vil·lain·ous (vil′ə nəs), *adj.* **1.** having a cruel, wicked, malicious nature. **2.** of, pertaining to, or befitting a villain: *villainous treachery.* **3.** outrageously base, wicked, or vile. **4.** objectionable or unpleasant; wretched: *a villainous storm.* [1300–50; ME; see VILLAIN, -OUS] —**vil′lain·ous·ly,** *adv.* —**vil′lain·ous·ness,** *n.*

vil·lain·y (vil′ə nē), *n., pl.* **-lain·ies. 1.** the actions or conduct of a villain; outrageous wickedness. **2.** a villainous act or deed. **3.** *Obs.* villeinage. [1175–1225; ME *vile(i)nie, vilainie* < OF. See VILLAIN, -Y[3]]

Vil·la-Lo·bos (vē′lä lō′bôs, -bōs, vil′ə-; *Port.* vē′lyä-lô′bo͝osh, -bo͝os), *n.* **Hei·tor** (ā′to͝oʀ), 1881–1959, Brazilian composer.

vil·la·nel·la (vil′ə nel′ə; *It.* vēl′lä nel′lä), *n., pl.* **-nel·le** (-nel′ē; *It.* -nel′le). a rustic Italian part song without accompaniment. [1590–1600; < It, fem. of *villanello* rural, rustic, equiv. to *villan(o)* peasant, boor (see VILLAIN) + *-ello* -ish]

vil·la·nelle (vil′ə nel′), *n. Pros.* a short poem of fixed form, written in tercets, usually five in number, followed by a final quatrain, all being based on two rhymes. [1580–90; < F < It; see VILLANELLA, -ELLE]

Vil·la·no·van (vil′ə nō′vən), *adj.* **1.** Also, **Vil′la·no′va.** of or pertaining to the early Iron Age culture of northern Italy, characterized by lake dwellings. —*n.* **2.** a member of this people. [after *Villanova,* a town in NE Italy; see -AN]

Vil′la Park′ (vil′ə), a city in NE Illinois, near Chicago. 23,185.

Vil·lard (vi lär′, -lärd′), *n.* **1. Henry** (*Ferdinand Heinrich Gustav Hilgard*) 1835–1900, U.S. railroad executive and publisher, born in Bavaria. **2. Oswald Garrison,** 1872–1949, U.S. journalist and author.

Vil·la′ri effect′ (vi lär′ē), *Physics.* the change in magnetic induction that takes place in certain substances when subjected to longitudinal stress. [named after E. *Villari,* 19th-century Italian physicist]

Vi·llar·ri·ca (bē′yär ʀē′kä; *Eng.* vē′ə rē′kə), *n.* a city in S central Paraguay. 18,300.

Vil·lars (vē lar′), *n.* **Claude Louis Hec·tor de** (klōd lwē ek tôʀ′ də), 1653–1734, marshal of France.

vil·lat·ic (vi lat′ik), *adj.* of or pertaining to the country or to a farm; rural. [1665–75; < L *villāticus.* See VILLA, -ATE[1], -IC]

Vi·lla·vi·cen·cio (bē′yä vē sen′syô), *n.* a city in central Colombia. 80,700.

-ville, a combining form extracted from place names ending in *-ville,* used in the coinage of informal nonce words, usu. pejorative, that characterize a place, person, group, or situation (*dullsville; disasterville; Mediaville*) or that name a condition (*embarrassmentville; gloomsville*). [ult. < F *ville* city; see BIDONVILLE]

Vi·lle·da Mo·ra·les (bē ye′thä mô ʀä′les), **Ra·món** (ʀä môn′), 1909?–71, Honduran diplomat and statesman: president 1957–63.

Ville-de-Pa·ris (vēl də pa ʀē′), *n.* a department in N France. 2,299,830; 41 sq. mi. (106 sq. km). *Cap.:* Paris.

vil·lein (vil′ən, -ān, vi lān′), *n.* a member of a class of partially free persons under the feudal system, who were serfs with respect to their lord but had the rights and privileges of freemen with respect to others. Also, **villain.** [1275–1325; ME; see VILLAIN]

vil·lein·age (vil′ə nij), *n.* **1.** the tenure by which a villein held land and tenements from a lord. **2.** the condition or status of a villein. Also, **villainage, villanage, vil′len·age.** [1275–1325; ME *vilenage* < AF, OF. See VILLEIN, -AGE]

vil′lein soc′age, *Medieval Hist.* land held by a tenant who rendered to a lord specified duties of a servile nature. Cf. **free socage.** [1760–70]

Ville·neuve (vēl nœv′), *n.* **Pierre Charles Jean Baptiste Sil·ves·tre de** (pyeʀ shaʀl zhän ba tēst′ sēl-ves′tʀ[e] də), 1763–1806, French admiral.

Ville·ur·banne (vēl yʀ ban′), *n.* a city in E France, near Lyons. 119,438.

Vil·liers (vil′ərz, vil′yərz), *n.* **1. Frederic,** 1852–1922, English artist and war correspondent. **2. George.** See **Buckingham, 1st Duke of. 3. George.** See **Buckingham, 2nd Duke of.**

vil·li·form (vil′ə fôrm′), *adj.* **1.** having the form of a villus. **2.** shaped and set so as to resemble the pile of velvet, as the teeth of certain fishes. [1840–50; < NL *villiformis.* See VILLUS, -I-, -FORM]

Vil·lon (vē yôn′), *n.* **1. Fran·çois** (fʀäɴ swa′), 1431–63?, French poet. **2. Jacques** (zhäk), (*Gaston Duchamp*), 1875–1963, French painter.

vil·lose (vil′ōs), *adj.* villous. [1720–30; < L *villōsus* shaggy. See VILLUS, -OSE[1]]

vil·los·i·ty (vi los′i tē), *n., pl.* **-ties. 1.** a villous surface or coating. **2.** a number of villi together. **3.** a villus. [1770–80; VILLOSE + -ITY]

vil·lous (vil′əs), *adj.* **1.** covered with or of the nature of villi. **2.** having villiform processes. **3.** *Bot.* pubescent with long and soft hairs that are not interwoven. [1350–1400; ME; see VILLOSE, -OUS] —**vil′lous·ly,** *adv.*

vil·lus (vil′əs), *n., pl.* **vil·li** (vil′ī). **1.** *Anat., Zool.* one of the minute, wormlike processes on certain membranes, esp. on the mucous membrane of the small intestine, where they serve in absorbing nutriment. **2.** *Bot.* one of the long, soft, straight hairs covering the fruit, flowers, and other parts of certain plants. [1695–1705; < L: shaggy hair, thick nap]

Vil·ma (vil′mə), *n.* a female given name, form of **Wilhelmina.**

Vil·ni·us (vil′nē o͝os′), *n.* a city in and the capital of Lithuania, in the SE part: formerly in the Soviet Union and earlier in Poland. 582,000. Polish, **Wilno.** Russian, **Vil·na** (vyēl′nə; *Eng.* vil′nə).

vim (vim), *n.* lively or energetic spirit; enthusiasm; vitality. [1835–45, *Amer.*; < L, acc. of *vīs* energy, force]
—**Syn.** vigor, pep, energy, dash.

vi·ma·na (vi mä′nə), *n.* a sanctuary of a Brahman temple. [1860–65; < Skt *vimāna*]

vi·men (vī′mən), *n., pl.* **vim·i·na** (vim′ə nə). *Bot.* a long, flexible shoot of a plant. [< L *vīmen* osier, withe, twig] —**vim·i·nal** (vim′ə nl), *adj.*

Vim·i·nal (vim′ə nl), *n.* one of the seven hills on which ancient Rome was built.

vi·min·e·ous (vi min′ē əs), *adj. Bot.* **1.** of, like, or producing long, flexible shoots. **2.** of or made of twigs. [1645–55; < L *vimineus* made of osiers, equiv. to *vīmin-* (s. of *vīmen*) osier + *-eus* -EOUS]

v. imp., verb impersonal.

vim·pa (vim′pə), *n. Rom. Cath. Ch.* a silk veil falling over the shoulders and extending down the arms and over the hands, worn by acolytes who carry the miter and crosier at a Pontifical Mass. [< ML < Gmc; see WIMPLE]

Vi·my (vim′ē, vē′mē; *Fr.* vē mē′), *n.* a town in N France, N of Arras: battle 1917.

Vin (vin), *n.* a male given name, form of **Vincent.**

vin (vaɴ), *n., pl.* ***vins*** (vaɴ). *French.* wine.

VIN, vehicle identification number.

vin-, var. of **vini-,** esp. before a vowel.

vin., (in prescriptions) wine. [< L *vīnum*]

vi·na (vē′nä, -nə), *n.* a musical stringed instrument of India, made of rosewood or ebony, consisting of a long, hollow, fretted stick to which one, two, or three gourds are attached to increase the resonance. Also, **veena.** [1780–90; < Skt *vīṇā*]

vina

vi·na·ceous (vī nā′shəs), *adj.* **1.** of, pertaining to, or resembling wine or grapes. **2.** of the color of red wine. [1680–90; < L *vīnāceus.* See WINE, -ACEOUS]

Vi·ña del Mar (bē′nyä thel mär′), a city in central Chile, near Valparaiso: seaside resort. 229,020.

vin·ai·grette (vin′ə gret′), *n.* **1.** Also, **vinegarette.** a small, ornamental bottle or box for holding aromatic vinegar, smelling salts, or the like. **2.** See **vinaigrette sauce.** —*adj.* **3.** (of a food, as asparagus or artichoke) served with a sauce made with vinegar or with vinaigrette sauce. [1690–1700; < F, equiv. to *vinaigre* VINEGAR + *-ette* -ETTE]

vinaigrette′ sauce′, a tart sauce of oil, vinegar, and seasonings, sometimes including chopped capers, pickles, etc., usually served cold with salads.

vi·nasse (vi nas′), *n. Distilling.* the residuum in a still after distillation; slop. [< F < Pr *vinassa* < L *vīnācea,* fem. of *vīnāceus* VINACEOUS]

Vin′a·ya Pit′aka (vin′ə yə), *Buddhism.* See under **Pali Canon.**

vin blanc (vaɴ bläɴ′), *pl.* ***vins blancs*** (vaɴ bläɴ′). *French.* See **white wine.**

vin·blas·tine (vin blas′tēn), *n. Pharm.* an alkaloid, $C_{46}H_{58}N_4O_9$, derived from the periwinkle *Vinca rosea,* used in the treatment of various malignant conditions, esp. in the management of lymphomas. [1960–65; < NL *Vin(ca)* a periwinkle genus + (LEUKO)BLAST + -INE[2]]

Vince (vins), *n.* a male given name, form of **Vincent.**

Vin·cennes (vin senz′; *for 2 also Fr.* vaɴ sen′), *n.* **1.** a city in SW Indiana, on the Wabash: the first permanent settlement in Indiana, 1702. 20,857. **2.** a city in N France, near Paris. 44,467.

Vin·cent (vin′sənt), *n.* **1. Saint,** died A.D. 304, Spanish martyr: patron saint of winegrowers. **2.** a male given name: from a Latin word meaning "conquering."

Vin·cent de Paul (vin′sənt də pôl′; *Fr.* vaɴ säɴ′ də pôl′), **Saint,** 1576–1660, French Roman Catholic priest noted for his work to aid the poor.

Vin·cen·tian (vin sen′shən), *Rom. Cath. Ch.* —*n.* **1.** Also called **Lazarist.** a member of the "Congregation of the Mission," founded in France in 1625, engaged chiefly in conducting missions and clerical seminaries. —*adj.* **2.** of or pertaining to St. Vincent de Paul or the Vincentians. [1850–55; VINCENT (DE PAUL) + -IAN]

Vin′cent's angi′na, *Pathol.* a disease characterized by ulceration of the mucosa of the tonsils, pharynx, and mouth, by the presence of abundant bacilli and spirochetes, and by the development of a membrane. Also called **Vin′cent's infec′tion, trench mouth.** [1900–05; named after J. H. *Vincent* (1862–1950), French physician]

Vin·ci (vin′chē; *It.* vēn′chē), *n.* **Le·o·nar·do da** (lē′ə-när′dō də, lā′-; *It.* le′ô näʀ′dô dä). See **Leonardo da Vinci.**

vin•ci•ble (vin′sə bəl), *adj.* capable of being conquered or overcome: *vincible fears.* [1540–50; < L *vincibilis,* equiv. to *vinc(ere)* to overcome + *-ibilis* -IBLE] —**vin′ci•bil′i•ty, vin′ci•ble•ness,** *n.*

vin•cit om•ni•a ve•ri•tas (wing′kit ôm′ni ä′ wā′ri-täs′; *Eng.* vin′sit om′nē ə ver′i tas′, -täs′), *Latin.* truth conquers all things.

vin•cris•tine (vin kris′tēn), *n. Pharm.* an alkaloid, $C_{46}H_{56}N_4O_{10}$, derived from the periwinkle, *Vinca rosea,* used in the management of leukemias and lymphomas. [1960–65; < NL *Vin(ca)* a periwinkle genus + L *crist(a)* CREST + -INE[2]]

vin•cu•lum (ving′kyə ləm), *n., pl.* **-la** (-lə). **1.** a bond signifying union or unity; tie. **2.** *Math.* a stroke or brace drawn over a quantity consisting of several members or terms, as $\overline{a + b}$, in order to show that they are to be considered together. [1655–65; < L: fetter, equiv. to *vinc(ire)* to bind + *-ulum* -ULE]

vin•cu•lum ma•tri•mo•ni•i (wing′kōō lōōm′ mä′tri-mō′ni ē′; *Eng.* ving′kyə ləm ma′tri mō′nē ī′), *Latin.* the bond of matrimony.

vin de pays (vaɴ də pā ē′), *pl.* ***vins de pays*** (vaɴ də pā ē′). *French.* the wine of a particular region, usually available only in the region where the wine is made; local wine. Also, ***vin du pays.***

Vin′dhya Hills′ (vind′yə), a mountain range in central India, N of the Narbada River.

Vin′dhya Pra•desh′ (prə dăsh′, -desh′), a former state in central India: now part of Madhya Pradesh.

vin•di•ca•ble (vin′di kə bəl), *adj.* capable of being vindicated: *a vindicable expedient.* [1625–35; < ML *vindicābilis,* equiv. to L *vindicā(re)* (see VINDICATE) + *-bilis* -BLE] —**vin′di•ca•bil′i•ty,** *n.*

vin•di•cate (vin′di kāt′), *v.t.,* **-cat•ed, -cat•ing. 1.** to clear, as from an accusation, imputation, suspicion, or the like: *to vindicate someone's honor.* **2.** to afford justification for; justify: *Subsequent events vindicated his policy.* **3.** to uphold or justify by argument or evidence: *to vindicate a claim.* **4.** to assert, maintain, or defend (a right, cause, etc.) against opposition. **5.** to claim for oneself or another. **6.** *Roman and Civil Law.* to regain possession, under claim of title of property through legal procedure, or to assert one's right to possession. **7.** to get revenge for; avenge. **8.** *Obs.* to deliver from; liberate. **9.** *Obs.* to punish. [1525–35; < L *vindicātus* (ptp. of *vindicāre* to lay legal claim to (property), to free (someone) from servitude (by claiming him as free), to protect, avenge, punish), equiv. to *vindic-* (s. of *vindex* claimant, protector, avenger) + *-ātus* -ATE[1]] —**vin′di•ca′tor,** *n.*
—**Syn. 1.** exonerate. **3, 4.** support.

vin•di•ca•tion (vin′di kā′shən), *n.* **1.** the act of vindicating. **2.** the state of being vindicated. **3.** defense; excuse; justification: *Poverty was a vindication for his thievery.* **4.** something that vindicates: *Subsequent events were her vindication.* [1475–85; < L *vindicātiōn-* (s. of *vindicātiō*), equiv. to *vindicāt(us)* (see VINDICATE) + *-iōn-* -ION]

vin•di•ca•to•ry (vin′di kə tôr′ē, -tōr′ē), *adj.* **1.** tending or serving to vindicate. **2.** punitive; retributive: *vindicatory killings.* Also, **vin•dic•a•tive** (vin dik′ə tiv, vin′di kā′-). [1640–50; VINDICATE + -ORY[1]]

vin•dic•tive (vin dik′tiv), *adj.* **1.** disposed or inclined to revenge; vengeful: *a vindictive person.* **2.** proceeding from or showing a revengeful spirit: *vindictive rumors.* [1610–20; < L *vindict(a)* vengeance + -IVE] —**vin•dic′tive•ly,** *adv.* —**vin•dic′tive•ness,** *n.*
—**Syn. 1.** unforgiving. See **spiteful.** —**Ant. 1.** forgiving.

vin du pays (vaɴ dʏ pā ē′), *pl.* ***vins du pays*** (vaɴ dʏ pā ē′). *French.* See ***vin de pays.***

vine (vīn), *n.* **1.** any plant having a long, slender stem that trails or creeps on the ground or climbs by winding itself about a support or holding fast with tendrils or claspers. **2.** the stem of any such plant. **3.** a grape plant. [1250–1300; ME < OF *vi(g)ne* < L *vīnea* vine(yard), equiv. to *vīn(um)* WINE + *-ea,* fem. of *-eus* -EOUS] —**vine′less,** *adj.* —**vine′like′,** *adj.*

vin•e•al (vin′ē əl), *adj.* **1.** of or pertaining to grapes or grapevines. **2.** of or pertaining to wine or winemaking. [1650–60; < L *vīneālis,* equiv. to *vīne(a)* VINE + *-ālis* -AL[1]]

vine′ cac′tus, the ocotillo, *Fouquieria splendens.*

vined (vīnd), *adj.* covered or decorated with vines or representations of vines: *a vined brick wall; vined wallpaper.* [1570–80; VINE + -ED[3]]

vine•dress•er (vīn′dres′ər), *n.* a person who tends or cultivates vines, esp. grapevines. [1550–60; VINE + DRESSER[1]]

vin•e•gar (vin′i gər), *n.* **1.** a sour liquid consisting of dilute and impure acetic acid, obtained by acetous fermentation from wine, cider, beer, ale, or the like: used as a condiment, preservative, etc. **2.** *Pharm.* a solution of a medicinal substance in dilute acetic acid, or vinegar. **3.** sour or irritable speech, manner, or countenance: *a note of vinegar in his voice.* **4.** *Informal.* vigor; high spirits; vim. [1250–1300; ME *vinegre* < OF, equiv. to *vin* WINE + *egre, aigre* sour (see EAGER[1])] —**vin′e•gar•like′,** *adj.*

vin′egar eel′, a minute nematode worm, *Anguillula aceti,* common in vinegar, fermenting paste, etc. Also called **vin′egar worm′.** [1830–40]

vin•e•gar•ette (vin′i gə ret′), *n.* vinaigrette (def. 1). [1850–55]

vin′egar fly′, any fly of the family Drosophilidae, the larvae of which feed on decaying fruit and vegetation. Also called **fruit fly, pomace fly.** [1900–05]

vin•e•gar•ish (vin′i gər ish), *adj.* resembling vinegar, as in sourness or acidity: *a vinegarish odor; a vinegarish disposition.* [1640–50; VINEGAR + -ISH[1]]

vin•e•gar•roon (vin′i gə rōōn′), *n.* a large, nonpoisonous whipscorpion, *Mastigoproctus giganteus,* of the southern U.S. and Mexico, which, when disturbed, emits a volatile fluid having a vinegary odor. [1850–55, *Amer.;* < MexSp *vinagrón,* equiv. to Sp *vinagr(e)* VINEGAR + *-ón* aug. suffix]

vin•e•gar•weed (vin′i gər wēd′), *n.* a plant, *Trichostema lanceolatum,* of the mint family, native to the western coast of the U.S., having clusters of blue flowers with long, protruding filaments and growing in dry, sandy soil. Also called **camphorweed.** [VINEGAR + WEED[1]]

vin•e•gar•y (vin′i gə rē), *adj.* **1.** of the nature of or resembling vinegar; sour; acid: *a vinegary taste.* **2.** having a disagreeable character or manner; crabbed; ill-tempered: *a vinegary person.* [1720–30; VINEGAR + -Y[1]]

vine•land (vīn′land′), *n.* land particularly suited to the growing of vines. [VINE + LAND]

Vine•land (vīn′lənd), *n.* **1.** a city in S New Jersey. 53,753. **2.** Vinland.

vine′ ma′ple, a maple, *Acer circinatum,* of the western coast of North America, often having vinelike or prostrate stems that form dense thickets. [1870–75, *Amer.*]

vin•er•y (vī′nə rē), *n., pl.* **-er•ies. 1.** a place or enclosure in which vines, esp. grapevines, are grown. **2.** vines collectively. [1375–1425; VINE + -ERY, r. late ME *vinary* < ML *vīnārium,* n. use of neut. of L *vīnārius* of WINE; see -ARY]

vine′ snake′, any of several slender, arboreal colubrid snakes of the genus *Oxybelis,* ranging from southern Arizona to Bolivia.

vine•yard (vin′yərd), *n.* **1.** a plantation of grapevines, esp. one producing grapes for winemaking. **2.** a sphere of activity, esp. on a high spiritual plane. [1300–50; ME (see VINE, YARD[2]); r. *win(e)yard,* OE *wīngeard*]

vine•yard•ist (vin′yər dist), *n.* a person who owns or operates a vineyard. [1840–50; VINEYARD + -IST]

vingt-et-un (*Fr.* vaɴ tā œɴ′), *n. Cards.* twenty-one (def. 4). [1775–85; < F: lit., twenty-one]

vini-, a combining form meaning "wine," used in the formation of compound words: *viniculture.* Also, **vin-, vino-.** [< L *vīni-,* comb. form of *vīnum*]

vi•nic (vī′nik, vin′ik), *adj.* of, pertaining to, found in, or derived from wine: *a vinic odor.* [1825–35; < L *vīn(um)* WINE + -IC]

vin•i•cul•ture (vin′i kul′chər, vī′ni-), *n.* the science or study of making wines. [1870–75; VINI- + CULTURE] —**vin′i•cul′tur•al,** *adj.* —**vin′i•cul′tur•ist,** *n.*

vi•nif•er•a (vi nif′ər ə, vi-), *adj.* **1.** of, pertaining to, or derived from a European grape, *Vitis vinifera,* widely cultivated for making wine and raisins and for table use. —*n.* **2.** a vinifera grape. [1895–1900; < NL, fem. of L *vinifer* wine-producing. See VINI-, -FER]

vi•nif•er•ous (vi nif′ər əs, vi-), *adj.* suitable for or used in winemaking: *a viniferous variety of grape.* [1825–35; < L *vinifer* (see VINI-, -FER) + -OUS]

vin•i•fi•ca•tion (vin′ə fi kā′shən), *n.* the process of making wine. [1875–80; VINI- + -FICATION]

vin•i•fi•ca•tor (vin′ə fi kā′tər), *n.* a condenser for alcohol vapors escaping from fermenting wine. [VINI- + L *-ficātor* maker (see -FIC, -ATE[1], -OR[2])]

vin•i•fy (vin′ə fī′), *v.,* **-fied, -fy•ing.** —*v.t.* **1.** to produce (a type of wine) by vinification: *to vinify champagne entirely from white grapes.* **2.** to convert (grapes or other fruit) into wine. —*v.i.* **3.** to make wine. **4.** to undergo the winemaking process: *Some juices vinify more quickly than others.* [1965–70; VINI- + -FY]

Vin•land (vin′lənd), *n.* a region in E North America variously identified as a place between Newfoundland and Virginia: visited and described by Norsemen ab. A.D. 1000. Also, **Vineland.**

Vin•ni•tsa (vin′it sə; *Russ.* vyē′nyi tsə), *n.* a city in central Ukraine, on the Bug River. 383,000.

Vin•ny (vin′ē), *n.* a male given name, form of **Vincent.** Also, **Vin′nie.**

vi•no (vē′nō), *n., pl.* **-nos.** *Informal.* wine; specifically, red Italian wine, as chianti. [1895–1900; < It: WINE]

vino-, var. of **vini-.**

vi•no de pas•to (vē′nō də pä′stō; *Sp.* bē′nô de päs′-tô), a pale, dry sherry of Spain. [1860–65; < Sp: lit., everyday (table) wine]

vi•nom•e•ter (vi nom′i tər, vī-), *n.* a hydrometer for measuring the percentage of alcohol in wine. [1860–65; VINO- + -METER]

vin or•di•naire (vaɴ nôr dē neʀ′), *pl.* ***vins or•di•naires*** (vaɴ zôr dē neʀ′). *French.* inexpensive table wine, usually of unspecified origin. [lit., ordinary wine]

vi•nos•i•ty (vi nos′i tē), *n.* the collective characteristics of a wine, esp. its distinctive taste. [1615–25; < LL *vīnōsitās* taste of wine, equiv. to L *vīnōs(us)* VINOUS + *-itās* -ITY]

vi•nous (vī′nəs), *adj.* **1.** of, resembling, or containing wine. **2.** of, pertaining to, or characteristic of wine: *a vinous fragrance.* **3.** produced by, indicative of, or given to indulgence in wine. **4.** wine red; wine-colored: *a vinous hue.* [1655–65; < L *vīnōsus,* equiv. to *vīn(um)* WINE + *-ōsus* -OUS]

vin rouge (vaɴ rōōzh′), *pl.* ***vins rouges*** (vaɴ rōōzh′). *French.* See **red wine.**

Vin•son (vin′sən), *n.* **Frederick Moore,** 1890–1953, U.S. jurist: Chief Justice of the U.S. 1946–53.

Vin′son Massif′, a mountain in Antarctica, near the Ronne Ice Shelf: highest point on Antarctica; discovered 1935. ab. 16,864 ft. (5140 m).

vin•tage (vin′tij), *n., adj., v.,* **-taged, -tag•ing.** —*n.* **1.** the wine from a particular harvest or crop. **2.** the annual produce of the grape harvest, esp. with reference to the wine obtained. **3.** an exceptionally fine wine from the crop of a good year. **4.** the time of gathering grapes, or of winemaking. **5.** the act or process of producing wine; winemaking. **6.** the class of a dated object with reference to era of production or use: *a hat of last year's vintage.* —*adj.* **7.** of or pertaining to wines or winemaking. **8.** being of a specified vintage: *Vintage wines are usually more expensive than nonvintage wines.* **9.** representing the high quality of a past time: *vintage cars; vintage movies.* **10.** old-fashioned or obsolete: *vintage jokes.* **11.** being the best of its kind: *They praised the play as vintage O'Neill.* —*v.t.* **12.** to gather or harvest (grapes) for wine-making: *The muscats were vintaged too early.* **13.** to make (wine) from grapes: *a region that vintages a truly great champagne.* —*v.i.* **14.** to harvest grapes for wine-making. [1400–50; late ME (n.) < AF, equiv. to *vint(er)* VINTNER + *-age* -AGE; r. ME *vindage, vendage* < AF; OF *vendange* < L *vīndēmia* grape-gathering, equiv. to *vīn(um)* grape, WINE + *-dēmia* a taking away (*dēm(ere)* to take from (see REDEEM) + *-ia* -Y[3])]

vin•tag•er (vin′tə jər), *n.* a person who helps in the harvest of grapes for winemaking. [1580–90; VINTAGE + -ER[1]]

vin′tage wine′, a wine, usually of superior quality, made from selected grapes of a certain type, region, and year, then dated and usually stored for aging.

vin′tage year′, 1. the year of production of a vintage wine. **2.** a year in which something of outstanding quality was produced or that was an especially happy or successful time. [1930–35]

vint•ner (vint′nər), *n.* a person who makes wine or sells wines. [1400–50; late ME *vint(e)ner,* deriv. of *vin(e)ter* < AF; OF *vinetier* < ML *vinētārius,* equiv. to L *vinēt(um)* vineyard (*vīn(um)* WINE + *-ētum* suffix denoting place where a given plant grows) + *-ārius* -ARY]

Vin•ton (vin′tn), *n.* a male given name.

vi•num (vī′nəm, vē′-), *n.* (in prescriptions) a solution of a medicinal substance in wine. [< L *vīnum* WINE]

vin•y (vī′nē), *adj.,* **vin•i•er, vin•i•est. 1.** of, pertaining to, of the nature of, or resembling vines: *viny tendrils.* **2.** abounding in or producing vines: *a viny region.* [1560–70; VINE + -Y[1]]

Vi•ny (vī′nē), *n.* a female given name.

vi•nyl (vīn′l), *adj.* **1.** *Chem.* containing the vinyl group. —*n.* **2.** any resin formed by polymerization of compounds containing the vinyl group or plastics made from such resins. [1860–65; < L *vīn(um)* WINE + -YL]

vi′nyl ac′etate, *Chem.* a colorless, easily polymerized, water-insoluble liquid, $C_4H_6O_2$, produced by the reaction of acetylene and acetic acid: used chiefly in the manufacture of plastics, films, paints, and adhesives.

vi•nyl•a•cet•y•lene (vīn′l ə set′l ēn′, -in), *n. Chem.* a colorless, volatile liquid, C_4H_4, used chiefly as an intermediate in the manufacture of the synthetic rubber neoprene. [VINYL + ACETYLENE]

vi′nyl al′cohol, *Chem.* an unstable liquid compound, C_2H_4O, found only in the form of its esters or as the polymer polyvinyl alcohol. [1870–75]

vi•nyl•ate (vīn′l āt′), *v.t.,* **-at•ed, -at•ing.** *Chem.* to subject to vinylation. [back formation from VINYLATION]

vi•nyl•a•tion (vīn′l ā′shən), *n. Chem.* the process of introducing the vinyl group into a compound by reaction with acetylene. [VINYL + -ATION]

vi•nyl•ben•zene (vīn′l ben′zēn, -ben zēn′), *n. Chem.* styrene. [VINYL + BENZENE]

vi′nyl chlo′ride, *Chem.* a colorless, easily liquefied, flammable, slightly water-soluble gas, C_2H_3Cl, having a pleasant, etherlike odor: used in the manufacture of plastics, as a refrigerant, and in the synthesis of polyvinyl chloride and other organic compounds. Also called **chloroethene, chloroethylene.**

vi′nyl e′ther, *Pharm.* a colorless, flammable, slightly water-soluble liquid, C_4H_6O, used as an inhalation anesthetic. Also called **divinyl ether.** [1935–40]

vi•nyl•eth•yl•ene (vīn′l eth′ə lēn′), *n. Chem.* butadiene. [VINYL + ETHYLENE]

vi′nyl group′, *Chem.* the univalent group C_2H_3, derived from ethylene. Also called **vi′nyl rad′ical.**

vi•nyl′i•dene chlo′ride (vī nil′i dēn′), *Chem.* a colorless, volatile, flammable liquid, C_2H_2Cl, that is copolymerized chiefly with vinyl chloride to form saran.

vinyl′idene group′, *Chem.* the bivalent group C_2H_2, derived from ethylene. Also, **vinyl′idene rad′ical.** [VINYL + -ID[3] + -ENE]

vinyl′idene res′in, *Chem.* any of the class of thermoplastic resins derived by the polymerization or copolymerization of a polyvinylidene compound, used similarly to the polyvinyl resins. Also called **polyvinylidene resin.** [1945–50]

Vi•nyl•ite (vīn′l īt′), *Trademark.* a brand name for a series of thermoplastic, nontoxic, acid-resistant, vinyl resins or plastics: used in coatings, adhesives, film, molded ware, and phonograph records.

vi′nyl pol′ymer, *Chem.* any of a group of compounds derived by polymerization from vinyl compounds, as vinyl acetate and styrene.

vi′nyl res′in, *Chem.* See **polyvinyl resin.**

vi•nyl•sty•rene (vīn′l stī′rēn, -stēr′ēn), *n. Chem.* divinylbenzene. [VINYL + STYRENE]

vi•ol (vī′əl), *n.* a bowed musical instrument, differing from the violin in having deeper ribs, sloping shoulders, a greater number of strings, usually six, and frets: common in the 16th and 17th centuries in various sizes from the treble viol to the bass viol. [1475–85; < MF *viole* (akin to OF *viel(l)e* > earlier E *viele*) < OPr *viola,* deriv. of *violar* to play the VIOLA[1] (perh. imit.)]

vi•o•la[1] (vē ō′lə), *n.* **1.** a four-stringed musical instrument of the violin family, slightly larger than the violin; a tenor or alto violin. **2.** a labial organ stop of eight-foot or four-foot pitch, giving tones of a penetrating stringlike quality. [1715–25; < It *viola* < OPr *viola;* see VIOL]

vi•o•la[2] (vī′ə lə, vī ō′-, vē-), *n.* **1.** any plant of the genus *Viola,* esp. a cultivated variety. Cf. **pansy** (def. 1), **violet** (defs. 1, 2). **2.** a pansy, *V. cornuta,* cultivated as a garden plant. [1400–50; late ME: violet < L: violet]

Vi•o•la (vī′ə lə, vē′-; vī ō′lə, vē-), *n.* a female given name.

vi•o•la•ble (vī′ə lə bəl), *adj.* capable of being violated: *a violable precept.* [1425–75; late ME: destructive < L *violābilis,* equiv. to *violā(re)* to VIOLATE + *-bilis* -BLE] —**vi′o•la•bil′i•ty, vi′o•la•ble•ness,** *n.* —**vi′o•la•bly,** *adv.*

vi•o•la•ceous (vī′ə lā′shəs), *adj.* **1.** belonging to the Violaceae, the violet family of plants. Cf. **violet family. 2.** of a violet color; bluish-purple. [1650–60; < NL *Violace(ae)* (see VIOLA[2], -ACEAE) + -OUS]

vi•o′la clef′ (vē ō′lə), *Music.* See **alto clef.**

vi•o•la da brac•cio (vē ō′lə də brä′chō), *pl.* **viola da braccios.** an old musical instrument of the viol family, held against the shoulder like a violin: superseded by the modern viola. [< It: lit., viola for the arm]

vi•o•la da gam•ba (vē ō′lə də gäm′bə, -gam′-), *pl.* **viola da gambas. 1.** an old musical instrument of the viol family, held on or between the knees: superseded by the modern violoncello; bass viol. **2.** an organ stop of eight-foot pitch giving a stringlike tone. [1590–1600; < It: lit., viol for the leg]

viola da gamba

vi•o•la d'a•mo•re (vē ō′lə dä môr′ā, -mōr′ā, -də-), *pl.* **viola d'amores.** a treble viol with numerous sympathetic strings and several gut strings, producing a resonant sound. [1690–1700; < It: lit., viol of love]

vi•o•late (vī′ə lāt′), *v.t.,* **-lat•ed, -lat•ing. 1.** to break, infringe, or transgress (a law, rule, agreement, promise, instructions, etc.). **2.** to break in upon or disturb rudely; interfere thoughtlessly with: *to violate his privacy.* **3.** to break through or pass by force or without right: *to violate a frontier.* **4.** to treat irreverently or disrespectfully; desecrate; profane: *violate a human right.* **5.** to molest sexually, esp. to rape. [1400–50; late ME < L *violātus,* ptp. of *violāre* to treat with violence, violate, appar. deriv. of *violentus* VIOLENT (taking *viol-* as base); see -ATE[1]] —**vi′o•la′tor, vi′o•lat′er,** *n.*

vi•o•la•tion (vī′ə lā′shən), *n.* **1.** the act of violating. **2.** the state of being violated. **3.** a breach, infringement, or transgression, as of a law, rule, promise, etc.: *He was fined for a traffic violation.* **4.** desecration; profanation: *the violation of a cemetery.* **5.** sexual molestation, esp. rape. **6.** a distortion of meaning or fact. [1400–50; late ME < L *violātiōn-* (s. of *violātiō*), equiv. to *violāt(us)* (see VIOLATE) + *-iōn-* -ION] —**vi′o•la′tion•al,** *adj.*
—**Syn. 3.** See **breach.**

vi•o•la•tive (vī′ə lā′tiv, vī′ə lə tiv), *adj.* involving violation. [1790–1800; VIOLATE + -IVE]

vi•o•lence (vī′ə ləns), *n.* **1.** swift and intense force: *the violence of a storm.* **2.** rough or injurious physical force, action, or treatment: *to die by violence.* **3.** an unjust or unwarranted exertion of force or power, as against rights or laws: *to take over a government by violence.* **4.** a violent act or proceeding. **5.** rough or immoderate vehemence, as of feeling or language: *the violence of his hatred.* **6.** damage through distortion or unwarranted alteration: *to do editorial violence to a text.* [1250–1300; ME < AF, OF < L *violentia;* see VIOLENT, -ENCE]
—**Syn. 1.** might, power, impact, fury.

vi•o•lent (vī′ə lənt), *adj.* **1.** acting with or characterized by uncontrolled, strong, rough force: *a violent earthquake.* **2.** caused by injurious or destructive force: *a violent death.* **3.** intense in force, effect, etc.; severe; extreme: *violent pain; violent cold.* **4.** roughly or immoderately vehement or ardent: *violent passions.* **5.** furious in impetuosity, energy, etc.: *violent haste.* **6.** of, pertaining to, or constituting a distortion of meaning or fact. [1300–50; ME < L *violentus,* equiv. to *vi-,* shortening (before a vowel) of base of *vīs* force, violence + *-olentus,* var. (after a vowel) of *-ulentus* -ULENT] —**vi′o•lent•ly,** *adv.*

vi′olent storm′, *Meteorol.* storm (def. 3). [1795–1805]

vi•o•les•cent (vī′ə les′ənt), *adj.* tending to a violet color: *a violescent twilight sky.* [1840–50; < L *viol(a)* violet + -ESCENT]

vi•o•let (vī′ə lit), *n.* **1.** any chiefly low, stemless or leafy-stemmed plant of the genus *Viola,* having purple, blue, yellow, white, or variegated flowers. Cf. **violet family. 2.** any such plant except the pansy and the viola. **3.** the flower of any native, wild species of violet, as distinguished from the pansy: the state flower of Illinois, New Jersey, and Rhode Island. **4.** any of various similar plants of other genera. **5.** reddish-blue, a color at the opposite end of the visible spectrum from red, an effect of light with a wavelength between 400 and 450 nm. —*adj.* **6.** of the color violet; reddish-blue: *violet hats.* [1300–50; ME < OF *violete,* equiv. to *viole* (< L *viola* violet) + *-ete* -ET]

Vi•o•let (vī′ə lit), *n.* a female given name. Also, **Vi•o•lette** (vī′ə let′, vī′ə lit), **Vi•o•let•ta** (vī′ə let′ə).

vi′olet fam′ily, the plant family Violaceae, characterized by herbaceous plants and some tropical shrubs and trees having alternate, usually simple leaves, solitary flowers with five usually irregular petals, the lower petal often spurred, and a berry or many-seeded capsule, and including the Johnny-jump-up, pansy, and numerous species of violet.

vi′olet i′ris, an iris, *Iris verna,* of the eastern U.S., having solitary, violet-blue flowers.

vi′olet wood′, kingwood. [1835–45]

violin

vi•o•lin (vī′ə lin′), *n.* **1.** the treble instrument of the family of modern bowed instruments, held nearly horizontal by the player's arm with the lower part supported against the collarbone or shoulder. **2.** a violinist or part for a violin. [1570–80; < It *violino,* equiv. to *viol(a)* (see VIOLA[1]) + *-ino* dim. suffix]

violin′ clef′, *Music.* See **treble clef.** [1875–80]

vi•o•lin•ist (vī′ə lin′ist), *n.* a person who plays the violin. [1660–70; < It *violinista.* See VIOLIN, -IST]

vi•o•lin•mak•er (vī′ə lin′mā′kər), *n.* a person who designs and constructs violins, esp. professionally. [1675–85; VIOLIN + MAKER]

violin′ spi′der. See **brown recluse spider.** [1965–70]

vi•ol•ist[1] (vī′ə list), *n.* a person who plays the viol. [1660–70; VIOL + -IST]

vi•o•list[2] (vē ō′list), *n.* a person who plays the viola. [VIOL(A)[1] + -IST]

Viol•let-le-Duc (vyô le′lə dʏk′), *n.* **Eu•gène Em•ma•nu•el** (œ zhen′ e mᴀ ɴʏ el′), 1814–79, French architect and writer.

vi•o•lon•cel•list (vē′ə lən chel′ist, vī′-), *n.* cellist. [1825–35; VIOLONCELL(O) + -IST]

vi•o•lon•cel•lo (vē′ə lən chel′ō, vī′-), *n., pl.* **-los.** cello. [1715–25; < It, equiv. to *violon(e)* VIOLONE + *-cello* dim. suffix]

vi•o•lo•ne (vē′ə lō′nā), *n.* **1.** a double bass. **2.** an organ pedal stop of 16-foot pitch, giving a tone resembling the violoncello. [1715–25; < It, equiv. to *viol(a)* bass viol + *-one* aug. suffix]

vi•os•ter•ol (vī os′tə rôl′, -rol′), *n. Biochem.* a vitamin D preparation produced by the irradiation of ergosterol. [(ULTRA)VI(OLET) + (ERG)OSTEROL]

VIP (vē′ī′pē′), *Informal.* very important person. Also, **V.I.P.** [1940–45]

vi•per (vī′pər), *n.* **1.** any of several venomous Old World snakes of the genus *Vipera,* esp. *V. berus,* a small snake common in northern Eurasia. **2.** any related snakes belonging to the family Viperidae, characterized by erectile, venom-conducting fangs. **3.** See **pit viper. 4.** any of various venomous or supposedly venomous snakes. **5.** a malignant or spiteful person. **6.** a false or treacherous person. **7.** (*cap.*) *Mil.* a 9-pound (4 kg), shoulder-launched, unguided U.S. Army antitank rocket with an effective range of 273 yds. (250 m). **8. to nourish a viper in one's bosom,** to befriend a person who proves to be treacherous. [1520–30; < L *vīpera,* haplological var. of **vīvipera,* n. use of fem. of **vīviper,* later (as re-formation) *vīviparus* VIVIPAROUS] —**vi′per•ish,** *adj.* —**vi′per•ish•ly,** *adv.*

vi•per•fish (vī′pər fish′), *n., pl.* (*esp. collectively*) **-fish,** (*esp. referring to two or more kinds or species*) **-fish•es.** any of several deep-sea fishes of the family Chauliodontidae, having a large mouth and fanglike teeth, some species having light-emitting organs on their bodies. [1890–95; VIPER + FISH]

vi•per•ine (vī′pər in, -pə rīn′), *adj.* of, pertaining to, or resembling a viper; venomous: *a gossip with a viperine tongue.* [1540–50; < L *vīperīnus.* See VIPER, -INE[1]]

vi•per•ous (vī′pər əs), *adj.* **1.** of the nature of or resembling a viper: *a viperous movement.* **2.** of or pertaining to vipers. **3.** characteristic of vipers. **4.** venomous. [1525–35; VIPER + -OUS] —**vi′per•ous•ly,** *adv.*

vi′per's bu′gloss, the blueweed. [1590–1600]

vir (vēr), *n. Latin.* husband (used chiefly in the legal phrase *et vir*).

vir•a•gin•i•ty (vir′ə jin′i tē), *n.* the qualities of a virago. [1840–50; < L *virāgin-* (s. of *virāgō* VIRAGO) + -ITY] —**vir•a•gi•nous** (vi raj′ə nəs), **vir′a•gin′i•an,** *adj.*

vi•ra•go (vi rä′gō, -rā′-), *n., pl.* **-goes, -gos. 1.** a loud-voiced, ill-tempered, scolding woman; shrew. **2.** *Archaic.* a woman of strength or spirit. [bef. 1000; ME, OE < L *virāgō,* equiv. to *vir* man + *-āgō* suffix expressing association of some kind, here resemblance]
—**Syn. 1.** scold, nag, termagant, harpy, Xanthippe.

vi•ral (vī′rəl), *adj.* of, pertaining to, or caused by a virus. [1935–40; VIR(US) + -AL[1]]

Vi•ra Sai•va (vir′ə sī′və), *n. Hinduism.* Lingayata. [< Skt, equiv. to *vīra* man + *śaiva* votary of Shiva]

Vi•ra•zole (vī′rə zōl′), *Pharm., Trademark.* a brand of ribavirin.

Vir•chow (fiʀ′ᴋʜō), *n.* **Ru•dolf** (ʀōō′dôlf), 1821–1902, German pathologist, anthropologist, and political leader.

vir•e•lay (vir′ə lā′), *n. Pros.* **1.** an old French form of short poem, composed of short lines running on two rhymes and having two opening lines recurring at intervals. **2.** any of various similar or other forms of poem, as one consisting of stanzas made up of longer and shorter lines, the lines of each kind rhyming together in each stanza, and having the rhyme of the shorter lines of one stanza forming the rhyme of the longer lines of the next stanza. **3.** a medieval song form providing a musical setting for a virelay but having a formal structure different from that of the poem. Also, **vir′e•lai′.** [1350–1400; ME < OF *virelai,* alter. (see LAY[4]) of *vireli, virli* jingle used as the refrain of a song]

vi•re•mi•a (vī rē′mē ə), *n. Pathol.* the presence of a virus in the blood. [1945–50; < NL; see VIRUS, -EMIA] —**vi•re′mic,** *adj.*

vir•e•o (vir′ē ō′), *n., pl.* **vir•e•os.** any of several small, insectivorous American birds of the family Vireonidae, having the plumage usually olive-green or gray above and white or yellow below. [1825–35; < NL; L *vireō* (Pliny), prob. the greenfinch, deriv. of *virēre* to be green]

red-eyed vireo,
Vireo olivaceus,
length 6 in. (15 cm)

vi•res•cence (vī res′əns, vi-), *n. Bot.* state of becoming somewhat, though usually not totally, green, due to the abnormal presence of chlorophyll. [1885–90; VIRESC(ENT) + -ENCE]

vi•res•cent (vī res′ənt, vi-), *adj.* **1.** turning green. **2.** tending to a green color; slightly greenish. [1820–30; < L *virēscent-* (s. of *virēscēns,* prp. of *virēscere* to become green), equiv. to *vir(ēre)* to be green + *-ēscent-* -ESCENT]

Virg., Virginia.

vir•ga (vûr′gə), *n.* (*used with a singular or plural v.*) *Meteorol.* streaks of water drops or ice particles falling out of a cloud and evaporating before reaching the ground (distinguished from *praecipitatio*). [1935–40; < L: rod, streak]

vir•gate[1] (vûr′git, -gāt), *adj.* shaped like a rod or wand; long, slender, and straight. [1815–25; < L *virgātus;* see VIRGA, -ATE[1]]

vir•gate[2] (vûr′git, -gāt), *n.* an early English measure of land of varying extent, usually considered equivalent to a quarter of a hide, or about 30 acres (12 hectares). Also called **yardland.** [1645–55; < ML *virgāta (terrae)* measure (of land), fem. of L *virgātus* pertaining to a rod; see VIRGATE[1]; trans. OE *gierd landes* yard-measure of land]

Vir•gil (vûr′jəl), *n.* **1.** Vergil. **2.** a male given name.

Vir•gil•i•an (vər jil′ē ən, -jil′yən), *adj.* Vergilian.

vir•gin (vûr′jin), *n.* **1.** a person who has never had sexual intercourse. **2.** an unmarried girl or woman. **3.** *Eccles.* an unmarried, religious woman, esp. a saint. **4. the Virgin,** Mary, the mother of Christ. **5.** *Informal.* any person who is uninitiated, uninformed, or the like: *He's still a virgin as far as hard work is concerned.* **6.** a female animal that has never copulated. **7.** an unfertilized insect. **8.** (*cap.*) *Astron., Astrol.* the constellation or sign of Virgo. —*adj.* **9.** being a virgin: *a virgin martyr.* **10.** of, pertaining to, or characteristic of a virgin: *virgin modesty.* **11.** pure; unsullied; undefiled: *virgin snow.* **12.** first: *the senator's virgin speech.* **13.** without admixture, alloy, or modification: *virgin gold.* **14.** not previously exploited, cultivated, tapped, or used: *virgin timberlands; virgin wool.* **15.** without experience of; not previously exposed to: *a mind virgin to such sorrows.* **16.** *Informal.* being a mixed drink resembling a specific cocktail but made without any alcoholic ingredient: *a virgin piña colada.* **17.** *Zool.* not fertilized. **18.** (of a metal) made directly from ore by smelting, rather than from scrap. **19.** noting the oil obtained, as from olives, by the first pressing without the application of heat. [1150–1200; ME *virgine* < AF, OF < L *virgin-,* s. of *virgō* maiden, virgin]
—**Syn. 2.** maid, maiden. **11.** chaste, unpolluted. **13.** unalloyed, unadulterated. **14.** fresh, new. —**Ant. 11.** defiled. **13.** mixed, adulterated.

vir•gin•al[1] (vûr′jə nl), *adj.* **1.** of, pertaining to, characteristic of, or befitting a virgin: *virginal purity.* **2.** continuing in a state of virginity. **3.** pure; unsullied; untouched: *a virginal mountain stream.* **4.** *Zool.* not fertilized. [1400–50; late ME < L *virginālis,* equiv. to *virgin-* VIRGIN + *-ālis* -AL[1]] —**vir′gin•al•ly,** *adv.*

vir•gin•al[2] (vûr′jə nl), *n.* Often, **virginals.** a rectangular harpsichord with the strings stretched parallel to the keyboard, the earlier types placed on a table: popular in the 16th and 17th centuries. [1520–30; appar. special use of VIRGINAL[1]] —**vir′gin•al•ist,** *n.*

virginal[2]

CONCISE ETYMOLOGY KEY: <, descended or borrowed from; >, whence; b., blend of, blended; c., cognate with; cf., compare; deriv., derivative; equiv., equivalent; imit., imitative; obl., oblique; r., replacing; s., stem; sp., spelling, spelled; resp., respelling, respelled; trans., translation; ?, origin unknown; *, unattested; ‡, probably earlier than. See the full key inside the front cover.

vir′gin birth′, 1. *Theol.* the doctrine or dogma that, by the miraculous agency of God, the birth of Christ did not impair or prejudice the virginity of Mary. Cf. **Immaculate Conception.** 2. *Zool.* parthenogenesis; parturition by a female who has not copulated. [1645–55]

Vir·gin·ia (vər jin′yə), *n.* 1. a state in the E United States, on the Atlantic coast: part of the historical South. 5,346,279; 40,815 sq. mi. (105,710 sq. km). *Cap.:* Richmond. *Abbr.:* VA (for use with zip code), Va. 2. a town in NE Minnesota. 11,056. 3. (*italics*) Merrimac. 4. a female given name: from a Roman family name.

Virgin′ia Beach′, a town in SE Virginia. 262,199.

Virgin′ia Cit′y, a mining town in W Nevada: famous for the discovery of the rich Comstock silver lode 1859.

Virgin′ia cow′slip, a wild plant, *Mertensia virginica,* of the borage family, native to the eastern U.S., grown as a garden plant for its handsome, nodding clusters of blue flowers. Also called **Roanoke bells.** [1905–10, *Amer.*]

Virgin′ia creep′er, a climbing plant, *Parthenocissus quinquefolia,* of the grape family, native to North America, having palmate leaves and bluish-black berries. Also called **American ivy, ivy vine.** [1660–70, *Amer.*]

Virgin′ia deer′, 1. the common white-tailed deer, *Odocoileus virginianus,* of eastern North America. 2. any related variety of white-tailed deer.

Virgin′ia fence′. See **snake fence.** Also called **rail fence, Virgin′ia rail′ fence′.** [1665–75, *Amer.*]

Virgin′ia ham′, a ham from a hog fed on corn and peanuts, cured in hickory smoke. [1625–35, *Amer.*]

Vir·gin·ian (vər jin′yən), *adj.* 1. of or pertaining to the state of Virginia. —*n.* 2. a native or inhabitant of Virginia. [1625–35; VIRGINI(A) + -AN]

Virgin′ia pine′, a pine tree, *Pinus virginiana,* of the eastern U.S., that grows in poor soil and has needles in groups of two. Also called **Jersey pine.** [1765–75]

Virgin′ia plan′, *Amer. Hist.* a plan, unsuccessfully proposed at the Constitutional Convention, providing for a legislature of two houses with proportional representation in each house and executive and judicial branches to be chosen by the legislature. Cf. **Connecticut Compromise, New Jersey plan.**

Virgin′ia rail′, a long-billed American rail, *Rallus limicola,* having blackish and reddish-brown plumage. See illus. under **rail**[3]. [1775–85, *Amer.*]

Virgin′ia reel′, an American country dance in which the partners start by facing each other in two lines.

Virgin′ia snake′root. See under **snakeroot** (def. 1).

Virgin′ia stock′, a plant, *Malcolmia maritima,* of the mustard family, native to the Mediterranean region, having oblong leaves on a weak, often reclining stem and reddish or white flowers.

Virgin′ia wil′low, a shrub, *Itea virginica,* of the eastern and southern U.S., having showy, fragrant, white flowers. Also called **sweet spire.** [1890–95, *Amer.*]

vir·gin·i·bus pu·er·is·que (wir gin′i bo͝os′ po͞o′er-ēs′kwe; *Eng.* vər jin′ə bəs pyo͞o′ə ris′kwē), *Latin.* for girls and boys.

Vir′gin Is′lands, a group of islands in the West Indies, E of Puerto Rico: comprises the Virgin Islands of the United States and the British Virgin Islands. *Abbr.:* V.I., VI

Vir′gin Is′lands Na′tional Park′, a national park on St. John Island, Virgin Islands: prehistoric Indian relics. 24 sq. mi. (62 sq. km).

Vir′gin Is′lands of the Unit′ed States′, a group of islands in the West Indies, including St. Thomas, St. John, and St. Croix: purchased from Denmark 1917. 96,569; 133 sq. mi. (345 sq. km). *Cap.:* Charlotte Amalie. Formerly, **Danish West Indies.**

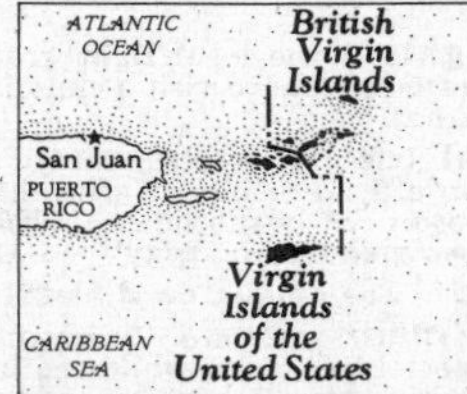

vir·gin·i·ty (vər jin′i tē), *n.* 1. the state or condition of being a virgin. 2. the state or condition of being pure, fresh, or unused. 3. *Informal.* any naive, uninitiated, or uninformed state. [1250–1300; ME *virginite* < AF, OF < L *virginitās.* See VIRGIN, -ITY]

vir·gin·i·um (vər jin′ē əm), *n. Chem.* (formerly) francium. *Symbol:* Vi [1925–30; VIRGINI(A) + -IUM]

Vir′gin Mar′y, 1. Mary (def. 1). 2. a Bloody Mary made without vodka or other liquor. [1250–1300; ME]

vir′gin met′al. See **primary metal.** [1660–70]

Vir′gin Queen′, Queen Elizabeth I of England.

vir·gin's-bow·er (vûr′jinz bou′ər), a climbing vine, *Clematis virginiana,* of eastern North America, having branching clusters of small, white flowers and seed pods with silky, grayish plumes. [1590–1600]

Vir·go (vûr′gō), *n., gen.* **Vir·gi·nis** (vûr′jə nis) for 1. 1. *Astron.* the Virgin, a zodiacal constellation between Leo and Libra, containing the bright star Spica. 2. *Astrol.* a. the sixth sign of the zodiac: the mutable earth sign. See illus. under **zodiac.** b. a person born under this sign, usually between August 23 and September 22. [bef. 1000; ME, OE *Virgō* < L: maiden]

Vir′go clus′ter, *Astron.* a cluster of about 2500 galaxies in the constellation Virgo, the nearest cluster to our galaxy.

vir·gu·late (vûr′gyə lit, -lāt′), *adj.* rod-shaped; virgate. [1830–40; < L *virgul(a)* rod (see VIRGA, -ULE) + -ATE[1]]

vir·gule (vûr′gyo͞ol), *n. Print.* 1. a short oblique stroke (/) between two words indicating that whichever is appropriate may be chosen to complete the sense of the text in which they occur: *The defendant and/or his/her attorney must appear in court.* 2. a dividing line, as in dates, fractions, a run-in passage of poetry to show verse division, etc.: *3/21/27; 3/4; Sweetest love I do not go/For weariness of thee.* Also called **diagonal, separatrix, shilling mark, slant, slash, solidus;** *esp. Brit.,* **stroke.** [1830–40; < F *virgule* comma, little rod < L *virgula;* see VIRGULATE]

vi·ri·cide (vī′rə sīd′), *n.* virucide. [1945–50; VIR(US) + -I- + -CIDE] —**vi′ri·cid′al,** *adj.*

vir·id (vir′id), *adj.* green or verdant: *the virid woodlands of spring.* [1590–1600; < L *viridis* green, for **viridus,* equiv. to *vir(ēre)* to be green + *-idus* -ID[4]]

vir·i·des·cent (vir′i des′ənt), *adj.* slightly green; greenish. [1840–50; < LL *viridēscent-* (s. of *viridēscēns,* prp. of *viridēscere* to become green), equiv. to *virid(is)* VIRID + *-ēscent-* -ESCENT] —**vir′i·des′cence,** *n.*

vi·rid·i·an (və rid′ē ən), *n.* a long-lasting, bluish-green pigment, consisting of a hydrated oxide of chromium. Also, **veridian.** [1880–85; < L *viridi(s)* green + -AN]

vi·rid·i·ty (və rid′i tē), *n.* 1. greenness; verdancy; verdure. 2. youth; innocence; inexperience. [1400–50; late ME < L *viriditās,* equiv. to *viridi(s)* green + *-tās* -TY[2]]

vir·ile (vir′əl or, *esp. Brit.,* -īl), *adj.* 1. of, pertaining to, characteristic of, or befitting a man; masculine; manly: *virile strength.* 2. having or exhibiting masculine energy, forcefulness, or strength in a marked degree. 3. characterized by a vigorous, masculine spirit: *a virile literary style.* 4. of, pertaining to, or capable of procreation. [1480–90; < L *virīlis* manly, equiv. to *vir* man (akin to OE *wer* man; see WEREWOLF) + *-īlis* -ILE]
—**Syn.** 2. vigorous. See **male.**

vir·il·ism (vir′ə liz′əm), *n.* a female disorder in which there is development of secondary male sexual characteristics, as hirsutism and lowered voice, caused by various conditions affecting hormone regulation. [1895–1900; VIRILE + -ISM]

vi·ril·i·ty (və ril′i tē), *n.* 1. the state or quality of being virile; manly character, vigor, or spirit; masculinity. 2. the power of procreation. [1580–90; < L *virīlitās,* equiv. to *virīli(s)* VIRILE + *-tās* -TY[2]]

vir·i·lo·cal (vir′ə lō′kəl), *adj. Anthropol.* living with or located near the husband's father's group; patrilocal. Cf. **matrilocal, neolocal.** [< L *viri-* (comb. form of *vir* man; see VIRILE) + LOCAL] —**vir′i·lo′cal·ly,** *adv.*

vi·ri·on (vī′rē on′, vir′ē-), *n.* the infectious form of a virus as it exists outside the host cell, consisting of a nucleic acid core, a protein coat, and, in some species, an external envelope. [< F *virion* (1959), equiv. to *viri(en)* viral (see VIRUS, -IAN) + *-on* -ON[1]]

virl (vûrl), *n. Scot.* ferrule (def. 1). [1400–50; syncopated var. of ME *virole* FERRULE] —**virled,** *adj.*

vi·roid (vī′roid), *n.* an infectious agent of plants similar to a virus but consisting of only a short, single strand of RNA without a protein coat. [1946; VIR(US) + -OID]

vi·rol·o·gy (vī rol′ə jē, vi-), *n.* the science dealing with the study of viruses and the diseases caused by them. [1930–35; VIR(US) + -O- + -LOGY] —**vi·ro·log·i·cal** (vī′rə loj′i kəl), *adj.* —**vi·rol′o·gist,** *n.*

Vi·ron (vī′rən), *n.* a male given name.

vi·ro·sis (vī rō′sis), *n. Med., Plant Pathol.* infection with a virus. [VIR(US) + -OSIS]

v. irr., irregular verb.

Vir·ta·nen (vir′tä nen), *n.* **Art·tu·ri Il·ma·ri** (ärt′to͞o-ri il′mä ri), 1895–1973, Finnish biochemist: Nobel prize 1945.

vir·tu (vər to͞o′, vûr′to͞o), *n.* 1. excellence or merit in objects of art, curios, and the like. 2. (*used with plural v.*) such objects or articles collectively. 3. a taste for or knowledge of such objects. Also, **vertu.** [1715–25; < It *virtù, vertù* VIRTUE]

vir·tu·al (vûr′cho͞o əl), *adj.* 1. being such in power, force, or effect, though not actually or expressly such: *a virtual dependence on charity.* 2. *Optics.* a. noting an image formed by the apparent convergence of rays geometrically, but not actually, prolonged, as the image formed by a mirror (opposed to *real*). b. noting a focus of a system forming virtual images. 3. temporarily simulated or extended by computer software: *a virtual disk in RAM; virtual memory on a hard disk.* [1350–1400; ME < ML *virtuālis,* equiv. to L *virtu(s)* VIRTUE + *-ālis* -AL[1]] —**vir′tu·al′i·ty,** *n.*

vir·tu·al·ly (vûr′cho͞o ə lē), *adv.* for the most part; almost wholly; just about: *He is virtually unknown.* [1400–50; late ME; see VIRTUAL, -LY]

vir′tual par′ticle, *Physics.* an elementary particle of transitory existence that does not appear as a free particle in a particular situation but that can transmit a force from one particle to another. [1970–75]

vir′tual real′ity, a realistic simulation of an environment, including three-dimensional graphics, by a computer system using interactive software and hardware. [1985–90]

vir′tual stor′age, *Computers.* a system whereby addressable memory is extended beyond main storage through the use of secondary storage managed by system software in such a way that programs can treat all of the designated storage as addressable main storage. Also called **vir′tual mem′ory.** Cf. **real storage.** [1970–75]

vir·tue (vûr′cho͞o), *n.* 1. moral excellence; goodness; righteousness. 2. conformity of one's life and conduct to moral and ethical principles; uprightness; rectitude. 3. chastity; virginity: *to lose one's virtue.* 4. a particular moral excellence. Cf. **cardinal virtues, natural virtue, theological virtue.** 5. a good or admirable quality or property: *the virtue of knowing one's weaknesses.* 6. effective force; power or potency: *a charm with the virtue of removing warts.* 7. **virtues,** an order of angels. Cf. **angel** (def. 1). 8. manly excellence; valor. 9. **by** or **in virtue of,** by reason of; because of: *to act by virtue of one's legitimate authority.* 10. **make a virtue of necessity,** to make the best of a difficult or unsatisfactory situation. [1175–1225; alter. (with *i* < L) of ME *vertu* < AF, OF < L *virtūt-* (s. of *virtūs*) maleness, worth, virtue, equiv. to *vir* man (see VIRILE) + *-tūt-* abstract n. suffix] —**vir′tue·less,** *adj.* —**vir′tue·less·ness,** *n.*
—**Syn.** 1. See **goodness.** 2. probity, integrity.
—**Ant.** 1. vice.

vir·tu·os·i·ty (vûr′cho͞o os′i tē), *n.* 1. the character, ability, or skill of a virtuoso. 2. a fondness for or interest in virtu. [1665–75; VIRTUOS(O) + -ITY]

vir·tu·o·so (vûr′cho͞o ō′sō), *n., pl.* **-sos, -si** (-sē), *adj.* —*n.* 1. a person who has special knowledge or skill in a field. 2. a person who excels in musical technique or execution. 3. a person who has a cultivated appreciation of artistic excellence, as a connoisseur or collector of objects of art, antiques, etc. 4. *Obs.* a scholar. —*adj.* 5. Also, **vir·tu·os·ic** (vûr′cho͞o os′ik). of, pertaining to, or characteristic of a virtuoso: *a virtuoso performance.* [1610–20; < It: versed, skilled < LL *virtuōsus* VIRTUOUS]

vir·tu·ous (vûr′cho͞o əs), *adj.* 1. conforming to moral and ethical principles; morally excellent; upright: *Lead a virtuous life.* 2. chaste: *a virtuous young person.* [1300–50; alter. (with *i* < L) of ME *vertuous* < AF < LL *virtuōsus,* equiv. to L *virtu(s)* VIRTUE + *-ōsus* -OUS] —**vir′tu·ous·ly,** *adv.* —**vir′tu·ous·ness,** *n.*

vir·tu·te et ar·mis (wir to͞o′te et är′mēs; *Eng.* vər-to͞o′tē et är′mis, -tyo͞o′-), *Latin.* by virtue and arms: motto of Mississippi.

vi·ru·cide (vī′rə sīd′), *n.* an agent for destroying viruses. [VIRU(S) + -CIDE] —**vi′ru·cid′al,** *adj.*

vir·u·lence (vir′yə ləns, vir′ə-), *n.* 1. quality of being virulent. 2. *Bacteriol.* a. the relative ability of a microorganism to cause disease; degree of pathogenicity. b. the capability of a microorganism to cause disease. 3. venomous hostility. 4. intense sharpness of temper. Also, **vir′u·len·cy.** [1655–65; < LL *vīrulentia* stench; see VIRULENT, -ENCE]

vir·u·lent (vir′yə lənt, vir′ə-), *adj.* 1. actively poisonous; intensely noxious: *a virulent insect bite.* 2. *Med.* highly infective; malignant or deadly. 3. *Bacteriol.* causing clinical symptoms. 4. violently or spitefully hostile. 5. intensely bitter, spiteful, or malicious: *a virulent attack.* [1350–1400; ME *verulent* < L *virulentus,* equiv. to *vīr(us)* poison (see VIRUS) + *-ulentus* -ULENT] —**vir′u·lent·ly,** *adv.*
—**Syn.** 1. venomous. 5. vicious, acerbic.

vi·rus (vī′rəs), *n., pl.* **-rus·es.** 1. an ultramicroscopic (20 to 300 nm in diameter), metabolically inert infectious agent that replicates only within the cells of living hosts, mainly bacteria, plants, and animals: composed of an RNA or DNA core, a protein coat, and, in more complex viruses, a surrounding envelope. 2. *Informal.* a viral disease. 3. a corrupting influence on morals or the intellect; poison: *the virus of intolerance.* 4. a segment of self-replicating code planted illegally in a computer program, often to damage or shut down a system or network. [1590–1600; < L *vīrus* slime, poison; akin to OOZE[2]] —**vi′rus·like′,** *adj.*

vi·rus·oid (vī′rə soid′), *n.* a small particle of RNA associated with the larger RNA of some infectious plant viruses. Compare **viroid.** [1980–85]

vis (wēs; *Eng.* vis), *n., pl.* **vi·res** (wē′rās; *Eng.* vī′rēz). *Latin.* strength; force; power.

Vis., 1. Viscount. 2. Viscountess.

vis., 1. visibility. 2. visual.

vi·sa (vē′zə), *n., pl.* **-sas,** *v.,* **-saed, -sa·ing.** —*n.* 1. an endorsement made by an authorized representative of one country upon a passport issued by another, permitting the passport holder entry into or transit through the country making the endorsement. —*v.t.* 2. to give a visa to; approve a visa for. 3. to put a visa on (a passport). Also, **visé.** [1825–35; < F, short for L *carta vīsa* the document (has been) examined; *vīsa,* ptp. fem. of *vīsere* to look into, see to, freq. of *vidēre* to see]

vis·age (viz′ij), *n.* 1. the face, usually with reference to features, expression, etc.; countenance. 2. aspect; appearance. [1250–1300; ME < AF, OF, equiv. to *vis* face (< L *vīsum* sight, appearance (VL: face), n. use of neut. ptp. of *vidēre* to see) + *-age* -AGE] —**vis′aged,** *adj.*
—**Syn.** 1. physiognomy, image. See **face.**

Vi·sa·kha·pat·nam (vi sä′kə put′nəm), *n.* a seaport in Andhra Pradesh, in E India, on the Bay of Bengal. 362,270.

Vi·sa·lia (vi sāl′yə), *n.* a city in central California. 49,729.

vis·ard (viz′ərd), *n.* vizard.

vis-à-vis (vē′zə vē′; *Fr.* vē zA vē′), *adv., adj., prep., n., pl.* **-vis** (-vēz′; *Fr.* -vē′). —*adv.* 1. face to face: *They sat vis-à-vis at the table.* —*adj.* 2. face-to-face: *a vis-à-vis encounter.* 3. *Numis.* (of a coin) having two portraits

CONCISE PRONUNCIATION KEY: act, cāpe, dâre, pärt; set, ēqual; *if,* ice; ox, ōver, ôrder, oil, bo͝ok, bo͞ot, out; up, ûrge; child; sing; shoe; thin, *that;* zh as in *treasure.* ə = a as in *alone,* e as in *system,* i as in *easily,* o as in *gallop,* u as in *circus;* ᵊ as in *fire* (fīᵊr), *hour* (ouᵊr). l and n can serve as syllabic consonants, as in *cradle* (krād′l), and *button* (but′n). See the full key inside the front cover.

facing each other. —*prep.* **4.** in relation to; compared with: *income vis-à-vis expenditures.* **5.** facing; opposite: *They were now vis-à-vis the most famous painting in the Louvre.* —*n.* **6.** a person face to face with or situated opposite to another: *He offered a cigarette to his vis-à-vis.* **7.** a date at a social affair: *She introduced her vis-à-vis to the hostess.* **8.** a person of equal authority, rank, or the like: *my vis-à-vis in the Louisville office.* **9.** a carriage in which the occupants sit face to face. **10.** *Furniture.* tête-à-tête (def. 2). [1745–55; < F: face to face; see VISAGE]

Vi•sa•yan (vi sī′ən), *n., pl.* **-yans,** (*esp. collectively*) **-yan. 1.** one of a Malay people, the most numerous native race of the Philippines. **2.** the language of this people, an Indonesian language of the Austronesian family. Also, **Bisayan.**

Visa′yan Is′lands, a group of islands in the central Philippines, including Panay, Negros, Cebú, Bohol, Leyte, Samar, Masbate, and smaller islands. Spanish, **Bisayas.**

Vis•by (viz′bē; *Swed.* vēs′bʏ), *n.* a seaport on the Swedish island of Gotland, in the Baltic: an important member of the Hanseatic League. 55,346. German, **Wisby.**

Visc., 1. Viscount. **2.** Viscountess.

vis•ca•cha (vi skä′chə), *n.* **1.** a burrowing rodent, *Lagostomus maximus,* about the size of a groundhog, inhabiting the pampas of Paraguay and Argentina, allied to the chinchilla. **2.** Also called **mountain viscacha.** a related rodent of the genus *Lagidium,* of the Andes, about the size of a squirrel, having rabbitlike ears and a squirrellike tail. Also, **vizcacha.** [1595–1605; < Sp < Quechua *wisk'acha*]

vis•cer•a (vis′ər ə), *n.pl., sing.* **vis•cus** (vis′kəs). **1.** *Anat., Zool.* the organs in the cavities of the body, esp. those in the abdominal cavity. **2.** (not used scientifically) the intestines; bowels. [1645–55; < L: internal organs, pl. of *viscus* flesh]

vis•cer•al (vis′ər əl), *adj.* **1.** of or pertaining to the viscera. **2.** affecting the viscera. **3.** of the nature of or resembling viscera. **4.** characterized by or proceeding from instinct rather than intellect: *a visceral reaction.* **5.** characterized by or dealing with coarse or base emotions; earthy; crude: *a visceral literary style.* [1565–75; < ML *viscerālis,* equiv. to *viscer-* (see VISCERA) + *-ālis* -AL] —**vis′cer•al•ly,** *adv.*

vis′ceral arch′, *Embryol.* See **branchial arch.** [1865–70]

vis′ceral cleft′, *Embryol.* See **branchial cleft.** [1870–75]

vis′ceral groove′, *Embryol.* See **branchial groove.**

vis′ceral leishmani′asis, *Pathol.* kala-azar.

vis•cer•o•mo•tor (vis′ə rō mō′tər), *adj.* of or pertaining to the normal movements of the viscera, esp. the digestive tract. [1885–90; VISCER(A) + -O- + MOTOR]

vis•cid (vis′id), *adj.* **1.** having a glutinous consistency; sticky; adhesive; viscous. **2.** *Bot.* covered by a sticky substance. [1625–35; < LL *viscidus,* equiv. to L *visc(um)* mistletoe, birdlime made from mistletoe + *-idus* -ID[4]; see VISCOUS] —**vis•cid′i•ty, vis′cid•ness,** *n.* —**vis′cid•ly,** *adv.*

vis•co•e•las•tic (vis′kō i las′tik), *adj. Physics.* pertaining to a substance having both viscous and elastic properties. [1930–35; VISC(OUS) + -O- + ELASTIC]

vis•coid (vis′koid), *adj.* somewhat viscous. Also, **vis•coi′dal.** [1875–80; VISC(OUS) + -OID]

vis•com•e•ter (vi skom′i tər), *n.* a device for measuring viscosity. Also, **vis•co•sim•eter** (vis′kō sim′i tər). [1880–85; syncopated var. of *viscosimeter;* see VISCOSE, -I-, -METER] —**vis•co•met•ric** (vis′kə me′trik), **vis•co•si•met•ric** (vis′kō si me′trik), *adj.* —**vis′co•met′ri•cal•ly,** *adv.* —**vis•com′e•try,** *n.*

Vis•con•ti (vēs kôn′tē), *n.* an Italian family that ruled Milan and Lombardy from 1277 to 1447.

vis•cose (vis′kōs), *n.* **1.** a viscous solution prepared by treating cellulose with caustic soda and carbon bisulfide: used in manufacturing regenerated cellulose fibers, sheets, or tubes, as rayon or cellophane. **2.** viscose rayon. —*adj.* **3.** of, pertaining to, or made from viscose. **4.** viscous. [1350–1400 for def. 4; 1895–1900 for def. 1; (in def. 4) < LL *viscōsus* VISCOUS (see -OSE[1]); (in def. 1) < L *visc(um)* birdlime + -OSE[2]]

vis•cos•i•ty (vi skos′i tē), *n., pl.* **-ties. 1.** the state or quality of being viscous. **2.** *Physics.* **a.** the property of a fluid that resists the force tending to cause the fluid to flow. **b.** the measure of the extent to which a fluid possesses this property. [1375–1425; late ME < ML *viscōsitās,* equiv. to L *viscōs(us)* VISCOUS + *-itās* -ITY]

viscos′ity in′dex, *Auto., Mach.* an arbitrary scale for lubricating oils that indicates the extent of variation in viscosity with variation of temperature. [1935–40]

vis•count (vī′kount′), *n.* **1.** a nobleman next below an earl or count and next above a baron. **2.** *Hist.* a deputy of a count or earl. **3.** (in England) a sheriff. [1350–1400; ME *viscounte* < AF; OF *visconte* (F *vicomte*), equiv. to *vis* VICE[3] + *counte* COUNT[2], trans. ML *vicecomes*]

vis•count•cy (vī′kount′sē), *n.* the rank or station of a viscount. Also, **vis′count•ship′.** [1865–70; VISCOUNT + -CY]

vis•count•ess (vī′koun′tis), *n.* **1.** the wife or widow of a viscount. **2.** a woman holding in her own right a rank equivalent to that of a viscount. [1425–75; late ME; see VISCOUNT, -ESS]
—**Usage.** See **-ess.**

vis•count•y (vī′koun′tē), *n., pl.* **-count•ies. 1.** viscountcy. **2.** *Hist.* the jurisdiction of a viscount or the territory under his authority. [1580–90; VISCOUNT + -Y[3]]

vis•cous (vis′kəs), *adj.* **1.** of a glutinous nature or consistency; sticky; thick; adhesive. **2.** having the property of viscosity. Also, **viscose.** [1350–1400; ME < LL *viscōsus,* equiv. to L *visc(um)* mistletoe, birdlime (made with mistletoe berries) + *-ōsus* -OUS] —**vis′cous•ly,** *adv.* —**vis′cous•ness,** *n.*

Visct., 1. Viscount. **2.** Viscountess.

vis•cus (vis′kəs), *n.* sing. of **viscera.**

vise (vīs), *n., v.,* **vised, vis•ing.** —*n.* **1.** any of various devices, usually having two jaws that may be brought together or separated by means of a screw, lever, or the like, used to hold an object firmly while work is being done on it. —*v.t.* **2.** to hold, press, or squeeze with or as with a vise. Also, **vice.** [1300–50; ME *vis* < OF: screw < L *vītis* vine (whose spiral form gave later sense)] —**vise′like′,** *adj.*

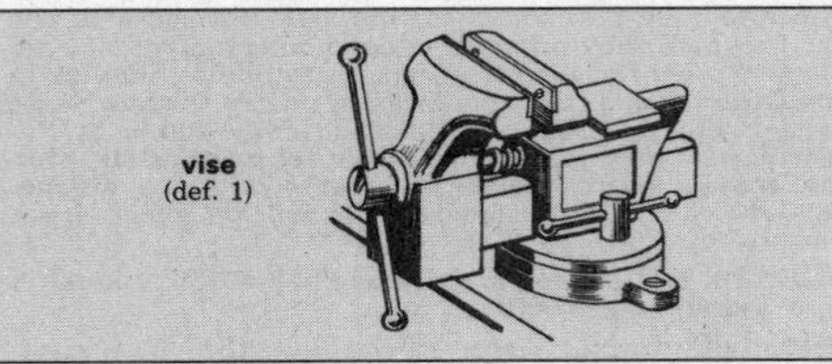

vise (def. 1)

vi•sé (vē′zā, vē zā′), *n., v.t.,* **vi•séed, vi•sé•ing.** visa. [< F, ptp. of *viser* to inspect, check; see VISA]

Vi•shin•sky (vi shin′skē; *Russ.* vi shin′skyĕ), *n.* **Andrei Ya•nu•a•rie•vich** (un dʀyä′ yi nōō ä′ʀyi vyich), 1883–1954, Soviet statesman. Also, **Vyshinsky.**

Vish•nev•ska•ya (vish nef′skä yə; *Russ.* vish nyef′skə yə), *n.* **Ga•li•na (Pa•vlov•na)** (gə lē′nə päv lōv′nə, pav-; *Russ.* gu lyē′nə pä′vləv nə), born 1926, Soviet operatic soprano, in the U.S. (wife of Mstislav Rostropovich).

Vish•nu (vish′nōō), *n. Hinduism.* **1.** (in later Hinduism) "the Preserver," the second member of the Trimurti, along with Brahma the Creator and Shiva the Destroyer. **2.** (in popular Hinduism) a deity believed to have descended from heaven to earth in several incarnations, or avatars, varying in number from nine to twenty-two, but always including animals. His most important human incarnation is the Krishna of the Bhagavad-Gita. **3.** "the Pervader," one of a half-dozen solar deities in the Rig-Veda, daily traversing the sky in three strides, morning, afternoon, and night. [< Skt *viṣṇu*] —**Vish′nu•ism,** *n.*

vis•i•bil•i•ty (viz′ə bil′i tē), *n.* **1.** the state or fact of being visible. **2.** the relative ability to be seen under given conditions of distance, light, atmosphere, etc.: *low visibility due to fog.* **3.** Also called **visual range.** *Meteorol.* the distance at which a given standard object can be seen and identified with the unaided eye. **4.** the ability to give a relatively large range of unobstructed vision: *a windshield with good visibility.* **5.** *Typography.* legibility (def. 2). [1575–85; < LL *vīsibilitās,* equiv. to L *vīsibili(s)* VISIBLE + *-tās* -TY[2]]

visibil′ity me′ter, any instrument for measuring the visual range through the atmosphere, as a transmissometer. [1955–60]

vis•i•ble (viz′ə bəl), *adj.* **1.** that can be seen; perceptible to the eye: *mountains visible in the distance.* **2.** apparent; manifest; obvious: *a man with no visible means of support.* **3.** being constantly or frequently in the public view; conspicuous: *a visible political position.* **4.** noting or pertaining to a system of keeping records or information on cards or sheets in such a way that the desired reference can be brought instantly to view: *a visible index.* **5.** *Com.* **a.** available or accessible; already existing, as goods in a warehouse or in transit as opposed to goods in production: *visible supply.* **b.** involving actual goods that have been recorded or accounted for: *visible trade.* **6.** prepared or converted for visual presentation; represented visually. [1300–50; ME < L *vīsibilis,* equiv. to *vīs(us)* (see VISION) + *-ibilis* -IBLE] —**vis′i•ble•ness,** *n.* —**vis′i•bly,** *adv.*
—**Syn. 1, 2.** discernible. **2.** evident.

vis′ible hori′zon, horizon (def. 1). [1695–1705]

vis′ible spec′trum, *Physics.* the range of wavelengths of electromagnetic radiation that is normally visible, from 380 to 760 nm.

vis′ible speech′, *Phonet.* **1.** the representation in graphic or pictorial form of characteristics of speech, as by means of sound spectrograms. **2.** the system of handwritten phonetic symbols invented by Melville Bell in 1867 to provide a visually comprehensible rendition of speech sounds. [1850–55]

Vis•i•goth (viz′i goth′), *n.* a member of the westerly division of the Goths, which formed a monarchy about A.D. 418, maintaining it in southern France until 507 and in Spain until 711. Cf. **Ostrogoth.** [1605–15; < LL *Visigothī* (pl.) < Gmc, equiv. to **wisi-* (c. WEST) + *goth-* GOTH] —**Vis′i•goth′ic,** *adj.*

Vi•sine (vī′zēn, vī zēn′), *Pharm., Trademark.* a brand of tetrahydrozoline.

vi•sion (vizh′ən), *n.* **1.** the act or power of sensing with the eyes; sight. **2.** the act or power of anticipating that which will or may come to be: *prophetic vision; the vision of an entrepreneur.* **3.** an experience in which a personage, thing, or event appears vividly or credibly to the mind, although not actually present, often under the influence of a divine or other agency: *a heavenly messenger appearing in a vision.* Cf. **hallucination** (def. 1). **4.** something seen or otherwise perceived during such an experience: *The vision revealed its message.* **5.** a vivid, imaginative conception or anticipation: *visions of wealth and glory.* **6.** something seen; an object of sight. **7.** a scene, person, etc., of extraordinary beauty: *The sky was a vision of red and pink.* **8.** See **computer vision.** —*v.t.* **9.** to envision: *She tried to vision herself in a past century.* [1250–1300; ME < L *vīsiōn-* (s. of *vīsiō*) a seeing, view, equiv. to *vīs(us),* ptp. of *vidēre* to see + *-iōn-* -ION] —**vi′sion•less,** *adj.*
—**Syn. 2.** perception, discernment. **4.** apparition, phantasm, chimera. See **dream.**

vi•sion•al (vizh′ə nl), *adj.* **1.** of or pertaining to visions. **2.** belonging to or seen in a vision. [1580–90; VISION + -AL[1]] —**vi′sion•al•ly,** *adv.*

vi•sion•ar•y (vizh′ə ner′ē), *adj., n., pl.* **-ar•ies.** —*adj.* **1.** given to or characterized by fanciful, not presently workable, or unpractical ideas, views, or schemes: *a visionary enthusiast.* **2.** given to or concerned with seeing visions. **3.** belonging to or seen in a vision. **4.** unreal; imaginary: *visionary evils.* **5.** purely idealistic or speculative; impractical; unrealizable: *a visionary scheme.* **6.** of, pertaining to, or proper to a vision. —*n.* **7.** a person of unusually keen foresight. **8.** a person who sees visions. **9.** a person who is given to audacious, highly speculative, or impractical ideas or schemes; dreamer. [1640–50; VISION + -ARY] —**vi′sion•ar′i•ness,** *n.*
—**Syn. 1.** impractical, impracticable. **4.** fancied, illusory, chimerical. **5.** unrealistic. —**Ant. 1.** practical.

vi′sion cloth′, *Theat.* a curtain with an inset scrim behind which a lighted scene appears, as a vision, dream, or the like.

vi•sioned (vizh′ənd), *adj.* **1.** pertaining to, seen in, or arising from a vision: *a visioned battle between good and evil.* **2.** gifted with prophetic vision. [1500–10; VISION + -ED[2], -ED[3]]

vi′sion quest′, *Anthropol.* (esp. among some North American Indians) the ritual seeking of personal communication with the spirit world through visions that are induced by fasting, prayer, and other measures during a time of isolation: typically undertaken by an adolescent male. [1920–25]

vis•it (viz′it), *v.t.* **1.** to go to and stay with (a person or family) or at (a place) for a short time for reasons of sociability, politeness, business, curiosity, etc.: *to visit a friend; to visit clients; to visit Paris.* **2.** to stay with as a guest. **3.** to come or go to: *to visit a church for prayer.* **4.** to go to for the purpose of official inspection or examination: *a general visiting his troops.* **5.** to come to in order to comfort or aid: *to visit the sick.* **6.** to come upon; assail; afflict: *The plague visited London in 1665.* **7.** to cause trouble, suffering, etc., to come to: *to visit him with sorrows.* **8.** to inflict, as punishment, vengeance, etc. (often fol. by *on* or *upon*). —*v.i.* **9.** to make a visit. **10.** to talk or chat casually: *to visit on the phone with a friend.* **11.** to inflict punishment. —*n.* **12.** the act of or an instance of visiting: *a nice, long visit.* **13.** a chat or talk: *We had a good visit on the way back from the grocery store.* **14.** a call paid to a person, family, etc. **15.** a stay or sojourn as a guest. **16.** an official inspection or examination. **17.** the act of an officer of a belligerent nation in boarding a vessel in order to ascertain the nature of its cargo, its nationality, etc.: *the right of visit and search.* [1175–1225; ME *visiten* (v.) (< OF *visiter*) < L *vīsitāre,* freq. of *vīsere* to go to see, itself freq. of *vidēre* to see]

vis•it•a•ble (viz′i tə bəl), *adj.* **1.** capable of, suitable for, or worthy of being visited: *a visitable island; a visitable museum.* **2.** liable or subject to official visitation. [1595–1605; VISIT + -ABLE]

vis•it•ant (viz′i tənt), *n.* **1.** a temporary resident; visitor; guest. **2.** a visitor to a place of religious or sightseeing interest; pilgrim. **3.** a being believed to come from the spirit world: *a ghostly visitant.* **4.** something, as a mood, feeling, emotion, etc., that overtakes a person from time to time: *Melancholy is an occasional visitant to all.* **5.** a migratory bird that has come to a place temporarily. —*adj.* **6.** visiting; paying a visit. [1590–1600; < L *visitant-* (s. of *visitāns*). See VISIT, -ANT]
—**Syn. 1.** See **visitor.**

vis•it•a•tion (viz′i tā′shən), *n.* **1.** the act of visiting. **2.** a formal visit, as one permitted by a court's granting of visitation rights or by parents invited to a school to observe the work of students. **3.** a visit for the purpose of making an official examination or inspection, as of a bishop to a diocese. **4.** (*usually cap.*) the visit of the Virgin Mary to her cousin Elizabeth. Luke 1:36–56. **5.** (*cap.*) a church festival, held on July 2, in commemoration of this visit. **6.** the administration of comfort or aid, or of affliction or punishment: *a visitation of the plague.* **7.** an affliction or punishment, as from God. **8.** the appearance or coming of a supernatural influence or spirit. [1275–1325; < L *vīsitātiōn-* (s. of *vīsitātiō*), equiv. to *vīsitāt(us)* (ptp. of *vīsitāre;* see VISIT, -ATE[1]) + *-iōn-* -ION; r. ME *visitacioun* < AF < L, as above] —**vis′it•a′tion•al,** *adj.*

visita′tion rights′, the legal right granted to a divorced or separated parent to visit a child in the custody of the other parent.

vis•it•a•to•ri•al (viz′i tə tôr′ē əl, -tōr′-), *adj.* **1.** of or pertaining to an official visitor or official visitation. **2.** having the power of visitation. [1680–90; < ML *visitātōri(us)* (see VISITATION, -TORY[1]) + -AL[1]]

vis′iting card′, See **calling card** (def. 1). [1775–85]

vis′iting fire′man, *Informal.* **1.** an influential person accorded special treatment while visiting an organization, industry, city, etc. **2.** a visitor, as a tourist or vacationer, in a city, presumed to be a big spender. [1935–40]

vis′iting nurse′, a registered nurse employed by a social service agency to give medical care to the sick in their homes or to implement other public health programs. [1920–25]

vis′iting profes′sor, a professor from another institution invited to teach at a university or college for a limited period, usually for a semester or one academic year. [1945–50]

vis′iting teach′er, a teacher in a public school system, assigned to give home instruction to sick or disabled pupils. [1920–25]

CONCISE ETYMOLOGY KEY: <, descended or borrowed from; >, whence; b., blend of, blended; c., cognate with; cf., compare; deriv., derivative; equiv., equivalent; imit., imitative; obl., oblique; r., replacing; s., stem; sp., spelling, spelled; resp., respelling, respelled; trans., translation; ?, origin unknown; *, unattested; ‡, probably earlier than. See the full key inside the front cover.

vis·i·tor (viz′i tər), *n.* a person who visits, as for reasons of friendship, business, duty, travel, or the like. [1400–50; late ME *visitour* < AF; OF *visiteor* < LL *visitātor*, equiv. to L *visitā(re)* to VISIT + *-tor* -TOR]
—**Syn.** VISITOR, CALLER, GUEST, VISITANT are terms for a person who comes to spend time with or stay with others, or in a place. A VISITOR often stays some time, for social pleasure, for business, sightseeing, etc.: *a visitor at our neighbor's house.* A CALLER comes for a brief (usually) formal visit: *The caller merely left her card.* A GUEST is anyone receiving hospitality, and the word has been extended to include anyone who pays for meals and lodging: *a welcome guest; a hotel guest.* VISITANT applies esp. to a migratory bird or to a supernatural being: *a warbler as a visitant.*

vis·i·to·ri·al (viz′i tôr′ē əl, -tōr′-), *adj.* of or pertaining to a visitor; visitatorial. [1805–15; VISITOR + -IAL]

vis ma·jor (vis′ mā′jər), *pl.* **vi·res ma·jo·res** (vī′rēz mə jôr′ēz, -jor′-), *Law.* See **force majeure.** [1595–1605; < L *vīs major* greater force]

vis·na (vis′nə), *n. Vet. Pathol.* a disease of sheep, caused by a quickly mutating lentivirus, and affecting the central nervous system. [1955–60; < ON *visna* to wither]

vi·sor (vī′zər), *n.* **1.** *Armor.* **a.** (on a close helmet) a piece having slits or holes for vision, situated above and pivoted with a beaver or a ventail and beaver. See diag. under **close helmet. b.** a similar piece of plate having holes or slits for vision and breathing, attached to or used with any of various other helmets, as the armet, sallet, basinet, or helm. **2.** the projecting front brim of a cap. **3.** a rigid adjustable flap on an automobile windshield that can shield the eyes of a driver from direct sunlight or glare. **4.** a means of concealment; disguise. —*v.t.* **5.** to protect or mask with a visor; shield. Also, **vizor.** [1250–1300; ME *viser* < AF (cf. OF *visiere*), equiv. to *vis* face (see VISAGE) + *-er* -ER[2]] —**vi′sor·less,** *adj.*

Vis·ser 't Hooft (vis′ərt hōft′), **Wil·lem A·dolf** (vil′-əm ä′dôlf), 1900–85, Dutch Protestant clergyman and writer: leader in ecumenical movement.

vis·ta (vis′tə), *n.* **1.** a view or prospect, esp. one seen through a long, narrow avenue or passage, as between rows of trees or houses. **2.** such an avenue or passage, esp. when formally planned. **3.** a far-reaching mental view: *vistas of the future.* [1650–60; < It: a viewing, n. use of fem. of *visto* (ptp. of *vedere* to see < L *vidēre*)] —**vis′·ta·less,** *adj.*
—**Syn. 1.** See **view. 3.** prospect, outlook, vision.

Vis·ta (vis′tə), *n.* a town in SW California. 35,834.

VISTA (vis′tə), *n.* a national program in the U.S., sponsored by ACTION, for sending volunteers into poor areas to teach various job skills. [*V(olunteers) i(n) S(ervice) t(o) A(merica)*]

vis·ta·dome (vis′tə dōm′), *Railroads. n.* **1.** dome (def. 7). —*adj.* **2.** having a vistadome or having cars with vistadomes: *a vistadome train.* [1945; VISTA + DOME]

vis·taed (vis′təd), *adj.* **1.** possessing or forming a vista or vistas. **2.** viewed in or as in a mental vista. [1825–35; VISTA + -ED[3]]

Vis·tu·la (vis′cho͝o lə), *n.* a river in Poland, flowing N from the Carpathian Mountains past Warsaw into the Baltic near Danzig. ab. 650 mi. (1050 km) long. Polish, **Wisła.** German, **Weichsel.**

vis·u·al (vizh′o͞o əl), *adj.* **1.** of or pertaining to seeing or sight: *a visual image.* **2.** used in seeing: *the visual sense.* **3.** optical. **4.** perceptible by the sense of sight; visible: *a visual beauty.* **5.** perceptible by the mind; of the nature of a mental vision: *a visual impression captured in a line of verse.* —*n.* **6.** Usually, **visuals. a.** the picture elements, as distinguished from the sound elements, in films, television, etc. **b.** photographs, slides, films, charts, or other visual materials, esp. as used for illustration or promotion. Cf. **audio, video. 7.** a rough, preliminary sketch of an advertising layout, showing possible arrangements of material. Cf. **comprehensive** (def. 5). **8.** any item or element depending on the sense of sight. [1375–1425; late ME < LL *visuālis*, equiv. to *vīsu(s)* sight (*vid(ēre)* to see + *-tus* suffix of v. action, with *dt* > *s*) + *-ālis* -AL[1]]

vis′ual acu′ity, *Ophthalm.* acuteness of the vision as determined by a comparison with the normal ability to define certain letters at a given distance, usually 20 ft. (6 m). *Abbr.:* V. [1885–90]

vis′ual aid′, any of various materials depending on the sense of sight, as films, slides, photographs, etc., used as aids in teaching. [1910–15]

vis′ual arts′, the arts created primarily for visual perception, as drawing, graphics, painting, sculpture, and the decorative arts.

vis′ual bi′nary, *Astron.* a binary star having components that are sufficiently separated to be resolved by a telescope. Cf. **spectroscopic binary.**

vis′ual cor′tex, the portion of the cerebral cortex of the brain that receives and processes impulses from the optic nerves.

vis′ual display′ ter′minal, *Computers.* See **video display terminal.** *Abbr.:* VDT

vis′ual display′ u′nit, *Chiefly Brit. Computers.* See **video display terminal.** *Abbr.:* VDU [1970–75]

vis′ual field′. See **field of vision.** [1880–85]

vis·u·al·ize (vizh′o͞o ə līz′), *v.,* **-ized, -iz·ing.** —*v.i.* **1.** to recall or form mental images or pictures. —*v.t.* **2.** to make visual or visible. **3.** to form a mental image of. **4.** to make perceptible to the mind or imagination. Also, *esp. Brit.,* **vis′u·al·ise′.** [1810–20; VISUAL + -IZE] —**vis′u·al·iz′a·ble,** *adj.* —**vis′u·al·i·za′tion,** *n.* —**vis′·u·al·iz′er, vis′u·al·ist,** *n.*

vis′ual lit′eracy, the ability to apprehend or interpret pictures or other visual images. [1970–75]

vis·u·al·ly (vizh′o͞o ə lē), *adv.* in a visual manner; with respect to sight; by sight. [1400–50; late ME; see VISUAL, -LY]

vis′ually impaired′, 1. (of a person) having reduced vision so severe as to constitute a handicap. **2.** visually impaired persons collectively (usually prec. by *the*): *a training program to aid the visually impaired.*

vis′ual mag′nitude, *Astron.* magnitude (def. 5a).

vis′ual pur′ple, *Biochem.* rhodopsin. [1895–1900]

vis′ual range′, *Meteorol.* visibility (def. 3). [1895–1900]

vis·u·o·spa·tial (vizh′o͞o ō spā′shəl), *adj.* pertaining to perception of the spatial relationships among objects within the field of vision. [1960–65; < L *vīsu(s)* sight (see VISUAL) + -O- + SPATIAL]

vi·ta (vī′tə, vē′-; *Lat.* wē′tä), *n., pl.* **vi·tae** (vī′tē, vē′tī; *Lat.* wē′tī). See **curriculum vitae** (def. 1). Also, **vi·tae** (vī′tē, vē′tī). [1920–25; < L: life]

Vi·ta (vē′tə), *n.* a female given name, form of **Davida.**

vi·ta·ceous (vī tā′shəs), *adj.* belonging to the Vitaceae, the grape family of plants. Cf. **grape family.** [< NL *Vitace(ae)* family name (*Vit(is)* genus name (L *vītis* vine) + *-aceae* -ACEAE) + -OUS]

vi·tal (vīt′l), *adj.* **1.** of or pertaining to life: *vital processes.* **2.** having remarkable energy, liveliness, or force of personality: *a vital leader.* **3.** being the seat or source of life: *the vital organs.* **4.** necessary to life: *vital fluids.* **5.** necessary to the existence, continuance, or well-being of something; indispensable; essential: *vital for a healthy society.* **6.** affecting the existence, well-being, truth, etc., of something: *a vital error.* **7.** of critical importance: *vital decisions.* **8.** destructive to life; deadly: *a vital wound.* [1350–1400; ME < L *vītālis*, equiv. to *vīt(a)* life (deriv. of *vīvere* to live; akin to Gk *bíesthai*, Skt *jīvati* (he) lives, E QUICK) + *-ālis* -AL[1]] —**vi′tal·ly,** *adv.* —**vi′tal·ness,** *n.*
—**Syn. 5.** important, critical.

vi′tal capac′ity, *Physiol.* the greatest amount of air that can be forced from the lungs after maximum inhalation. [1850–55]

vi′tal force′, the force that animates and perpetuates living beings and organisms. Also called **vi′tal prin′·ciple.**

vi′tal func′tion, *Physiol.* any function of the body that is essential for life. [1795–1805]

Vi·tal·ian (vi tāl′yən, -tā′lē ən), *n.* died A.D. 672, pope 657–672.

vi·tal·ism (vīt′l iz′əm), **1.** the doctrine that phenomena are only partly controlled by mechanical forces, and are in some measure self-determining. Cf. **dynamism** (def. 1), **mechanism** (def. 8). **2.** *Biol.* a doctrine that ascribes the functions of a living organism to a vital principle distinct from chemical and physical forces. [1815–25; VITAL + -ISM] —**vi′tal·ist,** *n., adj.* —**vi′tal·is′tic,** *adj.* —**vi′tal·is′ti·cal·ly,** *adv.*

vi·tal·i·ty (vī tal′i tē), *n., pl.* **-ties. 1.** exuberant physical strength or mental vigor: *a person of great vitality.* **2.** capacity for survival or for the continuation of a meaningful or purposeful existence: *the vitality of an institution.* **3.** power to live or grow: *the vitality of a language.* **4.** vital force or principle. [1585–95; < L *vītālitās*, equiv. to *vītāli(s)* VITAL + *-tās* -TY[2]]

vi·tal·ize (vīt′l īz′), *v.t.,* **-ized, -iz·ing. 1.** to give life to; make vital. **2.** to give vitality or vigor to; animate. Also, *esp. Brit.,* **vi′tal·ise′.** [1670–80; VITAL + -IZE] —**vi′tal·i·za′tion,** *n.* —**vi′tal·iz′er,** *n.*

Vi·tal·li·um (vī tal′ē əm), *Trademark.* a brand name for an alloy of cobalt, chromium, and molybdenum, having various dental and surgical applications.

vi·tals (vīt′lz), *n.pl.* **1.** those bodily organs that are essential to life, as the brain, heart, liver, lungs, and stomach. **2.** the essential parts of something: *the vitals of a democracy.* [1600–10; trans. of L *vītālia*; see VITAL]

vi′tal signs′, index of essential body functions, comprising pulse rate, body temperature, and respiration. [1915–20]

vi′tal statis′tics, 1. statistics concerning human life or the conditions affecting human life and the maintenance of population. **2.** *Facetious.* the measurements of a woman's figure, esp. the bust, waist, and hips. [1830–40; 1940–45 for def. 2]

vi·ta·min (vī′tə min; *Brit. also* vit′ə min), *n.* any of a group of organic substances essential in small quantities to normal metabolism, found in minute amounts in natural foodstuffs or sometimes produced synthetically: deficiencies of vitamins produce specific disorders. Also, **vi·ta·mine** (vī′tə min, -mēn′; *Brit. also* vit′ə min, -mēn′). [1912; earlier *vitamine* < L *vīt(a)* life + AMINE; coined by C. Funk, who thought they were amines] —**vi′ta·min′ic,** *adj.*

vitamin A, a yellow, fat-soluble, solid terpene alcohol, $C_{20}H_{30}O$, obtained from carotene and occurring in green and yellow vegetables, egg yolk, etc.: essential to growth, the protection of epithelial tissue, and the prevention of night blindness. Also called **vitamin A_1, retinol.** [1920–25]

vitamin A_2, a yellow oil, $C_{20}H_{28}O$, similar to vitamin A, obtained from fish liver.

vitamin A aldehyde, retinal.

vitamin B_1, thiamine. [1920–25]

vitamin B_2, riboflavin. [1925–30]

vitamin B_3, See **nicotinic acid.**

vitamin B_6, pyridoxine. [1930–35]

vitamin B_9, See **folic acid.**

vitamin B_{12}, a deep-red crystalline, water-soluble solid, $C_{63}H_{88}N_{14}O_{14}PCo$, obtained from liver, milk, eggs, fish, oysters, and clams: a deficiency causes pernicious anemia and disorders of the nervous system. Also called **cyanocobalamin, cobalamin, extrinsic factor.** [1945–50]

vitamin B complex, an important group of water-soluble vitamins containing vitamin B_1, vitamin B_2, etc. [1925–30]

vitamin C, See **ascorbic acid.** [1920–25]

vitamin D, any of the several fat-soluble, antirachitic vitamins D_1, D_2, D_3, occurring in milk and fish-liver oils, esp. cod and halibut, or obtained by irradiating provitamin D with ultraviolet light, essential for the formation of normal bones and teeth. [1920–25]

vitamin D_1, a mixture of lumisterol and calciferol, obtained by ultraviolet irradiation of ergosterol.

vitamin D_2, calciferol.

vitamin D_3, a D vitamin, $C_{27}H_{43}OH$, occurring in fish-liver oils, that differs from vitamin D_2 by slight structural differences in the molecule. Also called **cholecalciferol.**

vitamin E, a pale-yellow viscous fluid, abundant in vegetable oils, whole-grain cereals, butter, and eggs, and important as an antioxidant in the deactivation of free radicals and in maintenance of the body's cell membranes: deficiency is rare. Also called **alpha-tocopherol.** Cf. **tocopherol.** [1920–25]

vitamin G, riboflavin. [1925–30]

vitamin H, biotin. [1930–35]

vitamin K_1, a yellowish, oily, viscous liquid, $C_{31}H_{46}O_2$, occurring in leafy vegetables, rice, bran, hog liver, etc., or obtained esp. from alfalfa or putrefied sardine meat, or synthesized, that promotes blood clotting by increasing the prothrombin content of the blood. Also called **phylloquinone, phytonadione.** [1930–35]

vitamin K_2, a light-yellow, crystalline solid, $C_{41}H_{56}O_2$, having properties similar to those of vitamin K_1.

vitamin K_3, menadione.

vitamin M, See **folic acid.**

vitamin P, bioflavonoid. Also called **citrin.**

vi·ta·scope (vī′tə skōp′), *n.* one of the first motion-picture projectors, developed by Thomas Edison. [1890–95, *Amer.*; < L *vīta* life + -SCOPE] —**vi·ta·scop·ic** (vī′tə skop′ik), *adj.*

vite (vēt), *adv. Music.* briskly; lively. [< F: rapid, quickly, OF *viste*, of uncert. orig.]

Vi·tebsk (vē′tepsk; *Russ.* vyē′tyipsk), *n.* a city in NE Byelorussia (Belarus), on the Dvina River. 347,000.

vi·tel·lin (vi tel′in, vī-), *n. Biochem.* a phosphoprotein in the yolk of eggs. Also called **ovovitellin.** [1855–60; VITELL(US) + -IN[2]]

vi·tel·line (vi tel′in, -ēn, vī-), *adj.* **1.** of or pertaining to the egg yolk. **2.** having a yellow color resembling that of an egg yolk. [1375–1425; late ME < ML *vitellinus.* See VITELLUS, -INE[1]]

vitel′line mem′brane, the membrane surrounding the egg yolk. [1835–45]

vi·tel·lo·gen·e·sis (vi tel′ō jen′ə sis, vī-), *n. Embryol.* the process by which the yolk is formed and accumulated in the ovum. [1945–50; VITELL(US) + -O- + -GENESIS]

vi·tel·lus (vi tel′əs, vī-), *n., pl.* **-lus·es.** the yolk of an egg. [1720–30; < L]

vi·ti·a·ble (vish′ē ə bəl), *adj.* capable of being vitiated. [VITI(ATE) + -ABLE]

vi·ti·ate (vish′ē āt′), *v.t.,* **-at·ed, -at·ing. 1.** to impair the quality of; make faulty; spoil; mar. **2.** to impair or weaken the effectiveness of. **3.** to debase; corrupt; pervert. **4.** to make legally defective or invalid; invalidate: *to vitiate a claim.* [1525–35; < L *vitiātus* (ptp. of *vitiāre* to spoil), equiv. to *viti(um)* defect, blemish, VICE[1] + *-ātus* -ATE[1]] —**vi′ti·a′tion,** *n.* —**vi′ti·a′tor,** *n.*

vit·i·ce·tum (vit′ə sē′təm), *n., pl.* **-tums, -ta** (-tə). a place where vines, esp. grapevines, are cultivated. [< L *vīti(s)* vine + *-c-* by association with *vitic-* (s. of *vitex*) chaste tree + *-ētum* suffix denoting place where a given plant grows]

vit·i·cul·ture (vit′i kul′chər, vī′ti-), *n.* **1.** the culture or cultivation of grapevines; grape-growing. **2.** the study or science of grapes and their culture. [1870–75; < L *vīti(s)* vine + CULTURE] —**vit′i·cul′tur·al,** *adj.* —**vit′i·cul′tur·er, vit′i·cul′tur·ist,** *n.*

Vi·ti Le·vu (vē′tē lev′o͞o), the largest of the Fiji Islands, in the S Pacific. 395,060; 4053 sq. mi. (10,497 sq. km). *Cap.:* Suva.

vit·i·li·go (vit′l ī′gō, -ē′gō), *n. Pathol.* a skin disorder characterized by smooth, white patches on various parts of the body, caused by the loss of the natural pigment. Also called **leukoderma, piebald skin.** [1650–60; < L *vitilīgō* form of skin eruption, appar. equiv. to **vitil(is)* defective (*vit(ium)* blemish + *-ilis* -ILE) + *-īgō* n. suffix] —**vit·i·lig·i·nous** (vit′l ij′ə nəs), *adj.* —**vit′i·li′goid,** *adj.*

Vi·to (vē′tō), *n.* a male given name.

Vi·to·ria (vi tôr′ē ə, -tōr′-; *Sp.* bē tô′ryä), *n.* **1. Fran-**

cis·co de (fRän thes′kô the), c1480–1546, Spanish scholar and theologian. **2.** a city in N Spain: decisive defeat of the French forces in Spain 1813. 136,873.

Vi·tó·ri·a (vi tôr′ē ə, -tōr′-; *Port.* vi tô′Ryä), *n.* a seaport in and the capital of Espírito Santo, in E Brazil. 215,073.

vit·rain (vi′trān), *n.* the material of which the friable, vitreous layers in banded bituminous coal are composed. Cf. **clarain, durain.** [1915–20; < L *vitr(um)* glass + *-ain,* as in FUSAIN]

vit·rec·to·my (vi trek′tə mē), *n., pl.* **-mies.** the microsurgical procedure of removing the vitreous humor and replacing it with saline solution, performed to improve vision that has been impaired by opacities. [1965–70; VITR(EOUS HUMOR) + -ECTOMY]

vit·re·ous (vi′trē əs), *adj.* **1.** of the nature of or resembling glass, as in transparency, brittleness, hardness, glossiness, etc.: *vitreous china.* **2.** of or pertaining to glass. **3.** obtained from or containing glass. [1640–50; < L *vitreus,* equiv. to *vitr(um)* glass + *-eus* -EOUS] —**vit′re·ous·ly,** *adv.* —**vit′re·ous·ness, vit·re·os·i·ty** (vi′trē os′i tē), *n.*

vit′reous hu′mor, *Anat.* the transparent gelatinous substance filling the eyeball behind the crystalline lens. See diag. under **eye.** [1655–65]

vi·tres·cent (vi tres′ənt), *adj.* **1.** becoming glass. **2.** tending to become glass. **3.** capable of being formed into glass. [1750–60; < L *vitr(um)* glass + -ESCENT] —**vi·tres′cence,** *n.*

vi·tres·ci·ble (vi tres′ə bəl), *adj.* capable of being formed into or of becoming glass; vitrifiable. [1745–55; VITRESC(ENT) + -IBLE]

vit·re·um (vi′trē əm), *adj.* (in prescriptions) glass. [< L, n. use of neut. of *vitreus* VITREOUS]

vitri-, a combining form meaning "glass," used in the formation of compound words: *vitriform.* [comb. form of L *vitrum* glass]

vit·ric (vi′trik), *adj.* **1.** of or pertaining to glass. **2.** resembling glass. [< L *vitr(um)* glass + -IC]

vit·rics (vi′triks), *n.* **1.** (*used with a singular v.*) the art and technology of making glass products. **2.** (*used with a plural v.*) articles of glass or other vitreous materials. [1870–75; see VITRIC, -ICS]

vit·ri·fi·ca·tion (vi′trə fi kā′shən), *n.* **1.** act or process of vitrifying; state of being vitrified. **2.** something vitrified. Also, **vit·ri·fac·tion** (vi′trə fak′shən). [1720–30; VITRI(FY) + -FICATION]

vit·ri·form (vi′trə fôrm′), *adj.* having the form or appearance of glass. [1790–1800; VITRI- + -FORM]

vit·ri·fy (vi′trə fī′), *v.t., v.i.,* **-fied, -fy·ing. 1.** to convert or be converted into glass. **2.** to make or become vitreous. [1585–95; VITRI- + -FY; cf. F *vitrifier*] —**vit′ri·fi′a·bil′i·ty,** *n.* —**vit′ri·fi′a·ble,** *adj.*

vi·trine (vi trēn′), *n.* a glass cabinet or case, esp. for displaying art objects. [1875–80; < F, equiv. to *vitre* pane of glass + *-ine* -INE[2]]

vit·ri·ol (vi′trē əl), *n., v.,* **-oled, -ol·ing** or (*esp. Brit.*) **-olled, -ol·ling.** —*n.* **1.** *Chem.* any of certain metallic sulfates of glassy appearance, as copper sulfate or blue vitriol, iron sulfate or green vitriol, zinc sulfate or white vitriol, etc. **2.** oil of vitriol; sulfuric acid. **3.** something highly caustic or severe in effect, as criticism. —*v.t.* **4.** to treat with or as with vitriol, esp. sulfuric acid. [1350–1400; ME < ML *vitriolum, vitreolum,* equiv. to L *vitre(us)* VITREOUS + *-olum,* neut. of *-olus* -OLE[1]]

vit·ri·ol·ic (vi′trē ol′ik), *adj.* **1.** of, pertaining to, or resembling vitriol. **2.** obtained from vitriol. **3.** very caustic; scathing: *vitriolic criticism.* [1660–70; VITRIOL + -IC]
—**Syn. 3.** acid, bitter. —**Ant. 3.** bland, mild.

vit·ri·ol·ize (vi′trē ə līz′), *v.t.,* **-ized, -iz·ing. 1.** to treat with or change into vitriol. **2.** to injure or burn with sulfuric acid. Also, *esp. Brit.,* **vit′ri·ol·ise′.** [1685–95; VITRIOL + -IZE] —**vit′ri·ol·i·za′tion,** *n.*

vit·rum (vi′trəm), *n., pl.* **vit·ra** (vi′trə). (in prescriptions) glass. [1650–60; < L]

Vitru′vian scroll′, a scroll forming a stylized wave pattern. Also called **running dog, Vitru′vian wave′, wave scroll.** [1830–40; named after VITRUVIUS POLLIO]

Vi·tru′vi·us Pol′li·o (vi troo′vē əs pol′ē ō′), **Marcus,** fl. 1st century B.C., Roman architect, engineer, and author. —**Vi·tru′vi·an,** *adj.*

Vi·try (vē tRē′), *n.* **Phi·lippe de** (fē lēp′ də), 1290?–1361, French music theorist, composer, and poet.

vit·ta (vit′ə), *n., pl.* **vit·tae** (vit′ē). **1.** *Bot.* a tube or receptacle for oil, occurring in the fruits of most plants of the parsley family. **2.** *Zool., Bot.* a streak or stripe, as of color. [1685–95; < L: ribbon, fillet, akin to *viēre* to weave together]

vit·tate (vit′āt), *adj.* **1.** provided with or having a vitta or vittae. **2.** striped longitudinally. [1820–30; < L *vittātus,* equiv. to *vitt(a)* fillet + *-ātus* -ATE[1]]

vit·tle (vit′l), *n., v.t., v.i.,* victual. [1805–15]

Vit·to·ri·a (vi tôr′ē ə, -tōr′-; *It.* vēt tô′Rē ä′), *n.* a female given name, Italian form of **Victoria.**

Vit·to·rio (vi tôr′ē ō′, -tōr′-; *It.* vēt tô′Ryô), *n.* a male given name, Italian form of **Victor.**

vit·u·line (vich′ə lin′, -lin), *adj.* of, pertaining to, or resembling a calf or veal. [1650–60; < L *vitulīnus,* equiv. to *vitul(us)* calf + *-īnus* -INE[1]]

vi·tu·per·ate (vī too′pə rāt′, -tyoo′-, vi-), *v.i., v.t.,* **-at·ed, -at·ing.** to use or address with harsh or abusive language; revile. [1535–45; < L *vituperātus* (ptp. of *vituperāre* to spoil, blame), equiv. to *vituperā(re)* (*vitu-,* var. (before a labial) of *viti-,* s. of *vitium* blemish, VICE[1] + *-perāre,* comb. form of *parāre* to furnish, provide; see PREPARE) + *-tus* ptp. suffix; see -ATE[1]] —**vi·tu′per·a′tor,** *n.*
—**Syn.** censure, vilify, berate. —**Ant.** praise, commend.

vi·tu·per·a·tion (vī too′pə rā′shən, -tyoo′-, vi-), *n.* verbal abuse or castigation; violent denunciation or condemnation. [1475–85; < L *vituperātiōn-* (s. of *vituperātio*), equiv. to *vituperāt(us)* (see VITUPERATE) + *-iōn-* -ION]
—**Syn.** censure, vilification, spite, scolding, defamation, aspersion. —**Ant.** praise.

vi·tu·per·a·tive (vī too′pər ə tiv, -pə rā′tiv, -tyoo′-, vi-), *adj.* characterized by or of the nature of vituperation: *vituperative remarks.* [1720–30; VITUPERATE + -IVE] —**vi·tu′per·a·tive·ly,** *adv.*

vi·va[1] (vē′və; *It.* vē′vä; *Sp.* bē′vä), *interj.* **1.** *Italian, Spanish.* (an exclamation of acclaim or approval): *Viva Zapata!* —*n.* **2.** a shout of "viva." [1665–75; lit.: may (he) live! 3rd pers. sing. pres. subj. of It *vivere,* Sp *vivir* << L *vīvere* to live; see VITAL]

vi·va[2] (vī′və), *n.* (in British and European universities) an oral examination; viva voce. [1890–95; shortened form]

vi·va·ce (vi vä′chā; *It.* vē vä′che), *adv., adj.* (a musical direction) vivacious; lively. [1675–85; < It < L *vīvāc-,* s. of *vīvāx,* long-lived, lively; see VIVACITY]

vi·va·cious (vi vā′shəs, vī-), *adj.* lively; animated; gay: *a vivacious folk dance.* [1635–45; VIVACI(TY) + -OUS] —**vi·va′cious·ly,** *adv.* —**vi·va′cious·ness,** *n.*
—**Syn.** spirited, brisk. —**Ant.** languid.

vi·vac·i·ty (vi vas′i tē, vī-), *n., pl.* **-ties** for 1. **1.** the quality or state of being vivacious. **2.** liveliness; animation; sprightliness: *a people noted for their vivacity.* **3.** a vivacious act or statement. [1400–50; late ME < L *vīvācitās,* equiv. to *vīvāc-* (s. of *vīvāx* long-lived, lively, equiv. to *vīv(us)* alive (see VITAL) + *-āx* adj. suffix) + *-i-* -I- + *-tās* -TY[2]]

Vi·val·di (vi väl′dē; *It.* vē väl′dē), *n.* **An·to·nio** (an tō′nē ō′; *It.* än tô′nyô), 1678–1741, Italian violinist and composer.

vi·var·i·um (vī vâr′ē əm, vi-), *n., pl.* **-var·i·ums, -var·i·a** (-vâr′ē ə). a place, such as a laboratory, where live animals or plants are kept under conditions simulating their natural environment, as for research. [1590–1600; < L *vīvārium,* equiv. to *vīv(us)* living (see VITAL) + *-ārium* -ARY]

vi·va vo·ce (vī′və vō′sē, vē′və), **1.** by word of mouth; orally. **2.** Also, **viva.** (in British and European universities) the oral part of an examination. [1555–65; < ML *vīvā vōce* with living voice, L, abl. of *vīva vōx*] —**vi′va-vo′ce,** *adj.*

vi′vax malar′ia (vī′vaks), *Pathol.* the most common form of malaria, caused by the protozoan *Plasmodium vivax* and marked by the occurrence of attacks every other day. [1940–45; < NL (*Plasmodium*) *vivax* the protozoan species, L *vīvāx* long-lived, lively; see VIVACITY]

Vi·ve·ka·nan·da (vē′vi kə nun′də), *n.* (*Narendranath Datta*) 1863–1902, Hindu religious leader and teacher.

vive le roi (vēv lə RWA′), *French.* Long live the king!

vi·ver·rine (vī ver′īn, -in, vi-), *adj.* **1.** of or pertaining to the Viverridae, a family of small carnivorous mammals including the civets, genets, palm cats, etc. —*n.* **2.** a viverrine animal. [1790–1800; < NL *viverrīnus,* equiv. to *Viverr(a)* a genus name (L *vīverra* the ferret or a similar animal; akin to Lith *voverė̃,* ORuss *věveritsa,* OE *ācweorn,* OHG *eihhurno* squirrel) + *-īnus* -INE[1]]

vi·vers (vē′vərz), *n.pl. Chiefly Scot.* victuals; foodstuffs. [1530–40; < MF *vivres,* pl. of *vivre* food, n. use of *vivre* to live < L *vīvere;* cf. VIAND]

vives (vīvz), *n.* (*used with a singular v.*) *Vet. Pathol.* inflammation and swelling of the submaxillary gland in horses. [1515–25; earlier *avives* < MF < Sp *adibas* < Ar *al-dhi'bah* lit., the she-wolf]

vivi-, a combining form meaning "living," "alive," used in the formation of compound words: *vivisection.* [< L *vīvi-,* comb. form of *vīvus* alive; akin to *vīvere* to live (see VITAL)]

Viv·i·an (viv′ē ən), *n.* **1.** Also, **Viv′i·en.** *Arthurian Romance.* an enchantress, the mistress of Merlin: known as the Lady of the Lake. **2.** Also, **Vivien, Vi′v·ienne.** a male or female given name: from a Latin word meaning "alive."

Vi·vi·a·ni (vē vYA nē′), *n.* **Re·né** (Rə nā′), 1863–1925, French statesman: premier of France 1911–15.

viv·i·an·ite (viv′ē ə nīt′), *n.* a secondary mineral, hydrous ferrous phosphate, $Fe_3(PO_4)_2 \cdot 8H_2O$, occurring in the form of pale blue crystals or powder. [1815–25; named after J. G. Vivian, 19th-century English mineralogist, who found it; see -ITE[1]]

viv·id (viv′id), *adj.* **1.** strikingly bright or intense, as color, light, etc.: *a vivid green.* **2.** full of life; lively; animated: *a vivid personality.* **3.** presenting the appearance, freshness, spirit, etc., of life; realistic: *a vivid account.* **4.** strong, distinct, or clearly perceptible: *a vivid recollection.* **5.** forming distinct and striking mental images: *a vivid imagination.* [1630–40; < L *vīvidus* lively, equiv. to *vīv(ere)* to live (see VITAL) + *-idus* -ID[4]] —**viv′id·ly,** *adv.* —**viv′id·ness, vi·vid′i·ty,** *n.*
—**Syn. 1.** bright, brilliant, intense. **2.** spirited, vivacious, intense. **3.** See **picturesque.**

viv·i·fy (viv′ə fī′), *v.t.,* **-fied, -fy·ing. 1.** to give life to; animate; quicken. **2.** to enliven; brighten; sharpen. [1535–45; alter. (with -FY for *-ficate*) of late ME *vivificate* < L *vīvificātus* (ptp. of *vīvificāre*). See VIVI-, -FICATE] —**viv′i·fi·ca′tion,** *n.* —**viv′i·fi′er,** *n.*

vi·vip·a·rous (vī vip′ər əs, vi-), *adj.* **1.** *Zool.* bringing forth living young rather than eggs, as most mammals and some reptiles and fishes. **2.** *Bot.* producing seeds that germinate on the plant. [1640–50; < L *vīviparus* bringing forth living young. See VIVI-, -PAROUS] —**vi·vip′a·rism,** *n.* —**vi·vi·par·i·ty** (viv′ə par′i tē, vī′və-), **vi·vip′a·rous·ness,** *n.* —**vi·vip′a·rous·ly,** *adv.*

viv·i·sect (viv′ə sekt′, viv′ə sekt′), *v.t.* **1.** to dissect the living body of (an animal). —*v.i.* **2.** to practice vivisection. [1860–65; back formation from VIVISECTION] —**viv′i·sec′tor,** *n.*

viv·i·sec·tion (viv′ə sek′shən), *n.* **1.** the action of cutting into or dissecting a living body. **2.** the practice of subjecting living animals to cutting operations, esp. in order to advance physiological and pathological knowledge. [1700–10; VIVI- + SECTION] —**viv′i·sec′tion·al,** *adj.* —**viv′i·sec′tion·al·ly,** *adv.*

viv·i·sec·tion·ist (viv′ə sek′shə nist), *n.* **1.** a person who vivisects. **2.** a person who favors or defends the practice of vivisection. [1875–80; VIVISECTION + -IST]

Viv·yan (viv′yən), *n.* a male or female given name.

vix·en (vik′sən), *n.* **1.** a female fox. **2.** an ill-tempered or quarrelsome woman. [1375–1425; late ME (south); r. earlier *fixen,* ME (north), for OE *fyxe,* fem. of *fox* FOX (cf. *fyxen* (adj.) pertaining to a fox, OHG *fuhsin* (n.) vixen)] —**vix′en·ish, vix′en·ly,** *adj.*
—**Syn. 2.** shrew, scold, virago, harpy, termagant.

Vi·yel·la (vī el′ə), *Trademark.* a brand of fabric made of cotton and wool in twill weave. Also called **Viyel′la flan′nel.**

viz., videlicet.

viz·ard (viz′ərd), *n.* *Archaic.* a mask. Also, **visard.** [1545–55; var. of VISOR; see -ARD] —**viz′ard·ed,** *adj.*

viz·ca·cha (vi skä′chə), *n.* viscacha.

vi·zier (vi zēr′, viz′yər), *n.* (formerly) a high official in certain Muslim countries and caliphates, esp. a minister of state. Cf. **grand vizier.** Also, **vi·zir′.** [1555–65; < Turk *vezir* < Ar *wazīr*] —**vi·zier·ate** (vi zēr′it, -āt, viz′yər it, -yə rāt′), **vi·zier′ship,** *n.* —**vi·zier′i·al,** *adj.*

vi·zor (vī′zər), *n., v.t.* visor. —**vi′zor·less,** *adj.*

vizs·la (vizh′lo), *n.* (*sometimes cap.*) one of a Hungarian breed of medium-sized, powerful hunting dogs having a short, smooth, rusty-gold coat, a square muzzle, and a docked tail. Also called **Hungarian pointer.** [1940–45; < Hungarian; akin to Serbo-Croatian *vìžao,* Czech *vyžle, vyžel,* Pol *wyżeł,* Russ *výzhlets;* ult. source and direction of transmission uncert.]

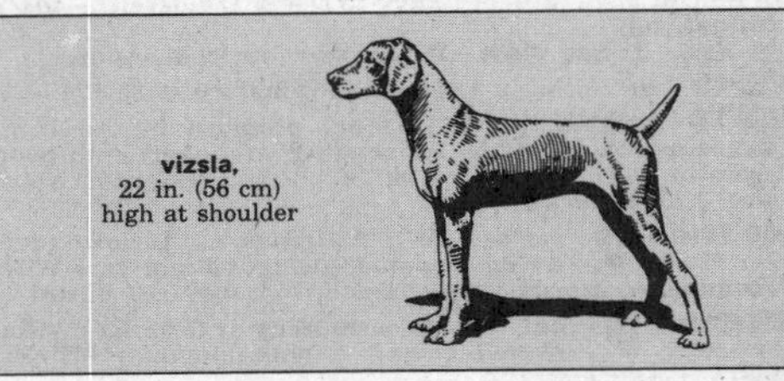
vizsla, 22 in. (56 cm) high at shoulder

VJ (vē′jā′), *Informal.* **1.** Also, **V.J.** See **video jockey. 2.** a video journalist; a person who works as a reporter in television news broadcasting.

V-J Day (vē′jā′), August 15, 1945, the day Japan accepted the Allied surrender terms in World War II. [*V-J:* victory over Japan]

V joint, *Masonry.* an angular, hollow mortar joint.

VL, Vulgar Latin.

v.l., varia lectio.

VLA, *Astron.* See **Very Large Array.**

Vlaar·ding·en (vlär′ding ən), *n.* a city in the W Netherlands, at the mouth of the Rhine. 79,100.

Vlach (vläk, vlak), *n.* **1.** a member of a people living in scattered communities in the Balkans. **2.** the Rumanian dialect of these people.

Vlad (vlad), *n.* a male given name, form of **Vladimir.**

Vla·di·kav·kaz (vlad′i kaf käz′; *Russ.* vlə dyi kuf käs′), *n.* a city in and the capital of the North Ossetian Autonomous Republic, in the Russian Federation in SE Europe. 300,000. Formerly (1944–91), **Ordzhonikidze.**

Vlad·i·mir (vlad′ə mēr′; *Russ.* vlu dyē′miR), *n.* **1. Saint.** Also, **Vladimir I, Wladimir.** (*Vladimir the Great*) A.D. c956–1015, first Christian grand prince of Russia 980–1015. **2.** a city in the W Russian Federation in Europe, E of Moscow. 343,000. **3.** a male given name.

Vla·di·vos·tok (vlad′ə vos′tok, -və stok′; *Russ.* vlə dyi vu stôk′), *n.* a seaport in the SE Russian Federation in Asia, on the Sea of Japan: eastern terminus of the Trans-Siberian Railroad. 648,000.

Vladivos′tok agree′ment, a preliminary arms control accord concluded by Soviet leader Leonid Brezhnev and U.S. President Gerald Ford in Vladivostok, U.S.S.R., in December 1974.

Vla·minck (vlA maNk′), *n.* **Mau·rice de** (mō Rēs′ də), 1876–1958, French painter.

CONCISE ETYMOLOGY KEY: <, descended or borrowed from; >, whence; b., blend of, blended; c., cognate with; cf., compare; deriv., derivative; equiv., equivalent; imit., imitative; obl., oblique; r., replacing; s., stem; sp., spelling, spelled; resp., respelling, respelled; trans., translation; ?, origin unknown; *, unattested; ‡, probably earlier than. See the full key inside the front cover.

VLBI, *Astron.* See **very long baseline interferometry.**

VLCC, a supertanker with a deadweight capacity of up to 250,000 tons. Cf. **ULCC** [*V*(*ery*) *L*(*arge*) *C*(*rude*) *C*(*arrier*)]

VLDL, *Biochem.* very-low-density lipoprotein: a plasma lipoprotein with a high lipid content, associated with atherosclerosis.

VLF, See **very low frequency.** Also, **vlf**

Vlis·sing·en (vlis′ing ən), *n.* Dutch name of **Flushing.**

Vlo·rë (vlôr′ə, vlōr′ə), *n.* a seaport in SW Albania. 58,400. Also, **Vlo′re, Vlo·na** (vlō′nə). Italian, **Valona.** Formerly, **Avlona.**

VLSI, very large scale integration: the technology for concentrating many thousands of semiconductor devices on a single integrated circuit. Cf. **MSI, LSI.**

Vl·ta·va (vl′tä vä), *n.* a river in the W Czech Republic, flowing N to the Elbe. 270 mi. (435 km) long. German, **Moldau.**

V-mail (vē′māl′), *n.* a mail system used by U.S. armed forces during World War II. [V: victory]

V.M.D., Doctor of Veterinary Medicine. [< NL *Veterinariae Medicinae Doctor*]

v.n., verb neuter.

V neck, a neckline V-shaped in front. [1900–05]

vo., verso.

V.O., very old (used esp. to indicate the age of whiskey or brandy, usually 6 to 8 years old).

VOA, 1. Also, **V.O.A.** See **Voice of America. 2.** See **Volunteers of America.**

vo-ag (vō′ag′), *adj. Informal.* vocational-agricultural: *the vo-ag curriculum.* [1950–55; by shortening]

voc., vocative.

vocab., vocabulary.

vo·ca·ble (vō′kə bəl), *n.* **1.** a word; term; name. **2.** a word considered only as a combination of certain sounds or letters, without regard to meaning. —*adj.* **3.** capable of being spoken. [1520–30; < L *vocābulum* a word, a name, equiv. to *vocā*(*re*) to call + *-bulum* n. suffix] —**vo′ca·bly,** *adv.*

vo·cab·u·lar·y (vō kab′yə ler′ē), *n., pl.* **-lar·ies. 1.** the stock of words used by or known to a particular people or group of persons: *His French vocabulary is rather limited. The scientific vocabulary is constantly growing.* **2.** a list or collection of the words or phrases of a language, technical field, etc., usually arranged in alphabetical order and defined: *Study the vocabulary in the fourth chapter.* **3.** the words of a language. **4.** any collection of signs or symbols constituting a means or system of nonverbal communication: *vocabulary of a computer.* **5.** any more or less specific group of forms characteristic of an artist, a style of art, architecture, or the like. [1525–35; < ML *vocābulārium,* n. use of neut. of *vocābulārius* of words, equiv. to L *vocābul*(*um*) VOCABLE + *-ārius* -ARY] —**vo·cab′u·lar′ied,** *adj.*

vocab′ulary en′try, (in dictionaries) a word, phrase, abbreviation, symbol, affix, name, etc., listed with its definition or explanation in alphabetical order or listed for identification after the word from which it is derived or to which it is related. [1930–35]

vo·cal (vō′kəl), *adj.* **1.** of, pertaining to, or uttered with the voice: *the vocal mechanism; vocal criticism.* **2.** rendered by or intended for singing: *vocal music.* **3.** having a voice: *A dog is a vocal, but not a verbal, being.* **4.** giving forth sound with or as with a voice. **5.** inclined to express oneself in words, esp. copiously or insistently: *a vocal advocate of reform.* **6.** *Phonet.* **a.** vocalic (def. 1). **b.** voiced. —*n.* **7.** a vocal sound. **8.** a musical piece for a singer, usually with instrumental accompaniment. Cf. **instrumental** (def. 6). [1350–1400; ME < L *vōcālis,* equiv. to *vōc-* (s. of *vōx*) VOICE + *-ālis* -AL[1]] —**vo·cal·i·ty** (vō kal′i tē), **vo′cal·ness,** *n.* —**vo′cal·ly,** *adv.*
—**Syn. 5.** vociferous, outspoken.

vo′cal cords′, *Anat.* either of the two pairs of folds of mucous membrane projecting into the cavity of the larynx. Cf. **true vocal cords, false vocal cords.**

vo′cal folds′. See **true vocal cords.**

vo·cal·ic (vō kal′ik), *adj.* **1.** of, pertaining to, or resembling a vowel. **2.** consisting of, characterized by, or containing vowels. [1805–15; VOCAL + -IC]

vocal′ic allitera′tion. See under **alliteration** (def. 1).

vo·ca·lise[1] (vō′kə lēz′), *n.* **1.** a musical composition consisting of the singing of melody with vowel sounds or nonsense syllables rather than text, as for special effect in classical compositions, in polyphonic jazz singing by special groups, or in virtuoso vocal exercises. **2.** any such singing exercise or vocalized melody. Cf. **doo-wop, melisma, scat singing, solfeggio.** [1870–75; < F *vocalise,* appar. n. deriv. of *vocaliser* to VOCALIZE, with *-ise* taken as a n. suffix (see -ISE[2])]

vo·cal·ise[2] (vō′kə līz′), *v.t., v.i.,* **-ised, is·ing.** *Chiefly Brit.* vocalize.

vo·cal·ism (vō′kə liz′əm), *n.* **1.** *Phonet.* **a.** a vowel, diphthong, triphthong, or vowel quality, as in a syllable. **b.** the system of vowels of a language. **2.** the use of the voice, as in speech or song. **3.** the act, principles, or art of singing. [1860–65; VOCAL + -ISM]

vo·cal·ist (vō′kə list), *n.* a singer. [1605–15; VOCAL + -IST]

vo·cal·ize (vō′kə līz′), *v.,* **-ized, -iz·ing.** —*v.t.* **1.** to make vocal; utter; articulate; sing. **2.** to endow with a voice; cause to utter. **3.** *Phonet.* **a.** to voice. **b.** to change into a vowel (contrasted with *consonantalize*). **4.** (of Hebrew, Arabic, and other writing systems that do not usually indicate vowels) to furnish with vowels or vowel points. —*v.i.* **5.** to use the voice, as in speech or song. **6.** to sing without uttering words, esp. to warm up the voice, practice vowel sounds, etc., before a performance. **7.** to sing scales, arpeggios, trills, or the like, usually to a solmization syllable or a vowel sound. **8.** *Phonet.* to become changed into a vowel. Also, *esp. Brit.,* **vocalise.** [1660–70; VOCAL + -IZE] —**vo′cal·i·za′tion,** *n.* —**vo′cal·iz′er,** *n.*

Vo′cal Mem′non, one of the two seated figures of the Colossus of Memnon: so called because it once emitted sounds when struck by the rays of the rising sun.

vocat., vocative.

vo·ca·tion (vō kā′shən), *n.* **1.** a particular occupation, business, or profession; calling. **2.** a strong impulse or inclination to follow a particular activity or career. **3.** a divine call to God's service or to the Christian life. **4.** a function or station in life to which one is called by God: *the religious vocation; the vocation of marriage.* [1400–50; late ME *vocacio(u)n* < L *vocātiōn-* (s. of *vocātiō*) a call, summons, equiv. to *vocāt*(*us*) ptp. of *vocāre* to call (see -ATE[1]) + *-iōn-* -ION]
—**Syn. 1.** employment, pursuit.

vo·ca·tion·al (vō kā′shə nl), *adj.* **1.** of, pertaining to, or connected with a vocation or occupation: *a vocational aptitude.* **2.** of, pertaining to, or noting instruction or guidance in an occupation or profession chosen as a career or in the choice of a career: *a vocational counselor.* [1645–55; VOCATION + -AL[1]] —**vo·ca′tion·al·ly,** *adv.*

voca′tional educa′tion, educational training that provides practical experience in a particular occupational field, as agriculture, home economics, or industry.

voca′tional guid′ance, the process of assisting a student to choose, prepare for, and enter an occupation for which he or she shows aptitude. [1925–30]

vo·ca·tion·al·ism (vō kā′shə nl iz′əm), *n.* the practice or policy of requiring vocational training of all college or high-school students. [1920–25; VOCATIONAL + -ISM] —**vo·ca′tion·al·ist,** *n.*

voca′tional school′, a school offering instruction in one or more skilled or semiskilled trades or occupations.

voc·a·tive (vok′ə tiv), *adj.* **1.** *Gram.* (in certain inflected languages, as Latin) noting or pertaining to a case used to indicate that a noun refers to a person or thing being addressed. **2.** of, pertaining to, or used in calling, specifying, or addressing. —*n. Gram.* **3.** the vocative case. **4.** a word in the vocative, as Latin *Paule* "O Paul." [1400–50; late ME < L *vocātīvus* (*cāsus*) calling (case), equiv. to *vocāt*(*us*) (see VOCATION) + *-īvus* -IVE] —**voc′a·tive·ly,** *adv.*

vo·cif·er·ance (vō sif′ər əns), *n.* vociferant utterance; vociferation. [1830–40; VOCIFER(ANT) + -ANCE]

vo·cif·er·ant (vō sif′ər ənt), *adj.* **1.** vociferating; noisy. —*n.* **2.** a person who vociferates. [1600–10; < L *vōciferant-* (s. of *vōciferāns*), prp. of *vōciferārī* to VOCIFERATE; see -ANT]

vo·cif·er·ate (vō sif′ə rāt′), *v.i., v.t.,* **-at·ed, -at·ing.** to speak or cry out loudly or noisily; shout; bawl. [1590–1600; < L *vōciferātus* (ptp. of *vōciferārī* to shout), equiv. to *vōci-,* s. of *vōx* VOICE + *fer*(*re*) to BEAR[1] + *-ātus* -ATE[1]] —**vo·cif′er·a′tor,** *n.*

vo·cif·er·a·tion (vō sif′ə rā′shən), *n.* noisy outcry; clamor. [1350–1400; ME < L *vōciferātiōn-* (s. of *vōciferātiō*), equiv. to *vōciferāt*(*us*) (see VOCIFERATE) + *-iōn* -ION]

vo·cif·er·ous (vō sif′ər əs), *adj.* **1.** crying out noisily; clamorous. **2.** characterized by or uttered with vociferation: *a vociferous manner of expression.* [1605–15; VOCIFER(ANT) + -OUS] —**vo·cif′er·ous·ly,** *adv.* —**vo·cif′er·ous·ness,** *n.*
—**Syn. 1.** loud, noisy, vocal, uproarious, boisterous.

vo·cod·er (vō′kō′dər), *n.* an electronic device that synthesizes speech. [1935–40]

vo·coid (vō′koid), *Phonet.* —*adj.* **1.** of or pertaining to a sound produced without stoppage or obstruction of the flow of air in the vocal tract; vowellike. —*n.* **2.** a vocoid sound. Cf. **contoid.** [1940–45; VOC(AL) + -OID]

vod·ka (vod′kə), *n.* an unaged, colorless, distilled spirit, originally made in Russia. [1795–1805; < Russ *vódka,* equiv. to *vod*(*á*) WATER + *-ka* n. suffix]

vo·dun (vō dōōn′), *n.* voodoo (def. 1). [1935–40; < Haitian Creole; see VOODOO]

Vo·gel (vō′gəl), *n.* **Sir Julius,** 1835–99, New Zealand statesman, born in England: prime minister 1873–75, 1876.

vo·gie (vō′gē, vog′ē), *adj. Scot.* **1.** conceited; proud. **2.** cheerful; merry. [1705–15; orig. uncert.]

vogue (vōg), *n.* **1.** something in fashion, as at a particular time: *Short hairdos were the vogue in the twenties.* **2.** popular currency, acceptance, or favor; popularity: *The book is having a great vogue.* [1565–75; < MF: wave or course of success < OIt *voga* a rowing, deriv. of *vogare* to row, sail < ?]
—**Syn. 1.** mode. See **fashion.**

vogue′ word′, a word or term that is fashionable for a time. [1920–25]

vo·guing (vō′ging), *n.* a dance consisting of a series of stylized poses struck in imitation of fashion models. Also, **vo·gueing.** [1985–90; after *Vogue,* a fashion magazine; see -ING[3]] —**vogue,** *v.i.,* **vogued, vo·guing** or **vo·gue·ing.**

vogu·ish (vō′gish), *adj.* **1.** being in vogue; fashionable; chic. **2.** briefly popular or fashionable; faddish. [1925–30; VOGUE + -ISH[1]] —**vogu′ish·ness,** *n.*

Vo·gul (vō′gōōl), *n.* Mansi. [1770–80; < Russ *vogúl* < Khanty *wojal′, wojat′* Mansi]

voice (vois), *n., v.,* **voiced, voic·ing,** *adj.* —*n.* **1.** the sound or sounds uttered through the mouth of living creatures, esp. of human beings in speaking, shouting, singing, etc. **2.** the faculty or power of uttering sounds through the mouth by the controlled expulsion of air; speech: *to lose one's voice.* **3.** a range of such sounds distinctive to one person, or to a type of person or animal. **4.** the condition or effectiveness of the voice for speaking or singing: *to be in poor voice.* **5.** a sound likened to or resembling vocal utterance: *the voice of the wind.* **6.** something likened to speech as conveying impressions to the mind: *the voice of nature.* **7.** expression in spoken or written words, or by other means: *to give voice to one's disapproval by a letter.* **8.** the right to present and receive consideration of one's desires or opinions: *We had no voice in the election.* **9.** an expressed opinion or choice: *a voice for compromise.* **10.** an expressed will or desire: *the voice of the people.* **11.** expressed wish or injunction: *obedient to the voice of God.* **12.** the person or agency through which something is expressed or revealed: *the voice of doom.* **13.** a singer: *one of our best voices.* **14.** a voice part: *a score for piano and voice.* **15.** *Phonet.* the audible result of phonation and resonance. **16.** *Gram.* **a.** a set of categories for which the verb is inflected in some languages, as Latin, and which is typically used to indicate the relation of the verbal action to the subject as performer, undergoer, or beneficiary of its action. **b.** a set of syntactic devices in some languages, as English, that is similar to this set in function. **c.** any of the categories of these sets: *the English passive voice; the Greek middle voice.* **17.** the finer regulation, as of intensity and color, in tuning, esp. of a piano or organ. **18. the still, small voice,** the conscience. **19. with one voice,** in accord; unanimously: *They arose and with one voice acclaimed the new president.*
—*v.t.* **20.** to give utterance or expression to; declare; proclaim: *to voice one's discontent.* **21.** *Music.* **a.** to regulate the tone of, as the pipes of an organ. **b.** to write the voice parts for (music). **22.** to utter with the voice. **23.** *Phonet.* to pronounce with glottal vibration. **24.** to interpret from sign language into spoken language.
—*adj.* **25.** *Computers.* of or pertaining to the use of human or synthesized speech: *voice-data entry; voice output.* **26.** *Telecommunications.* of or pertaining to the transmission of speech or data over media designed for the transmission of speech: *voice-grade channel.* [1250–1300; ME (n.) < AF *voiz, voice* (OF *voiz, vois*) < L *vōcem,* acc. of *vōx;* akin to *vocāre* to call, Gk *óps* voice, *épos* word (see EPIC), Skt *vakti* (he) speaks] —**voic′er,** *n.*
—**Syn. 5.** cry, call. **6.** sound, language, speech, tongue. **11.** order, command. **12.** mouthpiece, organ. **20.** reveal, disclose, publish.

voice-ac·ti·vat·ed (vois′ak′tə vā′tid), *adj.* (of a telephone answering machine or other device) operationally responsive to a human voice. Cf. **VOX**

voice′ box′, the larynx. [1910–15]

voice′ coil′, *Elect.* a moving coil that drives the diaphragm of a sound reproduction system, as a loudspeaker, by the interaction of a changing magnetic field that is produced by a current in the coil and a fixed magnetic field that is produced by permanent magnets.

voiced (voist), *adj.* **1.** having a voice of a specified kind (usually used in combination): *shrill-voiced.* **2.** expressed vocally: *his voiced opinion.* **3.** *Phonet.* pronounced with glottal vibrations; phonated (contrasted with *voiceless*): *"b," "v," and "z" are voiced.* [1590–1600; VOICE + -ED[2], -ED[3]] —**voic·ed·ness** (voi′sid nis, voist′-nis), *n.*

voice·ful (vois′fəl), *adj.* having a voice, esp. a loud voice; sounding; sonorous. [1605–15; VOICE + -FUL] —**voice′ful·ness,** *n.*

voice·less (vois′lis), *adj.* **1.** having no voice; mute. **2.** uttering no words; silent. **3.** having an unmusical voice. **4.** unspoken; unuttered: *voiceless sympathy.* **5.** having no vote or right of choice. **6.** *Phonet.* (of a speech sound) **a.** without voice; unvoiced; surd; aphonic (contrasted with *voiced*): *"p," "f," and "s" are voiceless.* **b.** uttered without phonation. [1525–35; VOICE + -LESS] —**voice′·less·ly,** *adv.* —**voice′less·ness,** *n.*
—**Syn. 1.** See **dumb.**

voice′ mail′, an electronic system enabling the recording and storage of (usually digitized) voice messages, which can subsequently be retrieved by the intended recipient. —**voice′-mail′,** *adj.*

Voice′ of Amer′ica, the division of the United States Information Agency that broadcasts daily programs of news and entertainment throughout the world. *Abbr.:* VOA, V.O.A.

voice-o·ver (vois′ō′vər), *n. Motion Pictures, Television.* **1.** the voice of an offscreen narrator, announcer, or the like. **2.** a televised sequence, as in a commercial, using such a voice. **3.** any offscreen voice, as that of a character in a narrative. [1945–50]

voice′ part′, *Music.* the melody or succession of tones for one of the voices or instruments in a harmonic or concerted composition. [1865–70]

voice·print (vois′print′), *n.* a graphic representation of a person's voice, showing the component frequencies as analyzed by a sound spectrograph. [1960–65; VOICE + PRINT] —**voice′print′ing,** *n.*

voice′ recogni′tion, *Computers.* See **speech recognition.**

voice′-stress an′alyzer (vois′stres′), a machine purported to detect stress in a human voice and to ascertain a person's truthfulness.

voice′ vote′, a vote based on estimation of the relative strength of ayes and noes called out rather than on a counting of ballots, a roll call, or a division. [1925–30]

void (void), *adj.* **1.** *Law.* having no legal force or effect; not legally binding or enforceable. **2.** useless; ineffectual; vain. **3.** devoid; destitute (usually fol. by *of*): *a life void of meaning.* **4.** without contents; empty. **5.** without an incumbent, as an office. **6.** *Math.* (of a set) empty. **7.** (in cards) having no cards in a suit. —*n.* **8.** an empty space; emptiness: *He disappeared into the void.* **9.** something experienced as a loss or privation: *His death left a great void in her life.* **10.** a gap or opening, as in a wall. **11.** a vacancy; vacuum. **12.** *Typography.* counter[3] (def. 10). **13.** (in cards) lack of cards in a suit: *a void in clubs.* —*v.t.* **14.** to make ineffectual; invalidate; nullify: *to void a check.* **15.** to empty; discharge;

CONCISE PRONUNCIATION KEY: *act, cāpe, dâre, pärt; set, ēqual; if, īce; ox, ōver, ôrder, oil, bŏŏk, bōōt, out; up, ûrge; child; sing; shoe; thin, that;* zh as in *treasure.* ə = *a* as in *alone, e* as in *system, i* as in *easily, o* as in *gallop, u* as in *circus;* ᵊ as in *fire* (fīᵊr), *hour* (ouᵊr). l and n can serve as syllabic consonants, as in *cradle* (krād′l), and *button* (but′n). See the full key inside the front cover.

evacuate: *to void excrement.* **16.** to clear or empty (often fol. by *of*): *to void a chamber of occupants.* **17.** *Archaic.* to depart from; vacate. —*v.i.* **18.** to defecate or urinate. [1250–1300; (adj.) ME *voide* < AF, OF < VL **vocita,* fem. of **vocitus,* dissimilated var. of L *vocivus,* itself var. of *vac(i)vus* empty; see VACUUM; (v.) ME *voiden* < AF *voider,* OF < VL **vocitāre,* deriv. of **vocitus;* (n.) deriv. of the adj.] —**void′ness,** *n.*
—**Syn. 3, 4.** See **empty. 5.** vacant, unoccupied.

void·a·ble (voi′də bəl), *adj.* **1.** capable of being nullified or invalidated. **2.** *Law.* capable of being adjudged void. [1475–85; VOID + -ABLE] —**void′a·ble·ness,** *n.*

void·ance (void′ns), *n.* **1.** the act of voiding. **2.** annulment, as of a contract. **3.** vacancy, as of a benefice. [1350–1400; ME, aph. var. of AVOIDANCE]

void·ed (voi′did), *adj.* **1.** having a void. **2.** having been made void: *a voided contract.* **3.** having a section or area that has been cut out or omitted: *a voided Greek cross.* **4.** *Heraldry.* (of a charge) depicted as if the center had been removed so as to leave only an outline: *an inescutcheon voided.* [1350–1400; ME; see VOID, -ED²]

void·er (voi′dər), *n.* **1.** a person or thing that voids. **2.** *Armor.* gusset (def. 3a). [1300–50; ME; see VOID, -ER¹]

voi·là (vwä lä′; *Fr.* vwa lᴀ′), *interj.* (used to express success or satisfaction). *Voilà, my new winter outfit!* Also, **voi·la′.** [1825–35; < F, equiv. to *voi* see! (2nd pers. sing. impv. of *voir* to see) + *la* there]

voile (voil; *Fr.* vwᴀl), *n.* a lightweight, semisheer fabric of wool, silk, rayon, or cotton constructed in plain weave. [1885–90; < F; AF *veile* VEIL]

voir dire (vwär′ dēr′; *Fr.* vwᴀʀ dēʀ′), *Law.* **1.** an oath administered to a proposed witness or juror by which he or she is sworn to speak the truth in an examination to ascertain his or her competence. **2.** the examination itself. [1670–80; < AF, equiv. to OF *voir* true, truly + *dire* to say]

Voit (foit), *n.* **Carl** or **Karl von** (kärl fən), 1831–1908, German physiologist.

voi·ture (vwä to͝or′, -tyo͝or′; *Fr.* vwᴀ tyʀ′), *n., pl.* **-tures** (*Fr.* -tyʀ′). a carriage, wagon, or other wheeled vehicle. [1690–1700; < F < L *vectūra,* equiv. to *vect(us)* (ptp. of *vehere* to carry) + *-ūra* -URE]

voi·vode (voi′vōd), *n.* (in Eastern European history) a local ruler or governor, esp. the semi-independent rulers of Transylvania, Wallachia, or Moldavia before c1700. Also, **vaivode.** [1550–60; << Slavic; cf. Pol *wojewoda,* Russ *voevóda,* Serbo-Croatian *vȍj(e)voda,* OCS *vojevoda* commander, governor (translating Gk *hēgemṓn* and *stratēgós*), equiv. to *voj-* base of *voinŭ* warrior + *-e-* var. (after *j*) of *-o-* -O- + *-voda,* n. deriv. of *voditi* to lead; *vaivode* < Hungarian *vajvoda* (now *vajda*) < Slavic]

voix cé·leste (vwä′ sā lest′), an organ stop having for each note two pipes tuned to slightly different pitches and producing a wavering, gentle tone. [< F: heavenly voice]

Voj·vo·di·na (voi′və din′ə, -dē′nə), *n.* an autonomous province within Serbia, in N Yugoslavia. 2,050,000; 8303 sq. mi. (21,506 sq. km). *Cap.:* Novi Sad.

vol., 1. volcano. **2.** volume. **3.** volunteer.

VO language, *Ling.* a type of language that has direct objects following the verb and that tends to have typological traits such as prepositions, prefixes, noun modifiers following nouns, adverbs following verbs, and auxiliary verbs preceding the main verb. Cf. **OV language.** [(*v*)*erb-o*(*bject*)]

Vo·lans (vō′lanz), *n., gen.* **Vo·lan·tis** (vō lan′tis). *Astron.* the Flying Fish, a southern constellation between Carina and Hydrus. [< L, prp. of *volāre* to fly]

vo·lant (vō′lənt), *adj.* **1.** engaged in or having the power of flight. **2.** moving lightly; nimble. —*n.* **3.** Also called **vo′lant piece′.** *Armor.* a reinforcing piece for the brow of a helmet. [1500–10; < F, prp. of *voler* to fly < L *volāre;* see -ANT]

vo·lan·te (vō län′tā; *It.* vô län′te), *adv., adj. Music.* moving lightly and quickly. [1785–95; < It: VOLANT]

Vo·la·pük (vō′lə pʏk′), *n.* one of the earliest of the artificially constructed international auxiliary languages, invented about 1879. Also, **Vo·la·puk** (vō′lə po͝ok′, vō′lə-). [1880–85; *vol,* repr. WORLD + *-a-* connecting vowel + *pük,* repr. SPEAK] —**Vo′la·puk′ist,** *n.*

vo·lar¹ (vō′lər), *adj.* of or pertaining to the palm of the hand or the sole of the foot. [1805–15; < L *vol(a)* palm of hand, sole of foot + -AR¹]

vo·lar² (vō′lər), *adj.* pertaining to or used for flight. [1830–40; < L *vol(āre)* to fly + -AR¹]

vo·la·ry (vō′lə rē, vol′ə-), *n., pl.* **-ries.** *Rare.* **1.** a large cage for confining birds; aviary. **2.** the birds in such a cage. **3.** a flight or flock of birds. [1620–30; < L *vol(āre)* to fly + -ARY]

vol·a·tile (vol′ə tl, -til *or, esp. Brit.,* -tīl′), *adj.* **1.** evaporating rapidly; passing off readily in the form of vapor: *Acetone is a volatile solvent.* **2.** tending or threatening to break out into open violence; explosive: *a volatile political situation.* **3.** changeable; mercurial; flighty: *a volatile disposition.* **4.** (of prices, values, etc.) tending to fluctuate sharply and regularly: *volatile market conditions.* **5.** fleeting; transient: *volatile beauty.* **6.** *Computers.* of or pertaining to storage that does not retain data when electrical power is turned off or fails. **7.** able to fly or flying. —*n.* **8.** a volatile substance, as a gas or solvent. [1250–1300; ME < L *volātilis,* equiv. to *volāt(us)* (ptp. of *volāre* to fly; see -ATE¹) + *-ilis* -ILE] —**vol·a·til·i·ty** (vol′ə til′i tē), **vol′a·tile·ness,** *n.*
—**Syn. 2.** eruptive, unstable, unsettled.

vol′atile oil′, a distilled oil, esp. one obtained from plant tissue, as distinguished from glyceride oils by their volatility and failure to saponify. [1790–1800]

CONCISE ETYMOLOGY KEY: <, descended or borrowed from; >, whence; b., blend of, blended; c., cognate with; cf., compare; deriv., derivative; equiv., equivalent; imit., imitative; obl., oblique; r., replacing; s., stem; sp., spelling, spelled; resp., respelling, respelled; trans., translation; ?, origin unknown; *, unattested; ‡, probably earlier than. See the full key inside the front cover.

MAJOR VOLCANOES OF THE WORLD

Volcano	Location	Height ft.	Height m	Last Major Eruption
Guallatiri	Northern Chile	19,882	6060	1959
Lascar	Northern Chile	19,652	5990	1951
Cotopaxi	Northern Central Ecuador	19,498	5943	Active
El Misti	Southern Peru	19,200	5880	Active
Demavend	Northern Iran	18,606	5670	Active
Tupungatito	Central Chile	18,504	5640	1959
Nevado del Ruiz	West Central Colombia	17,720	5401	1985
Sangay	Central Ecuador	17,159	5230	1946
Cotacachi	Northern Ecuador	16,197	4937	1955
Klyuchevskaya	Russian Federation, Kamchatka Peninsula	15,912	4850	1946
Puracé	Southern Colombia	15,420	4700	1950
Pasto	Southwestern Colombia	13,990	4265	Active
Mauna Loa	United States, Central Hawaii	13,680	4170	1984
Colima	Western Mexico	12,631	3850	Active
Fuji	Japan, Central Honshu	12,395	3778	1707
Nyiragongo	Zaire, Eastern Edge	11,385	3470	1948
Koryaksky	Russian Federation, Kamchatka Peninsula	11,339	3456	1957
Spurr	United States, South Central Alaska	11,069	3374	1992
Etna	Italy, Eastern Sicily	10,758	3280	1985
Torbert	United States, South Central Alaska	10,600	3231	1953
Lassen	United States, Northeastern California	10,465	3190	1921
Dempo	Indonesia, Southwestern Sumatra	10,364	3159	Active
Shishaldin	United States, Southwestern Alaska	9500	2896	Active
Poas	Central Costa Rica	8930	2722	Active
Pavlof	United States, Southwestern Alaska	8900	2712	1982
St. Helens	United States, Southwestern Washington	8364	2549	1990
Hualalai	United States, Western Hawaii	8269	2520	1800-01
Paricutín	West Central Mexico	8200	2500	1943-52
Katmai	United States, Southern Alaska	7500	2286	1962
Martin	United States, Alaska Peninsula	6100	1859	1960
Trident	United States, Alaska Peninsula	6010	1832	1960
Great Sitkin	United States, Aleutians	5740	1750	Active
Cleveland	United States, Aleutians	5675	1730	1944
Pelée	Martinique	4583	1397	1902
Kilauea	United States, South Central Hawaii	4040	1231	Active
Vesuvius	Italy, Bay of Naples	3900	1189	1944
El Chichón	Southern Mexico	3478	1060	1982
Capelinhos	Faial Island, Azores	3351	1021	Active
Stromboli	Italy, Lipari Islands	3040	927	1956
Asuncion	Marianas	2923	891	Active
Thera	Greece, Cyclades, Aegean Sea	1858	566	1866
Barren Island	Andaman Islands	1160	354	early 19th c.
White Island	New Zealand, Northern North Island	1075	328	Active
Surtsey	North Atlantic	568	173	1967

vol′atil′ity in′dex, *Stock Exchange.* beta (def. 6).

vol·a·til·ize (vol′ə tl īz′), *v.,* **-ized, -iz·ing.** —*v.i.* **1.** to become volatile; pass off as vapor. —*v.t.* **2.** to make volatile; cause to pass off as vapor. Also, *esp. Brit.,* **vol′a·til·ise′.** [1650–60; VOLATILE + -IZE] —**vol′a·til·iz′a·ble,** *adj.* —**vol′a·til·i·za′tion,** *n.* —**vol′a·til·iz′er,** *n.*

vol-au-vent (vô lō vän′), *n. Cookery.* a large shell of light, flaky pastry for filling with vegetable, fish, or meat mixtures, usually with a sauce. [1820–30; < F: lit., flight on the wind]

vol·can·ic (vol kan′ik), *adj.* **1.** of or pertaining to a volcano: *a volcanic eruption.* **2.** discharged from or produced by volcanoes: *volcanic mud.* **3.** characterized by the presence of volcanoes: *a volcanic area.* **4.** suggestive of or resembling a volcano; potentially explosive; volatile: *a volcanic temper.* [1765–75; VOLCAN(O) + -IC; cf. F *volcanique*] —**vol·can′i·cal·ly,** *adv.* —**vol·can·ic·i·ty** (vol′kə nis′i tē), *n.*

volcan′ic ash′, *Geol.* ash (def. 2). [1790–1800]

volcan′ic bomb′, *Geol.* bomb (def. 3). [1790–1800]

volcan′ic cone′, *Geol.* a conical hill produced by volcanic eruption of ash, cinders, or lava. Cf. **cinder cone.**

volcan′ic glass′, a natural glass produced when molten lava cools very rapidly; obsidian. [1830–40]

vol·can·i·clas·tic (vol kan′i klas′tik), *adj. Geol.* pyroclastic. Also, **vol·can·o·clas·tic** (vol kan′ə klas′tik). [1960–65; b. VOLCANIC and CLASTIC]

volcan′ic neck′, *Geol.* neck (def. 14).

volcan′ic tuff′, tuff². [1805–15]

vol·can·ism (vol′kə niz′əm), *n. Geol.* the phenomena connected with volcanoes and volcanic activity. Also, **vulcanism.** [1865–70; VOLCAN(O) + -ISM]

vol·ca·no (vol kā′nō), *n., pl.* **-noes, -nos. 1.** a vent in the earth's crust through which lava, steam, ashes, etc., are expelled, either continuously or at irregular intervals. **2.** a mountain or hill, usually having a cuplike crater at the summit, formed around such a vent from the ash and lava expelled through it. See table above. [1605–15; < It < L *Volcānus,* var. of *Vulcānus* VULCAN]

Volca′no Is′lands, three islands in the W Pacific, belonging to Japan: under U.S. administration 1945–68. Cf. **Iwo Jima.**

vol·can·ol·o·gy (vol′kə nol′ə jē), *n.* the scientific study of volcanoes and volcanic phenomena. Also, **vulcanology.** [1885–90; VOLCANO + -LOGY] —**vol·can·o·log·i·cal** (vol′kə nl oj′i kəl), **vol′can·o·log′ic,** *adj.* —**vol′can·ol′o·gist,** *n.*

vole¹ (vōl), *n.* any of several small mouselike or ratlike rodents of the genus *Microtus* and related genera, having short limbs and a short tail. [1795–1805; short for *volemouse* field mouse, perh. < Norw **vollmus,* equiv. to *voll* field (cf. WOLD¹) + *mus* MOUSE]

vole¹, *Microtus pennsylvanicus,* head and body 5 in. (13 cm); tail 2 in. (5 cm)

vole² (vōl), *n.* **1.** *Cards.* the winning by one player of all the tricks of a deal. **2. go the vole, a.** to venture everything on the chance of great rewards. **b.** to try one after another, as a variety of occupations: *He went the vole and finally settled on watchmaking.* [1670–80; < F, deriv. of *voler* to fly < L *volāre*]

Vol·ga (vol′gə, vōl′-; *Russ.* vôl′gə), *n.* a river flowing from the Valdai Hills in the W Russian Federation E and then S to the Caspian Sea: the longest river in Europe. 2325 mi. (3745 km).

Vol′ga Ta′tar. See under **Tatar** (def. 2). Also, **Vol′ga Tar′tar.**

Vol·go·grad (vol′gə grad′, vōl′-; *Russ.* vəl gu grät′), *n.* a city in the SW Russian Federation in Europe, on the Volga River: battles in World War II, 1942–1943. 999,000. Formerly, **Stalingrad, Tsaritsyn.**

vol·i·tant (vol′i tnt, -tənt), *adj.* **1.** engaged in or having the power of flight. **2.** active; moving. [1840–50; < L *volitant-* (s. of *volitāns*), prp. of *volitāre* to flutter, freq. of *volāre* to fly; see -ANT]

vol·i·ta·tion (vol′i tā′shən), *n.* the act or power of flying. [1640–50; < ML *volitātiōn-* (s. of *volitātiō*), equiv. to L *volitā(us)* (ptp. of *volitāre* to flutter; see VOLITANT, -ATE¹) + *-iōn-* -ION] —**vol′i·ta′tion·al,** *adj.*

vo·li·tion (vō lish′ən, və-), *n.* **1.** the act of willing, choosing, or resolving; exercise of willing: *She left of her own volition.* **2.** a choice or decision made by the will. **3.** the power of willing; will. [1605–15; < ML *volitiōn-* (s. of *volitiō*), equiv. to *vol-* (var. s. of *velle* to want, wish; see WILL¹) + *-itiōn-* -ITION] —**vo·li′tion·al, vo·li·tion·ar·y** (vō lish′ə ner′ē), *adj.* —**vo·li′tion·al·ly,** *adv.*
—**Syn. 1.** discretion, choice. See **will².**

vol·i·tive (vol′i tiv), *adj.* **1.** of, pertaining to, or characterized by volition. **2.** *Gram.* expressing a wish or permission: *a volitive construction.* [1650–60; VOLIT(ION) + -IVE]

Volks·deut·scher (fôlks′doi′chəʀ), *n., pl.* **-deut·sche** (-doi′chə). *German.* a member of the German people, esp. one of a community having its home outside of Germany, usually in central or eastern Europe.

volks·lied (fôlks′lēt′), *n., pl.* **-lied·er** (-lē′dər). a folk song. [< G]

vol·ley (vol′ē), *n., pl.* **-leys,** *v.,* **-leyed, -ley·ing.** —*n.* **1.** the simultaneous discharge of a number of missiles or firearms. **2.** the missiles so discharged. **3.** a burst or outpouring of many things at once or in quick succession: *a volley of protests.* **4.** *Tennis.* **a.** the flight of the ball before it hits the ground. **b.** the return of the ball before it hits the ground. **5.** *Soccer.* a kick of the ball before it bounces on the ground. **6.** *Cricket.* a ball so bowled that it hits the wicket before it touches the ground. **7.** *Mining.* the explosion of several charges at one time. —*v.t.* **8.** to discharge in or as in a volley. **9.** *Tennis.* to return (the ball) before it hits the ground. **10.** *Soccer.* to kick (the ball) before it bounces on the ground. **11.** *Cricket.* to bowl (a ball) in such a manner that it is pitched near the top of the wicket. —*v.i.* **12.** to fly or be discharged together, as missiles. **13.** to move or proceed with great rapidity, as in a volley. **14.** to fire a volley; sound together, as firearms. **15.** *Tennis, Soccer.* to return the ball before it touches the ground. [1565–75; < MF *volee* flight, n. use of fem. ptp. of *voler* to fly < L *volāre*] —**vol′ley·er,** *n.*

vol·ley·ball (vol′ē bôl′), *n.* **1.** a game for two teams in which the object is to keep a large ball in motion, from side to side over a high net, by striking it with the hands before it touches the ground. **2.** the ball used in this game. [1895–1900, *Amer.*; VOLLEY + BALL¹]

Vo·log·da (vô′ləg də), *n.* a city in the W Russian Federation in Europe, NNE of Moscow. 278,000.

Vo·los (vô′lôs), *n.* a seaport in E Thessaly, in E Greece: ancient ruins. 51,100.

vo·lost (vō′ləst), *n.* **1.** (formerly) a small administrative peasant division in Russia. **2.** a rural soviet. [< Russ *vólost′*; ORuss *volostĭ* region, state, authority, c. OCS *vlastĭ* sovereignty, power, authority, deriv. of Slavic **vald-* rule, c. Lith *valdýti,* Gothic *waldan,* OE *wealdan* to rule; cf. WIELD]

vol·plane (vol′plān′), *v.,* **-planed, -plan·ing,** *n.* —*v.i.* **1.** to glide toward the earth in an airplane, with no motor power or with the power shut off. —*n.* **2.** a glide in an airplane. [1905–10; < F *vol plané* glided flight, equiv. to *vol* flight (n. deriv. of *voler* < L *volāre* to fly) + *plané,* ptp. of *planer* to glide (see PLANE¹)] —**vol′plan′ist,** *n.*

vols., volumes.

Vol·sci (vol′sī, -sē, -shē), *n.pl.* an ancient people of Latium who were conquered by the Romans in the last part of the 4th century B.C.

Vol·scian (vol′shən), *adj.* **1.** of or pertaining to the Volsci or to their language. —*n.* **2.** one of the Volsci. [1505–15; < L *Volsc(us)* of the VOLSCI + -IAN]

Vol·stead (vol′sted, vōl′-), *n.* **Andrew Joseph,** 1860–1946, U.S. legislator.

Vol′stead Act′, an act of Congress, introduced in 1919 by Andrew J. Volstead to implement the Eighteenth Amendment of the Constitution, which forbade the sale of alcoholic beverages.

Vol·stead·ism (vol′sted iz′əm, vōl′-), *n.* **1.** the policy of prohibiting the sale of alcoholic beverages. **2.** the enforcement of this policy. [1915–20, *Amer.*; see VOLSTEAD ACT, -ISM] —**Vol·stead′i·an,** *adj.*

Vol·sung (vol′sŏŏng), *n.* (in the *Volsunga Saga*) **1.** a grandson of Odin and the father of Sigmund and Signy. **2.** any of his family.

Vol·sun·ga Sa·ga (vol′sŏŏng gə sä′gə), an Icelandic saga of the late 13th century, concerning the family of the Volsungs, the theft of the cursed treasure of Andvari, the adventures of Sigurd, his wooing of Brynhild, his enchantment and marriage to Gudrun, and his eventual murder. Also, ***Vol′sun·ga·sa′ga.*** Cf. ***Nibelungenlied.***

volt¹ (vōlt), *n. Elect.* the SI unit of potential difference and electromotive force, formally defined to be the difference of electric potential between two points of a conductor carrying a constant current of one ampere, when the power dissipated between these points is equal to one watt. *Abbr.:* V [1870–75; named after A. VOLTA]

volt² (vōlt), *n.* **1.** *Manège.* **a.** a circular or turning movement of a horse. **b.** a gait in which a horse going sideways turns around a center, with the head turned outward. **2.** *Fencing.* a sudden movement or leap to avoid a thrust. [1650–60; < F *volte* < It *volta,* n. deriv. of *voltare* to turn < VL **volvitare,* freq. of L *volvere* to turn; see VAULT²]

vol·ta (vōl′tə, vol′-; *It.* vôl′tä), *n., pl.* **-te** (-tā; *It.* -te). *Music.* turn; time (used in phrases): *una volta* ("once"); *prima volta* ("first time"). [1635–45; < It: a turn; see VOLT²]

Vol·ta (vōl′tə *or, It.* vôl′tä *for 1;* vol′tə, vōl′- *for 2*), *n.* **1. Count A·les·san·dro** (ä′les sän′drô), 1745–1827, Italian physicist. **2.** a river in W Africa, in Ghana, formed by the confluence of the Black Volta and the White Volta and flowing S into the Bight of Benin. ab. 250 mi. (400 km) long; with branches ab. 1240 mi. (1995 km) long.

Vol′ta effect′ (vōl′tə), *Elect.* See **contact potential.** [named after A. VOLTA]

volt·age (vōl′tij), *n. Elect.* electromotive force or potential difference expressed in volts. [1885–90; VOLT¹ + -AGE]

volt′age divid′er, *Elect.* a resistor or series of resistors connected to a voltage source and used to provide voltages that are fractions of that of the source. Also called **potential divider, potentiometer.** [1920–25]

volt′age reg′ulator, *Elect.* a device that controls or maintains the voltage of an electrical circuit. *Abbr.:* VR [1910–15]

vol·ta·ic (vol tā′ik, vōl-), *adj.* **1.** *Elect.* noting or pertaining to electricity or electric currents, esp. when produced by chemical action, as in a cell; galvanic. **2.** (*cap.*) of or pertaining to Alessandro Volta. [1805–15; after A. VOLTA; see -IC]

Vol·ta·ic (vol tā′ik), *n.* Gur.

volta′ic bat′tery, *Elect.* battery (def. 1a). [1805–15]

volta′ic cell′, *Elect.* cell (def. 7a). [1850–55]

volta′ic cou′ple, *Elect.* a pair of substances, as two different metals, that when placed in a proper solution produces an electromotive force by chemical action. Also called **galvanic couple.**

volta′ic electric′ity, electric current; moving electric charges. [1810–20]

volta′ic pile′, *Elect.* an early battery cell, consisting of several metal disks, each made of one of two dissimilar metals, arranged in an alternating series, and separated by pads moistened with an electrolyte. Also called **galvanic pile, pile, Vol′ta's pile′.** [1805–15]

Vol·taire (vōl târ′, vol-; *Fr.* vôl ter′), *n.* (*François Marie Arouet*), 1694–1778, French philosopher, historian, satirist, dramatist, and essayist. —**Vol·tair′e·an, Vol·tair′i·an,** *adj., n.*

vol·ta·ism (vōl′tə iz′əm, vol′-), *n.* the branch of electrical science that deals with the production of electricity or electric currents by chemical action. [1805–15; after A. VOLTA; see -ISM]

vol·tam·e·ter (vol tam′i tər, vōl-), *n.* a device for measuring the quantity of electricity passing through a conductor by the amount of electrolytic decomposition it produces, or for measuring the strength of a current by the amount of such decomposition in a given time. Also called **coulometer.** [1830–40; *volta* (see VOLT¹) + -METER] —**vol·ta·met·ric** (vol′tə me′trik, vōl′-), *adj.*

volt·am·me·ter (vōlt′am′mē′tər), *n.* an instrument for measuring voltage or amperage. [1885–90; VOLT-AM(PERE) + -METER]

volt-am·pere (vōlt′am′pēr, -am pēr′), *n. Elect.* an electric measurement unit, equal to the product of one volt and one ampere, equivalent to one watt for direct current systems and a unit of apparent power for alternating current systems. *Abbr.:* VA [1895–1900]

Vol·ta Re·don·da (vôl′tä ri dôn′dä), a city in SE Brazil, NW of Rio de Janeiro. 120,645.

volte-face (volt fäs′, vōlt-; *Fr.* vôltᵊ fas′), *n., pl.* **volte-face.** a turnabout, esp. a reversal of opinion or policy. [1810–20; < F < It *voltafaccia,* equiv. to *volta* turn (see VOLT²) + *faccia* FACE]

vol·ti (vôl′tē), *v. imperative. Music.* turn; turn over: a direction to turn the page. [< It]

volt·me·ter (vōlt′mē′tər), *n. Elect.* a calibrated instrument for measuring the potential difference between two points. [1880–85; VOLT¹ + -METER]

Vol·tur·no (vôl tŏŏr′nô), *n.* a river in S central Italy, flowing from the Apennines into the Tyrrhenian Sea. 110 mi. (175 km) long.

Vol·tur·nus (vol tûr′nəs, vol-), *n.* the ancient Roman personification of the east or southeast wind. Cf. **Eurus.**

vol·u·ble (vol′yə bəl), *adj.* characterized by a ready and continuous flow of words; fluent; glib; talkative: *a voluble spokesman for the cause.* [1565–75; < L *volūbilis* which turns easily, flowing, equiv. to *volū-,* base of *volvere* to turn + *-bilis* -BLE] —**vol′u·bil′i·ty, vol′u·ble·ness,** *n.* —**vol′u·bly,** *adv.*
—**Syn.** articulate, garrulous, loquacious. See **fluent.**
—**Ant.** taciturn.

vol·ume (vol′yo͞om, -yəm), *n.* **1.** a collection of written or printed sheets bound together and constituting a book. **2.** one book of a related set or series. **3.** a set of issues of a periodical, often covering one year. **4.** *Hist.* a roll of papyrus, parchment, or the like, or of manuscript. **5.** the amount of space, measured in cubic units, that an object or substance occupies. **6.** a mass or quantity, esp. a large quantity, of something: *a volume of mail.* **7.** amount; total: *the volume of sales.* **8.** the degree of sound intensity or audibility; loudness: *to turn up the volume on a radio.* **9.** fullness or quantity of tone. **10. speak volumes, a.** to be very evident or significant: *Her testimony spoke volumes.* **b.** to be expressive or meaningful: *Your eyes speak volumes.* [1350–1400; ME *volum(e)* < MF < L *volūmen* roll (of sheets), equiv. to *volū-,* base of *volvere* to roll + *-men* n. suffix]
—**Syn. 5.** See **size**¹.

vol·umed (vol′yo͞omd, -yəmd), *adj.* **1.** consisting of a volume or volumes (usually used in combination): *a many-volumed work.* **2.** in volumes of rolling or rounded masses, as smoke. [1590–1600; VOLUME + -ED³]

vo·lu·me·ter (və lo͞o′mi tər, vol′yə mē′tər), *n.* any of various instruments or devices for measuring volume, as of gases, liquids, or solids. [1820–30; VOLU(ME) + -METER]

vol·u·met·ric (vol′yə me′trik), *adj.* of or pertaining to measurement by volume. Also, **vol′u·met′ri·cal.** [1860–65; VOLU(ME) + -METRIC²] —**vol′u·met′ri·cal·ly,** *adv.* —**vo·lu·me·try** (və lo͞o′mi trē), *n.*

volumet′ric anal′ysis, *Chem.* **1.** determination of the concentration, by volume, of a substance in a solution, as by titration. **2.** determination of the volume of gases or changes in their volume during combination. Cf. **gravimetric analysis.** [1860–65]

vol′ume u′nit, a logarithmic unit used to measure the magnitude of a sound wave. [1935–40]

vol′ume veloc′ity, *Physics.* the movement caused by a sound wave of a unit volume of a sound-transmitting medium through a unit area per unit of time.

vo·lu·mi·nous (və lo͞o′mə nəs), *adj.* **1.** forming, filling, or writing a large volume or many volumes: *a voluminous edition.* **2.** sufficient to fill a volume or volumes: *a voluminous correspondence.* **3.** of great volume, size, or extent: *voluminous flow of lava.* **4.** of ample size, extent, or fullness: *voluminous petticoats.* **5.** having many coils, convolutions, or windings. [1605–15; < LL *volūminōsus* full of folds, equiv. to L *volūmin-* (s. of *volūmen*) VOLUME + *-ōsus* -OUS] —**vo·lu′mi·nous·ly,** *adv.* —**vo·lu′mi·nous·ness, vo·lu·mi·nos·i·ty** (və lo͞o′mə nos′i tē), *n.*
—**Syn. 3.** extensive, copious, ample.

Vo·lund (vō′lo͞ond), *n. Scand. Myth.* Wayland.

vol·un·ta·rism (vol′ən tə riz′əm), *n.* **1.** *Philos.* any theory that regards will as the fundamental agency or principle, in metaphysics, epistemology, or psychology. **2.** the principle or practice of supporting churches, schools, hospitals, etc., by voluntary contributions or aid instead of relying on government assistance. **3.** any policy or practice based on voluntary action. [1830–40; VOLUNTAR(Y) + -ISM] —**vol′un·ta·rist,** *n., adj.* —**vol′un·ta·ris′tic,** *adj.*

vol·un·tar·y (vol′ən ter′ē), *adj., n., pl.* **-tar·ies.** —*adj.* **1.** done, made, brought about, undertaken, etc., of one's own accord or by free choice: *a voluntary contribution.* **2.** of, pertaining to, or acting in accord with the will: *voluntary cooperation.* **3.** of, pertaining to, or depending on voluntary action: *voluntary hospitals.* **4.** *Law.* **a.** acting or done without compulsion or obligation. **b.** done by intention, and not by accident: *voluntary manslaughter.* **c.** made without valuable consideration: *a voluntary settlement.* **5.** *Physiol.* subject to or controlled by the will. **6.** having the power of willing or choosing: *a voluntary agent.* **7.** proceeding from a natural impulse; spontaneous: *voluntary laughter.* —*n.* **8.** something done voluntarily. **9.** a piece of music, frequently spontaneous and improvised, performed as a prelude to a larger work, esp. a piece of organ music performed before, during, or after an office of the church. [1350–1400; ME < L *voluntārius,* equiv. to *volunt(ās)* willingness, inclination (ult. repr. a formation with *-tās* -TY² on the prp. of *velle* to want, wish; see WILL¹, -ENT) + *-ārius* -ARY] —**vol·un·tar·i·ly** (vol′ən târ′ə lē, vol′ən ter′-), *adv.* —**vol′un·tar′i·ness,** *n.*
—**Syn. 1.** considered, purposeful, planned, intended, designed. See **deliberate. 7.** free, unforced, natural, unconstrained. VOLUNTARY, SPONTANEOUS agree in applying to something that is a natural outgrowth or natural expression arising from circumstances and conditions. VOLUNTARY implies having given previous consideration, or having exercised judgment: *a voluntary confession; a voluntary movement; The offer was a voluntary one.* Something that is SPONTANEOUS arises as if by itself from the nature of the circumstances or condition: *spontaneous applause, combustion, expression of admiration.*

vol′untary abor′tion, abortion (def. 1).

vol′untary associa′tion, a group of individuals joined together on the basis of mutual interest or common objectives, esp. a business group that is not organized or constituted as a legal entity.

vol·un·tar·y·ism (vol′ən ter′ē iz′əm), *n.* voluntarism (def. 2). [1825–35; VOLUNTARY + -ISM] —**vol′un·tar′y·ist,** *n.*

vol′untary mus′cle, *Anat.* muscle whose action is normally controlled by an individual's will; mainly skeletal muscle, composed of parallel bundles of striated, multinucleate fibers. [1780–90]

vol·un·teer (vol′ən tēr′), *n.* **1.** a person who voluntarily offers himself or herself for a service or undertaking. **2.** a person who performs a service willingly and without pay. **3.** *Mil.* a person who enters the service voluntarily rather than through conscription or draft, esp. for special or temporary service rather than as a member of the regular or permanent army. **4.** *Law.* **a.** a person whose actions are not founded on any legal obligation so to act. **b.** a person who intrudes into a matter that does not concern him or her, as a person who pays the debt of another where he or she is neither legally nor morally bound to do so and has no interest to protect in making the payment. **5.** *Agric.* a volunteer plant. **6.** (*cap.*) a native or inhabitant of Tennessee (used as a nickname). —*adj.* **7.** of, pertaining to, or being a volunteer or volunteers: *a volunteer fireman.* **8.** *Agric.* growing without being seeded, planted, or cultivated by a person; springing up spontaneously. —*v.i.* **9.** to offer oneself for some service or undertaking. **10.** to enter service or enlist as a volunteer. —*v.t.* **11.** to offer (oneself or one's services) for some undertaking or purpose. **12.** to give, bestow, or perform voluntarily: *to volunteer a song.* **13.** to say, tell, or communicate voluntarily: *to volunteer an explanation.* [1590–1600; < F *volontaire* < L *voluntārius* VOLUNTARY, with -EER for F *-aire*]

vol′unteer′ ar′my, a military force composed entirely of enlistees.

vol·un·teer·ism (vol′ən tēr′iz əm), *n.* **1.** voluntarism (def. 2). **2.** the policy or practice of volunteering one's time or talents for charitable, educational, or other worthwhile activities, esp. in one's community. [1835–45; VOLUNTEER + -ISM]

Volunteers′ in Serv′ice to Amer′ica. See **VISTA.**

Vol′unteers′ of Amer′ica, a religious reform and relief organization, similar to the Salvation Army, founded in New York City in 1896 by Ballington Booth, son of William Booth, the founder of the Salvation Army. *Abbr.:* VOA

Vol′unteer′ State′, Tennessee (used as a nickname).

vo·lup·tu·ar·y (və lup′cho͞o er′ē), *n., pl.* **-ar·ies,** *adj.* —*n.* **1.** a person whose life is devoted to the pursuit and enjoyment of luxury and sensual pleasure. —*adj.* **2.** of, pertaining to, or characterized by preoccupation with luxury and sensual pleasure: *voluptuary tastes.* [1595–1605; < LL *voluptuārius,* L *voluptārius* pertaining to (sensual) pleasure, equiv. to *volupt(ās)* pleasure + *-ārius* -ARY; for *-u-* see VOLUPTUOUS]

vo·lup·tu·ous (və lup′cho͞o əs), *adj.* **1.** full of, characterized by, or ministering to indulgence in luxury, pleasure, and sensuous enjoyment: *a voluptuous life.* **2.** derived from gratification of the senses: *voluptuous pleasure.* **3.** directed toward or concerned with sensuous enjoyment or sensual pleasure: *voluptuous desires.* **4.** sensuously pleasing or delightful: *voluptuous beauty.* [1325–75; ME < L *voluptuōsus,* equiv. to *volupt(ās)* pleasure + *-ōsus* -OUS; *-u-* prob. by assoc. with *sumptuōsus* SUMPTUOUS] —**vo·lup′tu·ous·ly,** *adv.* —**vo-**

CONCISE PRONUNCIATION KEY: *act, cāpe, dâre, pärt; set, ēqual; if, ice; ox, ōver, ôrder, oil, bo͝ok, bo͞ot, out; up, ûrge; child; sing; shoe; thin, that;* zh as in *treasure.* ə = *a* as in *alone, e* as in *system, i* as in *easily, o* as in *gallop, u* as in *circus;* ᵊ as in *fire* (fīᵊr), *hour* (ouᵊr). l and n can serve as syllabic consonants, as in *cradle* (krād′l), and *button* (but′n). See the full key inside the front cover.

lup′tu•ous•ness, vo•lup•tu•os•i•ty (və lup′cho͞o os′i tē), *n.*
—**Syn. 1.** See **sensual.**

vo•lute (və lo͞ot′), *n.* **1.** a spiral or twisted formation or object. **2.** *Archit.* a spiral ornament, found esp. in the capitals of the Ionic, Corinthian, and Composite orders. **3.** *Carpentry.* a horizontal scrolled termination to the handrail of a stair. **4.** *Zool.* **a.** a turn or whorl of a spiral shell. **b.** any of various tropical marine gastropods of the family Volutidae, many species of which have shells prized for their coloration. **5.** the spiral casing surrounding the impeller of a volute pump. —*adj.* **6.** having a volute or rolled-up form. **7.** *Mach.* **a.** spirally shaped or having a part so shaped. **b.** moving in a circular way, esp. if combined with a lateral motion. [1690–1700; (< F) < L *volūta,* fem. of *volūtus,* ptp. of *volvere* to turn. See REVOLVE] —**vo•lut′ed,** *adj.* —**vo•lu′tion,** *n.*

V, **volute** (def. 2) (on an Ionic capital)

volute′ spring′, a coil spring, conical in shape, extending in the direction of the axis of the coil. See illus. under **spring.** [1860–65]

vol•u•tin (vol′yə tin), *n. Cell Biol.* basophilic nucleoprotein granules in the cytoplasm or the vacuoles of certain microorganisms. [< G *Volutin* (1903), equiv. to (*Spirillum*) *volut(ans)* a species of bacteria + *-in* -IN[2]]

vol•va (vol′və), *n. Mycol.* the membranous envelope that encloses the base of various mushrooms formed when the velum ruptures. See diag. under **mushroom.** [1745–55; < L: covering, akin to *volvere* to roll, wrap] —**vol•vate** (vol′vit, -vāt), *adj.*

vol•velle (vol′vel), *n. Astron.* a medieval instrument consisting of a series of concentric rotating disks, used to compute the phases of the moon and its position in relation to that of the sun. [1400–50; late ME < ML *volvella,* equiv. to L *volv(ere)* to turn + *-ella* -ELLE]

vol•vent (vol′vənt), *n. Zool.* a small, pear-shaped nematocyst discharging a thread that entangles its prey. [< L *volvent-* (s. of *volvēns*), prp. of *volvere* to turn, twist; see -ENT]

vol•vox (vol′voks), *n.* any colonial, freshwater green algae of the genus *Volvox,* forming a hollow, greenish sphere of flagellated cells. [1790–1800; < NL, equiv. to L *volv(ere)* to turn, roll + *-ōx* (as in *ferōx*)]

vol•vu•lus (vol′vyə ləs), *n., pl.* **-lus•es.** *Pathol.* a torsion, or twisting, of the intestine, causing intestinal obstruction. [1670–80; < NL, equiv. to L *volv(ere)* to turn, twist + *-ulus* -ULE]

Volzh•sky (vôlsh′skē; *Russ.* vôlsh′skyə), *n.* a city in the SW Russian Federation in Europe, near Volgograd on the Volga River. 257,000. Also, **Volzh′skiy.**

vo•mer (vō′mər), *n. Anat.* a bone of the skull in most vertebrates, in humans forming a large part of the septum between the right and left cavities of the nose. [1695–1705; < L *vōmer* plowshare] —**vo•mer•ine** (vō′mə rīn′, -mər in, vom′ə rīn′, -ər in), *adj.*

vom•i•ca (vom′i kə), *n., pl.* **-i•cae** (-ə sē′). *Pathol.* **1.** a cavity, usually in the lungs, containing pus. **2.** the pus content of such a cavity. [1565–75; < L: a boil, ulcer, equiv. to *vom(ere)* to discharge (see VOMIT) + *-ica,* fem. of *-icus* -IC]

vom•it (vom′it), *v.i.* **1.** to eject the contents of the stomach through the mouth; regurgitate; throw up. **2.** to belch or spew with force or violence. —*v.t.* **3.** to eject from the stomach through the mouth; spew. **4.** to cast out or eject as if in vomiting; send out forcefully or violently: *The volcano vomited flames and molten rock.* **5.** to cause (a person) to vomit. —*n.* **6.** the act of vomiting. **7.** the matter ejected in vomiting. [1375–1425; late ME *vomiten* < L *vomitāre,* freq. of *vomere* to discharge, vomit; akin to Gk *emeîn* (see EMETIC)] —**vom′it•er,** *n.* —**vom′i•tive,** *adj.* —**vom′i•tous•ly,** *adv.*

vom•i•to (vom′i tō′, vō′mi-), *n. Pathol.* the black vomit of yellow fever. Also called **vom•i•to ne•gro** (vom′i tō′ nē′grō, nā′-, vō′mi-). [1825–35; < Sp *vómito* < L *vomitus* (see VOMITUS)]

vom•i•to•ri•um (vom′i tôr′ē əm, -tōr′-), *n., pl.* **-to•ri•a** (-tôr′ē ə, -tōr′-). vomitory (def. 5). [1745–55; < LL *vomitōrium*]

vom•i•to•ry (vom′i tôr′ē, -tōr′ē), *adj., n., pl.* **-ries.** —*adj.* **1.** inducing vomiting; emetic. **2.** of or pertaining to vomiting. —*n.* **3.** an emetic. **4.** an opening through which something is ejected or discharged. **5.** Also called **vomitorium.** an opening, as in a stadium or theater, permitting large numbers of people to enter or leave. [1595–1605; < L *vomitōrius,* equiv. to *vomi-,* var. s. of *vomere* to vomit + *-tōrius* -TORY[1]]

vom•i•tous (vom′i təs), *adj.* **1.** of, pertaining to, or causing vomiting. **2.** *Informal.* repugnant; disgusting; nauseating: *vomitous business methods.* [1950–55; VOMIT + -OUS]

vom•i•tu•ri•tion (vom′i cho͝o rish′ən), *n. Med.* **1.** ineffectual efforts to vomit. **2.** the vomiting of small amounts of matter. [1835–45; < L *vomit(us)* ptp. of *vomere* to discharge + *-urition,* prob. extracted from MICTURITION]

vom•i•tus (vom′i təs), *n., pl.* **-tus•es.** *Med.* **1.** the act of vomiting. **2.** vomited matter. [1880–85; < L, equiv. to *vomi-,* var. s. of *vomere* to VOMIT + *-tus* suffix of v. action]

von (von; *Ger.* fôn, *unstressed* fən), *prep.* from; of (used in German and Austrian personal names, originally to indicate place of origin and later to indicate nobility): *Paul von Hindenburg.*

Von Bé•ké•sy (von bā′kə shē; *Hung.* fôn bā′kā shi), **Ge•org** (gā′ôrg; *Hung.* ge′ôRG), 1899–1972, U.S. physicist, born in Hungary: Nobel prize for medicine 1961.

von Braun (von broun′; *Ger.* fən bRoun′). See **Braun, Wernher von.**

Von Kár•mán (von kär′män, -mən), **Theodore,** 1881–1963, U.S. scientist and aeronautical engineer, born in Hungary.

Von•ne•gut (von′i gət), *n.* **Kurt, Jr.,** born 1922, U.S. novelist.

Von Neu•mann (von noi′män, -mən), **John,** 1903–57, U.S. mathematician, born in Hungary.

von Stern•berg (von stûrn′bûrg), **Jo•sef** (jō′zəf, -səf) or **Joseph** (*Josef Stern*), 1894–1969, U.S. film director and screenwriter, born in Austria.

Von Stro•heim (von strō′hīm, shtrō′-; *Ger.* fən shtRō′hīm), **E•rich** (er′ik; *Ger.* ā′RIKH), 1885–1957, U.S. actor and director, born in Austria.

von Wil′le•brand's disease′ (fôn vil′ə bränts′), *Pathol.* an inherited autosomal recessive disease in which abnormally slow coagulation of blood may lead to spontaneous bleeding, excessive bleeding following an injury, and heavy menstrual flow. [1940–45; after Erik Adolf *von Willebrand* (1870–1949), Finnish physician]

voo•doo (vo͞o′do͞o), *n., pl.* **-doos,** *adj., v.,* **-dooed, -doo•ing.** —*n.* **1.** Also, **vodun.** a polytheistic religion practiced chiefly by West Indians, deriving principally from African cult worship and containing elements borrowed from the Catholic religion. **2.** a person who practices this religion. **3.** a fetish or other object of voodoo worship. **4.** a group of magical and ecstatic rites associated with voodoo. **5.** (not in technical use) black magic; sorcery. —*adj.* **6.** of, pertaining to, associated with, or practicing voodoo. **7.** *Informal* (*usually disparaging*). characterized by deceptively simple, almost magical, solutions or ideas: *voodoo politics.* —*v.t.* **8.** to affect by voodoo sorcery. [1810–20, *Amer.;* < LaF, earlier *vandoux, vandoo* < a West African source perh. akin to Ewe *vodū* demon]

voo•doo•ism (vo͞o′do͞o iz′əm), *n.* **1.** the voodoo religious rites and practices. **2.** the practice of sorcery. [1860–65, *Amer.;* VOODOO + -ISM] —**voo′doo•ist,** *n.* —**voo′doo•is′tic,** *adj.*

VOR, *Navig.* omnirange. [*v(ery high frequency) o(mni) r(ange)*]

-vora, a combining form meaning "ones that eat" what is specified by the initial element, used esp. in the names of zoological orders: *Carnivora.* [< L, neut. pl. of *-vorus* -VOROUS]

vo•ra•cious (vô rā′shəs, vō-, və-), *adj.* **1.** craving or consuming large quantities of food: *a voracious appetite.* **2.** exceedingly eager or avid: *voracious readers; a voracious collector.* [1625–35; VORACI(TY) + -OUS] —**vo•ra′cious•ly,** *adv.* —**vo•ra′cious•ness,** *n.*
—**Syn. 1.** See **ravenous. 2.** rapacious, insatiable.

vo•rac•i•ty (vô ras′i tē, vō-, və-), *n.* the condition or quality of being voracious. [1520–30; < L *vorācitās,* equiv. to *vorāc-* (s. of *vorāx*) gluttonous + *-itās* -ITY]

Vor•arl•berg (fōr′ärl′berk′), *n.* a province in W Austria. 305,615; 1004 sq. mi. (2600 sq. km). *Cap.:* Bregenz.

-vore, a combining form meaning "one that eats" what is specified by the initial element: *carnivore.* Cf. **-vora, -vorous.** [< F < L *-vorus* -VOROUS]

Vor•la•ge (fōr′lä′gə), *n., pl.* **-ge.** *German.* a position in which a skier leans forward but keeps the heels in contact with the skis.

Vo•ro•nezh (və rō′nish; *Russ.* vu Rô′nyish), *n.* a city in the SW Russian Federation in Europe. 887,000.

Vo•ro•noff (vôr′ə nôf′, -nof′; *Fr.* vô Rô nôf′; *Russ.* vô′Rə nəf), *n.* **Serge** (*Fr.* seRzh), 1866–1951, Russian physician.

Vo•ro•shi•lov (vôr′ə shē′ləf; *Russ.* və Ru shi′ləf), *n.* **1. Kli•ment E•fre•mo•vich** (klyi myent′ yi fRye′məvyich), 1881–1969, Soviet general: president of the Soviet Union 1953–60. **2.** former name of **Ussuriisk.**

Vo•ro•shi•lov•grad (vôr′ə shē′ləf grad′; *Russ.* və Rə-shi luf grät′), *n.* former name (1935–90) of **Lugansk.**

Vo•ro•shi•lovsk (vôr′ə shē′lôfsk, -lofsk; *Russ.* və Rə-shi′ləfsk), *n.* former name of **Stavropol.**

-vorous, a combining form meaning "eating, gaining sustenance from" that specified by the initial element: *carnivorous.* [< L *-vorus* devouring; see -OUS]

vor•spiel (fōr′shpēl, fôr′-), *n.* an introductory movement to a musical work, esp. a prelude or overture. [< G, equiv. to *vor-* pre-, FORE[1] + *Spiel* game, play]

Vor•ster (fôr′stər), *n.* **Balthazar Johannes,** 1915–83, South African political leader: prime minister 1966–78; president 1978–79.

vor•tex (vôr′teks), *n., pl.* **-tex•es, -ti•ces** (-tə sēz′). **1.** a whirling mass of water, esp. one in which a force of suction operates, as a whirlpool. **2.** a whirling mass of air, esp. one in the form of a visible column or spiral, as a tornado. **3.** a whirling mass of fire, flame, etc. **4.** a state of affairs likened to a whirlpool for violent activity, irresistible force, etc. **5.** something regarded as drawing into its powerful current everything that surrounds it: *the vortex of war.* **6.** (in Cartesian philosophy) a rapid rotatory movement of cosmic matter about a center, regarded as accounting for the origin or phenomena of bodies or systems of bodies in space. [1645–55; < L, var. of *vertex* VERTEX]

vor•ti•cal (vôr′ti kəl), *adj.* **1.** of or pertaining to a vortex. **2.** suggesting or resembling a vortex. **3.** moving in a vortex; whirling: *a vortical current.* [1645–55; < L *vortic-* (s. of *vortex* VORTEX) + -AL[1]] —**vor′ti•cal•ly,** *adv.*

vor•ti•cel•la (vôr′tə sel′ə), *n., pl.* **-cel•lae** (-sel′ē), **-cel•las.** any ciliated protozoan of the genus *Vorticella,* having a transparent, bell-shaped body with a retractile stalk. [1780–90; < NL; see VORTEX, -ELLA]

vor•ti•ces (vôr′tə sēz′), *n.* a pl. of **vortex.**

vor•ti•cism (vôr′tə siz′əm), *n.* (*sometimes cap.*) a short-lived avant-garde British art movement that was nurtured by Wyndham Lewis, derived from futurism and cubism, and reached its climax in an exhibition in London in 1915, dwindling in influence after World War I. [1910–15; < L *vortic-,* s. of *vortex* VORTEX + -ISM] —**vor′ti•cist,** *n., adj.*

vor•tic•i•ty (vôr tis′i tē), *n., pl.* **-ties.** *Mech.* a measure of the circulation of a fluid: a quantity equal to twice the angular momentum of a particle of the fluid around which there is circulation. [1890–95; < L *vortic-* (s. of *vortex;* see VORTEX) + -ITY]

vor•ti•cose (vôr′ti kōs′), *adj.* vortical; whirling. [1775–85; < L *vorticōsus* eddying. See VORTICAL, -OSE[1]] —**vor′ti•cose′ly,** *adv.*

vor•tig•i•nous (vôr tij′ə nəs), *adj.* resembling a vortex; whirling; vortical. [1665–75; var. of VERTIGINOUS]

Vosges (vōzh), *n.* **1.** a range of low mountains in NE France: highest peak, 4668 ft. (1423 m). **2.** a department in NE France. 397,957; 2279 sq. mi. (5905 sq. km). *Cap.:* Épinal.

Vos•khod (vos′kod, vos kod′; *Russ.* vu skhôd′), *n.* one of a series of Soviet spacecraft, carrying two or three cosmonauts. [1964; < Russ *Voskhód* lit., rising (of the sun, a planetary body, etc.)]

Vos•tok (vos′tok, vo stok′; *Russ.* vu stôk′), *n.* one of a series of Soviet spacecraft, carrying one cosmonaut, used to make the world's first manned spaceflights. [1961; < Russ *Vostók* lit., east]

vot•a•ble (vō′tə bəl), *adj.* capable of being voted upon; subject to a vote: *a votable issue.* Also, **voteable.** [1745–55; VOTE + -ABLE]

vo•ta•ress (vō′tər is), *n. Now Rare.* a woman who is a votary. [1580–90; VOTAR(Y) + -ESS]
—**Usage.** See **-ess.**

vo•ta•ry (vō′tə rē), *n., pl.* **-ries,** *adj.* —*n.* Also, **vo′ta•rist. 1.** a person who is bound by solemn religious vows, as a monk or a nun. **2.** an adherent of a religion or cult; a worshiper of a particular deity or sacred personage. **3.** a person who is devoted or addicted to some subject or pursuit: *a votary of jazz.* **4.** a devoted follower or admirer. —*adj.* **5.** consecrated by a vow. **6.** of or pertaining to a vow. [1540–50; < L *vōt(um)* a vow + -ARY]
—**Syn. 3.** buff, fan, admirer, devotee.

vote (vōt), *n., v.,* **vot•ed, vot•ing.** —*n.* **1.** a formal expression of opinion or choice, either positive or negative, made by an individual or body of individuals. **2.** the means by which such expression is made, as a ballot, ticket, etc. **3.** the right to such expression: *to give women the vote.* **4.** the decision reached by voting, as by a majority of ballots cast: *The vote was for the resolution.* **5.** a collective expression of will as inferred from a number of votes: *the labor vote.* **6.** an expression, as of some judgment: *a vote of confidence.* —*v.i.* **7.** to express or signify will or choice in a matter, as by casting a ballot: *to vote for president.* —*v.t.* **8.** to enact, establish, or determine by vote: *to vote a proposed bill into law.* **9.** to support by one's vote: *to vote the Republican ticket.* **10.** to advocate by or as by one's vote: *to vote that the report be accepted.* **11.** to declare or decide by general consent: *They voted the trip a success.* **12.** to encourage or cause to vote, esp. in a particular way. [1425–75; late ME (n.) < L *vōtum* a vow]

vote•a•ble (vō′tə bəl), *adj.* votable.

vo-tech (vō′tek′), *adj. Informal.* vocational-technical: used esp. of a school curriculum. [by shortening]

vote-get•ter (vōt′get′ər), *n.* a candidate or issue whose personality, policies, etc., are considered certain to attract many votes. Also, **vote′get′ter.** [1905–10, *Amer.*]

vote•less (vōt′lis), *adj.* **1.** lacking or without a vote. **2.** denied the right to vote, esp. in political elections. [1665–75; VOTE + -LESS]

vot•er (vō′tər), *n.* **1.** a person who votes. **2.** a person who has a right to vote; elector. [1570–80; VOTE (v.) + -ER[1]]

vot′ing machine′, a mechanical apparatus used in a polling place to register and count the votes. [1895–1900]

voting machine

vot′ing pa′per, *Brit.* a ballot. [1855–60]

vo•tive (vō′tiv), *adj.* **1.** offered, given, dedicated, etc., in accordance with a vow: *a votive offering.* **2.** performed, undertaken, etc., in consequence of a vow. **3.** of the nature of or expressive of a wish or desire. [1585–95; < L *vōtīvus,* equiv. to *vōt(um)* a vow + *-īvus* -IVE] —**vo′tive•ly,** *adv.* —**vo′tive•ness,** *n.*

CONCISE ETYMOLOGY KEY: <, descended or borrowed from; >, whence; b., blend of, blended; c., cognate with; cf., compare; deriv., derivative; equiv., equivalent; imit., imitative; obl., oblique; r., replacing; s., stem; sp., spelling, spelled; resp., respelling, respelled; trans., translation; ?, origin unknown; *, unattested; ‡, probably earlier than. See the full key inside the front cover.

vo′tive Mass′, *Rom. Cath. Ch.* a Mass that does not correspond with the office of the day but is said, as for a special intention, at the choice of the celebrant. [1730–40]

vo•tress (vō′tris), *n. Archaic.* a votaress.

Vo•ty•ak (vō′tē ak′), *n.* Udmurt. [< Russ *votyák,* deriv. of the collective name *vot′,* ORuss *oti* < Mari *odo,* akin to Udmurt *ud-;* see UDMURT]

vou., voucher.

vouch (vouch), *v.i.* **1.** to support as being true, certain, reliable, etc. (usually fol. by *for*): *Her record in office vouches for her integrity.* **2.** to attest; guarantee; certify (usually fol. by *for*): *to vouch for someone in a business transaction.* —*v.t.* **3.** to sustain or uphold by, or as if by, practical proof or demonstration. **4.** (formerly) to call or summon (a person) into court to make good a warranty of title. **5.** to adduce or quote in support, as extracts from a book or author; cite in warrant or justification, as authority, instances, facts, etc. **6.** *Archaic.* to warrant or attest; to support or authenticate with vouchers. **7.** *Archaic.* to declare as with warrant; vouch for. **8.** *Obs.* to call or take as a witness. —*n. Obs.* **9.** a vouching; an assertion. **10.** a formal attestation; a supporting warrant. [1275–1325; ME *vouchen* < AF, MF *vo(u)cher,* OF *avochier* < L *advocāre;* see ADVOCATE]

vouch•ee (vou chē′), *n.* the person for whom someone vouches. [1475–85; VOUCH + -EE]

vouch•er (vou′chər), *n.* **1.** a person or thing that vouches. **2.** a document, receipt, stamp, or the like, that gives evidence of an expenditure. **3.** a form authorizing a disbursement of cash or a credit against a purchase or expense to be made in the future. **4.** written authorization; credential. **5.** a piece of evidence or proof. **6.** *Early Eng. Law.* **a.** a person called into court to warrant another's title. **b.** the act of vouching another person to make good a warranty. —*v.t.* **7.** to pay for, guarantee, or authorize by voucher. **8.** to prepare a voucher for. [1525–35; < AF *voucher* to vouch; orig. F inf. used as n. but now taken as VOUCH + -ER[1]] —**vouch′er•a•ble,** *adj.*

vouch′er sys′tem, 1. *Accounting.* a procedure for controlling disbursements by means of vouchers. **2.** Also called **vouch′er plan′.** *Educ.* a plan in which each school-age child receives a publicly funded entitlement worth a fixed amount of money with which his or her parents can select a participating public or private school. [1880–85]

vouch•safe (vouch sāf′), *v.,* **-safed, -saf•ing.** —*v.t.* **1.** to grant or give, as by favor, graciousness, or condescension: *to vouchsafe a reply to a question.* **2.** to allow or permit, as by favor or graciousness: *They vouchsafed his return to his own country.* —*v.i.* **3.** to condescend; deign. [1275–1325; ME phrase *vouche sauf.* See VOUCH, SAFE] —**vouch•safe′ment,** *n.*
—**Syn. 1.** bestow, confer, accord.

vouge (vōōzh), *n.* an axlike, shafted weapon having a curved blade tapering to a point at the top, used by foot soldiers in the 14th century and after. [< F << Celtic; cf. Welsh *gwyddif* scythe, ML *vidubium*]

vous•soir (vōō swär′), *n. Archit.* any of the pieces, in the shape of a truncated wedge, that form an arch or vault. See diag. under **arch.** [1325–75; < F; r. ME *vousor(i)e* < AF; OF *volsoir* < VL **volsōrium,* equiv. to **volt(us)* (for L *volūtus*), ptp. of *volvere* to turn + *-tōrium* -TORY[2] with *tt* > *s*]

Vou•vray (vōōv rā′; *Fr.* vōō VRE′), *n.* **1.** a town in W central France, E of Tours. 2598. **2.** a medium dry, white wine of this region.

vow (vou), *n.* **1.** a solemn promise, pledge, or personal commitment: *marriage vows; a vow of secrecy.* **2.** a solemn promise made to a deity or saint committing oneself to an act, service, or condition. **3.** a solemn or earnest declaration. **4. take vows,** to enter a religious order or house. —*v.t.* **5.** to make a vow of; promise by a vow, as to God or a saint: *to vow a crusade or a pilgrimage.* **6.** to pledge or resolve solemnly to do, make, give, observe, etc.: *They vowed revenge.* **7.** to declare solemnly or earnestly; assert emphatically (often fol. by a clause as object): *She vowed that she would take the matter to court.* **8.** to dedicate or devote by a vow: *to vow oneself to the service of God.* —*v.i.* **9.** to make a vow. **10.** to make a solemn or earnest declaration. [1250–1300; ME < AF, OF *vo(u)* < L *vōtum,* neut. of *vōtus,* ptp. of *vovēre* to vow] —**vow′er,** *n.* —**vow′less,** *adj.*

vow•el (vou′əl), *n.* **1.** *Phonet.* **a.** (in English articulation) a speech sound produced without occluding, diverting, or obstructing the flow of air from the lungs (opposed to *consonant*). **b.** (in a syllable) the sound of greatest sonority, as *i* in *grill.* Cf. **consonant** (def. 1b). **c.** (in linguistic function) a concept empirically determined as a phonological element in structural contrast with consonant, as the (ē) of *be* (bē), *we* (wē), and *yeast* (yēst). **2.** a letter representing or usually representing a vowel, as, in English, *a, e, i, o, u,* and sometimes *w* and *y.* —*adj.* **3.** of or pertaining to a vowel. [1275–1325; ME < OF *vowel* < L *vōcālis* VOCAL] —**vow′el•less,** *adj.* —**vow′el•like′,** *adj.* —**vow′el•y, vow′el•ly,** *adv.*

vow′el frac′ture, *Phonol.* breaking[1].

vow′el har′mony, *Ling.* a phonological rule in some languages, as Hungarian and Turkish, requiring that the vowels of a word all share a specified feature, such as front or back articulation, thereby conditioning the form that affixes may take, as in forming the Turkish plurals *evler* "houses" from *ev* "house" and *adamlar* "men" from *adam* "man." [1895–1900]

vow•el•ize (vou′ə līz′), *v.t.,* **-ized, -iz•ing.** to provide (a Hebrew, Arabic, etc., text) with vowel points; vocalize. Also, *esp. Brit.,* **vow′el•ise′.** [1810–20; VOWEL + -IZE] —**vow′el•i•za′tion,** *n.*

vow′el point′, any of a group of auxiliary symbols, as small lines and dots, placed above or below consonant symbols to indicate vowels in a writing system, as that of Hebrew or Arabic, in which vowels are otherwise not written. [1755–65]

vow′el rhyme′, *Pros.* assonance (def. 2).

vow′el sys′tem, *Ling.* the vowel sounds of a language, esp. when considered as forming an interrelated and interacting group. Cf. **consonant system.** [1870–75]

VOX (voks), *n.* a device in certain types of telecommunications equipment, as telephone answering machines, that converts an incoming voice or sound signal into an electrical signal that turns on a transmitter or recorder that continues to operate as long as the incoming signal is maintained. [acronym from *voice-operated keying,* altered to conform to L *vōx* VOICE]

vox bar•ba•ra (voks′ bär′bər ə), a questionably unconventional word or term; barbarism: applied esp. to neo-Latin terms in botany, zoology, etc., that are formed from elements that are neither Latin nor Greek. [< L *vōx barbara* foreign word, speech]

vox et prae•te•re•a ni•hil (wōks′ et prī te′re ä′ ni′hil; *Eng.* voks′ et pri tĕr′ē ə nī′hil), *Latin.* a voice and nothing more.

vox hu•ma•na (voks′ hyōō mä′nə, -mā′-, -man′ə), a pipe-organ stop designed to produce tones resembling those of the human voice. [1720–30; < L *vōx hūmāna* human voice]

vox pop., vox populi.

vox po•pu•li (voks′ pop′yə lī′), the voice of the people; popular opinion. [< L *vōx populī*]

vox po•pu•li, vox De•i (wōks pō′pōō lē′ wōks de′ē; *Eng.* voks pop′yə lī′ voks dē′ī, dā′ē), *Latin.* the voice of the people (is) the voice of God.

voy•age (voi′ij), *n., v.,* **-aged, -ag•ing.** —*n.* **1.** a course of travel or passage, esp. a long journey by water to a distant place. **2.** a passage through air or space, as a flight in an airplane or space vehicle. **3.** a journey or expedition from one place to another by land. **4.** Often, **voyages.** journeys or travels as the subject of a written account, or the account itself: *the voyages of Marco Polo.* **5.** *Obs.* an enterprise or undertaking. —*v.i.* **6.** to make or take a voyage; travel; journey. —*v.t.* **7.** to traverse by a voyage: *to voyage the seven seas.* [1250–1300; ME *ve(i)age, viage, voyage* < AF, OF < L *viāticum* travel-money; see VIATICUM] —**voy′ag•er,** *n.*
—**Syn. 1.** cruise. See **trip**[1].

Voy•ag•er (voi′ə jər), *n.* one of a series of U.S. space probes that obtained scientific information while flying by the planets Jupiter, Saturn, and Uranus.

vo•ya•geur (vwä′yä zhûr′, voi′ə-; *Fr.* VWA YA ZHŒR′), *n., pl.* **-geurs** (-zhûrz′; *Fr.* -ZHŒR′). (in Canada) a person who is an expert woodsman, boatman, and guide in remote regions, esp. one employed by fur companies to transport supplies to and from their distant stations. [1785–95; < F: traveler, equiv. to *voyag(er)* to travel (deriv. of *voyage* journey; see VOYAGE) + *-eur* -EUR]

Voyageurs′ Na′tional Park′, a national park in N Minnesota. 343 sq. mi. (888 sq. km).

vo•yeur (vwä yûr′, voi-; *Fr.* VWA YŒR′), *n., pl.* **-yeurs** (-yûrz′; *Fr.* -YŒR′). a person who engages in voyeurism. Cf. **Peeping Tom.** [1915–20; < F, equiv. to *voi(r)* to see (< L *vidēre*) + *-eur* -EUR]

vo•yeur•ism (vwä yûr′iz əm, voi-, voi′ə riz′-), *n.* the practice of obtaining sexual gratification by looking at sexual objects or acts, esp. secretively. [VOYEUR + -ISM]

voy•eur•is•tic (vwä′yə ris′tic, voi′ə-), *adj.* of, pertaining to, or characteristic of a voyeur or of voyeurism. [VOYEUR + -IST + -IC] —**voy′eur•is′ti•cal•ly,** *adv.*

voy•euse (VWA YŒZ′), *n., pl.* **voy•euses** (VWA YŒZ′). *Fr. Furniture.* a chair of the 18th century used at game tables, having a padded top rail on which spectators could lean. [< F; fem. of VOYEUR]

Voz•ne•sen•sky (voz′nə sen′skē; *Russ.* vəz nyi syen′skē), *n.* **An•drei (An•dre•ie•vich)** (än′drā än drā′yə-vich; *Russ.* un DRYĀ′ un DRYE′yi vyich), born 1933, Soviet poet.

VP, 1. verb phrase. **2.** Also, **vp, v-p** vice president.

V.P., Vice President. Also, **V. Pres.**

v.p., passive verb. [< NL *verbum passīvum*]

VR, 1. virtual reality. **2.** voltage regulator.

V.R., Queen Victoria. [< L *Victōria Rēgīna*]

v.r., reflexive verb. [< NL *verbum reflexīvum*]

V region, *Immunol.* See **variable region.**

V. Rev., Very Reverend.

Vries (vrēs; *Du.* VRĒS), *n.* **Hu•go de** (hyōō′gō də; *Du.* HY′gō də). See **De Vries, Hugo.**

vrie•si•a (vrē′zhē ə, -zē ə, -zhə), *n.* any of numerous tropical American epiphytic bromeliads of the genus *Vriesia,* many species of which are cultivated for their rosettes of variegated leaves and showy flower spikes. [< NL (1843), after W.H. de *Vriese* (1806–62), Dutch botanist; see -IA]

Vri•tra (vrit′rə), *n. Hinduism.* a serpent-demon, the personification of evil and leader of the Danavas: conquered by Indra.

VRM, variable-rate mortgage.

vroom (vrōōm, vrŏŏm), *n.* **1.** the roaring sound made by a motor at high speed. —*v.i.* **2.** to make or move with such a sound. —*v.t.* **3.** to cause to make such a sound. Also, **varoom.** [1960–65; imit.]

vrouw (VROU; *Eng.* vrou), *n, pl.* **vrouw•en** (VROU′ən), *Eng.* **vrouws.** *Dutch.* **1.** a woman; wife; lady. **2.** (used as a title before the name of a married woman) Mrs.

vs., 1. verse. **2.** versus.

V.S., Veterinary Surgeon.

v.s., vide supra.

V-shaped (vē′shāpt′), *adj.* having the shape of the letter *V: a V-shaped flying formation.*

V sign, 1. a sign of victory formed by the raised index and middle fingers. **2.** this sign used as an indication of approval. [1940–45]

V-six (vē′siks′), *n. Auto.* a six-cylinder V-engine. Also, **V-6.** Cf. **V-eight.**

VSO language, *Ling.* a type of language that has basic verb-subject-object word order, as Welsh, classical Arabic, or Tagalog. Cf. **SOV language, SVO language.**

V.S.O.P., very superior old pale (used esp. to indicate a type of aged brandy, which under French law cannot be exported until it is at least four years old).

vss., versions.

V/STOL (vē′stôl′), *Aeron.* vertical and short takeoff and landing. Cf. **VTOL.**

VT, Vermont (approved esp. for use with zip code).

Vt., Vermont.

v.t., transitive verb. [< NL *verbum trānsitīvum*]

V.T.C., 1. Volunteer Training Corps. **2.** voting trust certificate.

Vte., Vicomte.

Vtesse., Vicomtesse.

VT fuze, a variable time fuze.

VTO, *Aeron.* vertical takeoff.

VTOL (vē′tôl′), *n. Aeron.* a convertiplane capable of taking off and landing vertically, having forward speeds comparable to those of conventional aircraft. [1965–70] [*v(ertical) t(ake)o(ff and) l(anding)*]

VTR, *Television.* See **videotape recorder.**

V′-type en′gine (vē′tīp′), *Auto.* an engine having the cylinders aligned in two banks at an angle to each other, forming a V.

vu, *Audio.* volume unit. Also, **VU**

Vuel•ta A•ba•jo (vwel′tə ə bä′hō; *Sp.* bwel′tä ä vä′hô), a region in W Cuba.

vug (vug, vŏŏg), *n. Geol.* a small cavity in a rock or vein, often lined with crystals. Also, **vugg, vugh.** [1810–20; < Cornish *vooga* cave; cf. L *fovea* pit] —**vug′gy,** *adj.*

Vuil•lard (vwē YAR′), *n.* **(Jean) É•douard** (zhän ā DWAR′), 1868–1940, French painter.

Vul., Vulgate.

Vul•can (vul′kən), *n.* **1.** the ancient Roman god of fire and metalworking, identified with the Greek Hephaestus. **2.** *Mil.* a six-barrel, 20mm U.S. Army antiaircraft gun system mounted on an armored personnel carrier and first deployed in 1968. **3.** *Astron.* a hypothetical planet nearest the sun whose existence was erroneously postulated to account for perturbations in Mercury's orbit. [1505–15; < L *Vulcānus*]

Vul•ca•ni•an (vul kā′nē ən), *adj.* **1.** of, pertaining to, or associated with Vulcan. **2.** (*l.c.*) volcanic. **3.** (*l.c.*) of or pertaining to metalworking. [1590–1600; < L *Vulcāni(us)* of Vulcan + -AN]

vul•can•ism (vul′kə niz′əm), *n. Geol.* volcanism. [1875–80; var. of VOLCANISM] —**vul′can•ist,** *n.*

vul•can•ite (vul′kə nīt′), *n.* a hard, readily cut and polished rubber, obtained by vulcanizing rubber with a large amount of sulfur, used in the manufacture of combs, buttons, and for electric insulation. Also called **ebonite.** [1830–40; VULCAN + -ITE[1]]

vul•can•i•zate (vul′kə nə zāt′), *n.* a vulcanized substance. [1925–30; VULCANIZE + -ATE[1]]

vul•can•ize (vul′kə nīz′), *v.t.,* **-ized, -iz•ing. 1.** to treat (rubber) with sulfur and heat, thereby imparting strength, greater elasticity, durability, etc. **2.** to subject (a substance other than rubber) to some analogous process, as to harden it. Also, *esp. Brit.,* **vul′can•ise′.** [1820–30; VULCAN + -IZE] —**vul′can•iz′a•ble,** *adj.* —**vul′can•i•za′tion,** *n.* —**vul′can•iz′er,** *n.*

vul′canized fi′ber, a leatherlike substance made by compression of layers of paper or cloth that have been treated with acids or zinc chloride, used chiefly for electric insulation. [1870–75]

vul•can•ol•o•gy (vul′kə nol′ə jē), *n.* volcanology. [1855–60; *vulcan-* (var. of *volcan-* as in VOLCANIC) + -O- + -LOGY] —**vul•can•o•log•i•cal** (vul′kə nl oj′i kəl), *adj.* —**vul′can•ol′o•gist,** *n.*

Vulg., Vulgate.

vulg., 1. vulgar. **2.** vulgarly.

vul•gar (vul′gər), *adj.* **1.** characterized by ignorance of or lack of good breeding or taste: *vulgar ostentation.* **2.** indecent; obscene; lewd: *a vulgar work; a vulgar gesture.* **3.** crude; coarse; unrefined: *a vulgar peasant.* **4.** of, pertaining to, or constituting the ordinary people in a society: *the vulgar masses.* **5.** current; popular; common: *a vulgar success; vulgar beliefs.* **6.** spoken by, or being in the language spoken by, the people generally; vernacular: *vulgar tongue.* **7.** lacking in distinction, aesthetic value, or charm; banal; ordinary: *a vulgar painting.* —*n.* **8.** *Archaic.* the common people. **9.** *Obs.* the vernacular. [1350–1400; ME < L *vulgāris,* equiv. to *vulg(us)* the general public + *-āris* -AR[1]] —**vul′gar•ly,** *adv.* —**vul′gar•ness,** *n.*
—**Syn. 1.** unrefined, inelegant, low, coarse, ribald. See **common. 3.** boorish, rude. **6.** colloquial.

vul′gar frac′tion. See **common fraction.** [1665–75]

vul•gar•i•an (vul gâr′ē ən), *n.* a vulgar person, esp. one whose vulgarity is the more conspicuous because of wealth, prominence, or pretensions to good breeding. [1640–50; VULGAR + -IAN]

vul•gar•ism (vul′gə riz′əm), *n.* **1.** vulgar behavior or character; vulgarity. **2.** a vulgar expression; a word or phrase used only in common colloquial, and esp. in coarse, speech. [1635–45; VULGAR + -ISM]

vul•gar•i•ty (vul gar′i tē), *n., pl.* **-ties.** **1.** the state or quality of being vulgar: *the vulgarity of his remark.* **2.** something vulgar, as an act or expression. [1570–80; < LL *vulgāritās* commonness, the public. See VULGAR, -ITY] —**Syn. 1.** tastelessness, crudeness, grossness, indelicacy.

vul•gar•ize (vul′gə rīz′), *v.t.,* **-ized, -iz•ing. 1.** to make vulgar or coarse; lower; debase: *to vulgarize standards of behavior.* **2.** to make (a technical or abstruse work) easier to understand and more widely known; popularize. **3.** to translate (a work) from a classical language into the vernacular. Also, *esp. Brit.,* **vul′gar•ise′.** [1595–1605; VULGAR + -IZE] —**vul′gar•i•za′tion,** *n.* —**vul′gar•iz′er,** *n.*

Vul′gar Lat′in, popular Latin, as distinguished from literary or standard Latin, esp. those spoken forms of Latin from which the Romance languages developed. *Abbr.:* VL [1810–20]

Vul•gate (vul′gāt, -git), *n.* **1.** the Latin version of the Bible, prepared chiefly by Saint Jerome at the end of the 4th century A.D., and used as the authorized version of the Roman Catholic Church. **2.** (*l.c.*) any commonly recognized text or version of a work. —*adj.* **3.** of or pertaining to the Vulgate. **4.** (*l.c.*) commonly used or accepted; common. [< LL *vulgāta* (*editiō*) popular (edition); *vulgāta,* fem. ptp. of *vulgāre* to make common, publish, deriv. of *vulgus* the public. See VULGAR, -ATE[1]]

vul•gus (vul′gəs), *n., pl.* **-gus•es** for 2. **1.** the common people; masses. **2.** an exercise in Latin formerly required of English public-school pupils. [1680–90; < L]

vul•ner•a•ble (vul′nər ə bəl), *adj.* **1.** capable of or susceptible to being wounded or hurt, as by a weapon: *a vulnerable part of the body.* **2.** open to moral attack, criticism, temptation, etc.: *an argument vulnerable to refutation; He is vulnerable to bribery.* **3.** (of a place) open to assault; difficult to defend: *a vulnerable bridge.* **4.** *Bridge.* having won one of the games of a rubber. [1595–1605; < LL *vulnerābilis,* equiv. to L *vulnerā(re)* to wound + *-bilis* -BLE; see VULNERARY] —**vul′ner•a•bil′i•ty, vul′ner•a•ble•ness,** *n.* —**vul′ner•a•bly,** *adv.*

CONCISE ETYMOLOGY KEY: <, descended or borrowed from; >, whence; b., blend of, blended; c., cognate with; cf., compare; deriv., derivative; equiv., equivalent; imit., imitative; obl., oblique; r., replacing; s., stem; sp., spelling, spelled; resp., respelling, respelled; trans., translation; ?, origin unknown; *, unattested; ‡, probably earlier than. See the full key inside the front cover.

vul•ner•ar•y (vul′nə rer′ē), *adj., n., pl.* **-ar•ies.** —*adj.* **1.** used to promote the healing of wounds, as herbs or other remedies. —*n.* **2.** a remedy for wounds. [1590–1600; < L *vulnerārius,* equiv. to *vulner-* (s. of *vulnus*) wound + *-ārius* -ARY]

Vul•pec•u•la (vul pek′yə lə), *n., gen.* **-lae** (-lē′). *Astron.* the Little Fox, a northern constellation between Cygnus and Aquila. [1865–70; < L *vulpēcula,* equiv. to *vulpē(s)* fox + *-cula* -CULE[1]]

vul•pec•u•lar (vul pek′yə lər), *adj.* pertaining to or resembling a fox; vulpine. [1880–85; < LL *vulpēculāris.* See VULPECULA, -AR[1]]

vul•pi•cide (vul′pə sīd′), *n. Brit.* **1.** the act of killing a fox other than by hunting it with hounds. **2.** a person who kills a fox by means other than hunting it with hounds. Also, **vul′pe•cide′.** [1820–30; < L *vulpi-* (s. of *vulpēs*) fox + -CIDE] —**vul′pi•cid′al,** *adj.* —**vul′pi•cid′ism,** *n.*

vul•pine (vul′pīn, -pin), *adj.* **1.** of or resembling a fox. **2.** cunning or crafty. [1620–30; < L *vulpīnus,* equiv. to *vulp(ēs)* fox + *-īnus* -INE[1]]

turkey vulture, *Cathartes aura,* length 2½ ft. (0.8 m); wingspread to 6 ft. (1.8 m)

vul•ture (vul′chər), *n.* **1.** any of several large, primarily carrion-eating Old World birds of prey of the family Accipitridae, often having a naked head and less powerful feet than those of the related hawks and eagles. **2.** any of several superficially similar New World birds of the family Cathartidae, as the turkey vulture. **3.** a person or thing that preys, esp. greedily or unscrupulously: *That vulture would sell out his best friend.* [1325–75; ME < L *vultur*] —**vul′ture•like′,** *adj.*

vul•tur•ine (vul′chə rīn′, -chər in), *adj.* **1.** of, pertaining to, or characteristic of a vulture. **2.** resembling a vulture, esp. in rapacious or predatory qualities: *a vulturine critic.* Also, **vul•tur•ous** (vul′chər əs). [1640–50; < L *vulturīnus.* See VULTURE, -INE[1]]

vul•va (vul′və), *n., pl.* **-vae** (-vē), **-vas.** *Anat.* the external female genitalia. [1540–50; < L] —**vul′val, vul′var,** *adj.* —**vul•vi•form** (vul′və fôrm′), **vul•vate** (vul′vāt, -vit), *adj.*

vul•vi•tis (vul vī′tis), *n. Pathol.* inflammation of the vulva. [1855–60; < NL; see VULVA, -ITIS]

vul•vo•vag•i•ni•tis (vul′vō vaj′ə nī′tis), *n. Pathol.* inflammation of the vulva and vagina. [1895–1900; VULV(A) + -O- + VAGINITIS]

VU meter, a meter used with sound-reproducing or recording equipment that indicates average sound levels.

vv., **1.** verses. **2.** violins.

v.v., vice versa.

vv.ll., variae lectiones.

V.W., Very Worshipful.

Vyat•ka (vyät′kə), *n.* former name of **Kirov.**

Vy•borg (vē′bôrg; *Russ.* vi′bərk), *n.* a seaport in the NW Russian Federation in Europe, on the Gulf of Finland: formerly in Finland. 79,000. Swedish, **Viborg.** Finnish, **Viipuri.**

Vy•cor (vī′kôr), *Trademark.* a brand of durable, highly heat-resistant glass containing approximately 96 percent silica, used chiefly for making laboratory vessels, as beakers, crucibles, and flasks.

Vyer•nyi (*Russ.* vyeʀ′nē), *n.* former name of **Alma-Ata.**

vy•ing (vī′ing), *adj.* **1.** competing; contending: *All vying swimmers come to the judge's desk.* —*v.* **2.** ppr. of **vie.** [VIE + -ING[2]] —**vy′ing•ly,** *adv.*

Vy•shin•sky (vi shin′skē; *Russ.* vi shin′skyē), *n.* **Andrei Yanuarievich.** See **Vishinsky, Andrei Yanuarievich.**

Vyv•yan (viv′yən), *n.* a male or female given name.

DEVELOPMENT OF MAJUSCULE						
NORTH SEMITIC	GREEK	ETR.	LATIN	MODERN		
				GOTHIC	ITALIC	ROMAN
SEE LETTERS F AND U				𝔚	*W*	W

DEVELOPMENT OF MINUSCULE					
ROMAN CURSIVE	ROMAN UNCIAL	CAROL. MIN.	MODERN		
			GOTHIC	ITALIC	ROMAN
—	ꟺ	—	𝔴	*w*	w

The twenty-third letter of the English alphabet, called "double-u," was created about the 11th century A.D. to distinguish two U's from a U and a V. (See **U, V.**) The *w*-sound was represented in North Semitic by *waw,* which in the Greek alphabet became *digamma* (**F**) and *upsilon* (**U**). (See **F.**)

W, w (dub′əl yo͞o′, -yo͞o; *rapidly* dub′yə), *n., pl.* **W's** or **Ws, w's** or **ws. 1.** the 23rd letter of the English alphabet, a semivowel. **2.** any spoken sound represented by the letter *W* or *w,* as in *way, bewitch,* or *row.* **3.** something having the shape of a W. **4.** a written or printed representation of the letter *W* or *w.* **5.** a device, as a printer's type, for reproducing the letter *W* or *w.*

W, 1. watt; watts. **2.** west. **3.** western. **4.** white. **5.** wide. **6.** widowed. **7.** width. **8.** withdrawn; withdrew. **9.** withheld.

W, *Symbol.* **1.** the 23rd in order or in a series, or, when *I* is omitted, the 22nd. **2.** *Chem.* tungsten. [< G *Wolfram* WOLFRAM] **3.** *Biochem.* tryptophan.

w, 1. watt; watts. **2.** withdrawn; withdrew. **3.** withheld.

W., 1. Wales. **2.** warden. **3.** warehouse. **4.** Washington. **5.** watt; watts. **6.** Wednesday. **7.** weight. **8.** Welsh. **9.** west. **10.** western. **11.** width. **12.** *Physics.* work.

w., 1. warden. **2.** warehouse. **3.** water. **4.** watt; watts. **5.** week; weeks. **6.** weight. **7.** west. **8.** western. **9.** wide. **10.** width. **11.** wife. **12.** with. **13.** won. **14.** *Physics.* work.

w/, with.

wa' (wô, wä), *n. Scot.* wall.

WA, 1. Washington (approved esp. for use with zip code). **2.** *Banking.* withholding agent.

W.A., 1. West Africa. **2.** Western Australia. **3.** *Marine Insurance.* with average.

WAAC (wak), *n.* **1.** *U.S. Mil.* **a.** Women's Army Auxiliary Corps: founded during World War II. **b.** a member of the Women's Army Auxiliary Corps. Cf. **Wac. 2.** *Brit.* **a.** Women's Army Auxiliary Corps: founded in 1917. **b.** a member of the Women's Army Auxiliary Corps. Cf. **WRAC.** Also, **W.A.A.C.** [1942 for def. 1]

Waadt (vät), *n.* German name of **Vaud.**

Waaf (waf), *n. Brit.* **1.** Women's Auxiliary Air Force: formed during World War II as an auxiliary of the Royal Air Force. **2.** a member of the Women's Auxiliary Air Force. Also, **W.A.A.F., WAAF** [1939]

Waal (väl), *n.* a river in the central Netherlands, flowing W to the Meuse River: the center branch of the lower Rhine. 52 mi. (84 km) long.

Waals (väls), *n.* **Jo·han·nes Di·de·rick van der** (yō hä′nəs dē′də rɪk vän dər), 1837–1923, Dutch physicist: Nobel prize 1910.

wab (wäb), *n. Scot. and North Eng.* web.

Wa·ba·na·ki (wä′bə nä′kē), *n., pl.* **-kis,** (*esp. collectively*) **-ki.** Abenaki.

Wa·bash (wô′bash), *n.* **1.** a river flowing from W Ohio through Indiana, along part of the boundary between Indiana and Illinois, into the Ohio River. 475 mi. (765 km) long. **2.** a city in N Indiana. 12,985.

wab·ble[1] (wob′əl), *v.i., v.t.,* **-bled, -bling.** wobble. **—wab′bler,** *n.* **—wab′bling·ly,** *adv.*

wab·ble[2] (wob′əl), *n.* the larva of a botfly, *Cuterebra emasculator,* that infests squirrels and other rodents, rendering the males sterile. [var. of WARBLE[2]]

wab·bly (wob′lē), *adj.,* **-bli·er, -bli·est.** wobbly. **—wab′bli·ness,** *n.*

Wac (wak), *n.* a member of the Women's Army Corps, an auxiliary of the U.S. Army. [1943]

Wace (wäs, wās; *Fr.* WAS), *n.* **Ro·bert** (rob′ərt; *Fr.* RÔ BER′), ("*Wace of Jersey*"), c1100–c1180, Anglo-Norman poet born on the Channel Island of Jersey.

wack[1] (wak), *Slang.* —*n.* **1.** wacko. —*adj.* **2.** very bad: *All drugs are bad, but crack is wack.* **3.** extreme; far-out. [1935–40; perh. back formation from WACKY]

wack[2] (wak), *v.t., v.i., n.* whack.

wack·e (wak′ə), *n.* a poorly sorted sandstone containing fragments of rock and minerals in a clayey matrix. Cf. **graywacke.** [1795–1805; < G: a kind of stone]

wacked-out (wakt′out′), *adj. Slang.* whacked-out.

wack·o (wak′ō), *n., pl.* **wack·os,** *adj. Slang.* —*n.* **1.** Also, **wack.** an eccentric, strange, or odd person. —*adj.* **2.** wacky. [1970–75, *Amer.*; see WACKY, -O]

wack·y (wak′ē), *adj.,* **wack·i·er, wack·i·est.** *Slang.* odd or irrational; crazy: *They had some wacky plan for selling more books.* Also, **whacky.** [1935–40; appar. WHACK (n., as in *out of whack*) + -Y[1]] **—wack′i·ly,** *adv.* **—wack′i·ness,** *n.*

Wa·co (wā′kō), *n.* a city in central Texas, on the Brazos River. 101,261.

wad[1] (wod), *n., v.,* **wad·ded, wad·ding.** —*n.* **1.** a small mass, lump, or ball of anything: *a wad of paper; a wad of tobacco.* **2.** a small mass of cotton, wool, or other fibrous or soft material, used for stuffing, padding, packing, etc. **3.** a roll of something, esp. of bank notes. **4.** *Informal.* a comparatively large stock or quantity of something, esp. money: *He's got a healthy wad salted away.* **5.** a plug of cloth, tow, paper, or the like, used to hold the powder or shot, or both, in place in a gun or cartridge. **6.** *Brit. Dial.* a bundle, esp. a small one, of hay, straw, etc. **7. shoot one's wad,** *Informal.* **a.** to spend all one's money: *He shot his wad on a new car.* **b.** to expend all one's energies or resources at one time: *She shot her wad writing her first novel and her second wasn't as good.* **c.** *Slang (vulgar).* (of a man) to have an orgasm. —*v.t.* **8.** to form (material) into a wad. **9.** to roll tightly (often fol. by *up*): *He wadded up his cap and stuck it into his pocket.* **10.** to hold in place by a wad: *They rammed and wadded the shot into their muskets.* **11.** to put a wad into; stuff with a wad. **12.** to fill out with or as if with wadding; stuff; pad: *to wad a quilt; to wad a speech with useless information.* —*v.i.* **13.** to become formed into a wad: *The damp tissues had wadded in his pocket.* [1530–40; < ML *wadda* < Ar *bāṭa'in* lining of a garment, batting; cf. F *ouate,* D *watte,* Sw *vadd*] **—wad′der,** *n.*

wad[2] (wod), *n.* a soft, earthy, black to dark-brown mass of manganese oxide minerals. [1605–15; orig. uncert.]

wad·a·ble (wā′də bəl), *adj.* that can be waded: *a wadable stream.* Also, **wade′a·ble.** [1605–15; WADE + -ABLE]

Wa·dai (wä dī′), *n.* a former independent sultanate of the Sudan, in N central Africa: now part of the Republic of Chad.

wad·ding (wod′ing), *n.* **1.** any fibrous or soft material for stuffing, padding, packing, etc., esp. carded cotton in specially prepared sheets. **2.** material used as wads for guns, cartridges, etc. **3.** *Surg.* any large dressing made of cotton or a similar absorbent material that is used to stanch the flow of blood or dress a wound. **4.** a wad or lump. [1620–30; WAD[1] + -ING[1]]

wad·dle (wod′l), *v.,* **-dled, -dling,** *n.* —*v.i.* **1.** to walk with short steps, swaying or rocking from side to side, as a duck. **2.** to move in any similar, slow, rocking manner; wobble: *The ship waddled into port.* —*n.* **3.** an act or instance of waddling, esp. a waddling gait. [1350–1400; ME; see WADE, -LE; cf. G *watteln*] **—wad′dler,** *n.* **—wad′dling·ly,** *adv.* **—wad′dly,** *adj.*

wad·dy[1] (wod′ē), *n., pl.* **-dies,** *v.,* **-died, -dy·ing.** *Australian.* —*n.* **1.** a heavy wooden war club of the Australian Aborigines. —*v.t.* **2.** to beat or strike with a waddy. [1795–1805; < Dharuk *wa-di* stick]

wad·dy[2] (wod′ē), *n., pl.* **-dies.** *Cowboy Slang, Western U.S.* a cowboy. [1895–1900, *Amer.*; orig. uncert.]

wade (wād), *v.,* **wad·ed, wad·ing,** *n.* —*v.i.* **1.** to walk in water, when partially immersed: *He wasn't swimming, he was wading.* **2.** to play in water: *The children were wading in the pool most of the afternoon.* **3.** to walk through water, snow, sand, or any other substance that impedes free motion or offers resistance to movement: *to wade through the mud.* **4.** to make one's way slowly or laboriously (often fol. by *through*): *to wade through a dull book.* **5.** *Obs.* to go or proceed. —*v.t.* **6.** to pass through or cross by wading; ford: *to wade a stream.* **7. wade in** or **into, a.** to begin energetically. **b.** to attack strongly: *to wade into a thoughtless child; to wade into a mob of rioters.* —*n.* **8.** an act or instance of wading: *We went for a wade in the shallows.* [bef. 900; ME *waden* to go, wade, OE *wadan* to go; c. G *waten,* ON *vatha;* akin to OE *wæd* ford, sea, L *vadum* shoal, ford, *vādere* to go, rush]
—Syn. 4. labor, toil, plod, plow, work.

Wade (wād), *n.* a male given name.

Wade′-Giles′ sys′tem (wād′jīlz′), a system of Romanization of Chinese, devised by Sir Thomas Francis Wade (1818–95) and adapted by Herbert Allen Giles (1845–1935), widely used in representing Chinese words and names in English, esp. before the adoption of pinyin. Also called **Wade′-Giles′.**

wad·er (wā′dər), *n.* **1.** a person or thing that wades. **2.** Also called **wading bird.** any of various large birds having long legs, long necks, and long bills, that are adapted for wading in shallow waters and living on fish, frogs, etc., as the crane, heron, stork, shoebill, ibis, and flamingo. **3.** *Brit.* any of various ground-nesting shorebirds of small to moderate size, as the gull, tern, skimmer, phalarope, and plover. **4. waders,** high, waterproof boots used for wading, as by fishermen, duck hunters, or laborers. [1665–75; WADE + -ER[1]]

wa·di (wä′dē), *n., pl.* **-dis.** (in Arabia, Syria, northern Africa, etc.) **1.** the channel of a watercourse that is dry except during periods of rainfall. **2.** such a stream or watercourse itself. **3.** a valley. Also, **wady.** [1830–40; < Ar *wādī*]

Wa·di Hal·fa (wä′dē häl′fə), a former town in the N Sudan, on the Nile: now under the waters of Lake Nasser, created by the Aswan High Dam in S Egypt.

wad′ing bird′, wader (def. 2). [1840–50]

wad′ing pool′, a small, shallow pool for children to wade and play in. [1920–25]

wad·mal (wod′məl), *n.* a bulky woolen fabric woven of coarse yarn and heavily napped, formerly much used in England and Scandinavia for the manufacture of durable winter garments. Also, **wad′maal, wad′mel, wad′mol, wad′moll.** [1350–1400; ME < ON *vathmāl,* equiv. to *vāth* cloth (c. OE *wæd;* see WEED[2]) + *māl* measure (see PIECEMEAL)]

Wad Me·da·ni (wäd mə dä′nē, med′n ē), a city in E central Sudan, on the Blue Nile. 81,904.

wad·na (wäd′nə), *Scot.* contraction of *would not.* [*wad,* var. of WOULD + NA]

Wads·worth (wodz′wərth), *n.* a city in N Ohio. 15,166.

wa·dy (wä′dē), *n., pl.* **-dies.** wadi.

wae (wā), *n. Scot. and North Eng.* woe.

wae·sucks (wā′suks), *interj. Scot.* alas. Also, **wae·suck** (wā′suk). [1765–75; *wae,* var. of WOE + *suck,* var. of SAKE[1]]

Waf (waf), *n.* a member of the Women in the Air Force, an auxiliary of the U.S. Air Force. [1948; *W(omen in the) A(ir) F(orce)*]

Wafd (wäft), *n.* a nationalist party in Egypt. [< Ar: lit., deputation] **—Wafd′ist,** *n., adj.*

CONCISE PRONUNCIATION KEY: act, cāpe, dâre, pärt; set, ēqual; *if,* īce; ox, ōver, ôrder, oil, bo͝ok, bo͞ot, out; up, ûrge; child; sing; shoe; thin, *th*at; zh as in *treasure.* ə = *a* as in *alone, e* as in *system, i* as in *easily, o* as in *gallop, u* as in *circus;* ˈ as in *fire* (fīˈr), *hour* (ouˈr). l and n can serve as syllabic consonants, as in *cradle* (krād′l), and *button* (but′n). See the full key inside the front cover.

wa·fer (wā′fər), *n.* **1.** a thin, crisp cake or biscuit, often sweetened and flavored. **2.** a thin disk of unleavened bread, used in the Eucharist, as in the Roman Catholic Church. **3.** a thin disk of dried paste, gelatin, adhesive paper, or the like, used for sealing letters, attaching papers, etc. **4.** *Med.* a thin sheet of dry paste or the like, used to enclose a powder to be swallowed. **5.** any small, thin disk, as a washer or piece of insulation. **6.** *Electronics.* a thin slice of semiconductor used as a base material on which single transistors or integrated-circuit components are formed. —*v.t.* **7.** to seal, close, or attach by means of a wafer or wafers: *to wafer a letter.* [1350–1400; ME *wafre* < MD *wafer,* var. of *wafel* WAFFLE[1]] —**wa′fer·like′, wa′fer·y,** *adj.*

wa·fer·board (wā′fər bôrd′, -bōrd′), *n.* a structural material made from wood wafers of controlled thickness and length bonded together with waterproof phenolic resin under extreme heat and pressure. [WAFER + BOARD]

wa·fer-thin (wā′fər thin′), *adj.* very thin: *a wafer-thin slice.*

waff (waf, wäf), *n. Scot. and North Eng.* **1.** a puff or blast of air, wind, etc. **2.** a brief view; glance. [1590–1600; deriv. of dial. *waff* to WAVE]

Waf·fen SS (vä′fən), the militarized formations of the SS, established by Nazi Germany between 1933 and 1945 and including some units of foreign nationals from occupied territories. [< G: military SS]

waf·fle[1] (wof′əl), *n.* **1.** a batter cake with a pattern of deep indentations on each side, formed by the gridlike design on each of the two hinged parts of the metal appliance (**waf′fle i′ron**) in which the cake is baked. —*adj.* **2.** Also, **waf′fled.** having a gridlike or indented lattice shape or design: *a waffle pattern.* [1735–45; < D *wafel*]

waf·fle[2] (wof′əl), *v.,* **-fled, -fling,** *n. Informal.* —*v.i.* **1.** to speak or write equivocally: *to waffle on an important issue.* —*v.t.* **2.** to speak or write equivocally about: *to waffle a campaign promise.* —*n.* **3.** waffling language. [1890–95; orig. dial. (Scots, N England): to wave about, flutter, waver, be hesitant; prob. WAFF + -LE] —**waf′fler,** *n.* —**waf′fling·ly,** *adv.* —**waf′fly,** *adj.*

waf·fle[3] (wof′əl), *v.i.,* **-fled, -fling.** *Brit.* to talk foolishly or without purpose; idle away time talking. [1695–1705; orig. dial. (N England); appar. *waff* to bark, yelp (imit.) + -LE]

waf′fle cloth′, honeycomb (def. 5a).

waf′fle slab′, *Building Trades.* a reinforced-concrete floor and roof construction employing a square grid of deep ribs with coffers in the interstices.

waf·fle·stomp·ers (wof′əl stom′pərz), *n.pl.* ankle boots with ridged soles, used esp. for hiking. [1970–75, *Amer.;* WAFFLE[1] + STOMPER + -S[3]]

waf′fle weave′, a textile weave that produces a textured pattern resembling the surface of a waffle.

W. Afr., 1. West Africa. **2.** West African.

WAFS, Women's Auxiliary Ferrying Squadron. Also, **W.A.F.S.** [1940, *Amer.*]

waft (waft, wäft), *v.t.* **1.** to carry lightly and smoothly through the air or over water: *The gentle breeze wafted the sound of music to our ears.* **2.** to send or convey lightly, as if in flight: *The actress wafted kisses to her admirers in the audience.* **3.** *Obs.* to signal to, summon, or direct by waving. —*v.i.* **4.** to float or be carried, esp. through the air: *The sound wafted on the breeze. The music wafted across the lake.* —*n.* **5.** a sound, odor, etc., faintly perceived: *a waft of perfume.* **6.** a wafting movement; light current or gust: *a waft of air.* **7.** the act of wafting. **8.** Also, **waif.** *Naut.* a signal given by waving a flag. [1535–45; back formation from late ME *waughter* armed escort vessel < D or LG *wachter* watchman; in some senses confused with WAFF] —**waft′er,** *n.*

waft·age (wäf′tij, waf′-), *n.* **1.** the act of wafting. **2.** the state of being wafted. [1550–60; WAFT + -AGE]

waf·ture (wäf′chər, waf′-), *n.* **1.** the act of wafting. **2.** something wafted: *waftures of incense.* [1595–1605; WAFT + -URE]

wag (wag), *v.,* **wagged, wag·ging,** *n.* —*v.t.* **1.** to move from side to side, forward and backward, or up and down, esp. rapidly and repeatedly: *a dog wagging its tail.* **2.** to move (the tongue), as in idle or indiscreet chatter. **3.** to shake (a finger) at someone, as in reproach. **4.** to move or nod (the head). —*v.i.* **5.** to be moved from side to side or one way and the other, esp. rapidly and repeatedly, as the head or the tail. **6.** to move constantly, esp. in idle or indiscreet chatter: *Her behavior caused local tongues to wag.* **7.** to get along; travel; proceed: *Let the world wag how it will.* **8.** to totter or sway. **9.** *Brit. Slang.* to play truant; play hooky. —*n.* **10.** the act of wagging: *a friendly wag of the tail.* **11.** a person given to droll, roguish, or mischievous humor; wit. [1175–1225; ME *waggen* < ON *vaga* to sway, or *vagga* cradle] —**wag′ger,** *n.*

wage (wāj), *n., v.,* **waged, wag·ing.** —*n.* **1.** Often, **wages.** money that is paid or received for work or services, as by the hour, day, or week. Cf. **living wage, minimum wage. 2.** Usually, **wages.** *Econ.* the share of the products of industry received by labor for its work (as distinct from the share going to capital). **3.** Usually, **wages.** (*used with a singular or plural v.*) recompense or return: *The wages of sin is death.* **4.** *Obs.* a pledge or security. —*v.t.* **5.** to carry on (a battle, war, conflict, argument, etc.): *to wage war against a nation.* **6.** *Chiefly Brit. Dial.* to hire. **7.** *Obs.* **a.** to stake or wager. **b.** to pledge. —*v.i.* **8.** *Obs.* to contend; struggle. [1275–1325; (n.) ME: pledge, security < AF; OF *guage* GAGE[1] < VL **wadium* < Gmc (see WED); (v.) ME *wagen* to pledge < AF *wagier;* OF *guagier* < VL **wadiāre,* deriv. of **wadium*] —**wage′less,** *adj.* —**wage′less·ness,** *n.*
—**Syn. 1.** earnings, emolument, compensation, remuneration. See **pay**[1]. **5.** undertake, prosecute.

wage′ earn′er, a person who works for wages, esp. a laborer. [1880–85]

wage′-push infla′tion (wāj′po͝osh′), an inflationary trend caused by wage increases that in turn cause rises in production costs and prices.

wa·ger (wā′jər), *n.* **1.** something risked or staked on an uncertain event; bet: *to place a wager on a soccer match.* **2.** the act of betting. **3.** the subject or terms of a bet. **4.** *Early Eng. Law.* a pledge to make good one's cause by the supporting oaths of others or by battle. —*v.t.* **5.** to risk (something) on the outcome of a contest or any uncertain event or matter; bet. **6.** *Hist.* to pledge oneself to (battle) for the decision of a cause. —*v.i.* **7.** to make or offer a wager; bet. [1275–1325; ME *wajour, wager* solemn pledge < AF *wageure,* equiv. to *wage(r)* to pledge (see WAGE) + *-ure* -URE] —**wa′ger·er,** *n.*
—**Syn. 1.** stake, hazard, risk. **5.** stake, venture.

wage′ scale′, 1. a schedule of wages paid workers performing related tasks in an industry or shop. **2.** a particular employer's wage schedule. [1900–05]

wage′ slave′, a person who works for a wage, esp. with total and immediate dependency on the income derived from such labor. [1885–90] —**wage′ slav′ery.**

wage·work·er (wāj′wûr′kər), *n.* a member of the laboring class; wage earner. [1875–80, *Amer.;* WAGE + WORKER] —**wage′work′ing,** *adj., n.*

Wag·ga Wag·ga (wog′ə wog′ə), a city in central New South Wales, in SE Australia. 32,510.

wag·ger·y (wag′ə rē), *n., pl.* **-ger·ies. 1.** the action, spirit, or language of a wag; roguish or droll humor: *the waggery of Shakespeare's clowns.* **2.** a waggish act; jest or joke. [1585–95; WAG + -ERY]

wag·gish (wag′ish), *adj.* **1.** like a wag; roguish in merriment and good humor; jocular: *Fielding and Sterne are waggish writers.* **2.** characteristic of or befitting a wag: *waggish humor.* [1580–90; WAG + -ISH[1]] —**wag′gish·ly,** *adv.* —**wag′gish·ness,** *n.*
—**Syn. 1.** jocund, mischievous, merry, jocose, droll, comical, funny. See **humorous.**

wag·gle (wag′əl), *v.,* **-gled, -gling,** *n.* —*v.i.* **1.** to wobble or shake, esp. while in motion: *The ball waggled slowly to a stop. The leaves of the tree waggled in the wind.* —*v.t.* **2.** to move up and down or from side to side in a short, rapid manner; wag: *to waggle one's head.* **3.** *Golf.* to make a waggle with (a golf club). —*n.* **4.** a waggling motion. **5.** *Golf.* a swinging movement made with a golf club to and fro over the ball prior to a stroke. [1585–95; WAG + -LE] —**wag′gling·ly,** *adv.*

wag′gle dance′, a series of patterned movements performed by a scouting bee, communicating to other bees of the colony the direction and distance of a food source or hive site.

wag·gly (wag′lē), *adj.* waggling; unsteady. [1890–95; WAGGLE + -Y[1]]

wag·gon (wag′ən), *n., v.t., v.i. Chiefly Brit.* wagon.

Wag·ner (wag′nər *for 1, 4, 5;* väg′nər *or, Ger.,* väg′nᴇʀ *for 2, 3*), *n.* **1. Ho·nus** (hō′nəs), (*John Peter*), 1874–1955, U.S. baseball player. **2. Ot·to** (ot′ō; *Ger.* ôt′ō), 1841–1918, Austrian architect. **3. Rich·ard** (rich′ərd; *Ger.* ʀɪᴋʜ′ärt), 1813–83, German composer. **4. Robert F(erdinand),** 1877–1953, U.S. politician. **5.** his son, **Robert F(erdinand), Jr.,** 1910–91, U.S. politician: mayor of New York City 1954–65.

Wag′ner Act′ (wag′nər). See **National Labor Relations Act.** [named after the legislation's sponsor, Robert F. WAGNER]

Wag·ne·ri·an (väg nēr′ē ən), *adj.* **1.** of, pertaining to, or characteristic of Richard Wagner or his works: *Wagnerian grandeur; a Wagnerian soprano.* —*n.* **2.** Also, **Wag·ner·ite** (väg′nə rīt′). a follower or admirer of the music or theories of Richard Wagner. [1870–75; WAGNER + -IAN]

Wag·ner-Jau·regg (väg′nᴇʀ you′rek), *n.* **Ju·li·us** (yo͞o′lē o͞os′), 1857–1940, Austrian psychiatrist: Nobel prize for medicine 1927.

wag·on (wag′ən), *n.* **1.** any of various kinds of four-wheeled vehicles designed to be pulled or having its own motor and ranging from a child's toy to a commercial vehicle for the transport of heavy loads, delivery, etc. **2.** *Informal.* See **station wagon. 3.** a police van for transporting prisoners; patrol wagon: *The fight broke up before the wagon arrived.* **4.** (*cap.*) *Astron.* Charles's Wain. See **Big Dipper. 5.** *Brit.* a railway freight car or flatcar. **6.** a baby carriage. **7.** *Archaic.* a chariot. **8. circle the wagons.** See **circle** (def. 21). **9. fix someone's wagon,** *Slang.* to get even with or punish someone: *He'd better mind his own business or I'll really fix his wagon.* **10. hitch one's wagon to a star,** to have a high ambition, ideal, or purpose: *It is better to hitch one's wagon to a star than to wander aimlessly through life.* **11. off the wagon,** *Slang.* again drinking alcoholic beverages after a period of abstinence. **12. on the wagon,** *Slang.* abstaining from alcoholic beverages. Also, **on the water wagon;** *Brit.,* **on the water cart.** —*v.t.* **13.** to transport or convey by wagon. —*v.i.* **14.** to proceed or haul goods by wagon: *It was strenuous to wagon up the hill.* Also, *esp. Brit.,* **waggon.** [1505–15; < D *wagen;* c. OE *wægn* WAIN] —**wag′on·less,** *adj.*
—**Syn. 1.** cart, van, wain, truck, dray, lorry.

wag·on·age (wag′ə nij), *n. Archaic.* **1.** transportation or conveyance by wagon. **2.** money paid for this. **3.** a group of wagons; wagon train. [1600–10; WAGON + -AGE]

wag′on boss′, a man in charge of a wagon train. Also called **wagon master.** [1870–75, *Amer.*]

wag·on·er (wag′ə nər), *n.* **1.** a person who drives a wagon. **2.** (*cap.*) *Astron.* the northern constellation Auriga. **3.** *Obs.* a charioteer. [1535–45; WAGON + -ER[1]]

wag·on·ette (wag′ə net′), *n.* a light, four-wheeled carriage, with or without a top, having a crosswise seat in front and two lengthwise seats facing each other at the back. [1855–60; WAGON + -ETTE]

wag·on-head·ed (wag′ən hed′id), *adj. Archit.* of the form of a round arch or a semicylinder, like the cover of a wagon when stretched over the bows, as a ceiling or roof. [1815–25]

wag′on job′ber. See **truck jobber.**

wa·gon-lit (*Fr.* va gôɴ lē′), *n., pl.* **wa·gons-lits** (va gôɴ lē′). (in continental European usage) a railroad sleeping car. [1880–85; < F, equiv. to *wagon* railway coach (< E) + *lit* bed (< L *lectus*)]

wag·on·load (wag′ən lōd′), *n.* the load carried by a wagon. [1715–25; WAGON + LOAD]

wag′on mas′ter, 1. See **wagon boss. 2.** Also, **wag′on·mas′ter.** a person hired or chosen to lead and guide a caravan of recreational vehicles, as campers, on a trip. **3.** *Facetious.* any leader, chief, commander, or the like: *the wagon master of the bill now before Congress.* [1635–45]

wag′on roof′. See **barrel vault.** [1865–70]

wag′on seat′, *Furniture.* a plain, unupholstered settee, usually with a slat back, for use either indoors or in a wagon. Also called **rumble seat.** [1850–55, *Amer.*]

wag′on sol′dier, *Mil. Slang.* a field-artillery soldier. [1865–70]

wag′on train′, *U.S. Hist.* a train of wagons and horses, as one carrying military supplies or transporting settlers in the westward migration. [1800–10]

wag′on vault′. See **barrel vault.** [1825–35]

Wa·gram (vä′gräm), *n.* a village in NE Austria: Napoleon defeated the Austrians here in 1809.

wag·tail (wag′tāl′), *n.* **1.** any of numerous small, chiefly Old World birds of the family Motacillidae, having a slender body with a long, narrow tail that is habitually wagged up and down. **2.** any of several similar birds, as the water thrushes of the genus *Seiurus.* [1500–10; WAG + TAIL[1]]

Wah·ha·bi (wə hä′bē, wä-), *n., pl.* **-bis.** *Islam.* a follower of ʻAbd al-Wahhab (1703–1792), who stringently opposed all practices not sanctioned by the Koran. The Wahhabis, founded in the 18th century, are the most conservative Muslim group and are today found mainly in Saudi Arabia. Also, **Wa·ha′bi, Wah·ha′bee, Wah·ha·bite, Wa·ha·bite** (wə hä′bīt, wä-). [1800–10; < Ar, equiv. to ʻAbd al-*Wahhab* + *-ī* suffix of appurtenance]

Wah·ha·bism (wə hä′biz əm, wä-), *n.* the group of doctrines or practices of the Wahhabis. Also, **Wah·ha·bi·ism** (wə hä′bē iz′əm, wä-), **Wa·ha′bism.** [1820–30; WAHHAB(I) + -ISM]

Wa·hi·a·wa (wä′hē ə wä′), *n.* a city on central Oahu, in central Hawaii. 41,562.

wa·hi·ne (wä hē′nē, -nā), *n., pl.* **-ne. 1.** (in Hawaii and Polynesia) a girl or young woman. **2.** *Slang.* a young woman surfer. [1835–45; < Polynesian]

wa·hoo[1] (wä ho͞o′, wä′ho͞o), *n., pl.* **-hoos.** any of various American shrubs or small trees, as the winged elm, *Ulmus alata,* or a linden, *Tilia heterophylla.* [1760–70, *Amer.;* orig. uncert.]

wa·hoo[2] (wä ho͞o′, wä′ho͞o), *n., pl.* **-hoos.** a shrub or small tree, *Euonymus atropurpurea,* of North America, having finely serrated, elliptical leaves and pendulous capsules that in opening reveal the bright-scarlet arils of the seeds. Also called **burning bush.** [1855–60, *Amer.;* < Dakota *waⁿhu,* equiv. to *waⁿ-* arrow + *hu* wood, shaft]

wa·hoo[3] (wä ho͞o′, wä′ho͞o), *n., pl.* **-hoos,** (*esp. collectively*) **-hoo.** a large, swift mackerel, *Acanthocybium solanderi,* widespread in warm seas, of a steel blue to greenish blue above and silver below, often leaping from the water and occasionally schooling in great numbers: valued as a food and game fish. Also called **peto.** [1905–10; orig. uncert.]

Wah·pe·ku·te (wä′pə ko͞o′tē), *n., pl.* **-tes,** (*esp. collectively*) **-te.** a member of a North American Indian people belonging to the Santee branch of the Dakota.

Wah·pe·ton (wô′pi tn), *n., pl.* **-tons,** (*esp. collectively*) **-ton.** a member of a North American Indian people belonging to the Santee branch of the Dakota.

wah-wah (wä′wä′), *adj.* **1.** producing a muted, bawling sound like that of a trumpet with the hand moved momentarily over the bell: *a wah-wah effect on a synthesizer; a guitar with a wah-wah pedal.* —*n.* **2.** a sound or effect like the muted sound of a trumpet, esp. in music. **3.** an electronic device or attachment to produce such a sound, often used with an electric guitar. Also, **wa-wa.** [1925–30; imit.]

Wai·chow (wī′jō′), *n. Older Spelling.* Huizhou.

waif (wāf), *n.* **1.** a person, esp. a child, who has no home or friends. **2.** something found, esp. a stray animal, whose owner is not known. **3.** a stray item or article: *to gather waifs of gossip.* **4.** *Naut.* waft (def. 8). [1350–1400; ME < AF, orig. lost, stray, unclaimed (cf. OF *guaif* stray beast) < Scand; cf. ON *veif* movement to and fro; see WAIVE]

Wai·ki·ki (wī′kē kē′, wī′kē kē′), *n.* a beach and resort area on SE Oahu, in central Hawaii; part of Honolulu.

wail (wāl), *v.i.* **1.** to utter a prolonged, inarticulate, mournful cry, usually high-pitched or clear-sounding, as in grief or suffering: *to wail with pain.* **2.** to make mournful sounds, as music or the wind. **3.** to lament or mourn bitterly. **4.** *Jazz.* to perform exceptionally well. **5.** *Slang.* to express emotion musically or verbally in an exciting, satisfying way. —*v.t.* **6.** to express deep sorrow for; mourn; lament; bewail: *to wail the dead; to wail one's fate.* **7.** to express in wailing; cry or say in lamentation: *to wail one's grief.* —*n.* **8.** the act of wailing. **9.** a wailing cry, as of grief, pain, or despair. **10.** any similar mournful sound: *the wail of an old tune.* [1300–50; ME *weile* (v. and n.), perh. deriv. of OE *weilā(wei)* WELL-

AWAY; cf. OE *wǣlan* to torment, ON *wǣla* to wail] **—wail′er,** *n.* **—wail′ing·ly,** *adv.*

wail·ful (wāl′fəl), *adj.* mournful; plaintive. [1535–45; WAIL + -FUL] **—wail′ful·ly,** *adv.*

Wail′ing Wall′. See **Western Wall.**

wail·some (wāl′səm), *adj. Archaic.* wailful. [1560–70; WAIL + -SOME[1]]

Wai·lu·ku (wī lo͞o′ko͞o), *n.* a town on NW Maui, in central Hawaii. 10,674.

wain (wān), *n.* **1.** (*cap.*) *Astron.* Charles's Wain. See **Big Dipper. 2.** a farm wagon or cart. [bef. 900; ME; OE *wægn, wǣn,* c. D *wagen,* G *Wagen.* See WEIGH[1]]

wain·scot (wān′skət, -skot, -skōt), *n., v.,* **-scot·ed, -scot·ing** or (*esp. Brit.*) **-scot·ted, -scot·ting.** **—*n.* 1.** wood, esp. oak and usually in the form of paneling, for lining interior walls. **2.** the lining itself, esp. as covering the lower portion of a wall. **3.** a dado, esp. of wood, lining an interior wall. **4.** *Brit.* oak of superior quality and cut, imported from the Baltic countries for fine woodwork. **—*v.t.* 5.** to line the walls of (a room, hallway, etc.) with or as if with woodwork: *a room wainscoted in oak.* [1325–75; ME < MLG or MD *wagenschot,* equiv. to *wagen* WAIN + *schot* (< ?)]

wain′scot chair′, *Eng. Furniture.* an armchair of the 17th century, made of oak and having a solid paneled back.

wain·scot·ing (wān′skō ting, -skot ing, -skə ting), *n.* **1.** paneling or woodwork with which rooms, hallways, etc., are wainscoted. **2.** wainscots collectively. Also, *esp. Brit.,* **wain·scot·ting** (wān′skə ting, -skot ing). [1570–80; WAINSCOT + -ING[1]]

wain·wright (wān′rīt′), *n.* a wagon maker. [bef. 1000; ME; OE *wǣnwyrhta;* see WAIN, WRIGHT]

Wain·wright (wān′rīt′), *n.* **Jonathan May·hew** (mā′hyo͞o), 1883–1953, U.S. general.

Wai·pa·hu (wī pä′ho͞o), *n.* a city in Hawaii, on S Oahu. 29,139.

WAIS (wās), *n.* Wechsler Adult Intelligence Scale. See under **Wechsler Scales.**

WAIS-R (wās′är′), *n.* Wechsler Adult Intelligence Scale—Revised. See under **Wechsler Scales.**

waist (wāst), *n.* **1.** the part of the body in humans between the ribs and the hips, usually the narrowest part of the torso. **2.** the part of a garment covering this part of the body. **3.** blouse (def. 1). **4.** the part of a one-piece garment covering the body from the neck or shoulders more or less to the waistline, esp. this part of a woman's or child's garment. **5.** a child's undergarment to which other articles of apparel may be attached. **6.** the part of an object, esp. a central or middle part, that resembles or is analogous to the human waist: *the waist of a violin.* **7.** *Naut.* the central part of a ship; that part of the deck between the forecastle and the quarterdeck. **8.** the constricted portion of the abdomen of certain insects, as a wasp. [1300–50; ME *wast,* apocopated var. of *wastum,* OE *wæstm* growth, form, figure; akin to WAX[2]] **—waist′less,** *adj.*

waist·band (wāst′band′, -bənd), *n.* a band encircling the waist, esp. as a part of a skirt or pair of trousers. [1575–85; WAIST + BAND[2]]

waist·cloth (wāst′klôth′, -kloth′), *n., pl.* **-cloths** (-klôthz′, -klothz′, -klôths′, -kloths′). a loincloth. [1605–15; WAIST + CLOTH]

waist·coat (wes′kət, wāst′kōt′), *n.* **1.** *Chiefly Brit.* vest (def. 1). **2.** an 18th-century garment for women that is similar to a man's vest, usually worn with a riding habit. **3.** a man's body garment, often quilted and embroidered and having sleeves, worn under the doublet in the 16th and 17th centuries. [1510–20; WAIST + COAT] **—waist′coat·ed,** *adj.*

waist·coat·ing (wes′kə ting, wāst′kō′ting), *n.* a fabric for making waistcoats. [1800–10; WAISTCOAT + -ING[1]]

waist-deep (wāst′dēp′), *adj.* being at or rising to the level of the waist. [1755–65]

waist·ed (wā′stid), *adj.* **1.** having a waist of a specified kind (usually used in combination): *long-waisted; high-waisted.* **2.** (of an object, a container, etc.) shaped like a waist; having concave sides: *a waisted vase.* [1575–85; WAIST + -ED[3]]

waist-high (wāst′hī′), *adj.* extending as high as the waist: *a waist-high hedge.* [1590–1600]

waist·line (wāst′līn′), *n.* **1.** the circumference of the body at the waist: *exercises to reduce the waistline.* **2.** the part of a garment that lies at or near the natural waistline, as the seam where the skirt and bodice of a dress are joined. **3.** an imaginary line encircling the waist. [1895–1900; WAIST + LINE[1]]

wait (wāt), *v.i.* **1.** to remain inactive or in a state of repose, as until something expected happens (often fol. by *for, till,* or *until*): *to wait for the bus to arrive.* **2.** (of things) to be available or in readiness: *A letter is waiting for you.* **3.** to remain neglected for a time: *a matter that can wait.* **4.** to postpone or delay something or to be postponed or delayed: *We waited a week and then bought the house. Your vacation will have to wait until next month.* **5.** to look forward to eagerly: *I'm just waiting for the day somebody knocks him down.* **—*v.t.* 6.** to continue as one is in expectation of; await: *to wait one's turn at a telephone booth.* **7.** to postpone or delay in expectation: *Don't wait supper for me.* **8.** *Archaic.* (of things) to be in readiness for; be reserved for; await: *Glory waits thee.* **9.** *Archaic.* to attend upon or escort, esp. as a sign of respect. **10. wait on, a.** to perform the duties of an attendant or servant for. **b.** to supply the wants of a person, as serving a meal or serving a customer in a store. **c.** to call upon or visit (a person, esp. a superior): *to wait on Her Majesty at the palace.* **d.** *Falconry.* (of a hawk) to soar over ground until prey appears. **e.** *Chiefly Midland and Southern U.S.* to wait for (a person); await. **f.** Also, **wait upon.** to await (an event). **11. wait table.** See **table** (def. 21). **12. wait up, a.** to postpone going to bed to await someone's arrival. **b.** *Informal.* to halt and wait for another to join one, as in running or walking: *Wait up, I can't walk so fast.* **—*n.* 13.** an act or instance of waiting or awaiting; delay; halt: *a wait at the border.* **14.** a period or interval of waiting: *There will be a long wait between trains.* **15.** *Theat.* **a.** the time between two acts, scenes, or the like. **b.** See **stage wait. 16.** *Brit.* **a. waits,** (formerly) a band of musicians employed by a city or town to play music in parades, for official functions, etc. **b.** a street musician, esp. a singer. **c.** one of a band of carolers. **d.** a piece sung by carolers, esp. a Christmas carol. **17.** *Obs.* a watchman. **18. lie in wait,** to wait in ambush: *The army lay in wait in the forest.* [1150–1200; (v.) early ME *waiten* < AF *waitier;* OF *guaitier* < Gmc; c. OHG *wahtēn* to watch, deriv. of *wahta* a watch (see WAKE[1]); (n.) late ME < AF deriv. of *waitier*]
—Syn. 1. await, linger, abide, delay. WAIT, TARRY imply pausing to linger and thereby putting off further activity until later. WAIT usually implies staying for a limited time and for a definite purpose, that is, for something expected: *to wait for a train.* TARRY is a somewhat archaic word for WAIT, but it suggests lingering, perhaps aimlessly delaying, or pausing (briefly) in a journey: *to tarry on the way home; to tarry overnight at an inn.*
—Usage. 10e, f. Sometimes considered objectionable in standard usage, the idiom WAIT ON meaning "to wait for, to await (a person)" is largely confined to speech or written representations of speech. It is most common in the Midland and Southern United States: *Let's not wait on Rachel, she's always late.* WAIT ON or UPON (an event) does not have a regional pattern and occurs in a wide variety of contexts: *We will wait on* (or *upon*) *his answer and make our decision then. The completion of the merger waits upon news of a drop in interest rates.*

wait-a-bit (wāt′ə bit′), *n.* any of various plants bearing thorns or prickly appendages, as the grapple plant or the greenbrier. [1775–85; trans. of Afrik *wag-'n-bietjie* < D *wacht een beetje*]

Waite (wāt), *n.* **Morrison Rem·ick** (rem′ik), 1816–88, U.S. jurist: Chief Justice of the U.S. 1874–88.

wait·er (wā′tər), *n.* **1.** a person, esp. a man, who waits on tables, as in a restaurant. **2.** a tray for carrying dishes, a tea service, etc.; salver. **3.** a person who waits or awaits. **4.** *Obs.* an attendant. **—*v.i.* 5.** to work or serve as a waiter: *to waiter in a restaurant.* [1350–1400; ME; see WAIT, -ER[1]] **—wait′er·less,** *adj.*
—Usage. See **-person.**

wait·er·ing (wā′tər ing), *n.* the occupation of a waiter. [1860–65; WAITER + -ING[1]]

wait·ing (wā′ting), *n.* **1.** a period of waiting; pause, interval, or delay. **2. in waiting,** in attendance, as upon a royal personage. **—*adj.* 3.** serving or being in attendance: *waiting man; waiting maid; waiting woman.* [1150–1200; ME (n.); see WAIT, -ING[1], -ING[2]] **—wait′ing·ly,** *adv.*

Wait′ing for Go·dot′ (gə dō′), a play (1952) by Samuel Beckett.

wait′ing game′, a stratagem in which action on a matter is reserved for or postponed to a later time, allowing one to wait for a more advantageous time to act or to see what develops in the meantime. [1885–90]

wait′ing list′, a list of persons waiting, as for reservations, appointments, living accommodations, or admission to a school. Also, **waitlist.** [1895–1900]

wait′ing pe′riod, 1. a specified delay, required by law, between officially stating an intention and acting on it, as between securing a marriage license and getting married. **2.** *Insurance.* the required delay between the date of inception of a claim and the date on which the indemnity becomes payable, as in workmen's compensation insurance or unemployment insurance.

wait′ing room′, a room for the use of persons waiting, as in a railroad station or a physician's office. [1675–85]

wait·list (wāt′list′), *v.t.* **1.** to place on a waiting list: *All they could do was to waitlist us for the afternoon flight.* **—*n.* 2.** See **waiting list.** [WAIT + LIST[1]]

wait·per·son (wāt′pûr′sən), *n.* a waiter or waitress. [WAIT(ER) or WAIT(RESS) + -PERSON]
—Usage. See **-person.**

wait·ress (wā′tris), *n.* **1.** a woman who waits on tables, as in a restaurant. **—*v.i.* 2.** to work or serve as a waitress: *She waitressed in a restaurant to help pay her way through college.* [1580–90; WAIT(E)R + -ESS]
—Usage. See **-ess, -person.**

wait·ress·ing (wā′trə sing), *n.* the occupation of a waitress. [1935–40; WAITRESS + -ING[1]]

wait·ron (wā′tron, -trən), *n.* a person of either sex who waits on tables; waiter or waitress. [1980–85, *Amer.;* WAIT(ER) or WAITR(ESS), appar. formed on analogy of PATRON]

waive (wāv), *v.t.,* **waived, waiv·ing. 1.** to refrain from claiming or insisting on; give up; forgo: *to waive one's right; to waive honors.* **2.** *Law.* to relinquish (a known right, interest, etc.) intentionally. **3.** to put aside for the time; defer; postpone; dispense with: *to waive formalities.* **4.** to put aside or dismiss from consideration or discussion: *waiving my attempts to explain.* [1250–1300; ME *weyven* < AF *weyver* to make a WAIF (of someone) by forsaking or outlawing (him or her)]
—Syn. 1. resign, renounce, surrender, remit.

waiv·er (wā′vər), *n. Law.* **1.** an intentional relinquishment of some right, interest, or the like. **2.** an express or written statement of such relinquishment. [1620–30; < AF *weyver,* n. use of *weyver* to WAIVE; see -ER[3]]

waiv′er of pre′mium, *Insurance.* a provision in a policy establishing specific conditions under which the policy will be kept in force without the policyholder's being required to continue to pay premiums.

wa·ka (wä′kə), *n., pl.* **-ka, -kas. 1.** *Pros.* tanka. **2.** poetry written in Japanese, as distinct from poetry written in Chinese by a Japanese writer, or poetry in other languages. [1875–80; < Japn: lit., Japanese song < MChin, equiv. to Chin *hé* harmony + *gē* song]

Wa·ka·ma·tsu (*Japn.* wä′kä mä′tso͞o), *n.* See under **Kitakyushu.**

Wa·kash·an (wä kash′ən, wô′kə shan′), *n.* a family of American Indian languages spoken in British Columbia and Washington and including esp. Kwakiutl and Nootka. [1895; coined by J.W. Powell from *Wakash,* used as the name of a Nootka subgroup but orig. a misapplication of Nootka *wa·ka·š* bravo!; see -AN]

Wa·ka·ya·ma (wä′kä yä′mä), *n.* a seaport on S Honshu, in S Japan. 401,462.

wake[1] (wāk), *v.,* **waked** or **woke, waked** or **wok·en, wak·ing,** *n.* **—*v.i.* 1.** to become roused from sleep; awake; awaken; waken (often fol. by *up*). **2.** to become roused from a tranquil or inactive state; awaken; waken: *to wake from one's daydreams.* **3.** to become cognizant or aware of something; awaken; waken: *to wake to the true situation.* **4.** to be or continue to be awake: *Whether I wake or sleep, I think of you.* **5.** to remain awake for some purpose, duty, etc.: *I will wake until you return.* **6.** to hold a wake over a corpse. **7.** to keep watch or vigil. **—*v.t.* 8.** to rouse from sleep; awake; awaken; waken (often fol. by *up*): *Don't wake me for breakfast. Wake me up at six o'clock.* **9.** to rouse from lethargy, apathy, ignorance, etc. (often fol. by *up*): *The tragedy woke us up to the need for safety precautions.* **10.** to hold a wake for or over (a dead person). **11.** to keep watch or vigil over. **—*n.* 12.** a watching, or a watch kept, esp. for some solemn or ceremonial purpose. **13.** a watch or vigil by the body of a dead person before burial, sometimes accompanied by feasting or merrymaking. **14.** a local annual festival in England, formerly held in honor of the patron saint or on the anniversary of the dedication of a church but now usually having little or no religious significance. **15.** the state of being awake: *between sleep and wake.* [bef. 900; (v.) in sense "to become awake" continuing ME *waken,* OE **wacan* (found only in past tense *wōc* and the compounds *onwacan, āwacan* to become awake; see AWAKE (v.)); in sense "to be awake" continuing ME *waken,* OE *wacian* (c. OFris *wakia,* OS *wakōn,* ON *vaka,* Goth *wakan*); in sense "to rouse from sleep" continuing ME *waken,* r. ME *wecchen,* OE *weccan,* prob. altered by assoc. with the other senses and with the *k* of ON *vaka;* (n.) ME: state of wakefulness, vigil (late ME: vigil over a dead body), prob. continuing OE **wacu* (found only in *nihtwacu* night-watch); all ult. < Gmc **wak-* be lively; akin to WATCH, VEGETABLE, VIGIL] **—wak′er,** *n.*
—Syn. 8. arouse. **9.** stimulate, activate, animate, kindle, provoke. **—Ant. 1.** sleep.

wake[2] (wāk), *n.* **1.** the track of waves left by a ship or other object moving through the water: *The wake of the boat glowed in the darkness.* **2.** the path or course of anything that has passed or preceded: *The tornado left ruin in its wake.* **3. in the wake of, a.** as a result of: *An investigation followed in the wake of the scandal.* **b.** succeeding; following: *in the wake of the pioneers.* [1540–50; < MLG, D *wake,* or ON *vǫk* hole in the ice]

Wake·field (wāk′fēld′), *n.* **1.** a city in West Yorkshire, in N England: battle 1460. 305,500. **2.** a town in E Massachusetts, near Boston. 24,895. **3.** an estate in E Virginia, on the Potomac River: birthplace of George Washington; restored as a national monument in 1932.

wake·ful (wāk′fəl), *adj.* **1.** unable to sleep; not sleeping; indisposed to sleep: *Excitement made the children wakeful.* **2.** characterized by absence of sleep: *a wakeful night.* **3.** watchful; alert; vigilant: *a wakeful foe.* [1540–50; WAKE[1] + -FUL] **—wake′ful·ly,** *adv.* **—wake′ful·ness,** *n.*
—Syn. 1. sleepless, awake, insomniac, restless. **3.** wary, observant. **—Ant. 1.** asleep, sleeping. **2.** sleepful.

Wake′ Is′land, an island in the N Pacific, belonging to the U.S.: air base. 3 sq. mi. (8 sq. km).

wake·less (wāk′lis), *adj.* (of sleep) sound; deep: *He lay in wakeless sleep.* [1815–25; WAKE[1] + -LESS]

wak·en (wā′kən), *v.t.* **1.** to rouse from sleep; wake; awake; awaken. **2.** to rouse from inactivity; stir up or excite; arouse; awaken: *to waken the reader's interest.* **—*v.i.* 3.** to wake, or become awake; awaken. [bef. 900; ME *waknen,* OE *wæcnan;* c. ON *vakna;* akin to WAKE[1]; see -EN[1]] **—wak′en·er,** *n.*

wak·en·ing (wā′kə ning), *n.* **1.** awakening. **2.** *Scots Law.* a revival of a legal action or the process by which this is done. [1350–1400; ME; see WAKEN, -ING[1]]

wake·rife (wāk′rīf′), *adj. Scot. and North Eng.* wakeful. [1470–80; WAKE[1] + RIFE] **—wake′rife′ness,** *n.*

wake-rob·in (wāk′rob′in), *n.* **1.** the cuckoopint. **2.** any of various plants belonging to the genus *Trillium,* native to eastern North America, of the lily family, as *T. erectum,* having rank-smelling purple, yellow, or white flowers. [1520–30]

wake-up (wāk′up′), *n.* **1.** an act or instance of waking up. **2.** an act or instance of being awakened: *I asked the hotel desk for a wake-up at 6.* **3.** a time of awaking or being awakened: *I'll need a 5 o'clock wake-up to make the early plane.* **4.** flicker[2]. **—*adj.* 5.** serving to wake one from sleep: *Leave a wake-up call at the front desk.* [1835–45; n., adj. use of v. phrase *wake up*]

Waks·man (waks′mən), *n.* **Sel·man Abraham** (sel′mən), 1888–1973, U.S. microbiologist: Nobel prize for medicine 1952.

Wal., 1. Wallachian. **2.** Walloon.

Wa·la·chi·a (wo lā′kē ə), *n.* Wallachia.

Wal·ays (wol′is), *n.* **Sir William.** See **Wallace, Sir William.**

Wał·brzych (väl′bzhiKH), *n.* a city in SW Poland, in Silesia. 128,000. German, **Waldenburg.**

Wal·bur·ga (väl bo͝or′gä), *n.* Walpurgis.

CONCISE PRONUNCIATION KEY: act, cāpe, dâre, pärt; set, ēqual; *if,* ice; ox, ōver, ôrder, oil, bo͝ok, bo͞ot, out; up, ûrge; child; sing; shoe; thin, *th*at; zh as in *treasure.* ə = *a* as in *alone, e* as in *system, i* as in *easily, o* as in *gallop, u* as in *circus;* ᵊ as in *fire* (fīᵊr), *hour* (ouᵊr). l and n can serve as syllabic consonants, as in *cradle* (krād′l), and *button* (but′n). See the full key inside the front cover.

Wal·che·ren (wäl′KHə rən, -rə, wäl′gə-), *n.* an island in SW Netherlands: part of Zeeland province. 82 sq. mi. (212 sq. km).

Wal·cott (wôl′kət, -kot), *n.* **Joe** (*Arnold Cream*) (*"Jersey Joe"*), born 1914, U.S. boxer: world heavyweight champion 1951–52.

Wald (wôld), *n.* **1. George,** born 1906, U.S. biochemist: Nobel prize for medicine 1967. **2. Lillian,** 1867–1940, U.S. social worker.

Wal·de·mar I (väl′də mär′), (*"the Great"*) 1131–82, king of Denmark 1157–82. Also, **Valdemar I.**

Wal·den (wôl′dən), *n.* a town in SE Ontario, in S Canada. 10,139.

Wal·den·burg (väl′dən bŏŏrk′), *n.* German name of **Wałbrzych.**

Wal′den, or Life′ in the Woods′ (wôl′dən), a book of philosophical observations (1854) by Thoreau.

Wal′den Pond′, a pond in NE Massachusetts, near Concord: site of Thoreau's cottage and inspiration for his book *Walden, or Life in the Woods.*

Wal·den·ses (wôl den′sēz, wol-), *n.* (*used with a singular v.*) a Christian sect that arose after 1170 in southern France, under the leadership of Pierre Waldo, a merchant of Lyons, and joined the Reformation movement in the 16th century. Also called **Vaudois.** [pl. of ME *Waldensis* < ML, after Pierre WALDO; see -ENSIS] —**Wal·den·si·an** (wôl den′sē ən, -shən, wol-), *adj., n.*

wald·glas (vält′gläs′), *n.* common medieval and Renaissance glassware, made from unrefined materials and characterized by a green color. [< G: lit., forest glass (so called from its being produced by glassmakers of the German forests)]

wald·grave (wôld′grāv), *n.* (in the Holy Roman Empire) an officer having jurisdiction over a royal forest. [< G *Waldgraf* (*Wald* forest + *Graf* count)]

Wald·heim (wôld′hīm′; *Ger.* vält′hīm′), *n.* **Kurt** (kûrt; *Ger.* kŏŏRt), born 1918, Austrian diplomat: secretary-general of the United Nations 1972–82; president of Austria 1986–92.

Wal·do (wôl′dō, wol′-), *n.* **Pierre** or **Peter,** died c1217, French merchant and religious reformer, declared a heretic: founder of the Waldenses.

Wal′dorf sal′ad (wôl′dôrf), a salad of celery, diced apples, nuts, and mayonnaise. [1900–05; after the *Waldorf*-Astoria Hotel in New York City]

Wald·stein (*Ger.* vält′shtīn′), *n.* **Al·brecht von** (*Ger.* äl′bReKHt fən). See **Wallenstein, Albrecht Wenzel Eusebius von.**

Wald·wick (wôld′wik), *n.* a city in N New Jersey. 10,802.

wale[1] (wāl), *n., v.,* **waled, wal·ing.** —*n.* **1.** a streak, stripe, or ridge produced on the skin by the stroke of a rod or whip; welt. **2.** the vertical rib in knit goods or a chain of loops running lengthwise in knit fabric (opposed to *course*). **3.** the texture or weave of a fabric. **4.** *Naut.* **a.** any of certain strakes of thick outside planking on the sides of a wooden ship. **b.** gunwale. **5.** Also called **breast timber, ranger, waling.** *Engin., Building Trades.* a horizontal timber or other support for reinforcing various upright members, as sheet piling or concrete form boards, or for retaining earth at the edge of an excavation. **6.** a ridge on the outside of a horse collar. —*v.t.* **7.** to mark with wales. **8.** to weave with wales. **9.** *Engin., Building Trades.* to reinforce or fasten with a wale or wales. [bef. 1050; (n.) ME; OE *walu* ridge, rib, WHEAL; c. ON *vǫlr,* Goth *walus* rod, wand; (v.) late ME, deriv. of the n.]

wale[2] (wāl), *n., v.,* **waled, wal·ing.** *Scot. and North Eng.* —*n.* **1.** something that is selected as the best; choice. —*v.t.* **2.** to choose; select. [1250–1300; ME *wal(e)* < ON *val* choice, *velja* to choose]

Wal·er (wā′lər), *n.* a horse bred in New South Wales, Australia, as a military saddle horse and exported in numbers during the 19th century to British India. [1840–50; after New South *Wales;* see -ER[1]]

Wales (wālz), *n.* a division of the United Kingdom, in SW Great Britain. 2,766,800; 8016 sq. mi. (20,760 sq. km). Medieval, **Cambria.**

Wa·łę·sa (və wen′sə), *n.* **Lech** (lek), born 1943, Polish labor leader: a leader of Solidarity 1980; president since 1990; Nobel peace prize 1983.

Wa·ley (wā′lē), *n.* **Arthur** (*Arthur David Schloss*), 1889–1966, British translator of Chinese and Japanese literature.

Wal′fish Bay′ (wôl′fish). See **Walvis Bay.**

Wal·hal·la (wal hal′ə, val-, wäl hä′lə, väl-), *n.* Valhalla. Also, **Wal·hall** (wal hal′, wal′hal).

CONCISE ETYMOLOGY KEY: <, descended or borrowed from; >, whence; b., blend of, blended; c., cognate with; cf., compare; deriv., derivative; equiv., equivalent; imit., imitative; obl., oblique; r., replacing; s., stem; sp., spelling, spelled; resp., respelling, respelled; trans., translation; ?, origin unknown; *, unattested; ‡, probably earlier than. See the full key inside the front cover.

wal·ing (wā′ling), *n. Engin., Building Trades.* **1.** a number of wales, taken as a whole. **2.** timber for use as wales. **3.** wale[1] (def. 5). [1830–40; WALE[1] + -ING[1]]

walk (wôk), *v.i.* **1.** to advance or travel on foot at a moderate speed or pace; proceed by steps; move by advancing the feet alternately so that there is always one foot on the ground in bipedal locomotion and two or more feet on the ground in quadrupedal locomotion. **2.** to move about or travel on foot for exercise or pleasure: *We can walk in the park after lunch.* **3.** (of things) to move in a manner suggestive of walking, as through repeated vibrations or the effect of alternate expansion and contraction: *He typed so hard that the lamp walked right off the desk.* **4.** *Baseball.* to receive a base on balls. **5.** *Slang.* **a.** to go on strike; stage a walkout: *The miners will walk unless they get a pay raise.* **b.** to be acquitted or to be released or fined rather than sentenced to jail: *If the prosecutor doesn't present his case well, the murderer may walk.* **6.** to go about on the earth, or appear to living persons, as a ghost: *to believe that spirits walk at night.* **7.** (of a tool, pointer, or pen of a recording device, etc.) to glide, slip, or move from a straight course, fixed position, or the like: *A regular drill bit may walk on a plastic surface when you first try to make a hole. When the earthquake started, the pen on the seismograph walked all over the paper.* **8.** to conduct oneself in a particular manner; pursue a particular course of life: *to walk humbly with thy God.* **9.** *Basketball.* (of a player in possession of the ball) to take more than two steps without dribbling or passing the ball. **10.** *Obs.* to be in motion or action.
—*v.t.* **11.** to proceed through, over, or upon at a moderate pace on foot: *walking London streets by night; walking the floor all night.* **12.** to cause to walk; lead, drive, or ride at a walk, as an animal: *We walked our horses the last quarter of a mile.* **13.** to force or help to walk, as a person: *They were walking him around the room soon after his operation.* **14.** to conduct or accompany on a walk: *He walked them about the park.* **15.** to move (a box, trunk, or other object) in a manner suggestive of walking, as by a rocking motion. **16.** *Baseball.* (of a pitcher) to give a base on balls to (a batter). **17.** to spend or pass (time) in walking (often fol. by *away*): *We walked the morning away along the beach.* **18.** to cause or accomplish by walking: *We saw them walking guard over the chain gang.* **19.** to examine, measure, etc., by traversing on foot: *to walk a track; to walk the boundaries of the property.* **20.** *Basketball.* to advance (the ball) by taking more than two steps without dribbling or passing. **21.** *Informal.* to send (a person who has a reservation at a hotel) to another hotel because of overbooking: *It's exasperating to find yourself walked when you arrive at a hotel late in the evening.* **22. walk off,** to get rid of by walking: *to walk off a headache.* **23. walk off with, a.** to remove illegally; steal. **b.** to win or attain, as in a competition: *to walk off with the first prize for flower arrangements.* **c.** to surpass one's competitors; win easily: *to walk off with the fight.* **24. walk out, a.** to go on strike. **b.** to leave in protest: *to walk out of a committee meeting.* **25. walk out on,** to leave unceremoniously; desert; forsake: *to walk out on one's family.* **26. walk out with,** *Brit.* to court or be courted by: *Cook is walking out with the chauffeur.* **27. walk (someone) through,** to guide or instruct carefully one step at a time: *The teacher will walk the class through the entire testing procedure before the real test begins.* **28. walk Spanish, a.** to be forced by another to walk on tiptoe. **b.** to walk cautiously. **c.** to be discharged or dismissed. **d.** to discharge or dismiss (someone). **29. walk the plank.** See **plank** (def. 5). **30. walk through,** *Theat., Television.* **a.** to rehearse (a play) by combining a reading aloud of the lines with the designated physical movements. **b.** *Informal.* to perform (a role, play, etc.) in a perfunctory manner. **c.** to make little or no effort in performing one's role: *He didn't like the script and walked through his part.* **31. walk up,** (of a hunter) to flush (game) by approaching noisily on foot and often with hunting dogs.
—*n.* **32.** an act or instance of walking or going on foot. **33.** a period of walking for exercise or pleasure: *to go for a walk.* **34.** a distance walked or to be walked, often in terms of the time required: *not more than ten minutes' walk from town.* **35.** the gait or pace of a person or an animal that walks. **36.** a characteristic or individual manner of walking: *It was impossible to mistake her walk.* **37.** a department or branch of activity, or a particular line of work: *They found every walk of life closed against them.* **38.** *Baseball.* See **base on balls. 39.** a path or way for pedestrians at the side of a street or road; sidewalk. **40.** a place prepared or set apart for walking. **41.** a path in a garden or the like. **42.** a passage between rows of trees. **43.** an enclosed yard, pen, or the like where domestic animals are fed and left to exercise. **44. the walk.** See **race walking. 45.** a sheepwalk. **46.** a ropewalk. **47.** (in the West Indies) a plantation of trees, esp. coffee trees. **48.** a group, company, or congregation, esp. of snipes. **49.** *Brit.* **a.** the route of a street vendor, tradesman, or the like. **b.** the district or area in which such a route is located. **c.** a tract of forest land under the charge of one forester or keeper. **50.** *Archaic.* manner of behavior; conduct; course of life. **51.** *Obs.* a haunt or resort. **52. take a walk,** *Informal.* to leave, esp. abruptly and without any intention or prospect of returning (often used imperatively to indicate dismissal): *If he doesn't get his way, he takes a walk. I don't need your advice, so take a walk.* [bef. 1000; (v.) ME *walken,* OE *wealcan* to roll, toss, *gewealcan* to go; c. D, G *walken* to full (cloth), ON *vālka* to toss; (n.) ME, deriv. of the v.]
—**Syn. 1.** step, stride, stroll, saunter, ambulate, perambulate, promenade. **32.** stroll, promenade, constitutional. **35.** step, carriage. **37.** sphere, area, field. **39, 40.** passage, footpath, alley, avenue. **43.** run.

walk·a·ble (wô′kə bəl), *adj.* **1.** capable of being traveled, crossed, or covered by walking: *a walkable road; a walkable distance.* **2.** suited to or adapted for walking: *walkable shoes.* [1730–40; WALK + -ABLE] —**walk′a·bil′i·ty,** *n.*

walk·a·bout (wôk′ə bout′), *n.* **1.** *Chiefly Brit.* **a.** a walking tour. **b.** an informal public stroll taken by members of the royal family or by a political figure for the purpose of greeting and being seen by the public. **2.** *Australian.* **a.** a brief, informal leave from work, taken by an Aborigine to wander the bush, visit relatives, or return to native life. **b.** absence from work. [1905–10; n. use of v. phrase *walk about*]

walk′a·round pay′ (wôk′ə round′), extra pay earned by an employee for accompanying an official inspector on a plant tour or around a job site.

walk·a·thon (wô′kə thon′), *n.* **1.** a long-distance walking race for testing endurance. **2.** such a contest held to raise funds for a charity or special cause, with supporters or sponsors pledging to donate a sum for a specific contestant or team for each mile walked or for the total miles covered. [1930–35; WALK + -ATHON]

walk·a·way (wôk′ə wā′), *n.* **1.** an easy victory or conquest. **2.** a patient or inmate who escapes from an institution by walking away when not being supervised or guarded. [1885–90; n. use of v. phrase *walk away*]

walk-be·hind (wôk′bi hīnd′), *adj.* **1.** being a motor-driven machine, as a power lawn mower or a snow-blower, designed for operation with the operator walking behind and guiding the machine by its handle controls. —*n.* **2.** a walk-behind machine. [adj., n. use of v. phrase *walk behind*]

walk-down (wôk′doun′), *n.* **1.** a store, living quarters, etc., located below the street level and approached by a flight of steps: *It was a dimly lit walk-down optimistically called a garden apartment.* —*adj.* **2.** (of a store, restaurant, apartment, etc.) located below the level of the sidewalk: *a popular walk-down nightclub in Greenwich Village.* [1905–10, *Amer.*; n., adj. use of v. phrase *walk down*]

walk·er (wô′kər), *n.* **1.** an enclosing framework on casters or wheels for supporting a baby who is learning to walk. **2.** a similar device, usually a waist-high four-legged framework of lightweight metal, for use by a weak or disabled person as a support while walking. **3.** (*usually cap.*) *Informal.* See **Walker hound. 4.** a person or thing that walks or likes to walk: *He's a great walker.* **5.** *Theater Slang.* an extra or supernumerary. **6.** *Slang.* a musician required by a union contract to be hired and paid full salary even when not needed for performance. [1325–75; ME; see WALK, -ER[1]]

walker (def. 2)

Walk·er (wô′kər), *n.* **1. David,** 1785–1830, U.S. abolitionist. **2. James John** (*Jimmy*), 1881–1946, U.S. politician: mayor of New York City 1926–32. **3. John,** born 1952, New Zealand track-and-field athlete. **4. Sarah Breed·love** (brĕd′luv′), 1867–1919, U.S. businesswoman and philanthropist. **5.** a city in W Michigan. 15,088. **6.** a male given name.

Walk′er hound′, an American foxhound having a black, tan, and white, or, sometimes, a tan and white coat. Also called **Walk′er fox′hound.** [1900–05, *Amer.*; after John W. *Walker* and his descendants, who bred the dog in Kentucky in the 19th century]

walk·ie-talk·ie (wô′kē tô′kē), *n. Radio.* a combined transmitter and receiver light enough to be carried by one person: developed originally for military use in World War II. Also, **walky-talky.** [1935–40, *Amer.*; see WALK, TALK, -IE]

walk-in (wôk′in′), *adj.* **1.** of or pertaining to persons who walk into a place from the street, esp. irregularly or without an appointment: *walk-in customers; walk-in sales; a walk-in patient.* **2.** large enough to be walked into: *a walk-in kitchen.* —*n.* **3.** a person, as a customer, patient, or interviewee, who arrives without an appointment: *Many of the clinic's patients are walk-ins who suddenly need help.* **4.** something large enough to be walked into, as a closet. **5.** an assured victory in an election or other contest. [1925–30; adj., n. use of v. phrase *walk in*]

walk′-in apart′ment, a ground-floor apartment having a private entrance directly from the street, rather than through a hallway of the building.

walk′-in clos′et, a closet that is large enough to walk around in.

walk·ing (wô′king), *adj.* **1.** considered as a person who can or does walk or something that walks: *The hospital is caring for six walking patients. He's walking proof that people can lose weight quickly.* **2.** used for or as an aid in walking: *She put on her walking shoes and went out.* **3.** suitable for, characterized by, or consisting of walking: *True sightseeing is a walking affair. We took a walking tour of Spain.* **4.** of or pertaining to an implement or machine drawn by a draft animal and operated or controlled by a person on foot: *a walking plow.* **5.** of or pertaining to a mechanical part that moves back and forth. —*n.* **6.** the act or action of a person or thing that walks: *Walking was the best exercise for him.* **7.** the manner or way in which a person walks. **8.** the state or condition of the surface, terrain, etc., on which a person walks: *The walking is dry over here.* **9.** See **race walking.** [1350–1400; ME; see WALK, -ING[2], -ING[1]]

walk′ing-a·round′ mon′ey (wô′king ə round′), **1.** money that is carried on the person for routine expenses and minor emergencies; pocket money. **2.** Also called **street money.** *Political Slang.* cash sums given by political managers, district leaders, or the like, to grassroots workers and others for expenses incurred while canvassing for votes or doing other chores before an election. [1975–80, for def. 2]

walk′ing bass′ (bās), (in jazz piano) a left-hand accompaniment consisting of a continuous rhythm of four beats to the measure, usually with a repetitive melodic pattern.

walk′ing beam′, *Mach.* an overhead oscillating lever, pivoted at the middle, for transmitting force from a vertical connecting rod below one end to a vertical connecting rod, pump rod, etc., below the other end. [1835–45, *Amer.*]

walk′ing cat′fish, an Asian catfish, *Clarias batrachus,* that can survive out of water and move overland from one body of water to another: introduced into Florida. [1965–70]

walk′ing del′egate, (formerly) an official appointed by a trade union to go from place to place to investigate working conditions, to ascertain whether union contracts were being fulfilled, and, sometimes, to negotiate contracts between employers and the union. [1890–95, *Amer.*]

walk′ing fern′, a fern, *Camptosorus rhizophyllus,* having simple, triangular fronds tapering into a prolongation that bends at the top and often takes root at the apex. Also called **walking leaf.** [1820–30]

walk′ing fish′, any of various fishes able to survive and move about for short periods of time on land, as the mudskipper or climbing perch. [1860–65]

walk′ing horse′. See **Tennessee walking horse.**

walk′ing leaf′, 1. See **leaf insect. 2.** See **walking fern.** [1650–60]

walk′ing line′, a line on the plan of a curving staircase on which all treads are of a uniform width and that is considered to be the ordinary path taken by persons on the stair.

walk′ing pa′pers, *Informal.* a notification of dismissal. [1815–25, *Amer.*]

walk′ing shorts′, medium to long shorts, often cut fuller than Bermuda shorts and used for walking or leisure activity. Also called **walk shorts.** [1960–65]

walk′ing stick′, 1. a stick held in the hand and used to help support oneself while walking. **2.** Also, **walk′·ing·stick′.** Also called **stick insect.** any of several insects of the family Phasmidae, having a long, slender, twiglike body. [1570–80]

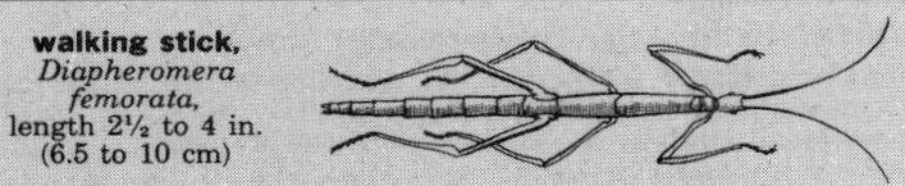
walking stick, *Diapheromera femorata,* length 2½ to 4 in. (6.5 to 10 cm)

walk′ing tick′et, *Informal.* See **walking papers.** [1825–35, *Amer.*]

walk′ing wound′ed, 1. casualties, as of a military conflict, who are wounded but ambulatory. **2.** *Informal.* persons who have been damaged or defeated psychologically or emotionally by their experiences in life. [1915–20]

walk′-in refrig′erator, a refrigerated storage room, as at a butcher shop.

Walk·man (wôk′mən, -man′), *Trademark.* a brand of small portable stereo cassette player, radio, or cassette player and radio used with headphones.

walk-off (wôk′ôf′, -of′), *n. Informal.* a person who escapes easily, esp. by walking away from a place of detention; a walkaway: *The guards rounded up the walk-offs from the prison farm.* [1935–40; n. use of v. phrase *walk off*]

walk-on (wôk′on′, -ôn′), *n.* **1.** Also called **walk′ing part′.** a small part in a play or other entertainment, esp. one without speaking lines. Cf. **bit**[2] (def. 6). **2.** an entertainer or actor who plays such a part. **3.** an athlete trying out for a team who has not been drafted, specifically invited, scouted, awarded a scholarship, etc. [1900–05; n. use of v. phrase *walk on*]

walk·out (wôk′out′), *n.* **1.** a strike by workers. **2.** the act of leaving or being absent from a meeting, esp. as an expression of protest. **3.** a doorway in a building or room that gives direct access to the outdoors: *a home with a sliding-glass walkout from the living room to the patio.* —*adj.* **4.** having a doorway that gives direct access to the outdoors: *a walkout basement.* Also, **walk′-out′.** [1885–90, *Amer.*; n., adj. use of v. phrase *walk out*]

walk·o·ver (wôk′ō′vər), *n.* **1.** *Racing.* a walking or trotting over the course by a contestant who is the only starter. **2.** an unopposed or easy victory. **3.** any task easily done. **4.** *Gymnastics.* a vertical rotation of the body from a standing position, performed by leaning forward to a brief handstand and bringing the legs over and back down to the floor one at a time **(front walkover)** or by arching backward to a similar handstand and returning the feet to the floor **(back walkover).** [1830–40; n. use of v. phrase *walk over*]

walk′ shorts′. See **walking shorts.**

walk-through (wôk′thrōō′), *n.* **1.** *Theat., Television.* **a.** a rehearsal in which physical action is combined with reading the lines of a play. **b.** a perfunctory performance of a script. **2.** *Television, Motion Pictures.* a rehearsal without cameras. **3.** a step-by-step demonstration of a procedure or process or a step-by-step explanation of it as a novice attempts it. **4.** a pedestrian passageway or arcade through the ground floor of a building connecting one street or building with another. —*adj.* **5.** designed to be walked through by an observer: *The zoo has a walk-through aviary where the birds are all around you.* **6.** activated by a person passing through: *a walk-through electronic scanner at the airport for detecting concealed weapons.* [1935–40; n., adj. use of v. phrase *walk through*]

walk-up (wôk′up′), *n.* **1.** an apartment above the ground floor in a building that has no elevator. **2.** a building, esp. an apartment house, that has no elevator. —*adj.* **3.** located above the ground floor in a building that has no elevator. **4.** having no elevator. **5.** accessible to pedestrians from the outside of a building: *a walk-up teller's window at a bank.* [1915–20, *Amer.*; n., adj. use of v. phrase *walk up*]

Wal·kü·re, Die (*Ger.* dē väl kʏ′rə). See ***Ring of the Nibelung.***

walk·way (wôk′wā′), *n.* **1.** any passage for walking, esp. one connecting the various areas of a ship, factory, park, etc. **2.** a garden path or walk. **3.** the front walk of a house, leading from the door to the sidewalk or road. **4.** skybridge (def. 2). [1785–95, *Amer.*; WALK + WAY[1]]

Wal·kyr·ie (wäl kēr′ē, -kī′rē, väl-, wäl′kēr ē, väl′-), *n.* Valkyrie.

walk·y-talk·y (wô′kē tô′kē), *n., pl.* **-talk·ies.** walkie-talkie.

wall (wôl), *n.* **1.** any of various permanent upright constructions having a length much greater than the thickness and presenting a continuous surface except where pierced by doors, windows, etc.: used for shelter, protection, or privacy, or to subdivide interior space, to support floors, roofs, or the like, to retain earth, to fence in an area, etc. **2.** Usually, **walls.** a rampart raised for defensive purposes. **3.** an immaterial or intangible barrier, obstruction, etc., suggesting a wall: *a wall of prejudice.* **4.** a wall-like, enclosing part, thing, mass, etc.: *a wall of fire; a wall of troops.* **5.** an embankment to prevent flooding, as a levee or sea wall. **6. the Wall.** See **Berlin Wall. 7.** the outermost film or layer of structural material protecting, surrounding, and defining the physical limits of an object: *the wall of a blood cell.* **8.** *Mining.* **a.** the side of a level or drift. **b.** the overhanging or underlying side of a vein; a hanging wall or footwall. **9. climb the walls** or **climb walls,** *Slang.* to become tense or frantic: *climbing the walls with boredom.* **10. drive** or **push to the wall,** to force into a desperate situation; humiliate or ruin completely: *Not content with merely winning the match, they used every opportunity to push the inferior team to the wall.* **11. go over the wall,** *Slang.* to break out of prison: *Roadblocks have been set up in an effort to capture several convicts who went over the wall.* **12. go to the wall, a.** to be defeated in a conflict or competition; yield. **b.** to fail in business, esp. to become bankrupt. **c.** to be put aside or forgotten. **d.** to take an extreme and determined position or measure: *I'd go to the wall to stop him from resigning.* **13. hit the wall,** (of long-distance runners) to reach a point in a race, usually after 20 miles, when the body's fuels are virtually depleted and willpower becomes crucial to be able to finish. **14. off the wall,** *Slang.* **a.** beyond the realm of acceptability or reasonableness: *The figure you quoted for doing the work is off the wall.* **b.** markedly out of the ordinary; eccentric; bizarre: *Some of the clothes in the fashion show were too off the wall for the average customer.* **15. up against the wall, a.** placed against a wall to be executed by a firing squad. **b.** in a crucial or critical position, esp. one in which defeat or failure seems imminent: *Unless sales improve next month, the company will be up against the wall.* **16. up the wall,** *Slang.* into an acutely frantic, frustrated, or irritated state: *The constant tension in the office is driving everyone up the wall.* —*adj.* **17.** of or pertaining to a wall: *wall space.* **18.** growing against or on a wall: *wall plants; wall cress.* **19.** situated, placed, or installed in or on a wall: *wall oven; a wall safe.* —*v.t.* **20.** to enclose, shut off, divide, protect, border, etc., with or as if with a wall (often fol. by *in* or *off*): *to wall the yard; to wall in the play area; He is walled in by lack of opportunity.* **21.** to seal or fill (a doorway or other opening) with a wall: *to wall an unused entrance.* **22.** to seal or entomb (something or someone) within a wall (usually fol. by *up*): *The workmen had walled up the cat quite by mistake.* [bef. 900; (n.) ME; OE *w(e)all* < L *vallum* palisade, deriv. of *vallus* stake, post; see WALE[1]; (v.) ME, deriv. of the n.] —**wall′-less,** *adj.* —**wall′-like′,** *adj.*
—**Syn. 2.** battlement, breastwork, bulwark, barrier, bastion. **5.** dike. **22.** immure.

wal·la (wä′lä, -lə), *n.* wallah.

wal·la·ba (wol′ə bə), *n.* **1.** any of several trees belonging to the genus *Eperua,* of the legume family, native to the Guianas and northern Brazil. **2.** the hard, heavy wood of any of these trees, used in the construction of buildings. [1815–25; < Arawak]

wal·la·by (wol′ə bē), *n., pl.* **-bies,** (*esp. collectively*) **-by.** any of various small and medium-sized kangaroos of the genera *Macropus, Thylogale, Petrogale,* etc., some of which are no larger than rabbits: several species are endangered. [1790–1800; < Dharuk *wa-la-ba*]

wallaby, *Macropus agilis,* height 2½ ft. (0.8 m); tail 20 in. (0.5 m)

Wal·lace (wol′is, wô′lis), *n.* **1. Alfred Rus·sel** (rus′-əl), 1823–1913, English naturalist, explorer, and author. **2. George Cor·ley** (kôr′lē), born 1919, U.S. politician: governor of Alabama 1963–67, 1971–79, and 1983–87. **3. Henry (A·gard)** (ā′gärd), 1888–1965, U.S. agriculturalist, author, and statesman: Secretary of Agriculture 1933–40; vice president of the U.S. 1941–45; Secretary of Commerce 1945–46. **4. Lewis** (*"Lew"*), 1827–1905, U.S. general and novelist. **5. Sir William.** Also, **Walays, Wallensis.** 1272?–1305, Scottish military leader and patriot. **6. (William Roy) De·Witt** (də wit′), 1889–1981, and his wife, **Lila Bell (Acheson),** 1889–1984, U.S. magazine publishers. **7.** a male given name: a Scottish family name meaning "Welshman, foreigner."

Wal·lace·burg (wol′is bûrg′, wô′lis-), *n.* a town in SE Ontario, in S Canada. 11,506.

Wal′lace's line′, *Zoogeog.* an imaginary line that separates the Oriental and Australian zoogeographical regions and passes between Bali and Lombok, west of Celebes, and east of the Philippines. [1865–70; after A. R. WALLACE]

Wal·lach (wol′ək; *Ger.* väl′äкн), *n.* **Ot·to** (ot′ō; *Ger.* ôt′ō), 1847–1931, German chemist: Nobel prize 1910.

Wal·la·chi·a (wo lā′kē ə), *n.* a former principality in SE Europe: united with Moldavia (Moldova) to form Rumania in 1861. 29,569 sq. mi. (76,585 sq. km). *Cap.:* Bucharest. Also, **Walachia.** —**Wal·la′chi·an,** *adj., n.*

wal·lah (wä′lä, -lə), *n. Anglo-Indian.* a person in charge of, employed at, or concerned with a particular thing (used in combination): *a book wallah; a ticket wallah.* [1770–80; < Hindi *-wālā* suffix of relation]

wal·la·roo (wol′ə rōō′), *n., pl.* **-roos,** (*esp. collectively*) **-roo.** any of several large kangaroos of the genus *Macropus (Osphranter),* of the grassy plains of Australia, esp. *M. robustus,* having a reddish-gray coat and inhabiting rocky hills. Also called **euro.** [1820–30; < Dharuk *wa-la-ru*]

Wal·la·sey (wol′ə sē), *n.* a city in Merseyside, in W England, on the Mersey estuary, opposite Liverpool. 97,061.

Wal·la Wal·la (wol′ə wol′ə), a city in SE Washington. 25,618.

wall·board (wôl′bôrd′, -bōrd′), *n.* material manufactured in large sheets for use in making or covering walls, ceilings, etc., as a substitute for wooden boards or plaster. [1905–10; WALL + BOARD]

wall′ box′, *Building Trades.* an enclosed iron or steel socket built into a masonry wall to support the end of a wooden beam. [1870–75]

wall·cov·er·ing (wôl′kuv′ər ing), *n.* a flexible sheet of sized paper, fabric, plastic, etc., usually laminated and printed with a repeat pattern, for pasting on a wall as decoration and protection. Also, **wall′ cov′ering.** [WALL + COVERING]

wall′ creep′er, a small, gray and crimson Old World bird, *Tichodroma muraria,* that inhabits cliffs in mountainous areas. [1660–70]

walled (wôld), *adj.* **1.** having walls (sometimes used in combination): *a high-walled prison.* **2.** enclosed or fortified with a wall: *a walled village.* [bef. 1000; ME; OE *geweallod*; see WALL, -ED[2], -ED[3]]

walled′ plain′, a circular or almost circular area on the moon, sometimes with a floor that is depressed, usually partially enclosed by walls that rise to varying heights and that are usually lower than those of a crater.

Wal·len·da (wo len′də; *Ger.* vä len′dä), *n.* **Karl** (kärl; *Ger.* kärl), 1905–78, German circus aerialist.

Wal·len·sis (wo len′sis), *n.* **Sir William.** See **Wallace, Sir William.**

Wal·len·stein (wol′ən stīn′; *for 1 also Ger.* väl′ən-shtīn′), *n.* **1.** Also, **Waldstein. Al·brecht Wen·zel Eu·se·bi·us von** (äl′brekнt ven′tsəl oi zā′bē ŏŏs′ fən), **Duke of Fried·land** (frēd′land′, -lənd; *Ger.* frēt′länt′), 1583–1634, Austrian general in the Thirty Years' War, born in Bohemia. **2. Alfred,** 1898–1983, U.S. cellist and conductor.

Wal·ler (wol′ər, wô′lər), *n.* **1. Edmund,** 1607–87, English poet. **2. Thomas** (*"Fats"*), 1904–43, U.S. jazz pianist and songwriter.

wal·let (wol′it, wô′lit), *n.* **1.** a flat, folding pocketbook, esp. one large enough to hold paper money, credit cards, driver's license, etc., and sometimes having a compartment for coins. **2.** *Chiefly Brit.* a bag for carrying food, clothing, toilet articles, etc., during a journey; knapsack or rucksack. [1350–1400; ME *walet* < ?]

wall·eye (wôl′ī), *n., pl.* **-eyes,** (*esp. collectively for 1, 2*) **-eye. 1.** Also called **walleyed pike, jack salmon.** a large game fish, *Stizostedion vitreum,* inhabiting the lakes and rivers of northeastern North America; pikeperch. **2.** any of various other fishes having large, staring eyes. **3.** an eye characteristic of a walleyed person or animal. 4. (*cap.*) *Mil.* a series of television-guided bombs with high-explosive warheads, in production since the 1960's. [1515–25; back formation from WALLEYED]

wall•eyed (wôl′īd′), *adj.* 1. having eyes in which there is an abnormal amount of the white showing, because of divergent strabismus. 2. having large, staring eyes, as some fishes. 3. marked by excited or agitated staring of the eyes, as in fear, rage, frenzy, or the like: *walleyed astonishment.* 4. having an eye or the eyes presenting little or no color, as the result of a light-colored or white iris or of white opacity of the cornea. [1300–50; ME *wawileghed, waugle eghed* < ON *vagleygr,* equiv. to *vagl-* (meaning uncert.; cf. Icel *vagl* film over the eye) + *-eygr* -eyed; see EYE; cf. OE *waldenīge*]

wall′eyed pike′, walleye (def. 1). [1865–70, *Amer.*]

wall′eye pol′lock, a cod, *Theragra chalcogramma,* ranging the northern Pacific, that is related to and resembles the pollock.

wall′ fern′, the polypody, esp. *Polypodium vulgare* or *P. virginianum.* [1515–25]

wall•flow•er (wôl′flou′ər), *n.* 1. a person who, because of shyness, unpopularity, or lack of a partner, remains at the side at a party or dance. 2. any person, organization, etc., that remains on or has been forced to the sidelines of any activity: *The firm was a wallflower in this year's bidding for government contracts.* 3. a European plant, *Cheiranthus cheiri,* of the mustard family, that, when growing wild on walls, cliffs, etc., has sweet-scented, usually yellow or orange flowers, but when cultivated has flowers varying in color from pale yellow to brown-red or purple. 4. any of several related plants of the genera *Cheiranthus* and *Erysimum.* [1570–80; WALL + FLOWER]

wall′ hang′ing, a tapestry, carpet, or similar object hung against a wall as decoration; arras. [1895–1900]

wall-hung (wôl′hung′), *adj.* designed to be hung from or attached to a wall: *a wall-hung medicine cabinet.*

Wal•ling•ford (wol′ing fərd), *n.* a town in S Connecticut. 37,274.

Wal•ling•ton (wol′ing tən), *n.* a town in NE New Jersey. 10,741.

Wal•lis (wol′is, wô′lis), *n.* 1. **Harold Brent** (brent), (*Hal*), 1899–1986, U.S. film producer. 2. **John,** 1616–1703, English mathematician. 3. a male given name, form of **Wallace.** 4. a female given name.

wall′ mold′ing. See **back molding.**

Wal•loon (wo lo͞on′), *n.* 1. one of a people inhabiting chiefly the southern and southeastern parts of Belgium and adjacent regions in France. 2. the French dialect spoken by the Walloons. —*adj.* 3. of or pertaining to the Walloons or their language. [< F *Wallon,* equiv. to *wall-* (<< Gmc **walh-* foreign; see WALNUT) + *-on* n. suffix]

Walloon′ sword′, pappenheimer.

wal•lop (wol′əp), *v.t.* 1. to beat soundly; thrash. 2. *Informal.* to strike with a vigorous blow; belt; sock: *Mantle walloped the ball out of the park.* 3. *Informal.* to defeat thoroughly, as in a game. 4. *Chiefly Scot.* to flutter, wobble, or flop about. —*v.i.* 5. *Informal.* to move violently and clumsily: *The puppy walloped down the walk.* 6. (of a liquid) to boil violently. 7. *Obs.* to gallop. —*n.* 8. a vigorous blow. 9. the ability to deliver vigorous blows, as in boxing: *That fist of his packs a wallop.* 10. *Informal.* a. the ability to effect a forceful impression; punch: *That ad packs a wallop.* b. a pleasurable thrill; kick: *The joke gave them all a wallop.* 11. *Informal.* a violent, clumsy movement; lurch. 12. *Obs.* a gallop. [1300–50; ME *walopen* to gallop, *wal(l)op* gallop < AF *waloper* (v.), *walop* (n.), OF *galoper, galop;* see GALLOP] —**wal′lop•er,** *n.*
—**Syn.** 3. trounce, rout, crush, best.

wal•lop•ing (wol′ə ping), *Informal.* —*n.* 1. a sound beating or thrashing. 2. a thorough defeat. —*adj.* 3. impressively big or good; whopping. —*adv.* 4. extremely; immensely: *We ran up a walloping big bill.* [1350–1400; ME; see WALLOP, -ING¹, -ING²]

wal•low (wol′ō), *v.i.* 1. to roll about or lie in water, snow, mud, dust, or the like, as for refreshment: *Goats wallowed in the dust.* 2. to live self-indulgently; luxuriate; revel: *to wallow in luxury; to wallow in sentimentality.* 3. to flounder about; move along or proceed clumsily or with difficulty: *A gunboat wallowed toward port.* 4. to surge up or billow forth, as smoke or heat: *Waves of black smoke wallowed into the room.* —*n.* 5. an act or instance of wallowing. 6. a place in which animals wallow: *hog wallow; an elephant wallow.* 7. the indentation produced by animals wallowing: *a series of wallows across the farmyard.* [bef. 900; ME *walwe,* OE *wealwian* to roll; c. Goth *walwjan;* akin to L *volvere*]
—**Syn.** 2. swim, bask.

wal•low•er (wol′ō ər), *n.* 1. a person or thing that wallows. 2. (in a windmill) a horizontal gear driven off the brake wheel. [1540–50; WALLOW + -ER¹]

wall′ paint′ing, mural painting executed by any of various techniques, as encaustic, tempera, fresco, or oil paint on canvas, often as an enhancement of the architecture of which the recipient wall is a part. [1850–55]

wall•pa•per (wôl′pā′pər), *n.* 1. paper, usually with printed decorative patterns in color, for pasting on and covering the walls or ceilings of rooms, hallways, etc. 2. any fabric, foil, vinyl material, etc., used as a wall or ceiling covering. —*v.t.* 3. to put wallpaper on (a wall, ceiling, etc.) or to furnish (a room, house, etc.) with wallpaper. [1820–30; WALL + PAPER]

wall′ plate′, 1. Also called **raising plate.** *Building Trades.* a horizontal member built into or laid along the top of a wall to support and distribute the pressure from joists, rafters, etc. 2. *Mach.* a vertical metal plate secured against a wall, as to attach a bracket. 3. *Mining.* one of the longer members of a set. Cf. **end plate.** 4. See **switch plate.** [1350–1400; ME]

wall′ plug′, an electrical outlet permanently mounted on a wall. [1895–1900]

wall•post•er (wôl′pō′stər), *n.* (in China) a usually lengthy notice, complaint, etc., handwritten in large characters and hung on walls in cities, as a means of communication and for criticizing or attacking government policy or politicians. [1965–70; WALL + POSTER¹]

wall′ rock′, *Mining.* the rock forming the walls of a vein. [1855–60, *Amer.*]

wall′ rue′, a small, delicate fern, *Asplenium ruta-muraria,* having fan-shaped leaflets and growing on walls and cliffs. [1540–50]

Walls•end (wôlz′end′), *n.* 1. a city in Tyne and Wear, NE England, near the mouth of the Tyne River. 45,793. 2. a type of coal widely used in Great Britain, esp. for domestic purposes.

wall′ sock′et, socket (def. 2b).

Wall′ Street′, 1. a street in New York City, in S Manhattan: the major financial center of the U.S. 2. the money market or the financiers of the U.S. [1820–30, *Amer.* for def. 2]

Wall′ Street′er, a person who is employed on Wall Street or in the financial district. [1880–85, *Amer.;* WALL STREET + -ER¹]

wall′ sys′tem, a modular system of shelves, some of which may be enclosed by doors, either mounted on a wall or arranged in freestanding units, for holding books, bric-a-brac, etc., and sometimes including such features as a drop-leaf desk or specially designed storage space, as to accommodate records or electronic equipment. Also called **wall′ u′nit.** [1965–70]

wall′ tent′, a tent having four perpendicular sides, usually larger and with more headroom than most pyramid-shaped tents. [1835–45, *Amer.*]

wall-to-wall (*adj., adv.* wôl′tə wôl′; *n.* wôl′tə wôl′), *adj.* 1. covering the entire floor from one wall to another: *wall-to-wall carpeting.* 2. *Informal.* occupying a space or period of time completely: *With no commercial interruptions, the telecast of the game was wall-to-wall action.* 3. *Informal.* being available everywhere; full of or saturated with something specified: *Las Vegas offers wall-to-wall gambling. Her life has been wall-to-wall misery.* —*adv.* 4. from one side to the other; to overflowing: *The store was jammed wall-to-wall with late shoppers.* —*n.* 5. a wall-to-wall carpet. [1945–50]

wal•ly (wā′lē), *adj. Scot.* 1. fine; splendid. 2. strong. [1490–1500; WALE² + -Y¹]

wal•ly•ball (wol′ē bôl′, wô′lē-), *n.* a game similar to volleyball played in a walled court so that the ball may be bounced against the walls. [1985–90; b. WALL and VOLLEYBALL]

wal•ly•drag (wā′lē drag′, -dräg′, wol′ē-), *n. Scot.* a feeble, dwarfed animal or person. Also called **wal•ly•drai•gle** (wā′lē drā′gəl, wol′ē-). [1500–10; perh. *wally* (var. of WALLOW) + DRAG]

wal•nut (wôl′nut′, -nət), *n.* 1. the edible nut of trees of the genus *Juglans,* of the North Temperate Zone. Cf. **walnut family.** 2. the tree itself. 3. the wood of such a tree. 4. *Northeastern U.S.* the hickory nut. 5. any of various fruits or trees resembling the walnut. 6. a somewhat reddish shade of brown, as that of the heartwood of the black walnut tree. [bef. 1050; ME; OE *wealh-hnutu* lit., foreign nut; see WELSH, NUT]

Wal′nut Creek′, a town in W California. 53,643.

wal′nut fam′ily, the plant family Juglandaceae, characterized by deciduous trees having alternate, pinnately compound leaves, male flowers in tassellike catkins and female flowers in clusters, and edible nuts enclosed in a thick-walled or leathery husk, and including the butternut, hickory, pecan, and walnut.

wal′nut husk′ fly′, any of several fruit flies, as *Rhagoletis completa,* the larvae of which feed on and discolor walnut husks.

Wal•pole (wôl′pōl′, wol′-), *n.* 1. **Horace, 4th Earl of Or•ford** (ôr′fərd), (*Horatio Walpole*), 1717–97, English novelist and essayist (son of Sir Robert Walpole). 2. **Sir Hugh Seymour,** 1884–1941, English novelist, born in New Zealand. 3. **Sir Robert, 1st Earl of Or•ford** (ôr′fərd), 1676–1745, British statesman: prime minister 1715–17; 1721–42. 4. a city in E Massachusetts. 18,859.

Wal•pur•gis (väl po͝or′gis), *n.* **Saint,** A.D. c710–780, English missionary and abbess in Germany: feast day May 1. Also, **Walburga, Wal•pur•ga** (väl po͝or′gä).

Walpur′gis Night′, (esp. in medieval German folklore) the evening preceding the feast day of St. Walpurgis, when witches congregated, esp. on the Brocken. German, ***Wal•pur•gis•nacht*** (väl po͝or′gis näKHt′).

Wal•ras (vAl RA′), *n.* **(Ma•rie Es•prit) Lé•on** (mA Rē′ e sprē′ lā ôN′), 1834–1910, French economist.

wal•rus (wôl′rəs, wol′-), *n., pl.* **-rus•es,** (*esp. collectively*) **-rus.** a large marine mammal, *Odobenus rosmarus,* of arctic seas, related to the seals, and having flippers, a pair of large tusks, and a tough, wrinkled skin. [1645–55; < D: lit., whale horse; c. G *Walross,* Dan *hvalros;* cf. OE *horshwæl* horse-whale]

Atlantic walrus, *Odobenus rosmarus rosmarus,* length to 11 ft. (3.4 m); tusks to 3 ft. (0.9 m)

wal′rus mus′tache, a thick, shaggy mustache hanging down loosely at both ends.

Wal•sall (wôl′sôl), *n.* a city in West Midlands, in central England, near Birmingham. 271,000.

Wal•sing•ham (wôl′sing əm), *n.* **Sir Francis** c1530–90, English statesman: Secretary of State 1573–90

Wal•ter (väl′tər *for 1;* wôl′tər *for 2, 3*), *n.* 1. **Bruno** (bro͞o′nō), (*Bruno Schlesinger*), 1876–1962, German opera and symphony conductor, in U.S. after 1939. 2. **Thomas U•stick** (yo͞o′stik), 1804–87, U.S. architect. 3. a male given name.

Wal′ter Mit′ty, *pl.* **Walter Mittys.** an ordinary timid person who is given to adventurous and self-aggrandizing daydreams or secret plans as a way of glamorizing a humdrum life. [from the title character of James Thurber's short story "The Secret Life of Walter Mitty" (1939)] —**Wal′ter Mit′tyish.**

Wal•tham (wôl′thəm *or, locally,* -tham), *n.* a city in E Massachusetts. 58,200.

Wal′tham For′est (wôl′təm, -thəm), a borough of Greater London, England. 228,200.

Wal•tham•stow (wôl′təm stō′, -thəm-), *n.* a former borough, now part of Waltham Forest, in SE England.

Wal•ther von der Vo•gel•wei•de (väl′tər fôn dər fō′gəl vī′də), c1170–c1230, German minnesinger and poet.

Wal•ton (wôl′tn), *n.* 1. **Ernest Thomas Sin•ton** (sin′tn), 1903–95, Irish physicist: Nobel prize 1951. 2. **I•zaak** (ī′zək), 1593–1683, English writer. 3. **Sir William (Turner),** 1902–83, English composer. —**Wal•to•ni•an** (wôl tō′nē ən), *n., adj.*

waltz (wôlts), *n.* 1. a ballroom dance, in moderately fast triple meter, in which the dancers revolve in perpetual circles, taking one step to each beat. 2. a piece of music for, or in the rhythm of, this dance. 3. *Informal.* an easy victory or accomplishment: *The game was a waltz—we won by four touchdowns. The math exam was a waltz.* —*adj.* 4. of, pertaining to, or characteristic of the waltz, as music, rhythm, or dance: *waltz tempo.* —*v.i.* 5. to dance or move in a waltz step or rhythm: *an invitation to waltz.* 6. *Informal.* a. to move breezily or casually: *to waltz in late for dinner.* b. to progress easily or successfully (often fol. by *through*): *to waltz through an exam.* —*v.t.* 7. to lead (a partner) in dancing a waltz. 8. *Informal.* to move or lead briskly and easily: *He waltzed us right into the governor's office.* 9. to fill (a period of time) with waltzing (often fol. by *away, through,* etc.): *They waltzed the night away.* [1775–85; back formation from G *Walzer* a waltz (taken as *walz* + -ER¹), deriv. of *walzen* to roll, dance; cf. obs. E *walt* unsteady, dial. *walter* to roll] —**waltz′er,** *n.* —**waltz′•like′,** *adj.*

waltz-length (wôlts′lengkth′, -length′, -lenth′), *adj.* having the hemline at mid calf: *a waltz-length nightgown.* [1955–60]

waltz′ time′. See **three-quarter time.**

Wal′vis Bay′ (wôl′vis), 1. an inlet of the S Atlantic Ocean, on the coast of Namibia, in SW Africa. 2. a seaport on this inlet. 3. an exclave of the Republic of South Africa around this seaport. 42,234; 347 sq. mi. (899 sq. km). Also, **Walfish Bay.**

WAM, wraparound mortgage.

wam•ble (wom′bəl, -əl, wam′-), *v.,* **-bled, -bling,** *n.* —*v.i.* 1. to move unsteadily. 2. to feel nausea. 3. (of the stomach) to rumble; growl. —*n.* 4. an unsteady or rolling movement. 5. a feeling of nausea. [1300–50; ME *wamle,* obscurely akin to Norw *vamla* to stagger] —**wam′bli•ness,** *n.* —**wam′bly,** *adj.*

wame (wām), *n. Scot. and North Eng.* belly. [1325–75; ME (north and Scots) *wayme,* var. of WOMB]

wam•mus (wom′əs), *n., pl.* **-mus•es.** wamus (def. 2).

Wam•pa•no•ag (wäm′pə nō′ag), *n., pl.* **-ags,** (*esp. collectively*) **-ag.** 1. a member of a once-powerful North American Indian people who inhabited the area east of Narragansett Bay from Rhode Island to Cape Cod, Martha's Vineyard, and Nantucket at the time of the Pilgrim settlement. 2. the Eastern Algonquian speech of the Wampanoag people, a dialect of Massachusett. [1670–80, *Amer.;* < Narragansett, equiv. to Proto-Algonquian **wa·pan(w)-* dawn + *-o·w-* person of + *-*aki* pl. suffix, i.e., easterners]

wam•pish (wam′pish, wäm′-), *v.i. Scot.* to wave about or flop to and fro. [1810–20; appar. of expressive orig.]

wam•pum (wom′pəm, wôm′-), *n.* 1. Also called **peag, seawan, sewan.** cylindrical beads made from shells, pierced and strung, used by North American Indians as a medium of exchange, for ornaments, and for ceremonial and sometimes spiritual purposes, esp. such beads when white but also including the more valuable black or dark-purple varieties. 2. *Informal.* money. [1630–40; short for WAMPUMPEAG]

wam•pum•peag (wom′pəm pēg′, wôm′-), *n.* wampum. [1620–30, *Amer.;* earlier also *wampampeak, wampompeage* < Massachusett (c. Eastern Abenaki *wápapəyak* wampum beads; equiv. to Proto-Algonquian **wa·p-* white + *-*a·py-* string + *-*aki* pl. suffix)]

wam•pus¹ (wom′pəs), *n., pl.* **-pus•es.** a strange or objectionable person; lout. [perh. extracted from CATAWAMPUS]

wam•pus² (wom′pəs), *n., pl.* **-pus•es.** wamus (def. 2).

wa•mus (wô′məs, wom′əs), *n., pl.* **-mus•es.** 1. a heavy cardigan jacket, loosely knit and belted. 2. Also, **wammus, wampus.** a durable, coarse, outer jacket. [1795–1805, *Amer.;* < D *wammes* (cf. G *Wams* vest, undershirt), MD *wambuis* < dial. OF *wambois* < Frankish **wamb-* belly (see WOMB) + F *-ois* -ESE; see GAMBESON]

wan¹ (won), *adj.,* **wan•ner, wan•nest,** *v.,* **wanned, wan•ning.** —*adj.* 1. of an unnatural or sickly pallor; pallid; lacking color: *His wan face suddenly flushed.* 2. showing or suggesting ill health, fatigue, unhappiness, etc.: *a wan look; a wan smile.* 3. lacking in forcefulness, competence, or effectiveness: *their wan attempts to organize*

CONCISE ETYMOLOGY KEY: <, descended or borrowed from; >, whence; b., blend of, blended; c., cognate with; cf., compare; deriv., derivative; equiv., equivalent; imit., imitative; obl., oblique; r., replacing; s., stem; sp., spelling, spelled; resp., respelling, respelled; trans., translation; ?, origin unknown; *, unattested; ‡, probably earlier than. See the full key inside the front cover.

the alumni. **4.** *Archaic.* **a.** dark or gloomy. **b.** pale in color or hue. —*v.i., v.t.* **5.** to become or make wan. [bef. 900; ME; OE *wann* dark, gloomy] —**wan′ly,** *adv.* —**wan′ness,** *n.*
—**Syn. 1.** ashen. See **pale**[1]. **3.** feeble, weak, half-hearted, lame. —**Ant. 1.** ruddy.

wan[2] (wän), *v. Obs.* a pt. of **win.**

WAN (wan), *n.* See **wide-area network.**

Wan•a•ma•ker (won′ə mā′kər), *n.* **John,** 1838–1922, U.S. merchant and philanthropist.

Wan•a•que (won′ə kyōō′, -kē′, wə nä′kwē, -kē), *n.* a town in NE New Jersey. 10,025.

Wan•chüan (*Chin.* wän′chyän′), *n. Wade-Giles.* former name of **Zhangjiakou.**

wand (wond), *n.* **1.** a slender stick or rod, esp. one used by a magician, conjurer, or diviner. **2.** a rod or staff carried as an emblem of one's office or authority. **3.** a slender shoot, stem, or branch of a shrub or tree. **4.** a small applicator for cosmetics, usually having a brush at the tip. **5.** *U.S. Archery.* a slat 6 ft. (183 cm) by 2 in. (5 cm) placed at a distance of 100 yd. (91 m) for men and 60 yd. (55 m) for women, and used as a target. **6.** Also called **wand reader.** an electronic device, in the form of a hand-held rod, that can optically read coded data, as on a merchandise label or tag. [1150–1200; ME < ON *vǫndr;* c. Goth *wandus*] —**wand′like′,** *adj.*

Wan•da (won′də), *n.* a female given name.

wan•der (won′dər), *v.i.* **1.** to ramble without a definite purpose or objective; roam, rove, or stray: *to wander over the earth.* **2.** to go aimlessly, indirectly, or casually; meander: *The river wanders among the rocks.* **3.** to extend in an irregular course or direction: *Foothills wandered off to the south.* **4.** to move, pass, or turn idly, as the hand or the eyes. **5.** (of the mind, thoughts, desires, etc.) to take one direction or another without conscious intent or control: *His attention wandered as the speaker droned on.* **6.** to stray from a path, place, companions, etc.: *During the storm the ship wandered from its course.* **7.** to deviate in conduct, belief, etc.; err; go astray: *Let me not wander from Thy Commandments.* **8.** to think or speak confusedly or incoherently. —*v.t.* **9.** to travel about, on, or through: *He wandered the streets.* —*n.* **10.** *Mech.* the drift of a gyroscope or a similar device. [bef. 900; ME *wandren,* OE *wandrian* (c. G *wandern*), freq. of *wendan* to WEND; see -ER[6]] —**wan′der•er,** *n.*
—**Syn. 1.** range, stroll. **2.** saunter. **6.** swerve, veer. **8.** ramble, rave.

Wan•der•er (won′dər ər), *n. Scot. Hist.* a Covenanter persecuted by Charles II and James II, esp. one who fled home to follow rebellious Presbyterian ministers who refused to accept episcopacy.

wan•der•ing (won′dər ing), *adj.* **1.** moving from place to place without a fixed plan; roaming; rambling: *wandering tourists.* **2.** having no permanent residence; nomadic: *a wandering tribe of Indians.* **3.** meandering; winding: *a wandering river; a wandering path.* —*n.* **4.** an aimless roving about; leisurely traveling from place to place: *a period of delightful wandering through Italy.* **5.** Usually, **wanderings. a.** aimless travels; meanderings: *Her wanderings took her all over the world.* **b.** disordered thoughts or utterances; incoherencies: *mental wanderings; the wanderings of delirium.* [bef. 1000; ME (n., adj.), OE *wandrigende* (adj.). See WANDER, -ING[2], -ING[1]] —**wan′der•ing•ly,** *adv.* —**wan′der•ing•ness,** *n.*

wan′dering al′batross, a large albatross, *Diomedea exulans,* of southern waters, having the plumage mostly white with dark markings. See illus. under **albatross.**

Wan′dering Jew′, 1. a legendary character condemned to roam without rest because he struck Christ on the day of the Crucifixion. **2.** Also, **wan′dering Jew′, Wan•der•ing-jew** (won′dər ing jōō′). Also called **inch plant.** any of various trailing or creeping plants, as *Zebrina pendula* or *Tradescantia fluminensis,* having green or variegated leaves: a popular houseplant. [1625–35]

Wan•der•jahr (vän′dər yär′), *n., pl.* **-jah•re** (-yä′rə). *German.* **1.** a year or period of travel, esp. following one's schooling and before practicing a profession. **2.** (formerly) a year in which an apprentice traveled and improved his skills before settling down to the practice of his trade.

wan•der•lust (won′dər lust′), *n.* a strong, innate desire to rove or travel about. [1850–55; < G, equiv. to *wander(n)* to WANDER + *Lust* desire; see LUST]

wan•der•oo (won′də rōō′), *n., pl.* **-der•oos. 1.** any of several purple-faced langurs, of Sri Lanka. **2.** a macaque, *Macacus silenus,* of southern India, having its face surrounded by long hair. [1675–85; < Sinhalese *wanduru* (pl.) < Skt *vānara* monkey]

w. & f., (in shipping) water and feed.

wan•doo (won dōō′), *n., pl.* **-doos. 1.** an Australian tree, *Eucalyptus redunca,* having hard, heavy wood valued as timber. **2.** the wood of this tree. [1880–85; < Nyungar *wando*]

Wan•do•ro•bo (wän′də rō′bō), *n., pl.* **-bos,** (*esp. collectively*) **-bo.** Dorobo.

wand′ read′er, wand (def. 6).

wands•man (wondz′mən), *n., pl.* **-men.** *Brit.* verger (def. 2). [1860–65; WAND + 's[1] + -MAN]

Wands•worth (wondz′wərth, -wûrth), *n.* a borough of Greater London, England. 288,400.

wane (wān), *v.,* **waned, wan•ing,** *n.* —*v.i.* **1.** to decrease in strength, intensity, etc.: *Daylight waned, and night came on. Her enthusiasm for the cause is waning.* **2.** to decline in power, importance, prosperity, etc.: *Colonialism began to wane after World War II.* **3.** to draw to a close; approach an end: *Summer is waning.* **4.** (of the moon) to decrease periodically in the extent of its illuminated portion after the full moon. Cf. **wax**[2] (def. 2). —*n.* **5.** a gradual decrease or decline in strength, intensity, power, etc. **6.** the drawing to a close of life, an era, a period, etc. **7.** the waning of the moon. **8.** a period of waning. **9.** a defect in a plank characterized by bark or insufficient wood at a corner or along an edge, due to the curvature of the log. **10. on the wane,** decreasing; diminishing: *The popularity of that song is on the wane.* [bef. 900; ME *wanen* (v.), OE *wanian* to lessen; c. MD, MHG *wanen,* ON *vana* to cause to wane, destroy]
—**Syn. 1, 2.** diminish, sink. **5.** diminution; failure.

wane•y (wā′nē), *adj.,* **wan•i•er, wan•i•est. 1.** wany (def. 1). **2.** (of a timber) having a wane or wanes. [1655–65; WANE + -Y[1]]

Wang Ching-wei (wäng′ jing′wā′), 1883–1944, Chinese political leader. Also, *Pinyin,* **Wang′ Jing′wei′.**

Wang•chuk (wäng′chŏŏk), *n.* **Jig•me Dor•ji** (jig′mā dôr′jē), 1929–72, king of Bhutan 1952–72.

wan•gle (wang′gəl), *v.,* **-gled, -gling,** *n.* —*v.t.* **1.** to bring about, accomplish, or obtain by scheming or underhand methods: *to wangle an invitation.* **2.** to falsify or manipulate for dishonest ends: *to wangle business records.* —*v.i.* **3.** to use contrivance, scheming, or underhand methods to obtain some goal or result. **4.** to manipulate something for dishonest ends. —*n.* **5.** an act or instance of wangling. [1810–20; b. WAG (the tongue) and DANGLE (about someone, i.e., hang around someone, court someone's favor)] —**wan′gler,** *n.*
—**Syn. 1.** maneuver, finagle, engineer, wheedle.

Wang Yang-ming (wäng′ yäng′ming′), *Wade-Giles, Pinyin.* (*Wang Shou-jen, Wang Shouren*) 1472–1529, Chinese scholar and philosopher.

Wan•hsien (*Chin.* wän′shyen′), *n. Wade-Giles.* Wanxian.

wan•i•gan (won′i gən), *n.* **1.** a lumberjack's trunk. **2.** a lumber camp's supply chest. **3.** a small house on wheels or tractor treads, used as an office or shelter in temporary lumber camps. **4.** (esp. in Alaska and the Pacific Northwest) a lean-to or other small addition built onto a house trailer, cabin, etc. Also, **wan•gan, wan•gun** (wang′gən), **wan′ni•gan.** [1840–50; < Ojibwa *wa·nikka·n* pit, deriv. of *wa·nikke·* to dig a hole < Proto-Algonquian **wa·θehke·* (**wa·θ-* hole + **-ehke·* make)]

wan′ing moon′, the moon at any time after full moon and before new moon (so called because its illuminated area is decreasing). Also called **old moon.** Cf. **waxing moon.** See diag. under **moon.** [bef. 1000; ME; OE]

wan•ion (won′yən), *n. Archaic.* curse; vengeance. [1540–50; alter. of *waniand,* ME: prp. of *wanien* to WANE (see -ING[2]), from the phrase *in the waniand* (*mone*) in the time of the waning (moon), i.e., in an unlucky hour]

wank (wangk), *v.i. Slang* (*vulgar*). to masturbate (often fol. by *off*). [1945–50; perh. b. WHACK and WHANG[2]] —**wank′er,** *n.*

Wan•kel (wäng′kəl, wang′-; *Ger.* väng′kəl), *n.* **Fe•lix** (fē′liks; *Ger.* fā′liks), born 1902, German engineer: inventor of rotary engine.

Wan′kel en′gine, an internal-combustion rotary engine that utilizes a triangular rotor that revolves in a chamber (rather than a conventional piston that moves up and down in a cylinder): it has fewer moving parts and is generally smaller and lighter for a given horsepower. Also called **Wan′kel.** [named after F. WANKEL]

wan•na (won′ə, wô′nə), *Pron. Spelling.* **1.** want to: *I wanna get out of here.* **2.** want a: *Wanna beer?*

wan•na•be (won′ə bē′, wô′nə-), *n., pl.* **-bes.** *Informal.* one who aspires, often vainly, to emulate another's success or attain eminence in some area. [1980–85; der. of (*I*) *wanna be . . .*]

wan•na•bee (won′ə bē′, wô′nə-), *n., pl.* **-bees.** wannabe.

Wan•ne-Eick•el (vä′nə ī′kəl), *n.* a city in the Ruhr region in W Germany. 100,300.

wan•nish (won′ish), *adj.* somewhat wan. [1375–1425; late ME; see WAN[1], -ISH[1]]

want (wont, wônt), *v.t.* **1.** to feel a need or a desire for; wish for: *to want one's dinner; always wanting something new.* **2.** to wish, need, crave, demand, or desire (often fol. by an infinitive): *I want to see you. She wants to be notified.* **3.** to be without or be deficient in: *to want judgment.* **4.** to fall short by (a specified amount): *The sum collected wants but a few dollars of the desired amount.* **5.** to require or need: *The house wants painting.* —*v.i.* **6.** to feel inclined; wish; like (often fol. by *to*): *We can stay home if you want.* **7.** to be deficient by the absence of some part or thing, or to feel or have a need (sometimes fol. by *for*): *He did not want for abilities.* **8.** to have need (usually fol. by *for*): *If you want for anything, let him know.* **9.** to be in a state of destitution, need, or poverty: *She would never allow her parents to want.* **10.** to be lacking or absent, as a part or thing necessary to completeness: *All that wants is his signature.* **11. want in** or **out,** *Chiefly Midland.* **a.** to desire to enter or leave: *The cat wants in.* **b.** *Informal.* to desire acceptance in or release from something specified. —*n.* **12.** something wanted or needed; necessity: *My wants are few.* **13.** something desired, demanded, or required: *a person of childish, capricious wants.* **14.** absence or deficiency of something desirable or requisite; lack: *plants dying for want of rain.* **15.** the state of being without something desired or needed; need: *to be in want of an assistant.* **16.** the state of being without the necessaries of life; destitution; poverty: *a country where want is virtually unknown.* **17.** a sense of lack or need of something: *to feel a vague want.* [1150–1200; ME *wante* < ON *vanta* to lack] —**want′er,** *n.* —**want′less,** *adj.* —**want′less•ness,** *n.*
—**Syn. 1.** require, crave. See **wish. 3.** need. See **lack. 12.** desideratum. **14.** dearth, scarcity, scarceness, inadequacy, insufficiency, paucity, meagerness. **16.** privation, penury, indigence. See **poverty.**

want′ ad′. See **classified ad.** [1885–90, *Amer.*]

want•age (won′tij, wôn′-), *n.* something, as an amount that is lacking, desired, or needed. [1820–30, *Amer.*; WANT + -AGE]

Wan•tagh (won′tô), *n.* a town on S Long Island, in SE New York. 19,817.

want•ing (won′ting, wôn′-), *adj.* **1.** lacking or absent: *a motor with some of the parts wanting.* **2.** deficient in some part, thing, or respect: *to be wanting in courtesy.* —*prep.* **3.** lacking; without: *a box wanting a lid.* **4.** less; minus: *a century wanting three years.* [1250–1300; ME (adj.); see WANT, -ING[2]]

want′ list′, a list of desired items, as stamps, coins, or books, circulated among dealers by a hobbyist, museum, or collector seeking to locate and purchase them.

wan•ton (won′tn), *adj.* **1.** done, shown, used, etc., maliciously or unjustifiably: *a wanton attack; wanton cruelty.* **2.** deliberate and without motive or provocation; uncalled-for; headstrong; willful: *Why jeopardize your career in such a wanton way?* **3.** without regard for what is right, just, humane, etc.; careless; reckless: *a wanton attacker of religious convictions.* **4.** sexually lawless or unrestrained; loose; lascivious; lewd: *wanton behavior.* **5.** extravagantly or excessively luxurious, as a person, manner of living, or style. **6.** luxuriant, as vegetation. **7.** *Archaic.* **a.** sportive or frolicsome, as children or young animals. **b.** having free play: *wanton breezes; a wanton brook.* —*n.* **8.** a wanton or lascivious person, esp. a woman. —*v.i.* **9.** to behave in a wanton manner; become wanton. —*v.t.* **10.** to squander, esp. in pleasure (often fol. by *away*): *to wanton away one's inheritance.* [1250–1300; ME *wantowen* lit., undisciplined, ill-reared, OE *wan-* not + *togen* ptp. of *tēon* to discipline, rear, c. G *ziehen,* L *dūcere* to lead; akin to TOW[1]] —**wan′ton•ly,** *adv.* —**wan′ton•ness,** *n.*
—**Syn. 1.** malicious. **2.** calculated. **3.** heedless, inconsiderate. **4.** licentious, dissolute, immoral, libidinous, concupiscent, lustful. **5.** lavish. **10.** waste. —**Ant. 3.** careful, considerate. **4, 5.** restrained.

Wan•xian (wän′shyän′), *n. Pinyin.* a city in E Sichuan province, in S central China, on the Chang Jiang. 175,000. Also, **Wanhsien.**

wan•y (wā′nē), *adj.,* **wan•i•er, wan•i•est. 1.** Also, **waney.** waning; decreasing; diminished in part. **2.** waney (def. 2). [WANE + -Y[1]]

wap (wop, wap), *v.t., v.i.,* **wapped, wap•ping,** *n.* whop.

wap•a•too (wop′ə tōō′), *n., pl.* **-toos.** an arrowhead plant, *Sagittaria latifolia.* [1805, *Amer.*; < Chinook Jargon; ulterior orig. uncert.]

wap•en•take (wop′ən tāk′, wap′-), *n.* (formerly in N England and the Midlands) a subdivision of a shire or county corresponding to a hundred. [bef. 1000; ME < ON *vāpnatak* (cf. OE *wǣpen-getæc*) show of weapons at public voting, equiv. to *vāpna* (gen. pl. of *vāpn* WEAPON) + *tak* taking; see TAKE]

wap•i•ti (wop′i tē), *n., pl.* **-tis,** (*esp. collectively*) **-ti.** elk (def. 2). [1806, *Amer.*; < Shawnee *wa·piti* lit., white rump (equiv. to Proto-Algonquian **wa·p-* white + **-etwiy-* rump); introduced as an E word by U.S. physician and naturalist Benjamin S. Barton]

wap•pen•shaw (wop′ən shô′, wap′-), *n.* a periodic muster or review of troops or persons under arms, formerly held in certain districts of Scotland to satisfy military chiefs that their men were properly armed and faithful to the local lord or chieftain. Also, **wap′pen•shaw′ing.** [1495–1505; short for *wappenshawing* (Scots), equiv. to *wappen* (OE *wǣpna,* gen. pl. of *wǣp(e)n* WEAPON) + *shawing* showing (see SHOW, -ING[1]); cf. D *wapenschouwing*]

wap•per•jaw (wop′ər jô′), *n. Informal.* a projecting underjaw. [*wapper* (< ?) + JAW[1]]

war[1] (wôr), *n., v.,* **warred, war•ring,** *adj.* —*n.* **1.** a conflict carried on by force of arms, as between nations or between parties within a nation; warfare, as by land, sea, or air. **2.** a state or period of armed hostility or active military operations: *The two nations were at war with each other.* **3.** a contest carried on by force of arms, as in a series of battles or campaigns: *the War of 1812.* **4.** active hostility or contention; conflict; contest: *a war of words.* **5.** aggressive business conflict, as through severe price cutting in the same industry or any other means of undermining competitors: *a fare war among airlines; a trade war between nations.* **6.** a struggle: *a war for men's minds; a war against poverty.* **7.** armed fighting, as a science, profession, activity, or art; methods or principles of waging armed conflict: *War is the soldier's business.* **8.** *Cards.* **a.** a game for two or more persons, played with a 52-card pack evenly divided between the players, in which each player turns up one card at a time with the higher card taking the lower, and in which, when both turned up cards match, each player lays one card face down and turns up another, the player with the higher card of the second turn taking all the cards laid down. **b.** an occasion in this game when both turned up cards match. **9.** *Archaic.* a battle. —*v.i.* **10.** to make or carry on war; fight: *to war with a neighboring nation.* **11.** to carry on active hostility or contention: *Throughout her life she warred with sin and corruption.* **12.** to be in conflict or in a state of strong opposition: *The temptation warred with his conscience.* —*adj.* **13.** of, belonging to, used in, or due to war: *war preparations; war hysteria.* [bef. 1150; (n.) ME, late OE *werre* < ONF < Gmc; c. OHG *werra* strife; (v.) ME, late OE *werrien* (transit.) to make war upon, deriv. of the n.; cf. OF *guerrer,* ONF *werreier;* akin to WAR[2]]

war[2] (wär), *adj., adv. Scot. and North Eng.* worse. [1150–1200; ME *werre* < ON *verri* WORSE]

war., warrant.

War′ and Peace′, a novel (1862–69) by Leo Tolstoy.

Wa•ran•gal (wôr′əng gəl), *n.* a city in N Andhra Pradesh, in SE India. 207,520.

war′ ba′by, 1. a child born or conceived in wartime. **2.** an illegitimate child born in wartime of a father in the armed forces. [1900–05]

War•beck (wôr′bek), *n.* **Per•kin** (pûr′kin), 1474–99, Flemish imposter who pretended to the throne of England.

CONCISE PRONUNCIATION KEY: *act, cāpe, dâre, pärt; set, ēqual; if, īce; ox, ōver, ôrder, oil, bŏŏk, bōōt, out; up, ûrge; child; sing; shoe; thin, that;* zh as in *treasure.* ə = *a* as in *alone, e* as in *system, i* as in *easily, o* as in *gallop, u* as in *circus;* ᵊ as in *fire* (fīᵊr), *hour* (ouᵊr). l and n can serve as syllabic consonants, as in *cradle* (krād′l), and *button* (but′n). See the full key inside the front cover.

War′ Between′ the States′, the American Civil War: used esp. in the South.

war·ble[1] (wôr′bəl), *v.*, **-bled, -bling,** *n.* —*v.i.* **1.** to sing or whistle with trills, quavers, or melodic embellishments: *The canary warbled most of the day.* **2.** to yodel. **3.** (of electronic equipment) to produce a continuous sound varying regularly in pitch and frequency. —*v.t.* **4.** to sing (an aria or other selection) with trills, quavers, or melodious turns. **5.** to express or celebrate in or as if in song; carol. —*n.* **6.** a warbled song or succession of melodic trills, quavers, etc. **7.** the act of warbling. [1300–50; ME *werble* a tune < ONF < Gmc; cf. OHG *werbel* something that turns, equiv. to *werb-* (c. OE *hweorf-* in *hweorfan* to turn) + *-el* n. suffix]

war·ble[2] (wôr′bəl), *n. Vet. Pathol.* **1.** a small, hard tumor on a horse's back, produced by the galling of the saddle. **2.** a lump in the skin of an animal's back, containing the larva of a warble fly. [1575–85; orig. uncert.; cf. obs. Sw *varbulde* boil] —**war′bled,** *adj.*

war′ble fly′, any of several stout, woolly flies of the family Oestridae, the larvae of which produce warbles in cattle and other animals. [1875–80]

war·bler (wôr′blər), *n.* **1.** any of several small, chiefly Old World songbirds of the subfamily Sylviidae. Cf. **blackcap** (def. 1), **reed warbler. 2.** Also called **wood warbler.** any of numerous small New World songbirds of the family Parulidae, many species of which are brightly colored. Cf. **yellow warbler. 3.** a person or thing that warbles. [1605–15; WARBLE[1] + -ER[1]]

war′bling vir′eo, a grayish-green American vireo, *Vireo gilvus,* characterized by its melodious warble. [1830–40, *Amer.*]

war′ bon′net, an American Indian headdress consisting of a headband with a tail of ornamental feathers. [1800–10]

war bonnet

war′ bride′, 1. a woman who marries a serviceman about to go overseas in wartime. **2.** a woman who marries a foreign serviceman and goes to live in his country. [1915–20]

War·burg (vär′bŏŏrk′; *Eng.* wôr′bûrg), *n.* **Ot·to Hein·rich** (ôt′ō hin′rɪкн), 1883–1970, German physiologist: Nobel prize for medicine 1931.

war′ chest′, money set aside or scheduled for a particular purpose or activity, as for a political campaign or organizational drive. [1900–05, *Amer.*]

war′ cloud′, something that threatens war; a harbinger of conflict. [1820–30]

war′ correspond′ent, a reporter or commentator assigned to send news or opinions directly from battle areas. [1860–65, *Amer.*]

war′ crime′, Usually, **war crimes.** crimes committed against an enemy, prisoners of war, or subjects in wartime that violate international agreements or, as in the case of genocide, are offenses against humanity. [1940–45] —**war′ crim′inal.**

war′ cry′, 1. a cry, word, phrase, etc., shouted in charging or in rallying to attack; battle cry. **2.** a slogan, phrase, or motto used to unite a political party, rally support for a cause, etc. [1740–50]

ward (wôrd), *n.* **1.** a division or district of a city or town, as for administrative or political purposes. **2.** one of the districts into which certain English and Scottish boroughs are divided. **3.** a division, floor, or room of a hospital for a particular class or group of patients: *a convalescent ward; a critical ward.* **4.** any of the separate divisions of a prison. **5.** a political subdivision of a parish in Louisiana. **6.** *Mormon Ch.* one of the subdivisions of a stake, presided over by a bishop. **7.** *Fort.* an open space within or between the walls of a castle or fortified place: *the castle's lower ward.* **8.** *Law.* **a.** a person, esp. a minor, who has been legally placed under the care of a guardian or a court. **b.** the state of being under the care or control of a legal guardian. **c.** guardianship over a minor or some other person legally incapable of managing his or her own affairs. **9.** the state of being under restraining guard or in custody. **10.** a person who is under the protection or control of another. **11.** a movement or posture of defense, as in fencing. **12.** a curved ridge of metal inside a lock, forming an obstacle to the passage of a key that does not have a corresponding notch. **13.** the notch or slot in the bit of a key into which such a ridge fits. **14.** the act of keeping guard or protective watch: *watch and ward.* **15.** *Archaic.* a company of guards or a garrison. —*v.t.* **16.** to avert, repel, or turn aside (danger, harm, an attack, an assailant, etc.) (usually fol. by *off*): *to ward off a blow; to ward off evil.* **17.** to place in a ward, as of a hospital or prison. **18.** *Archaic.* to protect; guard. [bef. 900; (n.) ME *warde,* OE *weard;* (v.) ME *warden,* OE *weardian;* c. MD *waerden,* G *warten;* cf. GUARD] —**ward′less,** *adj.*
—**Syn. 1.** precinct. **10.** protégé. **16.** parry, prevent.

Ward (wôrd), *n.* **1. (Aaron) Montgomery,** 1843–1913, U.S. merchant and mail-order retailer. **2. Ar·te·mas** (är′tə məs), 1727–1800, American general in the American Revolution. **3. Ar·te·mus** (är′tə məs), (*Charles Farrar Browne*), 1834–67, U.S. humorist. **4. Barbara** (*Baroness Jackson of Lodsworth*), 1914–81, English economist and author. **5. Mrs. Humphry** (*Mary Augusta Arnold*), 1851–1920, English novelist, born in Tasmania. **6. Sir Joseph George,** 1856–1930, New Zealand statesman, born in Australia: Prime Minister 1906–12, 1928–30. **7. Lester Frank,** 1841–1913, U.S. sociologist. **8. Nathaniel** (*"Theodore de la Guard"*), 1578?–1652, English clergyman, lawyer, and author in America. **9.** a male given name.

-ward, a native English suffix denoting spatial or temporal direction, as specified by the initial element: *toward; seaward; afterward; backward.* Also, **-wards.** [ME; OE *-weard* towards; c. G *-wärts;* akin to L *vertere* to turn (see VERSE)]
—**Usage.** Both -WARD and -WARDS occur in such words as *backward, forward, upward,* and *toward.* The -WARD form is by far the more common in edited American English writing.

war′ dance′, a dance preliminary to going into battle or in celebration of a victory, as formerly among American Indians. [1705–15, *Amer.*]

ward·ed (wôr′did), *adj.* having notches, slots, or wards, as in locks and keys. [1565–75; WARD (n.) + -ED[3]]

ward′ eight′, a mixed drink containing whiskey, lemon juice, grenadine, and often soda water, served in a tall glass with crushed ice and sometimes garnished with an orange slice and a cherry.

war·den (wôr′dn), *n.* **1.** a person charged with the care or custody of persons, animals, or things; keeper. **2.** the chief administrative officer in charge of a prison. **3.** any of various public officials charged with superintendence, as over a port or wildlife. **4.** See **air-raid warden. 5.** See **fire warden. 6.** (in Connecticut) the chief executive officer of a borough. **7.** (formerly) the principal official in a region, town, etc. **8.** *Brit.* **a.** (*cap.*) a traditional title of the president or governor of certain schools and colleges: *Warden of Merton College.* **b.** a member of a livery company of the City of London. **9.** *Canadian.* the head of certain county or local councils. **10.** a member of the governing body of a guild. **11.** a churchwarden. **12.** a gatekeeper. [1175–1225; ME *wardein* < OF (northeast dial.), equiv. to *ward-* (root of *warder* to guard; see WARD) + *-ein,* var. of *-ien, -enc* < Gmc *-ing* -ING[3]] —**ward′en·ship′,** *n.*
—**Syn. 1.** warder, guardian, guard, custodian, caretaker, superintendent.

War·den (wôr′dn), *n. Brit.* any of several pears having a crisp, firm flesh, used in cookery.

war·den·ry (wôr′dn rē), *n., pl.* **-ries.** the office, jurisdiction, or district of a warden. [1325–75; ME; see WARDEN, -RY]

War′ Depart′ment, *U.S. Hist.* the department of the federal government that, from 1789 until 1947, was responsible for defense and the military establishment: in 1947 it became the Department of the Army, which became part of the Department of Defense when it was established in 1949.

ward·er[1] (wôr′dər), *n.* **1.** a person who guards something, as a doorkeeper or caretaker. **2.** a soldier or other person set to guard an entrance. **3.** *Chiefly Brit.* an official having charge of prisoners in a jail. [1350–1400; ME *warder(e)* (see WARD, -ER[1]); cf. AF *wardere* < ME] —**ward′er·ship′,** *n.*

ward·er[2] (wôr′dər), *n.* a truncheon or staff of office or authority, used in giving signals. [1400–50; late ME < ?]

ward′ heel′er, *U.S. Politics.* a minor politician who canvasses voters and does other chores for a political machine or party boss. [1885–90, *Amer.*]

Ward′i·an case′ (wôr′dē ən), **1.** a type of terrarium having a top and sides of glass. **2.** a case used for transporting plants, having wood sides and a glass top protected by wood slats. [1835–45; named after Nathaniel B. *Ward* (1791–1868), English botanist; see -IAN]

ward·ress (wôr′dris), *n.* a woman who is a warder. [1815–25; WARD(E)R[1] + -ESS]
—**Usage.** See **-ess.**

ward·robe (wôr′drōb), *n., v.,* **-robed, -rob·ing.** —*n.* **1.** a stock of clothes or costumes, as of a person or of a theatrical company. **2.** a piece of furniture for holding clothes, now usually a tall, upright case fitted with hooks, shelves, etc. **3.** a room or place in which to keep clothes or costumes. **4.** the department of a royal or other great household charged with the care of wearing apparel. **5.** See **wardrobe trunk. 6.** a department in a motion-picture or television studio in charge of supplying and maintaining costumes: *Report to wardrobe right after lunch.* —*v.t.* **7.** to provide with a wardrobe. [1250–1300; ME *warderobe* < AF. See WARD (v.), ROBE]

ward′robe mis′tress, a woman in charge of keeping theatrical costumes cleaned, pressed, and in wearable condition. [1895–1900]

ward′robe trunk′, a large, upright trunk, usually with space on one side for hanging clothes and drawers or compartments on the other for small articles, shoes, etc. [1885–90, *Amer.*]

ward·room (wôrd′ro͞om′, -ro͝om′), *n.* (on a warship) **1.** the area serving as the living quarters for all commissioned officers except the commanding officer. **2.** the dining saloon and lounge for these officers. **3.** these officers collectively. [1795–1805; WARD + ROOM]

-wards, var. of **-ward:** *towards; afterwards.* [ME; OE *-weardes,* equiv. to *-weard* toward (see WARD) + *-es* -S[1]]
—**Usage.** See **-ward.**

ward·ship (wôrd′ship), *n.* **1.** guardianship; custody. **2.** *Law.* the guardianship over a minor or ward. [1425–75; late ME; see WARD, -SHIP]

ware[1] (wâr), *n.* **1.** Usually, **wares. a.** articles of merchandise or manufacture; goods: *a peddler selling his wares.* **b.** any intangible items, as services or products of artistic or intellectual creativity, that are salable: *an actor advertising his wares.* **2.** a specified kind or class of merchandise or of manufactured article (usually used in combination): *silverware; glassware.* **3.** pottery, or a particular kind of pottery: *delft ware.* **4.** *Archaeol.* a group of ceramic types classified according to paste and texture, surface modification, as burnish or glaze, and decorative motifs rather than shape and color. [bef. 1000; ME; OE *waru;* c. G *Ware*]

ware[2] (wâr), *adj., v.,* **wared, war·ing.** *Archaic.* —*adj.* **1.** watchful, wary, or cautious. **2.** aware; conscious. —*v.t.* **3.** to beware of (usually used in the imperative). [bef. 900; ME (adj. and v.); OE *wær* (adj.); c. G *gewahr* aware, ON *varr*]

ware[3] (wâr), *v.t.,* **wared, war·ing.** *Scot. and North Eng.* to spend; expend. [1300–50; ME < ON *verja* to spend, invest]

ware[4] (wâr), *n. Scot. and North Eng.* the first season in the year; spring. [1250–1300; ME < ON *vār* spring; perh. akin to L *vēr* (see VERNAL), Gk *éar* spring]

ware·house (*n.* wâr′hous′; *v.* wâr′houz′, -hous′), *n., pl.* **-hous·es** (-hou′ziz), *v.,* **-housed, -hous·ing.** —*n.* **1.** a building, or a part of one, for the storage of goods, merchandise, etc. **2.** *Brit.* a large retail store. **3.** a building, or a part of one, in which wholesalers keep large stocks of merchandise, which they display and sell to retailers. —*v.t.* **4.** to place, deposit, or store in a warehouse. **5.** to set aside or accumulate, as for future use. **6.** to place in a government or bonded warehouse, to be kept until duties are paid. **7.** *Informal.* to confine (the mentally ill) to large institutions for long-term custodial care. [1300–50; ME; see WARE[1], HOUSE]

ware·house·man (wâr′hous′mən), *n., pl.* **-men. 1.** a person who stores goods for others for pay. **2.** a person who is employed in or who manages a warehouse. [1625–35; WAREHOUSE + -MAN]

ware·hous·er (wâr′hou′zər), *n.* **1.** warehouseman. **2.** a person or company operating a warehouse or its services. **3.** a wholesaler with a large building for display and sale of goods. [1925–30; WAREHOUSE + -ER[1]]

ware′house receipt′, a receipt for goods placed in a warehouse. [1885–90]

ware·hous·ing (wâr′hou′zing), *n.* **1.** an act or instance of a person or company that warehouses something. **2.** the pledging as security, to a commercial bank, of a long-term mortgage for a short-term loan. [1785–95; WAREHOUSE + -ING[1]]

ware·room (wâr′ro͞om′, -ro͝om′), *n.* a room in which goods are stored or are displayed for sale. [1805–15; WARE[1] + ROOM]

war·fare (wôr′fâr′), *n.* **1.** the process of military struggle between two nations or groups of nations; war. **2.** armed conflict between two massed enemies, armies, or the like. **3.** conflict, esp. when vicious and unrelenting, between competitors, political rivals, etc. [1425–75; late ME *werefare,* i.e., a faring forth to war; see WAR[1], FARE]

war·fa·rin (wôr′fə rin), *n. Chem.* **1.** a colorless, crystalline, water-insoluble anticoagulant, $C_{19}H_{16}O_4$, used chiefly as a rodenticide. **2.** *Pharm.* a preparation of this used in the management of potential or existing clotting disorders. [1945–50; *W(isconsin) A(lumni) R(esearch) F(oundation)* (owners of patent) + (COUM)ARIN]

War·field (wôr′fēld′), *n.* **David,** 1866–1951, U.S. actor.

war′ foot′ing, the condition or status of a military force or other organization when operating under a state of war or as if a state of war existed. [1890–95]

war′ game′, *Mil.* a simulated military operation, carried out to test the validity of a war plan or operational concept: in its simplest form, two opposing teams of officers take part, and when necessary, military units of the required strength are employed. [1820–30]

war′ ham′mer. See **pole hammer.**

war′ hat′, *Armor.* See **chapel de fer.**

war′ hawk′, 1. hawk[1] (def. 4). **2.** (*caps.*) *U.S. Hist.* any of the congressmen from the South and West, led by Henry Clay and John Calhoun, who wanted war against Britain in the period leading up to the War of 1812.

war·head (wôr′hed′), *n.* the forward section of a self-propelled missile, bomb, torpedo, or the like, containing the explosive, chemical, or atomic charge. [1895–1900; WAR[1] + HEAD]

War·hol (wôr′hôl, -hol), *n.* **Andy,** 1928–87, U.S. artist.

war·horse (wôr′hôrs′), *n.* **1.** a horse used in war; charger. **2.** *Informal.* a veteran, as a soldier or politician, of many struggles and conflicts. **3.** a musical composition, play, etc., that has been seen, heard, or performed excessively. [1645–55; WAR[1] + HORSE]

war·i·ly (wâr′ə lē), *adv.* in a wary manner. [1545–55; WARY + -LY]

war·i·ness (wâr′ē nis), *n.* the state or quality of being wary. [1545–55; WARY + -NESS]

war·i·son (war′ə sən), *n.* a bugle call to assault. [1805; Walter Scott's misinterpretation of now obs. *warison* reward, wealth, possessions, ME < AF *warison* defense, possessions, OF *garison;* see GARRISON]

War′ La′bor Board′. See **National War Labor Board.**

war·less (wôr′lis), *adj.* unmarked by war: *The international conflict was followed by a warless decade.* [1400–50; late ME; see WAR[1], -LESS] —**war′less·ly,** *adv.* —**war′less·ness,** *n.*

war·like (wôr′līk′), *adj.* **1.** fit, qualified, or ready for war; martial: *a warlike fleet; warlike tribes.* **2.** threatening or indicating war: *a warlike tone.* **3.** of or pertaining to war: *a warlike expedition.* [1375–1425; late ME; see WAR[1], -LIKE]
—**Syn. 2.** bellicose, belligerent, hostile; inimical, unfriendly. —**Ant. 2.** peaceful.

war·lock (wôr′lok′), *n.* **1.** a man who practices the black arts; a male witch; sorcerer. **2.** a fortuneteller or conjurer. [bef. 900; ME *warloghe, -lach,* OE *wǣrloga* oathbreaker, devil, equiv. to *wǣr* covenant + *-loga* betrayer (deriv. of *lēogan* to lie)]

war•lord (wôr′lôrd′), *n.* **1.** a military leader, esp. of a warlike nation. **2.** a military commander who has seized power, esp. in one section of a country. **3.** tuchun. [1855–60; WAR[1] + LORD] **—war′lord′ism,** *n.*

warm (wôrm), *adj.,* **-er, -est,** *v., n.* **—***adj.* **1.** having or giving out a moderate degree of heat, as perceived by the senses: *a warm bath.* **2.** of or at a moderately high temperature; characterized by comparatively high temperature: *a warm oven; a warm climate; a warm summer.* **3.** having a sensation of bodily heat: *to be warm from fast walking.* **4.** conserving or maintaining warmth or heat: *warm clothes.* **5.** (of colors) suggestive of warmth; inclining toward red or orange rather than toward green or blue. **6.** characterized by or showing lively feelings, passions, emotions, sympathies, etc.: *a warm heart; warm interest.* **7.** strongly attached; intimate: *warm friends.* **8.** cordial or hearty: *a warm welcome.* **9.** heated, irritated, or angry: *to become warm when contradicted.* **10.** animated, lively, brisk, or vigorous: *a warm debate.* **11.** strong or fresh: *a warm scent.* **12.** close to something sought, as in a game. **13.** uncomfortable or unpleasant: *His opponents made things so warm that he decided to quit.* **14.** *Brit. Informal.* well off; in easy circumstances. **—***v.t.* **15.** to make warm; heat (often fol. by *up*): *to warm one's hands; to warm up a room.* **16.** to heat or cook (something) for reuse, as leftovers (usually fol. by *over* or *up*): *to warm up yesterday's stew.* **17.** to excite enthusiasm, ardor, cheerfulness, or vitality in (someone): *The wine soon warmed the company.* **18.** to inspire with kindly feeling; affect with lively pleasure: *It warms my soul to hear you say that.* **19.** to fill (a person, crowd, etc.) with strong feelings, as hatred, anger, or zeal: *Restrictions had warmed the crew to the point of mutiny.* **—***v.i.* **20.** to become warm or warmer (often fol. by *up*): *The room will warm up when the fire gets going.* **21.** to become ardent, enthusiastic, animated, etc. (often fol. by *up* or *to*): *The speaker quickly warmed to her subject.* **22.** to grow kindly, friendly, or sympathetically disposed (often fol. by *to* or *toward*): *My heart warms toward him.* **23. warm down,** to conclude or follow a period of strenuous physical exercise by walking or gentle stretching. **24. warm the bench,** *Sports.* to serve as a substitute who rarely plays in a game: *The young outfielder warmed the bench for the Yankees last season.* **25. warm up, a.** to prepare for a game, sports contest, dance, etc., by moderate exercise or practice beforehand. **b.** to increase in excitement, intensity, violence, etc.: *The racial situation was warming up.* **c.** to become friendlier or more receptive: *No matter how hard I tried, I just couldn't warm up to that proposal.* **d.** *Radio and Television.* to entertain (an audience) prior to a broadcast to increase receptiveness. **—***n.* **26.** *Informal.* a warming: *Sit by the fire and have a nice warm.* [bef. 900; (adj.) ME *werm, warm,* OE *wearm;* c. G *warm,* ON *varmr;* (v.) ME *warmen, wermen,* OE *werman, wirman* (transit.), *wearmian* (intransit.), both akin to the adj.; (n.) deriv. of the v.] **—warm′er,** *n.* **—warm′ish,** *adj.* **—warm′ly,** *adv.* **—warm′ness,** *n.*
—Syn. 1. lukewarm, tepid, heated. **6.** hearty, enthusiastic, fervent, fervid, emotional, ardent. **7.** friendly, close. **8.** fervent. **9.** annoyed, vexed, irate, furious. **10.** vehement. **17.** animate, excite, waken, stir, rouse, arouse. **—Ant. 1–3, 5, 8.** cool.

War′ Man′power Commis′sion, *U.S. Govt.* the board (1942–45) that regulated the most efficient use of labor during World War II. *Abbr.:* WMC

warm-blood•ed (wôrm′blud′id), *adj.* **1.** Also, **endothermic.** designating or pertaining to animals, as mammals and birds, whose blood ranges in temperatures from about 98° to 112°F (37° to 44°C) and remains relatively constant, irrespective of the temperature of the surrounding medium; homoiothermal. **2.** ardent, impetuous, or passionate: *young and warm-blooded valor.* [1785–95] **—warm′-blood′ed•ness,** *n.*

warm-down (wôrm′doun′), *n.* a tapering off or recovery from strenuous physical exercise, esp. running or racing, by slowing down or doing light stretches. [by analogy with WARMUP]

warmed-o•ver (wôrmd′ō′vər), *adj.* **1.** (of cooked foods) heated again: *warmed-over stew.* **2.** reworked or repeated without enthusiasm or introduction of new ideas; stale: *a warmed-over version of an old show.* [1885–90]

warmed-up (wôrmd′up′), *adj.* warmed-over (def. 1).

warm•er-up•per (wôr′mər up′ər), *n. Informal.* **1.** something that provides one with invigorating warmth: *Hot soup is a good warmer-upper after skiing.* **2.** something that serves to warm up an audience or group of participants before a main event: *Radio stations played martial music as a warmer-upper before the prime minister's speech.* [1940–45; *warm up* + -ER[1], applied pleonastically to both v. and particle]

warm′ front′, *Meteorol.* a transition zone between a mass of warm air and the colder air it is replacing. [1920–25]

warm-heart•ed (wôrm′här′tid), *adj.* having or showing sympathy, affection, kindness, cordiality, etc.: *a warm-hearted welcome.* Also, **warm′heart′ed.** [1490–1500] **—warm′-heart′ed•ly,** *adv.* **—warm′-heart′ed•ness,** *n.*
—Syn. sympathetic, compassionate, kind; enthusiastic, fervent.

warm′ing pan′, a long-handled, covered pan, usually of brass, filled with live coals or hot water for warming a cold bed. [1565–75]

war′min•ster broom′ (wôr′min′stər), a European shrub, *Cytisus praecox,* of the legume family, having yellowish-white or yellow, pealike flowers. [after *Warminster,* England]

war•mon•ger (wôr′mung′gər, -mong′-), *n.* a person who advocates, endorses, or tries to precipitate war. [1580–90; WAR[1] + MONGER]

war•mon•ger•ing (wôr′mung′gər ing, -mong′-), *n.* the practices and principles of a warmonger. [WARMONGER + -ING[1]]

war•mouth (wôr′mouth′), *n., pl.* **-mouths** (-mouthz′, -mouths′), (*esp. collectively*) **-mouth.** a freshwater sunfish, *Lepomis gulosus,* of the eastern U.S., having a patch of small teeth on its tongue. [1880–85, *Amer.;* orig. uncert.]

warm′ sec′tor, *Meteorol.* the region of warmest air bounded by the cold and warm fronts of a cyclone.

warm′ spot′, 1. *Physiol.* a sensory area in the skin that responds to an increase in temperature. **2.** *Informal.* a memory or group of memories that one regards with affection: *The good old days are a warm spot with most of us.* [1925–30]

warm′ spring′, a thermal spring having a temperature of up to 98°F (37°C). Cf. **hot spring.** [1740–50, *Amer.*]

Warm′ Springs′, a town in W Georgia: resort; site of foundation for treatment of poliomyelitis. 425.

warmth (wôrmth), *n.* **1.** the quality or state of being warm; moderate or gentle heat. **2.** the sensation of moderate heat. **3.** liveliness of feelings, emotions, or sympathies; ardor or fervor; enthusiasm or zeal: *She spoke her mind with great warmth. There was warmth in his greeting and in his handshake.* **4.** the quality of being intimate and attached: *All children need warmth and affection from their families.* **5.** an effect of brightness, cheerfulness, coziness, etc., achieved by the use of warm colors: *The room has warmth since it was redecorated.* **6.** the means or ability to produce a sensation of heat: *a jacket with little warmth.* **7.** slight anger or irritation: *Her denial betrayed some warmth.* [1125–75; ME *wermth.* See WARM, -TH[1]] **—warmth′less,** *adj.* **—warmth′less•ness,** *n.*
—Syn. 3. heat, fire, spirit, vigor. **4.** tenderness, kindness, affection.

warm′ tone′, *Photog.* a yellow, brown, olive, or reddish tinge in a black-and-white print. Cf. **cold tone.**

warm•up (wôrm′up′), *n.* **1.** an act or instance of warming up: *The spectators came early to watch the players go through their warmups. The dancers went through a quick warmup.* **2.** the period before a radio or television broadcast when the audience is entertained so that it will be more receptive to the actual program. **3.** Also, **warm′ up′.** the time lapse between turning on the power in an electronic component or device and the time it is operable. **4.** Often, **warmups.** any apparel, esp. a sweat suit, worn over other clothing for warmth, chiefly in sports or during preliminary exercise. Also, **warm′-up′.** [1840–50; n. use of v. phrase *warm up*]

warn (wôrn), *v.t.* **1.** to give notice, advice, or intimation to (a person, group, etc.) of danger, impending evil, possible harm, or anything else unfavorable: *They warned him of a plot against him. She was warned that her life was in danger.* **2.** to urge or advise to be careful; caution: *to warn a careless driver.* **3.** to admonish or exhort, as to action or conduct: *She warned her employees to be on time.* **4.** to notify, advise, or inform: *to warn a person of an intended visit.* **5.** to give notice to (a person, group, etc.) to go, keep at a distance, etc. (often fol. by *away, off,* etc.): *A sign warns trespassers off the grounds. A marker warned boats away from the dock.* **6.** to give authoritative or formal notice to (someone); order; summon: *to warn a person to appear in court.* **—***v.i.* **7.** to give a warning; caution: *to warn of further disasters.* [bef. 1000; ME *warnen,* OE *warnian;* c. G *warnen.* Cf. WARE[2]] **—warn′er,** *n.*
—Syn. 1. forewarn. WARN, CAUTION, ADMONISH imply attempting to prevent another from running into danger or getting into unpleasant or undesirable circumstances. To WARN is to speak plainly and usually in strong terms: *to warn him about danger and possible penalties.* To CAUTION is to advise about necessary precautions, to put one on one's guard about possibly harmful circumstances or conditions, thus emphasizing avoidance of undesirable consequences: *to caution him against driving in such weather.* ADMONISH suggests giving earnest, authoritative advice with only tacit references to danger or penalty: *to admonish a person for neglecting his duties.*

War•ner (wôr′nər), *n.* **1. Charles Dud•ley** (dud′lē), 1829–1900, U.S. editor and essayist. **2. Glenn Sco•bey** (skō′bē), ("*Pop*"), 1871–1954, U.S. football coach. **3. Jack L(eonard),** 1892–1978, U.S. film producer, born in Canada.

War′ner Rob′ins (rob′inz), a city in central Georgia. 39,893.

warn•ing (wôr′ning), *n.* **1.** the act or utterance of one who warns or the existence, appearance, sound, etc., of a thing that warns. **2.** something that serves to warn, give notice, or caution: *We fired a warning at the intruders.* **3.** *Meteorol.* an announcement from the U.S. National Weather Service alerting the public that a storm or other weather-related hazard is imminent and that immediate steps should be taken to protect lives and property. Cf. **advisory** (def. 5), **storm warning** (def. 2), **watch** (def. 23). **—***adj.* **4.** serving to warn, advise, caution: *a warning bell.* [bef. 900; ME (n.); OE *war(e)nung* precaution; see WARN, -ING[1], -ING[2]] **—warn′ing•ly,** *adv.*
—Syn. 2. caution, admonition, advice; omen, sign, portent, augury, presage.

warn′ing colora′tion, *Biol.* a bold, distinctive pattern of color characteristic of a poisonous or unpalatable organism, as the skunk or the monarch butterfly, that functions as a warning to and defense against predators. [1925–30]

warn′ing track′, *Baseball.* a strip, often consisting of a cinder or dirt track, bordering the outer edge of the outfield between the outfield turf and the stadium wall that alerts outfielders that the wall is near, esp. as they back up to catch a fly ball. [1965–70]

war′ nose′, the explosive forward section of a projectile, as of a torpedo or shell; warhead.

War′ of Amer′ican Independ′ence, *Brit.* See **American Revolution.**

War of 1812, the war between the United States and Great Britain from 1812 to 1815.

War′ of Independ′ence. See **American Revolution.**

war′ of nerves′, a conflict using psychological techniques, as propaganda, threats, and false rumors, rather than direct violence, in order to confuse, thwart, or intimidate an enemy. [1935–40]

War′ of Seces′sion. See **American Civil War.**

War′ of the Aus′trian Succes′sion, the war (1740–48) in which Austria, England, and the Netherlands opposed Prussia, France, and Spain over the selection of rulers for territories within the Austrian Empire. Cf. **King George's War.**

War′ of the Grand′ Alli′ance, the war (1689–97) in which England, the Netherlands, Spain, Sweden, and the Holy Roman Empire in league with Bavaria, Brandenburg, Savoy, and the Palatinate opposed France. Cf. **King William's War.**

War′ of the Na′tions. See **World War I.**

War′ of the Rebel′lion. See **American Civil War.**

War′ of the Span′ish Succes′sion, a war (1701–14) fought by Austria, England, the Netherlands, and Prussia against France and Spain, arising from disputes about the succession in Spain after the death of Charles II of Spain.

warp (wôrp), *v.t.* **1.** to bend or twist out of shape, esp. from a straight or flat form, as timbers or flooring. **2.** to bend or turn from the natural or true direction or course. **3.** to distort or cause to distort from the truth, fact, true meaning, etc.; bias; falsify: *Prejudice warps the mind.* **4.** *Aeron.* to curve or bend (a wing or other airfoil) at the end or ends to promote equilibrium or to secure lateral control. **5.** *Naut.* to move (a vessel) into a desired place or position by hauling on a rope that has been fastened to something fixed, as a buoy or anchor. **6.** *Agric.* to fertilize (land) by inundation with water that deposits alluvial matter. **—***v.i.* **7.** to become bent or twisted out of shape, esp. out of a straight or flat form: *The wood has warped in drying.* **8.** to be or become biased; hold or change an opinion due to prejudice, external influence, or the like. **9.** *Naut.* **a.** to warp a ship or boat into position. **b.** (of a ship or boat) to move by being warped. **10.** (of a stratum in the earth's crust) to bend slightly, to a degree that no fold or fault results. **—***n.* **11.** a bend, twist, or variation from a straight or flat form in something, as in wood that has dried unevenly. **12.** a mental twist, bias, or quirk, or a biased or twisted attitude or judgment. **13.** the set of yarns placed lengthwise in the loom, crossed by and interlaced with the weft, and forming the lengthwise threads in a woven fabric. See diag. under **weave.** **14.** See **time warp.** **15.** a situation, environment, etc., that seems characteristic of another era, esp. in being out of touch with contemporary life or attitudes, etc. **16.** Also called **spring, spring line.** *Naut.* a rope for warping or hauling a ship or boat along or into position. **17.** alluvial matter deposited by water, esp. water let in to inundate low land so as to enrich it. [bef. 900; (v.) ME *werpen,* OE *weorpan* to throw; c. G *werfen,* ON *verpa,* Goth *wairpan;* (n.) ME *warpe,* OE *wearp;* c. G *Warf,* ON *varp*] **—warp′age,** *n.*
—Syn. 1. turn, contort, distort. **2.** swerve, deviate. **—Ant. 1, 7.** straighten.

war′ paint′, 1. paint applied by American Indians to their faces and bodies before going to war. **2.** *Informal.* makeup; cosmetics. **3.** *Informal.* full dress; regalia. [1820–30, *Amer.*]

war′ par′ty, 1. *U.S. Hist.* a group of American Indians prepared for war. **2.** any political party or group that advocates war. [1745–55, *Amer.*]

war•path (wôr′path′, -päth′), *n., pl.* **-paths** (-pathz′, -päthz′, -paths′, -päths′). **1.** the path or course taken by American Indians on a warlike expedition. **2. on the warpath, a.** seeking, preparing for, or engaged in war or aggressive pursuit. **b.** in a state of anger or indignation; hostile. [1745–55, *Amer.;* WAR[1] + PATH]

warp′ beam′, a roller, located at the back of a loom, on which the warp ends are wound in preparation for weaving. Also called **warp′ roll′.** [1825–35]

warp•er (wôr′pər), *n.* **1.** a person or thing that warps. **2.** *Textiles.* a machine used to wind warp ends in preparation for weaving. [bef. 1000; OE *weorpere* thrower (in ME only in compounds); see WARP, -ER[1]]

warp′ i′kat. See under **ikat.**

warp′ing board′, a rectangular board containing evenly spaced pegs at each end on which the warp is wound in preparation for weaving. [1905–10]

warp′ing frame′, *n.* a wooden frame containing evenly spaced pegs on which the warp is wound in preparation for weaving. [1680–90]

warp′ knit′, a fabric or garment so constructed that runs do not occur: knitted from a warp beam that feeds yarn to the knitting frame.

warp-knit•ted (wôrp′nit′id), *adj.* designating a fabric made by warp knitting. [1915–20]

warp′ knit′ting, a knitting process in which the yarn is knitted vertically in a flat form. Cf. **weft knitting.**

war•plane (wôr′plān′), *n.* an airplane designed for, or used in, warfare. [1910–15; WAR[1] + PLANE[1]]

war′ pow′ers, the powers exercised by the president or by Congress during a war or a crisis affecting national security. [1760–70]

War′ Produc′tion Board′, *U.S. Govt.* the board (1942–45) that supervised and regulated the production and sale of matériel essential to the logistics of World War II. *Abbr.:* WPB, W.P.B.

warp′ speed′, an extremely rapid rate of speed: *rumors traveling at warp speed.* [alluding to the use in science fiction of spatial or temporal warps to travel interstellar distances]

warp•wise (wôrp′wīz′), *adv. Textiles.* in a vertical direction; at right angles to the filling; lengthwise. [WARP + -WISE]

war•rant (wôr′ənt, wor′-), *n.* **1.** authorization, sanction, or justification. **2.** something that serves to give reliable or formal assurance of something; guarantee, pledge, or security. **3.** something considered as having the force of a guarantee or as being positive assurance of a thing: *The cavalry and artillery were considered sure warrants of success.* **4.** a writing or document certifying or authorizing something, as a receipt, license, or commission. **5.** *Law.* an instrument, issued by a magistrate, authorizing an officer to make an arrest, seize property, make a search, or execute a judgment. **6.** the certificate of authority or appointment issued to an officer of the armed forces below the rank of a commissioned officer. **7.** a warehouse receipt. **8.** a written authorization for the payment or receipt of money: *a treasury warrant.* —*v.t.* **9.** to give authority to; authorize. **10.** to give reason or sanction for; justify: *The circumstances warrant such measures.* **11.** to give one's word for; vouch for (often used with a clause to emphasize something asserted): *I'll warrant he did!* **12.** to give a formal assurance, or a guarantee or promise, to or for; guarantee: *to warrant someone honorable treatment; to warrant payment; to warrant safe delivery.* **13.** to guarantee the quantity, quality, and other representations of (an article, product, etc.), as to a purchaser. **14.** to guarantee or secure title to (the purchaser of goods); assure indemnification against loss to. **15.** *Law.* to guarantee title of an estate or other granted property (to a grantee). [1175–1225; (n.) ME *warant* < AF; OF *guarant* < Gmc; cf. MLG *warend, -ent* warranty, n. use of prp. of *waren* to warrant; (v.) ME < AF *warantir;* OF *g(u)arantir,* deriv. of *guarant;* see GUARANTY] —**war′rant•less,** *adj.*
—**Syn. 2.** warranty, surety. **4.** permit, voucher, writ, order, chit. **11.** guarantee, attest.

war•rant•a•ble (wôr′ən tə bəl, wor′-), *adj.* **1.** capable of being warranted. **2.** (of deer) of a legal age for hunting. [1575–85; WARRANT + -ABLE]

war•ran•tee (wôr′ən tē′, wor′-), *n.* a person to whom a warranty is made. [1660–70; WARRANT(Y) or WARRANT(OR) + -EE]

war′rant of′ficer, 1. (in the U.S. Armed Forces) an officer of one of four grades ranking above enlisted personnel and below commissioned officers. **2.** a similar officer in other countries. [1685–95]

war•ran•tor (wôr′ən tôr′, -tər, wor′-), *n.* a person who warrants or makes a warranty. Also, **war•rant•er** (wôr′ən tər, wor′-). [1675–85; WARRANT + -OR[2]]

war•ran•ty (*n.* wôr′ən tē, wor′-; *v.* wôr′ən tē′, wor′-), *n., pl.* **-ties,** *v.,* **-tied, -ty•ing.** —*n.* **1.** an act or an instance of warranting; assurance; authorization; warrant. **2.** *Law.* **a.** a stipulation, explicit or implied, in assurance of some particular in connection with a contract, as of sale. **b.** Also called **covenant of warranty.** a covenant in a deed to land by which the party conveying assures the grantee that he or she will enjoy the premises free from interference by any person claiming under a superior title. Cf. **quitclaim deed, warranty deed. c.** (in the law of insurance) a statement or promise, made by the party insured, and included as an essential part of the contract, falsity or nonfulfillment of which renders the policy void. **d.** a judicial document, as a warrant or writ. **3.** a written guarantee given to the purchaser of a new appliance, automobile, etc., by the manufacturer or dealer, usually specifying that the manufacturer will make any repairs or replace defective parts free of charge for a stated period of time. —*v.t.* **4.** to provide a manufacturer's or dealer's warranty for: *The automaker warranties its new cars against exterior rust.* [1300–50; ME *warantie* < AF (OF *guarantie*). See WARRANT, -Y[3]]

war′ranty deed′, *Law.* a deed containing a covenant of warranty. Cf. **quitclaim deed.** [1770–80, *Amer.*]

war•ren (wôr′ən, wor′-), *n.* **1.** a place where rabbits breed or abound. **2.** a building or area containing many tenants in limited or crowded quarters. [1350–1400; ME *warenne* < AF; OF *g(u)arenne* < Gmc **warinne* game park, equiv. to **war-* (base of **warjan* to defend) + *-inne* fem. n. suffix]

War•ren (wôr′ən, wor′-), *n.* **1. Earl,** 1891–1974, U.S. lawyer and political leader: Chief Justice of the U.S. 1953–69. **2. Joseph,** 1741–75, American physician, statesman, and patriot. **3. Mercy Otis,** 1728–1814, U.S. historian and poet (sister of James Otis). **4. Robert Penn,** born 1905, U.S. novelist and poet: named the first U.S. poet laureate (1986–87). **5.** a city in SE Michigan, near Detroit. 161,134. **6.** a city in NE Ohio, NW of Youngstown. 56,629. **7.** a city in NW Pennsylvania. 12,146. **8.** a town in E Rhode Island. 10,640. **9.** a male given name: from a Germanic word meaning "protection."

war•ren•er (wôr′ə nər, wor′-), *n.* the keeper of a rabbit warren. [1250–1300; ME; see WARREN, -ER[1]]

War•rens•burg (wôr′inz bûrg′, wor′-), *n.* a town in central Missouri. 13,807.

War′rens•ville Heights′ (wôr′ənz vil′, wor′-), a city in NE Ohio. 16,565.

war•ri•gal (wôr′i gəl), *Australian.* —*n.* **1.** dingo. **2.** any large or ferocious dog. **3.** a wild horse. —*adj.* **4.** wild; ferocious; savage. [1840–50; < Dharuk *wa-ri-gal* wild dingo]

CONCISE ETYMOLOGY KEY: <, descended or borrowed from; >, whence; b., blend of, blended; c., cognate with; cf., compare; deriv., derivative; equiv., equivalent; imit., imitative; obl., oblique; r., replacing; s., stem; sp., spelling, spelled; resp., respelling, respelled; trans., translation; ?, origin unknown; *, unattested; ‡, probably earlier than. See the full key inside the front cover.

War•ring•ton (wôr′ing tən, wor′-), *n.* **1.** a city in Cheshire, in NW England, on the Mersey River. 164,800. **2.** a town in W Florida, on the Gulf of Mexico. 15,792.

war•ri•or (wôr′ē ər, wôr′yər, wor′ē ər, wor′yər), *n.* **1.** a person engaged or experienced in warfare; soldier. **2.** a person who shows or has shown great vigor, courage, or aggressiveness, as in politics or athletics. [1250–1300; ME *werreieor* < ONF, equiv. to *werrei(er)* to WAR[1] + *-eor* -OR[2]] —**war′ri•or•like′,** *adj.*

war′ risk′ insur′ance, life insurance for members of the armed forces.

war′ room′, 1. a room at a military headquarters in which strategy is planned and current battle situations are monitored. **2.** any room of similar function, as in a civilian or business organization.

warrty., warranty.

war•saw (wôr′sô), *n.* **1.** Also called **war′saw group′er.** a large grouper, *Epinephelus nigritus,* found in the warmer waters of the Atlantic Ocean. **2.** the jewfish, *Epinephelus itajara,* found off both coasts of tropical America. [1880–85, *Amer.;* < Sp *guasa*]

War•saw (wôr′sô), *n.* **1.** Polish, **Warszawa.** a city in and the capital of Poland, in the E central part, on the Vistula River. 1,436,000. **2.** a town in N Indiana. 10,649.

War′saw Conven′tion, a multilateral treaty on aviation set up chiefly to limit air carriers' liability to passengers and shippers on international flights in the event of an accident.

War′saw Trea′ty Organiza′tion, an organization formed in Warsaw, Poland (1955), comprising Bulgaria, Czechoslovakia, East Germany, Hungary, Poland, Rumania, and the U.S.S.R., for collective defense under a joint military command. Also called **War′saw Pact′.** Cf. **NATO.**

war•ship (wôr′ship′), *n.* a ship built or armed for combat purposes. Also called **war vessel.** [1525–35; WAR[1] + SHIP]

war•sle (wär′səl), *v.i., v.t.,* **-sled, -sling,** *n. Chiefly Scot.* wrestle. Also, **war′stle.** [1300–50; ME; OE **wǣrstlian,* metathetic var. (cf. *wǣrstlic* of wrestling) of *wrǣstlian* to WRESTLE]

Wars′ of the Ros′es, *Eng. Hist.* the civil struggle between the royal house of Lancaster, whose emblem was a red rose, and the royal house of York, whose emblem was a white rose, beginning in 1455 and ending with the accession of Henry VII in 1485 and the union of the two houses.

war′ sto′ry, 1. an account or anecdote concerning one's personal experiences, esp. in military combat, during a war. **2.** *Informal.* a story about hardships, ordeals, or adventures one has undergone. [1860–65]

war′ sur′plus, equipment, supplies, etc., originally used by or manufactured for the armed forces, but disposed of cheaply as surplus or obsolete: *He made his fortune in war surplus.* [1945–50]

War•sza•wa (vär shä′vä), *n.* Polish name of **Warsaw.**

wart (wôrt), *n.* **1.** a small, often hard, abnormal elevation on the skin, usually caused by a papomavirus. **2.** any small protuberance, as on the surface of certain plants, the skin of certain animals, etc. **3.** any unattractive detrimental feature or aspect: *the full story, warts and all.* **4.** See **venereal wart.** [bef. 900; ME; OE *wearte;* c. G *Warze,* ON *varta;* akin to L *verrūca* wart] —**wart′ed,** *adj.* —**wart′less,** *adj.*

War•ta (vär′tä), *n.* a river in Poland, flowing NW and W into the Oder. 445 mi. (715 km) long. German, **Warthe** (vär′tə).

Wart•burg (värt′bo͝ork′), *n.* a castle in E Germany, in Thuringia, near Eisenach: Luther translated the New Testament here 1521–22.

wart•hog (wôrt′hôg′, -hog′), *n.* an African wild swine, *Phacochoerus aethiopicus,* having large tusks and warty protuberances on the face. [1830–40; WART + HOG]

wart hog, *Phacochoerus aethiopicus,* 2½ ft. (0.8 m) high at shoulder; head and body 4½ ft. (1.4 m); tail 1½ ft. (0.5 m)

war•time (wôr′tīm′), *n.* **1.** a time or period of war: *Strict travel regulations apply only in wartime.* —*adj.* **2.** caused by, characteristic of, or occurring during war: *wartime shortages.* [1350–1400; ME; see WAR[1], TIME]

wart′ snake′, either of two stout, nonvenomous snakes of the family Acrochordidae, ranging from southeastern Asia to northern Australia, and having the skin covered with wartlike, three-pointed scales. [1875–80]

wart•y (wôr′tē), *adj.,* **wart•i•er, wart•i•est. 1.** having warts; covered with or as with warts. **2.** resembling a wart. [1475–85; WART + -Y[1]] —**wart′i•ness,** *n.*

war′ ves′sel, warship.

war-wea•ry (wôr′wēr′ē), *adj.* **1.** utterly exhausted and dejected by war, esp. after a prolonged conflict. **2.** (of an airplane) damaged beyond use except as scrap or as a source of spare parts. —**war′-wea′ri•ness,** *n.*

war′ whoop′, a yell uttered in making an attack: *the war whoop of the American Indian.* [1705–15, *Amer.*]

War•wick (wôr′ik, wor′- *or, for 4,* wôr′wik, wor′-), *n.* **1. Earl of** (*Richard Neville, Earl of Salisbury*) (*"the Kingmaker"*), 1428–71, English military leader and statesman. **2.** a town in Warwickshire in central England. 111,700. **3.** Warwickshire. **4.** a city in E Rhode Island. 87,123.

War•wick•shire (wôr′ik shēr′, -shər, wor′-), *n.* a county in central England. 471,800; 765 sq. mi. (1980 sq. km). Also called **Warwick.**

war•y (wâr′ē), *adj.,* **war•i•er, war•i•est. 1.** watchful; being on one's guard against danger. **2.** arising from or characterized by caution: *to give someone a wary look.* [1545–55; WARE[2] + -Y[1]] —**war′i•ly,** *adv.* —**war′i•ness,** *n.*
—**Syn. 1.** alert, vigilant, guarded, circumspect, prudent. See **careful.**

war′ zone′, (during wartime) a combat area in which the rights of neutrals are suspended, as such an area on the high seas, where ships flying a neutral flag are subject to attack. [1915–20]

was (wuz, woz; *unstressed* wəz), *v.* 1st and 3rd pers. sing. pt. indic. of **be.** [bef. 950; ME; OE *wæs,* past tense sing. of *wesan* to be; c. OFris, OHG, Goth *was,* ON *var;* cf. WASSAIL]

wa•sa•bi (wä′sə bē), *n.* **1.** an Asian plant, *Eutrema wasabi,* of the mustard family. **2.** the pungent, greenish root of this plant, which can be grated and used as a condiment. [(< NL) < Japn]

Wa′satch Range′ (wô′sach), a mountain range in N Utah and SE Idaho. Highest peak, Mt. Timpanogos, 12,008 ft. (3660 m).

wash (wosh, wôsh), *v.t.* **1.** to apply water or some other liquid to (something or someone) for the purpose of cleansing; cleanse by dipping, rubbing, or scrubbing in water or some other liquid. **2.** to remove (dirt, stains, paint, or any matter) by or as by the action of water (usually fol. by *out, off,* etc.): *to wash grime out of clothing.* **3.** to free from spiritual defilement or from sin, guilt, etc.: *to be washed whiter than the snow.* **4.** to bathe, wet, or moisten with water or other liquid: *a meadow newly washed with morning dew.* **5.** to flow through, over, or against: *a shore or cliff washed by waves.* **6.** to carry, bring, remove, or deposit (something) by means of water or any liquid, or as the water or liquid does (often fol. by *up, down,* or *along*): *The storm washed the boat up on the shore. A sailor was washed overboard.* **7.** to wear or diminish, as water does by flowing over or against a surface (often fol. by *out* or *away*): *The rain had washed away the lettering on the stone.* **8.** (of water) to form by flowing over and eroding a surface: *The flood had washed a new channel through the bottom lands.* **9.** *Mining.* **a.** to subject (earth or ore) to the action or force of water in order to separate valuable material. **b.** to separate (valuable material) in this way. **10.** to purify (a gas or gaseous mixture) by passage through or over a liquid. **11.** to cover with a watery or thin coat of color. **12.** to overlay with a thin coat or deposit of metal: *to wash brass with gold.* **13.** *Slang.* launder (def. 3).
—*v.i.* **14.** to wash oneself: *After using the insecticide spray they washed completely.* **15.** to wash clothes: *Monday is the day we wash.* **16.** to cleanse anything with or in water or other liquid. **17.** to undergo washing without injury, esp. shrinking or fading: *fabrics guaranteed to wash.* **18.** *Informal.* to be found true, valid, or real when tested or closely scrutinized; stand being put to the proof: *His honesty won't wash.* **19.** to be carried or driven by water (often fol. by *along* or *ashore*): *The boat had washed ashore in the night.* **20.** to flow or beat with a lapping sound, as waves on a shore. **21.** to move along in or as in waves, or with a rushing movement, as water. **22.** to be eroded, as by a stream or by rainfall: *a hillside that washes frequently.* **23.** to be removed by the action of water (often fol. by *away*): *Much of the topsoil washes away each spring.* **24. wash down, a.** to clean completely by washing: *to wash down a car.* **b.** to facilitate the swallowing of (food or medicine) by drinking water or other liquid: *to wash down a meal with a glass of wine.* **25. wash one's hands of.** See **hand** (def. 75). **26. wash out, a.** to be removed by washing: *The stain wouldn't wash out.* **b.** to damage or demolish by the action of water: *The embankment was washed out by the storm.* **c.** *Informal.* to fail to qualify or continue; be eliminated: *to wash out of graduate school.* **d.** to become dim, indistinct, or blurred: *The face of the watch washes out in sunlight.* **27. wash up, a.** to wash one's face and hands: *Aren't you going to wash up? Dinner is almost ready.* **b.** to wash (dishes, flatware, pots, etc.): *I'll wash up the dishes, don't bother. We had someone in to wash up after the party.* **c.** to end, esp. ignominiously (usually in the passive): *After that performance, he's all washed up as a singer.*
—*n.* **28.** the act or process of washing with water or other liquid: *to give the car a wash.* **29.** a quantity of clothes, linens, etc., washed, or to be washed, at one time: *a heavy wash.* **30.** a liquid with which something is washed, wetted, colored, overspread, etc.: *She gave the room a wash of pale blue.* **31.** the flow, sweep, dash, or breaking of water: *The wash of the waves had drenched us.* **32.** the sound made by this: *listening to the wash of the Atlantic.* **33.** water moving along in waves or with a rushing movement: *the wash of the incoming tide.* **34.** the rough or broken water left behind a moving ship, boat, etc.; wake: *The little boats tossed about in the wash from the liner's propellers.* **35.** *Aeron.* the disturbance in the air left behind by a moving airplane or any of its parts: *wing wash.* **36.** any of various liquids for grooming or cosmetic purposes: *a hair wash.* **37.** a lotion or other liquid having medicinal properties, as an antiseptic solution or the like (often used in combination): *to apply wash to a skinned knee; mouthwash; eyewash.* **38.** *Mining.* minerals from which valuable material can be extracted by washing. **39.** the wearing away of the shore by breaking waves. **40.** a tract of land washed by the action of the sea or a river. **41.** a marsh, fen, or bog. **42.** a small stream or shallow pool. **43.** a shallow arm of the sea or a shallow part of a river. **44.** a depression or channel formed by flowing water. **45.** *Geol.* alluvial matter transferred and deposited by flowing water. **46.** Also called **dry wash.** *Western U.S.* the dry bed of an intermittent stream. **47.** a broad, thin layer of color applied by a continuous movement of the brush, as in wa-

ter-color painting. **48.** Also called **watershed, weathering.** *Archit.* **a.** an upper surface so inclined as to shed rain water from a building. **b.** any member of a building having such a surface. **49.** Also, **washing.** a thin coat of metal applied in liquid form: *a gold wash.* **50.** waste liquid matter, refuse, food, etc., from the kitchen, as for hogs; swill (often used in combination): *hogwash.* **51.** washy or weak liquor or liquid food. **52.** the fermented wort from which the spirit is extracted in distilling. **53.** *Informal.* an action that yields neither gain nor loss: *The company's financial position is a wash compared with last year.* **54. come out in the wash, a.** to have a good or satisfactory result; turn out eventually: *The situation may look hopeless now, but it will all come out in the wash.* **b.** to be revealed; become known. —*adj.* **55.** capable of being washed without shrinking, fading, etc.; washable: *a wash dress.* [bef. 900; ME *washen* (v.), OE *wascan* (c. D *wasschen,* G *waschen,* ON *vaska*) < Gmc **watskan,* equiv. to **wat-* (root of WATER) + **-sk-* v. suffix + **-an* inf. suffix]
—**Syn. 1.** clean, lave, rinse, launder, mop, swab. **4.** bedew. **5.** bathe. **28.** ablution, cleansing, bathing. **41.** swamp, morass.

Wash (wosh, wôsh), *n.* **The,** a shallow bay of the North Sea, on the coast of E England. 20 mi. (32 km) long; 15 mi. (24 km) wide.

Wash., Washington (defs. 4, 5).

wash·a·ble (wosh′ə bəl, wô′shə-), *adj.* **1.** capable of being washed without shrinking, fading, or the like. —*n.* **2.** a washable garment. [1615–25; WASH + -ABLE] —**wash′a·bil′i·ty,** *n.*

wash-and-wear (wosh′ən wâr′, wôsh′-), *adj.* noting or pertaining to a garment that can be washed, that dries quickly, and that requires little or no ironing; drip-dry. [1955–60]

wash·a·te·ri·a (wosh′ə tēr′ē ə, wô′shə-), *n. Chiefly Southern U.S.* a launderette. Also, **washeteria.** [1935–40; WASH + (CAF)ETERIA, with *-a-* as var. sp. of (ə)]

wash·board (wosh′bôrd′, -bōrd′, wôsh′-), *n.* **1.** a rectangular board or frame, typically with a corrugated metallic surface, on which clothes are rubbed in the process of washing. **2.** a baseboard around the walls of a room. **3.** Also called **splashboard.** *Naut.* **a.** a thin, broad plank fastened to and projecting above the gunwale or side of a boat to keep out the spray and sea. **b.** a similar board on the sill of a port. —*adj.* **4.** resembling a washboard in being rough and bumpy: *a washboard roadbed.* [1735–45; WASH + BOARD] —**wash′board′y,** *adj.*

wash·bowl (wosh′bōl′, wôsh′-), *n.* a large bowl or basin used for washing one's hands and face, small articles of clothing, etc. Also called **wash·ba·sin** (wosh′bā′sən, wôsh′-). [1520–30; WASH + BOWL[1]]

wash·cloth (wosh′klôth′, -kloth′, wôsh′-), *n., pl.* **-cloths** (-klôthz′, -klothz′, -klôths′, -kloths′). a small cloth for washing one's face or body. Also called **facecloth, washrag.** [1900–05, *Amer.*; WASH + CLOTH]

wash·day (wosh′dā′, wôsh′-), *n.* the day set apart in a household for washing clothes: *Monday is always washday at our house.* [1840–50; WASH + DAY]

wash·down (wosh′doun′, wôsh′-), *n.* the act or process of washing down, as in cleaning something completely. [1945–50; n. use of v. phrase *wash down*]

wash′ draw′ing, a watercolor painting executed by applying a series of monochrome washes one over the other.

washed-out (wosht′out′, wôsht′-), *adj.* **1.** faded, esp. from washing. **2.** *Informal.* **a.** weary; exhausted. **b.** tired-looking; wan. [1830–40]

washed-up (wosht′up′, wôsht′-), *adj. Informal.* done for; having failed completely. [1920–25]

wash·er (wosh′ər, wô′shər), *n.* **1.** a person or thing that washes. **2.** See **washing machine. 3.** a flat ring or perforated piece of leather, rubber, metal, etc., used to give tightness to a joint, to prevent leakage, to distribute pressure, etc., as under the head of a nut or bolt. [1275–1325; ME; see WASH, -ER[1]] —**wash′er·less,** *adj.*

wash·er-dry·er (wosh′ər drī′ər, wô′shər-), *n.* a washing machine and a clothes dryer combined in one unit. [1965–70]

wash·er·man (wosh′ər mən, wô′shər-), *n., pl.* **-men. 1.** a man who washes clothes, linens, etc., for hire; laundryman. **2.** a man who operates a machine for washing, as in a phase of a manufacturing process. [1705–15; WASHER + -MAN]
—**Usage.** See **-man.**

wash·er·wom·an (wosh′ər wo͝om′ən, wô′shər-), *n., pl.* **-wom·en.** a woman who washes clothes, linens, etc., for hire; laundress. Also, **washwoman.** [1625–35; WASHER + -WOMAN]
—**Usage.** See **-woman.**

wash·e·te·ri·a (wosh′i tēr′ē ə, wô′shi-), *n.* washateria.

wash·foun·tain (wosh′foun′tn, wôsh′-), *n.* a large, usually circular wash basin, as in an industrial plant, in which a spray of water activated by foot pedal allows several workers to wash simultaneously. [WASH + FOUNTAIN]

wash′ goods′, textiles that will not fade or become weakened by washing.

wash·in (wosh′in′, wôsh′-), *n. Aeron.* a warp in an airfoil that gives an increase in the angle of attack toward the tip. Also, **wash′-in′.** Cf. **washout** (def. 3). [1930–35; n. use of v. phrase *wash in*]

wash·i·ness (wosh′ē nis, wô′shē-), *n.* the state or quality of being washy. [1625–35; WASHY + -NESS]

wash·ing (wosh′ing, wô′shing), *n.* **1.** the act of a person or thing that washes; ablution. **2.** clothes, linens, etc., washed or to be washed, esp. those washed at one time; wash. **3.** Often, **washings.** any liquid that has been used to wash something. **4.** matter removed or carried off in washing something or by the force of water: *The washings from numerous spring floods had clogged the mouth of the river.* **5.** *Mining.* **a.** material, as gold dust, obtained by washing earth, gravel, etc. **b.** the deposits so washed. **6.** wash (def. 49). **7.** the act of making a wash sale. [1175–1225; ME *wasschunge.* See WASH, -ING[1]]

wash′ing machine′, an apparatus, esp. a household appliance, for washing clothing, linens, etc. Also called **washer.** [1790–1800]

wash′ing so′da. See **sodium carbonate** (def. 2). [1840–50]

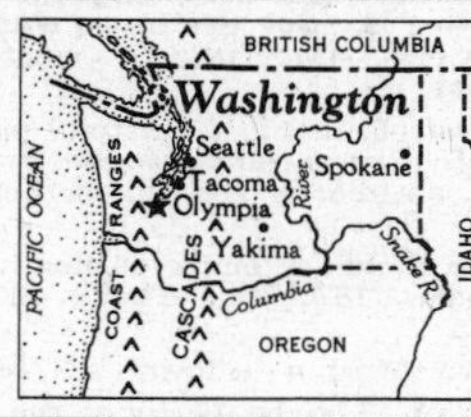

Wash·ing·ton (wosh′ing tən, wô′shing-), *n.* **1. Book·er T(al·ia·ferro)** (bo͝ok′ər tol′ə vər), 1856–1915, U.S. reformer, educator, author, and lecturer. **2. George,** 1732–99, U.S. general and political leader: 1st president of the U.S. 1789–97. **3. Martha** (*Martha Dandridge*), 1732–1802, wife of George. **4.** Also called **Washington, D.C.** the capital of the United States, on the Potomac between Maryland and Virginia: coextensive with the District of Columbia. 637,651. *Abbr.:* Wash. See map under **District of Columbia. 5.** Also called **Washington State.** a state in the NW United States, on the Pacific coast. 3,553,231; 68,192 sq. mi. (176,615 sq. km). *Cap.:* Olympia. *Abbr.:* WA (for use with zip code), Wash. **6.** a city in SW Pennsylvania. 18,363. **7.** a city in SW Indiana. 11,325. **8.** a town in central Illinois. 10,364. **9. Mount,** a mountain in N New Hampshire, in the White Mountains: highest peak in the NE United States. 6293 ft. (1918 m). **10. Lake,** a lake in W Washington, near Seattle. 20 mi. (32 km) long. **11.** a male given name.

Wash′ington clam′. See **butter clam.**

Wash′ington Court′ House′, a city in SW Ohio. 12,682.

Wash·ing·to·ni·an (wosh′ing tō′nē ən, wô′shing-), *adj.* **1.** living in or coming from Washington, D.C., or the state of Washington. —*n.* **2.** a native or inhabitant of Washington, D.C., or the state of Washington. [1780–90, *Amer.*; WASHINGTON + -IAN]

Wash′ington lil′y, a lily, *Lilium washingtonianum,* of the western coast of the U.S., having whorled leaves and fragrant, purple-spotted white flowers. [1865–70, *Amer.*]

Wash′ington pie′, a Boston cream pie with raspberry jam instead of custard between the layers. [1905–10, *Amer.*]

Wash′ington's Birth′day, 1. February 22, formerly observed as a legal holiday in most states of the U.S. in honor of the birth of George Washington. **2.** See **Presidents' Day.**

Wash′ington Square′, a short novel (1881) by Henry James.

Wash′ington State′, the state of Washington, esp. as distinguished from Washington, D.C.

Wash′ington thorn′, a dense tree, *Crataegus phaenopyrum,* of the rose family, native to the eastern coast of the U.S., having triangular leaves, small clusters of white flowers, and clusters of bright red fruit. [1840–50, *Amer.*]

Wash·i·ta (wosh′i tô′, wô′shi-), *n., pl.* **-tas,** (*esp. collectively*) **-ta.** Ouachita.

wash-leath·er (wosh′leth′ər, wôsh′-), *n.* a soft leather, usually sheepskin, dressed in imitation of chamois. Also, **wash′leath′er.** [1625–35]

Wash·o (wosh′ō, wô′shō), *n., pl.,* **Wash·os,** (*esp. collectively*) **Wash·o** for 1. **1.** a member of a tribe of North American Indians living in western Nevada and northeastern California. **2.** the Hokan language of the Washo.

Wash·oe (wosh′ō, wô′shō), *n.* b. 1965, female chimpanzee, first ape trained to communicate with humans by means of a sign language.

wash·out (wosh′out′, wôsh′-), *n.* **1.** a washing out of earth, gravel, etc., by water, as from an embankment or a roadway by heavy rain or by a flash flood. **2.** the hole, break, or erosion produced by such a washing out. **3.** Also, **wash′-out′.** *Aeron.* a warp in an airfoil that gives a decrease in the angle of attack toward the tip. Cf. **washin. 4.** rainout. **5.** *Informal.* an utter failure. **6.** *Informal.* a person who has failed a course of training or study: *air force washouts.* [1870–75; n. use of v. phrase *wash out*]

wash·rag (wosh′rag′, wôsh′-), *n.* washcloth. [1885–90, *Amer.*; WASH + RAG[1]]

wash·room (wosh′ro͞om′, -ro͝om′, wôsh′-), *n.* a room having washbowls and other toilet facilities. [1800–10, *Amer.*; WASH + ROOM]

wash′ sale′, 1. a sale of a stock at a loss and repurchase of the same or substantially identical stock within 30 days, for which the capital loss is disallowed for tax purposes. **2.** the simultaneous purchase and sale of large amounts of a stock or commodity by the same speculator so as to give a false appearance of wide market activity and interest in the stock or commodity. [1840–50, *Amer.*]

wash·stand (wosh′stand′, wôsh′-), *n.* **1.** a piece of furniture holding a basin, pitcher, etc., for use in washing one's hands and face. **2.** a stationary fixture having faucets with running water, for the same purpose. [1820–30; WASH + STAND]

wash·tub (wosh′tub′, wôsh′-), *n.* a tub for use in washing clothes, linens, etc. [1595–1605; WASH + TUB]

wash·up (wosh′up′, wôsh′-), *n.* **1.** an act of washing: *Allow five minutes for washup.* **2.** a place, as a bathroom, for washing. Also, **wash′-up′.** [1865–70; n. use of v. phrase *wash up*]

wash·wom·an (wosh′wo͝om′ən, wôsh′-), *n., pl.* **-wom·en.** washerwoman. [1580–90; WASH + -WOMAN]

wash·y (wosh′ē, wô′shē), *adj.,* **wash·i·er, wash·i·est. 1.** diluted too much; weak: *washy coffee.* **2.** pale, thin, or weak, as if from excessive dilution; pallid: *washy coloring.* [1560–70; WASH + -Y[1]]

was·n't (wuz′ənt, woz′-), contraction of *was not: I wasn't sure you heard me.*
—**Usage.** See **contraction.**
—**Pronunciation.** See **isn't.**

wasp (wosp), *n.* **1.** any of numerous social or solitary hymenopterous insects of the Vespidae, Sphecidae, and allied families, generally having a long, slender body and narrow waist and, in the female, a stinger. **2.** a person who is snappish or petulant. [bef. 900; ME *waspe,* OE *wæsp,* metathetic var. of *wæps,* itself var. of *wæfs,* akin to D *wesp,* G *Wespe,* L *vespa*] —**wasp′like′,** *adj.*

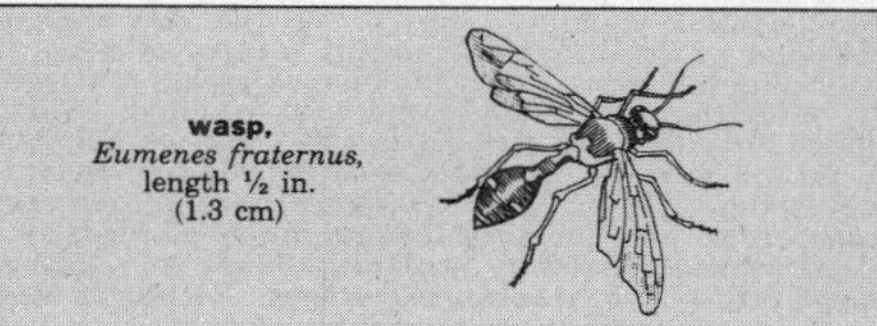
wasp, *Eumenes fraternus,* length ½ in. (1.3 cm)

WASP (wosp), *Sometimes Disparaging and Offensive.* —*n.* **1.** a white Anglo-Saxon Protestant. **2.** a member of the privileged, established white upper middle class in the U.S. —*adj.* **3.** Waspy. Also, **Wasp.** [1955–60]

WASP (wosp), *n.* a member of the Women's Air Force Service Pilots, an organization disbanded in 1944.

wasp·ish (wos′pish), *adj.* **1.** like or suggesting a wasp, esp. in behavior. **2.** quick to resent a trifling affront or injury; snappish. **3.** irascibly or petulantly spiteful: *waspish writing.* **4.** having a slight or slender build. [1560–70; WASP + -ISH[1]] —**wasp′ish·ly,** *adv.* —**wasp′ish·ness,** *n.*
—**Syn. 2.** resentful. **3.** testy, touchy.

Wasp·ish (wos′pish), *adj.* Waspy. Also, **WASP′ish.** [1965–70; WASP + -ISH[1]] —**Wasp′ish·ly, WASP′ish·ly,** *adv.* —**Wasp′ish·ness, WASP′ish·ness,** *n.*

Wasps, The, a satirical comedy (422 B.C.) by Aristophanes.

wasp′ waist′, a woman's slender waistline, esp. when the result of tight corseting. [1865–70] —**wasp′-waist′ed,** *adj.*

wasp·y (wos′pē), *adj.,* **wasp·i·er, wasp·i·est.** resembling a wasp; waspish. [1650–60; WASP + -Y[1]] —**wasp′i·ly,** *adv.* —**wasp′i·ness,** *n.*

Wasp·y (wos′pē), *adj.,* **Wasp·i·er, Wasp·i·est.** of, pertaining to, or characteristic of WASPs: *a Waspy country club.* Also, **WASP′y, Waspish.** [1965–70; WASP + -Y[1]]

was·sail (wos′əl, -āl, was′-, wo sāl′), *n.* **1.** a salutation wishing health to a person, used in England in early times when presenting a cup of drink or when drinking to the person. **2.** a festivity or revel with drinking of healths. **3.** liquor for drinking and wishing health to others on festive occasions, esp. spiced ale, as on Christmas Eve and Twelfth-night. **4.** *Archaic.* a song sung in wassailing. —*v.i.* **5.** to revel with drinking. —*v.t.* **6.** to drink to the health or success of; toast. [1175–1225; ME *was-hail,* equiv. to *was* be (OE *wæs,* var. of *wes,* impv. of *wesan* to be; akin to WAS) + *hail* HALE[1], in good health (< ON *heill* hale); r. OE *wæs hāl* be hale or whole. See WHOLE, HEAL] —**was′sail·er,** *n.*

Was·ser·mann (wä′sər mən; *Ger.* väs′ər män′), *n.* **1. Au·gust von** (ou′go͝ost fən), 1866–1925, German physician and bacteriologist. **2. Ja·kob** (yä′kôp), 1873–1934, German novelist.

Was′sermann an′tibody, *Immunol.* reagin (def. 1). [named after A. von WASSERMANN, who discovered its reaction in blood tests for syphilis]

Was′sermann test′, a diagnostic test for syphilis using the fixation of a complement by the serum of a syphilitic individual. Also called **Was′sermann reac′tion.** [1910–15; named after A. von WASSERMANN]

Was′si·ly chair′ (vä′sə lē, vas′ə-), a chair designed by Marcel Breuer in 1925, having a chromium-plated tubular steel frame over which strips of canvas or leather of varying widths are stretched to form the seat, back, and arms. Also called **Breuer chair, Was′sily lounge′ chair′.** [after *Wassily* Kandinsky, for whose house on the Bauhaus campus at Dessau the chair was designed]

wast (wost; *unstressed* wəst), *v. Archaic.* a 2nd pers. sing. pt. indic. of **be.**

wast·age (wā′stij), *n.* **1.** loss by use, wear, decay, etc. **2.** loss or losses as the result of wastefulness: *The annual wastage of time due to illness is appalling.* **3.** the action or process of wasting: *the steady wastage of erosion.* **4.** something that is wasted; waste or waste materials: *The river was befouled by factory wastage.* [1750–60; WASTE + -AGE]

waste (wāst), *v.,* **wast·ed, wast·ing,** *n., adj.* —*v.t.* **1.** to consume, spend, or employ uselessly or without adequate return; use to no avail or profit; squander: *to waste*

money; to waste words. **2.** to fail or neglect to use: *to waste an opportunity.* **3.** to destroy or consume gradually; wear away: *The waves waste the rock of the shore.* **4.** to wear down or reduce in bodily substance, health, or strength; emaciate; enfeeble: *to be wasted by disease or hunger.* **5.** to destroy, devastate, or ruin: *a country wasted by a long and futile war.* **6.** *Slang.* to kill or murder.
—*v.i.* **7.** to be consumed, spent, or employed uselessly or without giving full value or being fully utilized or appreciated. **8.** to become gradually consumed, used up, or worn away: *A candle wastes in burning.* **9.** to become physically worn; lose flesh or strength; become emaciated or enfeebled. **10.** to diminish gradually; dwindle, as wealth, power, etc.: *The might of England is wasting.* **11.** to pass gradually, as time.
—*n.* **12.** useless consumption or expenditure; use without adequate return; an act or instance of wasting: *The project was a waste of material, money, time, and energy.* **13.** neglect, instead of use: *waste of opportunity.* **14.** gradual destruction, impairment, or decay: *the waste and repair of bodily tissue.* **15.** devastation or ruin, as from war or fire. **16.** a region or place devastated or ruined: *The forest fire left a blackened waste.* **17.** anything unused, unproductive, or not properly utilized. **18.** an uncultivated tract of land. **19.** a wild region or tract of land; desolate country, desert, or the like. **20.** an empty, desolate, or dreary tract or extent: *a waste of snow.* **21.** anything left over or superfluous, as excess material or by-products, not of use for the work in hand: *a fortune made in salvaging factory wastes.* **22.** remnants, as from the working of cotton, used for wiping machinery, absorbing oil, etc. **23.** *Phys. Geog.* material derived by mechanical and chemical disintegration of rock, as the detritus transported by streams, rivers, etc. **24.** garbage; refuse. **25. wastes,** excrement. **26. go to waste,** to fail to be used or consumed; be wasted: *She hates to see good food go to waste.* **27. lay waste,** to devastate; destroy; ruin: *Forest fires lay waste thousands of acres yearly.*
—*adj.* **28.** not used or in use: *waste energy; waste talents.* **29.** (of land, regions, etc.) wild, desolate, barren, or uninhabited; desert. **30.** (of regions, towns, etc.) in a state of desolation and ruin, as from devastation or decay. **31.** left over or superfluous: *to utilize waste products of manufacture.* **32.** having served or fulfilled a purpose; no longer of use. **33.** rejected as useless or worthless; refuse: *to salvage waste products.* **34.** *Physiol.* pertaining to material unused by or unusable to the organism. **35.** designed or used to receive, hold, or carry away excess, superfluous, used, or useless material (often in combination): *a waste pipe; waste container.* **36.** *Obs.* excessive; needless. [1150–1200; 1960–65 for def. 6; (adj.) ME < ONF *wast* (OF *g(u)ast*) < L *vāstus* desolate; (v.) ME < ONF *waster* (OF *g(u)aster*) < L *vāstāre,* deriv. of *vāstus;* (n.) ME < ONF *wast(e)* (OF *g(u)aste*), partly < L *vāstum,* n. use of neut. of *vāstus,* partly deriv. of *waster;* ONF *w-*, OF *gu-* by influence of c. Frankish **wōsti* desolate (c. OHG *wuosti*)] —**wast′a·ble,** *adj.* —**waste′·less,** *adj.*
—**Syn. 1.** misspend, dissipate, fritter away, expend. **3.** erode. **5.** ravage, pillage, plunder, sack, spoil, despoil. **10.** decline, perish, wane, decay. **12.** dissipation. **14.** diminution, decline, emaciation, consumption. **15.** spoliation, desolation. **19.** See **desert**[1]. **24.** rubbish, trash. **27.** See **ravage. 30.** ruined, ghostly, destroyed. **31.** unused, useless, extra. —**Ant. 1.** save.

waste·bas·ket (wāst′bas′kit, -bä′skit), *n.* a standing basket for wastepaper, small items of trash, etc. Also called **waste′paper bas′ket.** [1855–60; WASTE + BASKET]

wast·ed (wā′stid), *adj.* **1.** waste (defs. 28–30). **2.** done to no avail; useless: *wasted efforts.* **3.** physically or psychologically exhausted; debilitated: *to be wasted by a long illness.* **4.** *Slang.* overcome by the influence of alcohol or drugs. **5.** *Archaic.* (of time) gone by. [1400–50; late ME; see WASTE, -ED[2]] —**wast′ed·ness,** *n.*

waste·ful (wāst′fəl), *adj.* **1.** given to or characterized by useless consumption or expenditure: *wasteful methods; a wasteful way of life.* **2.** grossly extravagant; prodigal: *a wasteful party.* **3.** devastating or destructive: *wasteful war.* [1250–1300; ME; see WASTE, -FUL] —**waste′ful·ly,** *adv.* —**waste′ful·ness,** *n.*

waste′ gate′, *Auto.* a valve in a turbocharger unit that automatically opens when a predetermined engine speed is reached, so that some of the exhaust gas to the turbine is diverted and the engine speed does not become excessive.

waste·land (wāst′land′), *n.* **1.** land that is uncultivated or barren. **2.** an area that is devastated, as by flood, storm, or war. **3.** something, as a period of history, phase of existence, or locality, that is spiritually or intellectually barren. [1630–40; WASTE + -LAND]

Waste′ Land′, The, a poem (1922) by T. S. Eliot.

waste·lot (wāst′lot′), *n.* *Chiefly Canadian.* a vacant lot, esp. one overgrown with weeds or covered with rubbish. [WASTE + LOT]

waste·pa·per (wāst′pā′pər), *n.* paper thrown away as useless. [1575–85; WASTE + PAPER]

waste′ pipe′, 1. a pipe for draining liquid waste or excess liquids. **2.** *Plumbing.* a pipe for draining away the wastes of a building other than those from water closets. Cf. **soil pipe.** [1505–15]

waste′ prod′uct, 1. material discarded as useless in the process of producing something. **2.** feces, urine, and other material excreted in the life process. [1930–35]

wast·er (wā′stər), *n.* **1.** a person or thing that wastes time, money, etc. **2.** a piece of ceramic ware warped, cracked, or melted during firing. **3.** a spendthrift or wastrel. **4.** a destroyer: *The Vandals were wasters of cities.* **5.** *Chiefly Brit.* wastrel (def. 2). [1300–50; ME < AF *wastere, wastour* (see -OR[2]); later understood as WASTE + -ER[1]]

waste·wa·ter (wāst′wô′tər, -wot′ər), *n.* water that has been used in washing, flushing, manufacturing, etc.; sewage. [1400–50; late ME *waste watre*]

waste′ well′. See **absorbing well.** [1895–1900]

wast·ing (wā′sting), *adj.* **1.** gradually reducing the fullness and strength of the body: *a wasting disease.* **2.** laying waste; devastating; despoiling: *the ravages of a wasting war.* —*n.* **3.** *Geol.* See **mass wasting.** [1200–50; ME; see WASTE, -ING[2], ING[1]] —**wast′ing·ly,** *adv.* —**wast′ing·ness,** *n.*

wast·rel (wā′strəl), *n.* **1.** a wasteful person; spendthrift. **2.** *Chiefly Brit.* **a.** refuse; waste. **b.** a waif; abandoned child. **c.** an idler or good-for-nothing. [1580–90; WASTE + -REL]

wat (wät), *n.* a Buddhist temple or monastery in Thailand or Cambodia. [1870–75; < Thai < Skt *vāṭa* enclosure]

Wa·tau·ga (wo tô′gə), *n.* a town in N Texas. 10,284.

watch (woch), *v.i.* **1.** to be alertly on the lookout, look attentively, or observe, as to see what comes, is done, or happens: *to watch while an experiment is performed.* **2.** to look or wait attentively and expectantly (usually fol. by *for*): *to watch for a signal; to watch for an opportunity.* **3.** to be careful or cautious: *Watch when you cross the street.* **4.** to keep awake, esp. for a purpose; remain vigilant, as for protection or safekeeping: *to watch with a sick person.* **5.** to keep vigil, as for devotional purposes. **6.** to keep guard: *She was assigned to watch at the door.* —*v.t.* **7.** to keep under attentive view or observation, as in order to see or learn something; view attentively or with interest: *to watch a play; to watch a football game.* **8.** to contemplate or regard mentally: *to watch his progress.* **9.** to look or wait attentively and expectantly for: *to watch one's opportunity.* **10.** to guard, tend, or oversee, esp. for protection or safekeeping: *to watch the baby.* **11. watch oneself, a.** to be cautious. **b.** to practice discretion or self-restraint. **12. watch out,** to be on one's guard; be cautious: *Watch out for cars when you cross the road.* **13. watch over,** to guard for protection or safekeeping: *She watched over us like a mother hen over her brood.* —*n.* **14.** close, continuous observation for the purpose of seeing or discovering something: *Their watch for the birds was unrewarding.* **15.** vigilant guard, as for protection or restraint: *to keep watch for prowlers.* **16.** a keeping awake for some special purpose: *a watch beside a sickbed.* **17.** a period of time for watching or keeping guard: *to stand the first watch.* **18.** a small, portable timepiece, as a wrist watch or pocket watch. **19.** a chronometer. **20.** *Naut.* **a.** a period of time, usually four hours, during which one part of a ship's crew is on duty, taking turns with another part. **b.** the officers and crew who attend to the working of a ship for an allotted period of time. **21.** one of the periods, usually three or four, into which the night was divided in ancient times, as by the Greeks or Hebrews: *the fourth watch of the night.* **22.** a person or group that watches, as a lookout, guard, or sentinel: *A watch was posted at sunset.* **23.** Also called **storm watch.** *Meteorol.* an announcement from the U.S. National Weather Service alerting the public that dangerous weather conditions are a possibility and that vigilance and precautionary preparations are advised: *hurricane watch, tornado watch.* Cf. **advisory** (def. 5), **warning** (def. 3). **24.** a flock of nightingales. **25. on the watch,** vigilant; alert: *The hunter was on the watch for game.* [bef. 900; 1580–90 for def. 18; (v.) ME *wacchen,* OE *wæccan,* doublet of *wacian* to be awake (see WAKE[1]); (n.) ME *wacche,* OE *wæcce,* deriv. of *wæccan*]
—**Syn. 1.** WATCH, LOOK, SEE imply being aware of things around one by perceiving them through the eyes. To WATCH is to be a spectator, to look on or observe, or to fix the attention upon during passage of time: *to watch while a procession passes.* To LOOK is to direct the gaze with the intention of seeing, to use the eyesight with attention: *to look for violets in the spring; to look at articles displayed for sale.* To SEE is to perceive with the eyes, to obtain a visual impression, with or without fixing the attention: *animals able to see in the dark.* **9.** await. **10.** protect. **14.** inspection, attention. **15.** vigil.

watch·a·ble (woch′ə bəl), *adj.* **1.** detectable; apparent. **2.** interesting or enjoyable to watch: *a watchable TV talk show.* [1605–15; WATCH + -ABLE] —**watch′a·bil′i·ty,** *n.*

watch′ and ward′, a continuous watch or vigil, by or as by night and by day, esp. for the purpose of guarding. [1350–1400; ME]

watch·band (woch′band′), *n.* a leather, metal, fabric, or plastic bracelet or strap attached to a wrist watch to hold it on the wrist. [1945–50, *Amer.*; WATCH + BAND[2]]

watch′ cap′, 1. *U.S. Navy.* a dark-blue, knitted woolen cap with a turned-up cuff worn by enlisted personnel on duty in cold weather. **2.** any wool or woollike cap resembling this and sold commercially in various colors. [1885–90]

watch·case (woch′kās′), *n.* the case or outer covering for the works of a watch. [1590–1600; WATCH + CASE[2]]

watch′ chain′, a chain, frequently of gold or silver, attached to a pocket watch, serving as an ornament and, when passed through a buttonhole in the vest, as a guard against loss or theft of the watch. [1730–40]

watch·dog (woch′dôg′, -dog′), *n., adj., v.,* **-dogged, -dog·ging.** —*n.* **1.** a dog kept to guard property. **2.** a watchful guardian: *a self-appointed watchdog of the public morals.* —*adj.* **3.** of, pertaining to, or characteristic of a watchdog. **4.** organized or functioning as a watchful guardian, esp. against illegal or unethical conduct: *a watchdog group in the legislature.* —*v.t.* **5.** to watch carefully, esp. so as to detect illegal or unethical conduct. [1600–10; WATCH + DOG]

watch·er (woch′ər), *n.* **1.** a person who watches or who keeps watch. **2.** an analytic observer of trends, fashions, events, celebrities, or the like: *Fashion watchers will have noted that pleats have become popular again.* **3.** a professional or experienced observer and analyst of political and historic trends and events, countries, or the like: *China watchers in the State Department predict a change in that country's trade policy.* **4.** See **poll watcher.** [1500–10; WATCH + -ER[1]]

watch·eye (woch′ī′), *n.* *Vet. Pathol.* an eye, esp. of a dog, with a whitish iris or a white opacity of the cornea; walleye. [1935–40; WATCH + EYE]

watch′ fire′, a fire maintained during the night as a signal and for providing light and warmth for guards. [1795–1805]

watch·ful (woch′fəl), *adj.* **1.** vigilant or alert; closely observant: *The sentry remained watchful throughout the night.* **2.** *Archaic.* wakeful. [1540–50; WATCH + -FUL] —**watch′ful·ly,** *adv.* —**watch′ful·ness,** *n.*
—**Syn. 1.** attentive, heedful, careful, circumspect, cautious, wary. See **alert.**

watch′ guard′, a short chain, cord, or ribbon for securing a watch when worn on the person. [1825–35]

watch·less (woch′lis), *adj.* **1.** not watchful or alert; lacking in vigilance: *an irresponsible and watchless sentry.* **2.** having no watch; without guards or sentries: *We welcomed the watchless nights of peacetime.* [1615–25; WATCH + -LESS] —**watch′less·ness,** *n.*

watch′ list′, a list of persons or things to watch for possible action in the future: *a watch list of possible growth stocks.* Also, **watch′list′.** [1970–75]

watch·mak·er (woch′mā′kər), *n.* a person whose occupation it is to make and repair watches. [1620–30; WATCH + MAKER] —**watch′mak′ing,** *n.*

watch·man (woch′mən), *n., pl.* **-men. 1.** a person who keeps guard over a building at night, to protect it from fire, vandals, or thieves. **2.** (formerly) a person who guards or patrols the streets at night. [1350–1400; late ME; see WATCH, MAN[1]] —**watch′man·ly,** *adj.*

watch′ meet′ing, a religious meeting or service on watch night, terminating on the arrival of the new year. Also called **watch′-night serv′ice** (woch′nīt′). [1895–1900]

watch′ night′, 1. the last night of the year, observed in a watch meeting. **2.** See **watch meeting.** [1735–45]

watch·out (woch′out′), *n.* the act of looking out for or anticipating something; lookout: *Keep a watchout for dishonest behavior.* [1880–85, *Amer.*; n. use of v. phrase *watch out*]

watch′ pock′et, a small pocket in a garment, as in a vest or trousers, for holding a pocket watch, change, etc. Cf. **fob**[1] (def. 1). [1830–40]

watch·tow·er (woch′tou′ər), *n.* a tower on which a sentinel keeps watch. [1535–45; WATCH + TOWER]

watch·word (woch′wûrd′), *n.* **1.** a word or short phrase to be communicated, on challenge, to a sentinel or guard; password or countersign. **2.** a word or phrase expressive of a principle or rule of action; slogan: *Conservation has been our watchword.* **3.** a rallying cry of a party, club, team, etc. [1350–1400; ME; see WATCH, WORD]
—**Syn. 1, 2.** shibboleth. **3.** motto.

Wa·ten·stedt-Salz·git·ter (*Ger.* vät′n shtet′zälts′git′ər), *n.* former name of **Salzgitter.**

wa·ter (wô′tər, wot′ər), *n.* **1.** a transparent, odorless, tasteless liquid, a compound of hydrogen and oxygen, H_2O, freezing at 32°F or 0°C and boiling at 212°F or 100°C, that in a more or less impure state constitutes rain, oceans, lakes, rivers, etc.: it contains 11.188 percent hydrogen and 88.812 percent oxygen, by weight. **2.** a special form or variety of this liquid, as rain. **3.** Often, **waters.** this liquid in an impure state as obtained from a mineral spring: *Last year we went to Marienbad for the waters.* **4.** the liquid content of a river, inlet, etc., with reference to its relative height, esp. as dependent on tide: *a difference of 20 feet between high and low water.* **5.** the surface of a stream, river, lake, ocean, etc.: *above, below, or on the water.* **6. waters, a.** flowing water, or water moving in waves: *The river's mighty waters.* **b.** the sea or seas bordering a particular country or continent or located in a particular part of the world: *We left San Diego and sailed south for Mexican waters.* **7.** a liquid solution or preparation, esp. one used for cosmetic purposes: *lavender water; lemon water.* **8.** Often, **waters.** *Med.* **a.** amniotic fluid. **b.** the bag of waters; amnion: *Her water broke at 2 A.M.* **9.** any of various solutions of volatile or gaseous substances in water: *ammonia water.* **10.** any liquid or aqueous organic secretion, exudation, humor, or the like, as tears, perspiration, or urine. **11.** *Finance.* fictitious assets or the inflated values they give to the stock of a corporation. **12.** a wavy, lustrous pattern or marking, as on silk fabrics or metal surfaces. **13.** (formerly) the degree of transparency and brilliancy of a diamond or other precious stone. **14. above water,** out of embarrassment or trouble, esp. of a financial nature: *They had so many medical bills that they could hardly keep their heads above water.* **15. break water, a.** to break the surface of the water by emerging from it. **b.** *Swimming.* to break the surface of the water with the feet, esp. in swimming the breaststroke doing the frog kick. **c.** *Med.* to break the amniotic sac prior to parturition. **16. by water,** by ship or boat: *to send goods by water.* **17. hold water, a.** to be logical, defensible, or valid: *That accusation won't hold water.* **b.** to check the movement of a rowboat by keeping the oars steady with the blades vertical. **18. dead in the water.** See **dead** (def. 36). **19. in deep water,** in great distress or difficulty: *Their marriage has been in deep water for some time.* **20. in hot water.** See **hot water. 21. like water,** lavishly; abundantly; freely: *The champagne flowed like water.* **22. make water, a.** (of a boat) to allow water to enter; leak. **b.** to urinate. **23. take water,** (of a boat) to allow water to enter through leaks or portholes or over the side. **24. tread water.** See **tread** (def. 12).

CONCISE ETYMOLOGY KEY: <, descended or borrowed from; >, whence; b., blend of, blended; c., cognate with; cf., compare; deriv., derivative; equiv., equivalent; imit., imitative; obl., oblique; r., replacing; s., stem; sp., spelling, spelled; resp., respelling, respelled; trans., translation; ?, origin unknown; *, unattested; ‡, probably earlier than. See the full key inside the front cover.

—*v.t.* **25.** to sprinkle, moisten, or drench with water: *to water the flowers; to water a street.* **26.** to supply (animals) with water for drinking. **27.** to furnish with a supply of water, as a ship. **28.** to furnish water to (a region), as by streams; supply (land) with water, as by irrigation: *The valley is watered by a branch of the Colorado River. Our land is watered by the All-American Canal.* **29.** to dilute, weaken, soften, or adulterate with, or as with, water (often fol. by *down*): *to water soup; to water down an unfavorable report.* **30.** *Finance.* to issue or increase the par value of (shares of stock) without having the assets to warrant doing so (often fol. by *down*). **31.** to produce a wavy, lustrous pattern, marking, or finish on (fabrics, metals, etc.): *watered silk.* —*v.i.* **32.** to discharge, fill with, or secrete water or liquid, as the eyes when irritated, or as the mouth at the sight or thought of tempting food. **33.** to drink water, as an animal. **34.** to take in a supply of water, as a ship: *Our ship will water at Savannah.* **35. make one's mouth water,** to excite a desire or appetite for something: *The roasting turkey made our mouths water.* —*adj.* **36.** of or pertaining to water in any way: *a water journey.* **37.** holding, or designed to hold, water: *a water jug.* **38.** worked or powered by water: *a water turbine.* **39.** heating, pumping, or circulating water (often used in combination): *hot-water furnace; city waterworks.* **40.** used in or on water: *water skis.* **41.** containing or prepared with water, as for hardening or dilution: *water mortar.* **42.** located or occurring on, in, or by water: *water music; water frontage.* **43.** residing by or in, or ruling over, water: *water people; water deities.* [bef. 900; (n.) ME; OE *wæter;* c. D *water,* G *Wasser;* akin to ON *vain,* Goth *wato,* Hittite *watar,* Gk *hýdōr;* (v.) ME *wateren,* OE *wæterian,* deriv. of the n.] —**wa′ter·er,** *n.* —**wa′ter·less,** *adj.* —**wa′ter·less·ly,** *adv.* —**wa′ter·less·ness,** *n.* —**wa′ter·like′,** *adj.*

wa′ter ar′um, an aquatic arum plant, *Calla palustris,* of the North Temperate Zone, having heart-shaped leaves, tiny green flowers, and red berries. Also called **wild calla.** [1810–20, *Amer.*]

wa′ter back′, a reservoir or arrangement of tubing at the back of certain stoves or fireplaces for containing water to be heated by the fire. [1860–65, *Amer.*]

wa′ter ballet′, synchronized movements, patterns, and other visual effects performed in the water by swimmers, usually to a musical accompaniment. [1925–30]

wa′ter-base paint′ (wô′tər bās′, wot′ər-). See **latex paint.** [1945–50]

wat′er bath′, **1.** a system for the control of temperature in which a vessel containing the material to be heated is set into or over one containing water and receiving the heat directly. **2.** a bath of water. [1815–25]

wa′ter bear′, *Zool.* a tardigrade. [1700–10]

Wa′ter Bear′er, *Astron., Astrol.* Aquarius. [1585–95]

wa·ter·bed (wô′tər bed′, wot′ər-), *n.* a bed having a liquid-filled rubber or plastic mattress in a rigid, often heated, waterproof frame, and providing a surface that conforms to the sleeper's body in any position. [1835–45; WATER + BED]

wa′ter bee′tle, any of various aquatic beetles, as a predaceous diving beetle. [1660–70]

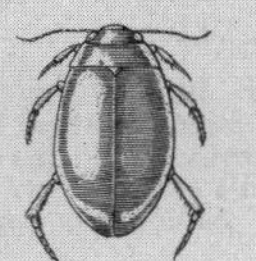

water beetle,
Captotomus interrogatus,
length ½ in.
(1.3 cm)

wa′ter bench′, a Pennsylvania Dutch dresser having a lower portion closed with doors for milk pails, an open shelf for water pails, and an upper section with shallow drawers. Also called **bucket bench, milk bench.**

wa′ter bird′, an aquatic bird; a swimming or wading bird. [1400–50; late ME]

wa′ter bis′cuit, a crackerlike biscuit prepared from flour and water. [1780–90]

wa′ter blis′ter, a blister that contains a clear, serous fluid, as distinguished from a blood blister, in which the fluid contains blood. [1890–95]

wa′ter boat′, a vessel for supplying ships with fresh water. [1720–30]

wa′ter boat′man, any of numerous aquatic insects of the family Corixidae, having paddlelike hind legs. Also called **boat bug.** [1805–15]

wa′ter bomb′, a bag filled with water and mischievously dropped from a height upon a passerby below.

wa·ter·borne (wô′tər bôrn′, -bōrn′, wot′ər-), *adj.* **1.** floating or moving on water; supported by water: *The ship was waterborne ten months after the keel was laid.* **2.** transported by ship or boat: *waterborne commerce.* **3.** communicated by water, esp. drinking water: *waterborne diseases.* [1550–60; WATER + BORNE]

wa′ter bou′get (bo͞o′jit), **1.** (formerly) a leather bag suspended at each end of a pole or yoke and used for carrying water. **2.** Also, **wa′ter budg′et.** *Heraldry.* a representation of a pair of these joined by a yoke, used as a charge. [1560–70; *bouget,* var. of BUDGET]

wa′ter boy′, **1.** a person who carries a canteen or bucket of drinking water to those too occupied to fetch it, as to soldiers, laborers, or football players. **2.** a person who sees that livestock is supplied with water, as by filling water troughs. [1645–55]

wa·ter·brain (wô′tər brān′, wot′ər-), *n. Vet. Pathol.* gid, in sheep. [WATER + BRAIN]

wa′ter brash′, *Pathol.* heartburn (def. 1). [1795–1805]

waterbuck,
Kobus ellipsiprymnus,
4 ft. (1.2 m)
high at shoulder;
horns 2½ ft. (0.8 m);
head and body
5 ft. (1.5 m);
tail 10 in. (25 cm)

wa·ter·buck (wô′tər buk′, wot′ər-), *n.* any of several large African antelopes of the genus *Kobus,* frequenting marshes and reedy places, esp. *K. ellipsiprymnus,* of eastern and central Africa. [1840–50; WATER + BUCK[1]]

wa′ter buf′falo, a buffalo, *Bubalus bubalis,* of the Old World tropics, having large, flattened, curved horns: wild populations are near extinction. Also called **water ox.** [1885–90]

water buffalo,
Bubalus bubalis,
5½ ft. (1.7 m)
high at shoulder;
length 9 ft. (2.7 m)

wa′ter bug′, **1.** any of various aquatic bugs, as of the family Belostomatidae **(giant water bug).** **2.** (loosely) a large cockroach, esp. the American cockroach. [1740–50]

Wa·ter·bur·y (wô′tər ber′ē, -bə rē, wot′ər-), *n.* a city in W Connecticut. 103,266.

wa·ter-bus (wô′tər bus′, wot′ər-), *n., pl.* **-bus·es, -bus·ses.** **1.** vaporetto. **2.** any small ship or boat serving as a passenger shuttle. [1925–30]

wa′ter can′non, a truck-mounted hose or pipe that shoots a jet of water through a nozzle at extremely high pressure, used esp. in dispersing rioters or demonstrators. [1965–70]

wa′ter car′rier, **1.** a person who carries water, as to a body of troops. **2.** a pipe, duct, or tank for conveying water. **3.** a ship that transports goods or persons by waterway or sea routes. [1645–55]

wa′ter chest′nut, **1.** any aquatic plant of the genus *Trapa,* bearing an edible, nutlike fruit, esp. *T. natans,* of the Old World. **2.** the fruit itself. Also called **wa′ter cal′trop.** [1850–55]

wa′ter chin′quapin, **1.** an American lotus, *Nelumbo lutea,* having pale-yellow flowers and an edible seed. **2.** the seed itself, similar in flavor to the chinquapin. [1830–40, *Amer.*]

wa′ter clock′, a device, as a clepsydra, for measuring time by the flow of water. [1595–1605]

wa′ter clos′et, **1.** an enclosed room or compartment containing a toilet bowl fitted with a mechanism for flushing. **2.** *Older Use.* a privy or bathroom. *Abbr.:* WC, w.c. [1745–55]

wa′ter clo′ver, a common freshwater fern, *Marsilea quadrifolia,* of lake edges and quiet ponds, having roots embedded in the bottom, very slender and often tangled stems, and floating, cloverlike leaves composed of four leaflets. Also called **pepperwort, water shamrock.**

wa·ter·col·or (wô′tər kul′ər, wot′ər-), *n.* **1.** a pigment for which water and not oil is used as the vehicle. **2.** the art or technique of painting with such pigments. **3.** a painting or design executed in such pigments by this technique. [1590–1600; WATER + COLOR] —**wa′·ter·col′or,** *adj.* —**wa′ter·col′or·ist,** *n.*

wa·ter-cool (wô′tər ko͞ol′, wot′ər-), *v.t.* to cool by means of water, esp. by water circulating in pipes or a water jacket, as an engine or machine gun. [1895–1900] —**wa′ter-cooled′,** *adj.*

wa′ter cool′er, **1.** a container for holding drinking water that is cooled and drawn off by a faucet or spigot. **2.** a drinking fountain in which water is cooled by mechanical refrigeration. [1840–50, *Amer.*]

wa·ter·course (wô′tər kôrs′, -kōrs′, wot′ər-), *n.* **1.** a stream of water, as a river or brook. **2.** the bed of a stream that flows only seasonally. **3.** a natural channel conveying water. **4.** a channel or canal made for the conveyance of water. [1500–10; WATER + COURSE]

wa·ter·craft (wô′tər kraft′, -kräft′, wot′ər-), *n.* **1.** skill in boating and water sports. **2.** any boat or ship. **3.** boats and ships collectively. [1560–70; WATER + CRAFT]

wa·ter·cress (wô′tər kres′, wot′ər-), *n.* **1.** a cress, *Nasturtium officinale,* of the mustard family, usually growing in clear, running streams and having pungent leaves. **2.** the leaves, used for salads, soups, and as a garnish. [1300–50; ME; c. MD, MLG *waterkerse.* See WATER, CRESS]

wa′ter cure′, **1.** hydropathy; hydrotherapy. **2.** a method of torture in which the victim is forced to drink great quantities of water. [1835–45]

wa′ter cur′tain, a sheet of water from a series of sprinklers for protecting the walls and roof of a building from fires outside the building.

wa′ter dog′, **1.** a dog that swims well or is trained to retrieve waterfowl in hunting. **2.** *Informal.* a person who feels at home in or on the water. **3.** waterdog. [1300–50; ME]

wa·ter·dog (wô′tər dôg′, -dog′, wot′ər-), *n.* any of several large salamanders, as a mudpuppy or hellbender. Also, **water dog.** [1855–60; WATER + DOG]

wa·tered (wô′tərd, wot′ərd), *adj.* **1.** having rivers or streams: *an amply watered area.* **2.** receiving rain or other precipitation. **3.** sprinkled, irrigated, etc., with water: *a poorly watered garden.* **4.** having a wavy, lustrous pattern or marking: *watered silk.* **5.** (of stock) issued in excess of a company's true worth. [1350–1400; ME; see WATER, -ED[2], -ED[3]]

wa·tered-down (wô′tərd doun′, wot′ərd-), *adj.* made weaker or less effective from or as from dilution with water: *a watered-down cocktail; Spectators saw a watered-down version of the famous opera.* [1895–1900]

Wa·ter·ee (wô′tə rē′, wot′ə-), *n.* a river in South Carolina, the lower portion of the Catawba River, joining with the Congaree River to form the Santee River. Cf. **Catawba** (def. 2).

wa′ter elm′. See **planer tree.** [1810–20, *Amer.*]

wa·ter·fall (wô′tər fôl′, wot′ər-), *n.* **1.** a steep fall or flow of water in a watercourse from a height, as over a precipice; cascade. See table on next page. **2.** a manner of arranging women's hair, as in long, loose waves. [bef. 1000; ME; OE *wætergefeall.* See WATER, FALL]

wa·ter-fast (wô′tər fast′, -fäst′, wot′ər-), *adj.* (of a color or dye) resistant to the effects caused by water; not changed or faded by the action of water. [1540–50]

wa′ter feath′er, **1.** a water milfoil, *Myriophyllum aquaticum.* **2.** a North American featherfoil, *Hottonia inflata.* [1810–20, *Amer.*]

wa·ter·find·er (wô′tər fīn′dər, wot′ər-), *n.* a dowser; water witch. [1880–85, *Amer.*; WATER + FINDER]

wa′ter flag′, a European iris, *Iris pseudacorus,* naturalized throughout eastern North America, with blue-green leaves and violet-veined, yellow flowers and growing in moist places. Also called **yellow flag.** [1570–80]

wa′ter flea′, any of various small crustaceans that move about in the water like fleas, as those of the genus *Daphnia.* [1575–85]

wa·ter·flood (wô′tər flud′, wot′ər-), *n.* (in the petroleum industry) a method of secondary recovery whereby water is pumped into reservoir rock to force out oil that has ceased to flow under its own pressure. [1925–30; WATER + FLOOD]

Wa·ter·ford (wô′tər fərd, wot′ər-), *n.* **1.** a county in Munster province, in the S Republic of Ireland. 50,190; 710 sq. mi. (1840 sq. km). **2.** its county seat: a seaport. 38,457. **3.** a town in SE Connecticut. 17,843.

Wa′terford glass′, fine cut or gilded glass made in Waterford, Ireland, having a slight blue cast due to the presence of cobalt. [1935–40]

wa′ter foun′tain, a drinking fountain, water cooler, or other apparatus supplying drinking water.

wa·ter·fowl (wô′tər foul′, wot′ər-), *n., pl.* **-fowls,** (*esp. collectively*) **-fowl.** **1.** a water bird, esp. a swimming bird. **2.** such birds taken collectively, esp. the swans, geese, and ducks. [1250–1300; ME; c. G *Wasservogel;* see WATER, FOWL]

wa·ter·front (wô′tər frunt′, wot′ər-), *n.* **1.** land on the edge of a body of water. **2.** a part of a city or town on such land; wharf or dock section. **3.** a container placed before a stove to heat water. [1760–70, *Amer.*; WATER + FRONT]

wa′ter gap′, a transverse gap in a mountain ridge, cut by and giving passage to a stream or river. [1750–60, *Amer.*]

wa′ter gas′, a toxic gaseous mixture consisting chiefly of carbon monoxide and hydrogen, prepared from steam and incandescent coke: used as an illuminant, fuel, and in organic synthesis. Also called **blue gas.** [1850–55] —**wa′ter-gas′,** *adj.*

wa′ter gate′, **1.** a gate for halting or controlling the flow of water in a watercourse; floodgate. **2.** a gateway leading to the edge of a body of water, as at a landing. [1350–1400; ME]

Wa·ter·gate (wô′tər gāt′, wot′ər-), *n.* **1.** a White House political scandal that came to light during the 1972 presidential campaign, growing out of a break-in at the Democratic party headquarters at the Watergate apartment-office complex in Washington, D.C., and, after Congressional hearings, culminating in the resignation of President Nixon in 1974. **2.** any scandal involving abuses of power, corruption, or the like, and attempts to cover them up.

wa′ter gauge′, any device for indicating the height of water in a reservoir, tank, boiler, or other vessel. [1700–10]

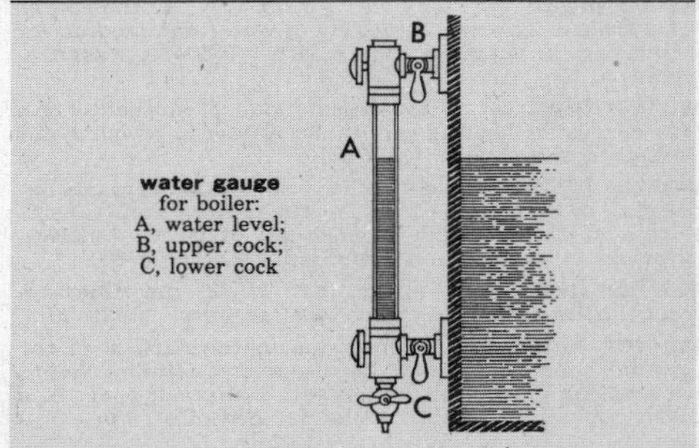

water gauge
for boiler:
A, water level;
B, upper cock;
C, lower cock

CONCISE PRONUNCIATION KEY: act, cāpe, dâre, pärt; set, ēqual; *if,* ice; ox, ōver, ôrder, oil, bo͝ok, bo͞ot, out; up, ûrge; child; sing; shoe; thin, *th*at; zh as in *treasure.* ə = *a* as in *alone, e* as in *system, i* as in *easily, o* as in *gallop, u* as in *circus;* ᵊ as in *fire* (fīᵊr), *hour* (ouᵊr). l and n can serve as syllabic consonants, as in *cradle* (krād′l), and *button* (but′n). See the full key inside the front cover.

NOTED WATERFALLS OF THE WORLD

Waterfall	Location (and Nearby City or Community)	River or Other Source of Water	Height ft.	Height m
Angel (1)	Southeastern Venezuela (Canaima)	Tributary of the Caroni	3212	979
Tugela (2)	Natal, South Africa (Durban)	Tugela	2810	856
Yosemite (3)	Yosemite National Park	Yosemite Creek	2526	770
Cuquenán (4)	Guyana-Venezuela Border (Santa Elena)	Tributary of the Arabopó	2000	610
Sutherland (5)	Southwest South Island, N.Z. (Milford Sound)	Into Arthur R.	1904	580
Kile (6)	Western Norway (Bergen)	Kile	1840	561
Wollomombi (7)	New South Wales, Australia (Armidale)	Macleay	1700	518
Ribbon (8)	Yosemite National Park	Ribbon Creek	1612	491
Upper Yosemite (9)	Yosemite National Park	Yosemite Creek	1436	438
Gavarnie (10)	Southern France (Lourdes)	Pyrenees Glaciers	1385	422
Krimmler	West Central Austria (Innsbruck)	Krimmler	1246	380
Takakkaw	Yoho National Park, B.C., Canada (Lake Louise)	Into Yoho R.	1200	366
Silver Strand	Yosemite National Park	(Stream)	1170	357
Staubbach	South Central Switzerland (Lauterbrunnen)	Staubbach	1000	305
Rjukan	Southern Norway (Skien)	Måne	983	300
Giessbach	South Central Switzerland (Brienz)	Giessbach	980	299
Trummelbach	South Central Switzerland (Lauterbrunnen)	Jungfrau Glaciers	950	290
Kalambo	Zambia-Tanzania Border (Mbala)	Kalambo	704	215
Bridalveil	Yosemite National Park	Bridalveil Creek	620	189
Multnomah	Northwestern Oregon (Bonneville)	Into Columbia R.	620	189
Nevada	Yosemite National Park	(Stream)	594	181
Toce	Northern Italy (Domodossola)	Toce	540	165
Vøring	Southwestern Norway (Eidfjord)	Bjoreia	535	163
Skjaggedals	Southwestern Norway (Odda)	Ringdal Lake	525	160
Tequendama	Central Columbia (Bogotá)	Bogotá	482	147
Victoria	Zambia-Zimbabwe Border (Livingstone)	Zambezi	420	122
Kabalega	Northwestern Uganda (Butiaba)	Victoria Nile	400	122
Glomach	Scotland (Inverness)	Elchaig	370	113
Illilouette	Yosemite National Park	Illilouette Creek	370	113
Granite	Northwestern Washington (Everett)	Stillaguamish	350	107
Lower Yosemite	Yosemite National Park	Yosemite Creek	320	98
Churchill	Western Labrador (Goose Bay)	Upper Hamilton	316	96
Lower Yellowstone	Yellowstone National Park	Yellowstone	308	94
Reichenbach, Upper	Central Switzerland (Grindelwald)	Rosenlaui Glacier	300	91
Iguassú	Argentina-Brazil Border (Puerto Iguassú)	Iguassú	210	64
Shoshone	Southern Idaho (Twin Falls)	Snake	210	64
Twin	Southern Idaho (Twin Falls)	Snake	180	55
Niagara	Western New York and Southern Ontario (Niagara Falls)	Niagara	167	51
Manitou	Northwestern Wisconsin (La Crosse)	Black	165	50
Pistyll Cain	Northern Wales (Dolgelley)	Cain	150	46
Tower	Yellowstone National Park	Yellowstone	132	40
Upper Yellowstone	Yellowstone National Park	Yellowstone	109	33
Rheinfall (Schaffhausen)	Northern Switzerland (Schaffhausen)	Rhine	100	30

Parenthetical numbers indicate rank of 10 highest waterfalls.

wa′ter glass′, 1. a drinking glass; tumbler. 2. a glass container for holding water, as for growing bulbs, plants, or the like. 3. a glass tube used to indicate water level, as in a boiler. 4. a device for observing objects beneath the surface of the water, consisting essentially of an open tube or box with a glass bottom. 5. See **sodium silicate.** Also, **wa′ter-glass′.** [1600–10]

wa′terglass paint′ing, stereochromy. [1860–65]

wa′ter gum′, any of several Australian trees of the myrtle family, growing near water. [1840–50]

wa′ter gun′. See **water pistol.** [1640–50]

wa′ter ham′mer, the concussion and accompanying noise that result when a volume of water moving in a pipe suddenly stops or loses momentum. [1795–1805]

wa·ter-hard·en (wô′tər här′dn, wot′ər-), *v.t. Metall.* to quench (steel) in water. Cf. **oil-harden.**

wa′ter haw′thorn. See **Cape pondweed.**

wa·ter·head (wô′tər hed′, wot′ər-), *n.* 1. the source of a river or stream. 2. a body of water dammed up for irrigation, to supply a garden, etc. [1560–70; WATER + HEAD]

wa′ter heat′er, a household appliance consisting of a gas or electric heating unit under a tank in which water is heated and stored. [1875–80]

wa′ter hem′lock, any of several poisonous plants belonging to the genus *Cicuta,* of the parsley family, as *C. virosa* of Europe, and *C. maculata* of North America, growing in swamps and marshy places. [1755–65]

wa′ter hen′, 1. moorhen (def. 1). 2. the American coot, *Fulica americana.* Also, **wa′ter-hen′.** [1520–30]

wa′ter hole′, 1. a depression in the surface of the ground, containing water. 2. a source of drinking water, as a spring or well in the desert. 3. a pond; pool. 4. a cavity containing water in the dry bed of a river. 5. a hole in the frozen surface of a lake, pond, stream, etc. [1645–55]

CONCISE ETYMOLOGY KEY: <, descended or borrowed from; >, whence; b., blend of, blended; c., cognate with; cf., compare; deriv., derivative; equiv., equivalent; imit., imitative; obl., oblique; r., replacing; s., stem; sp., spelling, spelled; resp., respelling, respelled; trans., translation; ?, origin unknown; *, unattested; ‡, probably earlier than. See the full key inside the front cover.

wa′ter hy′acinth, a floating aquatic plant, *Eichornia crassipes,* of tropical lakes and rivers, that grows so prolifically it often hinders the passage of boats. [1895–1900, *Amer.*]

wa′ter ice′, 1. ice formed by direct freezing of fresh or salt water, and not by compacting of snow. 2. a frozen dessert, similar to sherbet, made of water, sweetener, and fruit syrup or other flavorings. [1810–20]

wa·ter-inch (wô′tər inch′, wot′ər-), *n. Hydraulics.* the quantity of water (approx. 500 cubic feet) discharged in 24 hours through a circular opening of one inch diameter leading from a reservoir in which the water is constantly only high enough to cover the orifice. [1850–55]

wa·ter·i·ness (wô′tə rē nis, wot′ə-), *n.* the state or condition of being watery or diluted. [1350–1400; ME; see WATERY, -NESS]

wa·ter·ing (wô′tər ing, wot′ər-), *n.* 1. the act of a person or thing that waters. 2. a watered appearance on silk or other fabric. —*adj.* 3. supplying water or used to water. 4. pertaining to medicinal springs or to a seabathing resort. [bef. 1000; ME (n.); OE *wæterung.* See WATER, -ING[1], -ING[2]]

wa′tering can′, a container for water, typically of metal or plastic and having a spout with a perforated nozzle, for watering or sprinkling plants, flowers, etc. Also called **wa′tering pot′, sprinkling can.** [1685–95]

wa′tering hole′, *Informal.* a bar, nightclub, or other social gathering place where alcoholic drinks are sold. Also called **watering place, wa′tering spot′.**

wa′tering place′, 1. *Brit.* a seaside or lakeside vacation resort featuring bathing, boating, etc. 2. a health resort near mineral springs, a lake, or the sea, featuring therapeutic baths, water cures, or the like. 3. a place where drinking water may be obtained by humans or animals, as a spring or water hole. 4. See **watering hole.** [1400–50; late ME]

wa·ter·ish (wô′tər ish, wot′ər-), *adj.* somewhat, or tending to be, watery. [1520–30; WATER + -ISH[1]] —**wa′ter·ish·ly,** *adv.* —**wa′ter·ish·ness,** *n.*

wa′ter jack′et, a water-filled casing or compartment used to water-cool something, as an engine or machine gun. [1865–70]

wa·ter-jack·et (wô′tər jak′it, wot′ər-), *v.t.* to surround or fit with a water jacket. [1875–80]

wa·ter·jet (wô′tər jet′, wot′ər-), *n.* 1. a stream of water forced out through a small aperture. 2. Also, **wa′ter jet′.** waterpick. —*adj.* 3. of, pertaining to, or operated by a waterjet: *a waterjet pump.* [1825–35; WATER + JET[1]]

wa′ter jump′, any small body of water that a horse must jump over, as in a steeplechase. [1870–75]

wa·ter-laid (wô′tər lād′, wot′ər-), *adj. Ropemaking.* noting a rope laid left-handed from three or four plain-laid ropes, in the making of which water was used to wet the fibers instead of the more customary oil or tallow. [1855–60]

wa′ter leaf′, (in Greek architecture and sculpture) a motif of heart-shaped leaves having a conspicuous midrib. Also called **Lesbian leaf.** [1850–55]

wa·ter·leaf (wô′tər lēf′, wot′ər-), *n.* any of several North American plants of the genus *Hydrophyllum,* having clusters of bluish or white flowers and leaves often bearing marks resembling water stains. [1750–60; WATER + LEAF]

wa′terleaf fam′ily, the plant family Hydrophyllaceae, characterized by usually hairy herbaceous plants having lobed, divided, or compound leaves, five-parted blue or white flowers, and capsular fruit, and including baby-blue-eyes, phacelia, and waterleaf.

wa′ter lem′on. See **yellow granadilla.** [1775–85]

wa·ter·less (wô′tər lis, wot′ər-), *adj.* 1. devoid of water; dry. 2. needing no water, as for cooking. [bef. 950; ME *waterlees,* OE *wæterlēas.* See WATER, -LESS] —**wa′ter·less·ly,** *adv.* —**wa′ter·less·ness,** *n.*

wa′terless cook′er, 1. a tight-lidded kitchen utensil in which food can be cooked using only a small amount of water or only the juices emitted while cooking. 2. See **pressure cooker.**

wa′ter let′tuce, a floating aquatic plant, *Pistia stratiotes,* of the arum family, having a rosette of thick, spongy leaves. [1865–70]

wa′ter lev′el, 1. the surface level of any body of water. 2. the level to which a vessel is immersed; water line. [1555–65]

wa′ter lil′y, 1. any of various aquatic plants of the genus *Nymphaea,* species of which have large, disklike, floating leaves and showy flowers, esp. *N. odorata,* of America, or *N. alba,* of Europe. Cf. **water lily family.** 2. any related plant of the genus *Nuphar.* 3. a plant of the water lily family. 4. the flower of any such plant. [1540–50]

water lily, *Nymphaea odorata*

wa′ter lil′y fam′ily, the plant family Nymphaeaceae, characterized by aquatic herbaceous plants having usually broad leaves, solitary, often showy flowers, and fruit in a variety of forms, and including the lotus (genus *Nelumbo*), spatterdock, water lily, and water shield.

wa′ter lil′y tu′lip, a showy tulip, *Tulipa kaufmanniana,* of Turkestan, having spreading, white or pale-yellow flowers with red centers streaked with red.

wa′ter line′, 1. *Naut.* the part of the outside of a ship's hull that is just at the water level. 2. *Naval Archit.* any of a series of lines on the hull plans of a vessel representing the level to which the vessel is immersed or the bottom of the keel. Cf. **load line, Plimsoll line.** 3. the line in which water at its surface borders upon a floating body. 4. See **water level** (def. 2). 5. Also called **watermark.** a line indicating the former level or passage of water: *A water line all around the cellar served as a reminder of the flood.* 6. a pipe, hose, tube, or other line for conveying water. Also, **wa′ter·line′.** [1615–25]

wa·ter·locked (wô′tər lokt′, wot′ər-), *adj.* enclosed entirely, or almost entirely, by water: *a waterlocked nation.* [1910–15; WATER + *locked* (ptp. of LOCK[1])]

wa′ter lo′cust, a spiny tree, *Gleditsia aquatica,* of the legume family, native to the southeastern coastal U.S., having pinnate leaves, greenish-yellow, bell-shaped flowers, and long-stalked, thin pods. Also called **swamp locust.** [1800–10, *Amer.*]

wa·ter·log (wô′tər lôg′, -log′, wot′ər-), *v.,* **-logged, -log·ging.** —*v.t.* 1. to cause (a boat, ship, etc.) to become uncontrollable as a result of flooding. 2. to soak, fill, or saturate with water so as to make soggy or useless. —*v.i.* 3. to become saturated with water. [1770–80; appar. back formation from WATERLOGGED]

wa·ter·logged (wô′tər lôgd′, -logd′, wot′ər-), *adj.* 1. so filled or flooded with water as to be heavy or unmanageable, as a ship. 2. excessively saturated with or as if with water: *waterlogged ground; waterlogged with fatigue.* [1760–70; WATER + LOG[1] (appar. in v. sense "(of water) to accumulate in a ship") + -ED[2]]

Wa·ter·loo (wô′tər lo͞o′, wot′ər-, wô′tər lo͞o′, wot′ər-; *for 1 also Flem.* vä′tər lō′), *n.* 1. a village in central Belgium, south of Brussels: Napoleon decisively defeated here on June 18, 1815. See map on next page. 2. a decisive or crushing defeat: *The candidate met her Waterloo in the national elections.* 3. a city in E Iowa. 75,985. 4. a city in SE Ontario, in S Canada. 49,428.

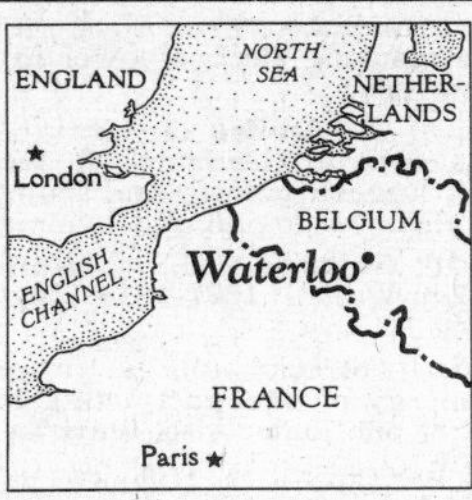

wa′ter loss′, evapotranspiration (def. 2).

wa′ter main′, a main pipe or conduit in a system for conveying water. [1795–1805]

wa•ter•man (wô′tər mən, wot′ər-), *n., pl.* **-men.** **1.** a person who manages or works on a boat; boatman. **2.** a person skilled in rowing or boating. **3.** *Chesapeake Bay Area.* a person with a general license to take any legal catch of fish and shellfish in Chesapeake Bay. [1350–1400; ME; see WATER, MAN[1]]

wa•ter•man•ship (wô′tər mən ship′, wot′ər-), *n.* **1.** the skill, duties, business, etc., of a waterman. **2.** skill in rowing or boating. [1880–85; WATERMAN + -SHIP]

wa•ter•mark (wô′tər märk′, wot′ər-), *n.* **1.** a mark indicating the height to which water rises or has risen, as in a river or inlet. **2.** See **water line** (def. 5). **3.** a figure or design impressed in some paper during manufacture, visible when the paper is held to the light. —*v.t.* **4.** to mark (paper) with a watermark. **5.** to impress (a design, pattern, etc.), as a watermark. [1625–35; WATER + MARK[1]]

wa′ter mead′ow, a meadow kept fertile by flooding. [1725–35]

wa•ter•meal (wô′tər mēl′, wot′ər-), *n.* any of several tiny floating aquatic plants of the genus *Wolffia.* [WATER + MEAL[2]]

wa•ter•mel•on (wô′tər mel′ən, wot′ər-), *n.* **1.** the large, roundish or elongated fruit of a trailing vine, *Citrullus lanata,* of the gourd family, having a hard, green rind and a sweet, juicy, usually pink or red pulp. **2.** the vine itself. [1605–15; WATER + MELON]

wa′ter me′ter, a device for measuring and registering the quantity of water that passes through a pipe or other outlet. [1855–60]

wa′ter mil′foil, any of various aquatic plants, chiefly of the genus *Myriophyllum,* the submerged leaves of which are very finely divided. [1570–80]

wa′ter mill′, a mill with machinery driven by water. [1375–1425; late ME]

wa′ter moc′casin, **1.** the cottonmouth. **2.** any of various similar but harmless snakes, as a water snake of the genus *Nerodia.* [1815–25, *Amer.*]

wa′ter mold′, *Mycol.* any of various aquatic fungi of the phylum Oomycota, free-living or parasitic in fish and other aquatic organisms. [1895–1900]

wa′ter mo′tor, any form of prime mover or motor that is operated by the kinetic energy, pressure, or weight of water, esp. a small turbine or waterwheel fitted to a pipe supplying water. [1880–85]

wa′ter nymph′, **1.** a nymph of the water, as a naiad, a Nereid, or an Oceanid. **2.** See **water lily.** **3.** any aquatic plant of the genus *Najas,* having narrow, opposite leaves. [1350–1400; ME]

wa′ter oak′, **1.** an oak, *Quercus nigra,* of the southern U.S., growing chiefly along streams and swamps. **2.** any of several other American oaks of similar habit. [1680–90, *Amer.*]

wa′ter oats′. See **wild rice.** [1810–20, *Amer.*]

wa′ter of constitu′tion, *Chem.* water present in a molecule that cannot be removed without disrupting the molecule. [1885–90]

wa′ter of crystalliza′tion, *Chem.* water of hydration, formerly thought necessary to crystallization: now usually regarded as affecting crystallization only as it forms new molecular combinations. [1785–95]

wa′ter of hydra′tion, *Chem.* the portion of a hydrate that is represented as, or can be expelled as, water: now usually regarded as being in true molecular combination with the other atoms of the compound, and not existing in the compound as water. [1885–90]

wa′ter on the brain′, hydrocephalus. [1780–90]

wa′ter on the knee′, *Pathol.* an accumulation of fluid in the knee cavity caused by inflammation and trauma to the cartilages or membranes of the knee joint. [1885–90]

wa′ter opos′sum, yapok. [1840–50]

wa′ter ou′zel, dipper (def. 4). [1615–25]

wa′ter ox′. See **water buffalo.** [1860–65]

wa′ter paint′, a pigment, as watercolor, in which water is used as the vehicle.

wa′ter part′ing, a watershed or divide. [1855–60]

wa•ter•pick (wô′tər pik′, wot′ər-) *n.* a portable electric appliance that uses a stream of water under force to remove food particles from between the teeth and to massage the gums. Also called **waterjet.** [WATER + PICK[2]; earlier as *Water Pik* a trademark (1963)]

wa′ter pill′, *Informal.* a diuretic pill.

wa′ter pim′pernel, **1.** the brookweed. **2.** the pimpernel, *Anagallis arvensis.*

wa′ter pipe′, **1.** a pipe for conveying water. **2.** a smoking apparatus, as a hookah or narghile, in which the smoke is drawn through a container of water and cooled before reaching the mouth. [1400–50; late ME]

wa′ter pip′it, a common, sparrow-sized pipit, *Anthus spinoletta,* of the Northern Hemisphere. [1880–85]

wa′ter pis′tol, a toy gun that shoots a stream of liquid. Also called **water gun, squirt gun.** [1900–05]

wa′ter plant′, a plant that grows in water. [1760–70]

wa′ter plat′ter, **1.** See **Santa Cruz water lily.** **2.** See **royal water lily.**

wa′ter plug′, a fireplug; hydrant.

wa′ter pock′et, **1.** a cavity at the foot of a cliff formed by the falling action of an intermittent stream. **2.** a plunge basin. [1885–90]

wa′ter po′lo, an aquatic game played by two teams of seven swimmers each, the object being to score goals by pushing, carrying, or passing an inflated ball and tossing it into the opponent's goal, defended by a goalkeeper. [1885–90]

wa′ter pop′py, a Brazilian, aquatic plant, *Hydrocleys nymphoides,* having yellow, poppylike flowers.

wa′ter pow′er, **1.** the power of water used, or capable of being used, to drive machinery, turbines, etc. **2.** a waterfall or descent in a watercourse capable of being so used. **3.** a water right possessed by a mill. Also, **wa′ter•pow′er.** [1820–30]

wa′ter pox′, *Pathol.* See **chicken pox.** [1815–25]

wa•ter•proof (wô′tər proof′, wot′ər-), *adj.* **1.** impervious to water. **2.** rendered impervious to water by some special process, as coating or treating with rubber: *a waterproof hat.* —*n.* **3.** *Chiefly Brit.* a raincoat or other outer coat impervious to water. **4.** any of several coated or rubberized fabrics that are impervious to water. —*v.t.* **5.** to make waterproof. [1730–40; WATER + -PROOF] —**wa′ter•proof′er,** *n.* —**wa′ter•proof′•ness,** *n.*

wa•ter•proof•ing (wô′tər proo′fing, wot′ər-), *n.* **1.** a substance by which something is made waterproof. **2.** the act or process of making something waterproof. [1835–45; WATERPROOF + -ING[1]]

wa′ter rail′, an Old World rail, *Rallus aquaticus,* having olive-brown plumage marked with black and a long, red bill. [1645–55]

wa′ter rat′, **1.** any of various rodents having aquatic habits. **2.** the muskrat, *Ondatra zibethica.* **3.** (in Australia and New Guinea) any of the aquatic rats of the subfamily Hydromyinae, esp. of the genus *Hydromys.* **4.** *Slang.* a vagrant or thief who frequents a waterfront. [1545–55]

wa•ter-re•pel•lent (wô′tər ri pel′ənt, wot′ər-), *adj.* having a finish that resists but is not impervious to water. [1895–1900]

wa•ter-re•sist•ant (wô′tər ri zis′tənt, wot′ər-), *adj.* resisting though not entirely preventing the penetration of water. [1920–25]

wa′ter rice′. See **wild rice.** [1810–20]

wa′ter right′, the right to make use of the water from a particular stream, lake, or irrigation canal. [1785–95, *Amer.*]

Wa•ters (wô′tərz, wot′ərz), *n.* **Ethel,** 1896–1977, U.S. singer and actress.

wa′ter sap′phire, a transparent variety of cordierite, found in Sri Lanka, Madagascar, and elsewhere, sometimes used as a gem. [1690–1700]

wa•ter•sav•er (wô′tər sā′vər, wot′ər-), *n.* a person, device, or practice that reduces water consumption, as during a drought. [WATER + SAVER]

wa•ter•scape (wô′tər skāp′, wot′ər-), *n.* a picture or view of the sea or other body of water. [1850–55; WATER + -SCAPE]

wa•ter•scor•pi•on (wô′tər skôr′pē ən, wot′ər-), *n.* any of several predaceous aquatic bugs of the family Nepidae, having clasping front legs and a long respiratory tube at the rear of the abdomen: capable of biting if handled. [1675–85; WATER + SCORPION]

wa′ter sham′rock. See **water clover.**

wa•ter•shed (wô′tər shed′, wot′ər-), *n.* **1.** *Chiefly Brit.* the ridge or crest line dividing two drainage areas; water parting; divide. **2.** the region or area drained by a river, stream, etc.; drainage area. **3.** *Archit.* wash (def. 48). **4.** an important point of division or transition between two phases, conditions, etc.: *The treaty to ban war in space may prove to be one of history's great watersheds.* —*adj.* **5.** constituting a watershed: *a watershed area; a watershed case.* [1795–1805; WATER + SHED[2]]

wa′ter shield′, **1.** Also called **water target.** an aquatic plant, *Brasenia schreberi,* of the water lily family, having purple flowers, floating, elliptic leaves, and a jellylike coating on the underwater stems and roots. **2.** a fanwort, esp. *Cabomba caroliniana.* See illus. under **dimorphism.** [1810–20]

wa•ter-sick (wô′tər sik′, wot′ər-), *adj. Agric.* (of soil) unproductive due to excessive watering or salt residues from irrigation.

wa•ter•side (wô′tər sīd′, wot′ər-), *n.* **1.** the margin, bank, or shore of a river, lake, ocean, etc. —*adj.* **2.** of, pertaining to, or situated at the waterside: *waterside insects; a waterside resort.* **3.** working by the waterside: *waterside police.* [1325–75; ME; see WATER, SIDE[1]]

wa′ter sign′, any of the three astrological signs, Cancer, Scorpio, and Pisces, that are grouped together because of the shared attributes of sensitivity and emotionalism. Cf. **triplicity.**

wa′ter ski′, a ski on which to water-ski, designed to plane over water: it is shorter and broader than the ski used on snow. [1930–35]

wa•ter-ski (wô′tər skē′, wot′ər-), *v.i.,* **-skied, -ski•ing.** to plane over water on water skis or a water ski by grasping a towing rope pulled by a speedboat. —**wa′•ter-ski′er,** *n.*

wa′ter snail′. See **Archimedes' screw.** [1555–65]

wa′ter snake′, **1.** any of numerous and widely distributed harmless snakes of the genus *Natrix,* inhabiting areas in or near fresh water. **2.** any of various other snakes living in or frequenting water. **3.** (*cap.*) *Astron.* the constellation Hydrus. [1595–1605]

wa•ter-soak (wô′tər sōk′, wot′ər-), *v.t.* to soak or saturate with water. [1785–95]

wa′ter sof′tener, any of a group of substances that when added to water containing calcium and magnesium ions cause the ions to precipitate or change their usual properties: used in the purification of water for the laboratory, and for giving water more efficient sudsing ability with soap. Also called **softener.**

wa•ter-sol•u•ble (wô′tər sol′yə bəl, wot′ər-), *adj.* capable of dissolving in water. [1920–25]

wa′ter span′iel, either of two breeds of spaniels, used for retrieving waterfowl. Cf. **American water spaniel, Irish water spaniel.** [1560–70]

Irish water spaniel, 2 ft. (0.6 m) high at shoulder

wa•ter•sport (wô′tər spôrt′, -spōrt′, wot′ər-), *n.* **1.** a sport played or practiced on or in water, as swimming, water polo, or surfing. **2. watersports,** (*used with a singular or plural v.*) *Slang.* sexual activity that typically involves urinating on or being urinated on by others. [1915–20; WATER + SPORT]

wa•ter•spout (wô′tər spout′, wot′ər-), *n.* **1.** Also called **rainspout.** a pipe running down the side of a house or other building to carry away water from the gutter of the roof. **2.** a spout, duct, or the like, from which water is discharged. **3.** a funnel-shaped or tubular portion of a cloud over the ocean or other body of water that, laden with mist and spray, resembles a solid column of water reaching upward to the cloud from which it hangs. Cf. **tornado** (def. 1). [1350–1400; 1730–40 for def. 3; ME; see WATER, SPOUT]

wa′ter sprite′, a sprite or spirit inhabiting the water, as an undine. [1790–1800]

wa′ter sprout′, **1.** a nonflowering shoot arising from a branch or axil of a tree or shrub. **2.** sucker (def. 9). [1890–95]

wa′ter strid′er, any of several aquatic bugs of the family Gerridae, having long, slender legs fringed with hairs, enabling the insects to dart about on the surface of the water. [1885–90]

wa′ter supply′, **1.** the supply of purified water available to a community. **2.** the facilities for storing and supplying this water, as reservoirs and pipelines. [1880–85] —**wa′ter-sup•ply′,** *adj.*

wa′ter sys′tem, **1.** a river and all its branches. **2.** a system of supplying water, as throughout a metropolitan area. [1825–35]

wa′ter ta′ble, **1.** the planar, underground surface beneath which earth materials, as soil or rock, are saturated with water. **2.** *Archit.* a projecting stringcourse or similar structural member placed so as to divert rain water from a building. Also, **wa′ter•ta′ble.** [1400–50; late ME]

wa′ter tar′get. See **water shield** (def. 1). [1805–15, *Amer.*]

wa′ter tax′i, a motorboat that transports passengers for a fare. [1925–30]

wa′ter thrush′, either of two North American warblers, *Seirus noveboracensis* or *S. motacilla,* usually living near streams. Also, **wa′ter•thrush′.** [1660–70]

wa′ter ti′ger, the larva of a predaceous diving beetle, of the genus *Dytiscus.* [1885–90]

wa•ter•tight (wô′tər tīt′, wot′ər-), *adj.* **1.** constructed or fitted so tightly as to be impervious to water: *The ship had six watertight compartments.* **2.** so devised or planned as to be impossible to defeat, evade, or nullify: *a watertight contract; a watertight alibi.* [1350–1400; ME; see WATER, TIGHT] —**wa′ter•tight′ness,** *n.*

Wa′ter•ton-Gla′cier Interna′tional Peace′ Park′ (wô′tər tən glā′shər, wot′ər-), an international park in SW Canada and NW Montana, jointly administered by Canada and the U.S. since 1932 and encompassing Waterton Lakes National Park (Canada) and Glacier National Park (U.S.). 1584 sq. mi. (4102 sq. km).

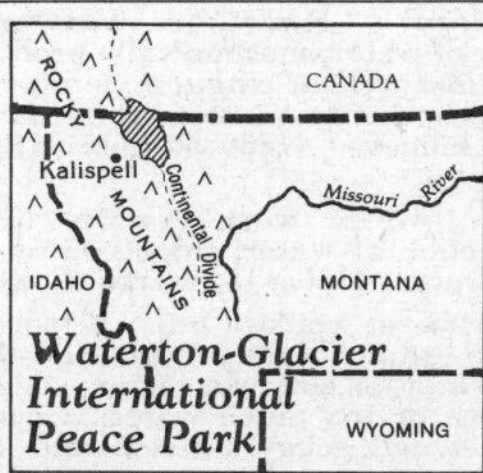

CONCISE PRONUNCIATION KEY: act, cāpe, dâre, pärt; set, ēqual; if, īce; ox, ōver, ôrder, oil, bŏŏk, bōōt, out; up, ûrge; child; sing; shoe; thin, *th*at; zh as in *treasure.* ə = *a* as in *alone, e* as in *system, i* as in *easily, o* as in *gallop, u* as in *circus;* ə as in *fire* (fīər), *hour* (ouər). l and n can serve as syllabic consonants, as in *cradle* (krād′l), and *button* (but′n). See the full key inside the front cover.

Wa′ter·ton Lakes′ Na′tional Park′ (wô′tər tən, wot′ər-), a national park in W Canada, in S Alberta. 220 sq. mi. (570 sq. km).

wa′ter tow′er, 1. a vertical pipe or tower into which water is pumped to a height sufficient to maintain a desired pressure for firefighting, distribution to customers, etc. **2.** a fire-extinguishing apparatus for throwing a stream of water on the upper parts of a tall burning building. [1880–85]

Wa·ter·town (wô′tər toun′, wot′ər-), *n.* **1.** a town in E Massachusetts, on the Charles River, near Boston: U.S. arsenal. 34,384. **2.** a city in N New York. 27,861. **3.** a town in NW Connecticut. 19,489. **4.** a city in SE Wisconsin. 18,113. **5.** a city in E South Dakota. 15,649.

wa′ter trap′, *Golf.* a pond, stream, or the like serving as a trap in a golf course.

wa′ter treat′ment, the act or process of making water more potable or useful, as by purifying, clarifying, softening, or deodorizing it. [1860–65]

wa′ter-tube boil′er (wô′tər to͞ob′, -tyo͞ob′, wot′ər-), a boiler for generating steam by passing water in tubes **(wa′ter tubes′)** through flames and hot gases. Cf. **fire-tube boiler.** [1870–75]

wa′ter tur′bine, a turbine driven by the momentum or reactive force of water. [1875–80]

wa′ter tur′key, anhinga. Also, **wa′ter-tur′key.** [1830–40, *Amer.*]

wa′ter va′por, a dispersion, in air, of molecules of water, esp. as produced by evaporation at ambient temperatures rather than by boiling. Cf. **steam** (def. 2). [1875–80]

wa′ter-vas′cu·lar sys′tem (wô′tər vas′kyə lər, wot′ər-), *Zool.* a system of closed, fluid-filled tubes and ducts of echinoderms used in clinging, locomotion, feeding, and respiration. [1865–70]

Wa·ter·ville (wô′tər vil′, wot′ər-), *n.* a city in SW Maine. 17,779.

Wa·ter·vliet (wô′tər vlēt′, wot′ər-), *n.* a city in E New York, on the Hudson: oldest U.S. arsenal. 11,354.

wa′ter wag′on, 1. a wagon used to transport water, as in military field operations or on a construction site. **2. on the water wagon.** See **wagon** (def. 12). [1805–15]

wa·ter·ward (wô′tər wərd, wot′ər-), *adv.* in the direction of water or a body of water. Also, **wa′ter·wards.** [1175–1225; ME; see WATER, -WARD]

wa′ter wave′, 1. a wave on the surface of a body of water. **2.** a wave combed or pressed into wet hair and then dried. [1550–60]

wa·ter-wave (wô′tər wāv′, wot′ər-), *v.t.,* **-waved, -wav·ing.** to set (hair) in a water wave. [1880–85, *Amer.*]

wa·ter·way (wô′tər wā′, wot′ər-), *n.* **1.** a river, canal, or other body of water serving as a route or way of travel or transport. **2.** *Shipbuilding.* (in a steel or iron vessel) a depressed gutter at the edge of the deck inside the bulwarks, used esp. when the decking is wooden. **3.** a channel for vessels, as a fairway in a harbor. [bef. 950; ME; OE *wæterweg.* See WATER, WAY[1]]

wa′terway plank′, *Naut.* See **margin plank.**

wa·ter·weed (wô′tər wēd′, wot′ər-), *n.* elodea. [1835–45; WATER + WEED[1]]

wa·ter·wheel (wô′tər hwēl′, -wēl′, wot′ər-), *n.* **1.** a wheel or turbine turned by the weight or momentum of water and used to operate machinery. **2.** a wheel with buckets for raising or drawing water, as a noria. **3.** the paddle wheel of a steamboat. Also, **wa′ter wheel′.** [1375–1425; late ME; see WATER, WHEEL]

wa′ter wil′low, any of several plants belonging to the genus *Justicia,* of the acanthus family, growing in water or wet places, esp. *J. americana,* of North America, having clusters of pale violet to white flowers. [1575–85]

wa′ter wings′, an inflatable contrivance shaped like a pair of wings, usually worn under the arms to keep the body afloat while one swims or learns to swim. [1900–10]

wa′ter witch′, 1. Also, **wa′ter witch′er.** a person skilled at water witching; dowser. **2.** a witch believed to haunt lakes, ponds, etc. [1810–20, *Amer.*]

wa·ter-witch (wô′tər wich′, wot′ər-), *v.i.* to practice water witching; work as a water witch.

wa′ter witch′ing, the supposed discovering of subterranean streams by means of a divining rod. [1875–80, *Amer.*]

wa·ter·works (wô′tər wûrks′, wot′ər-), *n., pl.* **-works. 1.** (*used with a singular or plural v.*) a complete system of reservoirs, pipelines, conduits, etc., by which water is collected, purified, stored, and pumped to urban users. **2.** (*used with a singular v.*) a pumping station or a purifying station of such a system. **3.** (*usually used with a plural v.*) Sometimes, **waterwork.** a spectacular display of water, mechanically produced, as for a pageant. **4.** (*used with a singular or plural v.*) *Slang.* tears, or the source of tears: *to turn on the waterworks.* **5.** *Slang.* the kidneys. [1400–50; late ME; see WATER, WORKS]

wa·ter·worn (wô′tər wôrn′, -wōrn′, wot′ər-), *adj.* worn by the action of water; smoothed by the force or movement of water. [1805–15; WATER + WORN]

wa·ter·y (wô′tə rē, wot′ə-), *adj.* **1.** pertaining to or connected with water: *watery Neptune.* **2.** full of or abounding in water, as soil or a region; soggy; boggy. **3.** containing much or too much water: *a watery paste; a watery batter.* **4.** soft, soggy, tasteless, etc., due to excessive water or overcooking: *watery vegetables; a watery stew.* **5.** tearful. **6.** of the nature of water: *watery vapor.* **7.** resembling water in appearance or color: *eyes of a watery blue.* **8.** resembling water in fluidity and absence of viscosity: *a watery fluid.* **9.** of poor or weak quality; thin, washy, or vapid: *watery prose.* **10.** consisting of water: *a watery grave.* **11.** discharging, filled with, or secreting a waterlike morbid substance. [bef. 1000; ME; OE *wæterig.* See WATER, -Y[1]] —**wa′ter·i·ly,** *adv.* —**wa′ter·i·ness,** *n.*
—**Syn. 3.** thin, weak, diluted, dilute.

CONCISE ETYMOLOGY KEY: <, descended or borrowed from; >, whence; b., blend of, blended; c., cognate with; cf., compare; deriv., derivative; equiv., equivalent; imit., imitative; obl., oblique; r., replacing; s., stem; sp., spelling, spelled; resp., respelling, respelled; trans., translation; ?, origin unknown; *, unattested; ‡, probably earlier than. See the full key inside the front cover.

Wat·kins (wot′kinz), *n.* a male given name.

Wat′kins Glen′, a village in W New York, on Seneca Lake: gorge and cascades. 2440.

Wat′ling Is′land (wot′ling). See **San Salvador** (def. 1).

WATS (wots), *n.* bulk-rate telephone service that enables a subscriber to make an unlimited number of long-distance telephone calls within a given service area for a fixed monthly charge or to receive calls from given areas with no charge to the caller. [*W*(*ide*) *A*(*rea*) *T*(*elecommunications*) *S*(*ervice*)]

Wat·son (wot′sən), *n.* **1. James Dewey,** born 1928, U.S. biologist: Nobel prize for medicine 1962. **2. John** ("*Ian Maclaren*"), 1850–1907, Scottish clergyman and novelist. **3. John Broa·dus** (brô′dəs), 1878–1958, U.S. psychologist. **4. John Christian,** 1867–1941, Australian statesman, born in Chile: prime minister 1904. **5. Thomas Augustus,** 1854–1934, U.S. electrical experimenter, associated with Alexander Graham Bell. **6. Thomas John,** 1874–1956, U.S. industrialist. **7. Thomas Stur·ges** (stûr′jis), (*Tom*), born 1949, U.S. golfer. **8. Sir William,** 1858–1935, English poet. **9.** a male given name.

Wat′son-Crick′ mod′el (wot′sən krik′), *Biochem.* a widely accepted model for the three-dimensional structure of DNA, featuring a double-helix configuration for the molecule's two hydrogen-bonded complementary polynucleotide strands. [1955–60; named after J. D. WATSON and F. H. C. CRICK]

Wat′son-Crick′ rules′. See **base-pairing rules.**

wat·so·ni·a (wot sō′nē ə), *n.* any of various iridaceous plants of the genus *Watsonia,* native to southern Africa, having sword-shaped leaves and spikes of white or reddish flowers. [< NL (1759); named after William *Watson* (1715–87), Scottish naturalist; see -IA]

Wat·son·ville (wot′sən vil′), *n.* a city in W California. 23,543.

Wat·son-Watt (wot′sən wot′), *n.* **Sir Robert Alexander,** 1892–1973, Scottish physicist: helped develop radar.

Wat·son-Went·worth (wot′sən went′wûrth′), *n.* **Charles, 2nd Marquis of Rock·ing·ham** (rok′ing əm), 1730–82, British statesman: prime minister 1765–66, 1782.

watt (wot), *n.* the SI unit of power, equivalent to one joule per second and equal to the power in a circuit in which a current of one ampere flows across a potential difference of one volt. *Abbr.:* W, w. [1882; named after J. WATT]

Watt (wot), *n.* **James,** 1736–1819, Scottish engineer and inventor.

watt·age (wot′ij), *n.* **1.** power, as measured in watts. **2.** the amount of power required to operate an electrical appliance or device. [1900–05; WATT + -AGE]

Wat·teau (wo tō′; *Fr.* VA tō′), *n.* **Jean An·toine** (zhän än twan′), 1684–1721, French painter.

Wat′teau back′, a loose, full back of a woman's gown, formed by wide box pleats hanging from a high shoulder yoke and extending to the hem in an unbroken line. [1895–1900; after a type of gown depicted in paintings by WATTEAU]

watt·er (wot′ər), *n. Informal.* a light bulb, radio station, etc., of specified wattage (usually used in combination): *This lamp takes a 60-watter.* [WATT + -ER[1]]

Wat·ter·son (wot′ər sən, wô′tər-), *n.* **Henry** ("*Marse Henry*"), 1840–1921, U.S. journalist and political leader.

watt-hour (wot′ouᵊr′, -ou′ər), *n.* a unit of energy equal to the energy of one watt operating for one hour, equivalent to 3600 joules. *Abbr.:* Wh Also, **watt′ hour′.** [1885–90]

wat·tle (wot′l), *n., v.,* **-tled, -tling,** *adj.* —*n.* **1.** Often, **wattles.** a number of rods or stakes interwoven with twigs or tree branches for making fences, walls, etc. **2. wattles,** a number of poles laid on a roof to hold thatch. **3.** (in Australia) any of various acacias whose shoots and branches were used by the early colonists for wattles, now valued esp. for their bark, which is used in tanning. **4.** a fleshy lobe or appendage hanging down from the throat or chin of certain birds, as the domestic chicken or turkey. —*v.t.* **5.** to bind, wall, fence, etc., with wattle or wattles. **6.** to roof or frame with or as if with wattles. **7.** to form into a basketwork; interweave; interlace. **8.** to make or construct by interweaving twigs or branches: *to wattle a fence.* —*adj.* **9.** built or roofed with wattle or wattles. [bef. 900; (n.) ME *wattel,* OE *watul* covering, akin to *wætla* bandage; (v.) ME *wattelen,* deriv. of the n.]

wat′tle and daub′, 1. Also, **wat′tle and dab′.** a building technique employing wattles plastered with clay and mud. **2.** a form of wall construction consisting of upright posts or stakes interwoven with twigs or tree branches and plastered with a mixture of clay and straw. [1800–10]

wat·tle·bird (wot′l bûrd′), *n.* **1.** any of several Australian honey eaters of the genus *Anthochaera,* most of which have fleshy wattles at the sides of the neck. **2.** any of three endemic New Zealand songbirds, of the family Callaeidae, all of which have brightly colored wattles at the corners of the mouth: *Callaeas cinerea* is endangered and *Heteralocha acutirostris* is believed to be extinct. [1765–75; WATTLE + BIRD]

watt′less compo′nent (wot′lis), *Elect.* See **reactive component.** [WATT + -LESS]

watt·me·ter (wot′mē′tər), *n. Elect.* a calibrated instrument for measuring electric power in watts. [1885–90; WATT + -METER]

Watts (wots), *n.* **1. An·dré** (än′drā), born 1946, U.S. concert pianist, born in Germany. **2. George Frederick,** 1817–1904, English painter and sculptor. **3. Isaac,** 1674–1748, English theologian and hymnist.

Watts-Dun·ton (wots′dun′tn), *n.* **(Walter) Theodore** (*Walter Theodore Watts*), 1832–1914, English poet, novelist, and critic.

watt-sec·ond (wot′sek′ənd), *n.* a unit of energy equal to the energy of one watt acting for one second; the equivalent of one joule. Also, **watt′ sec′ond.**

Wa·tu·si (wä to͞o′sē), *n., pl.* **-sis,** (*esp. collectively*) **-si.** Tutsi. Also, **Wa·tut·si** (wä to͞ot′sē).

Waugh (wô), *n.* **1. Alec** (*Alexander Raban*), 1898–1981, English novelist, traveler, and lecturer (son of Arthur, brother of Evelyn). **2. Arthur,** 1866–1943, English literary critic, publisher, and editor (father of Alec and Evelyn). **3. Evelyn (Arthur St. John),** 1903–66, English novelist, satirist, biographer, and author of books on travel (son of Arthur, brother of Alec). **4. Frederick Judd,** 1861–1940, U.S. painter and illustrator.

Wau·ke·gan (wô kē′gən), *n.* a city in NE Illinois, on Lake Michigan, N of Chicago. 67,653.

Wau·ke·sha (wô′ki shô′), *n.* a city in SE Wisconsin, W of Milwaukee. 50,319.

Wau·sau (wô′sô), *n.* a city in central Wisconsin. 32,426.

Wau·wa·to·sa (wô′wə tō′sə), *n.* a city in SE Wisconsin, near Milwaukee. 51,308.

wave (wāv), *n., v.,* **waved, wav·ing.** —*n.* **1.** a disturbance on the surface of a liquid body, as the sea or a lake, in the form of a moving ridge or swell. **2.** any surging or progressing movement or part resembling a wave of the sea: *a wave of the pulse.* **3.** a swell, surge, or rush, as of feeling or of a certain condition: *a wave of disgust sweeping over a person; a wave of cholera throughout the country.* **4.** a widespread feeling, opinion, tendency, etc.: *a wave of anti-intellectualism; the new wave of installment buying.* **5.** a mass movement, as of troops, settlers, or migrating birds. **6.** an outward curve, or one of a series of such curves, in a surface or line; undulation. **7.** an act or instance of waving. **8.** a fluttering sign or signal made with the hand, a flag, etc.: *a farewell wave.* **9.** natural waviness of the hair, or a special treatment to impart waviness: *to have a wave in one's hair; to get a shampoo and a wave.* **10.** a period or spell of unusually hot or cold weather. **11.** *Physics.* a progressive disturbance propagated from point to point in a medium or space without progress or advance by the points themselves, as in the transmission of sound or light. **12.** *Literary.* **a.** water. **b.** a body of water. **c.** the sea. **13.** (at sports events, esp. baseball games) a momentary standing and sitting back down by spectators in a sequential, lateral way to create, en masse, a wavelike effect visually. **14. make waves,** *Informal.* to disturb the status quo; cause trouble, as by questioning or resisting the accepted rules, procedures, etc.: *The best way to stay out of trouble at the office is not to make waves.*
—*v.i.* **15.** to move freely and gently back and forth or up and down, as by the action of air currents, sea swells, etc.: *The flags were waving in the wind.* **16.** to curve alternately in opposite directions; have an undulating form: *The road waved along the valley.* **17.** to bend or sway up and down or to and fro, as branches or plants in the wind. **18.** to be moved, esp. alternately in opposite directions: *The woman's handkerchief waved in encouragement.* **19.** to give a signal by fluttering or flapping something: *She waved to me with her hand.*
—*v.t.* **20.** to cause to flutter or have a waving motion in: *A night wind waves the tattered banners.* **21.** to cause to bend or sway up and down or to and fro: *The storm waved the heavy branches of the elm.* **22.** to give an undulating form to; cause to curve up and down or in and out. **23.** to give a wavy appearance or pattern to, as silk. **24.** to impart a wave to (the hair). **25.** to move, esp. alternately in opposite directions: *to wave the hand.* **26.** to signal to by waving a flag or the like; direct by a waving movement: *to wave a train to a halt; to wave traffic around an obstacle.* **27.** to signify or express by a waving movement: *to wave a last good-bye.* [1325–75; ME *waven* (v.), OE *wafian* to wave the hands; c. MHG *waben;* cf. WAVER[1]] —**wave′less,** *adj.* —**wave′less·ly,** *adv.* —**wav′ing·ly,** *adv.* —**wave′like′,** *adj.*
—**Syn. 1.** undulation, whitecap. WAVE, RIPPLE, BREAKER, SURF refer to a ridge or swell on the surface of water. WAVE is the general word: *waves in a high wind.* A RIPPLE is the smallest kind of wave, such as is caused by a stone thrown into a pool: *ripples in a brook.* A BREAKER is a wave breaking, or about to break, upon the shore or upon rocks: *the roar of breakers.* SURF is the collective name for breakers: *Heavy surf makes bathing dangerous.* **15.** undulate, flutter, float, sway, rock; fluctuate.

Wave (wāv), *n.* a member of the Waves. Also, **WAVE** [1942; see WAVES]

wave′ band′, *Radio and Television.* band[2] (def. 9). [1920–25]

wave′ cy′clone, *Meteorol.* a cyclone that forms on a front and, in maturing, produces an increasingly sharp, wavelike deformation of the front.

waved (wāvd), *adj.* having a form, outline, or appearance resembling waves; undulating. [1540–50; WAVE + -ED[3]]

wave′ drag′. See **aerodynamic wave drag.**

wave′ equa′tion, 1. *Math., Physics.* any differential equation that describes the propagation of waves or other disturbances in a medium. **2.** *Physics.* any of the fundamental equations of quantum mechanics whose solutions are possible wave functions of a particle. Cf. **Schrödinger equation.** [1925–30]

wave-form (wāv′fôrm′), *n. Physics.* the shape of a wave, a graph obtained by plotting the instantaneous values of a periodic quantity against the time. Also, **wave′form′.** [1840–50]

wave′ front′, *Physics.* a surface, real or imaginary, that is the locus of all adjacent points at which the phase of oscillation is the same. [1865–70]

wave′ func′tion, *Physics.* **1.** a solution of a wave equation. **2.** (in quantum mechanics) a mathematical function, found by solving a quantum-mechanical wave equation, that is used to predict the outcome of measurements on physical systems.

wave·guide (wāv′gīd′), *Electronics, Optics. n.* a conduit, as a metal tube, coaxial cable, or strand of glass fibers, used as a conductor or directional transmitter for various kinds of electromagnetic waves. Cf. **optical fiber.** [1930–35; WAVE + GUIDE]

wave·length (wāv′lengkth′, -length′, -lenth′), *n.* **1.** *Physics.* the distance, measured in the direction of propagation of a wave, between two successive points in the wave that are characterized by the same phase of oscillation. **2. on the same wavelength,** in sympathy or rapport: *We seemed to be on the same wavelength from the moment we met.* Also, **wave′ length′.** [1855–60; WAVE + LENGTH]

wave·let (wāv′lit), *n.* a small wave; ripple. [1800–10; WAVE + -LET]

Wa·vell (wā′vəl), *n.* **Archibald Percival, 1st Earl,** 1883–1950, British field marshal and author: viceroy of India 1943–47.

wa·vell·ite (wā′və līt′), *n. Mineral.* a hydrous aluminum fluorophosphate occurring as white to yellowish-green or brown aggregates of radiating fibers. [named in 1805 after W. *Wavell* (d. 1829), English physician, its discoverer; see -ITE[1]]

wave′ mechan′ics, *Physics.* a form of quantum mechanics formulated in terms of a wave equation, as the Schrödinger equation. Cf. **matrix mechanics.** [1925–30]

wave·me·ter (wāv′mē′tər), *n.* a device for measuring the wavelength or frequency of a radio wave. [1900–05; WAVE + -METER]

wave′ num′ber, the number of waves in one centimeter of light in a given wavelength; the reciprocal of the wavelength. [1900–05]

wave-off (wāv′ôf′, -of′), *n.* **1.** (on an aircraft carrier) the last-minute signaling to an aircraft making its final landing approach that it is not to land on that particular pass but is to go around and come in again. **2.** the postponement of a scheduled landing, as of a space shuttle, due to bad weather anticipated at the landing site. [n. use of v. phrase *wave off*]

wave′ of the fu′ture, a trend or development that may influence or become a significant part of the future: *Computerization is the wave of the future.* [phrase popularized as the title of an essay (1940) by Anne Morrow Lindbergh]

wa·ver[1] (wā′vər), *v.i.* **1.** to sway to and fro; flutter: *Foliage wavers in the breeze.* **2.** to flicker or quiver, as light: *A distant beam wavered and then disappeared.* **3.** become unsteady; begin to fail or give way: *When she heard the news her courage wavered.* **4.** to shake or tremble, as the hands or voice: *Her voice wavered.* **5.** to feel or show doubt, indecision, etc.; vacillate: *He wavered in his determination.* **6.** (of things) to fluctuate or vary: *Prices wavered.* **7.** to totter or reel: *The earth quaked and the tower wavered.* —*n.* **8.** an act of wavering, fluttering, or vacillating. [1275–1325; ME (see WAVE, -ER[6]); c. dial. G *wabern* to move about, ON *vafra* to toddle] —**wa′ver·er,** *n.* —**wa′ver·ing·ly,** *adv.*
—**Syn. 4.** quiver. **5.** WAVER, FLUCTUATE, VACILLATE refer to an alternation or hesitation between one direction and another. WAVER means to hesitate between choices: *to waver between two courses of action.* FLUCTUATE suggests irregular change from one side to the other or up and down: *The prices of stocks fluctuate when there is bad news followed by good.* VACILLATE is to make up one's mind and change it again suddenly; to be undecided as to what to do: *We must not vacillate but must set a day.*

wav·er[2] (wā′vər), *n.* **1.** a person who waves or causes something to wave: *Election time brings out the wavers of flags and haranguers of mobs.* **2.** a person who specializes in waving hair. **3.** something, as a curling iron, used for waving hair. [1550–60; WAVE + -ER[1]]

Waves (wāvz), *n.* (*used with a singular or plural v.*) the Women's Reserve of the U.S. Naval Reserve, the distinct force of women enlistees in the U.S. Navy, organized during World War II. Also, **WAVES** [1942; *W*(*omen*) *A*(*ccepted for*) *V*(*olunteer*) *E*(*mergency*) *S*(*ervice*)]

wave′ scroll′. See **Vitruvian scroll.**

wave′ the′ory, 1. Also called **undulatory theory.** *Physics.* the theory that light is transmitted as a wave, similar to oscillations in magnetic and electric fields. Cf. **corpuscular theory. 2.** *Historical Ling.* a theory that accounts for shared features among languages or dialects by identifying these features as innovations that spread from their points of origin to the speech of contiguous areas. Cf. **family-tree theory.** [1825–35]

wave′ train′, *Physics.* a series of successive waves spaced at regular intervals. [1895–1900]

wave′ trap′, *Radio.* a resonant-circuit filter between the antenna and the receiver for the suppression of unwanted frequencies. Cf. **resonance** (def. 5). [1920–25]

wa·vey (wā′vē), *n., pl.* **-veys.** a wild North American goose of the genus *Chen,* as the snow goose **(white wavey)** or blue goose **(blue wavey).** [1735–45; earlier *weywey* < Cree *we·hwe·w*]

wav·y[1] (wā′vē), *adj.,* **wav·i·er, wav·i·est. 1.** curving alternately in opposite directions; undulating: *a wavy course; wavy hair.* **2.** abounding in or characterized by waves: *the wavy sea.* **3.** resembling or suggesting waves: *a cotton material with a wavy pattern.* **4.** vibrating or tremulous; unsteady; wavering. [1555–65; WAVE + -Y[1]] —**wav′i·ly,** *adv.* —**wav′i·ness,** *n.*

wa·vy[2] (wā′vē), *n., pl.* **-vies.** wavey.

waw (väv, vôv), *n.* vav.

wāw (wou), *n.* the 27th letter of the Arabic alphabet. [1825–35; < Ar]

wa-wa (wä′wä′), *n.* wah-wah.

wax[1] (waks), *n.* **1.** Also called **beeswax.** a solid, yellowish, nonglycerine substance allied to fats and oils, secreted by bees, plastic when warm and melting at about 145°F, variously employed in making candles, models, casts, ointments, etc., and used by bees in constructing their honeycomb. **2.** any of various similar substances, as spermaceti or the secretions of certain insects and plants. Cf. **vegetable wax, wax insect. 3.** any of a group of substances composed of hydrocarbons, alcohols, fatty acids, and esters that are solid at ordinary temperatures. **4.** cerumen; earwax. **5.** a resinous substance used by shoemakers for rubbing thread. **6.** See **sealing wax. 7.** a person or object suggesting wax, as in manageability or malleability: *I am helpless wax in your hands.* **8. whole ball of wax,** *Slang.* **a.** the entire or overall plan, concept, action, result, or the like. **b.** everything of a similar or related nature: *They sold us skis, boots, bindings, poles—the whole ball of wax.* —*v.t.* **9.** to rub, smear, stiffen, polish, etc., with wax: *to wax the floor.* **10.** to fill the crevices of (ornamental marble) with colored material. **11.** *Informal.* to make a phonograph recording of. **12.** *Slang.* to defeat decisively; drub: *We waxed the competition.* —*adj.* **13.** pertaining to, made of, or resembling wax: *a wax candle; a wax doll.* [bef. 900; (n.) ME *wex, waxe,* OE *weax;* c. D *was,* G *Wachs,* ON *vax;* (v.) ME *wexen,* deriv. of the n.] —**wax′a·ble,** *adj.* —**wax′like′,** *adj.*

wax[2] (waks), *v.i.,* **waxed; waxed** or (*Literary*) **wax·en; wax·ing. 1.** to increase in extent, quantity, intensity, power, etc.: *Discord waxed at an alarming rate.* **2.** (of the moon) to increase in the extent of its illuminated portion before the full moon. Cf. **wane** (def. 4). **3.** to grow or become: *He waxed angry at the insinuation.* [bef. 900; ME *waxen,* OE *weaxan;* c. G *wachsen;* akin to WAIST]
—**Syn. 1.** extend, grow, lengthen, enlarge, dilate.

wax[3] (waks), *n. Chiefly Brit.* a fit of anger; rage. [1850–55; perh. special use of WAX[2]]

Wax·a·hach·ie (wôk′sə hach′ē), *n.* a city in NE central Texas. 14,624.

wax′ bean′, 1. a variety of string bean bearing yellowish, waxy pods. **2.** the pod of this plant, used for food. [1905–10, *Amer.*]

wax·ber·ry (waks′ber′ē, -bə rē), *n., pl.* **-ries. 1.** the wax myrtle or the bayberry. **2.** the snowberry. [1825–35; WAX[1] + BERRY]

wax·bill (waks′bil′), *n.* any of several small Old World finches, esp. of the genus *Estrilda,* that have white, pink, or red bills of waxy appearance and are often kept as cage birds. [1745–55; WAX[1] + BILL[2]]

waxed′ pa′per. See **wax paper.**

waxed′ tab′let. See **wax tablet.**

wax·en[1] (wak′sən), *adj.* **1.** made of or covered, polished, or treated with wax. **2.** resembling or suggesting wax: *Illness gave his face a waxen appearance.* **3.** weak, manageable, or impressionable: *The minds of young children are waxen.* [bef. 1000; ME; OE *weaxen;* see WAX[1], -EN[2]]

wax·en[2] (wak′sən), *v. Literary.* a pp. of **wax**[2].

wax·er (wak′sər), *n.* a person or appliance that polishes with or applies wax. [1870–75; WAX[1] + -ER[1]]

wax′ flow′er. See **Madagascar jasmine.** [1835–45]

wax′ gourd′, 1. a tropical Asian vine, *Benincasa hispida,* of the gourd family, having a brown, hairy stem, large, solitary, yellow flowers, and white, melonlike fruit. **2.** the fruit itself. Also called **Chinese watermelon, tunka, white gourd.**

wax·ing (wak′sing), *n.* **1.** the act or process of applying wax, as in polishing or filling. **2.** the manufacturing of a phonograph record. **3.** the act or technique of applying a depilatory wax to the body for removing hair. [1400–50; late ME; see WAX[1], -ING[1]]

wax′ing moon′, the moon at any time after new moon and before full moon, so called because its illuminated area is increasing. Cf. **waning moon.** See diag. under **moon.** [1660–70]

wax′ in′sect, any of several scale insects that secrete a commercially valuable waxy substance, esp. a Chinese scale insect, *Ericerus pe-la.* [1805–15]

wax′ jack′, a device for melting sealing wax, having a waxed wick fed through a plate from a reel. Also called **taper jack.**

wax′leaf priv′et (waks′lēf′), an evergreen shrub, *Ligustrum japonicum,* native to Japan and Korea, having leathery leaves and large clusters of small white flowers.

wax′ light′, a candle made of wax. [1690–1700]

wax′ moth′. See **bee moth.** [1760–70]

wax′ muse′um, a museum containing wax effigies of famous persons, esp. historical figures, usually in scenes associated with their lives. [1950–55]

wax′ myr′tle, an aromatic shrub, *Myrica cerifera,* of the southeastern U.S., bearing small berries coated with wax that is sometimes used in making candles. Cf. **bayberry.** [1800–10]

wax′ palm′, 1. a tall, pinnate-leaved palm, *Ceroxylon alpinum* (or *C. andicola*), of the Andes, whose stem and leaves yield a resinous wax. **2.** any of several other palms that are the source of wax, as the carnauba. [1820–30]

wax′ pa′per, a whitish, translucent wrapping paper made moistureproof by a paraffin coating. Also, **waxed paper.** [1835–45]

wax′ plant′, any climbing or trailing plant belonging to the genus *Hoya,* of the milkweed family, native to tropical Asia and Australia, having fleshy or leathery leaves and umbels of pink, white, or yellowish, waxy flowers. Also, **wax′plant′.** [1795–1805]

wax′ tab′let, a tablet made of bone, wood, etc., and covered with wax, used by the ancients for writing with a stylus. Also, **waxed tablet.** [1800–10]

wax·wing (waks′wing′), *n.* any of several songbirds of the family Bombycillidae, having a showy crest and certain feathers tipped with a red, waxy material, as *Bombycilla garrulus* **(Bohemian waxwing),** of the Northern Hemisphere. [1810–20; WAX[1] + WING]

wax·work (waks′wûrk′), *n.* **1.** a figure, ornament, or other object made of wax, or esp. the life-size effigy of a person. **2.** the bittersweet, *Celastrus scandens.* [1690–1700; WAX[1] + WORK] —**wax′work′er,** *n.*

wax·works (waks′wûrks′), *n., pl.* **-works.** (*usually used with a singular v.*) an exhibition of or a museum for displaying wax figures, ornaments, etc. [1690–1700; WAX[1] + WORKS]

wax·y[1] (wak′sē), *adj.,* **wax·i·er, wax·i·est. 1.** resembling wax in appearance or characteristics: *His face had a waxy shine.* **2.** abounding in, covered with, or made of wax: *Be careful! The floor is waxy.* **3.** pliable, yielding, or impressionable: *a waxy personality.* [1545–55; WAX[1] + -Y[1]] —**wax′i·ly,** *adv.* —**wax′i·ness,** *n.*

wax·y[2] (wak′sē), *adj.,* **wax·i·er, wax·i·est.** *Chiefly Brit.* angry. [1850–55; WAX[3] + -Y[1]]

way[1] (wā), *n.* **1.** manner, mode, or fashion: *a new way of looking at a matter; to reply in a polite way.* **2.** characteristic or habitual manner: *Her way is to work quietly and never complain.* **3.** a method, plan, or means for attaining a goal: *to find a way to reduce costs.* **4.** a respect or particular: *The plan is defective in several ways.* **5.** a direction or vicinity: *Look this way. We're having a drought out our way.* **6.** passage or progress on a course: *to make one's way on foot; to lead the way.* **7.** Often, **ways.** distance: *They've come a long way.* **8.** a path or course leading from one place to another: *What's the shortest way to town?* **9.** *Brit.* **a.** an old Roman or pre-Roman road: *Icknield Way.* **b.** a minor street in a town: *He lives in Stepney Way.* **10.** a road, route, passage, or channel (usually used in combination): *highway; waterway; doorway.* **11.** *Law.* a right of way. **12.** any line of passage or travel, used or available: *to blaze a way through dense woods.* **13.** space for passing or advancing: *to clear a way through the crowd.* **14.** Often, **ways.** a habit or custom: *The grandmother lived by the ways of the old country.* **15.** course or mode of procedure that one chooses or wills: *They had to do it my way.* **16.** condition, as to health, prosperity, or the like: *to be in a bad way.* **17.** range or extent of experience or notice: *the best device that ever came in my way.* **18.** a course of life, action, or experience: *The way of transgressors is hard.* **19.** *Informal.* business: *to be in the haberdashery way.* **20.** *Naut.* **a. ways,** two or more ground ways down which a hull slides in being launched. **b.** movement or passage through the water. **21.** *Mach.* a longitudinal strip, as in a planer, guiding a moving part along a surface. **22. by the way,** in the course of one's remarks; incidentally: *By the way, have you received that letter yet?* **23. by way of, a.** by the route of; through; via. **b.** as a method or means of: *to number articles by way of distinguishing them.* **c.** *Brit.* in the state or position of (being, doing, etc.); ostensibly: *He is by way of being an authority on the subject.* **24. come one's way,** to come to one; befall one: *A bit of good fortune came my way.* **25. give way, a.** to withdraw or retreat: *The army gave way before the advance of the enemy.* **b.** to collapse; yield; break down: *You will surely give way under the strain of overwork.* **26. give way to, a.** to yield to: *He gave way to their entreaties.* **b.** to become unrestrained or uninhibited; lose control of (one's temper, emotions, etc.): *I gave way to my rage and ordered them from the house.* **27. go all the way,** *Slang.* **a.** to do completely or wholeheartedly. **b.** to take a decisive action, esp. one from which no retreat is possible: *Neither side wants to go all the way with nuclear warfare.* **c.** to engage in sexual intercourse. **28. go out of one's way,** to do something that inconveniences one; make an unusual effort: *Please don't go out of your way on my account.* **29. have a way with,** to have a charming, persuasive, or effective manner of dealing with: *He has a way with children; to have a way with words.* **30. have one's way with,** (esp. of a man) to have sexual intercourse with, sometimes by intimidating or forcing one's partner. **31. in a family way,** pregnant. **32. in a way,** after a fashion; to some extent: *In a way, she's the nicest person I know.* **33. in someone's way,** forming a hindrance, impediment, or obstruction: *She might have succeeded in her ambition, had not circumstances been in her way.* Also, **in the way. 34. lead the way, a.** to go along a course in advance of others, as a guide. **b.** to take the initiative; be first or most prominent: *In fashion she has always led the way.* **35. make one's way, a.** to go forward; proceed: *to make one's way through the mud.* **b.** to achieve recognition or success; advance: *to make one's way in the world.* **36. make way, a.** to allow to pass; clear the way: *Make way for the king!* **b.** to relinquish to another; withdraw: *He resigned to make way for a younger man.* **c.** *Naut.* to make forward or astern progress even though engines are not running. **37. no way,** *Informal.* not under any circumstances; no: *Apologize to him? No way!* **38. out of the way, a.** in a state or condition so as not to obstruct or hinder. **b.** dealt with; disposed of: *I feel better, now that one problem is out of the way.* **c.** murdered: *to have a person put out of the way.* **d.** out of the frequented way; at a distance from the usual route. **e.** improper; amiss: *There was something decidedly out of the way about her explanation.* **f.** extraordinary; unusual: *Such behavior was out of the*

way for him. **39. pave the way to** or **for.** See **pave** (def. 2). **40. see one's way clear,** to regard as suitable or possible; consider seriously: *We couldn't see our way clear to spending so much money at once.* Also, **see one's way. 41. take one's way,** to start out; travel; go: *He took his way across the park and headed uptown.* [bef. 900; ME *wei(gh)e, wai,* OE *weg;* c. D, G *Weg,* ON *vegr,* Goth *wigs;* akin to L *vehere* to carry] **—way′less,** *adj.*
—Syn. 3. scheme, device. See **method. 4.** detail, part. **7.** space, interval. **10.** track. **14.** usage, practice, wont.

way[2] (wā), *adv.* **1.** Also, **'way.** away; from this or that place: *Go way.* **2.** to a great degree or at quite a distance; far: *way too heavy; way down the road.* [1175–1225; ME, aph. var. of AWAY]

way•bill (wā′bil′), *n.* **1.** a list of goods sent by a common carrier, as a railroad, with shipping directions. **2.** See **air waybill.** [1785–95; WAY[1] + BILL[1]]

way′ car′, *Railroads (older use).* caboose. [1875–80, *Amer.*]

Way•cross (wā′krôs′, -kros′), *n.* a city in SE Georgia. 19,371.

way•far•er (wā′fâr′ər), *n.* a traveler, esp. on foot. [1400–50; late ME *weyfarere.* See WAY[1], FARE, -ER[1]]

way•far•ing (wā′fâr′ing), *adj., n.* traveling, esp. on foot. [1530–40; WAY[1] + FARE + -ING[1]]

way′faring tree′, 1. a Eurasian shrub, *Viburnum lantana,* of the honeysuckle family, having finely toothed, ovate leaves and branching clusters of white flowers, growing along roadsides and cultivated as an ornamental in North America. **2.** the hobblebush. [1590–1600; short for *wayfaring man's tree*]

way•go•ing (wā′gō′ing), *n. Chiefly Scot. and North Eng.* the act of leaving; departure; leavetaking. [1625–35; WAY[1] + GOING]

way′going crop′, *Law.* See **away-going crop.** [1765–75]

way•laid (wā′lād′, wā lād′), *v.* pt. and pp. of **waylay.**

Way•land (wā′lənd), *n.* (in northern European folklore) the king of the elves, a smith and artificer: known in Scandinavia as Volund, in Germany as Wieland.

Way•land (wā′lənd), *n.* a city in NE Massachusetts. 12,170.

way•lay (wā′lā′, wā lā′), *v.t.,* **-laid, -lay•ing. 1.** to intercept or attack from ambush, as in order to rob, seize, or slay. **2.** to await and accost unexpectedly: *The actor was waylaid by a swarm of admirers.* [1505–15; WAY[1] + LAY[1], after MLG, MD *wegelagen* to lie in wait, deriv. of *wegelage* a lying in wait] **—way′lay′er,** *n.*

way•leave (wā′lēv′), *n. Law.* a right of way over or under another's ground or property, as for transporting minerals from a mine. [1400–50; late ME *waylefe.* See WAY[1], LEAVE[2]]

way•less (wā′lis), *adj.* lacking a way, road, or path; trackless: *wayless jungle.* [bef. 1100; ME; OE *weglēas.* See WAY[1], -LESS]

Wayne (wān), *n.* **1. Anthony** *("Mad Anthony"),* 1745–96, American Revolutionary War general. **2. John** *(Marion Michael Morrison) ("Duke"),* 1907–79, U.S. film actor. **3.** a township in N New Jersey. 46,474. **4.** a city in SE Michigan, near Detroit. 21,159. **5.** a male given name: from an Old English word meaning "wagonmaker."

Waynes•bor•o (wānz′bûr ō, -bur ō), *n.* a city in N Virginia. 15,329.

Way′ of All Flesh′, The, a novel (1903) by Samuel Butler.

way′ of the cross′. See **stations of the cross.** [1865–70]

Way′ of the World′, The, a comedy of manners (1700) by William Congreve.

way′ out′, 1. the means by which a predicament, dilemma, etc., may be solved. **2.** *Chiefly Brit.* an exit or exit door, as in a theater.

way-out (wā′out′), *adj. Informal.* **1.** advanced in style or technique: *way-out jazz.* **2.** exotic or esoteric in character: *way-out theories on nutrition.* [1950–55; adj. use of *way out* far off; see WAY[2], OUT]

way′ point′, 1. a place or point between major points on a route. **2.** See **way station.** [1875–80, *Amer.*]

ways (wāz), *n. (used with a singular v.)* way (defs. 7, 14, 20a). [ME *weyes,* OE *weges,* gen. sing. of *weg* WAY[1]]

-ways, a suffix appearing in native English adverbs: *always; sideways.* [ME; see WAY[1], -S[1]]

ways′ and means′, 1. legislation, methods, and means of raising revenue for the use of the government. **2.** methods and means of accomplishing or paying for something. [1400–50; late ME]

way•side (wā′sīd′), *n.* **1.** the side of the way; land immediately adjacent to a road, highway, path, etc.; roadside. **—adj. 2.** being, situated, or found at or along the wayside: *a wayside inn.* [1350–1400; ME; see WAY[1], SIDE[1]]

way′ sta′tion, a station intermediate between principal stations, as on a railroad. [1775–85, *Amer.*]

way•ward (wā′wərd), *adj.* **1.** turned or turning away from what is right or proper; willful; disobedient: *a wayward son; wayward behavior.* **2.** swayed or prompted by caprice; capricious: *a wayward impulse; to be wayward in one's affections.* **3.** turning or changing irregularly; irregular: *a wayward breeze.* [1350–1400; ME; aph. var. of *awayward.* See AWAY, -WARD] **—way′ward•ly,** *adv.* **—way′ward•ness,** *n.*
—Syn. 1. contrary, headstrong, stubborn, obstinate, unruly, refractory, intractable. See **willful. 3.** unsteady, inconstant, changeable.

way•worn (wā′wôrn′, -wōrn′), *adj.* worn or wearied by travel: *She was wayworn after the long trip.* [1770–80; WAY[1] + WORN]

Wa•zir•a•bad (wə zēr′ə bäd′), *n.* Balkh.

Wa•zir•i•stan (wə zēr′ə stän′, -stan′), *n.* a mountainous region in NW Pakistan.

Wb, *Elect.* weber; webers.

W/B, waybill. Also, **W.B.**

w.b., 1. warehouse book. **2.** water ballast. **3.** waybill. **4.** westbound.

wbfp, wood-burning fireplace.

WbN, west by north.

WbS, west by south.

WC, water closet.

W.C., 1. water closet. **2.** West Central (postal district in London, England).

w.c., 1. water closet. **2.** without charge.

W.C.T.U., Women's Christian Temperance Union.

wd, *Stock Exchange.* when distributed.

wd., 1. ward. **2.** word.

W/D, *Banking.* withdrawal.

W.D., War Department.

WDC, War Damage Corporation.

we (wē), *pron. pl., possessive* **our** or **ours,** *objective* **us. 1.** nominative pl. of **I. 2.** (used to denote oneself and another or others): *We have two children. In this block we all own our own houses.* **3.** (used to denote people in general): *the marvels of science that we take for granted.* **4.** (used to indicate a particular profession, nationality, political party, etc., that includes the speaker or writer): *We in the medical profession have moral responsibilities.* **5.** Also called **the royal *we.*** (used by a sovereign, or by other high officials and dignitaries, in place of *I* in formal speech): *We do not wear this crown without humility.* **6.** Also called **the editorial *we.*** (used by editors, writers, etc., to avoid the too personal or specific *I* or to represent a collective viewpoint): *As for this column, we will have nothing to do with shady politicians.* **7.** you (used familiarly, often with mild condescension or sarcasm, as in addressing a child, a patient, etc.): *We know that's naughty, don't we? It's time we took our medicine.* **8.** (used in the predicate following a copulative verb): *It is we who should thank you.* **9.** (used in apposition with a noun, esp. for emphasis): *We Americans are a sturdy lot.* [bef. 900; ME, OE *wē;* c. D *wij,* G *wir,* ON *vēr,* Goth *weis*]

weak (wēk), *adj.,* **-er, -est. 1.** not strong; liable to yield, break, or collapse under pressure or strain; fragile; frail: *a weak fortress; a weak spot in armor.* **2.** lacking in bodily strength or healthy vigor, as from age or sickness; feeble; infirm: *a weak old man; weak eyes.* **3.** not having much political strength, governing power, or authority: *a weak nation; a weak ruler.* **4.** lacking in force, potency, or efficacy; impotent, ineffectual, or inadequate: *weak sunlight; a weak wind.* **5.** lacking in rhetorical or creative force or effectiveness: *a weak reply to the charges; one of the author's weakest novels.* **6.** lacking in logical or legal force or soundness: *a weak argument.* **7.** deficient in mental power, intelligence, or judgment: *a weak mind.* **8.** not having much moral strength or firmness, resolution, or force of character: *to prove weak under temptation; weak compliance.* **9.** deficient in amount, volume, loudness, intensity, etc.; faint; slight: *a weak current of electricity; a weak pulse.* **10.** deficient, lacking, or poor in something specified: *a hand weak in trumps; I'm weak in spelling.* **11.** deficient in the essential or usual properties or ingredients: *weak tea.* **12.** unstressed, as a syllable, vowel, or word. **13.** (of Germanic verbs) inflected with suffixes, without inherited change of the root vowel, as English *work, worked,* or having a preterit ending in a dental, as English *bring, brought.* **14.** (of Germanic nouns and adjectives) inflected with endings originally appropriate to stems terminating in *-n,* as the adjective *alte* in German *der alte Mann* ("the old man"). **15.** (of wheat or flour) having a low gluten content or having a poor quality of gluten. **16.** *Photog.* thin; not dense. **17.** *Com.* characterized by a decline in prices: *The market was weak in the morning but rallied in the afternoon.* [1250–1300; ME *weik* < ON *veikr;* c. OE *wāc,* D *week,* G *weich;* akin to OE *wīcan* to yield, give way, ON *vīkja* to move, turn, draw back, G *weichen* to yield]
—Syn. 1. breakable, delicate. **2.** senile, sickly, unwell, invalid. WEAK, DECREPIT, FEEBLE, WEAKLY imply a lack of strength or of good health. WEAK means not physically strong, because of extreme youth, old age, illness, etc.: *weak after an attack of fever.* DECREPIT means old and broken in health to a marked degree: *decrepit and barely able to walk.* FEEBLE denotes much the same as WEAK, but connotes being pitiable or inferior: *feeble and almost senile.* WEAKLY suggests a long-standing sickly condition, a state of chronic bad health: *A weakly child may become a strong adult.* **4.** ineffective. **6.** unsound, ineffective, inadequate, illogical, inconclusive, unsustained, unsatisfactory, lame, vague. **7.** unintelligent, simple, foolish, stupid, senseless, silly. **8.** vacillating, wavering, unstable, irresolute, fluctuating, undecided, weak-kneed. **9.** slender, slim, inconsiderable, flimsy, poor, trifling, trivial. **11.** wanting, short, lacking. **—Ant. 1.** strong.

weak′ accumula′tion point′, *Math.* See **accumulation point.**

weak•en (wē′kən), *v.t.* **1.** to make weak or weaker. **2.** *Phonet.* to change (a speech sound) to an articulation requiring less effort, as from geminate to nongeminate or from stop to fricative. **—*v.i.*** **3.** to become weak or weaker. [1520–30; WEAK + -EN[1]] **—weak′en•er,** *n.*
—Syn. 1, 3. enfeeble, debilitate, enervate, undermine, sap, exhaust, deplete, lessen, diminish, lower, reduce, impair, minimize, invalidate. **—Ant. 1, 3.** strengthen.

weak′ end′ing, *Pros.* a verse ending in which the metrical stress falls on a word or syllable that would not be stressed in natural utterance, as a preposition, the object of which is carried over to the next line. [1855–60]

weak′er sex′, *Sometimes Offensive.* the female sex; women.

weak•fish (wēk′fish′), *n., pl. (esp. collectively)* **-fish,** *(esp. referring to two or more kinds or species)* **-fish•es.** any food fish of the genus *Cynoscion,* as *C. regalis,* inhabiting waters along the Atlantic and Gulf coasts of the U.S. [1790–1800, *Amer.;* < D *weekvis* (obs.), equiv. to *week* soft, WEAK + *vis* FISH]

weak′ force′, *Physics.* a force between elementary particles that causes certain processes that take place with low probability, as radioactive beta-decay and collisions between neutrinos and other particles. Also called **weak′ interac′tion force′.** Cf. **weak interaction.** [1965–70]

weak•hand•ed (wēk′han′did), *adj.* **1.** having weak hands. **2.** having insufficient help; shorthanded: *The flu epidemic didn't help the already weakhanded office.* [1530–40; WEAK + HANDED]

weak-head•ed (wēk′hed′id), *adj.* **1.** easily intoxicated by alcoholic beverages. **2.** prone to dizziness or giddiness. **3.** weak-minded. [1645–55] **—weak′-head′ed•ly,** *adv.* **—weak′-head′ed•ness,** *n.*

weak•heart•ed (wēk′här′tid), *adj.* without courage or fortitude; fainthearted. [1540–50; WEAK + HEARTED] **—weak′heart′ed•ly,** *adv.* **—weak′heart′ed•ness,** *n.*

weak′ interac′tion, *Physics.* the interaction between elementary particles and the intermediate vector bosons that carry the weak force from one particle to another. [1960–65]

weak•ish (wē′kish), *adj.* rather weak. [1585–95; WEAK + -ISH[1]] **—weak′ish•ly,** *adv.*

weak-kneed (wēk′nēd′), *adj.* yielding readily to opposition, pressure, intimidation, etc. [1860–65] **—weak′-kneed′ly,** *adv.* **—weak′-kneed′ness,** *n.*

weak•ling (wēk′ling), *n.* **1.** a person who is physically or morally weak. **—*adj.*** **2.** weak; not strong. [1520–30; WEAK + -LING[1]]
—Syn. 1. milksop, chicken, namby-pamby.

weak•ly (wēk′lē), *adj.,* **-li•er, -li•est,** *adv.* **—*adj.*** **1.** weak or feeble in constitution; not robust; sickly. **—*adv.*** **2.** in a weak manner. [1350–1400; ME *weekely.* See WEAK, -LY] **—weak′li•ness,** *n.*
—Syn. 1. See **weak.**

weak-mind•ed (wēk′mīn′did), *adj.* **1.** having or showing a lack of mental firmness; irresolute; vacillating. **2.** having or showing mental feebleness; foolish. [1775–85] **—weak′-mind′ed•ly,** *adv.* **—weak′-mind′ed•ness,** *n.*

weak•ness (wēk′nis), *n.* **1.** the state or quality of being weak; lack of strength, firmness, vigor, or the like; feebleness. **2.** an inadequate or defective quality, as in a person's character; slight fault or defect: *to show great sympathy for human weaknesses.* **3.** a self-indulgent liking or special fondness, as for a particular thing: *I've always had a weakness for the opera.* **4.** an object of special desire; something very difficult to resist: *Chocolates were her weakness.* [1250–1300; ME *weikenes.* See WEAK, -NESS]
—Syn. 1. fragility. **2.** flaw. See **fault. 3.** penchant, passion, hunger, appetite. **—Ant. 1.** strength.

weak′ safe′ty, *Football.* See **free safety.**

weak′ side′, *Football.* the side of the offensive line opposite the side with the tight end, thereby the side having the smaller number of players. [1925–30, *Amer.*]

weak′ sis′ter, *Informal.* **1.** a vacillating person; coward. **2.** a part or element that undermines the whole of something; a weak link. [1855–60]

weak-willed (wēk′wild′), *adj.* having or showing a want of firmness of will; easily swayed. [1880–85]

weal[1] (wēl), *n.* **1.** well-being, prosperity, or happiness: *the public weal; weal and woe.* **2.** *Obs.* wealth or riches. **3.** *Obs.* the body politic; the state. [bef. 900; ME *wele,* OE *wela;* akin to WELL[1]]

weal[2] (wēl), *n.* wheal. [var. of WALE[1], with *ea* of WHEAL]

weald (wēld), *n.* wooded or uncultivated country. [bef. 1150; ME *weeld,* OE *weald* forest; c. G *Wald;* cf. WOLD[1]]

Weald (wēld), *n.* **The,** a region in SE England, in Kent, Surrey, and Essex counties: once a forest area; now an agricultural region.

wealth (welth), *n.* **1.** a great quantity or store of money, valuable possessions, property, or other riches: *the wealth of a city.* **2.** an abundance or profusion of anything; plentiful amount: *a wealth of imagery.* **3.** *Econ.* **a.** all things that have a monetary or exchange value. **b.** anything that has utility and is capable of being appropriated or exchanged. **4.** rich or valuable contents or produce: *the wealth of the soil.* **5.** the state of being rich; prosperity; affluence: *persons of wealth and standing.* **6.** *Obs.* happiness. [1200–50; ME *welth* (see WELL[1], -TH[1]); modeled on HEALTH] **—wealth′less,** *adj.*
—Syn. 2. richness, amplitude, fullness. **3a.** possessions, assets, goods, property, money. **5.** opulence, fortune. **—Ant. 5.** poverty.

wealth•y (wel′thē), *adj.,* **wealth•i•er, wealth•i•est. 1.** having great wealth; rich; affluent: *a wealthy person; a wealthy nation.* **2.** characterized by, pertaining to, or suggestive of wealth: *a wealthy appearance.* **3.** rich in character, quality, or amount; abundant or ample: *a novel that is wealthy in its psychological insights.* [1325–75; ME; see WEALTH, -Y[1]] **—wealth′i•ly,** *adv.* **—wealth′i•ness,** *n.*
—Syn. 1. prosperous, well-to-do, moneyed. See **rich. 3.** copious. **—Ant. 1.** poor. **3.** scanty.

Weal·thy (wel′thē), *n.* a variety of red apple, grown in the U.S., ripening in early autumn. [orig. uncert.]

wean (wēn), *v.t.* **1.** to accustom (a child or young animal) to food other than its mother's milk; cause to lose the need to suckle or turn to the mother for food. **2.** to withdraw (a person, the affections, one's dependency, etc.) from some object, habit, form of enjoyment, or the like: *The need to reduce had weaned us from rich desserts.* [bef. 1000; ME *wenen,* OE *wenian;* c. D *wennen,* G *gewöhnen,* ON *venja* to accustom] **—wean·ed·ness** (wē′nid nis, wēnd′-), *n.*

wean·er (wē′nər), *n.* **1.** a recently weaned animal. **2.** *Stockbreeding.* a device placed over the mouth of an animal that is being weaned, to keep it from suckling. [1570–80; WEAN + -ER[1]]

wean·ling (wēn′ling), *n.* **1.** a child or animal newly weaned. *—adj.* **2.** newly weaned. [1525–35; WEAN + -LING[1]]

weap·on (wep′ən), *n.* **1.** any instrument or device for use in attack or defense in combat, fighting, or war, as a sword, rifle, or cannon. **2.** anything used against an opponent, adversary, or victim: *the deadly weapon of satire.* **3.** *Zool.* any part or organ serving for attack or defense, as claws, horns, teeth, or stings. *—v.t.* **4.** to supply or equip with a weapon or weapons: *to weapon aircraft with heat-seeking missiles.* [bef. 900; ME *wepen,* OE *wǣpen;* c. G *Waffe,* ON *vāpn,* Goth *wēpna* (pl.)] **—weap′oned,** *adj.* **—weap′on·less,** *adj.*

weap·on·eer (wep′ə nēr′), *n.* **1.** *Mil.* a person who prepares an atomic bomb for detonation. **2.** a person who designs nuclear weapons. [1945; WEAPON + -EER]

weap·on·ry (wep′ən rē), *n.* **1.** weapons or weaponlike instruments collectively. **2.** the invention and production of weapons. [1835–45; WEAPON + -RY]

weap′ons car′rier, *Mil.* a light truck for transporting weapons or munitions in the field. [1945–50]

wear (wâr), *v.,* **wore, worn, wear·ing,** *n.* *—v.t.* **1.** to carry or have on the body or about the person as a covering, equipment, ornament, or the like: *to wear a coat; to wear a saber; to wear a disguise.* **2.** to have or use on the person habitually: *to wear a wig.* **3.** to bear or have in one's aspect or appearance: *to wear a smile; to wear an air of triumph.* **4.** to cause (garments, linens, etc.) to deteriorate or change by wear: *Hard use has worn these gloves.* **5.** to impair, deteriorate, or consume gradually by use or any continued process: *Long illness had worn the bloom from her cheeks.* **6.** to waste or diminish gradually by rubbing, scraping, washing, etc.: *The waves have worn these rocks.* **7.** to make (a hole, channel, way, etc.) by such action. **8.** to bring about or cause a specified condition in (a person or thing) by use, deterioration, or gradual change: *to wear clothes to rags; to wear a person to a shadow.* **9.** to weary; fatigue; exhaust: *Toil and care soon wear the spirit.* **10.** to pass (time) gradually or tediously (usually fol. by *away* or *out*): *We wore the afternoon away in arguing.* **11.** *Naut.* to bring (a vessel) on another tack by turning until the wind is on the stern. **12.** *Brit. Dial.* to gather and herd (sheep or cattle) to a pen or pasture.
—v.i. **13.** to undergo gradual impairment, diminution, reduction, etc., from wear, use, attrition, or other causes (often fol. by *away, down, out,* or *off*). **14.** to retain shape, color, usefulness, value, etc., under wear, use, or any continued strain: *a strong material that will wear; colors that wear well.* **15.** (of time) to pass, esp. slowly or tediously (often fol. by *on* or *away*): *As the day wore on, we had less and less to talk about.* **16.** to have the quality of being easy or difficult to tolerate, esp. after a relatively long association: *It's hard to get to know him, but he wears well.* **17.** *Naut.* (of a vessel) to come round on another tack by turning away from the wind. **18.** *Obs.* to be commonly worn; to be in fashion. **19. wear down, a.** to reduce or impair by long wearing: *to wear down the heels of one's shoes.* **b.** to weary; tire: *His constant talking wears me down.* **c.** to prevail by persistence; overcome: *to wear down the opposition.* **20. wear off,** to diminish slowly or gradually or to diminish in effect; disappear: *The drug began to wear off.* **21. wear out, a.** to make or become unfit or useless through hard or extended use: *to wear out clothes.* **b.** to expend, consume, or remove, esp. slowly or gradually. **c.** to exhaust, as by continued strain; weary: *This endless bickering is wearing me out.* **22. wear thin, a.** to diminish; weaken: *My patience is wearing thin.* **b.** to become less appealing, interesting, tolerable, etc.: *childish antics that soon wore thin.*
—n. **23.** the act of wearing; use, as of a garment: *articles for winter wear; I've had a lot of wear out of this coat.* **24.** the state of being worn, as on the person. **25.** clothing or other articles for wearing, esp. when fashionable or appropriate for a particular function (often used in combination): *travel wear; sportswear.* **26.** gradual impairment, wasting, diminution, etc., as from use: *The carpet shows wear.* **27.** the quality of resisting deterioration with use; durability. [bef. 900; (v.) ME *weren* to have (clothes) on the body, waste, damage, suffer waste or damage, OE *werian;* c. ON *verja,* Goth *wasjan* to clothe; (n.) late ME *were* act of carrying on the body, deriv. of the v.; akin to L *vestis* clothing (see VEST)] **—wear′er,** *n.*
—Syn. 21c. tire, fatigue, drain.

wear·a·bil·i·ty (wâr′ə bil′i tē), *n.* the durability of clothing under normal wear. [1925–30; WEAR(ABLE) + -ABILITY]

wear·a·ble (wâr′ə bəl), *adj.* **1.** capable of being worn; appropriate, suitable, or ready for wearing. *—n.* **2.** Usually, **wearables.** that which may be worn; clothing. [1580–90; WEAR + -ABLE]

wear′ and tear′ (târ), damage or deterioration resulting from ordinary use; normal depreciation. Also, **wear′-and-tear′.** [1660–70]

wea·ri·ful (wēr′ē fəl), *adj.* **1.** full of weariness; fatigued; exhausted. **2.** causing weariness or fatigue; tedious; tiresome; annoying. [1425–75; late ME; see WEARY, -FUL] **—wea′ri·ful·ly,** *adv.* **—wea′ri·ful·ness,** *n.*

wea·ri·less (wēr′ē lis), *adj.* unwearying; tireless: *a weariless vigil.* [1400–50; late ME; see WEARY, -LESS] **—wea′ri·less·ly,** *adv.*

wear·ing (wâr′ing), *adj.* **1.** gradually impairing or wasting: *Reading small print can be wearing on the eyes.* **2.** wearying or exhausting: *a wearing task.* **3.** relating to or made for wear. [1805–15; WEAR + -ING[2]] **—wear′ing·ly,** *adv.*

wear′ing appar′el, clothing; garments. [1610–20]

wea·ri·some (wēr′ē səm), *adj.* **1.** causing weariness; fatiguing: *a difficult and wearisome march.* **2.** tiresome or tedious: *a wearisome person; a wearisome book.* [1400–50; late ME *werysom.* See WEARY, -SOME[1]] **—wea′ri·some·ly,** *adv.* **—wea′ri·some·ness,** *n.*
—Syn. 1. tiring. **2.** boring, monotonous, humdrum, dull, prosy, prosaic. **—Ant. 2.** interesting.

wear-out (wâr′out′), *n.* the act or fact of wearing out; a worn-out condition: *wear-out at the knees of pants.* Also, **wear′out′.** [1895–1900; n. use of v. phrase *wear out*]

wear·proof (wâr′pro͞of′), *adj.* resistant to damage or deterioration by normal use or wear. [WEAR + -PROOF]

wea·ry (wēr′ē), *adj.,* **-ri·er, -ri·est,** *v.,* **-ried, -ry·ing.** *—adj.* **1.** physically or mentally exhausted by hard work, exertion, strain, etc.; fatigued; tired: *weary eyes; a weary brain.* **2.** characterized by or causing fatigue: *a weary journey.* **3.** impatient or dissatisfied with something (often fol. by *of*): *weary of excuses.* **4.** characterized by or causing impatience or dissatisfaction; tedious; irksome: *a weary wait.* *—v.t., v.i.* **5.** to make or become weary; fatigue or tire: *The long hours of work have wearied me.* **6.** to make or grow impatient or dissatisfied with something or at having too much of something (often fol. by *of*): *The long drive had wearied us of desert scenery. We had quickly wearied at such witless entertainment.* [bef. 900; (adj.) ME *wery,* OE *wērig;* c. OS *-wōrig;* akin to OE *wōrian* to crumble, break down, totter; (v.) ME *werien,* OE *wēr(i)gian,* deriv. of the adj.] **—wea′ri·ly,** *adv.* **—wea′ri·ness,** *n.* **—wea′ry·ing·ly,** *adv.*
—Syn. 1. spent. See **tired**[1]. **4.** tiresome, wearisome. **5.** exhaust. **6.** irk; jade. **—Ant. 1.** energetic. **4.** interesting. **6.** interest.

wea·sand (wē′zənd), *n. Archaic.* **1.** throat. **2.** esophagus; gullet. **3.** trachea; windpipe. [bef. 1000; ME *wesand,* OE *wǣsend,* var. of *wāsend* gullet; c. OFris *wāsande* windpipe]

wea·sel (wē′zəl), *n., pl.* **-sels,** (*esp. collectively*) **-sel,** *v.* *—n.* **1.** any small carnivore of the genus *Mustela,* of the family Mustelidae, having a long, slender body and feeding chiefly on small rodents. **2.** any of various similar animals of the family Mustelidae. **3.** a cunning, sneaky person. **4.** a tracked vehicle resembling a tractor, used in snow. **5.** *Slang.* an informer; stool pigeon. *—v.i.* **6.** to evade an obligation, duty, or the like; renege (often fol. by *out*): *That's one invitation I'd like to weasel out of.* **7.** to use weasel words; be ambiguous; mislead: *Upon cross-examination the witness began to weasel.* **8.** *Slang.* to inform. [bef. 900; 1920–25 for def. 6; ME *wesele,* OE *wesle, weosule;* c. OHG *wisula,* G *Wiesel*]

weasel, *Mustela frenata,* head and body 10 in. (25 cm); tail 5 in. (13 cm)

wea·sel·ly (wē′zə lē), *adj.* resembling a weasel, esp. in features or manner: *a weaselly little clerk with furtive eyes.* [1830–40; WEASEL + -Y[1]]

wea′sel word′, a word used to temper the forthrightness of a statement; a word that makes one's views equivocal, misleading, or confusing. [1895–1900, *Amer.*] **—wea′sel-word′ed,** *adj.*

weath·er (weth′ər), *n.* **1.** the state of the atmosphere with respect to wind, temperature, cloudiness, moisture, pressure, etc. **2.** a strong wind or storm or strong winds and storms collectively: *We've had some real weather this spring.* **3.** a weathercast: *The radio announcer will read the weather right after the commercial.* **4.** Usually, **weathers.** changes or vicissitudes in one's lot or fortunes: *She remained a good friend in all weathers.* **5. under the weather,** *Informal.* **a.** somewhat indisposed; ailing; ill. **b.** suffering from a hangover. **c.** more or less drunk: *Many fatal accidents are caused by drivers who are under the weather.* *—v.t.* **6.** to expose to the weather; dry, season, or otherwise affect by exposure to the air or atmosphere: *to weather lumber before marketing it.* **7.** to discolor, disintegrate, or affect injuriously, as by the effects of weather: *These crumbling stones have been weathered by the centuries.* **8.** to bear up against and come safely through (a storm, danger, trouble, etc.): *to weather a severe illness.* **9.** *Naut.* (of a ship, mariner, etc.) to pass or sail to the windward of: *to weather a cape.* **10.** *Archit.* to cause to slope, so as to shed water. *—v.i.* **11.** to undergo change, esp. discoloration or disintegration, as the result of exposure to atmospheric conditions. **12.** to endure or resist exposure to the weather: *a coat that weathers well.* **13.** to go or come safely through a storm, danger, trouble, etc. (usually fol. by *through*): *It was a difficult time for her, but she weathered through beautifully.* [bef. 900; ME (n.), OE *weder;* c. D *weder,* G *Wetter,* ON *vethr*] **—weath′er·er,** *n.*

weath·er·a·bil·i·ty (weth′ər ə bil′i tē), *n.* the property of a material that permits it to endure or resist exposure to the weather. [1945–50; WEATHER + -ABILITY]

weath′er advi′sory, advisory (def. 5).

weath′er balloon′, *Meteorol.* See **sounding balloon.** [1935–40]

weath·er-beat·en (weth′ər bēt′n), *adj.* **1.** bearing evidences of wear or damage as a result of exposure to the weather. **2.** tanned, hardened, or otherwise affected by exposure to weather: *a weather-beaten face.* [1520–30]

weath·er·board (weth′ər bôrd′, -bōrd′), *n.* **1.** an early type of board used as a siding for a building. **2.** *Chiefly Brit.* any of various forms of board used as a siding for a building. **3.** *Naut.* the side of a vessel toward the wind. *—v.t.* **4.** to cover or furnish with weatherboards. [1530–40; WEATHER + BOARD]

weath·er·board·ing (weth′ər bôr′ding, -bōr′-), *n.* **1.** a covering or facing of weatherboards. **2.** weatherboards collectively. [1625–35; WEATHERBOARD + -ING[1]]

weath·er·bound (weth′ər bound′), *adj.* delayed or shut in by bad weather. [1580–90]

Weath′er Bu′reau, the former name of the U.S. National Weather Service.

weath·er·cast (weth′ər kast′, -käst′), *n.* a forecast of weather conditions, esp. on radio or television. [1865–70; WEATHER + (FORE)CAST]

weath·er·cast·er (weth′ər kas′tər, -kä′stər), *n.* an announcer on a radio or television station who delivers the weathercast. [WEATHERCAST + -ER[1]] **—weath′er·cast′ing,** *n.*

weath·er·coat (weth′ər kōt′), *n.* **1.** Also, **weath′er·coat′ing.** a weatherproof coating, applied esp. to the exterior of a building. **2.** *Chiefly Brit.* a waterproof coat for wear in bad weather. [1895–1900; WEATHER + COAT]

weath·er·cock (weth′ər kok′), *n.* **1.** a weather vane with the figure of a rooster on it. **2.** (loosely) any weather vane. **3.** a person who readily adopts the latest fads, opinions, etc.: *The count is the weathercock of the jet set.* [1250–1300; ME *wedercoc.* See WEATHER, COCK[1]]

weath′er deck′, (on a ship) the uppermost continuous deck exposed to the weather. [1840–50]

weath·ered (weth′ərd), *adj.* **1.** seasoned or otherwise affected by exposure to the weather. **2.** (of wood) artificially treated to seem discolored or stained by the action of air, rain, etc. **3.** (of rocks) worn, disintegrated, or changed in color or composition by weathering. **4.** *Archit.* made sloping or inclined, as a window sill, to prevent the lodgment of water. [1780–90; WEATHER + -ED[2]]

weath′er eye′, **1.** sensitivity and alertness to signs of change in the weather. **2.** a steady and astute watchfulness, esp. alertness to change. **3. keep one's** or **a weather eye open,** to be on one's guard; be watchful: *He kept a weather eye open for new political developments.* [1830–40]

weatherfish, *Misgurnus fossilis,* length 10 in. (25 cm)

weath·er·fish (weth′ər fish′), *n., pl.* (*esp. collectively*) **-fish,** (*esp. referring to two or more kinds or species*) **-fish·es.** any of several loaches of the genus *Misgurnus,* esp. the European *M. fossilis,* which shows increased activity in response to changes in barometric pressure. [1885–90; WEATHER + FISH]

Weath·er·ford (weth′ər fərd), *n.* a town in N Texas. 12,049.

weath′er gauge′, **1.** *Naut.* See under **gauge** (def. 17). **2.** the position of advantage; upper hand: *Having bought out her competitors, she now has the weather gauge in the industry.* [1890–95]

weath·er·glass (weth′ər glas′, -gläs′), *n.* any of various instruments, as a barometer or a hygroscope, designed to indicate the state of the atmosphere. [1620–30; WEATHER + GLASS]

weath·er·ing (weth′ər ing), *n.* **1.** *Archit.* wash (def. 48). **2.** material used as a weather strip. **3.** *Geol.* the various mechanical and chemical processes that cause exposed rock to decompose. [1655–65; WEATHER + -ING[1]]

weath·er·ize (weth′ə rīz′), *v.t.,* **-ized, -iz·ing.** to make (a house or other building) secure against cold or stormy weather, as by adding insulation, siding, and storm windows. Also, *esp. Brit.,* **weath′er·ise′.** [1940–45; WEATHER + -IZE] **—weath′er·i·za′tion,** *n.*

weath′er joint′, a mortar joint having a downward and outward slope. Also called **weath′ered joint′.**

weath·er·ly (weth′ər lē), *adj. Naut.* (of a ship or boat) making very little leeway when close-hauled. [1645–55; WEATHER + -LY] **—weath′er·li·ness,** *n.*

weath·er·man (weth′ər man′), *n., pl.* **-men.** **1.** a person who forecasts and reports the weather; meteorologist. **2.** a weathercaster. [1535–45; WEATHER + MAN[1]] **—Usage.** See **-man.**

weath′er map′, a map or chart showing weather conditions over a wide area at a particular time, compiled from simultaneous observations at different places. [1870–75, *Amer.*]

weath·er·per·son (weth′ər pûr′sən), *n.* a meteorologist or weathercaster. [WEATHER(MAN) + -PERSON] **—Usage.** See **-person.**

weath·er·proof (weth′ər pro͞of′), *adj.* **1.** able to withstand exposure to all kinds of weather. *—v.t.* **2.** to

CONCISE PRONUNCIATION KEY: act, cāpe, dâre, pärt; set, ēqual; *if,* ice; ox, ōver, ôrder, oil, bo͝ok, bo͞ot, out; up, ûrge; child; sing; shoe; thin, *th*at; zh as in *treasure.* ə = *a* as in *alone,* e as in *system,* i as in *easily,* o as in *gallop,* u as in *circus;* ᵊ as in *fire* (fīᵊr), *hour* (ouᵊr). l and n can serve as syllabic consonants, as in *cradle* (krād′l), and *button* (but′n). See the full key inside the front cover.

make (something) weatherproof. [1610–20; WEATHER + -PROOF] —**weath′er·proof′ness,** *n.*

weath·er·proof·er (weth′ər pro͞o′fər), *n.* **1.** a worker who weatherproofs houses and other buildings. **2.** a weatherproof material, as a sealant. [WEATHERPROOF + -ER[1]]

weath′er ra′dar, radar designed or suitable for use in detecting clouds and precipitation.

weath′er report′, a summary of weather conditions, often including predicted conditions, for an area. [1860–65]

weath·er-re·sist·ant (weth′ər ri zis′tənt), *adj.* resisting the effects of severe weather, as rain or cold: *weather-resistant cloth for topcoats.* [1930–35]

weath′er sat′ellite. See **meteorological satellite.** [1955–60]

weath′er ship′, a ship equipped for meteorological observation. [1945–50]

weath′er sig′nal, a visual signal, as a light or flag, indicating a weather forecast.

weath′er sta′tion, an installation equipped and used for meteorological observation. [1905–10]

weath′er strip′, a narrow strip of metal, wood, rubber, or the like placed between a door or window sash and its frame to exclude rain, wind, etc. [1840–50, *Amer.*]

weath·er-strip (weth′ər strip′), *v.t.*, **-stripped, -strip·ping.** to apply weather stripping to (something). [1890–95, *Amer.*]

weath′er strip′ping, 1. See **weather strip. 2.** a number of weather strips, taken collectively. [1940–45, *Amer.*]

weath′er tide′, *Naut.* a tide moving against the direction of the wind. [1805–15]

weath·er·tight (weth′ər tīt′), *adj.* secure against wind, rain, etc. [1895–1900; WEATHER + TIGHT] —**weath′er·tight′ness,** *n.*

weath′er vane′, a device, as a rod to which a freely rotating pointer is attached, for indicating the direction of the wind. Also, **weath′er·vane′.** Also called **vane, wind vane.** [1715–25]

weath·er-wise (weth′ər wīz′), *adj.* **1.** skillful in predicting weather. **2.** skillful in predicting reactions, opinions, etc.: *weather-wise political experts.* [1350–1400; late ME *wederwise.* See WEATHER, WISE[1]]

weath·er·wom·an (weth′ər wo͝om′ən), *n., pl.* **-wom·en.** a woman who works as a weathercaster. [1970–75; WEATHER(MAN) + -WOMAN]
—**Usage.** See **-woman.**

weath·er·worn (weth′ər wôrn′, -wōrn′), *adj.* weather-beaten. [1600–10; WEATHER + WORN]

weave (wēv), *v.,* **wove** or (*esp. for 5, 9*) **weaved; wo·ven** or **wove; weav·ing;** *n.* —*v.t.* **1.** to interlace (threads, yarns, strips, fibrous material, etc.) so as to form a fabric or material. **2.** to form by interlacing threads, yarns, strands, or strips of some material: *to weave a basket; to weave cloth.* **3.** to form by combining various elements or details into a connected whole: *to weave a tale; to weave a plan.* **4.** to introduce as an element or detail into a connected whole (usually fol. by *in* or *into*): *She wove an old folk melody into her latest musical composition.* **5.** to direct or move along in a winding or zigzag course; move from side to side, esp. to avoid obstructions: *to weave one's way through traffic.* —*v.i.* **6.** to form or construct something, as fabric, by interlacing threads, yarns, strips, etc. **7.** to compose a connected whole by combining various elements or details. **8.** to be or become formed or composed from the interlacing of materials or the combining of various elements: *The yarn wove into a beautiful fabric.* **9.** to move or proceed in a winding course or from side to side: *dancers weaving in time to the music.* —*n.* **10.** a pattern of or method for interlacing yarns. [bef. 900; ME *weven,* OE *wefan;* c. G *weben,* ON *vefa;* see WEB]
—**Syn. 3.** contrive, fabricate, construct, compose. **4.** insert, intermix, intermingle.

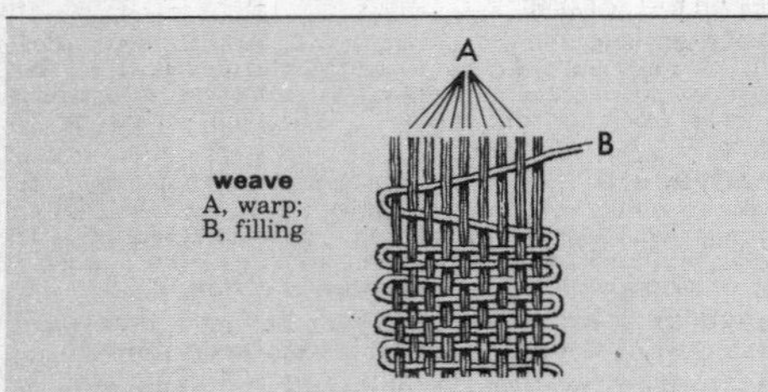

weave
A, warp;
B, filling

weave′ bead′, *Welding.* See under **bead** (def. 13).

weav·er (wē′vər), *n.* **1.** a person who weaves. **2.** a person whose occupation is weaving. **3.** a weaverbird. [1325–75; ME *wevere.* See WEAVE, -ER[1]]

Wea·ver (wē′vər), *n.* **1. James Baird,** 1833–1912, U.S. politician: congressman 1879–81, 1885–89. **2. Robert Clifton,** born 1907, U.S. economist and government official: first Secretary of Housing and Urban Development, 1966–68.

weav·er·bird (wē′vər bûrd′), *n.* any of numerous African and Asian finchlike birds of the family Ploceidae, noted for their elaborately woven nests and colonial habits. Also called **weav′er finch′.** [1820–30; WEAVER + BIRD]

CONCISE ETYMOLOGY KEY: <, descended or borrowed from; >, whence; b., blend of, blended; c., cognate with; cf., compare; deriv., derivative; equiv., equivalent; imit., imitative; obl., oblique; r., replacing; s., stem; sp., spelling, spelled; resp., respelling, respelled; trans., translation; ?, origin unknown; *, unattested; ‡, probably earlier than. See the full key inside the front cover.

weaverbird,
Ploceus cucullatus,
length 7 in. (18 cm)

weav′er's hitch′. See **sheet bend.** Also called **weav′er's knot′.** [1525–35]

web (web), *n., v.,* **webbed, web·bing.** —*n.* **1.** something formed by or as if by weaving or interweaving. **2.** a thin, silken material spun by spiders and the larvae of some insects, as the webworms and tent caterpillars; cobweb. **3.** *Textiles.* **a.** a woven fabric, esp. a whole piece of cloth in the course of being woven or after it comes from the loom. **b.** the flat woven strip, without pile, often found at one or both ends of an Oriental rug. **4.** something resembling woven material, esp. something having an interlaced or latticelike appearance: *He looked up at the web of branches of the old tree.* **5.** an intricate set or pattern of circumstances, facts, etc.: *The thief was convicted by a web of evidence. Who can understand the web of life?* **6.** something that snares or entangles; a trap: *innocent travelers caught in the web of international terrorism.* **7.** webbing. **8.** *Zool.* a membrane that connects the digits of an animal, as the toes of aquatic birds. **9.** *Ornith.* **a.** the series of barbs on each side of the shaft of a feather. See illus. under **feather. b.** the series on both sides, collectively. **10.** an integral or separate part of a beam, rail, truss, or the like, that forms a continuous, flat, narrow, rigid connection between two stronger, broader parallel parts, as the flanges of a structural shape, the head and foot of a rail, or the upper and lower chords of a truss. **11.** *Mach.* an arm of a crank, usually one of a pair, holding one end of a crankpin at its outer end. See illus. under **crankshaft. 12.** *Archit.* (in a vault) any surface framed by ribbing. **13.** a large roll of paper, as for continuous feeding of a web press. **14.** a network of interlinked stations, services, communications, etc., covering a region or country. **15.** *Informal.* a network of radio or television broadcasting stations. —*v.t.* **16.** to cover with or as if with a web; envelop. **17.** to ensnare or entrap. —*v.i.* **18.** to make or form a web. [bef. 900; ME (n.), OE; c. D, LG *webbe,* ON *vefr;* akin to WEAVE] —**web′less,** *adj.* —**web′like′,** *adj.*
—**Syn. 5.** network, tissue, tangle, maze.

web
of spider

Webb (web), *n.* **(Martha) Beatrice (Potter),** 1858–1943, and her husband, **Sidney (James), 1st Baron Pass·field** (pas′fēld′), 1859–1947, English economists, social reformers, authors, and socialists.

webbed (webd), *adj.* **1.** having the fingers or toes connected by a web or membrane: *the webbed foot of a duck or beaver.* **2.** connected or joined by a web, as the fingers or toes. **3.** formed like or with a web: *a webbed roof.* [1655–65; WEB + -ED[3]]

Web·be She·be·li (web′ā shi bā′lē). See **Webi Shebeli.** Also, **Web′be Shi·be′li.**

web·bing (web′ing), *n.* **1.** a strong, woven material of hemp, cotton, or jute, in bands of various widths, used for belts, carrying straps, harness, etc. **2.** such woven bands nailed on furniture under springs or upholstery, for support. **3.** *Zool.* the membrane forming a web or webs. **4.** something resembling this, as the leather thongs or piece connecting the sections for the thumb and forefinger in a baseball glove or mitt. **5.** any material or part formed from interlaced threads, thongs, branches, etc., or having a latticelike appearance, as the face of a tennis racket. **6. webbings,** *Chiefly Eastern New Eng. Older Use.* the reins or lines for controlling a horse or team of horses. [1400–50; late ME; see WEB, -ING[1]]

web′bing clothes′ moth′, a small brown moth, *Tineola bisselliella,* the larva of which feeds on woolens and spins a web when feeding.

web·by (web′ē), *adj.,* **-bi·er, -bi·est. 1.** pertaining to, of the nature of, or resembling a web. **2.** webbed. [1655–65; WEB + -Y[1]]

web·er (web′ər, vā′bər), *n. Elect.* the SI unit of magnetic flux and magnetic pole strength, equal to a flux that produces an electromotive force of one volt in a single turn of wire when the flux is uniformly reduced to zero in a period of one second; 10^8 maxwells. *Abbr.:* Wb [1875–80; named after W. E. WEBER]

We·ber (vā′bər *or, Ger.,* vā′bəʀ *for 1–3, 5;* web′ər *for 4*), *n.* **1. Ernst Hein·rich** (ernst hīn′ʀiKH), 1795–1878, German physiologist. **2. Baron Karl Ma·ri·a Frie·drich Ernst von** (kärl mä rē′ä fʀē′dʀiKH ernst fən), 1786–1826, German pianist, conductor, and composer. **3. Max** (maks; *Ger.* mäks), 1864–1920, German sociologist and political economist. **4. Max** (maks), 1881–1961, U.S. painter, born in Russia. **5. Wil·helm E·du·ard** (vil′helm ā′do͞o ärt′), 1804–91, German physicist (brother of Ernst Heinrich).

We·be′ri·an apparat′us (vā bēr′ē ən), *n.* (in certain fishes) a chain of small bones and ligaments connecting the inner ear with the air bladder. [1885–90; named after E. H. WEBER; see -IAN]

We·bern (vā′bərn; *Ger.* vā′bəʀn), *n.* **An·ton von** (än′tōn fən), 1883–1945, Austrian composer.

web-fed (web′fed′), *adj.* (of a printing press) fed by and designed to print a continuous roll of paper. Cf. **sheet-fed.** [1945–50]

web′ foot′, *Furniture.* a pad foot having the appearance of toes joined by a web. Also called **duck foot.**

web·foot (web′fo͝ot′), *n., pl.* **-feet. 1.** a foot with the toes joined by a web. **2.** (*cap.*) a native or inhabitant of Oregon (used as a nickname). **3.** an animal with webfeet. [1755–65; WEB + FOOT] —**web′-foot′ed,** *adj.*

Web′foot State′, Oregon (used as a nickname).

web′ frame′, *Naut.* a deep transverse frame reinforcing the hull of a ship. Also called **transverse.** [1895–1900]

We·bi She·be·li (wä′bē shi bā′lē), a river in E Africa, flowing SE from central Ethiopia to the Juba River, in the Somali Republic. ab. 700 mi. (1125 km) long. Also, **Webbe Shebeli, Webbe Shibeli, We′bi Shibe′li.**

web′ mem′ber, *Civ. Engin.* any of the structural members of a truss between the chords. [1885–90]

web′ press′, *Print.* a press into which paper is fed automatically from a large roll. Cf. **web** (def. 13). [1870–75, *Amer.*]

web′ spin′ner, any of several slender insects, of the order Embioptera, that nest in colonies in silken webs spun with secretions from the enlarged front legs. Also called **embiid.** [1905–10]

web·ster (web′stər), *n. Archaic.* a weaver. [bef. 1100; ME; OE *webbestre.* See WEB, -STER]

Web·ster (web′stər), *n.* **1. Daniel,** 1782–1852, U.S. statesman and orator. **2. John,** c1580–1625?, English dramatist. **3. Margaret,** 1905–72, British stage director, producer, and actress, born in the U.S. **4. Noah,** 1758–1843, U.S. lexicographer and essayist. **5. William H(edg·cock)** (hej′kok′), born 1924, U.S. judge and government official: director of the FBI since 1978. **6.** a city in central Massachusetts. 14,480.

Web′ster-Ash′bur·ton Trea′ty (web′stər ash′bûr tn), *U.S. Hist.* an agreement between the U.S. and England (1842) defining the boundary between British and American territory from Maine to present-day Minnesota. [named after D. WEBSTER and A. Baring, 1st Baron *Ashburton,* who negotiated it]

Web′ster Groves′, a city in E Missouri, near St. Louis. 23,097.

Web·ste·ri·an (web stēr′ē ən), *adj.* **1.** pertaining to or characteristic of Daniel Webster, his political theories, or his oratory. **2.** pertaining to or characteristic of Noah Webster or his dictionary. [1855–60, *Amer.;* WEBSTER + -IAN]

web·ster·ite (web′stə rīt′), *n. Mineral.* aluminite. [named after T. *Webster,* 19th-century Englishman; see -ITE[1]]

web-toed (web′tōd′), *adj.* web-footed.

web·worm (web′wûrm′), *n.* the larva of any of several moths, as *Hyphantria cunea* **(fall webworm)** or *Loxostege similalis* **(garden webworm),** which spins a web over the foliage on which it feeds. [1790–1800, *Amer;* WEB + WORM]

Wechs′ler Scales′ (weks′lər), *Psychol.* a group of intelligence tests, including the Wechsler Adult Intelligence Scale **(WAIS),** later revised **(WAIS-R);** the Wechsler Intelligence Scale for Children **(WISC),** later revised **(WISC-R);** the Wechsler Preschool and Primary Scale of Intelligence **(WPPSI);** and the Wechsler-Bellevue Scale, no longer used, all of which emphasize performance and verbal skills and give separate scores for subtests in vocabulary, arithmetic, memory span, assembly of objects, and other abilities. [named after David *Wechsler* (1896–1981), Rumanian-born U.S. psychologist, who developed them]

wed (wed), *v.,* **wed·ded** or **wed, wed·ding.** —*v.t.* **1.** to marry (another person) in a formal ceremony; take as one's husband or wife. **2.** to unite (a couple) in marriage or wedlock; marry. **3.** to bind by close or lasting ties; attach firmly: *She wedded herself to the cause of the poor.* **4.** to blend together or unite inseparably: *a novel that weds style and content perfectly.* —*v.i.* **5.** to contract marriage; marry. **6.** to become united or to blend: *a building that will wed with the landscape.* [bef. 900; ME *wedde,* OE *weddian* to pledge; c. G *wetten* to bet, ON *vethja* to pledge]
—**Syn. 4.** combine, fuse, merge.

we'd (wēd), contraction of *we had, we should,* or *we would.*
—**Usage.** See **contraction.**

Wed., Wednesday.

wed·ded (wed′id), *adj.* **1.** united in matrimony; married: *the wedded couple; a wedded woman.* **2.** of or pertaining to marriage or to those married: *the wedded state; wedded happiness.* **3.** attached or dedicated, esp. obstinately or unshakably: *a fearless person wedded to a just cause.* **4.** associated or bound together inseparably: *form and substance wedded in harmony.* [bef. 900; ME; OE *geweddode.* See WED, -ED[2]]

Wed′dell Sea′ (wed′l, wə del′), an arm of the Atlantic, E of Antarctic Peninsula.

wed·ding (wed′ing), *n.* **1.** the act or ceremony of marrying; marriage; nuptials. **2.** the anniversary of a marriage, or its celebration: *They invited guests to their silver wedding.* **3.** the act or an instance of blending or joining, esp. opposite or contrasting elements: *a perfect wedding of conservatism and liberalism.* **4.** *Business Slang.* a merger. —*adj.* **5.** of or pertaining to a wedding: *the wedding ceremony; a wedding dress.* [bef. 900; ME; OE *weddung.* See WED, -ING[1]] **—Syn. 1.** See **marriage.**

wed′ding anniver′sary, the annual commemoration of a couple's marriage: *a tenth wedding anniversary.* [1690–1700]

WEDDING ANNIVERSARIES AND GIFTS

Anniversary	Traditional Gift	Modern Gift
First	Paper	Clocks, plastics
Second	Cotton	China
Third	Leather	Crystal, glass
Fourth	Fruit, flowers*	Linen, appliances
Fifth	Wood	Silverware
Sixth	Candy**	Wood
Seventh	Wool	Copper, brass
Eighth	Bronze	Linen, lace
Ninth	Pottery	China, leather
Tenth	Tin, aluminum	Diamond jewelry
Eleventh	Steel	Fashion jewelry
Twelfth	Silk, linen	Pearls, colored gems
Thirteenth	Lace	Textiles
Fourteenth	Ivory	Gold jewelry
Fifteenth	Crystal	Glass, watches
Twentieth	China	Platinum
Twenty-fifth	Silver	Silver
Thirtieth	Pearl	Diamond
Thirty-fifth	Coral	Jade, coral
Fortieth	Ruby	Ruby
Forty-fifth	Sapphire	Sapphire
Fiftieth	Gold	Gold
Fifty-fifth	Emerald	Emerald
Sixtieth	Diamond	Diamond
Seventy-fifth	Diamond	Diamond

*Some references give this as Linen
**Some references give this as Iron

wed′ding cake′, **1.** a white cake, usually in tiered layers, covered with white icing and decorated. **2.** (in England) a fruit cake, similar in appearance. [1640–50]

wed·ding-cake (wed′ing kāk′), *adj.* highly ornate or overly elaborate: *wedding-cake architecture.* [1875–80]

wed′ding chest′, an ornamented chest for a trousseau. [1870–75]

wed′ding day′, **1.** the day of a wedding. **2.** the anniversary of a wedding. [1545–55]

wed′ding march′, a musical composition played during a wedding procession. [1840–50]

wed′ding ring′, **1.** a ring, usually of gold, platinum, or silver, given to the bride by the groom during a marriage ceremony. **2.** a ring similarly given to the groom by the bride. Also called **wed′ding band′.** [1350–1400; ME]

We·de·kind (vā′də kint′), *n.* **Frank** (fräŋk), 1864–1918, German poet and dramatist.

we·del (vād′l), *v.i.,* **-deled, -del·ing.** to engage in wedeln. [1960–65; back formation from WEDELN]

we·deln (vād′ln), *n.* a skiing technique first developed in Austria in the 1950's that consists of high-speed turns made in succession with both skis parallel while not noticeably setting the ski edges on a slope. [1955–60; < G: lit., wagging (the tail)]

wedge (wej), *n., v.,* **wedged, wedg·ing.** **—n. 1.** a piece of hard material with two principal faces meeting in a sharply acute angle, for raising, holding, or splitting objects by applying a pounding or driving force, as from a hammer. Cf. **machine** (def. 3b). **2.** a piece of anything of like shape: *a wedge of pie.* **3.** a cuneiform character or stroke of this shape. **4.** *Meteorol.* (formerly) an elongated area of relatively high pressure. **5.** something that serves to part, split, divide, etc.: *The quarrel drove a wedge into the party organization.* **6.** *Mil.* (formerly) a tactical formation generally in the form of a V with the point toward the enemy. **7.** *Golf.* a club with an iron head the face of which is nearly horizontal, for lofting the ball, esp. out of sand traps and high grass. **8.** *Optics.* See **optical wedge.** **9.** haček. **10.** *Chiefly Coastal Connecticut and Rhode Island.* a hero sandwich. **11.** a wedge heel or shoe with such a heel. **—v.t. 12.** to separate or split with or as if with a wedge (often fol. by *open, apart,* etc.): *to wedge open a log.* **13.** to insert or fix with a wedge. **14.** to pack or fix tightly: *to wedge clothes into a suitcase.* **15.** to thrust, drive, fix, etc., like a wedge: *He wedged himself through the narrow opening.* **16.** *Ceram.* to pound (clay) in order to remove air bubbles. **17.** to fell or direct the fall of (a tree) by driving wedges into the cut made by the saw. **—v.i. 18.** to force a way like a wedge (usually fol. by *in, into, through,* etc.). [bef. 900; ME *wegge* (n.), OE *wecg;* c. dial. G *Weck* (OHG *wecki*), ON *veggr*] **—wedge′like′,** *adj.* **—Syn. 14.** cram, jam, stuff, crowd, squeeze. **—Regional Variation. 10.** See **hero sandwich.**

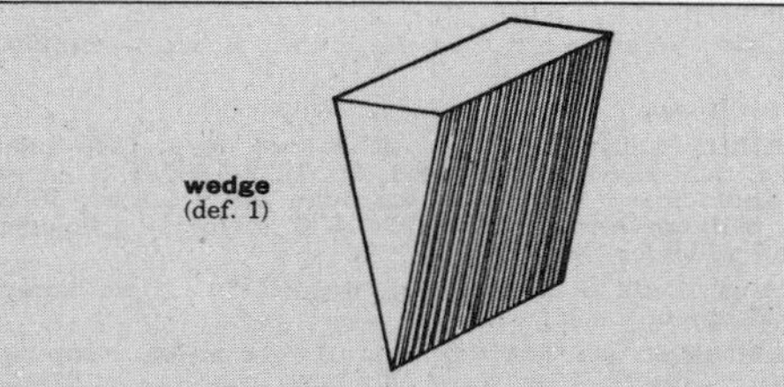
wedge (def. 1)

wedged (wejd), *adj.* having the shape of a wedge. [1545–55; WEDGE + -ED[3]]

wedge′ heel′, a heel formed by a roughly triangular or wedgelike piece that extends from the front or middle to the back of the sole, used on women's shoes.

wedg·ie (wej′ē), *n.* Often, **wedgies.** a shoe with a wedge heel. [WEDGE + -IE]

Wedg·wood (wej′wo͝od′), *n.* **1. Josiah,** 1730–95, English potter. **2.** *Trademark.* a brand of ceramic ware made by Josiah Wedgwood and his successors.

Wedg′wood blue′, a blue-gray color, esp. one characteristic of Wedgwood ceramic ware. [1895–1900] **—Wedg′wood-blue′,** *adj.*

wedg·y (wej′ē), *adj.,* **wedg·i·er, wedg·i·est.** resembling a wedge; wedgelike. [1790–1800; WEDGE + -Y[1]]

wed·lock (wed′lok′), *n.* the state of marriage; matrimony. [bef. 1100; ME *wedlok,* OE *wedlāc* lit., a pledging, equiv. to *wed* pledge (see WED) + *-lāc* verbal n. suffix]

Wednes·day (wenz′dā, -dē), *n.* the fourth day of the week, following Tuesday. [bef. 950; ME *Wednesdai,* OE **Wōdnesdæg,* mutated var. of *Wōdnesdæg* Woden's day; c. D *Woensdag,* Dan *onsdag;* trans. of L *Mercuriī diēs* day of Mercury]

Wednes·days (wenz′dāz, -dēz), *adv.* on or during Wednesdays; every Wednesday. [see WEDNESDAY, -S[1]]

wee (wē), *adj.,* **we·er, we·est. 1.** little; very small. **2.** very early: *in the wee hours of the morning.* [bef. 1150 for an earlier sense; ME *we,* var. of *wei* (small) quantity, OE *wēg,* Anglian form of *wǣge* weight, akin to *wegan* to WEIGH[1]] **—Syn. 1.** tiny, diminutive; minuscule.

weed[1] (wēd), *n.* **1.** a valueless plant growing wild, esp. one that grows on cultivated ground to the exclusion or injury of the desired crop. **2.** any undesirable or troublesome plant, esp. one that grows profusely where it is not wanted: *The vacant lot was covered with weeds.* **3.** *Informal.* a cigarette or cigar. **4.** *Slang.* a marijuana cigarette. **5.** a thin, ungainly person or animal. **6.** a wretched or useless animal, esp. a horse unfit for racing or breeding purposes. **7. the weed, a.** *Informal.* tobacco. **b.** *Slang.* marijuana. **—v.t. 8.** to free from weeds or troublesome plants; root out weeds from: *to weed a garden.* **9.** to root out or remove (a weed or weeds), as from a garden (often fol. by *out*): *to weed out crab grass from a lawn.* **10.** to remove as being undesirable, inefficient, or superfluous (often fol. by *out*): *to weed out inexperienced players.* **11.** to rid (something) of undesirable or superfluous elements. **—v.i. 12.** to remove weeds or the like. [bef. 900; ME *wede,* OE *wēod;* c. OS *wiod* weed, MD *wiet* fern] **—weed′less,** *adj.* **—weed′like′,** *adj.*

weed[2] (wēd), *n.* **1. weeds,** mourning garments: *widow's weeds.* **2.** a mourning band of black crepe or cloth, as worn on a man's hat or coat sleeve. **3.** Often, **weeds.** *Archaic.* **a.** a garment: *clad in rustic weeds.* **b.** clothing. [bef. 900; ME *wede,* OE *wǣd,* (ge)*wǣde* garment, clothing; c. OS *wād, gewādi,* OHG *wāt, gewāti* clothing; cf. WADMAL]

Weed (wēd), *n.* **Thur·low** (thûr′lō), 1797–1882, U.S. journalist and politician.

weed′ burn′er. See **flame cultivator.**

weed′ cut′ter, a hand implement, often powered by electricity or a gasoline motor, for cutting weeds or trimming grass and often utilizing a rotating nylon cord as the cutting blade. [1900–05]

weed·er (wē′dər), *n.* **1.** a person who removes weeds, as from a garden or lawn. **2.** a device, as a tool or machine, for removing weeds. [1400–50; late ME; see WEED[1], -ER[1]]

weed-kill·er (wēd′kil′ər), *n.* a herbicide. [1885–90]

weed·y (wē′dē), *adj.,* **weed·i·er, weed·i·est. 1.** full of or abounding in weeds. **2.** consisting of or pertaining to weeds. **3.** (of a plant, flower, etc.) growing poorly or in a straggling manner. **4.** (of a person or animal) scrawny or ungainly. [1375–1425; late ME; see WEED[1], -Y[1]] **—weed′i·ly,** *adv.* **—weed′i·ness,** *n.*

week (wēk), *n.* **1.** a period of seven successive days, usually understood as beginning with Sunday and ending with Saturday. **2.** a period of seven successive days that begins with or includes an indicated day: *the week of June 3; Christmas week.* **3.** (*often cap.*) a period of seven successive days devoted to a particular celebration, honor, cause, etc.: *National Book Week.* **4.** the working days or working portion of the seven-day period; workweek: *A 35-hour week is now commonplace.* **—adv. 5.** *Brit.* seven days before or after a specified day: *I shall come Tuesday week. He left yesterday week.* [bef. 900; ME *weke,* OE *wice;* c. D *week,* ON *vika* week, Goth *wikō* turn; akin to L *vicis* (gen.) turn (see VICE[3])]

week·day (wēk′dā′), *n.* **1.** any day of the week except Sunday or, often, Saturday and Sunday. **—adj. 2.** of or on a weekday: *weekday occupations.* [bef. 900; ME; OE *wicdæg.* See WEEK, DAY]

week·days (wēk′dāz′), *adv.* every day, esp. Monday through Friday, during the workweek: *Weekdays we're open from nine till five.* [see WEEK, DAY, -S[1]]

week·end (wēk′end′, -end′), *n.* **1.** the end of a week, esp. the period of time between Friday evening and Monday morning: *We spent the weekend at Virginia Beach.* **2.** this period as extended by one or more holidays, days off, or the like, that immediately precede or follow: *We're getting a three-day weekend at Christmas.* **3.** any two-day period taken or given regularly as a weekly rest period from one's work: *I have to work at the hospital on Saturdays and Sundays, so I take my weekends on Tuesdays and Wednesdays.* **—adj. 4.** of, for, or on a weekend: *a weekend pass; a weekend excursion.* **—v.i. 5.** to pass the weekend, as at a place: *They weekended at their country place.* [1875–80; WEEK + END[1]]

week′end bag′, weekender (def. 3). [1920–25]

week·end·er (wēk′en′dər), *n.* **1.** a person who goes on a weekend vacation. **2.** a weekend guest. **3.** a traveling bag large enough to carry the clothing and personal articles needed for a weekend trip. **4.** a small pleasure boat, esp. a sailboat, equipped to accommodate usually not more than four persons for a weekend cruise. **5.** a person who engages in a sport, hobby, or other activity occasionally, esp. on weekends. **6.** *Slang.* a minor offender sentenced to serve a weekend or series of weekends in jail. [1875–80; WEEKEND + -ER[1]]

week·ends (wēk′endz′), *adv.* every weekend; on or during weekends: *We go fishing weekends.* [1875–80; WEEKEND + -S[1]]

week′end war′rior, *Slang.* a reservist who attends weekend meetings of his or her unit in order to fulfill military obligations.

Week·ley (wēk′lē), *n.* **Ernest,** 1865–1954, English etymologist and lexicographer.

week·ly (wēk′lē), *adj., adv., n., pl.* **-lies. —adj. 1.** done, happening, appearing, etc., once a week, or every week: *a weekly appointment with an analyst.* **2.** computed or determined by the week: *a special weekly rate.* **3.** of or pertaining to a week or the working days in a week: *a day of respite from our weekly labors.* **—adv. 4.** once a week; by the week: *to visit someone weekly; to pay rent weekly.* **—n. 5.** a publication appearing once a week. [1425–75; late ME; see WEEK, -LY]

week·night (wēk′nīt′), *n.* **1.** any night of the week, usually except Saturday and Sunday. **—adj. 2.** Also, **week·night·ly** (wēk′nīt′lē). of, on, or for a weeknight: *the weeknight lineup of TV programs.* [1855–60; WEEK + NIGHT]

Weems (wēmz), *n.* **Mason Locke** ("*Parson Weems*"), 1759–1825, U.S. clergyman and biographer.

ween (wēn), *v.t., v.i. Archaic.* **1.** to think; suppose. **2.** to expect, hope, or intend. [bef. 900; ME *wenen,* OE *wēnan* to expect; c. G *wähnen* to imagine, ON *væna,* Goth *wēnjan* to hope, expect]

wee·nie (wē′nē), *n.* **1.** *Informal.* a wiener. **2.** *Slang.* penis. **3.** *Slang.* an insignificant, disliked person. Also, **weeny, wienie.** [WIEN(ER) + -IE; (def. 3) prob. influenced by or continuous with *weeny* small child, n. use of *weeny* tiny (see WEE, TEENY-WEENY)]

wee·ny (wē′nē), *n., pl.* **-nies.** *Informal.* weenie.

weep[1] (wēp), *v.,* **wept, weep·ing,** *n.* **—v.i. 1.** to express grief, sorrow, or any overpowering emotion by shedding tears; shed tears; cry: *to weep for joy; to weep with rage.* **2.** to let fall drops of water or other liquid; drip; leak: *The old water tank was weeping at the seams.* **3.** to exude water or liquid, as soil, a rock, a plant stem, or a sore. **—v.t. 4.** to weep for (someone or something); mourn with tears or other expression of sorrow: *He wept his dead brother.* **5.** to shed (tears); pour forth in weeping: *to weep tears of gratitude.* **6.** to let fall or give forth in drops: *trees weeping an odorous gum.* **7.** to pass, bring, put, etc., to or into a specified condition with the shedding of tears (usually fol. by *away, out,* etc.): *to weep one's eyes out; to weep oneself to sleep.* **—n. 8.** weeping, or a fit of weeping. **9.** the exudation of water or liquid. [bef. 900; ME *wepen,* OE *wēpan* to wail; c. Goth *wōpjan* to call, ON *æpa* to cry out] **—Syn. 1.** sob; wail, lament. **4.** bewail, bemoan, lament. **—Ant. 1.** laugh, rejoice.

weep[2] (wēp), *n. Brit. Dial.* the lapwing, *Vanellus vanellus,* of Europe. [imit.]

weep·er (wē′pər), *n.* **1.** a person who weeps. **2.** (formerly) a hired mourner at a funeral. **3.** something worn as a badge of mourning, as a widow's black veil. **4.** a wine bottle that has lost some of its contents through the cork. **5.** any of various loose-hanging, streamerlike objects, as a long, hanging hatband or a strand of moss hanging from a tree. **6.** *Informal.* a sad story, motion picture, song, or the like, that is apt to make one cry. [1350–1400; ME; see WEEP[1], -ER[1]]

weep′ hole′, *Building Trades.* a hole in a sill, retaining wall, or the like for draining off accumulated moisture, as from condensation or seepage. [1850–55; alter. of *weeping-hole*]

weep·ie (wē′pē), *n. Brit. Informal.* a tearjerker; weeper. [1925–30; WEEP[1] + -IE]

weep·ing (wē′ping), *adj.* **1.** expressing grief, sorrow, or any overwhelming emotion by shedding tears: *weeping multitudes.* **2.** tearful; weepy: *a weeping fit.* **3.** tending or liable to cry; given to crying. **4.** dripping or oozing liquid. **5.** (of trees, shrubs, etc.) having slender, drooping branches. [bef. 900; ME; OE *wepende.* See WEEP[1], -ING[2]] **—weep′ing·ly,** *adv.*

weep′ing fig′, a small tree, *Ficus benjamina,* of the mulberry family, native to southeastern Asia and Australia, having drooping branches and glossy leaves: widely cultivated as a houseplant. Also called **Java fig.**

weep′ing gold′en bell′, a Chinese shrub, *Forsythia suspensa,* of the olive family, having long, arching, pendulous, hollow branches that root at the tip in age, and golden-yellow flowers. Also called **weep′ing forsyth′ia.**

weep′ing love′grass. See under **lovegrass.**

weep′ing my′all. See under **myall.** [1895–1900]

weep′ing wil′low, an Asian willow, *Salix babylonica,* characterized by the drooping habit of its branches. [1725–35]

weep·y (wē′pē), *adj.,* **weep·i·er, weep·i·est. 1.** weeping or tending to weep; tearful; lachrymose. **2.** *Informal.* sad or sentimental, esp. to the point of causing one to weep: *a movie with a weepy ending.* **3.** exuding water or other moisture; leaky; seepy. [1595–1605; WEEP[1] + -Y[1]] **—weep′i·ness,** *n.*

wee·ver (wē′vər), *n.* **1.** either of two small, European, marine fishes of the genus *Trachinus, T. draco* **(greater**

CONCISE PRONUNCIATION KEY: act, cāpe, dâre, pärt; set, ēqual; if, ice; ox, ōver, ôrder, oil, bo͝ok, bo͞ot, out; up, ûrge; child; sing; shoe; thin, *th*at; zh as in *treasure.* ə = *a* as in *alone, e* as in *system, i* as in *easily, o* as in *gallop, u* as in *circus;* ə as in *fire* (fīər), *hour* (ouər). l and n can serve as syllabic consonants, as in *cradle* (krād′l), and *button* (but′n). See the full key inside the front cover.

weever) or *T. vipera* **(lesser weever),** having highly poisonous dorsal spines. **2.** any fish of the same family, Trachinidae. [1615–25; perh. continuing ME **wever,* OE *wifer* arrow (c. ON *vifr* sword); modern meaning by assoc. with obs. *wiver* viper; see WYVERN]

wee·vil (wē′vəl), *n.* **1.** Also called **snout beetle.** any of numerous beetles of the family Curculionidae, which have the head prolonged into a snout and which are destructive to nuts, grain, fruit, etc. **2.** any of numerous related beetles. [bef. 900; ME *wevel,* OE *wifel;* c. OHG *wibil* beetle; akin to WAVE]

wee·vil·y (wē′və lē), *adj.* infested with weevils. Also, **wee′vil·ly, wee·viled, wee·villed** (wē′vəld). [1750–60; WEEVIL + -Y¹]

wee·wee (wē′wē′), *n., v.,* **-weed, -wee·ing.** *Baby Talk.* —*n.* **1.** urine. —*v.i.* **2.** to urinate. Also, **wee′-wee′.** [1925–30]

weft (weft), *n.* **1.** *Textiles.* filling (def. 5). **2.** a woven fabric or garment. [bef. 900; ME, OE; akin to WEAVE]

weft′ i′kat. See under **ikat.**

weft-knit·ted (weft′nit′id), *adj.* noting or pertaining to a fabric made by weft knitting. Also, **weft′-knit′.** [1940–45]

weft′ knit′ting, a knitting process in which the yarn is knitted horizontally and in a circular form. Also called **filling knitting.** Cf. **warp knitting.**

weft·wise (weft′wīz′), *adv. Textiles.* in a horizontal direction; from selvage to selvage; crosswise. [WEFT + -WISE]

We·ge·ner (vā′gə nər), *n.* **Al·fred Lo·thar** (äl′frät lō′tär, lō tär′), 1880–1930, German meteorologist and geophysicist: originated theory of continental drift.

Wehr·macht (vâr′mäkht′; *Ger.* vār′mäkht′), *n.* the German armed forces of the years prior to and during World War II. [< G *Wehr* defense + *Macht* force]

Wei (wā), *n.* any of several dynasties that ruled in North China, esp. one ruling A.D. 220–265 and one ruling A.D. 386–534.

Weich·sel (vīk′səl), *n.* Vistula.

Weid·man (wīd′mən), *n.* **1. Charles Edward, Jr.,** 1901–75, U.S. dancer, choreographer, and teacher. **2. Jerome,** born 1913, U.S. author.

Wei·er·strass (vī′ər sträs′, -shträs′; *Ger.* vī′ər-shträs′), *n.* **Karl The·o·dor** (kärl tā′ō dôr′), 1815–97, German mathematician.

Wei′erstrass approxima′tion the′orem, *Math.* the theorem that for any continuous function on a closed interval, there is a polynomial such that the difference in values of the function and the polynomial at each point in the interval is less in absolute value than some positive number. [named after K. T. WEIERSTRASS]

Wei·fang (wā′fäng′), *n. Wade-Giles, Pinyin.* a city in N Shandong province, in NE China. 260,000.

wei·ge·la (wī gē′lə, -jē′-, wī′gə lə), *n.* any of various shrubby, eastern Asian plants belonging to the genus *Weigela,* of the honeysuckle family, having funnel-shaped white, pink, or crimson flowers. Also, **wei·ge·li·a** (wī gē′lē ə, -jē′-). [1840–50; < NL, named after C. E. *Weigel* (1748–1831), German physician; see -A²]

weigh¹ (wā), *v.t.* **1.** to determine or ascertain the force that gravitation exerts upon (a person or thing) by use of a balance, scale, or other mechanical device: *to weigh oneself; to weigh potatoes; to weigh gases.* **2.** to hold up or balance, as in the hand, in order to estimate the weight. **3.** to measure, separate, or apportion (a certain quantity of something) according to weight (usually fol. by *out*): *to weigh out five pounds of sugar.* **4.** to make heavy; increase the weight or bulk of; weight: *We weighed the drapes to make them hang properly.* **5.** to evaluate in the mind; consider carefully in order to reach an opinion, decision, or choice: *to weigh the facts; to weigh a proposal.* **6.** *Archaic.* to raise, lift, or hoist (something). **7.** *Obs.* to think important; esteem. —*v.i.* **8.** to have weight or a specified amount of weight: *to weigh less; to weigh a ton.* **9.** to have importance, moment, or consequence: *Your recommendation weighs heavily in his favor.* **10.** to bear down as a weight or burden (usually fol. by *on* or *upon*): *Responsibility weighed upon her.* **11.** to consider carefully or judicially: *to weigh well before deciding.* **12.** (of a ship) to raise the anchor and get under way: *The ship weighed early and escaped in the fog.* **13. weigh anchor,** *Naut.* to heave up a ship's anchor in preparation for getting under way. **14. weigh down, a.** to cause to become bowed under a weight: *snow and ice weighing down the trees.* **b.** to lower the spirits of; burden; depress: *This predicament weighs me down.* **15. weigh in,** *Sports.* **a.** (of a boxer or wrestler) to be weighed by a medical examiner on the day of a bout. **b.** to be of the weight determined by such a weighing: *He weighed in at 170 pounds.* **c.** (of a jockey) to be weighed with the saddle and weights after a race. **16. weigh one's words.** See **word** (def. 26). **17. weigh out,** *Horse Racing.* (of a jockey) **a.** to be weighed with the saddle and weights before a race. **b.** to be of the weight determined by such a weighing. [bef. 900; ME *weghen,* OE *wegan* to carry, weigh; c. D *wegen,* G *wägen,* ON *vega;* akin to L *vehere*] —**weigh′a·ble,** *adj.* —**weigh′er,** *n.*

—**Syn. 5.** ponder, contemplate. See **study¹.**

weigh² (wā), *n.* **under weigh,** *Naut.* in motion; under way. [1775–85; sp. var. of WAY¹ by assoc. with *weigh anchor*]

weigh·bridge (wā′brij′), *n.* a platform scale that stands flush with a road and is used for weighing trucks, livestock, etc. [1790–1800; WEIGH + BRIDGE¹]

CONCISE ETYMOLOGY KEY: <, descended or borrowed from; >, whence; b., blend of, blended; c., cognate with; cf., compare; deriv., derivative; equiv., equivalent; imit., imitative; obl., oblique; r., replacing; s., stem; sp., spelling, spelled; resp., respelling, respelled; trans., translation; ?, origin unknown; *, unattested; ‡, probably earlier than. See the full key inside the front cover.

weigh-in (wā′in′), *n. Sports.* the act or an instance of weighing in. [1865–70; n. use of v. phrase *weigh in*]

weigh·man (wā′mən), *n., pl.* **-men. 1.** a person whose occupation is weighing goods, produce, etc. **2.** *Mining.* a person who weighs coal extracted from a mine, esp. in mines where miners are paid according to the weight of the coal they dig. Cf. **checkweighman.** [1880–85; WEIGH + -MAN]

weight (wāt), *n.* **1.** the amount or quantity of heaviness or mass; amount a thing weighs. **2.** *Physics.* the force that gravitation exerts upon a body, equal to the mass of the body times the local acceleration of gravity: commonly taken, in a region of constant gravitational acceleration, as a measure of mass. **3.** a system of units for expressing heaviness or mass: *avoirdupois weight.* **4.** a unit of heaviness or mass: *The pound is a common weight in English-speaking countries.* **5.** a body of determinate mass, as of metal, for using on a balance or scale in weighing objects, substances, etc. **6.** a specific quantity of a substance that is determined by weighing or that weighs a fixed amount: *a half-ounce weight of gold dust.* **7.** any heavy load, mass, or object: *Put down that weight and rest your arms.* **8.** an object used or useful solely because of its heaviness: *the weights of a clock.* **9.** a mental or moral burden, as of care, sorrow, or responsibility: *Knowing you are safe takes a weight off my mind.* **10.** importance, moment, consequence, or effective influence: *an opinion of great weight.* **11.** *Statistics.* a measure of the relative importance of an item in a statistical population. **12.** (of clothing, textiles, etc.) **a.** relative heaviness or thickness as related to warmth or to seasonal use (often used in combination): *a winter-weight jacket.* **b.** relative heaviness or thickness as related to use: *a bolt of coat-weight woolen cloth.* **13.** *Print.* (of type) the degree of blackness or boldness. **14.** (esp. in boxing) a division or class to which a contestant belongs according to how much he weighs: *two brothers who fight professionally in the same weight.* **15.** the total amount the jockey, saddle, and leads must weigh on a racehorse during a race, according to the conditions of the race: *Jacinto has a weight of 122 pounds in the seventh race.* **16.** the stress or accent value given a sound, syllable, or word. **17. by weight,** according to measurement of heaviness or mass: *Rates are determined by weight.* **18. carry weight,** to have importance or significance; influence: *Her opinion is certain to carry weight.* **19. pull one's weight,** to contribute one's rightful share of work to a project or job: *We will finish in time if we each pull our weight.* Also, **pull one's own weight. 20. throw one's weight around** or **about,** to use one's power and influence, esp. beyond the bounds of propriety, to secure some personal gain. —*v.t.* **21.** to add weight to; load with additional weight: *to weight sacks before dumping them overboard.* **22.** to load (fabrics, threads, etc.) with mineral or other matter to increase the weight or bulk. **23.** to burden with or as if with weight (often fol. by *down*): *Financial worries have weighted that family down for years.* **24.** *Statistics.* to give a statistical weight to. **25.** to bias or slant toward a particular goal or direction; manipulate: *The teacher weighted the test so students who had read both books would make the highest marks.* **26.** to assign (a racehorse) a specific weight to carry in a race: *The handicapper weighted Dapper Dan with 128 pounds.* [bef. 1000; ME (n.); OE *wiht* (c. D *wicht,* G *Gewicht*); see WEIGH, -TH¹] —**weight′er,** *n.*

—**Syn. 10.** effect, power, efficacy, import, significance. **23.** oppress, encumber, saddle, load.

weight′ belt′, *Scuba Diving.* a belt worn to control a diver's buoyancy under water, on which slotted lead weights can be slipped according to the diver's body size and weight and having a quick-release buckle for emergency discarding. [1950–55]

weight′ den′sity, the weight per unit volume of a substance or object.

weight·ed (wā′tid), *adj.* **1.** having additional weight. **2.** burdened: *weighted with sorrow.* **3.** adjusted or adapted to a representative value, esp. in determining the value of a legislator's vote as proportionate to the population of that legislator's constituency. [1650–60; WEIGHT + -ED²] —**weight′ed·ly,** *adv.* —**weight′ed·ness,** *n.*

weight′ed mean′, *Statistics.* a mean that is computed with extra weight given to one or more elements of the sample. Also called **weight′ed av′erage.** [1835–45]

weight′ for age′, *Horse Racing.* the poundage assigned to be borne by a horse in a race, based on the age of the horse.

weight·ism (wā′tiz əm), *n.* bias or discrimination against people who are overweight. [1985–90] —**weight′ist,** *n., adj.*

weight·less (wāt′lis), *adj.* being without apparent weight, as a freely falling body. [1540–50; WEIGHT + -LESS] —**weight′less·ly,** *adv.* —**weight′less·ness,** *n.*

weight·lift·ing (wāt′lif′ting), *n.* the act, art, or sport of lifting barbells of given weights in a prescribed manner, as a competitive event or conditioning exercise. [1895–1900; WEIGHT + LIFTING] —**weight′lift′er,** *n.*

weight·man (wāt′man′), *n., pl.* **-men. 1.** a person whose work is to weigh goods or merchandise. **2.** Also, **weight′ man′.** *Track and Field.* a competitor in a field event who throws a weight, as a discus, shotput, or hammer. [1945–50; WEIGHT + MAN¹]

weight·room (wāt′ro͞om′, -ro͝om′), *n.* an exercise room with weightlifting equipment. Also, **weight′ room′.** [WEIGHT + ROOM]

weight·y (wā′tē), *adj.,* **weight·i·er, weight·i·est. 1.** having considerable weight; heavy; ponderous: *a weighty bundle.* **2.** burdensome or troublesome: *the weightier cares of sovereignty.* **3.** important or momentous: *weighty negotiations.* **4.** having or exerting influence, power, etc.; influential: *a weighty merchant of Boston.* [1480–90; see WEIGHT, -Y¹] —**weight′i·ly,** *adv.* —**weight′i·ness,** *n.*

—**Syn. 3.** significant, serious, grave, consequential. See **heavy.** —**Ant. 1, 3.** light. **3.** unimportant.

Wei·hai (wā′hī′), *n. Wade-Giles, Pinyin.* a seaport in NE Shandong province, in E China: district leased to Great Britain 1898–1930. 50,000; 285 sq. mi. (738 sq. km). Formerly, **Wei·hai·wei** (wā′hī′wā′).

Weill (wīl; *Ger.* vīl), *n.* **Kurt** (kûrt; *Ger.* ko͝ort), 1900–50, German composer, in the U.S. after 1935.

Weil's′ disease′ (vīlz, wīlz), *Med.* a type of leptospirosis in humans, characterized by fever and jaundice, caused by the spirochete *Leptospira icterohaemorrhagiae.* [named after Adolf *Weil* (1848–1916), German physician]

Wei·mar (vī′mär, wī′-), *n.* a city in Thuringia, in central Germany. 64,000. —**Wei·mar′i·an,** *adj., n.*

Wei·mar·an·er (vī′mə rä′nər, wī′-, wī′mə rā′-), *n.* one of a German breed of hunting dogs having a smooth silver-gray to dark-gray coat, a cropped tail, and blue-gray or amber eyes. [1940–45; < G, after WEIMAR; see -AN, -ER¹]

Wei′mar Repub′lic, the German republic (1919–33), founded at Weimar.

Wein·ber·ger (wīn′bûr gər), *n.* **1. Caspar W(illard)** ("Cap"), born 1917, U.S. government official: Secretary of Defense 1981–87. **2. Ja·ro·mir** (yär′ə mēr′), 1896–1967, Czech composer, in the U.S.

Wein′berg-Sa·lam′ the′ory (wīn′bərg sä läm′), *Physics.* See **electroweak theory.**

Wein·gart·ner (vīn′gärt′nər), *n.* **(Paul) Fe·lix (Ed·ler von Münz·berg)** (poul fā′liks äd′lər fən mynts′berk′), 1863–1942, Austrian composer, conductor, and writer.

weir (wēr), *n.* **1.** a small dam in a river or stream. **2.** a fence, as of brush or narrow boards, or a net set in a stream, channel, etc., for catching fish. [bef. 900; ME *were,* OE *wer,* deriv. of root of *werian* to defend, dam up]

weird (wērd), *adj.,* **-er, -est,** *n.* —*adj.* **1.** involving or suggesting the supernatural; unearthly or uncanny: *a weird sound; weird lights.* **2.** fantastic; bizarre: *a weird getup.* **3.** *Archaic.* concerned with or controlling fate or destiny. —*n. Chiefly Scot.* **4.** fate; destiny. **5.** fate (def. 6). [bef. 900; (n.) ME (northern form of *wird*), OE *wyrd;* akin to WORTH²; (adj.) ME, orig. attributive n. in phrase *werde sisters* the Fates (popularized as appellation of the witches in *Macbeth*)] —**weird′ly,** *adv.* —**weird′ness,** *n.*

—**Syn. 1.** unnatural, preternatural. WEIRD, EERIE, UNEARTHLY, UNCANNY refer to that which is mysterious and apparently outside natural law. WEIRD refers to that which is suggestive of the fateful intervention of supernatural influences in human affairs: *the weird adventures of a group lost in the jungle.* EERIE refers to that which, by suggesting the ghostly, makes one's flesh creep: *an eerie moaning from a deserted house.* UNEARTHLY refers to that which seems by its nature to belong to another world: *an unearthly light that preceded the storm.* UNCANNY refers to that which is mysterious because of its apparent defiance of the laws established by experience: *an uncanny ability to recall numbers.* —**Ant. 1.** natural.

weird·o (wēr′dō), *n., pl.* **weird·os.** *Informal.* **1.** an odd, eccentric, or unconventional person. **2.** a psychopath, esp. a dangerous or vicious one; psycho: *They caught the weirdo who attacked the children.* [1950–55; WEIRD + -O]

weird′ sis′ters, the Fates. [1350–1400; ME]

weird·y (wēr′dē), *n., pl.* **weird·ies.** *Informal.* weirdo. Also, **weird′ie.** [1795–1805; WEIRD + -Y²]

Weir·ton (wēr′tn), *n.* a city in N West Virginia, on the Ohio River. 24,736.

weis·en·heim·er (wī′zən hī′mər), *n.* wisenheimer.

Wei·ser (wī′zər), *n.* **(Johann) Conrad,** 1696–1760, American colonial Indian agent and interpreter, born in Germany.

Weis·mann (vīs′män′), *n.* **Au·gust** (ou′go͝ost), 1834–1914, German biologist.

Weis·mann·ism (vīs′män iz′əm), *n. Biol.* the theories of heredity as expounded by Weismann, esp. the theory that all inheritable characteristics are carried in the germ plasm, and that acquired characteristics cannot be inherited. [1890–95; WEISMANN + -ISM] —**Weis′·mann·i·an,** *adj., n.*

weiss′ beer′ (vīs, wīs), a light-colored, highly effervescent beer prepared largely from malted wheat. [< G *Weissbier,* equiv. to *weiss* WHITE + *Bier* BEER]

Weiss·horn (vīs′hôrn′), *n.* a mountain in S Switzerland, in the Alps. 14,804 ft. (4512 m).

Weiss·mul·ler (wīs′mul′ər), *n.* **Peter John** (*Johnny*), 1904–84, U.S. swimmer and film actor.

Weiz·mann (vīts′män′; *Eng.* wīts′mən, vīts′-), *n.* **Cha·im** (khī′im), 1874–1952, Israeli chemist and Zionist leader, born in Russia: 1st president of Israel 1948–52.

Weiz·säck·er (vīts′zek′ər), *n.* **Carl Frie·drich von** (kärl frē′drikh fən), born 1912, German physicist and cosmologist.

we·jack (wē′jak), *n.* fisher (def. 3). [1735–45; < Cree *oče·k* < Proto-Algonquian **wečye·ka*]

we·ka (wā′kə, wē′-), *n.* any of several large, flightless New Zealand rails of the genus *Gallirallus.* [1835–45; < Maori]

welch (welch, welsh), *v.i. Informal.* welsh. —**welch′·er,** *n.*

Welch (welch, welsh), *adj., n.* Welsh.

Welch (welch, welsh), *n.* **1. Joseph Nye,** 1890–1960, U.S. trial lawyer. **2. Robert, Jr.,** 1899–1985, U.S. candy manufacturer: founder of the John Birch Society 1958. **3. William Henry,** 1850–1934, U.S. medical pathologist and educator.

Welch·man (welch′mən, welsh′-), *n., pl.* **-men.** Welshman.

wel·come (wel′kəm), *interj., n., v.,* **-comed, -com·ing,** *adj.* —*interj.* **1.** (a word of kindly greeting, as to one whose arrival gives pleasure): *Welcome, stranger!* —*n.* **2.** a kindly greeting or reception, as to one whose arrival gives pleasure: *to give someone a warm welcome.* **3. wear out one's welcome,** to make one's visits so frequent or of such long duration that they become offensive. —*v.t.* **4.** to greet the arrival of (a person, guests, etc.) with pleasure or kindly courtesy. **5.** to receive or accept with pleasure; regard as pleasant or good: *to welcome a change.* **6.** to meet, accept, or receive (an action, challenge, person, etc.) in a specified, esp. unfriendly, manner: *They welcomed him with hisses and catcalls.* —*adj.* **7.** gladly received, as one whose arrival gives pleasure: *a welcome visitor.* **8.** agreeable, as something arriving, occurring, or experienced: *a welcome rest.* **9.** given full right by the cordial consent of others: *She is welcome to try it.* **10.** without obligation for the courtesy or favor received (used as a conventional response to expressions of thanks): *You're quite welcome.* [bef. 900; ME < Scand; cf. ON *velkominn,* equiv. to *vel* WELL[1] + *kominn* COME (ptp.); r. OE *wilcuma* one who is welcome, equiv. to *wil-* welcome (see WILL[2]) + *cuma* comer] —**wel′come·ness,** *n.* —**wel′com·er,** *n.*

wel′come mat′, **1.** a doormat, esp. one with the word "welcome" printed on it. **2. put out the welcome mat,** to extend a hearty welcome: *The club put out the welcome mat for new members.*

Wel′come Wag′on, *Trademark.* **1.** an organization sponsoring a service in which newcomers in an area are given information about the community, gifts, and sample products of local merchants. **2.** a vehicle dispensing such material.

weld[1] (weld), *v.t.* **1.** to unite or fuse (as pieces of metal) by hammering, compressing, or the like, esp. after rendering soft or pasty by heat, and sometimes with the addition of fusible material like or unlike the pieces to be united. **2.** to bring into complete union, harmony, agreement, etc. —*v.i.* **3.** to undergo welding; be capable of being welded: *a metal that welds easily.* —*n.* **4.** a welded junction or joint. **5.** the act of welding or the state of being welded. [1590–1600; var. of WELL[2] in obs. sense "to boil, weld"] —**weld′a·ble,** *adj.* —**weld′a·bil′i·ty,** *n.* —**weld′er, wel′dor,** *n.* —**weld′less,** *adj.*

weld[2] (weld), *n.* **1.** a mignonette, *Reseda luteola,* of southern Europe, yielding a yellow dye. **2.** the dye. Also, **wold, woald, would.** Also called **dyer's rocket.** [1325–75; ME *welde;* c. MLG *walde,* MD *woude*]

Weld (weld), *n.* **Theodore Dwight,** 1803–95, U.S. abolitionist leader.

weld′ed tuff′, *Petrol.* ignimbrite.

weld·ment (weld′mənt), *n.* a welded assembly. [1940–45; WELD[1] + -MENT]

wel·fare (wel′fâr′), *n.* **1.** the good fortune, health, happiness, prosperity, etc., of a person, group, or organization; well-being: *to look after a child's welfare; the physical or moral welfare of society.* **2.** See **welfare work. 3.** financial or other assistance to an individual or family from a city, state, or national government: *Thousands of jobless people in this city would starve if it weren't for welfare.* **4.** (*cap.*) *Informal.* a governmental agency that provides funds and aid to people in need, esp. those unable to work. **5. on welfare,** receiving financial aid from the government or from a private organization because of hardship and need. [1275–1325; ME, from phrase *wel fare.* See WELL[1], FARE]

wel′fare econom′ics, a branch of economics concerned with improving human welfare and social conditions chiefly through the optimum distribution of wealth, the relief or reduction of unemployment, etc.

wel′fare fund′, a fund set up by a union or employer, providing benefits to workers during a period of unemployment or disablement, as salary continuance while ill.

wel′fare hotel′, a hotel in which people receiving welfare assistance are temporarily housed until permanent quarters become available. [1970–75]

Wel′fare Is′land, a former name of **Roosevelt Island.**

wel′fare moth′er, the mother of dependent children who receives government welfare benefits. [1970–75]

wel′fare state′, a state in which the welfare of the people in such matters as social security, health and education, housing, and working conditions is the responsibility of the government. [1940–45]

wel′fare stat′ism, 1. the belief in or practices of a welfare state. **2.** the condition of being a welfare state. [1950–55; WELFARE STATE + -ISM]

wel′fare work′, the efforts or programs of an agency, community, business organization, etc., to improve living conditions, increase job opportunities, secure hospitalization, and the like, for needy persons within its jurisdiction. [1905–10] —**wel′fare work′er.**

wel·far·ism (wel′fâr′iz əm, -fâ riz′-), *n.* the set of attitudes and policies characterizing or tending toward the establishment of a welfare state. [1945–50; WELFARE + -ISM] —**wel′far·ist,** *n., adj.*

wel·kin (wel′kin), *n. Chiefly Literary.* the sky; the vault of heaven. [bef. 900; ME *welken(e),* OE *welcn,* var. of *wolcen* cloud, sky; c. G *Wolke* cloud]

well[1] (wel), *adv., adj., compar.* **bet·ter,** *superl.* **best,** *interj., n.* —*adv.* **1.** in a good or satisfactory manner: *Business is going well.* **2.** thoroughly, carefully, or soundly: *to shake well before using; listen well.* **3.** in a moral or proper manner: *to behave well.* **4.** commendably, meritoriously, or excellently: *a difficult task well done.* **5.** with propriety, justice, or reason: *I could not well refuse.* **6.** adequately or sufficiently: *Think well before you act.* **7.** to a considerable extent or degree: *a sum well over the amount agreed upon.* **8.** with great or intimate knowledge: *to know a person well.* **9.** certainly; without doubt: *I anger easily, as you well know.* **10.** with good nature; without rancor: *He took the joke well.* **11. as well, a.** in addition; also; too: *She insisted on directing the play and on producing it as well.* **b.** equally: *The town grew as well because of its location as because of its superb climate.* **12. as well as,** as much or as truly as; equally as: *Joan is witty as well as intelligent.* —*adj.* **13.** in good health; sound in body and mind: *Are you well? He is not a well man.* **14.** satisfactory, pleasing, or good: *All is well with us.* **15.** proper, fitting, or gratifying: *It is well that you didn't go.* **16.** in a satisfactory position; well-off: *I am very well as I am.* **17. leave well enough alone,** avoid changing something that is satisfactory. —*interj.* **18.** (used to express surprise, reproof, etc.): *Well! There's no need to shout.* **19.** (used to introduce a sentence, resume a conversation, etc.): *Well, who would have thought he could do it?* —*n.* **20.** well-being; good fortune; success: *to wish well to someone.* [bef. 900; ME, OE *wel(l)* (adj. and adv.); c. D *wel,* G *wohl,* ON *vel,* Goth *waila*]
—**Syn. 3.** properly, correctly. **4.** skillfully, adeptly, accurately, efficiently. **5.** suitably. **6.** fully, amply. **7.** rather, quite. **13.** healthy, hale, hearty. **14.** fine. **15.** suitable, befitting, appropriate. **16.** fortunate, happy.
—**Ant. 3.** poorly, badly. **13.** ill, sick.
—**Usage.** See **good.**
—**Note.** The lists at the bottom of this and following pages provide the spelling, syllabification, and stress for words whose meanings may be easily inferred by combining the meanings of WELL[1] and an attached base word, or base word plus a suffix. Appropriate parts of speech are also shown. Words formed with WELL[1] that have special meanings or uses are entered in their proper alphabetical places in the main vocabulary or as derived forms run on at the end of a main vocabulary entry.

well[2] (wel), *n.* **1.** a hole drilled or bored into the earth to obtain water, petroleum, natural gas, brine, or sulfur. **2.** a spring or natural source of water. **3.** an apparent reservoir or a source of human feelings, emotions, energy, etc.: *He was a well of gentleness and courtesy.* **4.** a container, receptacle, or reservoir for a liquid: *the well of ink in a fountain pen.* **5.** any sunken or deep, enclosed space, as a shaft for air or light, stairs, or an elevator, extending vertically through the floors of a building. **6.** *Naut.* **a.** a part of a weather deck between two superstructures, extending from one side of a vessel to the other. **b.** a compartment or enclosure around a ship's pumps to make them easily accessible and protect them from being damaged by the cargo. **7.** a hollow compartment, recessed area, or depression for holding a specific item or items, as fish in the bottom of a boat or the retracted wheels of an airplane in flight. **8.** any shaft dug or bored into the earth, as for storage space or a mine. —*v.i.* **9.** to rise, spring, or gush, as water, from the earth or some other source (often fol. by *up, out,* or *forth*): *Tears welled up in my eyes.* —*v.t.* **10.** to send welling up or forth: *a fountain welling its pure water.* —*adj.* **11.** like, of, resembling, from, or used in connection with a well. [bef. 900; (n.) ME *well(e),* OE *wylle, wella, welle;* c. G *Welle* wave; (v.) ME *wellen,* OE *wellan* (c. D *wellen,* ON *vella*); both n. and v. ult. akin to *weallan* to boil]
—**Syn. 3.** store, fund, mine, fount.

we'll (wēl; *unstressed* wil), contraction of *we will.*
—**Usage.** See **contraction.**

well-ad·vised (wel′əd vīzd′), *adj.* **1.** acting with caution, care, or wisdom: *They would be well-advised to sell*

CONCISE PRONUNCIATION KEY: *act, cāpe, dâre, pärt; set, ēqual; if, īce; ox, ōver, ôrder, oil, bo͝ok, bo͞ot, out; up, ûrge; child; sing; shoe; thin, that;* zh as in *treasure.* ə = *a* as in *alone, e* as in *system, i* as in *easily, o* as in *gallop, u* as in *circus;* ᵊ as in *fire* (fīᵊr), *hour* (ouᵊr). l and n can serve as syllabic consonants, as in *cradle* (krād′l), and *button* (but′n). See the full key inside the front cover.

well′-a·bol′ished, *adj.*
well′-a·bound′ing, *adj.*
well′-ab·sorbed′, *adj.*
well′-ac′cent·ed, *adj.*
well′-ac·cen′tu·at′ed, *adj.*
well′-ac·cept′ed, *adj.*
well′-ac·com′mo·dat′ed, *adj.*
well′-ac·com′pa·nied, *adj.*
well′-ac·com′plished, *adj.*
well′-ac·cord′ed, *adj.*
well′-ac·cred′it·ed, *adj.*
well′-ac·cu′mu·lat′ed, *adj.*
well′-ac·cus′tomed, *adj.*
well′-a·chieved′, *adj.*
well′-ac·knowl′edged, *adj.*
well′-ac·quaint′ed, *adj.*
well′-ac·quired′, *adj.*
well′-act′ed, *adj.*
well′-a·dapt′ed, *adj.*
well′-ad·dict′ed, *adj.*
well′-ad·dressed′, *adj.*
well′-ad·just′ed, *adj.*
well′-ad·min′is·tered, *adj.*
well′-ad·mit′ted, *adj.*
well′-a·dopt′ed, *adj.*
well′-a·dorned′, *adj.*
well′-ad·vanced′, *adj.*
well′-ad′ver·tised′, *adj.*
well′-ad′vo·cat′ed, *adj.*
well′-af·fect′ed, *adj.*
well′-aged′, *adj.*
well′-aimed′, *adj.*
well′-aired′, *adj.*
well′-al·lied′, *adj.*
well′-al·lot′ted, *adj.*
well′-al′tered, *adj.*
well′-a·mend′ed, *adj.*
well′-a·mused′, *adj.*
well′-an′a·lyzed′, *adj.*
well′-an′chored, *adj.*
well′-an′no·tat′ed, *adj.*
well′-an·nounced′, *adj.*
well′-a·noint′ed, *adj.*
well′-an′swered, *adj.*
well′-an·tic′i·pat′ed, *adj.*
well′-ap·par′eled, *adj.*
well′-ap·par′elled, *adj.*
well′-ap·pear′ing, *adj.*
well′-ap·plaud′ed, *adj.*
well′-ap·plied′, *adj.*
well′-ap·pre′ci·at′ed, *adj.*
well′-ap·proached′, *adj.*
well′-ap·pro′pri·at′ed, *adj.*
well′-ap·proved′, *adj.*
well′-ar′bi·trat′ed, *adj.*
well′-ar′gued, *adj.*
well′-armed′, *adj.*
well′-ar′mored, *adj.*
well′-a·roused′, *adj.*
well′-ar·ranged′, *adj.*
well′-ar·rayed′, *adj.*
well′-ar·tic′u·lat′ed, *adj.*
well′-as′cer·tained′, *adj.*
well′-as·sem′bled, *adj.*
well′-as·sert′ed, *adj.*
well′-as·sessed′, *adj.*
well′-as·signed′, *adj.*
well′-as·sim′i·lat′ed, *adj.*
well′-as·sist′ed, *adj.*
well′-as·so′ci·at′ed, *adj.*
well′-as·sort′ed, *adj.*
well′-as·sumed′, *adj.*
well′-as·sured′, *adj.*
well′-at·tached′, *adj.*
well′-at·tained′, *adj.*
well′-at·tempt′ed, *adj.*
well′-at·tend′ed, *adj.*
well′-at·tend′ing, *adj.*
well′-at·test′ed, *adj.*
well′-at·tired′, *adj.*
well′-at·trib′ut·ed, *adj.*
well′-au′dit·ed, *adj.*
well′-au·then′ti·cat′ed, *adj.*
well′-au′thor·ized′, *adj.*
well′-av′er·aged, *adj.*
well′-a·wak′ened, *adj.*
well′-a·ward′ed, *adj.*
well′-a·ware′, *adj.*
well′-backed′, *adj.*
well′-baked′, *adj.*
well′-baled′, *adj.*
well′-band′aged, *adj.*
well′-banked′, *adj.*
well′-bar′bered, *adj.*
well′-based′, *adj.*
well′-bathed′, *adj.*
well′-beat′en, *adj.*
well′-be·com′ing, *adj.*
well′-be·fit′ting, *adj.*
well′-be·got′ten, *adj.*
well′-be·gun′, *adj.*
well′-be·haved′, *adj.*
well′-be·known′, *adj.*
well′-be·lieved′, *adj.*
well′-bent′, *adj.*
well′-be·spo′ken, *adj.*
well′-be·stowed′, *adj.*
well′-blacked′, *adj.*
well′-blend′ed, *adj.*
well′-blessed′, *adj.*
well′-blood′ed, *adj.*
well′-bod′ing, *adj.*
well′-boiled′, *adj.*
well′-bond′ed, *adj.*
well′-boned′, *adj.*
well′-boot′ed, *adj.*
well′-bored′, *adj.*
well′-borne′, *adj.*
well′-bot′tled, *adj.*
well′-bought′, *adj.*
well′-bound′, *adj.*
well′-bowled′, *adj.*
well′-boxed′, *adj.*
well′-braced′, *adj.*
well′-braid′ed, *adj.*
well′-branched′, *adj.*
well′-brand′ed, *adj.*
well′-brewed′, *adj.*
well′-bro′ken, *adj.*
well′-browned′, *adj.*
well′-brushed′, *adj.*
well′-built′, *adj.*
well′-bur′ied, *adj.*
well′-burned′, *adj.*
well′-burnt′, *adj.*
well′-bus′ied, *adj.*
well′-but′toned, *adj.*
well′-cal′cu·lat′ed, *adj.*
well′-called′, *adj.*
well′-cam′ou·flaged′, *adj.*
well′-canned′, *adj.*
well′-can′vassed, *adj.*
well′-car′pet·ed, *adj.*
well′-carved′, *adj.*
well′-cased′, *adj.*
well′-cast′, *adj.*
well′-caught′, *adj.*
well′-cau′tioned, *adj.*
well′-cel′e·brat′ed, *adj.*
well′-ce·ment′ed, *adj.*
well′-cen′tered, *adj.*
well′-cer′ti·fied′, *adj.*
well′-changed′, *adj.*
well′-chap′er·oned′, *adj.*
well′-char′ac·ter·ized′, *adj.*
well′-charged′, *adj.*
well′-chart′ed, *adj.*
well′-chauf′feured, *adj.*
well′-checked′, *adj.*
well′-cheered′, *adj.*
well′-cher′ished, *adj.*
well′-chewed′, *adj.*
well′-chilled′, *adj.*
well′-chopped′, *adj.*
well′-churned′, *adj.*
well′-cir′cu·lat′ed, *adj.*
well′-cir′cum·stanced′, *adj.*
well′-civ′i·lized′, *adj.*
well′-clad′, *adj.*
well′-classed′, *adj.*
well′-clas′si·fied′, *adj.*
well′-cleansed′, *adj.*
well′-cleared′, *adj.*
well′-cloaked′, *adj.*
well′-clois′tered, *adj.*
well′-closed′, *adj.*
well′-clothed′, *adj.*
well′-coached′, *adj.*
well′-coat′ed, *adj.*
well′-coined′, *adj.*
well′-col·lect′ed, *adj.*
well′-col′o·nized′, *adj.*
well′-col′ored, *adj.*
well′-combed′, *adj.*
well′-com·bined′, *adj.*
well′-com·mand′ed, *adj.*
well′-com·menced′, *adj.*
well′-com·mend′ed, *adj.*
well′-com·mit′ted, *adj.*
well′-com·mu′ni·cat′ed, *adj.*
well′-com·pact′ed, *adj.*
well′-com·pared′, *adj.*
well′-com′pen·sat′ed, *adj.*
well′-com·piled′, *adj.*
well′-com·plet′ed, *adj.*
well′-com·plex′ioned, *adj.*
well′-com·posed′, *adj.*
well′-com′pre·hend′ed, *adj.*
well′-con·cealed′, *adj.*
well′-con·ced′ed, *adj.*
well′-con·ceived′, *adj.*
well′-con′cen·trat′ed, *adj.*
well′-con·cert′ed, *adj.*
well′-con·clud′ed, *adj.*
well′-con·coct′ed, *adj.*
well′-con·cord′ed, *adj.*
well′-con·densed′, *adj.*
well′-con·di′tioned, *adj.*
well′-con·duct′ed, *adj.*
well′-con·ferred′, *adj.*
well′-con·fid′ed, *adj.*
well′-con·firmed′, *adj.*
well′-con·nect′ed, *adj.*
well′-con·served′, *adj.*
well′-con·sid′ered, *adj.*
well′-con′sti·tut′ed, *adj.*
well′-con·strict′ed, *adj.*
well′-con·struct′ed, *adj.*
well′-con·tained′, *adj.*
well′-con·test′ed, *adj.*
well′-con·tin′ued, *adj.*
well′-con·tract′ed, *adj.*
well′-con·trast′ed, *adj.*
well′-con·trived′, *adj.*
well′-con·trolled′, *adj.*
well′-con·veyed′, *adj.*
well′-con·vinced′, *adj.*
well′-cooked′, *adj.*
well′-cooled′, *adj.*
well′-cop′ied, *adj.*
well′-corked′, *adj.*
well′-cor·rect′ed, *adj.*
well′-cor′set·ed, *adj.*
well′-cos′tumed, *adj.*
well′-couched′, *adj.*
well′-coun′seled, *adj.*
well′-coun′selled, *adj.*
well′-cou′pled, *adj.*
well′-court′ed, *adj.*
well′-cov′ered, *adj.*
well′-crammed′, *adj.*
well′-cred′it·ed, *adj.*
well′-crit′i·cized′, *adj.*
well′-cro·cheted′, *adj.*
well′-cropped′, *adj.*
well′-crossed′, *adj.*
well′-crushed′, *adj.*
well′-cul′ti·vat′ed, *adj.*
well′-cul′tured, *adj.*
well′-cured′, *adj.*
well′-curled′, *adj.*
well′-cur′ried, *adj.*
well′-curved′, *adj.*
well′-cush′ioned, *adj.*
well′-cut′, *adj.*
well′-danced′, *adj.*
well′-dark′ened, *adj.*
well′-darned′, *adj.*
well′-de·bat′ed, *adj.*
well′-de·ceived′, *adj.*
well′-de·cid′ed, *adj.*
well′-dec′o·rat′ed, *adj.*
well′-de·creed′, *adj.*
well′-de·fend′ed, *adj.*
well′-de·ferred′, *adj.*

the stock now. **2.** based on or showing wise consideration: *There was a well-advised delay in carrying out her plan.* [1350–1400; ME *well avysed*]

Wel·land (wel′ənd), *n.* a city in SE Ontario, in S Canada, on the Welland Ship Canal. 45,448.

Wel′land Ship′ Canal′, a ship canal in S Canada, in Ontario, connecting Lakes Erie and Ontario: 8 locks. 25 mi. (40 km) long. Formerly, **Wel′land Canal′.**

well-ap·point·ed (wel′ə poin′tid), *adj.* attractively equipped, arranged, or furnished, esp. for comfort or convenience: *a well-appointed room.* [1520–30]

well·a·way (wel′ə wā′), *interj. Archaic.* (used to express sorrow.) Also, **well·a·day** (wel′ə dā′). [bef. 900; ME *we(i)lawei,* OE *weilāwei* (*wei* < Scand; cf. ON *vei* WOE), r. OE *wā lā wā* woe! lo! woe!]

well-bal·anced (wel′bal′ənst), *adj.* **1.** rightly balanced, adjusted, or regulated: *a well-balanced diet.* **2.** sensible; sane: *a well-balanced mind.* [1620–30]

well-be·ing (wel′bē′ing), *n.* a good or satisfactory condition of existence; a state characterized by health, happiness, and prosperity; welfare: *to influence the well-being of the nation and its people.* [1605–15]

well-be·lov·ed (wel′bi luv′id, -luvd′), *adj.* **1.** loved deeply and sincerely: *my well-beloved fiancé.* **2.** highly respected and honored: *our well-beloved speaker.* —*n.* **3.** a person who is loved dearly: *in respect for the well-beloved.* [1350–1400; ME *wel biloved*]

well·born (wel′bôrn′), *adj.* **1.** born of a good, noble, or highly esteemed family. —*n.* **2.** (*used with a plural v.*) wellborn persons collectively (usually prec. by *the*): *the pride and assurance of the wellborn.* [bef. 950; ME; OE *welboren.* See WELL[1], BORN]

well-bred (wel′bred′), *adj.* **1.** well brought up; properly trained and educated: *a well-bred boy.* **2.** showing good breeding, as in behavior or manners. **3.** (of animals) of a desirable breed or pedigree. [1590–1600]

CONCISE ETYMOLOGY KEY: <, descended or borrowed from; >, whence; b., blend of, blended; c., cognate with; cf., compare; deriv., derivative; equiv., equivalent; imit., imitative; obl., oblique; r., replacing; s., stem; sp., spelling, spelled; resp., respelling, respelled; trans., translation; ?, origin unknown; *, unattested; ‡, probably earlier than. See the full key inside the front cover.

well-cho·sen (wel′chō′zən), *adj.* chosen with care, as for suitability or preciseness: *He entered at a well-chosen moment.* [1580–90]

well-con·tent (wel′kən tent′), *adj.* fully contented; satisfied. Also, **well′-con·tent′ed.** [1400–50; late ME]

well-de·fined (wel′di fīnd′), *adj.* sharply or clearly stated, outlined, described, etc.: *a well-defined character; a well-defined boundary.* [1695–1705]

well-dis·posed (wel′di spōzd′), *adj.* favorably, sympathetically, or kindly disposed: *The sponsors are well-disposed toward our plan.* [1350–1400; ME]

well·do·ing (wel′do͞o′ing), *n.* good conduct or action. [1300–50; ME; see WELL[1], DOING]

well-done (wel′dun′), *adj.* **1.** performed accurately and diligently; executed with skill and efficiency. **2.** (of meat) thoroughly cooked, esp. until all redness is gone. [1150–1200; ME]

well-dressed (wel′drest′), *adj.* attired in clothing that is of good quality, is properly fitted, and is appropriate and becoming. [1570–80]

well-dress·ing (wel′dres′ing), *n.* (in parts of rural Britain) a traditional ceremony of decorating wells with flowers in thanks for the blessing of an abundant supply of pure water. —**well′dress′er,** *n.*

Wel·ler (wel′ər), *n.* **Thomas Huck·le** (huk′əl), born 1915, U.S. physician: Nobel prize for medicine 1954.

Welles (welz), *n.* **1. (George) Orson,** 1915–85, U.S. actor, director, and producer. **2. Gideon,** 1802–78, U.S. journalist, legislator, and government official: Secretary of the Navy 1861–69. **3. Sumner,** 1892–1961, U.S. diplomat and government official.

Welles·ley (welz′lē), *n.* **1. Arthur.** See **Wellington, 1st Duke of. 2.** his brother **Robert Col·ley** (kol′ē), **1st Marquis,** 1760–1842, British statesman and administrator, born in Ireland: governor general of India 1797–1805. **3.** a city in E Massachusetts, near Boston. 27,209.

well-es·tab·lished (wel′i stab′lisht), *adj.* permanently founded; settled; firmly set: *a well-established business; a well-established habit.* [1700–10]

Wel·lesz (vel′es), *n.* **E·gon** (ā′gōn), 1885–1974, Austrian musicologist and composer.

well-fa·vored (wel′fā′vərd), *adj.* of pleasing appearance; good-looking; pretty or handsome. Also, *esp. Brit.,* **well′-fa′voured.** [1375–1425; late ME]

well-fed (wel′fed′), *adj.* fat; plump. [1325–75; ME]

well-fixed (wel′fikst′), *adj. Informal.* wealthy; prosperous; well-to-do; well-heeled. [1710–20]

well-formed (wel′fôrmd′), *adj.* **1.** rightly or pleasingly formed: *a well-formed contour.* **2.** *Ling.* (of an utterance) conforming to the rules of a language; grammatical (opposed to *ill-formed*). [1510–20] —**well-form·ed·ness** (wel′fôr′mid nis, -fôrmd′-), *n.*

well-found (wel′found′), *adj.* well-furnished with supplies, necessaries, etc.: *a well-found ship.* [1300–50 for earlier sense "welcome"; ME]

well-found·ed (wel′foun′did), *adj.* having a foundation in fact; based on good reasons, information, etc.: *well-founded suspicions.* [1325–75; ME]

well-groomed (wel′gro͞omd′, -gro͝omd′), *adj.* **1.** having the hair, skin, etc., well cared for; well-dressed, clean, and neat: *a well-groomed young man.* **2.** (of an animal) tended, cleaned, combed, etc., with great care. **3.** carefully cared for; neat; tidy: *a well-groomed lawn.* [1885–90]

well-ground·ed (wel′groun′did), *adj.* **1.** based on good reasons; well-founded: *His opposition to the scheme is well-grounded.* **2.** well or thoroughly instructed in the basic principles of a subject: *She is well-grounded in mathematics.* [1325–75; ME]

well-han·dled (wel′han′dld), *adj.* **1.** managed, directed, or completed with efficiency: *a well-handled political campaign.* **2.** treated with taste, discretion, etc.: *a delicate but well-handled subject.* **3.** having been handled or used much: *a sale of well-handled goods.* [1470–80]

well·head (wel′hed′), *n.* **1.** a fountainhead; source. **2.** Also called **wellhouse.** a shelter for a well. **3.** the assemblage of equipment attached to the opening of an oil or gas well. —*adj.* **4.** noting or pertaining to petroleum, natural gas, etc., at the place and time at which it leaves the ground: *a wellhead price.* [1300–50; ME *welleheved.* See WELL[2], HEAD]

well-heeled (wel′hēld′), *adj. Informal.* well-off; rich. [1895–1900]

well·hole (wel′hōl′), *n.* **1.** the shaft of a well. **2.** a tall, narrow opening surrounded by walls, as a stairwell. [1670–80; WELL[2] + HOLE]

well·house (wel′hous′), *n., pl.* **-hous·es** (-hou′ziz). wellhead (def. 2). [1590–1600; WELL[2] + HOUSE]

well-in·formed (wel′in fôrmd′), *adj.* having extensive knowledge, as in one particular subject or in a variety of subjects. [1400–50; late ME]

Wel·ling·ton (wel′ing tən), *n.* **1. 1st Duke of** (*Arthur Wellesley*) ("*the Iron Duke*"), 1769–1852, British general and statesman, born in Ireland: prime minister 1828–30. **2.** See **Wellington boot. 3.** a seaport in and the capital of New Zealand, on S North Island. 349,628. **4.** See **beef Wellington.**

Wel′lington boot′, 1. a leather boot with the front part of the top extending above the knee. **2.** a rubber or water-repellent leather boot extending to the knee or somewhat below it. **3.** See **half Wellington.** Also, **wel′·lington boot′.** Also called **Wellington, wel′ling·ton.** [1810–20; after the 1st Duke of WELLINGTON]

well-in·ten·tioned (wel′in ten′shənd), *adj.* well-meaning. [1590–1600]

well-knit (wel′nit′), *adj.* closely joined together or related; firmly constructed: *a well-knit society; a well-knit plot; a muscular, well-knit body.* Also, **well′-knit′ted.** [1400–50; late ME]

well-known (wel′nōn′), *adj.* **1.** clearly or fully known: *The well-known reasons are obvious.* **2.** generally or widely known: *a well-known painting.* [1425–75; late ME]
—**Syn. 2.** prominent, famous, noted, celebrated.

well′-de·layed′, *adj.*
well′-de·lib′er·at′ed, *adj.*
well′-de·lin′e·at′ed, *adj.*
well′-de·liv′ered, *adj.*
well′-dem′on·strat′ed, *adj.*
well′-de·pict′ed, *adj.*
well′-de·rived′, *adj.*
well′-de·scribed′, *adj.*
well′-de·served′, *adj.*
well′-de·serv′ed·ly, *adv.*
well′-des′ig·nat′ed, *adj.*
well′-de·signed′, *adj.*
well′-de·sign′ing, *adj.*
well′-de·sired′, *adj.*
well′-de·stroyed′, *adj.*
well′-de·vel′oped, *adj.*
well′-de·vised′, *adj.*
well′-di′ag·nosed′, *adj.*
well′-dif·fused′, *adj.*
well′-di·gest′ed, *adj.*
well′-di·rect′ed, *adj.*
well′-dis·bursed′, *adj.*
well′-dis′ci·plined, *adj.*
well′-dis·cussed′, *adj.*
well′-dis·guised′, *adj.*
well′-dis·persed′, *adj.*
well′-dis·played′, *adj.*
well′-dis·put′ed, *adj.*
well′-dis·sect′ed, *adj.*
well′-dis·sem′bled, *adj.*
well′-dis′si·pat′ed, *adj.*
well′-dis·tin′guished, *adj.*
well′-dis·trib′ut·ed, *adj.*
well′-di·ver′si·fied′, *adj.*
well′-di·vid′ed, *adj.*
well′-doc′u·ment′ed, *adj.*
well′-do·mes′ti·cat′ed, *adj.*
well′-dom′i·nat′ed, *adj.*
well′-dosed′, *adj.*
well′-drained′, *adj.*
well′-dram′a·tized′, *adj.*
well′-drawn′, *adj.*
well′-dried′, *adj.*
well′-drilled′, *adj.*
well′-driv′en, *adj.*
well′-dust′ed, *adj.*
well′-earned′, *adj.*
well′-eased′, *adj.*
well′-ed′it·ed, *adj.*
well′-ed′u·cat′ed, *adj.*
well′-ef·fect′ed, *adj.*
well′-e·lab′o·rat′ed, *adj.*
well′-el′e·vat′ed, *adj.*
well′-e·lim′i·nat′ed, *adj.*
well′-em·bod′ied, *adj.*
well′-em′pha·sized′, *adj.*
well′-em·ployed′, *adj.*
well′-en·act′ed, *adj.*
well′-en·cour′aged, *adj.*
well′-end′ed, *adj.*
well′-en·dorsed′, *adj.*
well′-en·dowed′, *adj.*
well′-en·forced′, *adj.*
well′-en′gi·neered′, *adj.*
well′-en·graved′, *adj.*
well′-en·light′ened, *adj.*
well′-en′tered, *adj.*
well′-en·ter·tained′, *adj.*
well′-en·ti′tled, *adj.*
well′-e·nu′mer·at′ed, *adj.*
well′-e·quipped′, *adj.*
well′-e·rect′ed, *adj.*
well′-es·cort′ed, *adj.*
well′-es·sayed′, *adj.*
well′-es·teemed′, *adj.*
well′-es′ti·mat′ed, *adj.*
well′-ev′i·denced, *adj.*
well′-ex·am′ined, *adj.*
well′-ex′e·cut′ed, *adj.*
well′-ex·em′pli·fied′, *adj.*
well′-ex′er·cised′, *adj.*
well′-ex·ert′ed, *adj.*
well′-ex·hib′it·ed, *adj.*
well′-ex·pend′ed, *adj.*
well′-ex·pe′ri·enced, *adj.*
well′-ex·plained′, *adj.*
well′-ex′pli·cat′ed, *adj.*
well′-ex·posed′, *adj.*
well′-ex·pressed′, *adj.*
well′-fab′ri·cat′ed, *adj.*
well′-fad′ed, *adj.*
well′-farmed′, *adj.*
well′-fash′ioned, *adj.*
well′-fas′tened, *adj.*
well′-fea′tured, *adj.*
well′-fenced′, *adj.*
well′-fer·ment′ed, *adj.*
well′-filled′, *adj.*
well′-filmed′, *adj.*
well′-fil′tered, *adj.*
well′-fi·nanced′, *adj.*
well′-fin′ished, *adj.*
well′-fit′ted, *adj.*
well′-fit′ting, *adj.*
well′-flanked′, *adj.*
well′-fla′vored, *adj.*
well′-flood′ed, *adj.*
well′-fo′cused, *adj.*
well′-fo′cussed, *adj.*
well′-fold′ed, *adj.*
well′-fol′lowed, *adj.*
well′-fooled′, *adj.*
well′-fore·seen′, *adj.*
well′-for′est·ed, *adj.*
well′-fore·warned′, *adj.*
well′-forged′, *adj.*
well′-for·got′ten, *adj.*
well′-for′mu·lat′ed, *adj.*
well′-for′ti·fied′, *adj.*
well′-fought′, *adj.*
well′-framed′, *adj.*
well′-freck′led, *adj.*
well′-fre·quent′ed, *adj.*
well′-fright′ened, *adj.*
well′-fu′eled, *adj.*
well′-fu′elled, *adj.*
well′-func′tion·ing, *adj.*
well′-fur′nished, *adj.*
well′-gained′, *adj.*
well′-gait′ed, *adj.*
well′-gar′dened, *adj.*
well′-gar′ment·ed, *adj.*
well′-gar′nished, *adj.*
well′-gath′ered, *adj.*
well′-geared′, *adj.*
well′-gift′ed, *adj.*
well′-got′ten, *adj.*
well′-gov′erned, *adj.*
well′-grad′ed, *adj.*
well′-grained′, *adj.*
well′-grat′i·fied′, *adj.*
well′-grav′eled, *adj.*
well′-grav′elled, *adj.*
well′-grav′en, *adj.*
well′-greased′, *adj.*
well′-greet′ed, *adj.*
well′-guard′ed, *adj.*
well′-guid′ed, *adj.*
well′-ham′mered, *adj.*
well′-hard′ened, *adj.*
well′-har′nessed, *adj.*
well′-hatched′, *adj.*
well′-haz′ard·ed, *adj.*
well′-head′ed, *adj.*
well′-heard′, *adj.*
well′-healed′, *adj.*
well′-heat′ed, *adj.*
well′-hedged′, *adj.*
well′-helped′, *adj.*
well′-hemmed′, *adj.*
well′-hewn′, *adj.*
well′-hid′den, *adj.*
well′-hinged′, *adj.*
well′-hit′, *adj.*
well′-housed′, *adj.*
well′-hu′mored, *adj.*
well′-hung′, *adj.*
well′-iced′, *adj.*
well′-i·den′ti·fied′, *adj.*
well′-ig·nored′, *adj.*
well′-il′lus·trat′ed, *adj.*
well′-i·mag′ined, *adj.*
well′-im′i·tat′ed, *adj.*
well′-im·mersed′, *adj.*
well′-im·plied′, *adj.*
well′-im·posed′, *adj.*
well′-im·pressed′, *adj.*
well′-im·proved′, *adj.*
well′-im′pro·vised′, *adj.*
well′-in·au′gu·rat′ed, *adj.*
well′-in·clined′, *adj.*
well′-in′dexed, *adj.*
well′-in′di·cat′ed, *adj.*
well′-in·hab′it·ed, *adj.*
well′-in·i′ti·at′ed, *adj.*
well′-in·spect′ed, *adj.*
well′-in·stalled′, *adj.*
well′-in′sti·tut′ed, *adj.*
well′-in·struct′ed, *adj.*
well′-in′su·lat′ed, *adj.*
well′-in·sured′, *adj.*
well′-in′te·grat′ed, *adj.*
well′-in′ter·est·ed, *adj.*
well′-in·ter′pret·ed, *adj.*
well′-in·tro·duced′, *adj.*
well′-in·vent′ed, *adj.*
well′-in·vest′ed, *adj.*
well′-in·ves′ti·gat′ed, *adj.*
well′-i′roned, *adj.*
well′-ir′ri·gat′ed, *adj.*
well′-i′tem·ized′, *adj.*
well′-joined′, *adj.*
well′-judged′, *adj.*
well′-jus′ti·fied′, *adj.*
well′-kept′, *adj.*
well′-kin′dled, *adj.*
well′-knot′ted, *adj.*
well′-la′bored, *adj.*
well′-laced′, *adj.*
well′-laid′, *adj.*
well′-lard′ed, *adj.*
well′-launched′, *adj.*
well′-laun′dered, *adj.*
well′-learned′, *adj.*
well′-leased′, *adj.*
well′-led′, *adj.*
well′-lent′, *adj.*
well′-let′tered, *adj.*
well′-lev′eled, *adj.*
well′-lev′elled, *adj.*
well′-light′ed, *adj.*
well′-liked′, *adj.*
well′-lined′, *adj.*
well′-linked′, *adj.*
well′-lit′, *adj.*
well′-load′ed, *adj.*
well′-locked′, *adj.*
well′-lodged′, *adj.*
well′-loft′ed, *adj.*
well′-loved′, *adj.*
well′-main·tained′, *adj.*
well′-man′aged, *adj.*
well′-manned′, *adj.*
well′-man′u·fac′tured, *adj.*
well′-ma·nured′, *adj.*
well′-mapped′, *adj.*
well′-marked′, *adj.*
well′-mar′ket·ed, *adj.*
well′-mar′ried, *adj.*
well′-masked′, *adj.*
well′-mas′tered, *adj.*
well′-matched′, *adj.*
well′-ma·tured′, *adj.*
well′-meas′ured, *adj.*
well′-mend′ed, *adj.*
well′-mer′it·ed, *adj.*
well′-meth′od·ized′, *adj.*
well′-milked′, *adj.*
well′-min′gled, *adj.*
well′-mixed′, *adj.*
well′-mod′u·lat′ed, *adj.*
well′-mo′ti·vat′ed, *adj.*
well′-mo′tived, *adj.*
well′-mount′ed, *adj.*
well′-named′, *adj.*
well′-nar′rat·ed, *adj.*
well′-nav′i·gat′ed, *adj.*
well′-need′ed, *adj.*
well′-ne·go′ti·at′ed, *adj.*
well′-not′ed, *adj.*
well′-nour′ished, *adj.*
well′-nursed′, *adj.*
well′-nur′tured, *adj.*
well′-o·beyed′, *adj.*
well′-ob·served′, *adj.*

well′ log′, log¹ (def. 7).

well′ log′ging, the process or technique of recording a well log.

well-made (wel′mād′), *adj.* **1.** skillfully built or constructed: *a well-made sofa.* **2.** strongly built; well-built: *sturdy, well-made youngsters.* [1250–1300; ME]

well-man•nered (wel′man′ərd), *adj.* polite; courteous. [1350–1400; ME]

well-mean•ing (wel′mē′ning), *adj.* **1.** meaning or intending well; having good intentions: *a well-meaning but tactless person.* **2.** Also, **well-meant** (wel′ment′). proceeding from good intentions: *Her well-meaning words were received in silence.* [1350–1400; ME]

well-met (wel′met′), *adj. Archaic.* (used as a salutation or part of a salutation). Cf. **hail-fellow.** [1580–90]

well•ness (wel′nis), *n.* the fact or condition of being in maximum physical and mental health. [1645–55; WELL¹ + -NESS]

well-nigh (wel′nī′), *adv.* very nearly; almost: *It's well-nigh bedtime.* [bef. 1150; ME; OE]
—**Syn.** See **almost.**

well-off (wel′ôf′, -of′), *adj.* **1.** having sufficient money for comfortable living; well-to-do. **2.** in a satisfactory, favorable, or good position or condition: *If you have your health, you are well-off.* [1725–35]
—**Syn. 1.** prosperous, wealthy, affluent, comfortable.

well-oiled (wel′oild′), *adj.* **1.** operating with efficiency: *a well-oiled department.* **2.** *Slang.* drunk. [1730–40]

well-or•dered (wel′ôr′dərd), *adj.* arranged, planned, or occurring in a desirable way, sequence, etc. [1600–10]

well′-ordered set′, *Math.* a totally ordered set in which every nonempty subset has a smallest element with the property that there is no element in the subset less than this smallest element. Cf. **partially ordered set, totally ordered set.**

well′-or′der•ing the′orem (wel′ôr′dər ing), *Math.* the theorem of set theory that every set can be made a well-ordered set.

well•point (wel′point′), *n. Engin., Building Trades.* a perforated tube driven into the ground to collect water from the surrounding area so that it can be pumped away, as to prevent an excavation from filling with ground water. [1940–45; WELL² + POINT]

well-pre•served (wel′pri zûrvd′), *adj.* having been maintained in good condition; preserving a good or healthy appearance: *a well-preserved manuscript; a well-preserved elderly couple.* [1850–55]

well-read (wel′red′), *adj.* having read extensively (sometimes fol. by *in*): *well-read in oceanography.* [1590–1600]

well-round•ed (wel′roun′did), *adj.* **1.** having desirably varied abilities or attainments. **2.** desirably varied: *a well-rounded curriculum.* **3.** fully developed; well-balanced. [1870–75]

Wells (welz), *n.* **1. Henry,** 1805–78, U.S. businessman: pioneered in banking, stagecoach services, and express shipping. **2. H(erbert) G(eorge),** 1866–1946, English novelist and historian. **3. Horace,** 1815–48, U.S. dentist: pioneered use of nitrous oxide as an anesthetic. **4. Ida Bell** (*Ida Bell Wells-Barnett*), 1862–1931, U.S. journalist and civil-rights leader. **5.** a historic town in E Somersetshire, in SW England: cathedral. 8586.

well-set (wel′set′), *adj.* **1.** firmly set or fixed. **2.** strongly formed: *a well-set human body.* [1300–50; ME]

well-spo•ken (wel′spō′kən), *adj.* **1.** speaking well, fittingly, or pleasingly: *The new chairwoman was very well-spoken.* **2.** polite in speech: *a well-spoken gentleman.* **3.** spoken in an apt, fitting, or pleasing manner: *a few well-spoken words on civic pride.* [1400–50; late ME]

well•spring (wel′spring′), *n.* **1.** the head or source of a spring, stream, river, etc.; fountainhead. **2.** a source or supply of anything, esp. when considered inexhaustible: *a wellspring of affection.* [bef. 900; ME *welle spring,* OE *wyllspring;* see WELL², SPRING]

well′ sweep′, sweep¹ (def. 29). [1820–30]

well-taken (wel′tā′kən), *adj.* soundly logical; worthy of consideration: *Her advice is well-taken.* [1755–65]

well-thought-of (wel′thôt′uv′, -ov′), *adj.* highly esteemed; of good reputation: *a well-thought-of scholar; This new book is well-thought-of.* [1570–80]

well-timed (wel′tīmd′), *adj.* fittingly or appropriately timed; opportune; timely: *a well-timed demand for new legislation.* [1625–35]

well-to-do (wel′tə do͞o′), *adj.* prosperous; rich; affluent. [1815–25]

well-turned (wel′tûrnd′), *adj.* **1.** gracefully shaped: *a well-turned ankle.* **2.** gracefully and concisely expressed: *a well-turned phrase.* [1610–20]

well-wish•er (wel′wish′ər), *n.* a person who wishes well to another person, a cause, etc. [1580–90]
—**well′-wish′ing,** *adj., n.*

well-worn (wel′wôrn′, -wōrn′), *adj.* **1.** showing the effects of extensive use or wear: *well-worn carpets.* **2.** trite, hackneyed, or stale: *a well-worn saying.* **3.** fittingly or becomingly worn or borne: *a well-worn reserve that never seems haughty.* [1615–25]

Wels′bach burn′er (welz′bak, -bäk; *Ger.* vels′bäKH), *Trademark.* a brand of gaslight consisting essentially of a Bunsen burner on which an incombustible mantle (**Wels′bach man′tle**) composed of thoria and some ceria becomes brilliantly incandescent when exposed to flame.

welsh (welsh, welch), *v.i. Informal (sometimes offensive).* **1.** to cheat by failing to pay a gambling debt: *You aren't going to welsh on me, are you?* **2.** to go back on one's word: *He welshed on his promise to help in the campaign.* Also, **welch.** [1855–60; perh. special use of WELSH] —**welsh′er,** *n.*

Welsh (welsh, welch), *adj.* **1.** of or pertaining to Wales, its people, or their language. —*n.* **2.** the inhabitants of Wales and their descendants elsewhere. **3.** Also called **Cymric, Kymric.** the Celtic language of Wales. **4.** one of a white, lop-eared breed of swine of Welsh origin that produces a large amount of lean meat. Also, **Welch.** [bef. 900; ME *Welische,* OE *Welisc,* deriv. of *Walh* Briton, foreigner (cf. L *Volcae* a Gallic tribe); c. G *welsch* foreign, Italian]

Welsh′ cor′gi, one of either of two Welsh breeds of dogs having short legs, erect ears, and a foxlike head. Cf. **Cardigan** (def. 2), **Pembroke** (def. 3). [1925–30]

Welsh corgi (Cardigan), 1 ft. (0.3 m) high at shoulder

Welsh′ dress′er, *Eng. Furniture.* a sideboard having drawers or compartments below and open, shallow shelves above. [1905–10]

Welsh•man (welsh′mən, welch′-), *n., pl.* **-men.** a native or inhabitant of Wales. Also, **Welchman.** [bef. 900; ME *Welische man,* OE *Wilisc mon;* see WELSH, MAN¹]

Welsh′ po′ny, one of a breed of small, sturdy ponies raised originally in Wales. [1765–75]

Welsh′ pop′py, a poppy, *Meconopsis cambrica,* of western Europe, having pale-green, slightly hairy foliage and pale-yellow flowers. [1735–45]

Welsh′ rab′bit, a dish of melted cheese, usually mixed with ale or beer, milk, and spices, served over toast. Also called **Welsh′ rare′bit.** [1715–25; prob. of jocular orig.; later *Welsh rarebit* by folk etym.]

Welsh′ spring′er span′iel, one of a Welsh breed of springer spaniels having a red and white coat. [1925–30]

Welsh′ ter′rier, one of a Welsh breed of terriers having a wiry, black-and-tan coat, resembling an Airedale but smaller. [1885–90]

Welsh terrier, 15 in. (38 cm) high at shoulder

CONCISE PRONUNCIATION KEY: act, cāpe, dâre, pärt; set, ēqual; if, ice; ox, ōver, ôrder, oil, bo͝ok, bo͞ot, out; up, ûrge; child; sing; shoe; thin, *th*at; zh as in *treasure.* ə = *a* as in *alone, e* as in *system, i* as in *easily, o* as in *gallop, u* as in *circus;* ᵊ as in *fire* (fīᵊr), *hour* (ouᵊr). l and n can serve as syllabic consonants, as in *cradle* (krād′l), and *button* (but′n). See the full key inside the front cover.

well′-oc′cu•pied′, *adj.*
well′-op′er•at′ed, *adj.*
well′-or′gan•ized′, *adj.*
well′-o′ri•ent′ed, *adj.*
well′-out′lined′, *adj.*
well′-packed′, *adj.*
well′-paid′, *adj.*
well′-paint′ed, *adj.*
well′-paired′, *adj.*
well′-par′a•graphed′, *adj.*
well′-parked′, *adj.*
well′-patched′, *adj.*
well′-pa•trolled′, *adj.*
well′-pa′tron•ized′, *adj.*
well′-paved′, *adj.*
well′-pay′ing, *adj.*
well′-pen′sioned, *adj.*
well′-peo′pled, *adj.*
well′-per•ceived′, *adj.*
well′-per•formed′, *adj.*
well′-per•suad′ed, *adj.*
well′-phi•los′o•phized′, *adj.*
well′-pho′to•graphed′, *adj.*
well′-picked′, *adj.*
well′-pi′lot•ed, *adj.*
well′-pitched′, *adj.*
well′-placed′, *adj.*
well′-planned′, *adj.*
well′-plant′ed, *adj.*
well′-played′, *adj.*
well′-pleased′, *adj.*
well′-plot′ted, *adj.*
well′-plowed′, *adj.*
well′-plucked′, *adj.*
well′-point′ed, *adj.*
well′-po•liced′, *adj.*
well′-pol′ished, *adj.*
well′-polled′, *adj.*
well′-pon′dered, *adj.*
well′-posed′, *adj.*
well′-po•si′tioned, *adj.*
well′-post′ed, *adj.*
well′-post•poned′, *adj.*
well′-prac′ticed, *adj.*
well′-pre•pared′, *adj.*
well′-pressed′, *adj.*
well′-priced′, *adj.*
well′-primed′, *adj.*
well′-prin′ci•pled, *adj.*
well′-print′ed, *adj.*
well′-prized′, *adj.*
well′-pro•longed′, *adj.*
well′-pro•nounced′, *adj.*
well′-pro•por′tioned, *adj.*
well′-pros′e•cut′ed, *adj.*
well′-pro•tect′ed, *adj.*
well′-proved′, *adj.*
well′-prov′en, *adj.*
well′-pro•vid′ed, *adj.*
well′-pub′lished, *adj.*
well′-pun′ished, *adj.*
well′-put′, *adj.*
well′-qual′i•fied′, *adj.*
well′-raised′, *adj.*
well′-rat′ed, *adj.*
well′-reared′, *adj.*
well′-rea′soned, *adj.*
well′-re•ceived′, *adj.*
well′-re•cit′ed, *adj.*
well′-rec′og•nized′, *adj.*
well′-rec′om•mend′ed, *adj.*
well′-re•cord′ed, *adj.*
well′-re•cov′ered, *adj.*
well′-re•ferred′, *adj.*
well′-re•fined′, *adj.*
well′-re•flect′ed, *adj.*
well′-re•freshed′, *adj.*
well′-re•gard′ed, *adj.*
well′-reg′u•lat′ed, *adj.*
well′-re•hearsed′, *adj.*
well′-re•marked′, *adj.*
well′-re•mem′bered, *adj.*
well′-ren′dered, *adj.*
well′-re•paid′, *adj.*
well′-re•paired′, *adj.*
well′-re•placed′, *adj.*
well′-re•plen′ished, *adj.*
well′-re•port′ed, *adj.*
well′-rep′re•sent′ed, *adj.*
well′-re•put′ed, *adj.*
well′-re•solved′, *adj.*
well′-re•spect′ed, *adj.*
well′-rest′ed, *adj.*
well′-re•stored′, *adj.*
well′-re•viewed′, *adj.*
well′-re•vised′, *adj.*
well′-re•ward′ed, *adj.*
well′-rhymed′, *adj.*
well′-rid′den, *adj.*
well′-rip′ened, *adj.*
well′-roast′ed, *adj.*
well′-rolled′, *adj.*
well′-root′ed, *adj.*
well′-rubbed′, *adj.*
well′-ruled′, *adj.*
well′-run′, *adj.*
well′-run′ning, *adj.*
well′-sac′ri•ficed′, *adj.*
well′-sail′ing, *adj.*
well′-salt′ed, *adj.*
well′-sanc′tioned, *adj.*
well′-sand′ed, *adj.*
well′-sat′is•fied′, *adj.*
well′-scat′tered, *adj.*
well′-scent′ed, *adj.*
well′-sched′uled, *adj.*
well′-schooled′, *adj.*
well′-scorched′, *adj.*
well′-scored′, *adj.*
well′-screened′, *adj.*
well′-scrubbed′, *adj.*
well′-sealed′, *adj.*
well′-searched′, *adj.*
well′-sea′soned, *adj.*
well′-seat′ed, *adj.*
well′-se•clud′ed, *adj.*
well′-se•cured′, *adj.*
well′-seed′ed, *adj.*
well′-se•lect′ed, *adj.*
well′-sep′a•rat′ed, *adj.*
well′-served′, *adj.*
well′-set′tled, *adj.*
well′-sewn′, *adj.*
well′-shad′ed, *adj.*
well′-shak′en, *adj.*
well′-shaped′, *adj.*
well′-sharp′ened, *adj.*
well′-shaved′, *adj.*
well′-shel′tered, *adj.*
well′-shod′, *adj.*
well′-shot′, *adj.*
well′-show′ered, *adj.*
well′-shown′, *adj.*
well′-sim′u•lat′ed, *adj.*
well′-sit′u•at′ed, *adj.*
well′-sized′, *adj.*
well′-sketched′, *adj.*
well′-skilled′, *adj.*
well′-soaked′, *adj.*
well′-sold′, *adj.*
well′-solved′, *adj.*
well′-sort′ed, *adj.*
well′-sound′ing, *adj.*
well′-spaced′, *adj.*
well′-speak′ing, *adj.*
well′-spent′, *adj.*
well′-spiced′, *adj.*
well′-sprayed′, *adj.*
well′-spun′, *adj.*
well′-stacked′, *adj.*
well′-staffed′, *adj.*
well′-staged′, *adj.*
well′-stained′, *adj.*
well′-stat′ed, *adj.*
well′-stirred′, *adj.*
well′-stitched′, *adj.*
well′-stocked′, *adj.*
well′-stored′, *adj.*
well′-straight′ened, *adj.*
well′-strained′, *adj.*
well′-strapped′, *adj.*
well′-stressed′, *adj.*
well′-stretched′, *adj.*
well′-stroked′, *adj.*
well′-strung′, *adj.*
well′-stud′ied, *adj.*
well′-stuffed′, *adj.*
well′-styled′, *adj.*
well′-sug′ared, *adj.*
well′-suit′ed, *adj.*
well′-sum′ma•rized′, *adj.*
well′-sun′burned′, *adj.*
well′-sun′burnt′, *adj.*
well′-sung′, *adj.*
well′-su′per•vised′, *adj.*
well′-sup′ple•ment′ed, *adj.*
well′-sup•plied′, *adj.*
well′-sup•port′ed, *adj.*
well′-sup•pressed′, *adj.*
well′-sus•tained′, *adj.*
well′-sys′tem•a•tized′, *adj.*
well′-tai′lored, *adj.*
well′-tamed′, *adj.*
well′-tanned′, *adj.*
well′-taught′, *adj.*
well′-taxed′, *adj.*
well′-tend′ed, *adj.*
well′-test′ed, *adj.*
well′-thought′, *adj.*
well′-thought′-out′, *adj.*
well′-thrashed′, *adj.*
well′-thrown′, *adj.*
well′-tied′, *adj.*
well′-tilled′, *adj.*
well′-tint′ed, *adj.*
well′-toast′ed, *adj.*
well′-told′, *adj.*
well′-toned′, *adj.*
well′-trained′, *adj.*
well′-trans•lat′ed, *adj.*
well′-trav′eled, *adj.*
well′-trav′elled, *adj.*
well′-treat′ed, *adj.*
well′-trod′, *adj.*
well′-trod′den, *adj.*
well′-trust′ed, *adj.*
well′-tuned′, *adj.*
well′-tu′tored, *adj.*
well′-typed′, *adj.*
well′-un′der•stood′, *adj.*
well′-u•nit′ed, *adj.*
well′-used′, *adj.*
well′-u′ti•lized′, *adj.*
well′-var′ied, *adj.*
well′-var′nished, *adj.*
well′-veiled′, *adj.*
well′-ven′ti•lat′ed, *adj.*
well′-ver′i•fied′, *adj.*
well′-vis′u•al•ized′, *adj.*
well′-voiced′, *adj.*
well′-vouched′, *adj.*
well′-warmed′, *adj.*
well′-warned′, *adj.*
well′-war′rant•ed, *adj.*
well′-washed′, *adj.*
well′-watched′, *adj.*
well′-wa′tered, *adj.*
well′-weighed′, *adj.*
well′-whipped′, *adj.*
well′-wind′ed, *adj.*
well′-win′dowed, *adj.*
well′-wired′, *adj.*
well′-wit′nessed, *adj.*
well′-won′, *adj.*
well′-wood′ed, *adj.*
well′-word′ed, *adj.*
well′-worked′, *adj.*
well′-wo′ven, *adj.*
well′-writ′ten, *adj.*
well′-wrought′, *adj.*
well′-yoked′, *adj.*

Welsh′ vault′. See **underpitch vault.** [1840–50]

Welsh·wom·an (welsh′wŏŏm′ən, welch′-), *n., pl.* **-wom·en.** a woman who is a native or inhabitant of Wales. [1400–50; late ME *Walsshwoman;* see WELSH, WOMAN]

welt (welt), *n.* **1.** a ridge or wale on the surface of the body, as from a blow of a stick or whip. **2.** a blow producing such a ridge or wale. **3.** *Shoemaking.* **a.** a strip, as of leather, set in between the outsole of a shoe and the edges of its insole and upper, through which these parts are joined by stitching or stapling. **b.** a strip, usually of leather, that ornaments a shoe. **4.** a strengthening or ornamental finish along a seam, the edge of a garment, etc. **5.** a seam in which one edge is cut close to the stitching line and covered by the other edge, which is stitched over it. —*v.t.* **6.** to beat soundly, as with a stick or whip. **7.** to furnish or supply (a shoe or garment) with a welt or welts; sew a welt on to. —*v.i.* **8.** to be marked with or develop welts. [1375–1425; late ME *welte, walt* shoemaker's welt, OE *wælt* (thigh) sinew]

Welt·an·schau·ung (velt′än′shou′ŏŏng), *n. German.* a comprehensive conception or image of the universe and of humanity's relation to it. [lit., world-view]

wel·ter[1] (wel′tər), *v.i.* **1.** to roll, toss, or heave, as waves or the sea. **2.** to roll, writhe, or tumble about; wallow, as animals (often fol. by *about*): *pigs weltering about happily in the mud.* **3.** to lie bathed in or be drenched in something, esp. blood. **4.** to become deeply or extensively involved, associated, entangled, etc.: *to welter in setbacks, confusion, and despair.* —*n.* **5.** a confused mass; a jumble or muddle: *a welter of anxious faces.* **6.** a state of commotion, turmoil, or upheaval: *the welter that followed the surprise attack.* **7.** a rolling, tossing, or tumbling about, as or as if by the sea, waves, or wind: *They found the shore through the mighty welter.* [1250–1300; ME, freq. (see -ER[6]) of *welten* to roll, OE *weltan;* c. MD *welteren,* LG *weltern* to roll]
—**Syn. 6.** confusion, tumult.

wel·ter[2] (wel′tər), *n.* **1.** *Informal.* a welterweight boxer or wrestler. —*adj.* **2.** (of a steeplechase or hurdle race) pertaining to, or noting a race in which the horses bear welterweights. [1785–95; WELT + -ER[1]]

wel·ter·weight (wel′tər wāt′), *n.* **1.** a boxer or other contestant intermediate in weight between a lightweight and a middleweight, esp. a professional boxer weighing up to 147 pounds (67 kg). **2.** (in a steeplechase or hurdle race) a weight of 28 pounds (13 kg) that is assigned to a horse in addition to the poundage assigned based on the age of the horse. **3.** a rider of steeplechase or hurdle-race horses who, though acting as a jockey, is of comparatively average weight and not small or lightweight as a professional jockey; heavyweight rider. [1815–25; WELTER[2] + WEIGHT]

Welt·schmerz (velt′shmerts′), *n. German.* sorrow that one feels and accepts as one's necessary portion in life; sentimental pessimism. Also, ***welt′schmerz′.*** [lit., world-pain]

Wel·ty (wel′tē), *n.* **Eu·do·ra** (yōō dôr′ə, -dōr′ə), born 1909, U.S. short-story writer and novelist.

Wem·bley (wem′blē), *n.* a former borough, now part of Brent, in SE England, near London.

Wemyss (wēmz), *n.* a parish in central Fife, in E Scotland, on the Firth of Forth: castle. 10,593.

wen[1] (wen), *n.* **1.** *Pathol.* a benign encysted tumor of the skin, esp. on the scalp, containing sebaceous matter; a sebaceous cyst. **2.** *Brit.* a large, crowded city or a crowded urban district: *London is the great wen of England.* [bef. 1000; ME, OE *wenn;* c. D *wen*]

wen[2] (wen), *n.* wynn.

We·natch·ee (wə nach′ē), *n.* a city in central Washington. 17,257.

Wen·ces·laus (wen′sis lôs′), *n.* **1.** Also, **Wen′ces·las′.** 1361–1419, emperor of the Holy Roman Empire 1378–1400; as Wenceslaus IV, king of Bohemia 1378–1419. **2. Saint** (*"Good King Wenceslaus"*), A.D. 903?–c935, duke of Bohemia 928–935. German, **Wenzel.**

wench (wench), *n.* **1.** a country lass or working girl: *The milkmaid was a healthy wench.* **2.** *Usually facetious.* a girl or young woman. **3.** *Archaic.* a strumpet. —*v.i.* **4.** to associate, esp. habitually, with promiscuous women. [1250–1300; ME, back formation from *wenchel,* OE *wencel* child, akin to *wancol* tottering, said of a child learning to walk; akin to G *wankeln* to totter] —**wench′er,** *n.*

Wen·chow (wen′chou′; *Chin.* wun′jō′), *n. Older Spelling.* Wenzhou. Also, *Wade-Giles,* **Wen′chou′.**

wend (wend), *v.,* **wend·ed** or (*Archaic*) **went; wend·ing.** —*v.t.* **1.** to pursue or direct (one's way). —*v.i.* **2.** to proceed or go. [bef. 900; ME *wenden,* OE *wendan;* c. D, G *wenden,* Goth *wandjan,* causative of *-windan* to WIND[2]]

Wend (wend), *n.* a member of a Slavic people of SE East Germany; Sorb. [1780–90; < G *Wende,* OHG *Winida;* c. OE *Winedas* (pl.)]

Wen·dell (wen′dl), *n.* a male given name.

Wend·ish (wen′dish), *adj.* **1.** of or pertaining to the Wends or their language; Sorbian. —*n.* **2.** Sorbian (def. 2). [1605–15; < G *wendisch,* equiv. to *Wende* WEND + *-isch* -ISH[1]]

Wen·dy (wen′dē), *n.* a female given name, form of **Gwendolyn.** Also, **Wen′die.**

Wen′dy house′, *Brit.* a child's playhouse. [1945–50; after the house that Peter Pan builds around Wendy in J. Barrie's *Peter Pan*]

CONCISE ETYMOLOGY KEY: <, descended or borrowed from; >, whence; b., blend of, blended; c., cognate with; cf., compare; deriv., derivative; equiv., equivalent; imit., imitative; obl., oblique; r., replacing; s., stem; sp., spelling, spelled; resp., respelling, respelled; trans., translation; ?, origin unknown; *, unattested; ‡, probably earlier than. See the full key inside the front cover.

wen·ny (wen′ē), *adj.,* **-ni·er, -ni·est. 1.** of the nature of or resembling a wen. **2.** having a wen or wens. [1590–1600; WEN[1] + -Y[1]]

We·no·nah (wi nō′nə), *n.* a female given name. Also, **We·no′na.**

Wens·ley·dale (wenz′lē dāl′), *n.* a rich, medium-hard, white cheese with blue veins, somewhat strong in flavor. Also called **Wens′leydale cheese′.** [1880–85; after *Wensleydale,* Yorkshire, England, where it is made]

went (went), *v.* **1.** pt. of **go. 2.** *Nonstandard.* a pp. of **go[1]. 3.** *Archaic.* a pt. and pp. of **wend.**

wen·tle·trap (wen′tl trap′), *n.* any of several marine gastropods of the family Epitonii (Scalariidae), having a whitish, spiraled shell. [1750–60; < D *wenteltrap,* earlier *wendeltrap* spiral staircase, equiv. to *wend(en)* to turn + freq. *-el-* (cf. *wentelen* to revolve) + *trap* TRAP[1])]

Went·worth (went′wûrth′), *n.* **1. Thomas, 1st Earl of Strafford.** See **Strafford, 1st Earl of. 2. William Charles,** 1793–1872, Australian political leader, author, and journalist.

wen-yen (wun′yun′), *n.* the formal, literary variety of written Chinese, as used in classical literature. Cf. **pai-hua.** [< Chin *wényán*]

Wen·zel (*Ger.* ven′tsəl), *n.* German form of **Wenceslaus.**

Wen·zhou (wœn′jō′), *n. Pinyin.* a seaport in SE Zhejiang province, in E China. 250,000. Also, **Wenchou, Wenchow.** Formerly, **Yongjia.**

wept (wept), *v.* pt. and pp. of **weep[1].**

were (wûr; *unstressed* wər; *Brit. also* wâr), *v.* a 2nd pers. sing. pt. indic., pl. pt. indic., and pt. subj. of **be.** [bef. 1000; ME; OE *wǣre* past subj., *wǣre* past ind. 2nd pers. sing. and *wǣron* past ind. pl. of *wesan* to be; c. D, G *waren,* Dan *var.* See WAS]
—**Usage.** See **subjunctive.**

we're (wēr), contraction of *we are: We're happy to see you.*
—**Usage.** See **contraction.**

were·n't (wûrnt, wûr′ənt), contraction of *were not: Weren't you surprised?*
—**Usage.** See **contraction.**

were·wolf (wâr′wŏŏlf′, wēr′-, wûr′-), *n., pl.* **-wolves** (-wŏŏlvz′). (in folklore and superstition) a human being who has changed into a wolf, or is capable of assuming the form of a wolf, while retaining human intelligence. Also, **werwolf.** [bef. 1000; ME *werwolf,* OE *werwulf,* equiv. to *wer* man (c. Goth *wair,* L *vir*) + *wulf* WOLF; c. MD *weerwolf,* OHG *werwolf*]

Wer·fel (*Ger.* ver′fəl), *n.* **Franz** (*Ger.* fränts), 1890–1945, Austrian novelist, poet, and dramatist, born in Czechoslovakia: in the U.S. after 1939.

wer·gild (wûr′gild, wer′-), *n.* (in Anglo-Saxon England and other Germanic countries) **1.** money paid to the relatives of a murder victim in compensation for loss and to prevent a blood feud. **2.** the amount of money fixed as compensation for the murder or disablement of a person, computed on the basis of rank. Also, **wer·geld** (wûr′geld, wer′-), **were′gild.** [1175–1225; ME (Scots) *weregylt,* OE *wer(e)gild,* equiv. to *wer* man (c. Goth *wair,* L *vir*) + *gild* GELD[2]; c. MD *weergelt,* OHG *wergelt;* see YIELD]

Wer·ner (wûr′nər; *for 1 also Ger.* ver′nər), *n.* **1. Al·fred** (al′fred, -frid; *Ger.* äl′frāt), 1866–1919, Swiss chemist: Nobel prize 1913. **2.** a male given name.

Wer·ne·ri·an (wûr nēr′ē ən, ver-), *adj.* pertaining to or characteristic of the views or the classificatory system of Alfred Werner. [WERNER + -IAN]

wer·ner·ite (wûr′nə rīt′), *n. Mineral.* a variety of scapolite. [1805–15; named after A. G. *Werner* (1750–1817), German mineralogist; see -ITE[1]]

Wer′nick·e-Kor′sa·koff syn′drome (vâr′ni kə-kôr′sə kôf′, -kof′), a disorder of the central nervous system characterized by abnormal eye movements, incoordination, confusion, and impaired memory and learning functions, caused by thiamine deficiency, and observed in chronic alcoholism. [1965–70; named after German neurologist Karl *Wernicke* (1848–1905) and Russian psychiatrist Sergeĭ Sergeevich *Korsakov* (1854–1900), who independently described it]

Wer′nick·e's apha′sia (vâr′ni kēz, -kəz), *Pathol.* a type of aphasia caused by a lesion in Wernicke's area of the brain and characterized by grammatical but more or less meaningless speech and an apparent inability to comprehend speech. [see WERNICKE'S AREA]

Wer′nick·e's ar′ea (vâr′ni kəz, -kēz), *Anat.* a portion of the left posterior temporal lobe of the brain, involved in the ability to understand words. [named after Karl *Wernicke* (1848–1905), German neurologist, who discovered it]

werste (vûrst, verst), *n.* verst.

wert (wûrt; *unstressed* wərt), *v. Archaic.* a 2nd pers. sing. pt. indic. and subj. of **be.**

wer·wolf (wâr′wŏŏlf′, wēr′-, wûr′-), *n., pl.* **-wolves** (-wŏŏlvz′). werewolf.

Wes (wes), *n.* a male given name, form of **Wesley.**

We·ser (vā′zər), *n.* a river in Germany, flowing N from S Lower Saxony into the North Sea. ab. 300 mi. (485 km) long.

We·ser·mün·de (*Ger.* vā′zər myn′də), *n.* former name of **Bremerhaven.**

wes·kit (wes′kit), *n.* a vest or waistcoat. [1855–60; phoneticized sp. of WAISTCOAT]

Wes·la·co (wes′lə kō′), *n.* a city in S Texas. 19,331.

Wes·ley (wes′lē, wez′-), *n.* **1. Charles,** 1707–88, English evangelist and hymnist. **2.** his brother **John,** 1703–91, English theologian and evangelist: founder of Methodism. **3.** a male given name.

Wes·ley·an (wes′lē ən, wez′-), *adj.* **1.** of or pertaining to John Wesley, founder of Methodism. **2.** pertaining to Methodism. —*n.* **3.** a follower of John Wesley. **4.** *Chiefly Brit.* a Methodist. [1765–75; WESLEY + -AN]

Wes·ley·an·ism (wes′lē ə niz′əm, wez′-), *n.* the evangelical principles taught by John Wesley; Methodism. Also, **Wes′ley·ism.** [1765–75; WESLEYAN + -ISM]

Wes′leyan Meth′odist, a member of any of the churches founded on the evangelical principles of John Wesley. [1790–1800]

Wes·sex (wes′iks), *n.* **1.** (in the Middle Ages) a kingdom, later an earldom, in S England. *Cap.:* Winchester. See map under **Mercia. 2.** the fictional setting of the novels of Thomas Hardy, principally identifiable with Dorsetshire.

Wes′sex cul′ture, *Archaeol.* an early Bronze Age culture of southern England, 1800–1400 B.C., known only from grave sites, grave goods, and megaliths and considered responsible for erecting the sarsen stones of the third building phase of Stonehenge.

west (west), *n.* **1.** a cardinal point of the compass, 90° to the left when facing north, corresponding to the point where the sun is seen to set. *Abbr.:* W **2.** the direction in which this point lies. **3.** (*usually cap.*) a region or territory situated in this direction, esp. the western part of the U.S., as distinguished from the East: *a vacation trip through the West.* **4.** (*cap.*) the western part of the world, as distinguished from the East or Orient; the Occident. **5.** (*cap.*) the non-Communist countries of Western Europe and the Americas. —*adj.* **6.** directed or proceeding toward the west. **7.** coming from the west: *a west wind.* **8.** lying toward or situated in the west. **9.** *Eccles.* designating, lying toward, or in that part of a church opposite to and farthest from the altar. —*adv.* **10.** to, toward, or in the west: *The car headed west.* **11.** from the west: *The wind blew west.* **12. go west,** *Informal.* to die. [bef. 900; ME, OE; c. D, G *west,* ON *vestr;* cf. F *ouest,* OF < OE]

West (west), *n.* **1. Benjamin,** 1738–1820, U.S. painter, in England after 1763. **2. Mae,** 1892?–1980, U.S. actress. **3. Nathanael** (*Nathan Wallenstein Weinstein*), 1902?–40, U.S. novelist. **4. Dame Rebecca** (*Cicily Isabel Fairfield Andrews*), 1892–1983, English novelist, journalist, and critic, born in Ireland.

West., western. Also, **west.**

West′ Al′lis (al′is), a city in SE Wisconsin, near Milwaukee. 63,982.

West·ar (wes′tär), *n.* one of a series of privately owned geostationary communications satellites that service commercial users in the U.S. [*West(ern Union st)ar*]

West′ Atlan′tic, a group of languages of W Africa constituting a branch of the Niger-Congo subfamily of languages, and including Fulani and Wolof.

West′ Bab′ylon, a city on S Long Island, in SE New York. 41,699.

West′ Bank′, an area in the Middle East, between the W bank of the Jordan River and the E frontier of Israel: occupied in 1967 and subsequently claimed by Israel; formerly held by Jordan.

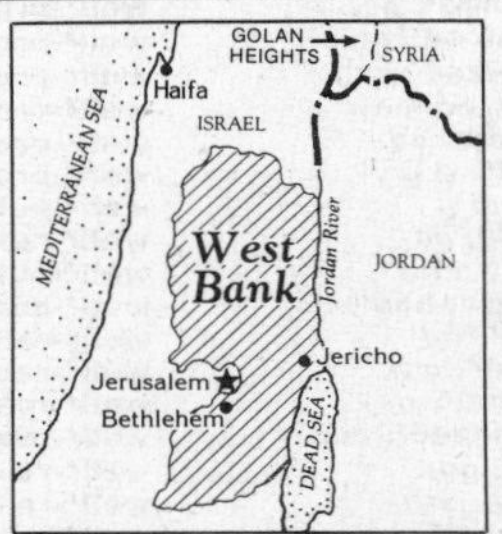

West′ Bend′, a town in SE Wisconsin. 21,484.

West′ Bengal′, a state in E India: formerly part of the province of Bengal. 50,900,000; 33,805 sq. mi. (87,555 sq. km). *Cap.:* Calcutta. Cf. **Bengal** (def. 1).

West′ Berlin′. See under **Berlin** (def. 2).

West·bor·ough (west′bûr′ō, -bur′ō), *n.* a town in central Massachusetts. 13,619.

west·bound (west′bound′), *adj.* proceeding or headed west. [1880–85, *Amer.;* WEST + -BOUND[2]]

West′ Brom′wich (brum′ij, -ich, brom′-), a city in West Midlands, in central England, near Birmingham. 166,626.

West·brook (west′brŏŏk′), *n.* a city in SW Maine. 14,976.

West·bur·y (west′ber′ē, -bə rē), *n.* a town on W Long Island, in SE New York. 14,644.

west′ by north′, *Navig., Survey.* a point on the compass 11°15′ north of west. *Abbr.:* WbN

west′ by south′, *Navig., Survey.* a point on the compass 11°15′ south of west. *Abbr.:* WbS

West′ Cald′well, a town in NE New Jersey. 11,407.

West′ Car′rollton, a town in W Ohio. 13,148.

West′ Ches′ter, a city in SE Pennsylvania. 17,435.

West·ches·ter (west′ches tər), *n.* a city in NE Illinois, near Chicago. 17,730.

West′ Chica′go, a town in NE Illinois. 12,550.

West′ Coast′, the western coast of the U.S., bordering the Pacific Ocean and comprising the coastal areas of California, Oregon, and Washington. —**West′-Coast′,** *adj.*

West′ Coast′ jazz′. See **cool jazz.** [1950–55]

West′ Colum′bia, a town in central South Carolina. 10,409.

West′ Covi′na, a city in SW California, E of Los Angeles. 80,094.

West′ Des Moines′, a city in S central Iowa, near Des Moines. 21,894.

west·er[1] (wes′tər), *n.* a wind or storm coming from the west. Cf. **northwester, southwester.** [1920–25; WEST + -ER[1]]

west·er[2] (wes′tər), *v.i.* **1.** (of heavenly bodies) to move or tend westward. **2.** to shift or veer toward the west. [1325–75; ME; see WEST, -ER[6]]

west·er·ing (wes′tər ing), *adj.* moving or shifting toward the west: *the westering sun; a westering wind.* [1375–1425; late ME; see WESTER[2], -ING[2]]

west·er·ly (wes′tər lē), *adj., adv., n., pl.* **-lies.** —*adj.* **1.** moving, directed, or situated toward the west: *the westerly end of the field.* **2.** (esp. of a wind) coming from the west: *a westerly gale.* —*adv.* **3.** toward the west: *to escape westerly.* **4.** from the west: *a sharp wind blowing westerly.* —*n.* **5.** a wind that blows from the west: *an occasional westerly that pommeled the island.* **6. westerlies,** (*used with a plural v.*) any semipermanent belt of westerly winds, esp. those that prevail at latitudes lying between the tropical and polar regions of the earth. [1570–80; WEST + *-erly*, as in *easterly*] —**west′er·li·ness,** *n.*

Wes·ter·ly (wes′tər lē), *n.* a town in SW Rhode Island. 18,580.

Wes·ter·marck (wes′tər märk′; *Fin.* ves′tər märk′), *n.* **Ed·ward Al·ex·an·der** (ed′wərd al′ig zan′dər, -zän′-; *Fin.* ed′värd ä′lek sän′dər), 1862–1939, Finnish sociologist.

west·ern (wes′tərn), *adj.* **1.** lying toward or situated in the west: *our company's western office.* **2.** directed or proceeding toward the west: *a western migration.* **3.** coming or originating from the west, as a wind. **4.** (*often cap.*) of, pertaining to, living in, or characteristic of the West, esp. the western U.S.: *a Western ranch.* **5.** (*usually cap.*) Occidental: *to adopt Western dress.* **6.** (*usually cap.*) of or pertaining to the non-Communist countries of Europe and the Americas: *Western trade agreements.* **7.** (*cap.*) of or pertaining to the Western Church. —*n.* **8.** (*often cap.*) a story, movie, or radio or television play about the U.S. West of the 19th century. **9.** See **western sandwich. 10.** a person or thing from a western region or country. [bef. 1050; 1905–10 for def. 8; ME, OE *westerne,* equiv. to *west* WEST + *-erne* -ERN]

West′ern Austral′ia, a state in W Australia. 1,273,624; 975,920 sq. mi. (2,527,635 sq. km). *Cap.:* Perth. —**West′ern Austral′ian.**

West′ern blot′, *Biol., Med.* a highly sensitive procedure for identifying and measuring the amount of a specific protein in a mixed extract, as in testing for AIDS virus protein in a blood sample: proteins are separated by gel electrophoresis and transferred to a special filter paper, on which the protein under investigation can be detected by a probe, as the binding of a labeled antibody. [orig. a facetious counterpart to SOUTHERN BLOT]

West′ern Church′, the Roman Catholic Church, sometimes with the Anglican Church, or, more broadly, the Christian churches of the West. [1620–30]

west′ern dia′mondback rat′tlesnake, an extremely venomous diamondback rattlesnake, *Crotalus atrox,* of the southwestern U.S. and Mexico.

West′ern Em′pire. See **Western Roman Empire.**

West·ern·er (wes′tər nər), *n.* (*sometimes l.c.*) a native or inhabitant of the West, esp. of the western U.S. [1830–40, *Amer.*; WESTERN + -ER[1]]

west′ern frame′. See **platform frame.**

West′ern Ghats′, a low mountain range in W India, along the W margin of the Deccan plateau and bordering on the Arabian Sea. ab. 1000 mi. (1600 km) long.

West′ern Han′. See **Earlier Han.**

West′ern Hem′isphere, 1. the western part of the terrestrial globe, including North and South America, their islands, and the surrounding waters. **2.** that half of the earth traversed in passing westward from the prime meridian to 180° longitude.

west′ern hem′lock, a tall, narrow hemlock, *Tsuga heterophylla,* of western North America: the state tree of Washington.

West′ern Hin′di, the vernacular of the western half of the Hindi-speaking area in India: the basis of Hindustani and of literary Hindi and Urdu.

West′ern In′dia States′, a former association of states in W India, largely on Kathiawar peninsula.

West′ern Is′lands, Hebrides.

west·ern·ism (wes′tər niz′əm), *n.* (*often cap.*) a word, idiom, or practice characteristic of people of the Occident or of the western U.S. [1830–40, *Amer.*; WESTERN + -ISM]

west·ern·ize (wes′tər nīz′), *v.t.,* **-ized, -iz·ing.** to influence with ideas, customs, practices, etc., characteristic of the Occident or of the western U.S. Also, *esp. Brit.,* **west′ern·ise′.** [1830–40; WESTERN + -IZE] —**west′·ern·i·za′tion,** *n.*

west′ern ju′niper, a round-headed tree, *Juniperus occidentalis,* of the western coast of the U.S., having scalelike leaves with a gland on the back and oval, blue-black fruit.

west′ern low′land goril′la. See under **gorilla.**

west′ern mead′owlark. See under **meadowlark.**

west·ern·most (wes′tərn mōst′ *or, esp. Brit.,* -məst), *adj.* most western or westerly; farthest west. [1695–1705; WESTERN + -MOST]

west′ern moun′tain ash′, a mountain ash, *Sorbus sitchensis,* of western North America.

West′ern O′cean, *Naut.* the North Atlantic Ocean.

west′ern om′elet, an omelet prepared with diced green peppers, onions, and ham. [1935–40]

west′ern red′ ce′dar, 1. an arborvitae, *Thuja plicata,* of western North America, grown as an ornamental. **2.** the soft, fragrant, reddish wood of this tree, used in the construction of houses, in shipbuilding, for making boxes, etc. [1900–05, *Amer.*]

West′ern Reserve′, a tract of land in NE Ohio reserved by Connecticut (1786) when its rights to other land in the western U.S. were ceded to the federal government; relinquished in 1800.

West′ern Ro′man Em′pire, the western portion of the Roman Empire after its division, A.D. 395, which became extinct A.D. 476. Also called **Western Empire.**

West′ern sad′dle, a heavy saddle having a deep seat, high cantle and pommel, pommel horn, wide leather flaps for protecting the rider's legs, and little padding. Also called **stock saddle.** See illus. under **saddle.** [1910–15, *Amer.*]

West′ern Sahar′a, a region in NW Africa on the Atlantic coast, bounded by Morocco, Algeria, and Mauritania: a former Spanish province comprising Río de Oro and Saguia el Hamra 1884–1976; divided between Morocco and Mauritania 1976; claimed entirely by Morocco 1979, but still under dispute. 165,000; ab. 102,700 sq. mi. (266,000 sq. km). Formerly, **Spanish Sahara.**

West′ern Samo′a, an independent country comprising the W part of Samoa: formerly a trust territory of New Zealand. 148,565; 1133 sq. mi. (2935 sq. km). *Cap.:* Apia. Cf. **Samoa, American Samoa.** —**West′ern Samo′an.**

west′ern sand′wich, a sandwich with a western omelet for a filling.

West′ern Slavs′. See under **Slav** (def. 1).

West′ern Springs′, a city in NE Illinois. 12,876.

west′ern tan′ager, a tanager, *Piranga ludoviciana,* of western North America, the male of which is black, yellow, and orange-red.

West′ern Thrace′. See under **Thrace** (def. 2).

West′ern Wall′, a wall in Jerusalem where Jews, on certain occasions, assemble for prayer and lamentation: traditionally believed to be the remains of the western wall of Herod's temple, destroyed by the Romans in A.D. 70. Also called **Wailing Wall.**

west′ern wool′. See **territory wool.**

west′ern yel′low pine′. See **ponderosa pine.** [1900–05, *Amer.*]

Wes·ter·ville (wes′tər vil′), *n.* a town in central Ohio. 23,414.

West·fa·len (vest fä′lən), *n.* German name of **Westphalia.**

West′ Far′go, a city in SE North Dakota: suburb of Fargo. 10,099.

West·field (west′fēld′), *n.* **1.** a city in S Massachusetts. 36,465. **2.** a city in NE New Jersey. 30,447.

West′ Flan′ders, a province in W Belgium. 1,071,604; 1249 sq. mi. (3235 sq. km). *Cap.:* Bruges.

West·ford (west′fərd), *n.* a city in NE Massachusetts. 13,434.

West′ Fri′sian Is′lands. See under **Frisian Islands.**

West′ German′ic, 1. a subbranch of Germanic that includes English, Frisian, Flemish, Dutch, Plattdeutsch, Yiddish, and German. *Abbr.:* WGmc **2.** of or pertaining to this subbranch of Germanic. [1890–95]

West′ Ger′many, a former republic in central Europe: created in 1949 by the coalescing of the British, French, and U.S. zones of occupied Germany established in 1945. 62,080,000; 96,025 sq. mi. (248,706 sq. km). *Cap.:* Bonn. Official name, **Federal Republic of Germany.** Cf. **Germany.** —**West′ Ger′man.**

West′ Glamor′gan, a county in S Wales. 371,700; 315 sq. mi. (815 sq. km).

West′ Goth′, a Visigoth. [erroneous trans. of LL *Visigothus* VISIGOTH]

West′ Green′land Cur′rent, an ocean current flowing northward along the west coast of Greenland.

West′ Ham′ (ham), a former borough, now part of Newham, in SE England, near London.

West′ Hart′ford, a town in central Connecticut. 61,301.

West′ Har′tle·pool (här′tl po͞ol′, härt′lē-), a former borough, now part of Hartlepool, in Cleveland County, in NE England, at the mouth of the Tees.

West′ Ha′ven, a town in S Connecticut, near New Haven. 53,184.

West′ Hel′e·na (hel′ə nə), a city in E Arkansas. 11,367.

West′ Hemp′stead, a city on W Long Island, in SE New York. 18,536.

West′ High′land, any of a breed of small, hardy, usually dun-colored, shaggy beef cattle with long, widespread horns, able to withstand the cold and sparse pasturage of its native western Scottish uplands. Also called **Scotch Highland, Kyloe;** *Brit.* **Highland.** [1870–75]

West′ High′land white′ ter′rier, one of a Scottish breed of small compact terriers having a white coat, erect ears and tail, originally developed as a hunting dog for small game. [1900–05]

West′ Hol′lywood, a city in SW California, near Los Angeles. 35,703.

West·ie (wes′tē), *n.* See **West Highland white terrier.**

West′ In′dian ce′dar. See **Spanish cedar.**

West′ In′dian gher′kin, gherkin (def. 2).

West′ In′dian kale′, malanga.

West′ In′dies, 1. Also called **the Indies.** an archipelago in the N Atlantic between North and South America, comprising the Greater Antilles, the Lesser Antilles, and the Bahamas. **2. Federation of.** Also called **West′ In′dies Federa′tion.** a former federation (1958–62) of the British islands in the Caribbean, comprising Barbados, Jamaica, Trinidad, Tobago, and the Windward and Leeward island colonies. —**West′ In′dian.**

West′ In′dies Asso′ciated States′, a former group (1967–81) of territorial islands in the West Indies in association with the United Kingdom: original members included Antigua, Dominica, Grenada, St. Kitts-Nevis-Anguilla, St. Lucia, and St. Vincent.

west·ing (wes′ting), *n.* **1.** *Navig.* the distance due west made good on any course tending westward; westerly departure. **2.** *Survey.* a distance west from a north-south reference line. [1620–30; WEST + -ING[1]]

West·ing·house (wes′ting hous′), *n.* **George,** 1846–1914, U.S. inventor and manufacturer.

West′inghouse brake′, a railroad air brake operated by compressed air. [named after G. WESTINGHOUSE, its inventor]

West′ I′ri·an (ēr′ē än′), a former name of **Irian Jaya.**

West′ I′slip, a city on S Long Island, in SE New York. 29,533.

West′ Jor′dan, a town in N central Utah. 26,794.

West′ Lafayette′, a city in central Indiana: suburb of Lafayette. 21,247.

West·lake (west′lāk′), *n.* a city in N Ohio. 19,483.

West·land (west′lənd), *n.* a city in SE Michigan, near Detroit. 84,603.

West′ Linn′ (lin), a town in NW Oregon. 12,956.

West′ Lo′thi·an (lō′thē ən), a historic county in S Scotland. Formerly, **Linlithgow.**

Westm., Westminster.

West·meath (west′mēth′, -mēth′), *n.* a county in Leinster in the N central Republic of Ireland. 61,300; 681 sq. mi. (1765 sq. km). *Co. seat:* Mullingar.

West′ Mem′phis, a city in E Arkansas, on the Mississippi. 28,138.

West′ Mid′lands, a metropolitan county in central England. 2,777,500; 347 sq. mi. (899 sq. km).

West′ Miff′lin (mif′lin), a city in W Pennsylvania, on the Monongahela River. 26,279.

West·min·ster (west′min′stər), *n.* **1.** a central borough (officially a city) of Greater London, England: Westminster Abbey, Houses of Parliament, Buckingham Palace. 214,000. **2.** a city in SW California. 71,133. **3.** a city in NE Colorado. 50,211.

West′minster Ab′bey, a Gothic church in London, England.

West′minster Assem′bly, a convocation that met at Westminster, London, 1643–49, and formulated the articles of faith **(West′minster Confes′sion of Faith′)** that are accepted as authoritative by most Presbyterian churches.

West′ Monroe′, a city in N Louisiana. 14,993.

West·mont (west′mont), *n.* a town in NE Illinois. 16,718.

West·more·land (west′môr′lənd, -mōr′-), *n.* **William Childs** (chīldz), born 1914, U.S. army officer: commander of U.S. forces in Vietnam and Thailand 1964–68.

West·mor·land (west′môr′lənd, -mōr′-; *Brit.* west′-mər lənd), *n.* a former county in NW England, now part of Cumbria, partially in the Lake District.

west·most (west′mōst′ *or, esp. Brit.,* -məst), *adj.* westernmost. [bef. 900; ME; r. ME, OE *westmest;* see WEST, -MOST]

West·mount (west′mount′), *n.* a city in S Quebec, in E Canada: suburb of Montreal. 20,480.

West′ New′ York′, a town in NE New Jersey, across the Hudson from New York City. 39,194.

West′ Nor′ri·ton (nôr′i tn, nor′-), a town in SE Pennsylvania. 14,034.

west-north·west (west′nôrth′west′; *Naut.* west′-nôr′west′), *Navig., Survey.* —*n.* **1.** a point on the compass midway between west and northwest. —*adj.* **2.** coming from this point: *a west-northwest wind.* **3.** directed toward this point: *a west-northwest course.* —*adv.* **4.** toward this point: *sailing west-northwest. Abbr.:* WNW [1400–50; late ME]

west-north·west·ward (west′nôrth′west′wərd; *Naut.* west′nôr′west′wərd), *Naut.* —*adj.* **1.** moving, bearing, facing, or situated toward the west-northwest. —*adv.* **2.** toward the west-northwest. Also, **west′-north′west′ward·ly.** [WEST-NORTHWEST + -WARD]

Wes·ton (wes′tən), *n.* **1. Edward,** 1886–1958, U.S. photographer. **2.** a city in NE Massachusetts. 11,169.

Wes′ton cell′, *Trademark.* a brand of cadmium cell. Also called **Wes′ton stand′ard cell′.**

West′ Or′ange, a town in NE New Jersey, near Newark. 39,510.

West′ Pa′kistan, a former province of British Pakistan, separated from East Pakistan (now Bangladesh) by N India: declared independence as Republic of Pakistan 1956.

West′ Palm′ Beach′, a city in SE Florida: winter resort. 62,530.

West′ Pat′erson, a town in NE New Jersey. 11,293.

West·pha·li·a (west fā′lē ə, -fāl′yə), *n.* a former province in NW Germany, now a part of North Rhine-

Westphalia: treaty ending the Thirty Years' War 1648. German, **Westfalen.** —**West·pha′li·an,** *adj., n.*

Westpha′lian ham′, a hard German ham with a distinctive flavor derived from being smoked over beechwood and juniper. [1655–65]

West′ Point′, a military reservation in SE New York, on the Hudson: U.S. Military Academy.

West·po·li·tik (vest′pō li tēk′), *n.* a policy of a Communist country of adopting trade and diplomatic relations with non-Communist nations. Cf. **Ostpolitik.** [1965–70; < G: Western policy]

West·port (west′pôrt′, -pōrt′), *n.* **1.** a town in SW Connecticut. 25,290. **2.** a city in SE Massachusetts. 13,763.

West′ Prus′sia, a former province of Prussia: since 1945 part of Poland. German, **West·preus·sen** (vest′-proi′sən). —**West′ Prus′sian.**

West′ Puen′te Val′ley (pwen′tē, -tā), a town in SW California. 20,445.

West′ Ri′ding (rī′ding), a former administrative division of Yorkshire, England.

West′ Sax′on, 1. the Old English dialect of the West Saxon kingdom, dominant after A.D. c850 and the medium of nearly all the literary remains of Old English. **2.** any of the English of the period before the Norman Conquest who lived in the region south of the Thames and west of Surrey and Sussex. **3.** a person whose native tongue was West Saxon. **4.** of or pertaining to the West Saxons or their dialect. [1350–1400; ME, for OE *Westseaxan* WESSEX; see WEST, SAXON]

West′ Sen′eca, a city in NW New York, near Buffalo. 51,210.

west-south·west (west′south′west′; *Naut.* west′-sou′west′), *Navig., Survey.* —*n.* **1.** a point on the compass midway between west and southwest. —*adj.* **2.** coming from this point: *a west-southwest wind.* **3.** directed toward this point: *a west-southwest course.* —*adv.* **4.** toward this point: *sailing west-southwest. Abbr.:* WSW [1350–1400; ME]

west-south·west·ward (west′south′west′wərd; *Naut.* west′sou′west′wərd), *Naut.* —*adj.* **1.** moving, bearing, facing, or situated toward the west-southwest. —*adv.* **2.** toward the west-southwest. Also, **west′-south′west′ward·ly.** [WEST-SOUTHWEST + -WARD]

West′ Spring′field, a city in SW Massachusetts, near Springfield. 27,042.

West St. Paul, a city in SE Minnesota, near St. Paul. 18,527.

West′ Suf′folk, a former administrative division of Suffolk, in E England.

West′ Sus′sex, a county in SE England. 623,100; 778 sq. mi. (2015 sq. km).

West′ Three′ Riv′ers, a town in S Quebec, in E Canada. 13,107. French, **Trois-Rivières-Ouest.**

West′ Univer′sity Place′, a city in SE Texas. 12,010.

West′ Virgin′ia, a state in the E United States. 1,949,644; 24,181 sq. mi. (62,629 sq. km). *Cap.:* Charleston. *Abbr.:* WV (for use with zip code), W.Va. —**West′ Virgin′ian.**

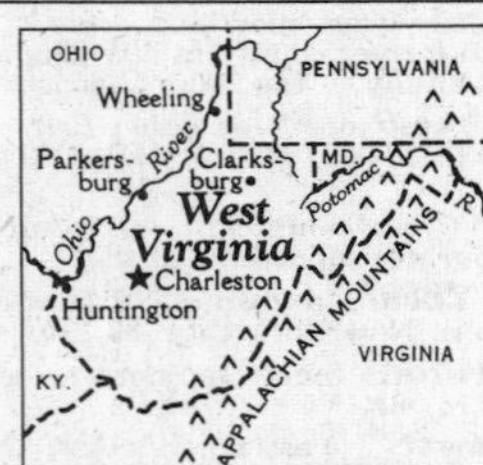

West·wall (west′wôl′; *Ger.* vest′väl′), *n.* See **Siegfried line.**

west·ward (west′wərd), *adj.* **1.** moving, bearing, facing, or situated toward the west: *a westward migration of farm workers.* —*adv.* **2.** Also, **west′wards.** toward the west; west: *a train moving westward.* —*n.* **3.** the westward part, direction, or point: *The wind had veered to the westward.* [bef. 900; ME; OE *westweard.* See WEST, -WARD]

west·ward·ly (west′wərd lē), *adj.* **1.** having a westward direction or situation: *the westwardly migration of the 1850's.* —*adv.* **2.** toward the west. [1510–20; WESTWARD + -LY]

West′ War′wick (wôr′ik, -wik, wor′-), a town in E Rhode Island, near Providence. 27,026.

West·we·go (west wē′gō), *n.* a town in SE Louisiana. 12,663.

West′ Wind′ Drift′ (wind). See **Antarctic Circumpolar Current.**

West·wood (west′wo͝od′), *n.* **1.** a city in E Massachusetts. 13,212. **2.** a town in NE New Jersey. 10,714.

west·work (west′wûrk′), *n.* (in German Romanesque architecture) a monumental western front to a church, treated as a tower or towers containing an entrance and vestibule below and a chapel above. [WEST + WORK]

West′ York′shire, a metropolitan county in N England. 2,082,600; 787 sq. mi. (2039 sq. km).

wet (wet), *adj.,* **wet·ter, wet·test,** *n., v.,* **wet** or **wet·ted, wet·ting.** —*adj.* **1.** moistened, covered, or soaked with water or some other liquid: *wet hands.* **2.** in a liquid form or state: *wet paint.* **3.** characterized by the presence or use of water or other liquid. **4.** moistened or dampened with rain; rainy: *Wet streets make driving hazardous.* **5.** allowing or favoring the sale of alcoholic beverages: *a wet town.* **6.** characterized by frequent rain, mist, etc.: *the wet season.* **7.** laden with a comparatively high percent of moisture or vapor, esp. water vapor: *There was a wet breeze from the west.* **8.** *Informal.* **a.** intoxicated. **b.** marked by drinking: *a wet night.* **9.** using water or done under or in water, as certain chemical, mining, and manufacturing processes. **10. all wet,** *Informal.* completely mistaken; in error: *He insisted that our assumptions were all wet.* **11. wet behind the ears,** immature; naive; green: *She was too wet behind the ears to bear such responsibilities.* —*n.* **12.** something that is or makes wet, as water or other liquid; moisture: *The wet from the earth had made the basement unlivable.* **13.** damp weather; rain: *Stay out of the wet as much as possible.* **14.** a person in favor of allowing the manufacture and sale of alcoholic beverages. **15.** *Informal (disparaging and offensive).* a wetback. —*v.t.* **16.** to make (something) wet, as by moistening or soaking (sometimes fol. by *through* or *down*): *Wet your hands before soaping them.* **17.** to urinate on or in: *The dog had wet the carpet.* —*v.i.* **18.** to become wet (sometimes fol. by *through* or *down*): *Dampness may cause plastered walls to wet. My jacket has wet through.* **19.** (of animals and children) to urinate. **20. wet out,** to treat (fabric) with a wetting agent to increase its absorbency. **21. wet one's whistle.** See **whistle** (def. 16). [bef. 900; ME *wett,* ptp. of *weten,* OE *wǣtan* to wet; r. ME *weet,* OE *wǣt,* c. OFris *wēt,* ON *vātr;* akin to WATER] —**wet′ly,** *adv.* —**wet′ness,** *n.* —**wet′ter,** *n.* —**wet′·tish,** *adj.*

—**Syn. 1.** dampened, drenched. **4.** misty, drizzling. **7.** humid. **12.** wetness, humidity, dampness, dankness. **13.** drizzle. **16.** WET, DRENCH, SATURATE, SOAK imply moistening something. To WET is to moisten in any manner with water or other liquid: *to wet or dampen a cloth.* DRENCH suggests wetting completely as by a downpour: *A heavy rain drenched the fields.* SATURATE implies wetting to the limit of absorption: *to saturate a sponge.* To SOAK is to keep in a liquid for a time: *to soak beans before baking.* —**Ant. 1.** dry.

wet·back (wet′bak′), *n. Disparaging and Offensive.* a Mexican laborer who enters the U.S. illegally, as by wading the Rio Grande. [1945–50, *Amer.;* WET + BACK[1]]

wet′ bar′, a small bar equipped with a sink and running water, for making and serving cocktails at home, in a hotel suite, or the like. [1965–70]

wet′ blan′ket, 1. a blanket dampened with water so as to extinguish a fire. **2.** a person or thing that dampens enthusiasm or enjoyment: *Nobody asked him to join the group because he's such a wet blanket.* [1655–65]

wet-blan·ket (wet′blang′kit), *v.t.* **1.** to extinguish (a fire) with a wet blanket. **2.** to dampen the enthusiasm or enjoyment of (a person, group, etc.). [1865–70]

wet′-bulb thermom′eter (wet′bulb′), a thermometer having a bulb that is kept moistened when humidity determinations are being made with a psychrometer. Cf. **dry-bulb thermometer.** [1840–50]

wet′ cell′, *Elect.* a cell whose electrolyte is in liquid form and free to flow.

wet′ collo′dion proc′ess, *Photog.* See **wet plate process.**

wet′ com′pass, *Navig.* a compass having a compass card floating in a liquid. Also called **liquid compass.** Cf. **dry compass.**

wet′ con′tact, *Elect.* a contact through which direct current flows.

wet′ dock′, *Naut.* a dock accessible only around the time of high tide and entered through locks or gates. [1620–30]

wet′ dream′. See **nocturnal emission.** [1850–55]

wet′ fly′, *Angling.* an artificial fly designed for use underwater. Cf. **dry fly.** [1870–75]

weth·er (weth′ər), *n.* **1.** a castrated male sheep. **2.** Also called **weth′er wool′.** wool from previously shorn sheep. [bef. 900; ME, OE; c. OS *withar,* OHG *widar,* ON *vethr,* Goth *withrus*]

Weth·ers·field (weth′ərz fēld′), *n.* a town in central Connecticut. 26,013.

wet·land (wet′land′), *n.* Often, **wetlands.** land that has a wet and spongy soil, as a marsh, swamp, or bog. [1770–80; WET + -LAND]

wet′ machine′, *Papermaking.* a machine for dewatering pulp.

wet′ mop′, a long-handled, absorbent mop designed to clean floors with water.

wet-mop (wet′mop′), *v.t.,* **-mopped, -mop·ping.** to clean (a floor) with a wet mop.

wet′ nurse′, a woman hired to suckle another's infant. [1610–20]

wet-nurse (wet′nûrs′), *v.t.,* **-nursed, -nurs·ing. 1.** to act as a wet nurse to (an infant). **2.** to give excessive care or attention to; treat as if helpless: *The warden is accused of wet-nursing his prisoners.* [1775–85]

wet′ pack′, *Med.* a type of bath in which wet sheets are applied to the patient.

wet′ plate′ proc′ess, a photographic process, in common use in the mid-19th century, employing a glass photographic plate coated with iodized collodion and dipped in a silver nitrate solution immediately before use. Also called **wet collodion process, collodion process.**

wet·proof (wet′pro͞of′), *adj.* waterproof. [WET + -PROOF]

wet′ pud′dling, *Metall.* puddling on a hearth rich in iron oxide so that carbon monoxide is generated, giving the iron the appearance of boiling. Also called **pig boiling.** Cf. **dry puddling.**

wet′-rice′ ag′riculture (wet′rīs′), the cultivation of rice by planting on dry land, transferring the seedlings to a flooded field, and draining the field before harvesting.

wet′ strength′, *Papermaking.* the relative resistance of paper to tearing when wet, resulting from the addition of resins during manufacture.

wet′ suit′, a close-fitting rubber garment worn by a skin diver in cold water that allows a thin, insulating layer of water to collect between the diver's skin and the suit in order to retain body heat. [1950–55]

wet·ta·bil·i·ty (wet′ə bil′i tē), *n.* **1.** the condition of being wettable. **2.** the degree or extent to which something absorbs or can be made to absorb moisture. [1925–30; WETT(ABLE) + -ABILITY]

wet·ta·ble (wet′ə bəl), *adj.* **1.** able to be wetted. **2.** made soluble or receptive to moisture, as by the addition of a chemical agent. [1880–85; WET + -ABLE]

Wet·ter·horn (vet′ər hôrn′), *n.* a mountain in S Switzerland, in the Bernese Alps. 12,149 ft. (3715 m).

wet′ting a′gent, *Chem.* any admixture to a liquid for increasing its ability to penetrate, or spread over the surface of, a given material, esp. cloth, paper, or leather. [1935–40]

wet′ wash′, laundry that has been washed but not dried or ironed. Cf. **dry wash** (def. 1). [1915–20]

we've (wēv), contraction of *we have: We've been here for an hour.*

—**Usage.** See **contraction.**

Wex·ford (weks′fərd), *n.* **1.** a county in Leinster province, in the SE Republic of Ireland. 99,016; 908 sq. mi. (2350 sq. km). **2.** its county seat: a seaport. 11,396.

wey (wā), *n., pl.* **weys. 1.** an old British unit of weight of various values, esp. 16 stones of 16 pounds each, or 256 pounds. **2.** an old Scotch-Irish unit of capacity equal to 40 U.S. bushels. [bef. 900; ME; OE *wǣge* weight. See WEIGH]

Wey·den (vīd′n), *n.* **Roger** or **Ro·gier** (*Flem.* RÔ GĒR′) **van der** (van dər; *Flem.* vän dər), 1400?–64, Flemish painter.

Wey·gand (vā gän′), *n.* **Ma·xime** (MAK sēm′), 1867–1965, French general.

Weyl (vīl), *n.* **Her·mann** (hûr′mən; *Ger.* heʀ′män), 1885–1955, German mathematician, in the U.S. after 1933.

Wey·mouth (wā′məth), *n.* a town in E Massachusetts, S of Boston. 55,601.

WF, white female.

wf, *Print.* See **wrong font.** Also, **w.f.**

WFTU, World Federation of Trade Unions. Also, **W.F.T.U.**

W.G., 1. water gauge. **2.** weight guaranteed. **3.** wire gauge. Also, **w.g.**

WGA, Writers Guild of America.

W. Ger., 1. West Germanic. **2.** West Germany.

WGmc, West Germanic. Also, **W. Gmc.**

WH, *Banking.* withholding.

Wh, watt-hour; watt-hours. Also, **wh, whr**

WHA, World Hockey Association.

wha·cha·ma·call·it (hwuch′ə mə kôl′it, hwoch′-, wuch′-, woch′-), *n. Informal.* an object or person whose name one does not know or cannot recall. Also, **what-chamacallit, what-you-may-call-it, what-do-you-call-it.** [1940–45; sp. of *what you may call it* reflecting affrication of *t* before *y* and reduction of vowels; cf. similar metric pattern and internal *əmə* in RIGAMAROLE, THINGAMAGIG]

whack (hwak, wak), *v.t.* **1.** to strike with a smart, resounding blow or blows. **2.** *Slang.* to divide into or take in shares (often fol. by *up*): *Whack the loot between us two.* —*v.i.* **3.** to strike a smart, resounding blow or blows. **4. whack off, a.** to cut off or separate with a blow: *The cook whacked off the fish's head.* **b.** *Slang (vulgar).* to masturbate. **5. whack out,** *Slang.* to produce quickly or, sometimes, carelessly: *She whacks out a short story every week or so.* —*n.* **6.** a smart, resounding blow: *a whack with his hand.* **7.** *Informal.* a trial or attempt: *to take a whack at a job.* **8.** *Slang.* a portion or share. **9. out of whack,** *Informal.* out of order or alignment; not in proper condition. [1710–20; orig. dial., Scots form of THWACK; cf. WHANG[2], WHITTLE] —**whack′er,** *n.*

—**Syn. 7.** try, go, turn.

whacked (hwakt, wakt), *adj. Chiefly Brit. Slang.* exhausted; tired out. [1915–20; WHACK + -ED[2]]

whacked-out (hwakt′out′, wakt′-), *adj. Slang.* **1.** tired; exhausted; worn-out. **2.** wacky; crazy. **3.** stupefied or crazed by narcotic drugs or alcohol; stoned. Also, **wacked-out.** [1965–70]

whack·ing (hwak′ing, wak′-), *adj. Informal.* large. [1800–10; WHACK + -ING[2]]

whack·o (hwak′ō, wak′ō), *n., pl.* **whack·os,** *adj. Slang.* —*n.* **1.** wacko. —*adj.* **2.** wacky. [1975–80; WHACK(Y) + -O]

whack·y (hwak′ē, wak′ē), *adj.,* **whack·i·er, whack·i·est.** *Slang.* wacky.

whale[1] (hwāl, wāl), *n., pl.* **whales,** (*esp. collectively*) **whale,** *v.,* **whaled, whal·ing.** —*n.* **1.** any of the larger marine mammals of the order Cetacea, esp. as distinguished from the smaller dolphins and porpoises, having

CONCISE ETYMOLOGY KEY: <, descended or borrowed from; >, whence; b., blend of, blended; c., cognate with; cf., compare; deriv., derivative; equiv., equivalent; imit., imitative; obl., oblique; r., replacing; s., stem; sp., spelling, spelled; resp., respelling, respelled; trans., translation; ?, origin unknown; *, unattested; ‡, probably earlier than. See the full key inside the front cover.

a fishlike body, forelimbs modified into flippers, and a head that is horizontally flattened. **2.** *Informal.* something big, great, or fine of its kind: *I had a whale of a time in Europe.* **3.** (*cap.*) *Astron.* the constellation Cetus. —*v.i.* **4.** to engage in whaling or whale fishing. [bef. 900; ME; OE *hwæl;* c. G *Wal-* in *Walfisch,* ON *hvalr;* perh. akin to L *squalus* kind of fish]

bowhead whale, *Balaena mysticetus,* length to 65 ft. (19.8 m)

whale[2] (hwāl, wāl), *v.,* **whaled, whal•ing.** to hit, thrash, or beat soundly. [1780–90; orig. uncert.]

whale•back (hwāl′bak′, wāl′-), *n.* **1.** *Naut.* **a.** a cargo vessel having a hull with a convex deck. **b.** a deck or cover curving upward. **2.** something shaped like the back of a whale, as a rounded hill or an ocean wave. [1885–90; WHALE[1] + BACK[1]]

whale•boat (hwāl′bōt′, wāl′-), *n.* a long, narrow boat designed for quick turning and use in rough seas: formerly used in whaling, now mainly for sea rescue. [1665–75; WHALE[1] + BOAT]

whale•bone (hwāl′bōn′, wāl′-), *n.* **1.** an elastic, horny substance growing in place of teeth in the upper jaw of certain whales, and forming a series of thin, parallel plates on each side of the palate; baleen. **2.** a thin strip of this substance, for stiffening a corset. [1175–1225; WHALE[1] + BONE]

whale′bone whale′, any whale of the suborder Mysticeti, having plates of whalebone on the sides of the upper jaw for filtering plankton from the water. Also called **baleen whale.** Cf. **toothed whale.** [1715–25]

whale•man (hwāl′mən, wāl′-), *n., pl.* **-men.** a person whose occupation is whaling; whaler. [1655–65, *Amer.;* WHALE[1] + -MAN]

whale′ oil′, oil rendered from whale blubber, formerly widely used as a fuel for lamps and for making soap and candles. [1400–50; late ME]

whal•er (hwā′lər, wā′-), *n.* a person or vessel employed in whaling. [1675–85; WHALE[1] + -ER[1]]

Whales (hwālz, wālz), *n.* **Bay of,** an inlet of the Ross Sea, in Antarctica: location of Little America.

whale′ shark′, a tropical shark, *Rhincodon typus,* ranging in size from 30 to 60 ft. (9 to 18 m), having small teeth and a sievelike structure over its gills for catching plankton. [1880–85]

whale•suck•er (hwāl′suk′ər, wāl′-), *n.* a large, blue remora, *Remora australis,* that attaches itself to whales and dolphins. [WHALE[1] + SUCKER]

whal•ing (hwā′ling, wā′-), *n.* the work or industry of capturing and rendering whales; whale fishing. [1680–90; WHALE[1] + -ING[1]]

whal′ing port′, a home port for whaling vessels.

wham (hwam, wam), *n., interj., v.,* **whammed, wham•ming,** *adv.* —*n.* **1.** a loud sound produced by an explosion or sharp impact: *the wham of a pile driver.* **2.** a forcible impact. —*interj.* **3.** (used as an exclamation suggestive of a loud slam, blow, or the like). —*v.t., v.i.* **4.** to hit or make a forcible impact, esp. one producing a loud sound: *The boat whammed into the dock. He whammed the door shut.* —*adv.* **5.** Also, **whammo.** abruptly; with startling suddenness: *The car ran wham up against the building.* [1730–40; imit.]

wham•mo (hwam′ō, wam′ō), *Informal.* —*interj.* **1.** (used to indicate the sound of a blow, collision, falling object, etc.). —*n.* **2.** immense energy; vigor: *a movie with plenty of whammo to please the kids.* —*adj.* **3.** characterized by such a strong effect: *a show with a whammo ending.* —*adv.* **4.** wham. [1930–35; WHAM + -o]

wham•my (hwam′ē, wam′ē), *n., pl.* **-mies.** *Informal.* **1.** the evil eye; jinx. **2.** bad luck or misfortune. **3.** a devastating blow, setback, or catastrophe: *The drought and the high price of fertilizer are a double whammy to farmers.* **4. put the whammy on, a.** to give the evil eye to; jinx. **b.** to destroy, end, or eradicate: *New controls will put the whammy on irresponsible spending.* [1935–40; WHAM + -Y[2], one of the methods of putting a whammy on someone being to strike the fist into the palm]

whang[1] (hwang, wang), *n. Informal.* **1.** a resounding blow. **2.** the sound produced by such a blow: *the whang of cymbals.* —*v.t.* **3.** to strike with a resounding blow. —*v.i.* **4.** to resound with such a blow. [1815–25; imit.]

whang[2] (hwang, wang), *n.* **1.** a thong, esp. of leather. **2.** Also called **thong leather.** rawhide. **3.** *Slang* (*often vulgar*). penis. [1530–40; orig. Scots form of *thwang,* early form of THONG (cf. WHACK, WHITTLE); sense "penis" perh. an unrelated expressive word (cf. DONG[2])]

whang•doo•dle (hwang′dōōd′l, wang′-), *n. Slang.* a fanciful creature of undefined nature. [1855–60, *Amer.;* nonsense formation; see WHANG[2], DOODLE]

whang•ee (hwang gē′, wang-), *n.* **1.** a bamboo of the genus *Phyllostachys,* of China. **2.** a walking stick or cane made from the stem of this plant. [1780–90; < Chin *huáng* hard bamboo + -ee < ?]

whap (whop, wop, hwap, wap), *v.t., v.i.,* **whapped, whap•ping,** *n.* whop.

whap•per (hwop′ər, wop′-), *n.* whopper.

whap•ping (whop′ing, wop′-), *adj.* whopping.

wharf (hwôrf, wôrf), *n., pl.* **wharves** (hwôrvz, wôrvz), **wharfs,** *v.* —*n.* **1.** a structure built on the shore of or projecting into a harbor, stream, etc., so that vessels may be moored alongside to load or unload or to lie at rest; quay; pier. **2.** *Obs.* **a.** a riverbank. **b.** the shore of the sea. —*v.t.* **3.** to provide with a wharf or wharves. **4.** to place or store on a wharf: *to wharf cargo.* **5.** to accommodate at or bring to a wharf: *The new structure will wharf several vessels.* —*v.i.* **6.** to tie up at a wharf; dock: *The ship wharfed in the morning.* [bef. 1050; ME (n.); OE *hwearf* embankment; c. MLG *warf;* akin to G *Werf* pier]

wharf•age (hwôr′fij, wôr′-), *n.* **1.** the use of a wharf: *to charge higher rates for wharfage.* **2.** storage of goods at a wharf: *conditions that make wharfage hazardous.* **3.** the charge or payment for the use of a wharf: *to pay one's wharfage monthly.* **4.** wharves collectively, esp. the number of wharves in a particular port. [1425–75; late ME; see WHARF, -AGE]

wharf•in•ger (hwôr′fin jər, wôr′-), *n.* one who owns or has charge of a wharf. Also called **wharf•mas•ter** (hwôrf′mas′ter, -mä′stər, wôrf′-). [1545–55; WHARFAGE + -ER[1], with *-n-* as in *passenger, messenger,* etc.]

wharf′ rat′, **1.** a large brown rat that is commonly found on wharves. **2.** a person who lives or loiters near wharves, often existing by pilfering from ships or warehouses. [1815–25, *Amer.*]

wharf′ shed′. See under **transit shed.** [1950–55]

Whar•ton (hwôr′tn, wôr′-), *n.* **Edith** 1862–1937, U.S. novelist.

wharve (hwôrv, wôrv), *n. Spinning.* a wheel or round piece of wood on a spindle, serving as a flywheel or as a pulley. [bef. 1000; ME *wherve,* OE *hweorfa;* deriv. of *hwerfan* to revolve]

wharves (hwôrvz, wôrvz), *n.* a pl. of **wharf.**

what (hwut, hwot, wut, wot; *unstressed* hwət, wət), *pron.* **1.** (used interrogatively as a request for specific information): *What is the matter?* **2.** (used interrogatively to inquire about the character, occupation, etc., of a person): *What does he do?* **3.** (used interrogatively to inquire as to the origin, identity, etc., of something): *What are those birds?* **4.** (used interrogatively to inquire as to the worth, usefulness, force, or importance of something): *What is wealth without friends?* **5.** (used interrogatively to request a repetition of words or information not fully understood, usually used in elliptical constructions): *You need what?* **6.** (used interrogatively to inquire the reason or purpose of something, usually used in elliptical constructions): *What of it?* **7.** how much?: *What does it cost?* **8.** (used relatively to indicate that which): *I will send what was promised.* **9.** whatever; anything that: *Say what you please. Come what may.* **10.** the kind of thing or person that: *He said what everyone expected he would. They are just what I was expecting.* **11.** as much as; as many as: *We should each give what we can.* **12.** the thing or fact that (used in parenthetic clauses): *He went to the meeting and, what was worse, insisted on speaking.* **13.** (used to indicate more to follow, additional possibilities, alternatives, etc.): *You know what? Shall we go or what?* **14.** (used as an intensifier in exclamatory phrases, often fol. by an indefinite article): *What luck! What an idea!* **15.** *Brit.* don't you agree?: *An unusual chap, what?* **16.** *Nonstandard.* that; which; who: *She's the one what told me.* **17. Say what?** *Slang.* (used especially among teenagers) What's that you say? Would you repeat that? **18. So what?** *Informal.* (an expression of disinterest, disinclination, or contempt.) **19. what have you,** other things of the same kind; so forth: *money, jewels, stocks, and what have you.* **20. what for, a.** why: *What are you doing that for?* **b.** a punishment or scolding. **21. what if,** what would be the outcome if; suppose that: *What if everyone who was invited comes?* **22. what it takes,** something that enables one to achieve success or attain a desired end, as good looks, ability, or money: *There's a young woman who has what it takes to get along in the world.* **23. what's what,** *Informal.* the true situation; all the facts: *It's high time you told him what's what.* —*n.* **24.** the true nature or identity of something, or the sum of its characteristics: *a lecture on the whats and hows of crop rotation.* —*adj.* **25.** (used interrogatively before nouns): *What news? What clothes shall I pack?* **26.** whatever: *Take what supplies you need.* —*adv.* **27.** to what extent or degree? how much?: *What does it matter?* **28.** (used to introduce a prepositional phrase beginning with *with*): *What with storms and all, their return was delayed.* **29.** *Obs.* for what reason or purpose? why? —*interj.* **30.** (used in exclamatory expressions, often fol. by a question): *What, no salt?* —*conj.* **31.** *Older Use.* as much as; as far as: *He helps me what he can.* **32. but what,** *Informal.* but that; but who; who or that . . . not: *Who knows but what the sun may still shine.* [bef. 900; ME; OE *hwæt;* c. G *was,* D *wat,* ON *hvat;* akin to Goth *hwa,* L *quod,* Gk *tí*]
—Usage. 31. See **doubt.**

what•cha•ma•call•it (hwuch′ə mə kôl′it, hwoch′-, wuch′-, woch′-), *n.* whachamacallit. Also, **what-do-you-call-it** (hwud′ə yə kôl′it, hwod′-, wud′-, wod′-).

what'd (hwut′id, hwot′-, wut′-, wot′-; hwud, wud), contraction of *what did: What'd you say?*
—Usage. See **contraction.**

what•e'er (hwut âr′, hwot-, hwət-, wut-, wot-, wət-), *pron., adj. Literary.* whatever.

what•ev•er (hwut ev′ər, hwot-, hwət-, wut-, wot-, wət-), *pron.* **1.** anything that (usually used in relative clauses): *Whatever you say is all right with me.* **2.** (used relatively to indicate a quantity of a specified or implied antecedent): *Take whatever you like of these.* **3.** no matter what: *Do it, whatever happens.* **4.** any or any one of a number of things whether specifically known or not: *papers, magazines, or whatever.* **5.** what (used interrogatively): *Whatever do you mean?* —*adj.* **6.** in any amount; to any extent: *whatever merit the work has.* **7.** no matter what: *whatever rebuffs he might receive.* **8.** being what or who it may be: *Whatever the reason, he refuses to go.* **9.** of any kind (used as an intensifier following the noun or pronoun it modifies): *any person whatever.* [1300–50; ME; see WHAT, EVER]

what-if (hwut′if′, hwot′-, wut′-, wot′-), *Informal.* —*adj.* **1.** hypothetical: *a what-if scenario.* —*n.* **2.** a hypothetical case or situation; conjecture: *a series of what-ifs.* [1980–85]

what'll (hwut′l, hwot′l, wut′l, wot′l), contraction of *what will: What'll I do and what'll she say?*
—Usage. See **contraction.**

what•not (hwut′not′, hwot′-, wut′-, wot′-), *n.* **1.** a stand with shelves for bric-a-brac, books, etc. **2.** something or anything of the same or similar kind: *sheets, pillowcases, towels, napkins, and whatnot.* [1530–40; from the phrase *what not?*]

what's (hwuts, hwots, wuts, wots; *unstressed* hwəts, wəts), **1.** contraction of *what is* or *what has: What's the matter? What's been done?* **2.** contraction of *what does: What's she do for a living?*
—Usage. See **contraction.**

whats•is (hwuts′is, hwots′-, wuts′-, wots′-), *n. Informal.* a thing or object whose name one does not know or cannot recall. [reduction of *what's this*]

whats•it (hwuts′it, hwots′-, wuts′-, wots′-), *n. Informal.* whatsis. [reduction of *what is it*]

what•so•e'er (hwut′sō âr′, hwot′-, wut′-, wot′-), *pron., adj. Literary.* whatsoever.

what•so•ev•er (hwut′sō ev′ər, hwot′-, wut′-, wot′-), *pron., adj.* (an intensive form of **whatever**): *whatsoever it be; in any place whatsoever.* [1200–50; ME, equiv. to *what so* whatever (OE *swā hwæt swā*) + *ever* EVER]

what've (hwut′əv, hwot′-, wut′-, wot′-), contraction of *what have: What've you done with the money?*
—Usage. See **contraction.**

what-you-may-call-it (hwuch′ə mə kôl′it, hwoch′-, wuch′-, woch′-), *n.* whachamacallit.

whaup (hwäp, hwôp, wäp, wôp), *n. Scot.* a curlew, *Numenius arquata.* [1505–15; perh. repr. earlier **whalp,* akin (by gradation) to OE *hwilpe* plover]

wheal (hwēl, wēl), *n.* **1.** a small, burning or itching swelling on the skin, as from a mosquito bite or from hives. **2.** a wale or welt. Also, **weal.** [bef. 900; akin to WHELK[2] and to obs. *wheal* (v.), OE *hwelian* to suppurate, develop wheals]

wheat (hwēt, wēt), *n.* **1.** the grain of any cereal grass of the genus *Triticum,* esp. *T. aestivum,* used in the form of flour for making bread, cakes, etc., and for other culinary and nutritional purposes. **2.** the plant itself. [bef. 900; ME *whete,* OE *hwǣte;* c. G *Weizen,* ON *hveiti,* Goth *hwaiteis;* akin to WHITE] **—wheat′less,** *adj.*

wheat′ ber′ry, the whole kernel of wheat, sometimes cracked or ground and used as a cereal or cooked food, or made into bread. [1535–45]

wheat′ cake′, a pancake made of wheat flour. [1765–75, *Amer.*]

wheat•ear (hwēt′ēr′, wēt′-), *n.* any of several small, chiefly Old World thrushes of the genus *Oenanthe,* having a distinctive white rump, esp. *O. oenanthe,* of Eurasia and North America. [1585–95; prob. back formation from *wheatears,* for **whiteers* white rump. See WHITE, ARSE]

wheat•en (hwēt′n, wēt′n), *adj.* **1.** made of wheat flour or grain. **2.** of or pertaining to wheat. **3.** of the color of wheat, esp. a pale yellow-brown color. [bef. 900; ME *wheten,* OE *hwǣten.* See WHEAT, -EN[2]]

wheat′en ter′rier, *Informal.* See **soft-coated wheaten terrier.** [1940–45]

wheat′ germ′, the embryo or nucleus of the wheat kernel, used in or on foods as a concentrated source of vitamins. [1900–05]

wheat•grass (hwēt′gras′, -gräs′, wēt′-), *n.* any of several wheatlike grasses of the genus *Agropyron,* grown for forage in the western U.S. [1810–20; WHEAT + GRASS]

Wheat•ley (hwēt′lē, wēt′-), *n.* **Phil•lis** (fil′is), 1753?–84, American poet, born in Africa; probably Senegal.

Whea•ton (hwēt′n, wēt′n), *n.* **1.** a town in central Maryland. 48,598. **2.** a city in NE Illinois, W of Chicago. 43,043.

Wheat′ Ridge′, a town in central Colorado, near Denver. 30,293.

wheat′ rust′, *Plant Pathol.* any of several diseases of wheat caused by rust fungi of the genus *Puccinia.* [1880–85]

Wheat•stone (hwēt′stōn′, wēt′- *or, esp. Brit.,* -stən), *n.* **Sir Charles,** 1802–75, English physicist and inventor.

Wheat′stone bridge′, *Elect.* a circuit for measuring an unknown resistance by comparing it with known resistances. Also, **Wheat′stone's bridge′.** Cf. **bridge** (def. 9), **null method.** [1870–75; named after C. WHEATSTONE]

wheat•worm (hwēt′wûrm′, wēt′-), *n.* a small nematode, *Tylenchus tritici,* that stunts growth and disrupts seed production in wheat. [1860–65; WHEAT + WORM]

whee (hwē, wē), *interj.* (used to express joy or delight). [1895–1900]

whee•dle (hwēd′l, wēd′l), *v.,* **-dled, -dling.** —*v.t.* **1.** to endeavor to influence (a person) by smooth, flattering, or beguiling words or acts: *We wheedled him incessantly, but he would not consent.* **2.** to persuade (a person) by such words or acts: *She wheedled him into going with her.* **3.** to obtain (something) by artful persuasions: *I wheedled a new car out of my father.* —*v.i.* **4.** to use beguiling or artful persuasions: *I always wheedle if I really need something.* [1655–65; orig. uncert.] **—whee′dler,** *n.* **—whee′dling•ly,** *adv.*
—Syn. **1.** flatter, cajole. **2, 3.** coax, beguile, inveigle.

wheel (hwēl, wēl), *n.* **1.** a circular frame or disk arranged to revolve on an axis, as on or in vehicles or machinery. **2.** any machine, apparatus, instrument, etc., shaped like this or having a circular frame, disk, or revolving drum as an essential feature: *a potter's wheel; roulette wheel; spinning wheel.* **3.** See **steering wheel.** **4.** *Naut.* **a.** a circular frame with an axle connecting to

CONCISE PRONUNCIATION KEY: act, cāpe, dâre, pärt; set, ēqual; *if,* ice; ox, ōver, ôrder, oil, bŏŏk, bōōt, out; up, ûrge; child; sing; shoe; thin, that; zh as in *treasure.* ə = *a* as in *alone, e* as in *system, i* as in *easily, o* as in *gallop, u* as in *circus;* ᵊ as in *fire* (fīᵊr), *hour* (ouᵊr). l and n can serve as syllabic consonants, as in *cradle* (krād′l), and *button* (but′n). See the full key inside the front cover.

the rudder of a ship, for steering: *He took the wheel during the storm.* **b.** a paddle wheel. **c.** a propeller. **5.** *Informal.* a bicycle. **6.** a round object, decoration, etc.: *a wheel of cheese; a design of red wheels and blue squares.* **7.** an old instrument of torture in the form of a circular frame on which the victim was stretched until disjointed. **8.** a circular firework that revolves rapidly while burning; pinwheel. **9.** a rotating instrument that Fortune is represented as turning in order to bring about changes or reverses in human affairs. **10. wheels, a.** moving, propelling, or animating agencies: *the wheels of commerce; the wheels of thought.* **b.** *Slang.* a personal means of transportation, esp. a car. **11.** a cycle, recurring action, or steady progression: *the wheel of days and nights.* **12.** a wheeling or circular movement: *the intricate wheels of the folk dances.* **13.** (formerly) a movement of troops, ships, etc., drawn up in line, as if turning on a pivot. **14.** *Informal.* someone active and influential, as in business, politics, etc.; an important person: *a big wheel.* **15. at the wheel, a.** at the helm of a ship, the steering wheel of a motor vehicle, etc. **b.** in command or control: *Her ambition is to be at the wheel of a large corporation by the age of 40.* **16. hell on wheels.** See **hell** (def. 16). **17. spin one's wheels,** *Informal.* to expend or waste effort to no avail: *He spun his wheels on that project for two years.* **18. wheels within wheels,** an involved interaction of motives or agencies operating to produce the final result: *Government agencies are a study of wheels within wheels.* —*v.t.* **19.** to cause to turn, rotate, or revolve, as on an axis. **20.** to perform (a movement) in a circular or curving direction. **21.** to move, roll, or convey on wheels, casters, etc.: *The servants wheel the tables out.* **22.** to provide (a vehicle, machine, etc.) with wheels. —*v.i.* **23.** to turn on or as on an axis or about a center; revolve, rotate, or pivot. **24.** to move in a circular or curving course: *pigeons wheeling above.* **25.** to turn so as to face in a different direction (often fol. by *about* or *around*): *He wheeled about and faced his opponent squarely.* **26.** to change one's opinion or procedure (often fol. by *about* or *around*): *He wheeled around and argued for the opposition.* **27.** to roll along on or as on wheels; travel along smoothly: *The car wheeled along the highway.* **28.** *Brit. Mil.* to turn: *Right wheel!* **29. wheel and deal,** *Informal.* to operate dynamically for one's own profit or benefit. [bef. 900; (n.) ME *whel(e),* OE *hwēol, hweohl;* c. D *wiel,* ON *hjōl;* akin to Gk *kýklos* (see CYCLE); (v.) ME, deriv. of the n.] —**wheel′less,** *adj.*

wheel′ and ax′le, a simple machine consisting, in its typical form, of a cylindrical drum to which a wheel concentric with the drum is firmly fastened: ropes are so applied that as one unwinds from the wheel, another rope is wound on to the drum. [1765–75]

wheel′ animal′cule, a rotifer. Also called **wheel′ an′imal.** [1825–35]

wheel′ back′, a chair back having the form of a circle or oval with spindles or bars meeting at the center. [1905–10]

wheel·bar·row (hwēl′bar′ō, wēl′-), *n.* **1.** a frame or box for conveying a load, supported at one end by a wheel or wheels, and lifted and pushed at the other by two horizontal shafts. —*v.t.* **2.** to move or convey in a wheelbarrow. [1300–50; ME; see WHEEL, BARROW[1]]

wheelbarrow (def. 1)

wheel′barrow race′, a race in which one member of each team of two walks on his or her hands while the legs are held up by the partner. [1830–40]

wheel·base (hwēl′bās′, wēl′-), *n. Auto.* the distance from the center of the front-wheel spindle to the center of the rear-wheel axle. [1885–90; WHEEL + BASE[1]]

wheel′ bug′, an assassin bug, *Arilus cristatus,* that has a toothed, semicircular crest on the pronotum and preys on other insects. [1805–15, *Amer.*]

wheel·chair (hwēl′châr′, wēl′-), *n.* a chair mounted on wheels for use by persons who cannot walk. [1690–1700; WHEEL + CHAIR]

wheeled (hwēld, wēld), *adj.* **1.** equipped with or having wheels (often used in combination): *a four-wheeled carriage.* **2.** moving or traveling on wheels: *wheeled transportation.* [1600–10; WHEEL + -ED[3]]

wheel·er (hwē′lər, wē′-), *n.* **1.** a person or thing that wheels. **2.** a person who makes wheels; wheelwright. **3.** something provided with a wheel or wheels (usually used in combination): *a four-wheeler; a stern-wheeler.* **4.** See **wheel horse** (def. 1). [1350–1400; ME; see WHEEL, -ER[1]]

Whee·ler (hwē′lər, wē′-), *n.* **1. Burton Kendall,** 1882–1975, U.S. political leader. **2. Joseph,** 1836–1906, U.S. Confederate officer and political leader. **3. William Al·mon** (al′mən, ôl′-), 1819–1887, vice president of the U.S. 1877–81.

wheel·er-deal·er (hwē′lər dē′lər, wē′-), *n. Informal.* a person who wheels and deals. Also, **wheel′er and deal′er.** [1950–55]

wheel′ horse′, 1. Also called **wheeler.** a horse, or one of the horses, harnessed behind others and nearest the front wheels of a vehicle. **2.** *Chiefly South Atlantic States.* the left-hand horse of a pair hitched to a wagon or plow. **3.** *Chiefly South Midland and Southern U.S.* a reliable, diligent, and strong worker. Also, **wheel′-horse′.** [1700–10]

wheel·house (hwēl′hous′, wēl′-), *n., pl.* **-hous·es** (-hou′ziz). pilothouse. [1805–15; WHEEL + HOUSE]

wheel·ie (hwē′lē, wē′-), *n.* **1.** a small, usually folding, metal frame with wheels for carrying luggage or small packages. **2.** a maneuver in which a bicycle, motorcycle, or car has its front wheel or wheels momentarily lifted off the ground. [1960–65; WHEEL + -IE]

wheel·ing (hwē′ling, wē′-), *n.* **1.** the act of a person who moves, travels, conveys, etc., on or as on wheels, esp. cycling. **2.** a rotating or circular motion: *the wheeling of birds.* **3.** the condition of a road for travel by wheeled vehicles: *A state highway is usually good wheeling.* [1475–85; WHEEL + -ING[1]]

Whee·ling (hwē′ling, wē′-), *n.* **1.** a city in N West Virginia, on the Ohio River. 43,070. **2.** a town in NE Illinois. 23,266.

wheel′ lock′, 1. an old type of gunlock in which sparks are produced by the friction of a small steel wheel against a piece of iron pyrites. **2.** a gun having such a gunlock. [1660–70]

wheel·man (hwēl′mən, wēl′-), *n., pl.* **-men. 1.** Also, **wheels·man** (hwēlz′mən, wēl′-). a helmsman or steersman. **2.** a rider of a bicycle, tricycle, or the like. **3.** *Slang.* **a.** a driver, esp. a chauffeur: *The mobster's wheelman was also his bodyguard.* **b.** a person who drives the getaway car in a holdup or robbery. [1860–65, *Amer.*; WHEEL + -MAN]

Whee·lock (hwē′lok, wē′-), *n.* **Eleazar,** 1711–79, U.S. clergyman and educator: founded Dartmouth College.

wheel′ of for′tune, 1. wheel (def. 9). **2.** a wheel-like gambling device that is rotated or spun to determine the winner of certain prizes. [1755–65]

wheel′ of life′, *Buddhism.* **1.** the symbol of the cycle of birth, death, and reincarnation. **2.** a pictorial representation of this.

wheel·spin (hwēl′spin′, wēl′-), *n.* the spinning of a wheel, esp. that of a drive wheel of a powered vehicle that has poor traction. [1925–30; WHEEL + SPIN]

wheel′ stat′ic, noise in an automobile radio induced by wheel rotation.

wheel′ win′dow, a rose window having prominent radiating mullions. Also called **Catherine wheel, marigold window.**

wheel·work (hwēl′wûrk′, wēl′-), *n.* a train of gears, as in a timepiece. [1660–70; WHEEL + WORK]

wheel·wright (hwēl′rīt′, wēl′-), *n.* a person whose trade it is to make or repair wheels, wheeled carriages, etc. [1250–1300; ME; see WHEEL, WRIGHT]

Wheel·wright (hwēl′rīt′, wēl′-), *n.* **John,** 1592?–1679, English clergyman in America.

wheen (hwēn, wēn), *Scot. and North Eng.* —*adj.* **1.** few. —*n.* **2.** a few persons or things. [1325–75; ME (north) *quheyn,* OE *hwēne,* instr. case of *hwōn* few, a few]

wheeze (hwēz, wēz), *v.,* **wheezed, wheez·ing,** *n.* —*v.i.* **1.** to breathe with difficulty and with a whistling sound: *Asthma caused him to wheeze.* **2.** to make a sound resembling difficult breathing: *The old locomotive wheezed into the station.* —*n.* **3.** a wheezing breath or sound. **4.** an old and frequently used joke, saying, story, etc. [1425–75; late ME *whese* (v.), prob. < ON *hvæsa* to hiss] —**wheez′er,** *n.* —**wheez′ing·ly,** *adv.*

wheez·y (hwē′zē, wē′-), *adj.,* **wheez·i·er, wheez·i·est.** afflicted with or characterized by wheezing: *wheezy breathing.* [1810–20; WHEEZE + -Y[1]] —**wheez′i·ly,** *adv.* —**wheez′i·ness,** *n.*

whelk[1] (hwelk, welk), *n.* any of several large, spiral-shelled, marine gastropods of the family Buccinidae, esp. *Buccinum undatum,* that is used for food in Europe. [bef. 900; late ME, aspirated var. of ME *welk,* OE *weoloc*]

whelk[1], *Buccinum undatum,* length 3 in. (8 cm)

whelk[2] (hwelk, welk), *n.* a pimple or pustule. [bef. 1000; ME *whelke,* OE *hwylca, hwelca;* akin to WHEAL]

whelked (hwelkt, welkt), *adj.* ridged like the shell of a snail: *a whelked horn.* [1550–60; WHELK[1] + -ED[3]]

whelm (hwelm, welm), *v.t.* **1.** to submerge; engulf. **2.** to overcome utterly; overwhelm: *whelmed by misfortune.* —*v.i.* **3.** to roll or surge over something, as in becoming submerged. [1250–1300; ME *whelme,* appar. b. dial. *whelve* (OE *gehwelfan* to bend over) and HELM[2] (v.) (OE *helmian* to cover)]

whelp (hwelp, welp), *n.* **1.** the young of the dog, or of the wolf, bear, lion, tiger, seal, etc. **2.** a youth, esp. an impudent or despised one. **3.** *Mach.* **a.** any of a series of longitudinal projections or ridges on the barrel of a capstan, windlass, etc. **b.** any of the teeth of a sprocket wheel. —*v.t., v.i.* **4.** (of a female dog, lion, etc.) to give birth to (young). [bef. 900; (n.) ME; OE *hwelp* (c. G *Welf*); (v.) ME *whelpen,* deriv. of the n.] —**whelp′less,** *adj.*
—**Syn. 2.** brat, urchin, whippersnapper.

whelp′ing ice′, *Newfoundland.* the ice on which a seal lies while giving birth in the spring. [1915–20]

when (hwen, wen; *unstressed* hwən, wən), *adv.* **1.** at what time or period? how long ago? how soon?: *When are they to arrive? When did the Roman Empire exist?* **2.** under what circumstances? upon what occasion?: *When is a letter of condolence in order? When did you ever see such a crowd?* —*conj.* **3.** at what time: *to know when to be silent.* **4.** at the time or in the event that: *when we were young; when the noise stops.* **5.** at any time; whenever: *He is impatient when he is kept waiting.* **6.** upon or after which; and then: *We had just fallen asleep when the bell rang.* **7.** while on the contrary; considering that; whereas: *Why are you here when you should be in school?* —*pron.* **8.** what time: *Till when is the store open?* **9.** which time: *They left on Monday, since when we have heard nothing.* —*n.* **10.** the time of anything: *the when and the where of an act.* [bef. 1000; ME *when(ne),* OE *hwenne;* c. G *wann* when, *wenn* if, when (cf. Goth *hwan* when, how); akin to WHO, WHAT]

when·as (hwen az′, wen-, hwən-, wən-), *conj.* **1.** *Archaic.* **a.** when. **b.** inasmuch as. **2.** *Obs.* whereas. [1375–1425; late ME; see WHEN, AS[1]]

whence (hwens, wens), —*adv.* **1.** from what place?: *Whence comest thou?* **2.** from what source, origin, or cause?: *Whence has he wisdom?* —*conj.* **3.** from what place, source, cause, etc.: *He told whence he came.* [1250–1300; ME *whennes, whannes,* equiv. to *whanne* (by syncope from OE *hwanone* whence) + *-s* -S[1]]
—**Usage.** Although sometimes criticized as redundant on the grounds that "from" is implied by the word WHENCE, the idiom FROM WHENCE is old in the language, well established, and standard. Among its users are the King James Bible, Shakespeare, Dryden, and Dickens: *Hilary finally settled in Paris, from whence she bombarded us with letters, postcards, and sketches.* FROM THENCE, a parallel construction, occurs infrequently.

whence·so·ev·er (hwens′sō ev′ər, wens′-), *adv., conj. Archaic.* from whatsoever place, source, or cause. [1505–15; modeled on WHERESOEVER; see WHENCE]

when'd (hwend, wend, hwen′əd, wen′əd), contraction of *when did: When'd that happen?*
—**Usage.** See **contraction.**

when·e'er (hwen âr′, wen-, hwən-, wən-), *conj. Literary.* whenever (def. 1).

when·ev·er (hwen ev′ər, wen-, hwən-, wən-), *conj.* **1.** at whatever time; at any time when: *Come whenever you like.* **2.** when? (used emphatically): *Whenever did he say that?* [1350–1400; ME; see WHEN, EVER]

when-is·sued (hwen ish′o͞od, wen-, hwən-, wən- *or, esp. Brit.,* -is′yo͞od), *adj.* of, pertaining to, or noting an agreement to buy securities paid for at the time of delivery. *Abbr.:* wi, w.i.

when'll (hwen′l, wen′l), contraction of *when will: When'll we meet again?*
—**Usage.** See **contraction.**

when're (hwen′ər, wen′ər), contraction of *when are: When're we having lunch?*
—**Usage.** See **contraction.**

when's (hwenz, wenz), **1.** contraction of *when is: When's the show over?* **2.** contraction of *when does: When's the next train leave?* **3.** contraction of *when has: When's he ever been an authority?*
—**Usage.** See **contraction.**

when·so·ev·er (hwen′sō ev′ər, wen′-), *adv., conj.* at whatsoever time. [1275–1325; ME, equiv. to *whenso* (modeled on *whereso;* see WHERESOEVER) + *ever* EVER]

when've (hwen′əv, wen′əv), contraction of *when have: When've you talked to her?*
—**Usage.** See **contraction.**

where (hwâr, wâr), *adv.* **1.** in or at what place?: *Where is he? Where do you live?* **2.** in what position or circumstances?: *Where do you stand on this question? Without money, where are you?* **3.** in what particular respect, way, etc.?: *Where does this affect us?* **4.** to what place, point, or end? whither?: *Where are you going?* **5.** from what source? whence?: *Where did you get such a notion?* —*conj.* **6.** in or at what place, part, point, etc.: *Find where he is. Find where the trouble is.* **7.** in or at the place, part, point, etc., in or at which: *The book is where you left it.* **8.** in a position, case, etc., in which: *Where ignorance is bliss, 'tis folly to be wise.* **9.** in any place, position, case, etc., in which; wherever: *Use the ointment where pain is felt.* **10.** to what or whatever place; to the place or any place to which: *I will go where you go.* **11.** in or at which place; and there: *They came to the town, where they lodged for the night.* **12. where it's at,** *Slang.* where the most exciting, prestigious, or profitable activity or circumstance is to be found. —*pron.* **13.** what place?: *Where did you come from?* **14.** the place in which; point at which: *This is where the boat docks. That was where the phone rang.* —*n.* **15.** a place; that place in which something is located or occurs: *the wheres and hows of job hunting.* [bef. 900; ME *quher, wher,* OE *hwǣr;* c. D *waar,* OHG *hwār;* akin to ON *hvar,* Goth *hwar*]
—**Usage.** WHERE . . . AT (*Where was he at?*) and WHERE . . . TO (*Where is this leading to?*) are often criticized as redundant because neither AT nor TO adds anything to the meaning of WHERE, and sentences like the preceding ones are perfectly clear and standard without the final AT or TO. This criticism does not apply to WHERE . . . FROM, which is fully standard: *Where does the money come from?* The constructions WHERE . . . AT and WHERE . . . TO occur in the speech of educated people but are rare in formal speech and edited writing.

where·a·bout (hwâr′ə bout′, wâr′-), *adv.* whereabouts. [1250–1300; ME; see WHERE, ABOUT]

where·a·bouts (hwâr′ə bouts′, wâr′-), *adv.* **1.** about where? where? —*conj.* **2.** near or in what place: *trying to find whereabouts in the world we were.* —*n.* **3.** (*used with a singular or plural v.*) the place where a person or thing is; the locality of a person or thing: *no clue as to his whereabouts.* [1400–50; late ME *whereaboutes,* equiv. to ME *whereaboute* (see WHEREABOUT) + *-s* -S[1]]

where·as (hwâr az′, wâr-), *conj., n., pl.* **where·as·es.** —*conj.* **1.** while on the contrary: *One arrived promptly, whereas the others hung back.* **2.** it being the case that, or considering that (used esp. in formal preambles). —*n.* **3.** a qualifying or introductory statement, esp. one having "whereas" as the first word: *to read the whereases in the will.* [1300–50; ME *wheras;* see WHERE, AS[1]]

where·at (hwâr at′, wâr-), *conj.* **1.** *Literary.* **a.** at

CONCISE ETYMOLOGY KEY: <, descended or borrowed from; >, whence; b., blend of, blended; c., cognate with; cf., compare; deriv., derivative; equiv., equivalent; imit., imitative; obl., oblique; r., replacing; s., stem; sp., spelling, spelled; resp., respelling, respelled; trans., translation; ?, origin unknown; *, unattested; ‡, probably earlier than. See the full key inside the front cover.

which: *a reception whereat many were present.* **b.** to which; whereupon: *a remark whereat she quickly angered.* —*adv.* **2.** *Archaic.* in reference to which. [1200–50; ME; see WHERE, AT[1]]

where·by (hwâr bī′, wâr-), *conj., adv.* **1.** by what or by which; under the terms of which. **2.** *Obs.* by what? how? [1150–1200; ME *wherby.* See WHERE, BY[1]]

where'd (hwârd, wârd), **1.** contraction of *where did: Where'd you go on your holiday?* **2.** contraction of *where would: Where'd you like to go?* —**Usage.** See **contraction.**

wher·e'er (hwâr âr′, wâr-), *conj., adv. Literary.* wherever.

where·fore (hwâr′fôr′, -fōr′, wâr′-), *adv.* **1.** *Archaic.* for what? why? **2.** for that cause or reason: *Wherefore let us be grateful.* —*n.* **3.** the cause or reason: *to study the whys and wherefores of a situation.* [1150–1200; ME; see WHERE, FOR] —**Syn. 2.** See **therefore.**

where·from (hwâr frum′, -from′, wâr-), *conj., adv.* from which; whence. [1480–90; WHERE + FROM]

where·in (hwâr in′, wâr-), *conj.* **1.** in what or in which. —*adv.* **2.** in what way or respect? [1200–50; ME *wherin.* See WHERE, IN]

where·in·to (hwâr in′to͞o, wâr-; hwâr′in to͞o′, wâr′-), *conj.* into which. [1530–40; WHERE + INTO]

where'll (hwârl, wârl), contraction of *where shall* or *where will: Where'll I be ten years from now?* —**Usage.** See **contraction.**

where·of (hwâr uv′, -ov′, wâr-), *adv., conj.* of what, which, or whom. [1150–1200; ME *wherof.* See WHERE, OF[1]]

where·on (hwâr on′, -ôn′, wâr-), *conj.* **1.** on what or which. —*adv.* **2.** *Archaic.* on what? [1175–1225; ME *wheron.* See WHERE, ON]

where're (hwâr′ər, wâr′-, hwâr, wâr), contraction of *where are: Where're you going?* —**Usage.** See **contraction.**

where's (hwârz, wârz), **1.** contraction of *where is: Where's my belt?* **2.** contraction of *where has: Where's he been all night?* **3.** contraction of *where does: Where's he study law?* —**Usage.** See **contraction.**

where·so·e'er (hwâr′sō âr′, wâr′-), *conj. Literary.* wheresoever.

where·so·ev·er (hwâr′sō ev′ər, wâr′-), *conj.* in or to whatsoever place; wherever. [1275–1325; ME, equiv. to *whereso* wherever (OE (*swā*) *hwǣr swā*) + *ever* EVER]

where·through (hwâr thro͞o′, wâr-), *conj.* through, during, or because of which. [1175–1225; ME *hwerthrough.* See WHERE, THROUGH]

where·to (hwâr to͞o′, wâr-), *conj., adv.* **1.** *Archaic.* to what or what place or end. **2.** to which. [1175–1225; ME *wherto.* See WHERE, TO]

where·un·to (hwâr un′to͞o, wâr-; hwâr′un to͞o′, wâr′-), *conj., adv. Archaic.* whereto. [1375–1425; late ME *quhareunto.* See WHERE, UNTO]

where·up·on (hwâr′ə pon′, -pôn′, wâr′-; hwâr′ə-pon′, -pôn′, wâr′-), *conj.* **1.** upon what or upon which. **2.** at or after which. **3.** *Archaic.* upon what? [1300–50; ME *wherupon.* See WHERE, UPON]

where've (hwârv, wârv, hwâr′əv, wâr′-), contraction of *where have: Where've you seen this before?* —**Usage.** See **contraction.**

wher·ev·er (hwâr ev′ər, wâr-), *conj.* **1.** in, at, or to whatever place. **2.** in any case or condition: *wherever it is heard of.* —*adv.* **3.** where? (used emphatically): *Wherever did you find that?* [bef. 1000; ME; OE *hwǣr ǣfre.* See WHERE, EVER]

where·with (hwâr with′, -with′, wâr-), *adv., conj.* **1.** *Literary.* with which; by means of which. **2.** *Archaic.* **a.** with what? **b.** because of which; by reason of which. **c.** whereupon; at which. —*pron.* **3.** *Archaic.* that by which; that with which. —*n.* **4.** *Rare.* wherewithal. [1150–1200; ME *wherwith.* See WHERE, WITH]

where·with·al (hwâr′with ôl′, -with-, wâr′-), *n.* **1.** that with which to do something; means or supplies for the purpose or need, esp. money: *the wherewithal to pay my rent.* —*adv.* **2.** by means of which; out of which. **3.** *Archaic.* wherewith. —*pron.* **4.** wherewith. [1525–35; WHERE + WITHAL]

wher·ry (hwer′ē, wer′ē), *n., pl.* **-ries,** *v.,* **-ried, -ry·ing.** —*n.* **1.** a light rowboat for one person; skiff. **2.** any of various barges, fishing vessels, etc., used locally in England. —*v.t., v.i.* **3.** to use, or transport in, a wherry. [1400–50; late ME *whery* < ?]

whet (hwet, wet), *v.,* **whet·ted, whet·ting,** *n.* —*v.t.* **1.** to sharpen (a knife, tool, etc.) by grinding or friction. **2.** to make keen or eager; stimulate: *to whet the appetite; to whet the curiosity.* —*n.* **3.** the act of whetting. **4.** something that whets; appetizer or drink. **5.** *Chiefly Southern U.S.* **a.** a spell of work. **b.** a while: *to talk a whet.* [bef. 900; ME *whetten* (v.), OE *hwettan* (deriv. of *hwæt* bold); c. G *wetzen,* ON *hvetja,* Goth *gahwatjan* to incite] —**whet′ter,** *n.*

wheth·er (hweth′ər, weth′-), *conj.* **1.** (used to introduce the first of two or more alternatives, and sometimes repeated before the second or later alternative, usually with the correlative *or*): *It matters little whether we go or stay. Whether we go or whether we stay, the result is the same.* **2.** (used to introduce a single alternative, the other being implied or understood, or some clause or element not involving alternatives): *See whether or not she has come. I doubt whether we can do any better.* **3.** *Archaic.* (used to introduce a question presenting alternatives, usually with the correlative *or*). **4. whether or no,** under whatever circumstances; regardless: *He threatens to go whether or no.* —*pron. Archaic.* **5.** which or whichever (of two)? [bef. 900; ME; OE *hwether, hwæther,* equiv. to *hwe-* (base of *hwā* WHO) + *-ther* comp. suffix; c. ON *hvatharr,* Goth *hwathar*] —**Usage.** See **if.**

whet·stone (hwet′stōn′, wet′-), *n.* **1.** a stone for sharpening cutlery or tools by friction. **2.** anything that sharpens: *a whetstone for dull wits.* [bef. 900; ME *whetston,* OE *hwetstān.* See WHET, STONE]

whew (hwyo͞o), *interj.* **1.** (a whistling exclamation or sound expressing astonishment, dismay, relief, etc.) —*n.* **2.** an utterance of "whew." [1505–15; imit.]

whew·ell·ite (hyo͞o′ə līt′), *n.* a white or colorless mineral of organic origin, calcium oxalate monohydrate, $Ca(C_2O_4)\cdot H_2O$, one of the main crystalline components of kidney stones and urinary precipitates; also found in coal deposits. [1850–55; named after William *Whewell* (1794–1866), English philosopher; see -ITE[1]]

whey (hwā, wā), *n.* a milk serum, separating as liquid from the curd after coagulation, as in cheese making. [bef. 900; ME *wheye,* OE *hwæg;* c. D, LG *wei*] —**whey′like′,** *adj.*

whey·ey (hwā′ē, wā′ē), *adj.* of, like, or containing whey. [1540–50; WHEY + -EY[1]]

whey·face (hwā′fās′, wā′-), *n.* a face that or a person who is pallid, as from fear. [1595–1605; WHEY + FACE] —**whey′faced′,** *adj.*

whey·ish (hwā′ish, wā′-), *adj.* rather like whey: *a mottled, wheyish complexion.* [1555–65; WHEY + -ISH[1]]

whf., wharf.

which (hwich, wich), *pron.* **1.** what one?: *Which of these do you want? Which do you want?* **2.** whichever: *Choose which appeals to you.* **3.** (used relatively in restrictive and nonrestrictive clauses to represent a specified antecedent): *The book, which I read last night, was exciting. The socialism which Owen preached was unpalatable to many. The lawyer represented five families, of which the Costello family was the largest.* **4.** (used relatively in restrictive clauses having *that* as the antecedent): *Damaged goods constituted part of that which was sold at the auction.* **5.** (used after a preposition to represent a specified antecedent): *the horse on which I rode.* **6.** (used relatively to represent a specified or implied antecedent) the one that; a particular one that: *You may choose which you like.* **7.** (used in parenthetic clauses) the thing or fact that: *He hung around for hours and, which was worse, kept me from doing my work.* **8.** *Nonstandard.* who or whom: *a friend which helped me move; the lawyer which you hired.* —*adj.* **9.** what one of (a certain number or group mentioned or implied)?: *Which book do you want?* **10.** whichever; any that: *Go which way you please, you'll end up here.* **11.** being previously mentioned: *It stormed all day, during which time the ship broke up.* [bef. 900; ME; OE *hwilc, hwelc,* equiv. to *hwe-* (base of *hwā* WHO) + *-līc* body, shape, kind (see LIKE[1]); c. OFris *hwelik,* D *welk,* G *welch,* Goth *hwileiks* lit., of what form] —**Usage.** The relative pronoun WHICH refers to inanimate things and to animals: *The house, which we had seen only from a distance, impressed us even more as we approached. The horses which pulled the coach were bay geldings.* Formerly, WHICH referred to persons, but this use, while still heard (*a man which I know*), is nonstandard. Contrary to the teachings of some usage guides, WHICH introduces both restrictive and nonrestrictive clauses. The "rule" that WHICH can be used only with nonrestrictive clauses has no basis in fact. In edited prose three-fourths of the clauses in which WHICH is the relative pronoun are restrictive: *A novel which he later wrote quickly became a bestseller.* See also **that.**

which·ev·er (hwich ev′ər, wich-), *pron.* **1.** any one that: *Take whichever you like.* **2.** no matter which: *Whichever you choose, the others will be offended.* —*adj.* **3.** no matter which: *whichever day; whichever ones you choose.* [1350–1400; ME; see WHICH, EVER]

which·so·ev·er (hwich′sō ev′ər, wich′-), *pron., adj.* whichever. [1400–50; late ME; WHICH, SOEVER]

which·way (hwich′wā′, wich′-), *adv.* See **every** (def. 6). [WHICH + WAY[1]]

whick·er (hwik′ər, wik′-), *Chiefly New Eng. and South Atlantic States.* —*v.i.* **1.** to whinny; neigh. —*n.* **2.** a whinny; neigh. [1650–60; *whick-* (cf. OE *hwicung* squeaking, said of mice) + -ER[6]; akin to G *wiehern* to neigh]

whid (hwid, hwud, wid, wud), *v.,* **whid·ded, whid·ding,** *n. Scot.* —*v.i.* **1.** to move quickly and quietly. —*n.* **2.** a quick, noiseless movement. [1580–90; appar. akin to OE *hwitha* a breeze (c. ON *hvitha* gust)]

whid·ah (hwid′ə, wid′ə), *n.* whydah.

whiff[1] (hwif, wif), *n.* **1.** a slight gust or puff of wind, air, vapor, smoke, or the like: *a whiff of fresh air.* **2.** a slight trace of odor or smell: *a whiff of onions.* **3.** a single inhalation or exhalation of air, tobacco smoke, or the like. **4.** a trace or hint: *a whiff of scandal.* **5.** a slight outburst: *a little whiff of temper.* —*v.i.* **6.** to blow or come in whiffs or puffs, as wind or smoke. **7.** to inhale or exhale whiffs, as in smoking tobacco. **8.** *Baseball Slang.* (of a batter) to strike out by swinging at and missing the pitch charged as the third strike. —*v.t.* **9.** to blow or drive with a whiff or puff, as the wind does. **10.** to inhale or exhale (air, tobacco smoke, etc.) in whiffs. **11.** to smoke (a pipe, cigar, etc.). **12.** *Baseball Slang.* (of a pitcher) to cause (a batter) to whiff. [1585–95; aspirated var. of ME *weffe* whiff (of steam or vapor)] —**whiff′er,** *n.*

whiff[2] (hwif, wif), *n.* any of several flatfishes having both eyes on the left side of the head, of the genus *Citharichthys,* as *C. cornutus* **(horned whiff),** inhabiting Atlantic waters from New England to Brazil. Cf. **lefteyed flounder.** [1705–15; orig. uncert.]

whif·fet (hwif′it, wif′-), *n. Informal.* an insignificant person; whippersnapper. [1795–1805, *Amer.;* WHIFF[1] + -ET, modeled on *whippet*]

whif·fle (hwif′əl, wif′-), *v.,* **-fled, -fling.** —*v.i.* **1.** to blow in light or shifting gusts or puffs, as the wind; veer or toss about irregularly. **2.** to shift about; vacillate; be fickle. —*v.t.* **3.** to blow with light, shifting gusts. [1550–60; WHIFF + -LE]

whif·fler[1] (hwif′lər, wif′-), *n.* **1.** a person who frequently shifts opinions, attitudes, interests, etc. **2.** a person who is vacillating or evasive in an argument. [1600–10; WHIFFLE + -ER[1]]

whif·fler[2] (hwif′lər, wif′-), *n. Hist.* an attendant who clears the way for a procession. [1530–40; earlier *wiffler* armed attendant, equiv. to *wiffle* (var. of ME *wifle,* OE *wifel* battle-ax) + -ER[1]]

whif·fle·tree (hwif′əl trē′, wif′-), *n. Northern U.S.* a crossbar, pivoted at the middle, to which the traces of a harness are fastened for pulling a cart, carriage, plow, etc. Also called **whippletree, singletree, swingletree.** Cf. **doubletree.** [1820–30; var. of WHIPPLETREE]

W, whiffletrees; D, doubletree

whig (hwig, wig), *v.i.,* **whigged, whig·ging.** *Scot.* to move along briskly. [1660–70; perh. Scots var. of dial. *fig* to move briskly; see FIDGET]

Whig (hwig, wig), *n.* **1.** *Amer. Hist.* **a.** a member of the patriotic party during the Revolutionary period; supporter of the Revolution. **b.** a member of a political party (c1834–1855) that was formed in opposition to the Democratic party, and favored economic expansion and a high protective tariff, while opposing the strength of the presidency in relation to the legislature. **2.** *Brit. Politics.* **a.** a member of a major political party (1679–1832) in Great Britain that held liberal principles and favored reforms: later called the Liberal party. **b.** (in later use) one of the more conservative members of the Liberal party. —*adj.* **3.** being a Whig. **4.** of, pertaining to, or characteristic of the Whigs. [1635–45; earlier, a Covenanter, hence an opponent of the accession of James II; of uncert. orig., though prob. in part a shortening of *whiggamaire* (later *whiggamore*), a participant in the *Whiggamore Raid* a march against the royalists in Edinburgh launched by Covenanters in 1648 (said to represent *whig* to spur on (cf. WHIG) + *maire* MARE[1])]

Whig·gish (hwig′ish, wig′-), *adj.* **1.** of, pertaining to, or characteristic of Whigs or Whiggism. **2.** inclined to Whiggism. [1670–80; WHIG + -ISH[1]] —**Whig′gish·ly,** *adv.* —**Whig′gish·ness,** *n.*

Whig·gism (hwig′iz əm, wig′-), *n.* the principles or practices of Whigs. Also, **Whig·ger·y** (hwig′ə rē, wig′-). [1660–70; WHIG + -ISM]

whig·ma·lee·rie (hwig′mə lēr′ē, wig′-), *n.* **1.** a whim; notion. **2.** a whimsical or fanciful ornament or contrivance; gimmick. [1720–30; orig. Scots, earlier *figmalirie,* perh. with *fig* (see FIDGET, WHIG); for *-ma-,* cf. RIGMAROLE, THINGAMAJIG]

whig·ma·lee·ry (hwig′mə lēr′ē, wig′-), *n., pl.* **-ries.** whigmaleerie.

while (hwīl, wīl), *n., conj., prep., v.,* **whiled, whil·ing.** —*n.* **1.** a period or interval of time: *to wait a long while; He arrived a short while ago.* **2.** *Archaic.* a particular time or occasion. **3. all the while,** at or during this time; all along: *She realized all the while that the cake would fall.* **4. worth one's while,** worth one's time, trouble, or expense: *The art exhibition that opened yesterday isn't worth your while.* —*conj.* **5.** during or in the time that. **6.** throughout the time that; as long as. **7.** even though; although: *While she appreciated the honor, she could not accept the position.* **8.** at the same time that (showing an analogous or corresponding action): *The floor was strewn with books, while magazines covered the tables.* —*prep.* **9.** *Archaic.* until. —*v.t.* **10.** to cause (time) to pass, esp. in some easy or pleasant manner (usually fol. by *away*). [bef. 900; ME; OE *hwīl;* c. D *wijl,* G *weile,* ON *hvīla,* Goth *hweila*]

whiles (hwīlz, wīlz), *adv.* **1.** *Chiefly Scot.* at times. **2.** *Obs.* in the meantime. —*conj.* **3.** *Archaic.* while. [1175–1225; ME; see WHILE, -S[1]]

whil·li·kers (hwil′i kərz, wil′-), *interj. Informal.* (used as an intensive after *gee* or *golly gee* to express astonishment, delight, etc.) Also, **whil·li·kins** (hwil′i kinz, wil′-). [orig. uncert.]

whi·lom (hwī′ləm, wī′-), *Archaic.* —*adj.* **1.** former; erstwhile: *whilom friends.* —*adv.* **2.** at one time. [bef. 900; ME; OE *hwīlum* at times, dat. pl. of *hwīl* WHILE (n.)]

whilst (hwīlst, wīlst), *conj.* while. [1325–75; ME *whilest,* equiv. to WHILES + parasitic *-t* as in *amongst, amidst*]

whim (hwim, wim), *n.* **1.** an odd or capricious notion or desire; a sudden or freakish fancy: *a sudden whim to take a midnight walk.* **2.** capricious humor: *to be swayed by whim.* [1635–45; short for WHIM-WHAM] —**Syn. 1.** whimsy, vagary, caprice.

whim·brel (hwim′brəl, wim′-), *n.* a curlew, *Numenius phaeopus,* of both the New and Old Worlds. [1520–30; *whim* (perh. imit.) + intrusive *-b-* + -REL]

whim·per (hwim′pər, wim′-), *v.i.* **1.** to cry with low,

plaintive, broken sounds. —*v.t.* **2.** to utter in a whimper. —*n.* **3.** a whimpering cry or sound. [1505–15; obs. *whimp* to whine + -ER[6]] —**whim′per·er,** *n.* —**whim′·per·ing·ly,** *adv.*
—**Syn. 1.** whine, weep, sob. **3.** whine, sob.

whim·sey (hwim′zē, wim′-), *n., pl.* **-seys.** whimsy.

whim·si·cal (hwim′zi kəl, wim′-), *adj.* **1.** given to whimsy or fanciful notions; capricious: *a pixyish, whimsical fellow.* **2.** of the nature of or proceeding from whimsy, as thoughts or actions: *Her writing showed whimsical notions of human behavior.* **3.** erratic; unpredictable: *He was too whimsical with regard to his work.* [1645–55; WHIMS(Y) + -ICAL] —**whim′si·cal·ly,** *adv.*

whim·si·cal·i·ty (hwim′zi kal′i tē, wim′-), *n., pl.* **-ties** for 2. **1.** Also, **whim′si·cal·ness.** whimsical quality or character. **2.** a whimsical notion, speech, or act. [1750–60; WHIMSICAL + -ITY]

whim·sy (hwim′zē, wim′-), *n., pl.* **-sies. 1.** capricious humor or disposition; extravagant, fanciful, or excessively playful expression: *a play with lots of whimsy.* **2.** an odd or fanciful notion. **3.** anything odd or fanciful; a product of playful or capricious fancy: *a whimsy from an otherwise thoughtful writer.* Also, **whimsey.** [1595–1605; WHIM(-WHAM) + -SY]
—**Syn. 2.** caprice, whim, humor.

whim-wham (hwim′hwam′, wim′wam′), *n.* **1.** any odd or fanciful object or thing; a gimcrack. **2. whim-whams,** *Informal.* nervousness; jitters: *He had the whim-whams after the accident.* [1490–1500; gradational compound; cf. FLIMFLAM, JIMJAMS, etc.]

whin (hwin, win), *n. Chiefly Brit.* any thorny or prickly shrub, esp. gorse. [1375–1425; late ME *whynne,* appar. < Scand; cf. Icel *hvingras* bent grass, Dan *hvene,* Sw *(h)ven*]

whin·chat (hwin′chat′, win′-), *n.* a small Old World thrush, *Saxicola rubetra,* having a buff-colored breast and white streaks in the tail. [1670–80; WHIN + CHAT]

whine (hwin, win), *v.,* **whined, whin·ing,** *n.* —*v.i.* **1.** to utter a low, usually nasal, complaining cry or sound, as from uneasiness, discontent, peevishness, etc.: *The puppies were whining from hunger.* **2.** to snivel or complain in a peevish, self-pitying way: *He is always whining about his problems.* —*v.t.* **3.** to utter with or as if with a whine: *I whined my litany of complaints.* —*n.* **4.** a whining utterance, sound, or tone. **5.** a feeble, peevish complaint. [bef. 1150; ME *whinen* (v.), OE *hwīnan* to whiz; c. ON *hvīna*] —**whin′er,** *n.* —**whin′ing·ly,** *adv.*
—**Syn. 1.** moan, whimper. **2.** See **complain.**

whing-ding (hwing′ding′, wing′-), *n.* wing-ding.

whinge (hwinj, winj), *v.i.,* **whinged, whing·ing.** *Australian Slang.* to complain; whine. [bef. 1150; dial. (Scots, N England), earlier Scots *quhynge,* OE *hwinsian* (not recorded in ME); c. OHG *winsōn* (G *winseln*); deriv. of Gmc base of WHINE] —**whing′er,** *n.*

whin·ny (hwin′ē, win′ē), *v.,* **-nied, -ny·ing,** *n., pl.* **-nies.** —*v.i.* **1.** to utter the characteristic cry of a horse; neigh. —*v.t.* **2.** to express by whinnying. —*n.* **3.** a whinnying sound. [1520–30; imit.; cf. earlier *whrinny,* L *hinnire*]

whin·stone (hwin′stōn′, win′-), *n. Chiefly Brit.* any of the dark-colored, fine-grained rocks, esp. igneous rocks, as dolerite and basalt. [1505–15; dial. (Scots and N England) *whin* whinstone (ME *quin* < ?) + STONE]

whin·y (hwī′nē, wī′-), *adj.,* **whin·i·er, whin·i·est.** complaining; fretful; cranky: *The baby is whiny because he missed his nap.* Also, **whin′ey.** [1850–55; WHINE + -Y[1]] —**whin′i·ness,** *n.*

whip (hwip, wip), *v.,* **whipped** or **whipt, whip·ping,** *n.* —*v.t.* **1.** to beat with a strap, lash, rod, or the like, esp. by way of punishment or chastisement; flog; thrash: *Criminals used to be whipped for minor offenses.* **2.** to strike with quick, repeated strokes of something slender and flexible; lash: *He impatiently whipped his leg with his riding crop.* **3.** to drive with lashes; urge or force on with, or as with, a lash, rod, etc. **4.** to lash or castigate with words. **5.** to unite, bring together, or bring into line: *The sergeant was ordered to whip the troops into line.* **6.** *Informal.* to defeat or overcome: *to whip the opposition; to whip a bad habit.* **7.** to hoist or haul by means of a whip. **8.** to move quickly and suddenly; pull, jerk, seize, or the like, with a sudden movement (often fol. by *out, in, into,* etc.): *He whipped his gun out of its holster.* **9.** to fish (a stream, lake, etc.) with rod and line, esp. by making repeated casts: *I whipped the stream all day and caught nothing.* **10.** to beat (eggs, cream, etc.) to a froth with an eggbeater, whisk, fork, or other implement in order to mix in air and cause expansion. **11.** to overlay or cover (cord, rope, etc.) with cord, thread, or the like wound about it: *to whip the end of a hawser.* **12.** to wind (cord, twine, thread, etc.) about something: *The tailor whipped the seams with heavy thread.* **13.** to use a light overcasting stitch in sewing. —*v.i.* **14.** to move or go quickly and suddenly; dart; whisk: *She whipped into the store for some milk.* **15.** to beat or lash about, as a pennant in the wind. **16.** to fish with rod and line, esp. by casting the line frequently. **17. whip in,** *Hunting.* to prevent from wandering, as hounds. **18. whip off,** *Informal.* to write hurriedly: *He whipped off three new songs last night.* **19. whip up,** *Informal.* **a.** to plan or assemble quickly: *to whip up a delicious dinner.* **b.** to incite; arouse; stir: *The crowd was whipped up to a frenzy.* —*n.* **20.** an instrument for striking, as in driving animals or in punishing, typically consisting of a lash or other flexible part with a more rigid handle. **21.** a whipping or lashing stroke or motion. **22.** a utensil for whipping; whisk. **23.** a dish made of cream or egg whites whipped to a froth with flavoring, often with fruit pulp or the like: *prune whip.* **24.** *Politics.* **a.** a party manager in a legislative body who secures attendance for voting and directs other members. **b.** (in Britain) a written call made on members of a party to be in attendance for voting. **25.** a windmill vane. **26.** *Hunting.* a whipper-in. **27.** a tackle consisting of a fall rove through a single standing block **(single whip)** so as to change the direction of hauling with no mechanical advantage, or consisting of a fall secured at one end and rove through a single running and a single standing block **(double whip)** so as to change the direction of hauling with a mechanical advantage of two, neglecting friction. Cf. **gun tackle.** See diag. under **tackle. 28.** the wrapping around the end of a whipped cord or the like. **29.** Also called **whirl.** *Mach.* eccentric rotation of a shaft having its center line slightly curved between supporting bearings. **30.** a branchless shoot of a woody plant, esp. one resulting from the first year's growth of a bud or graft. **31.** *Chiefly Brit.* a person who uses a whip as part of his or her work, as a driver of horses or a coachman. [1200–50; ME *w(h)ippe* (n.), *w(h)ippen* (v.); c. D *wippen* to swing, oscillate; cf. LG *wip(pe)* quick movement] —**whip′like′,** *adj.* —**whip′per,** *n.*
—**Syn. 1.** scourge, flagellate, switch, punish, chastise. **6.** beat, conquer. **8, 10.** whisk. **20.** switch.

whip′-and-tongue′ graft′ (hwip′ən tung′, wip′-), *Hort.* a graft prepared by cutting both the scion and the stock in a sloping direction and inserting a tongue in the scion into a slit in the stock. Also called **tongue graft.** Cf. **whip graft.**

whip·cord (hwip′kôrd′, wip′-), *n.* **1.** a cotton, woolen, or worsted fabric with a steep, diagonally ribbed surface. **2.** a strong, hard-twisted cord, sometimes used for the lashes of whips. **3.** a cord made from the intestines of animals; catgut. [1275–1325; ME *wyppe-cord.* See WHIP, CORD]

whip-crack·er (hwip′krak′ər, wip′-), *n.* **1.** a person who cracks a whip. **2.** a person who exerts authority, esp. excessively or ostentatiously.

whip′ graft′, *Hort.* a graft prepared by cutting both the scion and the stock in a sloping direction and securing them by tying or taping. Cf. **whip-and-tongue graft.** [1665–75]

whip′ hand′, 1. the hand that holds the whip, in driving. **2.** an advantageous or controlling position: *She had the whip hand throughout the debate.* [1670–80]

whip·lash (hwip′lash′, wip′-), *n.* **1.** the lash of a whip. **2.** an abrupt snapping motion or change of direction resembling the lash of a whip. **3.** Also, **whip′lash in′jury.** a neck injury caused by a sudden jerking backward, forward, or both, of the head: *Whiplash resulted when their car was struck from behind.* **4.** Also called **whip′lash curve′.** a connected series of reverse curves of more or less elliptical form, used as a major design motif in the Art Nouveau style. —*v.t.* **5.** to beat, hit, throw, etc., with or as if with a whiplash. **6.** to affect adversely, as by a sudden change: *new taxes whiplashing corporate earnings.* [1565–75; 1950–55 for def. 6; WHIP + LASH[1]]

whipped (hwipt, wipt), *adj.* **1.** having received a whipping. **2.** subdued or defeated as though by whipping: *whipped by poverty.* **3.** beaten into a froth: *whipped cream.* **4.** exhausted, tired, beat: *After all that weeding, I'm whipped.* [1540–50; WHIP + -ED[2]]

whip·per-in (hwip′ər in′, wip′-), *n., pl.* **whip·pers-in. 1.** *Fox Hunting.* a professional or honorary member of a hunt staff who assists the huntsman with the hounds. **2.** *Brit.* whip (def. 31). [1730–40]

whip·per·snap·per (hwip′ər snap′ər, wip′-), *n.* an unimportant but offensively presumptuous person, esp. a young one. [1665–75; prob. b. earlier *whipster* and *snippersnapper,* similar in sense; see WHIP, SNAP, -ER[1]]

whip·pet (whip′it, wip′-), *n.* **1.** one of a breed of small, swift dogs resembling a greyhound, used for hunting rabbits and for racing. **2.** Also called **whip′pet tank′.** a fast, light tank used by the British in World War I. [1490–1500; perh. alter. of phrase *whip it* move briskly]

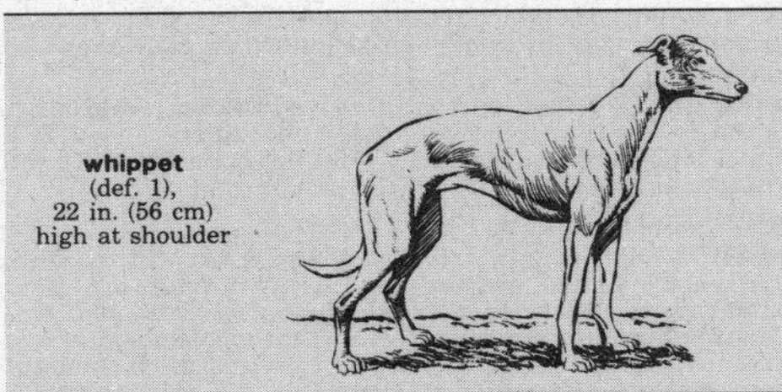
whippet (def. 1), 22 in. (56 cm) high at shoulder

whip·ping (hwip′ing, wip′-), *n.* **1.** a beating or flogging, esp. one administered with a whip or the like in punishment. **2.** a defeat, as in sports. **3.** an arrangement of cord, twine, or the like, whipped or wound about a thing, as to bind parts together or prevent unraveling, as at the end of a rope. [1530–40; WHIP + -ING[1]]

whip′ping boy′, 1. a person who is made to bear the blame for another's mistake; scapegoat. **2.** (formerly) a boy educated along with and taking punishment in place of a young prince or nobleman. [1640–50]

whip′ping cream′, cream with enough butterfat to allow it to be made into whipped cream.

whip′ping post′, a post to which persons are tied to undergo whipping as a legal penalty. [1590–1600]

Whip·ple (hwip′əl, wip′-), *n.* **1. Fred Lawrence,** born 1906, U.S. astronomer. **2. George Hoyt** (hoit), 1878–1976, U.S. pathologist: Nobel prize for medicine 1934.

whip·ple·tree (hwip′əl trē′, wip′-), *n. Northern U.S.* whiffletree. [1725–35; *whipple* (see WHIP, -LE) + TREE]

whip·poor·will (hwip′ər wil′, wip′-; hwip′ər wil′, wip′-), *n.* a nocturnal North American nightjar, *Caprimulgus vociferus,* having a variegated plumage of gray, black, white, and tawny. [1700–10, *Amer.*; imit.]

whip·py (hwip′ē, wip′ē), *adj.,* **-pi·er, -pi·est. 1.** of, pertaining to, or resembling a whip. **2.** bending and snapping back in the manner of a whip: *a whippy tree branch.* [1865–70; WHIP + -Y[1]]

whip·ray (hwip′rā′, wip′-), *n.* any ray having a long, whiplike tail, esp. a stingray. [1690–1700; WHIP + RAY[2]]

whip′ roll′, *Textiles.* a roller, located at the back of a loom, that guides the warp ends as they come up from the warp beam on their way to the harness. [1860–65]

whip·saw (hwip′sô′, wip′-), *n., v.,* **-sawed, -sawed** or **-sawn, -saw·ing.** —*n.* **1.** a saw for two persons, as a pitsaw, used to divide timbers lengthwise. —*v.t.* **2.** to cut with a whipsaw. **3.** to win two bets from (a person) at one turn or play, as at faro. **4.** to subject to two opposing forces at the same time: *The real-estate market has been whipsawed by high interest rates and unemployment.* —*v.i.* **5.** (of a trailer, railroad car, etc.) to swing suddenly to the right or left, as in rounding a sharp curve at high speed. [1530–40; WHIP + SAW[1]]

whip·sawed (hwip′sôd′, wip′-), *adj. Stock Exchange.* subjected to a double loss, as when an investor has bought a stock at a high price soon before it declines and then, in order to make good the loss, sells it short before it advances. [WHIPSAW + -ED[2]]

whip·scor·pi·on (hwip′skôr′pē ən, wip′-), *n.* any of numerous arachnids of the order Uropygi, of tropical and warm temperate regions, resembling a scorpion but having an abdomen that ends in a slender, nonvenomous whip. [1885–90; WHIP + SCORPION]

whip·snake (hwip′snāk′, wip′-), *n.* **1.** any of several long, slender New World snakes of the genus *Masticophis,* the tail of which resembles a whip. **2.** any of various similar or related snakes. Also, **whip′ snake′.** [1765–75; WHIP + SNAKE]

whip·stall (hwip′stôl′, wip′-), *Aeron.* —*n.* **1.** a stall during a vertical climb in which the nose of the airplane falls forward and downward in a whiplike movement. —*v.t.* **2.** to cause (an aircraft) to undergo whipstall. —*v.i.* **3.** (of an aircraft) to undergo whipstall. [1920–25; WHIP + STALL[1]]

whip·stitch (hwip′stich′, wip′-), *v.t.* **1.** to sew with stitches passing over an edge, in joining, finishing, or gathering. —*n.* **2.** one such stitch. **3. every whipstitch,** *Southern U.S.* at short intervals: *She drops in to see us every whipstitch.* [1585–95; WHIP + STITCH]

whip·stock (hwip′stok′, wip′-), *n.* the handle of a whip. [1520–30; WHIP + STOCK]

whip·tail (hwip′tāl′, wip′-), *n.* **1.** any of numerous New World lizards of the family Teiidae, esp. of the genus *Cnemidophorus,* characterized by great agility and alertness. **2.** any of various other whip-tailed animals, as the whipscorpion. [1765–75; WHIP + TAIL[1]]

whip-tailed (hwip′tāld′, wip′-), *adj.* having a long, slender tail like a whip. [WHIP + TAIL[1] + -ED[3]]

whip′-tailed ray′, a whipray. [1895–1900]

whip·worm (hwip′wûrm′, wip′-), *n.* any of several parasitic nematodes of the genus *Trichuris,* having a long, slender, whiplike anterior end. [1870–75; WHIP + WORM]

whir (hwûr, wûr), *v.,* **whirred, whir·ring,** *n.* —*v.i.* **1.** to go, fly, revolve, or otherwise move quickly with a humming or buzzing sound: *An electric fan whirred softly in the corner.* —*v.t.* **2.** to move or transport (a thing, person, etc.) with a whirring sound: *The plane whirred them away into the night.* —*n.* **3.** an act or sound of whirring: *the whir of wings.* Also, **whirr.** [1350–1400; ME *quirre* (Scots) < Scand; cf. Dan *hvirre,* Norw *kvirra.* See WHIRL]

whirl (hwûrl, wûrl), *v.i.* **1.** to turn around, spin, or rotate rapidly: *The merry-go-round whirled noisily.* **2.** to turn about or aside quickly: *He whirled and faced his pursuers.* **3.** to move, travel, or be carried rapidly along: *She whirled along the freeway in her new car.* **4.** to feel as though spinning rapidly; reel as from dizziness: *My head began to whirl.* —*v.t.* **5.** to cause to turn around, spin, or rotate rapidly. **6.** to send, drive, or carry in a circular or curving course. **7.** to drive, send, or carry along with great or dizzying rapidity. **8.** *Obs.* to hurl. —*n.* **9.** the act of whirling; rapid rotation or gyration. **10.** a whirling movement; quick turn or swing. **11.** a short drive, run, walk, or the like; spin. **12.** something that whirls; a whirling current or mass. **13.** a rapid round of events, affairs, etc.: *a whirl of meetings, conferences, and business lunches.* **14.** a state marked by dizziness or a dizzying succession of feelings, thoughts, etc. **15.** an attempt or trial, esp. one undertaken tentatively or experimentally: *Even if you don't agree with my plan, won't you give it a whirl?* **16.** *Mach.* whip (def. 29). [1250–1300; ME *whirlen* < ON *hvirfla* to whirl, akin to OE *hwyrflung* turning, revolving, *hwyrfel* circuit; see WHORL] —**whirl′er,** *n.* —**whirl′ing·ly,** *adv.*
—**Syn. 1.** gyrate, pirouette. **1, 5.** revolve, twirl, wheel. **9.** spin, revolution. **15.** try, go, fling, whack.

whirl·a·bout (hwûrl′ə bout′, wûrl′-), *n.* **1.** a whirling about. **2.** a whirligig. —*adj.* **3.** whirling about. [1585–95; WHIRL + ABOUT]

whirl·i·gig (hwûr′li gig′, wûr′-), *n.* **1.** something that whirls or revolves. **2.** a whirling motion or course: *the whirligig of fashion.* **3.** a giddy or flighty person. **4.** *Dial.* a merry-go-round or carrousel. **5.** a toy for whirling or spinning, as a top. [1400–50; late ME *whirlegigge.* See WHIRL, GIG[1]]

whirl′igig bee′tle, any of numerous aquatic beetles of the family Gyrinidae, commonly seen in groups circling about rapidly on the surface of the water. [1850–55]

whirl′ing der′vish, *Islam.* a member of a Turkish order of dervishes, or Sufis, whose ritual consists in part of a highly stylized whirling dance.

whirl·pool (hwûrl′po͞ol′, wûrl′-), *n.* **1.** water in swift, circular motion, as that produced by the meeting of opposing currents, often causing a downward spiraling ac-

CONCISE ETYMOLOGY KEY: <, descended or borrowed from; >, whence; b., blend of, blended; c., cognate with; cf., compare; deriv., derivative; equiv., equivalent; imit., imitative; obl., oblique; r., replacing; s., stem; sp., spelling, spelled; resp., respelling, respelled; trans., translation; ?, origin unknown; *, unattested; ‡, probably earlier than. See the full key inside the front cover.

tion. **2.** See **whirlpool bath.** **3.** *Heraldry.* gurge (def. 2). [1520–30; WHIRL + POOL[1]; cf. late OE *hwyrfepōl*]

whirl′pool bath′, **1.** a bath in which the body is immersed in swirling water as therapy or for relaxation. **2.** a device that swirls and often heats the water in such a bath. **3.** a tub or pool containing or equipped with such a device. Also called **whirlpool.** [1915–20]

whirl·wind (hwûrl′wind′, wûrl′-), *n.* **1.** any of several relatively small masses of air rotating rapidly around a more or less vertical axis and advancing simultaneously over land or sea, as a dust devil, tornado, or waterspout. **2.** anything resembling a whirlwind, as in violent action or destructive force. **3.** any circling rush or violent onward course. **4. reap the whirlwind,** to suffer the penalties for one's misdeeds. Hos. 8:7. —*adj.* **5.** like a whirlwind, as in speed or force: *a whirlwind visit to New York.* —*v.i.* **6.** to move or travel quickly. [1300–50; ME < ON *hvirfilvindr;* c. G *Wirbelwind*]
—**Syn. 5.** headlong, breakneck, hasty, impulsive.

whirl·y (hwûr′lē, wûr′-), *n., pl.* **whirl·ies.** a violent whirlwind carrying snow, occurring in Antarctica. [WHIRL + -Y[2]]

whirl·y·bird (hwûr′lē bûrd′, wûr′-), *n. Informal.* helicopter. [1950–55; WHIRL + -Y[1] + BIRD]

whirr (hwûr, wûr), *v.i., v.t., n.* whir.

whir·ry (hwûr′ē, wûr′ē), *v.,* **-ried, -ry·ing.** *Scot.* —*v.i.* **1.** to hurry; go rapidly. —*v.t.* **2.** to carry (something) or drive (cattle) swiftly. [1575–85; perh. b. WHIR and HURRY]

whish (hwish, wish), *v.i., v.t.* **1.** to make, or move with, a whiz or swish. —*n.* **2.** a whishing sound. [1510–20; imit.]

whisht (hwist, wist, hwisht, wisht), *interj., adj., n., v.i., v.t.* whist[2]. [1510–20; ult. imit.; cf. OE *hwiscettung* squeaking (said of mice)]

whisk (hwisk, wisk), *v.t.* **1.** to move with a rapid, sweeping stroke: *She whisked everything off the table with her arm.* **2.** to sweep (dust, crumbs, etc., or a surface) with a whisk broom, brush, or the like. **3.** to draw, snatch, carry, etc., lightly and rapidly: *He whisked the money into his pocket.* **4.** to whip (eggs, cream, etc.) to a froth with a whisk or beating instrument. —*v.i.* **5.** to sweep, pass, or go lightly and rapidly. —*n.* **6.** an act of whisking. **7.** a rapid, sweeping stroke; light, rapid movement. **8.** See **whisk broom.** **9.** a small bunch of grass, straw, hair, or the like, esp. for use in brushing. **10.** an implement, usually a bunch of wire loops held together in a handle, for beating or whipping eggs, cream, etc. [1325–75; (n.) ME (Scots) *wysk* rapid sweeping movement; (v.) earlier Scots *wisk, quhisk* < Scand; cf. ON, Norw *visk* wisp, Sw *viska* besom, wisp, to whisk (off), Dan *viske* to wipe (cf. OHG *wisken* to wipe, *wisc* wisp of hay); for development of *wh* cf. WHIP]

whisk′ broom′, a small, short-handled broom used chiefly to brush clothes. [1855–60]

whisk·er (hwis′kər, wis′-), *n.* **1. whiskers,** a beard. **2.** Usually, **whiskers.** See **side whiskers.** **3.** a single hair of the beard. **4.** *Archaic.* a mustache. **5.** one of the long, stiff, bristly hairs growing about the mouth of certain animals, as the cat or rat; vibrissa. **6.** Also called **whisk′er boom′, whisk′er pole′.** *Naut.* any spar for extending the clew or clews of a sail so that it can catch more wind. **7.** *Radio, Electronics.* See **cat whisker.** **8.** *Crystall.* a thin filament of a crystal, usually several millimeters long and one to two microns in diameter, having unusually great strength. **9. by a whisker,** by the narrowest margin: *She won the race by a whisker.* [1375–1425; late ME; see WHISK, -ER[1]] —**whisk′er·y,** *adj.*

whisk·ered (hwis′kərd, wis′-), *adj.* having, wearing, or covered with whiskers. [1755–65; WHISKER + -ED[3]]

whis·key (hwis′kē, wis′-), *n., pl.* **-keys,** *adj.* —*n.* **1.** an alcoholic liquor distilled from a fermented mash of grain, as barley, rye, or corn, and usually containing from 43 to 50 percent alcohol. **2.** a drink of whiskey. **3.** a word used in communications to represent the letter *W.* —*adj.* **4.** made of, relating to, or resembling whiskey. Also, **whisky.** [1705–15; short for *whiskybae* < Ir *uisce beatha* or ScotGael *uisge beatha,* ult. trans. of ML *aqua vitae* lit., water of life; cf. USQUEBAUGH]

whis′key jack′. See **gray jay.** [1735–45; var. of *whisky-John, whisky-Jonish,* by folk etym. < Eastmain Cree (dial. of Montagnais) *wi·skača·nis* Canada jay, dim. of *wi·skača·n* blacksmith, appar. alluding to the bird's smoky-gray color]

Whis′key Rebel′lion, *U.S. Hist.* a revolt of settlers in western Pennsylvania in 1794 against a federal excise tax on whiskey: suppressed by militia called out by President George Washington to establish the authority of the federal government.

whis′key sour′, a cocktail made with whiskey, lemon juice, and sugar. [1890–95, *Amer.*]

whis·ky (hwis′kē, wis′-), *n., pl.* **-kies,** *adj.* whiskey (used esp. for Scotch or Canadian whiskey).

whis·per (hwis′pər, wis′pər), *v.i.* **1.** to speak with soft, hushed sounds, using the breath, lips, etc., but with no vibration of the vocal cords. **2.** *Phonet.* to produce utterance substituting breath for phonation. **3.** to talk softly and privately (often implying gossip, slander, plotting, or the like): *The king knew that the courtiers were whispering.* **4.** (of trees, water, breezes, etc.) to make a soft, rustling sound like that of whispering. —*v.t.* **5.** to utter with soft, low sounds, using the breath, lips, etc.: *He whispered endearments to her.* **6.** *Phonet.* to utter (speech sounds) substituting breath for phonation. **7.** to say or tell in a whisper; tell privately. **8.** to speak to or tell (a person) in a whisper or privately. —*n.* **9.** the mode of utterance, or the voice, of a person who whispers: *to speak in a whisper.* **10.** a word or remark uttered by whispering. **11.** a rumor or insinuation: *Whispers circulated about the affair.* **12.** a soft, rustling sound like a whisper: *the whisper of leaves in the wind.* [bef. 950; ME *whisperen* (v.), OE *hwisprian;* c. G *wispern;* akin to ON *hviskra* to whisper, *hvísla* to whistle. See WHINE]

whis·pered (hwis′pərd, wis′-), *adj.* rumored; reported: *He is whispered to be planning to run for governor.* [1560–70; WHISPER + -ED[2]]

whis·per·er (hwis′pər ər, wis′-), *n.* **1.** a person or thing that whispers. **2.** a gossip, talebearer, rumormonger, or the like. [1540–50; WHISPER + -ER[1]]

whis·per·ing (hwis′pər ing, wis′-), *n.* **1.** whispered talk or conversation. **2.** rumor, hearsay, or gossip. **3.** a whispered sound. —*adj.* **4.** that whispers; making a sound like a whisper. **5.** like a whisper. **6.** given to whispering; gossipy. **7.** conversing in whispers. [bef. 1000; ME (n.), OE *hwisprunge.* See WHISPER, -ING[2], -ING[1]] —**whis′per·ing·ly,** *adv.*

whis′pering campaign′, the organized spreading of insinuations or rumors to destroy the reputation of a person, organization, etc. [1915–20]

whis′pering gal′lery, a space or gallery beneath a dome or broad arch in which low sounds produced at any of certain points are clearly audible at certain other distant points. [1690–1700]

whis·per·ous (hwis′pər əs, wis′-), *adj.* whispery. [1880–85; WHISPER + -OUS] —**whis′per·ous·ly,** *adv.*

whis·per·y (hwis′pə rē, wis′-), *adj.* **1.** like a whisper: *a soft, whispery voice.* **2.** abounding in whispers or other quiet, mysterious sounds: *dark, whispery streets.* [1825–35; WHISPER + -Y[1]]

whist[1] (hwist, wist), *n.* a card game, an early form of bridge, but without bidding. [1655–65; earlier *whisk,* perh. identical with WHISK, though sense relationship uncert.]

whist[2] (hwist, wist), *interj.* **1.** hush! silence! be still! —*adj.* **2.** hushed; silent; still. —*n.* **3.** *Chiefly Irish.* silence: *Hold your whist.* —*v.i.* **4.** *Brit. Dial.* to be or become silent. —*v.t.* **5.** *Brit. Dial.* to silence. Also, **whisht.** [1350–1400, ME; imit.]

whis·tle (hwis′əl, wis′-), *v.,* **-tled, -tling,** *n.* —*v.i.* **1.** to make a clear musical sound, a series of such sounds, or a high-pitched, warbling sound by the forcible expulsion of the breath through a small opening formed by contracting the lips, or through the teeth, with the aid of the tongue. **2.** to make such a sound or series of sounds otherwise, as by blowing on some device. **3.** to emit similar sounds from the mouth, as birds do. **4.** (of a device) to produce a similar sound when actuated by steam or the like: *This teakettle whistles when it boils.* **5.** to move, go, pass, etc., with a whistling or whizzing sound, as a bullet or the wind. —*v.t.* **6.** to produce by whistling: *to whistle a tune.* **7.** to call, direct, or signal by or as by whistling: *He whistled his dog over.* **8.** to send with a whistling or whizzing sound. **9. whistle for,** to demand or expect without success: *After promising to pay, he told us we could whistle for our money.* **10. whistle in the dark,** to attempt to summon up one's courage or optimism in a difficult situation: *He says his business will improve next year, but he's probably just whistling in the dark.* —*n.* **11.** an instrument for producing whistling sounds by means of the breath, steam, etc., as a small wooden or tin tube, a pipe, or a similar device with an air chamber containing a small ball that oscillates when air is forced through an opening, producing a high-pitched, warbling tone. **12.** a sound produced by whistling: *a prolonged whistle of astonishment.* **13.** a simple fipple flute. **14. blow the whistle,** to expose the existence of mischief or wrongdoing: *The agent was taking bribes until someone finally blew the whistle.* **15. blow the whistle on, a.** to bring a stop to; halt: *Congress has blown the whistle on all unnecessary expenditures for the program.* **b.** to expose (wrongdoing or wrongdoers): *to blow the whistle on corruption in high places.* **16. wet one's whistle,** *Informal.* to take a drink. [bef. 950; (v.) ME *whistlen,* OE *hwistlian;* akin to ON *hvísla* to whistle, *hviskra* to whisper; see WHINE; (n.) ME; OE *hwistle* instrument, akin to the v.] —**whis′tle·a·ble,** *adj.*

whis·tle-blow·er (hwis′əl blō′ər, wis′-), *n.* a person who informs on another or makes public disclosure of corruption or wrongdoing. Also, **whis′tle blow′er.** [1965–70] —**whis′tle-blow′ing,** *n.*

whis′tle pig′, *Chiefly Appalachian.* a woodchuck.

whis·tler (hwis′lər, wis′-), *n.* **1.** a person or thing that whistles. **2.** something that makes a sound like a whistle: *The windstorm was a 60-mile-an-hour whistler.* **3.** any of various birds whose wings whistle in flight, esp. the goldeneye. **4.** thickhead (def. 2). **5.** a large marmot, *Marmota caligata,* of mountainous northwestern North America, closely related to the woodchuck. **6.** a horse afflicted with whistling. **7.** *Radio.* a whistling sound heard on a radio, a type of interference caused by distant lightning. [bef. 1000; ME; OE *hwistlere.* See WHISTLE, -ER[1]]

Whis·tler (hwis′lər, wis′-), *n.* **James (Abbott) McNeill** (mək nēl′), 1834–1903, U.S. painter and etcher, in France and England after 1855. —**Whis·tle·ri·an** (hwis lēr′ē ən, wis-), *adj.*

Whis′tler's Moth′er, (formal name, *Arrangement in Gray and Black No. 1: Portrait of the Artist's Mother*) a painting (1871) by James McNeill Whistler.

whis′tles and bells′. See **bells and whistles.**

whis′tle stop′, **1.** a small, unimportant town, esp. one along a railroad line. **2.** a short talk from the rear platform of a train, esp. during a political campaign. **3.** a brief appearance, single performance, or the like, in a small town, as during a political campaign or theatrical tour. [1920–25, *Amer.*]

whis·tle-stop (hwis′əl stop′, wis′-), *v.,* **-stopped, -stop·ping,** *adj.* —*v.i.* **1.** to campaign for political office by traveling around the country, originally by train, stopping at small communities to address voters. **2.** to take a trip consisting of several brief, usually overnight, stops. —*adj.* **3.** occurring at a whistle stop; consisting of whistle stops: *a whistle-stop speech; a whistle-stop tour of the Northwest.* [1950–55]

whis·tling (hwis′ling, wis′-), *n.* **1.** the act of a person or thing that whistles. **2.** the sound produced. **3.** *Vet. Pathol.* a form of roaring characterized by a peculiarly shrill sound. [bef. 900; ME; OE *hwistlung.* See WHISTLE, -ING[1]]

whis′tling bu′oy, *Naut.* a buoy having a whistle operated by air trapped and compressed in an open-bottomed chamber by the rising and falling water level caused by natural wave action.

whis′tling duck′, any of several long-legged, chiefly tropical ducks of the genus *Dendrocygna,* most of which have whistling cries. [1690–1700]

whis′tling swan′, the small North American subspecies, *Cygnus columbianus columbianus,* of the tundra swan. [1775–85]

whit (hwit, wit), *n.* a particle; bit; jot (used esp. in negative phrases): *not a whit better.* [1470–80; perh. alter. of ME *wiht* WIGHT[1]]

Whit·a·ker (hwit′ə kər, wit′-), *n.* a male given name.

Whit·by (hwit′bē, wit′-), *n.* **1.** a port in SE Ontario, in S Canada, on Lake Ontario. 36,698. **2.** a seaport in E North Yorkshire, in NE England: ruins of an abbey; church council A.D. 664. 12,717.

Whit·church-Stouff·ville (hwit′chûrch′stō′vil, wit′-), *n.* a town in SW Ontario, in S Canada, N of Toronto. 12,884.

white (hwit, wit), *adj.,* **whit·er, whit·est,** *n., v.,* **whit·ed, whit·ing.** —*adj.* **1.** of the color of pure snow, of the margins of this page, etc.; reflecting nearly all the rays of sunlight or a similar light. **2.** light or comparatively light in color. **3.** (of human beings) marked by slight pigmentation of the skin, as of many Caucasoids. **4.** for, limited to, or predominantly made up of persons whose racial heritage is Caucasian: *a white club; a white neighborhood.* **5.** pallid or pale, as from fear or other strong emotion: *white with rage.* **6.** silvery, gray, or hoary: *white hair.* **7.** snowy: *a white Christmas.* **8.** lacking color; transparent. **9.** (politically) ultraconservative. **10.** blank, as an unoccupied space in printed matter: *Fill in the white space below.* **11.** *Armor.* composed entirely of polished steel plates without fabric or other covering; alwite. **12.** wearing white clothing: *a white monk.* **13.** *Slang.* decent, honorable, or dependable: *That's very white of you.* **14.** auspicious or fortunate. **15.** morally pure; innocent. **16.** without malice; harmless: *white magic.* **17.** (of wines) light-colored or yellowish, as opposed to red. **18.** *Brit.* (of coffee) containing milk. **19. bleed white,** *Informal.* to be or cause to be deprived of all one's resources: *Dishonesty is bleeding the union white.*
—*n.* **20.** a color without hue at one extreme end of the scale of grays, opposite to black. A white surface reflects light of all hues completely and diffusely. Most so-called whites are very light grays: fresh snow, for example, reflects about 80 percent of the incident light, but to be strictly white, snow would have to reflect 100 percent of the incident light. It is the ultimate limit of a series of shades of any color. **21.** a hue completely desaturated by admixture with white, the highest value possible. **22.** quality or state of being white. **23.** lightness of skin pigment. **24.** a person whose racial heritage is Caucasian. **25.** a white material or substance. **26.** the white part of something. **27.** *Biol.* a pellucid viscous fluid that surrounds the yolk of an egg; albumen. **28.** the white part of the eyeball: *He has a speck in the white of his eye.* **29. whites, a.** white or nearly white clothing. **b.** top-grade white flour. **30.** white wine: *Graves is a good white.* **31.** a type or breed that is white in color. **32.** Usually, **whites.** a blank space in printing. **33.** (*cap.*) a hog of any of several breeds having a white coat, as a Chester White. **34.** *Entomol.* any of several white-winged butterflies of the family Pieridae, as the common cabbage butterflies. **35.** white fabric. **36.** *Archery.* **a.** the outermost ring of the butt. **b.** an arrow that hits this portion of the butt. **c.** the central part of the butt or target, formerly painted white but now painted gold or yellow. **d.** *Archaic.* a target painted white. **37.** *Chess, Checkers.* the men or pieces that are light-colored. **38.** (*often cap.*) a member of a royalist, conservative, or reactionary political party. **39. in the white,** in an unfinished state or condition, as furniture wood that has not been stained or varnished.
—*v.t.* **40.** *Print.* **a.** to make white by leaving blank spaces (often fol. by *out*). **b.** to whiten (areas of artwork) in retouching preparatory to photoengraving (often fol. by *out*). **41.** *Archaic.* to make white; whiten. **42. white out, a.** to cover (errors in copy) with a white correction fluid. **b.** to censor, as by obliterating words or passages with white ink. [bef. 900; ME *whit(e),* OE *hwīt;* c. G *weiss,* ON *hvítr,* Goth *hweits;* akin to WHEAT]

White (hwīt, wīt), *n.* **1. Byron R(aymond)** ("*Whizzer*"), born 1917, U.S. lawyer and jurist: associate justice of the U.S. Supreme Court 1962–93. **2. Edward Douglass,** 1845–1921, U.S. jurist: Chief Justice of the U.S. 1910–21. **3. Edward H(ig·gins), II** (hig′inz), 1930–67, U.S. astronaut: first American to walk in space 1965. **4. E(l·wyn) B(rooks)** (el′win), 1899–1985, U.S. humorist and poet. **5. George Leonard,** 1838–95, U.S. choral conductor. **6. Gilbert,** 1720–93, English clergyman, naturalist, and writer. **7. Patrick (Victor Mar·tin·dale)** (mär′tn dāl′), 1912–90, Australian writer, born in England: Nobel prize 1973. **8. Stanford,** 1853–1906, U.S. architect. **9. Stewart Edward,** 1873–1946, U.S. novelist. **10. T(erence) H(an·bur·y)** (han′bə rē), 1896–1964, English novelist. **11. Walter Francis,** 1893–1955, U.S. civil-rights leader and writer: executive secretary of the NAACP 1931–55. **12. William A(l·an·son)** (al′ən sən), 1870–1937, U.S. neurologist, psychiatrist, and writer. **13. William Allen,** 1868–1944, U.S. journalist.

white·a·cre (hwīt′ā′kər, wīt′-), *n.* an arbitrary name for a piece of land used for purposes of supposition in legal argument or the like (often distinguished from *blackacre*). [1635–45; WHITE + ACRE]

white′ ad′miral. See under **purple** (def. 7).

CONCISE PRONUNCIATION KEY: act, cāpe, dâre, pärt; set, ēqual; if, īce; ox, ōver, ôrder, oil, bo͝ok, bo͞ot, out; up, ûrge; child; sing; shoe; thin, *th*at; zh as in *treasure.* ə = *a* as in *alone, e* as in *system, i* as in *easily, o* as in *gallop, u* as in *circus;* ᵊ as in *fire* (fīᵊr), *hour* (ouᵊr). l and n can serve as syllabic consonants, as in *cradle* (krād′l), and *button* (but′n). See the full key inside the front cover.

white′ al′der. See **sweet pepperbush.** [1855–60]

white′ alert′, **1.** (in military or civilian defense) an all-clear signal, directive, etc., indicating that the danger of air raid no longer exists. **2.** a return to normal conditions following an attack or a threat of attack. Cf. **blue alert, red alert, yellow alert.**

white′ al′kali, **1.** *Agric.* a whitish layer of mineral salts, esp. sodium sulfate, sodium chloride, and magnesium sulfate, often occurring on top of soils where rainfall is low. **2.** refined soda ash.

white′ ant′, termite. [1675–85]

white-ant (hwīt′ant′, wīt′-), *v.t. Australian Informal.* to undermine or subvert from within. [1915–20]

white′ ash′. See under **ash**² (def. 1). [1675–85]

white′ as′pen. See under **aspen** (def. 1).

white′ ba′con, *South Midland and Southern U.S.* bacon (def. 2). [1935–40]

white•bait (hwīt′bāt′, wīt′-), *n., pl.* **-bait. 1.** a young sprat or herring. **2.** *Cookery.* any small, delicate fish cooked whole without being cleaned, esp. the sprat. [1750–60; WHITE + BAIT, so called from use as bait]

white′ bass′ (bas), an edible freshwater fish, *Morone chrysops,* of the Great Lakes and Mississippi River drainage, silvery with yellow below and having the sides streaked with blackish lines. Also called **silver bass.**

white•beam (hwīt′bēm′, wīt′-), *n.* a European tree, *Sorbus aria,* of the rose family, having leathery leaves, showy, white flowers, and mealy, orange-red or scarlet fruit. [1695–1705; WHITE + BEAM]

white′ bear′. See **polar bear.** [1590–1600]

white•beard (hwīt′bērd′, wīt′-), *n.* an old man, esp. one with a white or gray beard. [1400–50; late ME; see WHITE, BEARD]

White′ Bear′ Lake′, a city in E Minnesota: summer resort. 22,538.

white′ belt′, *Martial Arts.* **1.** a white cloth waistband worn by a beginner in one of the martial arts, as judo or karate. **2.** a beginner or novice in one of the martial arts. **3.** the rank of beginner. Cf. **black belt** (def. 3), **brown belt.** —**white′-belt′,** *adj.*

white′ birch′, **1.** the European birch, *Betula pendula,* yielding a hard wood. **2.** See **paper birch.** [1780–90]

white′ blood′ cell′, any of various nearly colorless cells of the immune system that circulate mainly in the blood and lymph and participate in reactions to invading microorganisms or foreign particles, comprising the B cells, T cells, macrophages, monocytes, and granulocytes. Also called **leukocyte, white′ blood′ cor′puscle, white corpuscle, white′ cell′.** [1885–90]

white•board (hwīt′bôrd′, -bōrd′, wīt′-), *n.* a smooth, glossy sheet of white plastic that can be written on with a colored pen or marker in the manner of a blackboard. [1980–85]

white′ book′, an official report issued by a government, usually bound in white. [1400–50; late ME]

White•boys (hwīt′boiz′, wīt′-), *n.* (*used with a singular v.*) a secret agrarian peasant organization, active in Ireland during the early 1760's, whose members wore white shirts for recognition on their night raids to destroy crops, barns, and other property in redressing grievances against landlords and protesting the paying of tithes. [WHITE + BOY + -S³]

white′ bread′, any white or light-colored bread made from finely ground, usually bleached, flour. [1300–50; ME]

white-bread (hwīt′bred′, wīt′-), *adj. Informal* (*disparaging*). **1.** pertaining to or characteristic of the white middle class; bourgeois: *white-bread liberals.* **2.** bland; conventional. [1975–80]

white′ bucks′ (buks), casual oxford shoes made of white buckskin.

white′ cam′pion. See **evening campion.**

white•cap (hwīt′kap′, wīt′-), *n.* a wave with a broken and foaming white crest. [1660–70; WHITE + CAP¹]

white′ cast′ i′ron. See **white iron.**

white′ ce′dar, **1.** any of several chiefly coniferous trees valued for their wood, esp. *Chamaecyparis thyoides,* of the eastern U.S., or *Thuja occidentalis* (**northern white cedar**), of northeastern North America. **2.** the wood of any of these trees. [1665–75, *Amer.*]

White•chap•el (hwīt′chap′əl, wīt′-), *n.* a district in E London, England.

white′ chip′, *Poker.* a white-colored chip with the lowest value (contrasted with *blue chip*). [1895–1900]

white′ choc′olate, a chocolate-type product made of milk and sugar that are cooked together until highly condensed and then mixed with cocoa butter.

white′ cloud′, a small, brightly colored freshwater fish, *Tanichthys albonubes,* native to China: popular in home aquariums. [by ellipsis from *White Cloud Mountain fish,* after a hill (Chin *Báiyún shān*), NE of Canton, China, where the fish was discovered in 1932]

white′ clo′ver, a clover, *Trifolium repens,* having white flowers, common in pastures and meadows. See illus. under **clover.** [bef. 1100; ME; OE]

white′ coal′, *Informal.* water, as of a stream, used for power. [1880–85]

white•coat (hwīt′kōt′, wīt′-), *n.* a baby seal, usually less than four weeks old and still having its initial white fur. [1545–55; WHITE + COAT]

white-col•lar (hwīt′kol′ər, wīt′-), *adj.* **1.** belonging or pertaining to the ranks of office and professional workers whose jobs generally do not involve manual labor or the wearing of a uniform or work clothes. —*n.* **2.** a white-collar worker. Cf. **blue-collar.** [1920–25]

white′-collar crime′, any of various crimes, as embezzlement, fraud, or stealing office equipment, committed by business or professional people while working at their occupations. [1945–50] —**white′-collar crim′inal.**

white′ cor′puscle. See **white blood cell.** [1865–70]

white′ crab′. See **ghost crab.**

white′ crap′pie. See under **crappie.** [1925–30]

white′ croak′er, kingfish (def. 2).

white′-crowned spar′row (hwīt′kround′, wīt′-), a North American sparrow, *Zonotrichia leucophrys,* having black and white stripes on the head. [1830–40]

white•cup (hwīt′kup′, wīt′-), *n.* a creeping South American plant, *Nierembergia repens,* of the nightshade family, having bell-shaped, lilac- or blue-tinged, cream-white flowers. [WHITE + CUP]

whit•ed (hwī′tid, wī′-), *adj.* **1.** made white; bleached; blanched. **2.** covered with whitewash, whiting, or the like. [1300–50; ME; see WHITE, -ED²]

white′ damp′, a poisonous coal-mine gas composed chiefly of carbon monoxide. [1880–85]

whit′ed sep′ulcher, an evil person who feigns goodness; hypocrite. Matt. 23:27. [1575–85]

white′ dwarf′, *Astron.* a star, approximately the size of the earth, that has undergone gravitational collapse and is in the final stage of evolution for low-mass stars, beginning hot and white and ending cold and dark (**black dwarf**). Cf. **Chandrasekhar limit.** [1920–25]

white′ ear′drop, Dutchman's-breeches.

white′ el′ephant, **1.** a possession unwanted by the owner but difficult to dispose of: *Our Victorian bric-a-brac and furniture were white elephants.* **2.** a possession entailing great expense out of proportion to its usefulness or value. **3.** an abnormally whitish or pale elephant, usually found in Thailand; an albino elephant. [1850–55; from the perh. apocryphal tale that the King of Siam would award a disagreeable courtier a white elephant, the upkeep of which would ruin the courtier]

white′ en′sign, the British naval ensign, consisting of the red cross of St. George on a white field, with the British union occupying the upper quarter along the hoist. [1875–80]

white-eye (hwīt′ī′, wīt′-), *n., pl.* **-eyes.** any of numerous small, chiefly tropical Old World songbirds of the family Zosteropidae, most of which have a ring of white feathers around the eye: several species are endangered. Also called **silver-eye.** [1840–50]

white′-eyed vir′eo (hwīt′īd′, wīt′-), a vireo, *Vireo griseus,* of eastern North America, having olive, yellow, and white plumage, a yellow ring around each eye, and white irises. [1825–35, *Amer.*]

white•face (hwīt′fās′, wīt′-), *n.* **1.** a Hereford. **2.** *Theat.* **a.** a performer, as a clown, who appears in clown white. **b.** the white facial makeup used by such a performer. [1700–10; WHITE + FACE]

white-faced (hwīt′fāst′, wīt′-), *adj.* **1.** having a white or pale face. **2.** marked with white on the front of the head, as a horse. **3.** having a white front or surface. [1585–95]

white′-faced hor′net. See under **hornet.** [1890–95, *Amer.*]

white′ feath′er, *Chiefly Brit.* **1.** a symbol of cowardice. **2. show the white feather,** to behave in a cowardly manner. [1775–85; orig. from a white feather in a gamecock's tail, taken as a sign of inferior breeding and hence of poor fighting qualities]

White•field (hwit′fēld′, wit′-), *n.* **George,** 1714–70, English Methodist evangelist. —**White′field′i•an, White′field•ite′,** *n.*

white′ fir′, **1.** a tall, narrow fir, *Abies concolor,* of western North America, yielding a soft wood used for lumber, pulp, boxes, etc. **2.** the wood of this tree. **3.** any of various similar firs of western North America, or their wood. [1880–85, *Amer.*]

white•fish (hwīt′fish′, wīt′-), *n., pl.* (*esp. collectively*) **-fish,** (*esp. referring to two or more kinds or species*) **-fish•es. 1.** any of several fishes of the family Coregonidae, inhabiting northern waters of North America and Eurasia, similar to the trout but having a smaller mouth and larger scales. Cf. **lake whitefish, round whitefish. 2.** a marine food fish of California, *Caulolatilus princeps.* **3.** any of various silvery fishes of the minnow or carp family. **4.** the beluga, *Delphinapterus leucas.* [1425–75; late ME; see WHITE, FISH]

White′fish Bay′ (hwīt′fish′, wīt′-), a city in SE Wisconsin, N of Milwaukee. 14,930.

white′ flag′, **1.** an all-white banner or piece of cloth, used as a symbol of surrender or truce. **2. hoist, show,** or **wave the white flag,** to give up; weaken; yield. [1590–1600] —**white′-flag′,** *adj.*

white′-flow•ered gourd′ (hwīt′flou′ərd, wīt′-). See under **gourd.**

white•fly (hwīt′flī′, wīt′-), *n., pl.* **-flies.** any of several plant-sucking, homopterous insects of the family Aleyrodidae, having the body and wings dusted with a white, powdery wax, and being widely distributed chiefly in tropical regions where they are often serious crop pests, as *Dialeurodes citri* (**citrus whitefly**), commonly occurring on citrus trees, and *Trialeurodes vaporariorum* (**greenhouse whitefly**), inhabiting greenhouses. [1885–90; WHITE + FLY²]

white′-foot•ed mouse′ (hwīt′fo͝ot′id, wīt′-), any of several North American woodland mice of the genus *Peromyscus,* esp. *P. leucopus,* having white feet and undersides. Also called **deer mouse, vesper mouse, wood mouse.** [1855–60, *Amer.*]

white′ fox′. See **arctic fox.** [1690–1700]

White′ Fri′ar, a Carmelite friar: so called from th distinctive white cloak worn by the order. [1375–142 late ME]

White•fri•ars (hwīt′frī′ərz, wīt′-), *n.* a district in cen tral London, England.

white′-fringed bee′tle (hwīt′frinjd′, wīt′-), any o several weevils of the genus *Graphognathus,* native t South America and now of southeastern and mid-Atlar tic U.S., whose larvae feed on roots and cause seriou damage to a wide variety of plants. [1935–40]

white′-front•ed goose′ (hwīt′frun′tid, wīt′-), grayish-brown wild goose, *Anser albifrons,* of Eurasi and western North America, having a white patch on th front of the face. [1760–70]

white′ frost′, a heavy coating of frost. [1350–140 ME]

white′ gasoline′, unleaded and uncracked gasolin designed esp. for use in motorboats. [1925–30]

white′ gin′ger, a tall plant, *Hedychium coronariun* of the ginger family, native to tropical Asia, having lon broad leaves and showy, fragrant white flowers. Als called **ginger lily.**

white′ globe′ lil′y, a bulbous Californian plan *Calochortus albus,* of the lily family, having egg-shape white flowers with a purplish base.

white-glove (hwīt′gluv′, wīt′-), *adj. Informal.* **1** meticulous; painstaking; minute: *a white-glove inspec tion.* **2.** immaculate; spotless; sterile: *a white-glove en vironment.* Also, **white′-gloved′.**

white′ gold′, any of several gold alloys colored whit by the presence of nickel, palladium, or platinun [1660–70]

white′ goods′, **1.** household goods, as bed sheets, ta blecloths, and towels, formerly bleached and finished i white but now often patterned and colored. **2.** bleache goods, esp. cotton or linen fabrics. **3.** large househol appliances, as refrigerators, stoves, and washing ma chines. **4.** alcoholic liquors that are manufactured with out color, as vodka, gin, and tequila. [1870–75]

white′ gourd′. See **wax gourd.**

white-ground (hwīt′ground′, wīt′-), *adj.* pertainin to or designating a style of vase painting developed i Greece from the 6th to the 4th centuries B.C., character ized chiefly by a white background of slip onto whic were painted polychromatic figures.

white′ gum′, any of various Australian eucalyptuse having a whitish bark. [1735–45, *Amer.*]

white-haired (hwīt′hârd′, wīt′-), *adj.* **1.** havin white hair. **2.** white-headed (def. 3). [1350–1400; MI see WHITE, HAIR, -ED³]

white′ hake′, a food fish, *Urophycis tenuis,* inhabitin marine waters, esp. off the North Atlantic coast of th U.S.

White•hall (hwīt′hôl′, wīt′-), *n.* **1.** Also calle **White′hall Pal′ace.** a former palace in central Londo England, originally built in the reign of Henry III: exe cution of Charles I, 1649. **2.** the main thoroughfare i London, England, between Trafalgar Square and th Houses of Parliament. **3.** the British government or it policies. **4.** a city in central Ohio, near Columbu 21,299. **5.** a city in W Pennsylvania, near Pittsburgh 15,206.

white′-hand•ed gib′bon (hwīt′han′did, -han′ wīt′-), a gibbon, *Hylobates lar,* inhabiting Thailand, th Malay Peninsula, and northern Sumatra, varying fro black to light buff in color, and having white hands an feet: an endangered species. Also called **lar, lar gibbo**

white′ hat′, *Informal.* a virtuous hero, esp. in a cow boy movie; good guy. Cf. **black hat** (def. 1 —**white′-hat′, white′-hat′ted,** *adj.*

white•head (hwīt′hed′, wīt′-), *n.* a small pimple hav ing a white or yellowish head; milium. [1930–35; WHIT + HEAD]

White•head (hwīt′hed′, wīt′-), *n.* **Alfred Nort** 1861–1947, English philosopher and mathematician, i the U.S. after 1924.

white-head•ed (hwīt′hed′id, wīt′-), *adj.* **1.** white haired (def. 1). **2.** having fair or flaxen hair. **3.** bein especially favored; fair-haired: *He's the company white-headed boy.* [1515–25]

white′ heat′, **1.** a stage of intense activity, excite ment, feeling, etc.: *The sales campaign is at white hea* **2.** an intense heat at which a substance glows with whit light. [1700–10]

white′ hel′lebore. See **false hellebore.**

white′ hole′, **1.** pigeonhole (def. 3). **2.** *Astron.* a the oretical celestial object into which matter is funnele from a black hole.

white′ hope′, **1.** a person who is expected to accom plish much in a given field: *the white hope of the Ameri can theater.* **2.** *Sports.* (formerly) a white man who ha a good chance of winning the heavyweight boxing cham pionship from a black man. [1905–10]

white′ horse′, a white-topped wave; whitecap [1640–50]

White•horse (hwīt′hôrs′, wīt′-), *n.* a town in and th capital of the Yukon Territory, in NW Canada. 13,311.

white-hot (hwīt′hot′, wīt′-), *adj.* **1.** extremely ho **2.** showing white heat. **3.** exceedingly enthusiastic, ar dent, angry, devoted, etc.; impassioned; perfervid: *fierce, white-hot loyalty to the king.* [1810–20]

White′ House′, the, **1.** Also called **Executive Man sion.** the official residence of the President of the Unite States, in Washington, D.C.: a large, two-story, freeston building painted white. **2.** the executive branch of th U.S. federal government: *the White House's tax policy.*

white′ hunt′er, **1.** a white man who acts as guide o

CONCISE ETYMOLOGY KEY: <, descended or borrowed from; >, whence; b., blend of, blended; c., cognate with; cf., compare; deriv., derivative; equiv., equivalent; imit., imitative; obl., oblique; r., replacing; s., stem; sp., spelling, spelled; resp., respelling, respelled; trans., translation; ?, origin unknown; *, unattested; ‡, probably earlier than. See the full key inside the front cover.

African safaris and hunting expeditions. **2.** a white man who hunts big game in Africa. [1950–55]

white′ i′ron, cast iron having most or all of its carbon in the form of cementite and exhibiting a silvery fracture. Also called **white cast iron.** [1525–35]

white′ ker′ria, jetbead.

white′ knight′, **1.** a hero who comes to the rescue. **2.** a beleaguered champion who fights heroically for a cause, as in politics. **3.** *Informal.* a company that comes to the rescue of another, as to prevent a takeover. [1890–95]

white-knuckle (hwīt′nuk′əl, wīt′-), *adj. Informal.* **1.** causing fear, apprehension, or panic: *The plane made a white-knuckle approach to the fogged-in airport.* **2.** experiencing fear, terror, or apprehension: *The white-knuckle crowd loved that director's newest horror movie.* Also, **white′-knuck′led.**

white′-knuckle pad′dler, *Canadian.* an inexpert and timid canoeist.

white′ lead′ (led), **1.** a white, heavy powder, basic lead carbonate, $2PbCO_3 \cdot Pb(OH)_2$, used as a pigment, in putty, and in medicinal ointments for burns. **2.** the putty made from this substance in oil. [1400–50; late ME]

white′ leath′er, leather treated with chemicals, as alum or salt; tawed leather. Also, **whitleather.** [1400–50; late ME; cf. WHITLEATHER]

white′ lie′, a minor, polite, or harmless lie; fib.

white′ light′, light perceived by the eye as having the same color as sunlight at noon.

white′ light′ning, *Chiefly Midland and Southern U.S.* moonshine (def. 1). Also called **white mule.** [1910–15, *Amer.*]

white′ line′, **1.** a stripe of white paint, tiles, or the like, that marks the center or outer edge of a road. **2.** a white layer in a horse's hoof. **3.** any blank or white part, line, stripe, or margin. [1590–1600]

white·line (hwīt′līn′, wīt′-), *n. Naut.* codline. [WHITE + LINE¹]

white′ liq′uor, (in making wood pulp for paper) the chemicals used to digest the wood, basically sodium hydroxide and sodium hyposulfite. Cf. **black liquor.**

white′ list′, **1.** a list of novels, motion pictures, etc., deemed suitable for juveniles, members of a particular faith, or other specified groups of individuals. **2.** a list of persons thought by a business concern to be qualified or otherwise suitable for employment. **3.** a list of individuals, organizations, etc., having security clearance from government officials. **4.** a list of business establishments approved for patronage because of hiring practices, religious or political affiliations, etc. **5.** a list kept by a labor union, containing the names of employers who maintain working conditions approved by the union. Cf. **blacklist.** [1905–10]

white-liv·ered (hwīt′liv′ərd, wīt′-), *adj.* **1.** lacking courage; cowardly; lily-livered. **2.** lacking in vitality or spirit; pale; unhealthy. [1540–50]

white′ lo′tus. See under **Egyptian lotus** (def. 1).

white′ lung′, asbestosis.

white′ lu′pine. See under **lupine¹.**

white·ly (hwīt′lē, wīt′-), *adv.* with a white hue or color: *The sun shone whitely.* [1350–1400; late ME; see WHITE, -LY]

white′ mag′ic, magic used for good purposes, esp. to counteract evil (contrasted with *black magic*).

white′ mahog′any, **1.** an Australian eucalyptus, *Eucalyptus acmenioides.* **2.** the hard, heavy wood of this tree, used for making railroad ties, posts, etc. **3.** primavera (def. 2).

White·man (hwīt′mən, wīt′-), *n.* **Paul** (*"Pops"*), 1891–1967, U.S. orchestra conductor.

white′ man's′ bur′den, the alleged duty of the white race to care for subject peoples of other races in its colonial possessions. [after a poem of the same title by Rudyard Kipling (1899)]

white′ Maripo′sa, a Mariposa lily, *Calochortus venustus,* having white or pale lilac flowers.

white′ mar′ket, (in a system of rationing) the buying and selling of unused ration coupons at a fluctuating legal price based on the supply of and demand for the rationed commodity. Cf. **black market.** [1970–75] —**white′-mar′ket,** *adj.*

white′ mar′lin, a small marlin, *Tetrapterus albidus,* inhabiting the western Atlantic Ocean, pale blue above and silvery below.

white′ mat′ter, *Anat.* nerve tissue, esp. of the brain and spinal cord, which primarily contains myelinated fibers and is nearly white in color. Cf. **gray matter** (def. 1). [1830–40]

white′ meat′, **1.** any meat that is light-colored before cooking, as veal or chicken (distinguished from *red meat*). **2.** meat that is light-colored after cooking, as veal or breast of chicken or of turkey (distinguished from *dark meat*). **3.** *Slang* (*vulgar*). a white person considered as a sexual partner. **4.** *Southern U.S.* salt pork, fatback, or other pork without any lean. **5.** *Archaic.* food made from milk. Also called **light meat** (for defs. 1, 2). [1375–1425; late ME]

white′ mel′ilot, a Eurasian plant, *Melilotus alba,* of the legume family, naturalized in the U.S., having white flowers. Also called **Bokhara clover.**

white′ met′al, any of various light-colored alloys, as Babbitt metal or Britannia metal. [1605–15]

White′ Moun′tains, a mountain range in N New Hampshire, part of the Appalachian Mountains. Highest peak, Mt. Washington, 6293 ft. (1918 m).

white′ mul′berry. See under **mulberry** (def. 2). [1600–10]

white′ mule′, *Chiefly Midland and Southern U.S.* moonshine (def. 1). Also called **white lightning.** [1925–30, *Amer.*]

white′ mus′tard. See under **mustard** (def. 2). [1725–35]

whit·en (hwīt′n, wīt′n), *v.t., v.i.* to make or become white. [1250–1300; ME *whitenen;* see WHITE, -EN¹]
—**Syn.** WHITEN, BLANCH, BLEACH mean to make or become white. To WHITEN implies giving a white color or appearance by putting a substance of some kind on the outside: *to whiten shoes.* To BLANCH implies taking away natural or original color throughout: *to blanch celery by growing it in the dark.* To BLEACH implies making white by placing in (sun) light or by using chemicals: *to bleach linen, hair.* —**Ant.** blacken.

whit·en·er (hwīt′n ər, wīt′-), *n.* **1.** a preparation for making something white, as a bleach, dye, or polish: *a bottle of shoe whitener.* **2.** a person or thing that whitens. **3.** a person who applies whitener, as in a manufacturing process. [1605–15; WHITEN + -ER¹]

white·ness (hwīt′nis, wīt′-), *n.* **1.** the quality or state of being white. **2.** paleness. **3.** purity. **4.** a white substance. [bef. 1000; ME *whitenes,* OE *hwītnes.* See WHITE, -NESS]

White′ Nile′, the part of the Nile that flows NE to Khartoum, Sudan. ab. 500 mi. (800 km) long. Cf. **Nile.**

whit·en·ing (hwīt′n ing, wīt′-), *n.* **1.** a preparation for making something white; whiting. **2.** the act or process of making or turning white. [1595–1605; WHITEN + -ING¹]

white′ noise′, **1.** Also called **white sound.** a steady, unvarying, unobtrusive sound, as an electronically produced drone or the sound of rain, used to mask or obliterate unwanted sounds. **2.** *Physics.* random noise with a uniform frequency spectrum over a wide range of frequencies. [1965–70]

white′ oak′, **1.** an oak, *Quercus alba,* of eastern North America, having a light-gray to white bark and yielding a hard, durable wood: the state tree of Connecticut and Maryland. **2.** any of several other species of oak, as *Q. garryana* or *Q. lobata,* of western North America. **3.** the wood of any of these trees. [1625–35]

White′ Oak′, a town in central Maryland, near Washington, D.C. 13,700.

white·out (hwīt′out′, wīt′-), *n.* **1.** *Meteorol.* **a.** a condition, found in polar regions, in which uniform illumination from snow on the ground and from a low cloud layer makes features of the landscape indistinguishable. **b.** a condition of heavily falling or blowing snow in which visibility is very poor. **2.** an act or instance of whiting out with a correction fluid. **3.** a white correction fluid used for this: *a bottle of whiteout.* **4.** a mistake, as in typing, that has been whited out with a correction fluid. [1940–45; (defs. 2–4) n. use of v. phrase *white out;* (def. 1) WHITE + (BLACK)OUT]

white′ pag′es, the white pages of a telephone directory, or sometimes a separate volume, in which subscribers are listed alphabetically. Cf. **yellow pages.**

white paper (hwīt′ pā′pər, wīt′ *for 1;* hwīt′pā′pər, wīt′ *for 2–4*), **1.** paper bleached white. **2.** an official governmental report. **3.** an authoritative report issued by any organization: *The TV network presented its white paper on news coverage of major crimes.* **4.** an official British government publication on a specific subject prepared by a committee and presented to the House of Commons, usually reporting results of a recent investigation or summarizing policy. [1560–70]

White′ Pass′, a mountain pass in SE Alaska, near Skagway. 2888 ft. (880 m) high.

white′ pep′per, a condiment prepared from the husked dried berries of the pepper plant, used either whole or ground.

white′ perch′, **1.** a small game fish, *Morone americana,* greenish-gray above and silvery below, inhabiting streams along the Atlantic coast of the U.S. **2.** See **freshwater drum.** **3.** See **silver perch** (def. 2). [1765–75, *Amer.*]

white′ pine′, **1.** a large, irregularly branched pine, *Pinus strobus,* of eastern North America, having gray bark and yielding a light-colored, soft, light wood of great commercial importance. **2.** the wood itself. **3.** any of various other similar species of pine. [1675–85, *Amer.*]

white′-pine′ wee′vil (hwīt′pīn′, wīt′-), a brown beetle, *Pissodes strobi,* the larvae of which feed on the terminal buds and shoots of white pine and other conifers.

white′ plague′, tuberculosis, esp. pulmonary tuberculosis. [1865–70, *Amer.*]

White′ Plains′, a city in SE New York, near New York City: battle 1776. 46,999.

white′ pop′lar, **1.** Also called **abele.** an Old World poplar, *Populus alba,* widely cultivated in the U.S., having the underside of the leaves covered with a dense silvery-white down. **2.** the soft, straight-grained wood of this tree. [1765–75, *Amer.*]

white′ pota′to, potato (def. 1). [1785–95, *Amer.*]

white·print (hwīt′print′, wīt′-), *n. Print.* a proof print made by means of the diazo process. [1915–20; WHITE + PRINT, on the model of BLUEPRINT]

white′ rain′bow, fogbow.

white′ rat′, an albino variety of the Norway rat, *Rattus norvegicus,* used in biological experiments.

White′ Riv′er, **1.** a river flowing SE from NW Arkansas into the Mississippi River. 690 mi. (1110 km) long. **2.** a river flowing NE from NW Nebraska to the Missouri River in S South Dakota. 325 mi. (525 km) long.

white-robed (hwīt′rōbd′, wīt′-), *adj.* clothed in a white robe. [1615–25]

White′ Rock′, **1.** a city in SW British Columbia, in SW Canada, SE of Vancouver. 13,550. **2.** one of a variety of white Plymouth Rock chickens. [1940–45]

white′ rose′, *Eng. Hist.* emblem of the royal house of York. Cf. **red rose, Wars of the Roses.** [1550–60]

white′ rot′, **1.** a decay of wood caused by lignase-producing fungi, esp. *Phanerochaete chrysosporium.* **2.** a fungal disease of onions and related plants caused by *Sclerotinia cepivorum.* **3.** any of the several fungi causing white rot. [1905–10]

White′ Rus′sia, Byelorussia.

White′ Rus′sian, **1.** Byelorussian (def. 2). **2.** a Russian who fought against the Bolsheviks in the Russian Revolution. **3.** Byelorussian (def. 3). **4.** a cocktail of vodka, cream, and Kahlúa or crème de cacao. [1865–70]

White′ Rus′sian So′viet So′cialist Repub′lic, Byelorussia (def. 1).

white′ rust′, **1.** *Plant Pathol.* a disease of plants, characterized by pustules of white spores on affected parts that become yellow and malformed, caused by fungi of the genus *Albugo.* **2.** any fungus of the genus *Albugo.* [1880–85]

white′ sage′, **1.** Also called **greasewood.** a shrubby plant, *Salvia apiana,* of the mint family, native to southern California, having white, hairy foliage and spikes of white or pale lavender flowers. **2.** an aromatic, composite plant, *Artemisia ludoviciana,* of western North America, having leaves with a downy white undersurface. [1865–70, *Amer.*]

white′ sale′, a sale of sheets, pillowcases, and other white goods. [1920–25]

white′ salm′on, the yellowtail, *Seriola lalandei.* [1605–15]

white′ san′dalwood. See under **sandalwood** (def. 2).

White′ Sands′ Mis′sile Range′, a U.S. Army military testing ground for rockets and guided missiles in SW New Mexico, W of Alamogordo.

white′ sapo′te, a tropical American tree, *Casimiroa edulis,* of the rue family, having greenish, inconspicuous flowers and tomatolike fleshy fruit that is yellow on the inside and gray or yellowish-green on the outside. Also called **Mexican apple.**

white′ sap′phire, *Mineral.* a colorless variety of corundum, used as a gemstone.

white′ sauce′, a sauce made of butter, flour, seasonings, and milk or sometimes chicken or veal stock; béchamel. [1715–25]

White′ Sea′, an arm of the Arctic Ocean, in the NW Russian Federation in Europe. ab. 36,000 sq. mi. (93,240 sq. km).

white′ sea′ bass′ (bas), a large weakfish, *Atractoscion nobilis,* occurring along the Pacific coast of North America and popular as a sport and food fish. [1880–85]

White′ Set′tlement, a town in N Texas. 13,508.

white′ shark′. See **great white shark.** [1665–75]

white-shoe (hwīt′sho͞o′, wīt′-), *adj.* of or pertaining to members of the upper class who own or run large corporations: *white-shoe bankers; a conservative white-shoe image.* [1975–80; appar. from the white shoes popular as moderately formal wear among suburban men c1980]

white′ slave′, **1.** a woman who is sold or forced into prostitution. **2.** a white person held as a slave. [1825–35] —**white′-slave′,** *adj.*

White′ Slave′ Act′. See **Mann Act.**

white′ slav′er, a person engaged in white-slave traffic or business. [1910–15]

white′ slav′ery, the condition of or traffic in white slaves. [1815–25]

white-slav·ing (hwīt′slā′ving, wīt′-), *n.* traffic in white slaves.

white·smith (hwīt′smith′, wīt′-), *n.* a tinsmith. [1275–1325; ME, modeled on BLACKSMITH]

white′ snake′root, a North American boneset, *Eupatorium rugosum,* that has heads of white flowers and causes trembles and milk sickness. Also called **Indian sanicle.** [1810–20, *Amer.*]

white′ sound′. See **white noise.**

white′ space′, the unprinted area of a piece of printing, as of a newspaper page, or of a portion of a piece of printing, as of an advertisement; blank space. [1840–50]

white′ spruce′, **1.** a spruce, *Picea glauca,* of northern North America, having bluish-green needles and silvery-brown bark. **2.** the light, soft wood of this tree, used for pulp and for boxes, crates, etc. [1760–70]

white′ squall′, *Naut.* a whirlwind at sea or a violent disturbance of small radius not accompanied by clouds but indicated merely by whitecaps and turbulent water.

white′ stock′, a stock of veal bones, vegetables, herbs, and seasonings: used in sauces and soups.

white′ stork′, a large Eurasian stork, *Ciconia ciconia,* having white plumage with black in the wings and a red bill. See illus. under **stork.** [1785–95]

white′ stur′geon, a dark gray sturgeon, *Acipenser transmontanus,* inhabiting marine and fresh waters along the northwestern coast of North America, valued as a food and sport fish. Also called **Pacific sturgeon.**

white′ suprem′acy, the belief, theory, or doctrine that the white race is superior to all other races, esp. the black race, and should therefore retain control in all relationships. [1865–70, *Amer.*] —**white′ suprem′acist.**

white′-tailed deer′ (hwīt′tāld′, wīt′-), a common North American deer, *Odocoileus virginianus,* having a tail with a white underside. Also, **white′tail deer′.** Also called **white′tail′.** See illus. under **deer.** [1840–50, *Amer.*]

white′-tailed kite′, an American kite, *Elanus leucurus,* having gray plumage with a white head, breast, and tail.

white′-tailed sea′ ea′gle. See **gray sea eagle.**

white·thorn (hwīt′thôrn′, wīt′-), *n.* a hawthorn, *Crataegus laevigata,* having white flowers. [1225–75; ME, trans. of L *alba spīna*]

white·throat (hwīt′thrōt′, wīt′-), *n.* **1.** any of several small songbirds having white throats, esp. an Old World warbler, *Sylvia communis.* **2.** See **white-throated sparrow.** [1670–80; WHITE + THROAT]

white′-throat·ed spar′row (hwīt′thrō′tid, wīt′-), a common North American finch, *Zonotrichia albicollis,* having a white patch on the throat and a black and white striped crown. Also called **whitethroat.** [1805–15, *Amer.*]

white′ tie′, 1. formal evening dress for men (distinguished from *black tie*). **2.** a white bow tie for men, worn with formal evening dress.

white-tie (hwīt′tī′, wīt′-), *adj.* requiring that guests wear formal attire, esp. that men wear white bow ties with formal evening dress: *a white-tie embassy reception.* Cf. **black-tie.** [1950–55]

white′tip shark′ (hwīt′tip′, wīt′-), **1.** Also called **reef whitetip shark.** a smooth dogfish, *Triaenodon obseus,* having white-tipped dorsal and caudal fins and occurring inshore among the reefs in the Pacific and Indian oceans and the Red Sea. **2.** Also called **oceanic whitetip shark.** a large, predominantly tropical deepwater shark, *Carcharhinus longimanus,* inhabiting Atlantic and Pacific waters: considered to be the most dangerous of all sharks. Also, **white′-tipped shark′.** [WHITE + TIP[1]]

white′ trash′, *Slang (disparaging and offensive).* **1.** a member of the class of poor whites, esp. in the southern U.S. **2.** poor whites collectively. [1850–55, *Amer.*]

white′ truf′fle, an edible fungus, *Tuber magnatum pico,* occurring in certain parts of northern Italy, and considered a great delicacy.

white′ trum′pet lil′y, a lily, *Lilium longiflorum,* of Japan, having fragrant, pure white, trumpet-shaped flowers nearly 7 in. (18 cm) in length. [1850–55, *Amer.*]

white′ tur′nip, the turnip, *Brassica rapa.*

white′ vit′riol. See **zinc sulfate.**

White′ Vol′ta, a river in W Africa, in Ghana: a branch of the Volta River. ab. 550 mi. (885 km) long. Cf. **Volta** (def. 2).

white·wall (hwīt′wôl′, wīt′-), *n.* a rubber tire for an automobile, bicycle, etc., whose sidewall is colored white. Also called **white′wall tire′.** [1950–55; WHITE + (SIDE)WALL]

white′ wal′nut, butternut (def. 1). [1735–45, *Amer.*]

white·wash (hwīt′wosh′, -wôsh′, wīt′-), *n.* **1.** a composition, as of lime and water or of whiting, size, and water, used for whitening walls, woodwork, etc. **2.** anything, as deceptive words or actions, used to cover up or gloss over faults, errors, or wrongdoings, or absolve a wrongdoer from blame. **3.** *Sports Informal.* a defeat in which the loser fails to score. —*v.t.* **4.** to whiten with whitewash. **5.** to cover up or gloss over the faults or errors of; absolve from blame. **6.** *Sports Informal.* to defeat by keeping the opponent from scoring: *The home team whitewashed the visitors eight to nothing.* [1585–95; WHITE + WASH] —**white′wash′er,** *n.*
—**Syn. 5.** excuse, vindicate, exonerate.

white′ wa′ter, 1. frothy water, as in whitecaps and rapids. **2.** light-colored seawater over a shoal, sandy bottom, etc. [1580–90]

white·wa·ter (hwīt′wô′tər, -wot′ər, wīt′-), *adj.* of or moving over or through rapids: *whitewater rafting down the Colorado River.* Also, **white′-wa′ter.** [1900–05; from WHITE WATER]

White·wa·ter (hwīt′wô′tər, -wot′ər, wīt′-), *n.* a town in SE Wisconsin. 11,520.

white′ wa′ter lil′y, any water lily of the genus *Nymphaea,* esp. *N. odorata,* having fragrant, white flowers.

white′ wa′vey. See under **wavey.** [1775–85]

white′ wax′, a yellowish-white, somewhat translucent, tasteless solid, prepared by bleaching beeswax, used chiefly in pharmacy. [1535–45]

white′ whale′, beluga (def. 2). [1680–90]

white′ wine′, wine having a yellowish to amber color derived from the light-colored grapes used in production, or from dark grapes whose skins, pulp, and seeds have been removed before fermentation. [1250–1300; ME; cf. F *vin blanc*]

white·wing (hwīt′wing′, wīt′-), *n.* a person who wears a white uniform, esp. a public street cleaner. [1850–55; WHITE + WING]

white′-winged dove′ (hwīt′wingd′, wīt′-), a common dove, *Zenaida asiatica,* of the southwestern U.S. to Chile. [1850–55, *Amer.*]

white′-winged sco′ter, a blackish North American duck, *Melanitta deglandi,* having a white patch on each wing. [1890–95, *Amer.*]

white·wood (hwīt′wŏŏd′, wīt′-), *n.* **1.** any of numerous trees, as the tulip tree or the linden, yielding a white or light-colored wood. **2.** the wood of these trees. **3.** a cottonwood of the genus *Populus.* [1655–65; WHITE + WOOD[1]]

white′ wood′ as′ter, a composite plant, *Aster divaricatus,* of North America, having flat-topped clusters of white ray flowers and growing in dry woods. [1930–35]

white′ work′, needlework done in white on fine white cloth, esp. linen. Also, **white′work′.** [1860–65; WHITE + WORK]

whit·ey (hwī′tē, wī′-), *n. (sometimes cap.) Slang (disparaging and offensive).* a white person or white people collectively. Also, **whity.** [1820–30; WHITE + -EY[2]]

whith·er (hwith′ər, with′-), *adv.* **1.** to what place? where? **2.** to what end, point, action, or the like? to what? —*conj.* **3.** to which place. **4.** to whatever place. [bef. 900; ME, OE *hwider,* alter. of *hwæder* (c. Goth *hwadre*), modeled on *hider* HITHER]

whith·er·so·ev·er (hwith′ər sō ev′ər, with′-), *conj. Archaic.* to whatsoever place. [1200–50; ME, equiv. to *whitherso* whithersoever (OE *swā hwider swā*) + *ever* EVER]

whith·er·ward (hwith′ər wərd, with′-), *adv. Archaic.* toward what place; in what direction. Also, **whith′er·wards.** [1150–1200; ME; see WHITHER, -WARD]

whit·ing[1] (hwī′ting, wī′-), *n., pl. (esp. collectively)* **-ing,** *(esp. referring to two or more kinds or species)* **-ings. 1.** a slender food fish of the genus *Menticirrhus,* of the croaker family, inhabiting waters along the Atlantic coast of North America. **2.** the hake, *Merluccius bilinearis.* **3.** any of several European fishes of the cod family, esp. *Merlangus merlangus.* [1400–50; late ME, perh. alter. of OE *hwītling* kind of fish; cf. MD *witinc,* of which the E may be a trans.]

whit·ing[2] (hwī′ting, wī′-), *n.* pure-white chalk (calcium carbonate) that has been ground and washed, used in making putty, whitewash, silver polish, etc. [1400–50; late ME; cf. OE *hwīting-,* in *hwītingmelu;* see MEAL[2]. See WHITE, -ING[1]]

whit·ish (hwī′tish, wī′-), *adj.* somewhat white; tending to white. [1350–1400; ME; see WHITE, -ISH[1]] —**whit′ish·ness,** *n.*

whit·leath·er (hwit′leth′ər, wit′-), *n.* See **white leather.** [1325–75; ME *whitlether.* See WHITE, LEATHER]

whit·low (hwit′lō, wit′-), *n.* an inflammation of the deeper tissues of a finger or toe, esp. of the terminal phalanx, usually producing suppuration. Also called **felon.** [1350–1400; ME *whit(f)lowe, whitflawe.* See WHITE, FLAW[1]]

whit·low·wort (hwit′lō wûrt′, -wôrt′, wit′-), *n.* any of several small, tufted plants belonging to the genus *Paronychia,* of the pink family, native to temperate and warm regions, having opposite or whorled leaves and tiny, greenish flowers. [1640–50; WHITLOW + WORT[2]]

Whit·man (hwit′mən, wit′-), *n.* **1. Marcus,** 1802–47, U.S. missionary and pioneer. **2. Walt(er),** 1819–92, U.S. poet. **3.** a city in SE Massachusetts. 13,534.

Whit·mon·day (hwit′mun′dā, -dē, wit′-), *n.* the Monday following Whitsunday. [1550–60; modeled on WHITSUNDAY]

Whit·ney (hwit′nē, wit′-), *n.* **1. Eli,** 1765–1825, U.S. manufacturer and inventor. **2. John Hay,** 1904–82, U.S. diplomat and newspaper publisher. **3. Josiah Dwight,** 1819–96, U.S. geologist. **4. William Dwight,** 1827–94, U.S. philologist and lexicographer (brother of Josiah Dwight). **5. Mount,** a mountain in E California, in the Sierra Nevada. 14,495 ft. (4418 m). **6.** a male given name.

whit·rack (hwit′rak′, wit′-), *n. Brit. Dial.* a weasel; ermine or stoat. Also, **whit·ret** (hwit′rət, wit′-), **whit·ter·ick** (hwit′ər ik, wit′-). [dissimilated var. of ME *whitrat.* See WHITE, RAT]

Whit·sun (hwit′sən, wit′-), *adj.* **1.** of or pertaining to Whitsunday or Whitsuntide. —*n.* **2.** Whitsunday or Whitsuntide. [1250–1300; ME *Whitsone(n),* shortening of *whitsonenday* (by analysis as *whitsonen-day*); see WHITSUNDAY]

Whit·sun·day (hwit′sun′dā, -dē, wit′-; hwit′sən dā′, wit′-), *n.* the seventh Sunday after Easter, celebrated as a festival in commemoration of the descent of the Holy Spirit on the day of Pentecost. [bef. 1100; ME *whitsonenday,* OE *Hwīta Sunnandæg* white Sunday; prob. so called because the newly baptized wore white robes on that day]

Whit·sun·tide (hwit′sən tīd′, wit′-), *n.* the week beginning with Whitsunday, esp. the first three days of this week. Also called **Whit Week.** [1175–1225; ME *whitsone(n)tide.* See WHITSUN, TIDE[1]]

Whit·ta·ker (hwit′ə kər, wit′-), *n.* **Charles Evans,** 1901–73, U.S. jurist: associate justice of the U.S. Supreme Court 1957–62.

Whit·ti·er (hwit′ē ər, wit′-), *n.* **1. John Green·leaf** (grēn′lēf′), 1807–92, U.S. poet. **2.** a city in SW California, E of Los Angeles. 68,872.

Whit·ting·ton (hwit′ing tən, wit′-), *n.* **Richard** (*"Dick"*), 1358?–1423, English merchant and philanthropist: Lord Mayor of London 1398, 1406–07, 1419–20.

whit·tle (hwit′l, wit′l), *v.,* **-tled, -tling,** *n.* —*v.t.* **1.** to cut, trim, or shape (a stick, piece of wood, etc.) by carving off bits with a knife. **2.** to form by whittling: *to whittle a figure.* **3.** to cut off (a bit). **4.** to reduce the amount of, as if by whittling; pare down; take away by degrees (usually fol. by *down, away,* etc.): *to whittle down the company's overhead; to whittle away one's inheritance.* —*v.i.* **5.** to whittle wood or the like with a knife, as in shaping something or as a mere aimless diversion: *to spend an afternoon whittling.* **6.** to tire oneself or another by worrying or fussing. —*n.* **7.** *Brit. Dial.* a knife, esp. a large one, as a carving knife or a butcher knife. [1375–1425; late ME (n.), dial. var. of *thwitel* knife, OE *thwīt(an)* to cut + *-el* -LE] —**whit′·tler,** *n.*

Whit·tle (hwit′l, wit′l), *n.* **Sir Frank,** born 1907, English engineer and inventor.

whit·tling (hwit′ling, wit′-), *n.* **1.** the act of a person who whittles. **2.** Often, **whittlings.** a bit or chip whittled off. [1605–15; WHITTLE + -ING[1]]

Whit·tues·day (hwit′to͞oz′dā, -dē, -tyo͞oz′-, wit′-), *n.* the day following Whitmonday. [1770–80; modeled on WHITSUNDAY]

Whit′ Week′ (whit, wit), Whitsuntide. [1895–1900; modeled on WHITSUNDAY]

Whit·worth (hwit′wûrth′, wit′-), *n.* **Kathrynne Ann** (*Kathy*), born 1939, U.S. golfer.

whit·y (hwī′tē, wī′-), *adj.,* **whit·i·er, whit·i·est,** *n.* —*adj.* **1.** whitish. —*n.* **2.** *(sometimes cap.) Slang (disparaging and offensive).* whitey. [1585–95; WHITE + -Y[1]]

whiz[1] (hwiz, wiz), *v.,* **whizzed, whiz·zing,** *n.* —*v.i.* **1.** to make a humming, buzzing, or hissing sound, as an object passing swiftly through the air. **2.** to move or rush with such a sound: *The angry hornets whizzed by in a cloud.* —*v.t.* **3.** to cause to whiz. **4.** to treat with a whizzer. —*n.* **5.** *Informal.* a person who is quite good at a particular activity, in a certain field, etc.: *She's a whiz at math.* **6.** the sound of a whizzing object. **7.** a swift movement producing such a sound. Also, **whizz.** [1540–50; imit.; cf. FIZZ] —**whiz′zing·ly,** *adv.*

whiz[2] (hwiz, wiz), *n.* wizard (def. 3). [by shortening]

whiz-bang (*n.* hwiz′bang′, wiz′-; *adj.* hwiz′bang′, wiz′-), *n.* **1.** *Mil.* a small, high-speed shell whose sound as it flies through the air arrives almost at the same instant as its explosion. **2.** a firecracker with a similar effect. **3.** *Informal.* whiz[1] (def. 5). —*adj.* **4.** *Informal.* first-rate; topnotch: *a whiz-bang navigator.* Also, **whiz′·bang′, whizz′-bang′.** [1910–15; orig. imit.]

whiz′ kid′, *Informal.* a youthful and exceptionally intelligent, successful, or influential person in a given field: *the whiz kid of network programming.* [1940–45]

whiz-kid (hwiz′kid′, wiz′-), *adj.* of, pertaining to, or being a whiz kid: *a whiz-kid sales manager.* [1940–45]

whiz·zer (hwiz′ər, wiz′-), *n.* **1.** something that whizzes. **2.** a centrifugal machine for drying sugar, grain, clothes, etc. [1880–85; WHIZ[1] + -ER[1]]

whiz·zo (hwiz′ō, wiz′ō), *Brit. Slang.* —*adj.* **1.** absolutely first-rate; superb; excellent. —*interj.* **2.** (used as an exclamation of approval, wonder, or pleasure.) [WHIZ[1] + -O]

who (ho͞o), *pron.; possessive* **whose;** *objective* **whom. 1.** what person or persons?: *Who did it?* **2.** (of a person) of what character, origin, position, importance, etc.: *Who does she think she is?* **3.** the person that or any person that (used relatively to represent a specified or implied antecedent): *It was who you thought.* **4.** (used relatively in restrictive and nonrestrictive clauses to represent a specified antecedent, the antecedent being a person or sometimes an animal or personified thing): *Any kid who wants to can learn to swim.* **5.** *Archaic.* the person or persons who. **6. as who should say,** *Archaic.* in a manner of speaking; so to say. [bef. 900; ME; OE *hwā;* c. OHG *hwer,* Goth *hwas,* L *quis*]
—**Usage.** The typical usage guide statement about the choice between WHO and WHOM says that the choice must be determined by the grammar of the clause within which this pronoun occurs. WHO is the appropriate form for the subject of a sentence or clause: *Who are you? The voters who elected him have not been disappointed.* WHOM is the objective form: *Whom did you ask? To whom are we obliged for this assistance?* This method of selecting the appropriate form is generally characteristic of formal writing and is usually followed in edited prose.
In most speech and writing, however, since WHO or WHOM often occurs at the beginning of the sentence or clause, there is a strong tendency to choose WHO no matter what its function. Even in edited prose, WHO occurs at least ten times as often as WHOM, regardless of grammatical function. Only when it directly follows a preposition is WHOM more likely to occur than WHO: *Mr. Erickson is the man to whom you should address your request.*
In natural informal speech, WHOM is quite rare. *Who were you speaking to?* is far more likely to occur than the "correct" *To whom were you speaking?* or *Whom were you speaking to?* However, the notion that WHOM is somehow more "correct" or elegant than WHO leads some speakers to hypercorrect uses of WHOM: *Whom are you? The person whom is in charge has left the office.* See also **than.**

WHO, See **World Health Organization.**

whoa (hwō, wō), *interj.* stop! (used esp. to horses). [1615–25; dial. var. of HO[2]]

who'd (ho͞od), contraction of *who would: Who'd have thought it!*
—**Usage.** See **contraction.**

who·dun·it (ho͞o dun′it), *n. Informal.* a narrative dealing with a murder or a series of murders and the detection of the criminal; detective story. [1925–30; jocular formation from question *Who done it?,* for standard E *Who did it?*]

who·e'er (ho͞o âr′), *pron. Literary.* whoever.

CONCISE ETYMOLOGY KEY: <, descended or borrowed from; >, whence; b., blend of, blended; c., cognate with; cf., compare; deriv., derivative; equiv., equivalent; imit., imitative; obl., oblique; r., replacing; s., stem; sp., spelling, spelled; resp., respelling, respelled; trans., translation; ?, origin unknown; *, unattested; ‡, probably earlier than. See the full key inside the front cover.

who•ev•er (hōō ev′ər), *pron.; possessive* **whos•ev•er;** *objective* **whom•ev•er. 1.** whatever person; anyone that: *Whoever did it should be proud. Ask whoever is there. Tell it to whomever you like.* **2.** no matter who: *I won't do it, whoever asks.* **3.** who? what person? (used to express astonishment, disbelief, disdain, etc.): *Whoever is that? Whoever told you such a thing?* [1125–75; ME; see WHO, EVER]

whole (hōl), *adj.* **1.** comprising the full quantity, amount, extent, number, etc., without diminution or exception; entire, full, or total: *He ate the whole pie. They ran the whole distance.* **2.** containing all the elements properly belonging; complete: *We have a whole set of antique china.* **3.** undivided; in one piece: *to swallow a thing whole.* **4.** *Math.* integral, or not fractional. **5.** not broken, damaged, or impaired; intact: *Thankfully, the vase arrived whole.* **6.** uninjured or unharmed; sound: *He was surprised to find himself whole after the crash.* **7.** pertaining to all aspects of human nature, esp. one's physical, intellectual, and spiritual development: *education for the whole person.* **8. out of whole cloth,** without foundation in fact; fictitious: *a story made out of whole cloth.* —*n.* **9.** the whole assemblage of parts or elements belonging to a thing; the entire quantity, account, extent, or number: *He accepted some of the parts but rejected the whole.* **10.** a thing complete in itself, or comprising all its parts or elements. **11.** an assemblage of parts associated or viewed together as one thing; a unitary system. **12. as a whole,** all things included or considered; altogether: *As a whole, the relocation seems to have been beneficial.* **13. on** or **upon the whole, a.** in view of all the circumstances; after consideration. **b.** disregarding exceptions; in general: *On the whole, the neighborhood is improving.* [bef. 900; ME *hole, hool* (adj. and n.), OE *hāl* (adj.); c. D *heel,* G *heil,* ON *heill;* see HALE[1], HEAL; sp. with *w* reflects dial. form] —**whole′ness,** *n.*
—**Syn. 1.** undiminished, integral, complete. **5.** unimpaired, perfect. **9.** totality, aggregate. WHOLE, TOTAL mean the entire or complete sum or amount. The WHOLE is all there is; every part, member, aspect; the complete sum, amount, quantity of anything, not divided; the entirety: *the whole of one's property, family.* TOTAL also means whole, complete amount, or number, but conveys the idea of something added together or added up: *The total of their gains amounted to millions.* —**Ant. 1.** partial. **9.** part.

whole blood (hōl′ blud′ *for 1;* hōl′ blud′ *for 2*), **1.** blood directly from the body, from which none of the components have been removed, used in transfusions. **2.** relationship between persons through both parents. Cf. **half blood.** [1400–50; late ME]

whole′ broth′er, a brother whose parents are the same as one's own. [1350–1400; ME]

whole•food (hōl′fōōd′), *n. Brit.* food with little or no refining or processing and containing no artificial additives or preservatives; natural or organic food. [1955–60; WHOLE + FOOD]

whole′ gale′, *Meteorol.* a wind of 55–63 mph (24–28 m/sec). [1795–1805]

whole-grain (hōl′grān′), *adj.* of or being natural or unprocessed grain containing the germ and bran. [1955–60]

whole•heart•ed (hōl′här′tid), *adj.* fully or completely sincere, enthusiastic, energetic, etc.; hearty; earnest: *a wholehearted attempt to comply.* [1830–40, *Amer.;* WHOLE + HEARTED] —**whole′heart′ed•ly,** *adv.* —**whole′heart′ed•ness,** *n.*

whole′ hog′, *Informal.* **1.** the furthest extent; everything: *With them it was whole hog or nothing.* **2. go whole hog,** to do something completely or thoroughly: *The townspeople went whole hog for the celebration.* Also, **go the whole hog.**

whole-hog (hōl′hôg′, -hog′), *adj. Informal.* complete and thorough; wholehearted. [1820–30]

whole-length (*adj.* hōl′lengkth′, -length′; *n.* hōl′-lengkth′, -length′), *adj.* **1.** extended to or having its entire length; not shortened or abridged: *a whole-length report.* **2.** portraying, reflecting, or accommodating the full length of the human figure: *a whole-length sofa; a whole-length portrait of the general.* —*n.* **3.** a portrait or statue showing the full length of its subject: *The painting gallery had a roomful of whole-lengths.*

whole′ life′ insur′ance. See **ordinary life insurance.**

whole•meal (hōl′mēl′), *adj. Brit.* whole-wheat. [1610–20; WHOLE + MEAL[2]]

whole′ milk′, milk containing all its constituents as received from the cow or other milk-giving animal. [1965–70]

whole′ note′, *Music.* a note equivalent in duration to four quarter notes. See illus. under **note.** [1590–1600]

whole′ num′ber, *Math.* **1.** Also called **counting number.** one of the positive integers or zero; any of the numbers (0, 1, 2, 3, . . .). **2.** (loosely) integer (def. 1). [1550–60]

whole′ rest′, *Music.* a rest equivalent in duration to a whole note. See illus. under **rest**[2]. [1885–90]

whole•sale (hōl′sāl′), *n., adj., adv., v.,* **-saled, -sal•ing.** —*n.* **1.** the sale of goods in quantity, as to retailers or jobbers, for resale (opposed to *retail*). —*adj.* **2.** of, pertaining to, or engaged in sale by wholesale. **3.** extensive; broadly indiscriminate: *wholesale discharge of workers.* —*adv.* **4.** in a wholesale way; on wholesale terms: *I can get it for you wholesale.* **5.** in large quantities; on a large scale, esp. without discrimination: *Wild horses were slaughtered wholesale.* —*v.t., v.i.* **6.** to sell by wholesale. [1375–1425; late ME, from the phrase *by hole sale* in gross; see WHOLE, SALE] —**whole′sal′er,** *n.*
—**Syn. 3.** far-reaching, comprehensive, thorough, inclusive; undiscriminating, promiscuous.

whole•sal•ing (hōl′sā′ling), *n.* the business of selling to retailers, esp. in large quantities (distinguished from *retailing*). [1790–1800; WHOLESALE + -ING[1]]

whole′ sis′ter, a sister whose parents are the same as one's own.

whole′ snipe′, the common snipe. See under **snipe** (def. 1).

whole•some (hōl′səm), *adj.* **1.** conducive to moral or general well-being; salutary; beneficial: *wholesome recreation; wholesome environment.* **2.** conducive to bodily health; healthful; salubrious: *wholesome food; wholesome air; wholesome exercise.* **3.** suggestive of physical or moral health, esp. in appearance. **4.** healthy or sound. [1150–1200; ME *ho(o)lsom* (see WHOLE, -SOME[1]); c. OHG *heilsam,* ON *heilsamr*] —**whole′some•ly,** *adv.* —**whole′some•ness,** *n.*
—**Syn. 1.** helpful; good. **2.** nourishing, nutritious. **2, 3.** See **healthy.**

whole-souled (hōl′sōld′), *adj.* wholehearted; hearty. [1825–35, *Amer.*]

whole′ step′, *Music.* an interval of two semitones, as A-B or B-C♯; a major second. Also called **whole′ tone′.** [1895–1900]

whole•time (hōl′tīm′), *adj. Brit.* full-time. Also, **whole′-time′.** [1905–10; WHOLE + TIME]

whole′-tone scale′ (hōl′tōn′), *Music.* a scale progressing entirely by whole tones, as C, D, E, F♯, G♯, A♯, C.

whole-wheat (hōl′hwēt′, -wēt′), *adj.* prepared with the complete wheat kernel. [1875–80]

who•lism (hō′liz əm), *n.* holism. —**who•lis′tic,** *adj.*

who'll (hōōl), contraction of *who will* or *who shall: Who'll mind the store?*
—**Usage.** See **contraction.**

whol•ly (hō′lē, hōl′lē), *adv.* **1.** entirely; totally; altogether; quite. **2.** to the whole amount, extent, etc. **3.** so as to comprise or involve all. [1250–1300; ME *holliche.* See WHOLE, -LY]

whom (hōōm), *pron.* **1.** the objective case of **who:** *Whom did you call? Of whom are you speaking? With whom did you stay?* **2.** the dative case of **who:** *You gave whom the book?* [bef. 900; ME; OE *hwām,* dat. of *hwā* WHO]
—**Usage.** See **who.**

whom•ev•er (hōōm ev′ər), *pron.* the objective case of **whoever:** *She questioned whomever she met. Whomever she spoke to, she was invariably polite.* [1300–50; ME; see WHOM, EVER]

whomp (hwomp, womp), *Informal.* —*n.* **1.** a loud, heavy blow, slap, bang, or the like: *He fell with an awful whomp.* —*v.t.* **2.** to defeat (a person, opposing team, etc.) decisively: *We whomped the visiting team.* **3.** to slap or strike: *to whomp the kids.* —*v.i.* **4.** to make a banging or slapping noise: *Guns whomped in the distance.* **5. whomp up,** *Informal.* **a.** to make or create quickly: *to whomp up a new set of guidelines.* **b.** to stir up; rouse: *to whomp up public approval.* [1925–30; imit.]

whom•so (hōōm′sō), *pron.* the objective case of **whoso.**

whom•so•ev•er (hōōm′sō ev′ər), *pron.* the objective case of **whosoever:** *Ask whomsoever you like. Inquire of whomsoever you meet.* [1400–50; late ME, equiv. to *whomso* whomsoever (early ME *swā hwām swā;* see WHOM, SO[1]) + *ever* EVER]

whoof (hwōōf, wōōf, hwōōf, wōōf), *n.* **1.** a deep gruff sound. —*v.i.* **2.** to make such a sound. —*interj.* **3.** (used to express exultation or surprise). [1760–70; imit.]

whoop (hōōp, hōōp; *esp. for 1, 3–5, 7–12* hwōōp, hwōōp, wōōp, wōōp), *n.* **1.** a loud cry or shout, as of excitement or joy. **2.** the sound made by a person suffering from whooping cough. **3. not worth a whoop,** *Informal.* to be worthless: *Their promises aren't worth a whoop.* —*v.i.* **4.** to utter a loud cry or shout in expressing enthusiasm, excitement, etc. **5.** to cry as an owl, crane, or certain other birds. **6.** to make the characteristic sound accompanying the deep intake of air following a series of coughs in whooping cough. —*v.t.* **7.** to utter with or as if with a whoop. **8.** to whoop to or at. **9.** to call, urge, pursue, or drive with whoops: *to whoop dogs on.* **10. whoop it up,** *Informal.* **a.** to raise a disturbance, as to celebrate noisily: *They whooped it up after winning the big game.* **b.** to stir up enthusiasm, as for an idea or project: *Every spring they whoop it up for the circus.* **11. whoop up,** *Informal.* to promote or praise; extol: *a class reunion where they whoop up the good old days.* —*interj.* **12.** (used as a cry to attract attention from afar, or to show excitement, encouragement, enthusiasm, etc.) [1350–1400; ME *whopen,* OE *hwōpan* to threaten; c. Goth *hwopan* to boast]

whoop-de-do (hōōp′dē dōō′, -dōō′, hōōp′-, hwōōp′-, hwōōp′-, wōōp′-, wōōp′-), *n., pl.* **-dos.** *Informal.* **1.** lively and noisy festivities; merrymaking: *New Year's Eve whoop-de-do.* **2.** heated discussion or debate, esp. in public: *a whoop-de-do over the new tax bill.* **3.** extravagant publicity or fanfare: *the whoop-de-do of a movie premiere.* Also, **whoop′-de-doo′.** [1935–40; orig. uncert.; see WHOOP]

whoop•ee (*n.* hwōōp′ē, wōōp′ē, hwōō′pē, wōō′-; *interj.* hwōōp′ē′, wōōp′ē′, hwōō′pē′, wōō′-), *Informal.* —*n.* **1. make whoopee,** to engage in uproarious merrymaking. —*interj.* **2.** (used as a shout of exuberant joy.) Also, **whoop′ie.** [1875–80, *Amer.;* WHOOP + *-ee* of uncert. orig.; cf. YIPPEE]

whoop′ee cush′ion, a type of cushion or pillow used as a practical joke that, when sat upon, produces a loud noise resembling flatulence. Also, **whoop′ie cush′ion.** [1955–60]

whoop•er (hōō′pər, hwōō′-, wōō′-), *n.* **1.** a person or thing that whoops. **2.** See **whooper swan. 3.** *Informal.* See **whooping crane.** [1650–60; WHOOP + -ER[1]]

whoop′er swan′, a common, Old World swan, *Cygnus cygnus,* distinguished by a yellow patch at the base of its bill, noted for its whooping cry. [1875–80]

whoop′ing cough′ (hōō′ping, hōōp′ing), *Pathol.* an infectious disease of the respiratory mucous membrane, caused by *Bordetella pertussis,* characterized by a series of short, convulsive coughs followed by a deep inspiration accompanied by a whooping sound. Also called **pertussis.** [1730–40]

whoop′ing crane′, a white North American crane, *Grus americana,* having a loud, whooping call: an endangered species. See illus. under **crane.** [1720–30, *Amer.*]

whoop•la (hōōp′lä, hwōōp′-, wōōp′-), *n.* hoopla.

whoops (hwōōps, hwōōps, wōōps, wōōps), *interj.* (used to express surprise, mild embarrassment, etc., or as a casual apology.) [WHOOP + -s as in OOPS]

whoosh (hwōōsh, hwōōsh, wōōsh, wōōsh), *n.* **1.** a loud, rushing noise, as of air or water: *a great whoosh as the door opened.* —*v.i.* **2.** to move swiftly with a gushing or hissing noise: *gusts of wind whooshing through the trees.* —*v.t.* **3.** to move (an object, a person, etc.) with a whooshing motion or sound: *The storm whooshed the waves over the road.* Also, **woosh.** [1840–50; imit.]

whoo•sis (hōō′zis), *n., pl.* **-sis•es.** *Informal.* **1.** an object or person whose name is not known or cannot be recalled: *It's the whoosis next to the volume control.* **2.** a person or thing considered typical or illustrative: *the usual paragraph about the party given by Mme. Whoosis.* Also, **whosis.** [1920–25; alter. of phrase *who's this*]

whoo•sy (hōō′zē), *n., pl.* **-sies.** *Informal.* whoosis.

whop (hwop, wop), *v.,* **whopped, whop•ping,** *n. Informal.* —*v.t.* **1.** to strike forcibly. **2.** to defeat soundly, as in a contest. **3.** to put or pull violently; whip: *to whop out a book.* —*v.i.* **4.** to plump suddenly down; flop. —*n.* **5.** a forcible blow. **6.** the sound made by it. **7.** a bump; heavy fall. Also, **whap, wap.** [1350–1400; ME, var. of WAP]

whop•per (hwop′ər, wop′-), *n. Informal.* **1.** something uncommonly large of its kind. **2.** a big lie. Also, **whapper.** [1775–85; WHOP + -ER[1]]

whop•ping (hwop′ing, wop′-), *adj. Informal.* **1.** very large of its kind; thumping: *We caught four whopping trout.* —*adv.* **2.** extremely; exceedingly: *a whopping big lie.* Also, **whapping.** [1615–25; WHOP + -ING[2]]

whore (hôr, hōr *or, often,* hōōr), *n., v.,* **whored, whor•ing.** —*n.* **1.** a woman who engages in promiscuous sexual intercourse, usually for money; prostitute; harlot; strumpet. —*v.i.* **2.** to act as a whore. **3.** to consort with whores. —*v.t.* **4.** *Obs.* to make a whore of; corrupt; debauch. [bef. 1100; ME, OE *hōre;* c. G *Hure,* ON *hōra;* akin to Goth *hors* harlot, L *cārus* dear]

who're (hōō′ər), contraction of *who are: Who're the people at the next table?*
—**Usage.** See **contraction.**

whore•dom (hôr′dəm, hōr′- *or, often,* hōōr′-), *n.* **1.** the activity or state of whoring. **2.** *Bible.* idolatry. [1125–75; ME *hordom,* equiv. to OE *hōr* adultery + *-dōm* -DOM; cf. ON *hōrdōmr*]

whore•house (hôr′hous′, hōr′- *or, often,* hōōr′-), *n., pl.* **-hous•es** (-hou′ziz). a house or apartment in which prostitutes are available for hire; house of prostitution; brothel. [1300–50; ME *hoore-hows.* See WHORE, HOUSE]

whore′house cut′, *Cards.* a cut in which a pack is divided into two parts, each of which is divided again before the pack is reassembled.

whore•mon•ger (hôr′mung′gər, -mong′-, hōr′- *or, often,* hōōr′-), *n.* someone who consorts with whores; a lecher or pander. Also called **whore•mas•ter** (hôr′-mas′tər, -mä′stər, hōr′- *or, often,* hōōr′-). [1520–30; WHORE + MONGER] —**whore′mon′ger•ing, whore′-mas′ter•y,** *n.*

whore•son (hôr′sən, hōr′- *or, often,* hōōr′-), *n.* **1.** a bastard. **2.** wretch; scoundrel. —*adj.* **3.** wretched; scurvy. [1200–50; ME *horeson* SON of a WHORE]

Whorf (hwôrf, wôrf), *n.* **Benjamin Lee,** 1897–1941, U.S. linguist.

Whorf′i•an hypoth′esis (hwôr′fē ən, hwōr′-, wôr′-, wōr′-). See **Sapir-Whorf hypothesis.** [1960–65; WHORF + -IAN]

whor•ish (hôr′ish, hōr′- *or, often,* hōōr′-), *adj.* having the character or characteristics of a whore; lewd; unchaste. [1525–35; WHORE + -ISH[1]] —**whor′ish•ly,** *adv.* —**whor′ish•ness,** *n.*

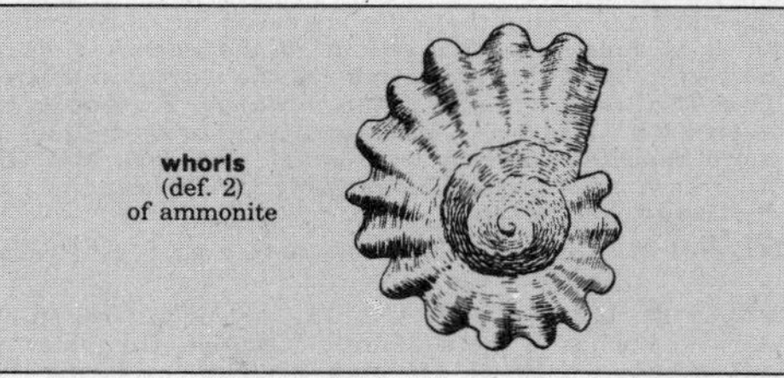
whorls (def. 2) of ammonite

whorl (hwûrl, hwôrl, wûrl, wôrl), *n.* **1.** a circular arrangement of like parts, as leaves or flowers, around a point on an axis; verticil. **2.** one of the turns or volutions of a spiral shell. **3.** anything shaped like a coil. **4.** one of the central ridges of a fingerprint, forming at least one complete circle. **5.** *Textiles.* a flywheel or pulley, as for a spindle. [1425–75; late ME *whorle, whorvil, wharwyl,* OE *hwyrfel,* equiv. to *hweorfa* whorl of a spindle + *-el* n. suffix]

whorled (hwûrld, hwôrld, wûrld, wôrld), *adj.* **1.** having a whorl or whorls. **2.** disposed in the form of a whorl, as leaves. [1770–80; WHORL + -ED[3]]

whorled′ loose′strife. See under **loosestrife** (def. 1).

CONCISE PRONUNCIATION KEY: *act, cāpe, dâre, pärt; set, ēqual; if, īce; ox, ōver, ôrder, oil, bo͝ok, bo͞ot, out; up, ûrge; child; sing; shoe; thin,* that; *zh as in treasure.* ə = *a* as in *alone, e* as in *system, i* as in *easily, o* as in *gallop, u* as in *circus;* ° as in *fire* (fī°r), *hour* (ou°r). l and n can serve as syllabic consonants, as in *cradle* (krād′l), and *button* (but′n). See the full key inside the front cover.

whorl′ foot′, *Furniture.* See **French foot** (def. 1).

whort (hwûrt, wûrt), *n.* the whortleberry. Also, **whor·tle** (hwûr′tl, wûr′-), **wort.** [1570–80; dial. var. of ME *hurte,* OE *horte* WHORTLEBERRY]

whor·tle·ber·ry (hwûr′tl ber′ē, wûr′-), *n., pl.* **-ries.** **1.** the edible black berry of a Eurasian shrub, *Vaccinium myrtillus,* of the heath family. **2.** the shrub itself. Also, **hurtleberry.** [1570–80; dial. var. of HURTLEBERRY]

who's (ho͞oz), **1.** contraction of *who is: Who's there?* **2.** contraction of *who has: Who's seen it?*

whose (ho͞oz), *pron.* **1.** (the possessive case of **who** used as an adjective): *Whose umbrella did I take? Whose is this one?* **2.** (the possessive case of **which** used as an adjective): *a word whose meaning escapes me; an animal whose fur changes color.* **3.** the one or ones belonging to what person or persons: *Whose painting won the third prize?* [bef. 900; ME *whos,* early ME *hwās;* r. *hwas,* OE *hwæs,* gen. of *hwā* WHO]
—Usage. Sometimes the phrase *of which* is used as the possessive of *which: Chicago is a city of which the attractions are many* or *Chicago is a city the attractions of which are many.* The use of this phrase can often seem awkward or pretentious, whereas WHOSE sounds more idiomatic: *Chicago is a city whose attractions are many.*

whose·so·ev·er (ho͞oz′sō ev′ər), *pron.* **1.** (the possessive case of **whosoever** used as an attributive adjective): *Whosesoever books are overdue will be fined.* **2.** the one or ones belonging to whomsoever: *Whosesoever are left here will be confiscated.* [1605–15; earlier *whoseso* whosesoever (see WHOSE, SO[1]) + EVER]

whos·ev·er (ho͞o zev′ər), *pron.* **1.** (the possessive case of **whoever** used as an adjective): *Whosever wagon this is, get it out of here. Whosever is this ridiculous hat?* **2.** the one or ones belonging to whomever: *Whosever will win, do you think?* [1730–40; WHOSE + EVER]

who·sis (ho͞o′zis), *n.* whoosis.

who·so (ho͞o′sō), *pron.; objective* **whom·so.** whosoever; whoever. [1125–75; ME, early ME *hwa swa,* OE (*swā*) *hwā swā.* See WHO, SO[1]]

who·so·ev·er (ho͞o′sō ev′ər), *pron.; possessive* **whose·so·ev·er;** *objective* **whom·so·ev·er.** whoever; whatever person: *Whosoever wants to apply should write to the bureau.* [1175–1225; ME; see WHOSO, EVER]

who's′ who′, **1.** a reference work containing short biographical entries on the outstanding persons in a country, industry, profession, etc.: *a who's who in automotive engineering.* **2.** the outstanding or influential persons in a community, industry, profession, or other group: *The who's who of racing will be there.* [1840–50]

WH-ques·tion (dub′əl yo͞o āch′kwes′chən), *n. Gram.* (in English) a question containing a WH-word, often in initial position, and calling for an item of information to be supplied, as *Where do you live?* Also, ***wh*-question.** Cf. **yes-no question.**

whr., watt-hour.

whse., warehouse. Also, **whs.**

whsle., wholesale.

whs. stk., warehouse stock.

whump (hwump, wump), *n., v.* thump. [1925–30; imit.]

whup (hwup, wup), *v.t.,* **whupped, whup·ping.** *South Midland and Southern U.S.* to whip; beat or defeat decisively: *The top seed whupped his opponent in three straight sets.* [1890–95; orig. Scots form of WHIP]

WH-word (dub′əl yo͞o āch′wûrd′), *n. Gram.* (in English) an interrogative or relative word that usually, but not always, begins with *wh-,* as *what, why, where, which, who,* or *how.* Also, ***wh*-word.**

why (hwī, wī), *adv., conj., n., pl.* **whys,** *interj.* **—adv. 1.** for what? for what reason, cause, or purpose?: *Why did you behave so badly?* **—conj. 2.** for what cause or reason: *I don't know why he is leaving.* **3.** for which; on account of which (usually after *reason* to introduce a relative clause): *the reason why he refused to go.* **4.** the reason for which: *That is why he returned.* **—n. 5.** a question concerning the cause or reason for which something is done, achieved, etc.: *a child's unending hows and whys.* **6.** the cause or reason: *the whys and wherefores of a troublesome situation.* **—interj. 7.** (used as an expression of surprise, hesitation, etc., or sometimes a mere expletive): *Why, it's all gone!* [bef. 900; ME; OE *hwī, hwȳ,* instr. case of *hwæt* WHAT; c. ON *hvī*]
—Usage. See **reason.**

Why·al·la (hwī al′ə, wī-), *n.* a city in S Australia. 29,962.

whyd·ah (hwid′ə, wid′ə), *n.* **1.** any of several small African finches of the subfamily Viduinae, the males of which have elongated, drooping tail feathers during the breeding season. **2.** any of several African weaverbirds of the genus *Euplectes,* the males of which have similar long tails. Also, **whidah.** Also called **widow bird.** [1775–85; alter. of WIDOW (BIRD) to make name agree with that of a town in Benin, West Africa, one of its haunts]

why'll (hwī′əl, wī′-), contraction of *why will* or *why shall: Why'll it take so long?*
—Usage. See **contraction.**

why're (hwī′ər, wī′-), contraction of *why are: Why're you so late?*
—Usage. See **contraction.**

why's (hwīz, wīz), contraction of *why is: Why's dinner so late?*
—Usage. See **contraction.**

CONCISE ETYMOLOGY KEY: <, descended or borrowed from; >, whence; b., blend of, blended; c., cognate with; cf., compare; deriv., derivative; equiv., equivalent; imit., imitative; obl., oblique; r., replacing; s., stem; sp., spelling, spelled; resp., respelling, respelled; trans., translation; ?, origin unknown; *, unattested; ‡, probably earlier than. See the full key inside the front cover.

Whyte′ classifica′tion (hwīt, wīt), a system for classifying steam locomotives according to the total number of wheels on the front trucks, drivers, and rear trucks, in that order. For example, a Pacific locomotive is designated as 4-6-2. See table. [after Frederic M. *Whyte,* engineer for the New York Central Railroad c1900, who devised the system]

WHYTE CLASSIFICATION

Locomotive Type	Whyte Symbol	Wheel Arrangement*
Forney	0-4-4	OOoo
Mogul	2-6-0	oOOO
Prairie	2-6-2	oOOOo
Consolidation	2-8-0	oOOOO
Mikado	2-8-2	oOOOOo
Berkshire	2-8-4	oOOOOoo
Decapod	2-10-0	oOOOOO
Santa Fe	2-10-2	oOOOOOo
American	4-4-0	ooOO
Atlantic	4-4-2	ooOOo
Ten-Wheeler	4-6-0	ooOOO
Pacific	4-6-2	ooOOOo
Hudson	4-6-4	ooOOOoo
Mountain	4-8-2	ooOOOOo
Northern	4-8-4	ooOOOOoo
"Big Boy" (Articulated)	4-8-8-4	ooOOOO-OOOOoo

*Front-to-back is shown from left to right, with each O or o representing a pair of wheels.

WI, Wisconsin (approved esp. for use with zip code).

wi, *Stock Exchange.* when-issued. Also, **w.i.**

W.I., 1. West Indian. **2.** West Indies.

WIA, *Mil.* wounded in action.

Wi·ak (wē yäk′), *n.* Biak.

wic·ca (wik′ə), *n.* (*sometimes cap.*) witchcraft, esp. benevolent, nature-oriented practices derived from pre-Christian religions. [1970–75; < OE *wicca* (male) sorcerer (ME *wicche,* mod. dial. *witch*); see WITCH]

wic·can (wik′ən), *n.* (*sometimes cap.*) a practitioner of wicca.

Wich·i·ta (wich′i tô′), *n., pl.* **-tas** for 1. **1.** a member of a tribe of North American Indians, originally of Kansas but relocated in Oklahoma after the Civil War. **2.** the Caddoan language of the Wichita. **3.** a city in S Kansas, on the Arkansas River. 279,272.

Wich′ita Falls′, a city in N Texas. 94,201.

wick[1] (wik), *n.* **1.** a twist or braid of soft threads, or a woven strip, as of cotton or asbestos, which in a candle, lamp, cigarette lighter, etc., serves to draw up the melted tallow or wax or the oil or other flammable liquid to be burned. **—v.t. 2.** to draw off (liquid) by capillary action. [bef. 1000; ME *wicke, weke,* OE *wice, wēoc*(*e*); c. MD *wiecke,* MLG *wēke,* OHG *wiohha* lint, wick (G *Wieke* lint); akin to Skt *vāgura* noose] **—wick′less,** *adj.*

wick[2] (wik), *n. Curling.* a narrow opening in the field, bounded by other players' stones. [orig. uncert.]

wick[3] (wik), *n.* **1.** *Brit. Dial.* a farm, esp. a dairy farm. **2.** *Archaic.* a village; hamlet. [bef. 900; ME *wik, wich,* OE *wīc* house, village (cf. OS *wīc,* OHG *wīch*) < L *vīcus* village, estate (see VICINITY); c. Gk *oîkos* house]

Wick (wik), *n.* a town in the Highland region, in N Scotland: herring fisheries. 7613.

wick·ed (wik′id), *adj.,* **-er, -est,** *adv.* **—adj. 1.** evil or morally bad in principle or practice; sinful; iniquitous: *wicked people; wicked habits.* **2.** mischievous or playfully malicious: *These wicked kittens upset everything.* **3.** distressingly severe, as a storm, wound, or cold: *a wicked winter.* **4.** unjustifiable; dreadful; beastly: *wicked prices; a wicked exam.* **5.** having a bad disposition; ill-natured; mean: *a wicked horse.* **6.** spiteful; malevolent; vicious: *a wicked tongue.* **7.** extremely troublesome or dangerous: *wicked roads.* **8.** unpleasant; foul: *a wicked odor.* **9.** *Slang.* wonderful; great; masterful; deeply satisfying: *He blows a wicked trumpet.* **—adv. 10.** *Slang.* very; really; totally: *That shirt is wicked cool.* [1225–75; ME *wikked,* equiv. to *wikke* bad (repr. adj. use of OE *wicca* wizard; cf. WITCH) + *-ed* -ED[3]] **—wick′ed·ly,** *adv.*
—Syn. 1. unrighteous, ungodly, godless, impious, profane, blasphemous; immoral, profligate, corrupt, depraved, dissolute; heinous; infamous, villainous.

wick·ed·ness (wik′id nis), *n.* **1.** the quality or state of being wicked. **2.** wicked conduct or practices. **3.** a wicked act or thing. [1250–1300; ME; see WICKED, -NESS]

wick·er (wik′ər), *n.* **1.** a slender, pliant twig; osier; withe. **2.** plaited or woven twigs or osiers as the material of baskets, chairs, etc.; wickerwork. **3.** something made of wickerwork, as a basket. **—adj. 4.** consisting or made of wicker: *a wicker chair.* **5.** covered with wicker: *a wicker jug.* [1300–50; ME < Scand; cf. dial. Sw *vikker* willow. See WEAK]

wick·er·work (wik′ər wûrk′), *n.* material or products consisting of plaited or woven twigs or osiers; articles made of wicker. [1705–15; WICKER + WORK]

wick·et (wik′it), *n.* **1.** a window or opening, often closed by a grating or the like, as in a door, or forming a place of communication in a ticket office, a teller's cage in a bank, etc. **2.** *Croquet.* a hoop or arch. **3.** a turnstile in an entrance. **4.** a small door or gate, esp. one beside, or forming part of, a larger one. **5.** a small gate by which a canal lock is emptied. **6.** a gate by which a flow of water is regulated, as to a waterwheel. **7.** *Cricket.* **a.** either of the two frameworks, each consisting of three stumps with two bails in grooves across the tops, at which the bowler aims the ball. **b.** the area between the wickets; the playing field. **c.** one batsman's turn at the wicket. **d.** the period during which two players bat together. **e.** a batsman's inning that is not completed or not begun. **8. to be on, have,** or **bat a sticky wicket** *Brit. Slang.* to be at or have a disadvantage. [1200–50; ME *wiket* < AF; OF *guischet* < Gmc; cf. MD *wike* wicket, equiv. to *wik-* (akin to OE *wīcan* to yield; see WEAK) + *-et* n. suffix]

wick·et·keep·er (wik′it kē′pər), *n. Cricket.* the player on the fielding side who stands immediately behind the wicket to stop balls that pass it. [1740–50; WICKET + KEEPER]

wick·ing (wik′ing), *n.* material for wicks. [1840–50; WICK[1] + -ING[1]]

wick·i·up (wik′ē up′), *n.* **1.** (in Nevada, Arizona, etc.) an American Indian hut made of brushwood or covered with mats. **2.** *Western U.S.* any rude hut. Also, **wick′y·up′, wikiup.** [1850–55, *Amer.;* earlier and still dialectally applied to the bark- or mat-covered wigwams of the Upper Great Lakes Indians < Fox *wi·kiya·pi* house < Proto-Algonquian **wi·kiwa·ʔmi;* cf. WIGWAM]

Wick·liffe (wik′lif), *n.* **1. John.** Also, **Wic′lif.** See **Wycliffe, John. 2.** a city in NE Ohio, near Cleveland. 16,790.

Wick·low (wik′lō), *n.* a county in Leinster province, in the E Republic of Ireland. 87,289; 782 sq. mi. (2025 sq km). *Co. seat:* Wicklow.

wic·o·py (wik′ə pē), *n., pl.* **-pies. 1.** the leatherwood, *Dirca palustris.* **2.** basswood. [1695–1705; < Western Abenaki *wigəbi* inner bark suitable for cordage]

wid., 1. widow. **2.** widower.

wid·der (wid′ər), *n. Dial.* widow. [by reduction of final vowel to ə and substitution of -ER[1]]

wid·der·shins (wid′ər shinz′), *adv. Chiefly Scot.* withershins.

wid·dy[1] (wid′ē), *n., pl.* **-dies.** *Chiefly Scot.* **1.** a band or rope, traditionally one made from intertwined willow twigs. **2.** a hangman's rope; noose. Also, **wid′die, woody.** [1400–50; late ME (north), var. of WITHY]

wid·dy[2] (wid′ē), *n., pl.* **-dies.** *Dial.* widow. [analogous to WIDDER, with -Y[2]]

wide (wīd), *adj.,* **wid·er, wid·est,** *adv., n.* **—adj. 1.** having considerable or great extent from side to side; broad: *a wide boulevard.* **2.** having a certain or specified extent from side to side: *three feet wide.* **3.** of great horizontal extent; extensive; vast; spacious: *the wide plains of the West.* **4.** of great range or scope; embracing a great number or variety of subjects, cases, etc.: *wide experience.* **5.** open to the full or a great extent; expanded; distended: *to stare with wide eyes.* **6.** apart or remote from a specified point or object: *a guess wide of the truth.* **7.** too far or too much to one side: *a shot wide of the mark.* **8.** *Baseball.* outside (def. 16): *The pitch was wide of the plate.* **9.** full, ample, or roomy, as clothing: *He wore wide, flowing robes.* **10.** *Phonet.* lax (def. 7). **11.** *Brit. Slang.* shrewd; wary. **—adv. 12.** to the full extent of opening: *Open your mouth wide.* **13.** to the utmost, or fully: *to be wide awake.* **14.** away from or to one side of a point, mark, purpose, or the like; aside; astray: *The shot went wide.* **15.** over an extensive space or region, or far abroad: *scattered far and wide.* **16.** to a great, or relatively great, extent from side to side: *The river runs wide here.* **—n. 17.** *Cricket.* a bowled ball that goes wide of the wicket, and counts as a run for the side batting. **18.** *Archaic.* a wide space or expanse. [bef. 900; ME; OE *wīd;* c. D *wijd,* G *weit,* ON *vīthr*] **—wide′ness,** *n.*
—Syn. 1. WIDE, BROAD refer to dimensions. They are often interchangeable, but WIDE especially applies to things of which the length is much greater than the width: *a wide road, piece of ribbon.* BROAD is more emphatic, and applies to things of considerable or great width, breadth, or extent, esp. to surfaces extending laterally: *a broad valley.* **3.** boundless; comprehensive.

-wide, a combining form of **wide,** forming from nouns adjectives with the general sense "extending or applying throughout a given space," as specified by the noun: *communitywide; countrywide; worldwide.*

wide-an·gle (wīd′ang′gəl), *adj. Photog.* **1.** of or pertaining to a lens having a relatively wide angle of view, generally 45° or more, and a focal length of less than 50 mm. **2.** employing, or made with, a wide-angle lens: *a wide-angle camera; a wide-angle shot.* [1875–80]

wide′-angle convert′er, *Photog.* See under **converter** (def. 8). Also called **wide′-angle convert′er lens′.**

wide′-angle glauco′ma, open-angle glaucoma. See under **glaucoma.**

wide′-ar′ea net′work, a computer network that spans a relatively large geographical area. Also called **WAN.**

wide-a·wake (wīd′ə wāk′), *adj.* **1.** fully awake; with the eyes wide open. **2.** alert, keen, or knowing: *a wide-awake young woman.* **—n. 3.** Also called **wide′-awake hat′.** a soft, low-crowned felt hat. **4.** the sooty tern. [1810–20] **—wide′-a·wake′ness,** *n.*
—Syn. 2. watchful, vigilant; sharp, quick, astute.

wide·bod·y (wīd′bod′ē), *n., pl.* **-bod·ies.** a jet airliner having a fuselage wide enough to allow passenger seating to be divided by two aisles running from front to back. Also, **wide′-bod′y.** [1965–70; WIDE + BODY]

wide-eyed (wīd′īd′), *adj.* with the eyes open wide, as in amazement, innocence, or sleeplessness. [1850–55]

wide·ly (wīd′lē), *adv.* **1.** to a wide extent. **2.** over a wide space or area: *a widely distributed plant.* **3.** by or among a large number of persons: *a widely known artist.* **4.** in many or various subjects, cases, etc.: *to be widely read.* **5.** greatly, very much, or very: *widely differing accounts of an event.* [1655–65; WIDE + -LY]

wide′mouth blind′cat (wīd′mouth′). See under **blindcat.** [WIDE + MOUTH]

wide·mouthed (wīd′mouthd′, -moutht′), *adj.* **1.** (of a person, object, body of water, etc.) having a wide mouth: *a widemouthed river.* **2.** (of a person) having the mouth opened wide, as in astonishment or horror. [1585–95; WIDE + MOUTH + -ED[3]]

wid·en (wīd′n), *v.t., v.i.* to make or become wide or wider; broaden; expand. [1600–10; WIDE + -EN[1]] —**wid′en·er,** *n.*

wide-o·pen (wīd′ō′pən), *adj.* **1.** opened to the full extent: *a wide-open window.* **2.** lacking laws or strict enforcement of laws concerning liquor, vice, gambling, etc.: *a wide-open town.* [1850–55]

wide-rang·ing (wīd′rān′jing), *adj.* extending over a large area; extensive or diversified in scope: *wide-ranging lands; a wide-ranging discussion.* [1810–20]

wide′ receiv′er, *Football.* an offensive player positioned wide of the formation, as a split end, used primarily as a pass receiver. [1965–70]

wide-screen (wīd′skrēn′), *adj.* of, noting, or pertaining to motion pictures projected on a screen having greater width than height, usually in a ratio of 1 to 2.5. [1950–55]

wide·spread (wīd′spred′), *adj.* **1.** spread over or open, or occupying a wide space. **2.** distributed over a wide region, or occurring in many places or among many persons or individuals: *widespread poverty.* [1695–1705; WIDE + SPREAD]
—**Syn. 2.** far-reaching, extensive, pervasive, far-flung.

wide-spread·ing (wīd′spred′ing), *adj.* **1.** spreading over or covering a large area: *wide-spreading showers; wide-spreading ivy.* **2.** affecting or reaching a large area: *a wide-spreading infection.* [1585–95]

widg·eon (wij′ən), *n., pl.* **-eons,** (*esp. collectively*) **-eon** for 1. **1.** any of several common freshwater ducks related to the mallards and teals in the genus *Anas,* having metallic green flight feathers, a white wing patch, and a buff or white forehead, including *A. penelope* of Eurasia and North Africa, *A. sibilatrix* of South America, and the baldpate, *A. americana,* of North America. **2.** *Obs.* a fool. Also, **wigeon.** [1505–15; perh. < an AF correspondent of F *vigeon* < VL; cf. ML *vipiō* kind of crane (deriv. of *vip-* imit. of bird's cry)]

widg·et (wij′it), *n.* **1.** a small mechanical device, as a knob or switch, esp. one whose name is not known or cannot be recalled; gadget: *a row of widgets on the instrument panel.* **2.** something considered typical or representative, as of a manufacturer's products: *the widgets coming off the assembly line.* [1925–30; perh. alter. of GADGET]

wid·ish (wī′dish), *adj.* rather wide; tending to be wide: *a widish bookcase; widish hips.* [1770–80; WIDE + -ISH[1]]

wid·ow (wid′ō), *n.* **1.** a woman who has lost her husband by death and has not remarried. **2.** *Cards.* an additional hand or part of a hand, as one dealt to the table. **3.** *Print.* **a.** a short last line of a paragraph, esp. one less than half of the full measure or one consisting of only a single word. **b.** the last line of a paragraph when it is carried over to the top of the following page away from the rest of the paragraph. Cf. **orphan** (def. 4). **4.** a woman often left alone because her husband devotes his free time to a hobby or sport (used in combination). Cf. **golf widow.** —*v.t.* **5.** to make (someone) a widow: *She was widowed by the war.* **6.** to deprive of anything cherished or needed: *A surprise attack widowed the army of its supplies.* **7.** *Obs.* **a.** to endow with a widow's right. **b.** to survive as the widow of. [bef. 900; (n.) ME *wid(e)we,* OE *widuwe, wydewe;* c. G *Witwe,* Goth *widuwo,* L *vidua* (fem. of *viduus* bereaved), Skt *vidhavā* widow; (v.) ME, deriv. of the n.] —**wid′ow·ly,** *adj.*

wid′ow bird′, whydah. [1765–75; trans. of NL *Vidua,* name of the genus (L: WIDOW). See WHYDAH]

wid·ow·er (wid′ō ər), *n.* a man who has lost his wife by death and has not remarried. [1325–75; late ME (see WIDOW, -ER[1]); r. widow (now dial.), OE *wydewa*] —**wid′·ow·ered,** *adj.* —**wid′ow·er·hood′,** *n.*

wid·ow·hood (wid′ō ho͝od′), *n.* the state or a period of being a widow or, sometimes, a widower. [bef. 900; ME *wid(e)wehood,* OE *widuwanhād,* equiv. to *widuwan,* gen. sing. of *widuwe* WIDOW + *-hād* -HOOD]

wid′ow's cruse′, an inexhaustible supply of something: in allusion to the miracle of the cruse of oil in I Kings 17:10–16 and II Kings 4:1–7.

wid′ow's mite′, a small contribution given cheerfully by one who can ill afford it. Mark 12:41–44. [1585–95]

wid′ow's peak′, a point formed in the hairline in the middle of the forehead. [1840–50]

wid′ow's walk′, a platform or walk atop a roof, as on certain coastal New England houses of the 18th and early 19th centuries: often used as a lookout for incoming ships. [1935–40, *Amer.*]

wid′ow wom′an, *Older Use.* a widow. Also called **wid′ow la′dy.** [1605–15]

width (width, witth *or, often,* with), *n.* **1.** extent from side to side; breadth; wideness. **2.** a piece of the full wideness, as of cloth. [1620–30; WIDE + -TH[1], modeled on *breadth,* etc.]

width·wise (width′wīz′, witth′-, *or, often,* with′-), *adv.* in the direction of the width. Also, **width·ways** (width′wāz′, witth′- *or, often,* with′-). [1880–85; WIDTH + -WISE]

Wi·du·kind (vē′do͞o kint′), *n.* Wittekind.

wie geht's (vē gāts′), *German.* how's it going?; how are you?

Wie·land (vē′länt′), *n.* **1. Chris·toph Mar·tin** (kris′tôf mär′tēn), 1733–1813, German poet, novelist, and critic. **2. Hein·rich** (hīn′rikh), 1877–1957, German chemist: Nobel prize 1927.

Wie·land (vē′länt′), *n. German Myth.* Wayland.

wield (wēld), *v.t.* **1.** to exercise (power, authority, influence, etc.), as in ruling or dominating. **2.** to use (a weapon, instrument, etc.) effectively; handle or employ actively. **3.** *Archaic.* to guide or direct. **4.** *Archaic.* to govern; manage. [bef. 900; ME *welden,* OE *wieldan* to control, deriv. of *wealdan* to rule; c. G *walten,* ON *valda,* Goth *waldan;* akin to L *valēre* to be strong, prevail] —**wield′a·ble,** *adj.* —**wield′er,** *n.*
—**Syn. 1.** exert, employ, utilize. **2.** manipulate, control.

wield·y (wēl′dē), *adj.,* **wield·i·er, wield·i·est.** readily wielded or managed, as in use or action. [1325–75; ME; see WIELD, -Y[1]]

Wien (vēn), *n.* **1. Wil·helm** (vil′helm), 1864–1928, German physicist: Nobel prize 1911. **2.** German name of **Vienna.**

wie·ner (wē′nər), *n.* **1.** frankfurter. **2.** See **Vienna sausage.** Also, **wie·ner·wurst** (wē′nər wûrst′, -wo͝orst′). [1865–70, *Amer.;* < G, short for *Wiener Wurst* Viennese sausage]

Wie·ner (wē′nər), *n.* **Norbert,** 1894–1964, U.S. mathematician: pioneer in cybernetics.

Wie·ner schnit·zel (vē′nər shnit′səl, shnit′səl), *Viennese, German Cookery.* a breaded veal cutlet, variously seasoned or garnished. [1860–65; < G, equiv. to *Wiener* Viennese + *Schnitzel* cutlet, chop]

wie·nie (wē′nē), *n. Informal.* weenie.

Wies·ba·den (vēs′bäd′n), *n.* the capital of Hesse in W Germany: health resort; mineral springs. 251,800.

Wie·sel (wi zel′), *n.* **El·ie** (el′ē), (*Eliezer*), born 1928, U.S. author, born in Rumania: Nobel peace prize 1986.

wife (wīf), *n., pl.* **wives** (wīvz), *v.,* **wifed, wif·ing.** —*n.* **1.** a woman joined in marriage to a man; a woman considered in relation to her husband; spouse. **2.** a woman (*archaic or dial.,* except in idioms): *old wives' tale.* **3. take to wife,** to marry (a particular woman): *He took an heiress to wife.* —*v.i., v.t.* **4.** *Rare.* wive. [bef. 900; ME, OE *wīf* woman; c. D *wijf,* G *Weib,* ON *vīf*] —**wife′dom,** *n.* —**wife′less,** *adj.* —**wife′less·ness,** *n.*

-wife, a combining form of **wife,** now unproductive, occurring in compound words that in general designate traditional roles or occupations of women: *fishwife; goodwife; housewife; midwife.*

wife·hood (wīf′ho͝od), *n.* **1.** the state of being a wife. **2.** wifely character or quality; wifeliness. [1350–1400; ME *wifhood,* OE *wīfhād.* See WIFE, -HOOD]

wife·like (wīf′līk′), *adj.* **1.** wifely. —*adv.* **2.** in a manner befitting a wife. [1590–1600; WIFE + -LIKE]

wife·ly (wīf′lē), *adj.,* **-li·er, -li·est.** of, like, or befitting a wife. Also, **wifelike.** [bef. 900; ME *wifly,* OE *wīflic.* See WIFE, -LY] —**wife′li·ness,** *n.*

wife′ swap′ping, sexual activity in which two or more married couples exchange partners. [1955–60]

wig (wig), *n., v.,* **wigged, wig·ging.** —*n.* **1.** an artificial covering of hair for all or most of the head, of either synthetic or natural hair, worn to be stylish or more attractive. **2.** a similar head covering, worn in one's official capacity, as part of a costume, disguise, etc. **3.** a toupee or hairpiece. **4.** *Brit. Informal.* a wigging. **5. flip one's wig,** *Slang.* See **lid** (def. 8). —*v.t.* **6.** to furnish with a wig. **7.** *Brit. Informal.* to reprimand or reprove severely; scold. **8. wig out,** *Slang.* **a.** to be intoxicated with narcotic drugs. **b.** to make or become wildly excited or enthusiastic: *She wigs out over every rock star that comes along.* [1665–75; short for PERIWIG] —**wig′·less,** *adj.* —**wig′like′,** *adj.*

wig·an (wig′ən), *n.* a stiff, canvaslike fabric for stiffening parts of garments. [1870–75; after WIGAN, where originally produced]

Wig·an (wig′ən), *n.* borough of Greater Manchester, in W England. 309,600.

wig·eon (wij′ən), *n., pl.* **-eons,** (*esp. collectively*) **-eon.** widgeon.

wigged (wigd), *adj.* wearing a wig: *The wigged justices entered the courtroom.* [WIG + -ED[3]]

wig·ger·y (wig′ə rē), *n., pl.* **-ger·ies. 1.** wigs or a wig; false hair. **2.** the wearing of wigs. [1765–75; WIG + -ERY]

Wig·gin (wig′in), *n.* **Kate Douglas,** 1856–1923, U.S. writer.

wig·ging (wig′ing), *n. Brit. Informal.* a scolding or reproof. [1805–15; WIG + -ING[1]]

wig·gle (wig′əl), *v.,* **-gled, -gling,** *n.* —*v.i.* **1.** to move or go with short, quick, irregular movements from side to side: *The puppies wiggled with delight.* —*v.t.* **2.** to cause to wiggle; move quickly and irregularly from side to side. —*n.* **3.** a wiggling movement or course. **4.** a wiggly line. **5.** a dish of creamed fish or shellfish and peas. **6. get a wiggle on,** *Informal.* to hurry up; get a move on. [1175–1225; ME *wiglen;* akin to OE *wegan* to move, *wēg* motion, *wicga* insect; cf. Norw *vigla* to totter, freq. of *vigga* to rock oneself, D, LG *wiggelen*]

wig′gle nail′, a fastener consisting of a piece of corrugated sheet steel with one wavy edge sharpened, for uniting two pieces of wood, as in a miter joint.

wig·gler (wig′lər), *n.* **1.** a person or thing that wiggles. **2.** wriggler (def. 2). **3.** *Southern U.S.* an earthworm. [1890–95; WIGGLE + -ER[1]]
—**Regional Variation.** See **earthworm.**

wig′gle room′, room to maneuver; latitude. [1985–90]

Wig·gles·worth (wig′əlz wûrth′), *n.* **Michael,** 1631–1705, U.S. theologian and author, born in England.

wig·gle-tail (wig′əl tāl′), *n.* wriggler (def. 2).

wig·gly (wig′lē), *adj.,* **-gli·er, -gli·est. 1.** wiggling: *a wiggly child.* **2.** undulating; wavy: *a wiggly line.* [1900–05; WIGGLE + -Y[1]]

wig·gy (wig′ē), *adj.,* **-gi·er, -gi·est.** *Slang.* **1.** crazy or eccentric. **2.** crazed or delirious. [1810–20; WIG + -Y[1]]

wight[1] (wīt), *n.* **1.** a human being. **2.** *Obs.* **a.** a supernatural being, as a witch or sprite. **b.** any living being; a creature. [bef. 900; ME, OE *wiht;* c. G *Wicht,* ON *vēttr,* Goth *waiht*]

wight[2] (wīt), *adj. Brit. Dial.* **1.** strong and brave, esp. in war. **2.** active; nimble. [1175–1225; ME < Scand; cf. ON *vīgt,* neut. of *vīgr* able to fight]

Wight (wīt), *n.* **Isle of,** an island off the S coast of England, forming an administrative division of Hampshire. 147 sq. mi. (381 sq. km). *Co. seat:* Newport.

Wight·man (wīt′mən), *n.* **Hazel Hotchkiss,** 1886–1974, U.S. tennis player.

wig·let (wig′lit), *n.* a small wig, esp. one used to supplement the existing hair. [1825–35; WIG + -LET]

wig·mak·er (wig′mā′kər), *n.* a person who makes or sells wigs. [1705–15; WIG + MAKER]

Wig·man (vig′män), *n.* **Mary,** 1886–1973, German dancer and choreographer.

Wig·ner (wig′nər), *n.* **Eugene Paul,** born 1902, U.S. physicist, born in Hungary: Nobel prize 1963.

Wig·town (wig′tən, -toun′), *n.* a historic county in SW Scotland. Also called **Wig·town·shire** (wig′tən shēr′, -shər, -toun′-).

wig·wag (wig′wag′), *v.,* **-wagged, -wag·ging,** *n.* —*v.t., v.i.* **1.** to move to and fro. **2.** *Naut.* to signal by movements of two flags or the like waved according to a code. —*n.* **3.** *Naut.* the act or process of sending messages by the movements of two flags or the like waved according to a code. **4.** a message so signaled. [1575–85; *wig* to wag (now dial.) + WAG; gradational compound, parallel to ZIGZAG, etc.] —**wig′wag′ger,** *n.*

wig·wam (wig′wom, -wôm), *n.* **1.** an American Indian dwelling, usually of rounded or oval shape, formed of poles overlaid with bark, mats, or skins. Cf. **lodge** (def. 9), **tepee. 2. the Wigwam.** See **Tammany Hall** (def. 2). [1620–30, *Amer.;* < Eastern Abenaki *wikəwam* house < Proto-Algonquian **wi·kiwa·ʔmi;* cf. WICKIUP]

wigwam (def. 1)

wik·i·up (wik′ē up′), *n.* wickiup.

Wil·ber·force (wil′bər fôrs′, -fōrs′), *n.* **William,** 1759–1833, British statesman, philanthropist, and writer.

Wil·bra·ham (wil′brə ham′), *n.* a city in SW Massachusetts. 12,053.

Wil·bur (wil′bər), *n.* **1. Richard,** born 1921, U.S. poet: U.S. poet laureate since 1987. **2.** Also, **Wil′ber.** a male given name: from an Old English word meaning "wild boar."

Wil·bur·ite (wil′bə rīt′), *n.* a member of a conservative body of Quakers formed in 1845 in protest against the evangelicalism of the Gurneyites. [1860–65, *Amer.;* after John *Wilbur* (1774–1856), American Quaker preacher; see -ITE[1]]

wil·co (wil′kō), *interj.* (esp. in radio transmission) an indication that the message just received will be complied with. [1935–40; short for *will comply*]

Wil·cox (wil′koks), *n.* **Ella Wheeler,** 1850–1919, U.S. poet.

wild (wīld), *adj.,* **-er, -est,** *adv., n.* —*adj.* **1.** living in a state of nature; not tamed or domesticated: *a wild animal; wild geese.* **2.** growing or produced without cultivation or the care of humans, as plants, flowers, fruit, or honey: *wild cherries.* **3.** uncultivated, uninhabited, or waste: *wild country.* **4.** uncivilized or barbarous: *wild tribes.* **5.** of unrestrained violence, fury, intensity, etc.; violent; furious: *wild strife; wild storms.* **6.** characterized by or indicating violent feelings or excitement, as actions or a person's appearance: *wild cries; a wild look.* **7.** frantic or distracted; crazy: *to drive someone wild.* **8.** violently or uncontrollably affected: *wild with rage; wild with pain.* **9.** undisciplined, unruly, or lawless: *a gang of wild boys.* **10.** unrestrained, untrammeled, or unbridled: *wild enthusiasm.* **11.** disregardful of moral restraints as to pleasurable indulgence: *He repented his wild youth.* **12.** unrestrained by reason or prudence: *wild schemes.* **13.** amazing or incredible: *Isn't that wild about Bill getting booted out of the club?* **14.** disorderly or disheveled: *wild hair.* **15.** wide of the mark: *He scored on a wild throw.* **16.** *Informal.* intensely eager or enthusiastic: *wild to get started; wild about the new styles.* **17.** *Cards.* (of a card) having its value decided by the wishes of the players. **18.** *Metall.* (of molten metal) generating large amounts of gas during cooling, so as to cause violent bubbling. —*adv.* **19.** in a wild manner; wildly. **20. blow wild,** (of an oil or gas well) to spout in an uncontrolled way, as in a blowout. Cf. **blowout** (def. 4). **21. run wild, a.** to grow unchecked: *The rambler roses are running wild.* **b.** to show lack of restraint or control: *Those children are allowed to run wild.* —*n.* **22.** Often, **wilds.** an uncultivated, uninhabited, or desolate region or tract; waste; wilderness; desert: *a cabin in the wild; a safari to the wilds of Africa.* [bef. 900; ME, OE *wilde;* c. D, G *wild,* ON *villr,* Sw *vild,* Goth *wiltheis*] —**wild′ly,** *adv.* —**wild′ness,** *n.*
—**Syn. 1.** undomesticated, untamed, unbroken; ferocious. **4.** barbarian, savage. **5.** tempestuous, stormy, frenzied, turbulent. **6.** boisterous. **7.** insane. **9.** self-willed, riotous, unrestrained, wayward. **10.** uncontrollable. **12.** reckless, rash, extravagant, impracticable. **13.** grotesque, bizarre, strange, fanciful. **14.** unkempt.
—**Ant. 1.** tame.

wild-and-wool·ly (wīld′n wo͝ol′ē), *adj.* unrestrained;

CONCISE PRONUNCIATION KEY: act, cāpe, dâre, pärt; set, ēqual; if, īce; ox, ōver, ôrder, oil, bo͝ok, bo͞ot, out; up, ûrge; child; sing; shoe; thin, *th*at; zh as in *treasure.* ə = *a* as in *alone, e* as in *system, i* as in *easily, o* as in *gallop, u* as in *circus;* ᵊ as in *fire* (fīᵊr), *hour* (ouᵊr). l and n can serve as syllabic consonants, as in *cradle* (krād′l), and *button* (but′n). See the full key inside the front cover.

lawless: *a wild-and-woolly frontier town.* [1885–90; perh. orig. referring to range-bred cattle]

wild′ ap′ricot, apricot (def. 4).

wild′ bean′, **1.** groundnut (def. 1). **2.** any of several other leguminous plants, esp. of the genus *Strophostyles.* [1770–80, *Amer.*]

wild′ ber′gamot, a plant, *Monarda fistulosa,* of the mint family, native to eastern North America, having a rounded cluster of lilac-colored or purple flowers, growing in dry places. [1835–45, *Amer.*]

wild′ bleed′ing-heart, a plant, *Dicentra eximia,* of the fumitory family, native to the eastern coast of the U.S., having elongated clusters of drooping, heart-shaped rose-colored or pink flowers.

wild′ boar′, a wild Old World swine, *Sus scrofa,* from which most of the domestic hogs are believed to be derived. [1475–85]

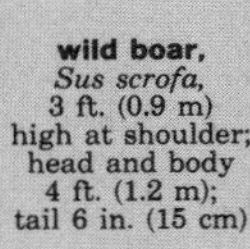

wild boar, *Sus scrofa,* 3 ft. (0.9 m) high at shoulder; head and body 4 ft. (1.2 m); tail 6 in. (15 cm)

wild′ bri′er, **1.** the dog rose, *Rosa canina.* **2.** the sweetbrier, *Rosa eglanteria.* **3.** any other brier growing wild.

wild′ buck′wheat. See **umbrella plant** (def. 3). [1875–80]

wild′ cal′la. See **water arum.** [1880–85, *Amer.*]

wild′ card′, **1.** *Cards.* a card having its value decided by the wishes of the players. **2.** a determining or important person or thing whose qualities are unknown, indeterminate, or unpredictable: *In a sailboat race the weather is the wild card.* **3.** *Tennis.* a player, usually without ranking, who is allowed to enter a tournament at the discretion of the tournament committee after regularly qualifying competitors have been selected. [1530–40]

wild-card (wīld′kärd′), *adj.* **1.** of, constituting, or including a wild card. **2.** *Informal.* of, being, or including an unpredictable or unproven element, person, item, etc. **3.** *Sports.* of, being, or including an unseeded or unproven participant or team, as a team in a championship tournament that has not placed first in its league or area. [1955–60]

wild′ car′rot. See **Queen Anne's lace.**

wild·cat (wīld′kat′), *n., pl.* **-cats,** (*esp. collectively*) **-cat** for 1–4, *adj., v.,* **-cat·ted, -cat·ting.** —*n.* **1.** any of several North American felines of the genus *Lynx.* Cf. **lynx.** **2.** a yellowish-gray, black-striped feline, *Felis sylvestris,* of Europe, western Asia, and northern Africa, resembling and closely related to the domestic cat, with which it interbreeds freely. **3.** a closely related feline, *Felis sylvestris libyca,* of northern Africa, believed to be the ancestor of the domestic cat. **4.** any of several other of the smaller felines, as the serval or ocelot. **5.** a domestic cat that has become feral. **6.** a quick-tempered or savage person. **7.** *Railroads.* a single locomotive operating without a train, as one switching cars. **8.** an exploratory well drilled in an effort to discover deposits of oil or gas; a prospect well. **9.** a reckless or unsound enterprise, business, etc. **10.** *Informal.* wildcatter (def. 2). **11.** *Naut.* a shaped drum on a windlass, engaging with the links of an anchor chain. **12.** *Informal.* See **wildcat strike.** —*adj.* **13.** characterized by or proceeding from reckless or unsafe business methods: *wildcat companies; wildcat stocks.* **14.** of or pertaining to an illicit enterprise or product. **15.** running without control or regulation, as a locomotive, or apart from the regular schedule, as a train. —*v.i.* **16.** to search an area of unknown or doubtful productivity for oil, ore, or the like, esp. as an independent prospector. **17.** *Slang.* to engage in a wildcat strike. —*v.t.* **18.** to search (an area of unknown or doubtful productivity) for oil, ore, or the like. [1375–1425; late ME *wilde cat;* cf. MLG *wildkatte*]

wild′cat bank′, a bank that issued notes without adequate security in the period before the establishment of the national banking system in 1864. [1830–40, *Amer.*]

wild′cat strike′, a labor strike that has not been called or sanctioned by the officials of the union. Also called **outlaw strike, quickie strike.** [1940–45, *Amer.*]

wild·cat·ter (wīld′kat′ər), *n.* **1.** an oil prospector. **2.** a person who promotes risky or unsound business ventures. **3.** a person who participates in a wildcat strike. [1880–85, *Amer.;* WILDCAT + -ER[1]]

wild′ cel′ery. See **tape grass.** [1850–55]

wild′ date′, a feather palm, *Phoenix sylvestris,* of India, having drooping, bluish-green or grayish leaves and small, orange-yellow fruit.

Wilde (wīld), *n.* **Oscar (Fin·gal O'Fla·her·tie Wills)** (fing′gəl ō flā′hər tē wilz′, ō flâr′tē), (*"Sebastian Melmoth"*), 1854–1900, Irish poet, dramatist, novelist, essayist, and critic.

Wild·e·an (wīl′dē ən), *adj.* of, pertaining to, characteristic of, or resembling the literary style of Oscar Wilde. [1920–25; WILDE + -AN]

wil·de·beest (wil′də bēst′, vil′-), *n., pl.* **-beests,** (*esp. collectively*) **-beest.** gnu. [1830–40; < Afrik *wildebees* < D *wildebeest,* equiv. to *wild* WILD + *beest* BEAST]

wil·der[1] (wil′dər), *Archaic.* —*v.t.* **1.** to cause to lose one's way. **2.** to bewilder. —*v.i.* **3.** to lose one's way. **4.** to be bewildered. [1605–15; perh. extracted from WILDERNESS; intrans. use prob. by assoc. with WANDER] —**wil′der·ment,** *n.*

wild·er[2] (wīl′dər), *adj.* comparative of **wild.**

Wil·der (wīl′dər), *n.* **1. Billy** (*Samuel Wilder*), born 1906, U.S. film director, producer, and writer; born in Austria. **2. Laura In·galls** (ing′gəlz), 1867–1957, U.S. writer of children's books. **3. Thorn·ton (Niv·en)** (thôrn′tn niv′ən), 1897–1975, U.S. novelist and playwright.

wil·der·ness (wil′dər nis), *n.* **1.** a wild and uncultivated region, as of forest or desert, uninhabited or inhabited only by wild animals; a tract of wasteland. **2.** a tract of land officially designated as such and protected by the U.S. government. **3.** any desolate tract, as of open sea. **4.** a part of a garden set apart for plants growing with unchecked luxuriance. **5.** a bewildering mass or collection. [1150–1200; ME; OE **wil(d)dēornes,* equiv. to either *wil(d)dēor* wild beast (see WILD, DEER) + *-nes* -NESS, or *wilddēoren* wild, savage (*wilddēor* + *-en* -EN[2]) + *(-n)es* -NESS; prob. reinforced by ME *wildernes,* gen. of *wildern* wilderness (n. use of OE *wilddēoren*), in phrases like *wildernes land* land of wilderness] —**Syn. 1.** See **desert**[1].

Wil·der·ness (wil′dər nis), *n.* a wooded area in NE Virginia: several battles fought here in 1864 between armies of Grant and Lee.

wil′derness ar′ea, a region whose natural growth is protected by legislation and whose recreational and industrial use is restricted. [1925–30, *Amer.*]

Wil′derness Road′, *Amer. Hist.* a 300-mile (500-km) route from eastern Virginia through the Cumberland Gap into Kentucky, explored by Daniel Boone in 1769 and marked as a trail by him and other pioneers in 1775: a major route for early settlers moving west.

wild-eyed (wīld′īd′), *adj.* **1.** having an angry, insane, or distressed expression in the eyes. **2.** extremely irrational, senseless, or radical: *a wild-eyed scheme.* [1810–20]

wild′ fig′, the caprifig. [1700–10]

wild·fire (wīld′fīər′), *n.* **1.** a highly flammable composition, as Greek fire, difficult to extinguish when ignited, formerly used in warfare. **2.** any large fire that spreads rapidly and is hard to extinguish. **3.** sheet lightning, unaccompanied by thunder. **4.** the ignis fatuus or a similar light. **5.** *Plant Pathol.* a disease of tobacco and soybeans, characterized by brown, necrotic spots, each surrounded by a yellow band, on the leaves and caused by a bacterium, *Pseudomonas tabaci.* **6.** *Pathol. Obs.* erysipelas or some similar disease. [bef. 1000; ME *wildefire,* OE *wildfȳr.* See WILD, FIRE]

wild·flow·er (wīld′flou′ər), *n.* **1.** the flower of a plant that normally grows in fields, forests, etc., without deliberate cultivation. **2.** the plant itself. Also, **wild′ flow′er.** [1790–1800; WILD + FLOWER]

wild·fowl (wīld′foul′), *n.* a game bird, esp. a wild duck, goose, or swan. [bef. 1000; ME *wilde foul,* OE *wildefugl.* See WILD, FOWL]

wild′ gera′nium, geranium (def. 2). [1880–85]

wild′ gin′ger, any of various plants belonging to the genus *Asarum,* of the birthwort family, esp. *A. canadense,* a woodland plant of eastern North America, having two heart-shaped leaves, a solitary reddish-brown flower, and a pungent rhizome. [1795–1805]

wild′ goose′, any undomesticated goose, esp. the greylag of Britain or the Canada goose. [bef. 1050; ME; OE]

wild′-goose′ chase′ (wīld′gōōs′), **1.** a wild or absurd search for something nonexistent or unobtainable: *a wild-goose chase looking for a building long demolished.* **2.** any senseless pursuit of an object or end; a hopeless enterprise: *Her scheme of being a movie star is a wild-goose chase.* [1585–95]

wild-head·ed (wīld′hed′id), *adj.* given to wild or exorbitant ideas.

wild′ hol′lyhock, checkerbloom.

wild′ hon′eysuckle. See **pinxster flower.** [1755–65, *Amer.*]

Wild′ Hunt′, (in northern European legend) a phantom hunt, conducted either in the sky or in forests.

Wild′ Hunts′man, the leader of the Wild Hunt, often associated with Odin. [1790–1800]

wild′ hy′acinth, any of several plants having usually blue flowers resembling those of a hyacinth, as *Camassia scilloides,* of the central U.S., or *Triteleia hyacinthina,* of western North America. [1840–50, *Amer.*]

wild′ hydran′gea, a shrub, *Hydrangea arborescens,* of the saxifrage family, common throughout the eastern half of the U.S., having egg-shaped leaves and a rounded cluster of white flowers. Also called **sevenbark.** [1885–90, *Amer.*]

wild′ in′digo, any of several plants belonging to the genus *Baptisia,* of the legume family, esp. *B. tinctoria,* having yellow flowers. [1735–45, *Amer.*]

wild·ing (wīl′ding), *n.* **1.** a wild apple tree. **2.** its fruit. **3.** any plant that grows wild. **4.** a plant, originally cultivated, that now grows wild; an escape. **5.** a wild animal. —*adj.* **6.** not cultivated or domesticated; wild. [1515–25; WILD + -ING[3]]

wild·ish (wīl′dish), *adj.* somewhat wild. [1705–15; WILD + -ISH[1]]

wild·land (wīld′land′), *n.* land that has not been cultivated, esp. land set aside and protected as a wilderness. [1805–15; WILD + -LAND]

wild′ leek′, ramp[2].

wild′ let′tuce, any of various uncultivated species of lettuce, growing as weeds in fields and waste places, esp. a North American species, *Lactuca canadensis.*

wild·life (wīld′līf′), *n.* **1.** undomesticated animals living in the wild, including those hunted for food, sport, or profit. —*adj.* **2.** of, for, or abounding in wildlife: *a wildlife preserve.* [1930–35; WILD + LIFE]

wild′ lil′y of the val′ley, a low-growing woodland plant, *Maianthemum canadense,* of the lily family, native to northeastern North America, having a cluster of small white flowers. Also called **Canada mayflower, false lily of the valley.** [1820–30, *Amer.*]

wild·ling (wīld′ling), *n.* a wild plant, flower, or animal. [1830–40; WILD + -LING[1]]

wild′ mad′der, madder[1] (defs. 1, 2).

wild′ man′, **1.** a person who is uncivilized; a savage. **2.** a person of violent temper, erratic behavior, etc. **3.** a person of extreme or outrageous political opinions. [1250–1300; ME]

wild′ man′drake, the May apple, *Podophyllum peltatum.*

wild′ monks′hood, a plant, *Aconitum uncinatum,* of the buttercup family, native to the eastern central U.S., having roundish leaves and hooded, blue flowers, growing in rich, moist soil.

wild′ mus′tard, any of several weedy plants belonging to the genus *Brassica,* of the mustard family, as charlock. [1590–1600]

wild′ oat′, **1.** any uncultivated species of *Avena,* esp. a common weedy grass, *A. fatua,* resembling the cultivated oat. **2.** a hardy plant, *Uvularia sessilifolia,* of the lily family, of eastern North America, having deep green, hairy leaves and greenish-yellow, tubular flowers. **3. sow one's wild oats,** to have a youthful fling at reckless and indiscreet behavior, esp. to be promiscuous before marriage. [1490–1500]

wild′ ol′ive, any tree resembling the olive in structure or fruit. [1800–10]

wild′ or′ange. See **laurel cherry.** [1795–1805]

wild′ pan′sy, any uncultivated or wild form of the common pansy, *Viola tricolor.* [1895–1900]

wild′ pars′ley, any of several uncultivated plants resembling the parsley in shape and structure.

wild′ pas′sionflow′er, the maypop, *Passiflora incarnata.*

wild′ pitch′, *Baseball.* a pitched ball that the catcher misses and could not be expected to catch, resulting in a base runner's or runners' advancing one or more bases or the batter's reaching first base safely. Cf. **passed ball.** [1865–70, *Amer.*]

wild′ poinset′tia. See **Mexican fire-plant.**

wild′ pota′to, **1.** a plant, *Solanum jamesii,* of the southwestern U.S., related to the edible cultivated potato. **2.** man-of-the-earth. [1765–75, *Amer.*]

wild′ pump′kin, calabazilla. [1925–30, *Amer.*]

wild′ rice′, **1.** a tall aquatic grass, *Zizania aquatica,* of northeastern North America. **2.** the grain of this plant, used for food. Also called **water oats, water rice.** [1740–50]

wild′ rose′, any native species of rose, usually having a single flower with the corolla consisting of one circle of five roundish, spreading petals. [1775–85]

wild′ rose′mary, a bog shrub, *Ledum palustre,* of the heath family, found from the North Temperate Zone to the Arctic Circle, having leaves that are rust-colored and hairy beneath with rolled margins, and dense clusters of white flowers. Also called **crystal tea.** [1825–35]

wild′ rub′ber, rubber obtained from trees growing wild.

wild′ rye′, any grass of the genus *Elymus,* somewhat resembling rye. [1745–55]

wild′ sarsaparil′la, a low plant, *Aralia nudicaulis,* of the ginseng family, native to eastern North America, having a single, long-stalked, compound leaf and a ball-like cluster of greenish-yellow flowers. [1805–15]

wild′ sen′na, a subshrubby senna, *Cassia marilandica,* of the eastern U.S., having yellow flowers. Also called **American senna.**

wild′ serv′ice tree′. See under **service tree** (def. 1).

wild′ silk′, **1.** tussah. **2.** *Brit.* See **raw silk.** [1790–1800, *Amer.*]

wild′ spin′ach, any of various plants of the genus *Chenopodium,* sometimes used in place of spinach.

wild′ sweet′ pota′to, man-of-the-earth. [1890–95, *Amer.*]

wild′ sweet′ wil′liam, **1.** See **blue phlox.** **2.** a plant, *Phlox maculata,* of the phlox family, native to eastern North America, having purple-spotted stems and elongated clusters of pink or purple flowers.

wild′ thyme′, mother-of-thyme.

wild′ tur′key, the ancestral species of the domesticated turkey. Cf. **turkey** (def. 1). [1605–15, *Amer.*]

wild′ type′, *Genetics.* **1.** an organism having an appearance that is characteristic of the species in a natural breeding population. **2.** the form or forms of a gene commonly occurring in nature in a given species. —**wild′-type′,** *adj.*

wild′ vanil′la. See **vanilla plant.** [1875–80, *Amer.*]

Wild′ Wea′sel, a nickname given various U.S. military aircraft fitted with radar-detection and jamming equipment and designed to suppress enemy air defenses with missiles that home on radar emissions.

Wild′ West′, the western frontier region of the U.S., before the establishment of stable government. [1850–55, *Amer.*]

Wild′ West′ show′, an entertainment, often as part

of a circus, representing scenes and events from the early history of the western U.S. and displaying feats of marksmanship, horseback riding, rope twirling, and the like. [1880–85]

wild•wood (wīld′wo͝od′), *n.* a wood growing in the wild or natural state; forest. [bef. 1150; ME *wilde wode,* OE *wilde wudu.* See WILD, WOOD[1]]

wild′ yam′, any of several uncultivated yams, esp. *Dioscorea villosa,* of the U.S., having a woody, tuberous root. [1835–45]

wile (wīl), *n., v.,* **wiled, wil•ing.** —*n.* **1.** a trick, artifice, or stratagem meant to fool, trap, or entice; device. **2.** **wiles,** artful or beguiling behavior. **3.** deceitful cunning; trickery. —*v.t.* **4.** to beguile, entice, or lure (usually fol. by *away, from, into,* etc.): *The music wiled him from his study.* **5.** **wile away,** to spend or pass (time), esp. in a leisurely or pleasurable fashion: *to wile away the long winter nights.* [1125–75; (n.) ME; late OE *wīl,* perh. < ON *vēl* artifice, earlier **wihl-*]
—**Syn. 1, 2.** deception, contrivance, maneuver. See **trick. 3.** chicanery, fraud.

Wil•fred (wil′frid), *n.* a male given name: from Old English words meaning "will" and "peace." Also, **Wil′•frid.**

wil•ful (wil′fəl), *adj.* willful. —**wil′ful•ly,** *adv.* —**wil′ful•ness,** *n.*

Wil•helm (wil′helm; *Ger.* vil′helm), *n.* a male given name, German form of **William.**

Wilhelm I. See **William I** (def. 3).

Wilhelm II. See **William II** (def. 2).

Wil•hel•mi•na (wil′ə mē′nə, wil′hel-; *Du.* vil′hel mē′nä), *n.* **1. Mount,** former name of **Trikora. 2.** a female given name: derived from *William.*

Wilhelmina I, (*Wilhelmina Helena Pauline Maria of Orange-Nassau*) 1880–1962, queen of the Netherlands 1890–1948 (mother of Juliana).

Wil•helm Meis•ter (vil′helm mī′stər), a novel (1795–1829) by Goethe.

Wil•helms•ha•ven (vil′helms hä′fən), *n.* a seaport in NW Germany, NW of Bremen, on the North Sea. 95,570.

Wil•helm•stras•se (vil′helm shträ′sə), *n.* **1.** a street in Berlin, Germany: location of the German foreign office and other government buildings until 1945. **2.** (formerly) the foreign office and policies of the German government.

Wilkes (wilks), *n.* **1. Charles,** 1798–1877, U.S. rear admiral and explorer. **2. John,** 1727–97, English political leader and journalist.

Wilkes-Bar•re (wilks′bar′ē, -bar′ə, -bâr′), *n.* a city in E Pennsylvania, on the Susquehanna River. 51,551.

Wilkes′ Land′, a coastal region of Antarctica, S of Australia.

Wil•kins (wil′kinz), *n.* **1. Sir George Hubert,** 1888–1958, Australian Antarctic explorer, aviator, and aerial navigator. **2. Mary Eleanor.** See **Freeman, Mary Eleanor. 3. Maurice Hugh Frederick,** born 1916, English biophysicist born in New Zealand: Nobel prize for medicine 1962. **4. Roy,** 1901–81, U.S. journalist and civil-rights leader: executive secretary of the NAACP, 1955–77.

Wil•kins•burg (wil′kinz bûrg′), *n.* a borough in SW Pennsylvania, near Pittsburgh. 23,669.

Wil•kin•son (wil′kin sən), *n.* **1. Geoffrey,** 1921–96, British chemist: Nobel prize 1973. **2. James,** 1757–1825, U.S. military officer, politician, and adventurer.

will[1] (wil), *auxiliary v.* and *v., pres. sing. 1st pers.* **will,** *2nd* **will** or (*Archaic*) **wilt,** *3rd* **will,** *pres. pl.* **will;** *past sing. 1st pers.* **would,** *2nd* **would** or (*Archaic*) **wouldst,** *3rd* **would,** *past pl.* **would;** *past part.* (*Obs.*) **wold** or **would;** *imperative, infinitive, and pres. participle lacking.* —*auxiliary verb.* **1.** am (is, are, etc.) about or going to: *I will be there tomorrow. She will see you at dinner.* **2.** am (is, are, etc.) disposed or willing to: *People will do right.* **3.** am (is, are, etc.) expected or required to: *You will report to the principal at once.* **4.** may be expected or supposed to: *You will not have forgotten him. This will be right.* **5.** am (is, are, etc.) determined or sure to (used emphatically): *You would do it. People will talk.* **6.** am (is, are, etc.) accustomed to, or do usually or often: *You will often see her sitting there. He would write for hours at a time.* **7.** am (is, are, etc.) habitually disposed or inclined to: *Boys will be boys. After dinner they would read aloud.* **8.** am (is, are, etc.) capable of; can: *This tree will live without water for three months.* **9.** am (is, are, etc.) going to: *I will bid you "Good night."* —*v.t., v.i.* **10.** to wish; desire; like: *Go where you will. Ask, if you will, who the owner is.* [bef. 900; ME *willen,* OE *wyllan;* c. D *willen,* G *wollen,* ON *vilja,* Goth *wiljan;* akin to L *velle* to wish]
—**Usage.** See **shall.**

will[2] (wil), *n., v.,* **willed, will•ing.** —*n.* **1.** the faculty of conscious and especially of deliberate action; the power of control the mind has over its own actions: *the freedom of the will.* **2.** power of choosing one's own actions: *to have a strong or a weak will.* **3.** the act or process of using or asserting one's choice; volition: *My hands are obedient to my will.* **4.** wish or desire: *to submit against one's will.* **5.** purpose or determination, often hearty or stubborn determination; willfulness: *to have the will to succeed.* **6.** the wish or purpose as carried out, or to be carried out: *to work one's will.* **7.** disposition, whether good or ill, toward another. **8.** *Law.* **a.** a legal declaration of a person's wishes as to the disposition of his or her property or estate after death, usually written and signed by the testator and attested by witnesses. **b.** the document containing such a declaration. **9. at will, a.** at one's discretion or pleasure; as one desires: *to wander at will through the countryside.* **b.** at one's disposal or command. —*v.t.* **10.** to decide, bring about, or attempt to effect or bring about by an act of the will: *He can walk if he wills it.* **11.** to purpose, determine on, or elect, by an act of will: *If he wills success, he can find it.* **12.** to give or dispose of (property) by a will or testament; bequeath or devise. **13.** to influence by exerting will power: *She was willed to walk the tightrope by the hypnotist.* —*v.i.* **14.** to exercise the will: *To will is not enough, one must do.* **15.** to decide or determine: *Others debate, but the king wills.* [bef. 900; (n.) ME *wille,* OE *will(e)*, OE *will(a);* c. D *wil,* G *Wille,* ON *vili,* Goth *wilja;* (v.) ME *willen,* OE *willian* to wish, desire, deriv. of the n.; akin to WILL[1]] —**will′er,** *n.*
—**Syn. 3.** choice. **4.** pleasure, disposition, inclination. **5.** resolution, decision. WILL, VOLITION refer to conscious choice as to action or thought. WILL denotes fixed and persistent intent or purpose: *Where there's a will there's a way.* VOLITION is the power of forming an intention or the incentive for using the will: *to exercise one's volition in making a decision.* **10.** determine. **12.** leave.

Will (wil), *n.* a male given name, form of **William.**

Wil•la (wil′ə), *n.* a female given name, form of **Wilhelmina.**

will•a•ble (wil′ə bəl), *adj.* capable of being willed or fixed by will. [1400–50; late ME; see WILL[2], -ABLE]

Wil•laert (wil′ärt, vil′-), *n.* **A•dri•an** (ä′drē ən, ä′drēän′), c1480–1562, Flemish composer.

Wil•lam•ette (wi lam′it), *n.* a river flowing N through NW Oregon into the Columbia River at Portland. ab. 290 mi. (465 km) long.

Wil•lard (wil′ərd), *n.* **1. Emma (Hart),** 1787–1870, U.S. educator and poet. **2. Frances Elizabeth Caroline,** 1839–98, U.S. educator, reformer, and author. **3. Jess,** 1883–1968, U.S. boxer: world heavyweight champion 1915–19. **4.** a male given name: from Germanic words meaning "hardy" and "will."

will-call (*n.* wil′kôl′; *adj.* wil′kôl′), *n.* **1.** an item of merchandise that is reserved for a customer, who takes possession of it when payments have been completed. **2.** a department in a store where such merchandise is held. **3.** See **layaway plan.** —*adj.* **4.** of or pertaining to merchandise held in will-call or on the layaway plan.

will′ con′test, legal proceedings to contest the authenticity or validity of a will.

willed (wild), *adj.* having a will (usually used in combination): *strong-willed; weak-willed.* [1350–1400; ME; see WILL[2], -ED[3]]

Wil•lem I (wil′əm; *Du.* vil′əm). See **William I** (def. 2).

wil•lem•ite (wil′ə mīt′), *n.* a mineral, a zinc silicate, Zn_2SiO_4, sometimes containing manganese, occurring in prismatic crystals or granular masses, usually greenish, sometimes white, brown, or red: a minor ore of zinc. [1835–45; named after King WILLEM I; see -ITE[1]]

Wil•lem•stad (vil′əm stät′), *n.* a seaport on the island of Curaçao, in the S West Indies: capital of the Netherlands Antilles. 152,000.

Wil•len•dorf (vil′ən dôrf′), *n.* a village in NE Austria, near Krems: site of an Aurignacian settlement where a 4½ in. (11 cm) limestone statuette **(Venus of Willendorf)** was found.

Willes•den (wilz′dən), *n.* a former borough, now part of Brent, in SE England, near London.

wil•let (wil′it), *n., pl.* **-lets,** (*esp. collectively*) **-let.** a large, eastern North American shorebird, *Catoptrophorus semipalmatus,* having a striking black and white wing pattern. [1700–10, *Amer.;* short for *pill-will-willet,* conventional imit. of its cry]

wil•ley (wil′ē), *n., v.t.* willy.

will•ful (wil′fəl), *adj.* **1.** deliberate, voluntary, or intentional: *The coroner ruled the death willful murder.* **2.** unreasonably stubborn or headstrong; self-willed. Also, **wilful.** [1150–1200; ME; OE *wilful* willing. See WILL[2], -FUL] —**will′ful•ly,** *adv.* —**will′ful•ness,** *n.*
—**Syn. 1.** volitional. **2.** intransigent; contrary, refractory, pigheaded, inflexible, obdurate, adamant. WILLFUL, HEADSTRONG, PERVERSE, WAYWARD refer to one who stubbornly insists upon doing as he or she pleases. WILLFUL suggests a stubborn persistence in doing what one wishes, esp. in opposition to those whose wishes or commands ought to be respected or obeyed: *that willful child who disregarded his parents' advice.* One who is HEADSTRONG is often foolishly, and sometimes violently, self-willed: *reckless and headstrong youths.* The PERVERSE person is unreasonably or obstinately intractable or contrary, often with the express intention of being disagreeable: *perverse out of sheer spite.* WAYWARD in this sense has the connotation of rash wrongheadedness that gets one into trouble: *a reform school for wayward girls.* —**Ant. 2.** obedient, tractable.

Wil•liam (wil′yəm), *n.* **1.** a word formerly used in communications to represent the letter *W.* **2.** a male given name: from Germanic words meaning "will" and "helmet."

William I, 1. (*"the Conqueror"*) 1027–87, duke of Normandy 1035–87; king of England 1066–87 (son of Robert I, duke of Normandy). **2.** Also, **Willem I.** (*William I of Orange*) (*"the Silent"*) 1533–84, Dutch leader, statesman, and revolutionary leader born in Germany: prince of Orange 1544–84; count of Nassau 1559–84; 1st stadholder of the United Provinces of the Netherlands 1578–84. **3.** Also, **Wilhelm I.** (*Wilhelm Friedrich Ludwig*) 1797–1888, King of Prussia 1861–88; emperor of Germany 1871–88 (brother of Frederick William IV).

William II, 1. (*William Rufus*) (*"the Red"*) 1056?–1100, King of England 1087–1100 (son of William I, duke of Normandy). **2.** Also, **Wilhelm II.** (*Frederick Wilhelm Viktor Albert*) 1859–1941, king of Prussia and emperor of Germany 1888–1918.

William III, (*William III of Orange*) 1650–1702, stadholder of the United Provinces of the Netherlands 1672–1702; king of England 1689–1702, joint ruler with his wife, Mary II.

William IV, (*"the Sailor-King"*) 1765–1837, king of Great Britain and Ireland 1830–37 (brother of George IV).

Wil′liam of Malmes′bur•y (mämz′ber′ē, -bə rē, -brē), c1090–1143?, English historian.

Wil•liams (wil′yəmz), *n.* **1. Ben Ames** (āmz), 1889–1953, U.S. novelist and short-story writer. **2. Bert** (*Egbert Austin Williams*), 1876?–1922, U.S. comedian and songwriter. **3. Betty (Smyth)** (smith), born 1943, Northern Irish peace activist: Nobel peace prize 1976. **4. Daniel Hale,** 1858–1931, U.S. surgeon and educator: performed first successful heart surgery 1893. **5. Em•lyn** (em′lin), born 1905, Welsh playwright and actor. **6. G. Men•nen** (men′ən), born 1911, U.S. politician and diplomat. **7. Hank,** 1923–53, U.S. country-and-western singer, musician, and composer. **8. Ralph Vaughan.** See **Vaughan Williams, Ralph. 9. Roger,** 1603?–83, English clergyman in America: founder of Rhode Island colony 1636. **10. Tennessee** (*Thomas Lanier Williams*), 1911–83, U.S. dramatist. **11. Theodore Samuel** (*Ted*), born 1918, U.S. baseball player. **12. William,** 1731–1811, U.S. merchant and revolutionary statesman. **13. William Car•los** (kär′lōs), 1883–1963, U.S. poet and novelist.

Wil•liams•burg (wil′yəmz bûrg′), *n.* a city in SE Virginia: colonial capital of Virginia; now restored to its original pre-Revolutionary style. 9870.

Wil•liams•port (wil′yəmz pôrt′, -pōrt′), *n.* a city in central Pennsylvania, on the Susquehanna River. 33,401.

Wil′liam Tell′, a legendary Swiss patriot forced by the Austrian governor to shoot an apple off his son's head with bow and arrow. German, **Wilhelm Tell.**

Wil′liam the Con′queror. See **William I** (def. 1).

Wil•lie (wil′ē), *n.* **1.** a male given name, form of **William. 2.** a female given name.

wil•lies (wil′ēz), *n.* (*used with a plural v.*) *Informal.* nervousness or fright; jitters; creeps (usually prec. by *the*): *That horror movie gave me the willies.* [1895–1900, *Amer.;* orig. obscure; cf. -s[3]]

Wil•li•man•tic (wil′ə man′tik), *n.* a city in NE Connecticut. 14,652.

will•ing (wil′ing), *adj.* **1.** disposed or consenting; inclined: *willing to go along.* **2.** cheerfully consenting or ready: *a willing worker.* **3.** done, given, borne, used, etc., with cheerful readiness. [1250–1300; ME. See WILL[2], -ING[2]] —**will′ing•ly,** *adv.* —**will′ing•ness,** *n.*
—**Syn. 1.** minded.

Wil•ling•don (wil′ing dən), *n.* **Freeman Free•man-Thom•as** (frē′mən tom′əs), **1st Marquis of,** 1866–1941, British colonial official: governor general of Canada 1926–31; viceroy and governor general of India 1931–36.

Wil•lis (wil′is), *n.* a male given name, form of **William.**

Wil•lis•ton (wil′ə stən), *n.* a city in NW North Dakota, on the Missouri River. 13,336.

wil•li•waw (wil′ē wô′), *n.* a violent squall that blows in near-polar latitudes, as in the Strait of Magellan, Alaska, and the Aleutian Islands. [1835–45; orig. uncert.]

Will•kie (wil′kē), *n.* **Wendell Lewis,** 1892–1944, U.S. executive, lawyer, and political leader.

will-less (wil′lis), *adj.* **1.** having or exerting no will: *a timid, will-less little man.* **2.** done or occurring without the will; involuntary: *a will-less compliance.* **3.** leaving no will; intestate: *to die will-less.* [1740–50] —**will′-less•ly,** *adv.* —**will′-less•ness,** *n.*

Will′mar Cit′y (wil′mär, -mər), a city in SW Minnesota. 15,895.

will-o'-the-wisp (wil′ə thə wisp′), *n.* **1.** See **ignis fatuus** (def. 1). **2.** anything that deludes or misleads by luring on. [1600–10; orig. *Will* (i.e., William) *with the wisp;* see WISP] —**will′o'-the-wisp′ish;** *esp. Brit.,* **will′-o'-the-wisp′y,** *adj.*

Wil•lough•by (wil′ə bē), *n.* **1.** a city in NE Ohio, near Cleveland. 19,329. **2.** a male given name.

wil•low (wil′ō), *n.* **1.** any tree or shrub of the genus *Salix,* characterized by narrow, lance-shaped leaves and dense catkins bearing small flowers, many species having tough, pliable twigs or branches used for wickerwork, etc. Cf. **willow family. 2.** the wood of any of these trees. **3.** *Informal.* something, esp. a cricket bat, made of willow wood. **4.** Also called **willower, willy.** a machine consisting essentially of a cylinder armed with spikes revolving within a spiked casing, for opening and cleaning cotton or other fiber. —*v.t.* **5.** to treat (textile fibers) with a willow. [bef. 900; ME *wilwe,* var. of *wilghe,* OE *welig;* c. OS *wilgia,* D *wilg,* LG *wilge*] —**wil′low•like′,** *adj.* —**wil′low•ish,** *adj.*

Wil•low•brook (wil′ō bro͝ok′), *n.* a city in SW California. 30,845.

wil•low•er (wil′ō ər), *n.* **1.** a person or a thing that willows. **2.** willow (def. 4). [1880–85; alter. of *willyer;* see WILLY, -ER[1]]

wil′low fam′ily, the plant family Salicaceae, characterized by deciduous trees and shrubs having simple, alternate leaves, hairy catkins of male and female flowers on separate plants, and capsular fruit, and including the aspen, cottonwood, poplar, and willow.

wil′low fly′catcher. See under **alder flycatcher.**

wil′low herb′, any of numerous plants belonging to the genus *Epilobium,* of the evening primrose family, having terminal clusters of purplish or white flowers. Cf. **fireweed.** [1570–80]

Wil•lo•wick (wil′ə wik), *n.* a city in NE Ohio, near Cleveland. 17,834.

wil′low-leaved jes′samine (wil′ō lēvd′), a Chilean shrub, *Cestrum parqui,* of the nightshade family, having willowlike leaves and clusters of whitish or yellowish flowers that are very fragrant at night.

wil′low oak′, an oak, *Quercus phellos,* of the southwestern U.S., having entire, narrow leaves, yielding a

CONCISE PRONUNCIATION KEY: *act, cāpe, dâre, pärt; set, ēqual; if, īce; ox, ōver, ôrder, oil, bo͝ok, bo͞ot, out; up, ûrge; child; sing; shoe; thin,* th*at;* zh *as in treasure.* ə = *a as in alone, e as in system, i as in easily, o as in gallop, u as in circus;* ᵊ *as in fire* (fīᵊr), *hour* (ouᵊr). l *and* n *can serve as syllabic consonants, as in cradle* (krād′l), *and button* (but′n). *See the full key inside the front cover.*

hard, heavy wood used in the construction of buildings. [1700–10, *Amer.*]

wil′low pat′tern, a decorative design in English ceramics, depicting chiefly a willow tree, small bridge, and two birds, derived from Chinese sources and introduced in approximately 1780: often executed in blue and white but sometimes in red and white. [1840–50]

wil′low ptar′migan, a ptarmigan, *Lagopus lagopus,* of arctic and subarctic regions of the New and Old Worlds, having brown, mottled plumage in summer and white plumage in winter. Cf. **red grouse.** [1870–75]

Wil′low Run′, a suburban area W of Detroit, Michigan, near Ypsilanti: airport.

wil·low·wacks (wil′ō waks′), *n. New Eng.* a wooded, uninhabited area. Also, **willywacks.** [of uncert. orig.]

wil′low war′bler, any of several usually grayish-green leaf warblers, esp. *Phylloscopus trochilus,* of Europe. [1840–50]

wil·low·ware (wil′ō wâr′), *n.* china using the willow pattern. [1850–55, *Amer.*; WILLOW + WARE[1]]

wil·low·y (wil′ō ē), *adj.,* **-low·i·er, -low·i·est. 1.** pliant; lithe. **2.** (of a person) tall, slender, and graceful. **3.** abounding with willows. [1760–70; WILLOW + -Y[1]]

will′ pow′er, control of one's impulses and actions; self-control. Also, **will′pow′er.** [1870–75]

Wills (wilz), *n.* **Helen New·ing·ton** (no͞o′ing tən, nyo͞o′-), born 1906, U.S. tennis player.

Will·stät·ter (vil′shtet′ər), *n.* **Rich·ard** (RIKH′ärt), 1872–1942, German chemist: Nobel prize 1915.

will′ to pow′er, (in the philosophy of Nietzsche) the self-assertive creative drive in all individuals, regarded as the supreme quality of the superman. [1895–1900]

wil·ly (wil′ē), *n., pl.* **-lies,** *v.,* **-lied, -ly·ing.** —*n.* **1.** willow (def. 4). —*v.t.* **2.** to willow (cotton). Also, **willey.** [1825–35; special use of dial. *willy,* OE *wilige* basket (orig. one made of willow twigs); akin to WILLOW]

Wil·ly (wil′ē), *n.* **1.** a male given name, form of **William. 2.** a female given name.

will·yard (wil′yərd), *adj. Scot. and North Eng.* obstinate; willful. Also, **will·yart** (wil′yərt). [1580–90; (earlier) wild, awkward, bewildered, deriv. of Scots, dial. *will* gone astray, perplexed (ME < ON *villr*), perh. with -ARD, though formation is unclear; later influenced by WILL[2] and WAYWARD]

wil·ly-nil·ly (wil′ē nil′ē), *adv.* **1.** in a disorganized or unplanned manner; sloppily. **2.** whether one wishes to or not; willingly or unwillingly: *He'll have to do it willy-nilly.* —*adj.* **3.** shilly-shallying; vacillating. **4.** disorganized, unplanned; sloppy: *willy-nilly work.* [1600–10; from the phrase *will ye, nill ye.* See WILL[1], NILL]

wil·ly·wacks (wil′ē waks′), *n.* willowwacks.

wil′ly wag′tail, a large black-and-white bird, *Rhipidura leucophrys,* of Australia and New Guinea, having bristles around the upper bill and a long, fanlike tail.

wil·ly-wil·ly (wil′ē wil′ē), *n., pl.* **-lies.** *Australian.* a severe tropical cyclone. [1890–95; of obscure orig.]

Wil·ma (wil′mə), *n.* a female given name, form of **Wilhelmina.**

Wil·mer (wil′mər), *n.* a male given name.

Wil·mette (wil met′), *n.* a city in NE Illinois, near Chicago. 28,229.

Wil·ming·ton (wil′ming tən), *n.* **1.** a seaport in N Delaware, on the Delaware River. 70,195. **2.** a seaport in SE North Carolina, on the Cape Fear River. 44,000. **3.** a city in NE Massachusetts. 17,471. **4.** a town in SW Ohio. 10,431. —**Wil·ming·to·ni·an** (wil′ming tō′nē ən), *n.*

Wil·mot (wil′mət), *n.* **1. David,** 1814–68, U.S. politician and jurist: congressman 1845–51; senator 1861–63. **2. John.** See **Rochester, John Wilmot, 2nd Earl of.**

Wil·no (vēl′nô), *n.* Polish name of **Vilnius.**

Wil·son (wil′sən), *n.* **1. Sir Angus (Frank Johnstone)** (jon′stən, -sən), 1913–91, English writer. **2. Charles Thom·son Rees** (tom′sən rēs), 1869–1959, Scottish physicist: Nobel prize 1927. **3. Edmund,** 1895–1972, U.S. literary and social critic. **4. Henry** (*Jeremiah Jones Colbath* or *Colbaith*), 1812–75, U.S. politician: vice president of the U.S. 1873–75. **5. James,** 1742–98, U.S. jurist, born in Scotland: associate justice of the U.S. Supreme Court 1789–98. **6. Sir (James) Harold,** 1916–95, British statesman: prime minister 1964–70, 1974–76. **7. John** (*"Christopher North"*), 1785–1854, Scottish poet, journalist, and critic. **8. Robert W(oodrow),** born 1936, U.S. radio astronomer: Nobel prize for physics 1978. **9. Sloan,** born 1920, U.S. journalist and novelist. **10. (Thomas) Woodrow,** 1856–1924, 28th president of the U.S. 1913–21: Nobel peace prize 1919. **11. Mount,** a mountain in SW California, near Pasadena: observatory. 5710 ft. (1740 m). **12.** a city in E North Carolina. 34,424.

Wil′son cloud′ cham′ber, *Physics.* See **cloud chamber.** Also called **Wil′son cham′ber.** [named after Charles T. R. WILSON]

Wil′son Dam′, a dam on the Tennessee River, in NW Alabama, at Muscle Shoals: a part of the Tennessee Valley Authority. 4862 ft. (1482 m) long; 137 ft. (42 m) high.

Wil·so·ni·an (wil sō′nē ən), *adj.* of, pertaining to, or characteristic of Woodrow Wilson. [1915–20, *Amer.*; WILSON + -IAN]

Wil·son·ism (wil′sə niz′əm), *n.* the theories, methods, or practices of Woodrow Wilson. Also, **Wil·so·ni·an·ism** (wil sō′nē ə niz′əm). [WILSON + -ISM]

Wil′son's disease′, *Pathol.* a rare hereditary disease in which copper accumulates in the brain and liver, gradually leading to tremors, muscular rigidity, kidney malfunction, and cognitive disturbances: marked by Kayser-Fleischer rings. [named after Samuel Alexander Kinnier *Wilson* (1878–1936), British neurologist, who described it in 1912]

Wil′son's phal′arope, a phalarope, *Phalaropus tricolor,* that breeds in the prairie regions of North America and winters in Argentina and Chile. [1820–30, *Amer.*; see WILSON'S STORM PETREL]

Wil′son's snipe′, a North American common snipe, *Gallinago (Capella) gallinago delicata.* See illus. under **snipe.** [1855–60, *Amer.*; see WILSON'S STORM PETREL]

Wil′son's storm′ pet′rel, a small petrel, *Oceanites oceanicus,* that breeds in the Southern Hemisphere but ranges into the North Atlantic and Pacific oceans. Also, **Wil′son's storm′-petrel.** Also called **Wil′son's pet′rel.** [named after Alexander *Wilson* (1766–1813), Scottish-American ornithologist]

Wil′son's thrush′, veery. [1830–40, *Amer.*; see WILSON'S STORM PETREL]

Wil′son's war′bler, a North American warbler, *Wilsonia pusilla,* having yellow plumage and a black patch on top of the head. Cf. **pileolated warbler.** [1900–05, *Amer.*; see WILSON'S STORM PETREL]

wilt[1] (wilt), *v.i.* **1.** to become limp and drooping, as a fading flower; wither. **2.** to lose strength, vigor, assurance, etc.: *to wilt after a day's hard work.* —*v.t.* **3.** to cause to wilt. —*n.* **4.** the act of wilting, or the state of being wilted: *a sudden wilt of interest in the discussion.* **5.** *Plant Pathol.* **a.** the drying out, drooping, and withering of the leaves of a plant due to inadequate water supply, excessive transpiration, or vascular disease. **b.** a disease so characterized, as fusarium wilt. **6.** a virus disease of various caterpillars, characterized by the liquefaction of body tissues. Also, **wilt′ disease′** (for defs. 5b, 6). [1685–95; dial. var. of *wilk* to wither, itself var. of *welk,* ME *welken,* prob. < MD *welken;* cf. G *welk* withered]
—**Syn. 2.** wane, droop; ebb, weaken.

wilt[2] (wilt), *v. Archaic.* second pers. sing. pres. ind. of **will**[1].

Wil·ton (wil′tn), *n.* a carpet woven like Brussels carpet, on a Jacquard loom but having the loops cut to form a velvet pile. Also called **Wil′ton car′pet, Wil′ton rug′.** [named after *Wilton,* town in Wiltshire, England]

Wil·ton (wil′tn), *n.* a town in SW Connecticut. 15,351.

Wil′ton Man′or, a town in S Florida. 12,742.

Wilt·shire (wilt′shēr, -shər), *n.* **1.** Also, **Wilts** (wilts). a county in S England. 511,600; 1345 sq. mi. (3485 sq. km). *Co. seat:* Salisbury. **2.** one of an English breed of white sheep having long, spiral horns. **3.** Also called **Wilt′shire cheese′.** a cylindrical, semihard cheese, moister and flakier than cheddar.

wil·y (wī′lē), *adj.,* **wil·i·er, wil·i·est.** full of, marked by, or proceeding from wiles; crafty; cunning. [1250–1300; ME; see WILE, -Y[1]] —**wil′i·ly,** *adv.* —**wil′i·ness,** *n.*
—**Syn.** artful, sly, designing, intriguing, tricky, foxy.

wim·ble (wim′bəl), *n., v.,* **-bled, -bling.** —*n.* **1.** a device used esp. in mining for extracting the rubbish from a bored hole. **2.** a marbleworker's brace for drilling. **3.** any of various other instruments for boring. —*v.t.* **4.** to bore or perforate with or as if with a wimble. [1250–1300; ME < MD or MLG *wimmel* auger; see GIMLET]

Wim·ble·don (wim′bəl dən), *n.* a former borough, now part of Merton, in SE England, near London: international tennis tournaments.

wim·min (wim′in), *n.pl. Eye Dialect.* women (sometimes also used as a feminist spelling to avoid the sequence *m-e-n*). [1910–15]

wimp (wimp), *Informal.* —*n.* **1.** a weak, ineffectual, timid person. —*v.* **2. wimp out, a.** to be or act like a wimp. **b.** to show timidity or cowardice; chicken out. [1915–20, *Amer.*; orig. uncert.; cf. WHIMPER]

WIMP (wimp), *n.* any of a group of weakly interacting elementary particles predicted by various unified field theories, as the W particle and Z-zero particle, that are characterized by relatively large masses. [1985–90; *W(eakly) I(nteracting) M(assive) P(article)*]

wim·ple (wim′pəl), *n., v.,* **-pled, -pling.** —*n.* **1.** a woman's headcloth drawn in folds about the chin, formerly worn out of doors, and still in use by some nuns. **2.** *Chiefly Scot.* **a.** a fold or wrinkle, as in cloth. **b.** a curve, bend, or turn, as in a road or river. —*v.t.* **3.** to cover or muffle with or as if with a wimple. **4.** to cause to ripple or undulate, as water. **5.** *Archaic.* to veil or enwrap. —*v.i.* **6.** to ripple, as water. **7.** *Archaic.* to lie in folds, as a veil. **8.** *Chiefly Scot.* to follow a curving course, as a road or river. [bef. 1100; (n.) ME *wimple, wimpel,* OE *wimpel;* c. D, LG *wimpel,* ON *vimpill;* (v.) ME: to wrap in a wimple, deriv. of the n.]

wimple (def. 1)

wimp·y (wim′pē), *adj.,* **wimp·i·er, wimp·i·est.** of, pertaining to, or characteristic of a wimp. Also, **wimp′ish.** [1965–70; WIMP + -Y[1]] —**wimp′i·ness,** *n.*

Wims′hurst machine′ (wimz′hûrst), *Elect.* a device for the production of electric charge by electrostatic induction, consisting of two oppositely rotating glass or mica disks carrying metal strips upon which charges are induced and subsequently removed by contact with metallic combs. Also called **Wims′hurst gen′erator.** [named after J. *Wimshurst* (d. 1903), English engineer]

win[1] (win), *v.,* **won, win·ning,** *n.* —*v.i.* **1.** to finish first in a race, contest, or the like. **2.** to succeed by striving or effort: *He applied for a scholarship and won.* **3.** to gain the victory; overcome an adversary: *The home team won.* —*v.t.* **4.** to succeed in reaching (a place, condition, etc.), esp. by great effort: *They won the shore through a violent storm.* **5.** to get by effort, as through labor, competition, or conquest: *He won his post after years of striving.* **6.** to gain (a prize, fame, etc.). **7.** to be successful in (a game, battle, etc.). **8.** to make (one's way), as by effort or ability. **9.** to attain or reach (a point, goal, etc.). **10.** to gain (favor, love, consent, etc.), as by qualities or influence. **11.** to gain the favor, regard, or adherence of. **12.** to gain the consent or support of; persuade (often fol. by *over*): *The speech won them over to our side.* **13.** to persuade to marry; gain in marriage. **14.** *Brit. Mining.* **a.** to obtain (ore, coal, etc.). **b.** to prepare (a vein, bed, mine, etc.) for working, by means of shafts or the like. **15. win out,** to win or succeed, esp. over great odds; triumph. —*n.* **16.** a victory, as in a game or horse race. **17.** the position of the competitor who comes in first in a horse race, harness race, etc. Cf. **place** (def. 27b), **show** (def. 29). [bef. 900; ME *winnen* (v.), OE *winnan* to work, fight, bear; c. G *gewinnen,* ON *vinna,* Goth *winnan*] —**win′na·ble,** *adj.*
—**Syn. 5.** obtain, secure, acquire, achieve, reach, procure. See **gain**[1]. **12.** convince.

win[2] (win), *v.t.,* **winned, win·ning.** *Scot. and North Eng.* to dry (hay, wood, etc.) by exposure to air and sun. [1550–60; perh. var. of WINNOW]

wince[1] (wins), *v.,* **winced, winc·ing,** *n.* —*v.i.* **1.** to draw back or tense the body, as from pain or from a blow; start; flinch. —*n.* **2.** a wincing or shrinking movement; a slight start. [1250–1300; ME *winsen,* var. of *winchen, wenchen* to kick < AF **wenc(h)ier;* OF *guenc(h)ier* < Gmc. Cf. WENCH, WINCH[1]] —**winc′er,** *n.* —**winc′ing·ly,** *adv.* —**winc′ing·ness,** *n.*
—**Syn. 1.** blench, quail. WINCE, RECOIL, SHRINK, QUAIL all mean to draw back from what is dangerous, fearsome, difficult, threatening, or unpleasant. WINCE suggests an involuntary contraction of the facial features triggered by pain, embarrassment, or a sense of revulsion: *to wince as a needle pierces the skin; to wince at coarse language.* RECOIL denotes a physical movement away from something disgusting or shocking or a similar psychological shutting out or avoidance: *to recoil from contact with a slimy surface; to recoil at the squalor and misery of the slum.* SHRINK may imply a fastidious or scrupulous avoidance of the distasteful or it may suggest cowardly withdrawal from what is feared: *to shrink from confessing a crime; to shrink from asking for a raise.* QUAIL suggests a loss of heart or courage in the face of danger or difficulty: *to quail before an angry mob.*

wince[2] (wins), *n.* winch[1] (def. 4).

winch[1] (winch), *n.* **1.** the crank or handle of a revolving machine. **2.** a windlass turned by a crank, for hoisting or hauling. **3.** any of various devices for cranking. **4.** Also, **wince.** *Textiles.* **a.** any machine equipped with rollers that guide cloth through a dye or finishing solution in an open vat. **b.** a roller between two dyeing vats for passing cloth from one vat to another. —*v.t.* **5.** to hoist or haul (a load) by means of a winch. [bef. 1050; ME *winche,* OE *wince* pulley] —**winch′er,** *n.*

winch[2] (winch), *v.i., n. Archaic.* wince[1].

Win·chell (win′chəl), *n.* **Walter,** 1897–1972, U.S. newspaper columnist and broadcaster.

Win·ches·ter (win′ches′tər, -chə stər), *n.* **1.** a city in Hampshire, in S England: cathedral; capital of the early Wessex kingdom and of medieval England. 88,700. **2.** a town in E Massachusetts, near Boston. 20,701. **3.** a city in N Virginia: Civil War battles 1862, 1864. 20,217. **4.** a city in E central Kentucky. 15,216. **5.** a town in NW Connecticut. 10,841. **6.** See **Winchester rifle. 7.** *Computers.* See **Winchester disk.**

Win′chester bush′el. See under **bushel**[1] (def. 1). [1695–1705; after WINCHESTER, England]

Win′chester disk′, *Computers.* a hard disk that is permanently mounted in its unit. Also called **Winchester.** [1970–75; orig. an IBM code name; the designation for a device containing two such disks was 3030 (each disk containing 30 megabytes), the same as the model number of a well-known Winchester rifle]

Win′chester ri′fle, a type of magazine rifle, first made in about 1866. [1870–75; named after D. F. *Winchester* (1810–80), American manufacturer]

Winck·el·mann (ving′kəl män′), *n.* **Jo·hann Jo·a·chim** (yō′hän yō′ä KHim), 1717–68, German archaeologist and art historian.

wind[1] (*n.* wind, *Literary* wīnd; *v.* wind), *n.* **1.** air in natural motion, as that moving horizontally at any velocity along the earth's surface: *A gentle wind blew through the valley. High winds were forecast.* **2.** a gale; storm; hurricane. **3.** any stream of air, as that produced by a bellows or fan. **4.** air that is blown or forced to produce a musical sound in singing or playing an instrument. **5.** See **wind instrument. 6.** wind instruments collectively. **7. the winds,** the members of an orchestra or band who play the wind instruments. **8.** breath or breathing: *to catch one's wind.* **9.** the power of breathing freely, as during continued exertion. **10.** any influential force or trend: *strong winds of public opinion.* **11.** a hint or intimation: *to catch wind of a stock split.* **12.** air carrying an animal's odor or scent. **13.** See **solar wind. 14.** empty talk; mere words. **15.** vanity; conceitedness. **16.** gas generated in the stomach and intestines. **17.** *Boxing Slang.* the pit of the stomach where a blow may cause a temporary shortness of breath; solar plexus. **18.** any direction of the compass. **19.** a state of unconcern, recklessness, or abandon: *to throw all caution to the winds.* **20. between wind and water, a.** (of a ship) at or near the water line. **b.** in a vulnerable or precarious spot: *In her profession one is always between wind and water.* **21. break wind,** to

CONCISE ETYMOLOGY KEY: <, descended or borrowed from; >, whence; b., blend of, blended; c., cognate with; cf., compare; deriv., derivative; equiv., equivalent; imit., imitative; obl., oblique; r., replacing; s., stem; sp., spelling, spelled; resp., respelling, respelled; trans., translation; ?, origin unknown; *, unattested; ‡, probably earlier than. See the full key inside the front cover.

expel gas from the stomach and bowels through the anus. **22. how the wind blows** or **lies,** what the tendency or probability is: *Try to find out how the wind blows.* Also, **which way the wind blows. 23. in the teeth of the wind,** sailing directly into the wind; against the wind. Also, **in the eye of the wind, in the wind's eye. 24. in the wind,** about to occur; imminent; impending: *There's good news in the wind.* **25. off the wind, a.** away from the wind; with the wind at one's back. **b.** (of a sailing vessel) headed into the wind with sails shaking or aback. **26. on the wind,** as close as possible to the wind. Also, **on a wind. 27. sail close to the wind, a.** Also, **sail close on a wind.** to sail as nearly as possible in the direction from which the wind is blowing. **b.** to practice economy in the management of one's affairs. **c.** to verge on a breach of propriety or decency. **d.** to escape (punishment, detection, etc.) by a narrow margin; take a risk. **28. take the wind out of one's sails,** to surprise someone, esp. with unpleasant news; stun; shock; flabbergast: *She took the wind out of his sails when she announced she was marrying someone else.* —*v.t.* **29.** to expose to wind or air. **30.** to follow by the scent. **31.** to make short of wind or breath, as by vigorous exercise. **32.** to let recover breath, as by resting after exertion. —*v.i.* **33.** to catch the scent or odor of game. [bef. 900; ME (n.), OE; c. D, G *Wind,* ON *vindr,* Goth *winds,* L *ventus*]

—Syn. 1. WIND, AIR, ZEPHYR, BREEZE, BLAST, GUST refer to a quantity of air set in motion naturally. WIND applies to any such air in motion, blowing with whatever degree of gentleness or violence. AIR, usually poetical, applies to a very gentle motion of the air. ZEPHYR, also poetical, refers to an air characterized by its soft, mild quality. A BREEZE is usually a cool, light wind. BLAST and GUST apply to quick, forceful winds of short duration; BLAST implies a violent rush of air, often a cold one, whereas a GUST is little more than a flurry. **16.** flatulence.

wind[2] (wīnd), *v.,* **wound** or (*Rare*) **wind•ed** (wīn′did); **wind•ing;** *n.* —*v.i.* **1.** to change direction; bend; turn; take a frequently bending course; meander: *The river winds through the forest.* **2.** to have a circular or spiral course or direction. **3.** to coil or twine about something: *The ivy winds around the house.* **4.** to proceed circuitously or indirectly. **5.** to undergo winding or winding up. **6.** to be twisted or warped, as a board. —*v.t.* **7.** to encircle or wreathe, as with something twined, wrapped, or placed about. **8.** to roll or coil (thread, string, etc.) into a ball, on a spool, or the like (often fol. by *up*). **9.** to remove or take off by unwinding (usually fol. by *off* or *from*): *She wound the thread off the bobbin.* **10.** to twine, fold, wrap, or place about something. **11.** to make (a mechanism) operational by tightening the mainspring with a key (often fol. by *up*): *to wind a clock; to wind up a toy.* **12.** to haul or hoist by means of a winch, windlass, or the like (often fol. by *up*). **13.** to make (one's or its way) in a bending or curving course: *The stream winds its way through the woods.* **14.** to make (one's or its way) by indirect, stealthy, or devious procedure: *to wind one's way into another's confidence.* **15. wind down, a.** to lessen in intensity so as to bring or come to a gradual end: *The war is winding down.* **b.** to calm down; relax: *He's too excited tonight to wind down and sleep.* **16. wind up, a.** to bring to a state of great tension; excite (usually used in the past participle): *He was all wound up before the game.* **b.** to bring or come to an end; conclude: *to wind up a sales campaign.* **c.** to settle or arrange in order to conclude: *to wind up one's affairs.* **d.** to become ultimately: *to wind up as a country schoolteacher.* **e.** *Baseball.* (of a pitcher) to execute a windup. —*n.* **17.** the act of winding. **18.** a single turn, twist, or bend of something wound: *If you give it another wind, you'll break the mainspring.* **19.** a twist producing an uneven surface. **20. out of wind,** (of boards, plasterwork, etc.) flat and true. [bef. 900; ME *winden,* OE *windan;* c. D, G *winden,* ON *vinda,* Goth *-windan;* akin to WEND, WANDER]

wind[3] (wīnd, wind), *v.t.,* **wind•ed** or **wound, wind•ing. 1.** to blow (a horn, a blast, etc.). **2.** to sound by blowing. **3.** to signal or direct by blasts of the horn or the like. [1375–1425; late ME; special use of WIND[1]]

WInd, West Indian. Also, **W.Ind.**

wind•a•ble (wīn′də bəl), *adj.* that can be wound. [WIND[2] + -ABLE]

wind•age (win′dij), *n.* **1.** the influence of the wind in deflecting a missile. **2.** the amount of such deflection. **3.** the degree to which a gunsight must be adjusted to correct for windage. **4.** a difference between the diameter of a projectile and that of the gun bore, for the escape of gas and the prevention of friction. **5.** *Naut.* that portion of a vessel's surface upon which the wind acts. **6.** *Mach.* friction between a rotor and the air within its casing, as in an electric generator. **7.** *Elect.* the resisting influence of air against the rotating armature of a dynamo, creating a power loss. [1700–10; WIND[1] + -AGE]

Win•daus (vin′dous), *n.* **A•dolf** (ä′dôlf), 1876–1959, German chemist: Nobel prize 1928.

wind•bag (wind′bag′), *n.* **1.** *Informal.* an empty, voluble, pretentious talker. **2.** the bag of a bagpipe. [1425–75; late ME; see WIND[1], BAG] **—wind′bag′ger•y,** *n.*

wind-bell (wind′bel′), *n.* **1.** a bell sounded by the action of the wind. **2.** See **wind chimes.** [1920–25]

wind•blast (wind′blast′, -bläst′, win′-), *n.* a strong, sudden gust of wind. [1940–45; WIND[1] + BLAST]

wind•blown (wind′blōn′), *adj.* **1.** blown by the wind: *windblown hair.* **2.** (of trees) growing in a certain shape because of strong prevailing winds. **3.** (of a hair style) bobbed short, with the ends combed toward the forehead. [1585–95; WIND[1] + BLOWN[1]]

wind-borne (wind′bôrn′, -bōrn′), *adj.* carried by the wind, as pollen or seed. [1900–05]

wind•bound (wind′bound′), *adj.* (of a sailing ship, sailboat, or the like) kept from sailing by a wind from the wrong direction or one of too high velocity. [1580–90; WIND[1] + -BOUND[1]]

wind•break (wind′brāk′), *n.* a growth of trees, a structure of boards, or the like, serving as a shelter from the wind. [1765–75; WIND[1] + BREAK]

Wind•break•er (wind′brā′kər), *Trademark.* a brand name for a jacket of wind-resistant material with close-fitting elastic hip band and cuffs.

wind-bro•ken (wind′brō′kən), *adj. Vet. Pathol.* (of horses) having the breathing impaired; affected with heaves. [1595–1605]

wind•burn (wind′bûrn′), *n.* an inflammation of the skin, esp. that of the face and hands, caused by overexposure to the wind. [1920–25; WIND[1] + BURN[1]] **—wind′burned′,** *adj.*

Wind′ Cave′ Na′tional Park′ (wind), a national park in SW South Dakota. 41½ sq. mi. (107 sq. km).

wind•cheat•er (wind′chē′tər), *n. Chiefly Brit.* a lightweight jacket for sports or other outdoor wear. [1945–50; WIND[1] + CHEATER]

wind•chest (wind′chest′), *n.* a chamber containing the air supply for the reeds or pipes of an organ. [1790–1800; WIND[1] + CHEST]

wind′chill fac′tor (wind′chil′, win′-), *Meteorol.* the apparent temperature felt on the exposed human body owing to the combination of temperature and wind speed. Also, **wind′ chill′ fac′tor, wind′-chill fac′tor.** Also called **chill factor, wind′ chill′, wind′chill in′dex.** [1945–50]

wind′ chimes′ (wind), an arrangement of bells, bamboo pipes, or glass or ceramic fragments hung so as to strike each other and tinkle when moved by the wind or, in orchestration, touched by the hand. [1925–30]

wind′ col′ic (wind), *Vet. Pathol.* (esp. in horses) flatulence caused by gases that result from the eating of fermenting vegetation; bloat. [1585–95]

wind′ cone′ (wind), windsock. [1915–20]

wind-down (wīnd′doun′), *n.* an act or instance of winding down, as in intensity: *a gradual wind-down in hostilities.* [1965–70; n. use of the v. phrase *wind down*]

wind•ed (win′did), *adj.* **1.** out of breath. **2.** having wind or breath of a specified kind (usually used in combination): *short-winded; broken-winded.* [1400–50; late ME; see WIND[1], -ED[3]] **—wind′ed•ness,** *n.*

wind′ en′ergy (wind). See **wind power.**

wind•er (wīn′dər), *n.* **1.** a person or thing that winds. **2.** a staircase step for changing direction. Cf. **flier** (def. 9). **3.** a plant that coils or twines itself about something. **4.** an instrument or a machine for winding thread or the like. [1545–55; WIND[2] + -ER[1]]

Win•der•mere (win′dər mēr′), *n.* **Lake,** a lake in NW England, between Westmorland and Lancashire: the largest lake in England. 10½ mi. (17 km) long; 5⅔ sq. mi. (15 sq. km).

wind′ ero′sion (wind), the erosion, transportation, and deposition of topsoil by the wind, esp. in dust storms. [1900–05]

wind•fall (wind′fôl′), *n.* **1.** an unexpected gain, piece of good fortune, or the like. **2.** something blown down by the wind, as fruit. —*adj.* **3.** accruing in unexpectedly large amounts: *windfall profits.* [1425–75; late ME; see WIND[1], FALL]

wind•farm (wind′färm′), *n. Energy.* a large grouping of wind generators or wind plants located at a site having dependable strong winds. Also, **wind′ farm′.** [1975–80; WIND[1] + FARM]

wind•flaw (wind′flô′), *n.* flaw[2] (def. 1). [1920–25; WIND[1] + FLAW[2]]

wind•flow•er (wind′flou′ər), *n.* any plant belonging to the genus *Anemone,* of the buttercup family, having divided leaves and showy, solitary flowers. [1545–55; trans. of Gk *amemṓnē* ANEMONE; see WIND[1], FLOWER]

wind•gall (wind′gôl′), *n. Vet. Pathol.* a puffy distention of the synovial bursa at the fetlock joint. [1515–25; WIND[1] + GALL[2]] **—wind′galled′,** *adj.*

wind′ gap′ (wind), a cut that indents only the upper part of a mountain ridge, usually a former water gap. [1760–70, *Amer.*]

wind′ gauge′ (wind), **1.** anemometer. **2.** a scale on the rear sight of a rifle by which the sight is adjusted to correct for windage. [1645–55]

wind′ gen′erator (wind), **1.** an electric generator situated on a tower and driven by the force of wind on blades or a rotor. **2.** a wind plant.

Wind•ham (win′dəm), *n.* **1.** a town in NE Connecticut. 21,062. **2.** a town in SW Maine. 11,282.

wind′ harp′ (wind). See **aeolian harp.** [1805–15]

Wind•hoek (vint′ho͝ok′), *n.* a city in and the capital of Namibia, in the central part. 62,000.

wind•hov•er (wind′huv′ər, -hov′-), *n.* the kestrel, *Falco tinnunculus.* [1665–75; WIND[1] + HOVER; from its hovering flight, head to the wind]

win•di•go (win′di gō′), *n.* **1.** (in the folklore of the Ojibwa and other Indians) a cannibalistic giant, the transformation of a person who has eaten human flesh. **2.** *Psychiatry.* a culture-specific syndrome occurring primarily among the Ojibwa and related Indian peoples and characterized by fever-induced delusions that one is being possessed by such a giant. Also called **witigo.** [1705–15; < Ojibwa *wi·ntiko·;* c. Cree *wi·htiko·w*]

wind′ in′dicator (wind), a large weather vane used at airports to indicate wind direction.

wind•ing (wīn′ding), *n.* **1.** the act of a person or thing that winds. **2.** a bend, turn, or flexure. **3.** a coiling, folding, or wrapping, as of one thing about another. **4.** something that is wound or coiled, or a single round of it. **5.** *Elect.* **a.** a symmetrically laid, electrically conducting current path in any device. **b.** the manner of such coiling: *a series winding.* —*adj.* **6.** bending or turning; sinuous. **7.** spiral, as stairs. [bef. 1050; ME (n.), OE *windung* (n.); see WIND[2], -ING[1], -ING[2]] **—wind′ing•ly,** *adv.* **—wind′ing•ness,** *n.*

wind′ing frame′, a machine on which yarn or thread is wound.

wind′ing num′ber, *Math.* the number of times a closed curve winds around a point not on the curve. Also called **index.**

wind′ing sheet′, 1. shroud (def. 1). **2.** a mass of tallow or wax that has run down and hardened on the side of a candle, sometimes considered an omen of misfortune. [1375–1425; late ME]

wind′ in′strument (wind), a musical instrument sounded by the breath or other air current, as the trumpet, trombone, clarinet, or flute. [1575–85]

wind•jam•mer (wind′jam′ər, win′-), *n. Informal.* **1.** (formerly) a merchant ship propelled by sails. **2.** any large sailing ship. **3.** a member of its crew. **4.** *Older Slang.* a long-winded person; a great talker. [1890–95, *Amer.*; WIND[1] + *jammer* (see JAM[1], -ER[1])]

wind•lass (wind′ləs), *n.* **1.** a device for raising or hauling objects, usually consisting of a horizontal cylinder or barrel turned by a crank, lever, motor, or the like, upon which a cable, rope, or chain winds, the outer end of the cable being attached directly or indirectly to the weight to be raised or the thing to be hauled or pulled; winch. —*v.t.* **2.** to raise, haul, or move (a load) by means of a windlass. [1350–1400; ME *wind(e)las* < ON *vindāss,* equiv. to *vinda* to WIND[2] + *āss* beam]

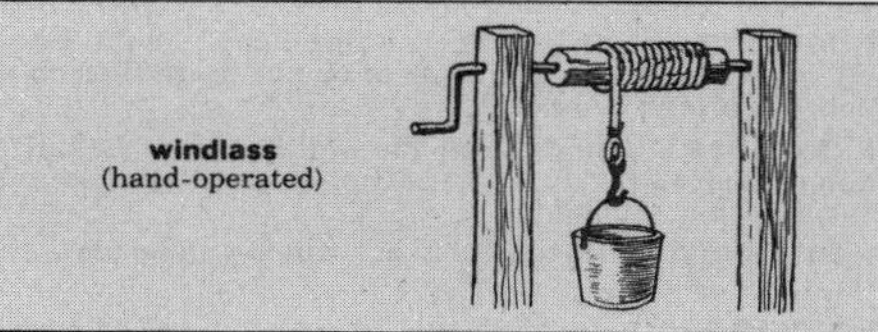

windlass
(hand-operated)

win•dle (win′dl, win′l), *n. Scot. and North Eng.* a measure of corn, wheat, or other commodities equal to approximately three bushels, but varying in different regions. [bef. 900; ME *wyndel,* OE *windel* box, basket; akin to WIND[2]]

wind•less (wind′lis), *adj.* **1.** without wind; calm: *a windless summer afternoon.* **2.** out of breath. [1350–1400; ME; see WIND[1], -LESS] **—wind′less•ly,** *adv.* **—wind′less•ness,** *n.*

win•dle•straw (win′dl strô′, win′l-), *n. Brit. Dial.* **1.** a withered stalk of any of various grasses. **2.** any of various long-stalked species of grass. **3.** any tall, thin person. **4.** any light or flimsy material or object. Also, *esp. Scot.,* **winlestrae.** [bef. 1000; OE *windelstrēaw* (not attested in ME). See WINDLE, STRAW]

wind•mill (wind′mil′), *n.* **1.** any of various machines for grinding, pumping, etc., driven by the force of the wind acting upon a number of vanes or sails. **2.** (loosely) a wind generator; wind plant. **3.** *Aeron.* a small air turbine with blades, like those of an airplane propeller, exposed on a moving aircraft and driven by the air, used to operate gasoline pumps, radio apparatus, etc. **4.** an imaginary opponent, wrong, etc. (in allusion to Cervantes' *Don Quixote*): *to tilt at windmills.* —*v.i., v.t.* **5.** *Aeron.* (of a propeller engine or turbojet engine) to rotate or cause to rotate solely under the force of a passing airstream. [1250–1300; ME; see WIND[1], MILL[1]]

windmill
(def. 1)

wind′mill grass′. See **finger grass.** [1885–90]

win•dow (win′dō), *n.* **1.** an opening in the wall of a building, the side of a vehicle, etc., for the admission of air or light, or both, commonly fitted with a frame in which are set movable sashes containing panes of glass. **2.** such an opening with the frame, sashes, and panes of glass, or any other device, by which it is closed. **3.** the frame, sashes, and panes of glass, or the like, intended to fit such an opening: *Finally the builders put in the windows.* **4.** a windowpane. **5.** anything likened to a window in appearance or function, as a transparent section in an envelope, displaying the address. **6.** a period of time regarded as highly favorable for initiating or completing something: *Investors have a window of perhaps six months before interest rates rise.* **7.** *Mil.* chaff[1] (def. 5). **8.** *Geol.* fenster. **9.** *Pharm.* the drug dosage range that results in a therapeutic effect, a lower dose being insufficient and a higher dose being toxic. **10.** *Aerospace.* **a.** See **launch window. b.** a specific area at the outer limits of the earth's atmosphere through which a spacecraft must reenter to arrive safely at its planned destination. **11.** *Computers.* a section of a display screen that can be created for viewing information from another part of a file or from another file: *The split screen feature enables a user to create two or more windows.* —*v.t.* **12.** to furnish with a window or windows. **13.**

CONCISE PRONUNCIATION KEY: act, cāpe, dâre, pärt; set, ēqual; *if,* īce; ox, ōver, ôrder, oil, bo͝ok, bo͞ot, out; up, ûrge; *child;* sing; shoe; thin, *that;* zh as in *treasure.* ə = *a* as in *alone, e* as in *system, i* as in *easily, o* as in *gallop, u* as in *circus;* ᵊ as in *fire* (fīᵊr), *hour* (ouᵊr). l and n can serve as syllabic consonants, as in *cradle* (krād′l), and *button* (but′n). See the full key inside the front cover.

Obs. to display or put in a window. [1175–1225; ME *windoge, windowe* < ON *vindauga,* equiv. to *vindr* WIND[1] + *auga* EYE] —**win′dow·less,** *adj.* —**win′dow·y,** *adj.*

win′dow back′, woodwork, esp. paneling, beneath the stool of a window.

win′dow blind′. See **window shade.** [1720–30]

win′dow board′, a thin board serving as a stool of a window. [1620–30]

win′dow box′, **1.** a box for growing plants, placed at or in a window. **2.** a hollow space in a window frame for a sash weight. [1880–85]

win′dow dress′er, a person employed to trim the display windows of a store. [1860–65]

win′dow dress′ing, **1.** the art, act, or technique of trimming the display windows of a store. **2.** misrepresentation of something, so as to give a favorable impression: *The company's list of assets included a great deal of window dressing.* [1780–90]

win′dow en′velope, an envelope with a transparent opening through which the address on the enclosure may be read. [1915–20]

win′dow·glass shell′ (win′dō glas′, -gläs′), capiz. [1965–70; WINDOW + GLASS]

win·dow·ing (win′dō ing), *n. Computers.* simultaneous display of different portions of one or more files on a screen. [WINDOW + -ING[1]]

win′dowless mon′ad, (in the philosophy of Leibniz) a monad having no direct causal or perceptual relation with any other monad.

win·dow·light (win′dō līt′), *n.* windowpane (def. 1). [1705–15; WINDOW + LIGHT[1]]

win·dow·pane (win′dō pān′), *n.* **1.** a plate of glass for filling a window sash within the frame. **2.** a flounder, *Scophthalmus aquosus,* occurring along the Atlantic coast of North America, characterized by the thinness and translucency of its body. —*adj.* **3.** designating or having a large, regular design of intersecting lines resembling a series of windowpanes: *a windowpane plaid sweater.* [1810–20; WINDOW + PANE]

win′dowpane shell′, capiz.

win′dow sash′, the frame holding the pane of a window. [1755–65]

win′dow seat′, **1.** a seat built beneath the sill of a recessed or other window. **2.** a bench having two arms and no back. [1745–55]

win′dow shade′, a shade or blind for a window, as a sheet of cloth or paper on a spring roller. Also called **blind, window blind.** [1800–10]
—**Regional Variation.** SHADE is used widely for WINDOW SHADE, although BLIND is common in the Midland U.S. (as well as in Great Britain), and CURTAIN is used chiefly in New England and the South Atlantic states.

win·dow-shop (win′dō shop′), *v.,* **-shopped, -shop·ping.** —*v.i.* **1.** to look at articles in the windows of stores without making any purchases. **2.** to examine or evaluate merchandise for possible purchase, use, etc.: *Russian delegations are window-shopping in European factories.* —*v.t.* **3.** to look at (merchandise) in the windows of stores without making any purchases: *to window-shop shoes.* [1925–30] —**win′dow-shop′per,** *n.*

win′dow sill′, the sill under a window. [1695–1705]

wind·pipe (wind′pīp′), *n.* the trachea of an air-breathing vertebrate. [1520–30; WIND[1] + PIPE[1]]

wind′ plant′ (wind), a grouping of devices, consisting of a tower, propellers, alternator, generator, and storage batteries, designed to produce electricity by converting the mechanical force of wind on blades or a rotor into electricity.

wind-pol·li·nat·ed (wind′pol′ə nā′tid), *adj. Bot.* being pollinated by airborne pollen. [1880–85] —**wind′-pol′li·na′tion,** *n.*

wind′ pop′py (wind), a Californian plant, *Stylomecon heterophylla,* of the poppy family, having satiny, brick-red flowers with purple centers.

wind′ pow′er (wind), power derived from wind: used to generate electricity or mechanical power. Also called **wind energy.** [1900–05]

wind·proof (wind′pro͞of′), *adj.* resisting wind, as fabric or a jacket or coat. [1610–20; WIND[1] + -PROOF]

wind′ pump′ (wind), a pump driven by a windmill. [1650–60]

Wind′ Riv′er Range′ (wind), a mountain range in W Wyoming, part of the Rocky Mountains. Highest peak, Gannett Peak, 13,785 ft. (4202 m).

wind·rode (wind′rōd′), *adj. Naut.* (of a moored vessel) riding with the force of the wind. [1625–35; WIND[1] + RODE]

wind′ rose′ (wind), **1.** a map symbol showing, for a given locality or area, the frequency and strength of the wind from various directions. **2.** a diagram showing the relation of wind direction to other weather conditions at a given location. [1590–1600]

wind·row (wind′rō′, win′-), *n.* **1.** a row or line of hay raked together to dry before being raked into heaps. **2.** any similar row, as of sheaves of grain, made for the purpose of drying. **3.** a row of dry leaves, dust, etc., swept together by the wind. —*v.t.* **4.** to arrange in a windrow. [1515–25; WIND[1] + ROW[1]]

wind·row·er (wind′rō′ər, win′-), *n.* a farm implement used to mow a field and arrange the mown crop in windrows. [1945–50; WINDROW + -ER[1]]

CONCISE ETYMOLOGY KEY: <, descended or borrowed from; >, whence; b., blend of, blended; c., cognate with; cf., compare; deriv., derivative; equiv., equivalent; imit., imitative; obl., oblique; r., replacing; s., stem; sp., spelling, spelled; resp., respelling, respelled; trans., translation; ?, origin unknown; *, unattested; ‡, probably earlier than. See the full key inside the front cover.

wind′ sail′ (wind), *Naut.* a sail rigged over a hatchway, ventilator, or the like, to divert moving air downward into the vessel. [1715–25]

wind′ scale′ (wind), a numerical scale, as the Beaufort scale, for designating relative wind intensities. [1905–10]

wind′ scor′pion. See **sun spider.** [1910–15]

wind-screen (wind′skrēn′, win′-), *n. Chiefly Brit.* windshield. [1855–60]

wind′ shaft′ (wind), the shaft driven by the sails of a windmill. [1815–25]

wind′ shake′ (wind), **1.** Also called **anemosis.** a flaw in wood supposed to be caused by the action of strong winds upon the trunk of the tree. **2.** such flaws collectively. Also called **cup shake.** [1535–45]

wind-shak·en (wind′shā′kən), *adj.* **1.** affected by windshake. **2.** shaken by the wind. [1540–50]

wind′ shear′ (wind), **1.** the rate at which wind velocity changes from point to point in a given direction. **2.** a condition, dangerous to aircraft, in which the speed or direction of the wind changes abruptly. Cf. **microburst.** [1940–45]

wind′ shelf′ (wind). See **smoke shelf.**

wind·shield (wind′shēld′, win′-), *n.* a shield of glass, in one or more sections, projecting above and across the dashboard of an automobile. Also called, *esp. Brit.,* **windscreen.** [1900–05; WIND[1] + SHIELD]

wind′shield wip′er, an electrically or pneumatically operated device consisting of a squeegee connected to a mechanical arm designed to wipe off rain, snow, etc., from a windshield or rear window.

wind′ ship′ (wind), a large sailing vessel. [1840–50, *Amer.*]

wind·sock (wind′sok′), *n.* a tapered, tubular cloth vane, open at both ends and having at the larger end a fixed ring pivoted to swing freely, installed at airports or elsewhere to indicate wind direction and approximate intensity. Also, **wind′ sock′.** Also called **air sleeve, air sock, wind cone, wind′ sleeve′.** [1925–30; WIND[1] + SOCK[1]]

Wind·sor (win′zər), *n.* **1.** (since 1917) a member of the present British royal family. Cf. **Saxe-Coburg-Gotha** (def. 1). **2. Duke of.** See **Edward VIII. 3. Wallis Warfield, Duchess of** (*Bessie Wallis Warfield Spencer Simpson*), 1896–1986, U.S. socialite: wife of Edward VIII of England, who abdicated the throne to marry her. **4.** Official name, **Wind′sor and Maid′enhead.** a city in E Berkshire, in S England, on the Thames: the site of the residence (**Wind′sor Cas′tle**) of English sovereigns since William the Conqueror. 134,700. **5.** a city in S Ontario, in SE Canada, opposite Detroit, Michigan. 196,526. **6.** a town in N central Connecticut. 25,204.

Wind′sor bench′, a bench similar in construction to a Windsor chair. Also called **Wind′sor settee′.**

Wind′sor chair′, (*sometimes l.c.*) a wooden chair of many varieties, having a spindle back and legs slanting outward: common in 18th-century England and in the American colonies. [1715–25]

Windsor chairs

Wind′sor knot′, a wide, triangular knot for tying a four-in-hand necktie. [1945–50]

Wind′sor Locks′, a town in N Connecticut. 12,190.

Wind′sor tie′, a wide, soft necktie of black silk, tied at the neck in a loose bow. [1895–1900]

wind′ sprint′ (wind), a sprint, usually run several times in succession as part of a conditioning program, to develop an athlete's wind, speed, and endurance. [1945–50]

wind·storm (wind′stôrm′), *n.* a storm with heavy wind but little or no precipitation. [1350–1400; ME; see WIND[1], STORM]

wind·suck·er (wind′suk′ər), *n. Vet. Pathol.* a horse afflicted with cribbing. [1680–90; WIND[1] + SUCKER]

wind·suck·ing (wind′suk′ing), *n. Vet. Pathol.* cribbing (def. 1). [1835–45]

wind·surf (wind′sûrf′), *v.i.* to engage in windsurfing. [1965–70; WIND[1] + SURF] —**wind′surf′er,** *n.*

wind·surf·ing (wind′sûr′fing), *n.* a form of sailing in which a flexible sail, free to move in any direction, is mounted on a surfboard and the craft guided by the standing rider. Also called **sailboarding.** [1965–70; WIND[1] + SURF + -ING[1]]

wind·swept (wind′swept′), *adj.* open or exposed to the wind: *a wind-swept beach.* [1805–15]

wind′ tee′ (wind), a large, T-shaped weather vane on or near an airfield. Also called **air tee, landing tee.** [1930–35, *Amer.*]

wind·tight (wind′tīt′), *adj.* so tight as to prevent passage of wind or air. [1500–10; WIND[1] + TIGHT]

wind′ tun′nel (wind), *Aeron.* a tubular chamber or structure in which a steady current of air can be maintained at a controlled velocity, equipped with devices for measuring and recording forces and moments on scale models of complete aircraft or of their parts or, sometimes, on full-scale aircraft or their parts. [1910–15, *Amer.*]

wind′ tur′bine (wind), a turbine powered by the wind. [1905–10]

wind·up (wīnd′up′), *n.* **1.** the conclusion of any action, activity, etc.; the end or close. **2.** a final act or part. **3.** *Baseball.* the preparatory movements of the arm before pitching a ball. Cf. **stretch** (def. 22). **4.** *Informal.* a mechanical object, as a toy or wristwatch, that is driven by a spring or similar mechanism that must be wound. **5.** an act or instance of winding up. Also, **wind′-up.′** [1565–75; n. use of v. phrase *wind up*]

wind′ vane′ (wind). See **weather vane.** [1715–25]

wind·ward (wind′wərd), *adv.* **1.** toward the wind; toward the point from which the wind blows. —*adj.* **2.** pertaining to, situated in, or moving toward the quarter from which the wind blows (opposed to *leeward*). —*n.* **3.** the point or quarter from which the wind blows. **4.** the side toward the wind. **5. to windward,** in a position of vantage: *We got to windward of the difficulty.* Also, **to the windward.** [1540–50; WIND[1] + -WARD] —**wind′ward·ness,** *n.*

Wind′ward Is′lands, a group of islands in the SE West Indies, consisting of the S part of the Lesser Antilles: includes British, French, and independent territories.

Wind′ward Pas′sage, a strait in the West Indies, between Cuba and Haiti. 50 mi. (80 km) wide.

wind·way (wind′wā′), *n.* **1.** a passage for air. **2.** *Music.* flue[1] (def. 4b). [1870–75; WIND[1] + WAY[1]]

wind·y (win′dē), *adj.,* **wind·i·er, wind·i·est.** **1.** accompanied or characterized by wind: *a windy day.* **2.** exposed to or swept by the wind: *a windy hill.* **3.** consisting of or resembling wind: *a windy tempest of activity.* **4.** toward the wind; windward. **5.** unsubstantial or empty. **6.** of the nature of, characterized by, or given to prolonged, empty talk; voluble; verbose; bombastic. **7.** characterized by or causing flatulence. **8.** *Chiefly Scot.* boastful. [bef. 900; ME; OE *windig.* See WIND[1], -Y[1]] —**wind′i·ly,** *adv.* —**wind′i·ness,** *n.*

Wind′y Cit′y, Chicago, Ill. (used as a nickname).

windz (winz), *n.* winze[1].

wine (wīn), *n., adj., v.,* **wined, win·ing.** —*n.* **1.** the fermented juice of grapes, made in many varieties, such as red, white, sweet, dry, still, and sparkling, for use as a beverage, in cooking, in religious rites, etc., and usually having an alcoholic content of 14 percent or less. **2.** a particular variety of such fermented grape juice: *port and sherry wines.* **3.** the juice, fermented or unfermented, of various other fruits or plants, used as a beverage, sauce, etc.: *gooseberry wine; currant wine.* **4.** a dark reddish color, as of red wines. **5.** *Pharm.* vinum. **6.** something that invigorates, cheers, or intoxicates like wine. **7.** *Brit.* **a.** a social gathering at which wine is the major beverage. **b.** a party, esp. one held by university students, for drinking wine. **8.** *Obs.* intoxication due to the drinking of wine. **9. new wine in old bottles,** something new placed in or superimposed on an old or existing form, system, etc. Matt. 9:17. —*adj.* **10.** dark red in color. —*v.t.* **11.** to supply with wine: *He wined his cellar with rare vintages.* —*v.i.* **12.** to drink wine. **13. wine and dine,** to entertain lavishly: *They wined and dined us in order to get us to sign the new contract.* [bef. 900; ME (n.), OE *wīn* (c. D *wijn,* G *Wein,* ON *vīn,* Goth *wein*) << L *vīnum* (c. Gk *oînos*)] —**wine′less,** *adj.* —**win′ish,** *adj.*

wine′ bag′, wineskin.

wine′ bar′, a bar, esp. of a café or restaurant, that features a variety of wines served by the glass. [1935–40]

wine·ber·ry (wīn′ber′ē, -bə rē), *n., pl.* **-ries.** **1.** a prickly shrub, *Rubus phoenicolasius,* of China and Japan, having pinkish or white flowers and small, red, edible fruit. **2.** the fruit of this plant. [bef. 1000; ME *winberie,* OE *winberige* grape. See WINE, BERRY]

wine·bib·ber (wīn′bib′ər), *n.* a person who drinks much wine. [1525–35; WINE + BIBBER] —**wine′bib′bing,** *n., adj.*

wine′ cel′lar, **1.** a cellar for the storage of wine. **2.** the wine stored there; a store or stock of wines. [1325–75; ME]

wine-col·ored (wīn′kul′ərd), *adj.* of the color of wine; dark red. [1825–35]

wine′ cool′er, **1.** a bucket for holding ice to chill a bottle of wine. **2.** a drink made of wine, fruit juice, carbonated water, and sometimes other flavorings. [1805–15]

wine′ gal′lon, a former English gallon of 160 fluid ounces: equal to the present U.S. standard gallon of 128 fluid ounces. [1650–60]

wine·glass (wīn′glas′, -gläs′), *n.* a drinking glass, as a goblet, having a foot and a stem and used specifically for serving wine. [1700–10; WINE + GLASS]

wine·glass·ful (wīn′glas fo͝ol′, -gläs-), *n., pl.* **-fuls.** the capacity of a wineglass, typically containing four to six fluid ounces. [1815–25; WINEGLASS + -FUL]
—**Usage.** See **-ful.**

wine·grow·er (wīn′grō′ər), *n.* **1.** a person who owns or works in a vineyard and winery. **2.** a winemaker. [1835–45; WINE + GROWER]

wine·grow·ing (wīn′grō′ing), *n.* **1.** the work or business of a winegrower. **2.** the industry of producing wine. Also called **winemaking.** [1840–50; WINE + GROWING]

wine·mak·er (wīn′mā′kər), *n.* **1.** an expert in the production of wines. **2.** a winegrower. [1350–1400; ME; see WINE, MAKER]

wine·mak·ing (wīn′mā′king), *n.* **1.** the procedures and processes carried out in the making and maturing of wine; viniculture; vinification. **2.** winegrowing. [1805–15; WINE + MAKING]

wine′ palm′, any of several palms from whose sap wine is made, as the coquito. [1675–85]

wine′ press′, a machine in which the juice from grapes is pressed for wine. Also, **wine′ press′er.** [1520–30]

win·er·y (wī′nə rē), *n., pl.* **-er·ies.** an establishment for making wine. [1880–85, *Amer.*; WINE + -ERY]

Wine·sap (wīn′sap′), *n.* (*sometimes l.c.*) a red variety of apple that ripens in the autumn. [1790–1800; WINE + SAP[1]]

Wines′burg, Ohi′o (wīnz′bûrg), a cycle of short stories (1919) by Sherwood Anderson.

wine·shop (wīn′shop′), *n.* a shop where wine is sold. [1840–50; WINE + SHOP]

wine·skin (wīn′skin′), *n.* a bag, usually of goatskin, for carrying wine and having a spigot from which one drinks. Also called **wine bag.** [1815–25; WINE + SKIN]

wine′ stew′ard, a waiter in a restaurant or club who is in charge of wine; sommelier. [1895–1900]

wine·tast·er (wīn′tā′stər), *n.* **1.** a critic, writer, buyer, or other professional who tests the quality of wine by tasting. **2.** a small, flat bowl, often of silver, used to hold a small amount of wine being tasted. [1625–35; WINE + TASTER]

wine·tast·ing (wīn′tā′sting), *n.* a gathering of critics, buyers, friends, etc., to taste a group of wines for comparative purposes. [1935–40; WINE + TASTE + -ING[1]]

wine·y (wī′nē), *adj.,* **win·i·er, win·i·est.** winy.

Win·field (win′fēld′), *n.* **1.** a town in S Kansas. 10,736. **2.** a male given name.

Win·fred (win′frid), *n.* a male given name: from an Old English word meaning "peaceful friend."

wing (wing), *n.* **1.** either of the two forelimbs of most birds and of bats, corresponding to the human arms, that are specialized for flight. **2.** either of two corresponding parts in flightless birds, which may be rudimentary, as in certain ratite birds, or adapted for swimming, as in penguins. **3.** one of the paired, thin, lateral extensions of the body wall of an insect, located on the mesothorax and the metathorax, by means of which it flies. **4.** a similar structure with which gods, angels, demons, etc., are conceived to be provided for the purpose of flying. **5.** *Slang.* an arm of a human being, esp. a baseball player's pitching or throwing arm. **6.** a means or instrument of flight, travel, or progress. **7.** the act or manner of flying. **8.** something resembling or likened to a bird's wing, as a vane or sail of a windmill. **9.** *Aeron.* **a.** one of a pair of airfoils attached transversely to the fuselage of an aircraft and providing lift. **b.** both airfoils, taken collectively. **10.** *Archit.* a part of a building projecting on one side of, or subordinate to, a central or main part. **11.** *Furniture.* either of two forward extensions of the sides of the back of an easy chair. **12.** either of the two side portions of an army or fleet, usually called right wing and left wing, and distinguished from the center; flank units. **13.** an administrative and tactical unit of the U.S. Air Force consisting of two or more groups, headquarters, and certain supporting and service units. **14.** (in flight formation) noting a position to the side and just to the rear of another airplane. **15.** *Fort.* either of the longer sides of a crownwork, uniting it to the main work. **16.** *Sports.* (in some team games) any one of the positions, or a player in such a position, on the far side of the center position, known as the left and right wings with reference to the direction of the opposite goal. **17.** *Theat.* **a.** the platform or space on the right or left of the stage proper. **b.** See **wing flat. 18.** *Anat.* an ala: *the wings of the sphenoid.* **19.** *Bot.* **a.** any leaflike expansion, as of a samara. **b.** one of the two side petals of a papilionaceous flower. See diag. under **papilionaceous. 20.** either of the parts of a double door, screen, etc. **21.** the feather of an arrow. **22.** a faction within a political party, as at one extreme or the other: *conflict between the right wing and the left wing.* **23.** *Naut.* one of the far side areas of the hold of a merchant vessel. **24.** *Brit.* a fender of an automobile, truck, bicycle, or other vehicle. **25. on the wing, a.** in flight, or flying: *a bird on the wing.* **b.** in motion; traveling; active: *Scouts are on the wing in search of a new talent.* **26. take wing, a.** to begin to fly; take to the air. **b.** to leave in haste; depart: *Our resolutions to economize swiftly took wing.* **27. under one's wing,** under one's protection, care, or patronage: *She took the orphan under her wing.* —*v.t.* **28.** to equip with wings. **29.** to enable to fly, move rapidly, etc.; lend speed or celerity to. **30.** to supply with a winglike part, a side structure, etc. **31.** to transport on or as on wings. **32.** to perform or accomplish by wings. **33.** to traverse in flight. **34.** to wound or disable in the wing: *to wing a bird.* **35.** to wound (a person) in an arm or other nonvital part. **36.** to bring down (as a flying bird) by a shot. **37.** *Informal.* to throw; lob: *He winged a ball through the neighbor's window.* **38.** to brush or clean with a wing. **39.** *Theat.* to perform (a part, role, etc.) relying on prompters in the wings. —*v.i.* **40.** to travel on or as if on wings; fly; soar: *They are winging to the coast.* **41. wing it,** *Informal.* to accomplish or execute something without sufficient preparation or experience; improvise: *He had no time to study, so he had to wing it.* [1125–75; ME *wenge* (pl. n.) < ODan *wingæ;* cf. Norw, Sw *vinge,* ON *vængr*]

wing′ and wing′, *Naut.* with a sail extended on each side, as with the foresail out on one side and the mainsail out on the other. [1775–85]

wing·back (wing′bak′), *n. Football.* **1.** an offensive back who lines up outside an end. **2.** the position played by this back. [1935–40; WING + BACK[1]]

wing′back forma′tion, *Football.* **1.** See **single wingback formation. 2.** See **double wingback formation.** [1930–35]

wing′ bar′, a line of contrasting color along the coverts of a bird's wing. [1850–55]

wing′ bit′, a flat bit projecting to one side near the end of a key.

wing′ bolt′, a bolt with a head like a wing nut.

wing′ bow′ (bō), (of poultry) the distinctively colored feathers on the shoulder or bend of the wing of a bird. [1865–70]

wing′ case′, *Entomol.* elytron. Also called **wing′ cov′er.** [1655–65]

wing′ chair′, a large upholstered chair having a back with wings. Also, **winged′ chair′.** [1900–05]

wing′ col′lar, a stand-up collar having the front edges or corners folded down, worn by men for formal or evening dress. [1910–15]

wing′ command′er, 1. *Brit.* an officer in the Royal Air Force equivalent in rank to a lieutenant colonel in the U.S. Air Force. **2.** an officer of the U.S. Navy or Air Force who commands a wing. [1910–15]

wing′ cov′erts, *Ornith.* the feathers that cover the bases of the quill feathers in birds. [1805–15]

wing′ dam′, a jetty for diverting the current of a stream. Also called **spur, spur dike.** [1800–10, *Amer.*]

wing-ding (wing′ding′), *n. Slang.* **1.** a noisy, exciting celebration or party. **2.** a fit, either induced by drugs or feigned. **3.** a fit of anger; a rage. Also, **wing′ ding′.** [1925–30, *Amer.*; rhyming compound, perh. based on WING]

winged (wingd *or, esp. Literary,* wing′id), *adj.* **1.** having wings. **2.** having a winglike part or parts: *a winged bone; a winged seed.* **3.** abounding with wings or winged creatures. **4.** moving or reaching swiftly on or as if on wings: *winged words.* **5.** rapid or swift. **6.** elevated or lofty: *winged sentiments.* **7.** disabled in the wing, as a bird. **8.** wounded in an arm or other nonvital part. [1350–1400; ME; see WING, -ED[3]] —**wing′ed·ly,** *adv.* —**wing′ed·ness,** *n.*

winged′ bean′, 1. a tropical Asian vine, *Psophocarpus tetragonolobus,* of the legume family, of which the pods, seeds, leaves, and flowers are edible and nutritious. **2.** the pod of this plant, having four flangelike longitudinal extensions. [1905–10]

winged′ elm′, a small tree, *Ulmus alata,* of southeastern North America, having twigs edged with flat, corky projections. Also called **wahoo.** [1810–20, *Amer.*]

winged′ everlast′ing, a bushy composite plant, *Ammobium alatum,* of Australia, having winged branches, javelin-shaped leaves, and white flowers.

Winged′ Horse′, *Astron.* the constellation Pegasus.

winged′ pea′, a trailing southern European plant, *Lotus tetragonolobus,* of the legume family, having purplish-red flowers and edible pods and seeds. [1730–40]

winged′ spin′dle tree′, a stiff, spreading shrub, *Euonymus alata,* of eastern Asia, having corky-winged twigs, yellowish flowers, and purplish fruit. Also called **winged′ euon′ymus.**

Winged′ Vic′tory, a Greek marble statue (c200 B.C.) of Nike found at Samothrace and now in the Louvre, Paris. Also called ***Nike of Samothrace, Victory of Samothrace, Winged′ Vic′tory of Sam′othrace.***

wing·er (wing′ər), *n.* **1.** (in Rugby, soccer, etc.) a person who plays a wing position. **2.** a right-winger. [1785–95; WING + -ER[1]]

wing′ flat′, *Theat.* a flat, esp. a two-fold, usually forming part of a unit of four panels of painted scenery. Also called **coulisse.**

wing-foot·ed (wing′fo͝ot′id), *adj.* **1.** having winged feet. **2.** swift. [1585–95]

wing′ for′mula, *Ornith.* a numerical representation of the relative lengths of the primary feathers of a bird's wing, used in identifying similar species, as flycatchers. [1935–40]

wing·less (wing′lis), *adj.* **1.** having no wings. **2.** having only rudimentary wings, as an apteryx. [1585–95; WING + -LESS] —**wing′less·ness,** *n.*

wing·let (wing′lit), *n.* **1.** a little wing. **2.** *Zool.* alula. **3.** *Aeron.* **a.** a small wing used mainly to carry external loads or to connect struts or gears to the fuselage. **b.** a short, near-vertical projection on a wing tip that reduces drag and improves fuel efficiency. [1605–15; WING + -LET]

wing·like (wing′līk′), *adj.* resembling a wing. [WING + -LIKE]

wing′ load′ing, *Aeron.* See under **loading** (def. 4). [1910–15]

wing′ nut′, a nut having two flat, widely projecting pieces such that it can be readily tightened with the thumb and forefinger. Also, **wing′nut′.** Also called **butterfly nut, thumbnut.** See illus. under **nut.** [1895–1900]

wing·o·ver (wing′ō′vər), *n. Aeron.* an airplane maneuver involving a steep, climbing turn to a near stall, then a sharp drop of the nose, a removal of bank, and a final leveling off in the opposite direction. [1925–30; WING + OVER]

wings (wingz), *n.* (*used with a plural v.*) **1.** Also called **aviation badge.** *Mil. Informal.* a badge bearing the image of a spread pair of bird's wings with a distinctive center design, awarded to an aircrewman on completion of certain requirements. **2.** a gold-embroidered green badge in the shape of a spread pair of bird wings worn by junior and cadette Girl Scouts to indicate previous membership in a Brownie troop.

wing′ shoot′ing, *Hunting.* the act or practice of shooting at birds in flight. [1880–85]

wing′ shot′, *Hunting.* **1.** a shot at a bird in flight. **2.** an expert in shooting birds in flight. [1880–85]

wing′ skid′, *Aeron.* a skid attached to the wing tip of an airplane to prevent it from touching the ground.

Wings′ of the Dove′, The (duv), a novel (1902) by Henry James.

wing·span (wing′span′), *n.* **1.** the distance between the wing tips of an airplane. **2.** wingspread. [1915–20; WING + SPAN[1]]

wing·spread (wing′spred′), *n.* the distance between the most outward tips of the wings when they are as extended as possible. [1895–1900; WING + SPREAD]

wing′ tip′, 1. Also, **wing′tip′.** the extreme outer edge of an airplane wing. **2.** a toecap, often with a perforated pattern, having a point at the center and a piece at each side extending back along the top and sides. **3.** a style of shoe with such a toe. **4.** the portion of a bird's folded wing formed by the part of the primary feathers extending beyond the secondary feathers. [1870–75]

wing-wea·ry (wing′wēr′ē), *adj.* tired from flying or traveling.

wing·y (wing′ē), *adj.,* **wing·i·er, wing·i·est. 1.** having wings. **2.** rapid; swift. [1590–1600; WING + -Y[1]]

Win·i·fred (win′ə frid), *n.* a female given name.

wink[1] (wingk), *v.i.* **1.** to close and open one or both eyes quickly. **2.** to close and open one eye quickly as a hint or signal or with some sly meaning (often fol. by *at*): *She winked at him across the room.* **3.** (of the eyes) to close and open thus; blink. **4.** to shine with little flashes of light; twinkle: *The city lights winked in the distance.* —*v.t.* **5.** to close and open (one or both eyes) quickly; execute or give (a wink). **6.** to drive or force by winking (usually fol. by *back* or *away*): *She attempted to wink back the tears.* **7.** to signal or convey by a wink. **8. wink at,** to ignore deliberately, as to avoid the necessity of taking action: *to wink at minor offenses.* —*n.* **9.** an act of winking. **10.** a winking movement, esp. of one eye in giving a hint or signal. **11.** a hint or signal given by winking. **12.** the time required for winking once; an instant or twinkling: *I'll be there in a wink.* **13.** a little flash of light; twinkle. **14.** the least bit: *I didn't sleep a wink last night.* [bef. 900; (v.) ME *winken,* OE *wincian;* c. G *winken* to wave, signal; (n.) ME: nap, deriv. of the v.] —**wink′ing·ly,** *adv.*
—**Syn. 1.** WINK, BLINK refer to rapid motions of the eyelid. To WINK is to close and open either one or both eyelids with a rapid motion. To BLINK suggests a sleepy, dazed, or dazzled condition in which it is difficult to focus the eyes or see clearly: *Bright sun makes one blink.* **4.** sparkle.

wink[2] (wingk), *n. Games.* a disk or similar small object used in tiddlywinks. [1890–95; extracted from TIDDLY-WINKS]

wink·er (wing′kər), *n.* **1.** a person or thing that winks. **2.** a blinker or blinder for a horse. **3.** *Informal.* an eyelash or an eye. [1540–50; WINK[1] + -ER[1]]

win·kle (wing′kəl), *n., v.,* **-kled, -kling.** *Brit.* —*n.* **1.** any of various marine gastropods; periwinkle. —*v.t.* **2.** *Informal.* to pry (something) out of a place, as winkle meat is dug out of its shell with a pin (usually fol. by *out*). [1575–85; short for PERIWINKLE]

win·le·strae (win′l strā′), *n. Chiefly Scot.* windlestraw.

win·na·ble (win′ə bəl), *adj.* that can be won: *a winnable war.* [1535–45; WIN + -ABLE] —**win′na·bil′i·ty,** *n.*

Win·ne·ba·go (win′ə bā′gō), *n., pl.* **-gos,** (*esp. collectively*) **-go** for 1. **1.** a member of a North American Indian tribe speaking a Siouan language closely related to Assiniboin, Teton, and Mandan, formerly located in Green Bay, Wis., now living in Green Bay and NE Nebraska. **2. Lake,** a lake in E Wisconsin. 30 mi. (48 km) long.

Win·ne·pe·sau·kee (win′ə pə sô′kē), *n.* Winnipesaukee.

win·ner (win′ər), *n.* **1.** a person or thing that wins; victor. **2. winner take all,** a situation or outcome whereby the winner receives all the prizes or rewards. [1325–75; ME; see WIN, -ER[1]]

win′ner's cir′cle, 1. a small, usually circular area or enclosure at a racetrack where awards are bestowed on winning mounts and their jockeys. **2.** any select group of winners, achievers, or those that have been accepted as worthy: *the winner's circle of fine wines.* [1950–55]

Win·net·ka (wi net′kə), *n.* a city in NE Illinois, near Chicago. 12,772.

Win·nie (win′ē), *n.* **1.** a male given name, form of **Winston. 2.** a female given name, form of **Winifred.**

Win·nie-the-Pooh (win′ē thə po͞o′), *n.* a collection of children's stories (1926) by A. A. Milne.

win·ning (win′ing), *n.* **1.** the act of a person or thing that wins. **2.** Usually, **winnings.** something that is won, esp. money. **3.** *Mining.* **a.** any opening by which coal is being or has been extracted. **b.** a bed of coal ready for mining. —*adj.* **4.** that wins; successful or victorious, as in a contest: *the winning team.* **5.** charming; engaging; pleasing: *a winning child; a winning smile.* [1250–1300; ME (n.); see WIN, -ING[1], -ING[2]] —**win′ning·ly,** *adv.* —**win′ning·ness,** *n.*
—**Syn. 5.** captivating, attractive, winsome.

win•ning•est (win′ing ist), *adj. Informal.* **1.** winning most often: *the winningest coach in college basketball.* **2.** most winning or charming: *the winningest smile in town.* [1970–75; WINNING + -EST]

win′ning gal′lery, *Court Tennis.* a winning opening on the hazard side, below the penthouse and farthest from the dedans. Cf. **dedans** (def. 1), **grille** (def. 5). [1875–80]

win′ning haz′ard. See under **hazard** (def. 7).

win′ning o′pening, *Court Tennis.* the dedans, winning gallery, or grille. [1875–80]

win′ning post′, a post on a racetrack, marking the goal of a race. [1810–20]

Win•ni•peg (win′ə peg′), *n.* **1.** a city in and the capital of Manitoba, in S Canada, on the Red River. 560,874. **2. Lake,** a lake in S Canada, in Manitoba. ab. 260 mi. (420 km) long; ab. 9300 sq. mi. (24,085 sq. km). **3.** a river in S Canada, flowing NW from the Lake of the Woods to Lake Winnipeg. ab. 200 mi. (320 km) long. —**Win′ni•peg′ger,** *n.*

Win•ni•pe•go•sis (win′ə pi gō′sis), *n.* **Lake,** a lake in S Canada, in W Manitoba, W of Lake Winnipeg. 2086 sq. mi. (5405 sq. km).

Win•ni•pe•sau•kee (win′ə pə sô′kē), *n.* **Lake,** a lake in central New Hampshire: summer resort. 25 mi. (40 km) long. Also, **Winnepesaukee.**

win•nock (win′ək), *n. Scot.* window. [1485–95; *windok,* Scots var. of ME *windoge* WINDOW]

win•now (win′ō), *v.t.* **1.** to free (grain) from the lighter particles of chaff, dirt, etc., esp. by throwing it into the air and allowing the wind or a forced current of air to blow away impurities. **2.** to drive or blow (chaff, dirt, etc.) away by fanning. **3.** to blow upon; fan. **4.** to subject to some process of separating or distinguishing; analyze critically; sift: *to winnow a mass of statements.* **5.** to separate or distinguish (valuable from worthless parts) (sometimes fol. by *out*): *to winnow falsehood from truth.* **6.** to pursue (a course) with flapping wings in flying. **7.** to fan or stir (the air) as with the wings in flying. —*v.i.* **8.** to free grain from chaff by wind or driven air. **9.** to fly with flapping wings; flutter. —*n.* **10.** a device or contrivance used for winnowing. **11.** an act of winnowing. [bef. 900; ME *win(d)wen* (v.), OE *windwian,* deriv. of *wind* WIND[1]] —**win′now•er,** *n.*

Win•ny (win′ē), *n.* **1.** a male given name, form of **Winston.** **2.** a female given name, form of **Winifred.**

win•o (wī′nō), *n., pl.* **win•os.** *Informal.* a person who is addicted to wine, esp. a derelict. [1915–20; WINE + -O]

Wi•no•na (wi nō′nə), *n.* **1.** a city in SE Minnesota, on the Mississippi. 25,075. **2.** a female given name.

Wins•low (winz′lō), *n.* **1. Edward,** 1595–1655, English colonist and author in America: governor of the Plymouth colony 1633, 1639, 1644. **2.** a male given name.

win•some (win′səm), *adj.* sweetly or innocently charming; winning; engaging: *a winsome smile.* [bef. 900; ME *winsom,* OE *wynsum,* equiv. to *wyn* joy (see WYNN) + *-sum* -SOME[1]] —**win′some•ly,** *adv.* —**win′some•ness,** *n.*

Win•sor (win′zər), *n.* **Justin,** 1831–97, U.S. librarian and historian.

Win•ston (win′stən), *n.* a male given name.

Win•ston-Sa•lem (win′stən sā′ləm), *n.* a city in N North Carolina. 131,885.

win•ter (win′tər), *n.* **1.** the cold season between autumn and spring in northern latitudes (in the Northern Hemisphere from the winter solstice to the vernal equinox; in the Southern Hemisphere from the summer solstice to the autumnal equinox). **2.** the months of December, January, and February in the U.S., and of November, December, and January in Great Britain. **3.** cold weather: *a touch of winter in northern Florida.* **4.** the colder half of the year (opposed to *summer*). **5.** a whole year as represented by this season: *a man of sixty winters.* **6.** a period like winter, as the last or final period of life; a period of decline, decay, inertia, dreariness, or adversity. —*adj.* **7.** of, pertaining to, or characteristic of winter: *a winter sunset.* **8.** (of fruit and vegetables) of a kind that may be kept for use during the winter. **9.** planted in the autumn to be harvested in the spring or early summer: *winter rye.* —*v.i.* **10.** to spend or pass the winter: *to winter in Italy.* **11.** to keep, feed, or manage during the winter, as plants or cattle: *plants wintering indoors.* [bef. 900; (n.) ME, OE; c. G *Winter,* ON *vetr,* Goth *wintrus;* (v.) ME, deriv. of the n.; akin to WET, WATER] —**win′ter•er,** *n.* —**win′ter•ish,** *adj.* —**win′ter•ish•ly,** *adv.* —**win′ter•less,** *adj.*

win′ter ac′onite, a small Old World plant, *Eranthis hyemalis,* of the buttercup family, often cultivated for its bright-yellow flowers, which appear very early in the spring. [1785–95]

win′ter bar′ley, barley that is planted in the autumn to be harvested in the spring or early summer. [1570–80]

win•ter•ber•ry (win′tər ber′ē), *n., pl.* **-ries. 1.** any of several North American hollies of the genus *Ilex,* having red berries that are persistent through the winter. **2.** See **black alder** (def. 1). [1750–60; WINTER + BERRY]

win•ter•bourne (win′tər bôrn′, -bōrn′, -bŏŏrn′), *n.* a channel filled only at a time of excessive rainfall. [bef. 950; OE *winterburna* (not recorded in ME). See WINTER, BURN[2]]

win′ter cher′ry, 1. Also called **Chinese lantern plant.** a Eurasian ground cherry, *Physalis alkekengi,* of the nightshade family, bearing fruit enclosed in a showy, orange-red, inflated calyx. **2.** the red, berrylike fruit of this plant. Also called **alkekengi.** [1540–50]

CONCISE ETYMOLOGY KEY: <, descended or borrowed from; >, whence; b., blend of, blended; c., cognate with; cf., compare; deriv., derivative; equiv., equivalent; imit., imitative; obl., oblique; r., replacing; s., stem; sp., spelling, spelled; resp., respelling, respelled; trans., translation; ?, origin unknown; *, unattested; ‡, probably earlier than. See the full key inside the front cover.

win′ter cress′, any cress belonging to the genus *Barbarea,* of the mustard family, having lyrate leaves and yellow flowers. [1540–50]

win′ter crook′neck, any of several winter varieties of squash, *Cucurbita moschata,* having elongated, curved necks. [1905–10]

win•ter•feed (win′tər fēd′), *v.,* **-fed, -feed•ing,** *n.* —*v.t.* **1.** to feed (cattle, sheep, etc.) during the winter when pasturage is not available. **2.** to supply (grain, hay, etc.) to livestock in winter. —*v.i.* **3.** to provide feed for livestock in winter. —*n.* **4.** the feed given to livestock during the winter. [1595–1605; WINTER + FEED]

win′ter floun′der. See under **lemon sole.** [1805–15]

Win′ter Games′, Olympic Games held every fourth winter and including skiing, ice-skating, bobsledding, and other primarily winter sports. Cf. **Summer Games.**

win′ter gar′den, 1. an outdoor garden maintained during the winter with hardy plants. **2.** a conservatory devoted to the cultivation of winter-blooming plants. [1775–85]

win•ter•green (win′tər grēn′), *n.* **1.** Also called **checkerberry.** a small, creeping, evergreen shrub, *Gaultheria procumbens,* of the heath family, common in eastern North America, having white, bell-shaped flowers, a bright-red, berrylike fruit, and aromatic leaves that yield a volatile oil. **2.** the oil of this shrub; wintergreen oil; methyl salicylate. **3.** the flavor of this oil or something flavored with it. **4.** any of various other plants of the same genus. **5.** any of various small evergreen herbs of the genera *Pyrola* and *Chimaphila.* [1540–50; trans. of D *wintergroen* or G *Wintergrün*]

win′tergreen bar′berry, a Chinese evergreen shrub, *Berberis julianae,* of the barberry family, having spiny leaves, dark green above, pale beneath, clusters of yellow flowers, and bluish-black fruit.

win′tergreen oil′. See **methyl salicylate.** [1835–45]

win•ter-har•dy (win′tər här′dē), *adj.* (esp. of plants, shrubs, or the like) able to survive the effects of cold weather. Also, **win′ter•har′dy.** —**win′ter-har′di•ness, win′ter•har′di•ness,** *n.*

Win′ter Ha′ven, a city in central Florida. 21,119.

win•ter•ize (win′tə rīz′), *v.,* **-ized, -iz•ing.** —*v.t.* **1.** to prepare (an automobile, house, etc.) for cold weather by (in automobiles) adding antifreeze and changing oil or (in houses) adding insulation, heating units, etc. —*v.i.* **2.** to winterize an automobile, house, etc. Also, *esp. Brit.,* **win′ter•ise′.** [1925–30; WINTER + -IZE] —**win′ter•i•za′tion,** *n.* —**win′ter•iz′er,** *n.*

win′ter jas′mine, a shrub, *Jasminum nudiflorum,* of China, having winter-blooming, yellow flowers.

win•ter•kill (win′tər kil′), *v.t., v.i.* **1.** to kill by or die from exposure to the cold of winter, as wheat. —*n.* **2.** an act or instance of winterkilling. **3.** death resulting from winterkilling. [1810–20; WINTER + KILL[1]]

win•ter•ly (win′tər lē), *adj.* **1.** of, pertaining to, or occurring in winter; hibernal. **2.** wintry. [bef. 1000; OE *winterlic* (not recorded in ME); see WINTER, -LY]

win′ter mel′on, a variety of late-keeping muskmelon, *Cucumis melo inodorus,* having a sweet, edible flesh. [1895–1900]

win′ter oats′, oats that are planted in the autumn to be harvested in the spring or early summer.

Win′ter Olym′pics. See **Winter Games.**

Win′ter Park′, a city in E Florida. 22,314.

win′ter purs′lane, a plant, *Montia perfoliata,* native to western North America, of the purslane family, having edible, egg-shaped leaves and clusters of small, white flowers. Also called **miner's lettuce.**

Win•ter•rei•se, Die (*Ger.* dē vin′tə rī′zə), a song cycle (1827) by Franz Schubert, consisting of 24 songs set to poems of Wilhelm Müller.

win′ter rose′. See **Christmas rose.** [1735–45]

Win•ters (win′tərz), *n.* **Y•vor** (ī′vôr), 1900–68, U.S. poet and critic.

win′ter sa′vory. See under **savory[2].** [1590–1600]

Win′ter's bark′, (*sometimes l.c.*) an evergreen tree, *Drimys winteri,* ranging from Mexico to Cape Horn, having aromatic leaves and cream-colored, jasmine-scented flowers. [1615–25; named after William *Winter,* 16th-century English captain]

Win•ter•set (win′tər set′), *n.* a drama in verse (1935) by Maxwell Anderson.

win′ter sol′stice, *Astron.* the solstice on or about December 21st that marks the beginning of winter in the Northern Hemisphere. [1625–35]

Win′ter Springs′, a town in central Florida. 10,475.

win′ter squash′, any of several varieties of *Cucurbita maxima* or *C. moschata* that mature in late autumn and are used, when ripe, as a vegetable. [1740–50]

Win′ter's Tale′, The, a drama (1610–11?) by Shakespeare.

win•ter•sweet (win′tər swēt′), *n.* a shrub, *Chimonanthus praecox,* native to China, having large leaves and fragrant yellow flowers. [1890–95; WINTER + SWEET]

Win•ter•thur (vin′tər tŏŏr′; *Ger.* vin′tər tōōr′), *n.* a city in Zurich canton, in N Switzerland, NE of Zurich. 91,000.

win•ter•tide (win′tər tīd′), *n. Literary.* wintertime. [bef. 900; ME; OE *wintertīd.* See WINTER, TIDE[1]]

win•ter•time (win′tər tīm′), *n.* the season of winter. [1350–1400; ME; r. ME *wintertide* WINTERTIDE]

win′ter vetch′. See **hairy vetch.**

win′ter wheat′, wheat that is planted in the autumn to be harvested in the spring or early summer. [1665–75]

win′ter wren′, (in the Western Hemisphere) a small wren, *Troglodytes troglodytes,* of coniferous forests. [1800–10, *Amer.*]

win•ter•y (win′tə rē, -trē), *adj.,* **-ter•i•er, -ter•i•est.** wintry.

Win•throp (win′thrəp), *n.* **1. John,** 1588–1649, English colonist in America: 1st governor of the Massachusetts Bay colony 1629–33, 1637–40, 1642–44, 1646–49. **2.** his son, **John,** 1606–76, English colonist in America: colonial governor of Connecticut 1657, 1659–76. **3. John** or **Fitz-John** (fits′jon′), 1638–1707, American soldier and statesman: colonial governor of Connecticut 1698–1707 (son of the younger John Winthrop). **4. John,** 1714–79, American astronomer, mathematician, and physicist. **5. Robert Charles,** 1809–94, U.S. politician: Speaker of the House 1847–49. **6.** a town in E Massachusetts, near Boston. 19,294. **7.** a male given name.

Win′throp desk′. See **Governor Winthrop desk.**

win•tle (win′tl), *n., v.,* **-tled, -tling.** *Scot.* —*n.* **1.** a rolling or staggering motion. —*v.i.* **2.** to roll or swing back and forth. **3.** to tumble over; capsize. [1775–85; < early D *windtelen* (D *wentelen*) to revolve, freq. of *winden* to WIND[2]]

win•try (win′trē), *adj.,* **-tri•er, -tri•est. 1.** of or characteristic of winter: *wintry blasts; wintry skies.* **2.** resembling winter weather; having snow, frost, cold, storms, etc.: *We had wintry weather well into May last year.* **3.** suggestive of winter, as in lack of warmth or cheer: *a wintry manner.* Also, **wintery.** [bef. 900; OE *wintrig* (not recorded in ME); see WINTER, -Y[1]] —**win′tri•ly,** *adv.* —**win′tri•ness,** *n.*
—**Syn. 3.** cold, bleak, cheerless.

Win•tu (win tōō′, win′tōō), *n., pl.* **-tus,** *esp. collectively* **-tu** for 1. **1.** a member of an American Indian people of the Sacramento River valley in California. **2.** the Wintun language of the Wintu. Also called **Wintun.**

Win•tun (win tōōn′, win′tōōn), *n.* **1.** Also called **Copehan.** a small family of North American Indian languages of Penutian stock spoken in northern California and including Wintu and Patwin. **2.** Wintu.

win-win (win′win′), *adj.* advantageous to both sides, as in a negotiation: *a win-win proposal; a win-win situation.* [1980–85]

win•y (wī′nē), *adj.,* **win•i•er, win•i•est. 1.** of, like, or characteristic of wine. **2.** affected by wine. Also, **winey.** [1350–1400; ME; see WINE, -Y[1]]

winze[1] (winz), *n. Mining.* a vertical or inclined shaft driven downward from a drift into an orebody. Also, **windz.** Cf. **raise** (def. 39). [1750–60; earlier *winds,* appar. deriv. of WIND[2] in obs. n. sense "apparatus for winding"]

winze[2] (winz), *n. Scot.* a curse. [1775–85; perh. < D *wens* wish, *wensen* to wish; see WISH]

WIP, 1. work in process. **2.** work in progress. Also, **W.I.P.**

wipe (wīp), *v.,* **wiped, wip•ing,** *n.* —*v.t.* **1.** to rub lightly with or on a cloth, towel, paper, the hand, etc., in order to clean or dry the surface of: *He wiped the furniture with a damp cloth.* **2.** to rub or draw (something) over a surface, as in cleaning or drying. **3.** to remove by rubbing with or on something (usually fol. by *away, off, out,* etc.): *Wipe the dirt off your shoes.* **4.** to remove as if by rubbing (usually fol. by *away, off,* etc.): *Wipe that smile off your face!* **5.** to erase, as from existence or memory (often fol. by *from*): *to wipe a thought from one's mind.* **6.** to erase (magnetic tape, a recording, etc.). **7.** *Plumbing.* **a.** to apply (solder in a semifluid state) by spreading with leather or cloth. **b.** to form (a joint) in this manner. **8.** *Mach.* (of a rotating shaft or the like) to melt the brasses of (a bearing) through friction. **9.** *Australian Slang.* to refuse to have anything to do with; reject; dismiss. **10. wipe out, a.** to destroy completely; demolish: *The entire city was wiped out.* **b.** *Informal.* to murder; kill: *They wiped him out to keep him from testifying.* **c.** *Slang.* to beat decisively, as in sports. **d.** *Slang.* (in sports) to be taken out of competition by a fall, accident, collision, etc. **e.** *Slang.* to intoxicate or cause to become high, esp. on narcotic drugs. **11. wipe up,** to clean completely by wiping: *to wipe up the mess on the floor.* —*n.* **12.** an act of wiping: *He gave a few quick wipes to the furniture.* **13.** a rub, as of one thing over another. **14.** Also called **wipe′-off′.** *Motion Pictures.* a technique in film editing by which the projected image of a scene appears to be pushed or wiped off the screen by the image that follows. **15.** a piece of absorbent material, as of paper or cloth, used for wiping. **16.** a sweeping stroke or blow. **17.** a gibe. **18.** *Mach.* wiper (def. 5). **19.** *Slang.* a handkerchief. [bef. 1000; ME (v.), OE *wīpian;* c. OHG *wīfan* to wind round, Goth *weipan* to crown; perh. akin to L *vibrāre* to move to and fro]
—**Syn. 4.** erase, eradicate, banish.

wiped-out (wīpt′out′), *adj. Slang.* **1.** completely exhausted. **2.** intoxicated; high. Also, **wiped.** [1960–65]

wipe•out (wīp′out′), *n.* **1.** *Informal.* destruction, annihilation, or murder. **2.** (in sports) *Informal.* a decisive defeat. **3.** a fall from a surfboard. **4.** *Slang.* a total or complete failure: *to suffer a wipeout in the stock market.* **5.** *Slang.* complete physical exhaustion. Also, **wipe′-out′.** [1920–25; n. use of v. phrase *wipe out*]

wip•er (wī′pər), *n.* **1.** a person or thing that wipes. **2.** the thing with which something is wiped, as a towel or squeegee. **3.** See **windshield wiper.** **4.** *Elect.* the portion of a selector or other similar device that makes contact with the terminals of a bank. **5.** Also, **wipe.** *Mach.* a projection or partial cam, as on a rotating shaft, moving to lift or dislodge another part, esp. so as to let it drop when released. [1545–50; WIPE + -ER[1]]

Wi•ra•dju•ri (wē′rä jŏŏr′ē), *n.* an Australian Aboriginal language, spoken over a wide area of central New South Wales.

wire (wīər), *n., adj., v.,* **wired, wir•ing.** —*n.* **1.** a slender, stringlike piece or filament of relatively rigid or flexible metal, usually circular in section, manufactured in a great variety of diameters and metals depending on its application. **2.** such pieces as a material. **3.** a length of such material, consisting either of a single filament or of several filaments woven or twisted together and usually insulated with a dielectric material, used as a conductor of electricity. **4.** a cross wire or a cross hair. **5.** a barbed-wire fence. **6.** a long wire or cable used in cable, telegraph, or telephone systems. **7.** *Naut.* a wire rope. **8.** *Informal.* **a.** a telegram. **b.** the telegraphic system: *to send a message by wire.* **9. wires,** a system of wires by which puppets are moved. **10.** a metallic string of a musical instrument. **11.** *Underworld Slang.* the member of a pickpocket team who picks the victim's pocket. Cf. **stall**[2] (def. 5). **12.** *Horse Racing.* a wire stretched across and above the track at the finish line, under which the horses pass. **13.** *Ornith.* one of the extremely long, slender, wirelike filaments or shafts of the plumage of various birds. **14.** a metal device for snaring rabbits and other small game. **15.** *Papermaking.* the woven wire mesh over which the wet pulp is spread in a papermaking machine. **16. down to the wire,** to the very last moment or the very end, as in a race or competition: *The candidates campaigned down to the wire.* **17. pull wires,** *Informal.* to use one's position or influence to obtain a desired result: *to pull wires to get someone a job.* **18. the wire,** the telephone: *There's someone on the wire for you.* **19. under the wire,** just within the limit or deadline; scarcely; barely: *to get an application in under the wire.* —*adj.* **20.** made of wire; consisting of or constructed with wires. **21.** resembling wire; wirelike. —*v.t.* **22.** to furnish with wires. **23.** to install an electric system of wiring in, as for lighting. **24.** to fasten or bind with wire: *He wired the halves together.* **25.** to put on a wire, as beads. **26.** to send by telegraph, as a message: *Please wire the money at once.* **27.** to send a telegraphic message to: *She wired him to come at once.* **28.** to snare by means of a wire. **29.** to equip with a hidden electronic device, as an eavesdropping device or an explosive. **30.** to connect (a receiver, area, or building) to a television cable and other equipment so that cable television programs may be received. **31.** *Informal.* to be closely connected or involved with: *a law firm wired into political circles.* **32.** *Informal.* to prepare, equip, fix, or arrange to suit needs or goals: *The sales force was wired for an all-out effort.* **33.** *Croquet.* to block (a ball) by placing it behind the wire of an arch. —*v.i.* **34.** to send a telegraphic message; telegraph: *Don't write; wire.* [bef. 900; ME *wir(e)* (n.), OE *wīr;* c. LG *wir,* ON *vīra-* wire, OHG *wiara* fine goldwork] —**wir′a·ble,** *adj.* —**wire′like′,** *adj.*

wire′ a′gency. See **wire service.**

wire′ brush′, a brush with steel bristles for removing rust, flaking paint, etc.

wire-brush (wīər′brush′), *v.t.* to clean or remove with a wire brush.

wire′ cloth′, a material of wires of moderate fineness, used for making strainers, manufacturing paper, etc. [1790–1800] —**wire′-cloth′,** *adj.*

wire′ cut′ter, any of various devices designed to cut wire. [1870–75]

wired (wīərd), *adj.* **1.** equipped with wires, as for electricity or telephone service. **2.** made of wire; consisting of or constructed with wires: *a wired barrier.* **3.** tied or secured with wires: *wired bales of wastepaper.* **4.** strengthened or supported with wires: *a sculpture of wired papier-mâché.* **5.** *Slang.* tense with excitement or anticipation; edgy. **6.** equipped so as to receive cable television. [1375–1425; late ME; see WIRE, -ED[3]]

wire·draw (wīər′drô′), *v.t.,* **-drew, -drawn, -draw·ing.** **1.** to draw (metal) out into wire, esp. by pulling forcibly through a series of holes of gradually decreasing diameter in a succession of dies. **2.** to draw out to great length, in quantity or time; stretch out to excess. **3.** to strain unwarrantably, as in meaning. [1590–1600; back formation from *wiredrawer;* see WIRE, DRAWER] —**wire·draw·er** (wīər′drô′ər), *n.*

wire·drawn (wīər′drôn′), *adj.* **1.** drawn out long and thin like a wire. **2.** (of ideas, comparisons, etc.) finely spun; extremely intricate; minute. [1595–1605; WIRE + DRAWN]

wire′ entan′glement, a barbed-wire obstacle, usually mounted on posts and zigzagged back and forth along a front, designed to channel, delay, or halt an advance by enemy foot soldiers. [1875–80]

wire′ gauge′, a gauge calibrated for determining the diameter of wire. [1825–35]

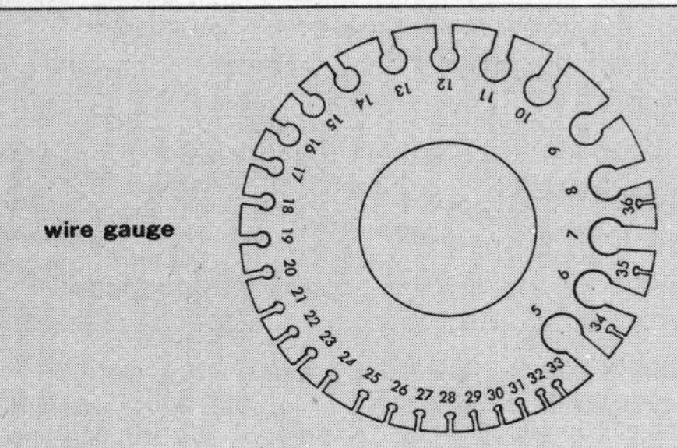
wire gauge

wire′ gauze′, a gauzelike fabric woven of very fine wires. [1810–20]

wire′ glass′, a pane or sheet of glass having a network of wire embedded within it as a reinforcement. [1895–1900]

wire′ grass′. See **Canada bluegrass.** [1745–55, *Amer.*]

wire·hair (wīər′hâr′), *n.* a fox terrier having a wiry coat. Also called **wire′-haired ter′rier.** [1880–85; WIRE + HAIR]

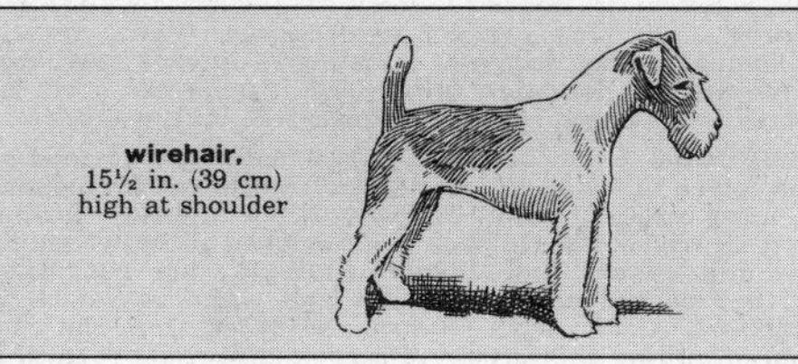
wirehair, 15½ in. (39 cm) high at shoulder

wire·haired (wīər′hârd′), *adj.* having coarse, stiff, wirelike hair. Also, **wire′-haired′.** [1795–1805; WIRE + HAIRED]

wire′haired point′ing grif′fon, griffon[2] (def. 2). [1925–30]

wire′ house′, *Stock Exchange.* a brokerage firm with branch offices connected with their main office by a private system of telephone, telegraph, and teletype wires. Also, **wire′house′.**

wire·less (wīər′lis), *adj.* **1.** having no wire. **2.** noting or pertaining to any of various devices that are operated with or actuated by electromagnetic waves. **3.** *Chiefly Brit.* radio. —*n.* **4.** wireless telegraphy or telephony. **5.** a wireless telegraph or telephone, or the like. **6.** a wireless message. **7.** *Chiefly Brit.* radio. —*v.t., v.i.* **8.** to telegraph or telephone by wireless. [1890–95; WIRE + -LESS] —**wire′less·ly,** *adv.* —**wire′less·ness,** *n.*

wire′less teleg′raphy, *Now Rare.* radiotelegraphy. [1895–1900] —**wire′less tel′egraph.**

wire′less teleph′ony, *Now Rare.* radiotelephony. —**wire′less tel′ephone.**

wire·man (wīər′mən), *n., pl.* **-men.** **1.** a person who installs and maintains electric wiring. **2.** *Slang.* a professional wiretapper. [1540–50; WIRE + -MAN]

wire′ net′ting, netting made of interwoven wire, coarser than wire gauze. [1850–55]

Wire·pho·to (wīər′fō′tō), *pl.* **-tos,** *v.,* **-toed, -to·ing.** **1.** *Trademark.* **a.** a device for transmitting photographs over distances by wire. **b.** a photograph so transmitted. —*v.t.* **2.** (*l.c.*) to transmit (a photograph) by means of a Wirephoto.

wire·pull·er (wīər′po͝ol′ər), *n.* **1.** a person or thing that pulls wires. **2.** a person who uses secret means to direct and control the actions of others, esp. for selfish ends; intriguer. **3.** snake (def. 3b). [1825–30, *Amer.;* WIRE + PULLER]

wire·pull·ing (wīər′po͝ol′ing), *n.* **1.** an act of pulling wires. **2.** the use of influence to manipulate persons or organizations, as political organizations, for one's own ends. [1825–35; WIRE + PULLING]

wir·er (wīər′ər), *n.* **1.** a person who wires. **2.** a person who uses wire to snare game. [1855–60; WIRE + -ER[1]]

wire′ record′er, a forerunner of the tape recorder that recorded sound on a steel wire by magnetizing the wire as it passed an electromagnet. [1940–45]

wire′ record′ing, **1.** a recording made on a wire recorder. **2.** an act or instance of recording on a wire recorder.

wire·room (wīər′ro͞om′, -ro͝om′), *n.* **1.** a bookmaking establishment, esp. one disguised as a lawful business. **2.** a room, as in a newspaper office or television station, containing a teletype or other equipment for receiving news. [WIRE + ROOM]

wire′ rope′, a rope made of or containing strands of wire twisted together. [1835–45]

wire′ serv′ice, a business organization that gathers news, news photos, the latest stock-market prices, etc., for distribution, usually by teletypewriter, to its subscribers, esp. newspapers: so called from the original transmission of news by telegraph wire. Also called **wire agency.** [1940–45]

wire′ side′, the wrong side of a sheet of paper; the side against the wire during manufacture. Cf. **felt side.**

wire·sonde (wīər′sond′), *n. Meteorol.* an instrument carried aloft by a captive balloon and sending temperature and humidity data over a wire cable. [WIRE + SONDE]

wire·spun (wīər′spun′), *adj.* **1.** drawn out as wire is. **2.** overly subtle; obscure. **3.** having too little substance. [WIRE + SPUN]

wire-stitch (wīər′stich′), *v.t. Bookbinding.* to stitch (the backs of gathered sections) by means of a machine that automatically forms staples from a continuous reel of wire. —**wire′-stitch′er,** *n.*

wire·tap (wīər′tap′), *n., v.,* **-tapped, -tap·ping,** *adj.* —*n.* **1.** an act or instance of tapping telephone or telegraph wires for evidence or other information. —*v.t.* **2.** to obtain (information, evidence, etc.) by tapping telephone or telegraph wires: *to wiretap conversations.* **3.** to listen in on by means of a wiretap: *to wiretap a telephone; to wiretap a conversation.* —*v.i.* **4.** to tap telephone or telegraph wires for evidence, information, etc. —*adj.* **5.** pertaining to or obtained by wiretap. [1950–55; back formation from WIRETAPPER]

wire·tap·per (wīər′tap′ər), *n.* **1.** a person who taps wires to learn the nature of messages passing over them. **2.** a swindler who professes to have betting tips or other information from tapped telephone wires. [1890–95; WIRE + TAPPER[2]]

wire′ trans′fer, an order transmitted by telephone, telegraph, or electronically from one bank to another to pay or credit money to a payee designated by a payer.

wire-trans·fer (wīər′trans fûr′, -trans′fər), *v.t.,* **-ferred, -fer·ring.** to transmit (money or credit) by wire transfer.

wire′ vine′, a twining vine, *Muehlenbeckia complexa,* of the buckwheat family, native to New Zealand, having wirelike stems and circular leaves. Also called **maidenhair-vine.**

wire·way (wīər′wā′), *n.* a prefabricated, enclosed passage for electrical wiring, as in a building. [1905–10; WIRE + WAY[1]]

wire wheel (wīər′ hwēl′, wēl′ *for 1;* wīər′ hwēl′, wēl′ *for 2*), **1.** a wheellike brush having stiff wire bristles and used esp. for finishing or cleaning metal. **2.** a wheel, as on a sports car, having wire spokes. [1905–10]

wire·work (wīər′wûrk′), *n.* fabrics or articles made of wire. [1580–90; WIRE + WORK]

wire·works (wīər′wûrks′), *n., pl.* **-works.** (*used with a singular or plural v.*) an establishment where wire is made or put to some industrial use. [1590–1600; WIRE + WORKS] —**wire′work′er,** *n.*

wire·worm (wīər′wûrm′), *n.* **1.** any of the slender, hard-bodied larvae of click beetles, many of which live underground and feed on the roots of plants. **2.** any of various small myriapods. **3.** See **stomach worm.** [1780–90; WIRE + WORM]

wire′-wound resis′tor (wīər′wound′), *Elect.* a resistor consisting of a wire with a high resistance wound in a coil around a cylindrical core of insulating material. Also, **wire′wound resis′tor.**

wire-wove (wīər′wōv′), *adj.* **1.** made of woven wire. **2.** noting fine, glazed paper used esp. as letter paper. [1790–1800; WIRE + WOVE]

wir·ing (wīər′ing), *n.* **1.** an act of a person who wires. **2.** *Elect.* the aggregate of wires in a lighting system, switchboard, radio, etc. [1800–10; WIRE + -ING[1]]

wir′ing har′ness, *Elect.* a system of insulated conducting wires bound together with insulating materials, used in the electrical system of a machine, as a motor vehicle or washing machine. Also called **harness.**

wir·ra (wir′ə), *interj. Irish Eng.* an exclamation of sorrow or lament. [1830–40; < Ir *A Mhuire!* Mary!, an appeal to the Virgin]

Wirtz (wûrts), *n.* **William Willard,** born 1912, U.S. lawyer and government official: Secretary of Labor 1962–69.

wir·y (wīər′ē), *adj.,* **wir·i·er, wir·i·est.** **1.** made of wire. **2.** in the form of wire. **3.** resembling wire, as in form, stiffness, etc.: *wiry grass.* **4.** lean and sinewy: *a wiry little person.* **5.** produced by or resembling the sound of a vibrating wire: *wiry tones.* [1580–90; WIRE + -Y[1]] —**wir′i·ly,** *adv.* —**wir′i·ness,** *n.*

wis (wis), *v.t., v.i. Archaic.* to know. [1500–10; by false analysis of IWIS as *I wis* I know; see WIT[2]]

Wis., Wisconsin. Also, **Wisc.**

Wis·by (vis′bē), *n.* German name of **Visby.**

WISC (wisk), Wechsler Intelligence Scale for Children. See under **Wechsler Scales.**

Wis·con·sin (wis kon′sən), *n.* **1.** a state in the N central United States: a part of the Midwest. 4,705,335; 56,154 sq. mi. (145,440 sq. km). *Cap.:* Madison. *Abbr.:* WI (for use with zip code), Wis., Wisc. **2.** a river flowing SW from N Wisconsin to the Mississippi. 430 mi. (690 km) long. **3.** the fourth stage of the glaciation of North America during the Pleistocene. Cf. **Würm.** —**Wis·con′sin·ite′,** *n.*

Wiscon′sin Rap′ids, a city in central Wisconsin. 17,995.

WISC-R (wisk′är′), Wechsler Intelligence Scale for Children—Revised. See under **Wechsler Scales.**

Wisd., Wisdom of Solomon.

wis·dom (wiz′dəm), *n.* **1.** the quality or state of being wise; knowledge of what is true or right coupled with just judgment as to action; sagacity, discernment, or insight. **2.** scholarly knowledge or learning: *the wisdom of the schools.* **3.** wise sayings or teachings; precepts. **4.** a wise act or saying. **5.** (*cap.*) *Douay Bible.* See **Wisdom of Solomon.** [bef. 900; ME, OE *wīsdōm;* c. ON *vīsdōmr,* G *Weistum.* See WISE[1], -DOM] —**wis′dom·less,** *adj.*
—**Syn. 1.** sense, understanding. **2.** sapience, erudition, enlightenment. See **information.** —**Ant. 1.** stupidity. **2.** ignorance.

Wis′dom of Je′sus, Son′ of Si′rach, Ecclesiasticus.

Wis′dom of Sol′omon, a book of the Apocrypha.

wis′dom tooth′, **1.** the third molar on each side of the upper and lower jaws: the last tooth to erupt. **2. cut one's wisdom teeth,** to attain maturity or discretion. [1660–70]

wise[1] (wīz), *adj.,* **wis·er, wis·est,** *v.,* **wised, wis·ing.** —*adj.* **1.** having the power of discerning and judging

properly as to what is true or right; possessing discernment, judgment, or discretion. **2.** characterized by or showing such power; judicious or prudent: *a wise decision.* **3.** possessed of or characterized by scholarly knowledge or learning; learned; erudite: *wise in the law.* **4.** having knowledge or information as to facts, circumstances, etc.: *We are wiser for their explanations.* **5.** *Slang.* informed; in the know: *You're wise, so why not give us the low-down?* **6.** *Archaic.* having knowledge of magic or witchcraft. **7. be** or **get wise to,** *Slang.* to be or become cognizant of or no longer deceived by; catch on: *to get wise to a fraud.* **8. get wise,** *Slang.* **a.** to become informed. **b.** to be or become presumptuous or impertinent: *Don't get wise with me, young man!* **9. put** or **set someone wise,** *Slang.* to inform a person; let a person in on a secret or generally unknown fact: *Some of the others put him wise to what was going on.* —*v.t.* **10.** *Slang.* to make wise or aware: *I'll wise you, kid.* **11. wise up,** *Slang.* to make or become aware of a secret or generally unknown fact, situation, attitude, etc.: *They wised him up on how to please the boss. She never wised up to the fact that the joke was on her.* [bef. 900; ME (adj.), OE *wīs;* c. D *wijs,* G *weise,* ON *viss,* Goth *-weis;* akin to WIT[1]] —**wise′ly,** *adv.*
—**Syn. 1, 2.** sage, sensible, sagacious, intelligent.
—**Ant. 1, 2.** foolish.

wise[2] (wīz), *n.* way of proceeding or considering; manner; fashion (usually used in combination or in certain phrases): *otherwise; in any wise; in no wise.* [bef. 900; ME, OE: way, manner; melody (OE); c. D *wijze,* G *Weise* manner, melody, ON *vīsa* short poem, Dan *vise* ballad; akin to Gk *eîdos* form, shape]

wise[3] (wīz), *v.t.,* **wised, wis•ing. 1.** *Chiefly Scot.* **a.** to instruct. **b.** to induce or advise. **c.** to show the way to; guide. **2.** *Scot.* to direct the course of; cause to turn. [bef. 900; ME *wisen,* OE *wīsian* to show the way, guide, direct, akin to *wīs* WISE[1]; c. OHG *wīsan,* ON *vīsa*]

Wise (wīz), *n.* **1. Isaac May•er** (mī′ər), 1819–1900, U.S. rabbi and educator, born in Bohemia: founder of Reform Judaism in the U.S. **2. Stephen Samuel,** 1874–1949, U.S. rabbi, theologian, and Zionist leader; born in Hungary.

-wise, a suffixal use of **wise**[2] in adverbs denoting manner, position, direction, reference, etc.: *counterclockwise; edgewise; marketwise; timewise.* Cf. **-ways.**
—**Usage.** The suffix -WISE is old in the language in adverbs referring to manner, direction, etc.: *crosswise; lengthwise.* Coinages like *marketwise, saleswise,* and *weatherwise* are often criticized, perhaps because of their association with the media: *Otherwise—or moneywise, as they were already saying in the motion-picture industry—Hollywood was at the crest of its supercolossal glory.* This suffix should not be confused with the adjective WISE[1], which appears in such compound words as *streetwise* and *worldly-wise.*

wise•a•cre (wīz′ā′kər), *n.* **1.** a person who possesses or affects to possess great wisdom. **2.** See **wise guy.** [1585–95; < MD *wijssager* prophet, trans. of MHG *wīssage,* late OHG *wīssago,* by popular etym. equiv. to *wīs* wise + *sago* sayer, from earlier *wīzzago* wise person; c. OE *wītega,* akin to WIT[2]]

wise-ass (wīz′as′), *Slang (sometimes vulgar).* —*adj.* **1.** Also, **wise′-assed′.** insolent; impertinent; smart-ass. —*n.* **2.** smart-ass. Also, **wise′ass′.** [1970–75]

wise•crack (wīz′krak′), *Informal.* —*n.* **1.** a smart or facetious remark. —*v.i.* **2.** to make wisecracks. —*v.t.* **3.** to say as a wisecrack. [1910–15, *Amer.;* WISE[1] + CRACK] —**wise′crack′er,** *n.*
—**Syn. 1.** jest, witticism, quip.

wise′ guy′, *Informal.* a cocksure, conceited, and often insolent person; smart aleck: *He has a reputation for being a wise guy.* Also called **wiseacre.** [1895–1900, *Amer.*] —**wise′-guy′,** *adj.*

Wise•man (wīz′mən), *n.* **Nicholas Patrick Stephen,** 1802–65, Irish cardinal and author, born in Spain.

wis•en•heim•er (wī′zən hī′mər), *n. Informal.* a wiseacre or smart aleck. Also, **weisenheimer.** [1915–20, *Amer.;* earlier also *wiseheimer,* equiv. to WISE[1] + *-(en)-heimer,* extracted from surnames with this ending]

wi•sent (vē′zənt), *n.* bison (def. 2). [1865–70; < G; OHG *wisunt;* cf. OE *wesend, weosend,* ON *visundr,* OPruss *wissambrs,* Gk *bíson* BISON]

wish (wish), *v.t.* **1.** to want; desire; long for (usually fol. by an infinitive or a clause): *I wish to travel. I wish that it were morning.* **2.** to desire (a person or thing) to be (as specified): *to wish the problem settled.* **3.** to entertain wishes, favorably or otherwise, for: *to wish someone well; to wish someone ill.* **4.** to bid, as in greeting or leave-taking: *to wish someone a good morning.* **5.** to request or charge: *I wish him to come.* —*v.i.* **6.** to desire; long; yearn (often fol. by *for*): *Mother says I may go if I wish. I wished for a book.* **7.** to make a wish: *She wished more than she worked.* **8. wish on, a.** to force or impose (usually used in the negative): *I wouldn't wish that awful job on my worst enemy.* **b.** Also, **wish upon.** to make a wish using some object as a magical talisman: *to wish on a star.* —*n.* **9.** an act or instance of wishing. **10.** a request or command: *I was never forgiven for disregarding my father's wishes.* **11.** an expression of a wish, often one of a kindly or courteous nature: *to send one's best wishes.* **12.** something wished or desired: *He got his wish—a new car.* [bef. 900; (v.) ME *wisshen,* OE *wȳscan;* c. G *wünschen,* ON *æskja;* akin to OE *wynn* joy (see WINSOME), L *venus* charm (see VENUS); (n.) ME, deriv. of the v.] —**wish′er,** *n.* —**wish′less,** *adj.*
—**Syn. 1.** crave. WISH, DESIRE, WANT indicate a longing for something. To WISH is to feel an impulse toward attainment or possession of something; the strength of the feeling may be of greater or lesser intensity: *I wish I could go home.* DESIRE, a more formal word, suggests a strong wish: *They desire a new regime.* WANT, usually colloquial in use, suggests a feeling of lack or need that imperatively demands fulfillment: *People all over the world want peace.* **5.** direct, order. **8.** will, want.

wish•bone (wish′bōn′), *n.* **1.** a forked bone, formed by the fusion of the two clavicles, in front of the breastbone in most birds; furcula. **2.** *Football.* an offensive formation in which the fullback is positioned directly behind the quarterback and the two halfbacks are positioned farther behind and to the left and right, respectively. [1850–55, *Amer.;* WISH + BONE; so called from the custom of pulling the furcula of a cooked fowl apart until it breaks, the person holding the longer (sometimes shorter) piece being granted a wish]

wish′bone flow′er, torenia.

wish•ful (wish′fəl), *adj.* having or showing a wish; desirous; longing. [1515–25; WISH + -FUL] —**wish′ful•ly,** *adv.* —**wish′ful•ness,** *n.*

wish′ fulfill′ment, 1. gratification of desires. **2.** *Psychoanal.* the drive to free oneself from tension caused by instinctual needs, as sex. [1905–10]

wish′ful think′ing, interpretation of facts, actions, words, etc., as one would like them to be rather than as they really are; imagining as actual what is not. [1925–30] —**wish′ful think′er.**

wish′ list′, a usually unwritten list of things one wishes for: *Money is on everyone's wish list.* [1970–75]

wish-wash (wish′wosh′, -wôsh′), *n.* **1.** a drink that is thin and weak. **2.** foolish talk or writing; claptrap. [1780–90; extracted from WISHY-WASHY]

wish•y-wash•y (wish′ē wosh′ē, -wô′shē), *adj.* **1.** lacking in decisiveness; without strength or character; irresolute. **2.** washy or watery, as a liquid; thin and weak. [1685–95; gradational compound based on WASHY] —**wish′y-wash′i•ly,** *adv.* —**wish′y-wash′i•ness,** *n.*

Wi•sła (vē′swä), *n.* Polish name of the **Vistula.**

Wis•mar (vis′mär), *n.* a seaport in N East Germany, on the Baltic. 56,948.

wisp (wisp), *n.* **1.** a handful or small bundle of straw, hay, or the like. **2.** any thin tuft, lock, mass, etc.: *wisps of hair.* **3.** a thin puff or streak, as of smoke; slender trace. **4.** a person or thing that is small, delicate, or barely discernible: *a mere wisp of a lad; a wisp of a frown.* **5.** a whisk broom. **6.** *Chiefly Brit. Dial.* **a.** a pad or twist of straw, as used to rub down a horse. **b.** a twisted bit of straw used as a torch. **7.** a will-o'-the-wisp or ignis fatuus. —*v.t.* **8.** to twist into a wisp. [1300–50; ME *wisp, wips;* akin to WIPE] —**wisp′like′,** *adj.*

wisp•y (wis′pē), *adj.,* **wisp•i•er, wisp•i•est.** being a wisp or in wisps; wisplike: *a wispy plant.* Also, **wisp′•ish.** [1710–20; WISP + -Y[1]] —**wisp′i•ly,** *adv.* —**wisp′i•ness,** *n.*

Wiss•ler (wis′lər), *n.* **Clark,** 1870–1947, U.S. anthropologist.

wist (wist), *v.* pt. and pp. of **wit**[2].

Wis•ter (wis′tər), *n.* **Owen,** 1860–1938, U.S. novelist.

wis•te•ri•a (wi stēr′ē ə), *n.* any climbing shrub belonging to the genus *Wisteria,* of the legume family, having showy, pendent clusters of blue-violet, white, purple, or rose flowers. Also, **wis•tar•i•a** (wi stēr′ē ə, -stâr′-). [< NL *Wistaria* (1818), named after Caspar *Wistar* (1761–1818), U.S. anatomist; see -IA]

wist•ful (wist′fəl), *adj.* **1.** characterized by melancholy; longing; yearning. **2.** pensive, esp. in a melancholy way. [1605–15; obs. *wist* quiet, silent, attentive (var. of WHIST[2]) + -FUL] —**wist′ful•ly,** *adv.* —**wist′ful•ness,** *n.*
—**Syn. 2.** reflective, musing, meditative, forlorn.

wit[1] (wit), *n.* **1.** the keen perception and cleverly apt expression of those connections between ideas that awaken amusement and pleasure. **2.** speech or writing showing such perception and expression. **3.** a person having or noted for such perception and expression. **4.** understanding, intelligence, or sagacity; astuteness. **5.** Usually, **wits. a.** powers of intelligent observation, keen perception, ingenious contrivance, or the like; mental acuity, composure, and resourcefulness: *using one's wits to get ahead.* **b.** mental faculties; senses: *to lose one's wits.* **6. at one's wit's end.** See **end**[1] (def. 23). **7. keep** or **have one's wits about one,** to remain alert and observant; be prepared for or equal to anything: *to keep your wits about you in a crisis.* **8. live by one's wits,** to provide for oneself by employing ingenuity or cunning; live precariously: *We traveled around the world, living by our wits.* [bef. 900; ME, OE: mind, thought; c. G *Witz,* ON *vit;* akin to WIT[2]]
—**Syn. 1.** drollery, facetiousness, waggishness, repartee. See **humor. 4.** wisdom, sense, mind.

wit[2] (wit), *v.t., v.i., pres. sing. 1st pers.* **wot,** *2nd* **wost,** *3rd* **wot,** *pres. pl.* **wit** or **wite;** *past and past part.* **wist;** *pres. part.* **wit•ting. 1.** *Archaic.* to know. **2. to wit,** that is to say; namely: *It was the time of the vernal equinox, to wit, the beginning of spring.* [bef. 900; ME *witen,* OE *witan;* c. D *weten,* G *wissen,* ON *vita,* Goth *witan* to know; akin to L *vidēre,* Gk *ideîn* to see, Skt *vidati* (he) knows. See WOT]

wit•an (wit′n, -än), *n. Early Eng. Hist.* **1.** the members of the national council or witenagemot. **2.** (*used with a singular v.*) the witenagemot. [1800–10; mod. E < OE, pl. of *wita* one who knows, councilor; akin to WIT[2]]

witch (wich), *n.* **1.** a person, now esp. a woman, who professes or is supposed to practice magic, esp. black magic or the black art; sorceress. Cf. **warlock. 2.** an ugly or mean old woman; hag: *the old witch who used to own this building.* **3.** a person who uses a divining rod; dowser. —*v.t.* **4.** to bring by or as by witchcraft (often fol. by *into, to,* etc.): *She witched him into going.* **5.** *Archaic.* to affect as if by witchcraft; bewitch; charm. —*v.i.* **6.** to prospect with a divining rod; dowse. —*adj.* **7.** of, pertaining to, or designed as protection against witches. [bef. 900; ME *wicche,* OE *wicce* (fem.; cf. *wicca* (masc.) wizard; see WICKED)] —**witch′hood,** *n.* —**witch′like′,** *adj.*

witch′ al′der, a shrub, *Fothergilla gardenii,* of the witch hazel family, native to the southeastern U.S., having spikes of white flowers that bloom before the leaves appear. [1810–20, *Amer.;* see WITCH HAZEL, WYCH ELM]

witch′ ball′, 1. a decorated blown glass ball. **2.** (in the 18th century) a hollow sphere of colored glass hung in the window of a house to protect it against witchcraft. [1865–70]

witch•craft (wich′kraft′, -kräft′), *n.* **1.** the art or practices of a witch; sorcery; magic. **2.** magical influence; witchery. [bef. 950; ME *wicchecraft,* OE *wiccecræft.* See WITCH, CRAFT]
—**Syn. 1.** See **magic.**

witch′ doc′tor, a person in some societies who attempts to cure sickness and to exorcise evil spirits by the use of magic. [1710–20]

witch•er•y (wich′ə rē), *n., pl.* **-er•ies. 1.** witchcraft; magic. **2.** magical influence; fascination; charm: *the witchery of her beauty.* [1540–50; WITCH + -ERY]

witch•es′-be•som (wich′iz bē′zəm), *n. Plant Pathol.* witches'-broom. [1865–70]

witch′es′ brew′, 1. a potent magical concoction supposedly prepared by witches. **2.** a harmful or threatening mixture; diabolical concoction: *a witches' brew of innuendo and rumor.* [1925–30]

witch•es′-broom (wich′iz brōōm′, -brŏŏm′), *n. Plant Pathol.* an abnormal, brushlike growth of small thin branches on woody plants, caused esp. by fungi, viruses, and mistletoes. [1865–70]

witch′es′ Sab′bath, *Demonology.* Sabbat. [1670–80]

witch′et•ty grub′ (wich′ə tē), the large white larva of any of several species of moth and beetle of Australia, esp. of the moth genus *Cossus,* occurring in decaying wood and traditionally used as food by Aborigines. [1890–95; < Adnyamadhanha (Australian Aboriginal language spoken around Lake Torrens, South Australia) *wityati* witchetty grub, perh. equiv. to v. base *witya* climb + *varti* grub, insect]

witch′ grass′, a panic grass, *Panicum capillare,* having a bushlike compound panicle, common as a weed in North America. [1780–90, *Amer.;* prob. alter. of QUITCH GRASS]

witch ha•zel (wich′ hā′zəl), **1.** a shrub, *Hamamelis virginiana,* of eastern North America, having toothed, egg-shaped leaves and small, yellow flowers. Cf. **witch hazel family. 2.** a liquid extraction from the leaves or bark of this plant mixed with water and alcohol, used externally as a liniment for inflammations and bruises and as an astringent. [1535–45; *witch,* var. of *wych* (see WYCH ELM)]

witch′ ha′zel fam′ily, the plant family Hamamelidaceae, characterized by trees and shrubs having alternate, simple leaves, flowers in clusters or heads, and fruit in the form of a double-beaked woody capsule, and including the sweet gum, witch alder, and witch hazel.

witch′ hob′ble, the hobblebush. [1830–40, *Amer.*]

witch′ hunt′, an intensive effort to discover and expose disloyalty, subversion, dishonesty, or the like, usually based on slight, doubtful, or irrelevant evidence. Also, **witch′-hunt′.** [1925–30] —**witch′ hunt′er.** —**witch′-hunt′ing,** *n.*

witch-hunt (wich′hunt′), *v.t.* to subject to a witch hunt. [1925–30]

witch•ing (wich′ing), *n.* **1.** the use or practice of witchcraft. **2.** fascination; charm; enchantment. —*adj.* **3.** of, characterized by, or suitable for sorcery or black magic: *a witching potion.* **4.** enchanting; fascinating. [bef. 1000; ME *wicching* (n. and adj.), OE *wiccung* (n.), deriv. of *wiccian* to practice witchcraft. See WITCH, -ING[1], -ING[2]] —**witch′ing•ly,** *adv.*

witch′ing hour′, midnight: *a rendezvous at the witching hour.* [1825–35]

witch′ moth′, any of several large noctuid moths of the genus *Erebus,* esp. the blackish *E. odora* (**black witch**) of Central and North America.

witch′ of A•gne′si (ä nyā′zē), *Geom.* a plane curve symmetrical about the *y*-axis and asymptotic to the *x*-axis, given by the equation $x^2y=4a^2(2a-y)$. Also called **versiera.** [1870–75; named after Maria Gaetana *Agnesi* (1718–99), Italian mathematician and philosopher]

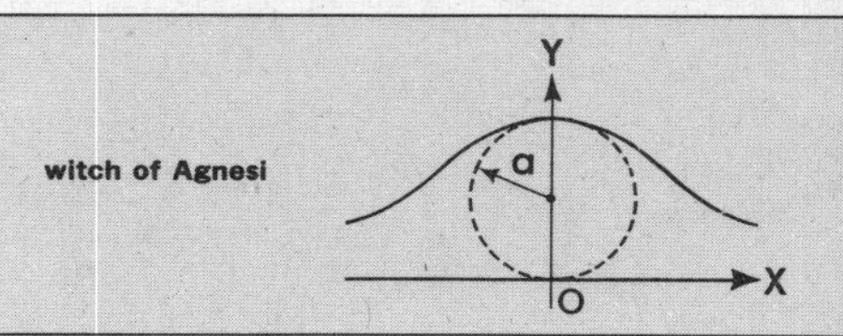

witch′'s mark′. See **devil's mark.** [1620–30]

witch•weed (wich′wēd′), *n.* an Old World parasitic plant of the genus *Striga,* introduced into the southern U.S.: a serious pest of corn and other grass crops. [1900–05; WITCH + WEED[1]]

witch•y (wich′ē), *adj.,* **witch•i•er, witch•i•est. 1.** accomplished by or as if by witchcraft: *strange, witchy sounds.* **2.** similar to or characteristic of a witch; witchlike: *a witchy enjoyment of mischief-making.* [1660–70; WITCH + -Y[1]]

wite[1] (wīt), *n., v.,* **wit•ed, wit•ing.** —*n.* **1.** (in Anglo-Saxon law) **a.** a fine imposed by a king or lord on a subject who committed a serious crime. **b.** a fee demanded for granting a special privilege. **2.** *Chiefly Scot.* responsibility for a crime, fault, or misfortune; blame. —*v.t.* **3.**

CONCISE ETYMOLOGY KEY: <, descended or borrowed from; >, whence; b., blend of, blended; c., cognate with; cf., compare; deriv., derivative; equiv., equivalent; imit., imitative; obl., oblique; r., replacing; s., stem; sp., spelling, spelled; resp., respelling, respelled; trans., translation; ?, origin unknown; *, unattested; ‡, probably earlier than. See the full key inside the front cover.

Chiefly Scot. to blame for; declare guilty of. Also, **wyte.** [bef. 900; (n.) ME, OE *wīte* penalty; c. OHG *wīzi,* ON *vīti;* (v.) ME *witen,* OE *wītan* to blame]

wite[2] (wīt), *v.* a pres. pl. of **wit**[2].

wit·e·na·ge·mot (wit′n ə gə mōt′), *n. Early Eng. Hist.* the assembly of the witan; the national council attended by the king, aldermen, bishops, and nobles. [1585–95; mod. E < OE, equiv. to *witena,* gen. pl. of *wita* councilor (see WITAN) + *gemōt* MOOT]

with (with, wit͟h), *prep.* **1.** accompanied by; accompanying: *I will go with you. He fought with his brother against the enemy.* **2.** in some particular relation to (esp. implying interaction, company, association, conjunction, or connection): *I dealt with the problem. She agreed with me.* **3.** characterized by or having: *a person with initiative.* **4.** (of means or instrument) by the use of; using: *to line a coat with silk; to cut with a knife.* **5.** (of manner) using or showing: *to work with diligence.* **6.** in correspondence, comparison, or proportion to: *Their power increased with their number. How does their plan compare with ours?* **7.** in regard to: *to be pleased with a gift.* **8.** (of cause) owing to: *to die with pneumonia; to pale with fear.* **9.** in the region, sphere, or view of: *It is day with us while it is night with the Chinese.* **10.** (of separation) from: *to part with a thing.* **11.** against, as in opposition or competition: *He fought with his brother over the inheritance.* **12.** in the keeping or service of: *to leave something with a friend.* **13.** in affecting the judgment, estimation, or consideration of: *Her argument carried a lot of weight with the trustees.* **14.** at the same time as or immediately after; upon: *And with that last remark, she turned and left.* **15.** of the same opinion or conviction as: *Are you with me or against me?* **16.** in proximity to or in the same household as: *He lives with his parents.* **17.** (used as a function word to specify an additional circumstance or condition): *We climbed the hill, with Jeff following behind.* **18. in with.** See **in** (def. 22). **19. with child,** pregnant. **20. with it,** *Slang.* **a.** knowledgeable about, sympathetic to, or partaking of the most up-to-date trends, fashions, art, etc. **b.** representing or characterized by the most up-to-date trends, fashions, art, etc. **21. with that.** See **that** (def. 10). [bef. 900; ME, OE: opposite, against (c. ON *vith*), appar. short var. of OE *wither* against; c. OS *withar,* OHG *widar,* ON *vithr,* Goth *withra*]
—**Syn. 4.** See **by.**

with-, a combining form of **with,** having a separative or opposing force: *withstand; withdraw.* [ME, OE. See WITH]

with·al (wit͟h ôl′, with-), *adv.* **1.** with it all; as well; besides. **2.** in spite of all; nevertheless. **3.** *Archaic.* with that; therewith. —*prep.* **4.** with (used after its object). [1150–1200; ME phrase *with al(le);* r. OE *mid ealle, mid eallum.* See WITH, ALL]

with·draw (wit͟h drô′, with-), *v.,* **-drew, -drawn, -draw·ing.** —*v.t.* **1.** to draw back, away, or aside; take back; remove: *She withdrew her hand from his. He withdrew his savings from the bank.* **2.** to retract or recall: *to withdraw an untrue charge.* **3.** to cause (a person) to undergo withdrawal from addiction to a substance. —*v.i.* **4.** to go or move back, away, or aside; retire; retreat: *to withdraw from the room.* **5.** to remove oneself from some activity, competition, etc.: *He withdrew before I could nominate him.* **6.** to cease using or consuming an addictive narcotic (fol. by *from*): *to withdraw from heroin.* **7.** *Parl. Proc.* to remove an amendment, motion, etc., from consideration. [1175–1225; ME *withdrawen.* See WITH-, DRAW] —**with·draw′a·ble,** *adj.* —**with·draw′er,** *n.* —**with·draw′ing·ness,** *n.*
—**Syn. 2.** revoke, rescind, disavow. **4.** See **depart.**

with·draw·al (wit͟h drô′əl, -drôl′, with-), *n.* **1.** Also, **with·draw′ment.** the act or condition of withdrawing. **2.** *Pharm.* the act or process of ceasing to use an addictive drug. **3.** coitus interruptus. [1740–50; WITHDRAW + -AL[2]]

withdraw′al syn′drome, *Pharm.* a spectrum of physical and behavioral symptoms following cessation from the continuous use of an addictive drug, the character and severity of the symptoms depending upon the particular drug and the daily dose.

withdraw′ing room′, *Archaic.* a room to withdraw or retire to; drawing room. [1585–95]

with·drawn (wit͟h drôn′, with-), *v.* **1.** pp. of **withdraw.** —*adj.* **2.** removed from circulation, contact, competition, etc. **3.** shy; retiring; reticent. —**with·drawn′·ness,** *n.*
—**Syn. 3.** quiet, reserved, aloof, detached.

with·drew (wit͟h dro͞o′, with-), *v.* pt. of **withdraw.**

withe (with, wit͟h, wīt͟h), *n., v.,* **withed, with·ing.** —*n.* **1.** a willow twig or osier. **2.** any tough, flexible twig or stem suitable for binding things together. **3.** an elastic handle for a tool, to lessen shock occurring in use. **4.** a partition dividing flues of a chimney. —*v.t.* **5.** to bind with withes. [bef. 1000; ME, OE *withthe;* akin to ON *vīthir* WITHY, Goth *kunawida* chain, L *viēre* to weave together]

with·er (wit͟h′ər), *v.i.* **1.** to shrivel; fade; decay: *The grapes had withered on the vine.* **2.** to lose the freshness of youth, as from age (often fol. by *away*). —*v.t.* **3.** to make flaccid, shrunken, or dry, as from loss of moisture; cause to lose freshness, bloom, vigor, etc.: *The drought withered the buds.* **4.** to affect harmfully: *Reputations were withered by the scandal.* **5.** to abash, as by a scathing glance: *a look that withered him.* [1250–1300; ME, perh. var. of WEATHER (v.)] —**with′ered·ness,** *n.* —**with′er·er,** *n.* —**with′er·ing·ly,** *adv.*
—**Syn. 1.** wrinkle, shrink, dry, decline, languish, droop, waste. WITHER, SHRIVEL imply a shrinking, wilting, and wrinkling. WITHER (of plants and flowers) is to dry up, shrink, wilt, fade, whether as a natural process or as the result of exposure to excessive heat or drought: *Plants withered in the hot sun.* SHRIVEL, used of thin, flat objects and substances, such as leaves, the skin, etc., means to curl, roll up, become wrinkled: *The leaves shrivel in cold weather. Paper shrivels in fire.* **5.** humiliate, shame.

With·er (wit͟h′ər), *n.* **George,** 1588–1667, English poet and pamphleteer. Also, **With·ers** (wit͟h′ərz).

with·er·ite (wit͟h′ə rīt′), *n.* a white to grayish mineral, barium carbonate, $BaCO_3$, occurring in crystals and masses: a minor ore of barium. [1785–95; named after W. *Withering* (1741–99), who first described it; see -ITE[1]]

withe′ rod′, either of two North American viburnums, *Viburnum cassinoides* or *V. nudum,* having tough, osierlike shoots. [1840–50, *Amer.*]

with·ers (wit͟h′ərz), *n.* (*used with a plural v.*) **1.** the highest part of the back at the base of the neck of a horse, cow, sheep, etc. See diag. under **dog, horse. 2. wring one's withers,** to cause one anxiety or trouble: *The long involved lawsuit is wringing his withers.* [1535–45; orig. uncert.]

with·er·shins (wit͟h′ər shinz′), *adv. Chiefly Scot.* in a direction contrary to the natural one, esp. contrary to the apparent course of the sun or counterclockwise: considered as unlucky or causing disaster. Also, **widdershins.** Cf. **deasil.** [1505–15; < MLG *weddersin(ne)s* < MHG *widdersinnes,* equiv. to *wider* (OHG *widar*) opposite (see WITH) + *sinnes,* gen. of *sin* way, course (c. OE *sīth*); see SEND, -S[1]]

With·er·spoon (wit͟h′ər spo͞on′), *n.* **John,** 1723–94, U.S. theologian and statesman, born in Scotland.

with·hold (with hōld′, wit͟h-), *v.,* **-held, -hold·ing.** —*v.t.* **1.** to hold back; restrain or check. **2.** to refrain from giving or granting: *to withhold payment.* **3.** to collect (taxes) at the source of income. **4.** to deduct (withholding tax) from an employee's salary or wages. —*v.i.* **5.** to hold back; refrain. **6.** to deduct withholding tax. [1150–1200; ME *withholden.* See WITH-, HOLD[1]] —**with·hold′er,** *n.*
—**Syn. 1, 2.** suppress, repress. See **keep.** —**Ant. 1, 2.** advance.

withhold′ing tax′, that part of an employee's tax liability withheld by the employer from wages or salary and paid directly to the government. Also called **withhold′ing.** [1940–45]

with·in (wit͟h in′, with-), *adv.* **1.** in or into the interior or inner part; inside. **2.** in or into a house, building, etc.; indoors: *The fire was burning on the hearth within.* **3.** on, or as regards, the inside; internally. **4.** inside an enclosed place, area, room, etc.: *He was startled by a cry from within.* **5.** in the mind, heart, or soul; inwardly. —*prep.* **6.** in or into the interior of or the parts or space enclosed by: *within city walls.* **7.** inside of; in. **8.** in the compass or limits of; not beyond: *within view; to live within one's income.* **9.** at or to some point not beyond, as in length or distance; not farther than: *within a radius of a mile.* **10.** at or to some amount or degree not exceeding: *within two degrees of freezing.* **11.** in the course or period of, as in time: *within one's memory; within three minutes.* **12.** inside of the limits fixed or required by; not transgressing: *within the law.* **13.** in the field, sphere, or scope of: *within the family; within one's power.* —*n.* **14.** the inside of a place, space, or building. [bef. 1000; ME *withinne* (prep. and adv.), OE *withinnan* (adv.), equiv. to *with* WITH- + *innan* from within, equiv. to *in* IN + *-an* suffix of motion from]

with·in·doors (wit͟h in′dôrz′, -dōrz′, with-), *adv.* into or inside the house. [1575–85; WITHIN + DOOR + -S[1]]

with·in-named (wit͟h in′nāmd′, with-), *adj.* that is named herein. [1560–70]

with·out (wit͟h out′, with-), *prep.* **1.** with the absence, omission, or avoidance of; not with; with no or none of; lacking: *without help; without shoes; without her helping me; without him to help.* **2.** free from; excluding: *a world without hunger.* **3.** not accompanied by: *Don't go without me.* **4.** at, on, or to the outside of; outside of: *both within and without the house or the city.* **5.** beyond the compass, limits, range, or scope of (now used chiefly in opposition to *within*): *whether within or without the law.* —*adv.* **6.** in or into an exterior or outer place; outside. **7.** outside a house, building, etc.: *The carriage awaits without.* **8.** lacking something implied or understood: *We must take this or go without.* **9.** as regards the outside; externally. —*n.* **10.** the outside of a place, region, area, room, etc. —*conj.* **11.** *Midland and Southern U.S.* unless. [bef. 900; ME *withouten,* OE *withūtan* (adv. and prep.), equiv. to *with* WITH + *-ūtan* from without, equiv. to *ūt* OUT + *-an* suffix of motion from]

with·out·doors (wit͟h out′dôrz′, -dōrz′, with-), *adv.* out of doors. [1610–20; WITHOUT + DOOR + -S[1]]

with·stand (with stand′, wit͟h-), *v.,* **-stood, -stand·ing.** —*v.t.* **1.** to stand or hold out against; resist or oppose, esp. successfully: *to withstand rust; to withstand the invaders; to withstand temptation.* —*v.i.* **2.** to stand in opposition; resist. [bef. 900; ME *withstanden,* OE *withstandan* (see WITH-, STAND); c. ON *vithstanda;* akin to G *widerstehen*] —**with·stand′er,** *n.* —**with·stand′ing·ness,** *n.*
—**Syn. 1.** confront, face. See **oppose.**

with·y (wit͟h′ē, with′ē), *n., pl.* **with·ies,** *adj.,* **with·i·er, with·i·est.** *Chiefly Brit.* —*n.* **1.** a willow. **2.** a pliable branch or twig, esp. a withe. **3.** a band, loop, halter, or rope of slender twigs; widdy. —*adj.* **4.** made of pliable branches or twigs, esp. of withes. **5.** flexible; pliable. [bef. 1000; ME, OE *withig;* akin to WITHE, ON *vīthir,* OHG *wīda,* Gk *itéa* willow, L *vītis* vine]

with·y·wind (wit͟h′ē wīnd′, with′-), *n.* traveler's-joy. [1570–80; WITHY + WIND[2]; r. *withwind,* ME, OE *withewinde* (see WITHE)]

wit·i·go (wit′i gō), *n.* windigo.

wit·less (wit′lis), *adj.* lacking wit or intelligence; stupid; foolish. [bef. 1000; ME; OE *witlēas.* See WIT[1], -LESS] —**wit′less·ly,** *adv.* —**wit′less·ness,** *n.*

wit·ling (wit′ling), *n.* a person who affects wittiness. [1685–95; WIT[1] + -LING[1]]

wit·loof (wit′lōf), *n.* endive (def. 2). [1880–85; < D, equiv. to *wit* white + *loof* foliage. See WHITE, LEAF]

wit·ness (wit′nis), *v.t.* **1.** to see, hear, or know by personal presence and perception: *to witness an accident.* **2.** to be present at (an occurrence) as a formal witness, spectator, bystander, etc.: *She witnessed our wedding.* **3.** to bear witness to; testify to; give or afford evidence of. **4.** to attest by one's signature: *He witnessed her will.* —*v.i.* **5.** to bear witness; testify; give or afford evidence. —*n.* **6.** an individual who, being present, personally sees or perceives a thing; a beholder, spectator, or eyewitness. **7.** a person or thing that affords evidence. **8.** a person who gives testimony, as in a court of law. **9.** a person who signs a document attesting the genuineness of its execution. **10.** testimony or evidence: *to bear witness to her suffering.* **11.** (*cap.*) a member of the Jehovah's Witnesses. [bef. 950; (n.) ME, OE *witnes* orig., knowledge, understanding; see WIT[1], -NESS; (v.) ME, deriv. of the n.] —**wit′ness·a·ble,** *adj.* —**wit′ness·er,** *n.*
—**Syn. 1.** perceive, watch, mark, notice, note. See **observe. 10.** proof, confirmation, substantiation.

wit·ness-box (wit′nis boks′), *n. Chiefly Brit.* See **witness stand.** [1800–10]

wit′ness cor′ner, *Survey.* a point, marked by a monument, situated at a known distance from and bearing relative to a corner that is used as a reference point but on which it is impossible to place a monument. Cf. **corner** (def. 10a). [1915–20, *Amer.*]

wit′ness stand′, the place occupied by a person giving testimony in a court. Also called, *esp. Brit.,* **witness-box.** [1880–85, *Amer.*]

Witt (wit), *n.* a male given name.

Wit·te (vit′ə; *Russ.* vyĕ′tyə), *n.* **Ser·gei Yu·lie·vich** (sûr gā′ yo͞ol′yə vich; *Russ.* syir gyā′ yo͞o′lyi vyich), 1849–1915, Russian statesman.

wit·ted (wit′id), *adj.* having wit or wits (usually used in combination): *quick-witted; slow-witted; dull-witted.* [1350–1400; ME; see WIT[1], -ED[3]] —**wit′ted·ness,** *n.*

Wit·te·kind (vit′ə kint′), *n.* died A.D. 807?, Westphalian chief: leader of the Saxons against Charlemagne. Also, **Widukind.**

Wit·ten·berg (wit′n bûrg′; *Ger.* vit′n berk′), *n.* a city in E central Germany, on the Elbe: Luther taught in the university here; beginnings of the Reformation 1517. 54,190.

Witt·gen·stein (vit′gən shtīn′, -stīn′), *n.* **Lud·wig (Jo·sef Jo·hann)** (lo͞ot′vikh yō′zef yō′hän, lo͞od′-), 1889–1951, Austrian philosopher. —**Witt′gen·stein′i·an,** *adj., n.*

wit·ti·cism (wit′ə siz′əm), *n.* a witty remark or sentence. [1645–55; deriv. of WITTY, modeled on *criticism*]
—**Syn.** joke, jest, quip, sally, wisecrack.

wit·ting (wit′ing), *adj.* **1.** knowing; aware; conscious. —*n.* **2.** *North Eng.* knowledge. [1250–1300; ME *witing.* See WIT[2], -ING[2], -ING[1]] —**wit′ting·ly,** *adv.*

wit·tol (wit′l), *n. Archaic.* a man who knows of and tolerates his wife's infidelity. [1400–50; late ME *wetewold,* equiv. to *wete* WIT[2] + (*coke*)*wold* CUCKOLD]

wit·ty (wit′ē), *adj.,* **-ti·er, -ti·est. 1.** possessing wit in speech or writing; amusingly clever in perception and expression: *a witty writer.* **2.** characterized by wit: *a witty remark.* **3.** *Brit. Dial.* intelligent; clever. [bef. 900; ME; OE *wittig* orig., wise. See WIT[1], -Y[1]] —**wit′ti·ly,** *adv.* —**wit′ti·ness,** *n.*
—**Syn. 1, 2.** droll, funny, original, sparkling, brilliant. See **humorous.** —**Ant. 1, 2.** dull, stupid.

Wit·wa·ters·rand (wit′wô′tərz rand′, -wot′ərz-), *n.* a rocky ridge in S Africa, in the Republic of South Africa, near Johannesburg. Also called **The Rand.**

wive (wīv), *v.,* **wived, wiv·ing.** —*v.i.* **1.** to take a wife; marry. —*v.t.* **2.** to take as wife; marry. **3.** to provide with a wife. [bef. 900; ME *wiven,* OE *wīfian,* deriv. of *wīf;* see WIFE]

wi·vern (wī′vərn), *n. Heraldry.* wyvern.

wives (wīvz), *n.* pl. of **wife.**

wiz (wiz), *n.* wizard (def. 3). [1900–05; by shortening]

wiz·ard (wiz′ərd), *n.* **1.** a person who practices magic; magician or sorcerer. **2.** a conjurer or juggler. **3.** Also, **whiz, wiz.** a person of amazing skill or accomplishment: *a wizard at chemistry.* —*adj.* **4.** of or pertaining to a wizard. **5.** magic. **6.** *Brit. Slang.* superb; excellent; wonderful: *That's wizard!* [1400–50; late ME *wysard.* See WISE[1], -ARD] —**wiz′ard·like′,** *adj.*
—**Syn. 1.** enchanter, necromancer, diviner.

wiz·ard·ly (wiz′ərd lē), *adj.* of, like, or befitting a wizard. [1580–90; WIZARD + -LY]

wiz·ard·ry (wiz′ər drē), *n.* the art, skill, or accomplishments of a wizard. [1575–85; WIZARD + -RY]

wiz·en (wiz′ən; wē′zən), *Brit. Dial.* —*v.i., v.t.* **1.** to wither; shrivel; dry up. —*adj.* **2.** wizened. [bef. 900; (v.) ME *wisenen,* OE *wisnian;* c. ON *visna* to wither; (adj.) shortened form of WIZENED]

wiz·ened (wiz′ənd; wē′zənd), *adj.* withered; shriveled: *a wizened old man; wizened features.* [1505–15; WIZEN + -ED[2]]

wk., **1.** week. **2.** work.

wkly., weekly.

wl, **1.** Also, **w.l.** water line. **2.** wavelength.

Wla·di·mir (vlad′ə mēr′; *Russ.* vlu dyē′myir), *n.* Vladimir.

WLB, War Labor Board.

w. long., west longitude.

WM, white male.

Wm., William.

CONCISE PRONUNCIATION KEY: act, cāpe, dâre, pärt; set, ēqual; if, īce; ox, ōver, ôrder, oil, bo͝ok, bo͞ot, out; up, ûrge; child; sing; shoe; thin, t͟hat; zh as in *treasure.* ə = *a* as in *alone, e* as in *system, i* as in *easily, o* as in *gallop, u* as in *circus;* ᵊ as in *fire* (fīᵊr), *hour* (ouᵊr). l and n can serve as syllabic consonants, as in *cradle* (krād′l), and *button* (but′n). See the full key inside the front cover.

w/m, (in shipping) weight and/or measurement.

WMC, See **War Manpower Commission.**

wmk., watermark.

WMO, World Meteorological Organization.

WNW, west-northwest.

wo (wō), *n., pl.* **wos,** *interj. Archaic.* woe.

WO, **1.** wait order. **2.** War Office. **3.** Warrant Officer. Also, **W.O.**

w/o, without.

woad (wōd), *n.* **1.** a European plant, *Isatis tinctoria,* of the mustard family, formerly cultivated for a blue dye extracted from its leaves. **2.** the dye extracted from this plant. [bef. 1000; ME *wode,* OE *wād* (c. G *Waid*); akin to F *guède,* ML *waizda* < Gmc]

woad·ed (wō′did), *adj.* dyed or colored blue with woad. [1570–80; WOAD + -ED[3]]

woad·wax·en (wōd′wak′sən), *n.* an ornamental Eurasian shrub, *Genista tinctoria,* whose flowers yield a yellow dye formerly used with woad to make a permanent green dye. Also, **woodwaxen.** Also called **dyer's-broom, dyer's greenweed, dyer's greenwood.** [1325–75; ME *wodewaxen,* equiv. to *wode* WOOD[1] + *waxen* grown (ptp. of *waxen* to WAX[2]); r. ME *wodewax,* OE *wuduweax*]

woald (wōld), *n.* weld[2].

w.o.b., (in shipping) washed overboard.

wob·be·gong (wob′ē gong′), *n. Australian.* the carpet shark. [1850–55; perh. < an Australian Aboriginal language]

wob·ble (wob′əl), *v.,* **-bled, -bling,** *n.* —*v.i.* **1.** to incline to one side and to the other alternately, as a wheel, top, or other rotating body when not properly balanced. **2.** to move unsteadily from side to side: *The table wobbled on its uneven legs.* **3.** to show unsteadiness; tremble; quaver: *His voice wobbled.* **4.** to vacillate; waver. —*v.t.* **5.** to cause to wobble. —*n.* **6.** a wobbling movement. Also, **wabble.** [1650–60; < LG *wabbeln;* akin to ON *vafla* to toddle, MHG *wabelen* to waver, OE *wæflian* to speak incoherently] —**wob′bler,** *n.*

wob′ble pump′, *Aeron.* an auxiliary hand pump for supplying fuel to the carburetor of an aircraft engine when the automatic pumping mechanism fails. [1925–30]

wob·bling (wob′ling), *adj.* that wobbles or causes to wobble. Also, **wabbling.** [1650–60; WOBBLE + -ING[2]] —**wob′bling·ly,** *adv.*

wob·bly (wob′lē), *adj.,* **-bli·er, -bli·est.** shaky; unsteady. Also, **wabbly.** [1850–55; WOBBLE + -Y[1]] —**wob′bli·ness,** *n.*

Wob·bly (wob′lē), *n., pl.* **-blies.** a member of the Industrial Workers of the World. [1910–15, *Amer.;* of uncert. orig.]

wo·be·gone (wō′bi gôn′, -gon′), *adj. Archaic.* woebegone.

Wo·burn (wō′bərn, wo͞o′-), *n.* a city in E Massachusetts, N of Boston. 36,626.

w.o.c., without compensation.

wo·cas (wō′kəs), *n.* a yellow pond lily, *Nuphar polysepalum,* of northwestern North America, having heart-shaped leaves and cup-shaped flowers. Also, **wokas, wokus.** [1875–80, *Amer.;* earlier, its seeds < Klamath *wokas;* cf. *woksʔam* the name of the plant]

Wode·house (wo͝od′hous′), *n.* **Sir P(el·ham) G(ren·ville)** (pel′əm), 1881–1975, U.S. novelist and humorist, born in England.

Wo·den (wōd′n), *n.* the chief god of the pagan Anglo-Saxons, identified with the Scandinavian Odin. Also, **Wo′dan.** [bef. 900; ME, OE *Wōden* (c. G *Wotan,* ON *Óthinn*), equiv. to *wōd* WOOD[2] + *-en* n. suffix marking headship; Woden was the leader of the Wild Hunt]

wodge (woj), *n. Brit. Informal.* **1.** a lump, chunk, or wad. **2.** an object having a lumpy, bulgy shape. [1905–10; perh. alter. of WEDGE] —**wodg′y,** *adj.*

woe (wō), *n.* **1.** grievous distress, affliction, or trouble: *His woe was almost beyond description.* **2.** an affliction: *She suffered a fall, among her other woes.* —*interj.* **3.** an exclamation of grief, distress, or lamentation. [bef. 900; ME *wo* (interj. and n.), OE *wā* (interj.) (cf. WELLAWAY); c. D *wee,* G *Weh,* ON *vei,* L *vae*]
—**Syn. 1.** anguish, tribulation, trial, wretchedness, melancholy. See **sorrow.** —**Ant. 1.** joy.

woe·be·gone (wō′bi gôn′, -gon′), *adj.* **1.** beset with woe; affected by woe, esp. in appearance. **2.** showing or indicating woe: *He always had a woebegone look on his face.* [1300–50; ME *wo begon* orig., woe (has or had) surrounded (someone); *wo* WOE + *begon,* ptp. of *begon,* OE *begān* to surround, besiege (see BE-, GO[1])] —**woe′be·gone′ness,** *n.*
—**Syn. 2.** suffering, troubled, forlorn, gloomy.

woe·ful (wō′fəl), *adj.* **1.** full of woe; wretched; unhappy: *a woeful situation.* **2.** affected with, characterized by, or indicating woe: *woeful melodies.* **3.** of wretched quality; sorry; poor: *a woeful collection of paintings.* Also, **wo′ful.** [1250–1300; ME; see WOE, -FUL] —**woe′ful·ly,** *adv.* —**woe′ful·ness,** *n.*
—**Syn. 3.** unpromising, unlikely, dreadful, awful.

woe·some (wō′səm), *adj. Archaic.* woeful. [1810–20; WOE + -SOME[1]]

wog (wog), *n. Chiefly Brit. Slang* (*disparaging and offensive*). any nonwhite, esp. a dark-skinned native of the Middle East or Southeast Asia. [1925–30; perh. shortening of GOLLIWOGG] —**wog′gish,** *adj.*

CONCISE ETYMOLOGY KEY: <, descended or borrowed from; >, whence; b., blend of, blended; c., cognate with; cf., compare; deriv., derivative; equiv., equivalent; imit., imitative; obl., oblique; r., replacing; s., stem; sp., spelling, spelled; resp., respelling, respelled; trans., translation; ?, origin unknown; *, unattested; ‡, probably earlier than. See the full key inside the front cover.

Wöh·ler (wûr′lər, vûr′-; *Ger.* vœ′lər), *n.* **Frie·drich** (frē′drikh), 1800–82, German chemist.

wok (wok), *n.* a large bowl-shaped pan used in cooking Chinese food. [1955–60; < dial. Chin (Guangdong) *wohk* pan, equiv. to Chin *huo*]

wo·kas (wō′kəs), *n.* wocas. Also, **wo′kus.**

woke (wōk), *v.* a pt. of **wake.**

wok·en (wō′kən), *v.* a pp. of **wake.**

Wol·cott (wo͝ol′kət), *n.* a town in S Connecticut. 13,008.

wold[1] (wōld), *n.* **1.** an elevated tract of open country. **2.** Often, **wolds.** an open, hilly district, esp. in England, as in Yorkshire or Lincolnshire. [bef. 900; ME; OE *w(e)ald* forest; c. G *Wald;* akin to WILD, ON *vǫllr* plain]

wold[2] (wōld), *n.* weld[2].

wold[3] (wôld), *v. Obs.* a pp. of **will**[1].

wolf (wo͝olf), *n., pl.* **wolves** (wo͝olvz), *v.* —*n.* **1.** any of several large carnivorous mammals of the genus *Canis,* of the dog family Canidae, esp. *C. lupus,* usually hunting in packs, formerly common throughout the Northern Hemisphere but now chiefly restricted to the more unpopulated parts of its range. **2.** the fur of such an animal. **3.** any of various wolflike animals of different families, as the thylacine. **4.** (*cap.*) *Astron.* the constellation Lupus. **5.** the larva of any of various small insects infesting granaries. **6.** a cruelly rapacious person. **7.** *Informal.* a man who makes amorous advances to many women. **8.** *Music.* **a.** the harsh discord heard in certain chords of keyboard instruments, esp. the organ, when tuned on some system of unequal temperament. **b.** a chord or interval in which such a discord appears. **c.** (in bowed instruments) a discordant or false vibration in a string due to a defect in structure or adjustment of the instrument. **9. cry wolf,** to give a false alarm: *Is she really sick or is she just crying wolf?* **10. keep the wolf from the door,** to avert poverty or starvation; provide sufficiently for: *Their small inheritance kept the wolf from the door.* **11. wolf in sheep's clothing,** a person who conceals his or her evil intentions or character beneath an innocent exterior. —*v.t.* **12.** to devour voraciously (often fol. by *down*): *He wolfed his food.* —*v.i.* **13.** to hunt for wolves. [bef. 900; ME; OE *wulf;* c. G *Wolf,* ON *ulfr,* Goth *wulfs,* Pol *wilk,* Lith *vilkas,* Skt *vṛka;* akin to L *lupus,* Gk *lýkos*] —**wolf′like′,** *adj.*

wolf, *Canis lupus,* 3 ft. (0.9 m) high at shoulder; head and body 4 ft. (1.2 m); tail 1½ ft. (0.46 m)

Wolf (vôlf), *n.* **1. Baron Christian von.** See **Wolff, Baron Christian von. 2. Frie·drich Au·gust** (frē′drikh ou′go͝ost), 1759–1824, German classical scholar. **3. Hu·go** (ho͞o′gō), 1860–1903, Austrian composer. **4.** a male given name.

wolf·ber·ry (wo͝olf′ber′ē, -bə rē), *n., pl.* **-ries.** a North American shrub, *Symphoricarpos occidentalis,* of the honeysuckle family, having gray, hairy, egg-shaped leaves and pinkish, bell-shaped flowers, and bearing white berries. [1825–35, *Amer.;* WOLF + BERRY]

wolf′ call′, a whistle, shout, or the like uttered by a male in admiration of a female's appearance.

wolf-child (wo͝olf′chīld′), *n., pl.* **-chil·dren.** a child who is thought to have been suckled or nurtured by wolves. [1855–60]

wolf′ cub′, *Brit.* a member of the junior division, for boys from 8 to 11, of the Boy Scouts; cub scout. [1810–20]

wolf′ dog′, **1.** any dog used in hunting wolves. **2.** a cross between a wolf and a domestic dog. **3.** an Eskimo dog. [1630–40]

Wolfe (wo͝olf), *n.* **1. Charles,** 1791–1823, Irish poet. **2. James,** 1727–59, English general. **3. Thomas (Clay·ton)** (klāt′n), 1900–38, U.S. novelist. **4.** a male given name.

Wolfe·bor·o (wo͝olf′bûr ō, -bur ō), *n.* a town in E New Hampshire, on Lake Winnipesaukee: summer resort. 3968.

wolf-eel (wo͝olf′ēl′), *n.* a large, eellike fish, *Anarrhichthys ocellatus,* inhabiting waters along the Pacific coast of North America. [1880–85, *Amer.*]

Wolff (vôlf; *Eng.* wo͝olf), *n.* **1. Chris·ti·an von** (kris′tē än′ fən), **Baron.** Also, **Wolf.** 1679–1754, German philosopher and mathematician. **2. Kas·par Frie·drich** (käs′pär frē′drikh), 1733–94, German anatomist and physiologist. —**Wolff′i·an,** *adj.*

Wolf-Fer·ra·ri (vôlf′fer rä′rē), *n.* **Er·man·no** (er-män′nô), 1876–1948, Italian composer.

Wolff′ian bod′y, *Embryol.* the mesonephros. [1835–45; named after Kaspar Friedrich WOLFF; see -IAN]

Wolff′ian duct′, (*sometimes l.c.*) *Embryol.* a duct, draining the mesonephros of the embryo, that becomes the vas deferens in males and vestigial in females. [1875–80; named after K. F. WOLFF; see -IAN]

wolf·fish (wo͝olf′fish′), *n., pl.* (*esp. collectively*) **-fish,** (*esp. referring to two or more kinds or species*) **-fish·es. 1.** any large fish of the genus *Anarhichas,* as *A. lupus* of the northern Atlantic, allied to the blenny and noted for its ferocious appearance and habits. **2.** lancetfish. [1560–70; WOLF + FISH]

Wölff·lin (*Ger.* vœlf′lin), *n.* **1. E·du·ard** (*Ger.* ā′do͞o-ärt′), 1831–1908, Swiss classical scholar. **2.** his son **Hein·rich** (*Ger.* hīn′rikh), 1864–1945, Swiss art historian.

Wolf·gang (wo͝olf′gang; *Ger.* vôlf′gäng), *n.* a male given name.

wolf′ her′ring, a voracious clupeoid fish, *Chirocentrus dorab,* inhabiting the tropical Indian and Pacific oceans. Also called **dorab.**

wolf·hound (wo͝olf′hound′), *n.* any of several large dogs used in hunting wolves. Cf. **borzoi, Irish wolfhound.** [1780–90; WOLF + HOUND[1]]

wolf·ish (wo͝olf′fish), *adj.* **1.** resembling a wolf, as in form or characteristics. **2.** characteristic of or befitting a wolf; fiercely rapacious. [1560–70; WOLF + -ISH[1]] —**wolf′ish·ly,** *adv.* —**wolf′ish·ness,** *n.*

wolf·man (wo͝olf′man′), *n., pl.* **-men.** *Folklore.* a man who turns into a wolf on certain occasions, as at the time of the full moon; werewolf. [1600–10; WOLF + MAN[1]]

wolf′ note′, wolf (defs. 8a, c).

Wolf′ num′ber (wo͝olf; *Fr.* vôlf), *Astron.* a number indicating the degree of sunspot activity on the sun as a factor of observer idiosyncrasies, the number of sunspot groups, and the number of individual sunspots. Also called **relative sunspot number, sunspot number.** [1975–80; after Rudolf *Wolf* (1816–93), Swiss astronomer]

wolf′ pack′, **1.** a group of submarines operating together in hunting down and attacking enemy convoys. **2.** a group of wolves hunting together. [1890–95 for def. 2; 1940–45 for def. 1]

wolf·ram (wo͝ol′frəm, vôl′-), *n.* **1.** *Chem.* tungsten. **2.** *Mineral.* wolframite. [1750–60; < G *Wolfram* orig., wolframite, prob. equiv. to *Wolf* WOLF + *-ram,* repr. MHG *rām* soot, dirt; formed on the model of personal names with initial *Wolf-,* as a contemptuous epithet for the mineral, which was considered worthless in comparison with tin ores, with which it is often found]

wolf·ram·ate (wo͝ol′frə māt′, vôl′-), *n. Chem.* tungstate. [1855–60; WOLFRAM + -ATE[2]]

wolf·ram·ic (wo͝ol fram′ik, vôl′-), *adj. Chem.* tungstic. [1855–60; WOLFRAM + -IC]

wolf·ram·ite (wo͝ol′frə mīt′, vôl′-), *n.* a mineral, iron manganese tungstate, $(Fe,Mn)WO_4$, occurring in heavy grayish-black to brownish-black tabular or bladed crystals: an important ore of tungsten. Also, **wolfram.** [1865–70; WOLFRAM + -ITE[1]]

Wolf·ram von Esch·en·bach (vôl′främ fən esh′ən bäkh′; *Eng.* wo͝ol′frəm von esh′ən bäkh′, -bäk′), c1170–c1220, German poet.

Wolf′-Ra·yet′ star′ (wo͝olf′rī ā′; *Fr.* vôlf ra ye′), a very hot (35,000–100,000 K) and luminous star in the early stages of evolution, with broad emission lines in its spectrum. Also called **W-R star.** [1885–90; after French astronomers Charles J. E. *Wolf* (1827–1918) and Georges *Rayet* (1839–1906)]

wolfs·bane (wo͝olfs′bān′), *n.* any of several plants in the aconite genus *Aconitum,* including *A. lycoctonum,* bearing stalks of hood-shaped purplish-blue flowers, the monkshood *A. napellus,* which yields a poisonous alkaloid used medicinally, and numerous garden varieties in various colors. [1540–50; WOLF + 'S[1] + BANE]

Wolfs·burg (wo͝olfs′bûrg; *Ger.* vôlfs′bo͝ork), *n.* a city in Lower Saxony, in N central Germany, near Brunswick. 124,900.

wolf′ spi′der, any of numerous ground spiders of the family Lycosidae, including the southern European tarantula, *Lycosa taretula,* that hunt their prey instead of using a web. [1600–10]

wolf′ whis′tle, a wolf call made by whistling, often characterized by two sliding sounds, a peal up to a higher note and then one up to a lower note and down. [1935–40]

Wol·las·ton (wo͝ol′ə stən), *n.* **William Hyde,** 1766–1828, English chemist and physicist.

wol·las·ton·ite (wo͝ol′ə stə nīt′), *n.* a mineral, calcium silicate, $CaSiO_3$, occurring usually in fibrous white masses. [1815–25; named after W. H. WOLLASTON; see -ITE[1]]

Wol′laston Lake′, a lake in NE Saskatchewan, in central Canada. ab. 796 sq. mi. (2062 sq. km).

Wol′laston wire′, extremely fine wire formed by a process **(Wol′laston proc′ess)** in which the metal, drawn as an ordinary wire, is encased in another metal and the two drawn together, after which the outer metal is stripped off or dissolved. [see WOLLASTONITE]

Wol·lon·gong (wo͝ol′ən gông′, -gong′), *n.* a seaport in E New South Wales, in E Australia. 232,510.

Wo·lof (wō′lof), *n.* a language of Senegal, a Niger-Congo language closely related to Fulani.

Wolse·ley (wo͝olz′lē), *n.* **Garnet Joseph, 1st Viscount,** 1833–1913, British field marshal.

Wol·sey (wo͝ol′zē), *n.* **Thomas,** 1475?–1530, English cardinal and statesman.

wolv·er (wo͝ol′vər), *n.* a person who hunts for wolves. [1585–95; see WOLF, -ER[1]]

Wol•ver•hamp•ton (wo͝ol′vər hamp′tən), *n.* a city in West Midlands, in W England. 269,000.

wol•ver•ine (wo͝ol′və rēn′, wo͝ol′və rēn′), *n.* **1.** Also called **carcajou.** a stocky, carnivorous North American mammal, *Gulo luscus,* of the weasel family, having blackish, shaggy hair with white markings. **2.** (*cap.*) a native or inhabitant of Michigan (the Wolverine State) (used as a nickname). [1565–75; alter. of earlier *wolvering* (with -INE[2] for -ING[3]), obscure deriv. of WOLF]

wolverine, *Gulo luscus,* head and body 3 ft. (0.9 m); tail 9 in. (23 cm)

Wol′verine State′, Michigan (used as a nickname).

wolves (wo͝olvz), *n.* pl. of **wolf.**

wom•an (wo͝om′ən), *n., pl.* **wom•en** (wim′in), *v., adj.* —*n.* **1.** the female human being (distinguished from *man*). **2.** an adult female person. **3.** a female attendant to a lady of rank. **4.** a wife. **5.** the nature, characteristics, or feelings often attributed to women; womanliness. **6.** a sweetheart or paramour; mistress. **7.** a female employee or representative: *A woman from the real estate agency called.* **8.** a female person who cleans house, cooks, etc.; housekeeper: *The woman will be in to clean today.* **9.** women collectively: *Woman is no longer subordinate to man.* **10. be one's own woman,** (of females) to be free from restrictions, control, or dictatorial influence; be independent. —*v.t.* **11.** to put into the company of a woman. **12.** to equip or staff with women. **13.** *Obs.* to cause to act or yield like a woman. —*adj.* **14.** of women; womanly. **15.** female: *a woman plumber.* [bef. 900; ME *womman, wimman,* OE *wifman,* equiv. to *wif* female + *man* human being; see WIFE, MAN[1]] —**wom′an•less,** *adj.*

—**Syn.** WOMAN, FEMALE, LADY are nouns referring to adult human beings who are biologically female; that is, capable of bearing offspring. WOMAN is the general term. It is neutral, lacking either favorable or unfavorable implication, and is the most commonly used of the three: *a wealthy woman; a woman of strong character, of unbridled appetites.* In scientific, statistical, and other objective use, FEMALE is the neutral contrastive term to MALE and may apply to plants and animals also: *104 females to every 100 males; Among lions, the female is the chief hunter.* FEMALE is sometimes used in disparaging contexts: *a gossipy female; a conniving female.* LADY meaning "refined, polite woman" is a term of approval or praise: *a real lady in all things; to behave like a lady.*

—**Usage. 2.** Although formerly WOMAN was sometimes regarded as demeaning and LADY was the term of courtesy, WOMAN is the designation preferred by most modern female adults: *League of Women Voters; American Association of University Women.* WOMAN is the standard feminine parallel to MAN. As a modifier of a plural noun, WOMAN, like MAN, is exceptional in that the plural form WOMEN is used: *women athletes; women students.* The use of LADY as a term of courtesy has diminished somewhat in recent years (*the lady of the house*), although it still survives in a few set phrases (*ladies' room; Ladies' Day*). LADY is also used, but decreasingly, as a term of reference for women engaged in occupations considered by some to be menial or routine: *cleaning lady; saleslady.* See also **girl, lady, -woman.**

-woman, a combining form of **woman:** *chairwoman; forewoman; spokeswoman.*

—**Usage.** Feminine compounds ending in -WOMAN are equivalent to the masculine compounds in -MAN. When the person referred to is a woman, the feminine form is often, but not always, used: *alderman, alderwoman; assemblyman, assemblywoman; chairman, chairwoman; congressman, congresswoman; spokesman, spokeswoman; businessman, businesswoman.* However, some forms ending in -MAN are applied to women, and occasionally terms in -MAN are specified by legal code: *Alderman Dorothy Lavelle.* In general, the practice in current edited written English is to avoid the -MAN form in reference to a woman or the plural -MEN when members of both sexes are involved. Instead, a sex-neutral term is used: *council members* rather than *councilmen* and *councilwomen; representative* or *legislator* rather than *congressman* or *congresswoman.* See also **chairperson, -man, -person.**

wom•an•chas•er (wo͝om′ən chā′sər), *n.* a philanderer; womanizer.

wom•an-day (wo͝om′ən dā′), *n., pl.* **-days.** a unit of measurement, esp. in accountancy; based on a standard number of woman-hours in a day of work.

wom•an•ful•ly (wo͝om′ən fə lē), *adv.* in a manner full of womanly spirit: *She struggled womanfully to complete the task.* [1815–25; WOMAN + (MAN)FULLY]

wom•an•hat•er (wo͝om′ən hā′tər), *n.* a person, esp. a man, who dislikes women; misogynist. [1600–10]

wom•an•hood (wo͝om′ən ho͝od′), *n.* **1.** the state of being a woman; womanly character or qualities. **2.** women collectively: *American womanhood.* [1325–75; ME; see WOMAN, -HOOD]

wom•an-hour (wo͝om′ən ouᵊr′, -ou′ər), *n.* a unit of measurement, esp. in accountancy, based on an ideal amount of work accomplished by one woman in an hour. [1960–65]

wom′an in the street′, the average woman: *a new magazine for the woman in the street.* [1925–30]

wom•an•ish (wo͝om′ə nish), *adj.* **1.** womanlike or feminine. **2.** weakly feminine; effeminate. [1325–75; ME; see WOMAN, -ISH[1]] —**wom′an•ish•ly,** *adv.* —**wom′an•ish•ness,** *n.*

—**Syn. 2.** See **womanly.**

wom•an•ize (wo͝om′ə nīz′), *v.,* **-ized, -iz•ing.** —*v.t.* **1.** to make effeminate. —*v.i.* **2.** to pursue or court women habitually. Also, *esp. Brit.,* **wom′an•ise′.** [1585–95; WOMAN + -IZE]

wom•an•iz•er (wo͝om′ə nī′zər), *n.* a philanderer. [1920–25; WOMANIZE + -ER[1]]

wom•an•kind (wo͝om′ən kīnd′), *n.* women, as distinguished from men; the female sex. [1325–75; ME; see WOMAN, KIND[2]]

wom•an•like (wo͝om′ən līk′), *adj.* like a woman; womanly. [1400–50; late ME; see WOMAN, -LIKE]

—**Syn.** See **womanly.**

wom•an•ly (wo͝om′ən lē), *adj.* **1.** like or befitting a woman; feminine; not masculine or girlish. —*adv.* **2.** in the manner of, or befitting, a woman. [1250–1300; ME *wommanli(che).* See WOMAN, -LY] —**wom′an•li•ness, wom′an•ness,** *n.*

—**Syn. 2.** WOMANLY, WOMANLIKE, WOMANISH mean having the traits or qualities that a culture regards as especially characteristic of or ideally appropriate to adult women. WOMANLY is usually a term of approval, suggesting the display of traits admired by the society, such as self-possession, modesty, motherliness, and calm competence: *a womanly consideration for others; with womanly skill and efficiency.* WOMANLIKE may be a neutral synonym for WOMANLY, or it may suggest mild disapproval: *a womanlike dignity; womanlike tears and recriminations.* WOMANISH is usually disparaging; applied to women it suggests traits not generally socially approved: *a womanish petulance; womanish disregard for the rules.* Applied to men it suggests traits culturally deemed inappropriate for men and (in what is now often regarded as a sexist notion) to be found in women: *a womanish shrillness in his speech; a womanish way of stamping his foot in anger.* See also **female.**

wom′an of let′ters, 1. a woman engaged in literary pursuits, esp. a professional writer. **2.** a woman of great learning; scholar.

wom′an of the house′. See **lady of the house.**

wom′an of the streets′, a prostitute; streetwalker. Also, **wom′an of the street′.** [1925–30]

wom′an of the world′, a woman experienced and sophisticated in the ways and manners of the world, esp. the world of society. [1570–80]

wom•an•pow•er (wo͝om′ən pou′ər), *n.* **1.** potential or actual power from the endeavors of women: *the utilization of womanpower during a great national emergency.* **2.** the influence exerted by women as a group, esp. in the work force and in social and political activities. [1940–45; WOMAN + POWER]

wom′an's rights′. See **women's rights.**

wom′an suf′frage, the right of women to vote; female suffrage. [1840–50] —**wom′an-suf′frage,** *adj.* —**wom′an-suf′fra•gist,** *n.*

wom•an-year (wo͝om′ən yēr′), *n.* a unit of measurement, esp. in accountancy, based on a standard number of woman-days in a year of work.

womb (wo͞om), *n.* **1.** the uterus of the human female and certain higher mammals. **2.** the place in which anything is formed or produced: *the womb of time.* **3.** the interior of anything. **4.** *Obs.* the belly. [bef. 900; ME, OE: belly, womb; c. D *wam,* G *Wamme,* Goth *wamba* belly; cf. WAMUS] —**wombed,** *adj.*

wom•bat (wom′bat), *n.* any of several stocky, burrowing, herbivorous marsupials of the family Vombatidae, of Australia, about the size of a badger. [1790–1800; < Dharuk *wom-bat*]

wombat, *Vombatus hirsutus,* length 3 ft. (0.9 m)

womb-to-tomb (wo͞om′tə to͞om′), *adj. Chiefly Brit.* extending from prebirth to death: said esp. of care under the National Health Service. [1970–75]

wom•en (wim′in), *n.* pl. of **woman.**

Wom′en at Point′ Sur′, The (sûr), a narrative poem (1927) by Robinson Jeffers.

wom•en•folk (wim′in fōk′), *n.* (*used with a plural v.*) **1.** women in general; all women. **2.** a particular group of women. Also, **wom′en•folks′.** [1825–35; WOMEN + FOLK]

Wom′en in Love′, a novel (1920) by D. H. Lawrence.

wom•en•kind (wim′in kīnd′), *n.* womankind. [1350–1400; ME *wommen kynde;* see WOMEN, KIND[2]]

wom•en's (wim′inz), *n., pl.* **-en's. 1.** a range of sizes usually from 38 to 44 for garments that fit larger than average women. **2.** a garment in this size range. **3.** the department or section of a store where these garments are sold.

wom′en's libera′tion, a movement to combat sexual discrimination and to gain full legal, economic, vocational, educational, and social rights and opportunities for women, equal to those of men. Also called **wom′en's libera′tion move′ment, wom′en's move′ment.** [1965–70] —**wom′en's libera′tionist.**

wom′en's rights′, the rights claimed for women, equal to those of men, with respect to suffrage, property, the professional fields, etc. Also, **woman's rights.** [1830–40]

wom′en's room′. See **ladies' room.** [1850–55]

wom′en's stud′ies, a program of studies concentrating on the role of women in history, learning, and culture. [1970–75]

wom′en's wear′, apparel and accessories for women. Also, **womenswear.** [1915–20]

wom•ens•wear (wim′inz wâr′), *n.* **1.** See **women's wear. 2.** cloth, esp. wool or wool-blend fabrics, used for women's tailored garments. [1975–80; WOMEN + 'S[1] + WEAR]

wom•er•a (wom′ər ə), *n.* woomera.

wom•yn (wim′in), *n.pl.* women (used chiefly in feminist literature as an alternative spelling to avoid the suggestion of sexism perceived in the sequence *m-e-n*). [1975–80]

won[1] (wun), *v.* pt. and pp. of **win.**

won[2] (wun, wo͝on, wōn), *v.i.,* **wonned, won•ning.** *Archaic.* to dwell; abide; stay. [bef. 900; ME *wonen,* OE *wunian;* c. G *wohnen;* see WONT]

won[3] (won), *n., pl.* **won.** the basic monetary unit of North and South Korea, equal to 100 chon. [1915–20; < Korean *wŏn* < MChin, equiv. to Chin *yuán* YUAN]

won•der (wun′dər), *v.i.* **1.** to think or speculate curiously: *to wonder about the origin of the solar system.* **2.** to be filled with admiration, amazement, or awe; marvel (often fol. by *at*): *He wondered at her composure in such a crisis.* **3.** to doubt: *I wonder if she'll really get here.* —*v.t.* **4.** to speculate curiously or be curious about; be curious to know: *to wonder what happened.* **5.** to feel wonder at: *I wonder that you went.* —*n.* **6.** something strange and surprising; a cause of surprise, astonishment, or admiration: *That building is a wonder. It is a wonder he declined such an offer.* **7.** the emotion excited by what is strange and surprising; a feeling of surprised or puzzled interest, sometimes tinged with admiration. **8.** miraculous deed or event; remarkable phenomenon. **9. for a wonder,** as the reverse of what might be expected; surprisingly: *For a wonder, they worked hard all day.* [bef. 900; (n.) ME; OE *wundor;* c. D *wonder,* G *Wunder,* ON *undr;* (v.) ME *wonderen,* OE *wundrian,* deriv. of the n.] —**won′der•er,** *n.* —**won′der•less,** *adj.*

—**Syn. 1.** conjecture, meditate, ponder, question. **5.** marvel. **7.** surprise, astonishment, amazement, bewilderment, awe.

won•der•ber•ry (wun′dər ber′ē), *n., pl.* **-ries.** the black, edible fruit of an improved garden variety of the black nightshade. Also called **sunberry.** [WONDER + BERRY]

won′der boy′, a young man who is unusually successful or especially popular.

won′der child′, an unusually intelligent or talented child; prodigy; wunderkind. [1895–1900; trans. of G *Wunderkind*]

won′der drug′, a new drug that is noted for its startling curative effect, as an antibiotic or sulfa drug. Also called **miracle drug.** [1935–40]

won•der•ful (wun′dər fəl), *adj.* **1.** excellent; great; marvelous: *We all had a wonderful weekend.* **2.** of a sort that causes or arouses wonder; amazing; astonishing: *The storm was wonderful to behold.* [bef. 1100; ME; OE *wundorful* (see WONDER, -FUL); c. G *wundervoll*] —**won′der•ful•ly,** *adv.* —**won′der•ful•ness,** *n.*

—**Syn. 1.** awesome, wondrous, miraculous, prodigious, astonishing, amazing, astounding, phenomenal.

won•der•ing (wun′dər ing), *adj.* expressing admiration or amazement; marveling. [1585–95; WONDER + -ING[2]] —**won′der•ing•ly,** *adv.*

won•der•land (wun′dər land′), *n.* **1.** a land of wonders or marvels. **2.** a wonderful country or region: *a wonderland of rare plants and flowers; a winter wonderland.* [1780–90; WONDER + -LAND]

won•der•ment (wun′dər mənt), *n.* **1.** wondering or wonder. **2.** a cause or occasion of wonder. [1525–35; WONDER + -MENT]

won•der-strick•en (wun′dər strik′ən), *adj.* struck or affected with wonder. Also, **won•der-struck** (wun′dər-struk′). [1590–1600]

won•der•work (wun′dər wûrk′), *n.* a wonderful work; marvel; miracle. [bef. 1000; ME *wonder werk,* OE *wundorweorc.* See WONDER, WORK]

won•der•work•er (wun′dər wûr′kər), *n.* a worker or performer of wonders or marvels. [1590–1600] —**won′der-work′ing,** *adj.*

won•drous (wun′drəs), *adj.* **1.** wonderful; remarkable. —*adv.* **2.** *Archaic.* wonderfully; remarkably. [1490–1500; metathetic var. of ME *wonders* (gen. of WONDER) wonderful; c. G *Wunders;* sp. conformed to -OUS] —**won′drous•ly,** *adv.* —**won′drous•ness,** *n.*

wong•a•wong•a (wong′ə wong′ə), *n.* a woody Australian vine, *Pandorea pandorana,* of the bignonia family, having showy clusters of yellowish-white flowers streaked with purple. [1890–95; by ellipsis from *wonga-wonga vine,* perh. to be identified with *wonga-wonga* a kind of pigeon < Dharuk *wa-ŋa-wa-ŋa*]

Wŏn•ju (wun′jo͞o′), *n.* a city in N South Korea, E of Seoul. 110,188.

wonk (wongk), *n. Slang.* **1.** a student who spends much time studying and has little or no social life; grind. **2.** a stupid, boring, or unattractive person. [1960–65, *Amer.;* of expressive orig.; nautical slang *wonk* "a midshipman," Australian slang: "white person, homosexual" are prob. independent formations]

won•ky (wong′kē), *adj.,* **-ki•er, -ki•est. 1.** *Brit. Slang.* **a.** shaky, groggy, or unsteady. **b.** unreliable; not trustworthy. **2.** *Slang.* stupid; boring; unattractive. [1920–25; perh. var. of dial. *wanky,* equiv. to *wank(le)* (ME *wankel,* OE *wancol;* see WENCH) + -Y[1]; def. 1 prob. represents a different word (see WONK)]

won•na (wun′nə), *Scot.* contraction of *will not.*

CONCISE PRONUNCIATION KEY: *act, cāpe, dâre, pärt; set, ēqual; if, ice; ox, ōver, ôrder, oil, bo͝ok, bo͞ot, out; up, ûrge; child; sing; shoe; thin, that;* zh as in *treasure.* ə = *a* as in *alone, e* as in *system, i* as in *easily, o* as in *gallop, u* as in *circus;* ᵊ as in *fire* (fīᵊr), *hour* (ouᵊr). l and n can serve as syllabic consonants, as in *cradle* (krād′l), and *button* (but′n). See the full key inside the front cover.

Wŏn•san (wœn′sän′), *n.* a seaport in E North Korea. 300,000.

wont (wônt, wōnt, wunt), *adj., n., v.,* **wont, wont** or **wont•ed, wont•ing.** —*adj.* **1.** accustomed; used (usually fol. by an infinitive): *He was wont to rise at dawn.* —*n.* **2.** custom; habit; practice: *It was her wont to walk three miles before breakfast.* —*v.t.* **3.** to accustom (a person), as to a thing. **4.** to render (a thing) customary or usual (usually used passively). —*v.i.* **5.** *Archaic.* to be wont. [1300–50; (adj.) ME *wont, woned,* OE *gewunod,* ptp. of *gewunian* to be used to (see WON[2]); c. G *gewöhnt;* (v.) ME, back formation from WONTED or *wont* (ptp.); (n.) appar. from conflation of *wont* (ptp.) with obs. *wone* wish, in certain stereotyped phrases] —**wont′less,** *adj.*
—**Syn. 1.** habituated, wonted. **2.** use. —**Ant. 1.** unaccustomed.

won't (wōnt, wunt), contraction of *will not: He won't see you now.*
—**Usage.** See **contraction.**

wont•ed (wôn′tid, wōn′-, wun′-), *adj.* **1.** accustomed; habituated; used. **2.** customary, habitual, or usual: *He took his wonted place in the library.* [1375–1425; WONT (n.) + -ED[3], or by extension (see -ED[2]) of *wont* (ptp.; see WONT (adj.))] —**wont′ed•ly,** *adv.* —**wont′ed•ness,** *n.*
—**Syn. 1.** wont.

won ton (won′ ton′), **1.** (in Chinese cooking) a dumpling filled with minced pork and spices, usually boiled in and served with soup but sometimes fried as a side dish. **2.** a soup containing won tons. Also, **won′ton′.** [1930–35; < dial. Chin (Guangdong) *wàhn tān,* akin to Chin *húntun* dumpling]

woo (wo͞o), *v.t.* **1.** to seek the favor, affection, or love of, esp. with a view to marriage. **2.** to seek to win: *to woo fame.* **3.** to invite (consequences, whether good or bad) by one's own action; court: *to woo one's own destruction.* **4.** to seek to persuade (a person, group, etc.), as to do something; solicit; importune. —*v.i.* **5.** to make love to a woman; court: *He went wooing.* **6.** to solicit favor or approval; entreat: *Further attempts to woo proved useless.* [bef. 1050; ME *wowe,* OE *wōgian*] —**woo′er,** *n.* —**woo′ing•ly,** *adv.*
—**Syn. 4.** petition, sue, address, entreat.

wood[1] (wo͝od), *n.* **1.** the hard, fibrous substance composing most of the stem and branches of a tree or shrub, and lying beneath the bark; the xylem. **2.** the trunks or main stems of trees as suitable for architectural and other purposes; timber or lumber. **3.** firewood. **4.** the cask, barrel, or keg, as distinguished from the bottle: *aged in the wood.* **5.** See **wood block** (def. 1). **6.** *Music.* **a.** a woodwind instrument. **b.** the section of a band or orchestra composed of woodwinds. **7.** Often, **woods.** (*used with a singular or plural v.*) a large and thick collection of growing trees; a grove or forest: *They picnicked in the woods.* **8.** *Golf.* a club with a wooden head, as a driver, brassie, spoon, or baffy for hitting long shots. Cf. **iron** (def. 5). **9. have the wood on,** *Australian Slang.* to have an advantage over or have information that can be used against. **10. out of the woods, a.** out of a dangerous, perplexing, or difficult situation; secure; safe. **b.** no longer in precarious health or critical condition; out of danger and recovering. —*adj.* **11.** made of wood; wooden. **12.** used to store, work, or carry wood: *a wood chisel.* **13.** dwelling or growing in woods: *wood bird.* —*v.t.* **14.** to cover or plant with trees. **15.** to supply with wood; get supplies of wood for. —*v.i.* **16.** to take in or get supplies of wood (often fol. by *up*): *to wood up before the approach of winter.* [bef. 900; ME; OE *wudu,* earlier *widu;* c. ON *vithr,* OHG *witu,* OIr *fid*] —**wood′less,** *adj.*
—**Syn. 7.** See **forest.**

wood[2] (wo͝od), *adj. Archaic.* **1.** wild, as with rage or excitement. **2.** mad; insane. [bef. 900; ME; OE *wōd;* c. ON *ōthr;* akin to G *Wut* rage, OE *wōth* song]

Wood (wo͝od), *n.* **1. Grant,** 1892–1942, U.S. painter. **2. Leonard,** 1860–1927, U.S. military doctor and political administrator.

wood′ al′cohol. See **methyl alcohol.** [1860–65]

wood′ anem′one, any of several anemones, esp. *Anemone nemorosa,* of the Old World, or *A. quinquefolia,* of the U.S. [1650–60]

wood′ bet′ony, 1. the betony, *Stachys officinalis.* **2.** a hairy lousewort, *Pedicularis canadensis,* native to eastern North America, having deeply lobed leaves and a dense cluster of yellow or red tubular flowers. [1650–60]

wood•bin (wo͝od′bin′), *n.* a bin, box, or the like for storing wood fuel. Also called **wood•box** (wo͝od′boks′). [WOOD[1] + BIN]

wood•bine (wo͝od′bīn′), *n.* any of several climbing vines, as a European honeysuckle, *Lonicera periclymenum,* or the Virginia creeper of North America. [bef. 900; ME *wodebinde,* OE *wudubind,* equiv. to *wudu* WOOD[1] + *bind* binding; see BIND]

wood•block (wo͝od′blok′), *n.* **1.** a block of wood engraved in relief, for printing from; woodcut. **2.** a print or impression from such a block. **3.** a hollow block of hard wood struck with a wooden stick or mallet and used in the percussion section of an orchestra. —*adj.* **4.** made from a woodblock: *woodblock prints.* [1830–40; WOOD[1] + BLOCK]

wood•bor•er (wo͝od′bôr′ər, -bōr′-), *n.* **1.** a tool, operated by compressed air, for boring wood. **2.** *Zool.* **a.** borer (def. 3a). **b.** borer (def. 3b). [1840–50; WOOD[1] + BORER] —**wood′bor′ing,** *adj.*

Wood•bridge (wo͝od′brij′), *n.* a city in NE New Jersey. 90,074.

Wood•burn (wo͝od′bərn), *n.* a town in NW Oregon. 11,196.

CONCISE ETYMOLOGY KEY: <, descended or borrowed from; >, whence; b., blend of, blended; c., cognate with; cf., compare; deriv., derivative; equiv., equivalent; imit., imitative; obl., oblique; r., replacing; s., stem; sp., spelling, spelled; resp., respelling, respelled; trans., translation; ?, origin unknown; *, unattested; ‡, probably earlier than. See the full key inside the front cover.

Wood•bur•y (wo͝od′ber′ē, -bə rē), *n.* a city in SW New Jersey. 10,353.

wood•carv•er (wo͝od′kär′vər), *n.* a person whose occupation is woodcarving. [1855–60; WOOD[1] + CARVE + -ER[1]]

wood•carv•ing (wo͝od′kär′ving), *n.* **1.** the art or technique of carving objects by hand from wood or of carving decorations into wood. **2.** something made or decorated in such a manner. [1840–50; WOOD[1] + CARVE + -ING[1]]

wood•chat (wo͝od′chat′), *n.* **1.** Also, **wood′chat shrike′.** a shrike, *Lanius senator,* of Europe and northern Africa, having a black forehead and a chestnut crown, nape, and mantle. **2.** any of various Asiatic thrushes, esp. of the genus *Larvivora.* [1695–1705; WOOD[1] + CHAT]

wood•chip (wo͝od′chip′), *n.* **1.** a small chip of wood, esp. one that flakes off when felling a tree or splitting a log. **2. woodchips,** chips of wood, esp. fir or other pine, used as a winter mulch on plants and shrubs. [1955–60; WOOD[1] + CHIP[1]]

wood•chop•per (wo͝od′chop′ər), *n.* a person who chops wood, esp. one who fells trees. [1770–80, *Amer.;* WOOD[1] + CHOPPER] —**wood′chop′ping,** *n.*

wood•chuck (wo͝od′chuk′), *n.* a stocky North American burrowing rodent, *Marmota monax,* that hibernates in the winter. Also called **chuck, groundhog.** [1665–75, *Amer.;* presumably a reshaping by folk etym. of a word in a Southern New England Algonquian language; cf. Narragansett (E sp.) *ockqutchaun* woodchuck]

woodchuck, *Marmota monax,* head and body 17 in. (43 cm); tail 6 in. (15 cm)

wood′ coal′, 1. brown coal; lignite. **2.** charcoal. [1645–55]

wood•cock (wo͝od′kok′), *n., pl.* **-cocks,** (*esp. collectively*) **-cock** for 1, 2. **1.** either of two plump, short-legged migratory game birds of variegated brown plumage, the Eurasian *Scolopax rusticola* and the smaller American *Philohela minor.* **2.** any of various pileated or ivory-billed woodpeckers. **3.** *Archaic.* a simpleton. [bef. 1050; ME *wodecok,* OE *wuducoc.* See WOOD[1], COCK[1]]

wood•craft (wo͝od′kraft′, -kräft′), *n.* **1.** skill in anything that pertains to the woods or forest, esp. in making one's way through the woods or in hunting, trapping, etc. **2.** forestry (defs. 1, 2). **3.** the art of making or carving wooden objects. [1300–50; ME; see WOOD[1], CRAFT]

wood•craft•er (wo͝od′kraf′tər, -kräf′-), *n.* a person who makes or carves wooden objects. [WOODCRAFT + -ER[1]]

wood•crafts•man (wo͝od′krafts′mən, -kräfts′-), *n., pl.* **-men.** a person who is skilled in woodcraft. [WOOD[1] + CRAFTSMAN]

wood•creep•er (wo͝od′krē′pər), *n.* any of numerous New World tropical songbirds of the family Dendrocolaptidae, having stiffened tail feathers and creeperlike habits. Also called **woodhewer.** [WOOD[1] + CREEPER]

wood′ cud′weed, a weedy, composite plant, *Gnaphalium sylvaticum,* of the North Temperate Zone, having woolly foliage and numerous, dirty-white flowerheads in a leafy spike. Also called **chafeweed.**

wood•cut (wo͝od′kut′), *n.* **1.** a carved block of wood from which prints are made. **2.** a print or impression from such a block. [1655–65; WOOD[1] + CUT]

wood•cut•ter (wo͝od′kut′ər), *n.* **1.** a person who cuts down trees for firewood. **2.** a person who makes woodcuts. [1755–65, *Amer.;* WOOD[1] + CUTTER] —**wood′cut′ting,** *n.*

Wood′ Dale′, a town in NE Illinois. 11,251.

wood′ duck′, a North American duck, *Aix sponsa,* that nests in trees, the male of which has a long crest and black, chestnut, green, purple, and white plumage. [1770–80, *Amer.*]

wood duck, *Aix sponsa,* length 1½ ft. (0.5 m)

wood′ ear′. See **tree ear.**

wood•ed (wo͝od′id), *adj.* covered with or abounding in woods or trees. [1595–1605; WOOD[1] + -ED[3]]

wood•en (wo͝od′n), *adj.* **1.** consisting or made of wood; wood: *a wooden ship.* **2.** stiff, ungainly, or awkward: *a wooden gait.* **3.** without spirit, animation, or awareness. **4.** dull or stupid. **5.** indicating the fifth event of a series, as a wedding anniversary. [1530–40; WOOD[1] + -EN[2]] —**wood′en•ly,** *adv.* —**wood′en•ness,** *n.*
—**Syn. 3.** expressionless, vacant, lifeless, impassive.

wood′ engrav′ing, 1. the art or process of engraving designs in relief with a burin on the end grain of wood, for printing. **2.** a block of wood so engraved. **3.** a print or impression from it. [1810–20] —**wood′ engrav′er.**

wood•en•head (wo͝od′n hed′), *n. Informal.* a stupid person; blockhead. [1825–35; WOODEN + HEAD]

wood•en-head•ed (wo͝od′n hed′id), *adj. Informal.* thick-headed, dull; stupid. [1850–55] —**wood′en-head′ed•ness,** *n.*

Wood′en Horse′. See **Trojan Horse** (def. 1). [1615–25]

wood′en In′dian, 1. a carved wooden statue of a standing American Indian, formerly found before many cigar stores as an advertisement. **2.** (*often l.c.*) *Informal.* a person who appears emotionless and unresponsive; a poker face. [1875–80, *Amer.*]

wood′en shoe′, sabot (def. 1). [1600–10]

wood′en tongue′, *Vet. Pathol.* actinobacillosis. [1910–15, *Amer.*]

wood•en•ware (wo͝od′n wâr′), *n.* vessels, utensils, etc., made of wood. [1640–50; WOODEN + WARE[1]]

wood′ fern′, any of several shield ferns of the genus *Dryopteris.* [1880–85]

wood′ frog′, a typically light-brown frog, *Rana sylvatica,* inhabiting moist woodlands of eastern North America, having a dark, masklike marking on the head. [1690–1700]

wood•grain (wo͝od′grān′), *n.* **1.** a material or finish that imitates the natural grain of wood in pattern, color, and sometimes texture. **2.** of or pertaining to woodgrain. [WOOD[1] + GRAIN] —**wood′grain′ing,** *n.*

wood′ grouse′, the capercaillie. [1770–80]

Wood•ha•ven (wo͝od′hā′vən), *n.* a city in SE Michigan. 10,902.

wood•henge (wo͝od′henj′), *n. Archaeol.* a henge monument consisting of circles of upright timber posts. [1925–30; WOOD[1] + (STONE)HENGE]

wood•hew•er (wo͝od′hyo͞o′ər), *n.* woodcreeper. [WOOD[1] + HEWER]

wood′ hoo′poe, any of several tropical, African birds of the family Phoeniculidae, having metallic, blackish plumage and slender, curved bills.

wood•house (wo͝od′hous′), *n., pl.* **-hous•es** (-hou′ziz). a house or shed in which wood is stored. [1225–75; ME; see WOOD[1], HOUSE]

Wood•hull (wo͝od′hul′), *n.* **Victoria Claf•lin** (klaf′lin), 1838–1927, U.S. social reformer, newspaper publisher, and women's-rights advocate.

wood′ hy′acinth, bluebell (def. 2). [1870–75]

wood′ i′bis, any of several storks of the subfamily Mycteriinae, esp. *Mycteria americana,* of the warm parts of America, and *Ibis ibis,* of Africa, having chiefly white plumage and a featherless head and resembling the true ibises in having curved bills: *M. Americana* is endangered. Also called **wood stork.** [1775–85, *Amer.*]

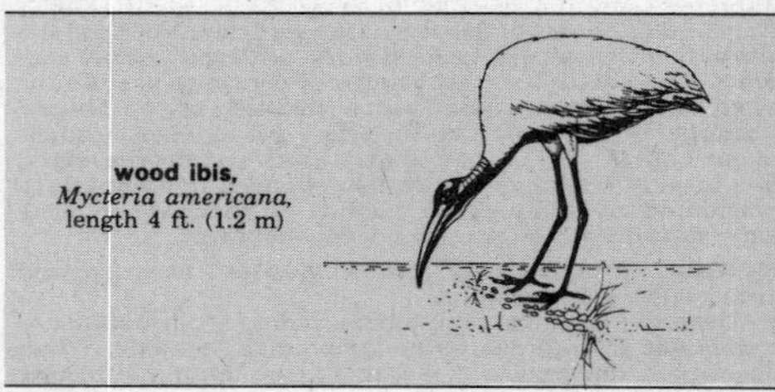
wood ibis, *Mycteria americana,* length 4 ft. (1.2 m)

wood•land (*n.* wo͝od′land′, -lənd; *adj.* wo͝od′lənd), *n.* **1.** land covered with woods or trees. —*adj.* **2.** of, pertaining to, or inhabiting the woods; sylvan: *a woodland nymph.* [bef. 900; OE *wuduland.* See WOOD[1], LAND]

Wood•land (wo͝od′lənd), *n.* a city in N central California. 30,235.

wood′land car′ibou, a variety of caribou inhabiting the bogs and forests of eastern Canada, having large, palmate antlers. [1950–55]

Wood′land cul′ture, *Archaeol.* a long pre-Columbian tradition characterized by the corded pottery of a hunting and later agricultural people of the eastern U.S. noted for the construction of burial mounds and other structures and dating from c1000 B.C. to A.D 1700.

wood•land•er (wo͝od′lən dər), *n.* an inhabitant of the woods. [1765–75; WOODLAND + -ER[1]]

wood•lark (wo͝od′lärk′), *n.* a small, European songbird, *Lullula arborea,* noted for its song in flight. [1275–1325; ME *wodelarke.* See WOOD[1], LARK[1]]

wood′ lil′y, a lily, *Lilium philadelphicum,* of eastern North America, having orange-red flowers. [1350–1400; ME: meadow saffron]

wood′ lot′, a tract, esp. on a farm, set aside for trees. Also, **wood′lot′.** [1635–45, *Amer.*]

wood′ louse′, *Zool.* any of certain small, terrestrial crustaceans of the genera *Oniscus, Armadillidium,* etc., having a flattened, elliptical body. [1605–15]

wood•man (wo͝od′mən), *n., pl.* **-men. 1.** woodsman (def. 1). **2.** a person who fells timber, esp. for fuel. **3.** *Brit.* **a.** a forester having charge of the king's woods. **b.** a woodcutter. **c.** a dealer in wood, esp. one who sells kindling wood. **4.** *Obs.* a hunter of forest game. [bef. 1000; ME *wodeman,* OE *wudumann.* See WOOD[1], MAN[1]] —**wood•man•craft** (wo͝od′mən kraft′, -kräft′), *n.*

wood′ mead′ow grass′, a coarse, spreading grass, *Poa nemoralis,* of Eurasia, having flowers in long, narrow clusters.

Wood•mere (wo͝od′mēr), *n.* a city on SW Long Island, in SE New York. 17,205.

wood′ mouse′, 1. any of various mice living in woodlands. 2. See **white-footed mouse.** [1595–1605]

wood•note (wo͝od′nōt′), *n.* a wild or natural musical tone, as that of a forest bird. [1625–35; WOOD[1] + NOTE]

wood′ nymph′, 1. (esp. in legend) a nymph of the woods; dryad. 2. a brown satyr butterfly, *Minois alope,* having a broad yellow band and black-and-white eyespots on each front wing. 3. any of several Central and South American hummingbirds, esp. of the genus *Thalurania.* [1570–80]

wood•peck•er (wo͝od′pek′ər), *n.* any of numerous climbing birds of the family Picidae, having a hard, chisellike bill that it hammers repeatedly into wood in search of insects, stiff tail feathers to assist in climbing, and usually more or less boldly patterned plumage. [1520–30; WOOD[1] + PECKER]

wood′ pe′wee, either of two small North American flycatchers, the western *Contopus sordidulus* or the eastern *C. virens.* Also **wood′-pe′wee.** [1800–10]

wood′ pi′geon, 1. Also called **ringdove.** a European pigeon, *Columba palumbus,* having a whitish patch on each side of the neck. 2. See **band-tailed pigeon.** [1660–70]

wood•pile (wo͝od′pīl′), *n.* a pile or stack of firewood. [1545–55; WOOD[1] + PILE[1]]

wood′ pitch′, the final product of the destructive distillation of wood.

wood•print (wo͝od′print′), *n.* woodcut. [1810–20; WOOD[1] + PRINT]

wood′ pulp′, wood reduced to pulp through mechanical and chemical treatment for use in the manufacture of certain kinds of paper. [1865–70]

wood′ puss′y, *Facetious.* a skunk. [1895–1900, *Amer.*]

wood′ rab′bit, a cottontail. [1890–95]

wood′ rat′. See **pack rat** (def. 1). [1750–60]

wood′ ray′. See **xylem ray.** [1920–25]

Wood•ridge (wo͝od′rij′), *n.* a city in NE Illinois. 22,322.

Wood′ Riv′er, a city in SW Illinois. 12,449.

wood′ rose′, the dried seed pod of the Ceylon morning glory.

Wood•row (wo͝od′rō), *n.* a male given name.

wood•ruff (wo͝od′rəf, -ruf′), *n.* any of several plants belonging to the genus *Asperula* or *Galium,* of the madder family, as *G. odoratum* **(sweet woodruff),** a fragrant plant with small white flowers. [bef. 1000; ME *woderove,* OE *wudurofe, wudurife,* equiv. to *wudu* WOOD[1] + *-rofe, -rife,* element of uncert. meaning; cf. G *Rübe* carrot]

Wood•ruff (wo͝od′rəf), *n.* **Hiram,** 1817–67, Canadian driver, trainer, and breeder of harness-racing horses.

Wood′ruff key′, *Mach.* a key having the form of a nearly semicircular disk fitting into a recess in a shaft. [appar. after the proper name]

Woods (wo͝odz), *n.* **Lake of the.** See **Lake of the Woods.**

wood′ screw′, any of various screws that have a slotted head and a gimlet point that permit them to be driven into wood with a screwdriver. [1725–35]

wood•shed (wo͝od′shed′), *n., v.,* **-shed•ded, -shed•ding.** —*n.* 1. a shed for storing wood for fuel. —*v.i.* 2. *Slang.* to practice a musical instrument assiduously and with a specific goal in mind. [1835–45; WOOD[1] + SHED[1]]

wood′ shot′, 1. (in tennis, badminton, and other racket games) a shot hit off the neck or frame of the racket instead of the strings. 2. *Golf.* a shot made with a wood. [1925–30]

wood•si•a (wo͝od′zē ə), *n.* any of various small ferns of the genus *Woodsia,* of northern temperate, alpine, and arctic regions, having short, stout stalks, usually lance-shaped fronds, and often covered with fine hairs: common on mountains in rocky ledges and crevices. [< NL (1815), after Joseph Woods (1776–1864), English botanist; see -IA]

woods•man (wo͝odz′mən), *n., pl.* **-men.** 1. Also, **woodman.** a person accustomed to life in the woods and skilled in the arts of the woods, as hunting or trapping. 2. a lumberman. [1680–90; WOOD[1] + -S[3] + MAN[1]]

Wood's′ met′al, *Trademark.* a fusible alloy of 50 percent bismuth, 25 percent lead, 12.5 percent tin, and 12.5 percent cadmium; melts at 158°F (70°C): used in the valves of sprinkler systems.

Wood•son (wo͝od′sən), *n.* **Carter Godwin,** 1875–1950, U.S. historian and publisher: pioneer in modern black studies.

wood′ sor′rel, any of numerous plants of the genus *Oxalis,* esp. *O. acetosella,* of Eurasia, having heart-shaped, trifoliolate leaves and white, pink-veined flowers. [1515–25; trans. of F *sorrel de bois*; r. *woodsour,* so called from sour taste of the leaves]

wood′ spir′it, 1. See **methyl alcohol.** 2. (esp. in folklore) a supernatural, incorporeal being believed to inhabit the forest. [1835–45]

Wood•stock (wo͝od′stok′), *n.* 1. a town in NE Illinois. 11,725. 2. a village in SE New York, NW of Kingston. 1073. 3. a rock music festival held in August of 1969 near Bethel, N.Y.: originally scheduled to be held at Woodstock, N.Y.

wood′ stork′. See **wood ibis.** [1880–85]

wood′ sug′ar, *Chem.* a white, crystalline, water-soluble powder, $C_5H_{10}O_5$, the dextrorotatory form of xylose: used chiefly in dyeing and tanning. [1895–1900]

wood•swal•low (wo͝od′swol′ō), *n.* any of several slate-colored songbirds of the family Artamidae, of southeastern Asia, Australia, and New Guinea, having long, pointed wings and noted for their swift, soaring flight. [1850–55]

woods•y (wo͝od′zē), *adj.,* **woods•i•er, woods•i•est.** of, or characteristic or suggestive of, the woods: *a woodsy fragrance.* [1855–60, *Amer.*; WOOD[1] + -S[3] + -Y[1]; cf. -SY]

wood′ tar′, a dark viscid product obtained from wood by distillation or by slow burning without flame, used in its natural state to preserve timber, rope, etc., or subjected to further distillation to yield creosote, oils, and a final residuum, wood pitch. [1855–60]

wood′ thrush′, a large thrush, *Hylocichla mustelina,* common in woodlands of eastern North America, and noted for its melodious song. See illus. under **thrush**[1]. [1785–95]

wood′ tick′. See **American dog tick.** [1660–70]

wood•tone (wo͝od′tōn′), *adj.* 1. having a finish painted, dyed, printed, etc., to imitate the pattern or color of wood; woodgrain: *a woodtone instrument panel in a car.* —*n.* 2. a woodtone finish. [WOOD[1] + TONE]

wood•turn•er (wo͝od′tûr′nər), *n.* a person whose occupation is wood turning. [1830–40; WOOD[1] + TURNER[1]]

wood′ turn′ing, the forming of wood articles upon a lathe. [1875–80] —**wood′-turn′ing,** *adj.*

wood′ tur′pentine, turpentine obtained from pine trees. [1905–10]

wood′ vin′egar. See **pyroligneous acid.** [1830–40]

wood′ war′bler, 1. warbler (def. 2). 2. a yellowish-green European warbler, *Phylloscopus sibilatrix.* [1810–20]

Wood•ward (wo͝od′wərd), *n.* 1. **Robert Burns,** 1917–79, U.S. chemist: Nobel prize 1965. 2. a town in NW Oklahoma. 13,610.

wood•wax•en (wo͝od′wak′sən), *n.* woadwaxen.

wood•wind (wo͝od′wind′), *n.* 1. a musical wind instrument of the group comprising the flutes, clarinets, oboes, bassoons, and occasionally, the saxophones. 2. **woodwinds,** the section of an orchestra or band comprising the woodwind instruments. —*adj.* 3. of, relating to, or composed of woodwinds. [1875–80; WOOD[1] + WIND[3]]

wood•wool (wo͝od′wo͝ol′), *n.* fine wood shavings, usually of pine, or chemically treated wood fibers: used for surgical dressings, as an insulating material, as a binder in plaster, for packing breakable objects, etc. [1550–60]

wood•work (wo͝od′wûrk′), *n.* 1. objects or parts made of wood. 2. the interior wooden fittings, esp. of a house, as doors, stairways, or moldings. 3. **come out of the woodwork,** *Informal.* to appear or materialize suddenly and unexpectedly: *Since mortgage rates declined, prospective buyers have been coming out of the woodwork.* [1640–50; WOOD[1] + WORK]

wood•work•er (wo͝od′wûr′kər), *n.* a worker in wood, as a carpenter, joiner, or cabinetmaker. [1870–75; WOOD[1] + WORKER]

wood•work•ing (wo͝od′wûr′king), *n.* 1. the act or art of working wood. —*adj.* 2. pertaining to or used for shaping wood: *woodworking tools.* [1870–75; WOOD[1] + WORKING]

wood•worm (wo͝od′wûrm′), *n.* a worm or larva that breeds in or bores into wood. [1530–40; WOOD[1] + WORM]

wood•y[1] (wo͝od′ē), *adj.,* **wood•i•er, wood•i•est.** 1. abounding with woods; wooded. 2. belonging or pertaining to the woods; sylvan. 3. consisting of or containing wood; ligneous. 4. resembling wood, as in appearance, texture, or toughness: *a woody vegetable.* [1325–75; ME; see WOOD[1], -Y[1]] —**wood′i•ness,** *n.*

wood•y[2] (wo͝od′ē), *n., pl.* **wood•ies.** *Slang.* a station wagon having wood or simulated-wood panels on the outside of the body. [1960–65; WOOD[1] + -Y[2]]

wood•y[3] (wud′ē, wo͞o′dē), *n., pl.* **wood•ies,** *adj.,* **wood•i•er, wood•i•est.** *Chiefly Scot.* widdy[1].

Wood•y (wo͝od′ē), *n.* a male given name, form of **Woodrow.**

wood′y night′shade, bittersweet (def. 3). [1570–80]

woof[1] (wo͝of, wo͞of), *n.* 1. filling (def. 5). 2. texture; fabric. 3. *Brit.* warp (def. 13). [bef. 900; ME *oof, owf,* OE *ōwef, āwef* (cf. *gewef*), equiv. to *ō-, ā-* A-[3] + *wef* (akin to WEB); modern *w-* from WEFT, WARP, WEAVE, etc.]

woof[2] (wo͝of), *interj.* (used to imitate the bark of a dog).

woof•er (wo͝of′ər), *n. Audio.* a loudspeaker designed for the reproduction of low-frequency sounds. [1935–40; WOOF[2] + -ER[1]]

wool (wo͝ol), *n.* 1. the fine, soft, curly hair that forms the fleece of sheep and certain other animals, characterized by minute, overlapping surface scales that give it its felting property. 2. fabrics and garments of such wool. 3. yarn made of such wool. 4. any of various substances used commercially as substitutes for the wool of sheep or other animals. 5. any of certain vegetable fibers, as cotton or flax, used as wool, esp. after preparation by special process **(vegetable wool).** 6. any finely fibrous or filamentous matter suggestive of the wool of sheep: *glass wool; steel wool.* 7. any coating of short, fine hairs or hairlike processes, as on a caterpillar or a plant; pubescence. 8. *Informal.* the human hair, esp. when short, thick, and crisp. 9. **all wool and a yard wide,** genuine; excellent; sincere: *He was a real friend, all wool and a yard wide.* 10. **dyed in the wool,** inveterate; confirmed: *a dyed in the wool sinner.* 11. **pull the wool over someone's eyes,** to deceive or delude someone: *The boy thought that by hiding the broken dish he could pull the wool over his mother's eyes.* [bef. 900; ME *wolle,* OE *wull(e),* c. D *wol,* G *Wolle,* ON *ull,* Goth *wulla;* akin to L *lāna,* Skt *ūrṇā,* Welsh *gwlân* wool, L *vellus* fleece, Gk *oúlos* woolly] —**wool′like′,** *adj.*

wool′ clip′, the total yield of wool shorn during one season from the sheep of a particular region. [1890–95]

wool•en (wo͝ol′ən), *n.* 1. any cloth of carded wool yarn of which the fibers vary in length: bulkier, looser, and less regular than worsted. 2. **woolens,** wool cloth or clothing. —*adj.* 3. made or consisting of wool: *woolen cloth.* 4. of or pertaining to wool or woolen fabrics. Also, *esp. Brit.,* **wool′len.** [bef. 1050; ME *wollen* (adj. and n.), OE *wullen, wyllen* (n.). See WOOL, -EN[2]]

wool•er (wo͝ol′ər), *n.* a domestic animal raised for its wool. [WOOL + -ER[1]]

Woolf (wo͝olf), *n.* **Virginia** (*Adeline Virginia Stephen Woolf*), 1882–1941, English novelist, essayist, and critic.

wool′ fat′, lanolin. [1890–95]

wool•fell (wo͝ol′fel′), *n.* the skin of a wool-bearing animal with the fleece still on it. [1375–1425; late ME *wolle fell.* See WOOL, FELL[4]]

wool•gath•er (wo͝ol′gath′ər), *v.i.* to engage in woolgathering. [1840–50; by back formation from WOOLGATHERING] —**wool′gath′er•er,** *n.*

wool•gath•er•ing (wo͝ol′gath′ər ing), *n.* 1. indulgence in idle fancies and in daydreaming; absentmindedness: *His woolgathering was a handicap in school.* 2. gathering of the tufts of wool shed by sheep and caught on bushes. [1545–55; WOOL + GATHERING]

wool•grow•er (wo͝ol′grō′ər), *n.* a person who raises sheep or other animals for the production of wool. [1800–10; WOOL + GROWER] —**wool′grow′ing,** *n.*

Wooll•cott (wo͝ol′kət), *n.* **Alexander,** 1887–1943, U.S. essayist and journalist.

Wool•ley (wo͝ol′ē), *n.* **Sir (Charles) Leonard,** 1880–1960, English archaeologist and explorer.

wool•ly (wo͝ol′ē), *adj.,* **-li•er, -li•est,** *n., pl.* **-lies.** —*adj.* 1. consisting of wool: *a woolly fleece.* 2. resembling wool in texture or appearance: *woolly hair.* 3. clothed or covered with wool or something resembling it: *a woolly caterpillar.* 4. *Bot.* covered with a pubescence of long, soft hairs resembling wool. 5. like the rough, vigorous atmosphere of the early West in America: *wild and woolly.* 6. fuzzy; unclear; disorganized: *woolly thinking.* —*n.* 7. *Western U.S.* a wool-bearing animal; sheep. 8. Usually, **woollies.** a knitted undergarment of wool or other fiber. 9. any woolen garment, as a sweater. 10. *Dial.* a dust ball. Also, **wooly.** [1580–90; WOOL + -Y[1]] —**wool′li•ness,** *n.*
—**Regional Variation.** 10. See **dust ball.**

wool′ly a′phid, 1. any plant louse of the family Aphididae, characterized by a waxy secretion that appears like a jumbled mass of fine, curly, white cottony or woolly threads, as *Eriosoma lanigerum* **(wool′ly ap′ple a′phid** or **American blight)** and *Prociphilus tessellatus* **(wool′ly al′der a′phid).** 2. any of various aphids that produce white waxy threads, as *Adelges piceae* **(balsam woolly aphid).** [1835–45]

wool′ly bear′, the caterpillar of any of several moths, as a tiger moth, having a dense coat of woolly hairs. [1835–45]

wool•ly•butt (wo͝ol′ē but′), *n.* any of several Australian trees of the genus *Eucalyptus,* esp. *E. longifolia,* having rough, often fibrous bark. [1835–45; WOOLLY + BUTT[1]]

wool•ly-head•ed (wo͝ol′ē hed′id), *adj.* 1. having hair of a woolly texture or appearance. 2. marked by fuzzy thinking; muddleheaded; dim-witted. [1640–50] —**wool′ly-head′ed•ness,** *n.*

wool′ly mam′moth, a shaggy-coated mammoth, *Mammuthus primigenius,* that lived in cold regions across Eurasia and North America during the Ice Age, known from fossils, cave paintings, and well-preserved frozen carcasses. Also called **Siberian mammoth.** See illus. under **mammoth.** [1965–70]

wool′ly manza•ni′ta, a tree or shrub, *Arctostaphylos tomentosa,* of the heath family, common from British Columbia to California, having broad leaves, with the underside covered with white hairs, and white flowers.

wool′ly mon′key, either of two large New World monkeys *Lagothrix lagotricha,* with black skin and dark, woolly fur, and *L. flavicauda,* similar but with a buffy face patch and a yellow-banded tail, native to forests of the Amazon and Orinoco basins: *L. lagotricha* is endangered and *L. flavicauda* threatened. [1875–80]

wool′ly worm′, *Midland U.S.* See **woolly bear.** [1910–15, *Amer.*]

wool•man (wo͝ol′mən), *n., pl.* **-men.** a person who buys and sells wool; wool dealer. [1350–1400; ME; see WOOL, MAN[1]]

wool•pack (wo͝ol′pak′), *n.* 1. a coarse fabric, usually of jute, in which raw wool is packed for transport. 2. the package in which raw wool is done up for transport. 3. something resembling such a package, as a fleecy cloud. 4. *Meteorol.* a cumulus cloud of fleecy appearance with a horizontal base. [1250–1300; ME; see WOOL, PACK[1]]

wool•sack (wo͝ol′sak′), *n.* 1. a sack or bag of wool. 2. *Brit.* a. (in the House of Lords) one of a number of cloth-covered seats or divans stuffed with wool, for the use of judges, esp. one for the Lord Chancellor. b. the Lord Chancellor's office. [1250–1300; ME; see WOOL, SACK[1]]

wool•shed (wo͝ol′shed′), *n.* a building in which sheep are sheared and wool is gathered and prepared for market. [1840–50; WOOL + SHED[1]]

wool•skin (wo͝ol′skin′), *n.* a sheepskin with the wool still attached. [1400–50; late ME; see WOOL, SKIN]

wool′sort•ers' disease′ (wo͝ol′sôr′tərz), *Pathol.* pulmonary anthrax in humans, caused by inhaling the spores of *Bacillus anthracis,* which may contaminate wool fleece. [1875–80; WOOL + SORTER + 'S[1]]

wool′ sponge′, a commercial sponge, *Hippiospongia lachne,* of Florida and the West Indies, the surface of which resembles the fleece of a sheep. Also called **sheepswool sponge.** [1875–80, *Amer.*]

CONCISE PRONUNCIATION KEY: *act, cāpe, dâre, pärt; set, ēqual; if, ice; ox, ōver, ôrder, oil, bo͝ok, bo͞ot, out; up, ûrge; child; sing; shoe; thin, that; zh as in treasure.* ə = *a* as in *alone, e* as in *system, i* as in *easily, o* as in *gallop, u* as in *circus;* ᵊ as in *fire* (fīᵊr), *hour* (ouᵊr). l and n can serve as syllabic consonants, as in *cradle* (krād′l), and *button* (but′n). See the full key inside the front cover.

wool′ sta′pler, **1.** a dealer in wool. **2.** a person who sorts wool, according to the staple or fiber. [1700–10] —**wool′sta′pling,** *adj.*

Wool·wich (wo͝ol′ij, -ich), *n.* a former borough of Greater London, England, now part of Greenwich and Newham: royal military academy and arsenal.

Wool·worth (wo͝ol′wûrth′), *n.* **Frank Win·field** (win′fēld′), 1852–1919, U.S. merchant.

wool·y (wo͝ol′ē), *adj.,* **wool·i·er, wool·i·est,** *n., pl.* **wool·ies.** woolly. —**wool′i·ness,** *n.*

woo·mer·a (wo͝om′ər ə), *n.* a notched stick used by Australian Aborigines to propel spears or darts. Also, **womera.** [1810–20; < Dharuk *wu-ma-ra*]

woom·er·ang (wo͞o′mə rang′), *n. Australian Obs.* boomerang. [1840–50; < Dharuk *wu-ma-rāŋ*]

Woon·sock·et (wo͞on sok′it), *n.* a city in NE Rhode Island. 45,914.

woops (wo͝ops, wo͞ops), *interj.* whoops.

Woop Woop (wo͝op′ wo͝op′), *Australian Slang (disparaging).* an imaginary remote town or district symbolizing isolation and backwardness. Also, **woop′ woop′.** [1925–30; jocular coinage mimicking placenames of Aboriginal orig.]

woo·ra·li (wo͞o rä′lē), *n.* curare.

woosh (wo͞osh, wo͝osh), *n., v.i., v.t.* whoosh.

Woos·ter (wo͝os′tər), *n.* **1. David,** 1711–77, American Revolutionary War general. **2.** a city in N Ohio. 19,289.

wooz·y (wo͞o′zē, wo͝oz′ē), *adj.,* **wooz·i·er, wooz·i·est.** **1.** stupidly confused; muddled: *woozy from a blow on the head.* **2.** physically out of sorts, as with dizziness, faintness, or slight nausea: *He felt woozy after the flu.* **3.** drunken. [1895–1900, *Amer.*; perh. short for *boozy-woozy,* rhyming compound based on BOOZY] —**wooz′i·ly,** *adv.* —**wooz′i·ness,** *n.*

wop (wop), *n. Slang (disparaging and offensive).* an Italian or a person of Italian descent. [1910–15, *Amer.*; < It (Neapolitan dial.) *guappo* swaggerer < Sp *guapo* pimp, ruffian, via dial. F < L *vappa* wine that has gone flat, worthless person; initial *w* perh. by assoc. with a related Gmc word]

Worces·ter (wo͝os′tər), *n.* **1. Joseph Emerson,** 1784–1865, U.S. lexicographer. **2.** a city in central Massachusetts. 161,799. **3.** a city in Hereford and Worcester, in W England, on the Severn: cathedral; Cromwell's defeat of the Scots 1651. 74,300. **4.** Worcestershire.

Worces′ter chi′na, *Trademark.* a soft-paste porcelain containing very little clay or none at all, made at Worcester, England, since 1751. Also called **Royal Worcester, Worces′ter por′celain.** [1795–1805]

Worces·ter·shire (wo͝os′tər shēr′, -shər), *n.* a former county in W central England, now part of Hereford and Worcester.

Worces′tershire sauce′, a sharp sauce made with soy, vinegar, spices, etc., originally made in Worcester, England. [1680–90]

word (wûrd), *n.* **1.** a unit of language, consisting of one or more spoken sounds or their written representation, that functions as a principal carrier of meaning. Words are composed of one or more morphemes and are either the smallest units susceptible of independent use or consist of two or three such units combined under certain linking conditions, as with the loss of primary accent that distinguishes *black′bird′* from *black′ bird′.* Words are usually separated by spaces in writing, and are distinguished phonologically, as by accent, in many languages. **2. words, a.** speech or talk: *to express one's emotion in words; Words mean little when action is called for.* **b.** the text or lyrics of a song as distinguished from the music. **c.** contentious or angry speech; a quarrel: *We had words and she walked out on me.* **3.** a short talk or conversation: *Marston, I'd like a word with you.* **4.** an expression or utterance: *a word of warning.* **5.** warrant, assurance, or promise: *I give you my word I'll be there.* **6.** news; tidings; information: *We received word of his death.* **7.** a verbal signal, as a password, watchword, or countersign. **8.** an authoritative utterance, or command: *His word was law.* **9.** Also called **machine word.** *Computers.* a string of bits, characters, or bytes treated as a single entity by a computer, particularly for numeric purposes. **10.** *(cap.)* Also called **the Word, the Word of God. a.** the Scriptures; the Bible. **b.** the Logos. **c.** the message of the gospel of Christ. **11.** a proverb or motto. **12. at a word,** in immediate response to an order or request; in an instant: *At a word they came to take the situation in hand.* **13. be as good as one's word,** to hold to one's promises. **14. eat one's words,** to retract one's statement, esp. with humility: *They predicted his failure, but he made them eat their words.* **15. have a word,** to talk briefly: *Tell your aunt that I would like to have a word with her.* **16. have no words for,** to be unable to describe: *She had no words for the sights she had witnessed.* **17. in a word,** in summary; in short: *In a word, there was no comparison.* Also, **in one word. 18. in so many words,** in unequivocal terms; explicitly: *She told them in so many words to get out.* **19. keep one's word,** to fulfill one's promise: *I said I'd meet the deadline, and I kept my word.* **20. man of his word** or **woman of her word,** a person who can be trusted to keep a promise; a reliable person. **21. of few words,** laconic; taciturn: *a woman of few words but of profound thoughts.* **22. of many words,** talkative; loquacious; wordy: *a person of many words but of little wit.* **23. put in a good word for,** to speak favorably of; commend: *He put in a good word for her with the boss.* Also, **put in a word for. 24. take one at one's word,** to take a statement to be literal and true. **25. take the words out of one's mouth,** to say exactly what another person was about to say. **26. weigh one's words,** to choose one's words carefully in speaking or writing: *It was an important message, and he was weighing his words.*
—*v.t.* **27.** to express in words; select words to express; phrase: *to word a contract with great care.*
—*interj.* **28. my word!** or **upon my word!** (used as an exclamation of surprise or astonishment.) [bef. 900; ME, OE; c. D *woord,* G *Wort,* ON *orth,* Goth *waurd;* akin to OPruss *wirds,* L *verbum* word, Lith *var̃das* name]
—**Syn. 4.** statement, declaration. **5.** pledge. **6.** message, report, account. **7.** catchword, shibboleth.

word′ ac′cent, *Phonet.* See **word stress.** [1900–05]

word·age (wûr′dij), *n.* **1.** words collectively. **2.** quantity or amount of words: *The wordage of the document exceeds a million.* **3.** verbiage; wordiness. **4.** choice of words; wording: *His wordage betrayed his lack of knowledge on the subject.* [1820–30; WORD + -AGE]

word′ associa′tion, stimulation of an associative pattern by a word.

word′ associa′tion test′, *Psychol.* a technique for determining a subject's associative pattern by providing a verbal stimulus to which a verbal response is required. [1945–50]

word-blind (wûrd′blīnd′), *adj.* having alexia. [1895–1900]

word′ blind′ness, alexia. [1880–85]

word·book (wûrd′bo͝ok′), *n.* **1.** a book of words, usually with definitions, explanations, etc.; a dictionary. **2.** the libretto of an opera. [1590–1600; WORD + BOOK]

word′ class′, *Gram.* a group of words all of which are members of the same form class or part of speech. [1920–25]

word′ deaf′ness, *Pathol.* inability to comprehend the meanings of words though they are heard, caused by lesions of the auditory center of the brain. [1885–90] —**word′-deaf′,** *adj.*

word′ for word′, **1.** in exactly the same words; verbatim. **2.** one word at a time, without regard for the sense of the whole: *She translated the book word for word.* [1350–1400; ME] —**word′-for-word′,** *adj.*

word′ game′, any game or contest involving skill in using, forming, guessing, or changing words or expressions, such as anagrams or Scrabble.

word-hoard (wûrd′hôrd′, -hōrd′), *n.* a person's vocabulary. [1890–95; literal mod. rendering of OE *word-hord*]

word·ing (wûr′ding), *n.* **1.** the act or manner of expressing in words; phrasing. **2.** the particular choice of words in which a thing is expressed: *He liked the thought but not the wording.* [1555–65; WORD + -ING[1]]
—**Syn.** See **diction.**

word·less (wûrd′lis), *adj.* **1.** speechless, silent, or mute. **2.** not put into words; unexpressed. [1150–1200; ME; see WORD, -LESS] —**word′less·ly,** *adv.* —**word′less·ness,** *n.*

word-lore (wûrd′lôr′, -lōr′), *n.* **1.** a study of words and derivations. **2.** the vocabulary of a particular language and the history of its words. Also, **word′lore′.** [1865–70]

word·mon·ger (wûrd′mung′gər, -mong′-), *n.* a writer or speaker who uses words pretentiously or with careless disregard for meaning. [1580–90; WORD + MONGER] —**word′mon′ger·ing,** *n.*

Word′ of God′, the, word (def. 10). [1520–30]

word′ of hon′or, a pledge of one's honor that a specified condition, bargain, etc., will be fulfilled; oath; promise. [1805–15]

word′ of mouth′, informal oral communication: *The rumor spread rapidly by word of mouth.* [1545–55] —**word′-of-mouth′,** *adj.*

word′ or′der, the way in which words are arranged in sequence in a sentence or smaller construction: *In Latin, word order is freer than in English.* [1890–95]

word′ paint′ing, **1.** an effective verbal description. **2.** See **tone painting.** [1865–70] —**word′ paint′er.**

word′ pic′ture, a description in words, esp. one that is unusually vivid: *She drew a word picture of a South Pacific sunset.* [1855–60]

word·play (wûrd′plā′), *n.* **1.** clever or subtle repartee; verbal wit. **2.** a play on words; pun. [1870–75; WORD + PLAY]

word′ proc′essing, writing, editing, and production of documents, as letters, reports, and books, through the use of a computer program or a complete computer system designed to facilitate rapid and efficient manipulation of text. *Abbr.:* WP Also, **word′-proc′ess·ing.** [1970–75]

word′ proc′essor, **1.** a computer program or computer system designed for word processing. **2.** a person who performs word processing. [1975–80]

word′ sal′ad, incoherent speech consisting of both real and imaginary words, lacking comprehensive meaning, and occurring in advanced schizophrenic states. [1910–15]

word·smith (wûrd′smith′), *n.* **1.** an expert in the use of words. **2.** a person, as a journalist or novelist, whose vocation is writing. [1895–1900; WORD + SMITH]

word′ square′, a set of words such that when arranged one beneath another in the form of a square they read alike horizontally and vertically. [1875–80]

word square

S A T E D
A T O N E
T O A S T
E N S U E
D E T E R

word′ stress′, the stress pattern or patterns associated with the words of a particular language when they are considered in isolation. Also called **word accent.** Cf. **sentence stress.** [1910–15]

Words·worth (wûrdz′wûrth′), *n.* **William,** 1770–1850, English poet: poet laureate 1843–50. —**Words·worth′i·an,** *adj., n.* —**Words·worth′i·an·ism,** *n.*

word′ time′, *Computers.* the time required to transfer a machine word, esp. one stored serially, from one memory unit to another. Cf. **access time.**

word′ wrap′, a feature of word-processing systems and some electronic typewriters that automatically moves a word to a new line to avoid overrunning the margin. Also called **wraparound.** [1975–80]

word·y (wûr′dē), *adj.,* **word·i·er, word·i·est.** **1.** characterized by or given to the use of many, or too many, words; verbose: *She grew impatient at his wordy reply.* **2.** pertaining to or consisting of words; verbal. [bef. 1100; ME; OE *wordig.* See WORD, -Y[1]] —**word′i·ly,** *adv.* —**word′i·ness,** *n.*
—**Syn. 1.** diffuse, talkative, loquacious, voluble. WORDY, PROLIX, REDUNDANT, PLEONASTIC all mean using more words than necessary to convey a desired meaning. WORDY, the broadest and least specific of these terms, may, in addition to indicating an excess of words, suggest a garrulousness or loquaciousness: *a wordy, gossipy account of a simple incident.* PROLIX refers to speech or writing extended to great and tedious length with inconsequential details: *a prolix style that tells you more than you need or want to know.* REDUNDANT and PLEONASTIC both refer to unnecessary repetition of language. REDUNDANT has also a generalized sense of "excessive" or "no longer needed": *the dismissal of redundant employees.* In describing language, it most often refers to overelaboration through the use of expressions that repeat the sense of other expressions in a passage: *a redundant text crammed with amplifications of the obvious.* PLEONASTIC, usually a technical term, refers most often to expressions that repeat something that has been said before: *"A true fact" and "a free gift" are pleonastic expressions.*

wore (wôr, wōr), *v.* pt. of **wear.**

wore-out (wôr′out′, wōr′-), *adj. Chiefly Midland and Southern U.S.* worn-out.

work (wûrk), *n., adj., v.,* **worked** or *(Archaic except for 35, 37, 40)* **wrought; working.** —*n.* **1.** exertion or effort directed to produce or accomplish something; labor; toil. **2.** something on which exertion or labor is expended; a task or undertaking: *The students finished their work in class.* **3.** productive or operative activity. **4.** employment, as in some form of industry, esp. as a means of earning one's livelihood: *to look for work.* **5.** one's place of employment: *Don't phone him at work.* **6.** materials, things, etc., on which one is working or is to work. **7.** the result of exertion, labor, or activity; a deed or performance. **8.** a product of exertion, labor, or activity: *musical works.* **9.** an engineering structure, as a building or bridge. **10.** a building, wall, trench, or the like, constructed or made as a means of fortification. **11. works, a.** *(used with a singular or plural v.)* a place or establishment for manufacturing (often used in combination): *ironworks.* **b.** the working parts of a machine: *the works of a watch.* **c.** *Theol.* righteous deeds. **12.** *Physics.* force times the distance through which it acts; specifically, the transference of energy equal to the product of the component of a force that acts in the direction of the motion of the point of application of the force and the distance through which the point of application moves. **13. at work, a.** working, as at one's job: *He's at work on a new novel.* **b.** in action or operation: *to see the machines at work.* **14. gum up the works,** *Slang.* to spoil something, as through blundering or stupidity: *The surprise party was all arranged, but her little brother gummed up the works and told her.* **15. in the works,** in preparation or being planned: *A musical version of the book is in the works.* **16. make short work of,** to finish or dispose of quickly: *We made short work of the chocolate layer cake.* **17. out of work,** unemployed; jobless: *Many people in the area were out of work.* **18. shoot the works,** *Slang.* to spend all one's resources: *Let's shoot the works and order the crêpes suzette.* **19. the works,** *Informal.* **a.** everything; all related items or matters: *a hamburger with the works.* **b.** harsh or cruel treatment: *to give someone the works.*
—*adj.* **20.** of, for, or concerning work: *work clothes.* **21.** working (def. 18).
—*v.i.* **22.** to do work; labor. **23.** to be employed, esp. as a means of earning one's livelihood: *He hasn't worked for six weeks.* **24.** to be in operation, as a machine. **25.** to act or operate effectively: *The pump will not work. The plan works.* **26.** to attain a specified condition, as by repeated movement: *The nails worked loose.* **27.** to have an effect or influence, as on a person or on the mind or feelings of a person. **28.** to move in agitation, as the features under strong emotion. **29.** to make way with effort or under stress: *The ship works to windward.* **30.** *Naut.* to give slightly at the joints, as a vessel under strain at sea. **31.** *Mach.* to move improperly, as from defective fitting of parts or from wear. **32.** to undergo treatment by labor in a given way: *This dough works slowly.* **33.** to ferment, as a liquid.
—*v.t.* **34.** to use or manage (an apparatus, contrivance, etc.): *She can work many business machines.* **35.** to bring about (any result) by or as by work or effort: *to work a change.* **36.** to manipulate or treat by labor: *to work butter.* **37.** to put into effective operation. **38.** to operate (a mine, farm, etc.) for productive purposes: *to work a coal mine.* **39.** to carry on operations in (a district or region). **40.** to make, fashion, or execute by work. **41.** to achieve or win by work or effort: *to work one's passage.* **42.** to keep (a person, a horse, etc.) at work: *She works her employees hard.* **43.** to influence or persuade, esp. insidiously: *to work other people to one's will.* **44.** *Informal.* to exploit (someone or something) to one's advantage: *See if you can work your uncle for a new car. He worked his charm in landing a new job.* **45.** to make or decorate by needlework or embroidery: *She worked a needlepoint cushion.* **46.** to cause fermentation in. **47. work in** or **into, a.** to bring or put in; add, merge, or blend: *The tailor worked in the patch*

skillfully. Work the cream into the hands until it is completely absorbed. **b.** to arrange a time or employment for: *The dentist was very busy, but said she would be able to work me in late in the afternoon. They worked him into the new operation.* **48. work off, a.** to lose or dispose of, as by exercise or labor: *We decided to work off the effects of a heavy supper by walking for an hour.* **b.** to pay or fulfill by working: *He worked off his debt by doing odd jobs.* **49. work on** or **upon,** to exercise influence on; persuade; affect: *I'll work on her, and maybe she'll change her mind.* **50. work out, a.** to bring about by work, effort, or action. **b.** to solve, as a problem. **c.** to arrive at by or as by calculation. **d.** to pay (a debt) by working instead of paying money. **e.** to exhaust, as a mine. **f.** to issue in a result. **g.** to evolve; elaborate. **h.** to amount to (a total or specified figure); add up (to): *The total works out to 176.* **i.** to prove effective or successful: *Their marriage just didn't work out.* **j.** to practice, exercise, or train, esp. in order to become proficient in an athletic sport: *The boxers are working out at the gym tonight.* **51. work over, a.** to study or examine thoroughly: *For my term paper I worked over 30 volumes of Roman history.* **b.** *Informal.* to beat unsparingly, esp. in order to obtain something or out of revenge: *They threatened to work him over until he talked.* **52. work through,** to deal with successfully; come to terms with: *to work through one's feelings of guilt.* **53. work up, a.** to move or stir the feelings; excite. **b.** to prepare; elaborate: *Work up some plans.* **c.** to increase in efficiency or skill: *He worked up his typing speed to 70 words a minute.* **54. work up to,** rise to a higher position; advance: *He worked up to the presidency.* [bef. 900; (n.) ME *worke,* OE *worc,* r. ME *werk(e),* OE *weorc,* c. OFris, OS *werk,* OHG *werah, werc* (G *Werk*), ON *verk,* Gk *érgon;* (v.) ME *worken,* deriv. of the n., r. ME *wyrchen,* OE *wyrcean;* c. G *wirken,* ON *verkja,* Goth *waurkjan*]
—Syn. 1. WORK, DRUDGERY, LABOR, TOIL refer to exertion of body or mind in performing or accomplishing something. WORK is the general word and may apply to exertion that is either easy or hard: *fun work; heavy work.* DRUDGERY suggests continuous, dreary, and dispiriting work, esp. of a menial or servile kind: *the drudgery of household tasks.* LABOR particularly denotes hard manual work: *labor on a farm, in a steel mill.* TOIL suggests wearying or exhausting labor: *toil that breaks down the worker's health.* **2.** enterprise, project, job, responsibility. **3.** industry, occupation, business. **4.** job, trade, calling, vocation, profession. **7.** product, achievement, feat. **22.** toil, drudge. **34.** operate, manipulate, handle. **35.** accomplish, effect, produce, achieve. **40.** finish, form, shape. **43.** move. **—Ant. 1.** play, rest.

Work (wûrk), *n.* **Henry Clay,** 1832–84, U.S. songwriter.

work•a•ble (wûr′kə bəl), *adj.* **1.** practicable or feasible: *He needs a workable schedule.* **2.** capable of or suitable for being worked. [1535–45; WORK + -ABLE] **—work′a•bil′i•ty, work′a•ble•ness,** *n.*

work•a•day (wûr′kə dā′), *adj.* **1.** of or befitting working days; characteristic of a workday and its occupations. **2.** ordinary; commonplace; everyday; prosaic. [1150–1200; alter. (prob. after NOWADAYS) of earlier *worky-day* workday, alter. (by assoc. with HOLIDAY) of ME *werkeday,* obscurely derived from WORK and DAY]

work•a•hol•ic (wûrk′ə hô′lik, -hol′ik), *n.* a person who works compulsively at the expense of other pursuits. [1965–70; WORK + -AHOLIC] **—work′a•hol′ism,** *n.*

work•bag (wûrk′bag′), *n.* a bag for holding implements and materials for work, esp. needlework. [1765–75; WORK + BAG]

work•bas•ket (wûrk′bas′kit, -bä′skit), *n.* a basket used to hold needlework paraphernalia. [1735–45; WORK + BASKET]

work•bench (wûrk′bench′), *n.* a sturdy table at which an artisan works. [1775–85; WORK + BENCH]

work•boat (wûrk′bōt′), *n.* a boat used for work or trade rather than sport, public transportation, or military purposes. [1935–40; WORK + BOAT]

work•book (wûrk′bo͝ok′), *n.* **1.** a manual of operating instructions. **2.** a book designed to guide the work of a student by inclusion of questions, exercises, etc. **3.** a book in which a record is kept of work completed or planned. [1905–10; WORK + BOOK]

work•box (wûrk′boks′), *n.* a box to hold instruments and materials for work, esp. needlework. [1805–15; WORK + BOX[1]]

work′ camp′, 1. a camp for prisoners sentenced to labor, esp. to outdoor labor such as roadbuilding or farming. **2.** a volunteer project in which members of a church, service organization, etc., work together in aid of some worthy cause. [1930–35]

work•day (wûrk′dā′), *n.* **1.** a day on which work is done; working day. **2.** the part of a day during which one works. **3.** the length of time during a day on which one works: *a seven-hour workday.* **—***adj.* **4.** workaday. [1400–50; late ME *werkday,* OE *weorcdæg.* See WORK, DAY]

worked (wûrkt), *adj.* that has undergone working. [1700–10; WORK + -ED[2]]
—Syn. WORKED, WROUGHT both apply to something on which effort has been applied. WORKED implies expended effort of almost any kind: *a worked silver mine.* WROUGHT implies fashioning, molding, or making, esp. of metals: *wrought iron.*

worked-up (wûrkt′up′), *adj.* wrought-up. [1900–05]

work•er (wûr′kər), *n.* **1.** a person or thing that works. **2.** a laborer or employee: *steel workers.* **3.** a person engaged in a particular field, activity, or cause: *a worker in psychological research; a worker for the Republican party.* **4.** *Entomol.* **a.** a member of a caste of sexually underdeveloped, nonreproductive bees, specialized to collect food and maintain the hive. See illus. under **bee. b.** a similar member of a specialized caste of ants, termites, or wasps. **5.** *Print.* one of a set of electrotyped plates used to print from (contrasted with *molder*). **6.** any of several rollers covered with card clothing that work in combination with the stripper rollers and the cylinder in the carding of fibers. [1300–50; ME *werker, worcher.* See WORK, -ER[1]]

work•er-priest (wûr′kər prēst′), *n.* (in France) a Roman Catholic priest who, in addition to his priestly duties, works part-time in a secular job. [1945–50]

work′ers' compensa′tion insur′ance, insurance required by law from employers for the protection of employees while engaged in the employer's business. [1975–80]

work′ eth′ic, a belief in the moral benefit and importance of work and its inherent ability to strengthen character. [1950–55]

work•fare (wurk′fâr′), *n.* a governmental plan under which welfare recipients are required to accept public-service jobs or to participate in job training. [1965–70; WORK + (WEL)FARE]

work′ farm′, a farm to which juvenile offenders are sent for a period to work, for disciplinary purposes or rehabilitation. [1950–55]

work•flow (wûrk′flō′), *n.* the flow or amount of work to and from an office, department, or employee. [1945–50; WORK + FLOW]

work•folk (wûrk′fōk′), *n. pl.* people who work for a wage, salary, commission, etc., esp. rural or agricultural employees. Also, **work′folks′.** [1425–75; late ME; see WORK, FOLK]

work′ force′, 1. the total number of workers in a specific undertaking: *a holiday for the company's work force.* **2.** the total number of persons employed or employable: *a sharp increase in the nation's work force.* Also, **work′force′.** Also called **labor force.** [1940–45]

work′ func′tion, 1. *Physics.* the least energy necessary to free an electron from a metal surface. **2.** *Thermodynam.* See **Helmholtz function.**

work•fur•lough (wûrk′fûr′lō), *adj.* work-release. [1955–60]

work•horse (wûrk′hôrs′), *n.* **1.** a horse used for plowing, hauling, and other heavy labor, as distinguished from a riding horse, racehorse, etc. **2.** a person who works tirelessly at a task, assumes extra duties, etc. [1535–45; WORK + HORSE]

work•hour (wûrk′ouᵊr′, -ou′ər), *n.* any of the hours of a day during which work is done, as in an office, usually between 9 A.M. and 5 P.M. Also, **work′hour′, working hour.** [1840–50]

work•house (wûrk′hous′), *n., pl.* **-hous•es** (-hou′ziz). **1.** a house of correction. **2.** *Brit.* (formerly) a poorhouse in which paupers were given work. **3.** *Obs.* a workshop. [bef. 1100; ME *werkhous,* OE *weorchūs* workshop. See WORK, HOUSE]

work•ing (wûr′king), *n.* **1.** the act of a person or thing that works. **2.** operation; action: *the involuted workings of his mind.* **3.** the process of shaping a material: *the working of damp clay.* **4.** the act of manufacturing or building a thing. **5.** Usually, **workings.** a part of a mine, quarry, or the like, in which work is carried on. **6.** the process of fermenting, as of yeasts. **7.** a slow advance involving exertion. **8.** disturbed or twisting motions: *The working of his limbs revealed the disease.* **9.** repeated movement or strain tending to loosen a structural assembly or part. **—***adj.* **10.** that works. **11.** doing some form of work, esp. manual, mechanical, or industrial work, as for a living: *a working person.* **12.** operating; producing effects, results, etc. **13.** pertaining to, connected with, or used in operating or working. **14.** serving to permit or facilitate continued work: *a working model; a working majority.* **15.** adequate for usual or customary needs: *a working knowledge of Spanish.* **16.** large enough for working or being worked: *a working sample.* **17.** done, taken, etc., while conducting or discussing business: *a working lunch.* **18.** Also, **work.** (of a face or edge, as of a timber or a metal casting) shaped and planed as a reference for further shaping and planing. [1250–1300; ME *werking.* See WORK, -ING[1], -ING[2]]
—Syn. 15. usable, practical, operative, functioning.

work′ing as′set, *Accounting.* invested capital that is comparatively liquid. [1910–15]

work′ing cap′ital, 1. the amount of capital needed to carry on a business. **2.** *Accounting.* current assets minus current liabilities. **3.** liquid capital assets as distinguished from fixed capital assets. [1900–05]

work′ing-cap•i•tal fund′ (wûr′king kap′i tl), a fund established to finance operating activities in an industrial enterprise.

work′ing class′, 1. those persons working for wages, esp. in manual labor. **2.** the social or economic class composed of these workers. [1805–15] **—work′•ing-class′,** *adj.*

work′ing day′, 1. the amount of time that a worker must work for an agreed daily wage. **2.** a day ordinarily given to working (distinguished from *holiday*). **3.** the daily period of hours for working. [1525–35]

work•ing-day (wûr′king dā′), *adj.* workaday; everyday. [1470–80]

work′ing dog′, one of any of several breeds of usually large dogs developed to perform a practical function, as herding, guarding, or pulling heavy loads, as the collie, Doberman pinscher, and Siberian Husky. [1890–95]

work′ing draw′ing, an accurately measured and detailed drawing of a structure, machine, detail, etc., used as a guide to workers in constructing it. [1825–35]

work′ing face′, *Mining.* face (def. 18).

work′ing flu′id, *Mech.* a liquid or gaseous working substance. [1900–05]

work′ing girl′, 1. a woman who works. **2.** *Slang.* a prostitute. [1860–65, for def. 1; 1965–70, for def. 2]
—Usage. See **girl.**

work′ing hour′, work-hour.

work′ing hypoth′esis. See under **hypothesis** (def. 1).

work•ing•man (wûr′king man′), *n., pl.* **-men.** a man of the working class; a man, whether skilled or unskilled, who earns his living at some manual or industrial work. [1630–40; WORKING + MAN[1]]
—Usage. See **-man.**

work′ing or′der, the condition of a mechanism when it is functioning properly: *a stove in working order.* [1835–45]

work′ing pa′pers, 1. legal papers often required for employment, as by an alien. **2.** legal papers enabling a minor in the U.S. to work under certain conditions. [1925–30]

work•ing•per•son (wûr′king pûr′sən), *n.* a workingman or workingwoman.
—Usage. See -PERSON.

work′ing rail′. See **fly rail** (def. 2).

work′ing sub′stance, a substance, usually a fluid, that undergoes changes in pressure, temperature, volume, or form as part of a process for accomplishing work. [1895–1900]

work•ing•wom•an (wûr′king wo͝om′ən), *n., pl.* **-wom•en.** a woman who is regularly employed. [1850–55; WORKING + WOMAN]
—Usage. See **-woman.**

work′ load′, the amount of work that a machine, employee, or group of employees can be or is expected to perform. [1940–45]

work•man (wûrk′mən), *n., pl.* **-men. 1.** a man employed or skilled in some form of manual, mechanical, or industrial work. **2.** a male worker. [bef. 900; ME *werkman,* OE *weorcman.* See WORK, MAN[1]]
—Usage. See **-man.**

work•man•like (wûrk′mən līk′), *adj.* **1.** like or befitting a workman. **2.** skillful; well executed: *a workmanlike piece of writing.* Also, **work′man•ly.** [1400–50; late ME *werkmanlike.* See WORKMAN, -LIKE]

work•man•ship (wûrk′mən ship′), *n.* **1.** the art or skill of a workman or workwoman. **2.** the quality or mode of execution, as of a thing made. **3.** the product or result of labor and skill; work executed. [1325–75; ME *werkmanschipe.* See WORKMAN, -SHIP]

work′men's compensa′tion insur′ance. See **workers' compensation insurance.**

work′ of art′, 1. a piece of creative work in the arts, esp. a painting or sculpture. **2.** a product that gives aesthetic pleasure and that can be judged separately from any utilitarian considerations. [1825–35]

work′ or′der, an order authorizing specific work, repairs, etc., to be done.

work•out (wûrk′out′), *n.* **1.** a trial or practice session in athletics, as in running, boxing, or football. **2.** a structured regime of physical exercise: *She goes to the gym for a workout twice a week.* **3.** any trial or practice session. **4.** an act or instance of working something out. [1890–95; n. use of v. phrase *work out*]

work•peo•ple (wûrk′pē′pəl), *n.pl.* people employed at work or labor; workers; employees. [1700–10; WORK + PEOPLE]

work•piece (wûrk′pēs′), *n.* a piece of work being machined. [1925–30; WORK + PIECE]

work•place (wûrk′plās′), *n.* **1.** a person's place of employment. **2.** any or all places where people are employed: *a bill to set safety standards for the workplace.* [1820–30; WORK + PLACE]

work•print (wûrk′print′), *n. Motion Pictures.* the first positive print of a film, assembled from the dailies: used in the editing process. [1935–40; WORK + PRINT]

Work′ Proj′ects Administra′tion. See **WPA.**

work-re•lease (wûrk′ri lēs′), *adj.* of or pertaining to a program under which prisoners may work outside of prison while serving their sentences. [1955–60]

work•room (wûrk′ro͞om′, -ro͝om′), *n.* a room in which work is carried on. [1820–30; WORK + ROOM]

work′ rules′, a set of rules, usually established by one or more unions in an agreement with management, specifying the tasks to be done by each employee. [1960–65]

works′ coun′cil, *Chiefly Brit.* **1.** an elected body of employee representatives that deals with management regarding grievances, working conditions, wages, etc. **2.** a joint council or committee representing employer and employees that discusses working conditions, wages, etc., within a plant or business. [1925–30]

work′ sheet′, 1. a sheet of paper on which work schedules, working time, special instructions, etc., are recorded. **2.** a piece or scrap of paper on which problems, ideas, or the like, are set down in tentative form. **3.** Also, **work′sheet′.** *Accounting.* a sheet of paper on which is printed a series of columns and into which tentative figures are entered as a preliminary step in preparing the adjusted or final statement. [1920–25]

work•shop (wûrk′shop′), *n.* **1.** a room, group of rooms, or building in which work, esp. mechanical work, is carried on. **2.** a seminar, discussion group, or the like, that emphasizes exchange of ideas and the demonstration and application of techniques, skills, etc.: *a theater workshop; opera workshop.* [1555–65; WORK + SHOP]

work•shop•per (wôrk′shop′ər), *n. Informal.* a person who has a workshop, esp. in a home, for working with tools, usually as a hobby. [WORKSHOP + -ER[1]]

work′ song′, a folk song sung by workers, with a rhythm like that of their work. [1920–25]

work•space (wûrk′spās′), *n.* space used or required for one's work, as in an office or home. [1955–60; WORK + SPACE]

CONCISE PRONUNCIATION KEY: act, cāpe, dâre, pärt; set, ēqual; *if,* īce; ox, ōver, ôrder, oil, bo͝ok, bo͞ot, out; up, ûrge; child; sing; shoe; thin, *th*at; zh as in *treasure.* ə = *a* as in *alone, e* as in *system, i* as in *easily, o* as in *gallop, u* as in *circus;* ᵊ as in *fire* (fīᵊr), *hour* (ouᵊr). l and n can serve as syllabic consonants, as in *cradle* (krād′l), and *button* (but′n). See the full key inside the front cover.

Works′ Prog′ress Administra′tion. See **WPA.**

work′ sta′tion, **1.** a work or office area assigned to one person, often one accommodating a computer terminal or other electronic equipment. **2.** a computer terminal or microcomputer connected to a mainframe, minicomputer, or data-processing network. **3.** a powerful microcomputer, often with a high-resolution display, used for computer-aided design, electronic publishing, or other graphics-intensive processing. Also, **work′sta′tion.** [1930–35]

work′ stop′page, the collective stoppage of work by employees in a business or an industry to protest working conditions. [1940–45]

work′-stud′y pro′gram (wûrk′stud′ē, -stud′ē), a program enabling high-school or college students to combine academic work with actual job experience. [1945–50]

work•ta•ble (wûrk′tā′bəl), *n.* a table with a work surface, often with drawers. [1790–1800; WORK + TABLE]

work′ train′, a train that transports railroad workers, building materials, etc., to construction or maintenance assignments on the railroad. [1880–85, *Amer.*]

work-up (wûrk′up′), *n. Print.* an undesirable deposit of ink on a surface being printed, caused by the forcing into type-high position of quads or other spacing material. [n. use of v. phrase *work up*]

work•up (wûrk′up′), *n.* **1.** a thorough medical diagnostic examination including laboratory tests and x-rays. **2.** a tentative plan or proposal. [1935–40; n. use of v. phrase *work up*]

work•week (wûrk′wēk′), *n.* the total number of regular working hours or days in a week. [1920–25; WORK + WEEK]

work•wom•an (wûrk′wo͝om′ən), *n., pl.* **-wom•en. 1.** a female worker. **2.** a woman employed or skilled in some manual, mechanical, or industrial work. [1520–30; WORK + WOMAN]
—Usage. See **-woman.**

world (wûrld), *n.* **1.** the earth or globe, considered as a planet. **2.** (*often cap.*) a particular division of the earth: *the Western world.* **3.** the earth or a part of it, with its inhabitants, affairs, etc., during a particular period: *the ancient world.* **4.** humankind; the human race; humanity. **5.** the public generally: *The whole world knows it.* **6.** the class of persons devoted to the affairs, interests, or pursuits of this life: *The world worships success.* **7.** a particular class of people, with common interests, aims, etc.: *the fashionable world.* **8.** any sphere, realm, or domain, with all pertaining to it: *the world of dreams; the insect world.* **9.** everything that exists; the universe; the macrocosm. **10.** any complex whole conceived as resembling the universe: *the world of the microcosm.* **11.** one of the three general groupings of physical nature: *animal world; mineral world; vegetable world.* **12.** any period, state, or sphere of existence: *this world; the world to come.* **13.** Often, **worlds.** a great deal: *That vacation was worlds of fun.* **14.** any indefinitely great expanse. **15.** any heavenly body: *the starry worlds.* **16. bring into the world, a.** to give birth to; bear. **b.** to deliver (a baby). **17. come into the world,** to be born. **18. for all the world, a.** for any consideration, however great: *She wouldn't come to visit us for all the world.* **b.** in every respect; precisely: *You look for all the world like my Aunt Mary.* **19. in the world, a.** at all; ever: *I never in the world would have believed such an obvious lie.* **b.** from among all possibilities: *Where in the world did you find that hat?* **20. on top of the world.** See **top**[1] (def. 25). **21. out of this** or **the world,** exceptional; fine: *The chef prepared a roast duck that was out of this world.* **22. set the world on fire,** to achieve great fame and success. **23. think the world of,** to like or admire greatly: *His coworkers think the world of him.* **24. world without end,** for all eternity; for always. [bef. 900; ME; OE *world, weorold;* c. D *wereld,* G *Welt,* ON *verǫld,* all < Gmc **wer-ald-* lit., age of man]
—Syn. 1. See **earth.**

World′ Bank′, an international bank established in 1944 to help member nations reconstruct and develop, esp. by guaranteeing loans: a specialized agency of the United Nations. Official name, **International Bank for Reconstruction and Development.**

world′ beat′, (*sometimes caps.*) any of various styles of popular music combining traditional, indigenous forms with elements of another culture's music, esp. of Western rock and pop. Also called **world′ mu′sic.** [1985–90]

world•beat•er (wûrld′bē′tər), *n.* a person or thing that surpasses all others of like kind, as in quality, ability, or endurance. Also, **world′-beat′er.** [1885–90; WORLD + BEATER]

world′ car′, an automobile designed to be built with standard parts manufactured in various countries and sold, with few changes, throughout the world. [1975–80]

world-class (wûrld′klas′, -kläs′), *adj.* **1.** ranking among the world's best; outstanding: *a world-class orchestra.* **2.** attracting or comprising world-class players, performers, etc.: *a world-class tennis tournament.* **3.** *Informal.* being a notorious example of its kind: *a world-class slob.* Also, **world′class′.** [1945–50]

World′ Commun′ion Sun′day, the first Sunday in October, during which members of ecumenical churches throughout the world celebrate Holy Communion, esp. to affirm their unity in Christ.

World′ Coun′cil of Church′es, an ecumenical organization formed in 1948 in Amsterdam, The Netherlands, comprising more than 160 Protestant and Eastern churches in over 48 countries, for the purpose of cooperative, coordinated action in theological, ecclesiastical, and secular matters.

CONCISE ETYMOLOGY KEY: <, descended or borrowed from; >, whence; b., blend of, blended; c., cognate with; cf., compare; deriv., derivative; equiv., equivalent; imit., imitative; obl., oblique; r., replacing; s., stem; sp., spelling, spelled; resp., respelling, respelled; trans., translation; ?, origin unknown; *, unattested; ‡, probably earlier than. See the full key inside the front cover.

World′ Court′, an international tribunal established under the Covenant of the League of Nations and replaced in 1945 by the International Court of Justice. Official name, **Permanent Court of International Justice.**

World′ Cup′, *Soccer.* **1.** a trophy emblematic since 1930 of the world championship in soccer and competed for every four years by finalists from more than 150 national teams. **2.** the quadrennial championship match for this trophy between the two finalists emergent from 24 qualifying teams.

World′ Day′ of Prayer′ (prâr), the first Friday in Lent, during which Christians belonging to ecumenical communions pray for foreign missions.

world′ exposi′tion, (*often caps.*) See **world's fair.**

world-fa•mous (wûrld′fā′məs), *adj.* famous throughout the world: *a world-famous film.* [1830–40]

world′ fed′eralism, 1. federalism on a worldwide level. **2.** (*caps.*) the movement, doctrines, and aims of World Federalists. [1945–50]

world′ fed′eralist, 1. a promoter or supporter of world federalism. **2.** (*caps.*) a member of a movement, active since 1947, proposing a world government on a federal basis, having powers of maintaining order and peace among the nations. [1950–55]

World′ Health′ Organiza′tion, an agency of the United Nations, established in 1948, concerned with improving the health of the world's people and preventing or controlling communicable diseases on a worldwide basis through various technical projects and programs. *Abbr.:* WHO

world′line′, *Physics.* (in relativity) the path of a particle in space-time. [1915–20]

world•ling (wûrld′ling), *n.* a person devoted to the interests and pleasures of this world; a worldly person. [1540–50; WORLD + -LING[1]]

world•ly (wûrld′lē), *adj.,* **-li•er, -li•est,** *adv.* **—adj. 1.** of or pertaining to this world as contrasted with heaven, spiritual life, etc.; earthly; mundane. **2.** experienced; urbane; sophisticated: *worldly wisdom.* **3.** devoted to, directed toward, or connected with the affairs, interests, or pleasures of this world. **4.** of or pertaining to the people or laity; secular; neither ecclesiastical nor religious. **5.** *Obs.* of, pertaining to, or existing on earth. **—adv. 6.** in a worldly manner (archaic except in combination): *worldly-wise; worldly-minded.* [bef. 900; ME; OE *wor(u)ldlic.* See WORLD, -LY] **—world′li•ness,** *n.*
—Syn. 1. temporal. See **earthly. 2.** cosmopolitan.

world•ly-mind•ed (wûrld′lē mīn′did), *adj.* having or showing devotion to the affairs and interests of this world. [1595–1605] **—world′ly-mind′ed•ness,** *n.*

world•ly-wise (wûrld′lē wīz′), *adj.* wise as to the affairs of this world. [1350–1400; ME]

world′ point′, *Physics.* (in relativity) a point in space-time, specified by three space coordinates and a time coordinate. Cf. **event** (def. 4). [1920–25]

world′ pow′er, a nation, organization, or institution so powerful that it is capable of influencing or changing the course of world events. [1880–85]

world′ premiere′, the first public performance of a play, motion picture, musical work, etc. [1920–25]

world′ proc′ess, *Philos.* **1.** change within time, regarded as meaningful in relation to a transcendent principle or plan. **2.** *Hegelianism.* change, regarded as the temporal expression and fulfillment of the absolute idea.

World′ Sav′ior, *Zoroastrianism.* Saoshyant.

World′ Se′ries, *Baseball.* an annual series of games between the winning teams of the two major leagues: the first team to win four games being champions of the U.S. Also, **World's′ Se′ries.** [1885–90, *Amer.*]

world's′ fair′, a large international exposition with exhibitions of arts, crafts, industrial and agricultural products, scientific achievements, etc. [1840–50, *Amer.*]

world-shak•er (wûrld′shā′kər), *n.* something of sufficient importance to affect the entire world.

world-shak•ing (wûrld′shā′king), *adj.* of sufficient size or importance to affect the entire world: *the world-shaking effects of an international clash.* [1590–1600]

world's′ old′est profes′sion, prostitution.

world′ soul′, the animating principle or the moving force of the universe; world spirit. [1840–50]

world′ spir′it, 1. (*often caps.*) God. **2.** See **world soul.**

world-view (wûrld′vyo͞o′), *n.* Weltanschauung. [1855–60; trans. of G WELTANSCHAUUNG]

world′ war′, a war that involves most of the principal nations of the world. [1910–15]

World War I, the war fought mainly in Europe and the Middle East, between the Central Powers and the Allies, beginning on July 28, 1914, and ending on November 11, 1918, with the collapse of the Central Powers. *Abbr.:* WWI Also called **Great War, War of the Nations.**

World War II, the war between the Axis and the Allies, beginning on September 1, 1939, with the German invasion of Poland and ending with the surrender of Germany on May 8, 1945, and of Japan on August 14, 1945. *Abbr.:* WWII

World War III, a hypothetical world war of the future, often conceived as a nuclear war resulting in the total destruction of the human race.

world-wea•ry (wûrld′wēr′ē), *adj.* weary of the world; bored with existence, material pleasures, etc. [1760–70] **—world′-wea′ri•ness,** *n.*

world•wide (wûrld′wīd′), *adj.* extending or spread throughout the world. Also, **world′-wide′.** [1625–35]

worm (wûrm), *n.* **1.** *Zool.* any of numerous long, slender, soft-bodied, legless, bilaterally symmetrical invertebrates, including the flatworms, roundworms, acanthocephalans, nemerteans, gordiaceans, and annelids. **2.** (loosely) any of numerous small creeping animals with more or less slender, elongated bodies, and without limbs or with very short ones, including earthworms, tapeworms, insect larvae, and adult forms of some insects. **3.** something resembling or suggesting a worm in appearance, movement, etc. **4.** *Informal.* a groveling, abject, or contemptible person. **5.** the spiral pipe in which the vapor is condensed in a still. **6.** (not in technical use) See **screw thread** (def. 1). **7.** See **screw conveyor. 8.** a rotating cylinder or shaft, cut with one or more helical threads, that engages with and drives a worm wheel. **9.** something that penetrates, injures, or consumes slowly or insidiously, like a gnawing worm. **10. worms,** (*used with a singular v.*) *Pathol., Vet. Pathol.* any disease or disorder arising from the presence of parasitic worms in the intestines or other tissues; helminthiasis. **11.** (*used with a plural v.*) *Metall.* irregularities visible on the surfaces of some metals subject to plastic deformation. **12.** the lytta of a dog or other carnivorous animal. **13.** computer code planted illegally in a software program so as to destroy data in any system that downloads the program, as by reformatting the hard disk. **—v.i. 14.** to move or act like a worm; creep, crawl, or advance slowly or stealthily. **15.** to achieve something by insidious procedure (usually fol. by *into*): *to worm into another's favor.* **16.** *Metall.* craze (def. 8a). **—v.t. 17.** to cause to move or advance in a devious or stealthy manner: *The thief wormed his hand into my coat pocket.* **18.** to get by persistent, insidious efforts (usually fol. by *out* or *from*). **19.** to insinuate (oneself or one's way) into another's favor, confidence, etc.: *to worm his way into the king's favor.* **20.** to free from worms: *He wormed the puppies.* **21.** *Naut.* to wind yarn or the like spirally round (a rope) so as to fill the spaces between the strands and render the surface smooth. [bef. 900; ME (n.); OE *wyrm,* dragon, serpent, worm; c. D *worm,* G *Wurm,* ON *ormr;* akin to L *vermis*] **—worm′er,** *n.* **—worm′like′, worm′ish,** *adj.*

worm′ drive′, *Mach.* a drive mechanism utilizing a worm gear. [1905–10]

worm-eat•en (wûrm′ēt′n), *adj.* **1.** eaten into or gnawed by worms. **2.** impaired by time; decayed or antiquated. [1350–1400; ME *wormeten;* see WORM, EAT, -EN[3]]

worm′ fence′. See **snake fence.** [1645–55]

worm•fish (wûrm′fish′), *n., pl.* (*esp. collectively*) **-fish,** (*esp. referring to two or more kinds or species*) **-fish•es.** any of several small, slender, tropical fishes of the family Microdesmidae. [WORM + FISH]

worm′ gear′, 1. a mechanism consisting of a worm engaging with and driving a worm wheel, the two axes usually being at right angles, used where a relatively low speed and a relatively large amplification of power are desired. **2.** Also called **worm wheel.** a gear wheel driven by a worm. Also, **worm′gear′.** [1875–80]

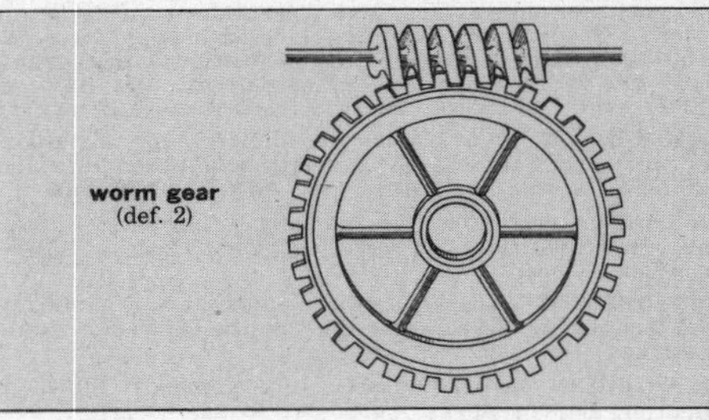
worm gear (def. 2)

worm′ grass′, the pinkroot, *Spigelia marilandica.* [1570–80]

worm•hole (wûrm′hōl′), *n.* **1.** a hole made by a burrowing or gnawing worm, as in timber, nuts, etc. **2.** a theoretical passageway in space between a black hole and a white hole. [1585–95; WORM + HOLE]

worm′ liz′ard, any of numerous burrowing, primarily legless lizards of the suborder Amphisbaenia, mostly inhabiting tropical areas and resembling an earthworm in shape.

Worms (wûrmz; *Ger.* vôRms), *n.* **1.** a city in E Rhineland-Palatinate, in SW Germany. 71,827. **2. Diet of,** the council, or diet, held here (1521) at which Luther was condemned as a heretic.

worm•seed (wûrm′sēd′), *n.* **1.** the dried, unexpanded flower heads of a wormwood, *Artemisia cina* (**Levant wormseed**), or the fruit of certain goosefoots, esp. *Chenopodium anthelminticum* (or *C. ambrosioides*), the Mexican tea or American wormseed, used as an anthelmintic drug. **2.** any of these plants. [1350–1400; ME *wyrmsed.* See WORM, SEED]

worm′seed oil′. See **chenopodium oil.** [1820–30]

worm's′-eye view′ (wûrmz′ī′), a perspective seen from below or from a low or inferior position: *The new man will get a worm's-eye view of the corporate structure.* [1910–15; on the model of *bird's-eye view*]

worm′ snake′, 1. any of several small, wormlike snakes, esp. *Carphophis amoenus,* of the eastern and central U.S. **2.** See **blind snake.** [1880–85, *Amer.*]

worm′ wheel′. See **worm gear** (def. 2). [1670–80] **—worm′-wheel′,** *adj.*

worm•wood (wûrm′wo͝od′), *n.* **1.** any composite herb or low shrub of the genus *Artemisia.* **2.** a bitter, aromatic plant, *A. absinthium,* of the Old World, used as a vermifuge and a tonic, and as an ingredient in absinthe. **3.** something bitter, grievous, or extremely unpleasant. [1350–1400; late ME *wormwode* (see WORM, WOOD[1]); r. ME *wermode,* OE *wermōd;* c. G *Wermut;* see VERMOUTH]

worm•y (wûr′mē), *adj.,* **worm•i•er, worm•i•est. 1.** containing a worm or worms; contaminated with worms.

2. damaged or bored into by worms; worm-eaten. 3. wormlike; groveling; low. [1400–50; late ME; see WORM, -Y[1]] —**worm′i•ness,** *n.*

worn (wôrn, wōrn), *v.* 1. pp. of **wear.** —*adj.* 2. diminished in value or usefulness through wear, use, handling, etc.: *worn clothing; worn tires.* 3. wearied; exhausted. —**worn′ness,** *n.*
—**Syn.** 3. fatigued, tired, spent.

worn-out (wôrn′out′, wōrn′-), *adj.* 1. worn or used beyond repair. 2. depleted of energy, strength, or enthusiasm; exhausted; fatigued. [1585–95]

wor•ried (wûr′ēd, wur′-), *adj.* 1. having or characterized by worry; concerned; anxious: *Their worried parents called the police.* 2. indicating, expressing, or attended by worry: *worried looks.* [1550–60; WORRY + -ED[2]] —**wor′ried•ly,** *adv.*

wor•ri•ment (wûr′ē mənt, wur′-), *n. Informal.* 1. the act or an instance of worrying; anxiety. 2. a source or cause of trouble or annoyance. [1825–35; WORRY + -MENT]

wor•ri•some (wûr′ē səm, wur′-), *adj.* 1. worrying, annoying, or disturbing; causing worry: *a worrisome problem.* 2. inclined to worry. [1835–45; WORRY + -SOME[1]] —**wor′ri•some•ly,** *adv.*
—**Syn.** 1. vexing, troublesome, trying, irksome.

wor•ry (wûr′ē, wur′ē), *v.,* **-ried, -ry•ing,** *n., pl.* **-ries.** —*v.i.* 1. to torment oneself with or suffer from disturbing thoughts; fret. 2. to move with effort: *an old car worrying uphill.* —*v.t.* 3. to torment with cares, anxieties, etc.; trouble; plague. 4. to seize, esp. by the throat, with the teeth and shake or mangle, as one animal does another. 5. to harass by repeated biting, snapping, etc. 6. **worry along** or **through,** *Informal.* to progress or succeed by constant effort, despite difficulty: *to worry through an intolerable situation.* —*n.* 7. a worried condition or feeling; uneasiness or anxiety. 8. a cause of uneasiness or anxiety; trouble. 9. act of worrying. 10. *Fox Hunting.* the action of the hounds in tearing to pieces the carcass of a fox. [bef. 900; ME *weryen, werwen, wyrwyn* to strangle, bite, harass, OE *wyrgan* to strangle; c. G *würgen*] —**wor′ri•er,** *n.* —**wor′ri•less,** *adj.* —**wor′ry•ing•ly,** *adv.*
—**Syn.** 3. tease, harry, hector, badger, disquiet. WORRY, ANNOY, HARASS all mean to disturb or interfere with someone's comfort or peace of mind. To WORRY is to cause anxiety, apprehension, or care: *to worry one's parents.* To ANNOY is to vex or irritate by continued repetition of interferences: *to annoy the neighbors.* HARASS implies long-continued worry and annoyance: *Cares of office harass a president.* 7. apprehension, solicitude, disquiet, misgiving, fear. See **concern.**

wor′ry beads′, a string of beads manipulated to relieve worry and tension. [1955–60]

wor•ry•wart (wûr′ē wôrt′, wur′-), *n.* a person who tends to worry habitually and often needlessly; pessimist; fussbudget. [1930–35; WORRY + WART]

worse (wûrs), *adj., comparative of* **bad** *and* **ill.** 1. bad or ill in a greater or higher degree; inferior in excellence, quality, or character. 2. more unfavorable or injurious. 3. in less good condition; in poorer health. —*n.* 4. that which is worse. —*adv.* 5. in a more evil, wicked, severe, or disadvantageous manner. 6. with more severity, intensity, etc.; in a greater degree. [bef. 900; ME (adj., adv., and n.); OE *wiersa* (comp. adj.), *wiers* (adv.); c. ON *verri,* Goth *wairsiza;* see WAR[2]]

wors•en (wûr′sən), *v.t., v.i.* to make or become worse. [1175–1225; ME *worsenen.* See WORSE, -EN[1]]
—**Syn.** decline, deteriorate, slip, sink.

wors•er (wûr′sər), *adj., adv. Nonstandard.* worse.

wor•set (wûr′sit), *n., adj. Brit. Dial.* worsted. Also, **worssett.**

wor•ship (wûr′ship), *n., v.,* **-shiped, -ship•ing** or (*esp. Brit.*) **-shipped, -ship•ping.** —*n.* 1. reverent honor and homage paid to God or a sacred personage, or to any object regarded as sacred. 2. formal or ceremonious rendering of such honor and homage: *They attended worship this morning.* 3. adoring reverence or regard: *excessive worship of business success.* 4. the object of adoring reverence or regard. 5. (*cap.*) *Brit.* a title of honor used in addressing or mentioning certain magistrates and others of high rank or station (usually prec. by *Your, His,* or *Her*). —*v.t.* 6. to render religious reverence and homage to. 7. to feel an adoring reverence or regard for (any person or thing). —*v.i.* 8. to render religious reverence and homage, as to a deity. 9. to attend services of divine worship. 10. to feel an adoring reverence or regard. [bef. 900; (n.) ME *wors(c)hipe, worthssipe,* OE *worthscipe,* var. of *weorthscipe;* see WORTH, -SHIP; (v.) ME, deriv. of the n.] —**wor′ship•er,** *n.* —**wor′ship•ing•ly,** *adv.*
—**Syn.** 3. honor, homage, adoration, idolatry. 7. honor, venerate, revere, adore, glorify, idolize, adulate.

wor•ship•ful (wûr′ship fəl), *adj.* 1. feeling or showing worship. 2. (*cap.*) *Brit.* a formal title of honor used in announcing or mentioning certain highly regarded or respected persons or groups (usually prec. by *the*). [1250–1300; ME; see WORSHIP, -FUL]

wors•sett (wûr′sit), *n., adj. Brit. Dial.* worset.

worst (wûrst), *adj., superlative of* **bad** *and* **ill.** 1. bad or ill in the highest, greatest, or most extreme degree: *the worst person.* 2. most faulty, unsatisfactory, or objectionable: *the worst paper submitted.* 3. most unfavorable or injurious. 4. in the poorest condition: *the worst house on the block.* 5. most unpleasant, unattractive, or disagreeable: *the worst personality I've ever known.* 6. most lacking in skill; least skilled: *the worst typist in the group.* 7. **in the worst way,** *Informal.* in an extreme degree; very much: *She wanted a new robe for Christmas in the worst way.* Also, **the worst way.** —*n.* 8. that which is worst. 9. **at worst,** if the worst happens; under the worst conditions: *He will be expelled from school, at worst.* Also, **at the worst.** 10. **get the worst of something,** to be defeated by; lose: *to get the worst of a fight.* 11. **if worst comes to worst,** if the very worst happens: *If worst comes to worst, we still have some money in reserve.* —*adv.* 12. in the most evil, wicked, severe, or disadvantageous manner. 13. with the most severity, intensity, etc.; in the greatest degree. —*v.t.* 14. to defeat; beat: *He worsted him easily.* [bef. 900; ME *worste* (adj., adv., and n.), OE *wur(re)sta, wyr(re)st, wer(re)sta* (adj. and adv.); c. ON *verstr;* see WORSE, -EST[1]]

worst-case (wûrst′kās′), *adj.* of the worst possibility; being the worst result that could be expected under the circumstances: *a worst-case scenario.* Cf. **best-case.** [1960–65]

wor•sted (wŏŏs′tid, wûr′stid), *n.* 1. firmly twisted yarn or thread spun from combed, stapled wool fibers of the same length, for weaving, knitting, etc. Cf. **woolen.** 2. wool cloth woven from such yarns, having a hard, smooth surface and no nap. —*adj.* 3. consisting or made of worsted. [1250–1300; ME *worsted(e),* special use of *Worstede* Worstead (OE *Wurthestede*), name of parish in Norfolk, England, where the cloth was made]

wort[1] (wûrt, wôrt), *n.* the unfermented or fermenting infusion of malt that after fermentation becomes beer or mash. [bef. 1000; ME; OE *wyrt;* c. G *Würze* spice; akin to WORT[2]]

wort[2] (wûrt, wôrt), *n.* a plant, herb, or vegetable (now usually used only in combination): *figwort.* [bef. 900; ME; OE *wyrt* root, plant; c. OHG *wurz,* ON *urt* herb, Goth *waurts* root; akin to ROOT[1], ON *rōt,* L *rādix,* Gk *rhíza*]

wort[3] (wûrt), *n.* whort.

worth[1] (wûrth), *prep.* 1. good or important enough to justify (what is specified): *advice worth taking; a place worth visiting.* 2. having a value of, or equal in value to, as in money: *This vase is worth 12 dollars.* 3. having property to the value or amount of: *They are worth millions.* —*n.* 4. excellence of character or quality as commanding esteem: *women of worth.* 5. usefulness or importance, as to the world, to a person, or for a purpose: *Your worth to the world is inestimable.* 6. value, as in money. 7. a quantity of something of a specified value: *ten cents' worth of candy.* 8. wealth; riches; property or possessions: *net worth.* 9. **for all one is worth,** *Informal.* to the utmost: *He ran for all he was worth.* [bef. 900; ME; OE *weorth, wurth;* c. OHG *werd* (G *wert*), ON *verthr,* Goth *wairths*]
—**Syn.** 4. See **merit.** 6. See **value.**

worth[2] (wûrth), *v.i. Archaic.* to happen or betide: *woe worth the day.* [bef. 900; ME *worthen,* OE *wurthan, weorthan;* c. G *werden,* ON *vertha,* Goth *wairthan* to become, L *vertere* to turn (see VERSE)]

Worth (wûrth), *n.* a town in NE Illinois. 11,592.

worth•ful (wûrth′fəl), *adj.* 1. full of worth or merit. 2. highly respected; esteemed. [bef. 900; ME; OE *weorthful;* see WORTH[1], -FUL]

Wor•thing•ton (wûr′thing tən), *n.* 1. a town in central Ohio. 15,016. 2. a town in SW Minnesota. 10,243.

worth•less (wûrth′lis), *adj.* without worth; of no use, importance, or value; good-for-nothing: *a worthless person; a worthless contract.* [1580–90; WORTH[1] + -LESS] —**worth′less•ly,** *adv.* —**worth′less•ness,** *n.*

worth•while (wûrth′hwīl′, -wīl′), *adj.* such as to repay one's time, attention, interest, work, trouble, etc.: *a worthwhile book.* [1865–70; WORTH[1] + WHILE] —**worth′while′ness,** *n.*
—**Syn.** valuable, rewarding, beneficial.

wor•thy (wûr′thē), *adj.,* **-thi•er, -thi•est,** *n., pl.* **-thies.** —*adj.* 1. having adequate or great merit, character, or value: *a worthy successor.* 2. of commendable excellence or merit; deserving: *a book worthy of praise; a person worthy to lead.* —*n.* 3. a person of eminent worth, merit, or position: *The town worthies included two doctors.* [1175–1225; ME; see WORTH[1], -Y[1]] —**wor′thi•ly,** *adv.* —**wor′thi•ness,** *n.*
—**Syn.** 2. meritorious, worthwhile, estimable, excellent, exemplary, righteous, upright, honorable.

-worthy, a combining form of **worthy,** occurring in adjectives that have the general sense "deserving of, fit for" (*blameworthy; newsworthy; noteworthy; trustworthy*), "capable of travel in or on" (*airworthy; roadworthy; seaworthy*), as specified by the first word of the compound.

wot (wot), *v. Archaic.* first and third pers. sing. pres. of **wit**[2]. [ME *woot,* OE *wāt;* c. G *weiss,* ON *veit,* Goth *wait,* Gk *oîda,* I have seen, I know, Skt *veda;* see WIT[2]]

Wo•tan (vô′tän, vō′-), *n.* a Germanic god corresponding to the Scandinavian Odin.

Wot•ton (wot′n), *n.* **Henry,** 1568–1639, English poet and diplomat.

Wouk (wōk), *n.* **Herman,** born 1915, U.S. novelist.

would[1] (wŏŏd; *unstressed* wəd), *v.* 1. a pt. and pp. of **will**[1]. 2. (used to express the future in past sentences): *He said he would go tomorrow.* 3. (used in place of *will,* to make a statement or form a question less direct or blunt): *That would scarcely be fair. Would you be so kind?* 4. (used to express repeated or habitual action in the past): *We would visit Grandma every morning up at the farm.* 5. (used to express an intention or inclination): *Nutritionists would have us all eat whole grains.* 6. (used to express a wish): *Would he were here!* 7. (used to express an uncertainty): *It would appear that he is guilty.* 8. (used in conditional sentences to express choice or possibility): *They would come if they had the fare. If the temperature were higher, the water would evaporate.* 9. **would have,** (used with a past participle to express unfulfilled intention or preference): *I would have saved you some but Jimmy took it all.* 10. **would like,** (used to express desire): *I would like to go next year.* 11. **would rather.** See **rather** (def. 7). [bef. 900; ME, OE *wolde.* See WILL[1]]
—**Usage.** See **should.**

would[2] (wōld), *n.* weld[2].

would-be (wŏŏd′bē′), *adj.* 1. wishing or pretending to be: *a would-be wit.* 2. intended to be: *a would-be kindness.* —*n.* 3. a person who wishes or pretends to be something: *Opera singers and would-bes should practice at least four hours a day.* [1250–1300; ME (adj.)]

would•n't (wŏŏd′nt), contraction of *would not: I wouldn't ask her.*
—**Usage.** See **contraction.**

wouldst (wŏŏdst, wŏŏtst), *v. Archaic.* 2nd pers. sing. past of **will**[1]. Also, **would•est** (wŏŏd′ist).

wound[1] (wōōnd; *Older Use and Literary* wound), *n.* 1. an injury, usually involving division of tissue or rupture of the integument or mucous membrane, due to external violence or some mechanical agency rather than disease. 2. a similar injury to the tissue of a plant. 3. an injury or hurt to feelings, sensibilities, reputation, etc. 4. **lick one's wounds,** to attempt to heal one's injuries or soothe one's hurt feelings after a defeat. —*v.t.* 5. to inflict a wound upon; injure; hurt. —*v.i.* 6. to inflict a wound. [bef. 900; (n.) ME; OE *wund;* c. OHG *wunta* (G *Wunde*), ON *und,* Goth *wunds;* (v.) ME *wounden,* OE *wundian,* deriv. of the n.] —**wound′ed•ly,** *adv.* —**wound′ing•ly,** *adv.*
—**Syn.** 1. cut, stab, laceration, lesion, trauma. See **injury.** 3. insult, pain, anguish. 5. harm, damage; cut, stab, lacerate.

wound[2] (wound), *v.* a pt. and pp. of **wind**[2] and **wind**[3].

wound•ed (wōōn′did), *adj.* 1. suffering injury or bodily harm, as a laceration or bullet wound: *to bandage a wounded hand.* 2. marred; impaired; damaged: *a wounded reputation.* —*n.* 3. wounded persons collectively (often prec. by *the*): *to treat the wounded.* [bef. 1000; ME; OE *gewundode.* See WOUND[1], -ED[2]]

Wound′ed Knee′, a village in SW South Dakota: site of a massacre of about 300 Oglala Sioux Indians on Dec. 29, 1890.

wound•fin (wōōnd′fin′), *n.* a slender, scaleless cyprinid fish, *Plagopterus argentissimus,* inhabiting the tributaries of the Colorado River system, having sharp spines in front of the dorsal fin and each pelvic fin: an endangered species. [WOUND[1] + FIN]

wound•wort (wōōnd′wûrt′, -wôrt′), *n.* 1. any of several plants of the genus *Stachys,* belonging to the mint family, esp. *S. palustris,* having hairy stems and leaves and whorled clusters of small, reddish flowers. 2. See **kidney vetch.** [1540–50; WOUND[1] + WORT[2]]

wou•ra•li (wōō rä′lē), *n.* curare.

wove (wōv), *v.* a pt. and pp. of **weave.**

wo•ven (wō′vən), *v.* a pp. of **weave.**

wove′ pa′per, paper that exhibits a pattern of fine mesh when held up to the light. Cf. **laid paper.** [1805–15]

Wo•vo•ka (wə vō′kə), *n.* c1856–1932, Paiute religious leader: originator of the ghost dance religion.

wow[1] (wou), *Informal.* —*interj.* 1. (an exclamation of surprise, wonder, pleasure, or the like): *Wow! Look at that!* —*v.t.* 2. to gain an enthusiastic response from; thrill. —*n.* 3. an extraordinary success: *His act is a real wow.* 4. excitement, interest, great pleasure, or the like: *a car that will add some wow to your life.* [1890–95; perh. identical with Scots *wow!* exclamation of surprise or admiration]

wow[2] (wou), *n.* 1. *Audio.* a slow wavering of pitch in sound recording or reproducing equipment caused by uneven speed of the turntable or the tape. Cf. **flutter** (def. 12). 2. *Scot. and North Eng. Dial.* a howl, wail, bark, whine, or mew. —*v.i.* 3. *Scot. and North Eng. Dial.* to howl, wail, bark, whine, or mew. [1800–10 for defs. 2–3; 1930–35 for def. 1; imit.; the audio term is prob. an independent formation]

wow•ser (wou′zər), *n. Australia and New Zealand.* an excessively puritanical person. [1895–1900; orig. uncert.]

WP, word processing.

wp., *Baseball.* wild pitch; wild pitches.

W.P., 1. weather permitting. 2. wire payment. 3. working pressure. Also, **WP, w.p.**

WPA, Work Projects Administration: the former federal agency (1935–43) charged with instituting and administering public works in order to relieve national unemployment. Originally, **Works Progress Administration.**

W particle, *Physics.* either of two types of charged intermediate vector bosons, one having a positive charge and the other a negative charge. *Symbols:* W^+, W^- [1970–75; appar. for *weak*]

WPB, See **War Production Board.** Also, **W.P.B.**

WPI, wholesale price index.

wpm, words per minute.

wpn, weapon.

WPPSI (wip′sē), *n.* Wechsler Preschool and Primary Scale of Intelligence. See under **Wechsler Scales.**

w.r., 1. warehouse receipt. 2. *Insurance.* war risk.

WRA, War Relocation Authority.

WRAC, *Brit.* Women's Royal Army Corps. Also, **W.R.A.C.**

wrack[1] (rak), *n.* 1. wreck or wreckage. 2. damage or destruction: *wrack and ruin.* 3. a trace of something destroyed: *leaving not a wrack behind.* 4. seaweed or other vegetation cast on the shore. —*v.t.* 5. to wreck: *He wracked his car up on the river road.* [bef. 900; ME *wrak* (n.), OE *wræc* vengeance, misery, akin to *wracu* vengeance, misery, *wrecan* to WREAK]

wrack[2] (rak), *n., v.i.* rack[4].

wrack·ful (rak′fəl), *adj.* ruinous. [1550–60; WRACK[1] + -FUL]

WRAF (raf), *Brit.* Women's Royal Air Force. Also, **W.R.A.F.**

wraith (rāth), *n.* **1.** an apparition of a living person supposed to portend his or her death. **2.** a visible spirit. [1505–15; originally Scots; orig. uncert.] —**wraith′like′,** *adj.*

Wran·gel (rang′gəl; *Russ.* VRÄN′gyil), *n.* a Russian island in the Arctic Ocean, off the coast of the NE Soviet Union in Asia: meteorological station. ab. 2000 sq. mi. (5180 sq. km).

Wran·gell (rang′gəl), *n.* **Mount,** an active volcano in SE Alaska, in the Wrangell Mountains. 14,006 ft. (4269 m).

Wran′gell Moun′tains, a mountain range in SE Alaska. Highest peak, Mt. Bona, 16,420 ft. (5005 m).

Wran·gell-St. E·li·as National Park (rang′gəl-sānt′ i lī′əs), a national park in E Alaska. 12,730 sq. mi. (32,970 sq. km).

wran·gle (rang′gəl), *v.,* **-gled, -gling,** *n.* —*v.i.* **1.** to argue or dispute, esp. in a noisy or angry manner. —*v.t.* **2.** to argue or dispute. **3.** to tend or round up (cattle, horses, or other livestock). **4.** to obtain, often by contrivance or scheming; wangle: *He wrangled a job through a friend.* —*n.* **5.** a noisy or angry dispute; altercation. [1350–1400; ME, appar. < LG *wrangeln,* freq. of *wrangen* to struggle, make an uproar; akin to WRING] —**Syn. 1, 5.** quarrel, brawl. **5.** argument.

wran·gler (rang′glər), *n.* **1.** a cowboy, esp. one in charge of saddle horses. **2.** a person who wrangles or disputes. **3.** (at Cambridge University, England) a person placed in the first class in the mathematics tripos. [1505–15; WRANGLE + -ER[1]; (def. 1) orig. *horse-wrangler,* prob. partial trans. of MexSp *caballerango* groom, stable boy, with *-erango* suggesting *wrangler*]

wrap (rap), *v.,* **wrapped** or **wrapt, wrap·ping,** *n., adj.* —*v.t.* **1.** to enclose in something wound or folded about (often fol. by *up*): *She wrapped her head in a scarf.* **2.** to enclose and make fast (an article, bundle, etc.) within a covering of paper or the like (often fol. by *up*): *He wrapped the package in tissue.* **3.** to wind, fold, or bind (something) about as a covering. **4.** to protect with coverings, outer garments, etc. (usually fol. by *up*). **5.** to surround, envelop, shroud, or hide. **6.** to fold or roll up. **7.** *Motion Pictures, Television.* to finish the filming of (a motion picture). —*v.i.* **8.** to wrap oneself (usually fol. by *up*). **9.** to become wrapped, as about something; fold. **10.** *Motion Pictures, Television.* to complete the filming of a motion picture: *We hope to wrap in time for Christmas.* **11. wrapped up in, a.** intensely absorbed in: *wrapped up in one's work.* **b.** involved in; bound up with: *Peace is wrapped up in willingness to compromise.* **12. wrap up,** to conclude; finish work on: *to wrap up a project.* —*n.* **13.** something to be wrapped about the person, esp. in addition to the usual indoor clothing, as a shawl, scarf, or sweater: *an evening wrap.* **14.** a beauty treatment in which a part or all of the body is covered with cream, lotion, herbs, or the like and then wrapped snugly with cloth. **15.** *Motion Pictures, Television.* **a.** the completion of photography on a film or an individual scene. **b.** the termination of a working day during the shooting of a film. **16. under wraps,** *Informal.* secret: *a research project kept under wraps.* —*adj.* **17.** wraparound in style: *a wrap skirt.* [1275–1325; ME (v.), of obscure orig.; cf. dial. Dan *vravle* to wind]

wrap′account′, a personally managed investment account where charges are levied on the basis of the account's total assets.

wrap·a·round (rap′ə round′), *adj.* **1.** (of a garment) made to fold around or across the body so that one side of the garment overlaps the other forming the closure. **2.** extending in a curve from the front around to the sides: *a wraparound windshield.* **3.** of, pertaining to, or arranged under a wraparound mortgage: *wraparound financing.* **4.** all-inclusive; comprehensive: *a wraparound insurance plan.* —*n.* **5.** a wraparound object. **6.** outsert. **7.** *Print.* a thin metal, plastic, or rubber plate made flat and then wrapped around a cylinder for printing on a rotary press. **8.** See **word wrap. 9.** *Brit.* See **book jacket.** Also, **wrap′-a-round′.** [1965–70; adj., n. use of v. phrase *wrap around* (something)]

wrap′around mort′gage, a mortgage, as a second mortgage, that includes payments on a previous mortgage that continues in effect. [1970–75]

wrap·per (rap′ər), *n.* **1.** a person or thing that wraps. **2.** a covering or cover. **3.** a long, loose outer garment. **4.** a loose bathrobe; negligee. **5.** *Brit.* See **book jacket. 6.** the tobacco leaf used for covering a cigar. **7.** *Armor.* a supplementary beaver reinforcing the chin and mouth area of an armet of the 15th century. [1425–75; late ME; see WRAP, -ER[1]]

wrap·ping (rap′ing), *n.* Often, **wrappings.** the covering in which something is wrapped. [1350–1400; ME; see WRAP, -ING[1]]

wrap′ping pa′per, heavy paper used for wrapping packages, parcels, etc. [1760–70]

wrapt (rapt), *v.* a pt. and pp. of **wrap.**

wrap-up (rap′up′), *n.* **1.** a final report or summary: *a wrap-up of the evening news.* **2.** the conclusion or final result: *the wrap-up of the election campaign.* **3.** *Australian Slang.* an enthusiastic recommendation or flattering account. [1950–55; n. use of v. phrase *wrap up*]

wrasse (ras), *n.* any of various marine fishes of the family Labridae, esp. of the genus *Labrus,* having thick, fleshy lips, powerful teeth, and usually a brilliant color, certain species being valued as food fishes. [1665–75; appar. orig. a pl. of dial. (Cornwall) *wrah, wraugh, wrath* < Cornish *wragh,* lenited form of *gwragh* lit., old woman, hag; cf. Welsh *gwrach(en),* Breton *gwrac'h,* also with both senses]

CONCISE ETYMOLOGY KEY: <, descended or borrowed from; >, whence; b., blend of, blended; c., cognate with; cf., compare; deriv., derivative; equiv., equivalent; imit., imitative; obl., oblique; r., replacing; s., stem; sp., spelling, spelled; resp., respelling, respelled; trans., translation; ?, origin unknown; *, unattested; ‡, probably earlier than. See the full key inside the front cover.

wras·tle (ras′əl), *v.i., v.t.,* **-tled, -tling,** *n. Dial.* wrestle. Also, **rassle, rastle.** [1200–50; ME *wrastlen,* var. of *wrestlen* to WRESTLE]

wrath (rath, räth *or, esp. Brit.,* rôth), *n.* **1.** strong, stern, or fierce anger; deeply resentful indignation; ire. **2.** vengeance or punishment as the consequence of anger. —*adj.* **3.** *Archaic.* wroth. [bef. 900; (n.) ME *wraththe,* OE *wrǣththo,* equiv. to *wrāth* WROTH + *-tho* -TH[1]; (adj.) var. of WROTH by assoc. with the n.] —**Syn. 1.** rage, resentment, fury, choler.

wrath·ful (rath′fəl, räth′- *or, esp. Brit.,* rôth′-), *adj.* **1.** very angry; ireful; full of wrath: *They trembled before the wrathful queen.* **2.** characterized by or showing wrath: *wrathful words.* [1250–1300; ME; see WRATH, -FUL] —**wrath′ful·ly,** *adv.* —**wrath′ful·ness,** *n.* —**Syn. 1.** irate, furious, raging, incensed, enraged.

wrath·y (rath′ē, rä′thē *or, esp. Brit.,* rô′thē), *adj.,* **wrath·i·er, wrath·i·est.** *Informal.* wrathful; angry. [1820–30, *Amer.*; WRATH + -Y[1]] —**wrath′i·ly,** *adv.*

wreak (rēk), *v.t.* **1.** to inflict or execute (punishment, vengeance, etc.): *They wreaked havoc on the enemy.* **2.** to carry out the promptings of (one's rage, ill humor, will, desire, etc.), as on a victim or object: *He wreaked his anger on the office staff.* [bef. 900; ME *wreken,* OE *wrecan;* c. G *rächen* to avenge, ON *reka* to drive, avenge, Goth *wrikan* to persecute; akin to L *urgēre* to drive, push] —**wreak′er,** *n.* —**Syn. 1.** visit, vent, unleash.

wreath (rēth), *n., pl.* **wreaths** (rēthz, rēths), *v.* —*n.* **1.** a circular band of flowers, foliage, or any ornamental work, for adorning the head or for any decorative purpose; a garland or chaplet. **2.** any ringlike, curving, or curling mass or formation: *a wreath of clouds.* **3.** (in stair building) **a.** a curved section of a handrail. **b.** Also called **wreath′piece′.** a curved section of a string. —*v.t., v.i.* **4.** to wreathe. [bef. 1000; ME *wrethe,* OE *writha* something wound or coiled; akin to WRITHE] —**wreath′like′,** *adj.*

wreathe (rēth), *v.,* **wreathed; wreathed** or (*Archaic*) **wreath·en; wreath·ing.** —*v.t.* **1.** to encircle or adorn with or as with a wreath. **2.** to form as a wreath by twisting or twining. **3.** to surround in curving or curling masses or form. **4.** to envelop: *a face wreathed in smiles.* —*v.i.* **5.** to take the form of a wreath or wreaths. **6.** to move in curving or curling masses, as smoke. [1520–30; earlier *wrethe,* partly v. use of WREATH, partly back formation from *wrethen,* obs. ptp. of WRITHE] —**wreath′er,** *n.*

wreathed′ col′umn, a column having a twisted or spiral form. [1615–25]

wreath·y (rē′thē, -thē), *adj.* having the shape of a wreath: *wreathy clouds.* [1635–45; WREATH + -Y[1]]

wreck (rek), *n.* **1.** any building, structure, or thing reduced to a state of ruin. **2.** wreckage, goods, etc., remaining above water after a shipwreck, esp. when cast ashore. **3.** the ruin or destruction of a vessel in the course of navigation; shipwreck. **4.** a vessel in a state of ruin from disaster at sea, on rocks, etc. **5.** the ruin or destruction of anything: *the wreck of one's hopes.* **6.** a person of ruined health; someone in bad shape physically or mentally: *The strain of his work left him a wreck.* —*v.t.* **7.** to cause the wreck of (a vessel); shipwreck. **8.** to involve in a wreck. **9.** to cause the ruin or destruction of: *to wreck a car.* **10.** to tear down; demolish: *to wreck a building.* **11.** to ruin or impair severely: *Fast living wrecked their health.* —*v.i.* **12.** to be involved in a wreck; become wrecked: *The trains wrecked at the crossing.* **13.** to act as a wrecker; engage in wrecking. [1200–50; (n.) ME *wrec, wrech, wrek* < ODan *wrækæ* wreck; (v.) late ME, deriv. of the n.] —**Syn. 9.** destroy, devastate, shatter. See **spoil.**

wreck·age (rek′ij), *n.* **1.** act of wrecking; state of being wrecked. **2.** remains or fragments of something that has been wrecked: *They searched the wreckage for survivors.* [1830–40; WRECK + -AGE]

wreck·er (rek′ər), *n.* **1.** a person or thing that wrecks. **2.** a person, car, or train employed in removing wreckage, debris, etc., as from railroad tracks. **3.** Also called **tow car, tow truck.** a vehicle equipped with a mechanical apparatus for hoisting and pulling, used to tow wrecked, disabled, or stalled automobiles. **4.** Also called **housewrecker.** a person whose business it is to demolish and remove houses or other buildings, as in clearing sites for other use. **5.** a person or vessel employed in recovering salvage from wrecked or disabled vessels. **6.** a person who plunders wrecks, esp. after exhibiting false signals in order to cause shipwrecks. [1795–1805; WRECK + -ER[1]]

wreck′er's ball′, a heavy metal ball swung on a cable from a crane and used in demolition work. Also, **wreck′ing ball′.** [1965–70, *Amer.*]

wreck·fish (rek′fish′), *n., pl.* **-fish·es,** (*esp. collectively*) **-fish.** a large brown fish, *Polyprion americanus,* of the sea bass family, inhabiting the Mediterranean Sea and tropical Atlantic Ocean, often occurring in groups near wrecks. Also called **stone bass.** [1875–80; WRECK + -FISH]

wreck·ful (rek′fəl), *adj. Archaic.* causing wreckage. [1590–1600; WRECK + -FUL]

wreck·ing (rek′ing), *n.* **1.** the act, work, or business of a wrecker. —*adj.* **2.** employed or for use in wrecking: *a wrecking crew.* [1795–1805; WRECK + -ING[1]]

wreck′ing bar′. See **pinch bar.** [1940–45]

wreck′ing car′, *Railroads.* a car that is equipped as a wrecker. Cf. **wrecker** (def. 2). [1860–65, *Amer.*]

wreck′ing crane′, *Railroads.* a crane for lifting and removing wrecked rolling stock. [1870–75, *Amer.*]

wren (ren), *n.* **1.** any of numerous small, active songbirds of the family Troglodytidae, esp. *Troglodytes troglodytes,* of the Northern Hemisphere, having dark-brown plumage barred with black and a short, upright tail. Cf. **house wren, marsh wren, rock wren, winter wren. 2.** any of various similar, unrelated birds, esp. any of several Old World warblers. [bef. 900; ME *wrenn(e),* OE *wrenna,* obscurely akin to OHG *wrendilo,* ON *rindill*]

house wren, *Troglodytes aedon,* length 5 in. (13 cm)

Wren (ren), *n.* **1. Sir Christopher,** 1632–1723, English architect. **2. Percival Christopher,** 1885–1941, English novelist.

Wren (ren), *n.* (*sometimes l.c.*) *Chiefly Brit. Informal.* a member of the Wrens. [1915–20]

wrench (rench), *v.t.* **1.** to twist suddenly and forcibly; pull, jerk, or force by a violent twist: *He wrenched the prisoner's wrist.* **2.** to overstrain or injure (the ankle, knee, etc.) by a sudden, violent twist: *When she fell, she wrenched her ankle.* **3.** to affect distressingly as if by a wrench. **4.** to wrest, as from the right use or meaning: *to wrench the facts out of context.* —*v.i.* **5.** to twist, turn, or move suddenly aside: *He wrenched away.* **6.** to give a wrench or twist at something. —*n.* **7.** a wrenching movement; a sudden, violent twist: *With a quick wrench, she freed herself.* **8.** a painful, straining twist, as of the ankle or wrist. **9.** a sharp, distressing strain, as to the feelings. **10.** a twisting or distortion, as of meaning. **11.** a tool for gripping and turning or twisting the head of a bolt, a nut, a pipe, or the like, commonly consisting of a bar of metal with fixed or adjustable jaws. [bef. 1050; ME *wrenchen* (v.), OE *wrencan* to twist, turn; c. G *renken*] —**wrench′er,** *n.* —**wrench′ing·ly,** *adv.* —**Syn. 4.** distort, twist, warp.

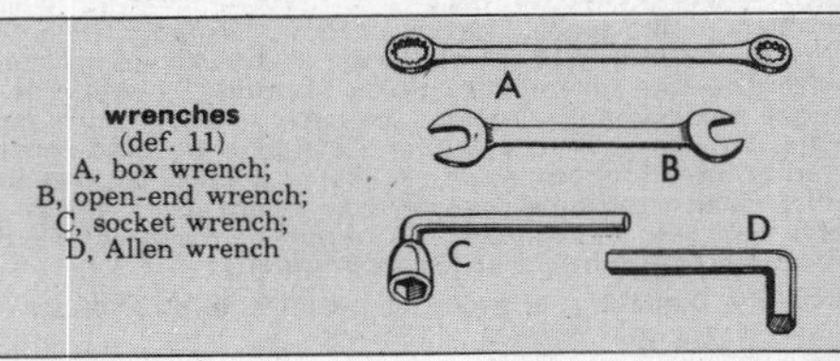

wrenches (def. 11) A, box wrench; B, open-end wrench; C, socket wrench; D, Allen wrench

Wrens (renz), *n.* (*used with a singular or plural v.*) *Chiefly Brit. Informal.* the Women's Royal Naval Service: established in 1917 as an auxiliary to the Royal Navy. [pronounced form of the initial letters, with placement of vowel suggested by *wren*]

wren-tit (ren′tit′), *n.* a small, brown bird, *Chamaea fasciata,* of the western U.S., resembling a wren and a titmouse, and having a long, tapered tail. Also, **wren′-tit′.** [1870–75, *Amer.*]

wrest (rest), *v.t.* **1.** to twist or turn; pull, jerk, or force by a violent twist. **2.** to take away by force: *to wrest a knife from a child.* **3.** to get by effort: *to wrest a living from the soil.* **4.** to twist or turn from the proper course, application, use, meaning, or the like; wrench. —*n.* **5.** a wresting; twist or wrench. **6.** a key or small wrench for tuning stringed musical instruments, as the harp or piano, by turning the pins to which the strings are fastened. [bef. 1000; (v.) ME *wresten,* OE *wrǣstan;* c. ON *reista;* akin to WRIST; (n.) ME: a wresting, deriv. of the v.] —**wrest′er,** *n.* —**Syn. 1, 3.** wring. **3.** See **extract.**

wres·tle (res′əl), *v.,* **-tled, -tling,** *n.* —*v.i.* **1.** to engage in wrestling. **2.** to contend, as in a struggle for mastery; grapple: *to wrestle with one's conscience.* —*v.t.* **3.** to contend with in wrestling. **4.** to force by or as if by wrestling. **5.** to throw (a calf or other animal) for branding. —*n.* **6.** an act of or a bout at wrestling. **7.** a struggle. [bef. 1100; ME *wrestlen, wrastlen* (v.), OE **wrǣstlian* (cf. OE *wrǣstlere* wrestler), freq. of *wrǣstan* to WREST; c. MD, MLG *worstelen*] —**wres′tler,** *n.*

wres·tling (res′ling), *n.* **1.** a sport in which two opponents struggle hand to hand in order to pin or press each other's shoulders to the mat or ground, with the style, rules, and regulations differing widely in amateur and professional matches. Cf. **catch-as-catch-can** (def. 3), **Greco-Roman** (def. 3). **2.** the act of a person who wrestles. [bef. 1100; ME; OE *wrǣstlunge.* See WRESTLE, -ING[1]]

wrest′ pin′, peg (def. 5). [1780–90]

wretch (rech), *n.* **1.** a deplorably unfortunate or unhappy person. **2.** a person of despicable or base character. [bef. 900; ME *wrecche,* OE *wrecca* exile, adventurer; c. G *Recke* warrior, hero, ON *rekkr* man]

wretch·ed (rech′id), *adj.,* **-er, -est. 1.** very unfortunate in condition or circumstances; miserable; pitiable. **2.** characterized by or attended with misery and sorrow. **3.** despicable, contemptible, or mean: *a wretched miser.* **4.** poor, sorry, or pitiful; worthless: *a wretched job of sewing.* [1150–1200; ME *wrecchede.* See WRETCH, -ED[3]] —**wretch′ed·ly,** *adv.* —**wretch′ed·ness,** *n.* —**Syn. 1.** dejected, distressed, afflicted, woeful, woebegone, forlorn, unhappy. **2.** WRETCHED, MISERABLE, SORRY refer to that which is unhappy, afflicted, or distressed. WRETCHED refers to a condition of extreme affliction or distress, esp. as outwardly apparent: *wretched hovels.* MISERABLE refers more to the inward feeling of unhappiness or distress: *a miserable life.* SORRY applies to distressed, often poverty-stricken outward circumstances but it has connotations of unworthiness, incongruousness, or the like, so that the beholder feels more contempt than pity: *in a sorry plight.* **3.** base, vile.

wrick (rik), *v.t., v.i., n.* wrench; strain. [1275–1325; ME *wrikken* to make abrupt movements; perh. akin to WRINKLE, WRENCH]

wri·er (rī′ər), *adj.* comparative of **wry.**

wri·est (rī′ist), *adj.* superlative of **wry.**

wrig·gle (rig′əl), *v.,* **-gled, -gling,** *n.* —*v.i.* **1.** to twist to and fro; writhe; squirm. **2.** to move along by twisting and turning the body, as a worm or snake. **3.** to make one's way by shifts or expedients (often fol. by *out*): *to wriggle out of a difficulty.* —*v.t.* **4.** to cause to wriggle: *to wriggle one's hips.* **5.** to bring, get, make, etc., by wriggling: *to wriggle one's way through a narrow opening.* —*n.* **6.** act of wriggling; a wriggling movement. [1485–95; < MLG *wriggelen* (c. D *wriggelen*), freq. of **wriggen* to twist, turn, akin to OE *wrigian* to twist; see WRY] —**wrig′gling·ly,** *adv.*

wrig·gler (rig′lər), *n.* **1.** a person or thing that wriggles. **2.** Also called **wiggler, wiggle-tail.** the larva of a mosquito. [1625–35; WRIGGLE + -ER[1]]

wrig·gle·work (rig′əl wûrk′), *n.* decorative engraving of a metal surface with repeated zigzags. [WRIGGLE + WORK]

wrig·gly (rig′lē), *adj.,* **-gli·er, -gli·est. 1.** twisting; writhing; squirming: *a wriggly caterpillar.* **2.** evasive; shifty: *a wriggly character.* [1865–70; WRIGGLE + -Y[1]]

wright (rīt), *n.* a worker, esp. a constructive worker (used chiefly in combination): *a wheelwright; a playwright.* [bef. 900; ME; OE *wryhta,* metathetic var. of *wyrhta* worker; akin to WORK]

Wright (rīt), *n.* **1. Frances** or **Fanny,** 1795–1852, U.S. abolitionist and social reformer, born in Scotland. **2. Frank Lloyd,** 1867–1959, U.S. architect. **3. Joseph** (*"Wright of Derby"*), 1734–97, English painter. **4. Joseph,** 1855–1935, English philologist and lexicographer. **5. Mary Kathryn** (*"Mickey"*), born 1935, U.S. golfer. **6. Or·ville** (ôr′vil), 1871–1948, and his brother **Wilbur,** 1867–1912, U.S. aeronautical inventors. **7. Richard,** 1908–60, U.S. novelist. **8. Rus·sel** (rus′əl), 1904–76, U.S. industrial designer. **9. Willard Huntington** (*"S. S. Van Dine"*), 1888–1939, U.S. journalist, critic, and author. **10.** a male given name.

Wrig·ley (rig′lē), *n.* **William, Jr.,** 1861–1932, U.S. chewing-gum manufacturer and baseball team owner.

wring (ring), *v.,* **wrung, wring·ing,** *n.* —*v.t.* **1.** to twist forcibly: *He wrung the chicken's neck.* **2.** to twist and compress, or compress without twisting, in order to force out water or other liquid (often fol. by *out*): *to wring clothes.* **3.** to extract or expel by twisting or compression (usually fol. by *out* or *from*). **4.** to affect painfully by or as if by some contorting or compressing action. **5.** to clasp tightly with or without twisting: *to wring one's hands in pain.* **6.** to force (usually fol. by *off*) by twisting. **7.** to extract or get by forceful effort or means (often fol. by *out*). —*v.i.* **8.** to perform the action of wringing something. **9.** to writhe, as in anguish. —*n.* **10.** a wringing; forcible twist or squeeze. [bef. 900; ME *wringen,* OE *wringan;* c. G *ringen* to wrestle]

wring·er (ring′ər), *n.* **1.** a person or thing that wrings. **2.** an apparatus or machine for squeezing liquid out of anything wet, as two rollers through which an article of wet clothing may be squeezed. **3.** a painful, difficult, or tiring experience; ordeal (usually prec. by *through the*): *His child's illness really put him through the wringer.* [1250–1300; ME; see WRING, -ER[1]]

wrin·kle[1] (ring′kəl), *n., v.,* **-kled, -kling.** —*n.* **1.** a small furrow or crease in the skin, esp. of the face, as from aging or frowning. **2.** a temporary slight ridge or furrow on a surface, due to contraction, folding, crushing, or the like. —*v.t.* **3.** to form wrinkles in; corrugate; crease: *Don't wrinkle your dress.* —*v.i.* **4.** to become wrinkled. [1375–1425; late ME (n.), back formation from *wrinkled,* OE *gewrinclod,* ptp. of *gewrinclian* to wind round; perh. akin to WRICK, WRENCH]

wrin·kle[2] (ring′kəl), *n. Informal.* an ingenious trick or device; a clever innovation: *a new advertising wrinkle.* [1375–1425; late ME, equiv. to *wrinc* trick (OE *wrenc;* see WRENCH) + -LE]

wrin·kly (ring′klē), *adj.,* **-kli·er, -kli·est.** having wrinkles or tending to wrinkle; creased; puckery: *a wrinkly material.* [1565–75; WRINKLE + -Y[1]]

wrist (rist), *n.* **1.** the carpus or lower part of the forearm where it joins the hand. **2.** the joint or articulation between the forearm and the hand. **3.** the part of an article of clothing that fits around the wrist. **4.** *Mach.* See **wrist pin.** [bef. 950; ME, OE; c. G *Rist* back of hand, ON *rist* instep; akin to WRITHE]

wrist·band (rist′band′), *n.* **1.** the band of a sleeve, esp. that of a shirt sleeve, that covers the wrist. **2.** a strap attached to a wrist watch and worn around the wrist. **3.** a sweatband worn on the wrist to absorb perspiration. [1565–75; WRIST + BAND[2]]

wrist·drop (rist′drop′), *n. Pathol.* paralysis of the extensor muscles of the hand causing it to droop, due to injuries or some poisons, as lead or arsenic. Also, **wrist′-drop′.** [1835–45; WRIST + DROP]

wrist·let (rist′lit), *n.* **1.** a band worn around the wrist, esp. to protect it from cold. **2.** a bracelet. **3.** *Slang.* a handcuff. [1840–50; WRIST + -LET]

wrist·lock (rist′lok′), *n. Wrestling.* a hold in which an opponent's wrist is grasped and twisted. [1920–25; WRIST + LOCK[1]]

wrist′ pin′, *Mach.* a pin joining the end of a connecting rod to a trunk piston or the end of a piston rod. [1870–75]

wrist′ plate′, *Mach.* a platelike part of a mechanism, oscillating in its own plane, to which links or rods are attached by pins.

wrist′ watch′, a watch attached to a strap or band worn about the wrist. Also, **wrist′watch′.** [1895–1900]

wrist′ wres′tling, a form of arm wrestling in which two contenders interlock thumbs and try to force each other's hands to touch the table on which they are competing. Also, **wrist′wres′tling.** [1965–70]

wrist·y (ris′tē), *adj.* using or involving extensive or strong movement of the wrist: *a wristy forehand.* [1885–90; WRIST + -Y[1]]

writ[1] (rit), *n.* **1.** *Law.* **a.** a formal order under seal, issued in the name of a sovereign, government, court, or other competent authority, enjoining the officer or other person to whom it is issued or addressed to do or refrain from some specified act. **b.** (in early English law) any formal document in letter form, under seal, and in the sovereign's name. **2.** something written; a writing: *sacred writ.* [bef. 900; ME, OE; c. ON *rit* writing, Goth *writs* letter. See WRITE]

writ[2] (rit), *v. Archaic.* a pt. and pp. of **write.**

write (rīt), *v.,* **wrote** or (*Archaic*) **writ; writ·ten** or (*Archaic*) **writ; writ·ing.** —*v.t.* **1.** to trace or form (characters, letters, words, etc.) on the surface of some material, as with a pen, pencil, or other instrument or means; inscribe: *Write your name on the board.* **2.** to express or communicate in writing; give a written account of. **3.** to fill in the blank spaces of (a printed form) with writing: *to write a check.* **4.** to execute or produce by setting down words, figures, etc.: *to write two copies of a letter.* **5.** to compose and produce in words or characters duly set down: *to write a letter to a friend.* **6.** to produce as author or composer: *to write a sonnet; to write a symphony.* **7.** to trace significant characters on, or mark or cover with writing. **8.** to cause to be apparent or unmistakable: *Honesty is written on his face.* **9.** *Computers.* to transfer (information, data, programs, etc.) from storage to secondary storage or an output medium. **10.** *Stock Exchange.* to sell (options). **11.** to underwrite. —*v.i.* **12.** to trace or form characters, words, etc., with a pen, pencil, or other instrument or means, or as a pen or the like does: *He writes with a pen.* **13.** to write as a profession or occupation: *She writes for the* Daily Inquirer. **14.** to express ideas in writing. **15.** to write a letter or letters, or communicate by letter: *Write if you get work.* **16.** to compose or work as a writer or author. **17.** *Computers.* to write into a secondary storage device or output medium. **18. write down, a.** to set down in writing; record; note. **b.** to direct one's writing to a less intelligent reader or audience: *He writes down to the public.* **19. write in, a.** to vote for (a candidate not listed on the ballot) by writing his or her name on the ballot. **b.** to include in or add to a text by writing: *Do not write in corrections on the galley.* **c.** to request something by mail: *If interested, please write in for details.* **20. write off, a.** to cancel an entry in an account, as an unpaid and uncollectable debt. **b.** to regard as worthless, lost, obsolete, etc.; decide to forget: *to write off their bad experience.* **c.** to amortize: *The new equipment was written off in three years.* **21. write out, a.** to put into writing. **b.** to write in full form; state completely. **c.** to exhaust the capacity or resources of by excessive writing: *He's just another author who has written himself out.* **22. write up, a.** to put into writing, esp. in full detail: *Write up a report.* **b.** to present to public notice in a written description or account. **c.** *Accounting.* to make an excessive valuation of (an asset). [bef. 900; ME *writen,* OE *wrītan;* c. OS *wrītan* to cut, write, G *reissen* to tear, draw, ON *rīta* to score, write]
—**Syn. 6.** compose, pen, author, draft, create.

write-down (rīt′doun′), *n. Accounting.* **1.** a reduction of the entered value of an asset account. **2.** the procedure of reducing the recorded value of an asset, either by estimate or as a plan. [1930–35; n. use of v. phrase *write down*]

write-in (rīt′in′), *n.* **1.** a candidate or vote for a candidate not listed on the printed ballot but written onto it by the voter: *Write-ins may swing the election.* —*adj.* **2.** of, pertaining to, or for such a candidate or vote or a ballot so marked: *a write-in campaign.* [1930–35]

write-off (rīt′ôf′, -of′), *n.* **1.** a cancellation from the accounts as a loss. **2.** an uncollectable account. **3.** a reduction in book value; depreciation. **4.** *Informal.* a person or thing that is given up as hopeless or pointless: *Joe's college career is a write-off.* [1745–55; n. use of v. phrase *write off*]

writ·er (rī′tər), *n.* **1.** a person engaged in writing books, articles, stories, etc., esp. as an occupation or profession; an author or journalist. **2.** a clerk, scribe, or the like. **3.** a person who commits his or her thoughts, ideas, etc., to writing: *an expert letter writer.* **4.** (in a piece of writing) the author (used as a circumlocution for "I," "me," "my," etc.): *The writer wishes to state. . . .* **5.** a person who writes or is able to write: *a writer in script.* **6.** *Stock Exchange.* someone who sells options. **7.** *Scot.* a lawyer or solicitor. [bef. 900; ME, OE *writere.* See WRITE, -ER[1]]

writ′er's block′, a usually temporary condition in which a writer finds it impossible to proceed with the writing of a novel, play, or other work. [1945–50]

writ′er's cramp′, spasmodic, painful contractions of the muscles of the thumb, forefinger, and forearm during writing.

write-up (rīt′up′), *n.* **1.** a written description or account, as in a newspaper or magazine: *The play got a terrible write-up.* **2.** *Accounting.* an increase in the book value of a corporation that is not warranted by the true assets of the corporation. [1880–85, *Amer.*; n. use of v. phrase *write up*]

writhe (rīth), *v.,* **writhed, writh·ing,** *n.* —*v.i.* **1.** to twist the body about, or squirm, as in pain, violent effort, etc. **2.** to shrink mentally, as in acute discomfort. —*v.t.* **3.** to twist or bend out of shape or position; distort; contort. **4.** to twist (oneself, the body, etc.) about, as in pain. —*n.* **5.** a writhing movement; a twisting of the body, as in pain. [bef. 900; ME *writhen* (v.), OE *wrīthan* to twist, wind; c. ON *rītha* to knit, twist; akin to WREATH, WRY] —**writh′er,** *n.* —**writh′ing·ly,** *adv.*
—**Syn. 1.** thresh, flail, contort, wriggle.

writh·en (rith′ən), *adj. Archaic.* twisted. [bef. 900; ME, OE; see WRITHE, -EN[2]]

writ·ing (rī′ting), *n.* **1.** the act of a person or thing that writes. **2.** written form: *to commit one's thoughts to writing.* **3.** that which is written; characters or matter written with a pen or the like: *His writing is illegible.* **4.** such characters or matter with respect to style, kind, quality, etc. **5.** an inscription. **6.** a letter. **7.** any written or printed paper, as a document or deed. **8.** literary or musical style, form, quality, technique, etc.: *Her writing is stilted.* **9.** a literary composition or production. **10.** the profession of a writer: *He turned to writing at an early age.* **11. the Writings,** Hagiographa. **12. writing on the wall.** See **handwriting** (def. 4). [1175–1225; ME; see WRITE, -ING[1]]

writ′ing desk′, 1. a piece of furniture with a surface for writing, with drawers and pigeonholes for writing materials. **2.** a portable case that when opened forms a surface on which to write. [1605–15]

writ′ing pa′per, 1. paper on which to write. **2.** stationery; notepaper. [1540–50]

writ′ of assist′ance, *Amer. Hist.* a writ issued by a superior colonial court authorizing officers of the British crown to summon aid and enter and search any premises. [1700–10]

writ′ of certiora′ri, *Law.* certiorari. [1815–25]

writ′ of elec′tion, a writ by an executive authority requiring the holding of an election, esp. one issued by a governor to require a special election for filling a vacancy in the representation from a state.

writ′ of er′ror, *Law.* a writ issued by an appellate court to the court of record where a case was tried, requiring that the record of the trial be sent to the appellate court for examination of alleged errors.

writ′ of extent′, *Eng. Law.* extent (def. 4a). [1860–65]

writ′ of prohibi′tion, *Law.* a command by a higher court that a lower court shall not exercise jurisdiction in a particular case. [1875–80]

writ′ of right′, 1. *Eng. Law.* a writ directed to a person who presided over a feudal court, directing him to render justice between his vassals in a dispute as to ownership of land: usually led to a trial in a royal court if feudal ownership was involved. **2.** *Law.* a common-law writ to restore land to its rightful owner or tenants.

writ′ of sum′mons, *Law.* a writ requiring one to appear in court to answer a complaint. [1835–45]

writ·ten (rit′n), *v., adj.* —*v.* **1.** a pp. of **write.** —*adj.* **2.** expressed in writing (distinguished from *spoken*).

W.R.N.S., *Brit.* Women's Royal Naval Service.

wrnt., warrant.

Wroc·law (vrôts′läf), *n.* **1.** a province in SW Poland. **2.** a city in and the capital of this province, on the Oder River: formerly in Germany. 576,000. German, **Breslau.**

wrong (rông, rong), *adj.* **1.** not in accordance with what is morally right or good: *a wrong deed.* **2.** deviating from truth or fact; erroneous: *a wrong answer.* **3.** not correct in action, judgment, opinion, method, etc., as a person; in error: *You are wrong to blame him.* **4.** not proper or usual; not in accordance with requirements or recommended practice: *the wrong way to hold a golf club.* **5.** out of order; awry; amiss: *Something is wrong with the machine.* **6.** not suitable or appropriate: *He always says the wrong thing.* **7.** (of clothing) that should be worn or kept inward or under: *You're wearing the sweater wrong side out.* —*n.* **8.** that which is wrong, or not in accordance with morality, goodness, or truth; evil: *I committed many wrongs.* **9.** an injustice: *The wrongs they suffered aged them.* **10.** *Law.* **a.** an invasion of another's right, to his damage. **b.** a tort. **11. get in wrong,** *Slang.* to cause to come into disfavor: *We are forever getting in wrong with the people next door.* **12. in the wrong,** to blame; in error: *He knew he was in the wrong but refused to concede the point.* —*adv.* **13.** in a wrong manner; not rightly; awry; amiss: *You did it wrong again.* **14. go wrong, a.** to go amiss; fail: *Everything is going wrong today.* **b.** to pursue an immoral course; become depraved: *Bad friends caused him to go wrong.* —*v.t.* **15.** to do wrong to; treat unfairly or unjustly; harm. **16.** to impute evil to (someone) unjustly; malign. [bef. 1100; (adj.) ME *wrong, wrang,* OE *wrang,* perh. < ODan *wrang;* cf. Dan *vrang* wrong, ON *rangr* awry; (v. and adv.) ME, deriv. of the adj.; (n.) ME; OE *wrang,* deriv. of the adj.; akin to WRING] —**wrong′er,** *n.* —**wrong′ly,** *adv.* —**wrong′ness,** *n.*
—**Syn. 1.** bad, evil, wicked, sinful, immoral, iniquitous, reprehensible, crooked. **2.** inaccurate, incorrect, false, untrue, mistaken. **6.** improper, unsuitable. **8.** misdoing, wickedness, sin, vice. **15.** maltreat, abuse, oppress, cheat, defraud, dishonor.

wrong·do·er (rông′do͞o′ər, -do͞o′-, rong′-), *n.* a person who does wrong, esp. a sinner or transgressor. [1350–1400; ME; see WRONG, DOER]
—**Syn.** evildoer, culprit, offender.

wrong·do·ing (rông′do͞o′ing, -do͞o′-, rong′-), *n.* **1.** behavior or action that is wrong, evil, or blameworthy. **2.** an act that is wrong, evil, or blameworthy; misdeed; sin. [1470–80; WRONG + DOING]

wronged (rôngd, rongd), *adj.* treated unfairly or unjustly: *the wronged party in the dispute.* [1540–50; WRONG + -ED[2]]

wrong′ font′, *Print.* the improper font, or size and style of type, for its place. *Abbr.:* wf, w.f.

wrong·ful (rông′fəl, rong′-), *adj.* **1.** unjust or unfair: *a wrongful act; a wrongful charge.* **2.** having no legal right; unlawful: *The court ruled it was a wrongful diversion of trust income.* [1275–1325; ME; see WRONG, -FUL] —**wrong′ful·ly,** *adv.* —**wrong′ful·ness,** *n.*

CONCISE PRONUNCIATION KEY: *act, cāpe, dâre, pärt; set, ēqual; if, ice; ox, ōver, ôrder, oil, bo͝ok, bo͞ot, out; up, ûrge; child; sing; shoe; thin, that;* zh *as in treasure.* ə = *a as in alone, e as in system, i as in easily, o as in gallop, u as in circus;* ᵊ *as in fire* (fīᵊr), *hour* (ouᵊr). l and n can serve as syllabic consonants, as in *cradle* (krād′l), and *button* (but′n). See the full key inside the front cover.

wrong′ful death′, *Law.* the death of a person wrongfully caused, as comprising the grounds of a damage suit.

wrong·head·ed (rông′hed′id, rong′-), *adj.* wrong in judgment or opinion; misguided and stubborn; perverse. Also, **wrong′-head′ed.** [1725–35; WRONG + HEADED] —**wrong′head′ed·ly,** *adv.* —**wrong′head′ed·ness,** *n.*

wrong′ num′ber, 1. (in telephoning) **a.** a call made to a number other than the one intended. **b.** the number or person reached through such a call. **2.** *Slang.* **a.** the wrong person for a particular task, role, or situation: *Me cook a gourmet dinner?—You've got the wrong number!* **b.** an inadequate, disagreeable, or repulsive person: *She's OK, but her brother's a wrong number.*

Wron·ski·an (rän′skē ən, vrän′-), *n. Math.* the determinant of order *n* associated with a set of *n* functions, in which the first row consists of the functions, the second row consists of the first derivatives of the functions, the third row consists of their second derivatives, and so on. [after *Józef Wroński* (1778–1853), Polish mathematician]

wrote (rōt), *v.* a pt. of **write.**

wroth (rôth, roth *or, esp. Brit.,* rōth), *adj.* **1.** angry; wrathful (usually used predicatively): *He was wroth to see the damage to his home.* **2.** stormy; violent; turbulent: *the wroth sea.* [bef. 900; ME; OE *wrāth;* c. D *wreed* cruel, ON *reithr* angry; akin to WRITHE]

wrought (rôt), *v.* **1.** *Archaic except in some senses.* a pt. and pp. of **work.** —*adj.* **2.** worked. **3.** elaborated; embellished. **4.** not rough or crude. **5.** produced or shaped by beating with a hammer, as iron or silver articles. [1200–50; ME *wroght,* metathetic var. of *worht,* ptp. of *worchen* to WORK]
—**Syn. 2.** See **worked.**

wrought′ i′ron, a form of iron, almost entirely free of carbon and having a fibrous structure including a uniformly distributed slag content, that is readily forged and welded. [1670–80] —**wrought′-i′ron,** *adj.*

wrought-up (rôt′up′), *adj.* excited; perturbed. Also, **worked-up.** [1800–10]

W.R.S.S.R., White Russian Soviet Socialist Republic.

W-R star, *Astron.* See **Wolf-Rayet star.**

wrung (rung), *v.* pt. and pp. of **wring.**

wry (rī), *adj.,* **wri·er, wri·est. 1.** produced by a distortion or lopsidedness of the facial features: *a wry grin.* **2.** abnormally bent or turned to one side; twisted; crooked: *a wry mouth.* **3.** devious in course or purpose; misdirected. **4.** contrary; perverse. **5.** distorted or perverted, as in meaning. **6.** bitterly or disdainfully ironic or amusing: *a wry remark.* [1515–25; adj. use of *wry* to twist, ME *wryen,* OE *wrigian* to go, strive, tend, swerve; c. D *wrijgen* to twist; akin to OE *wrigels,* L *rīcula* veil, Gk *rhoikós* crooked] —**wry′ly,** *adv.* —**wry′ness,** *n.*
—**Syn. 2.** awry, askew. —**Ant. 2.** straight.

wry·mouth (rī′mouth′), *n., pl.* (*esp. collectively*) **-mouth,** (*esp. referring to two or more kinds or species*) **-mouths** (-mouthz′). **1.** any blennioid fish of the family Stichaeidae, having a large, upturned mouth, esp. *Cryptacanthodes maculatus,* a bottom fish of the Atlantic Ocean. **2.** any of several related fishes. Also called **ghostfish.** [1645–55; WRY + MOUTH]

wry·neck (rī′nek′), *n.* **1.** *Informal.* **a.** torticollis. **b.** a person having torticollis. **2.** any of several small Old World climbing birds of the subfamily Jynginae, of the woodpecker family, noted for the peculiar habit of twisting the head and neck. [1575–85; WRY + NECK]

wry-necked (rī′nekt′), *adj. Informal.* afflicted with wryneck. Also, **wry′necked′.** [1590–1600]

W.S., West Saxon.

WSA, War Shipping Administration.

WSW, west-southwest.

wt., weight.

W-2 (dub′əl yoo too′, -yə-), a standard tax form showing the total wages paid to an employee and the taxes withheld during the calendar year: prepared by an employer for each employee. Also called **W-2 form.**

Wu (wo͞o), *n.* **1.** a dynasty that ruled in China A.D. 222–80. **2.** a Chinese language having several dialects, spoken widely in Anhwei, Chekiang, and Kiangsu provinces and including the dialect of Shanghai.

Wu·chang (wo͞o′chäng′), *n. Pinyin, Wade-Giles.* a former city in E Hubei province, in E China: now part of Wuhan.

wud (wo͝od), *adj. Chiefly Scot.* wood; mad. [see WOOD[2]]

Wu Di (*Chin.* wo͞o′ dē′), *Pinyin.* See **Han Wu Ti.**

wu·du (wo͞o do͞o′), *n. Islam.* ritual ablution. [< Ar *wuḍū′*]

Wu·han (wo͞o′hän′), *n. Pinyin, Wade-Giles.* a conglomerate city in and the capital of Hubei province, in E China, at the junction of the Han Shui and Chang Jiang: comprises the former cities of Hankou, Hanyang, and Wuchang. 4,400,000. Also called **Han Cities.**

Wu·hsi (*Chin.* wo͞o′shē′), *n. Wade-Giles.* Wuxi.

Wu·hsien (*Chin.* wo͞o′shyen′), *n. Wade-Giles.* Wuxian.

Wu·hu (wo͞o′ho͞o′), *n. Pinyin, Wade-Giles.* a port in E Anhui province, in E China, on the Chang Jiang. 300,000.

Wu·jin (*Chin.* wʏ′jin′), *n. Pinyin.* former name of **Changzhou.** Also, *Wade-Giles,* **Wu′chin′, Wutsin.**

wul·fen·ite (wo͝ol′fə nīt′), *n.* a lead molybdate mineral, $PbMoO_4$, occurring usually in tabular crystals, and varying in color from grayish to bright-yellow or red; yellow lead ore. [1840–50; named after F. X. von *Wulfen* (1728–1805), Austrian scientist; see -ITE[1]]

Wul·fi·la (wo͝ol′fə lə), *n.* Ulfilas.

Wu·lu·mu·qi (*Chin.* wʏ′lʏ′mʏ′chœ′), *n. Pinyin.* Ürümqi. Also, *Wade-Giles,* **Wu′lu′mu′chi′.**

wun·der·kind (vo͝on′dər kind′, wun′-; *Ger.* vo͝on′dəʀ-kint′), *n., pl.* **-kinds,** *Ger.* **-kin·der** (-kin′dəʀ). **1.** a wonder child or child prodigy. **2.** a person who succeeds, esp. in business, at a comparatively early age. [1890–95; < G, equiv. to *Wunder* WONDER + *Kind* child]

Wundt (vo͝ont), *n.* **Wil·helm Max** (vil′helm mäks′), 1832–1920, German physiologist and psychologist. —**Wundt′i·an,** *adj.*

Wup·per·tal (vo͝op′ər täl′), *n.* a city in North Rhine-Westphalia, in W Germany, in the Ruhr Valley: formed by the union of Barmen, Elberfeld, and smaller communities 1929. 365,500.

wur·ley (wûr′lē), *n., pl.* **-leys, -lies.** *Australian.* **1.** an Aborigine's shelter, made of branches and leaves. **2.** a nest, esp. a rat's nest. [1840–50; < Kaurna (Australian Aboriginal language, now extinct, spoken at the present site of Adelaide), recorded as *wa(d)li*]

Würm (vo͝orm, wo͝orm, wûrm; *Ger.* vʏʀm), *n.* the fourth stage of the glaciation of Eurasia during the Pleistocene. Cf. **Wisconsin** (def. 3). [< G (1909), after a river in Bavaria, joining the Starnberger See and the river Amper]

wurst (wûrst, wo͝orst), *n.* sausage (def. 1). [1890–95; < G *Wurst*]

Würt·tem·berg (wûr′təm bûrg′; *Ger.* vʏʀ′təm berk′), *n.* a former state in SW Germany: now part of Baden-Württemberg.

wurtz·i·lite (wûrt′sə līt′), *n.* a massive black bituminous substance, similar to asphalt but having a high degree of elasticity. [1890–95, *Amer.;* named after Henry *Wurtz* (d. 1910), American mineralogist; see -I-, -LITE]

wurtz·ite (wûrt′sīt), *n. Mineral.* a dimorph of sphalerite, zinc sulfide, ZnS, similar in structure to greenockite and brownish-black in color. [1865–70; < F, named after Charles *Wurtz* (1817–84), French chemist; see -ITE[1]] —**wurtz·it·ic** (wərt sit′ik), *adj.*

Würz·burg (wûrts′bûrg; *Ger.* vʏʀts′bo͝oʀk′), *n.* a city in NW Bavaria, in S Germany, on the Main River. 123,500.

wu shu (wo͞o′ sho͞o′), Chinese martial arts collectively. [1970–75; < Chin *wǔshù* = *wǔ* military + *shù* art]

wuss (wo͝os), *n. Slang.* a weakling; wimp. [1980–85; perh. b. WIMP and PUSS[1]]

Wu·su·li Jiang (*Chin.* wʏ′sʏ′lē′ jyäng′), *Pinyin.* Ussuri.

wuth·er (wuth′ər), *v.i. Brit Dial.* (of wind) to blow fiercely. [1846; var. of dial. and Scots *whither,* ME (Scots) *quhediren;* cf. ON *hvitha* squall of wind]

Wuth′er·ing Heights′ (wuth′ər ing), a novel (1846) by Emily Brontë.

Wu Ti (*Chin.* wo͞o′ dē′). See **Han Wu Ti.** Also, **Wu Di.**

Wu·tsin (*Chin.* wo͞o′dzin′), *n. Older Spelling.* Wujin.

wu-wei (wo͞o′wā′), *n.* (in philosophical Taoism) action accomplishing its purpose in accordance with the natures of things and events. Cf. **yu-wei.** [< Chin *wúwéi* lit., without action]

Wu·xi (wʏ′shœ′), *n. Pinyin.* a city in S Jiangsu province, in E China. 900,000. Also, **Wuhsi;** *Older Spelling,* **Wu′sih′.**

Wu·xian (*Chin.* wʏ′shyän′), *n. Pinyin.* former name of **Suzhou** (def. 1). Also, **Wuhsien.**

WV, West Virginia (approved esp. for use with zip code).

W.Va., West Virginia.

W.V.S., *Brit.* Women's Voluntary Service.

WW, 1. World War. **2.** *Real Estate.* wall-to-wall. Also, **W/W**

ww, *Stock Exchange.* with warrants (offered to the buyer of a given stock or bond).

WWI, See **World War I.**

WWII, See **World War II.**

WY, Wyoming (approved esp. for use with zip code).

Wy., Wyoming.

Wy·an·dot (wī′ən dot′), *n., pl.* **-dots,** (*esp. collectively*) **-dot** for 1. **1.** an Indian of the former Huron confederacy. **2.** a dialect of the Huron language, esp. as used by those elements of the Huron tribe regrouped in Oklahoma. Also, **Wyandotte.**

Wy·an·dotte (wī′ən dot′), *n., pl.* **-dottes** for 2, 3; (*esp. collectively for 3*) **-dotte. 1.** a city in SE Michigan, on the Detroit River. 34,006. **2.** one of an American breed of chickens, raised for meat and eggs. **3.** Wyandot.

Wy·att (wī′ət), *n.* **1. James,** 1746–1813, English architect. **2.** Sir Thomas, 1503?–42, English poet and diplomat. **3.** a male given name. Also, **Wy′at** (for defs. 2, 3).

wych′ elm′ (wich), an elm, *Ulmus glabra,* of northern and western Europe, having large, coarse leaves. [1620–30; *wych* wych elm, ME *wyche,* OE *wice*]

Wych·er·ley (wich′ər lē), *n.* **William,** c1640–1716, English dramatist and poet.

Wyc·liffe (wik′lif), *n.* **John,** c1320–84, English theologian, religious reformer, and Biblical translator. Also, **Wyc′lif, Wickliffe, Wiclif.** —**Wyc′liff·ism, Wyc′lif·ism,** *n.*

Wyc·lif·fite (wik′li fīt′), *adj.* **1.** of or pertaining to Wycliffe or the Wycliffites. —*n.* **2.** a follower of John Wycliffe; Lollard. Also, **Wyc′lif·ite′.** [1570–80; < ML *Wyclefita.* See WYCLIFFE, -ITE[1]]

wye (wī), *n., pl.* **wyes. 1.** the letter Y, or something with a similar shape. **2.** *Elect.* a three-phase, Y-shaped circuit arrangement. **3.** *Railroads.* a track arrangement with three switches and three legs for reversing the direction of a train. [1855–60; a sp. of the letter name]

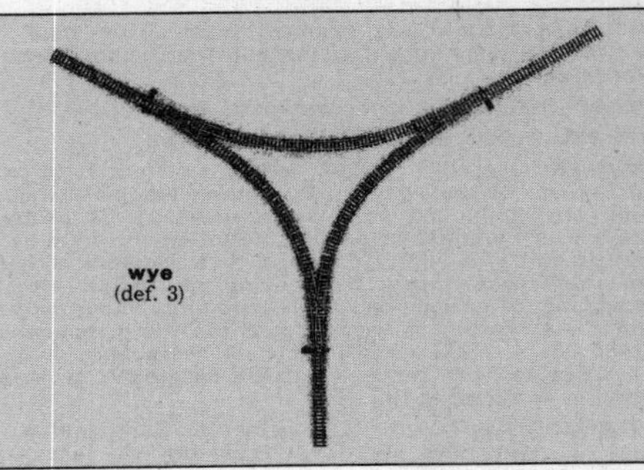
wye (def. 3)

Wye (wī), *n.* a river flowing from central Wales through SW England into the Severn estuary. 130 mi. (210 km) long.

wye′ lev′el, *Survey.* an instrument, consisting of a spirit level mounted under and parallel to a telescope, that can be rotated in its Y-shaped supports for adjustment.

Wy·eth (wī′əth), *n.* **1. Andrew New·ell** (no͞o′əl, nyo͞o′-), born 1917, U.S. painter. **2.** his son **James Browning,** born 1946, U.S. painter. **3. Newell Con·vers** (kon′vərz), (father of Andrew Newell), 1882–1945, U.S. illustrator and painter.

Wyld (wīld), *n.* **Henry Cecil Kennedy,** 1870–1945, English lexicographer and linguist.

Wy·ler (wī′lər), *n.* **William,** 1902–81, U.S. film director, born in Germany.

Wy·lie (wī′lē), *n.* **1. Elinor** (*Elinor Morton Hoyt*), 1885–1928, U.S. poet and novelist. **2. Philip,** 1902–71, U.S. novelist and critic.

wy·lie·coat (wī′lē kōt′), *n. Scot. and North Eng.* **1.** a woolen or flannel undergarment, as a warm undershirt. **2.** a petticoat. [1470–80; orig. uncert.; see COAT]

wynd (wīnd), *n. Chiefly Scot.* a narrow street or alley. [1375–1425; late ME (Scots) *wynde,* OE *gewind* winding path. See WIND[2]]

Wynd·ham (win′dəm), *n.* **John** (*John Benyon Harris*), 1903–69, British science-fiction writer.

wynn (win), *n.* a character (ƿ) representing the sound (w) in Old English and early Middle English manuscripts, based on a rune with the same phonetic value. Also, **wen.** [bef. 1100; ME *wen,* OE *wyn(n),* special use of *wyn(n)* joy (see WINSOME, WISH)]

Wynn (win), *n.* **Ed** (*Isaiah Edwin Leopold*), 1886–1966, U.S. comedian.

Wyo., Wyoming.

Wy·o·ming (wī ō′ming), *n.* **1.** a state in the NW United States. 470,816; 97,914 sq. mi. (253,595 sq. km). *Cap.:* Cheyenne. *Abbr.:* WY (for use with zip code), Wyo., Wy. **2.** a city in W Michigan, near Grand Rapids. 59,616. —**Wy·o·ming·ite** (wī ō′ming īt′), *n.*

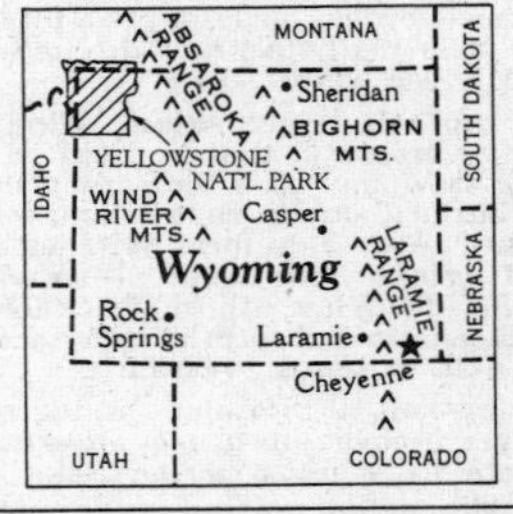

Wyo′ming Val′ley, a valley in NE Pennsylvania, along the Susquehanna River: Indian massacre 1778.

WYSIWYG (wiz′ē wig′), *Computers.* —*adj.* **1.** of, pertaining to, or noting a screen display that shows text exactly as it will appear in printed output, including underlining, various typefaces, as italics, line spacing, end-of-line breaks, and paragraph indentations. —*n.* **2.** a WYSIWYG display: *This program won't give you true WYSIWYG, but it does show boldface text and underlining.* [*w(hat) y(ou) s(ee) i(s) w(hat) y(ou) g(et)*]

Wy·szyń·ski (vi shin′skē), *n.* **Ste·fan** (stef′än), **Cardinal,** 1901–81, Polish Roman Catholic clergyman: archbishop of Gniezno and Warsaw and primate of Poland 1949–81; cardinal 1953–81.

wyte (wīt), *v.,* **wyt·ed, wyt·ing,** *n. Chiefly Scot.* wite[1].

Wythe (with), *n.* **George,** 1729–1806, U.S. jurist and statesman.

wy·vern (wī′vərn), *n. Heraldry.* a two-legged winged dragon having the hinder part of a serpent with a barbed tail. Also, **wivern.** [1600–10; alter. (with unexplained -*n*) of earlier *wyver,* ME < AF *wivre* (OF *guivre*) < L *vipera* VIPER]

wyvern

CONCISE ETYMOLOGY KEY: <, descended or borrowed from; >, whence; b., blend of, blended; c., cognate with; cf., compare; deriv., derivative; equiv., equivalent; imit., imitative; obl., oblique; r., replacing; s., stem; sp., spelling, spelled; resp., respelling, respelled; trans., translation; ?, origin unknown; *, unattested; ‡, probably earlier than. See the full key inside the front cover.

DEVELOPMENT OF MAJUSCULE								
NORTH SEMITIC	GREEK		ETR.	LATIN		MODERN		
						GOTHIC	ITALIC	ROMAN
—	—	X	—	—	X	X	*X*	X

DEVELOPMENT OF MINUSCULE					
ROMAN CURSIVE	ROMAN UNCIAL	CAROL. MIN.	MODERN		
			GOTHIC	ITALIC	ROMAN
x	x	x	x	*x*	x

The twenty-fourth letter of the English alphabet originated in form with North Semitic *taw,* where it signified the *t*-sound. It was adopted by Classical Greek for the *KH*-sound (as in Scottish *loch*) and in some local scripts for the *ks*-sound. In the latter representation it passed from Latin into English and has been maintained, despite its redundancy, for the letter combination KS.

X, x (eks), *n., pl.* **X's** or **Xs, x's** or **xs. 1.** the 24th letter of the English alphabet, a consonant. **2.** any spoken sound or combination of sounds represented by the letter *X* or *x,* as in *xylene, box,* or *exact.* **3.** something having the shape of an X. **4.** a written or printed representation of the letter *X* or *x.* **5.** a device, as a printer's type, for reproducing the letter *X* or *x.*

x (eks), *v.t.,* **x-ed** or **x'd** (ekst), **x-ing** or **x'ing** (ek′sing). **1.** to cross out or mark with or as if with an *x* (often fol. by *out*): *to x out an error.* **2.** to indicate choice, as on a ballot or examination (often fol. by *in*): *to x in the candidate of your choice.* [1840–50]

X, 1. experimental. **2.** extra. **3.** extraordinary.

X, *Symbol.* **1.** the 24th in order or in a series, or, when *I* is omitted, the 23rd. **2.** (*sometimes l.c.*) the Roman numeral for 10. Cf. **Roman numerals. 3.** Christ. **4.** Christian. **5.** cross. **6.** *Elect.* reactance. **7.** *Slang.* a ten-dollar bill. **8.** (in the U.S.) a rating of the Motion Picture Association of America for movies with subject matter that is suitable for adults only: persons who are under age (usually 17) will not be admitted. Cf. **G** (def. 7), **PG, PG-13, R** (def. 5). **9.** (in Great Britain) a designation for a film recommended for adults only. Cf. **A** (def. 11), **AA** (def. 5), **U** (def. 5). **10.** a person, thing, agency, factor, etc., of unknown identity. **11.** *Chem.* (formerly) xenon.

x, 1. ex[1] (def. 1). **2.** excess. **3.** *Stock Exchange.* **a.** (of stock trading) ex dividend. **b.** (of bond trading) See **ex interest. 4.** experimental. **5.** extra.

x, *Symbol.* **1.** an unknown quantity or a variable. **2.** (used at the end of letters, telegrams, etc., to indicate a kiss.) **3.** (used to indicate multiplication) times: $8 \times 8 = 64$. **4.** (used between figures indicating dimensions) by: 3″ × 4″ (read: "three by four inches"); 3″ × 4″ × 5″ (read: "three by four by five inches"). **5.** power of magnification: *a 50x telescope.* **6.** (used as a signature by an illiterate person.) **7.** cross. **8.** crossed with. **9.** (used to indicate a particular place or point on a map or diagram.) **10.** out of; foaled by: *a colt by Flag-a-way x Merrylegs.* **11.** (used to indicate choice, as on a ballot, examination, etc.) **12.** (used to indicate an error or incorrect answer, as on a test.) **13.** *Math.* (in Cartesian coordinates) the x-axis. **14.** *Chess.* captures. **15.** a person, thing, agency, factor, etc., of unknown identity.

Xan•a•du (zan′ə dōō′, -dyōō′), *n.* a place of great beauty, luxury, and contentment. [S.T. Coleridge's modification, in the poem "Kubla Khan" (1797), of *Xandu* (17th century sp.), modern Shangtu, the site of Kublai Khan's summer residence in SE Mongolia]

Xan•ax (zan′aks), *n. Pharm. Trademark.* a brand of alprazolam.

xanth-, var. of **xantho-** before a vowel: *xanthoma.*

xan•than (zan′thən), *n. Nutrition.* a water-soluble natural gum produced by the fermentation of sugar with certain microorganisms and used as a binder, extender, or stabilizer in foods and other products. Also called **xan′than gum′.** [1960–65; prob. *Xanth*(*omonas campestris*) bacterium which produces the gum + *-an,* var. of -ANE]

xan•thate (zan′thāt), *n. Chem.* a salt or ester of xanthic acid. [1825–35; XANTH(IC ACID) + -ATE[2]] **—xan•tha′tion,** *n.*

Xan•the (zan′thē), *n.* a female given name.

xan•the•in (zan′thē in), *n.* the part of the coloring matter in yellow flowers that is soluble in water. Cf. **xanthin** (def. 1). [1855–60; < F *xanthéine,* equiv. to Gk *xanth*(*ós*) yellow + F *-éine,* extension of *-ine* to distinguish it from F *xanthine* XANTHIN]

xan•thene (zan′thēn), *n. Chem.* a yellow, crystalline substance, $C_{13}H_{10}O$, soluble in ether and slightly soluble in alcohol, used in organic synthesis and as a fungicide. [1905–10; earlier *xanthen;* see XANTHO-, -ENE]

xan′thene dye′, *Chem.* any of a group of dyes having a molecular structure related to that of xanthene in which the aromatic (C_6H_4) groups are the chromophore. [1925–30]

Xan•thi•an (zan′thē ən), *adj.* of or pertaining to the ancient city of Xanthus. [1675–85; XANTH(US) + -IAN]

xan•thic (zan′thik), *adj.* **1.** of or pertaining to a yellow or yellowish color. **2.** *Chem.* of or derived from xanthine or xanthic acid. [1810–20; < F *xanthique.* See XANTHO-, -IC]

xan′thic ac′id, *Chem.* an unstable organic acid, $C_3H_6S_2O$, the methyl and ethyl esters of which are colorless, oily liquids with a penetrating odor. [1825–35]

xan•thin (zan′thin), *n.* **1.** the part of the coloring matter in yellow flowers that is insoluble in water. Cf. **xanthein. 2.** a yellow coloring matter in madder. [1830–40; < F *xanthine* or < G *Xanthin.* See XANTHO-, -IN[2]]

xan•thine (zan′thēn, -thin), *n. Biochem., Chem.* **1.** a crystalline, nitrogenous compound, $C_5H_4N_4O_2$, related to uric acid, occurring in urine, blood, and certain animal and vegetable tissues. **2.** any derivative of this compound. [1855–60; < F; see XANTHO-, -INE[2]]

Xan•thip•pe (zan tip′ē), *n.* **1.** fl. late 5th century B.C., wife of Socrates. **2.** a scolding or ill-tempered wife; a shrewish woman. Also, **Xantippe.**

xantho-, a combining form meaning "yellow," used in the formation of compound words: *xanthophyll.* Also, *esp. before a vowel,* **xanth-.** [comb. form of Gk *xanthós* yellow]

xan•tho•ma (zan thō′mə), *n., pl.* **-mas, -ma•ta** (-mə tə). *Pathol.* a yellow papule or nodule in the skin, containing lipid deposits. [1875–80; XANTH- + -OMA]

xan•tho•phyll (zan′thə fil), *n. Biochem.* lutein (def. 1). Also, **xan′tho•phyl.** [1830–40; < F *xanthophylle.* See XANTHO-, -PHYLL] **—xan•tho•phyl′lous,** *adj.*

xan•tho•sid•er•ite (zan′thə sid′ə rit′), *n.* a mineral, hydrous iron oxide, $Fe_2O_3 \cdot 2H_2O$. [1865–70; XANTHO- + SIDERITE]

xan•thous (zan′thəs), *adj.* **1.** yellow. **2.** yellowish. [1820–30; < Gk *xanth*(*ós*) yellow + -OUS]

Xan•thus (zan′thəs), *n.* an ancient city of Lycia, in SW Asia Minor, near the mouth of the Xanthus River: site of archaeological remains.

Xan•tip•pe (zan tip′ē), *n.* Xanthippe.

xat (KHät), *n.* a carved totem pole of various North American Indian peoples. [< Haida *ḥa·d* carved memorial column]

Xave′rian Broth′er, a member of a congregation of Roman Catholic laymen bound by simple vows and dedicated to education.

Xa•vi•er (zā′vē ər, zav′ē-, zā′vyər), *n.* **1. Saint Francis** (*Francisco Javier*) (*"the Apostle of the Indies"*), 1506–52, Spanish Jesuit missionary, esp. in India and Japan. **2.** a male given name: from an Arabic word meaning "bright." **—Xa•ve•ri•an** (zā vēr′ē ən, za-), *adj.*

x-ax•is (eks′ak′sis), *n., pl.* **x-ax•es** (eks′ak′sēz). *Math.* **1.** Also called **axis of abscissas.** (in a plane Cartesian coordinate system) the axis, usually horizontal, along which the abscissa is measured and from which the ordinate is measured. See diag. under **abscissa. 2.** (in a three-dimensional Cartesian coordinate system) the axis along which values of *x* are measured and at which both *y* and *z* equal zero. [1925–30]

xc, *Stock Exchange.* without coupon. Also, **xcp** [x (def. 1) + *c*(*oupon*)]

X-C, cross-country: *X-C skiing.*

X chromosome, *Genetics.* a sex chromosome of humans and most mammals that determines femaleness when paired with another X chromosome and that occurs singly in males. Cf. **Y chromosome.** [1910–15]

xcl, *Insurance.* excess current liabilities.

xd, *Stock Exchange.* ex dividend. Also, **xdiv.**

x-dis•ease (eks′di zēz′), *n. Vet. Pathol.* **1.** Also, **X-disease.** hyperkeratosis (def. 2). **2.** See **blue comb.** [1915–20]

Xe, *Symbol, Chem.* xenon.

xe•bec (zē′bek), *n.* a small, three-masted vessel of the Mediterranean, formerly much used by corsairs, now employed to some extent in commerce. Also, **chebeck, zebec, zebeck.** [1750–60; alter. of earlier *chebec* < F < Catalan *xabec* or Sp *xabeque* (now *jabeque*), both < Ar *shabbāk*]

xe•ni•a (zē′nē ə, zēn′yə), *n. Bot.* the influence or effect of pollen on a structure other than the embryo, as the seed or fruit. [1895–1900; < NL < Gk *xenía* hospitality. See XEN-, -IA] **—xe′ni•al,** *adj.*

Xe•ni•a (zē′nē ə, zēn′yə), *n.* **1.** a city in W Ohio. 24,653. **2.** a female given name.

xe′nic ac′id (zē′nik, zen′ik), *Chem.* the aqueous solution of xenon trioxide, a stable weak acid and strong oxidizing agent. [XEN(ON) + -IC]

xeno-, a combining form meaning "alien," "strange," "guest," used in the formation of compound words: *xenogamy, xenolith.* Also, *esp. before a vowel,* **xen-.** [comb. form of Gk *xénos* stranger, guest (n.); alien, foreign, strange (adj.)]

xen•o•bi•ot•ic (zen′ə bī ot′ik, -bē-, zē′nə-), *n.* a chemical or substance that is foreign to an organism or biological system. [1915–20; XENO- + BIOTIC]

Xe•noc•ra•tes (zə nok′rə tēz′), *n.* 396–314 B.C., Greek philosopher. **—Xen•o•crat•ic** (zen′ə krat′ik), **Xe•noc′•ra•te′an,** *adj.*

xen•o•cryst (zen′ə krist, zē′nə-), *n. Mineral.* a rock or crystal engulfed by magma and retained as an inclusion in the resulting igneous rock. [XENO- + CRYST(AL)] **—xen′o•crys′tic,** *adj.*

xen•o•cur•ren•cy (zen′ə kûr′ən sē, -kur′-), *n.* currency circulating or traded in money markets of countries outside its country of issue. [1975–80; XENO- + CURRENCY]

xen•o•di•ag•no•sis (zen′ə dī′əg nō′sis, zē′nə-), *n. Med.* a method of diagnosing certain diseases caused by insects, ticks, or other vectors, by allowing uninfected vectors to feed on the patient and later examining them for infections. [1925–30; XENO- + DIAGNOSIS] **—xen•o•di•ag•nos•tic** (zen′ə dī′əg nos′tik, zē′nə-), *adj.*

xe•nog•a•my (zə nog′ə mē), *n. Bot.* pollination of the stigma of a flower by pollen from a flower on another plant. Cf. **geitonogamy.** [1875–80; XENO- + -GAMY]

xen•o•gen•e•sis (zen′ə jen′ə sis, zē′nə-), *n. Biol.* **1.** heterogenesis (def. 1). **2.** the supposed generation of offspring completely and permanently different from the parent. Also, **xe•nog•e•ny** (zə noj′ə nē). [1865–70; XENO- + -GENESIS] **—xen•o•ge•net•ic** (zen′ə jə net′ik, zē′nə-), **xen′o•gen′ic,** *adj.*

xen•o•graft (zen′ə graft′, -gräft′, zē′nə-), *n. Surg.* a graft obtained from a member of one species and transplanted to a member of another species. Also called **heterograft.** Cf. **allograft, autograft, syngraft.** [1960–65; XENO- + GRAFT[1]]

xen•o•lith (zen′l ith), *n. Petrog.* a rock fragment foreign to the igneous rock in which it is embedded. Also called **inclusion.** [1900–05; XENO- + -LITH] —**xen′o•lith′ic,** *adj.*

xen•o•mor•phic (zen′ə môr′fik, zē′nə-), *adj.* **1.** Also, **allotriomorphic.** *Petrog.* noting or pertaining to a mineral grain that does not have its characteristic crystalline form but has a form impressed on it by surrounding grains; anhedral. **2.** in an unusual form; having a strange form. [1885–90; XENO- + -MORPHIC] —**xen′o•mor′phi•cal•ly,** *adv.*

xe•non (zē′non, zen′on), *n. Chem.* a heavy, colorless, chemically inactive, monatomic gaseous element used for filling radio, television, and luminescent tubes. *Symbol:* Xe; *at. wt.:* 131.30; *at. no.:* 54. [1898; < Gk *xénon,* neut. of *xénos* strange (see -ON[2]); name introduced by William Ramsay, the element's discoverer]

xe′non arc′, an electric arc between two metal electrodes enclosed in a quartz bulb and contained in a xenon atmosphere, used mainly as a high-intensity light source in motion-picture projectors and studio spotlights. Cf. **arc light.** [1970–75]

xe′non hexafluo′ride, *Chem.* a colorless, crystalline compound, XeF_6, that melts at 50°C to a yellow liquid, and boils at 75°C.

xe′non tetrafluo′ride, *Chem.* a colorless, crystalline compound, XeF_4, prepared by heating a gaseous mixture of fluorine and xenon.

xe′non triox′ide, *Chem.* a colorless, nonvolatile solid, XeO_3, explosive when dry: in solution it is called xenic acid.

Xe•noph•a•nes (zə nof′ə nēz′), *n.* c570–c480 B.C., Greek philosopher and poet. —**Xe•noph′a•ne′an,** *adj.*

xen•o•phile (zen′ə fīl′, zē′nə-), *n.* a person who is attracted to foreign peoples, cultures, or customs. [1945–50; XENO- + -PHILE]

xen•o•phil•i•a (zen′ə fil′ē ə, zē′nə-), *n.* an attraction to foreign peoples, cultures, or customs. [1955–60; XENO- + -PHILIA] —**xen′o•phil′ic,** *adj.*

xen•o•phobe (zen′ə fōb′, zē′nə-), *n.* a person who fears or hates foreigners, strange customs, etc. [1910–15; XENO- + -PHOBE]

xen•o•pho•bi•a (zen′ə fō′bē ə, zē′nə-), *n.* an unreasonable fear or hatred of foreigners or strangers or of that which is foreign or strange. [1900–05; XENO- + -PHOBIA] —**xen′o•pho′bic,** *adj.*

Xen•o•phon (zen′ə fən, -fon′), *n.* 434?–355? B.C., Greek historian and essayist. —**Xen•o•phon•te•an** (zen′ə fon′tē ən, -fon tē′-), **Xen•o•phon•ti•an** (zen′ə-fon′tē ən), **Xen•o•phon•tine** (zen′ə fon′tin, -tin), *adj.*

xe•rarch (zēr′ärk), *adj. Ecol.* (of a sere) originating in a dry habitat. [1935–40; XER- + -ARCH]

Xe•res (*Sp.* he′res), *n.* former name of **Jerez.**

xe•ric (zēr′ik), *adj.* of, pertaining to, or adapted to a dry environment. [1926; < Gk *xēr(ós)* dry + -IC[1]] —**xe′ri•cal•ly,** *adv.*

xe•ri•scap•ing (zēr′i skā′ping), *n.* environmental design of residential and park land using various methods for minimizing the need for water use. Also, **xe′ri•scape′.** [1980–85; XER(IC) + *(land)scaping*]

xero-, a combining form meaning "dry," used in the formation of compound words: *xerophyte.* Also, *esp. before a vowel,* **xer-.** [comb. form of Gk *xērós* dry]

xe•ro•der•ma (zēr′ə dûr′mə), *n. Pathol.* a disease in which the skin becomes dry, hard, and scaly. [1840–50; XERO- + -DERMA]

xeroder′ma pig•men•to′sum (pig′mən tō′səm), *Pathol.* a rare inherited disease characterized by sensitivity to ultraviolet light, exposure resulting in lesions and tumors of the skin and eyes. [1880–85; < NL: pigmented xeroderma; see PIGMENT, -OSE[1]]

xe•rog•ra•phy (zi rog′rə fē), *n.* an electrostatic printing process for copying text or graphics whereby areas on a sheet of paper corresponding to the image areas of the original are sensitized with a charge of static electricity so that, when powdered with a toner carrying an opposite charge, only the charged areas retain the toner, which is then fused to the paper to make it permanent. [1945–50; XERO- + -GRAPHY] —**xe•ro•graph•ic** (zēr′ə-graf′ik), *adj.* —**xe′ro•graph′i•cal•ly,** *adv.*

xe•roph•a•gy (zi rof′ə jē), *n., pl.* **-gies.** a Lenten fast observed esp. during Holy Week, constituting the strictest fast in the Eastern Church. Also, **xe•ro•pha•gia** (zēr′ə fā′jə, -jē ə). [1650–60; < LL *xerophagia* < Gk *xērophagía,* deriv. of *xērophageîn* to eat dry food. See XERO-, -PHAGY]

xe•roph•i•lous (zi rof′ə ləs), *adj.* **1.** *Bot.* growing in or adapted to dry, esp. dry and hot, regions. **2.** *Zool.* living or flourishing in a dry environment. [1860–65; XERO- + -PHILOUS] —**xe•roph′i•ly,** *n.*

xe•roph•thal•mi•a (zēr′of thal′mē ə, -op-), *n. Ophthalm.* abnormal dryness of the eyeball characterized by conjunctivitis, caused by a deficiency of tears and attributed to a lack of vitamin A. [1650–60; XER- + OPHTHALMIA] —**xe′roph•thal′mic,** *adj.*

xe•ro•phyte (zēr′ə fīt′), *n.* a plant adapted for growth under dry conditions. [1895–1900; XERO- + -PHYTE] —**xe•ro•phyt•ic** (zēr′ə fit′ik), *adj.* —**xe′ro•phyt′i•cal•ly,** *adv.* —**xe•ro•phyt•ism** (zēr′ə fī′tiz əm, -fī tiz′-), *n.*

CONCISE ETYMOLOGY KEY: <, descended or borrowed from; >, whence; b., blend of, blended; c., cognate with; cf., compare; deriv., derivative; equiv., equivalent; imit., imitative; obl., oblique; r., replacing; s., stem; sp., spelling, spelled; resp., respelling, respelled; trans., translation; ?, origin unknown; *, unattested; ‡, probably earlier than. See the full key inside the front cover.

xe•ro•ra•di•o•graph (zēr′ō rā′dē ə graf′, -gräf′), *n.* an x-ray utilizing a specially coated plate that allows a picture to be developed without the use of liquid chemicals. [XERO- + RADIOGRAPH] —**xe•ro•ra•di•og•ra•phy** (zēr′ō rā′dē og′rə fē), *n.*

xe•ro•sere (zēr′ə sēr′), *n. Ecol.* a sere occurring on dry soil. [1925–30; XERO- + SERE[2]]

xe•ro•sis (zi rō′sis), *n. Med.* **1.** abnormal dryness, as of the eye or skin. **2.** normal sclerosis of the tissue in an aged person. [1885–90; XER- + -OSIS] —**xe•rot•ic** (zi-rot′ik), *adj.*

xe•ro•sto•mi•a (zēr′ə stō′mē ə), *n. Pathol.* dryness of the mouth caused by diminished function of the salivary glands due to aging, disease, drug reaction, etc. [1885–90; XERO- + NL *-stomia* a condition of the mouth, as specified by the 1st element; see -STOME, -IA]

xe•ro•ther•mic (zēr′ə thûr′mik), *adj.* **1.** of or pertaining to the condition of being dry and hot: *a xerothermic climate.* **2.** adapted to an environment that is dry and hot: *a xerothermic organism.* [1900–05; XERO- + THERMIC]

Xe•rox (zēr′oks), **1.** *Trademark.* a brand name for a copying machine for reproducing printed, written, or pictorial matter by xerography. —*n.* **2.** (*sometimes l.c.*) a copy made on a xerographic copying machine. —*v.t., v.i.* **3.** (*sometimes l.c.*) to print or reproduce by xerography.

xe•rus (zēr′əs), *n.* an African ground squirrel of the genus *Xerus,* having spiny fur, very short ears, and a long tail, and including the species *X. rutilus* of northeastern Africa and *X. erythropus* of western and central Africa. [< NL (1833), appar. < Gk *xērós* dry, perh. in reference to its rough fur]

Xerx•es I (zûrk′sēz), 519?–465 B.C., king of Persia 486?–465 (son of Darius I).

x-height (eks′hīt′), *n. Typography.* the height of a lowercase *x.* [1945–50] —**x-high** (eks′hī′), *adj.*

Xho•sa (kō′sə, -zə, kô′-), *n., pl.* **-sas,** (*esp. collectively*) **-sa** for 1. **1.** a member of a Nguni people of eastern Cape Province, Republic of South Africa. **2.** the Bantu language of the Xhosa. Also, **Xosa.**

xi (zī, sī; *Gk.* ksē), *n., pl.* **xis. 1.** the 14th letter of the Greek alphabet (Ξ, ξ). **2.** the group of consonant sounds represented by this letter.

Xia (*Chin.* shyä), *n. Pinyin.* Hsia.

Xia•men (shyä′mœn′), *n. Pinyin.* **1.** an island near the Chinese mainland in the Taiwan Strait. **2.** a seaport on this island. 350,000. Also, **Hsiamen.** Also called **Amoy.**

xian (*Chin.* shyän), *n.* hsien.

Xi•an (shē′än′), *n. Pinyin.* a city in and the capital of Shaanxi province, in central China: capital of the ancient Chinese Empire. 1,600,000. Also, **Sian, Singan, Xi′an′.** Formerly, **Changan.**

Xiang•gang (*Chin.* shyäng′gäng′), *n. Pinyin.* **1.** See **Hong Kong. 2.** Victoria (def. 4).

Xiang•tan (shyäng′tän′), *n. Pinyin.* a city in E Hunan, in S China. 300,000. Also, **Hsiangt′an, Siangtan.**

Xi Jiang (shē′ jyäng′), *Pinyin.* a river in S China, flowing E from Yunnan province to the South China Sea near Canton. 1250 mi. (2012 km) long. Also, **Hsi Chiang, Si Kiang.**

Xi•kang (shē′käng′), *n. Pinyin.* a former province in W China, now part of Sichuan. Also, **Sikang.**

Xi•me•nes (*Sp.* hē me′nes), *n.* See **Jiménez de Cisneros.**

x in, *Stock Exchange.* ex interest.

Xing, crossing (used esp. on road signs): *deer Xing; school Xing.* Also, **XING, xing.**

Xin•gú (shing gōō′), *n.* a river flowing N through central Brazil to the Amazon. 1300 mi. (2090 km) long.

Xin•hai•lian (*Chin.* shin′hī′lyän′), *n. Pinyin.* former name of **Lianyungang.** Also, **Hsinhailien, Sinhailien.**

Xin•hua (shin′hwä′), *n.* the official press agency of the People's Republic of China. [< Chin *Xīnhuá* lit., New China]

Xi•ning (shē′ning′), *n. Pinyin.* a city in and the capital of Qinghai province, in W central China. 250,000. Also, **Hsining, Sining.**

Xin•jiang Uy•gur (shin′jyäng′ wē′gər), *n.* an administrative division in westernmost China, bordering Tibet, India, the Soviet Union, and Mongolia: formerly a province. 7,270,000; 635,829 sq. mi. (1,646,797 sq. km). *Cap.:* Ürümqi. Also, **Sinkiang Uighur.** Official name, **Xin′jiang′ Uy′gur Auton′omous Re′gion.**

Xin•xiang (shin′shyäng′), *n. Pinyin.* a city in N Henan province, in E China. 300,000. Also, **Hsinhsiang, Sinsiang.**

-xion, *Chiefly Brit.* var. of **-tion:** *connexion; inflexion.*

xi′ par′ticle, *Physics.* any of a family of baryons having strangeness −2 and isotopic spin ½. *Symbol:* Ξ Cf. **cascade particle.** [1960–65]

Xi•pe (shē′pā; *Sp.* hē′pe), *n.* the Aztec god of sowing or planting. Also called **Xi•pe To•tec** (shē′pā tō′tek; *Sp.* hē′pe tô′tek). [< Nahuatl *Xīpeuh Totēuc; xīpeuh* peeled, skinned; *totēuc, totēcuh* our lord, equiv. to *to-* our + *tēuc(tli), tēcuh(tli)* lord]

xiph•i•ster•num (zif′ə stûr′nəm), *n., pl.* **-na** (-nə). *Anat.* the lowermost of the three segments of the sternum. Cf. **gladiolus** (def. 2), **manubrium** (def. 2a). [1855–60; < NL *xiphi-* (comb. form of Gk *xíphos* sword) + *sternum* STERNUM] —**xiph′i•ster′nal,** *adj.*

xiph•oid (zif′oid), *adj.* **1.** *Anat., Zool.* sword-shaped; ensiform. —*n.* **2.** the xiphisternum. [1740–50; < NL *xiphoīdēs* < Gk *xiphoeidḗs* swordlike, equiv. to *xíph(os)* sword + *-oeidēs* -OID]

xiph•o•su•ran (zif′ə sŏŏr′ən), *adj.* **1.** belonging or pertaining to the order Xiphosura, comprising the horseshoe crabs. —*n.* **2.** an arthropod of the order Xiphosura; a horseshoe crab. [1830–40; < NL *Xiphosur(a)* order name (irreg. < Gk *xíphos* sword + *-oura,* neut. pl. of *-ouros* -tailed, deriv. of *ourá* tail) + -AN]

Xi•zang (*Chin.* shē′zäng′), *n. Pinyin.* Tibet.

XL, 1. extra large. **2.** extra long.

x-line (eks′līn′), *n. Print.* See **mean line.**

X-linked (eks′lingkt′), *adj. Genetics.* **1.** of or pertaining to a trait controlled by a gene or genes on the X chromosome. **2.** of or pertaining to a gene on an X chromosome. [1945–50]

Xmas (kris′məs *or, often,* eks′məs), Christmas. —**Usage.** The abbreviation XMAS for Christmas dates from the mid 16th century. The X is the Greek letter chi, the initial in the word *Χριστός* (*Christos*) "Christ." In spite of a long and respectable history, today XMAS is offensive to many, perhaps because of its associations with advertising. It is not used in formal writing.

Xn., Christian.

Xnty., Christianity.

xo•a•non (zō′ə non′), *n., pl.* **-na** (-nə). *Gk. Antiq.* a simple, carved image, esp. one in which the original block of stone or wood is readily apparent. [1700–10; < Gk *xóanon* carved image; akin to *xeîn* to scrape, carve]

Xo•sa (kō′sə, -zə, kô′-), *n., pl.* **-sas,** (*esp. collectively*) **-sa.** *n.* Xhosa.

x pr, *Stock Exchange.* without privileges.

XQ, cross question. Also, **xq**

xr, *Stock Exchange.* ex rights.

x-ra•di•a•tion (eks′rā′dē ā′shən), *n.* **1.** exposure to x-rays. **2.** radiation in the form of x-rays. [1895–1900]

X-rat•ed (eks′rā′tid), *adj.* **1.** (of a motion picture) having a rating of X; intended for adults only. **2.** obscene; sexually explicit: *X-rated language.* [1970–75]

x-ray (eks′rā′), *n.* Also, **x ray, X ray. 1.** *Physics.* **a.** Often, **x-rays.** a form of electromagnetic radiation, similar to light but of shorter wavelength and capable of penetrating solids and of ionizing gases. **b.** such radiation having wavelengths in the range of approximately 0.1–10 nm. **2.** a radiograph made by x-rays. **3.** (*cap.*) a word in communications to represent the letter *X.* —*v.t.* **4.** to examine, photograph, or treat with x-rays. —*adj.* **5.** of or pertaining to x-rays. Also, **X′-ray′.** [1895–1900; trans. of G *X-Strahl* (1895), the name orig. given to the rays by Röntgen, their discoverer, *x* signifying their unknown nature]

x′-ray astron′omy, the study of celestial objects by means of the x-rays emitted by them. Cf. **x-ray** (def 1b). [1960–65] —**x′-ray astron′omer.**

x′-ray burst′er, *Astron.* a celestial source from which bursts of x-rays are received. Also called **burster.**

x′-ray crystallog′raphy, *Crystall.* the determination of the structure of a crystal by the use of x-ray diffraction. [1925–30]

x′-ray diffrac′tion, *Physics.* diffraction of x-rays by the regularly spaced atoms of a crystal, useful for determining the arrangement of the atoms. [1940–45]

x′-ray pho′tograph, a radiograph made with x-rays. [1905–10] —**x′-ray photog′raphy.**

x′-ray star′, a star, usually a binary star, that is a strong emitter of x-rays, as Cygnus X-1. [1960–65]

x′-ray techni′cian, a technician who specializes in taking and processing x-rays, esp. in a hospital or clinic.

x′-ray ther′apy, *Med.* treatment of a disease using controlled quantities of x-rays. [1925–30]

x′-ray tube′, an electronic tube for producing x-rays, essentially a cathode-ray tube in which a metal target is bombarded with high-energy electrons. [1905–10]

XS, extra small.

x-stretch•er (eks′strech′ər), *n. Furniture.* a stretcher having the form of an X.

Xt., Christ.

Xtian., Christian.

Xty., Christianity.

xu (sōō), *n., pl.* **xu.** an aluminum coin and monetary unit of Vietnam, the 100th part of a dong. [1945–50; < Vietnamese < F *sou* SOU]

Xuan Tong (*Chin.* shyän′ tông′), *Pinyin.* Hsüan T'ung.

Xuan Zong (*Chin.* shyän′ zông′), *Pinyin.* See **Hsüan Tsung.**

x-u•nit (eks′yōō′nit), *n.* a unit formerly used to express the wavelength of x-rays and gamma rays, equal to approximately 10^{-11} cm. *Abbr.:* Xu, XU

Xu•zhou (shy′jō′), *n. Pinyin.* a city in N Jiangsu province, in E China. 1,000,000. Also, **Hsüchou, Süchow.** Formerly, **Tongshan.**

X-wave (eks′wāv′), *n. Radio.* See **extraordinary wave.**

XX, See **powdered sugar.**

XXXX, See **confectioners' sugar.**

xy•lan (zī′lan), *n. Chem.* the pentosan occurring in woody tissue that hydrolyzes to xylose: a source of furfural. [1890–95; < Gk *xýl(on)* wood + *-an,* var. of -ANE]

xy•lem (zī′ləm, -lem), *n. Bot.* a compound tissue in vascular plants that helps provide support and that conducts water and nutrients upward from the roots, consisting of tracheids, vessels, parenchyma cells, and woody fibers. [1870–75; < G, equiv. to Gk *xýl(on)* wood + *-ēma* (see PHLOEM)]

xy′lem ray′, a vascular ray extending into or located entirely within the secondary xylem. Also called **wood ray.** [1870–75]

xy•lene (zī′lēn), *n. Chem.* any of three oily, colorless water-insoluble, flammable, toxic, isomeric liquids C_8H_{10}, of the benzene series, obtained mostly from coal tar: used chiefly in the manufacture of dyes. Also, **xy•lo**

(zī′lôl, -lol). Also called **dimethylbenzene.** [1850–55; < Gk *xýl(on)* wood + -ENE]

xy′lic ac′id (zī′lik, zil′ik), *Chem.* any of six colorless, crystalline, isomeric acids having the formula $C_9H_{10}O_2$, derived from xylene. [1870–75; XYL(ENE) + -IC]

xy•li•dine (zī′li dēn′, -din, zil′i-), *n.* **1.** any of six isomeric compounds that have the formula $C_8H_{11}N$, are derivatives of xylene, and resemble aniline: used in dye manufacture. **2.** an oily liquid consisting of a mixture of certain of these compounds, used commercially in making dyes. [1840–50; XYL(ENE) + -ID[3] + -INE[2]]

xy•li•tol (zī′li tôl′, -tol′), *n. Biochem.* a naturally occurring pentose sugar alcohol, $C_5H_{12}O_5$, used as a sugar substitute. [< G *Xylit* (1891), equiv. to *Xyl(ose)* XYLOSE + *-it* -ITE[1]; see -ITOL]

xylo-, a combining form meaning "wood," used in the formation of compound words: *xylophilous.* [comb. form of Gk *xýlon*]

xy•lo•graph (zī′lə graf′, -gräf′), *n.* an engraving on wood. [1860–65; XYLO- + -GRAPH]

xy•log•ra•phy (zī log′rə fē), *n.* the art of engraving on wood, or of printing from such engravings. [1810–20; < F *xylographie.* See XYLO-, -GRAPHY] **—xy•log′ra•pher,** *n.* **—xy•lo•graph•ic** (zī′lə graf′ik), **xy′lo•graph′i•cal,** *adj.* **—xy′lo•graph′i•cal•ly,** *adv.*

xy•loid (zī′loid), *adj.* resembling wood; ligneous. [1850–55; < Gk *xýl(on)* wood + -OID]

xy•lo•phage (zī′lə fāj′), *n.* a wood-eating insect. [1875–80; XYLO- + -PHAGE]

xy•loph•a•gous (zī lof′ə gəs), *adj.* **1.** feeding on wood, as certain insects or insect larvae. **2.** perforating or destroying timber, as certain mollusks, crustaceans, and fungi. [1835–45; < Gk *xylophágos.* See XYLO, -PHAGOUS]

xy•loph•i•lous (zī lof′ə ləs), *adj.* growing in or living on wood: *xylophilous fungi.* [1860–65; XYLO- + -PHILOUS]

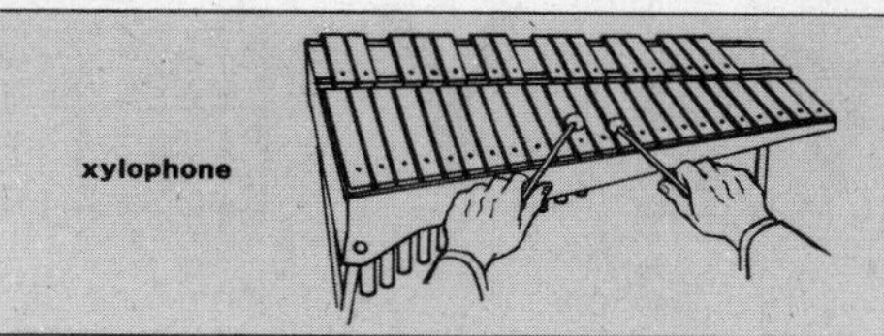
xylophone

xy•lo•phone (zī′lə fōn′), *n.* a musical instrument consisting of a graduated series of wooden bars, usually sounded by striking with small wooden hammers. [1865–70; XYLO- + -PHONE] **—xy•lo•phon•ic** (zī′lə fon′ik), *adj.* **—xy•lo•phon•ist** (zī′lə fō′nist, zī lof′ə nist, zi-), *n.*

xy•lose (zī′lōs), *n. Chem.* a colorless, crystalline pentose sugar, $C_5H_{10}O_5$, derived from xylan, straw, corncobs, etc., by treating with heated dilute sulfuric acid, and dehydrating to furfural if stronger acid is used. [1890–95; < Gk *xýl(on)* wood + -OSE[2]]

xy•lo•stro•ma (zī′lə strō′mə), *n., pl.* **-ma•ta** (-mə tə). *Mycol.* the felted, blackish stroma of some species of wood-destroying fungi. [< NL; see XYLO-, STROMA] **—xy′lo•stro′ma•toid′,** *adj.*

xy•lot•o•mous (zī lot′ə məs), *adj.* boring into or cutting wood, as certain insects. [XYLO- + -TOMOUS]

xyst (zist), *n.* **1.** (in ancient Greek and Roman architecture) a covered portico, as a promenade. **2.** (in an ancient Roman villa) a garden walk planted with trees. Also, **xystum, xystus.** [1655–65; < L *xystus* garden terrace, shaded walk < Gk *xystós* a covered colonnade]

xys•ter (zis′tər), *n.* a surgical instrument for scraping bones. [< NL < Gk *xystḗr* scraping tool, equiv. to *xys-* (s. of *xýein* to scrape) + *-tēr* instrumental n. suffix]

xys•tum (zis′təm), *n., pl.* **-ta** (-tə). xyst.

xys•tus (zis′təs), *n., pl.* **-ti** (-tī). xyst.

Xys•tus I (zis′təs). See **Sixtus I.**

Xystus II. See **Sixtus II.**

Xystus III. See **Sixtus III.**

CONCISE PRONUNCIATION KEY: act, cāpe, dâre, pärt; set, ēqual; if, īce; ox, ōver, ôrder, oil, bŏŏk, bōōt, out; up, ûrge; child; sing; shoe; thin, *th*at; zh as in *treasure.* ə = *a* as in *alone, e* as in *system, i* as in *easily, o* as in *gallop, u* as in *circus;* ᵊ as in *fire* (fīᵊr), *hour* (ouᵊr). l and n can serve as syllabic consonants, as in *cradle* (krād′l), and *button* (but′n). See the full key inside the front cover.

DEVELOPMENT OF MAJUSCULE						
NORTH SEMITIC	GREEK	ETR.	LATIN	MODERN		
				GOTHIC	ITALIC	ROMAN
SEE LETTER U			Y	𝔜	*Y*	Y

DEVELOPMENT OF MINUSCULE					
ROMAN CURSIVE	ROMAN UNCIAL	CAROL. MIN.	MODERN		
			GOTHIC	ITALIC	ROMAN
y	y	—	𝔶	*y*	y

The twenty-fifth letter of the English alphabet, as a consonant, developed from North Semitic *yodh,* whence it was adopted into Greek as a vowel (*iota*) and became English I. (See **I.**) The Y-form goes back to Greek Y, a variant of North Semitic *waw.* (See **U, V, W.**) After the conquest of Greece by the Romans in the 1st century B.C., it was used in Latin for transliterating the Greek *y*-sound (as in French *pure,* German *über*) in such words as *zephyros.*

Y, y (wī), *n., pl.* **Y's** or **Ys, y's** or **ys. 1.** the 25th letter of the English alphabet, a semivowel. **2.** any spoken sound represented by the letter *Y* or *y,* as in *yet, city,* or *rhythm.* **3.** something having the shape of a Y. **4.** a written or printed representation of the letter *Y* or *y.* **5.** a device, as a printer's type, for reproducing the letter Y or y.

Y (wī), **the Y,** *Informal.* the YMCA, YWCA, YMHA, or YWHA.

Y, yen[1] (def. 1).

Y, *Symbol.* **1.** the 25th in order or in a series, or, when *I* is omitted, the 24th. **2.** (*sometimes l.c.*) the medieval Roman numeral for 150. Cf. **Roman numerals. 3.** (*sometimes l.c.*) *Elect.* admittance. **4.** *Chem.* yttrium. **5.** *Biochem.* tyrosine.

y, *Symbol, Math.* **1.** an unknown quantity. **2.** (in Cartesian coordinates) the y-axis.

y-, a prefix occurring in certain obsolete words (*ywis*) and esp. in archaic past participles: *yclad.* Also, **i-.** [ME *y-, i-* (reduced var. *a-*), OE *ge-,* prefix with perfective, intensifying, or collective force; c. OFris, OS *ge-, gi-,* Goth *ga-,* G *ge-;* cf. perh. L *com-* COM-]

-y[1], a native English suffix of adjectives meaning "characterized by or inclined to" the substance or action of the word or stem to which the suffix is attached: *juicy; grouchy; rumbly; dreamy.* Also, **-ey[1].** [OE *-ig;* c. G *-ig;* cf. perh. L *-icus,* Gk *-ikos*]

-y[2], a noun-forming suffix with a variety of functions in contemporary English, added to monosyllabic bases to create words that are almost always informal. Its earliest use, probably still productive, was to form endearing or familiar names or common nouns from personal names, other nouns, and adjectives (*Billy; Susie; birdie; doggie; granny; sweetie; tummy*). The hypocoristic feature is absent in recent coinages, however, which are simply informal and sometimes pejorative (*boonies; cabby; groupie; hippy; looie; Okie; preemie; preppy; rookie*). Another function of **-y[2] (-ie)** is to form from adjectives nouns that denote exemplary or extreme instances of the quality named by the adjective (*baddie; biggie; cheapie; toughie*), sometimes focusing on a restricted, usually unfavorable sense of the adjective (*sharpie; sickie; whitey*). A few words in which the informal character of **-y[2] (-ie)** has been lost are now standard in formal written English (*goalie; movie*). Also, **-ie.** Cf. **-o, -sy.** [late ME (Scots), orig. in names; of uncert. orig.; BABY and PUPPY, now felt as having this suffix, may be of different derivation]

-y[3], a suffix of various origins used in the formation of action nouns from verbs (*inquiry*), also found in other abstract nouns: *carpentry; infamy.* [repr. L *-ia, -ium;* Gk *-ia, -eia, -ion;* F *-ie;* G *-ie*]

y., 1. yard; yards. **2.** year; years.

ya (yə), *pron. Pron. Spelling.* **1.** you: *Give me a hand, will ya?* **2.** your: *Where's ya brother?*

yā (yä), *n.* the 28th letter of the Arabic alphabet. [< Ar]

yab·ber (yab′ər), *n. Australian.* jabber. [1870–75; perh. alter., by assoc. with JABBER, of a word based on *ya-* speak, talk, in Gabi (Australian Aboriginal language spoken in the Maryborough district, S Queensland)]

yab·by (yab′ē), *n.* a small Australian crayfish, of the genus *Cherax,* inhabiting streams and water holes. [1890–95; < Wergaia (Australian Aboriginal language spoken around Wimmera, Victoria) *yabij*]

Ya′blo·no·vyy Range′ (yä′blə nə vē), a mountain range in the SE Russian Federation in Asia, E of Lake Baikal. Also, **Ya′blo·no·vy Range′.**

CONCISE ETYMOLOGY KEY: <, descended or borrowed from; >, whence; b., blend of, blended; c., cognate with; cf., compare; deriv., derivative; equiv., equivalent; imit., imitative; obl., oblique; r., replacing; s., stem; sp., spelling, spelled; resp., respelling, respelled; trans., translation; ?, origin unknown; *, unattested; ‡, probably earlier than. See the full key inside the front cover.

yacht (yot), *n.* **1.** a vessel used for private cruising, racing, or other noncommercial purposes. —*v.i.* **2.** to sail, voyage, or race in a yacht. [1550–60; < early D *jaght,* short for *jaghtschip* hunting ship, equiv. to D *jacht* hunt (deriv. of *jagen* to hunt) + *schip* SHIP] —**yacht′y,** *adj.*

yacht′ chair′, a folding armchair consisting of a wooden frame across which are stretched strips of canvas to form the seat and back.

yacht′ club′, an organization of yachtsmen and yachtswomen for the purpose of encouraging and directing the sport of yachting. [1830–40]

yacht·ing (yot′ing), *n.* the practice or sport of sailing or voyaging in a yacht. [1830–40; YACHT + -ING[1]]

yachts·man (yots′mən), *n., pl.* **-men.** a person who owns or sails a yacht, or who is devoted to yachting. [1860–65; YACHT + 's[1] + -MAN] —**yachts′man·ship′, yacht′man·ship′,** *n.*
—**Usage.** See **-man.**

yachts·wom·an (yots′wo͝om′ən), *n., pl.* **-wom·en.** a woman who owns or sails a yacht, or who is devoted to yachting. [1885–90; YACHT + 's[1] + -WOMAN]
—**Usage.** See **-woman.**

yack (yak), *v.i., n. Slang.* yak[2]. —**yack′er,** *n.*

yack·e·ty-yak (yak′i tē yak′), *v.i.,* **-yakked, -yak·king,** *n. Slang.* yak[2]. Also, **yack′ety-yack′, yakety-yak, yakity-yak.** [1945–50; appar. imit.]

yad (*Seph.* yäd; *Ashk.* yôd), *n., pl.* ***ya·dim*** (*Seph.* yä dēm′; *Ashk.* yô′dim). *Hebrew.* a tapered, usually ornamented rod, usually of silver, with the tip of the tapered part forming a fist with the index finger extended, used by the reader of a scroll of the Torah as a place marker. [*yādh* lit., hand]

Yad·kin (yad′kin), *n.* a part of the Pee Dee River that flows SE through central North Carolina.

Yad Va·shem (yäd′ vä shem′), *Hebrew.* **1.** the official authority in Israel for the commemoration of the Holocaust and its victims. **2.** the memorial shrine administered by this authority. Also, ***Yad′ va-Shem′.***

yaff (yaf), *v.i. Scot. and North Eng.* to bark; yelp. [1600–10; perh. b. dial. *waff* bark and YAP or YAWP]

Ya·fo (yä′fō), *n.* Jaffa.

YAG (yag), *n.* a synthetic yttrium aluminum garnet, used for infrared lasers and as a gemstone. [1960–65; *y*(*ttrium*) *a*(*luminum*) *g*(*arnet*)]

ya·ge (yä′hā), *n.* a mildly hallucinogenic drug obtained from a South American vine, *Banisteriopsis caapi.* Also, **yaje.** [1920–25; < AmerSp *yagé,* appar. < an indigenous language of SE Colombia or NE Peru]

ya·ger (yä′gər), *n.* jaeger (defs. 2, 3).

Ya′gi anten′na (yä′gē, yag′ē), *Radio.* a sharply directional antenna array, consisting of one or two dipoles connected to the transmitting or receiving circuit, and several insulated dipoles all parallel and about equally spaced in a line. [1940–45; named after Hidetsugu *Yagi* (1886–1976), Japanese electrical engineer]

yah (yä, yâ), *interj.* an exclamation of impatience or derision.

Ya·ha·ta (*Japn.* yä′hä tä′), *n.* Yawata.

Yah·gan (yä′gən), *n., pl.* **-gans,** (*esp. collectively*) **-gan** for 1. **1.** a member of an Indian people of the southern coast of Tierra del Fuego and adjacent islands. **2.** the language of the Yahgan.

Ya·hoo (yä′ho͞o, yā′-, yä ho͞o′), *n., pl.* **-hoos. 1.** (in Swift's *Gulliver's Travels*) one of a race of brutes, having the form and all the vices of humans, who are subject to the Houyhnhnms. **2.** (*l.c.*) an uncultivated or boorish person; lout; philistine; yokel. **3.** (*l.c.*) a coarse or brutish person. [coined by Swift in *Gulliver's Travels* (1726)] —**ya′hoo·ism,** *n.*

Yahr·zeit (yär′tsīt, yôr′-), *n. Judaism.* the anniversary of the death of a parent, sibling, child, or spouse, observed by lighting a memorial lamp or candle the night before and reciting the *Kaddish* at the evening service of the day before and at the morning and afternoon services of the day itself. Also, **Jahrzeit.** [1850–55; < Yiddish *yortsayt,* equiv. to *yor* YEAR + *tsayt* time (see TIDE[1]); cf. MHG *jārzīt* anniversary]

Yah·weh (yä′we), *n.* a name of God, transliterated by scholars from the Tetragrammaton and commonly rendered Jehovah. Also, **Yah′we, Yah·veh, Yah·ve** (yä′ve), **Jahveh, Jahve, Jahweh, Jahwe.**

Yah·wism (yä′wiz əm), *n.* the worship of Yahweh or the religious system based on such worship. Also, **Yahvism** (yä′viz əm), **Jahvism, Jahwism.** [1865–70; YAHW(EH) + -ISM]

Yah·wist (yä′wist), *n.* a writer of the earliest major source of the Hexateuch, in which God is characteristically referred to as Yahweh rather than Elohim. Also, **Yah·vist** (yä′vist), **Jahvist, Jahwist.** Cf. **Elohist.** [YAHW(EH) + -IST]

Yah·wis·tic (yä wis′tik), *adj.* **1.** of, pertaining to, or characteristic of the Yahwist. **2.** of or pertaining to Yahwism. Also, **Yah·vis·tic** (yä vis′tik), **Jahvistic, Jahwistic.** [YAHWIST + -IC]

ya·je (yä′hā), *n.* yage.

Yaj·ur-Ve·da (yuj′o͝or vā′də, -vē′-), *n. Hinduism.* a Samhita, containing a collection of sacrificial formulas. Cf. **Veda.** [< Skt *yajus* term for ritual formulas not in strict metrical composition + *veda* VEDA]

yak[1] (yak), *n.* **1.** a large, stocky, shaggy-haired wild ox, *Bos grunniens,* of the Tibetan highlands, having long, curved horns: endangered. **2.** a domesticated variety of this animal. [1785–95; < Tibetan, sp. *gyag*]

yak[1], *Bos grunniens,* 6 ft. (1.8 m) high at shoulder; head and body to 11 ft. (3.4 m); tail 3 ft. (0.9 m)

yak[2] (yak), *v.,* **yakked, yak·king,** *n. Slang.* —*v.i.* **1.** to talk, esp. uninterruptedly and idly; gab; chatter: *They've been yakking on the phone for over an hour.* —*n.* **2.** incessant idle or gossipy talk. Also, **yack, yackety-yak.** [1945–50, *Amer.*; appar. of expressive orig.] —**yak′ker,** *n.*

yak[3] (yak), *n., v.i., v.t.,* **yakked, yak·king.** *Slang.* yuk[1].

yak·e·ty-yak (yak′i tē yak′), *v.i.,* **-yakked, -yak·king,** *n. Slang.* yak[2]. Also, **yak′i·ty-yak′.**

Yak·i·ma (yak′ə mô′, -mə), *n., pl.* **-mas,** (*esp. collectively*) **-ma** for 3. **1.** a city in S Washington. 49,826. **2.** a river in S central Washington. 203 mi. (327 km) long. **3.** a member of a North American Indian people of Washington. **4.** the Sahaptin language of the Yakima.

ya·ki·to·ri (yä′ki tôr′ē, -tōr′ē), *n. Japanese Cookery.* a dish of small pieces of boneless chicken, usually marinated, skewered, and grilled. [1960–65; < Japn, equiv. to *yaki* broil + *tori* fowl]

yak·ka (yak′ə), *n. Australian.* work, esp. hard work. [1885–90; earlier sp. *yacker, yakker;* of obscure orig.]

yak·ow (yak′ou), *n.* **1.** a hybrid animal, produced by rossbreeding yaks with cows. **2.** the meat of such an nimal. [1970–75; b. YAK[1] and COW[1]]

a·kut (yə ko͝ot′), *n., pl.* **-kuts,** (*esp. collectively*) **-kut** or 1. **1.** a member of a Turkic-speaking people of the ena River valley and adjacent areas of eastern Siberia. . the Turkic language of the Yakut.

akut′ Auton′omous Repub′lic, *n.* an autono-ous republic in the NE Russian Federation in Asia. ,081,000; 1,198,146 sq. mi. (3,103,200 sq. km). *Cap.:* Ya-utsk.

a·kutsk (yə ko͞otsk′), *n.* the capital of the Yakut Au-onomous Republic in the NE Russian Federation in sia, on the Lena River. 187,000.

a·ku·za (yä′ko͞o zä′), *n., pl.* **-za. 1.** any of various ightly knit Japanese criminal organizations having a itualistic, strict code of honor. **2.** such organizations ollectively. **3.** a member of such an organization; gang-ter. [1960–65; < Japn: racketeer, gambler, good-for-othing, useless, from the name of a game in which the orst hand is of three cards marked *ya* eight, *ku* nine (< MChin, equiv. to Chin *jiǔ*), and *-za* three (comb. form of *a(n)* < MChin, equiv. to Chin *sān*)]

ale (yāl), *n.* **1. Elihu,** 1648–1721, English colonial offi-ial, born in America: governor of Madras 1687–92; prin-ipal benefactor of the Collegiate School at Saybrook, onnecticut (now Yale University). **2.** a male given ame.

'all (yôl), *pron.* you-all.

al·ow (yal′ō), *n.* **Ros·a·lyn (Suss·man)** (roz′ə lin us′mən), born 1921, U.S. medical physicist: Nobel prize or medicine 1977.

al·ta (yôl′tə; *Russ.* yäl′tə), *n.* a seaport in the Cri-nea, S Ukraine, on the Black Sea: site of wartime con-erence of Roosevelt, Churchill, and Stalin February –12, 1945. 83,000.

'a·lu (yä′lo͞o′; *Chin.* yä′ly′), *n. Pinyin, Wade-Giles.* a iver in E Asia, forming part of the boundary between Manchuria and North Korea and flowing SW to the Yel-ow Sea. 300 mi. (483 km) long. Also called, *Wade-Giles,* **'a′lu′ Chiang′** (jyäng); *Pinyin,* **Ya′lu′ Jiang′** (jyäng).

am (yam), *n.* **1.** the starchy, tuberous root of any of various climbing vines of the genus *Dioscorea,* cultivated or food in warm regions. **2.** any of these plants. **3.** the weet potato. **4.** *Scot.* potato (def. 1). [1580–90; cf. Gul-ah *nyam,* Jamaican E *nyaams,* Sranan *jamsi* < sources in ne or more West African languages (cf. Wolof *nam(nam),* ulani *nami* to eat, Twi *ɛnãm* flesh, *ànyinam, ayam′kàw-dé* kinds of yam; earlier E forms < Pg *inhame* or Sp *(i)ñame*]

'a·ma (yum′ə), *n. Hindu Myth.* the Vedic god presid-ng over the underworld. [< Skt *yama*]

'a·ma·ga·ta (yä′mä gä′tä), *n.* **Prince A·ri·to·mo** ä′RE tô′mô), 1838–1922, Japanese field marshal and tatesman.

'a·ma·mo·to (yä′mä mô′tô), *n.* **I·so·ro·ku** (ē′sô RÔ′-o͞o), 1884–1943, Japanese naval officer.

'a·ma·ni (yä mä′nē), *n.* **Sheik Ah·med Zak·i** äKH′med zak′ē), born 1930, Saudi Arabian govern-ment official: minister of petroleum 1962–86.

'a·ma·sa·ki (yä′mə sä′kē), *n.* **Mi·no·ru** (mi nôr′o͞o, nōr′-), 1912–86, U.S. architect.

'a·ma·shi·ta (yä′mä shē′tä), *n.* **To·mo·yu·ki** (tô′mô-o͞o′kē), (*"the Tiger of Malaya"*), 1885–1946, Japanese general.

'a·ma·to-e (yä′mä tô e′), *n. Japanese.* a narrative style of painting developed from the 12th to the 14th century, characterized chiefly by continuous illustrations often executed on long scrolls.

'a·men (yä′mən), *n.* (in the Chinese Empire) the resi-dence or office of a public official. [1820–30; < Chin *yámen* (*yá* office + *mén* gate)]

'a·mi (yä′mē), *n., pl.* **-mis,** (*esp. collectively*) **-mi** for 1. **1.** a member of an Indonesian people of Hungtow Island, off the southeastern coast of Taiwan. **2.** the Austrone-sian language of the Yami.

'a·mim to·vim (*Yiddish.* yôn toi′vim; *Seph. Heb.* yä-mēm′ tô vēm′; *Ashk. Heb.* yô′mim tō′vim), a pl. of ***yom tov.***

'am·mer (yam′ər), *Informal.* —*v.i.* **1.** to whine or complain. **2.** to make an outcry or clamor. **3.** to talk loudly and persistently. —*v.t.* **4.** to utter clamorously, persistently, or in complaint: *They yammered their com-plaints until she let them see the movie.* —*n.* **5.** the act or noise of yammering. [1275–1325; ME *yameren* (v.) < MD *jam(m)eren,* r. ME *yomeren,* OE *gēomrian* to com-plain, deriv. of *gēomor* sad; akin to G *Jammer* lamenta-tion] **—yam′mer·er,** *n.* **—yam′mer·ing·ly,** *adv.*

'a·mous·sou·kro (yä′mə so͞o′krō), *n.* a city in and the capital of the Ivory Coast, in the S central part. 120,000.

'am·pee (yam′pē), *n.* a vine, *Dioscorea trifida,* of South America, having large leaves and edible tubers. Also called **cush-cush.** [1790–1800; perh. ult. of West African orig.; cf. Vai (Mande language of Liberia and Si-erra Leone) *džambi* wild yam]

'a·na (yä′nə), *n., pl.* **-nas,** (*esp. collectively*) **-na** for 1. **1.** a member of a North American Indian people who once resided in the eastern portion of the upper Sacra-mento River valley in California. **2.** the now extinct Hokan language of the Yana, best known for a system-atic differentiation between men's and women's speech.

'an·an (yä′nän′), *n. Pinyin.* a city in N Shaanxi prov-ince, in N central China: the headquarters of Chinese Communists 1937–47. 45,000. Also, **Yan′an′, Yenan.** Formerly, **Fushih.**

'ang (yäng, yang), *n.* See under **yin and yang.**

'ang Chen Ning (yäng′ chen′ ning′), born 1922, Chinese physicist in the U.S.: Nobel prize 1957.

'an·gon (yang gon′, -gôn′), *n.* the capital of Burma (Myanmar), in the S part. 2,459,000. Formerly, **Rangoon.**

'ang·qu (yäng′chy′), *n. Pinyin.* former name of **Tai-yuan.** Also, *Older Spelling,* **Yang·kü** (yäng′ky′).

Yang·quan (yäng′chwän′), *n. Pinyin.* a city in E Shanxi province, in NE China. 177,400. Also, *Wade-Giles,* **Yang′chuan′.**

Yang Shang·kun (yäng′ shäng′ko͞on′), *n.* born 1907, Chinese Communist leader: president since 1988.

Yang-shao (yäng′shou′), *adj. Archaeol.* of or desig-nating a Neolithic culture of N China c5000–3000 B.C., characterized by dwellings with sunken floors, domesti-cation of the pig, and fine pottery. Also, **Yang′ Shao′.** [after the type site at the village of *Yang-shao* (Chin *Yǎngshāo cūn*), western Henan, excavated in 1921]

yang tao (yäng′ tou′). See **Chinese gooseberry.** [< Chin *yángtáo,* equiv. to *yáng* sheep + *táo* peach]

Yang·tze (yang′sē′, -tsē′; *Chin.* yäng′tse′), *n. Older Spelling.* See **Chang Jiang.** Also called **Yang′tze′ Kiang′** (kyäng).

Yang·zhou (yäng′jō′), *n. Pinyin.* a city in central Jiangsu province, in E China. 180,200. Also, *Wade-Giles,* **Yang′chou′;** *Older Spelling,* **Yang′chow′.**

Ya·ni·na (yä′nē nä′), *n.* Ioannina. Also, **Yannina.**

yank (yangk), *v.t., v.i.* **1.** to pull or remove abruptly and vigorously: *Yank down on the bell rope. He was yanked out of school.* —*n.* **2.** an abrupt, vigorous pull; jerk. [1810–20; orig. uncert.]
—Syn. 1. pluck, tug, tear.

Yank (yangk), *n., adj. Informal.* Yankee. [1770–80, *Amer.*; shortened form]

Yan·kee (yang′kē), *n.* **1.** a native or inhabitant of the United States. **2.** a native or inhabitant of New Eng-land. **3.** a native or inhabitant of a northern U.S. state, esp. of one of the northeastern states that sided with the Union in the American Civil War. **4.** a federal or north-ern soldier in the American Civil War. **5.** a word used in communications to represent the letter *Y.* **6.** *Mil.* the NATO name for a class of Soviet ballistic missile subma-rine, nuclear powered, with up to 16 missile launchers. —*adj.* **7.** of, pertaining to, or characteristic of a Yankee or Yankees: *Yankee ingenuity.* [1750–60, *Amer.*; perh. back formation from D *Jan Kees* John Cheese, nickname (mistaken for plural) applied by the Dutch of colonial New York to English settlers in Connecticut]

Yan′kee bond′, a bond issued by a foreign corpora-tion or country designed for sale in the U.S.

Yan·kee·dom (yang′kē dəm), *n.* **1.** the region inhab-ited by Yankees. **2.** Yankees collectively. [1835–45, *Amer.*; YANKEE + -DOM]

Yan′kee Doo′dle (do͞od′l), **1.** (*italics*) a song with a melody of apparent British origin, popular with Ameri-can troops during the Revolutionary War. **2.** a Yankee.

Yan·kee·fy (yang′kē fī′, -ki-), *v.t.,* **-fied, -fy·ing.** to cause to acquire Yankee traits or characteristics: *She was afraid that a year in a Connecticut college had Yan-keefied her speech.* [YANKEE + -FY]

Yan·kee·ism (yang′kē iz′əm), *n.* **1.** Yankee charac-ter or characteristics. **2.** a Yankee peculiarity, as of speech. [1785–95, *Amer.*; YANKEE + -ISM]

Yan·kee·land (yang′kē land′), *n.* **1.** *Chiefly South-ern U.S.* the northern states of the U.S. **2.** *Chiefly Brit.* the U.S. **3.** *Chiefly Northern U.S.* New England. [1780–90, *Amer.*; YANKEE + LAND]

Yank·ton (yangk′tən), *n., pl.* **-tons,** (*esp. collectively*) **-ton** for 1. **1.** a member of one of two tribes of Dakota Indian people who inhabited the northern Great Plains in the 18th and 19th centuries. Cf. **Yanktonai. 2.** a town in SE South Dakota. 12,011.

Yank·to·nai (yangk′tə nī′), *n., pl.* **-nais,** (*esp. collec-tively*) **-nai.** a member of one of two tribes of Dakota Indian people who inhabited the northern Great Plains in the 18th and 19th centuries. Cf. **Yankton** (def. 1).

Yan·ni·na (yä′nē nä′), *n.* Ioannina.

Ya·no·ma·ma (yä′nə mä′mə), *n., pl.* **-mas,** (*esp. col-lectively*) **-ma.** Yanomamo.

Ya·no·ma·mo (yä′nə mä′mō), *n., pl.* **-mos,** (*esp. col-lectively*) **-mo** for 1. **1.** a member of an indigenous peo-ple of southern Venezuela and neighboring Brazil who live in scattered villages in the rain forests and conduct warfare against one another continually. **2.** the family of languages spoken by the Yanomamo. Also, **Yanomama.**

yan·qui (yäng′kē), *n., pl.* ***-quis*** (-kēs). (*often cap.*) *Spanish.* (in Latin America) Yankee; a citizen of the U.S.

Yan·tai (yän′tī′), *n. Pinyin.* a seaport in NE Shandong province, in E China. 180,000. Also, **Yentai.** Formerly, **Zhifu.**

Yan Xi·shan (*Chin.* yän′ shē′shän′), *Pinyin.* See **Yen Hsi-shan.**

Yao (you), *n. Wade-Giles, Pinyin.* a legendary emperor of China who, with his successor **(Shun),** was a paragon of good government.

Yao (you), *n., pl.* **Yaos,** (*esp. collectively*) **Yao** for 1. **1.** a member of an indigenous people of Malawi, Mozam-bique, and Tanzania. **2.** the Bantu language of the Yao.

Ya·oun·dé (*Fr.* yA o͞on dā′), *n.* a city in and the capi-tal of Cameroon, in the SW part. 180,000. Also, **Yaunde.**

yap (yap), *v.,* **yapped, yap·ping,** *n.* —*v.i.* **1.** to bark sharply, shrilly, or snappishly; yelp. **2.** *Slang.* to talk shrilly, noisily, or foolishly. —*v.t.* **3.** to utter by yap-ping. —*n.* **4.** a sharp, shrill, or snappish bark; yelp. **5.** *Slang.* **a.** shrill, noisy, or foolish talk. **b.** the mouth: *Keep your yap shut.* **6.** *Slang.* an uncouth or stupid per-son; bumpkin; fool. [1595–1605; 1900–05 for def. 5b; imit.] **—yap′per,** *n.* **—yap′ping·ly,** *adv.*

Yap (yäp, yap), *n.* one of the Caroline Islands, in the W Pacific: part of the Federated States of Micronesia. 8482 including adjacent islands; 83 sq. mi. (215 sq. km).

ya·pok (yə pok′), *n.* an aquatic Central and South American opossum, *Chironectes variegatus,* having webbed hind feet and a grayish coat. Also called **water opossum.** [1820–30; after *Oyapok,* a river forming the border between French Guiana and N Brazil]

ya·pon (yô′pon), *n.* yaupon.

yapp (yap), *n.* See **circuit binding.** Also called **yapp′ bind′ing.** [1880–85; named after William *Yapp,* 19th-century English bookseller]

Ya·qui (yä′kē), *n., pl.* **-quis,** (*esp. collectively*) **-qui** for 1. **1.** a member of an American Indian people of Sonora, Mexico. **2.** the Uto-Aztecan language of the Yaqui. **3.** a river in NW Mexico, flowing into the Gulf of California. 420 mi. (676 km) long.

yar (yär, yâr), *adj.* yare (defs. 1, 2).

yar·ak (yar′ak), *n. Falconry.* a state of prime fitness in a hawk. [1850–55; perh. < Pers *yārakī* strength]

Yar·bor·ough (yär′bûr′ō, -bur′ō *or, esp. Brit.,* -bər ə), *n. Whist, Bridge.* a hand in which no card is higher than a nine. [1895–1900; after the 2nd Earl of *Yarbor-ough* (d. 1897), said to have bet 1000 to 1 against its oc-currence]

yard[1] (yärd), *n.* **1.** a common unit of linear measure in English-speaking countries, equal to 3 feet or 36 inches, and equivalent to 0.9144 meter. **2.** *Naut.* a long spar, supported more or less at its center, to which the head of a square sail, lateen sail, or lugsail is bent. **3.** yard-of-ale. **4.** *Informal.* a large quantity or extent. **5.** *Slang.* one hundred or, usually, one thousand dollars. **6. the whole nine yards,** *Informal.* **a.** everything that is perti-nent, appropriate, or available. **b.** in all ways; in every respect; all the way: *I'll be with you the whole nine yards.* [bef. 900; ME *yerd(e),* OE (Anglian) *gerd* orig., straight twig; c. D *gard,* G *Gerte* rod]

yard[2] (yärd), *n.* **1.** the ground that immediately adjoins or surrounds a house, public building, or other structure. **2.** an enclosed area outdoors, often paved and sur-rounded by or adjacent to a building; court. **3.** an out-door enclosure designed for the exercise of students, in-mates, etc.: *a prison yard.* **4.** an outdoor space sur-rounded by a group of buildings, as on a college campus. **5.** a pen or other enclosure for livestock. **6.** an enclo-sure within which any work or business is carried on (often used in combination): *navy yard; a brickyard.* **7.** an outside area used for storage, assembly, or the like. **8.** *Railroads.* a system of parallel tracks, crossovers, switches, etc., where cars are switched and made up into trains and where cars, locomotives, and other rolling stock are kept when not in use or when awaiting repairs. **9.** a piece of ground set aside for cultivation; garden; field. **10.** the winter pasture or browsing ground of moose and deer. **11. the Yard,** *Brit.* See **Scotland Yard** (def. 2). —*v.t.* **12.** to put into, enclose, or store in a yard. [bef. 900; ME *yerd,* OE *geard* enclosure; c. D *gaard* garden, ON *garthr* yard, Goth *gards* house, L *hor-tus* garden, OIr *gort* field; akin to GARDEN]

yard·age[1] (yär′dij), *n.* measurement, or the amount measured in yards; length or extent in yards. [1875–80; YARD[1] + -AGE]

yard·age[2] (yär′dij), *n.* **1.** the use of a yard or enclo-sure, as in loading livestock at a railroad station. **2.** the charge for such use. [1860–65; YARD[2] + -AGE]

yar·dang (yär′däng), *n. Geol.* a keel-shaped crest or ridge of rock, formed by the action of the wind, usually parallel to the prevailing wind direction. [earlier *jar-dang,* term introduced by Sven Hedin (1904); perh. a compound with Uigur *yar* cliff, precipice, or a cognate Turkic word]

yard·arm (yärd′ärm′), *n. Naut.* either of the outer portions of the yard of a square sail. [1545–55; YARD[1] + ARM[1]]

yard·bird (yärd′bûrd′), *n. Slang.* **1.** a convict or pris-oner. **2.** an army recruit. **3.** a soldier confined to camp and assigned to menial tasks as punishment. [1940–45, *Amer.*; YARD[2] + BIRD, by analogy with JAILBIRD]

yard′ goods′. See **piece goods.** [1900–05]

yard·land (yärd′land′), *n.* virgate[2]. [1400–50; late ME *yerdlonde.* See YARD[1], LAND]

yard′-long bean′ (yärd′lông′, -long′). See **aspara-gus bean.**

yard·man[1] (yärd′mən), *n., pl.* **-men.** *Naut.* a sailor assigned to the yards. [1885–90; YARD[1] + -MAN]

yard·man[2] (yärd′mən), *n., pl.* **-men. 1.** a person who works in a railroad yard, boatyard, lumberyard, or the like. **2.** a person employed to care for the yard of a house, public building, etc., as by mowing the lawn and trimming shrubbery. [1815–25; YARD[2] + -MAN]

yard·mas·ter (yärd′mas′tər, -mä′stər), *n.* a person who superintends all or part of a railroad yard. [1870–75; YARD[2] + MASTER]

yard-of-ale (yärd′əv āl′), *n.* **1.** a trumpet-shaped glass about 3 ft. (1 m) long with a bulb at the closed end, for serving ale or beer. **2.** the amount contained in such a glass. Also called **aleyard, yard.** [1885–90]

yard′ sale′. See **garage sale.** [1970–75]

yard·stick (yärd′stik′), *n.* **1.** a stick a yard long, com-monly marked with subdivisions, used for measuring. **2.** any standard of measurement or judgment: *Test scores are not the only yardstick of academic achievement.* [1810–20, *Amer.*; YARD[1] + STICK[1]]

yare (yâr *or, esp. for 1, 2,* yär), *adj.,* **yar·er, yar·est. 1.** quick; agile; lively. **2.** (of a ship) quick to the helm; eas-ily handled or maneuvered. **3.** *Archaic.* **a.** ready; pre-pared. **b.** nimble; quick. Also, **yar** (for defs. 1, 2). [bef. 900; ME; OE *gearu, gearo,* equiv. to *ge-* Y- + *earu* ready; c. D *gaar,* G *gar* done, dressed (as meat)] **—yare′ly,** *adv.*

Yar·kand (yär kand′, -känd′), *n.* Shache. Also, **Yar·kend** (yär kend′).

Yar·mouth (yär′məth), *n.* **1.** a city in SE Massachusetts. 18,449. **2.** a seaport in SW Nova Scotia, in SE Canada: summer resort. 7801. **3. Great.** See **Great Yarmouth.**

Yar·muk (yär mo͝ok′), *n.* a river in NW Jordan, flowing W into the Jordan River. 50 mi. (80 km) long.

yar·mul·ke (yär′məl kə, -mə-, yä′-), *n. Judaism.* a skullcap worn, esp. during prayer and religious study, by Jewish males, esp. those adhering to Orthodox or Conservative tradition. Also, **yar′mel·ke, yar′mul·ka.** [1940–45; < Yiddish *yarmlke* < Polish *jarmułka* (earlier *jałmurka, jamułka*) or Ukrainian *yarmúlka* < Turkic; cf. Turk *yağmurluk* rain apparel, equiv. to *yağmur* rain + *-luk* n. suffix of appurtenance]

yarn (yärn), *n.* **1.** thread made of natural or synthetic fibers and used for knitting and weaving. **2.** a continuous strand or thread made from glass, metal, plastic, etc. **3.** the thread, in the form of a loosely twisted aggregate of fibers, as of hemp, of which rope is made **(rope yarn). 4.** a tale, esp. a long story of adventure or incredible happenings: *He spun a yarn that outdid any I had ever heard.* —*v.i.* **5.** *Informal.* to spin a yarn; tell stories. [bef. 1000; ME; OE *gearn;* c. G *Garn;* akin to ON *gǫrn* gut, Gk *chordḗ* intestine, CHORD[1], Lith *žarnà* entrails, L *hernia* a rupture, Skt *hirā* vein]

yarn-dyed (yärn′dīd′), *adj.* (of fabrics) woven from yarns previously dyed (opposed to *piece-dyed*). [1880–85]

Ya·ro·slavl (yär′ə slä′vəl; *Russ.* yi RU slävl′), *n.* a city in the W Russian Federation in Europe, on the Volga. 634,000.

yar·o·vize (yär′ə vīz′), *v.t.,* **-vized, -viz·ing.** jarovize. Also, *esp. Brit.,* **yar′o·vise′.** —**yar′o·vi·za′tion,** *n.*

yar·ra·man (yar′ə mən), *n., pl.* **-men.** *Australian Archaic.* horse. [1840–50; perh. < Dhurga (Australian Aboriginal language spoken on the New South Wales coast, from Jervis Bay to Bermagui) *yara-* teeth + *-may* n. suffix; borrowed into Australian pidgins, used by white settlers, thence into other Aboriginal languages]

yar·row (yar′ō), *n.* **1.** a composite plant, *Achillea millefolium,* of Eurasia, having fernlike leaves and flat-topped clusters of whitish flowers, naturalized in North America. **2.** any of various other plants of the genus *Achillea,* some having yellow flowers. [bef. 900; ME *yar(o)we,* OE *gearwe;* c. G *Garbe* sheaf]

Yar·row (yar′ō), *n.* a river in SE Scotland, flowing into the Tweed. 14 mi. (23 km) long.

yash·mak (yäsh mäk′, yash′mak), *n.* the veil worn by Muslim women to cover the face in public. Also, **yash·mac′.** [1835–45; < Turk *yaşmak*]

Yasht (yasht, yusht), *n. Zoroastrianism.* **1.** a hymn to a deity. **2. Yashts,** hymns to various deities, forming part of the Avesta. [< Avestan *yashtay*]

Yas·min (yaz′min, yäs′mēn), *n.* a female given name: from an Arabic word meaning "jasmine."

Yas·na (yus′nə), *n. Zoroastrianism.* a part of the Avesta including the Gathas and other liturgical texts. —**Yas·ni·an** (yus′nē ən), *adj.*

Yas·sy (yä′sē), *n.* Jassy.

yat·a·ghan (yat′ə gan′, -gən; *Turk.* yä′tä gän′), *n.* a Turkish saber having a doubly curved blade, concave toward the hilt, and a hilt with a prominent pommel and no guard. Also, **ataghan, yat′a·gan′.** [1810–20; < Turk *yatağan*]

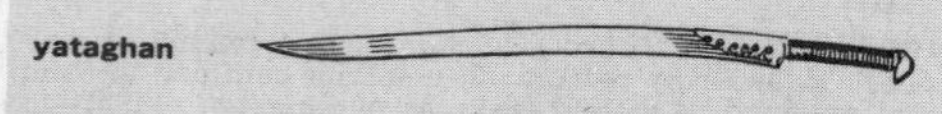
yataghan

ya·ta·ta (yä′tə tə, yat′ə tə), *n. Slang.* empty conversation. [1945–50, *Amer.;* imit.]

yat·ter (yat′ər), *Informal.* —*v.i.* **1.** to chatter or jabber. —*n.* **2.** chatter; idle talk. [1865–70; perh. YA(P) + (CHA)TTER]

Yau·co (you′kô), *n.* a city in SW Puerto Rico. 14,594.

yaud (yôd, yäd), *n. Scot. and North Eng.* a mare, esp. an old, worn-out one. [1350–1400; ME *yald* < ON *jalda* mare]

yauld (yôd, yôld, yäd, yäld), *adj. Scot. and North Eng.* active; vigorous. [1780–90; orig. uncert.]

Yaun·de (youn′dā), *n.* Yaoundé.

yaup (yôp, yäp), *v.i., n.* yawp. —**yaup′er,** *n.*

yau·pon (yô′pon), *n.* a holly shrub or small tree, *Ilex vomitoria,* of the southern U.S., having bitter leaves that are sometimes brewed as a tea. Also, **yapon.** [1700–10, *Amer.;* < Catawba *yą́pą,* equiv. to *yą-* wood, tree + *pą* leaf]

yau·ti·a (you tē′ə), *n.* a stemless plant, *Xanthosoma sagittifolium,* of the arum family, cultivated in tropical America for its tuberous, starchy root, cooked and eaten like potatoes. [1900–05; < AmerSp < Taino]

Ya·va·pai (yav′ə pī′, yä′və-), *n., pl.* **-pais,** (*esp. collectively*) **-pai** for 1. **1.** a member of a tribe of North American Indians who live in Arizona. **2.** the Yuman language of the Yavapai.

Ya·va·rí (yä′vä RĒ′), *n.* Spanish name of **Javari.**

yaw[1] (yô), *v.i.* **1.** to deviate temporarily from a straight course, as a ship. **2.** (of an aircraft) to have a motion about its vertical axis. **3.** (of a rocket or guided missile) to deviate from a stable flight attitude by oscillation of the longitudinal axis in the horizontal plane. —*v.t.* **4.** to cause to yaw. —*n.* **5.** a movement of deviation from a direct course, as of a ship. **6.** a motion of an aircraft about its vertical axis. **7.** an angle, to the right or left, determined by the direction of motion of an aircraft or spacecraft and its vertical and longitudinal plane of symmetry. **8.** (of a rocket or guided missile) **a.** the act of yawing. **b.** the angular displacement of the longitudinal axis due to yawing. [1540–50; orig. uncert.]

yaw[2] (yô), *n. Pathol.* one of the lesions of yaws. [1735–45; back formation from YAWS]

Ya·wa·ta (*Japn.* yä′wä tä′), *n.* See under **Kitakyushu.** Also, **Yahata.**

yaw·ey (yô′ē), *adj.* of or pertaining to yaws. [YAW[2] + -EY[1]]

yawl[1] (yôl), *n.* **1.** a ship's small boat, rowed by a crew of four or six. **2.** a two-masted, fore-and-aft-rigged sailing vessel having a large mainmast and a smaller jiggermast or mizzenmast stepped abaft the sternpost. Cf. **ketch.** [1660–70; < D *jol* kind of boat < ?]

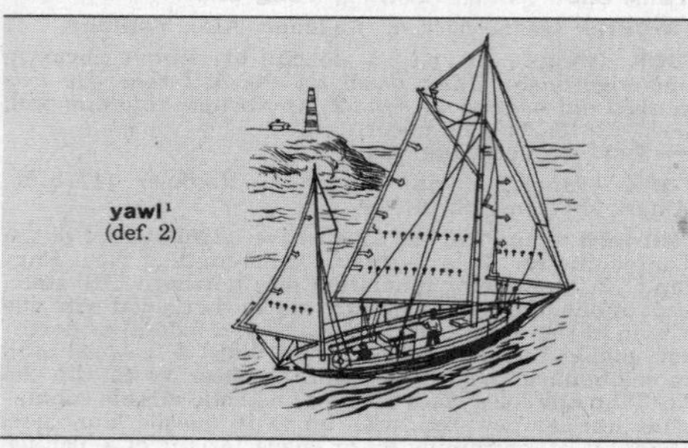
yawl[1] (def. 2)

yawl[2] (yôl), *n., v.i., v.t. Brit. Dial.* yowl; howl. [1300–50; ME; cf. YOWL]

yawl-rigged (yôl′rigd′), *adj.* rigged in the manner of a yawl. [1880–85]

yaw·me·ter (yô′mē′tər), *n. Aeron.* an instrument that measures the yaw of an aircraft. [1920–25; YAW[1] + -METER]

yawn (yôn), *v.i.* **1.** to open the mouth somewhat involuntarily with a prolonged, deep inhalation and sighing or heavy exhalation, as from drowsiness or boredom. **2.** to open wide like a mouth. **3.** to extend or stretch wide, as an open and deep space. —*v.t.* **4.** to say with a yawn. **5.** *Archaic.* to open wide, or lay open, as if by yawning. —*n.* **6.** an act or instance of yawning. **7.** an opening; open space; chasm. **8.** Also, **yawner.** *Informal.* something so boring as to make one yawn: *Critics say the new fashions are one big yawn.* [bef. 900; ME *yanen, yonen* (v.), alter. of *yenen,* OE *ge(o)nian;* akin to OE *gānian, ginan,* ON *gīna,* G *gähnen,* L *hiāre* (see HIATUS), Gk *chainein* to gape (see CHASM)] —**Syn. 1–3.** gape.

yawn·er (yô′nər), *n.* **1.** a person who yawns. **2.** yawn (def. 8). [1680–90; YAWN + -ER[1]]

yawn·ful (yôn′fəl), *adj.* causing or arousing yawns, esp. as the result of boredom, tedium, or the like: *a yawnful story about her childhood.* [YAWN + -FUL] —**yawn′ful·ly,** *adv.*

yawn·ing (yô′ning), *adj.* **1.** being or standing wide open; gaping: *the yawning mouth of a cave.* **2.** indicating by yawns one's weariness or indifference: *The lecturer was oblivious to his yawning audience.* [bef. 900; ME; OE *geniendum.* See YAWN, -ING[2]] —**yawn′ing·ly,** *adv.*

yawn·y (yô′nē), *adj.,* **yawn·i·er, yawn·i·est.** emitting or causing yawns: *yawny spectators; a yawny debate.* [1795–1805; YAWN + -Y[1]]

yawp (yôp, yäp), *v.i.* **1.** to utter a loud, harsh cry; to yelp, squawk, or bawl. **2.** *Slang.* to talk noisily and foolishly or complainingly. —*n.* **3.** a harsh cry. **4.** *Slang.* **a.** raucous or querulous speech. **b.** a noisy, foolish utterance. Also, **yaup.** [1300–50; ME *yolpen;* akin to YELP] —**yawp′er,** *n.*

yaws (yôz), *n.* (*used with a singular v.*) *Pathol.* an infectious, nonvenereal tropical disease, primarily of children, characterized by raspberrylike eruptions of the skin and caused by a spirochete, *Treponema pertenue,* that is closely related to the agent of syphilis. Also called **frambesia, pian.** Cf. **mother yaw.** [1670–80; < Carib; see -S[3]]

Yax·chi·lán (yäs′chē län′, yäsh′-), *n.* the ruins of an ancient Mayan city, in Chiapas state, Mexico, famous for its many carved lintels depicting ceremonial and military scenes. Also, **Yax′chi·lan′, Yax′chil·lan′.**

y-ax·is (wī′ak′sis), *n., pl.* **y-ax·es** (wī′ak′sēz). *Math.* **1.** Also called **axis of ordinates.** (in a plane Cartesian coordinate system) the axis, usually vertical, along which the ordinate is measured and from which the abscissa is measured. See diag. under **ordinate. 2.** (in a three-dimensional Cartesian coordinate system) the axis along which values of *y* are measured and at which both *x* and *z* equal zero. [1925–30]

Ya·yoi (yä yoi′), *adj.* of or pertaining to a cultural period in Japan, c300 B.C.–A.D. c300, characterized by unglazed reddish clay pottery **(Yayoi′ ware′)** made on a wheel and noted for its restrained, undecorated style, haniwa figures, raised-floor dwellings, wet-rice agriculture, and the first use of bronze and iron. [< Japn *Yayoi* site of a tumulus where the pottery was discovered in 1884]

ya·za·ta (yä zä′tə), *n.* any of the lesser ancient Iranian gods. [< Avestan: being worthy of veneration, god]

Yazd (yäzd), *n.* Yezd.

Yaz·oo (yaz′o͞o, ya zo͞o′), *n.* **1.** a city in W central Mississippi. 12,426. **2.** a river flowing SW from N Mississippi into the Mississippi River at Vicksburg. 188 m (303 km) long.

Yb, *Symbol, Chem.* ytterbium.

Y.B., yearbook. Also, **YB**

Y chromosome, *Genetics.* a sex chromosome of hu mans and most mammals that is present only in male and is paired with an X chromosome. Cf. **X chrom some.** [1920–25]

Y.C.L., Young Communist League.

y·clad (ē klad′), *v. Archaic.* pp. of **clothe.** [1300–5 ME; see Y-, CLAD[1]]

y·clept (ē klept′), *v.* a pp. of **clepe.** Also, **y·cleped** [bef. 1000; ME *ycleped,* OE *geclypod,* ptp. of *clypia cleopian* to CLEPE]

YD., (in the People's Democratic Republic of Yeme dinar; dinars.

yd., yard; yards.

yds., yards.

ye[1] (yē), *pron.* **1.** *Archaic (except in some elevated ecclesiastical prose), Literary, or Brit. Dial.* **a.** (use nominatively as the plural of **thou,** esp. in rhetorical, d dactic, or poetic contexts, in addressing a group of pe sons or things): *O ye of little faith; ye brooks and hill* **b.** (used nominatively for the second person singula esp. in polite address): *Do ye not know me?* **c.** (used ob jectively in the second person singular or plural): *I ha something to tell ye. Arise, the enemy is upon ye!* **2** (used with mock seriousness in an invocation, mild oat or the like): *Ye gods and little fishes!* [bef. 900; ME; OI *gē;* c. D *gij,* G *ihr,* ON *ēr,* Goth *jus*]

ye[2] (t͟hē; *spelling pron.* yē), *definite article. Archai* the[1].
—**Usage.** The word YE[2], as in *Ye Olde Booke Shoppe,* simply an archaic spelling of the definite article *the.* Th use of the letter *Y* was a printer's adaptation of th thorn, þ, the character in the Old English alphab representing the *th-* sounds (th) and (t͟h) in Modern Eng lish; *Y* was the closest symbol in the Roman alphabe Originally, the form would have been rendered as ʸ̇ or y The pronunciation (yē) today is a spelling pronunciation.

yea (yā), *adv.* **1.** yes (used in affirmation or assent). **2** indeed: *Yea, and he did come.* **3.** not only this but eve *a good, yea, a noble man.* —*n.* **4.** an affirmation; a affirmative reply or vote. **5.** a person who votes in th affirmative. [bef. 900; ME *ye, ya,* OE *gēa;* c. D, G, ON Goth *ja*]

Yea·don (yād′n), *n.* a city in SE Pennsylvania. 11,72

Yea·ger (yā′gər), *n.* **Charles (Elwood)** (*"Chuck"* born 1923, U.S. aviator and test pilot: the first person t fly faster than the speed of sound (1947).

yeah (yâ), *adv. Informal.* yes. [1900–05; var. of YEA o YES]

yeal·ing (yē′lin), *n. Scot.* a person of the same age a oneself. [1720–30; perh. E(VEN) + *eil(d)ing* age]

yean (yēn), *v.i.* (of a sheep or goat) to bring fort young. [1375–1425; late ME *yenen,* prob. continuing O **geēanian* to bring forth young, equiv. to *ge-* Y- + *ēanian* to yean, akin to L *agnus,* Gk *ámnos* lamb]

yean·ling (yēn′ling), *n.* **1.** the young of a sheep o goat; a lamb or kid. —*adj.* **2.** just born; infant. [1630 40; YEAN + -LING[1]]

year (yēr), *n.* **1.** a period of 365 or 366 days, in th Gregorian calendar, divided into 12 calendar month now reckoned as beginning Jan. 1 and ending Dec. 3 **(calendar year** or **civil year).** Cf. **common year, lea year. 2.** a period of approximately the same length i other calendars. **3.** a space of 12 calendar months calc lated from any point: *This should have been finishe a year ago.* **4.** *Astron.* **a.** Also called **lunar year.** a divi sion of time equal to 12 lunar months. **b.** Also called **as tronomical year, equinoctial year, solar year, trop cal year.** a division of time equal to about 365 days, hours, 48 minutes, and 46 seconds, representing the in terval between one vernal equinox and the next. **c.** Als called **sidereal year.** a division of time equal to the equinoctial year plus 20 minutes, representing the tim required for the earth to complete one revolution aroun the sun, measured with relation to the fixed stars. Cf **anomalistic year. 5.** the time in which any plane completes a revolution round the sun: *the Martian year* **6.** a full round of the seasons. **7.** a period out of ever 12 months, devoted to a certain pursuit, activity, or th like: *the academic year.* **8. years, a.** age. **b.** old age: *a man of years.* **c.** time; period: *the years of hardship an frustration.* **d.** an unusually long period of time of in definite length: *I haven't spoken to them in years.* **9.** a group of students entering school or college, graduating or expecting to graduate in the same year; class. **10. a year and a day,** a period specified as the limit of time in various legal matters, as in determining a right or a lia bility, to allow for a full year by any way of counting. **11. from the year one,** for a very long time; as long as anyone remembers: *He's been with the company from the year one.* **12. year in and year out,** regularly through the years; continually: *Year in and year out they went to Florida for the winter.* Also, **year in, year out.** [bef 900; ME *yeer,* OE *gēar;* c. D *jaar,* G *Jahr,* ON *ār,* Goth *jēr,* Gk *hṓros* season, part of a day, hour]

year-a·round (yēr′ə round′), *adj.* year-round.

year·book (yēr′bo͝ok′), *n.* **1.** a book published annually, containing information, statistics, etc., about the past year: *an encyclopedia yearbook.* **2.** a book published by the graduating class of a high school or college, containing photographs of class members and commemorating school activities. [1580–90; YEAR + BOOK]

year-end (yēr′end′), *n.* **1.** year's end; the end of a calendar year. —*adj.* **2.** taking place or done at the year-end: *a year-end sale; a year-end audit.* Also, **year′end′.** [1870–75]

year·ling (yēr′ling), *n.* **1.** an animal in its second year. **2.** a horse one year old, dating from January 1 of the

CONCISE ETYMOLOGY KEY: <, descended or borrowed from; >, whence; b., blend of, blended; c., cognate with; cf., compare; deriv., derivative; equiv., equivalent; imit., imitative; obl., oblique; r., replacing; s., stem; sp., spelling, spelled; resp., respelling, respelled; trans., translation; ?, origin unknown; *, unattested; ‡, probably earlier than. See the full key inside the front cover.

year after the year of foaling. —*adj.* **3.** being a year old. **4.** of a year's duration or standing: *a yearling bride.* [1425–75; late ME; see YEAR, -LING[1]; c. G *Jährling*]

year·long (yēr′lông′, -long′), *adj.* lasting for a year. [1805–15; YEAR + LONG[1]]

year·ly (yēr′lē), *adj., adv., n., pl.* **-lies.** —*adj.* **1.** pertaining to a year or to each year. **2.** done, made, happening, appearing, coming, etc., once a year or every year: *a yearly medical examination.* **3.** computed or determined by the year. **4.** continuing or lasting for a year. —*adv.* **5.** once a year; annually. —*n.* **6.** a publication appearing once a year. [bef. 900; ME *yeerly*, OE *gēarlic.* See YEAR, -LY]

Year′ly Meet′ing, any of several associations of local Quaker congregations.

yearn (yûrn), *v.i.* **1.** to have an earnest or strong desire; long: *to yearn for a quiet vacation.* **2.** to feel tenderness; be moved or attracted: *They yearned over their delicate child.* [bef. 900; ME *yernen*, OE *giernan* deriv. of *georn* eager; akin to ON *girna* to desire, Gk *chaírein* to rejoice, Skt *háryati* (he) desires] —**yearn′er,** *n.*
—**Syn. 1.** YEARN, LONG, HANKER, PINE all mean to feel a powerful desire for something. YEARN stresses the depth and passionateness of a desire: *to yearn to get away and begin a new life; to yearn desperately for recognition.* LONG implies a wholehearted desire for something that is or seems unattainable: *to long to relive one's childhood; to long for the warmth of summer.* HANKER suggests a restless or incessant craving to fulfill some urge or desire: *to hanker for a promotion; to hanker after fame and fortune.* PINE adds the notion of physical or emotional suffering as a result of the real or apparent hopelessness of one's desire: *to pine for one's native land; to pine for a lost love.*

yearn·ing (yûr′ning), *n.* **1.** deep longing, esp. when accompanied by tenderness or sadness: *a widower's yearning for his wife.* **2.** an instance of such longing. [bef. 900; ME; OE *gierninge.* See YEARN, -ING[1]] —**yearn′ing·ly,** *adv.*
—**Syn. 1.** See **desire.**

Year′ of Confu′sion, (in ancient Rome) the year of 445 days preceding the introduction, in 46 B.C., of the Julian calendar: lengthened to compensate for the cumulative errors of the Roman calendar.

year′ of grace′, a specified year of the Christian era: *this year of grace; the year of grace 1982.*

year-round (yēr′round′), *adj.* continuing, active, operating, etc., throughout the year: *a year-round vacation spot.* Also, **year-around.** [1920–25]

year-round·er (yēr′roun′dər), *n.* **1.** a person who is a year-round resident, as at a seasonal resort. **2.** something that is designed for use throughout the year: *My new suit is a year-rounder.* [YEAR-ROUND + -ER[1]]

year's′ mind′, a Requiem Mass said one year after a person's death or burial. [bef. 1100; ME; OE]

yea·say·er (yā′sā′ər), *n.* **1.** a person with an optimistic and confident outlook. **2.** a person who habitually agrees with or is submissive to others. [1915–20; YEA + (NAY)SAYER]

yeast (yēst), *n.* **1.** any of various small, single-celled fungi of the phylum Ascomycota that reproduce by fission or budding, the daughter cells often remaining attached, and that are capable of fermenting carbohydrates into alcohol and carbon dioxide. **2.** any of several yeasts of the genus *Saccharomyces*, used in brewing alcoholic beverages, as a leaven in baking breads, and in pharmacology as a source of vitamins and proteins. Cf. **bottom yeast, brewer's yeast, top yeast. 3.** spume; foam. **4.** ferment; agitation. **5.** something that causes ferment or agitation. —*v.i.* **6.** to ferment. **7.** to be covered with froth. [bef. 1000; ME *ye(e)st* (n.), OE *gist, gyst;* c. D *gist*, G *Gischt* yeast, foam, ON *jastr* yeast, Gk *zestós* boiled, Skt *yásati* (it) boils] —**yeast′less,** *adj.* —**yeast′like′,** *adj.*

yeast′ cake′, 1. a small cake of compacted yeast for baking or the like. **2.** a cake or sweet bread containing yeast as a leavening agent. [1785–95]

yeast′ nucle′ic ac′id, *Biochem.* See **RNA.**

yeast·y (yē′stē), *adj.,* **yeast·i·er, yeast·i·est. 1.** of, containing, or resembling yeast. **2.** frothy; foamy. **3.** youthful; exuberant; ebullient. **4.** trifling; frivolous. **5.** characterized by agitation, excitement, change, etc.: *the yeasty years immediately following college.* [1590–1600; YEAST + -Y[1]] —**yeast′i·ly,** *adv.* —**yeast′i·ness,** *n.*

Yeats (yāts), *n.* **William Butler,** 1865–1939, Irish poet, dramatist, and essayist: Nobel prize 1923. —**Yeats′i·an,** *adj.*

yech (yeKH, yek, yuKH, yuk), *interj. Slang.* yuck[1]. Also, **yecch.**

yech·y (yeKH′ē, yek′ē, yuKH′ē, yuk′ē), *adj.,* **yech·i·er, yech·i·est.** *Slang.* yucky. [YECH + -Y[1]]

yed′do haw′thorn (yed′ō), a Japanese shrub, *Raphiolepis umbellata*, of the rose family, having leathery leaves and dense, hairy clusters of fragrant white flowers. [after *Yeddo*, sp. var. of YEDO]

Ye·do (yed′ō; *Japn.* ye′dô), *n.* a former name of **Tokyo.**

yegg (yeg), *n. Slang.* **1.** a safecracker. **2.** an itinerant burglar. **3.** a thug. [1925–30, *Amer.;* of obscure orig.; the proposals that the word is < G *Jäger* "hunter" or that it is the surname of a well-known safecracker are both very dubious]

yegg·man (yeg′mən), *n., pl.* **-men.** yegg. [1900–05, *Amer.;* appar. YEGG + -MAN, though the appearance of *yegg* as an independent word is later]

Yeisk (yāsk), *n.* a seaport in the SW RSFSR, in the SW Soviet Union in Europe, on the Sea of Azov. 73,000. Also, **Eisk, Eysk.**

Ye Jian·ying (yu′jyän′ying′), 1898–1986, Chinese marshal and Communist leader: defense minister 1971–78. Also, *Wade-Giles,* **Yeh Chien-ying** (yu′ jyun′ying′).

Ye·ka·te·rin·burg (yə kat′ər in bûrg′; *Russ.* yi kə-tyi Ryin bōōRk′), *n.* Ekaterinburg.

Ye·ka·te·ri·no·dar (yə kat′ə rē′nə där′; *Russ.* yi kə-tyi Ryi nu däR′), *n.* a former name of **Krasnodar.**

Ye·ka·te·ri·no·slav (yə kät′ə rē′nə släv′, -släf′; *Russ.* yi kə tyi Ryi nu släf′), *n.* a former name of **Dnepropetrovsk.**

yeld (yeld), *adj. Scot. and North Eng.* **1.** barren; sterile. **2.** (of a cow) not giving milk, from being in calf or from age. [bef. 1100; ME; OE *gelde* barren; c. G *Gelt;* akin to GELD[1]]

Ye·lets (yə lets′; *Russ.* yi lyets′), *n.* a city in the W Russian Federation in Europe, SE of Moscow. 112,000. Also, **Elets.**

Ye·li·za·vet·grad (yə liz′ə vet′grad; *Russ.* yi lyi zə-vyit grät′), *n.* a former name of **Kirovograd.**

Ye·li·za·vet·pol (yə liz′ə vet′pōl; *Russ.* yi lyi zə vyit-pôl′), *n.* a former name of **Kirovabad.**

yelk (yelk), *n. Older Use.* yolk.

yell (yel), *v.i.* **1.** to cry out or speak with a strong, loud, clear sound; shout: *He always yells when he is angry.* **2.** to scream with pain, fright, etc. —*v.t.* **3.** to utter or tell by yelling: *to yell an order to the troops.* —*n.* **4.** a cry uttered by yelling. **5.** a cheer or shout of fixed words or syllables, as one adopted by a school or college to encourage a team. [bef. 1000; (v.) ME *yellen*, OE *gellan, giellan;* c. G *gellen* to resound, D *gillen;* akin to OE *galan* to sing (see NIGHTINGALE); (n.) ME, deriv. of the v.]

yel·low (yel′ō), *n., adj.,* **-er, -est,** *v.* —*n.* **1.** a color like that of egg yolk, ripe lemons, etc.; the primary color between green and orange in the visible spectrum, an effect of light with a wavelength between 570 and 590 nm. **2.** the yolk of an egg. **3.** a yellow pigment or dye. **4.** *Informal.* See **yellow light. 5.** *Slang.* See **yellow jacket** (def. 2). —*adj.* **6.** of the color yellow. **7.** *Often Offensive.* **a.** designating or pertaining to an Oriental person or Oriental peoples. **b.** designating or pertaining to a person of mixed racial origin, esp. of black and white heritage, whose skin is yellowish or yellowish brown. **8.** having a sallow or yellowish complexion. **9.** *Informal.* cowardly. **10.** (of journalism, a newspaper, etc.) **a.** sensational, esp. morbidly or offensively so: *That yellow rag carried all the gory details.* **b.** dishonest in editorial comment and the presentation of news, esp. in sacrificing truth for sensationalism: *Objective reporting isn't always a match for yellow journalism.* **11.** jealous; envious. —*v.t., v.i.* **12.** to make or become yellow: *Yellow the sheets with dye. The white stationery had yellowed with age.* [bef. 900; 1895–1900 for def. 9; ME *yelou* (adj. and n.), OE *geolo, geolu* (adj.); c. D *geel*, G *gelb*, L *helvus* pale-yellow; akin to ON *gulr*] —**yel′low·ly,** *adv.* —**yel′low·ness,** *n.*
—**Syn. 9.** craven, timorous, fearful.

yel′low alert′, 1. (in military or civilian defense) the first alert given when enemy aircraft are discovered approaching a military installation, city, coastline, etc. Cf. **blue alert, red alert, white alert. 2.** the signal or alarm sounded for this alert. **3.** any primary stage of alert, as when toxic chemicals have escaped in a particular area and a potential hazard exists. [1965–70]

yel′low av′ens. See **herb bennet.**

yel·low·back (yel′ō bak′), *n.* **1.** (formerly) an inexpensive, often lurid, novel bound in yellow cloth or paper. **2.** a gold certificate. [1790–1800; YELLOW + BACK[1]]

yel·low-bel·lied (yel′ō bel′ēd), *adj.* **1.** having a yellow abdomen or underside. **2.** *Slang.* cowardly; lily-livered. [1700–10]

yel′low-bellied sap′sucker, a woodpecker, *Sphyrapicus varius*, of eastern North America, having a red patch on the forehead and black and white plumage with a pale-yellow abdomen, and feeding on sap from trees. [1905–10, *Amer.*]

yel·low·bel·ly (yel′ō bel′ē), *n., pl.* **-lies.** *Slang.* a person who is without courage, fortitude, or nerve; coward. [1790–1800; YELLOW + BELLY]

yel′low bile′, one of the four elemental bodily humors of medieval physiology, regarded as causing anger; choler. [1880–85]

yel′low-billed cuck′oo (yel′ō bild′), a North American cuckoo, *Coccyzus americanus*, that has a yellow bill and, unlike many cuckoos, constructs its own nest and rears its own young. [1805–15, *Amer.*]

yel′low-billed mag′pie. See under **magpie** (def. 1). [1855–60, *Amer.*]

yel′low birch′, 1. a North American birch, *Betula alleghaniensis* (or *B. lutea*), having yellowish or silvery gray bark. **2.** the hard, light, reddish-brown wood of this tree, used in the construction of furniture, buildings, boxes, etc. [1765–75]

yel·low·bird (yel′ō bûrd′), *n.* **1.** *Brit. Dial.* any of various yellow or golden birds, as the golden oriole of Europe. **2.** any of several American goldfinches. **3.** See **yellow warbler.** [1695–1705; YELLOW + BIRD]

yel′low-breast·ed chat′ (yel′ō bres′tid), an American warbler, *Icteria virens*, having a yellow throat and breast and greenish-brown upper parts and noted for imitating the songs of other species. [1720–30, *Amer.*]

yel·low·cake (yel′ō kāk′), *n.* a processed oxide of uranium, U_3O_8, extracted and concentrated from uranium ore: used as the raw material for commercial nuclear materials, esp. fuel elements in nuclear reactors. Also, **yel′low cake′.** [1945–50; YELLOW + CAKE]

yel′low cop′per ore′, chalcopyrite. [1790–1800]

yel′low-crowned night′ her′on (yel′ō kround′). See under **night heron.** [1805–15, *Amer.*]

yel′low dai′sy, the black-eyed Susan, *Rudbeckia hirta.* [1890–95]

yel′low dog′, a cowardly, despicable person; a craven. [1825–35]

yel′low-dog′ con′tract (yel′ō dôg′, -dog′), a contract between a worker and an employer in which, as a condition of employment, the worker agrees not to remain in or join a union. [1915–20, *Amer.*]

Yel′low Em′peror. See **Huang Ti.**

yel′low-eye rock′fish (yel′ō ī′), a red rockfish, *Sebastes ruberrimus*, of waters along the Pacific coast of North America, having yellow eyes and sawlike, bony ridges on the head. [YELLOW + EYE]

yel′low fe′ver, *Pathol.* an acute, often fatal, infectious febrile disease of warm climates, caused by an RNA virus transmitted by a mosquito, esp. *Aedes aegypti*, and characterized by liver damage and jaundice. Also called **yellow jack.** [1730–40]

yel′low-fe′ver mosqui′to (yel′ō fē′vər), a mosquito, *Aedes aegypti*, that transmits yellow fever and dengue. [1900–05, *Amer.*]

yel·low·finch (yel′ō finch′), *n.* any of several tropical American finches of the genus *Sicalis*, most of which are bright yellow in color. [YELLOW + FINCH]

yel′low·fin tu′na (yel′ō fin′), an important food fish, *Thunnus albacares*, inhabiting warm seas. Also called **yellowfin.** [1935–40; YELLOW + FIN]

yel′low flag′, 1. *Naut.* See **quarantine flag. 2.** See **water flag.** [1775–85]

yel′low-flow·ered gourd′ (yel′ō flou′ərd). See under **gourd.**

yel′low gen′tian, a plant, *Gentiana lutea*, of Europe and Asia Minor, having yellow flowers, the rootstock yielding a bitter tonic.

yel′low goat′fish, a schooling goatfish, *Mulloidichthys martinicus*, inhabiting the Atlantic Ocean from Florida to Panama.

yel′low granadil′la, a climbing vine, *Passiflora laurifolia*, of tropical America, having red-spotted white flowers nearly 4 in. (10 cm) wide, with a white and violet-colored crown, and edible yellow fruit. Also called **Jamaica honeysuckle, water lemon.**

yel·low-green (yel′ō grēn′), *n.* **1.** a color containing both yellow and green. —*adj.* **2.** of the color yellow-green. [1760–70]

yel′low-green al′gae, *Biol.* a group of common single-celled and colonial algae of the phylum Chrysophyta, having mostly yellow and green pigments, occurring in soil and on moist rocks and vegetation and also as a slime or scum on ponds and stagnant waters. Also, **yel′low green′ al′gae.** [1925–30]

yel′low gum′, 1. any of several Australian eucalyptuses, as *Eucalyptus melliodora*, having yellowish bark. **2.** any of several tupelos.

yel·low·ham·mer (yel′ō ham′ər), *n.* **1.** a common European bunting, *Emberiza citrinella*, the male of which is marked with bright yellow. **2.** *Chiefly Southern U.S.* a flicker, *Colaptes auratus*, having yellow wing and tail linings. [1550–60; earlier also *yelamber, yelambre*, prob. continuing OE **geolu-amore*, equiv. to *geolu* YELLOW + *amore* presumably, the bunting (c. OS *amer*, OHG *amaro;* see EMBERIZINE); forms with *-h-* perh. reflect blending with another etymon, later conformed to HAMMER (cf. dial. *yellowham*)]

Yel′low Hats′, the sect of Tibetan Buddhist monks established after religious reforms in the 14th century. Also called **Gelugpa.** Cf. **Red Hats.**

yel′low-head·ed black′bird (yel′ō hed′id), a North American blackbird, *Xanthocephalus xanthocephalus*, having a yellow head. [1840–50, *Amer.*]

yel′low hon′eysuckle, a spreading, twining vine, *Lonicera flava*, of the southern and eastern U.S., having fragrant, tubular, orange-yellow flowers. [1830–40, *Amer.*]

yel·low·ish (yel′ō ish), *adj.* somewhat yellow; tinged with yellow; yellowy. [1350–1400; ME; see YELLOW, -ISH[1]]

yel′low jack′, *pl.* (*esp. collectively*) **jack,** (*esp. referring to two or more kinds or species*) **jacks** for 3. **1.** *Informal.* See **quarantine flag. 2.** *Pathol.* See **yellow fever. 3.** any carangoid fish, esp. a Caribbean food fish, *Caranx bartholomaei.* [1830–40, *Amer.*]

yel′low jack′et, 1. any of several paper wasps of the family Vespidae, having black and bright yellow bands. **2.** *Slang.* a yellow capsule of phenobarbital. [1790–1800, *Amer.*]

yellow jacket, *Vespula maculifrons,* length ¾ in. (1.9 cm)

yel′low jas′mine. See **Carolina jessamine.** Also, **yel′low jes′samine.** [1700–10]

Yel·low·knife (yel′ō nīf′), *n.* a city in and the capital of the Northwest Territories, in N central Canada, on Great Slave Lake. 10,394.

yel′low la′dy's-slipper, a showy orchid, *Cypripedium calceolus*, of eastern North America, having purple-tinged yellow flowers with an inflated lip petal. [1730–40, *Amer.*]

yel′low lead′ ore′ (led), *Mineral.* wulfenite.

yel·low·legs (yel′ō legz′), *n.* (*used with a singular v.*)

either of two American shorebirds having yellow legs, *Tringa melanoleuca* **(greater yellowlegs)** or *T. flavipes* **(lesser yellowlegs)**. [1765–75, *Amer.*; YELLOW + LEGS]

yel′low light′, a yellow traffic light, usually preceding a signal halting traffic in a particular direction. [1970–75]

yel′low lo′cust. See **black locust.** [1800–10, *Amer.*]

yel′low man′darin. See under **mandarin** (def. 5).

yel′low mercu′ric ox′ide. See under **mercuric oxide.**

yel′low mom·bin′ (mōm bēn′), a tropical American tree, *Spondias mombin,* having yellowish-white flowers and yellow, oval, edible fruit. Also called **hog plum.** [*mombin* < F (or < AmerSp *mombín*) < Carib]

Yel′low New′town, a variety of yellow apple that ripens in the autumn.

Yellow No. 5, a yellow dye used in food, drugs, cosmetics, and other products: required by FDA regulations to be identified on food labels because of possible allergic reactions in sensitive individuals. Also called **tartrazine.**

yel′low pad′, a scratch pad of yellow, lined paper.

yel′low pag′es, (*often caps.*) a classified telephone directory or section of a directory, listing subscribers by the type of business or service they offer, usually printed on yellow paper. Cf. **white pages.** [1950–55]

yel′low paril′la. See **Canada moonseed.**

yel′low perch′. See under **perch**[2] (def. 1). [1795–1805, *Amer.*]

yel′low per′il, *Usually Offensive.* **1.** the alleged danger that Western civilizations and populations could be overwhelmed by numerically superior Oriental peoples. **2.** the Oriental peoples regarded as presenting such a danger. [1895–1900]

yel′low pike′perch, the walleye, *Stizostedion vitreum.* [1795–1805]

yel′low pine′, **1.** any of several North American pines yielding a strong, yellowish wood. **2.** the wood of any such tree. [1700–10, *Amer.*]

yel′low pitch′er plant′, trumpets.

yel′low poincian′a. See under **poinciana** (def. 2).

yel′low pop′lar, **1.** See **tulip tree.** **2.** the wood of the tulip tree. [1765–75, *Amer.*]

yel′low prus′siate of pot′ash. See **potassium ferrocyanide.**

yel′low puccoon′, a plant, *Lithospermum incisum,* of central and western North America, having numerous branches and fringed yellow flowers. [1885–90, *Amer.*]

yel′low rain′, small, powdery yellow deposits containing the fungal toxin tricothecene, found on leaves and other surfaces in Southeast Asia in the early 1980's and alleged by some to be a chemical weapon but claimed by others to be contaminated bee excrement. [1975–80]

Yel′low Riv′er. See **Huang He.**

yel′low-rumped war′bler (yel′ō rumpt′), a common North American wood warbler, *Dendroica coronata,* having yellow spots on the rump, crown, and sides, including a white-throated eastern subspecies **(myrtle warbler)** and a yellow-throated western subspecies **(Audubon's warbler).** [1775–85, *Amer.*]

yel′low rust′, *Plant Pathol.* See **stripe rust.** [1905–10]

yel·lows (yel′ōz), *n.* (*used with a singular v.*) **1.** *Plant Pathol.* a disease of plants, characterized by stunting and the loss of chlorophyll. **2.** *Vet. Pathol.* jaundice. **3.** *Obs.* jealousy. [1555–65; YELLOW (n.) + -S[3]]

yel′low sage′. See **red sage.**

Yel′low Sea′, an arm of the Pacific N of the East China Sea, between China and Korea. Also called **Huang Hai, Hwang Hai.**

yel′low spot′, *Ophthalm.* macula (def. 2b). [1865–70]

Yel·low·stone (yel′ō stōn′), *n.* a river flowing from NW Wyoming through Yellowstone Lake and NE through Montana into the Missouri River in W North Dakota. 671 mi. (1080 km) long.

Yel′lowstone Falls′, two waterfalls of the Yellowstone River, in Yellowstone National Park: upper falls, 109 ft. (33 m) high; lower falls, 308 ft. (94 m) high.

Yel′lowstone Lake′, a lake in NW Wyoming, in Yellowstone National Park. 20 mi. (32 km) long; 140 sq. mi. (363 sq. km).

Yel′lowstone Na′tional Park′, a park in NW Wyoming and adjacent parts of Montana and Idaho: geysers, hot springs, falls, canyon. 3458 sq. mi. (8955 sq. km).

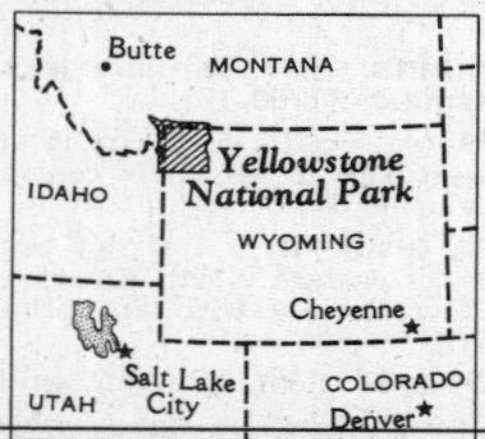

CONCISE ETYMOLOGY KEY: <, descended or borrowed from; >, whence; b., blend of, blended; c., cognate with; cf., compare; deriv., derivative; equiv., equivalent; imit., imitative; obl., oblique; r., replacing; s., stem; sp., spelling, spelled; resp., respelling, respelled; trans., translation; ?, origin unknown; *, unattested; ‡, probably earlier than. See the full key inside the front cover.

yel′low streak′, *Informal.* a trait of cowardice in a person's character. [1910–15, *Amer.*]

yel·low·tail (yel′ō tāl′), *n., pl.* **-tails,** (*esp. collectively*) **-tail.** **1.** a game fish, *Seriola lalandei,* of California. **2.** Also called **yel′lowtail snap′per.** a small West Indian snapper, *Ocyurus chrysurus.* **3.** See **yellowtail flounder.** **4.** any of several other fishes with a yellow caudal fin. [1600–10; YELLOW + TAIL[1]]

yel′lowtail floun′der, a spotted, righteyed flounder, *Limanda ferruginea,* of the Atlantic coast of North America, having a yellowish tail fin: once commercially important, now greatly reduced in number.

yel·low·throat (yel′ō thrōt′), *n.* any of several American warblers of the genus *Geothlypis,* having a yellow throat, esp. the common yellowthroat, *G. trichas.* [1695–1705; YELLOW + THROAT]

yel′low-throat·ed vir′eo (yel′ō thrō′tid), an olive-green vireo, *Vireo flavifrons,* of eastern North America, having a bright yellow throat and breast. [1830–40]

yel′low war′bler, a small American warbler, *Dendroica petechia,* the male of which has yellow plumage streaked with brown on the underparts. Also called **golden warbler.** [1775–85, *Amer.*]

yel′low wa′ter lil′y, any of several water lilies, as the spatterdock, *Nuphar luteum,* having yellow flowers.

yel·low·weed (yel′ō wēd′), *n.* **1.** any of certain coarse goldenrods. **2.** the European ragwort, *Senecio jacobaea.* [1750–60; YELLOW + WEED[1]]

yel·low·wood (yel′ō wo͝od′), *n.* **1.** a tree, *Cladrastis lutea,* of the legume family, native to the southeastern U.S., having clusters of fragrant, white flowers and wood that yields a yellow dye. **2.** any of several other trees having yellowish wood or yielding a yellow substance, as *Podocarpus elongatus* or *P. henkelii,* of Africa. **3.** the wood of any of these trees. [1660–70; YELLOW + WOOD[1]]

yel·low·y (yel′ō ē), *adj.* somewhat yellow; yellowish. [1660–70; YELLOW + -Y[1]]

yelp (yelp), *v.i.* **1.** to give a quick, sharp, shrill cry, as a dog or fox. **2.** to call or cry out sharply: *The boy yelped in pain when the horse stepped on his foot.* —*v.t.* **3.** to utter or express by or as if by yelping. —*n.* **4.** a quick, sharp bark or cry. [bef. 900; (v.) ME *yelpen,* OE *gielpan* to boast; c. LG *galpen* to croak; (n.) ME: boasting, OE *gielp,* deriv. of the v.] —**yelp′er,** *n.*

Yel·tsin (yelt′sin), *n.* **Bo·ris Ni·ko·la·ye·vich** (bôr′is nik′ə lī′ ə vich, bōr′-, bor′-; *Russ.* bu ryes′ nyi ku lä′-yi vyich), born 1931, president of the Russian Federation since 1991.

Yem·en (yem′ən, yā′mən), *n.* **1. Republic of,** a country in S Arabia, formed in 1990 by the merger of the Yemen Arab Republic and the People's Democratic Republic of Yemen. 12,000,000; 207,000 sq. mi. (536,130 sq. km). *Cap. (political):* San'a. *Cap. (economic):* Aden. **2.** Also called **North Yemen.** a former country in SW Arabia: since 1990 a part of the Republic of Yemen. *Cap.:* San'a. **3.** Also called **South Yemen.** a former country in S Arabia: since 1990 a part of the Republic of Yemen. *Cap.:* Aden.

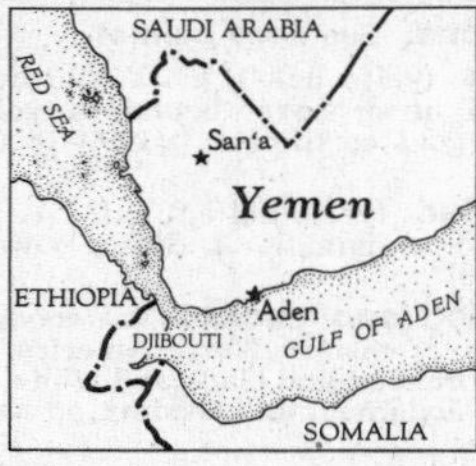

Yem·en·ite (yem′ə nīt′), *n.* **1.** a native or inhabitant of Yemen. —*adj.* **2.** of or pertaining to Yemen or its people. Also, **Yem·e·ni** (yem′ə nē). [YEMEN + -ITE[1]]

yen[1] (yen), *n., pl.* **yen.** **1.** an aluminum coin and monetary unit of Japan, equal to 100 sen or 1000 rin. *Symbol:* ; *Abbr.:* Y **2.** a former silver coin of Japan. [1870–75; < Japn (*y*)*en* < Chin *yuán* YUAN]

yen[2] (yen), *n., v.,* **yenned, yen·ning.** *Informal.* —*n.* **1.** a desire or craving: *a yen for apple pie.* —*v.i.* **2.** to have a craving; yearn. [1905–10, *Amer.*; prob. < dial. Chin (Guangdong) *yáhn,* akin to Chin *yǐn* craving, addiction] —**Syn. 1.** longing, hankering, hunger, appetite.

Ye·na·ki·ye·vo (yen′ə kē′yə və; *Russ.* yi nä′kyi yivə), *n.* a city in E Ukraine: suburb of Donetsk. 114,000. Formerly, **Ordzhonikidze.**

Yen·an (*Chin.* yen′än′), *n.* *Wade-Giles.* Yanan.

Yen Hsi-shan (yun′ shē′shän′), 1882–1960, Chinese general.

Ye·ni·sei (yen′ə sā′), *n.* a river in the Russian Federation in Asia, flowing N from the Sayan Mountains to the Kara Sea. 2566 mi. (4080 km) long.

Yen·i·sei·an (yen′ə sā′ən), *n.* a group of languages spoken in Siberia, the only surviving member of which is Ket. [YENISEI + -AN, trans. of Russ *yeniséĭskiĭ*]

Yen·i·sei′ Os′ty·ak (yen′ə sā′ os′tē ak′), Ket.

yen·ta (yen′tə), *n. Slang.* a person, esp. a woman, who is a busybody or gossip. [1930–35; < Yiddish *yente,* orig. a female personal name, earlier *Yentl* << OIt; cf. It *gentile* kind, amiable, orig., noble, highborn; see GENTLE]

Yen·tai (*Chin.* yen′tī′), *n.* *Wade-Giles.* Yantai.

yeo., yeomanry.

yeo·man (yō′mən), *n., pl.* **-men,** *adj.* —*n.* **1.** a petty officer in a navy, having chiefly clerical duties in the U.S. Navy. **2.** *Brit.* a farmer who cultivates his own land. **3.** *Hist.* one of a class of lesser freeholders, below the gentry, who cultivated their own land, early admitted in England to political rights. **4.** *Archaic.* **a.** a servant, attendant, or subordinate official in a royal or other great household. **b.** a subordinate or assistant, as of a sheriff or other official or in a craft or trade. —*adj.* **5.** of, pertaining to, composed of, or characteristic of yeomen: *the yeoman class.* **6.** performed or rendered in a loyal, valiant, useful, or workmanlike manner, esp. in situations that involve a great deal of effort or labor: *He did a yeoman job on the problem.* [1300–50; ME *yeman, yoman,* prob. reduced forms of *yengman, yongman, yungman,* with similar sense; see YOUNG, MAN[1]]

yeo·man·ly (yō′mən lē), *adj.* **1.** of the condition or rank of a yeoman. **2.** pertaining to or befitting a yeoman; loyal, staunch, sturdy, etc. —*adv.* **3.** like or as befits a yeoman. [1350–1400; ME *yemanly.* See YEOMAN, -LY]

yeo′man of the guard′, a member of the bodyguard of the English sovereign, instituted in 1485, which now consists of 100 men, including officers, having purely ceremonial duties. Also called **Yeo′man of the Roy′al Guard′.** [1475–85]

yeo·man·ry (yō′mən rē), *n.* **1.** yeomen collectively. **2.** a British volunteer cavalry force, formed in 1761, originally composed largely of yeomen, that became part of the British Territorial Army in 1907. [1325–75; ME *yemanry;* see YEOMAN, -RY]

yeo′man's serv′ice, good, useful, or workmanlike service: *His trusty sword did him yeoman's service.* Also, **yeo′man serv′ice.** [1595–1605]

yep (yep), *adv., n. Informal.* yes. [1830–40; see YUP]

-yer, var. of **-er**[1] after *w: bowyer; lawyer; sawyer.*

Yer·ba Bue·na (yâr′bə bwā′nə, yûr′bə), **1.** an island in San Francisco Bay between Oakland and San Francisco, California: a 500 ft. (152 m) two-story tunnel across this island connects the two spans of the San Francisco-Oakland bridge. **2.** (*l.c.*) a trailing plant, *Satureja douglasii,* of the mint family, native to the Pacific coast of North America, having egg-shaped leaves, solitary white flowers, and branches that root at the tips, used formerly in medicine as an anthelmintic and emmenagogue.

yer·ba ma·té (yâr′bə mä′tā, mat′ā, mä tā′, yûr′bə; *Sp.* yeʀ′bä mä te′), maté. [< Amer Sp: lit., maté herb]

Ye·re·van (yer′ə vän′; *Russ.* yi ʀyi vän′), *n.* a city in and the capital of Armenia, in the W part. 1,199,000. Also, **Erevan, Erivan.**

yerk (yûrk), *Chiefly Brit. Dial.* —*v.t.* **1.** to strike or whip. **2.** to stir up; arouse; excite. **3.** to jerk. **4.** to move (a part of one's body) with a jerk. **5.** to pull (stitches) tight or bind tightly. —*v.i.* **6.** to kick. **7.** to rise suddenly. **8.** to enter into something eagerly. —*n.* **9.** a kick or jerk. **10.** a thud or blow, as from a stick. [1400–50; late ME < ?]

Yer·kes (yûr′kēz), *n.* **1. Charles Tyson,** 1837–1905, U.S. financier and mass-transit magnate. **2. Robert Mearns** (mûrnz), 1876–1956, U.S. psychologist and psychobiologist: pioneered in studies of the great apes.

Yer′kes Observ′atory, an astronomical observatory located in Williams Bay, Wisconsin, affiliated with the University of Chicago, and having a 40-in. (102-cm) refracting telescope, the largest refractor in the world.

Yer·kish (yûr′kish), *n.* an experimental language for communicating with apes, using symbols consisting of geometric shapes. [1970–75; *Yerk(es)* (Regional Primate Research Center, at Emory University, Atlanta, Georgia) + -ISH[1]]

yes (yes), *adv., n., pl.* **yes·es,** *v.,* **yessed, yes·sing.** —*adv.* **1.** (used to express affirmation or assent or to mark the addition of something emphasizing and amplifying a previous statement): *Do you want that? Yes, I do.* **2.** (used to express an emphatic contradiction of a previously negative statement or command): *Don't do that! Oh, yes I will!* **3.** (used, usually interrogatively, to express hesitation, uncertainty, curiosity, etc.): *"Yes?" he said as he opened the door. That was a marvelous show! Yes?* **4.** (used to express polite or minimal interest or attention.) —*n.* **5.** an affirmative reply. —*v.t.* **6.** to give an affirmative reply to; give assent or approval to. [bef. 900; ME *yes, yis,* OE *gēse* (adv. and n.), prob. equiv. to *gēa* YEA + *sī* be it (pres. subj. sing. of *bēon* to be)]

ye'se (yēs), *Scot. Archaic.* contraction of *ye shall.*

Ye·se·nin (yə sā′nin; *Russ.* yi sye′nyin), *n.* **Ser·gey A·le·ksan·dro·vich** (syiʀ gyā′ u lyi ksän′dʀə vyich), 1895–1925, Russian poet. Also, **Esenin.**

ye·shi·va (yə shē′və), *n.* **1.** an Orthodox Jewish school for the religious and secular education of children of elementary school age. **2.** an Orthodox Jewish school of higher instruction in Jewish learning, chiefly for students preparing to enter the rabbinate. Also, **ye·shi′vah.** [1925–30; < Heb (post-Biblical) *yəshībhāh* lit., a sitting]

Ye·şil·köy (ye′shēl koi′), *n.* a town in Turkey, near Istanbul. Formerly, **San Stefano.**

yes-man (yes′man′), *n., pl.* **-men.** a person who, regardless of actual attitude, always expresses agreement with his or her supervisor, superior, etc.; sycophant. [1910–15]

yes′-no′ ques′tion (yes′nō′), *Gram.* a question calling for an answer of *yes* or *no,* as *Are you ready?* Cf. **WH-question.** [1955–60]

yes·ter (yes′tər), *adj. Archaic.* of or pertaining to yesterday. Also, **yestern.** [1570–80; back formation from YESTERDAY, etc.]

yester-, a combining form, now unproductive, occurring in words that denote an extent of time one period prior to the present period, the nature of the period being specified by the second element of the compound: *yesterweek.* [ME; OE *geostran, giestron;* c. D *gisteren,* G *gestern;* akin to L *hesternus* of yesterday]

yes·ter·day (yes′tər dā′, -dē), *adv.* **1.** on the day preceding this day. **2.** a short time ago: *Yesterday your money went further.* —*n.* **3.** the day preceding this day. **4.** time in the immediate past. —*adj.* **5.** belonging or pertaining to the day before or to a time in the immediate past: *yesterday morning.* [bef. 950; ME; OE *geostran dæg.* See YESTER-, DAY] —**yes′ter·day·ness,** *n.*

ɛs·ter·eve (yes′tər ēv′), *n., adv. Archaic.* yestereve-ng. [1595–1605; YESTER- + EVE]

ɛs·ter·eve·ning (yes′tər ēv′ning), *Archaic.* —*n.* **1.** ɛsterday evening. —*adv.* **2.** during yesterday evening. 705–15; YESTER- + EVENING]

ɛs·ter·morn·ing (yes′tər môr′ning), *Archaic.* —*n.* . yesterday morning. —*adv.* **2.** during yesterday ɔrning. [1645–55; YESTER- + MORNING]

ɛs·tern (yes′tərn), *adj. Archaic.* yester. [1855–60; ter. of YESTER, perh. with -ERN]

ɛs·ter·night (yes′tər nīt′), *Archaic.* —*n.* **1.** last ight. —*adv.* **2.** during last night. [bef. 900; ME; OE *ystran niht.* See YESTER-, NIGHT]

ɛs·ter·noon (yes′tər no͞on′), *Archaic.* —*n.* **1.** yes-ɛrday noon. —*adv.* **2.** at noon yesterday. [1850–55; ESTER- + NOON]

ɛs·ter·week (yes′tər wēk′), *Archaic.* —*n.* **1.** last eek. —*adv.* **2.** during last week. [1830–40; YESTER- + 'EEK]

ɛs·ter·year (yes′tər yēr′, -yûr′), *n.* **1.** last year. **2.** ɛ recent years; time not long past. —*adv.* **3.** during me not long past. [YESTER- + YEAR; appar. introduced y D.G. Rossetti (1870) to render MF *antan* (Villon)]

ɛs·treen (ye strēn′), *Scot. and North Eng.* —*n.* **1.** esterday evening; last evening. —*adv.* **2.** during yes-ɛrday evening. [1325–75; ME. See YESTER-, EVEN[2]]

ɛt (yet), *adv.* **1.** at the present time; now: *Don't go yet. re they here yet?* **2.** up to a particular time; thus far: *'hey had not yet come.* **3.** in the time still remaining; efore all is done: *There is yet time.* **4.** from the preced-g time; as previously; still: *He came here on a vacation 0 years ago, and he is here yet.* **5.** in addition; again: *'he mail brought yet another reply.* **6.** moreover: *I've ever read it nor yet intend to.* **7.** even; still (used to mphasize a comparative): *a yet milder tone; yet greater ower.* **8.** though the case be such; nevertheless: *strange nd yet very true.* **9. as yet.** See **as**[1] (def. 27). —*conj.* **0.** though; still; nevertheless: *It is good, yet it could be mproved.* [bef. 900; ME *yet(e)* (adv. and conj.), OE *iet(a)* (adv.); c. MHG *ieze* yet, now > G *jetzt* now] —**Syn. 10.** See **but**[1].

ɛt·i (yet′ē), *n.* (*sometimes cap.*) See **Abominable nowman.** [1950–55; < the Tibetan language of the herpas]

ɛtt (yet), *n. Chiefly Scot.* gate. [Scots form of GATE[1]]

ɛt·ta (yet′ə), *n.* a female given name.

ɛuk (yo͝ok), *Scot.* —*v.i.* **1.** to itch. —*n.* **2.** an itching ensation. [1375–1425; late ME *yuke* < MD *jeuken* to ch; r. ME (north) *yeke, yike;* see ITCH] —**yeuk′y,** *adj.*

ɛv·tu·shen·ko (yev′to͝o sheng′kō; *Russ.* yif to͞o-shen′kə), *n.* **Yev·ge·ny A·le·xan·dro·vich** (yiv gye′nyē lyi ksän′drə vyich), born 1933, Russian poet. Also, **Evtushenko.**

ɛw[1] (yo͞o), *n.* **1.** any of several evergreen, coniferous rees and shrubs of the genera *Taxus* and *Torreya,* constituting the family Taxaceae, of the Old World, North America, and Japan, having needlelike or scalelike foli-ge and seeds enclosed in a fleshy aril. **2.** the fine-rained, elastic wood of any of these trees. **3.** an rcher's bow made of this wood. **4.** this tree or its ranches as a symbol of sorrow, death, or resurrection. bef. 900; ME *ew(e),* OE *ēow, i(o)w;* c. OHG *iga, īwa* MHG *iwe,* G *Eibe*), ON *ýr,* MIr *eó* yew (OIr: stem, shaft), Velsh *ywen* yew tree, Russ *íva* willow]

ɛw[2] (yo͞o; *unstressed* yo͝o), *pron. Eye Dial.* you.

é-yé (ye′ye′), *adj. Informal.* **1.** of, pertaining to, or characteristic of the rock-'n'-roll music, fashions, enter-ainment, etc., of the 1960's, esp. in France. **2.** of or per-aining to the people associated with these trends. **3.** aving exuberance, optimism, and enthusiasm for cur-ent fads, as a teenager or young adult. [1960–65; < F < E YEAH-YEAH]

'ezd (yezd), *n.* a city in central Iran. 122,000. Also, **'azd.**

'e·zo (*Japn.* ye′zô), *n.* former name of **Hokkaido.**

'gg·dra·sil (ig′drə sil, yg′-), *n. Scand. Myth.* an ev-ergreen ash tree, the three roots of which bind together Asgard, Midgard, and Niflheim. Also, **Yg′dra·sil.**

'HA, Youth Hostels Association.

'HVH, a transliteration of the Tetragrammaton. Also, **YHWH, JHVH, JHWH** [< Heb *yhwh* God]

i (yē), *n.* (in Chinese ethical philosophy) faithful per-formance of one's specified duties to society. [< Chin *yì*]

'i (yē), *n., pl.* **Yis,** (*esp. collectively*) **Yi.** Lolo (def. 1).

'i·bin (yē′bin′), *n. Pinyin.* a city in SE Sichuan prov-ince, in central China, on the Chang Jiang. 275,000. Also, **pin.** Formerly, **Suzhou.**

'i·chang (yē′chäng′), *n. Pinyin.* a port in SW Hubei province, in central China, on the Chang Jiang. 160,000. Also, **Ichang.**

'id (yid), *n. Slang (disparaging and offensive).* a Jew. [1885–90; < Yiddish *yid* JEW; cf. MHG *jude, jüde*]

'id·dish (yid′ish), *n.* **1.** a High German language with an admixture of vocabulary from Hebrew and the Slavic languages, written in Hebrew letters, and spoken mainly by Jews from eastern and central Europe. —*adj.* **2.** of, pertaining to, or characteristic of Yiddish. [1885–90; < Yiddish *yidish;* see YID, -ISH[1]]

'id·dish·ism (yid′i shiz′əm), *n.* **1.** a word, phrase, or linguistic feature characteristic of or peculiar to Yiddish. **2.** the advocacy of Yiddish language and literature. [1925–30; YIDDISH + -ISM] —**Yid′dish·ist,** *n.*

'id·dish·keit (yid′ish kit′), *n. Yiddish.* Jewish tradi-tion, culture, character, or heritage.

ield (yēld), *v.t.* **1.** to give forth or produce by a natu-ral process or in return for cultivation: *This farm yields enough fruit to meet all our needs.* **2.** to produce or fur-nish (payment, profit, or interest): *a trust fund that yields ten percent interest annually; That investment will yield a handsome return.* **3.** to give up, as to superior power or authority: *They yielded the fort to the enemy.* **4.** to give up or surrender (oneself): *He yielded himself to temptation.* **5.** to give up or over; relinquish or re-sign: *to yield the floor to the senator from Ohio.* **6.** to give as due or required: *to yield obedience.* **7.** to cause; give rise to: *The play yielded only one good laugh.* —*v.i.* **8.** to give a return, as for labor expended; produce; bear. **9.** to surrender or submit, as to superior power: *The reb-els yielded after a week.* **10.** to give way to influence, entreaty, argument, or the like: *Don't yield to their out-rageous demands.* **11.** to give place or precedence (usu-ally fol. by *to*): *to yield to another; Will the senator from New York yield?* **12.** to give way to force, pressure, etc., so as to move, bend, collapse, or the like. —*n.* **13.** the act of yielding or producing. **14.** something yielded. **15.** the quantity or amount yielded. **16.** *Chem.* the quantity of product formed by the interaction of two or more substances, generally expressed as a percentage of the quantity obtained to that theoretically obtainable. **17.** the income produced by a financial investment, usu-ally shown as a percentage of cost. **18.** a measure of the destructive energy of a nuclear explosion, expressed in kilotons of the amount of TNT that would produce the same destruction. [bef. 900; (v.) ME *y(i)elden,* OE *g(i)el-dan* to pay; c. G *gelten* to be worth, apply to; (n.) late ME, deriv. of the v.] —**yield′er,** *n.*
—**Syn. 1.** furnish, supply, render, bear. **3.** abandon, abdicate, waive, forgo. YIELD, SUBMIT, SURRENDER mean to give way or give up to someone or something. To YIELD is to concede under some degree of pressure, but not necessarily to surrender totally: *to yield ground to an enemy.* To SUBMIT is to give up more completely to au-thority, superior force, etc., and to cease opposition, al-though usually with reluctance: *to submit to control.* To SURRENDER is to give up complete possession of, relin-quish, and cease claim to: *to surrender a fortress, one's freedom, rights.* **6.** render. **10.** give in, comply, bow. **14.** fruit. See **crop.** —**Ant. 4.** resist.

yield·a·bil·i·ty (yēl′də bil′i tē), *n., pl.* **-ties.** the abil-ity to yield or produce a yield: *a hybrid seed with greatly increased yieldability.* [YIELD + -ABILITY]

yield·a·ble (yēl′də bəl), *adj.* capable of yielding or of producing a yield. [1570–80; YIELD + -ABLE]

yield·ing (yēl′ding), *adj.* **1.** inclined to give in; sub-missive; compliant: *a timid, yielding man.* **2.** tending to give way, esp. under pressure; flexible; supple; pliable: *a yielding mattress.* **3.** (of a crop, soil, etc.) producing a yield; productive. [1300–50; ME: owing; see YIELD, -ING[2]] —**yield′ing·ly,** *adv.* —**yield′ing·ness,** *n.*

yield′ man′agement, the process of frequently ad-justing the price of a product in response to various mar-ket factors, as demand or competition. [1980–85]

yield′ strength′, *Physics.* the stress necessary to produce a given inelastic strain in a material. [1930–35]

yield′ to matu′rity, *Finance.* the rate of return on a bond expressed as a percentage that accounts for the difference between the interest earned based on current market value and that earned if the bond is held to ma-turity. Also called **maturity yield.**

YIG (yig), *n.* a synthetic yttrium iron garnet, used in electronics in filters and amplifiers. [*y(ttrium) i(ron) g(arnet)*]

Yig·dal (yig däl′, yēg-), *n. Judaism.* a liturgical prayer or hymn expressing the faith of Israel in God, usually sung responsively by the cantor and congrega-tion at the close of the evening service on the Sabbath and festivals. [< Heb *yighdal* may He be magnified]

Yi Jing (*Chin.* yē′ jĭng′), *Pinyin.* See **I Ching.**

yill (yil), *n. Scot.* ale.

Yi·ma (yē′mä), *n. Zoroastrianism.* a legendary king who, having reigned under the protection of Ahura Mazda in perfect happiness, sinned and lost for the world the immortality it had enjoyed.

yin[1] (yin), *n.* See under **yin and yang.** [1890–95]

yin[2] (yin), *adj., n., pron. Scot.* one.

Yin (yin), *n.* Shang.

yin′ and yang′, (in Chinese philosophy and religion) two principles, one negative, dark, and feminine **(yin),** and one positive, bright, and masculine **(yang),** whose interaction influences the destinies of creatures and things. [1930–35; < Chin *yīn-yáng*]

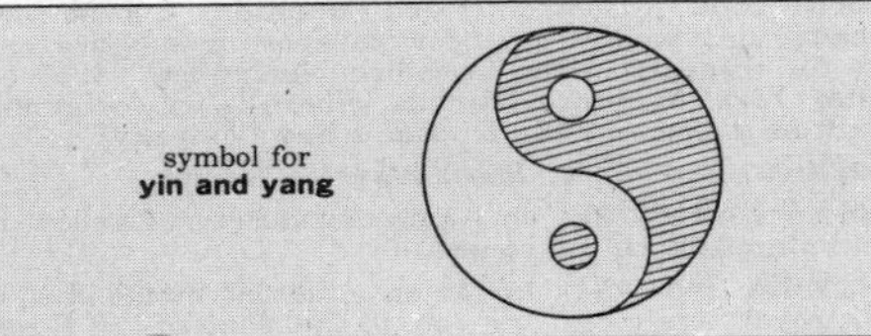

symbol for **yin and yang**

Yin·chuan (yin′chwän′), *n. Pinyin.* a city in and the capital of Ningxia Hui region, in N China. 100,000. Also, *Wade-Giles,* **Yin′ch'uan′;** *Older Spelling,* **Yin′chwan′.**

Ying·kou (ying′kō′), *n. Pinyin, Wade-Giles.* a port in Liaoning province, in NE China, near the Gulf of Liao-dong. 215,000. Also, *Older Spelling,* **Ying·kow** (ying′-kou′, -kō′). Formerly, **Niuzhuang.**

Ying·lish (ying′glish *or, often,* -lish), *n.* English char-acterized by a large number of Yiddish words and ex-pressions. [1950–55, *Amer.;* b. YIDDISH and ENGLISH]

Yin·xian (*Chin.* yin′shyän′), *n. Pinyin.* former name of **Ningbo.** Also, **Ninghsien;** *Wade-Giles,* **Yin·hsien** (yin′shyun′).

Yin′-Yang′ School′ (yin′yäng′, -yang′), a school of ancient Chinese philosophers who interpreted history in terms of the influence of the seasons and of five ele-ments: earth, wood, metal, fire, and water. Also called **Five-Elements School.**

yip (yip), *v.,* **yipped, yip·ping,** *n.* —*v.i.* **1.** to bark sharply, as a young dog. —*n.* **2.** a sharp bark; yelp. [1400–50; late ME *yippe,* perh. alter. of *yilpe* YELP]

yipe (yīp), *interj.* (an expression or exclamation of fright, surprise, pain, etc.) [perh. var. of YAP]

yip·pee (yip′ē, yip′ē′), *interj.* (an exclamation used to express joy, exultation, or the like.) [1910–15, *Amer.;* ex-pressive word of uncert. orig.; cf. *-ee* in WHOOPEE]

yip·pie (yip′ē), *n.* a member of a group of radical, politically active hippies. Also, **Yip′pie.** [1965–70, *Amer.; Y(outh) I(nternational) P(arty)* + -IE, on the model of HIPPIE]

yird (yird), *n. Scot. and North Eng.* earth.

yirr (yir), *Scot.* —*v.i.* **1.** to snarl or growl, as a dog does. —*n.* **2.** a growl or snarl, as of a dog. [1780–90; perh. to be identified with OE *georran* to make a harsh sound]

Yiz·kor (*Seph.* yēz kôr′; *Ashk.* yis′kər, yiz′-; *Eng.* yis′kər), *n. Hebrew.* the Jewish service for com-memorating the dead, held on Yom Kippur, Shemini At-zereth, the second day of Shavuoth, and the last day of Passover. [*yizkōr* may He be mindful]

-yl, *Chem.* a suffix used in the names of radicals: *ethyl.* [< F *-yle* < Gk *hýlē* matter, wood, substance]

y·lang-y·lang (ē′läng ē′läng), *n.* **1.** an aromatic tree, *Cananga odorata,* of the annona family, native to the Philippines, Java, etc., having fragrant, drooping flowers that yield an oil used in perfumery. **2.** the oil or per-fume. Also, **ilang-ilang.** [1875–80; < Tagalog *ilang-ilang*]

y·lem (ī′ləm), *n.* the initial substance of the universe from which all matter is said to be derived. [1948; adop-tion, in modern astrophysics, of ME *ylem* (Gower) < ML *(h)ylem,* acc. of *hylē* < Gk *hýlē* matter, wood]

YMCA, Young Men's Christian Association. Also, **Y.M.C.A.**

Y.M.Cath.A., Young Men's Catholic Association.

YMHA, Young Men's Hebrew Association. Also, **Y.M.H.A.**

Y·mir (ē′mir, ɪ′mir), *n. Scand. Myth.* the earliest being and the progenitor of the giants, killed by Odin and his brothers. From his flesh the earth was made, from his blood the waters, and from his skull the heav-ens. Also, **Y·mer** (ē′mər).

Yng·ling (ing′ling), *n. Scand. Myth.* a member of a royal family of Sweden and Norway, claiming descent from Ing, the god of fertility. [< ON *Ynglingr*]

yo (yō), *interj.* **1.** (used as an exclamation to get some-one's attention, express excitement, greet someone, etc.) **2.** here; present: used esp. in answer to a roll call. [1375–1425; late ME]

y.o., year old; years old.

yob (yob), *n. Brit. Slang.* a teenage lout or hooligan. [1855–60; a consciously reversed form of BOY]

y.o.b., year of birth.

yob·bo (yob′ō), *n., pl.* **-bos.** *Brit. Slang.* yob. [1920–25; YOB + -O]

yock (yok), *n., v.i., v.t. Slang.* yuk[1].

yod (yo͝od; *Heb.* yôd), *n.* **1.** the 10th letter of the He-brew alphabet. **2.** any of the sounds represented by this letter. Also, **yodh.** [1725–35; < Heb *yōdh,* akin to *yādh* hand]

yo·del (yōd′l), *v.,* **-deled, -del·ing,** or (*esp. Brit.*) **-delled, -del·ling,** *n.* —*v.t., v.i.* **1.** to sing with frequent changes from the ordinary voice to falsetto and back again, in the manner of Swiss and Tyrolean mountain-eers. **2.** to call or shout in a similar fashion. —*n.* **3.** a song, refrain, etc., so sung. **4.** a call or shout so uttered. Also, **yodle.** [1865–70; < G *jodeln*] —**yo′del·er,** *n.*

yo·dle (yōd′l), *v.t., v.i.,* **-dled, -dling,** *n.* yodel.

yo·ga (yō′gə), *n.* (*sometimes cap.*) **1.** a school of Hindu philosophy advocating and prescribing a course of physi-cal and mental disciplines for attaining liberation from the material world and union of the self with the Su-preme Being or ultimate principle. **2.** any of the meth-ods or disciplines prescribed, esp. a series of postures and breathing exercises practiced to achieve control of the body and mind, tranquillity, etc. **3.** union of the self with the Supreme Being or ultimate principle. [1810–20; < Skt] —**yo·gic** (yō′gik), *adj.* —**yo′gism,** *n.*

yogh (yōKH), *n.* the letter used in the writing of Middle English to represent a palatal fricative, as in *ung* (Modern English *young*) or a velar fricative, as in *li tliche* (Modern English *lightly*). [1250–1300; ME *yogh, yok*]

yo·gi (yō′gē), *n., pl.* **-gis** (-gēz). a person who practices yoga. Also, **yo·gin** (yō′gin). [1610–20; < Skt *yogī,* nom. sing. of *yogin,* deriv. of *yoga* YOGA]

yo·gi·ni (yō′gə nē), *n.* a woman who practices yoga. [1880–85; < Skt *yoginī,* fem. deriv. of *yogin* YOGI]

yo·gurt (yō′gərt), *n.* a prepared food having the con-sistency of custard, made from milk curdled by the ac-tion of cultures, sometimes sweetened or flavored. Also, **yo′ghurt, yo′ghourt.** [1615–25; < Turk *yoğurt*]

yo-heave-ho (yō′hēv′hō′), *interj.* (a chant formerly shouted by sailors to maintain a steady rhythm when hauling something together.) [1795–1805]

yo·him·be (yō him′bā, -bē), *n.* a tropical African tree, *Corynanthe johimbe,* whose bark is a source of the alka-loid yohimbine. [(< NL) << a language of Cameroon, where specimens were first procured]

yo·him·bine (yō him′bēn), *n. Pharm.* an alkaloid, $C_{21}H_{26}N_2O_3$, extracted from the bark of *Corynanthe jo-himbe* or *Rauwolfia serpentina,* used as a selective al-pha-adrenergic receptor antagonist: purported to have

CONCISE PRONUNCIATION KEY: *act, cāpe, dâre, pärt; set, ēqual; if, ice; ox, ōver, ôrder, oil, bo͝ok, bo͞ot, out; up, ûrge; child; sing; shoe; thin, that;* zh as in *treasure.* ə = *a* as in *alone, e* as in *system, i* as in *easily, o* as in *gallop, u* as in *circus;* ′ as in *fire* (fī′r), *hour* (ou′r). l and n can serve as syllabic consonants, as in *cradle* (krād′l), and *button* (but′n). See the full key inside the front cover.

aphrodisiac properties. [1895–1900; YOHIMB(E) + -INE[2]; perh. orig. formed in G]

yo-ho (yō hō′), *interj., v.,* **-hoed, -ho·ing.** —*interj.* **1.** (used as a call or shout to attract attention, accompany effort, etc.) —*v.i.* **2.** to shout "yo-ho!" [1760–70]

yoicks (yoiks), *interj.* **1.** *Fox Hunting.* (used as a cry by the huntsman to encourage the hounds.) **2.** (used as a cry of high spirits or encouragement.) [1765–75; cf. earlier *hoick(s)* < ?]

yok (yok), *n., v.i., v.t.,* **yokked, yok·king.** *Slang.* yuk[1].

yoke[1] (yōk), *n., pl.* **yokes** for 1, 3–20, **yoke** for 2; *v.,* **yoked, yok·ing.** —*n.* **1.** a device for joining together a pair of draft animals, esp. oxen, usually consisting of a crosspiece with two bow-shaped pieces, each enclosing the head of an animal. Cf. **harness** (def. 1). **2.** a pair of draft animals fastened together by a yoke: *five yoke of oxen.* **3.** something resembling a yoke or a bow of a yoke in form or use. **4.** a frame fitting the neck and shoulders of a person, for carrying a pair of buckets or the like, one at each end. **5.** an agency of oppression, subjection, servitude, etc. **6.** an emblem or symbol of subjection, servitude, slavery, etc., as an archway under which prisoners of war were compelled to pass by the ancient Romans and others. **7.** something that couples or binds together; a bond or tie. **8.** *Mach.* a viselike piece gripping two parts firmly together. **9.** Also called **fork.** a forklike termination for a rod or shaft, inside which another part is secured. **10.** a fitting for the neck of a draft animal for suspending the tongue of a cart, carriage, etc., from a harness. **11.** a crosshead attached to the upper piston of an opposed-piston engine with rods to transmit power to the crankshaft. **12.** (in an airplane) a double handle, somewhat like a steering wheel in form, by which the elevators are controlled. **13.** *Naut.* a crossbar on the head of the rudder of a small boat, having lines or chains attached to the ends so as to permit the steering of the boat from forward. **14.** See **spreader beam. 15.** a shaped piece in a garment, fitted about or below the neck and shoulders or about the hips, from which the rest of the garment hangs. **16.** a horizontal piece forming the top of a window frame. See diag. under **double-hung. 17.** a Y-shaped piece connecting branch pipes with a main soil pipe. **18.** *Television.* an electromagnetic assembly placed around the neck of a cathode-ray tube to produce and control the scanning motion of electron beams inside the tube. **19.** *Brit. Dial.* (esp. in Kent) **a.** the time during which a plowman and team work without stopping; a period of plowing. **b.** a measure or area of land equal to over 50 but less than 60 acres. **20.** a word formerly used in communications to represent the letter *Y.* —*v.t.* **21.** to put a yoke on; join or couple by means of a yoke. **22.** to attach (a draft animal) to a plow or vehicle: *to yoke oxen.* **23.** to harness a draft animal to (a plow or vehicle): *to yoke a wagon.* **24.** to join, couple, link, or unite. **25.** *Obs.* to bring into subjection or servitude. —*v.i.* **26.** to be or become joined, linked, or united. [bef. 900; (n.) ME *yok(e),* OE *geoc;* c. D *juk,* G *Joch,* ON *ok,* L *jugum,* Gk *zygón,* Hittite *yugan,* Skt *yuga;* (v.) ME *yoken,* OE *geocian,* deriv. of the n.] —**yoke′less,** *adj.*
—**Syn. 2.** See **pair.**

Y, yoke[1] (def. 1)

yoke[2] (yōk), *n.* yolk.

yoke·fel·low (yōk′fel′ō), *n.* **1.** an associate or companion, esp. at work; partner. **2.** a spouse. Also, **yoke·mate** (yōk′māt′). [1520–30; YOKE[1] + FELLOW, trans. of Gk *sýzygos*]

yoke′ front′. See **oxbow front.** [1885–90]

yo·kel (yō′kəl), *n.* a rustic; a country bumpkin. [1805–15; orig. uncert.] —**yo′kel·ish,** *adj.*

Yok·ka·i·chi (yôk′kä ē′chē), *n.* a city on S Honshu, in central Japan. 255,442.

Yo·ko·ha·ma (yō′kə hä′mə; *Japn.* yô′kô hä′mä), *n.* a seaport on SE Honshu, in central Japan, on Tokyo Bay: destructive earthquake 1923. 2,773,822.

Yo·ko·su·ka (yō′kə sōō′kə, yə kōōs′kə; *Japn.* yô′kô-sōō′kä), *n.* a seaport on SE Honshu, in central Japan, on Tokyo Bay: naval base. 421,112.

Yo·kuts (yō′kuts), *n., pl.* **-kuts** for 1. **1.** a member of a North American Indian group of small tribes speaking related dialects and occupying the San Joaquin Valley of California and the adjoining eastern foothill regions. Nearly all the Valley Yokuts are extinct; some foothill groups remain. **2.** a Penutian family of languages spoken by the Yokuts.

Yo·lan·de (yō lan′də; *Fr.* yô länd′), *n.* a female given name. Also, **Yo·lan·da** (yō lan′də, -län′-).

yol·dring (yol′drin, yōl′-), *n. Scot. and North Eng.* a yellowhammer. [1780–90; earlier *yowl(o)ring,* equiv. to *yowlo(w),* var. of YELLOW + RING[1]]

yolk (yōk, yōlk), *n.* **1.** the yellow and principal substance of an egg, as distinguished from the white. **2.** *Embryol.* the part of the contents of the egg of an animal that enters directly into the formation of the embryo, together with any material that nourishes the embryo during its formation. **3.** the essential part; the inner core. **4.** a natural grease exuded from the skin of sheep. Also, **yoke.** [bef. 1000; ME *yolke, yelke,* OE *geoloca,* deriv. of *geolu* YELLOW] —**yolked,** *adj.* —**yolk′less,** *adj.* —**yolk′y,** *adj.*

CONCISE ETYMOLOGY KEY: <, descended or borrowed from; >, whence; b., blend of, blended; c., cognate with; cf., compare; deriv., derivative; equiv., equivalent; imit., imitative; obl., oblique; r., replacing; s., stem; sp., spelling, spelled; resp., respelling, respelled; trans., translation; ?, origin unknown; *, unattested; ‡, probably earlier than. See the full key inside the front cover.

yolk′ sac′, *Embryol.* **1.** an extraembryonic membrane that encloses the yolk of eggs in birds, reptiles, and marsupials and that circulates nourishment from the yolk to the developing embryo. **2.** a similar membrane in placental mammals that encloses a mostly hollow space and loses its nutritive function entirely as the placenta develops. [1860–65]

yolk′ stalk′, a tubular connection between the yolk sac and the embryonic gut in the developing embryo. [1895–1900]

Yom Kip·pur (yôm kip′ər, yōm, yom; *Seph. Heb.* yôm′ kē pōōr′; *Ashk. Heb.* yōm ki′pər), a Jewish high holy day observed on the 10th day of the month of Tishri by fasting and by the recitation of prayers of repentance. Also called **Day of Atonement.** [< Heb, equiv. to *yōm* day + *kippūr* atonement]

Yom′ Kip′pur War′, a war that began on Yom Kippur in 1973 with the attack of Israel by Egypt, Syria, and Iraq: Israel recovered most of its initial losses.

yom tov (*Yiddish.* yôn′ təv, təf; *Eng.* yun′ təv, təf; *Seph. Heb.* yôm′ tôv′; *Ashk. Heb.* yōm′ tōv′), *pl. Eng.* **yom tovs** (yun′ təvz, təfs), ***ya·mim to·vim, yo·mim to·vim*** (*Yiddish.* yôn toi′vim; *Seph. Heb.* yä mēm′ tô-vēm′; *Ashk. Heb.* yô′mim tō′vim). *Yiddish and Hebrew.* holiday. [lit., good day]

yon (yon), *Older Use.* —*adj., adv.* **1.** yonder. —*pron.* **2.** that or those yonder. [bef. 900; ME; OE *geon;* akin to D *gene,* G *jener,* ON *enn, inn* the, Goth *jains* that]

yond (yond), *adv., adj. Archaic.* yonder. [bef. 900; ME; OE *geond;* akin to D *ginds,* Goth *jaind.* See YON]

yon·der (yon′dər), *adj.* **1.** being in that place or over there; being that or those over there: *That road yonder is the one to take.* **2.** being the more distant or farther: *yonder side.* —*adv.* **3.** at, in, or to that place specified or more or less distant; over there. [1250–1300; ME *yonder, yender,* equiv. to YOND + *-er* as in HITHER, THITHER, etc.; akin to D *ginder,* Goth *jaindre*]

Yong·jia (*Chin.* yông′jyä′), *n. Pinyin.* former name of **Wenzhou.** Also, **Yungchia, Yungkia.**

Yong Lo (yông′ lō′), *Pinyin.* (*Zhu Di*) See **Yung Lo.**

Yong·ning (*Chin.* yông′ning′), *n. Pinyin.* former name of **Nanning.** Also, **Yungning.**

yo·ni (yō′nē), *n.* (in Shaktism) the external female genitals regarded as the symbol of Shakti. Cf. **lingam** (def. 2). [1790–1800; < Skt]

Yon·kers (yong′kərz), *n.* a city in SE New York, on the Hudson, near New York City. 195,351. —**Yon′kers·ite′,** *n.*

Yonne (yôn), *n.* a department in central France. 299,851; 2881 sq. mi. (7460 sq. km). *Cap.:* Auxerre.

yoo-hoo (yōō′hōō′), *interj.* **1.** (used as an exclamation to get someone's attention, in calling to another person, or the like.) —*v.i.* **2.** to get or attempt to get someone's attention by or as if by calling "yoo-hoo": *yoo-hooing across the back fence.* [‡1920–25, *Amer.*; of expressive orig.]

Yor·ba Lin·da (yôr′bə lin′də, yōr′bə), a city in SW California. 28,254.

yore (yôr, yōr), *n.* **1.** *Chiefly Literary.* time past: *knights of yore.* —*adv.* **2.** *Obs.* of old; long ago. [bef. 900; ME; OE *geāra*]

York (yôrk), *n.* **1.** a member of the royal house of England that ruled from 1461 to 1485. **2. 1st Duke of** (*Edmund of Langley*), 1341–1402, progenitor of the house of York (son of Edward III). **3. Alvin Cul·lum** (kul′əm) (*Sergeant*), 1887–1964, U.S. soldier. **4.** Yorkshire (def. 1). **5.** Ancient, **Eboracum.** a city in North Yorkshire, in NE England, on the Ouse: the capital of Roman Britain; cathedral. 102,700. **6.** a city in SE Pennsylvania: meeting of the Continental Congress 1777–78. 44,619. **7.** an estuary in E Virginia, flowing SE into Chesapeake Bay. 40 mi. (64 km) long. **8. Cape,** a cape at the NE extremity of Australia.

York′ boat′, (*sometimes l.c.*) *Canadian.* a large rowboat or heavy canoe used for transporting supplies, esp. by fur trappers in the Canadian Northwest. [1860–65; after *York,* Manitoba, Canada, where it was originally built as a canoe by the Hudson's Bay Company]

York·ie (yôr′kē), *n.* See **Yorkshire terrier.**

York′ Imper′ial, an American variety of yellow or green apple with red stripes.

York·ist (yôr′kist), *n.* **1.** an adherent or member of the royal family of York, esp. in the Wars of the Roses. —*adj.* **2.** belonging or pertaining to the English royal family of York. **3.** of or pertaining to the Yorkists. [1595–1605; YORK + -IST]

York′ rite′, one of the two advanced divisions of Masonic membership, leading to the Knights Templar degree. Cf. **Scottish rite.** [1905–10]

York·shire (yôrk′shēr, -shər), *n.* **1.** Also called **York, Yorks** (yôrks). a former county in N England, now part of Humberside, North Yorkshire, South Yorkshire, Cleveland, and Durham. **2.** one of an English breed of white hogs having erect ears.

York′shire bond′. See **flying bond.** [1890–95]

York′shire chair′. See **Derbyshire chair.** [1905–10]

York′shire pud′ding, a pudding made of an unsweetened batter of flour, salt, eggs, and milk, baked under meat as it roasts to catch the drippings or baked separately with a small amount of meat drippings. [1740–50]

York′shire ter′rier, one of an English breed of toy terriers having a long, silky, straight coat that is dark steel blue from the back of the skull to the tail and tan on the head, chest, and legs. [1880–85]

Yorkshire terrier, 8 in. (20 cm) high at shoulder

York·ton (yôrk′tən), *n.* a city in SE Saskatchewan, S Canada. 14,119.

York·town (yôrk′toun′), *n.* a village in SE Virgini surrender (October 19, 1781) of Cornwallis to Washin ton in the American Revolution.

Yo·ru·ba (yôr′ə bə, yōr′-), *n., pl.* **-bas,** (*esp. colle tively*) **-ba** for 1. **1.** a member of a numerous West Afr can coastal people. **2.** the language of the Yoruba, Kwa language. —**Yo′ru·ban,** *adj.*

Yo·ru·ba·land (yôr′ə bə land′, yōr′-), *n.* a form kingdom in W Africa, in the E part of the Slave Coas now a region in SW Nigeria.

Yo·sem·i·te (yō sem′i tē), *n.* a valley in E Californi in the Sierra Nevada Mountains: a part of Yosemite N tional Park. 7 mi. (11 km) long.

Yosem′ite Falls′, a series of falls in Yosemite N tional Park: upper falls, 1436 ft. (438 m) high; middl 626 ft. (190 m) high; lower, 320 ft. (98 m) high. Tot height (including rapids), 2526 ft. (770 m).

Yosem′ite Na′tional Park′, a national park in California. 1182 sq. mi. (3060 sq. km).

Yo·shi·hi·to (yō′shə hē′tō; *Japn.* yô′shē hē′tō), 1879–1926, emperor of Japan 1912–26 (son of Mutsuhit

Yo·shkar-O·la (*Russ.* yu shkär′u lä′), *n.* Ioshkar Ola.

Yŏ·su (yu′sōō′), *n.* a city in S South Korea. 111,455.

you (yōō; *unstressed* yŏŏ, yə), *pron., poss.* **your** o **yours,** *obj.* **you,** *pl.* **you;** *n., pl.* **yous.** —*pron.* **1.** the pronoun of the second person singular or plural, used c the person or persons being addressed, in the nominativ or objective case: *You are the highest bidder. It is yo who are to blame. We can't help you. This package cam for you. Did she give you the book?* **2.** one; anyone; peo ple in general: *a tiny animal you can't even see.* **3.** (use in apposition with the subject of a sentence, sometime repeated for emphasis following the subject): *You chil dren pay attention. You rascal, you!* **4.** *Informal.* (use in place of the pronoun *your* before a gerund): *There's n sense in you getting upset.* **5.** *Archaic.* **a.** yourself; your selves: *Get you home. Make you ready.* **b.** a pl. form o the pronoun **ye.** —*n.* **6.** something or someone closel identified with or resembling the person addressed *Don't buy the bright red shirt—it just isn't you. It wa like seeing another you.* **7.** the nature or character o the person addressed: *Try to discover the hidden you* [bef. 900; ME; OE *ēow* (dat., acc. of *gē* YE[1]); c. OFris *ju* OS *iu,* D *u,* OHG *iu, eu*]
—**Usage.** In American English the pronoun YOU ha been supplemented by additional forms to make clea the distinction between singular and plural. YOU-ALL often pronounced as one syllable, is a widespread spoke form in the South Midland and Southern United States Its possessive is often *you-all's* rather than *your.* YOU-UNS (from *you* + *ones*) is a South Midland form most often found in uneducated speech; it is being replaced by YOU-ALL. YOUSE (*you* + the plural *-s* ending of nouns) probably of Irish-American origin, is most common in the North, especially in urban centers like Boston, New York, and Chicago. It is rare in educated speech. *You guys* is a common informal expression among younger speakers; it can include persons of both sexes or even a group of women only. See also **me.**

you-all (yōō ôl′, yôl), *pron. Chiefly South Midland and Southern U.S.* (used in direct address to two or more persons, or to one person who represents a family, organization, etc.): *You-all come back now, hear? Tell your mother it's time you-all came to to visit us.* Also, **y'all.** [1815–25, *Amer.*]
—**Usage.** See **you.**

You′ Can't′ Go′ Home′ Again′, a novel (1940) by Thomas Wolfe.

you'd (yōōd; *unstressed* yŏŏd, yəd), contraction of *you had* or *you would: You'd be foolish to pass up such an offer.*
—**Usage.** See **contraction.**

you'll (yōōl; *unstressed* yŏŏl, yəl), contraction of *you will: You'll never guess who was here.*
—**Usage.** See **contraction.**

You•lou (yōō′lōō), *n.* **Ful•bert** (fōōl′bərt), 1917–72, African political leader: president of the Republic of Congo (now People's Republic of the Congo) 1959–63.

young (yung), *adj.,* **young•er** (yung′gər), **young•est** (yung′gist), *n.* —*adj.* **1.** being in the first or early stage of life or growth; youthful; not old: *a young woman.* **2.** having the appearance, freshness, vigor, or other qualities of youth. **3.** of or pertaining to youth: *in one's young days.* **4.** inexperienced or immature. **5.** not far advanced in years in comparison with another or others. **6.** junior, as applied to the younger of two persons having the same name: *the young Mr. Smith.* **7.** being in an early stage generally, as of existence, progress, operation, development, or maturity; new; early: *a young wine; It is a young company, not yet firmly established.* **8.** representing or advocating recent or progressive tendencies, policies, or the like. —*n.* **9.** those who have youth; young persons collectively: *the educated young of today; a game for young and old.* **10.** young offspring: *a mother hen protecting her young.* **11. with young,** (of an animal) pregnant. [bef. 900; ME *yong(e),* OE *geong;* c. D *jong,* G *jung,* ON *ungr,* Goth *jungs;* akin to L *juvenis*]
—**Syn. 1.** growing. YOUNG, YOUTHFUL, JUVENILE all refer to lack of age. YOUNG is the general word for that which is undeveloped, immature, and in process of growth: *a young colt, child; young shoots of wheat.* YOUTHFUL has connotations suggesting the favorable characteristics of youth, such as vigor, enthusiasm, and hopefulness: *youthful sports, energy, outlook.* JUVENILE may suggest less desirable characteristics, such as childishness, petulance, idleness, selfishness, or heedlessness (*juvenile behavior*), or it may refer simply to the years, up to the later teens, before legal responsibility: *juvenile delinquency; juvenile court; juvenile books.* —**Ant. 1.** mature, old.

Young (yung), *n.* **1. Andrew (Jackson, Jr.),** born 1932, U.S. clergyman, civil-rights leader, politician, and diplomat: mayor of Atlanta, Georgia, since 1981. **2. Ar•t(hur Henry),** 1866–1944, U.S. cartoonist and author. **3. Brigham,** 1801–77, U.S. Mormon leader. **4. Charles,** 1864–1922, U.S. army colonel: highest-ranking black officer in World War I. **5. Denton T. (Cy),** 1867–1955, U.S. baseball player. **6. Edward,** 1683–1765, English poet. **7. Ella,** 1867–1956, Irish poet and mythologist in the U.S. **8. Owen D.,** 1874–1962, U.S. lawyer, industrialist, government administrator, and financier. **9. Stark,** 1881–1963, U.S. drama critic, novelist, and playwright. **10. Thomas,** 1773–1829, English physician, physicist, mathematician, and Egyptologist. **11. Whitney M., Jr.,** 1921–71, U.S. social worker and educator: executive director of the National Urban League 1961–71.

young′ adult′, **1.** a teenager (used esp. by publishers and librarians). **2.** a person in the early years of adulthood.

young•ber•ry (yung′ber′ē, -bə rē), *n., pl.* **-ries.** *Hort.* a blackberry that is a cultivated variety of *Rubus ursinus* of the southwestern U.S. [1930–35; named after B. M. Young, U.S. hybridizer, who developed it c1900]

young′ blood′, **1.** youthful people. **2.** fresh new ideas, practices, etc.; vigor. [1620–30]

young•blood (yung′blud′), *adj.* youthful, vigorous, and fresh in ideas or practices: *an aging company badly in need of youngblood management.* [1620–30; attributive use of YOUNG BLOOD]

young•er (yung′gər), *adj.* **1.** compar. of **young. 2.** (*usually cap.*) (used to designate the junior of two related persons bearing the same name): *Charles the Younger ruled after his father abdicated.* —*n.* **3.** the junior of two persons in age (often used with a possessive pronoun): *Her brother is seven years her younger.*

Young•er (yung′gər), *n.* **Thomas Coleman ("Cole"),** 1844–1916, U.S. outlaw, associated with Jesse James.

Young′er Ed′da. See under **Edda.**

young•est (yung′gist), *adj.* **1.** superl. of **young.** —*n.* **2.** a person who is the least old of a group, as the youngest member of a family: *Their youngest is still in high school.*

young-eyed (yung′īd′), *adj.* **1.** clear-eyed; bright-eyed. **2.** having a youthful outlook; enthusiastic; fresh. [1590–1600]

young′ fus′tic, **1.** fustet (def. 2). **2.** the dye obtained from dyewood of the fustet.

young′ hy′son. See under **hyson.**

young•ish (yung′ish), *adj.* somewhat young. [1660–70; YOUNG + -ISH[1]]

Young′ It′aly, a political society in Italy advocating the unification of Italy, founded by Mazzini in 1831 to replace the Carbonari.

young′ la′dy, **1.** a young, usually unmarried woman of refinement, grace, etc. **2.** any young woman. **3.** a girlfriend; sweetheart; fiancée. [1375–1425; late ME]

young•ling (yung′ling), *n.* **1.** a young person. **2.** anything young, as a young animal. **3.** a novice; a beginner. —*adj.* **4.** young; youthful. [bef. 900; ME *yongling,* OE *geongling;* c. D *jongeling,* G *Jüngling.* See YOUNG, -LING[1]]

young′ man′, **1.** a male in early manhood. **2.** a boyfriend; sweetheart; fiancé. [bef. 1000; 1850–55 for def. 2; ME; OE]

young one (yung′ ən, wən), a child or offspring: *They have five young ones and another on the way.* [1525–35]

Young′ plan′, a plan reducing the reparations provided by the Dawes plan, devised by an international committee headed by Owen D. Young and put into effect in 1929.

Young′ Pretend′er. See **Stuart, Charles Edward.**

Young's′ mod′ulus, *Physics.* a coefficient of elasticity of a substance, expressing the ratio between a stress that acts to change the length of a body and the fractional change in length caused by this force. [1860–65; named after Thomas YOUNG, who derived it]

young•ster (yung′stər), *n.* **1.** a child. **2.** a young person. **3.** a young horse or other animal. **4.** (in the British navy) a midshipman of less than four years' standing. **5.** (in the U.S. Naval Academy) a midshipman in the second year. [1580–90; YOUNG + -STER]
—**Syn. 2.** youth, lad, stripling, boy; girl.

Youngs•town (yungz′toun′), *n.* a city in NE Ohio. 115,436.

young′ thing′, **1.** a young person. **2.** a young animal.

Young′ Turk′, **1.** a member of a Turkish reformist and nationalist party that was founded in the latter part of the 19th century and was the dominant political party in Turkey in the period 1908–18. **2.** an insurgent in a political party, esp. one belonging to a group or faction that supports liberal or progressive policies: *The leadership of the party passed from the cautious old-line conservatives to the zealous Young Turks.* **3.** Also, **young′ Turk′, young′ turk′.** any person aggressively or impatiently advocating reform within an organization. [1900–05]

youn•ker (yung′kər), *n.* **1.** a youngster. **2.** *Obs.* a young noble or gentleman. [1495–1505; < MD *jonchere,* equiv. to *jonc* YOUNG + *here* lord; c. G *Junker*]

your (yŏŏr, yôr, yōr; *unstressed* yər), *pron.* **1.** (a form of the possessive case of **you** used as an attributive adjective): *Your jacket is in that closet. I like your idea.* Cf. **yours. 2.** one's (used to indicate that one belonging to oneself or to any person): *The consulate is your best source of information. As you go down the hill, the library is on your left.* **3.** (used informally to indicate all members of a group, occupation, etc., or things of a particular type): *Take your factory worker, for instance. Your power brakes don't need that much servicing.* [bef. 900; ME; OE *ēower* (gen. of *gē* YE[1]); c. G *euer*]
—**Usage.** See **me.**

you're (yŏŏr; *unstressed* yər), contraction of *you are: You're certain that's right?*
—**Usage.** See **contraction.**

yourn (yŏŏrn, yôrn, yōrn), *pron. Nonstandard.* yours. Also, **your'n.** [1350–1400; ME, equiv. to YOUR + *-n,* as in MINE[1]]

yours (yŏŏrz, yôrz, yōrz), *pron.* **1.** (a form of the possessive case of **you** used as a predicate adjective): *Which cup is yours? Is she a friend of yours?* **2.** that which belongs to you: *Yours was the first face I recognized.* [1250–1300; ME, equiv. to YOUR + *-s,* as in HIS]

your•self (yŏŏr self′, yôr-, yōr-, yər-), *pron., pl.* **-selves** (-selvz′). **1.** (an emphatic appositive of **you** or **ye**): *a letter you yourself wrote.* **2.** a reflexive form of **you** (used as the direct or indirect object of a verb or the object of a preposition): *Don't blame yourself. Did you ever ask yourself "why"? You can think for yourself.* **3.** *Informal.* (used in place of **you,** esp. in compound subjects, objects, and complements): *Ted and yourself have been elected. We saw your sister and yourself at the game. People like yourselves always feel like that.* **4.** (used in absolute constructions): *Yourself having so little money, how could they expect you to help?* **5.** your normal or customary self: *You'll soon be yourself again.* **6.** (used in place of **you** after *as, than,* or *but*): *scholars as famous as yourselves; a girl no older than yourself.* **7.** oneself: *The surest way is to do it yourself.* [1275–1325; ME; see YOUR, SELF]
—**Usage.** See **myself.**

yours′ tru′ly, **1.** a conventional phrase used at the end of a letter. **2.** *Informal.* I; myself; me: *I'm only in business to profit yours truly.* [1790–1800]

yous[1] (yōōz), *n.* pl. of **you.**

yous[2] (yōōz; *unstressed* yəz, yiz), *pron.* youse.

youse (yōōz; *unstressed* yəz, yiz), *pron. Nonstandard.* you (usually used in addressing two or more people).
—**Usage.** See **you.**

Yous•ke•vitch (yōōs kā′vich), *n.* **I•gor** (ē′gôr), born 1912, U.S. ballet dancer, born in Russia.

youth (yōōth), *n., pl.* **youths** (yōōths, yōōthz), (*collectively*) **youth. 1.** the condition of being young. **2.** the appearance, freshness, vigor, spirit, etc., characteristic of one who is young. **3.** the time of being young; early life: *His youth was spent on the farm.* **4.** the period of life from puberty to the attainment of full growth; adolescence. **5.** the first or early period of anything: *The business, even in its youth, showed great potential.* **6.** young persons collectively. **7.** a young person, esp. a young man or male adolescent. [bef. 900; ME *youthe,* OE *geoguth;* c. D *jeugd,* G *Jugend*] —**youth′less,** *adj.*
—**Syn. 3.** minority, immaturity. **7.** youngster, teenager, adolescent, stripling, lad, boy. —**Ant. 1, 3.** maturity.

youth-and-old-age (yōōth′ən ōld′āj′, -ənd), *n.* a stiff-growing, erect composite plant, *Zinnia elegans,* of Mexico, having large, solitary flowers with yellow-to-purple disks and usually red rays. [1890–95, *Amer.*]

youth•en (yōō′thən), *v.t.* **1.** to make youthful; to restore youth to (someone or something). —*v.i.* **2.** to become youthful. [1880–85; YOUTH + -EN[1]]

youth•ful (yōōth′fəl), *adj.* **1.** characterized by youth; young. **2.** of, pertaining to, or befitting youth: *youthful enthusiasm.* **3.** having the appearance, freshness, vigor, etc., of youth: *She is 60 but her optimism has kept her youthful.* **4.** in an early period of existence; early in time. **5.** *Physical Geog.* (of topographical features) having undergone erosion to a slight extent only. [1555–65; YOUTH + -FUL] —**youth′ful•ly,** *adv.* —**youth′ful•ness,** *n.*
—**Syn. 1–3.** See **young.**

youth′ful offend′er, a young delinquent, esp. a first offender, usually from 14 to 21 years old, whom the court tries to correct and guide rather than to punish as a criminal. Also, **youth′ offend′er.**

youth′ group′, an organization of young people, as for social purposes, usually under the sponsorship of a church, political organization, or the like. [1945–50]

youth′ hos′tel, hostel (def. 1). [1935–40]

youth′ hos′teler, a person who stays at youth hostels during travels. [1930–35; YOUTH HOSTEL + -ER[1]]

you-uns (yunz, yōō′ənz), *pron. Nonstandard.* you (used in direct address usually to two or more persons).
—**Usage.** See **you.**

you've (yōōv; *unstressed* yŏŏv, yəv), contraction of *you have: You've already been there.*
—**Usage.** See **contraction.**

yow (you), *interj., n.* (an exclamation or shout of pain, dismay, etc.) [1400–50; late ME]

yowl (youl), *v.i.* **1.** to utter a long, distressful or dismal cry, as an animal or a person; howl. —*n.* **2.** a yowling cry; a howl. [1175–1225; ME *yuhele, yule, youle,* appar. from a cry of pain or distress *yuhele;* cf. OE *geoh-* (in *geohthu* grief)]

yowl•er (you′lər), *n.* **1.** a person who yowls; a howler. **2.** See **ocean pout.** [YOWL + -ER[1]]

yo-yo (yō′yō), *n., pl.* **-yos,** *adj., v.* —*n.* **1.** a spoollike toy consisting of two thick wooden, plastic, or metal disks connected by a dowel pin in the center to which a string is attached, one end being looped around the player's finger so that the toy can be spun out and reeled in by wrist motion. **2.** something that fluctuates or moves up and down, esp. suddenly or repeatedly. **3.** *Slang.* a stupid, foolish, or incompetent person. —*adj.* **4.** *Informal.* moving up and down or back and forth; fluctuating; vacillating: *yo-yo prices; a yo-yo foreign policy.* —*v.i.* **5.** *Informal.* to move up and down or back and forth; fluctuate or vacillate: *Mortgage rates are still yo-yoing.* —*v.t.* **6.** *Informal.* to cause to yo-yo. [earlier, a U.S. trademark for such a toy (1932); recorded in 1915 as the name of a Philippine toy; of undetermined orig.]

Y•pres (*Fr.* ē′pʀᵊ; *Brit. or facetious* wī′pərz), *n.* a town in W Belgium: battles 1914–18. 34,758. Flemish, **Ieper.**

Y.P.S.C.E., Young People's Society of Christian Endeavor.

Yp•si•lan•ti (ip′sə lan′tē), *n.* **1. Alexander,** 1792–1828, Greek patriot and revolutionary leader. **2.** his brother **De•me•tri•os** (di mē′trē əs; *Gk.* t͟hē mē′tʀē ôs), 1793–1832, Greek patriot and revolutionary leader. **3.** a city in SE Michigan, W of Detroit. 24,031. Also, **Yp•si•lan•tis, Yp•se•lan•tes** (*Gk.* ē′psē län′dēs) (for defs. 1, 2).

Y•quem (ē kem′), *n.* **Château d',** a sweet white wine from the estate of Château d'Yquem in the Sauternes region of France.

yr., **1.** year; years. **2.** your.

yrbk., yearbook.

yrs., **1.** years. **2.** yours.

Y•sa•ÿe (*Fr.* ē zä ē′), *n.* **Eu•gène** (œ zhen′), 1858–1931, Belgian violinist, composer, and conductor.

Ys•bad•da•den Chief-gi•ant (is ba t͟had′n chēf′jī′ənt), *Welsh Legend.* the father of Olwen.

Y•ser (*Fr.* ē zeʀ′), *n.* a river flowing from N France through NW Belgium into the North Sea: battles 1914–18. 55 mi. (89 km) long.

Y•seult (i sōōlt′), *n.* **1.** German, **Y•sol•de** (ē zôl′də). Iseult. **2.** a female given name, form of **Iseult.**

Y.T., Yukon Territory.

YTD, *Accounting.* year to date.

yt•ter•bi•a (i tûr′bē ə), *n. Chem.* a colorless compound, Yb_2O_3, used in certain alloys and ceramics. Also called **ytter′bium ox′ide.** [1875–80; < NL, named after *Ytterby,* a quarry near Stockholm, Sweden, where found; see -IA]

yt•ter•bi•um (i tûr′bē əm), *n. Chem.* a rare metallic element found in gadolinite and forming compounds resembling those of yttrium. *Symbol:* Yb; *at. wt.:* 173.04; *at. no.:* 70; *sp. gr.:* 6.96. Cf. **rare-earth element.** [1875–80; < NL; see YTTERBIA, -IUM] —**yt•ter′bic, yt•ter′•bous,** *adj.*

yt•tri•a (i′trē ə), *n. Chem.* a white, water-insoluble powder, Y_2O_3, used chiefly in incandescent gas and acetylene mantles. Also called **yt′trium ox′ide.** [1790–1800; < NL, named after *Ytterby.* See YTTERBIA]

yt•trif•er•ous (i trif′ər əs), *adj.* yielding or containing yttrium. [1875–80; YTTRI(UM) + -FEROUS]

yt•tri•um (i′trē əm), *n. Chem.* a rare trivalent metallic element, found in gadolinite and other minerals. *Symbol:* Y; *at. wt.:* 88.905; *at. no.:* 39; *sp. gr.:* 4.47. Cf. **rare-earth element.** [1815–25; < NL, named after *Ytterby.* See YTTERBIA, -IUM] —**yt′tric,** *adj.*

yt′trium met′al, *Chem.* any of a subgroup of rare-earth elements, of which the cerium and terbium metals comprise the other two subgroups.

yt•tro•tan•ta•lite (i′trō tan′tl īt′), *n.* a mineral, tantalite and niobate of yttrium and various elements, as iron, and cerium, occurring in the form of brown-black crystals. [1800–10; *yttro-* (comb. form of YTTRIUM) + TANTALITE]

CONCISE PRONUNCIATION KEY: act, cāpe, dâre, pärt; set, ēqual; *if,* ice; ox, ōver, ôrder, oil, bŏŏk, bōōt, out; up, ûrge; child; sing; shoe; thin, t͟hat; zh as in *treasure.* ə = *a* as in *alone, e* as in *system, i* as in *easily, o* as in *gallop, u* as in *circus;* ᵊ as in *fire* (fīᵊr), *hour* (ouᵊr). l and n can serve as syllabic consonants, as in *cradle* (krād′l), and *button* (but′n). See the full key inside the front cover.

Yü (yʏ), *n.* a legendary Chinese emperor who drained the land and made the mountains. Also, *Pinyin,* **Yu.**

yu·an (yo͞o än′; *Chin.* yʏän), *n., pl.* **-an. 1.** Also called **yuan′ dol′lar.** a copper coin of the Republic of China, equal to 100 cents; dollar. **2.** a paper money, brass or cupronickel coin, and monetary unit of the People's Republic of China, equal to 10 jiao or 100 fen. [1915–20; < Chin *yuán* lit., round, circular; cf. YEN]

Yu·an (yo͞o än′; *Chin.* yʏän), *n.* (*sometimes l.c.*) (in the Republic of China) a department of government; council.

Yü·an (yo͞o än′; *Chin.* yʏän), *n.* **1.** the Mongol dynasty in China, 1260–1368, founded by Kublai Khan. **2.** Yüen. Also, *Pinyin,* **Yuan.**

Yüan Shih-kai (yʏän′ shē′kī′), 1859–1916, president of China 1912–16. Also, *Pinyin,* **Yuan′ Shi′kai′.**

Yu′ba Cit′y (yo͞o′bə), a city in N central California. 18,736.

yuc·a (yuk′ə), *n.* cassava. [1545–55; < Sp, said to be < Carib]

Yu·cai·pa (yo͞o kī′pə), *n.* a town in S California. 23,345.

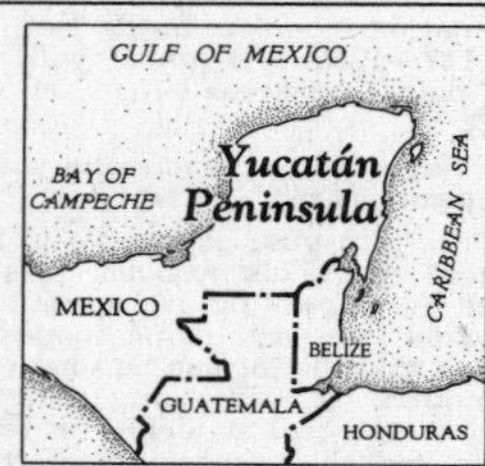

Yu·ca·tán (yo͞o′kə tan′; *Sp.* yo͞o′kä tän′), *n.* **1.** a peninsula in SE Mexico and N Central America comprising parts of SE Mexico, N Guatemala, and Belize. **2.** a state in SE Mexico, in N Yucatán Peninsula. 904,000; 14,868 sq. mi. (38,510 sq. km). *Cap.:* Mérida. Also, **Yu·ca·tan** (yo͞o′kə tan′).

Yu·ca·tec (yo͞o′kə tek′), *n., pl.* **-tecs,** (*esp. collectively*) **-tec. 1.** a member of an American Indian people of Yucatán, Mexico. **2.** Also called **Yu′catec Ma′yan.** the Mayan language of these people. **3.** a native or inhabitant of Yucatán, Mexico. **—Yu′ca·tec′an,** *adj., n.*

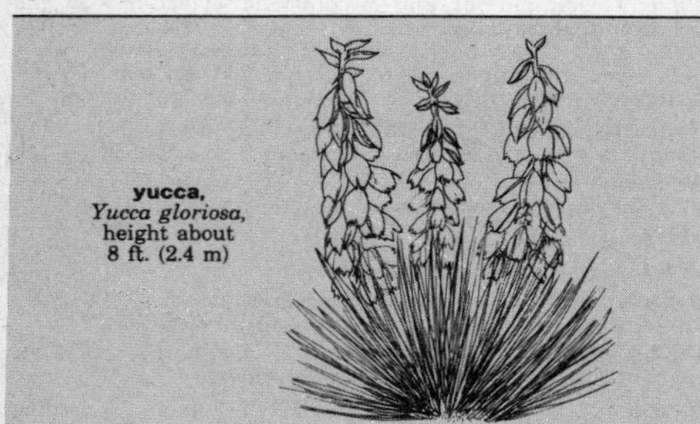

yucca, *Yucca gloriosa,* height about 8 ft. (2.4 m)

yuc·ca (yuk′ə), *n.* any plant belonging to the genus *Yucca,* of the agave family, native to the warmer regions of America, having pointed, usually rigid, sword-shaped leaves and clusters of white, waxy flowers: the state flower of New Mexico. [1655–65; < NL, appar. < Sp; perh. orig. identical with *yuca* YUCA]

yuc′ca moth′, any of several white moths of the genus *Tegeticula* that pollinate the yucca plant, the larvae of which develop in the ovary of the plant. [1890–95]

yuch (yuᴋʜ, yuk), *interj. Slang.* yuck[1]. Also, **yucch.**

yuch·y (yuᴋʜ′ē, yuk′ē), *adj.,* **yuch·i·er, yuch·i·est.** *Slang.* yucky. [YUCH + -Y[1]]

yuck[1] (yuk), *interj. Slang.* (used to express disgust or repugnance.) [1965–70, *Amer.;* expressive word]

yuck[2] (yuk), *n., v.i., v.t. Slang.* yuk[1].

yuck·y (yuk′ē), *adj.,* **yuck·i·er, yuck·i·est.** *Slang.* disgusting or repugnant. [1965–70; YUCK[1] + -Y[1]]

Yü·en (yo͞o en′; *Chin.* yʏen), *n.* a river in S China, flowing NE to Tungting. 540 mi. (869 km) long. Also, **Yüan.**

Yu·ga (yo͝og′ə), *n. Hinduism.* **1.** an age of time. **2.** any of four ages, the Satya, the Treta, the Dvapara, and the Kali, each worse than the last, forming a cycle due to begin again when the Kali has come to an end. [1775–85; < Skt]

CONCISE ETYMOLOGY KEY: <, descended or borrowed from; >, whence; b., blend of, blended; c., cognate with; cf., compare; deriv., derivative; equiv., equivalent; imit., imitative; obl., oblique; r., replacing; s., stem; sp., spelling, spelled; resp., respelling, respelled; trans., translation; ?, origin unknown; *, unattested; ‡, probably earlier than. See the full key inside the front cover.

Yugo., Yugoslavia.

Yu·go·slav (yo͞o′gō släv′, -slav′), *n.* **1.** a native or inhabitant of Yugoslavia. **2.** a southern Slav; a member of the southern group of Slavic peoples. Cf. **Slav.** **—*adj.*** **3.** of or pertaining to the Yugoslavs. Also, **Jugoslav.** [1850–55; earlier *Jugo-Slav* < G *Jugoslawe* < Serbo-Croatian *Jugoslòvēn, Jugoslàvēn,* equiv. to *jùg* south + -o- -o- + *Slovēn, Slavēn* SLAV]

Yu·go·sla·vi·a (yo͞o′gō slä′vē ə), *n.* **1.** a federal republic in S Europe: since 1992 comprised of Serbia and Montenegro. 10,392,000; 39,449 sq. mi. (102,173 sq. km). *Cap.:* Belgrade. **2.** Formerly (1918–29), **Kingdom of the Serbs, Croats, and Slovenes.** a republic in S Europe on the Adriatic: formed 1918 from the kingdoms of Serbia and Montenegro and part of Austria-Hungary; a federal republic 1945–91 comprised of Bosnia and Herzegovina, Croatia, Macedonia, Montenegro, Serbia, and Slovenia. Also, **Jugoslavia. —Yu′go·sla′vi·an,** *adj., n.* **—Yu′go·slav′ic,** *adj.*

yuk[1] (yuk), *n., v.,* **yukked, yuk·king.** *Slang.* **—*n.*** **1.** a loud, hearty laugh. **2.** a joke evoking such a laugh. **—*v.i., v.t.*** **3.** to laugh or joke: *The audience really yukked it up at the movie.* Also, **yuck, yock, yok, yak.** [imit.]

yuk[2] (yuk), *interj.* (used in repetition to indicate pleasure or amused malice.)

yuk[3] (yuk), *interj. Slang.* yuck[1].

Yu·ka·ghir (yo͞o′kə gēr′), *n., pl.* **-ghirs,** (*esp. collectively*) **-ghir** for 1. **1.** a member of a Mongoloid people of northeastern Siberia. **2.** the Paleosiberian language of the Yukaghir.

Yu·ka·gir (yo͞o′kə gēr′), *n., pl.* **-girs,** (*esp. collectively*) **-gir.** Yukaghir.

yu·ka·ta (yo͞o kä′tä), *n., pl.* **-ta.** a Japanese dressing gown or lounging robe of soft, lightweight cotton. [1815–25; < Japn: lit., a bathrobe, shortened form of *yukatabira,* equiv. to *yu* hot water + *kata* side + *-bira,* comb. form of *hira* (earlier *fira,* **pira*) flat thing]

Yu·ka·wa (yo͞o kä′wä), *n.* **Hi·de·ki** (hē′de kē), 1907–81, Japanese physicist: Nobel prize 1949.

Yuka′wa me′son, *Physics.* a hypothetical elementary particle with finite rest mass, whose exchange between nucleons would account for the strong short-range forces between nucleons: subsequently identified as the pion. [1960–65; after H. YUKAWA]

yuk·ky (yuk′ē), *adj.,* **-ki·er, -ki·est.** *Slang.* yucky. [1965–70; YUK[3] + -Y[1]]

Yu·kon (yo͞o′kon), *n.* **1.** a river flowing NW and then SW from NW Canada through Alaska to the Bering Sea. ab. 2000 mi. (3220 km) long. **2.** a territory in NW Canada. 21,392; 207,076 sq. mi. (536,325 sq. km). *Cap.:* Whitehorse. **3.** a town in central Oklahoma. 17,112. **—Yu′kon·er,** *n.*

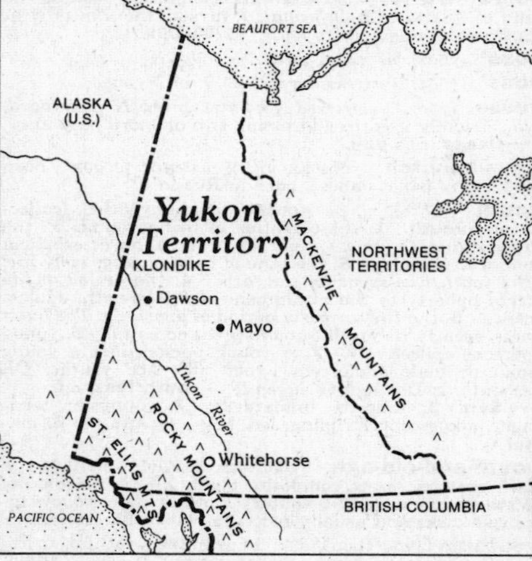

Yu′kon time′. See under **standard time.** Also called **Yu′kon Stand′ard Time′.** [1945–50]

yu·lan (yo͞o′lan; *Chin.* yʏ′län′), *n.* a magnolia tree, *Magnolia heptapeta,* native to China, having large, fragrant white flowers and cylindrical brownish fruit. [1815–25; < Chin *yùlan* (*yù* jade + *lán* orchid)]

yule (yo͞ol), *n.* Christmas, or the Christmas season. [bef. 900; ME *yole,* OE *geōl(a)* Christmastide; c. ON *jōl;* akin to Goth *jiuleis*]

yule′ log′, a large log of wood that traditionally formed the backlog of the fire at Christmas. Also called **yule′ block′, yule′ clog′.** [1715–25]

yule·tide (yo͞ol′tīd′), *n.* **1.** the Christmas season. **—*adj.*** **2.** of or pertaining to the Christmas season. [1425–75; late ME; see YULE, TIDE[1]]

yum (yum), *interj.* yum-yum.

Yu·ma (yo͞o′mə), *n., pl.* **-mas** (*esp. collectively*) **-ma** for 1. **1.** a member of an American Indian people of Arizona. **2.** the Yuman dialect of the Yuma Indians, mutually intelligible with the dialect of the Mohave Indians. **3.** a city in SW Arizona, on the Colorado River. 42,433.

Yu·man (yo͞o′mən), *n.* **1.** a family of languages including the language shared by the Yuma and Mohave Indians and several other languages of the lower valley of the Colorado River. **—*adj.*** **2.** of or pertaining to Yuman. [1890–95; YUM(A) + -AN]

yum·my (yum′ē), *adj.,* **-mi·er, -mi·est,** *n., pl.* **-mies.** *Informal.* **—*adj.*** **1.** very pleasing, esp. to the taste; delicious: *yummy desserts.* **2.** extremely attractive or appealing. **—*n.*** **3.** an item of food that is particularly delicious: *a tray of yummies.* **4.** anything that is extremely attractive or appealing. [1925–30; YUM + -Y[1]]

Yum·pie (yum′pē), *n.* (*sometimes l.c.*) a young, well-educated person who has a professional career and aspires to a higher social and economic status; yuppie. Also, **Yumpy.** [1980–85, *Amer.; y(oung) u(pwardly) m(obile) p(rofessional)* or *p(erson)*) + -IE; cf. YUPPIE]

Yum·py (yum′pē), *n., pl.* **-pies.** Yumpie.

yum-yum (yum′yum′), *interj.* (used to express enjoyment or satisfaction, esp. in the taste of food.) Also, **yum.** [1880–85]

Yung·kia (yo͝ong′kyä′), *n. Older Spelling.* Yongjia. Also, *Wade-Giles,* **Yung′chia′.**

Yung Lo (yo͝ong′ lô′), (*Chu Ti*) 1360–1424, Chinese emperor 1403–25. Also called **Ch'eng Tsu.**

Yung·ning (yo͝ong′ning′), *n. Wade-Giles.* Yongning.

Yun·nan (yo͞o nan′, -nän′; *Chin.* yʏn′nän′), *n. Pinyin.* **1.** a province in S China. 20,510,000; 168,417 sq. mi. (436,200 sq. km). *Cap.:* Kunming. **2.** former name of **Kunming.** Also, *Wade-Giles,* **Yün′nan′.**

yup (yup), *adv., n. Informal.* yes. Also, **yep.** [form of YEAH as an isolated or emphatic utterance, with *p* repr. closing of the lips, creating, in effect, an unreleased labial stop (and perh. also lowering the vowel); cf. the parallel use of *p* in NOPE]

Yu·pik (yo͞o′pik), *n.* **1.** a member of any of three groups of Eskimos inhabiting western coastal Alaska from Prince William Sound north to Norton Sound, and St. Lawrence Island and the coast of the Chukchi Peninsula of Siberia. **2.** any of the Eskimo-Aleut languages spoken by the Yupik.

yup·pie (yup′ē), *n.* (*often cap.*) a young, ambitious, and well-educated city-dweller who has a professional career and an affluent lifestyle. Also, **yuppy.** [1980–85, *Amer.; y(oung) u(rban) p(rofessional)* + -IE]

yup′pie flu′, *Informal.* See **chronic fatigue syndrome.** [1985–90]

yup·py (yup′ē), *n., pl.* **-pies.** (*often cap.*) yuppie.

Yu·rak (yə rak′), *n.* Nenets. [1880–85; < Russ *yurák; yur-,* akin to Komi *jaran* Samoyed (cf. Mansi *jorin,* Khanty *jarən, jaran, jaryan*), with suffix as in Russ *permyák* Komi, *votyák* Udmurt (see VOTYAK)]

Yu·rev (yo͞o′ryif), *n.* Russian name of **Tartu.**

Yu·ri·ma·guas (yo͞o′rē mä′gwäs), *n.* a city in N Peru. 12,000.

yurt (yo͝ort), *n.* a tentlike dwelling of the Mongol and Turkic peoples of central Asia, consisting of a cylindrical wall of poles in a lattice arrangement with a conical roof, covered by felt or skins. [1885–90; < Russ *yurt* < Turkic; cf. Turk *yurt* home, fatherland, with cognates meaning "abode, dwelling" in all branches of Turkic]

yu-wei (yo͞o′wā′), *n.* (in philosophical Taoism) action of an artificial or arbitrary kind. Cf. **wu-wei.** [< Chin *yǒuwéi* lit., having action]

Yu·zhno-Sa·kha·linsk (yo͞ozh′nə säᴋʜ′ə linsk′; *Russ.* yo͞o′zhnə sə ᴋʜu lyēnsk′), *n.* a city in the SE Russian Federation in Asia, on S Sakhalin Island. 140,000. Formerly, **Toyohara.**

Yu·zov·ka (*Russ.* yo͞o′zəf kə), *n.* a former name of **Donetsk.**

Yve·lines (ēv lēn′), *n.* a department in N France. 1,082,255; 877 sq. mi. (2271 sq. km). *Cap.:* Versailles.

Y·vette (i vet′, ē vet′), *n.* a female given name, form of **Yvonne.**

Y·vonne (i von′, ē von′; *Fr.* ē vôn′), *n.* a female given name.

YWCA, Young Women's Christian Association. Also, **Y.W.C.A.**

YWHA, Young Women's Hebrew Association. Also, **Y.W.H.A.**

y·wis (i wis′), *adv. Archaic.* iwis.

DEVELOPMENT OF MAJUSCULE								
NORTH SEMITIC	GREEK		ETR.	LATIN		MODERN		
						GOTHIC	ITALIC	ROMAN
I	I	Z	I	—	Z	Z	Z	Z

Z

DEVELOPMENT OF MINUSCULE					
ROMAN CURSIVE	ROMAN UNCIAL	CAROL. MIN.	MODERN		
			GOTHIC	ITALIC	ROMAN
z	Z	—	z	z	z

The twenty-sixth letter of the English alphabet developed from the seventh letter of the North Semitic alphabet, *zayin.* Adopted into Greek as *zeta* (ζ), it passed on to the Etruscans. It does not appear in Latin until after the conquest of Greece by the Romans in the 1st century B.C., when it was used to transliterate the Greek *z*-sound in words like *Zephyrus* and *zona.* Placed at the end of the alphabet together with Greek-derived Y, it passed in this position to all Western European alphabets.

Z, z (zē or, *esp. Brit.,* zed; *Archaic* iz′ərd), *n., pl.* **Z's** or **Zs, z's** or **zs. 1.** the 26th letter of the English alphabet, a consonant. **2.** any spoken sound represented by the letter Z or z, as in *zero, zigzag,* or *buzzer.* **3.** something having the shape of a Z. **4.** a written or printed representation of the letter Z or z. **5.** a device, as a printer's type, for reproducing the letter Z or z.

Z, 1. *Astron.* zenith distance. **2.** zone.

Z, *Symbol.* **1.** the 26th in order or in a series, or, when *I* is omitted, the 25th. **2.** (*sometimes l.c.*) the medieval Roman numeral for 2000. Cf. **Roman numerals. 3.** *Chem., Physics.* atomic number. **4.** *Elect.* impedance.

z, zone.

z, *Symbol, Math.* **1.** an unknown quantity or variable. **2.** (in Cartesian coördinates) the *z*-axis.

z., zero.

Z°, *Symbol, Physics.* Z-zero particle.

za (zä), *n. Slang.* pizza. [1965–70, *Amer.*; by shortening and alter.]

zā (zä), *n.* the 11th letter of the Arabic alphabet. [< Ar *zā(y)*]

ẓā (zä), *n.* the 17th letter of the Arabic alphabet. [< Ar]

za·ba·glio·ne (zä′bəl yō′nē; *It.* dzä′bä lyô′ne), *n. Italian Cookery.* a foamy, custardlike mixture of egg yolks, sugar, and Marsala wine, usually served hot or chilled as a dessert. Also, **za·ba·io·ne, za·ba·jo·ne** (zä′bə yō′nē; *It.* dzä′bä yô′ne). Also called **sabayon.** [1895–1900; < It, var. of *zabaione,* perh. < LL *sabai(a)* an Illyrian drink + It *-one* aug. suffix]

Zab·rze (zäb′zhe), *n.* a city in SW Poland: formerly in Germany. 203,000. German, **Hindenburg.**

Zab·u·lon (zab′yŏŏ lən, zə byŏŏ′lən), *n. Douay Bible.* Zebulun.

za·bu·ton (zə bŏŏ′ton, -byŏŏ′-), *n.* a large, flat cushion, used in Japan for sitting or kneeling on the floor. [1885–90; < Japn, equiv. to *za* seat (< MChin, equiv. to Chin *zuò* sit) + *-buton,* comb. form of *futon* FUTON]

Za·ca·te·cas (sä′kä te′käs), *n.* **1.** a state in central Mexico. 1,097,000; 28,125 sq. mi. (72,845 sq. km). **2.** the capital of this state. 56,829.

Zach (zak), *n.* a male given name, form of **Zachary** or **Zachariah.** Also, **Zack.**

Zach·a·ri·ah (zak′ə rī′ə), *n.* **1.** the father of John the Baptist. Luke 1:5. **2.** a man referred to as a martyr by Jesus. Matt. 23:35; Luke 11:51. **3.** a male given name: from a Hebrew word meaning "God is renowned." Also, **Zacharias, Zachary** (for defs. 1, 2).

Zach·a·ri·as (zak′ə rī′əs), *n.* **1.** *Douay Bible.* Zechariah. **2. Saint.** Also, **Zachary.** died 752, Greek ecclesiastic, born in Italy: pope 741–752. **3.** Zachariah (defs. 1, 2). **4.** a male given name, form of **Zachariah.**

Za·cha·ry (zak′ə rē), *n.* **1.** Zacharias (def. 2). **2.** *Douay Bible.* Zachariah (defs. 1, 2). **3.** a male given name, form of **Zachariah.**

Za·cyn·thus (zə kin′thəs, -sin′-), *n.* Latin name of **Zante.**

Za·dar (zä′där), *n.* a seaport in W Croatia, on the Adriatic coast: formerly, with surrounding territory, an exclave of Italy. 116,174. Formerly, **Zara.**

zad·dik (*Seph.* tsä dēk′; *Ashk., Eng.* tsä′dik), *n., pl.* **zad·di·kim** (*Seph.* tsä dē kēm′; *Ashk., Eng.* tsä dē′kim, -dik′im). *Hebrew.* **1.** a person of outstanding virtue and piety. **2.** the leader of a Hasidic group. Also, **tzaddik.** [*ṣaddīq* lit., righteous]

Zad·kine (zäd kēn′), *n.* **Os·sip** (o sēp′), 1890–1967, Russian sculptor, in France.

Za·dok (zā′dok), *n.* a priest at the time of David and Solomon. I Sam. 15:34–37; I Kings 1:7, 8.

zaf·fer (zaf′ər), *n.* an artificial mixture, resembling smalt, containing cobalt oxide and, usually, silica, used to produce a blue color in glass and in ceramic glazes. Also, **zaf′fre.** [1655–65; < It *zaffera,* perh. < L *sapphira* SAPPHIRE]

zaf·tig (zäf′tik, -tig), *adj. Slang.* **1.** (of a woman) having a pleasantly plump figure. **2.** full-bodied; well-proportioned. Also, **zoftig.** [1935–40; < Yiddish *zaftik* lit., juicy, succulent; cf. MHG *saftec,* deriv. of *saf(t),* OHG *saf* (G *Saft*) SAP¹, juice]

zag (zag), *v.i.,* **zagged, zag·ging.** to move in one of the two directions followed in a zigzag course: *First we zigged, then we zagged, trying to avoid the bull.* [1785–95; extracted from ZIGZAG]

Za·ga·zig (zä′gä zēg′), *n.* a city in NE Egypt, on the Nile delta. 195,100. Also, **Zaqaziq.**

Zagh·lul Pa·sha (zäg′lōōl pä′shä), **Saad** (säd), c1860–1927, Egyptian political leader: first prime minister 1924–27.

Za·gorsk (zə gôrsk′; *Russ.* zu gôrsk′), *n.* former name (1930–91) of **Sergiyev Posad.**

Za·greb (zä′greb), *n.* a city in and the capital of Croatia, in the NW part. 1,174,512. German, **Agram.**

Zag′ros Moun′tains (zag′rəs), a mountain range in S and SW Iran, extending along parts of the borders of Turkey and Iraq. Highest peak, Zardeh Kuh, 14,912 ft. (4545 m).

Za·har·i·as (zə hâr′ē əs, -har′-), *n.* **Mildred Did·rik·son** (did′rik sən), ("*Babe*"), 1914–56, U.S. track-and-field athlete and golfer.

Za·he·dan (zä′hē dän′), *n.* a city in E Iran. 42,000. Also, **Za′hi·dan′.**

zai·ba·tsu (zī′bä tsōō′), *n., pl.* **-tsu.** a great industrial or financial combination of Japan. [1935–40; < Japn, equiv. to *zai* wealth (< MChin, equiv. to Chin *cái*) + *batsu,* deriv. of *bat* clique (< MChin, equiv. to Chin *fá*)]

Zai·di (zī′dē), *n. Islam.* Zaydi. [< Ar *Zayd* an imam of the 8th century + *-i* suffix of appurtenance]

za·ire (zä ēr′, zä′ēr), *n., pl.* **za·ire.** a paper money and monetary unit of Zaire, equal to 100 makuta.

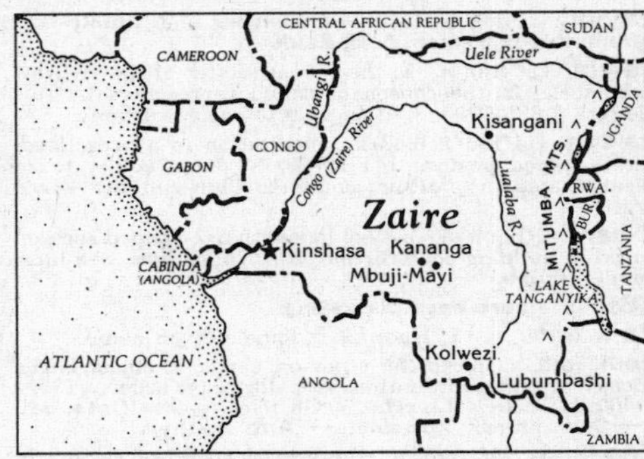

Za·ire (zä ēr′, zä′ēr), *n.* **1. Republic of.** Formerly, **Democratic Republic of the Congo, Belgian Congo, Congo Free State.** a republic in central Africa: a former Belgian colony; gained independence 1960. 27,100,000; 905,063 sq. mi. (2,344,113 sq. km). *Cap.:* Kinshasa. **2.** Official name within Zaire of the Congo River (the term Congo River is more widely used elsewhere). Also, **Za·ïre′.**

Za·ir·i·an (zä ēr′ē ən), *adj.* **1.** of or pertaining to Zaire or its people. —*n.* **2.** a native or inhabitant of Zaire. Also, **Za·ir′e·an.** [1970–75; ZAIRE + -IAN]

Zak (zak), *n.* a male given name, form of **Zachary** or **Zachariah.**

za·kat (zə kät′), *n. Islam.* a tax, comprising percentages of personal income of every kind, levied as almsgiving for the relief of the poor: the third of the Pillars of Islam. Also, **za·kah** (zə kä′). Also called **sadaqat.** [1800–05; < Turk *zekât* or Pers *zakāt* < Ar *zakāh*]

Za·ki·ya (zä kē′yə), *n.* a female given name: from a Swahili word meaning "intelligent." Also, **Za·kiy′ya.**

za·kus·ka (zə kōōs′kə), *n., pl.* **-ki** (-kē), **-ka.** *Russian Cookery.* an hors d'oeuvre. [1880–85; < Russ *zakúska* (usually in pl.), deriv. of *zakusít′* to snack, have a bite, equiv. to *za-* v. prefix + *-kusit′,* deriv. of *kusát′* to bite]

Za·kyn·thos (zä′kēn thôs; *Eng.* zə kin′thəs), *n.* Greek name of **Zante.**

Za·ma (zā′mə, zä′mä), *n.* an ancient town in N Africa, SW of Carthage: the Romans defeated Hannibal near here in the final battle of the second Punic War, 202 B.C.

za·mar·ra (zə mär′ə), *n.* a sheepskin coat of the kind worn by shepherds in Spain. [1835–45; < Sp < Basque *zamar* sheepskin]

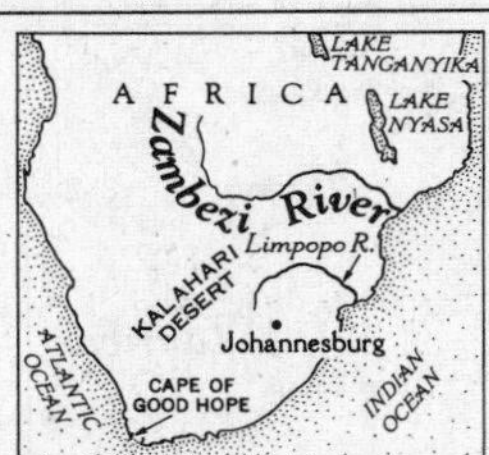

Zam·be·zi (zam bē′zē), *n.* a river in S Africa, flowing S and W from Zambia through E Angola and Zambia and then E along the border between Zambia and Zimbabwe into and through central Mozambique to the Indian Ocean. 1650 mi. (2657 km) long. —**Zam·be′zi·an,** *adj.*

Zam·bi·a (zam′bē ə), *n.* a republic in S Africa: formerly a British protectorate and part of the Federation of Rhodesia and Nyasaland; gained independence 1964; a member of the Commonwealth of Nations. 5,500,000; 288,130 sq. mi. (746,256 sq. km). *Cap.:* Lusaka. Formerly, **Northern Rhodesia.** —**Zam′bi·an,** *adj., n.*

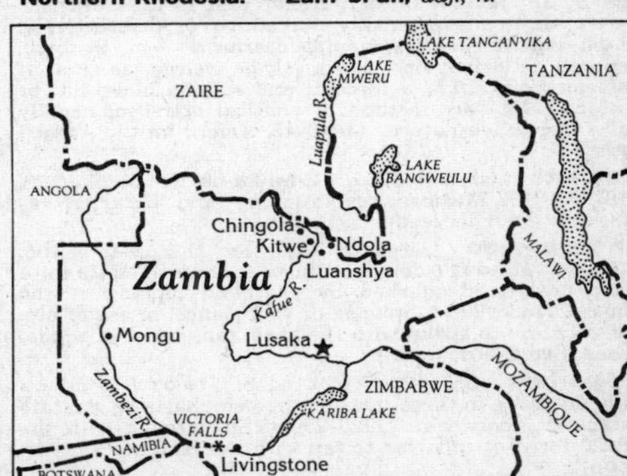

CONCISE PRONUNCIATION KEY: act, cāpe, dâre, pärt; set, ēqual; if, īce; ox, ōver, ôrder, oil, bŏŏk, bōōt, out; up, ûrge; child; sing; shoe; thin, *th*at; zh as in *treasure.* ə = *a* as in *alone, e* as in *system, i* as in *easily, o* as in *gallop, u* as in *circus;* ° as in *fire* (fī°r), *hour* (ou°r). l and n can serve as syllabic consonants, as in *cradle* (krād′l), and *button* (but′n). See the full key inside the front cover.

zam•bo (zam′bō), *n., pl.* **-bos.** sambo.

Zam•bo•an•ga (zam′bō äng′gə), *n.* a seaport on SW Mindanao, in the S Philippines. 343,722.

za•mi•a (zā′mē ə), *n.* any of various plants of the genus *Zamia,* chiefly of tropical and subtropical America, having a short, tuberous stem and a crown of palmlike pinnate leaves. [1810–20; < NL, misreading of L (Pliny) (*nucēs*) *azāniae* (pl.) pine cone (nuts)]

za•min•dar (zə mēn där′), *n.* **1.** (in British India) a landlord required to pay a land tax to the government. **2.** (in Mogul India) a collector of farm revenue, who paid a fixed sum on the district assigned to him. Also, **zemindar.** [1675–85; < Hindi < Pers *zamīndār* landholder, equiv. to *zamīn* earth, land + *-dār* holding, holder]

Za•mo•ra (thä mô′rä, sä-), *n.* **Al•ca•lá** (äl′kä lä′), (*Niceto Alcalá Zamora y Torres*), 1877–1949, Spanish statesman: 1st president of the Republic 1931–36.

Zan•de (zan′dē), *n., pl.* **-des,** (*esp. collectively*) **-de.** Azande.

zan•der (zan′dər), *n., pl.* **-ders,** (*esp. collectively*) **-der.** a freshwater pikeperch, *Stizostedion* (*Lucioperca*) *lucioperca,* of central Europe, valued as a food fish. [1850–55; < G < LG *Sander, Sandart, Zanat, Sanat,* of uncert. orig. (Pol *sandacz* prob. < LG)]

Zane (zān), *n.* a male given name, form of **John.**

Zanes•ville (zānz′vil), *n.* a city in SE Ohio. 28,655.

Zang•will (zang′wil), *n.* **Israel,** 1865–1926, English novelist and playwright.

Zan•te (zän′tē, -tä, zan′-), *n.* **1.** a Greek island, off the W coast of Greece: southernmost of the Ionian Islands. 30,156; 157 sq. mi. (407 sq. km). **2.** a seaport on and the capital of this island. 9281. Greek, **Zakynthos.** Latin, **Zacynthus.**

Zan•uck (zan′ək), *n.* **Dar•ryl F(rancis)** (dar′əl), 1902–79, U.S. motion-picture producer.

za•ny (zā′nē), *adj.,* **-ni•er, -ni•est,** *n., pl.* **-nies.** —*adj.* **1.** ludicrously or whimsically comical; clownish. —*n.* **2.** one who plays the clown or fool in order to amuse others. **3.** a comically wild or eccentric person. **4.** a secondary stock character in old comedies who mimicked his master. **5.** a professional buffoon; clown. **6.** a silly person; simpleton. **7.** a slavish attendant or follower. [1560–70; (< MF) < It *zan(n)i* (later *zanno*) a servant character in the commedia dell'arte, perh. orig. the character's name, the Upper Italian form of Tuscan *Gianni,* for *Giovanni* John] —**za′ni•ly,** *adv.* —**za′ni•ness, za′ny•ism,** *n.* —**za′ny•ish,** *adj.*
—**Syn. 3.** kook, crazy, lunatic.

Zan•zi•bar (zan′zə bär′, zan′zə bär′), *n.* **1.** an island off the E coast of Africa: with Pemba and adjacent small islands it formerly comprised a sultanate under British protection; became independent in 1963; now part of Tanzania. 421,000; 640 sq. mi. (1658 sq. km). **2.** a seaport on W Zanzibar, Tanzania. —**Zan′zi•ba′ri,** *adj., n.*

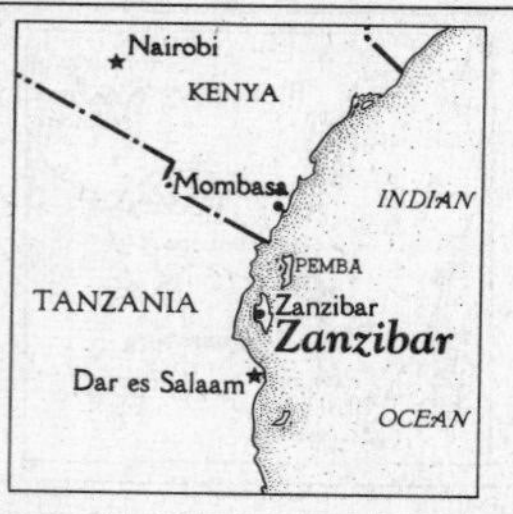

zap (zap), *v.,* **zapped, zap•ping,** *n. Informal.* —*v.t.* **1.** to kill or shoot. **2.** to attack, defeat, or destroy with sudden speed and force. **3.** to bombard with electrical current, radiation, laser beams, etc. **4.** to strike or jolt suddenly and forcefully. **5.** to cook in a microwave oven. **6.** to skip over or delete (TV commercials), as by switching channels or pushing a fast-forward button on a playback device: *We recorded the show on our VCR but zapped all the commercials.* **7.** to add a sudden infusion of energy, verve, color, attractiveness, or the like (often fol. by *up*): *just the thing to zap up your spring wardrobe.* —*v.i.* **8.** to move quickly, forcefully, or destructively: *high-voltage currents zapping overhead.* —*n.* **9.** force, energy, or drive; zip. **10.** a jolt or charge, as or as if of electricity. **11.** a forceful and sudden blow, hit, or attack. **12.** any method of political activism, usually of a disruptive nature. [1940–45, *Amer.*; imit.] —**zap′per,** *n.*

Za•pa•ta (sä pä′tä), *n.* **E•mi•lia•no** (e′mē lyä′nô), 1877?–1919, Mexican revolutionary and agrarian reformer: guerrilla leader 1911–16.

za•pa•te•a•do (zä′pə tē ä′dō; *Sp.* thä′pä te ä′thô, sä′-), *n., pl.* **-dos** (-dōz; *Sp.* -thôs). a Spanish dance for a solo performer, marked by rhythmic tapping of the heels. [1885–90; < Sp: clog or shoe dance, n. use of ptp. of *zapatear* to strike with the shoe, tap, deriv. of *zapato* shoe. See SABOT, -ADE[1]]

za•pa•te•o (*Sp.* sä′pä te′ô), *n., pl.* **-te•os** (-te′ôs). a Cuban dance in three-quarter time emphasizing staccato stamping footwork. [1920–25; < Sp: tapping with the feet, deriv. of *zapatear* to tap with the feet; see ZAPATEADO]

CONCISE ETYMOLOGY KEY: <, descended or borrowed from; >, whence; b., blend of, blended; c., cognate with; cf., compare; deriv., derivative; equiv., equivalent; imit., imitative; obl., oblique; r., replacing; s., stem; sp., spelling, spelled; resp., respelling, respelled; trans., translation; ?, origin unknown; *, unattested; ‡, probably earlier than. See the full key inside the front cover.

Za•po•ro•zhye (zä′pə rô′zhə; *Russ.* zə pu RÔ′zhye), *n.* a city in SE Ukraine, on the Dnieper River. 884,000. Formerly, **Aleksandrovsk.**

Za•po•tec (zap′ə tek′, zä′pə-; *Sp.* sä′pô tek′), *n., pl.* **-tecs,** (*esp. collectively*) **-tec** for 1, *adj.* —*n.* **1.** a member of an American Indian people living in the Mexican state of Oaxaca. **2.** the Oto-Manguean language of the Zapotecs, consisting of a number of highly divergent dialects. —*adj.* **3.** *Archaeol.* of or pertaining to a Mesoamerican Indian civilization of the Oaxaca region of Mexico c600 B.C. to A.D. 1000, characterized by a bar-and-dot system of enumeration, a calendar of Mayan derivation, ball courts, and underground frescoed tombs. [< MexSp *zapoteco* < Nahuatl *tzapotēcah,* pl. of *tzapotēcatl* person from *Tzapotlān* (*tzapo(tl)* sapodilla + *-tēcatl* suffix of personal nouns, *-tlān* locative suffix)]

zap•py (zap′ē), *adj.,* **-pi•er, -pi•est.** *Informal.* energetic, lively, or fast-moving; zippy. [1965–70; ZAP + -Y[1]]

zap•ti•ah (zup tē′ä), *n.* a Turkish police officer. Also, **zap•ti•eh** (zup tē′e). [1865–70; < Turk *zaptiye* < Ar *ḍabtīyah* police]

Za•qa•ziq (zä′kä zēk′), *n.* Zagazig.

Za•ra (zär′ə; *It.* dzä′Rä), *n.* former name of **Zadar.**

Za•ra•go•za (thä′Rä gô′thä, sä′Rä gô′sä), *n.* Spanish name of **Saragossa.**

Zar•a•thus•tra (zar′ə thōō′strə), *n.* Zoroaster. —**Zar•a•thus•tri•an** (zar′ə thōō′strē ən), *adj., n.* —**Zar′a•thus′tric,** *adj.*

zar•a•tite (zar′ə tīt′), *n.* a mineral, hydrated basic nickel carbonate, occurring in the form of emerald-green incrustations on chromite and magnetite. [1855–60; < Sp *zaratita,* after *Zarate* Spanish surname; see -ITE[1]]

Zar•deh Kuh (zär′də kōō′), *n.* a mountain in W Iran: the highest peak of the Zagros Mountains, 14,921 ft. (4550 m). Also, **Zard Kuh** (zärd′ kōō′).

za•re•ba (zə rē′bə), *n.* (in the Sudan and adjoining regions) a protective enclosure, as of thorn bushes. Also, **za•ree′ba.** [1840–50; < Ar *zarībah* pen]

zarf

zarf (zärf), *n.* (in the Levant) a holder, usually of ornamental metal, for a coffee cup without a handle. Also, **zurf.** [1830–40; < Ar *ẓarf* vessel, sheath]

Za•ri•a (zär′ē ə), *n.* a city in N central Nigeria. 224,000.

Zar•qa (zär′kə), *n.* a city in N Jordan, N of Amman. 226,000. Also, **Az-Zarqa.**

zar•zue•la (zär zwā′lə, -zwē′-; *Sp.* thär thwe′lä, särswe′-), *n., pl.* **-las** (-ləz; *Sp.* -läs). a Spanish opera having spoken dialogue and often a satirically treated, topical theme. [1885–90; < Sp, after *La Zarzuela,* palace near Madrid where first performance took place (1629)]

zas•tru•ga (zas′trə gə, zä′strə-, za strōō′-, zä-), *n., pl.* **-gi** (-gē). sastruga.

Za•ti•shye (*Russ.* zu tyē′shyə), *n.* former name of **Elektrostal.**

Zá•to•pek (zä′tô pek), *n.* **E•mil** (e′mil), born 1922, Czechoslovakian long-distance runner.

zax (zaks), *n.* a hatchetlike tool for cutting and punching nail holes in roofing slate. [dial. var. of SAX[2]]

z-ax•is (zē′ak′sis), *n., pl.* **z-ax•es** (zē′ak′sēz). *Math.* (in a three-dimensional Cartesian coordinate system) the axis along which values of *z* are measured and at which both *x* and *y* equal zero. [1945–50]

Zay•di (zī′dē), *n. Islam.* a member of a Shi'ite sect prominent in Yemen. Also, **Zaidi.**

za•yin (zä′yin), *n.* **1.** the seventh letter of the Hebrew alphabet. **2.** the consonant sound represented by this letter. [1895–1900; < Heb, akin to *zayin* weapon]

za•zen (zä′zen′), *n. Zen.* meditation in a prescribed, cross-legged posture. [1720–30; < Japn, equiv. to *za* seat, seated (< MChin, equiv. to Chin *zuò* sit) + *zen* ZEN]

Z-bar (zē′bär′), *n.* a steel bar with a Z-shaped section, used in building construction. Also called **zee.** See illus. under **shape.**

ZBB, See **zero-base budgeting.**

Ze•a (zē′ə), *n.* **1.** Keos. **2.** a female given name.

zeal (zēl), *n.* fervor for a person, cause, or object; eager desire or endeavor; enthusiastic diligence; ardor. [1350–1400; ME *zele* < LL *zēlus* < Gk *zêlos*] —**zeal′less,** *adj.*
—**Syn.** intensity, passion. —**Ant.** apathy.

Zea•land (zē′lənd), *n.* the largest island of Denmark: Copenhagen is located here. 2,055,040; 2709 sq. mi. (7015 sq. km). Also, **Seeland.** Danish, **Sjaelland.** —**Zea′land•er,** *n.*

zeal•ot (zel′ət), *n.* **1.** a person who shows zeal. **2.** an excessively zealous person; fanatic. **3.** (*cap.*) a member of a radical, warlike, ardently patriotic group of Jews in Judea, particularly prominent from A.D. 69 to 81, advocating the violent overthrow of Roman rule and vigorously resisting the efforts of the Romans and their supporters to heathenize the Jews. [1530–40; earlier *zelote* < LL *zēlōtēs* < Gk *zēlōtḗs,* equiv. to *zēlō-* (var. s. of *zēloûn* to be zealous; see ZEAL) + *-tēs* agent suffix]
—**Syn. 2.** extremist, crank, bigot. See **fanatic.**

zeal•ot•ry (zel′ə trē), *n.* undue or excessive zeal; fanaticism. [1650–60; ZEALOT + -RY]

zeal•ous (zel′əs), *adj.* full of, characterized by, or due to zeal; ardently active, devoted, or diligent. [1520–30; < ML *zēlōsus.* See ZEAL, -OUS] —**zeal′ous•ly,** *adv.* —**zeal′ous•ness,** *n.*
—**Syn.** enthusiastic, eager, fervid, fervent, intense, passionate, warm.

ze•a•tin (zē′ə tin), *n.* a cytokinin occurring in corn, spinach, and peas. [1963; < NL *Zea* the maize genus (see ZEIN) + *-t-* (of uncert. derivation) + -IN[2]]

ze•bec (zē′bek), *n. Naut.* xebec. Also, **ze′beck.**

Zeb•e•dee (zeb′i dē′), *n.* the father of the apostles James and John. Matt. 4:21.

Ze•bo•im (zi bō′im), *n.* one of the cities destroyed along with Sodom and Gomorrah. Deut. 29:23.

zebra, *Equus burchelli,* 4 ft. (1.2 m) high at shoulder; head and body 6½ ft. (2 m); tail 1½ ft. (0.5 m)

ze•bra (zē′brə; *Brit. also* zeb′rə), *n., pl.* **-bras,** (*esp. collectively*) **-bra. 1.** any of several horselike African mammals of the genus *Equus,* each species having a characteristic pattern of black or dark-brown stripes on a whitish background: all zebra species are threatened or endangered. **2.** Also called **ze′bra but′terfly.** a tropical butterfly, *Heliconius charithonius,* having black wings barred with yellow. **3.** (*cap.*) a word formerly used in communications to represent the letter Z. **4.** *Football Slang.* an official, who usually wears a black and white striped shirt. **5.** See **zebra crossing.** [1590–1600; 1975–80 for def. 4; < Pg *zebra, zebro* the Iberian wild ass (Sp *cebra*), perh. < L *equiferus* (Pliny) kind of wild horse, equiv. to *equi-* (comb. form of *equus* horse) + *ferus* wild] —**ze′bra•like′, ze•bra•ic** (zi brā′ik), *adj.* —**ze•brine** (zē′brīn, -brin), *adj.*

ze′bra cross′ing, a street crossing marked with white stripes. Also called **zebra.** [1950–55]

ze′bra finch′, a small Australian waxbill, *Poephila guttata,* that has black-and-white barred plumage and a chestnut ear patch: popular as a cage bird. [1885–90]

ze•bra•fish (zē′brə fish′; *Brit. also* zeb′rə-), *n., pl.* **-fish•es,** (*esp. collectively*) **-fish.** a small, slender freshwater fish, *Brachydanio rerio,* having luminous bluish-black and silvery-gold horizontal stripes: popular in home aquariums. [1765–75; ZEBRA + FISH]

ze′bra la′bel, *Library Science.* a label with a coded series of short, black lines affixed to each book in a library and to each borrower's card for purposes of identification and prevention of theft.

ze′bra plant′, any of several plants having conspicuously striped or veined foliage, as *Calathea zebrina,* of Brazil.

ze•brass (zē′bras′), *n.* the offspring of a zebra and an ass. [ZEBR(A) + ASS[1]]

ze′bra swal′lowtail, a swallowtail butterfly, *Papilio marcellus,* having black and greenish-white stripes on the wings. [1890–95, *Amer.*]

ze′bra-tailed liz′ard (zē′brə tāld′; *Brit. also* zeb′rə-), a lizard, *Callisaurus draconoides,* inhabiting sandy deserts of Mexico and the southwestern U.S., having a long tail marked with black bands. Also called **gridiron-tailed lizard.**

ze•bra•wood (zē′brə wo͝od′; *Brit. also* zeb′rə-), *n.* **1.** any of several trees, esp. *Connarus guianensis,* of tropical America, yielding a striped, hard wood used for making furniture. **2.** the wood of any of these trees. [1775–85; ZEBRA + WOOD[1]]

ze•bru•la (zē′brōō lə; *Brit. also* zeb′rōō-), *n.* the offspring of a female horse and a male zebra. Also, **zebrule** (zē′brōōl; *Brit. also* zeb′rōōl). [1900–05; ZEBR(A) + L (*m*)*ūla* MULE]

ze•bu (zē′byōō, -bōō), *n.* one of a domesticated form of cattle, *Bos taurus indicus,* of India, having a large hump over the shoulders and a large dewlap. [1765–75; < F *zébu,* of obscure orig.]

zebu, *Bos taurus indicus,* 6 ft. (1.8 m) high at shoulder; head and body 10 ft. (3 m); tail 2½ ft. (0.75 m)

Zeb•u•lon (zeb′yə lon′, -lən), *n.* a male given name.

Zeb•u•lun (zeb′yo͝o lən, zə byōō′lən), *n.* **1.** a son of Jacob and Leah. Gen. 30:20. **2.** one of the 12 tribes of Israel.

Zeb•u•lun•ite (zeb′yə lə nīt′), *n.* a member of the tribe of Zebulun. Num. 26:27. [ZEBULUN + -ITE[1]]

zec•chi•no (zə kē′nō; *It.* tsek kē′nô), *n., pl.* **-ni** (-nē). sequin (defs. 2–4). Also, **zech•in** (zek′in). [1610–20; < It. See SEQUIN]

Zech., Zechariah.

Zech•a•ri•ah (zek′ə rī′ə), *n.* **1.** a Minor Prophet of the

..h century B.C. **2.** a book of the Bible bearing his name. ..bbr.: Zech.

..d (zed), *n. Chiefly Brit.* **1.** the letter Z or *z.* **2.** a ..-bar. [1400–50; late ME < MF *zede* < L *zēta* < Gk *zêta* ..ETA]

..d (zed), *n.* a male given name, form of **Zedekiah.**

..-da•kah (*Seph.* tsə dä kä′; *Ashk.* tsə dô′kə), *n. He-..rew.* tzedakah.

..d-bar (zed′bär′), *n. Chiefly Brit.* a Z-bar.

..d•e•ki•ah (zed′i kī′ə), *n.* **1.** Also, **Zidkijah.** the last ..ing of Judah. II Kings 24, 25; Jer. 52:1–11. **2.** a male ..ven name.

..d•o•a•ry (zed′ō er′ē), *n.* an East Indian drug con-..sting of the rhizome of either of two species of cur-..uma, *Curcuma zedoaria* or *C. aromatica,* used as a ..imulant. [1425–75; late ME *zeduarye* < ML *zeduāria* .. Ar *zadwār* (< Pers) + L *-ia* -Y[3]]

..•donk (zē′dongk, -dôngk, -dungk), *n.* the offspring ..f a zebra and a donkey. [1970–75; ZE(BRA) + DONK(EY)]

..e (zē), *n.* **1.** the letter Z or *z.* **2.** Z-bar. [1665–75; by ..nalogy with the names of other consonant letters; cf. ..ED]

..e•brug•ge (zē′brŏŏg′ə; *Flem.* zā′brœkh′ə), *n.* a ..eaport in NW Belgium: part of the city of Bruges; Ger-..an submarine base in World War I.

..e•land (zē′lənd; *Du.* zā′länt′), *n.* a province in the ..W Netherlands, consisting largely of islands. 351,662; ..041 sq. mi. (2695 sq. km). *Cap.:* Middelburg. —**Zee′•..and•er,** *n.*

..e•man (zā′män′), *n.* **Pie•ter** (pē′tər), 1865–1943, ..utch physicist: Nobel prize 1902.

..e′man effect′, *Physics, Optics.* the dividing of a ..pectral line or lines as a result of placing a radiation ..ource in a magnetic field. The division consists of three ..qually spaced lines **(normal Zeeman effect)** in sys-..ems for which the spin quantum number is zero, or of ..hree or more unequally spaced lines **(anomalous Zee-..an effect)** in systems for which the spin quantum ..umber is not zero. Also called **Zee′man split′ting.** Cf. ..aschen-Back effect. [1895–1900; named after P. ZEE-..AN]

..EG, zero economic growth.

..•in (zē′in), *n.* **1.** *Biochem.* a soft, yellow powder of ..imple proteins obtained from corn, used chiefly in the ..anufacture of textile fibers, plastics, and paper coat-..ngs. **2.** a synthetic fiber produced from this protein. ..1815–25; < NL *Ze(a)* the maize genus (L: emmer < Gk ..eiá barley, wheat; c. Skt *yáva* grain) + -IN[2]]

..eist (zīst), *n.* a city in the central Netherlands. 61,784.

..eit•ge•ber (tsīt′gā′bər), *n.* an environmental cue, as ..he length of daylight or the degree of temperature, that ..elps to regulate the cycles of an organism's biological ..lock. [1970–75; < G (1954), lit., time-giver, on the ..nodel of *Taktgeber* an electronic synchronization device]

..eit•geist (tsīt′gīst′), *n. German.* the spirit of the ..ime; general characteristics of a particular period.

..eke (zēk), *n.* a male given name, form of **Ezekiel.**

..el•da (zel′də), *n.* a female given name, form of **Gri-..selda.**

..e•le•no•grad (zyi lyi nu grät′; *Eng.* zə lē′nə grad′), ... a city in the NW RSFSR, in central Soviet Union in ..urope, NW of Moscow. 127,000.

..e•lig (zē′lig, zel′ig), *n.* a male given name: from a ..ermanic word meaning "blessed."

..el•ko•va (zel′kə və, zel kō′-), *n.* any of several trees ..f the genus *Zelkova,* native to Asia, related to and ..esembling the elms. [< NL (1841) < Russ *dzél′kva,* ..zél′kova, presumably < a language of Transcaucasia, ..here the tree is native]

..el•os (zel′os), *n.* the ancient Greek personification of ..eal or emulation: the son of the Titan Pallas and of ..tyx, and the brother of Bia, Cratus, and Nike.

..e•min•dar (zə mēn där′), *n.* zamindar.

..e•mi•roth (*Seph.* zə mē rôt′; *Ashk.* zə mi′rōs, zmi′-..əs), *n.pl. Hebrew.* traditional songs sung by Jews dur-..ng Sabbath meals. Also, **ze•mi•rot′.** [*zəmirōth* songs, ..ymns]

..em•stvo (zemst′vō; *Russ.* zyem′stvə), *n., pl.* **zem-..stvos** (zemst′vōz). *Russ. Hist.* one of a system of ..lected local assemblies established in 1864 by Alexander ..I to administer local affairs after the abolition of serf-..dom: became the core of the liberal movement from 1905 ..o 1917. [1860–65; < Russ *zémstvo,* deriv. of *zemlyá* ..and, earth; see HUMUS]

..em•zem (zem′zem), *n. Islam.* the sacred well located ..near the Ka'ba at Mecca.

..en (zen), *n.* **1.** Chinese, **Ch'an.** *Buddhism.* a Maha-..yana movement, introduced into China in the 6th cen-..tury A.D. and into Japan in the 12th century, that em-..phasizes enlightenment for the student by the most ..direct possible means, accepting formal studies and ob-..servances only when they form part of such means. Cf. ..koan, mondo. **2.** the discipline and practice of this sect. ..Also called **Zen Buddhism.** [< Japn < MChin, equiv. to ..Chin *chán,* transliteration of Pali *jhāna* < Skt *dhyāna*] ..—**Zen′ic,** *adj.*

..e•na•na (ze nä′nə), *n.* (in India) **1.** the part of the ..house in which the women and girls of a family are se-..cluded. **2.** its occupants collectively. [1755–65; < Hindi ..< Pers *zanāna,* female, pertaining to women, adj. deriv. ..of *zan* woman; c. Skt *jani* woman, wife, Gk *gynḗ,* OCS ..žena, OE *cwēn* woman, wife; see QUEEN]

..en′ Bud′dhism, Zen. —**Zen′ Bud′dhist.**

..end (zend), *n.* **1.** *Zoroastrianism.* a translation and ..exposition of the Avesta in Pahlavi. **2.** *Archaic.* Avestan ..(def. 1). [1690–1700; see ZEND-AVESTA] —**Zend′ic,** *adj.*

..end-A•ves•ta (zend′ə ves′tə), *n. Zoroastrianism.* the ..Avesta together with the Zend. [< Pahlavi *avastāk-u-..zend* the text and its interpretation]

..en•do (zen′dō), *n., pl.* **-dos.** the meditation room of a ..Zen monastery. [1955–60; < Japn *zendō,* equiv. to *zen* ZEN + *-dō* (earlier *dau, daū* < MChin, equiv. to Chin *táng* hall, meeting hall; cf. TONG[2])]

ze′ner di′ode (zē′nər), *Electronics.* a semiconductor diode across which the reverse voltage remains almost constant over a wide range of currents, used esp. to regulate voltage. Also, **Ze′ner di′ode.** [1955–60; after U.S. physicist Clarence Melvin Zener (born 1905)]

Zeng•er (zeng′ər, -gər), *n.* **John Peter,** 1697–1746, American journalist, printer, and publisher, born in Germany: his libel trial and eventual acquittal (1735) set a precedent for establishing freedom of the press in America.

Zeng Guo•fan (*Chin.* zung′ gwô′fän′), *Pinyin.* See **Tseng Kuo-fan.**

Ze•ni•a (zē′nē ə, zēn′yə), *n.* a female given name: from a Greek word meaning "hospitality."

Zen•ist (zen′ist), *n.* a person who advocates or practices Zen. [ZEN + -IST]

ze•nith (zē′nith *or, esp. Brit.,* zen′ith), *n.* **1.** the point on the celestial sphere vertically above a given position or observer. Cf. **nadir.** **2.** a highest point or state; culmination. [1350–1400; ME *cenith* < ML < OSp *zenit,* scribal error for *zemt* < Ar *samt* road, incorrectly read as *senit* by medieval scribes (cf. Ar *samt ar-rās* road above (over) one's head, the opposite of *nadir*)] —**Syn. 2.** apex, summit. —**Ant. 1, 2.** nadir.

ze•nith•al (zē′nə thəl *or, esp. Brit.,* zen′ə-), *adj.* **1.** of or pertaining to the zenith; situated at or near the zenith. **2.** (of a map) drawn to indicate the actual direction of any point from the center point. [1855–60; ZENITH + -AL[1]]

ze′nithal equidis′tant projec′tion. See **azimuthal equidistant projection.**

ze′nith dis′tance, *Astron.* the angular distance from the zenith of a point on the celestial sphere to the sphere, measured along a great circle that is perpendicular to the horizon; the complement of the altitude. [1595–1705]

ze′nith tube′, *Astron.* a telescope mounted to point only at the zenith, used at some observatories for measuring time by the stars. Also called **ze′nith tel′escope.** [1830–40]

Ze•no (zē′nō), *n.* **1.** See **Zeno of Citium.** **2.** See **Zeno of Elea.**

Ze•no•bi•a (zə nō′bē ə), *n.* **1.** (*Septimia Bathzabbai*) died after A.D. 272, queen of Palmyra in Syria A.D. 267–272. **2.** a female given name.

Ze′no of Ci′ti•um (sish′ē əm), c340–c265 B.C., Greek philosopher, born in Cyprus. Also called **Zeno, Ze′no the Sto′ic.**

Ze′no of E′lea, c490–c430 B.C., Greek philosopher. Also called **Zeno.**

Ze′no's par′adox, *Math.* any of various versions of a paradox regarding the relation of the discrete to the continuous and requiring the concept of limit for its satisfactory explanation. [after ZENO OF ELEA]

ze•o•lite (zē′ə līt′), *n. Mineral.* any of a group of hydrated silicates of aluminum with alkali metals, commonly occurring as secondary minerals in cavities in basic volcanic rocks: used for their molecular sieve properties because they undergo dehydration with little or no change in crystal structure. [1770–80; < Gk *ze(in)* to boil + -o- + -LITE] —**ze•o•lit•ic** (zē′ə lit′ik), *adj.*

Zeph., Zephaniah.

Zeph•a•ni•ah (zef′ə nī′ə), *n.* **1.** a Minor Prophet of the 7th century B.C. **2.** a book of the Bible bearing his name. *Abbr.:* Zeph.

Zeph•i•ran (zef′ə ran′), *Trademark.* a brand of benzalkonium chloride.

zeph•yr (zef′ər), *n.* **1.** a gentle, mild breeze. **2.** (*cap.*) *Literary.* the west wind. **3.** any of various things of fine, light quality, as fabric, yarn, etc. [bef. 1000 for def. 2; ME < L *zephyrus* < Gk *zéphyros* the west wind; r. ME *zeferus, zephirus,* OE *zefferus* < L as above] —**Syn. 1.** See **wind**[1].

zeph•yr•an•thes (zef′ə ran′thēz), *n.* any of various bulbous plants belonging to the genus *Zephyranthes,* of the amaryllis family, as *Z. grandiflora,* having showy rose or pink flowers. Also called **fairy lily, zeph′yr lil′y.** [< NL < Gk *zéphyr(os)* ZEPHYR + *-anthēs* having flowers of the given kind, deriv. of *ánthos* flower]

zeph′yr cloth′, a lightweight worsted cloth. [1855–60]

zeph•yr•e•an (zef′ə rē′ən), *adj.* of, pertaining to, or like a zephyr; full of or containing light breezes. Also, **ze•phyr•i•an** (zi fēr′ē ən), **zeph•yr•ous** (zef′ər əs). [1830–40; ZEPHYR + -EAN]

Zeph•y•ri•nus (zef′ə rī′nəs), *n.* **Saint,** pope A.D. 198?–217.

Zeph•y•rus (zef′ər əs), *n. Class. Myth.* the west wind personified. Also, **Zeph•y•ros** (zef′ə ros′).

zeph′yr wor′sted, lightweight worsted yarn. [1860–65]

zeph′yr yarn′, any of various soft, lightweight yarns, often of silk, rayon, or a combination of natural and synthetic fibers, for woven and knit goods. [1860–65]

zep•pe•lin (zep′ə lin), *n.* **1.** (*often cap.*) a large dirigible balloon consisting of a long, cylindrical, covered framework containing compartments or cells filled with gas, and of various structures for holding the engines, passengers, etc. **2.** any rigid airship or dirigible. [1900; after Count von ZEPPELIN]

zeppelin (def. 1)

Zep•pe•lin (tsep′ə lēn′, tsep′ə lēn′; *Eng.* zep′ə lin), *n.* **Count Fer•di•nand von** (fer′di nänt′ fən), 1838–1917, German general and aeronaut: designer and manufacturer of the zeppelin.

Zer•matt (*Ger.* tser mät′), *n.* a village in S Switzerland, near the Matterhorn: resort. 3101; 5315 ft. (1620 m) above sea level.

Zer′me•lo's ax′iom (tser′mə lōz′), *Math.* See **axiom of choice.** [after Ernst E.F. *Zermelo* (1871–1953), German mathematician]

Zer•ni•ke (zâr′ni kə, zûr′-; *Du.* zer′ni kə), *n.* **Frits** (frits; *Du.* frits), 1888–1966, Dutch physicist: Nobel prize 1953.

ze•ro (zēr′ō), *n., pl.* **-ros, -roes,** *v.,* **-roed, -ro•ing,** *adj.* —*n.* **1.** the figure or symbol 0, which in the Arabic notation for numbers stands for the absence of quantity; cipher. **2.** the origin of any kind of measurement; line or point from which all divisions of a scale, as a thermometer, are measured in either a positive or a negative direction. **3.** a mathematical value intermediate between positive and negative values. **4.** naught; nothing. **5.** the lowest point or degree. **6.** *Ling.* the absence of a linguistic element, as a phoneme or morpheme, in a position in which one previously existed or might by analogy be expected to exist, often represented by the symbol Ø: *Inflectional endings were reduced to zero. The alternant of the plural morpheme in "sheep" is zero.* **7.** *Ordn.* a sight setting for both elevation and windage on any particular range causing a projectile to strike the center of the target on a normal day, under favorable light conditions, with no wind blowing. **8.** *Math.* **a.** the identity element of a group in which the operation is addition. **b.** (of a function, esp. of a function of a complex variable) a point at which a given function, usually a function of a complex variable, has the value zero; a root. **9.** (*cap.*) a single-engine Japanese fighter plane used in World War II. —*v.t.* **10.** to adjust (an instrument or apparatus) to a zero point or to an arbitrary reading from which all other readings are to be measured. **11.** to reduce to zero. **12.** *Slang.* to kill (a congressional bill, appropriation, etc.): *The proposed tax increase has been zeroed for the time being.* **13. zero in,** to aim (a rifle, etc.) at the precise center or range of a target. **14. zero in on, a.** to aim directly at (a target). **b.** to direct one's attention to; focus on; concentrate on. **c.** to converge on; close in on. —*adj.* **15.** amounting to zero: *a zero score.* **16.** having no measurable quantity or magnitude; not any: *zero economic growth.* **17.** *Ling.* noting a hypothetical morphological element that is posited as existing by analogy with a regular pattern of inflection or derivation in a language, but is not represented by any sequence of phonological elements: *the zero allomorph of "-ed" in "cut"; "Deer" has a zero plural.* **18.** *Meteorol.* **a.** (of an atmospheric ceiling) pertaining to or limiting vertical visibility to 50 ft. (15.2 m) or less. **b.** of, pertaining to, or limiting horizontal visibility to 165 ft. (50.3 m) or less. **19.** *Finance.* zero-coupon. **20.** being or pertaining to the precise time when something must or does happen, as the explosion of a nuclear weapon. [1595–1605; < It < ML *zephirum* < Ar *ṣifr* CIPHER]

ze•ro-base (zēr′ō bās′), *adj., v.,* **-based, -bas•ing.** —*adj.* **1.** Also, **ze′ro-based′.** without reference to a base figure or to previous practice; according to present needs only, as opposed to a percentage increase or decrease of previous figures: *zero-base planning; zero-base inventory.* —*v.t.* **2.** to apply zero-base methods to. [1965–70]

ze′ro-base budg′eting, a process in government and corporate finance of justifying an overall budget or individual budgeted items each fiscal year or each review period rather than dealing only with proposed changes from a previous budget. *Abbr.:* ZBB Also, **ze′ro-based budg′eting.** [1970]

ze•ro-cou•pon (zēr′ō kōō′pon, -kyōō′-), *adj.* of or pertaining to a debt obligation that bears no interest but that is sold substantially below its face value. [1975–80]

ze′ro de′fects, quality control that strives for a perfect production process.

ze•ro-di•vi•sor (zēr′ō di vī′zər), *n. Math.* a nonzero element of a ring such that its product with some other nonzero element of the ring equals zero.

ze′ro grav′ity, *Physics.* the condition in which the apparent effect of gravity is zero, as in the case of a body in free fall or in orbit. Also, **ze•ro-g, ze•ro-G** (zēr′ō jē′).

ze′ro hour′, **1.** the time set for the beginning of a military attack or operation. **2.** the time set for the beginning of any event or action. **3.** a decisive or critical time. [1915–20]

ze′ro-point en′ergy (zēr′ō point′), *Physics.* energy in a substance at the temperature of absolute zero. [1930–35]

ze′ro popula′tion growth′, the maintenance of a population at a constant level by limiting the number of live births to that needed to replace the existing population. [1965–70]

ze•ro-sum (zēr′ō sum′), *adj.* of or denoting a system in which the sum of the gains equals the sum of the losses: *a zero-sum economy.* [1955–60]

ze′ro-sum game′, *Math.* a game in which the sum of the winnings and losses of the various players is always zero, the losses being counted negatively. [1940–45]

ze•roth (zēr′ōth), *adj.* coming in a series before the first: *the zeroth level of energy.* [1895–1900; ZERO + -TH[2]]

ze′roth law′ of thermodynam′ics (zēr′ōth), the principle that any two systems in thermal equilibrium

CONCISE PRONUNCIATION KEY: act, cāpe, dâre, pärt; set, ēqual; *if,* īce; ox, ōver, ôrder, oil, bŏŏk, bōōt, out; up, ûrge; child; sing; shoe; thin, *that;* zh as in *treasure.* ə = *a* as in *alone,* *e* as in *system,* *i* as in *easily,* *o* as in *gallop,* *u* as in *circus;* ᵊ as in *fire* (fīᵊr), *hour* (ouᵊr). l and n can serve as syllabic consonants, as in *cradle* (krād′l), and *button* (but′n). See the full key inside the front cover.

with a third system are in thermal equilibrium with each other. Cf. **law of thermodynamics** (def. 2). [1955–60]

ze′ro till′age, no-tillage. Also, **ze′ro-till′.** [1960–65]

ze′ro vec′tor, *Math.* a vector of which all the components are zero. [1900–05]

ze·ro-ze·ro (zēr′ō zēr′ō), *adj. Meteorol.* (of atmospheric conditions) having or characterized by zero visibility in both horizontal and vertical directions. [1935–40]

Ze·rub·ba·bel (zə rub′ə bəl), *n.* a leader of the Jews on their return to Jerusalem after the Babylonian captivity. Ezra 2:1, 2; 3:2–13. Also, **Zorobabel.**

Zer·van (zûr′vən), *n.* Zurvan.

Zer·van·ism (zûr′və niz′əm), *n.* Zurvanism. —**Zer′·van·ite′,** *n.*

zest (zest), *n.* **1.** keen relish; hearty enjoyment; gusto. **2.** an agreeable or piquant flavor imparted to something. **3.** anything added to impart flavor, enhance one's appreciation, etc. **4.** piquancy; interest; charm. **5.** liveliness or energy; animating spirit. **6.** the peel, esp. the thin outer peel, of a citrus fruit used for flavoring: *lemon zest.* —*v.t.* **7.** to give zest, relish, or piquancy to. [1665–75; < F *zest* (now *zeste*) orange or lemon peel used for flavoring < ?] —**zest′less,** *adj.*
—**Syn. 4.** spice, tang.

zest·ful (zest′fəl), *adj.* **1.** full of zest. **2.** characterized by keen relish, hearty enjoyment, etc. [1840–50; ZEST + -FUL] —**zest′ful·ly,** *adv.* —**zest′ful·ness,** *n.*

zest·y (zes′tē), *adj.,* **zest·i·er, zest·i·est. 1.** full of zest; piquant: *a zesty salad dressing.* **2.** energetic; active: *zesty trading in growth stocks.* [1925–30; ZEST + -Y[1]]

ze·ta (zā′tə, zē′-), *n.* **1.** the sixth letter of the Greek alphabet (Z, ζ). **2.** the consonant sound represented by this letter. [1820–30; < Gk *zêta*]

Ze·thar (zē′thär), *n.* one of the seven eunuchs who served in the court of King Ahasuerus. Esther 1:10.

Zet·land (zet′lənd), *n.* former name of **Shetland Islands.**

zeug·ma (zo͞og′mə), *n. Gram., Rhet.* the use of a word to modify or govern two or more words when it is appropriate to only one of them or is appropriate to each but in a different way, as in *to wage war and peace* or *On his fishing trip, he caught three trout and a cold.* Cf. **syllepsis.** [1515–25; < Gk *zeûgma* a yoking, equiv. to *zeug(nýnai)* to YOKE[1] + *-ma* n. suffix of result] —**zeug·mat·ic** (zo͞og mat′ik), *adj.* —**zeug·mat′i·cal·ly,** *adv.*

Zeus (zo͞os), *n.* the supreme deity of the ancient Greeks, a son of Cronus and Rhea, brother of Demeter, Hades, Hera, Hestia, and Poseidon, and father of a number of gods, demigods, and mortals; the god of the heavens, identified by the Romans with Jupiter.

Zeux·is (zo͞ok′sis), *n.* fl. c430–c400 B.C., Greek painter.

Zhang·jia·kou (jäng′jyä′kō′), *n. Pinyin.* a city in NW Hebei province, in NE China: capital of the former Qahar province. 1,000,000. Also, **Changchiak'ou.** Also called **Kalgan.** Formerly, **Wanchüan.**

Zhang·zhou (jäng′jō′), *n. Pinyin.* a city in S Fujian province, in SE China. 300,000. Also, **Changchou.** Formerly, **Longxi.**

Zhang Zuo·lin (*Chin.* jäng′ zwô′lin′), *Pinyin.* See **Chang Tso-lin.**

Zhao Kuang·yin (*Chin.* jou′ kwäng′yin′), *Pinyin.* See **Chao K'uang-yin.**

Zhao Zi·yang (jou′ zœ′yäng′), born 1919, Chinese Communist leader: premier 1980–87; general secretary of the Communist Party 1987–89.

Zhda·nov (zhdä′nəf), *n.* former name (1948–89) of **Mariupol.**

Zhe·jiang (jœ′jyäng′), *n. Pinyin.* a province in E China, on the East China Sea. 28,320,000; 39,768 sq. mi. (102,999 sq. km). *Cap.:* Hangzhou. Also, **Chekiang.**

Zheng·zhou (jœng′jō′), *n. Pinyin.* a city in and the capital of Henan province, in E China. 1,500,000. Also, **Chengchow.**

Zhen·jiang (jœn′jyäng′), *n. Pinyin.* a port in S Jiangsu province, in E China, on the Chang Jiang. 250,000. Also, **Chenchiang, Chinkiang.**

Zhi·fu (*Chin.* jœ′fy′), *n. Pinyin.* former name of **Yantai.** Also, **Chefoo.**

Zhi·to·mir (zhi tô′myir), *n.* a city in central Ukraine, W of Kiev. 244,000.

Zhiv·kov (zhif′kôf), *n.* **To·dor** (tô′dôr), born 1911, Bulgarian political leader: prime minister 1962–71, president 1971–89.

zhlob (zhlôb, zhlub), *n. Slang.* a clumsy, stupid person. Also, **zhlub, schlub.** [< Yiddish *zhlob, zhlub* yokel, boor < Pol *żłób* (gen. *żłoba*) blockhead, lit., trough, manger, c. Czech *žlab,* Russ *zhëlob* gutter, channel]

Zhou (*Chin.* jō), *n. Pinyin.* Chou.

Zhou En·lai (jō′ en lī′; *Chin.* jō′ un′lī′), 1898–1976, Chinese Communist leader: premier 1949–76. Also, **Chou En-lai.**

Zhou·kou·dian (jō′gō′dyän′), *n.* **1.** the site of fossil-bearing caves near Peking, China, dating from the middle Pleistocene, in one of which were found the physical remains of Peking man together with stone tools and evidence of fire use. **2.** a chopper and flake stone-tool industry of the middle Pleistocene found at this site. Also, **Choukoutien.**

CONCISE ETYMOLOGY KEY: <, descended or borrowed from; >, whence; b., blend of, blended; c., cognate with; cf., compare; deriv., derivative; equiv., equivalent; imit., imitative; obl., oblique; r., replacing; s., stem; sp., spelling, spelled; resp., respelling, respelled; trans., translation; ?, origin unknown; *, unattested; ‡, probably earlier than. See the full key inside the front cover.

Zhuang·zi (*Chin.* zhyäng′zœ′), *n. Pinyin.* Chuang-tzu.

Zhu De (jo͞o′ du′), 1886–1976, Chinese military and Communist leader.

Zhu Jiang (jy′ jyäng′), *Pinyin.* a river in SE China, in S Guangdong province, flowing E and S from Canton and forming an estuary near Hong Kong. ab. 110 mi. (177 km) long. Also, **Chu Kiang.** Also called **Canton River, Pearl River.**

Zhu·kov (zho͞o′kəf), *n.* **Ge·or·gi Kon·stan·ti·no·vich** (gyi ôr′gyē kən stun tyē′nə vyich), 1896–1974, Russian marshal.

Zhu Xi (jy′ shē′), *Pinyin.* See **Chu Hsi.**

Zhu·zhou (jy′jō′), *n. Pinyin.* a city in NE Hunan province, in SE China. 350,000. Also, **Chuchow.**

ZI, *Mil.* Zone of the Interior.

Zi·a-ul-Haq (zē′ä o͝ol häk′), *n.* **Mohammed,** 1924–88, Pakistani army general and political leader: president 1978–88.

zib·el·ine (zib′ə līn′, -lēn′, -lin), *adj.* **1.** of or pertaining to the sable. —*n.* **2.** the fur of the sable. **3.** a thick woolen cloth with a flattened hairy nap. Also, **zib′el·line′.** [1575–85; < MF < It *zibellino,* ult. from the same source as SABLE; cf. OF, OPr *sebelin*]

zib·et (zib′it), *n.* a civet, *Viverra zibetha,* of India, the Malay Peninsula, and other parts of Asia. [1585–95; < ML *zibethum* or It *zibetto* < Ar *zabād;* see CIVET]

Zi·bo (zœ′bō′), *n. Pinyin.* a city in central Shandong province, in NE China. 806,000. Also, **Tzepo, Tzupo.**

Zid·ki·jah (zid kī′jə), *n.* Zedekiah (def. 1).

zi·do·vu·dine (zī dō′vyo͞o dēn′), *n. Pharm.* the international generic term for azidothymidine. Cf. **AZT.**

Zieg·feld (zig′feld), *n.* **Flor·enz** (flôr′ənz, flor′-), 1867–1932, U.S. theatrical producer.

Zie·gler (zē′glər; *Ger.* tsē′glər), *n.* **Karl** (kärl; *Ger.* kärl), 1897–1973, German chemist: Nobel prize 1963.

Zif (zif), *n. Chiefly Biblical.* Ziv.

zig (zig), *v.i.,* **zigged, zig·ging.** to move in one of the two directions followed in a zigzag course: *He zigged when he should have zagged.* [1785–95; extracted from ZIGZAG]

zig·gu·rat (zig′o͝o rat′), *n.* (among the ancient Babylonians and Assyrians) a temple of Sumerian origin in the form of a pyramidal tower, consisting of a number of stories and having about the outside a broad ascent winding round the structure, presenting the appearance of a series of terraces. Also, **zik·ku·rat, zik·u·rat** (zik′o͝o rat′). [1875–80; < Akkadian *ziqqurratu*]

Zi·gong (zœ′gông′), *n. Pinyin.* a city in S Sichuan province, in central China. 350,000. Also, **Tzekung, Tzukung.**

Zi·guin·chor (*Fr.* zē gan shôr′), *n.* a seaport in SW Senegal. 45,772.

zig·zag (zig′zag′), *n., adj., adv., v.,* **-zagged, -zag·ging.** —*n.* **1.** a line, course, or progression characterized by sharp turns first to one side and then to the other. **2.** one of a series of such turns, as in a line or path. —*adj.* **3.** proceeding or formed in a zigzag: *zigzag stitches.* —*adv.* **4.** with frequent sharp turns from side to side; in a zigzag manner: *The child ran zigzag along the beach.* —*v.t.* **5.** to make (something) zigzag, as in form or course; move or maneuver (something) in a zigzag direction: *They zigzagged their course to confuse the enemy.* —*v.i.* **6.** to proceed in a zigzag line or course. [1705–15; < F; r. earlier *ziczac* < F < G *zickzack,* gradational compound based on *Zacke* TACK[1]] —**zig·zag′ged·ness** (zig′zag′id nis), *n.*

zig·zag·ger (zig′zag′ər), *n.* **1.** a person or thing that zigzags. **2.** an attachment on a sewing machine for making zigzag stitches. [ZIGZAG + -ER[1]]

zig′zag rule′, a rule composed of light strips of wood joined by rivets so as to be foldable, all the opening and closing parts being in parallel planes. Also called **folding rule.**

zikr (zik′ər), *n. Islam.* dhikr.

zilch (zilch), *n. Slang.* zero; nothing: *The search came up with zilch.* [1965–70, *Amer.*; perh. continuous with earlier *zilch* snafu, *Mr. Zilch* a character in *Ballyhoo,* a humor magazine first published in 1931; for sense cf. ZIP[3]]

zil·lah (zil′ə), *n.* (in British India) any of the districts into which a province was divided for administrative purposes. [1790–1800; < Hindi *zila* < Pers *ẓila'* < Ar *ḍil'* part]

Zil·lah (zil′ə), *n.* one of the two wives of Lamech. Gen. 4:19.

zil·lion (zil′yən), *n., pl.* **-lions,** (*as after a numeral*) **-lion,** *adj. Informal.* —*n.* **1.** an extremely large, indeterminate number. —*adj.* **2.** of, pertaining to, or amounting to a zillion. [1930–35; jocular alter. of *million, billion,* etc.]

zil·lion·aire (zil′yə nâr′), *n. Informal.* a person of incalculably great wealth. [1945–50; ZILLION + (MILLION)-AIRE]

Zil·pah (zil′pə), *n.* the mother of Gad and Asher. Gen. 30:10–13.

zi·mar·ra (zi mär′ə), *n. Rom. Cath. Ch.* a cassock with a small cape attached. Also called **simar.** [< It; see SIMAR]

Zim·bab·we (zim bäb′wā, -wē), *n.* **1.** Formerly, **Southern Rhodesia, Rhodesia.** a republic in S Africa: a former British colony and part of the Federation of Rhodesia and Nyasaland; gained independence 1980. 7,200,000; 150,330 sq. mi. (389,362 sq. km). *Cap.:* Harare. **2.** the site of stone ruins **(Great Zimbabwe)** discovered c1870 in Rhodesia, probably built by a Bantu people, consisting of three main groups of ruins, and dating between the 9th and 15th centuries A.D. —**Zim·bab′we·an,** *adj., n.*

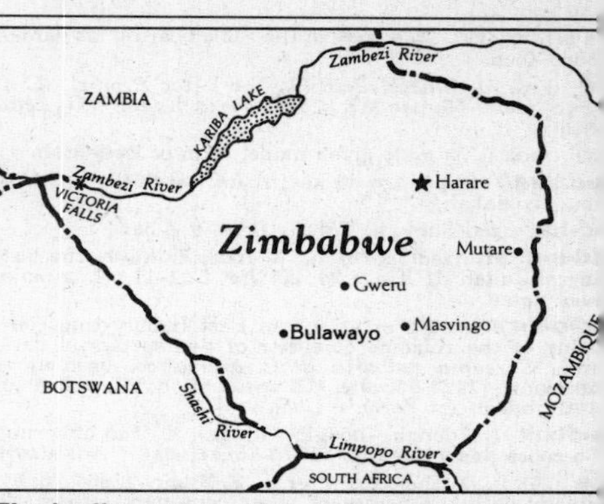

Zim·ba·list (zim′bə list) *n.* **1. Ef·rem** (ef′rəm), 1889–1985, U.S. violinist and composer, born in Russia. **2.** his son, **Efrem, Jr.,** born 1923, U.S. actor.

zim·ba·lon (zim′bə lon′), *n.* cymbalom.

zinc (zingk), *n., v.,* **zincked** or **zinced** (zingkt), **zincking** or **zinc·ing** (zing′king). —*n.* **1.** *Chem.* a ductile bluish-white metallic element: used in making galvanized iron, brass, and other alloys, and as an element in voltaic cells. *Symbol:* Zn; *at. wt.:* 65.37; *at. no.:* 30; *sp. gr.* 7.14 at 20°C. **2.** a piece of this metal used as an element in a voltaic cell. —*v.t.* **3.** to coat or cover with zinc. [1635–45; < G *Zink,* perh. deriv. of *Zinke(n)* prong, tine, from the spikelike form it takes in a furnace] —**zinck·y, zinc′y, zink′y,** *adj.* —**zinc′oid,** *adj.*

zinc·ate (zing′kāt), *n. Chem.* a salt derived from H_2ZnO_2, the acid form of amphoteric zinc hydroxide. [1870–75; ZINC + -ATE[2]]

zinc′ blende′, *Mineral.* sphalerite. [1835–45]

zinc′ chlo′ride, *Chem.* a white, crystalline, deliquescent, water-soluble, poisonous solid, $ZnCl_2$, used chiefly as a wood preservative, as a disinfectant and antiseptic, and in the manufacture of vulcanized fiber, parchment paper, and soldering fluxes. [1880–85]

zinc′ green′. See **cobalt green** (def. 2). [1945–50]

zinc·ic (zing′kik), *adj.* pertaining to or containing zinc. [1855–60; ZINC + -IC]

zinc·if·er·ous (zing kif′ər əs, zin sif′-), *adj.* yielding or containing zinc. [1810–20; ZINC + -I- + -FEROUS]

zinc·i·fy (zing′kə fī′), *v.t.,* **-fied, -fy·ing.** to cover or impregnate with zinc. [1795–1805; ZINC + -I- + -FY] —**zinc′i·fi·ca′tion,** *n.*

zinc·ite (zing′kīt), *n.* a brittle, deep-red to orange-yellow mineral, native zinc oxide, ZnO, usually massive or granular: formerly an important ore of zinc. Also called **red oxide of zinc.** [1850–55; ZINC + -ITE[1]]

zinck·en·ite (zing′kə nīt′), *n. Mineral.* zinkenite.

zin·co·graph (zing′kə graf′, -gräf′), *n.* **1.** (formerly) a zinc plate produced by zincography. **2.** a print from such a plate. [1885–90; ZINC + -O- + -GRAPH]

zin·cog·ra·phy (zing kog′rə fē), *n.* the art or process of producing a printing surface on a zinc plate, esp. of producing one in relief by etching away unprotected parts with acid. [1825–35; ZINC + -O- + -GRAPHY] —**zin·cog′ra·pher,** *n.* —**zin·co·graph·ic** (zing′kə graf′ik), **zin′co·graph′i·cal,** *adj.*

zinc′ oint′ment, *Pharm.* an ointment composed of mineral oil and zinc oxide, used in medicine in the treatment of skin conditions. [1835–45]

zinc·ous (zing′kəs), *adj.* zincic. [1835–45; ZINC + -OUS]

zinc′ ox′ide, *Chem., Pharm.* a white or yellowish white, amorphous, odorless, water-insoluble powder, ZnO, used chiefly as a paint pigment, in cosmetics, dental cements, matches, white printing inks, and opaque glass, and in the treatment of skin conditions. Also called **flowers of zinc, zinc′ white′.** [1840–50]

zinc′ phos′phide, *Chem.* a dark-gray, gritty, water-insoluble, poisonous powder, Zn_3P_2, used chiefly as a rodenticide.

zinc′ ste′arate, *Chem.* a white, fine, soft, water-insoluble powder, $Zn(C_{18}H_{35}O_2)_2$, used in the manufacture of cosmetics, ointments, and lacquers, as a drying agent for rubber, and as a waterproofing agent for textiles, paper, etc.

zinc′ sul′fate, *Chem.* a colorless, crystalline, water-soluble powder, $ZnSO_4{\cdot}7H_2O$, used for preserving skins and wood, in the electrodeposition of zinc, in the bleaching of paper, as a mordant in calico printing, and in medicine as an astringent, styptic, and emetic. Also called **white vitriol, zinc′ vit′riol.** [1850–55]

zinc′ sul′fide, *Chem.* a white to yellow, crystalline powder, ZnS, soluble in acids, insoluble in water, occurring naturally as wurtzite and sphalerite: used as a pigment and as a phosphor on x-ray and television screens. [1880–85]

Zin·der (zin′dər), *n.* a city in S Niger. 39,000.

'zine or **zine** (zēn), *n.* fanzine. [by shortening]

zin·eb (zin′eb), *n.* a light tan, water-insoluble compound, $C_4H_6N_2S_4Zn$, used as a fungicide for fruits and vegetables. [1945–50; *zin(c)e(thylene) b(isdithiocarbamate)* an alternate chemical name]

zin·fan·del (zin′fən del′), *n.* **1.** a black vinifera grape, grown in California. **2.** a dry red wine made from this grape in California. [1895–1900; orig. uncert.]

zing (zing), *n.* **1.** vitality, animation, or zest. **2.** a quality or characteristic that excites the interest, enthusiasm, etc.: *a tourist town with lots of zing.* **3.** a sharp singing or whining noise, as of a bullet passing through the air. —*v.i.* **4.** to move or proceed with a sharp singing or whining noise: *The cars zinged down the highway.* **5.** to move or proceed with speed or vitality; zip. —*v.t.* **6.** to cause to move with or as with a sharp, singing or whining noise: *The pitcher zinged a slider right over the plate.* **7.** *Slang.* to blame or criticize severely: *City Hall always gets zinged when crime increases.* [1910–15; imit.]

zin·ga·ra (tsēng′gä rä) *n., pl.* ***-re*** (-re). *Italian.* a female Gypsy.

zin·ga·ro (tsēng′gä rô), *n., pl.* ***-ri*** (-rē). *Italian.* a Gypsy.

zing·er (zing′ər), *n. Informal.* **1.** a quick, witty, or pointed remark or retort: *During the debate she made a couple of zingers that deflated the opposition.* **2.** a surprise, shock, or piece of electrifying news: *The President's resignation was a real zinger.* **3.** a person or thing that has vitality or animation or produces startling results. [1950–55; ZING + -ER[1]]

zin·gi·ber·a·ceous (zin′jə bə rā′shəs), *adj.* belonging to the Zingiberaceae, the ginger family of plants. Also, **zinziberaceous.** Cf. **ginger family.** [1840–50; < NL *Zingiberac(ae)* family name (see GINGER, -ACEAE) + -OUS]

zing·y (zing′ē), *adj.* **zing·i·er, zing·i·est.** full of zing; lively; zesty; exciting: *a zingy new musical comedy.* Also, **zing′ing.** [1940–45; ZING + -Y[1]]

Zin·jan·thro·pus (zin jan′thrə pəs, zin′jan thrō′-), *n.* the genus to which *Australopithecus boisei* was formerly assigned. [< NL (1959) < Ar *zinj* East Africa + Gk *ánthrōpos* man]

zin·ken·ite (zing′kə nīt′), *n.* a steel-gray mineral with metallic luster, lead antimony sulfide, $Pb_6Sb_{14}S_{27}$. Also, **zinckenite.** [1825–35; < G *Zinkenit,* named after J. K. L. Zincken (1790–1862), German mineralogist and mining director; see -ITE[1]]

zin·ni·a (zin′ē ə), *n.* any of several composite plants of the genus *Zinnia,* native to Mexico and adjacent areas, esp. the widely cultivated species *Z. elegans,* having variously colored, many-rayed flower heads. [1760–70; < NL, named after J. G. Zinn (1727–59), German botanist; see -IA]

zinn·wald·ite (tsin′väl tīt′), *n. Mineral.* a yellow-brown variety of mica containing iron, found with tin ores. [1860–65; named after *Zinnwald,* village in Czechoslovakia where first found; see -ITE[1]]

Zi·no·viev (zi nō′vē ef′, -nov′yef; *Russ.* zyi nô′vyif), *n.* **Gri·go·ri Ev·se·e·vich** (gryi gô′ryĕ yif sye′yi vyich), 1883–1936, Russian Bolshevik leader.

Zi·no·vievsk (zi nō′vē efsk, -nov′yefsk; *Russ.* zyi nô′vyifsk), *n.* a former name of **Kirovograd.**

Zins·ser (zin′sər), *n.* **Hans** (hanz, hänz), 1878–1940, U.S. bacteriologist.

Zin·zen·dorf (tsin′tsən dôrf′), *n.* **Count Ni·ko·laus Lud·wig von** (nē′kō lous′ lōōt′vikh fən, lōōd′-), 1700–60, German religious leader: reformer and organizer of the Moravian Church.

zin·zi·ber·a·ceous (zin′zə bə rā′shəs), *adj.* zingiberaceous.

Zi·on (zī′ən), *n.* **1.** a hill in Jerusalem, on which the Temple was built (used to symbolize the city itself, esp. as a religious or spiritual center). **2.** the Jewish people. **3.** Palestine as the Jewish homeland and symbol of Judaism. **4.** heaven as the final gathering place of true believers. **5.** a city in NE Illinois. 17,861. Also, **Sion** (for defs. 1–4). [bef. 1000; < Heb *ṣiyyōn*; r. ME, OE *Sion* < LL (Vulgate) *Siōn* < Gk (Septuagint) *Seiṓn* < Heb, as above]

Zi·on·ism (zī′ə niz′əm), *n.* a worldwide Jewish movement that resulted in the establishment and development of the state of Israel. [1895–1900; ZION + -ISM] —**Zi′·on·ist,** *n., adj.* —**Zi′on·is′tic,** *adj.* —**Zi·on·ite** (zī′ə nīt′), *n.*

Zi′on Na′tional Park′, a park in SW Utah. 148 sq. mi. (383 sq. km).

zip[1] (zip), *n., v.,* **zipped, zip·ping.** —*n.* **1.** a sudden, brief hissing sound, as of a bullet. **2.** *Informal.* energy; vim; vigor. —*v.i.* **3.** to move with a zipping sound. **4.** *Informal.* to act or move with speed or energy: *I'll just zip upstairs.* —*v.t. Informal.* **5.** to convey with speed and energy: *I'll zip you downtown on my motorcycle.* **6.** to add vitality or zest to (usually fol. by *up*): *A little garlic zips up a salad.* [1850–55; of expressive orig.] —**Syn. 2.** pep, dash, verve, vivacity, vitality.

zip[2] (zip), *v.,* **zipped, zip·ping,** *n., adj.* —*v.t.* **1.** to fasten or unfasten with a zipper: *Zip your jacket. Zip open the traveling case.* **2.** to enclose or free by doing up or undoing a zipper: *Zip this money into your wallet.* —*v.i.* **3.** to become fastened or unfastened by means of a zipper: *a handy purse that zips shut.* **4.** to do up or undo a zipper. —*n.* **5.** a zipper. —*adj.* **6.** utilizing or having a zipper: *a coat with a zip front.* [1935–40, *Amer.*; back formation from ZIPPER] —**zip′less,** *adj.*

zip[3] (zip), *n., v.,* **zipped, zip·ping.** *Slang.* —*n.* **1.** zero or nothing: *The score of last night's hockey game was 4-zip.* —*v.t.* **2.** (in sports) to defeat by keeping an opponent from scoring: *The home team was zipped again yesterday.* [1895–1900; *Amer.*; appar. an expressive word, with *z-* of ZERO; cf. ZILCH]

zip[4] (zip), *n., v.,* **zipped, zip·ping.** *Informal.* —*n.* **1.** See **zip code.** —*v.t.* **2.** to zip-code. [by ellipsis]

zip′ code′, a system used in the U.S. to facilitate the delivery of mail, consisting of a five- or nine-digit code printed directly after the address, the first five digits **(initial code)** indicating the state and post office or postal zone, the last four **(expanded code)** the box section or number, portion of a rural route, building, or other specific delivery location. Also, **ZIP′ code′, Zip′ code′.** [1960–65, *Amer.*; Z(one) I(mprovement) P(rogram)]

zip-code (zip′kōd′), *v.t.,* **-cod·ed, -cod·ing.** to provide or mark with a zip code: *Zip-code all mail.* Also, **ZIP′-code′, Zip′-code′.**

zip′ fas′tener, *Brit.* a zipper. [1925–30]

zip′ gun′, a homemade pistol, typically consisting of a metal tube taped to a wooden stock and firing a .22-caliber bullet. [1945–50]

zip-in (zip′in′), *adj.* capable of being inserted or attached by means of a zipper: *a coat with a zip-in lining.* [1970–75; adj. use of v. phrase *zip in*]

Zip·loc (zip′lok′), *Trademark.* a brand of plastic bag made with interlocking ridges near the edges, so as to be easily closed or sealed by pressing one side of the opening against the other.

zip-out (zip′out′), *adj.* capable of being removed or detached by means of a zipper. [1960–65; adj. use of v. phrase *zip out*]

zip·per (zip′ər), *n.* **1.** Also called **slide fastener.** a device used for fastening clothing, valises, etc., consisting of two toothed tracks or spiral metal or plastic coils, each bordering one of two edges to be joined, and a piece that either interlocks or separates them when pulled. **2.** a person or thing that zips. **3.** a rubber and fabric boot or overshoe fastened up the leg by a zipper. **4.** a large illuminated display of news bulletins or advertisements that rapidly and continuously flash by on an upper part of a building. —*v.t., v.i.* **5.** zip[2]. [1920–25, *Amer.*; formerly a trademark; see ZIP[1], -ER[1]] —**zip′per·less,** *adj.*

zip·pered (zip′ərd), *adj.* fastened or fitted with a zipper or zippers: *zippered slipcovers.* [1940–45; ZIPPER + -ED[3]]

ZIP + 4 (zip′ plus′ fôr′, fōr′), a zip code of nine digits, used to facilitate accurate and prompt delivery of mail.

Zip·po·rah (zi pôr′ə, -pōr′ə, zip′ər ə), *n.* the daughter of Jethro and the wife of Moses. Ex. 2:21.

zip·py (zip′ē), *adj.,* **-pi·er, -pi·est.** *Informal.* lively; peppy. [1915–20; ZIP[1] + -Y[1]]

zi·ram (zī′ram), *n. Chem.* a white crystalline powder, $C_6H_{12}N_2S_4Zn$, almost insoluble in water, soluble in acetone and chloroform: used as a fungicide and rubber accelerator. [1945–50; *zi(nc dimethyl dithioca)r(b)am(ate)* an alternate chemical name]

Zir·co·loy (zûr′kə loi′), *Trademark.* a zirconium alloy used in structural elements or tubing in nuclear reactors.

zir·con (zûr′kon), *n.* a common mineral, zirconium silicate, $ZrSiO_4$, occurring in small tetragonal crystals or grains of various colors, usually opaque: used as a refractory when opaque and as a gem when transparent. [1785–95; < G *Zirkon;* see JARGON[2]]

zir·co·ni·um (zûr kō′nē əm), *n. Chem.* a metallic element found combined in zircon, baddeleyite, etc., resembling titanium chemically: used in steel metallurgy, as a scavenger, as a refractory, and as an opacifier in vitreous enamels. *Symbol:* Zr; *at. wt.:* 91.22; *at. no.:* 40; *sp. gr.:* 6.49 at 20°C. [1800–10; < NL; see ZIRCON, -IUM] —**zir·con·ic** (zûr kon′ik), *adj.*

zirco′nium ox′ide, *Chem.* a white, heavy, amorphous, infusible, water-insoluble powder, ZrO_2, used chiefly as a pigment for paints, an abrasive, and in the manufacture of refractory crucibles. Also called **zir·co·ni·a** (zûr kō′nē ə), **zirco′nium diox′ide.** [1865–70]

zir·co·nyl (zûr′kə nil), *adj. Chem.* containing the group ZrO=, as zirconyl bromide, $ZrOBr_2$. [ZIRCON + -YL]

Zis·ka (*Ger.* tsis′kä), *n.* **Jo·hann** (yō′hän). See **Žižka, Jan.**

zit (zit), *n. Slang.* a pimple; skin blemish. [1960–65; orig. uncert.]

zith·er (zith′ər, zith′-), *n.* a musical instrument, consisting of a flat sounding box with numerous strings stretched over it, that is placed on a horizontal surface and played with a plectrum and the fingertips. [1840–50; < G < L *cithara* < Gk *kithára;* see KITHARA] —**zith′er·ist,** *n.*

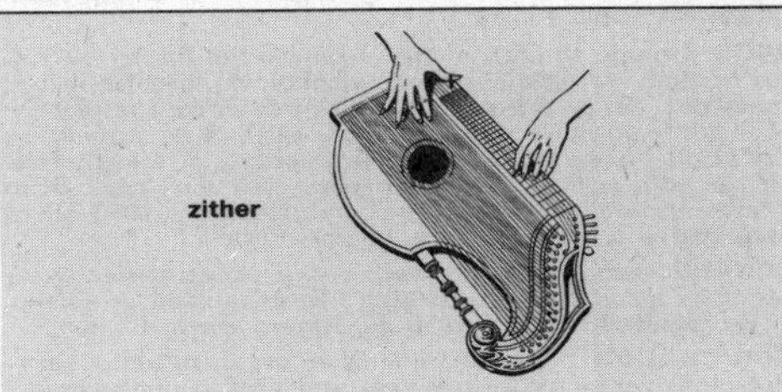
zither

zith·ern (zith′ərn, zith′-), *n.* **1.** cittern. **2.** zither.

zi·ti (zē′tē), *n. Italian Cookery.* a tubular pasta in short pieces, similar to rigatoni. Also, **zit′ti.** [1925–30; < It *zite, ziti,* pl. of *zita, zito,* of uncert. orig.]

zit·tern (zit′ərn), *n.* cittern.

Zi·u·su·dra (zē′ōō sōō′drə), *n.* a legendary Sumerian king who built a boat in which to escape the Deluge. Cf. **Atrahasis.**

Ziv (ziv; *Heb.* zēv), *n. Chiefly Biblical.* a month equivalent to Iyar of the modern Jewish calendar. I Kings 6:1. [< Heb: lit., radiance]

Zi·wiye (zē′wē), *n.* an ancient city in W Iran: large collection of ivory, gold, and bronze artifacts, dating from c675 to c600 B.C., found here in 1946. Also, **Zi·wi·ye** (zē′wē yə).

zi·zith (*Seph. Heb.* tsē tsēt′; *Ashk. Heb.* tsi′tsis), *n.* (*used with a singular or plural v.*) *Judaism.* the fringes or tassels formerly worn at the corners of the outer garment and now worn at the four corners of the tallith and the *arba kanfoth.* Also, **tzitzith.** [1895–1900; < Heb *ṣiṣith*]

Žiž·ka (*Czech.* zhish′kä), *n.* **Jan** (yän), c1370–1424, Bohemian Hussite military leader. German, **Ziska.**

Zl., zloty.

Zla·to·ust (zlə tu ōōst′), *n.* a city in the W Russian Federation in Asia, in the Ural Mountains. 198,000.

zlo·ty (zlô′tē), *n., pl.* **-tys,** (*collectively*) **-ty.** a nickel coin and monetary unit of Poland, equal to 100 groszy. *Abbr.:* Zl. [1915–20; < Pol *złoty* lit., of gold, golden, adj. deriv. of *złoto* GOLD]

Zn, *Symbol, Chem.* zinc.

Zna·nie·cki (znä nyets′kē), *n.* **Flo·ri·an** (flô rē′än), 1882–1958, Polish sociologist.

zo-, var. of **zoo-** before a vowel: *zooid.*

zo·a (zō′ə), *n.* pl. of **zoon.**

-zoa, a combining form meaning "animals," "organisms" of the kind specified by the initial element, used in the names of classes in zoology: *Protozoa.* [< NL < Gk *zôia,* pl. of *zôion* animal; see ZOON]

Zo·an (zō′an, -ən), *n.* Biblical name of **Tanis.**

zo·an·thro·py (zō an′thrə pē), *n. Psychiatry.* a mental disorder in which one believes oneself to be an animal. [1855–60; zo- + *-anthropy* < NL *-anthrōpia* < Gk; see ANTHROPO-, -Y[3]]

Zo·ar (zō′ər, -är), *n.* the city where Lot and his family took refuge during the destruction of Sodom and Gomorrah. Gen. 19:20–30.

zó·ca·lo (sô′kä lô′; *Eng.* sō′kə lō′), *n., pl.* ***-los*** (-lôs′; *Eng.* -lōz). *Mexican Spanish.* a public square or plaza, esp. in the center of a city or town.

zod., zodiac.

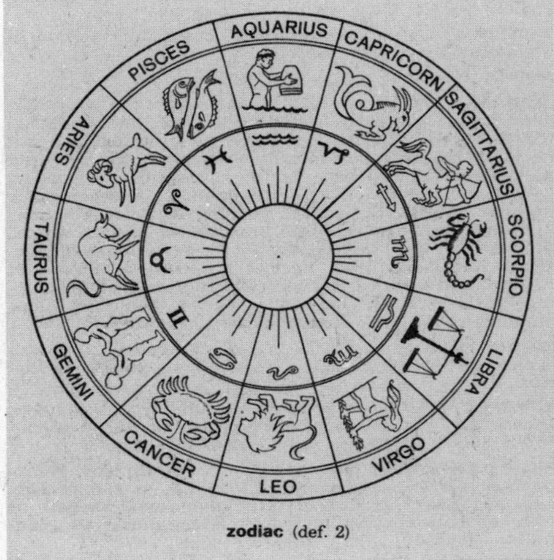

zodiac (def. 2)

zo·di·ac (zō′dē ak′), *n.* **1.** an imaginary belt of the heavens, extending about 8° on each side of the ecliptic, within which are the apparent paths of the sun, moon, and principal planets. It contains twelve constellations and hence twelve divisions called signs of the zodiac. Each division, however, because of the precession of the equinoxes, now contains the constellation west of the one from which it took its name. Cf. **sign of the zodiac. 2.** a circular or elliptical diagram representing this belt, and usually containing pictures of the animals, human figures, etc., that are associated with the constellations and signs. **3.** a circuit or round. [1350–1400; ME *zodiaque* < L *zōdiacus* < Gk *zōidiakòs* (*kýklos*) signal (circle), equiv. to *zṓidi(on)* animal sign (*zô(ion)* animal + *-idion* dim. suffix) + *-akos* -AC] —**zo·di·a·cal** (zō dī′ə kəl), *adj.*

zodi′acal light′, a luminous tract in the sky, seen in the west after sunset or in the east before sunrise and thought to be the light reflected from a cloud of meteoric matter revolving round the sun. [1725–35]

Zo·e (zō′ē, zō), *n.* a female given name: from a Greek word meaning "life." Also, **Zo′ë.**

zo·e·a (zō ē′ə), *n., pl.* **-e·ae** (-ē′ē), **-e·as.** *Zool.* any of the free-swimming larva of certain crustaceans, as the crab, having rudimentary legs and a spiny carapace. [1820–30; < NL, equiv. to Gk *zō(ḗ)* life + NL *-ea* -EA] —**zo·e′al,** *adj.*

zo·e·trope (zō′ē trōp′), *n.* a device for giving an illusion of motion, consisting of a slitted drum that, when whirled, shows a succession of images placed opposite the slits within the drum as one moving image. [1865–70; irreg. < Gk *zōḗ* life + *tropḗ* turn]

zof·tig (zof′tik, -tig), *adj. Slang.* zaftig.

Zog I (zōg), (*Ahmed Bey Zogu*) 1895–1961, king of Albania 1928–39. Also, **Zo·gu I** (zō′gōō).

Zo·har (zō′här), *n.* a medieval mystical work, consisting chiefly of interpretations of and commentaries on the Pentateuch: the definitive work of Jewish cabala.

zois·ite (zoi′sīt), *n. Mineral.* an orthorhombic dimorph of clinozoisite. [1795–1805; named after Baron S. Zois von Edelstein (1747–1819), Slovenian nobleman who discovered it; see -ITE[1]]

CONCISE PRONUNCIATION KEY: *act, cāpe, dâre, pärt; set, ēqual; if, īce; ox, ōver, ôrder, oil, bŏŏk, bōōt, out; up, ûrge; child; sing; shoe; thin, that;* zh as in *treasure.* ə = *a* as in *alone, e* as in *system, i* as in *easily, o* as in *gallop, u* as in *circus;* ᵊ as in *fire* (fīᵊr), *hour* (ouᵊr). l and n can serve as syllabic consonants, as in *cradle* (krād′l), and *button* (but′n). See the full key inside the front cover.

Zo•la (zō′lə; *Fr.* zô lȧ′), *n.* **É•mile** (ā mēl′), 1840–1902, French novelist. —**Zo′la•esque′,** *adj.*

Zol′ling•er-El′li•son syn′drome (zol′ing ər el′ə sən), *Pathol.* a condition in which a gastrin-secreting tumor of the pancreas or small intestine causes excessive secretion of gastric juice, leading to intractable peptic ulcers. [after Robert Milton *Zollinger* (born 1903) and Edwin Homer *Ellison* (1918–1970), U.S. surgeons, who described it in 1955]

Zoll′ner illu′sion (tsul′nər; *Ger.* tsœl′nər), *Psychol.* a spatial illusion in which parallel lines intersected by short oblique lines are perceived as converging or diverging. [1950–55; named after J. K. F. *Zöllner,* 19th-century German physicist]

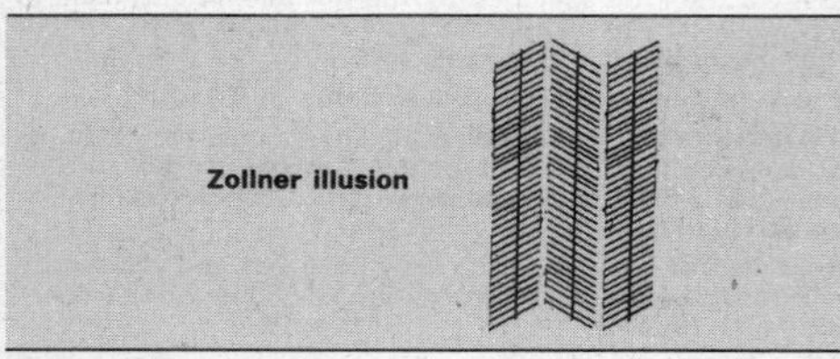
Zollner illusion

Zoll•ver•ein (tsôl′fer īn′; *Eng.* tsōl′fə rīn′), *n.* **1.** (in the 19th century) a union of German states for the maintenance of a uniform tariff on imports from other countries, and of free trading among themselves. **2.** any similar arrangement; customs union. [1835–45; < G, equiv. to *Zoll* custom, duty, tariff + *Verein* union]

Zom•ba (zom′bə), *n.* a city in and former capital of Malawi in the S part. 22,000.

zom•bi (zom′bē), *n., pl.* **-bis.** zombie.

zom•bie (zom′bē), *n.* **1.** (in voodoo) **a.** the body of a dead person given the semblance of life, but mute and will-less, by a supernatural force, usually for some evil purpose. **b.** the supernatural force itself. **2.** *Informal.* **a.** a person whose behavior or responses are wooden, listless, or seemingly rote; automaton. **b.** an eccentric or peculiar person. **3.** a snake god worshiped in West Indian and Brazilian religious practices of African origin. **4.** a tall drink made typically with several kinds of rum, citrus juice, and often apricot liqueur. **5.** *Canadian Slang.* an army conscript assigned to home defense during World War II. [1810–20; appar. < Kongo or Kimbundu *nzambi* god] —**zom′bi•ism,** *n.*

zom•bi•fy (zom′bə fī′), *v.t.,* **-fied, -fy•ing.** to turn (someone) into a zombie. [1980–85] —**zom′bi•fi•ca′•tion,** *n.*

zon•al (zōn′l), *adj.* **1.** of or pertaining to a zone or zones. **2.** of the nature of a zone. Also, **zon•ar•y** (zō′nə rē). [1865–70; ZONE + -AL[1]] —**zon′al•ly,** *adv.*

zon′al gera′nium, a widely cultivated plant, *Pelargonium hortorum,* having white, pink, or red flowers and rounded leaves that are sometimes banded or blotched with contrasting colors. Also called **fish geranium.** [1905–10]

zo•na pel•lu•ci•da (zō′nə pə lo͞o′si də, pel yo͞o′-), *pl.* **zo•nae pel•lu•ci•dae** (zō′nē pə lo͞o′si dē′, pel yo͞o′-). *Anat.* the transparent, noncellular layer surrounding the ovum of mammals, often having radial striations. [1835–45; < NL; see ZONE, PELLUCID]

zon•ate (zō′nāt), *adj.* **1.** marked with zones, as of color, texture, or the like. **2.** arranged in zones. Also, **zon′at•ed.** [1795–1805; ZONE + -ATE[1]]

zo•na•tion (zō nā′shən), *n.* **1.** the state or condition of being zonate. **2.** arrangement or distribution in zones. [1900–05; ZONE + -ATION]

Zond (zônd), *n.* one of a series of Soviet space probes that photographed the moon and returned to earth. [1964; < Russ: orig., surgical probe < F *sonde* SONDE; *z-* perh. due to G *Sonde* (< F)]

zone (zōn), *n., v.,* **zoned, zon•ing.** —*n.* **1.** any continuous tract or area that differs in some respect, or is distinguished for some purpose, from adjoining tracts or areas, or within which certain distinctive circumstances exist or are established. **2.** *Geog.* any of five great divisions of the earth's surface, bounded by lines parallel to the equator and named according to the prevailing temperature. Cf. **North Frigid Zone, North Temperate Zone, South Frigid Zone, South Temperate Zone, Torrid Zone.** See illus. in next column. **3.** *Biogeog.* an area characterized by a particular set of organisms, whose presence is determined by environmental conditions, as an altitudinal belt on a mountain. **4.** *Geol.* a horizon. **5.** *Geom.* a part of the surface of a sphere included between two parallel planes. **6.** a specific district, area, etc., within which a uniform charge is made for transportation, mail delivery, or other service. **7.** the total number of available railroad terminals within a given circumference around a given shipping center. **8.** an area or district in a city or town under special restrictions as to the type, size, purpose, etc., of existing or proposed buildings. **9.** See **time zone. 10.** Also called **postal delivery zone.** (in the U.S. postal system) any of the numbered districts into which a city or metropolitan area was formerly divided for expediting the sorting and delivery of mail. **11.** *Sports.* a particular portion of a playing area: *The wing was trapped with the puck in his own defensive zone.* **12.** *Archaic.* a girdle or belt; cincture. —*v.t.* **13.** to mark with zones or bands. **14.** to divide into zones, tracts, areas, etc., as according to existing characteristics or as distinguished for some purpose. **15.** to divide (a city, town, neighborhood, etc.) into areas subject to special restrictions on any existing or proposed buildings. **16.** to encircle or surround with a zone, girdle, belt, or the like. —*v.i.* **17.** to be formed into zones. [1490–1500; < L *zōna* < Gk *zṓnē* belt] —**zone′less,** *adj.*
—**Syn. 1.** region. See **belt. 16.** gird, band.

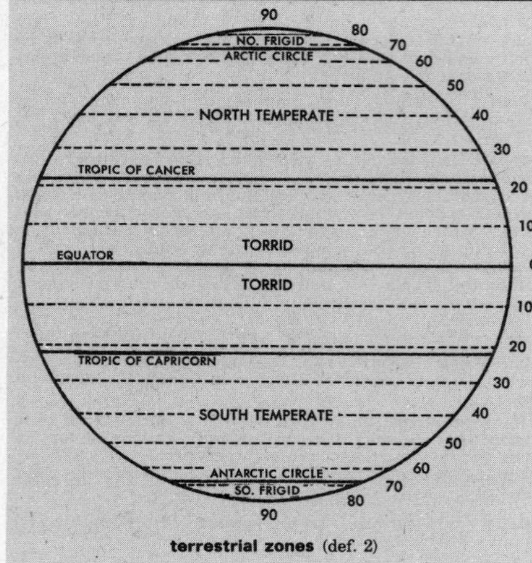

terrestrial zones (def. 2)

zone′ defense′, *Sports.* a method of defense, esp. in basketball and football, in which each member of the defensive team guards a specified portion of the playing area. Cf. **man-to-man defense.** [1925–30]

zone′ line′, *Ice Hockey.* See **blue line.**

zone′ melt′ing, a process of purifying any of various metals and other materials, as germanium or silicon, by passing it in bar form through an induction coil. Also called **zone′ refin′ing.** Cf. **cage zone melting.** [1955–60]

zone′ of avoid′ance, *Astron.* the area of the sky in the plane of the Milky Way where interstellar dust obscures visible light so that no distant galaxies can be observed.

zone′ of fire′, *Mil.* the area within which a unit is prepared to place its fire. [1875–80]

zone′ of inte′rior, the part of a theater of war not included in the theater of operations. [1930–35]

zone′ plate′, *Optics.* a plate or screen with alternating opaque and transparent concentric rings that focus light by diffraction. [1895–1900]

zone′ sys′tem, *Photog.* a system for envisioning the values to appear in a black-and-white print and for determining exposure and development, based on a scale of shades ranging from 0 (black) to IX (white). [1970–75]

zone′ time′, standard time as applied at sea, reckoned according to the system of time zones. [1905–10]

Zon•i•an (zō′nē ən), *n.* **1.** a U.S. citizen living in the Canal Zone. —*adj.* **2.** of or pertaining to the Zonians. [(CANAL) ZONE + -IAN]

zon•ing (zō′ning), *adj.* (esp. in city planning) of or pertaining to the division of an area into zones, as to restrict the number and types of buildings and their uses: *zoning laws.* [1810–20; ZONE + -ING[2]]

zo•nite (zō′nīt), *n.* a body segment of a diplopod. [1855–60; ZONE + -ITE[1]]

zonk (zongk, zôngk), *Slang.* —*v.i.* (often fol. by *out*) **1.** to become unconscious from alcohol or narcotic drugs; pass out. **2.** to fall soundly asleep or relax completely: *I've got to go home and zonk out.* —*v.t.* **3.** to stupefy, as by alcohol or narcotic drugs. **4.** to sedate or anesthetize: *If the pain gets too bad the doctors will zonk you.* **5.** to strike or defeat soundly; knock out; clobber. [1945–50; of expressive orig.; *-onk* perh. copies CONK[2]]

zonked (zongkt, zôngkt), *adj. Slang.* **1.** stupefied by or as if by alcohol or drugs; high. **2.** exhausted or asleep. Also, **zonked′ out′.** [1955–60, *Amer.*; ZONK + -ED[2]]

Zon′ta Club′ (zon′tə), one of an organization of service clubs composed of business and professional women, founded in 1919, and a member chapter of a worldwide organization **(Zon′ta Interna′tional)** dedicated to promoting world peace and fellowship. [< Lakhota *zǫta* honest, trustworthy]

Zon•ti•an (zon′tē ən), *n.* **1.** a member of a Zonta Club. —*adj.* **2.** of or pertaining to a Zonta Club or its members. [ZONT(A) + -IAN]

zon•ule (zōn′yo͞ol), *n.* a little zone, belt, band, or the like. [1825–35; < NL *zōnula.* See ZONE, -ULE] —**zon•u•lar** (zōn′yə lər), *adj.*

zoo (zo͞o), *n., pl.* **zoos. 1.** Also called **zoological garden.** a parklike area in which live animals are kept in cages or large enclosures for public exhibition. **2.** *Informal.* a place, activity, or group marked by chaos or unrestrained behavior. [1840–50; first two syllables of *zoological garden* taken as one syllable]

zoo-, a combining form meaning "living being," "animal," used in the formation of compound words: *zoometry; zooplankton.* Also, *esp. before a vowel,* **zo-.** [comb. form repr. Gk *zôion* animal]

zoochem., zoochemistry.

zo•o•chem•is•try (zō′ə kem′i strē), *n.* the branch of chemistry dealing with the constituents of the animal body; animal chemistry. [1860–65; ZOO- + CHEMISTRY] —**zo•o•chem•i•cal** (zō′ə kem′i kəl), *adj.*

zo•o•chore (zō′ə kôr′, -kōr′), *n. Bot.* a plant whose structure adapts it for dispersion by animals. [1900–05; zoo- + *-chore,* comb. form repr. Gk *chōreîn* to make way]

zo•o•flag•el•late (zō′ə flaj′ə lit, -lāt′), *n.* any flagellated protozoan that lacks photosynthetic pigment and feeds on organic matter: often parasitic. [1955–60; ZOO- + FLAGELLATE]

zo•o•gam•ete (zō′ə gam′ēt, -gə mēt′), *n.* planogamete. [1875–80; ZOO- + GAMETE]

zo•o•gen•ic (zō′ə jen′ik), *adj.* **1.** produced or caused by animals. **2.** pertaining or related to animal development or evolution. Also, **zo•og•e•nous** (zō oj′ə nəs). [1860–65; ZOO- + -GENIC] —**zo•o•gen•e•sis** (zō′ə jen′ə sis), **zo•og•e•ny** (zō oj′ə nē), *n.*

zoogeog., zoogeography.

zo•o•ge•og•ra•phy (zō′ə jē og′rə fē), *n.* **1.** the science dealing with the geographical distribution of animals. **2.** the study of the causes, effects, and other relations involved in such distributions. [1865–70; ZOO- + GEOGRAPHY] —**zo′o•ge•og′ra•pher,** *n.* —**zo•o•ge•o•graph•ic** (zō′ə jē′ə graf′ik), **zo′o•ge′o•graph′i•cal,** *adj.* —**zo′o•ge′o•graph′i•cal•ly,** *adv.*

zo•o•gle•a (zō′ə glē′ə), *n., pl.* **-gle•as, -gle•ae** (-glē′ē). *Bacteriol.* a jellylike mass of microorganisms. Also, **zo′•o•gloe′a.** [1875–80; ZOO- + NL *gloea* gum < Gk *gloía* glue] —**zo′o•gle′al,** *adj.*

zo•o•graft•ing (zō′ə graf′ting, -gräf′-), *n.* zooplasty. [ZOO- + GRAFTING]

zo•og•ra•phy (zō og′rə fē), *n.* the branch of zoology dealing with the description of animals. [1585–95; ZOO- + -GRAPHY] —**zo•og′ra•pher,** *n.* —**zo•o•graph•ic,** (zō′ə graf′ik), **zo′o•graph′i•cal,** *adj.*

zo•oid (zō′oid), *Biol.* —*n.* **1.** any organic body or cell capable of spontaneous movement and of an existence more or less apart from or independent of the parent organism. **2.** any animal organism or individual capable of separate existence, and produced by fission, gemmation, or some method other than direct sexual reproduction. **3.** any one of the recognizably distinct individuals or elements of a compound or colonial animallike organism, whether or not detached or detachable. —*adj.* **4.** Also, **zo•oi′dal.** pertaining to, resembling, or of the nature of an animal. [1850–55; ZO- + -OID]

zoo•keep•er (zo͞o′kē′pər), *n.* a person who feeds and tends animals in a zoo. [1920–25; ZOO + KEEPER] —**zoo′keep′ing,** *n.*

zooks (zo͝oks, zo͞oks), *interj.* (used in exclamatory phrases as a mild oath.) [1625–35; short for GADZOOKS]

zool., 1. zoological. **2.** zoologist. **3.** zoology.

zo•ol•a•try (zō ol′ə trē), *n.* the worship of or excessive attention to animals. [1810–20; ZOO- + -LATRY] —**zo•ol′a•ter,** *n.* —**zo•ol′a•trous,** *adj.*

zo•o•log•i•cal (zō′ə loj′i kəl), *adj.* **1.** of or pertaining to zoology. **2.** relating to or concerned with animals. Also, **zo′o•log′ic.** [1800–10; ZOOLOG(Y) + -ICAL] —**zo′•o•log′i•cal•ly,** *adv.*

zo′olog′ical gar′den, zoo (def. 1). [1820–30]

zo•ol•o•gist (zō ol′ə jist), *n.* a specialist in zoology. [1655–65; ZOOLOG(Y) + -IST]

zo•ol•o•gy (zō ol′ə jē), *n., pl.* **-gies. 1.** the science or branch of biology dealing with animals. **2.** a treatise on zoology. **3.** the animal life of a particular region. [1660–70; ZOO- + -LOGY]

zoom (zo͞om), *v.i.* **1.** to move quickly or suddenly with a loud humming or buzzing sound: *cars zooming by on the freeway.* **2.** to fly an airplane suddenly and sharply upward at great speed for a short distance, as in regaining altitude, clearing an obstacle, or signaling. **3.** *Motion Pictures, Television.* to bring a subject, scene, etc., into closeup or cause it to recede into a long shot using a zoom lens and while maintaining focus. **4.** *Informal.* to increase or rise suddenly and sharply: *Rents would zoom without rent control laws.* —*v.t.* **5.** to cause (an airplane) to zoom. **6.** to fly over (an obstacle) by zooming. **7. zoom in (on), a.** to bring (a subject, scene, etc.) into closeup by using a zoom lens: *to zoom in for a look at the injured man; to zoom in on a candidate at a political convention.* **b.** to examine more closely or in greater detail; focus on: *The panel zoomed in on the subject of abortion.* —*n.* **8.** the act or process of zooming. **9.** a zooming sound. **10.** *Informal.* See **zoom lens. 11.** Also called **zoom shot.** *Motion Pictures, Television.* a shot in which a subject, scene, or action is brought closer or made to recede by the use of a zoom lens. [1885–90; imit.]
—**Syn. 1.** buzz, speed, streak, flash.

zo•om•e•try (zō om′i trē), *n.* measurement of the proportionate lengths or sizes of the parts of animals. [1875–80; ZOO- + -METRY] —**zo•o•met•ric** (zō′ə me′trik), **zo′o•met′ri•cal,** *adj.*

zoom′ lens′, (in a camera or motion-picture projector) a lens assembly whose focal length can be continuously adjusted to provide various degrees of magnification without any loss of focus, thus combining the features of wide-angle, normal, and telephoto lenses. [1935–40]

zo•o•mor•phic (zō′ə môr′fik), *adj.* **1.** of or pertaining to a deity or other being conceived of as having the form of an animal. **2.** characterized by a highly stylized or conventionalized representation of animal forms. **3.** representing or using animal forms. [1870–75; ZOO- + -MORPHIC] —**zo′o•morph′,** *n.*

zo•o•mor•phism (zō′ə môr′fiz əm), *n.* **1.** zoomorphic representation, as in ornament. **2.** zoomorphic conception, as of a deity. [1830–40; ZOOMORPH(IC) + -ISM]

zoom′ shot′, zoom (def. 11).

zo•on (zō′on), *n., pl.* **zo•a** (zō′ə). *Biol. Rare.* **1.** any of the individuals of a compound organism. **2.** any individual, or the individuals collectively, produced from a single egg. **3.** zooid. [1860–65; < NL *zōon* < Gk *zôion* animal] —**zo•on•al** (zō′ə nl), *adj.*

-zoon, a combining form meaning "animal," "organism" of the kind specified by the initial element, often corre-

CONCISE ETYMOLOGY KEY: <, descended or borrowed from; >, whence; b., blend of, blended; c., cognate with; cf., compare; deriv., derivative; equiv., equivalent; imit., imitative; obl., oblique; r., replacing; s., stem; sp., spelling, spelled; resp., respelling, respelled; trans., translation; ?, origin unknown; *, unattested; ‡, probably earlier than. See the full key inside the front cover.

ponding to zoological class names ending in **-zoa,** with **zoon** used to name a single member of such a class: *protozoon.* [see ZOON]

o·on·o·sis (zō on′ə sis, zō′ə nō′sis), *n., pl.* **-ses** (-sēz′, sēz). *Pathol.* any disease of animals communicable to umans. [1875–80; < NL, irreg. < Gk *zōio-* ZOO- + *ιόsos* sickness, with ending appar. conformed to -SIS]

o·o·par·a·site (zō′ə par′ə sīt′), *n.* **1.** any parasitic animal or protozoan. **2.** a parasite of animals. [1895–1900; ZOO- + PARASITE] **—zo·o·par·a·sit·ic** (zō′ə par′ə-sit′ik), *adj.*

o·oph·a·gous (zō of′ə gəs), *adj.* carnivorous. [1825–35; ZOO- + -PHAGOUS]

o·o·phil·i·a (zō′ə fil′ē ə), *n.* **1.** the state of being zoophilous. **2.** *Psychol.* an abnormal fondness or preference for animals. [1895–1900; ZOO- + -PHILIA]

o·oph·i·lous (zō of′ə ləs), *adj.* **1.** *Bot.* adapted to pollination by animals, esp. those other than insects. **2.** having an affinity for animals. Also, **zo·o·phil·ic** (zō′ə-fil′ik). [1885–90; ZOO- + -PHILOUS]

o·o·pho·bi·a (zō′ə fō′bē ə), *n.* abnormal fear of animals. [1900–05; ZOO- + -PHOBIA]

o·oph·o·rus (zō of′ər əs), *n., pl.* **-o·ri** (-ə rī′). zophorus. **—zo·o·phor·ic** (zō′ə fôr′ik, -for′-), *adj.*

o·o·phyte (zō′ə fīt′), *n.* any of various invertebrate animals resembling a plant, as a coral. [1615–25; < NL *zōophyton* < Gk *zōióphyton.* See ZOO-, -PHYTE] **—zo·o·phyt·ic** (zō′ə fit′ik), **zo′o·phyt′i·cal,** *adj.*

o·o·plank·ton (zō′ə plangk′tən), *n.* the aggregate of animal or animallike organisms in plankton, as protozoans. Cf. **phytoplankton.** [1900–05; ZOO- + PLANKTON]

o·o·plas·ty (zō′ə plas′tē), *n. Surg.* the transplantation of living tissue to the human body from an animal of another species. Also called **zoografting.** [ZOO- + -PLASTY] **—zo′o·plas′tic,** *adj.*

o·o·prax·i·scope (zō′ə prak′sə skōp′), *n. Motion Pictures.* an early type of motion-picture projector, designed by Eadweard Muybridge, in which the images were drawings or photographs placed along the rim of a circular glass plate, the shutter was a rotating opaque disk with radial slots, and a limelight source was used. [ZOO- + *praxi-* as comb. form of Gk *práxis* action, PRAXIS + -SCOPE; term introduced by Muybridge about 1881, r. his own earlier term *zoogyriscope*]

o·o·se·mi·ot·ics (zō′ə sē′mē ot′iks, -sē′mī-, -sem′ē-, -sem′ī-), *n.* (*used with a singular v.*) the study of the sounds and signals used by animals in communication. [1960–65; ZOO- + SEMIOTICS]

o·o·sperm (zō′ə spûrm′), *n.* **1.** *Bot., Mycol. Archaic.* zoospore. **2.** *Zool.* spermatozoon. [1830–40; ZOO- + -SPERM] **—zo·o·sper·mat·ic** (zō′ə spər mat′ik), *adj.*

o·o·spo·ran·gi·um (zō′ə spə ran′jē əm), *n., pl.* **-gi·a** (-jē ə). *Bot.* a sporangium or spore case in which zoospores are produced. [1870–75; ZOO- + SPORANGIUM] **—zo′o·spo·ran′gi·al,** *adj.*

zo·o·spore (zō′ə spôr′, -spōr′), *n.* **1.** *Bot., Mycol.* an asexual spore produced by certain algae and some fungi, capable of moving about by means of flagella. **2.** *Zool.* any of the minute motile flagelliform or ameboid bodies that issue from the sporocyst of certain protozoans. [1840–50; ZOO- + SPORE] **—zo·o·spor·ic** (zō′ə spôr′ik, -spor′-), **zo·os·por·ous** (zō os′pər əs, zō′ə spôr′-, -spōr′-), *adj.*

zo·ot·o·my (zō ot′ə mē), *n.* **1.** the anatomy, esp. the comparative anatomy, of animals. **2.** the dissection of animals. [1655–65; < NL *zōotomia.* See ZOO-, -TOMY] **—zo·o·tom·ic** (zō′ə tom′ik), **zo′o·tom′i·cal,** *adj.* **—zo′o·tom′i·cal·ly,** *adv.* **—zo·ot′o·mist,** *n.*

zo·o·tox·in (zō′ə tok′sin), *n.* any toxin of animal origin, as a snake or scorpion venom, or serum produced by means of such toxin. [1975–80; ZOO- + TOXIN]

zoot′ suit′ (zo͞ot), a man's suit with baggy, tight-cuffed, sometimes high-waisted trousers and an over-sized jacket with exaggeratedly broad, padded shoulders and wide lapels, often worn with suspenders and a long watch chain and first popularized in the early 1940's. [1940–45, *Amer.*; rhyming compound based on SUIT]

zoot′ suit′er, a person who wears a zoot suit. [1940–45; ZOOT SUIT + -ER[1]]

zoot·y (zo͞o′tē), *adj. Slang.* characteristic of a zoot suiter; extreme or flamboyant in style or appearance: *a zooty new convertible.* [1945–50; ZOOT (SUIT) + -Y[1]]

Zo·phar (zō′fər), *n.* a friend of Job. Job 2:11.

zo·pho·rus (zō′fər əs), *n., pl.* **-pho·ri** (-fə rī′). a frieze having representations of people or animals. Also, **zoophorus.** [1555–65; < L *zōphorus* < Gk *zōiophóros.* See ZOO-, -PHORE]

Zo·ra (zôr′ə, zōr′ə), *n.* a female given name.

Zo·rach (zôr′äk, -äKH, -ak, zōr′-), *n.* **William,** 1887–1966, U.S. sculptor and painter, born in Lithuania.

Zo·ran·a (zō ran′ə, zō-), *n.* a female given name.

zo·ri (zôr′ē), *n., pl.* **zo·ri.** a Japanese sandal, often made of straw or rubber and consisting of a flat sole held on the foot by a thong passing between the first and second toes. [1895–1900; < Japn *zōri,* earlier *zau-ri* < MChin, equiv. to Chin *cǎo* grass + *lǐ* footgear]

zor·il (zôr′il, zor′-), *n.* a weasellike African animal, *Ictonyx striatus,* resembling a skunk in coloration and habits. Also, **zo·ril·la** (zə ril′ə), **zo·rille** (zə ril′). [1765–75; < F *zorille* < Sp *zorrilla, zorillo,* equiv. to *zorra, zorro* fox + *-illa, -illo* dim. suffix]

Zorn (sôRn), *n.* **An·ders Le·on·hard** (än′dərs lā′ô-närd′), 1860–1920, Swedish painter and sculptor.

Zorn's′ lem′ma (zôrnz), *Math.* a theorem of set theory that if every totally ordered subset of a nonempty partially ordered set has an upper bound, then there is an element in the set such that the set contains no element greater than the specified given element. [1945–50; after Max August *Zorn* (born 1906), German mathematician]

Zo·ro·as·ter (zôr′ō as′tər, zōr′-, zôr′ō as′tər, zōr′-), *n.* fl. 6th century B.C., Persian religious teacher. Also called **Zarathustra.**

Zo·ro·as·tri·an (zôr′ō as′trē ən, zōr′-), *adj.* **1.** of or pertaining to Zoroaster or to Zoroastrianism. **—***n.* **2.** one of the adherents of Zoroastrianism. [1735–45; < L *Zōroastr(ēs)* (< Gk *Zōroástrēs* < Avestan *zaraθuštra* ZARATHUSTRA) + -IAN]

Zo·ro·as·tri·an·ism (zôr′ō as′trē ə niz′əm, zōr′-), *n.* an Iranian religion, founded c600 B.C. by Zoroaster, the principal beliefs of which are in the existence of a supreme deity, Ahura Mazda, and in a cosmic struggle between a spirit of good, Spenta Mainyu, and a spirit of evil, Angra Mainyu. Also, **Zo′ro·as′trism.** Also called **Mazdaism.** [1850–55; ZOROASTRIAN + -ISM]

Zo·rob·a·bel (zō rob′ə bəl, zō-), *n. Douay Bible.* Zerubbabel.

Zor·ri·lla y Mo·ral (thôR Rē′lyä ē mō Räl′, sôR Rē′-yä), **Jo·sé** (hō se′), 1817–93, Spanish poet and dramatist.

Zo·ser (zō′sər), *n.* fl. c2800 B.C., Egyptian ruler of the 3rd dynasty.

Zo·si·mus (zos′ə məs), *n.* **Saint,** pope 417–418.

zos·ter (zos′tər), *n.* **1.** Also called **herpes zoster.** *Pathol.* shingles. **2.** *Gk. Antiq.* a belt or girdle. [1595–1605; < L *zōstēr* < Gk *zōstḗr* girdle]

Zou·ave (zo͞o äv′, zwäv), *n.* **1.** (*sometimes l.c.*) one of a former body of infantry in the French army, composed originally of Algerians, distinguished for their dash, hardiness, and picturesque Oriental uniform. **2.** a member of any body of soldiers adopting a similar dress and drill, esp. a soldier serving in any of certain regiments in the American Civil War. [1820–30; < F < Ar *zawāwah,* prob. < Berber *igowawen,* the name of a Berber group]

zouk (zo͝ok), *n.* a style of dance music that originated in Guadeloupe and Martinique, featuring Caribbean rhythms over a disco beat and played with electric guitars and synthesizers. [1985–90; appar. < Lesser Antillean Creole French; said to mean lit. "place to dance, party"]

zounds (zoundz), *interj. Archaic.* (used as a mild oath.) [1590–1600; var. of 'SWOUNDS]

Zo·vi·rax (zō vī′raks), *Pharm., Trademark.* a brand name for acyclovir.

zow·ie (zou′ē), *interj.* (used to express keen pleasure, astonishment, approval, etc.) [1935–40, *Amer.*]

zoy·si·a (zoi′sē ə, -zē ə, -shə, -zhə), *n.* any low-growing grass of the genus *Zoysia,* esp. *Z. matrella,* native to tropical Asia and widely used for lawns. [1920–25; named after Karl von Zois (d. 1800), German botanist; see -IA]

Z particle. See **Z-zero particle.**

ZPG, zero population growth.

Zr, *Symbol, Chem.* zirconium.

z's (zēz), *n.* (*used with a plural v.*) *Slang.* sleep (often used with *grab, catch,* etc.): *to grab some z's before dinner.* Also, **Z's.** [1960–65; from the conventional use of a series of z's to represent snoring]

Zsig·mon·dy (zhig′môn dē), *n.* **Rich·ard** (RiKH′ärt), 1865–1929, German chemist, born in Austria: Nobel prize 1925.

Z twist, a direction of the twist in yarns, from top right to bottom left, resembling the long stroke of the letter Z. Cf. **S twist.** [1975–80]

Zuc·ca·ri (tso͞ok′kä Rē), *n.* **Fe·de·ri·co** (fe′de Rē′kô), 1543?–1609, and his brother **Tad·de·o** (täd de′ô), 1529–66, Italian painters. Also, **Zuc·ca·ro** (tso͞ok′kä Rô), **Zuc·che·ro** (tso͞ok′ke Rô).

zuc·chet·to (zo͞o ket′ō; *It.* tso͞ok ket′tô), *n., pl.* **-tos,** *It.* **-ti** (-tē). a small, round skullcap worn by Roman Catholic ecclesiastics, a priest's being black, a bishop's violet, a cardinal's red, and the pope's white; calotte. [1850–55; < It, var. of *zucchetta,* dim. of *zucca* gourd, head, perh. < pre-IE *tjukka gourd]

zucchini, *Cucurbita pepo melopepo*

zuc·chi·ni (zo͞o kē′nē), *n., pl.* **-ni, -nis. 1.** a variety of summer squash that is shaped like a cucumber and that has a smooth, dark-green skin. **2.** the plant bearing this fruit. Also called, *esp. Brit.,* **courgette.** [1925–30, *Amer.*; < It, pl. of *zucchino,* equiv. to *zucc(a)* gourd (see ZUCCHETTO) + *-ino* dim. suffix]

Zug (tso͞ok), *n.* **1.** a canton in central Switzerland. 72,800. 92 sq. mi. (238 sq. km). **2.** the capital of this canton, on the Lake of Zug. 22,200. **3. Lake of,** a lake in this canton. 15 sq. mi. (39 sq. km).

zug·zwang (tso͞ok′tsväng′), *n. Chess.* a situation in which a player is limited to moves that cost pieces or have a damaging positional effect. [1900–05; < G, equiv. to *Zug* move + *Zwang* constraint, obligation]

Zui·der Zee (zī′dər zā′, zē′; *Du.* zœi′dəR zā′), a former shallow inlet of the North Sea in central Netherlands. Cf. **IJsselmeer.** Also, **Zuyder Zee.**

Zu·kor (zo͞o′kər), *n.* **Adolph,** 1873–1976, U.S. film producer, born in Hungary.

Zu·lei·ka (zo͞o lā′kə, -lī′-), *n.* a female given name.

Zu 'l-hij·jah (zo͞ol hij′ä). See **Dhu l-hijjah.**

Zu 'l·ka·'dah (zo͞ol kä′dä). See **Dhu 'l-Qa'da.**

Zu·lo·a·ga (thō͞o′lô ä′gä, so͞o′-), *n.* **Ig·na·cio** (ēg nä′-thyô, -syô), 1870–1945, Spanish painter.

Zu·lu (zo͞o′lo͞o), *n., pl.* **-lus,** (*esp. collectively*) **-lu** for 1, *adj.* **—***n.* **1.** a member of a Nguni people living mainly in Natal, Republic of South Africa. **2.** the Bantu language of the Zulu. **3.** a word used in communications to represent the letter Z. **—***adj.* **4.** of or pertaining to the Zulus or their language.

Zu·lu·land (zo͞o′lo͞o land′), *n.* a territory in NE Natal, in the Republic of South Africa.

Zu·ni (zo͞o′nē), *n., pl.* **-nis,** (*esp. collectively*) **-ni** for 1. **1.** a member of a group of North American Indians inhabiting the largest of the Indian pueblos, in western New Mexico. **2.** the language of the Zuni. Also, **Zu·ñi** (zo͞o′-nē, zo͞on′yē). [1830–35, *Amer.*; earlier *Zuñi* < AmerSp < Acoma Keresan *sí·ni* (pronounced *sə̂i·nʸi*) or a cognate] **—Zu′ni·an, Zu′ñi·an,** *adj., n.*

zup·pa (zo͞o′pə; *It.* tso͞op′pä), *n. Italian Cookery.* a soup or chowder. [1960–65; < It: SOUP]

zup·pa in·gle·se (zo͞o′pə ing glā′zä; *It.* tso͞op′pä eng-gle′ze), *Italian Cookery.* tiered layers of sponge cake sprinkled with rum or liqueur, then spread with custard or other cream filling. [1940–45; < It: lit., English soup]

Zur·ba·rán (tho͞oR′bä Rän′, zo͞oR′-), *n.* **Fran·cis·co de** (fRän thēs′kô the, -sēs′-), 1598–1663?, Spanish painter.

zurf (zûrf), *n.* zarf.

Zu·rich (zo͝or′ik), *n.* **1.** a canton in N Switzerland. 1,118,200; 668 sq. mi. (1730 sq. km). **2.** the capital of this canton, on the Lake of Zurich. 389,600. **3. Lake of,** a lake in N Switzerland. 25 mi. (40 km) long; 34 sq. mi. (88 sq. km). German, **Zü·rich** (tsʏ′RiKH) (for defs. 1, 2).

Zur·van (zûr′vən), *n.* the ancient Iranian god of time and fate. Also, **Zervan.** Cf. **Zurvanism.**

Zur·van·ism (zûr′və niz′əm), *n.* a Zoroastrian heresy according to which both Ahura Mazda and Angra Mainyu were offspring of Zurvan. Also, **Zervanism.** [ZURVAN + -ISM] **—Zur′van·ite′,** *n.*

Zuy·der Zee (zī′dər zā, zē′; *Du.* zœi′dəR zā′). See **Zuider Zee.**

Zweig (zwīg, swīg; *Ger.* tsvīk), *n.* **1. Ar·nold** (är′nəld; *Ger.* är′nôlt), 1887–1968, German novelist, essayist, and dramatist. **2. Ste·fan** (stef′ən, -än; *Ger.* shte′fän), 1881–1942, Austrian dramatist, critic, biographer, and novelist.

Zwick·au (tsvik′ou), *n.* a city in W Saxony, in E Germany. 123,000.

Zwick·y (tsvik′ē), *n.* **Fritz** (fRits), 1898–1974, Swiss astrophysicist, born in Bulgaria, in the U.S. after 1925.

zwie·back (zwī′bak′, -bäk′, zwē′-, swī′-, swē′-; *Ger.* tsvē′bäk′), *n.* a special egg bread made into rusks. [1890–95, *Amer.*; < G: twice-baked, equiv. to *zwie* twice + *backen* to bake. See TWI-, BAKE; cf. BISCUIT]

Zwing·li (zwing′glē, swing′-; *Ger.* tsving′lē), *n.* **Ul·rich** (o͝ol′RiKH) or **Hul·dreich** (ho͝ol′dRiKH), 1484–1531, Swiss Protestant reformer.

Zwing·li·an (zwing′glē ən, swing′-, tsving′lē-), *adj.* **1.** of or pertaining to Ulrich Zwingli or his doctrines, largely agreeing with those of Luther. **—***n.* **2.** a follower of Zwingli. [1525–35; ZWINGLI + -AN] **—Zwing′li·an·ism,** *n.* **—Zwing′li·an·ist,** *n., adj.*

zwit·ter·i·on (tsvit′ər ī′ən), *n. Physical Chem.* an ion with both a positive and a negative charge. [< G *Zwitterion* (1897), equiv. to *Zwitter* hybrid, hermaphrodite + *Ion* ION] **—zwit·ter·i·on·ic** (tsvit′ər ī on′ik), *adj.*

Zwol·le (zvôl′ə), *n.* a city in central Netherlands. 83,711.

Zwor·y·kin (zwôr′i kin), *n.* **Vlad·i·mir Kos·ma** (vlad′-ə mēr′ koz′mə), 1889–1982, U.S. physicist and inventor, born in Russia: known as the "father of television."

zy·de·co (zī′di kō′), *n.* a blues-influenced type of Cajun dance music popular in Louisiana and Texas, and usually played on accordion, guitar, and violin. [1955–60, *Amer.*; said to represent LaF *les haricots* in the dance-tune title *Les haricots sont pas salés*]

zyg·a·poph·y·sis (zig′ə pof′ə sis, zī′gə-), *n., pl.* **-ses** (-sēz′). *Anat.* one of the four processes of a vertebra, occurring in pairs that interlock each vertebra with the vertebrae above and below. [1850–55; ZYG- + APOPHYSIS] **—zyg·ap·o·phys·e·al, zyg·ap·o·phys·i·al** (zig′ap-ə fiz′ē əl, zī′gap-), *adj.*

zygo-, a combining form meaning "yoke," "yoked," "yoke-shaped," used in the formation of compound words: *zygomorphic.* Also, *esp. before a vowel,* **zyg-.** [comb. form of Gk *zygón* YOKE]

zy·go·dac·tyl (zī′gə dak′til, zig′ə-), *adj.* **1.** Also, **zy′·go·dac′ty·lous.** (of a bird) having the toes of each foot arranged in pairs, with two toes in front and two behind. **—***n.* **2.** a zygodactyl bird. [1825–35; ZYGO- + -DACTYL] **—zy′go·dac′tyl·ism,** *n.*

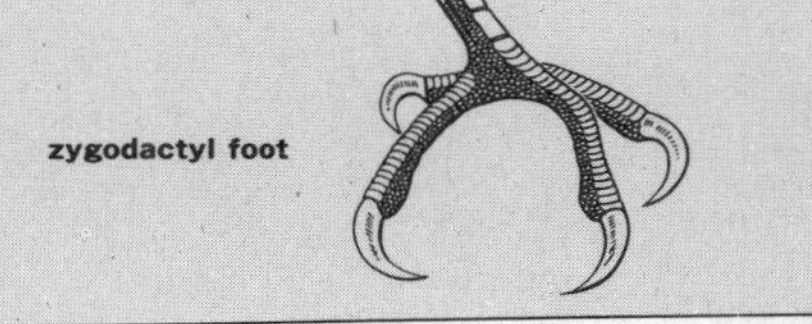

zygodactyl foot

zy·go·gen·e·sis (zī′gō jen′ə sis, zig′ō-), *n. Biol.* **1.** the formation of a zygote. **2.** reproduction by means of gametes. [1945–50; ZYGO- + -GENESIS] **—zy·go·ge·net·ic** (zī′gō jə net′ik), *adj.*

zy·go·ma (zī gō′mə, zi-), *n., pl.* **-ma·ta** (-mə tə). *Anat.* **1.** See **zygomatic arch. 2.** the zygomatic process of the temporal bone. **3.** See **zygomatic bone.** [1675–85; < NL *zygōma* < Gk *zýgōma* bolt, bar, equiv. to *zygó-,* var. s. of *zygoûn* to YOKE (see ZYGO-) + *-ma* n. suffix of result]

CONCISE PRONUNCIATION KEY: act, cāpe, dâre, pärt; set, ēqual; *if,* ice; ox, ōver, ôrder, oil, bo͝ok, bo͞ot, out; up, ûrge; child; sing; shoe; thin, *th*at; zh as in *treasure.* ə = a as in *alone,* e as in *system,* i as in *easily,* o as in *gallop,* u as in *circus;* ə as in *fire* (fīər), *hour* (ouər). l and n can serve as syllabic consonants, as in *cradle* (krād′l), and *button* (but′n). See the full key inside the front cover.

zy·go·mat·ic (zī′gə mat′ik, zig′ə-), *Anat.* —*adj.* **1.** of, pertaining to, or situated near the zygoma. —*n.* **2.** See **zygomatic bone.** [1700–10; *zygomat-* (comb. form of ZYGOMA) + -IC]

zy′gomat′ic arch′, *Anat.* the bony arch at the outer border of the eye socket, formed by the union of the cheekbone and the zygomatic process of the temporal bone. See diag. under **skull.** [1815–25]

zy′gomat′ic bone′, *Anat.* a bone on each side of the face below the eye, forming the prominence of the cheek; cheekbone. Also called **malar, malar bone.** See diag. under **skull.** [1700–10]

zy′gomat′ic proc′ess, *Anat.* any of several bony processes that articulate with the cheekbone. [1735–45]

zy·go·mor·phic (zī′gə môr′fik, zig′ə-), *adj. Biol.* having bilateral symmetry; divisible lengthwise into similar or symmetrical halves. Also, **zy′go·mor′phous.** [1870–75; ZYGO- + -MORPHIC] —**zy′go·mor′phism, zy′go·mor′phy,** *n.*

zy·go·my·cete (zī′gə mī′sēt, -mī sēt′, zig′ə-), *n. Mycol.* any of a wide variety of common fungi constituting the phylum Zygomycota of the kingdom Fungi (or the class Zygomycetes of the kingdom Plantae), in which sexual reproduction is by the formation of zygospores. [< NL *Zygomycetes* (1874), var. name of the class; see ZYGO-, -MYCETE]

zy·go·my·co·ta (zī′gə mī kō′tə), *n. Mycol.* the zygomycetes considered as belonging to the phylum Zygomycota of the kingdom Fungi. [< NL; see ZYGOMYCETE, -OTA]

zy·go·phore (zī′gə fôr′, -fōr′, zig′ə-), *n. Mycol.* (in certain fungi) any of several specialized branches of hyphae, bearing the isogametes that unite to produce a zygospore. [1900–05; ZYGO- + -PHORE] —**zy·go·phor·ic** (zī′gə fôr′ik, -for′-, zig′ə-), *adj.*

zy·go·phyl·la·ceous (zī′gō fə lā′shəs, zig′ō-), *adj.* belonging to the Zygophyllaceae, the caltrop family of plants. Cf. **caltrop family.** [1885–90; < NL *Zygophyllace(ae)* family name (*Zygophyll(um)* the type genus (see ZYGO-, -PHYLL) + *aceae* -ACEAE) + -OUS]

CONCISE ETYMOLOGY KEY: <, descended or borrowed from; >, whence; b., blend of, blended; c., cognate with; cf., compare; deriv., derivative; equiv., equivalent; imit., imitative; obl., oblique; r., replacing; s., stem; sp., spelling, spelled; resp., respelling, respelled; trans., translation; ?, origin unknown; *, unattested; ‡, probably earlier than. See the full key inside the front cover.

zy·go·phyte (zī′gə fīt′, zig′ə-), *n.* a plant that reproduces by means of zygospores. [1880–85; ZYGO- + -PHYTE]

zy·gop·ter·an (zī gop′tər ən), *adj.* **1.** belonging or pertaining to the suborder Zygoptera, comprising the damselflies. —*n.* **2.** any member of this suborder. [< NL *Zygopter(a)* (see ZYGO-, -PTERA) + -AN]

zy·go·sis (zī gō′sis, zi-), *n. Biol.* the union of two gametes; conjugation. [1875–80; < NL *zygōsis* < Gk *zygōsis* a yoking. See ZYGOTE, -SIS] —**zy·gose** (zī′gōs, zig′ōs), *adj.*

zy·gos·i·ty (zī gos′i tē, zi-), *n. Genetics.* **1.** the characterization of an individual's hereditary traits in terms of gene pairing in the zygote from which it developed. Cf. **homozygous, heterozygous. 2.** the characterization of twinning and multiple births in terms of the combination of alleles for particular hereditary traits. Cf. **monozygotic, dizygotic.** [1945–50; ZYG- + -OSITY or ZYGOS(IS) + -ITY]

zy·go·spo·ran·gi·um (zī′gō spô ran′jē əm, -spō-, zig′ō-), *n., pl.* **-gi·a** (-jē ə). *Mycol.* a sporangium that bears a zygospore. [ZYGO- + SPORANGIUM]

zy·go·spore (zī′gə spôr′, -spōr′, zig′ə-), *n. Bot., Mycol.* a cell formed by fusion of two similar gametes, as in certain algae and fungi. [1860–65; ZYGO- + -SPORE] —**zy·go·spor·ic** (zī′gə spôr′ik, -spor′-, zig′ə-), *adj.*

zy·gote (zī′gōt, zig′ōt), *n. Biol.* the cell produced by the union of two gametes, before it undergoes cleavage. [1885–90; < Gk *zygōtós* yoked, equiv. to *zygō-*, var. s. of *zygoûn* to yoke, join together (deriv. of *zygón* YOKE[1]) + *-tos* adj. suffix]

zy·go·tene (zī′gə tēn′, zig′ə-), *n. Cell Biol.* the second stage of prophase in meiosis, during which strands of homologous chromosomes line up and become pairs. [1925–30; < F *zygotène*; see ZYGO-, -TENE]

zy·got·ic (zī got′ik), *adj. Biol.* **1.** of or pertaining to a zygote. **2.** having zygosity. [1905–10; ZYGOTE + -IC] —**zy·got′i·cal·ly,** *adv.*

zy·mase (zī′mās), *n. Biochem.* the complex of enzymes obtained from yeast, also occurring in bacteria and other organisms, that acts in alcoholic fermentation and other forms of glycolysis. [1870–75; < F < Gk *zȳm(ē)* leaven + F *-ase* -ASE]

zyme (zīm), *n. Archaic.* the specific principle regarded as the cause of a zymotic disease. Cf. **zymosis.** [1880–85; < Gk *zȳmē* leaven]

zymo-, a combining form meaning "ferment," "leaven," used in the formation of compound words: *zymology.* Also, *esp. before a vowel,* **zym-.** [comb. form repr. Gk *zȳmē* leaven]

zy·mo·gen (zī′mə jən, -jen′), *n. Biochem.* any of various enzyme precursor molecules that may change into an enzyme as a result of catalytic change. Also called **proenzyme.** [< G (1875); see ZYMO-, -GEN]

zy·mol·o·gy (zī mol′ə jē), *n. Biochem.* (formerly) the science dealing with fermentation and the action of enzymes; enzymology. [1745–55; ZYMO- + -LOGY] —**zy·mo·log·ic** (zī′mə loj′ik), *adj.* —**zy·mol′o·gist,** *n.*

zy·mol·y·sis (zī mol′ə sis), *n. Biochem.* the digestive and fermentative action of enzymes. [1885–90; ZYMO- + -LYSIS] —**zy·mo·lyt·ic** (zī′mə lit′ik), *adj.*

zy·mom·e·ter (zī mom′i tər), *n.* an instrument for measuring the degree of fermentation. [1695–1705; ZYMO- + -METER]

zy·mo·sis (zī mō′sis), *n., pl.* **-ses** (-sēz). **1.** fermentation. **2.** an infectious or contagious disease. [1835–45; < NL *zȳmōsis* < Gk *zȳmōsis,* equiv. to *zȳmō-*, var. s. of *zȳmoûn* to leaven, ferment (deriv. of *zȳmē* leaven) + -sis -SIS]

zy·mot·ic (zī mot′ik), *adj.* **1.** pertaining to or caused by or as if by fermentation. **2.** of or pertaining to zymosis. [1835–45; < Gk *zȳmōtikós* causing fermentation; see ZYMOSIS, -TIC] —**zy·mot′i·cal·ly,** *adv.*

zy·mur·gy (zī′mûr jē), *n.* the branch of applied chemistry dealing with fermentation, as in winemaking, brewing, the preparation of yeast, etc. [1865–70; ZYM- + -URGY]

Zyr·yan (zēr′yən, -yän), *n., pl.* **-yans,** (*esp. collectively*) **-yan.** Komi. Also, **Zyr·yen·i·an** (zēr yen′ē ən). [1885–90; < Russ *zyryánin* (pl. *zyryáne*), ORuss *syryanin, seryanin,* perh. akin to Mansi *saran* a Komi]

ZZ, zigzag approach.

zz, zigzag.

Zz., ginger. Also, **zz.** [< L *zingiber*]

Z′-ze′ro par′ticle (zē′zēr′ō), *Physics.* one of three particles, called intermediate vector bosons, that are believed to transmit the weak force. *Symbol:* Z^0

ZZZ, (used to represent the sound of a person snoring.) Also, **zzz**

BASIC MANUAL OF STYLE

This basic manual offers concise guidelines to common stylistic practices in academic, business, and scholarly writing. Although individual publishing firms, newspapers, and periodicals often establish detailed rules of their own, the practices described below are general ones prevalent in the United States and considered standard.

USE OF PUNCTUATION

PERIOD (.)

Use a period:

1. To end a declarative or imperative sentence (but not an exclamatory sentence).

    The meeting was amicable and constructive.
    Please pass the salt.
    Read the next two chapters by Friday.

2. To end an indirect question.

    We should find out when the plane is leaving.

3. To end a response.

    Not at all.
    In a manner of speaking.
    Yes.

4. To follow many abbreviations.
5. To end a polite request phrased as a question.

    Will you please vote by raising your hands.

ELLIPSIS (. . . or . . . .)

Use ellipsis points (three or four consecutive periods) to indicate that part of a quoted sentence has been omitted.

1. If the omission occurs at the beginning or in the middle of the sentence, use three periods in the ellipsis.

    ". . . the book is lively . . . and well written."

2. If the last part of the sentence is omitted or if entire sentences are omitted, add a fourth period to the ellipsis to mark the end of the sentence.

    "He left his home. . . . Years later he returned to find that everything had changed. . . ."

3. Other punctuation may precede or follow the ellipsis points to clarify the overall sense:

    She named three factors: . . . and (c) unemployment.

QUESTION MARK (?)

Use a question mark:

1. To end a sentence, clause, or phrase (or after a single word) that asks a question.

    Who invited him to the party?
    "Is something wrong?" she asked.
    Who said "Now"?
    Whom shall we elect? Stein? Conroy?

2. To indicate doubt or uncertainty.

    The manuscript dates back to 560(?) B.C.

EXCLAMATION POINT (!)

Use an exclamation point:

1. To end a sentence, clause, or phrase (or after a single word) that expresses strong emotion, as surprise, joy, or anger, or that indicates a cry of distress, a forceful command, etc.

    Go away!
    What a day this has been!
    "Hey, there!" he shouted.
    "Wow!"

2. In parentheses, to indicate the writer's amazement, outrage, or amusement at what precedes. This practice is not recommended for use in formal writing.

    She extolled the perfection (!) of the memo.
    The room was 21 feet wide, 88 feet long (!), and 18 feet high.

COMMA (,)

Use a comma:

1. To separate words, phrases, and clauses that are part of a series of three or more items or attributes.

    We found the Danes to be friendly, generous, and hospitable people.
    The chief agricultural products of Denmark are butter, eggs, potatoes, beets, barley, and oats.

    It is permissible to omit the final comma, or so-called series comma, before the *and* in a series of words as long as its absence does not interfere with clarity of meaning. The final commas in the examples above, while desirable, are not essential.

    In many cases, however, the omission of a comma before the conjunction can materially affect the meaning. In the following sentence, its omission might indicate that the tanks were amphibious.

    Their equipment included airplanes, helicopters, artillery, amphibious vehicles, and tanks.

    Do not use a comma to separate two items considered a single unit within a series.

    For breakfast he ordered orange juice, bacon and eggs, and coffee.

    But

    At the supermarket he bought orange juice, coffee, bacon, and eggs.

    In a series of phrases or dependent clauses, place a comma before the conjunction.

    He sold his business, rented his house, gave up his car, paid his creditors, and set off for Africa.
    They strolled along the city streets, browsed in the bookshops, and dined at their favorite café.

2. Do not use commas to separate adjectives so integral to the sense of a phrase that they appear to form a single element with the noun they modify. Adjectives that refer to the number, age (*old, young, new*), size, color, affiliation, nationality, or location of the noun often fall within this category. A simple test can usually determine the appropriateness of a comma in such instances: If *and* cannot replace the comma without creating a clumsy, almost meaningless effect, it is safe to conclude that a comma is also out of place.

    twenty happy little youngsters
    a dozen large blue dresses
    several old Western mining towns

    But commas must be used in the following cases, where clarity demands separation of the items in a series:

    a dozen large blue, red, yellow, and green dresses
    twenty old, young, and middle-aged spectators

3. To separate independent clauses joined by the coordinating conjunctions *and, but, yet, for, or, nor.*

    Almost anyone knows how to earn money, but not one in a million knows how to spend it.

    The comma may be omitted in sentences consisting of two short independent clauses.

    We missed the train but we caught the bus in time.

4. To separate a long introductory phrase or subordinate clause from the rest of the sentence.

    Having rid themselves of their former rulers, the people now disagreed on the new leadership.
    Although the details have not been fully developed, we will be making the trip.

5. To set off words of direct address, interjections, or transitional words used to introduce a sentence (*oh, yes, no, however, nevertheless, still, anyway, well, why, frankly, really, moreover, incidentally,* etc.).

    Jennifer, where have you been?
    Oh, here's our new neighbor.
    Why, you can't mean that!
    Still, you must agree that she knows her business.
    Fine, we'll get together.

6. To set off an introductory modifier (adjective, adverb, participle, participial phrase), even if it consists of only one word or a short phrase.

    Politically, our candidate has proved to be inept.
    Hurt, he left the room quickly.
    Pleased with the result, she beamed at her painting.

7. To set off a nonrestrictive clause or phrase (an element not essential to the basic meaning of the sentence). Place commas both before and after the nonrestrictive portion.

    The hotel, which had housed visiting celebrities for a century, remained largely unchanged.

8. To set off appositives or appositive phrases. Place commas both before and after the appositive.

    March, the month of crocuses, can still bring snow and ice.
    One of our major problems, narcotics, remains unsolved.
    Mrs. Polonski, a member of the committee, refused to comment.

9. To set off parenthetical words and phrases and words of direct address.

    You may, if you insist, demand a retraction.
    The use of pesticides, however, has its disadvantages.
    She knew, nevertheless, that all was lost.
    Mr. Brown, far younger in spirit than his eighty years, delighted in his great-grandchildren.
    You realize, Mary, that we may never return to Paris.

10. To set off quoted matter from the rest of the sentence. (See *Quotation Marks* below.)
11. To set off items in dates. A date given in the order of month, day, and year is also followed by a comma.

    Both John Adams and Thomas Jefferson died on July 4, 1826, just fifty years after the signing of the Declaration of Independence.

    An intermediary comma may or may not be used when only two items are given in a date.

    Washington was born in February, 1732, in Virginia.

    or

    Washington was born in February 1732, in Virginia.

12. To set off elements in addresses and geographical locations when the items are written on the same line.

    35 Fifth Avenue, New York, N.Y.
    1515 Halsted Street, Chicago, Illinois
    He lived in Lima, Peru, for fifteen years.

13. To set off titles of individuals.

    Dr. Ellen Sachs, Dean of Admissions
    Mr. John Winthrop, President, will be there.
    Charles I, Duke of Albany, Duke of York, Prince of Wales

14. To set off the salutation in a personal letter.

    Dear Sam,

15. To set off the closing in a letter.

    Sincerely yours,
    Very truly yours,

16. To denote an omitted, understood word or words in one or more parallel constructions

within a sentence, usually a sentence containing a semicolon.

John is studying Greek; Sarah, Latin.

SEMICOLON (;)

Use a semicolon:

1. **To separate closely or implicitly related independent clauses not joined by a conjunction.**

   The house burned down; it was the last shattering blow.

   The struggle must continue; we will be satisfied only with victory.

2. **To separate independent clauses that are joined by such conjunctive adverbs as *hence, however, therefore,* and *thus.***

   The funds are inadequate; therefore, the project will close down.

   Enrollments exceed all expectations; however, there is a teacher shortage.

3. **To separate long or possibly ambiguous items in a series, especially when the items already include commas.**

   The elected officers are Jonathan Adelmann, president; Frances Glenn, vice president; Edward Morrell, treasurer; and Susan Stone, secretary.

4. **To separate elements that are closely related but cannot be joined unambiguously with a comma.**

   Poverty is unbearable; luxury, insufferable.

5. **To precede a word, phrase, or abbreviation that introduces explanatory information or an offered example, as before *i.e., e.g.,* or *that is.* A comma may sometimes be used instead of a semicolon.**

   On the advice of her broker, after much deliberation, she chose to invest in major industries; i.e., steel, automobiles, and oil.

   He organized his work well; for example, by putting correspondence in folders of different colors to indicate degrees of urgency.

COLON (:)

Use a colon:

1. **To introduce a series or list of items, examples, or the like that follows but is not part of the sentence. Thus a colon need not follow a main verb when the series completes (or is the predicate of) the sentence.**

   The three committees are as follows: membership, finance, and nominations.

   He named his five favorite poets: Byron, Keats, Tennyson, Hardy, and Auden.

   Her favorite ballplayers were Winfield, Rose, and Seaver.

2. **To introduce a long statement, quotation, or question or one made in a formal or forceful way.**

   This I believe: All men are created equal and must enjoy equally the rights that are inalienably theirs.

   Richards replied: "You are right. There can be no unilateral peace just as there can be no unilateral war. No one will contest that view."

   This is the issue: Can an employer dismiss someone simply because he or she laughs loudly?

   Note that the first word of the complete sentence following the colon is capitalized, but practice varies here.

3. **To follow a formal salutation, as in a business letter or speech.**

   Gentlemen:
   Dear Mrs. Armbruster:
   My Fellow Americans:
   To Whom It May Concern:

4. **To follow the name of the speaker in a play.**

   Ghost: Revenge his foul and most unnatural murder.
   Hamlet: Murder!

5. **To separate parts of a citation, such as volume, chapter, page, and verse.**

   Genesis 3:2.
   Journal of Astronomy 15:261–327.

6. **To separate hours, minutes, and seconds in indicating time.**

   1:30 P.M.
   His marathon time was 2:18:33.

7. **To indicate that an initial clause in a sentence will be further explained or illustrated by what follows the colon. In effect, the colon is a substitute for such phrases (after a semicolon or comma) as *e.g., that is, for example,* and *namely.***

   It was a city notorious for its inadequacies: its schools were antiquated, its administration was corrupt, and everyone felt the burden of its taxes.

APOSTROPHE (')

Use an apostrophe:

1. **To denote the omission of letters or numerals.**

   a. **The contraction of a word:**

nat'l	m'f'g	ne'er
ma'am	couldn't	won't
I'm	you're	he's
she's	we're	they're

   Do not confuse *it's* (contraction of *it is*) with the possessive *its,* which does not contain an apostrophe.

   b. **The contraction of a number, usually a date:**

   the devastating hurricane of '28
   the Spirit of '76
   the class of '48

   c. **The omission of letters in indicating or quoting dialect:**

   "I ain't goin' back 'cause I'm doin' mighty fine now."

2. **To denote the possessive case of nouns.**

   a. **To form the possessive of most singular and plural nouns or of indefinite pronouns not ending in *s,* add an apostrophe and an *s.***

   the city's industries
   the children's room
   someone's car
   bachelor's degree

   b. **To form the possessive of *singular* nouns (both common and proper) ending in *s* or the sound of *s,* add an apostrophe and an *s* in most instances.**

   the bus's signal light
   the horse's mane
   Tennessee Williams's plays
   Kansas's schools
   Texas's governor
   the class's average
   Francis's promotion

   But if the addition of an *s* would produce an awkward or strained sound or a visually odd spelling, add only an apostrophe.

   Socrates' concepts
   Aristophanes' comedies
   for goodness' sake
   for old times' sake

   In some cases either form is acceptable.

   Mr. Jones's *or* Jones' employees
   Keats's *or* Keats' poetry

   c. **To form the possessive of *plural* nouns (both common and proper) ending in *s,* add only an apostrophe.**

farmers' problems	judges' opinions
students' views	the Smiths' travels
critics' reviews	the Joneses' relatives
two weeks' vacation	three months' delay

   Note, however, that plurals not ending in *s* form their possessive by adding the apostrophe and *s.*

   men's clothing
   women's basketball teams
   the phenomena's aspects

   d. **To denote possession in most compound constructions, add the apostrophe and *s* to the last word of the compound.**

   anyone else's property
   one another's books
   brother-in-law's job
   the attorney general's office

   e. **To denote close association, joint involvement, or possession in the case of two or more proper names, add the apostrophe and *s* to the last name only.**

   Brown, Ross and King's law firm
   Japan and Germany's agreement
   Lewis and Clark's expedition

   f. **To denote individual ownership by two or more proper names, add the apostrophe and an *s* to both names.**

   Paula's and Rick's skis.

3. **To form the plurals of letters or figures add an apostrophe and an *s.* Some authorities and editors prefer to use no apostrophe in such cases, but using one may make it clearer that the added *s* is not part of the abbreviated form or initialism itself.**

   Dot the i's and cross the t's.

figure 8's	PC's
P's and Q's	CEO's
the 1890's	V.I.P.'s
the 20's	GI's

QUOTATION MARKS (" ")

Use quotation marks:

1. **To distinguish spoken words from other matter, as in reporting dialogue.**

   "God bless us every one!" said Tiny Tim.

2. **To mark single words, sentences, paragraphs, or poetic stanzas that are quoted verbatim from the original.**

   Portia's speech on "the quality of mercy" is one of the most quoted passages from Shakespeare.

   It was Shaw who wrote: "All great truths begin as blasphemies."

3. **To enclose a quotation within a quotation, in which case single quotation marks are used.**

   Reading Jill's letter, Pat said, "Listen to this! 'I've just received notice that I made dean's list.' Isn't that great?"

4. **To enclose titles of newspaper and magazine articles, essays, stories, poems (if they are not long or major works), and chapters of books. The quotation marks distinguish such literary pieces from the books or periodicals (these are italicized) in which they appear.**

   Our anthology contains such widely assorted pieces as Bacon's essay "Of Studies," Poe's "The Gold Bug," Keats's "Ode to a Nightingale," and an article on literary criticism from *The American Scholar.*

5. **To enclose titles of short musical compositions and songs, as distinguished from symphonies and operas, which are italicized.**

   Our national anthem is "The Star-Spangled Banner."

   Even the youngsters laughed at the "Figaro" aria from *The Barber of Seville.*

6. **To enclose titles of works of art, such as paintings, drawings, photographs, and sculpture; especially when italics are not available.**

   Most people recognize Da Vinci's "Mona Lisa" (or "La Gióconda") or Rodin's "The Thinker."

7. **To enclose titles of radio and television programs or series.**

   "The Six O'Clock News"
   "Star Trek"

8. **To enclose titles of plays *only* if they are referred to as part of a larger collection. Referred to as single volumes, they are italicized.**

   "The Wild Duck" is the Ibsen play included in this edition of *Modern European Plays.*

9. **To enclose names of ships and airplanes, especially when italics are not available.**

   Lindbergh flew across the Atlantic in the "Spirit of St. Louis."

   My parents sailed to Europe on the "Queen Elizabeth."

10. **To emphasize a word or phrase that is itself the subject of discussion. Italics may also be used for this purpose.**

    The words "imply" and "infer" are not synonymous.

    Such Freudian terms as "ego," "superego," "id," and "libido" are not used by all therapists.

11. **To draw attention to an uncommon word or phrase, a technical term, or a usage very different in style (dialect, extreme slang) from**

the context. This practice should be used with discretion.

Teachers need not be dismayed when students smirk at "uncool" traditions.

In glassblowing, the molten glass is called "metal."

12. To suggest ironic use of a word or phrase.

The radio blasting forth John's favorite "music" is to his grandfather an instrument of torture.

Doris's skiing "vacation" consisted of three weeks with her leg in a cast.

NOTE: The placement of quotation marks next to commas, periods, etc., is determined by certain arbitrary rules and varies with the different marks of punctuation.

1. Use quotation marks both before and after a quoted word, phrase, or longer passage.
2. Use a comma between the quoted matter and such phrases as "according to the speaker," "he said," "she replied," and "they asked" whenever these phrases introduce a quotation, are used parenthetically, or follow a quotation that, in its original form, would end with a period.

John asked, "Why not this week?"

According to the Declaration of Independence, "all men are created equal."

"Well," announced Peggy's father, "we are all going on vacation."

"The merger is imminent," replied the new chairperson.

3. Whenever a phrase such as "he said," "she replied," or "he asked" follows a question or an exclamation, use the corresponding punctuation before the closing quotation mark.

"Why can't we go to the movies this week?" asked Arlene.

"We simply can't buy you a car. And that's final!" replied the boy's mother.

4. Always place the closing quotation mark *before* a colon or semicolon.

She remembered that the girls had always called Gail "the brain"; she began to wonder if the reputation endured.

There were several reasons why Tom was acknowledged as "the champ": physical strength, intellectual superiority, and qualities of leadership.

5. Place the closing quotation mark *after* a question mark or exclamation point only when the latter is part of the quoted passage.

"Hurry, please, before it's too late!" she cried.

"Is there any hope of recovering the property?" he asked.

In all other cases, place the quotation mark *before* the exclamation point or question mark.

Did Pangloss really mean it when he said, "This is the best of all possible worlds"?

How absurd of him to say "This is the best of all possible worlds"!

6. If a quotation consists of two or more consecutive paragraphs, use quotation marks at the beginning of each paragraph, but place them at the end of the last paragraph only.

PARENTHESES ( )

Use parentheses:

1. To enclose material that is not part of the main sentence but is too relevant to omit.

Copies of Faulkner's novels (published by Random House) were awarded as prizes.

Mr. Johnson (to the chairman): Will you allow that question to pass unanswered?

The data (see Table 13) were very impressive.

2. To enclose part of a sentence that, if enclosed by commas, would be confusing.

The authors he advised (none other than Hemingway, Lewis, and Cather) would have been delighted to honor him today.

3. To enclose an item of clarifying or explanatory information.

Her new cottage in Woodstock (New York) was lovely.

4. To set off a sobriquet or nickname within a proper name.

Charles (The Bald) of France
Stan ("The Man") Musial

5. To enclose numbers or letters that designate each item in a series.

The project is (1) too expensive, (2) too time-consuming, and (3) poorly staffed.

He was required to take courses in (a) mathematics, (b) English, (c) history, and (d) geology.

6. To enclose a numerical figure used to confirm a spelled-out number that precedes it.

Enclosed is a check for ten dollars ($10.00) to cover the cost of the order.

BRACKETS [ ]

Brackets are used in pairs to enclose figures, phrases, or sentences that are inserted into the context—usually to set apart interpolated matter from a direct quotation.

Use brackets:

1. To set off a notation, explanation, or editorial comment that is inserted in quoted material and is not part of the original text.

According to the *Globe* critic, "This [*Man and Superman*] is one of Shaw's greatest plays."

Or substitute the bracketed proper name for the pronoun:

"[*Man and Superman*] is one of Shaw's. . . ."

"Young as they are," he writes, "these students are afflicted with cynicism, world-weariness, and *a total disregard for tradition and authority.*" [Emphasis is mine.]

2. To correct an error in a quotation.

"It was on April 25, 1944 [1945—Ed.] that delegates representing forty-six countries met in San Francisco."

3. To indicate that an error in fact, spelling, punctuation, or language usage is quoted deliberately in an effort to reproduce the original statement with complete accuracy. The questionable fact or expression is followed by the Latin word *sic*, meaning "thus," which is enclosed in brackets.

"George Washington lived during the seventeenth [*sic*] century."

"The governor of Missisipi [*sic*] addressed the student body."

4. To enclose stage directions, which are usually italicized, in plays. Parentheses may also be used for this purpose.

Juliet: [*Snatching Romeo's dagger*] . . . O happy dagger! This is thy sheath; [*Stabs herself*] there rest and let me die.

5. To enclose comments, responses, observations, etc., regarding a verbatim transcription of a speech, debate, or testimony.

Sen. Eaton: The steady rise in taxes must be halted. [*Applause*]

6. To substitute for parentheses within material already enclosed by parentheses. Although it is not seen frequently, this is a convention in footnotes.

[1]See "René Descartes" (M. C. Beardsley, *The European Philosophers from Descartes to Nietzsche* [New York, 1960]).

7. To enclose the publication date, inserted by the editor, of an item appearing in an earlier issue of a periodical. This is conventionally done in letters to the editor or in articles written on subjects previously reported. Parentheses may also be used for this purpose.

Dear Sir: Your excellent article on China [April 15] brings to mind my recent experience . . .

When removing old wallpaper [*House Crafts Monthly*, March 1987] some do-it-yourselfers neglect to . . .

DASH (—)

Use a dash:

1. To mark an abrupt change in thought or grammatical construction in the middle of a sentence.

He won the game—but I'm getting ahead of the story.

2. To suggest halting or hesitant speech.

"Well—er—ah—it's very hard to explain," he faltered.

3. To indicate a sudden break or interruption before a sentence is completed.

"Harvey, don't climb up that —." It was too late.

4. To add emphasis to parenthetical material or to mark an emphatic separation between parenthetical material and the rest of a sentence.

His influence—he was a powerful figure in the community—was a deterrent to effective opposition.

The excursions for school groups—to museums, zoos, and theatres—are less expensive.

5. To set off an appositive or appositive phrase when commas would provide less than the desired emphasis or result in confusion (because of commas within the appositive phrase).

The premier's promise of changes—land reform, higher wages, reorganization of industry—was not easily fulfilled.

6. To replace an offensive word or part of one.

Where's that son of a —?
Where the h— is he?

7. To signal informally the end or breaking off of a brief introductory phrase, salutation, dateline, etc.

Jack—
Be back at 2:30.
Grace
Washington, May 2—

HYPHEN (-)

The hyphenation of compound nouns and modifiers is often arbitrary, inconsistent, and subject to change. Practices vary, often changing as a term becomes more widely used. To determine current usage as well as traditional forms, it is best to consult the Dictionary.

Use a hyphen:

1. To form certain compound nouns:

a. Nouns consisting of two or more words denoting the combination of two or more constituents, qualities, or functions in one person or thing.

secretary-treasurer city-state
teacher-counselor AFL-CIO

b. Nouns made up of two or more words or word elements, including other parts of speech and suffixes.

cease-fire fourth-grader
court-martial hand-me-down
cure-all has-been
do-gooder jack-in-the-pulpit
do-it-yourselfer

Do not hyphenate compound nouns denoting chemical terms or certain governmental positions or military ranks.

hydrogen sulfide brigadier general
sodium chloride lieutenant junior grade
carbon tetrachloride
lieutenant governor attorney general
justice of the peace private first class
sergeant at arms

2. To connect the elements of a compound modifier when used *before* the noun it modifies. In most cases, the same modifier is not hyphenated if it *follows* the noun it modifies.

They engaged in hand-to-hand combat.
They fought hand to hand.
They endured a hand-to-mouth existence.
They lived hand to mouth.
a well-known expert
an expert who is well known

Do not hyphenate a compound modifier that includes an adverb ending in *ly* even when it is used before the noun.

her loose-fitting jacket
her loosely fitting jacket
a well-guarded secret
a carefully guarded secret

3. To distinguish a near homonym from a more commonly used word.

COMMON FORM:	HYPHENATED FORM:
a recreation hall	re-creation of a scene
to recover from an illness	re-cover the couch
to reform a sinner	re-form their lines
a job well done	a steak well-done

4. To prevent possible confusion in pronunciation when a prefix results in the doubling of a letter, especially a vowel, or if a suffix results in the tripling of a consonant.

    anti-intellectual
    de-emphasize
    de-energize
    trill-like

5. To join certain prefixes with *proper* nouns or adjectives.

anti	anti-American, anti-British
mid	mid-Victorian, mid-Atlantic, mid-August
neo	neo-Nazi, neo-Darwinism
non	non-European, non-Asian, non-Christian
pan	Pan-American, Pan-African
pro	pro-French, pro-American
un	un-American, un-British

With few exceptions, these prefixes are joined to common nouns without hyphenation:

anticlimax	midsummer	proslavery
nonintervention	neoclassic	unambiguous

Words beginning with *co-* are usually not hyphenated.

coordinate	coauthor
coworker	cobelligerent
co-host	co-manage
coaction	coanchor
cofactor	cosigner

6. To join the following prefixes and suffixes with the main word of a compound.

ex-	ex-sergeant, ex-mayor, ex-wife, ex-premier
self-	self-preservation, self-defeating, self-explanatory, self-educated
-elect	president-elect, governor-elect

7. To form most compound nouns and adjectives that begin with the word elements listed below. For words not listed, it is best to consult the Dictionary.

all-	all-around	all-embracing
	all-day	all-expense
cross-	cross-examine	cross-fertilize
	cross-purposes	cross-stitch
double-	double-breasted	double-edged
	double-jointed	double-park
great-	(always used in family relationships)	
	great-grandfather	great-grandchild
heavy-	heavy-handed	heavy-hearted
	heavy-duty (but heavyweight)	
ill-	ill-disposed	ill-organized
	ill-timed	
light-	light-fingered	light-footed
	light-duty	light-year
single-	single-breasted	single-handed
	single-minded	
well-	well-behaved	well-balanced
	well-preserved	well-wisher

For words beginning with *half-*, it is best to consult the Dictionary.

half-blooded	halfway
halfhearted	half-share
half title	halftime

8. To spell out a word or name.

    r-e-a-s-o-n
    G-a-e-l-i-c

9. To divide a word into syllables.

    hal-lu-ci-na-tion

10. To mark the division of a word of more than one syllable at the end of a line, indicating that the word is completed on the following line.

    It is difficult to estimate the damaging psycholog-
    ical effects of poverty.

11. To separate the parts (when spelling out numerals) of a compound number from twenty-one to ninety-nine.

    thirty-six inches to the yard
    Fifty-second Street
    nineteen hundred and forty-three

12. To separate (when spelling out numerals) the numerator from the denominator of a fraction, especially a fraction used adjectivally.

    One-half cup of milk
    a two-thirds majority

    While some writers, editors, and publications avoid hyphenating fractions used as nouns, the practice is not uncommon.

    Three fourths (or three-fourths) of his constituents
    One fifth (or one-fifth) of the class

    Do not use a hyphen to indicate a fraction if either the numerator or denominator is already hyphenated.

    one thirty-second
    forty-five hundredths
    twenty-one thirty-sixths

DIVISION OF WORDS

If it is necessary to divide a word at the end of a line, follow the syllabification shown in the Dictionary.

Do not syllabify a word so that only one letter stands alone at the end or beginning of a line. Do not divide a one-syllable word, including words ending in *-ed* (such as *walked, saved, hurled*). Avoid the division of a word that carries only two letters over to the next line. The following terminal parts of words should never be divided: *-able, -ible, -cial, -sial, -tial; -cion, -sion, -tion; -gion; -ceous, -cious, -tious; -geous.*

If a word that already has a hyphen must be broken, hyphenate only at the hyphen.

	mother- in-law	mother-in- law
but not	moth- er-in-law	

ABBREVIATIONS

In standard academic, scientific, business, or other formal writing, abbreviations are generally avoided unless they are the commonly required ones and are specifically known and accepted terms within a particular discipline or trade.

Some abbreviations that are acceptable in journalistic or business writing may not be appropriate in extremely formal announcements or invitations in which even dates may be spelled out.

Abbreviations are often used in ordering and billing, catalogs, tabulations, telephone books, classified advertising, recordkeeping, scorekeeping, and similar cases where brevity is essential.

In some cases, the decision to use an abbreviation is a matter of individual preference. It is usually prudent to use the spelled-out form the first time the term is used in a piece of writing. Thereafter one should be consistent in using either the written-out or the abbreviated form. As in all writing, it is most important to maintain consistency of usage within any single written document, whether it be a letter or a treatise. Use abbreviations in writing:

1. The following titles and forms of address whenever they precede a proper name: *Mr., Mrs., Ms., Dr., Mme., Mlle., M.* Do not spell out these titles even in the most formal contexts.

Mlle. Modiste	Dr. Jekyll
Mr. Hyde	Mme. Marie Curie
Ms. O'Hara	Mrs. Lopez

2. Titles of the clergy, government officials, officers of organizations, and military personnel, except in an extremely formal context and provided that the title is followed by a first name or initial as well as a surname. If the title is followed only by a surname, it should be spelled out.

Gen. George Armstrong Custer	General Custer
Sgt. Leon Greene	Sergeant Greene
Prof. Barbara Page	Professor Page
Gov. Mario Cuomo	Governor Cuomo
Rev. John McDermott	The Reverend John McDermott *or* The Reverend Dr. (*or* Mr.) McDermott
Hon.	The Honorable Harvey Douglas *or* The Honorable Mr. Douglas

Note above that in very formal writing, the title *Honorable* or *Reverend* is spelled out and is preceded by *The.* When the first name or initial is omitted, the title *Mr.* or *Dr.* is substituted.

3. *Jr.* or *Sr.* following a name. These abbreviations should be added only when the names preceding them include a first name or initial.

4. *Esq.* following a name. Not a common usage in the United States, this abbreviation should not be used with any other title.

    James Grant, Esq. (*not* Mr. James Grant, Esq.)

5. Academic degrees: *B.A.* (Bachelor of Arts) *M.A.* (Master of Arts); *M.S.* (Master of Science); *Ph.D.* (Doctor of Philosophy); *M.D.* (Doctor of Medicine), etc. When a person's name is followed by a scholastic degree or by the abbreviations of religious or fraternal orders (e.g., BPOE) it should not be preceded by *Mr., Miss, Dr.,* or any other title.

6. The terms used to describe business firms (*Co., Corp., Inc., Bro.* or *Bros., Ltd., R.R.* or *Ry.*) only when these abbreviations are part of the legally authorized name. In all other cases (except for brevity in tables, listings, etc.), *Company, Corporation, Incorporated, Brothers, Limited, Railroad,* and *Railway* should be spelled out.

7. Except in formal writing, the names of states, territories, or possessions that immediately follow the name of a city, mountain, airport, or other specific geographic location. Check the dictionary for all such abbreviations. In addressing mail, authorized postal abbreviations (e.g., CA) should be used.

    Detroit, Mich.
    San Juan, P.R.

8. Certain expressions derived from Latin and more common in their abbreviated forms.

    i.e. (*id est*), that is
    e.g. (*exempli gratia*), for example
    et al. (*et alii*), and others
    etc. (et cetera), and so forth

Do not abbreviate:

1. Names of countries, except:
    a. The U.S.S.R. (Union of Soviet Socialist Republics) because of its exceptional length.
    b. U.S. (United States) when preceding the name of an American ship. The abbreviation *U.S.* may also be used in tables, footnotes, etc., or, in all but the most formal writing, as an attributive modifier: *U.S. Congress, U.S. Post Office, U.S. economic policies,* etc.

2. The days of the week or the months of the year except in the most informal situations or in tables.

3. Weights and measures except in lists of items, technical writing, etc.

    I had hoped to lose ten pounds.
    We used ten yards of cloth.

Do not use a period after the following abbreviations or shortened forms:

1. After a contraction, which is not to be confused with an abbreviation. Contractions contain apostrophes that indicate omitted letters; they never end with a period.

sec't'y or sec'y	sec.
Nat'l	natl.

2. After chemical symbols.

    H_2O NaCl

3. After *percent.*

4. After specific military terms.

USA	United States Army
USMC	United States Marine Corps
USN	United States Navy
USNR	United States Naval Reserve

USCG United States Coast Guard
USNG United States National Guard
MP military police
SP shore patrol
POW prisoner of war
APO Army post office

5. After the initials of certain governmental agencies or call letters of television and radio stations.

NATO, UNICEF, CIA, CARE, OPEC, KCTS Seattle, WQXR New York.

6. After letters that are used as symbols rather than initials.

Let us assume that A and B are playing opposite C and D.

7. After listed items (as in catalogs, outlines, or syllabi), if none of the items is a complete sentence. If the list includes only one complete sentence, use a period after this and all other items on the list, including those which are not complete sentences. Consistency is essential: a period after each item or no end punctuation whatever.

8. After points of the compass.

NE SW
ESE E by NE

CAPITALIZATION

Many writers have a tendency to use capitals unnecessarily. When in doubt, one can usually learn whether a particular word is generally capitalized—written with an initial capital letter—by consulting the dictionary. A safe guideline is to capitalize only when there is specific need or reason to do so.

1. Capitalize the first word of a sentence. Capitalize, also, any word (or the first word of a phrase) that stands independently, such as an exclamation or the beginning of a minor sentence.

He is the new president of the club.
Where is the chess set?
Hurrah! No school!

Capitalize the first word of each line of poetry (unless the poet specifically rejects this convention in his or her verse).

Her pretty feet
Like snails did creep
A little out, and then,
As if they started at Bo-Peep,
Did soon draw in again.

Capitalize the first word of a direct quotation within a sentence (unless the quotation is a fragment).

He replied, "He prefers to enter in the fall."
"George," she asked, "don't you want to join us for dinner?"
He denied that he was "a neurotic editor."

2. Always capitalize the interjection *O* or the pronoun *I*. None of the other pronouns is capitalized unless it occurs at the beginning of a sentence, refers to the Deity, or deifies or personifies a thing.

Here I am. Exult, O Shores!

3. Capitalize all proper nouns and adjectives:

Italians Scottish
Emily Dickinson Edwardian
the Cabot family Martha
Australia Shavian
Chicago Chaucerian

4. The German *von* and the Dutch *van* in proper names are commonly not written with a capital when part of a name, but usage varies.

Paul von Hindenburg Vincent van Gogh
James Van Allen Martin Van Buren

The French particles *de* and *du* and the Italian *di* and *da* are commonly written in lowercase when they are preceded by a first name or title. Without title or first name, the particle is sometimes dropped, sometimes capitalized.

Marquis de Lafayette Count de Mirabeau
(De) Lafayette (De) Mirabeau

In English or American names these particles are commonly capitalized in all instances:

William De Morgan Lee De Forest
De Morgan De Forest

5. Do not capitalize words derived from proper nouns but now having a meaning distinct from that of the proper name:

antimacassar china
pasteurize macadam

6. Capitalize recognized geographical names:

Ohio River Strait of Juan de Fuca
Cascade Mountains Gulf of Mexico

Capitalize the following when they follow a single proper name and are written in the singular:

Basin Desert Peninsula
Butte Forest Plateau
Canal Gap Pond
Canyon Glacier Range
County Harbor River
Creek Head Tract
Delta Ocean Valley

For example, the *Sacramento River,* but the *Tennessee and Cumberland rivers.*

Capitalize the following in the singular and plural when they follow a proper name:

Hill Mountain
Island Narrows

Capitalize the following in the singular whether placed before or after the name.

Bay Cape Lake
Point Mount Peak
Strait Gulf Plain
Sea Isle

7. Capitalize compass directions when they designate particular regions. Capitalize also the nicknames or special names for regions or districts:

East Tennessee the South
Middle Atlantic States the Near East
the New World the Dust Bowl
the West Coast the Midwest

Exception: Do not capitalize merely directional parts of states or countries.

eastern Washington southern Indiana

8. Capitalize months, days of the week, and religious and secular holidays.

February Thanksgiving
Tuesday Passover

9. Capitalize the names of districts, streets, parks, buildings, etc.:

Fifth Avenue Golden Gate Park
the Loop Sears Tower

Exceptions: Do not capitalize such categories of buildings as *library, post office,* or *museum,* written without a proper name, unless local custom makes the classification equivalent to a proper name.

10. Capitalize the various names of God or the Christian Trinity, both nouns and adjectives, and all pronouns clearly referring to the Deity. Capitalize also words that refer to the Bible or other sacred personages or writings, such as those of Islam or Hinduism, as well as words for religious adherents.

the Word Holy Bible
the Savior the Koran
the Messiah Ten Commandments
the Almighty Buddhist

11. Capitalize all personifications.

Come, gentle Death!

12. Capitalize the names of organizations, institutions, political parties, alliances, movements, classes, religious groups, nationalities, races, etc.:

Democratic party Royalist Spain
Labor party Axis powers
Republicans Soviet Russia
Protestants University of Wisconsin
United Nations Lutherans
American Legion

13. Capitalize divisions, departments, and offices of government when the official name is used.

Do not capitalize incomplete or generalized designations:

Department of Commerce
Circuit Court of Marion County
Bureau of Labor Statistics
Congress
Senate
House of Burgesses
United States Army
Board of Aldermen
the council
the lower house (of Congress)
the bureau
the legislature

14. Capitalize the names of wars, battles, treaties, documents, prizes, and important periods or events:

Tet Offensive
Declaration of Independence
Nobel Prize
Revolutionary War
Congress of Vienna
Black Death
Vietnam War
Golden Age of Pericles
Middle Ages
Treaty of Versailles

Do not capitalize *war* or *treaty* when used without the distinguishing name.

Capitalize the numerals used with royal or imperial personages, dynasties, or organizations. Numerals preceding the name are ordinarily spelled out; those following the name are commonly put in Roman numerals:

Second World War World War II
Nineteenth Amendment Third Army
Forty-eighth Congress Henry IV

15. Capitalize titles, military or civil ranks of honor, academic degrees, decorations, etc., when written with the name, and all honorific titles when used for specific persons in place of the name:

General Grant
the Senator from Ohio
the Earl of Rochester
King George
the Archbishop of Canterbury
Your Highness

16. Capitalize the main words (nouns, verbs, adjectives, adverbs) of the titles of books, articles, poems, plays, musical compositions, etc., and always the first word and the last.

Catch-22
All's Well That Ends Well
"The Moonlight Sonata"

17. Titles of chapters in a book are usually capitalized. Capitalize also any sections of a specific book, such as *Bibliography, Index, Table of Contents,* etc.

In expressions of time, *A.M., P.M., A.D.,* and *B.C.* are usually written or typed in capitals without space between them.

9:40 A.M. 42 B.C.
3 P.M. A.D. 750

It is equally acceptable to show *a.m.* and *p.m.* in lowercase letters. When A.M., P.M., A.D., and B.C. are to be typeset, one may mark them with double-underlining to indicate that small capitals are to be used.

ITALICS

Italics (usually indicated in manuscript by underlining) are occasionally used to emphasize a particular word, phrase, or statement. Done with restraint, this use of italics can be effective. Done to excess, it gives the text a flickering, confusing appearance.

Italics are used for titles of books, magazines, newspapers, motion pictures and plays, longer musical compositions, works of art, ships, individual aircraft and spacecraft, and book-length poems.

A Separate Peace *Hamlet*
Reader's Digest Beethoven's *Ninth Symphony*
the *Washington Post* *Guernica*
The Wizard of Oz

Rodin's *The Thinker*	*Enola Gay*
	Mariner 2
the *Titanic*	*Paradise Lost*

While the names of single spacecraft, satellites, or space missions, such as *Sputnik II,* are italicized, those for projects, programs, or types of rockets are not.

Foreign words and phrases that have not been fully adopted into English should be italicized.

In her younger days she was considered quite a *femme du monde.*
I'll be there, *deo volente.*
She has a lot of panache.

Use italics when referring to a letter, number (except after "number"), word, or expression as such. Quotation marks are sometimes used instead of italics.

The word *fantastic* is her favorite adjective.
Do not pronounce the final *e* in *Hecate.*
She drew a large *4* on the blackboard.
He wrote a small number five on the pad.

Use italics for parenthesized stage directions in a play.

HEIDI (*turning to* ANITA): Did he call me?
ANITA: I didn't hear him. *(She picks up a magazine.)*

NUMERALS

In general, numbers that can be stated in only one or two words are spelled out.

There were twelve girls and twenty-six boys there.
The sweater cost sixty dollars.
He gave one-tenth of his income to charity.

Other numbers are usually shown in figures.

There are 392 members in the association.
The radio cost him $136.50.
The population of Chicago in 1980 was 3,005,072.

Any numeral at the beginning of a sentence is usually spelled out. If this is awkwardly long or difficult to read, rewrite the sentence to avoid beginning with a numeral.

Three hundred and sixty students attended the dance.
Twenty-six million votes were cast for him.
Six thousand dollars was stolen from the safe.

It is important to be consistent in the treatment of numbers when they appear in the same series or in the same sentence or paragraph. When they are in close sequence, do not spell some out and use figures for others.

The three chairs are 36, 72, and 122 years old.
He spent $800 on rent, $90 on food, and $265 on clothes.

Use figures (generally) for dates, decades, pages, dimensions, decimals, percentages, measures, statistical data, exact amounts of money, designations of time when followed by *A.M.* or *P.M.*, and addresses.

June 24, 1945	2.5 om	£12.95
the 1920's	0.9631	96.8°
124 B.C.	23 percent	86%
p. 263	75 pounds	8:30 A.M.
p. xxvi	93 miles	3:20 P.M.
2′ × 4′	$369.27	4262 B Street

Spell out ordinal numbers whenever possible.

sixteenth century	Fifth Avenue
Eighty-second Congress	Third Republic
Third Assembly District	Twenty-third Psalm

A common rule for the styling of numbers that is used by many magazines, newspapers, and editorial departments is to spell out only numbers from one through ten and larger round or approximate numbers.

MANUSCRIPT PREPARATION

The manuscript should be typewritten, *double-spaced,* on white medium-weight paper. The sheets should be of the standard 8½″ × 11″ size and of good enough quality to permit clear markings in ink. The paper should not be the glossy, erasable variety. If a computer is used, the manuscript should be printed in letter quality. Some publishers will accept dot-matrix print if it is highly legible, but they generally prefer manuscripts without such enhancements as bold print (for emphasis) or justified text. Margins should be about one inch on each side and at the top and bottom. All pages should be numbered consecutively, preferably at the top.

A quotation that will run three lines or more is usually set off as a single-spaced, double-indented paragraph.

IMPORTANT: The author should always retain a complete copy of the manuscript, not only to facilitate correspondence between the editor and author but to serve as insurance against loss of the original. Publishers are usually very careful not to lose or damage a manuscript, but it is always wise to take precautions.

FOOTNOTES

Footnotes serve a variety of purposes: to indicate the source of a fact, opinion, or quotation; to provide additional or explanatory material that, although relevant, would interrupt the flow of the main text; and to cross-refer the reader to another part of the text. Excessive use of footnotes, however, is usually distracting; it is the sign, generally, of spurious scholarship or of pedantry.

Material in the text to which footnotes are to be keyed should be numbered with superscript Arabic numerals ([1], [2], [3], [4], etc.). These numerals are usually placed without intervening space at the close of the sentence, quotation, or paragraph, unless doing so would cause confusion or ambiguity (in which case the numeral is placed within the sentence, after the specific word, phrase, or name to which it refers).

Footnote numbers should continue consecutively throughout an article or chapter, with the numbering beginning again in each chapter.

Some writers prefer to use special symbols (*, †, ‡, §, ||, ¶, etc.) instead of superscript numerals. Because this system of symbols is limited and confusing, it is preferably avoided.

Footnotes are placed at the bottom of the page under a straight line that extends from the left to the right margins. (Some style manuals suggest that this line extend only two or three inches in from the left margin.) One line of space is left blank above this separation line and two lines of space are left blank below it. The footnote, which begins with the appropriate superscript number without a space after it, is usually typed single-space. The first line of the footnote is the same indention used throughout the text itself; subsequent lines are typed to the same margins as the text itself. Avoid carrying footnotes onto a following page if at all possible.

BOOKS: FIRST FOOTNOTE REFERENCES

When a book is first mentioned in a footnote, the bibliographical information should be as complete as possible. The information should appear in the following order:

1. AUTHOR'S NAME OR AUTHORS' NAMES. Normal word order is used. The given name or initials are given first, using the form in which the name is generally encountered, the surname being followed by a comma.
2. TITLE OF THE CHAPTER OR PART. When reference is made to an article in a collection, symposium, or the like, the title of the article appears within quotation marks, the final quotation mark being preceded by a comma.
3. TITLE OF THE BOOK. The title is underlined (to indicate italics) and followed by a comma unless the next information is in parentheses; in such a case, the comma follows the closing parenthesis. If the title is exceptionally long, it may be shortened by omissions (indicated by three ellipsis points in each case). The title should be given as it is shown on the title page of the book cited.
4. EDITOR'S OR TRANSLATOR'S NAME. The name of the editor or translator, given in its full and normal form, is preceded by "ed." or "trans." It is followed by a comma unless the next material is in parentheses.
5. EDITION USED. If the edition is other than the first one, the edition is identified in Arabic numerals, followed by a comma unless the next material is in parentheses.
6. SERIES TITLE. The name of the series is shown without underlining or quotation marks. It is followed by the specific number of the work in the series, preceded and followed by commas. If the next material is in parentheses, the second comma is placed after the closing parenthesis.
7. NUMBER OF VOLUMES. If there is more than one volume in the work and it appears relevant to indicate this fact, the number is shown in Arabic numerals.
8. PLACE OF PUBLICATION. This information, plus the name of the publisher and date of publication, is shown within one set of parentheses. The place of publication is usually found on the title page; if more than one city is shown, it is necessary only to show the publisher's main place of activity. If the city is not well known or might be confused with another of the same name, add the state or nation. The place of publication is followed by a colon.
9. NAME OF THE PUBLISHER. The name of the company, institution, etc., that published the work is shown next, followed by a comma.
10. DATE OF PUBLICATION. The date of publication is usually found on the copyright page or title page. If no date is shown on either, write "n.d." (without quotation marks) to indicate "no date." The parentheses containing the place of publication, publisher's name, and date of publication is followed by a comma. When several dates are shown on a copyright page only the earliest need be given. But the date of the latest *edition* is always pertinent.
11. VOLUME NUMBER. If there are two or more volumes in the work, give the volume number in capital Roman numerals, enclosed by commas. If this information is followed by the page number, omit "Vol." and give the volume number only, followed by a comma.
12. PAGE NUMBER OR NUMBERS. The page number (preceded by "p.") is shown in Arabic numerals (unless the original uses Roman numerals), followed by a period. However, if the volume number has been given, the "p." may be omitted. In the case of a reference to several sequential pages, "pp." rather than "p." is used.

ARTICLES IN PERIODICALS: FIRST FOOTNOTE REFERENCES

When a magazine or newspaper article is referred to in a footnote for the first time, the bibliographical information is given in the following order:

1. AUTHOR'S NAME OR AUTHORS' NAMES. The name is given in normal order and usual form, followed by a comma.
2. TITLE OF THE ARTICLE. The title is given in full, enclosed by quotation marks, with a comma preceding the closing quotation mark.
3. NAME OF THE PERIODICAL. The name of the periodical, underlined to indicate italics, is followed by a comma. If there is a familiar abbreviation of the name of the periodical, it may be used.
4. VOLUME NUMBER. The volume number in capital Roman numerals is followed by a comma unless the next item is within parentheses.
5. ISSUE NUMBER OR NAME. If the pagination of each issue is separate and the issue is not designated by month, give the issue number or name.
6. YEAR AND MONTH. The month (if necessary) and year of the volume are enclosed by parentheses followed by a comma.
7. PAGE NUMBER OR NUMBERS. The page number (preceded by "p.") or numbers (preceded by "pp.") are given in Arabic numerals (unless the original text uses Roman numerals) and terminated with a period. However, if the

volume number has been given, the "p." may be omitted.

UBSEQUENT FOOTNOTE EFERENCES

fter the first footnote reference to a book, artile, or the like, it is unnecessary to repeat all the ibliographical information in each reference to he same work.

If a footnote reference is the same work as the receding footnote, use "ibid." (Latin: *ibidem* "in he same place") in place of all bibliographical nformation. If a different volume or page of the ame work is to be indicated, this information ollows "ibid." and a comma.

If "ibid." might be used if it were not for the ntervention of references to other works, some riters use either "op. cit." (Latin: *opere citato* in the work cited") or "loc. cit." (*loco citato* "in he cited place") after the author's surname to void restatement of all the bibliographical data hen the volume (and, with "loc. cit.," page) is he same as that of the first footnote reference to he work.

Many writers prefer to avoid "op. cit." and "loc. it." as well as "ibid." by simply giving the auhor's surname, followed by the year of publicaion and page number, in parentheses in the body f the text. The page number may be preceded by ither a comma or a colon.

(Taylor 1980, 944)
(Dilworth 1986:328–333)

When the author's name is part of the text, the ear and page number form the parenthetical eference.

This information can be found in Lazarsfeld et al. (1944:61), and is substantiated by . . .

COMMON ABBREVIATIONS IN OOTNOTES

he following abbreviations are commonly enountered in footnotes:

anon.	anonymous
ch. (chs.)	chapter (chapters)
chap. (chaps.)	chapter (chapters)
col.	column
comp.	compiled
ed.	editor; edition
esp.	especially
f. (ff.)	and the following page (pages)
n.d.	no date
no. (nos.)	number (numbers)
n.s.	new series
p. (pp.)	page (pages)
pass.	*(passim)* throughout
repr.	reprint; reprinted
rev.	revised
ser.	series
supp., suppl.	supplement
tr., trans.	translator; translation
vol. (vols.)	volume (volumes)

SAMPLE FOOTNOTES: FIRST REFERENCE

A book by one author, first edition:

[4]Telford Taylor, *Munich: The Price of Peace* (New York: Vintage Books, 1980), p. 944.

A book by one author, revised or later edition:

[2]James B. Dilworth, *Production and Operations Management,* 3d ed. (New York: Random House, 1986), pp. 328–333.

A book by two or more authors:

[2]Mary Luisa and Jack Denton Scott, *The Complete Rice Cookbook* (New York: Times Books, 1985), p. 68.

[3]P. F. Lazarsfeld, B. Berelson, and H. Gaudet, *The People's Choice* (New York: Duell, Sloan, and Pearce, 1944), pp. 61–3.

A book having one or more editors:

[4]Peter Russell, ed., *An Examination of Ezra Pound* (Norfolk, Conn.: New Directions, 1950), pp. 14–23.

[5]William Van O'Connor and Edward Stone, eds., *A Casebook on Ezra Pound* (New York: Thomas Y. Crowell, 1959), p. 137.

A book having an author and an editor:

[3]Thomas Robert Malthus, *On Population,* ed. Gertrude Himmelfarb (New York: The Modern Library, 1960), p. xxvii.

A book having a translator:

[4]Andrei Amalrik, *Notes of a Revolutionary,* trans. Guy Daniels (New York: Alfred A. Knopf, 1982), p.193.

A book in several volumes:

[1]Dennis Sherman, ed., *Western Civilization: Images and Interpretations* (New York: Alfred A. Knopf, 1983), II, pp. 104–106.

A book in a series:

[3]Arthur S. Link, *Woodrow Wilson and the Progressive Era, 1910–1917,* New American Nation Series (New York: Harper, 1954), pp. 16–31.

An article in an edited collection of contributions:

[2]Herbert H. Rowen, "Kingship and Republicanism in the Seventeenth Century: Some Reconsiderations," in *From the Renaissance to the Counter-Reformation,* ed. by Charles H. Carter (New York: Random House, 1965), p. 430.

An unsigned article in an encyclopedia:

[3]"Rivers and Lakes," *The Random House Encyclopedia,* 1983, p. 258.

A signed article in an encyclopedia:

[2]Edgar Frederick Carritt, "Aesthetics," *Encyclopaedia Britannica,* 1956, I, 265–267.

An unsigned article in a periodical:

[3]"About the MLA Convention," *PMLA,* CI (November, 1986), pp. 932–937.

A signed article in a periodical:

[12]Roger I. Glass, "New Prospects for Epidemiologic Investigations," *Science,* Vol. 234, No. 4779 (Nov. 21, 1986), pp. 951–955.

A bulletin report or pamphlet:

[13]United Nations, *Measures for the Economic Development of Under-Developed Countries* (New York: United Nations, 1951), pp. 8–9.

[14]*Education: An Answer to Poverty,* The Office of Education and the Office of Economic Opportunity (Washington, D.C.: Government Printing Office, 1965), pp. 68–70.

An unpublished thesis or dissertation:

[3]L. S. Yorick, "The Myth of Anchises in Shakespeare's *Hamlet*" (unpublished Ph.D. dissertation, Department of English, University of Chicago), p. 9.

A private communication:

[10]Information in a letter to the author from Professor John R. Perry, University of Chicago, September 14, 1987.

SAMPLE FOOTNOTES: SUBSEQUENT REFERENCE

General:

[17]Taylor, p. 947.
[18]Dilworth, pp. 118–32.
[19]Luisa and Scott, p. 112.

(Alternative) Same work and page as in footnote immediately preceding:

[20]Ibid.

(Alternative) Same work as in footnote immediately preceding but different page:

[3]Ibid., p. 321.

(Alternative) Same work as previously cited but not in footnote immediately preceding:

[6]Taylor, op. cit., p. 31.

(Alternative) Same work (same page) as previously cited but not in footnote immediately preceding:

[7]Taylor, loc. cit.

BIBLIOGRAPHIES

Although bibliographies may be organized by subject, types of publications cited, chronological sequence, or alphabetical order, alphabetical arrangement by author is, by far, most common. Within the list, a given author's works may be arranged chronologically.

The bibliography should be typed so that the first line of each item begins flush with the left margin and succeeding lines are indented several spaces. The material is usually single-spaced (but double-spaced between items).

The content of bibliographical entries is the same as that of footnotes with only these major differences:

1. AUTHOR'S NAME. The surname comes first, followed by a comma; then the given name, followed by a period.
2. TITLE. The title is closed by a period.
3. PUBLICATION DATA. The place of publication, name of the publisher, and date of publication are not enclosed by parentheses; a period is placed after the date.

SAMPLE ENTRIES

"Controversies in Education: The American High School." *Phi Delta Kappan,* XL (November, 1958), pp. 3–126.

Gide, André. *The André Gide Reader.* Edited by David Littlejohn. New York: Alfred A. Knopf, 1971.

Baum, Andrew, Jeffrey D. Fisher, and Jerome E. Singer. *Social Psychology.* New York: Random House, 1985.

Johnson, E. L. "Cooperation in Higher Education." *Liberal Education,* XLVIII (December 1962).

Russell, Peter (ed.). *An Examination of Ezra Pound.* Norfolk, Conn.: New Directions, 1950.

Schwartz, Harry. *Russia's Soviet Economy.* 2d ed. Englewood Cliffs, N.J.: Prentice-Hall, 1954.

White, Newman Ivey. *Shelley.* 2 vols. New York: Alfred A. Knopf, 1940.

When writing for a specific publication or publisher, the author should ask whether there is a preferred house style or style manual to be followed. Among the widely used style manuals are *A Manual of Style* (published by the University of Chicago Press), *The MLA Style Sheet* (published by the Modern Language Association), and *Words into Type* (published by Prentice-Hall).

WRITING A RÉSUMÉ

A résumé is a formal summary of a person's professional or business experience and qualifications. Its purpose is to interest potential employers in a candidate's background, capabilities, and suitability for a particular position as effectively and concisely as possible. It is usually accompanied by a brief covering letter, explaining why the résumé is being submitted and informing the employer of the applicant's unique qualifications for the job.

The importance of the résumé cannot be overestimated. It is a convenient credential that can be left with or mailed to employment agencies, personnel (or human resources) departments, or specific executives or potential employers. It can serve as a door-opener and help you get an interview. At the interview itself, it constitutes a handy capsule working biography that can save the interviewer's time and lead to more detailed and more focused questions and discussion. Finally, even when a suitable job is not available, a résumé may be kept on file by a firm and serve as a standing job application for future openings.

PREPARATION

Make up a list or work sheet containing all relevant or possibly useful career data before drafting the actual résumé. This will give you a better idea of what information, and how much, belongs on the résumé and what the best format might be.

The first thing to be considered is your immediate job objective. Next, your long-range career goals should be considered. One or both of these should be addressed in the résumé itself.

The work sheet should list: your name, address, and telephone number(s); your current job title and/or description of your present work; your previous work experience, listed in reverse chronological order, including dates, names of the companies worked for, and positions held. Also include relevant part-time jobs; professional accomplishments, such as special certificates or awards; membership in professional or civic organizations, etc.; special skills that may be relevant, such as typing, ability to use various computer programs, knowledge of a foreign language, and the like; educational background, including degrees earned and institutions attended, major fields of study, etc.; and military or other national service. (Information about age, sex, marital status, etc., is not required, and employers now prefer not to have it on a résumé in order to avoid any suspicion of bias in choice of job applicants.) You may also want to state when you will be available to start work and whether you are willing to relocate. The résumé usually ends with names and addresses of people who will serve as references, or with the line "References available on request." Desired salary is best discussed at an interview.

FORMAT

The résumé can be organized in any of various ways. Although it is good to have a résumé for general use, suitable for distribution to numerous, possibly different kinds of companies, it may be to your advantage to tailor your résumé to have maximum appeal to an employer whom you know to have a particular job opening or for whom you may especially want to work.

The format also depends on three other factors: (1) the nature of your profession, trade, or business, (2) the amount and variety of your work experience, and (3) personal preference or taste. The résumé of a successful business executive will be markedly different from that of a recently graduated student, and it in turn will usually differ in format and style from that of a free-wheeling journalist or commercial artist. Regardless of which format is chosen, your name, address, telephone number(s), and specific profession or job title should always appear at the top of the résumé.

The key to choosing the best format for your résumé is to emphasize what shows off your experience and skills to best advantage. Decide whether it is best to highlight your promotions within a company or from job to job, the diversity of your training or skills, the name of a prestigious company for which you have worked, or your creative or artistic bent. The two formats described below lend themselves to such different approaches.

A résumé may be written either as an outline, with tabular arrangements of data in brief groupings, or in full paragraphs and complete sentences. A typical résumé will be about one page, though some may run to three pages.

Two standard formats are the Chronological Résumé and the Functional Résumé.

Chronological Résumé This very common format stresses step-by-step job history. A person's successive positions are listed in reverse chronological order, with the current or most recent job listed first. The chronological format itemizes factual detail and dates, giving the résumé a concise, orderly, and formal look. It lets the facts (e.g., companies, positions held, and responsibilities) speak for themselves.

MICHAEL SMITH

11 River Lane
Albuquerque, New Mexico 87139
(505) 220-8801

POSITION DESIRED:	Assistant Editor	
EDUCATION:	University of New Mexico, Albuquerque Bachelor of Arts, May 1987 Major: English; Minor: Fine Arts Graduated Cum Laude	
EXPERIENCE:		
Summer 1986	*Modern Arts Magazine,* New York, N.Y. Editorial Assistant Read manuscripts and gave preliminary evaluations. Typed correspondence for editors. Worked on IBM-PC.	
September 1986–May 1987	University of New Mexico (work-study program) Library Clerk Checked books in and out. Assisted with cataloging.	
Summer 1985	Albuquerque Institute of the Arts Museum Volunteer Assisted staff in setting up a photography exhibit of local photographers.	
ACTIVITIES:		
1985–1987	University of New Mexico Photography Club President	
1985–1987	Wrote an art column for University of New Mexico student newspaper	
REFERENCES:	Professor John Sher English Dept. University of New Mexico Albuquerque, NM 87139	Ms. Alice Smirnoff Modern Arts Magazine 777 W. 3 St. New York, N.Y. 10007

Functional Résumé This type of résumé is organized according to different job functions in which a person is experienced or skilled—with a view to responsibilities desired in a future position. With chronology secondary but with dates of employment always indicated, the writer singles out for emphasis specific qualifications—for example, experience both as a manager and as a researcher, or in both public-health nursing and industrial nursing. Basically, this format gives discrete summaries of varied capabilities, usually in descending order of importance.

The functional résumé is best designed by correlating particulars of the position desired with relevant accomplishments in your job experience. Thus skills learned in different jobs can be extracted for emphasis in a way not possible in a chronological, company-by-company résumé. This format is usually not the best choice if you are just out of school or have limited work experience.

SARAH COLBERT
2000 Riverside Drive
New York, New York 10057
(212) 292-2727

CAREER OBJECTIVE:	MARKETING VICE PRESIDENT
MANAGERIAL EXPERIENCE:	Managed Kitchen Bazaar retail chain of food and gourmet equipment stores in SW United States for 13 years. Planned and executed expansion into new market areas, opening 3 new stores. Did buying and marketing of gourmet equipment for home use, increasing volume by over 600%. Hired and trained a staff of 25.
SALES EXPERIENCE:	Headed Contemporary Furniture Designs, Inc., sales staff of 9 persons (as well as design staff of 5 persons) for corporate and residential furniture. Sales and marketing representative in the New York City market for newly created kitchen products. Increased sales to over $4 million yearly.
ADVERTISING EXPERIENCE:	Copywriter for kitchen products and athletic shoes, writing advertisements and promotional materials for major magazines, newspapers, television, and radio, as well as direct mail. Wrote a training manual for furniture sales staff. Produced 16mm sales films. Designed and set up booths for trade shows. Did marketing and public relations for a public utility.
WORK HISTORY:	
1985–Present	CONTEMPORARY FURNITURE DESIGNS, INC. 17 E. Bayside Street, New York, NY 10016 Sales and Marketing

1 of 2

1983–85	Sales and Marketing Self-employed consultant to major food products companies.
1970–83	KITCHEN BAZAAR 302 N. Canal Road, Phoenix, AZ 85069 Manager
1968–70	EASTERN GAS AND ELECTRIC CO. 781 Patterson Highway, Newark, NJ 08709 Marketing and Public Relations
1960–68	AMERICAN ATHLETIC SHOE COMPANY 188 Bayside Road, Bayside, NY 10479 Copywriter
EDUCATION:	Bachelor of Arts, CCNY, New York, NY 1960 Major: English
MEMBERSHIP:	New York City Marketing Association; Furniture Sales Association of the United States (vice president, 1986–87)

Good knowledge of sales contacts in the East and SW United States; willing to relocate.

References available on request

2 of 2

HEADINGS

Headings or subheadings are integral to a résumé. They subdivide the nformation into distinct sections, making it easier to understand, and help to catch the reader's eye. The wording of the heads and subheads should be concise, and should be appropriate to the nature and format of he résumé.

COMPLETION

Take great care that the final typed or printed résumé is as good as it can e in every detail. Any mistake in grammar or spelling or any strikeover r smudge indicates incompetence or carelessness, exactly the opposite of what a résumé should convey.

The page size should be a standard 8½ × 11 inches, and the paper preferably white and of good quality. Whether a typewriter or word processor-printer is used, the print should be clear and all spacing even or balanced. If the résumé is for short-term use only, a month/year date may be added in the upper corner, if desired, to emphasize its currency or "freshness."

Remember that your résumé should be (1) businesslike, literate, and neat; (2) succinctly organized to be specific and complete, with all important details but no irrelevant ones; (3) focused on your immediate or long-term career goal; and (4) accompanied, when mailed, by a brief covering letter. Conversely, it should not be vague, wordy, exaggerated or self-important in its claims or style, or visually hard to read from excessive data, insufficient margins, or poor typing or photocopying.

WRITING A TERM PAPER

A term paper, or any research paper, calls upon the writer to focus on an ssigned or chosen topic, gather and interpret source materials, marshal rguments, and organize, document, and express ideas forcefully.

A term paper may be a factual inquiry, an analysis of causes and effects, r an account or interpretation of events, ideas, or themes. It may explain r analyze a phenomenon or describe an experience. But whether it is asically informative, argumentative, or narrative, it should always be (1) lear in purpose, (2) unslanted (not omitting contrary evidence), (3) concise nd to the point, and (4) well documented, with sources acknowledged in ootnotes and/or a bibliography.

Begin the assignment as early as possible, to allow time for proper reearch, for rethinking the subject or approach, and for reorganizing and evising the paper.

THE SUBJECT

The subject and scope of the term paper should be neither too ambitious nor oo narrow or technical in scope. Do not pose a question whose answer is bvious or address an issue whose solution is self-evident. First make sure hat adequate information on the topic is conveniently available. If there s a choice of topics, make a preliminary visit to the library for exploratory eading and research before making the final choice.

Remember that the term paper has not only a subject but a thesis. Your houghts and conclusions, not those of other writers, are the essence of the aper. These personal thoughts and conclusions, however, must be well rganized and supported by the research.

RESEARCH

The student who knows how to use the library and all its resources will void many problems in researching. Although primary sources and direct nformation (as from interviews) are valuable for certain topics, it is usually he books, journals, microfilm, etc., available in the reference room of the ibrary that form the backbone of the term paper.

Particularly useful sources, in addition to books on the subject, are (1) ncyclopedias; (2) the *Readers' Guide to Periodical Literature* (for leads to ertinent magazine and journal articles); (3) book bibliographies and crosseferences that lead to other usable sources; and, with some subjects, (4) overnment agencies and private organizations and their publications. Make a preliminary list of sources that promise to be helpful; the paper's nal bibliography will come from this list. Many librarians will do on-line esearch for you (often for a fee), giving you access to material in electronic atabases.

While reading, take systematic notes, organizing and explaining various spects of the topic. Taking notes on index cards will facilitate the sorting nd rearranging of information. If you prefer using a notebook, write on one ide only of each page so that the pages can be pulled out and rearranged ater. Some students enter their notes into a computer, so that they may ake advantage of electronic or word-processing programs to organize their ata.

While taking notes, record not only factual information but also relevant uotations, questions that come to mind, and personal observations and deas. It is also helpful to summarize various points as you go along—in your wn words, not those of the authors consulted. This will make the actual writing of the paper easier and lessen the risk of inadvertent plagiarism. Research sources (with title, author, page number, and all necessary bibliographic information) for both quotations and paraphrases should be written own carefully on first reading, to avoid having to recheck later.

OUTLINE

An outline helps the writer not only to plan the overall paper but also to organize and develop individual sections and ideas. Based on the research notes and sequentially arranged, the outline helps to crystallize the major and supporting points to be made and the step-by-step presentation required. Preparing the outline will also help you decide how best to organize the material: chronologically, by category, or in some other logical way.

Many students make a sketchy outline early in their research stage, then revise and expand it as the research continues. A topic outline, indicating the sequence of ideas and subtopics, may later be expanded into a paragraph outline, which expresses these points as complete, final units and which may grow into the final term paper.

WRITING

Before beginning the actual writing, have a clear idea of the intended approach of the paper. How formal is it to be? Should it be completely objective and factual, somewhat argumentative, or strong and impassioned?

Beginning the actual writing often seems the hardest part of the term paper. Begin at all costs, even if not satisfied with the opening sentence or paragraph; this can be improved later. (Some find it easier to start in the middle of the paper or even with the conclusion, and to write the beginning later.)

There are four standard openings with which to begin a term paper: a summary sentence, a defining statement, a quotation, or a posed question. As you write, remember: (1) The thesis should be made clear to the reader at the very beginning of the paper. What are you setting out to discuss or prove? (2) The purport of each paragraph should be made clear by a topic, or key, sentence, usually the first sentence of the paragraph. (3) Depending on the nature of the paper, first-person references—such as "I" and "me"—should be avoided or minimized.

Do not expect to write a good term paper in just one draft. A second and third draft will almost always be necessary. In the first draft concentrate on substance and organization. Grammar, sentence construction, and spelling can be corrected later. Leave nothing of substance out of the first draft; it will be easier to shorten the paper later than to add to it. If you are typing rather than using a word processor or computer, triple-space your early drafts and use wide margins to allow for corrections and additions. (See the earlier sections of this Manual of Style for proper manuscript preparation, footnotes and bibliography, etc.)

After the first draft has been read and reread, it should be rewritten and reorganized as much as necessary. Use of scissors and tape or glue can be helpful in reordering or inserting material; a word processor or computer can ease this part of the process.

The final manuscript should be as perfect as you can make it in all ways: in organization, clarity, and style; in grammar, punctuation, and spelling; and in exactness of quotations, footnotes, and bibliography. It should be clear and to the point, and free of pretentious words, of overly long sentences, and of digressions. Footnotes or parenthetical acknowledgments should be scrupulously incorporated wherever there is a debt to another source for a specific idea or quotation, or to another writer's statement of "fact" that is clearly debatable or controversial. On the other hand, do not quote or footnote excessively: a term paper is meant to be a documented presentation of your themes or ideas, not a dense, pedantic recitation of material from other sources. It is the use of research material, the process of reasoning, personal insights, and writing skills that are the essence of the term paper.

AVOIDING INSENSITIVE AND OFFENSIVE LANGUAGE

This essay is intended as a general guide to language that can, intentionally r not, cause offense or perpetuate discriminatory values and practices by mphasizing the differences between people or implying that one group is uperior to another.

Several factors complicate the issue. A group may disagree within itself s to what is acceptable and what is not. Many seemingly inoffensive terms levelop negative connotations over time and become dated or go out of style s awareness changes. A "within the group" rule often applies, which allows a member of a group to use terms freely that would be considered ffensive if used by an outsider.

While it is true that some of the more extreme attempts to avoid offending language have resulted in ludicrous obfuscation, it is also true that heightened sensitivity in language indicates a precision of thought and is a positive move toward rectifying the unequal social status between one group and another.

Suggestions for avoiding insensitive or offensive language are given in the following pages. The suggested terms are given on the right. While these suggestions can reflect trends, they cannot dictate or predict the preferences of each individual.

Sexism

Sexism is the most difficult bias to avoid, in part because of the convention of using *man* or *men* and *he* or *his* to refer to people of either sex. Other, more disrespectful conventions include giving descriptions of women in terms of age and appearance while describing men in terms of accomplishment.

Replacing man or men

Man may refer to a male or to a human in general, an ambiguity often thought to be slighting of women.

Instead of	*Use*
mankind, man	human beings, humans, humankind, humanity, people, society, men and women
man-made	synthetic, artificial
man in the street	average person, ordinary person

Using gender-neutral terms for occupations, positions, roles, etc.

Terms that specify a particular sex can perpetuate stereotypes when used generically.

Instead of	*Use*
anchorman	anchor
bellman, bellboy	bellhop
businessman	businessperson, executive, manager business owner, retailer, etc.
chairman	chair, chairperson
cleaning lady, girl, maid	housecleaner, housekeeper, cleaning person, office cleaner
clergyman	member of the clergy, rabbi, priest, etc.
clergymen	the clergy
congressman	representative, member of Congress, legislator
fireman	firefighter
forefather	ancestor
girl/gal Friday	assistant
housewife	homemaker
insurance man	insurance agent
layman	layperson, nonspecialist, nonprofessional
mailman, postman	mail carrier, letter carrier
policeman	police officer, law enforcement officer
salesman, saleswoman, saleslady, salesgirl	salesperson, sales representative, clerk
spokesman	spokesperson, representative
stewardess, steward	flight attendant
weatherman	weather reporter, weathercaster meteorologist
workman	worker
actress	actor

Replacing the pronoun he

Like *man*, the generic use of *he* can be seen to exclude women.

Instead of

When a driver approaches a red light, he must prepare to stop.

Use

When drivers approach a red light, they must prepare to stop.

When a driver approaches a red light, he or she must prepare to stop.

When approaching a red light, a driver must prepare to stop.

Referring to members of both sexes with parallel names, titles, or descriptions

Don't be inconsistent unless you are trying to make a specific point.

Instead of	*Use*
men and ladies	men and women, ladies and gentlemen

Instead of

Betty Schmidt, an attractive 49-year-old physician, and her husband, Alan Schmidt, a noted editor

Use

Betty Schmidt, a physician, and her husband, Alan, an editor

Instead of	*Use*
Mr. David Kim and Mrs. Betty Harrow	Mr. David Kim and Ms. Betty Harrow (unless *Mrs.* is her known preference)
man and wife	husband and wife
Dear Sir:	Dear Sir/Madam: Dear Madam or Sir: To whom it may concern:
Mrs. Whitman and President Clinton	Governor Whitman and President Clinton

Race, Ethnicity, and National Origin

Some words and phrases that refer to racial and ethnic groups are clearly offensive. Other words (e.g., *Oriental*, *colored*) are outdated or inaccurate. *Hispanic* is generally accepted as a broad term for Spanish-speaking people of the Western Hemisphere, but more specific terms (*Latino*, *Mexican American*) are also acceptable and in some cases preferred.

Instead of	*Use*
Negro, colored, Afro-American	black, African-American (generally preferred to *Afro-American*)
Oriental, Asiatic	Asian, or more specific designations such as Pacific Islander, Korean
Indian	*Indian* properly refers to people who live in or come from India. *American Indian*, *Native American*, or more specific designations (Chinook, Hopi), are usually preferred when referring to the native peoples of the Western Hemisphere.
Eskimo	Inuit, Alaska natives
native (n.)	native peoples, early inhabitants, aboriginal peoples (but not *aborigines*)

Age

The concept of aging is changing as people are living longer and more active lives. Be aware of word choices that reinforce stereotypes (*decrepit*, *senile*) and avoid mentioning age unless it is relevant.

Instead of

elderly, aged, old, geriatric, the elderly, the aged

Use

older person, senior citizen, older people, senior citizens, seniors

Sexual Orientation

The term *homosexual* to describe a man or a woman is increasingly replaced by the terms *gay* for men and *lesbian* for women. *Homosexual* as a noun is sometimes used only in reference to a male. Among homosexuals, certain terms (such as *queer* and *dyke*) that are usually considered offensive have been gaining currency in recent years, However, it is still prudent to avoid these terms in standard contexts.

Avoiding Depersonalization of Persons with Disabilities or Illnesses

Terminology that emphasizes the person rather than the disability is generally preferred. *Handicap* is used to refer to the environmental barrier that affects the person. (Stairs handicap a person who uses a wheelchair.) While words such as *crazy*, *demented*, and *insane* are used in facetious or informal contexts, these terms are not used to describe people with clinical diagnoses of mental illness. The euphemisms *challenged*, *differently abled*, and *special* are preferred by some people, but are often ridiculed and are best avoided.

Instead of	*Use*
Mongoloid	person with Down Syndrome
wheelchair-bound person	who uses a wheelchair

Instead of

AIDS sufferer, person afflicted with AIDS, AIDS victim

Use

person living with AIDS, P.W.A., HIV+ (one who tests positive for HIV but does not show symptoms of AIDS)

Instead of	*Use*
polio victim	has/had polio
the handicapped, the disabled, cripple	persons with disabilities, person with a disability *or* person who uses crutches *or* more specific description
deaf-mute, deaf and dumb	deaf person

Avoiding Patronizing or Demeaning Expressions

Instead of

girls (when referring to adult women), the fair sex

Use

women

Instead of

sweetie, dear, dearie, honey

Use

(usually not appropriate with strangers or in public situations)

Instead of	*Use*
old maid, spinster, bachelorette	single woman, divorced woman (but only if one would specify "divorced man" in the same context)
the little woman, old lady, ball and chain	wife
boy (when referring to an adult man)	man, sir

Avoiding Language that Excludes or Unnecessarily Emphasizes Differences

References to age, sex, religion, race, and the like should only be included if they are relevant.

Instead of	*Use*
lawyers and their wives	lawyers and their spouses
a secretary and her boss	a secretary and boss, a secretary and his or her boss
the male nurse	the nurse
Arab man denies assault charge	Man denies assault charge
the articulate black student	the articulate student
Marie Curie was a great woman scientist.	Marie Curie was a great scientist. (unless the intent is to compare her only with other women in the sciences)
Christian name	given name, personal name, first name

PROOFREADER'S MARKS

The marks shown below are used in (1) preparing a manuscript to be typeset or (2) proofreading or revising printed material. The mark should be written in the margin, directly in line with the sentence or part of the text in which the change is being made, and the line of text should also be marked to indicate the exact place of the change.

When more than one change is being made in the same line, diagonal or vertical slashes are used in the margin to separate the respective marks.

Marks that are actual words, such as "OK?," "run over," and "set?," as well as editorial comments or queries noted in the margin, are often circled to distinguish them from textual corrections (words to be inserted) themselves.

In practice, these marks often differ slightly from person to person. For example, some proofreaders use slash marks even when making only one correction in a line. In all cases, however, the marks must be legible and carefully placed to avoid creating uncertainty or introducing new errors.

LETTERS, WORDS, SPACING, AND QUERIES

Mark in margin	*Indication in text*	*Instruction or comment*
a	Peter left town in^ hurry.	Insert at caret (^)
a/r	Peter left town in^ hurfy.	Insert at carets
ꝺ or ɣ	Joan sent me ~~the~~ the book.	Delete
⁀	ma ke	Close up; no space
ꝺ	I haven't seen the*e*m in years.	Delete and close up
stet	They phoned ~~both~~ Betty and Jack.	Let it stand; disregard indicated deletion or change
¶	up the river.^Two years	Start new paragraph
no ¶ or run in	many unnecessary additives. The most dangerous one	No new paragraph
tr	Ptu the book on the table. Put the book table on the. Put the table on the book.	Transpose
trup or tr↑	to Betty Steinberg, who was traveling abroad. Mrs. Steinberg, an actress,	Transpose to place indicated above
tr down or tr↓	in the clutch. The final score was 6–5. He pitched the last three innings but didn't have it.	Transpose to place indicated below
sp	Lunch cost me (6) dollars.	Spell out; use letters
fig	There were (eighteen) members present.	Set in figures; use numbers
#	It was a small^village.	Insert one letter space
##	too late.^After the dance	Insert two letter spaces
hr#	jerob^oam	Insert hair space (very thin space, as between letters)
line #	Oscar Picks This year's Academy Awards nomination.	Insert line space
eq#	Ronnie got rid of the dog.	Equalize spacing between words or between lines
=	thre^e d_a ys later	Align horizontally
‖	from one hand to another without spilling it	Align vertically
run over	enhance production. 2. It will	Start new line
□	□Rose asked the price.	Indent or insert one em (space)
□□	□□The Use of the Comma	Indent or insert two ems
⊏	⊏What's Ellen's last name?	Move left
⊐	April 2, 1945⊐	Move right
⊓	Please go now.	Move up
⊔	Well, that's that!	Move down
⊐ ⊏	⊐"The Birth of Atomic Energy"⊏	Center (heading, title, etc.)
fl	⊏2. Three (3) skirts	Flush left; no indention
fr	Total: $89.50⊐	Flush right; no indention
sent/? [the specific word that appears to be missing]	He^the copy.	Insert this word here?
(OK?) or (?)	by Francis G. Kellsey. (She) wrote	Query or verify; is this correct?
(out: see copy)	the discovery of^but near the hull	Something left out in typesetting
(set?)	arrived in 1922 (wrong date) and	Is this part of the copy, to be set (or a marginal note)?

PUNCTUATION

Mark in margin	*Indication in text*	*Instruction or comment*
⊙	Christine teaches fifth grade^	Insert period (.)
^,^	We expect Eileen^ Tom, and Ken.	Insert comma (,)
^;^	I came; I saw^ I conquered.	Insert semicolon (;)
(:)	Jenny worked until 6^30 P.M.	Insert colon (:)
=	Douglas got a two^thirds majority.	Insert hyphen (-)
=	Douglas got a two= thirds majority.	End-of-line hyphen is part of word

Mark in Margin	Indication in text	Instruction or comment
1/M	Mike then left^very reluctantly.	Insert one-em dash or long dash (—)
1/N	See pages 96^124.	Insert one-en dash or short dash (-)
’	Don't mark the authors^ copy. / Don't mark the authors^ copy.	Insert apostrophe (’)
!	Watch out^	Insert exclamation point (!)
?	Did Seth write to you^	Insert question mark (?)
“/”	I always liked^Stopping by Woods on a Snowy Evening.^	Insert quotation marks (“ ”)
‘/’	She said, “Read^The Raven^tonight.”	Insert single quotation marks (‘ ’)
(/) or ⊂/⊃	Dorothy paid 8 pesos^800 centavos^for it.	Insert parentheses (( ))
[/] or ⊏/⊐	The “portly and profane author^Dickson, presumably^in his cups” was noticed by nobody else.	Insert brackets ([ ])

TYPOGRAPHIC CASE, STYLE, AND ADJUSTMENT

Mark in Margin	Indication in text	Instruction or comment
ital	I've read <u>Paradise Lost</u> twice.	Set in *italic* (not roman) type
bf	See the definition at peace.	Set in **boldface** (heavier) type
lf	She repaired (the) motor easily.	Set in lightface (standard) type
rom	(*Gregory drove to Winnipeg.*)	Set in roman (not *italic*) type
cap or caps or uc or u/c	the italian role in Nato	Set as CAPITAL letter(s)
sc	He lived about 350 <u>B.C.</u>	Set as SMALL CAPITAL letter(s)
lc or l/c	Arlene enjoys Reading. I do NOT.	Set in lowercase; not capitalized
u+lc or c+lc or uc+lc	STOP! STOP!	Set in uppercase and lowercase
^2	H2O	Set as subscript; inferior figure
v2	A² + B2	Set as superscript; superior figure
X	They drove to (M)iami.	Broken (damaged) letter of type
wf	Turn (R)ight	Wrong font; not the proper typeface style or size
9	(H)ert proofread the book	Turn inverted (upside-down) letter

FORMS OF ADDRESS

Titles and salutations are given below for government, civic, religious, academic, and professional persons commonly addressed in correspondence. While an exhaustive list is not possible here, the forms shown should help the reader to determine how to address officials not included in the table.

As a general rule, when an individual's name is followed by the initials of a professional or academic degree, the name is not preceded by an honorific, such as "Professor" or "Dr." In almost all cases, the proper way to greet a particular individual in person can be determined by the forms given in the "Salutation" column. For the complimentary close in a letter, "Respectfully," or "Very truly yours," or, more informally, "Sincerely yours," may be used.

THE FEDERAL EXECUTIVE BRANCH

Addressee	Addressed on Letter and Envelope	Salutation
The President	The Honorable (full name) President of the United States The White House Washington, D.C. 20500 *or* The President The White House Washington, D.C. 20500	Dear Mr./Madam President: *or* Mr./Madam President:
Wife or Husband of the President	Mrs./Mr. (full name) The White House Washington, D.C. 20500	Dear Mrs./Mr. (surname):
The Vice President	The Honorable (full name) Vice President of the United States United States Senate Washington, D.C. 20510 *or* The Vice President United States Senate Washington, D.C. 20510	Dear Mr./Madam Vice President: *or* Sir/Madam:
Cabinet Member (Secretary of ______)	The Honorable (full name) Secretary of ______ *or* The Secretary of ______	Dear Mr./Madam Secretary: *or* Sir/Madam:
Attorney General	The Honorable (full name) Attorney General of the United States Washington, D.C. 20530	Dear Mr./Madam Attorney General: *or* Sir/Madam:
Postmaster General	The Honorable (full name) Postmaster General U.S. Postal Service Washington, D.C. 20260	Dear Mr./Madam Postmaster General: *or* Sir/Madam:

THE CONGRESS

Addressee	Addressed on Letter and Envelope	Salutation
Senator (in Washington)	The Honorable (full name) United States Senate Washington, D.C. 20510	Dear Senator (surname): *or* Sir/Madam:
(away from Washington)	The Honorable (full name) United States Senator (local address)	Dear Senator (surname): *or* Sir/Madam:
Committee Chairperson, Senate	The Honorable (full name) Chairman, Committee on ______ United States Senate Washington, D.C. 20510	Dear Mr./Madam Chairman: (*or, in person,* Senator)
Speaker of the House of Representatives	The Honorable (full name) Speaker of the House of Representatives Washington, D.C. 20515 *or* The Honorable Speaker of the House of Representatives	Dear Mr./Madam Speaker: *or* Dear Mr./Ms./Miss/Mrs. (surname): *or* Sir/Madam:
Representative (in Washington)	The Honorable (full name) House of Representatives Washington, D.C. 20515	Dear Mr./Ms./Miss/Mrs. (surname): *or* Dear Representative (surname):
(away from Washington)	The Honorable (full name) Member, United States House of Representatives (local address) *or* The Honorable (full name) Representative in Congress (local address)	Dear Mr./Ms./Miss/Mrs. (surname): *or* Dear Representative (surname):
Former Senator, Representative, or Government Official	The Honorable (full name) (local address)	Dear Senator/Mr./Ms./Miss/Mrs. (surname):

Addressee	*Addressed on Letter and Envelope*	*Salutation*
Committee Chairperson, House of Representatives	The Honorable (full name) Chairman/Chairwoman, Committee on ____ House of Representatives Washington, D.C. 20515	Dear Mr./Madam Chairman:

THE FEDERAL JUDICIARY

Addressee	*Addressed on Letter and Envelope*	*Salutation*
Chief Justice	The Honorable (full name) The Chief Justice of the United States The Supreme Court of the United States Washington, D.C. 20543 *or* The Chief Justice The Supreme Court Washington, D.C. 20543	Dear Mr./Madam Chief Justice: *or* Sir/Madam:
ssociate Justice	The Honorable Justice (surname) The Supreme Court of the United States Washington, D.C. 20543 *or* The Honorable (full name) Justice of the United States Supreme Court	Dear Justice: *or* Dear Justice (surname): *or* Sir/Madam:
udge of a Federal Court	The Honorable (full name) Judge of the (name of court; if a district, give district) (local address)	Dear Judge (surname): *or* Sir/Madam:

OTHER FEDERAL OFFICIALS

Addressee	*Addressed on Letter and Envelope*	*Salutation*
ibrarian of Congress	The Honorable (full name) Librarian of Congress Library of Congress Washington, D.C. 20540	Dear Mr./Ms./Miss/Mrs. (surname):
irector or Head of an Agency	The Honorable (full name) (title, name of organization) Washington, D.C.	Dear Mr./Ms./Miss/Mrs. (surname):

DIPLOMATIC OFFICIALS

Addressee	*Addressed on Letter and Envelope*	*Salutation*
merican Ambassador	The Honorable (full name) American Ambassador*	Dear Mr./Madam Ambassador: *or* Sir/Madam:
merican Minister	The Honorable (full name) American Minister to ____	Dear Mr./Madam Minister: *or* Sir/Madam:
oreign Ambassador in the United States	His/Her Excellency (full name) Ambassador of ____	Dear Mr./Madam Ambassador: *or* Excellency:
ritish Ambassador	His/Her Excellency The Right Honorable (full name) British Ambassador	Dear Mr./Madam Ambassador: *or* Excellency:
oreign Minister in the United States	The Honorable (full name) Minister of ____	Dear Mr./Madam Minister: *or* Sir/Madam:
oreign Chargé d'Affaires in the United States	Mr./Ms./Miss/Mrs. (full name) Chargé d'Affaires of ____	Dear Mr./Madam Chargé d'Affaires:
nerican Chargé d'Affaires	(full name), Esq. American Chargé d'Affaires	Dear Mr./Ms./Miss/Mrs. (surname): *or* Sir/Madam:
nerican Consul	(full name), Esq. American Consul *or* The American Consul	Dear Mr./Ms./Miss/Mrs. (surname): *or* Sir/Madam:
reign Consul	The Honorable (full name) Consul of ____ *or* ____ Consul *or* The Consul of ____	Dear Mr./Ms./Miss/Mrs. (surname): *or* Sir/Madam:

*An acceptable alternative to "American" in this title and in similar titles below is "United ates" or ". . . of the United States." The latter variant forms are used particularly for officials rving in South and Central America.

Addressee	*Addressed on Letter and Envelope*	*Salutation*
Secretary General of the United Nations	His/Her Excellency (full name) Secretary General of the United Nations New York, N.Y. 10017	Dear Mr./Madam Secretary General: *or* Dear Mr./Ms./Miss/Mrs. (surname): *or* Sir/Madam: *or* Excellency:
American Representative to the United Nations	The Honorable (full name) United States Representative to the United Nations New York, N.Y. 10017	Dear Mr./Ms./Miss/Mrs. (surname): *or* Sir/Madam:

STATE AND LOCAL OFFICIALS

Addressee	*Addressed on Letter and Envelope*	*Salutation*
Governor	The Honorable (full name) Governor of ____	Dear Governor (surname): *or* Sir/Madam:
Lieutenant Governor	The Honorable (full name) Lieutenant Governor of ____ *or* The Honorable Lieutenant Governor of ____	Dear Mr./Ms./Miss/Mrs. (surname): *or* Sir/Madam:
Secretary of State	The Honorable (full name) Secretary of State of ____ *or* The Honorable Secretary of State of ____	Dear Mr./Madam Secretary: *or* Sir/Madam:
Chief Justice of the State Supreme Court	The Honorable (full name) Chief Justice Supreme Court of the State of ____	Dear Mr./Madam Chief Justice: *or* Sir/Madam:
Attorney General of a State	The Honorable (full name) Attorney General State of ____	Dear Mr./Madam Attorney General: *or* Sir/Madam:
President of the State Senate	The Honorable (full name) President of the Senate of the State of ____	Dear Mr./Ms./Miss/Mrs. (surname):
State Senator	The Honorable (full name) ____ Senate *or* State Senator (full name)	Dear Mr./Ms./Miss/Mrs. (surname): *or* Dear Senator (surname):
Treasurer, Comptroller, or Auditor of a State	The Honorable (full name) State Treasurer/Comptroller/Auditor State of ____	Dear Mr./Ms./Miss/Mrs. (surname):
Speaker of the House of Representatives/Assembly/House of Delegates of a State**	The Honorable (full name) Speaker of the House of Representatives/Assembly/House of Delegates of the State of ____	Dear Mr./Ms./Miss/Mrs. (surname):
Representative, Assemblyman, or Delegate**	The Honorable (full name) ____ House of Representatives/Assembly/House of Delegates	Dear Mr./Ms./Miss/Mrs. (surname): *or* Sir/Madam:
State Judge	The Honorable (full name) Judge of the ____ Court	Dear Judge (surname): *or* Sir/Madam:
Local Judge	The Honorable (full name) Judge of the ____ Court of ____	Dear Judge (surname):
County Clerk or County Treasurer	The Honorable (full name) Clerk of ____ County	Dear Mr./Ms./Miss/Mrs. (surname):
Court Clerk	(full name), Esq. Clerk of the Court of ____	Dear Mr./Ms./Miss/Mrs. (surname):
Mayor	The Honorable (full name) Mayor of ____	Dear Mayor (surname): *or* Sir/Madam: *or* Dear Mr./Madam Mayor:
City Attorney	The Honorable (full name) (title) for the City of ____	Dear Mr./Ms./Miss/Mrs. (surname):

**The lower branch of the state legislature is usually called the House of Representatives. In California, Nevada, New Jersey, New York, and Washington, the lower branch is called the Assembly. In Maryland, Virginia, and West Virginia, the lower branch is called the House of Delegates. The state legislature of Nebraska is not divided into branches; its legislators are addressed as Senators.

Addressee	*Addressed on Letter and Envelope*	*Salutation*
President of a Board of Commissioners	The Honorable (full name) President, Board of Commissioners of _____	Dear Mr./Ms./Miss/Mrs. (surname):
Councilperson or Alderperson	The Honorable (full name) Councilman *or* Councilwoman/Alderman *or* Alderwoman *or* Councilman *or* Councilwoman/Alderman *or* Alderwoman (full name)	Dear Mr./Ms./Miss/Mrs. (surname): *or* Dear Councilman *or* Councilwoman/Alderman *or* Alderwoman (surname):
Superintendent of Schools	Dr./Mr./Ms./Miss/Mrs. (full name) Superintendent of Schools	Dear Superintendent (surname): *or* Dear Dr./Mr./Ms./Miss/Mrs. (surname):

CANADIAN GOVERNMENT

Addressee	*Addressed on Letter and Envelope*	*Salutation*
The Governor General	His/Her Excellency (full name) Governmental House Ottawa, Ontario K1A0A1	Dear Governor General: *or* Sir/Madam:
The Prime Minister	The Right Honourable (full name), P.C., M.P. Prime Minister of Canada Prime Minister's Office Ottawa, Ontario K1A0A2	Dear Mr./Madam Prime Minister: *or* Madam/Dear Sir:
Members of the Cabinet	The Honourable (full name) Minister of _____ House of Commons Parliament Buildings Ottawa, Ontario K1A0A2	Dear Mr./Ms./Miss/Mrs. (surname): *or* Madam/Dear Sir:
Senator	The Honourable (full name) The Senate Parliament Buildings Ottawa, Ontario K1A0A4	Dear Senator: *or* Madam/Dear Sir:
Member of the House of Commons	Mr./Ms./Miss/Mrs. (full name), M.P. House of Commons Parliament Buildings Ottawa, Ontario K1A0A6	Dear Mr./Ms./Miss/Mrs. (surname): *or* Madam/Dear Sir:
Chief Justice of Canada	The Right Honourable (full name) Chief Justice of Canada Supreme Court Building Ottawa, Ontario K1A0J1	Madam/Dear Sir: *or* Madam/Sir:
Canadian Ambassador	Mr./Ms./Miss/Mrs. (full name) Canadian Ambassador to _____	Dear Mr./Ms./Miss/Mrs. (surname): *or* Madam/Dear Sir:
Canadian Minister	Mr./Ms./Miss/Mrs. (full name) Canadian Minister to _____	Dear Mr./Ms./Miss/Mrs. (surname): *or* Sir/Madam:
The Premier of a Province	The Honourable (full name), M.L.A.* Premier of the Province of _____**	Dear Mr./Ms./Miss/Mrs. (surname): *or* Madam/Dear Sir:
Members of Provincial Governments	Mr./Ms./Miss/Mrs. (full name), M.L.A.* Member of the Legislative Assembly _____ Building	Dear Mr./Ms./Miss/Mrs. (surname): *or* Madam/Dear Sir:
Mayor	His/Her Worship Mayor (full name) City Hall	Madam/Dear Sir:

ROYALTY AND FOREIGN LEADERS

Addressee	*Addressed on Letter and Envelope*	*Salutation*
King	The Private Secretary to His Majesty the King	May it please your Majesty: (*or, in person,* Your Majesty)
Queen	The Private Secretary to Her Majesty the Queen	May it please your Majesty: (*or, in person,* Your Majesty)
President of a Republic	His/Her Excellency (full name) President of _____	Dear Mr./Madam President: *or* Excellency: (*or, in person,* Your Excellency)
Premier	His/Her Excellency (full name) Premier of _____	Dear Mr./Madam Premier: *or* Excellency: (*or, in person,* Mr./Ms./Miss/Mrs. (surname))
Prime Minister	His/Her Excellency (full name) Prime Minister of _____	Dear Mr./Madam Prime Minister: *or* Excellency: (*or, in person,* Mr./Ms./Miss/Mrs. (surname))
Royal Prince	His Royal Highness, The Prince (given name), Prince of _____	Your Royal Highness:
Royal Princess	Her Royal Highness, The Princess of _____ *or* Her Royal Highness, The Princess (given name), Mrs. (husband's full name)	Your Royal Highness:
Royal Duke	His Royal Highness, The Duke of _____	Your Royal Highness:
Royal Duchess	Her Royal Highness, The Duchess of _____	Your Royal Highness:
Duke	The Duke of _____	Dear Duke of _____: *or* Dear Duke:
Duchess	The Duchess of _____	Dear Duchess of _____ *or* Dear Duchess:
Earl	The Earl of _____	Dear Lord _____:
Countess	The Countess of _____	Dear Lady _____:

ACADEMIC AND OTHER PROFESSIONAL PEOPLE

Addressee	*Addressed on Letter and Envelope*	*Salutation*
President of a University or College (with doctoral degree)	President (full name) *or* Dr. (full name) President, (institution name)	Dear Dr. (surname): *or* Dear Sir/Madam:
President of a University or College (without doctoral degree)	President (full name) *or* Mr./Ms./Miss/Mrs. (full name) President, (institution name)	Dear Mr./Ms./Miss/Mr (surname):
Chancellor of a University or College	Dr. or Mr./Ms./Miss/Mrs. (full name) Chancellor	Dear Dr. or Mr./Ms./Miss/Mrs. (surname)
Dean of a University, College, or School (with doctoral degree)	Dean (full name) *or* Dean, (school name) (institution name)	Dear Dr. (surname): *or* Dear Dean (surname):
Dean of a University, College, or School (without doctoral degree)	Dean (full name) *or* Mr./Ms./Miss/Mrs. (full name) Dean, (name of school, if any) (institution name)	Dear Mr./Ms./Miss/M (surname): *or* Dear Dean (surname):
Professor (with doctoral degree)	Dr. (full name) Department of _____ *or* Professor (full name) Department of _____ *or* Dr. (full name) Professor of _____	Dear Dr. (surname): *or* Professor (surname): *or* Dear Professor (surname):
Professor (without doctoral degree)	Mr./Ms./Miss/Mrs. (full name) Department of _____ *or* Professor (full name) Department of _____ *or* Mr./Ms./Miss/Mrs. (full name) Professor of _____	Dear Professor (surname):

*For Ontario, use M.P.P. (Member of the Provincial Parliament); for Quebec, use M.N.A. (Member of the National Assembly).

**For Quebec, use "Prime Minister."

ssee	Addressed on Letter and Envelope	Salutation
ate or Assistan fessor	Dr. or Mr./Ms./Miss/Mrs. (full name) Associate/Assistant Professor Department of ______ *or* Dr. or Mr./Ms./Miss/Mrs. (full name) Associate/Assistant Professor of ______	Dear Professor (surname):
cian	(full name), M.D. *or* Dr. (full name)	Dear Dr. (surname):
st	(full name), D.D.S./D.M.D. *or* Dr. (full name)	Dear Dr. (surname):
inarian	(full name), D.V.M. *or* Dr. (full name)	Dear Dr. (surname):
er	Mr./Ms./Miss/Mrs. (full name) Attorney at Law *or* (full name), Esq.	Dear Mr./Ms./Miss/Mrs. (surname):
er (having J.D. ree)	Dr. (full name)	Dear Dr. (surname):

RELIGIOUS LEADERS

	His Holiness Pope ______ *or* His Holiness the Pope	Your Holiness: *or* Most Holy Father:
arch	His Beatitude the Patriarch of ______	Most Reverend Lord:
bishop of Canterby	The Most Reverend (full name) Archbishop of Canterbury *or* The Most Reverend Archbishop of Canterbury	Dear Archbishop (surname): (*or, in person,* Your Grace)
bi (with doctoral gree)	Rabbi (full name) *or* r. (full name)	Dear Rabbi (surname): *or* Dear Dr. (surname):
bi (without doctoral gree)	bbi (full name)	Dear Rabbi (surname):
an Catholic Cardinal	Eminence (given name) rdinal (surname) A ishop of ______	Dear Cardinal (surname): *or* Your Eminence:
an Catholic rchbishop	The st Reverend (full na Arch op of ______ *or* The M Reverend Arch op of ______	Dear Archbishop (surname): *or* Your Excellency:
an Catholic Bishop	The Mo everend (full name) Bishop o ______	Dear Bishop (surname): *or* Your Excellency:
an Catholic Monsignor igher rank)	The Right verend Monsign ull name)	Dear Monsignor (surname): *or* Right Reverend Monsignor:

Addressee	Addressed on Letter and Envelope	Salutation
Roman Catholic Monsignor (lower rank)	The Very Reverend Monsignor (full name)	Dear Monsignor (surname): *or* Very Reverend Monsignor:
Roman Catholic Priest	The Reverend (full name), (initials of order, if any)	Dear Father (surname): *or* Reverend Sir:
Roman Catholic Mother Superior	The Reverend Mother (full name) *or* The Reverend Mother Superior, S.C.* *or* Mother (full name), (initials of order, if used) Superior, (name of institution)	Dear Mother (given name): *or* Reverend Mother:
Roman Catholic Sister	Sister (full name) (name of organization)	Dear Sister (full name): *or* My dear Sister (full name):
Roman Catholic Brother	Brother (full name) (name of organization)	Dear Brother (given name):
Mormon Bishop	Bishop (full name) Church of Jesus Christ of Latter-day Saints	Dear Bishop (surname): *or* Dear Mr. (surname): *or* Sir:
Anglican Archbishop	The Most Reverend (full name) Archbishop of ______	Dear Archbishop (surname):
Protestant Episcopal Bishop	The Right Reverend (full name) Bishop of ______	Dear Bishop (surname): *or* Right Reverend Sir: *or* My dear Bishop (surname):
Protestant Episcopal Dean (of a cathedral)	The Very Reverend (full name) Dean of ______ *or* Dean (full name)	Dear Dean (surname): *or* Very Reverend Sir/Madam: *or* My dear Dean (surname):
Bishop (other Protestant denominations)	The Reverend (full name)	Dear Bishop (surname): *or* Reverend Sir:
Protestant Episcopal Archdeacon	The Venerable (full name)	Dear Archdeacon (surname):
Minister, Pastor, or Rector (with doctoral degree)	The Reverend Dr. (full name)	Dear Dr. (surname):
Minister, Pastor, or Rector (without doctoral degree)	The Reverend (full name)	Dear Mr./Ms./Miss/Mrs. (surname): *or* My dear Mr./Ms./Miss/Mrs. (surname):
Military Chaplain	Chaplain (full name) (rank, service, designation)	Dear Chaplain (surname):

*Initials such as *S.C.* (Sacred Congregation) or *S.J.* (Society of Jesus) commonly follow the name of a member of a holy order.

WORDS COMMONLY CONFUSED

accept*—to take
except—to exclude

adapt—to make fit
adopt—to take as one's own

adverse*—unfavorable
averse—disinclined

advice—recommendation (noun)
advise—to recommend (verb)

affect*—to influence
effect—to accomplish; result

aid—help
aide—assistant

alley—narrow back street
ally—confederate

all ready—completely ready
already*—previously; so soon

altar—platform in a church
alter—to change

amend—to modify
emend—to edit or correct

ante-—before
anti-—against

appraise—to estimate the value of
apprise—to notify

bloc—political grouping
block—obstruction

born—given birth
borne*—carried, supported, produced, etc.

bough—tree branch
bow—to bend or yield

brake—to slow and stop
break—to fracture, damage, etc; to stop work temporarily

breach—a break
breech—the buttocks

callous—unfeeling
callus—hardened skin

Calvary—site of Jesus' crucifixion
cavalry—mounted soldiers

cannon—gun
canon—law

canvas—cloth
canvass—to solicit opinions, votes, etc.

capital*—economic resources; government seat
capitol—legislature building

censer—container for incense
censor—one who checks for objectionable material

cession—act of ceding
session—meeting

chafe—to rub
chaff—worthless matter

chord—musical tones
cord—thin rope

climactic—referring to a climax
climatic—referring to a climate

complement*—something that completes or balances
compliment—praise

compose—to make up
comprise*—to include or consist of

consul—diplomat
council*—assembly
counsel—advice; a lawyer

corporal—of the body
corporeal—material, tangible

corps—group of people
corpse—dead body

credible—believable
creditable—praiseworthy

cue—hint; rod used in billiards
queue—line

desert—arid region; to leave or abandon
dessert—final course of a meal

dialectal*—of a dialect
dialectic—of logical argumentation

discomfit—to confuse, frustrate
discomfort—to make uncomfortable

discreet—circumspect, prudent
discrete—separate

dual—of two, double
duel—fight

emigrate—to leave a country
immigrate—to enter and settle in a country

eminent—renowned
immanent—inherent
imminent—about to happen

equable—uniform
equitable—fair, just

flair—aptitude, style
flare—to burn, burst out

flaunt*—to make boastful display
flout—to treat with contempt

flounder—to struggle awkwardly
founder—to sink, fail

forceful—powerful
forcible—done by force

foreword—introduction to written work
forward—onward, ahead

fortuitous*—happening by chance
fortunate—lucky

gamble—to bet
gambol—to frolic

hangar—shed for airplanes
hanger—frame for hanging clothes

hyper-—excessive, above
hypo-—insufficient, under

idle—inactive
idol—image of a god

incredible—extraordinary, unbelievable
incredulous—skeptical

inter-—between, among
intra-—within

its—belonging to it
it's—it is

lay*—to place or put; past tense of *lie*
lie—to recline

lead—a metal; to guide
led—past tense of *lead*

loath—reluctant
loathe—to hate

loose—not tight or bound; to make loose
lose—to experience loss

luxuriant—abundant, lush
luxurious—sumptuous

mean—intermediate value of number sequ
median—middle number in number seque

miner—one who mines
minor—underage person

moral—ethical; lesson
morale—spirit

naval—of the navy
navel—umbilicus

ordinance—law
ordnance—military supply

palate—roof of mouth taste
palette—artist's board
pallet—crude bed; platform

peace—calmness; lack of hostility
piece—a part

pedal—foot lever
peddle—to sell

persecute—to hound
prosecute—to institute legal proceed against

perspective—vision, view
prospective—future

plain—simple
plane—airplane; to smoot

practicable—feasible
practical—suited to actu conditions; sensi

precede—to go before
proceed—to continue

prescribe—to recommd
proscribe—to prohibi

principal*—chief; he person; capital sum
principle—rule

prophecy—predicti (noun)
prophesy—to pred (verb)

prostate—gland
prostrate—lying

quiet—still
quite—very

role—a part
roll—to turn; mall bread

seasonable—propriate to the season; time
seasonal*—ending on the season

shear—to c
sheer—tra rent; utter

stationary xed
stationer paper supplies

than—as "greater than"
then—a at time

to—tow
too—a excessive
two— ber

troop—soldier or police officer
trou—actor; dependable person

ven corrupt
ver—pardonable

w er—state of atmosphere
w her—if

s—who is
se—belonging to whom

r—belonging to you
u're—you are

*These words have Usage notes at their entries in the Dictionary discussing the asterisked word and the lar word with which it is paired here.

WEIGHTS AND MEASURES

U.S. SYSTEM

LINEAR MEASURE

12 inches	=	1 foot
3 feet	=	1 yard
5½ yards	=	1 rod
40 rods	=	1 furlong
8 furlongs (5280 feet)	=	1 statute mile

MARINERS' MEASURE

6 feet	=	1 fathom
1000 fathoms (approx.)	=	1 nautical mile
3 nautical miles	=	1 league

SQUARE MEASURE

144 square inches	=	1 square foot
9 square feet	=	1 square yard
30¼ square yards	=	1 square rod
160 square rods	=	1 acre
640 acres	=	1 square mile

CUBIC MEASURE

1728 cubic inches	=	1 cubic foot
27 cubic feet	=	1 cubic yard

SURVEYORS' MEASURE

7.92 inches	=	1 link
100 links	=	1 chain

LIQUID MEASURE

4 gills	=	1 pint
2 pints	=	1 quart
4 quarts	=	1 gallon
31½ gallons	=	1 barrel
2 barrels	=	1 hogshead

APOTHECARIES' FLUID MEASURE

60 minims	=	1 fluid dram
8 fluid drams	=	1 fluid ounce
16 fluid ounces	=	1 pint
2 pints	=	1 quart
4 quarts	=	1 gallon

DRY MEASURE

2 pints	=	1 quart
8 quarts	=	1 peck
4 pecks	=	1 bushel

WOOD MEASURE

16 cubic feet	=	1 cord foot
8 cord feet	=	1 cord

TIME MEASURE

60 seconds	=	1 minute
60 minutes	=	1 hour
24 hours	=	1 day
7 days	=	1 week
4 weeks (28-31 days)	=	1 month
12 months (365-366 days)	=	1 year
100 years	=	1 century

ANGULAR AND CIRCULAR MEASURE

60 seconds	=	1 minute
60 minutes	=	1 degree
90 degrees	=	1 right angle
180 degrees	=	1 straight angle
360 degrees	=	1 circle

TROY WEIGHT

24 grains	=	1 pennyweight
20 pennyweights	=	1 ounce
12 ounces	=	1 pound

AVOIRDUPOIS WEIGHT

$27\frac{11}{32}$ grains	=	1 dram
16 drams	=	1 ounce
16 ounces	=	1 pound
100 pounds	=	1 short hundredweight
20 short hundredweight	=	1 short ton

APOTHECARIES' WEIGHT

20 grains	=	1 scruple
3 scruples	=	1 dram
8 drams	=	1 ounce
12 ounces	=	1 pound

METRIC SYSTEM

LINEAR MEASURE

10 millimeters	=	1 centimeter
10 centimeters	=	1 decimeter
10 decimeters	=	1 meter
10 meters	=	1 decameter
10 decameters	=	1 hectometer
10 hectometers	=	1 kilometer

SQUARE MEASURE

100 sq. millimeters	=	1 sq. centimeter
100 sq. centimeters	=	1 sq. decimeter
100 sq. decimeters	=	1 sq. meter
100 sq. meters	=	1 sq. decameter
100 sq. decameters	=	1 sq. hectometer
100 sq. hectometers	=	1 sq. kilometer

CUBIC MEASURE

1000 cu. millimeters	=	1 cu. centimeter
1000 cu. centimeters	=	1 cu. decimeter
1000 cu. decimeters	=	1 cu. meter

LIQUID MEASURE

10 milliliters	=	1 centiliter
10 centiliters	=	1 deciliter
10 deciliters	=	1 liter
10 liters	=	1 decaliter
10 decaliters	=	1 hectoliter
10 hectoliters	=	1 kiloliter

WEIGHTS

10 milligrams	=	1 centigram
10 centigrams	=	1 decigram
10 decigrams	=	1 gram
10 grams	=	1 decagram
10 decagrams	=	1 hectogram
10 hectograms	=	1 kilogram
100 kilograms	=	1 quintal
10 quintals	=	1 ton

METRIC AND U.S. EQUIVALENTS

LINEAR MEASURE

U.S. Unit		*Metric Unit*
1 inch	=	25.4 millimeters 2.54 centimeters
1 foot	=	30.48 centimeters 3.048 decimeters 0.3048 meter
1 yard	=	0.9144 meter
1 mile	=	1609.3 meters 1.6093 kilometers
0.03937 inch	=	1 millimeter
0.3937 inch	=	1 centimeter
3.937 inches	=	1 decimeter
39.37 inches 3.2808 feet 1.0936 yards	=	1 meter
3280.8 feet 1093.6 yards 0.62137 mile	=	1 kilometer

DRY MEASURE

U.S. Unit		*Metric Unit*
1 quart	=	1.1012 liters
1 peck	=	8.8098 liters
1 bushel	=	35.239 liters
0.90808 quart 0.11351 peck 0.028378 bushel	=	1 liter

LIQUID MEASURE

U.S. Unit		*Metric Unit*
1 fluid ounce	=	29.573 milliliters
1 quart	=	9.4635 deciliters 0.94635 liter
1 gallon	=	3.7854 liters
0.033814 fluid ounce	=	1 milliliter
3.3814 fluid ounces	=	1 deciliter
33.814 fluid ounces 1.0567 quarts 0.26417 gallon	=	1 liter

WEIGHTS

U.S. Unit		*Metric Unit*
1 grain	=	0.064799 gram
1 avoirdupois ounce	=	28.350 grams
1 troy ounce	=	31.103 grams
1 avoirdupois pound	=	0.45359 kilogram
1 troy pound	=	0.37324 kilogram
1 short ton (0.8929 long ton)	=	907.18 kilograms 0.90718 metric ton
1 long ton (1.1200 short tons)	=	1016.0 kilograms 1.0160 metric tons
15.432 grains 0.035274 avoirdupois ounce 0.032151 troy ounce	=	1 gram
2.2046 avoirdupois pounds	=	1 kilogram
0.98421 long ton 1.1023 short tons	=	1 metric ton

CUBIC MEASURE

U.S. Unit		*Metric Unit*
1 cubic inch	=	16.387 cubic centimeters 0.016387 liter
1 cubic foot	=	0.028317 cubic meter
1 cubic yard	=	0.76455 cubic meter
1 cubic mile	=	4.16818 cubic kilometers
0.061023 cubic inch	=	1 cubic centimeter
61.023 cubic inches	=	1 cubic decimeter
35.315 cubic feet 1.3079 cubic yards	=	1 cubic meter
0.23990 cubic mile	=	1 cubic kilometer

SQUARE MEASURE

U.S. Unit		*Metric Unit*
1 square inch	=	645.16 square millimeters 6.4516 square centimeters
1 square foot	=	929.03 square centimeters 9.2903 square decimeters 0.092903 square meter
1 square yard	=	0.83613 square meter
1 square mile	=	2.5900 square kilometers
0.0015500 square inch	=	1 square millimeter
0.15500 square inch	=	1 square centimeter
15.500 square inches 0.10764 square foot	=	1 square decimeter
1.1960 square yards	=	1 square meter
0.38608 square mile	=	1 square kilometer